TABLE OF CONTENTS–Continued

Page No.

Drum Brakes (Volume 1)..................18-1
Electric Cooling Fans (Volume 1)............11-1
Engine Cooling Fans (Volume 1)............11-1
Engine Rebuilding Specifications (Volume 1)...27-1
Fans, Engine Cooling (Volume 1)...........11-1
Front Wheel Drive Axle (Volume 1)..........23-1
Hydraulic Brake Systems (Volume 1)........19-1
Machine Shop Specifications (Volume 1)......27-1
Passive Restraint Systems..................4-1
Power Brake Units (Volume 1)..............20-1
Power Steering (Volume 1)................16-1
Speed Control Systems....................2-1

Starter Motors (Volume 1)
Steering
  Power Steering (Volume 1)..............16-1
  Steering Columns (Volume 1)...........15-1
Steering Columns (Volume 1)..............15-1
Tire Pressure Monitoring Systems............6-1
Transfer Cases (Volume 1).................22-1
Universal Joints (Volume 1)................26-1
Vacuum Pumps (Volume 1)................21-1
Variable Speed Fans (Volume 1)............11-1
Warning Indicators.......................1-1
Wiper Systems...........................3-1

FORD MOTOR COMPANY–TAB 2

Page No.

FORD

Econoline (Volume 1)......................1-1
Escape incl. hybrid model (Volume 1).........2-1
E-Super Duty (Volume 1)...................1-1
Excursion (Volume 1).....................1-1
Expedition (Volume 1)....................1-1
Explorer (Volume 1)......................3-1
Explorer Sport/Sport Trac (Volume 1).........3-1
E150–550 Vans (Volume 1)................1-1
Freestar (Volume 1)......................4-1
Full-Size Pickup Trucks (Volume 1)..........1-1
Full-Size Vans (Volume 1).................1-1
F-Super Duty (Volume 1)..................1-1
F150–550 (Volume 1)....................1-1
Ranger (Volume 1).......................3-1
Windstar (Volume 1).....................6-1

LINCOLN

Aviator (Volume 1).......................3-1
Blackwood (Volume 1)....................1-1
Mark LT (Volume 1)......................1-1
Navigator (Volume 1).....................1-1

MERCURY

Mariner incl. hybrid model (Volume 1).........2-1
Monterey (Volume 1) 4-1
Mountaineer (Volume 1)...................3-1
Villager (Volume 1)......................5-1

GENERAL SERVICE

Active Suspension System 6-1
Air Bag Systems.........................4-1
Air Conditioning (Volume 1) 7-1
All Wheel Drive (Volume 1) 21-1
Alternators (Volume 1)...................10-1
Anti-Lock Brake Systems 5-1

Page No.

Axles, Drive (Volume 1) 22-1
Axles, Front Wheel Drive (Volume 1) 20-1
Brakes
  Anti-Lock Brake Systems................5-1
  Disc Brakes (Volume 1) 14-1
  Drum Brakes (Volume 1) 15-1
  Hydraulic Brake Systems (Volume 1) 16-1
  Power Brake Units (Volume 1)...........17-1
Cooling Fans (Volume 1)..................8-1
Cruise Control Systems 2-1
Dash Gauges..........................1-1
Dash Panel Service (Volume 1)............11-1
Disc Brakes (Volume 1)..................14-1
Drive Axles (Volume 1)..................22-1
Drum Brakes (Volume 1).................15-1
Electronic Level Control..................6-1
Engine Cooling Fans (Volume 1)...........8-1
Engine Rebuilding Specifications (Volume 1)...24-1
Fans, Variable Speed (Volume 1).............8-1
Front Wheel Drive Axles (Volume 1)........20-1
Hydraulic Brake Systems (Volume 1)........16-1
Machine Shop Specifications (Volume 1) 24-1
Passive Restraint System 4-1
Power Brake Units (Volume 1).............17-1
Power Steering (Volume 1) 13-1
Speed Control Systems...................2-1
Starter Motors (Volume 1)................9-1
Steering
  Power Steering (Volume 1)..............13-1
  Steering Columns (Volume 1)...........12-1
Steering Columns (Volume 1)..............12-1
Tire Pressure Monitoring Systems............7-1
Transfer Cases (Volume 1)................19-1
Universal Joints (Volume 1)...............23-1
Vacuum Pumps (Volume 1)...............18-1
Variable Speed Fans (Volume 1)............8-1
Warning Indicators......................1-1
Wiper Systems 3-1

GENERAL MOTORS CORPORATION—TAB 3

Page No.

BUICK
Rainier (Volume 1) 5-1
Rendezvous (Volume 1) 7-1
Terraza (Volume 1) 13-1

CADILLAC
Escalade (Volume 1)........................ 3-1
Escalade ESV (Volume 1)................... 3-1
Escalade EXT (Volume 1)................... 1-1
SRX (Volume 1) 11-1

CHEVROLET
Astro (Volume 1) 9-1
Avalanche (Volume 1)...................... 1-1
Blazer (Volume 1) 5-1
Colorado (Volume 1)....................... 4-1
Equinox (Volume 1)........................ 6-1
Express/Van (Volume 1) 2-1
HHR (Volume 1) 8-1
Pickup Trucks (Volume 1) 3-1
S-10 (Volume 1)........................... 4-1
Silverado (Volume 1) 1-1
SSR (Volume 1) 1-1
Suburban (Volume 1) 3-1
Tahoe (Volume 1) 3-1
Tracker (Volume 1) 12-1
TrailBlazer (Volume 1) 5-1
Uplander (Volume 1)....................... 13-1
Venture (Volume 1) 10-1

GMC
Canyon (Volume 1) 4-1
Envoy (Volume 1) 5-1
Jimmy (Volume 1).......................... 5-1
Safari (Volume 1) 9-1
Savana (Volume 1) 2-1
Sierra (Volume 1) 1-1
Sonoma (Volume 1) 4-1
Suburban (Volume 1) 3-1
Yukon (Volume 1) 3-1
Yukon XL (Volume 1) 3-1

HUMMER
H2 (Volume 1) 14-1
H3 (Volume 1) 14-1

OLDSMOBILE
Bravada (Volume 1) 5-1
Silhouette (Volume 1)..................... 10-1

PONTIAC
Aztek (Volume 1) 7-1
Montana (Volume 1) 10-1

Page No.

Montana SV6 (Volume 1) 13-1
Torrent (Volume 1) 6-1

SATURN
Relay (Volume 1).......................... 13-1
VUE (Volume 1)............................ 15-1

GENERAL SERVICE
Active Suspension Systems 6-1
Air Bag Systems........................... 4-1
Air Conditioning (Volume 1)............... 16-1
All-Wheel Drive (Volume 1)................ 30-1
Alternators (Volume 1).................... 19-1
Anti-Lock Brake Systems 5-1
Axles, Drive (Volume 1) 31-1
Axles, Front Wheel Drive (Volume 1) 29-1
Brakes
   Anti-Lock Brake Systems 5-1
   Disc Brakes (Volume 1) 23-1
   Drum Brakes (Volume 1) 24-1
   Hydraulic Brake Systems (Volume 1) 25-1
   Power Brake Units (Volume 1)......... 26-1
Cooling Fans (Volume 1) 17-1
Cruise Control Systems.................... 2-1
Dash Gauges 1-1
Dash Panel Service (Volume 1) 20-1
Disc Brakes (Volume 1) 23-1
Drive Axles (Volume 1).................... 31-1
Drum Brakes (Volume 1) 24-1
Electric Cooling Fans (Volume 1) 17-1
Electronic Level Controls 6-1
Engine Cooling Fans (Volume 1) 17-1
Engine Rebuilding Specifications (Volume 1) ... 33-1
Fans, Engine Cooling (Volume 1) 17-1
Front Wheel Drive Axle (Volume 1)......... 29-1
Hydraulic Brake Systems (Volume 1) 25-1
Machine Shop Specifications (Volume 1) 33-1
Passive Restraint Systems 4-1
Power Brake Units (Volume 1) 26-1
Power Steering (Volume 1) 22-1
Speed Control Systems.................... 2-1
Starter Motors (Volume 1)................. 18-1
Steering
   Power Steering (Volume 1) 22-1
   Steering Columns (Volume 1) 21-1
Steering Columns (Volume 1) 21-1
Tire Pressure Monitoring Systems......... 7-1
Transfer Cases (Volume 1)................. 28-1
Universal Joints (Volume 1) 32-1
Vacuum Pumps (Volume 1) 27-1
Variable Speed Fans (Volume 1) 17-1
Warning Indicators....................... 1-1
Wiper Systems 3-1

MOTOR

CHEK-CHART

INFORMATION IS OUR MIDDLE NAME.
www.MOTOR.com

LIGHT TRUCK & VAN REPAIR MANUAL

ABS/ELECTRICAL
20th Edition, Volume 2
First Printing

FOR INFORMATION ON MOTOR PRODUCTS CALL
1-800-4A-MOTOR
(1-800-426-6867)

MOTOR IS A TRADEMARK OF HEARST BUSINESS PUBLISHING, INC.

PUBLISHED BY MOTOR INFORMATION SYSTEMS, A DIVISION OF HEARST BUSINESS PUBLISHING, INC. A UNIT OF THE HEARST CORPORATION

560 CROOKS ROAD, TROY, MI 48098

PRINTED IN THE U.S.A.
COPYRIGHT © 2006 HEARST BUSINESS PUBLISHING, INC.
ALL RIGHTS RESERVED
ISBN -58251-278-7

COLLISION DATABASE PRODUCTS
Virginia Hudson, ASE, Team Manager
Robert J. Toles, ASE, SAE, Labor Development Coordinator

SENIOR ANALYST
Jeni Witte

ASSOCIATE ANALYSTS
Norman Lentine
Garry A. Mackew, SAE
Harry Narsesian
Gary Ratiu
Brian Robertson, ASE
Doug Sajor, ASE

ANALYSTS
Steven A. Bielecki, SAE
Deborah Person
Andrew Rundell
James Santo
Helmut H. Schneid, ASE
Jacqueline M. Scruggs
Randy Smith
Richard J. Tracy, ASE

CONTENT PRODUCTION
Joel Van Deven, Senior Analyst

CUSTOMER SUPPORT SERVICES
Holly Wright, National Account Services Manager

ASSOCIATE ANALYSTS
Pieter Dijkstra
Brian Martin
Jeffrey Short

ANALYST
Staranne Maxson

MANUFACTURING & DISTRIBUTION
Donna Kijek

INFORMATION PROCUREMENT
Sheri Aquisto

OFFICE MANAGER
Vita Green

SERVICE & REPAIR PRODUCTS
Kelly L. McKinstry, Team Manager

SENIOR ANALYST
Richard G. Glover, SAE

ASSOCIATE ANALYST
Ron Lathrop

ANALYSTS
Jason Baker
Joe Damron
Anthony W. Dutton
Alan McGregor
Uche-Uwa Ogu
Ken Pakkala, ASE
Daniel G. Paalanen, ASE

CONTENT PRODUCTION
Julie Andrews
Susan J. Porzondek

NATIONAL ACCOUNT PRODUCTS
SENIOR ANALYSTS
Richard C. Grunz, SAE
Jim Jackovatz, ASE
Warren Schildknecht, SAE
Michael A. Zimmerman, ASE

Keith Naszradi, Electronic Data Lead

ANALYSTS
Melissa Campbell
Marquel Cherry
Sherry Ciechorski
Jeff Finamore
Scott Gordon
Ken Hinton
Denise Masterson
Richard Sparkes, ASE

CONTENT PRODUCTION
Amy E. Bouchard
Dawn Finamore
Elaine Finamore
Luisa Harrington
Catherine Starzyk
Jill Zimmerman

CHEK-CHART PRODUCTS
James Pirkola, ASE, Team Manager

ANALYSTS
Joseph DeStefanis
Eric Rogowski, ASE
Marcus Teague

MECHANICAL DATABASE PRODUCTS
Paul M. Schmidt, SAE, Team Manager

SENIOR ANALYSTS
Dennis Green, SAE
Scott Hansen, Content Standards
Daniel W. Owen, ASE, SAE
David Williams, ASE, SAE

ASSOCIATE ANALYST
Robert Basler

GRAPHIC SERVICES
Randy Harwood, Art Director
Michele Hawley
Frank Jannaro
Hilarie McMullen

COMPOSITION
Rose Ahee
Christopher Mallory

MEDIA PRODUCTION
Robert Jaramillo, Chief Information Officer
Steven J. Hollowell, MCP, IT Manager
Tina Wrubel, Manager, Product Development/Technical Support

Victor F. Ganzi
President & Chief Executive Officer, The Hearst Corporation
Frank A. Bennack, Jr.
Vice Chairman, The Hearst Corporation
William M. Wright
Executive Vice President & Deputy Group Head, Hearst Business Media
Kevin F. Carr
President, Motor Information Systems
Philip C. Cunningham
Director of Database Development
John Lypen
Director, Data Content Services

George R. Hearst, Jr.
Chairman, The Hearst Corporation
Richard P. Malloch
President & Group Head, Hearst Business Media
Robert D. Wilbanks
Vice President & Group Controller, Hearst Business Media
Richard B. Laimbeer
Publisher, Motor Manuals
Marian A. Maasshoff
Director of Product Development

VEHICLE IDENTIFICATION
INDEX

	PAGE NO.	FIG. NO.
DaimlerChrysler:		
Chrysler	0-2	1
Dodge	0-2	2
Jeep	0-3	3
Ford Motor Co.:		
Ford	0-4	4
Lincoln	0-5	5
Mercury	0-5	6
General Motors Corp.:		
Buick	0-5	7
Cadillac	0-6	8
Chevrolet	0-6	9
GMC	0-7	10
Oldsmobile	0-8	11
Pontiac	0-8	12
Saturn	0-8	13

DIGIT 1 — Country Of Origin
1 = USA
2 = Canada

DIGIT 2 — Make
A = Chrysler
C = Chrysler

DIGIT 3 — Vehicle Type
4 = Multipurpose Passenger Vehicle
8 = Multipurpose Passenger Vehicle w/Side Airbags

DIGIT 4 — GVWR
F = 4001-5000 Lbs
G = 5001-6000 Lbs

DIGIT 5 — Line
F = Pacifica AWD
H = Town & Country FWD
J = Voyager FWD
J = Grand Voyager FWD
K = Town & Country AWD
M = Pacifica FWD
P = Town & Country FWD
T = Town & Country AWD
Y = Town & Country

DIGIT 6 — Series
1 = eC
2 = Base
2 = LX - Fleet
3 = eL
4 = LX
4 = SE
4 = LX LWB
4 = Base
4 = Base SWB
5 = Touring
5 = Touring LWB
5 = SX
5 = LXi
5 = LX
5 = Base
6 = Limited
6 = Limited LWB
6 = LXi
6 = Touring
6 = FWD/AWD
7 = Limited
7 = EX

DIGIT 7 — Body Type
4 = Extended Wagon
5 = Wagon
8 = Sport Utility 4D

DIGIT 8 — Engine
3 = 3.3L V6 SFI
3 = 3.0L V6 MPI
3 = 3.0L V6 EFI
4 = 3.5L V6 MPI SOHC
B = 2.4L I-4 EFI DOHC
G = 3.3L V6 SFI Flex
G = 3.3L V6 MPI Flex
L = 3.8L V6 SFI
L = 3.8L V6 OHV SMPI
R = 3.3L V6 SFI
R = 3.3L V6 SFI SOHC

DIGIT 10 — Model Year
1 = 2001
2 = 2002
3 = 2003
4 = 2004
5 = 2005

DIGIT 10 — Model Year
6 = 2006
L = 1990
M = 1991
N = 1992
P = 1993
R = 1994
S = 1995
T = 1996
V = 1997
W = 1998
Y = 2000

DIGIT 11 — Assembly Plant
B = St. Louis Assembly South, Fenton, MO, USA
R = Windsor, ON, Canada
X = St. Louis, MO, USA

LTV0500000000567

Fig. 1 DaimlerChrysler. Chrysler

DIGIT 1 — Country Of Origin
1 = USA
2 = Canada
3 = Mexico
J = Japan

DIGIT 1-3 — World Manufacturer Identifier
WD1 = Sprinter Cab Chassis
WD2 = Freightliner Cargo Van
WD5 = Freightliner Multipurpose Passenger Vehicle
WDI = Sprinter Cab Chassis
WDX = Sprinter Cab Chassis

DIGIT 2 — Make
B = Dodge
D = Dodge

DIGIT 3 — Vehicle Type
3 = Truck
3 = Truck w/Side Airbags
4 = Multi-Purpose Passenger Vehicle
5 = Bus
5 = Truck w/Side Airbags
6 = Incomplete Vehicle
7 = Truck w/o Side Airbags
7 = Truck
7 = Multi-Purpose Passenger Vehicle w/Side Airbags

DIGIT 4 — GVWR/Brake System
B = Manual Seat Belt
D = 1-3000 Lbs, Hydraulic
E = 3001-4000 Lbs, Hydraulic
F = 4001-5000 Lbs, Hydraulic
G = 5001-6000 Lbs, Hydraulic
H = 6001-7000 Lbs, Hydraulic
J = 7001-8000 Lbs, Hydraulic
K = 8001-9000 Lbs, Hydraulic
L = 9001-10000 Lbs, Hydraulic
L = 4001-5000 Lbs, Hydraulic
M = 10001-14000 Lbs, Hydraulic
M = 5001-6000 Lbs, Hydraulic
W = Hydraulic Brakes
W = Bus's & Incomplete Vehicles w/Hydraulic Brakes
W = Bus Or Incomplete Vehicle
W = Bus

DIGIT 4* — Body Type
P = 4X2
W = Wagon
Y = Cargo Van

DIGIT 5 — Line
A = Ram Pickup 4X2
B = Wagon/Van
B = Durango 4X4
B = Ram Van 3500
C = Ram Pickup 4X2
D = Caravan AWD
D = Dodge Ramcharger 4X2
D = Durango 4X2
D = Grand Caravan AWD
D = Ram Pickup 4X2
E = Dodge Ramcharger 4X2
E = Ram Pickup 4X2
E = Dakota 4X2
F = Ram Pickup 4X4
G = Dakota 4X4
H = Grand Caravan FWD
H = Caravan FWD
K = Ram 50 4X4
K = Mini Ram Van
K = Grand Caravan FWD
K = Grand Caravan AWD
K = Caravan FWD

DIGIT 5 — Line
K = Caravan AWD
L = Dakota 4X2
M = Dodge Ramcharger 4X4
M = Ram Pickup 4X4
N = Dakota 4X2
P = Grand Caravan FWD
P = Ram 50
P = Caravan FWD
R = Ram Pickup 4X2
R = Durango 4X2
R = Dakota 4X4
S = Durango 4X4
S = Ram 50
S = Ram Pickup 4X4
T = Power Ram 50
T = Grand Caravan WD
U = Ram Pickup 4X
W = Dakota 4X4
W = Dodge Ramcharger 4X4
W = Ram Pickup 4
Z = Rampage

DIGIT 5-6 — Line/Sees
D1 = 118-Inch, 85 Lbs
D1 = 118-Inch, 80 Lbs
D2 = 140-Inch, 80 Lbs
D2 = 140-Inch, 80 Lbs
D3 = 158-Inch, 50 Lbs
D3 = 158-Inch, 50 Lbs
D4 = 140-Inch, 990 Lbs
D4 = 140-Inch, 990 Lbs
D5 = 158-Inch, 990 Lbs
D5 = 158-Inch, 990 Lbs
D6 = 140-Inch, 8550 Lbs
D6 = 140-Inch, 8550 Lbs
D7 = 158-Inch, 8550 Lbs
D7 = 158-Inch, 8550 Lbs
D8 = 140-Inch, 10,200 Lbs
D8 = 140-Inch, 10,200 Lbs
D9 = 158-Inch, 10,200 Lbs
D9 = 158-Inch, 10,200 Lbs
J4 = Ram
J4 = Ram
L2 = Ram 50
L2 = Ram 50
L4 = Ram 50 Custom
L4 = Ram 50 Custom
L4 = Ram 50 SE
L4 = Ram 50 SE
L5 = Ram 50 LE
L5 = Ram 50 LE
L5 = Ram 50 Sport
L5 = Ram 50 Sport
M2 = Ram 50 4X4
M2 = Ram 50 4X4
M4 = Ram 50 SE 4X4
M4 = Ram 50 Custom 4X4
M4 = Ram 50 Custom 4X4
M4 = Ram 50 SE 4X4
M5 = Ram 50 Sport 4X4
M5 = Ram 50 Sport 4X4
M5 = Ram 50 LE 4X4
M5 = Ram 50 LE 4X4

DIGIT — Series
0 = 150S Job Rated
0 = Ramcharger
0 = 100 Job Rated
1 = Ramcharger
1 = 100 Job Rated
1 = 150 Job Rated
= Cargo

LTV0500000000568

Fig. 2 DaimlerChrysler (Part 1 o3). Dodge

DIGIT 6	Series
1	= Dakota
1	= Dakota Base
1	= Dakota "S"
1	= eC
1	= Dodge Ram "150 Job Rated"
1	= Dodge Ram 1500
2	= Low
2	= SE
2	= Durango
2	= Dodge Ram 2500
2	= Dakota ST
2	= Dakota R/T Sport
2	= Dakota
2	= 250 Job Rated
2	= Base
3	= 350 Job Rated
3	= Dakota Sport
3	= Dodge Ram 3500
3	= Dodge Ram 3500 w/SRW
3	= Durango Sport
3	= eL
3	= Durango ST
3	= SE
3	= Durango SXT
4	= Dodge Ram 3500 w/DRW
4	= SXT
4	= Sport
4	= SE
4	= Rampage
4	= Durango SLT
4	= Dodge 3500 Quad Cab 4WD DRW
4	= Dakota SLT
4	= Base
4	= 450 Job Rated
4	= High
5	= Durango SLT+
5	= ES
5	= LE
5	= Dakota Laramie
5	= 550 Job Rated
5	= Premium
5	= Durango Limited
6	= Dakota Sport
6	= Rampage 2.2
6	= Royal
7	= ES
7	= EX
7	= Durango R/T
7	= Dakota R/T Sport
9	= Shelby Dakota

DIGIT 7	Body Type
0	= Extended Van
0	= Extended Wagon
1	= Conventional Cab - Short
1	= Extended Wagon
1	= Van
1	= Wagon
2	= Club Cab 2D
2	= Club Cab
2	= Conventional Cab - Long
2	= Sport Utility
3	= Club Cab
3	= Club Cab 4D
3	= Extended Cargo Van
3	= Quad Cab - Half Rear Doors
3	= Quad Cab 4D
3	= Van
3	= 3D Metal Top
4	= Conventional Cab
4	= Van
4	= Extended Wagon/Van
4	= Extended Wagon
4	= Conventional Cab - Short
4	= Extended Van
5	= Club Cab
5	= Extended Cab
5	= Wagon
6	= Reg Cab
6	= Conventional Cab
6	= Conventional Cab/Chassis Cab
7	= Sport Utility 2D
8	= Quad Cab - Full Rear Doors
8	= Quad Cab 4D
8	= Sport Utility 4D
9	= Conventional Cab - Long
9	= Convertible
A	= Quad Cab 4D

DIGIT 7-8	Engine
41	= 2.7L I-5 DI Dsl
43	= 2.7L I-5 DI Dsl
44	= 2.7L I-5 DI Dsl

DIGIT 8	Engine
1	= 5.9L V8 4BBL
3	= 3.0L V6 EFI
3	= 3.0L V6 MPI
3	= 3.3L V6 SFI
3	= 3.3L V6 SFI Flex
5	= 5.9L V8 MPI
5	= 2.0L I-4 2BBL
5	= 5.9L V8 MPI HD
5	= 5.9L V8 MPI HDC
6	= 5.9L I-6 FI TDsl
7	= 2.6L I-4 2BBL
7	= 5.9L I-6 FI TDsl HO
8	= 5.9L I-6 Dsl
8	= 5.9L I-6 FI Dsl
B	= 2.2L I-4 2BBL
B	= 2.4L I-4 MPI
B	= 2.4L I-4 MPI DOHC
C	= 5.9L I-6 FI TDsl HO
C	= 5.9L I-6 FI TDSL
C	= 2.2L I-4 2BBL
D	= 2.0L I-4 2BBL
D	= 5.7L V8 HEMI SMPI
D	= 5.7L V8 MPI
D	= 5.7L V8 SMPI Hemi Magnum
D	= 5.9L V6 MPI TDsl
E	= 2.6L I-4 2BBL
E	= 3.3L V6 SFI Flex
E	= 3.7L I-6 1BBL SD
G	= 3.3L V6 MPI Flex
G	= 2.6L I-4 2BBL
G	= 2.5L I-4 TBI
G	= 2.4L I-4 MPI
H	= 8.3L V10 SFI
H	= 3.7L I-6 1BBL SD
J	= 2.5L I-4 FI Tbo
J	= 3.3L V6 MPI CNG
J	= 2.3L I-4 TDsl
J	= 4.7L V8 MPI HO
K	= 3.7L V6 MPI
K	= 3.7L V6 SFI
K	= 2.5L I-4 TBI
K	= 2.5L I-4 EFI
L	= 3.8L V6 MPI
M	= 3.9L V6 2BBL
N	= 4.7L V8 MPI
N	= 3.7L I-6 1BBL
P	= 2.5L I-4 MPI
P	= 5.2L V8 2BBL SD
P	= 4.7L V8 FFV

LTV0500000000569

Fig. 2 DaimlerChrysler (Part 2 of 3). Dodge

DIGIT 8	Engine
P	= 2.5L I-4 EFI
R	= 3.3L V6 MPI
R	= 3.3L V6 SFI
R	= 3.3L V6 SMPI
R	= 5.2L V8 4BBL HD
S	= 3.0L V6 EFI
S	= 3.0L V6 MPI
S	= 5.9L V8 2BBL SD
T	= 5.2L V8 MPI CNG
T	= 5.9L V8 4BBL SD
T	= 5.2L V8 EFI CNG
T	= 5.2L V8 2BBL SD
T	= 5.2L V8 2BBL
U	= 5.9L V8 4BBL
U	= 5.9L V8 4BBL HD Sngl Exh
U	= 5.2L V8 4BBL SD
V	= 5.9L V8 4BBL
V	= 5.9L V8 4BBL HD Dual Exh
W	= 2.4L I-4 EFI
W	= 3.7L I-6 2BBL SD
W	= 5.9L V8 4BBL
W	= 8.0L V10 MPI
X	= 3.9L V6 SFI
X	= 2.4L I-4 EFI DOHC
X	= 3.9L V6 MPI
X	= 3.9L V6 TBI
X	= 3.9L V6 EFI
Y	= 5.2L V8 EFI
Y	= 5.2L V8 MPI
Y	= 5.2L V8 SFI
Y	= 5.2L V8 SMPI
Y	= 5.2L V8 TBI
Z	= 5.9L V8 EFI LD
Z	= 5.9L V8 MPI
Z	= 5.9L V8 MPI LD
Z	= 5.9L V8 MPI LDC
Z	= 5.9L V8 SFI

DIGIT 10	Model Year
1	= 2001
2	= 2002
3	= 2003
4	= 2004
5	= 2005
6	= 2006
B	= 1981
C	= 1982
D	= 1983
E	= 1984
F	= 1985
G	= 1986
H	= 1987
J	= 1988
K	= 1989
L	= 1990
M	= 1991
N	= 1992
P	= 1993
R	= 1994
S	= 1995
T	= 1996
V	= 1997
W	= 1998
X	= 1999
Y	= 2000

DIGIT 11	Assembly Plant
5	= Dusseldorf
A	= Outer Drive, USA
A	= Lynch Road, USA
B	= St. Louis South, MO, USA
D	= Belvidere, IL, USA
F	= Newark, DE, USA
G	= Saltillo, Mexico
G	= Saltillo Assembly - Saltillo, Mexico
J	= Nagoya #3, Japan
J	= St. Louis Assembly North - Fenton, MO, USA
K	= Windsor, ON, Canada
K	= Pillette, Canada
L	= Toledo #1, OH, USA
M	= Lago Alberto Assembly - Mexico City, Mexico
P	= Toledo #2, OH, USA
P	= Nagoya #2, Japan
R	= Windsor, ON, Canada
S	= Dodge City Assembly - Warren, MI, USA
T	= Toluca, Mexico
T	= Warren #2, MI, USA
U	= Mizushima, Japan
U	= Mizushima #1, Japan
V	= Warren #3, MI, USA
W	= Toledo #3, OH, USA
X	= St. Louis #2, MO, USA
Y	= Nagoya #1, Japan
Y	= Nagoya, Japan
Z	= Okazaki, Japan

LTV0500000000570

Fig. 2 DaimlerChrysler (Part 3 of 3). Dodge

DIGIT 1	Country Of Origin
1	= USA
2	= Canada

DIGIT 2	Manufacturer
B	= American Motors Canada
J	= Jeep

DIGIT 3	Vehicle Type
4	= MPV
7	= Truck
8	= MPV w/Side Airbags
C	= Multi-Purpose Vehicle
C	= Multi-purpose Vehicle {MPV}
T	= Truck

DIGIT 4	Engine
B	= 2.5L I-4 2BBL
B	= 2.5L I-4 2BBL
B	= 2.1L I-4 FI TDsl
B	= 2.1L I-4 FI TDsl
C	= 4.2L I-6 2BBL
C	= 4.2L I-6 2BBL
E	= 3001-4000 Lbs, Hydraulic
E	= 3001-4000 Lbs, Hydraulic
F	= 4001-5000 Lbs, Hydraulic
F	= 4001-5000 Lbs, Hydraulic
G	= 5001-6000 Lbs, Hydraulic
G	= 5001-6000 Lbs, Hydraulic
H	= 2.5L I-4 TBI
H	= 6001-7000 Lbs, Hydraulic
H	= 5.0L V8 2BBL
H	= 2.5L I-4 TBI
H	= 6001-7000 Lbs, Hydraulic
H	= 5.0L V8 2BBL
M	= 4.0L I-6 MPI
M	= 4.2L I-6 2BBL
M	= 4.2L I-6 MPI
M	= 4.2L I-6 MPI
M	= 4.0L I-6 MPI
M	= 4.2L I-6 2BBL
N	= 5.9L V8 2BBL
N	= 5.9L V8 2BBL
U	= 2.5L I-4 1BBL
U	= 2.5L I-4 1BBL
W	= 2.8L V6 2BBL
W	= 2.8L V6 2BBL

DIGIT 5	Line
2	= Grand Cherokee 2WD
2	= Grand Cherokee 2WD
4	= Wrangler 4WD
4	= Wrangler 4WD
A	= 3 Spd At Column/Quadra Trac 4WD
A	= 3 Spd At Column/Quadra-Trac 4WD
A	= 3 Spd At Column
A	= Wrangler 4WD
A	= 3 Spd At Column/Quadra-Trac 4WD
A	= 3 Spd At Column/Quadra Trac 4WD
A	= 3 Spd At Column
A	= Wrangler 4WD
B	= 3-Spd At Floor/PT Time 4WD
B	= 3 Spd At Floor/PT Time 4WD
B	= 3-sp At Floor, PT Time 4WD
B	= 3-sp At Floor, PT Time 4WD
B	= 3 Spd At Floor/PT Time 4WD
B	= 3-Spd At Floor/PT Time 4WD
B	= Cherokee 2WD RHD
B	= Cherokee 2WD RHD
C	= 3-sp At Floor, Sel-trac 4WD
C	= 3 Spd At Floor/Selec-Trac 4WD
C	= 3-sp At Floor, Sel-trac 4WD
C	= 3 Spd At Floor/Selec-Trac 4WD
D	= 3 Spd At Floor
D	= 3 Spd At Floor
E	= 3 Spd At Column/PT Time 4WD
E	= 3 Spd At Column/PT Time 4WD
F	= 5 Spd Mt Floor/PT Time 4WD
F	= Cherokee 4WD LHD
F	= 5 Spd Floor/PT Time 4WD
F	= Cherokee 4WD LHD
F	= 5 Spd Mt Floor/PT Time 4WD
F	= 5 Spd Floor/PT Time 4WD
G	= 4 Spd At Column
G	= 4 Spd At Column
H	= Wrangler 4WD
H	= Wrangler 4WD
J	= 3 Spd At Column/Selec-Trac 4WD
J	= 3 Spd At Column/Selec-Trac 4WD
J	= Cherokee 4WD LHD
J	= Cherokee 4WD LHD
K	= Liberty 2WD LHD
K	= Liberty 2WD LHD
L	= 5 Spd Mt Floor/PT Time 4WD
L	= 5-sp Floor, PT Time 4WD
L	= Liberty 4WD LHD
L	= 5-sp Floor, PT Time 4WD
L	= Liberty 4WD LHD
L	= 5 Spd Mt Floor/PT Time 4WD
M	= 4 Spd Manual Floor/PT Time 4WD
M	= 4 Spd Mt Floor/PT Time 4WD
M	= 4 Spd Manual Floor/PT Time 4WD
M	= 4 Spd Mt Floor/PT Time 4WD
N	= Cherokee 4WD RHD
N	= 5 Spd Mt Floor/PT Time 4WD
N	= 5 Spd Mt Floor/PT Time 4WD
N	= 5 Spd Mt Floor/Selec-Trac 4WD
N	= Cherokee 4WD RHD
N	= 5 Spd Mt Floor/Selec-Trac 4WD
P	= 4 Spd At Column/PT Time 4WD
P	= 4 Spd At Column/PT Time 4WD
R	= 4 Spd At Floor/PT Time 4WD
R	= Grand Cherokee 4WD
R	= 4 Spd At Floor/PT Time 4WD
R	= Grand Cherokee 4WD
S	= 4 Spd Mt Floor
S	= Grand Cherokee 2WD
S	= 4 Spd Mt Floor
S	= Grand Cherokee 2WD
T	= Cherokee 2WD LHD
T	= Cherokee 2WD LHD
T	= 4 Spd At Floor/Selec-Trac 4WD
T	= 4 Spd At Floor/Selec-Trac 4WD
U	= 4 Spd At Floor
U	= 4 Spd At Floor
V	= 5 Spd Mt Floor/PT Time 4WD
V	= 5 Spd Mt Floor/PT Time 4WD
W	= Grand Cherokee 4WD
W	= 5 Spd Mt Floor
W	= 5 Spd Mt Floor
W	= Grand Cherokee 4WD
X	= Grand Cherokee 2WD
X	= 4 Spd Mt Floor/PT Time 4WD
X	= Grand Cherokee 2WD
X	= 4 Spd AT Floor/PT Time 4WD
X	= 4 Spd AT Floor/PT Time 4WD
X	= 4 Spd Mt Floor/PT Time 4WD
Y	= Wrangler 4WD
Y	= Wrangler 4WD
Z	= Grand Cherokee 4WD
Z	= 3 Spd At Column/PT Time 4WD
Z	= Grand Cherokee 4WD
Z	= 3 Spd At Column/PT Time 4WD

DIGIT 5-6	Line/Series
J2	= Cherokee 4WD

LTV0500000000577

Fig. 3 DaimlerChrysler (Part 1 of 4). Jeep

DIGIT 5-6	Line/Series
J2	= Comanche 4WD
J2	= Comanche Eliminator 4WD
J2	= Comanche Pioneer 4WD
J3	= Comanche Pioneer 4WD
J3	= Comanche Eliminator 4WD
J3	= Comanche 4WD
J3	= Cherokee Pioneer 4WD
J5	= Cherokee Laredo 4WD
J6	= Comanche Eliminator 4WD
J7	= Cherokee Limited 4WD
J8	= Cherokee 4WD
J8	= Cherokee Sport 4WD
N7	= Cherokee Wagoneer Limited 4WD
N7	= Cherokee Briarwood 4WD
S5	= Grand Wagoneer 4WD
T2	= Comanche 2WD
T2	= Comanche Eliminator 2WD
T2	= Comanche Pioneer 2WD
T2	= Cherokee 2WD
T3	= Cherokee Pioneer 2WD
T3	= Comanche 2WD
T3	= Comanche Eliminator 2WD
T3	= Comanche Pioneer 2WD
T5	= Cherokee Laredo 2WD
T6	= Comanche Eliminator 2WD
T8	= Cherokee 2WD
T8	= Cherokee Sport 2WD
Y1	= Wrangler 4WD
Y1	= Wrangler S 4WD
Y2	= Wrangler 4WD
Y2	= Wrangler S 4WD
Y3	= Wrangler Islander 4WD
Y4	= Wrangler Sahara 4WD
Y5	= Wrangler Laredo 4WD
Y5	= Wrangler Renegade 4WD
Y6	= Wrangler Renegade 4WD

DIGIT 6	Series
1	= Wrangler S
1	= Wrangler Sport
1	= Wrangler Rio Grande
2	= Cherokee SE
2	= Wrangler
2	= Wrangler SE
2	= Wrangler Sport
2	= Wrangler Unlimited LWB
2	= Cherokee
3	= Renegade
3	= Wrangler X
3	= Wrangler Rocky Mountain
3	= Rocky Mountain
3	= Sport
4	= Cherokee Sport
4	= Wrangler Unlimited
4	= Laredo
4	= Rocky Mountain
4	= Special Edition
4	= Sport
4	= Wrangler Sahara
4	= Wrangler Sport
5	= Cherokee Classic
5	= Classic
5	= Laredo
5	= Limited
5	= TSi
5	= Wrangler Sahara
6	= SE
6	= Wrangler Renegade
6	= Overland
6	= Limited
6	= Cherokee Limited
6	= Cherokee Classic
6	= Base
6	= Wrangler Rubicon
6	= Cherokee Sport
7	= Orvis
7	= Cherokee Country
7	= Cherokee Limited
7	= Limited
8	= 5.9 Limited
8	= Grand Wagoneer

DIGIT 6-7	Body Type
15	= Grand Wagoneer 4D Wagon 109 W.B.
16	= Cherokee 2D Wagon 109 W.B.
17	= Cherokee 2D Wagon 109 W.B.
18	= Cherokee 4D Wagon 109 W.B.
25	= Jeep Truck J10 w/Box 119 W.B.
25	= Jeep Truck J20 w/Box 119 W.B.
26	= Jeep Truck J10 w/Box 131 W.B.
27	= Jeep Truck J20 w/Box 131 W.B.
63	= Comanche 4WD 113 W.B.
64	= Comanche 2WD 113 W.B.
65	= Comanche 4WD 120 W.B.
66	= Comanche 2WD 120 W.B.
73	= Cherokee 2D Wagon 2WD 101 W.B.
74	= Cherokee 4D Wagon 2WD 101 W.B.
75	= Cherokee Wagoneer 4D Wagon 4WD 101 W.B.
75	= Wagoneer 4D Wagon 4WD 101 W.B.
77	= Cherokee 2D Wagon 4WD 101 W.B.
78	= Cherokee 4D Wagon 4WD 101 W.B.
81	= 2D Open Body 93.5 W.B.
85	= CJ-5 Open Body 83.5 W.B.
87	= CJ-7 Open Body 93.5 W.B.
88	= CJ-8 Scrambler Open Body 103.5 W.B.
88	= Scrambler Open Body 103.5 W.B.

DIGIT 7	Body Type
4	= 2D Open Body LWB
6	= Conventional Cab
7	= Sport Utility 2D
8	= Sport Utility 4D
9	= 2D Open Body

DIGIT 8	Engine
1	= Comanche 4001-5000#
1	= Cherokee Base, 4001-5000 Lbs
1	= 2.4L I-4 MPI
1	= Wrangler Base, 5001-5000 Lbs
1	= Cherokee Base, 4001-5000 Lbs
1	= Wrangler Base, 5001-5000 Lbs
1	= 2.4L I-4 MPI
1	= Comanche 4001-5000#
2	= Cherokee Pioneer, 4001-5000 Lbs
2	= Wrangler Sahara, 4001-5000 Lbs
2	= 5.7L V8 SFI Hemi
2	= Wrangler Sahara, 4001-5000 Lbs
2	= Cherokee Pioneer, 4001-5000 Lbs
2	= 5.7L V8 SFI Hemi
3	= Cherokee Chief, 4001-5000 Lbs
3	= Wrangler Sport, 4001-5000 Lbs
3	= Wrangler Sport, 4001-5000 Lbs
3	= Cherokee Chief, 4001-5000 Lbs
4	= Wrangler Laredo, 4001-5000 Lbs
4	= Wrangler Laredo, 4001-5000 Lbs
4	= Cherokee Laredo, 4001-5000 Lbs
4	= Cherokee Laredo, 4001-5000 Lbs
5	= Wagoneer, 4001-5000 Lbs
5	= 2.8L I-4 Turbo Diesel
5	= Comanche Eliminator 4001-5000#
5	= Wagoneer, 4001-5000 Lbs
5	= 2.8L I-4 Turbo Diesel
5	= Comanche Eliminator 4001-5000#
6	= Wagoneer Limited, 4001-5000 Lbs

LTV0500000000578

Fig. 3 DaimlerChrysler (Part 2 of 4). Jeep

DIGIT 8	Engine
6	= Wagoneer Limited, 4001-5000 Lbs
7	= 5.9L V8 2BBL
7	= Comanche X 4001-5000#
7	= 5.9L V8 2BBL
7	= Comanche X 4001-5000#
9	= Cherokee Limited, 4001-5000 Lbs
9	= Comanche XLS 4001-5000#
9	= Cherokee Limited, 4001-5000 Lbs
9	= Comanche XLS 4001-5000#
A	= CJ-7, 3001-4000 Lbs
A	= CJ-5, 3001-4000 Lbs
A	= CJ-7, 3001-4000 Lbs
A	= CJ-5, 3001-4000 Lbs
A	= CJ-8 Scrambler, 4001-5000 Lbs
A	= CJ-8 Scrambler, 4001-5000 Lbs
C	= Cherokee Chief, 5001-6000 Lbs
C	= Cherokee Chief, 5001-6000 Lbs
D	= Cherokee Laredo, 5001-6000 Lbs
D	= Cherokee Laredo, 5001-6000 Lbs
E	= 2.5L I-4 TBI
E	= CJ-7, 4001-5000 Lbs
E	= CJ-5, 4001-5000 Lbs
E	= CJ-8 Scrambler, 4001-5000 Lbs
E	= CJ-8 Scrambler, 4001-5000 Lbs
E	= CJ-7, 4001-5000 Lbs
E	= CJ-5, 4001-5000 Lbs
E	= 2.5L I-4 TBI
F	= Comanche Custom 5001-6000#
F	= Comanche 5001-6000#
F	= Comanche Custom 5001-6000#
F	= Comanche 5001-6000#
G	= Comanche X 5001-6000#
G	= Comanche X 5001-6000#
J	= 4.7L V8 MPI HO
J	= Wrangler Base, 3001-4000 Lbs
J	= Comanche XLS 5001-6000#
J	= Comanche XLS 5001-6000#
J	= Cherokee Base, 3001-4000 Lbs
J	= 4.7L V8 MPI HO
J	= Wrangler Base, 3001-4000 Lbs
J	= Cherokee Base, 3001-4000 Lbs
K	= Cherokee Base, 3001-4000 Lbs
K	= Wrangler Sport, 3001-4000 Lbs
K	= 3.7L V6 MPI
K	= 3.7L V6 SFI
K	= Cherokee Pioneer, 3001-4000 Lbs
K	= 3.7L V6 SFI
K	= 3.7L V6 MPI
K	= Cherokee Base, 3001-4000 Lbs
K	= Cherokee Pioneer, 3001-4000 Lbs
K	= Wrangler Sport, 3001-4000 Lbs
L	= Cherokee Pioneer, 3001-4000 Lbs
L	= Cherokee Laredo, 3001-4000 Lbs
L	= 4.0L I-6 MPI
L	= Wrangler Laredo, 3001-4000 Lbs
L	= Cherokee Laredo, 3001-4000 Lbs
L	= 4.0L I-6 MPI
L	= Cherokee Pioneer, 3001-4000 Lbs
L	= Wrangler Laredo, 3001-4000 Lbs
M	= Cherokee Laredo, 3001-4000 Lbs
M	= Wrangler Sahara, 3001-4000 Lbs
M	= 4.2L I-6 2BBL
M	= Cherokee Laredo, 3001-4000 Lbs
M	= Wrangler Sahara, 3001-4000 Lbs
M	= 4.2L I-6 2BBL
N	= 4.7L V8 SFI SOHC
N	= Cherokee, 5001-6000 Lbs
N	= Grand Wagoneer 5001-6000 Lbs
N	= Truck J10, 5001-6000 Lbs
N	= Truck J10, 6001-7000 Lbs
N	= Truck J20, 6001-7000 Lbs

DIGIT 8	Engine
N	= Truck J10, 6001-7000 Lbs
N	= Truck J20, 5001-6000 Lbs
N	= Truck J20, 5001-6000 Lbs
N	= 4.7L V8 MPI
N	= Truck J10, 5001-6000 Lbs
N	= Grand Wagoneer 5001-6000 Lbs
N	= Cherokee, 5001-6000 Lbs
N	= 4.7L V8 SFI SOHC
N	= 4.7L V8 MPI
N	= Truck J20, 6001-7000 Lbs
P	= 2.5L I-4 MPI
P	= Comanche Pioneer 4001-5000#
P	= Truck J20, 6001-7000 Lbs
P	= Comanche Pioneer 4001-5000#
P	= 2.5L I-4 SFI
P	= 2.5L I-4 SFI
P	= 2.5L I-4 MPI
P	= Truck J20, 6001-7000 Lbs
R	= Comanche Pioneer 5001-6000#
R	= Cherokee Chief, 6001-7000 Lbs
R	= Comanche Pioneer 5001-6000#
R	= Cherokee Chief, 6001-7000 Lbs
S	= Truck J20, 7001-8000 Lbs
S	= 4.0L I-6 MPI
S	= 4.0L I-6 SFI
S	= Wrangler S, 3001-4000 Lbs
S	= Comanche Chief 4001-5000#
S	= Wrangler S, 3001-4000 Lbs
S	= 4.0L I-6 MPI
S	= 4.0L I-6 SFI
S	= Comanche Chief 4001-5000#
S	= Truck J20, 7001-8000 Lbs
T	= 4.2L I-6 2BBL
T	= Cherokee Laredo, 6001-7000 Lbs
T	= 4.2L I-6 2BBL
T	= Comanche Laredo 4001-5000#
T	= Cherokee Laredo, 6001-7000 Lbs
T	= Comanche Laredo 4001-5000#
U	= Truck J10, 6001-7000 Lbs
U	= Truck J20, 6001-7000 Lbs
U	= Grand Wagoneer 6001-7000 Lbs
U	= Grand Wagoneer 6001-7000 Lbs
U	= Truck J20, 6001-7000 Lbs
U	= Truck J10, 6001-7000 Lbs
Y	= Truck J20, 8001-9000 Lbs
Y	= Truck J20, 8001-9000 Lbs
Y	= 5.2L V8 MPI
Y	= 5.2L V8 MPI
Z	= 5.9L V8 MPI
Z	= 5.9L V8 MPI

DIGIT 10	Model Year
1	= 2001
2	= 2002
3	= 2003
4	= 2004
5	= 2005
6	= 2006
B	= 1981
C	= 1982
D	= 1983
E	= 1984
F	= 1985
G	= 1986
H	= 1987
J	= 1988
K	= 1989
L	= 1990
M	= 1991
N	= 1992
P	= 1993
R	= 1994

LTV0500000000579

Fig. 3 DaimlerChrysler (Part 3 of 4). Jeep

DIGIT 10	Model Year
S	= 1995
T	= 1996
V	= 1997
W	= 1998
X	= 1999
Y	= 2000

DIGIT 11	Assembly Plant
B	= Brampton, ON, Canada
C	= Detroit, MI, USA
J	= Brampton, ON, Canada
L	= Toledo #1, OH, USA
P	= Toledo #2, OH, USA
T	= Toledo, OH, USA
W	= Toledo North Assembly, Ohio, USA
W	= Toledo North Assembly, OH, USA
W	= Toledo #3, OH, USA
W	= Toledo-North, OH, USA

LTV0500000000580

Fig. 3 DaimlerChrysler (Part 4 of 4). Jeep

DIGIT 1-3	World Manufacturer Identifier
1F1	= Ford Motor Co., USA, MPV-Limousine
1FB	= Ford Motor Co., USA, Bus
1FC	= Ford Motor Co., USA, Truck Stripped Chassis
1FD	= Ford Motor Co., USA, Incomplete Vehicle
1FD	= Ford Motor Co., USA, Truck (Incomplete Vehicle)
1FM	= Ford Motor Co., USA, Multipurpose Vehicle
1FT	= Ford Motor Co., USA, Truck {Complete Vehicle}
2FD	= Ford Motor Co., Canada, Truck (Incomplete Vehicle)
2FD	= Ford Motor Co., Canada, Truck {Incomplete Vehicle}
2FM	= Ford Motor Co., Canada, Multipurpose Vehicle
2FT	= Ford Motor Co., Canada, Truck (Complete Vehicle)
3FD	= Ford Motor Co., Mexico, Incomplete Vehicle
3FT	= Ford Motor Co., Mexico, Truck {Complete Vehicle}
JC2	= Toyo Kogyo Of Japan, Truck {Complete Vehicle}
JC4	= Toyo Kogyo Of Japan, Truck {Incomplete Vehicle}

DIGIT 4	Brake Type/GVWR Class
B	= Hydraulic, 3001-4000 Lbs
C	= Hydraulic, 4001-5000 Lbs
D	= Hydraulic, 5001-6000 Lbs
E	= Hydraulic, 6001-7000 Lbs
F	= Hydraulic, 7001-8000 Lbs
G	= Hydraulic, 8001-8500 Lbs
H	= Hydraulic, 8501-9000 Lbs
J	= Hydraulic, 9001-10000 Lbs
K	= Hydraulic, 10001-14000 Lbs
L	= Hydraulic, 14001-16000 Lbs

DIGIT 4*	Brake Type/GVWR Class/Restraint
B	= Hydraulic, 3001-4000 Lbs, Dual Front & Front Side Airbags
C	= Hydraulic, 4001-5000 Lbs, Dual Front & Front Side Airbags
D	= Hydraulic, 5001-6000 Lbs, Dual Front & Front Side Airbags
E	= Hydraulic, 6001-7000 Lbs, Dual Front & Front Side Airbags
F	= Hydraulic, 7001-8000 Lbs, Dual Front & Front Side Airbags
G	= Hydraulic, 8001-8500 Lbs, No Airbags
H	= Hydraulic, 8501-9000 Lbs, No Airbags
J	= Hydraulic, 9001-10000 Lbs, Without Airbags
J	= Hydraulic, 9001-10000 Lbs, No Airbags
K	= Hydraulic, 10001-14000 Lbs, Without Airbags
N	= Hydraulic, 8501-9000 Lbs, Dual Front Airbags
P	= Hydraulic, 7001-8000 Lbs, Dual Front Airbags
R	= Hydraulic, 6001-7000 Lbs, Dual Front Airbags
S	= Hydraulic, 9001-10000 Lbs, Dual Front Airbags
U	= Hydraulic, 3001-4000 Lbs, Dual Front Airbags
V	= Hydraulic, 8001-8500 Lbs, Dual Front Airbags
W	= Hydraulic, 10001-14000 Lbs, Dual Front Airbags
W	= Hydraulic, 10001-14000 Lbs, Without Airbags
X	= Hydraulic, 14001-16000 Lbs, Dual Front Airbags
Y	= Hydraulic, 4001-5000 Lbs, Dual Front Airbags
Z	= Hydraulic, 5001-6000 Lbs, Dual Front Airbags

DIGIT 4-6	Line, Series, Chassis, Cab Or Body
UA1	= Courier Pickup 2WD, 106.9 WB
UA2	= Courier Pickup 2WD, 112.8 WB

DIGIT 5-7	Line, Series, Chassis, Cab Or Body
A11	= Aerostar Wagon
A14	= Aerostar Cargo Van
A15	= Aerostar Window Van
A21	= Aerostar Wagon 4WD
A24	= Aerostar Cargo Van 4WD
A25	= Aerostar Window Van 4WD
A31	= Aerostar Extended Wagon
A34	= Aerostar Extended Cargo Van
A35	= Aerostar Extended Window Van
A41	= Aerostar Extended Wagon 4WD
A44	= Aerostar Extended Cargo Van 4WD
A45	= Aerostar Extended Window Van 4WD
A50	= Windstar LX Wagon
A50	= Windstar LX 3D Wagon
A50	= Windstar Base Wagon
A50	= Freestar S 4D Wagon
A51	= Freestar SE 4D Wagon

DIGIT 5-7	Line, Series, Chassis, Cab Or Body
A51	= Windstar LX 4D Wagon
A51	= Windstar LX Wagon
A51	= Windstar Wagon
A52	= Windstar SE 4D Wagon
A52	= Freestar SEL 4D Wagon
A53	= Windstar Limited 4D Wagon
A53	= Windstar SEL 4D Wagon
A54	= Windstar Cargo Van
A54	= Freestar Cargo Van
A56	= Windstar SEL 4D Wagon
A57	= Windstar SE Sport 4D Wagon
A57	= Freestar SES 4D Wagon
A58	= Windstar Limited 4D Wagon
A58	= Freestar Limited 4D Wagon
E01	= E100 Club Wagon
E04	= E100 Cargo Van
E05	= E100 Window Van
E06	= E100 Display Van
E11	= E150 Wagon
E14	= E150 Cargo Van
E15	= E150 Window Van
E16	= E150 Display Van
E21	= E250 Club Wagon
E24	= E250 Cargo Van
E25	= E250 Window Van
E25	= E250 HD Cargo Van
E26	= E250 Display Van
E31	= E350 Club Wagon
E34	= E350 Cargo Van
E35	= E350 Window Van
E35	= E350SD Base Cutaway
E36	= E350 Display Van
E37	= E350 Super Duty Commercial Cutaway
E37	= E350 Parcel Delivery Van
E39	= E350SD Commercial Stripped Chassis
F02	= F150 Pickup Regular Cab Flareside 2WD
F04	= F150 Pickup Regular Cab Flareside 4WD
F07	= F150 Pickup Regular Cab Flareside 2WD
F08	= F150 Pickup Regular Cab Flareside 4WD
F10	= F100 Pickup Regular Cab 2WD
F12	= F150 Pickup Regular Cab Styleside 2WD
F14	= F150 Pickup Regular Cab Styleside 4WD
F15	= F150 Pickup Regular Cab Styleside 2WD
F17	= F150 Pickup Regular Cab Styleside 2WD
F18	= F150 Pickup Regular Cab Styleside 4WD
F20	= F250 Super Duty Pickup Regular Cab Styleside 2WD
F21	= F250 Super Duty Pickup Regular Cab Styleside 4WD
F25	= F250HD Pickup Regular Cab Styleside 2WD
F25	= F250 Pickup Regular Cab Styleside 2WD
F26	= F250HD Pickup Regular Cab Styleside 4WD
F26	= F250 Pickup Regular Cab Styleside 4WD
F27	= F250 Pickup Regular Cab Styleside 2WD
F28	= F250 Pickup Regular Cab Styleside 4WD
F30	= F350 Super Duty Pickup Regular Cab 2WD
F31	= F350 Super Duty Pickup Regular Cab 4WD
F32	= F350 Super Duty Pickup Regular Cab 2WD DRW
F33	= F350 Super Duty Pickup Regular Cab 4WD DRW
F35	= F350 Pickup Regular Cab Styleside 2WD
F36	= F350 Pickup Regular Cab Styleside 4WD
F46	= F450 Super Duty Chassis Cab Regular Cab 2WD DRW
F47	= F450 Super Duty Chassis Cab Regular Cab 4WD DRW
F47	= F-Super Duty Chassis Cab Regular Cab 2WD
K01	= Freestyle SE 4D Utility FWD
K02	= Freestyle SEL 4D Utility FWD
K03	= Freestyle Limited 4D Utility FWD
K04	= Freestyle SE 4D Utility AWD
K05	= Freestyle SEL 4D Utility AWD
K06	= Freestyle Limited 4D Utility AWD
R10	= Ranger Regular Cab 2WD
R11	= Ranger Regular Cab 4WD
R14	= Ranger Supercab 2WD

LTV0500000000571

Fig. 4 Ford Motor Company (Part 1 of 3). Ford

DIGIT 5-7	Line, Series, Chassis, Cab Or Body
R15	= Ranger Supercab 4WD
R44	= Ranger 4D Supercab 2WD
R45	= Ranger 4D Supercab 4WD
S11	= E150 Super Club Wagon
S14	= E150 Super Cargo Van
S15	= E150 Super Window Van
S16	= E150 Super Display Van
S21	= E250 Super Club Wagon
S24	= Extended Cargo Van
S24	= E250 Extended Cargo Van
S24	= E250 Super Cargo Van
S25	= E250 Super Window Van
S26	= E250 Super Display Van
S31	= E350 Super Club Wagon
S31	= E350 Super Duty Extended Club Wagon
S34	= E350 Super Cargo Van
S34	= E350 Super Duty Extended Cargo Van
S35	= E350 Super Window Van
S36	= E350 Super Display Van
U01	= Escape XLS 4D Utility 2WD
U02	= Escape XLS 4D Utility 2WD
U02	= Escape XLS 4D Utility 4WD
U03	= Escape XLT 4D Utility 2WD
U04	= Escape XLT 4D Utility 4WD
U04	= Escape Limited 4D Utility 2WD
U04	= Escape Limited 4D Utility 4WD
U12	= Bronco II 2WD
U13	= Expedition XLS 4D Utility 2WD
U14	= Bronco II 4WD
U14	= Expedition XLS 4D Utility 4WD
U15	= Bronco 4WD
U15	= Expedition XLT 4D Utility 2WD
U16	= Expedition XLT 4D Utility 4WD
U17	= Expedition King Ranch 4D Utility 2WD
U17	= Expedition 4D Utility 2WD
U17	= Expedition Eddie Bauer 4D Utility 2WD
U18	= Expedition 4D Utility 4WD
U18	= Expedition Eddie Bauer 4D Utility 4WD
U18	= Expedition King Ranch 4D Utility 4WD
U19	= Expedition Limited 4D Utility 2WD
U20	= Expedition Limited 4D Utility 4WD
U22	= Explorer 2D Utility 2WD
U24	= Explorer 2D Utility 4WD
U32	= Explorer 4D Utility 2WD
U34	= Explorer 4D Utility 4WD
U35	= Explorer 4D Utility AWD
U40	= Excursion XLT 4D Utility 2WD
U40	= Excursion XLS 4D Utility 2WD
U41	= Excursion XLS 4D Utility 4WD
U41	= Excursion XLT 4D Utility 4WD
U42	= Excursion Limited 4D Utility 2WD
U43	= Excursion Limited 4D Utility 4WD
U44	= Excursion Eddie Bauer 4D Utility 2WD
U45	= Excursion Eddie Bauer 4D Utility 4WD
U60	= Explorer Sport 2D Utility 2WD
U61	= Explorer XL 4D Utility 2WD
U62	= Explorer XLS 4D Utility 2WD
U63	= Explorer XLT 4D Utility 2WD
U64	= Explorer Eddie Bauer 4D Utility 2WD
U65	= Explorer Limited 4D Utility 2WD
U67	= Explorer Sport Trac 4D Utility 2WD
U70	= Explorer Sport 2D Utility 4WD
U71	= Explorer XL 4D Utility 4WD
U72	= Explorer XLS 4D Utility 4WD
U73	= Explorer XLT 4D Utility 4WD
U74	= Explorer Eddie Bauer 4D Utility 4WD
U75	= Explorer Limited 4D Utility 4WD
U77	= Explorer Sport Trac 4D Utility 4WD
U82	= Explorer XLS 4D Utility AWD
U83	= Explorer XLT 4D Utility AWD
U84	= Explorer Eddie Bauer 4D Utility AWD

DIGIT 5-7	Line, Series, Chassis, Cab Or Body
U85	= Explorer Limited 4D Utility AWD
U92	= Escape XLS 4D Utility 4WD
U93	= Escape XLT 4D Utility 4WD
U94	= Escape Limited 4D Utility 4WD
U95	= Escape Hybrid 4D Utility 2WD
U96	= Escape Hybrid 4D Utility 4WD
W07	= F150 Pickup SuperCrew 2WD
W08	= F150 Pickup SuperCrew 4WD
W12	= F150 Pickup SuperCrew 2WD
W14	= F150 Pickup SuperCrew 4WD
W20	= F250 Super Duty Pickup Crew Cab 2WD
W21	= F250 Super Duty Pickup Crew Cab 4WD
W25	= F250HD Pickup Crew Cab 2WD
W25	= F250 Pickup Crew Cab 2WD
W26	= F250HD Pickup Crew Cab 4WD
W26	= F250 Pickup Crew Cab 4WD
W30	= F350 Super Duty Pickup Crew Cab 2WD
W31	= F350 Super Duty Pickup Crew Cab 4WD
W32	= F350 Super Duty Pickup Crew Cab 2WD DRW
W33	= F350 Super Duty Pickup Crew Cab 4WD DRW
W35	= F350 Pickup Crew Cab 2WD
W36	= F350 Pickup Crew Cab 4WD
W46	= F450 Super Duty Chassis Cab Crew Cab 2WD DRW
W47	= F450 Super Duty Chassis Cab Crew Cab 4WD DRW
X02	= F150 Pickup Supercab Flareside 2WD
X04	= F150 Pickup Supercab Flareside 4WD
X07	= F150 Pickup Supercab Flareside 2WD
X08	= F150 Pickup Supercab Flareside 4WD
X12	= F150 Pickup Supercab Styleside 2WD
X14	= F150 Pickup Supercab Styleside 4WD
X15	= F150 Pickup Supercab Styleside 2WD
X17	= F150 Pickup Supercab Styleside 2WD
X18	= F150 Pickup Supercab Styleside 4WD
X20	= F250 Super Duty Pickup Supercab Styleside 2WD
X21	= F250 Super Duty Pickup Supercab Styleside 4WD
X23	= F250 Pickup Supercab Styleside 2WD
X25	= F250HD Pickup Supercab Styleside 2WD
X26	= F250 Pickup Supercab Styleside 4WD
X26	= F250HD Pickup Supercab Styleside 4WD
X27	= F250 Pickup Supercab Styleside 2WD
X28	= F250 Pickup Supercab Styleside 4WD
X30	= F350 Super Duty Pickup Supercab 2WD
X31	= F350 Super Duty Pickup Supercab 4WD
X32	= F350 Super Duty Pickup Supercab 2WD DRW
X33	= F350 Super Duty Pickup Supercab 4WD DRW
X35	= F350 Pickup Supercab Styleside 2WD
X46	= F450 Super Duty Chassis Cab Supercab 2WD DRW
X47	= F450 Super Duty Chassis Cab Supercab 4WD DRW

DIGIT 7	GVWR
1	= Class B: 3001-4000 Lbs
2	= Class C: 4001-5000

DIGIT 8	Engine
1	= 2.0L I-4 2BBL
1	= 3.0L V6 DOHC
1	= 3.0L V6 SFI DOHC
1	= 6.9L V8 Dsl
1	= 3.0L Duratec 4V V6
2	= 4.2L V6 EFI OHV
2	= 4.2L V6 SPI
2	= 2.3L I-4 2BBL
3	= 5.4L V8 EFI SOHC S/C
3	= 3.8L V6 2BBL
4	= 3.8L V6 EFI OHV
5	= 5.4L V8 EFI SOHC
5	= 5.4L V8 3V SOHC
6	= 4.6L V8 EFI SOHC
6	= 3.9L V6 SPI
9	= 4.9L I-6 EFI LPG
A	= 2.3L I-4 EFI
A	= 2.3L I-4 1BBL

LTV0500000000572

Fig. 4 Ford Motor Company (Part 2 of 3). Ford

DIGIT 8 Engine

B	= 2.0L I-4 SFI DOHC
C	= 7.3L V8 IDI TDsl
C	= 2.0L I-4 NFC
C	= 2.0L I-4 2BBL IFM
C	= 2.5L I-4 EFI SOHC
C	= 2.0L I-4 1BBL
C	= 7.3L V8 DI TDsl
D	= 4.2L V8 2BBL
E	= 4.0L V6 EFI SOHC
E	= 4.9L I-6 1BBL
E	= 2.5L I-4 TDsl
F	= 5.0L V8 2BBL
F	= 7.3L V8 DI TDsl
G	= 7.5L V8 EFI
G	= 5.8L V8 2BBL
H	= 5.8L V8 EFI HO
H	= 5.8L V8 EFI
H	= 2.3L I-4 w/AC Synchronous Motor
H	= 5.8L V8 4BBL HO
K	= 4.0L V6 EFI SOHC FFV
K	= 4.0L V6 EFI SOHC
K	= 7.3L V8 IDI TDsl
L	= 7.5L V8 4BBL
L	= 5.4L V8 EFI SOHC
M	= 7.3L V8 Dsl
M	= 5.4L V8 EFI SOHC CNG
N	= 5.0L V8 EFI
P	= 2.2L I-4 Dsl
P	= 5.0L V8 EFI
P	= 6.0L V8 DI TDsl
P	= 6.0L V8 FI Dsl
R	= 5.8L V8 EFI HP
S	= 6.8L V10 EFI SOHC
S	= 2.8L V6 2BBL
T	= 2.9L V6 EFI
U	= 3.0L V6 EFI
V	= 3.0L V6 EFI Flex Fuel Ethanol
W	= 4.6L V8 EFI
X	= 4.0L V6 EFI
Y	= 6.8L V10 EFI SOHC
Y	= 4.9L I-6 EFI
Y	= 4.9L I-6 1BBL
Z	= 5.4L V8 EFI SOHC GFP
Z	= 6.6L V8 2BBL
Z	= 4.9L I-6 EFI GFP
Z	= 2.3L I-4 DOHC

DIGIT 10 Model Year

1	= 2001
2	= 2002
3	= 2003
4	= 2004
5	= 2005
6	= 2006
B	= 1981
C	= 1982
D	= 1983
E	= 1984
F	= 1985
G	= 1986
H	= 1987
J	= 1988
K	= 1989
L	= 1990
M	= 1991
N	= 1992
P	= 1993
R	= 1994
S	= 1995
T	= 1996
V	= 1997

DIGIT 10 Model Year

W	= 1998
X	= 1999
Y	= 2000

DIGIT 11 Assembly Plant

0	= Hiroshima, Japan
0	= Detroit, MI, USA
B	= Oakville, ON, Canada
C	= Ontario Truck: Oakville, ON, Canada
D	= Avon Lake, OH, USA
E	= Kentucky Truck: Jefferson County, KY, USA
F	= Dearborn: Dearborn, MI, USA
G	= Chicago, Illinois
H	= Lorain, OH, USA
K	= Michigan Truck: Wayne, MI, USA
K	= Kansas City: Claycomo, MO, USA
K	= Kansas City: Claycomo, MO, USA
L	= Michigan Truck: Wayne, MI, USA
M	= Cuautitlan, Mexico
N	= Norfolk, VA, USA
P	= Twin Cities: St. Paul, MN, USA
R	= San Jose, CA, USA
T	= Edison, NJ, USA
U	= Louisville, KY, USA
V	= Kentucky Truck: Jefferson County, KY, USA
W	= Wayne, MI, USA
Z	= St. Louis: Hazelwood, MO, USA

LTV0500000000573

Fig. 4 Ford Motor Company (Part 3 of 3). Ford

DIGIT 1-3 World Manufacturer Identifier

5L1	= Ford Motor Co., USA, Limo
5LM	= Ford Motor Co., USA, MPV
5LT	= Ford Motor Co., USA, Truck (Complete Vehicle)

DIGIT 4 GVWR/Brake System

E	= 6001-7000 Lbs, Hydraulic
F	= 7001-8000 Lbs, Hydraulic
P	= 7001-8000 Lbs, Hydraulic
P	= 7000-8001 Lbs, Hydraulic
R	= 6001-7000 Lbs, Hydraulic

DIGIT 5-7 Line/Series/Body Type

U27	= Navigator 4D Utility 2WD
U28	= Navigator 4D Utility 4WD
U68	= Aviator 4D Utility 2WD
U78	= Aviator 4D Utility AWD
U88	= Aviator 4D Utility AWD
W05	= Blackwood 4D 2WD
W16	= Mark LT Supercrew 2WD
W18	= Mark LT Supercrew 4WD

DIGIT 8 Engine

5	= 5.4L V8 3V SOHC
5	= 5.4L V8 EFI DOHC
A	= 5.4L V8 EFI DOHC
H	= 4.6L V8 EFI
L	= 5.4L V8 EFI
R	= 5.4L V8 EFI DOHC

DIGIT 10 Model Year

1	= 2001
2	= 2002
3	= 2003
4	= 2004
5	= 2005
6	= 2006
W	= 1998
X	= 1999
Y	= 2000

DIGIT 11 Assembly Plant

F	= Dearborn, MI, USA
K	= Kansas City: Claycomo, MO, USA
L	= Wayne, MI, USA
Z	= St. Louis: Hazelwood, MO, USA

LTV0500000000581

Fig. 5 Ford Motor Company. Lincoln

DIGIT 1-3 World Manufacturer Identifier

2MR	= Ford Motor Company of Canada - Mercury, MPV
4M2	= Ford Motor Co., USA, MPV
4M3	= Ford Motor Co., USA, Incomplete Vehicle
4M4	= Ford Motor Co., USA, Truck (Completed Vehicle)

DIGIT 4 GVWR/Brake System

C	= 4001-5000 Lbs, Hydraulic
C	= 4001-5000 Lbs, Hydraulic, Dual Front Airbags w/Manual Bel
D	= 5001-6000 Lbs, Hydraulic
X	= 5001-6000 Lbs, Hydraulic
Y	= 4001-5000 Lbs, Hydraulic, Dual Front & Side Airbags w/Man
Y	= 4001-5000 Lbs, Hydraulic
Z	= 5001-6000 Lbs, Hydraulic

DIGIT 4* Brake Type/GVWR Class/Restraint

D	= Hydraulic, 5001-6000 Lbs, Dual Front & Front Side Airbags
Z	= Hydraulic, 5001-6000 Lbs, Dual Front Airbags

DIGIT 5-7 Line/Series/Body Type

A20	= Monterey 4D Wagon
A21	= Monterey 4D Wagon
A22	= Monterey 4D Wagon
A23	= Monterey 4D Wagon
U36	= Mountaineer 4D Utility - Convenience 2WD
U37	= Mountaineer 4D Utility - Luxury 2WD
U38	= Mountaineer 4D Utility - Premier 2WD
U46	= Mountaineer 4D Utility - Convenience AWD
U47	= Mountaineer 4D Utility - Luxury AWD
U48	= Mountaineer 4D Utility - Premier AWD
U52	= Mountaineer 4D Utility 2WD
U54	= Mountaineer 4D Utility 4WD
U55	= Mountaineer 4D Utility AWD
U56	= Mariner 4D Utility 2WD
U57	= Mariner 4D Utility AWD
U66	= Mountaineer 4D Utility 2WD
U66	= Mariner 4D Utility AWD
U76	= Mountaineer 4D Utility 4WD
U86	= Mountaineer 4D Utility AWD
V11	= Villager Wagon
V12	= Villager Sport Wagon
V14	= Villager Estate Wagon
V14	= Villager Cargo Van

DIGIT 8 Engine

1	= 3.0L V6 MPI
1	= 3.0L Duratec V6
2	= 4.2L V6 SPI
E	= 4.0L V6 EFI SOHC
K	= 4.0L V6 EFI SOHC FFV
P	= 5.0L V8 EFI
T	= 3.3L V6 MPI SOHC
W	= 3.0L V6 MPI SOHC
W	= 4.6L V8 EFI SOHC
Z	= 2.3L I4

DIGIT 10 Model Year

1	= 2001
2	= 2002
3	= 2003
4	= 2004
5	= 2005
6	= 2006
P	= 1993
R	= 1994
S	= 1995
T	= 1996
V	= 1997
W	= 1998
X	= 1999
Y	= 2000

DIGIT 11 Assembly Plant

B	= Oakville, Ontario, Canada

DIGIT 11 Assembly Plant

D	= Avon Lake, OH, USA
D	= Ohio Assembly Plant, Avon Lake, Ohio
U	= Louisville, KY, USA
Z	= St Louis: Hazelwood, MO

LTV0500000000582

Fig. 6 Ford Motor Company. Mercury

DIGIT 1 Country Of Origin

3	= Mexico
5	= USA

DIGIT 2 Manufacturer

G	= General Motors Corporation

DIGIT 3 Vehicle Type

5	= Buick MPV
A	= Buick MPV

DIGIT 4 GVWR/Brake System

D	= 5001-6000 Lbs, Hydraulic
E	= 6001-7000 Lbs, Hydraulic

DIGIT 5-6 Line Chassis/Series

A0	= Utility 4X2
B0	= Utility 4X4
S1	= Utility 4X2
T1	= Utility 4X4
V1	= Incomplete Mobility 4X2
V2	= Terraza CX 4X2
V3	= Terraza CXL 4X2
X2	= Terraza CX 4X4
X3	= Terraza CXL 4X4

DIGIT 7 Body Type

3	= 4D Utility

DIGIT 8 Engine

1	= 3.9L V6 SFI
7	= 3.6L V6 SFI DOHC
E	= 3.4L V6 MPI HO
L	= 3.5L V6 SFI
M	= 5.3L V8 SFI
P	= 5.3L V8 SFI
S	= 4.2L I6 MPI DOHC

DIGIT 10 Model Year

2	= 2002
3	= 2003
4	= 2004
5	= 2005
6	= 2006

DIGIT 11 Assembly Plant

2	= Moraine, OH, USA
D	= Doraville, GA, USA
S	= Ramos Arizpe, Mexico

LTV0500000000562

Fig. 7 General Motors Corporation. Buick

Fig. 8 — General Motors Corporation. Cadillac

DIGIT 1	Country Of Origin
1	= USA
3	= Mexico

DIGIT 2	Manufacturer
G	= General Motors Corporation

DIGIT 3	Vehicle Type
Y	= Cadillac MPV

DIGIT 4	GVWR/Brake System
D	= 5001-6000 Lbs, Hydraulic
E	= 6001-7000 Lbs, Hydraulic
F	= 7001-8000 Lbs, Hydraulic

DIGIT 5	Line & Chassis
C	= Conventional Cab 4X2
K	= Conventional Cab 4X4

DIGIT 5-6	Line Chassis/Series
E6	= SRX

DIGIT 6	Series
1	= 1/2 Ton
4	= 1/2 Ton Platinum
6	= 1/2 Ton Luxury

DIGIT 7	Body Type
2	= Sport Utility Truck
3	= 4D Utility
6	= Escalade ESV

DIGIT 8	Engine
7	= 3.6L V6 SFI
A	= 4.6L V8 SFI
N	= 6.0L V8 SFI
R	= 5.7L V8 CPI
T	= 5.3L V8 SFI

DIGIT 10	Model Year
2	= 2002
3	= 2003
4	= 2004
5	= 2005
6	= 2006
X	= 1999
Y	= 2000

DIGIT 11	Assembly Plant
0	= Grand River, MI, USA
0	= Lansing, MI, USA
B	= Lansing, MI, USA
G	= Silao, Mexico
L	= Lansing, MI, USA
R	= Arlington, TX, USA

LTV0500000000563

Fig. 8   General Motors Corporation. Cadillac

Fig. 9 — General Motors Corporation (Part 1 of 3). Chevrolet

DIGIT 1	Country Of Origin
1	= USA
2	= Canada
3	= Mexico
J	= Japan

DIGIT 2	Manufacturer
8	= Isuzu
C	= Cami/GM Of Canada/Suzuki J.V.
G	= General Motors Corp.

DIGIT 3	Vehicle Type/Make
8	= Chevrolet MPV
A	= Chevrolet Bus (Van W/4th Seat)
B	= Chevrolet Truck (Incomplete Vehicle)
C	= Chevrolet Truck (Complete Vehicle)
N	= Chevrolet MPV
Y	= Chevrolet Luv (Incomplete Vehicle)
Z	= Chevrolet Luv (Complete Vehicle)

DIGIT 4	GVWR/Brake System
B	= 10001-14000 Lbs, Hydraulic
C	= 3001-4000 Lbs, Hydraulic
C	= 4001-5000 Lbs, Hydraulic
D	= 5001-6000 Lbs, Hydraulic
E	= 6001-7000 Lbs, Hydraulic
F	= 7001-8000 Lbs, Hydraulic
F	= 7000-8000 Lbs, Hydraulic
G	= 8001-9000 Lbs, Hydraulic
H	= 9001-10000 Lbs, Hydraulic
J	= 10001-14000 Lbs, Hydraulic
K	= 1400-16000 Lbs, Hydraulic
L	= 16001-19500 Lbs, Hydraulic
M	= 19501-26000 Lbs, Air/Hydraulic

DIGIT 5	Series
4	= 4500 Series
4	= 4500 Series
C	= Conventional Cab 4X2
C	= Conventional Cab 4X2
E	= Compact Cab 4x2
E	= Compact Cab 4x2
G	= Van, Sport Van
G	= Van
G	= Van, Sport Van
J	= Compact Cab 4X4
J	= Compact Cab 4X4
K	= Conventional Cab 4X4
K	= Conventional Cab 4X4
L	= Luv 4X2
L	= Small Van 4X4
L	= Luv 4X2
M	= Small Van 4X2
M	= Small Van 4X2
P	= Forward Control 4X2
P	= Forward Control 4X2
R	= Conventional Cab 4X2
R	= Luv 4X4
R	= Luv 4X4
S	= Small Cab 4X2
S	= Small Cab 4X2
T	= Small Cab 4X4
T	= Small Cab 4X4
U	= All Purpose Vehicle
U	= All Purpose Vehicle
V	= Conventional Cab 4X4
V	= Conventional Cab 4X4
W	= EL Camino
W	= EL Camino
X	= All Purpose Vehicle - Extended Wheelbase
X	= All Purpose Vehicle - Extended Wheelbase

DIGIT 5-6	Line Chassis/Series
C1	= Astro 4X2
C1	= Full Size Truck 4X2, 1500
C2	= Full Size Truck 4X2, 2500
C3	= Full Size Truck 4X2, 3500
C6	= Full Size Truck 4X2, 1500 Luxury
C7	= Full Size Truck 4X2, 2500 Luxury
C8	= Full Size Truck 4X2, 3500 Luxury
C8	= Full Size Truck 4X2, Luxury 3500
E1	= Tracker 4X2
E6	= Tracker 4X2 LT
G1	= Express 4X2 1500
G2	= Express 4X2 2500
G3	= Express 4X2 3500
G6	= Express 4X2 1500, Luxury
G7	= Express 4X2 2500, Luxury
G8	= Express 4X2 3500, Luxury
H1	= Express 4X4 1500
H2	= Express 4X4 2500
J1	= Tracker 4X4
J6	= Tracker 4X4 LT
J7	= Tracker 4X4 ZR2 Sport
K1	= Astro 4X4
K1	= Full Size Truck 4X4, 1500
K2	= Full Size Truck 4X4, 2500
K3	= Full Size Truck 4X4, 3500
K6	= Full Size Truck 4X4, 1500 Luxury
K7	= Full Size Truck 4X4, 2500 Luxury
K8	= Full Size Truck 4X4, Luxury 3500
K8	= Full Size Truck 4X4, 3500 Luxury
L1	= Astro 4X4
L1	= Equinox 4X2 LS
L1	= Equinox 4X2
L2	= Equinox 4X4
L2	= Equinox 4X4 LS
L6	= Astro 4X4 Luxury
L6	= Equinox 4X2 LT
L7	= Equinox 4X4 LT
M1	= Astro 4X2
M6	= Astro 4X2 Luxury
P3	= P30 Aluminum Body, Step Van
S0	= Blazer 4X2, Base
S0	= Full Size Truck 4X2 - 1SA Trim
S0	= Trailblazer 4X2, Base
S1	= Full Size Truck 4X2 - 1SB Trim
S1	= S10 4X2
S1	= Colorado 4X2
S1	= Blazer 4X2, LS
S1	= Blazer 4X2
S1	= Full Size Truck 4X2
S2	= Trailblazer 4X2
S2	= Trailblazer 4X2, LT
S6	= S10 4X2 Luxury
T0	= Blazer 4X4, Base
T0	= Full Size Truck 4X2 - 1SA Trim
T0	= Trailblazer 4X4, Base
T1	= Blazer 4X4
T1	= Trailblazer 4X4, LS
T1	= Trailblazer 4X4
T1	= S10 4X4
T1	= Full Size Truck 4X2, LS
T1	= Blazer 4X4, LS
T1	= Colorado 4X4
T2	= Trailblazer 4X4, LT
T6	= S10 4X4 Luxury
U0	= Venture APV 4X2
U0	= Uplander APV 4X2, Base
U1	= Uplander APV 4X2, Cargo
U1	= Venture APV 4X2 Luxury
U2	= Venture APV 4X2 Economy
U2	= Uplander APV 4X2, Economy

LTV0500000000564

Fig. 9   General Motors Corporation (Part 1 of 3). Chevrolet

Fig. 9 — General Motors Corporation (Part 2 of 3). Chevrolet

DIGIT 5-6	Line Chassis/Series
U3	= Uplander APV 4X2, LT
V0	= Uplander APV 4X2, Base Ext
V0	= Venture APV 4X2 Extended
V0	= Venture APV 4X4
V1	= Venture APV 4X4 Luxury
V1	= Uplander APV 4X2, Cargo Ext
V1	= Venture APV 4X2 Extended Cargo
V2	= Venture APV 4X4 Economy
V2	= Uplander APV 4X2, LS Ext
V2	= Venture APV 4X2 Extended Economy
V3	= Uplander APV 4X2, LT Ext
V3	= Venture APV 4X2 Extended Luxury
X0	= Uplander APV AWD, Base
X0	= Venture APV 4X2 Extended
X1	= Uplander, APV AWD, Cargo
X1	= Venture APV 4X2 Luxury Extended
X2	= Venture APV 4X2 Economy Extended
X2	= Uplander, APV AWD, LS
X3	= Uplander, APV AWD, LT

DIGIT 6	Truck Line & Cab Type
0	= All Purpose Vehicle
0	= All Purpose Vehicle
1	= 1/2 Ton
1	= 1/2 Ton
2	= 3/4 Ton
2	= 3/4 Ton
3	= 1 Ton
3	= 1 Ton
8	= 1/2 Ton
8	= 1/2 Ton
B	= Forward/Tiltmaster Medium, Tilt, 67.9 BBC
B	= Forward/Tiltmaster Medium, Tilt, 67.9 BBC

DIGIT 7	Body Type
0	= Chassis Cab
0	= Sedan Pickup
1	= Hi-cube/Cutaway
1	= Forward Control
2	= Sport Utility Truck
3	= 4D All Purpose Vehicle
3	= 4D Cab/Utility
3	= 4D Utility
3	= Crew Cab
4	= 4D Cab
4	= 2D Cab
4	= Ext Cab
4	= Extended Cab
5	= Van
6	= Suburban
6	= All Purpose Vehicle
6	= 4D Extended Utility
8	= 2D Utility
9	= Extended Cab
9	= Extended Van

DIGIT 7*	Chassis Type
1	= 4X2 (2 Axles - 1 Driving)

DIGIT 8	Engine
1	= 6.6L V8 FI DSL
2	= 6.6L V8 OHV Tbo Dsl
2	= 6.6L V8 FI DSL
4	= 2.2L I-4 MPI
4	= 2.5L V6 MPI
4	= 2.2L I-4 SFI Flex Fuel
6	= 3.5L I5 DOHC MPI
6	= 1.6L I-4 MPI
8	= 2.8L I4 DOHC MPI
9	= 3.4L V6 SFI OHV
A	= 3.8L V6 2BBL
A	= 2.5L I4 TBI
A	= 1.9L I-4 2BBL
B	= 5.3L V8 SFI
B	= 2.8L V6 2BBL
B	= 4.3L V6 EFI HO
C	= 6.2L V8 Dsl
C	= 6.2L V8 FI DSL
C	= 2.0L I-4 2BBL
D	= 4.1L I-4 2BBL
D	= 3.1L V6 TBI
E	= 8.1L V8 MPI
E	= 5.0L V8 TBI
E	= 3.4L V6 SFI HO
E	= 3.4L V6 MPI
F	= 2.5L I-4 TBI
F	= 6.5L V8 FI TDsl HO
F	= 3.4L V6 SFI
F	= 5.0L V8 4BBL
F	= 6.5L V8 FI TDSL
G	= 8.1L V8 MFI
G	= 8.1L V8 SFI OHV
G	= 5.0L V8 2BBL
H	= 2.2L I-4 MFI
H	= 5.0L V8 4BBL
H	= 5.0L V8 TBI
H	= 6.0L OHV SFI V8
J	= 6.2L V8 FI DSL
J	= 6.2L V8 DSL
J	= 7.4L V8 MPI HO
K	= 4.4L V8 4BBL
K	= 3.8L V6 2BBL
K	= 5.7L V8 TBI
K	= 5.7L V8 TBI CNG Capable
L	= 5.7L V8 4BBL
L	= 3.5L V6 SFI
L	= 3.8L V6 MPI
M	= 5.3L V8 SFI OHV
M	= 5.7L V8 4BBL
M	= 5.0L V8 MPI
M	= 5.0L V8 CPI
M	= 5.7L V8 4BBL
N	= 1.8L I-4 2BBL
N	= 4.3L V6 4BBL
N	= 5.7L V8 FI DSL
N	= 6.0L V8 MFI HO
N	= 6.0L V8 SFI
N	= 7.4L V8 TBI
P	= 5.3L V8 SFI Alum
P	= 6.5L V8 FI DSL
R	= 5.7L V8 CPI
R	= 5.7L V8 TBI
R	= 5.7L V8 SFI
R	= 5.7L V8 SFI CNG Capable
S	= 2.8L V6 TBI
S	= 6.5L V8 FI TDsl
S	= 2.2L I-4 DSL
S	= 2.2L I-4 FI DSL
S	= 4.2L I-6 MPI DOHC
S	= 6.5L V8 FI TDsl HO
T	= 5.3L V8 SFI
T	= 4.8L I-6 1BBL
T	= 5.3L V8 SFI
U	= 6.0L V8 MFI
V	= 4.8L V8 SFI
W	= 5.0L V8 CPI
W	= 7.4L V8 4BBL
X	= 4.3L V6 MFI
X	= 4.3L V6 CPI
X	= 4.3L V6 SFI

LTV0500000000565

Fig. 9   General Motors Corporation (Part 2 of 3). Chevrolet

Fig. 9 — General Motors Corporation (Part 3 of 3). Chevrolet

DIGIT 8	Engine
Y	= 2.0L I-4 2BBL
Y	= 6.5L V8 Dsl HO
Y	= 6.5L V8 FI Dsl HO
Z	= 4.3L V6 CPI
Z	= 4.3L V6 TBI
Z	= 5.3L V8 SFI Flex Fuel
Z	= 5.7L V8 FI DSL

DIGIT 10	Model Year
1	= 2001
2	= 2002
3	= 2003
4	= 2004
5	= 2005
6	= 2006
B	= 1981
C	= 1982
D	= 1983
E	= 1984
F	= 1985
G	= 1986
H	= 1987
J	= 1988
K	= 1989
L	= 1990
M	= 1991
N	= 1992
P	= 1993
R	= 1994
S	= 1995
T	= 1996
V	= 1997
W	= 1998
X	= 1999
Y	= 2000

DIGIT 11	Assembly Plant
P	= Pontiac, MI, USA
R	= Arlington, TX, USA
S	= St. Louis, MO, USA
S	= Ramos Arizpe, Mexico
T	= Tarrytown, NY, USA
U	= Hamtramck, MI, USA
V	= Pontiac, MI, USA
W	= Willow Run, MI, USA
Z	= Ft. Wayne, IN, USA

DIGIT 11	Assembly Plant
0	= Pontiac West, MI, USA
0	= Lansing, MI, USA
1	= Wentzville, MO, USA
1	= Oshawa, ON, Canada
1	= Oshawa #2, ON, Canada
2	= Moraine, OH, USA
3	= Detroit, MI, USA
3	= St. Eustache, PQ, Canada
4	= Orion, MI, USA
4	= Scarborough, ON, Canada
5	= Bowling Green, KY, USA
5	= London, ON, Canada
6	= Ingersoll, ON, Canada
6	= Oklahoma City, OK, USA
7	= Lordstown, OH, USA
8	= Fujusawa, Japan
8	= Shreveport, LA, USA
8	= Oshawa #1, ON, Canada
A	= Lakewood, GA, USA
A	= Baltimore, MD, USA
B	= Lansing, MI, USA
C	= Charlotte, Nc, USA
C	= Southgate, CA, USA
C	= Lansing, MI, USA
D	= Doraville, GA, USA
E	= Linden, NJ, USA
E	= Pontiac East, MI, USA
F	= Flint, MI, USA
G	= Silao, Mexico
H	= Flint, MI, USA
J	= Janesville, WI, USA
K	= Linden, NJ, USA
L	= Van Nuys, CA, USA
M	= Toluca, Mexico

LTV0500000000566

Fig. 9   General Motors Corporation (Part 3 of 3). Chevrolet

Fig. 10 Part 1 of 3

DIGIT 1   Country Of Origin
1 = USA
2 = Canada
3 = Mexico

DIGIT 2   Manufacturer
G = General Motors Corp.

DIGIT 3   Vehicle Type
0 = GMC Van w/4th Seat
5 = GMC MPV
D = GMC Truck (Incomplete Vehicle)
J = GMC Bus (Van W/4th Seat)
K = GMC MPV
T = GMC Truck (Complete Vehicle)

DIGIT 4   GVWR/Brake System
B = 3001-4000 Lbs, Hydraulic
B = 10001-14000 Lbs, Hydraulic
C = 4001-5000 Lbs, Hydraulic
D = 5001-6000 Lbs, Hydraulic
E = 6001-7000 Lbs, Hydraulic
F = 7001-8000 Lbs, Hydraulic
G = 8001-9000 Lbs, Hydraulic
H = 9001-10000 Lbs, Hydraulic
J = 10001-14000 Lbs, Hydraulic
K = 14001-16000 Lbs, Hydraulic

DIGIT 5   Series
4 = 4500 Series
4 = 4500 Series
C = Conventional Cab 4X2
C = Conventional Cab 4X2
G = Van
G = Van
K = Conventional Cab 4X4
K = Conventional Cab 4X4
L = Small Van 4X4
L = Small Van 4X4
M = Small Van 4X2
M = Small Van 4X2
P = Forward Control
P = Forward Control
R = Conventional Cab 4X2
R = Conventional Cab 4X2
S = Small Cab 4X2
S = Small Cab 4X2
T = Small Cab 4X4
T = Small Cab 4X4
V = Conventional Cab 4X4
V = Conventional Cab 4X4
W = Caballero 4X2
W = Caballero 4X2

DIGIT 5-6   Line Chassis/Series
C1 = Full Size Truck 4X2, 1500
C2 = Full Size Truck 4X2, 2500
C3 = Full Size Truck 4X2, 3500
C6 = Full Size Truck 4X2, 1500 Luxury
C7 = Full Size Truck 4X2, 2500 Luxury
C7 = Full Size Truck 4X2, Luxury 2500
C8 = Full Size Truck 4X2, Luxury 3500
C8 = Full Size Truck 4X2, 3500 Luxury
G1 = Savana 4X2, 1500
G2 = Savana 4X2, 2500
G3 = Savana 4X2, 3500
G3 = G3500
G6 = Savana 4X2, 1500 Luxury
G7 = Savana 4X2, 2500 Luxury
G8 = Savana 4X2, 3500 Luxury
H1 = Savana 4X4, 1500
H2 = Savana 4X4, 2500
H6 = Savana 4X4, 1500 Luxury
H7 = Savana 4X4, 2500 Luxury

DIGIT 5-6   Line Chassis/Series
K1 = Full Size Truck 4X4, 1500
K2 = Full Size Truck 4X4, 2500
K3 = Full Size Truck 4X4, 3500
K6 = Full Size Truck 4X4, 1500 Luxury
K7 = Full Size Truck 4X4, Luxury 2500
K7 = Full Size Truck 4X4, 2500 Luxury
K8 = Full Size Truck 4X4, 3500 Luxury
K8 = Full Size Truck 4X4, Luxury 3500
L1 = Safari 4X4
L6 = Safari 4X4 Luxury
M1 = Safari 4X2
M6 = Safari 4X2 Luxury
P3 = P3500 Aluminum Body Step Van
S0 = Canyon Z85 SL 4X2
S0 = Envoy 4X2 SLE
S1 = Envoy XUV 4X2
S1 = Canyon 4X2
S1 = Canyon Z85 SLE 4X2
S1 = Envoy 4X2
S1 = Envoy XL 4X2
S1 = Jimmy 4X2
S1 = Sonoma 4X2
S1 = Envoy 4X2 SLE
S2 = Canyon Z71 SL 4X2
S2 = Envoy 4X2 SLT
S3 = Canyon Z71 SLE 4X2
S3 = Envoy 4X2 SLT
S6 = Canyon 4X2 Luxury
S6 = Envoy 4X2 Luxury
S6 = Sonoma 4X2 Luxury
S6 = Jimmy 4X2 Luxury
S6 = Envoy 4X2 Denali
S6 = Envoy XL 4X2 Luxury
S6 = Envoy XUV 4X2 Luxury
T0 = Canyon Z85 SL 4X4
T0 = Envoy 4X4 SLE
T1 = Envoy 4X4
T1 = Sonoma 4X4
T1 = Jimmy 4X4
T1 = Envoy XUV 4X4
T1 = Envoy 4X4 SLE
T1 = Canyon Z85 SLE 4X4
T1 = Envoy 4X4
T1 = Envoy XL 4X4
T2 = Canyon Z71 SL 4X4
T2 = Envoy 4X4 SLT
T3 = Envoy 4X4 SLT
T3 = Canyon Z71 SLE 4X4
T6 = Canyon 4X4 Luxury
T6 = Envoy 4X4 Luxury
T6 = Envoy XL 4X4 Luxury
T6 = Envoy XUV 4X4 Luxury
T6 = Jimmy 4X4 Luxury
T6 = Sonoma 4X4 Luxury
T6 = Envoy 4X4 Denali

DIGIT 6   Series
1 = 1/2 Ton
1 = 1/2 Ton
2 = 3/4 Ton
2 = 3/4 Ton
3 = 1 Ton
3 = 1 Ton
8 = 1/2 Ton
8 = 1/2 Ton
B = Forward/Tiltmaster Medium, Tilt 67.9 BBC
B = Forward/Tiltmaster Medium, Tilt 67.9 BBC

DIGIT 7   Body Type
0 = Sedan Pickup
1 = Commercial Special & RV Cutaway
2 = Envoy XUV

LTV0500000000574

Fig. 10 General Motors Corporation (Part 1 of 3).
GMC

Fig. 10 Part 2 of 3

DIGIT 7   Body Type
2 = Forward Control
3 = 4D Utility
3 = Crew Cab
3 = 4D Crew Cab
3 = 4D Cab/Utility
4 = 2D Cab
5 = Van
6 = Envoy XL
6 = Suburban
6 = Yukon XL
7 = 2D Utility
9 = Extended Cab
9 = Extended Van

DIGIT 7*   Chassis Type
1 = 4X2 (2 Axles - 1 Driving)

DIGIT 8   Engine
1 = 6.6L V8 FI DSL
2 = 6.6L V8 FI DSL
4 = 2.2L I-4 MPI
5 = 2.2L I-4 SFI Flex Fuel
6 = 3.5L I5 DOHC MPI
8 = 2.8L I4 DOHC MPI
A = 2.5L I-4 FI
A = 3.8L V6 2BBL
A = 1.9L I-4 2BBL
B = 4.3L V6 EFI HO
B = 5.3L V8 SFI H/O
B = 2.8L V6 2BBL
C = 6.2L V8 DSL
C = 6.2L V8 FI CSL
D = 4.1L I-6 2BBL
E = 8.1L V8 MFI
E = 2.5L I-4 FI
E = 2.5L I-4 TBI
E = 5.0L V8 TBI
F = 5.0L V8 4BBL
F = 6.5L V8 FI TDSL
F = 6.5L V8 FI TDsl HO
F = 6.5L V8 FI TSDL HO
G = 5.0L V8 4BBL
G = 8.1L V8 MFI
G = 5.0L V8 2BBL
G = 8.1L V8 SFI
H = 2.2L I-4 MPI
H = 5.0L V8 4BBL
H = 5.0L V8 TBI
J = 6.2L V8 FI DSL
J = 4.4L V8 2BBL
J = 6.2L V8 Dsl
J = 7.4L V8 MPI HO
K = 5.7L V8 TbI/LPG
K = 3.8L V6 2B3L
K = 5.7L V8 TBI CNG Capable
L = 5.7L V8 4B3L
L = 5.7L V8 4B3L
E = 5.7L V8 4B3L
M = 5.7L V8 4B3L
M = 5.0L V8 CPI
M = 5.0L V8 MFI
M = 5.0L V8 SFI
M = 5.3L V8 SFI
N = 5.7L V8 DSL
N = 6.0L V8 SFI
N = 7.4L V8 FI
N = 7.4L V8 TBI
N = 4.3L V6 4BBL
P = 4.8L V8 SFI
P = 5.3L V8 SFI
P = 5.7L V8 MPI
P = 6.5L V8 FI DSL

DIGIT 8   Engine
P = 5.7L V8 MFI
R = 5.7L V8 SFI CNG Capable
R = 5.7L V8 SFI
R = 5.7L V8 CPI
R = 2.8L V6 TBI
R = 2.8L V6 FI
S = 6.5L V8 FI TDsl HO
S = 6.5L V8 FI TDsl
S = 2.2L I-4 FI DSL
S = 4.2L I-6 MPI DOHC
T = 4.8L I-6 1BBL
T = 5.3L V8 MFI
T = 5.3L V8 SFI
T = 5.3L V8 MFI
U = 6.0L V8 MPI
V = 4.8L V8 SFI
V = 4.8L V8 SFI
W = 4.3L V6 MPI
W = 4.3L V6 MPI
W = 7.4L V8 MFI
X = 4.3L V6 CPI
X = 4.3L V6 MPI
Y = 6.5L V8 FI DSL
Y = 6.5L V8 FI Dsl HO
Y = 2.0L I-4 2BBL
Z = 5.7L V8 DSL
Z = 4.3L V6 CPI
Z = 4.3L V6 TBI
Z = 5.3L V8 SFI Flex Fuel

DIGIT 10   Model Year
1 = 2001
2 = 2002
3 = 2003
4 = 2004
5 = 2005
6 = 2006
B = 1981
C = 1982
D = 1983
E = 1984
F = 1985
G = 1986
H = 1987
J = 1988
K = 1989
L = 1990
M = 1991
N = 1992
P = 1993
R = 1994
S = 1995
T = 1996
V = 1997
W = 1998
X = 1999
Y = 2000

DIGIT 11   Assembly Plant
0 = Pontiac West, MI, USA
1 = Oshawa #2, ON, Canada
1 = Oshawa (T&B), ON, Canada
1 = Oshawa, ON, Canada
1 = Wentzville, MO, USA
2 = Moraine, OH, USA
3 = Detroit, MI, USA
3 = St. Eustache, PQ, Canada
4 = Scarborough, ON, Canada
6 = Oklahoma City, OK, USA

LTV0500000000575

Fig. 10 General Motors Corporation (Part 2 of 3).
GMC

DIGIT 11   Assembly Plant

7 = Lordstown, OH, USA
8 = Shreveport, LA, USA
9 = Oshawa #1, ON, Canada
B = Baltimore, MD, USA
E = Pontiac East, MI, USA
E = Pontiac East, USA
E = Pontiac, MI, USA
F = Flint, MI, USA
G = Silao, Mexico
H = Flint, MI, USA
J = Janesville, WI, USA
K = Linden, NJ, USA
L = Van Nuys, CA, USA
R = Arlington, TX, USA
S = Ramos Arizpe, Mexico
S = St. Louis, MO, USA
V = Pontiac, MI, USA
Z = Ft. Wayne, IN, USA

LTV0500000000576

Fig. 10 General Motors Corporation (Part 3 of 3). GMC

DIGIT 1   Country Of Origin
1   = USA

DIGIT 2   Manufacturer
G   = General Motors Corporation

DIGIT 3   Vehicle Type
H   = Oldsmobile APV/MPV

DIGIT 4   GVWR/Brake System
C   = 4001-5000 Lbs, Hydraulic
D   = 5001-6000 Lbs, Hydraulic

DIGIT 5   Line & Chassis
T   = Small Conventional Cab 4X4
U   = All Purpose Vehicle 4X2
X   = All Purpose Vehicle Ext 4X2

DIGIT 5-6   Line Chassis/Series
S1   = Bravada 4X2
S6   = Bravada 4X2 Luxury
T1   = Bravada 4X4
T6   = Bravada 4X4 Luxury
V0   = Silhouette 4X4
V1   = Silhouette 4X4 Luxury
V2   = Silhouette 4X4 Economy
X0   = Silhouette 4X2 Ext
X1   = Silhouette 4X2 Luxury Ext
X2   = Silhouette 4X2 Economy Ext

DIGIT 6   Series
0   = APV
1   = 1/2 Ton

DIGIT 7   Body Type
3   = 4D Utility
6   = All Purpose Vehicle

DIGIT 8   Engine
D   = 3.1L V6 TBI
E   = 3.4L V6 SFI
L   = 3.8L V6 MFI
S   = 4.2L I-6 MFI, DOHC
S   = 4.2L I-6 SFI
W   = 4.3L V6 CPI
Z   = 4.3L V6 TBI

DIGIT 10   Model Year
1   = 2001
2   = 2002
3   = 2003
4   = 2004
L   = 1990
M   = 1991
N   = 1992
P   = 1993
R   = 1994
S   = 1995
T   = 1996
V   = 1997
W   = 1998
X   = 1999
Y   = 2000

DIGIT 11   Assembly Plant
2   = Moraine, OH, USA
D   = Doraville, GA, USA
J   = Janesville, WI, USA
T   = Tarrytown, NY, USA

LTV0500000000583

Fig. 11   General Motors Corporation. Oldsmobile

DIGIT 1   Country Of Origin
1   = USA
3   = Mexico

DIGIT 2   Manufacturer
G   = General Motors Corporation

DIGIT 3   Vehicle Type
7   = APV
M   = APV

DIGIT 4   GVWR/Brake System
C   = 4001-5000 Lbs, Hydraulic
D   = 5001-6000 Lbs, Hydraulic

DIGIT 5   Line & Chassis
U   = All Purpose Vehicle 2WD
X   = All Purpose Vehicle Ext 2WD

DIGIT 5-6   Line Chassis/Series
A0   = Aztek SRV 4X2
B0   = Aztek SRV 4X4
U0   = Montana 4X2
U1   = Montana 4X2 Luxury
U2   = Montana 4X2 Economy
V0   = Montana 4X2 Ext Economy
V0   = Montana 4X2
V1   = Montana 4X4 Luxury
V1   = Montana 4X2 Ext Cargo
V2   = Montana 4X4 Economy
V2   = Montana 4X2 Ext Luxury
V3   = Montana 4X2 Ext
X0   = Montana 4X2 Ext
X1   = Montana 4X2 Ext Luxury
X2   = Montana 4X4 Ext Economy
X2   = Montana 4X2 Ext Economy
X3   = Montana 4X4 Ext Luxury

DIGIT 6   Series
0   = All Purpose Vehicle

DIGIT 7   Body Type
3   = 4D APV
6   = All Purpose Vehicle
6   = APV

DIGIT 8   Engine
D   = 3.1L V6 TBI
E   = 3.4L V6 SFI
L   = 3.5L V6 SFI
L   = 3.8L V6 MFI

DIGIT 10   Model Year
1   = 2001
2   = 2002
3   = 2003
4   = 2004
5   = 2005
L   = 1990
M   = 1991
N   = 1992
P   = 1993
R   = 1994
S   = 1995
T   = 1996
V   = 1997
W   = 1998
X   = 1999
Y   = 2000

DIGIT 11   Assembly Plant
D   = Doraville, GA, USA
S   = Ramos Arizpe, Mexico
T   = Tarrytown, NY, USA

LTV0500000000584

Fig. 12   General Motors Corporation. Pontiac

DIGIT 1-3   World Manufacturer Identifier
1G8   = Saturn MPV
5GZ   = Saturn MPV

DIGIT 4   GVWR/Brake System
C   = 4001-5000 Lbs, Hydraulic
D   = 5001-6000 Lbs, Hydraulic
Z   = Saturn SL

DIGIT 5-6   Line & Chassis
S5   = FWS 6 Cylinder SL
U0   = Level 2 Wagon
U1   = Level 2 Wagon
U2   = Level 2 Wagon
U3   = Level 2 Wagon
V0   = Level 3 Wagon
V1   = Level 3 Wagon
V2   = Level 3 Wagon
V3   = Level 3 Wagon
X0   = Level 3 AWD Wagon
X1   = Level 3 AWD Wagon
X2   = Level 3 AWD Wagon
X3   = Level 3 AWD Wagon
Z2   = FWD Manual
Z3   = FWD Auto
Z4   = AWD 4 Cylinder
Z5   = FWD 6 Cylinder
Z6   = AWD 6 Cylinder

DIGIT 7   Body Type
2   = FWD
3   = 4D All-Purpose Vehicle

DIGIT 8   Engine
4   = 3.5L V6 MPI SOHC
8   = 3.0L MFI DOHC HO V6 - Flt
B   = 3.0L V6 MPI DOHC
D   = 2.2L I-4 MPI DOHC
L   = 3.5L V6 SFI OHV

DIGIT 10   Model Year
2   = 2002
3   = 2003
4   = 2004
5   = 2005
6   = 2006

DIGIT 11   Assembly Plant
D   = Doraville, GA, USA
S   = Spring Hill, TN, USA
Y   = Wilmington, DE, USA
Z   = Spring Hill, TN, USA

LTV0500000000585

Fig. 13   Saturn

TABLE OF CONTENTS

	Page No.		Page No.
DAIMLERCHRYSLER	0-9	GENERAL MOTORS CORP.	0-15
FORD MOTOR CO.	0-9		

DaimlerChrysler

INDEX

	Page No.
Arming	0-9
Disarming	0-9

DISARMING

1. Place ignition switch in Lock position.
2. Disconnect and isolate battery ground cable.
3. **Wait at least 2 minutes after disconnecting battery ground cable before performing any further repairs on vehicle. The system is designed to retain enough voltage to deploy air bags for a short time even after battery has been disconnected.**

ARMING

1. **Ensure no one is inside vehicle.**
2. Connect battery ground cable.
3. Turn ignition switch to On position, **from a safe position below or at the sides of air bag modules.**
4. SRS warning lamp should light for 6–8 seconds, then remain off for at least 45 seconds to indicate SRS is functioning properly.
5. If air bag warning lamp fails to light, or goes on and stays on, there is a system fault. Refer to **MOTOR's "Air Bag Manual" or "Air Bag Diagnostics CD."**

Ford Motor Co.

INDEX

	Page No.		Page No.		Page No.
Arming	0-11	F150	0-13	Expedition & Navigator	0-10
Aviator	0-11	Mark LT	0-14	Explorer & Mountaineer	0-10
Blackwood	0-11	Ranger	0-14	Explorer Sport & Explorer	
Econoline	0-12	Villager	0-14	Sport-Trac	0-10
Escape & Mariner	0-12	Windstar	0-14	F150	0-11
Excursion & F-Super Duty		Disarming	0-9	Freestar & Monterey	0-11
250-350	0-12	Aviator	0-9	Mark LT	0-11
Expedition & Navigator	0-12	Blackwood	0-9	Ranger	0-11
Explorer & Mountaineer	0-13	Econoline	0-10	Villager	0-11
Explorer Sport & Explorer		Escape & Mariner	0-10	Windstar	0-11
Sport-Trac	0-13	Excursion & F-Super Duty			
Freestar & Monterey	0-13	250-350	0-10		

DISARMING

Aviator

To avoid accidental deployment and possible personal injury, the back-up power supply must be depleted before repairing or replacing any air bag supplemental restraint system component.

1. Ensure all vehicle accessories are in Off position.
2. Ensure ignition switch is in Off position.
3. Remove restraints control module (RCM) fuse F2.12 (15A) from central junction box (CJB).
4. Turn ignition switch to On position and visually monitor air bag indicator for 30 seconds. Air bag indicator will remain lit continuously if correct RCM fuse has been removed. Remove correct RCM fuse as required.
5. Turn ignition switch to Off position.
6. Disconnect battery ground cable and wait at least 1 minute prior to any service or repair.

Blackwood

1. Move and tilt front seats to highest and rearmost position.
2. Disconnect battery ground cable and isolate.
3. **On models equipped with auxiliary batteries and power supplies,** disconnect ground cables and isolate.
4. **On all models,** wait at least one minute for back-up power supply to deplete stored energy.

5. Remove driver air bag module as outlined under "Component Service."
6. Connect restraint system diagnostic tool No. 105-R0012, or equivalent, to clockspring side of driver side air bag module electrical connector.
7. Remove instrument panel relay cover from top of instrument panel.
8. Remove passenger air bag module as outlined under "Component Service."
9. Connect restraint system diagnostic tool No. 105-R0012, or equivalent, in place of passenger air bag module.
10. **On models less side impact air bag modules, do not disconnect side impact air bag bridge resistors.**
11. **On models equipped with side impact air bags modules,** proceed as follows:
    a. Disconnect driver and passenger side impact air bag module electrical connectors located under seats.
    b. Connect restraint system diagnostic tools Nos. 40-009, or equivalent, to side impact air bag modules' electrical connectors.
12. **On all models,** disconnect seat belt retractor and pretensioner electrical connectors behind B-pillar.
13. Connect restraint system diagnostic tools No. 40-009, or equivalent, to seat belt retractor and pretensioner electrical connectors.
14. Connect battery ground cable.

Econoline

To avoid accidental deployment and possible personal injury, the back-up power supply must be depleted before repairing or replacing any air bag supplemental restraint system component.
1. Ensure all vehicle accessories are in Off position.
2. Ensure ignition switch is in Off position.
3. **On 2002–03 models,** remove electronic crash sensor (ECS) module fuse F2.19 (10A) and F2.38 (10A) from central junction box (CJB).
4. **On 2004–06 models,** remove restraints control module (RCM) fuse F2.20 (10A) from central junction box (CJB).
5. **On all models,** turn ignition switch to On position and visually monitor air bag indicator for 30 seconds. Air bag indicator will remain lit continuously if correct RCM fuse has been removed. Remove correct RCM fuse as required.
6. Turn ignition switch to Off position.
7. Disconnect battery ground cable and wait at least 1 minute prior to any service or repair.

Escape & Mariner .

To avoid accidental deployment and possible personal injury, the back-up power supply must be depleted before repairing or replacing any air bag supplemental restraint system component.

For Hybrid models, refer to "High-Voltage Traction Battery Systems De-Powering" in "2.3L Engine" section of chassis chapter for required safety precautions
1. Ensure all vehicle accessories are in Off position.
2. Ensure ignition switch is in Off position.
3. **On 2002–04 models,** remove restraints control module (RCM) fuses F2.5 (5A) and F2.7 (10A) from central junction box (CJB).
4. **On 2005–06 models,** remove restraints control module (RCM) fuse F33 (15A) from central junction box (CJB).
5. **On all models,** turn ignition switch to On position and visually monitor air bag indicator for 30 seconds. Air bag indicator will remain lit continuously if correct RCM fuse has been removed. Remove correct RCM fuse as required.
6. Turn ignition switch to Off position.
7. Disconnect battery ground cable and wait at least 1 minute prior to any service or repair.

Excursion & F-Super Duty 250-350

To avoid accidental deployment and possible personal injury, the back-up power supply must be depleted before repairing or replacing any air bag supplemental restraint system component.
1. Ensure all vehicle accessories are in Off position.
2. Ensure ignition switch is in Off position.
3. Remove restraints control module (RCM) fuse F2.26 (10A) from central junction box (CJB).
4. Turn ignition switch to On position and visually monitor air bag indicator for 30 seconds. Air bag indicator will remain lit continuously if correct RCM fuse has been removed. Remove correct RCM fuse as required.
5. Turn ignition switch to Off position.
6. Disconnect battery ground cable and wait at least 1 minute prior to any service or repair.

Expedition & Navigator

To avoid accidental deployment and possible personal injury, the back-up power supply must be depleted before repairing or replacing any air bag supplemental restraint system component.
1. Ensure all vehicle accessories are in Off position.
2. Ensure ignition switch is in Off position.
3. **On 2002 models,** remove restraints control module (RCM) fuse F22 (10A) from central junction box (CJB).
4. **On 2003–06 models,** remove restraints control module (RCM) fuse F1.19 (10A) from central junction box (CJB).
5. **On all models,** turn ignition switch to On position and visually monitor air bag indicator for 30 seconds. Air bag indicator will remain lit continuously if correct RCM fuse has been removed.

Remove correct RCM fuse as required.
6. Turn ignition switch to Off position.
7. Disconnect battery ground cable and wait at least 1 minute prior to any service or repair.

Explorer & Mountaineer

To avoid accidental deployment and possible personal injury, the back-up power supply must be depleted before repairing or replacing any air bag supplemental restraint system component.
1. Ensure all vehicle accessories are in Off position.
2. Ensure ignition switch is in Off position.
3. **On models built up to March 2002,** remove restraints control module (RCM) fuse F2.28 (10A) from central junction box (CJB).
4. **On models built from March 2002–05,** remove restraints control module (RCM) fuse F2.19 (10A) from central junction box (CJB).
5. **On 2006 models,** remove restraints control module (RCM) fuse F17 (10A) from central junction box (CJB).
6. **On all models,** turn ignition switch to On position and visually monitor air bag indicator for 30 seconds. Air bag indicator will remain lit continuously if correct RCM fuse has been removed. Remove correct RCM fuse as required.
7. Turn ignition switch to Off position.
8. Disconnect battery ground cable and wait at least 1 minute prior to any service or repair.

Explorer Sport & Explorer Sport-Trac

To avoid accidental deployment and possible personal injury, the back-up power supply must be depleted before repairing or replacing any air bag supplemental restraint system component.
1. Ensure all vehicle accessories are in Off position.
2. Ensure ignition switch is in Off position.
3. **On models built up to February 17, 2002,** remove restraints control module (RCM) fuse F2.6 (7.5A less rear blower, 15A w/rear blower) from central junction box (CJB).
4. **On models built from February 17, 2002** remove restraints control module (RCM) fuse F2.12 (15A) from central junction box (CJB).
5. **On 2003 models,** remove restraints control module (RCM) fuse F2.14 (10A) from central junction box (CJB).
6. **On 2004–05 models,** remove restraints control module (RCM) fuse F2.10 (10A) from central junction box (CJB).
7. **On all models,** turn ignition switch to On position and visually monitor air bag indicator for 30 seconds. Air bag indicator will remain lit continuously if correct RCM fuse has been removed.

Remove correct RCM fuse as required.
8. Turn ignition switch to Off position.
9. Disconnect battery ground cable and wait at least 1 minute prior to any service or repair.

F150

To avoid accidental deployment and possible personal injury, the back-up power supply must be depleted before repairing or replacing any air bag supplemental restraint system component.
1. Ensure all vehicle accessories are in Off position.
2. Ensure ignition switch is in Off position.
3. **On 2002–03 models,** remove restraints control module (RCM) fuse F2.22 (10A) from central junction box (CJB).
4. **On 2004–06 models,** remove restraints control module (RCM) fuse F2.19 (10A) from central junction box (CJB).
5. **On all models,** turn ignition switch to On position and visually monitor air bag indicator for 30 seconds. Air bag indicator will remain lit continuously if correct RCM fuse has been removed. Remove correct RCM fuse as required.
6. Turn ignition switch to Off position.
7. Disconnect battery ground cable and wait at least 1 minute prior to any service or repair.

Freestar & Monterey

To avoid accidental deployment and possible personal injury, the back-up power supply must be depleted before repairing or replacing any air bag supplemental restraint system component.
1. Ensure all vehicle accessories are in Off position.
2. Ensure ignition switch is in Off position.
3. Remove restraints control module (RCM) fuse F2.17 (10A) from central junction box (CJB).
4. Turn ignition switch to On position and visually monitor air bag indicator for 30 seconds. Air bag indicator will remain lit continuously if correct RCM fuse has been removed. Remove correct RCM fuse as required.
5. Turn ignition switch to Off position.
6. Disconnect battery ground cable and wait at least 1 minute prior to any service or repair.

Mark LT

To avoid accidental deployment and possible personal injury, the back-up power supply must be depleted before repairing or replacing any air bag supplemental restraint system component.
1. Ensure all vehicle accessories are in Off position.
2. Ensure ignition switch is in Off position.
3. Remove restraints control module (RCM) fuse F2.19 (10A) from central junction box (CJB).
4. Turn ignition switch to On position and

visually monitor air bag indicator for 30 seconds. Air bag indicator will remain lit continuously if correct RCM fuse has been removed. Remove correct RCM fuse as required.
5. Turn ignition switch to Off position.
6. Disconnect battery ground cable and wait at least 1 minute prior to any service or repair.

Ranger

To avoid accidental deployment and possible personal injury, the back-up power supply must be depleted before repairing or replacing any air bag supplemental restraint system component.
1. Ensure all vehicle accessories are in Off position.
2. Ensure ignition switch is in Off position.
3. **On 2002–03 models,** remove restraints control module (RCM) fuses F2.2 (10A) and F2.26 (10A) from central junction box (CJB).
4. **On 2004–06 models,** remove restraints control module (RCM) fuse F2.8 (10A) from central junction box (CJB).
5. **On all models,** turn ignition switch to On position and visually monitor air bag indicator for 30 seconds. Air bag indicator will remain lit continuously if correct RCM fuse has been removed. Remove correct RCM fuse as required.
6. Turn ignition switch to Off position.
7. Disconnect battery ground cable and wait at least 1 minute prior to any service or repair.

Villager

1. Disconnect and isolate battery ground cable.
2. Wait at least three minutes for air bag diagnostic monitor back-up power supply to deplete.
3. Remove cover panel at lower portion of steering wheel to access driver side air bag electrical connector.
4. Disconnect driver air bag electrical connector.
5. Connect air bag simulator tool No. T94P-50-A, or equivalent, to driver air bag module vehicle harness connector.
6. Disconnect passenger air bag module electrical connector, then install Rotunda air bag simulator tool No. T96P-50-A, or equivalent, in place of passenger air bag module.
7. Connect battery ground cable.

Windstar

To avoid accidental deployment and possible personal injury, the back-up power supply must be depleted before repairing or replacing any air bag supplemental restraint system component.
1. Ensure all vehicle accessories are in Off position.
2. Ensure ignition switch is in Off position.
3. Remove restraints control module (RCM) fuse F2.26 (10A) from central

junction box (CJB).
4. Turn ignition switch to On position and visually monitor air bag indicator for 30 seconds. Air bag indicator will remain lit continuously if correct RCM fuse has been removed. Remove correct RCM fuse as required.
5. Turn ignition switch to Off position.
6. Disconnect battery ground cable and wait at least 1 minute prior to any service or repair.

ARMING

Aviator

The restraint system diagnostic tool is for restraint system service only. Remove tool from vehicle prior to road use. Failure to remove could result in injury and possible violation of vehicle safety standards.
1. Turn ignition switch from Off to On position.
2. Install RCM fuse F2.12 (15A) to CJB.
3. **Ensure that nobody is in vehicle and that there is nothing blocking or set in front of any air bag module when battery ground cable is connected.** Connect battery ground cable.
4. Prove out SRS system as follows:
   a. Turn ignition from On to Off position.
   b. Wait 10 seconds, then turn key back to On position and monitor air bag indicator with air bag modules installed.
   c. Air bag indicator will light continuously for 6 seconds and then turn Off.
   d. If air bag SRS fault is present, air bag indicator will fail to light, remain lit continuously or flash.
   e. Flashing might not occur until 30 seconds after ignition switch has been turned from Off to On position.
   f. This is time required for RCM to complete testing of SRS.
   g. If air bag indicator is inoperative and a SRS fault exists, a chime will sound in a pattern of 5 sets of 5 beeps.
   h. If this occurs, air bag indicator and any SRS fault discovered must be diagnosed and repaired.
   i. Clear all continuous DTC's from RCM using a suitable scan tool. Refer to **MOTOR's "Air Bag Manual"** or **"Air Bag Diagnostics CD."**

Blackwood

1. Disconnect battery ground cable and isolate.
2. **On models equipped with auxiliary batteries and power supplies,** disconnect ground cables and isolate.
3. **On all models,** wait at least one minute for back-up power supply to deplete stored energy.
4. Remove restraint system diagnostic tools from seat belt retractor and pretensioner electrical connectors.

5. Connect seat belt retractor and pretensioner electrical connectors.
6. **On models equipped with side impact air bag modules,** proceed as follows:
   a. Remove restraint system diagnostic tools from side impact air bag module electrical connectors.
   b. Connect side impact air bag module electrical connectors.
7. **On all models,** remove restraint system diagnostic tool from passenger air bag module.
8. Install passenger air bag module as outlined under "Component Service."
9. Remove restraint system diagnostic tool from driver side air bag module.
10. Install driver air bag module as outlined under "Component Service."
11. Connect battery ground cable.
12. Prove out SRS system as follows:
    a. Turn ignition from On to Off position.
    b. Wait 10 seconds, then turn key back to On position and monitor air bag indicator with air bag modules installed.
    c. Air bag indicator will light continuously for 6 seconds and then turn Off.
    d. If air bag SRS fault is present, air bag indicator will fail to light, remain lit continuously or flash.
    e. Flashing might not occur until 30 seconds after ignition switch has been turned from Off to On position.
    f. This is time required for RCM to complete testing of SRS.
    g. If air bag indicator is inoperative and a SRS fault exists, a chime will sound in a pattern of 5 sets of 5 beeps.
    h. If this occurs, air bag indicator and any SRS fault discovered must be diagnosed and repaired.
    i. Clear all continuous DTC's from RCM using a suitable scan tool. Refer to **MOTOR's "Air Bag Manual"** or **"Air Bag Diagnostics CD."**

Econoline

The restraint system diagnostic tool is for restraint system service only. Remove tool from vehicle prior to road use. Failure to remove could result in injury and possible violation of vehicle safety standards.
1. Turn ignition switch from Off to On position.
2. **On 2002–03 models,** install ECS fuses F2.19 (10A) and F2.38 (10A) to CJB and install cover.
3. **On 2004–06 models,** install RCM fuse F2.20 (10A) to CJB and install cover.
4. **On all models, ensure that nobody is in vehicle and that there is nothing blocking or set in front of any air bag module when battery ground cable is connected.** Connect battery ground cable.
5. Prove out SRS system as follows:
   a. Turn ignition from On to Off position.
   b. Wait 10 seconds, then turn key back to On position and monitor air

bag indicator with air bag modules installed.
   c. Air bag indicator will light continuously for 6 seconds and then turn Off.
   d. If air bag SRS fault is present, air bag indicator will fail to light, remain lit continuously or flash.
   e. Flashing might not occur until 30 seconds after ignition switch has been turned from Off to On position.
   f. This is time required for ECS or RCM to complete testing of SRS.
   g. If air bag indicator is inoperative and a SRS fault exists, a chime will sound in a pattern of 5 sets of 5 beeps.
   h. If this occurs, air bag indicator and any SRS fault discovered must be diagnosed and repaired.
   i. Clear all continuous DTC's from RCM using a suitable scan tool. Refer to **MOTOR's "Air Bag Manual"** or **"Air Bag Diagnostics CD."**

Escape & Mariner

The restraint system diagnostic tool is for restraint system service only. Remove tool from vehicle prior to road use. Failure to remove could result in injury and possible violation of vehicle safety standards.
1. Turn ignition switch from Off to On position.
2. **On 2002–04 models,** install RCM fuses F2.5 (5A) and F2.7 (10A) to CJB and install cover.
3. **On 2005–06 models,** install RCM fuse F33 (15A) to CJB and install cover.
4. **On all models, ensure that nobody is in vehicle and that there is nothing blocking or set in front of any air bag module when battery ground cable is connected.** Connect battery ground cable.
5. Prove out SRS system as follows:
   a. Turn ignition from On to Off position.
   b. Wait 10 seconds, then turn key back to On position and monitor air bag indicator with air bag modules installed.
   c. Air bag indicator will light continuously for 6 seconds and then turn Off.
   d. If air bag SRS fault is present, air bag indicator will fail to light, remain lit continuously or flash.
   e. Flashing might not occur until 30 seconds after ignition switch has been turned from Off to On position.
   f. This is time required for RCM to complete testing of SRS.
   g. If air bag indicator is inoperative and a SRS fault exists, a chime will sound in a pattern of 5 sets of 5 beeps.
   h. If this occurs, air bag indicator and any SRS fault discovered must be diagnosed and repaired.
   i. Clear all continuous DTC's from RCM using a suitable scan tool. Refer to **MOTOR's "Air Bag Manual"** or **"Air Bag Diagnostics CD."**

Excursion & F-Super Duty 250-350

The restraint system diagnostic tool is for restraint system service only. Remove tool from vehicle prior to road use. Failure to remove could result in injury and possible violation of vehicle safety standards.
1. Turn ignition switch from Off to On position.
2. Install RCM fuse F2.26 (10A) to CJB and install cover.
3. **Ensure that nobody is in vehicle and that there is nothing blocking or set in front of any air bag module when battery ground cable is connected.** Connect battery ground cable.
4. Prove out SRS system as follows:
   a. Turn ignition from On to Off position.
   b. Wait 10 seconds, then turn key back to On position and monitor air bag indicator with air bag modules installed.
   c. Air bag indicator will light continuously for 6 seconds and then turn Off.
   d. If air bag SRS fault is present, air bag indicator will fail to light, remain lit continuously or flash.
   e. Flashing might not occur until 30 seconds after ignition switch has been turned from Off to On position.
   f. This is time required for RCM to complete testing of SRS.
   g. If air bag indicator is inoperative and a SRS fault exists, a chime will sound in a pattern of 5 sets of 5 beeps.
   h. If this occurs, air bag indicator and any SRS fault discovered must be diagnosed and repaired.
   i. Clear all continuous DTC's from RCM using a suitable scan tool. Refer to **MOTOR's "Air Bag Manual"** or **"Air Bag Diagnostics CD."**

Expedition & Navigator

The restraint system diagnostic tool is for restraint system service only. Remove tool from vehicle prior to road use. Failure to remove could result in injury and possible violation of vehicle safety standards.
1. Turn ignition switch from Off to On position.
2. **On 2002 models,** install RCM fuse F22 (10A) to CJB and install cover.
3. **On 2003–06 models,** install RCM fuse F1.19 (10A) to CJB and install cover.
4. **On all models, ensure that nobody is in vehicle and that there is nothing blocking or set in front of any air bag module when battery ground cable is connected.** Connect battery ground cable.
5. Prove out SRS system as follows:
   a. Turn ignition from On to Off position.

b. Wait 10 seconds, then turn key back to On position and monitor air bag indicator with air bag modules installed.

c. Air bag indicator will light continuously for 6 seconds and then turn Off.

d. If air bag SRS fault is present, air bag indicator will fail to light, remain lit continuously or flash.

e. Flashing might not occur until 30 seconds after ignition switch has been turned from Off to On position.

f. This is time required for RCM to complete testing of SRS.

g. If air bag indicator is inoperative and a SRS fault exists, a chime will sound in a pattern of 5 sets of 5 beeps.

h. If this occurs, air bag indicator and any SRS fault discovered must be diagnosed and repaired.

i. Clear all continuous DTC's from RCM using a suitable scan tool. Refer to **MOTOR's "Air Bag Manual" or "Air Bag Diagnostics CD."**

Explorer & Mountaineer

The restraint system diagnostic tool is for restraint system service only. Remove tool from vehicle prior to road use. Failure to remove could result in injury and possible violation of vehicle safety standards.

1. Turn ignition switch from Off to On position.
2. **On models built up to March 2002,** install RCM fuse F2.28 (10A) to CJB and install cover.
3. **On models built from March 2002–05,** install RCM fuse F2.19 (10A) to CJB and install cover.
4. **On 2006 models,** install RCM fuse F17 (10A) to CJB and install cover.
5. **On all models, ensure that nobody is in vehicle and that there is nothing blocking or set in front of any air bag module when battery ground cable is connected.** Connect battery ground cable.
6. Prove out SRS system as follows:
   a. Turn ignition from On to Off position.
   b. Wait 10 seconds, then turn key back to On position and monitor air bag indicator with air bag modules installed.
   c. Air bag indicator will light continuously for 6 seconds and then turn Off.
   d. If air bag SRS fault is present, air bag indicator will fail to light, remain lit continuously or flash.
   e. Flashing might not occur until 30 seconds after ignition switch has been turned from Off to On position.
   f. This is time required for RCM to complete testing of SRS.
   g. If air bag indicator is inoperative and a SRS fault exists, a chime will sound in a pattern of 5 sets of 5 beeps.
   h. If this occurs, air bag indicator and

any SRS fault discovered must be diagnosed and repaired.
   i. Clear all continuous DTC's from RCM using a suitable scan tool. Refer to **MOTOR's "Air Bag Manual" or "Air Bag Diagnostics CD."**

Explorer Sport & Explorer Sport-Trac

The restraint system diagnostic tool is for restraint system service only. Remove tool from vehicle prior to road use. Failure to remove could result in injury and possible violation of vehicle safety standards.

1. Turn ignition switch from Off to On position.
2. **On models built up to February 17, 2002,** install RCM fuse F2.6 (7.5A less rear blower, 15A w/rear blower) from central junction box (CJB).
3. **On models built from February 17, 2002–03** install RCM fuse F2.12 (15A) from central junction box (CJB).
4. **On 2003 models,** install RCM fuse F2.14 (10A) from central junction box (CJB).
5. **On 2004–05 models,** install RCM fuse F2.10 (10A) from central junction box (CJB).
6. **On all models, ensure that nobody is in vehicle and that there is nothing blocking or set in front of any air bag module when battery ground cable is connected.** Connect battery ground cable.
7. Prove out SRS system as follows:
   a. Turn ignition from On to Off position.
   b. Wait 10 seconds, then turn key back to On position and monitor air bag indicator with air bag modules installed.
   c. Air bag indicator will light continuously for 6 seconds and then turn Off.
   d. If air bag SRS fault is present, air bag indicator will fail to light, remain lit continuously or flash.
   e. Flashing might not occur until 30 seconds after ignition switch has been turned from Off to On position.
   f. This is time required for RCM to complete testing of SRS.
   g. If air bag indicator is inoperative and a SRS fault exists, a chime will sound in a pattern of 5 sets of 5 beeps.
   h. If this occurs, air bag indicator and any SRS fault discovered must be diagnosed and repaired.
   i. Clear all continuous DTC's from RCM using a suitable scan tool. Refer to **MOTOR's "Air Bag Manual" or "Air Bag Diagnostics CD."**

F150

The restraint system diagnostic tool is for restraint system service only. Remove tool from vehicle prior to road use. Failure to remove could result in injury and possible violation of vehicle safety standards.

1. Turn ignition switch from Off to On position.
2. **On 2002–03 models,** install RCM fuse F2.22 (10A) from central junction box (CJB).
3. **On 2004–06 models,** install RCM fuse F2.19 (10A) from central junction box (CJB).
4. **On all models, ensure that nobody is in vehicle and that there is nothing blocking or set in front of any air bag module when battery ground cable is connected.** Connect battery ground cable.
5. Prove out SRS system as follows:
   a. Turn ignition from On to Off position.
   b. Wait 10 seconds, then turn key back to On position and monitor air bag indicator with air bag modules installed.
   c. Air bag indicator will light continuously for 6 seconds and then turn Off.
   d. If air bag SRS fault is present, air bag indicator will fail to light, remain lit continuously or flash.
   e. Flashing might not occur until 30 seconds after ignition switch has been turned from Off to On position.
   f. This is time required for RCM to complete testing of SRS.
   g. If air bag indicator is inoperative and a SRS fault exists, a chime will sound in a pattern of 5 sets of 5 beeps.
   h. If this occurs, air bag indicator and any SRS fault discovered must be diagnosed and repaired.
   i. Clear all continuous DTC's from RCM using a suitable scan tool. Refer to **MOTOR's "Air Bag Manual" or "Air Bag Diagnostics CD."**

Freestar & Monterey

The restraint system diagnostic tool is for restraint system service only. Remove tool from vehicle prior to road use. Failure to remove could result in injury and possible violation of vehicle safety standards.

1. Turn ignition switch from Off to On position.
2. Install RCM fuse F2.17 (10A) from central junction box (CJB).
3. **Ensure that nobody is in vehicle and that there is nothing blocking or set in front of any air bag module when battery ground cable is connected.** Connect battery ground cable.
4. Prove out SRS system as follows:
   a. Turn ignition from On to Off position.
   b. Wait 10 seconds, then turn key back to On position and monitor air bag indicator with air bag modules installed.
   c. Air bag indicator will light continuously for 6 seconds and then turn Off.
   d. If air bag SRS fault is present, air bag indicator will fail to light, remain lit continuously or flash.
   e. Flashing might not occur until 30

seconds after ignition switch has been turned from Off to On position.

f. This is time required for RCM to complete testing of SRS.

g. If air bag indicator is inoperative and a SRS fault exists, a chime will sound in a pattern of 5 sets of 5 beeps.

h. If this occurs, air bag indicator and any SRS fault discovered must be diagnosed and repaired.

i. Clear all continuous DTC's from RCM using a suitable scan tool. Refer to **MOTOR's "Air Bag Manual" or "Air Bag Diagnostics CD."**

Mark LT

The restraint system diagnostic tool is for restraint system service only. Remove tool from vehicle prior to road use. Failure to remove could result in injury and possible violation of vehicle safety standards.

1. Turn ignition switch from Off to On position.
2. Install RCM fuse F2.19 (10A) from central junction box (CJB).
3. **Ensure that nobody is in vehicle and that there is nothing blocking or set in front of any air bag module when battery ground cable is connected.** Connect battery ground cable.
4. Prove out SRS system as follows:
   a. Turn ignition from On to Off position.
   b. Wait 10 seconds, then turn key back to On position and monitor air bag indicator with air bag modules installed.
   c. Air bag indicator will light continuously for 6 seconds and then turn Off.
   d. If air bag SRS fault is present, air bag indicator will fail to light, remain lit continuously or flash.
   e. Flashing might not occur until 30 seconds after ignition switch has been turned from Off to On position.
   f. This is time required for RCM to complete testing of SRS.
   g. If air bag indicator is inoperative and a SRS fault exists, a chime will sound in a pattern of 5 sets of 5 beeps.
   h. If this occurs, air bag indicator and any SRS fault discovered must be diagnosed and repaired.
   i. Clear all continuous DTC's from RCM using a suitable scan tool. Refer to **MOTOR's "Air Bag Manual" or "Air Bag Diagnostics CD."**

Ranger

The restraint system diagnostic tool is for restraint system service only. Remove tool from vehicle prior to road use. Failure to remove could result in injury and possible violation of vehicle safety standards.

1. Turn ignition switch from Off to On position.
2. **On 2002–03 models,** install RCM fuses F2.2 (10A) and F2.26 (10A) from central junction box (CJB).
3. **On 2004–06 models,** install RCM fuse F2.8 (10A) from central junction box (CJB).
4. **On all models, ensure that nobody is in vehicle and that there is nothing blocking or set in front of any air bag module when battery ground cable is connected.** Connect battery ground cable.
5. Prove out SRS system as follows:
   a. Turn ignition from On to Off position.
   b. Wait 10 seconds, then turn key back to On position and monitor air bag indicator with air bag modules installed.
   c. Air bag indicator will light continuously for 6 seconds and then turn Off.
   d. If air bag SRS fault is present, air bag indicator will fail to light, remain lit continuously or flash.
   e. Flashing might not occur until 30 seconds after ignition switch has been turned from Off to On position.
   f. This is time required for RCM to complete testing of SRS.
   g. If air bag indicator is inoperative and a SRS fault exists, a chime will sound in a pattern of 5 sets of 5 beeps.
   h. If this occurs, air bag indicator and any SRS fault discovered must be diagnosed and repaired.
   i. Clear all continuous DTC's from RCM using a suitable scan tool. Refer to **MOTOR's "Air Bag Manual" or "Air Bag Diagnostics CD."**

Villager

1. Disconnect and isolate battery ground cable.
2. Wait at least three minutes for air bag diagnostic monitor back-up power supply to deplete.
3. Remove air bag simulator from driver air bag connector.
4. Connect driver air bag connector to driver air bag module, then install cover on steering wheel.

5. Remove air bag simulator from passenger air bag module connector.
6. Connect passenger air bag module electrical connector and install passenger air bag module.
7. Connect battery ground cable and prove out system as follows:
   a. Cycle ignition switch from Off to Run **from a safe location at side of or below air bag modules** and visually monitor air bag indicator.
   b. Air bag indicator lamp should light continuously for approximately seven seconds, then go out. Refer to **MOTOR's "Air Bag Manual" or "Air Bag Diagnostics CD."**

Windstar

The restraint system diagnostic tool is for restraint system service only. Remove tool from vehicle prior to road use. Failure to remove could result in injury and possible violation of vehicle safety standards.

1. Turn ignition switch from Off to On position.
2. Install RCM fuse F2.26 (10A) from central junction box (CJB).
3. **Ensure that nobody is in vehicle and that there is nothing blocking or set in front of any air bag module when battery ground cable is connected.** Connect battery ground cable.
4. Prove out SRS system as follows:
   a. Turn ignition from On to Off position.
   b. Wait 10 seconds, then turn key back to On position and monitor air bag indicator with air bag modules installed.
   c. Air bag indicator will light continuously for 6 seconds and then turn Off.
   d. If air bag SRS fault is present, air bag indicator will fail to light, remain lit continuously or flash.
   e. Flashing might not occur until 30 seconds after ignition switch has been turned from Off to On position.
   f. This is time required for RCM to complete testing of SRS.
   g. If air bag indicator is inoperative and a SRS fault exists, a chime will sound in a pattern of 5 sets of 5 beeps.
   h. If this occurs, air bag indicator and any SRS fault discovered must be diagnosed and repaired.
   i. Clear all continuous DTC's from RCM using a suitable scan tool. Refer to **MOTOR's "Air Bag Manual" or "Air Bag Diagnostics CD."**

General Motors Corp.

INDEX

	Page No.		Page No.		Page No.
Arming	0-30	Relay, SV6, Terraza &		Zone 3	0-22
Astro & Safari	0-30	Uplander	0-41	Zone 5	0-22
2002	0-30	Zone 10	0-41	Zone 6	0-22
2003–05	0-30	Zone 12	0-42	Zone 8	0-22
Avalanche, Escalade ESV,		Zone 1	0-41	Express & Savana	0-22
Escalade EXT, Sierra,		Zone 2	0-41	2002	0-22
Silverado, Suburban, SSR,		Zone 3	0-41	2003–06	0-22
Tahoe & Yukon	0-31	Zone 5	0-41	HHR	0-23
2002	0-31	Zone 6	0-41	Zone 1	0-23
2003–06	0-31	Zone 7	0-41	Zone 2	0-23
Aztek & Rendezvous	0-32	Zone 9	0-41	Zone 3	0-23
2002	0-32	SRX	0-42	Zone 5	0-23
2003–06	0-32	Zone 1	0-42	Zone 6	0-24
Blazer, Sonoma & S10	0-33	Zone 2	0-42	Zone 8	0-24
2002	0-33	Zone 3	0-42	Hummer H2	0-24
2003–04	0-33	Zone 5	0-42	Zone 1	0-24
Bravada, Envoy, Rainier &		Zone 6	0-42	Zone 3	0-24
Trailblazer	0-34	Zone 7	0-42	Zone 5	0-24
2002	0-34	Zone 8	0-42	Zone 7	0-24
2003–06	0-34	Zone 9	0-43	Hummer H3	0-24
Canyon & Colorado	0-35	Tracker	0-43	Zone 1	0-24
Zone 1	0-35	2002	0-43	Zone 2	0-24
Zone 2	0-35	2003–04	0-43	Zone 3	0-25
Zone 3	0-35	Vue	0-43	Zone 5	0-25
Zone 5	0-35	Zone 2	0-43	Zone 6	0-25
Zone 6	0-35	Zone 3	0-43	Zone 8	0-25
Zone 8	0-36	Zone 5	0-43	Montana, Silhouette & Venture	0-25
Equinox & Torrent	0-36	Zone 6	0-43	2002	0-25
Zone 1	0-36	Zone 8	0-44	2003–05	0-25
Zone 2	0-36	**Disarming**	0-16	Relay, SV6, Terraza &	
Zone 3	0-36	Astro & Safari	0-16	Uplander	0-26
Zone 5	0-36	2002	0-16	Zone 10	0-27
Zone 6	0-36	2003–05	0-16	Zone 12	0-27
Zone 8	0-36	Avalanche, Escalade ESV,		Zone 1	0-26
Express & Savana	0-37	Escalade EXT, Sierra,		Zone 2	0-26
2002	0-37	Silverado, Suburban, SSR,		Zone 3	0-26
2003–06	0-37	Tahoe & Yukon	0-16	Zone 5	0-26
HHR	0-38	2002	0-16	Zone 6	0-27
Zone 1	0-38	2003–06	0-16	Zone 7	0-27
Zone 2	0-38	Aztek & Rendezvous	0-17	Zone 9	0-27
Zone 3	0-38	2002	0-17	SRX	0-27
Zone 5	0-38	2003–06	0-18	Zone 1	0-27
Zone 6	0-38	Blazer, Sonoma & S10	0-19	Zone 2	0-27
Zone 8	0-38	2002	0-19	Zone 3	0-27
Hummer H2	0-38	2003–05	0-19	Zone 5	0-28
Zone 1	0-38	Bravada, Envoy, Rainier &		Zone 6	0-28
Zone 3	0-39	Trailblazer	0-19	Zone 7	0-28
Zone 5	0-39	2002	0-19	Zone 8	0-28
Zone 7	0-39	2003–06	0-19	Zone 9	0-28
Hummer H3	0-39	Canyon & Colorado	0-20	Tracker	0-28
Zone 1	0-39	Zone 1	0-20	2002	0-28
Zone 2	0-39	Zone 2	0-20	2003–04	0-28
Zone 3	0-39	Zone 3	0-21	Vue	0-29
Zone 5	0-39	Zone 5	0-21	Zone 2	0-29
Zone 6	0-39	Zone 6	0-21	Zone 3	0-29
Zone 8	0-39	Zone 8	0-21	Zone 5	0-29
Montana, Silhouette & Venture	0-40	Equinox & Torrent	0-21	Zone 6	0-29
2002	0-40	Zone 1	0-21	Zone 8	0-30
2003–06	0-40	Zone 2	0-21		

DISARMING

The inflatable restraint sensing and diagnostic module (SDM) maintains a reserved energy supply. The reserved energy supply provides deployment power for the air bags. Deployment power is available for as much as 1 minute after disconnecting the vehicle power. Disabling the SIR system prevents deployment of the air bags from the reserved energy supply.

Astro & Safari

2002

1. Ensure front wheels are in straight ahead position.
2. Turn ignition switch to Off position.
3. Remove key from ignition.
4. Remove AIR BAG fuse from fuse block. **With AIR BAG fuse removed and ignition On, AIR BAG indicator illuminates. This is normal operation and does not indicate an SIR system fault.**
5. Remove driver side insulator panel.
6. Remove connector position assurance (CPA) from driver air bag module yellow 2-way connector located at base of steering column.
7. Disconnect driver air bag module yellow 2-way connector.
8. Remove passenger side insulator panel.
9. Remove CPA from passenger air bag module yellow 2-way connector located under instrument panel insulator panel.
10. Disconnect passenger air bag module yellow 2-way connector.

2003–05

ZONE 1

1. Ensure front wheels are in straight ahead position.
2. Turn ignition switch to Off position.
3. Remove key from ignition.
4. Remove AIR BAG fuse from fuse block. **With AIR BAG fuse removed and ignition On, AIR BAG indicator illuminates. This is normal operation and does not indicate an SIR system fault.**
5. Raise and support vehicle using suitable lift or jack.
6. Remove connector position assurance (CPA) from front end discriminating sensor connector located on frame crossmember.
7. Disconnect front end discriminating sensor connector.

ZONE 3

1. Ensure front wheels are in straight ahead position.
2. Turn ignition switch to Off position.
3. Remove key from ignition.
4. Remove driver side knee bolster.
5. Remove AIR BAG fuse from fuse block. **With AIR BAG fuse removed and ignition On, AIR BAG indicator illuminates. This is normal opera-**

tion and does not indicate an SIR system fault.
6. Remove connector position assurance (CPA) from driver air bag module yellow 2-way connector located left of steering column near knee bolster.
7. Disconnect driver air bag module yellow 2-way connector.

ZONE 5

1. Ensure front wheels are in straight ahead position.
2. Turn ignition switch to Off position.
3. Remove key from ignition.
4. Remove passenger side knee bolster.
5. Remove AIR BAG fuse from fuse block. **With AIR BAG fuse removed and ignition On, AIR BAG indicator illuminates. This is normal operation and does not indicate an SIR system fault.**
6. Remove connector position assurance (CPA) from passenger air bag module connector located behind instrument panel support.
7. Disconnect passenger air bag module yellow 2-way connector.

ZONE 7

1. Ensure front wheels are in straight ahead position.
2. Turn ignition switch to Off position.
3. Remove key from ignition.
4. Remove passenger and driver side knee bolster.
5. Remove AIR BAG fuse from fuse block. **With AIR BAG fuse removed and ignition On, AIR BAG indicator illuminates. This is normal operation and does not indicate an SIR system fault.**
6. Remove connector position assurance (CPA) from driver air bag module yellow 2-way connector located left of steering column near knee bolster.
7. Disconnect driver air bag module yellow 2-way connector.
8. Remove CPA from passenger air bag module yellow 2-way connector located behind instrument panel support.
9. Disconnect passenger air bag module yellow 2-way connector.

Avalanche, Escalade ESV, Escalade EXT, Sierra, Silverado, Suburban, SSR, Tahoe & Yukon

2002

1. Ensure front wheels are in straight ahead position.
2. Turn ignition switch to Off position.
3. Remove key from ignition.
4. Remove AIR BAG fuse from fuse block. **With AIR BAG fuse removed and ignition On, AIR BAG indicator illuminates. This is normal operation and does not indicate an SIR system fault.**

5. Remove connector position assurance (CPA) from driver air bag module yellow 2-way connector at base of steering column.
6. Disconnect driver air bag module yellow 2-way connector at base of steering column.
7. Open glove compartment door beyond support stops to access passenger air bag module yellow 2-way connector located behind main instrument panel support.
8. Remove CPA from passenger air bag module yellow 2-way connector.
9. Disconnect passenger air bag module yellow 2-way connector.
10. **On Avalanche, Suburban, Tahoe and Yukon models,** remove and disconnect CPA from driver side impact air bag module yellow 2-way connector from under driver seat.
11. **On Avalanche, Suburban, Tahoe and Yukon models,** remove and disconnect CPA from passenger side impact air bag module yellow 2-way connector from under passenger seat.

2003–06

ZONE 1

1. Ensure steering wheel is in straight ahead position.
2. Turn ignition switch to Off position.
3. Remove key from gnition.
4. Remove SIR fuse from fuse block. **With SIR fuse removed and ignition On, AIR BAG indicator illuminates. This is normal operation and does not indicate an SIR system fault.**
5. Remove connector position assurance (CPA) from both front end sensor connectors from frame crossmember. **This vehicle is equipped with two inflatable restraint front end sensors. Remove both front end sensors.**
6. Disconnect both front end sensor connectors.

ZONE 2

1. Ensure steering wheel is in straight ahead position.
2. Turn ignition switch to Off position.
3. Remove key from ignition.
4. Remove SIR fuse from fuse block. **With SIR fuse removed and ignition On, AIR BAG indicator illuminates. This is normal operation and does not indicate an SIR system fault.**
5. Remove driver side door trim panel using a suitable flat-bladed tool.
6. Remove connector position assurance (CPA) from side impact sensor yellow 2-way connector located at bottom left-hand side of door.
7. Disconnect side impact sensor yellow 2-way connector.
8. **On SSR models,** proceed as follows:
   a. Remove lock pillar trim panel using suitable flat-bladed tool.
   b. Disconnect electrical connector.
   c. Remove CPA from seat belt pretensioner lefthand connector.
   d. Disconnect seat belt pretensioner lefthand connector from vehicle harness connector.

ZONE 3

1. Ensure steering wheel is in straight ahead position.
2. Turn ignition switch to Off position.
3. Remove key from ignition.
4. **On SSR models,** remove knee bolster trim panel.
5. **On all models,** remove SIR fuse from fuse block. **With SIR fuse removed and ignition On, AIR BAG indicator illuminates. This is normal operation and does not indicate an SIR system fault.**
6. Remove connector position assurance (CPA) from driver air bag module yellow 4-way connector located left of steering column near knee bolster.
7. Disconnect driver air bag module yellow 4-way connector.

ZONE 5

1. Ensure steering wheel is in straight ahead position.
2. Turn ignition switch to Off position.
3. Remove key from ignition.
4. Remove SIR fuse from fuse block. **With SIR fuse removed and ignition On, AIR BAG indicator illuminates. This is normal operation and does not indicate an SIR system fault.**
5. Remove connector position assurance (CPA) from passenger air bag module yellow 4-way connector located behind instrument panel support.
6. Disconnect passenger air bag module yellow 4-way connector.

ZONE 6

1. Ensure steering wheel is in straight ahead position.
2. Turn ignition switch to Off position.
3. Remove key from ignition.
4. Remove SIR fuse from fuse block. **With SIR fuse removed and ignition On, AIR BAG indicator illuminates. This is normal operation and does not indicate an SIR system fault.**
5. Remove passenger side door trim panel using a suitable flat-bladed tool.
6. Remove connector position assurance (CPA) from side impact sensor yellow 2-way connector located at bottom of righthand door.
7. Disconnect side impact sensor yellow 2-way connector.
8. **On SSR models,** proceed as follows:
   a. Remove lock pillar trim panel using suitable flat-bladed tool.
   b. Disconnect electrical connector.
   c. Remove CPA from seat belt pretensioner righthand connector.
   d. Disconnect seat belt pretensioner righthand connector from vehicle harness connector.

ZONE 7

Except SSR

1. Ensure steering wheel is in straight ahead position.
2. Turn ignition switch to Off position.
3. Remove key from ignition.
4. Remove SIR fuse from fuse block. **With SIR fuse removed and ignition On, AIR BAG indicator illuminates.**

This is normal operation and does not indicate an SIR system fault.

5. Remove connector position assurance (CPA) from driver air bag module yellow 4-way connector located left of steering column near knee bolster.
6. Disconnect driver air bag module yellow 4-way connector.
7. Remove CPA from passenger air bag module yellow 4-way connector located behind instrument panel support.
8. Disconnect passenger air bag module yellow 4-way connector.
9. **On Avalanche and 2003–04 Escalade, Suburban, Tahoe and Yukon models,** proceed as follows:
   a. Remove CPA from passenger side impact air bag module yellow 2-way connector located under passenger seat.
   b. Disconnect passenger side impact air bag module yellow 2-way connector.
   c. Remove CPA from driver side impact air bag module yellow 2-way connector located under driver seat.
   d. Disconnect driver side impact air bag module yellow 2-way connector.

SSR

1. Ensure steering wheel is in straight ahead position.
2. Turn ignition switch to Off position.
3. Remove key from ignition.
4. Remove SIR fuse from fuse block. **With SIR fuse removed and ignition On, AIR BAG indicator illuminates. This is normal operation and does not indicate an SIR system fault.**
5. Remove connector position assurance (CPA) from driver side impact air bag module yellow 2-way connector located under driver seat.
6. Disconnect driver side impact air bag module yellow 2-way connector.

ZONE 8

1. Ensure steering wheel is in straight ahead position.
2. Turn ignition switch to Off position.
3. Remove key from ignition.
4. Remove SIR fuse from fuse block. **With SIR fuse removed and ignition On, AIR BAG indicator illuminates. This is normal operation and does not indicate an SIR system fault.**
5. Remove connector position assurance (CPA) from driver air bag module yellow 4-way connector located left of steering column near knee bolster.
6. Disconnect driver air bag module yellow 4-way connector located left of steering column near knee bolster.
7. Remove CPA from passenger air bag module yellow 4-way connector located behind instrument panel support.
8. Disconnect passenger air bag module yellow 4-way connector.
9. Remove CPA from passenger side impact air bag module yellow 2-way connector located under passenger seat.
10. Disconnect passenger side impact air bag module yellow 2-way connector.

11. Remove lock pillar trim panel using suitable flat-bladed tool.
12. Remove CPA from seat belt pretensioner righthand side connector.
13. Disconnect seat belt pretensioner righthand side connector from vehicle harness connector.
14. Remove CPA from driver side impact air bag module yellow 2-way connector located under driver seat.
15. Disconnect driver side impact air bag module yellow 2-way connector.
16. Remove lock pillar trim panel using suitable flat-bladed tool.
17. Remove CPA from seat belt pretensioner lefthand side connector.
18. Disconnect seat belt pretensioner lefthand side connector from vehicle harness connector.

ZONE 9

1. Ensure steering wheel is in straight ahead position.
2. Turn ignition switch to Off position.
3. Remove key from ignition.
4. Remove SIR fuse from fuse block. **With SIR fuse removed and ignition On, AIR BAG indicator illuminates. This is normal operation and does not indicate an SIR system fault.**
5. Remove connector position assurance (CPA) from passenger side impact air bag module yellow 2-way connector located under passenger seat.
6. Disconnect passenger side impact air bag module yellow 2-way connector.

Aztek & Rendezvous

2002

1. Ensure front wheels are in straight ahead position.
2. Turn ignition switch to Off position.
3. Remove key from ignition.
4. Remove SIR fuse from fuse block. **With SIR fuse removed and ignition On, AIR BAG indicator illuminates. This is normal operation and does not indicate an SIR system fault.**
5. Remove driver side insulator panel.
6. Remove connector position assurance (CPA) from driver air bag module coil connector located at base of steering column.
7. Disconnect driver air bag module coil connector.
8. Remove passenger side insulator panel.
9. Remove CPA from passenger air bag module connector located behind insulator panel.
10. Disconnect passenger air bag module connector.
11. Remove CPA from driver side impact air bag module connector located under driver seat.
12. Disconnect driver side impact air bag module connector.
13. Remove CPA from passenger side impact air bag module connector located under passenger seat.
14. Disconnect passenger side impact air bag module connector.

AIR BAG SYSTEM PRECAUTIONS

2003-06

ZONE 1

1. Ensure front wheels are in straight ahead position.
2. Turn ignition switch to Off position.
3. Remove key from ignition.
4. Remove SIR fuse from fuse block. **With SIR fuse removed and ignition On, AIR BAG indicator illuminates. This is normal operation and does not indicate an SIR system fault.**
5. Remove connector position assurance (CPA) from front end sensor harness connector.
6. Disconnect harness connector from front end sensor.

ZONE 2

1. Ensure front wheels are in straight ahead position.
2. Turn ignition switch to Off position.
3. Remove key from ignition.
4. Remove SIR fuse from fuse block. **With SIR fuse removed and ignition On, AIR BAG indicator illuminates. This is normal operation and does not indicate an SIR system fault.**
5. Remove connector position assurance (CPA) from driver side impact sensor and pretensioner yellow 2-way harness connectors.
6. Disconnect driver side impact sensor and pretensioner wiring harness connectors.

ZONE 3

1. Ensure front wheels are in straight ahead position.
2. Turn ignition switch to Off position.
3. Remove key from ignition.
4. Remove SIR fuse from fuse block. **With SIR fuse removed and ignition On, AIR BAG indicator illuminates. This is normal operation and does not indicate an SIR system fault.**
5. Remove driver side insulator panel.
6. Remove connector position assurance (CPA) from driver air bag module coil connector located at base of steering column.
7. Disconnect driver air bag module coil connector.

ZONE 5

1. Ensure front wheels are in straight ahead position.
2. Turn ignition switch to Off position.
3. Remove key from ignition.
4. Remove SIR fuse from fuse block. **With SIR fuse removed and ignition On, AIR BAG indicator illuminates. This is normal operation and does not indicate an SIR system fault.**
5. Remove passenger side insulator panel.
6. Remove connector position assurance (CPA) from passenger air bag module connector located behind insulator panel.
7. Disconnect passenger air bag module connector.

ZONE 6

1. Ensure front wheels are in straight ahead position.

---

2. Turn ignition switch to Off position.
3. Remove key from ignition.
4. Remove SIR fuse from fuse block. **With SIR fuse removed and ignition On, AIR BAG indicator illuminates. This is normal operation and does not indicate an SIR system fault.**
5. Remove connector position assurance (CPA) from passenger side impact sensor and pretensioner yellow 2-way harness connector.
6. Disconnect passenger side impact sensor and pretensioner wiring harness connectors.

ZONE 7

1. Ensure front wheels are in straight ahead position.
2. Turn ignition switch to Off position.
3. Remove key from ignition.
4. Remove SIR fuse from fuse block. **With SIR fuse removed and ignition On, AIR BAG indicator illuminates. This is normal operation and does not indicate an SIR system fault.**
5. **On 2003 models,** remove connector position assurance (CPA) from driver side impact air bag module connector located under driver seat.
6. **On 2003 models,** disconnect driver side impact air bag module connector.
7. **On 2004-06 models,** remove both CPA's from driver side impact air bag module yellow connector located under driver seat.
8. **On 2004-06 models,** disconnect vehicle harness yellow connector from driver side impact air bag module yellow connector.

ZONE 9

2003

1. Ensure front wheels are in straight ahead position.
2. Turn ignition switch to Off position.
3. Remove key from ignition.
4. Remove SIR fuse from fuse block. **With SIR fuse removed and ignition On, AIR BAG indicator illuminates. This is normal operation and does not indicate an SIR system fault.**
5. **To disable entire SIR system,** proceed as follows:
   a. Remove driver side insulator panel.
   b. Remove connector position assurance (CPA) from driver air bag module coil connector located at base of steering column.
   c. Disconnect driver air bag module coil connector.
   d. Remove passenger side insulator panel.
   e. Remove CPA from passenger air bag module connector located behind insulator panel.
   f. Disconnect passenger air bag module connector.
   g. Remove CPA from driver side impact air bag module connector located under driver seat.
   h. Disconnect driver side impact air bag module connector.
   i. Remove CPA from passenger side impact air bag module connector located under passenger seat.

---

   j. Disconnect passenger side impact air bag module connector.
6. **To disable passenger side impact air bag module,** proceed as follows:
   a. Remove CPA from passenger side impact air bag module connector located under passenger seat.
   b. Disconnect passenger side impact air bag module connector.

2004

1. Ensure front wheels are in straight ahead position.
2. Turn ignition switch to Off position.
3. Remove key from ignition.
4. Remove SIR fuse from fuse block. **With SIR fuse removed and ignition On, AIR BAG indicator illuminates. This is normal operation and does not indicate an SIR system fault.**
5. Remove both connector position assurance (CPA) from passenger side impact air bag module yellow connector located under passenger seat.
6. Disconnect vehicle harness yellow connector from passenger side impact air bag module yellow connector.

2005-06

1. Ensure front wheels are in straight ahead position.
2. Turn ignition switch to Off position.
3. Remove key from ignition.
4. Remove SIR fuse from fuse block. **With SIR fuse removed and ignition On, AIR BAG indicator illuminates. This is normal operation and does not indicate an SIR system fault.**
5. **To disable entire SIR system,** proceed as follows:
   a. Remove connector position assurance (CPA) from driver side impact sensor and pretensioner harness connectors.
   b. Disconnect driver side impact sensor and pretensioner wiring harness connectors.
   c. Remove CPA from driver side impact air bag module connector located under driver seat.
   d. Disconnect vehicle harness connector from driver side impact air bag module connector.
   e. Remove driver side insulator panel.
   f. Remove CPA from driver air bag module coil connector located at base of steering column.
   g. Disconnect driver air bag module coil connector.
   h. Remove passenger side insulator panel.
   i. Remove CPA from passenger air bag module connector.
   j. Disconnect passenger air bag module connector.
   k. Remove CPA from passenger side impact sensor and pretensioner harness connectors.
   l. Disconnect passenger side impact sensor and pretensioner wiring harness connectors.
   m. Remove CPA from passenger side impact air bag module connector located under passenger seat.

n. Disconnect vehicle harness connector from passenger side impact air bag module connector.

6. **To disable passenger side impact air bag module,**
   a. Remove CPA from passenger side impact air bag module connector located under passenger seat.
   b. Disconnect vehicle harness connector from passenger side impact air bag module connector.

Blazer, Sonoma & S10

2002

1. Ensure front wheels are in straight ahead position.
2. Turn ignition switch to Off position.
3. Remove key from ignition.
4. Remove SIR fuse from fuse block. **With SIR fuse removed and ignition On, AIR BAG indicator illuminates. This is normal operation and does not indicate an SIR system fault.**
5. Remove driver side knee bolster and sound insulator panels.
6. Remove connector position assurance (CPA) from driver air bag module yellow 2-way connector located at base of steering column.
7. Disconnect driver air bag module yellow 2-way connector.
8. Open glove compartment door, lift stop and allow door to fully open.
9. Remove CPA from passenger air bag module yellow 2-way connector located behind glove compartment.
10. Disconnect passenger air bag module yellow 2-way connector.

2003-05

ZONE 1

1. Ensure front wheels are in straight ahead position.
2. Turn ignition switch to Off position.
3. Remove key from ignition.
4. Remove SIR fuse from fuse block. **With SIR fuse removed and ignition On, AIR BAG indicator illuminates. This is normal operation and does not indicate an SIR system fault.**
5. Raise and support vehicle using a suitable jack or lift.
6. Remove connector position assurance (CPA) from both inflatable restraints front end discriminating sensor connectors located on frame crossmember.
7. Disconnect inflatable restraints front end discriminating sensor connectors.

ZONE 3

1. Ensure front wheels are in straight ahead position.
2. Turn ignition switch to Off position.
3. Remove key from ignition.
4. Remove knee bolster.
5. Remove SIR fuse from fuse block. **With SIR fuse removed and ignition On, AIR BAG indicator illuminates. This is normal operation and does not indicate an SIR system fault.**

6. Remove connector position assurance (CPA) from driver air bag module yellow 2-way connector located left of steering column near knee bolster.
7. Disconnect driver air bag module yellow 2-way connector.

ZONE 5

1. Ensure front wheels are in straight ahead position.
2. Turn ignition switch to Off position.
3. Remove key from ignition.
4. Remove SIR fuse from fuse block. **With SIR fuse removed and ignition On, AIR BAG indicator illuminates. This is normal operation and does not indicate an SIR system fault.**
5. Remove connector position assurance (CPA) from passenger air bag module yellow 2-way connector located behind instrument panel support.
6. Disconnect passenger air bag module yellow 2-way connector.

ZONE 8

1. Ensure front wheels are in straight ahead position.
2. Turn ignition switch to Off position.
3. Remove key from ignition.
4. Remove driver panel knee bolster
5. Remove SIR fuse from fuse block. **With SIR fuse removed and ignition On, AIR BAG indicator illuminates. This is normal operation and does not indicate an SIR system fault.**
6. Remove connector position assurance (CPA) from driver air bag module yellow 2-way connector located left of steering column near knee bolster.
7. Disconnect driver air bag module yellow 2-way connector.
8. Remove CPA from passenger air bag module yellow 2-way connector located behind instrument panel support.
9. Disconnect passenger air bag module yellow 2-way connector.

Bravada, Envoy, Rainier & Trailblazer

2002

1. Ensure front wheels are in straight ahead position.
2. Turn ignition switch to Off position.
3. Remove key from ignition.
4. Remove AIR BAG fuse from fuse block. **With AIR BAG fuse removed and ignition On, AIR BAG indicator illuminates. This is normal operation and does not indicate an SIR system fault.**
5. Remove connector position assurance (CPA) from driver air bag module yellow 2-way connector located at base of steering column.
6. Disconnect driver air bag module yellow 2-way connector.
7. Access passenger air bag module yellow 2-way connector located behind instrument panel support by opening glove compartment door and allow to open fully.
8. Remove CPA from passenger air bag module yellow 2-way connector locat-

ed behind instrument panel support.
9. Disconnect passenger air bag module yellow 2-way connector.
10. Remove CPA from driver side impact air bag module yellow 2-way connector located under driver seat.
11. Disconnect driver side impact air bag module yellow 2-way connector.
12. Remove CPA from passenger side impact air bag module yellow 2-way connector located under passenger seat.
13. Disconnect passenger side impact air bag module yellow 2-way connector.

2003-06

ZONE 1

1. Ensure front wheels are in straight ahead position.
2. Turn ignition switch to Off position.
3. Remove key from ignition.
4. Remove SIR fuse from fuse block. **With SIR fuse removed and ignition On, AIR BAG indicator illuminates. This is normal operation and does not indicate an SIR system fault.**
5. Remove front grille assembly.
6. Remove sensor bracket from bumper.
7. Remove connector position assurance (CPA) from both electronic frontal sensor connectors. **This vehicle is equipped with two inflatable restraint electronic frontal sensors (EFS). Remove both front end sensors.**
8. Disconnect both EFS connectors.

ZONE 2

1. Ensure front wheels are in straight ahead position.
2. Turn ignition switch to Off position.
3. Remove key from ignition.
4. Remove SIR fuse from fuse block. **With SIR fuse removed and ignition On, AIR BAG indicator illuminates. This is normal operation and does not indicate an SIR system fault.**
5. Remove driver door trim panel using suitable flat-bladed tool.
6. Remove connector position assurance (CPA) from driver side impact sensor yellow 2-way connector located near bottom lefthand corner of door.
7. Disconnect driver side impact sensor yellow 2-way connector.

ZONE 3

1. Ensure front wheels are in straight ahead position.
2. Turn ignition switch to Off position.
3. Remove key from ignition.
4. Remove driver side lower instrument panel trim panel.
5. Remove SIR fuse from fuse block. **With SIR fuse removed and ignition On, AIR BAG indicator illuminates. This is normal operation and does not indicate an SIR system fault.**
6. Remove connector position assurance (CPA) from driver air bag module yellow 4-way connector located left of steering column near knee bolster.
7. Disconnect driver air bag module yellow 4-way connector.

AIR BAG SYSTEM PRECAUTIONS

ZONE 5

1. Ensure front wheels are in straight ahead position.
2. Turn ignition switch to Off position.
3. Remove key from ignition.
4. Remove SIR fuse from fuse block. **With SIR fuse removed and ignition On, AIR BAG indicator illuminates. This is normal operation and does not indicate an SIR system fault.**
5. Remove connector position assurance (CPA) from passenger air bag module yellow 4-way connector located behind instrument panel support.
6. Disconnect passenger air bag module yellow 4-way connector.

ZONE 6

1. Ensure front wheels are in straight ahead position.
2. Turn ignition switch to Off position.
3. Remove key from ignition.
4. Remove SIR fuse from fuse block. **With SIR fuse removed and ignition On, AIR BAG indicator illuminates. This is normal operation and does not indicate an SIR system fault.**
5. Remove passenger door trim panel using suitable flat-bladed tool.
6. Remove connector position assurance (CPA) from passenger side impact sensor yellow 2-way connector located near bottom of righthand corner of door.
7. Disconnect passenger side impact sensor yellow 2-way connector.

ZONE 7

2003-04

1. Ensure front wheels are in straight ahead position.
2. Turn ignition switch to Off position.
3. Remove key from ignition.
4. Remove SIR fuse from fuse block. **With SIR fuse removed and ignition On, AIR BAG indicator illuminates. This is normal operation and does not indicate an SIR system fault.**
5. Remove connector position assurance (CPA) from driver side impact air bag module yellow 2-way connector located under driver seat.
6. Disconnect driver side impact air bag module yellow 2-way connector.

2005-06

1. Ensure front wheels are in straight ahead position.
2. Turn ignition switch to Off position.
3. Remove key from ignition.
4. Remove SIR fuse from fuse block. **With SIR fuse removed and ignition On, AIR BAG indicator illuminates. This is normal operation and does not indicate an SIR system fault.**
5. Remove connector position assurance (CPA) from driver seat belt pretensioner yellow 2-way connector located under driver seat.
6. Disconnect driver seat belt pretensioner yellow 2-way connector.

ZONE 8

2003-04

1. Ensure front wheels are in straight ahead position.
2. Turn ignition switch to Off position.
3. Remove key from ignition.
4. Remove driver side lower instrument panel trim panel.
5. Remove SIR fuse from fuse block. **With SIR fuse removed and ignition On, AIR BAG indicator illuminates. This is normal operation and does not indicate an SIR system fault.**
6. Remove connector position assurance (CPA) from driver air bag module yellow 4-way connector located left of steering column near knee bolster.
7. Disconnect driver air bag module yellow 4-way connector.
8. Remove CPA from passenger air bag module yellow 4-way connector located behind instrument panel support.
9. Disconnect passenger air bag module yellow 4-way connector.
10. Remove CPA from passenger side impact air bag module yellow 2-way connector located under passenger seat.
11. Disconnect passenger side impact air bag module yellow 2-way connector.
12. Remove CPA from driver side impact air bag module yellow 2-way connector located under driver seat.
13. Disconnect driver side impact air bag module yellow 2-way connector.

2005-06

1. Ensure front wheels are in straight ahead position.
2. Turn ignition switch to Off position.
3. Remove key from ignition.
4. Remove driver side lower instrument panel trim panel.
5. Remove SIR fuse from fuse block. **With SIR fuse removed and ignition On, AIR BAG indicator illuminates. This is normal operation and does not indicate an SIR system fault.**
6. Remove connector position assurance (CPA) from driver air bag module yellow 4-way connector located left of steering column near knee bolster.
7. Disconnect driver air bag module yellow 4-way connector.
8. Remove CPA from passenger air bag module yellow 4-way connector located behind instrument panel support.
9. Disconnect passenger air bag module yellow 4-way connector.
10. Remove CPA from passenger seat belt pretensioner yellow 2-way connector located under passenger seat.
11. Disconnect passenger seat belt pretensioner yellow 2-way connector.
12. Remove passenger side center pillar trim panel.
13. Remove CPA from passenger roof panel air bag module yellow 2-way connector.
14. Disconnect passenger roof panel air bag module yellow 2-way connector from vehicle harness connector.
15. Remove CPA from driver seat belt pretensioner yellow 2-way connector located under driver seat.
16. Disconnect driver seat belt pretensioner yellow 2-way connector.
17. Remove driver side center pillar trim panel.
18. Remove CPA from driver roof panel air bag module yellow 2-way connector.
19. Disconnect driver roof panel air bag module yellow 2-way connector from vehicle harness connector.

ZONE 9

2003-04

1. Ensure front wheels are in straight ahead position.
2. Turn ignition switch to Off position.
3. Remove key from ignition.
4. Remove SIR fuse from fuse block. **With SIR fuse removed and ignition On, AIR BAG indicator illuminates. This is normal operation and does not indicate an SIR system fault.**
5. Remove connector position assurance (CPA) from passenger side impact air bag module yellow 2-way connector located under passenger seat.
6. Disconnect passenger side impact air bag module yellow 2-way connector.

2005-06

1. Ensure front wheels are in straight ahead position.
2. Turn ignition switch to Off position.
3. Remove key from ignition.
4. Remove SIR fuse from fuse block. **With SIR fuse removed and ignition On, AIR BAG indicator illuminates. This is normal operation and does not indicate an SIR system fault.**
5. Remove connector position assurance (CPA) from passenger seat belt pretensioner yellow 2-way connector located under passenger seat.
6. Disconnect passenger seat belt pretensioner yellow 2-way connector.

Canyon & Colorado

ZONE 1

1. Ensure front wheels are in straight ahead position.
2. Turn ignition switch to Off position.
3. Remove key from ignition.
4. Remove SIR fuse from fuse block. **With SIR fuse removed and ignition On, AIR BAG indicator illuminates. This is normal operation and does not indicate an SIR system fault.**
5. Remove connector position assurance (CPA) from both front end sensor connectors from frame crossmember. **This vehicle is equipped with two inflatable restraint front end sensors. Remove both front end sensors.**
6. Disconnect both front end sensor connectors.

ZONE 2

1. Ensure front wheels are in straight ahead position.
2. Turn ignition switch to Off position.
3. Remove key from ignition.
4. Remove SIR fuse from fuse block. **With SIR fuse removed and ignition On, AIR BAG indicator illuminates.**

This is normal operation and does not indicate an SIR system fault.

5. Remove driver front door trim panel using suitable flat-bladed tool.
6. Remove connector position assurance (CPA) from driver side impact sensor yellow 2-way connector located near middle of door.
7. Disconnect driver side impact sensor yellow 2-way connector.
8. **On models equipped with crew cab,** remove lower center pillar trim panel.
9. **On models equipped with extended cab,** remove rear access door wiring harness grommet to access connector.
10. **On models equipped with regular cab,** remove lower body rear corner trim panel.
11. **On all models,** remove CPA from driver seat belt pretensioner connector.
12. Disconnect driver seat belt pretensioner connector from vehicle harness connector.
13. Remove driver windshield garnish molding trim panel.
14. Disconnect driver roof panel air bag module from vehicle harness.

ZONE 3

1. Ensure front wheels are in straight ahead position.
2. Turn ignition switch to Off position.
3. Remove key from ignition.
4. Remove driver knee bolster panel.
5. Remove SIR fuse from fuse block. **With SIR fuse removed and ignition On, AIR BAG indicator illuminates. This is normal operation and does not indicate an SIR system fault.**
6. Remove connector position assurance (CPA) from driver air bag module yellow 4-way connector located left of steering column above lefthand hinge pillar trim panel.
7. Disconnect driver air bag module yellow 4-way connector.

ZONE 5

1. Ensure front wheels are in straight ahead position.
2. Turn ignition switch to Off position.
3. Remove key from ignition.
4. Remove SIR fuse from fuse block. **With SIR fuse removed and ignition On, AIR BAG indicator illuminates. This is normal operation and does not indicate an SIR system fault.**
5. Remove connector position assurance (CPA) from passenger air bag module yellow 4-way connector C208 located above driver kick panel.
6. Disconnect passenger air bag module yellow 4-way connector C208.

ZONE 6

1. Ensure front wheels are in straight ahead position.
2. Turn ignition switch to Off position.
3. Remove key from ignition.
4. Remove SIR fuse from fuse block. **With SIR fuse removed and ignition On, AIR BAG indicator illuminates. This is normal operation and does not indicate an SIR system fault.**
5. Remove passenger front door trim

panel using suitable flat-bladed tool.
6. Remove connector position assurance (CPA) from passenger side impact sensor yellow 2-way connector located near middle of door.
7. Disconnect passenger side impact sensor yellow 2-way connector.
8. **On models equipped with crew cab,** remove lower center pillar trim panel.
9. **On models equipped with extended cab,** remove rear access door wiring harness grommet to access connector.
10. **On models equipped with regular cab,** remove lower body rear corner trim panel.
11. **On all models,** remove CPA from passenger seat belt pretensioner connector.
12. Disconnect passenger seat belt pretensioner connector from vehicle harness connector.
13. Remove passenger windshield garnish molding trim panel.
14. Disconnect passenger roof panel air bag module from vehicle harness.

ZONE 8

1. Ensure front wheels are in straight ahead position.
2. Turn ignition switch to Off position.
3. Remove key from ignition.
4. Remove knee bolster trim panel.
5. Remove SIR fuse from fuse block. **With SIR fuse removed and ignition On, AIR BAG indicator illuminates. This is normal operation and does not indicate an SIR system fault.**
6. Remove connector position assurance (CPA) from driver air bag module yellow 4-way connector located left of steering column above lefthand hinge pillar trim panel.
7. Disconnect driver air bag module yellow 4-way connector.
8. Remove driver door trim panel.
9. Remove CPA from driver side impact sensor yellow 2-way connector located near middle of door.
10. Disconnect driver side impact sensor yellow 2-way connector.
11. **On models equipped with crew cab,** remove driver side lower center pillar trim panel.
12. **On models equipped with extended cab,** remove driver side rear access door wiring harness grommet to access connector.
13. **On models equipped with regular cab,** remove driver side lower body rear corner trim panel.
14. **On all models,** remove CPA from driver seat belt pretensioner connector.
15. Disconnect driver seat belt pretensioner connector from vehicle harness connector.
16. Remove driver side windshield pillar garnish molding.
17. Disconnect driver roof panel air bag module connector from vehicle harness.
18. Remove CPA passenger air bag module yellow 4-way connector C208 located above driver side kick panel.
19. Disconnect passenger air bag module yellow 4-way connector C208.

20. Remove passenger door trim panel.
21. Remove CPA from passenger side impact sensor yellow 2-way connector located near middle of door.
22. Disconnect passenger side impact sensor yellow 2-way connector.
23. **On models equipped with crew cab,** remove passenger side lower center pillar trim panel.
24. **On models equipped with extended cab,** remove passenger side rear access door wiring harness grommet to access connector.
25. **On models equipped with regular cab,** remove passenger side lower body rear corner trim panel.
26. **On all models,** remove CPA from passenger seat belt pretensioner connector.
27. Disconnect passenger seat belt pretensioner connector from vehicle harness connector.
28. Remove passenger side windshield pillar garnish molding.
29. Disconnect passenger roof panel air bag module connector from vehicle harness.

Equinox & Torrent

ZONE 1

1. Ensure front wheels are in straight ahead position.
2. Turn ignition switch to Off position.
3. Remove key from ignition.
4. Remove AIR BAG fuse from fuse block. **With AIR BAG fuse removed and ignition On, AIR BAG indicator illuminates. This is normal operation and does not indicate an SIR system fault.**
5. Open hood and locate front end sensor.
6. Remove connector position assurance (CPA) from electronic frontal sensor (EFS).
7. Remove EFS connector from EFS.

ZONE 2

1. Ensure front wheels are in straight ahead position.
2. Turn ignition switch to Off position.
3. Remove key from ignition.
4. Remove AIR BAG fuse from fuse block. **With AIR BAG fuse removed and ignition On, AIR BAG indicator illuminates. This is normal operation and does not indicate an SIR system fault.**
5. **To disable driver roof panel air bag module,** proceed as follows:
   a. Remove upper rear window molding.
   b. Remove lefthand and righthand rear corner trim panels.
   c. Remove rear headliner push-in retainers.
   d. Remove rear coat hooks.
   e. Pull down lefthand rear corner of headliner to access driver roof panel air bag module.
   f. Remove connector position assurance (CPA) from driver roof panel air bag module connector.
   g. Disconnect driver roof panel air bag

module connector from vehicle harness connector.

6. **To disable driver side impact sensor and driver seat belt pretensioner,** proceed as follows:
   a. Remove driver side lower center pillar trim panel.
   b. Remove CPA from driver seat belt pretensioner connector.
   c. Disconnect driver seat belt pretensioner connector from vehicle harness connector.
   d. Remove CPA from driver side impact sensor connector.
   e. Disconnect driver side impact sensor from vehicle harness connector.

ZONE 3

1. Ensure front wheels are in straight ahead position.
2. Turn ignition switch to Off position.
3. Remove key from ignition.
4. Remove AIR BAG fuse from fuse block. **With AIR BAG fuse removed and ignition On, AIR BAG indicator illuminates. This is normal operation and does not indicate an SIR system fault.**
5. Remove connector position assurance (CPA) from driver air bag module coil connector.
6. Disconnect driver air bag module coil connector from vehicle harness connector.

ZONE 5

1. Ensure front wheels are in straight ahead position.
2. Turn ignition switch to Off position.
3. Remove key from ignition.
4. Remove AIR BAG fuse from fuse block. **With AIR BAG fuse removed and ignition On, AIR BAG indicator illuminates. This is normal operation and does not indicate an SIR system fault.**
5. Remove connector position assurance (CPA) from passenger air bag module connector.
6. Disconnect passenger air bag module connector from vehicle harness connector.

ZONE 6

1. Ensure front wheels are in straight ahead position.
2. Turn ignition switch to Off position.
3. Remove key from ignition.
4. Remove AIR BAG fuse from fuse block. **With AIR BAG fuse removed and ignition On, AIR BAG indicator illuminates. This is normal operation and does not indicate an SIR system fault.**
5. **To disable passenger roof panel air bag module,** proceed as follows:
   a. Remove upper rear window molding.
   b. Remove lefthand and righthand rear corner trim panels.
   c. Remove rear headliner push-in retainers.
   d. Remove rear coat hooks.

e. Pull down righthand rear corner of headliner to access passenger roof panel air bag module.
   f. Remove connector position assurance (CPA) from passenger roof panel air bag module connector.
   g. Disconnect passenger roof panel air bag module connector from vehicle harness connector.

6. **To disable passenger side impact sensor and passenger seat belt pretensioner,** proceed as follows:
   a. Remove passenger side lower center pillar trim panel.
   b. Remove CPA from passenger seat belt pretensioner connector.
   c. Disconnect passenger seat belt pretensioner connector from vehicle harness connector.
   d. Remove CPA from passenger side impact sensor connector.
   e. Disconnect passenger side impact sensor from vehicle harness connector.

ZONE 8

1. Ensure front wheels are in straight ahead position.
2. Turn ignition switch to Off position.
3. Remove key from ignition.
4. Remove AIR BAG fuse from fuse block. **With AIR BAG fuse removed and ignition On, AIR BAG indicator illuminates. This is normal operation and does not indicate an SIR system fault.**
5. Remove upper rear window molding.
6. Remove lefthand and righthand rear corner trim panels.
7. Remove rear headliner push-in retainers.
8. Remove rear coat hooks.
9. Pull down righthand rear corner to access passenger roof panel air bag module connector.
10. Remove connector position assurance (CPA) from passenger roof panel air bag module connector.
11. Disconnect passenger roof panel air bag module connector from vehicle harness connector.
12. Remove passenger side lower center trim panel.
13. Remove CPA from passenger seat belt pretensioner connector.
14. Disconnect passenger seat belt pretensioner connector from vehicle harness connector.
15. Remove CPA from passenger air bag module connector.
16. Disconnect passenger air bag module connector from vehicle harness connector.
17. Remove CPA from driver air bag module coil connector.
18. Disconnect driver air bag module coil connector from vehicle harness connector.
19. Remove driver side lower center trim panel.
20. Remove CPA from driver seat belt pretensioner connector.
21. Disconnect driver seat belt preten-

sioner connector from vehicle harness connector.
22. Pull down lefthand rear corner to access driver roof panel air bag module connector.
23. Remove CPA from driver roof panel air bag module connector.
24. Disconnect driver roof panel air bag module connector from vehicle harness connector.

Express & Savana
2002

1. Ensure front wheels are in straight ahead position.
2. Turn ignition switch to Off position.
3. Remove key from ignition.
4. Remove AIR BAG fuse from fuse block. **With AIR BAG fuse removed and ignition On, AIR BAG indicator illuminates. This is normal operation and does not indicate an SIR system fault.**
5. Remove driver side knee bolster.
6. Remove connector position assurance (CPA) from driver air bag module yellow 2-way connector located at base of steering column.
7. Disconnect driver air bag module yellow 2-way connector.
8. Remove passenger side knee bolster.
9. Remove CPA from passenger air bag module yellow 2-way connector located under instrument panel extension.
10. Disconnect passenger air bag module yellow 2-way connector.

2003–06
ZONE 1

1. Ensure front wheels are in straight ahead position.
2. Turn ignition switch to Off position.
3. Remove key from ignition.
4. Remove SIR fuse from fuse block. **With SIR fuse removed and ignition On, AIR BAG indicator illuminates. This is normal operation and does not indicate an SIR system fault.**
5. Raise and support vehicle using suitable jack or lift.
6. Remove connector position assurance (CPA) from front end sensor connector located on frame crossmember.
7. Disconnect front end sensor connector.

ZONE 3

1. Ensure front wheels are in straight ahead position.
2. Turn ignition switch to Off position.
3. Remove key from ignition.
4. Remove SIR fuse from fuse block. **With SIR fuse removed and ignition On, AIR BAG indicator illuminates. This is normal operation and does not indicate an SIR system fault.**
5. Remove connector position assurance (CPA) from driver air bag module yellow 4-way connector located left of steering column near knee bolster.
6. Disconnect driver air bag module yellow 4-way connector.

ZONE 5

1. Ensure front wheels are in straight ahead position.
2. Turn ignition switch to Off position.
3. Remove key from ignition.
4. Remove SIR fuse from fuse block. **With SIR fuse removed and ignition On, AIR BAG indicator illuminates. This is normal operation and does not indicate an SIR system fault.**
5. Remove righthand side panel knee bolster bracket.
6. Remove connector position assurance (CPA) from passenger air bag module yellow 4-way connector located behind instrument panel support.
7. Disconnect passenger air bag module yellow 4-way connector.

ZONE 7

2003

1. Ensure front wheels are in straight ahead position.
2. Turn ignition switch to Off position.
3. Remove key from ignition.
4. Remove SIR fuse from fuse block. **With SIR fuse removed and ignition On, AIR BAG indicator illuminates. This is normal operation and does not indicate an SIR system fault.**
5. Remove connector position assurance (CPA) from driver air bag module yellow 4-way connector located left of steering column near knee bolster.
6. Disconnect driver air bag module yellow 4-way connector.
7. Remove righthand side panel knee bolster bracket.
8. Remove CPA from passenger air bag module yellow 4-way connector located behind instrument panel support.
9. Disconnect passenger air bag module yellow 4-way connector.
10. Remove CPA from passenger seat belt pretensioner yellow 2-way connector located under passenger seat.
11. Disconnect passenger seat belt pretensioner yellow 2-way connector.
12. Remove CPA from driver seat belt pretensioner yellow 2-way connector located under driver seat.
13. Disconnect driver seat belt pretensioner yellow 2-way connector.

2004-05

1. Ensure front wheels are in straight ahead position.
2. Turn ignition switch to Off position.
3. Remove key from ignition.
4. Remove SIR fuse from fuse block. **With SIR fuse removed and ignition On, AIR BAG indicator illuminates. This is normal operation and does not indicate an SIR system fault.**
5. Remove connector position assurance (CPA) from driver air bag module yellow 4-way connector located left of steering column near knee bolster.
6. Disconnect driver air bag module yellow 4-way connector.
7. Remove righthand side knee bolster bracket.
8. Remove CPA from passenger air bag module yellow 4-way connector locat-

ed behind instrument panel support.
9. Disconnect passenger air bag module yellow 4-way connector.

2006

1. Ensure front wheels are in straight ahead position.
2. Turn ignition switch to Off position.
3. Remove key from ignition.
4. Remove SIR fuse from fuse block. **With SIR fuse removed and ignition On, AIR BAG indicator illuminates. This is normal operation and does not indicate an SIR system fault.**
5. Remove connector position assurance (CPA) from driver air bag module yellow 4-way connector located left of steering column near knee bolster.
6. Disconnect driver air bag module yellow 4-way connector.
7. Remove CPA from driver seat belt pretensioner yellow 2-way connector located under driver seat.
8. Disconnect driver seat belt pretensioner yellow 2-way connector.
9. Remove righthand side knee bolster bracket.
10. Remove CPA from passenger air bag module yellow 4-way connector located behind instrument panel support.
11. Disconnect passenger air bag module yellow 4-way connector.
12. Remove CPA from passenger seat belt pretensioner yellow 2-way connector located under passenger seat.
13. Disconnect passenger seat belt pretensioner yellow 2-way connector.

ZONE 9

1. Ensure front wheels are in straight ahead position.
2. Turn ignition switch to Off position.
3. Remove key from ignition.
4. Remove SIR fuse from fuse block. **With SIR fuse removed and ignition On, AIR BAG indicator illuminates. This is normal operation and does not indicate an SIR system fault.**
5. Remove connector position assurance (CPA) from passenger seat belt pretensioner yellow 2-way connector located under passenger seat.
6. Disconnect passenger seat belt pretensioner yellow 2-way connector.

HHR

ZONE 1

1. Ensure front wheels are in straight ahead position.
2. Turn ignition switch to Off position.
3. Remove key from ignition.
4. Remove AIR BAG and SDM fuses from fuse block. **With AIR BAG and SDM fuses removed and ignition On, AIR BAG indicator illuminates. This is normal operation and does not indicate an SIR system fault.**
5. Open hood and locate front end sensor.
6. Remove connector position assurance (CPA) from front end sensor connector.
7. Remove front end sensor connector from front end sensor.

ZONE 2

1. Ensure front wheels are in straight ahead position.
2. Turn ignition switch to Off position.
3. Remove key from ignition.
4. Remove AIR BAG and SDM fuses from fuse block. **With AIR BAG and SDM fuses removed and ignition On, AIR BAG indicator illuminates. This is normal operation and does not indicate an SIR system fault.**
5. Remove driver door trim panel.
6. Remove water deflector shield to access driver side impact sensor.
7. Remove connector position assurance (CPA) from driver side impact sensor connector.
8. Disconnect driver side impact sensor connector from sensor.
9. Remove driver side lower center pillar trim.
10. Remove CPA from driver seat belt pretensioner connector.
11. Disconnect driver seat belt pretensioner connector from vehicle harness connector.
12. Remove driver rear quarter upper trim panel.
13. Remove CPA from driver roof panel air bag module connector.
14. Disconnect driver roof panel air bag module connector from vehicle harness connector.

ZONE 3

1. Ensure front wheels are in straight ahead position.
2. Turn ignition switch to Off position.
3. Remove key from ignition.
4. Remove AIR BAG and SDM fuses from fuse block. **With AIR BAG and SDM fuses removed and ignition On, AIR BAG indicator illuminates. This is normal operation and does not indicate an SIR system fault.**
5. Remove driver outer trim panel from instrument panel.
6. Remove connector position assurance (CPA) from driver air bag module coil connector.
7. Disconnect driver air bag module coil connector from vehicle harness connector.

ZONE 5

1. Ensure front wheels are in straight ahead position.
2. Turn ignition switch to Off position.
3. Remove key from ignition.
4. Remove AIR BAG and SDM fuses from fuse block. **With AIR BAG and SDM fuses removed and ignition On, AIR BAG indicator illuminates. This is normal operation and does not indicate an SIR system fault.**
5. Slide connector position assurance (CPA) of passenger air bag module connector to release position located above righthand side hinge pillar trim panel.
6. Disconnect passenger air bag module connector from vehicle harness connector.

AIR BAG SYSTEM PRECAUTIONS

ZONE 6

1. Ensure front wheels are in straight ahead position.
2. Turn ignition switch to Off position.
3. Remove key from ignition.
4. Remove AIR BAG and SDM fuses from fuse block. **With AIR BAG and SDM fuses removed and ignition On, AIR BAG indicator illuminates. This is normal operation and does not indicate an SIR system fault.**
5. Remove passenger door trim panel.
6. Remove water deflector shield to access passenger side impact sensor.
7. Remove connector position assurance (CPA) from passenger side impact sensor connector.
8. Disconnect passenger side impact sensor connector from sensor.
9. Remove passenger lower center pillar trim.
10. Remove CPA from passenger seat belt pretensioner connector.
11. Disconnect passenger seat belt pretensioner connector from vehicle harness connector.
12. Remove passenger rear quarter upper trim panel.
13. Remove CPA from passenger roof panel air bag module connector.
14. Disconnect passenger roof panel air bag module connector from vehicle harness connector.

ZONE 8

1. Ensure front wheels are in straight ahead position.
2. Turn ignition switch to Off position.
3. Remove key from ignition.
4. Remove AIR BAG and SDM fuses from fuse block. **With AIR BAG and SDM fuses removed and ignition On, AIR BAG indicator illuminates. This is normal operation and does not indicate an SIR system fault.**
5. Remove passenger door trim panel.
6. Remove water deflector shield to access passenger side impact sensor.
7. Remove connector position assurance (CPA) from passenger side impact sensor connector.
8. Disconnect passenger side impact sensor connector from sensor.
9. Slide CPA of passenger air bag module connector to release position located above righthand hinge pillar trim.
10. Disconnect passenger air bag module connector from vehicle harness connector.
11. Remove passenger lower center pillar trim panel.
12. Remove CPA from passenger seat belt pretensioner connector.
13. Disconnect passenger seat belt pretensioner connector from vehicle harness connector.
14. Remove passenger rear quarter upper trim molding from upper lock pillar.
15. Remove CPA from passenger roof panel air bag module connector.
16. Disconnect passenger roof panel air bag module connector from vehicle harness connector.
17. Remove driver door trim panel.
18. Remove water deflector shield to access driver side impact sensor.
19. Remove CPA from driver side impact sensor connector.
20. Disconnect driver side impact sensor connector from sensor.
21. Remove driver outer trim panel from instrument panel.
22. Remove CPA from driver air bag module coil connector.
23. Disconnect driver air bag module coil connector from vehicle harness connector.
24. Remove driver lower center pillar trim.
25. Remove CPA from driver seat belt pretensioner connector.
26. Disconnect driver seat belt pretensioner connector from vehicle harness connector.
27. Remove driver rear quarter upper trim panel.
28. Remove CPA from driver roof panel air bag module connector.
29. Disconnect driver roof panel air bag module connector from vehicle harness connector.

Hummer H2

ZONE 1

1. Ensure front wheels are in straight ahead position.
2. Turn ignition switch to Off position.
3. Remove key from ignition.
4. Remove engine protection shield.
5. Remove SIR fuse from fuse block. **With SIR fuse removed and ignition On, AIR BAG indicator illuminates. This is normal operation and does not indicate an SIR system fault.**
6. Raise and support vehicle using suitable lift or jack.
7. Remove connector position assurance (CPA) from both front end sensor connectors located on frame crossmember.
8. Disconnect both front end sensor connectors.

ZONE 3

1. Ensure front wheels are in straight ahead position.
2. Turn ignition switch to Off position.
3. Remove key from ignition.
4. Remove engine protection shield.
5. Remove SIR fuse from fuse block. **With SIR fuse removed and ignition On, AIR BAG indicator illuminates. This is normal operation and does not indicate an SIR system fault.**
6. Remove connector position assurance (CPA) from driver air bag module yellow 2-way connector located left of steering column near knee bolster.
7. Disconnect driver air bag module yellow 2-way connector.

ZONE 5

1. Ensure front wheels are in straight ahead position.
2. Turn ignition switch to Off position.
3. Remove key from ignition.
4. Remove engine protection shield.
5. Remove SIR fuse from fuse block. **With SIR fuse removed and ignition On, AIR BAG indicator illuminates.**

This is normal operation and does not indicate an SIR system fault.

6. Remove connector position assurance (CPA) from passenger air bag module yellow 2-way connector located behind air bag module.
7. Disconnect passenger air bag module yellow 2-way connector.

ZONE 7

1. Ensure front wheels are in straight ahead position.
2. Turn ignition switch to Off position.
3. Remove key from ignition.
4. Remove engine protection shield.
5. Remove SIR fuse from fuse block. **With SIR fuse removed and ignition On, AIR BAG indicator illuminates. This is normal operation and does not indicate an SIR system fault.**
6. Remove connector position assurance (CPA) from driver air bag module yellow 2-way connector located left of steering column near knee bolster.
7. Disconnect driver air bag module yellow 2-way connector.
8. Remove connector position assurance (CPA) from passenger air bag module yellow 2-way connector located behind air bag module.
9. Disconnect passenger air bag module yellow 2-way connector.

Hummer H3

ZONE 1

1. Ensure front wheels are in straight ahead position.
2. Turn ignition switch to Off position.
3. Remove key from ignition.
4. Remove engine protection shield.
5. Remove AIR BAG fuse from fuse block. **With AIR BAG fuse removed and ignition On, AIR BAG indicator illuminates. This is normal operation and does not indicate an SIR system fault.**
6. Remove connector position assurance (CPA) from both front end sensor connectors.
7. Disconnect both front end sensor connectors.

ZONE 2

1. Ensure front wheels are in straight ahead position.
2. Turn ignition switch to Off position.
3. Remove key from ignition.
4. Remove engine protection shield.
5. Remove AIR BAG fuse from fuse block. **With AIR BAG fuse removed and ignition On, AIR BAG indicator illuminates. This is normal operation and does not indicate an SIR system fault.**
6. Remove driver door trim panel.
7. Remove connector position assurance (CPA) from driver side impact sensor yellow 2-way connector located near middle of door.
8. Disconnect driver side impact sensor yellow 2-way connector.
9. Remove driver lower center pillar trim panel.

10. Remove CPA from driver seat belt pretensioner connector.
11. Disconnect driver seat belt pretensioner connector from vehicle harness connector.
12. Remove driver windshield pillar trim panel.
13. Disconnect driver roof panel air bag module connector from vehicle harness connector.

ZONE 3

1. Ensure front wheels are in straight ahead position.
2. Turn ignition switch to Off position.
3. Remove key from ignition.
4. Remove engine protection shield.
5. Remove AIR BAG fuse from fuse block. **With AIR BAG fuse removed and ignition On, AIR BAG indicator illuminates. This is normal operation and does not indicate an SIR system fault.**
6. Remove driver knee bolster trim panel.
7. Remove connector position assurance (CPA) from driver air bag module yellow 4-way connector located left of steering column and above left hinge pillar trim panel.
8. Disconnect driver air bag module yellow 4-way connector.

ZONE 5

1. Ensure front wheels are in straight ahead position.
2. Turn ignition switch to Off position.
3. Remove key from ignition.
4. Remove engine protection shield.
5. Remove AIR BAG fuse from fuse block. **With AIR BAG fuse removed and ignition On, AIR BAG indicator illuminates. This is normal operation and does not indicate an SIR system fault.**
6. Access passenger air bag module inline connector C208 above driver kick panel.
7. Remove connector position assurance (CPA) from passenger air bag module yellow 4-way inline connector located above driver kick panel.
8. Disconnect passenger air bag module yellow 4-way inline connector.

ZONE 6

1. Ensure front wheels are in straight ahead position.
2. Turn ignition switch to Off position.
3. Remove key from ignition.
4. Remove engine protection shield.
5. Remove AIR BAG fuse from fuse block. **With AIR BAG fuse removed and ignition On, AIR BAG indicator illuminates. This is normal operation and does not indicate an SIR system fault.**
6. Remove passenger door trim panel.
7. Remove connector position assurance (CPA) from passenger side impact sensor yellow 2-way connector located near middle of door.
8. Disconnect passenger side impact sensor yellow 2-way connector.
9. Remove passenger lower center pillar trim panel.

10. Remove CPA from passenger seat belt pretensioner connector.
11. Disconnect passenger seat belt pretensioner connector from vehicle harness connector.
12. Remove passenger windshield pillar trim panel.
13. Disconnect passenger roof panel air bag module connector from vehicle harness connector.

ZONE 8

1. Ensure front wheels are in straight ahead position.
2. Turn ignition switch to Off position.
3. Remove key from ignition.
4. Remove engine protection shield.
5. Access passenger air bag module inline connector C208 above driver kick panel.
6. Remove AIR BAG fuse from fuse block. **With AIR BAG fuse removed and ignition On, AIR BAG indicator illuminates. This is normal operation and does not indicate an SIR system fault.**
7. Remove connector position assurance (CPA) from driver air bag module yellow 4-way connector located left of steering column above left hinge pillar trim panel.
8. Disconnect driver air bag module yellow 4-way connector.
9. Remove driver door trim panel.
10. Remove CPA from driver side impact sensor yellow 2-way connector located near middle of door.
11. Disconnect driver side impact sensor yellow 2-way connector.
12. Remove driver lower center pillar trim panel.
13. Remove CPA from driver seat belt pretensioner connector.
14. Disconnect driver seat belt pretensioner connector from vehicle harness connector.
15. Remove driver windshield pillar trim panel.
16. Disconnect driver roof panel air bag module connector from vehicle harness connector.
17. Remove CPA from passenger air bag module yellow 4-way inline connector located above driver kick panel.
18. Disconnect passenger air bag module yellow 4-way inline connector C208.
19. Remove passenger door trim panel.
20. Remove CPA from passenger side impact sensor yellow 2-way connector located near middle of door.
21. Disconnect passenger side impact sensor yellow 2-way connector.
22. Remove passenger lower center pillar trim panel.
23. Remove CPA from passenger seat belt pretensioner connector.
24. Disconnect passenger seat belt pretensioner connector from vehicle harness connector.
25. Remove passenger windshield pillar trim panel.
26. Disconnect passenger roof panel air bag module connector from vehicle harness connector.

Montana, Silhouette & Venture

2002

1. Ensure front wheels are in straight ahead position.
2. Turn ignition switch to Off position.
3. Remove key from ignition.
4. Remove SDM fuse from fuse block. **With SDM fuse removed and ignition On, AIR BAG indicator illuminates. This is normal operation and does not indicate an SIR system fault.**
5. Remove driver insulator panel.
6. Remove connector position assurance (CPA) from driver air bag module coil connector located at base of steering column.
7. Disconnect driver air bag module coil connector.
8. Remove passenger insulator panel.
9. Remove CPA from passenger air bag module connector located behind insulator panel.
10. Disconnect passenger air bag module connector.
11. Remove CPA from driver side impact air bag module connector located under driver seat.
12. Disconnect driver side impact air bag module connector.
13. Remove CPA from driver seat belt pretensioner connector located under driver seat.
14. Disconnect driver seat belt pretensioner connector.
15. Remove CPA from passenger side impact air bag module connector located under passenger seat.
16. Disconnect passenger side impact air bag module connector.
17. Remove CPA from passenger seat belt pretensioner connector located under passenger seat.
18. Disconnect passenger seat belt pretensioner connector.

2003–05

ZONE 1

1. Ensure front wheels are in straight ahead position.
2. Turn ignition switch to Off position.
3. Remove key from ignition.
4. Remove SIR fuse from fuse block. **With SIR fuse removed and ignition On, AIR BAG indicator illuminates. This is normal operation and does not indicate an SIR system fault.**
5. Remove connector position assurance (CPA) from both front end sensor connectors from frame crossmember. **This vehicle is equipped with two inflatable restraint front end sensors. Remove both front end sensors.**
6. Disconnect both front end sensor connectors.

ZONE 2

1. Ensure front wheels are in straight ahead position.
2. Turn ignition switch to Off position.
3. Remove key from ignition.

4. Remove SIR fuse from fuse block. **With SIR fuse removed and ignition On, AIR BAG indicator illuminates. This is normal operation and does not indicate an SIR system fault.**
5. Remove driver seat belt retractor trim cover.
6. Remove connector position assurance (CPA) from driver side impact sensor yellow 2-way connector located near bottom of B-pillar.
7. Disconnect driver side impact sensor yellow 2-way connector from sensor.

ZONE 3

1. Ensure front wheels are in straight ahead position.
2. Turn ignition switch to Off position.
3. Remove key from ignition.
4. Remove SIR fuse from fuse block. **With SIR fuse removed and ignition On, AIR BAG indicator illuminates. This is normal operation and does not indicate an SIR system fault.**
5. Remove driver insulator panel.
6. Remove connector position assurance (CPA) from driver air bag module coil yellow 4-way connector located at base of steering column.
7. Disconnect driver air bag module coil yellow 4-way connector.

ZONE 5

1. Ensure front wheels are in straight ahead position.
2. Turn ignition switch to Off position.
3. Remove key from ignition.
4. Remove SIR fuse from fuse block. **With SIR fuse removed and ignition On, AIR BAG indicator illuminates. This is normal operation and does not indicate an SIR system fault.**
5. Remove glove compartment assembly and disconnect electrical connectors.
6. Remove connector position assurance (CPA) from passenger air bag module yellow 4-way connector located behind passenger insulator panel.
7. Disconnect passenger air bag module yellow 4-way connector.

ZONE 6

1. Ensure front wheels are in straight ahead position.
2. Turn ignition switch to Off position.
3. Remove key from ignition.
4. Remove SIR fuse from fuse block. **With SIR fuse removed and ignition On, AIR BAG indicator illuminates. This is normal operation and does not indicate an SIR system fault.**
5. Remove passenger seat belt retractor trim cover.
6. Remove connector position assurance (CPA) from passenger side impact sensor yellow 2-way connector located near bottom of B-pillar.
7. Disconnect passenger side impact sensor yellow 2-way connector from sensor.

ZONE 7

1. Ensure front wheels are in straight ahead position.
2. Turn ignition switch to Off position.

3. Remove key from ignition.
4. Remove SIR fuse from fuse block. **With SIR fuse removed and ignition On, AIR BAG indicator illuminates. This is normal operation and does not indicate an SIR system fault.**
5. Remove connector position assurance (CPA) from driver side impact air bag module yellow 2-way connector located under driver seat.
6. Disconnect driver side impact air bag module yellow 2-way connector.
7. Remove CPA from driver seat belt pretensioner yellow 2-way connector located under driver seat.
8. Disconnect driver seat belt pretensioner yellow 2-way connector.

ZONE 9

1. Ensure front wheels are in straight ahead position.
2. Turn ignition switch to Off position.
3. Remove key from ignition.
4. Remove SIR fuse from fuse block. **With SIR fuse removed and ignition On, AIR BAG indicator illuminates. This is normal operation and does not indicate an SIR system fault.**
5. Remove driver insulator panel.
6. Remove connector position assurance (CPA) from driver air bag module coil yellow 4-way connector located at base of steering column.
7. Disconnect driver air bag module coil yellow 4-way connector.
8. Remove glove compartment assembly and disconnect electrical connectors.
9. Remove CPA from passenger air bag module 4-way connector located behind passenger insulator panel.
10. Disconnect passenger air bag module yellow 4-way connector.
11. Remove CPA from driver side impact air bag module yellow 2-way connector located under driver seat.
12. Disconnect driver side impact air bag module yellow 2-way connector.
13. Remove CPA from driver seat belt pretensioner yellow 2-way connector located under driver seat.
14. Disconnect driver seat belt pretensioner yellow 2-way connector.
15. Remove CPA from passenger side impact air bag module yellow 2-way connector located under passenger seat.
16. Disconnect passenger side impact air bag module yellow 2-way connector.
17. Remove CPA from passenger seat belt pretensioner yellow 2-way connector located under passenger seat.
18. Disconnect passenger seat belt pretensioner yellow 2-way connector.

Relay, SV6, Terraza & Uplander

ZONE 1

1. Ensure front wheels are in straight ahead position.
2. Turn ignition switch to Off position.
3. Remove key from ignition.
4. Remove AIR BAG fuse from fuse block. **With AIR BAG fuse removed and ignition On, AIR BAG indicator**

illuminates. This is normal operation and does not indicate an SIR system fault.**
5. Open hood and locate both electronic front end sensors.
6. Remove connector position assurance (CPA) from both front end sensors.
7. Disconnect both front end sensor harness connectors from sensors.

ZONE 2

1. Ensure front wheels are in straight ahead position.
2. Turn ignition switch to Off position.
3. Remove key from ignition.
4. Remove AIR BAG fuse from fuse block. **With AIR BAG fuse removed and ignition On, AIR BAG indicator illuminates. This is normal operation and does not indicate an SIR system fault.**
5. Remove driver lower center pillar trim cover.
6. Remove driver side impact sensor from center pillar.
7. Remove connector position assurance (CPA) from driver side impact sensor connector.
8. Disconnect driver side impact sensor harness connector from sensor.
9. Remove CPA from driver seat belt pretensioner connector.
10. Remove vehicle harness connector from driver seat belt pretensioner.

ZONE 3

1. Ensure front wheels are in straight ahead position.
2. Turn ignition switch to Off position.
3. Remove key from ignition.
4. Remove AIR BAG fuse from fuse block. **With AIR BAG fuse removed and ignition On, AIR BAG indicator illuminates. This is normal operation and does not indicate an SIR system fault.**
5. Remove driver knee bolster insulator panel.
6. Remove connector position assurance (CPA) from driver air bag module coil yellow connector located at base of steering column.
7. Disconnect driver air bag module coil connector.

ZONE 5

1. Ensure front wheels are in straight ahead position.
2. Turn ignition switch to Off position.
3. Remove key from ignition.
4. Remove AIR BAG fuse from fuse block. **With AIR BAG fuse removed and ignition On, AIR BAG indicator illuminates. This is normal operation and does not indicate an SIR system fault.**
5. Remove passenger knee bolster insulator panel.
6. Remove connector position assurance (CPA) from passenger air bag module yellow connector.
7. Disconnect passenger air bag module connector.

ZONE 6

1. Ensure front wheels are in straight ahead position.
2. Turn ignition switch to Off position.
3. Remove key from ignition.
4. Remove AIR BAG fuse from fuse block. **With AIR BAG fuse removed and ignition On, AIR BAG indicator illuminates. This is normal operation and does not indicate an SIR system fault.**
5. Remove passenger lower center pillar trim cover.
6. Remove passenger side impact sensor from center pillar.
7. Remove connector position assurance (CPA) from passenger side impact sensor connector.
8. Disconnect passenger side impact sensor harness connector from sensor.
9. Remove CPA from passenger seat belt pretensioner connector.
10. Remove vehicle harness connector from passenger seat belt pretensioner.

ZONE 7

1. Ensure front wheels are in straight ahead position.
2. Turn ignition switch to Off position.
3. Remove key from ignition.
4. Remove AIR BAG fuse from fuse block. **With AIR BAG fuse removed and ignition On, AIR BAG indicator illuminates. This is normal operation and does not indicate an SIR system fault.**
5. Remove connector position assurance (CPA) from driver front side impact air bag module yellow connector located under driver seat.
6. Disconnect vehicle harness connector from driver front side impact air bag module connector.

ZONE 9

1. Ensure front wheels are in straight ahead position.
2. Turn ignition switch to Off position.
3. Remove key from ignition.
4. Remove AIR BAG fuse from fuse block. **With AIR BAG fuse removed and ignition On, AIR BAG indicator illuminates. This is normal operation and does not indicate an SIR system fault.**
5. **To disable entire SIR system,** proceed as follows:
   a. Remove driver lower center pillar trim cover.
   b. Remove connector position assurance (CPA) from driver seat belt pretensioner connector.
   c. Remove vehicle harness connector from driver seat belt pretensioner.
   d. Remove driver knee bolster insulator panel.
   e. Remove CPA from driver air bag module coil yellow connector located at base of steering column.
   f. Disconnect driver air bag module coil connector.
   g. Remove CPA from driver front side impact air bag module yellow connector located under driver seat.

h. Disconnect vehicle harness connector from driver front side impact air bag module connector.
   i. Remove CPA from driver rear side impact air bag module yellow connector located under driver rear seat.
   j. Disconnect vehicle harness connector from driver rear side impact air bag module connector.
   k. Remove passenger knee bolster insulator panel.
   l. Remove CPA from passenger air bag module yellow connector.
   m. Disconnect passenger air bag module connector.
   n. Remove passenger lower center pillar trim cover.
   o. Remove CPA from passenger seat belt pretensioner connector.
   p. Remove vehicle harness connector from passenger seat belt pretensioner.
   q. Remove CPA from passenger rear side impact air bag module yellow connector located under passenger rear seat.
   r. Disconnect vehicle harness connector from passenger rear side impact air bag module connector.
   s. Remove CPA from passenger front side impact air bag module yellow connector located under passenger seat.
   t. Disconnect vehicle harness connector from passenger front side impact air bag module connector.
6. **To disable passenger front side impact air bag module,** proceed as follows:
   a. Remove CPA from passenger front side impact air bag module yellow connector located under passenger seat.
   b. Disconnect vehicle harness connector from passenger front side impact air bag module connector.

ZONE 10

1. Ensure front wheels are in straight ahead position.
2. Turn ignition switch to Off position.
3. Remove key from ignition.
4. Remove AIR BAG fuse from fuse block. **With AIR BAG fuse removed and ignition On, AIR BAG indicator illuminates. This is normal operation and does not indicate an SIR system fault.**
5. Remove connector position assurance (CPA) from driver rear side impact air bag module yellow connector located under driver rear seat.
6. Disconnect vehicle harness connector from driver rear side impact air bag module connector.

ZONE 12

1. Ensure front wheels are in straight ahead position.
2. Turn ignition switch to Off position.
3. Remove key from ignition.
4. Remove AIR BAG fuse from fuse block. **With AIR BAG fuse removed and ignition On, AIR BAG indicator illuminates. This is normal opera-**

tion and does not indicate an SIR system fault.
5. Remove connector position assurance (CPA) from passenger rear side impact air bag module yellow connector located under passenger rear seat.
6. Disconnect vehicle harness connector from passenger rear side impact air bag module connector.

SRX

ZONE 1

1. Ensure front wheels are in straight ahead position.
2. Turn ignition switch to Off position.
3. Remove key from ignition.
4. Place passenger rear seat in farthest back position.
5. Pull carpet away from rear seat to access fuse block.
6. Remove SIR fuse from fuse block. **With SIR fuse removed and ignition On, AIR BAG indicator illuminates. This is normal operation and does not indicate an SIR system fault.**
7. Open hood and remove both connector position assurance (CPA) from front end sensor connectors.
8. Remove both connectors from front end sensors.

ZONE 2

1. Ensure front wheels are in straight ahead position.
2. Turn ignition switch to Off position.
3. Remove key from ignition.
4. Place passenger rear seat in farthest back position.
5. Pull carpet away from rear seat to access fuse block.
6. Remove SIR fuse from fuse block. **With SIR fuse removed and ignition On, AIR BAG indicator illuminates. This is normal operation and does not indicate an SIR system fault.**
7. **To disable driver roof panel air bag module,** proceed as follows:
   a. Remove driver carpet retainer trim, lift carpet to access driver roof panel air bag module connector.
   b. Remove connector position assurance (CPA) from driver roof panel air bag module yellow connector.
   c. Disconnect driver roof panel air bag module connector from air bag module.
8. **To disable driver side impact sensor,** proceed as follows:
   a. Remove driver center pillar trim panel.
   b. Remove driver side impact sensor CPA from sensor connector.
   c. Remove driver side impact sensor connector from sensor.

ZONE 3

1. Ensure front wheels are in straight ahead position.
2. Turn ignition switch to Off position.
3. Remove key from ignition.
4. Place passenger rear seat in farthest back position.
5. Pull carpet away from rear seat to access fuse block.

6. Remove SIR fuse from fuse block. **With SIR fuse removed and ignition On, AIR BAG indicator illuminates. This is normal operation and does not indicate an SIR system fault.**
7. Remove driver insulator panel from side of instrument panel.
8. Remove connector position assurance (CPA) from driver air bag module coil yellow connector.
9. Disconnect driver air bag module coil yellow connector from vehicle harness yellow connector.

ZONE 5

1. Ensure front wheels are in straight ahead position.
2. Turn ignition switch to Off position.
3. Remove key from ignition.
4. Place passenger rear seat in farthest back position.
5. Pull carpet away from rear seat to access fuse block.
6. Remove SIR fuse from fuse block. **With SIR fuse removed and ignition On, AIR BAG indicator illuminates. This is normal operation and does not indicate an SIR system fault.**
7. Remove passenger insulator panel from side of instrument panel.
8. Remove connector position assurance (CPA) from passenger air bag module yellow connector.
9. Disconnect passenger air bag module yellow connector from vehicle harness yellow connector.

ZONE 6

1. Ensure front wheels are in straight ahead position.
2. Turn ignition switch to Off position.
3. Remove key from ignition.
4. Place passenger rear seat in farthest back position.
5. Pull carpet away from rear seat to access fuse block.
6. Remove SIR fuse from fuse block. **With SIR fuse removed and ignition On, AIR BAG indicator illuminates. This is normal operation and does not indicate an SIR system fault.**
7. **To disable passenger roof panel air bag module,** proceed as follows:
   a. Remove passenger carpet retainer trim, lift carpet to access passenger roof panel air bag module connector.
   b. Remove connector position assurance (CPA) from passenger roof panel air bag module yellow connector.
   c. Disconnect passenger roof panel air bag module connector from air bag module.
8. **To disable passenger side impact sensor,** proceed as follows:
   a. Remove passenger center pillar trim panel.
   b. Remove passenger side impact sensor CPA from sensor connector.
   c. Remove passenger side impact sensor connector from sensor.

ZONE 7

1. Ensure front wheels are in straight ahead position.
2. Turn ignition switch to Off position.
3. Remove key from ignition.
4. Place passenger rear seat in farthest back position.
5. Pull carpet away from rear seat to access fuse block.
6. Remove SIR fuse from fuse block. **With SIR fuse removed and ignition On, AIR BAG indicator illuminates. This is normal operation and does not indicate an SIR system fault.**
7. Remove both connector position assurance (CPA) from driver side impact air bag module and seat belt pretensioner yellow connectors located under driver seat.
8. Disconnect driver side impact air bag module and pretensioner yellow connectors from vehicle harness yellow connector.

ZONE 8

1. Ensure front wheels are in straight ahead position.
2. Turn ignition switch to Off position.
3. Remove key from ignition.
4. Place passenger rear seat in farthest back position.
5. Pull carpet away from rear seat to access fuse block.
6. Remove SIR fuse from fuse block. **With SIR fuse removed and ignition On, AIR BAG indicator illuminates. This is normal operation and does not indicate an SIR system fault.**
7. Remove passenger carpet retainer trim.
8. Remove connector position assurance (CPA) from passenger roof panel air bag module yellow connector.
9. Disconnect passenger roof panel air bag module connector from air bag module.
10. Remove passenger insulator panel from side of instrument panel.
11. Remove CPA from passenger air bag module yellow connector.
12. Disconnect passenger air bag module yellow connector from vehicle harness yellow connector.
13. Remove both CPA locks from passenger side impact air bag module and seat belt pretensioner yellow connector located under passenger seat.
14. Disconnect passenger side impact air bag module and pretensioner yellow connector from vehicle harness yellow connector.
15. Remove driver insulator panel from side of instrument panel.
16. Remove CPA from driver air bag module coil yellow connector.
17. Disconnect driver air bag module coil yellow connector from vehicle harness yellow connector.
18. Remove both CPA locks from driver side impact air bag module and seat belt pretensioner yellow connector located under driver seat.
19. Disconnect driver side impact air bag module and pretensioner yellow connector from vehicle harness yellow connector.
20. Remove driver carpet retainer trim.
21. Remove CPA from driver roof panel air bag module yellow connector.
22. Disconnect driver roof panel air bag module connector from air bag module.

ZONE 9

1. Ensure front wheels are in straight ahead position.
2. Turn ignition switch to Off position.
3. Remove key from ignition.
4. Place passenger rear seat in farthest back position.
5. Pull carpet away from rear seat to access fuse block.
6. Remove SIR fuse from fuse block. **With SIR fuse removed and ignition On, AIR BAG indicator illuminates. This is normal operation and does not indicate an SIR system fault.**
7. Remove both connector position assurance (CPA) from passenger side impact air bag module and seat belt pretensioner yellow connector located under passenger seat.
8. Disconnect passenger side impact air bag module and pretensioner yellow connector from vehicle harness yellow connector.

Tracker

2002

1. Ensure front wheels are in straight ahead position.
2. Turn ignition switch to Off position.
3. Remove key from ignition.
4. Remove AIR BAG fuse from fuse block. **With AIR BAG fuse removed and ignition On, AIR BAG indicator illuminates. This is normal operation and does not indicate an SIR system fault.**
5. Remove driver knee bolster trim plate.
6. Remove driver air bag module connector position assurance (CPA).
7. Remove driver air bag module yellow 2-way connector and unlock connector.
8. Remove glove compartment door.
9. Remove CPA and yellow 2-way connector from passenger air bag module and unlock connector.

2003-04

ZONE 3

1. Ensure front wheels are in straight ahead position.
2. Turn ignition switch to Off position.
3. Remove key from ignition.
4. Remove AIR BAG fuse from fuse block. **With AIR BAG fuse removed and ignition On, AIR BAG indicator illuminates. This is normal operation and does not indicate an SIR system fault.**
5. Remove driver knee bolster trim panel.
6. Remove driver air bag module connector position assurance (CPA).
7. Remove driver air bag module yellow 2-way connector and unlock connector.

ZONE 5

1. Ensure front wheels are in straight ahead position.
2. Turn ignition switch to Off position.
3. Remove key from ignition.
4. Remove AIR BAG fuse from fuse block. **With AIR BAG fuse removed and ignition On, AIR BAG indicator illuminates. This is normal operation and does not indicate an SIR system fault.**
5. Remove glove compartment door.
6. Remove CPA and yellow 2-way connector from passenger air bag module and unlock connector.

ZONE 8

1. Ensure front wheels are in straight ahead position.
2. Turn ignition switch to Off position.
3. Remove key from ignition.
4. Remove AIR BAG fuse from fuse block. **With AIR BAG fuse removed and ignition On, AIR BAG indicator illuminates. This is normal operation and does not indicate an SIR system fault.**
5. Remove driver knee bolster trim panel.
6. Remove driver air bag module connector position assurance (CPA).
7. Remove driver air bag module yellow 2-way connector and unlock connector.
8. Remove glove compartment door.
9. Remove CPA and yellow 2-way connector from passenger air bag module and unlock connector.

Vue

ZONE 2

2002-03

1. Ensure front wheels are in straight ahead position.
2. Turn ignition switch to Off position.
3. Remove key from ignition.
4. Remove AIR BAG fuse from fuse block. **With AIR BAG fuse removed and ignition On, AIR BAG indicator illuminates. This is normal operation and does not indicate an SIR system fault.**
5. Remove rear window upper trim panel.
6. Remove both lefthand and righthand rear corner trim panels.
7. Remove rear headliner push-in retainers.
8. Remove rear coat hooks.
9. Pull down corner of headliner to access driver roof panel air bag module connector.
10. Remove connector position assurance (CPA) from driver roof panel air bag module connector.
11. Disconnect driver roof panel air bag module connector from vehicle harness connector.

2004-06

1. Ensure front wheels are in straight ahead position.
2. Turn ignition switch to Off position.
3. Remove key from ignition.
4. Remove AIR BAG fuse from fuse

block. **With AIR BAG fuse removed and ignition On, AIR BAG indicator illuminates. This is normal operation and does not indicate an SIR system fault.**
5. **To disable driver roof panel air bag module and driver seat belt pretensioner,** proceed as follows:
   a. Remove upper rear window trim panel.
   b. Remove both lefthand and righthand rear corner trim panels.
   c. Remove rear headliner push-in retainers.
   d. Remove rear coat hooks.
   e. Pull down lefthand rear corner of headliner to access driver roof panel air bag module connector.
   f. Remove connector position assurance (CPA) from driver roof panel air bag module connector.
   g. Disconnect driver roof panel air bag module connector from vehicle harness connector.
   h. Remove driver lower center pillar trim panel.
   i. Remove CPA from driver seat belt pretensioner connector.
   j. Disconnect driver seat belt pretensioner connector.
6. **To disable driver roof panel air bag module,** proceed as follows:
   a. Remove upper rear window trim panel.
   b. Remove both lefthand and righthand rear corner trim panels.
   c. Remove rear headliner push-in retainers.
   d. Remove rear coat hooks.
   e. Pull down lefthand rear corner of headliner to access driver roof panel air bag module connector.
   f. Remove connector position assurance (CPA) from driver roof panel air bag module connector.
   g. Disconnect driver roof panel air bag module connector from vehicle harness connector.

ZONE 3

1. Ensure front wheels are in straight ahead position.
2. Turn ignition switch to Off position.
3. Remove key from ignition.
4. Remove AIR BAG fuse from fuse block. **With AIR BAG fuse removed and ignition On, AIR BAG indicator illuminates. This is normal operation and does not indicate an SIR system fault.**
5. Remove connector position assurance (CPA) from driver air bag module coil connector.
6. Disconnect driver air bag module coil connector from vehicle harness connector.

ZONE 5

1. Ensure front wheels are in straight ahead position.
2. Turn ignition switch to Off position.
3. Remove key from ignition.
4. Remove AIR BAG fuse from fuse block. **With AIR BAG fuse removed and ignition On, AIR BAG indicator illuminates. This is normal opera-

tion and does not indicate an SIR system fault.**
5. Remove connector position assurance (CPA) from passenger air bag module connector.
6. Disconnect passenger air bag module connector from vehicle harness connector.

ZONE 6

2002-03

1. Ensure front wheels are in straight ahead position.
2. Turn ignition switch to Off position.
3. Remove key from ignition.
4. Remove AIR BAG fuse from fuse block. **With AIR BAG fuse removed and ignition On, AIR BAG indicator illuminates. This is normal operation and does not indicate an SIR system fault.**
5. Remove upper rear window trim panel.
6. Remove both lefthand and righthand corner trim panels.
7. Remove rear headliner push-in retainers.
8. Remove rear coat hooks.
9. Pull down righthand corner of headliner to access passenger roof panel air bag module connector.
10. Remove connector position assurance (CPA) from passenger roof panel air bag module connector.
11. Disconnect passenger roof panel air bag module connector from vehicle harness connector.

2004-06

1. Ensure front wheels are in straight ahead position.
2. Turn ignition switch to Off position.
3. Remove key from ignition.
4. Remove AIR BAG fuse from fuse block. **With AIR BAG fuse removed and ignition On, AIR BAG indicator illuminates. This is normal operation and does not indicate an SIR system fault.**
5. **To disable passenger roof panel air bag module and passenger seat belt pretensioner,** proceed as follows:
   a. Remove upper rear window trim panel.
   b. Remove both lefthand and righthand rear corner trim panels.
   c. Remove rear headliner push-in retainers.
   d. Remove rear coat hooks.
   e. Pull down righthand rear corner of headliner to access passenger roof panel air bag module connector.
   f. Remove connector position assurance (CPA) from passenger roof panel air bag module connector.
   g. Disconnect passenger roof panel air bag module connector from vehicle harness connector.
   h. Remove passenger lower center pillar trim panel.
   i. Remove CPA from passenger seat belt pretensioner connector.
   j. Disconnect passenger seat belt pretensioner connector.
6. **To disable passenger roof panel air

bag module, proceed as follows:

a. Remove upper rear window trim panel.
b. Remove both lefthand and righthand rear corner trim panels.
c. Remove rear headliner push-in retainers.
d. Remove rear coat hooks.
e. Pull down right rear corner of headliner to access passenger roof panel air bag module connector.
f. Remove connector position assurance (CPA) from passenger roof panel air bag module connector.
g. Disconnect passenger roof panel air bag module connector from vehicle harness connector.

ZONE 8

2002-03

1. Ensure front wheels are in straight ahead position.
2. Turn ignition switch to Off position.
3. Remove key from ignition.
4. Remove AIR BAG fuse from fuse block. **With AIR BAG fuse removed and ignition On, AIR BAG indicator illuminates. This is normal operation and does not indicate an SIR system fault.**
5. Remove upper rear window trim panel.
6. Remove both lefthand and righthand rear corner trim panels.
7. Remove rear headliner push-in retainers.
8. Remove rear coat hooks.
9. Pull down corner of headliner to access passenger roof panel air bag module connector.
10. Remove connector position assurance (CPA) from passenger roof panel air bag module.
11. Disconnect passenger roof panel air bag module connector from vehicle harness connector.
12. Remove CPA from passenger air bag module connector.
13. Disconnect passenger air bag module connector from vehicle harness connector.
14. Remove CPA from driver air bag module coil connector.
15. Disconnect driver air bag module coil connector from vehicle harness connector.
16. Remove CPA from driver roof panel air bag module connector.
17. Disconnect driver roof panel air bag module connector from vehicle harness connector.

2004-06

1. Ensure front wheels are in straight ahead position.
2. Turn ignition switch to Off position.
3. Remove key from ignition.
4. Remove AIR BAG fuse from fuse block. **With AIR BAG fuse removed and ignition On, AIR BAG indicator illuminates. This is normal operation and does not indicate an SIR system fault.**
5. Remove rear upper window trim panel.
6. Remove both lefthand and righthand side rear corner trim panels.

7. Remove rear headliner push-in retainers.
8. Remove rear coat hooks.
9. Pull down righthand rear corner to access passenger roof panel air bag module connector.
10. Remove connector position assurance (CPA) from passenger roof panel air bag module connector.
11. Disconnect passenger roof panel air bag module connector from vehicle harness connector.
12. Remove passenger lower center pillar trim panel.
13. Remove CPA from passenger seat belt pretensioner connector.
14. Disconnect passenger seat belt pretensioner connector.
15. Remove CPA from passenger air bag module connector.
16. Disconnect passenger air bag module connector from vehicle harness connector.
17. Remove CPA from driver air bag module coil connector.
18. Disconnect driver air bag module coil connector from vehicle harness connector.
19. Remove driver lower center pillar trim panel.
20. Remove CPA from driver seat belt pretensioner connector.
21. Disconnect driver seat belt pretensioner connector.
22. Pull down lefthand rear corner of headliner to access driver roof panel air bag module connector.
23. Remove CPA from driver roof panel air bag module connector.
24. Disconnect driver roof panel air bag module connector from vehicle harness connector.

ARMING

Astro & Safari

2002

1. Remove key from ignition.
2. Connect passenger air bag module yellow 2-way connector located under instrument panel insulator panel.
3. Install CPA to passenger air bag module yellow 2-way connector.
4. Install instrument panel insulator panel.
5. Connect driver air bag module yellow 2-way connector located at base of steering column.
6. Install CPA to driver air bag module yellow 2-way connector.
7. Install driver side insulator panel.
8. Install AIR BAG fuse into fuse block.
9. From a position away from air bag modules, turn On ignition with engine Off.
10. AIR BAG indicator will flash seven times, then AIR BAG indicator will then turn Off.
11. If AIR BAG indicator does not operate as outlined, refer to **MOTOR's "Air Bag Manual" or "Air Bag Diagnostics CD."**

2003-05

ZONE 1

1. Remove key from ignition.
2. Connect front end discriminating sensor connector to front end discriminating sensor located on frame crossmember.
3. Install CPA to front end discriminating sensor connector.
4. Install AIR BAG fuse into fuse block.
5. From a position away from air bag modules, turn On ignition with engine Off.
6. AIR BAG indicator will flash seven times, then AIR BAG indicator will turn Off.
7. If AIR BAG indicator does not operate as outlined, refer to **MOTOR's "Air Bag Manual" or "Air Bag Diagnostics CD."**

ZONE 3

1. Remove key from ignition.
2. Connect driver air bag module yellow 2-way connector located left of steering column near knee bolster.
3. Install CPA to driver air bag module yellow 2-way connector.
4. Install AIR BAG fuse into fuse block.
5. Install driver side knee bolster.
6. From a position away from air bag modules, turn On ignition with engine Off.
7. AIR BAG indicator will flash seven times, then AIR BAG indicator will then turn Off.
8. If AIR BAG indicator does not operate as outlined, refer to **MOTOR's "Air Bag Manual" or "Air Bag Diagnostics CD."**

ZONE 5

1. Remove key from ignition.
2. Connect passenger air bag module yellow 2-way connector located behind instrument panel support.
3. Install CPA to passenger air bag module yellow 2-way connector.
4. Install passenger side knee bolster.
5. Install AIR BAG fuse into fuse block.
6. From a position away from air bag modules, turn On ignition with engine Off.
7. AIR BAG indicator will flash seven times, then AIR BAG indicator will then turn Off.
8. If AIR BAG indicator does not operate as outlined, refer to **MOTOR's "Air Bag Manual" or "Air Bag Diagnostics CD."**

ZONE 7

1. Remove key from ignition.
2. Connect passenger air bag module yellow 2-way connector located behind instrument panel support.
3. Install CPA to passenger air bag module yellow 2-way connector.
4. Connect driver air bag module yellow 2-way connector located left of steering column near knee bolster.
5. Install CPA to driver air bag module yellow 2-way connector.
6. Install AIR BAG fuse into fuse block.

7. Install passenger and driver side knee bolster.
8. From a position away from air bag modules, turn On ignition with engine Off.
9. AIR BAG indicator will flash seven times, then AIR BAG indicator will then turn Off.
10. If AIR BAG indicator does not operate as outlined, refer to **MOTOR's "Air Bag Manual" or "Air Bag Diagnostics CD."**

Avalanche, Escalade ESV, Escalade EXT, Sierra, Silverado, Suburban, SSR, Tahoe & Yukon

2002

1. Remove key from ignition.
2. **On Avalanche, Suburban, Tahoe and Yukon models,** proceed as follows:
   a. Connect passenger side impact air bag module yellow 2-way connector located under passenger seat.
   b. Install CPA to passenger side impact air bag module yellow 2-way connector located under passenger seat.
   c. Connect driver side impact air bag module yellow 2-way connector located under driver seat.
   d. Install CPA to driver side impact air bag module yellow 2-way connector located under driver seat.
3. **On all models,** connect passenger air bag module yellow 2-way connector located behind main instrument panel support.
4. Install CPA to passenger air bag module yellow 2-way connector located behind instrument panel support.
5. Connect driver air bag module yellow 2-way connector at base of steering column.
6. Install CPA to driver air bag module yellow 2-way connector at base of steering column.
7. Install AIR BAG fuse into fuse block.
8. From a position away from air bag modules, turn On ignition with engine Off.
9. AIR BAG indicator will flash 7 times, then AIR BAG indicator will then turn Off.
10. If AIR BAG indicator does not operate as outlined, refer to **MOTOR's "Air Bag Manual" or "Air Bag Diagnostics CD."**

2003–06

ZONE 1

1. Remove key from ignition.
2. Connect front end sensor connectors to both front end sensors.
3. Install CPA's to both front end sensor connectors.
4. Install SIR fuse into fuse block.
5. From a position away from air bag modules, turn On ignition with engine Off.
6. AIR BAG indicator will flash 7 times, then AIR BAG indicator will then turn Off.
7. If AIR BAG indicator does not operate as outlined, refer to **MOTOR's "Air Bag Manual" or "Air Bag Diagnostics CD."**

ZONE 2

1. Remove key from ignition.
2. **On SSR models,** connect seat belt pretensioner lefthand connector to vehicle harness connector.
3. **On SSR models,** install lock pillar trim panel.
4. **On all models,** connect side impact sensor yellow 2-way connector located at middle of door.
5. Install CPA to side impact sensor yellow 2-way connector.
6. Install driver side door trim panel.
7. Install SIR fuse into fuse block.
8. From a position away from air bag modules, turn On ignition with engine Off.
9. AIR BAG indicator will flash 7 times, then AIR BAG indicator will then turn Off.
10. If AIR BAG indicator does not operate as outlined, refer to **MOTOR's "Air Bag Manual" or "Air Bag Diagnostics CD."**

ZONE 3

1. Remove key from ignition.
2. Connect driver air bag module yellow 4-way connector located left of steering column near knee bolster.
3. Install CPA to driver air bag module yellow 4-way connector.
4. Install SIR fuse into fuse block.
5. From a position away from air bag modules, turn On ignition with engine Off.
6. AIR BAG indicator will flash 7 times, then AIR BAG indicator will then turn Off.
7. If AIR BAG indicator does not operate as outlined, refer to **MOTOR's "Air Bag Manual" or "Air Bag Diagnostics CD."**

ZONE 5

1. Remove key from ignition.
2. Connect passenger air bag module yellow 4-way connector located behind instrument panel support.
3. Install CPA to passenger air bag module yellow 4-way connector.
4. Install SIR fuse into fuse block.
5. From a position away from air bag modules, turn On ignition with engine Off.
6. AIR BAG indicator will flash 7 times, then AIR BAG indicator will then turn Off.
7. If AIR BAG indicator does not operate as outlined, refer to **MOTOR's "Air Bag Manual" or "Air Bag Diagnostics CD."**

ZONE 6

1. Remove key from ignition.
2. **On SSR models,** connect seat belt pretensioner righthand connector to vehicle harness connector.
3. **On SSR models,** install lock pillar trim panel.
4. **On all models,** connect side impact sensor yellow 2-way connector located in middle of righthand side door.
5. Install CPA to side impact sensor yellow 2-way connector.
6. Install passenger side door trim panel.
7. Install SIR fuse into fuse block.
8. From a position away from air bag modules, turn On ignition with engine Off.
9. AIR BAG indicator will flash 7 times, then AIR BAG indicator will then turn Off.
10. If AIR BAG indicator does not operate as outlined, refer to **MOTOR's "Air Bag Manual" or "Air Bag Diagnostics CD."**

ZONE 7

Except SSR

1. Remove key from ignition.
2. Connect driver air bag module yellow 4-way connector located left of steering column at knee bolster.
3. Install CPA to driver air bag module yellow 4-way connector.
4. Connect passenger air bag module yellow 4-way connector located behind instrument panel support.
5. Install CPA to passenger air bag module yellow 4-way connector.
6. **On Avalanche and 2003–04 Escalade, Suburban, Tahoe and Yukon models,** proceed as follows:
   a. Connect passenger side impact air bag module yellow 2-way connector located under passenger seat.
   b. Install CPA to passenger side impact air bag module yellow 2-way connector.
   c. Connect driver side impact air bag module yellow 2-way connector located under driver seat.
   d. Install CPA to driver side impact air bag module yellow 2-way connector.
7. **On all models,** install SIR fuse into fuse block.
8. From a position away from air bag modules, turn On ignition with engine Off.
9. AIR BAG indicator will flash 7 times, then AIR BAG indicator will then turn Off.
10. If AIR BAG indicator does not operate as outlined, refer to **MOTOR's "Air Bag Manual" or "Air Bag Diagnostics CD."**

SSR

1. Remove key from ignition.
2. Connect driver side impact air bag module yellow 2-way connector located under driver seat.
3. Install CPA to driver side impact air bag module yellow 2-way connector.
4. Install SIR fuse into fuse block.

5. From a position away from air bag modules, turn On ignition with engine Off.
6. AIR BAG indicator will flash 7 times, then AIR BAG indicator will then turn Off.
7. If AIR BAG indicator does not operate as outlined, refer to **MOTOR's "Air Bag Manual" or "Air Bag Diagnostics CD."**

ZONE 8

1. Remove key from ignition.
2. Connect driver air bag module yellow 4-way connector located left of steering column and near knee bolster.
3. Install CPA to driver air bag module yellow 4-way connector.
4. Connect passenger air bag module yellow 4-way connector located behind instrument panel support.
5. Install CPA to passenger air bag module yellow 4-way connector.
6. Connect passenger side impact air bag module yellow 2-way connector located under passenger seat.
7. Install CPA to passenger side impact air bag module yellow 2-way connector.
8. Connect righthand side seat belt pretensioner and install CPA.
9. Install lock pillar trim panel.
10. Connect driver side impact module yellow 2-way connector located under driver seat.
11. Install CPA to driver side impact air bag module yellow 2-way connector.
12. Connect lefthand side seat belt pretensioner and install CPA.
13. Install lock pillar trim panel.
14. Install SIR fuse into fuse block.
15. From a position away from air bag modules, turn On ignition with engine Off.
16. AIR BAG indicator will flash 7 times, then AIR BAG indicator will then turn Off.
17. If AIR BAG indicator does not operate as outlined, refer to **MOTOR's "Air Bag Manual" or "Air Bag Diagnostics CD."**

ZONE 9

1. Remove key from ignition.
2. Connect passenger side impact air bag module yellow 2-way connector located under passenger seat.
3. Install CPA to passenger side impact air bag module yellow 2-way connector.
4. Install SIR fuse into fuse block.
5. From a position away from air bag modules, turn On ignition with engine Off.
6. AIR BAG indicator will flash 7 times, then AIR BAG indicator will then turn Off.
7. If AIR BAG indicator does not operate as outlined, refer to **MOTOR's "Air Bag Manual" or "Air Bag Diagnostics CD."**

Aztek & Rendezvous

2002

1. Connect passenger side impact air bag module connector locate under passenger seat.
2. Install CPA to passenger side air bag module connector.
3. Connect driver side impact air bag module connector located under driver seat.
4. Install CPA to driver side impact air bag module connector.
5. Connect passenger air bag module connector located behind passenger side insulator panel.
6. Install CPA to passenger air bag module connector.
7. Install passenger side insulator panel.
8. Connect driver air bag module coil connector located at base of steering column.
9. Install CPA to driver air bag module coil connector.
10. Install driver side insulator panel.
11. Install SIR fuse into fuse block.
12. From a position away from air bag modules, turn On ignition with engine Off.
13. AIR BAG indicator will flash seven times, then AIR BAG indicator will then turn Off.
14. If AIR BAG indicator does not operate as outlined, refer to **MOTOR's "Air Bag Manual" or "Air Bag Diagnostics CD."**

2003–06

ZONE 1

1. Remove key from ignition.
2. Connect harness connector to front end sensor.
3. Install CPA to front end sensor harness connector.
4. Install SIR fuse into fuse block.
5. From a position away from air bag modules, turn On ignition with engine Off.
6. AIR BAG indicator will flash, then AIR BAG indicator will then turn Off.
7. If AIR BAG indicator does not operate as outlined, refer to **MOTOR's "Air Bag Manual" or "Air Bag Diagnostics CD."**

ZONE 2

1. Remove key from ignition.
2. Connect CPA to driver side impact sensor and pretensioner yellow 2-way harness connectors.
3. Install CPA to yellow sensor and pretensioner harness connectors.
4. Install SIR fuse into fuse block.
5. From a position away from air bag modules, turn On ignition with engine Off.
6. AIR BAG indicator will flash seven times, then AIR BAG indicator will then turn Off.
7. If AIR BAG indicator does not operate as outlined, refer to **MOTOR's "Air Bag Manual" or "Air Bag Diagnostics CD."**

ZONE 3

1. Remove key from ignition.
2. Connect driver air bag module coil connector.
3. Install CPA to driver air bag module coil connector located at base of steering column.
4. Install driver side insulator panel.
5. Install SIR fuse into fuse block.
6. From a position away from air bag modules, turn On ignition with engine Off.
7. AIR BAG indicator will flash seven times, then AIR BAG indicator will then turn Off.
8. If AIR BAG indicator does not operate as outlined, refer to **MOTOR's "Air Bag Manual" or "Air Bag Diagnostics CD."**

ZONE 5

1. Remove key from ignition.
2. Connect passenger air bag module connector.
3. Install CPA to passenger air bag module connector located behind passenger side insulator panel.
4. Install passenger side insulator panel.
5. Install SIR fuse into fuse block.
6. From a position away from air bag modules, turn On ignition with engine Off.
7. AIR BAG indicator will flash seven times, then AIR BAG indicator will then turn Off.
8. If AIR BAG indicator does not operate as outlined, refer to **MOTOR's "Air Bag Manual" or "Air Bag Diagnostics CD."**

ZONE 6

1. Remove key from ignition.
2. Connect CPA to passenger side impact sensor and pretensioner yellow 2-way harness connectors.
3. Install CPA to passenger side impact sensor and pretensioner.
4. Install SIR fuse into fuse block.
5. From a position away from air bag modules, turn On ignition with engine Off.
6. AIR BAG indicator will flash seven times, then AIR BAG indicator will then turn Off.
7. If AIR BAG indicator does not operate as outlined, refer to **MOTOR's "Air Bag Manual" or "Air Bag Diagnostics CD."**

ZONE 7

1. Remove key from ignition.
2. **On 2003 models,** connect driver side impact air bag module connector.
3. **On 2003 models,** install connector position assurance (CPA) from driver side impact air bag module connector located under driver seat.
4. **On 2004–06 models,** connect vehicle harness yellow connector from driver side impact air bag module yellow connector.
5. **On 2004–06 models,** install both CPA's from driver side impact air bag module yellow connector located under driver seat.

6. **On all models,** install SIR fuse into fuse block.
7. From a position away from air bag modules, turn On ignition with engine Off.
8. AIR BAG indicator will flash seven times, then AIR BAG indicator will then turn Off.
9. If AIR BAG indicator does not operate as outlined, refer to **MOTOR's "Air Bag Manual"** or **"Air Bag Diagnostics CD."**

ZONE 9
2003

1. Remove key from ignition.
2. **To enable entire SIR system,** proceed as follows:
   a. Connect passenger air bag module connector located behind passenger side insulator panel.
   b. Install CPA to passenger air bag module connector.
   c. Install passenger side insulator panel.
   d. Connect driver air bag module coil connector located at base of steering column.
   e. Install CPA to driver air bag module coil connector.
   f. Install driver side insulator panel.
   g. Connect driver side impact air bag module connector located under driver seat.
   h. Install CPA to driver side impact air bag module connector.
   i. Connect passenger side impact air bag module connector located under passenger seat.
   j. Install CPA to passenger side impact air bag module connector.
3. **To enable passenger side impact air bag module,** proceed as follows:
   a. Connect passenger side impact air bag module connector located under passenger seat.
   b. Install CPA to passenger side impact air bag module connector.
4. **On all models,** install SIR fuse into fuse block.
5. From a position away from air bag modules, turn On ignition with engine Off.
6. AIR BAG indicator will flash seven times, then AIR BAG indicator will then turn Off.
7. If AIR BAG indicator does not operate as outlined, refer to **MOTOR's "Air Bag Manual"** or **"Air Bag Diagnostics CD."**

2004

1. Remove key from ignition.
2. Connect vehicle harness yellow connector to passenger side impact sensor yellow connector.
3. Install both CPA's to passenger side impact module yellow connector.
4. Install SIR fuse into fuse block.
5. From a position away from air bag modules, turn On ignition with engine Off.
6. AIR BAG indicator will flash seven times, then AIR BAG indicator will then turn Off.

7. If AIR BAG indicator does not operate as outlined, refer to **MOTOR's "Air Bag Manual"** or **"Air Bag Diagnostics CD."**

2005-06

1. Remove key from ignition.
2. **To enable entire SIR system,** proceed as follows:
   a. Connect CPA to driver side impact sensor and pretensioner harness connectors.
   b. Install CPA to driver side impact sensor and pretensioner harness connectors.
   c. Connect driver air bag module coil connector.
   d. Install CPA to driver air bag module coil connector located at base of steering column.
   e. Install driver side insulator panel.
   f. Connect passenger air bag module connector.
   g. Install CPA to passenger air bag module connector.
   h. Install passenger side insulator panel.
   i. Connect passenger side impact sensor and pretensioner harness connectors.
   j. Install CPA to passenger side impact sensor and pretensioner harness connectors.
   k. Connect vehicle harness connector to passenger side impact air bag module connector.
   l. Install CPA to passenger side impact air bag module yellow connector.
3. **To enable passenger side impact air bag module,** proceed as follows:
   a. Connect vehicle harness connector to passenger side impact air bag module connector.
   b. Install CPA to passenger side impact air bag module yellow connector.
4. **On all models,** install SIR fuse into fuse block.
5. From a position away from air bag modules, turn On ignition with engine Off.
6. AIR BAG indicator will flash, then AIR BAG indicator will then turn Off.
7. If AIR BAG indicator does not operate as outlined, refer to **MOTOR's "Air Bag Manual"** or **"Air Bag Diagnostics CD."**

Blazer, Sonoma & S10

2002

1. Remove key from ignition.
2. Connect passenger air bag module yellow 2-way connector located behind glove compartment.
3. Install CPA to passenger air bag module yellow 2-way connector.
4. Close glove compartment door.
5. Connect driver air bag module yellow 2-way connector located at base of steering column.
6. Install CPA to driver air bag module

yellow 2-way connector.
7. Install knee bolster and sound insulator panel.
8. Install SIR fuse into fuse block.
9. From a position away from air bag modules, turn On ignition with engine Off.
10. AIR BAG indicator will flash 7 times, then AIR BAG indicator will then turn Off.
11. If AIR BAG indicator does not operate as outlined, refer to **MOTOR's "Air Bag Manual"** or **"Air Bag Diagnostics CD."**

2003-04

ZONE 1

1. Remove key from ignition.
2. Connect inflatable restraint front end discriminating sensor connectors to inflatable restraints front end discriminating sensor.
3. Install CPA to inflatable restraints front end discriminating sensor connectors.
4. Install SIR fuse into fuse block.
5. From a position away from air bag modules, turn On ignition with engine Off.
6. AIR BAG indicator will flash 7 times, then AIR BAG indicator will then turn Off.
7. If AIR BAG indicator does not operate as outlined, refer to **MOTOR's "Air Bag Manual"** or **"Air Bag Diagnostics CD."**

ZONE 3

1. Remove key from ignition.
2. Connect driver air bag module yellow 2-way connector located left of steering column near knee bolster.
3. Install CPA to driver air bag module yellow 2-way connector.
4. Install SIR fuse into fuse block.
5. Install knee bolster.
6. From a position away from air bag modules, turn On ignition with engine Off.
7. AIR BAG indicator will flash 7 times, then AIR BAG indicator will then turn Off.
8. If AIR BAG indicator does not operate as outlined, refer to **MOTOR's "Air Bag Manual"** or **"Air Bag Diagnostics CD."**

ZONE 5

1. Remove key from ignition.
2. Connect passenger air bag module yellow 2-way connector located behind main instrument panel support.
3. Install CPA to passenger air bag module yellow 2-way connector.
4. Install SIR fuse into fuse block.
5. From a position away from air bag modules, turn On ignition with engine Off.
6. AIR BAG indicator will flash 7 times, then AIR BAG indicator will then turn Off.
7. If AIR BAG indicator does not operate as outlined, refer to **MOTOR's "Air Bag Manual"** or **"Air Bag Diagnostics CD."**

ZONE 8

1. Remove key from ignition.
2. Connect passenger air bag module yellow 2-way connector located behind main instrument panel support.
3. Install CPA to passenger air bag module yellow 2-way connector.
4. Connect driver air bag module yellow 2-way connector located left of steering column near knee bolster.
5. Install CPA to driver air bag module yellow 2-way connector.
6. Install SIR fuse into fuse block.
7. Install knee bolster.
8. From a position away from air bag modules, turn On ignition with engine Off.
9. AIR BAG indicator will flash 7 times, then AIR BAG indicator will then turn Off.
10. If AIR BAG indicator does not operate as outlined, refer to **MOTOR's "Air Bag Manual" or "Air Bag Diagnostics CD."**

Bravada, Envoy, Rainier & Trailblazer

2002

1. Remove key from ignition.
2. Connect passenger side impact air bag module yellow 2-way connector located under passenger seat.
3. Install CPA to passenger side impact air bag module yellow 2-way connector.
4. Connect driver side impact air bag module yellow 2-way connector located under driver seat.
5. Install CPA to driver side impact air bag module yellow 2-way connector.
6. Connect passenger air bag module yellow 2-way connector located behind instrument panel support.
7. Install CPA to passenger air bag module yellow 2-way connector.
8. Connect driver air bag module yellow 2-way connector located at base of steering column.
9. Install CPA to driver air bag module yellow 2-way connector.
10. Install AIR BAG fuse into fuse block.
11. From a position away from air bag modules, turn On ignition with engine Off.
12. AIR BAG indicator will flash 7 times, then AIR BAG indicator will then turn Off.
13. If AIR BAG indicator does not operate as outlined, refer to **MOTOR's "Air Bag Manual" or "Air Bag Diagnostics CD."**

2003-06

ZONE 1

1. Remove key from ignition.
2. Connect EFS connectors to both EFS's.
3. Install CPA's to EFS connectors.
4. Install sensor bracket to bumper.
5. Install grille.
6. Install SIR fuse into fuse block.
7. From a position away from air bag

---

modules, turn On ignition with engine Off.
8. AIR BAG indicator will flash 7 times, then AIR BAG indicator will then turn Off.
9. If AIR BAG indicator does not operate as outlined, refer to **MOTOR's "Air Bag Manual" or "Air Bag Diagnostics CD."**

ZONE 2

1. Remove key from ignition.
2. Connect driver side impact sensor yellow 2-way connector located near bottom lefthand corner of door.
3. Install CPA to driver side impact sensor yellow 2-way connector.
4. Install driver side door trim panel.
5. Install SIR fuse into fuse block.
6. From a position away from air bag modules, turn On ignition with engine Off.
7. AIR BAG indicator will flash 7 times, then AIR BAG indicator will then turn Off.
8. If AIR BAG indicator does not operate as outlined, refer to **MOTOR's "Air Bag Manual" or "Air Bag Diagnostics CD."**

ZONE 3

1. Remove key from ignition.
2. Connect driver air bag module yellow 4-way connector located left of steering column near knee bolster.
3. Install CPA to driver air bag module yellow 4-way connector.
4. Install SIR fuse into fuse block.
5. From a position away from air bag modules, turn On ignition with engine Off.
6. AIR BAG indicator will flash 7 times, then AIR BAG indicator will then turn Off.
7. If AIR BAG indicator does not operate as outlined, refer to **MOTOR's "Air Bag Manual" or "Air Bag Diagnostics CD."**

ZONE 5

1. Remove key from ignition.
2. Connect passenger air bag module yellow 4-way connector located behind main instrument panel support.
3. Install CPA to passenger air bag module yellow 4-way connector.
4. Install SIR fuse into fuse block.
5. From a position away from air bag modules, turn On ignition with engine Off.
6. AIR BAG indicator will flash 7 times, then AIR BAG indicator will then turn Off.
7. If AIR BAG indicator does not operate as outlined, refer to **MOTOR's "Air Bag Manual" or "Air Bag Diagnostics CD."**

ZONE 6

1. Remove key from ignition.
2. Connect passenger side impact sensor yellow 2-way connector located near bottom of righthand corner of door.
3. Install CPA to passenger side impact sensor yellow 2-way connector.

---

4. Install SIR fuse into fuse block.
5. From a position away from air bag modules, turn On ignition with engine Off.
6. AIR BAG indicator will flash 7 times, then AIR BAG indicator will then turn Off.
7. If AIR BAG indicator does not operate as outlined, refer to **MOTOR's "Air Bag Manual" or "Air Bag Diagnostics CD."**

ZONE 7

2003-04

1. Remove key from ignition.
2. Connect driver side impact air bag module yellow 2-way connector located under driver seat.
3. Install CPA to driver side impact air bag module yellow 2-way connector.
4. Install SIR fuse into fuse block.
5. From a position away from air bag modules, turn On ignition with engine Off.
6. AIR BAG indicator will flash 7 times, then AIR BAG indicator will then turn Off.
7. If AIR BAG indicator does not operate as outlined, refer to **MOTOR's "Air Bag Manual" or "Air Bag Diagnostics CD."**

2005-06

1. Remove key from ignition.
2. Connect driver seat belt pretensioner yellow 2-way connector located under driver seat.
3. Install CPA to driver seat belt pretensioner yellow 2-way connector.
4. Install SIR fuse into fuse block.
5. From a position away from air bag modules, turn On ignition with engine Off.
6. AIR BAG indicator will flash 7 times, then AIR BAG indicator will then turn Off.
7. If AIR BAG indicator does not operate as outlined, refer to **MOTOR's "Air Bag Manual" or "Air Bag Diagnostics CD."**

ZONE 8

2003-04

1. Remove key from ignition.
2. Connect driver air bag module yellow 4-way connector located left of steering column near knee bolster.
3. Install CPA to driver air bag module yellow 4-way connector.
4. Connect passenger air bag module yellow 4-way connector located behind instrument panel support.
5. Install CPA to passenger air bag module yellow 4-way connector.
6. Connect passenger side impact air bag module yellow 2-way connector located under passenger seat.
7. Install CPA to passenger side impact air bag module yellow 2-way connector.
8. Connect driver side impact air bag module yellow 2-way connector located under driver seat.
9. Install CPA to driver side impact air bag

module yellow 2-way connector.

10. Install SIR fuse into fuse block.
11. From a position away from air bag modules, turn On ignition with engine Off.
12. AIR BAG indicator will flash 7 times, then AIR BAG indicator will then turn Off.
13. If AIR BAG indicator does not operate as outlined, refer to **MOTOR's "Air Bag Manual" or "Air Bag Diagnostics CD."**

2005–06

1. Remove key from ignition.
2. Connect driver air bag module yellow 4-way connector located left of steering column near knee bolster.
3. Install CPA to driver air bag module yellow 4-way connector.
4. Connect passenger air bag module yellow 4-way connector located behind instrument panel support.
5. Install CPA to passenger air bag module yellow 4-way connector.
6. Connect passenger seat belt pretensioner yellow 2-way connector located under passenger seat.
7. Install CPA to passenger seat belt pretensioner yellow 2-way connector.
8. Connect passenger roof panel air bag module yellow 2-way connector and install CPA.
9. Install passenger side center pillar trim panel.
10. Connect driver seat belt pretensioner yellow 2-way connector located under driver seat.
11. Install CPA to driver seat belt pretensioner yellow 2-way connector.
12. Connect driver roof panel air bag module yellow 2-way connector and install CPA.
13. Install driver side center pillar trim panel.
14. Install SIR fuse into fuse block.
15. From a position away from air bag modules, turn On ignition with engine Off.
16. AIR BAG indicator will flash 7 times, then AIR BAG indicator will then turn Off.
17. If AIR BAG indicator does not operate as outlined, refer to **MOTOR's "Air Bag Manual" or "Air Bag Diagnostics CD."**

ZONE 9
2003–04

1. Remove key from ignition.
2. Connect passenger side impact air bag module yellow 2-way connector located under passenger seat.
3. Install CPA to passenger side impact air bag module yellow 2-way connector.
4. Install SIR fuse into fuse block.
5. From a position away from air bag modules, turn On ignition with engine Off.
6. AIR BAG indicator will flash 7 times, then AIR BAG indicator will then turn Off.
7. If AIR BAG indicator does not operate

as outlined, refer to **MOTOR's "Air Bag Manual" or "Air Bag Diagnostics CD."**

2005–06

1. Remove key from ignition.
2. Connect passenger seat belt pretensioner yellow 2-way connector located under passenger seat.
3. Install CPA to passenger seat belt pretensioner yellow 2-way connector.
4. Install SIR fuse into fuse block.
5. From a position away from air bag modules, turn On ignition with engine Off.
6. AIR BAG indicator will flash 7 times, then AIR BAG indicator will then turn Off.
7. If AIR BAG indicator does not operate as outlined, refer to **MOTOR's "Air Bag Manual" or "Air Bag Diagnostics CD."**

Canyon & Colorado

ZONE 1

1. Remove key from ignition.
2. Connect both front end sensor connectors.
3. Install SIR fuse into fuse block.
4. From a position away from air bag modules, turn On ignition with engine Off.
5. AIR BAG indicator will flash 7 times, then AIR BAG indicator will then turn Off.
6. If AIR BAG indicator does not operate as outlined, refer to **MOTOR's "Air Bag Manual" or "Air Bag Diagnostics CD."**

ZONE 2

1. Remove key from ignition.
2. Connect driver roof panel air bag module and install trim panel.
3. Connect driver seat belt pretensioner and install CPA.
4. **On models equipped with crew cab,** install lower center pillar trim panel.
5. **On models equipped with extended cab,** install rear access door wiring harness grommet to access connector.
6. **On models equipped with regular cab,** install lower body rear corner trim panel.
7. **On all models,** connect driver side impact sensor yellow 2-way connector located near middle of door.
8. Install CPA to driver side impact sensor yellow 2-way connector.
9. Install driver front door trim panel.
10. Install SIR fuse into fuse block.
11. From a position away from air bag modules, turn On ignition with engine Off.
12. AIR BAG indicator will flash 7 times, then AIR BAG indicator will then turn Off.
13. If AIR BAG indicator does not operate as outlined, refer to **MOTOR's "Air Bag Manual" or "Air Bag Diagnostics CD."**

ZONE 3

1. Remove key from ignition.
2. Connect driver air bag module yellow 4-way connector located left of steering column above left hinge pillar trim panel.
3. Install CPA to driver air bag module yellow 4-way connector.
4. Install SIR fuse into fuse block.
5. From a position away from air bag modules, turn On ignition with engine Off.
6. AIR BAG indicator will flash 7 times, then AIR BAG indicator will then turn Off.
7. If AIR BAG indicator does not operate as outlined, refer to **MOTOR's "Air Bag Manual" or "Air Bag Diagnostics CD."**

ZONE 5

1. Remove key from ignition.
2. Connect passenger air bag module 4-way connector C208 located above driver kick panel.
3. Install CPA to passenger air bag module yellow 4-way connector C208.
4. Install SIR fuse into fuse block.
5. From a position away from air bag modules, turn On ignition with engine Off.
6. AIR BAG indicator will flash 7 times, then AIR BAG indicator will then turn Off.
7. If AIR BAG indicator does not operate as outlined, refer to **MOTOR's "Air Bag Manual" or "Air Bag Diagnostics CD."**

ZONE 6

1. Remove key from ignition.
2. Connect passenger roof panel air bag module connector and install trim panel.
3. Connect passenger seat belt pretensioner connector and install CPA.
4. **On models equipped with crew cab,** install lower center pillar trim panel.
5. **On models equipped with extended cab,** install rear access door wiring harness grommet to access connector.
6. **On models equipped with regular cab,** install lower body rear corner trim panel.
7. **On all models,** connect passenger side impact sensor yellow 2-way connector located near middle of door.
8. Install CPA to passenger side impact sensor yellow 2-way connector.
9. Install passenger front door trim panel.
10. Install SIR fuse into fuse block.
11. From a position away from air bag modules, turn On ignition with engine Off.
12. AIR BAG indicator will flash 7 times, then AIR BAG indicator will then turn Off.
13. If AIR BAG indicator does not operate as outlined, refer to **MOTOR's "Air Bag Manual" or "Air Bag Diagnostics CD."**

ZONE 8

1. Remove key from ignition.
2. Connect driver air bag module yellow 4-way connector located left of steering column above left hinge pillar trim panel.
3. Install CPA to driver air bag module yellow 4-way connector.
4. Connect driver roof panel air bag module connector and install trim panel.
5. Connect driver seat belt pretensioner and install CPA.
6. **On models equipped with crew cab,** install driver side lower center pillar trim panel.
7. **On models equipped with extended cab,** install driver side rear access door wiring harness grommet to access connector.
8. **On models equipped with regular cab,** install driver side lower body rear corner trim panel.
9. **On all models,** connect driver side impact sensor yellow 2-way connector located near middle of door.
10. Install CPA to driver side impact sensor yellow 2-way connector.
11. Install driver door trim panel.
12. Connect passenger air bag module yellow 4-way connector C208 located above driver kick panel.
13. Install CPA to passenger air bag module yellow 4-way connector C208.
14. Connect passenger roof panel air bag module connector and install trim panel.
15. Connect passenger seat belt pretensioner and install CPA.
16. **On models equipped with crew cab,** install passenger side lower center pillar trim panel.
17. **On models equipped with extended cab,** install passenger side rear access door wiring harness grommet to access connector.
18. **On models equipped with regular cab,** install passenger side lower body rear corner trim panel.
19. **On all models,** connect passenger side impact sensor yellow 2-way connector located near middle of door.
20. Install passenger door trim panel.
21. Install SIR fuse into fuse block.
22. From a position away from air bag modules, turn On ignition with engine Off.
23. AIR BAG indicator will flash 7 times, then AIR BAG indicator will then turn Off.
24. If AIR BAG indicator does not operate as outlined, refer to **MOTOR's "Air Bag Manual" or "Air Bag Diagnostics CD."**

Equinox & Torrent

ZONE 1

1. Remove key from ignition.
2. Connect EFS connector to EFS.
3. Install CPA to EFS connector.
4. Install AIR BAG fuse into fuse block.
5. From a position away from air bag modules, turn On ignition with engine Off.

6. AIR BAG indicator will flash, then AIR BAG indicator will then turn Off.
7. If AIR BAG indicator does not operate as outlined, refer to **MOTOR's "Air Bag Manual" or "Air Bag Diagnostics CD."**

ZONE 2

1. Remove key from ignition.
2. **To enable driver roof panel air bag module,** proceed as follows:
   a. Connect driver roof panel air bag module connector to vehicle harness connector.
   b. Install CPA to driver roof panel air bag module connector.
   c. Install rear coat hooks.
   d. Install rear headliner push-in retainers.
   e. Install lefthand and righthand rear corner trim panels.
   f. Install upper rear window molding.
3. **To enable driver side impact sensor and driver seat belt pretensioner,** proceed as follows:
   a. Connect driver seat belt pretensioner connector to vehicle harness connector and install CPA.
   b. Connect driver side impact sensor to vehicle harness connector and install CPA.
   c. Install driver side lower center pillar trim.
4. Install AIR BAG fuse into fuse block.
5. From a position away from air bag modules, turn On ignition with engine Off.
6. AIR BAG indicator will flash, then AIR BAG indicator will then turn Off.
7. If AIR BAG indicator does not operate as outlined, refer to **MOTOR's "Air Bag Manual" or "Air Bag Diagnostics CD."**

ZONE 3

1. Remove key from ignition.
2. Connect driver air bag module coil connector to vehicle harness connector.
3. Install CPA to driver air bag module coil connector.
4. Install AIR BAG fuse into fuse block.
5. From a position away from air bag modules, turn On ignition with engine Off.
6. AIR BAG indicator will flash, then AIR BAG indicator will then turn Off.
7. If AIR BAG indicator does not operate as outlined, refer to **MOTOR's "Air Bag Manual" or "Air Bag Diagnostics CD."**

ZONE 5

1. Remove key from ignition.
2. Connect passenger air bag module connector to vehicle harness connector.
3. Install CPA to passenger air bag module connector.
4. Install AIR BAG fuse into fuse block.
5. From a position away from air bag modules, turn On ignition with engine Off.
6. AIR BAG indicator will flash, then AIR BAG indicator will then turn Off.
7. If AIR BAG indicator does not operate

as outlined, refer to **MOTOR's "Air Bag Manual" or "Air Bag Diagnostics CD."**

ZONE 6

1. Remove key from ignition.
2. **To enable passenger roof panel air bag module,** proceed as follows:
   a. Connect passenger roof panel air bag module connector to vehicle harness connector.
   b. Install CPA to passenger roof panel air bag module connector.
   c. Install rear coat hooks.
   d. Install rear headliner push-in retainers.
   e. Install lefthand and righthand rear corner trim panels.
   f. Install upper rear window molding.
3. **To enable passenger side impact sensor and passenger seat belt pretensioner,** proceed as follows:
   a. Connect passenger seat belt pretensioner connector to vehicle harness connector and install CPA.
   b. Connect passenger side impact sensor to vehicle harness connector and install CPA.
   c. Install passenger side lower center pillar trim.
4. Install AIR BAG fuse into fuse block.
5. From a position away from air bag modules, turn On ignition with engine Off.
6. AIR BAG indicator will flash, then AIR BAG indicator will then turn Off.
7. If AIR BAG indicator does not operate as outlined, refer to **MOTOR's "Air Bag Manual" or "Air Bag Diagnostics CD."**

ZONE 8

1. Remove key from ignition.
2. Connect driver air bag module coil connector to vehicle harness connector.
3. Install CPA to driver air bag module coil connector.
4. Connect driver seat belt pretensioner connector to vehicle harness connector and install CPA.
5. Install driver side lower center pillar trim.
6. Connect driver roof panel air bag module connector to vehicle harness connector.
7. Install CPA to driver roof panel air bag module connector.
8. Connect passenger air bag module connector to vehicle harness connector.
9. Install CPA to passenger air bag module connector.
10. Connect passenger seat belt pretensioner connector to vehicle harness connector and install CPA.
11. Install passenger side lower center pillar trim.
12. Connect passenger roof panel air bag module connector to vehicle harness connector.
13. Install CPA to passenger roof panel air bag module connector.
14. Install rear coat hooks.
15. Install rear headliner push-in retainers.

16. Install lefthand and righthand rear corner moldings.
17. Install upper rear window molding.
18. Install AIR BAG fuse into fuse block.
19. From a position away from air bag modules, turn On ignition with engine Off.
20. AIR BAG indicator will flash, then AIR BAG indicator will then turn Off.
21. If AIR BAG indicator does not operate as outlined, refer to **MOTOR's "Air Bag Manual" or "Air Bag Diagnostics CD."**

Express & Savana

2002

1. Remove key from ignition.
2. Connect passenger air bag module yellow 2-way connector located under instrument panel extension.
3. Install CPA to passenger air bag module yellow 2-way connector.
4. Install passenger side knee bolster.
5. Connect driver air bag module yellow 2-way connector located at base of steering column.
6. Install CPA to driver air bag module yellow 2-way connector.
7. Install driver side knee bolster.
8. Install AIR BAG fuse into fuse block.
9. From a position away from air bag modules, turn On ignition with engine Off.
10. AIR BAG indicator will flash 7 times, then AIR BAG indicator will then turn Off.
11. If AIR BAG indicator does not operate as outlined, refer to **MOTOR's "Air Bag Manual" or "Air Bag Diagnostics CD."**

2003-06

ZONE 1

1. Remove key from ignition.
2. Connect front end sensor connector to front end sensor.
3. Install CPA to front end sensor connector.
4. Install SIR fuse into fuse block.
5. From a position away from air bag modules, turn On ignition with engine Off.
6. AIR BAG indicator will flash 7 times, then AIR BAG indicator will then turn Off.
7. If AIR BAG indicator does not operate as outlined, refer to **MOTOR's "Air Bag Manual" or "Air Bag Diagnostics CD."**

ZONE 3

1. Remove key from ignition.
2. Connect driver air bag module yellow 4-way connector located left of steering column near knee bolster.
3. Install CPA to driver air bag module yellow 4-way connector.
4. Install SIR fuse into fuse block.
5. From a position away from air bag modules, turn On ignition with engine Off.

6. AIR BAG indicator will flash 7 times, then AIR BAG indicator will then turn Off.
7. If AIR BAG indicator does not operate as outlined, refer to **MOTOR's "Air Bag Manual" or "Air Bag Diagnostics CD."**

ZONE 5

1. Remove key from ignition.
2. Connect passenger air bag module yellow 4-way connector located behind main instrument panel support.
3. Install CPA to passenger air bag module yellow 4-way connector.
4. Install righthand side knee bolster bracket.
5. Install SIR fuse into fuse block.
6. From a position away from air bag modules, turn On ignition with engine Off.
7. AIR BAG indicator will flash 7 times, then AIR BAG indicator will then turn Off.
8. If AIR BAG indicator does not operate as outlined, refer to **MOTOR's "Air Bag Manual" or "Air Bag Diagnostics CD."**

ZONE 7

2003

1. Remove key from ignition.
2. Connect driver air bag module yellow 4-way connector located left of steering column near knee bolster.
3. Install CPA to driver air bag module yellow 4-way connector.
4. Connect passenger air bag module yellow 4-way connector located behind instrument panel support.
5. Install CPA to passenger air bag module yellow 4-way connector.
6. Install righthand side knee bolster bracket.
7. Connect passenger seat belt pretensioner yellow 2-way connector located under passenger seat.
8. Install CPA to passenger seat belt pretensioner yellow 2-way connector.
9. Connect driver seat belt pretensioner yellow 2-way connector located under driver seat.
10. Install CPA to driver seat belt pretensioner yellow 2-way connector.
11. Install SIR fuse into fuse block.
12. From a position away from air bag modules, turn On ignition with engine Off.
13. AIR BAG indicator will flash 7 times, then AIR BAG indicator will then turn Off.
14. If AIR BAG indicator does not operate as outlined, refer to **MOTOR's "Air Bag Manual" or "Air Bag Diagnostics CD."**

2004-05

1. Remove key from ignition.
2. Connect driver air bag module yellow 4-way connector located left of steering column near knee bolster.
3. Install CPA to driver air bag module yellow 4-way connector.

4. Connect passenger air bag module yellow 4-way connector located behind instrument panel support.
5. Install CPA to passenger air bag module yellow 4-way connector.
6. Install righthand side knee bolster bracket.
7. Install SIR fuse into fuse block.
8. From a position away from air bag modules, turn On ignition with engine Off.
9. AIR BAG indicator will flash 7 times, then AIR BAG indicator will then turn Off.
10. If AIR BAG indicator does not operate as outlined, refer to **MOTOR's "Air Bag Manual" or "Air Bag Diagnostics CD."**

2006

1. Remove key from ignition.
2. Connect driver air bag module yellow 4-way connector located left of steering column near knee bolster.
3. Install CPA to driver air bag module yellow 4-way connector.
4. Connect driver seat belt pretensioner yellow 2-way connector located under driver seat.
5. Install CPA to driver seat belt pretensioner yellow 2-way connector.
6. Connect passenger air bag module yellow 4-way connector located behind instrument panel support.
7. Install CPA to passenger air bag module yellow 4-way connector.
8. Install righthand side knee bolster bracket.
9. Connect passenger seat belt pretensioner yellow 2-way connector located under passenger seat.
10. Install CPA to passenger seat belt pretensioner yellow 2-way connector.
11. Install SIR fuse into fuse block.
12. From a position away from air bag modules, turn On ignition with engine Off.
13. AIR BAG indicator will flash 7 times, then AIR BAG indicator will then turn Off.
14. If AIR BAG indicator does not operate as outlined, refer to **MOTOR's "Air Bag Manual" or "Air Bag Diagnostics CD."**

ZONE 9

1. Remove key from ignition.
2. Connect passenger seat belt pretensioner yellow 2-way connector located under passenger seat.
3. Install CPA to passenger seat belt pretensioner yellow 2-way connector.
4. Install SIR fuse into fuse block.
5. From a position away from air bag modules, turn On ignition with engine Off.
6. AIR BAG indicator will flash 7 times, then AIR BAG indicator will then turn Off.
7. If AIR BAG indicator does not operate as outlined, refer to **MOTOR's "Air Bag Manual" or "Air Bag Diagnostics CD."**

AIR BAG SYSTEM PRECAUTIONS

HHR

ZONE 1

1. Remove key from ignition.
2. Connect front end sensor connector to front end sensor.
3. Connect CPA to front end sensor connector.
4. Install AIR BAG and SDM fuses into fuse block.
5. From a position away from air bag modules, turn On ignition with engine Off.
6. AIR BAG indicator will flash, then AIR BAG indicator will then turn Off.
7. If AIR BAG indicator does not operate as outlined, refer to **MOTOR's "Air Bag Manual" or "Air Bag Diagnostics CD."**

ZONE 2

1. Remove key from ignition.
2. Connect driver roof panel air bag module connector to vehicle harness connector.
3. Install CPA to driver roof panel air bag module connector.
4. Install driver rear quarter upper trim panel.
5. Connect driver seat belt pretensioner connector.
6. Install CPA to seat belt pretensioner connector.
7. Install driver lower center pillar trim panel.
8. Install driver side impact sensor connector to sensor.
9. Install CPA to driver side impact sensor connector.
10. Install driver door water deflector.
11. Install driver door trim panel.
12. Install AIR BAG and SDM fuses into fuse block.
13. From a position away from air bag modules, turn On ignition with engine Off.
14. AIR BAG indicator will flash, then AIR BAG indicator will then turn Off.
15. If AIR BAG indicator does not operate as outlined, refer to **MOTOR's "Air Bag Manual" or "Air Bag Diagnostics CD."**

ZONE 3

1. Remove key from ignition.
2. Connect driver air bag module coil connector to vehicle harness connector.
3. Install CPA to driver air bag module coil connector.
4. Install driver outer trim panel to instrument panel.
5. Install AIR BAG and SDM fuses into fuse block.
6. From a position away from air bag modules, turn On ignition with engine Off.
7. AIR BAG indicator will flash, then AIR BAG indicator will then turn Off.
8. If AIR BAG indicator does not operate

as outlined, refer to **MOTOR's "Air Bag Manual" or "Air Bag Diagnostics CD."**

ZONE 5

1. Remove key from ignition.
2. Connect passenger air bag module connector to vehicle harness connector.
3. Engage CPA of passenger air bag module connector.
4. Install AIR BAG and SDM fuses into fuse block.
5. From a position away from air bag modules, turn On ignition with engine Off.
6. AIR BAG indicator will flash, then AIR BAG indicator will then turn Off.
7. If AIR BAG indicator does not operate as outlined, refer to **MOTOR's "Air Bag Manual" or "Air Bag Diagnostics CD."**

ZONE 6

1. Remove key from ignition.
2. Connect passenger roof panel air bag module connector to vehicle harness connector.
3. Install CPA to passenger roof panel air bag module connector.
4. Install passenger rear quarter upper trim panel.
5. Connect passenger seat belt pretensioner connector.
6. Install CPA to passenger seat belt pretensioner connector.
7. Install passenger lower center pillar trim panel.
8. Install passenger side impact sensor connector to sensor.
9. Install CPA to passenger side impact sensor connector.
10. Install passenger door water deflector.
11. Install passenger door trim panel.
12. Install AIR BAG and SDM fuses into fuse block.
13. From a position away from air bag modules, turn On ignition with engine Off.
14. AIR BAG indicator will flash, then AIR BAG indicator will then turn Off.
15. If AIR BAG indicator does not operate as outlined, refer to **MOTOR's "Air Bag Manual" or "Air Bag Diagnostics CD."**

ZONE 8

1. Remove key from ignition.
2. Connect driver roof panel air bag module connector to vehicle harness connector.
3. Install CPA to driver roof panel air bag module connector.
4. Install driver rear quarter upper trim molding to lock pillar.
5. Connect driver seat belt pretensioner connector.
6. Install CPA to driver seat belt pretensioner connector.
7. Install driver lower center pillar trim panel.

8. Connect driver air bag module coil connector to vehicle harness connector.
9. Install CPA to driver air bag module coil connector.
10. Install driver outer trim cover to instrument panel.
11. Install driver side impact sensor connector to sensor.
12. Install CPA to driver side impact sensor connector.
13. Install driver door water deflector shield.
14. Install driver door trim panel.
15. Connect passenger air bag module connector to vehicle harness connector.
16. Engage CPA to passenger air bag module connector.
17. Connect passenger seat belt pretensioner connector.
18. Install CPA to passenger seat belt pretensioner connector.
19. Install passenger lower center pillar trim panel.
20. Connect passenger roof panel air bag module connector to vehicle harness connector.
21. Install CPA to passenger air bag module connector.
22. Install passenger rear quarter upper trim molding to lock pillar.
23. Install passenger side impact sensor connector to sensor.
24. Install CPA to passenger side impact sensor connector.
25. Install passenger door water deflector shield.
26. Install passenger door trim panel.
27. Install AIR BAG and SDM fuses into fuse block.
28. From a position away from air bag modules, turn On ignition with engine Off.
29. AIR BAG indicator will flash, then AIR BAG indicator will then turn Off.
30. If AIR BAG indicator does not operate as outlined, refer to **MOTOR's "Air Bag Manual" or "Air Bag Diagnostics CD."**

Hummer H2

ZONE 1

1. Remove key from ignition.
2. Connect both front end sensor connectors to sensors.
3. Install CPA to both front end sensor connectors.
4. Install SIR fuse into fuse block.
5. Install engine protection shield.
6. From a position away from air bag modules, turn On ignition with engine Off.
7. AIR BAG indicator will flash seven times, then AIR BAG indicator will then turn Off.
8. If AIR BAG indicator does not operate as outlined, refer to **MOTOR's "Air Bag Manual" or "Air Bag Diagnostics CD."**

ZONE 3

1. Remove key from ignition.
2. Connect driver air bag module yellow 2-way connector located left of steering column near knee bolster.
3. Install CPA to driver air bag module yellow 2-way connector.
4. Install SIR fuse into fuse block.
5. Install engine protection shield.
6. From a position away from air bag modules, turn On ignition with engine Off.
7. AIR BAG indicator will flash seven times, then AIR BAG indicator will then turn Off.
8. If AIR BAG indicator does not operate as outlined, refer to **MOTOR's "Air Bag Manual" or "Air Bag Diagnostics CD."**

ZONE 5

1. Remove key from ignition.
2. Connect passenger air bag module yellow 2-way connector located behind air bag module.
3. Install CPA to passenger air bag module yellow 2-way connector.
4. Install SIR fuse into fuse block.
5. Install engine protection shield.
6. From a position away from air bag modules, turn On ignition with engine Off.
7. AIR BAG indicator will flash seven times, then AIR BAG indicator will then turn Off.
8. If AIR BAG indicator does not operate as outlined, refer to **MOTOR's "Air Bag Manual" or "Air Bag Diagnostics CD."**

ZONE 7

1. Remove key from ignition.
2. Connect driver air bag module yellow 2-way connector located left of steering column near knee bolster.
3. Install CPA to driver air bag module yellow 2-way connector.
4. Connect passenger air bag module yellow 2-way connector located behind air bag module.
5. Install CPA to passenger air bag module yellow 2-way connector.
6. Install SIR fuse into fuse block.
7. Install engine protection shield.
8. From a position away from air bag modules, turn On ignition with engine Off.
9. AIR BAG indicator will flash seven times, then AIR BAG indicator will then turn Off.
10. If AIR BAG indicator does not operate as outlined, refer to **MOTOR's "Air Bag Manual" or "Air Bag Diagnostics CD."**

Hummer H3

ZONE 1

1. Remove key from ignition.
2. Connect sensor connectors to both front end sensors.
3. Install CPA's to both sensor connectors.
4. Install SIR fuse into fuse block.

5. Install engine protection shield.
6. From a position away from air bag modules, turn On ignition with engine Off.
7. AIR BAG indicator will flash seven times, then AIR BAG indicator will then turn Off.
8. If AIR BAG indicator does not operate as outlined, refer to **MOTOR's "Air Bag Manual" or "Air Bag Diagnostics CD."**

ZONE 2

1. Remove key from ignition.
2. Connect driver roof panel air bag module connector and install windshield pillar trim panel.
3. Connect driver seat belt pretensioner and install CPA.
4. Install driver lower center pillar trim panel.
5. Connect driver side impact sensor yellow 2-way connector located near middle of door.
6. Install CPA to driver side impact sensor yellow 2-way connector.
7. Install driver door trim panel.
8. Install SIR fuse into fuse block.
9. Install engine protection shield.
10. From a position away from air bag modules, turn On ignition with engine Off.
11. AIR BAG indicator will flash seven times, then AIR BAG indicator will then turn Off.
12. If AIR BAG indicator does not operate as outlined, refer to **MOTOR's "Air Bag Manual" or "Air Bag Diagnostics CD."**

ZONE 3

1. Remove key from ignition.
2. Connect driver air bag module yellow 4-way connector located left of steering column above left hinge pillar trim panel.
3. Install CPA to driver air bag module yellow 4-way connector.
4. Install SIR fuse into fuse block.
5. Install engine protection shield.
6. From a position away from air bag modules, turn On ignition with engine Off.
7. AIR BAG indicator will flash seven times, then AIR BAG indicator will then turn Off.
8. If AIR BAG indicator does not operate as outlined, refer to **MOTOR's "Air Bag Manual" or "Air Bag Diagnostics CD."**

ZONE 5

1. Remove key from ignition.
2. Connect passenger air bag module yellow 4-way inline connector C208 located above driver kick panel.
3. Install CPA to passenger air bag module yellow 4-way inline connector.
4. Install SIR fuse into fuse block.
5. Install engine protection shield.
6. From a position away from air bag modules, turn On ignition with engine Off.
7. AIR BAG indicator will flash seven times, then AIR BAG indicator will then turn Off.

8. If AIR BAG indicator does not operate as outlined, refer to **MOTOR's "Air Bag Manual" or "Air Bag Diagnostics CD."**

ZONE 6

1. Remove key from ignition.
2. Connect passenger roof panel air bag module connector and install windshield pillar trim panel.
3. Connect passenger seat belt pretensioner and install CPA.
4. Install passenger lower center pillar trim panel.
5. Connect passenger side impact sensor yellow 2-way connector located near middle of door.
6. Install CPA to passenger side impact sensor yellow 2-way connector.
7. Install passenger door trim panel.
8. Install SIR fuse into fuse block.
9. Install engine protection shield.
10. From a position away from air bag modules, turn On ignition with engine Off.
11. AIR BAG indicator will flash seven times, then AIR BAG indicator will then turn Off.
12. If AIR BAG indicator does not operate as outlined, refer to **MOTOR's "Air Bag Manual" or "Air Bag Diagnostics CD."**

ZONE 8

1. Remove key from ignition.
2. Connect driver air bag module yellow 4-way connector located left of steering column above left hinge pillar trim panel.
3. Install CPA to driver air bag module yellow 4-way connector.
4. Connect driver roof panel air bag module connector and install windshield pillar trim panel.
5. Connect driver seat belt pretensioner and install CPA.
6. Install driver lower center pillar trim panel.
7. Connect driver side impact sensor yellow 2-way connector located near middle of door.
8. Install CPA to driver side impact sensor yellow 2-way connector.
9. Install driver door trim panel.
10. Connect passenger air bag module yellow 4-way inline connector C208 located above driver kick panel.
11. Install CPA to passenger air bag module yellow 4-way inline connector.
12. Connect passenger roof panel air bag module connector and install windshield pillar trim panel.
13. Connect passenger seat belt pretensioner and install CPA.
14. Install passenger lower center pillar trim panel.
15. Connect passenger side impact sensor yellow 2-way connector located near middle of door.
16. Install CPA to passenger side impact sensor yellow 2-way connector.
17. Install passenger door trim panel.
18. Install SIR fuse into fuse block.
19. Install engine protection shield.
20. From a position away from air bag

modules, turn On ignition with engine Off.

21. AIR BAG indicator will flash seven times, then AIR BAG indicator will then turn Off.

22. If AIR BAG indicator does not operate as outlined, refer to **MOTOR's "Air Bag Manual" or "Air Bag Diagnostics CD."**

Montana, Silhouette & Venture

2002

1. Connect passenger seat belt pretensioner connector located under passenger seat.
2. Install CPA to passenger seat belt pretensioner connector.
3. Connect passenger side impact air bag module connector located under passenger seat.
4. Install CPA to passenger side impact air bag module connector.
5. Connect driver seat belt pretensioner connector located under driver seat.
6. Install CPA to driver seat belt pretensioner connector.
7. Connect driver side impact air bag module connector located under driver seat.
8. Install CPA to driver side impact air bag module connector.
9. Connect passenger air bag module connector located behind insulator panel.
10. Install CPA to passenger air bag module connector.
11. Install passenger insulator panel.
12. Connect driver air bag module coil connector located at base of steering column.
13. Install CPA to driver air bag module coil connector.
14. Install driver insulator panel.
15. Install SDM fuse into fuse block.
16. From a position away from air bag modules, turn On ignition with engine Off.
17. AIR BAG indicator will flash seven times, then AIR BAG indicator will then turn Off.
18. If AIR BAG indicator does not operate as outlined, refer to **MOTOR's "Air Bag Manual" or "Air Bag Diagnostics CD."**

2003-06

ZONE 1

1. Remove key from ignition.
2. Connect both front end sensor connectors to front end sensors.
3. Install CPA to both front end sensor connectors.
4. Install SIR fuse into fuse block.
5. From a position away from air bag modules, turn On ignition with engine Off.
6. AIR BAG indicator will flash seven times, then AIR BAG indicator will then turn Off.
7. If AIR BAG indicator does not operate as outlined, refer to **MOTOR's "Air**

Bag Manual" or "Air Bag Diagnostics CD."

ZONE 2

1. Remove key from ignition.
2. Connect driver side impact sensor yellow 2-way connector to sensor located near bottom of B-pillar.
3. Install CPA to driver side impact sensor yellow 2-way connector.
4. Install driver seat belt retractor trim cover.
5. Install SIR fuse into fuse block.
6. From a position away from air bag modules, turn On ignition with engine Off.
7. AIR BAG indicator will flash seven times, then AIR BAG indicator will then turn Off.
8. If AIR BAG indicator does not operate as outlined, refer to **MOTOR's "Air Bag Manual" or "Air Bag Diagnostics CD."**

ZONE 3

1. Remove key from ignition.
2. Connect driver air bag module coil yellow 4-way connector located at base of steering column.
3. Install CPA to driver air bag module coil yellow 4-way connector.
4. Install driver insulator panel.
5. Install SIR fuse into fuse block.
6. From a position away from air bag modules, turn On ignition with engine Off.
7. AIR BAG indicator will flash seven times, then AIR BAG indicator will then turn Off.
8. If AIR BAG indicator does not operate as outlined, refer to **MOTOR's "Air Bag Manual" or "Air Bag Diagnostics CD."**

ZONE 5

1. Remove key from ignition.
2. Connect passenger air bag module yellow 4-way connector located behind passenger insulator panel.
3. Install CPA to passenger air bag module yellow 4-way connector.
4. Connect electrical connectors and install glove compartment.
5. Install SIR fuse into fuse block.
6. From a position away from air bag modules, turn On ignition with engine Off.
7. AIR BAG indicator will flash seven times, then AIR BAG indicator will then turn Off.
8. If AIR BAG indicator does not operate as outlined, refer to **MOTOR's "Air Bag Manual" or "Air Bag Diagnostics CD."**

ZONE 6

1. Remove key from ignition.
2. Connect passenger side impact sensor yellow 2-way connector to sensor located near bottom of B-pillar.
3. Install CPA to passenger side impact sensor yellow 2-way connector.
4. Install passenger seat belt retractor trim cover.
5. Install SIR fuse into fuse block.
6. From a position away from air bag

modules, turn On ignition with engine Off.

7. AIR BAG indicator will flash seven times, then AIR BAG indicator will then turn Off.
8. If AIR BAG indicator does not operate as outlined, refer to **MOTOR's "Air Bag Manual" or "Air Bag Diagnostics CD."**

ZONE 7

1. Remove key from ignition.
2. Connect driver seat belt pretensioner yellow 2-way connector located under driver seat.
3. Install CPA to driver seat belt pretensioner yellow 2-way connector.
4. Connect driver side impact air bag module yellow 2-way connector located under driver seat.
5. Install CPA to driver side impact air bag module yellow 2-way connector.
6. Install SIR fuse into fuse block.
7. From a position away from air bag modules, turn On ignition with engine Off.
8. AIR BAG indicator will flash seven times, then AIR BAG indicator will then turn Off.
9. If AIR BAG indicator does not operate as outlined, refer to **MOTOR's "Air Bag Manual" or "Air Bag Diagnostics CD."**

ZONE 9

1. Remove key from ignition.
2. Connect passenger air bag module yellow 4-way connector located behind passenger insulator panel.
3. Install CPA to passenger air bag module yellow 4-way connector.
4. Connect electrical connectors and install glove compartment.
5. Connect driver air bag module coil yellow 4-way connector located at base of steering column.
6. Install CPA to driver air bag module coil yellow 4-way connector.
7. Install driver insulator panel.
8. Connect driver seat belt pretensioner yellow 2-way connector located under driver seat.
9. Install CPA to driver seat belt pretensioner yellow 2-way connector.
10. Connect driver side impact air bag module yellow 2-way connector located under driver seat.
11. Install CPA to driver side impact air bag module yellow 2-way connector.
12. Connect passenger seat belt pretensioner yellow 2-way connector located under passenger seat.
13. Install CPA to passenger seat belt pretensioner yellow 2-way connector.
14. Connect passenger side impact air bag module yellow 2-way connector located under passenger seat.
15. Install CPA to passenger side impact air bag module yellow 2-way connector.
16. Install SIR fuse into fuse block.
17. From a position away from air bag modules, turn On ignition with engine Off.
18. AIR BAG indicator will flash seven

times, then AIR BAG indicator will then turn Off.
19. If AIR BAG indicator does not operate as outlined, refer to **MOTOR's "Air Bag Manual" or "Air Bag Diagnostics CD."**

Relay, SV6, Terraza & Uplander

ZONE 1

1. Remove key from ignition.
2. Connect both front end sensor harness connectors to front end sensors.
3. Install CPA's to both front end sensor connectors.
4. Install AIR BAG fuse into fuse block.
5. From a position away from air bag modules, turn On ignition with engine Off.
6. AIR BAG indicator will flash, then AIR BAG indicator will then turn Off.
7. If AIR BAG indicator does not operate as outlined, refer to **MOTOR's "Air Bag Manual" or "Air Bag Diagnostics CD."**

ZONE 2

1. Remove key from ignition.
2. Connect vehicle harness connector to driver seat belt pretensioner.
3. Install CPA to driver seat belt pretensioner connector.
4. Connect driver side impact sensor harness connector to sensor.
5. Install CPA to driver side impact sensor connector.
6. Install driver side impact sensor to center pillar and tighten sensor fasteners.
7. Install driver lower center pillar trim cover.
8. Install AIR BAG fuse into fuse block.
9. From a position away from air bag modules, turn On ignition with engine Off.
10. AIR BAG indicator will flash, then AIR BAG indicator will then turn Off.
11. If AIR BAG indicator does not operate as outlined, refer to **MOTOR's "Air Bag Manual" or "Air Bag Diagnostics CD."**

ZONE 3

1. Remove key from ignition.
2. Connect driver air bag module coil yellow connector.
3. Install CPA to driver air bag module coil connector located at base of steering column.
4. Install driver knee bolster insulator panel.
5. Install AIR BAG fuse into fuse block.
6. From a position away from air bag modules, turn On ignition with engine Off.
7. AIR BAG indicator will flash, then AIR BAG indicator will then turn Off.
8. If AIR BAG indicator does not operate as outlined, refer to **MOTOR's "Air Bag Manual" or "Air Bag Diagnostics CD."**

ZONE 5

1. Remove key from ignition.
2. Connect passenger air bag module yellow connector.
3. Install CPA to passenger air bag module connector.
4. Install passenger knee bolster insulator panel.
5. Install AIR BAG fuse into fuse block.
6. From a position away from air bag modules, turn On ignition with engine Off.
7. AIR BAG indicator will flash, then AIR BAG indicator will then turn Off.
8. If AIR BAG indicator does not operate as outlined, refer to **MOTOR's "Air Bag Manual" or "Air Bag Diagnostics CD."**

ZONE 6

1. Remove key from ignition.
2. Connect vehicle harness connector to passenger seat belt pretensioner.
3. Install CPA to passenger seat belt pretensioner connector.
4. Connect passenger side impact sensor harness connector to sensor.
5. Install CPA to passenger side impact sensor connector.
6. Install passenger side impact sensor to center pillar and tighten sensor fasteners.
7. Install passenger lower center pillar trim cover.
8. Install AIR BAG fuse into fuse block.
9. From a position away from air bag modules, turn On ignition with engine Off.
10. AIR BAG indicator will flash, then AIR BAG indicator will then turn Off.
11. If AIR BAG indicator does not operate as outlined, refer to **MOTOR's "Air Bag Manual" or "Air Bag Diagnostics CD."**

ZONE 7

1. Remove key from ignition.
2. Connect vehicle harness connector to driver front side impact air bag module yellow connector.
3. Install CPA to driver front side impact air bag module connector.
4. Install AIR BAG fuse into fuse block.
5. From a position away from air bag modules, turn On ignition with engine Off.
6. AIR BAG indicator will flash, then AIR BAG indicator will then turn Off.
7. If AIR BAG indicator does not operate as outlined, refer to **MOTOR's "Air Bag Manual" or "Air Bag Diagnostics CD."**

ZONE 9

1. Remove key from ignition.
2. **To enable entire SIR system,** proceed as follows:
   a. Connect vehicle harness connector to driver seat belt pretensioner.
   b. Install CPA to driver seat belt pretensioner connector.
   c. Install driver lower center pillar trim cover.
   d. Connect driver air bag module coil

yellow connector.
   e. Install CPA to driver air bag module coil connector located at base of steering column.
   f. Install driver knee bolster insulator panel.
   g. Connect vehicle harness connector to driver front side impact air bag module yellow connector.
   h. Install CPA to driver front side impact air bag module connector.
   i. Connect vehicle harness connector to driver rear side impact air bag module yellow connector.
   j. Install CPA to driver rear side impact air bag module connector.
   k. Connect passenger air bag module yellow connector.
   l. Install CPA to passenger air bag module connector.
   m. Install passenger knee bolster insulator panel.
   n. Connect vehicle harness connector to passenger seat belt pretensioner.
   o. Install CPA to passenger seat belt pretensioner connector.
   p. Install passenger lower center pillar trim cover.
   q. Connect vehicle harness connector to passenger rear side impact air bag module yellow connector.
   r. Install CPA to passenger rear side impact air bag module connector.
   s. Connect vehicle harness connector to passenger front side impact air bag module yellow connector.
   t. Install CPA to passenger front side impact air bag module connector.
3. **To enable passenger front side impact air bag module,** proceed as follows:
   a. Connect vehicle harness connector to passenger front side impact air bag module yellow connector.
   b. Install CPA to passenger front side impact air bag module connector.
4. Install AIR BAG fuse into fuse block.
5. From a position away from air bag modules, turn On ignition with engine Off.
6. AIR BAG indicator will flash, then AIR BAG indicator will then turn Off.
7. If AIR BAG indicator does not operate as outlined, refer to **MOTOR's "Air Bag Manual" or "Air Bag Diagnostics CD."**

ZONE 10

1. Remove key from ignition.
2. Connect vehicle harness connector to driver rear side impact air bag module yellow connector.
3. Install CPA to driver rear side impact air bag module connector.
4. Install AIR BAG fuse into fuse block.
5. From a position away from air bag modules, turn On ignition with engine Off.
6. AIR BAG indicator will flash, then AIR BAG indicator will then turn Off.
7. If AIR BAG indicator does not operate as outlined, refer to **MOTOR's "Air Bag Manual" or "Air Bag Diagnostics CD."**

AIR BAG SYSTEM PRECAUTIONS

ZONE 12

1. Remove key from ignition.
2. Connect vehicle harness connector to passenger rear side impact air bag module yellow connector.
3. Install CPA to passenger rear side impact air bag module connector.
4. Install AIR BAG fuse into fuse block.
5. From a position away from air bag modules, turn On ignition with engine Off.
6. AIR BAG indicator will flash, then AIR BAG indicator will then turn Off.
7. If AIR BAG indicator does not operate as outlined, refer to **MOTOR's "Air Bag Manual" or "Air Bag Diagnostics CD."**

SRX

ZONE 1

1. Remove key from ignition.
2. Connect both connectors to front end sensors.
3. Install both CPA's to front end sensor connectors.
4. Close hood.
5. Install SIR fuse into fuse block.
6. Install fuse cover and place carpet back under seat.
7. From a position away from air bag modules, turn On ignition with engine Off.
8. AIR BAG indicator will flash, then AIR BAG indicator will then turn Off.
9. If AIR BAG indicator does not operate as outlined, refer to **MOTOR's "Air Bag Manual" or "Air Bag Diagnostics CD."**

ZONE 2

1. Remove key from ignition.
2. **To enable driver side impact sensor,** proceed as follows:
   a. Connect driver side impact sensor connector to sensor.
   b. Connect CPA to driver side impact sensor connector.
   c. Install driver center pillar trim panel.
3. **To enable driver roof panel air bag module,** proceed as follows:
   a. Connect driver roof panel air bag module yellow connector to air bag module.
   b. Install CPA to driver roof panel air bag module connector.
   c. Install driver carpet retainer trim.
4. Install SIR fuse into fuse block.
5. Install fuse cover and place carpet back under seat.
6. From a position away from air bag modules, turn On ignition with engine Off.
7. AIR BAG indicator will flash, then AIR BAG indicator will then turn Off.
8. If AIR BAG indicator does not operate as outlined, refer to **MOTOR's "Air Bag Manual" or "Air Bag Diagnostics CD."**

ZONE 3

1. Remove key from ignition.
2. Connect driver air bag module coil yellow connector to vehicle harness yellow connector.
3. Install CPA to driver air bag module coil yellow connector.
4. Install driver insulator panel to side of instrument panel.
5. Install SIR fuse into fuse block.
6. Install fuse cover and place carpet back under seat.
7. From a position away from air bag modules, turn On ignition with engine Off.
8. AIR BAG indicator will flash, then AIR BAG indicator will then turn Off.
9. If AIR BAG indicator does not operate as outlined, refer to **MOTOR's "Air Bag Manual" or "Air Bag Diagnostics CD."**

ZONE 5

1. Remove key from ignition.
2. Connect passenger air bag module yellow connector to vehicle harness yellow connector.
3. Install CPA to passenger air bag module yellow connector.
4. Install passenger insulator panel to side of instrument panel.
5. Install SIR fuse into fuse block.
6. Install fuse cover and place carpet back under seat.
7. From a position away from air bag modules, turn On ignition with engine Off.
8. AIR BAG indicator will flash, then AIR BAG indicator will then turn Off.
9. If AIR BAG indicator does not operate as outlined, refer to **MOTOR's "Air Bag Manual" or "Air Bag Diagnostics CD."**

ZONE 6

1. Remove key from ignition.
2. **To enable passenger side impact sensor,** proceed as follows:
   a. Connect passenger side impact sensor connector to sensor.
   b. Connect CPA to passenger side impact sensor connector.
   c. Install passenger center pillar trim panel.
3. **To enable passenger roof panel air bag module,** proceed as follows:
   a. Connect passenger roof panel air bag module yellow connector to air bag module.
   b. Install CPA to passenger roof panel air bag module connector.
   c. Install passenger carpet retainer trim.
4. Install SIR fuse into fuse block.
5. Install fuse cover and place carpet back under seat.
6. From a position away from air bag modules, turn On ignition with engine Off.
7. AIR BAG indicator will flash, then AIR BAG indicator will then turn Off.
8. If AIR BAG indicator does not operate as outlined, refer to **MOTOR's "Air Bag Manual" or "Air Bag Diagnostics CD."**

ZONE 7

1. Remove key from ignition.
2. Connect driver side impact air bag module and pretensioner yellow connector to vehicle harness yellow connector.
3. Install both CPA locks to driver side impact air bag module and pretensioner yellow connector.
4. Install SIR fuse into fuse block.
5. Install fuse cover and place carpet back under seat.
6. From a position away from air bag modules, turn On ignition with engine Off.
7. AIR BAG indicator will flash, then AIR BAG indicator will then turn Off.
8. If AIR BAG indicator does not operate as outlined, refer to **MOTOR's "Air Bag Manual" or "Air Bag Diagnostics CD."**

ZONE 8

1. Remove key from ignition.
2. Connect driver roof panel air bag module yellow connector to air bag module.
3. Install CPA to driver roof panel air bag module connector.
4. Install driver carpet retainer trim.
5. Connect driver side impact air bag module and seat belt pretensioner yellow connector to vehicle harness yellow connector located under driver seat.
6. Install both CPA locks to driver side impact air bag module and pretensioner yellow connector.
7. Connect driver air bag module coil yellow connector to vehicle harness yellow connector.
8. Install CPA to driver air bag module coil yellow connector.
9. Install driver insulator panel to side of instrument panel.
10. Connect passenger air bag module yellow connector to vehicle harness yellow connector.
11. Install CPA to passenger air bag module yellow connector.
12. Install passenger insulator panel to side of instrument panel.
13. Connect passenger side impact air bag module and seat belt pretensioner yellow connector to vehicle harness yellow connector located under passenger seat.
14. Install both CPA locks to passenger side impact air bag module and pretensioner yellow connector.
15. Connect passenger roof panel air bag module yellow connector to air bag module.
16. Install CPA to passenger roof panel air bag module connector.
17. Install passenger carpet retainer trim.
18. Install SIR fuse into fuse block.
19. Install fuse cover and place carpet back under seat.
20. From a position away from air bag modules, turn On ignition with engine Off.
21. AIR BAG indicator will flash, then AIR BAG indicator will then turn Off.
22. If AIR BAG indicator does not operate as outlined, refer to **MOTOR's "Air Bag Manual" or "Air Bag Diagnostics CD."**

ZONE 9

1. Remove key from ignition.
2. Connect passenger side impact air bag module and pretensioner yellow connector to vehicle harness yellow connector.
3. Install both CPA locks to passenger side impact air bag module and pretensioner yellow connector.
4. Install SIR fuse into fuse block.
5. Install fuse cover and place carpet back under seat.
6. From a position away from air bag modules, turn On ignition with engine Off.
7. AIR BAG indicator will flash, then AIR BAG indicator will then turn Off.
8. If AIR BAG indicator does not operate as outlined, refer to **MOTOR's "Air Bag Manual" or "Air Bag Diagnostics CD."**

Tracker

2002

1. Remove key from ignition.
2. Install yellow 2-way connector and CPA to passenger air bag module connector.
3. Install glove compartment door.
4. Install yellow 2-way connector and CPA to driver air bag module connector.
5. Install driver knee bolster trim plate.
6. Install AIR BAG fuse into fuse block.
7. From a position away from air bag modules, turn On ignition with engine Off.
8. AIR BAG indicator will flash seven times, then AIR BAG indicator will then turn Off.
9. If AIR BAG indicator does not operate as outlined, refer to **MOTOR's "Air Bag Manual" or "Air Bag Diagnostics CD."**

2003-04

ZONE 3

1. Remove key from ignition.
2. Install yellow 2-way connector and CPA to driver air bag module connector.
3. Install driver knee bolster trim panel.
4. Install AIR BAG fuse into fuse block.
5. From a position away from air bag modules, turn On ignition with engine Off.
6. AIR BAG indicator will flash seven times, then AIR BAG indicator will then turn Off.
7. If AIR BAG indicator does not operate as outlined, refer to **MOTOR's "Air Bag Manual" or "Air Bag Diagnostics CD."**

ZONE 5

1. Remove key from ignition.
2. Install yellow 2-way connector and CPA to passenger air bag module connector.
3. Install glove compartment door.
4. Install AIR BAG fuse into fuse block.
5. From a position away from air bag

modules, turn On ignition with engine Off.
6. AIR BAG indicator will flash seven times, then AIR BAG indicator will then turn Off.
7. If AIR BAG indicator does not operate as outlined, refer to **MOTOR's "Air Bag Manual" or "Air Bag Diagnostics CD."**

ZONE 8

1. Remove key from ignition.
2. Install yellow 2-way connector and CPA to passenger air bag module connector.
3. Install glove compartment door.
4. Install yellow 2-way connector and CPA to driver air bag module connector.
5. Install driver knee bolster trim panel.
6. Install AIR BAG fuse into fuse block.
7. From a position away from air bag modules, turn On ignition with engine Off.
8. AIR BAG indicator will flash seven times, then AIR BAG indicator will then turn Off.
9. If AIR BAG indicator does not operate as outlined, refer to **MOTOR's "Air Bag Manual" or "Air Bag Diagnostics CD."**

Vue

ZONE 2

2002-03

1. Remove key from ignition.
2. Connect driver roof panel air bag module connector to vehicle harness connector.
3. Install CPA to driver air bag module connector.
4. Install rear coat hooks.
5. Install rear headliner push-in retainers.
6. Install both lefthand and righthand rear corner trim panels.
7. Install upper rear window trim panels.
8. Install AIR BAG fuse into fuse block.
9. From a position away from air bag modules, turn On ignition with engine Off.
10. AIR BAG indicator will flash, then AIR BAG indicator will then turn Off.
11. If AIR BAG indicator does not operate as outlined, refer to **MOTOR's "Air Bag Manual" or "Air Bag Diagnostics CD."**

2004-06

1. Remove key from ignition.
2. **To enable driver roof panel air bag module,** proceed as follows:
   a. Connect driver roof panel air bag module connector to vehicle harness connector.
   b. Install CPA to driver roof panel air bag module connector.
   c. Install rear coat hooks.
   d. Install rear headliner push-in retainers.
   e. Install both lefthand and righthand rear corner trim panels.
   f. Install upper rear window trim panel.
3. **To enable driver roof panel air bag**

module and driver seat belt pretensioner, proceed as follows:
   a. Connect driver roof panel air bag module connector to vehicle harness connector.
   b. Install CPA to driver roof panel air bag module connector.
   c. Install rear coat hooks.
   d. Install rear headliner push-in retainers.
   e. Install both lefthand and righthand rear corner trim panels.
   f. Install upper rear window trim panel.
   g. Connect driver seat belt pretensioner connector and install CPA.
   h. Install driver lower center pillar trim panel.
4. Install AIR BAG fuse into fuse block.
5. From a position away from air bag modules, turn On ignition with engine Off.
6. AIR BAG indicator will flash, then AIR BAG indicator will then turn Off.
7. If AIR BAG indicator does not operate as outlined, refer to **MOTOR's "Air Bag Manual" or "Air Bag Diagnostics CD."**

ZONE 3

1. Remove key from ignition.
2. Connect driver air bag module coil connector to vehicle harness connector.
3. Install CPA to driver air bag module coil connector.
4. Install AIR BAG fuse into fuse block.
5. From a position away from air bag modules, turn On ignition with engine Off.
6. AIR BAG indicator will flash, then AIR BAG indicator will then turn Off.
7. If AIR BAG indicator does not operate as outlined, refer to **MOTOR's "Air Bag Manual" or "Air Bag Diagnostics CD."**

ZONE 5

1. Remove key from ignition.
2. Connect passenger air bag module connector to vehicle harness connector.
3. Install CPA to passenger air bag module connector.
4. Install AIR BAG fuse into fuse block.
5. From a position away from air bag modules, turn On ignition with engine Off.
6. AIR BAG indicator will flash, then AIR BAG indicator will then turn Off.
7. If AIR BAG indicator does not operate as outlined, refer to **MOTOR's "Air Bag Manual" or "Air Bag Diagnostics CD."**

ZONE 6

2002-03

1. Remove key from ignition.
2. Connect passenger roof panel air bag module connector to vehicle harness connector.
3. Install CPA to passenger air bag module connector.
4. Install rear coat hooks.
5. Install rear headliner push-in retainers.

6. Install both lefthand and righthand rear corner trim panels.
7. Install upper rear window trim panel.
8. Install AIR BAG fuse into fuse block.
9. From a position away from air bag modules, turn On ignition with engine Off.
10. AIR BAG indicator will flash, then AIR BAG indicator will then turn Off.
11. If AIR BAG indicator does not operate as outlined, refer to **MOTOR's "Air Bag Manual" or "Air Bag Diagnostics CD."**

2004-06

1. Remove key from ignition.
2. **To enable passenger roof panel air bag module and passenger seat belt pretensioner,** proceed as follows:
   a. Connect passenger roof panel air bag module connector to vehicle harness connector.
   b. Install CPA to passenger roof panel air bag module connector.
   c. Install rear coat hooks.
   d. Install rear headliner push-in retainers.
   e. Install both lefthand and righthand rear corner trim panels.
   f. Install upper rear window trim panel.
   g. Connect passenger seat belt pretensioner connector and install CPA.
   h. Install passenger lower center pillar trim panel.
3. **To enable passenger roof panel air bag module,** proceed as follows:
   a. Connect passenger roof panel air bag module connector to vehicle harness connector.
   b. Install CPA to passenger roof panel air bag module connector.
   c. Install rear coat hooks.
   d. Install rear headliner push-in retainers.
   e. Install both lefthand and righthand rear corner trim panels.

f. Install upper rear window trim panel.
4. Install AIR BAG fuse into fuse block.
5. From a position away from air bag modules, turn On ignition with engine Off.
6. AIR BAG indicator will flash, then AIR BAG indicator will then turn Off.
7. If AIR BAG indicator does not operate as outlined, refer to **MOTOR's "Air Bag Manual" or "Air Bag Diagnostics CD."**

ZONE 8

2002-03

1. Remove key from ignition.
2. Connect driver air bag module coil connector to vehicle harness connector.
3. Install CPA to driver air bag module coil connector.
4. Connect driver roof panel air bag module connector to vehicle harness connector.
5. Install CPA to driver roof panel air bag module connector.
6. Connect passenger air bag module connector to vehicle harness connector.
7. Install CPA to passenger air bag module connector.
8. Connect passenger roof panel air bag module connector to vehicle harness connector.
9. Install CPA to passenger roof panel air bag module connector.
10. Install rear coat hooks.
11. Install rear headliner push-in retainers.
12. Install both lefthand and righthand rear corner trim panels.
13. Install upper rear window trim panel.
14. Install AIR BAG fuse into fuse block.
15. From a position away from air bag modules, turn On ignition with engine Off.
16. AIR BAG indicator will flash, then AIR BAG indicator will then turn Off.
17. If AIR BAG indicator does not operate

as outlined, refer to **MOTOR's "Air Bag Manual" or "Air Bag Diagnostics CD."**

2004-06

1. Remove key from ignition.
2. Connect driver air bag module coil connector to vehicle harness connector.
3. Install CPA to driver air bag module coil connector.
4. Connect driver seat belt pretensioner connector and install CPA.
5. Install driver lower center pillar trim panel.
6. Connect driver roof panel air bag module connector to vehicle harness connector.
7. Install CPA to driver roof panel air bag module connector.
8. Connect passenger air bag module connector to vehicle harness connector.
9. Install CPA to passenger air bag module connector.
10. Connect passenger seat belt pretensioner connector and install CPA.
11. Install passenger lower center pillar trim panel.
12. Connect passenger roof panel air bag module connector to vehicle harness connector.
13. Install CPA to passenger roof panel air bag module connector.
14. Install rear coat hooks.
15. Install rear headliner push-in retainers.
16. Install both lefthand and righthand rear corner trim panels.
17. Install upper rear window trim panel.
18. Install AIR BAG fuse into fuse block.
19. From a position away from air bag modules, turn On ignition with engine Off.
20. AIR BAG indicator will flash, then AIR BAG indicator will then turn Off.
21. If AIR BAG indicator does not operate as outlined, refer to **MOTOR's "Air Bag Manual" or "Air Bag Diagnostics CD."**

GENERAL MOTORS CORP.

INDEX

	Page No.		Page No.		Page No.
DaimlerChrysler Corp.	0-45	Transaxle Quick Learn		VCM	0-46
Controller Anti-Lock Brakes (CAB)	0-45	Procedure	0-45	Passlock Learn Procedure	0-47
Dakota, Durango, Ram Pick-Up & Ram Van	0-45	**Description**	0-45	Auto Learn Passlock Procedure	0-47
Engine Performance	0-45	**Ford Motor Co.**	0-46	With Techline Terminal & Scan Tool	0-47
Pinion Factor Procedure	0-46	**General Motors Corp.**	0-46	TDC Offset Adjustment	0-46
Powertrain Control Module (PCM)	0-45	Crankshaft Position System Variation Learn	0-46	C & K Series w/Diesel Engine	0-46
Shift Quality	0-46	Engine Performance	0-46		
Theft Alarm	0-46	PCM/VCM	0-46		
		Body Control Module (BCM)	0-46		
		PCM	0-46		

DESCRIPTION

A computer relearn procedure may be required on any vehicle equipped with body, engine or transmission control computers whenever battery power to the computer is interrupted. These computers gather and store information on vehicle operation. They use this information to provide maximum driveability and vehicle performance.

DAIMLERCHRYSLER CORP.

Engine Performance

The PCM receives input signals from various switches and sensors. Based on these inputs, the PCM adjusts fuel injector pulse width, idle speed, ignition timing and canister purge operation. If the battery is disconnected, the PCM will need to relearn values sent by the sensors and switches. During the PCM relearning period, a change may be noted in vehicle performance. To allow the PCM to relearn its values, ensure engine is at operating temperature. Drive the vehicle at part throttle, with moderate acceleration and idle conditions until normal performance returns.

Transaxle Quick Learn Procedure

The transaxle quick learn procedure requires the use of a DRB III scan tool, or equivalent. This program allows the electronic transaxle system to calibrate itself. Use the following procedure whenever the transaxle assembly, transaxle control module, solenoid pack, clutch plate, clutch plate seal or valve body are replaced.
1. To perform the quick learn procedure, the following conditions must be met:
   a. Brakes must be applied.

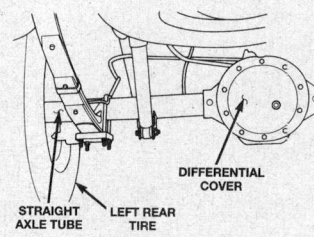
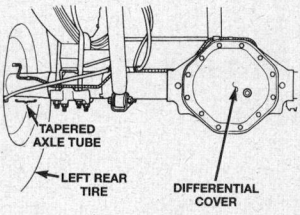
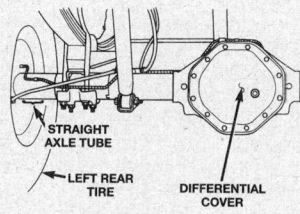
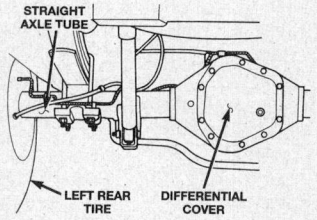

Fig. 1 Rear axle identification. Dakota, Durango, Ram Pick-Up & Ram Van

8.25" REAR AXLE = 104 TONE RING TEETH

9.25" LD REAR AXLE = 108 TONE RING TEETH

9.25" HD REAR AXLE = 117 TONE RING TEETH

DANA REAR AXLE = 120 TONE RING TEETH

CR1139900886000X

   b. Engine speed must be above 500 RPM.
   c. Throttle angle (TPS) must be less than 3°F.
   d. Shift lever position must remain same except when prompted to change position by scan tool.
   e. Calculated oil temperature must be below 200°F and above 60°F.
2. Connect scan tool to Data Link Connector (DLC).
3. Go to transmission screen.
4. Go to miscellaneous screen.
5. Select quick learn procedure.
6. Follow scan tool instructions to perform procedure.

Powertrain Control Module (PCM)

When the PCM is replaced, the new PCM must be programmed using the DRB, or equivalent, scan tool with the original vehicles identification number and the vehicles original miles.

Controller Anti-Lock Brakes (CAB)

DAKOTA, DURANGO, RAM PICK-UP & RAM VAN

If the CAB unit is replaced, the rear axle type and tire revolutions per mile must be programmed into the new CAB unit. Failure to properly program a new CAB unit will result in a blinking ABS light.
1. Place ignition in Off position.
2. Replace CAB unit.
3. Inspect connectors and clean and repair if required.
4. Connect DRB, or equivalent, scan tool to Data Link Connector (DLC).
5. If tire size and rear axle are known,

Fig. 1, select MISC, then MODULE REPLACEMENT.

6. If tire size and rear axle are not known, proceed as follows:
   a. Select MISC, then SET PINION FACTOR on DRB.
   b. If vehicle does not have standardized tires listed on DRB menu, install production size tires.
   c. If size of tires is not known, inspect rear tires for size printed on side wall.
   d. Place ignition in On position with engine Off.
   e. Program tire size into DRB.
   f. Program correct rear axle into DRB.
   g. Road test vehicle above 30 mph for two minutes, then inspect for DTC's. If DTC's are present, refer to "Anti-Lock Brakes" chapter in this manual.

Pinion Factor Procedure

The pinion factor must be set any time the transaxle control module is replaced. This will ensure speedometer readings are correct. The DRB III scan tool, or equivalent, is required to perform this procedure. Failure to perform this procedure could result in an inoperative speedometer. Perform the pinion factor procedure as follows:
1. Connect scan tool to Data Link Connector (DLC).
2. Select transmission menu.
3. Select miscellaneous menu.
4. Select Pinion Factor.
5. Follow scan tool instructions to perform procedure.

Shift Quality

This procedure must be performed whenever battery voltage is interrupted to the Transmission Control Module (TCM) or any transmission internal components are replaced. A Chrysler Diagnostic Readout Box (DRB), or equivalent, scan tool with the specified transmission cartridge must be used to perform this procedure.
1. To perform shift quality reset procedure, following conditions must exist:
   a. Transmission oil temperature must be between 60–200°F (16–94°C).
   b. Engine speed greater than 500 RPM.
   c. Throttle angle less than 3°F.
2. Connect DRB, or equivalent, scan tool to DLC. DLC is located under lefthand side of instrument panel, near top of brake pedal.
3. With correct cartridge installed, select "ADJUSTMENTS" function.
4. Apply brakes and select "QUICK LEARN" function.
5. Place gearshift in NEUTRAL, then "OD" when indicated.
6. Wait until "TEST COMPLETE" is indicated by DRB.
7. Place gearshift in PARK, release brakes and disconnect DRB.

Theft Alarm

This procedure must be done any time the battery is disconnected or the battery is boosted. If the theft alarm is not reset, the alarm system will power up and the vehicle will not start.
1. Before reconnecting battery or connecting booster cables to battery, insert door key into driver side door lock.
2. Connect battery or booster cables and cycle driver door lock once.
3. Vehicle can now be started.

FORD MOTOR CO.

Disconnect battery ground for a minimum of five minutes. After clearing memory, it is required to drive vehicle a minimum of 10 miles to allow processor time to relearn values.

GENERAL MOTORS CORP.

Engine Performance

The PCM/VCM has a learning ability which allows it to make corrections for minor variations in the fuel system to improve driveability. If the battery is disconnected, the learning process resets and begins again. A change may be noted in the vehicle performance. To enact PCM/VCM relearn procedures, ensure engine is at operating temperature. Drive the vehicle at part throttle, with moderate acceleration and idle conditions until normal performance returns. To relearn idle, the engine should be idled in Drive with all accessories off until the vehicle reaches operating temperature and the cooling fan cycles twice.

PCM/VCM

PCM

C & K TRUCKS w/DIESEL ENGINE

1. Perform set up.
   a. Battery is charged.
   b. Ignition is on.
   c. Battery/cigar lighter connection secure.
   d. Data Link Connector attached.
2. Perform programming. Refer to up to date Techline terminal/equipment, or equivalent, for user instructions.
3. After vehicle has been programmed, operate vehicle until coolant temperature is greater than 170°F. This will allow TDC Offset to be programmed.
4. Inspect data list for a TDC Offset.
5. If PCM fails to reprogram, proceed as follows:
   a. Inspect all PCM connections.
   b. Inspect Techline terminal/equipment, or equivalent, for latest software version.
   c. Try again to reprogram PCM. If it fails again, replace PCM.

BODY CONTROL MODULE (BCM)

The BCM must be programmed with proper RPO configurations. The BCM stores information regarding vehicle options and if not programmed properly, the BCM will not control features properly.
1. Ensure following conditions:
   a. Battery is fully charged.
   b. Ignition switch is in Run position.
   c. Data Link Connector (DLC) is accessible.
2. Follow instructions on Techline Terminal and scan tool to program BCM.
3. If BCM fails to accept program, proceed as follows:
   a. Inspect all BCM connections.
   b. Ensure Techline Terminal and scan tool have latest software version.

VCM

EEPROM

1. Perform set up.
   a. Battery is charged.
   b. Ignition is on.
   c. Battery/cigar lighter connection secure.
   d. Data Link Connector attached.
2. Perform programming. Refer to up to date Techline terminal/equipment, or equivalent, for user instructions.
3. If VCM fails to reprogram, proceed as follows:
   a. Inspect all VCM connections.
   b. Inspect Techline terminal/equipment, or equivalent, for latest software version.
   c. Try again to reprogram VCM. If it fails again, replace VCM.

TDC Offset Adjustment

C & K SERIES w/DIESEL ENGINE

The PCM will automatically activate the TDC offset program when the engine coolant is greater than 170°F. If the PCM is not programmed with a TDC offset, a DTC P1214 will set.

Crankshaft Position System Variation Learn

While the learn procedure is in progress, release throttle immediately when the engine starts to decelerate. The engine control is returned to the operator and the engine will respond to throttle position after the learn procedure is complete.

If the CKP system variation learn procedure cannot be completed successfully, refer to the **MOTOR's "Domestic Engine Performance & Driveability Manual"** for DTC P1336 for more information.
1. Install scan tool, then apply parking brake.
2. Block drive wheels and close hood.
3. Place vehicle in Park or Neutral.

4. Idle engine until coolant temperature reaches 150°F.
5. Turn Off all accessories, then enable "Crankshaft Position System Variation Learn Procedure" with scan tool.
6. Apply brakes for duration of procedure, then slowly raise engine speed to 4000 RPM.
7. Immediately release throttle when engine speed decreases, then turn Off ignition for 15 seconds after learn procedure is completed successfully.

Passlock Learn Procedure

WITH TECHLINE TERMINAL & SCAN TOOL

Follow instructions displayed on Techline Terminal in Service Programming System (SPS) and the scan tool for programming procedure.

AUTO LEARN PASSLOCK PROCEDURE

1. Place ignition to RUN position.
2. Turn ignition to CRANK position, then release to RUN position. **Do not start vehicle.**
3. After ignition has been in RUN position for 10 minutes, security indicator lamp will cycle from On to Off.
4. Repeat steps 2 and 3 two more times.
5. After three consecutive cycles of ignition switch are completed, vehicle will learn new component on next ignition lock cylinder cycle from Off position to CRANK position, then to RUN position. Vehicle will then start.
6. Erase Diagnostic Trouble Codes (DTC).

TABLE OF CONTENTS

	Page No.		Page No.
DAIMLERCHRYSLER	0-48	**GENERAL MOTORS CORP.**	0-57
FORD MOTOR CO.	0-54		

DaimlerChrysler

INDEX

	Page No.		Page No.		Page No.
Air Bag Indicator Lamp	0-48	1980	0-49	1989–93	0-51
Anti-Lock Brake System		1981–87	0-49	Ram Raider	0-51
Warning Indicators	0-48	1988	0-49	1988	0-51
Jeep	0-48	1989	0-49	1989	0-51
Light Trucks & Vans	0-48	1990–99	0-49	Malfunction Indicator Light	0-50
Check CARB Lamp	0-48	Jeep	0-50	1993–94 w/California Emissions	
1980 4-151 CJ	0-48	1981–83 CJ 2.5L & Scrambler		& 1995–99	0-50
California Models	0-48	California Models	0-50	Ram Raider & Ram 50	0-50
Check Engine Lamp	0-48	1988–90 Comanche,		Transmission Temperature	
Fuel Injected Engine	0-48	Cherokee, Wagoneer &		Indicator Lamp	0-51
Less Fuel Injected Engine	0-49	Wrangler	0-50	Dodge	0-51
Emission Maintenance		1991–92 Comanche,		Vehicle Information Center	
Reminder Indicator	0-49	Cherokee & Wrangler	0-50	(VIC)	0-51
Chrysler Town & Country,		Maintenance Reminder		Grand Cherokee	0-51
Dodge B Series Vans,		Lamp/Indicator	0-50	1998	0-51
Caravan, Dakota, D & W		1985–87 Ram 50 & 1987 Ram		1999–2006	0-51
100–400 & 3500 Series, Mini		Raider	0-50	Vehicle Maintenance Monitor	0-51
Ram Van, Ramcharger,		Maintenance Required Lamp	0-51	1993–95 Grand Cherokee &	
Plymouth Trailduster &		Ram 50	0-51	Grand Wagoneer	0-51
Voyager	0-49	1988	0-51	Wait-To-Start Lamp	0-51

AIR BAG INDICATOR LAMP

The air bag indicator lamp lights for 6–8 seconds each time the ignition switch is turned on. The light indicates a system self-test is being performed by the air bag control module. If the lamp remains on after the self-test or comes on while driving, an air bag system fault has been detected and the air bag may be inoperative.

ANTI-LOCK BRAKE SYSTEM WARNING INDICATORS

Light Trucks & Vans

The amber lamp monitors anti-lock brake system condition. The lamp will be on during engine starting, but should go off when the self-diagnostic system determines proper system operation. If the lamp remains On, a fault in the anti-lock brake system is indicated. After diagnosis and repair of the system, the lamp may be turned off by disconnecting and reconnecting the anti-lock brake system control module electrical connector or the battery ground cable. The anti-lock brake system control module is located in the passenger compartment and can be accessed after removing the righthand cowl cover.

Jeep

Red and yellow indicator lamps are used to warn of system faults. The red lamp warns of such faults as low brake fluid level, parking brake On, system pressure differential and other system faults. The red indicator lamp will be illuminated for approximately two seconds during engine starting and should go off, unless parking brake is applied or a problem in the brake system exist. The red indicator lamp will reset after repairs to system have been completed and system has returned to normal operation.

The yellow lamp monitors anti-lock brake system condition. The yellow lamp will be On during engine starting, but should go off when the self-diagnostic system determines proper system operation. If the yellow lamp remains On, a fault in the anti-lock brake system is indicated. After diagnosis and repair of the system, the yellow lamp may be turn off by cycling the ignition switch off then on. If yellow lamp remains on, it may be required to disconnect and reconnect the battery ground cable.

CHECK CARB LAMP

1980 4-151 CJ

CALIFORNIA MODELS

When the C4 self-diagnostic system detects a problem, the Check Carb lamp on the instrument will be illuminated. After diagnosing and servicing the vehicle, the Check Carb lamp can be reset by disconnecting and reconnecting the battery ground cable.

CHECK ENGINE LAMP

Fuel Injected Engine

The Check Engine lamp will be illuminated for approximately three seconds after

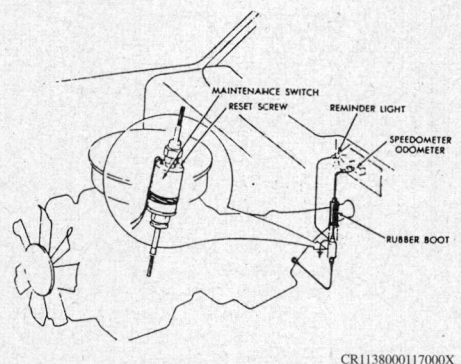

Fig. 1 Emission maintenance reminder system (mechanical type). 1980 Dodge & Plymouth

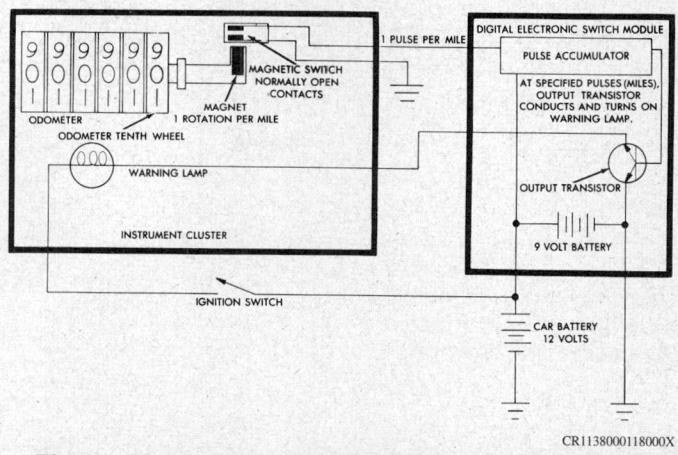

Fig. 2 Emission maintenance reminder system (electronic type). 1980–87 Dodge & Plymouth

the ignition switch has been placed in the On position as a bulb inspection. If incorrect or no signals are received by the Single Module Engine Controller (SMEC) from various sensors, the engine controller will illuminate the Check Engine lamp. After diagnosing and servicing the fuel injection system or emission related systems, the memory will be cleared after approximately 20–100 ignition key on-off cycles or by using the Diagnosis Readout Box II (DRB II) and selecting the fault code erasure mode.

Less Fuel Injected Engine

Refer to "Malfunction Indicator Light" for procedure.

EMISSION MAINTENANCE REMINDER INDICATOR

Chrysler Town & Country, Dodge B Series Vans, Caravan, Dakota, D & W 100–400 & 3500 Series, Mini Ram Van, Ramcharger, Plymouth Trailduster & Voyager

1980

At 30,000 mile intervals, an instrument panel warning lamp will light to indicate need for oxygen sensor replacement. The reminder can either be mechanical, **Fig. 1,** or electronic, **Fig. 2.** After performing the required service, the reminder lamp must be reset.

On the mechanical system, rotate the reset screw located on the switch counterclockwise until it stops, **Fig. 3.**

On the electronic system, remove nine volt battery from module, which is located under the lefthand side of the instrument panel. Insert a suitable rod into hole on module case to reset switch. After resetting switch, install a replacement nine volt battery.

1981-87

This reminder **Fig. 4,** uses mileage impulse counting contacts to calculate maintenance intervals. On front wheel drive van models, the module is located in the upper center of the instrument cluster behind the fuel gauge. On Dakota models, the module is located to the right of the glove compartment. On rear wheel drive van models, the module is located on or near the brake pedal support, **Fig. 5.** On 1981–86 D and W Series pickup trucks and Ramcharger and Trailduster models, the module is located to the right of the steering column. On 1987 D and W Series pickup trucks and Ramcharger models, the module is located to the right of the glove compartment, **Fig. 6.**

After required emission maintenance has been performed, reset module as follows:
1. Slide module from bracket.
2. Insert a small screwdriver into small hole on module case and close switch.
3. Remove module battery cover and install a replacement nine volt battery.
4. Position module on mounting bracket.

1988

This reminder system uses ignition "On" time to calculate maintenance intervals. On front wheel drive van models less tachometer, the module is located in the upper center of the instrument cluster behind the fuel gauge, **Fig. 7.** On front wheel drive van models equipped with tachometer, the module is located behind the tachometer. On Dakota models, the module is located behind the instrument panel on a bracket below the headlamp switch. On rear wheel drive van models, the module is located on or near the brake pedal support, **Fig. 5.** On D and W Series pickup trucks and Ramcharger models, the module is located to the right of the glove compartment, **Fig. 6.**

After required emission maintenance has been performed, reset module by inserting a small screwdriver blade into the hole on module case to depress the reset button.

1989

This reminder system uses ignition "On" time to calculate maintenance intervals. After required emission maintenance has been performed, connect Diagnosis Read-Out Box II (DRB II) to the on-board diagnostic connector, **Figs. 8 through 12.** Follow instructions indicated by DRB II tool.

1990-99

This Emission Maintenance Reminder System (Maintenance Required Lamp) is incorporated into the engine controller. The controller stores vehicle mileage into its memory every eight miles, then at 60,000, 82,500 or 120,000 miles it will light the EMR (Maintenance Required) lamp. When the indicated mileage is reached or the EMR lamp is on at all times the following components must be replaced and the EMR lamp reset.
1. At 60,00 miles, proceed as follows:
   a. Replace EGR valve.
   b. Clean EGR passage.
   c. Replace PCV valve.
2. At 82,500 miles, replace oxygen sensor.
3. At 120,000 miles, proceed as follows:
   a. Replace EGR valve.
   b. Clean EGR passage.
   c. Replace PCV valve.
4. **On 1990–95 models,** after required emission maintenance has been performed, connect Diagnosis Read-Out Box II (DRB II) to the on board diagnosis connector, **Figs. 8 through 13.**
5. **On 1996–99 models,** after required emission maintenance has been performed, connect Diagnosis Read-Out Box II (DRB II) to the on board DLC located under lefthand side of instrument panel.
6. **On all models,** follow instructions indicated by DRB II tool.

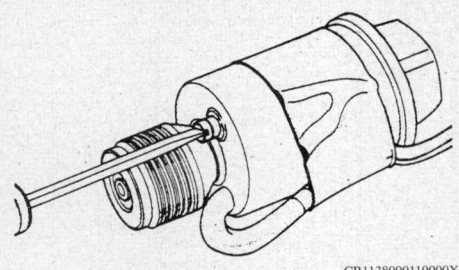

Fig. 3 Resetting maintenance reminder switch (mechanical type). 1980 Dodge & Plymouth

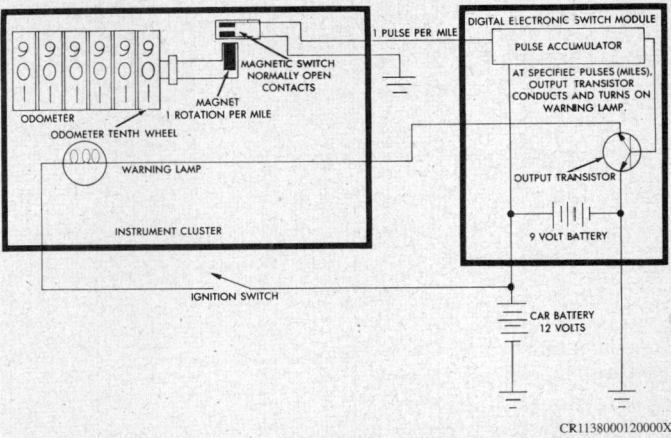

Fig. 4 Emission maintenance reminder system. 1984–87 Dodge Caravan, Dakota, Mini Ram Van & Plymouth Voyager

Jeep

1981–83 CJ 2.5L & SCRAMBLER CALIFORNIA MODELS

At 30,000 mile intervals, an instrument panel warning lamp will light to indicate oxygen sensor service. After performing the required service, the reminder lamp may be reset by rotating the reset screw located on the switch counterclockwise ¼ turn, **Fig. 3.**

1988-90 COMANCHE, CHEROKEE, WAGONEER & WRANGLER

The emission maintenance timer will light an instrument cluster indicator lamp when vehicle mileage has reached 82,500 miles. At this time, the oxygen sensor and PCV valve should be replaced, in addition to the other required emission maintenance scheduled for this mileage.

If the timer should fail before vehicle has accumulated 82,500 miles, the timer and oxygen sensor should both be replaced to maintain a proper sensor replacement interval.

After performing the required service, replace the emission maintenance timer as follows:

1. **On Comanche, Cherokee and Wagoneer models,** emission maintenance timer is located under instrument panel to right of steering column. On Wrangler models, timer is located under instrument panel to the right of accelerator pedal.
2. **On Comanche, Cherokee and Wagoneer models,** remove cruise control module attaching screws, then remove module, if equipped.
3. **On all models,** remove emission maintenance timer to instrument panel bracket attaching screws.
4. Remove timer, then disconnect electrical connector, **Figs. 14 and 15.**
5. Connect electrical connector to replacement timer, then position timer to dash panel and install and tighten attaching screws.

1991–92 COMANCHE, CHEROKEE & WRANGLER

The emission maintenance timer will

light an indicator lamp on the instrument cluster when vehicle mileage has reached 82,500 miles. At this time, the oxygen sensor and other scheduled emission maintenance is required.

If the timer should fail before vehicle has accumulated 82,500 miles, the timer and oxygen sensor should both be replaced to maintain a proper sensor replacement interval. After required emission maintenance has been performed, connect Diagnosis Read-Out Box II (DRB II) to the on board diagnosis connector, **Figs. 16 and 17.** Follow instructions indicated by DRB II tool.

MALFUNCTION INDICATOR LIGHT

1993-94 w/California Emissions & 1995-99

The Powertrain Control Module (PCM) performs an On-Board Diagnostic (OBD) inspection of the EGR system on all California Vehicles. The diagnostic system uses the electronic EGR Transducer (EET) for the system tests.

The OBD inspection activates only during selected engine/driving conditions. When the conditions are met, the PCM energizes the EET solenoid to disable the EGR. The PCM inspects for a change in the oxygen sensor signal. If the air/fuel mixture goes lean, the PCM will attempt to enrich the mixture. The PCM registers a Diagnostic Trouble Code (DTC) if the EGR system has failed or degraded. After registering a DTC, the PCM turns the MALFUNCTION INDICATOR LAMP (MIL) on. (The malfunction indicator lamp was formerly referred to as the Check Engine Lamp). The MIL indicates the need for immediate service.

If a fault is indicated by the MIL and a DTC for the EGR system was set, inspect for proper operation of the EGR system. If the EGR system tests properly, inspect the system using the DRB II scan tool.

Ram Raider & Ram 50

The malfunction indicator light will come on when an irregularity is found in one or more of the following components: engine control unit, injector, fuel pump, or in the oxygen, air flow, intake air temperature, throttle position, engine coolant temperature, crank angle, top dead center or barometric pressure sensors.

When an irregular signal returns to normal or is repaired and the engine control unit judges that it has returned to normal, the malfunction indicator light will turn Off. When the ignition switch is turned Off then malfunction indicator light will turn off until such time as the irregular signal is detected again.

MAINTENANCE REMINDER LAMP/ INDICATOR

1985-87 Ram 50 & 1987 Ram Raider

An EGR warning light on the dash will become illuminated at 50,000 miles to alert the driver to have EGR system inspected and/or serviced.

Following inspection and performance of any needed maintenance, reset mileage sensor. Reset switch is located on the back of instrument panel either to the left of or below speedometer cable junction, **Figs. 18 through 20.** Slide switch to the opposite position to reset sensor lamp.

VEHICLE INFORMATION CENTER (VIC)

Grand Cherokee

1998

The Vehicle Information Center (VIC) is optional on these models and mounts in the instrument panel lower center stack area, above the ashtray and below the HVAC controls. Among its features are reminders for service and distances to the next service interval.

The VIC receives inputs from hard-wired sensors and over the Chrysler Collision Detection (CCD) data bus network.

The "Perform Service" message will display if "Miles/Kms To Service" is zero to indicate that regular service and maintenance are due. The "xxx Miles to Service" message will light each time the vehicle is started.

To reset the counter, turn the ignition On, momentarily press the SELECT button (only if "Miles/Kms To Service" is not currently displayed), then press and hold the SET button for at least two seconds.

This device cannot be repaired. If it has been damaged or proven faulty, the entire module will need replacement.

1999–2006

1. Place ignition in On position.
2. Depress and release menu push button to display first programmable feature.
3. Momentarily depress and release menu push button to step through programmable features list.
4. Momentarily depress and release step push button to step through available options for the following programmable features:
   a. Language.
   b. Display U.S. or metric.
   c. Auto door locks.
   d. Remote unlock.
   e. Remote linked to memory.
   f. Sound horn on lock?
   g. Flash lights with lock?
   h. Headlamp delay and headlamps on with wipers.
   i. Service Intervals.
   j. Reset service distance?
   k. Low fuel chime?
   l. Easy exit seat.
5. Option that lasts appears in display with programmable feature before exiting programming mode becomes newly selected programmable feature option.
6. Electronic Vehicle Information Center (EVIC) exits programming mode and

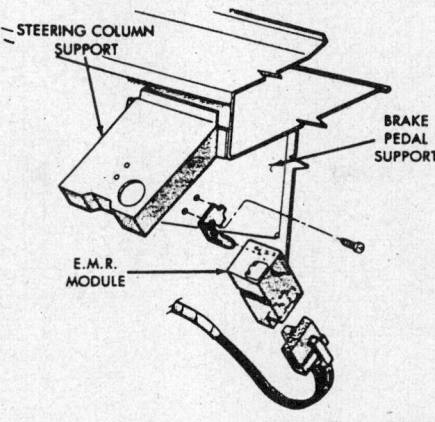

Fig. 5 Emission maintenance reminder module location. Dodge & Plymouth B Series rear wheel drive vans

returns to normal operating mode when C/T button is depressed or when end of programmable features menu list is reached.

VEHICLE MAINTENANCE MONITOR

1993–95 Grand Cherokee & Grand Wagoneer

The vehicle maintenance monitor will display a "Perform Service" message at intervals ranging from 2000–7500 miles, depending on the initial operator system setup. To reset the "Perform Service" message after repairs have been performed, depress the SELECT button, then press the SET button.

MAINTENANCE REQUIRED LAMP

Ram Raider

1988

At mileage intervals of 50,000 and 100,000 the Maintenance Required lamp will be illuminated. At 100,000 miles, the bulb should be removed from the Maintenance Required lamp. After performing the required service, reset switch located at rear of instrument cluster to turn lamp off, **Fig. 19.**

1989

At mileage intervals of 50,000, 80,000 and 100,000 the Maintenance Required lamp will be illuminated. At mileage above 120,000 miles, the bulb should be removed from the Maintenance Required lamp. After performing the required service, reset switch located at rear of instrument cluster to turn lamp off, **Fig. 19.**

Ram 50

1988

At mileage intervals of 50,000 and 100,000 the Maintenance Required lamp will be illuminated. At 100,000 miles, the bulb should be removed from the Maintenance Required lamp. After performing the required service, reset switch located at front of instrument cluster to turn lamp off, **Fig. 20.**

1989–93

At mileage intervals of 50,000, 80,000 and 100,000 the Maintenance Required lamp will be illuminated. At mileage above 120,000 miles, the bulb should be removed from the Maintenance Required lamp. After performing the required service, reset switch located at front of instrument cluster to turn lamp off, **Fig. 20.**

TRANSMISSION TEMPERATURE INDICATOR LAMP

Dodge

This indicator lamp is used on some models equipped with snow plow package. When this lamp is illuminated while operating the vehicle, operate engine at idle speed or fast idle with transmission in Neutral until lamp goes off. If lamp is frequently or continually illuminated, transmission service may be required.

WAIT-TO-START LAMP

The wait-to-start lamp is used on diesel engine models. The lamp is lit by the PCM after the ignition switch is turned to the On position. It gives the driver an indication to wait until the intake manifold air heater grid has had sufficient time to warm the intake air for a good quality start. The intake manifold air preheat cycle is controlled by an electronic air heater control module. The lamp will be turned off when the heating cycle is complete or if the ignition is turned to the Start position prior to the end of the heating cycle.

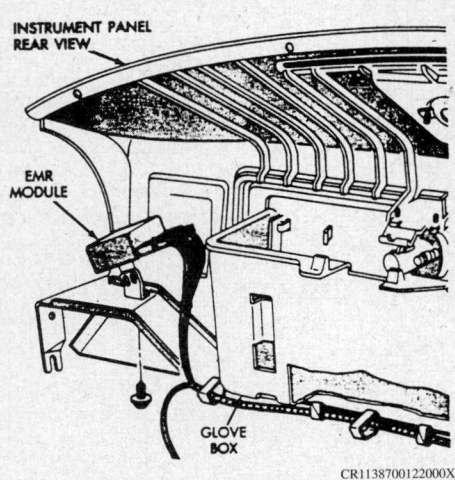

Fig. 6 Emission maintenance reminder module location. 1987–88 Dodge D & W Series

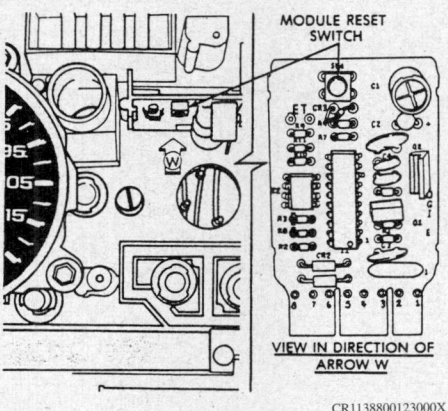

Fig. 7 Emission maintenance reminder module reset switch location. 1988 Dodge Caravan & Plymouth Voyager

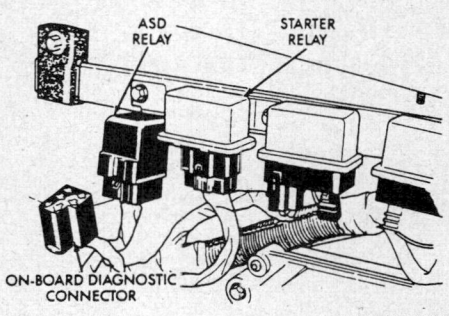

Fig. 8 On board diagnosis connector location. 1989–90 Dodge Caravan & Plymouth Voyager

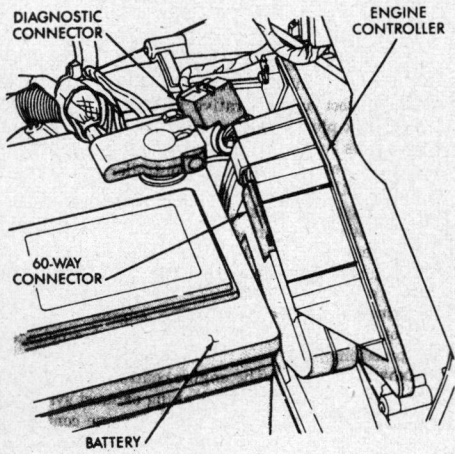

Fig. 9 On board diagnosis connector location. 1991–92 Chrysler Town & Country, Dodge Caravan & Plymouth Voyager

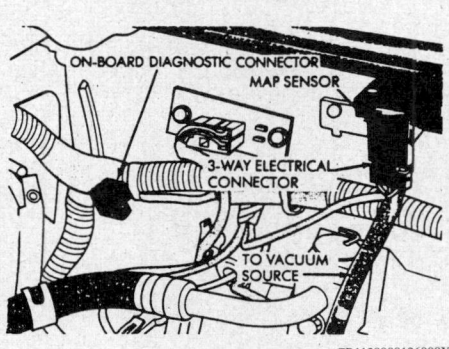

Fig. 10 On board diagnosis connector location. 1989–92 Dodge Dakota

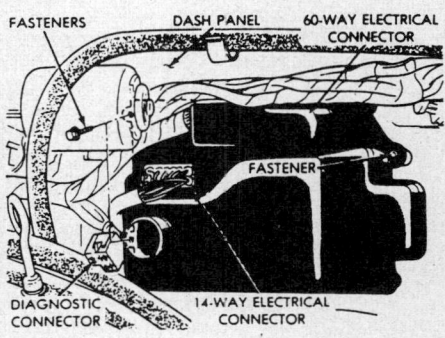

Fig. 11 On board diagnosis connector location. 1989–93 Dodge B Series Vans

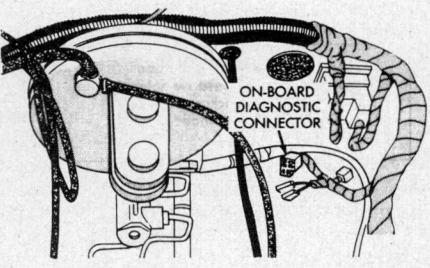

Fig. 12 On board diagnosis connector location. 1989–93 D & W Series & Ramcharger

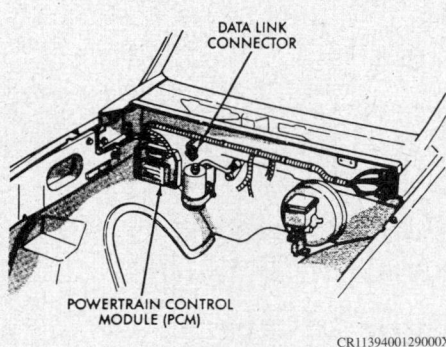

Fig. 13 Data link connector location. 1994–95 Ram Truck 1500–3500

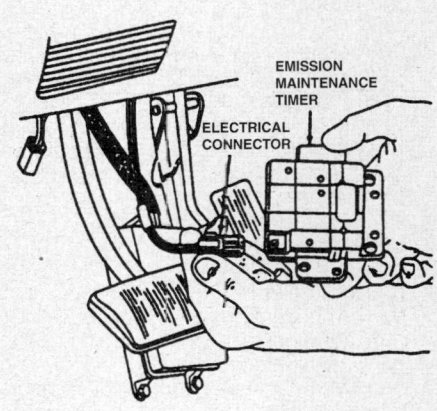

Fig. 14 Emission maintenance timer location. 1988–90 Jeep Cherokee, Comanche & Wagoneer

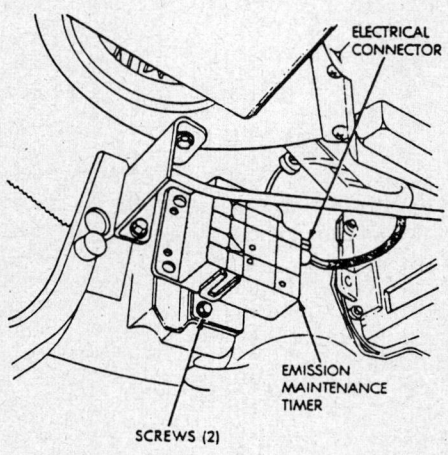

Fig. 15 Emission maintenance timer location. 1988–90 Jeep Wrangler

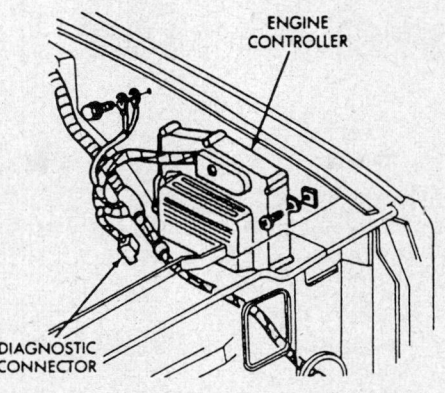

Fig. 16 Diagnostic connector location. 1991–92 Jeep Cherokee & Comanche

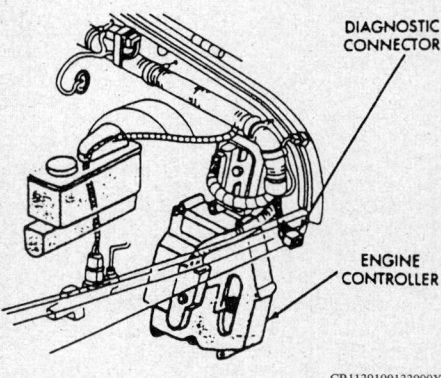

Fig. 17 Diagnostic connector location. 1991–92 Jeep Wrangler

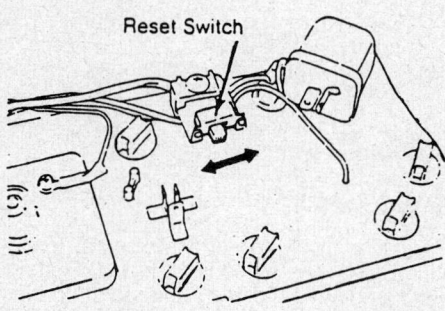

Fig. 18 EGR maintenance reminder lamp reset. 1985–86 Ram 50

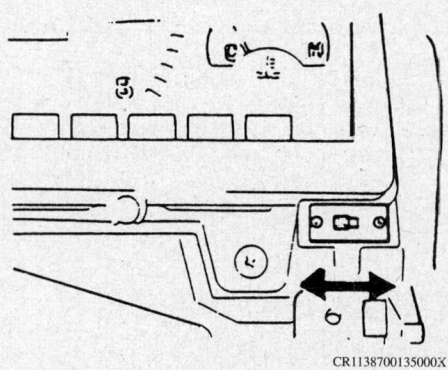

Fig. 19 Resetting EGR/ Maintenance Required reminder lamp. 1987–89 Ram Raider

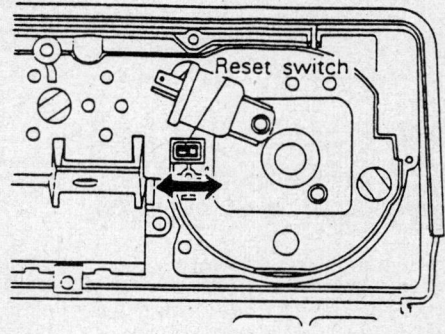

Fig. 20 Resetting EGR/ Maintenance Required reminder lamp. 1987–93 Ram 50

Ford Motor Co.

INDEX

	Page No.
Anti-Lock Or Rear Anti-Lock Brake System Warning	0-54
Change Oil Soon Lamp	0-54
Windstar	0-54
Charge System Warning Indicator	0-54
Check Engine Or Malfunction Indicator Lamp (MIL)	0-54
DI Turbo Diesel	0-54
New Generation Star (NGS) Scan Tool	0-54
Star II Tester	0-54
EEC-IV	0-54

	Page No.
1988–91	0-54
1992–97	0-54
EEC-V	0-55
KAM	0-55
PCM	0-55
EEC	0-54
Except Malfunction Light (MIL)	0-54
Malfunction Indicator Light	0-54
EGR Indicator Lamp	0-55
Courier	0-55
Emission Maintenance Reminder Lamp	0-55

	Page No.
Fuel Filter Warning Lamp	0-55
Diesel Engine	0-55
Fuel Reset	0-55
Low Coolant Lamp	0-55
Low Fuel Indicator	0-56
Low Oil Level Warning Indicator	0-56
Rear Load Leveling (CHECK SUSP)	0-56
Service Engine Soon	0-56
Water In Fuel Warning Lamp	0-56
Diesel Engine	0-56

ANTI-LOCK OR REAR ANTI-LOCK BRAKE SYSTEM WARNING

Red and yellow indicator lamps are used to warn of system faults. The red lamp warns of such faults as low brake fluid level, parking brake On, system pressure differential and other system faults. The red indicator lamp will be illuminated for approximately two seconds during engine starting and should go off, unless parking brake is applied or a problem in the brake system exist. The red indicator lamp will reset after repairs to system have been completed and system has returned to normal operation.

The yellow lamp monitors anti-lock brake system condition. The yellow lamp will be on during engine starting, but should go off when the self-diagnostic system determines proper system operation. If yellow lamp remains On, a fault in the anti-lock brake system is indicated. After diagnosis and repair of the system, the yellow may be turn off by cycling the ignition switch Off then On.

CHARGE SYSTEM WARNING INDICATOR

The charge system warning indicator lamps are used to warn of no alternator output. When ignition switch contacts are closed, current flows through charge indicator and parallel resistor to voltage indicator and the indicator lights. When alternator builds enough voltage to energize a circuit in voltage regulator, the indicator will go out.

CHANGE OIL SOON LAMP

Windstar

1. Press RESET and SETUP buttons at same time to activate service mode.
2. Press SETUP to access system in-

spection, then press RESET to start system inspection.
3. Press and hold RESET button.
4. Press RESET and SETUP buttons for personalized setting.
5. After successfully reset, message center will display oil life reset to 100%.

CHECK ENGINE OR MALFUNCTION INDICATOR LAMP (MIL)

DI Turbo Diesel

STAR II TESTER

Unlatching STAR tester during "fast" code transmission will clear all codes in the PCM. They will be stored in the STAR tester for viewing.

NEW GENERATION STAR (NGS) SCAN TOOL

Select RETRIEVE/CLEAR option from NGS menu for the appropriate test, then press CLEAR ALL button. Diagnostic trouble codes will be cleared from memory.

EEC

EXCEPT MALFUNCTION INDICATOR LIGHT (MIL)

When using NGS tool No. 007-00500, or equivalent, select Diagnostic Test Mode Results, then press CLEAR. Or, disconnect battery ground cable. Codes will be erased from back-up memory after 24 hours.

MALFUNCTION INDICATOR LIGHT

1. Activate diagnostic test mode.
2. Disconnect diagnostic connector.
3. Jump BL/W and GY/BL wires using suitable jumper wires.
4. Wait about two seconds.

5. Remove jumper wire and reconnect diagnostic connector.
6. MIL will stay on, and codes will be erased.

EEC-IV

1988–91

This lamp will be illuminated when the ignition switch is placed in the On position. After engine is started the lamp should go off, unless a problem has been detected by the EEC-IV system. After diagnosis and repair, the Check Engine/MIL lamp will automatically reset when stored codes are cleared from the EEC-IV system memory. After diagnosis and repair, EEC-IV memory may be cleared of stored codes as follows:

1. With ignition switch in Off position, connect a jumper wire between Self Test and Self Test Input (STI) connectors, **Fig. 1.** On Aerostar, Self Test and STI connectors are gray in color and are located on lefthand fender apron, near Electronic Engine Control (EEC) relay. On Bronco and F-Series, Self Test and STI connectors and are located in area of EEC system charcoal canister. On Bronco II, Explorer and Ranger, Self Test connector and STI connector are red in color and they are both located on righthand fender apron near Electronic Engine Control (EEC) relay. On E-Series, Self Test and STI connectors are located on righthand fender apron in area of MAP sensor and starter motor relay.
2. Position ignition switch in On position, then disconnect jumper wire from test connector terminals. Disconnect jumper as soon as Check Engine lamp starts flashing.

1992–97

CONTINUOUS MEMORY

This lamp will be illuminated when the ignition switch is placed in the On position. After the engine is started the lamp should go off, unless a problem has been detected by the EEC-IV system. After diagnosis and

repair, the Check Engine/MIL lamp will automatically reset when stored diagnostic trouble codes (DTC's) are cleared from the EEC-IV system memory as follows:

1. Perform Key On Engine Off (KOEO) Self-Test using Super Star II Tester, or equivalent scan tool.
2. When DTC's begin to be displayed, deactivate self-test as follows:
   a. Unlatch center button using **Super Star II Tester.**
   b. Push stop button using **scan tool.**
   c. Remove jumper wire from between self-test input (STI) connector and signal return pin of DLC on all others.

KEEP ALIVE MEMORY (KAM)

Disconnecting the battery ground cable for at least five minutes will also clear PCM memory but will also clear Keep Alive Memory (KAM) which stores certain emission related DTC's. Whenever KAM is cleared, the vehicle must be driven 10 miles or more to allow the PCM to relearn values for optimum driveability.

EEC-V

Codes must be cleared either by performing the PCM reset function of an OBD II scan tool or by disconnecting the battery ground cable for a minimum of five minutes. **Disconnecting the battery ground cable will also clear Keep Alive Memory (KAM) which stores certain emission related DTC's.** Whenever KAM is cleared, the vehicle must be driven 10 miles or more to allow the PCM to relearn values for optimum driveability.

PCM

The PCM Reset allows the scan tool to command the PCM to clear all emission-related diagnostic information. When resetting the PCM, a DTC P1000 will be stored in the PCM until all the OBD II system monitors or components have been tested to satisfy a Trip without any other faults occurring.

1. Following results occur when resetting PCM:
   a. Clears number of DTC's.
   b. Clears DTC's.
   c. Clears freeze frame data.
   d. Clears oxygen sensor test data.
   e. Resets status of OBD II system monitors.
   f. Sets DTC P1000.
2. To reset PCM, perform following:
   a. Connect scan tool to DLC.
   b. Select Vehicle and Engine Selection menu (OPTIONAL).
   c. Select year, model with appropriate qualifier, if needed (transmission, 499 state, California, OPTIONAL).
   d. Follow operating instructions from menu (turn key On).
   e. Select GENERIC OBD II FUNCTIONS. Press CONT button if all OBD II monitors are not complete.
   f. Turn key On.
   g. Select CLEAR DIAGNOSTIC CODES.

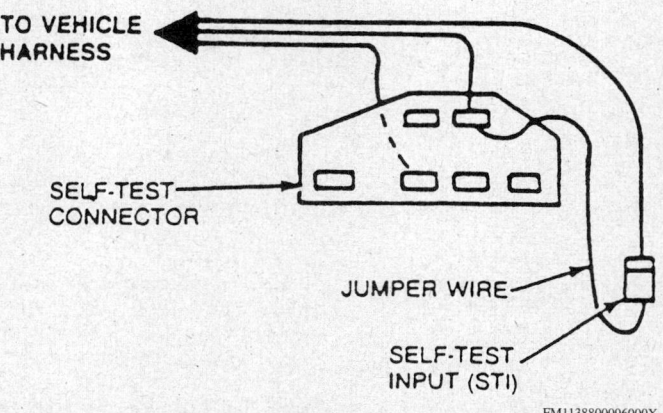

CHECK ENGINE LIGHT (WITH JUMPER WIRE)

TO VEHICLE HARNESS

SELF-TEST CONNECTOR

JUMPER WIRE

SELF-TEST INPUT (STI)

FM1138800096000X

Fig. 1 Jumper wire connections for resetting check engine lamp. EEC-IV

KAM

Disconnect the battery ground cable for a minimum of five minutes (this will also result in PCM reset). Resetting KAM will also clear learned values the PCM has stored for adaptive systems such as idle and Fuel systems. Once the vehicle is driven, the PCM will relearn new adaptive values. It will take a few miles and may run rough until the values are relearned.

EGR INDICATOR LAMP

Courier

After performing the required EGR system maintenance, reset the lamp as follows:

1. Locate switch, which is installed behind speedometer.
2. Remove switch cover, then slide switch knob to opposite position.

EMISSION MAINTENANCE REMINDER LAMP

This lamp will be illuminated after approximately 60,000 miles of operation, **Fig. 2.** The amber lens lamp is located on the instrument panel and has the word Emissions, Emiss or EGR printed on it. On 1988 Ranger models with 2.0L engine, the lamp lens will indicate Check Engine. After performing the required emission control maintenance, the module must be replaced or reset, depending on type of module used. On module equipped with reset feature, reset the module as follows:

1. Place ignition switch in Off position.
2. Insert a suitable Phillips head screwdriver through .2 inch diameter hole located on module near reset sticker and lightly press down and hold.
3. While still lightly pressing down on screwdriver, turn ignition switch to Run position. Emissions maintenance lamp

should remain illuminated for as long as screwdriver is pressing down. Hold screwdriver in position for approximately five seconds.
4. Remove screwdriver, lamp should go out after approximately two to five seconds, indicating module has been reset. If lamp fails to go out, repeat reset procedure. Place ignition switch in Off position.
5. Turn ignition switch to Run position and inspect to ensure emission maintenance lamp is illuminated for two to five seconds. After approximately two to five seconds lamp should turn off.

FUEL FILTER WARNING LAMP

Diesel Engine

The fuel filter indicator will be illuminated when fuel filter replacement is required. A vacuum switch located on the fuel filter head, activates the instrument panel lamp. If the lamp is illuminated, replace fuel filter. After replacing fuel filter, the lamp will automatically reset.

FUEL RESET

The FUEL RESET indicator is grounded through the inertia switch whenever vehicle is in a high force situation. The Inertia Fuel Shutoff (IFS) switch cuts off the fuel pump motor. The FUEL RESET indicator illuminates when IFS switch has been tripped.

LOW COOLANT LAMP

This lamp will be illuminated when engine coolant level in the radiator drops below a pre-determined level. To turn lamp off, inspect cooling system, then add coolant to bring system to proper level.

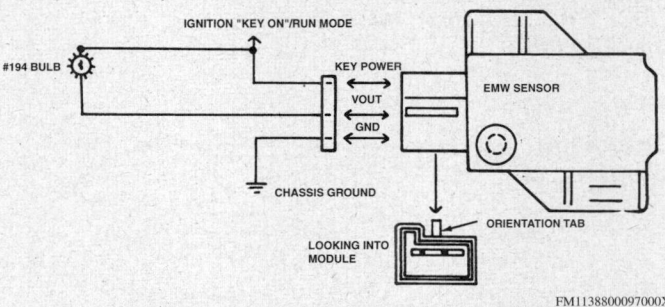

Fig. 2   Emission maintenance reminder lamp system

LOW FUEL INDICATOR

When fuel level drops below a predetermined level, the CHECK GAUGE indicator will light. The CHECK GAUGE indicator will light if engine oil pressure drops below 6 psi, fuel level drops below 1–2 gallons or engine temperature exceeds 250° F.

LOW OIL LEVEL WARNING INDICATOR

This system is used to indicate a low engine oil level condition. The lamp will be illuminated during engine starting. If oil level is sufficient, the lamp will go off when engine is operating. If oil level is low the lamp will remain on until engine oil is added and the ignition switch is placed in the Off position. The module may take a few minutes to reset. If the engine is started during this period, the last recorded reading will be displayed.

REAR LOAD LEVELING (CHECK SUSP)

The CHECK SUSP indicator lights when there is a fault of the rear load leveling system or if the air suspension switch is in the Off position.

SERVICE ENGINE SOON

After the engine is started, the SERVICE ENGINE SOON indicator will cycle for three seconds. If the instrument cluster does not receive a message from the Powertrain Control Module (PCM) within five seconds, the instrument cluster will send two messages to the PCM and attempt to establish communication. If instrument cluster is unable to establish communication it will light the SERVICE ENGINE SOON indicator and record a Diagnostic Trouble Code (DTC).

WATER IN FUEL WARNING LAMP
Diesel Engine

The water in fuel indicator will be illuminated when excessive water has entered the fuel system. As water collects in the fuel filter, a probe located at the water separator section of the filter, will activate the instrument panel lamp. If the lamp is illuminated, drain fuel filter. After fuel filter has been drained, the lamp will automatically reset. If lamp illuminates after drain fuel filter, replacement of fuel filter and or purging of fuel tank may be required.

General Motors Corp.

INDEX

Page No.

Brake Warning Lamp............ 0-57
  Tracker 0-57
Check Engine Or Service
Engine Soon Indicator Lamp.... 0-57
  Diesel Electronic Control
  System 0-57
  Electronic Engine Controls Or
    Electronic Fuel Injection....... 0-57
    Except Luv & Tracker......... 0-57
    Luv......................... 0-57

Page No.

  Tracker 0-57
Choke Or Oil/Choke Warning
Lamp.......................... 0-57
  Carbureted Engine............. 0-57
DaimlerChrysler Corp........... 0-79
Emission Or Sensor
Maintenance Reminder Flag..... 0-58
  1980 Caballero & El Camino.... 0-58
Engine Oil Life Monitor......... 0-58
Ford Motor Co. 0-79

Page No.

General Motors Corp. 0-79
Low Coolant Lamp 0-58
Malfunction Indicator Lamp
(MIL) 0-58
  Tracker w/Federal Emissions ... 0-58
    1989–91 0-58
    1992–95 0-58
Water In Fuel Or Drain Fuel
Filter Warning Lamp 0-58
  Diesel Engine................... 0-58

CHECK ENGINE OR SERVICE ENGINE SOON INDICATOR LAMP

Diesel Electronic Control System

The Check Engine Lamp will be illuminated when the ignition switch is placed in the On position. When the engine is started, the lamp should go off. If the lamp remains on after the engine is started, the self diagnosis system has detected a problem and has stored a code in the system Electronic Control Module (ECM). After diagnosis and repair, the ECM memory can be cleared of codes by disconnecting the battery ground cable for approximately 30 seconds with ignition switch in Off position. It should be noted, when battery ground cable is disconnected to clear codes, components such as clocks, electronically tuned radios etc., will have to be reset.

Electronic Engine Controls Or Electronic Fuel Injection

EXCEPT LUV & TRACKER

The Check Engine Lamp will be illuminated when the ignition switch is placed in the On position. When the engine is started, the lamp should go off. If the lamp remains on for 10 seconds or constantly after the engine is started, the self diagnosis system has detected a problem and has stored a code in the system Electronic Control Module (ECM) or Powertrain Control Module (PCM). After diagnosis and repair, the ECM/PCM memory can be cleared of codes either by using a scan tool (OBD II systems) or by disconnecting the battery ground cable for approximately 30 seconds with the ignition switch in the Off position. It should be noted that if the battery ground cable is disconnected to clear codes, components such as clocks, electronically tuned radios etc., will have to be reset.

LUV

The check engine lamp will be illuminated when the ignition switch is in the On position with engine not operating. When engine is started, the Check Engine lamp should go off. If lamp remains on, a code has been stored by the Electronic Control Module (ECM). After diagnosis and repair, place ignition switch in Off position, then clear codes stored in the ECM memory by removing the Emission or ECM fuse, located on the fuse box in engine compartment, for approximately ten seconds.

TRACKER

FEDERAL MODELS

The Check Engine lamp will be illuminated when the ignition switch is in the On position with engine not operating. When engine is started, the Check Engine lamp should go off. If lamp remains on, either a service interval is indicated or a code has been stored by the Electronic Control Module (ECM) memory.

At mileage intervals of 50,000, 80,000 and 100,000 miles, the Check Engine lamp will be illuminated indicating required service and maintenance is to be performed. After performing the required service, the lamp may be turned off by resetting the cancel switch located on the instrument panel.

If a service code has been stored in the ECM memory, perform diagnosis and repair, then place ignition switch in Off position and clear codes stored in the ECM memory by disconnecting the battery ground cable for approximately 20 seconds.

CALIFORNIA MODELS

The Check Engine lamp will be illuminated when the ignition switch is in the On position with engine not operating. When engine is started, the Check Engine lamp should go off. If lamp remains on, a code has been stored by the Electronic Control Module (ECM) memory. After diagnosis and repair, place ignition switch in Off position, then clear codes stored in the ECM memory by disconnecting the battery ground cable, for approximately 20 seconds.

BRAKE WARNING LAMP

Tracker

The electronic brake control module (EBCM) contains the rear wheel anti-lock (RWAL) self-diagnosis programming. Should a failure be detected, the EBCM sets a trouble code and will cause the "BRAKE" warning lamp to illuminate and the RWAL brake system operation will cease its operation.

After the RWAL system is repaired, erase codes by enabling flash code diagnostics as follows:

1. Release parking brake and block drive wheels.
2. Ensure brake fluid level in reservoir is adequate.
3. Turn ignition switch to On position.
4. Connector together for more than two seconds using a jumper wire, short terminals 3 and 5 of diagnostic.
5. After flash code diagnostic mode has been entered, turn ignition switch to Off position.

CHOKE OR OIL/CHOKE WARNING LAMP

Carbureted Engine

On models less gauges, the oil/choke warning indicator lamp should be illuminated when the ignition switch is in the Run or Start position. When the engine is started, the choke warning indicator lamp should go off. If the lamp fails to illuminate with ignition switch in Run or Start position, with engine not operating, a burnt out bulb or fuse or defect in choke electrical system is indicated. If lamp remains on after engine has been started, a problem in the engine oil pressure system or electrical choke system exist.

On models equipped with gauges, the choke warning indicator lamp should be illuminated when the ignition switch is in the Run or Start position. When the engine is started, the choke warning indicator lamp should go off. If the lamp fails to illuminate

with ignition switch in Run or Start position, with engine not operating, a burnt out bulb or fuse or defect in choke electrical system is indicated. If lamp remains on after engine has been started, a problem in the alternator circuit is indicated.

After service has been completed, the lamp operation should return to normal.

EMISSION OR SENSOR MAINTENANCE REMINDER FLAG

1980 Caballero & El Camino

At 30,000 mile intervals, an Emission or Sensor reminder flag, if equipped, will appear across the odometer to indicate the need for oxygen sensor replacement. After performing the required service, the flag must be reset for the next 30,000 mile interval. This is accomplished by gaining access to the speedometer head and removing the speedometer lens. Using a suitable pointed tool, rotate edge of flag wheel detents downward, until flag wheel can no longer be rotated. Flag wheel alignment mark should center in odometer.

LOW COOLANT LAMP

This lamp will be illuminated when engine coolant level in the radiator drops below a pre-determined level. To turn lamp off, inspect cooling system, then add coolant to bring system to proper level.

MALFUNCTION INDICATOR LAMP (MIL)

Tracker w/Federal Emissions

The MIL lamp will flash or illuminate at 50,000, 80,000 and 100,000 miles to indicate emission maintenance is required.

1989-91

After performing the required maintenance the MIL lamp may be reset by moving cancel switch to opposite position. The MIL cancel switch is located behind the access panel below the steering column.

1992-95

After performing the required maintenance, reset the MIL cancel switch. The MIL cancel switch is located behind the instrument panel (attached to instrument panel next to left speaker).

WATER IN FUEL OR DRAIN FUEL FILTER WARNING LAMP

Diesel Engine

The water in fuel indicator will be illuminated when excessive water has entered the fuel system. As the fuel filter becomes plugged, a low pressure sensor activates the lamp. The lamp will be illuminated during engine starting as a bulb inspect. Once the engine has started, the lamp should go off. If the lamp is illuminated intermittently, drain fuel filter. If lamp remains illuminated, drain fuel filter. If the lamp still remains on after fuel filter has been drained, replace fuel filter. If lamp is illuminated during high speed operation or during heavy acceleration, replace fuel filter. If after starting, the engine stalls and will not restart and lamp remains illuminated, inspect for plugged fuel filter or fuel lines. If this condition occurs immediately after refueling, inspect fuel tank for large concentration of water in fuel, and if required purge fuel tank and replace fuel filter. After performing the required service, the increased fuel pressure through the fuel filter will reset the water in fuel lamp.

ENGINE OIL LIFE MONITOR

The engine oil life monitor will indicate when to change engine oil usually between 3000–10,000 miles since last oil change. Under severe conditions, the CHANGE OIL SOON light may be displayed before 3000 miles. Vehicle must not be driven more than 10,000 miles or 12 months without an oil change. After oil has been changed, reset oil life monitor as follows:

1. Turn ignition to Run position.
2. Fully push and release accelerator pedal three times within five seconds.
3. If CHANGE OIL SOON light flashes two times, system is reset.
4. If CHANGE OIL SOON light comes on and stays on for five seconds, system did not reset. Repeat procedure until system resets.

MODULE CONFIGURATION PROCEDURE

TABLE OF CONTENTS

Page No.

FORD MOTOR CO. 0-59

Ford Motor Co.

Some modules will require configuration after being installed on the vehicle. All configurable modules will be packaged in a kit which contains a warning label and multi-language sheet which lists requirements to configure the modules.

There are two types of configuration data. The first type is used by the module so that it can interact with the vehicle correctly. The second type is customer preference driven. These are items that the customer may or may not want to have enabled. To program customer driven preferences, a Ford service function card (FSF) and the New Generation Star Tester (NGS), tool No. 007-00500, or equivalents, must be used to toggle preferences On or Off.

The New Generation Star Tester (NGS), tool No. 007-00500, or equivalent, must be used to retrieve configuration data from the old module before it is removed from the vehicle. This information will be transferred into the new module so that the new module will contain the same settings as the old module.

On some vehicles the following modules require configuration when being replaced; ABS control module, ABS control module with traction control, interactive vehicle dynamic (IVD) module, instrument cluster, instrument cluster with message center, rear electronic module (REM), front electronic module (FEM), driver door module (DDM), dual automatic temperature control (DATC) module, remote emergency satellite cellular unit (RESCU) module, and the steering column lock module (SCLM) when PCM is replaced on manual transmission equipped models. If configuring PCM, the NGS tester flash cable tool No. 007-00531, or equivalent, must be used.

To perform the configuration process, proceed as follows:

1. Connect New Generation Star Tester tool No. 007-00500 or equivalent, with Ford service function (FSF) card to vehicle DLC.
2. Follow scan tool instructions to upload configuration data.
3. Install new module. **NGS will not retain configuration data for more than 24 hours.**
4. Download stored configuration information to new module using FSF card and NGS tester.
5. If unable to carry out configuration process, proceed as follows:
   a. Inspect for signs of electrical damage.
   b. If NGS does not communicate with vehicle, ensure program card is correctly installed, vehicle connections are secure and that ignition switch is in run position.
   c. If NGS still does not communicate with vehicle, diagnose module communications network concern.

TABLE OF CONTENTS

	Page No.			Page No.
DAIMLERCHRYSLER	0-60	**FORD MOTOR CO.**		0-63
		GENERAL MOTORS CORP.		0-68

DaimlerChrysler

INDEX

	PAGE NO.	FIG. NO.		PAGE NO.	FIG. NO.
Caravan	0-61	3	Liberty	0-62	9
Commander	0-62	8	Pacifica	0-61	5
Dakota	0-61	4	PT Cruiser	0-61	6
Durango	0-61	4	Ram Pickups	0-60	1
Grand Caravan	0-61	3	Ram Vans	0-60	2
Grand Cherokee:			Town & Country	0-61	3
2002–04	0-62	7	Voyager	0-61	3
2005–06	0-62	8	Wrangler	0-62	7

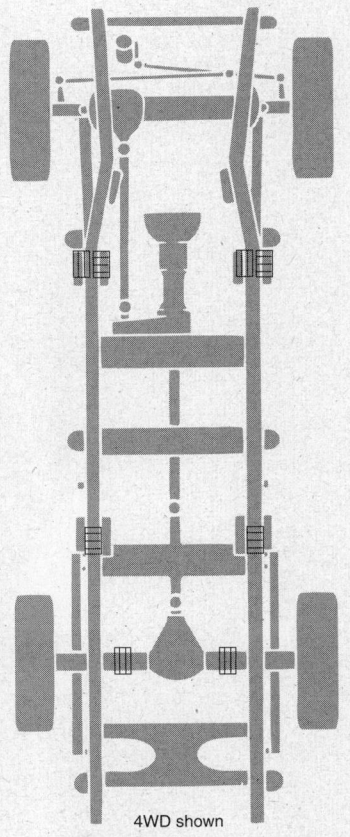

ALDT00007

Fig. 1   Dodge Ram Pickups 1500, 2500 & 3500

4WD shown

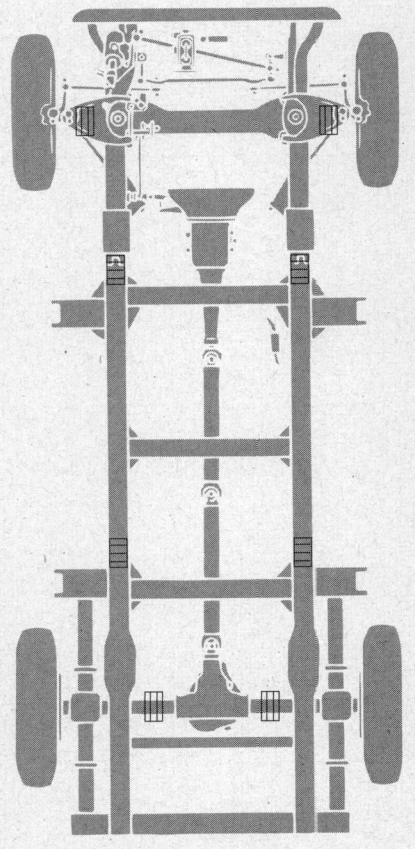

ALDT00003

Fig. 2   Dodge Ram Vans

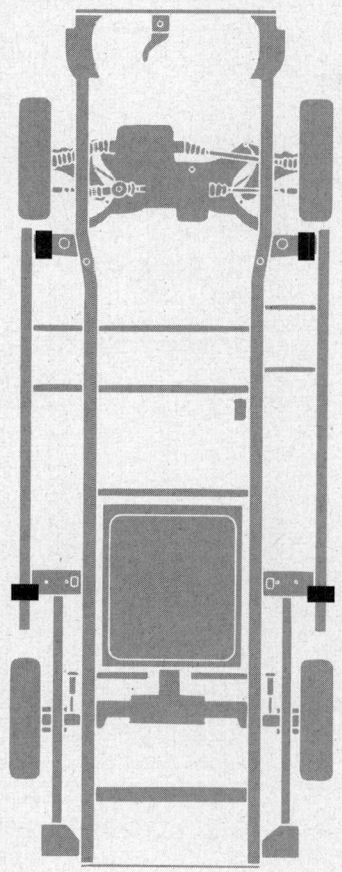

ALDT00004

Fig. 3   Caravan, Grand Caravan, Town & Country & Voyager

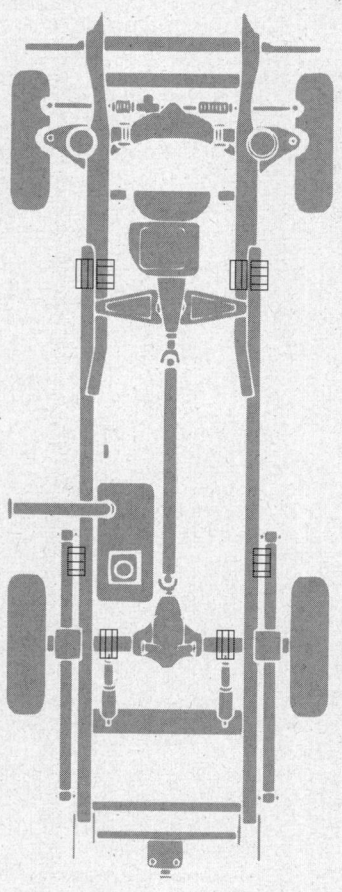

ALDT00005

Fig. 4   Dakota & Durango

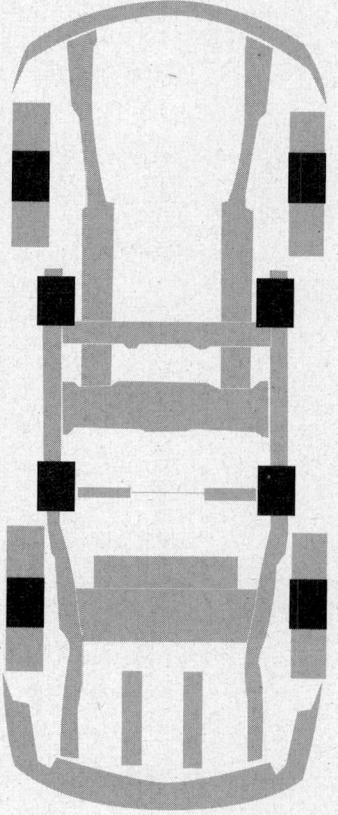

ALCR040008

Fig. 5   Pacifica

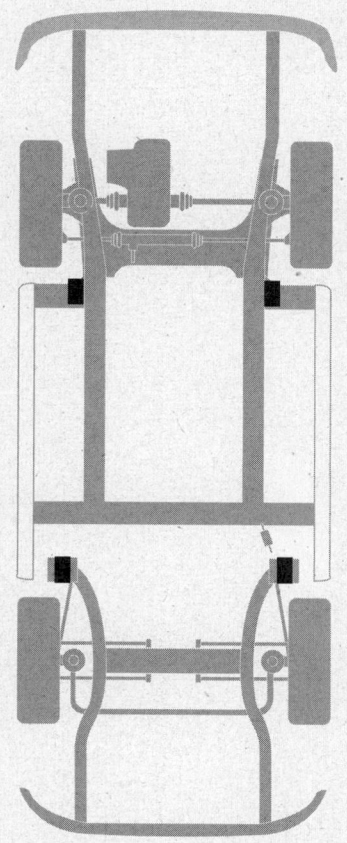

ALCR00006

Fig. 6   PT Cruiser

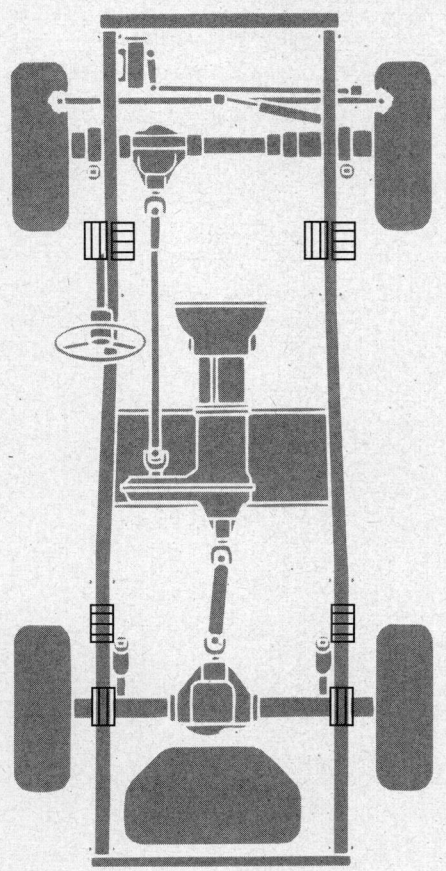

ALJP00005

Fig. 7 Wrangler & 2002–04 Grand Cherokee

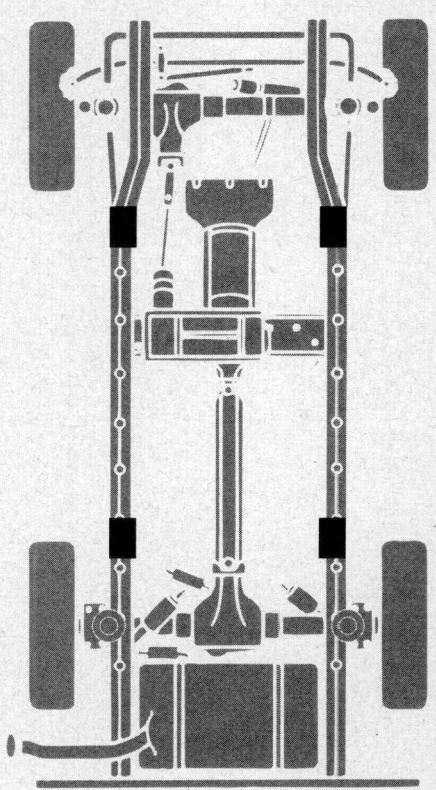

ALJP00008

Fig. 8 Commander & 2005–06 Grand Cherokee

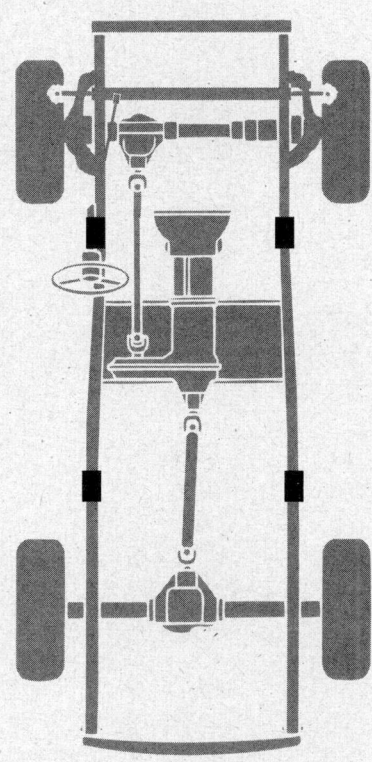

ALJP00006

Fig. 9 Liberty

Ford Motor Co.

INDEX

	PAGE NO.	FIG. NO.
Aviator	0-65	5
Blackwood	0-64	4
Escape	0-63	1
E-Series Vans	0-63	2
Excursion	0-64	3
Expedition	0-64	4
Explorer	0-65	5
Explorer Sport	0-65	6
Explorer Sport-Trac	0-65	6
Freestar	0-67	9

	PAGE NO.	FIG. NO.
F150	0-64	4
F250HD	0-64	3
F350	0-64	3
Mariner	0-63	1
Monterey	0-67	9
Mountaineer	0-65	5
Navigator	0-64	4
Ranger	0-65	6
Villager	0-66	7
Windstar	0-66	8

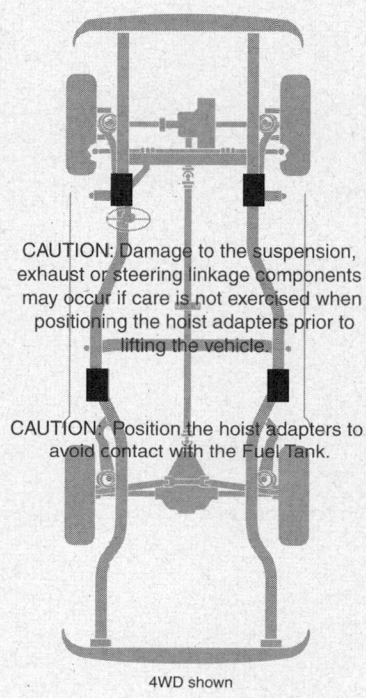

CAUTION: Damage to the suspension, exhaust or steering linkage components may occur if care is not exercised when positioning the hoist adapters prior to lifting the vehicle.

CAUTION: Position the hoist adapters to avoid contact with the Fuel Tank.

4WD shown

ALTF00010

Fig. 1   Escape & Mariner

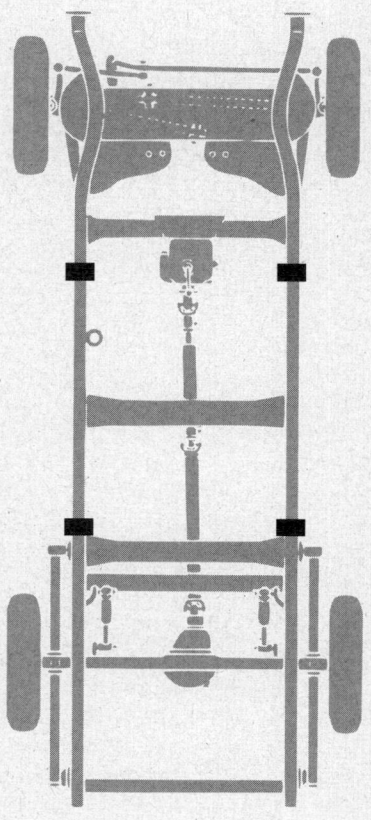

ALTF00002

Fig. 2   E-Series Vans

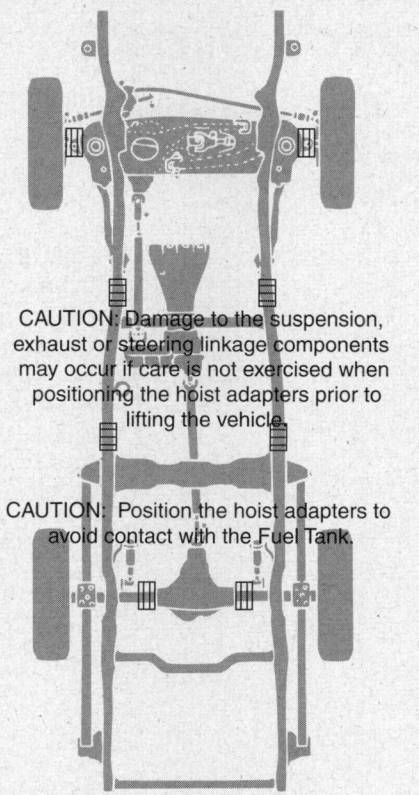

CAUTION: Damage to the suspension, exhaust or steering linkage components may occur if care is not exercised when positioning the hoist adapters prior to lifting the vehicle.

CAUTION: Position the hoist adapters to avoid contact with the Fuel Tank.

ALTF00004

Fig. 3   Excursion, F250HD & F350

CAUTION: Damage to the suspension, exhaust or steering linkage components may occur if care is not exercised when positioning the hoist adapters prior to lifting the vehicle.

CAUTION: Position the hoist adapters to avoid contact with the Fuel Tank.

AIR SUSPENSION
Turn air suspension off
(switch located behind access panel
underneath passenger side dashboard)
before jacking or hoisting vehicle.

4WD shown

ALTF00008

**Fig. 4   Blackwood, Expedition, F150 Pickups &
Navigator**

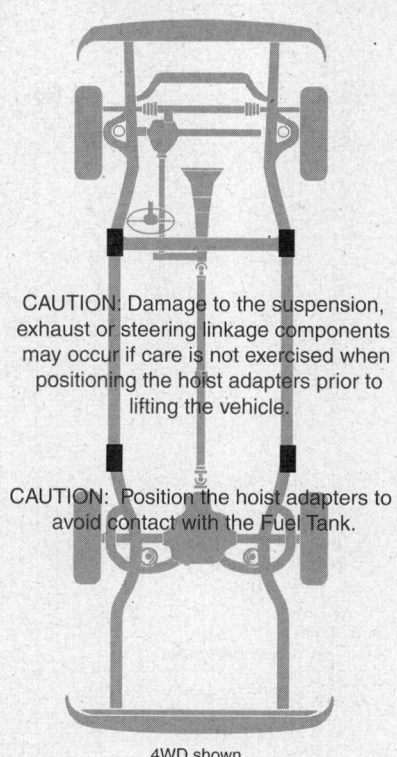

CAUTION: Damage to the suspension, exhaust or steering linkage components may occur if care is not exercised when positioning the hoist adapters prior to lifting the vehicle.

CAUTION: Position the hoist adapters to avoid contact with the Fuel Tank.

4WD shown

ALTF00011

Fig. 5 Aviator, Explorer & Mountaineer

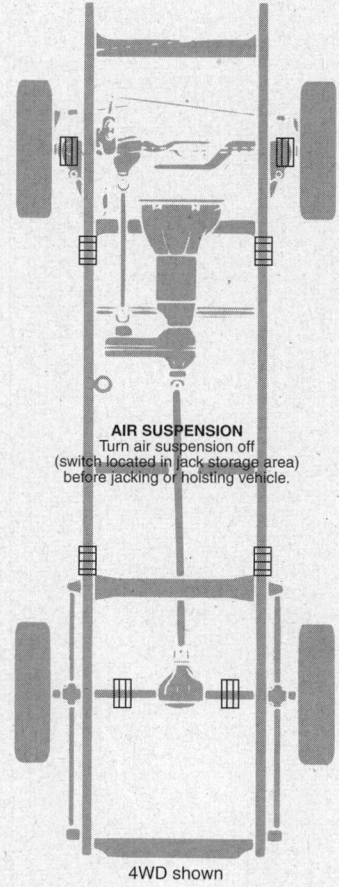

AIR SUSPENSION
Turn air suspension off
(switch located in jack storage area)
before jacking or hoisting vehicle.

4WD shown

ALTF0001

Fig. 6 Explorer Sport, Explorer Sport-Trac & Ranger

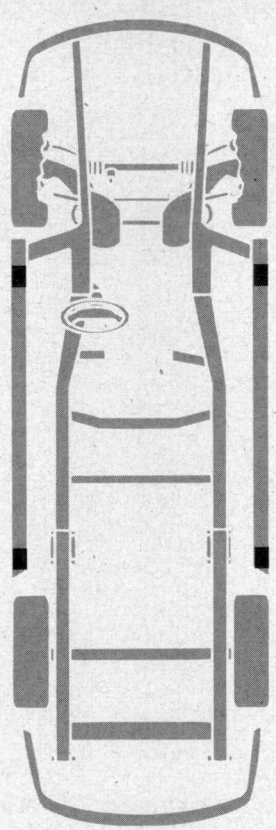

ALND00012

Fig. 7   Villager

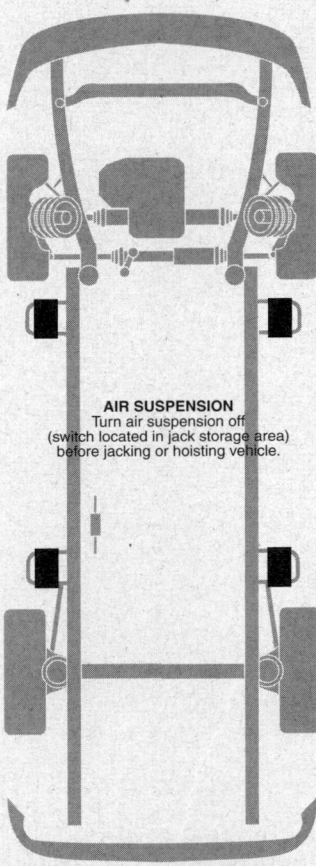

AIR SUSPENSION
Turn air suspension off
(switch located in jack storage area)
before jacking or hoisting vehicle.

ALFD00011

Fig. 8   Windstar

AIR SUSPENSION
Turn air suspension off
(switch located in trunk on right side or
jack storage area)
before jacking or hoisting vehicle.
On 1996-99 Sable/Taurus models
use a cushioned pad on rear
contact pad to prevent paint damage.

ALFD00007

Fig. 9   Freestar & Monterey

General Motors Corp.

INDEX

	PAGE NO.	FIG. NO.		PAGE NO.	FIG. NO.
Astro	0-69	1	Safari	0-69	1
Avalanche	0-71	5	Savana	0-71	6
Aztek	0-69	2	Sierra	0-71	5
Bravada	0-69	1	Silhouette	0-69	2
Canyon	0-69	1	Silverado	0-71	5
Colorado	0-69	1	Sonoma	0-69	1
Denali	0-71	5	SRX	0-72	8
Envoy	0-69	1	SSR	0-69	1
Equinox	0-72	7	Suburban	0-71	5
Escalade	0-71	5	S-Blazer	0-69	1
Escalade ESV	0-71	5	S-10	0-69	1
Escalade EXT	0-71	5	Tahoe	0-71	5
Express	0-71	6	Terraza	0-69	2
HHR	0-73	9	Torrent	0-72	7
Hummer H2	0-71	5	Trailblazer	0-69	1
Hummer H3	0-71	5	Uplander	0-69	2
Montana	0-69	2	Venture	0-69	2
Rainer	0-69	1	Vue	0-70	3
Relay	0-70	4	Yukon	0-71	5
Rendezvous	0-69	2	Yukon XL	0-71	5

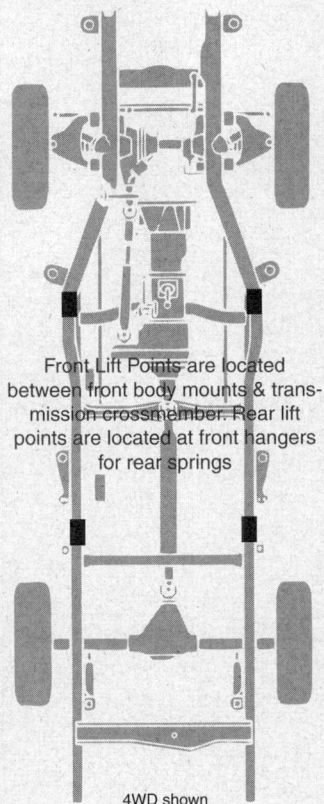

Front Lift Points are located between front body mounts & transmission crossmember. Rear lift points are located at front hangers for rear springs

4WD shown

ALCT00001

Fig. 1 Astro, Bravada, Canyon, Colorado, Envoy, Rainer, Safari, Sonoma, S-Blazer, SSR, S-10 & Trailblazer

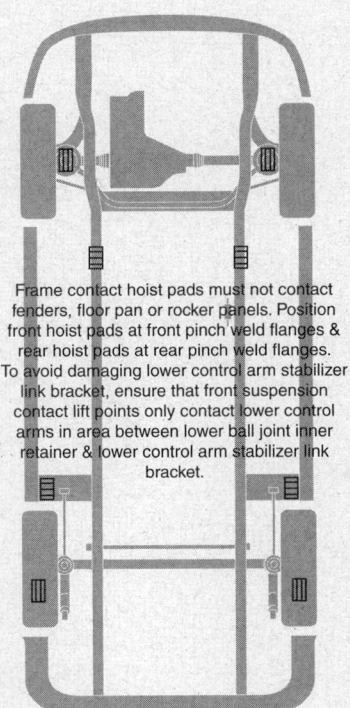

Frame contact hoist pads must not contact fenders, floor pan or rocker panels. Position front hoist pads at front pinch weld flanges & rear hoist pads at rear pinch weld flanges. To avoid damaging lower control arm stabilizer link bracket, ensure that front suspension contact lift points only contact lower control arms in area between lower ball joint inner retainer & lower control arm stabilizer link bracket.

ALGM00031

Fig. 2 Aztek, Montana, Rendezvous, Silhouette, Terraza, Uplander & Venture

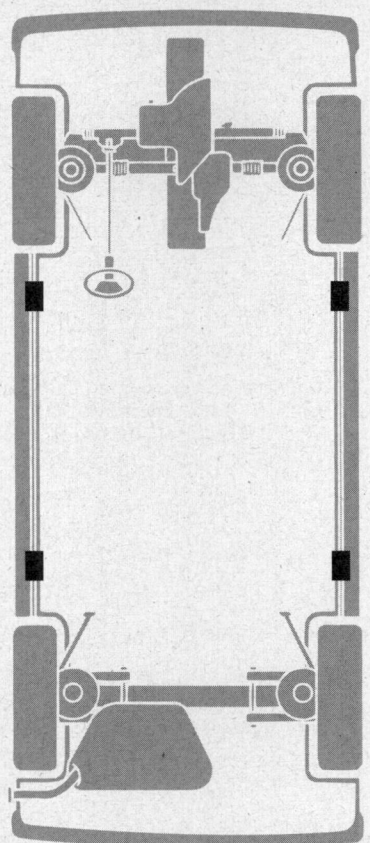

ALTA00007

Fig. 3   Vue

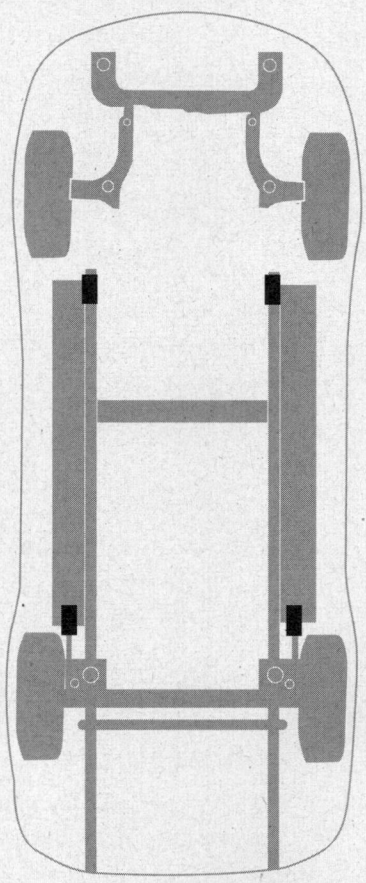

ALSN04003

Fig. 4   Relay

Frame contact hoist pads must not contact rocker panels, fenders or floor. When using tip-up hoist pad, position front frame contact hoist pads under front frame between lower control arm & frame pad or front frame pad. On models with rear leaf springs, position rear frame contact tip-up hoist pad under rear spring just behind hanger.

4WD Shown

ALCT00008

Fig. 5   Avalanche, Denali, Escalade, Escalade ESV, Escalade EXT, Hummer H2, Hummer H3, Sierra, Silverado, Suburban, Tahoe, Yukon & Yukon XL

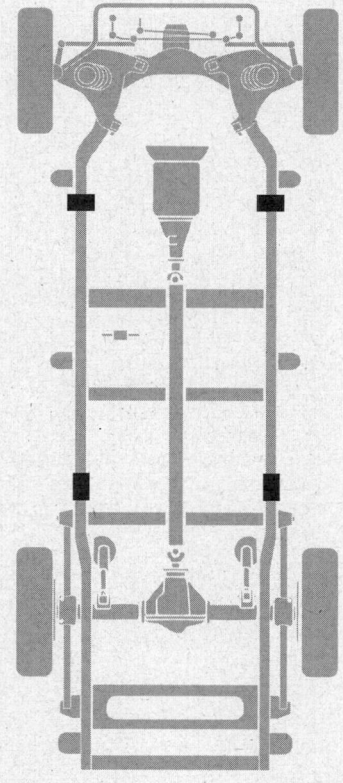

ALCT00007

Fig. 6   Express & Savana

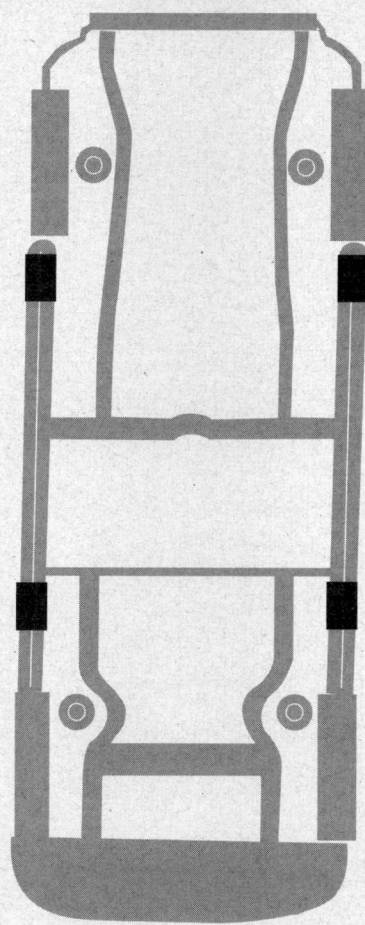

Fig. 7   Equinox & Torrent

ALGM04040

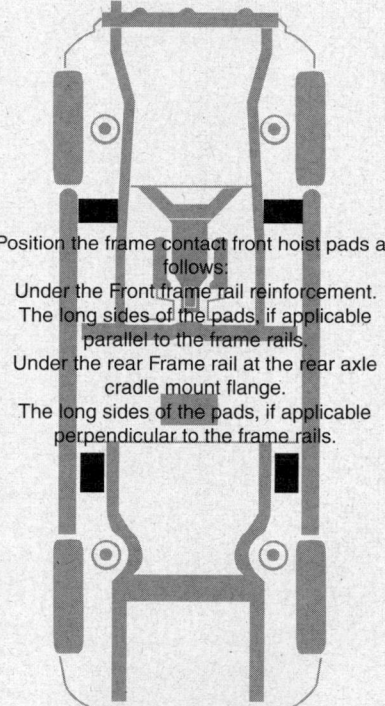

Position the frame contact front hoist pads as follows:
Under the Front frame rail reinforcement.
The long sides of the pads, if applicable parallel to the frame rails.
Under the rear Frame rail at the rear axle cradle mount flange.
The long sides of the pads, if applicable perpendicular to the frame rails.

ALGM00035

Fig. 8   SRX

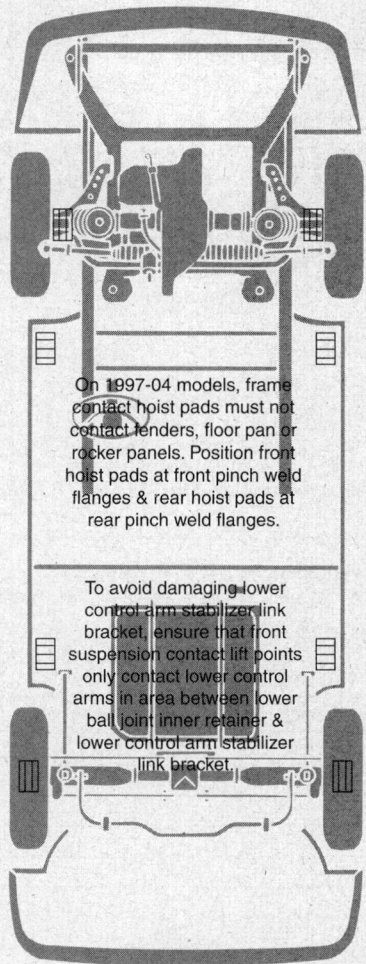

On 1997-04 models, frame contact hoist pads must not contact fenders, floor pan or rocker panels. Position front hoist pads at front pinch weld flanges & rear hoist pads at rear pinch weld flanges.

To avoid damaging lower control arm stabilizer link bracket, ensure that front suspension contact lift points only contact lower control arms in area between lower ball joint inner retainer & lower control arm stabilizer link bracket.

ALGM00018

Fig. 9   HHR

NON-STANDARD TIRE & WHEEL SIZE ADJUSTMENT TO RIDE HEIGHT SPECIFICATIONS & TIRE SIZE ADJUSTMENT CHARTS

INDEX

	Page No.		Page No.		Page No.
Aspect Ratio Adjustment For Alpha-Numeric Radial Ply Tires	0-75	Aspect Ratio Adjustment For P225–275 Metric Radial & Bias Ply Tires	0-75	Section Width Adjustment For Alpha-Numeric Radial Ply Tires	0-75
Aspect Ratio Adjustment For P145–215 Metric Radial & Bias Ply Tires	0-74	Section Width Adjustment For Alpha-Numeric Bias Ply Tires	0-75	Section Width Adjustment for Metric Radial & Bias Ply Tires	0-74

SECTION WIDTH ADJUSTMENT FOR METRIC RADIAL & BIAS PLY TIRES

These specifications are approximate and are only intended for use in making approximate ride height inspections and adjustments on models with non-standard tires. These specifications should not be used in place of those recommended by the vehicle manufacturer.

Standard Tire	Optional Tire, Tire Section Width Change Adjustment To Ride Height Specification, Inch													
	P145	P155	P165	P175	P185	P195	P205	P215	P225	P235	P245	P255	P265	P275
P145	0	+.25	+.50	—	—	—	—	—	—	—	—	—	—	—
P155	−.25	0	+.25	+.50	—	—	—	—	—	—	—	—	—	—
P165	−.50	−.25	0	+.25	+.50	—	—	—	—	—	—	—	—	—
P175	—	−.50	−.25	0	+.25	+.50	—	—	—	—	—	—	—	—
P185	—	—	−.50	−.25	0	+.25	+.50	—	—	—	—	—	—	—
P195	—	—	—	−.50	−.25	0	+.25	+.50	—	—	—	—	—	—
P205	—	—	—	—	−.50	−.25	0	+.25	+.50	—	—	—	—	—
P215	—	—	—	—	—	−.50	−.25	0	+.25	+.50	—	—	—	—
P225	—	—	—	—	—	—	−.50	−.25	0	+.25	+.50	—	—	—
P235	—	—	—	—	—	—	—	−.50	−.25	0	+.25	+.50	—	—
P245	—	—	—	—	—	—	—	—	−.50	−.25	0	+.25	+.50	—
P255	—	—	—	—	—	—	—	—	—	−.50	−.25	0	+.25	+.50
P265	—	—	—	—	—	—	—	—	—	—	−.50	−.25	0	+.25
P275	—	—	—	—	—	—	—	—	—	—	—	−.50	−.25	0

ASPECT RATIO ADJUSTMENT FOR P145-215 METRIC RADIAL & BIAS PLY TIRES

These specifications are approximate and are only intended for use in making approximate ride height inspections and adjustments on models with non-standard tires. These specifications should not be used in place of those recommended by the vehicle manufacturer.

Standard Tire	Optional Tire, Tire Aspect Ratio Change to Ride Height Specification, Inch				
	60	65	70	75	80
60	0	+.38	+.75	—	—
65	−.38	0	+.38	+.75	—
70	−.75	−.38	0	+.38	+.75
75	—	−.75	−.38	0	+.38
80	—	—	−.75	−.38	0

ASPECT RATIO ADJUSTMENT FOR P225-275 METRIC RADIAL & BIAS PLY TIRES

These specifications are approximate and are only intended for use in making approximate ride height inspections and adjustments on models with non-standard tires. These specifications should not be used in place of those recommended by the vehicle manufacturer.

Standard Tire	Optional Tire, Tire Aspect Ratio Change to Ride Height Specification, Inch				
	60	65	70	75	80
60	0	+.50	+1.00	—	—
65	−.50	0	+.50	+1.00	—
70	−1.00	−.50	0	+.50	+1.00
75	—	−.75	−.50	0	+.50
80	—	—	−1.00	−.50	0

SECTION WIDTH ADJUSTMENT FOR ALPHA-NUMERIC RADIAL PLY TIRES

These specifications are approximate and are only intended for use in making approximate ride height inspections and adjustments on models with non-standard tires. These specifications should not be used in place of those recommended by the vehicle manufacturer.

Standard Tire	Optional Tire, Tire Section Width Change Adjustment To Ride Height Specification, Inch						
	DR	ER	FR	GR	HR	JR	LR
DR	0	+.19	+.44	—	—	—	—
ER	−.19	0	+.25	+.50	—	—	—
FR	−.44	−.25	0	+.25	+.63	—	—
GR	—	−.50	−.25	0	+.31	+.50	—
HR	—	—	−.63	−.31	0	+.19	+.44
JR	—	—	—	−.50	−.19	0	+.25
LR	—	—	—	—	−.44	−.25	0

ASPECT RATIO ADJUSTMENT FOR ALPHA-NUMERIC RADIAL PLY TIRES

These specifications are approximate and are only intended for use in making approximate ride height inspections and adjustments on models with non-standard tires. These specifications should not be used in place of those recommended by the vehicle manufacturer.

Standard Tire	Optional Tire, Change Adjustment to Ride Height Specification, Inch		
	60	70	78
60	0	+.50	+.62
70	−.50	0	+.13
78	−.62	−.13	0

SECTION WIDTH ADJUSTMENT FOR ALPHA-NUMERIC BIAS PLY TIRES

These specifications are approximate and are only intended for use in making approximate ride height inspections and adjustments on models with non-standard tires. These specifications should not be used in place of those recommended by the vehicle manufacturer.

Standard Tire	Optional Tire, Change Adjustment To Ride Height Specifications, Inch							
	A	B	C	D	E	F	G	H
A	0	+.25	+.50	—	—	—	—	—
B	−.25	0	+.25	+.38	—	—	—	—
C	−.50	−.25	0	+.13	+.37	—	—	—
D	—	−.37	−.13	0	+.25	+.50	—	—
E	—	—	−.38	−.25	0	+.25	+.50	—
F	—	—	—	−.50	−.25	0	+.25	+.56
G	—	—	—	—	−.50	−.25	0	+.31
H	—	—	—	—	—	−.56	−.31	0

TABLE OF CONTENTS

	Page No.		Page No.
ELECTRICAL SYMBOL IDENTIFICATION	0-76	**WIRE COLOR CODE IDENTIFICATION**	0-79

Electrical Symbol Identification

INDEX

	PAGE NO.	FIG. NO.		PAGE NO.	FIG. NO.
DaimlerChrysler	0-76	1	Escape, Explorer Sport, Explorer Sport-Trac & Villager	0-77	3
Ford Motor Co.:			**General Motors Corp.**	0-78	4
Except Escape, Explorer Sport, Explorer Sport-Trac & Villager	0-76	2			

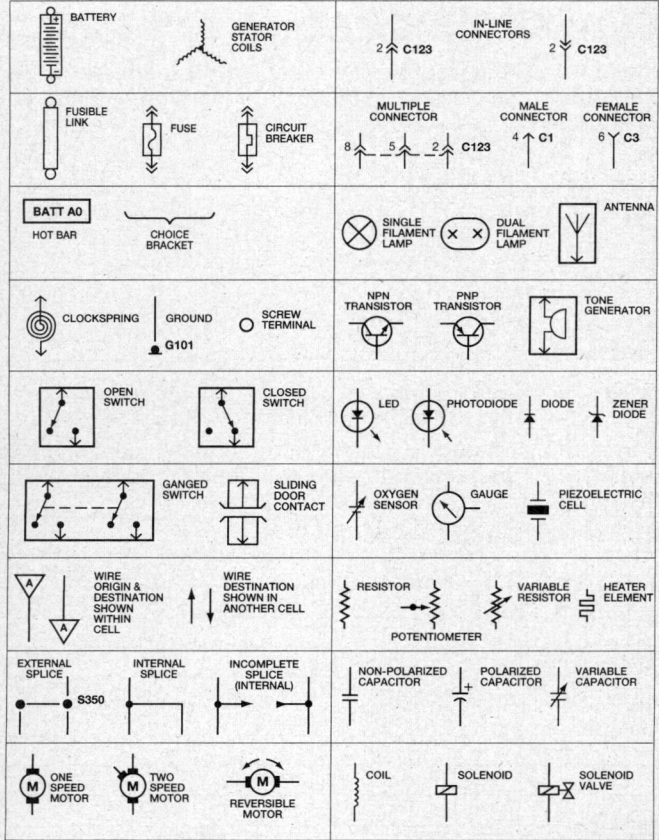

JP1139900033000X

Fig. 1   DaimlerChrysler

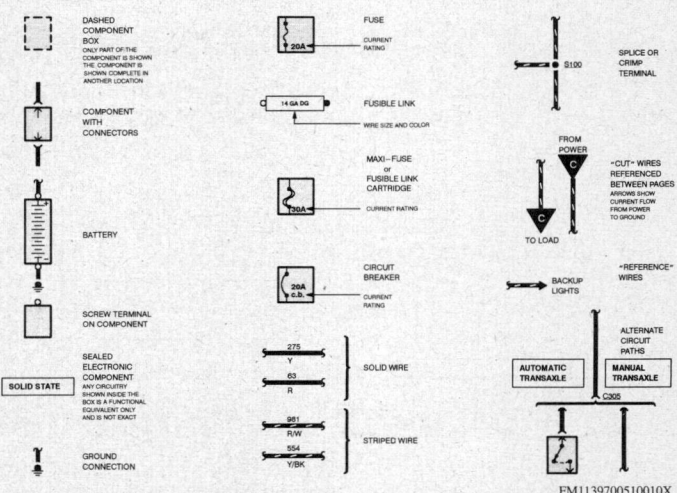

FM1139700510010X

Fig. 2   Ford Motor Co. (Part 1 of 2). Except Escape, Explorer Sport, Explorer Sport-Trac & Villager

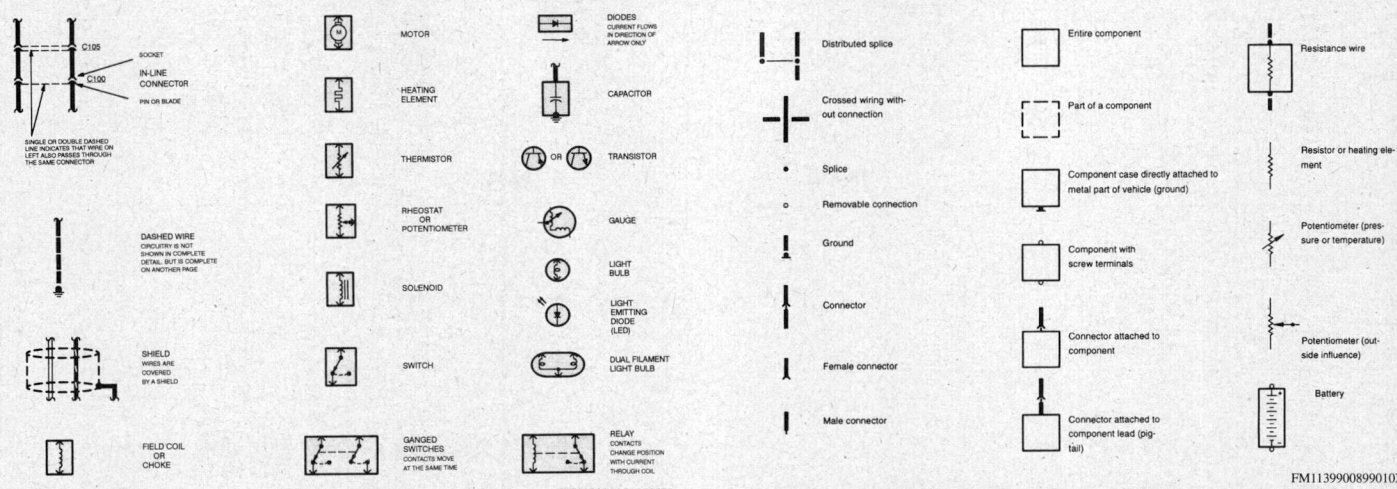

FM1139700510020X

FM1139900899010X

Fig. 2   Ford Motor Co. (Part 2 of 2). Except Escape, Explorer Sport, Explorer Sport-Trac & Villager

Fig. 3   Ford Motor Co. (Part 1 of 4). Escape, Explorer Sport, Explorer Sport-Trac & Villager

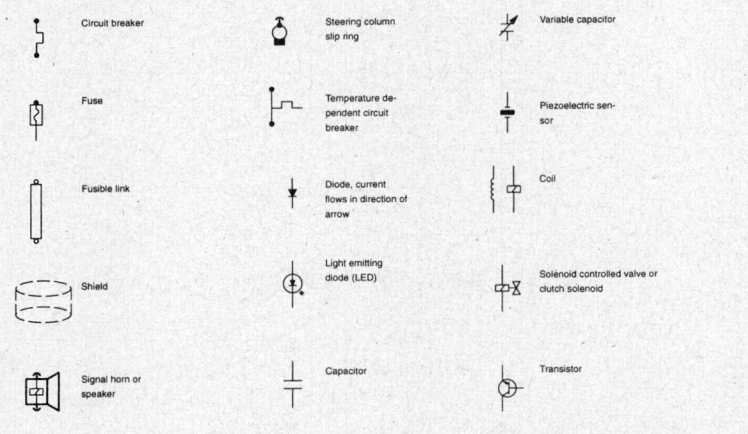

FM1139900899020X

Fig. 3   Ford Motor Co. (Part 2 of 4). Escape, Explorer Sport, Explorer Sport-Trac & Villager

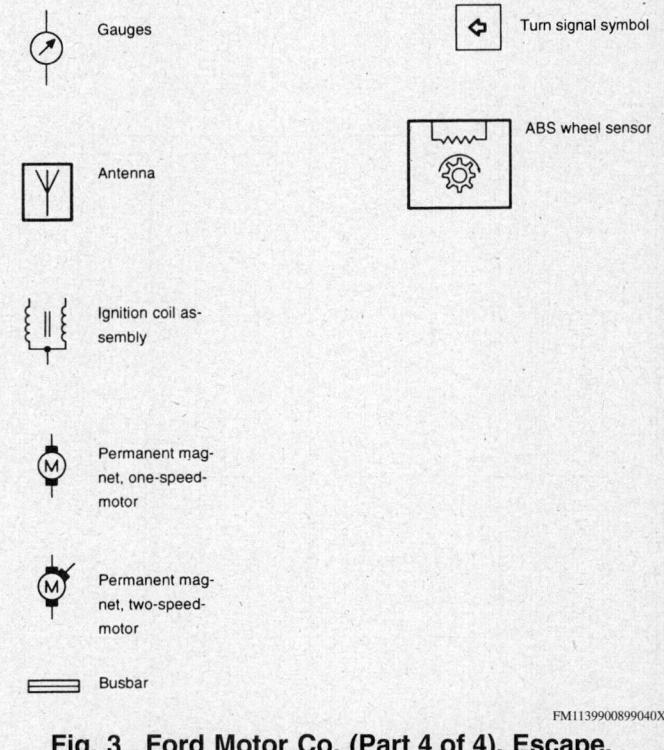

FM1139900899040X

Fig. 3   Ford Motor Co. (Part 4 of 4). Escape, Explorer Sport, Explorer Sport-Trac & Villager

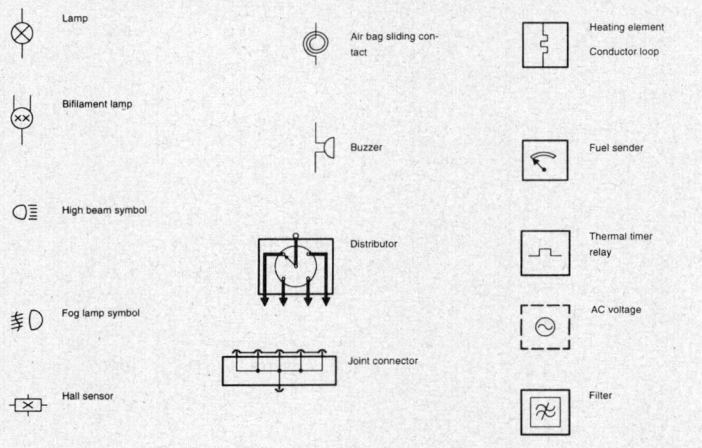

FM1139900899030X

Fig. 3   Ford Motor Co. (Part 3 of 4). Escape, Explorer Sport, Explorer Sport-Trac & Villager

ELECTRICAL SYMBOL & WIRE COLOR CODE IDENTIFICATION

Symbol	Description
	Supplemental Inflatable Restraint (SIR) or Supplemental Restraint System (SRS) Icon This icon is used to alert the technician that the system contains SIR/SRS components that require certain precautions before servicing. Refer to *SIR Handling Caution* in Cautions and Notices.
	On-Board Diagnostic (OBD II) Icon This icon is used to alert the technician that the circuit is essential for proper OBD II emission controls circuit operation. Any circuit which, if it fails, causes the malfunction indicator lamp (MIL) to turn on, is identified as an OBD II circuit.
	Important Icon This icon is used to alert the technician that there is additional information that will aid in servicing a system.
Hot At All Times / Hot In Run / Hot In Start / Hot In Acc And Run / Hot In Run And Start / Hot In Run, Bulb Test And Start / Hot With Headlamp Switch In Park Or Head / Hot In Retained Accessory Power (RAP)	**Voltage Indicator Boxes** These boxes are used on schematics to indicate when voltage is present at a fuse.
	Partial Component When a component is represented in a dashed box, the component or its wiring is not shown in its entirety.

Symbol	Description
	Entire Component When a component is represented in a solid box the component or its wiring is shown in its entirety.
	Fuse
	Circuit Breaker
	Fusible Link
12	Connector Attached to Component

Fig. 4 General Motors Corp. (Part 1 of 4)

Symbol	Description
12	Pigtail Connector
	Bolt On or Screw On Eyelet Terminal
12 C100	Inline Harness Connector
S100	Splice
P100	Pass Through the Grommet

Symbol	Description
G100	Chassis Ground
	Case Ground
	Single Filament Light Bulbs
	Double Filament Light Bulb
	Light Emitting Diodes

Fig. 4 General Motors Corp. (Part 2 of 4)

Symbol	Description
	Capacitor
	Battery
	Variable Battery
	Resistor
	Variable Resistor

Symbol	Description
	Position Sensor
	I/O Resistors
	I/O Switches
	Diode
	Crystal

Fig. 4 General Motors Corp. (Part 3 of 4)

Symbol	Description
	Heating Elements
	Motor
	Solenoid
	Coil
	Antenna

Symbol	Description
	Shield
	Switches
	Single Pole Single Throw Relay
	Single Pole Double Throw Relay

Fig. 4 General Motors Corp. (Part 4 of 4)

Wire Color Code Identification

DAIMLERCHRYSLER

Color	Code
Black	BK
Blue	BL
Brown	BR
Dark Blue	DB
Dark Green	DG
Gray	GY
Light Blue	LB
Light Green	LG
Orange	OR
Pink	PK
Red	RD
Silver	SR
Tan	TN
Violet	VT
White	WH
White	WT
Yellow	YE
Yellow	YL

GENERAL MOTORS CORP.

Color	Code
Black	BLK
Blue	BLU
Brown	BRN
Dark Blue	DKBLU
Dark Green	DKGRN
Gray	GR
Green	GRN
Light Blue	LGTBLU
Light Green	LGTGRN
Orange	ORN
Pink	PNK
Purple	PPL
Red	RED
Tan	TAN
White	WHT
Yellow	YEL

FORD MOTOR CO.

Color	Code
Black	BK
Blue	BU
Brown	BN
Dark Blue	DB
Dark Green	DG
Gray	GY
Green	GN
Light Blue	LB
Light Green	LG
Natural	NA
Orange	OG
Pink	PK
Red	RD
Silver	SR
Tan	TN
Violet	VT
White	WH
Yellow	YE

VEHICLE MAINTENANCE SCHEDULES

TABLE OF CONTENTS

	Page No.
DAIMLERCHRYSLER	0-81
FORD MOTOR CO.	0-102
GENERAL MOTORS CORP.	0-110

DaimlerChrysler

INDEX

	Page No.
Caravan, Pacifica, Town & Country & Voyager	0-81
Dakota & Durango	0-84
Full Size Pickups	0-86
Full Size Vans	0-92
Jeep	0-94
PT Cruiser	0-98
Sprinter	0-100

CARAVAN, PACIFICA, TOWN & COUNTRY & VOYAGER

Service Interval In Miles①

Recommended Service & Intervals (Months)	7,500	15,000	22,500	30,000	37,500	45,000	52,500	60,000	67,500	75,000	82,500	90,000	97,500	105,000
BODY														
Replace Cabin Air Filter	Every 12 Months Or 12,000 Miles													
BRAKES														
Inspect Brake Connections, Hoses & Lines, 2002	Normal Service Every 12 Months Or 7500 Miles; Severe Service 3000 Miles													
Inspect Brake Connections, Hoses & Lines, 2003–06	At Every Oil Change Interval													
Inspect Brake Drums, Linings & Rotors, 2002	S	S	N		X		S	S	N	S		S		
Inspect Brake Drums, Linings & Rotors, 2003–05	Normal Service Every 18,000 Miles; Severe Service Every 9000 Miles													
Inspect Brake Drums, Linings & Rotors, 2006	Normal Service Every 18,000 Miles; Severe Service Every 12,000 Miles													
CLUTCH & TRANSMISSION														
Adjust Bands 3 Speed Transaxle	Every 15,000 Miles													
Change Automatic Transaxle Fluid & Filter, 2002–03②	No Normal Service; Severe Service Every 48,000 Miles													
Change Automatic Transaxle Fluid & Filter, 2004–06②	No Normal Service; Severe Service Every 60,000 Miles													
Change AWD Overrunning Clutch & Driveline Module/Rear Carrier Lubricants				S				S				S		
Change AWD Power Transfer Unit Lubricant②		S		S		S		S		S		S		
DRIVESHAFT & CV JOINTS														
Inspect CV & Driveshaft Joint Boots	X	X	X	X	X	X	X	X			X	X	X	X

CARAVAN, PACIFICA, TOWN & COUNTRY & VOYAGER—Continued

Service Interval In Miles①

Recommended Service & Intervals (Months)	Interval / Notes
ENGINE	
Change Engine Coolant, 2002–05	Every 60 Months Or 100,000 Miles
Change Engine Coolant, 2006	Normal Service Every 60 Months Or 102,000 Miles; Severe Service Every 60 Months Or 100,000 Miles
Change Engine Oil & Filter, 2002	Normal Service Every 6 Months Or 7500 Miles; Severe Service Every 3000 Miles
Change Engine Oil & Filter, 2003–06	Normal Service Every 6 Months Or 6000 Miles; Severe Service Every 3 Months Or 3000 Miles
Inspect Coolant Level	At Every Engine Oil Change
Inspect Cooling System & Protection Level	X (at intervals noted)
Inspect Alternator Drive Belt, 2002 2.4L	Inspect Every 30,000 Miles
Inspect Alternator Drive Belt, 2003–06 2.4L	Normal Service Inspect Every 42,000 Miles; Severe Service Inspect Every 15,000 Miles
Inspect Drive Belts, 2002	S (at intervals noted)
Inspect PCV Valve③	S / X (at intervals noted)
Inspect Power Steering Pump Drive Belt, 2003–06 2.4L	Normal Service Every 30,000 Miles; Severe Service Every 15,000 Miles
Inspect Serpentine Belt	X / S (at intervals noted)
Replace Engine Air & PCV Filters	S (at intervals noted)
Replace Ignition Cables Except, 2.4L & 2002 3.3L & 3.8L	Every 60,000 Miles
Replace Ignition Cables, 2002–03 3.3L & 3.8L	Every 100,000 Miles
Replace Ignition Cables, 2004–06 3.3L & 3.8L	Normal Service Every 100,000 Miles; Severe Service Every 75,000 Miles
Replace PCV Valve, 2002	At 60,000 Miles & 120,000 Miles, Or When Emissions Maintenance Lamp Remains Lit w/Ignition On
Replace PCV Valve, 2003–06	Normal Service Inspect At 60,000 Miles & Replace If Necessary; Severe Service Inspect Every 30,000 Miles & Replace If Necessary Or When Emissions Maintenance Lamp Remains Lit w/Ignition On
Replace Spark Plugs, 2003–06 2.4L	Every 30,000 Miles
Replace Spark Plugs, 2002 2.4L & 3.0L	X (at interval noted)
Replace Spark Plugs, 2003 3.3L & 3.8L & 2004–06 3.5L	Normal Service Every 100,000 Miles; Severe Service Every 75,000 Miles

CARAVAN, PACIFICA, TOWN & COUNTRY & VOYAGER—Continued

Service Interval In Miles①

Recommended Service & Intervals (Months)	36000	39000	42000	45000	48000	51000	54000	57000	60000	63000	66000	69000	72000	75000	78000	81000	84000	87000	90000	93000	96000	99000
ENGINE																						
Replace Timing Belt, 2.4L	Normal Service Every 120,000 Miles; Severe Service Every 90,000 Miles																					
Replace Timing Belt, 2.5L																			X			
Replace Timing Belt, 3.0L	Normal Service Every 90,000 Miles																					
STEERING, SUSPENSION & TIRES																						
Inspect Ball Joints (Every 24 Mos.)									X										X			
Inspect Bushings, Arms, Seals, Springs & Jounce Bumpers	S	X	S	X	S	X	S	X	S	X	S	X	S	X	S	X	S	X	S	X	S	X
Inspect Power Steering Belt & Tensioner, 2.4L	Every 30,000 Miles																					
Lubricate Front Suspension Ball Joints, Steering Linkage & Wheel Stops (Every 24 Mos.)									X										X			
Rotate Tires & Adjust Pressure, 2002	S	N	S	N	S	N	S	N	S	N	S	N	S	N	S	N	S	N	S	N	S	N
Rotate Tires & Adjust Pressure, 2003-06	Every 6000 Miles																					

AWD — All Wheel Drive
N — Normal Service
S — Severe Service
X — Normal Or Severe Service

① — After vehicle passes 99,000 mile mark return to beginning of mileage table & start cycle over again.

② — Operating vehicle more than 50% heavy traffic during hot weather, above 90°F, using vehicle for police, taxi, limousine type operation, or trailer towing require more frequent transaxle & AWD service. Perform these services if vehicle is usually operated under these conditions.

③ — This maintenance is recommended by DaimlerChrysler to owner but is not required to maintain warranty on PCV valve.

DAKOTA & DURANGO

Service Interval In Miles①

Recommended Service & Intervals (Months)

Service interval columns (miles): 3000, 6000, 9000, 12000, 15000, 18000, 21000, 24000, 27000, 30000, 33000, 36000, 39000, 42000, 45000, 48000, 51000, 54000, 57000, 60000, 63000, 66000, 69000, 72000, 75000, 78000, 81000, 84000, 87000, 90000, 93000, 96000, 99000

BRAKES

Service	Interval / Service Codes
Inspect Brake Connections, Hoses & Lines	Normal Service Every 6 Months Or 7500 Miles; Severe Service Every 3 Months Or 3000 Miles
Inspect Brake Drums & Rotors	S at 15000, 30000, 45000, 60000, 75000, 90000
Inspect Brake Pads & Shoes	S at 15000, 30000, 60000, 75000; X at 45000, 90000

CLUTCH & TRANSMISSION

Service	Interval / Service Codes
Change Automatic Transmission Fluid & Filter, 2002–04 Dakota & 4.7L & 5.7L Durango	Normal Service Every 100,000 Miles; Severe Service Every 30,000 Miles
Change Automatic Transmission Fluid & Filter, 2004 Durango 3.7L	Normal Service Every 100,000 Miles; Severe Service At 60,000 Miles Then Every 30,000 Miles Thereafter
Change Automatic Transmission Fluid & Filter, 2005–06 3.7L, 4.7L & 5.7L	Severe Service Every 60,000 Miles
Change Transfer Case Lubricant, 2002–03	Normal Service Inspect Every 60,000 Miles; Drain And Refill Every 120,000 Miles; Severe Service Every 60,000 Miles
Change Transfer Case Lubricant, 2004–06	Normal Service Inspect Every 60,000 Miles; Drain And Refill Every 120,000 Miles; Severe Service Inspect Every 30,000 Miles; Drain & Refill Every 120,000 Miles
Lubricate Clutch Bellcrank	X at 30000, 60000, 90000

DRIVE AXLE & DRIVESHAFT

Service	Interval / Service Codes
Change Differential Lubricants, Except 2004 Dakota & 2005–06 All	S at 15000, 30000, 45000, 60000, 75000, 90000
Change Differential Lubricants, 2004 Dakota & 2005–06 All	S at 30000, 45000, 60000, 75000, 90000
Inspect CV & Driveshaft Joint Boots	X at 15000, 30000, 45000, 60000, 75000, 90000
Lubricate Driveshaft U-Joints, Slip Splines & Yokes②	S at 3000, 9000, 15000, 21000, 27000, 33000, 39000, 45000, 51000, 57000, 63000, 69000, 75000, 81000, 87000, 93000, 99000; X at 6000, 12000, 18000, 24000, 30000, 36000, 42000, 48000, 54000, 60000, 66000, 72000, 78000, 84000, 90000, 96000

ENGINE

Service	Interval / Service Codes
Change Engine Coolant, 2002–04 Except 2004 Durango	Every 60 Months Or 100,000 Miles
Change Engine Coolant, 2004 Durango & 2005–06 All	Every 60 Months Or 102,000 Miles
Change Engine Oil & Filter, 2002	Normal Service Every 6 Months Or 7500 Miles; Severe Service Every 3000 Miles

DAKOTA & DURANGO—Continued

Service Interval In Miles①

Recommended Service & Intervals (Months)	Service Interval In Miles
ENGINE	
Change Engine Oil & Filter, 2003–06	Normal Service Every 6 Months Or 6000 Miles; Severe Service Every 3000 Miles
Inspect Air Filter, 2003–06	Normal Service Every 30,000 Miles; Severe Service Every 15,000 Miles
Inspect Cooling System & Protection Level	X marks at regular intervals
Inspect Drive Belts	X marks at regular intervals
Inspect Ignition Cables, 5.7L	X marks at regular intervals
Inspect PCV Valve③	S marks
Replace Air Filter, 2002	Every 60,000 Miles
Replace Ignition Cables, 2.5L, 3.9L, 5.2L & 5.9L	Every 30,000 Miles
Replace Spark Plugs	Every 60,000 Miles
Replace Timing Belt, 2.5L	X marks
STEERING, SUSPENSION & TIRES	
Inspect Bushings, Arms, Seals, Springs & Jounce Bumpers	S X S X S X S X S X S X S X S X S X S X S
Inspect Front Wheel Bearings (Clean & Repack If Required)	Every 18 Months Or 22,500 Miles
Lubricate Ball Joints (Every 18 Mos.)	X marks
Lubricate Steering Linkage (Every 12 Mos.)	X marks
Rotate Tires & Adjust Pressure, 2002	S N S N S N S N S N S N S N S N
Rotate Tires & Adjust Pressure, 2003–06	Every 6000 Miles

AWD — All Wheel Drive
N — Normal Service
S — Severe Service
X — Normal Or Severe Service
① — After vehicle passes 99,000 mile mark return to beginning of mileage table & start cycle over again.
② — Lubricate slip splines daily if travelling through water.
③ — Inspect and replace as necessary. This maintenance is recommended by DaimlerChrysler Corporation to the owner, but not required to maintain the warranty of the PCV Valve.

FULL SIZE PICKUPS

Service Interval In Miles ①

Recommended Service & Intervals (Months)

Grid mileage columns (in thousands of miles): 30, 60, 90, 120, 150, 180, 210, 240, 270, 300, 330, 360, 390, 420, 450, 480, 510, 540, 570, 600, 630, 660, 690, 720, 750, 780, 810, 840, 870, 900, 930, 960, 990

BRAKES

Service	Schedule / Interval
Inspect Brake Connections, Hoses & Lines	Normal Service Every 6 Months Or 7500 Miles; Severe Service Every 3000 Miles
Inspect Brake Linings, 2002 HD	Normal Service Every 18,000 Miles; Severe Service Every 12,000 Miles
Inspect Brake Linings, 2002 MD	S / N marks at odometer columns (S = Severe, N = Normal)
Inspect Brake Linings, 2002 1500, 2500 & 3500 LD	S / N marks at odometer columns
Inspect Brake Linings 2003–05 1500, 2500 & 3500	Normal Service Every 18,000 Miles; Severe Service Every 12,000 Miles
Inspect Brake Linings 2006 1500, 2500 & 3500	Normal Service Every 24,000 Miles; Severe Service Every 18,000 Miles
Inspect Brake Linings, Diesel	Normal Service Every 22,500 Miles; Severe Service Every 15,000 Miles
Lubricate Parking Brake Ratio Lever Pivot	X marks at odometer columns

CLUTCH & TRANSMISSION

Service	Schedule / Interval
Change Automatic Transmission Filter, Fluid & Adjust Bands, Diesel, 2002–03	Normal Service Every 100,000 Miles; Severe Service Every 30,000 Miles
Change Automatic Transmission Filter, Fluid & Adjust Bands, Diesel, 2004–06 (48RE)	Normal Service Every 100,000 Miles; Severe Service Every 30,000 Miles
Change Automatic Transmission Filter, Fluid & Adjust Bands, Diesel, 2004–06 (54RFE)	Severe Service Every 60,000 Miles
Change Automatic Transmission Filter, Fluid & Adjust Bands, 2002 1500, 2500 & 3500 LD	Normal Service Every 100,000 Miles; Severe Service Every 30,000 Miles
Change Automatic Transmission Filter, Fluid & Adjust Bands, 2003–04 1500, 2500 & 3500	Normal Service Every 100,000 Miles; Severe Service Every 30,000 Miles
Change Automatic Transmission Filter, Fluid & Adjust Bands, 2005 Gasoline Except SRT 10	Normal Service Every 120,000 Miles; Severe Service Every 60,000 Miles

Recommended Service & Intervals (Months)

Service Interval In Miles①

Mileage interval columns: 3000, 6000, 7500, 9000, 12000, 15000, 18000, 21000, 24000, 27000, 30000, 33000, 36000, 39000, 42000, 45000, 48000, 51000, 54000, 57000, 60000, 63000, 66000, 69000, 72000, 75000, 78000, 81000, 84000, 87000, 90000, 93000, 96000, 99000

CLUTCH & TRANSMISSION

Service	Interval
Change Automatic Transmission Filter, Fluid & Adjust Bands, 2002 MD, Gasoline④	Normal Service Every 100,000 Miles; Severe Service Every 24,000 Miles
Change Automatic Transmission Filter, Fluid & Adjust Bands, 2002 HD, Gasoline④	Normal Service Every 100,000 Miles; Severe Service Every 30,000 Miles
Change Automatic Transmission Filter, Fluid & Adjust Bands, 2005 Gasoline SRT 10②	Normal Service Every 100,000 Miles; Severe Service Every 30,000 Miles
Change Automatic Transmission Filter, Fluid & Adjust Bands, 2006 Gasoline Except SRT 10	Severe Service Every 60,000 Miles
Change Transfer Case Lubricant, 2002 1500 LD	Normal Service Inspect Every 30,000 Miles, Drain And Refill At 90,000 Miles; Severe Service Drain And Refill Every 60,000 Miles
Change Transfer Case Lubricant, 2002 2500 & 3500 HD	Normal Service At 36,000 Miles, Then Every 18,000 Miles Thereafter; Severe Service Every 18,000 Miles
Change Transfer Case Lubricant, 2002 2500 & 3500 LD & MD	Normal Service Inspect Every 30,000 Miles, Drain And Refill Every 120,000 Miles; Severe Service Drain And Refill Every 60,000 Miles
Change Transfer Case Lubricant, 2003–04	Normal Service, Inspect Every 30,000 Miles & Drain And Refill Every 90,000 Miles; Severe Service Inspect Every 30,000 Miles And Drain And Refill Every 60,000 Miles
Change Transfer Case Lubricant, 2005–06	Normal Service, Inspect Every 30,000 Miles & Drain And Refill Every 120,000 Miles; Severe Service Inspect Every 30,000 Miles And Drain And Refill Every 60,000 Miles
Change 6 Speed Manual Transmission Fluid, 2005–06 Diesel	Severe Service Every 75,000 Miles
Change 6 Speed Manual Transmission Fluid, 2005–06 Gasoline	Severe Service Every 60,000 Miles
Lubricate Clutch Bellcrank	X at 45,000; X at 60,000; X at 90,000
Lubricate O/D 4 Gearshift Mechanism	X at 45,000; X at 60,000; X at 90,000

DRIVE AXLE & DRIVESHAFT

Service	Interval
Change Differential Lubricant, 2002	S at 15,000; S at 30,000; S at 45,000; S at 60,000; S at 75,000; S at 90,000

FULL SIZE PICKUPS—Continued

Service Interval In Miles ①

The table below lists each recommended service, its interval note, and (where shown) per‑mileage‑column service marks (X = service, S = severe‑service interval, N = normal‑service interval).

Recommended Service & Intervals (Months)	Service Interval / Notes
DRIVE AXLE & DRIVESHAFT	
Change Differential Lubricant, 2003–06	Severe Service Every 15,000 Miles
Change Front (4X4) & Rear Axle Fluid, 2002 1500	Severe Service Every 12,000 Miles
Change Front (4X4) & Rear Axle Fluid, 2004–06 1500	Severe Service Every 15,000 Miles
Inspect CV & Driveshaft Joint Boots	X marks across mileage columns
Inspect Differential Lubricant Level	At Every Engine Oil Change
Lubricate Driveshaft U-Joints, Slip Splines & Yokes ③	S X S X S X S X S X S X S X S (severe/normal marks across mileage columns)
ENGINE	
Adjust Engine Valve Clearance, 2004–06 Diesel	Every 135,000 Miles
Change Engine Coolant, 2002 1500 LD	Normal Service At 60 Months Or 75,000 Miles Then Every 25,000 Miles Thereafter; Severe Service Every 100,000 Miles
Change Engine Coolant, 2002 2500 & 3500 LD	Normal Service At 36 Months Or 45,000 Miles Then Every 24 Months Or 30,000 Miles; Severe Service Every 51,000 Miles
Change Engine Coolant, 2006 Diesel	Every 60 Months Or 100,000 Miles
Change Engine Coolant, 2003–04 1500, 2500 & 3500	Every 60 Months Or 100,000 Miles
Change Engine Coolant, 2005–06 1500, 2500 & 3500	Every 60 Months Or 102,000 Miles
Change Engine Coolant, 2002 MD Gasoline	Green IAT Coolant Every 36 Months Or 48,000 Miles
Change Engine Coolant, 2002 MD Gasoline	Green Coolant Every 48,000 Miles
Change Engine Coolant, 2002 Diesel	Every 36 Months Or 52,500 Miles
Change Engine Oil, LD (Normal Service Every 6 Mos.), 2002	S S N S S N S S N ... (severe/normal marks across mileage columns)
Change Engine Oil, MD & HD Gasoline (Normal Service Every 6 Mos.), 2002	S X S X S X S X ... (severe/normal marks across mileage columns)
Change Engine Oil, 2002 Diesel	Normal Service Every 6 Months Or 7500 Miles; Severe Service Every 3 Months Or 3750 Miles

FULL SIZE PICKUPS—Continued

Service Interval In Miles①

Recommended Service & Intervals (Months): 3, 6, 9, 12, 15, 18, 21, 24, 27, 30, 33, 36, 39, 42, 45, 48, 51, 54, 57, 60, 63, 66, 69, 72, 75, 78, 81, 84, 87, 90, 93, 96, 99

Service Interval In Miles: 3000, 6000, 9000, 12000, 15000, 18000, 21000, 24000, 27000, 30000, 33000, 36000, 39000, 42000, 45000, 48000, 51000, 54000, 57000, 60000, 63000, 66000, 69000, 72000, 75000, 78000, 81000, 84000, 87000, 90000, 93000, 96000, 99000

ENGINE

Service Item	Service Notes
Change Engine Oil, 2003–06 Gasoline	Normal Service Every 6 Months Or 6000 Miles; Severe Service Every 3 Months Or 3000 Miles
Change Engine Oil, 2003–04 Diesel Tier 1 EPA (250HO Or 305HP)	Normal Service Every 12 Months Or 15,000 Miles; Severe Service Every 7500 Miles
Change Engine Oil, 2003–04 Diesel, California LEV (235HP)	Normal Service Every 6 Months Or 7500 Miles; Severe Service Every 3750 Miles
Change Engine Oil, 2005–06 Diesel	Normal Service Every 12 Months Or 15,000 Miles; Severe Service Every 7500 Miles
Change Engine Oil Filter, 2002 1500, 2500 & 3500 LD	Normal Service Every 6 Months Or 7500 Miles; Severe Service Every 3000 Miles
Change Engine Oil Filter, 2003–06 Gasoline	Normal Service Every 6000 Miles; Severe Service Every 3000 Miles
Change Engine Oil Filter, 2002 Diesel	Normal Service Every 6 Months Or 7500 Miles; Severe Service Every 3750 Miles
Change Engine Oil Filter, 2002 MD & HD	Normal Service Every 6 Months Or 6000 Miles; Severe Service Every 3000 Miles
Change Engine Oil Filter, 2003–04 Diesel Tier 1 EPA (250HP Or 305HP)	Normal Service Every 12 Months Or 15,000 Miles; Severe Service Every 7500 Miles
Change Engine Oil Filter, 2003–04 Diesel, California LEV (235HP)	Normal Service Every 6 Months Or 7500 Miles; Severe Service Every 3750 Miles
Change Engine Oil Filter, 2005–06 Diesel	Normal Service Every 12 Months Or 15,000 Miles; Severe Service Every 7500 Miles
Clean & Lubricate Crankcase Inlet Air Filter, 2002 HD 5.9L Gasoline	S
Drain Crankcase Breather Bottle, 2002 Diesel	Normal Service Every 15,000 Miles; Severe Service Every 3750 Miles
Inspect Coolant Pump Weep Hole For Blockage, Diesel	Every 15,000 Miles
Inspect Cooling System & Protection Level, Gasoline	X
Inspect Drive Belts, Replace As Necessary, Diesel	Every 22,500 Miles
Inspect Drive Belts, Replace As Necessary, 2002–03 Gasoline	Every 60,000 Miles

FULL SIZE PICKUPS—Continued

Service Interval In Miles ①

Recommended Service & Intervals (Months)	Service Interval In Miles ①
ENGINE	
Inspect Drive Belts, Replace As Necessary, 2004–06 Gasoline	Normal Service Every 90,000 Miles; Severe Service Every 75,000 Miles
Inspect Engine Air Filter, 2003–06	Normal Service Every 30,000 Miles; Severe Service Every 15,000 Miles & Replace As Necessary
Inspect Exhaust System	X (at regular intervals through 90,000 Miles)
Inspect Fan Hub & Dampener, Diesel	Every 30,000 Miles
Inspect PCV Valve, 2002 1500 & 2003 1500, 2500 & 3500	Every 60,000 Miles
Inspect PCV Valve, 2004 1500, 2500 & 3500	Normal Service Every 60,000 Miles; Severe Service Every 30,000 Miles
Inspect PCV Valve, 2005–06 1500, 2500 & 3500	Every 60,000 Miles
Lubricate Manifold Heat Riser Valve, 3.9L & 5.2L	X (54,000)
Replace Distributor Cap & Rotor, 2002 HD 5.9L Gasoline	X (57,000)
Replace Engine Air Filter, 2002 LD & MD Gasoline	S / X (S at intermediate intervals; X at 30,000 & 60,000)
Replace Fuel Filter & Clean Strainer, Diesel, 2002–03	Normal Service At 15,000 Miles & Every 15,000 Thereafter; Severe Service Every 7500 Miles
Replace Fuel Filter & Clean Strainer, Diesel, 2004–06	Every 15,000 Miles
Replace Ignition Cables, 2002 5.9L 1500	Every 60,000 Miles
Replace Ignition Cables, 2003–06 5.7L, 5.9L & 8.0L	Every 60,000 Miles
Replace O2 Sensor, 2002 HD 5.9L Gasoline	X (82,500)
Replace PCV Valve, 2003–06	Normal Service Inspect Every 60,000 Miles And Replace If Necessary; Severe Service Inspect Every 30,000 Miles
Replace Spark Plugs	X (30,000)
STEERING, SUSPENSION & TIRES	
Change Power Steering Fluid, 2003–06	Drain And Replace At 100,000 Miles
Inspect Bushings, Arms, Seals, Springs & Jounce Bumpers ③	S / X (inspect at regular intervals — S = severe, X = normal — from 7,500 through 90,000 Miles)
Inspect & Repack Front Wheel Bearings, 2002 2WD Diesel	X (at regular intervals)

FULL SIZE PICKUPS—Continued

Service Interval In Miles ①

Recommended Service & Intervals (Months)	7500	15000	22500	30000	37500	45000	52500	60000	67500	75000	82500	90000	97500
STEERING, SUSPENSION & TIRES													
Inspect & Repack Front Wheel Bearings, 2002 2WD LD		S	N		S	N		S	N		S	N	
Inspect & Repack Front Wheel Bearing, 2002 2WD MD & HD			X			X			X			X	
Lubricate Center Link	Every 24 Months Or 22,500 Miles												
Lubricate Steering Linkage, 2002	Normal Service Every 6 Months Or 7500 Miles; Severe Service Every 3000 Miles												
Rotate Tires & Adjust Pressure, 2002 LD & Diesel	Inspect For Wear & Rotate Every 7500 Miles												
Rotate Tires & Adjust Pressure, 2002 MD & HD	Inspect For Wear & Rotate Every 6000 Miles												
Rotate Tires & Adjust Pressure, 2003–06 Diesel	Inspect For Wear & Rotate Every 7500 Miles												
Rotate Tires & Adjust Pressure, 2003–06 Gasoline	Inspect For Wear & Rotate Every 6000 Miles												

GVWR — Gross Vehicle Weight Rating
LD — Light Duty 2002 2500 models except 8.0L engine.
MD — Medium Duty 2002 2500 & 3500 models w/CA emissions & 8.0L engine.
HD — Heavy Duty 2002 2500 models w/FED emissions & 8.0L HD engine & 3500 models w/FED emissions & 5.9L & 8.0L engines.
Mos. — Months
N — Normal Service
S — Severe Service
X — Normal Or Severe Service
2WD — Two Wheel Drive
4WD — Four Wheel Drive

① — After vehicle passes 99,000 mile mark return to beginning of mileage table & start cycle over again.
② — If used for frequent wide open throttle upshifts (Drag Racing etc.) every 15,000 miles.
③ — Lubricate slip splines daily if travelling through water.
④ — Off-the-highway operation, trailer towing, snow plowing or prolonged operation w/heavy loading, especially in hot weather require more frequent transmission service. Perform these services if vehicle is usually operated under these conditions.

FULL SIZE VANS

Service Interval In Miles ①

The mileage column headings run across the top of the grid (3600, 7500, 9000 … up to 99000). The entries below give the recommended service for each item, either as a marked interval (X or S) or as a descriptive note.

Recommended Service & Intervals (Months)	Service Interval In Miles ①
BRAKES	
Inspect Brake Connections, Hoses & Lines, 2002	Normal Service Every 6 Months Or 7500 Miles; Severe Service Every 3000 Miles
Inspect Brake Connections, Hoses & Lines, 2003	Normal Service Every 18,000 Miles; Severe Service Every 12,000 Miles
Lubricate Brake Booster Bellcrank Pivot	X — at 15,000 / 37,500 / 60,000 / 82,500 Miles
Lubricate Parking Brake Ratio Lever Pivot	X — at 22,500 / 45,000 / 67,500 / 90,000 Miles
CLUTCH & TRANSMISSION	
Change Automatic Transmission Fluid, Filter & Adjust Bands	Normal Service Every 100,000 Miles; Severe Service Every 30,000 Miles
DRIVE AXLE & DRIVESHAFT	
Change Differential Lubricants	S — Severe Service intervals marked
Lubricate Driveshaft U-Joints, Slip Splines & Yokes	S / X — marked at recurring intervals
ENGINE	
Change Engine Coolant, 2002 Gasoline	Normal Service Every 45,000 Miles Then Every 30,000 Miles Thereafter; Severe Service At 51,000 Miles Then Every 30,000 Miles Thereafter
Change Engine Coolant, 2003 Gasoline	Normal Service At 36 Months Or 60,000 Miles Then Every 24 Months Or 30,000 Miles Thereafter; Severe Service At 51,000 Miles Then Every 30,000 Miles Thereafter
Change Engine Oil Filter, 2002	Normal Service Every 6 Months Or 7500 Miles; Severe Service Every 3000 Miles
Change Engine Oil Filter, 2003	Normal Service Every 6 Months Or 6000 Miles; Severe Service Every 3000 Miles
Inspect Cooling System & Protection Level	X — marked at recurring intervals
Inspect Exhaust System	X — marked at recurring intervals
Inspect PCV Valve ②	S — marked at recurring intervals
Lubricate Manifold Heat Riser Valve, 3.9L & 5.2L	X — marked
Replace Drive Belts	Inspect And/Or Replace At 60,000 Miles & Then Inspect Every 15,000 Miles Thereafter
Replace Engine Air Filter	Normal Service Every 30,000 Miles; Severe Service Inspect Every 15,000 Miles & Replace As Necessary
Replace Fuel Filter, Van w/FED Emissions	S — marked
Replace PCV Valve ②	S / X — marked
Replace Spark Plugs	X — marked

STEERING, SUSPENSION & TIRES

Recommended Service & Intervals (Months) — Service Interval In Miles①	6000	7500	9000	12000	15000	18000	21000	24000	27000	30000	33000	36000	39000	42000	45000	48000	51000	54000	57000	60000	63000	66000	69000	72000	75000	78000	81000	84000	87000	90000	93000	96000	97500	99000
Inspect Bushings, Arms, Seals, Springs & Jounce Bumpers	S	X	S	S	X	S	S	S	S	X	S	S	S	S	X	S	S	S	S	X	S	S	S	S	X	S	S	S	S	X	S	S	X	S
Inspect & Repack Front Wheel Bearings, 2002								S	N							S	N							S	N					S	N			

Interval-based items:

- Lubricate Front Suspension Ball Joints, 2002 — Every 18 Months Or 22,500 Miles
- Lubricate Front Suspension Ball Joints, 2003 — Every 21,000 Miles
- Lubricate Steering Linkage, 2002 — Every 12 Months Or 15,000 Miles
- Lubricate Steering Linkage, 2003 — Normal Service Every 12,000 Miles; Severe Service Every 3000 Miles
- Rotate Tires, 2002 — Normal Service Every 7500 Miles; Severe Service Every 6000 Miles
- Rotate Tires, 2003 — Normal Service Every 6000 Miles

Mos. — Months
N — Normal Service
S — Severe Service
X — Normal Or Severe Service
① — After vehicle passes 99,000 mile mark return to beginning of mileage table & start cycle over again.
② — This maintenance is recommended by DaimlerChrysler Corporation to the customer but it is not required to maintain warranty on PCV valve.

JEEP

Service Interval In Miles①

(Column headings are a row of mileage intervals printed vertically across the top of the grid.)

Recommended Service	Service Interval / Notes
BODY	
Lubricate Body Components	X — Every 60,000 Miles
BRAKES	
Drain & Replace Brake Fluid, Grand Cherokee	X
Inspect Brake Connections, Hoses & Lines, 2002	Normal Service Every 6 Months Or 7500 Miles; Severe Service Every 3000 Miles
Inspect Brake Connections, Hoses & Lines, 2003–06	Normal Service Every 18,000 Miles; Severe Service Every 12,000 Miles
Inspect Brake Drums & Rotors	S … N S … S N S (marks at various intervals)
Inspect Brake Pads & Shoes Except Liberty Diesel	S … N S … S N S (marks at various intervals)
Inspect Brake Pads & Shoes, Liberty Diesel	Normal Service Every 25,000 Miles; Severe Service Every 12,500 Miles
Inspect Brake System	X … X … X
CLUTCH, TRANSMISSION & TRANSFER CASE	
Change Automatic Transmission Fluid & Filter, 2002 Grand Cherokee, Liberty & Wrangler	Normal Service Every 100,000 Miles; Severe Service Every 30,000 Miles
Change Automatic Transmission Fluid & Filter, 2003–04 Grand Cherokee, Liberty & Wrangler	Normal Service Every 102,000 Miles; Severe Service Every 30,000 Miles
Change Automatic Transmission Fluid & Filter, 2005–06 Grand Cherokee, Liberty & Wrangler & 2006 Commander	Gasoline Engine Models Severe Service Every 60,000 Miles; Diesel Engine Models Severe Service Every 62,500 Miles
Change Transfer Case Lubricant, Grand Cherokee	②
Change Transfer Case Lubricant, Liberty Diesel	Normal Service Inspect Every 12,500 Miles; Severe Service Every 62,500 Miles
Change Transfer Case Lubricant, 2002 Liberty	No Normal Service; Severe Service Every 60,000 Miles
Change Transfer Case Lubricant, 2002–03 Wrangler & 2003–06 Liberty Except Diesel	Normal Service At 120,000 Miles; Severe Service Every 60,000 Miles
Change Transfer Case Lubricant, 2006 Commander	Every 60,000 Miles

JEEP—Continued

Service Interval In Miles①

CLUTCH, TRANSMISSION & TRANSFER CASE

Recommended Service	Service Interval / Notes
Inspect Manual Transmission Lubricant, 2006 Liberty Diesel	At 12,500 Miles Then Every 62,500 Miles

DRIVE AXLE & DRIVESHAFT

Recommended Service	Service Interval / Notes
Change Differential Lubricants, Wrangler④	Severe Service Every 12,000 Miles
Change Differential Lubricants, 2006 Commander. Grand Cherokee, Liberty Except Diesel④	Severe Service Every 12,500 Miles
Change Differential Lubricants, 2006 Liberty Diesel④	Severe Service Every 15,000 Miles
Inspect & Lubricate Driveshaft U-Joints & Slip Splines	S S N S S X S S N S S X S S N S S X S S N S

ENGINE

Recommended Service	Service Interval / Notes
Change Engine Coolant, 2002–04	Every 60 Months Or 100,000 Miles
Change Engine Coolant, 2005–06	Every 60 Months Or 102,000 Miles
Change Engine Oil & Filter, Liberty Diesel	Normal Service Every 12,500 Miles; Severe Service Every 6250 Miles
Change Engine Oil & Filter, 2002	Normal Service Every 7500 Miles; Severe Service Every 3000 Miles
Change Engine Oil & Filter, 2003–06 Gasoline Engine	Normal Service Every 6000 Miles; Severe Service Every 3000 Miles
Inspect & Adjust Manually Tensioned Drive Belts, 2002 Grand Cherokee	4.0L At 60,000 Miles & Every 15,000 Miles Thereafter; 4.7L At 90,000 Miles & Every 15,000 Miles Thereafter.
Inspect & Adjust Manually Tensioned Drive Belts, 2002 Wrangler	(marked X at designated intervals)
Inspect Coolant Level	At Every Engine Oil Change
Inspect Cooling System & Protection Level	(marked X at designated intervals)
Inspect Drive Belts, 2002–04 Liberty & 2003–04 Grand Cherokee	Normal Service At 60,000 Miles & Every 15,000 Miles Thereafter; Severe Service At 45,000 Miles & Every 15,000 Miles Thereafter
Inspect Drive Belts, 2003	Normal Service At 75,000 Miles & Every 15,000 Miles Thereafter; Severe Service At 60,000 Miles & Every 15,000 Miles Thereafter

JEEP—Continued

Service Interval In Miles①

Recommended Service

ENGINE

Recommended Service	Service Interval In Miles
Inspect Drive Belts, 2005	Normal Service At 60,000 Miles & Every 12,000 Miles Thereafter; Severe Service At 45,000 Miles & Every 15,000 Miles Thereafter
Inspect Drive Belts, 2006	Normal Service At 60,000 Miles & Every 30,000 Miles Thereafter; Severe Service At 60,000 Miles & Every 15,000 Miles Thereafter
Inspect Exhaust System	At Every Engine Oil Change
Inspect PCV Valve	Normal Service At 60,000 Miles & Every 30,000 Miles Thereafter; Severe Service Every 30,000 Miles
Inspect PCV Valve, Grand Cherokee, 2002 4.7L & 2003–06 Grand Cherokee, Liberty, Wrangler & 2006 Commander③	Normal Service Inspect Every 60,000 Miles; Severe Service Every 30,000 Miles
Replace Boost Pressure Solenoid Filter, 2006 Liberty Diesel	Every 50,000 Miles
Replace Drive Belts, Liberty Diesel	Normal Service Every 62,500 Miles; Severe Service Every 37,500 Miles
Replace Engine Air Filter, Liberty Diesel	Normal Service Every 25,000 Miles; Severe Service Every 12,500 Miles
Replace Engine Air Filter, 2002 Cherokee, Grand Cherokee, Wrangler & Liberty	S … X … S … X (per mileage grid)
Replace Engine Air Filter, 2003 Grand Cherokee, Liberty & Wrangler	Inspect Every 30,000 Miles & Replace As Necessary
Replace Engine Air Filter, 2004–06 Grand Cherokee, Liberty Except Diesel, Wrangler & 2006 Commander	Normal Service Inspect Every 30,000 Miles & Replace As Necessary; Severe Service Inspect Every 15,000 Miles & Replace As Necessary
Replace Fuel Filter/Water Separator Unit, Liberty Diesel	Every 25,000 Miles
Replace Ignition Cables 2002–05 Wrangler, 2.5L & 2003–06 2.4L Liberty & Wrangler	Every 60,000 Miles
Replace Spark Plugs	X … X (per mileage grid)
Replace Timing Belt & Idler Pulleys, 2006 Liberty Diesel③	Every 100,000 Miles
Replace Timing Belt, 2.4L③	Normal Service Every 120,000 Miles; Severe Service Every 90,000 Miles

STEERING, SUSPENSION & TIRES

Recommended Service	Service Interval In Miles
Inspect Chassis Components	X … X (per mileage grid)

JEEP—Continued

Service Interval In Miles [1]

Recommended Service	3000	6000	7500	9000	12000	15000	18000	21000	22500	24000	27000	30000	33000	36000	37500	39000	42000	45000	48000	51000	52500	54000	57000	60000	63000	66000	67500	69000	72000	75000	78000	81000	82500	84000	87000	90000	93000	96000	97500	99000
STEERING, SUSPENSION & TIRES																																								
Inspect Power Steering Fluid Level	At Every Engine Oil Change																																							
Inspect & Lubricate Steering Gear & Linkage, & Suspension Ball Joints	S	S	N	S	S	X	S	S	N	S	S	X	S	S	N	S	S	X	S	S	N	S	S	X	S	S	N	S	S	X	S	S	N	S	S	X	S	S	N	S
Rotate Tires & Adjust Pressure		S	N		S	N	S		N	S		X		S	N		S	N	S		N	S		X		S	N		S	N	S		N	S		X		S	N	

Mos. — Months
N — Normal Service
S — Severe Service
X — Normal Or Severe Service

① — After vehicles passes 99,000 mile mark return to beginning of mileage table & start cycle over again.
② — Quadra Trac drain and refill every 30,000 miles. Select Trac inspect every 30,000 miles, Severe Service drain & refill every 60,000 miles.
③ — This maintenance is recommended to customer but is not required to maintain emissions warranty.
④ — Off highway operation, trailer towing, snow plowing or prolonged operation w/heavy loading, especially in hot weather require more frequent transmission service. Perform services if vehicle is usually operated under these conditions.

PT CRUISER

Service Interval In Miles ①

Service intervals run in 3,000-mile increments (with corresponding Recommended Service & Intervals in Months). Marks: **S** = Severe Service, **N** = Normal Service, **X** = Service due.

Recommended Service & Intervals	Schedule / Notes
BRAKES	
Inspect Brake Connections, Hoses & Lines	Normal Service Every 6 Months Or 7500 Miles; Severe Service Every 3 Months Or 3000 Miles
Inspect Brake Drums & Rotors, 2002	(S / N at intervals)
Inspect Brake Drums & Rotors, 2003–06	Normal Service Every 18,000 Miles; Severe Service Every 12,000 Miles
Inspect Brake Pads & Linings, 2002	(S / N at intervals)
Inspect Brake Pads & Linings, 2003–06	Normal Service Every 18,000 Miles; Severe Service Every 12,000 Miles
Replace Brake Fluid ③	S
CLUTCH & TRANSMISSION	
Change Automatic Transmission Fluid & Filter, 2002–04	Severe Service Replace Every 48,000 Miles
Change Automatic Transmission Fluid & Filter, 2005–06	Severe Service Replace Every 60,000 Miles
Change Manual Transmission Lubricant	Severe Service Replace Every 48,000 Miles
Check Transmission Lubricant & Level Condition	Severe Service At Every Oil Change
DRIVE AXLE & DRIVESHAFT	
Inspect CV & Driveshaft Joint Boots	X (at intervals)
ENGINE	
Adjust Alternator Drive Belt Tension	Every 24 Months Or 30,000 Miles
Change Engine Coolant, 2002–04	Every 60 Months Or 100,000 Miles
Change Engine Coolant, 2005–06	Every 60 Months Or 102,000 Miles
Change Engine Oil & Filter, 2002	S (every interval)
Change Engine Oil & Filter, 2003–06 Non-Turbo	Normal Service Every 6 Months Or 6000 Miles; Severe Service Every 3000 Miles
Change Engine Oil, Turbo	Normal Service Every 6 Months Or 5000 Miles; Severe Service Every 3000 Miles

PT CRUISER—Continued

Recommended Service & Intervals (Months)	Service Interval In Miles① 3000	6000	7500	9000	12000	15000	18000	21000	22500	24000	27000	30000	33000	36000	37500	39000	42000	45000	48000	51000	52500	54000	57000	60000	63000	66000	67500	69000	72000	75000	78000	81000	82500	84000	87000	90000	93000	96000	97500	99000
ENGINE																																								
Inspect Coolant Level, Hoses & Clamps	At Every Oil Change																																							
Inspect Drive Belts						S						X						S						X						S						X				
Inspect Engine Air Filter & PCV Filter	Normal Service Every 30,000 Miles; Severe Service Every 15,000 Miles																																							
Inspect Exhaust System	At Every Oil Change																																							
Inspect PCV Valve②												S												X												S				
Replace Ignition Cables	Every 60,000 Miles																																							
Replace PCV Filter	Normal Service Inspect at 60,000 Miles, Severe Service Inspect At 30,000 & Every 30,000 Thereafter. Replace If Necessary																																							
Replace Spark Plugs												X												X												X				
Replace Timing Belt, 2002–04	Every 102,000 Miles																																							
Replace Timing Belt, 2005–06	Normal Service Every 105,000 Miles; Severe Service Every 90,000 Miles																																							
STEERING, SUSPENSION & TIRES																																								
Inspect Bushings, Arms, CV Joints, Seals, Springs & Jounce Bumpers	S	X		S	X	S	X	S		X	S	X	S	X		S	X	S	X	S		X	S	X	S	X		S	X	S	X	S		X	S	X	S	X		S
Inspect Tie Rod Ends & Boot Seals	Every 30,000 Miles																																							
Lubricate Ball Joints (Every 18 Mos.)									X									X									X									X				
Lubricate Steering Linkage (Every 12 Mos.)						X						X						X						X						X						X				
Rotate Tires & Adjust Pressure, 2002		S	N		S	N	S		N	S		X		S	N		S	N	S		N	S		X		S	N		S	N	S		N	S		X		S	N	
Rotate Tires & Adjust Pressure, 2003–06 Non-Turbo	Every 6000 Miles																																							
Rotate Tires & Adjust Pressure, 2003–06 Turbo	Every 5000 Miles																																							

N — Normal Service
S — Severe Service
X — Normal Or Severe Service
① — After vehicle passes 99,000 mile mark return to beginning of mileage table & start cycle over again.
② — This maintenance is recommended by DaimlerChrysler Corporation to the owner, but not required to maintain the warranty of the PCV Valve.
③ — If vehicle is used for trailer towing.

SPRINTER

Service Interval In Miles ①

Recommended Service & Intervals (Months)	Service
BODY	
Inspect Body And Paint For Damage And Corrision	Every 24 Months
Inspect Headlamp Aiming②	Schedule B
Inspect Seat Belts②	Schedule B
Lubricate Hood Hinges And Latches ②	Schedules A And B
BRAKES	
Inspect Brake Connections, Hoses & Lines②	Schedule B
Inspect Brake Drums & Rotors	Schedule B
Inspect Brake Pads & Linings②	Schedules A And B
Inspect Parking Brake②	Schedule B
CLUTCH & TRANSMISSION	
Change Automatic Transmission Fluid & Filter	Replace At 80,000 Miles, After This Change, Automatic Transmission Fluid Is Changed For Life
Check Transmission Lubricant & Level Condition②	Schedules A And B
DRIVE AXLE & DRIVESHAFT	
Inspect Driveshaft Flex Discs	Every 48 Months Or 50,000 Miles
Rear Axle Fluid②	At Fourth Maintenance Service
ENGINE	
Change Engine Coolant	Every 60 Months Or 100,000 Miles
Change Engine Oil & Filter②	Schedules A And B; Normal Service Every 12 Months Or 10,000 Miles
Inspect Coolant Level, Hoses & Clamps②	Schedules A And B
Inspect Drive Belts②	Schedule B
Inspect Exhaust System②	Schedule B
Replace Air Filter	Every 36 Months Or 30,000 Miles
Replace Fuel Filter	At Oil Change Intervals
Replace Spark Plugs	Every 60 Months Or 100,000 Miles
STEERING, SUSPENSION & TIRES	
Inspect Chassis Components For Damage And Corrision	Every 48 Months
Inspect Front Ball Joints And Boots②	Schedule B

SPRINTER—Continued

Recommended Service & Intervals (Months)

Service Interval In Miles①

Service Interval In Miles (thousands): 6000, 7500, 9000, 12000, 15000, 18000, 21000, 24000, 27000, 30000, 33000, 36000, 39000, 42000, 45000, 48000, 51000, 54000, 57000, 60000, 63000, 66000, 69000, 72000, 75000, 78000, 81000, 84000, 87000, 90000, 93000, 96000, 99000

STEERING, SUSPENSION & TIRES

Item	Schedule
Inspect Steering Components And Boots②	Schedule B
Inspect Tires②	Schedules A And B
Rotate Tires②	Schedule B

N — Normal Service
S — Severe Service
X — Normal Or Severe Service

① — After vehicle passes 99,000 mile mark return to beginning of mileage table & start cycle over again.

② — There are two FSS symbols that will appear in the main odometer display when oil service is necessary... Service Schedule B is represented by two wrench symbols which indicates maintenace service is necessary. Service Schedule A is represented by one wrench symbol which indicates oil service is necessary. Service Schedule B for second service interval. Schedule A for first service interval. Schedule B for second service interval and so on. If the display shows the number of days a clock sysmbol will appear and the maintenance should be performed in the stated period/distance. The service indicator will be reset after an oil service and or maintenance service has been performed.

Ford Motor Co.

INDEX

Page No.

Aviator, Blackwood, E-Series, Excursion, Expedition, F-Series & F-Super
Duty, Mark LT & Navigator 0-103
Escape, Explorer, Marnier, Mountaineer & Ranger 0-106

Page No.

Freestar, Monterey & Windstar 0-108
Villager 0-109

AVIATOR, BLACKWOOD, E-SERIES, EXCURSION, EXPEDITION, F-SERIES & F-SUPER DUTY, MARK LT & NAVIGATOR

Service Interval In Miles ①

Recommended Service	12500	18000	24500	27000	36500	42000	45800	60000
BODY								
Inspect Instrument Panel Warning Lamps & Gauges	At Every Engine Oil Change							
Inspect & Replace Damaged Or Missing Vehicle Noise Shields, Diesel					X			X
Lubricate Body Hardware & Hinges	X						X	
Replace Cabin Air Filter	Every 15,000 Miles, If Equipped							
Replace Climate Control Seat Filter, Blackwood, Navigator & Aviator				X				X
BRAKES								
Inspect Brake Systems	Normal Service Every 15,000 Miles; Severe Service Every 5000 Miles							
Inspect Parking Brake System Operation					X			X
CLUTCH & TRANSMISSION								
Change Automatic Transmission Fluid & Filter, 2004–06 4RTOW & 4R100	Normal Service Inspect Every 15,000 Miles Change At 150,000 Miles; Severe Service Replace Every 30,000 Miles							
Change Automatic Transmission Fluid & Filter	Inspect Every 15,000 Miles; Replace Every 30,000 Miles							
Change Automatic Transmission Fluid & Remote Filter Element, 2005–06 Torqushift	Inspect Fluid Level Every 15,000 Miles; Replace Every 30,000 Miles							
Change Manual Transmission	Normal Service Every 60,000 Miles; Severe Service 60,000 Miles Or Less If Required							
Change Transfer Case Lubricant	Normal Service Every 60,000 Miles; Severe Service Every 60,000 Miles							
Inspect & Lubricate Automatic Transmission Shift Linkage	Normal Service Every 150,000 Miles; Severe Service Every 60,000 Miles							
Lubricate Throttle Kickdown Or TV Lever Ball Studs			S		X		S	X
Lubricate Transfer Case Shift Lever Pivot Bolt & Control Rod Connecting Pins		X				X		
DRIVE AXLE & DRIVESHAFT								
Change Differential Lubricant	At Every Engine Oil Change ③							
Driveshaft U-Joints & Slip Yoke Grease Fittings								
Lubricate RH Front Drive Axle Slip Yoke, 4WD								X

VEHICLE MAINTNENACE SCHEDULES, FORD MOTOR CO.

AVIATOR, BLACKWOOD, E-SERIES, EXCURSION, EXPEDITION, F-SERIES & F-SUPER DUTY, MARK LT & NAVIGATOR—Continued

Recommended Service	Service Interval In Miles①																														
	3000	5000	6000	7500	9000	10000	12000	15000	18000	20000	21000	22500	24000	25000	27000	30000	33000	35000	36000	37500	39000	40000	42000	45000	48000	50000	51000	52500	54000	55000	57000	60000
ENGINE																																
Change Engine Coolant, 2002–03	Green Coolant, Every 45,000 Miles, Then Every 30,000 Miles Thereafter. Replace Orange Coolant, Every 150,000 Miles, Replace Yellow Coolant, Every 5 Years Or 100,000 Miles																															
Change Engine Coolant, 2004–06	Replace Premium Gold Coolant, Every 5 Years Or 100,000 Miles Thereafter Replace Every 36 Months Or 50,000 Miles																															
Change Engine Oil & Filter	S	N	S		S	N	S	X	S	N	S		S	N	S	X	S	N	S		S	N	S	X	S	N	S		S	N	S	X
Drain Coalescent Filter Bowl, 2002–04, NGV	Every 120,000 Miles And Inspect NGV Tanks																															
Drain Coalescent Filter Bowl, 2005–06, NGV	Every 125,000 Miles And Inspect NGV Tanks																															
Drain Water From Diesel Fuel Filter Bowl & Water Separator		X				X		X		X				X		X		X				X		X		X				X		X
Inspect Drive Belts, Ambulance		X				X		X		X				X		X		X				X		X		X				X		X
Inspect Drive Belts, Except Ambulance								X								X								X								X
Inspect Engine Air Induction System, Fan & Shrouds, E-350 & F-350 w/10,000 Lb. GVWR & Over																X																X
Inspect Exhaust System & Instrument Panel Warning Lamps & Gauges	At Every Engine Oil Change																															
Inspect Thermactor Or Secondary Air Injection Hoses, Clamps & System Operation																X																X
Replace Engine Air & Crankcase Filter Elements, Except Diesel																X																X
Replace Engine Air Filter Element, Diesel	Every 30,000 Miles Or When Restriction Gauge Enters Red Zone																															
Replace Fuel Filter, 2002–03②	Every 30,000 Miles																															
Replace Fuel Filter, 2004–06②	Normal Service Every 30,000 Miles; Severe Service Every 15,000 Miles																															
Replace Fuel Filter, 2002–03 Diesel	Every 15,000 Miles Or When Filter Restriction Lamp Lights																															
Replace PCV Valve																																X
Replace Spark Plugs, Expedition, Navigator & F-150 & E-Series Except NGV	Normal Service Every 100,000 Miles; Severe Service Every 60,000 Miles																															
Replace Spark Plugs, E-Series NGV																																X
Replace Spark Plug Wires																																X

AVIATOR, BLACKWOOD, E-SERIES, EXCURSION, EXPEDITION, F-SERIES & F-SUPER DUTY, MARK LT & NAVIGATOR—Continued

Recommended Service	Service Interval In Miles①
STEERING, SUSPENSION & TIRES	
Inspect Hub Lock & Spindle Needle Bearing Lubrication, 4WD	X … X
Lubricate Front Axle Spindle Pins & Steering Linkage	Normal Service Every 15,000 Miles; Severe Service As Required
Tighten Wheel Lugnuts	500 Miles After Rotation Or Wheel Removal, Then At Every Engine Oil Change
Rotate Tires	Normal Service Inspect For Wear & Rotate Every 5000 Miles

GVWR — Gross Vehicle Weight Rating
HD — Heavy Duty, GVWR of 8501 lbs. or more
LD — Light Duty, GVWR of 8500 lbs. or less
N — Normal Service
NGV — Natural Gas Vehicle
S — Severe Service
X — Normal Or Severe Service
① — After vehicle has passed 60,000 mile mark return to beginning of mileage table & start cycle over again.
② — On models equipped w/California emission service is recommended but not required.
③ — **Normal Vehicle Axle Maintenance:** Front axle, rear axle and power take off (PTO) units containing synthetic lubricant and light duty trucks equipped with Ford-design axles are lubricated for life. These lubricants are not to be checked or changed unless a leak is suspected, service is required or the axle assembly has been submerged in water. The axle lubricant and PTO lubricant should be changed anytime the axle and PTO has been submerged in water. Non-synthetic rear axle lubricants should be replaced every 100,000 miles under normal operating conditions. Non-synthetic rear axle lubricants should be replaced every 3000 miles or 3 months, whichever occurs first, during extended trailer tow operation above (70°F) ambient and wide open throttle for extended periods above 45 mph. The 3000 mile lube change interval may be waived if the axle was filled with 75W140 synthetic gear lubricant meeting Ford specification WSL-M2C192–A, part number F1TZ-19580–B or equivalent. Add four ounces of additive friction modifier C8AZ-19B546–A (EST-M2C118–A) or equivalent for complete refill of Traction-Lok rear axles. The rear axle lubricant should be changed anytime the axle has been submerged in water.
Police and Taxi Vehicle Axle Maintenance: Replace rear axle lubricant every 160,000km (100,000 miles). Rear axle lubricant change may be waived if the axle was filled with 75W140 synthetic gear lubricant meeting Ford specification WSL-M2C192–A. Add four ounces of additive friction modifier C8AZ-19B546–A(EST-M2C118–A) or equivalent for complete refill of Traction-Lok rear axles. The rear axle lubricant should be changed anytime the axle has been submerged in water.

ESCAPE, EXPLORER, MARNIER, MOUNTAINEER & RANGER

Service Interval In Miles①

Service interval columns (in miles): 3500, 6000, 9000, 10000, 11000, 12000, 15000, 18000, 20000, 21000, 24000, 25000, 27000, 30000, 33000, 35000, 36000, 39000, 40000, 42000, 45000, 48000, 50000, 51000, 54000, 55000, 57000, 60000

Recommended Service	Service Schedule / Interval
BRAKES	
Inspect Brake Hoses & Lines	X (at 15,000; 45,000 mile intervals)
Inspect Disc & Drum Brake System, Lubricate Caliper Slide Rails	Normal Service Every 15,000 Miles; Severe Service Every 5000 Miles
Inspect Parking Brake Operation	X (Every 15,000 Miles)
Replace Cabin Air Filter, If Equipped	Every 15,000 Miles
CLUTCH & TRANSMISSION	
Change Automatic Transmission Fluid & Filter, Explorer, Mountaineer & Ranger⑤	Normal Service Inspect Every 15,000 Miles, Change Every 150,000 Miles; Severe Service Change Every 30,000 Miles
Change Automatic Transmission Fluid, 2002–03 Explorer & Mountaineer②	Inspect Every 15,000 Miles; Every 30,000 Miles — X
Change Manual Transmission Lubricant	Normal Service Every 150,000 Miles; Severe Service Every 60,000 Miles — X
Change Transfer Case Fluid	N / S
Inspect & Lubricate Automatic Transmission Cable Linkage	N / S — X
Lubricate Transfer Case Shift Lever Pivot Bolt & Control Rod Connecting Pins	X
DRIVE AXLE & DRIVESHAFT	
Change Differential Lubricant	⑥
Lubricate Driveshaft Grease Fittings, Double Cardan Joint Centering Ball & Slip Yoke	N / S … S / N … S
Lubricate RH Front Drive Axle Shaft Slip Yoke, 4WD Models	X
ENGINE	
Change Engine Coolant, 2002–03	Green Coolant, Every 45,000 Miles, Then Every 30,000 Miles Thereafter. Replace Orange Coolant, Every 150,000 Miles, Replace Yellow Coolant, Every 5 Years Or 100,000 Miles
Change Engine Coolant, 2004–06	Replace Premium Gold Coolant, Every 5 Years Or 100,000 Miles Thereafter Replace Every 36 Months Or 50,000 Miles
Change Engine Oil & Filter	S / N / S / N / S / N / S / N / S / N / S / N / S
Inspect Cooling System & Protection Level	X
Inspect Drive Belts	Every 100,000 Miles
Inspect Exhaust System	N / S / N / S / N / S / N / S
Inspect NGV Tanks, 2002–03④	Every 30,000 Miles
Inspect NGV Tanks, 2004–06④	Every 3 Years From Date Of Tank Manufacture
Inspect Spark Plug Wires	X
Replace Engine Air Filter & Crankcase Emission Filter Elements	X — Normal Service Every 30,000 Miles; Severe Service Every 15,000 Miles
Replace Fuel Filter③	Every 15 Years From Date Of Tank Manufacture
Replace NGV Tanks, 2004–06④	4 Cylinder Every 60,000 Miles; Except 4 Cylinder Every 100,000 Miles
Replace PCV Valve	Every 100,000 Miles
Replace Spark Plugs	Normal Service Every 100,000 Miles; Severe Service Every 60,000 Miles

ESCAPE, EXPLORER, MARNIER, MOUNTAINEER & RANGER—Continued

Service Interval In Miles①

Recommended Service	3000	6000	9000	12000	15000	18000	21000	24000	27000	30000	33000	36000	39000	42000	45000	48000	51000	54000	57000	60000
STEERING, SUSPENSION & TIRES																				
Inspect Power Steering Fluid Level	At Every Engine Oil Change																			
Inspect Spindle Needle Bearing Thrust Bearing & Hub Lock Lubrication										X										X
Lubricate Steering Linkage	S	S	S	S	N	S	S	S	S	N	S	S	S	S	N	S	S	S	S	N
Repack Front Wheel Bearings										X										X
Rotate Tires & Inspect Wheel Lug Nut Security	Normal Service Inspect For Wear And Rotate Every 5000 Miles																			

N — Normal Service
S — Severe Service
X — Normal Or Severe Service
① — After vehicle has passed 60,000 mile mark return to beginning of mileage table & start cycle over again.
② — On models equipped w/4R70W or 4R100 automatic transmissions.
③ — On models equipped with California emissions.
④ — On natural gas equipped models.
⑤ — Except models equipped w/4R70W or 4R100 automatic transmission.
⑥ — **Normal Vehicle Axle Maintenance:** Rear axle and power take off (PTO) units containing synthetic lubricant and light duty trucks equipped with Ford-design axles are lubricated for life. These lubricants are not to be checked or changed unless a leak is suspected, service is required or the axle assembly has been submerged in water. The axle lubricant and PTO lubricant should be changed anytime the axle and PTO has been submerged in water. Non-synthetic rear axle lubricants should be replaced every 3000 miles or 3 months, whichever occurs first, during extended trailer tow operation above (70°F) ambient and wide open throttle for extended periods above 45 mph. The 3000 mile lube change interval may be waived if the axle was filled with 75W140 synthetic gear lubricant meeting Ford specification WSL-M2C192–A, part number F1TZ-19580–B or equivalent. Add four ounces of additive friction modifier C8AZ-19B546–A (EST-M2C118–A) or equivalent for complete refill of Traction-Lok rear axles. The rear axle lubricant should be changed anytime the axle has been submerged in water. **Police and Taxi Vehicle Axle Maintenance:** Replace rear axle lubricant every 160,000km (100,000 miles). Rear axle lubricant change may be waived if the axle was filled with 75W140 synthetic gear lubricant meeting Ford specification WSL-M2C192–A. Add four ounces of additive friction modifier C8AZ-19B546–A(EST-M2C118–A) or equivalent for complete refill of Traction-Lok rear axles. The rear axle lubricant should be changed anytime the axle has been submerged in water.

FREESTAR, MONTEREY & WINDSTAR

Service Interval In Miles①

Recommended Service	3000	6000	9000	12000	15000	18000	21000	24000	27000	30000	33000	36000	39000	42000	45000	48000	51000	54000	57000	60000
BRAKES																				
Inspect Brake Drums, Linings, Pads & Rotors	Normal Service Every 15,000 Miles; Severe Service Every 5000 Miles																			
Inspect Brake Lines & Hoses										X										
Replace Cabin Air Filter	Every 15,000 Miles																			
CLUTCH & TRANSMISSION																				
Change Automatic Transaxle Fluid & Filter, 2002–04	Inspect Every 15,000 Miles; Replace Every 30,000 Miles																			
Change Automatic Transaxle Fluid & Filter, 2005–06	Inspect Every 15,000 Miles; Replace Every 30,000 Miles																			
ENGINE																				
Change Engine Coolant, 2002–03	Replace Green Coolant Every 45,000 Miles, Then Every 30,000 Miles Thereafter. Replace Orange Coolant Every 150,000 Miles, Replace Yellow Coolant, Every 5 Years Or 100,000 Miles																			
Change Engine Coolant, 2004–06	Replace Premium Gold Coolant, Every 5 Years Or 100,000 Miles Thereafter Replace Every 36 Months Or 50,000 Miles																			
Change Engine Oil & Filter	S	N	S	N	S	N	S	N	S	N	S	N	S	N	S	N	S	N	S	N
Inspect Cooling System & Protection Level										X										X
Inspect Drive Belts	Every 100,000 Miles																			
Inspect Exhaust System										X										X
Replace Engine Air Filter Element										X										X
Replace Fuel Filter②	Normal Service Every 30,000 Miles; Severe Service Every 15,000 Miles																			
Replace PCV Valve	Every 100,000 Miles																			
Replace Spark Plugs	Normal Service Every 100,000 Miles; Severe Service Every 60,000 Miles																			
STEERING, SUSPENSION & TIRES																				
Rotate Tires	Normal Service Inspect For Wear & Rotate Every 5000 Miles																			
Tighten Wheel Lugnuts	500 Miles After Rotation Or Wheel Removal																			

N — Normal Service
S — Severe Service
X — Normal Or Severe Service
① — After vehicle has passed 60,000 mile mark return to beginning of mileage table & start cycle over again.
② — On models equipped with California emissions. Service is recommended but not required.

VILLAGER

Service Interval In Miles [1]

Recommended Service	Service Interval
BODY	
Replace Cabin Air Filter	Every 15,000 Miles
BRAKES	
Inspect Brake Drums, Linings, Pads & Rotors	Normal Service Every 15,000 Miles; Severe Service Every 5000 Miles
Inspect Brake Lines & Hoses	X
CLUTCH & TRANSMISSION	
Change Automatic Transaxle Fluid & Filter	Normal Service Inspect Every 15,000 Miles, Change Every 150,000 Miles; Severe Service Change Every 30,000 Miles
ENGINE	
Change Engine Coolant	Replace Green Coolant, Every 45,000 Miles, Then Every 30,000 Miles Thereafter, Replace Orange Coolant Every 150,000 Miles, Replace Yellow Coolant Every 5 Years Or 100,000 Miles
Change Engine Oil & Filter	S / N
Inspect Cooling System & Protection Level	S / N
Inspect Drive Belts	S / N
Replace Accessory Drive Belts	Every 60,000 Miles
Replace Drive Belts	At 120,000 Miles
Replace Engine Air Filter Element	X
Inspect Exhaust System	X
Replace Fuel Filter [2]	Every 30,000 Miles
Replace Spark Plugs	Every 100,000 Miles
Replace Timing Belt	Every 105,000 Miles
STEERING, SUSPENSION & TIRES	
Rotate Tires	Normal Service Inspect For Wear And Rotate Every 5000 Miles

N — Normal Service
S — Severe Service
X — Normal Or Severe Service
[1] — After vehicle has passed 60,000 mile mark return to beginning of mileage table & start cycle over again.
[2] — On models equipped w/California emissions.

General Motors Corp.

INDEX

	Page No.
Astro & Safari	0-111
Avalanche	0-113
Aztek & Rendezvous	0-115
Blazer/Jimmy S-Series, Sonoma, SSR, S-10 & S-15	0-117
Bravada, Envoy, Rainer & TrailBlazer	0-120
Canyon & Colorado	0-122
Denali, Escalade, Escalade ESV & EXT, Sierra, Silverado, Suburban, Tahoe, Yukon & Yukon XL	0-123

	Page No.
Equinox & Torrent	0-127
G Series	0-128
HHR	0-132
Hummer H2 & H3	0-133
Montana, Relay, Silhouette, Terraza, Uplander & Venture	0-135
SRX	0-137
Tracker	0-139
Vue	0-142

ASTRO & SAFARI

Recommended Service — Service Interval In Miles ①

Service intervals shown across the top: 3000, 6000, 7500, 9000, 12000, 15000, 18000, 21000, 24000, 27000, 30000, 33000, 36000, 39000, 42000, 45000, 48000, 51000, 54000, 57000, 60000, 63000, 66000, 69000, 72000, 75000, 78000, 81000, 84000, 87000, 90000, 93000, 96000

BODY

Recommended Service	Service Interval
Clean Power Antenna Mast, Inspect Neutral Safety & BTSI Operation	At Least Once Every 3 Months
Flush Vehicle Underside, Inspect Drain Holes	At Least Once Every 12 Months, Especially In Winter & Springtime
Inspect Lamps, Seat Belts & Warning Devices	At Least Once Every 6 Months
Inspect Noise Shields & Underhood Insulation	X — At Engine Oil Changes Or At Least Every 12 Months
Lubricate Hinges, Latches, Lock Cylinders & Strikers	At Engine Oil Changes Or At Least Every 12 Months

BRAKES

Recommended Service	Service Interval
Inspect Brake System	At Tire Rotation Or At Least Every 6 Months
Lubricate Brake Cable Guides	S S N S S S S X S S S N S S S S X S S S N S S S S X S S S N S S S

CLUTCH & TRANSMISSION

Recommended Service	Service Interval
Adjust Clutch Pedal Freeplay	At Least Once Every 6 Months
Change Automatic Transmission Fluid & Filter	Normal Service Every 50,000 Miles; Severe Service Every 15,000 Miles
Change Transfer Case Fluid	Every 50,000 Miles
Lubricate Transfer Case & Transmission Linkage, Pedal Pivots & Springs	S S N S S S S X S S S N S S S S X S S S N S S S S X S S S N S S S

DRIVE AXLE

Recommended Service	Service Interval
Lubricate Driveshaft	S S N S S S S X S S S N S S S S X S S S N S S S S X S S S N S S S

ENGINE

Recommended Service	Service Interval
Change Engine Coolant	Every 60 Months Or 150,000 Miles
Change Engine Oil & Filter	S S N S S S S X S S S N S S S S X S S S N S S S S X S S S N S S S
Inspect Drive Belts, Emission & Fuel System Connections, Hoses, Lines, Filler Cap & Tank	X
Inspect Engine Air Filter Element	S S X S S S S S S X S S S S S X S S S S S X S S S S S X S S S S S
Inspect Exhaust System	At Engine Oil Changes
Inspect PCV System & Valve	Every 100,000 Miles
Inspect Spark Plug Wires, Distributor Cap & Rotor	Every 30,000 Miles & At Spark Plug Replacements

VEHICLE MAINTNENACE SCHEDULES, GENERAL MOTORS CORP.

ASTRO & SAFARI—Continued

Service Interval In Miles①

ENGINE

Recommended Service	Interval / Marks
Inspect Thermostatically Controlled Air Cleaner Operation	X at 12000, 24000, 36000, 48000, 60000, 72000, 84000
Inspect Throttle Linkage Operation	At Engine Oil Or Air Filter Element Changes
Replace Engine Air & PCV Inlet Filter Elements, 2002–04	X at 30000, 60000, 90000
Replace Engine Air & PCV Inlet Filter Elements, 2005	X at 45000, 90000
Replace Fuel Filter	X at 30000, 60000, 90000
Replace Spark Plugs	Every 100,000 Miles

STEERING, SUSPENSION & TIRES

Recommended Service	Interval / Marks
Lubricate Steering & Suspension Grease Fittings	Marked S (Severe Service) / N (Normal Or Severe Service) / X across intervals
Lubricate Steering Kingpins & Bushings	Normal Service Every 3000 Miles; Severe Service Every 1500 Miles
Repack Front Wheel Bearings, 2WD Only	S at 30000, 60000, 90000
Rotate Tires	Normal Service Every 7500 Miles; Severe Service Every 6000 Miles

BTSI — Brake Transmission Shift Interlock
CDRV — Crankcase Depression Regulator Valve
EPR — Exhaust Pressure Regulator
EVR — Electronic Vacuum Regulator N — Normal Service
S — Severe Service
X — Normal Or Severe Service
① — After vehicle passes 99,000 mile mark return to beginning of mileage table & start cycle over again.

AVALANCHE

Service Interval In Miles ①

Mileage columns (in thousands): 3,000 · 6,000 · 7,500 · 9,000 · 12,000 · 15,000 · 18,000 · 21,000 · 24,000 · 27,000 · 30,000 · 33,000 · 36,000 · 39,000 · 45,000 · 48,000 · 51,000 · 54,000 · 57,000 · 60,000 · 63,000 · 66,000 · 69,000 · 72,000 · 75,000 · 78,000 · 81,000 · 84,000 · 87,000 · 90,000 · 93,000 · 96,000 · 99,000

Recommended Service	Interval / Notes
BODY	
Inspect Lamps, Seat Belts & Warning Devices	At Least Once Every 6 Months
Lubricate Hinges, Latches, Lock Cylinders & Strikers	At Engine Oil Changes Or At Least Every 12 Months
Replace Passenger Compartment Air Filter	Normal Service Every 15,000 Miles; Severe Service Every 10,000 Miles
BRAKES	
Inspect Brake System	At Tire Rotation Or At Least Every 6 Months
CLUTCH & TRANSMISSION	
Adjust Clutch Pedal Freeplay (Models w/Mechanical Linkage)	At Least Once Every 6 Months
Change Automatic Transmission Fluid & Filter, 2002–03	Every 100,000 Miles
Change Automatic Transmission Fluid & Filter, 2004–06	Normal Service Every 100,000 Miles; Severe Service, Every 50,000 Miles
Change Transfer Case Fluid	Every 50,000 Miles
Manual Transmission Fluid	Does Not Require Change
DRIVE AXLE	
Change Rear Axle Lubricant, Trailor Towing	After The First 500 Miles (Break In Period) Of Trailer Towing
Inspect Axle Seals & CV Joints	Normal Service Every 7500 Miles; Severe Service, Every 3000 Miles Or Every 3 Months
Inspect Front & Rear Axle Lubricant Level	Normal Service Every 7500 Miles; Severe Service, Every 3000 Miles Or Every 3 Months
Lubricate Driveshaft Fittings	Normal Service Every 7500 Miles; Severe Service Every 3 Months Or 3000 Miles
ENGINE	
Change Engine Coolant	Every 150,000 Miles Or 60 Months
Change Engine Oil & Filter, 2002	(See chart — marked S / N / X across mileage columns)
Change Engine Oil & Filter, 2003–06	Engine Oil Life Monitor Will Indicate When To Change Oil Filter, Vehicle Must Not Be Driven More Than 12 Months Or 10,000 Miles Without An Oil & Filter Change
Inspect Air Intake System & Filter	(See chart — marked X across mileage columns)
Inspect Drive Belts, 2002–03	(See chart — marked X / S across mileage columns)
Inspect Drive Belts, 2004–06	Every 150,000 Miles

VEHICLE MAINTENANCE SCHEDULES, GENERAL MOTORS CORP.

AVALANCHE—Continued

Service Interval In Miles①

The schedule is laid out as a grid of mileage‑interval columns with N / S / X marks. The service intervals indicated for each item are transcribed below.

ENGINE

Recommended Service	Service Interval
Inspect Emission & Fuel System Connections, Hoses, Lines, Filler Cap & Tank, 2002–03	Severe Service (S)
Inspect Evaporative Control System, 2004–06	Every 50,000 Miles
Inspect Exhaust System, 2002–03	At Engine Oil Changes
Inspect Exhaust System, 2004–06	Every 25,000 Miles
Inspect Fuel System For Damage & Leaks, 2004–06	Every 25,000 Miles
Inspect PVC, 2003–04 Except 8.1L V8	At 100,000 Miles
Inspect Thermostatically Controlled Cooling Fan System	Marked (X) at intervals in mileage chart
Inspect Throttle Linkage Operation	At Air Filter Element Changes
Replace Engine Air Filter, 2002–03	Every 30,000 Miles
Replace Engine Air Filter, 2004②	Every 25,000 Miles
Replace Engine Air Filter, 2005–06②	Every 50,000 Miles
Replace Fuel Filler Cap, 2002	Severe Service Every 25,000 Miles
Replace Fuel Filter, 2002–03	Marked (X) at intervals in mileage chart
Replace Spark Plugs	At 100,000 Miles

STEERING, SUSPENSION & TIRES

Recommended Service	Service Interval
Lubricate Steering & Suspension Grease Fittings	Marked (S / N) per mileage in chart
Rotate Tires	At Engine Oil Change Intervals

N — Normal Service
S — Severe Service
X — Normal Or Severe Service
① — After vehicle passes 150,000 mile mark return to beginning of mileage table & start cycle over again.
② — Models less filter restriction indicator.

AZTEK & RENDEZVOUS

Service Interval In Miles①

Recommended Service	Service Interval / Notes
BODY	
Inspect Lamps, Seat Belts & Warning Devices	At Least Once Every 6 Months
Lubricate Hinges, Latches, Lock Cylinders & Strikers	
Replace Passenger Comparment Air Filter	At Engine Oil Changes Or At Least Every 12 Months
BRAKES	
Inspect Brake System, 2002–03	Every 7500 Miles
Inspect Brake System, 2004–06	At Engine Oil Changes Or At Least Every 12 Months
CLUTCH & TRANSMISSION	
Change Automatic Transmission Fluid & Filter	Normal Service Every 100,000 Miles; Severe Service Every 50,000 Miles
DRIVE AXLE	
Change Differential Lubricant, 2002 AWD	Trailer Tow At 7500 Miles Only
ENGINE	
Change Engine Coolant	Every 60 Months Or 150,000 Miles
Change Engine Oil & Filter	The Engine Oil Life Monitor Will Indicate When To Change Engine Oil. The Engine Oil & Filter Must Be Changed At Least Once a Year
Inspect Accessory Drive Belt, 2002	Every 60,000 Miles
Inspect Accessory Drive Belt, 2003–06	Every 150,000 Miles
Inspect Emission & Fuel System Connections, Hoses, Lines, Filler Cap & Tank	
Inspect Engine Air Filter	Severe Service Every 15,000 Miles
Inspect Exhaust System, 2002–03	At Engine Oil Changes
Inspect Exhaust System, 2004–06	Every 25,000 Miles
Inspect Fuel System, 2004–06	Every 25,000 Miles
Inspect Spark Plug Wires	Every 100,000 Miles
Replace Engine Air Filter, 2002–03	Every 25,000 Miles
Replace Engine Air Filter, 2004	Every 25,000 Miles

AZTEK & RENDEZVOUS—Continued

Service Interval In Miles①

Mileage intervals (thousands of miles): 3000, 6000, 7500, 9000, 12000, 15000, 18000, 21000, 24000, 27000, 30000, 36000, 45000, 50000, 60000, 67500, 75000, 82500, 90000, 93000, 96000, 99000

Recommended Service	Service Interval
ENGINE	
Replace Engine Air Filter, 2005–06	Every 50,000 Miles
Replace Spark Plugs	Every 100,000 Miles
STEERING, SUSPENSION & TIRES	
Rotate Tires, 2002–03	At Engine Oil Changes Or At Least Every 12 Months
Rotate Tires, 2004–06	Every 7500 Miles

N — Normal Service
S — Severe Service
X — Normal Or Severe Service
① — If equipped, the engine oil life monitor will indicate when to change engine oil, ususally 3000–10,000 miles. Under severe driving conditions, engine oil may need to be changed before 3000 miles. If vehicle is driven in a dusty area, change engine oil every 3000 miles.

BLAZER/JIMMY S-SERIES, SONOMA, SSR, S-10 & S-15

Service Interval In Miles①

Interval columns (in miles): 3000, 6000, 7500, 9000, 12000, 15000, 18000, 21000, 24000, 27000, 30000, 33000, 36000, 39000, 42000, 45000, 48000, 51000, 54000, 57000, 60000, 63000, 66000, 69000, 72000, 75000, 78000, 81000, 84000, 87000, 90000, 93000, 96000, 99000

Recommended Service	Interval / Marks
BODY	
Inspect Lamps, Seat Belts & Warning Devices	At Least Once Every 6 Months
BRAKES	
Inspect Brake System & CV Joint Boots	At Tire Rotation Or At Least Every 6 Months
Lubricate Brake Cable Guides	S S N S S X S S N S S X S S N S S X S S N S S X S S N S S X S S N S
CLUTCH & TRANSMISSION	
Adjust Clutch Pedal Freeplay (Models w/Mechanical Linkage)	At Least Once Every 6 Months
Change Automatic Transfer Case Only	Every 50,000 Miles
Change Automatic Transmission Fluid & Filter, Blazer, Jimmy, S-10 & Sonoma	Normal Service Every 50,000 Miles; Severe Service Every 15,000 Miles
Change Automatic Transmission Fluid & Filter, 2003 SSR	Normal Service Every 60,000 Miles; Severe Service At 30,000 Miles Then Every 60,000 Miles Thereafter
Change Automatic Transmission Fluid & Filter, 2004–05 SSR	Normal Service Every 50,000 Miles; Severe Service Every 25,000 Miles
Lubricate Transfer Case & Transmission Linkage, Pedal Pivots & Springs, Except Sonoma GT, Syclone & Typhoon	S S N S S X S S N S S X S S N S S X S S N S S X S S N S S X S S N S
Lubricate Transfer Case & Transmission Linkage, Pedal Pivots & Springs, Sonoma GT, Syclone & Typhoon	Initial Service At 2500 Miles, Then Every 3 Months Or 3000 Miles Thereafter
DRIVE AXLE & DRIVESHAFT	
Check Front & Rear Axle Fluid Level, 2003	Every 7500 Miles
Lubricate Driveshaft, Except Sonoma GT, Syclone & Typhoon	S S N S S X S S N S S X S S N S S X S S N S S X S S N S S X S S N S
Lubricate Driveshaft, Sonoma GT, Syclone & Typhoon	Initial Service At 2500 Miles, Then Every 3 Months Or 3000 Miles Thereafter
Locking Differential Lubrication	Drain & Refill At First Oil Change Interval Then, Normal Service Inspect & Add As Needed Every 15,000 Miles; Severe Service Drain & Refill Every 15,000 Miles

VEHICLE MAINTNENACE SCHEDULES, GENERAL MOTORS CORP.

BLAZER/JIMMY S-SERIES, SONOMA, SSR, S-10 & S-15—Continued

Service Interval In Miles①

The mileage columns run in 7,500-mile increments (7,500 through 195,000). Symbols (S, N, X) are marked in the applicable columns for each service.

Recommended Service	Service Interval / Notes
DRIVE AXLE & DRIVESHAFT	
Standard Differential Lubrication	Normal Service Inspect & Add As Needed Every 15,000 Miles; Severe Service Drain & Refill Every 15,000 Miles
ENGINE	
Change Engine Coolant	150,000 Miles
Change Engine Oil & Filter, Except Sonoma GT, Syclone & Typhoon	Marked (S / N / X) across service interval columns
Change Engine Oil & Filter, Sonoma GT, Syclone & Typhoon	Initially At 2500 Miles, Then Every 3 Months Or 3000 Miles Thereafter
Change Engine Oil & Filter, SSR	Every 3 Months Or 3000 Miles Or As Indicated By Oil Life Monitor
Inspect Drive Belts, Emission & Fuel System	Marked (S) in service interval columns
Inspect Engine Air & PCV Inlet Filter Elements	Marked (X / S) in service interval columns
Inspect Engine Drive Belt, 2003–05	Every 150,000 Miles
Inspect Exhaust System	At Engine Oil Changes
Inspect Fuel System, 2004–05	Every 25,000 Miles
Inspect PCV System & Valve	Every 100,000 Miles
Inspect Spark Plug Wires, Distributor Cap & Rotor	Every 30,000 Miles
Inspect Spark Plug Wires, 2003–05	Every 100,000 Miles
Replace Engine Air Filter, 2003	Every 30,000 Miles
Replace Engine Air Filter, 2004	Every 25,000 Miles
Replace Engine Air Filter, 2005 Except SSR	Every 45,000 Miles
Replace Engine Air Filter, 2005 SSR	Every 50,000 Miles
Replace Fuel Filter, Except 2002–03 4.3L	Every 90,000 Miles
Replace Fuel Filter, 4.3L & 2003 SSR	Every 30,000 Miles
Replace Fuel Filter, 2004 SSR	Every 25,000 Miles
Replace Spark Plugs	Every 100,000 Miles

BLAZER/JIMMY S-SERIES, SONOMA, SSR, S-10 & S-15—Continued

Recommended Service	Service Interval In Miles①																													
	3000	6000	7500	9000	12000	15000	21000	24000	27000	30000	33000	36000	42000	45000	48000	51000	54000	57000	63000	66000	69000	72000	75000	78000	81000	84000	87000	90000	93000	96000
STEERING, SUSPENSION & TIRES																														
Clean & Repack Front Wheel Bearings, 2002–03 2WD S-10 & Sonoma	Every 30,000 Miles																													
Inspect Steering & Suspension System Components	At Engine Oil Change Intervals																													
Lubricate Steering & Suspension Grease Fittings, Sonoma GT, Syclone & Typhoon	Initial Service At 2500 Miles, Then Every 3 Months Or 3000 Miles Thereafter																													
Lubricate Steering & Suspension Grease Fittings, S & T Except Sonoma GT, Syclone & Typhoon	S	S	N	S	S	X	S	S	N	S	S	X	S	S	N	S	S	X	S	S	N	S	S	X	S	S	N	S	S	X
Rotate Tires	At Engine Oil Change Intervals																													

BTSI — Brake Transmission Shift Interlock
EPR — Exhaust Pressure Regulator
N — Normal Service
S — Severe Service
X — Normal Or Severe Service
① — After vehicle passes 99,000 mile mark return to beginning of mileage table & start cycle over again.

VEHICLE MAINTNENACE SCHEDULES, GENERAL MOTORS CORP.

BRAVADA, ENVOY, RAINER & TRAILBLAZER①

Service Interval In Miles

Mileage columns: 3000, 6000, 7500, 9000, 12000, 15000, 18000, 21000, 24000, 27000, 30000, 33000, 36000, 39000, 42000, 45000, 48000, 51000, 54000, 57000, 60000, 63000, 66000, 69000, 72000, 75000, 78000, 81000, 84000, 87000, 90000, 93000, 96000, 99000

Recommended Service	Service Interval / Notes
BODY	
Inspect Lamps, Seat Belts & Warning Devices	At Least Once Every 6 Months
Inspect Restraint System	At Oil Change Intervals
Lubricate Body Components	At Oil Change Intervals
BRAKES	
Inspect Brake System	At Tire Rotation Or At Least Every 6 Months
CLUTCH & TRANSMISSION	
Change Automatic Transfer Case Fluid	Every 50,000 Miles
Change Automatic Transmission Fluid & Filter	Normal Service Every 100,000 Miles; Severe Service Every 50,000 Miles
DRIVE AXLE & DRIVESHAFT	
Check Front & Rear Axle Fluid Level, 2002–03	Every 7500 Miles
Check Front & Rear Axle Fluid Level, 2004–06	At Oil Change Intervals
ENGINE	
Change Engine Coolant	Every 60 Months Or 150,000 Miles
Change Engine Oil & Filter	Engine Oil Life Monitor Will Indicate When To Change Oil Filter, Vehicle Must Not Be Driven More Than 12 Months Or 10,000 Miles Without An Oil & Filter Change
Inspect Cooling System	At Oil Change Intervals
Inspect Drive Belts	Every 150,000 Miles
Inspect Engine Air Filter	At Oil Change Intervals
Inspect Exhaust System	Every 25,000 Miles
Inspect Fuel System	Every 25,000 Miles
Inspect PCV Valve, 5.3L	Every 100,000 Miles
Inspect Spark Plug Wire, 5.3L	Every 100,000 Miles
Replace Engine Air Filter, 2002–03	Every 30,000 Miles
Replace Engine Air Filter, 2004	Every 25,000 Miles
Replace Engine Air Filter, 2005–06	Every 50,000 Miles
Replace Fuel Filter, 2002–03	Every 30,000 Miles
Replace Fuel Filter, 2004–05	Every 25,000 Miles

BRAVADA, ENVOY, RAINER & TRAILBLAZER—Continued

Service Interval In Miles[1]

Recommended Service	3000	6000	7500	9000	12000	15000	18000	21000	22500	24000	27000	30000	33000	36000	37500	39000	42000	45000	48000	51000	52500	54000	57000	60000	63000	66000	67500	69000	72000	75000	78000	81000	82500	84000	87000	90000	93000	96000	97500	99000
ENGINE																																								
Replace Spark Plugs	Every 100,000 Miles																																							
STEERING, SUSPENSION & TIRES																																								
Inspect Suspension And Steering Components	At Oil Change Intervals																																							
Lubricate Steering & Suspension Grease Fittings	At Oil Change Intervals																																							
Rotate Tires, 2002–03	Every 7500 Miles																																							
Rotate Tires, 2004–06	At Oil Change Intervals																																							

BTSI — Brake Transmission Shift Interlock
EPR — Exhaust Pressure Regulator
N — Normal Service
S — Severe Service
X — Normal Or Severe Service
[1] — After vehicle passes 99,000 mile mark return to beginning of mileage table & start cycle over again.

CANYON & COLORADO

Service Interval In Miles①

3000, 6000, 9000, 12000, 15000, 18000, 21000, 24000, 27000, 30000, 33000, 36000, 39000, 42000, 45000, 48000, 51000, 54000, 57000, 60000, 63000, 66000, 69000, 72000, 75000, 78000, 81000, 84000, 87000, 90000, 93000, 96000, 99000

Recommended Service	Interval
BODY	
Inspect Lamps, Seat Belts & Warning Devices	At Least Once Every 6 Months
Inspect Restraint System	At Oil Change Intervals
Lubricate Body Components	At Oil Change Intervals
BRAKES	
Inspect Brake System	At Tire Rotation Or At Least Every 6 Months
CLUTCH & TRANSMISSION	
Change Automatic Transmission Fluid & Filter	Normal Service Every 100,000 Miles; Severe Service Every 50,000 Miles
ENGINE	
Change Engine Coolant	Every 60 Months Or 150,000 Miles
Change Engine Oil & Filter	Engine Oil Life Monitor Will Indicate When To Change Oil Filter, Vehicle Must Not Be Driven More Than 12 Months Or 10,000 Miles Without An Oil & Filter Change
Inspect Cooling System	At Oil Change Intervals
Inspect Drive Belts	Every 150,000 Miles
Inspect Engine Air Filter	At Oil Change Intervals
Inspect Exhaust System	Every 25,000 Miles
Inspect Fuel System For Damage And Leaks	Every 25,000 Miles
Replace Engine Air Filter	Every 50,000 Miles
Replace Fuel Filter, 2005–06	Every 25,000 Miles
Replace Spark Plugs	Every 100,000 Miles
STEERING, SUSPENSION & TIRES	
Inspect Suspension And Steering Components	At Oil Change Intervals
Rotate Tires	At Oil Change Intervals

BTSI — Brake Transmission Shift Interlock
EPR — Exhaust Pressure Regulator
N — Normal Service
S — Severe Service
X — Normal Or Severe Service
① — After vehicle passes 99,000 mile mark return to beginning of mileage table & start cycle over again.

DENALI, ESCALADE, ESCALADE ESV & EXT, SIERRA, SILVERADO, SUBURBAN, TAHOE, YUKON & YUKON XL

Service Interval In Miles①

Recommended Service	Interval
BODY	
Inspect Lamps, Seat Belts & Warning Devices	At Least Once Every 6 Months
Inspect Noise Shields & Underhood Insulation, w/Diesel	Every 10,000 Miles
Lubricate Hinges, Latches, Lock Cylinders & Strikers	At Engine Oil Changes Or At Least Every 12 Months
Replace Passenger Compartment Air Filter, w/Diesel	Every 10,000 Miles
Replace Passenger Compartment Air Filter, w/Gasoline Engine	Every 15,000 Miles
BRAKES	
Inspect Brake System	At Tire Rotation Or At Least Every 6 Months
CLUTCH & TRANSMISSION	
Adjust Clutch Pedal Freeplay (Models w/Mechanical Linkage)	At Least Once Every 6 Months
Change Automatic Transfer Case Fluid, w/Gasoline Engine	Every 50,000 Miles
Change Automatic Transmission External Main Control Filter, w/ Allison Transmission	At First Maintenance Service Performed On Vehicle
Change Automatic Transmission Fluid & Filter, w/Allison Transmission	Normal Service Every 50,000 Miles; Severe Service Every 25,000 Miles
Change Automatic Transmission Fluid & Filter, GVW Under 8600 Lbs.	Normal Service Every 100,000 Miles; Severe Service Every 50,000 Miles
Change Automatic Transmission Fluid & Filter, GVW Over 8600 Lbs., Less Allison Transmission	Every 50,000 Miles
Change Clutch Fluid, 2004–05 6 Speed Manual Transmission	Every 24 Months Or 25,000 Miles

VEHICLE MAINTNENACE SCHEDULES, GENERAL MOTORS CORP.

DENALI, ESCALADE, ESCALADE ESV & EXT, SIERRA, SILVERADO, SUBURBAN, TAHOE, YUKON & YUKON XL—Continued

Service Interval In Miles①

Recommended Service	Interval / Notes
CLUTCH & TRANSMISSION	
Change 5 Speed Manual Transmission 4300 V6, 4800 V8, 2003 Silerado 4WD	At 100,000 Miles
Change 5 Speed Manual Transmission 6000 V8, 2003 Silverado 4WD	At 200,000 Miles
Change 5 Speed Manual Transmission, 2004–06	At 150,000 Miles
DRIVE AXLE	
Change Rear Axle Lubricant, Trailor Towing, 2002	After The First 500 Miles (Break In Period) Of Trailer Towing
Inspect Axle Seals & CV Joints, w/Diesel	
Inspect Axle Seals & CV Joints, w/Gasoline Engine	Normal Service Every 7500 Miles; Severe Service, Every 8000 Miles Or Every 3 Months
Inspect Front & Rear Axle Lubricant Level, w/Diesel	Every 5000 Miles
Inspect Front & Rear Axle Lubricant Level, w/Gasoline Engine	Normal Service Every 7500 Miles; Severe Service Every 8000 Miles Or Every 3 Months
Lubricate Driveshaft Fittings, w/Gasoline Engine	Normal Service Every 7500 Miles; Severe Service Every 3 Months Or 8000 Miles
Lubricate Driveshaft Fitting, w/Diesel	Every 5000 Miles
ENGINE	
Change Engine Coolant	Every 150,000 Miles Or 60 Months
Change Engine Oil & Filter, 2002 w/Gasoline Engine & All 2003–06②	Every 12 Months Or As Indicated By Oil Life Monitor
Change Engine Oil & Filter, 2002 w/Diesel	Every 3 Months Or 5000 Miles
Inspect Air Intake System & Filter, w/Gasoline Engine	X (at intervals)
Inspect Air Intake System & Filter Housing, w/Diesel	Every 10,000 Miles
Inspect CDRV System, w/Diesel	X

DENALI, ESCALADE, ESCALADE ESV & EXT, SIERRA, SILVERADO, SUBURBAN, TAHOE, YUKON & YUKON XL—Continued

Service Interval In Miles①

ENGINE

Recommended Service	Interval / Notes
Inspect Drive Belts, w/Diesel 2002–03	S (at intervals)
Inspect Drive Belts, 2004–06	Every 150,000 Miles
Inspect EGR System	X (at intervals)
Inspect Emission & Fuel System Connections, Hoses, Lines, Filler Cap & Tank	S (at intervals)
Inspect Engine Idle Speed, w/Diesel	Initially At 5000 & 30,000 Miles, Then Every 30,000 Miles Thereafter
Inspect Evaporative System, 2005–06	Every 50,000 Miles
Inspect Exhaust System, 2002–03	At Engine Oil Changes
Inspect Exhaust System, 2004–06	Every 25,000 Miles
Inspect Fuel System, 2004–06	Every 25,000 Miles
Inspect PCV System & Valve	Every 100,000 Miles
Inspect Spark Plug Wires, Distributor Cap & Rotor	Every 30,000 Miles
Inspect Thermostatically Controlled Cooling Fan System	X (at intervals)
Inspect Thermostatically Controlled Cooling Fan System, w/Diesel	Every 12 Months Or 10,000 Miles
Inspect Throttle Linkage Operation	At Air Filter Element Changes
Replace Engine Air Filter, 2003	Every 30,000 Miles
Replace Engine Air Filter, 2004	Every 25,000 Miles
Replace Engine Air Filter, 2005–06③	Every 50,000 Miles
Replace External Main Control Filter, 2003 Silverado w/Allison Transmission	At 7500 Miles
Replace Fuel Filler Cap, 2002	Severe Service Every 25,000 Miles
Replace Fuel Filter	X (at intervals)
Replace PCV Inlet Filter Elements	Replace Every 100,000 Miles

DENALI, ESCALADE, ESCALADE ESV & EXT, SIERRA, SILVERADO, SUBURBAN, TAHOE, YUKON & YUKON XL—Continued

Recommended Service	Service Interval In Miles①																												
	3375	6750	10125	13500	16875	20250	23625	27000	30375	33750	37125	40500	43875	47250	50625	54000	57375	60750	64125	67500	70875	74250	77625	81000	84375	87750	91125	94500	97875
ENGINE																													
Replace Spark Plugs, 2002 4.3L							X																		X				
Replace Spark Plugs, Except 2002 4.3L	Every 100,000 Miles																												
STEERING, SUSPENSION & TIRES																													
Lubricate Steering & Suspension Grease Fittings, w/Diesel	Every 3 Months Or 5000 Miles																												
Lubricate Steering & Suspension Grease Fittings, w/Gasoline Engine	At Engine Oil Changes																												
On 2WD, Clean & Repack Wheel Bearings, 2002–04	Normal Service Every 30,000 Miles; Severe Service Every 15,000 Miles																												
Rotate Tires	At Engine Oil Changes																												

BTSI — Brake Transmission Shift Interlock
CDRV — Crankcase Depression Regulator Valve
EPR — Exhaust Pressure Regulator
EVR — Electronic Vacuum Regulator
GVWR — Gross Vehicle Weight Rating
N — Normal Service
S — Severe Service
X — Normal Or Severe Service
① — After vehicle passes 99,000 mile mark return to beginning of mileage table & start cycle over again.
② — The engine Oil Life Monitor will indicate when to change the engine oil. Reset the indicator after the oil has been changed.
③ — Vehicles without filter restriction indicator.

EQUINOX & TORRENT

Service Interval In Miles①

Recommended Service	3000	6000	7500	9000	12000	15000	18000	21000	24000	27000	30000	33000	36000	39000	42000	45000	48000	51000	54000	57000	60000	63000	66000	69000	72000	75000	78000	81000	84000	87000	90000	93000	96000	99000
BODY																																		
Inspect Seat Belts & Restraint Systems	*At Least Once Every 6 Months*																																	
Inspect Wiper Blades & Inserts	*At Least Once Every 6 Months*																																	
Lubricate Door Check Straps & Hinges	*At Engine Oil Change Intervals*																																	
Lubricate Headlamp Doors	*At Engine Oil Change Intervals*																																	
Lubricate Hood Latch	*At Engine Oil Change Intervals*																																	
Replace Cabin Air Filter	*Every 12 Months Or 12,000 Miles. In Dusty Areas Change More Often*																																	
BRAKES																																		
Inspect Brake Drums & Shoes						X					X					X					X					X					X			
Inspect Brake Hoses, Lines & Connections						X					X					X					X					X					X			
Inspect Disc Brake Calipers For Freedom Of Movement (Lubricate If Required)						X					X					X					X					X					X			
Inspect Disc Brake Pads & Rotors						X					X					X					X					X					X			
CLUTCH & TRANSAXLE																																		
Change Automatic Transaxle Fluid & Filter	*Normal Service Every 100,000 Miles; Severe Service Every 50,000 Miles*																																	
DRIVESHAFT																																		
Inspect CV Joint Boots	X	X	X	X	X	X	X	X	X	X	X	X	X	X	X	X	X	X	X	X	X	X	X	X	X	X	X	X	X	X	X	X	X	X
ENGINE																																		
Change Engine Coolant	*Every 60 Months Or 150,000 Miles*																																	
Change Engine Oil & Filter②	*The Engine Oil Life Monitor Will Indicate When To Change Engine Oil. The Engine Oil & Filter Must Be Changed At Least Once a Year*																																	
Inspect Air Filter	*Severe Service Every 15,000 Miles*																																	
Inspect Cooling System & Protection Level						X										X										X								
Inspect Drive Belts	*Every 150,000 Miles*																																	
Inspect Exhaust System	*Every 25,000 Miles*																																	
Inspect Fuel System	*Every 25,000 Miles*																																	
Inspect Fuel Tank Filler Cap																										X								
Inspect Throttle System	*At Engine Oil Change Intervals*																																	
Replace Air Filter	*Every 50,000 Miles*																																	
Replace Spark Plugs	*Every 100,000 Miles*																																	

VEHICLE MAINTNENACE SCHEDULES, GENERAL MOTORS CORP.

EQUINOX & TORRENT—Continued

Service Interval In Miles①

Recommended Service	3000	6000	7500	9000	12000	15000	18000	21000	24000	27000	30000	33000	36000	39000	42000	45000	48000	51000	54000	57000	60000	63000	66000	69000	72000	75000	78000	81000	84000	87000	90000	93000	96000	99000

STEERING, SUSPENSION & TIRES

Recommended Service	
Inspect Ball Joint Seals	At Engine Oil Change Intervals
Inspect Suspension	At Engine Oil Change Intervals
Rotate Tires	Every 6000 Miles

BTSI — Brake Transaxle Shift Interlock
N — Normal Service
S — Severe Service
X — Normal Or Severe Service
① — After vehicle passes 100,000 mile mark return to beginning of mileage table & start cycle over again.
② — On models equipped with Engine Oil Life Moniter, change engine oil when message appears in message display center. Never drive vehicle more then 6000 miles or 6 months without changing oil and filter.

G SERIES

Service Interval In Miles①

Recommended Service	3000	6000	7500	9000	12000	15000	18000	21000	24000	27000	30000	33000	36000	39000	42000	45000	48000	51000	54000	57000	60000	63000	66000	69000	72000	75000	78000	81000	84000	87000	90000	93000	96000	99000

BODY

Recommended Service	
Inspect Lamps, Seat Belts & Warning Devices	At Least Once Every 6 Months
Inspect Noise Shields & Underhood Insulation, w/Diesel	Every 10,000 Miles
Lubricate Hinges, Latches, Lock Cylinders & Strikers	At Engine Oil Changes Or At Least Every 12 Months
Replace Cabin Air Filter	Every 15,000 Miles

BRAKES

Recommended Service	
Inspect Brake System	Every 6 Months
Lubricate Brake Cable Guides, w/Diesel	Normal Service Every 12 Months Or 5000 Miles; Severe Service Every 3 Months Or 2500 Miles

Recommended Service	3000	6000	7500	9000	12000	15000	18000	21000	24000	27000	30000	33000	36000	39000	42000	45000	48000	51000	54000	57000	60000	63000	66000	69000	72000	75000	78000	81000	84000	87000	90000	93000	96000	99000
Lubricate Brake Cable Guides, w/Gasoline Engine	S	S	N	S	S	X	S	S	S	N	S	S	X	S	S	S	N	S	S	X	S	S	S	N	S	S	X	S	S	S	N	S	S	S

G SERIES—Continued

Service Interval In Miles①

Recommended Service	3750	7500	11250	15000	18750	22500	26250	30000	33750	37500	41250	45000	48750	52500	56250	60000	63750	67500	71250	75000	78750	82500	86250	90000
CLUTCH & TRANSMISSION																								
Adjust Clutch Pedal Freeplay (Models w/Mechanical Linkage)	At Least Once Every 6 Months																							
Change Automatic Transmission Fluid & Filter	Normal Service Every 100,000 Miles; Severe Service Every 50,000 Miles																							
Lubricate Transfer Case & Transmission Linkage, Pedal Pivots & Springs, w/Diesel	Normal Service Every 12 Months Or 5000 Miles; Severe Service Every 3 Months Or 2500 Miles																							
Lubricate Transfer Case & Transmission Linkage, Pedal Pivots & Springs, w/Gasoline Engine	S	S	S	N	S	S	S	S	S	N	S	S	S	S	S	N	S	S	S	S	S	N	S	S
DRIVE AXLE																								
Change Differential Lubricant	Normal Service Once Only At Initial Engine Oil Change; Severe Service Every 15,000 Miles																							
Change Differential Lubricant, Except 3500HD				S				S				S				S				S				S
Change Differential Lubricant, Locking Type, Models Less Dana 70/80 Axle	S	N		S				S				S				S				S				S
Change Differential Lubricant, 3500HD				S				S				S				S				S				S
Lubricate Driveshaft, w/Diesel	Normal Service Every 12 Months Or 5000 Miles; Severe Service Every 3 Months Or 2500 Miles																							
Lubricate Driveshaft, w/Gasoline Engine	S	S	S	N	S	S	S	S	S	N	S	S	S	S	S	N	S	S	S	S	S	N	S	S
ENGINE																								
Change Engine Oil & Filter, w/Diesel	Normal Service Every 12 Months Or 5000 Miles; Severe Service Every 3 Months Or 2500 Miles																							
Change Engine Oil & Filter, w/Gasoline Engine②	Normal Service Every 12 Months Or 5000 Miles; Severe Service Every 3 Months Or 2500 Miles																							
Inspect Air Intake System & Filter, Gasoline w/HD Emissions				X				X				X				X				X				X
Inspect Air Intake System & Filter Housing, w/Diesel																								
Inspect CDRV System, w/Diesel	Every 10,000 Miles																							
Inspect Drive Belts, 2002	Every 60,000 Miles																X							
Inspect Drive Belts, 2003–06	Every 150,000 Miles																							

G SERIES—Continued

Service Interval In Miles①

The service-interval columns span: 3600, 7500, 15000, 18000, 21000, 24000, 27000, 30000, 33000, 36000, 39000, 42000, 45000, 48000, 51000, 54000, 57000, 60000, 63000, 66000, 69000, 72000, 75000, 78000, 81000, 84000, 87000, 90000, 93000, 96000, 99000

ENGINE

Recommended Service	Service Interval / Marked Miles
Inspect EGR System, w/Gasoline Engines & VIN S Diesel	X at 66,000
Inspect Emission & Fuel System Connections, Hoses, Lines, Filler Cap & Tank	S at 24,000; 66,000; 87,000
Inspect Engine Idle Speed, w/Diesel	Initially At 5000 & 30,000 Miles, Then Every 30,000 Miles Thereafter
Inspect Evaporative Emission Control System, 2005–06	Every 50,000 Miles
Inspect Exhaust System, 2002–04	At Engine Oil Changes
Inspect Exhaust System, 2005–06	Every 25,000 Miles
Inspect Fuel System, 2005–06	Every 25,000 Miles
Inspect PCV System & Valve	Every 100,000 Miles
Inspect Spark Plug Wires, Distributor Cap & Rotor	Every 30,000 Miles
Inspect Thermostatically Controlled Air Cleaner Operation, Gasoline Engines w/LD Emissions	X at 15,000; 30,000; 45,000; 60,000; 75,000; 90,000
Inspect Thermostatically Controlled Air Cleaner Operation, Gasoline Engines w/HD Emissions	X at 18,000; 30,000; 42,000; 54,000; 66,000; 78,000; 90,000
Inspect Thermostatically Controlled Air Cleaner Operation, w/Diesel	Every 10,000 Miles
Inspect Thermostatically Controlled Cooling Fan System, w/Diesel	Every 12 Months Or 10,000 Miles
Inspect Thermostatically Controlled Cooling Fan System, w/Gasoline Engine	X at 15,000; 45,000; 66,000; 87,000
Inspect Throttle Linkage Operation	At Air Filter Element Changes
Replace Engine Air Filter, 2002–04	Every 30,000 Miles

G SERIES—Continued

Service Interval In Miles ①

The mileage-interval grid across the top of the table runs in 3,000-mile steps (with intermediate service points) from 3,000 up to 99,000 miles.

Recommended Service	Service Interval / Marks
ENGINE	
Replace Engine Air Filter, 2005–06 Less Filter Restriction Indicator	Every 50,000 Miles
Replace Fuel Filter, w/Diesel	X — 30,000; 60,000; 90,000 Miles
Replace Fuel Filter, w/Gasoline	X — 30,000; 60,000; 90,000 Miles
Replace PCV Inlet Filter Elements	Replace Every 100,000 Miles
Replace Spark Plugs, Standard Tip	X — 30,000; 60,000; 90,000 Miles
Replace Spark Plugs, Platinum Tip	Every 100,000 Miles
STEERING, SUSPENSION & TIRES	
Lubricate Steering Kingpins & Bushings	Normal Service Every 3000 Miles; Severe Service Every 1500 Miles
Lubricate Steering & Suspension Grease Fittings, w/Diesel	Normal Service Every 12 Months Or 5000 Miles; Severe Service Every 3 Months Or 2500 Miles
Lubricate Steering & Suspension Grease Fittings, w/Gasoline Engine	S (Severe) at 3000-mile points; N (Normal) at 7500-mile points, across all intervals
Repack Front Wheel Bearings, Except Diesel	S/X across intervals (X — Normal Or Severe)
Rotate Tires, Except Diesel	At Oil Change Intervals
Rotate Tires, w/Diesel	Normal Service Every 7500 Miles; Severe Service Every 5000 Miles

---

BTSI — Brake Transmission Shift Interlock
CDRV — Crankcase Depression Regulator Valve
EPR — Exhaust Pressure Regulator
EVR — Electronic Vacuum Regulator
GVWR — Gross Vehicle Weight Rating
HD — Heavy Duty, GVWR of 8501 lbs. or more
LD — Light Duty, GVWR of 8500 lbs. or less
N — Normal Service
S — Severe Service
X — Normal Or Severe Service

① — After vehicle passes 99,000 mile mark return to beginning of mileage table & start cycle over again.

② — On models equipped with engine Oil Life Monitor, change oil when message appears in display center. Reset oil monitor when oil has been changed. Vehicle must not be driven more than 10,000 miles or 12 months without an oil and filter change.

HHR

Service Interval In Miles①

Mileage column headings (left → right): 3000, 6000, 7500, 9000, 12000, 15000, 18000, 21000, 24000, 27000, 30000, 33000, 36000, 39000, 42000, 45000, 48000, 51000, 54000, 57000, 60000, 63000, 66000, 69000, 72000, 75000, 78000, 81000, 84000, 87000, 90000, 93000, 96000, 99000

Recommended Service	Interval
BODY	
Inspect Lamps, Seat Belts & Warning Devices	At Least Once Every 6 Months
Inspect Restraint System	At Oil Change Intervals
Lubricate Body Components	At Oil Change Intervals
BRAKES	
Inspect Brake System	At Tire Rotation Or At Least Every 6 Months
CLUTCH & TRANSMISSION	
Change Automatic Transmission Fluid & Filter	Severe Service Every 50,000 Miles
ENGINE	
Change Engine Coolant	Every 60 Months Or 150,000 Miles
Change Engine Oil & Filter	Engine Oil Life Monitor Will Indicate When To Change Oil Filter, Vehicle Must Not Be Driven More Than 12 Months Or 10,000 Miles Without An Oil & Filter Change
Inspect Cooling System	At Oil Change Intervals
Inspect Drive Belts	Every 150,000 Miles
Inspect Engine Air Filter	At Oil Change Intervals
Inspect Exhaust System	Every 25,000 Miles
Inspect Fuel System For Damage And Leaks	Every 25,000 Miles
Replace Engine Air Filter	Every 50,000 Miles
Replace Fuel Filter	Every 25,000 Miles
Replace Spark Plugs	Every 100,000 Miles
STEERING, SUSPENSION & TIRES	
Inspect Suspension And Steering Components	At Oil Change Intervals
Rotate Tires	At Oil Change Intervals

N — Normal Service
S — Severe Service
X — Normal Or Severe Service
BTSI — Brake Transmission Shift Interlock
EPR — Exhaust Pressure Regulator
① — After vehicle passes 99,000 mile mark return to beginning of mileage table & start cycle over again.

HUMMER H2 & H3

Service Interval In Miles①

The mileage interval columns run (in thousands): 3, 6, 7.5, 9, 12, 15, 18, 21, 24, 27, 30, 33, 36, 39, 42, 45, 48, 51, 54, 57, 60, 63, 66, 69, 72, 75, 78, 81, 84, 87, 90, 93, 96, 99 thousand miles.

Recommended Service	Service Interval / Notes
BODY	
Inspect Lamps, Seat Belts & Warning Devices	At Least Once Every 6 Months
Lubricate Hinges, Latches, Lock Cylinders & Strikers	At Engine Oil Changes Or At Least Every 12 Months
Replace Passenger Compartment Air Filter	Normal Service Every 15,000 Miles; Severe Service Every 10,000 Miles
BRAKES	
Inspect Brake System	At Tire Rotation Or At Least Every 6 Months
CLUTCH & TRANSMISSION	
Change Automatic Transmission Fluid & Filter	Normal Service Every 100,000 Miles; Severe Service, Every 50,000 Miles
Change Transfer Case Fluid	Every 50,000 Miles
DRIVE AXLE	
Inspect Axle Seals & CV Joints	Normal Service Every 7500 Miles; Severe Service, Every 3000 Miles Or Every 3 Months
Inspect Front & Rear Axle Lubricant Level	Normal Service Every 7500 Miles; Severe Service, Every 3000 Miles Or Every 3 Months
Lubricate Driveshaft Fittings	Normal Service Every 7500 Miles; Severe Service Every 3 Months Or 3000 Miles
ENGINE	
Change Engine Coolant	Every 150,000 Miles Or 60 Months
Change Engine Oil & Filter③	Engine Oil Life Monitor Will Indicate When To Change Oil Filter, Vehicle Must Not Be Driven More Than 12 Months Or 10,000 Miles Without An Oil & Filter Change, Reset Oil Life System (X marked at intervals)
Inspect Air Intake System & Filter	X marked at intervals
Inspect Drive Belts	Every 150,000 Miles
Inspect Emission & Fuel System Connections, Hoses, Lines, Filler Cap & Tank	Every 25,000 Miles
Inspect Exhaust System	Every 25,000 Miles
Inspect Fuel System For Damage & Leaks	Every 25,000 Miles
Inspect PVC, 2003	At 100,000 Miles
Inspect Thermostatically Controlled Cooling Fan System	X marked at intervals
Inspect Throttle Linkage Operation	At Air Filter Element Changes
Replace Engine Air Filter, 2003	Every 30,000 Miles

VEHICLE MAINTNENACE SCHEDULES, GENERAL MOTORS CORP.

HUMMER H2 & H3—Continued

Recommended Service — Service Interval In Miles①

Recommended Service	Service Interval
ENGINE	
Replace Engine Air Filter, 2004-05 ②	At 100,000 Miles
Replace Engine Air Filter, 2006 ②	Every 50,000 Miles
Replace Fuel Filter, 2003 H2	Every 30,000 Miles
Replace Spark Plugs	At 100,000 Miles
STEERING, SUSPENSION & TIRES	
Lubricate Steering & Suspension Grease Fittings	S S N S S X S S N S S S N S S X S S N S S S N S S X S S N S (at service intervals: 3000, 6000, 7500, 9000, 12000, 15000, 21000, 24000, 27000, 30000, 36000, 37500, 39000, 45000, 48000, 51000, 54000, 57000, 60000, 63000, 67500, 69000, 72000, 75000, 78000, 81000, 84000, 87000, 90000, 97500 miles)
Rotate Tires	Every 7500 Miles

N — Normal Service
S — Severe Service
X — Normal Or Severe Service

① — After vehicle passes 150,000 mile mark return to beginning of mileage table & start cycle over again.

② — Models less filter restriction indicator.

③ — If equipped, the engine oil life monitor will indicate when to change engine oil, usually 3000–10,000 miles. Under severe driving conditions, engine oil may need to be changed before 3000 miles. If vehicle is driven in a dusty area, change engine oil every 3000 miles.

MONTANA, RELAY, SILHOUETTE, TERRAZA, UPLANDER & VENTURE

Service Interval In Miles①

Recommended Service	Interval / Notes
BODY	
Change Passenger Compartment Air Filter	Every 15,000 Miles
Clean Power Antenna Mast, Inspect Neutral Safety & BTSI Operation	At Least Once Every 3 Months
Flush Vehicle Underside, Inspect Drain Holes	At Least Once Every 12 Months, Especially In Winter & Springtime
Inspect Lamps, Seat Belts & Warning Devices	At Least Once Every 6 Months
Lubricate Hinges, Latches, Lock Cylinders & Strikers	At Engine Oil Changes Or At Least Every 12 Months
BRAKES	
Inspect Brake System	At Tire Roatations
Lubricate Brake Cable Guides	S S N S S S X S S S N S S S X S S S N S S S X S S S N S S S X S S S N S
CLUTCH & TRANSMISSION	
Change Automatic Transmission Fluid & Filter, 2002	No Normal Service Required; Severe Service Change Every 50,000 Miles
Change Automatic Transmission Fluid & Filter, 2003–06	Normal Service Every 100,000 Miles; Severe Service Change Every 50,000 Miles
DRIVE AXLE & DRIVESHAFT	
Change Rear Axle Fluid, AWD Models, 2002④	Severe Service At 7500 Miles
Lubricate Driveshaft	S S N S S S N S S S X S S S N S S S X S S S N S S S X S S S N S S S X S S S N S
ENGINE	
Change Engine Coolant	150,000 Miles
Change Engine Oil & Filter③	Every 12 Months Or As Indicated By Oil Life Monitor
Inspect Accessory Drive Belts, 2003–06	Every 150,000 Miles
Inspect Drive Belts, 2002	Every 60,000 Miles
Inspect Emission & Fuel System Connections, Hoses, Lines, Filler Cap & Tank, 2002–03	S … X … S
Inspect Exhaust System, 2002–03	At Engine Oil Changes

MONTANA, RELAY, SILHOUETTE, TERRAZA, UPLANDER & VENTURE—Continued

Service Interval In Miles ①

Recommended Service	3000	6000	9000	12500	15000	18000	21000	24500	27000	30000	33000	36000	39000	42000	45500	48000	51000	54000	57500	60000	63000	66000	69000	72500	75000	78000	81000	84000	87500	90000	93000	96000	99000
ENGINE																																	
Inspect Exhaust System, 2004–06										Every 25,000 Miles																							
Inspect EVR Valve & Ignition Timing																				X													
Inspect Fuel System, 2004–06										Every 25,000 Miles																							
Replace Engine Air Filter, 2004										Every 25,000 Miles																							
Replace Engine Air Filter, 2005–06										Every 50,000 Miles																							
Replace Engine Air & PCV Inlet Filter Elements, 2002–03 ②					S					X					S					X					S					X			
Replace Spark Plugs										Every 100,000 Miles																							
STEERING, SUSPENSION & TIRES																																	
Lubricate Steering & Suspension Grease Fittings										At Engine Oil Changes																							
Rotate Tires			S	N		S	N		S	N		S	X		S	N		S	N		S	X		S	N		S	N		S	X		S	N

BTSI — Brake Transmission Shift Interlock
EPR — Exhaust Pressure Regulator
N — Normal Service
S — Severe Service
X — Normal Or Severe Service
① — After vehicle passes 99,000 mile mark return to beginning of mileage table & start cycle over again.
② — Inspect & replace even more frequently in severe dusty conditions, possibly as often as every 3000 miles.
③ — This vehicle is equipped with a GM Oil Life System and will show when to change the engine oil and oil filter. This occurs usually between 3000 miles and 10,000 miles since last oil change. Do not exceed 12 months between oil changes. Severe conditions change every 3000 miles or sooner if the CHANGE OIL SOON light comes on. Reset Oil Life System when the oil and filter have been changed.
④ — If vehicle is used to pull a trailer, change at 7500 miles.

SRX

Service Interval In Miles[1]

Recommended Service	7,500	15,000	22,500	30,000	37,500	45,000	52,500	60,000	67,500	75,000	82,500	90,000	97,500
BODY													
Flush Vehicle Underside, Inspect Drain Holes — *At Least Every 12 Months, Especially In Winter & Springtime*													
Inspect Lamps, Seat Belts & Warning Devices — *At Least Once Every 6 Months*													
Lubricate Hinges, Latches, Lock Cylinders & Strikers — *At Engine Oil Changes Or At Least Every 12 Months*													
Replace Passenger Compartment Air Filter		X		X		X		X		X		X	
BRAKES													
Inspect Brake System — *At Engine Oil Changes Or At Least Every 12 Months*													
Inspect Parking Brake Operation — *At Least Once Every 12 Months*													
Lubricate Parking Brake Cable Guides (S)				X				X				X	
Lubricate Parking Brake Cable Guides (N)								X					
CLUTCH & TRANSAXLE/TRANSMISSION													
Change Automatic Transmission Fluid & Filter — *Normal Service Every 100,000 Miles; Severe Service Every 50,000 Miles*													
Change Transfer Case Fluid — *Trailer Tow Operation Only Every 50,000 Miles*													
Inspect Neutral Safety & BTSI Operation (S)			X			X			X			X	
Inspect Neutral Safety & BTSI Operation (N)						X						X	
Lubricate Transmission Shift Linkage (S)			X			X			X			X	
Lubricate Transmission Shift Linkage (N)						X						X	
ENGINE													
Change Engine Coolant — *Every 60 Months Or 150,000 Miles*													
Change Engine Oil & Filter[2] — *As Indicated By Oil Life System. Do Not Exceed 12 Months Between Oil And Filter Change Intervals*													
Inspect Air Cleaner Element		X									X		
Inspect Drive Belts — *At 150,000 Miles*													
Inspect EGR System										X			
Inspect Exhaust System — *Every 25,000 Miles*													
Inspect Fuel Filler Cap										X			
Inspect Fuel System Hoses, Lines & Connections — *Every 25,000 Miles*													
Inspect Spark Plug Wires — *At Spark Plug Changes*													
Replace Air Filter — *Every 50,000 Miles*													
Replace Spark Plugs — *Every 100,000 Miles*													

SRX—Continued

Service Interval In Miles①

Recommended Service	3000	6000	9000	12000	15000	18000	21000	24000	27000	30000	33000	36000	39000	42000	45000	48000	51000	54000	57000	60000	63000	66000	69000	72000	75000	78000	81000	84000	87000	90000	93000	96000	99000

STEERING, SUSPENSION & TIRES

Recommended Service	3000	6000	9000	12000	15000	18000	21000	24000	27000	30000	33000	36000	39000	42000	45000	48000	51000	54000	57000	60000	63000	66000	69000	72000	75000	78000	81000	84000	87000	90000	93000	96000	99000
Inspect Steering & Suspension System	At Tire Rotations																																
Lubricate Chassis & Suspension	S	N	S	N	X	S	N	S	N	X	S	N	S	N	X	S	N	S	N	X	S	N	S	N	X	S	N	S	N	X	S	N	S
Rotate Tires	Initial Service At 5000 Miles, Then Every 10,000 Miles Thereafter																																

BTSI — Brake Transmission Shift Interlock
IAC — Idle Air Control
ISC — Idle Speed Control System
N — Normal Service
S — Severe Service
X — Normal Or Severe Service
① — After vehicle passes 99,000 mile mark return to beginning of mileage table & start cycle over again.
② — If equipped, the engine oil life monitor will indicate when to change engine oil, usually 3000–10,000 miles. Under severe driving conditions, engine oil may need to be changed before 3000 miles. If vehicle is driven in a dusty area, change engine oil every 3000 miles.

TRACKER

Service Interval In Miles ①

The recommended service intervals (in miles) across the chart are:
3000, 6000, 7500, 9000, 12000, 15000, 18000, 21000, 22500, 24000, 27000, 30000, 33000, 36000, 37500, 39000, 42000, 45000, 48000, 51000, 52500, 54000, 57000, 60000, 63000, 66000, 67500, 69000, 72000, 75000, 78000, 81000, 82500, 84000, 87000, 90000, 93000, 96000, 97500, 99000.

BODY

Recommended Service	Schedule / Notes
Inspect Seat Belt Pretensioners & Supplemental Restraint System	10 Years From Vehicle Build Date
Inspect Warning Lamps & Devices	S / N / X at listed service intervals
Lubricate Door Hinges	At listed service intervals
Lubricate Lock Cylinders	At listed service intervals
Replace AC Evaporator Filter	At Every Engine Oil Change — At Least Once Every 12 Months
Tighten Body Fasteners	Every 30,000 Miles

BRAKES

Recommended Service	Schedule / Notes
Change Brake Fluid	(at listed interval)
Inspect Brake Connections, Drums, Hoses, Lines, Pads, Rotors & Shoes	At Tire Rotation

CLUTCH & TRANSMISSION

Recommended Service	Schedule / Notes
Change Automatic Transmission Fluid & Filter	Normal Service Every 100,000 Miles; Severe Service Every 15,000 Miles
Change Transfer Case & Manual Transmission Lubricants	S / X at listed service intervals
Inspect Clutch	S / N / X at listed service intervals
Inspect Clutch Pedal Freeplay	S / N at listed service intervals
Inspect Neutral Safety & Shift Interlock Switch Operation	At Least Once Every 12 Months
Lubricate Transmission Shift Control Lever & Shaft & Inspect Operation	At Every Engine Oil Change
Replace Automatic Transmission Fluid Cooler Hoses	X (at listed interval)

VEHICLE MAINTNENACE SCHEDULES, GENERAL MOTORS CORP.

TRACKER—Continued

Service Interval In Miles ①

Note (Change Engine Oil & Filter): Normal Service Every 7.5 Months Or 7500 Miles; Severe Service Every 3 Months Or 3000 Miles

Recommended Service	3000	6000	7500	9000	12000	15000	18000	21000	22500	24000	27000	30000	33000	36000	37500	39000	42000	45000	48000	51000	52500	54000	57000	60000	63000	66000	67500	69000	72000	75000	78000	81000	82500	84000	87000	90000	93000	96000	97500	99000
DRIVE AXLE																																								
Change Differential Lubricant						X						X						X						X						X						X				
Inspect CV Joint Boots & Wheel Bearings	S	S	N	S	S	N	S	S	N	S	S	N	S	S	N	S	S	N	S	S	N	S	S	N	S	S	N	S	S	N	S	S	N	S	S	N	S	S	N	S
Inspect & Lubricate Driveshafts			S			X			S			X			S			X			S			X			S			X			S			X			S	
ENGINE																																								
Change Engine Coolant																					X																			
Change Engine Oil & Filter	Normal Service Every 7.5 Months Or 7500 Miles; Severe Service Every 3 Months Or 3000 Miles																																							
Inspect Carburetor Or Fuel Injector & Catalytic Converter	Every 100,000 Miles																																							
Inspect Carburetor Or TBI Unit Fastener Security		S	N																																					
Inspect Cooling System & Protection Level						X						X						X						X						X						X				
Inspect Distributor Cap & Rotor						S						S						S						S						S						S				
Inspect Drive Belts						S						S						S						S						S						S				
Inspect ECM & Related Sensors	Every 100,000 Miles																																							
Inspect EGR System	Every 100,000 Miles																																							
Inspect Emission System Hoses & Tubes						S						S						S						S						S						S				
Inspect Engine Air Filter Element	S	S		S	S	S	S	S		S	S	S	S	S		S	S	S	S	S		S	S	S	S	S		S	S	S	S	S		S	S	S	S	S		S
Inspect Fuel & Vapor System & Idle Speed						X						X						X						X						X						X				
Inspect Ignition Coils						X						X						X						X						X						X				
Inspect Ignition Timing						X						X						X						X						X						X				
Inspect PCV Valve						S						S						S						S						S						S				
Inspect Spark Plug Wires						S						S						S						S						S						S				
Inspect Thermostatic Air Cleaner System Operation						X						X						X						X						X						X				
Inspect Underhood Wiring Harness & Connections						X						X						X						X						X						X				
Replace Drive Belts																								X															S	
Replace Engine Air Filter Element												X												X												X				

TRACKER—Continued

Recommended Service	Service Interval In Miles①																																							
	3000	6000	7500	9000	12000	15000	18000	21000	22500	24000	27000	30000	33000	36000	37500	39000	42000	45000	48000	51000	52500	54000	57000	60000	63000	66000	67500	69000	72000	75000	78000	81000	82500	84000	87000	90000	93000	96000	97500	99000
ENGINE																																								
Replace EVAP Canister, 2002	Every 100,000 Miles																																							
Replace EVAP Canister, 2003–04	Every 120,000 Miles																																							
Replace Exhaust System Hangers																								X																
Replace Fuel Filter	Every 30 Months Or 30,000 Miles																																							
Replace Fuel Hoses, Connections & Filler Cap & Spark Plug Wires																								X																
Replace Spark Plugs												X												X												X				
Replace O2 Sensor	Every 80,000 Miles																																							
Replace PCV Valve	Every 50,000 Miles																																							
Replace Timing Belt	②																																							
STEERING, SUSPENSION & TIRES																																								
Clean & Repack Front Wheel Bearings, 2WD	At 30,000 Miles Or At Brake Relinings																																							
Inspect Leaf Springs						S						X						S						X						S						X				
Inspect Power Steering & Steering & Suspension System		S	N		S	N	S		N	S		X		S	N		S	N	S		N	S		X		S	N		S	N	S		N	S		X		S	N	
Inspect Shock Absorbers			X			X						X						X						X						X						X				
Inspect Steering Wheel Freeplay, Gearbox Lubricant & Linkage	S	S		S	S	S	S	S		S	S	S	S	S		S	S	S	S	S		S	S	S	S	S		S	S	S	S	S		S	S	S	S	S		S
Inspect Wheel Discs & Free-Wheeling Hubs			X			X			X			X			X			X			X			X			X			X			X			X			X	
Rotate Tires		S	N		S	N	S		N	S		X		S	N		S	N	S		N	S		X		S	N		S	N	S		N	S		X		S	N	
Tighten Chassis & Suspension Fasteners		S	N		S	N	S			S		X		S			S	N	S			S		X		S			S	N	S			S		X		S		

N — Normal Service
S — Severe Service
X — Normal Or Severe Service
① — After vehicle passes 99,000 mile mark return to beginning of mileage table & start cycle over again.
② — Inspect every 60,000 miles, then replace at 100,000 miles.

VUE

Service Interval In Miles①

Recommended Service	3750	7500	11250	15000	18750	22500	26250	30000	33750	37500	41250	45000	48750	52500	56250	60000	63750	67500	71250	75000	78750	82500	86250	90000	93750	97500	101250	105000
BODY																												
Inspect Seat Belts & Restraint Systems	At Least Once Every 6 Months																											
Inspect Wiper Blades & Inserts	At Least Once Every 6 Months																											
Lubricate Door Check Straps & Hinges				X				X				X				X				X				X				X
Lubricate Headlamp Doors		X		X		X		X		X		X		X		X		X		X		X		X		X		X
Lubricate Hood Latch		X		X		X		X		X		X		X		X		X		X		X		X		X		X
Lubricate Sunroof		X		X		X		X		X		X		X		X		X		X		X		X		X		X
Replace Cabin Air Filter	Every 12 Months Or 12,000 Miles; In Dusty Areas Change More Often																											
BRAKES																												
Inspect Brake Drums & Shoes	At Oil Change Intervals																											
Inspect Brake Hoses, Lines & Connections	At Oil Change Intervals																											
Inspect Disc Brake Calipers For Freedom Of Movement (Lubricate If Required)	At Oil Change Intervals																											
Inspect Disc Brake Pads & Rotors	At Oil Change Intervals																											
CLUTCH & TRANSAXLE																												
Add DEX-CVT Additive To VTi Variable Transmission	Every 50,000 Miles																											
Change Automatic Or VTi Transaxle Fluid & Filter, 2002–03	No Normal Service; Severe Service Every 50,000 Miles																											
Change Automatic Transmission Fluid, 2004–06	Normal Service Every 100,000 Miles; Severe Service Every 25,000 Miles																											
Change VTi VariableTransaxle Fluid & Filter	Normal Service Every 100,000 Miles; Severe Service Every 50,000 Miles																											
DRIVESHAFT																												
Change Engine Coolant & Inspect Pressure Cap, 2002–03	Every 60 Months Or 100,000 Miles																											
Change Engine Coolant & Inspect Pressure Cap, 2004–06	Every 60 Months Or 150,000 Miles																											
Change Engine Oil & Filter②	S	X	S	X	S	X	S	X	S	X	S	X	S	X	S	X	S	X	S	X	S	X	S	X	S	X	S	X
Change Rear Drive Module Fluid, 3.5L	Normal Service Every 100,000 Miles; Severe Service Every 50,000 Miles																											

Service Interval In Miles ①

Recommended Service	36000	37500	39000	42000	45000	48000	51000	54000	57000	60000	63000	66000	69000	72000	75000	78000	81000	84000	87000	90000	93000	96000	99000
DRIVESHAFT																							
Change Rear Drive Module & Power Take Off Unit Fluid, 2.2L	Normal Service Every 100,000 Miles; Severe Service Every 50,000 Miles																						
Change Transfer Assembly Fluid, 3.5L	Normal Service At 100,000 Miles Then Every 50,000 Miles Thereafter; Severe Service Every 25,000 Miles																						
ENGINE																							
Inspect Air Filter	Severe Service Every 15,000 Miles																						
Inspect Cooling System & Protection Level					X															X			
Inspect CV Joint Boots	X			X		X		X		X		X		X		X		X		X		X	
Inspect Drive Belts & Coolant Hoses, 2002–03	Every 18,000 Miles																						
Inspect Drive Belts & Coolant Hoses, 2004–06	Every 25,000 Miles																						
Inspect Emission Hoses, Lines & Connections, 2002–03	Every 30,000 Miles																						
Inspect Exhaust System, 2002–03	X			X		X		X		X		X		X		X		X		X		X	
Inspect Exhaust System, 2004–06	Every 25,000 Miles																						
Inspect Fuel System	Every 25,000 Miles																						
Inspect Fuel Hoses, Lines & Connections							X								X								
Inspect Fuel Tank Filler Cap							X								X								
Inspect Valve Clearance, 3.5L	Every 100,000 Miles																						
Replace Air Filter, 2002–03	Normal Service Every 30,000 Miles; More Frequently In Severe Service Or Dusty Conditions																						
Replace Air Filter, 2004	Every 25,000 Miles																						
Replace Air Filter, 2005–06	Every 50,000 Miles																						
Replace Fuel Filter	Every 100,000 Miles																						
Replace Spark Plugs	Every 100,000 Miles																						
Replace Timing Belt, 3.0L, 2002–03	Every 100,000 Miles																						
Replace Timing Belt, 3.5L, 2004–06	Normal Service Every 100,000 Miles; Severe Service Every 50,000 Miles																						
STEERING, SUSPENSION & TIRES																							
Inspect Ball Joint Seals	X			X		X		X		X		X		X		X		X		X		X	
Inspect Suspension	X			X		X		X		X		X		X		X		X		X		X	
Rotate Tires	Every 6000 Miles																						

VEHICLE MAINTENANCE SCHEDULES, GENERAL MOTORS CORP.

BTSI — Brake Transaxle Shift Interlock
N — Normal Service
S — Severe Service
X — Normal Or Severe Service
① — After vehicle passes 100,000 mile mark return to beginning of mileage table & start cycle over again.
② — On models equipped with Engine Oil Life Moniter, change engine oil when message appears in message display center. Do not exceed 12 months between oil and filter change intervals.

DAIMLERCHRYSLER CORP./JEEP

Page No.

CHRYSLER

Pacifica (Volume 1). 4-1
PT Cruiser (Volume 1) 5-1
Town & Country (Volume 1). 2-1
Voyager (Volume 1). 2-1

DODGE

Caravan (Volume 1) 2-1
Dakota (Volume 1) 3-1
Durango (Volume 1) 3-1
Full-Size Vans (Volume 1) 1-1
Ram 1500–3500 Pickups (Volume 1). 1-1
Sprinter (Volume 1). 6-1

JEEP

Commander (Volume 1). 8-1
Grand Cherokee (Volume 1) 8-1
Liberty (Volume 1) 9-1
Wrangler (Volume 1). 7-1

GENERAL SERVICE

Air Bag Systems 4-1
Air Conditioning (Volume 1). 10-1
All-Wheel Drive (Volume 1). 24-1
Alternators (Volume 1). 13-1
Anti-Lock Brake Systems 5-1
Axles, Drive (Volume 1). 25-1
Axles, Front Wheel Drive (Volume 1) 23-1
Brakes
    Anti-Lock Brake Systems 5-1
    Disc Brakes (Volume 1) 17-1

Page No.

    Drum Brakes (Volume 1) 18-1
    Hydraulic Brake Systems (Volume 1). 19-1
    Power Brake Units (Volume 1) 20-1
Cooling Fans (Volume 1). 11-1
Cruise Control Systems 2-1
Dash Gauges 1-1
Dash Panel Service (Volume 1) 14-1
Disc Brakes (Volume 1). 17-1
Drive Axles (Volume 1) 25-1
Drum Brakes (Volume 1). 18-1
Electric Cooling Fans (Volume 1). 11-1
Engine Cooling Fans (Volume 1) 11-1
Engine Rebuilding Specifications (Volume 1). . . 27-1
Fans, Engine Cooling (Volume 1) 11-1
Front Wheel Drive Axle (Volume 1). 23-1
Hydraulic Brake Systems (Volume 1). 19-1
Machine Shop Specifications (Volume 1) 27-1
Passive Restraint Systems 4-1
Power Brake Units (Volume 1). 20-1
Power Steering (Volume 1) 16-1
Speed Control Systems 2-1
Starter Motors (Volume 1) 12-1
Steering
    Power Steering (Volume 1). 16-1
    Steering Columns (Volume 1) 15-1
Steering Columns (Volume 1) 15-1
Tire Pressure Monitoring Systems. 6-1
Transfer Cases (Volume 1). 22-1
Universal Joints (Volume 1). 26-1
Vacuum Pumps (Volume 1) 21-1
Variable Speed Fans (Volume 1) 11-1
Warning Indicators. 1-1
Wiper Systems 3-1

DAIMLERCHRYSLER CORP./JEEP

Page No.

CHRYSLER

Pacifica (Volume 1)............................. 4-1
PT Cruiser (Volume 1) 5-1
Town & Country (Volume 1).................... 2-1
Voyager (Volume 1)............................ 2-1

DODGE

Caravan (Volume 1) 2-1
Dakota (Volume 1) 3-1
Durango (Volume 1) 3-1
Full-Size Vans (Volume 1) 1-1
Ram 1500–3500 Pickups (Volume 1)............ 1-1
Sprinter (Volume 1)........................... 6-1

JEEP

Commander (Volume 1)....................... 8-1
Grand Cherokee (Volume 1) 8-1
Liberty (Volume 1) 9-1
Wrangler (Volume 1).......................... 7-1

GENERAL SERVICE

Air Bag Systems 4-1
Air Conditioning (Volume 1) 10-1
All-Wheel Drive (Volume 1).................... 24-1
Alternators (Volume 1)........................ 13-1
Anti-Lock Brake Systems 5-1
Axles, Drive (Volume 1)....................... 25-1
Axles, Front Wheel Drive (Volume 1) 23-1
Brakes
    Anti-Lock Brake Systems 5-1
    Disc Brakes (Volume 1) 17-1

Page No.

    Drum Brakes (Volume 1) 18-1
    Hydraulic Brake Systems (Volume 1)........ 19-1
    Power Brake Units (Volume 1)............. 20-1
Cooling Fans (Volume 1)..................... 11-1
Cruise Control Systems 2-1
Dash Gauges 1-1
Dash Panel Service (Volume 1) 14-1
Disc Brakes (Volume 1)...................... 17-1
Drive Axles (Volume 1) 25-1
Drum Brakes (Volume 1)..................... 18-1
Electric Cooling Fans (Volume 1)............. 11-1
Engine Cooling Fans (Volume 1) 11-1
Engine Rebuilding Specifications (Volume 1)... 27-1
Fans, Engine Cooling (Volume 1) 11-1
Front Wheel Drive Axle (Volume 1)............ 23-1
Hydraulic Brake Systems (Volume 1).......... 19-1
Machine Shop Specifications (Volume 1) 27-1
Passive Restraint Systems 4-1
Power Brake Units (Volume 1)................ 20-1
Power Steering (Volume 1) 16-1
Speed Control Systems...................... 2-1
Starter Motors (Volume 1) 12-1
Steering
    Power Steering (Volume 1)................. 16-1
    Steering Columns (Volume 1) 15-1
Steering Columns (Volume 1) 15-1
Tire Pressure Monitoring Systems............. 6-1
Transfer Cases (Volume 1)................... 22-1
Universal Joints (Volume 1) 26-1
Vacuum Pumps (Volume 1) 21-1
Variable Speed Fans (Volume 1).............. 11-1
Warning Indicators.......................... 1-1
Wiper Systems 3-1

DASH GAUGES & WARNING INDICATORS

NOTE: On Air Bag Equipped Models, Refer To "Air Bag System Precautions" Located In The Front Of This Manual For System Disarming & Arming Procedures.

NOTE: Refer To The "Electronic Instrumentation" Section In MOTOR's "Domestic Engine Performance & Driveability Manual" For Information Related To Electronic Instrumentation.

NOTE: Refer To "Computer Relearn Procedures" Located In The Front Of This Manual When Battery Power To The Computer Has Been Interrupted.

INDEX

	Page No.		Page No.		Page No.
Diagnostic Trouble Code		Lamp	1-1	Durango	1-1
Interpretation	1-1	Check Engine Warning Lamp	1-1	Full Size Pickup	1-1
Precautions	1-1	Low Fuel Warning Lamp	1-1	Full Size Van	1-1
Air Bag Systems	1-1	Oil Pressure Indicator Lamp	1-1	Grand Cherokee	1-2
Battery Ground Cable	1-1	Safety Belt Warning Lamp	1-1	Liberty	1-2
Troubleshooting	1-1	Wiring Diagrams	1-1	PT Cruiser	1-2
Air Bag Warning Lamp	1-1	Caravan, Town & Country &		Pacifica	1-2
Anti-Lock Brake Warning Lamp	1-1	Voyager	1-1	Sprinter	1-2
Brake System Warning Lamp	1-1	Commander	1-1	Wrangler	1-2
Charging System Warning		Dakota	1-1		

PRECAUTIONS

AIR BAG SYSTEMS

Refer to "Air Bag System Precautions" in the front of this manual for system disarming and arming procedures.

BATTERY GROUND CABLE

Prior to service disconnect battery ground cable and isolate as required.

TROUBLESHOOTING

AIR BAG WARNING LAMP

Air bag warning lamp illuminates when there is an air bag system concern.
Refer to MOTOR's "Air Bag Quick Reference Guide" or "Air Bag Diagnostics CD."

ANTI-LOCK BRAKE WARNING LAMP

The Anti-lock brake warning lamp will illuminate if the system controller detects any fault in the anti-lock brake system. Normal brake system operation will remain operational, but wheels could lock during panic stop. Refer to "Anti-Lock Brake" chapter.

BRAKE SYSTEM WARNING LAMP

1. Brake fluid level switch.
2. Low brake fluid level.
3. Park brake system.

4. Wiring circuits and bulb.
5. Instrument cluster printed circuits.

CHARGING SYSTEM WARNING LAMP

1. Wiring circuits and bulb.
2. Inspect BCM.
3. Inspect for corroded terminals.
4. Alternator.
5. Instrument cluster printed circuits.

CHECK ENGINE WARNING LAMP

Check engine or malfunction indicator lamp (MIL) indicator is illuminated by Powertrain Control Module (PCM). Refer to MOTOR's "Domestic Engine Performance & Driveability Manual" for lamp diagnosis.

LOW FUEL WARNING LAMP

1. Fuel gauge and indicator bulb.
2. Low fuel level switch.
3. Inspect sensor.
4. Instrument cluster printed circuits.

OIL PRESSURE INDICATOR LAMP

1. Wiring circuits, bulb and fuse.
2. Oil pressure switch.
3. Low engine oil level.
4. Instrument cluster printed circuits.

SAFETY BELT WARNING LAMP

1. Seat belt switch and fuse.

2. Wiring circuits and bulb.
3. Instrument cluster printed circuits.

DIAGNOSTIC TROUBLE CODE INTERPRETATION

Refer to **Fig. 1** for DTC interpretation.

WIRING DIAGRAMS

CARAVAN, TOWN & COUNTRY & VOYAGER

Refer to **Figs. 2 and 3** for wiring diagrams.

COMMANDER

Refer to **Fig. 4** for wiring diagrams.

DAKOTA

Refer to **Figs. 5 and 6** for wiring diagrams.

DURANGO

Refer to **Figs. 7 and 8** for wiring diagrams.

FULL SIZE PICKUP

Refer to **Figs. 9 and 10** for wiring diagrams.

FULL SIZE VAN

Refer to **Fig. 11** for wiring diagrams.

DASH GAUGES & WARNING INDICATORS

GRAND CHEROKEE

Refer to **Figs. 12 and 13** for wiring diagrams.

LIBERTY

Refer to **Figs. 14 and 15** for wiring diagrams.

PACIFICA

Refer to **Fig. 16** for wiring diagrams.

PT CRUISER

Refer to **Figs. 17 and 18** for wiring diagrams.

SPRINTER

Refer to **Fig. 19** for wiring diagrams.

WRANGLER

Refer to **Fig. 20** for wiring diagrams.

Code	Interpretation
B1200	Air Bag Warning Indicator Circuit Low
B1201	Air Bag Warning Indicator Circuit Open
B123F	Menu Switch Stuck
B1240	Step Switch Stuck
B1241	C/T Switch Stuck
B1242	Reset Switch Stuck
B1243	Rear Park Assist Disable Switch Stuck
B1612	Panel Illumination Control Circuit
B1613	Panel Illumination Control Circuit Low
B1615	Panel Illumination Control Circuit Open
B210D	Battery Voltage Low
B211A	Ignition RUN/ACC/SPAD Control Circuit Low
B211B	Ignition RUN/ACC/SPAD Control Circuit High
B2107	Ignition Switch Sense Input Circuit/Performance
B2122	Ignition Run Control Circuit Low
B2123	Ignition Run Control Circuit High
B2213	CCN Internal
B222C	Vehicle Configuration Not Programmed
U0019	CAN B BUS
U0141	Lost Communication With Front Control Module
U0151	Lost Communication With Occupant Restraint Controller
U0154	Lost Communication With Occupant Classification Module
U0156	Lost Communication With EOM
U0159	Lost Communication With Parking Assist Control Module
U0164	Lost Communication With HVAC Control Module
U0168	Lost Communication With Vehicle Security Control Module (SKREEM/WCM)
U0169	Lost Communication With Sunroof Control Module
U0184	Lost Communication With Radio
U0186	Lost Communication With Audio Amplifier
U0195	Lost Communication With SDARS
U0196	Lost Communication With Vehicle Entertainment Control Module
U0197	Lost Communication With Hands Free Phone Module
U0199	Lost Communication With Drivers Door Module
U0200	Lost Communication With Passenger Door Module
U0208	Lost Communication With Heated Seat Control Module
U0209	Lost Communication With Memory Seat Control Module
U0212	Lost Communication With SCCM CAN B
U0231	Lost Communication With Rain Sensing Module
U0241	Lost Communication With Auto High Beam Headlamp Control Module
U1008	LIN 1 BUS
U1121	Lost Communication With LIN ECU 1
U1122	Lost Communication With LIN ECU 2

Fig. 1   DTC interpretation

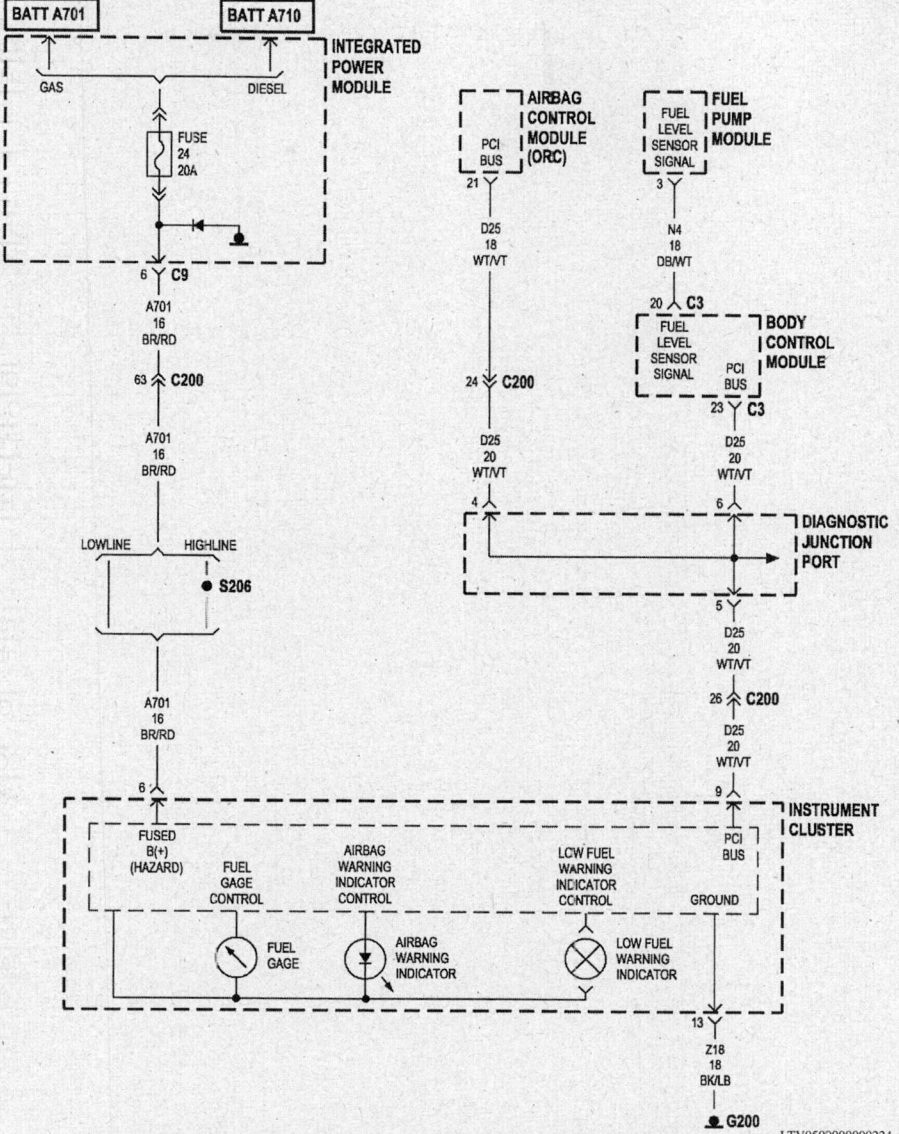

Fig. 2 Instrument Cluster (Part 1 of 10). 2002–04 Caravan, Town & Country & Voyager

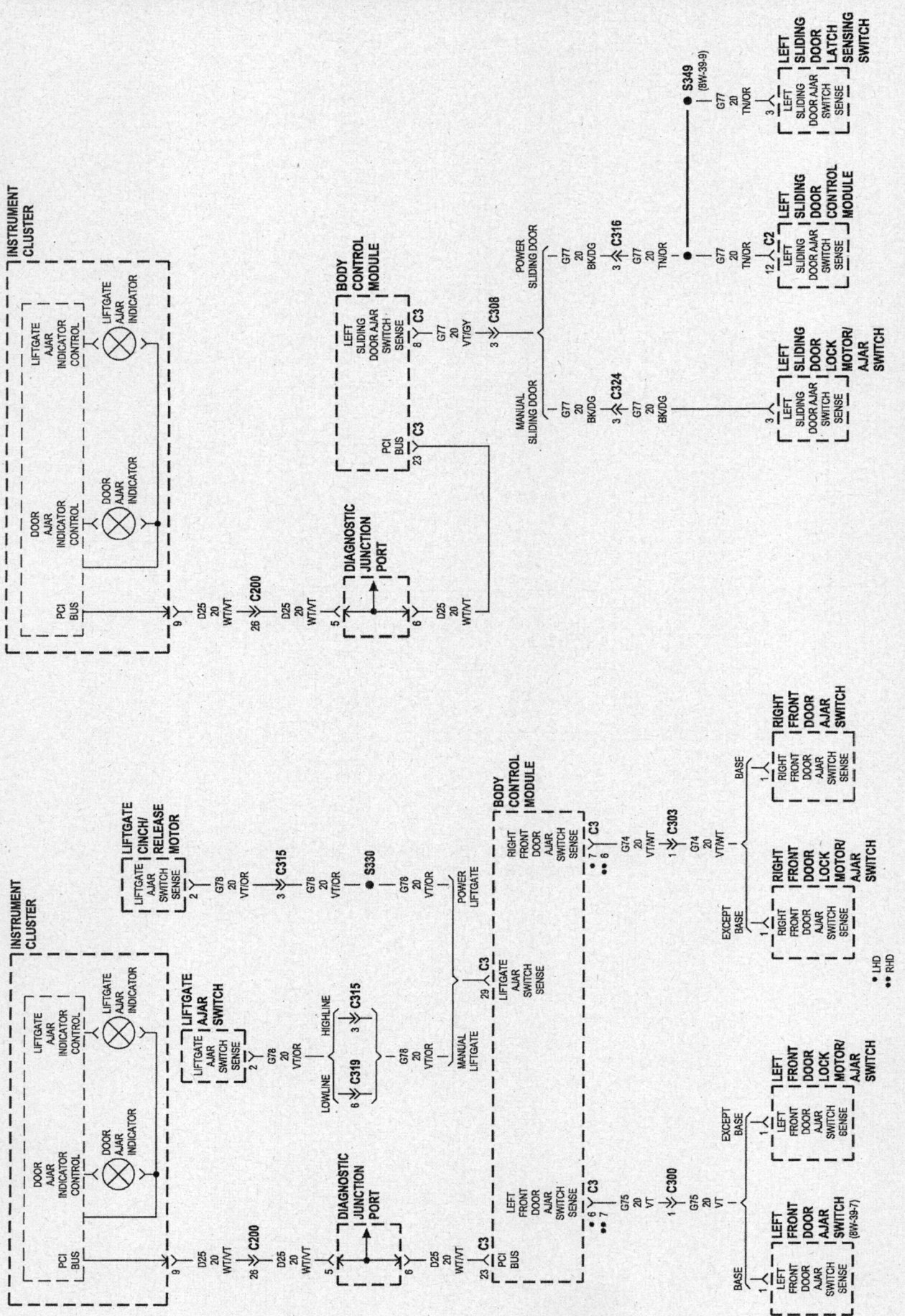

Fig. 2 Instrument Cluster (Part 3 of 10). 2002–04 Caravan, Town & Country & Voyager

Fig. 2 Instrument Cluster (Part 2 of 10). 2002–04 Caravan, Town & Country & Voyager

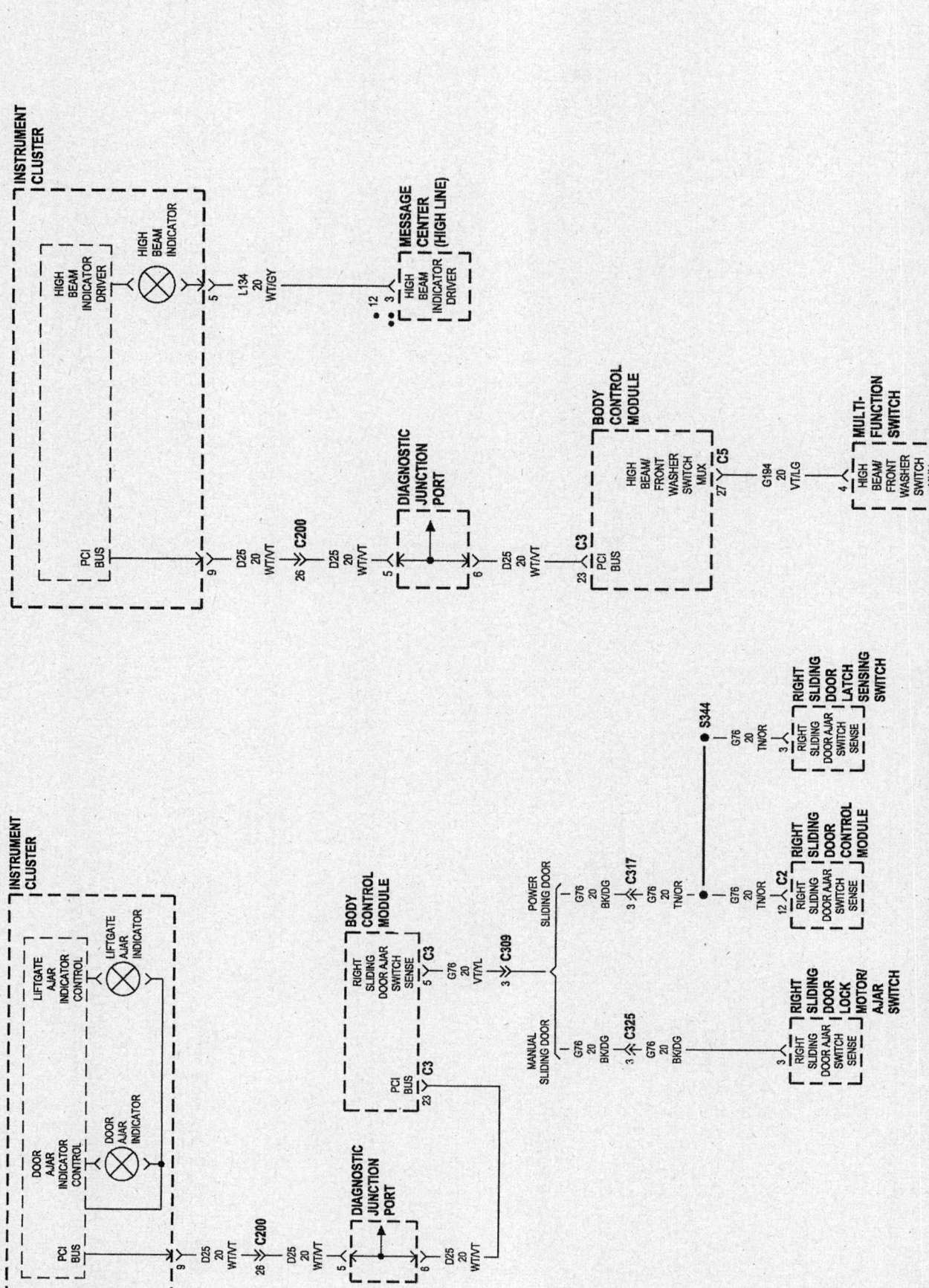

Fig. 2   Instrument Cluster (Part 5 of 10). 2002-04 Caravan, Town & Country & Voyager

Fig. 2   Instrument Cluster (Part 4 of 10). 2002-04 Caravan, Town & Country & Voyager

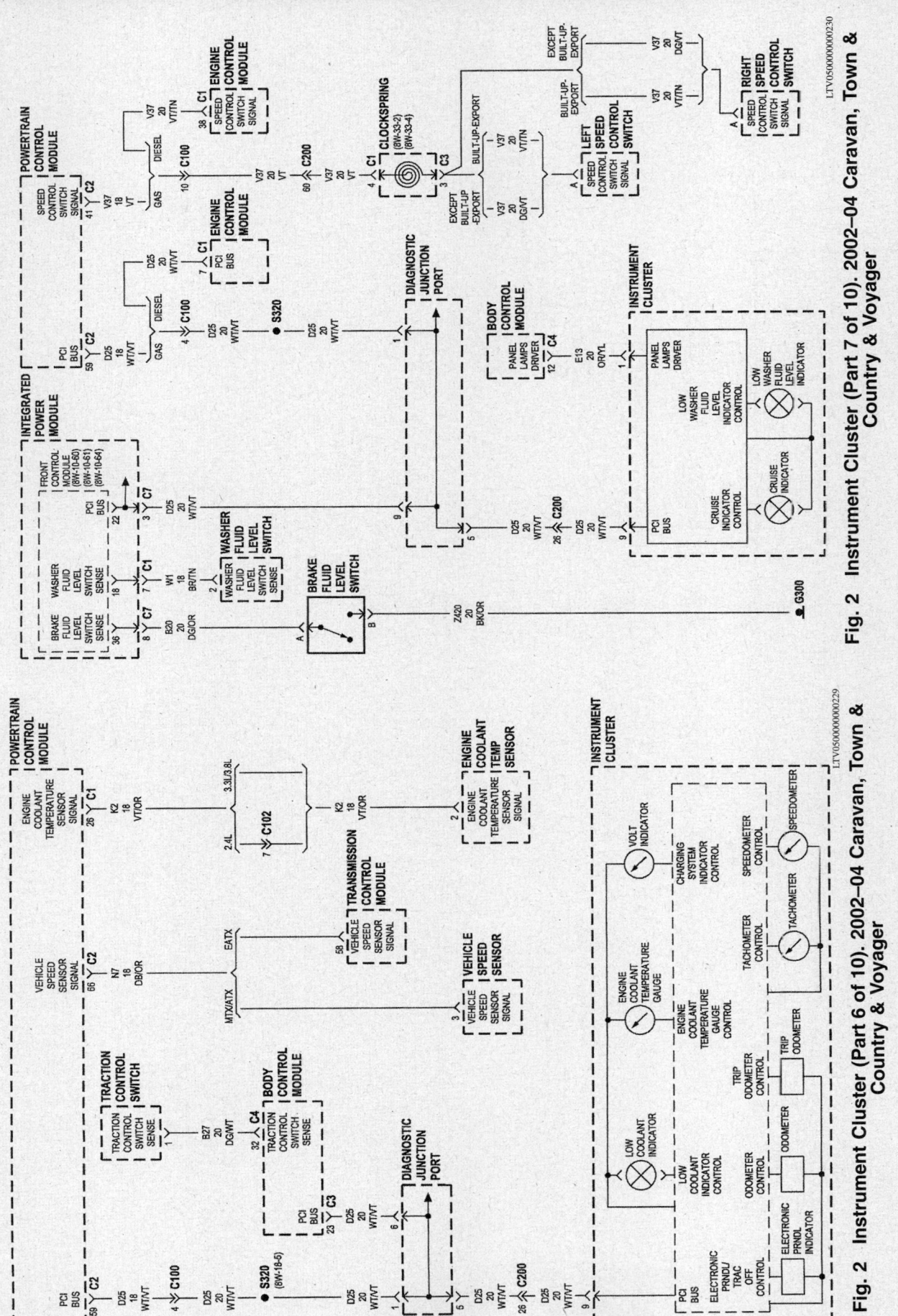

Fig. 2   Instrument Cluster (Part 7 of 10). 2002-04 Caravan, Town & Country & Voyager

Fig. 2   Instrument Cluster (Part 6 of 10). 2002-04 Caravan, Town & Country & Voyager

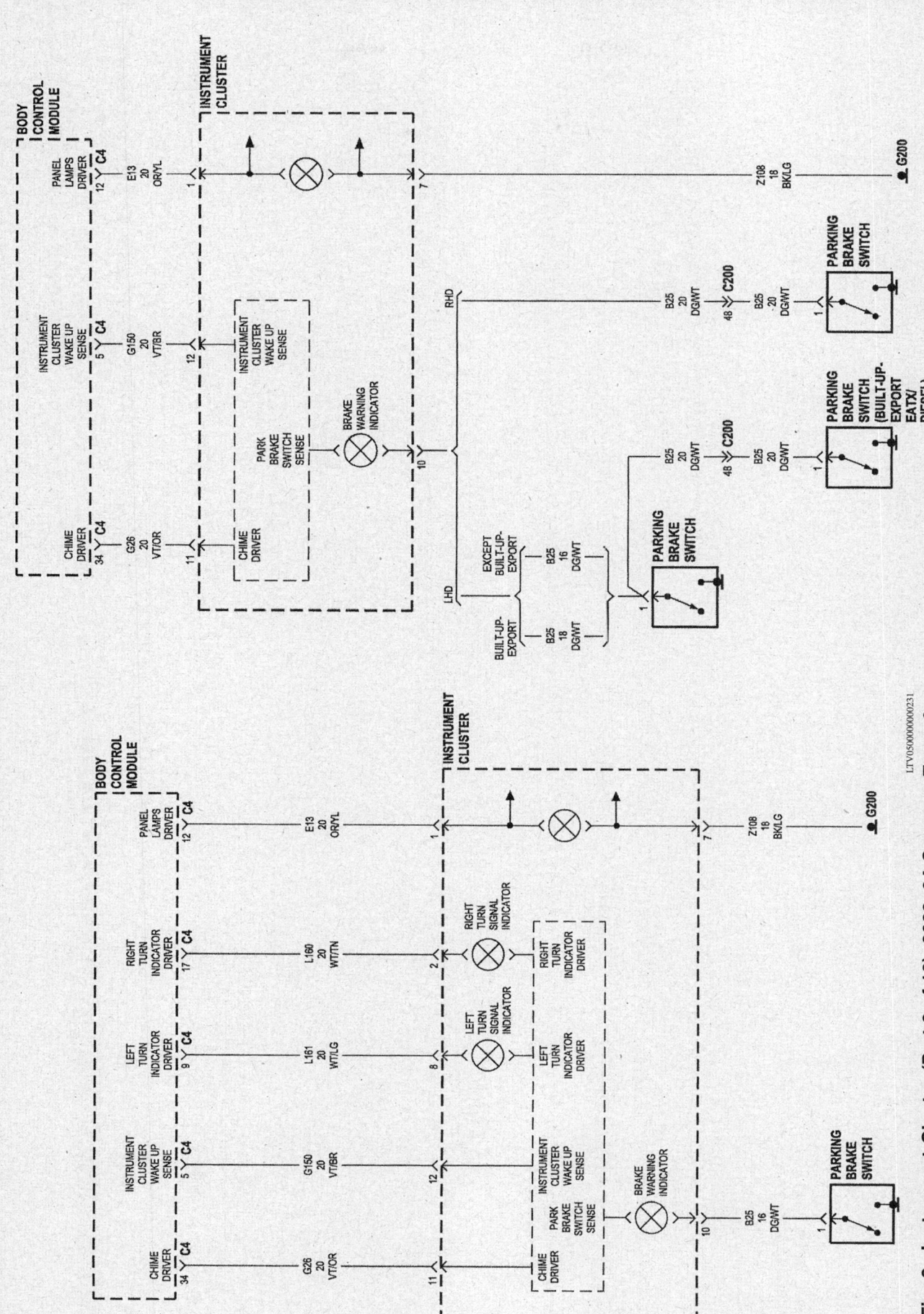

Fig. 2 Instrument Cluster (Part 9 of 10). 2002-04 Caravan, Town & Country & Voyager

Fig. 2 Instrument Cluster (Part 8 of 10). 2002-04 Caravan, Town & Country & Voyager

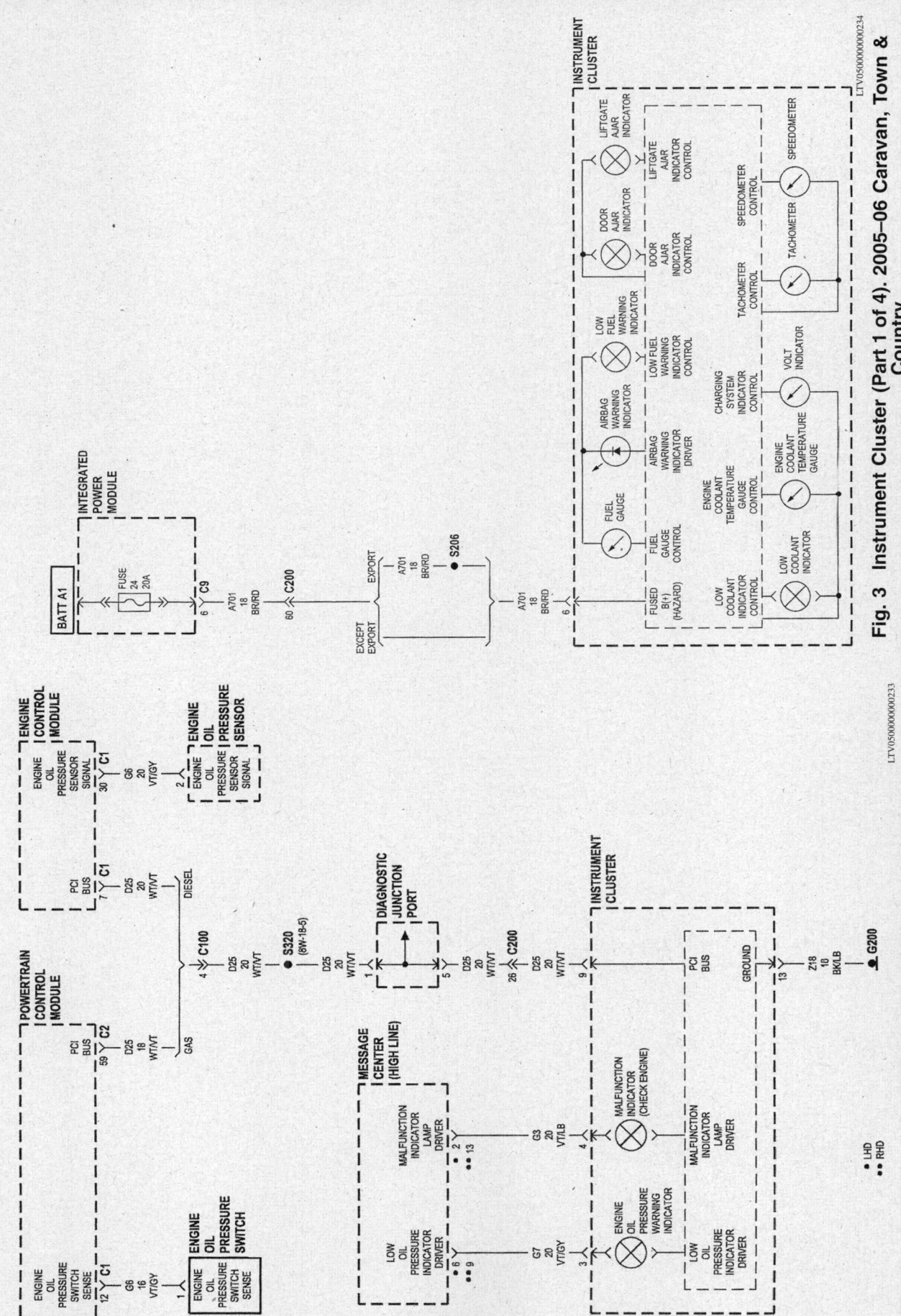

Fig. 3 Instrument Cluster (Part 1 of 4). 2005-06 Caravan, Town & Country

Fig. 2 Instrument Cluster (Part 10 of 10). 2002-04 Caravan, Town & Country & Voyager

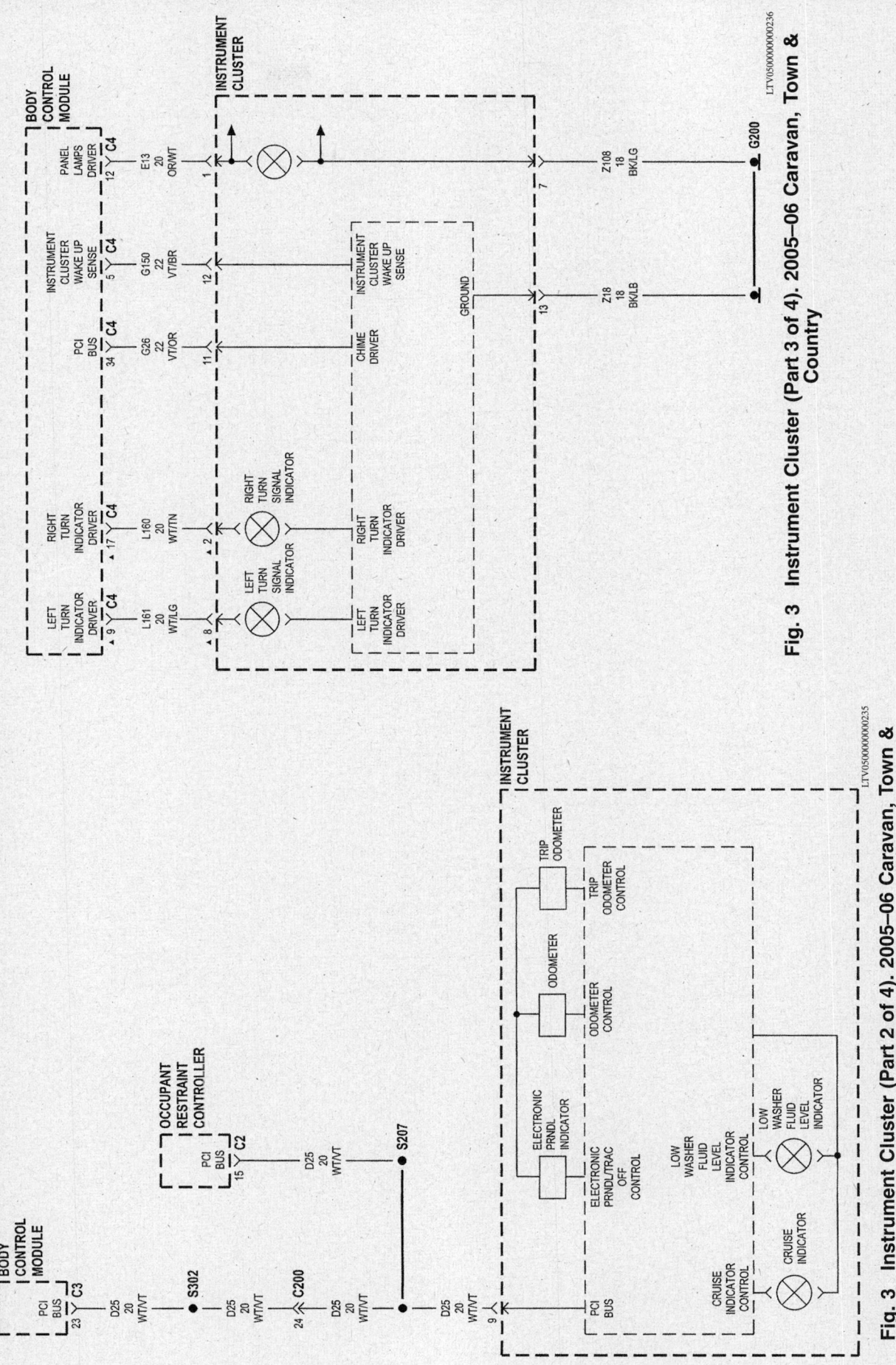

Fig. 3 Instrument Cluster (Part 3 of 4). 2005–06 Caravan, Town & Country

Fig. 3 Instrument Cluster (Part 2 of 4). 2005–06 Caravan, Town & Country

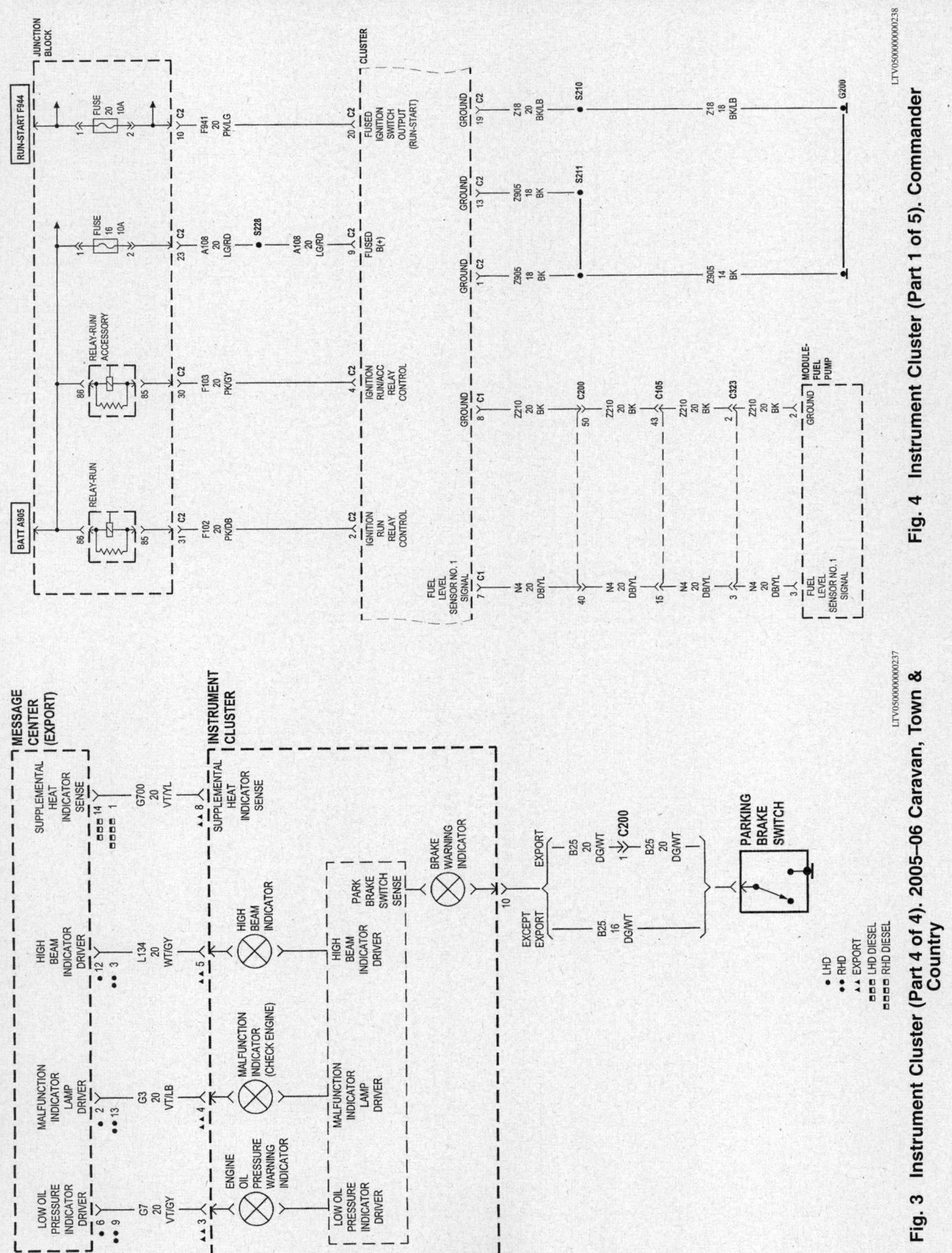

Fig. 4 Instrument Cluster (Part 1 of 5). Commander

Fig. 3 Instrument Cluster (Part 4 of 4). 2005–06 Caravan, Town & Country

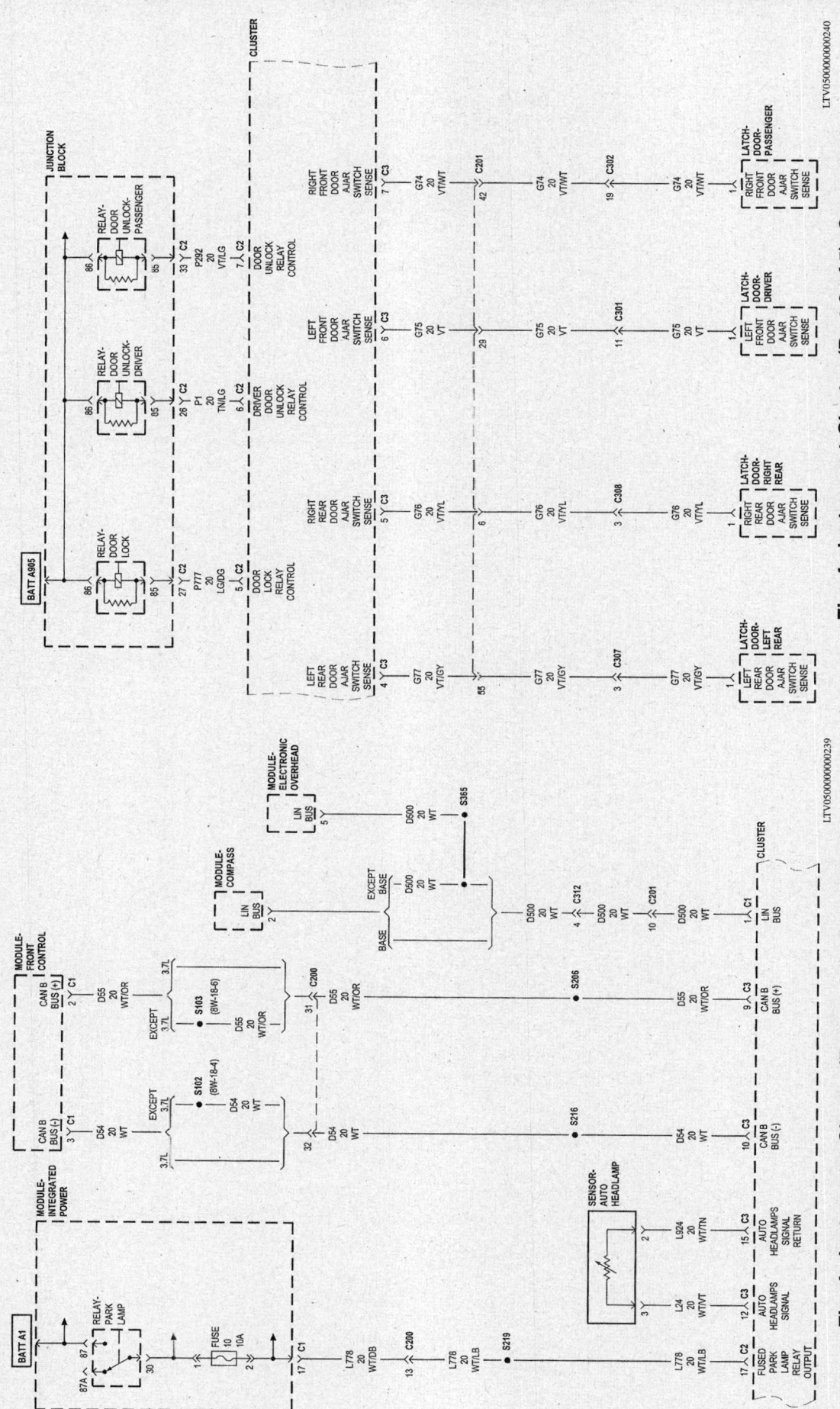

Fig. 4 Instrument Cluster (Part 3 of 5). Commander

Fig. 4 Instrument Cluster (Part 2 of 5). Commander

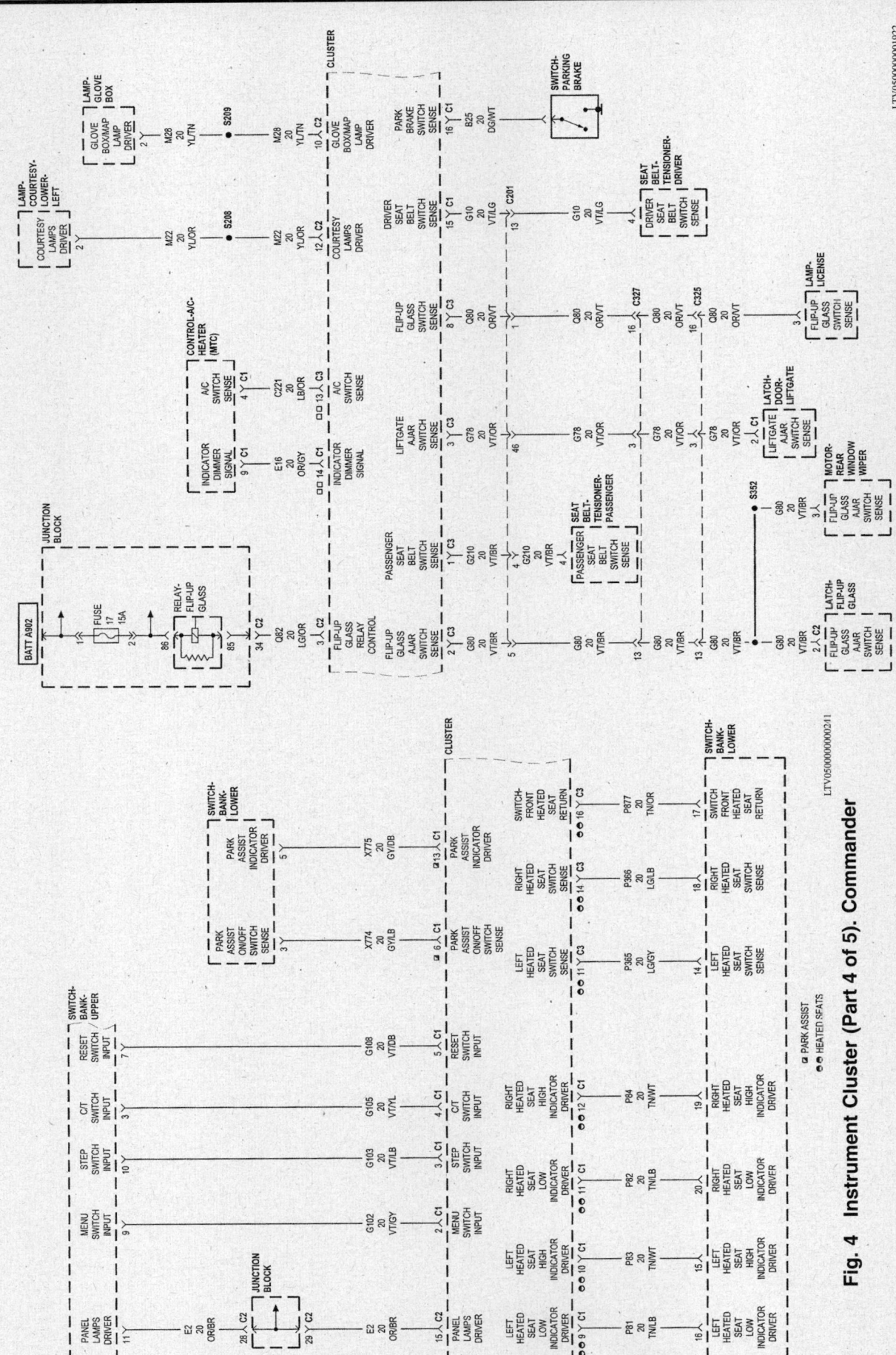

Fig. 4 Instrument Cluster (Part 5 of 5). Commander

Fig. 4 Instrument Cluster (Part 4 of 5). Commander

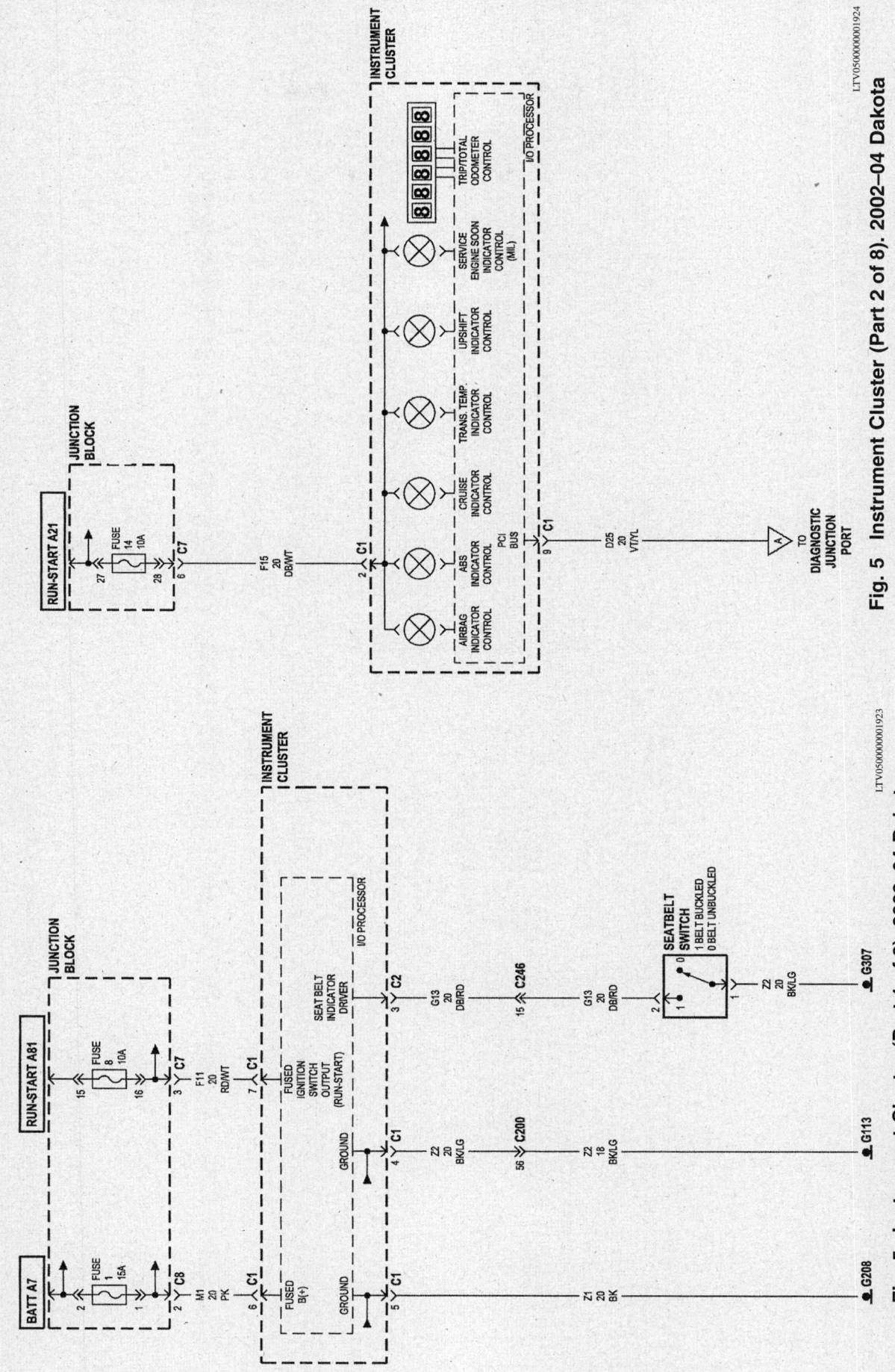

Fig. 5 Instrument Cluster (Part 2 of 8). 2002–04 Dakota

Fig. 5 Instrument Cluster (Part 1 of 8). 2002–04 Dakota

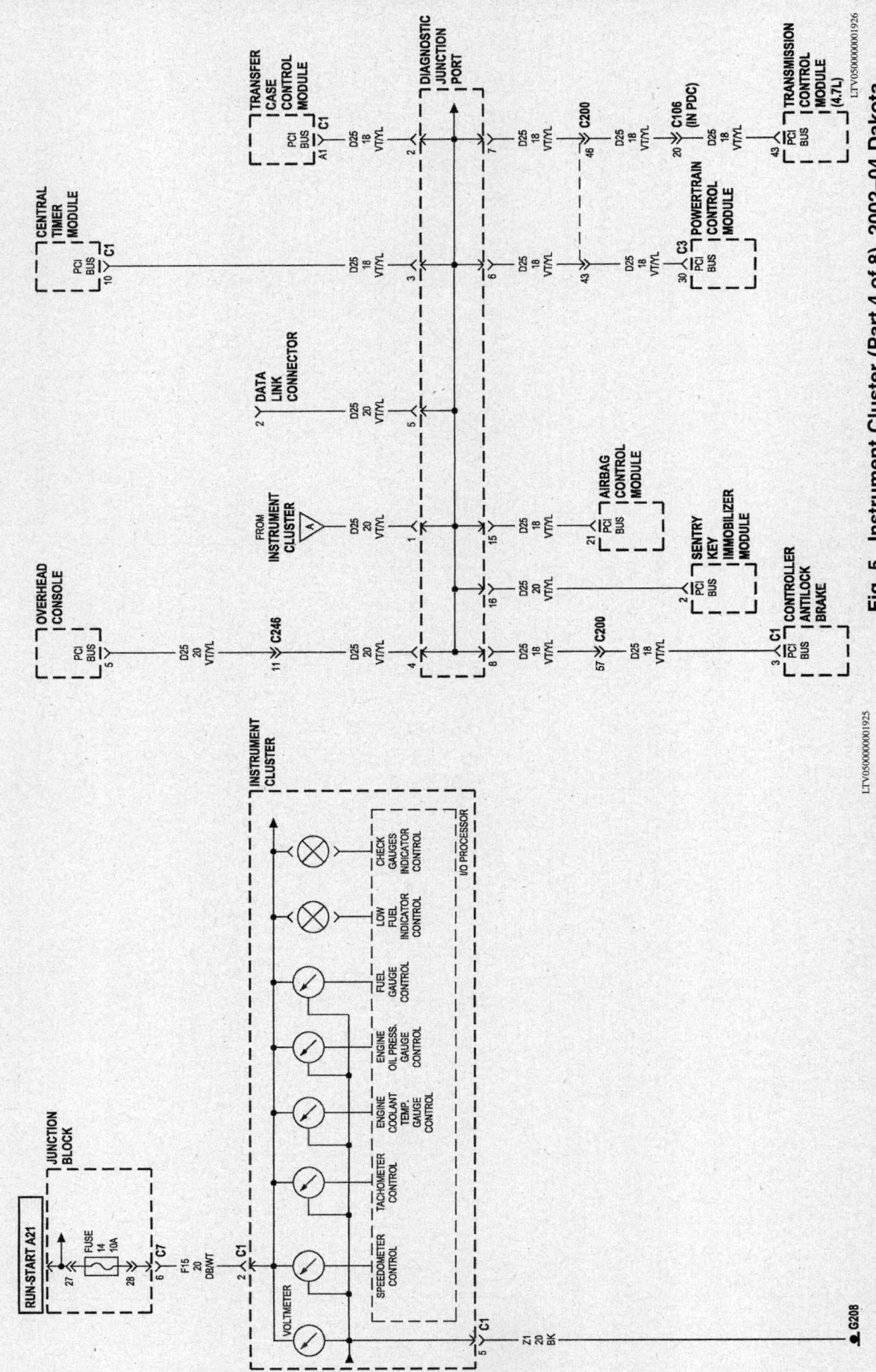

Fig. 5 Instrument Cluster (Part 4 of 8). 2002–04 Dakota

Fig. 5 Instrument Cluster (Part 3 of 8). 2002–04 Dakota

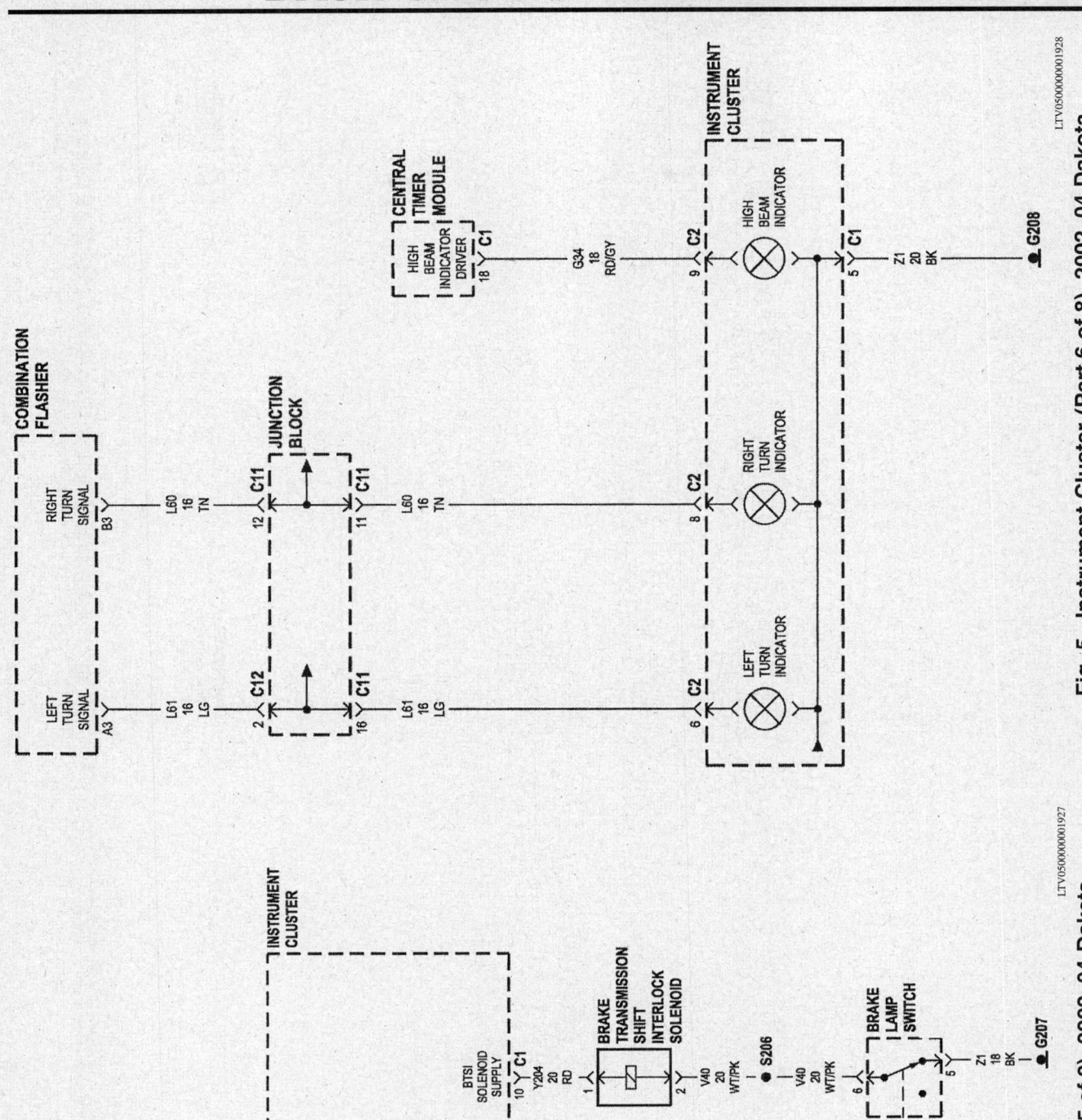

Fig. 5 Instrument Cluster (Part 6 of 8). 2002–04 Dakota

Fig. 5 Instrument Cluster (Part 5 of 8). 2002–04 Dakota

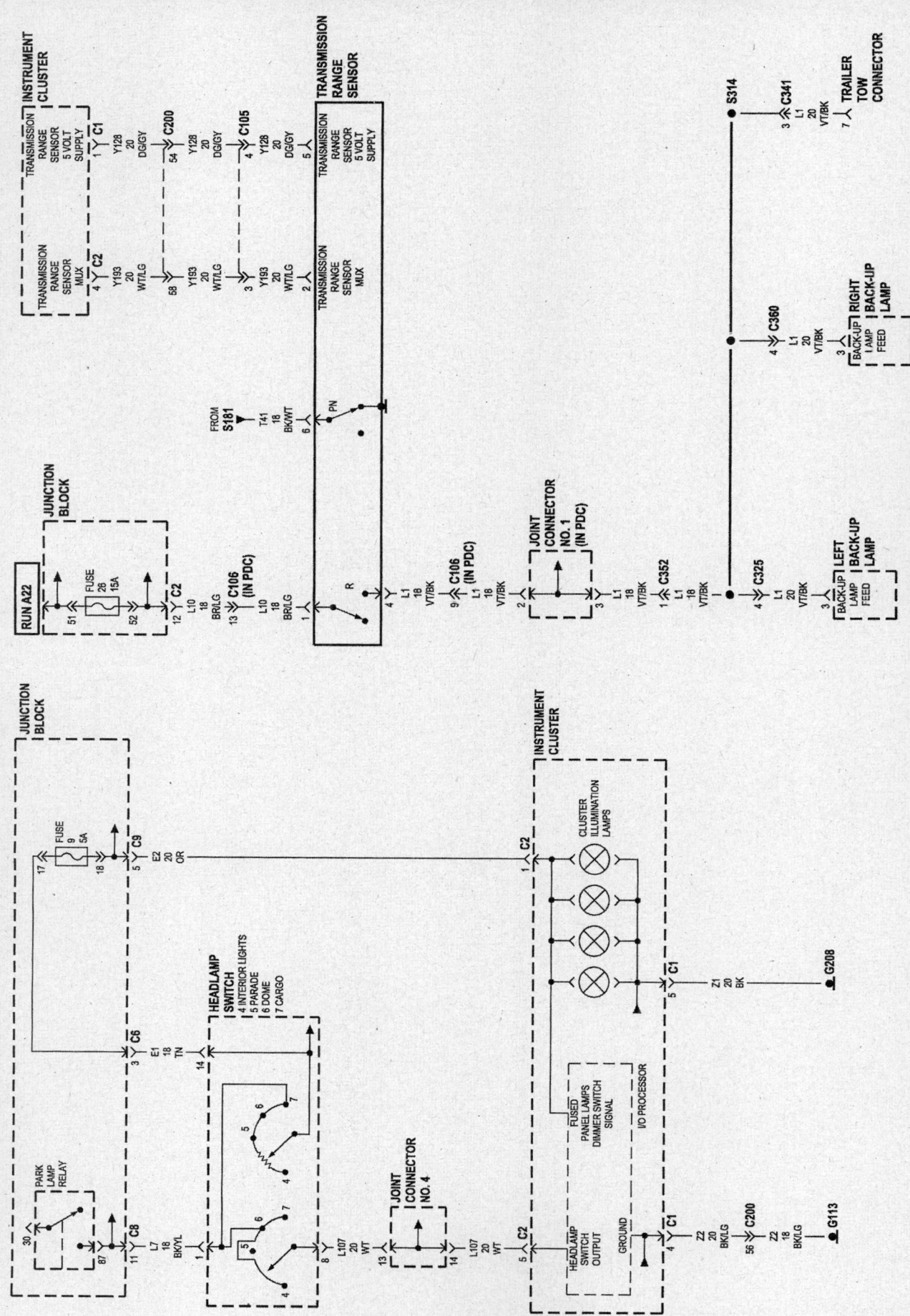

Fig. 5 Instrument Cluster (Part 8 of 8). 2002–04 Dakota

Fig. 5 Instrument Cluster (Part 7 of 8). 2002–04 Dakota

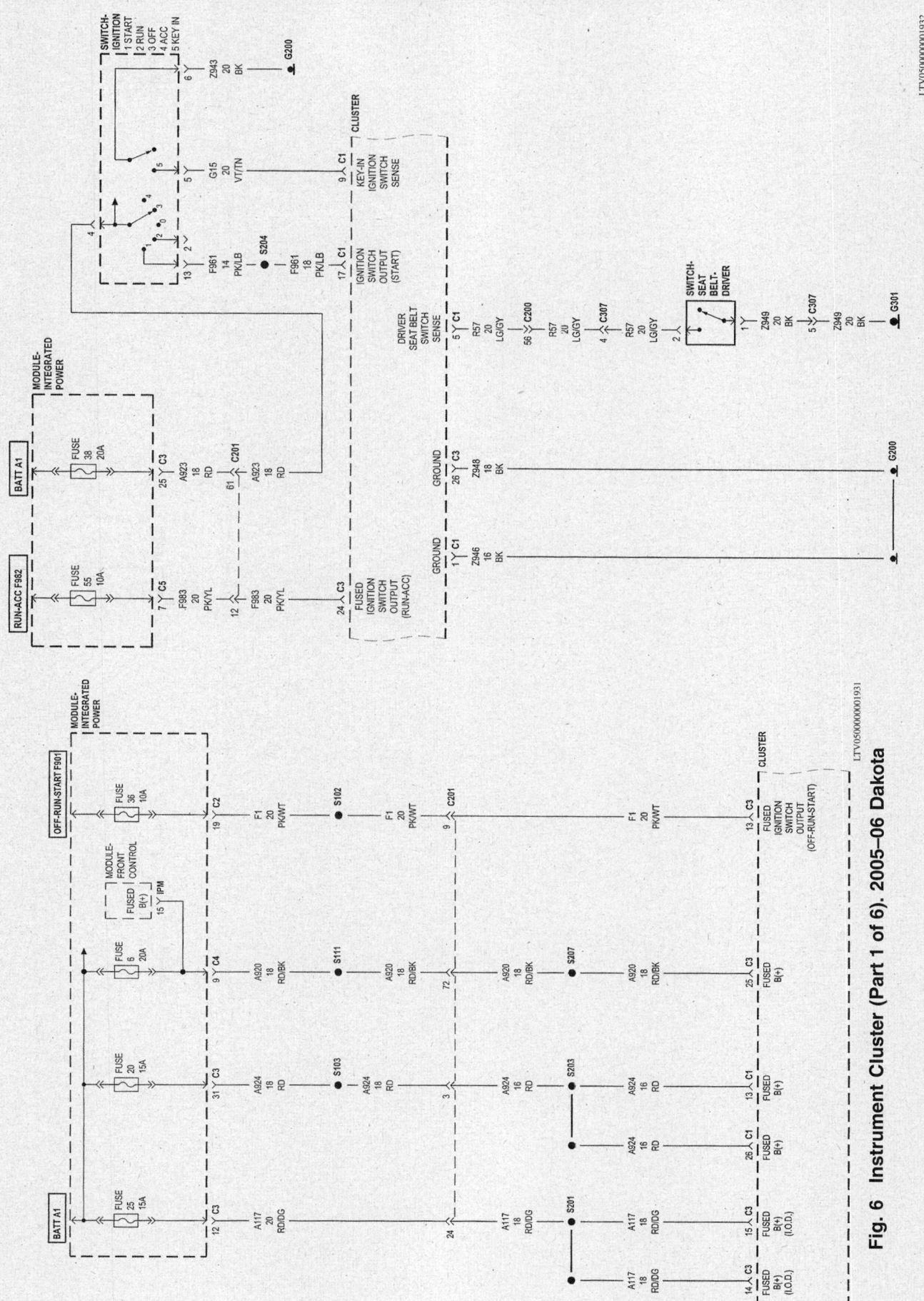

Fig. 6 Instrument Cluster (Part 2 of 6). 2005–06 Dakota

Fig. 6 Instrument Cluster (Part 1 of 6). 2005–06 Dakota

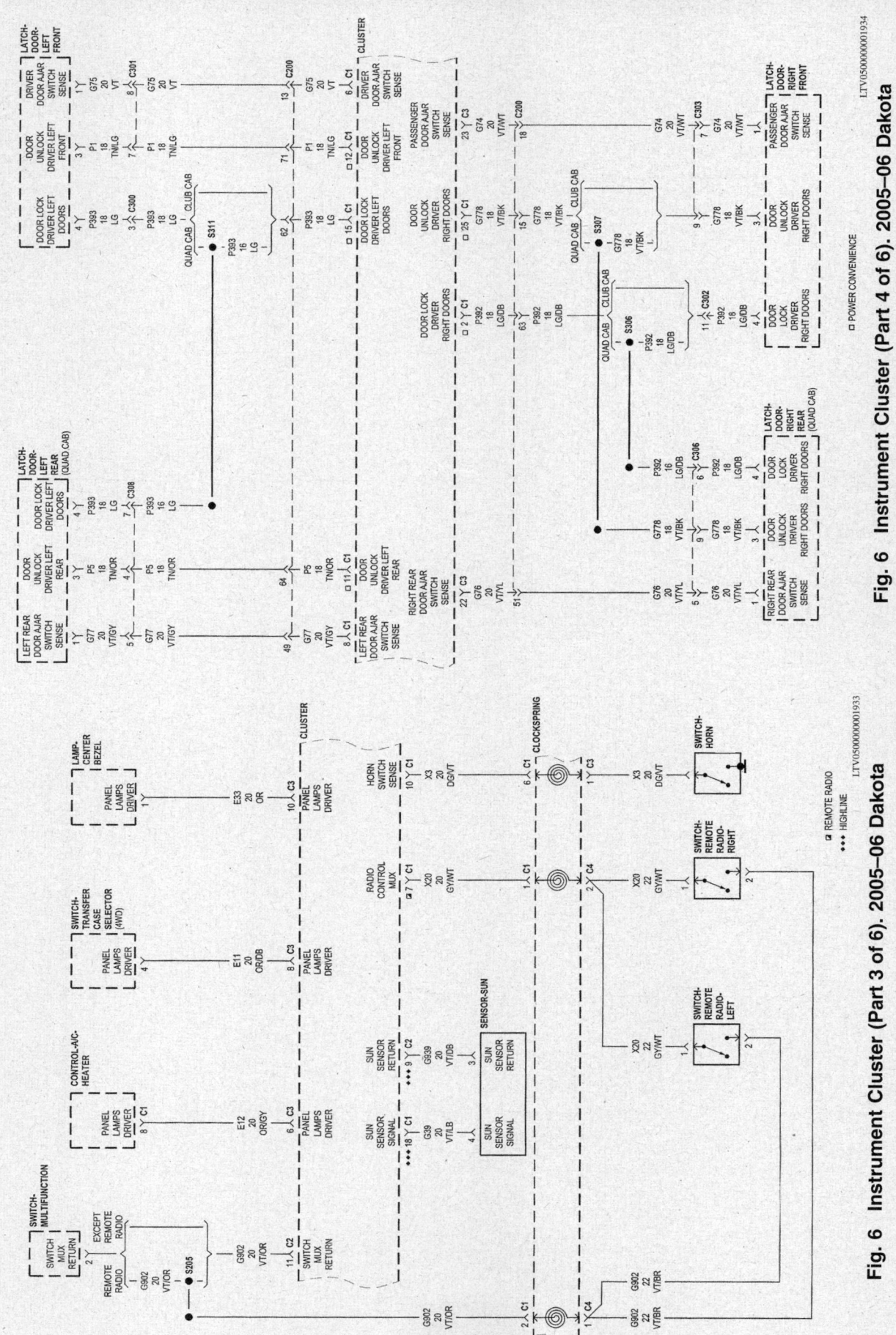

Fig. 6 Instrument Cluster (Part 4 of 6). 2005–06 Dakota

Fig. 6 Instrument Cluster (Part 3 of 6). 2005–06 Dakota

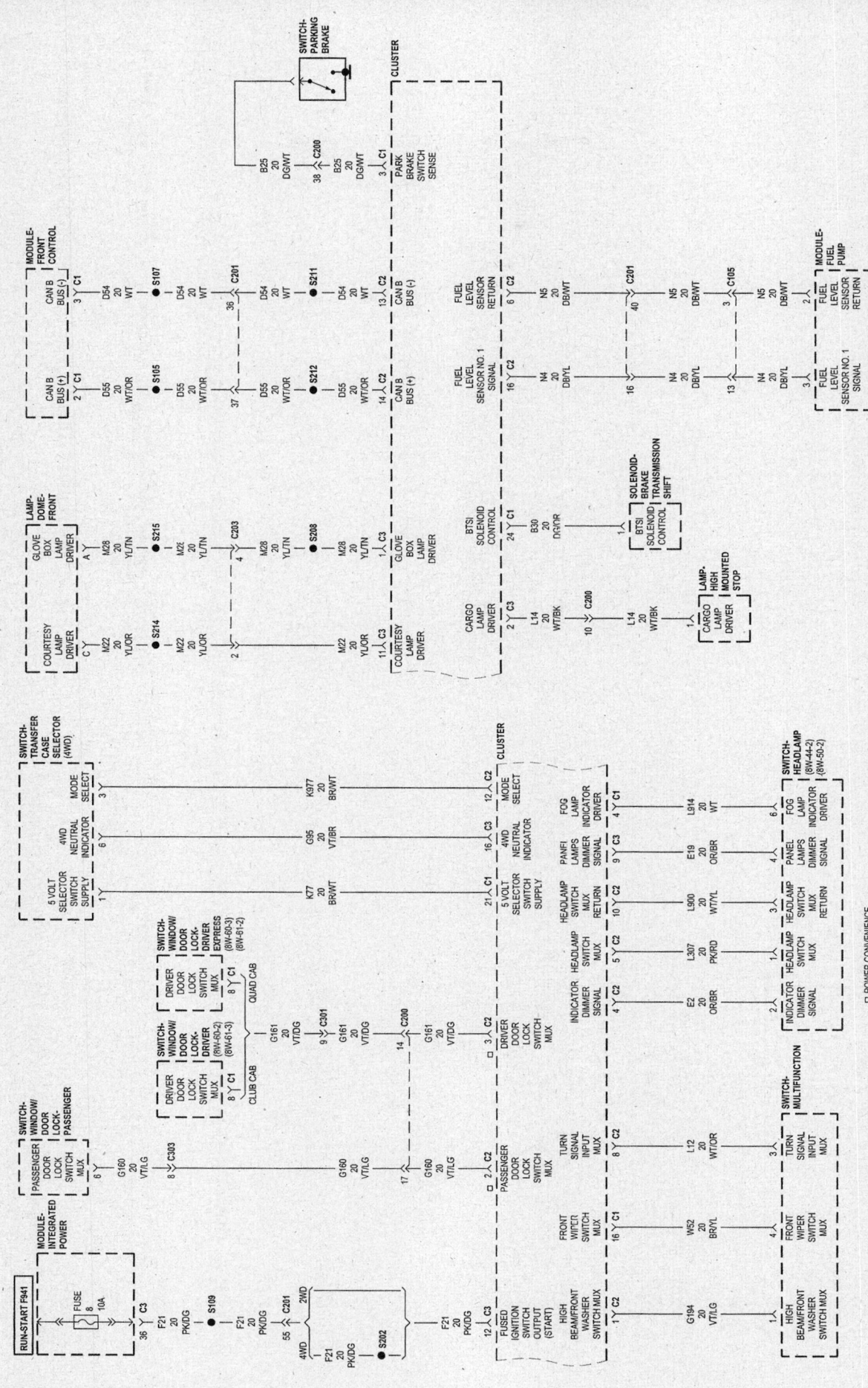

Fig. 6 Instrument Cluster (Part 6 of 6). 2005–06 Dakota

Fig. 6 Instrument Cluster (Part 5 of 6). 2005–06 Dakota

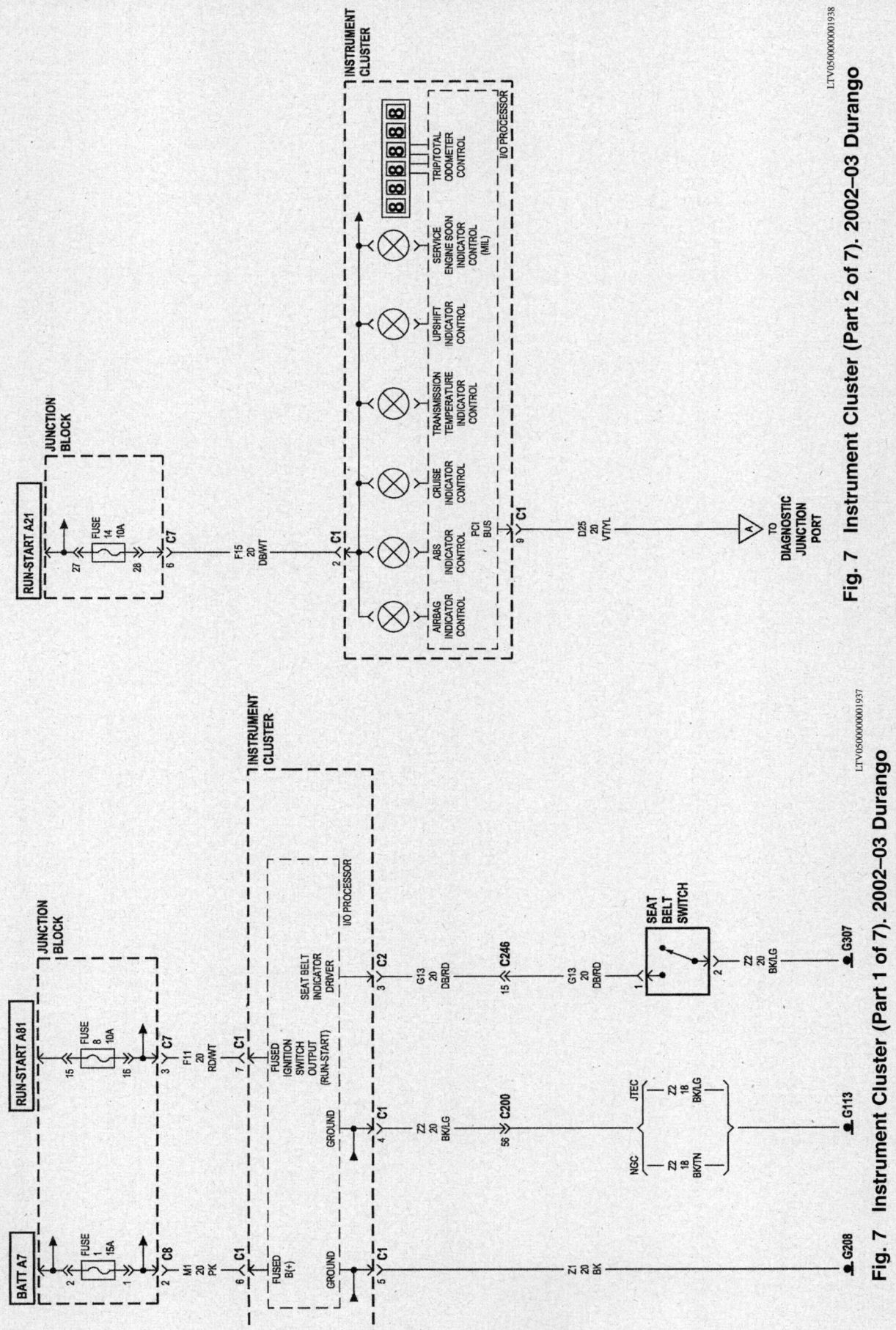

Fig. 7 Instrument Cluster (Part 2 of 7). 2002–03 Durango

Fig. 7 Instrument Cluster (Part 1 of 7). 2002–03 Durango

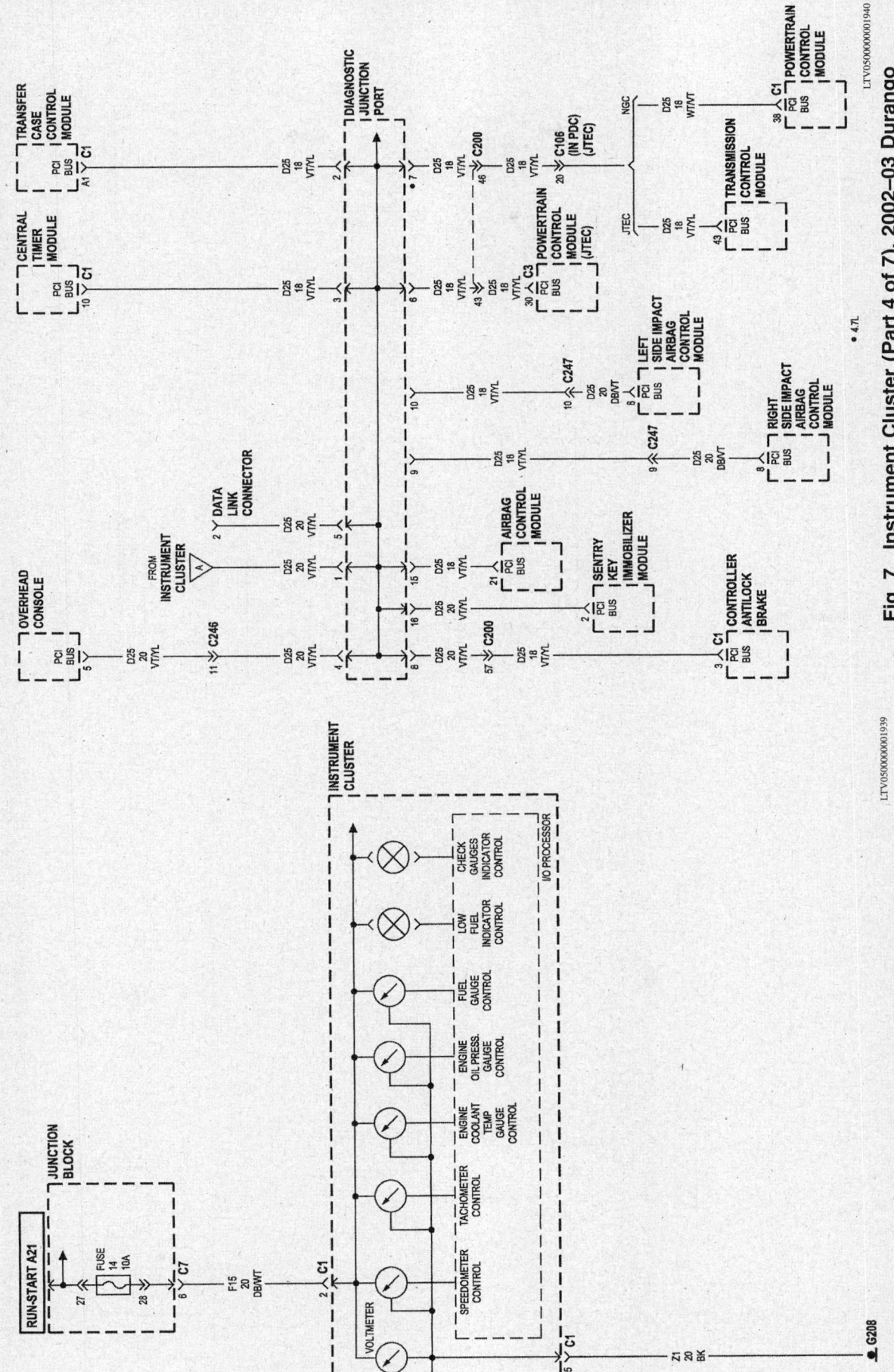

Fig. 7 Instrument Cluster (Part 4 of 7). 2002-03 Durango

Fig. 7 Instrument Cluster (Part 3 of 7). 2002-03 Durango

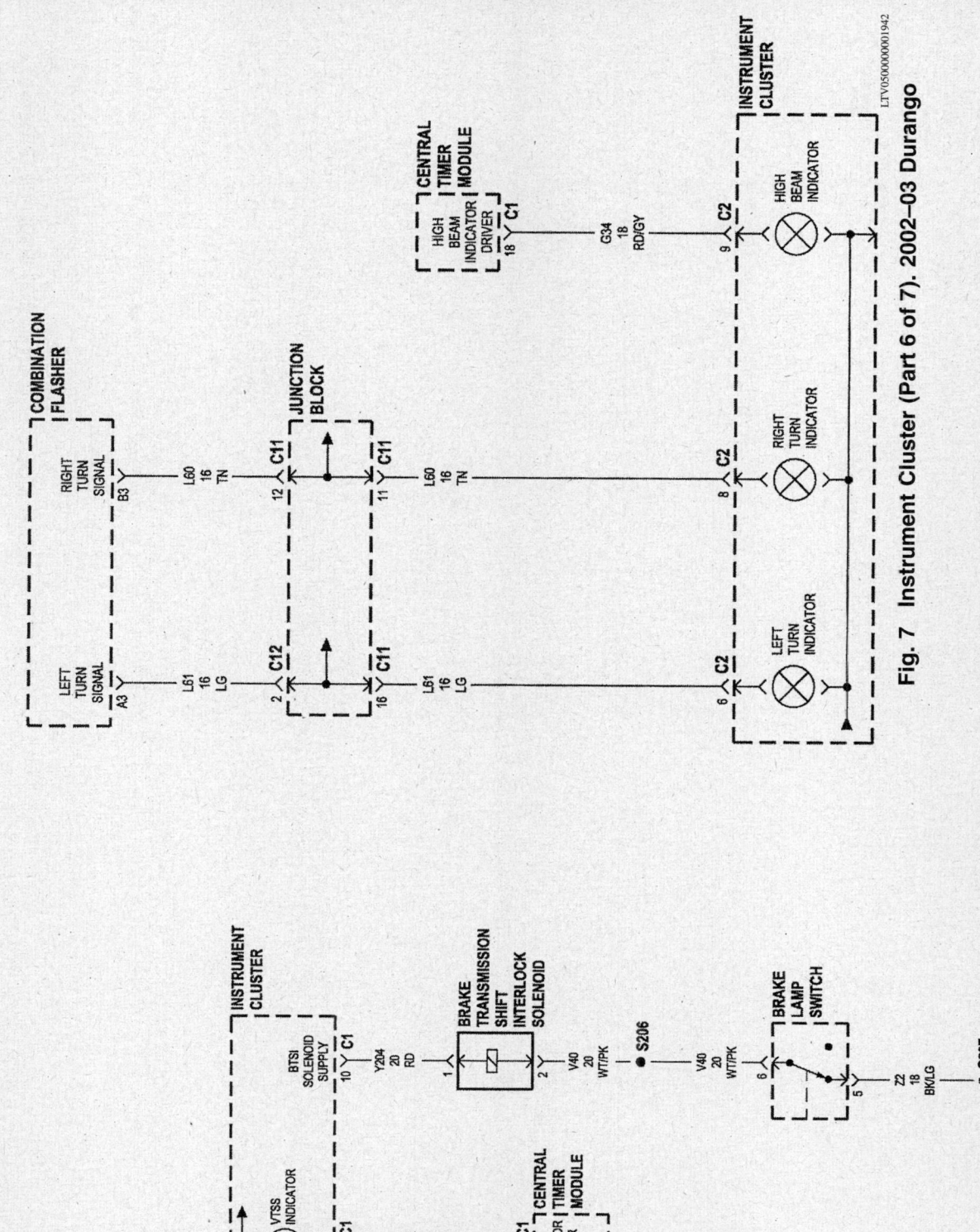

Fig. 7 Instrument Cluster (Part 6 of 7). 2002–03 Durango

Fig. 7 Instrument Cluster (Part 5 of 7). 2002–03 Durango

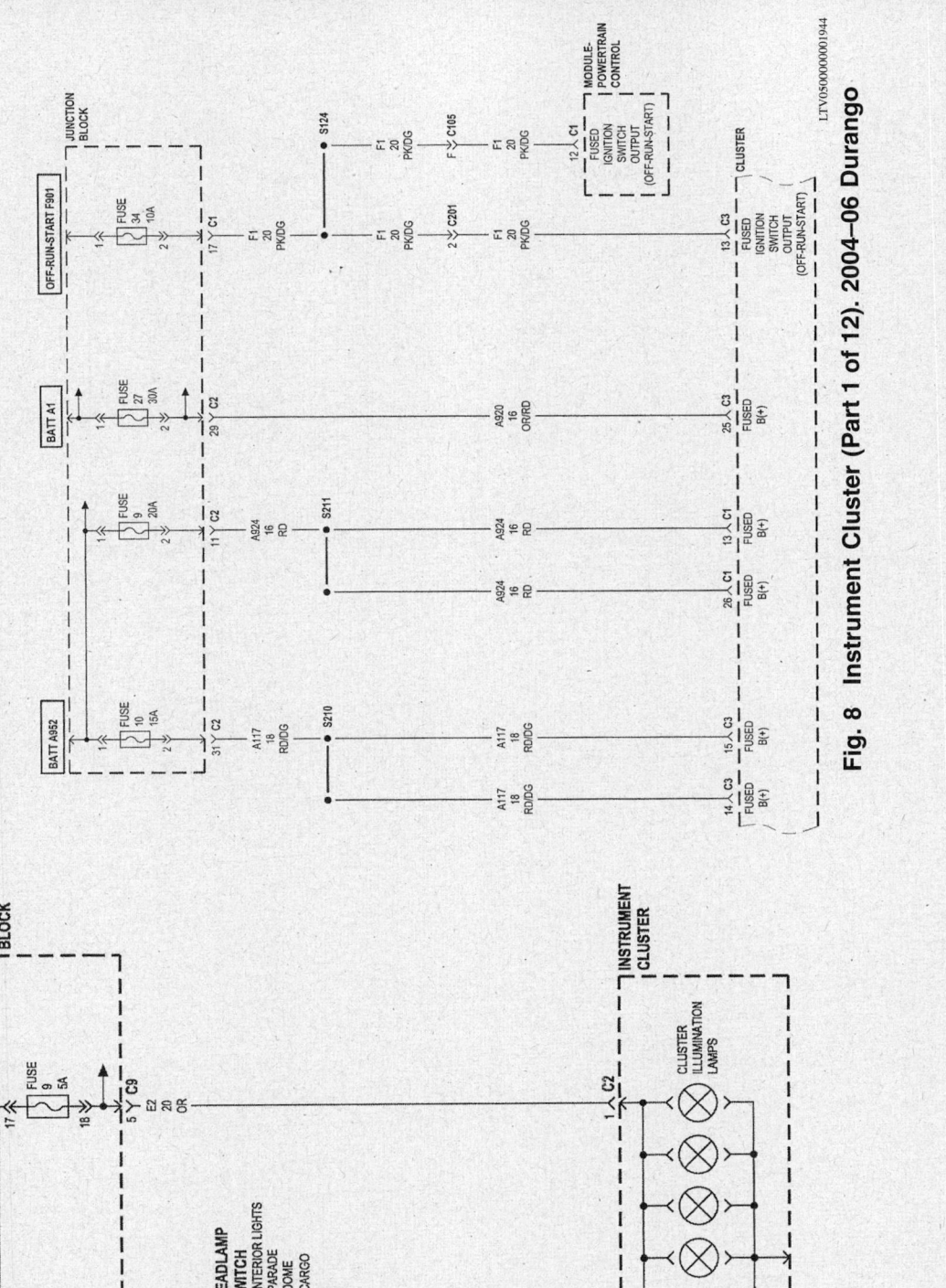

Fig. 8 Instrument Cluster (Part 1 of 12). 2004–06 Durango

Fig. 7 Instrument Cluster (Part 7 of 7). 2002–03 Durango

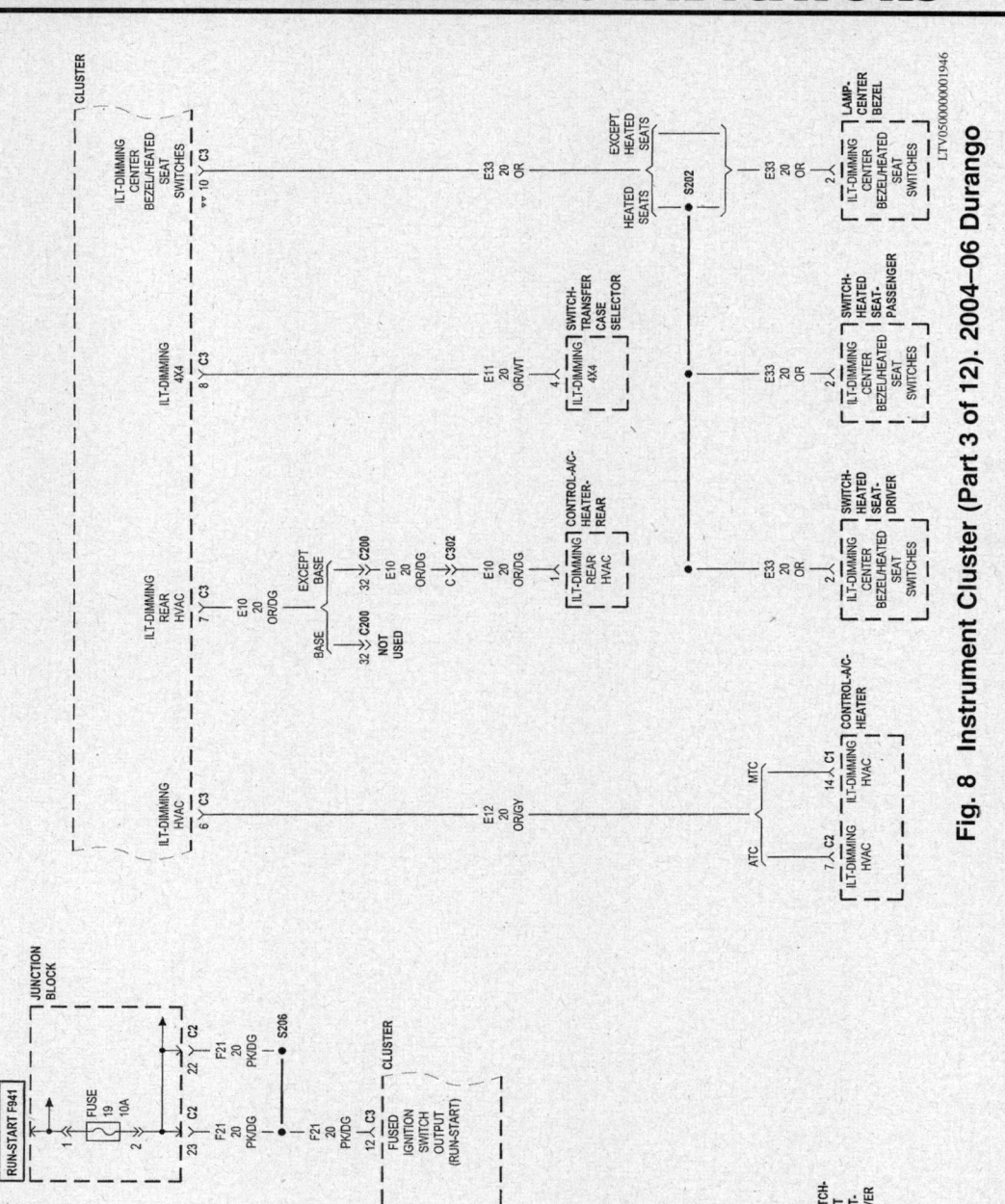

Fig. 8 Instrument Cluster (Part 3 of 12). 2004–06 Durango

Fig. 8 Instrument Cluster (Part 2 of 12). 2004–06 Durango

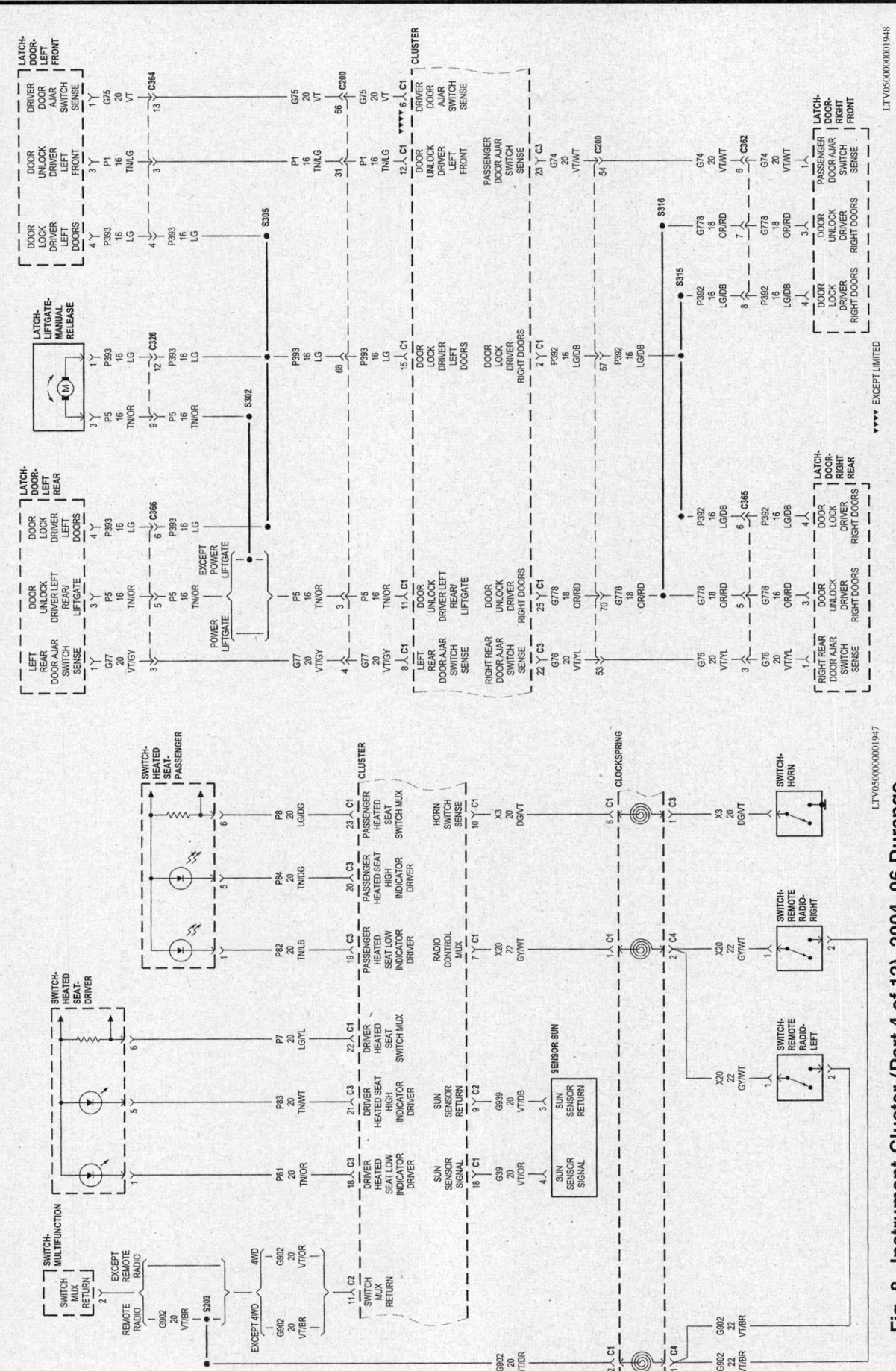

Fig. 8 Instrument Cluster (Part 5 of 12). 2004–06 Durango

Fig. 8 Instrument Cluster (Part 4 of 12). 2004–06 Durango

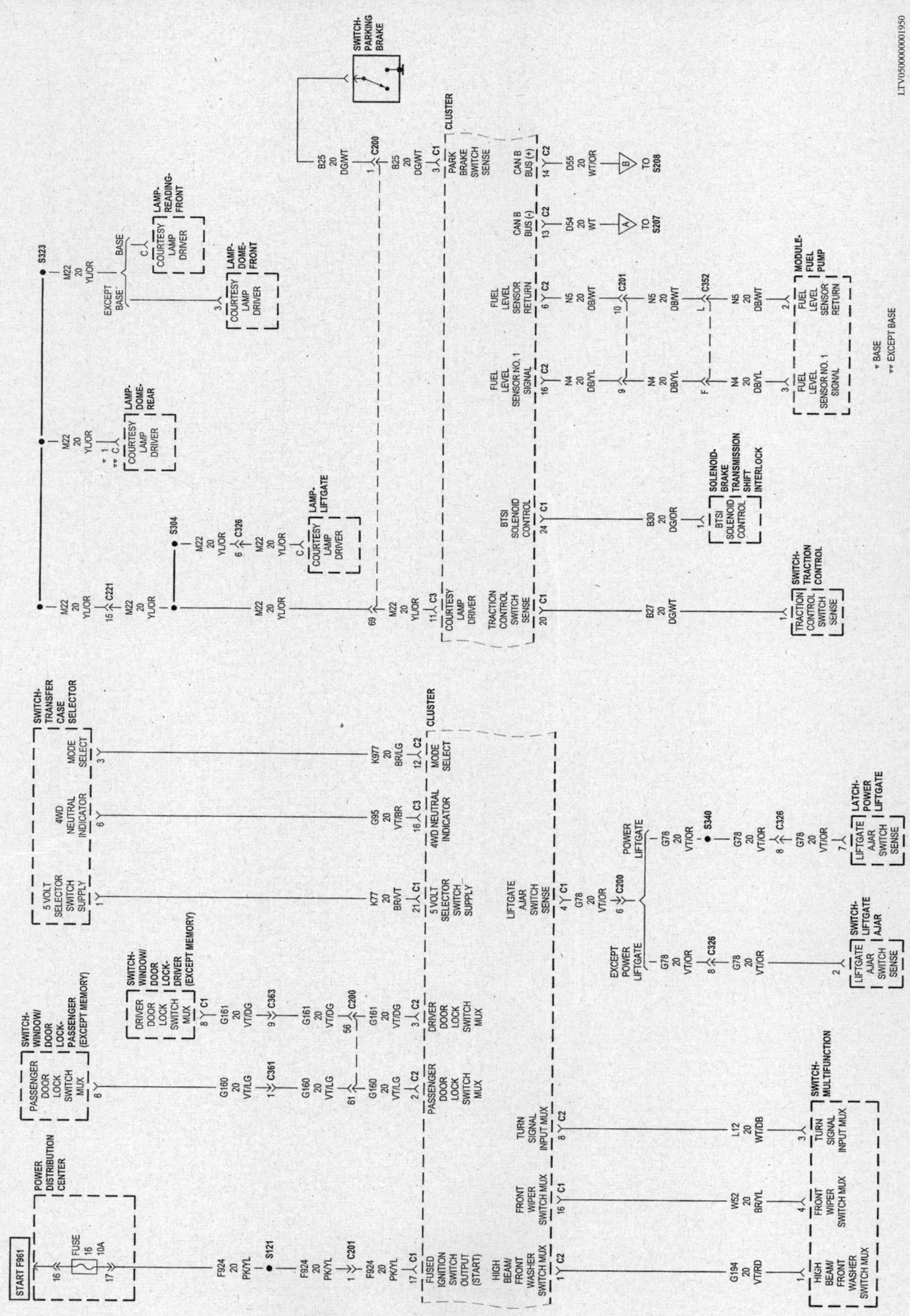

Fig. 8 Instrument Cluster (Part 7 of 12). 2004–06 Durango

Fig. 8 Instrument Cluster (Part 6 of 12). 2004–06 Durango

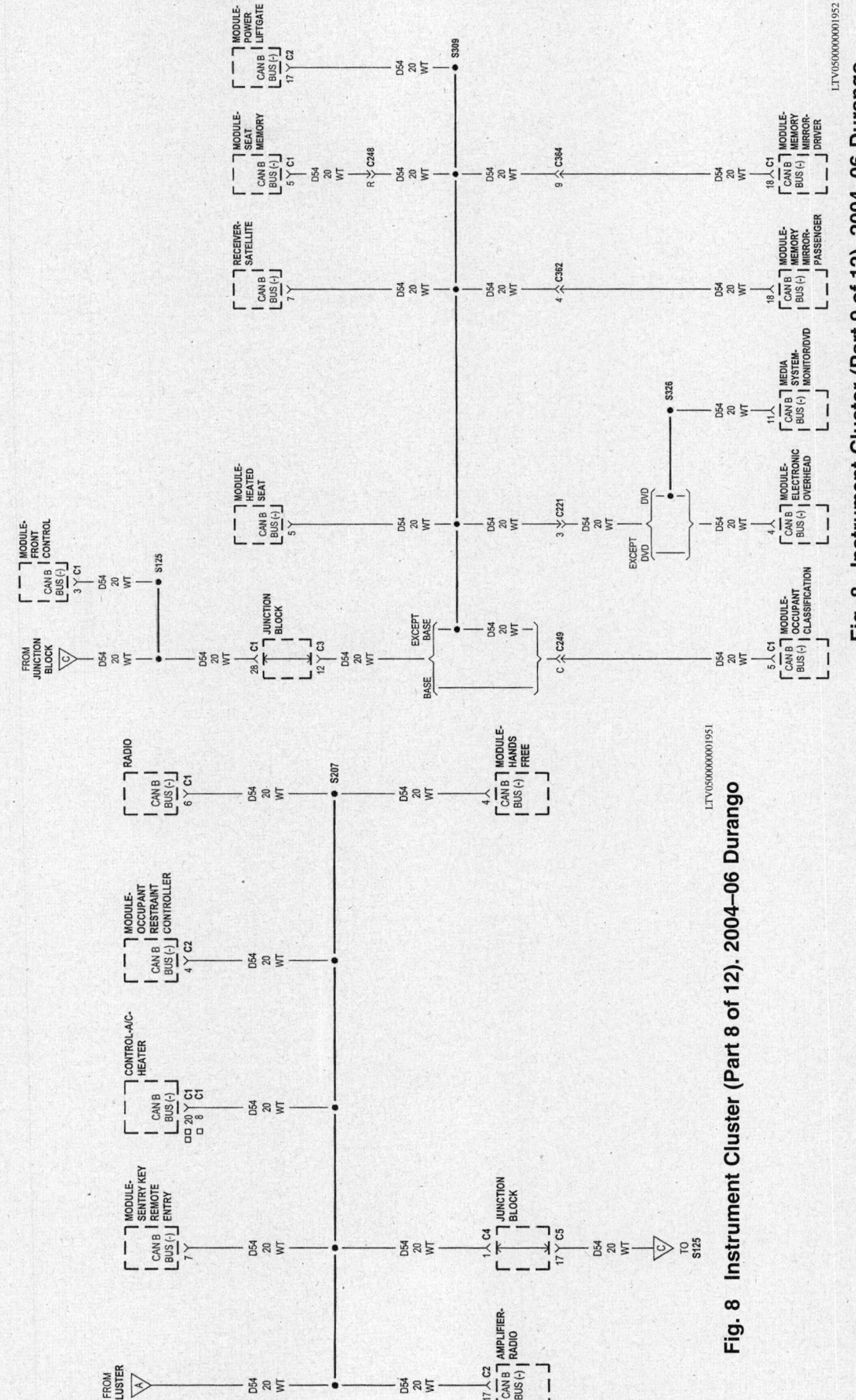

Fig. 8 Instrument Cluster (Part 9 of 12). 2004-06 Durango

Fig. 8 Instrument Cluster (Part 8 of 12). 2004-06 Durango

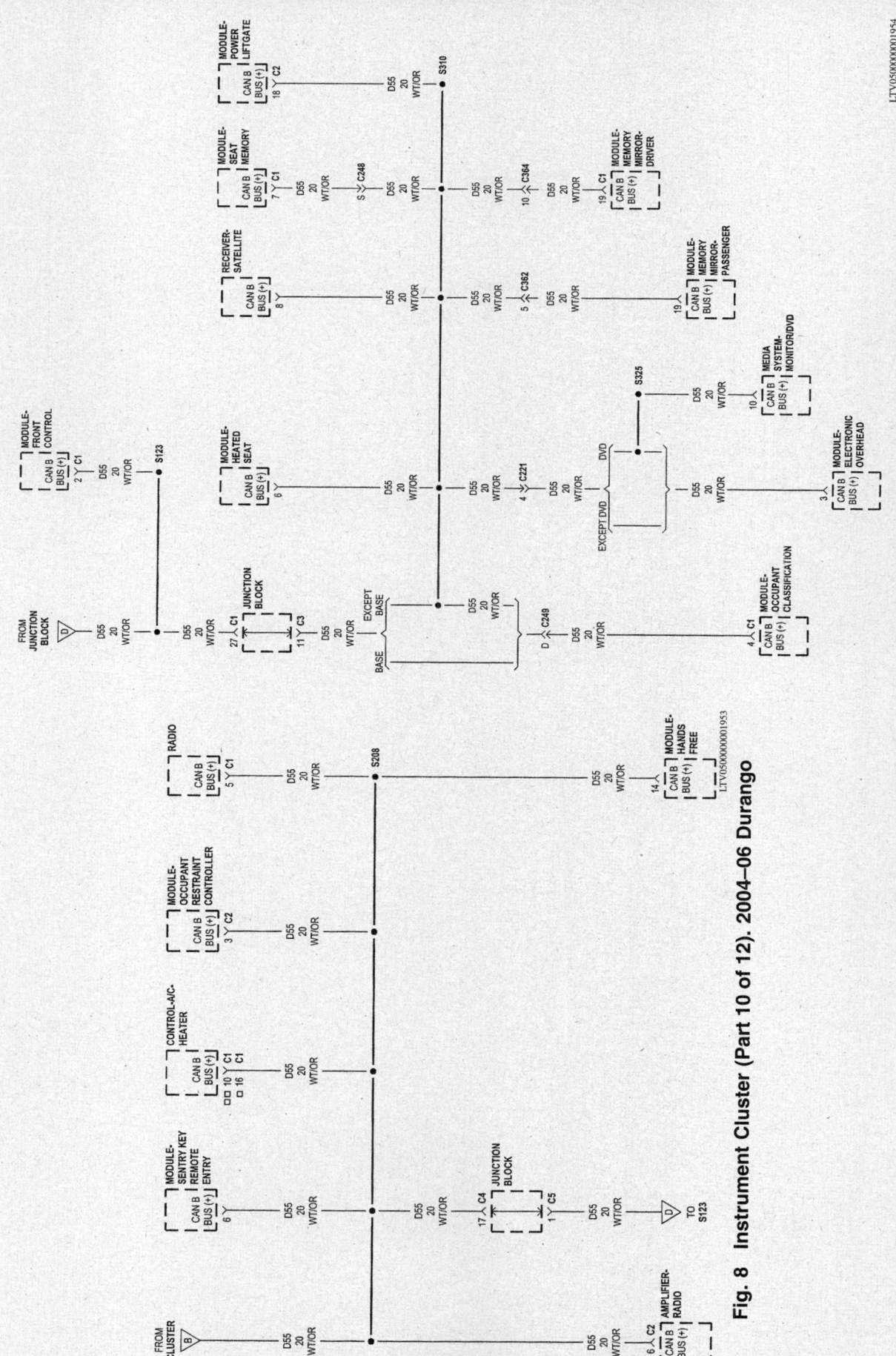

Fig. 8   Instrument Cluster (Part 11 of 12). 2004–06 Durango

Fig. 8   Instrument Cluster (Part 10 of 12). 2004–06 Durango

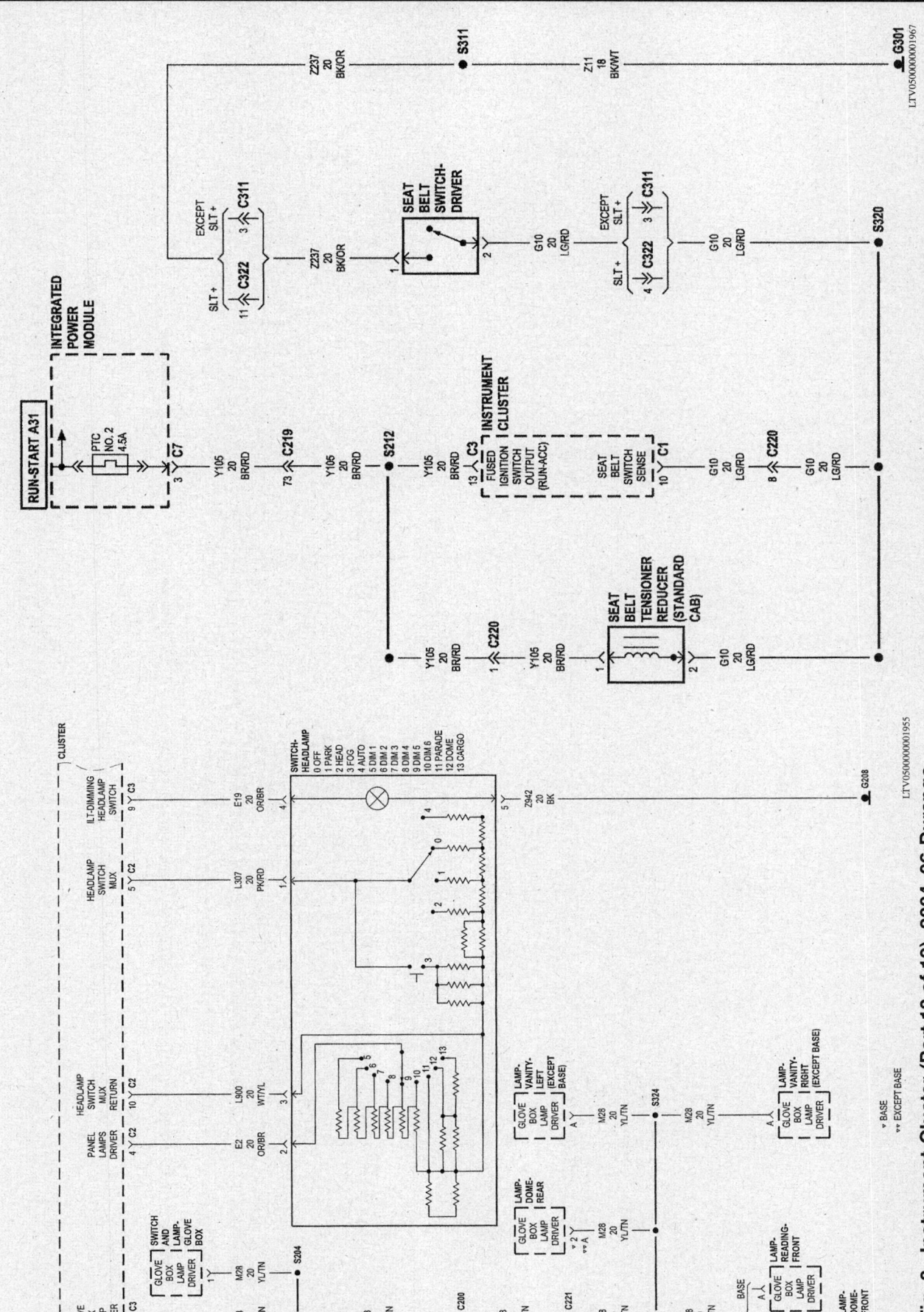

Fig. 9 Instrument Cluster (Part 1 of 11). 2002–04 Full Size Pickup

Fig. 8 Instrument Cluster (Part 12 of 12). 2004–06 Durango

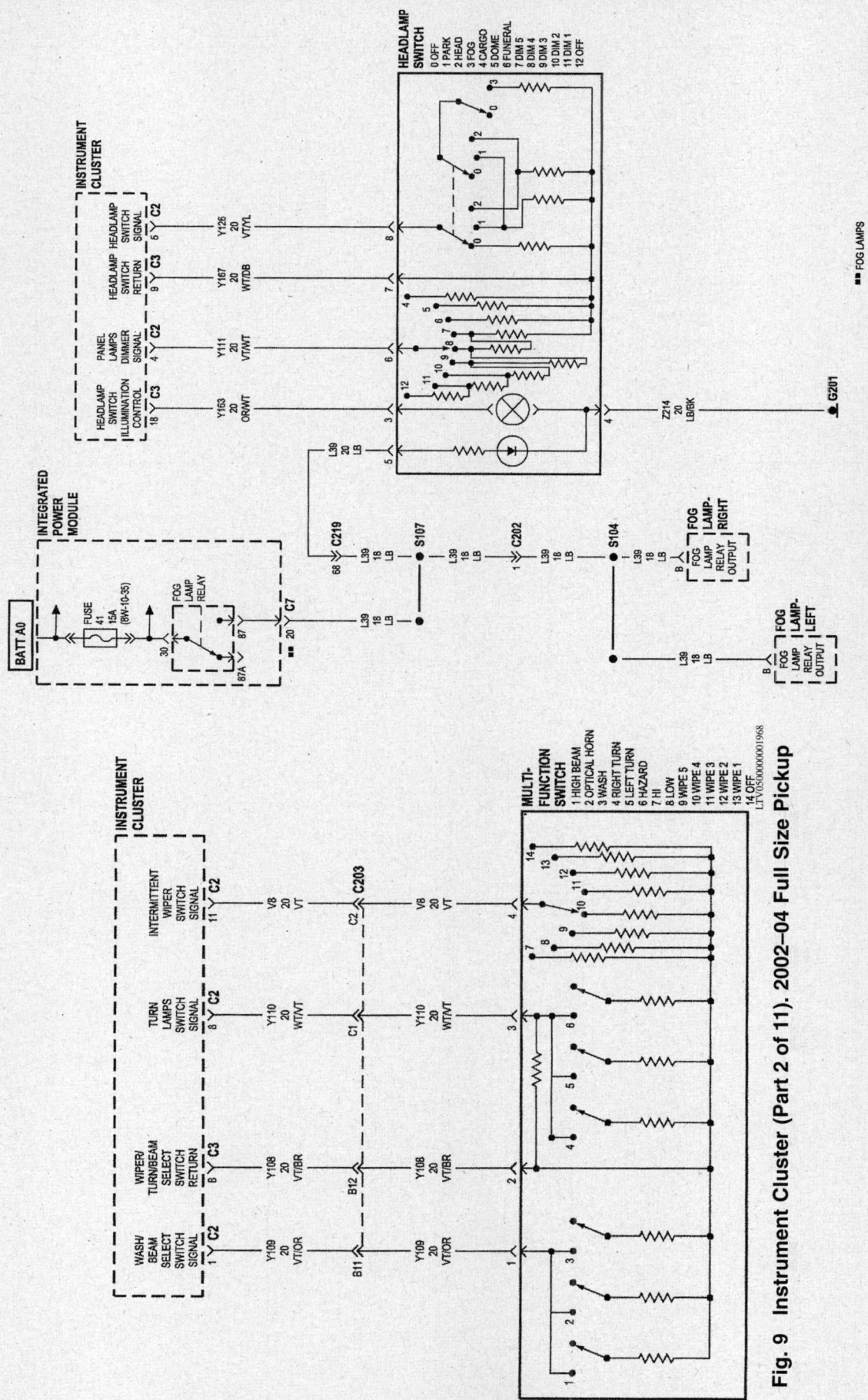

Fig. 9 Instrument Cluster (Part 3 of 11). 2002-04 Full Size Pickup

Fig. 9 Instrument Cluster (Part 2 of 11). 2002-04 Full Size Pickup

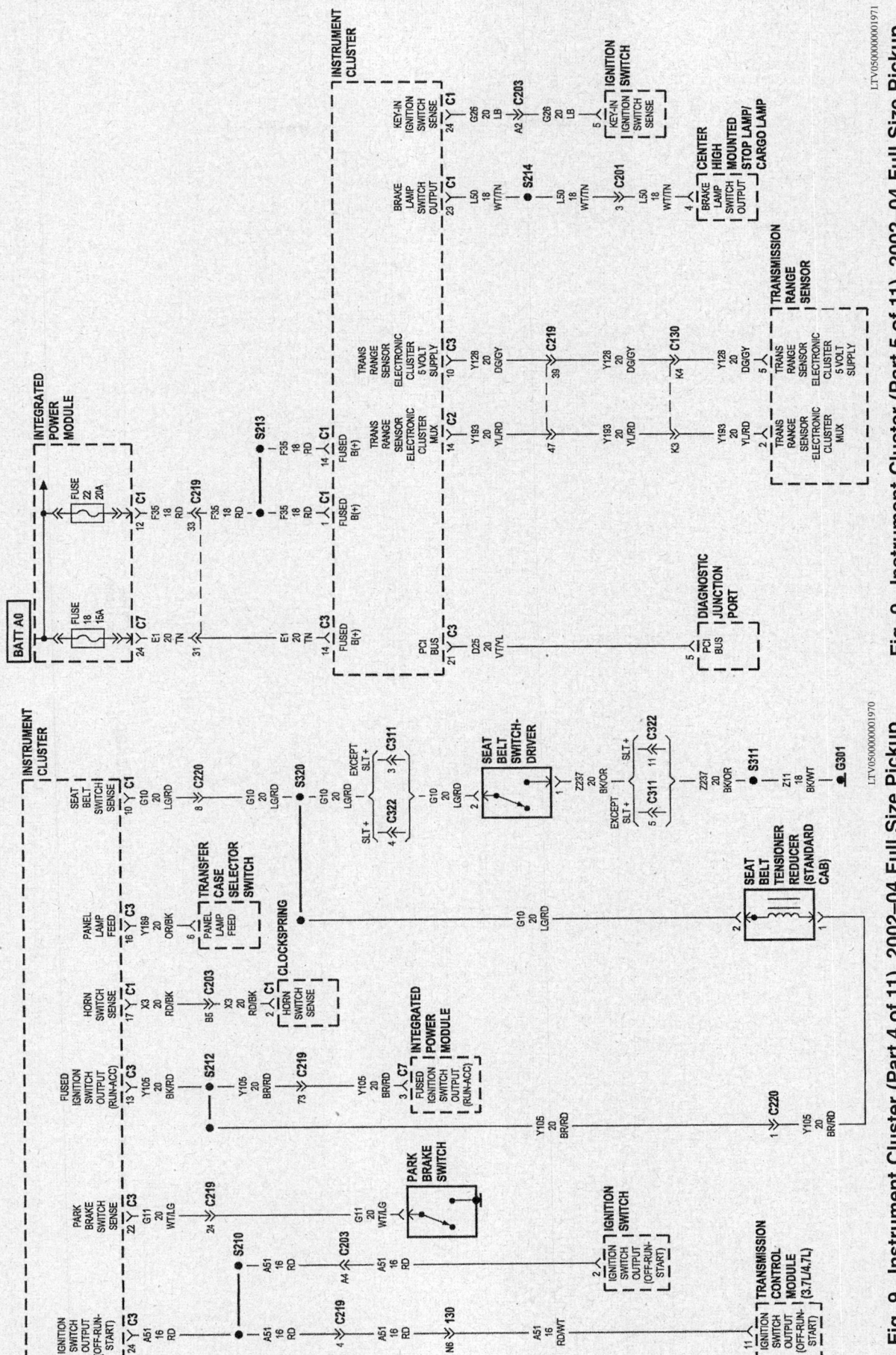

Fig. 9 Instrument Cluster (Part 5 of 11). 2002–04 Full Size Pickup

Fig. 9 Instrument Cluster (Part 4 of 11). 2002–04 Full Size Pickup

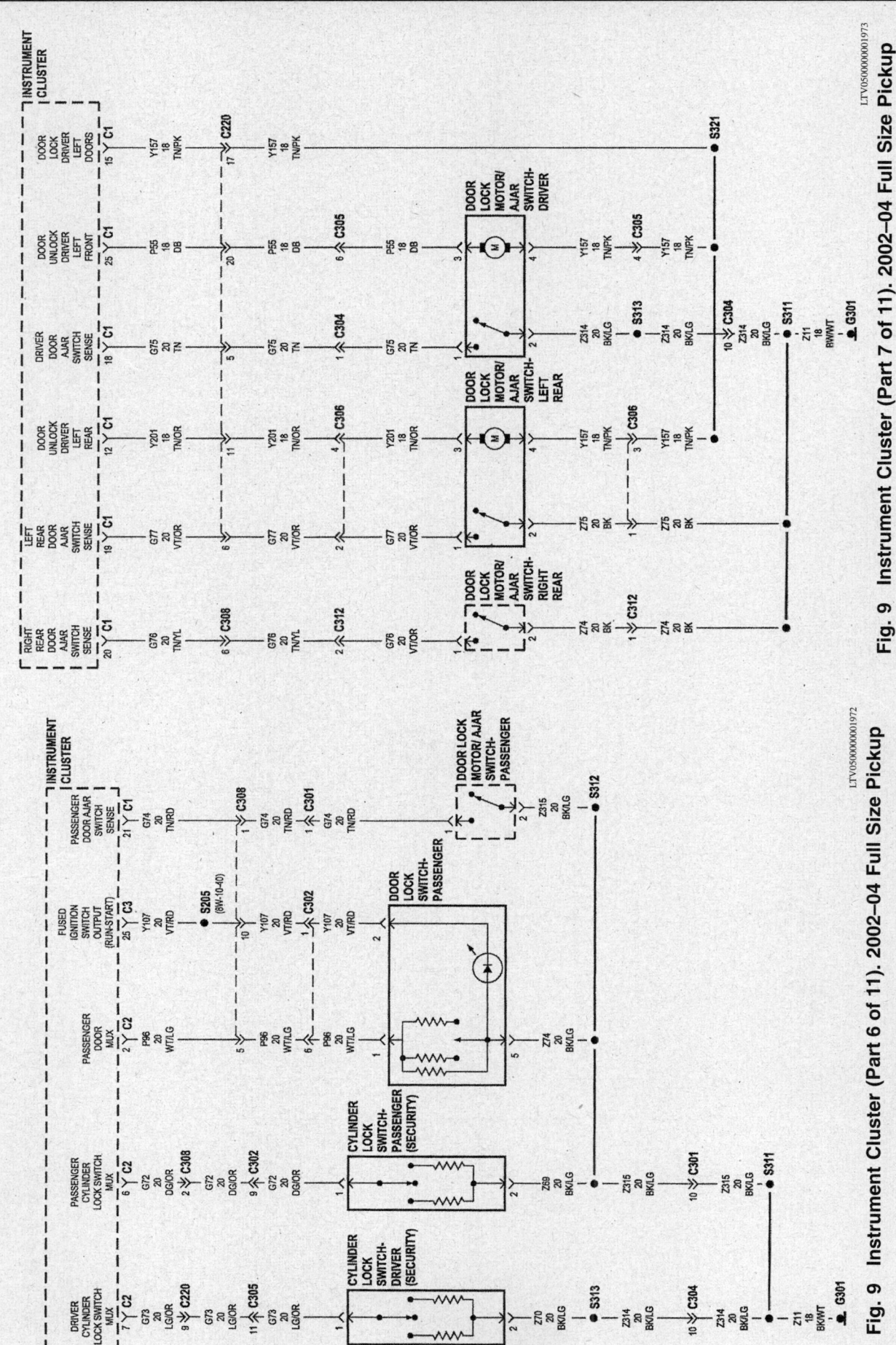

Fig. 9   Instrument Cluster (Part 7 of 11). 2002–04 Full Size Pickup

Fig. 9   Instrument Cluster (Part 6 of 11). 2002–04 Full Size Pickup

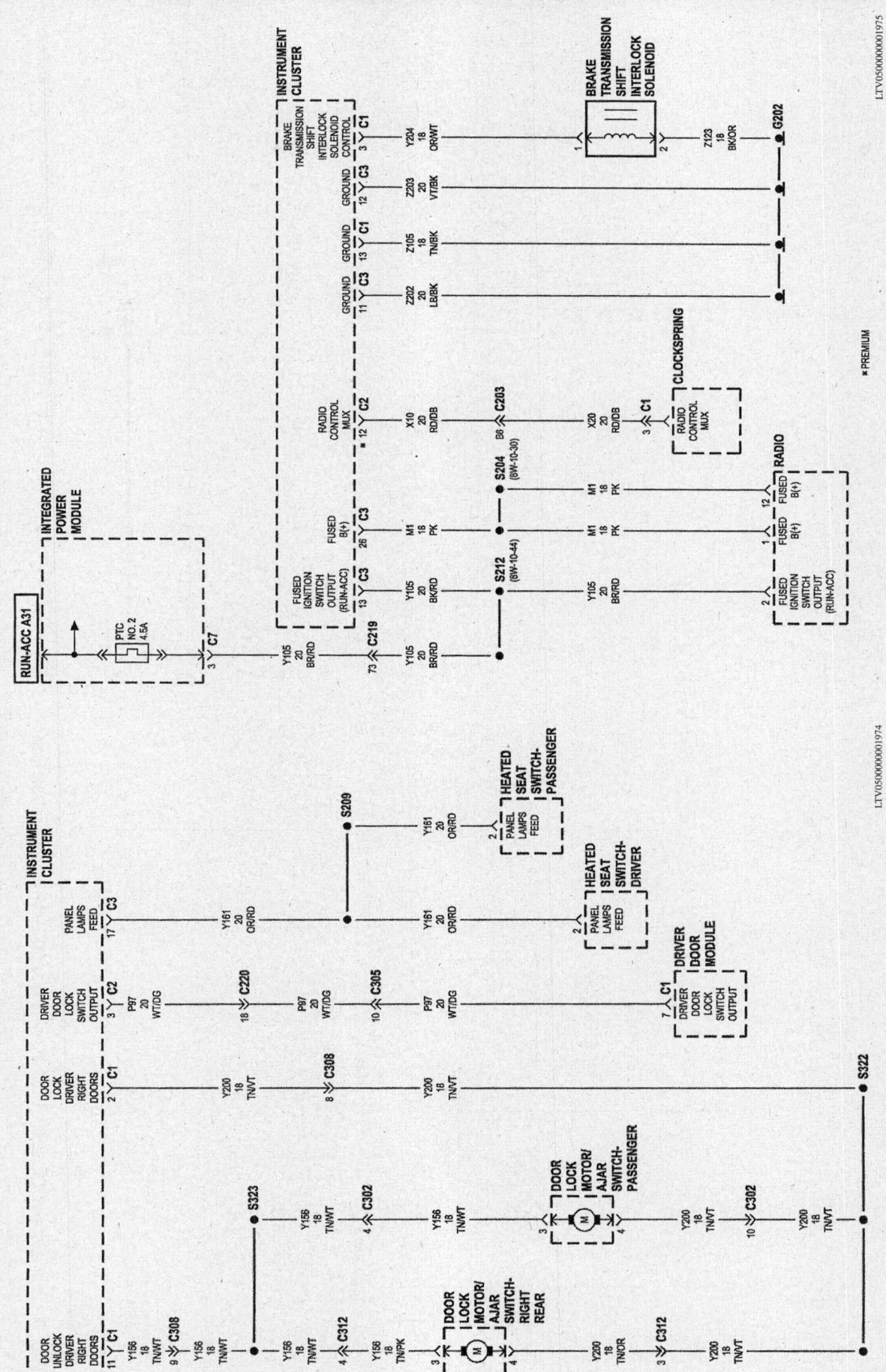

Fig. 9 Instrument Cluster (Part 9 of 11). 2002-04 Full Size Pickup

Fig. 9 Instrument Cluster (Part 8 of 11). 2002-04 Full Size Pickup

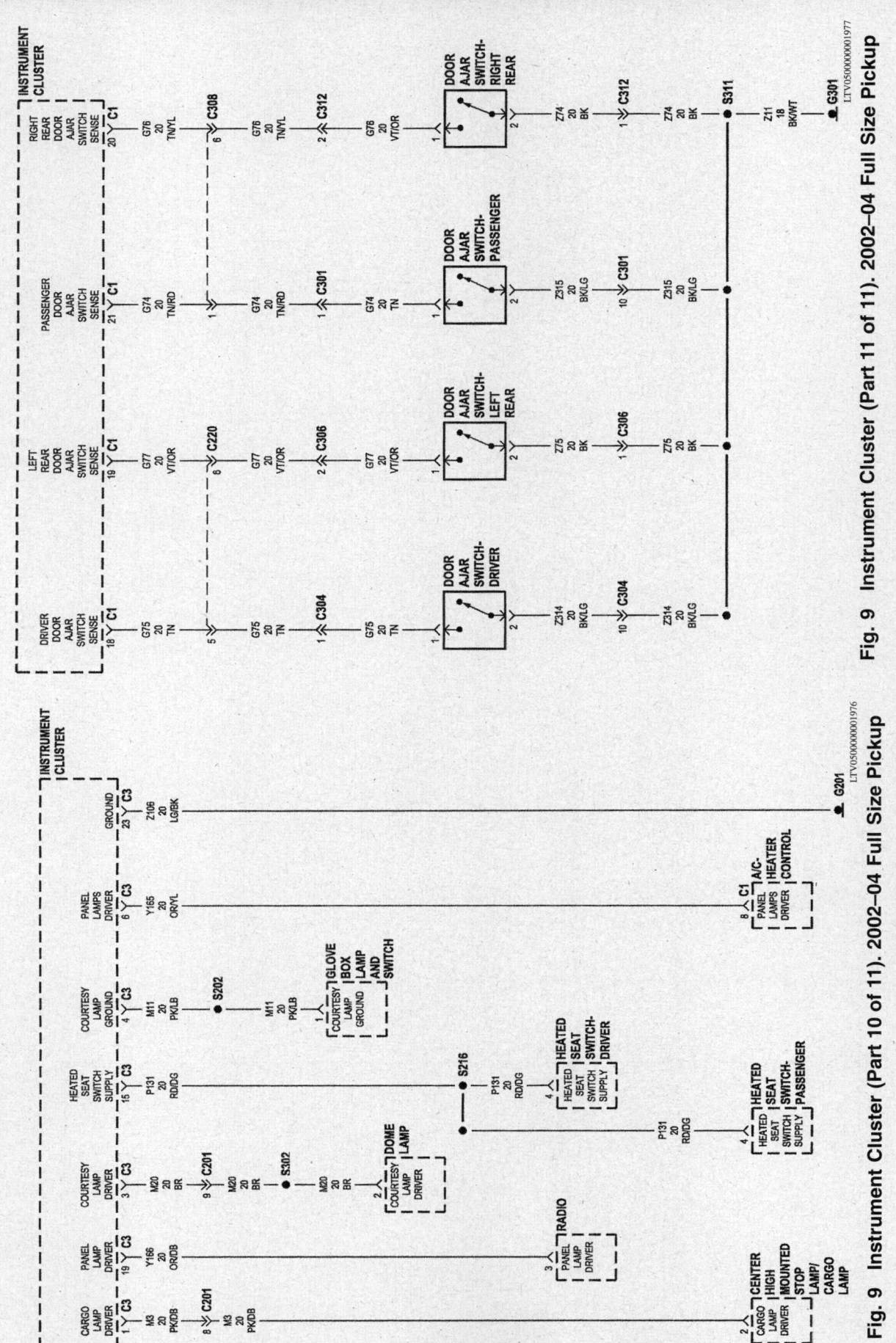

Fig. 9   Instrument Cluster (Part 11 of 11). 2002–04 Full Size Pickup

Fig. 9   Instrument Cluster (Part 10 of 11). 2002–04 Full Size Pickup

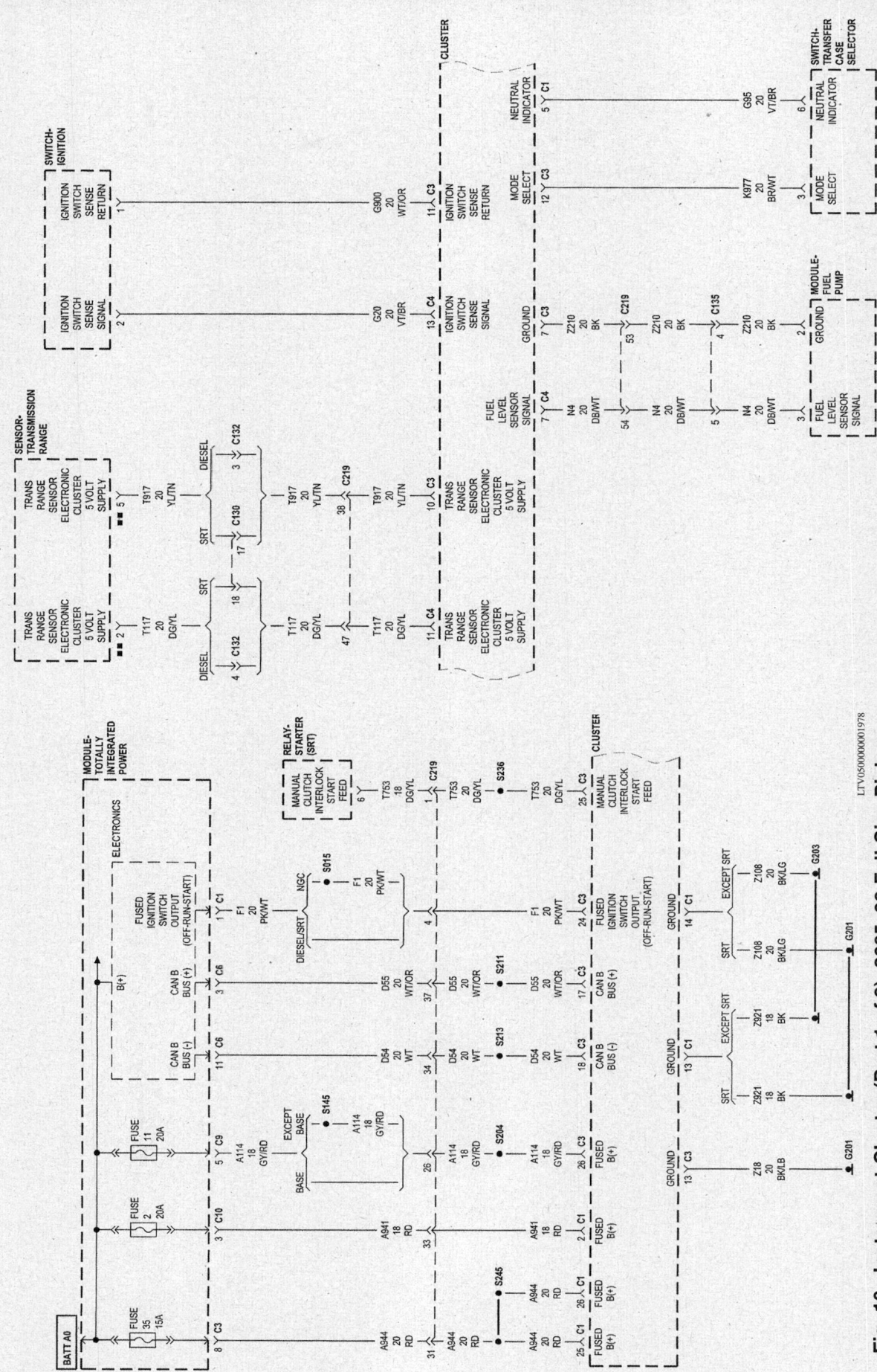

Fig. 10 Instrument Cluster (Part 2 of 9). 2005-06 Full Size Pickup

Fig. 10 Instrument Cluster (Part 1 of 9). 2005-06 Full Size Pickup

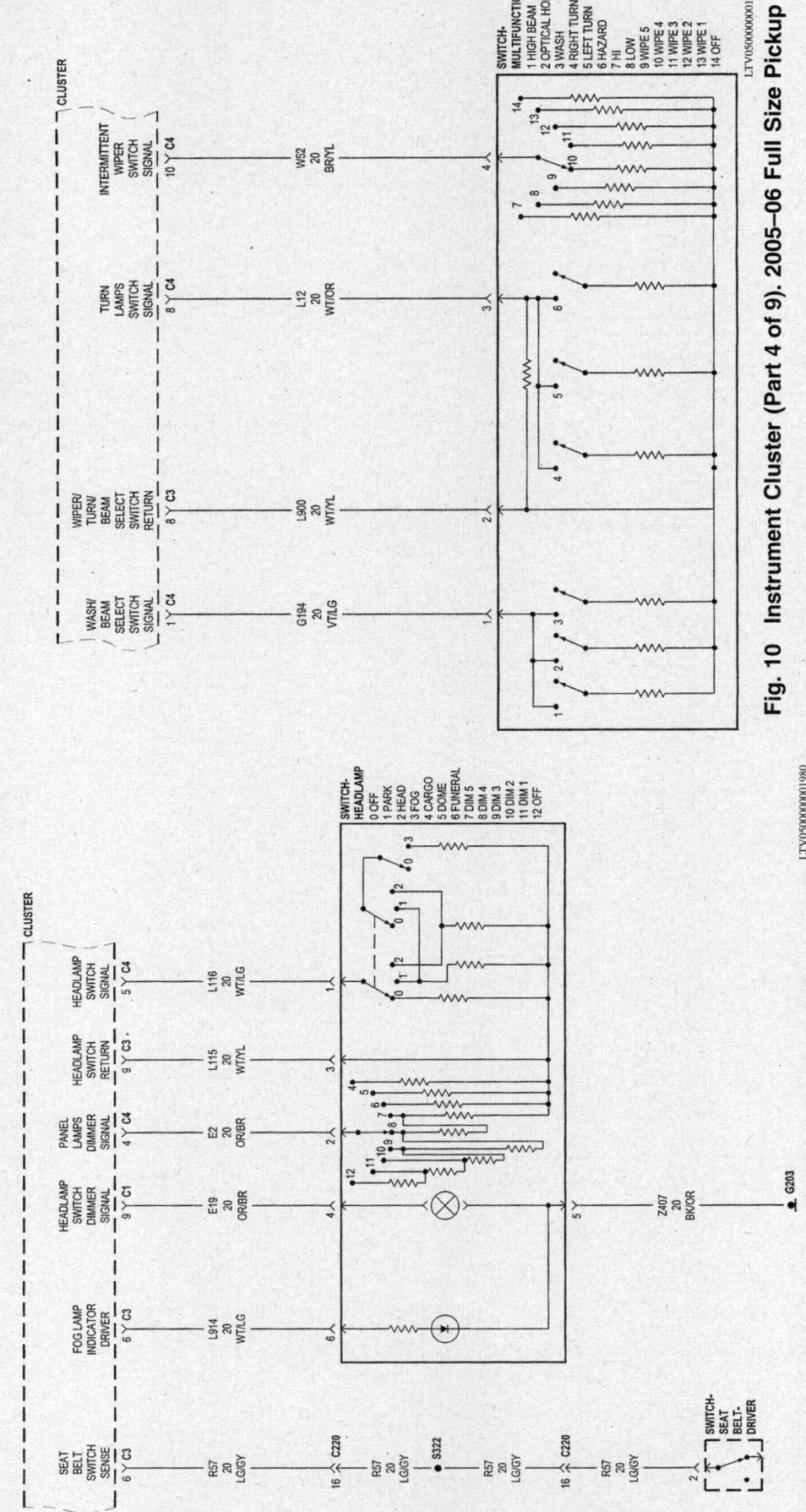

Fig. 10 Instrument Cluster (Part 4 of 9). 2005–06 Full Size Pickup

Fig. 10 Instrument Cluster (Part 3 of 9). 2005–06 Full Size Pickup

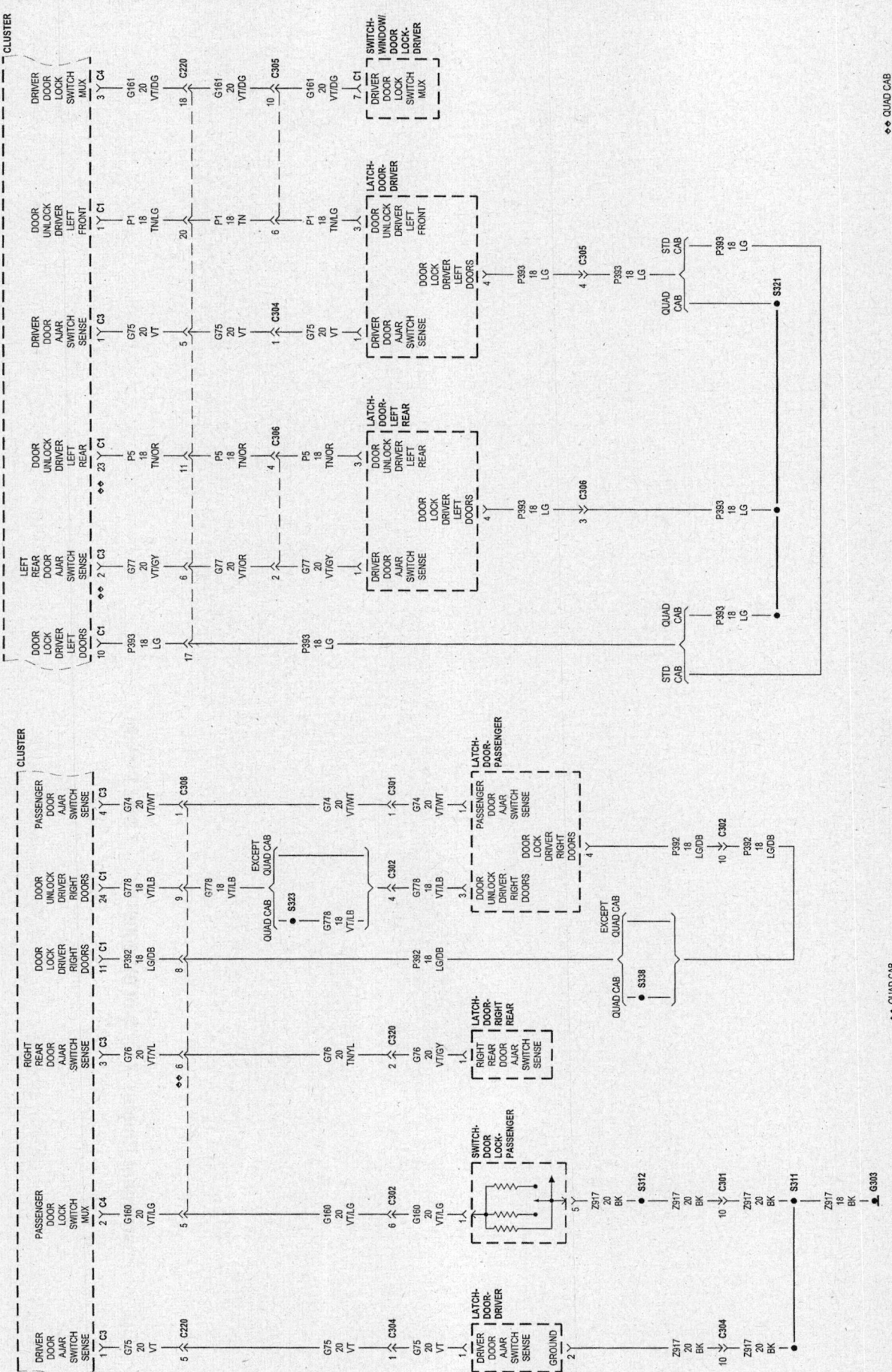

Fig. 10 Instrument Cluster (Part 6 of 9). 2005–06 Full Size Pickup

Fig. 10 Instrument Cluster (Part 5 of 9). 2005–06 Full Size Pickup

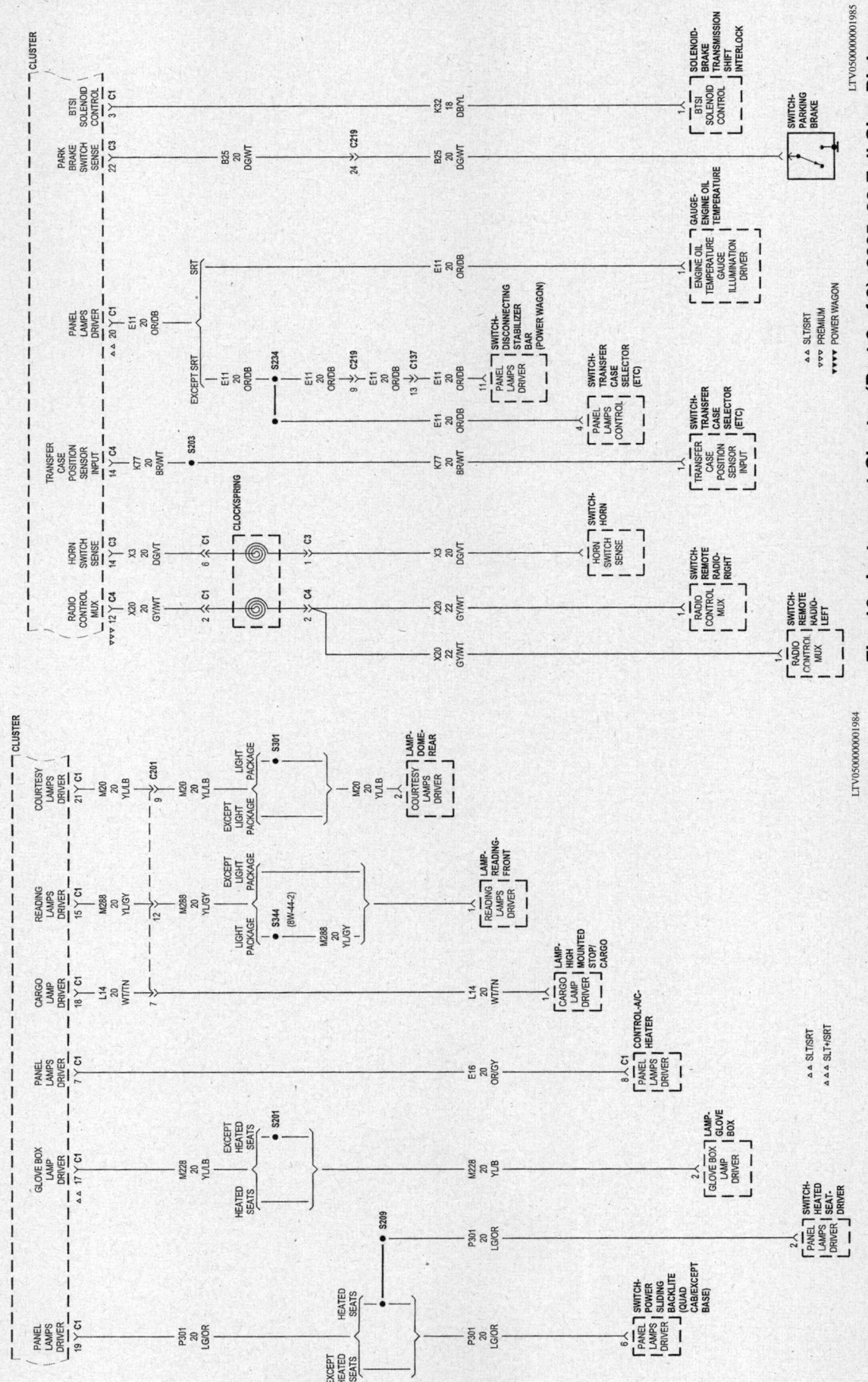

Fig. 10   Instrument Cluster (Part 8 of 9). 2005–06 Full Size Pickup

Fig. 10   Instrument Cluster (Part 7 of 9). 2005–06 Full Size Pickup

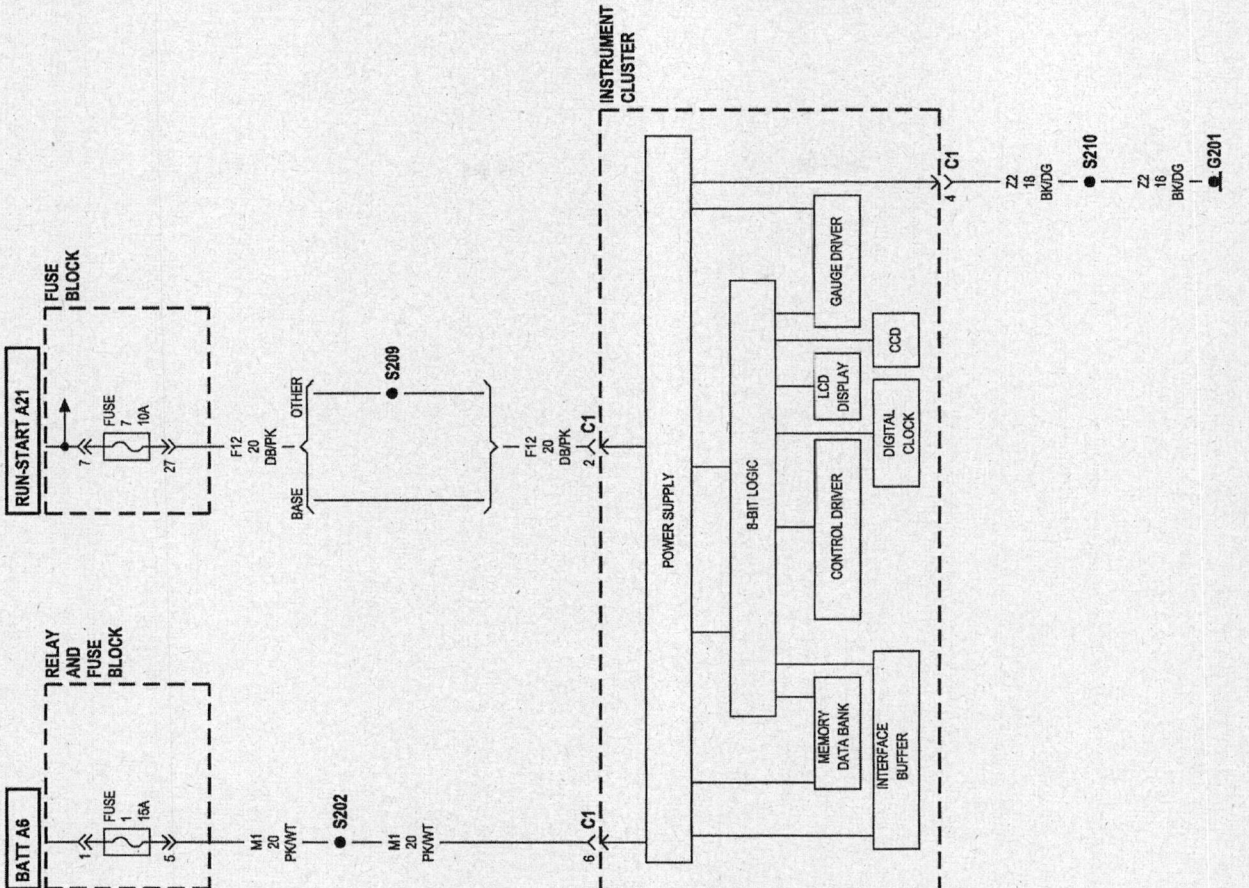

Fig. 11 Instrument Cluster (Part 1 of 6). Full Size Van

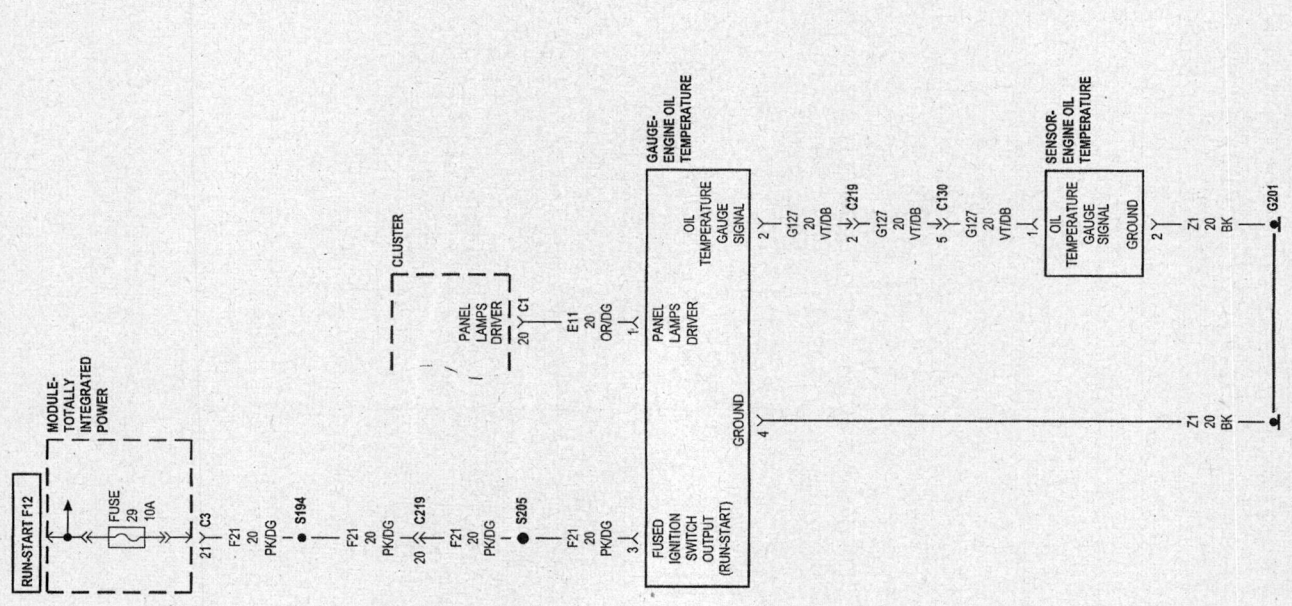

Fig. 10 Instrument Cluster (Part 9 of 9). 2005–06 Full Size Pickup

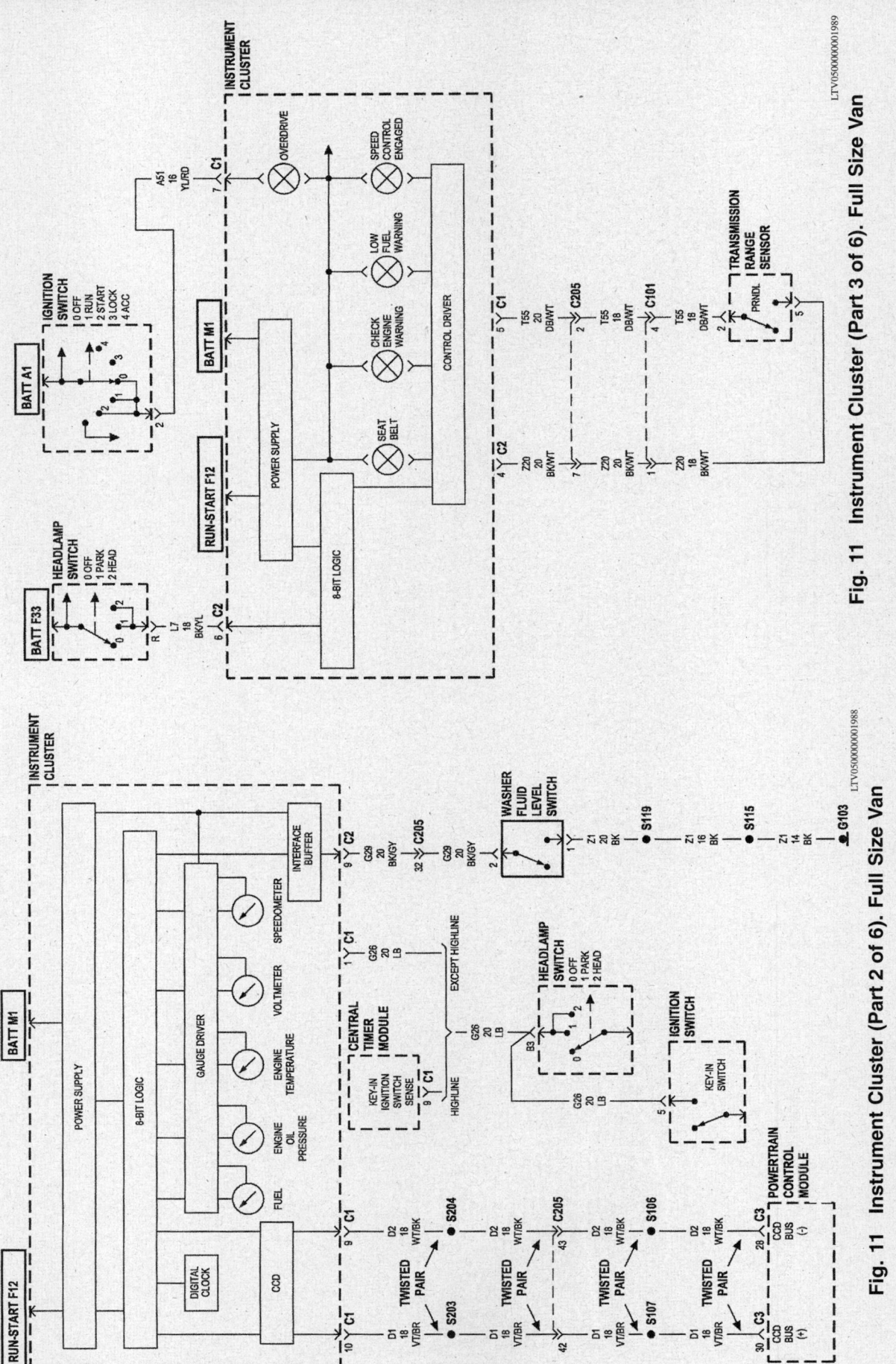

Fig. 11 Instrument Cluster (Part 3 of 6). Full Size Van

Fig. 11 Instrument Cluster (Part 2 of 6). Full Size Van

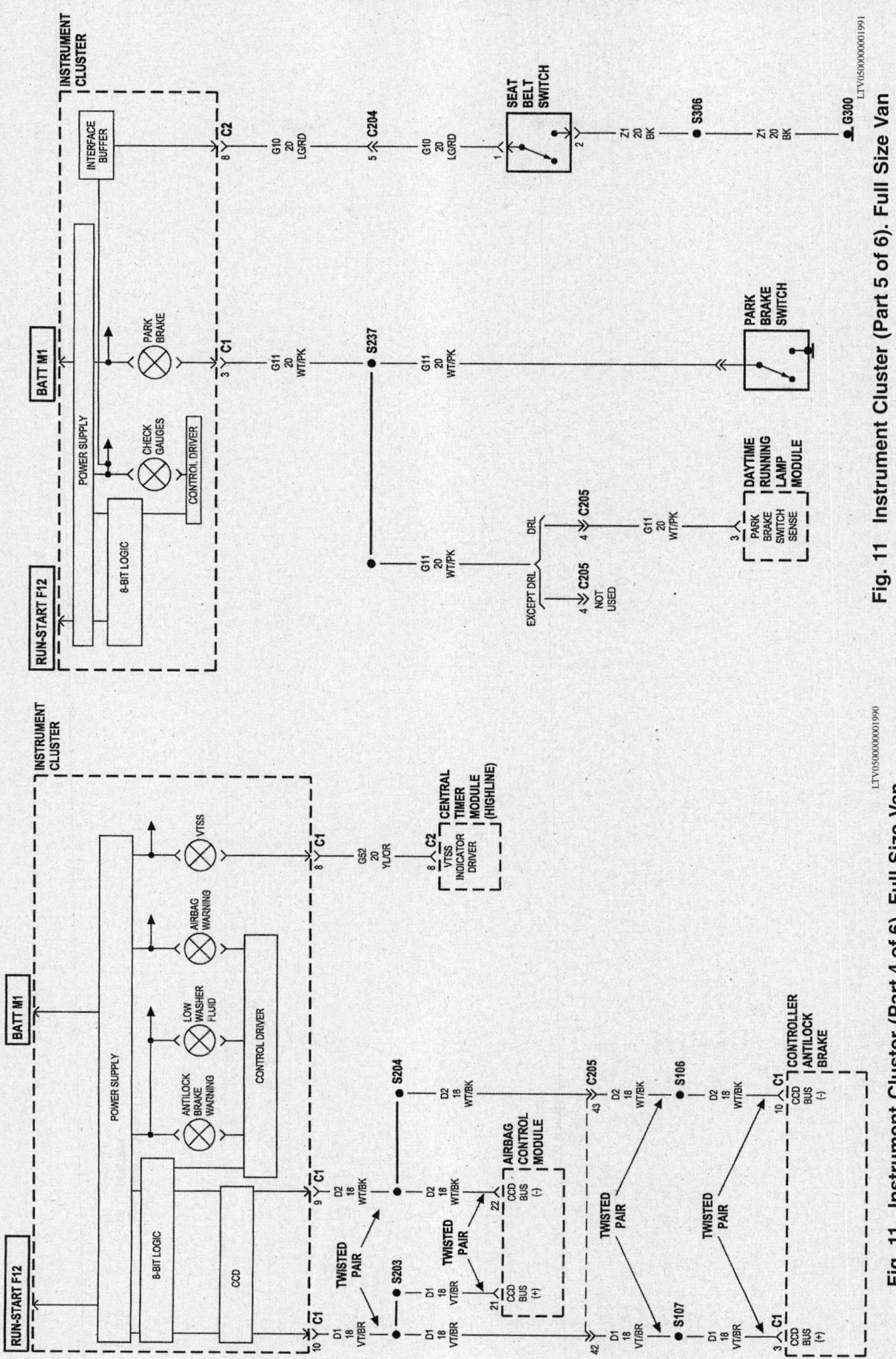

Fig. 11 Instrument Cluster (Part 5 of 6). Full Size Van

Fig. 11 Instrument Cluster (Part 4 of 6). Full Size Van

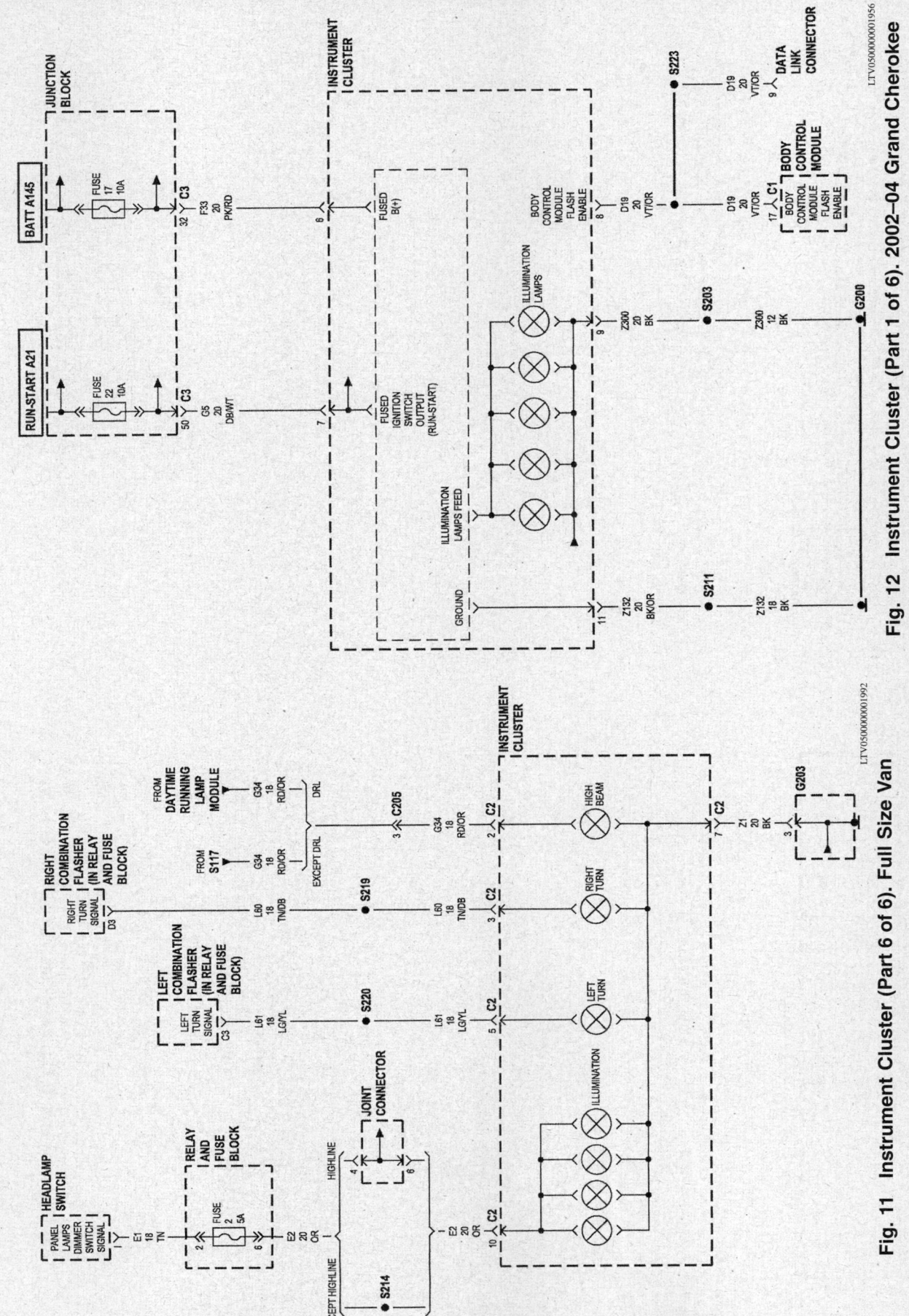

Fig. 12 Instrument Cluster (Part 1 of 6). 2002–04 Grand Cherokee

Fig. 11 Instrument Cluster (Part 6 of 6). Full Size Van

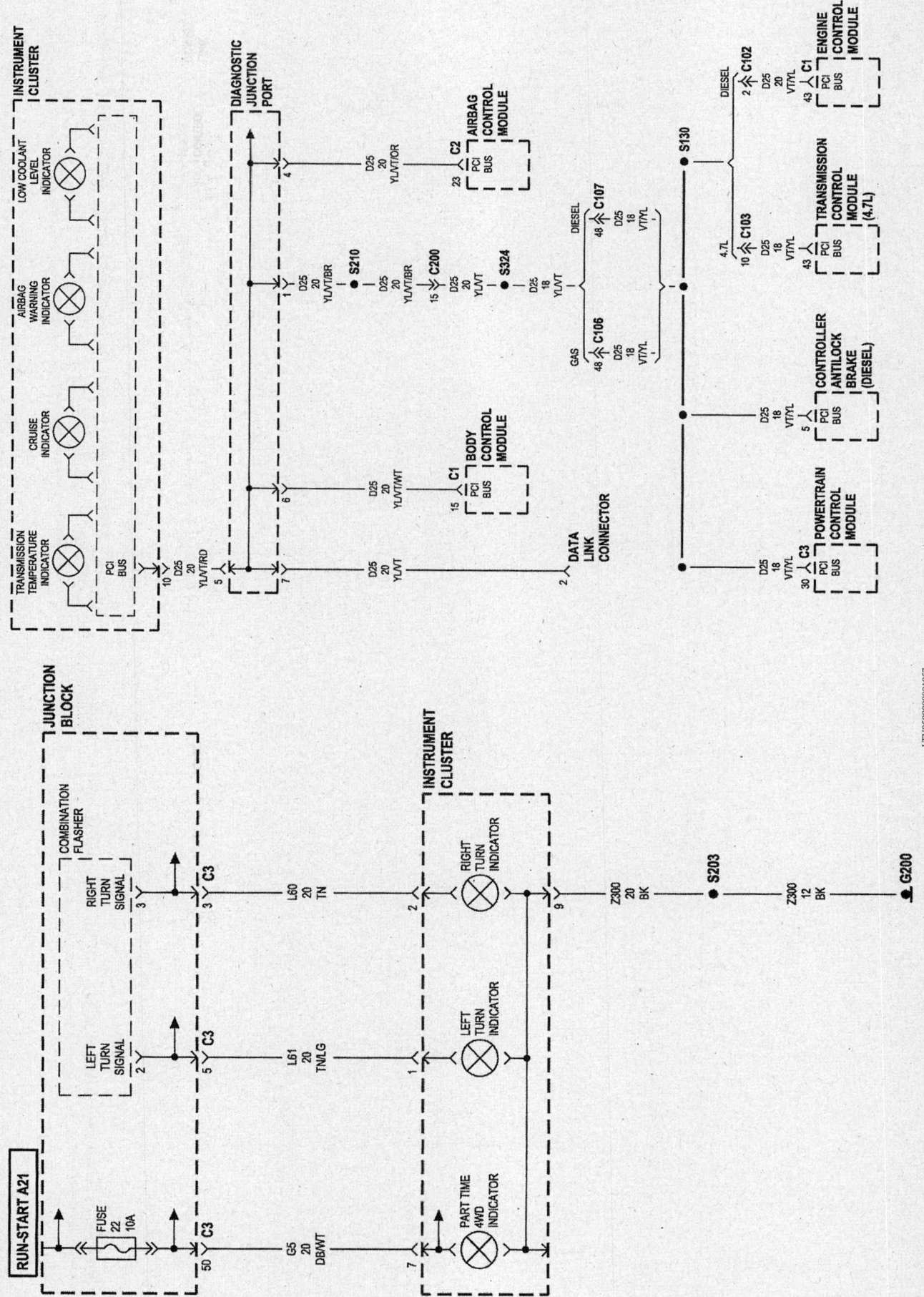

Fig. 12 Instrument Cluster (Part 3 of 6). 2002–04 Grand Cherokee

Fig. 12 Instrument Cluster (Part 2 of 6). 2002–04 Grand Cherokee

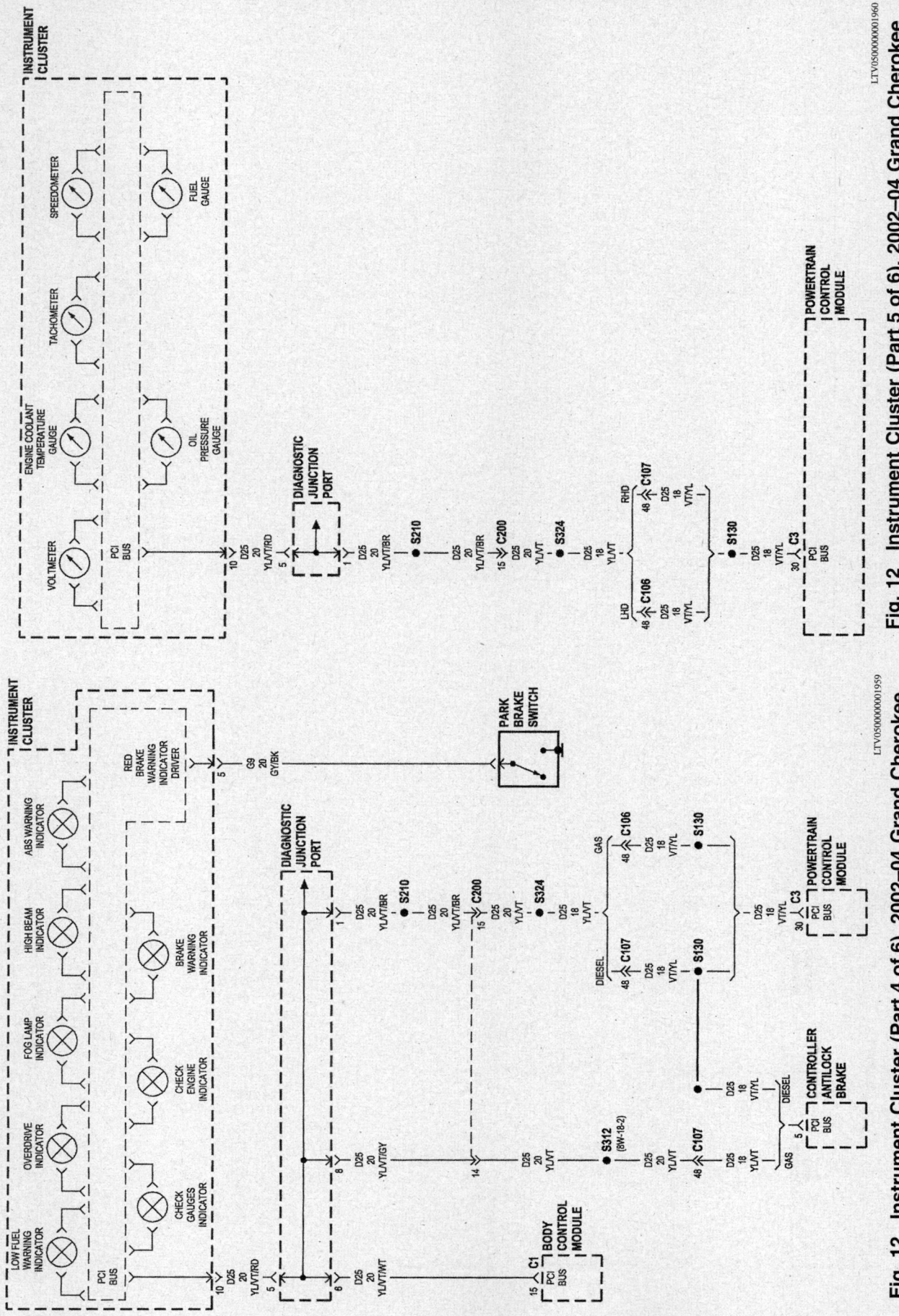

Fig. 12 Instrument Cluster (Part 5 of 6). 2002–04 Grand Cherokee

Fig. 12 Instrument Cluster (Part 4 of 6). 2002–04 Grand Cherokee

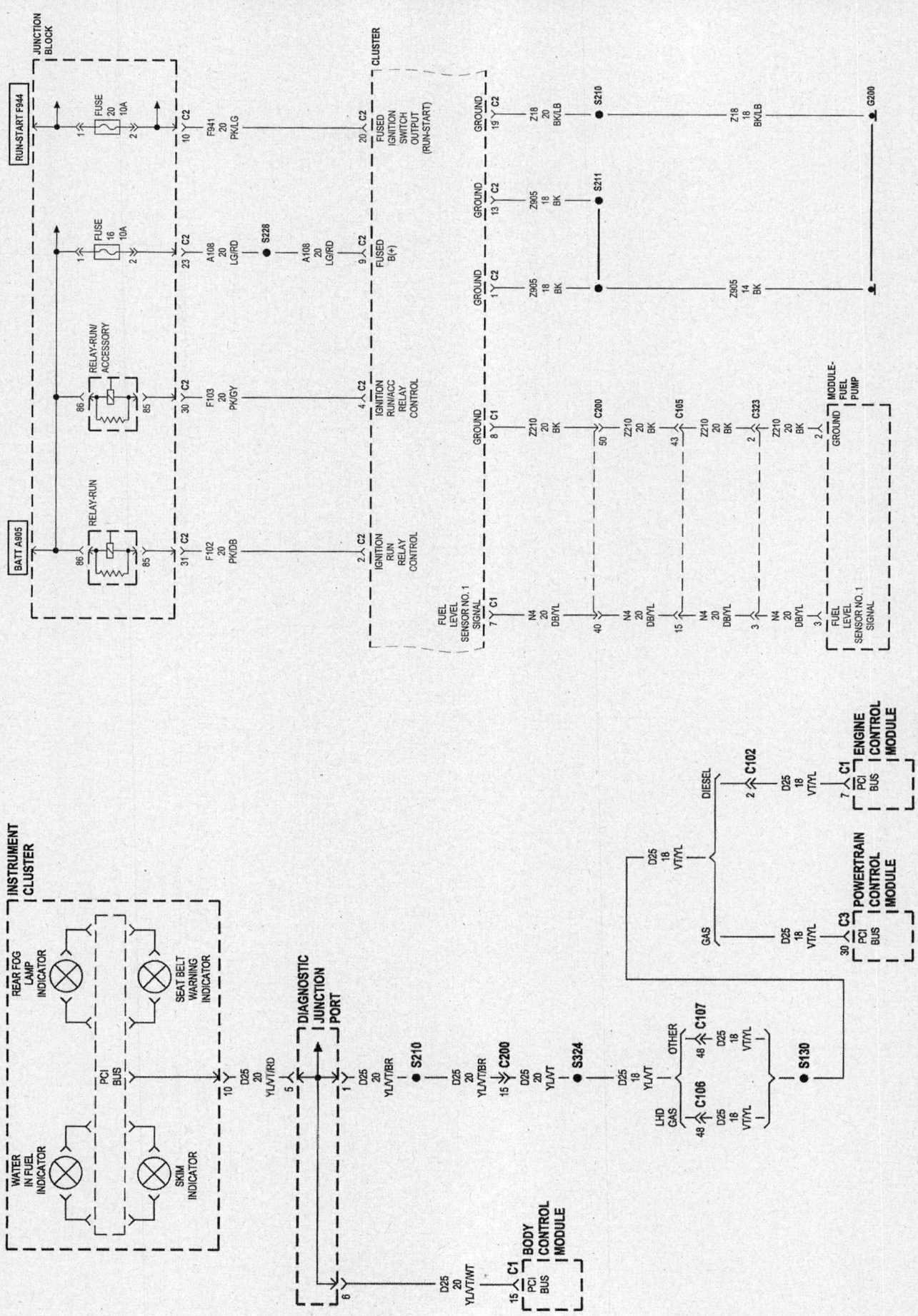

Fig. 13 Instrument Cluster (Part 1 of 5). 2005–06 Grand Cherokee

Fig. 12 Instrument Cluster (Part 6 of 6). 2002–04 Grand Cherokee

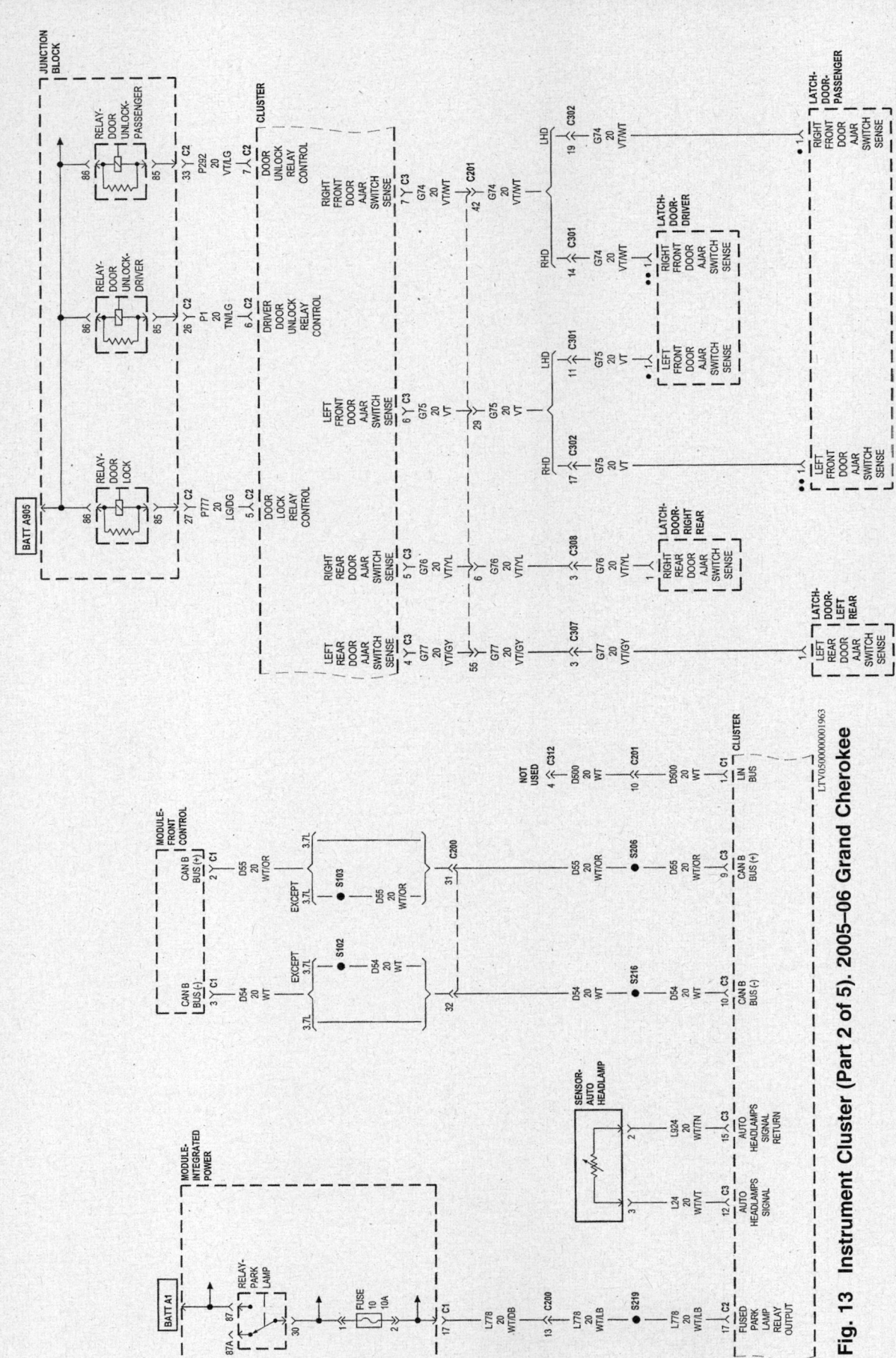

Fig. 13 Instrument Cluster (Part 3 of 5). 2005–06 Grand Cherokee

Fig. 13 Instrument Cluster (Part 2 of 5). 2005–06 Grand Cherokee

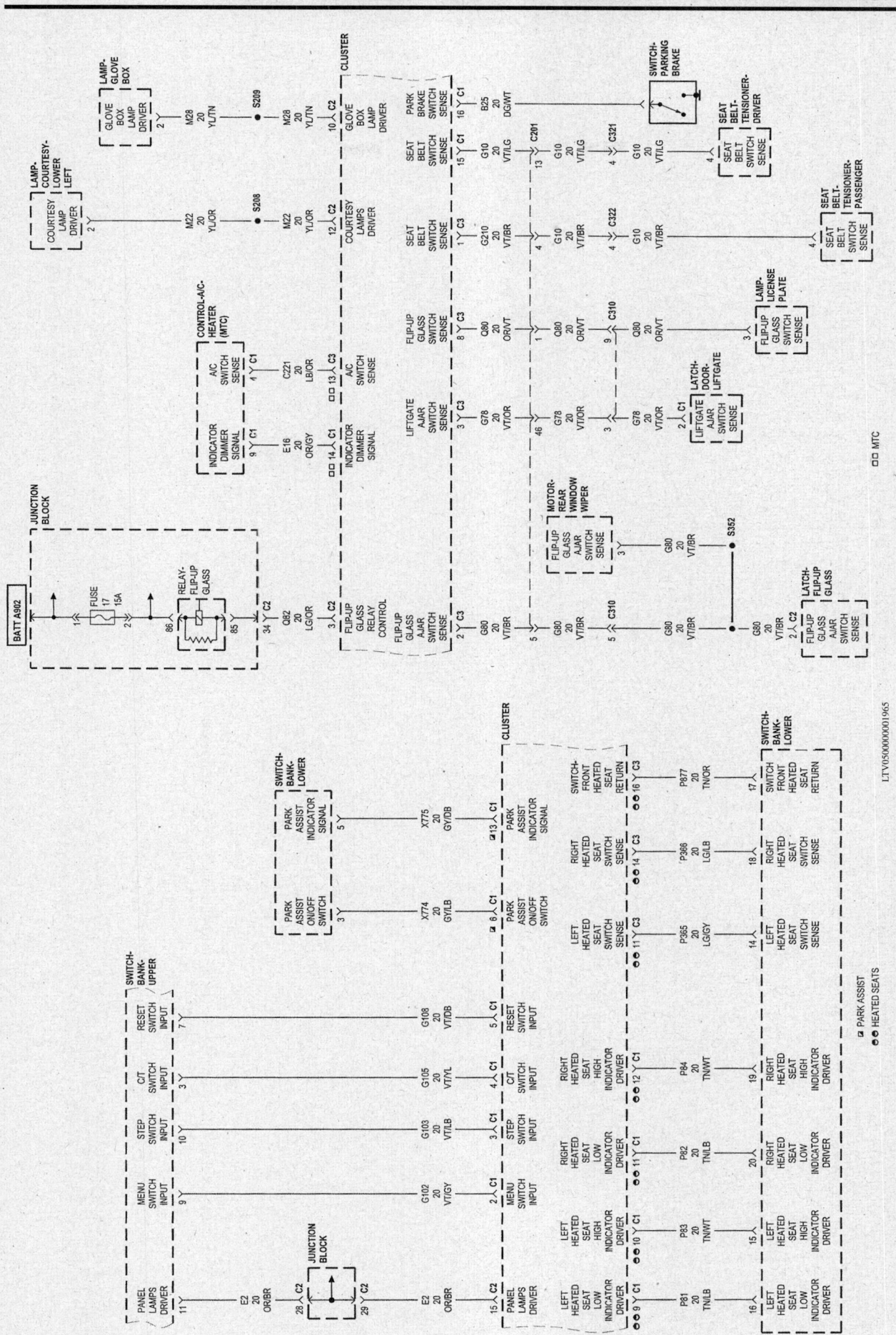

Fig. 13   Instrument Cluster (Part 5 of 5). 2005–06 Grand Cherokee

Fig. 13   Instrument Cluster (Part 4 of 5). 2005–06 Grand Cherokee

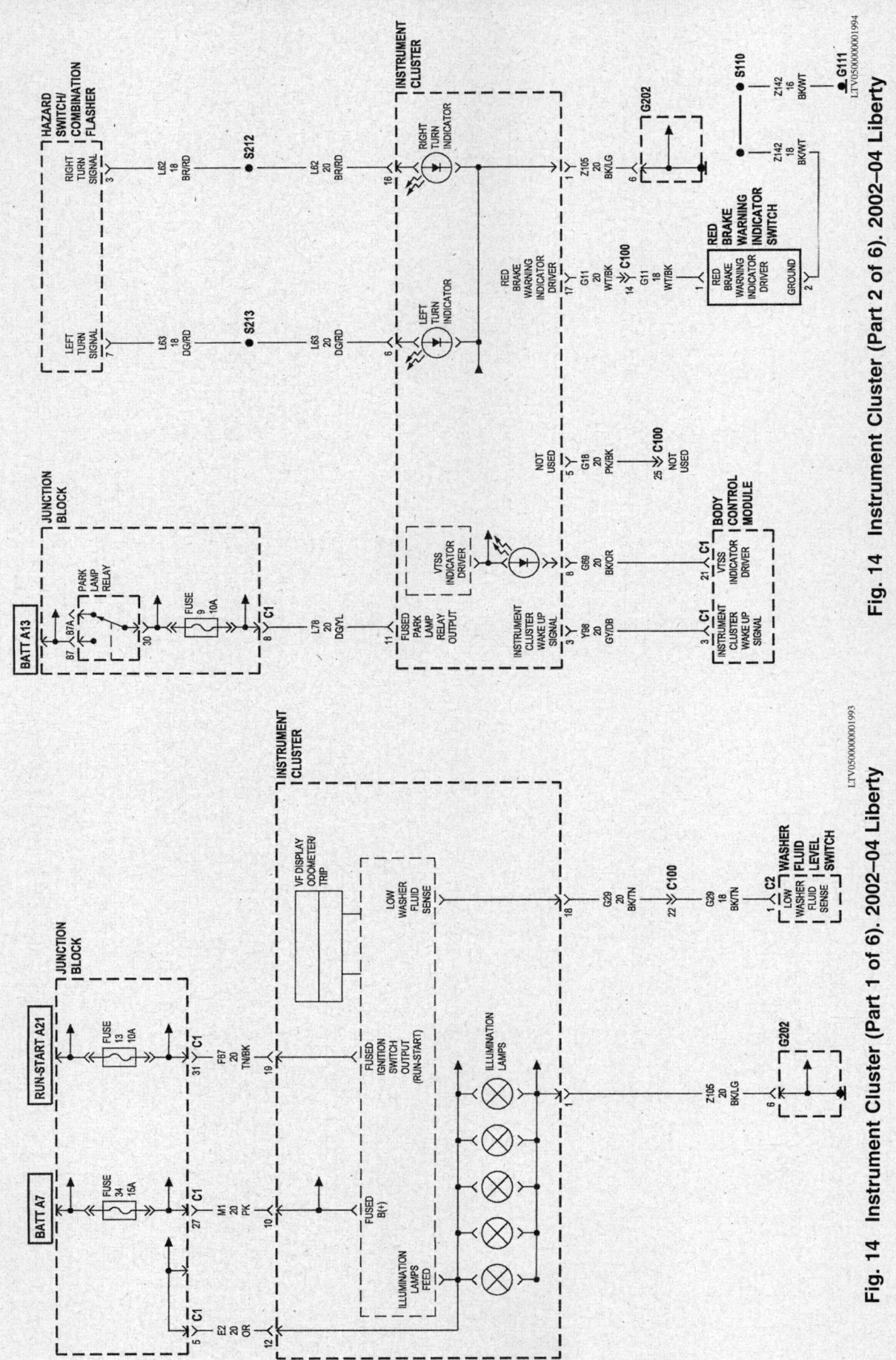

Fig. 14 Instrument Cluster (Part 2 of 6). 2002–04 Liberty

Fig. 14 Instrument Cluster (Part 1 of 6). 2002–04 Liberty

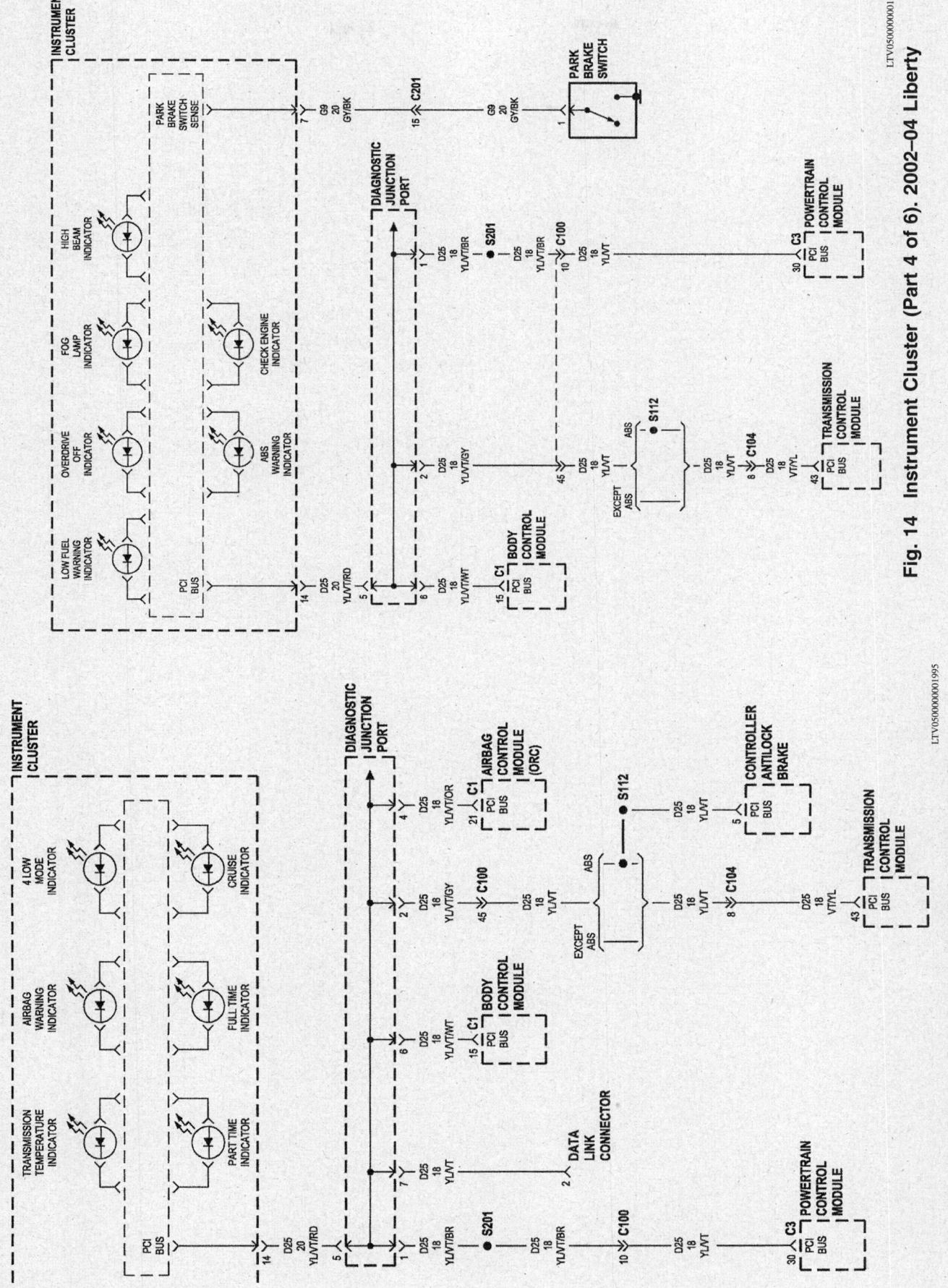

Fig. 14 Instrument Cluster (Part 4 of 6). 2002–04 Liberty

Fig. 14 Instrument Cluster (Part 3 of 6). 2002–04 Liberty

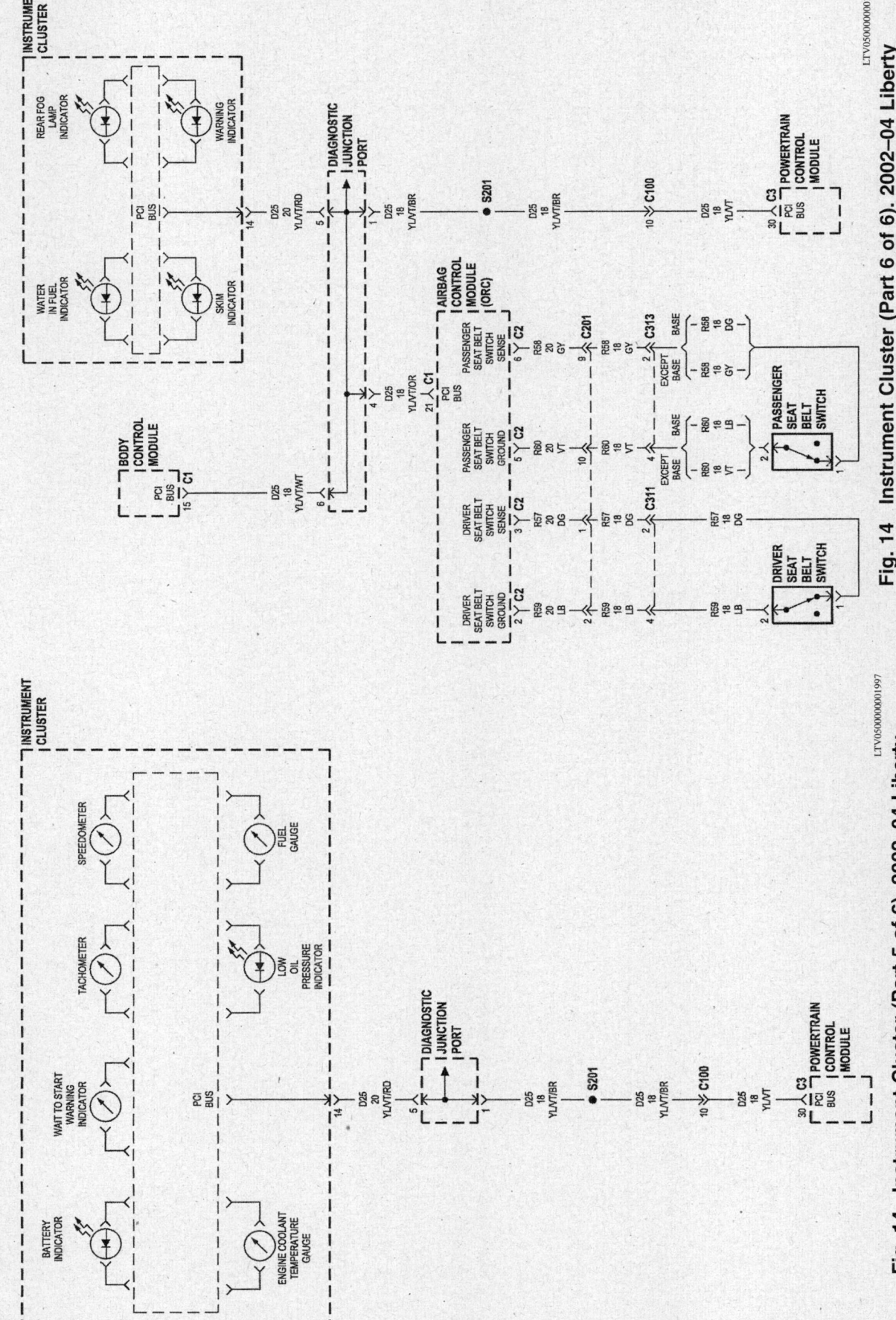

Fig. 14 Instrument Cluster (Part 6 of 6). 2002–04 Liberty

Fig. 14 Instrument Cluster (Part 5 of 6). 2002–04 Liberty

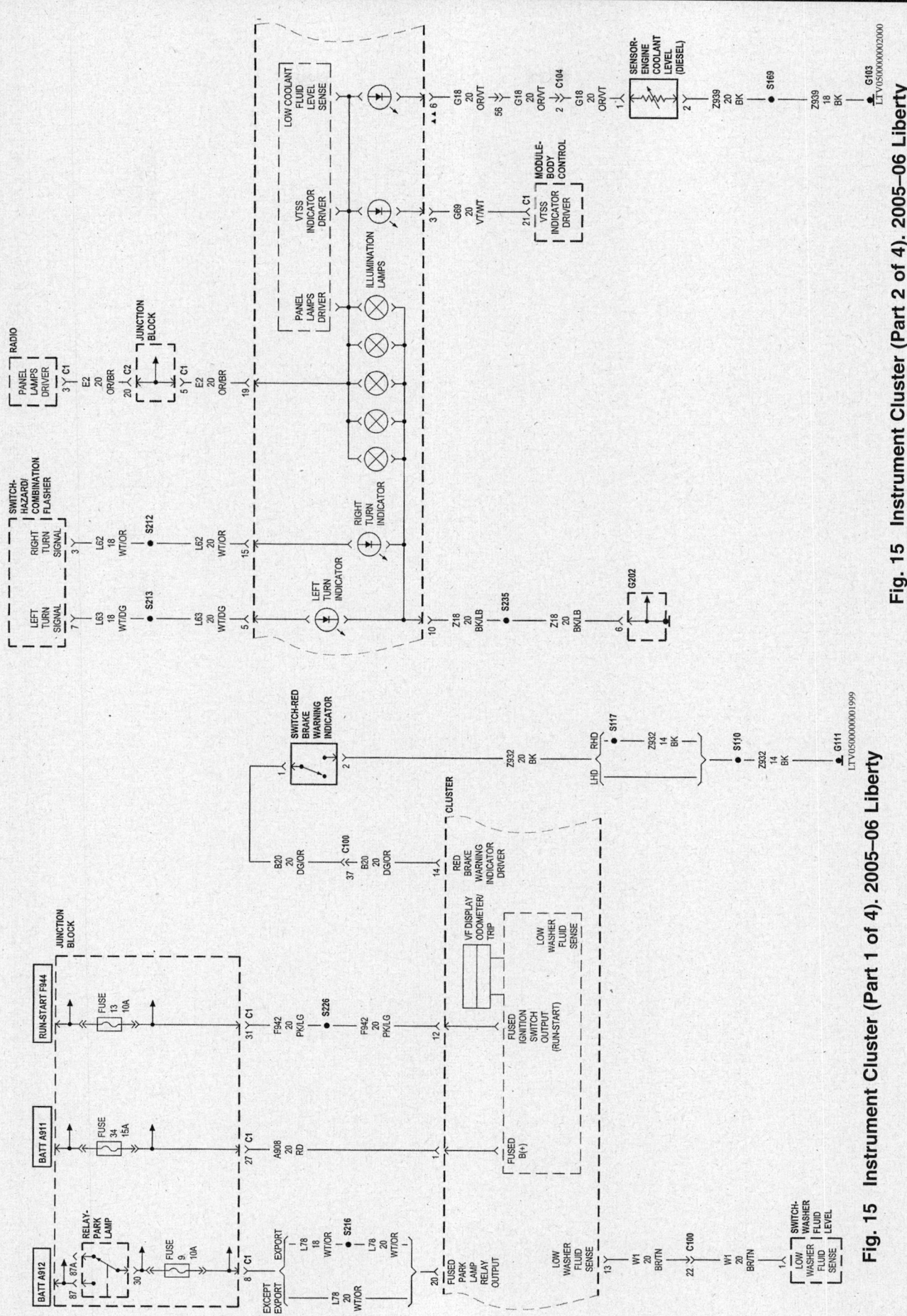

Fig. 15 Instrument Cluster (Part 2 of 4). 2005–06 Liberty

Fig. 15 Instrument Cluster (Part 1 of 4). 2005–06 Liberty

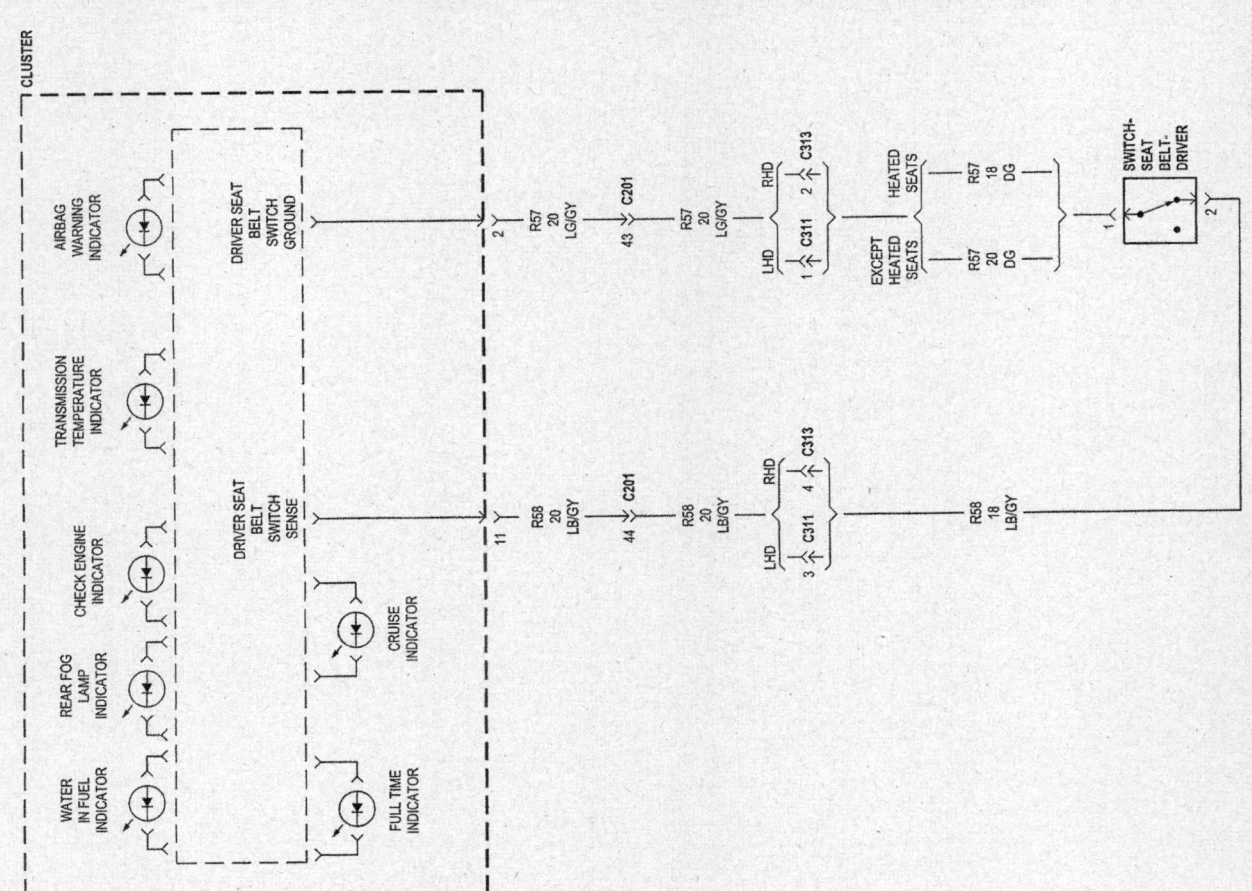

Fig. 15 Instrument Cluster (Part 4 of 4). 2005–06 Liberty

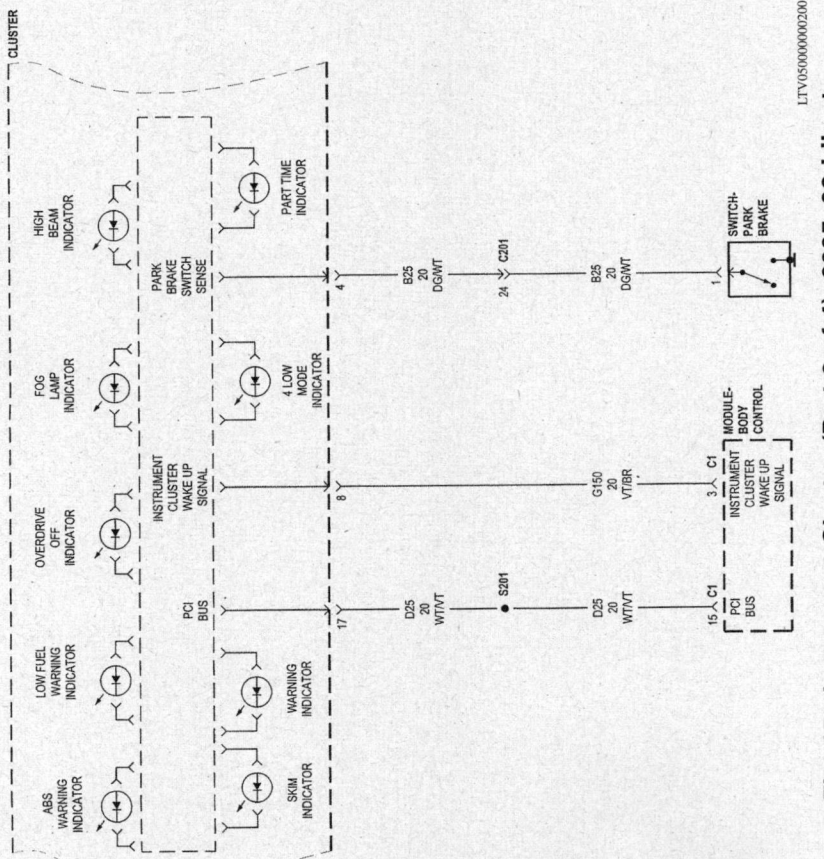

Fig. 15 Instrument Cluster (Part 3 of 4). 2005–06 Liberty

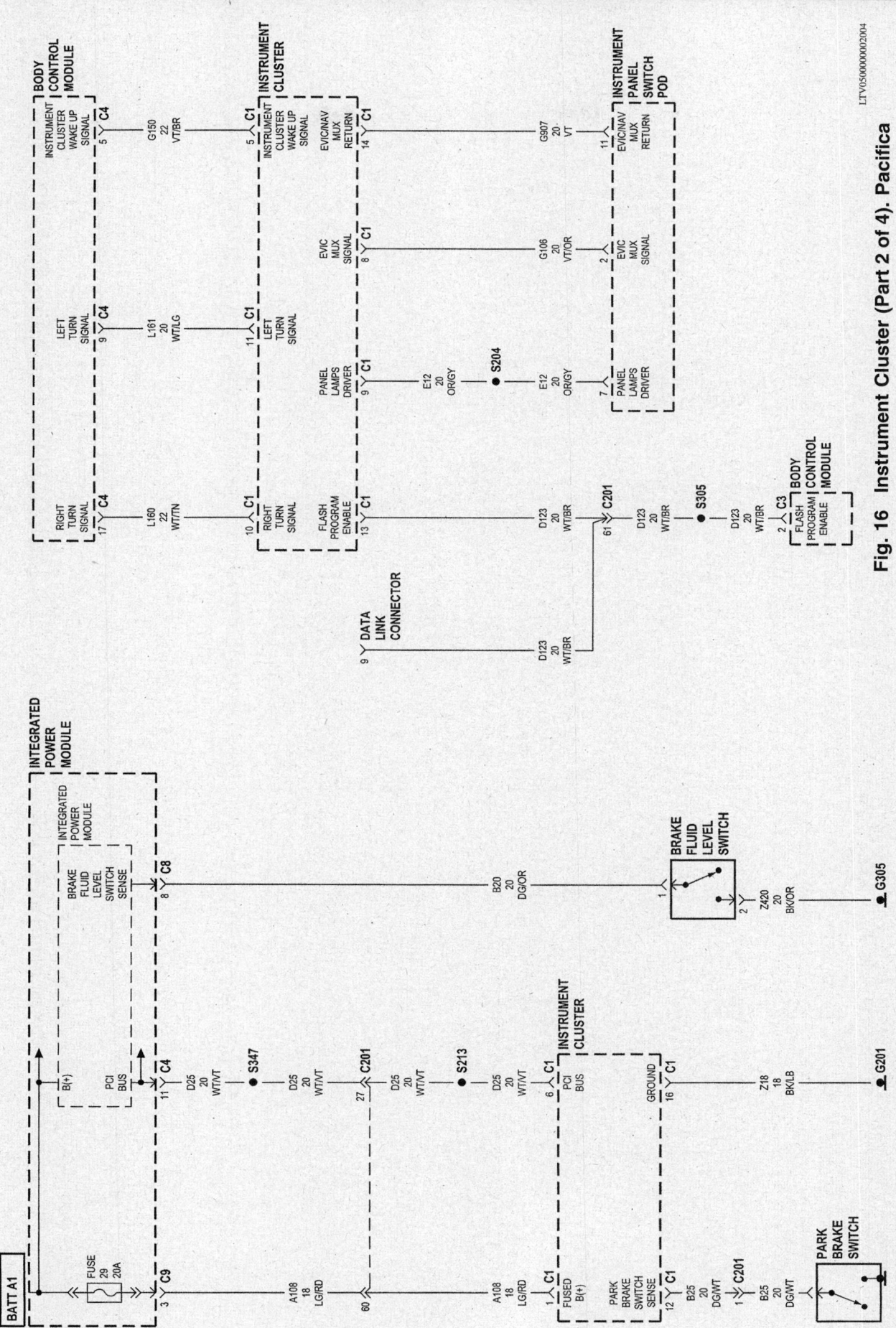

Fig. 16 Instrument Cluster (Part 2 of 4). Pacifica

Fig. 16 Instrument Cluster (Part 1 of 4). Pacifica

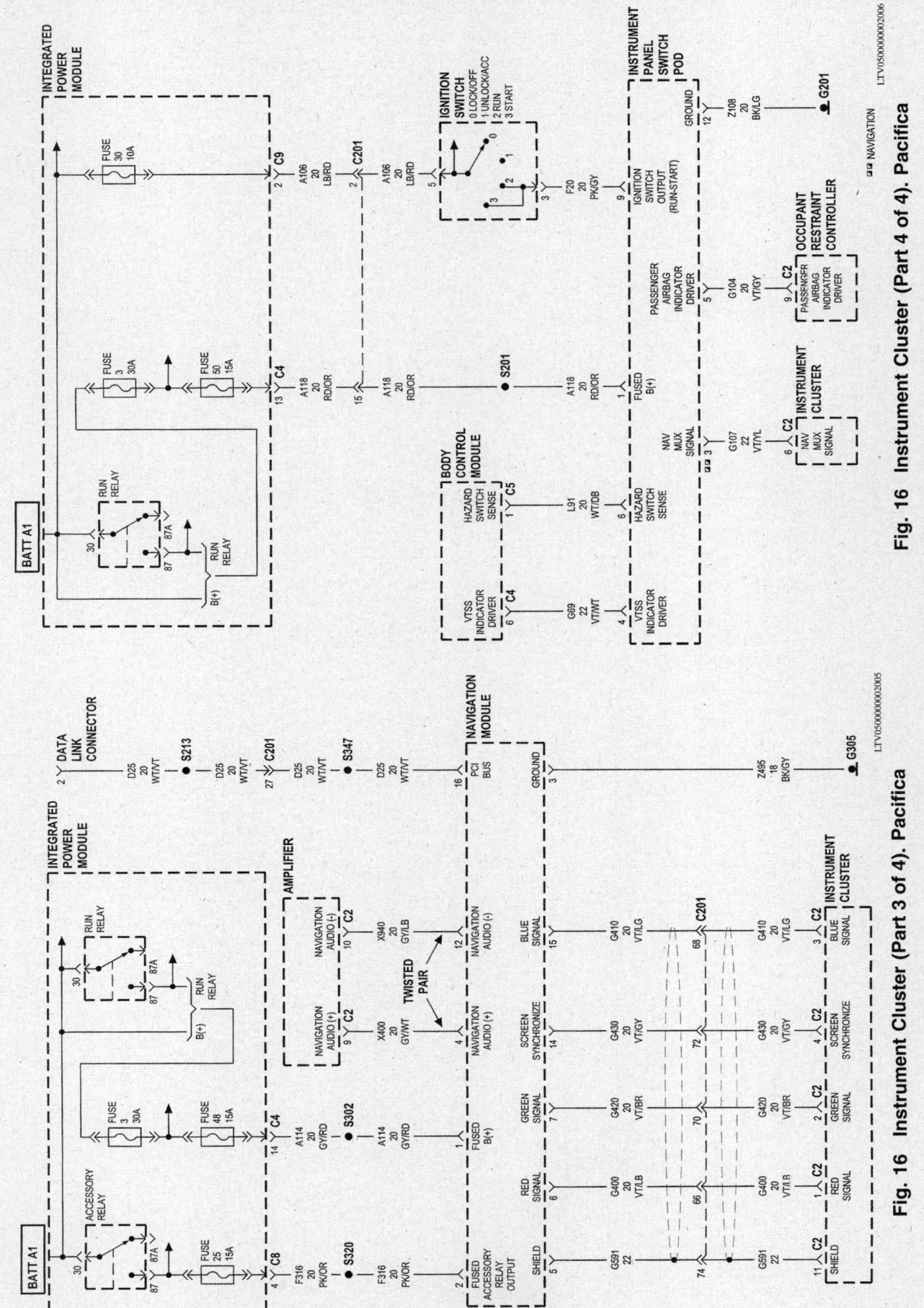

Fig. 16 Instrument Cluster (Part 4 of 4). Pacifica

Fig. 16 Instrument Cluster (Part 3 of 4). Pacifica

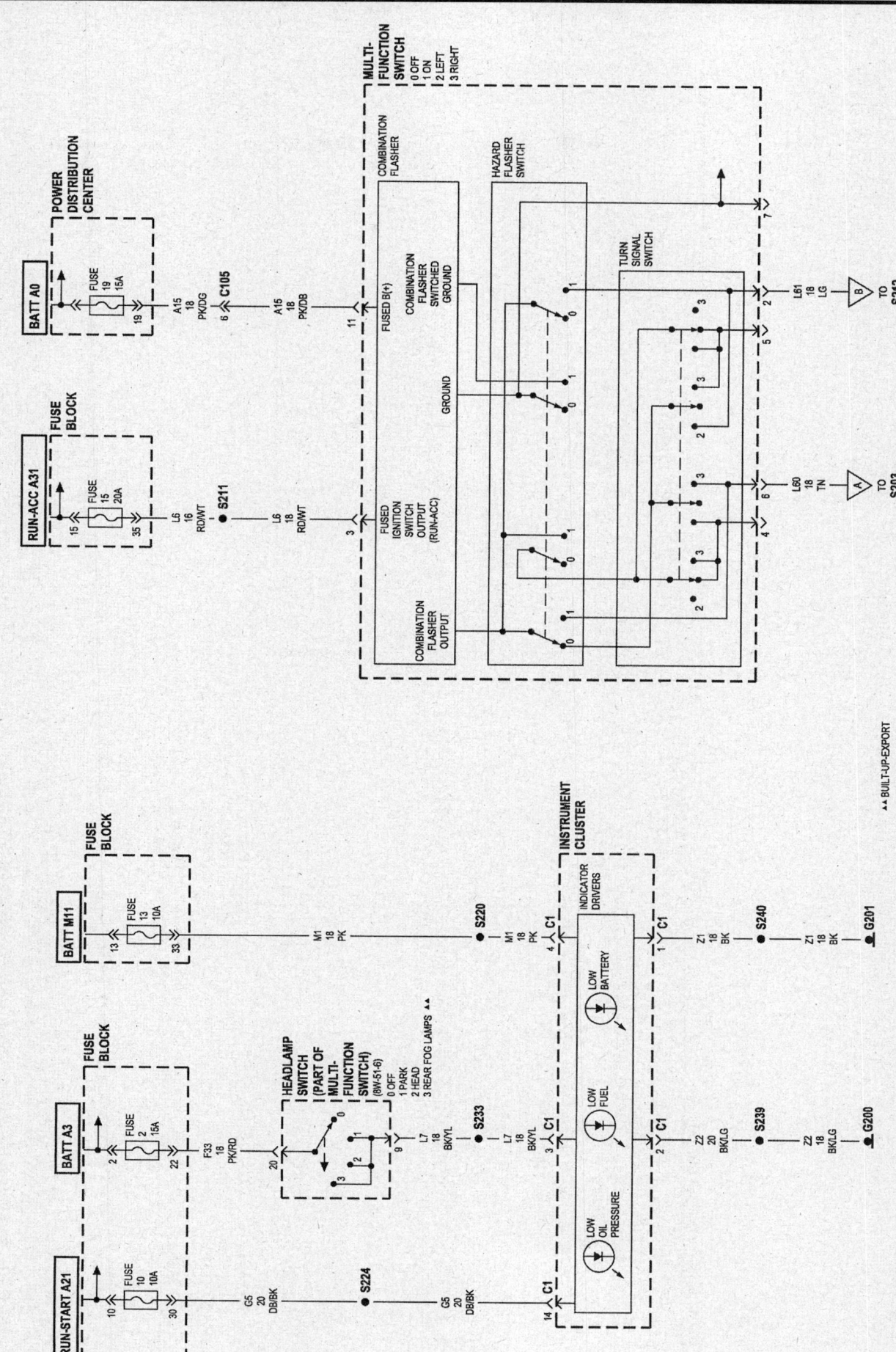

Fig. 17 Instrument Cluster (Part 2 of 13). 2002–04 PT Cruiser

Fig. 17 Instrument Cluster (Part 1 of 13). 2002–04 PT Cruiser

▲▲ BUILT-UP-EXPORT

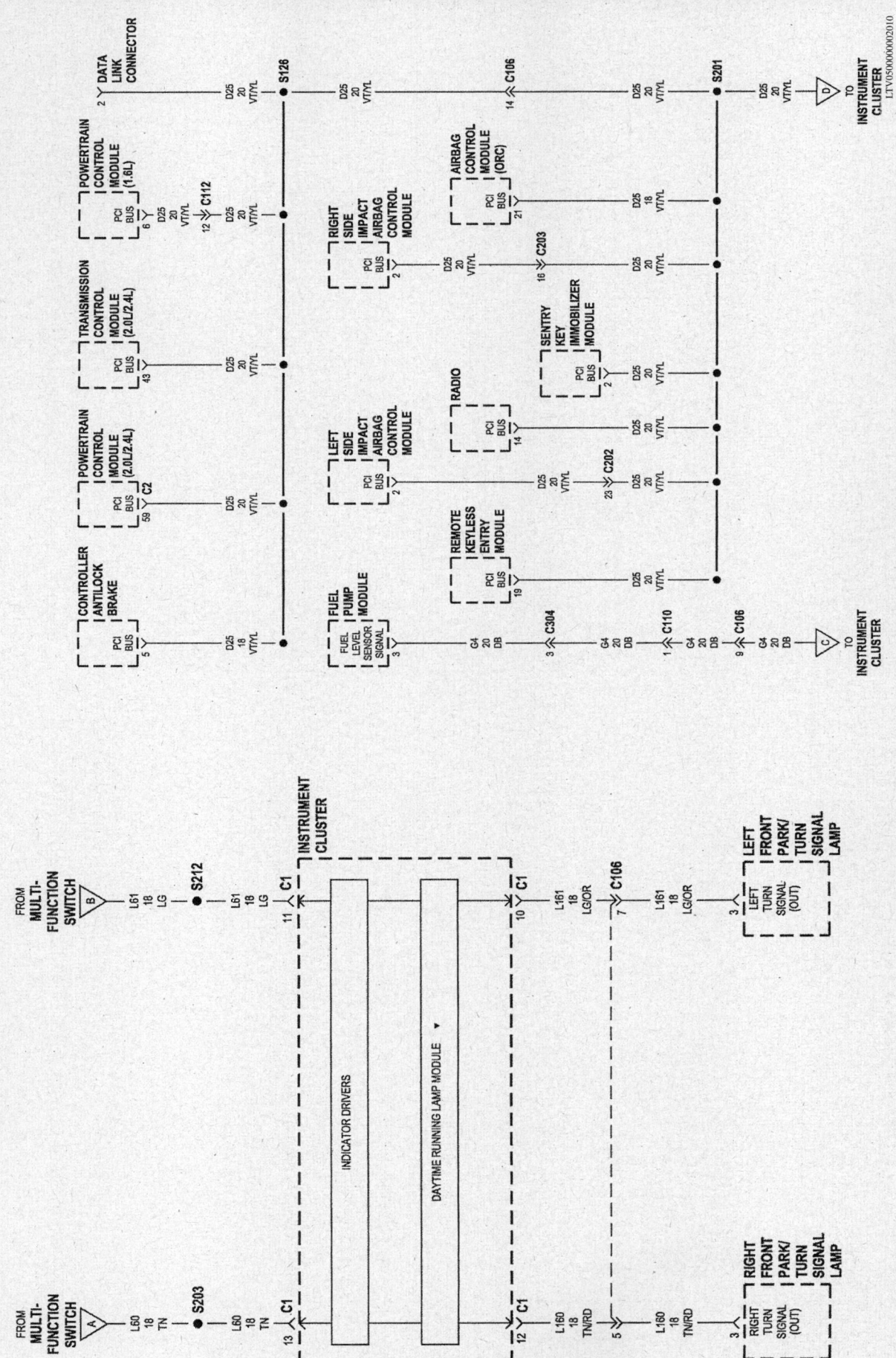

Fig. 17 Instrument Cluster (Part 4 of 13). 2002–04 PT Cruiser

Fig. 17 Instrument Cluster (Part 3 of 13). 2002–04 PT Cruiser

▼ CANADA ONLY

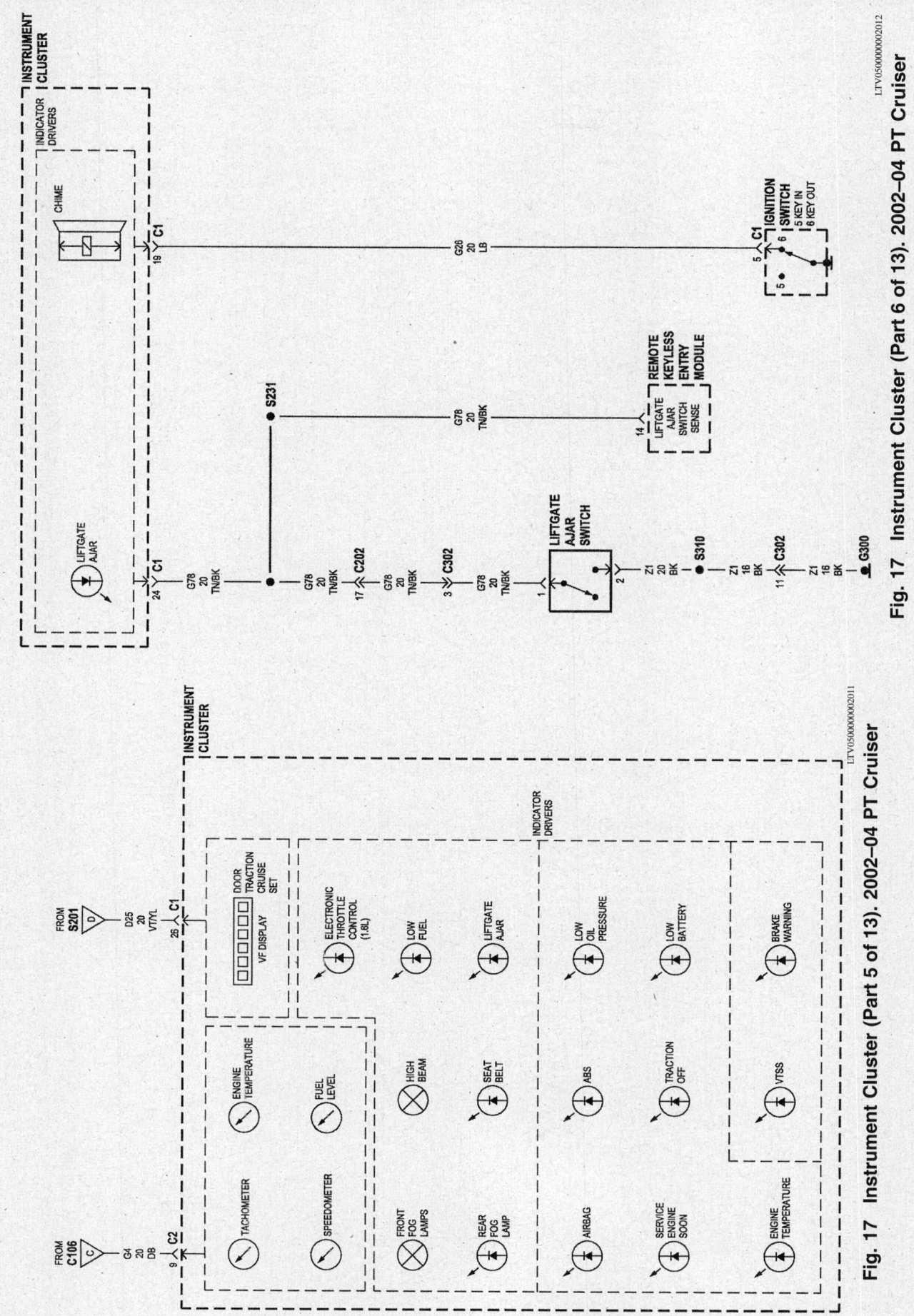

Fig. 17 Instrument Cluster (Part 6 of 13). 2002–04 PT Cruiser

Fig. 17 Instrument Cluster (Part 5 of 13). 2002–04 PT Cruiser

Fig. 17 Instrument Cluster (Part 5 of 13). 2002–04 PT Cruiser

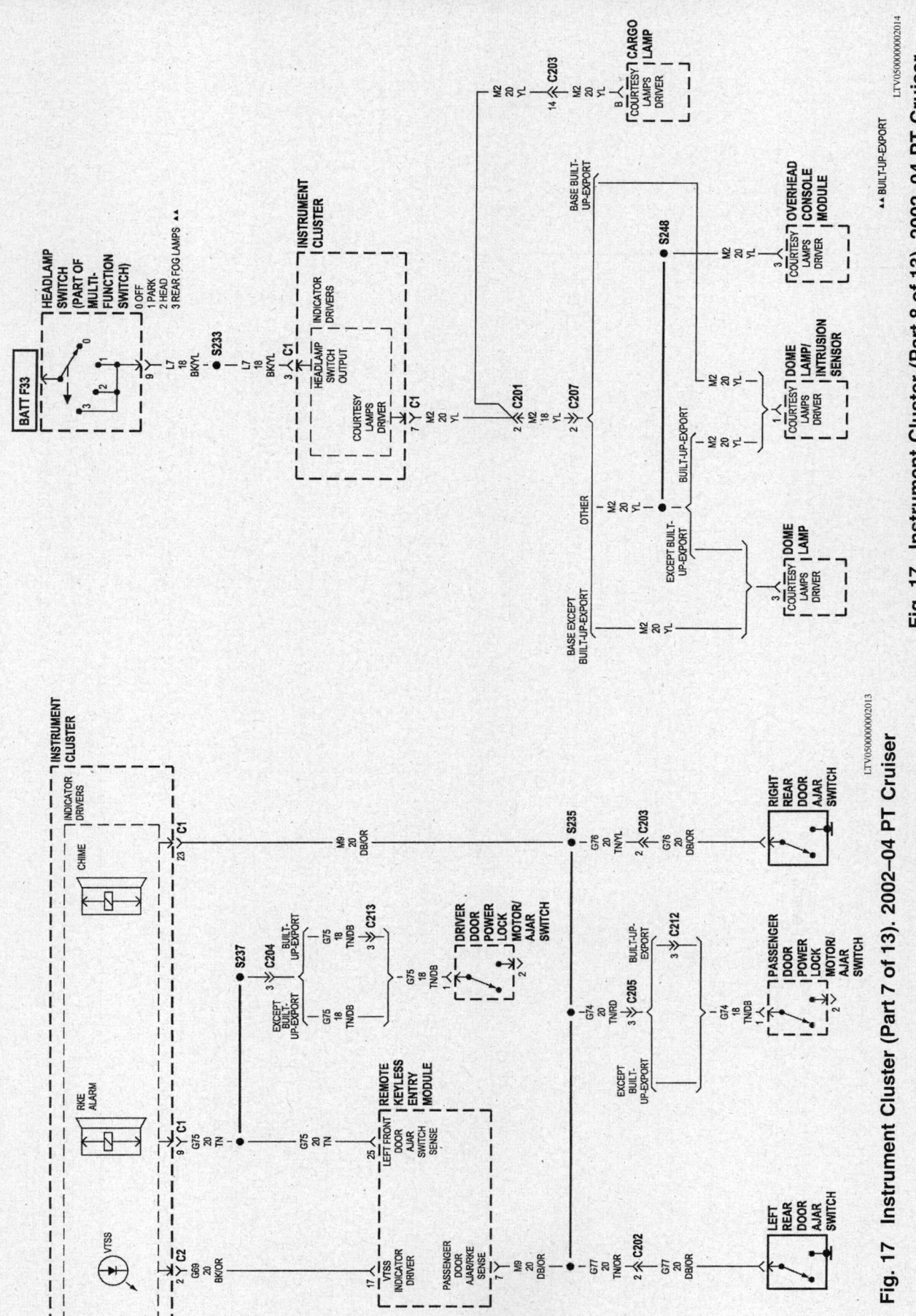

Fig. 17 Instrument Cluster (Part 8 of 13). 2002–04 PT Cruiser

Fig. 17 Instrument Cluster (Part 7 of 13). 2002–04 PT Cruiser

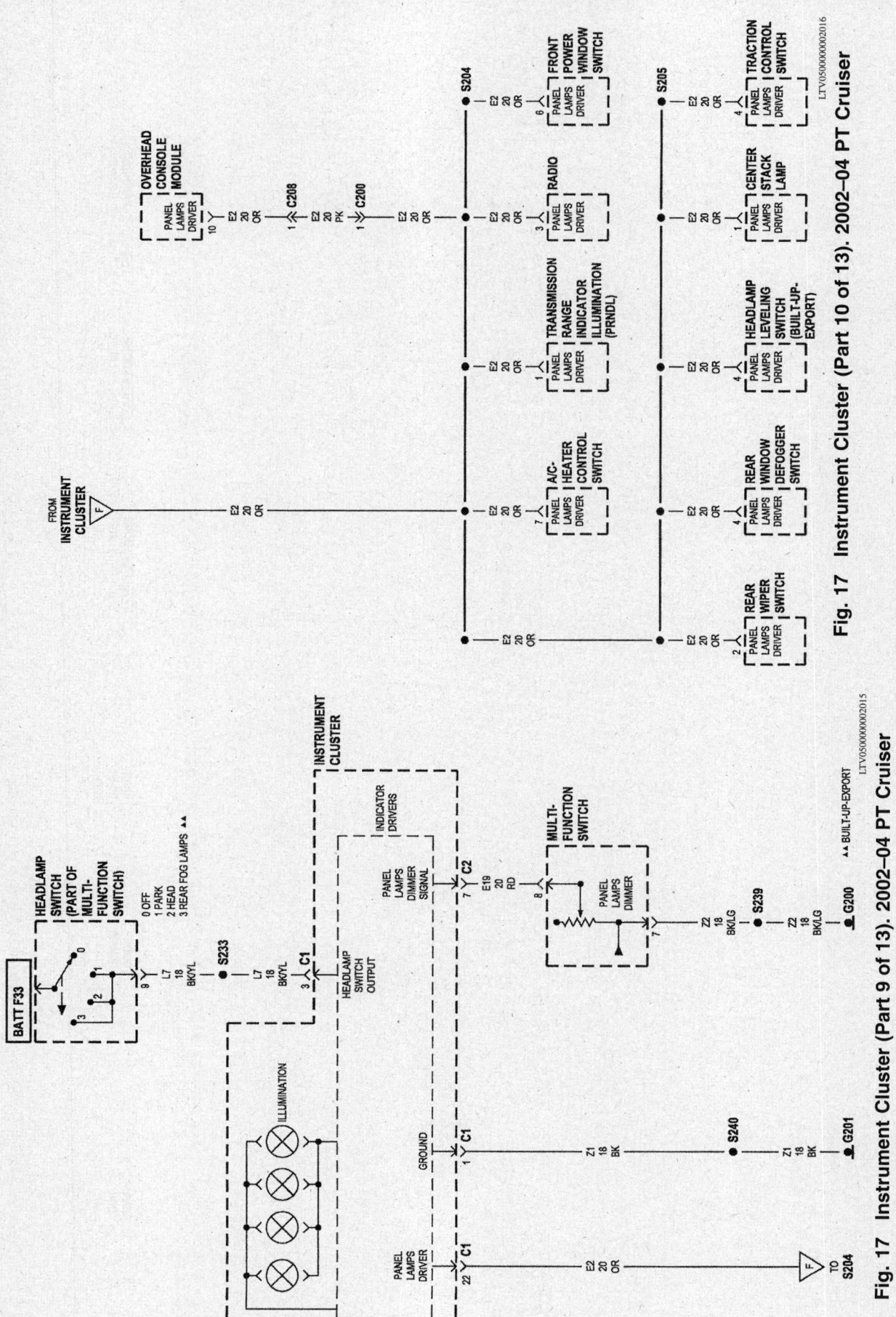

Fig. 17   Instrument Cluster (Part 10 of 13). 2002–04 PT Cruiser

Fig. 17   Instrument Cluster (Part 9 of 13). 2002–04 PT Cruiser

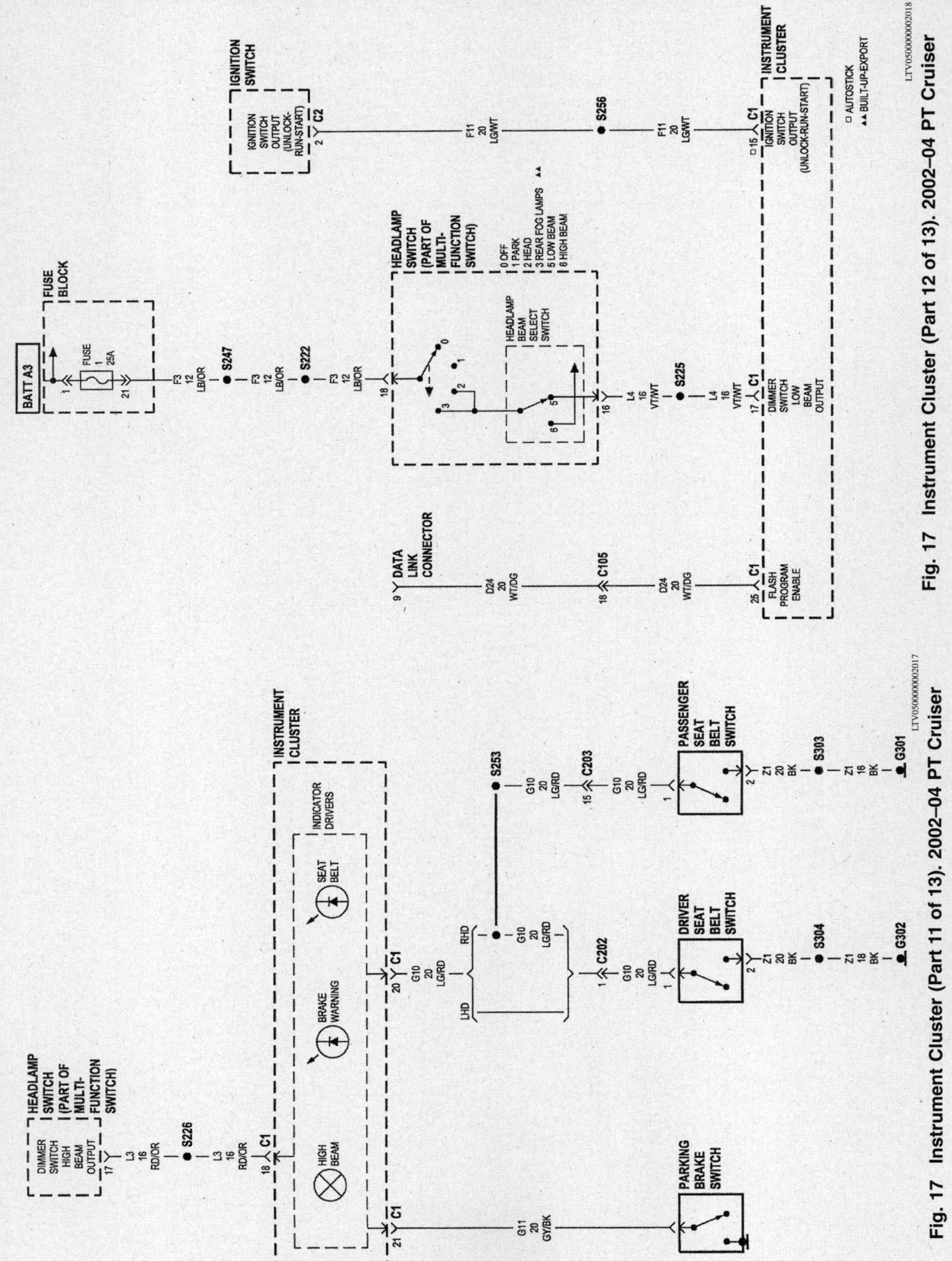

Fig. 17 Instrument Cluster (Part 12 of 13). 2002–04 PT Cruiser

Fig. 17 Instrument Cluster (Part 11 of 13). 2002–04 PT Cruiser

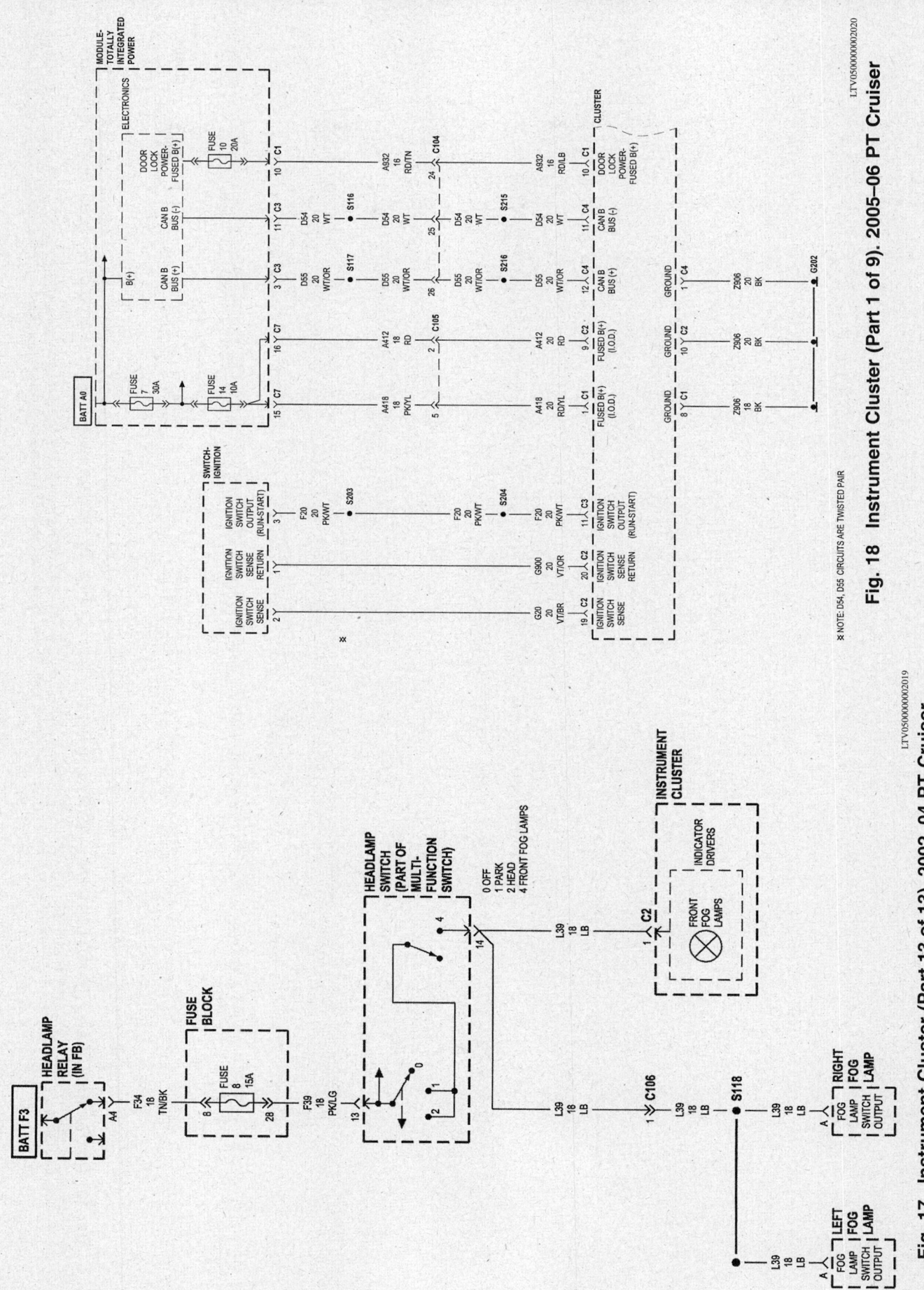

Fig. 18 Instrument Cluster (Part 1 of 9). 2005-06 PT Cruiser

Fig. 17 Instrument Cluster (Part 13 of 13). 2002-04 PT Cruiser

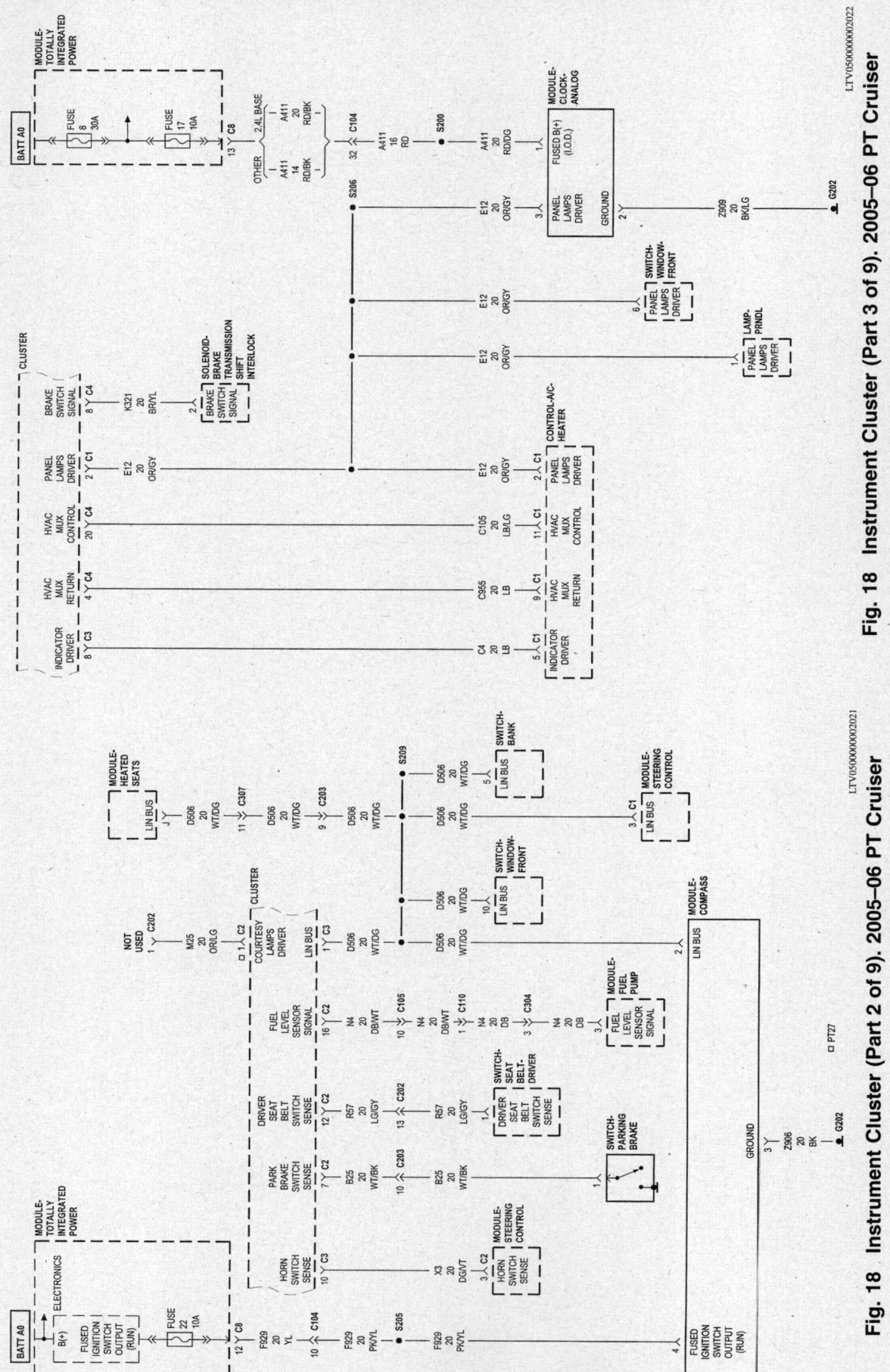

Fig. 18 Instrument Cluster (Part 3 of 9). 2005–06 PT Cruiser

Fig. 18 Instrument Cluster (Part 2 of 9). 2005–06 PT Cruiser

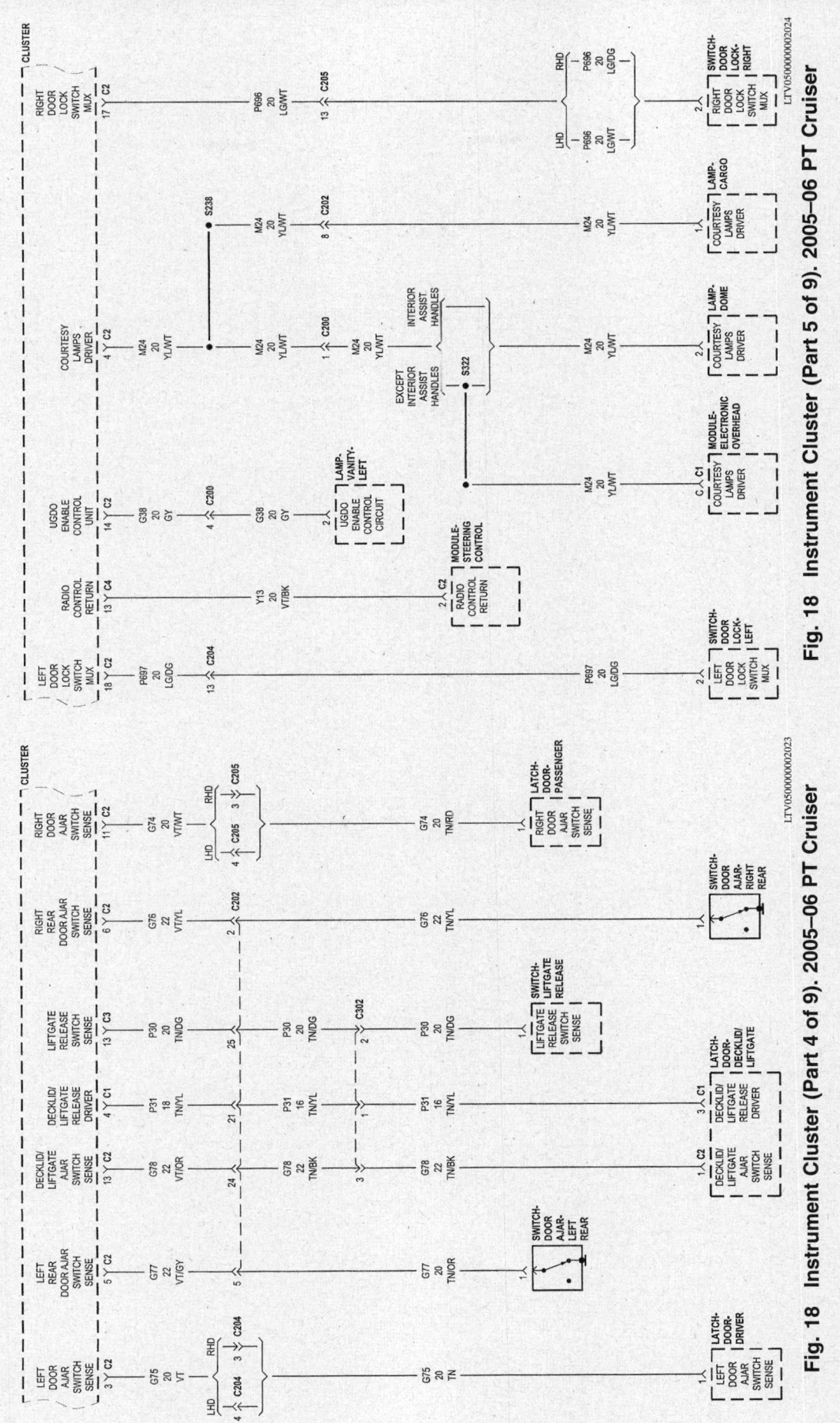

Fig. 18 Instrument Cluster (Part 5 of 9). 2005–06 PT Cruiser

Fig. 18 Instrument Cluster (Part 4 of 9). 2005–06 PT Cruiser

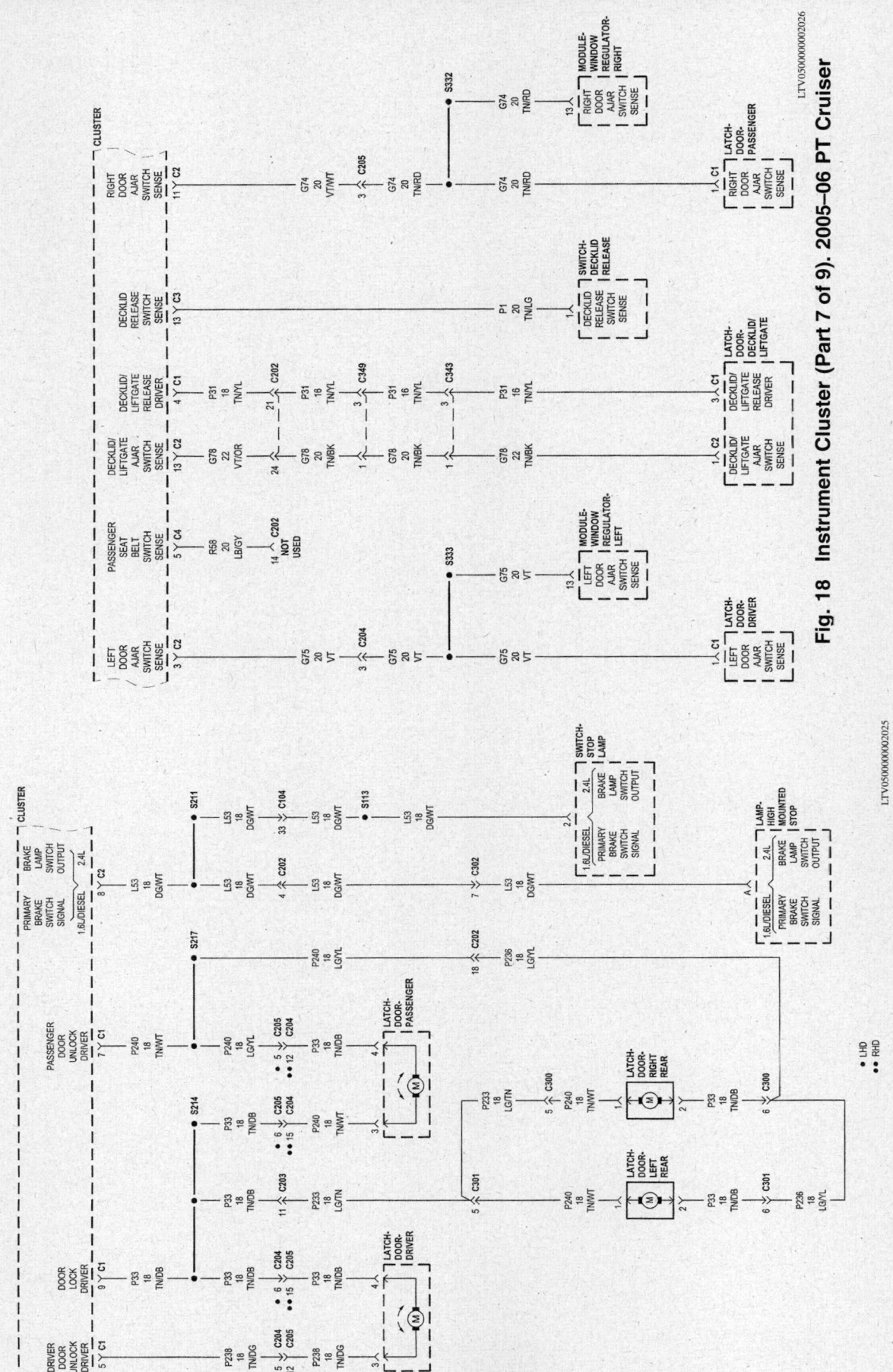

Fig. 18 Instrument Cluster (Part 7 of 9). 2005–06 PT Cruiser

Fig. 18 Instrument Cluster (Part 6 of 9). 2005–06 PT Cruiser

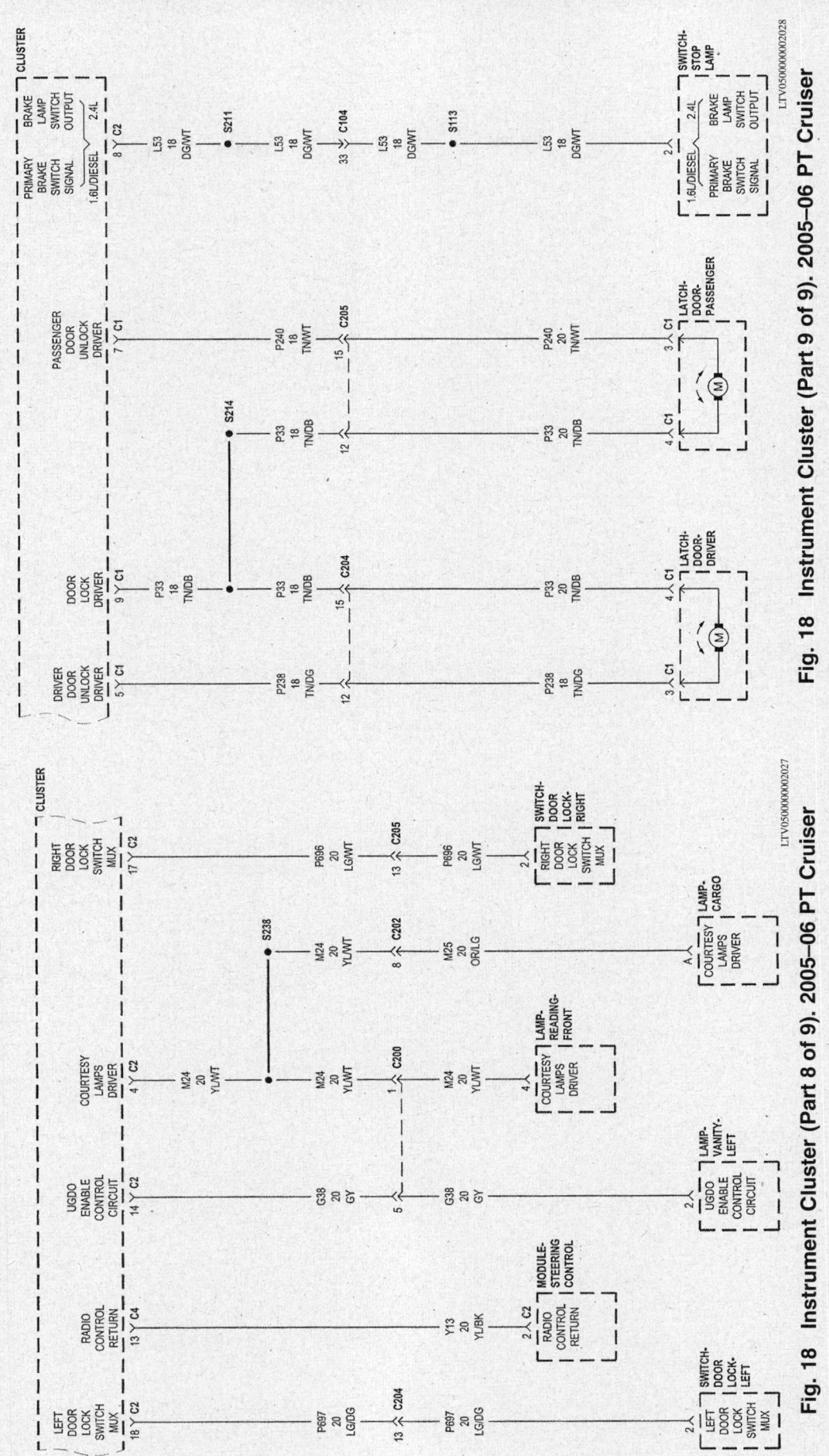

Fig. 18 Instrument Cluster (Part 9 of 9). 2005–06 PT Cruiser

Fig. 18 Instrument Cluster (Part 8 of 9). 2005–06 PT Cruiser

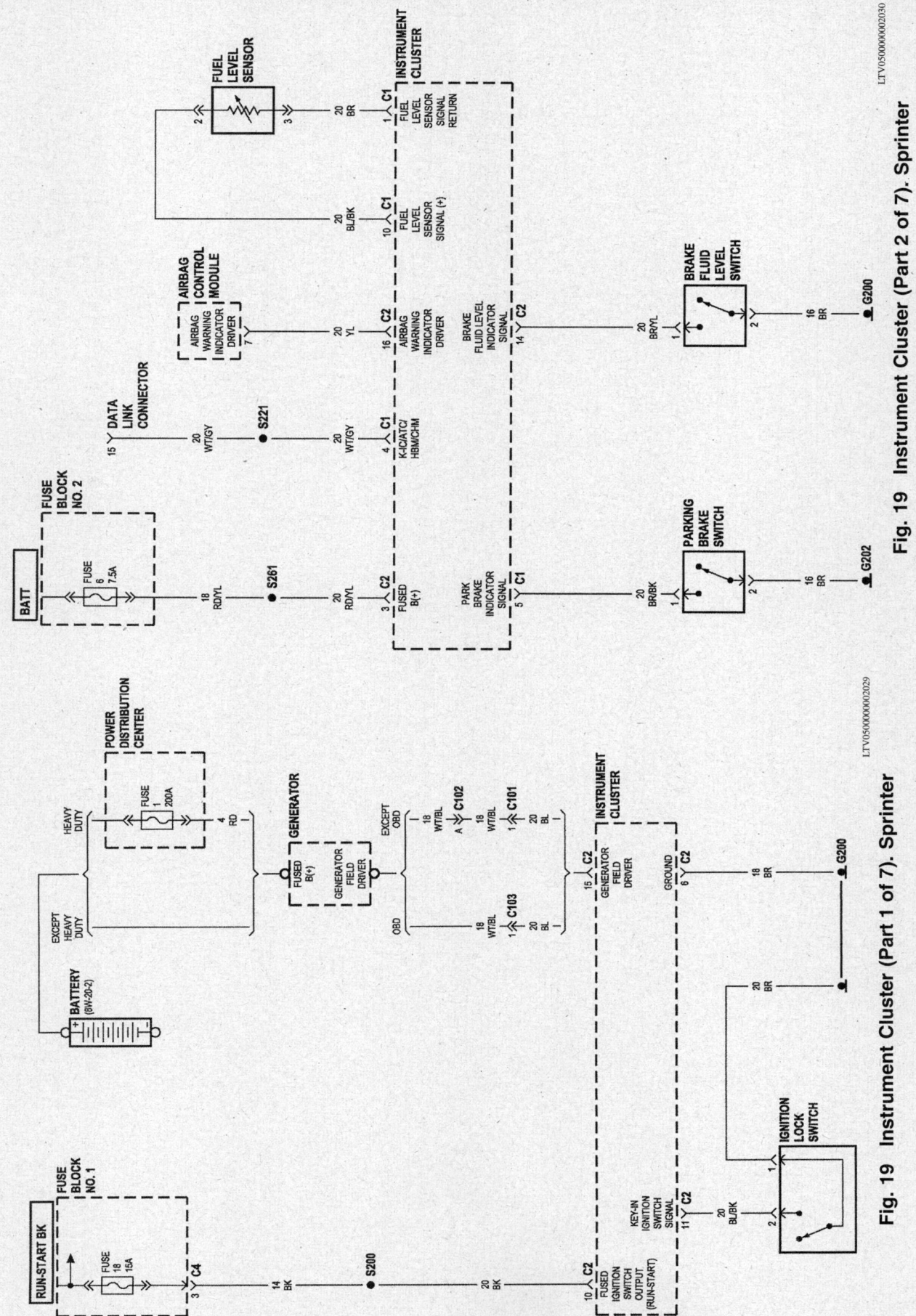

Fig. 19   Instrument Cluster (Part 2 of 7). Sprinter

Fig. 19   Instrument Cluster (Part 1 of 7). Sprinter

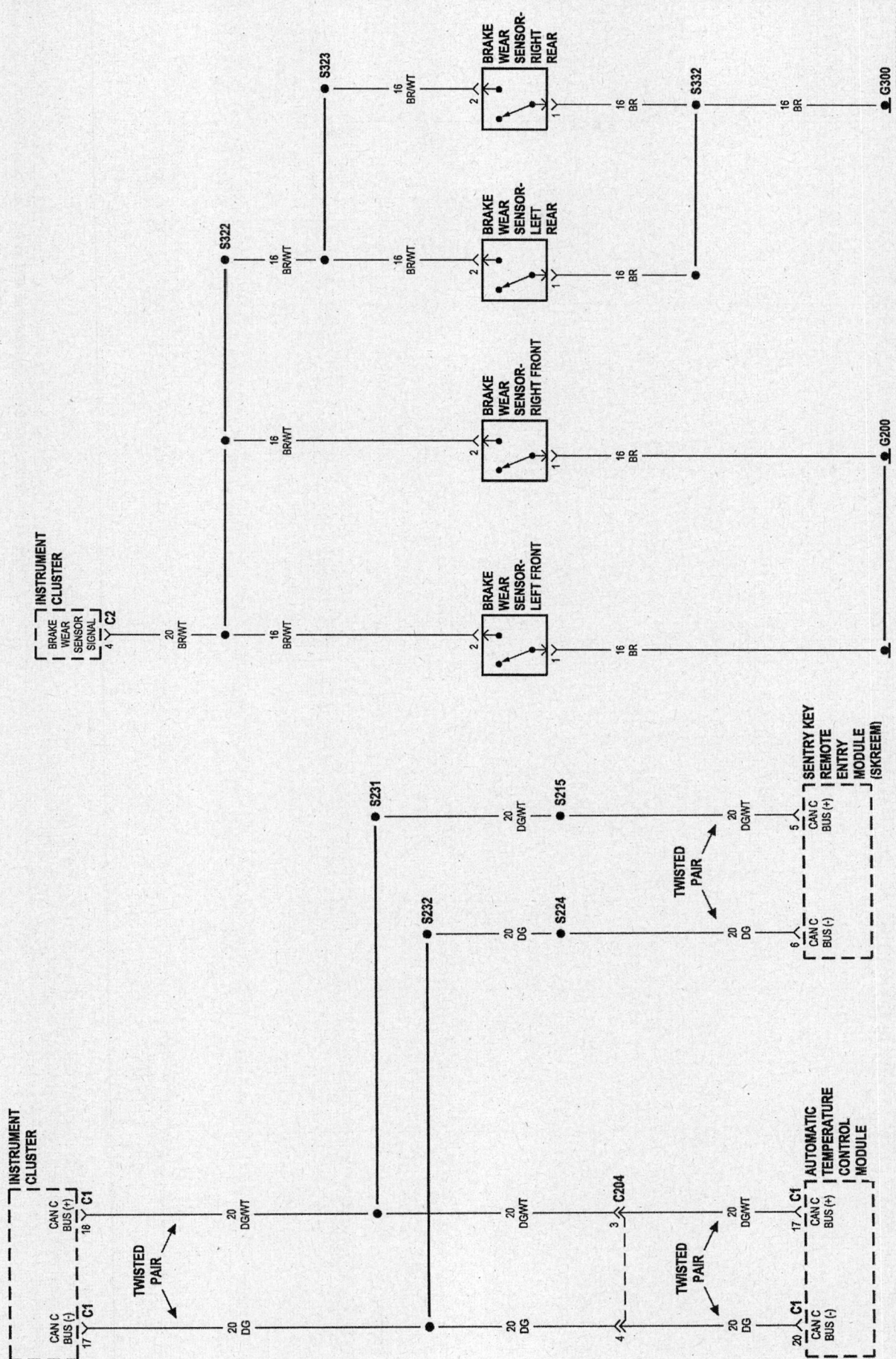

Fig. 19 Instrument Cluster (Part 4 of 7). Sprinter

Fig. 19 Instrument Cluster (Part 3 of 7). Sprinter

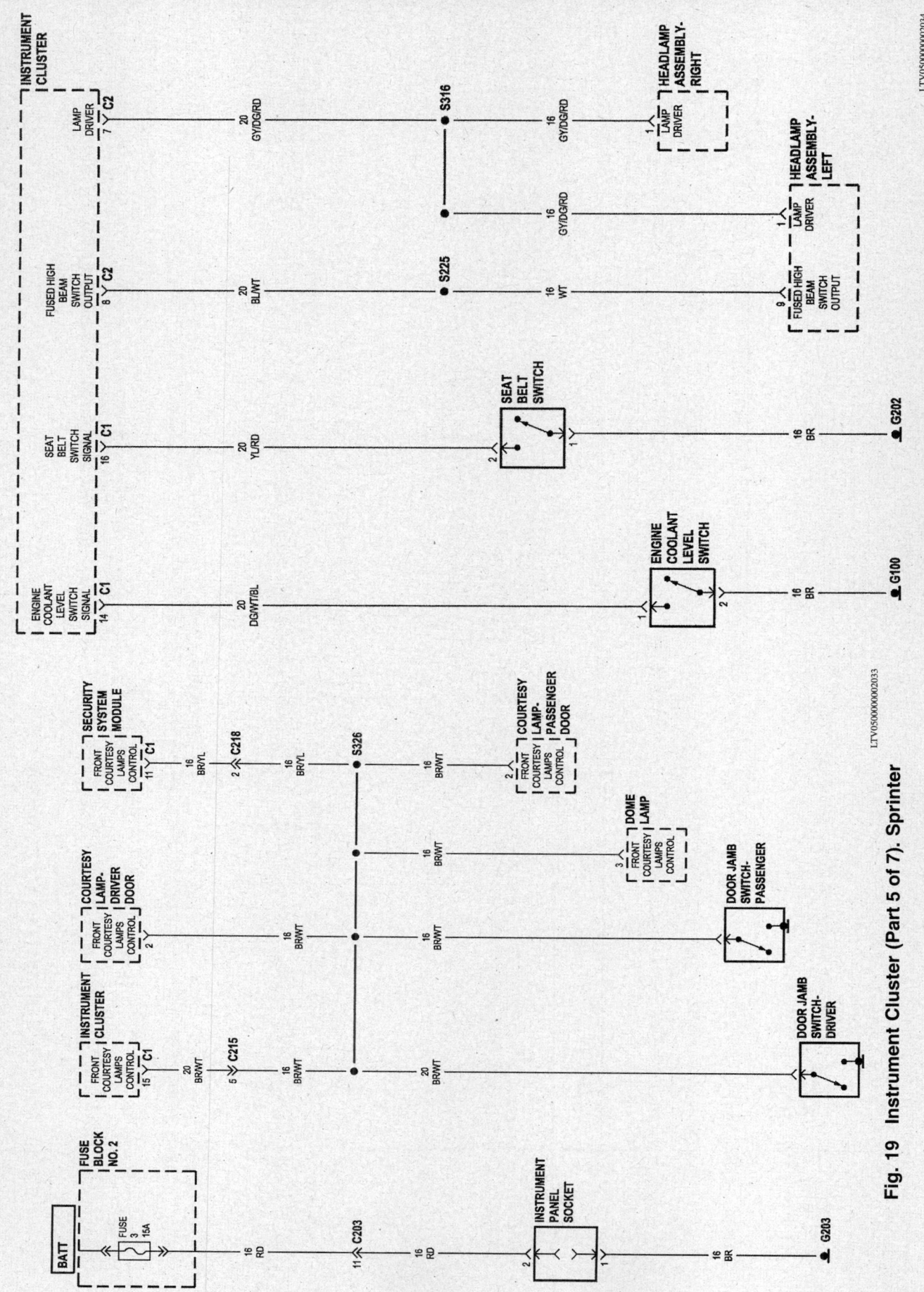

Fig. 19   Instrument Cluster (Part 6 of 7). Sprinter

Fig. 19   Instrument Cluster (Part 5 of 7). Sprinter

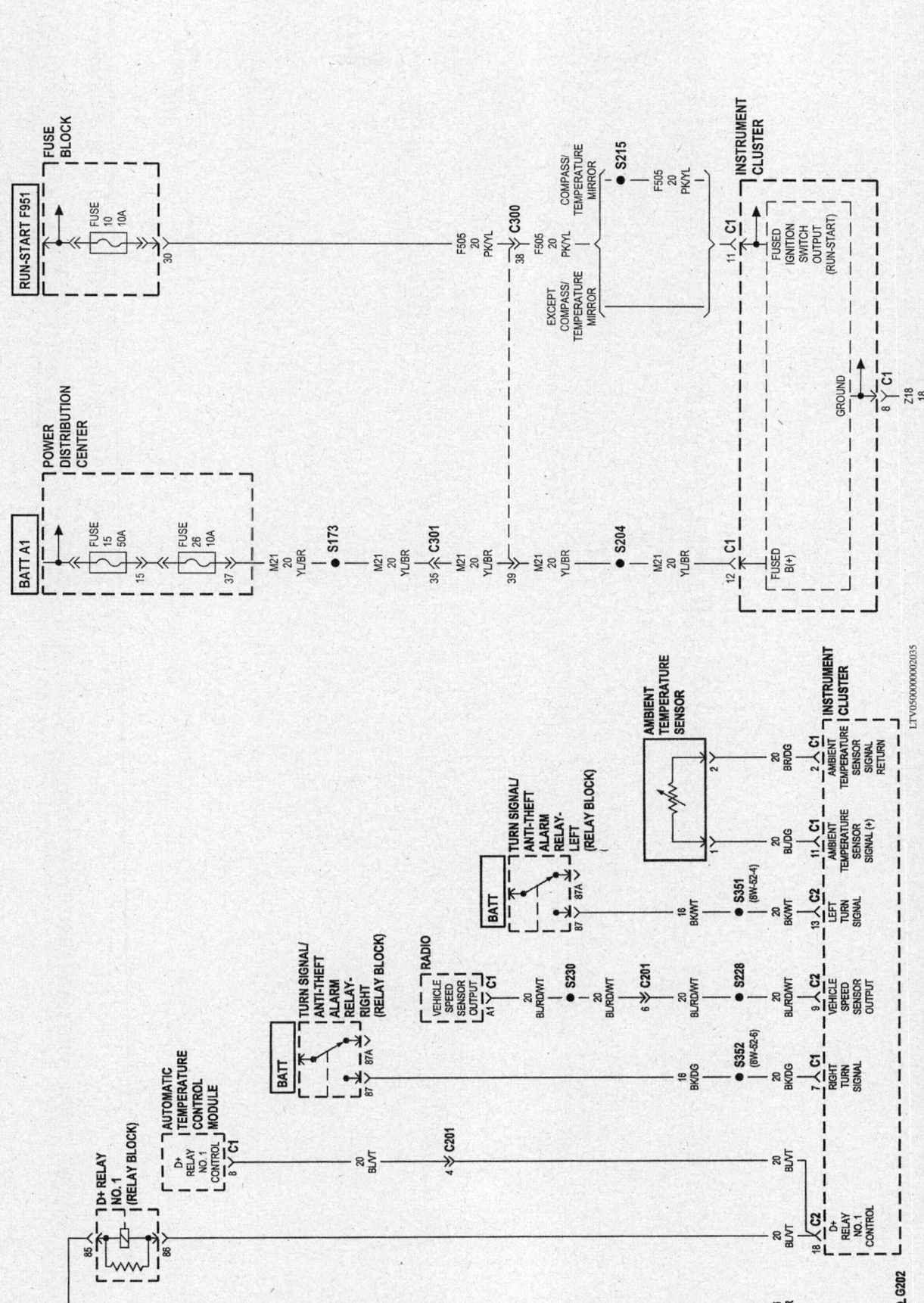

Fig. 20 Instrument Cluster (Part 1 of 9). Wrangler

Fig. 19 Instrument Cluster (Part 7 of 7). Sprinter

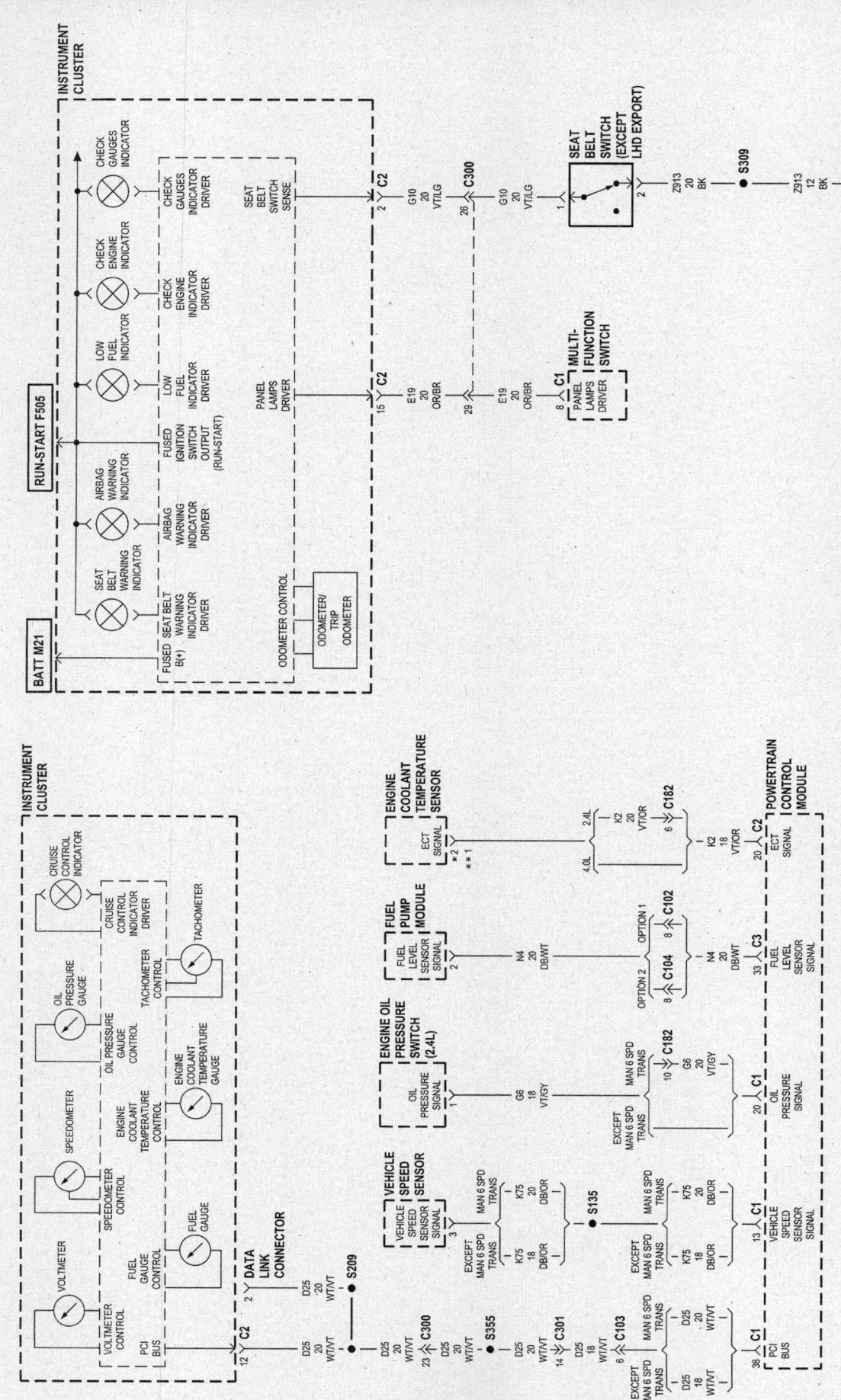

Fig. 20 Instrument Cluster (Part 3 of 9). Wrangler

Fig. 20 Instrument Cluster (Part 2 of 9). Wrangler

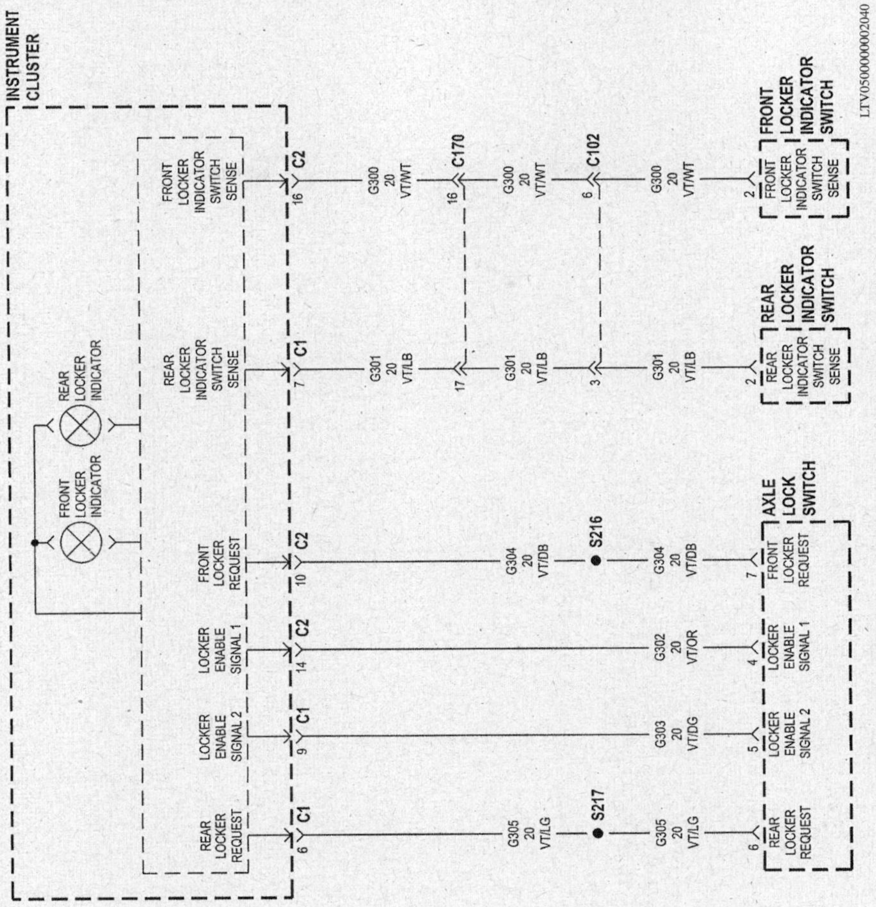

Fig. 20 Instrument Cluster (Part 5 of 9). Wrangler

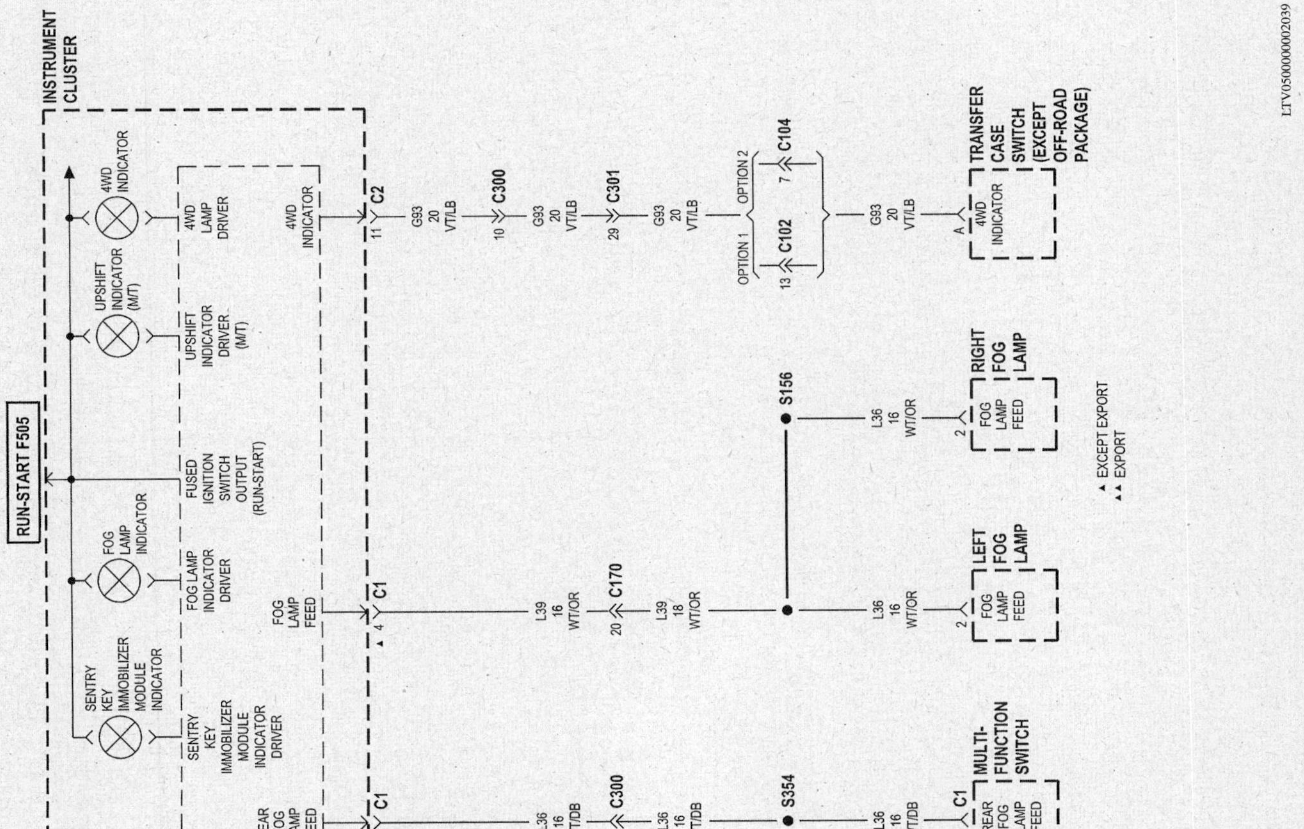

LTV050000002040

Fig. 20 Instrument Cluster (Part 4 of 9). Wrangler

LTV050000002039

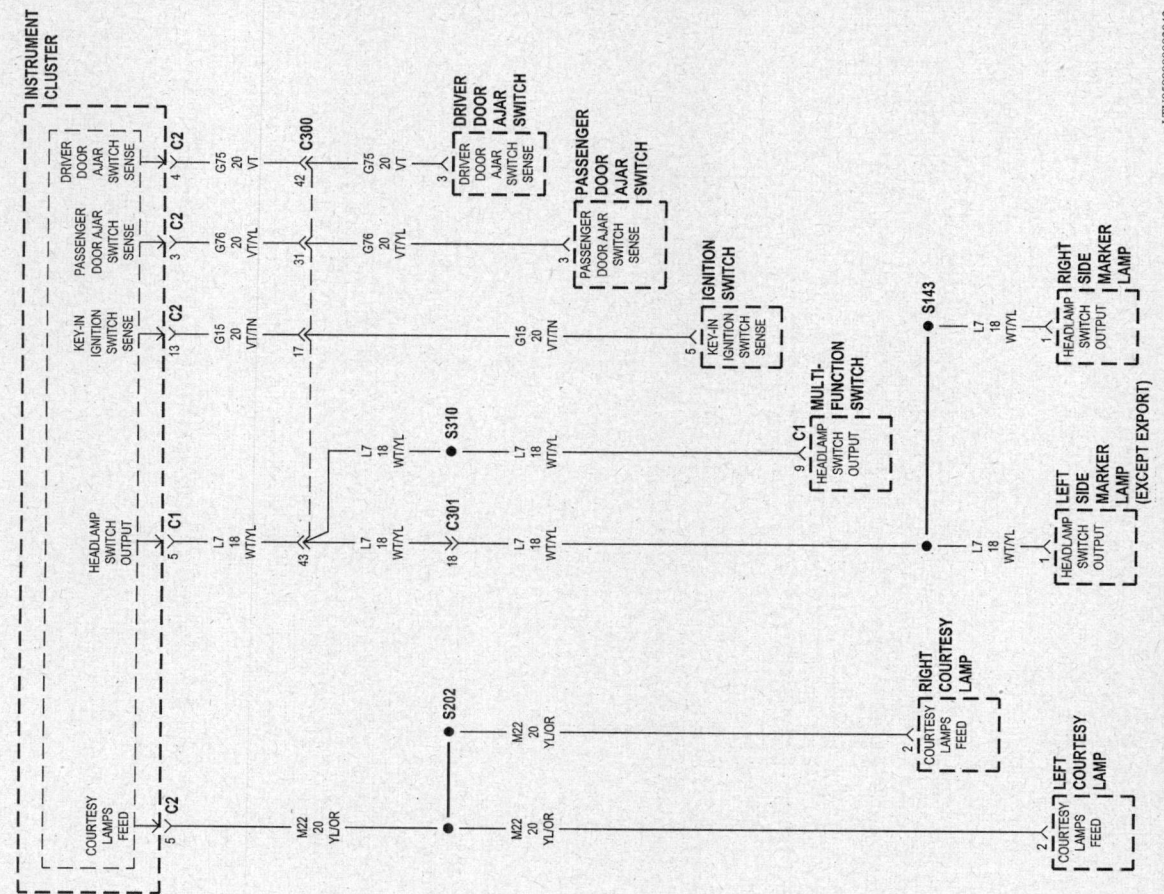

Fig. 20 Instrument Cluster (Part 7 of 9). Wrangler

Fig. 20 Instrument Cluster (Part 6 of 9). Wrangler

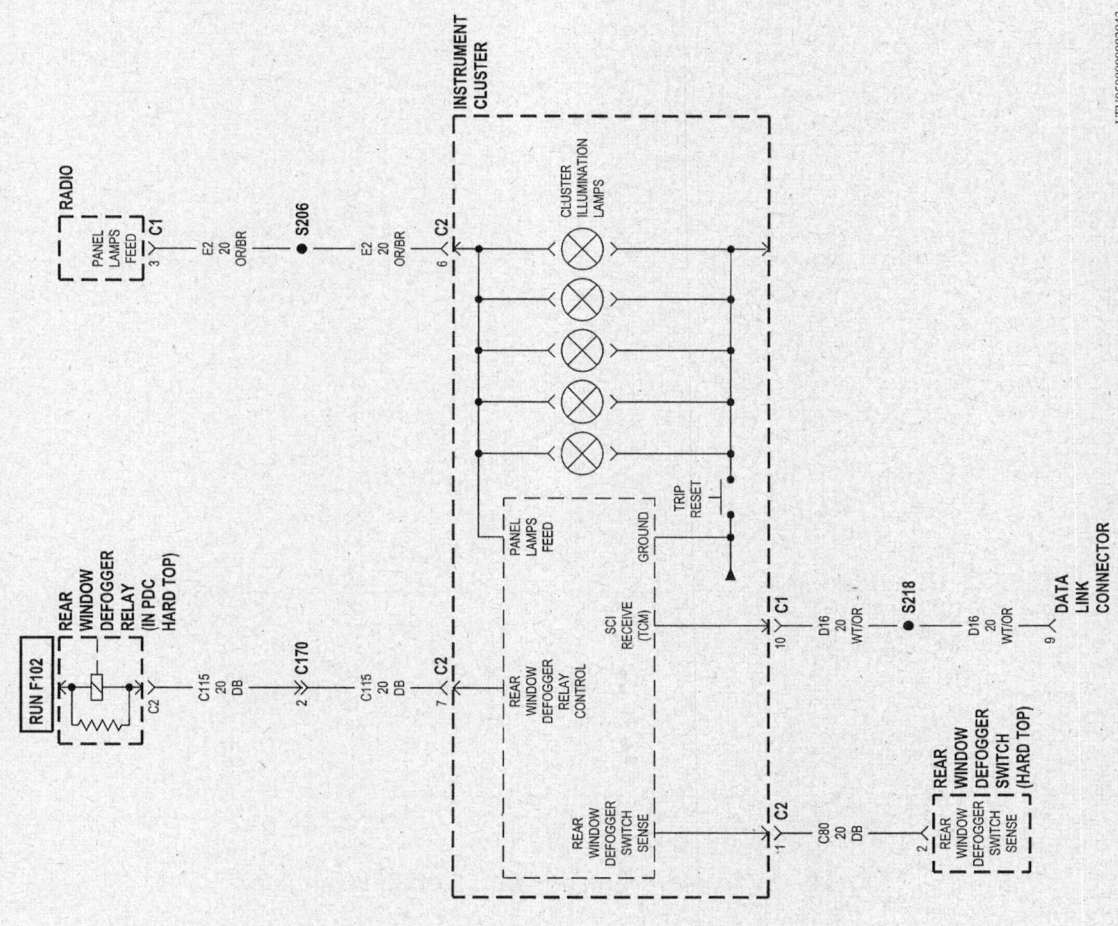

Fig. 20 Instrument Cluster (Part 8 of 9). Wrangler

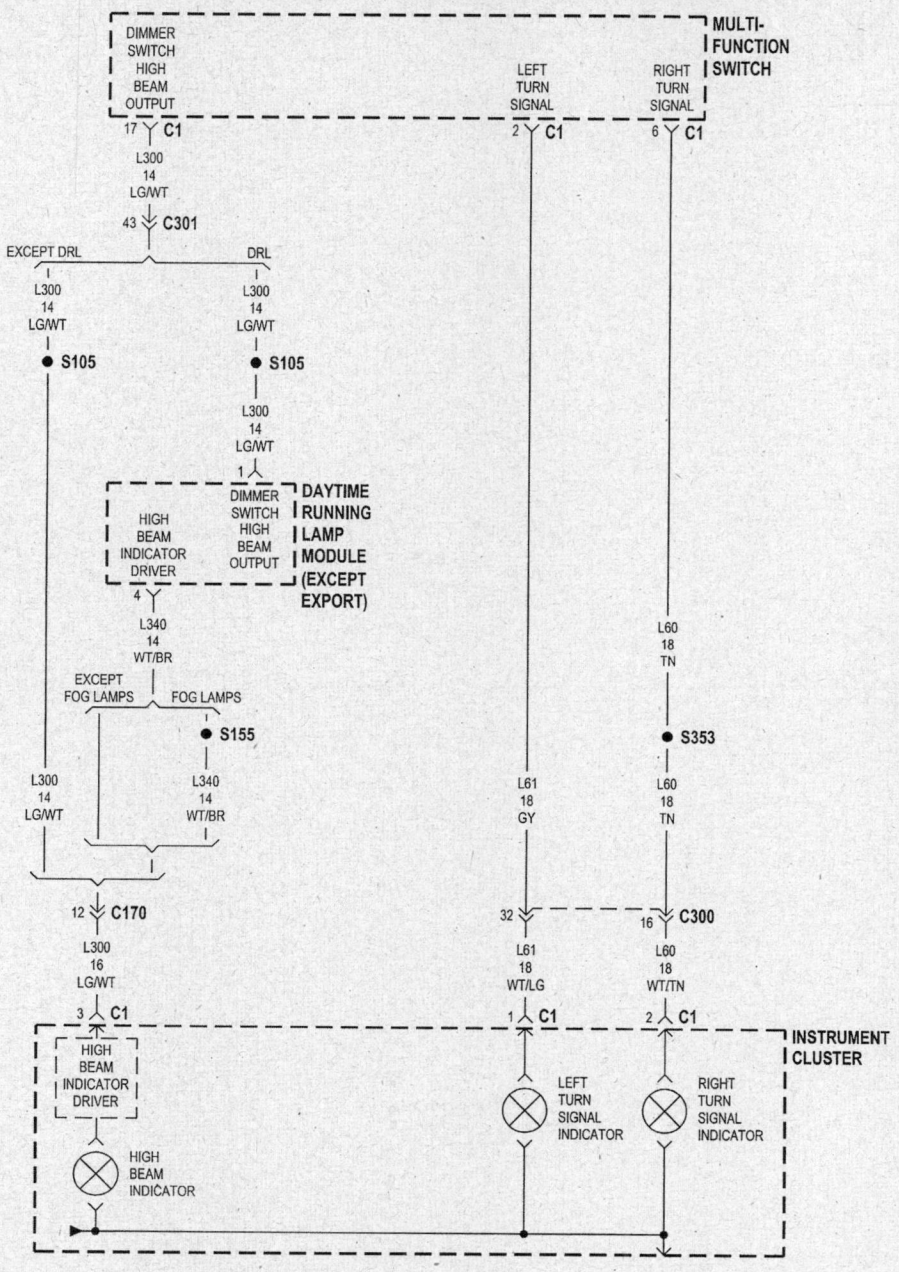

Fig. 20   Instrument Cluster (Part 9 of 9). Wrangler

LTV0500000002044

SPEED CONTROL SYSTEMS

INDEX

	Page No.
Component Diagnosis & Testing	2-2
Caravan, Town & Country & Voyager	2-2
Powertrain Control Module (PCM) Test	2-2
Speed Control Servo Test	2-2
Speed Control Switch Test	2-3
Stop Lamp Switch Test	2-3
Vacuum Supply Test	2-3
Dakota, Durango, Full Size Pickup & Van	2-4
Powertrain Control Module Test	2-4
Speed Control Servo Test	2-4
Speed Control Switch Test	2-4
Stop Lamp Switch Test	2-4
Vacuum Supply Test	2-5
Grand Cherokee & Wrangler	2-5
Powertrain Control Module Test	2-5
Speed Control Servo Test	2-5

	Page No.
Speed Control Switch Test	2-6
Stop Lamp Switch Test	2-6
Vacuum Supply Test	2-6
Component Replacement	2-6
Servo Throttle Cable Assembly	2-7
Caravan, Town & Country & Voyager	2-7
Dakota, Durango, Grand Cherokee & Wrangler	2-8
Full Size Pickup & Van	2-7
PT Cruiser	2-8
Speed Control Servo	2-6
Caravan, Town & Country & Voyager	2-6
Commander	2-6
Full Size Pickup, Liberty & Wrangler	2-6
Full Size Pickup	2-7
Grand Cherokee	2-6
PT Cruiser	2-7
Pacifica	2-7
Sprinter	2-7

	Page No.
Speed Control Switch	2-8
Caravan, Town & Country & Voyager	2-8
Commander, Dakota, Full Size Van, Grand Cherokee, Liberty, Pacifica & Wrangler	2-8
Full Size Pickup	2-8
PT Cruiser	2-8
Sprinter	2-8
Description	2-1
Diagnostic Trouble Code Interpretation	2-1
Precautions	2-1
Air Bag Systems	2-1
Battery Ground Cable	2-1
System Diagnosis & Testing	2-1
Body Code Identification Chart	2-1
Diagnostic Tests	2-2
Wiring Diagrams	2-1
Troubleshooting	2-1

DESCRIPTION

The speed control system is electrically controlled and vacuum operated. Two types of controls are used. One is mounted on the steering column, the other is mounted on the steering wheel. The control lever on the steering column incorporates a slide switch which has three positions: Off/On, Resume/Accel and Set/Decel. The controls on the steering wheel use On/Off and momentary type switches. The Set button is located at the end of the three position slide switch. The system is designed to operate at speeds exceeding 35 mph.

The engine controller monitors critical input and output circuits within the speed control system, making sure they are operating correctly. If a problem is sensed by the controller often enough to be considered a fault, it is stored in the controller memory in the form of a diagnostic trouble code message. These messages are short descriptions of a faulty condition that exists or of a certain circuit experiencing a fault. If the problem is repaired or ceases to occur, the controller will cancel the message after 50 ignition key On/Off cycles.

To engage the speed control when desired speed is achieved, depress and release the Set button to engage the system. Speed will be maintained at this level. Moving the slide switch from Off to On position while vehicle is in motion establishes memory without system engagement.

To disengage speed control, a normal brake application or soft tap on the brake pedal will disengage system without erasing speed memory. Moving the slide switch to Off position also disengages the system, but will erase the speed memory.

PRECAUTIONS

Air Bag Systems

Refer to "Air Bag System Precautions" in the front of this manual for system disarming and arming procedures.

Battery Ground Cable

Prior to service disconnect battery ground cable and isolate as required.

TROUBLESHOOTING

Refer to **Figs. 1 and 2** when troubleshooting the speed control system.

DIAGNOSTIC TROUBLE CODE INTERPRETATION

Refer to **Fig. 3** for DTC interpretation.

SYSTEM DIAGNOSIS & TESTING

Body Code Identification Chart

Refer to **Fig. 4** for the body code identification chart when using wiring diagrams or diagnostic tests.

Wiring Diagrams

Refer to **Figs. 5 through 22** for speed control system wiring diagrams.

Diagnostic Tests

Before starting test procedures, visually inspect speed control system for disconnected vacuum hoses, corroded electrical connectors and improper cable operation. After visual inspection, perform the test procedures using the following guidelines:

1. Always start at first diagnostic test. Starting at any other test may give incorrect results.
2. At the end of each test, reconnect all wires and hoses.
3. Ensure vehicle being tested has a fully charged battery.
4. When inspecting voltage or continuity at the engine controller 60-way connector, use the terminal side (not wire side) of the connector. **Use caution when performing electrical tests to prevent accidental shorting of terminals; shorts can damage fuses or engine controller.**

COMPONENT DIAGNOSIS & TESTING

Caravan, Town & Country & Voyager

SPEED CONTROL SERVO TEST

1. Turn ignition switch and speed control switch to the On position.
2. Set voltmeter to read battery voltage. Connect negative lead to chassis ground.
3. Disconnect connector at servo, Pin 2 should read approximately battery voltage. If not, inspect for loose connections or repair main harness as required.
4. If voltage reading is satisfactory, inspect fuse.
5. Disconnect connector from stop lamp switch, then test pin 3 for battery voltage. If voltage is satisfactory, perform "Stop Lamp Switch Test."
6. If Stop Lamp Switch test is satisfactory, repair wire between servo and stop lamp switch.
7. If voltage is not present at pin 3, disconnect speed control connector, then test pin 1 for battery voltage.
8. If voltage is present, perform "Speed Control Switch Test."
9. If no voltage is present at pin 1, test pin 2 of stop lamp switch connector for battery voltage.
10. If voltage is not present, repair wiring as required.
11. If speed control switch is satisfactory, inspect clockspring for continuity.
12. If clockspring continuity is satisfactory, repair wire between stop lamp switch and clockspring.
13. If voltage is not present at pin 1 of speed control switch connector, inspect for battery voltage between ignition and fuse.
14. Inspect continuity between fuse and clockspring.

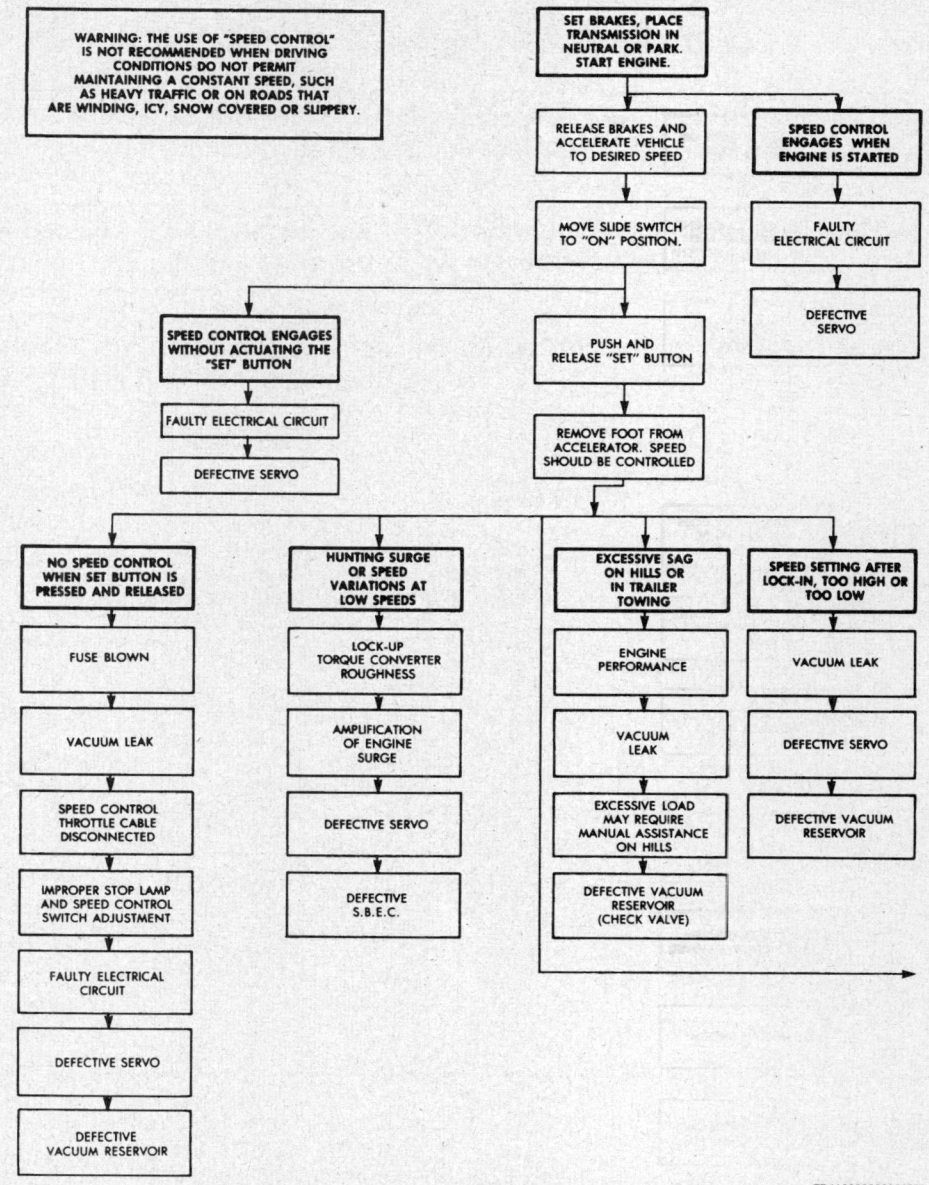

Fig. 1 System troubleshooting (Part 1 of 2). Gasoline engine

CR1108800002010X

15. Connect jumper wire between pin 2 of connector and pin 2 of speed control servo. Pin 1, 3 and 4 of the servo should show battery voltage.
16. If these terminals do not measure as specified, replace servo.
17. Connect negative lead to chassis ground, then positive lead to pin 1 of the four-way connector of the main harness.
18. Ohmmeter should show continuity. If not, repair ground circuit as required.

POWERTRAIN CONTROL MODULE (PCM) TEST

1. Disconnect connector at engine controller, then remove speed control switch and disconnect connector.
2. Inspect continuity between PCM connector terminal No. 23, and speed control switch harness terminal No. 4. If no continuity is present, then repair wire circuit as required. If continuity is satis-

factory, then perform speed control switch test.
3. Connect connector to speed control switch, then connect negative lead of voltmeter to body ground near PCM connector and place ignition switch in On position.
4. Place speed control switch in Off position, then place positive lead of voltmeter to terminal No. 53 of PCM connector. Voltmeter should indicate zero volts.
5. With speed control switch in the On position, voltmeter should indicate battery voltage.
6. If voltage is not as specified, then inspect for voltage at terminal No. 3 of speed control servo. If on voltage is present perform speed control servo test. If voltage is satisfactory, then repair wire between terminal No. 3 of servo and terminal No. 5 of PCM connector.

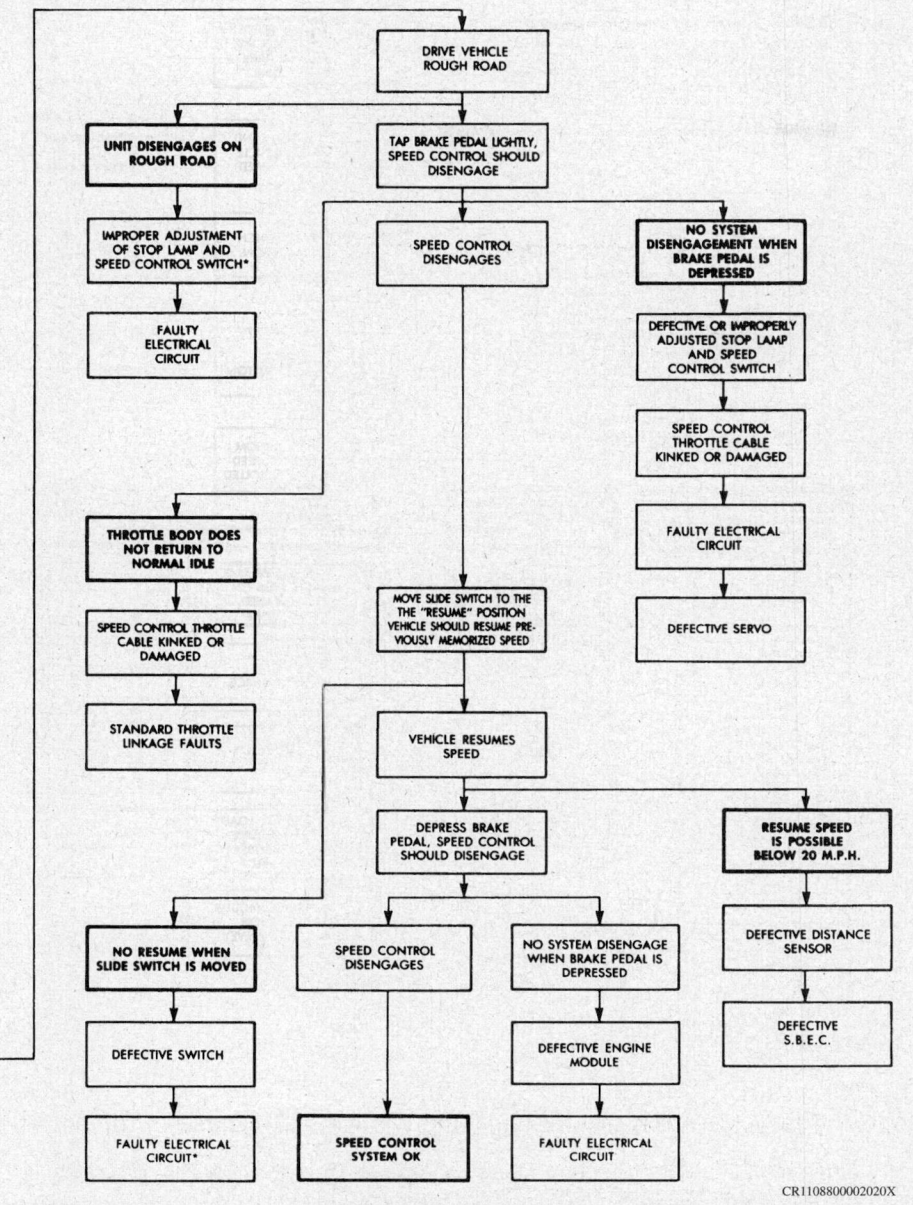

Fig. 1 System troubleshooting (Part 2 of 2). Gasoline engine

7. Place positive lead of voltmeter to terminal No. 33 of PCM connector. With the speed control switch in the Off position, voltmeter should indicate zero volts.
8. With speed control switch in the On position, voltmeter should indicate battery voltage.
9. If no voltage is present, then inspect for voltage at terminal No. 4 of servo. If no voltage is present, then perform speed control servo test. If voltage is satisfactory, then repair wire between terminal No. 33 of PCM connector and terminal No. 4 of servo.
10. Connect one lead to body ground, then to terminal 29 of PCM connector With the brake pedal released, the meter should indicate continuity. When pedal is depressed, the meter should indicate no continuity. If no continuity is present proceed as follows:

a. Inspect for continuity between terminal No. 29 of PCM connector and terminal No. 1 of stop lamp switch connector.
b. If no continuity is present, then repair as required.
c. If continuity is present, then perform stop lamp test.
d. If stop lamp test is satisfactory, then test continuity between terminal No. 2 of stop lamp switch and ground.
11. Touch one lead of ohmmeter to a good body ground and the other lead to terminal 30.
12. With transmission in D, meter should show continuity. When in P or N, meter should not show continuity.
13. If above results are not measured, test neutral start and back-up switch using DRB scan tool.

SPEED CONTROL SWITCH TEST

1. Remove speed control On/Off and Set switch assembly, then disconnect electrical connector.
2. Inspect resistance between terminal No. 1 and No. 3. of On/Off and Set switch. Resistance should be as specified in **Fig. 23**.
3. Remove speed control Resume/Accel, Cancel and Decel switch assembly, then disconnect electrical connector.
4. Inspect resistance between terminals 1 and 2 of Resume/Accel, Cancel and Decel switch. Resistance should be as specified in **Fig. 23**.
5. If resistance is not as specified, then replace switch.
6. If On indicator does not illuminate connect battery voltage to terminal No. 2 and ground to terminal No. 3 of On/Off and Set switch. On indicator should illuminate. If indicator is not as specified, then replace switch.
7. If On indicator illuminates, then inspect speed control dimmer module as follows:
   a. Remove top cover shroud to access turn signal combination switch.
   b. Remove speed control dimmer module from back side of turn signal combination switch.
   c. Inspect for continuity between dimmer module terminal No. 1 and No. 3, then between terminal No. 3 and No. 4.
   d. If no continuity is present, then replace dimmer module. If continuity is satisfactory then refer to wiring diagram and inspect wire circuit V32 for open or short.

STOP LAMP SWITCH TEST

1. Remove stop lamp switch, then inspect for continuity between terminal No. 5 and No. 6 with plunger released. Continuity should exist.
2. Inspect for continuity between terminal No. 1 and No. 2 with plunger depressed. Continuity should exist.
3. Inspect for continuity between terminal No. 3 and No. 4 with plunger depressed. Continuity should exist.
4. If continuity is not as specified, then stop lamp switch is out of adjustment or faulty.

VACUUM SUPPLY TEST

1. Disconnect vacuum hose from servo, then install a vacuum gauge into hose.
2. Start engine and run at idle. Vacuum gauge should read 10 inches Hg.
3. Turn ignition switch to the Off position. Vacuum should hold at 10 inches Hg.
4. If vacuum gauge reads below 10 inches Hg, or does not hold, inspect for vacuum leaks, or poor engine performance.

SPEED CONTROL SYSTEMS

Dakota, Durango, Full Size Pickup & Van

SPEED CONTROL SERVO TEST

1. Start engine, then disconnect electrical connector at servo.
2. Place speed control switch in On position, then inspect for battery voltage at pin No. 3. Battery voltage should be present when brake is released and not present when brake pedal is depressed.
3. If voltage is not as specified, then inspect stop lamp switch adjustment and inspect for continuity between stop lamp switch and servo.
4. Connect a jumper wire between pin No. 3 of connector and pin No. 3 of servo.
5. Inspect for battery voltage at pins 1, 2 and 4 of servo. Battery voltage should be present.
6. If voltage is not as specified, then replace servo.
7. Place ignition switch In Off position, then inspect for continuity between servo harness connector pin No. 4 and ground. Continuity should exist.
8. If continuity is not as specified, then repair open to ground as required.

POWERTRAIN CONTROL MODULE TEST

1. Disconnect connector at engine controller.
2. Connect negative lead of voltmeter to ground near controller, then turn ignition switch to the On position.
3. Connect positive lead of voltmeter to cavity of terminal 53. With the speed control switch in the Off position, voltmeter should indicate zero volts.
4. With speed control switch in the On position, voltmeter should indicate battery voltage. If not, repair main harness as required.
5. Place positive lead of voltmeter to cavity of terminal 33. With the speed control switch in the Off position, voltmeter should indicate zero volts.
6. With speed control switch in the On position, voltmeter should indicate battery voltage.
7. If no voltage is present, repair wire between terminal 33 and terminal 4 of speed control servo.
8. Connect positive lead of voltmeter to cavity 48. With the speed control switch in the Off position, voltmeter should indicate zero volts.
9. With speed control switch in the On position, voltmeter should indicate battery voltage.
10. Press the Set button. This should cause the voltmeter to switch from indicating battery voltage to zero volts for as long as the switch is held. If not, perform "Speed Control Switch Test." If the switch is satisfactory, repair wire

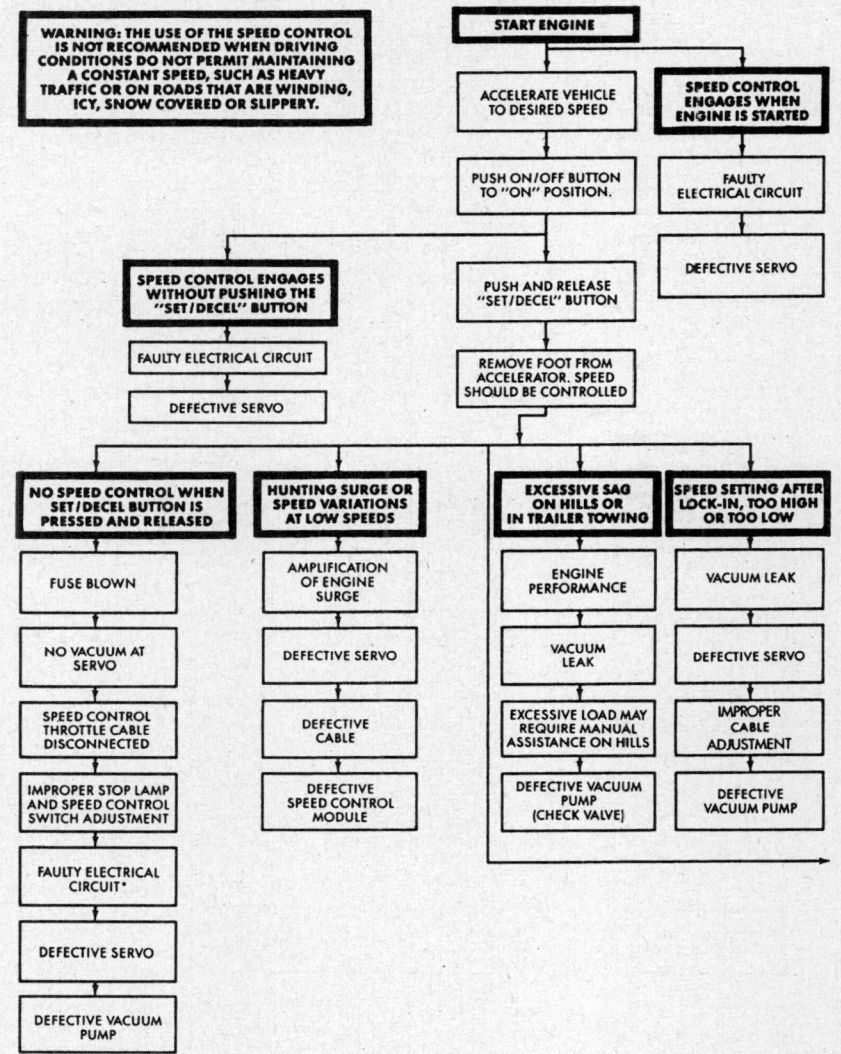

Fig. 2   System troubleshooting (Part 1 of 2). Diesel engine

between pin 48 and speed control switch.
11. Place positive lead of voltmeter to cavity of terminal 50. With the speed control switch in the On or Off position, voltmeter should indicate zero volts.
12. With switch in the On position, press Resume button. Battery voltage should be read as long as button is held. If not, perform "Speed Control Switch Test."
13. If switch is satisfactory, repair wire between pin 50 and speed control switch.
14. Place positive lead of voltmeter to cavity of terminal 49. With switch in the Off position, voltmeter should indicate zero volts.
15. With switch in the On position, voltmeter should indicate battery voltage.
16. If voltage is not indicated, repair wire between terminal 49 and speed control switch.
17. Connect one lead to body ground, then the cavity of terminal 29.
18. With the brake pedal released, the meter should indicate continuity. When pedal is depressed, the meter should indicate an open circuit.

SPEED CONTROL SWITCH TEST

1. Remove speed control switch.
2. Inspect switch continuity as outlined in **Fig. 24.**
3. If continuity is not as specified, replace switch.

STOP LAMP SWITCH TEST

1. Remove stop lamp switch from mounting bracket, then disconnect switch from wiring harness.
2. Ensure switch continuity is as follows:
   a. With switch plunger released, continuity should exist between pins 5 and 6.
   b. With switch plunger depressed, continuity should exist between pins 1 and 2 and between pins 3 and 4.
3. If switch continuity is as specified, switch is satisfactory; if not, replace switch.

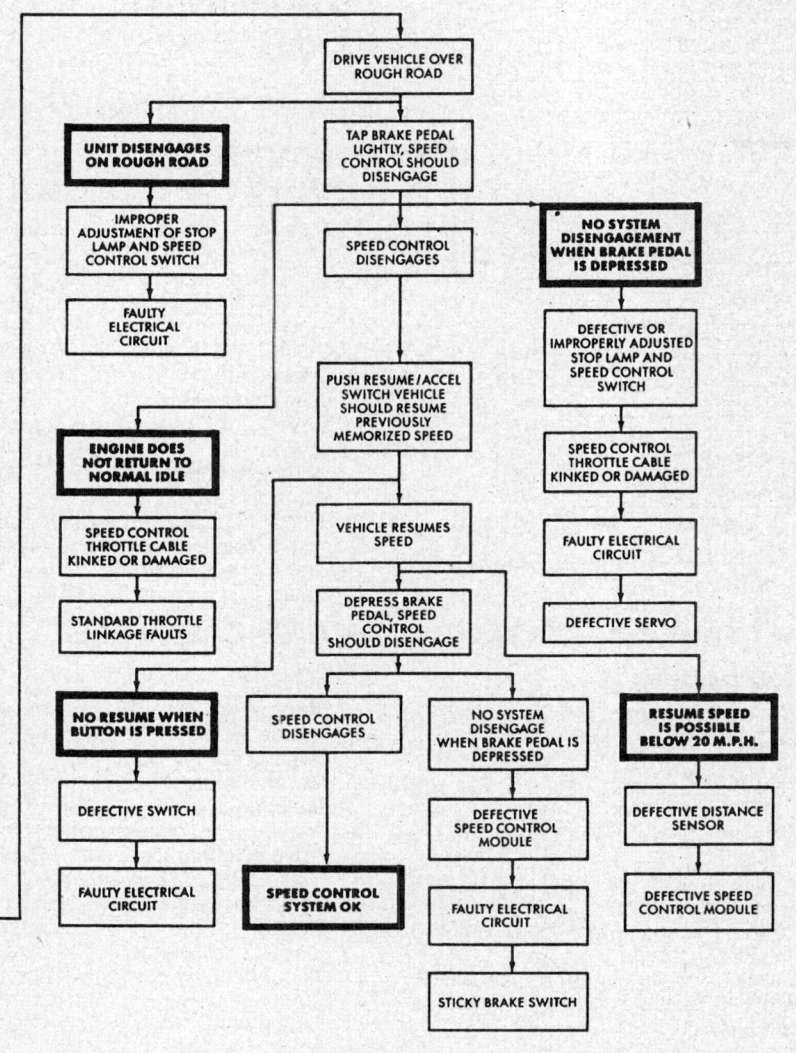

Fig. 2 System troubleshooting (Part 2 of 2). Diesel engine

VACUUM SUPPLY TEST

1. Disconnect vacuum hose from servo, then install a vacuum gauge into hose.
2. Start engine and run at idle. Vacuum gauge should read 10 inches Hg.
3. Turn ignition switch to the Off position. Vacuum should hold at 10 inches Hg.
4. If vacuum gauge reads below 10 inches Hg or does not hold, inspect for vacuum leaks and for poor engine performance.

Grand Cherokee & Wrangler

SPEED CONTROL SERVO TEST

1. Start engine, then disconnect electrical connector at servo.
2. Place speed control switch in On position, then inspect for battery voltage at pin No. 3. Battery voltage should be present when brake is released and not present when brake pedal is depressed.
3. If voltage is not as specified, inspect stop lamp switch adjustment and inspect for continuity between stop lamp switch and servo.
4. Connect a jumper wire between pin No. 3 of connector and pin No. 3 of servo.
5. Inspect for battery voltage at pin No. 1, 2 and 4 of servo. Battery voltage should be present.
6. If voltage is not as specified, replace servo.
7. Place ignition switch In Off position, then inspect for continuity between servo harness connector pin No. 4 and ground. Continuity should exist.
8. If continuity is not as specified, then repair open to ground as required.

POWERTRAIN CONTROL MODULE TEST

GRAND CHEROKEE

1. Disconnect connector at engine controller.
2. Connect negative lead of voltmeter to ground near controller, then turn ignition switch to the On position.
3. Place positive lead of voltmeter to cavity of terminal 33. With speed control switch in Off position, voltmeter should indicate zero volts.
4. With speed control switch in On position, voltmeter should indicate battery voltage.
5. If no voltage is present, repair wire between terminal 33 and terminal 4 of speed control servo.
6. Place positive lead of voltmeter to cavity of terminal 53. With the speed control switch in the Off position, voltmeter should indicate zero volts.
7. With speed control switch in the On position, voltmeter should indicate battery voltage. If not, repair main harness as required.
8. Connect positive lead of voltmeter to cavity 48. With the speed control switch in the Off position, voltmeter should indicate zero volts.
9. With speed control switch in the On position, voltmeter should indicate battery voltage.
10. Press the Set button. This should cause the voltmeter to switch from indicating battery voltage to zero volts for as long as the switch is held. If not, perform "Speed Control Switch Test." If the switch is satisfactory, repair wire between pin 48 and speed control switch.
11. Place positive lead of voltmeter to cavity of terminal 50. With the speed control switch in the On or Off position, voltmeter should indicate zero volts.
12. With switch in the On position, press Resume button. Battery voltage should be read as long as button is held. If not, perform "Speed Control Switch Test."
13. If switch is satisfactory, repair wire between pin 50 and speed control switch.
14. Place positive lead of voltmeter to cavity of terminal 49. With switch in the Off position, voltmeter should indicate zero volts.
15. With switch in the On position, voltmeter should indicate battery voltage.
16. If voltage is not indicated, repair wire between terminal 49 and speed control switch.
17. Connect one lead to body ground, then the cavity of terminal 29.
18. With the brake pedal released, the meter should indicate continuity. When pedal is depressed, the meter should indicate an open circuit.

WRANGLER

1. Disconnect connector at engine controller.
2. Connect negative lead of voltmeter to ground near controller, then turn ignition switch to the On position.
3. Place positive lead of voltmeter to cavity of terminal 53. With the speed control switch in the Off position, voltmeter should indicate zero volts.
4. With speed control switch in the On position, voltmeter should indicate battery voltage. If not, repair main harness as required.
5. Connect positive lead of voltmeter to cavity 48. With the speed control switch in the Off position, voltmeter should indicate zero volts.

SPEED CONTROL SYSTEMS

Code	Interpretation
P0579	Speed Control Switch #1 Performance
P0580	Speed Control Switch Voltage Low
P0581	Speed Control Switch Voltage High
P0582	Speed Control Vacuum Solenoid Circuit
P0585	Speed Control Switch #1 And #2 Correlation
P0586	Speed Control Vent Solenoid Circuit
P0587	Speed Control Vent Driver Voltage Low
P0588	Speed Control Vent Driver Voltage High
P0591	Speed Control Switch #2 Performance
P0592	Speed Control Switch #2 Low
P0593	Speed Control Switch #2 High
P0594	Speed Control Servo Power Circuit
P1593	Speed Control Switch Stuck
P1595	Speed Control Solenoid Circuits
P1596	Speed Control Switch Always High
P1597	Speed Control Switch Always Low
P1683	Speed Control Power Relay Or Speed Control 12V Driver Circuit

Fig. 3 DTC interpretation

6. With speed control switch in the On position, voltmeter should indicate battery voltage.
7. Press the Set button. This should cause the voltmeter to switch from indicating battery voltage to zero volts for as long as the switch is held. If not, perform "Speed Control Switch Test." If the switch is satisfactory, repair wire between pin 48 and speed control switch.
8. Place positive lead of voltmeter to cavity of terminal 50. With the speed control switch in the On or Off position, voltmeter should indicate zero volts.
9. With switch in the On position, press Resume button. Battery voltage should be read as long as button is held. If not, perform "Speed Control Switch Test."
10. If switch is satisfactory, repair wire between pin 50 and speed control switch.
11. Place positive lead of voltmeter to cavity of terminal 49. With switch in the Off position, voltmeter should indicate zero volts.
12. With switch in the On position, voltmeter should indicate battery voltage.
13. If voltage is not indicated, repair wire between terminal 49 and speed control switch.
14. Connect one lead to body ground, then the cavity of terminal 29.
15. With the brake pedal released, the meter should indicate continuity. When pedal is depressed, the meter should indicate an open circuit.

SPEED CONTROL SWITCH TEST

1. Remove speed control switch.
2. Inspect switch continuity as outlined in **Fig. 25.**
3. If continuity is not as specified, replace switch.

STOP LAMP SWITCH TEST
GRAND CHEROKEE

1. Remove stop lamp switch from mounting bracket, then disconnect switch from wiring harness.
2. Ensure switch continuity is as follows:
   a. With switch plunger released, continuity should exist between pins 5 and 6.
   b. With switch plunger depressed, continuity should exist between pins 1 and 2 and between pins 3 and 4.
3. If switch continuity is as specified, switch is satisfactory; if not, replace switch.

WRANGLER

1. Disconnect electrical connector from stop lamp switch pigtail.
2. Inspect for continuity at switch side of connector with brake pedal released.
3. Continuity should be present between the black wire and white/pink, yellow/red and dark blue/red wires.
4. Continuity should not be present between the pink and white wires.
5. With brake pedal depressed, there should be continuity between the pink and white wires. There should be no continuity between black and white/pink, yellow/red and dark blue/red wires.
6. If the above results are not obtained, adjust or replace stop lamp switch as required.

VACUUM SUPPLY TEST

1. Disconnect vacuum hose from servo, then install a vacuum gauge into hose.
2. Start engine and run at idle. Vacuum gauge should read 10 inches Hg.
3. Turn ignition switch to the Off position. Vacuum should hold at 10 inches Hg.
4. If vacuum gauge reads below 10 inches Hg or does not hold, inspect for vacuum leaks and poor engine performance.

COMPONENT REPLACEMENT
Speed Control Servo
CARAVAN, TOWN & COUNTRY & VOYAGER

1. Disconnect throttle and speed control cable ends from throttle body.
2. Depress lock tabs holding speed control and throttle cable casing to cable mount bracket.
3. Disconnect vacuum line from speed control servo that leads to battery tray/vacuum reservoir.
4. Remove battery tray/vacuum reservoir.
5. Remove speed control servo, then bracket.
6. Disconnect wire harness electrical connector from speed control servo.
7. Remove speed control servo.
8. Reverse procedure to install.

GRAND CHEROKEE
2002-04

1. Remove air cleaner housing at top of throttle body and disconnect servo cable at throttle body.
2. Remove battery from battery tray, then disconnect wiring at battery tray.
3. Disconnect positive battery cable at Power Distribution Center (PDC).
4. Loosen PDC at battery tray.
5. Remove 4 battery tray bolts.
6. Disconnect battery temperature sensor electrical connector at sensor.
7. Disconnect vacuum line at servo vacuum hose fitting.
8. Disconnect electrical connector at servo.
9. Remove two mounting nuts holding servo cable sleeve to bracket.
10. Remove speed control cable retaining clip.
11. Remove servo.
12. Reverse procedure to install.

2005-06

Refer to "Commander" for "Speed Control Servo" replacement procedure.

COMMANDER

1. Disconnect vacuum line at servo.
2. Disconnect electrical connector at servo.
3. Remove servo mounting bolt.
4. Disconnect servo cable at throttle body.
5. Remove two mounting nuts holding servo cable sleeve to bracket.
6. Remove speed control cable retaining clip.
7. Remove servo from mounting bracket.
8. Reverse procedure to install.

FULL SIZE PICKUP, LIBERTY & WRANGLER

1. **On Full Size Pickup models,** remove lefthand wheel house splash shield.
2. **On all models,** disconnect vacuum line at servo.

3. Disconnect electrical connector at servo.
4. Remove three servo mounting screws.
5. **On Liberty models,** remove coolant bottle nuts/bolts, then position bottle forward a few inches.
6. **On all models,** disconnect servo cable at throttle body.
7. Remove two mounting nuts holding servo cable sleeve to bracket.
8. Remove speed control cable retaining clip.
9. Remove servo from mounting bracket.
10. Reverse procedure to install.

FULL SIZE PICKUP

3.9L, 5.2 & 5.9L ENGINES

1. Disconnect servo vacuum hose and electrical connector, then remove cable sleeve nuts and pull speed control cable aside to access cable hairpin clip.
2. Remove hairpin clip, then separate servo from mounting bracket.
3. Reverse procedure to install. **Torque** servo nuts to 72–84 inch lbs.

5.9L DIESEL & 8.0L GASOLINE ENGINES

1. Remove battery hold down clamp and heat shield, then lift battery out of vehicle and remove battery tray assembly mounting nuts and bolts.
2. Position tray aside to access servo electrical connector, then unplug connector and remove cable sleeve nuts.
3. Pull speed control cable aside to access hairpin clip, then remove clip and separate servo from mounting bracket.
4. Reverse procedure to install, noting the following:
   a. **Torque** servo nuts to 72–84 inch lbs.
   b. **Torque** battery tray mounting bolts and nuts to 11–12 ft. lbs., and battery hold down clamp bolt to 35 inch lbs.

PACIFICA

1. Remove servo bracket bolt.
2. Remove speed control cable from throttle cam by sliding clasp out hole used for throttle cable.
3. Disconnect electrical connectors and vacuum hose.
4. Remove two nuts attaching mounting bracket and speed control cable to servo.
5. Pull cable away from servo to expose retaining clip and remove clip attaching cable to servo.
6. Remove servo.
7. Reverse procedure to install.

PT CRUISER

EXCEPT 2.4L TURBO

1. Remove air cleaner lid, then makeup air hose.
2. Remove two nuts attaching speed control cable and mounting bracket to servo.
3. Remove servo from mounting bracket.
4. Disconnect electrical connectors and vacuum hose, then remove engine cover.

Model	Year	Body Code
Caravan	2002–06	RS
Commander	2006	XK
Dakota	2002–04	AN
	2005–06	ND
Durango	2002–03	DN
	2004–06	HB
Full Size Van	2002–03	AB
Full Size Pickup	2002–06	DR
Grand Cherokee	2002–04	WJ
	2005–06	WK
Liberty	2002–06	KJ
Pacifica	2004–06	CS
PT Cruiser	2002–06	PT
Sprinter	2004–06	VA
Town & Country	2002–06	RS
Voyager	2002–03	RS
Wrangler	2002–06	TJ

Fig. 4 Body code identification chart

5. Remove cable from throttle cam, then two push nuts.
6. Remove clip attaching cable to servo.
7. Reverse procedure to install.

2.4L TURBO

1. Remove throttle control shield.
2. Remove speed control cable from throttle body lever.
3. Remove vacuum line from speed control servo.
4. Remove two nuts from speed control servo studs.
5. Push and pull up speed control servo from mounting bracket.
6. Unlock and disconnect speed control servo electrical connector.
7. Remove two push clips and discard.
8. Remove retaining clip holding cable to servo.
9. Reverse procedure to install.

SPRINTER

This is a cable-less, servo-less system. The speed control system is electronically controlled by the Engine Control Module

Servo Throttle Cable Assembly

CARAVAN, TOWN & COUNTRY & VOYAGER

1. Disconnect throttle and speed control cable ends from throttle body.
2. Depress lock tabs holding speed control cable casing to cable mount bracket.
3. Remove tie wrap holding vacuum line, throttle cable and speed control cable together.
4. Remove nuts holding speed control cable case to servo, then cable case from servo.
5. Remove hairpin clip holding cable end to servo diaphragm.
6. Remove speed control cable.
7. Reverse procedure to install.

FULL SIZE PICKUP & VAN

3.9L, 5.2L & 5.9L ENGINES

1. Remove air cleaner.
2. Disconnect cable from servo, then remove cable assembly.
3. Hold throttle open by rotating cable remaining cam, then remove cable slug from throttle lever cam.
4. Remove cable from bracket at throttle body.
5. Remove two nuts from servo mounting bracket, then pull servo away from mounting bracket.
6. Remove and discard push nuts on servo studs, then pull speed control cable away from servo to exposed servo retaining clip.
7. Disconnect cable from servo, then remove cable assembly.
8. To install, locate cable through servo mounting bracket.
9. Connect cable sleeve to servo stud, align holes, then install clip.
10. Insert servo studs through holes in cable and holes in bracket, then install new nuts on servo studs.
11. Route cable from servo, through cable support bracket and clip, then install cable end on stud of throttle body.
12. Replace air cleaner.

5.9L DIESEL & 8.0L GASOLINE ENGINES

1. Remove hairpin clip and washer retaining cables to bellcrank.
2. Remove servo throttle cable from bellcrank.
3. Disconnect cable from servo, then remove cable assembly.
4. To install, insert servo stud through servo mounting bracket.
5. Connect cable sleeve to servo stud, align holes, then install hairpin clip.
6. Insert servo studs through holes in cable, then install new push nuts on servo studs.
7. Insert servo studs through holes in bracket, then install nut washers and **torque** to 48 inch lbs.

8. Route cable from servo to cable support bracket.
9. Install cable end on bellcrank rod, then the washer and hairpin clip on end of bellcrank rod.

DAKOTA, DURANGO, GRAND CHEROKEE & WRANGLER

EXCEPT 4.7L ENGINE

1. Remove speed control cable connector at throttle body bellcrank by pushing connector off bellcrank pin using finger pressure. Do not pull connector off perpendicular to bellcrank pin.
2. Squeeze two tabs on sides of speed control cable at throttle body mounting bracket, then push cable out of bracket.
3. Remove cable from cable guide at top of valve cover.
4. Remove servo cable from servo.
5. Reverse procedure to install.

3.7L, 4.7L, 5.7L & 8.3L ENGINES

1. Remove air box housing from throttle body.
2. With finger pressure, disconnect accelerator cable connector at throttle body bellcrank pin by pushing connector from bell crank. **Do not try to pull connector off perpendicular to bell crank.**
3. Lift accelerator cable from top of cable cam.
4. Press tab to release plastic cable mount from bracket.
5. Slide plastic mount toward righthand side to remove cable from bracket.
6. With finger pressure, disconnect speed control cable connector at throttle body bellcrank pin by pushing connector from bell crank. **Do not try to pull connector off perpendicular to bell crank.**
7. Slide speed control cable plastic mount toward righthand side to remove cable from bracket.
8. Remove cable from servo.
9. Reverse procedure to install.

PT CRUISER

1. Remove air cleaner lid, then makeup air hose.
2. Remove engine cover and throttle control shield.
3. Remove two nuts attaching speed control cable and mounting bracket to servo.
4. Remove servo from mounting bracket.
5. Disconnect electrical connectors and vacuum hose.
6. Remove retaining clip holding cable to servo.
7. Remove throttle cable clasp from throttle body cam.
8. Remove speed control cable from throttle cam by sliding clasp out hole used for throttle cable.
9. Compress retaining tabs on cables and slide cables out of bracket.
10. Reverse procedure to install.

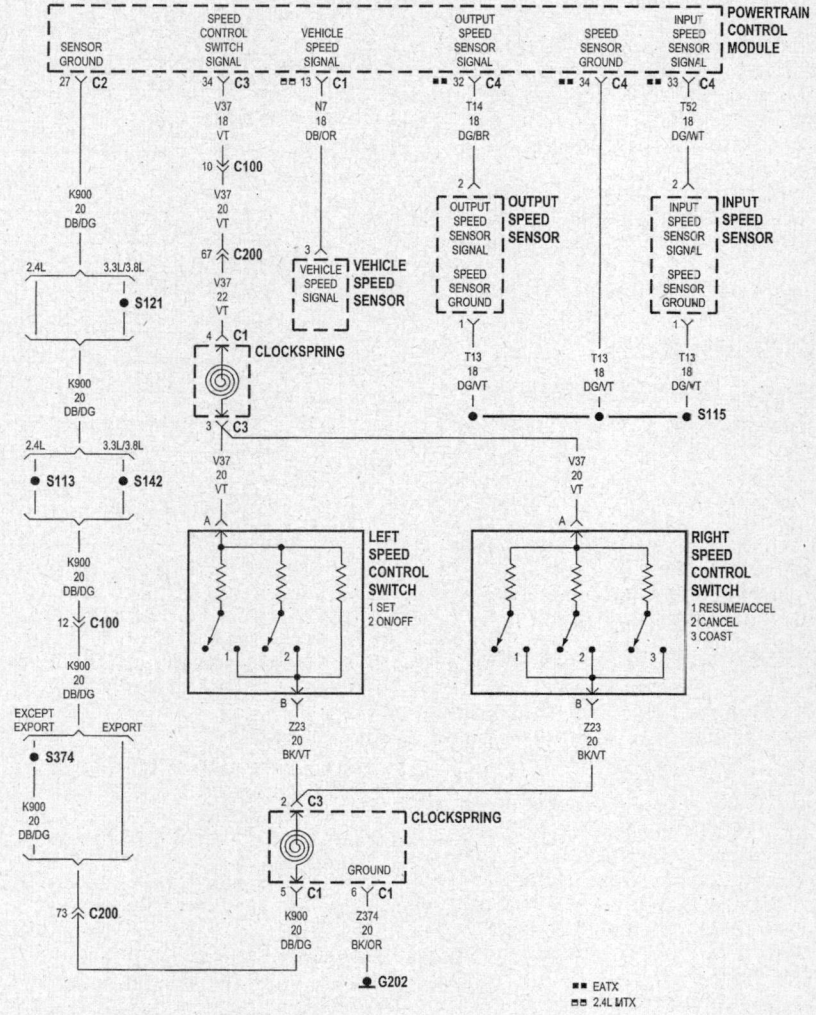

Fig. 5 Wiring diagram (Part 1 of 3). Caravan, Town & Country & Voyager

Speed Control Switch

CARAVAN, TOWN & COUNTRY & VOYAGER

1. Remove air bag/horn pad from steering wheel.
2. Disconnect electrical connector from horn, air bag and speed control switches.
3. Remove speed control switches from air bag/horn pad.
4. Reverse procedure to install.

COMMANDER, DAKOTA, FULL SIZE VAN, GRAND CHEROKEE, LIBERTY, PACIFICA & WRANGLER

1. Remove air bag module.
2. Disconnect electrical connector.
3. Remove speed control switch mounting screw, then switch
4. Reverse procedure to install.

FULL SIZE PICKUP

1. Remove switch mounting screw.

2. Pull switch from steering wheel.
3. Disconnect switch electrical connector.
4. Reverse procedure to install.

PT CRUISER

1. Remove air cleaner lid, then disconnect inlet air temperature sensor and makeup air hose.
2. Remove air bag, then switch top mounting screw.
3. Rotate steering wheel so that switch is in 6 o'clock position, then remove two screws from back of speed control switch.
4. Disconnect electrical connector, then remove switch.
5. Reverse procedure to install.

SPRINTER

1. Remove multi-function switch.
2. Remove switch mounting screw.
3. Remove speed control switch from multi-function switch.
4. Disconnect pigtail electrical connector from instrument panel wiring harness.
5. Reverse procedure to install.

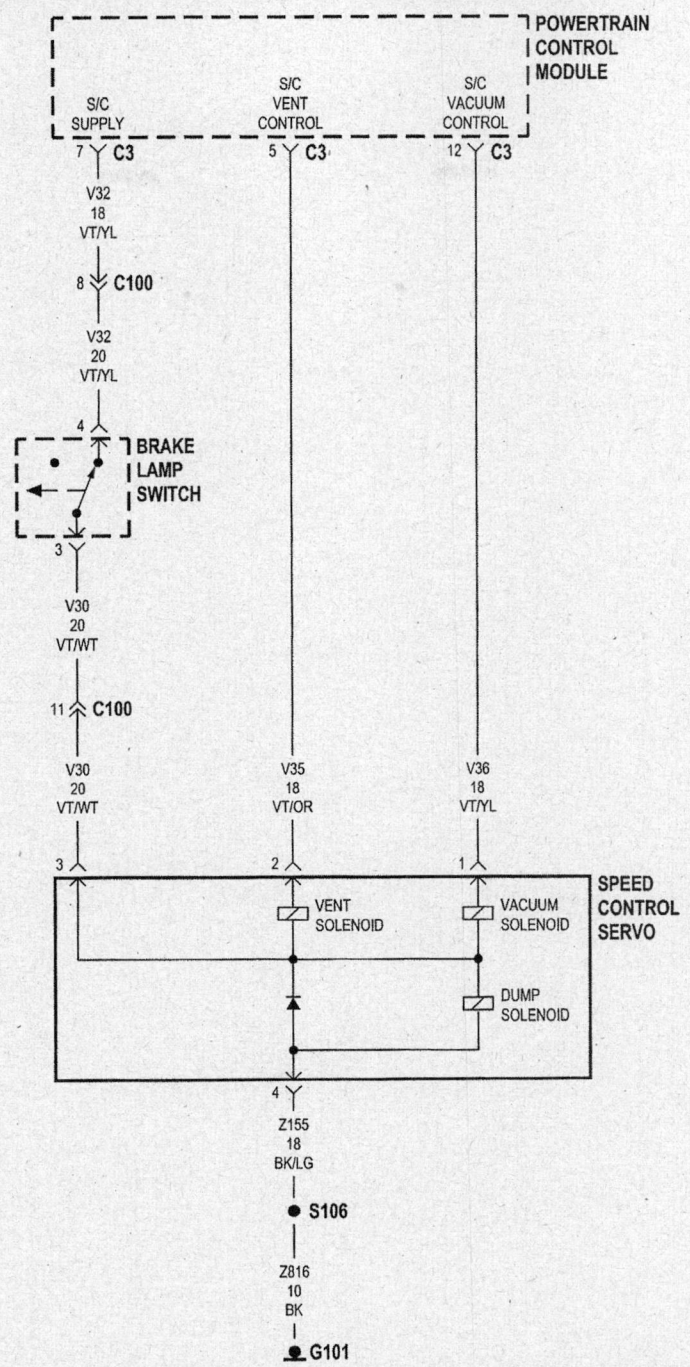

Fig. 5 Wiring diagram (Part 2 of 3). Caravan, Town & Country & Voyager

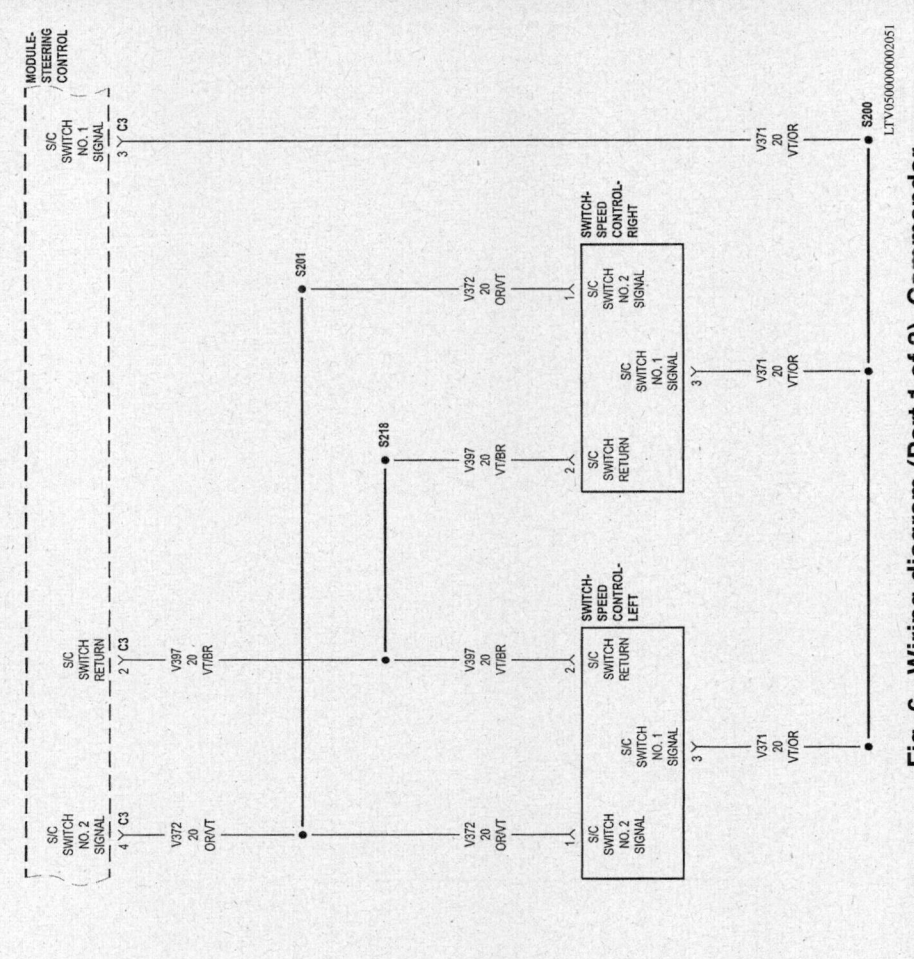

Fig. 6 Wiring diagram (Part 1 of 3). Commander

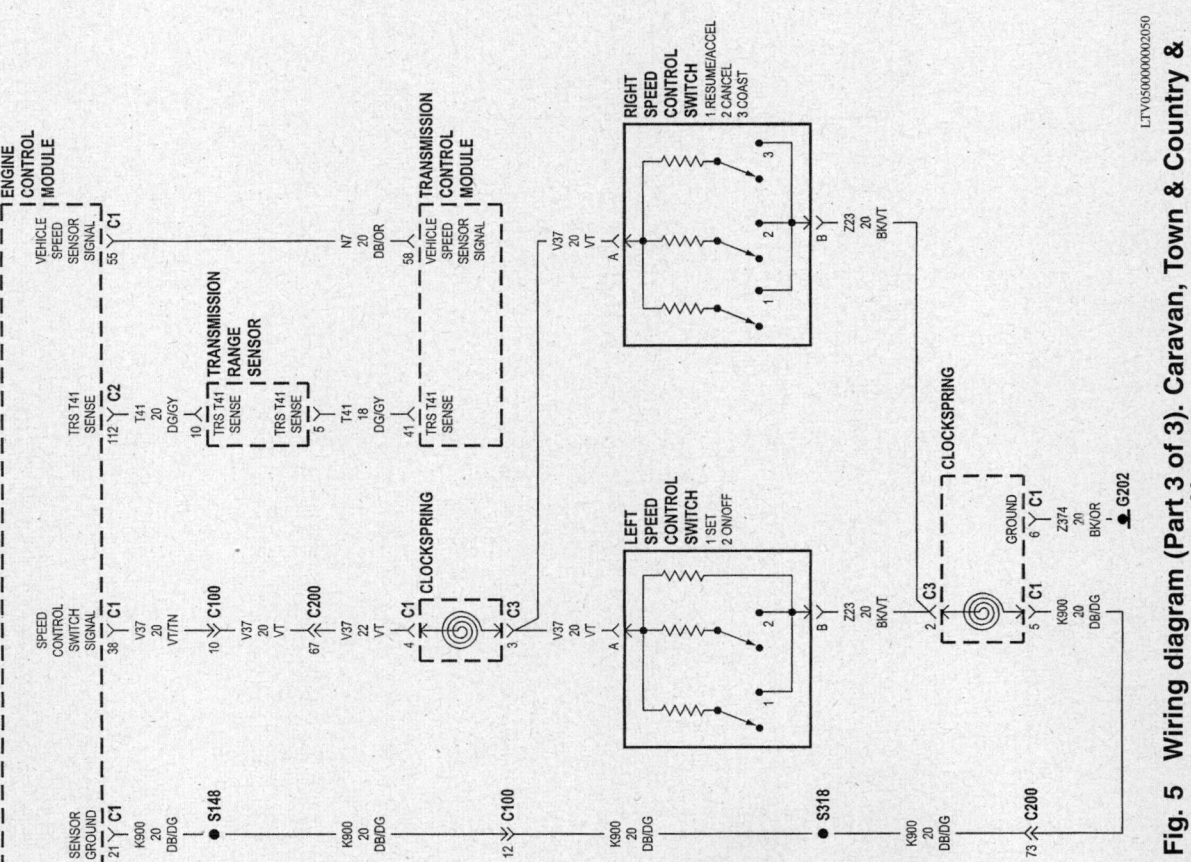

Fig. 5 Wiring diagram (Part 3 of 3). Caravan, Town & Country & Voyager

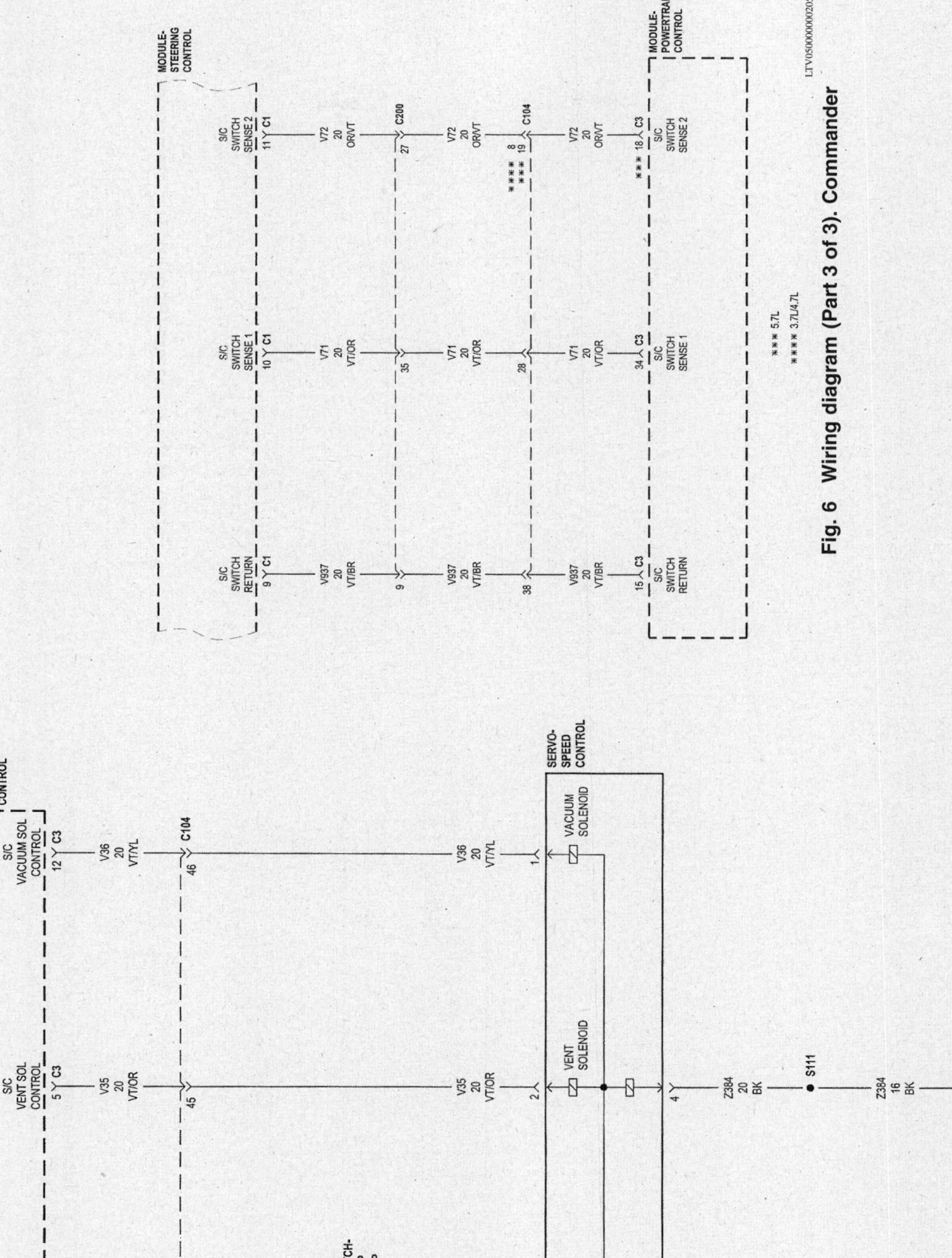

Fig. 6 Wiring diagram (Part 3 of 3). Commander

Fig. 6 Wiring diagram (Part 2 of 3). Commander

SPEED CONTROL SYSTEMS

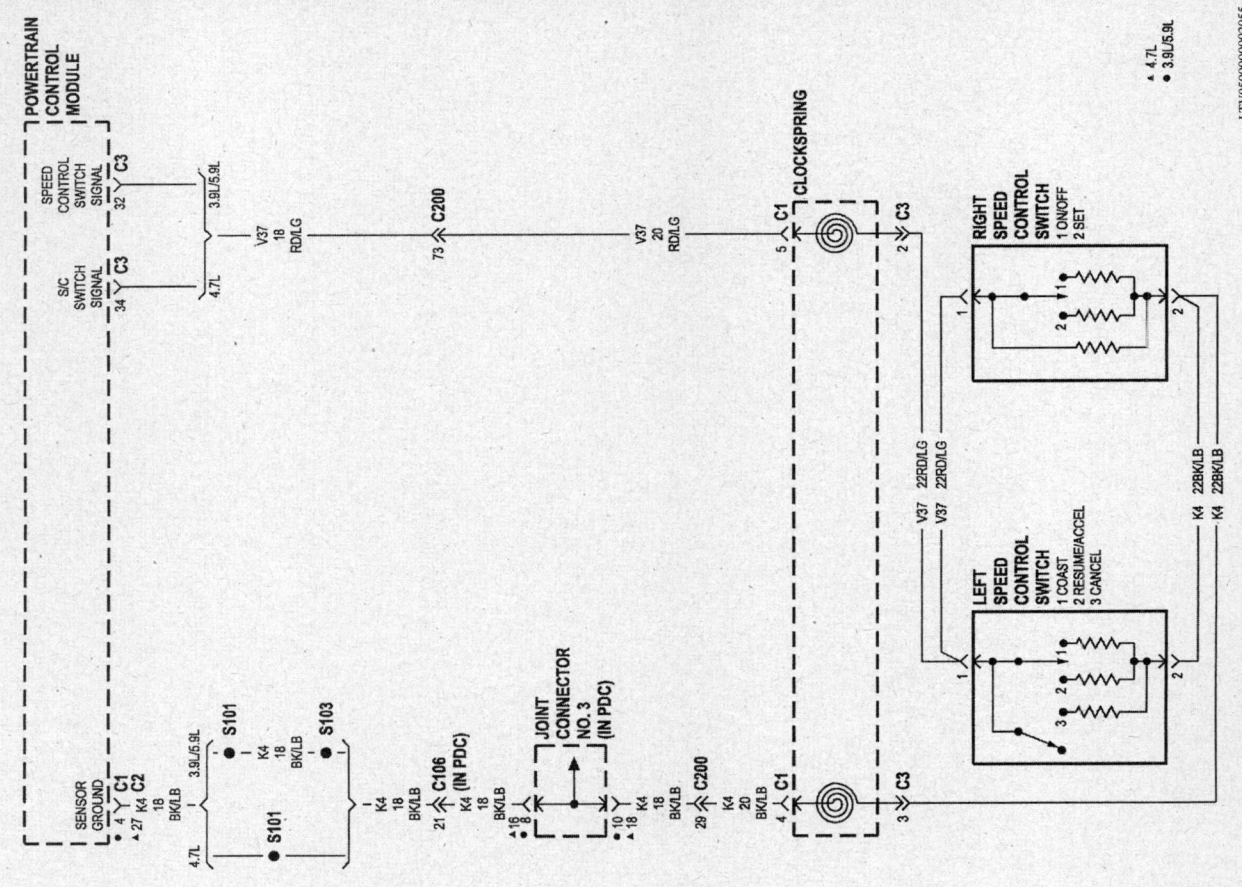

Fig. 7 Wiring diagram (Part 2 of 2). 2002–04 Dakota

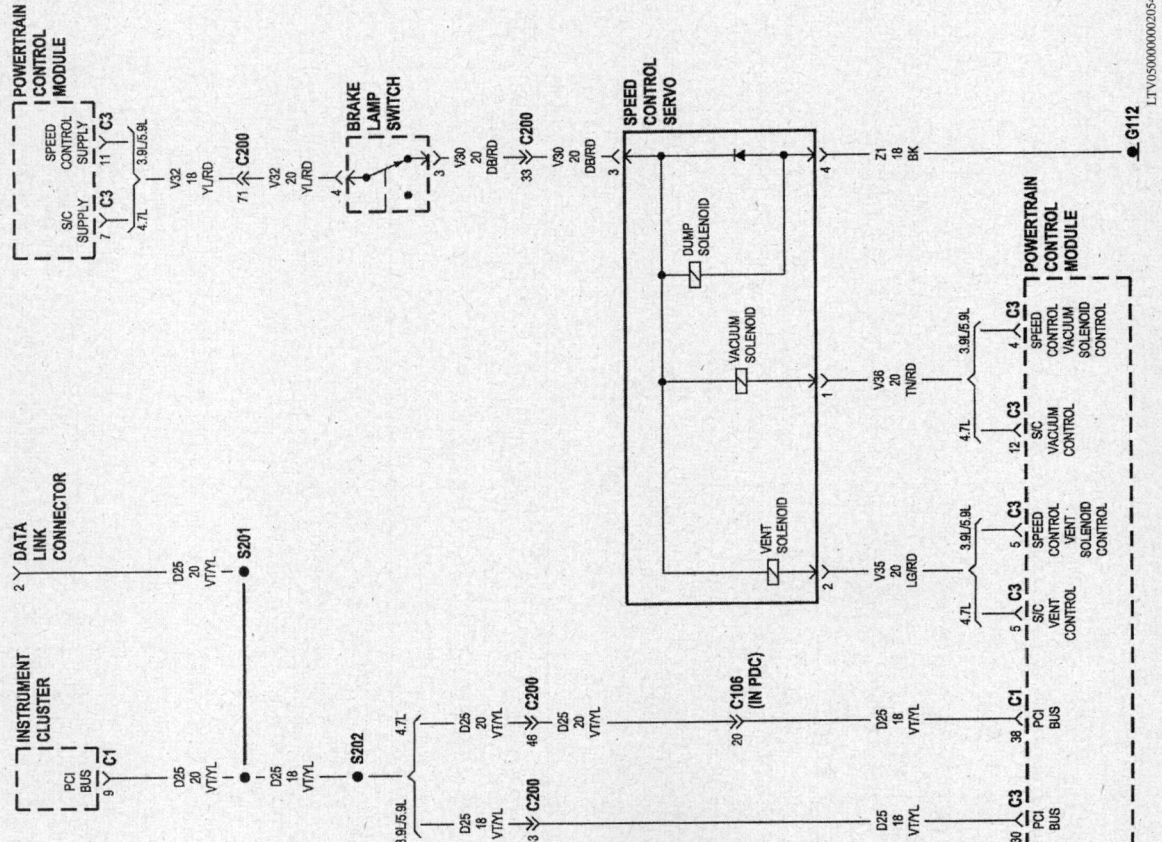

Fig. 7 Wiring diagram (Part 1 of 2). 2002–04 Dakota

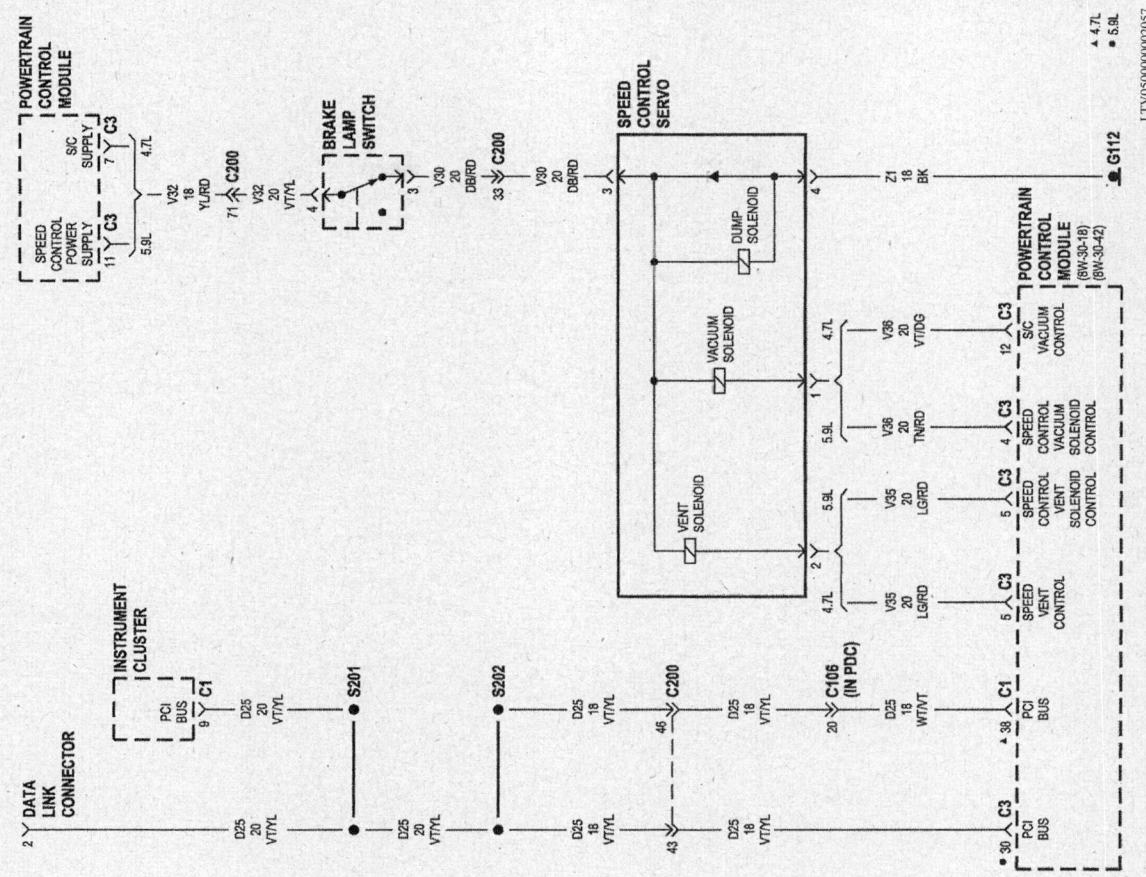

Fig. 9 Wiring diagram (Part 1 of 2). 2002–03 Durango

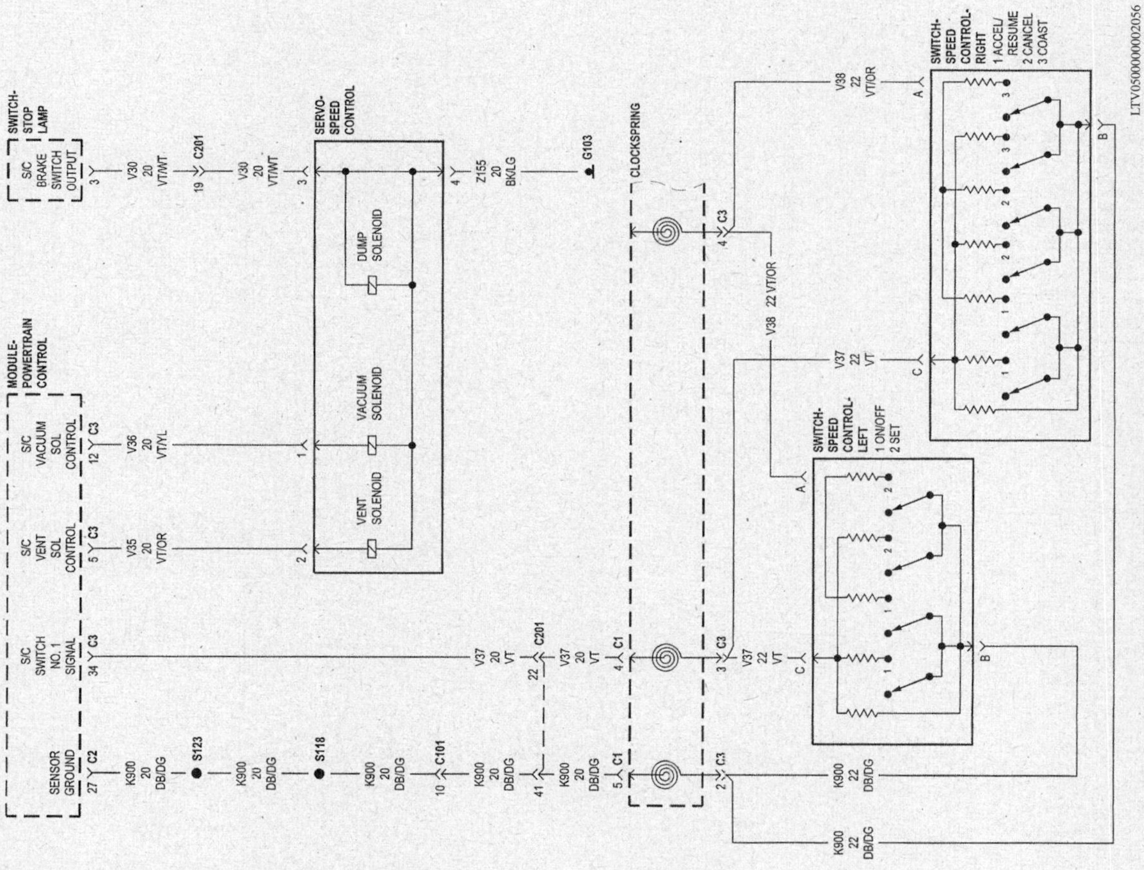

Fig. 8 Wiring diagram. 2005–06 Dakota

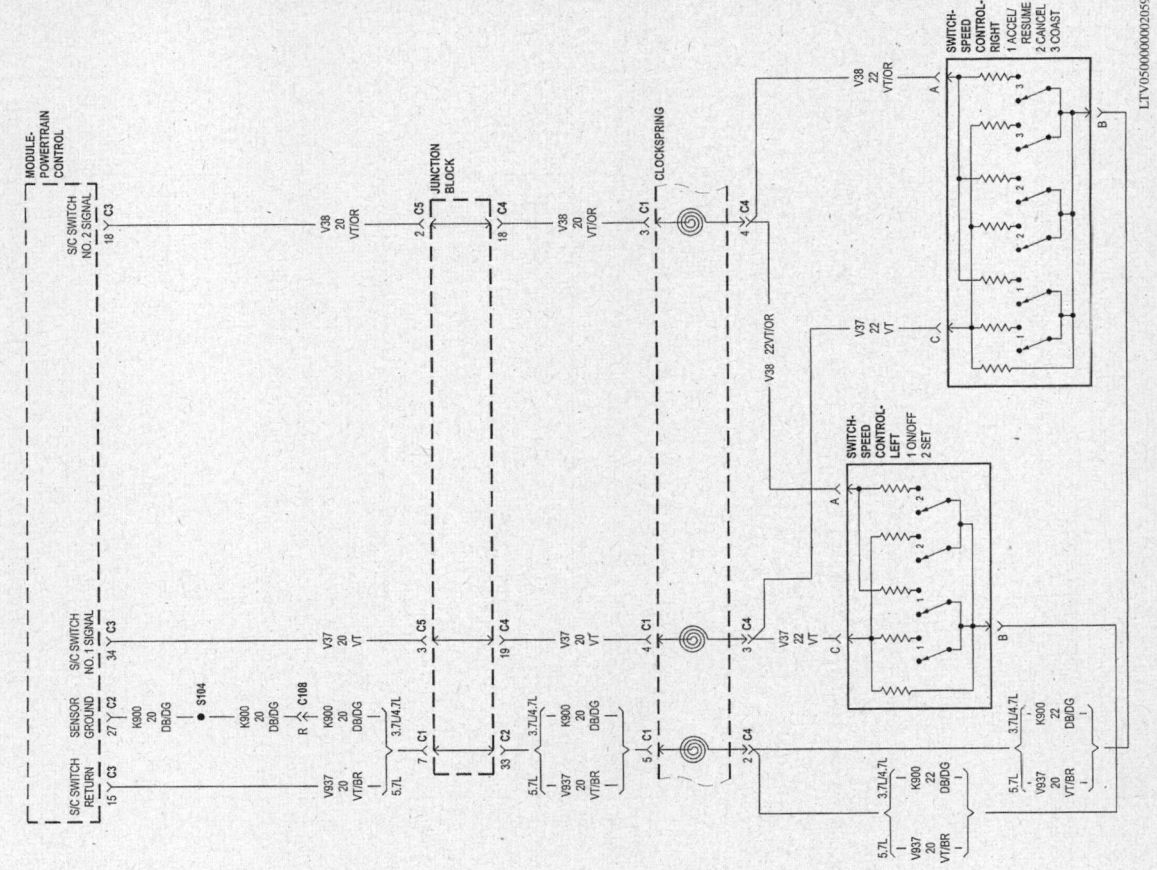

Fig. 10 Wiring diagram (Part 1 of 3). 2004–06 Durango

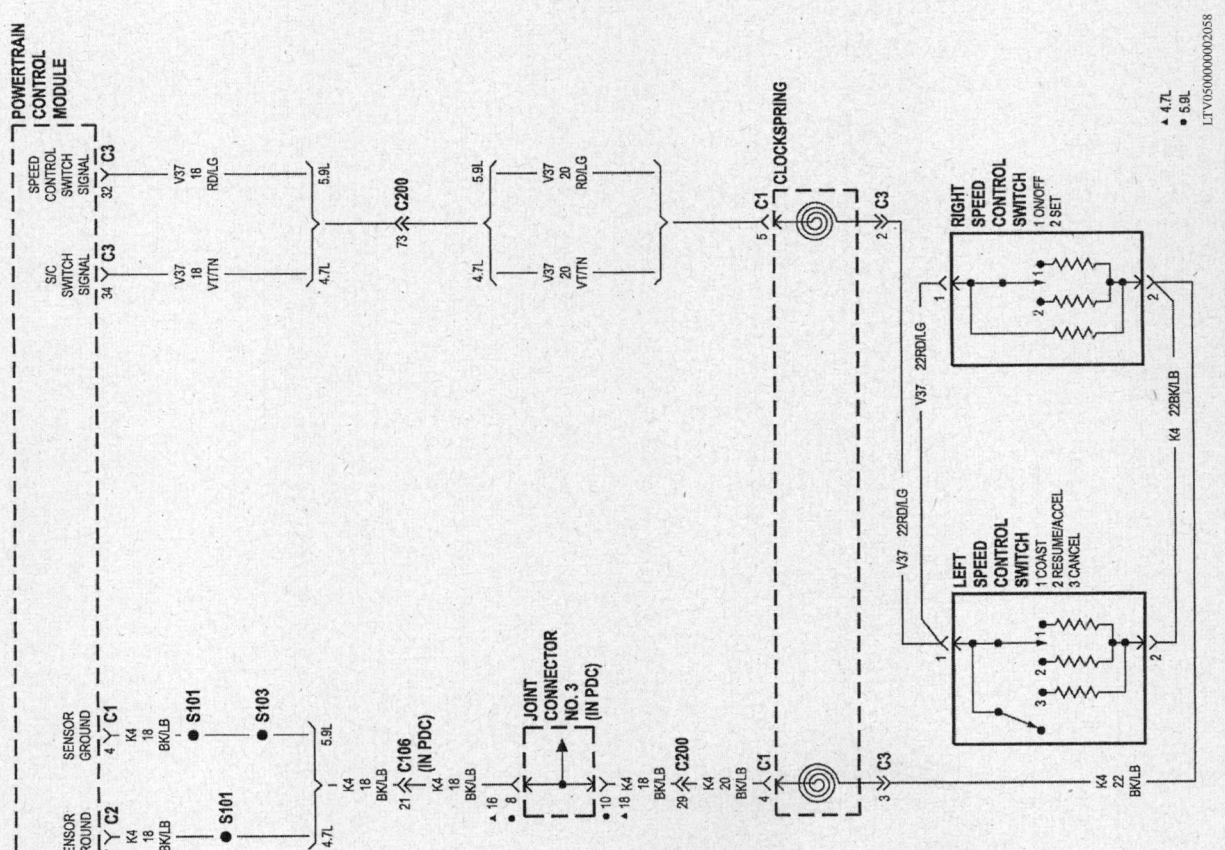

Fig. 9 Wiring diagram (Part 2 of 2). 2002–03 Durango

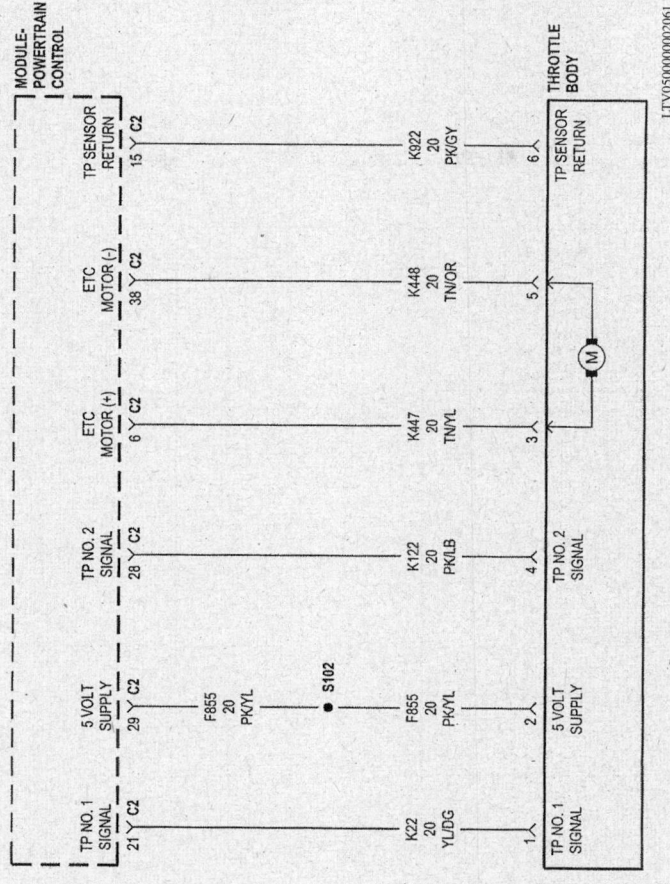

MODULE-POWERTRAIN CONTROL

Signal	Pin	Wire		Throttle Body
TP SENSOR RETURN	15 C2	K922 20 PK/GY		TP SENSOR RETURN 6
ETC MOTOR (-)	38 C2	K448 20 TN/OR		5
ETC MOTOR (+)	6 C2	K447 20 TN/YL		3
TP NO. 2 SIGNAL	28 C2	K122 20 PK/LB		TP NO. 2 SIGNAL 4
5 VOLT SUPPLY	29 C2	F855 20 PK/YL — S102 — F855 20 PK/YL		5 VOLT SUPPLY 2
TP NO. 1 SIGNAL	21 C2	K22 20 YL/DG		TP NO. 1 SIGNAL 1

THROTTLE BODY

M

LTV050000002061

Fig. 10 Wiring diagram (Part 3 of 3). 2004–06 Durango

LTV050000002060

SWITCH-STOP LAMP
S/C BRAKE SWITCH OUTPUT 3

V30 20 VT/WT

JUNCTION BLOCK
22 C4 — 6 C5

V30 20 VT/WT

SERVO-SPEED CONTROL
3

DUMP SOLENOID

VACUUM SOLENOID

VENT SOLENOID

4

Z155 20 BK/LG

G112

1 — V36 20 VT/YL — 12 C3 — **MODULE-POWERTRAIN CONTROL** S/C VACUUM SOLENOID CONTROL

2 — V35 20 VT/OR — 5 C3 — S/C VENT SOLENOID CONTROL

Fig. 10 Wiring diagram (Part 2 of 3). 2004–06 Durango

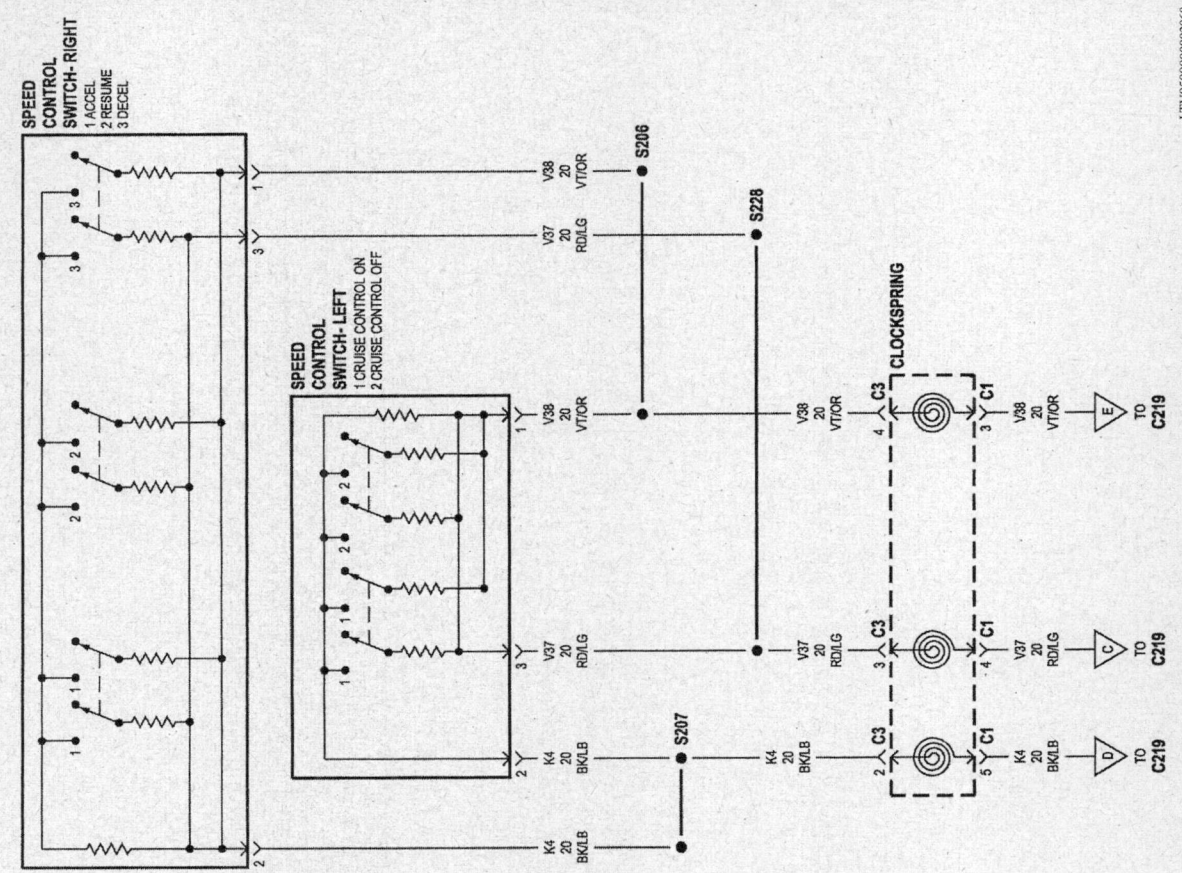

Fig. 11   Wiring diagram (Part 2 of 4). 2002–03 Full Size Pickup

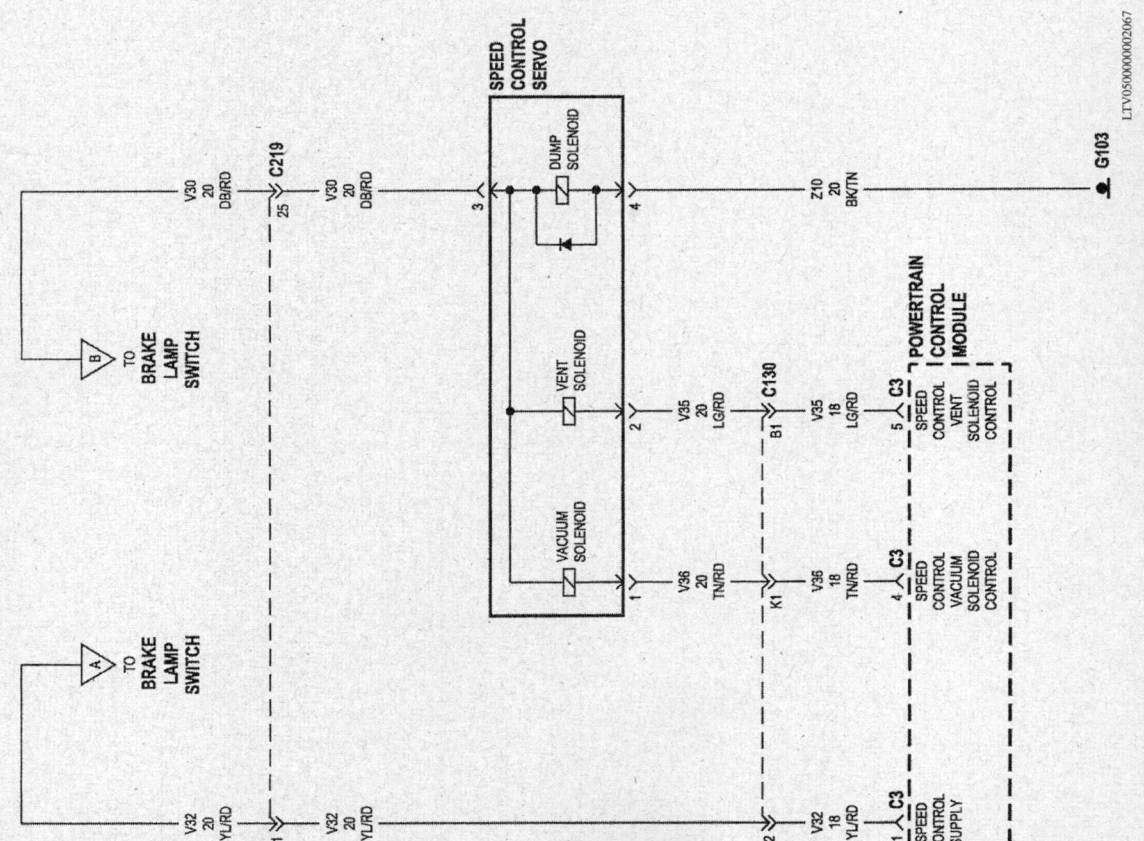

Fig. 11   Wiring diagram (Part 1 of 4). 2002–03 Full Size Pickup

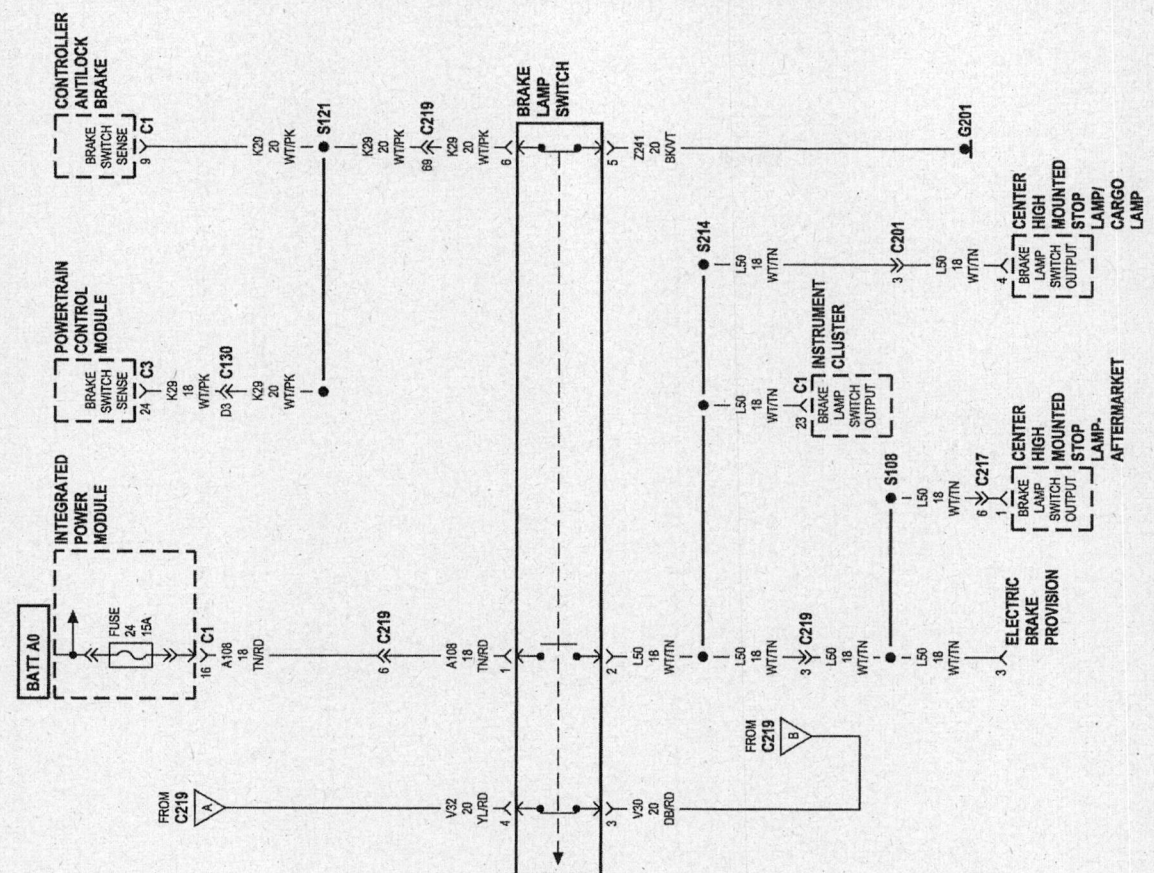

Fig. 11 Wiring diagram (Part 4 of 4). 2002–03 Full Size Pickup

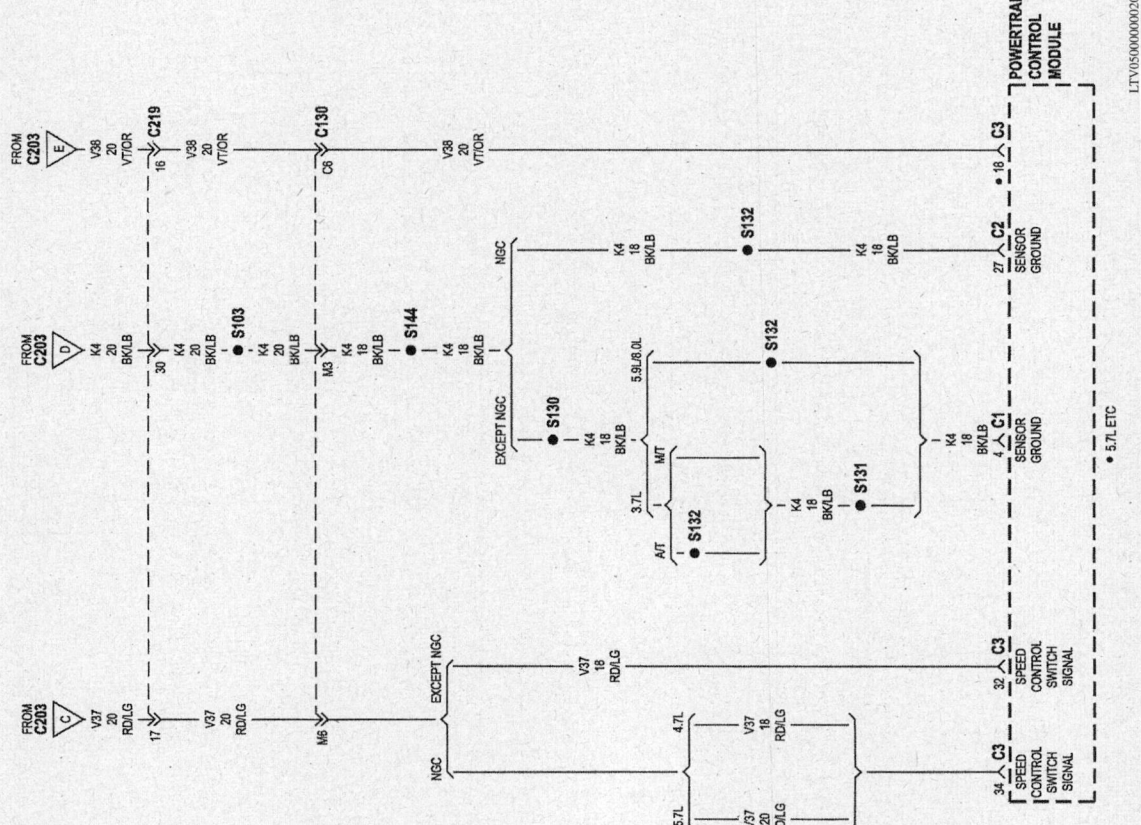

Fig. 11 Wiring diagram (Part 3 of 4). 2002–03 Full Size Pickup

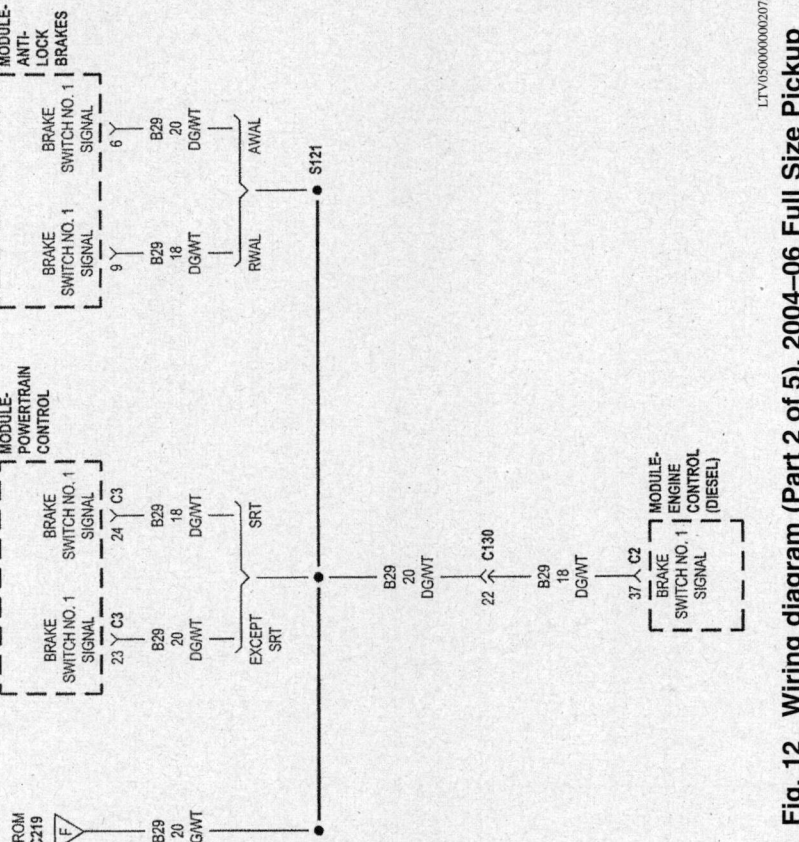

Fig. 12 Wiring diagram (Part 2 of 5). 2004–06 Full Size Pickup

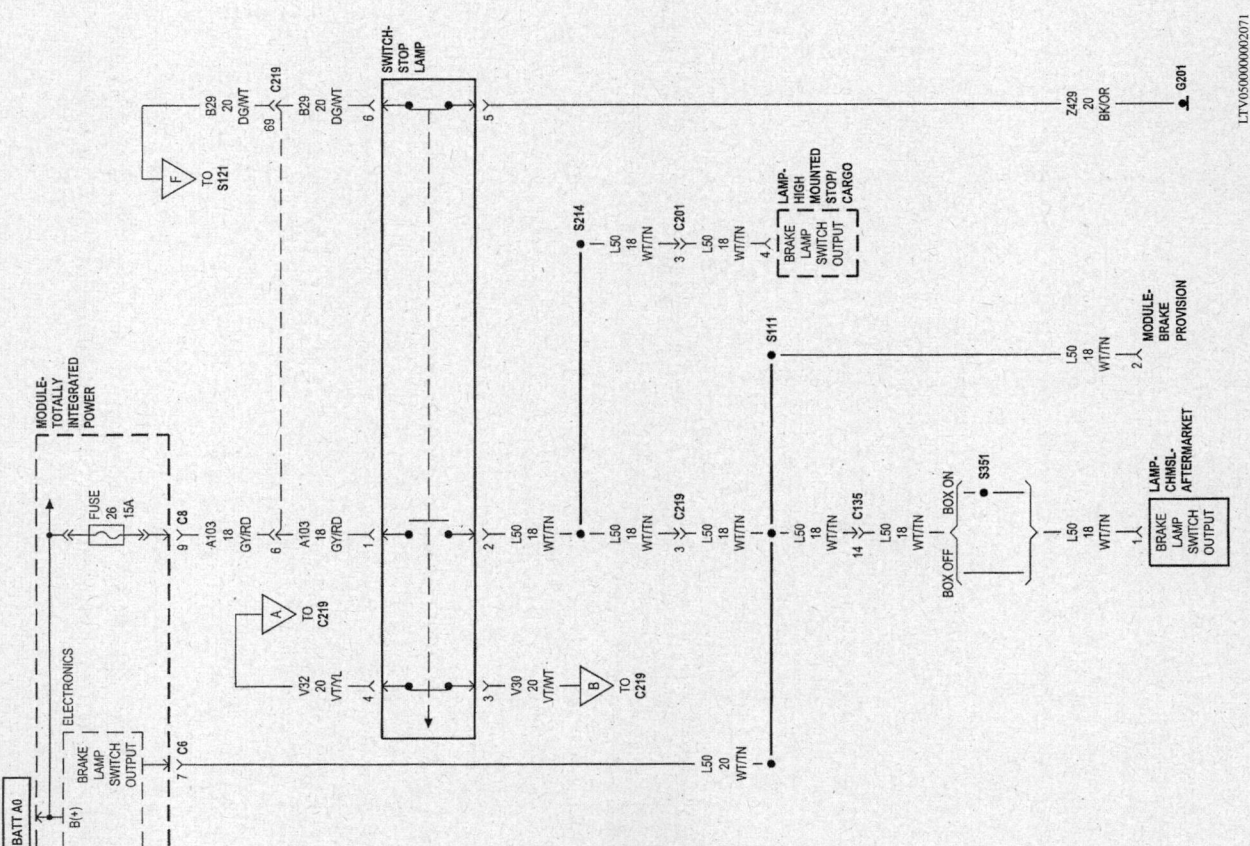

Fig. 12 Wiring diagram (Part 1 of 5). 2004–06 Full Size Pickup

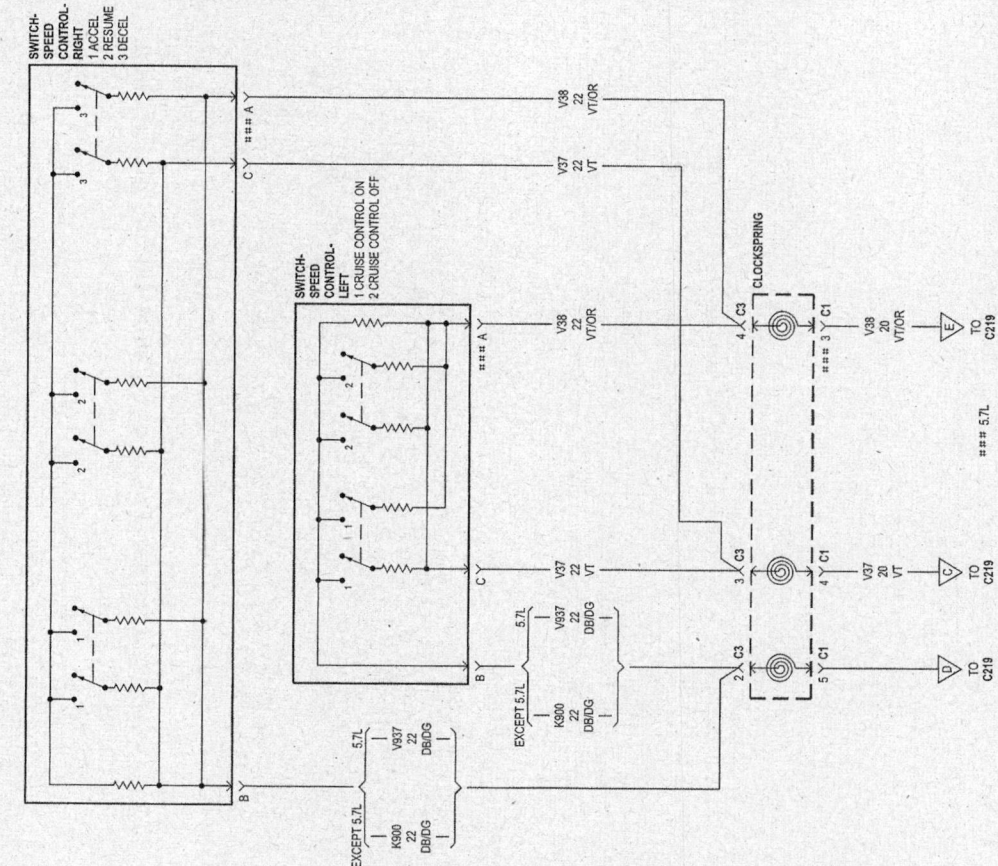

Fig. 12 Wiring diagram (Part 4 of 5). 2004–06 Full Size Pickup

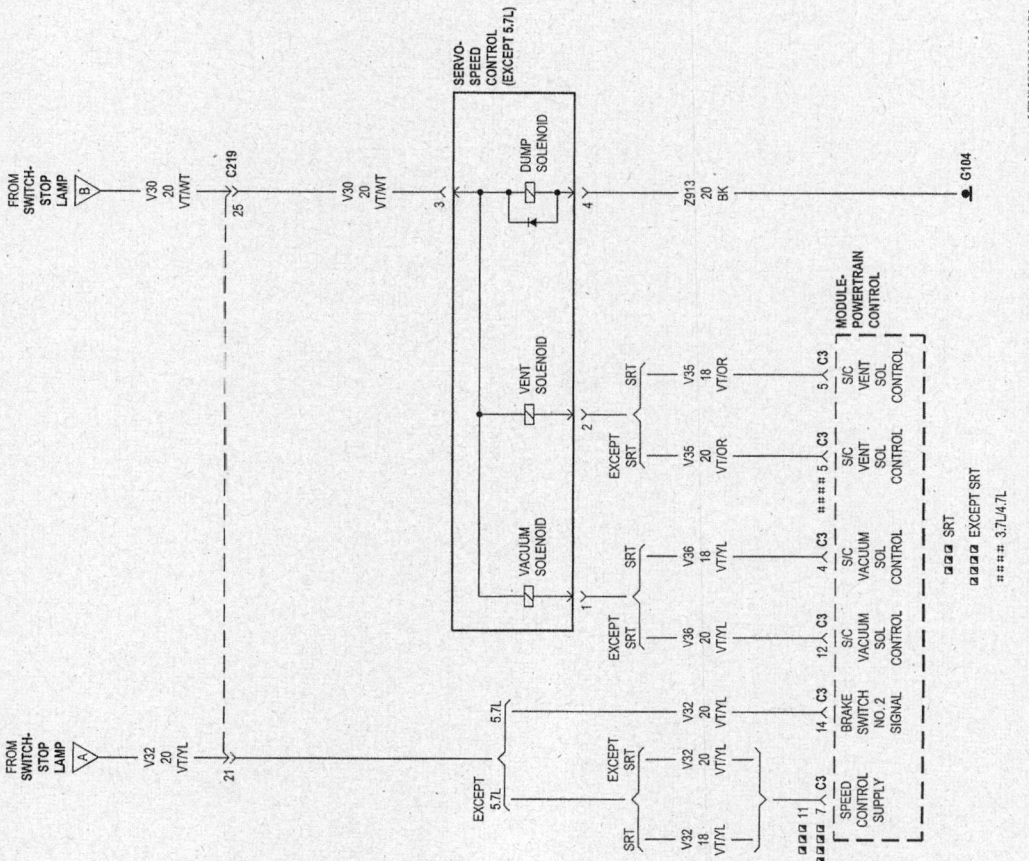

Fig. 12 Wiring diagram (Part 3 of 5). 2004–06 Full Size Pickup

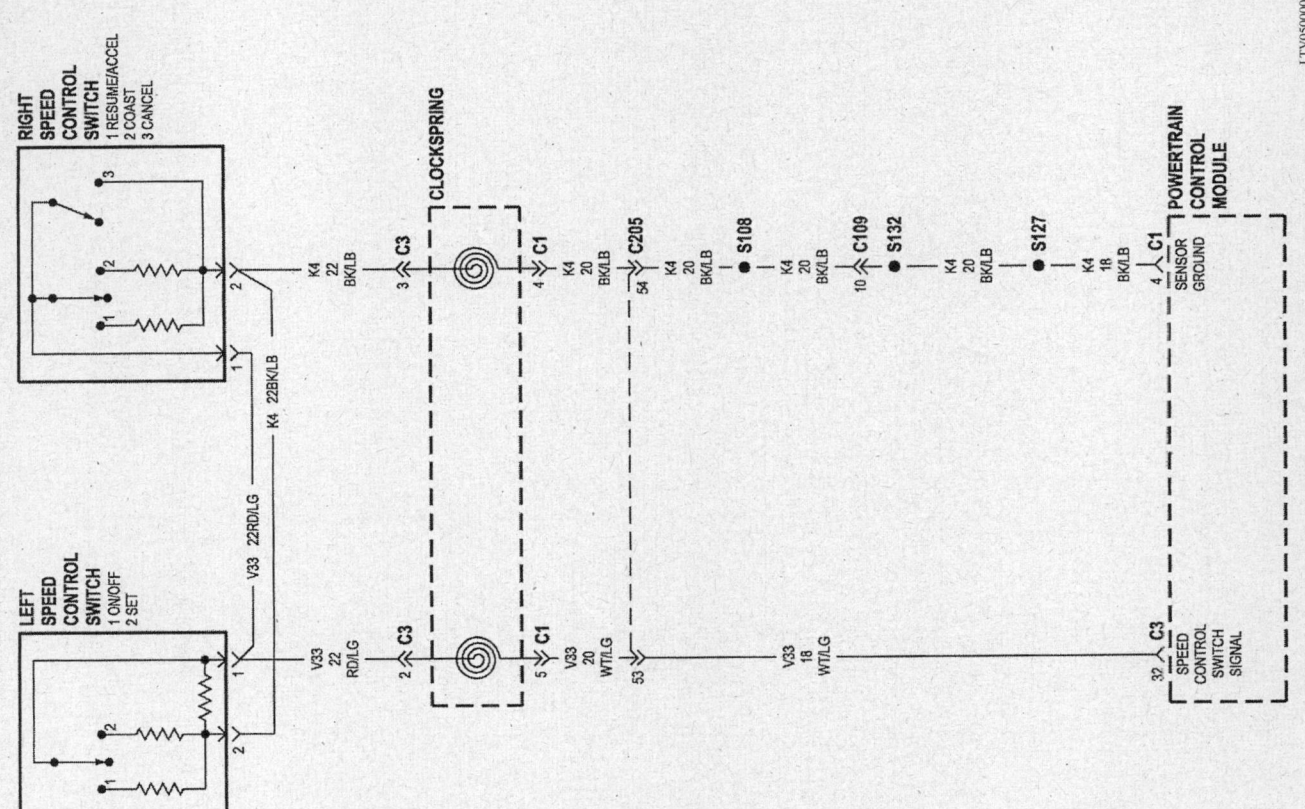

Fig. 13 Wiring diagram (Part 1 of 2). Full Size Van

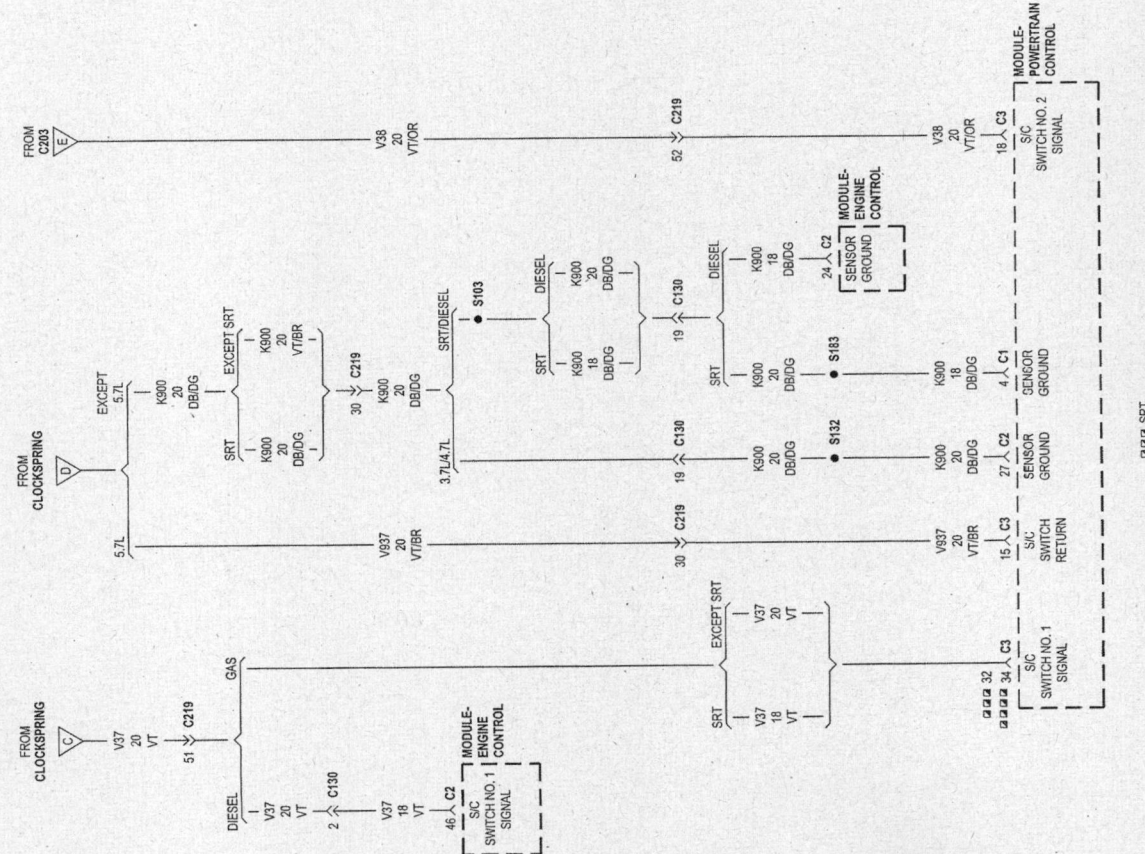

Fig. 12 Wiring diagram (Part 5 of 5). 2004–06 Full Size Pickup

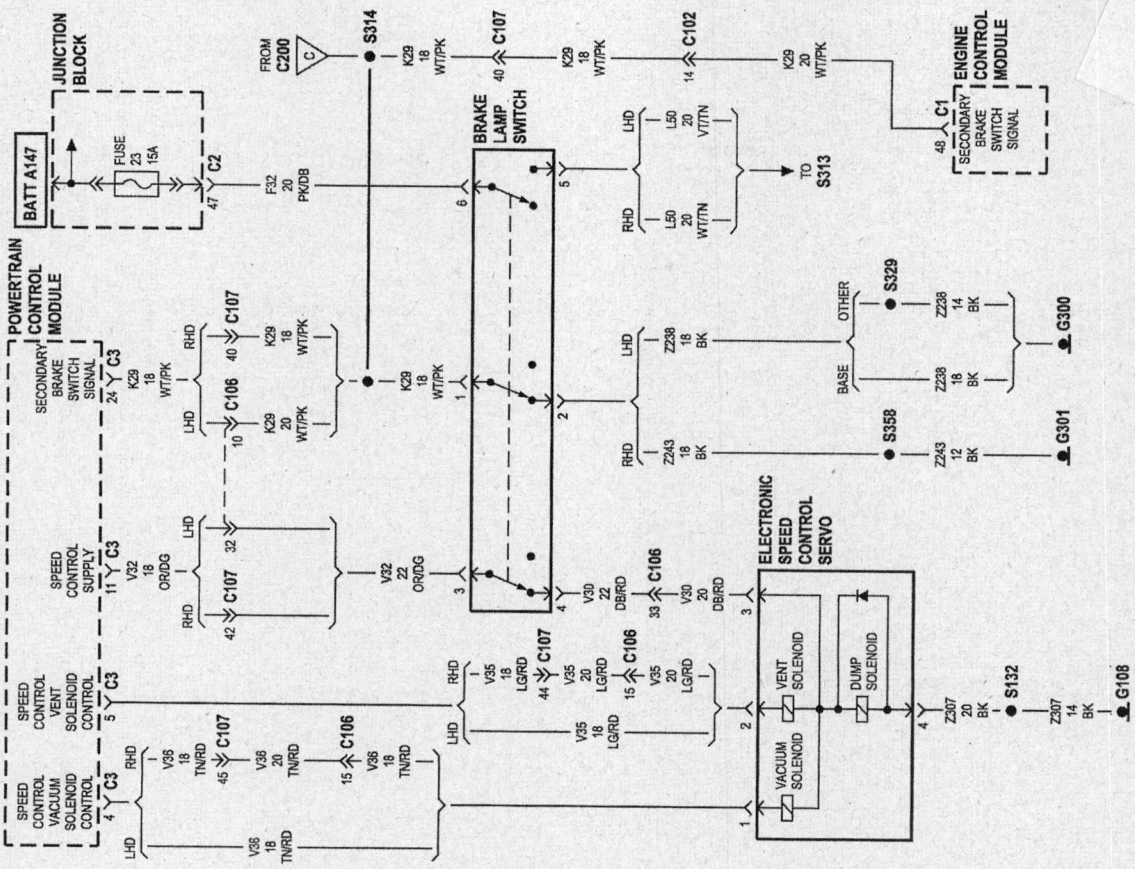

Fig. 14 Wiring diagram (Part 1 of 3). 2002–04 Grand Ch

L1V05000000002077

Fig. 13 Wiring diagram (Part 2 of 2). Full Size Van

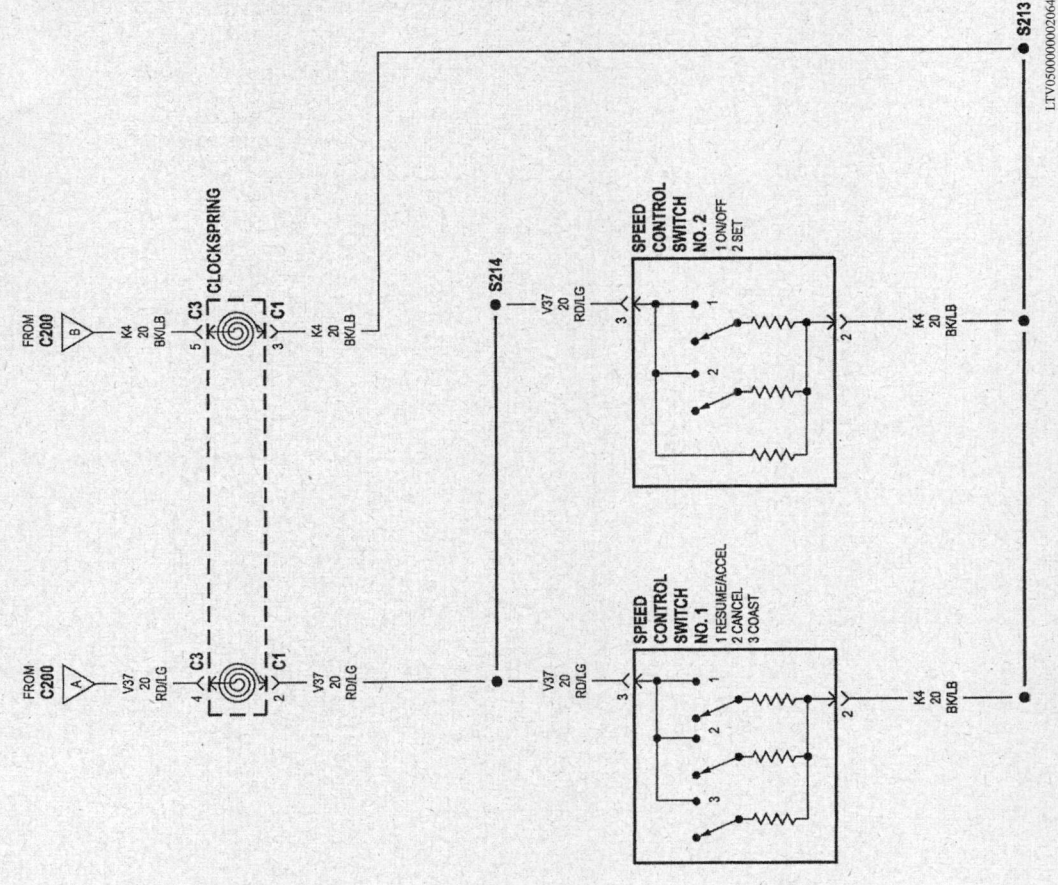

Fig. 14   Wiring diagram (Part 3 of 3). 2002–04 Grand Cherokee

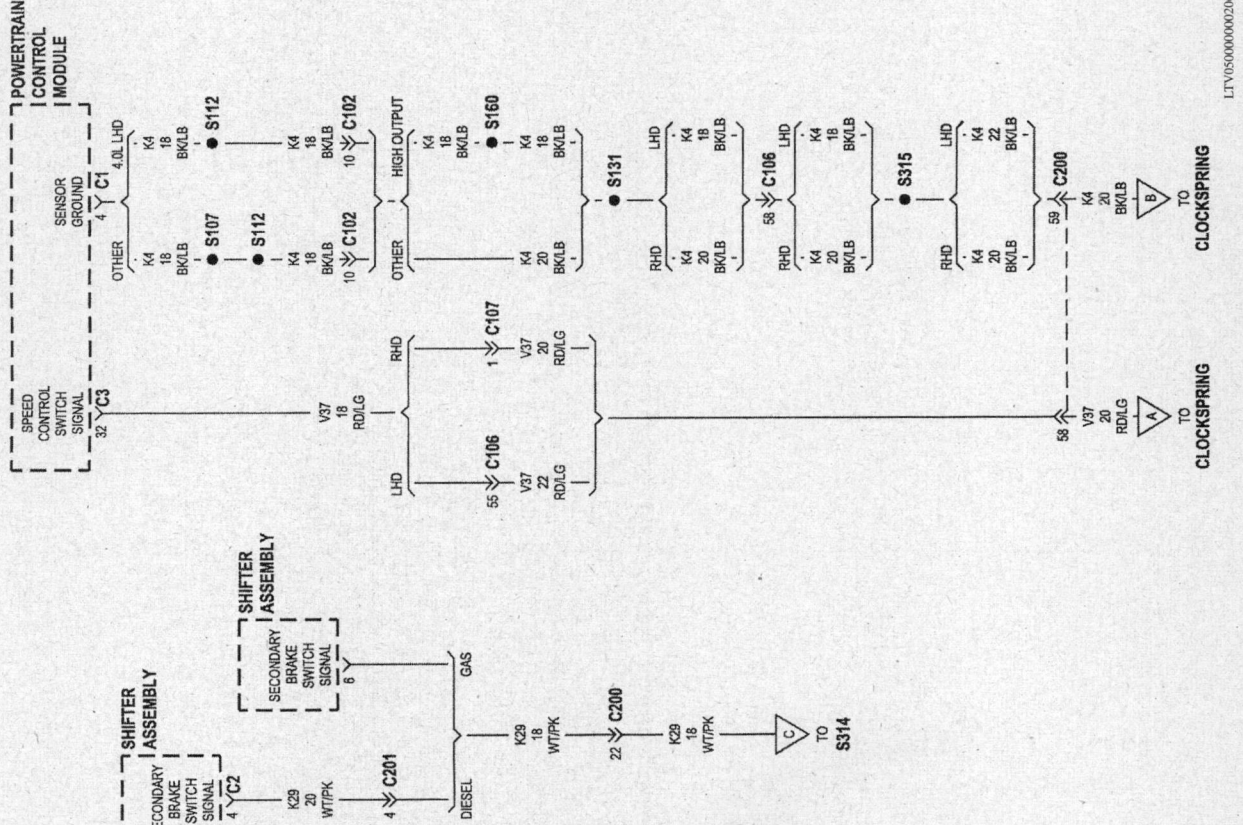

Fig. 14   Wiring diagram (Part 2 of 3). 2002–04 Grand Cherokee

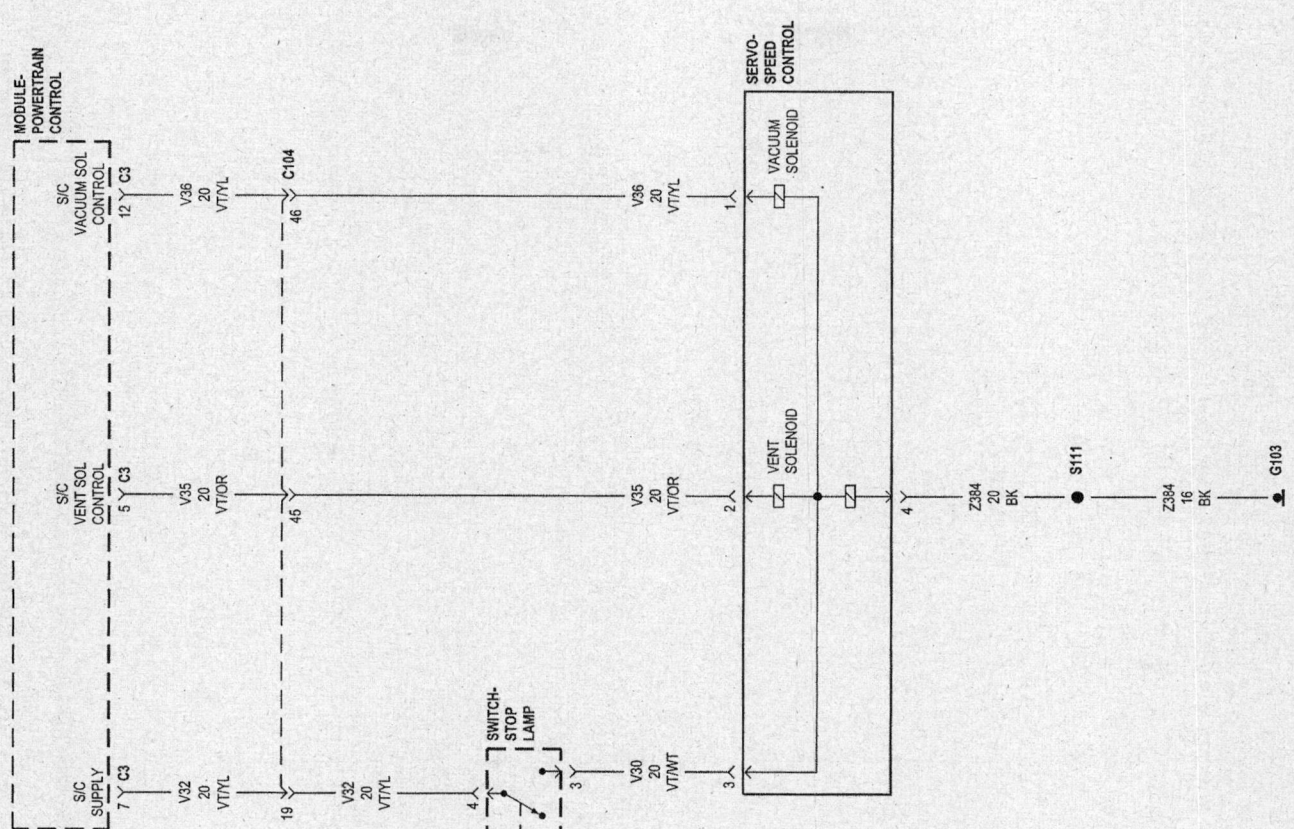

Fig. 15 Wiring diagram (Part 2 of 2). 2005-06 Grand Cherokee

Fig. 15 Wiring diagram (Part 1 of 2). 2005-06 Grand Cherokee

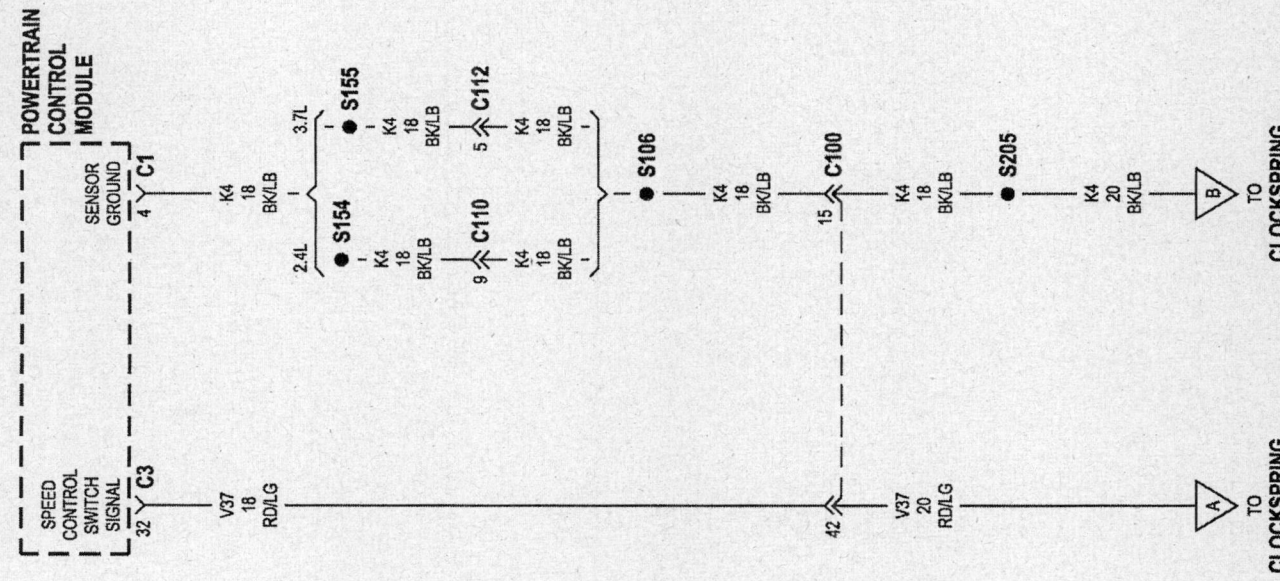

Fig. 16 Wiring diagram (Part 2 of 3). 2002–04 Liberty

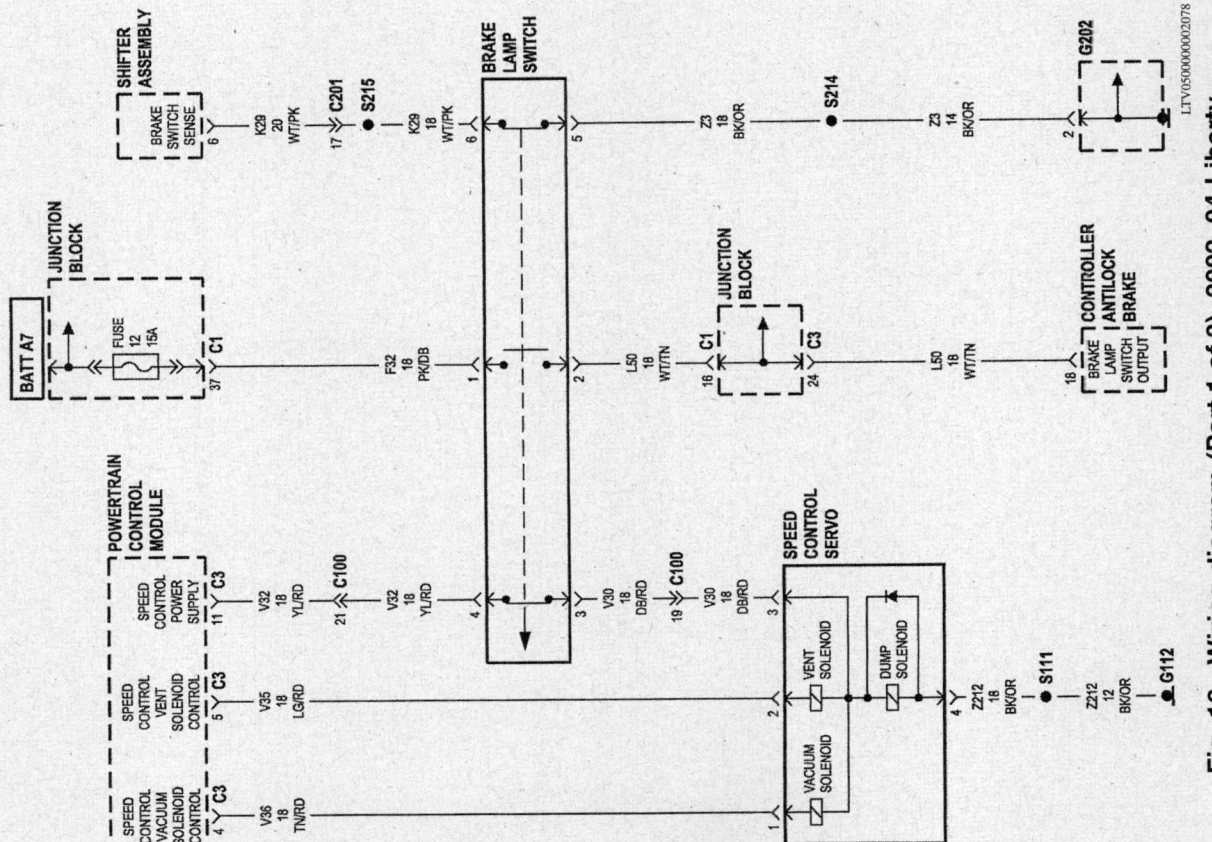

Fig. 16 Wiring diagram (Part 1 of 3). 2002–04 Liberty

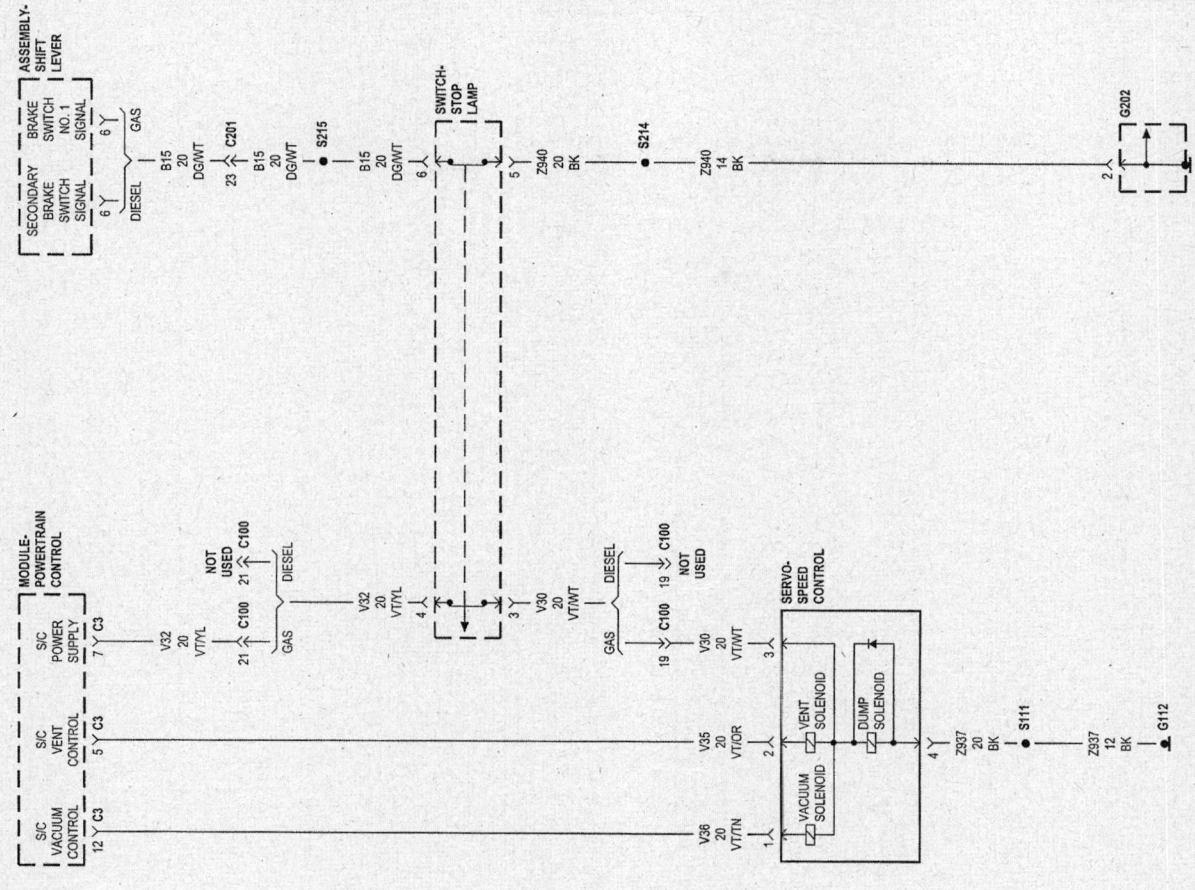

Fig. 17 Wiring diagram (Part 1 of 3). 2005–06 Liberty

Fig. 16 Wiring diagram (Part 3 of 3). 2002–04 Liberty

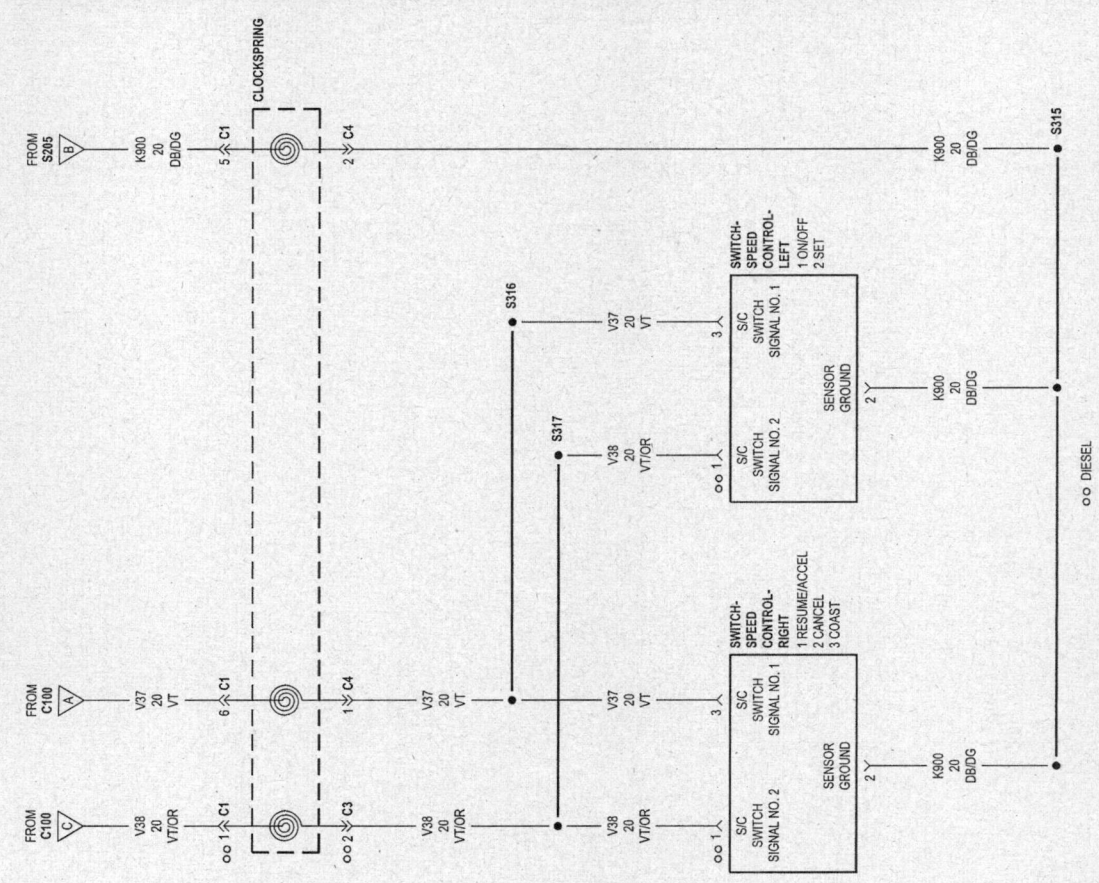

Fig. 17 Wiring diagram (Part 3 of 3). 2005–06 Liberty

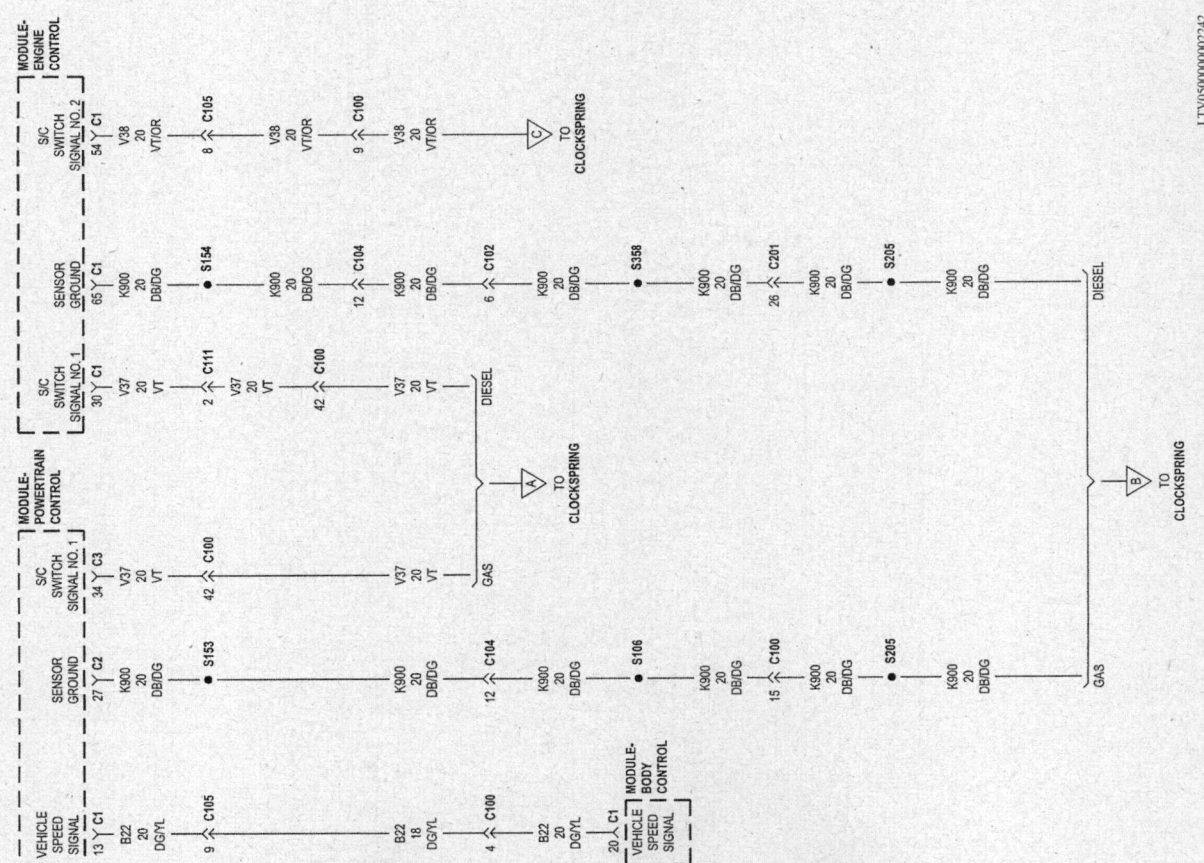

Fig. 17 Wiring diagram (Part 2 of 3). 2005–06 Liberty

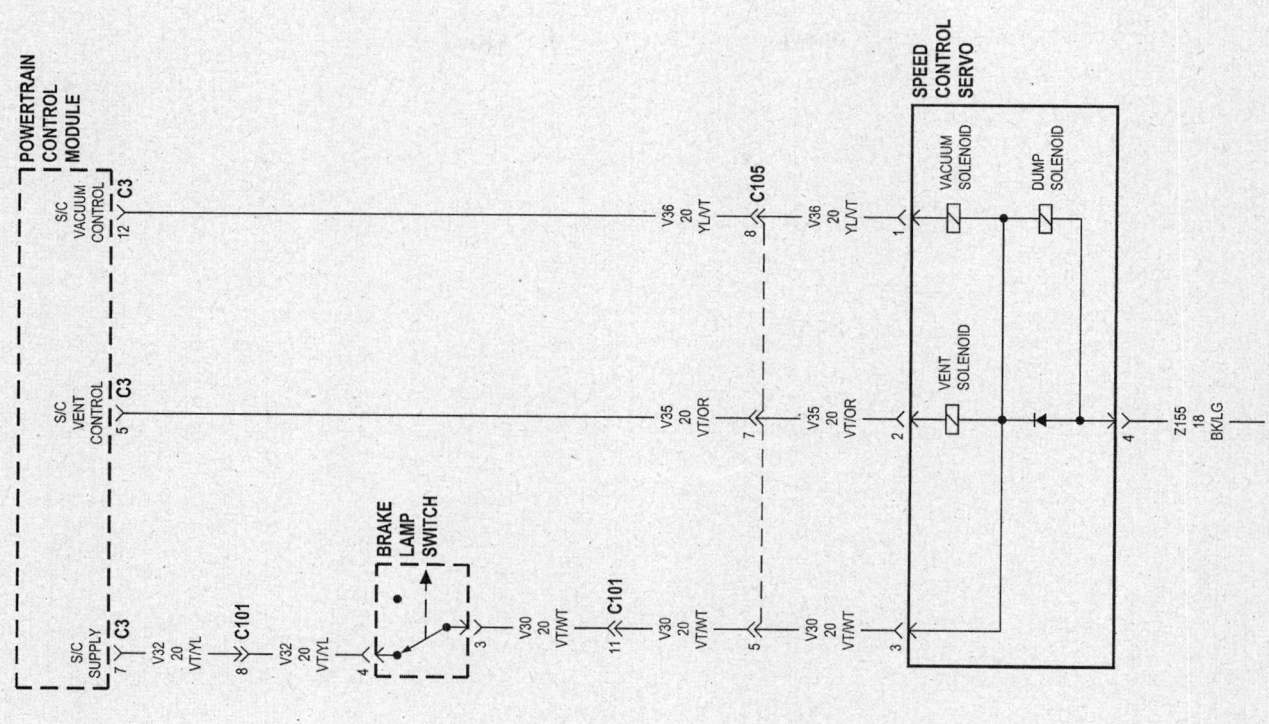

Fig. 18 Wiring diagram (Part 2 of 3). 2004–06 Pacifica

Fig. 18 Wiring diagram (Part 1 of 3). 2004–06 Pacifica

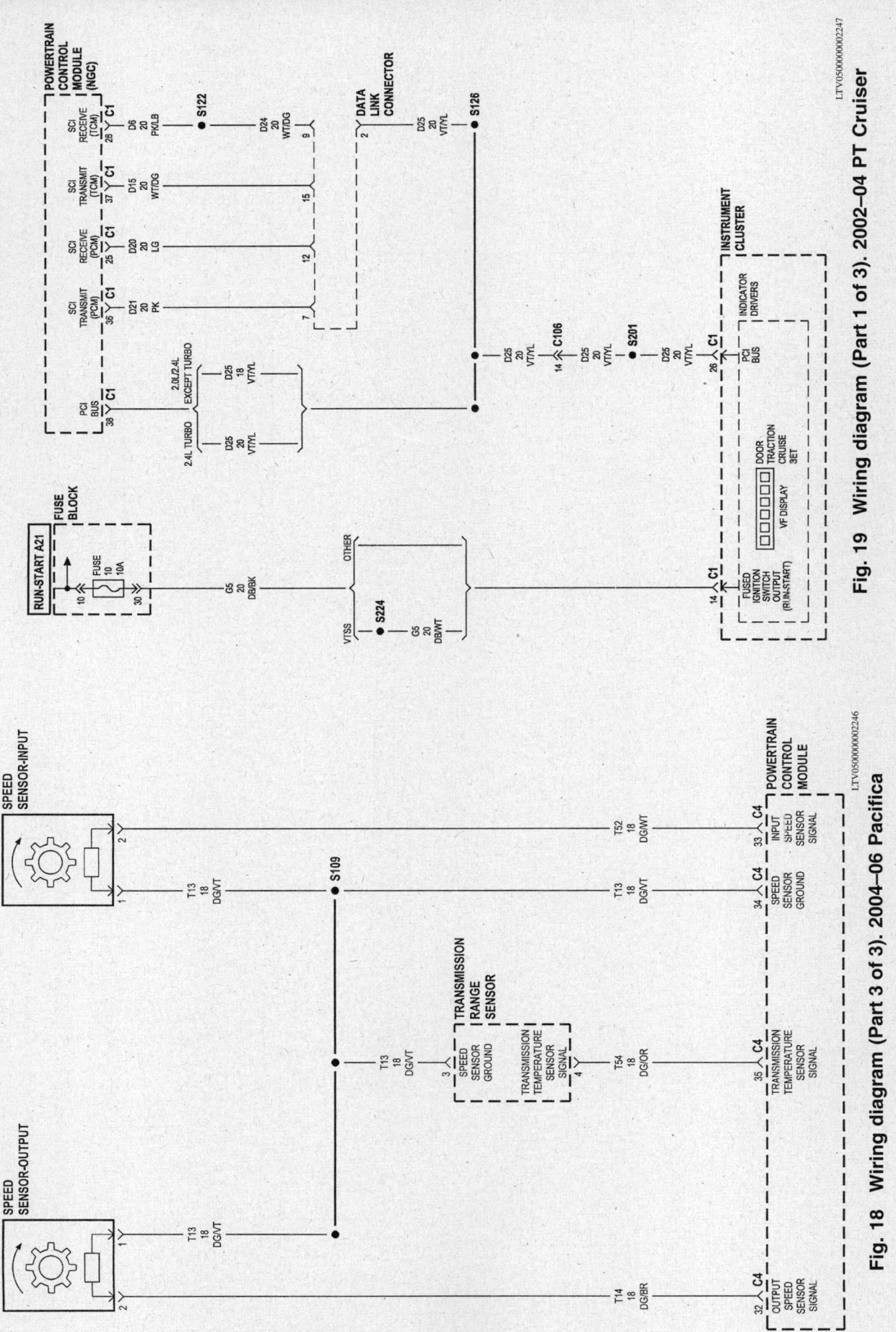

Fig. 19 Wiring diagram (Part 1 of 3). 2002–04 PT Cruiser

Fig. 18 Wiring diagram (Part 3 of 3). 2004–06 Pacifica

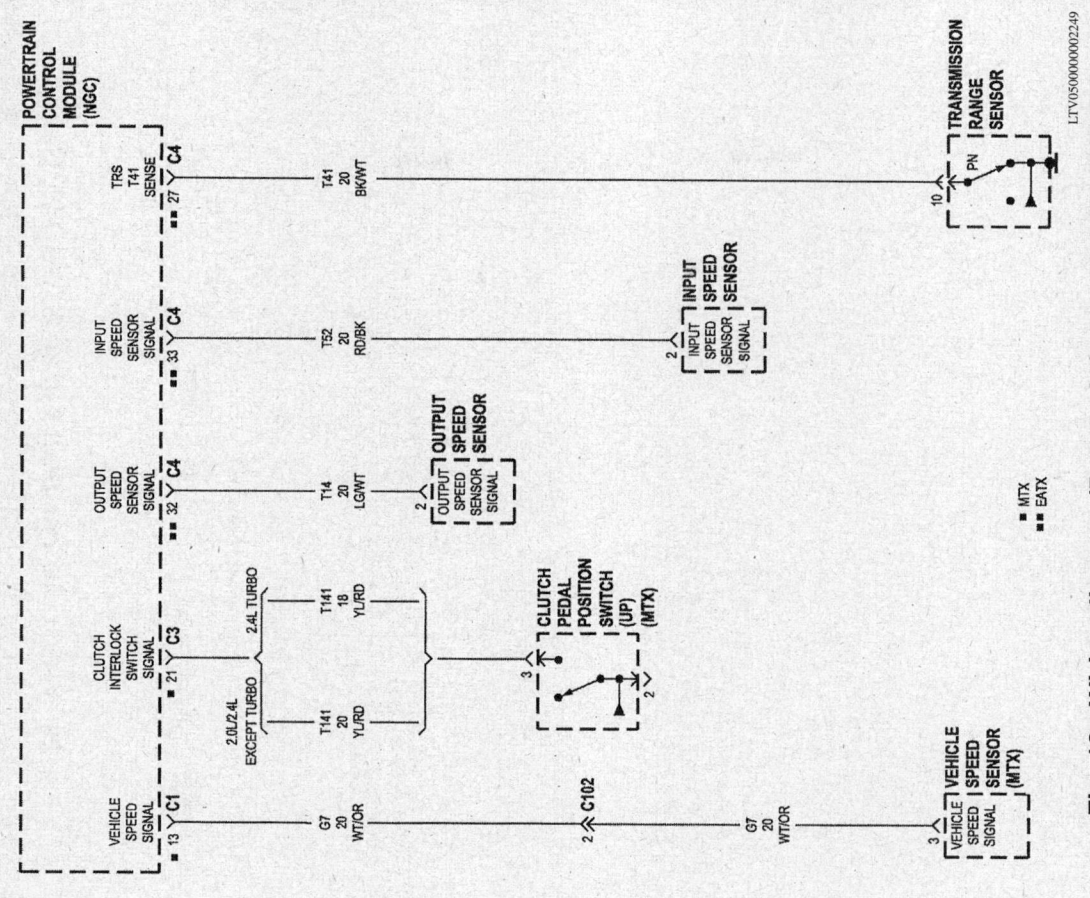

Fig. 19 Wiring diagram (Part 3 of 3). 2002–04 PT Cruiser

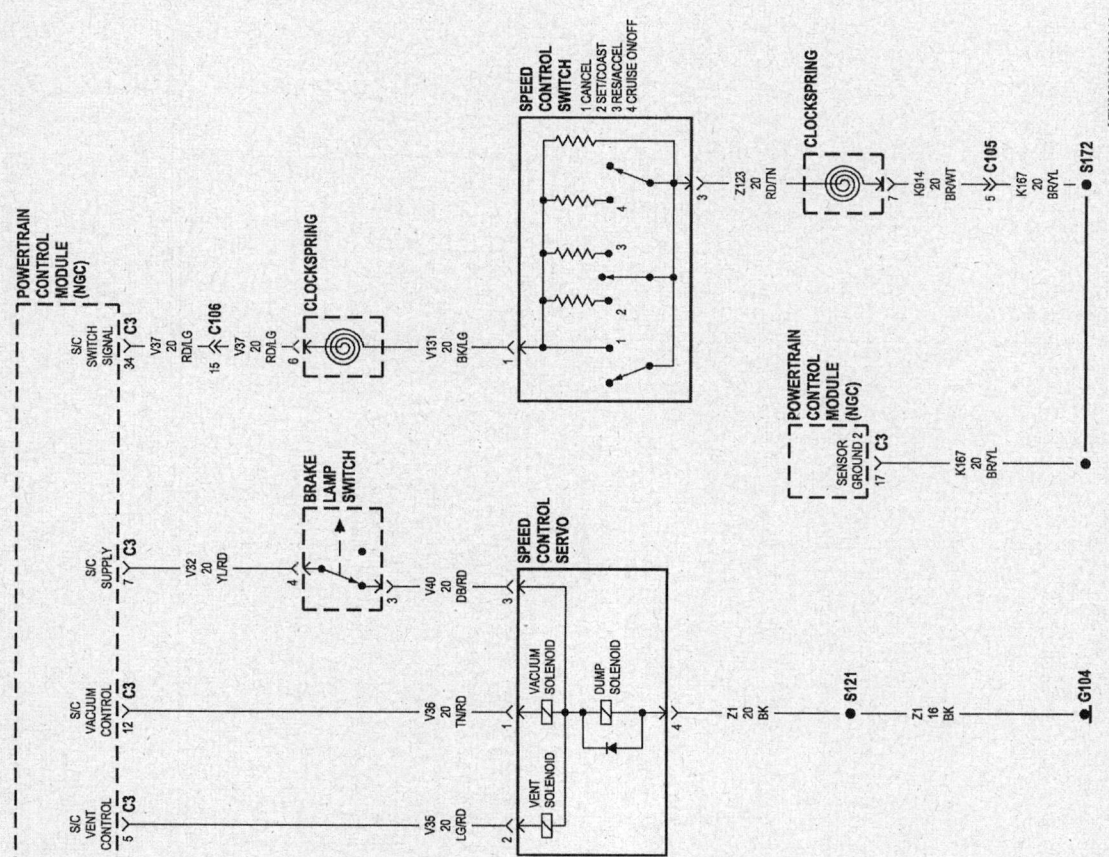

Fig. 19 Wiring diagram (Part 2 of 3). 2002–04 PT Cruiser

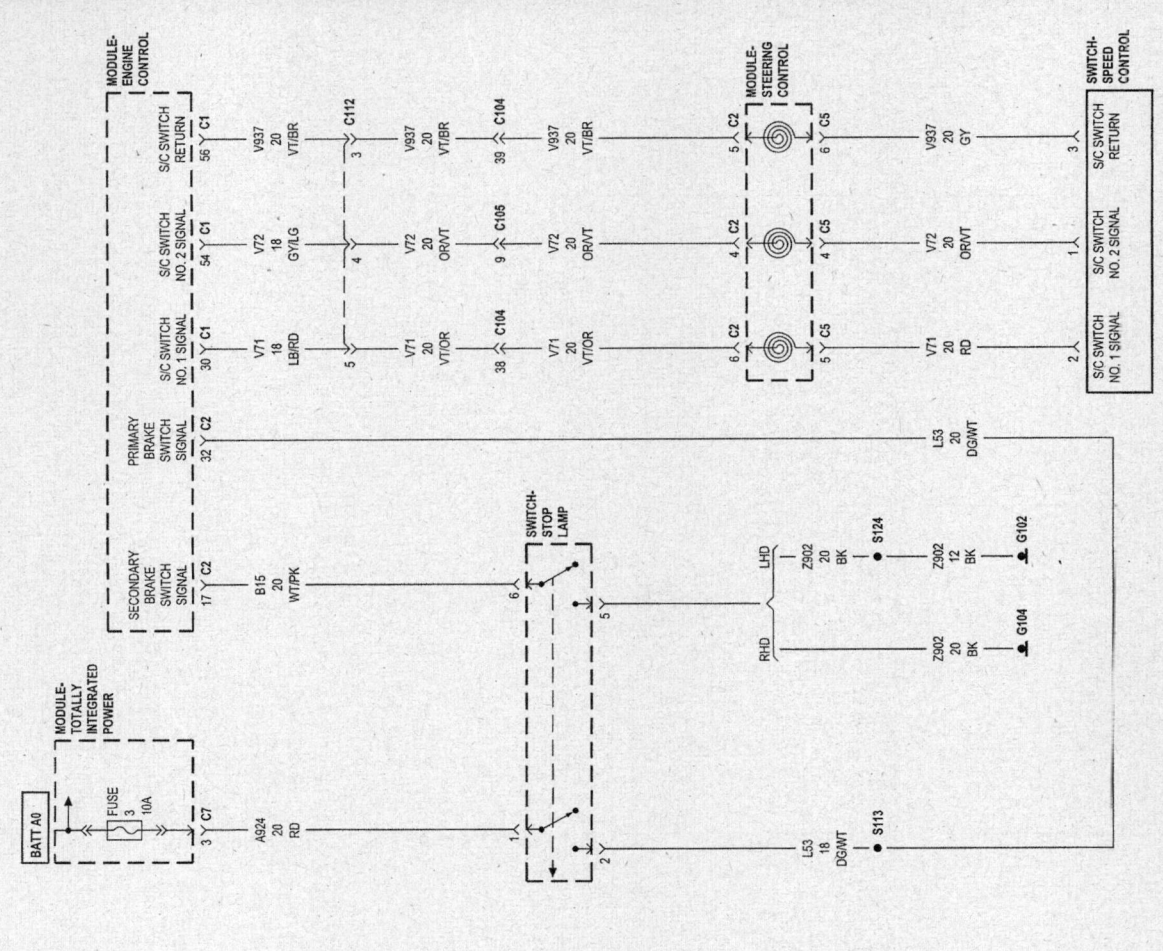

Fig. 20 Wiring diagram (Part 2 of 3). 2005–06 PT Cruiser

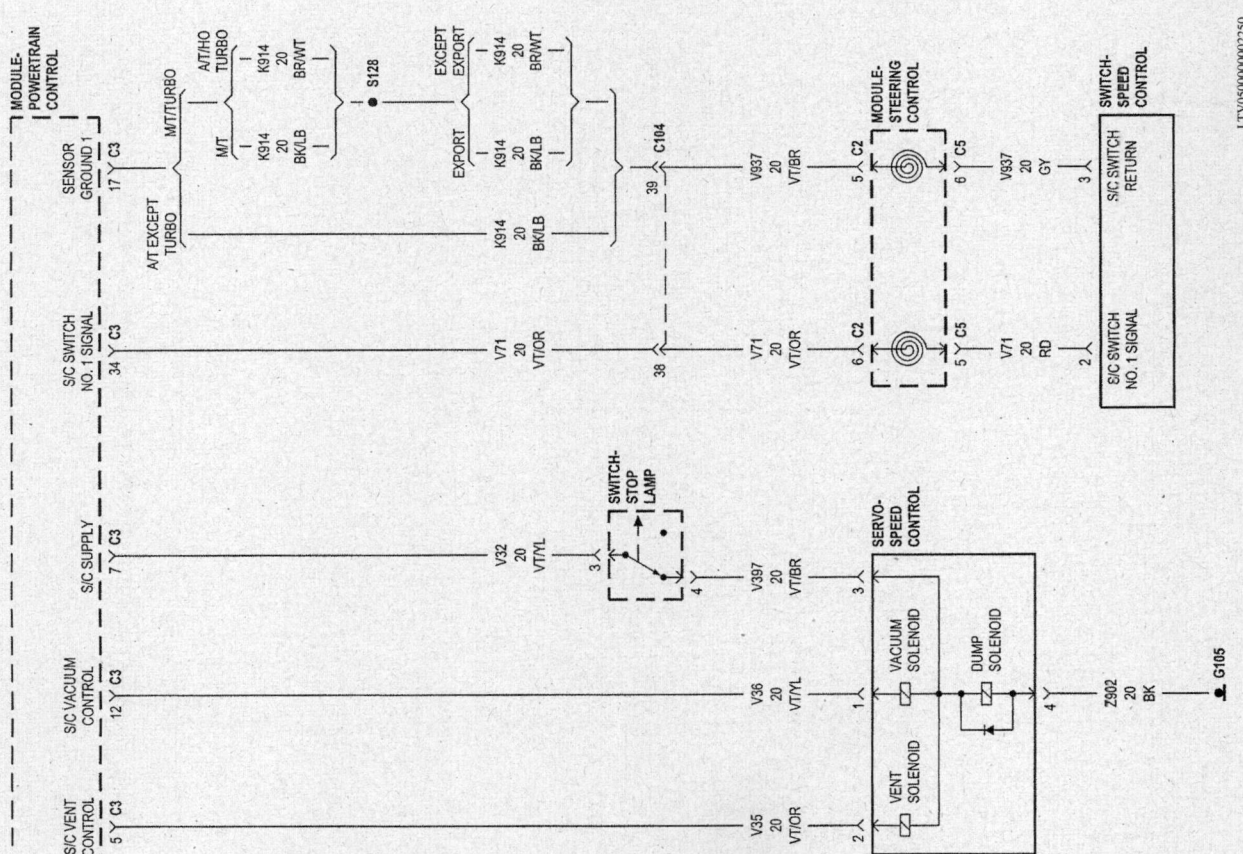

Fig. 20 Wiring diagram (Part 1 of 3). 2005–06 PT Cruiser

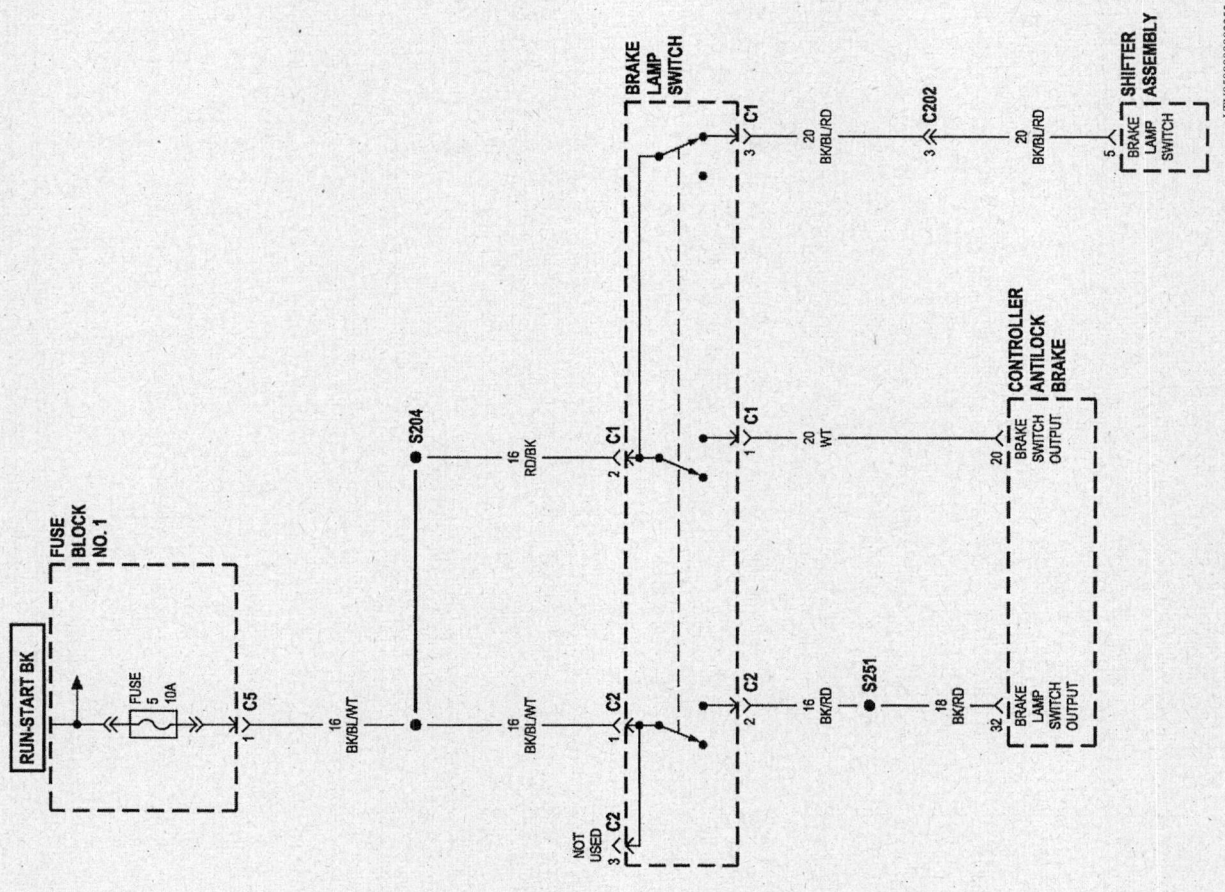

Fig. 21 Wiring diagram (Part 1 of 2). Sprinter

Fig. 20 Wiring diagram (Part 3 of 3). 2005–06 PT Cruiser

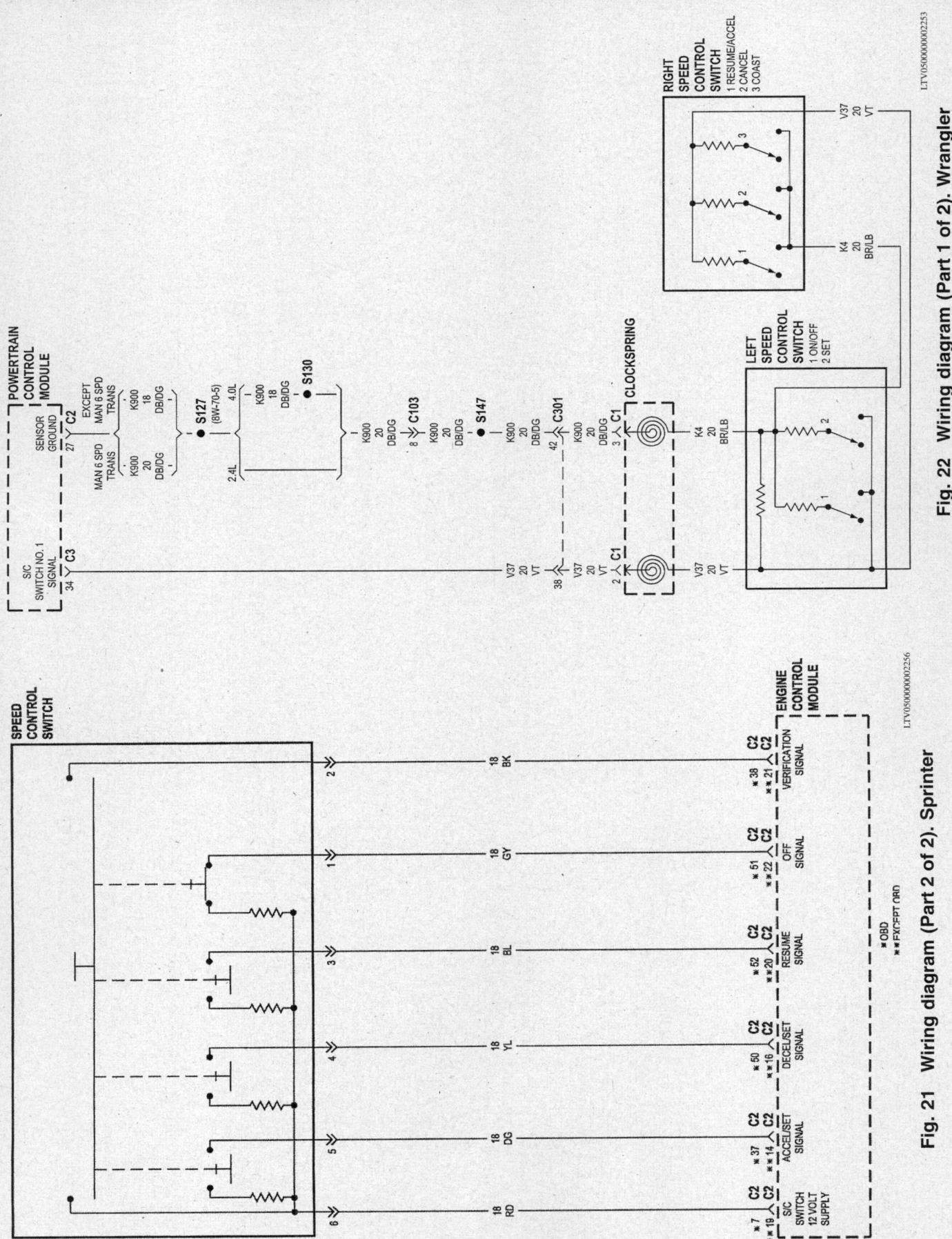

Fig. 22 Wiring diagram (Part 1 of 2). Wrangler

Fig. 21 Wiring diagram (Part 2 of 2). Sprinter

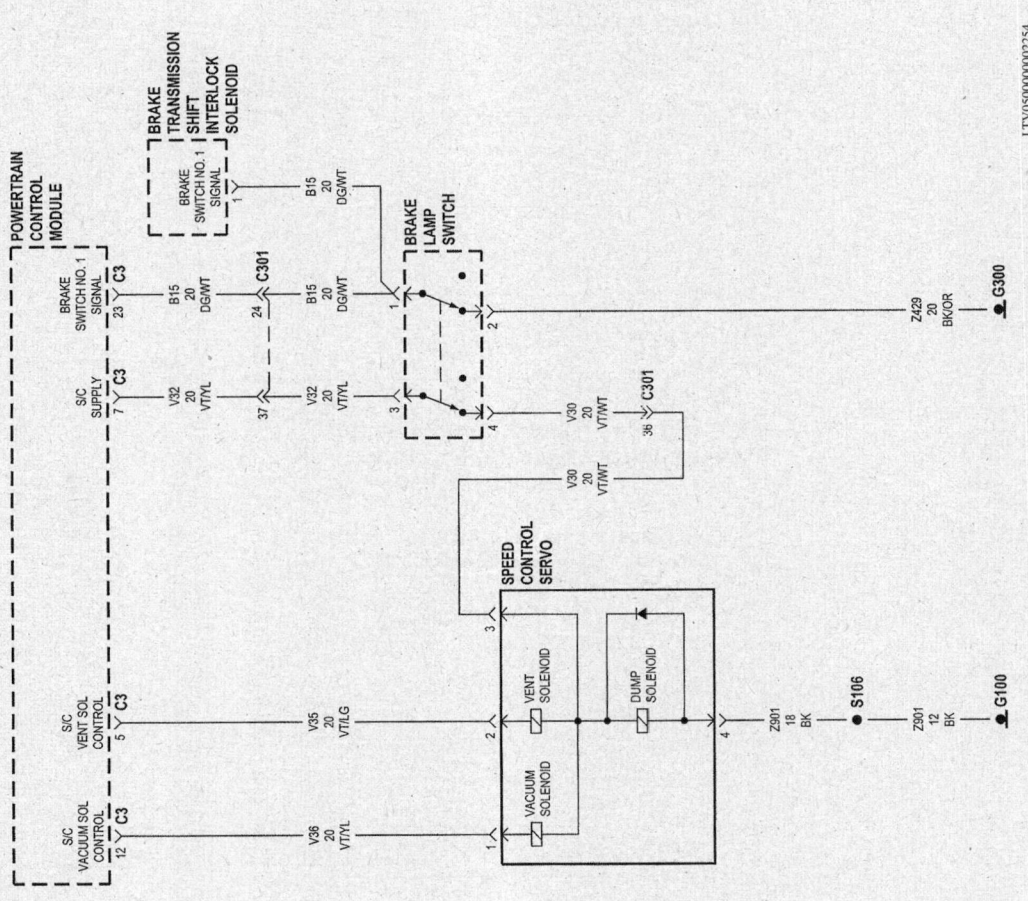

Fig. 22 Wiring diagram (Part 2 of 2). Wrangler

Condition	Resistance, Ohms
No Switches Depressed	No Continuity
On/Off Switch Depressed	0–.5
Set Switch Depressed	6583–6717
Resume/Accel Switch Depressed	15,246–15,554
Cancel Switch Depressed	899–919
Decel Switch Depressed	2910–2970

Fig. 23 Speed Control Switch Inspection. Caravan, Town & Country & Voyager

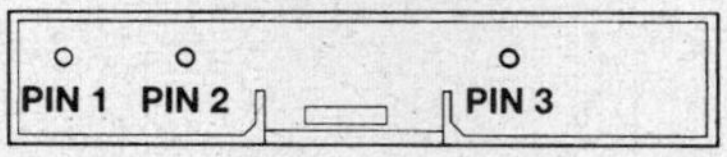

REAR VIEW OF SWITCH

PIN 1 PIN 2   PIN 3

SWITCH POSITION	RESISTANCE BETWEEN PINS 2 AND 3	RESISTANCE BETWEEN PINS 1 AND 2
NO SWITCHES DEPRESSED	OPEN CIRCUIT	806 ohms +/- 8 ohms
ON	909 ohms +/- 9 ohms	
RESUME/ACCEL	15,400 ohms +/- 154 ohms	
SET/COAST	6650 ohms +/- 66 ohms	

CR1109600495000X

Fig. 24 Speed control switch inspection. Dakota, Durango, Full Size Pickup & Van

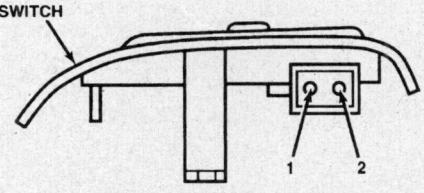

SWITCH

SWITCH POSITION	RESISTANCE BETWEEN PINS 1 AND 2
ON	909 ohms +/- 9 ohms
SET	6650 ohms +/- 66 ohms
RESUME/ACCEL	15.4000 ohms +/- 1540 ohms
CANCEL	0 ohms (CLOSED CIRCUIT)
COAST	2940 ohms +/- 29 ohms

CR1109600498000X

Fig. 25 Speed control switch inspection. Grand Cherokee & Wrangler

WIPER SYSTEMS

TABLE OF CONTENTS

	Page No.		Page No.
DAIMLERCHRYSLER	3-1	**JEEP**	3-25

DaimlerChrysler

NOTE: On Air Bag Equipped Models, Refer To "Air Bag System Precautions" Located In The Front Of This Manual For System Disarming & Arming Procedures.

NOTE: Refer To "Computer Relearn Procedures" Located In The Front Of This Manual When Battery Power To The Computer Has Been Interrupted.

NOTE: "Electrical Symbol & Wire Color Code Identification" Located In The Front Of This Manual May Be Used As An Aid When Using Wiring Circuits Found In This Section.

INDEX

	Page No.		Page No.		Page No.
Component Diagnosis &		**Precautions**	3-1	Connector Pin Identification	3-1
Testing	3-2	Air Bag Systems	3-1	Diagnostic Tests	3-1
Front Wiper Motor	3-2	Battery Ground Cable	3-1	Diagnostic Trouble Code	
Front Wiper/Washer Switch	3-2	**System Diagnosis & Testing**	3-1	Interpretation	3-1
Liftgate Wiper Switch	3-2	Accessing Diagnostic Trouble		Wiring Diagrams	3-1
Washer System	3-2	Codes	3-1		
Description	3-1	Clearing Diagnostic Trouble			
		Codes	3-1		

PRECAUTIONS

Air Bag Systems

Refer to "Air Bag System Precautions" in the front of this manual for system disarming and arming procedures.

Battery Ground Cable

Prior to service, disconnect battery ground cable and isolate as required.

DESCRIPTION

An electrically operated intermittent wiper and washer system is standard equipment. The wiper and washer system includes: Check valve, Totally Integrated Power Module (TIPM), Instrument cluster, Multi-function switch, Washer fluid level switch, Washer nozzle, Washer plumbing, Washer pump/motor, Washer reservoir, Wiper arm and blade and Wiper module.

SYSTEM DIAGNOSIS & TESTING

Accessing Diagnostic Trouble Codes

Connect a suitably programmed scan tool to Data Link Connector (DLC) and follow scan tool manufacturer's instructions.

Diagnostic Trouble Code Interpretation

Refer to **Fig. 1** for diagnostic trouble code interpretation.

Connector Pin Identification

Refer to **Figs. 2 through 17** for connector pin identification.

Wiring Diagrams

Refer to **Figs. 18 through 27** for wiring diagrams.

Diagnostic Tests

Refer to **Figs. 28 through 32** for diagnostic test procedures.

Clearing Diagnostic Trouble Codes

Connect a suitably programmed scan tool to Data Link Connector (DLC) and follow scan tool manufacturer's instructions.

Code	Interpretation
B210D	Battery Voltage Low (RSM)
B210E	Battery Voltage High (RSM)
B2211	Rain Sensor Module Initialization Performance
B221D	(RSM) Rain Sensor Module Internal
B2301	Wiper Mode Switch Input Circuit Low (SCM)
B2302	Wiper Mode Switch Input Circuit High (SCM)
B2304	Wiper Park Switch Input Circuit Low
B2305	Wiper Park Switch Input Circuit High
B230A	Rear Wiper Switch Input Circuit Low (SCM)
B230B	Rear Wiper Switch Input Circuit High (SCM)
B2313	Wiper On/Off Control Circuit Low
B2314	Wiper On/Off Control Circuit High
B2315	Wiper On/Off Control Circuit Open
B2317	Wiper Hi/Low Control Circuit Low
B2318	Wiper Hi/Low Control Circuit High
B2319	Wiper Hi/Low Control Circuit Open
B231F	Front/Rear Washer Motor Control Circuit Low
B2320	Front/Rear Washer Motor Control Circuit High
B2328	Washer Fluid Level Sensor Input Circuit High
B2329	Rain Sensor Optical Path 1 Performance
B232A	Rain Sensor Optical Path 2 Performance
B232B	Rain Sensor Optical Path 3 Performance
B232C	Rain Sensor Optical Path 4 Performance
B232D	Washer Switch Stuck
B232E	Rear Washer Switch Stuck
B232F	Mist Switch Stuck
U0141	Lost Communication With Front Control Module
U0155	Lost Communication With Cluster/CCN
U0212	Lost Communication With SCCM-CAN-B

Fig. 1   Diagnostic trouble code interpretation

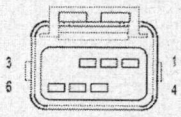

FRONT WIPER MOTOR

CAV	CIRCUIT	FUNCTION
1	V6 18DB	FUSED IGNITION SWITCH OUTPUT (RUN-ACC)
2	V5 18DG	FRONT WIPER PARK SWITCH SENSE
3	-	
4	Z1 18BK	GROUND
5	V45 18VT	FRONT WIPER LOW SPEED
6	V48 18RD/GY	FRONT WIPER HIGH SPEED

LTV0500000002270

Fig. 4   Connector pin identification (Front wiper motor). 2002–04 Dakota & 2002–03 Durango

COMPONENT DIAGNOSIS & TESTING

Front Wiper Motor

Refer to **Fig. 33** for front wiper motor tests.

Front Wiper/Washer Switch

Refer to **Fig. 34** for front wiper/washer switch continuity test.

Liftgate Wiper Switch

1. Remove switch from instrument panel leaving connected, then turn ignition switch to On.

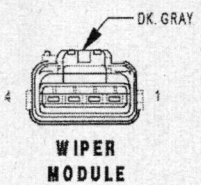

WIPER MODULE

CAV	CIRCUIT	FUNCTION
1	W3 14BR/WT	FRONT WIPER HIGH/LOW RELAY LOW SPEED OUTPUT
2	W7 20BR/GY	FRONT WIPER PARK SWITCH SENSE
3	W4 14BR/OR	FRONT WIPER HIGH/LOW RELAY HIGH SPEED OUTPUT
4	Z103 14BK/WT	GROUND

LTV0500000002257

Fig. 2   Connector pin identification (Wiper module). Caravan, Town & Country & Voyager

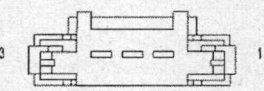

REAR WIPER MOTOR

CAV	CIRCUIT	FUNCTION
1	W13 18BR/LG	REAR WIPER MOTOR CONTROL
2	F302 18GY/PK	FUSED ACCESSORY RELAY OUTPUT
3	Z213 18BK/LG	GROUND

LTV0500000002258

Fig. 3   Connector pin identification (Rear wiper motor). Caravan, Town & Country & Voyager

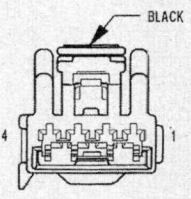

SWITCH-MULTIFUNCTION

CAV	CIRCUIT	FUNCTION
1	G194 20LB/RD	HIGH BEAM/FRONT WASHER SWITCH MUX
2	G902 20VT/OR	SWITCH MUX RETURN
3	L12 20WT/OR	TURN SIGNAL INPUT MUX
4	W52 20BR/YL	FRONT WIPER SWITCH MUX

LTV0500000002273

Fig. 5   Connector pin identification (Multi-function switch). 2005–06 Dakota & 2004–06 Durango

2. Inspect for battery voltage at pin Nos. 1 and 2 using suitable voltmeter, **Fig. 35.** If satisfactory, go to step 4. If not satisfactory go to step 3.
3. Inspect wiper fuse in fuse block and 40 amp cartridge fuse in PDC. If fuses are satisfactory, inspect wiring circuit.
4. Inspect pin 5 with switch in On position, there should be battery voltage and no voltage in Off position. If not satisfactory, Replace switch.

Washer System

Refer to **Fig. 36** for washer system tests.

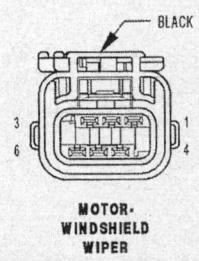

MOTOR-
WINDSHIELD
WIPER

CAV	CIRCUIT	FUNCTION
1	-	-
2	W7 20BR/GY	FRONT WIPER PARK SWITCH SENSE
3	-	-
4	Z103 14BK/WT	GROUND
5	W3 14BR/WT	FRONT WIPER HIGH/LOW RELAY LOW SPEED OUTPUT
6	W4 14BR/OR	FRONT WIPER HIGH/LOW RELAY HIGH SPEED OUTPUT

LTV0500000002274

Fig. 6   Connector pin identification (Wiper motor). 2005–06 Dakota & 2004–06 Durango

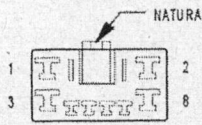

INTERMITTENT
WIPE MODULE
(BASE/MIDLINE)

CAV	CIRCUIT	FUNCTION
1	V6 18DB	FUSED IGNITION SWITCH OUTPUT (RUN-ACC)
2	V7 18DG/WT	WIPER SWITCH MODE SENSE
3	V5 18DG	WIPER PARK SWITCH SENSE
4	Z2 18BK/DG	GROUND
5	-	-
6	V9 18WT/BR	WIPER SWITCH MODE SIGNAL
7	V10 18BR	WASHER SWITCH SENSE
8	-	-

LTV0500000002285

Fig. 8   Connector pin identification (Intermittent wiper module). Full Size Van

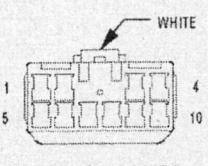

WIPER/WASHER
SWITCH

CAV	CIRCUIT	FUNCTION
1	G902 20VT/OR	MULTI-FUNCTION SWITCH MUX RETURN
2	-	-
3	W33 22BR/DG	FRONT WASHER SIGNAL
4	-	-
5	W26 20BR/DB	REAR WIPER SWITCH MUX
6	W27 22DB/BR	REAR WIPER SWITCH DELAY
7	G902 20VT/OR	MULTI-FUNCTION SWITCH MUX RETURN
8	W52 22BR/YL	FRONT WIPER SWITCH MUX
9	W35 22BR/LG	FRONT WIPER HIGH/LOW SWITCH SENSE
10	-	-

LTV0500000002304

Fig. 10   Connector pin identification (Wiper switch). Pacifica

MOTOR-
WINDSHIELD WIPER

CAV	CIRCUIT	FUNCTION
A	W4 16BR/OR (EXCEPT SRT)	WIPER RELAY HIGH SPEED OUTPUT
A	W4 14 BR/OR (SRT)	WIPER RELAY HIGH SPEED OUTPUT
B	W3 16BR/WT (EXCEPT SRT)	WIPER RELAY LOW SPEED OUTPUT
B	W3 14 BR/WT (SRT)	WIPER RELAY LOW SPEED OUTPUT
C	Z103 18BK/WT	GROUND
D	W7 20BR/GY	WIPER PARK SWITCH SENSE

LTV0500000002281

Fig. 7   Connector pin identification (Wiper motor). Full Size Pickup

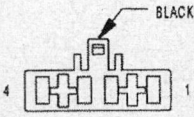

WIPER MOTOR

CAV	CIRCUIT	FUNCTION
1	V3 18BR/WT	LOW SPEED WIPER SWITCH OUTPUT
2	V6 18DB	FUSED IGNITION SWITCH OUTPUT (RUN-ACC)
3	V5 18DG	WIPER PARK SWITCH SENSE
4	V4 18RD/LB	HIGH SPEED WIPER SWITCH OUTPUT

LTV0500000002286

Fig. 9   Connector pin identification (Wiper motor). Full Size Van

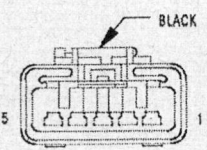

WIPER
MODULE-FRONT

CAV	CIRCUIT	FUNCTION
1	Z103 12BK/WT	GROUND
2	W7 20BR/GY	FRONT WIPER PARK SWITCH SENSE
3	-	-
4	W3 12BR/WT	FRONT WIPER HIGH/LOW RELAY LOW SPEED OUTPUT
5	W4 12BR/OR	FRONT WIPER HIGH/LOW RELAY HIGH SPEED OUTPUT

LTV0500000002305

Fig. 11   Connector pin identification (Front wiper module). Pacifica

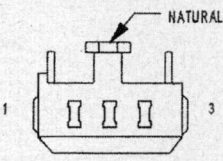

WIPER MODULE-REAR

CAV	CIRCUIT	FUNCTION
1	Z213 18BK/OR	GROUND
2	W17 20BR/LG	REAR WIPER PARK SWITCH SENSE
3	W13 18BR/WT	REAR WIPER MOTOR CONTROL

LTV0500000002306

Fig. 12   Connector pin identification (Rear wiper module). Pacifica

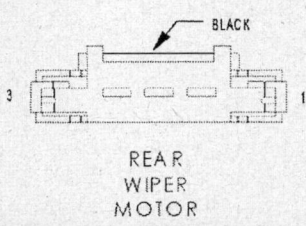

REAR WIPER MOTOR

CAV	CIRCUIT	FUNCTION
1	V13 18BR/LG	REAR WIPER MOTOR CONTROL
2	V23 18BR/PK	FUSED IGNITION SWITCH OUTPUT (RUN-ACC)
3	Z1 18BK	GROUND

LTV0500000002311

Fig. 14   Connector pin identification (Rear wiper motor). PT Cruiser

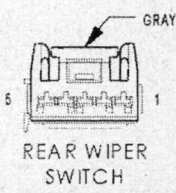

REAR WIPER SWITCH

CAV	CIRCUIT	FUNCTION
1	V20 18BK/WT	REAR WASHER MOTOR CONTROL
2	E2 20OR	PANEL LAMPS DRIVER
3	Z1 18BK	GROUND
4	V23 18BR/PK	FUSED IGNITION SWITCH OUTPUT (RUN-ACC)
5	V13 18BR/LG	REAR WIPER MOTOR CONTROL

LTV0500000002313

Fig. 16   Connector pin identification (Rear wiper switch). PT Cruiser

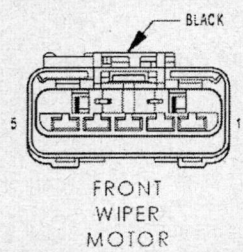

FRONT WIPER MOTOR

CAV	CIRCUIT	FUNCTION
1	Z1 16BK	GROUND
2	V5 16DG	WIPER SWITCH MODE SENSE
3	F88 16RD/WT	FUSED IGNITION SWITCH OUTPUT (RUN-ACC)
4	V3 16BR/WT	WIPER SWITCH LOW SPEED OUTPUT
5	V4 16RD/YL	WIPER SWITCH HIGH SPEED OUTPUT

LTV0500000002310

Fig. 13   Connector pin identification (Front wiper motor). PT Cruiser

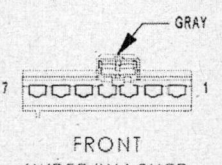

FRONT WIPER/WASHER SWITCH

CAV	CIRCUIT	FUNCTION
1	V5 16DG	WIPER SWITCH MODE SENSE
2	Z1 18BK	GROUND
3	V10 18BR	WASHER SWITCH SENSE
4	F88 16DB	FUSED IGNITION SWITCH OUTPUT (RUN-ACC)
5	V4 16RD/YL	WIPER SWITCH HIGH SPEED OUTPUT
6	V3 16BR/WT	WIPER SWITCH LOW SPEED OUTPUT
7	-	-

LTV0500000002312

Fig. 15   Connector pin identification (Front wiper/washer switch). PT Cruiser

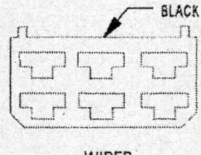

WIPER MOTOR-FRONT

CAV	CIRCUIT	FUNCTION
1	16BR	GROUND
2	16BR/BK	WIPER ON/OFF RELAY OUTPUT
3	16BK/VT	FUSED IGNITION SWITCH OUTPUT (RUN-START)
4	-	-
5	16BK	WIPER MOTOR CONTROL
6	16BK/GY/RD	WIPER SWITCH OUTPUT

LTV0500000002317

Fig. 17   Connector pin identification (Wiper motor). Sprinter

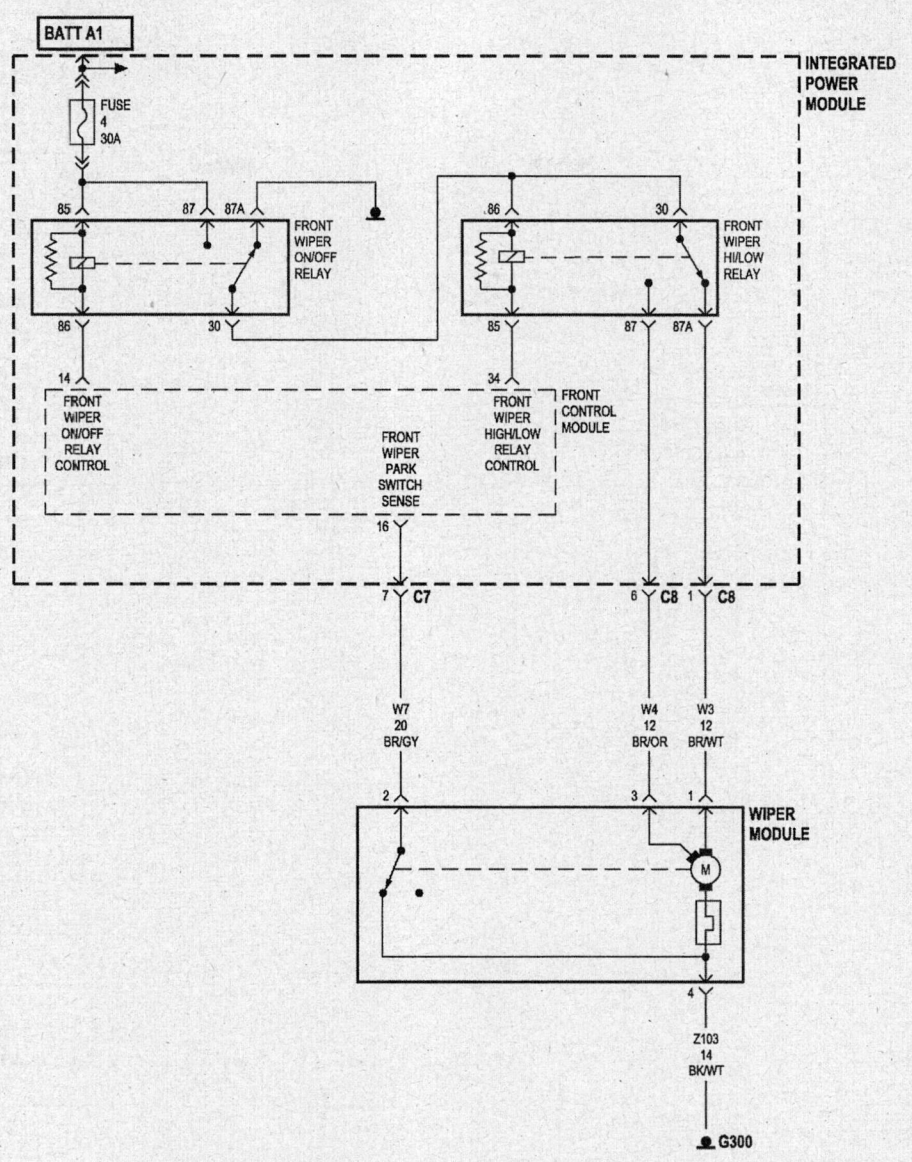

Fig. 18   Wiring diagram (Part 1 of 6). Caravan, Town & Country & Voyager

LTV0500000002259

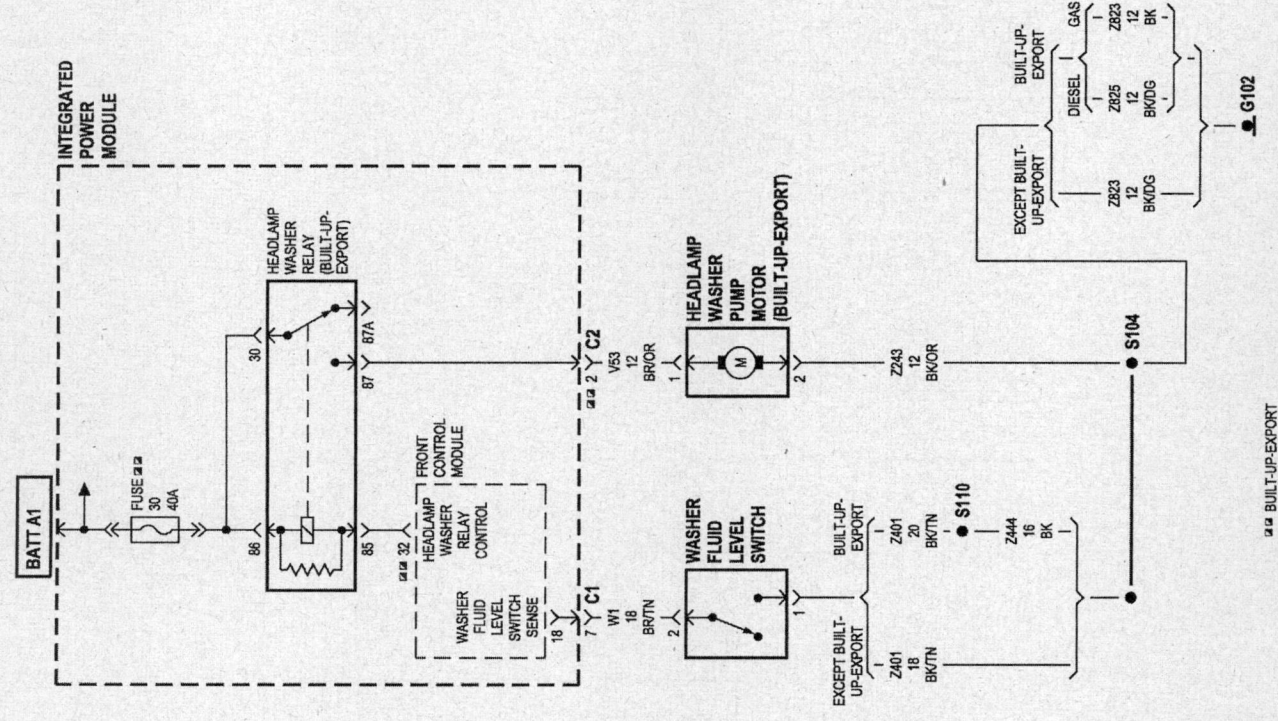

Fig. 18 Wiring diagram (Part 3 of 6). Caravan, Town & Country & Voyager

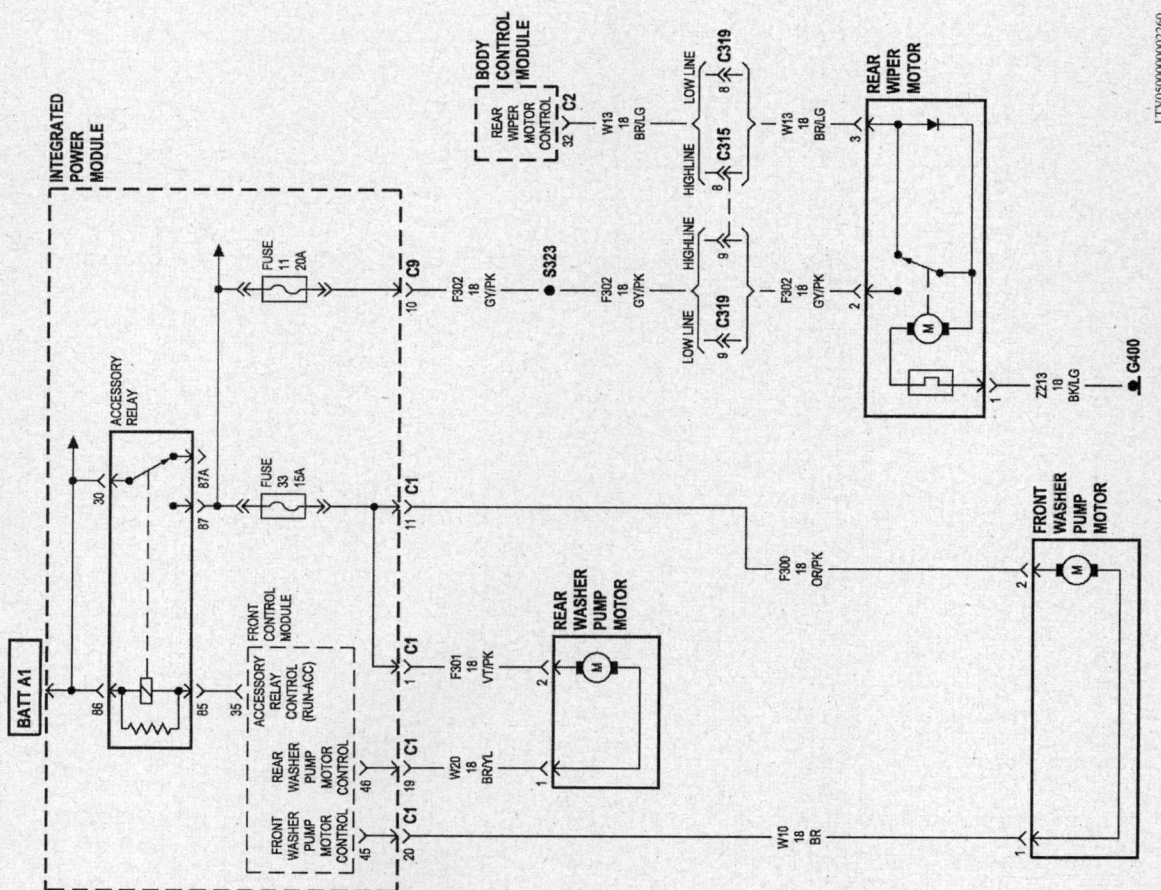

Fig. 18 Wiring diagram (Part 2 of 6). Caravan, Town & Country & Voyager

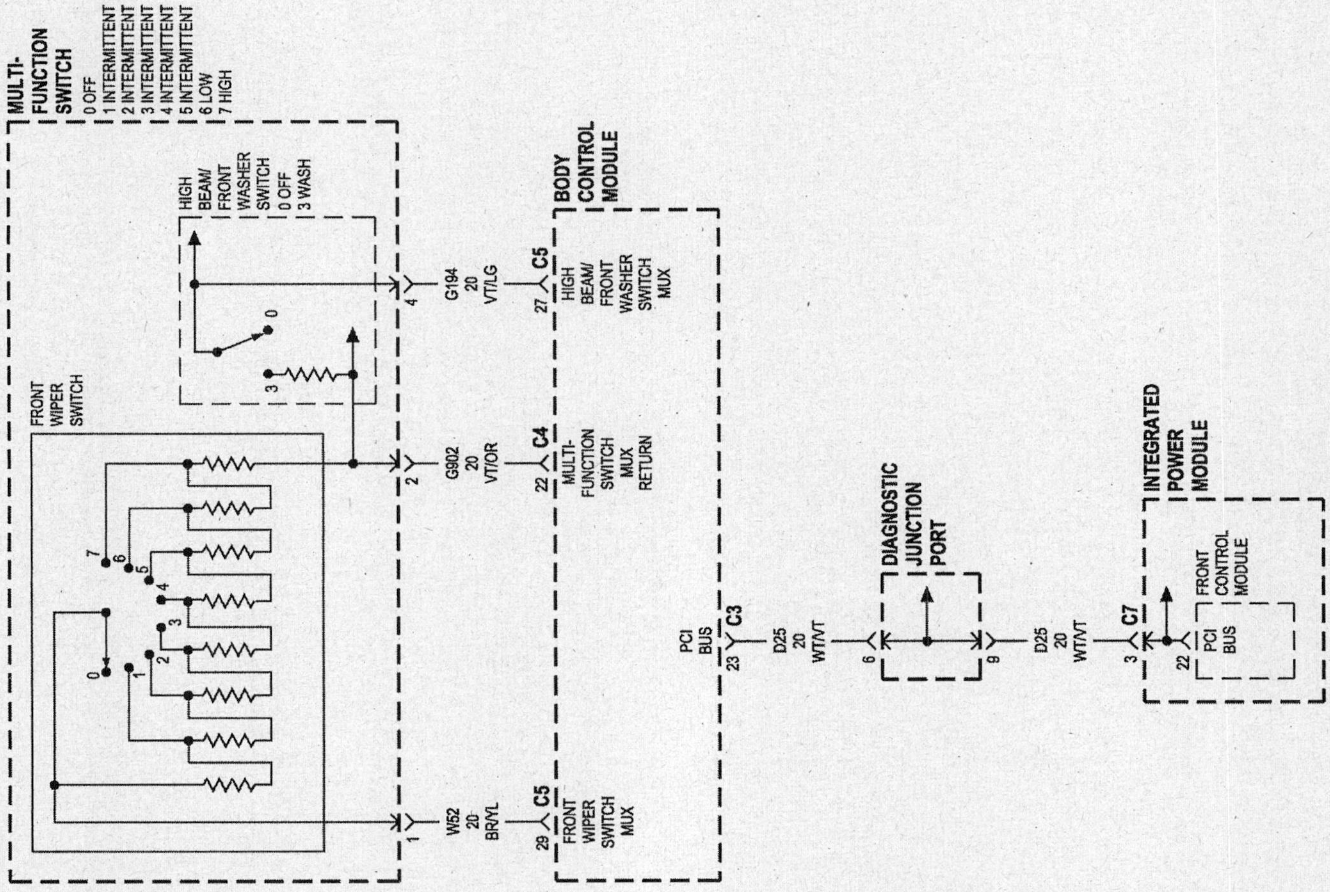

LTV0500000002262

Fig. 18 Wiring diagram (Part 4 of 6). Caravan, Town & Country & Voyager

LTV0500000002263

Fig. 18 Wiring diagram (Part 5 of 6). Caravan, Town & Country & Voyager

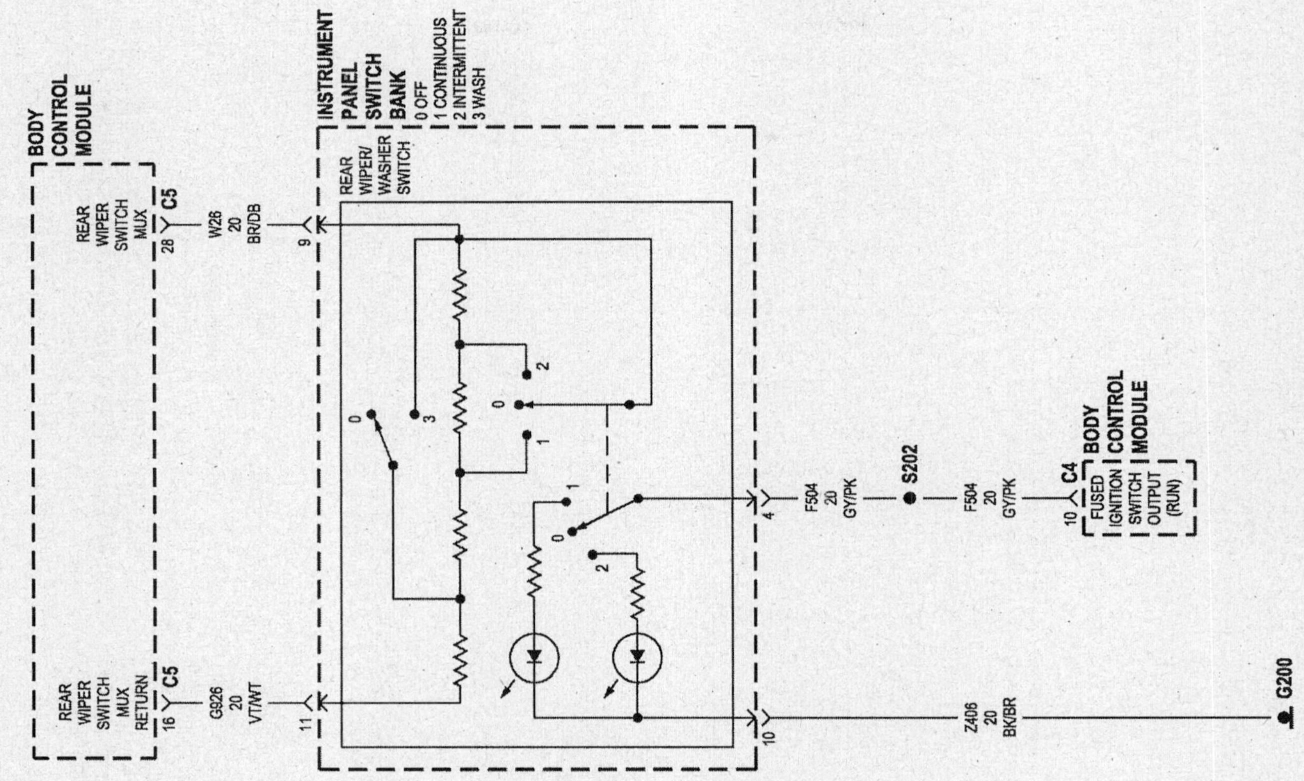

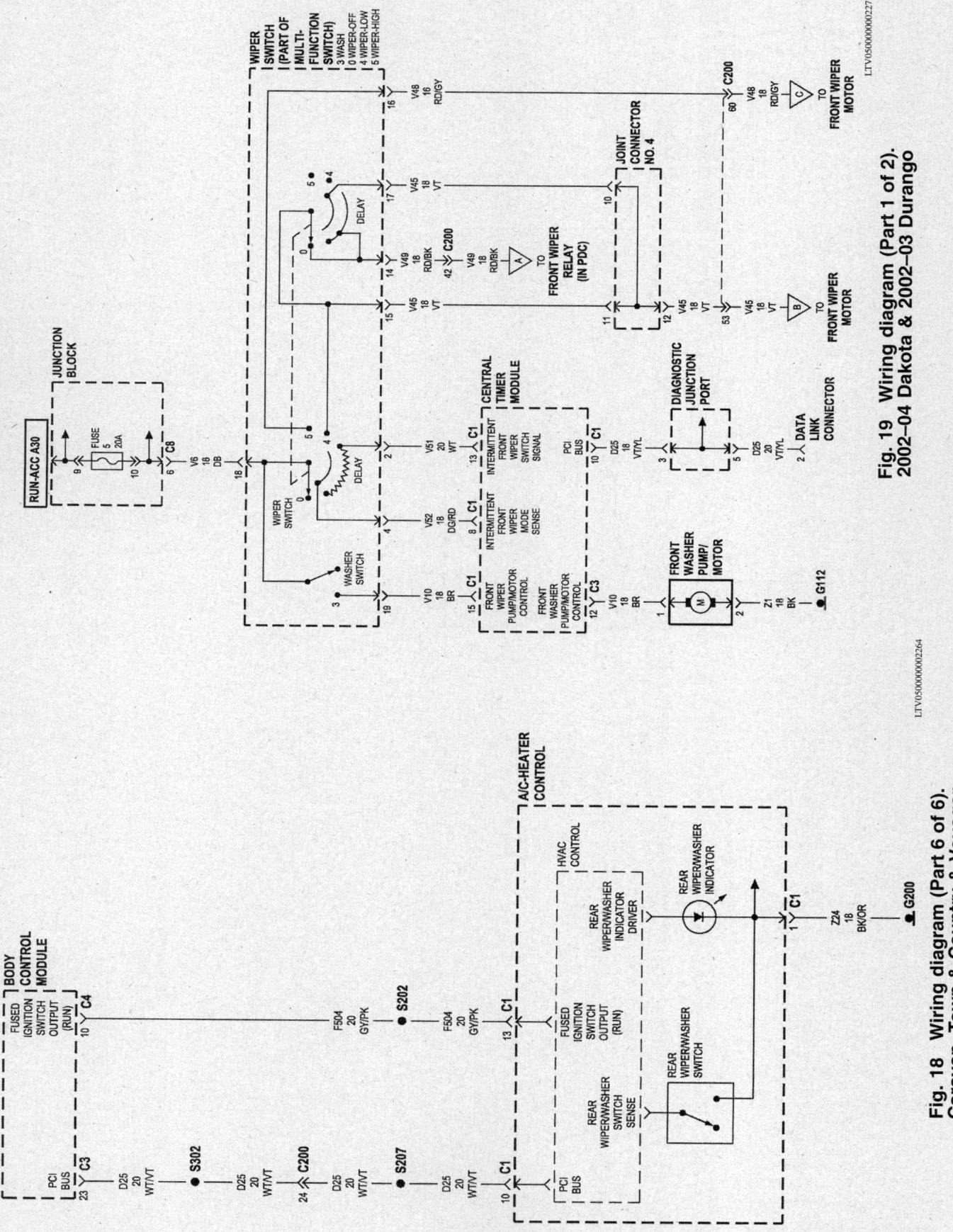

Fig. 19 Wiring diagram (Part 1 of 2). 2002–04 Dakota & 2002–03 Durango

Fig. 18 Wiring diagram (Part 6 of 6). Caravan, Town & Country & Voyager

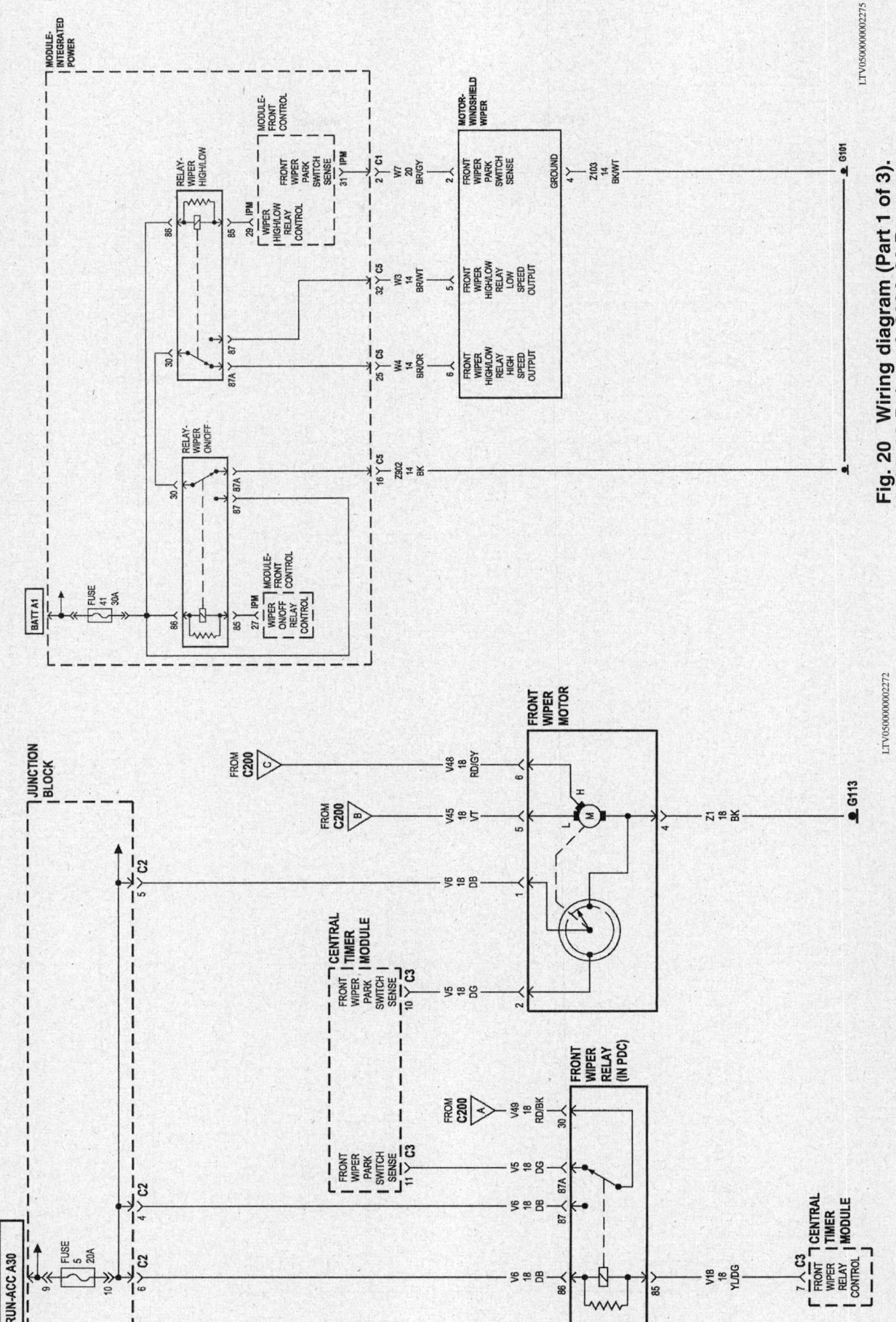

Fig. 20 Wiring diagram (Part 1 of 3).
2005–06 Dakota & 2004–06 Durango

Fig. 19 Wiring diagram (Part 2 of 2).
2002–04 Dakota & 2002–03 Durango

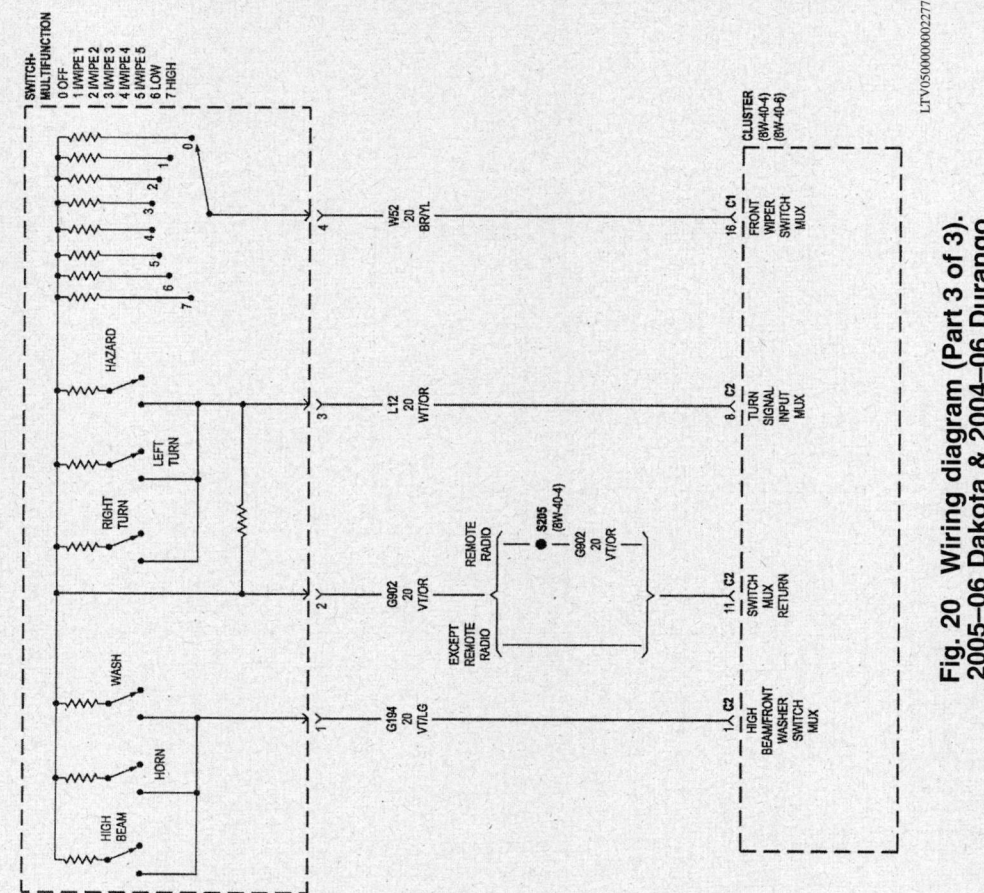

Fig. 20 Wiring diagram (Part 3 of 3). 2005–06 Dakota & 2004–06 Durango

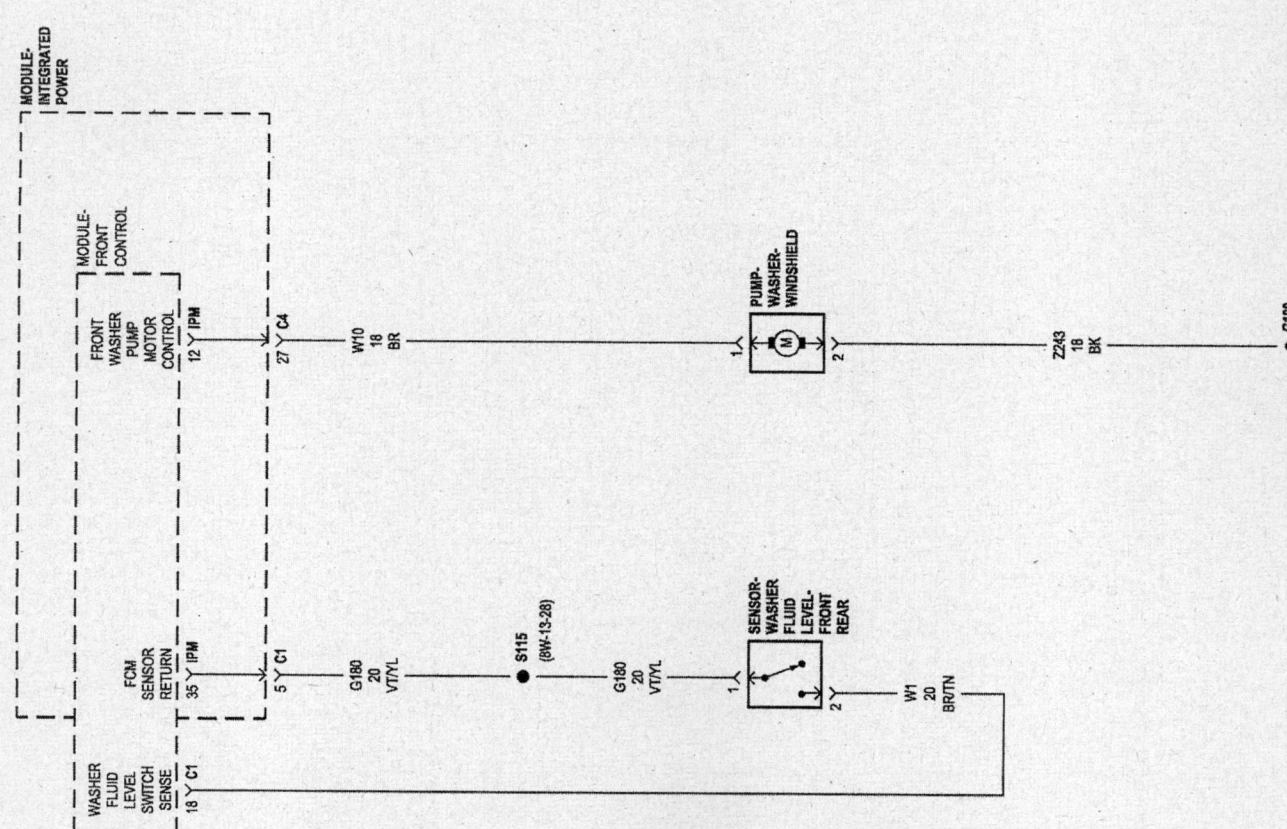

Fig. 20 Wiring diagram (Part 2 of 3). 2005–06 Dakota & 2004–06 Durango

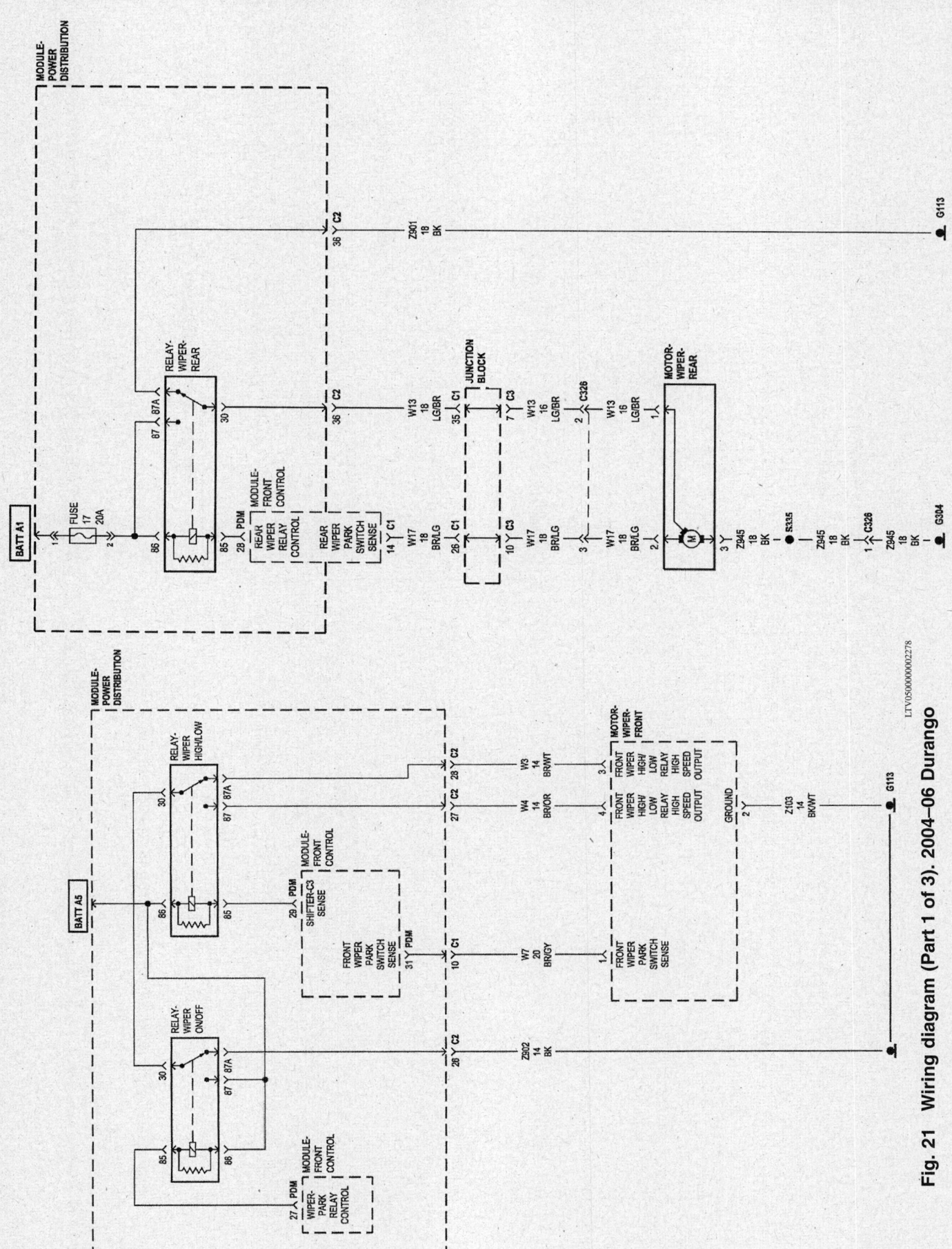

Fig. 21 Wiring diagram (Part 2 of 3). 2004–06 Durango

Fig. 21 Wiring diagram (Part 1 of 3). 2004–06 Durango

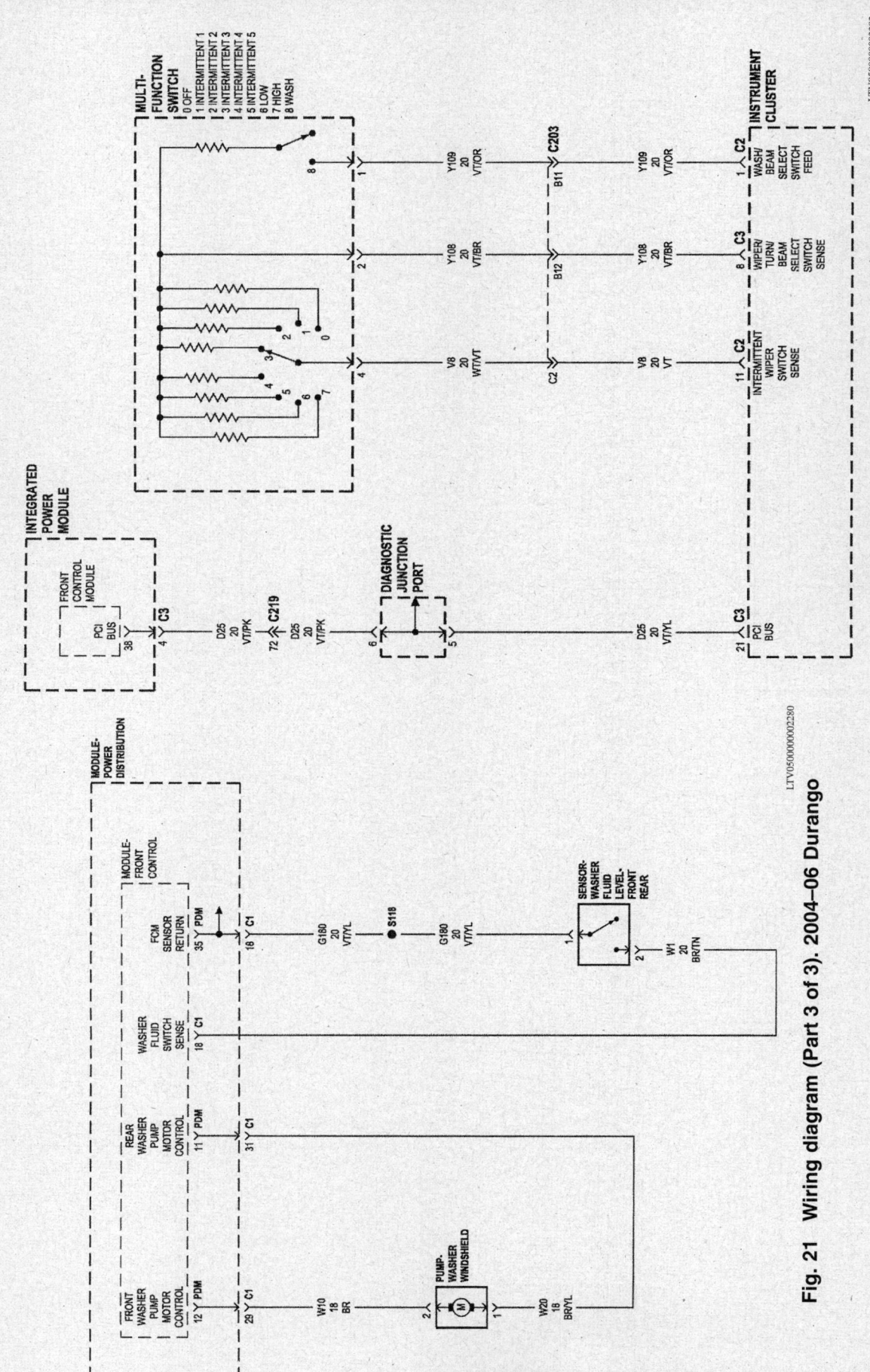

Fig. 22 Wiring diagram (Part 1 of 3). Full Size Pickup

Fig. 21 Wiring diagram (Part 3 of 3). 2004–06 Durango

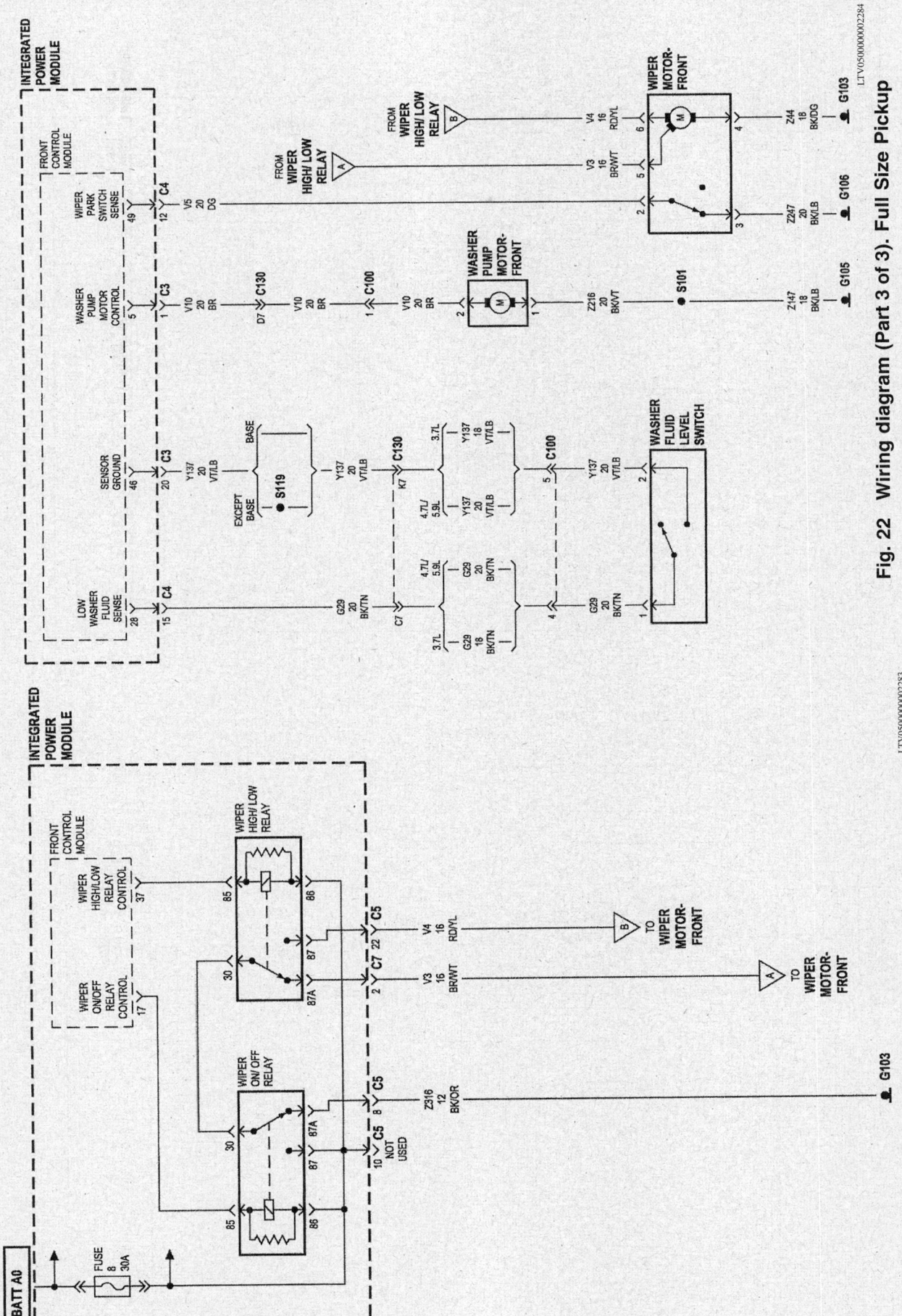

Fig. 22 Wiring diagram (Part 3 of 3). Full Size Pickup

Fig. 22 Wiring diagram (Part 2 of 3). Full Size Pickup

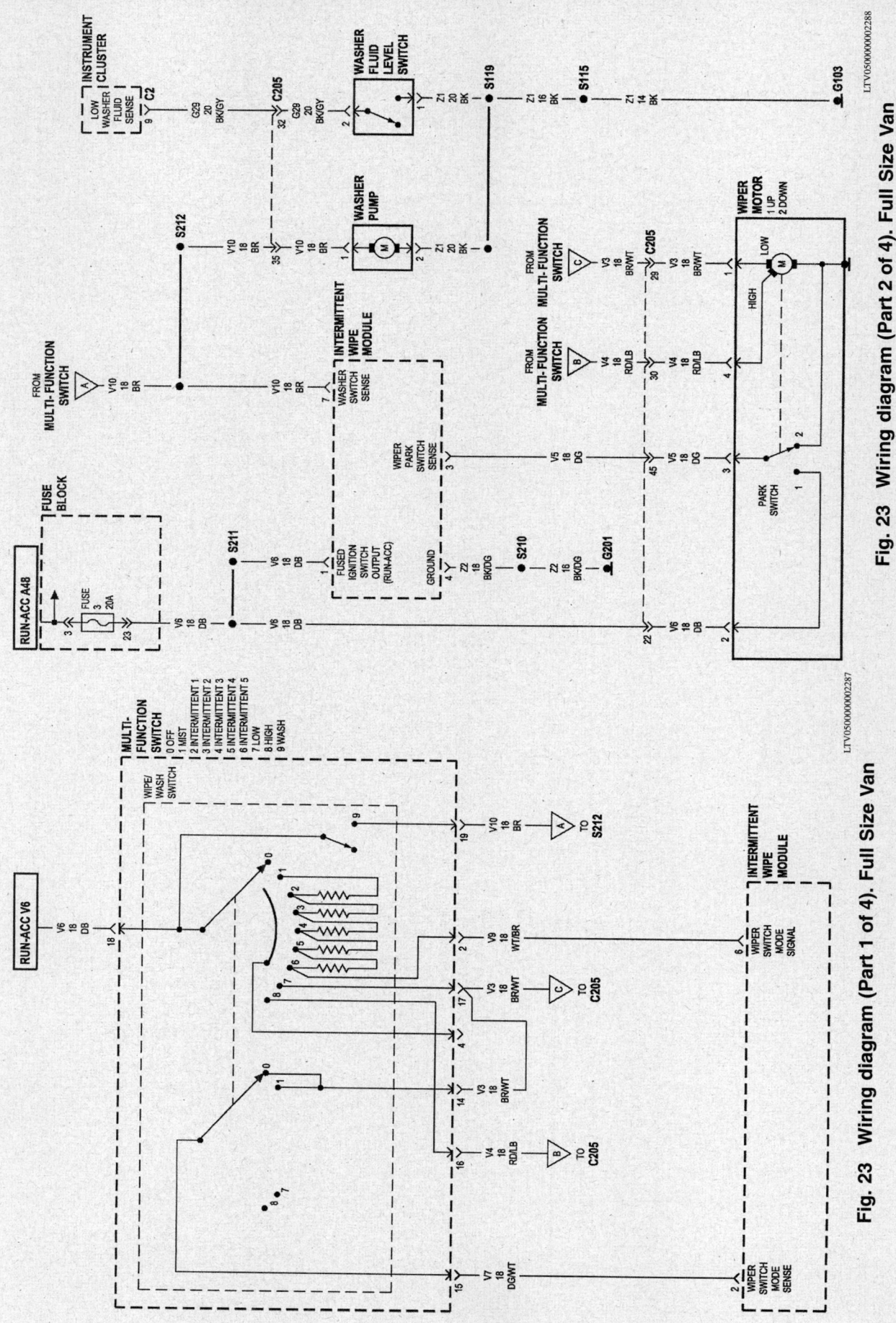

Fig. 23 Wiring diagram (Part 2 of 4). Full Size Van

Fig. 23 Wiring diagram (Part 1 of 4). Full Size Van

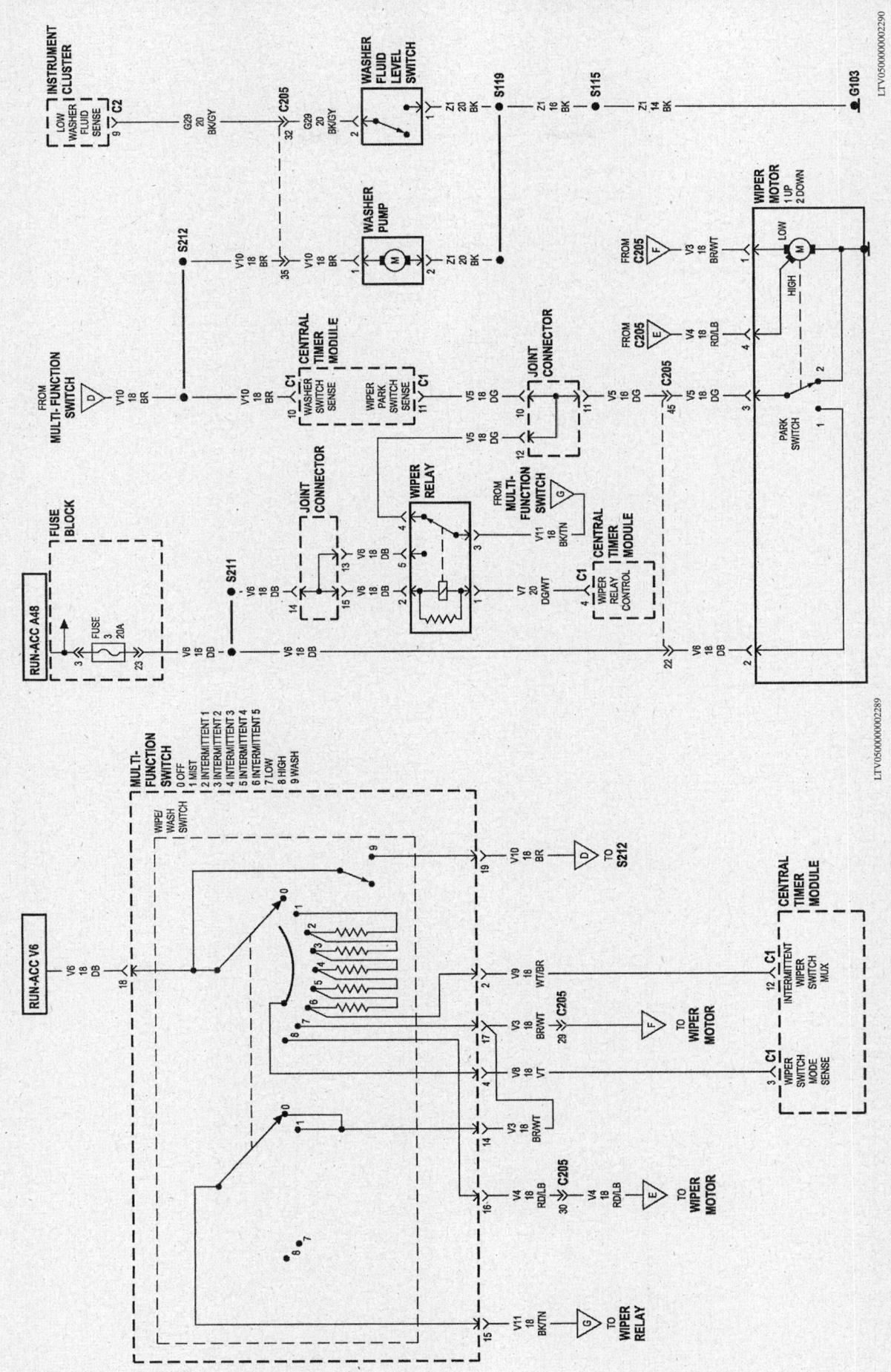

Fig. 23   Wiring diagram (Part 4 of 4). Full Size Van

Fig. 23   Wiring diagram (Part 3 of 4). Full Size Van

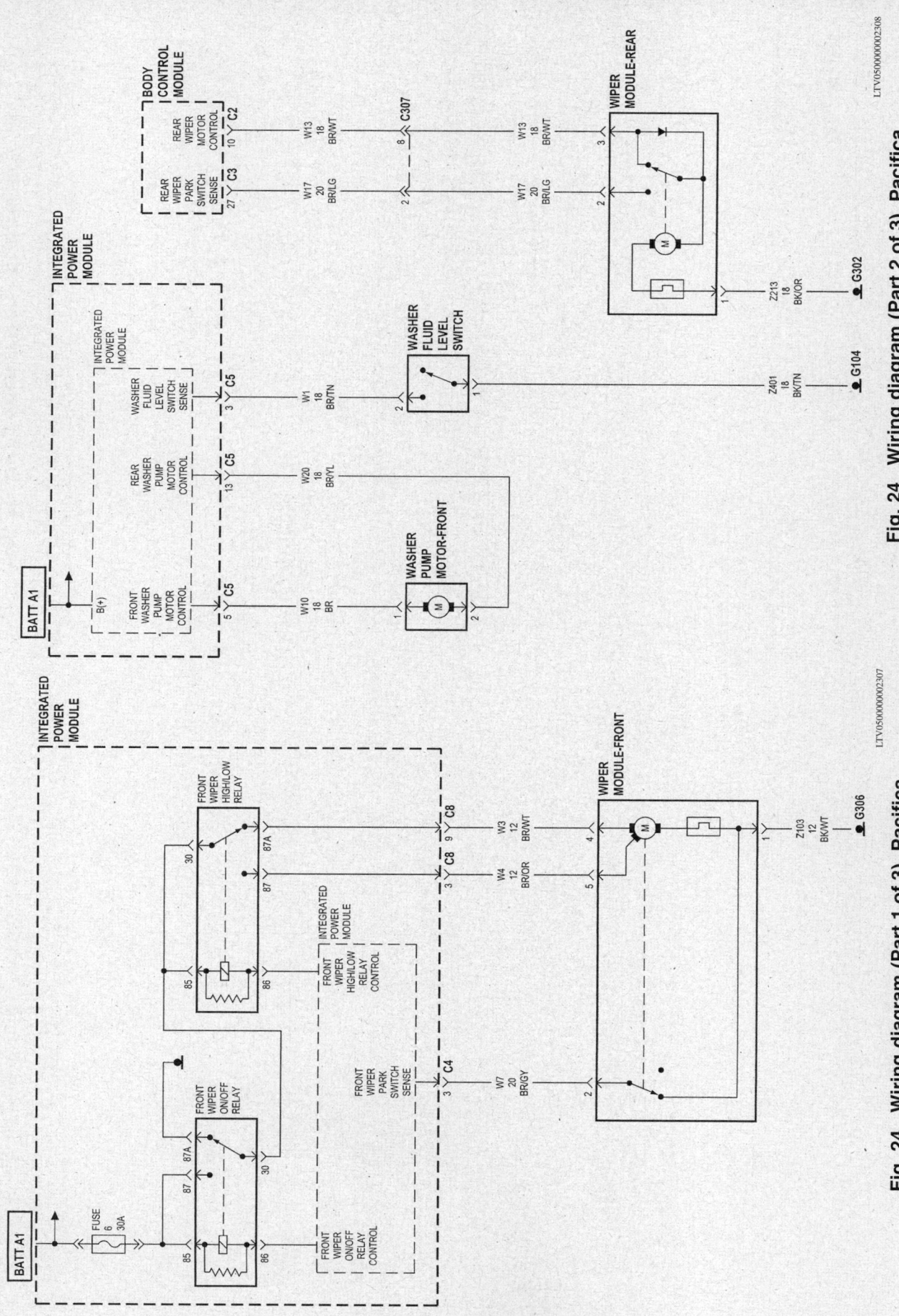

Fig. 24 Wiring diagram (Part 2 of 3). Pacifica

Fig. 24 Wiring diagram (Part 1 of 3). Pacifica

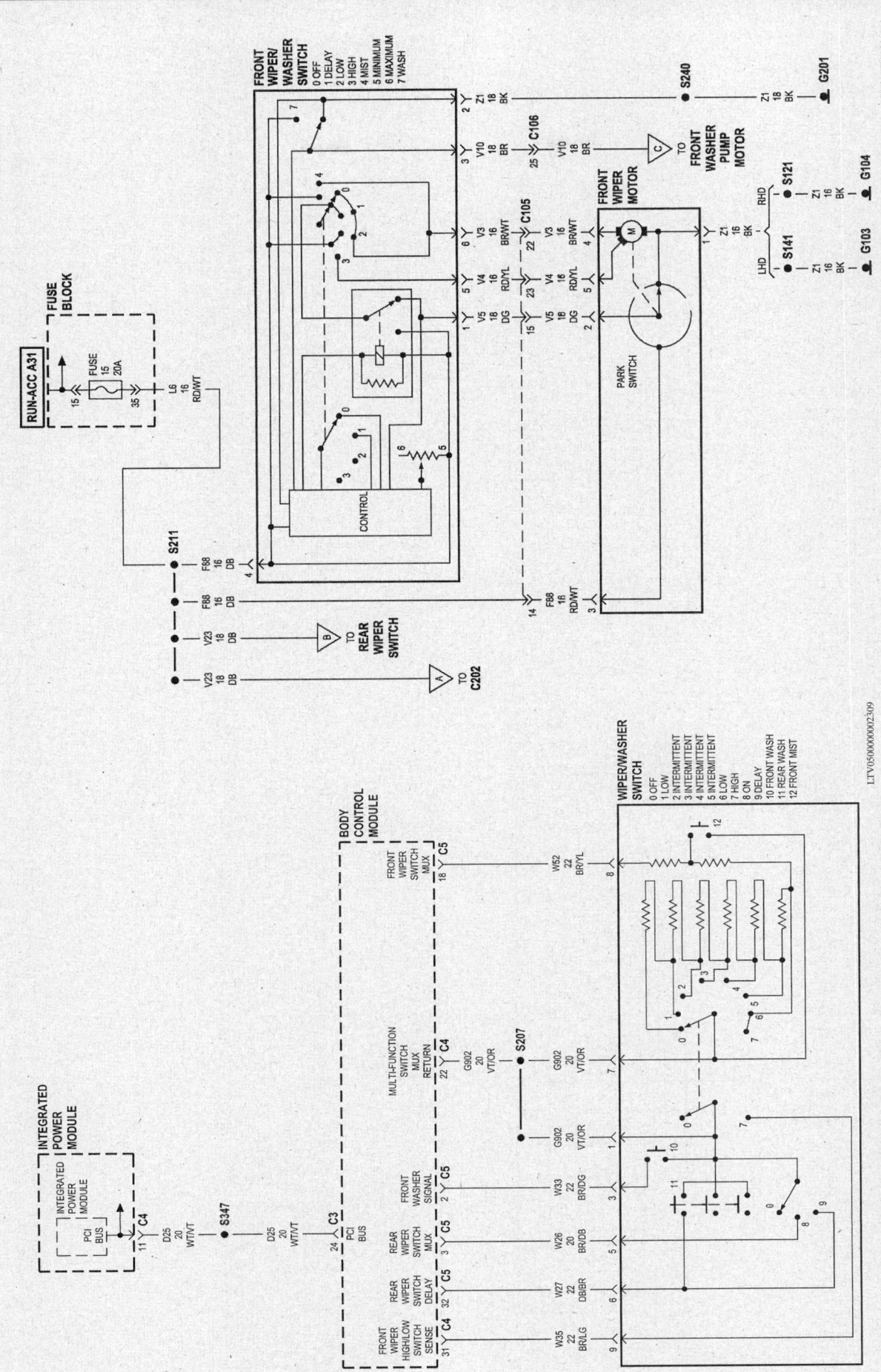

Fig. 25 Wiring diagram (Part 1 of 2). 2002–04 PT Cruiser

Fig. 24 Wiring diagram (Part 3 of 3). Pacifica

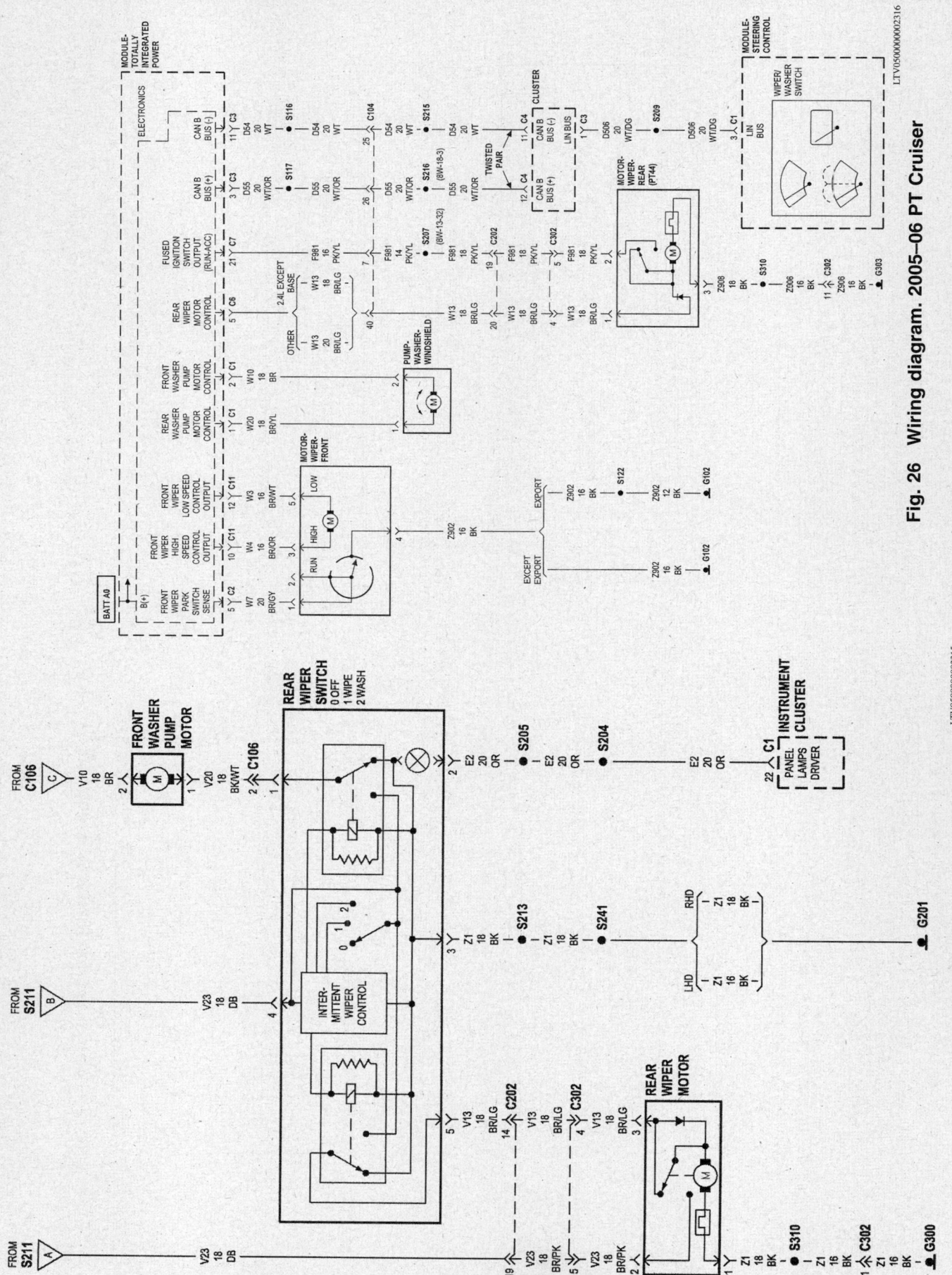

Fig. 26 Wiring diagram. 2005–06 PT Cruiser

Fig. 25 Wiring diagram (Part 2 of 2). 2002–04 PT Cruiser

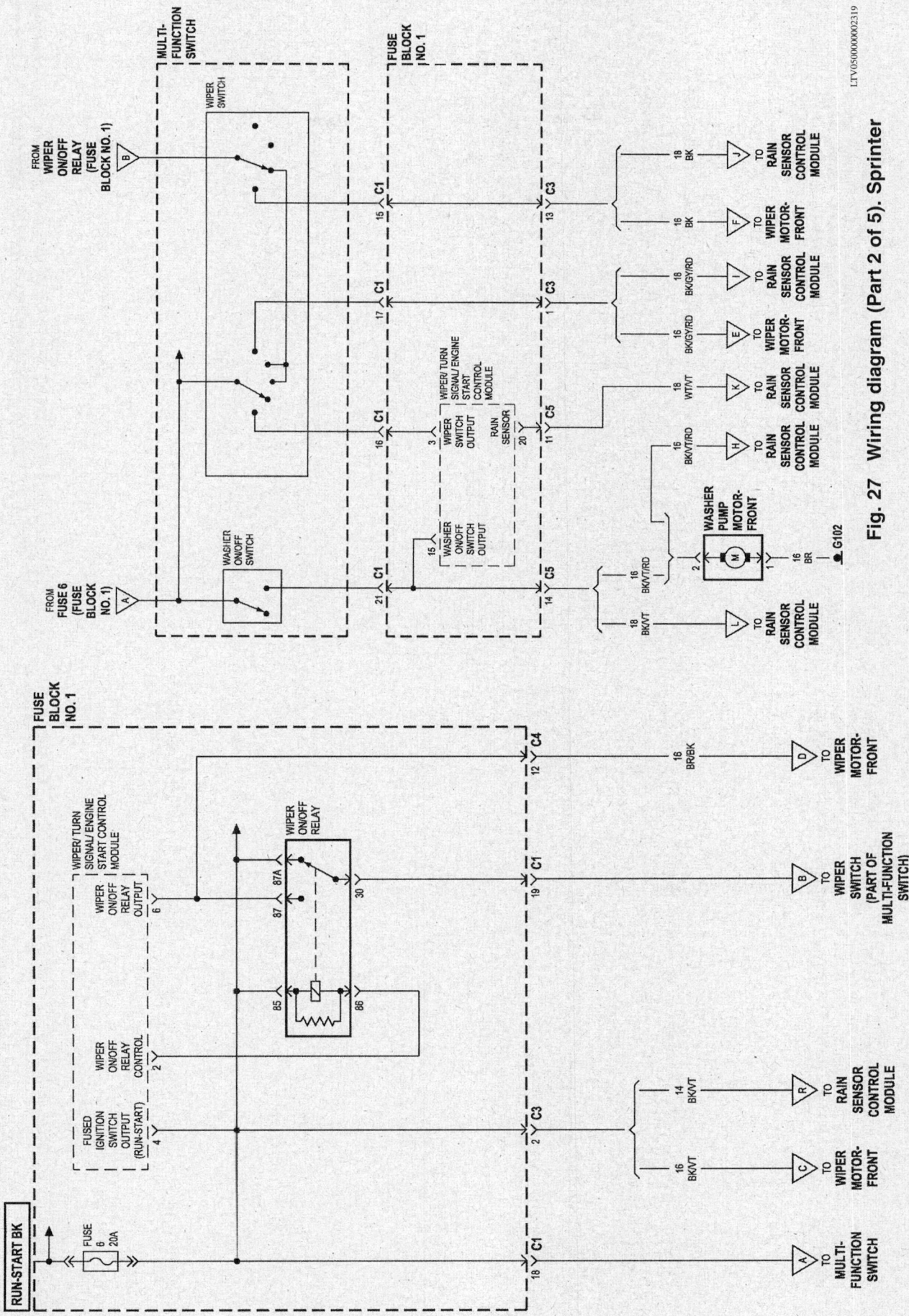

Fig. 27 Wiring diagram (Part 2 of 5). Sprinter

Fig. 27 Wiring diagram (Part 1 of 5). Sprinter

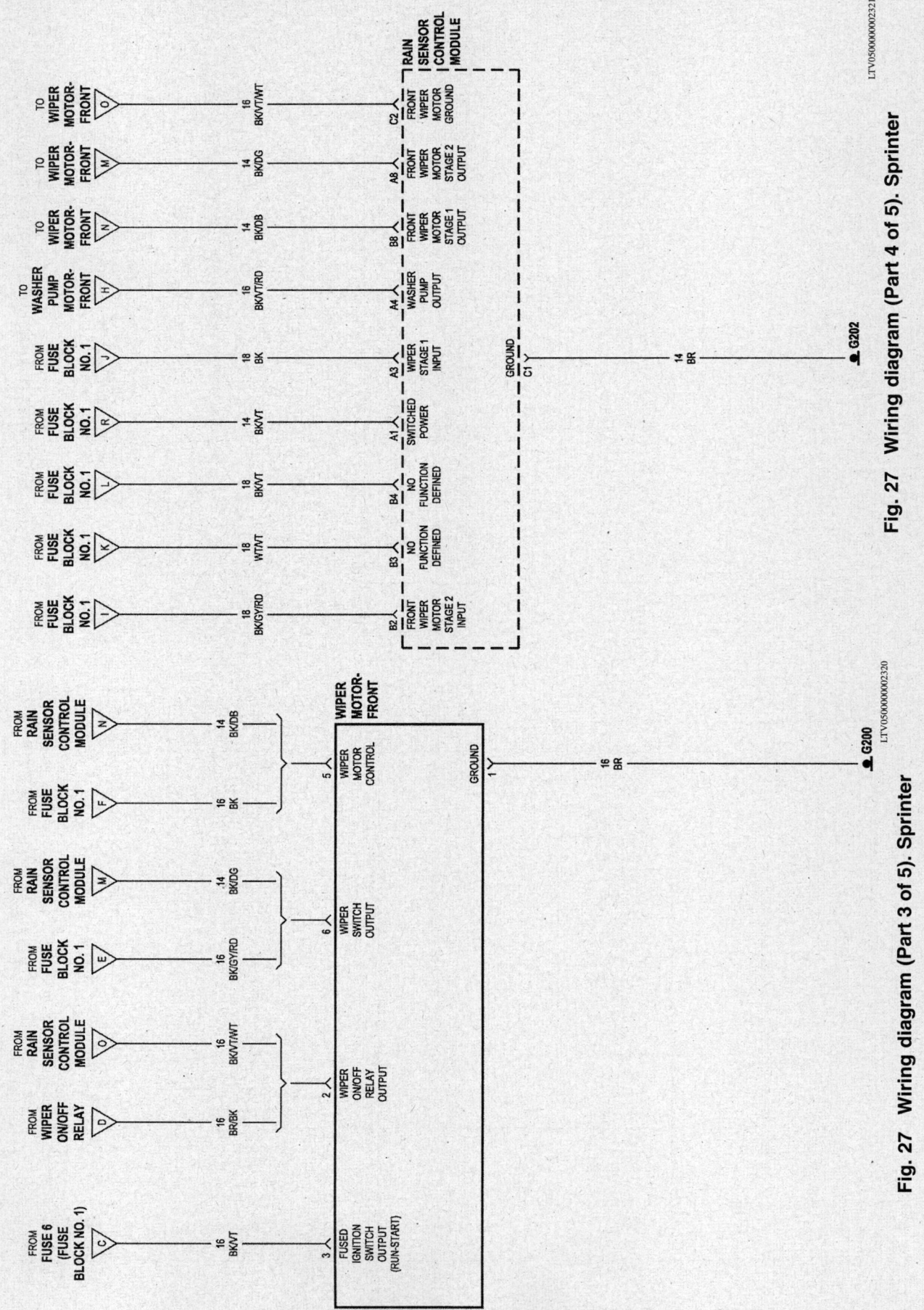

Fig. 27 Wiring diagram (Part 4 of 5). Sprinter

Fig. 27 Wiring diagram (Part 3 of 5). Sprinter

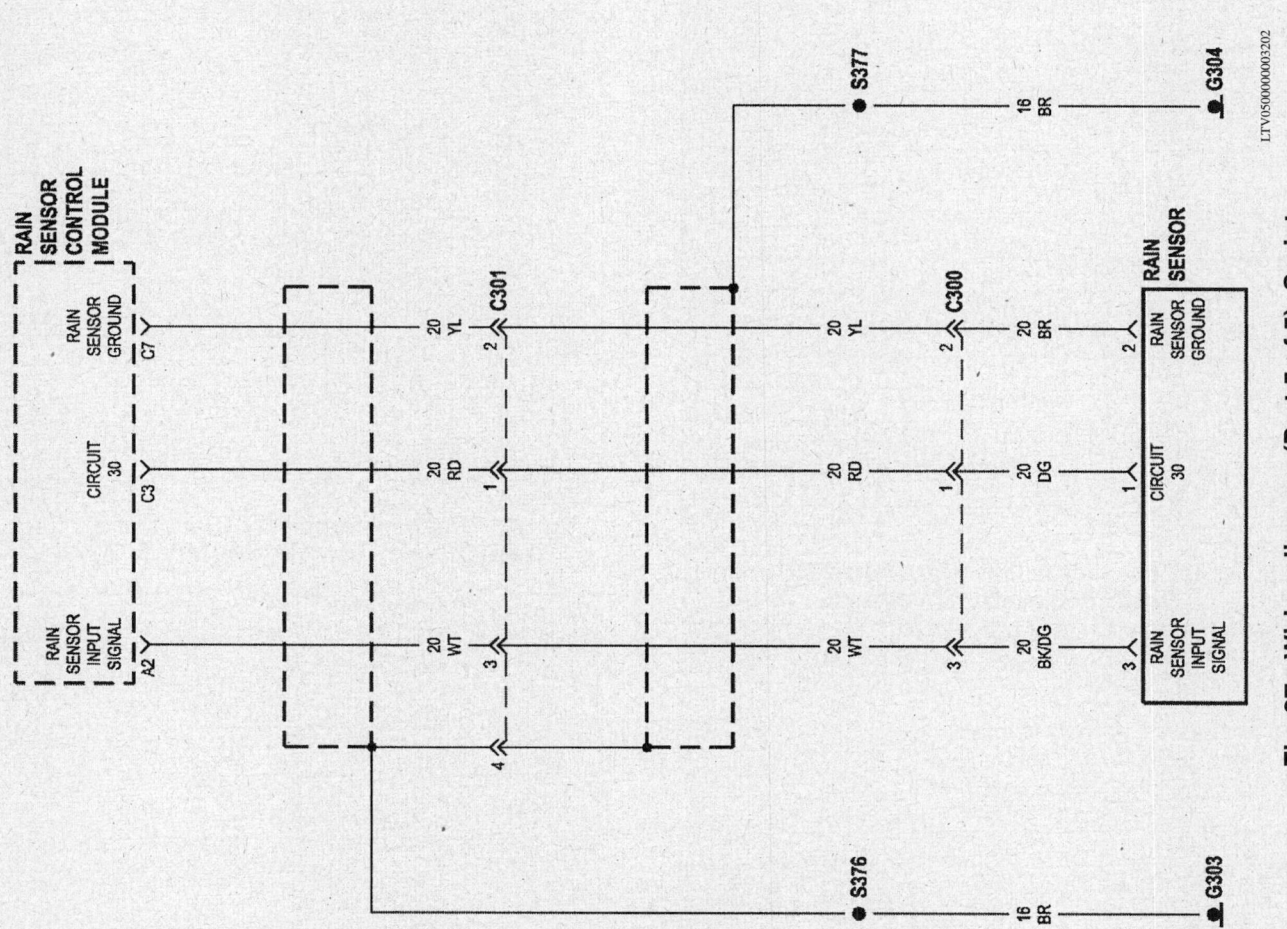

Fig. 27 Wiring diagram (Part 5 of 5). Sprinter

LTVU50000003202

CONDITION	POSSIBLE CAUSES	CORRECTION
WIPER BLADES DO NOT PARK PROPERLY	1. WIPER ARMS IMPROPERLY PARKED.	1. REMOVE WIPER ARMS AND REPARK.
	2. WIPER ARMS ARE LOOSE ON PIVOT SHAFT.	2. REMOVE WIPER ARM AND REPARK.
	3. MOTOR CRANK LOOSE AT OUTPUT SHAFT.	3. REMOVE WIPER ARM, RUN WIPER MOTOR TO PARK POSITION AND REMOVE THE MODULE. WITHOUT ROTATING THE MOTOR OUTPUT SHAFT, REMOVE THE CRANK AND CLEAN ANY FOREIGN MATTER FROM THE MOTOR SHAFT. INSTALL THE MOTOR CRANK IN ITS ORIGINAL POSITION.
	4. STRIPPED WIPER ARM HEAD.	4. REPLACE WIPER ARM.
MOTOR STOPS IN ANY POSITION WHEN THE SWITCH IS TURNED OFF	OPEN PARK CIRCUIT.	CHECK PARK SWITCH BY DISCONNECTING THE WIRE CONNECTOR AND APPLY BATTERY VOLTAGE TO PIN 4. PLACE A JUMPER WIRE FROM PIN 2 TO PIN 3 AND THEN TO AN EXTERNAL GROUND. REPLACE MOTOR IF MOTOR DOES NOT PARK.
MOTOR WILL NOT STOP WHEN THE SWITCH IS TURNED OFF	1. FAULTY SWITCH.	1. CHECK SWITCH IN LOW, HIGH AND INTERMITTENT POSITION.
	2. LACK OF DYNAMIC BRAKE ON WET GLASS.	2. ENSURE PARK SWITCH HAS CLEAN GROUND.
WIPER BLADES SLAP AGAINST COWL SCREEN OR WINDOW MOLDINGS.	WIPER ARMS ARE PARKED INCORRECTLY.	PARK WIPER ARMS.
BLADES CHATTER	1. FOREIGN SUBSTANCE SUCH AS POLISH ON GLASS OR BLADES.	1. CLEAN GLASS AND BLADE ELEMENT WITH NON-ABRASIVE CLEANER.
	2. ARMS TWISTED, BLADE AT WRONG ANGLE OR GLASS.	2. REPLACE ARM.
	3. BLADE STRUCTURE BENT.	3. REPLACE BLADE.
	4. BLADE ELEMENT HAS PERMANENT SET.	4. REPLACE BLADE.
WIPER KNOCK AT REVERSAL	1. LINKAGE BUSHINGS WORN.	1. REPLACE WORN LINK.
	2. ARMATURE ENDPLAY IN MOTOR.	2. REPLACE WIPER MOTOR.
WIPER MOTOR WILL NOT RUN	1. BLOWN FUSE.	1. REPLACE FUSE, AND RUN SYSTEM.
	2. NEW FUSE BLOWS.	2. CHECK FOR SHORT IN WIRING OR SWITCH.
	3. NEW FUSE BLOWS.	3. REPLACE FUSE, REMOVE MOTOR CONNECTOR, TURN SWITCH ON, FUSE DOES NOT BLOW, REPLACE MOTOR.
	4. NO VOLTAGE AT MOTOR.	4. CHECK SWITCH AND WIRING HARNESS.
	5. POOR GROUND.	5. REPAIR GROUND WIRE CONNECTION AS NECESSARY.

LTV0500000003210

Fig. 28 Wiper motor test. Caravan, PT Cruiser, Town & Country & Voyager

CONDITION	POSSIBLE CAUSES	CORRECTION
WASHER MOTOR	1. IPM FUSE #33 BLOWN OR DEFECTIVE.	1. CHECK FUSE #33 IN THE IPM. REPLACE IF NOT OK.
	2. IPM FUSE #33 LOOSE.	2. PROPERLY INSTALL IPM FUSE #33 IN SOCKET.
BLOWN FUSE WHEN IGNITION SWITCH IS IN THE RUN OR ACCESSORY POSITION.	1. SHORT IN IPM BETWEEN FUSE #33 AND PIN 11 OR PIN 1.	1. PERFORM IPM DIAGNOSTIC
	2. SHORT IN MOTOR POWER CIRCUIT.	2. SHORT OR DEFECTIVE CIRCUIT BETWEEN IPM PIN 11 AND WASHER MOTOR CONNECTOR POSITIVE TERMINAL 2. IF NOT OK, REPAIR CIRCUIT.
	3. SHORT IN WASHER PUMP MOTOR.	3. REPLACE WASHER PUMP MOTOR.
WASHER MOTOR RUNS WHEN IGNITION SWITCH IN RUN OR ACCESSORY POSITION.	1. SHORT IN IPM BETWEEN WASHER PUMP MOTOR LSD AND PIN 20.	1. PERFORM IPM DIAGNOSTIC
	2. DEFECTIVE FRONT WASHER LSD IN IPM.	2. PERFORM IPM DIAGNOSTIC
	3. SHORT IN MOTOR GROUND CIRCUIT.	3. SHORT OR DEFECTIVE CIRCUIT BETWEEN IPM PIN 20 AND MOTOR CONNECTOR NEGATIVE TERMINAL 1. IF NOT OK, REPAIR CIRCUIT.
WASHER SYSTEM WILL NOT FLOW WASHER FLUID.	1. NO WASHER FLUID IN RESERVOIR.	1. FILL WASHER RESERVOIR.
	2. IPM FUSE #33 BLOWN.	2. SHORT OR DEFECTIVE CIRCUIT BETWEEN IPM PIN 11 AND WASHER PUMP MOTOR CONNECTOR POSITIVE TERMINAL 2. INTERNAL SHORT IN IPM. IF NOT OK, REPAIR CIRCUIT OR PERFORM IPM DIAGNOSTIC
	3. WASHER HOSE NOT FLOWING WASHER FLUID.	3. ASSURE WASHER HOSE IS NOT PINCHED, LOOSE, BROKEN OR DISCONNECTED. IF NOT OK, PROPERLY ROUTE OR REPAIR WASHER HOSE.
	4. MOTOR CONNECTOR LOOSE.	4. PROPERLY SEAT AND LOCK CONNECTOR TO MOTOR.
	5. MOTOR CONNECTOR TERMINALS BENT.	5. REPAIR TERMINALS AND PROPERLY SEAT CONNECTOR TO MOTOR.
	6. OPEN OR DEFECTIVE CIRCUIT TO OR FROM WASHER SELECT SWITCH (EXPORT AND ATC EQUIPPED VEHICLES ONLY).	6. OPEN OR DEFECTIVE CIRCUIT BETWEEN IPM BODY CONTROLLER PIN 27 AND WASHER SELECT SWITCH PIN 4, OR OPEN OR DEFECTIVE CIRCUIT BETWEEN IPM BODY CONTROLLER PIN 22 AND WASHER SELECT SWITCH PIN 2. IF NOT OK, REPAIR CIRCUIT.
	7. OPEN OR DEFECTIVE WASHER SELECT SWITCH.	7. PERFORM THE PROPER BODY DIAGNOSTIC PROCEDURES INFORMATION ON MANUAL TEMPERATURE CONTROLS.
	8. OPEN POWER CIRCUIT TO MOTOR.	8. OPEN OR DEFECTIVE CIRCUIT BETWEEN IPM CONNECTOR TERMINAL 11 AND WASHER MOTOR CONNECTOR POSITIVE TERMINAL 2. INTERNAL OPEN IN IPM. IF NOT OK, REPAIR CIRCUIT OR PERFORM IPM DIAGNOSTIC

LTV0500000003211

Fig. 29 Washer pump test (Part 1 of 3). Caravan, PT Cruiser, Town & Country & Voyager

CONDITION	POSSIBLE CAUSES	CORRECTION
	9. OPEN OR DEFECTIVE MOTOR GROUND CIRCUIT.	9. OPEN OR DEFECTIVE CIRCUIT BETWEEN IPM CONNECTOR TERMINAL 20 AND WASHER MOTOR CONNECTOR NEGATIVE TERMINAL 1. INTERNAL OPEN IN IPM. IF NOT OK, REPAIR CIRCUIT OR PERFORM IPM DIAGNOSTIC
	10. OPEN CIRCUIT IN MOTOR.	10. CHECK FOR OPEN CIRCUIT IN MOTOR BETWEEN POSITIVE TERMINAL 2 AND NEGATIVE TERMINAL 1. IF NOT OK, REPLACE WASHER MOTOR.
	11. SEIZED MOTOR BEARINGS.	11. APPLY DIRECT BATTERY VOLTAGE TO MOTOR TERMINALS. IF MOTOR DOES NOT RUN, REPLACE MOTOR.
	12. NO BUS MESSAGE FROM MTC CONTROL (MANUAL TEMP. CONTROL ONLY).	12. CHECK FOR CORRECT PCI BUS MESSAGE WITH DRBIII®.
COWL GRILLE NOZZLE WILL NOT FLOW.	1. FROZEN NOZZLE.	1. MOVE VEHICLE INTO HEATED AREA TO ALLOW TIME TO THAW NOZZLE. ASSURE WASHER FLUID IS PROPERLY BLENDED FOR AMBIENT OUTSIDE TEMPERATURES.
	2. NOZZLE HOSE NOT FLOWING.	2. ASSURE NOZZLE HOSE IS NOT PINCHED, LOOSE, BROKEN, OR DISCONNECTED. IF NOT OK, PROPERLY ROUTE OR REPAIR NOZZLE HOSE.
	3. NOZZLE HOSE PLUGGED BY CONTAMINATION.	3. CLEAN NOZZLE HOSE OF CONTAMINATION, DETERMINE SOURCE OF CONTAMINATION. INSPECT RESERVOIR FOR EXCESSIVE CONTAMINATION. CLEAN SYSTEM AS REQUIRED.
	4. NOZZLE PLUGGED BY CONTAMINATION.	4. CLEAN NOZZLE OF CONTAMINATION OR REPLACE NOZZLE. DETERMINE SOURCE OF CONTAMINATION. INSPECT RESERVOIR FOR EXCESSIVE CONTAMINATION. CLEAN SYSTEM AS REQUIRED.
	5. DEFECTIVE WASHER HOSE CHECK VALVE.	5. REPLACE COWL GRILLE PANEL WASHER HOSE/CHECK VALVE ASSEMBLY.
WASHER FLUID OUTPUT IS LOW.	1. PARTIALLY PINCHED HOSE.	1. ASSURE WASHER HOSE IS NOT PARTIALLY PINCHED. IF NOT OK, PROPERLY ROUTE HOSE.
	2. FRONT REAR VALVE DEFECTIVE.	2. REPLACE WASHER PUMP.
	3. WORN OUT WASHER PUMP.	3. REPLACE WASHER PUMP.
COWL GRILLE NOZZLE STREAM OVERSHOOTS WINDSHIELD.	1. NOZZLE NOT SEATED IN COWL GRILLE.	1. ASSURE NOZZLE IS SNAPPED IN PLACE.

LTV0500000003212

Fig. 29 Washer pump test (Part 2 of 3). Caravan, PT Cruiser, Town & Country & Voyager

CONDITION	POSSIBLE CAUSES	CORRECTION
WIPER WILL NOT CYCLE WHEN WASHER SELECT SWITCH IS DEPRESSED.	1. DEFECTIVE IPM.	1 PERFORM IPM DIAGNOSTIC
	2. DEFECTIVE IPM/BODY CONTROLLER.	2. PERFORM IPM/BODY CONTROLLER DIAGNOSTIC
	3. REAR WIPER OUTPUT SHORT FAULT.	3. A GROUND SHORT DETECTED BETWEEN BCM AND REAR WIPER MOTOR. CLEAR FAULT. IF IT WON'T CLEAR, REPAIR SHORT
	4. REAR WIPER OUTPUT OPEN FAULT.	4. AN OPEN CIRCUIT DETECTED BETWEEN BCM AND REAR WIPER MOTOR. CLEAR FAULT. IF IT WON'T CLEAR, REPAIR OPEN CIRCUIT.
	5. NO BUS MESSAGE FROM MTC CONTROL (MANUAL TEMP. CONTROL ONLY).	5. CHECK PROPER MESSAGE STATUS.
WASHER OPERATES INTERMITTENTLY.	1. INTERMITTENT MOTOR GROUND.	1. INTERMITTENT GROUND BETWEEN MOTOR CONNECTOR TERMINAL 1 AND IPM PIN 20.
	2. INTERMITTENT OPEN IN WASHER SELECT SWITCH.	2. DIAGNOSE EXTERIOR/MULTI-FUNCTION SWITCH
	3. DEFECTIVE WASHER MOTOR.	3. REPLACE WASHER PUMP.
LOW WASHER FLUID LEVEL INDICATOR INOPERATIVE.	1. LOOSE FLUID LEVEL SENSOR CONNECTOR.	1. PROPERLY SEAT CONNECTOR TO LOW FLUID LEVEL SENSOR AND LOCK.
	2. OPEN POWER CIRCUIT TO FLUID LEVEL SENSOR.	2. OPEN OR DEFECTIVE CIRCUIT BETWEEN IPM CONNECTOR TERMINAL 7 AND THE LOW FLUID LEVEL SENSOR CONNECTOR TERMINAL 2. IF NOT OK, REPAIR CIRCUIT.
	3. OPEN GROUND CIRCUIT.	3. OPEN OR DEFECTIVE CIRCUIT BETWEEN FLUID LEVEL SENSOR CONNECTOR TERMINAL 1 AND FLOOR GROUND 1.
	4. DEFECTIVE IPM.	4. PERFORM IPM DIAGNOSTIC
	5. FLUID LEVEL SENSOR SWITCH OPEN OR DEFECTIVE.	5. APPLY OHMMETER TO THE SWITCH TERMINALS TO CHECK FOR COMPLETE CIRCUIT. CYCLE SWITCH FLOAT BACK AND FORTH BY FILLING AND DEPLETING RESERVOIR OF WASHER FLUID TO CHECK FOR PROPER SWITCH FUNCTION. IF NOT OK, REPLACE LOW FLUID LEVEL SENSOR SWITCH.
LEAKING WASHER FLUID.	1. PUMP OR SENSOR GROMMET DEFECTIVE.	1. PROPERLY SEAT PUMP OR SENSOR IN GROMMET. IF NOT OK, REPLACE PUMP OR SENSOR GROMMET.
	2. LEAKING WASHER PUMP.	2. REPLACE WASHER PUMP.
	3. LEAKING FLUID LEVEL SENSOR.	3. REPLACE FLUID LEVEL SENSOR.
	4. LEAKING OR DEFECTIVE RESERVOIR BODY.	4. REPLACE RESERVOIR BODY.

LTV0500000003213

Fig. 29 Washer pump test (Part 3 of 3). Caravan, PT Cruiser, Town & Country & Voyager

CONDITION	POSSIBLE CAUSE	CORRECTION
WIPER OPERATES IN LOW SPEED OR INTERMITTENT ONLY.	1. HI/LO RELAY DEFECTIVE.	1. CHECK HI/LO RELAY WITH KNOWN GOOD RELAY. IF NOT OK, REPLACE HI/LO RELAY.
	2. OPEN OR DEFECTIVE CONTROL CIRCUIT IN BCM.	2. OPEN OR DEFECTIVE CIRCUIT BETWEEN HI/LO RELAY CAVITY "C" AND BCM CONNECTOR TERMINAL #12C. DEFECTIVE BCM. IF NOT OK, REPAIR CIRCUIT OR PERFORM BCM DIAGNOSTIC.
	3. DEFECTIVE WIPER SWITCH.	3. PERFORM WIPER SWITCH DIAGNOSTIC.
	4. OPEN HIGH SPEED CIRCUIT.	4. OPEN OR DEFECTIVE CIRCUIT BETWEEN HI/LO RELAY CAVITY "D" AND WIPER MOTOR CONNECTOR TERMINAL #1. IF NOT OK, REPAIR CIRCUIT.
	5. DEFECTIVE MOTOR.	5. APPLY BATTERY JUMPER OVER TO WIPER TERMINAL #1 AND GROUND TERMINAL #5. IF NOT OK, REPLACE MOTOR.
WIPER OPERATES IN INTERMITTENT MODE ONLY.	1. DEFECTIVE WIPER SWITCH.	1. PERFORM WIPER SWITCH DIAGNOSTIC
WIPER OPERATES IN HIGH SPEED ONLY.	1. DEFECTIVE HI/LO RELAY.	1. CHECK WIPER HI/LO RELAY WITH KNOWN GOOD RELAY. REPLACE IF NOT OK.
	2. DEFECTIVE CONTROL CIRCUIT TO BCM.	2. CONTINUOUS SHORT BETWEEN HI/LO RELAY CAVITY "C" AND BCM CONNECTOR TERMINAL #12C. IF NOT OK, REPAIR CIRCUIT.
	3. DEFECTIVE BCM.	3. PERFORM BCM DIAGNOSTIC.
	4. OPEN LOW SPEED CIRCUIT.	4. OPEN OR DEFECTIVE CIRCUIT BETWEEN HI/LO RELAY CAVITY "E" AND WIPER MOTOR CONNECTOR TERMINAL #2. IF NOT OK, REPAIR CIRCUIT.
	5. DEFECTIVE MOTOR.	5. APPLY BATTERY JUMPER POWER TO WIPER TERMINAL #2 AND GROUND TERMINAL #5. IF NOT OK, REPLACE MOTOR.
WIPER OPERATION SWITCHES BETWEEN LOW AND HIGH SPEED OPERATION.	1. DEFECTIVE CONTROL CIRCUIT TO BCM.	1. INTERMITTENT SHORT BETWEEN HI/LO RELAY CAVITY "C" AND BCM CONNECTOR TERMINAL #12C. IF NOT OK, REPAIR CIRCUIT.
	2. DEFECTIVE BCM.	2. PERFORM BCM DIAGNOSTIC.

LTV0500000003214

Fig. 30   Wiper motor test (Part 1 of 4). Pacifica

CONDITION	POSSIBLE CAUSE	CORRECTION
WIPER WILL NOT PARK.	1. OPEN WIPER MOTOR PARK CIRCUIT.	1. OPEN OR DEFECTIVE CIRCUIT BETWEEN WIPER MOTOR CONNECTOR TERMINAL #4 AND BCM TERMINAL #3C. IF NOT OK, REPAIR CIRCUIT.
	2. DEFECTIVE BCM.	2. PERFORM BCM DIAGNOSTIC
	3. DEFECTIVE WIPER MOTOR.	3. APPLY BATTERY JUMPER POWER TO WIPER TERMINAL #2 (LOW SPEED) AND GROUND TERMINAL #5 (COMMON GROUND). POSITION AN OHMMETER ACROSS MOTOR PARK TERMINAL #4 AND COMMON GROUND. THE OHMMETER MUST INDICATE ONE SHORT, ONCE EVERY MOTOR REVOLUTION. OR WITH MOTOR IN "PARK" POSITION, CHECK FOR CONTINUITY BETWEEN MOTOR TERMINAL #4 AND 5. IF NOT OK, REPLACE MOTOR.
WIPER WILL NOT RUM TO PARK AFTER IGNITION OFF.	1. DEFECTIVE BCM.	1 PERFORM BCM DIAGNOSTIC
WIPER RUNS THRU PARK POSITION ON WINDSHIELD.	1. DEFECTIVE ON/OFF RELAY.	1. CHECK WIPER ON/OFF RELAY WITH KNOWN GOOD RELAY. IF NOT OK, REPLACE RELAY.
	2. OPEN ON/OFF RELAY GROUND CIRCUIT.	2. OPEN OR DEFECTIVE CIRCUIT BETWEEN ON/OFF RELAY CAVITY "E" AND LEFT HEADLAMP GROUND #5 OR ENGINE GROUND #1 OR 2.
WIPER RUNS CONTINUOUSLY OR INTERMITTENTLY IN LOW SPEED WITH IGNITION OR ACCESSORY ON AND WIPER SWITCH OFF.	1. DEFECTIVE ON/OFF RELAY.	1. CHECK WIPER ON/OFF RELAY WITH KNOWN GOOD RELAY. IF NOT OK, REPLACE RELAY.
	2. DEFECTIVE CONTROL CIRCUIT TO BCM.	2. INTERMITTENT OR CONTINUOUS SHORT BETWEEN ON/OFF RELAY CAVITY "C" AND BCM CONNECTOR TERMINAL #4C. IF NOT OK, REPAIR CIRCUIT.
	3. DEFECTIVE BCM.	3. PERFORM BCM DIAGNOSTIC
WIPER MOTOR POWER FEED FUSE OPEN.	1. POWER DISTRIBUTION CENTER (PDC) FUSE "M" DEFECTIVE.	1. CHECK FUSE "M". IF NOT OK, REPLACE FUSE.
WIPER SWITCH POWER FEED FUSE OPEN.	1. JUNCTION BLOCK FUSE #5 DEFECTIVE.	1. CHECK FUSE #5. IF NOT OK, REPLACE FUSE.

LTV0500000003215

Fig. 30   Wiper motor test (Part 2 of 4). Pacifica

CONDITION	POSSIBLE CAUSE	CORRECTION
WIPER SYSTEM WILL NOT RUN.	1. PDC FUSE "M" BLOWN.	1. SHORT CIRCUIT BETWEEN PDC FUSE "M" AND ON/OFF RELAY CAVITY "A" OR "D" OR HI/LO RELAY CAVITY "A". SHORT CIRCUIT IN ON/OFF RELAY OR HI/LO RELAY. SHORT CIRCUIT BETWEEN ON/OFF RELAY CAVITY "B" AND HI/LO RELAY CAVITY "B". IF NOT OK, REPLACE ON/OFF RELAY OR REPAIR CIRCUIT(S).
	2. JUNCTION BLOCK FUSE #5 BLOWN.	2. SHORT CIRCUIT BETWEEN JUNCTION BLOCK FUSE #5 AND WIPER SWITCH TERMINAL #1. SHORT IN WIPER SWITCH. IF NOT OK, REPAIR CIRCUIT OR PERFORM WIPER SWITCH DIAGNOSTIC
	3. ON/OFF RELAY DEFECTIVE.	3. CHECK WITH A KNOWN GOOD RELAY. IF NOT OK, REPLACE RELAY.
	4. MOTOR CONNECTOR DEFECTIVE (LOOSE, BENT OR CORRODED).	4. CHECK MOTOR CONNECTOR FOR BENT, LOOSE, OR CORRODED CONNECTOR.
	5. OPEN POWER CIRCUIT TO MOTOR.	5. OPEN OR DEFECTIVE CIRCUIT BETWEEN PDC FUSE "M" AND ON/OFF RELAY CAVITY "A" OR "D". OPEN OR DEFECTIVE CIRCUIT BETWEEN ON/OFF RELAY CAVITY "B" AND HI/LO RELAY CAVITY "B". IF NOT OK, REPLACE ON/OFF RELAY OR REPAIR CIRCUIT(S).
	6. BCM CONNECTORS "B" AND "C" (LOOSE, BENT OR CORRODED).	6. CHECK BCM CONNECTORS "B" AND "C" FOR BENT, LOOSE, OR CORRODED CONNECTORS.
	7. OPEN OR DEFECTIVE CONTROL CIRCUIT TO BCM.	7. OPEN OR DEFECTIVE CIRCUIT BETWEEN ON/OFF RELAY CAVITY "C" AND BCM CONNECTOR TERMINAL #4C. OPEN OR DEFECTIVE CIRCUIT BETWEEN WIPER SWITCH TERMINAL #5 AND BCM CONNECTOR TERMINAL #5B. DEFECTIVE BCM. IF NOT OK, REPAIR CIRCUIT(S) OR PERFORM BCM DIAGNOSTIC
	8. OPEN OR DEFECTIVE MOTOR GROUND CIRCUIT.	8. OPEN OR DEFECTIVE CIRCUIT BETWEEN WIPER MOTOR CONNECTOR GROUND TERMINAL #5 AND LEFT HEADLAMP GROUND #5 OR ENGINE GROUND #1 OR 2.
	9. OPEN CIRCUIT IN MOTOR.	9. CHECK FOR OPEN CIRCUIT IN MOTOR BETWEEN LO SPEED TERMINAL #2 AND GROUND TERMINAL #5 OR BETWEEN HI SPEED TERMINAL #1 AND GROUND TERMINAL #5. IF NOT OK, REPLACE WIPER MOTOR.
	10. STRIPPED GEARS IN MOTOR.	10. APPLY BATTERY VOLTAGE TO MOTOR HI SPEED OR LO SPEED CIRCUIT. IF MOTOR RUNS AND OUTPUT CRANK RUNS INTERMITTENTLY OR DOES NOT RUN, REPLACE MOTOR.
	11. SEIZED MOTOR BEARINGS.	11. APPLY BATTERY VOLTAGE TO MOTOR HI SPEED OR LO SPEED CIRCUIT. IF MOTOR DOES NOT RUN, REPLACE MOTOR.
WIPER SYSTEM MAKES REVERSAL NOISE.	1. LOOSE ARM TO BLADE CONNECTION.	1. INSPECT CONNECTION FOR DAMAGE, BENDING, EXCESSIVE WARE. REPLACE ARM OR BLADE IF NOT OK.
	2. LOOSE MASTER LINK.	2. REPLACE MASTER LINK IF NOT OK.
	3. LOOSE SLAVE LINK.	3. REPLACE SLAVE LINK IF NOT OK.
	4. LOOSE LINKAGE PIVOT(S).	4. REPLACE LINKAGE FRAME IF NOT OK.
	5. LOOSE MOTOR CRANK.	5. TIGHTEN CRANK NUT TO SPECIFICATION.
	6. EXCESSIVE MOTOR GEARBOX "BACKLASH" OR LOOSE ARMATURE.	6. REPLACE WIPER MOTOR.

LTV0500000003216

Fig. 30   Wiper motor test (Part 3 of 4). Pacifica

CONDITION	POSSIBLE CAUSE	CORRECTION
WIPER ARM(S) CHATTER ON WINDSHIELD.	1. PERMANENT HI OR LO TEMPERATURE SET OF BLADE ELEMENT EDGE.	1. INSPECT RUBBER ELEMENT FOR PERMANENT SET. IF NOT OK, REPLACE RUBBER ELEMENT.
	2. BENT OR DAMAGED BLADE STRUCTURE.	2. INSPECT BLADE. IF NOT OK, REPLACE BLADE.
	3. BENT OR DAMAGED ARM.	3. INSPECT ARM. IF NOT OK, REPLACE ARM.
DRIVER AND/OR PASSENGER ARM WILL NOT CYCLE (OPERATE).	1. LOOSE ARM TO PIVOT SHAFT.	1. CHECK ARM TO PIVOT SHAFT CONNECTION FOR LOOSENESS. TORQUE NUT TO SPECIFICATION.
	2. STRIPPED ARM TO PIVOT SHAFT.	2. CHECK ARM TO PIVOT SHAFT FOR STRIPPING. TORQUE NUT TO SPECIFICATION. IF NOT OK, REPLACE ARM.
DRIVER AND/OR PASSENGER ARM OR BLADE HITS COWL SCREEN OR WINDSHIELD MOLDINGS.	1. ARM(S) OUT OF POSITION.	1. REMOVE ARM OFF PIVOT SHAFT, CYCLE MODULE TO PARK. REPOSITION ARM/BLADE TO LOCATION MARKS ON WINDSHIELD. SECURE ARM TO PIVOT SHAFT AND TORQUE TO SPECIFICATION.
WIPER BLADE(S) STREAK.	1. CONTAMINATION ON BLADE ELEMENT OR WINDSHIELD.	1. CLEAN BLADE ELEMENT EDGE WITH MILD SOAP OR ALCOHOL AND WATER. CLEAN WINDSHIELD WITH MILD SOAP OR NON-ABRASIVE CLEANSER AND WATER. CHECK FOR PROPER WIPE QUALITY. IF NOT OK, REPLACE BLADE ELEMENT.
	2. BLADE ELEMENT DAMAGED.	2. REPLACE BLADE ELEMENT.
POOR COLD TEMPERATURE WIPE QUALITY.	1. NO WASHER FLUID FOR WASH/WIPE CYCLE.	1. ADD WASHER FLUID TO RESERVOIR.
	2. POOR WINDSHIELD DEFROST PERFORMANCE.	2. CHECK WINDSHIELD DEFROSTER FOR PROPER FUNCTION AND PERFORMANCE.
	3. PERMANENT HI OR LO TEMPERATURE SET OF BLADE ELEMENT EDGE.	3. INSPECT RUBBER ELEMENT FOR PERMANENT SET. IF NOT OK, REPLACE RUBBER ELEMENT.
	4. LOW ARM FORCE.	4. CHECK FOR PROPER ARM FORCE. IF NOT OK, REPLACE ARM.

LTV0500000003217

Fig. 30   Wiper motor test (Part 4 of 4). Pacifica

CONDITION	POSSIBLE CAUSES	CORRECTION
WIPERS INOPERATIVE IN ALL SWITCH POSITIONS	1. Faulty or missing fuse.	1. Test and replace the fuse as required.
	2. Faulty wiper motor ground circuit.	2. Test and repair the open ground circuit as required.
	3. Faulty wiper motor.	3. Test and replace the wiper motor as required.
	4. Faulty multi-function switch feed circuit.	4. Test and repair the open fused ignition switch output circuit between the fuse and the multi-function switch as required.
	5. Faulty multi-function switch.	5. Test and replace the multi-function switch as required.
	6. Faulty rain sensor control module ground circuit.	6. Test and repair the open ground circuit as required.
	7. Faulty rain sensor control module feed circuit.	7. Test and repair the open fused ignition switch output circuit between the fuse and the rain sensor control module as required.
	8. Faulty rain sensor control module.	8. Test and replace the rain sensor control module as required.
AUTOMATIC WIPE INOPERATIVE (WITH ACKNOWLEDGE-MENT WIPE)	1. Faulty rain sensor shielding ground circuits.	1. Test and repair the open shielding circuits as required.
	2. Faulty rain sensor ground circuit.	2. Test and repair the open ground circuit between the rain sensor and the control module as required.
	3. Faulty faulty rain sensor feed circuit.	3. Test and repair the open feed circuit between the rain sensor and the control module as required.
	4. Faulty rain sensor signal circuit.	4. Test and repair the open or shorted signal circuit between the rain sensor and the control module as required.
	5. Faulty rain sensor.	5. Test and replace the rain sensor as required.
AUTOMATIC WIPE INOPERATIVE (NO ACKNOWLEDGE-MENT WIPE)	1. Faulty rain sensor control module.	1. Test and replace the rain sensor control module as required.
WIPERS INOPERATIVE IN LOW POSITION AND NO PULSE FEATURE	1. Faulty low speed request circuit.	1. Test and repair the open low speed request circuit between the multi-function switch and the rain sensor control module as required.
	2. Faulty multi-function switch.	2. Test and replace the multi-function switch as required.
	3. Faulty low speed control circuit.	3. Test and repair the open low speed control circuit between the rain sensor control module and the wiper motor as required.
	4. Faulty wiper low speed brush.	4. Test and replace the wiper motor as required.

LTV0500000003218

Fig. 31 Automatic wiper system test (Part 1 of 2). Sprinter

CONDITION	POSSIBLE CAUSES	CORRECTION
WIPERS INOPERATIVE IN ALL SWITCH POSITIONS	1. Faulty or missing fuse.	1. Test and replace the fuse as required.
	2. Faulty wiper motor ground circuit.	2. Test and repair the open ground circuit as required.
	3. Faulty multi-function switch feed circuit.	3. Test and repair the open fused ignition switch output circuit between the fuse and the multi-function switch as required.
	4. Faulty multi-function switch.	4. Test and replace the multi-function switch as required.
	5. Faulty wiper motor.	5. Test and replace the wiper motor as required.
WIPERS INOPERATIVE IN INTERMITTENT POSITION AND NO WIPE AFTER WASH FEATURE	1. Faulty wiper relay.	1. Test and replace the wiper relay as required.
	2. Faulty multi-function switch.	2. Test and replace the multi-function switch as required.
	3. Faulty intermittent wipe logic circuit.	3. Replace the steering column fuse block as required.
WIPERS INOPERATIVE IN LOW POSITION AND NO PULSE FEATURE	1. Faulty low speed circuit.	1. Test and repair the open low speed circuit between the multi-function switch and the wiper motor as required.
	2. Faulty multi-function switch.	2. Test and replace the multi-function switch as required.
	3. Faulty wiper low speed brush.	3. Test and replace the wiper motor as required.
WIPERS INOPERATIVE IN HIGH POSITION	1. Faulty high speed circuit.	1. Test and repair the open high speed circuit between the multi-function switch and the wiper motor as required.
	2. Faulty multi-function switch.	2. Test and replace the multi-function switch as required.
	3. Faulty wiper high speed brush.	3. Test and replace the wiper motor as required.
WIPERS DO NOT PARK AFTER OPERATING	1. Faulty motor feed circuit.	1. Test and repair the open fused ignition switch output circuit to the wiper motor as required.
	2. Faulty park switch output circuit.	2. Test and repair the open or shorted circuit between the wiper park switch and the wiper relay as required.
	3. Faulty wiper relay.	3. Test and replace the wiper relay as required.
	4. Faulty park switch.	4. Test and replace the wiper motor as required.
WASHERS INOPERATIVE	1. Faulty washer pump ground circuit.	1. Test and repair the open ground circuit as required.
	2. Faulty washer pump feed circuit.	2. Test and repair the open circuit between the multi-function switch and the washer pump as required.
	3. Faulty washer pump motor.	3. Test and replace the washer pump as required.
	4. Faulty multi-function switch.	4. Test and replace the multi-function switch as required.

LTV0500000003220

Fig. 32 Intermittent wiper system test. Sprinter

CONDITION	POSSIBLE CAUSES	CORRECTION
WIPERS INOPERATIVE IN HIGH POSITION	1. Faulty high speed request circuit.	1. Test and repair the open high speed request circuit between the multi-function switch and the rain sensor control module as required.
	2. Faulty multi-function switch.	2. Test and replace the multi-function switch as required.
	3. Faulty high speed control circuit.	3. Test and repair the open high speed control circuit between the rain sensor control module and the wiper motor as required.
	3. Faulty wiper high speed brush.	3. Test and replace the wiper motor as required.
WIPERS DO NOT PARK AFTER OPERATING	1. Faulty park switch output circuit.	1. Test and repair the open or shorted circuit between the wiper park switch and the rain sensor control module as required.
	2. Faulty wiper relay output circuit.	2. Test and repair the open or shorted circuit between the rain sensor control module and the wiper relay as required.
	3. Faulty wiper relay.	3. Test and replace the wiper relay as required.
	4. Faulty park switch.	4. Test and replace the wiper motor as required.
	5. Faulty intermittent wipe logic circuit.	5. Replace the steering column fuse block as required.
WASHERS INOPERATIVE	1. Faulty washer pump ground circuit.	1. Test and repair the open ground circuit as required.
	2. Faulty washer pump request circuit.	2. Test and repair the open washer pump request circuit between the multi-function switch and the rain sensor control module as required.
	3. Faulty muli-function switch.	3. Test and replace the multi-function switch as required.
	4. Faulty washer pump control circuit.	4. Test and repair the open washer pump control circuit between the rain sensor control module and the washer pump as required.
	5. Faulty washer pump motor.	5. Test and replace the washer pump as required.

LTV0500000003219

Fig. 31 Automatic wiper system test (Part 2 of 2). Sprinter

CONDITION	POSSIBLE CAUSES	CORRECTION
WIPER BLADES DO NOT PARK PROPERLY.	(1) WIPER ARMS IMPROPERLY PARKED. (2) WIPER ARMS ARE LOOSE ON PIVOT SHAFT. (3) MOTOR CRANK LOOSE AT OUTPUT SHAFT.	(1) REMOVE WIPER ARMS AND REPARK. (2) REMOVE WIPER ARM AND REPARK. (3) REMOVE WIPER ARM, RUN WIPER MOTOR TO PARK POSITION AND REMOVE THE MODULE. WITHOUT ROTATING THE MOTOR OUTPUT SHAFT, REMOVE THE CRANK AND CLEAN ANY FOREIGN MATTER FROM THE MOTOR SHAFT. INSTALL THE MOTOR CRANK IN ITS ORIGINAL POSITION.
MOTOR STOPS IN ANY POSITION WHEN THE SWITCH IS TURNED OFF.	(1) OPEN PARK CIRCUIT.	(1) CHECK PARK SWITCH BY DISCONNECTING THE WIRE CONNECTOR AND APPLY BATTERY VOLTAGE TO PIN 3. PLACE A JUMPER WIRE FROM PIN 2 TO PIN 4 AND THEN TO AN EXTERNAL GROUND TO PIN 1. REPLACE MOTOR IF IT DOES NOT PARK.
MOTOR WILL NOT STOP WHEN THE SWITCH IS TURNED OFF.	(1) FAULTY SWITCH.	(1) CHECK SWITCH IN LOW, HIGH AND INTERMITTENT POSITION. (2) ENSURE PARK SWITCH HAS CLEAN GROUND.
WIPER BLADES SLAP AGAINST COWL SCREEN OR WINDOW MOLDINGS.	(1) WIPER ARMS ARE PARKED INCORRECTLY.	(1) PARK WIPER ARMS.
BLADES CHATTER.	(1) FOREIGN SUBSTANCE SUCH AS POLISH ON GLASS OR BLADES. (2) ARMS TWISTED, BLADE AT WRONG ANGLE ON GLASS. (3) BLADE STRUCTURE BENT. (4) BLADE ELEMENT HAS PERMANENT SET.	(1) CLEAN GLASS AND BLADE ELEMENT WITH NON-ABRASIVE CLEANER. (2) REPLACE ARM. (3) REPLACE BLADE. (4) REPLACE BLADE ELEMENT.
WIPER KNOCK AT REVERSAL.	(1) LINKAGE BUSHINGS WORN. (2) ARMATURE ENDPLAY IN MOTOR.	(1) REPLACE WORN LINK. (2) REPLACE WIPER MOTOR.

CR9020000432010X

Fig. 33 Front wiper motor tests (Part 1 of 2). PT Cruiser

CONDITION	POSSIBLE CAUSES	CORRECTION
WIPER MOTOR WILL NOT RUN.	(1) BLOWN FUSE. (2) NEW FUSE BLOWS. (3) NEW FUSE BLOWS. (4) NO VOLTAGE AT MOTOR. (5) POOR GROUND.	(1) REPLACE FUSE, AND RUN SYSTEM. (2) CHECK FOR SHORT IN WIRING OR SWITCH. (3) REPLACE FUSE, REMOVE MOTOR CONNECTOR, TURN SWITCH ON, FUSE DOES NOT BLOW, REPLACE MOTOR. (4) CHECK SWITCH AND WIRING HARNESS. REFER TO WIRING DIAGRAMS. (5) REPAIR GROUND WIRE CONNECTION AS NECESSARY.

CR9020000432020X

Fig. 33 Front wiper motor tests (Part 2 of 2). PT Cruiser

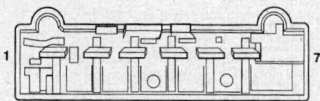

SWITCH POSITION	MODE	CONTINUITY BETWEEN
WIPER	OFF	PIN C-1 AND C-6
	LOW/MIST	PIN C-4 AND C-6
	HIGH	PIN C-4 AND C-5
	WASH	PIN C-4 AND C-3
	INTERMITTENT	CANNOT BE CHECKED

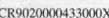

CR9020000433000X

Fig. 34 Front wiper/washer switch continuity test. PT Cruiser

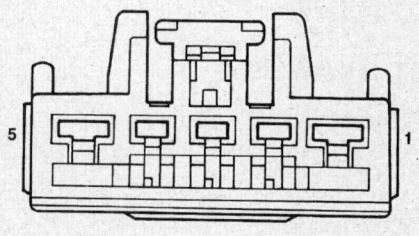

CR9020000435000X

Fig. 35 Rear wiper switch harness connector. PT Cruiser

CONDITION	POSSIBLE CAUSES	CORRECTION
PUMP RUNS NO FLUID FLOWING.	1. NO FLUID IN THE RESERVOIR. 2. NOZZLE PLUGGED OR FROZEN. 3. BROKEN, LOOSE OR PINCHED HOSE. 4. FAULTY PUMP.	1. FILL RESERVOIR. 2. THAW AND CHECK FLOW IF BLOCKED 3. CHECK FLOW THROUGH HOSE CONNECTIONS. 4. APPLY BATTERY VOLTAGE TO MOTOR TERMINALS, REPLACE IF PUMP DOES NOT RUN.
SYSTEM OPERATES INTERMITTENTLY.	1. LOOSE WIRE CONNECTION. 2. FAULTY SWITCH.	1. CHECK WIRE CONNECTIONS. 2. DISCONNECT WIRE HARNESS USE VOLTMETER TO CHECK SWITCH.
SYSTEM OUTPUT IS LOW.	1. PINCHED HOSE. 2. HOSE BLOCKED.	1. CHECK FLOW THROUGH HOSE CONNECTION. 2. DISCONNECT HOSE AT NOZZLE CHECK FOR FLOW. REPLACE AS NECESSARY.

CR9020000434000X

Fig. 36 Washer system tests. PT Cruiser

Jeep

NOTE: On Air Bag Equipped Models, Refer To "Air Bag System Precautions" Located In The Front Of This Manual For System Disarming & Arming Procedures.

NOTE: Refer To "Computer Relearn Procedures" Located In The Front Of This Manual When Battery Power To The Computer Has Been Interrupted.

NOTE: "Electrical Symbol & Wire Color Code Identification" Located In The Front Of This Manual May Be Used As An Aid When Using Wiring Circuits Found In This Section.

INDEX

	Page No.		Page No.		Page No.
Description	3-26	Codes	3-26	Wrangler	3-26
Precautions	3-26	Clearing Diagnostic Trouble		Diagnostic Trouble Code	
Air Bag Systems	3-26	Codes	3-27	Interpretation	3-26
Battery Ground Cable	3-26	Connector Pin Identification	3-26	Wiring Diagrams	3-26
System Diagnosis & Testing	3-26	Diagnostic Tests	3-26		
Accessing Diagnostic Trouble		Multi-Function Switch	3-26		

PRECAUTIONS

Air Bag Systems

Refer to "Air Bag System Precautions" in the front of this manual for system disarming and arming procedures.

Battery Ground Cable

Prior to service, disconnect battery ground cable and isolate as required.

DESCRIPTION

Wiper and washer system operation is completely controlled by the SCM and FCM logic circuits, and that logic will only allow these systems to operate when the ignition switch is in the Accessory or On positions.

SYSTEM DIAGNOSIS & TESTING

Accessing Diagnostic Trouble Codes

Connect a suitably programmed scan tool to Data Link Connector (DLC) and follow manufacturer's instructions.

Diagnostic Trouble Code Interpretation

Refer to **Fig. 1** for diagnostic trouble code interpretation.

Connector Pin Identification

Refer to **Figs. 2 through 11** for connector pin identification.

Wiring Diagrams

Refer to **Figs. 12 through 15** for wiring diagrams.

Diagnostic Tests

MULTI-FUNCTION SWITCH

COMMANDER & 2005–06 GRAND CHEROKEE

1. Remove righthand multi-function switch from Steering Control Module (SCM).
2. Test resistance between terminals of switch as outlined in three function tests tables, **Fig. 16.**
3. If switch fails any of tests, replace ineffective righthand multi-function switch.

2002–04 GRAND CHEROKEE

1. Disconnect battery ground cable.
2. Remove righthand multi-function switch from steering column and disconnect instrument panel wire harness connector for switch from switch connector receptacle.

Code	Interpretation
B210D	Battery Voltage Low (RSM)
B210E	Battery Voltage High (RSM)
B2211	Rain Sensor Module Initialization Performance
B221D	(RSM) Rain Sensor Module Internal
B2301	Wiper Mode Switch Input Circuit Low (SCM)
B2302	Wiper Mode Switch Input Circuit High (SCM)
B2304	Wiper Park Switch Input Circuit Low
B2305	Wiper Park Switch Input Circuit High
B230A	Rear Wiper Switch Input Circuit Low (SCM)
B230B	Rear Wiper Switch Input Circuit High (SCM)
B2313	Wiper On/Off Control Circuit Low
B2314	Wiper On/Off Control Circuit High
B2315	Wiper On/Off Control Circuit Open
B2317	Wiper Hi/Low Control Circuit Low
B2318	Wiper Hi/Low Control Circuit High
B2319	Wiper Hi/Low Control Circuit Open
B231F	Front/Rear Washer Motor Control Circuit Low
B2320	Front/Rear Washer Motor Control Circuit High
B2328	Washer Fluid Level Sensor Input Circuit High
B2329	Rain Sensor Optical Path 1 Performance
B232A	Rain Sensor Optical Path 2 Performance
B232B	Rain Sensor Optical Path 3 Performance
B232C	Rain Sensor Optical Path 4 Performance
B232D	Washer Switch Stuck
B232E	Rear Washer Switch Stuck
B232F	Mist Switch Stuck
U0141	Lost Communication With Front Control Module
U0155	Lost Communication With Cluster/CCN
U0212	Lost Communication With SCCM-CAN-B

Fig. 1   Diagnostic trouble code interpretation

3. Inspect righthand multi-function switch continuity and resistances at switch terminals using suitable ohmmeter as outlined in righthand multi-function switch test chart, **Fig. 17.**
4. If righthand multi-function switch fails any of continuity or resistance tests, replace righthand multi-function switch.

WRANGLER

FRONT WIPER SYSTEM

1. Inspect front wiper and washer system fuse, if not OK, repair shorted circuit or component as required and replace faulty fuse.
2. Turn ignition switch to On position, inspect for battery voltage at front wiper and washer system fuse, if not OK, repair open fused ignition switch output (run-acc) circuit between fuse block and ignition switch as required.
3. Disconnect battery ground cable, then disconnect cross body wire harness connector for righthand multi-function switch from switch connector receptacle.
4. Inspect for continuity between ground circuit cavity of cross body wire harness connector for righthand multi-function switch and a good ground.
5. Turn ignition switch to Off position, remove righthand multi-function switch from steering column and inspect

switch continuity, if not OK replace faulty switch.
6. Disconnect cross body wire harness connector for front wiper motor from wiper motor pigtail wire connector.
7. Inspect for continuity between ground circuit cavity in cross body wire harness connector for front wiper motor and a good ground, if not OK, repair open ground circuit to ground.
8. Reconnect battery ground cable and turn ignition switch to ON position, inspect for battery voltage at fused ignition switch output (run-acc) circuit cavity of cross body wire harness connector for front wiper motor. If not OK, repair open circuit between front wiper motor and fuse block.
9. Turn ignition switch to Off position and disconnect battery ground cable, inspect each of following circuits at proper cavity of cross body wire harness connector for front wiper motor for continuity to ground. In each case, there should be no continuity.
   a. Wiper park switch sense.
   b. Wiper switch low speed output.
   c. Wiper switch high speed output.
10. Inspect continuity of following circuits between proper cavities of cross body wire harness connectors for front wiper motor and righthand multi-function switch. In each case, there should be continuity. If OK, replace the faulty front wiper module.

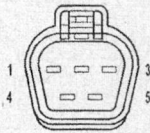

MOTOR-
WINDSHIELD
WIPER

CAV	CIRCUIT	FUNCTION
1	W7 20BR/GY	FRONT WIPER PARK SWITCH SENSE
2	-	-
3	W4 16BR/OR	FRONT WIPER HIGH/LOW RELAY HIGH SPEED OUTPUT
4	Z103 16BK/WT	GROUND
5	W3 16BR/WT	FRONT WIPER HIGH/LOW RELAY LOW SPEED OUTPUT

LTV0500000002265

Fig. 2   Connector pin identification (Front). Commander & 2005–06 Grand Cherokee

MOTOR-
REAR
WINDOW
WIPER

CAV	CIRCUIT	FUNCTION
1	Z800 16BK	GROUND
2	W13 20BR/LG	REAR WIPER MOTOR CONTROL
3	G80 20VT/BR	FLIP-UP GLASS AJAR SWITCH SENSE
4	W14 20BR/LB	REAR WIPER MOTOR DELAY SIGNAL
5	A46 18RD/GY	REAR WIPER RELAY OUTPUT
6		

LTV0500000002266

Fig. 3   Connector pin identification (Rear). Commander & 2005–06 Grand Cherokee

a. Wiper park switch sense
b. Wiper switch low speed output.
c. Wiper switch high speed output.

FRONT WIPER WASHER SYSTEM

1. Disconnect battery ground cable, then disconnect headlamp and dash wire harness electrical connector for front washer pump/motor from connector receptacle.
2. Inspect for continuity between ground circuit cavity of headlamp and dash wire harness connector for front washer pump/motor and a good ground. There should be continuity.
3. Reconnect battery ground cable and turn ignition switch to On position.
4. Inspect for battery voltage at washer pump control switch output circuit cavity of headlamp and dash wire harness connector for front washer pump/motor while pulling righthand multi-function switch control stalk toward steering wheel to close washer switch, if OK, replace faulty front washer pump/motor.
5. Turn ignition to OFF position and disconnect battery ground cable.
6. Disconnect cross body wire harness connector for righthand multi-function switch from switch connector receptacle.
7. Inspect for continuity between washer pump control switch output circuit cavity of headlamp and dash wire harness connector for front washer pump/motor and a good ground. There should be no continuity.
8. Inspect for continuity between washer pump control switch output circuit cavities of headlamp and dash wire harness connector for front washer pump/motor and cross body wire harness connector for righthand multi-function switch. There should be continuity. If OK, replace faulty righthand multi-function switch.

REAR WIPER SYSTEM

1. Inspect the rear wiper and washer fuse, if not OK, repair shorted circuit or component as required and replace faulty fuse.

2. Turn ignition switch to On position. Inspect for battery voltage at rear wiper and washer fuse, if not OK, repair open circuit between fuse block and ignition switch as required.
3. Turn ignition switch to Off position and disconnect battery ground cable.
4. Disconnect instrument panel wire harness connector for rear wiper and washer switch from switch connector receptacle.
5. Reconnect battery ground cable and turn ignition switch to ON position, inspect for battery voltage at fused ignition switch output circuit cavity of instrument panel wire harness connector for rear wiper and washer switch. If not OK, repair open circuit between rear wiper and washer switch and fuse block as required.
6. Turn ignition switch to Off position and disconnect battery ground cable.
7. Inspect for continuity between ground circuit cavity of instrument panel wire harness connector for rear wiper and washer switch and a good ground. There should be continuity.
8. Test rear wiper and washer switch continuity, if not OK, replace faulty rear wiper and washer switch.
9. Disconnect hardtop wire harness connector for rear wiper motor from motor pigtail wire connector.
10. Reconnect battery ground cable and turn ignition switch to ON position, inspect for battery voltage at circuit cavity of hardtop wire harness connector for rear wiper motor. If not OK, repair open circuit between rear wiper motor and fuse block.
11. Turn ignition switch to Off position and disconnect battery ground cable.
12. Inspect for continuity between ground circuit cavity of hardtop wire harness connector for rear wiper motor and a good ground. There should be continuity.
13. Inspect for continuity between rear wiper motor control circuit cavity of hardtop wire harness connector for rear wiper motor and a good ground.
14. Inspect for continuity between rear wiper motor control circuit cavities of hardtop wire harness connector for

rear wiper motor and instrument panel wire harness connector for rear wiper and washer switch. There should be continuity. If OK, replace faulty rear wiper motor.

REAR WIPER WASHER SYSTEM

1. Turn ignition switch to Off position and disconnect battery ground cable.
2. Disconnect rear body wire harness connector from rear pump/motor connector receptacle.
3. Inspect for continuity between ground circuit cavity of rear body wire harness connector for rear washer pump/motor and a good ground. If not OK, repair open ground circuit to ground
4. Reconnect battery ground cable and turn ignition switch to ON position.
5. Inspect for battery voltage at rear washer motor control circuit cavity of rear body wire harness connector for rear washer pump/motor while rear wiper and washer switch rocker is actuated to wash position, if OK, replace faulty rear washer pump/motor unit.
6. Turn ignition switch to Off position and disconnect battery ground cable.
7. Disconnect instrument panel wire harness connector for rear wiper and washer switch from switch connector receptacle.
8. Inspect for continuity between rear washer motor control circuit cavities of rear body wire harness connector for rear washer pump/motor and instrument panel wire harness connector for rear wiper and washer switch.
9. If not OK, repair open rear washer motor control circuit between rear wiper and washer switch and rear washer pump/motor.
10. Test rear wiper and washer switch continuity, if not OK, replace faulty rear wiper and washer switch.

Clearing Diagnostic Trouble Codes

Connect a suitably programmed scan tool to Data Link Connector (DLC) and follow manufacturer's instructions.

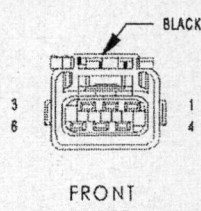

FRONT
WIPER
MOTOR

CAV	CIRCUIT	FUNCTION
1	V6 16DB	FUSED IGNITION SWITCH OUTPUT (RUN-ACC)
2	V55 16TN/RD	WIPER PARK SWITCH SENSE
3	-	-
4	Z141 16BK	GROUND
5	V3 16BR/WT	WIPER HIGH/LOW RELAY LOW SPEED OUTPUT
6	V4 16RD/YL	WIPER HIGH/LOW RELAY HIGH SPEED OUTPUT

LTV0500000002291

**Fig. 4 Connector pin identification
(Front wiper motor). 2002–04 Grand Cherokee**

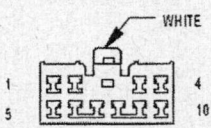

RIGHT MULTI-
FUNCTION
SWITCH

CAV	CIRCUIT	FUNCTION
1	V23 20BR/PK	FUSED IGNITION SWITCH OUTPUT (RUN-ACC)
2	V20 18BK/WT	REAR WASHER PUMP MOTOR CONTROL
3	V10 20BR	WASHER PUMP SWITCH SENSE
4	-	-
5	V13 18BR/LG	REAR WIPER MOTOR CONTROL
6	V22 18BR/YL	REAR WIPER MOTOR DELAY CONTROL
7	V9 20WT/BK	WINDSHIELD WIPER SWITCH RETURN
8	V52 20DG/RD	WINDSHIELD WIPER SWITCH MUX
9	V48 20RD/GY	WIPER HIGH CONTROL
10	-	-

LTV0500000002293

**Fig. 6 Connector pin identification
(Multi-function switch). 2002–04 Grand Cherokee**

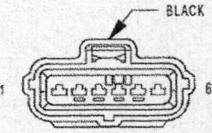

REAR
WIPER
MOTOR

CAV	CIRCUIT	FUNCTION
1	Z213 18BK/OR	GROUND
2	W13 20BR/LG	REAR WIPER ON DRIVER
3	G80 20VT/YL	FLIP-UP GLASS AJAR SWITCH SENSE
4	W27 20DB/BR	REAR WIPER INTERMITTENT DRIVER
5	A44 18BR/OR	FUSED B(+)
6	-	-

LTV0500000002299

**Fig. 8 Connector pin identification
(Front wiper motor). Liberty**

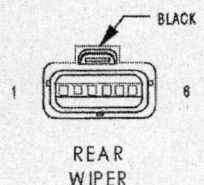

REAR
WIPER
MOTOR

CAV	CIRCUIT	FUNCTION
1	Z309 18BK	GROUND
2	V13 18BR/LG	REAR WIPER MOTOR CONTROL
3	G80 20VT/YL	LIFTGATE FLIP-UP AJAR SWITCH SENSE
4	V22 18BR/YL	REAR WIPER MOTOR DELAY CONTROL
5	F70 18PK	FUSED B(+)
6	-	-

LTV0500000002292

**Fig. 5 Connector pin identification
(Rear wiper motor). 2002–04 Grand Cherokee**

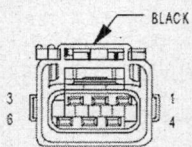

FRONT WIPER
MOTOR

CAV	CIRCUIT	FUNCTION
1	A5 16RD/VT	FUSED IGNITION SWITCH OUTPUT (RUN-ACC)
2	W7 16BR/GY	FRONT WIPER PARK SWITCH SENSE
3	-	-
4	Z931 16BK	GROUND
5	W3 16BR/WT	FRONT WIPER HIGH/LOW RELAY LOW SPEED OUTPUT
6	W4 16BR/OR	FRONT WIPER HIGH/LOW RELAY HIGH SPEED OUTPUT

LTV0500000002298

**Fig. 7 Connector pin identification
(Front wiper motor). Liberty**

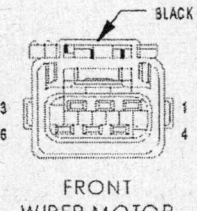

FRONT
WIPER MOTOR

CAV	CIRCUIT	FUNCTION
1	V6 16PK/BK	FUSED IGNITION SWITCH OUTPUT (RUN-ACC)
2	V5 16DG/YL	WIPER PARK SWITCH SENSE
3	-	-
4	Z1 18BK	GROUND
5	V3 16BR/WT	LOW SPEED WIPER SWITCH OUTPUT
6	V4 16RD/YL	WIPER SWITCH HIGH SPEED OUTPUT

LTV0500000003203

**Fig. 9 Connector pin identification
(Front wiper motor). Wrangler**

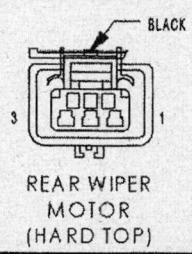

REAR WIPER MOTOR (HARD TOP)

CAV	CIRCUIT	FUNCTION
1	V23 18BR/PK	FUSED IGNITION SWITCH OUTPUT (RUN)
2	Z1 16BK	GROUND
3	V13 18BK/LG	REAR WIPER MOTOR CONTROL

LTV0500000003204

Fig. 10   Connector pin identification (Rear wiper motor). Wrangler

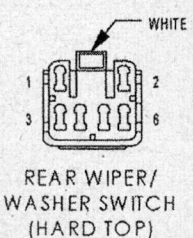

REAR WIPER/ WASHER SWITCH (HARD TOP)

CAV	CIRCUIT	FUNCTION
1	Z1 18BK	GROUND
2	V20 18VT/OR	REAR WASHER MOTOR CONTROL
3	E2 20OR	FUSED PANEL LAMPS DIMMER SWITCH SIGNAL
4	V13 18BR/LG	REAR WIPER MOTOR CONTROL
5	V23 18BR/PK	FUSED IGNITION SWITCH OUTPUT (RUN)
6	-	-

LTV0500000003205

Fig. 11   Connector pin identification (Rear wiper/washer switch). Wrangler

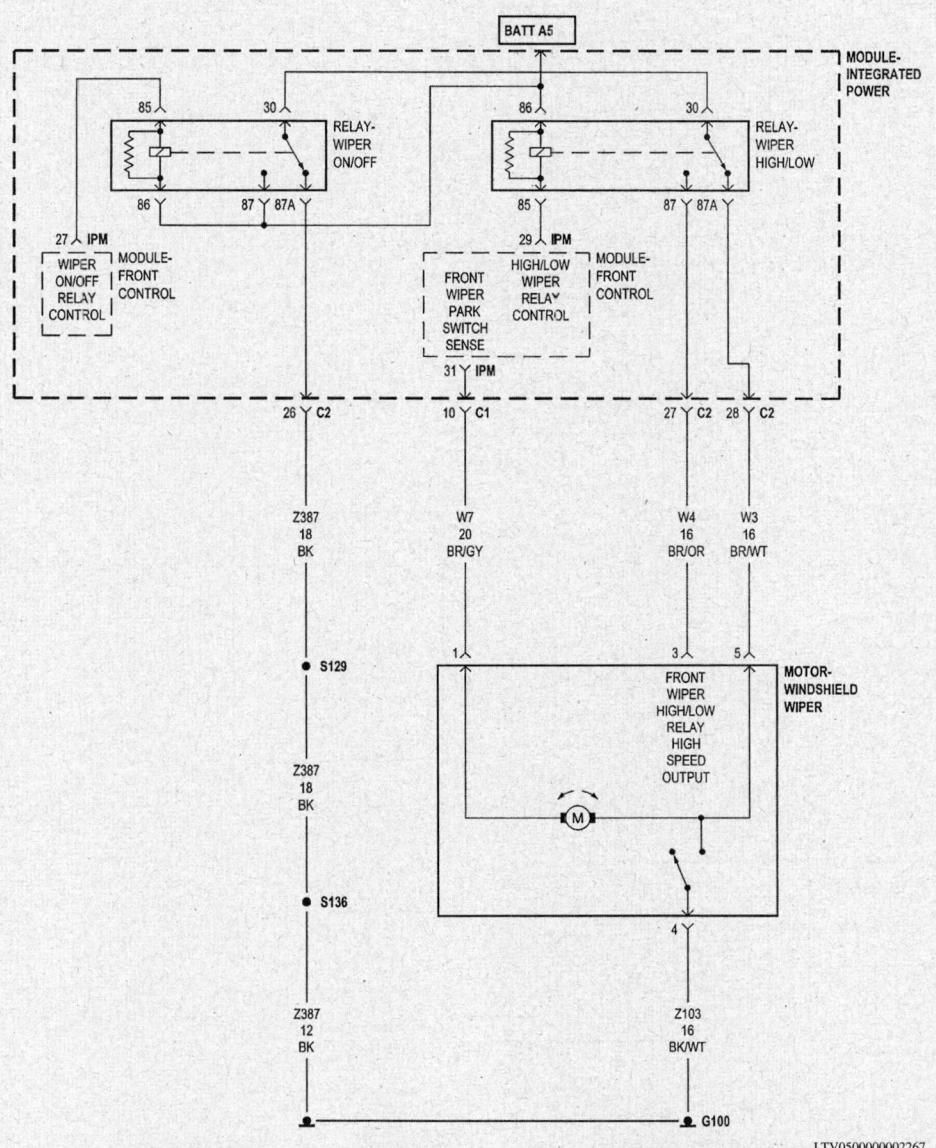

LTV0500000002267

Fig. 12   Wiring diagram (Part 1 of 3). Commander & 2005–06 Grand Cherokee

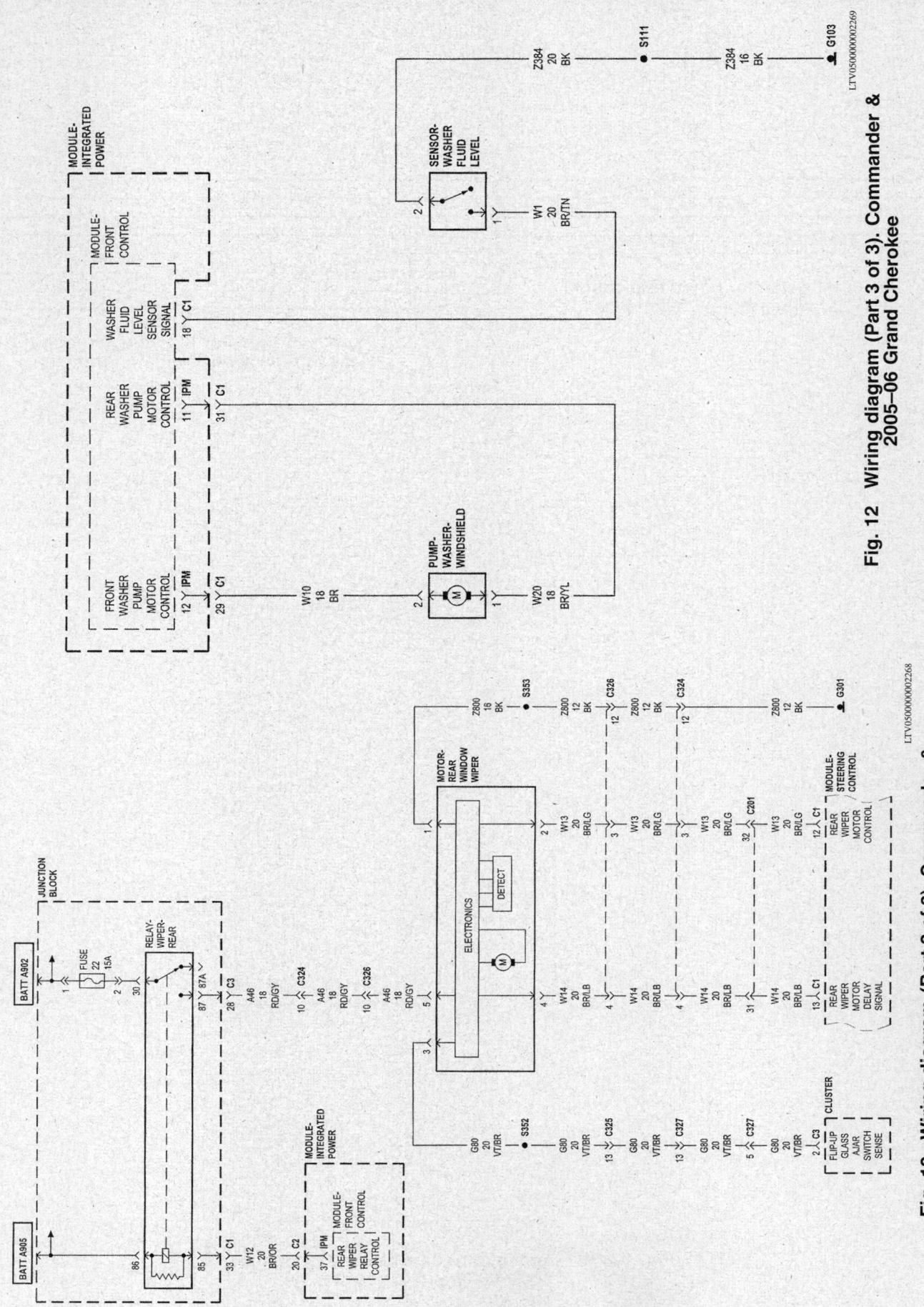

Fig. 12 Wiring diagram (Part 3 of 3). Commander & 2005–06 Grand Cherokee

Fig. 12 Wiring diagram (Part 2 of 3). Commander & 2005–06 Grand Cherokee

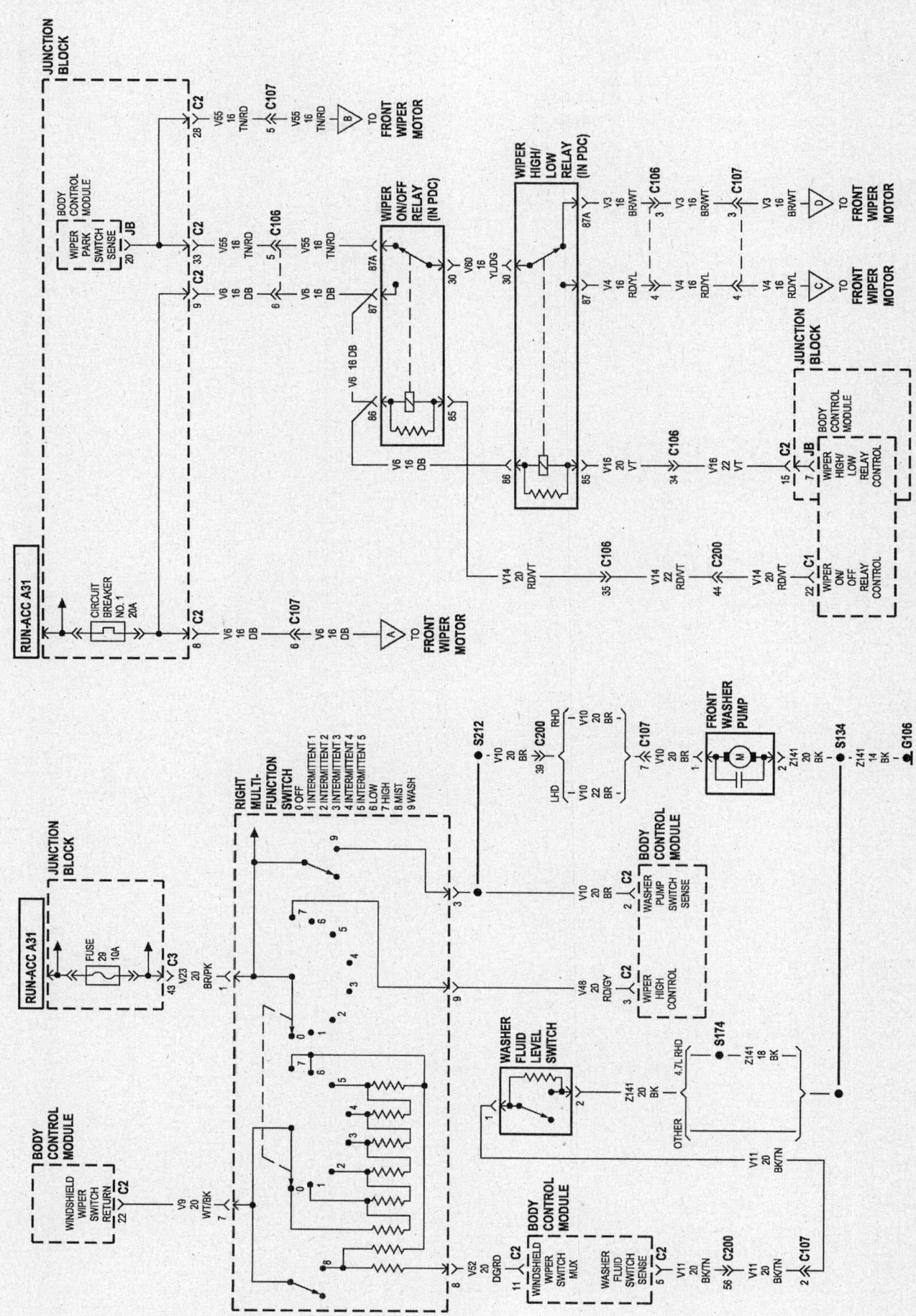

Fig. 13 Wiring diagram (Part 2 of 4). 2002–04 Grand Cherokee

Fig. 13 Wiring diagram (Part 1 of 4). 2002–04 Grand Cherokee

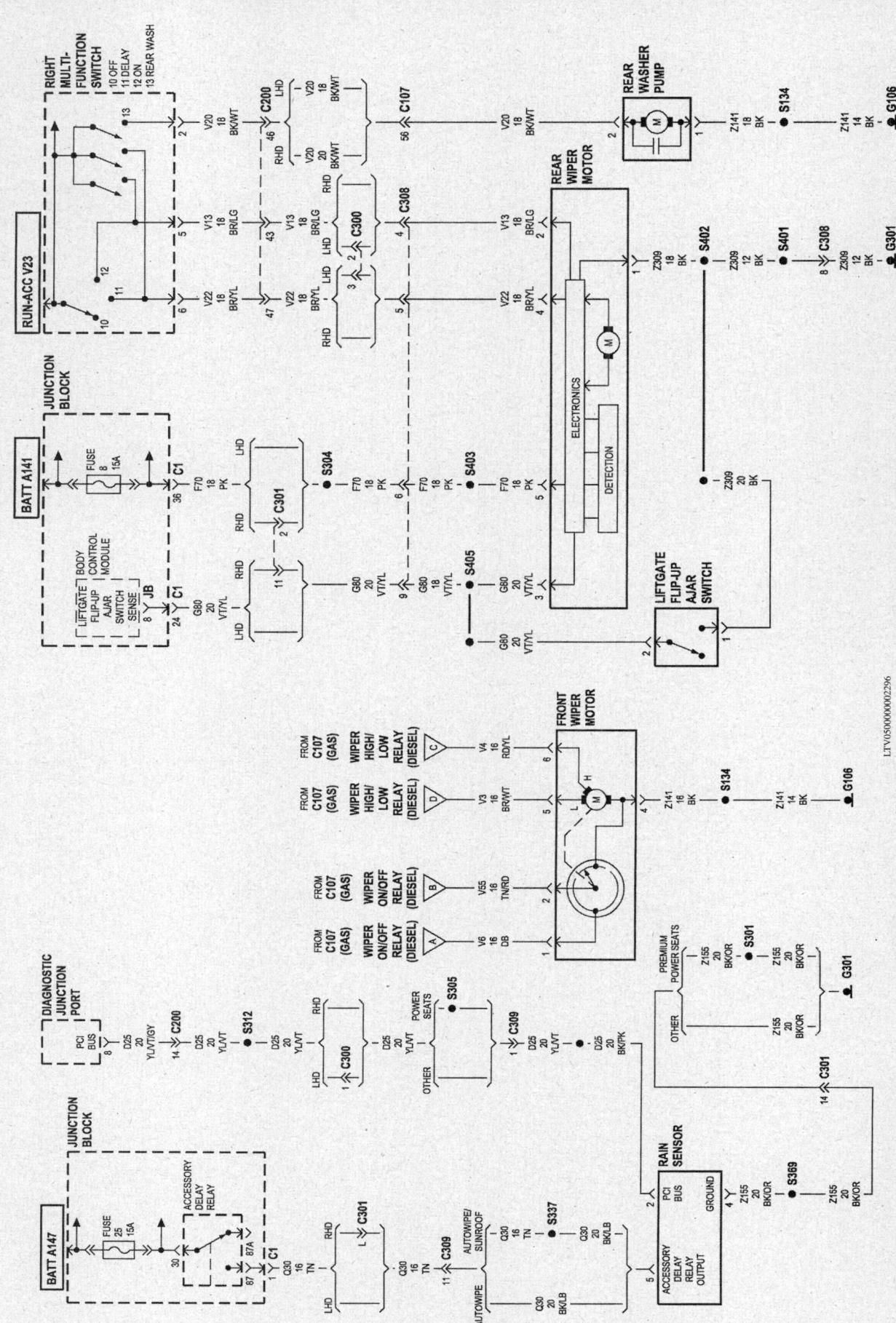

Fig. 13 Wiring diagram (Part 4 of 4). 2002–04 Grand Cherokee

Fig. 13 Wiring diagram (Part 3 of 4). 2002–04 Grand Cherokee

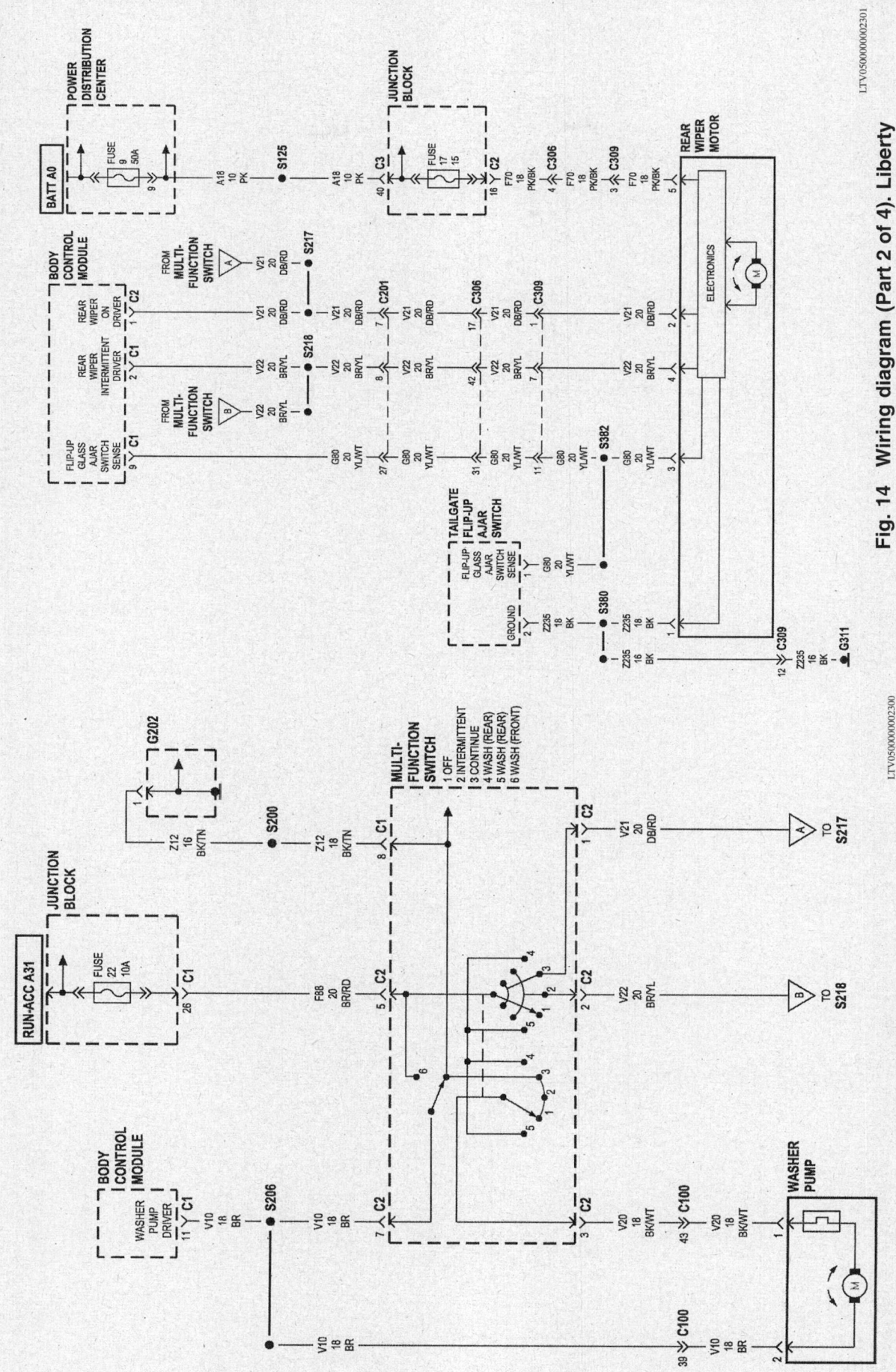

Fig. 14 Wiring diagram (Part 2 of 4). Liberty

Fig. 14 Wiring diagram (Part 1 of 4). Liberty

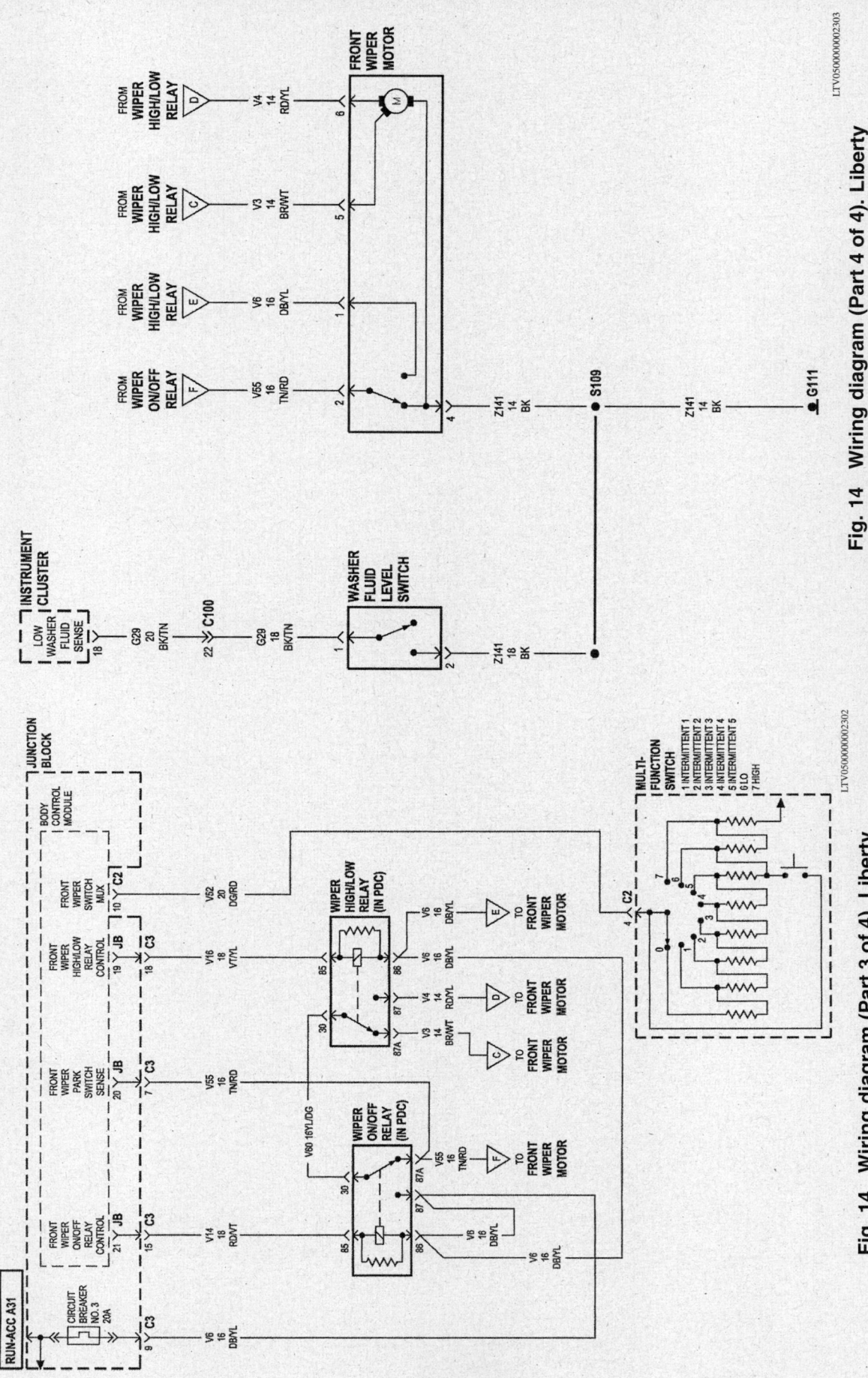

Fig. 14 Wiring diagram (Part 4 of 4). Liberty

Fig. 14 Wiring diagram (Part 3 of 4). Liberty

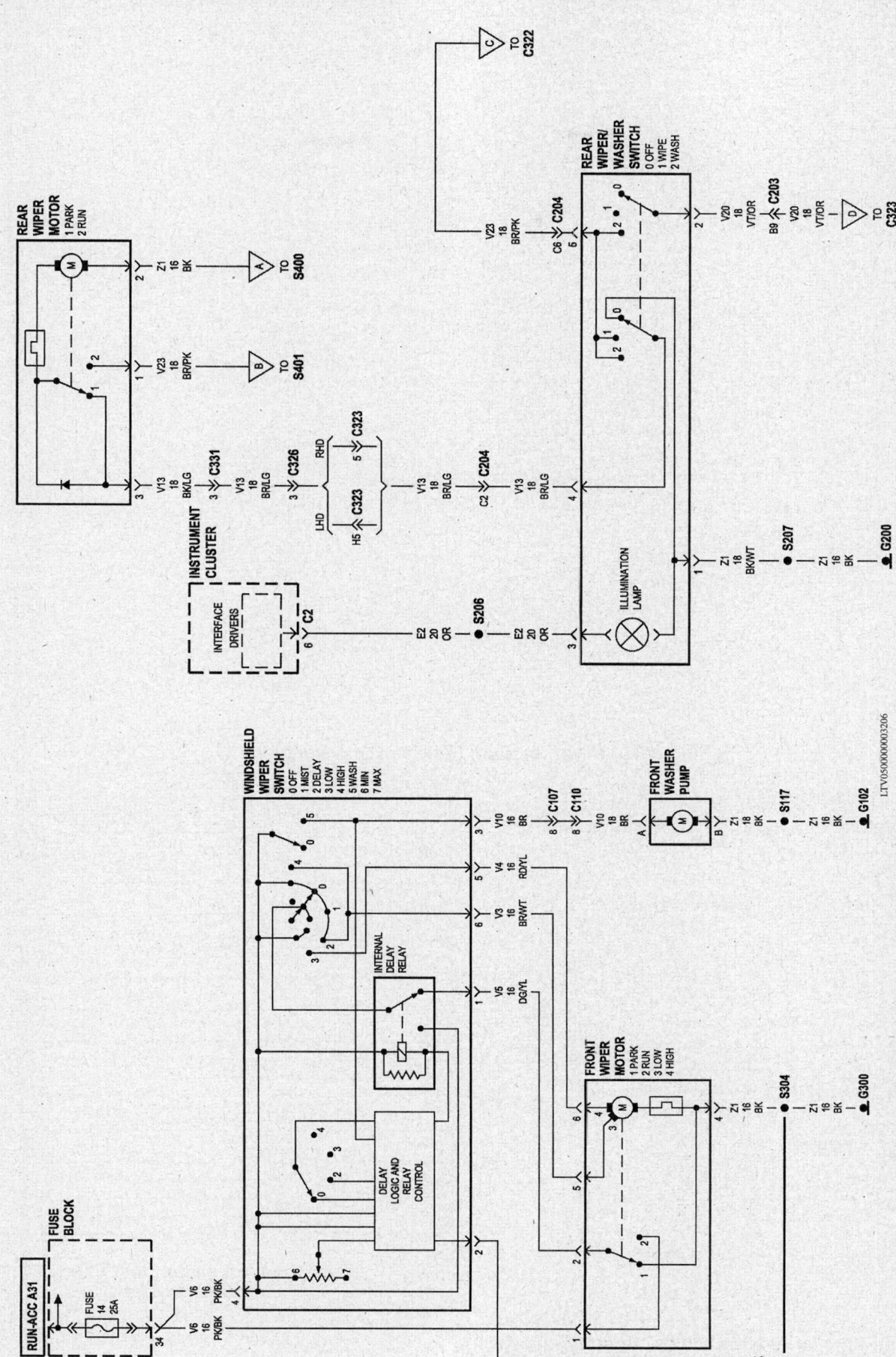

Fig. 15 Wiring diagram (Part 2 of 3). Wrangler

Fig. 15 Wiring diagram (Part 1 of 3). Wrangler

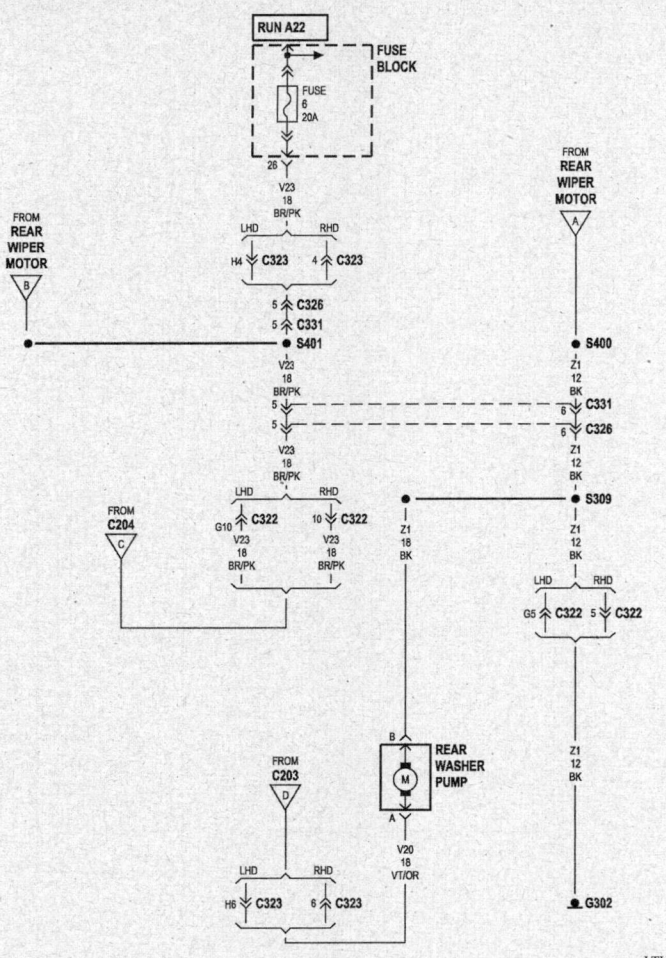

Fig. 15 Wiring diagram (Part 3 of 3). Wrangler

CONTROL STALK FUNCTION TESTS			
FUNCTION	**CAVITIES**		**RESISTANCE**
	1	**2**	
Front Wash	X	X	0 Ohms
Front Mist	X	X	650 Ohms

CONTROL KNOB FUNCTION TESTS			
FUNCTION	**CAVITIES**		**RESISTANCE**
	7	**9**	
Off	X	X	1581 Ohms
Front Delay/Sensitivity 1	X	X	695 Ohms
Front Delay/Sensitivity 2	X	X	463 Ohms
Front Delay/Sensitivity 3	X	X	323 Ohms
Front Delay/Sensitivity 4	X	X	232 Ohms
Front Delay/Sensitivity 5	X	X	169 Ohms
Front Wiper Low	X	X	96 Ohms
Front Wiper High	X	X	0 Ohms

CONTROL SLEEVE FUNCTION TESTS			
FUNCTION	**CAVITIES**		**RESISTANCE**
	4	**5**	
Rear Wash	X	X	0 Ohms
Off	X	X	1045 Ohms
Intermittent Rear Wipe	X	X	382 Ohms
Continuous Rear Wipe	X	X	174 Ohms
Rear Wash	X	X	0 Ohms

LTV0500000003221

Fig. 16 Multi-function switch tables. Commander & 2005–06 Grand Cherokee

RIGHT (WIPER) MULTI-FUNCTION SWITCH			
FRONT WIPER/WASHER SWITCH TESTS			
SWITCH POSITION	**CONTINUITY BETWEEN**	**RESISTANCE BETWEEN**	**RESISTANCE RANGE (OHMS)**
Off	-	Pins 7 & 8	4286-4379
Intermittent Wipe or Sensitivity Position 1	-	Pins 7 & 8	1445-1480
Intermittent Wipe or Sensitivity Position 2	-	Pins 7 & 8	847-870
Intermittent Wipe or Sensitivity Position 3	-	Pins 7 & 8	556-573
Intermittent Wipe or Sensitivity Position 4	-	Pins 7 & 8	367-380
Intermittent Wipe or Sensitivity Position 5	-	Pins 7 & 8	218-229
Low Speed	-	Pins 7 & 8	99-106
High Speed	Pins 7 & 9	Pins 7 & 8	99-106
Mist	-	Pins 7 & 8	49-56
Wash	Pins 1 & 3	-	-
REAR WIPER/WASHER SWITCH TESTS			
SWITCH POSITION	**CONTINUITY BETWEEN**	**RESISTANCE BETWEEN**	**RESISTANCE BETWEEN**
Off	-	-	-
Delay	Pins 1 & 6	-	-
On	Pins 1 & 5	-	-
Wash	Pins 1 & 5 & 6 & 2	-	-

LTV0500000003222

Fig. 17 Multi-function switch test chart. 2002–04 Grand Cherokee

LTV0500000003208

PASSIVE RESTRAINT SYSTEMS
Air Bag System

NOTE: Refer To "Computer Relearn Procedures" Located In The Front Of This Manual When Battery Power To The Computer Has Been Interrupted.

INDEX

	Page No.
Air Bag System Disarming & Arming	4-2
Arming	4-2
Disarming	4-2
Collision Inspection	4-2
Caravan, Town & Country & Voyager	4-2
2002	4-2
2003–06	4-2
Commander	4-3
Components	4-3
Dakota	4-3
2002–04	4-3
2005–06	4-3
Durango	4-3
2002–03	4-3
2004–06	4-4
Full Size Pickup	4-4
Full Size Van	4-4
Components	4-4
Grand Cherokee	4-4
Liberty	4-4
Components	4-4
PT Cruiser	4-4
Components	4-4
Pacifica	4-4
Sprinter	4-4
Components	4-4
Wrangler	4-4
2002	4-4
2003–06	4-5
Component Locations	4-2
Component Service	4-5
Air Bag Control Module (ACM), Replace	4-10
Dakota & Durango	4-10
Full Size Van	4-10
Grand Cherokee	4-10
Liberty	4-10
Sprinter	4-10
Wrangler	4-10
Air Bag Module Disposal	4-12
Clockspring, Replace	4-9
Driver Air Bag Module, Replace	4-5
Caravan, Pacifica, Town & Country & Voyager	4-5

	Page No.
Commander	4-5
Dakota, Durango, Full Size Pickup, Full Size Van, Grand Cherokee & Wrangler	4-5
Liberty & Sprinter	4-5
PT Cruiser	4-5
Front Impact Sensor, Replace	4-10
Caravan, Town & Country & Voyager	4-10
Except Caravan, Town & Country & Voyager	4-10
PT Cruiser	4-11
Pacifica	4-11
Knee Blocker Air Bag Module, Replace	4-5
Caravan, Pacifica, Town & Country & Voyager	4-5
PT Cruiser	4-5
Occupant Classification Module, Replace	4-11
Caravan, Pacifica, PT Cruiser & Town & Country	4-11
Commander & Grand Cherokee	4-11
Dakota, Durango & Liberty	4-11
Occupant Restraint Controller, Replace	4-11
Caravan, Town & Country & Voyager	4-11
Commander & PT Cruiser	4-11
Dakota	4-11
Durango & 2005–06 Grand Cherokee	4-11
Full Size Pickup	4-11
Pacifica	4-11
Passenger Air Bag Module, Replace	4-6
2002–04 Dakota & 2002–03 Durango	4-6
2005–06 Dakota & 2004–06 Durango	4-6
Caravan, Town & Country & Voyager	4-6
Commander	4-6
Full Size Pickup	4-6
Full Size Van	4-7

	Page No.
Grand Cherokee	4-7
Liberty	4-7
PT Cruiser	4-7
Pacifica	4-7
Sprinter	4-7
Wrangler	4-7
Passenger Side Air Bag On/Off Switch, Replace	4-11
Dakota	4-11
Full Size Pickup	4-11
Full Size Van & Wrangler	4-11
Roof Panel Air Bag Module, Replace	4-7
Caravan, Town & Country & Voyager	4-7
Commander	4-7
Dakota	4-8
Durango	4-8
Full Size Pickup	4-8
Grand Cherokee	4-8
Liberty	4-8
Pacifica	4-9
Sprinter	4-9
Side Impact Air Bag Module	4-9
PT Cruiser	4-9
Side Impact Sensor, Replace	4-11
Caravan, PT Cruiser & Town & Country	4-11
Commander, Grand Cherokee & Pacifica	4-12
Dakota	4-12
Durango	4-12
Full Size Pickup	4-12
Liberty	4-12
Sprinter	4-12
Steering Control Module	4-9
Commander, Grand Cherokee & PT Cruiser	4-9
Description & Operation	4-2
Diagnosis & Testing	4-2
General Inspection	4-2
Precautions	4-2
Tightening Specifications	4-13

AIR BAG SYSTEM DISARMING & ARMING

Disarming

Refer to "Air Bag System Precautions" in the front of this manual for air bag system disarming and arming procedures.

Arming

Refer to "Air Bag System Precautions" in the front of this manual for air bag system disarming and arming procedures.

DESCRIPTION & OPERATION

The Supplemental Restraint System (SRS) is designed to supplement drivers and passengers seat belts to help reduce risk or severity of injury to front seat occupants by activating and deploying a driver, and, if equipped, passenger air bag in certain frontal collisions.

DaimlerChrysler and Jeep light duty trucks and vans use three types of air bag control modules (ACM). The Air Bag System Diagnostic Module (ASDM) is mechanically triggered, using two front impact sensors and a sensor inside the ACM. The Air Bag Electronic Control Module (AECM) used on the Full Size Van is electronically triggered, using an ACM internal sensor, only. The Occupant Restraint Controller (ORC) is used on PT Cruiser, Pacifica, Commander, Full Size Pick Up, Grand Cherokee, Liberty, Caravan, Town & Country, Voyager, Sprinter and Wangler. The other major SRS components are air bag modules, clocksprings and impact sensors. If any of these parts should fail, they must be replaced, as they cannot be repaired.

The ASDM systems are designed so that the air bag(s) will deploy when the safing sensor plus either impact sensor simultaneously activate while ignition switch in On position. The AECM SRS air bag(s) will deploy when the internal electronic sensor is triggered.

The fasteners, screws and bolts used for air bag components have special coatings and are specifically designed for air bag systems. They must not be replaced with substitutes. If fastener replacement is required, use correct fasteners provided in service package.

PRECAUTIONS

Always wear safety glasses when servicing an air bag equipped vehicle or when handling an air bag module.

Because this system is a sensitive, complex electro-mechanical unit, before attempting to diagnose, remove or install any air bag system component, you must first disarm air bag system as outlined under "Air Bag System Disarming & Arming."

The fasteners, screws and bolts used for air bag components have special coatings and are specifically designed for air bag

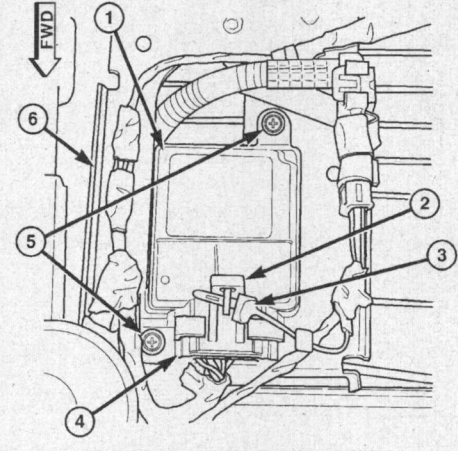

1 - OCCUPANT CLASSIFICATION MODULE (OCM)
2 - LOCK TOWER
4 - CONNECTOR
5 - SCREW (2)
6 - BRACKET

LTV0500000003223

Fig. 1 OCM location. Caravan, Town & Country & Voyager

system. They must not be replaced with substitutes. If fastener replacement is required, use correct fasteners provided in service package.

COMPONENT LOCATIONS

Refer to **Figs. 1 through 18** for air bag system component locations.

DIAGNOSIS & TESTING

GENERAL INSPECTION

Refer to **MOTOR's "Air Bag Manual"** or **"Air Bag Diagnostics CD"** for air bag system diagnosis and testing procedures.

A visual inspection consists of physically looking for possible cause of a malfunction. A careful and thorough visual inspection of components may quickly identify malfunction cause and eliminate need for diagnostic testing. If a malfunction is not resolved by visual inspection, proceed with diagnostic testing.

1. **On models equipped with front impact sensors,** ensure both sensors are properly install with three fasteners each.
2. **On all models,** turn ignition switch to On.
3. If air bag warning lamp does not light, proceed with diagnostic testing.
4. If air bag warning lamp fails to go out after ten seconds, proceed with diagnostic testing.
5. Check air bag control module (ACM) case and brackets for dents, cracks or deformities.
6. Check ACM connectors and lock levers for damage and terminals for deformities.
7. Remove air bag module as outlined under "Component Service."
8. **Never attempt to measure circuit resistance of air bag module even with a specified tester.**

9. Check air bag pad cover for dents, cracks or deformities.
10. Check air bag module for dents, cracks or deformities.
11. Check hooks and connectors for damage, terminals for deformities and harness for binds.

COLLISION INSPECTION

On vehicles that have experienced air bag deployment, certain SRS components must be replaced.

After all collisions, minor or major, inspect system as outlined under "Diagnosis & Testing," section using "General Inspection" procedure.

Caravan, Town & Country & Voyager

2002
COMPONENTS
Inspection

All other air bag and vehicle components should be closely inspected following any air bag deployment, and should be replaced when visible damage is incurred.

Replacement

The following components are mandatory replacement items following an air bag deployment according to current vehicle manufacturer recommendations.
1. Complete steering column assembly.
2. Lower steering column coupler.
3. Steering wheel.
4. Clockspring.
5. Driver air bag module.
6. Passenger air bag module.
7. Upper instrument panel with pad.

2003-06
COMPONENTS
Inspection

All air bag and vehicle components should be closely inspected following any air bag deployment, and should be replaced when visible damage is incurred

Replacement

The following components are mandatory replacement items following a driver air bag deployment according to current vehicle manufacturer recommendations.
1. Driver air bag module.
2. Clockspring assembly.
3. Steering wheel.
4. Complete steering column assembly w/lower steering column coupler.

The following components are mandatory replacement items following a passenger air bag deployment according to current vehicle manufacturer recommendations.
1. Passenger air bag module.
2. Instrument panel and pad assembly.

The following components are mandatory replacement items following a Knee blocker air bag deployment according to current vehicle manufacturer recommendations.

1. Knee blocker air bag.
2. Instrument panel and pad assembly.

The following components are mandatory replacement items following a roof air bag deployment according to current vehicle manufacturer recommendations.

1. roof air bag assembly.
2. Headliner.
3. A, B, and C-pillar trim on deployed side.

After an impact event, either front, rear, or side, the OCS system components need to be inspected and replaced if found to be damaged.

1. Belt tension sensor.
2. Occupant classification module (OCM).
3. Passenger air bag ON/Off indicator.
4. Seat weight bladder and sensor.

Commander

COMPONENTS

INSPECTION

The following components must be inspected for damage and replaced if necessary, following a collision.

1. Front impact sensors.
2. ORC mounting brackets
3. Side impact sensors.
4. Sunroof drain tubes and hoses following a side roof air bag deployment.
5. Squib 1 and squib 2 circuits.

Replacement

The following components are mandatory replacement items following a driver air bag deployment according to current vehicle manufacturer recommendations.

1. Driver air bag module.
2. Steering control module.
3. Seat belt tensioners.

The following components are mandatory replacement items following a passenger air bag deployment according to current vehicle manufacturer recommendations.

1. Instrument panel top pad.
2. Passenger air bag module.
3. Seat belt tensioners.

The following components are mandatory replacement items following a roof air bag deployment according to current vehicle manufacturer recommendations.

1. roof air bag module.
2. Headliner.
3. Upper A, B, C and D-pillar trim.

Dakota

2002-04

COMPONENTS

Inspection

All vehicle components should be closely inspected following any supplemental restraint deployment, but are to be replaced only as required by the extent of the visible

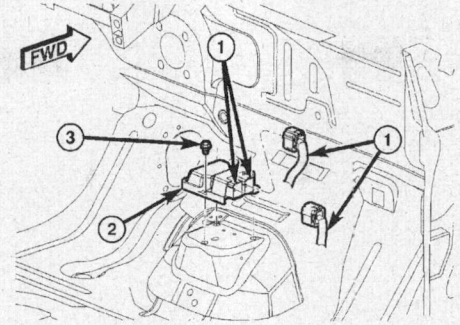

1 - ORC ELECTRICAL CONNECTORS
2 - ORC
3 - ORC MOUNTING SCREWS

LTV0500000003224

Fig. 2 ORC location. Caravan, Town & Country & Voyager

damage incurred. It is critical that the mounting surfaces and/or mounting bracket for the Air Bag Control Module (ACM) be closely inspected and restored to its original condition following any vehicle impact damage. Because the ACM contains the impact sensors that are used by the supplemental restraint system to monitor or confirm the direction and severity of a vehicle impact, improper orientation or insecure fastening of this component may cause air bags not to deploy when required, or to deploy when not required. All other vehicle components should be closely inspected following any supplemental restraint deployment, but are to be replaced only as required by the extent of the visible damage incurred.

Replacement

The following components are mandatory replacement items following an air bag deployment according to current vehicle manufacturer recommendations.

1. Air bag modules.
2. Clockspring.
3. Instrument panel.
4. Steering column assembly
5. Seat belt tensioners.

2005-06

COMPONENTS

Inspection

All vehicle components should be closely inspected following any supplemental restraint deployment, but are to be replaced only as required by the extent of the visible damage incurred. On vehicles with an optional sunroof, the sunroof drain tubes and hoses must be closely inspected following a side roof air bag deployment. It is also critical that the mounting surfaces and mounting brackets for the Occupant Restraint Controller (ORC), side impact sensors, and front impact sensors be closely inspected and restored to their original conditions following any vehicle impact damage. Because the ORC and each front and side impact sensor are used by the supplemental restraint system to monitor or confirm the direction and severity of a vehicle impact, improper orientation or insecure fastening of these components may cause air bags not to deploy when required, or to de-

ploy when not required. Multistage air bags with multiple initiators (squibs) must be checked to determine that all squibs were used during the deployment event.

Replacement

The following components are mandatory replacement items following a driver air bag deployment according to current vehicle manufacturer recommendations.

1. Drivers air bag module.
2. Clockspring.
3. Seat belt tensioners.

The following components are mandatory replacement items following a passenger air bag deployment according to current vehicle manufacturer recommendations.

1. Passenger air bag module.
2. Passenger air bag door.
3. Seat belt tensioners.

The following components are mandatory replacement items following a roof air bag deployment according to current vehicle manufacturer recommendations.

1. roof air bag module.
2. Headliner.
3. A, B, and C/D-pillar trim on deployed side.

Durango

2002-03

COMPONENTS

Inspection

It is critical that the mounting surfaces and/or mounting brackets for the Air Bag Control Module (ACM) and Side Impact Air bag Control Module (SIACM) be closely inspected and restored to their original conditions following any vehicle impact damage. Because the ACM and SIACM each contain impact sensors that are used by the supplemental restraint system to monitor or confirm the direction and severity of a vehicle impact, improper orientation or insecure fastening of these components may cause air bags not to deploy when required, or to deploy when not required. All other vehicle components should be closely inspected following any supplemental restraint deployment, but are to be replaced only as required by the extent of the visible damage incurred.

Replacement

The following components are mandatory replacement items following a driver air bag deployment according to current vehicle manufacturer recommendations.

1. Drivers air bag module.
2. Clockspring.
3. Seat belt tensioners.
4. Steering column assembly.

The following components are mandatory replacement items following a passenger air bag deployment according to current vehicle manufacturer recommendations.

1. Passenger air bag module.
2. Seat belt tensioners.

The following components are mandatory replacement items following a roof air

PASSIVE RESTRAINT SYSTEMS

bag deployment according to current vehicle manufacturer recommendations.
1. roof air bag module.
2. Headliner.
3. A, B, and C-pillar trim on deployed side.

2004-06

Refer to "2005–06 Dakota" for inspection and replacement requirements not covered in this section.

Full Size Pickup

Refer to "2005–06"section of "Dakota" for inspection and replacement requirements not covered in this section.

Full Size Van

COMPONENTS

INSPECTION

All vehicle components should be closely inspected following any supplemental restraint deployment, but are to be replaced only as required by the extent of the visible damage incurred.

REPLACEMENT

The following components are mandatory replacement items following a driver air bag deployment according to current vehicle manufacturer recommendations.
1. Clockspring.
2. Driver air bag module.
3. Seat belt tensioners.
4. Steering column.

The following components are mandatory replacement items following a passenger air bag deployment according to current vehicle manufacturer recommendations.
1. Passenger air bag module.
2. Passenger air bag door.
3. Seat belt tensioners.

Grand Cherokee

Refer to "Commander" for inspection and replacement requirements not covered in this section.

Liberty

COMPONENTS

INSPECTION

All vehicle components should be closely inspected following any supplemental restraint deployment, but are to be replaced only as required by the extent of the visible damage incurred. On vehicles with an optional sunroof, the sunroof drain tubes and hoses must be closely inspected following a side roof air bag deployment. It is also critical that the mounting surfaces and/or mounting brackets for the Air Bag Control Module (ACM), side impact sensors, and front impact sensors be closely inspected and restored to their original conditions following any vehicle impact damage. Because the ACM and each front and side impact sensor are used by the supplemen-

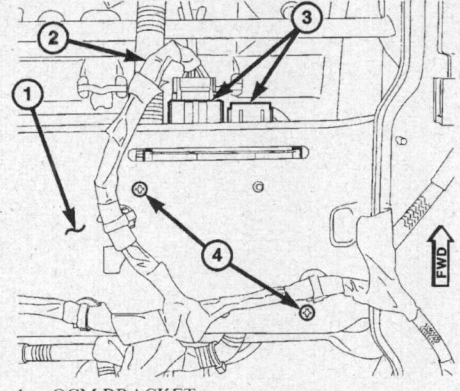

1- OCM BRACKET
2- ELECTRICAL CONNECTORS
3- OCM
4- MOUNTING SCREWS

LTV0500000003225

Fig. 3   OCM location. Commander

tal restraint system to monitor or confirm the direction and severity of a vehicle impact, improper orientation or insecure fastening of these components may cause air bags not to deploy when required, or to deploy when not required. Multistage air bags with multiple initiators (squibs) must be checked to determine that all squibs were used during the deployment event.

Replacement

The following components are mandatory replacement items following a drivers air bag deployment according to current vehicle manufacturer recommendations.
1. Drivers air bag module.
2. Clockspring.
3. Seat belt tensioners.

The following components are mandatory replacement items following a passenger air bag deployment according to current vehicle manufacturer recommendations.
1. Passenger air bag module.
2. Passenger air bag door.
3. Passenger air bag mounting brackets.
4. Seat belt tensioners.

The following components are mandatory replacement items following a roof air bag deployment according to current vehicle manufacturer recommendations.
1. Roof air bag module.
2. Headliner.
3. Upper A, B, C and D-pillar trim.

Pacifica

Refer to "2003–06" section of "Caravan, Town & Country & Voyager" for inspection and replacement requirements not covered in this section.

PT Cruiser

COMPONENTS

INSPECTION

All air bag and vehicle components should be closely inspected following any air bag deployment, and should be replaced when visible damage is incurred.

Replacement

After a seat air bag has been deployed due to a collision, the following MUST be replaced.

Refer to "2003–06 Caravan & Town & Country" for additional replacement requirements not covered in this section.
1. Side impact air bag module.

Sprinter

COMPONENTS

INSPECTION

It is critical that the mounting surfaces and/or mounting brackets for the Air Bag Control Module (ACM) and the side impact sensors be closely inspected and restored to their original conditions following any vehicle impact damage. Because the ACM and each impact sensor are used by the supplemental restraint system to monitor or confirm the direction and severity of a vehicle impact, improper orientation or insecure fastening of these components may cause air bags not to deploy when required, or to deploy when not required

Replacement

The following components are mandatory replacement items following a Drivers air bag deployment according to current vehicle manufacturer recommendations.
1. Drivers air bag module.
2. Clockspring.
3. Seat belt tensioners.
4. Steering wheel.

The following components are mandatory replacement items following a passenger air bag deployment according to current vehicle manufacturer recommendations.
1. Instrument Panel.
2. Passenger air bag module.
3. Seat belt tensioners.

Wrangler

2002

COMPONENTS

Inspection

All vehicle air bag components should be closely inspected, but are to be replaced only as required by the extent of the visible damage incurred.

Replacement

The following components are mandatory replacement items following an air bag deployment according to current vehicle manufacture recommendations.
1. Clockspring.
2. Drivers and Passenger air bag modules.
3. Driver air bag trim cover.
4. Horn switch.
5. Passenger air bag door.

2003-06
COMPONENTS
Inspection

It is critical that the mounting surfaces and/or mounting bracket for the Air Bag Control Module (ACM) be closely inspected and restored to its original condition following any vehicle impact damage. Because the ACM contains impact sensors that are used by the supplemental restraint system to monitor or confirm the direction and severity of a vehicle impact, improper orientation or insecure fastening of this component may cause air bags not to deploy when required, or to deploy when not required. All other vehicle components should be closely inspected following any supplemental restraint deployment, but are to be replaced only as required by the extent of the visible damage incurred.

Replacement

The following components are mandatory replacement items following a driver air bag deployment according to current vehicle manufacture recommendations.
1. Clockspring.
2. Driver air bag module.

The following components are mandatory replacement items following a passenger air bag deployment according to current vehicle manufacturer recommendations.
1. Passenger air bag module.
2. Passenger air bag door.

COMPONENT SERVICE

Driver Air Bag Module, Replace

CARAVAN, PACIFICA, TOWN & COUNTRY & VOYAGER

1. Disarm air bag as outlined under "Air Bag System Disarming & Arming."
2. Remove two screws retaining driver air bag to steering wheel.
3. Disconnect wire connectors from back of driver air bag module.
4. **On models equipped with steering wheel mounted speed control,** disconnect 4–way harness connector from speed control/horn harness to clockspring.
5. **On models equipped with steering wheel mounted radio controls,** disconnect 2–way connector from remote radio control harness.
6. **On all models,** remove driver air bag from vehicle.
7. Reverse procedure to install.

COMMANDER

1. Disarm air bag as outlined under "Air Bag System Disarming & Arming."
2. Remove air bag module attaching screws from back of steering wheel.
3. Pull driver air bag away from steering

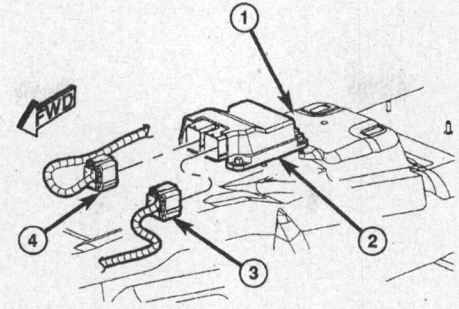

1- TRANSMISSION TUNNEL
2- ORC
3- INSTRUMENT PANEL CONNECTOR
4- BODY HARNESS CONNECTOR

LTV0500000003226

Fig. 4 ORC location. Commander

wheel far enough to access electrical connections at back of air bag housing.
4. Disconnect driver air bag jumper harness connector for horn switch, cruise control switches and remote radio switches on back of driver air bag trim cover from receptacles on upper clockspring rotor.
5. Disconnect driver air bag pigtail electrical connectors. Connectors are secured by an integral lock to air bag inflator connector receptacles. Firmly grasp and pull lock straight out from connector insulator, then pull insulators straight out from air bag inflator to disconnect.
6. Remove driver air bag from steering wheel.
7. Reverse procedure to install.

DAKOTA, DURANGO, FULL SIZE PICKUP, FULL SIZE VAN, GRAND CHEROKEE & WRANGLER

1. Disarm air bag as outlined under "Air Bag System Disarming & Arming."
2. Remove air bag module attaching nuts from steering wheel back.
3. Pull air bag module away from steering wheel, then disconnect wire harness horn switch feed connector from horn switch feed pigtail.
4. Disconnect clockspring driver air bag wire harness connector insulator from air bag inflator connector.
5. Remove driver air bag from steering wheel.
6. Reverse procedure to install.

LIBERTY & SPRINTER

1. Disarm air bag as outlined under "Air Bag System Disarming & Arming."
2. Remove air bag module attaching nuts from steering wheel back.
3. Pull driver air bag module away from steering wheel far enough to access three electrical connections on back of air bag housing.
4. Disconnect electrical connector for horn switch from horn switch feed pigtail wire connector.
5. Disconnect clockspring driver air bag pigtail wire connectors.
6. Remove driver air bag module from

steering wheel.
7. Reverse procedure to install.

PT CRUISER
2002-05

1. Disarm air bag as outlined under "Air Bag System Disarming & Arming."
2. Remove upper and lower steering column shrouds.
3. Using suitable 90° internal snap ring pliers, pry open retaining clip on back of steering wheel to release retaining pin. Pull or press rearward on air bag module to release pin slightly.
4. Using suitable 90° internal snap ring pliers, pry open retaining clip at the same time gently pry pin away from retaining clip.
5. With driver air bag module released from steering wheel, pull module rearward and disconnect electrical connectors.
6. Remove driver side air bag module.
7. Reverse procedure to install.

2006

1. Disarm air bag as outlined under "Air Bag System Disarming & Arming."
2. Insert tip of a small flat bladed screwdriver into one of top two access holes.
3. Ensure screwdriver is behind driver air bag loop then turn in either direction to release loop from hook.
4. Repeat for additional access holes.
5. Disconnect squib connectors and speed control connector.
6. Remove air bag module from steering wheel.
7. Reverse procedure to install.

Knee Blocker Air Bag Module, Replace

CARAVAN, PACIFICA, TOWN & COUNTRY & VOYAGER

1. Disarm air bag as outlined under "Air Bag System Disarming & Arming."
2. Remove steering column opening cover retaining screws.
3. Disconnect knee blocker air bag electrical connector.
4. Remove knee blocker air bag retaining bolts from air bag.
5. Remove knee blocker air bag from vehicle.
6. Reverse procedure to install.

PT CRUISER

1. Disarm air bag as outlined under "Air Bag System Disarming & Arming."
2. Tilt steering column to full upwards position.
3. Gently pry out on upper corners of under column cover on each side of steering column using a trim stick or equivalent.
4. Push down and pull out slightly on under steering column cover so loop tabs may be undone.
5. Remove screw to left instrument panel end cap, then unsnap cap.

6. Disconnect power mirror electrical connector.
7. Remove upper screws to knee blocker air bag trim cover.
8. Disconnect trim cover hook and loop retainers through access hole to left of knee blocker air bag module.
9. Remove knee blocker air bag to instrument panel mounting bolts.
10. Disconnect knee blocker air bag electrical connector, then remove module.
11. Reverse procedure to install.

Passenger Air Bag Module, Replace

CARAVAN, TOWN & COUNTRY & VOYAGER

1. Disarm air bag as outlined under "Air Bag System Disarming & Arming."
2. Remove center console bin between front seats.
3. Remove lefthand and righthand front door sill plates.
4. Remove lefthand and righthand cowl panels.
5. Remove lower steering column cover.
6. Disconnect parking brake lever from knee blocker reinforcement.
7. Remove Data Link Connector (DLC) from knee blocker.
8. Remove knee blocker mounting screws.
9. Remove lefthand and righthand A-pillar lower extension trim panels.
10. Remove three lefthand instrument panel A-pillar retaining bolts and loosen instrument panel roll down bolt.
11. Remove brake pedal support bracket to instrument panel mounting nuts.
12. Remove lefthand upper A-pillar trim.
13. Remove six screws and two wiring electrical connectors to lower instrument panel cubby bin at bottom of center stack.
14. Remove lefthand and righthand instrument panel center stack support to floor retaining nuts.
15. Remove righthand instrument panel end cap.
16. Remove three righthand instrument panel A-pillar retaining bolts and loosen instrument panel roll down bolt.
17. Remove righthand upper A-pillar trim.
18. Open glove box, pinch in sides and roll down towards floor. With a firm pull, snap glove box door off hinges and remove.
19. Pry up on rear of instrument panel top cover using suitable trim stick and then pull rearward and out.
20. Pry off filler bezel just above cup holder using suitable trim stick to expose lower screws to center bezel
21. Remove two screws and then using a trim stick or equivalent, gently pry off instrument panel center bezel.
22. Remove center bezel wiring electrical connectors to HVAC control and switch assembly.
23. Slide cup holder assembly from instrument panel.
24. Remove nineteen screws to right lower instrument panel trim (glove box sur-

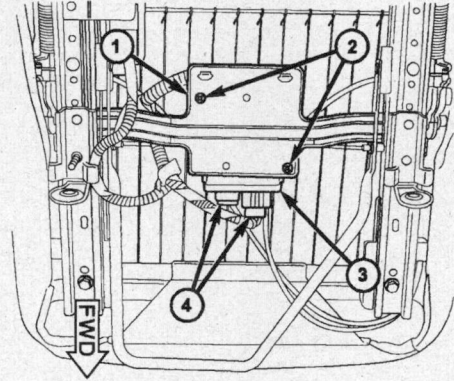

1- OCM BRACKET
2- MOUNTING SCREWS
3- OCCUPANT CLASSIFICATION MODULE
4- ELECTRICAL CONNECTORS

LTV0500000003227

Fig. 5   OCM location. Dakota

round), unplug glove box lamp wire connector, and remove panel.
25. Remove radio.
26. Remove one far left instrument panel speaker retaining screw.
27. Remove four screws along top front edge of instrument panel cover/pad.
28. Remove seven lower instrument panel cover/pad retaining screws starting from righthand side of vehicle and only removing these seven.
29. Remove six upper fence line instrument panel retaining bolts.
30. Roll back instrument panel just enough to increase access to passenger air bag retaining bolts at reinforcement. Lift instrument panel up slightly so as not to damage air distribution to HVAC unit seal
31. Disconnect passenger air bag electrical connector, then separate electrical connector from instrument panel reinforcement.
32. Remove two passenger air bag to instrument panel cover/pad retaining screws.
33. Remove three passenger air bag to instrument panel reinforcement retaining bolts.
34. Pull rearward slightly on instrument panel cover/pad to maneuver passenger air bag out from reinforcement and instrument panel.
35. Reverse procedure to install.

COMMANDER

1. Disarm air bag as outlined under "Air Bag System Disarming & Arming."
2. Remove instrument panel as outlined under "Dash Panel, Replace."
3. Place instrument panel on a suitable work surface with top pad facing down.
4. Disconnect passenger air bag pigtail electrical connector from instrument panel wire harness connector for air bag.
5. Remove air bag mounting bracket to instrument panel structural support attaching screws.
6. Remove top pad from instrument panel.
7. Disengage each of hooks of air bag

housing from windows in forward and rearward vertical walls of air bag retainer on underside of top pad.
8. Lift housing, inflator, and cushion as a unit from retainer receptacle.
9. Reverse procedure to install.

2002-04 DAKOTA & 2002-03 DURANGO

1. Disarm air bag as outlined under "Air Bag System Disarming & Arming."
2. Remove glove box module from instrument panel.
3. Remove radio from instrument panel.
4. Disconnect passenger air bag electrical connector from pigtail wire connector through radio opening in instrument panel.
5. Disengage passenger air bag pigtail wire connector retainers from instrument panel armature.
6. Remove passenger air bag front brackets to instrument panel armature mounting screws.
7. Remove passenger air bag rear brackets to glove box opening upper reinforcement attaching screws.
8. Gently pry top of passenger air bag door away from instrument panel far enough to disengage five snap features on air bag door from receptacles in instrument panel.
9. Remove passenger air bag module and air bag door from instrument panel as a unit.
10. Reverse procedure to install.

2005-06 DAKOTA & 2004-06 DURANGO

1. Disarm air bag as outlined under "Air Bag System Disarming & Arming."
2. Remove defroster grille from top of instrument panel.
3. Remove glove box from instrument panel.
4. Remove screws that secure passenger air bag lower bracket to instrument panel support structure through opening in instrument panel between upper glove box reinforcement and cross car beam.
5. Gently pry top of passenger air bag door away from instrument panel far enough to disengage snap features on air bag door from receptacles in instrument panel.
6. Pull passenger air bag module out of instrument panel far enough to access and disconnect instrument panel wire harness connector from air bag inflator pigtail.
7. Remove passenger air bag module from instrument panel as a unit.
8. Reverse procedure to install.

FULL SIZE PICKUP

1. Disarm air bag as outlined under "Air Bag System Disarming & Arming."
2. Remove glove box, then upper trim strip from instrument panel.
3. Remove four screws securing plastic support brackets of air bag module door panel to upper reinforcement.
4. Reach through glove box opening and disconnect air bag module connector.

5. Remove two screws securing air bag module front bracket to instrument panel.
6. Remove three screws securing air bag module rear bracket to glove box opening upper reinforcement.
7. Using trim stick or other suitable tool, start at left lower edge and gently pry air bag module door away from instrument panel top cover to disengage retainers.
8. Remove air bag door and module from instrument panel.
9. Reverse procedure to install and tighten to specifications.

FULL SIZE VAN

1. Disarm air bag as outlined under "Air Bag System Disarming & Arming."
2. Lower glove box from instrument panel.
3. Remove two large and three small screws securing air bag module rear bracket and door lower flange to glove box opening upper reinforcement.
4. Reach through glove box opening and disconnect air bag module harness connector.
5. Reach through glove box opening and remove two screws securing air bag module front bracket to instrument panel armature.
6. Using trim stick or other suitable tool, gently pry air bag module door away from instrument panel top cover to disengage five snap retainers.
7. Remove air bag door and module from instrument panel.
8. Reverse procedure to install and tighten to specifications.

GRAND CHEROKEE

2002-04

1. Disarm air bag as outlined under "Air Bag System Disarming & Arming."
2. Remove instrument panel top pad.
3. Remove air bag module mounting screws from front and rear air bag mounting bracket.
4. Unplug air bag wiring connect and remove air bag module.
5. If air bag is deployed, remove rear air bag mounting bracket as follows:
   a. Remove screws attaching instrument panel wiring trough to rear air bag mounting bracket.
   b. Remove heater-A/C controls.
   c. Through heater-A/C control opening, remove lefthand rear air bag mounting bracket bolts.
   d. Remove righthand mounting bolts.
   e. Remove bracket righthand end first through lower instrument panel opening.
6. Reverse procedure to install and tighten screws and bolts to specifications.

2005-06

Refer to "Commander" for air bag replacement procedures.

LIBERTY

1. Disarm air bag as outlined under "Air Bag System Disarming & Arming."
2. Remove passenger air bag door from

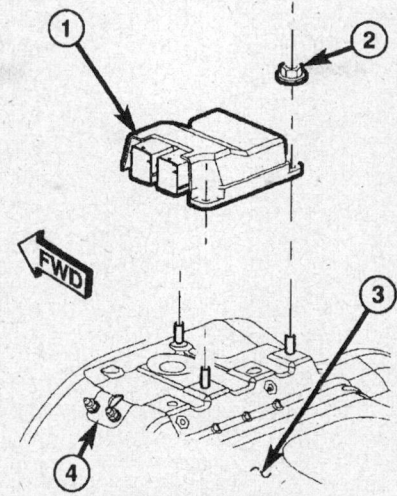

1- OCCUPANT RESTRAINT MODULE
2- RETAINING NUT
3- TRANSMISSION TUNNEL
4- ORC MOUNT

LTV0500000003228

Fig. 6 ORC location. Dakota

instrument panel.
3. Remove mounting screws on each side of passenger air bag housing that secure passenger air bag module to metal brackets on instrument panel support structure.
4. Disconnect passenger air bag module electrical connector from retainer.
5. Pull passenger air bag module away from instrument panel far enough to access wire harness connectors for air bag.
6. Disconnect passenger air bag module electrical connectors.
7. Remove passenger air bag module from instrument panel as a unit.
8. Reverse procedure to install.

PACIFICA

1. Disarm air bag as outlined under "Air Bag System Disarming & Arming."
2. Remove glove box assembly.
3. Remove passenger air bag module to instrument panel pad and door mounting screws.
4. Remove passenger air bag module to crosscar beam mounting screws.
5. Disconnect passenger air bag module electrical connector.
6. Pull passenger air bag rearward and down to remove through glove box opening.
7. Reverse procedure to install.

PT CRUISER

1. Disarm air bag as outlined under "Air Bag System Disarming & Arming."
2. Remove instrument panel top cover.
3. Open glove box, then push in on sides and lower to floor.
4. Remove right instrument panel end cap.
5. Remove four passenger air bag cover screws along bottom end of air bag cover.
6. Remove two passenger air bag cover screws along top edge of air bag cover.

7. Remove two nuts retaining passenger air bag to instrument panel inside glove box opening.
8. Lift module up until electrical connector is visible, then disconnect.
9. Remove passenger air bag module.
10. Reverse procedure to install.

SPRINTER

1. Disarm air bag as outlined under "Air Bag System Disarming & Arming."
2. Remove instrument panel top cover.
3. Remove passenger air bag door upper clips to instrument panel base trim mounting screws.
4. Remove screws that secure flange of passenger air bag housing to bracket on instrument panel structural support.
5. Pull passenger air bag unit rearward to disengage air bag door from lower clips and far enough to access electrical connection on right end of unit.
6. Disconnect passenger air bag module electrical connectors.
7. Remove passenger air bag module and air bag door from instrument panel as a unit.
8. Reverse procedure to install.

WRANGLER

1. Remove instrument panel as outlined under "Dash Panel, Replace."
2. Place instrument panel face down on suitable work bench, then remove three nuts securing air bag module to instrument panel armature.
3. Remove air bag module.
4. Reverse procedure to install and tighten to specifications.

Roof Panel Air Bag Module, Replace

CARAVAN, TOWN & COUNTRY & VOYAGER

1. Disarm air bag as outlined under "Air Bag System Disarming & Arming."
2. Remove headliner from vehicle.
3. Disconnect roof air bag squib connector.
4. Remove bolt from roof air bag front tether and unclip from A-pillar.
5. Remove screws that secure roof air bag to spring nuts in roof side rail.
6. Remove bolt from roof air bag inflator mounting bracket.
7. Remove bolts retaining roof air bag to roof rail in D-pillar area.
8. Grasp roof air bag, using suitable trim stick, gently pry out push fasteners to disengage roof air bag and remove it from its mounting location in side roof rail.
9. Remove roof air bag from vehicle as a unit.
10. Reverse procedure to install.

COMMANDER

1. Disarm air bag as outlined under "Air Bag System Disarming & Arming."
2. Remove headliner from vehicle.
3. Disconnect body wire harness connector from connector receptacle at

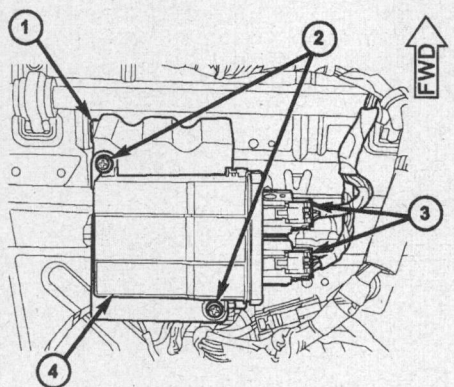

1- OCM BRACKET
2- MOUNTING SCREWS
3- ELECTRICAL CONNECTORS
4- OCM

LTV0500000003229

Fig. 7 OCM location. Durango

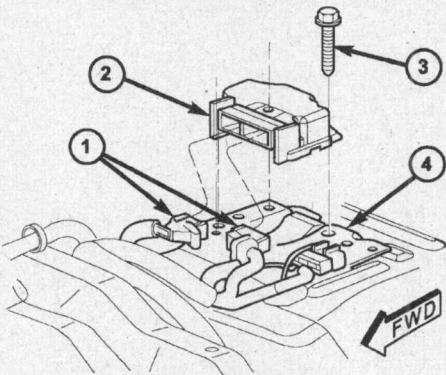

1- ELECTRICAL CONNECTORS
2- OCCUPANT RESTRAINT CONTROLLER
3- MOUNTING SCREW
4- ORC BRACKET

LTV0500000003230

Fig. 8 ORC location. Durango

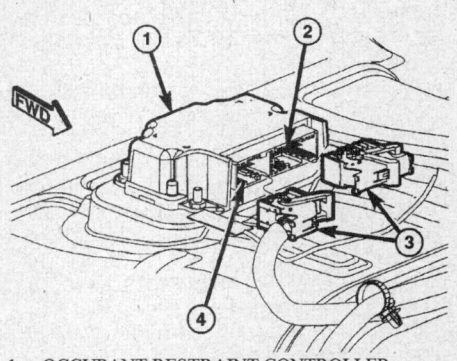

1- OCCUPANT RESTRAINT CONTROLLER
2- CONNECTOR RECEPTACLE
3- ELECTRICAL CONNECTORS
4- CONNECTOR RECEPTACLE

LTV0500000003231

Fig. 9 ORC location. Full Size Pickup

back of inflator on roof side rail between B and C-pillars.
4. Remove side roof air bag rear roof rod to U-nut mounting screw in inner quarter panel near D-pillar.
5. Remove side roof air bag rear tab to U-nut mounting screw in inner D-pillar near liftgate opening upper header panel.
6. Disengage two plastic retainers, then hook that secures side roof air bag front tether to inner A-pillar.
7. Remove eight screws that secure side roof air bag channel to box nuts in inner roof side rail.
8. Disengage two plastic push-in fasteners that secure channel to roof side rail above B-pillar.
9. Remove two screws that secure inflator mounting bracket to U-nuts in roof side rail between B and C-pillars.
10. Disengage integral hook on inflator from locating hole in roof side rail.
11. Remove side roof air bag from vehicle as a unit.
12. Reverse procedure to install.

DAKOTA

1. Disarm air bag as outlined under "Air Bag System Disarming & Arming."
2. Remove headliner and rest upon seat backs.
3. Disengage metal clip that secures side roof air bag rear tether to cab roof rear header.
4. Disengage side roof air bag front tether to inner A-pillar retainers.
5. Remove screws that secure side roof air bag to U-nuts.
6. Disconnect body wire harness electrical connector.
7. Disengage two plastic retainers from inner roof rail.
8. Remove side roof air bag from vehicle as a unit.
9. Reverse procedure to install.

DURANGO

2002–03

1. Disarm air bag as outlined under "Air Bag System Disarming & Arming."

2. Remove headliner from vehicle.
3. Remove hook that secures side roof air bag tether from slot at base of A-pillar.
4. Disengage two side roof air bag tether plastic retainer clips from A-pillar.
5. Disconnect electrical connector for side roof air bag from connector at air bag inflator.
6. Remove side roof air bag inflator and manifold tube/channel brackets to U-nuts retaining screws in roof rail.
7. Pull extruded plastic side roof air bag channel straight away from roof rail far enough to disengage all fasteners.
8. Remove side roof air bag from vehicle as a unit.
9. Reverse procedure to install.

2004–06

1. Disarm air bag as outlined under "Air Bag System Disarming & Arming."
2. Remove headliner from vehicle.
3. Remove B-pillar lower trim.
4. Disconnect side roof air bag pigtail wire connector from body electrical connector.
5. Disengage pigtail plastic retainers from inner B-pillar.
6. Remove screw that secures side roof air bag to U-nut near top D-pillar.
7. Remove screw that secures side roof air bag front tether to inner A-pillar.
8. Remove remaining screws that secure side roof air bag to U-nuts in inner roof rail and D-pillar.
9. Disengage three front tether plastic retainers from inner A-pillar.
10. Disengage four air bag plastic retainers from inner roof rail.
11. Remove side roof air bag module from vehicle through liftgate opening as a unit
12. Reverse procedure to install.

FULL SIZE PICKUP

1. Disarm air bag as outlined under "Air Bag System Disarming & Arming."
2. Remove headliner from vehicle.
3. **On mega cab models only,** remove screw and disengage retainers that secure side roof air bag rear tether to inner C-pillar.

4. **On all models,** remove screw that secures roof air bag front tether retainer to base of A-pillar.
5. Disengage roof air bag front tether plastic retainer clips from A-pillar.
6. Disconnect wire harness electrical connector.
7. Working from front to rear, remove screws that secure roof air bag inflator and manifold tube brackets to spring nuts in roof rail.
8. Remove roof air bag module from vehicle as a unit.
9. Reverse procedure to install.

GRAND CHEROKEE

1. Disarm air bag as outlined under "Air Bag System Disarming & Arming."
2. Remove headliner from vehicle.
3. Disconnect wire harness electrical connector for side roof air bag from connector at back of inflator near D-pillar.
4. Disconnect two plastic retainers, then hook that secure side roof air bag front tether to inner A-pillar.
5. Remove side roof air bag channel to box nuts retaining screws.
6. Disconnect plastic push-in fasteners that secure channel to roof side rail at top of B & C-pillars.
7. Remove inflator mounting bracket to U-nuts retaining screws.
8. Disconnect integral hooks on inflator mounting bracket from locating holes in roof side rail.
9. Remove side roof air bag module from vehicle as a unit.
10. Reverse procedure to install.

LIBERTY

1. Disarm air bag as outlined under "Air Bag System Disarming & Arming."
2. Remove lower B-pillar trim.
3. Remove headliner from vehicle.
4. Remove side roof air bag tether retainer to base of A-pillar retaining screw.
5. Disengage side roof air bag tether plastic retainer clips from A-pillar.
6. Disconnect side roof air bag pigtail electrical connector from connector at base of B-pillar.
7. Disconnect side roof air bag pigtail

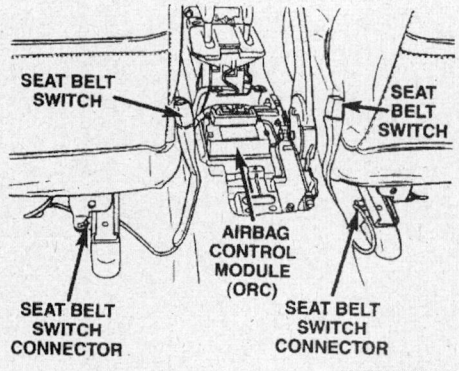

Fig. 10 ORC location. Grand Cherokee

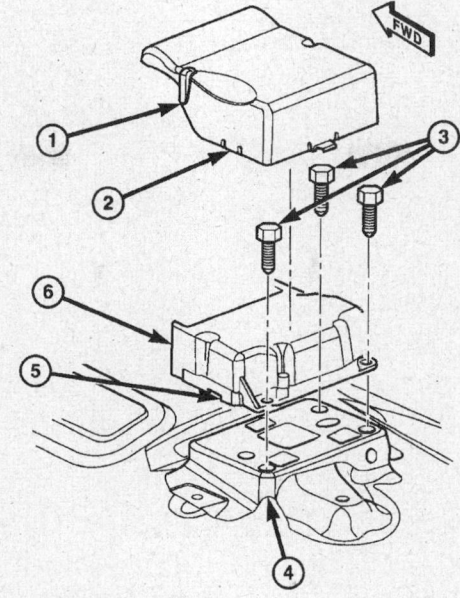

1- COVER
2- LATCH (2)
3- SCREW (3)
4- BRACKET
5- SLOT (2)
6- AIRBAG CONTROL MODULE

LTV0500000003233

Fig. 11 ACM location. Liberty

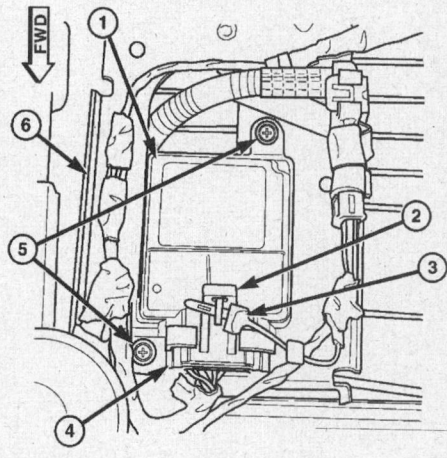

1 - OCCUPANT CLASSIFICATION MODULE
2 - LOCK TOWER
3 - LOCK PIN
4 - CONNECTOR
5 - SCREW (2)
6 - BRACKET

LTV0500000003234

Fig. 12 OCM location. Liberty

wire retainer clips from B-pillar.
8. Remove side roof air bag manifold tube brackets to U-nuts retaining screws.
9. Remove side roof air bag inflator bracket to U-nuts retaining screws.
10. Firmly pull side roof air bag channel straight away from roof rail far enough to disengage plastic push-in fasteners.
11. Remove side roof air bag module from vehicle as a unit.
12. Reverse procedure to install.

PACIFICA

1. Disarm air bag as outlined under "Air Bag System Disarming & Arming."
2. Remove headliner from vehicle.
3. Remove roof air bag to spring nuts mounting screws.
4. Disconnect roof air bag squib connector.
5. Disconnect roof air bag front tether plastic retainer from hole in upper A-pillar.
6. Firmly pull side roof air bag channel straight away from roof rail far enough to disengage plastic push-in fasteners.
7. Remove roof air bag from vehicle as a unit.
8. Reverse procedure to install.

SPRINTER

1. Disarm air bag as outlined under "Air Bag System Disarming & Arming."
2. Remove pinch welt from front door opening.
3. Remove B-pillar trim.
4. Remove grab handle from headliner.
5. Carefully remove trim from A-pillar that conceals side roof air bag front tether.
6. Disconnect pigtail wire connector on B-pillar, then cut tie strap.
7. Remove screw that secures side roof air bag tether retainer to base of A-pillar.
8. Remove screw that secures front of side roof air bag module to A-pillar.
9. Remove screw that secures rear of side roof air bag module to B-pillar.
10. Disengage lug that secures side roof air bag bracket and remove unit from vehicle.
11. Reverse procedure to install.

Side Impact Air Bag Module
PT CRUISER

1. Disarm air bag as outlined under "Air Bag System Disarming & Arming."
2. Remove front seat from vehicle.
3. Remove plastic back panel from seat back.
4. Disengage seat back trim cover J-strap from upper, lower and air bag side of seat back.
5. Disconnect side impact air bag module electrical connector.
6. Remove side impact air bag module retaining nuts.
7. Grasp upper air bag side of seat back trim cover and pull trim cover and cushion over top of seat back frame.
8. Working between seat back trim cover/cushion and frame carefully unhook seat air bag studs from nylon sleeve and slide air bag out of sleeve. **NOTE: Be certain not to tear the seat air bag nylon sleeve during removal.**
9. Reverse procedure to install.

Steering Control Module
COMMANDER, GRAND CHEROKEE & PT CRUISER

The clockspring for this vehicle is internal to and serviced as a unit with the Steering Control Module (SCM).
1. Place front wheels in straight ahead position.
2. Disarm air bag as outlined under "Air

Bag System Disarming & Arming."
3. Remove driver air bag module as outlined under **Driver Air Bag Module, Replace.**
4. Disconnect steering wheel wire harness connectors from upper clockspring rotor connector.
5. Remove steering wheel from steering column.
6. Remove steering column covers.
7. Remove righthand multi-function switch from SCM.
8. Remove lefthand multi-function switch from SCM.
9. Remove hazard switch from SCM.
10. Disconnect instrument panel wire harness connectors from back of SCM case.
11. Remove SCM to steering column housing mounting screws.
12. Remove SCM.
13. Reverse procedure to install.

Clockspring, Replace

1. Disarm air bag as outlined under "Air Bag System Disarming & Arming."
2. Set front wheels in straight ahead position.
3. Remove air bag module as outlined under "Driver Air Bag Module, Replace."
4. Disconnect wire connectors from back of driver air bag.
5. **On models equipped with steering wheel mounted radio controls,** disconnect 2-way connector from remote radio control harness.
6. **On models equipped with steering wheel mounted speed controls,** disconnect 4-way harness connector from speed control/horn harness to clockspring.
7. **On all models,** remove steering wheel attaching nut, then remove steering wheel with suitable puller.
8. Remove steering column shrouds and disconnect traction control wire electrical connector if equipped.

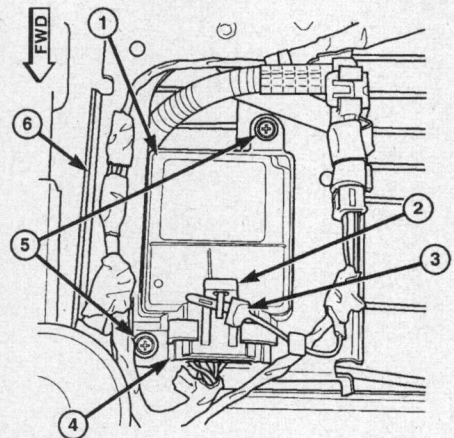

1 - OCCUPANT CLASSIFICATION MODULE (OCM)
2 - LOCK TOWER
3 - LOCK PIN
4 - CONNECTOR
5 - SCREW (2)
6 - BRACKET

LTV0500000003235

Fig. 13 OCM location. Pacifica

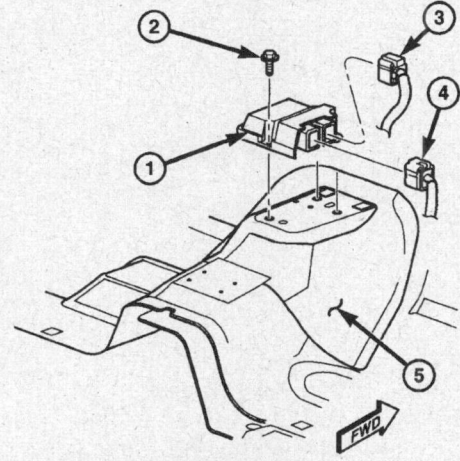

1 - OCCUPANT RESTRAINT CONTROLLER (ORC)
2 - ORC RETAINING SCREWS (3)
3 - INSTRUMENT PANEL HARNESS ORC CONNECTOR
4 - BODY HARNESS ORC CONNECTOR
5 - FLOOR TUNNEL

LTV0500000003236

Fig. 14 ORC location. Pacifica

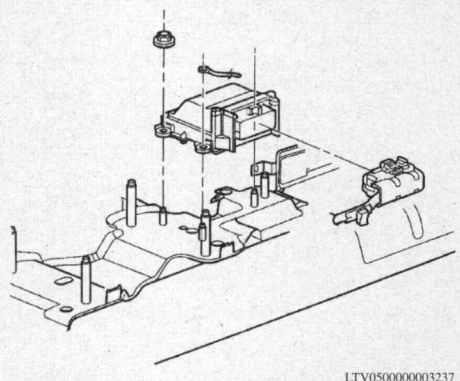

LTV0500000003237

Fig. 15 ORC location. PT Cruiser

9. Disconnect 4-way and 6-way connectors between clockspring and instrument panel wiring harness.
10. Remove clockspring from column assembly by removing two retaining screws that attach clock spring to column.
11. Reverse procedure to install.

Air Bag Control Module (ACM), Replace

DAKOTA & DURANGO

1. Disarm air bag as outlined under "Air Bag System Disarming & Arming."
2. Remove floor duct adapter to bottom of heater-air conditioner housing attaching screw, from righthand side of floor panel transmission tunnel.
3. Remove floor duct adapter.
4. Pull carpet on righthand and lefthand sides of floor panel transmission tunnel rearward far enough to access Air Bag Control Module (ACM).
5. Remove screws that secure ACM to righthand and lefthand sides of bracket on floor panel transmission tunnel.
6. Lift ACM upward far enough to disengage locating pin, then pull ACM out from under instrument panel far enough to access wire harness connector.
7. Disconnect instrument panel wire harness connector for ACM from ACM connector receptacle.
8. Remove ACM from instrument panel.
9. Reverse procedure to install.

FULL SIZE VAN

1. Disarm air bag as outlined under "Air Bag System Disarming & Arming."
2. Adjust driver's power seat to full forward and upward position, then unplug seat belt switch and power seat adjuster connectors, if equipped.
3. Remove seat riser rear and lift shields,

then remove seat riser nuts, seat and riser.
4. Remove ACM trim cover screws and cover.
5. Unplug ACM connectors.
6. Remove ACM mounting screws and ACM.
7. Reverse procedure to install and tighten screws to specifications.

GRAND CHEROKEE

2002-04

1. Disarm air bag as outlined under "Air Bag System Disarming & Arming."
2. Remove center console.
3. Remove center console bracket retaining nuts just forward of ACM, then remove bracket.
4. Disconnect air bag electrical connector from ACM.
5. Disconnect instrument panel wire harness electrical connector from ACM.
6. Remove ACM mounting screws, then ACM.
7. Reverse procedure to install.

LIBERTY

1. Disarm air bag as outlined under "Air Bag System Disarming & Arming."
2. Remove center console, then ACM cover.
3. Remove ACM mounting screws.
4. Disconnect electrical connectors.
5. Remove ACM.
6. Reverse procedure to install.

SPRINTER

1. Disarm air bag as outlined under "Air Bag System Disarming & Arming."
2. Move driver side seat to its most forward position.
3. Remove seat riser covers.
4. Remove screws that secure control module bracket to top of seat riser under driver side seat.
5. Remove control module bracket from top of driver seat riser.
6. Locate ACM in right rear corner of driver seat riser. Firmly grasp and pull up-

ward on molded plastic cover to unsnap it from over ACM.
7. Remove ACM to bracket mounting screws.
8. Lift ACM up far enough to disconnect electrical connectors, then remove ACM.
9. Reverse procedure to install.

WRANGLER

1. Disarm air bag as outlined under "Air Bag System Disarming & Arming."
2. Pull back carpeting over transmission tunnel under heater housing.
3. **On vehicles equipped with ABS,** remove acceleration switch and bracket.
4. **On all models,** remove four screws securing ACM to transmission tunnel.
5. Pull ACM and bracket out far enough to access harness connector.
6. Disconnect ACM harness connector, then remove ACM and bracket as an assembly.
7. Reverse procedure to install and tighten to specifications.

Front Impact Sensor, Replace

CARAVAN, TOWN & COUNTRY & VOYAGER

1. Disarm air bag as outlined under "Air Bag System Disarming & Arming."
2. Raise and support vehicle.
3. Disconnect sensor electrical connector.
4. Remove two screws attaching front impact sensor to outer rails.
5. Remove sensor from vehicle.
6. Reverse procedure to install.

EXCEPT CARAVAN, TOWN & COUNTRY & VOYAGER

1. Disarm air bag as outlined under "Air Bag System Disarming & Arming."
2. Disconnect headlamp and dash wire harness electrical connector from side of sensor being replaced.
3. Remove two nuts that secure sensor to studs on back of radiator support vertical member.
4. Remove impact sensor.
5. Reverse procedure to install.

PACIFICA

1. Disarm air bag as outlined under "Air Bag System Disarming & Arming."
2. Remove headlamp unit.
3. Remove impact sensor mounting screws through headlamp opening.
4. Disconnect electrical connector, then remove sensor.
5. Reverse procedure to install.

PT CRUISER

1. Disarm air bag as outlined under "Air Bag System Disarming & Arming."
2. Remove front lower grille.
3. Disconnect impact sensor electrical connector.
4. Remove sensor mounting screws, then sensor.
5. Reverse procedure to install.

Occupant Restraint Controller, Replace

CARAVAN, TOWN & COUNTRY & VOYAGER

1. Disarm air bag as outlined under "Air Bag System Disarming & Arming."
2. Remove storage bin from instrument panel.
3. Remove ORC to floor bracket mounting bolts.
4. Disconnect ORC wire electrical connectors.
5. Remove ORC from vehicle.
6. Reverse procedure to install.

COMMANDER & PT CRUISER

1. Disarm air bag as outlined under "Air Bag System Disarming & Arming."
2. Remove center console.
3. Disconnect electrical connectors from ORC.
4. Remove ORC mounting screws, then ORC.
5. Reverse procedure to install.

DAKOTA

1. Disarm air bag as outlined under "Air Bag System Disarming & Arming."
2. Remove floor distribution duct from bottom of heater-air conditioner housing.
3. Disconnect instrument panel and body wire harness connectors from Occupant Restraint Controller (ORC).
4. Remove ORC retaining nuts.
5. Remove ORC from ORC mount.
6. Reverse procedure to install.

DURANGO & 2005-06 GRAND CHEROKEE

1. Disarm air bag as outlined under "Air Bag System Disarming & Arming."
2. Remove center console.
3. Disconnect OCM electrical connectors.
4. Remove ORC to ORC bracket mounting screws.
5. Remove ORC from vehicle.
6. Reverse procedure to install.

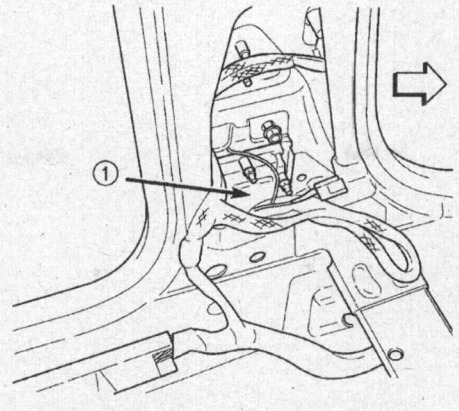

1- SIDE IMPACT AIRBAG CONTROL MODULE

LTV0500000003238

Fig. 16 Side Impact Module location. PT Cruiser

FULL SIZE PICKUP

1. Disarm air bag as outlined under "Air Bag System Disarming & Arming."
2. Remove front seat mounting bolts and position seat for access to ORC protective cover.
3. Remove ORC protective cover.
4. Disconnect ORC electrical connections.
5. Remove ORC to ORC bracket retaining nuts, then ORC.
6. Reverse procedure to install.

PACIFICA

1. Disarm air bag as outlined under "Air Bag System Disarming & Arming."
2. Remove lefthand and righthand forward console closeout panels.
3. From righthand side of vehicle, disconnect ORC electrical connectors.
4. Remove ORC retaining screws, then ORC.
5. Reverse procedure to install.

Occupant Classification Module, Replace

CARAVAN, PACIFICA, PT CRUISER & TOWN & COUNTRY

1. Disarm air bag as outlined under "Air Bag System Disarming & Arming."
2. Reach under front edge of passenger side front seat cushion to access and remove lock pin from connector lock tower on OCM.
3. Disconnect passenger front seat wire harness connector for OCM.
4. Remove OCM to OCM bracket mounting screws.
5. Remove OCM from under passenger front seat.
6. Reverse procedure to install.

COMMANDER & GRAND CHEROKEE

1. Disarm air bag as outlined under "Air Bag System Disarming & Arming."

2. Remove passenger side front seat from vehicle.
3. Disconnect seat wire harness connector from OCM connector receptacle.
4. Remove screws that secure OCM to bracket on underside of passenger side front seat riser frame.
5. Remove OCM from passenger side front seat.
6. Reverse procedure to install.

DAKOTA, DURANGO & LIBERTY

1. Disarm air bag as outlined under "Air Bag System Disarming & Arming."
2. Reach under front edge of passenger side front seat cushion and disconnect body wire harness and seat wire harness connectors from OCM.
3. Remove OCM to OCM bracket mounting screws.
4. Remove OCM.
5. Reverse procedure to install.

Passenger Side Air Bag On/Off Switch, Replace

DAKOTA

1. Remove bezel from instrument panel.
2. Remove three screws securing switch to back of instrument panel lower bezel, then switch.
3. Reverse procedure to install.

FULL SIZE PICKUP

1. Disarm air bag as outlined under "Air Bag System Disarming & Arming."
2. Remove cluster bezel from instrument panel.
3. Remove screws that attach passenger side air bag On/Off switch to back of switch plate, then remove the switch.
4. Reverse procedure to install.

FULL SIZE VAN & WRANGLER

1. Disarm air bag as outlined under "Air Bag System Disarming & Arming."
2. Remove accessory switch plate from instrument panel.
3. Remove screws that attach passenger side air bag On/Off switch to back of switch plate, then remove the switch.
4. Reverse procedure to install.

Side Impact Sensor, Replace

CARAVAN, PT CRUISER & TOWN & COUNTRY

B-pillar Mounted

1. Disarm air bag as outlined under "Air Bag System Disarming & Arming."
2. Remove B-pillar lower trim.
3. Disconnect electrical connector from impact sensor.
4. Remove retaining screws to impact sensor bracket.

5. Remove impact sensor from vehicle.
6. Reverse procedure to install.

Sliding Door Opening Mounted

1. Disarm air bag as outlined under "Air Bag System Disarming & Arming."
2. Open sliding door to fullest open position.
3. Remove two retaining screws to impact sensor.
4. Disconnect electrical connector from impact sensor.
5. Remove impact sensor from vehicle.
6. Reverse procedure to install.

Quarter Panel Mounted

1. Disarm air bag as outlined under "Air Bag System Disarming & Arming."
2. Remove quarter trim panel.
3. Remove two retaining screws to impact sensor.
4. Disconnect electrical connector from impact sensor.
5. Remove impact sensor from vehicle.
6. Reverse procedure to install.

COMMANDER, GRAND CHEROKEE & PACIFICA

B-Pillar Mounted

1. Disarm air bag as outlined under "Air Bag System Disarming & Arming."
2. Remove lower B-pillar trim on side of vehicle sensor is being replaced.
3. Disconnect electrical connector from side impact sensor.
4. Remove impact sensor mounting screws, then sensor.
5. Reverse procedure to install.

C-Pillar Mounted

1. Disarm air bag as outlined under "Air Bag System Disarming & Arming."
2. Remove lower C-pillar quarter trim panel.
3. Disconnect electrical connector from side impact sensor.
4. Remove impact sensor mounting screws, then sensor.
5. Reverse procedure to install.

D-Pillar Mounted

1. Disarm air bag as outlined under "Air Bag System Disarming & Arming."
2. Remove quarter trim panel near D-pillar.
3. Disconnect body wire harness electrical connector from side impact sensor.
4. Remove impact sensor mounting screws, then sensor.
5. Reverse procedure to install.

DAKOTA

1. Disarm air bag as outlined under "Air Bag System Disarming & Arming."
2. Remove front door sill plate.
3. Lift floor carpet upward from sill far enough to access side impact sensor.
4. Remove side impact sensor to floor panel mounting screws.
5. Disconnect body wire harness electrical connector, then remove sensor.
6. Reverse procedure to install.

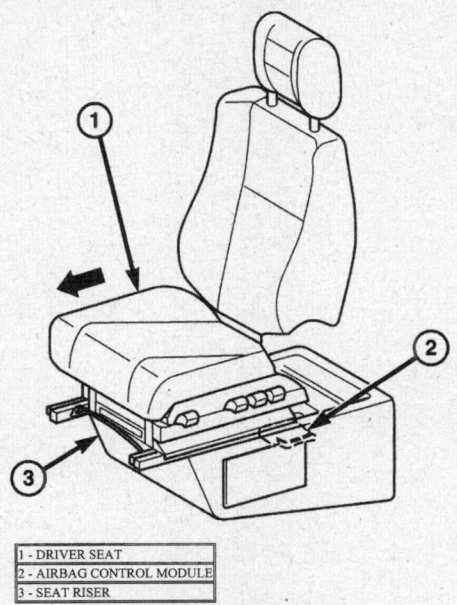

1 - DRIVER SEAT
2 - AIRBAG CONTROL MODULE
3 - SEAT RISER

LTV0500000003239

Fig. 17 ACM location. Sprinter

DURANGO

C-pillar Mounted

1. Disarm air bag as outlined under "Air Bag System Disarming & Arming."
2. Remove quarter trim panel from lower C-pillar.
3. Remove side impact sensor to C-pillar mounting screw.
4. Disconnect impact sensor electrical connector, then remove sensor.
5. Reverse procedure to install.

D-pillar Mounted

1. Disarm air bag as outlined under "Air Bag System Disarming & Arming."
2. Remove quarter trim panel from lower D-pillar.
3. Remove side impact sensor mounting screw.
4. Disconnect impact sensor electrical connector, then remove sensor.
5. Reverse procedure to install.

Front Door Mounted

1. Disarm air bag as outlined under "Air Bag System Disarming & Arming."
2. Remove front door trim panel.
3. Remove impact sensor mounting screw through large opening in inner door.
4. Disconnect impact sensor electrical connector, then remove sensor.
5. Reverse procedure to install.

FULL SIZE PICKUP

1. Disarm air bag as outlined under "Air Bag System Disarming & Arming."
2. Remove B-pillar trim panel.
3. Remove side impact sensor to inner B-pillar retaining nut.
4. Reach through large hole to access side impact sensor and disconnect anti-rotation pin and mounting stud from holes in inner B-pillar.
5. Pull side impact sensor out through

large hole in B-pillar far enough to access and disconnect wire harness electrical connector, then remove sensor.
6. Reverse procedure to install.

LIBERTY

1. Disarm air bag as outlined under "Air Bag System Disarming & Arming."
2. Remove lower B-pillar trim panel.
3. Remove impact sensor mounting screw.
4. Disconnect impact sensor electrical connector, then remove sensor.
5. Reverse procedure to install.

SPRINTER

1. Disarm air bag as outlined under "Air Bag System Disarming & Arming."
2. Remove front door step well trim panel.
3. Disconnect side impact sensor electrical connector.
4. Remove impact sensor mounting screws, then sensor.
5. Reverse procedure to install.

Air Bag Module Disposal

After deployment, air bag module should be placed in a plastic bag and disposed of in same manner as any other scrap parts, except that following points should be carefully noted during disposal.
1. **When handling deployed air bag assembly, face shield and rubber gloves should be worn.**
2. There may be material adhered to air bag module that could irritate eyes and/or skin. Note following: **If any irritation develops, seek medical attention.**
   a. If sinus or throat irritation is encountered during air bag removal, exit vehicle and breathe fresh air.
   b. If material does come in contact with eyes and/or skin, immediately rinse affected area with a large amount of cool, clean water.
   c. If sinus, throat, skin or any other type of irritation continues, consult a physician.
3. After handling a deployed air bag assembly, wash hands and rinse thoroughly with water.
4. **Inflator will be quite hot immediately after deployment, wait 30 minutes to allow air bag to cool.**
5. Do not put water or oil on air bag after deployment.
6. Put deployed air bag in a hermetically sealed container and discard it.
7. Use a vacuum cleaner to remove any residual powder from vehicle interior as follows
   a. Work from outside to center of vehicle.
   b. Vacuum A/C, vent, defroster and heater ducts.
   c. Run blower motor on low speed and vacuum any powder expelled from plenum.
   d. It may be necessary to vacuum interior of vehicle a second time to

ensure all powder is recovered.

8. An air bag that has been deployed should be removed as outlined under "Driver Air Bag Assembly, Replace" or "Passenger Air Bag Assembly, Replace."

9. Prior to removing a deployed air bag assembly, place tape over air bag exhaust vents.

10. Before disposing of a vehicle equipped with air bag(s), or prior to disposing of air bag module, module must be deployed as follows:

   a. If vehicle is to be scrapped, deploy air bag(s) inside vehicle.

   b. If vehicle is to continue in service, air bags must be removed and deployed outside vehicle.

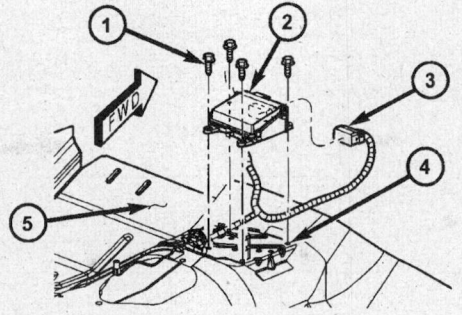

1 - SCREW (4)
2 - AIRBAG CONTROL MODULE
3 - WIRE HARNESS CONNECTOR
4 - MOUNTING BRACKET
5 - FRONT FLOOR PANEL

LTV0500000003240

Fig. 18 ACM location. Wrangler

TIGHTENING SPECIFICATIONS

Year	Component	Torque, Inch Lbs.
CARAVAN, TOWN & COUNTRY & VOYAGER		
2002–06	Air Bag Module, Driver	90
	Air Bag Module To Crosscar Beam, Passenger	90–105
	Air Bag Module To Instrument Panel Pad , Passenger	24–29
	Front Impact Sensor Nuts	62
	Occupant Classification Module	20
	Occupant Restraint Controller	65–85
	Side Impact Sensor	62
COMMANDER & GRAND CHEROKEE		
2002–06	Air Bag Module, Driver	90
	Air Bag Module, Passenger	105
	Air Bag Module, Roof Panel	50
	Front Impact Sensors	70
	Occupant Classification Module	20
	Occupant Restraint Controller	120
	Side Impact Sensor	70
DAKOTA		
2002–06	Air Bag Module, Driver	80–100
	Air Bag Module, Passenger	55
	Air Bag Module, Roof Panel	50
	Front Impact Sensor	90
	Occupant Classification Module	15
	Occupant Restraint Controller	50
	Side Impact Sensor	75
DURANGO		
2002–06	Air Bag Module, Driver	90
	Air Bag Module, Passenger	55
	Air Bag Module, Roof Panel	50
	Front Impact Sensor	55
	Occupant Classification Module	15
	Occupant Restraint Controller	96
	Side Impact Sensor	50

AIR BAG SYSTEM

Continued

TIGHTENING
SPECIFICATIONS—Continued

Year	Component	Torque, Inch Lbs.
FULL SIZE PICKUP		
2002–06	Air Bag Module, Driver	90
	Air Bag Module, Passenger	55
	Air Bag Module, Roof Panel	50
	Front Impact Sensor	90
	Side Impact Sensor	70
	Occupant Restraint Controller	84
FULL SIZE VAN		
2002–03	Air Bag Control Module	65
	Air Bag Door	17
	Air Bag Module, Driver	80–100
	Air Bag Module, Passenger	75
PACIFICA		
2004–06	Air Bag Module To Crosscar Beam, Passenger	90–105
	Air Bag Module To Instrument Panel Pad, Passenger	24–29
	Front Impact Sensor	75
	Occupant Classification Module	20
	Occupant Restraint Controller	128
	Side Impact Sensor	62–65
PT CRUISER		
2002–06	Air Bag Module, Knee Blocker	93
	Air Bag Module, Passenger	239
	Air Bag Module, Side Impact	93
	Front Impact Sensor	62
	Occupant Restraint Controller	93
SPRINTER		
2004–06	Air Bag Control Module	105
	Air Bag Module, Driver	53
	Air Bag Module, Passenger	89
	Air Bag Module, Roof Panel (Front)	204
	Air Bag Module, Roof Panel (Rear)	44
WRANGLER		
2002–06	Air Bag Control Module	125
	Air Bag Door	20
	Air Bag Module, Driver	90
	Air Bag Module, Passenger	105

ANTI-LOCK BRAKES

TABLE OF CONTENTS

	Page No.		Page No.
CARAVAN, TOWN & COUNTRY & VOYAGER	5-1	FULL SIZE VAN	5-80
		JEEP	5-102
DAKOTA	5-44	PACIFICA	5-83
DURANGO	5-57	PT CRUISER	5-18
FULL SIZE PICKUP	5-76	SPRINTER	5-86

Caravan, Town & Country & Voyager

NOTE: On Air Bag Equipped Models, Refer To "Air Bag System Precautions" Located In The Front Of This Manual For System Disarming & Arming Procedures.

NOTE: Refer To "Computer Relearn Procedures" Located In The Front Of This Manual When Battery Power To The Computer Has Been Interrupted.

NOTE: "Electrical Symbol & Wire Color Code Identification" Located In The Front Of This Manual May Be Used As An Aid When Using Wiring Circuits Found In This Section.

INDEX

	Page No.		Page No.		Page No.
Description	5-2	Intermittents & Poor Connections	5-2	Brake System Bleed	5-2
Diagnosis & Testing	5-2	Symptom Tests	5-2	Component Replacement	5-2
Accessing Diagnostic Trouble Codes	5-2	Wiring Diagrams	5-2	Controller Anti-Lock Brake (CAB)	5-2
Clearing Diagnostic Trouble Codes	5-2	Diagnostic Chart Index	5-6	Front Wheel Speed Sensor	5-2
Connector Pin Identification	5-2	Precautions	5-1	Integrated Control Unit (ICU)	5-3
Diagnostic Tests	5-2	Air Bag Systems	5-1	Pump/Motor	5-3
Diagnostic Trouble Code Interpretation	5-2	Battery Ground Cable	5-1	Rear Wheel Speed Sensor	5-3
		General Service Precautions	5-1		
		System Service	5-2		

PRECAUTIONS

Air Bag Systems

Refer to "Air Bag System Precautions" in the front of this manual for system disarming and arming procedures.

Battery Ground Cable

Prior to service disconnect battery ground cable and isolate as required.

General Service Precautions

Certain components of the anti-lock brake system are not intended to be serviced individually. Attempting to remove or disconnect components of this type may result in personal injury and/or improper system operation. Only the components with removal and installation procedures should be serviced.

Observe the following general precautions when servicing the anti-lock brake system:

1. If any welding work is to be performed using an arc welder, Controller Anti-Lock Brake (CAB) should be disconnected.
2. When ignition switch is in On position, CAB electrical connector should not be disconnected or connected.
3. Some components of ABS system are not serviced separately and must be serviced as complete assemblies. Do not disassemble any component which is designated as non-serviceable.

ANTI-LOCK BRAKES

DESCRIPTION

When wheel slip is detected during a brake application, the ABS enters anti-lock mode. During anti-lock braking, hydraulic pressure in the individual wheel circuits is controlled to prevent any wheel from slipping. A separate hydraulic line and specific solenoid valves are provided for each wheel. The ABS can decrease, hold, or increase hydraulic pressure to each wheel brake. The ABS cannot, however, increase hydraulic pressure above the amount which is transmitted by the master cylinder during braking.

During anti-lock braking, a series of rapid pulsations is felt in the brake pedal. These pulsations are caused by the rapid changes in position of the individual solenoid valves as the EBCM responds to wheel speed sensor inputs and attempts to prevent wheel slip. These pedal pulsations are present only during anti-lock braking and stop when normal braking is resumed or when the vehicle comes to a stop. A ticking or popping noise may also be heard as the solenoid valves cycle rapidly. During anti-lock braking on dry pavement, intermittent chirping noises may be heard as the tires approach slipping. These noises and pedal pulsations are considered normal during anti-lock operation.

Vehicles equipped with ABS may be stopped by applying normal force to the brake pedal. Brake pedal operation during normal braking is no different than that of previous non-ABS systems. Maintaining a constant force on the brake pedal provides the shortest stopping distance while maintaining vehicle stability.

DIAGNOSIS & TESTING

Accessing Diagnostic Trouble Codes

Connect a suitably programmed scan tool to Data Link Connector (DLC) and follow manufacturer's instructions.

Diagnostic Trouble Code Interpretation

Refer to "Diagnostic Chart Index" for diagnostic trouble code interpretation.

Connector Pin Identification

Refer to **Figs. 1 and 2** for connector terminal identification.

Wiring Diagrams

Refer to **Figs. 3 and 4** for wiring diagrams.

Diagnostic Tests

Refer to **Figs. 5 and 6** for diagnostic tests.

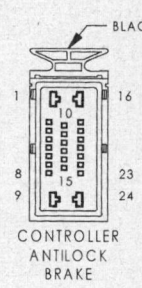

CAV	CIRCUIT	FUNCTION
1	Z107 12BK/DG	GROUND
2	B1 18DG/OR	RIGHT REAR WHEEL SPEED SENSOR 12 VOLT SUPPLY
3	B2 18DG/LB	RIGHT REAR WHEEL SPEED SENSOR SIGNAL
4	-	-
5	D25 18WT/VT	PCI BUS
6	B6 18DG/WT	RIGHT FRONT WHEEL SPEED SENSOR 12 VOLT SUPPLY
7	B7 18DG/VT	RIGHT FRONT WHEEL SPEED SENSOR SIGNAL
8	-	-
9	A111 12DG/RD	FUSED B(+)
10	F500 18DG/PK	FUSED IGNITION SWITCH OUTPUT
11	-	-
12	-	-
13	-	-
14	-	-
15	-	-
16	Z127 12BK/DG	GROUND

CE4020102190010X

Fig. 1   Controller Anti-Lock Brake (CAB) connector terminal identification (Part 1 of 2). 2002

Symptom Tests

Refer to **Figs. 7 through 28** for diagnostic tests.

Clearing Diagnostic Trouble Codes

Connect a suitably programmed scan tool to Data Link Connector (DLC) and follow manufacturer's instructions.

Intermittents & Poor Connections

Most Intermittents are caused by faulty electrical connections or wiring, although a sticking relay or solenoid can also cause an intermittent condition. Inspect wiring and connectors for the following:

1. Poor mating of connector halves, or terminals not fully seated in connector body.
2. Dirt or corrosion on terminals.
3. Damaged connector body.
4. Improperly formed or damaged terminals.
5. Poor terminal to wire connection.
6. Rubbed through wiring insulation.
7. Wiring broken inside insulation.

SYSTEM SERVICE

Brake System Bleed

The base brake system must be bled anytime air is permitted to enter the hydraulic system. However, anti-lock brake system components should only be bled if the hydraulic control unit has been removed or if there is reason to believe that air has entered the unit. **The ABS portion of the braking system must be bled separately.** Under most circumstances, only the base brake system will require bleeding, refer to the "Hydraulic Brake Systems" chapter for procedure. If the anti-lock brake system must be bled, proceed as follows:

1. Ensure all brake system components are installed and all hydraulic lines are connected securely.
2. Connect DRB diagnostic scan tool to diagnostic connector, then ensure Controller Anti-Lock Brake (CAB) has no stored diagnostic trouble codes.
3. Bleed base brake system as outlined in "Hydraulic Brake Systems" chapter, then select "Bleed ABS" routine on diagnostic scan tool.
4. Apply firm pressure to brake pedal and initiate ABS bleed cycle one time, then release pedal.
5. Bleed base brake system once again, then repeat ABS bleed cycle and base brake system bleed until brake fluid flow (as established in "Hydraulic Brake Systems" bleed procedure) is free of bubbles. **Ensure all bleeder valves are closed tightly after bleed sequence is completed.**
6. Road test vehicle to ensure base hydraulic system and anti-lock brake system operate properly.

Component Replacement

CONTROLLER ANTI-LOCK BRAKE (CAB)

1. Disconnect battery cables, then remove battery.
2. Disconnect vacuum hose connector at tank built into battery tray, then remove battery tray.
3. Pull up on CAB connector lock, then disconnect 24-way electrical connector and pump motor connector from CAB.
4. Remove screws securing CAB, then the CAB.
5. Reverse procedure to install, noting the following:
   a. **Torque** mounting screws to 17 inch lbs.
   b. Initialize system using DRB scan tool.

FRONT WHEEL SPEED SENSOR

1. Raise and support vehicle, then remove wheel.
2. Remove sensor cable routing clamp screws.

CONTROLLER ANTILOCK BRAKE - BLACK 24 WAY

CAV	CIRCUIT	FUNCTION
17	-	-
18	L50 18WT/TN	BRAKE LAMP SWITCH OUTPUT
19	B3 18DG/YL	LEFT REAR WHEEL SPEED SENSOR 12 VOLT SUPPLY
20	B4 18DG/GY	LEFT REAR WHEEL SPEED SENSOR SIGNAL
21	-	-
22	B8 18DG/TN	LEFT FRONT WHEEL SPEED SENSOR 12 VOLT SUPPLY
23	B9 18DG/LG	LEFT FRONT WHEEL SPEED SENSOR SIGNAL
24	A107 12TN/RD	FUSED B(+)

CR4020102190020X

Fig. 1 Controller Anti-Lock Brake (CAB) connector terminal identification (Part 2 of 2). 2002

3. Remove speed sensor cable grommets from intermediate bracket on strut.
4. Disconnect speed sensor cable from vehicle wiring harness behind fender well shield.
5. Remove wheel speed sensor head mounting bolt.
6. Remove sensor head from steering knuckle. If sensor has seized due to corrosion, use hammer and a punch to tap on edge of sensor ear, rocking sensor side-to-side until free. **Do not use pliers on sensor head.**
7. Remove wheel speed sensor from vehicle.
8. Reverse procedure to install, noting the following:
   a. Ensure wheel speed sensor cables are installed in retainers.
   b. **Torque** wheel speed sensor head mounting bolt to 105 inch lbs.

INTEGRATED CONTROL UNIT (ICU)

The hydraulic control unit (HCU) and the controller antilock brake (CAB) used with this antilock brake system are combined into one unit which is called the integrated control unit (ICU), **Fig. 29.**
1. Remove battery and battery tray.
2. Using suitable prop, depress brake pedal past 1 inch of travel and lock into position. **This will prevent brake fluid from draining out of master cylinder when brake tubes are removed.**
3. Disconnect speed control servo electrical connector.
4. Remove speed control servo mounting nuts and position servo aside.
5. Disconnect 24 way connector from CAB, then thoroughly clean all surfaces of ICU.
6. Remove brake tubes from inlet and outlet ports on HCU.
7. Center and prop steering wheel.
8. Remove pinch bolt and disconnect steering shaft coupling.
9. Remove dash seal.
10. Remove ICU to mounting bracket bolts.
11. Remove ICU.
12. Separate CAB from HCU.
13. Reverse procedure to install, noting the following:
   a. Bleed ABS system as outlined

under "System Service."
   b. Road test vehicle and ensure proper brake operation.

PUMP/MOTOR

The pump/motor cannot be serviced independently from the modulator (hydraulic control unit). If it is not function properly, the entire unit must be replaced.

REAR WHEEL SPEED SENSOR

AWD

1. Raise and support vehicle.
2. Remove grommet from floor pan of vehicle, then disconnect speed sensor cable from vehicle wiring harness.
3. Carefully remove speed sensor cable from press-in routing clips along brake hose and tubing.
4. Remove bolt securing wheel speed sensor cable metal clip to rear axle. If sensor has seized due to corrosion, use hammer and a punch to tap on edge of sensor ear, rocking sensor side-to-side until free. **Do not use pli-**

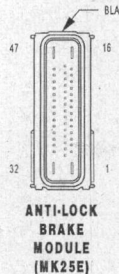

BLACK

47 — 16

32 — 1

ANTI-LOCK BRAKE MODULE (MK25E)

ANTI-LOCK BRAKE MODULE (MK25E) - BLACK 47 WAY

CAV	CIRCUIT	FUNCTION
1	A107 12TN/RD	FUSED B(+) (PUMP)
2	-	-
3	-	-
4	-	-
5	-	-
6	L50 18WT/TN (DIESEL)	PRIMARY BRAKE SWITCH SIGNAL
6	L50 18WT/TN (GAS)	BRAKE LAMP SWITCH OUTPUT
7	-	-
8	F500 18DG/PK	FUSED IGNITION SWITCH OUTPUT (RUN)
9	-	-
10	-	-
11	D25 18WT/VT	PCI BUS
12	-	-
13	-	-
14	-	-
15	-	-
16	Z127 12BK/DG	GROUND
17	-	-
18	-	-
19	-	-
20	-	-
21	-	-
22	-	-
23	-	-
24	-	-
25	-	-
26	-	-
27	-	-
28	-	-
29	-	-
30	-	-
31	-	-
32	A111 12DG/RD	FUSED B(+) (VALVE)
33	B6 18DG/WT	RIGHT FRONT WHEEL SPEED SENSOR SIGNAL
34	B7 18DG/VT	RIGHT FRONT WHEEL SPEED SENSOR 12 VOLT SUPPLY
35	-	-
36	B4 18DG/GY	LEFT REAR WHEEL SPEED SENSOR 12 VOLT SUPPLY
37	B3 18DG/YL	LEFT REAR WHEEL SPEED SENSOR SIGNAL
38	-	-
39	-	-
40	-	-
41	-	-
42	B1 18DG/OR	RIGHT REAR WHEEL SPEED SENSOR SIGNAL
43	B2 18DG/LB	RIGHT REAR WHEEL SPEED SENSOR 12 VOLT SUPPLY
44	-	-
45	B9 18DG/LG	LEFT FRONT WHEEL SPEED SENSOR 12 VOLT SUPPLY
46	B8 18DG/TN	LEFT FRONT WHEEL SPEED SENSOR SIGNAL
47	Z107 12BK/DG	GROUND

LTV0500000003241

Fig. 2 Controller Anti-Lock Brake (CAB) connector terminal identification. 2003–06

ers on sensor head.
5. Remove wheel speed sensor head bolt.
6. Remove wheel speed sensor head from axle, then the sensor from vehicle.
7. Reverse procedure to install, noting the following:
   a. Ensure wheel speed sensor cables are installed in retainers.
   b. Prior to installing mounting bolt, ensure plastic anti-rotating pin is fully seated into bearing flange.
   c. **Torque** mounting bolt to 105 inch lbs.
   d. Air gap between face of wheel speed sensor and top surface of tone wheel must be .016–.047 inch.

FWD

1. Raise and support vehicle.
2. Remove grommet from floor pan of vehicle, then disconnect speed sensor cable connector from vehicle wiring harness.
3. Carefully remove speed sensor cable

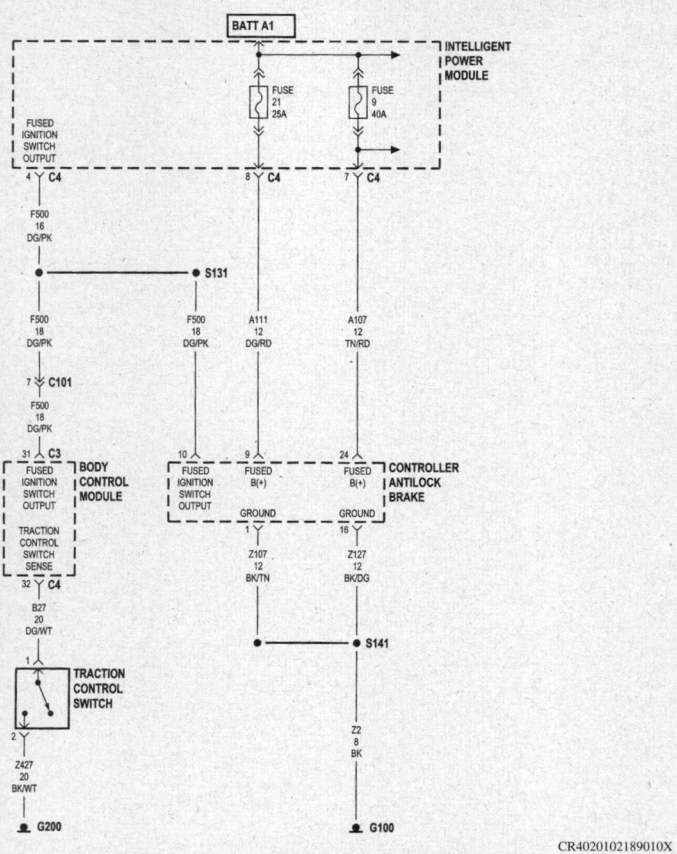

Fig. 3 Wiring diagram (Part 1 of 3). 2002

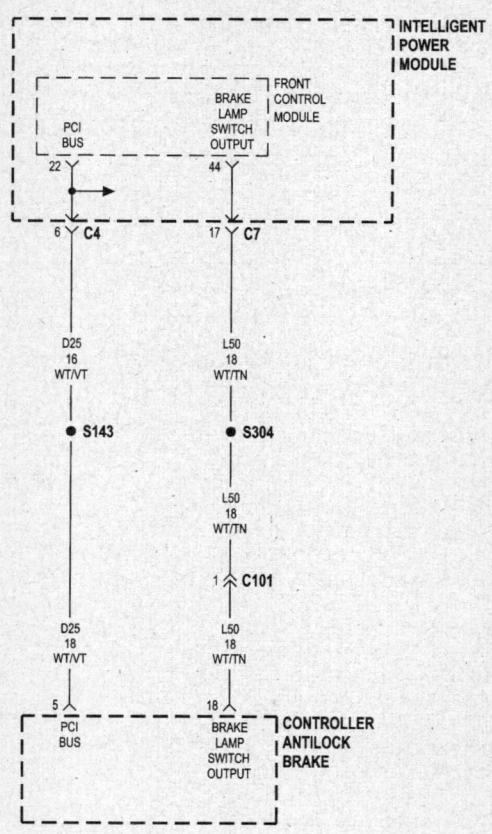

Fig. 3 Wiring diagram (Part 2 of 3). 2002

from press-in routing clips.

4. Remove bolt securing metal routing clip to rear of axle, then the sensor cable from metal clip.

5. Remove secondary yellow retaining clip at rear of wheel speed sensor head.

6. Push up on metal retaining clip until it bottoms to release wheel speed sensor head from hub and bearing.

7. While holding metal clip up, pull back on wheel speed sensor head and remove from hub and bearing.

8. Reverse procedure to install, noting the following:

   a. Ensure cable is installed in routing retainers.

   b. Install wheel speed sensor head into rear of hub and bearing aligning index tab with notch in top of mounting hole. Push sensor in until it snaps into place on metal retaining clip.

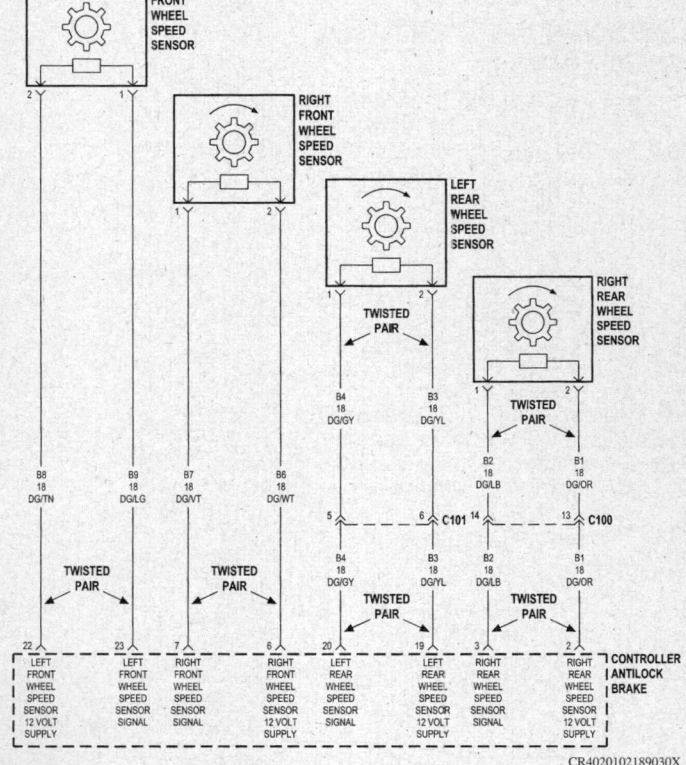

Fig. 3 Wiring diagram (Part 3 of 3). 2002

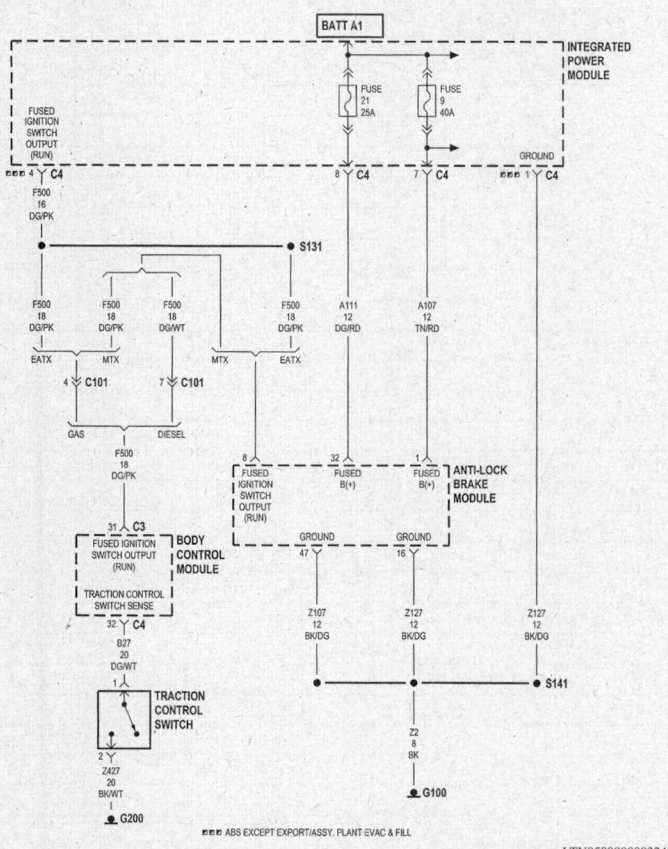

Fig. 4 Wiring diagram (Part 1 of 3). 2003–06

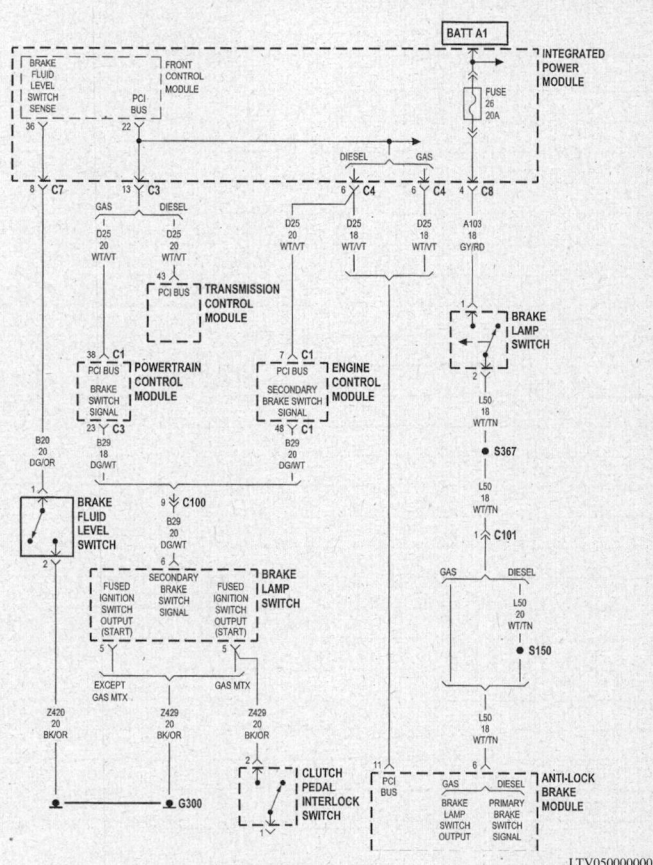

Fig. 4 Wiring diagram (Part 2 of 3). 2003–06

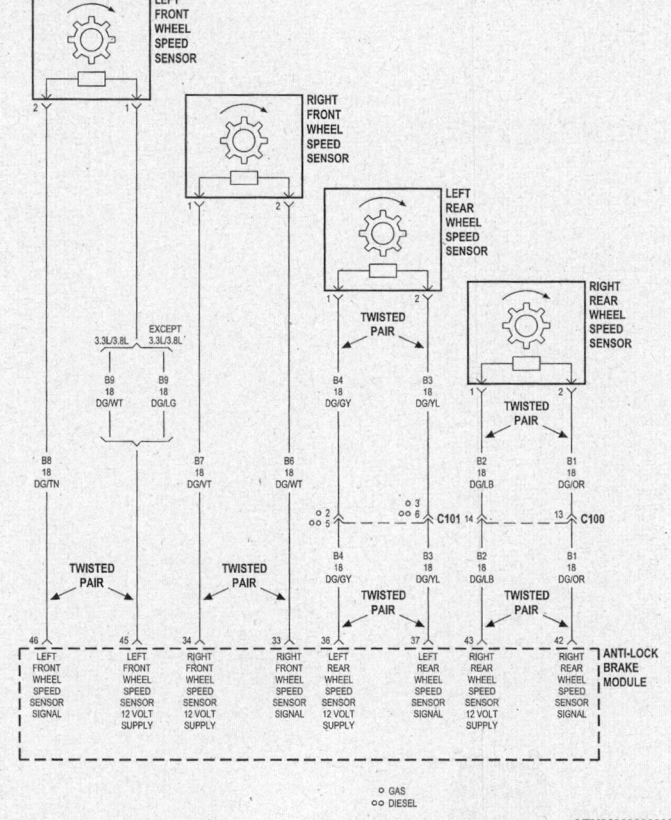

Fig. 4 Wiring diagram (Part 3 of 3). 2003–06

DIAGNOSTIC CHART INDEX

Code	Description	Page No.	Fig. No.
—	Brake Lamp Switch	5-7	7
—	Bus System Communication Failure. 2002	5-7	8
—	CAB Internal Failure. 2002	5-7	9
—	Cluster Lamp Failure	5-8	10
—	Left Front, Left Rear, Right Front & Right Rear Sensor Circuit Failure. 2002	5-8	11
—	Left Front Wheel Speed Signal Failure. 2002	5-9	12
—	Left Rear Wheel Speed Signal Failure. 2002	5-9	13
—	Pump Circuit Failure. 2002	5-9	14
—	Right Front Wheel Speed Signal Failure. 2002	5-10	15
—	Right Rear Wheel Speed Signal Failure. 2002	5-10	16
—	System Overvoltage	5-11	17
—	System Undervoltage. 2002	5-11	18
—	Valve Power Feed Failure. 2002	5-12	19
—	Verification Test	5-12	20
—	Bus System Communication Failure	5-13	21
—	Cab Internal Failure	5-13	22
—	Incorrect Tone Wheel Failure	5-13	23
—	Left Front, Left Rear, Right Front & Right Rear Sensor Circuit Failure	5-14	24
—	Left Front, Left Rear, Right Front & Right Rear Speed Signal Failure	5-15	25
—	Pump Circuit Failure	5-16	26
—	System Undervoltage	5-17	27
—	Valve Power Feed Failure	5-17	28
P0572	Brake Switch # 1 Circuit Low	5-6	5
P0573	Brake Switch # 1 Circuit High	5-7	6

When Monitored and Set Condition:

P0572-BRAKE SWITCH #1 CIRCUIT LOW

When Monitored: Ignition on.

Set Condition: When the PCM recognizes Brake Switch is mechanically stuck in the low/on position. One Trip Fault. Three Global Good Trips to Clear.

POSSIBLE CAUSES
GOOD TRIP EQUAL TO ZERO
BRAKE LAMP SWITCH OPERATION
(K29) BRAKE SWITCH SIGNAL CIRCUIT SHORTED TO GROUND
PCM

TEST	ACTION
1	NOTE: Verify battery voltage is greater than 10 volts. Record Freeze Frame Data that was set by the related DTC before continuing. With the DRBIII®, read DTCs and record the related Freeze Frame data. Is the Good Trip Counter displayed and equal to zero? Yes → Go To 2 No → Refer to the INTERMITTENT CONDITIONS Perform POWERTRAIN VERIFICATION TEST VER - 5.
2	Turn the ignition off. Remove the Brake Lamp Switch and disconnect the harness connector. Measure the resistance between the (Z1) Ground circuit terminal and the (K29) Brake Switch Signal terminal at the Brake Lamp Switch. Apply and release the brake pedal plunger while monitoring the ohmmeter. Does the resistance change from below 5.0 ohms to an open circuit? Yes → Go To 3 No → Replace the Brake Lamp Switch. Perform POWERTRAIN VERIFICATION TEST VER - 5.
3	Turn the ignition off. Disconnect the PCM harness connectors. Measure the resistance between ground and the (K29) Brake Switch Signal circuit in the Brake Lamp Switch harness connector. Is the resistance below 100 ohms? Yes → Repair the short to ground in the (K29) Brake Switch Signal circuit. Perform POWERTRAIN VERIFICATION TEST VER - 5. No → Go To 4

LTV0500000003268

Fig. 5   Code P0572: Brake Switch # 1 Circuit Low (Part 1 of 2). 2003–06

TEST	ACTION
4	NOTE: Before continuing, check the PCM harness connector terminals for corrosion, damage, or terminal push out. Repair as necessary. Using the schematics as a guide, inspect the wire harness and connectors. Pay particular attention to all Power and Ground circuits. If there are no possible causes remaining, view repair. Repair Replace and program the Powertrain Control Module Perform POWERTRAIN VERIFICATION TEST VER - 5.

LTV0500000003269

Fig. 5   Code P0572: Brake Switch # 1 Circuit Low (Part 2 of 2). 2003–06

When Monitored and Set Condition:

P0573-BRAKE SWITCH #1 CIRCUIT HIGH

When Monitored: Ignition on.

Set Condition: When the PCM recognizes Brake Switch is stuck in the high/off position. One Trip Fault. Three good trips to turn off the MIL.

POSSIBLE CAUSES
GOOD TRIP EQUAL TO ZERO
BRAKE LAMP SWITCH OPERATION
(K29) BRAKE SWITCH SIGNAL CIRCUIT OPEN
(Z1) GROUND CIRCUIT OPEN
PCM

TEST	ACTION
1	Ignition on, engine not running. With the DRBIII®, read DTCs and record the related Freeze Frame data. Is the Good Trip Counter displayed and equal to zero? Yes → Go To 2 No → Refer to the INTERMITTENT CONDITIONS Perform POWERTRAIN VERIFICATION TEST VER - 5.
2	Turn the ignition off. Disconnect the Brake Lamp Switch harness connector. Measure the resistance between the (Z1) Ground circuit terminal and the (K29) Brake Switch Signal circuit terminal in the Brake Lamp Switch. Apply and release the brake pedal while monitoring the ohmmeter. Does the resistance change from below 5.0 ohms to an open circuit? Yes → Go To 3 No → Replace the Brake Lamp Switch. Perform POWERTRAIN VERIFICATION TEST VER - 5.

LTV0500000003270

Fig. 6 Code P0573: Brake Switch # 1 Circuit High (Part 1 of 2). 2003–06

POSSIBLE CAUSES
CHECK BRAKE LAMP SWITCH OUTPUT
BRAKE LAMP SWITCH B+ OPEN
BRAKE LAMP SWITCH OUTPUT CIRCUIT SHORT OR OPEN
BRAKE LAMP SWITCH OPEN
CAB -- INTERNAL OPEN

TEST	ACTION
1	With the DRBIII® in Inputs/Outputs, read the Brake Lamp Switch state. Press and release the brake pedal. Does the DRBIII® display PRESSED and RELEASED? Yes → The Brake Lamp Switch is OK. Perform ABS VERIFICATION TEST - VER 1. No → Go To 2
2	Disconnect the Brake Lamp Switch harness connector. Using a 12-volt test light connected to ground, check the Brake Lamp Switch Fused B+ circuit. Does the test light illuminate brightly ? Yes → Go To 3 No → Repair the Brake Lamp Switch Fused B+ circuit for an open. Perform ABS VERIFICATION TEST - VER 1.
3	Disconnect the Brake Lamp Switch harness connector. Connect a jumper wire between the Brake Lamp Switch B+ and Output circuits. With the DRBIII® in Inputs/Outputs, read the Brake Lamp Switch state. Does the DRBIII® display PRESSED? Yes → Replace the Brake Lamp Switch Perform ABS VERIFICATION TEST - VER 1. No → Go To 4
4	Disconnect the CAB harness connector. Disconnect the Brake Lamp Switch harness connector. Check the Brake Lamp Switch Output circuit for a short to voltage and an open. Is the Brake Lamp Switch Output circuit shorted or open? Yes → Repair the Brake Lamp Switch Output circuit for a short to voltage or an open. Perform ABS VERIFICATION TEST - VER 1. No → Replace the Controller Anti-Lock Brake Perform ABS VERIFICATION TEST - VER 1.

CR4020102203000X

Fig. 7 Brake Lamp Switch

TEST	ACTION
3	Turn the ignition off. Disconnect the PCM harness connectors. **CAUTION: DO NOT PROBE THE PCM HARNESS CONNECTORS. PROBING THE PCM HARNESS CONNECTORS WILL DAMAGE THE PCM TERMINALS RESULTING IN POOR TERMINAL TO PIN CONNECTION. INSTALL MILLER SPECIAL TOOL #8815 TO PERFORM DIAGNOSIS.** Measure the resistance of the (K29) Brake Switch Signal circuit from the Brake Lamp Switch harness connector to the appropriate terminal of special tool #8815. Is the resistance below 5.0 ohms? Yes → Go To 4 No → Repair the open in the (K29) Brake Switch Signal circuit. Perform POWERTRAIN VERIFICATION TEST VER - 5.
4	Measure the resistance between the (Z2) Ground circuit and ground at the Brake Lamp Switch harness connector. Is the resistance below 5.0 ohms? Yes → Go To 5 No → Repair the open in the (Z1) Ground circuit. Perform POWERTRAIN VERIFICATION TEST VER - 5.
5	**NOTE: Before continuing, check the PCM harness connector terminals for corrosion, damage, or terminal push out. Repair as necessary.** Using the schematics as a guide, inspect the wire harness and connectors. Pay particular attention to all Power and Ground circuits. If there are no possible causes remaining, view repair. Repair Replace and program the Powertrain Control Module Perform POWERTRAIN VERIFICATION TEST VER - 5.

LTV0500000003271

Fig. 6 Code P0573: Brake Switch # 1 Circuit High (Part 2 of 2). 2003–06

When Monitored and Set Condition:

BUS SYSTEM COMMUNICATION FAILURE

When Monitored: Ignition ON, every 7 ms.

Set Condition: When the CAB does not receive a message from the instrument cluster for 10 seconds.

POSSIBLE CAUSES
CHECK COMMUNICATION TO MIC
CAB-- INTERNAL FAULT

TEST	ACTION
1	Turn the ignition on. With the DRBIII®, attempt to communicate with the MIC Was the DRB able to I/D or communicate with the MIC? Yes → Go To 2 No → Perform the symptom Bus +/- Signals Open from the Controller Anti-Lock Brake. Perform ABS VERIFICATION TEST - VER 1.
2	With the DRB, erase DTC's. Turn the ignition on and wait approximately 1 minute. With the DRB, read DTC's. Did this DTC reappear? Yes → Replace the Controller Anti-Lock Brake Perform ABS VERIFICATION TEST - VER 1. No → Test Complete.

CR4020102191000X

Fig. 8 Bus System Communication Failure. 2002

When Monitored and Set Condition:

CAB INTERNAL FAILURE

When Monitored: Ignition on. The CAB monitors its internal microprocessors for correct operation.

Set Condition: If the CAB detects an internal fault, the DTC is set.

POSSIBLE CAUSES
CAB - INTERNAL CONCERN

TEST	ACTION
1	The only possible cause is a CAB internal concern. If there are no possible causes remaining, view repair. View repair. Replace the Controller Antilock Brake Perform ABS VERIFICATION TEST - VER 1.

CR4020102192000X

Fig. 9 CAB Internal Failure. 2002

When Monitored and Set Condition:

CLUSTER LAMP FAILURE

When Monitored: Key ON. After Key-ON bulb check.

Set Condition: When the instrument cluster informs the CAB that the cluster cannot turn on the ABS Lamp.

POSSIBLE CAUSES
CLUSTER DTC PRESENT
CLUSTER INTERNAL FAULT
CAB -- NO ABS INDICATOR MESSAGE
CAB -- ABS INDICATOR FAULT

TEST	ACTION
1	Turn the ignition on. With the DRBIII®, read DTCs. Are there any Instrument Cluster DTCs present? Yes → Diagnose INSTRUMENT CLUSTER Perform ABS VERIFICATION TEST - VER 1. No → Go To 2
2	Turn the ignition off. Observe the instrument cluster indicators. Turn the ignition on. Did the ABS Indicator illuminate for several seconds and then go out? Yes → Go To 3 No → Go To 4
3	NOTE: The DRBIII® communication with the CAB must be operational for the result of this test to be valid. Turn the ignition off. Remove Fuse 21 (ABS valve power) from the IPM. Perform the Key-on Bulb Check. Does the ABS Indicator remain on after the bulb check? Yes → Test Complete. No → Replace the Controller Antilock Brake Perform ABS VERIFICATION TEST - VER 1.

CR4020102193010X

Fig. 10 Cluster Lamp Failure (Part 1 of 2)

When Monitored and Set Condition:

LEFT FRONT SENSOR CIRCUIT FAILURE

When Monitored: Ignition on. The CAB monitors the wheel speed circuit every 7 milliseconds (ms).

Set Condition: If the CAB detects an open or shorted wheel speed sensor circuit, the Diagnostic Trouble Code (DTC) will set.

LEFT REAR SENSOR CIRCUIT FAILURE

When Monitored: Ignition on. The CAB monitors the wheel speed circuit every 7 milliseconds (ms).

Set Condition: If the CAB detects an open or shorted wheel speed sensor circuit, the Diagnostic Trouble Code (DTC) will set.

RIGHT FRONT SENSOR CIRCUIT FAILURE

When Monitored: Ignition on. The CAB monitors the wheel speed circuit every 7 milliseconds (ms).

Set Condition: If the CAB detects an open or shorted wheel speed sensor circuit, the Diagnostic Trouble Code (DTC) will set.

RIGHT REAR SENSOR CIRCUIT FAILURE

When Monitored: Ignition on. The CAB monitors the wheel speed circuit every 7 milliseconds (ms).

Set Condition: If the CAB detects an open or shorted wheel speed sensor circuit, the Diagnostic Trouble Code (DTC) will set.

POSSIBLE CAUSES
SENSOR OR CONNECTOR DAMAGE
WHEEL SPEED SENSOR FAULT
SENSOR CIRCUITS SHORTED OR OPEN

CR4020102194010X

Fig. 11 Left Front, Left Rear, Right Front & Right Rear Sensor Circuit Failure (Part 1 of 3). 2002

TEST	ACTION
4	NOTE: The purpose of this test is to perform the Instrument Cluster self test. Turn the ignition on. Depress and hold the Odometer Reset Button. Turn the Key from OFF to ON and then back to OFF. Release the Odometer Reset Button. Do the Instrument Cluster Indicators and Gauges activate and deactivate? Yes → Replace the Controller Antilock Brake Perform ABS VERIFICATION TEST - VER 1. No → Replace the Instrument Cluster Perform ABS VERIFICATION TEST - VER 1.

CR4020102193020X

Fig. 10 Cluster Lamp Failure (Part 2 of 2)

POSSIBLE CAUSES
CAB - INTERNAL FAULT
INTERMITTENT CIRCUIT DTC

TEST	ACTION
1	Turn the ignition on. With the DRBIII®, record and erase DTC's. Turn the ignition off. Turn the ignition on. With the DRBIII®, read DTC's. Does the DRBIII® display a Wheel Speed Sensor Circuit Failure DTC? Yes → Go To 2 No → Go To 5
2	Turn the ignition off. Inspect the affected Wheel Speed Sensor and Connector. Is the Sensor or Connector Damaged? Yes → Repair as necessary. Perform ABS VERIFICATION TEST - VER 1. No → Go To 3
3	Turn the ignition off. Disconnect the affected Wheel Speed Sensor connector. **Note: Check connector - Clean/repair as necessary.** Turn the ignition on. Using a 12-volt test light connected to ground, check the Sensor 12 volt Supply circuit. Measure the resistance between ground and the Sensor Signal circuit. Was the test light bright and the resistance between 100 and 300 ohms? Yes → Replace the Wheel Speed Sensor Perform ABS VERIFICATION TEST - VER 1. No → Go To 4
4	Turn the ignition off. Disconnect the affected Wheel Speed Sensor connector. **Note: Check connector - Clean/repair as necessary.** Disconnect the CAB connector. **Note: Check connector - Clean/repair as necessary.** Turn the ignition on. Check the Wheel Speed Sensor 12 volt Supply and Signal circuits for a short to battery, ground, to each other and for an open. For the purposes of this test, a short to ground must be below 15k ohms. Was any circuit short or open found? Yes → Repair the Wheel Speed Sensor circuit short or open. Perform ABS VERIFICATION TEST - VER 1. No → Replace the Controller Antilock Brake Perform ABS VERIFICATION TEST - VER 1.

CR4020102194020X

Fig. 11 Left Front, Left Rear, Right Front & Right Rear Sensor Circuit Failure (Part 2 of 3). 2002

TEST	ACTION
5	Turn the ignition off. Visually inspect the related wiring harness. Look for any chafed, pierced, pinched, or partially broken wires. Visually inspect the related wire harness connectors. Look for broken, bent, pushed out, or corroded terminals. Refer to any Hotline letters or Technical Service Bulletins that may apply. Were any problems found? Yes → Repair as necessary. Perform ABS VERIFICATION TEST - VER 1. No → Test Complete.

CR4020102194030X

Fig. 11 Left Front, Left Rear, Right Front & Right Rear Sensor Circuit Failure (Part 3 of 3). 2002

When Monitored and Set Condition:

LEFT FRONT WHEEL SPEED SIGNAL FAILURE

When Monitored: Wheel speed comparison is checked at drive off or every 7 milliseconds (ms). Sensor signal continuity is checked every 7 milliseconds. Wheel speed phase length supervision is checked every 7 milliseconds.

Set Condition: If, during an ABS stop, the CAB commands any valve solenoid on for an extended length of time, and does not see a corresponding wheel speed change, the Diagnostic Trouble Code (DTC) is set. The DTC can also set if the signal is missing or erratic.

POSSIBLE CAUSES
SENSOR OR TONE WHEEL CONCERN
DTC INTERMITTENT
LEFT FRONT WHEEL SPEED SENSOR INOPERATIVE
INTERMITTENT SIGNAL DTC

TEST	ACTION
1	With the DRBIII®, erase DTCs. Turn the ignition off. Start the engine. Slowly accelerate as straight as possible from a stop to 24 km/h (15 mph). Using the DRBIII®, monitor the Left Front Wheel Speed Sensor while an assistant drives the vehicle. With the DRBIII®, monitor all wheel speed sensors. Is Left Front WSS Signal 0 km/h (0 mph) or differing from others by more than 5 km/h (3 mph)? Yes → Go To 2 No → Go To 3
2	Inspect the Left Front Wheel Speed Sensor, Connector and Tone Wheel. **NOTE: Inspect components for damage and correct installation.** Are there any visible Sensor, Connector or Tone Wheel concerns? Yes → Correct the sensor, connector or tone wheel concern as necessary. The vehicle must be driven at 25 km/h (15 mph) to extinguish the ABS indicator. Perform ABS VERIFICATION TEST - VER 1. No → Replace the Left Front Wheel Speed Sensor The vehicle must be driven at 25 km/h (15 mph) to extinguish the ABS indicator. Perform ABS VERIFICATION TEST - VER 1.

CR4020102195010X

Fig. 12 Left Front Wheel Speed Signal Failure (Part 1 of 2). 2002

When Monitored and Set Condition:

LEFT REAR WHEEL SPEED SIGNAL FAILURE

When Monitored: Wheel speed comparison is checked at drive off or every 7 milliseconds (ms). Wheel speed circuit continuity is checked every 7 milliseconds. Wheel speed phase length supervision is checked every 7 milliseconds.

Set Condition: If, during an ABS stop, the CAB commands any valve solenoid on for an extended length of time, and does not see a corresponding wheel speed change, the Diagnostic Trouble Code (DTC) is set. The DTC can also set if the signal is missing or erratic.

POSSIBLE CAUSES
SENSOR OR TONE WHEEL CONCERN
DTC INTERMITTENT
LEFT REAR WHEEL SPEED SENSOR INOPERATIVE
INTERMITTENT SIGNAL DTC

TEST	ACTION
1	With the DRBIII®, erase DTCs. Turn the ignition off. Start the engine. Slowly accelerate as straight as possible from a stop to 24 km/h (15 mph). Using the DRBIII®, monitor the Left Rear Wheel Speed Sensor while an assistant drives the vehicle. With the DRBIII®, monitor all wheel speed sensors. Is Left Rear WSS Signal 0 km/h (0 mph) or differing from others by more than 5 km/h (3 mph)? Yes → Go To 2 No → Go To 3
2	Inspect the Left Rear Wheel Speed Sensor, Connector and Tone Wheel. **NOTE: Inspect components for damage and correct installation.** Are there any visible Sensor, Connector or Tone Wheel concerns? Yes → Correct the sensor, connector or tone wheel concern as necessary. The vehicle must be driven at 25 km/h (15 mph) to extinguish the ABS indicator. Perform ABS VERIFICATION TEST - VER 1. No → Replace the Left Rear Wheel Speed Sensor The vehicle must be driven at 25 km/h (15 mph) to extinguish the ABS indicator. Perform ABS VERIFICATION TEST - VER 1.

CR4020102196010X

Fig. 13 Left Rear Wheel Speed Signal Failure (Part 1 of 2). 2002

TEST	ACTION
3	With the DRBIII®, read DTCs. Did the DTC reoccur? Yes → Replace the Wheel Speed Sensor Perform ABS VERIFICATION TEST - VER 1. No → Go To 4
4	Turn the ignition off. Visually inspect wheel speed sensor. Visually inspect tone wheel. Visually inspect wiring harness. Visually inspect brakes for locking up due to lining contamination or overheating. Inspect all Components for defects which may cause a Signal DTC to set. Is any Component Damaged? Yes → Repair as necessary. The vehicle must be driven at 25 km/h (15 mph) to extinguish the ABS indicator. Perform ABS VERIFICATION TEST - VER 1. No → Test Complete.

CR4020102195020X

Fig. 12 Left Front Wheel Speed Signal Failure (Part 2 of 2). 2002

TEST	ACTION
3	With the DRBIII®, read DTCs. Did the DTC reoccur? Yes → No → Go To 4
4	Turn the ignition off. Visually inspect wheel speed sensor. Visually inspect tone wheel. Visually inspect wiring harness. Visually inspect brakes for locking up due to lining contamination or overheating. Inspect all Components for defects which may cause a Signal DTC to set. Is any Component Damaged? Yes → Repair as necessary. The vehicle must be driven at 25 km/h (15 mph) to extinguish the ABS indicator. Perform ABS VERIFICATION TEST - VER 1. No → Test Complete.

CR4020102196020X

Fig. 13 Left Rear Wheel Speed Signal Failure (Part 2 of 2). 2002

When Monitored and Set Condition:

PUMP CIRCUIT FAILURE

When Monitored: Ignition on. The CAB commands the pump on at 20 km/h (12 mph) to check its operation, if the brake switch is not applied. If the brake is applied, the test will run at 40 km/h (25 mph). The CAB monitors pump voltage every 7 milliseconds.

Set Condition: The DTC is stored when the CAB detects: 1) Improper voltage decay after the pump was turned off. 2) Pump not energized by the CAB, but voltage is present for 3.5 seconds. 3) Pump is turned on by the CAB, but without sufficient voltage to operate it.

POSSIBLE CAUSES
PUMP HARNESS DISCONNECTED
CAB - PUMP MOTOR RUNNING CONTINUOUSLY
ABS PUMP MOTOR INTERMITTENT DTC
GROUND CIRCUIT HIGH RESISTANCE
FUSED B(+) CIRCUIT OPEN
GROUND CIRCUIT OPEN
CAB - INTERNAL FAULT
CAB - SETTING FALSE CODE

TEST	ACTION
1	Turn the ignition off. Turn the ignition on. Monitor the pump motor for continuous operation. Is the pump motor running continuously? Yes → Replace the Controller Anti-Lock Brake The vehicle must be driven at 25 km/h (15 mph) to extinguish the ABS indicator. Perform ABS VERIFICATION TEST - VER 1. No → Go To 2
2	Turn the ignition on. With the DRBIII®, read DTC's. With the DRBIII®, erase DTC's. Turn the ignition off. Turn the ignition on. With the DRBIII®, actuate the ABS pump motor. Did the Pump Motor operate when actuated? Yes → Go To 3 No → Go To 4

CR4020102197010X

Fig. 14 Pump Circuit Failure (Part 1 of 3). 2002

TEST	ACTION
3	Turn the ignition off. Visually inspect the related wiring harness. Look for any chafed, pierced, pinched, or partially broken wires. Visually inspect the related wire harness connectors. Look for broken, bent, pushed out, or corroded terminals. Refer to any Hotline letters or Technical Service Bulletins that may apply. Were any problems found? Yes → Repair as necessary. The vehicle must be driven at 25 km/h (15 mph) to extinguish the ABS indicator. Perform ABS VERIFICATION TEST - VER 1. No → Replace the Controller Anti-Lock Brake The vehicle must be driven at 25 km/h (15 mph) to extinguish the ABS indicator. Perform ABS VERIFICATION TEST - VER 1.
4	Check the short Wiring Harness between the ABS Pump and the CAB. Check for disconnect and damage. Is the harness disconnected or damaged? Yes → Reconnect or repair the Pump Harness as necessary. Perform ABS VERIFICATION TEST - VER 1. No → Go To 5
5	Turn the ignition off. Disconnect CAB Connector. Note: Check connector - Clean/repair as necessary. Measure the resistance of the CAB ground circuits. Is the resistance below 1.0 ohm? Yes → Go To 6 No → Repair the ground circuit for an open. The vehicle must be driven at 25 km/h (15 mph) to extinguish the ABS indicator. Perform ABS VERIFICATION TEST - VER 1.
6	Turn the ignition on. With the DRBIII®, enable pump motor actuation. NOTE: Pump motor will not operate, but voltage will be applied. Measure the voltage drop across the ABS ground circuit connection, with pump motor actuation enabled. Is the voltage below 0.1 volt? Yes → Go To 7 No → Repair the Ground circuit for high resistance. The vehicle must be driven at 25 km/h (15 mph) to extinguish the ABS indicator. Perform ABS VERIFICATION TEST - VER 1.

CR4020102197020X

Fig. 14   Pump Circuit Failure (Part 2 of 3). 2002

When Monitored and Set Condition:

RIGHT FRONT WHEEL SPEED SIGNAL FAILURE

When Monitored: Wheel speed comparison is checked at drive off or every 7 milliseconds (ms). Wheel speed continuity is checked every 7 milliseconds. Wheel speed phase length supervision is checked every 7 milliseconds.

Set Condition: If, during an ABS stop, the CAB commands any valve solenoid on for an extended length of time, and does not see a corresponding wheel speed change, the Diagnostic Trouble Code (DTC) is set. The DTC can also set if the signal is missing or erratic.

POSSIBLE CAUSES
SENSOR OR TONE WHEEL CONCERN
DTC INTERMITTENT
RIGHT FRONT WHEEL SPEED SENSOR INOPERATIVE
CAB - WON'T RESPOND TO RIGHT FRONT WHEEL SPEED SENSOR SIGNAL
INTERMITTENT SIGNAL DTC

TEST	ACTION
1	With the DRBIII®, erase DTCs. Turn the ignition off. Start the engine. Slowly accelerate as straight as possible from a stop to 24 km/h (15 mph). Using the DRBIII®, monitor the Right Front Wheel Speed Sensor while an assistant drives the vehicle. With the DRBIII®, monitor all wheel speed sensors. Is Right Front WSS Signal 0 km/h (0 mph) or differing from others by more than 5 km/h (3 mph)? Yes → Go To 2 No → Go To 3
2	Inspect the Right Front Wheel Speed Sensor, Connector and Tone Wheel. NOTE: Inspect components for damage and correct installation. Are there any visible Sensor, Connector or Tone Wheel concerns? Yes → Correct the sensor, connector or tone wheel concern as necessary. The vehicle must be driven at 25 km/h (15 mph) to extinguish the ABS indicator. Perform ABS VERIFICATION TEST - VER 1. No → Replace the Right Front Wheel Speed Sensor The vehicle must be driven at 25 km/h (15 mph) to extinguish the ABS indicator. Perform ABS VERIFICATION TEST - VER 1.

CR4020102198010X

Fig. 15   Right Front Wheel Speed Signal Failure (Part 1 of 2). 2002

TEST	ACTION
7	Turn the ignition off. Disconnect the CAB connector. Note: Check connector - Clean/repair as necessary. Turn the ignition on. Using a 12-volt test light connected to ground, check the Pump Motor Fused B+ circuit. Does the test light illuminate brightly? Yes → Go To 8 No → Repair the Fused B(+) circuit for an open. The vehicle must be driven at 25 km/h (15 mph) to extinguish the ABS indicator. Perform ABS VERIFICATION TEST - VER 1.
8	If there are no possible causes remaining, view repair. Repair Replace the Controller Anti-Lock Brake The vehicle must be driven at 25 km/h (15 mph) to extinguish the ABS indicator. Perform ABS VERIFICATION TEST - VER 1.

CR4020102197030X

Fig. 14   Pump Circuit Failure (Part 3 of 3). 2002

TEST	ACTION
3	With the DRBIII®, read DTCs. Did the DTC reoccur? Yes → Replace the Controller Antilock Brake The vehicle must be driven at 25 km/h (15 mph) to extinguish the ABS indicator. Perform ABS VERIFICATION TEST - VER 1. No → Go To 4
4	Turn the ignition off. Visually inspect wheel speed sensor. Visually inspect tone wheel. Visually inspect wiring harness. Visually inspect brakes for locking up due to lining contamination or overheating. Inspect all Components for defects which may cause a Signal DTC to set. Is any Component Damaged? Yes → Repair as necessary. The vehicle must be driven at 25 km/h (15 mph) to extinguish the ABS indicator. Perform ABS VERIFICATION TEST - VER 1. No → Test Complete.

CR4020102198020X

Fig. 15   Right Front Wheel Speed Signal Failure (Part 2 of 2). 2002

When Monitored and Set Condition:

RIGHT REAR WHEEL SPEED SIGNAL FAILURE

When Monitored: Wheel speed comparison is checked at drive off or every 7 milliseconds (ms). Wheel speed circuit continuity is checked every 7 milliseconds. Wheel speed phase length supervision is checked every 7 milliseconds.

Set Condition: If, during an ABS stop, the CAB commands any valve solenoid on for an extended length of time, and does not see a corresponding wheel speed change, the Diagnostic Trouble Code (DTC) is set. The DTC can also set if the signal is missing or erratic.

POSSIBLE CAUSES
SENSOR OR TONE WHEEL CONCERN
DTC INTERMITTENT
RIGHT REAR WHEEL SPEED SENSOR INOPERATIVE
INTERMITTENT SIGNAL DTC

TEST	ACTION
1	With the DRBIII®, erase DTCs. Turn the ignition off. Start the engine. Slowly accelerate as straight as possible from a stop to 24 km/h (15 mph). Using the DRBIII®, monitor the Right Rear Wheel Speed Sensor while an assistant drives the vehicle. With the DRBIII®, monitor all wheel speed sensors. Is Right Rear WSS Signal 0 km/h (0 mph) or differing from others by more than 5 km/h (3 mph)? Yes → Go To 2 No → Go To 3
2	Inspect the Right Rear Wheel Speed Sensor, Connector and Tone Wheel. NOTE: Inspect components for damage and correct installation. Are there any visible Sensor, Connector or Tone Wheel concerns? Yes → Correct the sensor, connector or tone wheel concern as necessary. The vehicle must be driven at 25 km/h (15 mph) to extinguish the ABS indicator. Perform ABS VERIFICATION TEST - VER 1. No → Replace the Left Rear Wheel Speed Sensor The vehicle must be driven at 25 km/h (15 mph) to extinguish the ABS indicator. Perform ABS VERIFICATION TEST - VER 1.

CR4020102199010X

Fig. 16   Right Rear Wheel Speed Signal Failure (Part 1 of 2). 2002

TEST	ACTION
3	With the DRBIII®, read DTCs. Did the DTC reoccur? Yes → No → Go To 4
4	Turn the ignition off. Visually inspect wheel speed sensor. Visually inspect tone wheel. Visually inspect wiring harness. Visually inspect brakes for locking up due to lining contamination or overheating. Inspect all Components for defects which may cause a Signal DTC to set. Is any Component Damaged? Yes → Repair as necessary. The vehicle must be driven at 25 km/h (15 mph) to extinguish the ABS indicator. Perform ABS VERIFICATION TEST - VER 1. No → Test Complete.

CR4020102199020X

Fig. 16 Right Rear Wheel Speed Signal Failure (Part 2 of 2). 2002

TEST	ACTION
3	Turn the ignition off. Disconnect the CAB connector. **Note: Check connector - Clean/repair as necessary.** Start the engine. Raise engine speed above 1,800 RPM. Measure the battery voltage. Is the voltage above 16.5 volts ? Yes → Refer to appropriate service information for charging system testing and repair. Perform ABS VERIFICATION TEST - VER 1. No → Go To 4
4	Turn the ignition off. Disconnect the CAB connector. **Note: Check connector - Clean/repair as necessary.** Measure the resistance of the ground circuits. Is the resistance below 1.0 ohm? Yes → Go To 5 No → Repair the Ground circuit for an open. Perform ABS VERIFICATION TEST - VER 1.
5	If there are no potential causes remaining, view repair. Repair Replace the Controller Antilock Brake. Perform ABS VERIFICATION TEST - VER 1.
6	Turn the ignition off. Visually inspect the related wiring harness. Look for any chafed, pierced, pinched, or partially broken wires. Visually inspect the related wire harness connectors. Look for broken, bent, pushed out, or corroded terminals. Refer to any Hotline letters or Technical Service Bulletins that may apply. Were any problems found? Yes → Repair as necessary Perform ABS VERIFICATION TEST - VER 1. No → Test Complete.

CR4020102200020X

Fig. 17 System Overvoltage (Part 2 of 2)

When Monitored and Set Condition:

SYSTEM OVERVOLTAGE

When Monitored: Ignition on. The CAB monitors the Fused B(+) circuit at all times for proper system voltage.

Set Condition: If the voltage is above 16.5 volts for greater than 420 milliseconds (ms), the Diagnostic Trouble Code (DTC) is set.

POSSIBLE CAUSES
BATTERY OVERCHARGED
FUSED IGNITION SWITCH OUTPUT HIGH
GROUND CIRCUIT OPEN
CAB - INTERNAL FAULT
INTERMITTENT DTC

TEST	ACTION
1	Turn the ignition on. With the DRBIII®, erase DTC's. Turn the ignition off. Turn the ignition on. Start the engine. With the DRBIII®, read DTC's. Does the DRBIII® display System Overvoltage DTC? Yes → Go To 2 No → Go To 6
2	Turn the ignition off. Inspect for battery charger connected to battery. Is a battery charger connected to the battery? Yes → Charge battery to proper level. Disconnect the battery charger. Clear DTC's. Perform ABS VERIFICATION TEST - VER 1. No → Go To 3

CR4020102200010X

Fig. 17 System Overvoltage (Part 1 of 2)

When Monitored and Set Condition:

SYSTEM UNDERVOLTAGE

When Monitored: Ignition on. The CAB monitors the Fused Ignition Switch Output circuit voltage above 10 km/h (6 mph) every 7 milliseconds for proper system voltage.

Set Condition: If the voltage is below 9.5 volts, the Diagnostic Trouble Code (DTC) is set.

POSSIBLE CAUSES
BATTERY VOLTAGE LOW
INTERMITTENT DTC
FUSED IGNITION SWITCH OUTPUT CIRCUIT HIGH RESISTANCE
CAB - INTERNAL FAULT

TEST	ACTION
1	Turn the ignition on. With the DRBIII®, erase DTC's. Turn the ignition off. Turn the ignition on. Start the engine. Drive the vehicle above 16 km/h (10 mph) for at least 20 seconds. Stop the vehicle With the DRBIII®, read DTC's. Does the DRBIII® display System Undervoltage DTC? Yes → Go To 2 No → Go To 5
2	Engine Running. Measure the battery voltage. Is the battery voltage below 10 volts? Yes → Refer to appropriate service information for charging system testing and repair. Perform ABS VERIFICATION TEST - VER 1. No → Go To 3
3	Disconnect the CAB harness connector. Turn the ignition on. Measure the voltage of the Fused Ignition Switch circuit. Is the voltage above 10 volts? Yes → Go To 4 No → Repair the Fused Ignition Switch Output Circuit for high resistance Perform ABS VERIFICATION TEST - VER 1.

CR4020102201010X

Fig. 18 System Undervoltage (Part 1 of 2). 2002

TEST	ACTION
4	If there are no potential causes remaining, view repair. Repair Replace the Controller Antilock Brake. Perform ABS VERIFICATION TEST - VER 1.
5	Turn the ignition off. Visually inspect the related wiring harness. Look for any chafed, pierced, pinched, or partially broken wires. Visually inspect the related wire harness connectors. Look for broken, bent, pushed out, or corroded terminals. Refer to any Hotline letters or Technical Service Bulletins that may apply. Were any problems found? Yes → Repair as necessary. Perform ABS VERIFICATION TEST - VER 1. No → Test Complete.

CR4020102201020X

Fig. 18 System Undervoltage (Part 2 of 2). 2002

TEST	ACTION
3	Turn the ignition off. Remove the ABS Fuse 21 from the IPM. Disconnect the CAB harness connector. Note: Check connector - Clean/repair as necessary. Using a test light connected to 12 volts, probe the Fused B(+) Circuit. Does the test light illuminate brightly? Yes → Repair the Fused B(+) Circuit short to ground. Perform ABS VERIFICATION TEST - VER 1. No → Go To 4
4	Turn the ignition off. Remove the ABS Fuse 21 from the IPM. The CAB must be connected for the results of this test to be valid. Using a test light connected to 12 volts, probe the Fused B(+) Circuit at the IPM fuse terminal. Does the test light illuminate brightly? Yes → Replace the Controller Antilock Brake Perform ABS VERIFICATION TEST - VER 1. No → Go To 5
5	Turn the ignition off. If there are no potential causes remaining, view repair. Continue Replace the Fuse. Perform ABS VERIFICATION TEST - VER 1.
6	Remove the ABS Fuse 21 from the IPM. Turn the ignition on. Measure the voltage of the Fused B+ supply to Fuse 21 in the IPM. Is the voltage above 10 volts? Yes → Go To 7 No → Repair the B+ Supply circuit for an open. Perform ABS VERIFICATION TEST - VER 1.
7	Turn the ignition off. Remove the ABS Fuse 21 from the IPM. Disconnect the CAB harness connector. Note: Check connector - Clean/repair as necessary. Measure the resistance of the Fused B(+) circuit between IPM Fuse terminal 21 and the CAB connector. Is the resistance below 5 ohms? Yes → Go To 8 No → Repair the Fuse B+ circuit for an open. Perform ABS VERIFICATION TEST - VER 1.
8	If there are no possible causes remaining, view repair. Repair Replace the Controller Antilock Brake in accordance with the Service Information. Perform ABS VERIFICATION TEST - VER 1.

CR4020102202020X

Fig. 19 Valve Power Feed Failure (Part 2 of 3). 2002

When Monitored and Set Condition:

VALVE POWER FEED FAILURE

When Monitored: Ignition ON for at least 3.5 seconds. ABS Power Relay closed. Valve command for a particular solenoid not present.

Set Condition: Low feedback voltage from the low side of all the solenoids for over 20 consecutive controller checks spaced 5 ms apart.

POSSIBLE CAUSES
INTERMITTENT DTC
BLOWN FUSE - FUSED B(+) CIRCUIT
NO B+ SUPPLY TO FUSE
FUSED B(+) CIRCUIT OPEN
B(+) CIRCUIT SHORTED TO GROUND
CAB - FUSED B(+) CIRCUIT OPEN
CAB - FUSED B(+) CIRCUIT SHORTED TO GROUND

TEST	ACTION
1	Turn the ignition on. With the DRBIII®, erase DTC's. Turn the ignition off. Turn the ignition on. Drive the vehicle above 25 km/h (15 mph) for at least 10 seconds. Stop the vehicle. With the DRBIII®, read DTC's. Does the DRBIII® display Valve Power Feed Circuit DTC present right now? Yes → Go To 2 No → Go To 9
2	Turn the ignition off. Remove and Inspect the ABS Fuse 21 in the IPM. Is the Fuse blown? Yes → Go To 3 No → Go To 6

CR4020102202010X

Fig. 19 Valve Power Feed Failure (Part 1 of 3). 2002

TEST	ACTION
9	Turn the ignition off. Visually inspect the related wiring harness. Look for any chafed, pierced, pinched, or partially broken wires. Visually inspect the related wire harness connectors. Look for broken, bent, pushed out, or corroded terminals. Refer to any Hotline letters or Technical Service Bulletins that may apply. Were any problems found? Yes → Repair as necessary. Perform ABS VERIFICATION TEST - VER 1. No → Test Complete.

CR4020102202030X

Fig. 19 Valve Power Feed Failure (Part 3 of 3). 2002

ABS VERIFICATION TEST - VER 1
1. Turn the ignition off. 2. Connect all previously disconnected components and connectors. 3. Ensure all accessories are turned off and the battery is fully charged. 4. Ensure that the Ignition is on, and with the DRBIII, erase all Diagnostic Trouble Codes from ALL modules. Start the engine and allow it to run for 2 minutes and fully operate the system that was malfunctioning. 5. Turn the ignition off and wait 5 seconds. Turn the ignition on and using the DRBIII, read DTC's from ALL modules. 6. If any Diagnostic Trouble Codes are present, return to Symptom list and troubleshoot new or recurring symptom. 7. If no DTC's present after turning ignition on, road test the vehicle for at least 5 minutes. Perform several antilock braking stops. 8. Caution: Ensure braking capability is available before road testing. 9. Again, with the DRBIII® read DTC's. If any DTC's are present, return to Symptom list. 10. If there are no Diagnostic Trouble Codes (DTC's) present, and the customer's concern can no longer be duplicated, the repair is complete. Are any DTC's present or is the original concern still present?   Yes → Repair is not complete, refer to appropriate symptom.   No → Repair is complete.

CR4020102204000X

Fig. 20 Verification Test

When Monitored and Set Condition:

BUS SYSTEM COMMUNICATION FAILURE

When Monitored: Ignition ON, continuously.

Set Condition: When the CAB does not receive a message from the instrument cluster for 10 seconds.

POSSIBLE CAUSES
INTERMITTENT CONDITION
ELECTRO-MECHANICAL INSTRUMENT CLUSTER DTC PRESENT
BUS CIRCUIT OPEN
CAB - INTERNAL FAILURE

TEST	ACTION
1	Turn the ignition on. With the DRBIII®, read DTCs. With the DRBIII®, read Freeze Frame information. With the DRBIII®, erase DTCs. Turn the ignition off. Turn the ignition on. With the DRBIII®, read DTCs. Does the DRBIII® display BUS SYSTEM COMMUNICATION FAILURE? Yes → Go To 2 No → Go To 4
2	Turn the ignition on. With the DRBIII®, read EMIC DTCs. Does the DRBIII® display NO ABS MESSAGE RECEIVED? Yes → Refer to symptom NO ABS MESSAGE RECEIVED Perform ABS VERIFICATION TEST - VER 1. No → Go To 3

LTV0500000003245

Fig. 21 Bus System Communication Failure (Part 1 of 2). 2003–06

When Monitored and Set Condition:

CAB INTERNAL FAILURE

When Monitored: Ignition on. The CAB monitors its internal microprocessors for correct operation.

Set Condition: If the CAB detects an internal fault, the DTC is set.

POSSIBLE CAUSES
INTERMITTENT DTC
DAMAGED CAB/CAB HARNESS CONNECTOR
CAB - GROUND CIRCUIT OPEN
ABS VALVE FUSED B(+) CIRCUIT OPEN
ABS PUMP FUSED B(+) CIRCUIT OPEN
CAB - INTERNAL FAULT

TEST	ACTION
1	Turn the ignition on. With the DRBIII®, read DTCs. With the DRBIII®, erase DTCs. Turn the ignition off. Turn the ignition on. With the DRBIII®, read DTCs. Does the DRBIII® display CAB INTERNAL FAILURE? Yes → Go To 2 No → Go To 6
2	Turn the ignition off. Disconnect the CAB harness connector. Inspect the CAB/CAB harness connector for damage. Is there any broken, bent, pushed out, corroded or spread terminals? Yes → Repair as necessary. Perform ABS VERIFICATION TEST - VER 1. No → Go To 3
3	Turn the ignition off. Disconnect the CAB harness connector. Using a 12-volt test light connected to 12-volts, probe the CAB harness connector ground circuits. Did the test light illuminate? Yes → Go To 4 No → Repair the CAB Ground circuit for an open. Perform ABS VERIFICATION TEST - VER 1.

LTV0500000003247

Fig. 22 Cab Internal Failure (Part 1 of 2). 2003–06

TEST	ACTION
3	Turn the ignition off. Disconnect the negative (-) battery cable. Disconnect the CAB harness connector. NOTE: check connector - Clean/repair as necessary. Measure the resistance of the Bus circuit between the CAB connector and the Data Link Connector (DLC). Is the resistance below 5.0 ohms? Yes → Replace the Controller Antilock Brake Perform ABS VERIFICATION TEST - VER 1. No → Repair the Bus circuit for an open. Perform ABS VERIFICATION TEST - VER 1.
4	Turn the ignition off. Visually inspect the related wiring harness. Look for any chafed, pierced, pinched, or partially broken wires. Visually inspect the related wire harness connectors. Look for broken, bent, pushed out, or corroded terminals. Were any problems found? Yes → Repair as necessary. Perform ABS VERIFICATION TEST - VER 1. No → Test Complete.

LTV0500000003246

Fig. 21 Bus System Communication Failure (Part 2 of 2). 2003–06

TEST	ACTION
4	Turn the ignition off. Using a 12-volt test light connected to ground, probe the ABS Valve Fused B(+) circuit at the CAB harness connector. Did the test light illuminate? Yes → Go To 5 No → Repair the ABS Valve Fused B(+) circuit for an open. Perform ABS VERIFICATION TEST - VER 1.
5	Turn the ignition off. Using a 12-volt test light connected to ground, probe the ABS Pump Fused B(+) circuit at the CAB harness connector. Did the test light illuminate? Yes → Replace the Controller Antilock Brake Perform ABS VERIFICATION TEST - VER 1. No → Repair the ABS Pump Fused B(+) circuit for an open. Perform ABS VERIFICATION TEST - VER 1.
6	Turn the ignition off. Visually inspect the related wiring harness. Look for any chafed, pierced, pinched, or partially broken wires. Visually inspect the related wire harness connectors. Look for broken, bent, pushed out, or corroded terminals. Refer to any Hotline letters or Technical Service Bulletins that may apply. Were any problems found? Yes → Repair as necessary. Perform ABS VERIFICATION TEST - VER 1. No → Test Complete.

LTV0500000003248

Fig. 22 Cab Internal Failure (Part 2 of 2). 2003–06

When Monitored and Set Condition:

INCORRECT TONE WHEEL FAILURE

When Monitored: Ignition ON. Vehicle speed above 40 km/h (25 mph) for 2 minutes.

Set Condition: When the CAB detects an unexpected wheel speed condition caused by a tire size that does not meet vehicle specification.

POSSIBLE CAUSES
INCORRECT TIRES ON VEHICLE
INCORRECT TONE WHEEL ON VEHICLE

TEST	ACTION
1	Inspect the tire sizes on the vehicle. Is a smaller than production tire, mini spare, or two mini spares installed on both front wheels? Yes → Replace the incorrect tire(s) size with production size tire(s). Perform ABS VERIFICATION TEST - VER 1. No → Go To 2
2	Count the number of tone wheel teeth on both of the front driveshafts. Does one or both tone wheel(s) have (56 or 40) teeth? Yes → Replace the front driveshaft(s) with the incorrect number of tone wheel teeth. Perform ABS VERIFICATION TEST - VER 1. No → Test Complete.

LTV0500000003249

Fig. 23 Incorrect Tone Wheel Failure. 2003–06

Test Note: All symptoms listed above are diagnosed using the same tests. The title for the tests will be LEFT FRONT SENSOR CIRCUIT FAILURE.

When Monitored and Set Condition:

LEFT FRONT SENSOR CIRCUIT FAILURE

When Monitored: Ignition on. The CAB monitors the wheel speed circuit continuously.

Set Condition: If the CAB detects an open or shorted wheel speed sensor circuit, the Diagnostic Trouble Code (DTC) will set.

LEFT REAR SENSOR CIRCUIT FAILURE

When Monitored: Ignition on. The CAB monitors the wheel speed circuit continuously.

Set Condition: If the CAB detects an open or shorted wheel speed sensor circuit, the Diagnostic Trouble Code (DTC) will set.

RIGHT FRONT SENSOR CIRCUIT FAILURE

When Monitored: Ignition on. The CAB monitors the wheel speed circuit continuously.

Set Condition: If the CAB detects an open or shorted wheel speed sensor circuit, the Diagnostic Trouble Code (DTC) will set.

RIGHT REAR SENSOR CIRCUIT FAILURE

When Monitored: Ignition on. The CAB monitors the wheel speed circuit continuously.

Set Condition: If the CAB detects an open or shorted wheel speed sensor circuit, the Diagnostic Trouble Code (DTC) will set.

POSSIBLE CAUSES
INTERMITTENT CONDITION
WHEEL SPEED SENSOR OR CONNECTOR DAMAGE
WHEEL SPEED SENSOR SIGNAL CIRCUIT FAULT
WHEEL SPEED SENSOR 12 VOLT SUPPLY CIRCUIT SHORT TO GROUND
WHEEL SPEED SENSOR 12 VOLT SUPPLY CIRCUIT OPEN
WHEEL SPEED SENSOR SIGNAL CIRCUIT SHORT TO GROUND
WHEEL SPEED SENSOR SIGNAL CIRCUIT OPEN

LTV0500000003250

Fig. 24 Left Front, Left Rear, Right Front & Right Rear Sensor Circuit Failure (Part 1 of 5). 2003–06

POSSIBLE CAUSES
CAB - 12 VOLT SUPPLY CIRCUIT FAULT
CAB - SIGNAL CIRCUIT FAULT
WHEEL SPEED SENSOR 12 VOLT SUPPLY SHORT TO GROUND
WHEEL SPEED SENSOR SIGNAL CIRCUIT INOPERATIVE

TEST	ACTION

1	Turn the ignition on.
	With the DRBIII®, read DTCs.
	With the DRBIII®, read the Freeze Frame information.
	With the DRBIII®, erase DTCs.
	Turn the ignition off.
	Turn the ignition on.
	With the DRBIII®, read DTCs.
	NOTE: The CAB must sense all four wheels at 25km/h (15 mph) before it will extinguish the ABS indicators.
	Does the DRBIII® display SENSOR CIRCUIT FAILURE?
	  Yes → Go To 2
	  No → Go To 13

2	Turn the ignition off.
	Inspect the CAB connector, affected Wheel Speed Sensor, and affected Wheel Speed Sensor connector.
	Is the affected Wheel Speed Sensor or any of the connectors damaged?
	  Yes → Repair as necessary.
	       Perform ABS VERIFICATION TEST - VER 1.
	  No → Go To 3

3	Turn the ignition off.
	Disconnect the affected Wheel Speed Sensor connector.
	Note: Check connector - Clean/repair as necessary.
	Turn the ignition on.
	Measure the voltage between affected Wheel Speed Sensor 12 Volt Supply circuit and ground.
	Is the voltage above 10 volts?
	  Yes → Go To 6
	  No → Go To 4

4	Turn the ignition off.
	Disconnect the CAB harness connector.
	Disconnect the affected Wheel Speed Sensor connector.
	Using a 12-volt test light connected to 12-volts, probe the affected Wheel Speed Sensor 12 Volt Supply circuit.
	Does the test light illuminate?
	  Yes → Repair the affected Wheel Speed Sensor 12 Volt Supply circuit for a short to ground.
	       Perform ABS VERIFICATION TEST - VER 1.
	  No → Go To 5

LTV0500000003251

Fig. 24 Left Front, Left Rear, Right Front & Right Rear Sensor Circuit Failure (Part 2 of 5). 2003–06

TEST	ACTION

5	Turn the ignition off.
	Disconnect the CAB harness connector.
	Disconnect the affected Wheel Speed Sensor connector.
	Connect a jumper wire between affected Wheel Speed Sensor 12 Volt Supply circuit and ground.
	Using a 12-volt test light connected to 12-volts, probe the affected Wheel Speed Sensor 12 Volt Supply circuit.
	Does the test light illuminate?
	  Yes → Go To 6
	  No → Repair the affected Wheel Speed Sensor 12 Volt Supply circuit for an open.
	       Perform ABS VERIFICATION TEST - VER 1.

6	Turn the ignition off.
	Disconnect the affected Wheel Speed Sensor connector.
	NOTE: Check connector - Clean/repair as necessary.
	Turn the ignition on.
	Measure the voltage between affected Wheel Speed Sensor Signal circuit and ground.
	Is the voltage above 1 volt?
	  Yes → Repair the affected Wheel Speed Sensor Signal circuit for a short to voltage.
	       Perform ABS VERIFICATION TEST - VER 1.
	  No → Go To 7

7	Turn the ignition off.
	Disconnect the CAB harness connector.
	Disconnect the affected Wheel Speed Sensor connector.
	Using a 12-volt test light connected to 12-volts, probe the affected Wheel Speed Sensor Signal circuit.
	Does the test light illuminate?
	  Yes → Repair the affected Wheel Speed Sensor Signal circuit for a short to ground.
	       Perform ABS VERIFICATION TEST - VER 1.
	  No → Go To 8

8	Turn the ignition off.
	Disconnect the CAB harness connector.
	Disconnect the affected Wheel Speed Sensor connector.
	Connect a jumper wire between affected Wheel Speed Sensor Signal circuit and ground.
	Using a 12-volt test light connected to 12-volts, probe the affected Wheel Speed Sensor Signal circuit.
	Does the test light illuminate?
	  Yes → Go To 9
	  No → Repair the affected Wheel Speed Sensor Signal circuit for an open.
	       Perform ABS VERIFICATION TEST - VER 1.

LTV0500000003252

Fig. 24 Left Front, Left Rear, Right Front & Right Rear Sensor Circuit Failure (Part 3 of 5). 2003–06

TEST	ACTION

9	Turn the ignition off.
	Remove the CAB harness strain relief to access wires.
	Reconnect the CAB harness connector.
	Turn the ignition on.
	Measure the voltage between affected Wheel Speed Sensor 12 Volt Supply circuit and ground.
	Is the voltage above 10 volts?
	  Yes → Go To 10
	  No → Replace the Controller Antilock Brake
	
	       Perform ABS VERIFICATION TEST - VER 1.

10	Turn the ignition off.
	Remove the CAB harness strain relief to access wires.
	Reconnect the CAB harness connector.
	Turn the ignition on.
	Measure the voltage between affected Wheel Speed Sensor 12 Volt Supply circuit and affected Wheel Speed Sensor Signal circuit.
	Is the voltage above 10 volts?
	  Yes → Go To 11
	  No → Replace the Controller Antilock Brake
	
	       Perform ABS VERIFICATION TEST - VER 1.

11	Turn the ignition off.
	Reconnect ALL affected Wheel Speed Sensor circuit connectors.
	Disconnect the affected Wheel Speed Sensor connector.
	Turn the ignition on.
	Measure the voltage of the affected Wheel Speed Sensor 12 Volt Supply circuit in the affected Wheel Speed Sensor connector while reconnecting the sensor connector.
	Did the affected Wheel Speed Sensor 12 Volt Supply circuit drop voltage to 0 DC volts?
	  Yes → Replace the affected Wheel Speed Sensor
	
	       Perform ABS VERIFICATION TEST - VER 1.
	  No → Go To 12

12	Turn the ignition off.
	Reconnect ALL affected Wheel Speed Sensor circuit connectors.
	Turn the ignition on.
	Measure the DC voltage of the Wheel Speed Sensor Signal circuit in the affected Wheel Speed Sensor connector.
	Slowly rotate the wheel.
	Does the DC voltage toggle between 1.6 volts to .8 volts?
	  Yes → Go To 13
	  No → Replace the affected Wheel Speed Sensor
	
	       Perform ABS VERIFICATION TEST - VER 1.

LTV0500000003253

Fig. 24 Left Front, Left Rear, Right Front & Right Rear Sensor Circuit Failure (Part 4 of 5). 2003–06

TEST	ACTION
13	Turn the ignition off. Visually inspect the related wiring harness. Look for any chafed, pierced, pinched, or partially broken wires. Visually inspect the related wire harness connectors. Look for broken, bent, pushed out, or corroded terminals. Refer to any Hotline letters or Technical Service Bulletins that may apply. Were any problems found? Yes → Repair as necessary. Perform ABS VERIFICATION TEST - VER 1. No → Test Complete.

LTV0500000003254

Fig. 24 Left Front, Left Rear, Right Front & Right Rear Sensor Circuit Failure (Part 5 of 5). 2003–06

POSSIBLE CAUSES
WHEEL SPEED SIGNAL FAILURE DTC PRESENT
AFFECTED WHEEL SPEED SENSOR SIGNAL INOPERATIVE
AFFECTED WHEEL SPEED SENSOR CONNECTOR DAMAGED
AFFECTED WHEEL SPEED SENSOR TONE WHEEL DAMAGED
AFFECTED WHEEL SPEED SENSOR AIR GAP FAULT
WHEEL BEARING FAULT
BRAKE LINING FAULT
AFFECTED WHEEL SPEED SENSOR CIRCUIT ELECTRICAL FAULT

TEST	ACTION
1	Turn the ignition on. With the DRBIII®, read DTCs. With the DRBIII®, read Freeze Frame information. **NOTE: The CAB must sense ALL 4 wheels at 25 km/h (15 mph) before it will extinguish the ABS indicators.** Does the DRBIII® display WHEEL SPEED/SIGNAL FAILURE and SENSOR CIRCUIT FAILURE? Yes → Refer to the affected Wheel Speed SENSOR CIRCUIT FAILURE Perform ABS VERIFICATION TEST - VER 1. No → Go To 2
2	Turn the ignition on. With the DRBIII® in Sensors, monitor ALL the Wheel Speed Sensor Signals while an assistant drives the vehicle. Slowly accelerate as straight as possible from a stop to 24 km/h (15 mph). Is the affected Wheel Speed Signal showing 0 km/h (0 mph)? Yes → Go To 3 No → The condition is not present at this time. Monitor DRBIII® parameters while wiggling the related wiring harness. Refer to any Technical Service Bulletins (TSB) that may apply. Visually inspect the related wiring harness and connector terminals. Perform ABS VERIFICATION TEST - VER 1.
3	Turn the ignition off. Inspect the CAB connector, affected Wheel Speed Sensor, and affected Wheel Speed Sensor connector. Is the Wheel Speed Sensor or any connector damaged? Yes → Repair as necessary. Perform ABS VERIFICATION TEST - VER 1. No → Go To 4

LTV0500000003256

Fig. 25 Left Front, Left Rear, Right Front & Right Rear Speed Signal Failure (Part 2 of 3). 2003–06

When Monitored and Set Condition:

LEFT FRONT WHEEL SPEED SIGNAL FAILURE

When Monitored: Wheel speed are checked and verified at drive off and continuously thereafter.

Set Condition: If, during an ABS stop, the CAB commands any valve solenoid on for an extended length of time, and does not see a corresponding wheel speed change, the Diagnostic Trouble Code (DTC) is set. The DTC can also set if the signal is missing or erratic.

LTV0500000003255

Fig. 25 Left Front, Left Rear, Right Front & Right Rear Speed Signal Failure (Part 1 of 3). 2003–06

TEST	ACTION
4	Turn ignition off. Inspect the affected Tone Wheel for damaged, missing teeth, cracks, or looseness. **NOTE: The Tone Wheel teeth should be perfectly square, not bent, or nicked.** Is the affected Tone Wheel OK? Yes → Go To 5 No → Replace the Tone Wheel Perform ABS VERIFICATION TEST - VER 1.
5	Turn the ignition off. Using a Feeler Gauge, measure the affected Wheel Speed Sensor Air Gap. **NOTE: Refer to the appropriate service information, if necessary, for procedures or specifications.** Is the Air Gap OK? Yes → Go To 6 No → Repair as necessary. Perform ABS VERIFICATION TEST - VER 1.
6	Turn the ignition off. Inspect the wheel bearings for excessive runout or clearance. **NOTE: Refer to the appropriate service information, if necessary, for procedures or specifications.** Is the bearing clearance OK? Yes → Go To 7 No → Repair as necessary. Perform ABS VERIFICATION TEST - VER 1.
7	Turn the ignition off. Visually inspect brakes for locking up due to lining contamination or overheating. Inspect all Components for defects which may cause a Signal DTC to set. Is any Component Damaged? Yes → Repair as necessary. Perform ABS VERIFICATION TEST - VER 1. No → Refer to symptom SENSOR CIRCUIT FAILURE for further diagnostics. Perform ABS VERIFICATION TEST - VER 1.

LTV0500000003257

Fig. 25 Left Front, Left Rear, Right Front & Right Rear Speed Signal Failure (Part 3 of 3). 2003–06

When Monitored and Set Condition:

PUMP CIRCUIT FAILURE

When Monitored: Ignition on. The CAB commands the pump on at 20 km/h (12 mph) to check its operation, if the brake switch is not applied. If the brake is applied, the test will run at 40 km/h (25 mph).

Set Condition: The DTC is stored when the CAB detects: 1) Improper voltage decay after the pump was turned off. 2) Pump not energized by the CAB, but voltage is present for 3.5 seconds. 3) Pump is turned on by the CAB, but without sufficient voltage to operate it.

POSSIBLE CAUSES
CAB - PUMP MOTOR RUNNING CONTINUOUSLY
ABS PUMP FUSE
ABS PUMP MOTOR INTERMITTENT DTC
DAMAGED CAB/CAB HARNESS CONNECTOR
ABS PUMP FUSED B(+) CIRCUIT INTERMITTENT SHORT TO GROUND
ABS PUMP FUSED B(+) CIRCUIT SHORT TO GROUND
CAB - INTERNAL FAULT
ABS PUMP MOTOR INOPERATIVE
ABS PUMP MOTOR OPEN
ABS PUMP MOTOR B(+) CIRCUIT OPEN
ABS PUMP MOTOR GROUND CIRCUIT OPEN
CAB - INTERNAL FAULT

TEST	ACTION
1	Turn the ignition off. Turn the ignition on. Monitor the ABS Pump Motor for continuous operation. **NOTE: The CAB must sense ALL wheels at 25 km/h (15 mph) before it will extinguish the ABS indicators.** Is the ABS Pump Motor running continuously? Yes → Replace the Controller Antilock Brake Perform ABS VERIFICATION TEST - VER 1. No → Go To 2

LTV0500000003258

Fig. 26 Pump Circuit Failure (Part 1 of 4). 2003–06

TEST	ACTION
7	Turn the ignition off. Reconnect the CAB harness connector. Using a 12-volt test light connected to 12-volts, probe the ABS Pump Fused B(+) circuit fuse terminal. Does the test light illuminate? Yes → Replace the Controller Antilock Brake Perform ABS VERIFICATION TEST - VER 1. No → Replace the ABS Pump fuse. If the fuse is open make sure to check for a short to ground. Perform ABS VERIFICATION TEST - VER 1.
8	Turn the ignition off. Disconnect the CAB harness connector. Inspect the CAB and CAB harness connector for damage. Is there any broken, bent, pushed out, corroded, or spread terminals? Yes → Repair as necessary. Perform ABS VERIFICATION TEST - VER 1. No → Go To 9
9	Turn the ignition off. Reinstall the ABS Pump fuse. Disconnect the ABS Pump Motor connector. Check connectors - Clean/repair as necessary. Connect a 10 gauge 40 amp fused jumper wire between the ABS Pump Fused B(+) terminal in the CAB harness connector to the ABS Pump Motor connector RED wired terminal. Connect a 10 gauge jumper wire between the Ground circuit terminal in the CAB harness connector to the ABS Pump Motor connector BLACK wired terminal. Did the ABS Pump Motor operate? Yes → Replace the Controller Antilock Brake Perform ABS VERIFICATION TEST - VER 1. No → Go To 10
10	Turn the ignition off. Disconnect the ABS Pump Motor connector. Check connectors - Clean/repair as necessary. Connect a 10 gauge 40 amp fused jumper wire between the ABS Pump Motor connector RED wired terminal and an alternate 40 amp capable B(+) source. Connect a 10 gauge jumper wire between the ABS Pump Motor connector BLACK wired terminal and ground. Did the ABS Pump Motor operate? Yes → Go To 11 No → Replace the Hydraulic Control Unit Perform ABS VERIFICATION TEST - VER 1.

LTV0500000003260

Fig. 26 Pump Circuit Failure (Part 3 of 4). 2003–06

TEST	ACTION
2	Turn the ignition off. Turn the ignition on. With the DRBIII®, read DTCs. With the DRBIII®, erase DTCs. Turn the ignition off. Turn the ignition on. With the DRBIII®, actuate the ABS Pump Motor. Did the ABS Pump Motor operate? Yes → Go To 3 No → Go To 4
3	Turn the ignition off. Visually inspect the related wiring harness. Look for any chafed, pierced, pinched, or partially broken wires. Make sure the Pump Motor connecter is secure. Visually inspect the related wire harness connectors. Look for broken, bent, pushed out, or corroded terminals. Refer to any Hotline letters or Technical Service Bulletins that may apply. Were any problems found? Yes → Repair as necessary. Perform ABS VERIFICATION TEST - VER 1. No → Test Complete.
4	Turn the ignition off. Remove and inspect the ABS Pump fuse. Is the ABS Pump fuse open? Yes → Go To 5 No → Go To 8
5	Turn the ignition off. Visually inspect the ABS Pump Fused B(+) circuit in the wiring harness. Look for any sign of an intermittent short to ground. Is the wiring harness OK? Yes → Go To 6 No → Repair the ABS Pump Fused B(+) circuit for a short to ground. Perform ABS VERIFICATION TEST - VER 1.
6	Turn the ignition off. Disconnect the CAB harness connector. Check connectors - Clean/repair as necessary. Using a 12-volt test light connected to 12-volts, probe the ABS Pump Fused B(+) circuit fuse terminal. Does the test light illuminate? Yes → Repair the ABS Pump Fused B(+) circuit for a short to ground. Perform ABS VERIFICATION TEST - VER 1. No → Go To 7

LTV0500000003259

Fig. 26 Pump Circuit Failure (Part 2 of 4). 2003–06

TEST	ACTION
11	Turn the ignition off. Disconnect the ABS Pump Motor connector. Check connectors - Clean/repair as necessary. Connect a 10 gauge 40 amp fused jumper wire between the ABS Pump Fused B(+) terminal in the CAB harness connector to the ABS Pump Motor connector RED wired terminal. Connect a 10 gauge jumper wire between the ABS Pump Motor connector BLACK wired terminal and ground. Did the ABS Pump Motor operate? Yes → Repair the ABS Pump Motor Fused B(+) circuit for an open. Perform ABS VERIFICATION TEST - VER 1. No → Repair the ABS Pump Motor Ground circuit for an open. Perform ABS VERIFICATION TEST - VER 1.

LTV0500000003261

Fig. 26 Pump Circuit Failure (Part 4 of 4). 2003–06

When Monitored and Set Condition:

SYSTEM UNDER VOLTAGE

When Monitored: Ignition on. The CAB monitors the Fused Ignition Switch Output circuit voltage above 10 km/h (6 mph) for proper system voltage.

Set Condition: If the voltage is below 9.5 volts, the Diagnostic Trouble Code (DTC) is set.

POSSIBLE CAUSES
INTERMITTENT DTC
DAMAGED CAB/CAB HARNESS CONNECTOR
RUNNING BATTERY VOLTAGE LOW
CAB - GROUND CIRCUIT OPEN
FUSED IGNITION SWITCH OUTPUT (RUN) CIRCUIT OPEN
CAB - INTERNAL FAULT

TEST	ACTION
1	Turn the ignition on. With the DRBIII®, read DTC's. With the DRBIII®, erase DTC's. Turn the ignition off. Turn the ignition on. Start the engine. Drive the vehicle above 16 km/h (10 mph) for at least 20 seconds. Stop the vehicle With the DRBIII®, read DTC's. Does the DRBIII® display SYSTEM UNDER VOLTAGE ? Yes → Go To 2 No → Go To 6
2	Engine Running. Measure the battery voltage. Is the battery voltage below 10 volts? Yes → Diagnose charging system. Perform ABS VERIFICATION TEST - VER 1. No → Go To 3

LTV0500000003262

Fig. 27 System Undervoltage (Part 1 of 2). 2003–06

When Monitored and Set Condition:

VALVE POWER FEED FAILURE

When Monitored: Ignition ON. ABS Power Relay closed. Valve command for a particular solenoid not present.

Set Condition: Low feedback voltage from the low side of all the solenoids.

POSSIBLE CAUSES
INTERMITTENT DTC
ABS VALVE FUSE
ABS VALVE FUSED B(+) SUPPLY CIRCUIT OPEN
ABS VALVE FUSED B(+) CIRCUIT OPEN
ABS VALVE FUSED B(+) CIRCUIT INTERMITTENT SHORT TO GROUND
ABS VALVE FUSED B(+) CIRCUIT SHORT TO GROUND
DAMAGED CAB/CAB HARNESS CONNECTOR
CAB - GROUND CIRCUIT OPEN
CAB - INTERNAL FAULT

TEST	ACTION
1	Turn the ignition on. With the DRBIII®, read DTC's. With the DRBIII®, erase DTC's. Turn the ignition off. Turn the ignition on. With the DRBIII®, read DTC's. Does the DRBIII® display VALVE POWER FEED FAILURE? Yes → Go To 2 No → Go To 10
2	Turn the ignition off. Remove and Inspect the ABS Valve fuse. Is the ABS Valve fuse open? Yes → Go To 3 No → Go To 4

LTV0500000003264

Fig. 28 Valve Power Feed Failure (Part 1 of 3).
2003–06

TEST	ACTION
3	Turn the ignition off. Disconnect the CAB harness connector. Inspect the CAB and CAB harness connector for damage. Is there any broken, bent, pushed out, corroded, or spread terminals? Yes → Repair as necessary. Perform ABS VERIFICATION TEST - VER 1. No → Go To 4
4	Turn the ignition off. Disconnect the CAB harness connector. Using a 12-volt test light connected to 12-volts, probe the Ground circuits. Does the test light illuminate? Yes → Go To 5 No → Repair the Ground circuit for an open. Perform ABS VERIFICATION TEST - VER 1.
5	Turn the ignition on. Using a 12-volt test light connected to ground, probe the Fused Ignition Switch Output (RUN) circuit. Does the test light illuminate? Yes → Replace the Controller Antilock Brake Perform ABS VERIFICATION TEST - VER 1. No → Repair the Fused Ignition Switch Output (RUN) circuit for an open. Perform ABS VERIFICATION TEST - VER 1.
6	Turn the ignition off. Visually inspect the related wiring harness. Look for any chafed, pierced, pinched, or partially broken wires. Visually inspect the related wire harness connectors. Look for broken, bent, pushed out, or corroded terminals. Refer to any Hotline letters or Technical Service Bulletins that may apply. Ensure the battery is fully charged. Inspect the vehicle for aftermarket accessories that may exceed the Generator System output. Using the wiring diagram/schematic as a guide, inspect the wiring and connectors. Were any problems found? Yes → Repair as necessary. Perform ABS VERIFICATION TEST - VER 1. No → Test Complete.

LTV0500000003263

Fig. 27 System Undervoltage (Part 2 of 2). 2003–06

TEST	ACTION
3	Turn the ignition off. Visually inspect the ABS Valve Fused B(+) circuit in the wiring harness. Look for any sign of an intermittent short to ground. Is the wiring harness OK? Yes → Go To 4 No → Repair the ABS Valve Fused B(+) circuit for a short to ground. Perform ABS VERIFICATION TEST - VER 1.
4	Turn the ignition off. Disconnect the CAB harness connector. **Note: Check connector - Clean/repair as necessary.** Using a test light connected to 12 volts, probe the ABS Valve Fused B(+) circuit fuse terminal. Did the test light illuminate? Yes → Repair the ABS Valve Fused B(+) circuit for a short to ground. Perform ABS VERIFICATION TEST - VER 1. No → Go To 5
5	Turn the ignition off. Reconnect the CAB harness connector. **NOTE: The CAB harness connector must be reconnected for the results of this test to be valid.** Using a test light connected to 12 volts, probe the ABS Valve Fused B(+) circuit fuse terminal. Did the test light illuminate? Yes → Replace the Controller Antilock Brake Perform ABS VERIFICATION TEST - VER 1. No → Replace the ABS Valve Fused B(+) fuse. If the fuse is open make sure to check for a short to ground. Perform ABS VERIFICATION TEST - VER 1.
6	Turn the ignition off. Disconnect the CAB harness connector. Inspect the CAB and CAB harness connector for damage. Is there any broken, bent, pushed out, corroded or spread terminals? Yes → Repair as necessary. Perform ABS VERIFICATION TEST - VER 1. No → Go To 7
7	Turn the ignition off. Using a 12-volt test light connected to ground, probe the B(+) supply at the ABS Valve fuse terminal. Did the test light illuminate? Yes → Go To 8 No → Repair the ABS Valve Fused B(+) supply circuit for an open. Perform ABS VERIFICATION TEST - VER 1.

LTV0500000003265

Fig. 28 Valve Power Feed Failure (Part 2 of 3).
2003–06

TEST	ACTION
8	Reinstall the ABS Valve fuse. Disconnect the CAB harness connector. Using a 12-volt test light connected to ground, probe the ABS Valve Fused B(+) circuit at the CAB harness connector. Did the test light illuminate? Yes → Go To 9 No → Repair the ABS Valve Fused B(+) circuit for an open. Perform ABS VERIFICATION TEST - VER 1.
9	Turn the ignition off. Using a 12-volt test light connected to 12-volts, probe the ground circuits at the CAB harness connector. Did the test light illuminate? Yes → Replace the Controller Antilock Brake Perform ABS VERIFICATION TEST - VER 1. No → Repair the CAB Ground circuit for an open. Perform ABS VERIFICATION TEST - VER 1.
10	Turn the ignition off. Visually inspect the related wiring harness. Look for any chafed, pierced, pinched, or partially broken wires. Visually inspect the related wire harness connectors. Look for broken, bent, pushed out, or corroded terminals. Refer to any Hotline letters or Technical Service Bulletins that may apply. Were any problems found? Yes → Repair as necessary. Perform ABS VERIFICATION TEST - VER 1. No → Test Complete.

LTV0500000003266

Fig. 28   Valve Power Feed Failure (Part 3 of 3).
2003–06

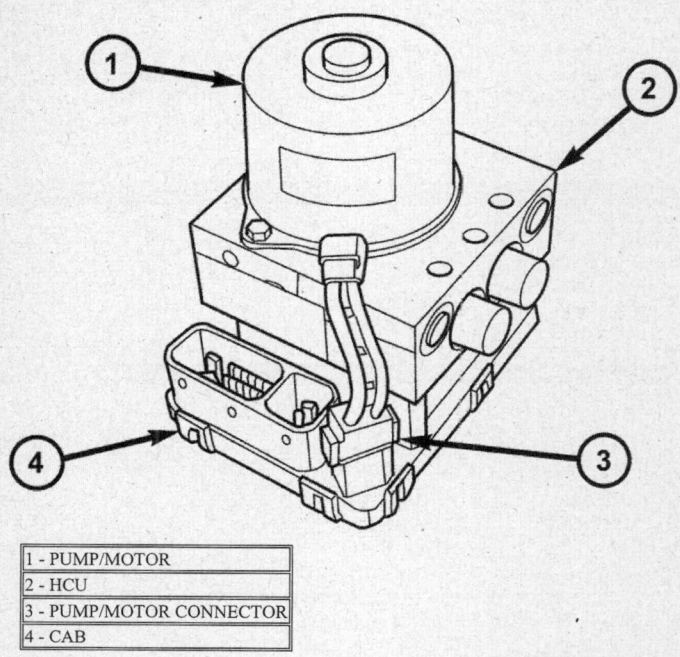

1 - PUMP/MOTOR
2 - HCU
3 - PUMP/MOTOR CONNECTOR
4 - CAB

LTV0500000003267

Fig. 29   Integrated control unit

PT Cruiser

NOTE: On Air Bag Equipped Models, Refer To "Air Bag System Precautions" Located In The Front Of This Manual For System Disarming & Arming Procedures.

NOTE: Refer To "Computer Relearn Procedures" Located In The Front Of This Manual When Battery Power To The Computer Has Been Interrupted.

NOTE: "Electrical Symbol & Wire Color Code Identification" Located In The Front Of This Manual May Be Used As An Aid When Using Wiring Circuits Found In This Section.

INDEX

	Page No.		Page No.		Page No.
Description	5-19	Intermittents & Poor		Brake System Bleed	5-20
Diagnosis & Testing	5-19	Connections	5-19	Component Replacement	5-20
Accessing Diagnostic Trouble		Symptom Tests	5-19	Controller Anti-Lock Brake	
Codes	5-19	Wiring Diagrams	5-19	(CAB)	5-20
Clearing Diagnostic Trouble		**Diagnostic Chart Index**	5-23	Front Wheel Speed Sensor	5-20
Codes	5-19	**Precautions**	5-19	Integrated Control Unit (ICU)	5-21
Connector Pin Identification	5-19	Air Bag Systems	5-19	Pump/Motor	5-21
Diagnostic Tests	5-19	Battery Ground Cable	5-19	Rear Wheel Speed Sensor	5-21
Diagnostic Trouble Code		General Service Precautions	5-19		
Interpretation	5-19	**System Service**	5-20		

PRECAUTIONS

Air Bag Systems

Refer to "Air Bag System Precautions" in the front of this manual for system disarming and arming procedures.

Battery Ground Cable

Prior to service disconnect battery ground cable and isolate as required.

General Service Precautions

Certain components of the anti-lock brake system are not intended to be serviced individually. Attempting to remove or disconnect components of this type may result in personal injury and/or improper system operation. Only the components with removal and installation procedures should be serviced.

Observe the following general precautions when servicing the anti-lock brake system:

1. If any welding work is to be performed using an arc welder, Controller Anti-Lock Brake (CAB) should be disconnected.
2. When ignition switch is in On position, CAB electrical connector should not be disconnected or connected.
3. Some components of ABS system are not serviced separately and must be serviced as complete assemblies. Do not disassemble any component which is designated as non-serviceable.

DESCRIPTION

When wheel slip is detected during a brake application, the ABS enters anti-lock mode. During anti-lock braking, hydraulic pressure in the individual wheel circuits is controlled to prevent any wheel from slipping. A separate hydraulic line and specific solenoid valves are provided for each wheel. The ABS can decrease, hold, or increase hydraulic pressure to each wheel brake. The ABS cannot, however, increase hydraulic pressure above the amount which is transmitted by the master cylinder during braking.

During anti-lock braking, a series of rapid pulsations is felt in the brake pedal. These pulsations are caused by the rapid changes in position of the individual solenoid valves as the EBCM responds to wheel speed sensor inputs and attempts to prevent wheel slip. These pedal pulsations are present only during anti-lock braking and stop when normal braking is resumed or when the vehicle comes to a stop. A ticking or popping noise may also be heard as the solenoid valves cycle rapidly. During anti-lock braking on dry pavement, intermittent chirping noises may be heard as the tires approach slipping. These noises and pedal pulsations are considered normal during anti-lock operation.

CAV	CIRCUIT	FUNCTION
1	B8 18RD/DB	LEFT FRONT WHEEL SPEED SENSOR SIGNAL
2	B9 18RD	LEFT FRONT WHEEL SPEED SENSOR 12 VOLT SUPPLY
3	-	-
4	F12 18DB/WT	FUSED IGNITION SWITCH OUTPUT (RUN-START)
5	B3 18LG/DB	LEFT REAR WHEEL SPEED SENSOR SIGNAL
6	B4 18LG	LEFT REAR WHEEL SPEED SENSOR 12 VOLT SUPPLY
7	-	-
8	Z1 12BK	GROUND
9	A20 12RD/DB	FUSED B(+)
10	D25 18VT/YL	PCI BUS
11	-	-
12	-	-
13	-	-
14	-	-
15	B27 18RD/YL	TRACTION CONTROL SWITCH SENSE
16	-	-
17	-	-
18	L50 18WT/TN	BRAKE LAMP SWITCH OUTPUT
19	B6 18WT/DB	RIGHT FRONT WHEEL SPEED SENSOR SIGNAL
20	B7 18WT	RIGHT FRONT WHEEL SPEED SENSOR 12 VOLT SUPPLY
21	-	-
22	B2 18YL	RIGHT REAR WHEEL SPEED SENSOR 12 VOLT SUPPLY
23	B1 18YL/DB	RIGHT REAR WHEEL SPEED SENSOR SIGNAL
24	Z1 12BK	GROUND
25	A10 12RD/DG	FUSED B(+)

CR4020002025000X

Fig. 1 Controller Anti-Lock Brake (CAB) connector & terminal identification. 2002–04

Vehicles equipped with ABS may be stopped by applying normal force to the brake pedal. Brake pedal operation during normal braking is no different than that of previous non-ABS systems. Maintaining a constant force on the brake pedal provides the shortest stopping distance while maintaining vehicle stability.

DIAGNOSIS & TESTING

Accessing Diagnostic Trouble Codes

Connect a suitably programmed scan tool to Data Link Connector (DLC) and follow manufacturer's instructions.

Diagnostic Trouble Code Interpretation

Refer to "Diagnostic Chart Index" for diagnostic trouble code interpretation.

Connector Pin Identification

Refer to **Figs. 1 and 2** for pin connector and terminal identification.

Wiring Diagrams

Refer to **Figs. 3 and 4** for wiring diagrams.

Diagnostic Tests

Refer to **Figs. 5 through 19** for diagnostic tests.

Symptom Tests

Refer to **Figs. 20 through 42** for diagnostic tests.

Clearing Diagnostic Trouble Codes

Connect a suitably programmed scan tool to Data Link Connector (DLC) and follow manufacturer's instructions.

Intermittents & Poor Connections

Most Intermittents are caused by faulty electrical connections or wiring, although a sticking relay or solenoid can also cause an intermittent condition. Inspect wiring and connectors for the following:

1. Poor mating of connector halves, or terminals not fully seated in connector body.
2. Dirt or corrosion on terminals.

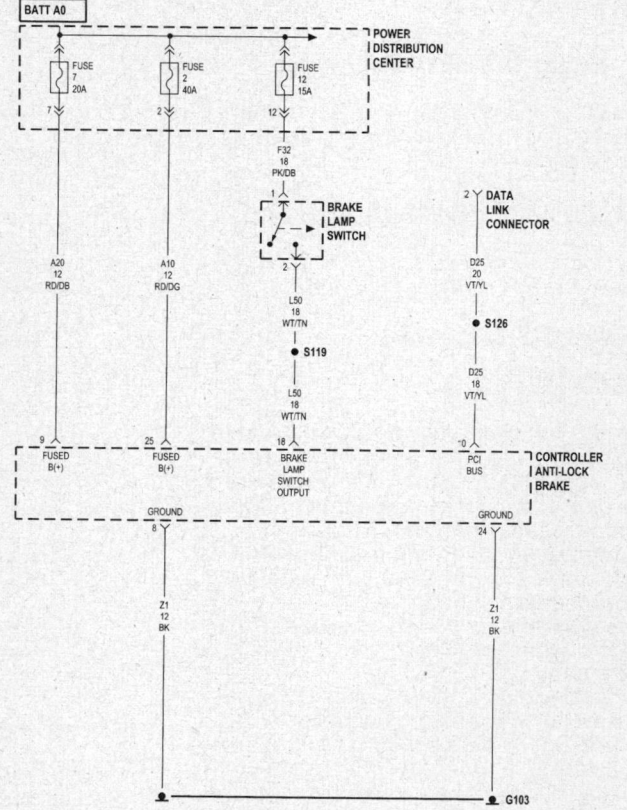

MODULE-ANTI-LOCK BRAKES - 47 WAY

CAV	CIRCUIT	FUNCTION
1	A921 12RD	FUSED B(+) (PUMP)
2	-	-
3	-	-
4	-	-
5	-	-
6	L53 18DG/WT (1.6L/DIESEL)	PRIMARY BRAKE SWITCH SIGNAL
6	L53 18DG/WT (2.4L)	BRAKE LAMP SWITCH OUTPUT
7	-	-
8	F20 20PK/WT	IGNITION SWITCH OUTPUT (RUN-START)
9	-	-
10	-	-
11	-	-
12	D65 20WT/LG	CAN C BUS (+)
13	D64 20WT/LB	CAN C BUS (-)
14	-	-
15	-	-
16	Z902 12BK	GROUND
17	-	-
18	-	-
19	-	-
20	-	-
21	-	-
22	-	-
23	-	-
24	-	-
25	-	-
26	-	-
27	-	-
28	-	-
29	-	-
30	-	-
31	-	-
32	A922 12RD	FUSED B(+) (VALVE)
33	B6 20WT/DB	RIGHT FRONT WHEEL SPEED SENSOR SIGNAL
34	B7 20WT	RIGHT FRONT WHEEL SPEED SENSOR 12 VOLT SUPPLY
35	-	-
36	B4 20LG	LEFT REAR WHEEL SPEED SENSOR 12 VOLT SUPPLY
37	B3 20LG/DB	LEFT REAR WHEEL SPEED SENSOR SIGNAL
38	-	-
39	-	-
40	-	-
41	-	-
42	B1 20YL/DB	RIGHT REAR WHEEL SPEED SENSOR SIGNAL
43	B2 20YL	RIGHT REAR WHEEL SPEED SENSOR 12 VOLT SUPPLY
44	-	-
45	B9 20RD	LEFT FRONT WHEEL SPEED SENSOR 12 VOLT SUPPLY
46	B8 20RD/DB	LEFT FRONT WHEEL SPEED SENSOR SIGNAL
47	Z902 12BK	GROUND

LTV0500000003275

CR4020002024010X

Fig. 2 Controller Anti-Lock Brake (CAB) connector & terminal identification. 2005–06

Fig. 3 Wiring diagram (Part 1 of 3). 2002–04

3. Damaged connector body.
4. Improperly formed or damaged terminals.
5. Poor terminal to wire connection.
6. Rubbed through wiring insulation.
7. Wiring broken inside insulation.

SYSTEM SERVICE

Brake System Bleed

The base brake system must be bled anytime air is permitted to enter the hydraulic system. However, anti-lock brake system components should only be bled if the hydraulic control unit has been removed or if there is reason to believe that air has entered the unit. **The ABS portion of the braking system must be bled separately.** Under most circumstances, only the base brake system will require bleeding, refer to the "Hydraulic Brake Systems" chapter for procedure. If the anti-lock brake system must be bled, proceed as follows:

1. Ensure all brake system components are installed and all hydraulic lines are connected securely.
2. Connect DRB diagnostic scan tool to diagnostic connector, then ensure CAB has no stored diagnostic trouble codes.
3. Bleed base brake system as outlined in "Hydraulic Brake Systems" chapter, then select "Anti-Lock Brakes" fol-

lowed by "Miscellaneous" then "Bleed Brakes" routine on diagnostic scan tool.
4. Bleed base brake system once again, then repeat ABS bleed cycle and base brake system bleed until brake fluid flow (as established in "Hydraulic Brake Systems" bleed procedure) is free of bubbles. **Ensure all bleeder valves are closed tightly after bleed sequence is completed.**
5. Road test vehicle to ensure base hydraulic system and anti-lock brake system operate properly.

Component Replacement

CONTROLLER ANTI-LOCK BRAKE (CAB)

1. Remove ICU as outlined in this section.
2. Disconnect pump motor electrical connector from CAB.
3. Remove four bolts attaching CAB to ICU.
4. Remove CAB from ICU.
5. Reverse procedure to install. Bleed brake system as outlined under "System Service."

FRONT WHEEL SPEED SENSOR

1. Raise and support vehicle, then re-

move front wheel.
2. Remove two bolts securing cable channel bracket and grommet retainer to outer frame rail, then pull cable grommet and connector through hole in strut tower.
3. Disconnect sensor cable from wiring harness, then remove wheel speed sensor head to steering knuckle bolt.
4. Remove sensor head from steering knuckle. **If sensor has corroded and seized, do not use pliers to loosen. Use a suitable punch and hammer to tap edge of sensor ear and rock side to side until free.**
5. Remove sensor grommets from retaining bracket, then the sensor assembly from vehicle.
6. Reverse procedure to install, noting the following:
   a. When installing sensor cable, ensure it is installed properly in retainer and is not pinched.
   b. **Torque** cable channel bracket bolts to 96 inch lbs. and speed sensor bolt to 105 inch lbs.
   c. Clearance between sensor and tone wheel should be .012–.059 inch and tone wheel runout must not exceed .009 inch.
   d. Road test vehicle after installation to ensure ABS and base brake systems function properly.

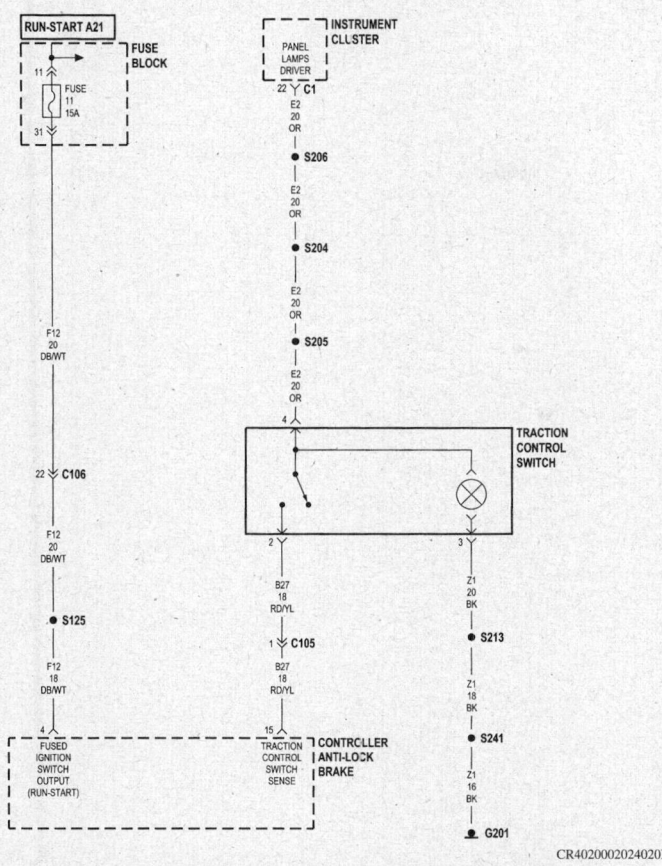

Fig. 3 Wiring diagram (Part 2 of 3). 2002–04

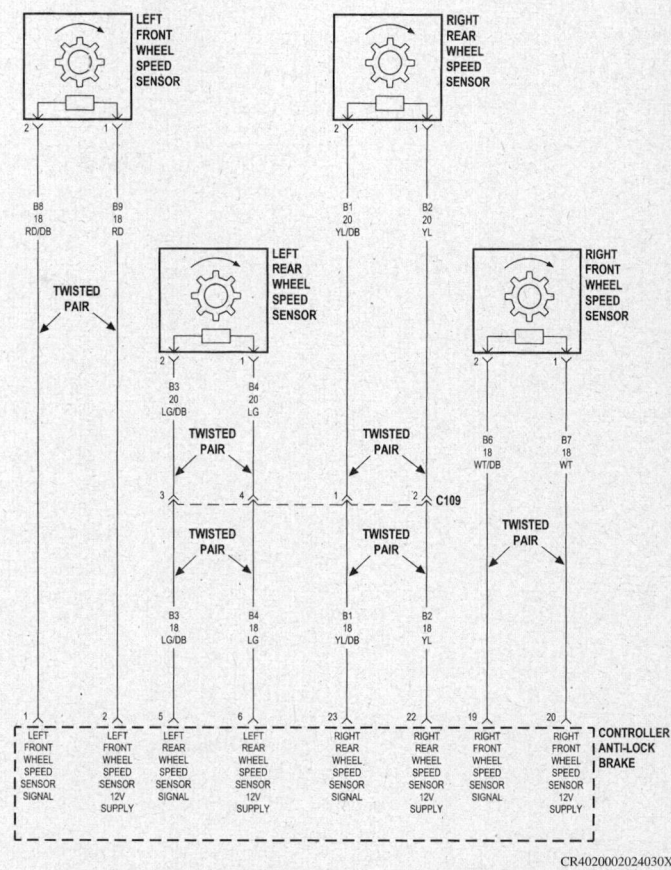

Fig. 3 Wiring diagram (Part 3 of 3). 2002–04

INTEGRATED CONTROL UNIT (ICU)

CAUTION: Vacuum in the power brake booster must be pumped down before removing the master cylinder to prevent booster from becoming contaminated. Pumping the brake pedal while the engine is not running until a firm brake pedal is achieved.

1. Remove air cleaner assembly and set aside.
2. Unlatch and remove Power Distribution Center (PDC).
3. Remove wiring harness connector from brake fluid level switch in master cylinder brake fluid reservoir.
4. Tag brake tubes from master cylinder as primary and secondary.
5. Disconnect brake tubes from master cylinder ports, install plugs in all open brake tube outlets on master cylinder.
6. Disconnect and remove brake tubes coming from master cylinder.
7. Clean area around master cylinder and power brake booster, then remove two nuts attaching master cylinder to power brake booster.
8. Slide master cylinder straight out of power brake booster.
9. Disconnect brake tubes from HCU.
10. Disconnect 24–way connector from CAB.

11. Remove three bolts attaching ICU to mounting bracket.
12. Remove ICU from vehicle.
13. Reverse procedures to install, noting the following:
    a. **Torque** three ICU mounting bolts to 97 inch lbs.
    b. Ensure 25–way electrical connector seal is properly installed in connector.
    c. **Torque** four brake tube nuts to 12 ft. lbs.
    d. **Torque** both master cylinder mounting nuts to 21 ft. lbs.

PUMP/MOTOR

The pump/motor cannot be serviced independently from the modulator (hydraulic control unit). If it does function properly, the entire unit must be replaced.

REAR WHEEL SPEED SENSOR

1. Raise and support vehicle, then remove rear wheel.
2. Remove floor pan grommet, then disconnect speed sensor cable connector at vehicle wiring harness.
3. Disengage speed sensor cable from rear brake flex hose clips.
4. If right rear speed sensor is to be removed, remove cable grommet from axle flange, then disengage brake tube

clip and routing clip from track bar bracket.
5. Remove two sensor cable and brake tube routing clips, then disengage cable from routing clips on rear brake tube.
6. Remove wheel speed sensor head to rear bearing bolt. **If sensor has seized or if sensor head will not come loose, do not use pliers to loosen. Use only a hammer and suitable punch to tap gently until free.**
7. Remove sensor head from rear bearing, then the entire assembly from vehicle.
8. Reverse procedure to install, noting the following:
    a. Ensure plastic anti-rotational pin is fully seated prior to installing sensor head attaching bolt.
    b. **Torque** sensor head attaching bolt to 105 inch lbs.
    c. Ensure sensor cable is routed properly and is not pinched.
    d. Clearance between sensor and tone wheel should be .019–.049 inch and tone wheel runout must not exceed .009 inch.
    e. After installation is complete, road test vehicle to ensure ABS and base brake systems function properly.

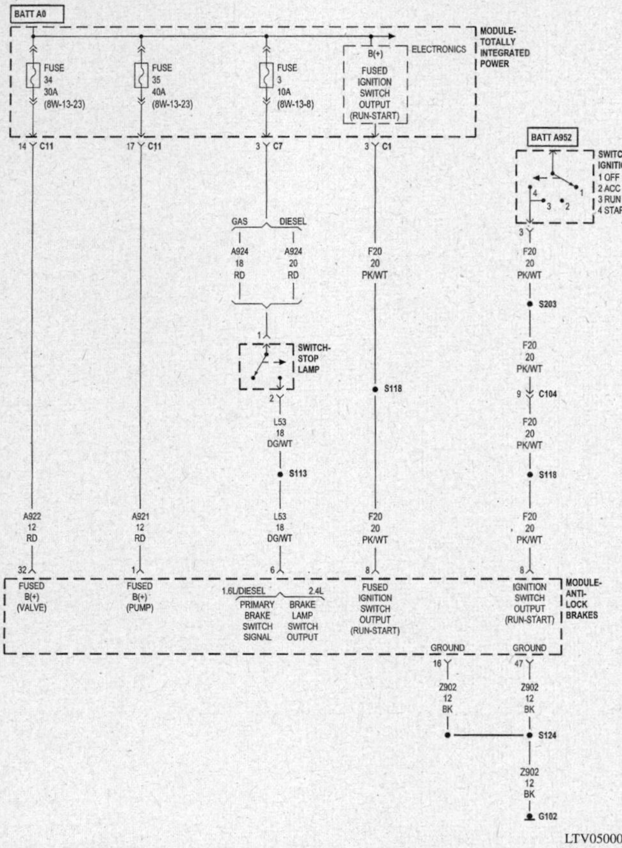

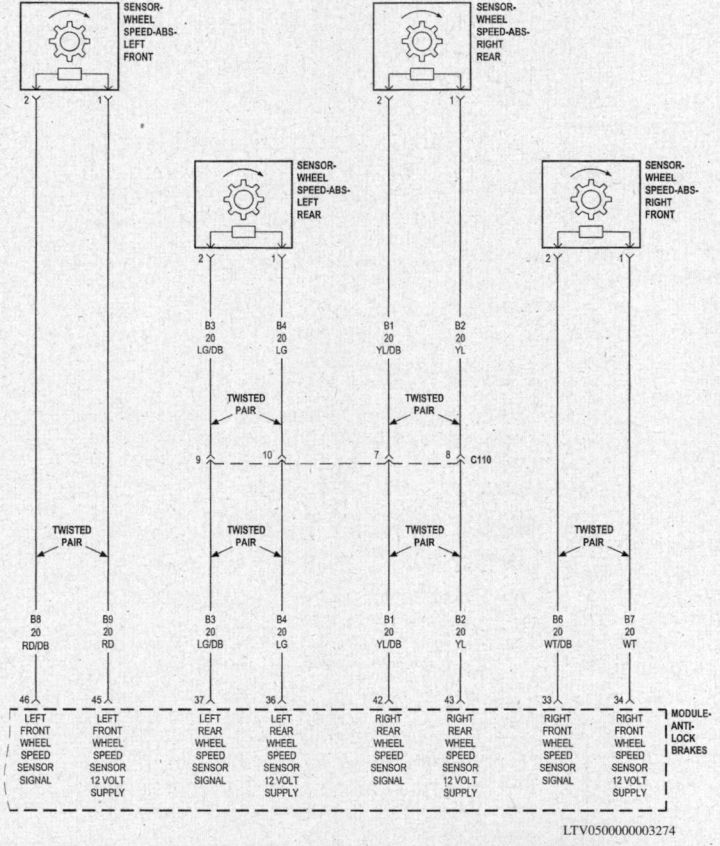

LTV0500000003272

Fig. 4   Wiring diagram (Part 1 of 3). 2005–06

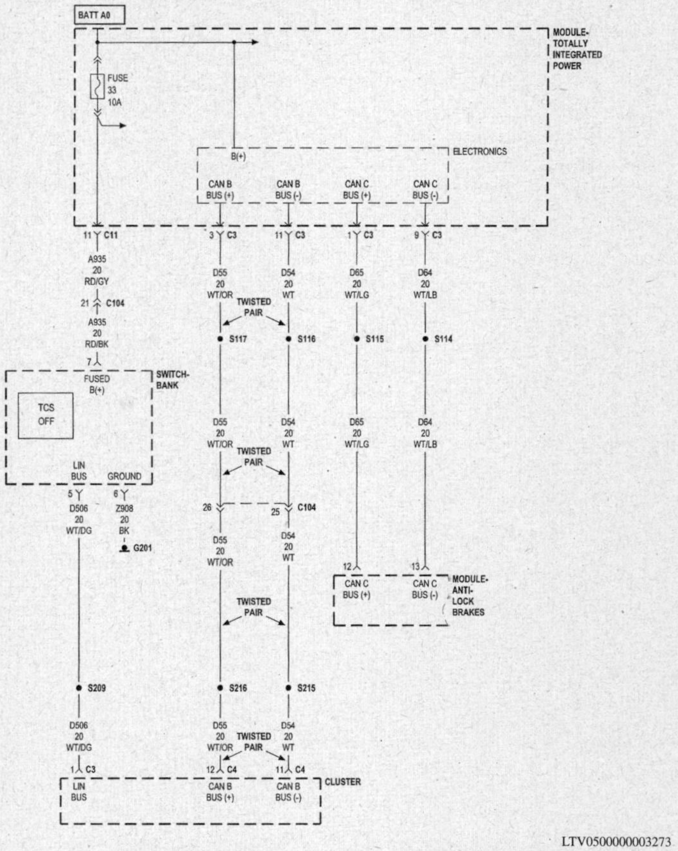

LTV0500000003273

Fig. 4   Wiring diagram (Part 2 of 3). 2005–06

LTV0500000003274

Fig. 4   Wiring diagram (Part 3 of 3). 2005–06

DIAGNOSTIC CHART INDEX

Code	Description	Page No.	Fig. No.
—	ABS Intermittent Condition	5-24	5
—	ABS Verification Test	5-33	19
—	ABM Internal	5-33	20
—	Bus System Communication Failure	5-33	21
—	BCM Message Not Received	5-34	22
—	CAB Internal Failure	5-34	23
—	CAB Power Feed Circuit	5-34	24
—	Cluster Fault	5-35	25
—	Cluster Lamp Failure	5-35	26
—	Controller Failure	5-36	27
—	Incorrect Tone Wheel	5-36	28
—	Instrument Cluster Bulb	5-36	29
—	Left Front, Left Rear, Right Front & Right Rear Sensor Circuit Failure	5-36	30
—	PCI Bus Communication	5-37	31
—	PCI Bus Communication	5-38	32
—	PCI Bus Loopback	5-38	33
—	PCI Bus Shorted To Ground	5-39	34
—	PCI Bus Shorted To Voltage	5-39	35
—	PCI Hardware	5-40	36
—	Pump Not Working Properly	5-40	37
—	Pump Motor Circuit	5-41	38
—	System Overvoltage	5-42	39
—	System Undervoltage	5-42	40
—	Valve Power Feed Failure	5-42	41
—	Verification Tests	5-43	42
C1007	Brake Fluid Level Circuit Low	5-24	6
C1008	Brake Fluid Level Circuit High	5-24	7
C1015	Wheel Speed Sensor Circuit	5-25	8
C1020	Wheel Speed Sensor Circuit	5-25	8
C100A	Wheel Speed Sensor Circuit	5-25	8
C102B	Wheel Speed Sensor Circuit	5-25	8
C1027	Wheel Speed Sensor Signal Erratic Performance	5-26	9
C1032	Wheel Speed Sensor Signal Erratic Performance	5-26	9
C1011	Wheel Speed Sensor Signal Erratic Performance	5-26	9
C101C	Wheel Speed Sensor Signal Erratic Performance	5-26	9
C1035	Wheel Speed Comparative Performance	5-27	10
C1014	Wheel Speed Comparative Performance	5-27	10
C101F	Wheel Speed Comparative Performance	5-27	10
C102A	Wheel Speed Comparative Performance	5-27	10
C1041	Tone Wheel Performance	5-28	11
C1042	Tone Wheel Performance	5-28	11
C1043	Tone Wheel Performance	5-28	11
C1044	Tone Wheel Performance	5-28	11
C1046	Wheel Pressure Phase Monitoring	5-28	12
C1047	Wheel Pressure Phase Monitoring	5-28	12
C1048	Wheel Pressure Phase Monitoring	5-28	12
C1049	Wheel Pressure Phase Monitoring	5-28	12
C1073	ABS Pump Motor Control Circuit	5-29	13
C1078	Tire Revolutions Range Performance	5-30	14
C2100	Battery Voltage Low	5-30	15
C2116	ABS Pump Motor Supply Low Voltage	5-30	16
C2200	Anti-lock Brake Module Internal	5-31	17
C2206	Vehicle Configuration Mismatch	5-32	18

POSSIBLE CAUSES
INTERMITTENT CONDITION

1. INTERMITTENT CONDITION

NOTE: The conditions that set the DTC are not present at this time. The following list may help in identifying the intermittent condition.

WARNING: When the engine is operating, do not stand in direct line with the fan. Do not put your hands near the pulleys, belts, or fan. Do not wear loose clothing. Failure to follow these instructions can result in personal injury or death.

Refer to any Technical Service Bulletins (TSBs) that may apply.
Review the scan tool Freeze Frame information. If possible, try to duplicate the conditions under which the DTC set.
Turn the ignition off.
Visually inspect the related wire harness. Wiggle the related wire harness and look for an interrupted signal on the affected circuit. Disconnect all the related harness connectors. Look for any chafed, pierced, pinched, partially broken wires and broken, bent, pushed out, or corroded terminals.
Perform a voltage drop test on the related circuits between the suspected component and the Anti-Lock Brake Module.
Inspect and clean all PCM, ABS, engine, and chassis grounds that are related to the most current DTC.
If numerous trouble codes were set, use a wire schematic and look for any common ground or supply circuits
For any Relay DTCs, actuate the Relay with the scan tool and wiggle the related wire harness to try to interrupt the actuation.

Use the scan tool to perform a System Test if one applies to failing component.
A co-pilot, data recorder, and/or lab scope should be used to help diagnose intermittent conditions.

Were any problems found during the above inspections?

Yes

- Perform the necessary repairs.
- Perform ABS VERIFICATION TEST.

No

- Test Complete.

LTV0500000003276

Fig. 5 ABS Intermittent Condition

3. BRAKE FLUID LEVEL SENSOR INTERNAL FAILURE

Turn the ignition off.
Disconnect the Brake Fluid Level Sensor harness connector
Turn the ignition on.
With the scan tool, read the Brake Fluid Level Sensor voltage

Is the voltage approximately 5 volts?

Yes

- Replace the Brake Fluid Level Sensor
- Perform ABS VERIFICATION TEST.

No

- Go To4

4. CHECK THE (B20) BRAKE FLUID LEVEL SENSOR SIGNAL CIRCUIT FOR SHORT TO GROUND

Turn the ignition off.
Disconnect the Totally Integrated Power Module harness connector.
Disconnect the Brake Fluid Level Sensor harness connector.
Measure the resistance of the (B20) Brake Fluid Level circuit in the Brake Fluid Level Sensor harness connector to ground.

Is the resistance below 100 ohms?

Yes

- Repair the (B20) Brake Fluid Level circuit for a short to ground.
- Perform ABS VERIFICATION TEST

No

- Replace and program the Totally Integrated Power Module
- Perform ABS VERIFICATION TEST.

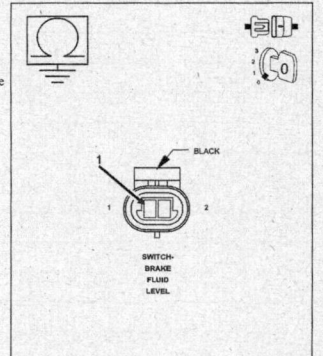

LTV0500000003278

Fig. 6 Code C1007: Brake Fluid Level Circuit Low (Part 2 of 2)

Diagnostic Test

1. BRAKE FLUID LEVEL SENSOR SIGNAL VOLTAGE BELOW 0.10 VOLTS

NOTE: This DTC must be active for the results of this test to be valid.

Turn the ignition on.
With the scan tool, read Brake Fluid Level Sensor Signal voltage.

Is the voltage below 0.10 volt?

Yes

- Go To 2

No

- Refer to the INTERMITTENT CONDITION diagnostic procedure.
- Perform ABS VERIFICATION TEST.

2. CHECK BRAKE FLUID LEVEL

NOTE: Visually inspect for worn brake linings or undersized rotors.

Was low brake fluid level found?

Yes

- Repair as needed.
- Perform ABS VERIFICATION TEST

No

- Go To 3

LTV0500000003277

Fig. 6 Code C1007: Brake Fluid Level Circuit Low (Part 1 of 2)

Diagnostic Test

1. BRAKE FLUID LEVEL SWITCH SIGNAL VOLTAGE ABOVE 4.9 VOLTS

NOTE: This DTC must be active for the results of this test to be valid.

Turn the ignition on.
With the scan tool, read Fuel Level Switch Signal voltage.

Is the voltage above 4.9 volts?

Yes

- Go To 2

No

- Refer to the INTERMITTENT CONDITIONS
- Refer to the ABS-INTERMITTENT CONDITION TEST.

2. (B20) BRAKE FLUID LEVEL SWITCH SIGNAL CIRCUIT FOR SHORT TO BATTERY VOLTAGE

Turn the ignition off.
Disconnect the Brake Fluid Level Switch harness connector.
Turn the ignition on.
Measure the voltage of the (B20) Brake Fluid Level signal circuit in the Brake Fluid Level Switch harness connector to ground.

Is the voltage above 5.2 volts?

Yes

- Repair the (B20) Brake Fluid Level signal circuit for a short to voltage.
- Perform ABS VERIFICATION TEST.

No

- Go To 3

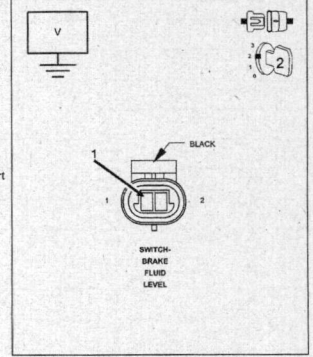

LTV0500000003279

Fig. 7 Code C1008: Brake Fluid Level Circuit High (Part 1 of 3)

3. BRAKE FLUID LEVEL SWITCH INTERNAL FAILURE

Turn the ignition off.
Connect a jumper wire between the (B20) Brake Fluid Level signal circuit and the (Z902) Brake Fluid Level ground circuit in the Brake Fluid Level Switch harness connector
Turn the ignition on.
With the scan tool, read the Brake Fluid Level Switch voltage

Is the voltage below 1.0 volt?

Yes

- Replace the Brake Fluid Level Switch

- Perform ABS VERIFICATION TEST.

No

- Go To 4

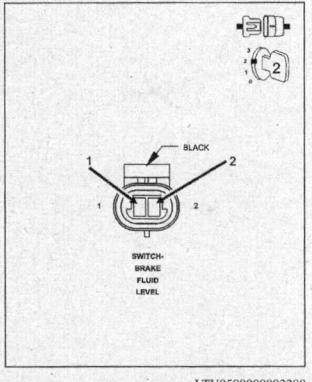

LTV0500000003280

Fig. 7   Code C1008: Brake Fluid Level Circuit High (Part 2 of 3)

Diagnostic Test

1. CHECK FOR DTC C100A–LEFT FRONT WHEEL SPEED SENSOR CIRCUIT

NOTE: This DTC must be active for the results of this test to be valid.

Turn the ignition on.
With the scan tool, record and erase DTCs.
Cycle the ignition switch from off to on.
With the scan tool, read DTCs.

NOTE: The Anti-Lock Brake Module must sense ALL 4 wheels at 12 km/h (7.5 mph) before it will extinguish the ABS indicators.

Does the scan tool display: C100A–LEFT FRONT WHEEL SPEED SENSOR CIRCUIT?

Yes

- Go To 2

No

- The condition that caused the symptom is currently not present. Inspect the related wiring for a possible intermittent condition. Look for any chafed, pierced, pinched, or partially broken wires.
- Refer to the ABS-INTERMITTENT CONDITION TEST.

2. CHECK CONNECTOR/TERMINAL FOR DAMAGE

NOTE: Check all terminals for broken, bent, pushed out, or corroded terminals.

Turn the ignition off.
Inspect the Anti-Lock Brake Module harness connector, Left Front WSS, and Left Front WSS harness connector.

Is the Left Front WSS or any of the connectors/terminals damaged?

Yes

- Repair as necessary.
- Perform ABS VERIFICATION TEST.

No

- Go To 3

LTV0500000005522

Fig. 8   Code C1015, C1020, C100A & C102B: Wheel Speed Sensor Circuit (Part 1 of 5)

4. (B20) BRAKE FLUID LEVEL SWITCH CIRCUIT OPEN

Turn the ignition off.
Disconnect the Brake Fluid Level Switch.
Disconnect the TIPM harness connector.
Measure the resistance of the (B20) Brake Fluid Level signal circuit between the Brake Fluid Level Switch harness connector and the TIPM harness connector.

Is the resistance below 5 ohms?

Yes

- Go To 5

No

- Repair the open in the (B20) Brake Fluid Level Switch signal circuit.
- Perform ABS VERIFICATION TEST.

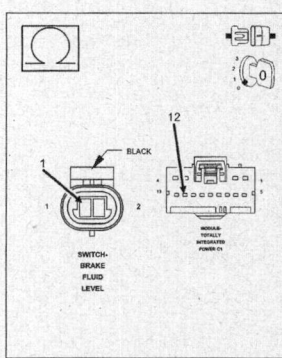

5. (Z902) SENSOR GROUND CIRCUIT OPEN

Turn the ignition off.
Disconnect the Brake Fluid Level Switch harness connector.
Reconnect the TIPM harness connector.
Measure the resistance of the (Z902) Brake Fluid Level Switch ground circuit between the Brake Fluid Level Switch harness connector and ground.

Is the resistance below 5.0 ohms?

Yes

- Replace and program the Totally Integrated Power Module

- Perform ABS VERIFICATION TEST.

No

- Repair the open in the (Z902) Sensor ground circuit .
- Perform POWERTRAIN VERIFICATION TEST

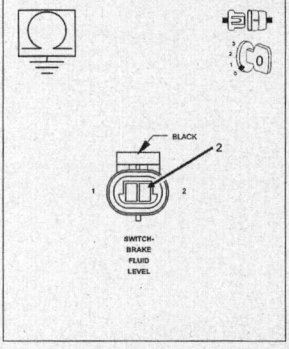

LTV0500000003281

Fig. 7   Code C1008: Brake Fluid Level Circuit High (Part 3 of 3)

3. CHECK (B9) LEFT FRONT WSS SUPPLY CIRCUIT VOLTAGE

Disconnect the Left Front WSS harness connector.
Turn the ignition on.
Measure the voltage between the (B9) Left Front WSS Supply circuit and ground.

Is the voltage above 10 volts?

Yes

- Go To 5

No

- Go To 4

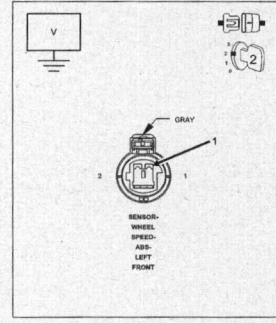

4. CHECK (B9) LEFT FRONT WSS SUPPLY CIRCUIT SHORT TO GROUND

Disconnect the Anti-Lock Brake Module harness connector.
Using a 12-volt test light connected to 12-volts, probe the (B9) Left Front WSS Supply circuit.

Does the test light illuminate brightly?

Yes

- Repair the (B9) Left Front WSS Supply circuit for a short to ground.
- Perform ABS VERIFICATION TEST.

No

- Go To 5

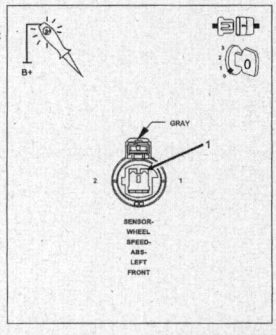

LTV0500000005523

Fig. 8   Code C1015, C1020, C100A & C102B: Wheel Speed Sensor Circuit (Part 2 of 5)

5. CHECK (B9) LEFT FRONT WSS SUPPLY CIRCUIT OPEN

Connect a jumper wire between ground and the (B9) Left Front WSS Supply circuit in the Anti-Lock Brakes Module harness connector.
Using a 12-volt test light connected to 12-volts, probe the (B9) Left Front WSS Supply circuit.

Does the test light illuminate brightly

Yes

- Go To 6

No

- Repair the (B9) Left Front WSS Supply circuit for an open.
- Perform ABS VERIFICATION TEST.

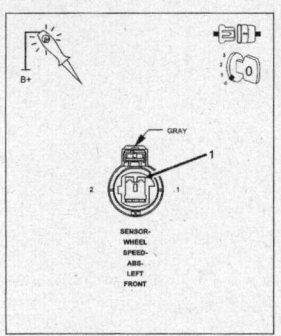

6. CHECK (B8) LEFT FRONT WSS SIGNAL CIRCUIT SHORT TO VOLTAGE

Turn the ignition on.
Using a 12-volt test light connected between the (B8) Left Front WSS Signal circuit and ground.

Does the test lioght illuminate brightly?

Yes

- Repair the (B8) Left Front WSS Signal circuit for a short to voltage.
- Perform ABS VERIFICATION TEST.

No

- Go To7

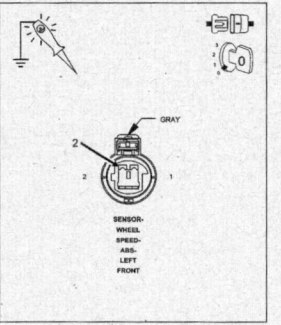

LTV0500000005524

Fig. 8   Code C1015, C1020, C100A & C102B: Wheel Speed Sensor Circuit (Part 3 of 5)

9. CHECK (B8) LEFT FRONT WSS SIGNAL CIRCUIT AND (B9) LEFT FRONT WSS SUPPLY CIRCUIT SHORT TOGETHER

Remove all jumper wires.
Measure the resistance between the (B8) Left Front WSS Signal circuit and the (B9) Left Front WSS Supply circuit.

Is the resistance above 5.0 ohms?

Yes

- Go To 10

No

- Repair the (B8) Left Front WSS Signal circuit and the (B9) Left Front WSS Supply circuit for a short together.
- Perform ABS VERIFICATION TEST.

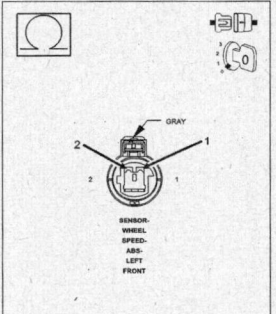

10. LEFT FRONT WHEEL SPEED SENSOR

Replace the Left Front Wheel Speed Sensor
Perform ABS VERIFICATION TEST.

CAUTION: Ensure brake capability is available before road testing.

Road test the vehicle over 40 km/h (25 m.p.h.).

NOTE: Vehicle must be driven above 40 km/h (25 m.p.h.) for set conditions to be meet.

With the scan tool, read ABS DTCs.

NOTE: The Anti-Lock Brake Module must sense ALL 4 wheels at 12 km/h (7.5 mph) before it will extinguish the ABS indicators.

Did DTC C100A–LEFT FRONT WHEEL SPEED SENSOR CIRCUIT reset?

Yes

- Replace the Anti-Lock Brakes Module
- Perform ABS VERIFICATION TEST.

LTV0500000005526

Fig. 8   Code C1015, C1020, C100A & C102B: Wheel Speed Sensor Circuit (Part 5 of 5)

7. CHECK (B8) LEFT FRONT WSS SIGNAL CIRCUIT SHORT TO GROUND

Turn the ignition off.
If not done previously, disconnect the Anti-Lock Brake Module harness connector.
Using a 12-volt test light connected to 12-volts, probe the (B8) Left Front WSS Signal circuit.

Does the test light illuminate brightly?

Yes

- Repair the (B8) Left Front WSS Signal circuit for a short to ground.
- Perform ABS VERIFICATION TEST.

No

- Go To 8

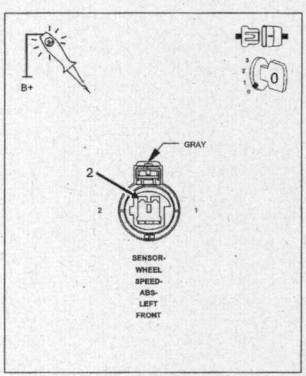

8. CHECK (B8) LEFT FRONT WSS SIGNAL CIRCUIT OPEN

Connect a jumper wire between ground and the (B8) Left Front WSS Signal circuit in the Anti-Lock Brakes Module harness connector.
Using a 12-volt test-light connected to 12-volts, probe the (B8) Left Front WSS Signal circuit.

Does the test light illuminate brightly?

Yes

- Go To 9

No

- Repair the (B8) Left Front WSS Signal circuit for an open.
- Perform ABS VERIFICATION TEST.

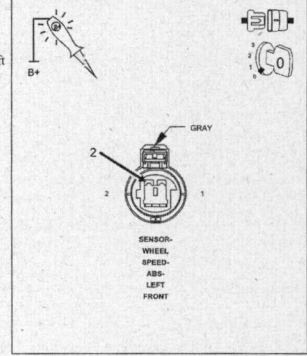

LTV0500000005525

Fig. 8   Code C1015, C1020, C100A & C102B: Wheel Speed Sensor Circuit (Part 4 of 5)

Diagnostic Test

1. CHECK FOR DTC C1011-LEFT FRONT WHEEL SPEED SENSOR SIGNAL ERRATIC PERFORMANCE

NOTE: This DTC must be active for the results of this test to be valid.

NOTE: If DTC C100A Left Front Wheel Speed Sensor Circuit is present it must be repaired before continuing.

Turn the ignition on.
With the scan tool, record and erase DTCs.
Road test the vehicle over 40 km/h (25 m.p.h.).

NOTE: Vehicle must be driven above 40 km/h (25 m.p.h.) for set conditions to be meet.

With the scan tool, read DTCs.

NOTE: The Anti-Lock Brake Module must sense ALL 4 wheels at 12 km/h (7.5 mph) before it will extinguish the ABS indicators.

Does the scan tool display: C1011-LEFT FRONT WHEEL SPEED SENSOR SIGNAL ERRATIC PERFORMANCE?

Yes

- Go To 2
-

No

- The condition that caused the symptom is currently not present. Inspect the related wiring for a possible intermittent condition. Look for any chafed, pierced, pinched, or partially broken wires.
- Refer to the ABS-INTERMITTENT CONDITION TEST.

LTV0500000005527

Fig. 9   Code C1027, C1032, C1011 & C101C: Wheel Speed Sensor Signal Erratic Performance (Part 1 of 4)

2. CHECK WHEEL SPEED SENSOR SIGNALS

Turn the ignition on.
With the scan tool, monitor and graph ALL the WSS speeds and compare graph while an assistant drives the vehicle.

NOTE: If graph shows periodic dropouts pay close attention to the tone wheel.

Slowly accelerate as straight as possible from a stop to 40 km/h (25 m.p.h.).

Is the Left Front WSS speed showing 0 km/h (0 m.p.h.) or not matching other wheel speeds?

Yes

- Go To 3

No

- Refer to the INTERMITTENT CONDITIONS
- Perform ABS VERIFICATION TEST.

3. CHECK FOR IMPROPER LEFT FRONT TIRE PRESSURE/MISMATCHED TIRES

Turn the ignition off.
Check and adjust the Left Front Tire pressure.
Check and adjust all other tire pressures.
Inspect for mismatched tires on vehicle.

Is the Left Front Tire improperly inflated or mismatched tires on vehicle?

Yes

- Repair as necessary
- Perform ABS VERIFICATION TEST.

No

- Go To 4

LTV0500000005528

Fig. 9 Code C1027, C1032, C1011 & C101C: Wheel Speed Sensor Signal Erratic Performance (Part 2 of 4)

6. CHECK LEFT FRONT WHEEL BEARING FOR DAMAGE

Inspect the Left Front wheel bearing for excessive runout or clearance.

NOTE: Refer to the appropriate service information, if necessary, for procedures or specifications.

Is the Left Front Wheel Bearing Damaged?

Yes

- Repair as necessary
- Perform ABS VERIFICATION TEST.

No

- Go To 7

7. LEFT FRONT WHEEL SPEED SENSOR

Replace the Left Front Wheel Speed Sensor
Perform ABS VERIFICATION TEST.
Road test the vehicle over 40 km/h (25 m.p.h.).

NOTE: Vehicle must be driven above 40 km/h (25 m.p.h.) for set conditions to be meet.

With the scan tool, read ABS DTCs.

NOTE: The Anti-Lock Brake Module must sense ALL 4 wheels at 12 km/h (7.5 mph) before it will extinguish the ABS indicators.

Did DTC C1011-LEFT FRONT WHEEL SPEED SENSOR SIGNAL ERRATIC PERFORMANCE reset?

Yes

- Replace the Anti-Lock Brakes Module
- Perform ABS VERIFICATION TEST.

No

- Test Complete.

LTV0500000005530

Fig. 9 Code C1027, C1032, C1011 & C101C: Wheel Speed Sensor Signal Erratic Performance (Part 4 of 4)

4. CHECK LEFT FRONT WSS LOOSENESS, INSPECT B8, B9 CIRCUITS/TERMINALS FOR DAMAGE

NOTE: Check all terminals for broken, bent, pushed out, or corroded terminals

Inspect the Anti-Lock Brake Module harness connector, Left Front WSS, and Left Front WSS harness connector
Inspect the Left Front WSS for looseness, excessive corrosion and not properly fastened.
Inspect the (B8) Left Front WSS Signal and (B9) Left Front WSS Supply circuits between the Left Front WSS and Anti-Lock Brake Module for damage.

Is the Left Front WSS loose or any of the wiring/connectors/terminals damaged?

Yes

- Repair as necessary
- Perform ABS VERIFICATION TEST.

No

- Go To 5

5. CHECK LEFT FRONT TONE WHEEL FOR DAMAGE

Inspect the Left Front Tone Wheel for damage, missing teeth, cracks, or looseness.

NOTE: The Tone Wheel teeth should be perfectly square, not bent, or nicked.

Is the Left Front Tone Wheel damaged?

Yes

- Repair as necessary
- Perform ABS VERIFICATION TEST.

No

- Go To 6

LTV0500000005529

Fig. 9 Code C1027, C1032, C1011 & C101C: Wheel Speed Sensor Signal Erratic Performance (Part 3 of 4)

Diagnostic Test

1. CHECK FOR DTC C1014-LEFT FRONT WHEEL SPEED COMPARATIVE PERFORMANCE

NOTE: This DTC must be active for the results of this test to be valid.

Turn the ignition on.
With the scan tool, record and erase DTCs.
Road test the vehicle over 40 km/h (25 m.p.h.).

NOTE: Vehicle must be driven above 40 km/h (25 m.p.h.) for set conditions to be meet.

With the scan tool, read DTCs.

NOTE: The Anti-Lock Brake Module must sense ALL 4 wheels at 12 km/h (7.5 mph) before it will extinguish the ABS indicators.

Does the scan tool display: C1014-LEFT FRONT WHEEL SPEED COMPARATIVE PERFORMANCE?

Yes

- Go To 3

No

- Go To 2

2. CHECK WHEEL SPEED SENSOR SIGNALS

Turn the ignition on.
With the scan tool, monitor and graph ALL the WSS speeds and compare graph while an assistant drives the vehicle.

NOTE: If graph shows periodic dropouts pay close attention to the tone wheel.

Slowly accelerate as straight as possible from a stop to 40 km/h (25 m.p.h.).

Is the Left Front WSS speed showing 0 km/h (0 m.p.h.) or not matching other wheel speeds?

Yes

- Go To 3

No

- The condition that caused the symptom is currently not present. Inspect the related wiring for a possible intermittent condition. Look for any chafed, pierced, pinched, or partially broken wires.
- Refer to the ABS-INTERMITTENT CONDITION TEST.

LTV0500000005531

Fig. 10 Code C1035, C1014, C101F & C102A: Wheel Speed Comparative Performance (Part 1 of 3)

3. CHECK FOR IMPROPER LEFT FRONT TIRE PRESSURE/MISMATCHED TIRES

Turn the ignition off.
Check and adjust the Left Front Tire pressure.
Check and adjust all other tire pressures.
Inspect for mismatched tires on vehicle.

Is the Left Front Tire improperly inflated or mismatched tires on vehicle?

Yes

- Repair as necessary
- Perform ABS VERIFICATION TEST.

No

- Go To 4

4. CHECK LEFT FRONT WSS LOOSENESS, INSPECT B8, B9 CIRCUITS/TERMINALS FOR DAMAGE

NOTE: Check all terminals for broken, bent, pushed out, or corroded terminals

Inspect the Anti-Lock Brake Module harness connector, Left Front WSS, and Left Front WSS harness connector
Inspect the Left Front WSS for looseness, excessive corrosion and not properly fastened.
Inspect the (B8) Left Front WSS Signal and (B9) Left Front WSS Supply circuits between the Left Front WSS and Anti-Lock Brake Module for damage.

Is the Left Front WSS loose or any of the wiring/connectors/terminals damaged?

Yes

- Repair as necessary
- Perform ABS VERIFICATION TEST.

No

- Go To 5

LTV0500000005532

Fig. 10 Code C1035, C1014, C101F & C102A: Wheel Speed Comparative Performance (Part 2 of 3)

Diagnostic Test

1. CHECK FOR A DTC C1041-LEFT FRONT TONE WHEEL PERFORMANCE

NOTE: This DTC must be active for the results of this test to be valid.

Turn the ignition on.
With the scan tool, read DTCs.
Record DTC and Freeze Frame information.
With the scan tool, erase DTCs.
Cycle the ignition switch off then on.

WARNING: To avoid personal injury or death, check brake capability is available before road testing.

Test drive the vehicle in a straight line to 40 Km/h (25 mph).

NOTE: Vehicle must be driven above 40 km/h (25 m.p.h.) for set conditions to be meet.

With the scan tool, read DTCs.

Does the scan tool display: C1041-LEFT FRONT TONE WHEEL PERFORMANCE?

Yes

- Replace the Left Front Tone Wheel
- Perform ABS VERIFICATION TEST.

No

- Refer to the INTERMITTENT CONDITIONS
- Refer to the ABS-INTERMITTENT CONDITION TEST.

LTV0500000005534

Fig. 11 Code C1041, C1042, C1043 & C1044: Tone Wheel Performance

5. CHECK LEFT FRONT TONE WHEEL FOR DAMAGE

Inspect the Left Front Tone Wheel for damage, missing teeth, cracks, or looseness.

NOTE: The Tone Wheel teeth should be perfectly square, not bent, or nicked.

Is the Left Front Tone Wheel damaged?

Yes

- Repair as necessary
- Perform ABS VERIFICATION TEST.

No

- Go To 6

6. LEFT FRONT WHEEL SPEED SENSOR

Replace the Left Front Wheel Speed Sensor
Perform ABS VERIFICATION TEST. (Refer to 5 - BRAKES - STANDARD PROCEDURE).
Road test the vehicle over 40 km/h (25 m.p.h.).

NOTE: Vehicle must be driven above 40 km/h (25 m.p.h.) for set conditions to be meet.

With the scan tool, read ABS DTCs.

NOTE: The Anti-Lock Brake Module must sense ALL 4 wheels at 12 km/h (7.5 mph) before it will extinguish the ABS indicators.

Did DTC C1011-LEFT FRONT WHEEL SPEED SENSOR SIGNAL ERRATIC PERFORMANCE reset?

Yes

- Replace the Anti-Lock Brakes Module
- Perform ABS VERIFICATION TEST.

No

- Test Complete.

LTV0500000005533

Fig. 10 Code C1035, C1014, C101F & C102A: Wheel Speed Comparative Performance (Part 3 of 3)

Diagnostic Test

1. COMPARE WHEEL SPEED SENSOR SIGNALS

WARNING: To avoid personal injury or death, check brake capability is available before road testing.

With the scan tool, monitor ALL the WSS speeds while an assistant drives the vehicle.
Slowly accelerate as straight as possible from a stop to 40 km/h (25 m.p.h.).

Does the Left Front WSS speed differ from the other WSS speeds by 8 Km/h (5 m.p.h.) or show NO speed?

Yes

- Go To 2

No

- Perform the ABS Intermittent Condition diagnostic procedure
- Refer to the ABS-INTERMITTENT CONDITION TEST.

2. INSPECT TONE WHEEL/BEARING

Turn the ignition off.
Visually inspect the tone wheel and bearing for damage.

- Check the tone wheel teeth for missing teeth, cracks, and looseness. The teeth must be perfectly square, not bent, or nicked. Check the wheel bearing for worn/looseness.

Were any problems found?

Yes

- Repair as necessary.
- Perform ABS VERIFICATION TEST.

No

- Go To 3

LTV0500000005535

Fig. 12 Code C1046, C1047, C1048 & C1049: Wheel Pressure Phase Monitoring (Part 1 of 2)

3. CHECK WHEEL SPEED SENSOR WIRING

Check the Anti-Lock Brakes Module and Wheel Speed Sensors harness connectors for incorrectly wired connectors.

Were any problems found?

Yes

- Repair as necessary.
- Perform ABS VERIFICATION TEST.

No

- Go To 4

4. LEFT FRONT WHEEL SPEED SENSOR

Replace the Left Front Wheel Speed Sensor
Perform ABS VERIFICATION TEST.

WARNING: To avoid personal injury or death, check brake capability is available before road testing.

Road test the vehicle over 40 km/h (25 m.p.h.).

NOTE: Vehicle must be driven above 40 km/h (25 m.p.h.) for set conditions to be meet.

With the scan tool, read ABS DTCs.

NOTE: The Anti-Lock Brake Module must sense ALL 4 wheels at 12 km/h (7.5 mph) before it will extinguish the ABS indicators.

Did DTC C1046–LEFT FRONT WHEEL PRESSURE PHASE MONITORING reset?

Yes

- Replace the Anti-Lock Brakes Module
- Perform ABS VERIFICATION TEST.

No

- Test Complete.

LTV0500000005536

Fig. 12   Code C1046, C1047, C1048 & C1049: Wheel Pressure Phase Monitoring (Part 2 of 2)

3. CHECK THE ABS PUMP MOTOR FUSED B+ FOR AN OPEN

Turn the ignition off.
Remove and visually inspect the ABS Pump Motor B+ fuse.

Is the ABS Pump Motor B+ fuse open?

Yes

- Go To 4

No

- Go To 6

4. CHECK THE (A921) FUSED B(+) FOR A SHORT TO GROUND

Turn the ignition off.
Disconnect the Anti-Lock Brake Module harness connector.
Using a 12–volt test light connected to 12–volts, probe the (A921) Fused B+ circuit.

Does the test light illuminate brightly?

Yes

- Repair the (A921) Fused B(+) circuit for a short to ground.
- Perform ABS VERIFICATION TEST.

No

- Go To 5

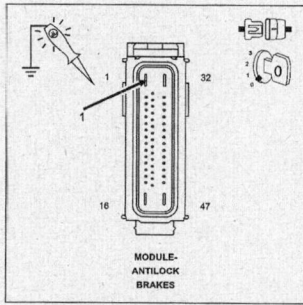

MODULE-
ANTILOCK
BRAKES

LTV0500000005538

Fig. 13   Code C1073: ABS Pump Motor Control Circuit (Part 2 of 4)

Diagnostic Test

1. CHECK FOR A DTC C1073-ABS PUMP MOTOR CONTROL CIRCUIT

NOTE: This DTC must be active for the results of this test to be valid.

Turn the ignition on.
With the scan tool, record and erase DTCs.
Cycle the ignition switch from off to on.
Road test the vehicle over 40 km/h (25 m.p.h.).

NOTE: Vehicle must be driven above 40 km/h (25 m.p.h.) for set conditions to be meet.

With the scan tool, read DTCs

NOTE: The Anti-Lock Brake Module must sense ALL 4 wheels at 12 km/h (7.5 mph) before it will extinguish the ABS indicators.

Does the scan tool display: C1073-ABS PUMP MOTOR CONTROL CIRCUIT?

Yes

- Go To 2

No

- Refer to the INTERMITTENT CONDITIONS
- Refer to the ABS-INTERMITTENT CONDITION TEST.

2. INSPECT RELATED WIRING HARNESS, TERMINALS, & CONNECTORS

Turn the ignition off.
Visually inspect the related wiring harness. Look for any pinched, chafed, pierced, and partially broken wires.
Visually inspect the related wiring harness connectors. Look for broken, bent, pushed out, and corroded terminals.

Were any problems found?

Yes

- Repair as necessary.
- Perform ABS VERIFICATION TEST.

No

- Go To 3

LTV0500000005537

Fig. 13   Code C1073: ABS Pump Motor Control Circuit (Part 1 of 4)

5. CHECK THE (A921) FUSED B(+) CIRCUIT

Turn the ignition off.
Visually inspect the (A921) Fused B(+) circuit in the wiring harness.
Look for any signs of intermittent short to ground.

Is the wiring harness OK?

Yes

- Go To 6

No

- Repair the (A921) Fused B(+) circuit for a short to ground.
- Perform ABS VERIFICATION TEST.

6. CHECK THE VOLTAGE ON THE (A921) FUSED B(+) CIRCUIT

Turn the ignition off.
Disconnect the Anti-Lock Brake Module harness connector.
Measure the voltage of the (A921) Fused B(+) circuit in the Anti-Lock Brake Module harness connector.

Is the voltage above 10 volts?

Yes

- Go To 7

No

- Repair the (A921) Fused B(+) circuit for an open.
- Perform ABS VERIFICATION TEST.

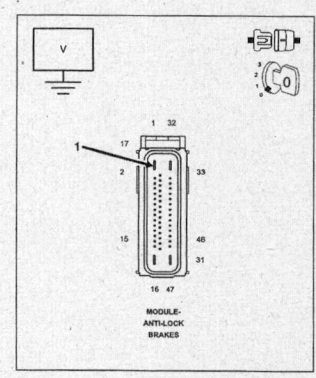

MODULE-
ANTILOCK
BRAKES

LTV0500000005539

Fig. 13   Code C1073: ABS Pump Motor Control Circuit (Part 3 of 4)

7. CHECK THE (Z902) GROUND CIRCUIT FOR AN OPEN

Measure the resistance of the (Z902) Ground circuits between the Anti-Lock Brake Module harness connector and ground

Is the resistance below 5.0 ohms?

Yes

- Replace the ICU per service information.
- Perform ABS VERIFICATION TEST.

No

- Repair the high resistance in the affected circuit.
- Perform ABS VERIFICATION TEST.

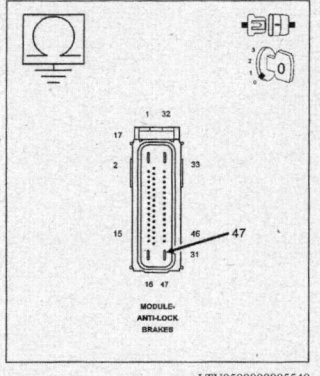

LTV0500000005540

Fig. 13 Code C1073: ABS Pump Motor Control Circuit (Part 4 of 4)

Diagnostic Test

1. DTCS IN THE PCM

NOTE: This DTC must be active for the results of this test to be valid.

Turn the ignition on.
With the scan tool, read and record DTCs from the PCM.
With the scan tool, read and record Freeze Frame information.
With the scan tool, erase DTCs.
Start the engine.
With the scan tool, read and record DTCs.
With the scan tool read DTCs from the PCM.

Are any charging system codes present?

Yes

- Repair the charging system DTC in the PCM.
- Perform ABS VERIFICATION TEST.

No

- Go To 2

2. CHARGING SYSTEM FAILURE

Start the engine.
Connect voltmeter to vehicle battery.

Is the vehicle battery voltage under 8.2 volts?

No

- Go To 3

Yes

- Repair the charging system
- Perform ABS VERIFICATION TEST.

LTV0500000005542

Fig. 15 Code C2100: Battery Voltage Low (Part 1 of 2)

3. CHARGING POWER SUPPLY VOLTAGE

With a scan tool read Power Supply Voltage.

Is Power Supply Voltage under 8.2 volts?

No

- Perform the ABS Intermittent Condition diagnostic procedure in this Section.
- Refer to the ABS-INTERMITTENT CONDITION TEST.

Yes

- Replace the Anti-Lock Brakes Module in accordance with the Service Information.
- Perform ABS VERIFICATION TEST.

LTV0500000005543

Fig. 15 Code C2100: Battery Voltage Low (Part 2 of 2)

Diagnostic Test

1. INCORRECT VALUE PROGRAMMED INTO TIPM

TIRE SIZE	BODY STYLE	ENGINE SIZE	SALES CODE	TIRE CIRCUMFERENCE (HEX)
P195/65R15 89T BSW AS Touring	PT	ALL	TNC	$0791
P195/65R15 91H BSW Perf.	PT	ALL	TNR	$079a
P205/50R17XL 93W BSW Perf.	PT	ALL	TPD	$07b7
P205/50R17XL 93H BSW AS Perf.	PT	ALL	TPJ	$079a
P205/55R16 89T BSW AS Touring	PT	ALL	TP1	$0788
P205/55R16 91H BSW Perf. Touring	PT	ALL	TVR	$0792

Verify the correct Tire/wheel information is programmed in the TIPM.

Is the correct value programmed in the TIPM according to the chart?

Yes

- Test complete.
- Perform ABS VERIFICATION TEST.

No

- Program the correct Tire/Wheel information in the TIPM.
- Perform ABS VERIFICATION TEST.

LTV0500000005541

Fig. 14 Code C1078: Tire Revolutions Range Performance

Diagnostic Test

1. CHECK FOR A DTC C2116-ABS PUMP MOTOR SUPPLY LOW VOLTAGE

NOTE: This DTC must be active for the results of this test to be valid.

Turn the ignition on.
With the scan tool, read and record DTCs.
With the scan tool, read and record Freeze Frame information.
With the scan tool, erase DTCs.

CAUTION: Ensure braking capability is available before road testing.

Drive the vehicle over 40 km/h (25 mph).
Park the vehicle and cycle the ignition switch from off to on.
With the scan tool, read and record DTCs

Does the scan tool display: C2116-ABS PUMP MOTOR SUPPLY LOW VOLTAGE?

Yes

- Go To 2

No

- Refer to the INTERMITTENT CONDITION diagnostic procedure.
- Refer to the ABS-INTERMITTENT CONDITION TEST.

2. CHECK ABS PUMP OPERATION WITH SCAN TOOL

Cycle the ignition from off to on.
With the scan tool, actuate the ABS Pump Motor.

Did the ABS Pump Motor operate?

Yes

- Perform the ABS Intermittent Condition diagnostic procedure.
- Refer to the ABS-INTERMITTENT CONDITION TEST.

No

- Go To 3

LTV0500000005544

Fig. 16 Code C2116: ABS Pump Motor Supply Low Voltage (Part 1 of 4)

3. CHECK THE ABS PUMP MOTOR FUSE FOR AN OPEN

Turn the ignition off.
Remove and visually inspect the ABS Pump Motor fuse.

Is the ABS Pump Motor fuse open?

Yes

- Go To 4

No

- Go To 5

4. CHECK THE (A921) FUSED B(+) FOR A SHORT TO GROUND

Turn the ignition off.
Visually inspect the (A921) Fused B(+) circuit in the wiring harness.
Look for any signs of intermittent short to ground.

Is the wiring harness OK?

Yes

- Go To 5

No

- Repair the (A921) Fused B(+) circuit for a short to ground.
- Perform ABS VERIFICATION TEST.

LTV0500000005545

**Fig. 16   Code C2116: ABS Pump Motor Supply Low
Voltage (Part 2 of 4)**

7. CHECK THE (Z902) GROUND CIRCUIT FOR AN OPEN

Turn the ignition off.
Disconnect the Anti-Lock Brake Module harness connector.
Measure the resistance of the (Z902) Ground circuit between the
Anti-Lock Brake Module harness connector and ground

Is the resistance below 5.0 ohms?

Yes

- Replace the Anti-Lock Brake Module in accordance with
  the Service Information.
- Perform ABS VERIFICATION TEST.

No

- Repair the (Z902) Ground circuit for an open.
- Perform ABS VERIFICATION TEST.

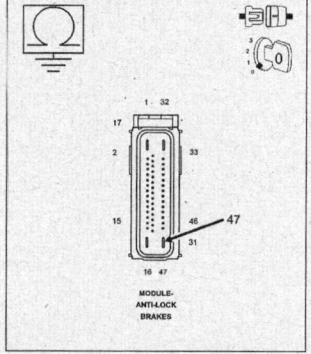

LTV0500000005547

**Fig. 16   Code C2116: ABS Pump Motor Supply Low
Voltage (Part 4 of 4)**

5. CHECK THE WIRING HARNESS, TERMINALS, AND CONNECTORS

NOTE: Check all related wiring for bruised, chafed, pierced, or partially broken wires.

NOTE: Check all related connectors for broken, bent, pushed out, or corroded terminals.

Turn the ignition off.
Visually inspect the Anti-Lock Brake Module harness connector and (A921) Fused B(+) circuit in the wiring harness for
damage.

Were any problems found?

Yes

- Repair as necessary.
- Perform ABS VERIFICATION TEST.

No

- Go To 6

6. CHECK THE VOLTAGE ON THE (A921) FUSED B(+) CIRCUIT

Turn the ignition off.
Disconnect the Anti-Lock Brake Module harness connector.
Measure the voltage of the (A921) Fused B(+) circuit in the Anti-
Lock Brake Module harness connector.

Is the voltage above 10 volts?

Yes

- Go To 7

No

- Repair the (A921) Fused B(+) circuit for an open.
- Perform ABS VERIFICATION TEST.

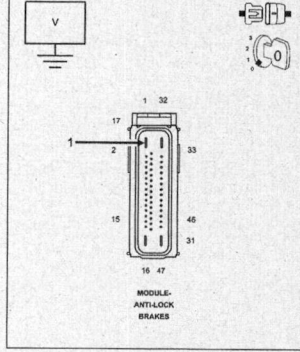

LTV0500000005546

**Fig. 16   Code C2116: ABS Pump Motor Supply Low
Voltage (Part 3 of 4)**

Diagnostic Test

1. CHECK FOR A DTC C2200-ANTI-LOCK BRAKE MODULE INTERNAL

NOTE: This DTC must be active for the results of this test to be valid.

Turn the ignition on.
With the scan tool, read and record DTCs.
With the scan tool, read and record Freeze Frame information.
With the scan tool, erase DTCs.
Cycle the ignition switch from off to on.
With the scan tool, read and record DTCs.

Does the scan tool display: C2200-ANTI-LOCK BRAKE MODULE INTERNAL?

Yes

- Go To 2

No

- Refer to the INTERMITTENT CONDITION diagnostic procedure.
- Refer to the ABS-INTERMITTENT CONDITION TEST.

2. CHECK THE WIRING HARNESS, TERMINALS, AND CONNECTORS

Visually inspect the related wiring harness. Look for any bruised, chafed, pierced, or partially broken wires.
Visually inspect the related wiring harness connectors. Look for broken, bent, pushed out, or corroded terminals.

Were any problems found?

Yes

- Repair as necessary.
- Perform ABS VERIFICATION TEST.

No

- Go To 3

LTV0500000005548

**Fig. 17   Code C2200: Anti-lock Brake Module
Internal (Part 1 of 4)**

3. CHECK THE VOLTAGE ON THE (A922) FUSED B(+) CIRCUIT

Turn the ignition off.
Disconnect the Anti-Lock Brake Module harness connector.
Measure the voltage of the (A922) Fused B(+) circuit in the Anti-Lock Brake Module harness connector.

Is the voltage above 10 volts?

Yes

- Go To 7

No

- Go To 4

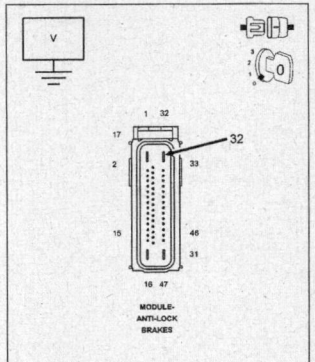

4. CHECK THE (A922) FUSED B(+) CIRCUIT FOR A SHORT TO GROUND

Turn the ignition off.
Disconnect the Anti-Lock Brake Module harness connector.
Using a 12-volt test light connected to 12-volts, check the (A922) Fused B(+) circuit.

Does the test light illuminate brightly?

Yes

- Repair the (A922) Fused B(+) circuit for a short to ground.
- Perform ABS VERIFICATION TEST.

No

- Go To 5

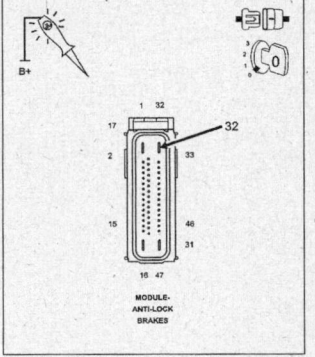

LTV0500000005549

Fig. 17   Code C2200: Anti-lock Brake Module Internal (Part 2 of 4)

7. CHECK THE (Z902) GROUND CIRCUIT FOR AN OPEN

Turn the ignition off.
Disconnect the Anti-Lock Brake Module harness connector.
Measure the resistance between the (Z902) Ground circuit and ground.

Is the resistance below 5.0 ohms?

Yes

- Replace the Anti-Lock Brake Module in accordance with the Service Information.
- Perform ABS VERIFICATION TEST.

No

- Repair the (Z902) Ground circuit for an open.
- Perform ABS VERIFICATION TEST.

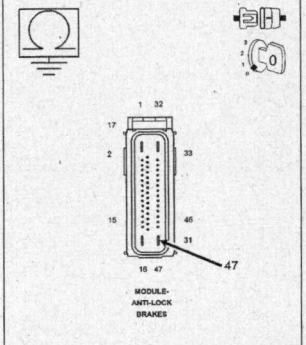

LTV0500000005551

Fig. 17   Code C2200: Anti-lock Brake Module Internal (Part 4 of 4)

5. CHECK THE (A922) FUSED B(+) CIRCUIT FOR A SHORT TO VOLTAGE

Turn the ignition off.
Disconnect the Anti-Lock Brake Module harness connector.
Using a 12-volt test light connected to ground, check the (A922) Fused B(+) circuit.

Does the test light illuminate brightly?

Yes

- Repair the (A922) Fused B(+) circuit for a short to voltage.
- Perform ABS VERIFICATION TEST.

No

- Go To 6

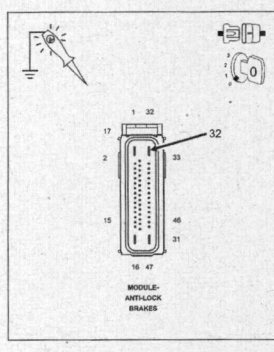

6. CHECK THE (A922) FUSED B(+) CIRCUIT FOR AN OPEN

Turn the ignition off.
Remove the Anti-Lock Brake Module Fused B(+) fuse.
Disconnect the Anti-Lock Brake Module harness connector.
Connect a jumper wire between the (A922) Fused B(+) circuit and ground.
Using a 12-volt test light connected to 12-volts, check the (A922) Fused B(+) circuit.

Does the test light illuminate brightly?

Yes

- Replace the Integrated Power Module in accordance with the Service Information.
- Perform ABS VERIFICATION TEST.

No

- Repair the (A922) Fused B(+) circuit for an open.
- Perform ABS VERIFICATION TEST.

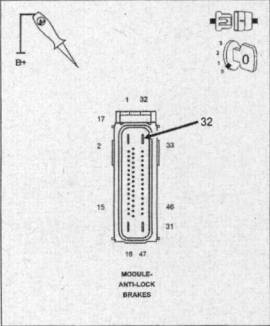

LTV0500000005550

Fig. 17   Code C2200: Anti-lock Brake Module Internal (Part 3 of 4)

Diagnostic Test

1. CHECK FOR A DTC C2206-VEHICLE CONFIGURATION MISMATCH

NOTE: This DTC must be active for the results of this test to be valid.

NOTE: This DTC will be active when a new module is installed until initialization is performed.

Turn the ignition on.
With the scan tool, read and record DTCs.
With the scan tool, read and record Freeze Frame information.
With the scan tool, erase DTCs.
Perform ECU initialization with drive test on ABM. Refer to ABS VERIFICATION TEST.

Cycle the ignition switch from off to on.
With the scan tool, read and record DTCs.

Does the scan tool display: C2206-VEHICLE CONFIGURATION MISMATCH?

Yes

- Go To 2

No

- Perform the ABS Intermittent Condition diagnostic procedure
- Refer to the ABS-INTERMITTENT CONDITION TEST.

2. VERIFY THAT THE FCM/PCM IS CONFIGURED CORRECTLY

Turn the ignition on.
Check the following data to ensure the TIPM/PCM is configured correctly. Engine Displacement (PCM), XWD 4x2, 4x4, all Wheel Drive, (TIPM), Axle ratio (TIPM), Vehicle Line (TIPM), Brake type 0= ABS 1=ESP (TIPM).

NOTE: The DTC will be active when a new controller is installed until initialization is performed.

Was the TIPM/PCM configured correctly?

Yes

- Replace the Anti-Lock Brake Module
- Perform ABS VERIFICATION TEST.

No

- Reprogram the appropriate module.
- Perform ABS or PCM VERIFICATION TEST.

LTV0500000005552

Fig. 18   Code C2206: Vehicle Configuration Mismatch

1. ABS VERIFICATION TEST

WARNING: To avoid personal injury or death, check brake capability is available before road testing.

NOTE: If the ABM (Anti-Lock Brake Module), SAS (Steering Angle Sensor), Dynamics Sensor was replaced, it must be initialized using the scan tool. If not initialized, the ABS indicator will flash continuously with no DTCs. To initialize the ABM and clear offsets have wheels pointing straight ahead and follow the directions on the scan tool. The drive test requires a 90° turn. If the Dynamics Sensor was replaced, test drive the vehicle by turning the vehicle left or right in a curving manner at a velocity between 10 and 25 km/hr (6 and 15 m.p.h.).

1. Turn the ignition off.
2. Connect all previously disconnected components and connectors.
3. Verify all accessories are turned off and the battery is fully charged.
4. Verify that the ignition is on, with the scan tool, erase all Diagnostic Trouble Codes from All modules. Start the engine and allow it to run for 2 minutes and fully operate the system that was indicating the failure.
5. Turn the ignition off and wait 5 seconds. Turn the ignition on and using the scan tool, read DTCs from all modules.
6. If any Diagnostic Trouble Codes are present, return to symptom list and trouble shoot new or recurring symptom.
NOTE: For Sensor Signal and Pump Motor faults, the ABM must sense all 4 wheels at 12 km/h (7.5 mph) before it will extinguish the ABS indicator.
7. If there are no DTCs present after turning ignition on, road test the vehicle for at least 5 minutes. Perform several anti-lock braking stops.
8. Again, with the scan tool read DTCs . If any DTCs are present, refer to the Table of Contents in the applicable Section for the diagnostic test procedure and troubleshoot the new or recurring symptom.
9. If there are no Diagnostic Trouble Codes (DTCs) present, and the customer's concern can no longer be duplicated, the repair is complete.

Are any DTCs present or is the original concern still present?

Yes

- Repair is not complete, refer to appropriate symptom.

No

- Repair is complete.

LTV0500000005553

Fig. 19 ABS Verification Test

TEST	ACTION
3	Turn the ignition off. Disconnect the ABM harness connector. Turn the ignition on. Measure the voltage of the Fused Run Relay Output circuit. Is the voltage above 10 volts? Yes → Go To 4 No → Repair the Fused Run Relay Output circuit for an open. Perform ABS VERIFICATION TEST - VER 1.
4	Turn the ignition off. Disconnect the ABM harness connector. Measure the voltage of the ABS Valve Fused B(+) circuit. Is the voltage above 10 volts? Yes → Go To 5 No → Repair the ABS Valve Fused B(+) circuit for an open. Perform ABS VERIFICATION TEST - VER 1.
5	Turn the ignition off. Disconnect the ABM harness connector. Measure the voltage of the ABS Pump Fused B(+) circuit. Is the voltage above 10 volts? Yes → Go To 6 No → Repair the ABS Pump Fused B(+) circuit for an open. Perform ABS VERIFICATION TEST - VER 1.
6	Turn the ignition off. Disconnect the ABM harness connector. Measure the resistance of the ground circuits. Is the resistance below 5.0 ohms? Yes → Replace the Anti-Lock Brake Module Perform ABS VERIFICATION TEST - VER 1. No → Repair the ground circuit(s) for an open. Perform ABS VERIFICATION TEST - VER 1.
7	Turn the ignition off. Visually inspect the related wiring harness. Look for any chafed, pierced, pinched, or partially broken wires. Visually inspect the related wire harness connectors. Look for broken, bent, pushed out, or corroded terminals. Refer to any Hotline letters or Technical Service Bulletins that may apply. Were any problems found? Yes → Repair as necessary. Perform ABS VERIFICATION TEST - VER 1. No → Test Complete.

LTV0500000005558

Fig. 20 ABM Internal (Part 2 of 2). 2005–06

POSSIBLE CAUSES
INTERMITTENT DTC
DAMAGED ABM/ABM HARNESS CONNECTOR
FUSED RUN RELAY OUTPUT CIRCUIT OPEN
ABS VALVE FUSED B(+) CIRCUIT OPEN
ABS PUMP FUSED B(+) CIRCUIT OPEN
ABM - GROUND CIRCUIT OPEN
ABM - INTERNAL FAULT

TEST	ACTION
1	Turn the ignition on. With the DRBIII®, read DTCs. With the DRBIII®, erase DTCs. Turn the ignition off. Turn the ignition on. With the DRBIII®, read DTCs. Does the DRBIII® display ABM INTERNAL? Yes → Go To 2 No → Go To 7
2	Turn the ignition off. Disconnect the ABM harness connector. Inspect the ABM/ABM harness connector for damage. Is there any broken, bent, pushed out, corroded or spread terminals? Yes → Repair as necessary. Perform ABS VERIFICATION TEST - VER 1. No → Go To 3

LTV0500000005557

Fig. 20 ABM Internal (Part 1 of 2). 2005–06

POSSIBLE CAUSES
INTERMITTENT CONDITION
ELECTRO-MECHANICAL INSTRUMENT CLUSTER DTC PRESENT
BUS CIRCUIT OPEN
CAB - INTERNAL FAILURE

TEST	ACTION
1	Turn the ignition on. With the DRBIII®, read DTCs. With the DRBIII®, read Freeze Frame information. With the DRBIII®, erase DTCs. Turn the ignition off. Turn the ignition on. With the DRBIII®, read DTCs. Does the DRBIII® display BUS SYSTEM COMMUNICATION FAILURE? Yes → Go To 2 No → Go To 4
2	Turn the ignition off. With the DRBIII®, read EMIC DTCs. Does the DRBIII® display ABS MESSAGE NOT RECEIVED? Yes → Refer to symptom ABS MESSAGE NOT RECEIVED Perform ABS VERIFICATION TEST - VER 1. No → Go To 3

LTV0500000005559

Fig. 21 Bus System Communication Failure
(Part 1 of 2). 2004

TEST	ACTION
3	Turn the ignition off. Disconnect the negative (-) battery cable. Disconnect the CAB harness connector. **NOTE: check connector - Clean/repair as necessary.** Measure the resistance of the Bus circuit between the CAB connector and the Data Link Connector (DLC). Is the resistance below 5.0 ohms? Yes → Replace the Controller Antilock Brake Perform ABS VERIFICATION TEST - VER 1. No → Repair the Bus circuit for an open. Perform ABS VERIFICATION TEST - VER 1.
4	Turn the ignition off. Visually inspect the related wiring harness. Look for any chafed, pierced, pinched, or partially broken wires. Visually inspect the related wire harness connectors. Look for broken, bent, pushed out, or corroded terminals. Were any problems found? Yes → Repair as necessary. Perform ABS VERIFICATION TEST - VER 1. No → Test Complete.

LTV0500000005560

Fig. 21 Bus System Communication Failure
(Part 2 of 2). 2004

POSSIBLE CAUSES
ATTEMPT TO COMMUNICATE WITH THE BCM
BODY CONTROL MODULE

TEST	ACTION
1	Turn the ignition on. With the DRBIII®, attempt to communicate with the Body Control Module. Was the DRBIII® able to I/D or communicate with the BCM? Yes → Go To 2 No → Refer to the Communication category for the related symptom(s). Perform BODY VERIFICATION TEST - VER 1.
2	With the DRBIII®, erase DTC's. Cycle the ignition switch from off to on and wait approximately 1 minute. With the DRBIII®, read DTC's. Did this DTC reset? Yes → Replace the Body Control Module Perform BODY VERIFICATION TEST - VER 1. No → Test Complete.

LTV0500000005561

Fig. 22   BCM Message Not Received. 2005

TEST	ACTION
3	Turn the ignition off. Disconnect the CAB harness connector. Using a 12-volt test light connected to 12-volts, probe the CAB harness connector ground circuits. Did the test light illuminate? Yes → Go To 4 No → Repair the CAB Ground circuit for an open. Perform ABS VERIFICATION TEST - VER 1.
4	Turn the ignition off. Disconnect the CAB harness connector. Using a 12-volt test light connected to ground, probe the ABS Valve Fused B(+) circuit at the CAB harness connector. Did the test light illuminate? Yes → Go To 5 No → Repair the ABS Valve Fused B(+) circuit for an open. Perform ABS VERIFICATION TEST - VER 1.
5	Turn the ignition off. Disconnect the CAB harness connector. Using a 12-volt test light connected to ground, probe the ABS Pump Fused B(+) circuit at the CAB harness connector. Did the test light illuminate? Yes → Replace the Controller Antilock Brake Perform ABS VERIFICATION TEST - VER 1. No → Repair the ABS Pump Fused B(+) circuit for an open. Perform ABS VERIFICATION TEST - VER 1.
6	Turn the ignition off. Visually inspect the related wiring harness. Look for any chafed, pierced, pinched, or partially broken wires. Visually inspect the related wire harness connectors. Look for broken, bent, pushed out, or corroded terminals. Refer to any Hotline letters or Technical Service Bulletins that may apply. Were any problems found? Yes → Repair as necessary. Perform ABS VERIFICATION TEST - VER 1. No → Test Complete.

LTV0500000005563

Fig. 23   CAB Internal Failure (Part 2 of 2). 2004

When Monitored and Set Condition:

CAB INTERNAL FAILURE

When Monitored: Ignition on. The CAB monitors the Fused B(+) circuit at all times for proper system voltage.

Set Condition: If the Fused B(+) voltage is missing when the CAB detects that an internal main driver is not "on", the Diagnostic Trouble Code (DTC) is set.

POSSIBLE CAUSES
INTERMITTENT DTC
DAMAGED CAB/CAB HARNESS CONNECTOR
CAB - GROUND CIRCUIT OPEN
ABS VALVE FUSED B(+) CIRCUIT OPEN
ABS PUMP FUSED B(+) CIRCUIT OPEN
CAB - INTERNAL FAULT

TEST	ACTION
1	Turn the ignition on. With the DRBIII®, read DTCs. With the DRBIII®, erase DTCs. Turn the ignition off. Turn the ignition on. With the DRBIII®, read DTCs. Does the DRBIII® display CAB INTERNAL FAILURE? Yes → Go To 2 No → Go To 6
2	Turn the ignition off. Disconnect the CAB harness connector. Inspect the CAB/CAB harness connector for damage. Is there any broken, bent, pushed out, corroded or spread terminals? Yes → Repair as necessary. Perform ABS VERIFICATION TEST - VER 1. No → Go To 3

LTV0500000005562

Fig. 23   CAB Internal Failure (Part 1 of 2). 2004

POSSIBLE CAUSES
INTERMITTENT DTC
FUSE BLOWN - FUSED B(+) CIRCUIT
FUSED B(+) CIRCUIT OPEN
FUSED B(+) CIRCUIT SHORTED TO GROUND
FUSED B(+) CIRCUIT INTERMITTENTLY SHORTED TO GROUND
CAB - FUSED B(+) CIRCUIT OPEN
CAB - FUSED B(+) CIRCUIT SHORTED TO GROUND

TEST	ACTION
1	Turn the ignition on. With the DRBIII®, erase DTC's. Turn the ignition off. Turn the ignition on. With the DRBIII®, read DTC's. Is the CAB Power Feed Circuit DTC present right now? Yes → Go To 2 No → Go To 10
2	Turn the ignition off. Remove and Inspect ABS SOL Fuse in the PDC. Is the Fuse blown? Yes → Go To 3 No → Go To 8
3	Turn the ignition off. Visually inspect the Fused B(+) Circuit in the wiring harness from the PDC to the CAB. Look for any sign of an intermittent short to ground. Is the wiring harness OK? Yes → Go To 4 No → Repair the Fused B(+) Circuit Shorted to Ground. Perform ABS VERIFICATION TEST.

CR4020002026010X

**Fig. 24   CAB Power Feed Circuit (Part 1 of 3).
2002–03**

TEST	ACTION
4	Turn the ignition off. Disconnect the ABS SOL Fuse from the PDC. Disconnect the CAB connector. **Note: Check connector - Clean/repair as necessary.** Using a test light connected to 12 volts, probe the Fused B(+) Circuit. Is the test light on? Yes → Repair the Fused B(+) Circuit Shorted to Ground. Perform ABS VERIFICATION TEST. No → Go To 5
5	Turn the ignition off. Disconnect the ABS SOL Fuse from the PDC. Disconnect the CAB connector. **Note: Check connector - Clean/repair as necessary.** Measure the resistance of the Fused Ignition Switch Output circuit between the Fuse and the CAB connector. Is the resistance below 5 ohms? Yes → Go To 6 No → Repair Fused B(+) Circuit Open. Perform ABS VERIFICATION TEST.
6	Turn the ignition off. Disconnect the ABS SOL Fuse from the PDC. Using a test light connected to 12 volts, probe the Fused B(+) Circuit. Is the test light on? Yes → Replace the CAB. Perform ABS VERIFICATION TEST. No → Go To 7
7	Turn the ignition off. If there are no potential causes remaining, replace the Fuse. View repair options. Repair Replace the Fuse. Perform ABS VERIFICATION TEST.
8	Turn the ignition off. Disconnect the ABS SOL Fuse from the PDC. Disconnect the CAB connector. **Note: Check connector - Clean/repair as necessary.** Measure the resistance of the Fused Ignition Switch Output circuit between the Fuse and the CAB connector. Is the resistance below 5 ohms? Yes → Go To 9 No → Repair Fused B(+) Circuit Open. Perform ABS VERIFICATION TEST.
9	If there are no potential causes remaining, replace the CAB. View repair options. Repair Replace the CAB. Perform ABS VERIFICATION TEST.

CR4020002026020X

Fig. 24 CAB Power Feed Circuit (Part 2 of 3). 2002–03

POSSIBLE CAUSES
INSTRUMENT CLUSTER OR ABS DTC PRESENT
INSTRUMENT CLUSTER
CAB - NO DTC SIGNAL TO THE INSTRUMENT CLUSTER
CAB - NO KEY-ON BULB CHECK SIGNAL
CAB - PERMANENT FAULT SIGNAL

TEST	ACTION
1	Turn the ignition on. With the DRBIII®, read DTCs. Are there any Instrument Cluster or ABS DTCs present? Yes → Refer to the appropriate category for the related symptom(s). Perform ABS VERIFICATION TEST - VER 1. No → Go To 2
2	Turn the ignition off. Perform the Key-on Bulb Check. Does the ABS Warning Indicator light and then go out after a few seconds? Yes → Go To 3 No. Light remains after bulb check. Replace the Controller Antilock Brake Perform ABS VERIFICATION TEST - VER 1. No. Indicator never comes on. Go To 4

LTV0500000005555

Fig. 26 Cluster Lamp Failure (Part 1 of 2). 2004–06

TEST	ACTION
10	Turn the ignition off. Visually inspect the related wiring harness. Look for any chafed, pierced, pinched, or partially broken wires. Visually inspect the related wire harness connectors. Look for broken, bent, pushed out, or corroded terminals. Refer to any Hotline letters or Technical Service Bulletins that may apply. Were any problems found? Yes → Repair as necessary. Perform ABS VERIFICATION TEST. No → Test Complete.

CR4020002026030X

Fig. 24 CAB Power Feed Circuit (Part 3 of 3). 2002–03

POSSIBLE CAUSES
CLUSTER FAILURE DTC PRESENT
INTERMITTENT DTC

TEST	ACTION
1	With the DRBIII®, erase DTCs. With the DRBIII®, read DTCs. Does the DRBIII® display Cluster Failure? Yes → Replace the Instrument Cluster Perform ABS VERIFICATION TEST - VER 1. No → Go To 2
2	Turn the ignition off. Visually inspect the related wiring harness. Look for any chafed, pierced, pinched, or partially broken wires. Visually inspect the related wire harness connectors. Look for broken, bent, pushed out, or corroded terminals. Refer to any Hotline letters or Technical Service Bulletins that may apply. Were any problems found? Yes → Repair as necessary. Perform ABS VERIFICATION TEST - VER 1. No → Test Complete.

LTV0500000005554

Fig. 25 Cluster Fault. 2002–03

TEST	ACTION
3	**NOTE: The DRBIII® communication with the CAB must be operational for the result of this test to be valid.** Turn the ignition off. Remove ABS Valve fuse. Perform the Key-on Bulb Check. Does the ABS Indicator remain on after the bulb check? Yes → Test Complete. No → Replace the Controller Antilock Brake Perform ABS VERIFICATION TEST - VER 1.
4	**NOTE: The following steps will initiate the Instrument Cluster self test.** Turn the ignition off. Press and hold the odometer reset button. Turn the ignition to RUN. Observe the Instrument Cluster indicators. Release the odometer reset button. Did the ABS Indicator illuminate during the Instrument Cluster self test? Yes → Replace the Controller Antilock Brake Perform ABS VERIFICATION TEST - VER 1. No → Replace the Instrument Cluster Perform ABS VERIFICATION TEST - VER 1.

LTV0500000005556

Fig. 26 Cluster Lamp Failure (Part 2 of 2). 2004–06

POSSIBLE CAUSES
GROUND CIRCUIT CONNECTION POOR
GROUND CIRCUIT OPEN
CAB - GROUND CIRCUIT OPEN
GROUND CIRCUIT RADIO FREQUENCY INTERFERENCE

TEST	ACTION
1	Turn the ignition off. Disconnect the CAB harness connector. **Note: Check connector - Clean/repair as necessary.** Measure the resistance between ground and both of the ground circuits. Is the resistance below 1.0 ohm for both measurements? Yes → Go To 2 No → Repair the Ground circuit(s) for an open. Perform ABS VERIFICATION TEST.
2	Turn the ignition on. With the DRBIII®, actuate the pump motor. Measure the voltage drop across the CAB ground circuit connection with the pump motor running. Is the voltage above 0.10 volts? Yes → Repair Ground Circuit Poor Connection. Perform ABS VERIFICATION TEST. No → Go To 3

CR4020002028010X

Fig. 27   Controller Failure (Part 1 of 2). 2002–03

POSSIBLE CAUSES
INCORRECT TONE WHEEL
INCORRECT TIRES

TEST	ACTION
1	Inspect the tire sizes on the vehicle. Is a smaller than production tire, or two mini spares installed on both front wheels? Yes → Replace the incorrect tire(s) size with production size tire(s). Perform ABS VERIFICATION TEST. No → Go To 2
2	Count the number of tone wheel teeth on both of the front driveshafts. Does one or both of the front driveshaft teeth have 40 teeth? Yes → Replace the front driveshaft(s) with the incorrect number of tone wheel teeth. Note: Driveshafts for 1997 and earlier vehicles can not be used on this vehicle, because the number of tone wheel teeth are different between the Bendix and Teves systems. Perform ABS VERIFICATION TEST. No → Test Complete.

CR4020002029000X

Fig. 28   Incorrect Tone Wheel. 2002–03

TEST	ACTION
3	Turn the ignition off. Turn the ignition on. With the DRBIII®, record and erase DTC's. **NOTE: If you have other DTCs, repair other DTCs first before continuing.** Turn the ignition off. Remove ABS Valve fuse. Perform the Key-on Bulb Check. Does the ABS, Brake, and TCS (if equipped) Indicators remain on after the 4 second bulb check? Yes → Reinstall the ABS Valve fuse. With the DRBIII®, erase Instrument Cluster DTCs. Test Complete. Perform ABS VERIFICATION TEST - VER 1. No → Go To 4
4	Reinstall the ABS Valve fuse, if removed. Turn the ignition off. Turn the ignition to RUN. Perform the Instrument Cluster self test. **NOTE: Refer to Body information for the related test(s).** Did the indicators illuminate during the Instrument Cluster self test? Yes → Replace the Anti-Lock Brake module Perform ABS VERIFICATION TEST - VER 1. No → Go To 5
5	Turn the ignition off. Turn the ignition to RUN. Perform the Instrument Cluster self test. **NOTE: Refer to Body information for the related test(s).** Do the indicators turn on for 4 seconds, shut off for 5-10 seconds then illuminate? Yes → Test Complete. No → Ensure the ABS indicator bulb is installed or good in the Instrument Cluster. If verified working, replace the Instrument Cluster in accordance with the Service Information. Perform ABS VERIFICATION TEST - VER 1.

LTV0500000005565

Fig. 29   Instrument Cluster Bulb (Part 2 of 2). 2005–06

TEST	ACTION
3	Turn the ignition off. Disconnect the CAB connector. **Note: Check connector - Clean/repair as necessary.** Turn the ignition on. Turn on all accessories. Measure the voltage of the ground circuit at the CAB. Measure the voltage of the ground circuit. Is the voltage below 1.0 volts? Yes → Go To 4 No → Repair as necessary. Unsplice any accessories connected to the CAB ground circuit. Reroute and shield any high voltage cables away from the CAB ground circuit. Perform ABS VERIFICATION TEST.
4	If there are no potential causes remaining, replace the CAB. View repair options. Repair Replace the CAB. Perform ABS VERIFICATION TEST.

CR4020002028020X

Fig. 27   Controller Failure (Part 2 of 2). 2002–03

POSSIBLE CAUSES
INSTRUMENT CLUSTER OR ABM DTC PRESENT
CHECKING INSTRUMENT CLUSTER OPERATION
INSTRUMENT CLUSTER SELF-TEST
INSTRUMENT CLUSTER INTERNAL FAULT
ABM - INTERNAL FAULT

TEST	ACTION
1	Turn the ignition on. With the DRBIII®, read DTCs. Are there any Instrument Cluster or ABM DTCs present? Yes → Refer to the appropriate category for the related symptom(s). Perform ABS VERIFICATION TEST - VER 1. No → Go To 2
2	Turn the ignition off. Perform the Key-on Bulb Check. Does the ABS, Brake, or TCS (if equipped) indicators light and then go out after four seconds? Yes → Go To 3 No. Light remains after bulb check. Go To 4 No. Indicator never came on. Go To 5

LTV0500000005564

Fig. 29   Instrument Cluster Bulb (Part 1 of 2). 2005–06

POSSIBLE CAUSES
INTERMITTENT CONDITION
WHEEL SPEED SENSOR OR CONNECTOR DAMAGE
WHEEL SPEED SENSOR SIGNAL CIRCUIT FAULT
WHEEL SPEED SENSOR 12 VOLT SUPPLY CIRCUIT SHORT TO GROUND
WHEEL SPEED SENSOR 12 VOLT SUPPLY CIRCUIT OPEN
WHEEL SPEED SENSOR SIGNAL CIRCUIT SHORT TO GROUND
WHEEL SPEED SENSOR SIGNAL CIRCUIT OPEN
CAB - 12 VOLT SUPPLY CIRCUIT FAULT

LTV0500000005566

Fig. 30   Left Front, Left Rear, Right Front & Right Rear Sensor Circuit Failure (Part 1 of 5)

POSSIBLE CAUSES
CAB - SIGNAL CIRCUIT FAULT
WHEEL SPEED SENSOR 12 VOLT SUPPLY SHORT TO GROUND
WHEEL SPEED SENSOR SIGNAL CIRCUIT INOPERATIVE

TEST	ACTION
1	Turn the ignition on. With the DRBIII®, read DTCs. With the DRBIII®, read the Freeze Frame information. With the DRBIII®, erase DTCs. Turn the ignition off. Turn the ignition on. With the DRBIII®, read DTCs. **NOTE: The CAB must sense all four wheels at 25km/h (15 mph) before it will extinguish the ABS indicators.** Does the DRBIII® display SENSOR CIRCUIT FAILURE? Yes → Go To 2 No → Go To 13
2	Turn the ignition off. Inspect the CAB connector, affected Wheel Speed Sensor, and affected Wheel Speed Sensor connector. Is the affected Wheel Speed Sensor or any of the connectors damaged? Yes → Repair as necessary. Perform ABS VERIFICATION TEST - VER 1. No → Go To 3
3	Turn the ignition off. Disconnect the affected Wheel Speed Sensor connector. **Note: Check connector - Clean/repair as necessary.** Turn the ignition on. Measure the voltage between affected Wheel Speed Sensor 12 Volt Supply circuit and ground. Is the voltage above 10 volts? Yes → Go To 6 No → Go To 4
4	Turn the ignition off. Disconnect the CAB harness connector. Disconnect the affected Wheel Speed Sensor connector. Using a 12-volt test light connected to 12-volts, probe the affected Wheel Speed Sensor 12 Volt Supply circuit. Does the test light illuminate? Yes → Repair the affected Wheel Speed Sensor 12 Volt Supply circuit for a short to ground. Perform ABS VERIFICATION TEST - VER 1. No → Go To 5

LTV0500000005567

Fig. 30   Left Front, Left Rear, Right Front & Right Rear Sensor Circuit Failure (Part 2 of 5)

TEST	ACTION
9	Turn the ignition off. Remove the CAB harness strain relief to access wires. Reconnect the CAB harness connector. Turn the ignition on. Measure the voltage between affected Wheel Speed Sensor 12 Volt Supply circuit and ground. Is the voltage above 10 volts? Yes → Go To 10 No → Replace the Controller Antilock Brake Perform ABS VERIFICATION TEST - VER 1.
10	Turn the ignition off. Remove the CAB harness strain relief to access wires. Reconnect the CAB harness connector. Turn the ignition on. Measure the voltage between affected Wheel Speed Sensor 12 Volt Supply circuit and affected Wheel Speed Sensor Signal circuit. Is the voltage above 10 volts? Yes → Go To 11 No → Replace the Controller Antilock Brake Perform ABS VERIFICATION TEST - VER 1.
11	Turn the ignition off. Reconnect ALL affected Wheel Speed Sensor circuit connectors. Disconnect the affected Wheel Speed Sensor connector. Turn the ignition on. Measure the voltage of the affected Wheel Speed Sensor 12 Volt Supply circuit in the affected Wheel Speed Sensor connector while reconnecting the sensor connector. Did the affected Wheel Speed Sensor 12 Volt Supply circuit drop voltage to 0 DC volts? Yes → Replace the affected Wheel Speed Sensor Perform ABS VERIFICATION TEST - VER 1. No → Go To 12
12	Turn the ignition off. Reconnect ALL affected Wheel Speed Sensor circuit connectors. Turn the ignition on. Measure the DC voltage of the Wheel Speed Sensor Signal circuit in the affected Wheel Speed Sensor connector. Slowly rotate the wheel. Does the DC voltage toggle between 1.6 volts to .8 volts? Yes → Go To 13 No → Replace the affected Wheel Speed Sensor Perform ABS VERIFICATION TEST - VER 1.

LTV0500000005569

Fig. 30   Left Front, Left Rear, Right Front & Right Rear Sensor Circuit Failure (Part 4 of 5)

TEST	ACTION
5	Turn the ignition off. Disconnect the CAB harness connector. Disconnect the affected Wheel Speed Sensor connector. Connect a jumper wire between affected Wheel Speed Sensor 12 Volt Supply circuit and ground. Using a 12-volt test light connected to 12-volts, probe the affected Wheel Speed Sensor 12 Volt Supply circuit. Does the test light illuminate? Yes → Go To 6 No → Repair the affected Wheel Speed Sensor 12 Volt Supply circuit for an open. Perform ABS VERIFICATION TEST - VER 1.
6	Turn the ignition off. Disconnect the affected Wheel Speed Sensor connector. **NOTE: Check connector - Clean/repair as necessary.** Turn the ignition on. Measure the voltage between affected Wheel Speed Sensor Signal circuit and ground. Is the voltage above 1 volt? Yes → Repair the affected Wheel Speed Sensor Signal circuit for a short to voltage. Perform ABS VERIFICATION TEST - VER 1. No → Go To 7
7	Turn the ignition off. Disconnect the CAB harness connector. Disconnect the affected Wheel Speed Sensor connector. Using a 12-volt test light connected to 12-volts, probe the affected Wheel Speed Sensor Signal circuit. Does the test light illuminate? Yes → Repair the affected Wheel Speed Sensor Signal circuit for a short to ground. Perform ABS VERIFICATION TEST - VER 1. No → Go To 8
8	Turn the ignition off. Disconnect the CAB harness connector. Disconnect the affected Wheel Speed Sensor connector. Connect a jumper wire between affected Wheel Speed Sensor Signal circuit and ground. Using a 12-volt test light connected to 12-volts, probe the affected Wheel Speed Sensor Signal circuit. Does the test light illuminate? Yes → Go To 9 No → Repair the affected Wheel Speed Sensor Signal circuit for an open. Perform ABS VERIFICATION TEST - VER 1.

LTV0500000005568

Fig. 30   Left Front, Left Rear, Right Front & Right Rear Sensor Circuit Failure (Part 3 of 5)

TEST	ACTION
13	Turn the ignition off. Visually inspect the related wiring harness. Look for any chafed, pierced, pinched, or partially broken wires. Visually inspect the related wire harness connectors. Look for broken, bent, pushed out, or corroded terminals. Refer to any Hotline letters or Technical Service Bulletins that may apply. Were any problems found? Yes → Repair as necessary. Perform ABS VERIFICATION TEST - VER 1. No → Test Complete.

LTV0500000005570

Fig. 30   Left Front, Left Rear, Right Front & Right Rear Sensor Circuit Failure (Part 5 of 5)

POSSIBLE CAUSES
INTERMITTENT CONDITION
ELECTRO-MECHANICAL INSTRUMENT CLUSTER DTC PRESENT
PCI BUS CIRCUIT OPEN
CAB - INTERNAL FAILURE

TEST	ACTION
1	Turn the ignition on. With the DRBIII®, read DTCs. With the DRBIII®, read Freeze Frame information. With the DRBIII®, erase DTCs. Turn the ignition off. Turn the ignition on. With the DRBIII®, read DTCs. Does the DRBIII® display PCI BUS COMMUNICATION? Yes → Go To 2 No → Go To 4
2	Turn the ignition off. With the DRBIII®, read EMIC DTCs. Does the DRBIII® display ABS MESSAGE NOT RECEIVED? Yes → Refer to symptom ABS MESSAGE NOT RECEIVED Perform ABS VERIFICATION TEST - VER 1. No → Go To 3

LTV0500000005571

Fig. 31   PCI Bus Communication (Part 1 of 2). 2002–04

TEST	ACTION

3	Turn the ignition off.
	Disconnect the negative (-) battery cable.
	Disconnect the CAB harness connector.
	NOTE: check connector - Clean/repair as necessary.
	Measure the resistance of the PCI Bus circuit between the CAB connector and the Data Link Connector (DLC).
	Is the resistance below 5.0 ohms?
	
	    Yes → Replace the Controller Antilock Brake
	
	          Perform ABS VERIFICATION TEST - VER 1.
	
	    No → Repair the PCI Bus circuit for an open.
	          Perform ABS VERIFICATION TEST - VER 1.

4	Turn the ignition off.
	Visually inspect the related wiring harness. Look for any chafed, pierced, pinched, or partially broken wires.
	Visually inspect the related wire harness connectors. Look for broken, bent, pushed out, or corroded terminals.
	Were any problems found?
	
	    Yes → Repair as necessary.
	          Perform ABS VERIFICATION TEST - VER 1.
	
	    No → Test Complete.

LTV0500000005572

Fig. 31 PCI Bus Communication (Part 2 of 2). 2002–04

TEST	ACTION

3	Turn the ignition off.
	Disconnect the ABM harness connector.
	Turn the ignition on.
	Measure the voltage of the Fused Run Relay Output circuit.
	Is the voltage above 10 volts?
	
	    Yes → Go To 4
	
	    No → Repair the Fused Run Relay Output circuit for an open.
	          Perform ABS VERIFICATION TEST - VER 1.

4	Turn the ignition off.
	Disconnect the ABM harness connector.
	Measure the voltage of the ABS Valve Fused B(+) circuit.
	Is the voltage above 10 volts?
	
	    Yes → Go To 5
	
	    No → Repair the ABS Valve Fused B(+) circuit for an open.
	          Perform ABS VERIFICATION TEST - VER 1.

5	Turn the ignition off.
	Disconnect the ABM harness connector.
	Measure the resistance of the ground circuits.
	Is the resistance below 5.0 ohms?
	
	    Yes → Go To 6
	
	    No → Repair the ground circuit(s) for an open.
	          Perform ABS VERIFICATION TEST - VER 1.

6	Turn the ignition off.
	Disconnect the ABM harness connector.
	Turn the ignition on.
	Measure the voltage of the PCI Bus circuit.
	Is there any voltage present?
	
	    Yes → Repair the PCI Bus circuit for a short to voltage.
	          Perform ABS VERIFICATION TEST - VER 1.
	
	    No → Go To 7

7	Turn the ignition off.
	Disconnect the ABM harness connector.
	Measure the resistance between ground and the PCI Bus circuit.
	Is the resistance below 5.0 ohms?
	
	    Yes → Repair the PCI Bus circuit for a short to ground.
	          Perform ABS VERIFICATION TEST - VER 1.
	
	    No → Go To 8

LTV0500000005574

Fig. 32 PCI Bus Communication (Part 2 of 3). 2005–06

POSSIBLE CAUSES
INTERMITTENT DTC
DAMAGED ABM/ABM HARNESS CONNECTOR
FUSED RUN RELAY OUTPUT CIRCUIT OPEN
ABS VALVE FUSED B(+) CIRCUIT OPEN
ABM - GROUND CIRCUIT OPEN
PCI BUS CIRCUIT OPEN
ABM - INTERNAL FAULT
PCI BUS CIRCUIT SHORT TO VOLTAGE
PCI BUS CIRCUIT SHORT TO GROUND

TEST	ACTION

1	Turn the ignition on.
	With the DRBIII®, read DTCs.
	With the DRBIII®, erase DTCs.
	Turn the ignition off.
	Turn the ignition on.
	With the DRBIII®, read DTCs.
	Does the DRBIII® display PCI BUS COMMUNICATION?
	
	    Yes → Go To 2
	
	    No → Go To 9

2	Turn the ignition off.
	Disconnect the ABM harness connector.
	Inspect the ABM/ABM harness connector for damage.
	Is there any broken, bent, pushed out, corroded or spread terminals?
	
	    Yes → Repair as necessary.
	          Perform ABS VERIFICATION TEST - VER 1.
	
	    No → Go To 3

LTV0500000005573

Fig. 32 PCI Bus Communication (Part 1 of 3). 2005–06

TEST	ACTION

8	Turn the ignition off.
	Disconnect the ABM harness connector.
	Measure the resistance of the PCI Bus circuit between the ABM harness connector and the Data Link connector.
	Is the resistance over 5.0 ohms?
	
	    Yes → Repair the PCI Bus circuit for an open.
	          Perform ABS VERIFICATION TEST - VER 1.
	
	    No → Replace the Anti-Lock Brake Module
	
	          Perform ABS VERIFICATION TEST - VER 1.

9	Turn the ignition off.
	Visually inspect the related wiring harness. Look for any chafed, pierced, pinched, or partially broken wires.
	Visually inspect the related wire harness connectors. Look for broken, bent, pushed out, or corroded terminals.
	Refer to any Hotline letters or Technical Service Bulletins that may apply.
	Were any problems found?
	
	    Yes → Repair as necessary.
	          Perform ABS VERIFICATION TEST - VER 1.
	
	    No → Test Complete.

LTV0500000005575

Fig. 32 PCI Bus Communication (Part 3 of 3). 2005–06

POSSIBLE CAUSES
INTERMITTENT DTC
DAMAGED ABM/ABM HARNESS CONNECTOR
FUSED RUN RELAY OUTPUT CIRCUIT OPEN
ABS VALVE FUSED B(+) CIRCUIT OPEN
ABM - GROUND CIRCUIT OPEN
ABM - INTERNAL FAULT

TEST	ACTION

1	Turn the ignition on.
	With the DRBIII®, read DTCs.
	With the DRBIII®, erase DTCs.
	Turn the ignition off.
	Turn the ignition on.
	With the DRBIII®, read DTCs.
	Does the DRBIII® display PCI BUS LOOPBACK?
	
	    Yes → Go To 2
	
	    No → Go To 6

2	Turn the ignition off.
	Disconnect the ABM harness connector.
	Inspect the ABM/ABM harness connector for damage.
	Is there any broken, bent, pushed out, corroded or spread terminals?
	
	    Yes → Repair as necessary.
	          Perform ABS VERIFICATION TEST - VER 1.
	
	    No → Go To 3

3	Turn the ignition off.
	Disconnect the ABM harness connector.
	Turn the ignition on.
	Measure the voltage of the Fused Run Relay Output circuit.
	Is the voltage above 10 volts?
	
	    Yes → Go To 4
	
	    No → Repair the Fused Run Relay Output circuit for an open.
	          Perform ABS VERIFICATION TEST - VER 1.

LTV0500000005576

Fig. 33 PCI Bus Loopback (Part 1 of 2). 2005–06

TEST	ACTION
4	Turn the ignition off. Disconnect the ABM harness connector. Measure the voltage of the ABS Valve Fused B(+) circuit. Is the voltage above 10 volts? Yes → Go To 5 No → Repair the ABS Valve Fused B(+) circuit for an open. Perform ABS VERIFICATION TEST - VER 1.
5	Turn the ignition off. Disconnect the ABM harness connector. Measure the resistance of the ground circuits. Is the resistance below 5.0 ohms? Yes → Replace the Anti-Lock Brake Module Perform ABS VERIFICATION TEST - VER 1. No → Repair the ground circuit(s) for an open. Perform ABS VERIFICATION TEST - VER 1.
6	Turn the ignition off. Visually inspect the related wiring harness. Look for any chafed, pierced, pinched, or partially broken wires. Visually inspect the related wire harness connectors. Look for broken, bent, pushed out, or corroded terminals. Refer to any Hotline letters or Technical Service Bulletins that may apply. Were any problems found? Yes → Repair as necessary. Perform ABS VERIFICATION TEST - VER 1. No → Test Complete.

LTV0500000005577

Fig. 33 PCI Bus Loopback (Part 2 of 2). 2005–06

TEST	ACTION
3	Turn the ignition off. Disconnect the ABM harness connector. Turn the ignition on. Measure the voltage of the Fused Run Relay Output circuit. Is the voltage above 10 volts? Yes → Go To 4 No → Repair the Fused Run Relay Output circuit for an open. Perform ABS VERIFICATION TEST - VER 1.
4	Turn the ignition off. Disconnect the ABM harness connector. Measure the voltage of the ABS Valve Fused B(+) circuit. Is the voltage above 10 volts? Yes → Go To 5 No → Repair the ABS Valve Fused B(+) circuit for an open. Perform ABS VERIFICATION TEST - VER 1.
5	Turn the ignition off. Disconnect the ABM harness connector. Measure the resistance of the ground circuits. Is the resistance below 5.0 ohms? Yes → Go To 6 No → Repair the ground circuit(s) for an open. Perform ABS VERIFICATION TEST - VER 1.
6	Turn the ignition off. Disconnect the ABM harness connector. Turn the ignition on. Measure the voltage of the PCI Bus circuit. Is there any voltage present? Yes → Repair the PCI Bus circuit for a short to voltage. Perform ABS VERIFICATION TEST - VER 1. No → Go To 7
7	Turn the ignition off. Disconnect the ABM harness connector. Measure the resistance between ground and the PCI Bus circuit. Is the resistance below 5.0 ohms? Yes → Repair the PCI Bus circuit for a short to ground. Perform ABS VERIFICATION TEST - VER 1. No → Go To 8

LTV0500000005579

Fig. 34 PCI Bus Shorted To Ground (Part 2 of 3). 2005–06

POSSIBLE CAUSES
INTERMITTENT DTC
DAMAGED ABM/ABM HARNESS CONNECTOR
FUSED RUN RELAY OUTPUT CIRCUIT OPEN
ABS VALVE FUSED B(+) CIRCUIT OPEN
ABM - GROUND CIRCUIT OPEN
PCI BUS CIRCUIT OPEN
ABM - INTERNAL FAULT
PCI BUS CIRCUIT SHORT TO VOLTAGE
PCI BUS CIRCUIT SHORT TO GROUND

TEST	ACTION
1	Turn the ignition on. With the DRBIII®, read DTCs. With the DRBIII®, erase DTCs. Turn the ignition off. Turn the ignition on. With the DRBIII®, read DTCs. Does the DRBIII® display PCI BUS SHORTED TO GROUND? Yes → Go To 2 No → Go To 9
2	Turn the ignition off. Disconnect the ABM harness connector. Inspect the ABM/ABM harness connector for damage. Is there any broken, bent, pushed out, corroded or spread terminals? Yes → Repair as necessary. Perform ABS VERIFICATION TEST - VER 1. No → Go To 3

LTV0500000005578

Fig. 34 PCI Bus Shorted To Ground (Part 1 of 3). 2005–06

TEST	ACTION
8	Turn the ignition off. Disconnect the ABM harness connector. Measure the resistance of the PCI Bus circuit between the ABM harness connector and the Data Link connector. Is the resistance over 5.0 ohms? Yes → Repair the PCI Bus circuit for an open. Perform ABS VERIFICATION TEST - VER 1. No → Replace the Anti-Lock Brake Module Perform ABS VERIFICATION TEST - VER 1.
9	Turn the ignition off. Visually inspect the related wiring harness. Look for any chafed, pierced, pinched, or partially broken wires. Visually inspect the related wire harness connectors. Look for broken, bent, pushed out, or corroded terminals. Refer to any Hotline letters or Technical Service Bulletins that may apply. Were any problems found? Yes → Repair as necessary. Perform ABS VERIFICATION TEST - VER 1. No → Test Complete.

LTV0500000005580

Fig. 34 PCI Bus Shorted To Ground (Part 3 of 3). 2005–06

POSSIBLE CAUSES
INTERMITTENT DTC
DAMAGED ABM/ABM HARNESS CONNECTOR
FUSED RUN RELAY OUTPUT CIRCUIT OPEN
ABS VALVE FUSED B(+) CIRCUIT OPEN
ABM - GROUND CIRCUIT OPEN
PCI BUS CIRCUIT OPEN
ABM - INTERNAL FAULT
PCI BUS CIRCUIT SHORT TO VOLTAGE
PCI BUS CIRCUIT SHORT TO GROUND

TEST	ACTION
1	Turn the ignition on. With the DRBIII®, read DTCs. With the DRBIII®, erase DTCs. Turn the ignition off. Turn the ignition on. With the DRBIII®, read DTCs. Does the DRBIII® display PCI BUS SHORTED TO VOLTAGE? Yes → Go To 2 No → Go To 9
2	Turn the ignition off. Disconnect the ABM harness connector. Inspect the ABM/ABM harness connector for damage. Is there any broken, bent, pushed out, corroded or spread terminals? Yes → Repair as necessary. Perform ABS VERIFICATION TEST - VER 1. No → Go To 3

LTV0500000005581

Fig. 35 PCI Bus Shorted To Voltage (Part 1 of 3). 2005–06

TEST	ACTION
3	Turn the ignition off. Disconnect the ABM harness connector. Turn the ignition on. Measure the voltage of the Fused Run Relay Output circuit. Is the voltage above 10 volts? Yes → Go To 4 No → Repair the Fused Run Relay Output circuit for an open. Perform ABS VERIFICATION TEST - VER 1.
4	Turn the ignition off. Disconnect the ABM harness connector. Measure the voltage of the ABS Valve Fused B(+) circuit. Is the voltage above 10 volts? Yes → Go To 5 No → Repair the ABS Valve Fused B(+) circuit for an open. Perform ABS VERIFICATION TEST - VER 1.
5	Turn the ignition off. Disconnect the ABM harness connector. Measure the resistance of the ground circuits. Is the resistance below 5.0 ohms? Yes → Go To 6 No → Repair the ground circuit(s) for an open. Perform ABS VERIFICATION TEST - VER 1.
6	Turn the ignition off. Disconnect the ABM harness connector. Turn the ignition on. Measure the voltage of the PCI Bus circuit. Is there any voltage present? Yes → Repair the PCI Bus circuit for a short to voltage. Perform ABS VERIFICATION TEST - VER 1. No → Go To 7
7	Turn the ignition off. Disconnect the ABM harness connector. Measure the resistance between ground and the PCI Bus circuit. Is the resistance below 5.0 ohms? Yes → Repair the PCI Bus circuit for a short to ground. Perform ABS VERIFICATION TEST - VER 1. No → Go To 8

LTV0500000005582

Fig. 35   PCI Bus Shorted To Voltage (Part 2 of 3). 2005–06

POSSIBLE CAUSES
INTERMITTENT DTC
DAMAGED ABM/ABM HARNESS CONNECTOR
FUSED RUN RELAY OUTPUT CIRCUIT OPEN
ABS VALVE FUSED B(+) CIRCUIT OPEN
ABM - GROUND CIRCUIT OPEN
ABM - INTERNAL FAULT

TEST	ACTION
1	Turn the ignition on. With the DRBIII®, read DTCs. With the DRBIII®, erase DTCs. Turn the ignition off. Turn the ignition on. With the DRBIII®, read DTCs. Does the DRBIII® display PCI HARDWARE? Yes → Go To 2 No → Go To 6
2	Turn the ignition off. Disconnect the ABM harness connector. Inspect the ABM/ABM harness connector for damage. Is there any broken, bent, pushed out, corroded or spread terminals? Yes → Repair as necessary. Perform ABS VERIFICATION TEST - VER 1. No → Go To 3
3	Turn the ignition off. Disconnect the ABM harness connector. Turn the ignition on. Measure the voltage of the Fused Run Relay Output circuit. Is the voltage above 10 volts? Yes → Go To 4 No → Repair the Fused Run Relay Output circuit for an open. Perform ABS VERIFICATION TEST - VER 1.

LTV0500000005584

Fig. 36   PCI Hardware (Part 1 of 2). 2005–06

TEST	ACTION
8	Turn the ignition off. Disconnect the ABM harness connector. Measure the resistance of the PCI Bus circuit between the ABM harness connector and the Data Link connector. Is the resistance over 5.0 ohms? Yes → Repair the PCI Bus circuit for an open. Perform ABS VERIFICATION TEST - VER 1. No → Replace the Anti-Lock Brake Module Perform ABS VERIFICATION TEST - VER 1.
9	Turn the ignition off. Visually inspect the related wiring harness. Look for any chafed, pierced, pinched, or partially broken wires. Visually inspect the related wire harness connectors. Look for broken, bent, pushed out, or corroded terminals. Refer to any Hotline letters or Technical Service Bulletins that may apply. Were any problems found? Yes → Repair as necessary. Perform ABS VERIFICATION TEST - VER 1. No → Test Complete.

LTV0500000005583

Fig. 35   PCI Bus Shorted To Voltage (Part 3 of 3). 2005–06

TEST	ACTION
4	Turn the ignition off. Disconnect the ABM harness connector. Measure the voltage of the ABS Valve Fused B(+) circuit. Is the voltage above 10 volts? Yes → Go To 5 No → Repair the ABS Valve Fused B(+) circuit for an open. Perform ABS VERIFICATION TEST - VER 1.
5	Turn the ignition off. Disconnect the ABM harness connector. Measure the resistance of the ground circuits. Is the resistance below 5.0 ohms? Yes → Replace the Anti-Lock Brake Module Perform ABS VERIFICATION TEST - VER 1. No → Repair the ground circuit(s) for an open. Perform ABS VERIFICATION TEST - VER 1.
6	Turn the ignition off. Visually inspect the related wiring harness. Look for any chafed, pierced, pinched, or partially broken wires. Visually inspect the related wire harness connectors. Look for broken, bent, pushed out, or corroded terminals. Refer to any Hotline letters or Technical Service Bulletins that may apply. Were any problems found? Yes → Repair as necessary. Perform ABS VERIFICATION TEST - VER 1. No → Test Complete.

LTV0500000005585

Fig. 36   PCI Hardware (Part 2 of 2). 2005–06

POSSIBLE CAUSES
CAB - PUMP MOTOR RUNNING CONTINUOUSLY
ABS PUMP MOTOR INTERMITTENT DTC
FUSED B(+) CIRCUIT INTERMITTENTLY SHORTED TO GROUND
FUSED B(+) CIRCUIT SHORTED TO GROUND
CAB - FUSED B(+) CIRCUIT SHORTED TO GROUND
FUSE BLOWN - PUMP MOTOR CIRCUIT
NO B+ SUPPLY TO FUSE
ABS PUMP MOTOR INOPERATIVE
FUSED B(+) CIRCUIT OPEN
GROUND CIRCUIT OPEN
GROUND CIRCUIT HIGH RESISTANCE
CAB - INTERNAL FAULT

TEST	ACTION
1	Turn the ignition off. Reconnect all connectors. Turn the ignition on. Monitor the pump motor for continuous operation. Is the pump motor running continuously? Yes → Replace the Controller Anti-Lock Brake Perform ABS VERIFICATION TEST - VER 1. No → Go To 2

LTV0500000005586

Fig. 37   Pump Not Working Properly (Part 1 of 4). 2002–04

TEST	ACTION
2	Turn the ignition on. With the DRBIII®, read DTC's. With the DRBIII®, erase DTC's. Turn the ignition off. Turn the ignition on. With the DRBIII®, actuate the ABS pump motor. Did the Pump Motor operate when actuated? No → Go To 3 Yes → Go To 14
3	Turn the ignition off. Remove and inspect the ABS Pump fuse 2 in the PDC. Is the Fuse blown? Yes → Go To 4 No → Go To 8
4	Turn the ignition off. Make sure the Pump Motor connector is secure. Visually inspect the Fused B(+) Circuit in the wiring harness from the PDC to the CAB. Look for any sign of an Intermittent Short to Ground. Is the wiring harness OK? Yes → Go To 5 No → Repair the Fused B(+) Circuit shorted to ground. Perform ABS VERIFICATION TEST - VER 1.
5	Turn the ignition off. Remove the ABS PUMP Fuse 2 from the Power Distribution Center (PDC). Disconnect the CAB connector. Make sure the Pump Motor connector is secure. **Note: Check connector - Clean/repair as necessary.** Using a test light connected to 12 volts, probe the Fused B (+) Circuit. Is the test light on? Yes → Repair the Fused B(+) circuit short to ground. Perform ABS VERIFICATION TEST - VER 1. No → Go To 6
6	Turn the ignition off. Make sure the Pump Motor connector is secure. Remove the ABS PUMP Fuse 2 from the PDC. The CAB must be connected for the results of this test to be valid. Using a test light connected to 12 volts, probe the Fused B (+) circuit in the PDC. Is the test light on? Yes → Replace the Controller Anti-Lock Brake Perform ABS VERIFICATION TEST - VER 1. No → Go To 7

LTV0500000005587

Fig. 37   Pump Not Working Properly (Part 2 of 4). 2002–04

TEST	ACTION
7	Turn the ignition off. Make sure the Pump Motor connector is secure If there are no potential causes remaining, replace the Fuse. If there are no possible causes remaining, view repair. Repair Replace the ABS Pump Motor Fuse. Perform ABS VERIFICATION TEST - VER 1.
8	Turn the ignition off. Remove the ABS PUMP Fuse 2 from the Power Distribution Center (PDC). Disconnect the CAB connector. **Note: Check connector - Clean/repair as necessary.** Measure the resistance of the Fused B (+) circuit between the PDC Fuse Terminal and the CAB connector. Is the resistance below 10 ohms? Yes → Go To 9 No → Repair the Fused B(+) circuit for an open. Perform ABS VERIFICATION TEST - VER 1.
9	Turn the ignition on. Using a 12-volt test light connected to ground, check the B+ supply to Fuse 2 in the PDC. Is the B+ supply OK? Yes → Go To 10 No → Repair the B+ supply for an open. Perform ABS VERIFICATION TEST - VER 1.
10	Turn the ignition off. Disconnect Pump Motor Connector. Connect a 10 gauge jumper wire between pump motor Fused B (+) circuit and a 40 Amp Fused B (+) circuit. Connect a 10 gauge jumper wire between pump motor ground circuit and a known good body ground. Monitor Pump Motor operation. Is the pump motor running? Yes → Go To 11 No → Replace the ABS Pump Motor/Hydraulic Control Unit assembly. Perform ABS VERIFICATION TEST - VER 1.
11	Turn the ignition off. Disconnect CAB Connector. **Note: Check connector - Clean/repair as necessary.** Measure the resistance of the CAB ground circuits. Is the resistance below 1.0 ohm? Yes → Go To 12 No → Repair the ground circuit circuit for an open. Perform ABS VERIFICATION TEST - VER 1.

LTV0500000005588

Fig. 37   Pump Not Working Properly (Part 3 of 4). 2002–04

TEST	ACTION
12	Make sure the Pump Motor connector is secure. Turn the ignition on. With the DRBIII®, enable pump motor actuation. **NOTE: Pump motor will not operate, but voltage will be applied.** Measure the voltage drop across the ABS ground circuit connection, with pump motor actuation enabled. Is the voltage below 0.1 volt? Yes → Go To 13 No → Repair the Ground circuit for an open. Perform ABS VERIFICATION TEST - VER 1.
13	If there are no possible causes remaining, view repair. Repair Replace the Controller Anti-Lock Brake in accordance with the Service Information. Perform ABS VERIFICATION TEST - VER 1.
14	Turn the ignition off. Visually inspect the related wiring harness. Look for any chafed, pierced, pinched, or partially broken wires. Make sure the Pump Motor connector is secure. Visually inspect the related wire harness connectors. Look for broken, bent, pushed out, or corroded terminals. Refer to any Hotline letters or Technical Service Bulletins that may apply. Were any problems found? Yes → Repair as necessary. Perform ABS VERIFICATION TEST - VER 1. No → Test Complete.

LTV0500000005589

Fig. 37   Pump Not Working Properly (Part 4 of 4). 2002–04

POSSIBLE CAUSES
INTERMITTENT DTC
DAMAGED ABM/ABM HARNESS CONNECTOR
ABS PUMP FUSED B(+) CIRCUIT OPEN
PUMP MOTOR GROUND CIRCUITS OPEN
ABM - INTERNAL FAULT

TEST	ACTION
1	Turn the ignition off. Turn the ignition on. With the DRBIII®, read DTCs. With the DRBIII®, erase DTCs. Turn the ignition off. Turn the ignition on. With the DRBIII®, read DTCs. Does the DRBIII® display PUMP MOTOR CIRCUIT? Yes → Go To 4 No → Go To 2
2	Turn the ignition off. Turn the ignition on. With the DRBIII®, actuate the Pump. Did the Pump operate? Yes → Go To 3 No → Go To 4

LTV0500000005590

Fig. 38   Pump Motor Circuit (Part 1 of 2). 2005–06

TEST	ACTION
3	Turn the ignition off. Visually inspect the related wiring harness. Look for any chafed, pierced, pinched, or partially broken wires. Make sure the ABM harness connecter is secure. Visually inspect the related wire harness connectors. Look for broken, bent, pushed out, or corroded terminals. Refer to any Hotline letters or Technical Service Bulletins that may apply. Were any problems found? Yes → Repair as necessary. Perform ABS VERIFICATION TEST - VER 1. No → Test Complete.
4	Turn the ignition off. Disconnect the ABM harness connector. Inspect the ABM and ABM harness connector for damage. Is there any broken, bent, pushed out, corroded, or spread terminals? Yes → Repair as necessary. Perform ABS VERIFICATION TEST - VER 1. No → Go To 5
5	Turn the ignition off. Disconnect the ABM harness connector. Check connectors - Clean/repair as necessary. Measure the voltage of the ABS Pump Fused B(+) circuit. Is the voltage above 10 volts? Yes → Go To 6 No → Repair the ABS Pump Fused B(+) circuit for an open. Perform ABS VERIFICATION TEST - VER 1.
6	Turn the ignition off. Disconnect the ABM harness connector. Check connectors - Clean/repair as necessary. Measure the resistance of the ground circuits. Is the resistance below 5.0 ohms? Yes → Replace the Anti-Lock Brake Module Perform ABS VERIFICATION TEST - VER 1. No → Repair the Pump Motor ground circuit(s) for an open. Perform ABS VERIFICATION TEST - VER 1.

LTV0500000005591

Fig. 38 Pump Motor Circuit (Part 2 of 2). 2005–06

TEST	ACTION
4	Turn the ignition off. Visually inspect the related wiring harness. Look for any chafed, pierced, pinched, or partially broken wires. Visually inspect the related wire harness connectors. Look for broken, bent, pushed out, or corroded terminals. Refer to any Hotline letters or Technical Service Bulletins that may apply. Were any problems found? Yes → Repair as necessary. Perform ABS VERIFICATION TEST. No → Test Complete.

CR4020002040020X

Fig. 39 System Overvoltage (Part 2 of 2)

TEST	ACTION
3	Turn ignition off. Disconnect the CAB connector. **Note: Check connector - Clean/repair as necessary.** Start the engine. Raise engine RPM's above 1800. Measure the voltage of the Fused Ignition Switch Output circuit. Is the voltage below 13 volts ? Yes → Refer to appropriate service information for charging system testing and repair. Perform ABS VERIFICATION TEST. No → Test Complete.
4	Turn the ignition off. Visually inspect the related wiring harness. Look for any chafed, pierced, pinched, or partially broken wires. Visually inspect the related wire harness connectors. Look for broken, bent, pushed out, or corroded terminals. Refer to any Hotline letters or Technical Service Bulletins that may apply. Were any problems found? Yes → Repair as necessary. Perform ABS VERIFICATION TEST. No → Test Complete.

CR4020002041020X

Fig. 40 System Undervoltage (Part 2 of 2)

POSSIBLE CAUSES
INTERMITTENT DTC
BATTERY OVERCHARGED
FUSED IGNITION SWITCH OUTPUT CIRCUIT OVERVOLTAGE

TEST	ACTION
1	Turn the ignition on. With the DRBIII®, erase DTC's. Turn the ignition off. Turn the ignition on. Start the engine. With the DRBIII®, read DTC's. Is the System Overvoltage DTC present? Yes → Go To 2 No → Go To 4
2	Turn ignition off. Inspect for battery charger connected to battery. Is a battery charger connected to the battery? Yes → Charge battery to proper level. Disconnect the battery charger. Clear DTC's. Perform ABS VERIFICATION TEST. No → Go To 3
3	Turn ignition off. Disconnect the CAB connector. **Note: Check connector - Clean/repair as necessary.** Start the engine. Raise engine RPM's above 1800. Measure the voltage of the Fused Ignition Switch Output Circuit. Is the voltage above 16.5 volts ? Yes → Refer to appropriate service information for charging system testing and repair. Perform ABS VERIFICATION TEST. No → Test Complete.

CR4020002040010X

Fig. 39 System Overvoltage (Part 1 of 2)

POSSIBLE CAUSES
INTERMITTENT DTC
FUSED IGNITION SWITCH OUTPUT CIRCUIT HIGH RESISTANCE
FUSED IGNITION SWITCH OUTPUT CIRCUIT UNDERVOLTAGE

TEST	ACTION
1	Turn the ignition on. With the DRBIII®, erase DTC's. Turn the ignition off. Turn the ignition on. Start the engine. With the DRBIII®, read DTC's. Is the System Undervoltage DTC present? Yes → Go To 2 No → Go To 4
2	Turn ignition on. With the DRBIII®, select Sensors. With the DRBIII®, read the "Ignition Voltage" status and record. Measure the voltage at the battery and record. Compare voltage measurements. Does the DRBIII® display ignition voltage within one volt of the battery voltage? Yes → Go To 3 No → Repair the Fused Ignition Switch Output Circuit for high resistance Perform ABS VERIFICATION TEST.

CR4020002041010X

Fig. 40 System Undervoltage (Part 1 of 2)

POSSIBLE CAUSES
INTERMITTENT DTC
ABS VALVE FUSE
ABS VALVE FUSED B(+) SUPPLY CIRCUIT OPEN
ABS VALVE FUSED B(+) CIRCUIT OPEN
ABS VALVE FUSED B(+) CIRCUIT INTERMITTENT SHORT TO GROUND
ABS VALVE FUSED B(+) CIRCUIT SHORT TO GROUND
DAMAGED CAB/CAB HARNESS CONNECTOR
CAB - GROUND CIRCUIT OPEN
CAB - INTERNAL FAULT

TEST	ACTION
1	Turn the ignition on. With the DRBIII®, read DTC's. With the DRBIII®, erase DTC's. Turn the ignition off. Turn the ignition on. With the DRBIII®, read DTC's. Does the DRBIII® display VALVE POWER FEED FAILURE? Yes → Go To 2 No → Go To 10
2	Turn the ignition off. Remove and Inspect the ABS Valve fuse. Is the ABS Valve fuse open? Yes → Go To 3 No → Go To 6

LTV0500000005592

Fig. 41 Valve Power Feed Failure (Part 1 of 3). 2004

TEST	ACTION
3	Turn the ignition off. Visually inspect the ABS Valve Fused B(+) circuit in the wiring harness. Look for any sign of an intermittent short to ground. Is the wiring harness OK? Yes → Go To 4 No → Repair the ABS Valve Fused B(+) circuit for a short to ground. Perform ABS VERIFICATION TEST - VER 1.
4	Turn the ignition off. Disconnect the CAB harness connector. **Note: Check connector - Clean/repair as necessary.** Using a test light connected to 12 volts, probe the ABS Valve Fused B(+) circuit fuse terminal. Did the test light illuminate? Yes → Repair the ABS Valve Fused B(+) circuit for a short to ground. Perform ABS VERIFICATION TEST - VER 1. No → Go To 5
5	Turn the ignition off. Reconnect the CAB harness connector. **NOTE: The CAB harness connector must be reconnected for the results of this test to be valid.** Using a test light connected to 12 volts, probe the ABS Valve Fused B(+) circuit fuse terminal. Did the test light illuminate? Yes → Replace the Controller Antilock Brake Perform ABS VERIFICATION TEST - VER 1. No → Replace the ABS Valve Fused B(+) fuse. If the fuse is open make sure to check for a short to ground. Perform ABS VERIFICATION TEST - VER 1.
6	Turn the ignition off. Disconnect the CAB harness connector. Inspect the CAB and CAB harness connector for damage. Is there any broken, bent, pushed out, corroded or spread terminals? Yes → Repair as necessary. Perform ABS VERIFICATION TEST - VER 1. No → Go To 7
7	Turn the ignition off. Using a 12-volt test light connected to ground, probe the B(+) supply at the ABS Valve fuse terminal. Did the test light illuminate? Yes → Go To 8 No → Repair the ABS Valve Fused B(+) supply circuit for an open. Perform ABS VERIFICATION TEST - VER 1.

LTV0500000005593

Fig. 41 Valve Power Feed Failure (Part 2 of 3). 2004

TEST	ACTION
8	Reinstall the ABS Valve fuse. Disconnect the CAB harness connector. Using a 12-volt test light connected to ground, probe the ABS Valve Fused B(+) circuit at the CAB harness connector. Did the test light illuminate? Yes → Go To 9 No → Repair the ABS Valve Fused B(+) circuit for an open. Perform ABS VERIFICATION TEST - VER 1.
9	Turn the ignition off. Using a 12-volt test light connected to 12-volts, probe the ground circuits at the CAB harness connector. Did the test light illuminate? Yes → Replace the Controller Antilock Brake Perform ABS VERIFICATION TEST - VER 1. No → Repair the CAB Ground circuit for an open. Perform ABS VERIFICATION TEST - VER 1.
10	Turn the ignition off. Visually inspect the related wiring harness. Look for any chafed, pierced, pinched, or partially broken wires. Visually inspect the related wire harness connectors. Look for broken, bent, pushed out, or corroded terminals. Refer to any Hotline letters or Technical Service Bulletins that may apply. Were any problems found? Yes → Repair as necessary. Perform ABS VERIFICATION TEST - VER 1. No → Test Complete.

LTV0500000005594

Fig. 41 Valve Power Feed Failure (Part 3 of 3). 2004

ABS VERIFICATION TEST - VER 1

1. Turn the ignition off.
2. Connect all previously disconnected components and connectors.
3. Ensure all accessories are turned off and the battery is fully charged.
4. Ensure that the Ignition is on, and with the DRBIII, erase all Diagnostic Trouble Codes from ALL modules. Start the engine and allow it to run for 2 minutes and fully operate the system that was malfunctioning.
5. Turn the ignition off and wait 5 seconds. Turn the ignition on and using the DRBIII®, read DTC's from ALL modules.
6. If any Diagnostic Trouble Codes are present, return to Symptom list and troubleshoot new or recurring symptom.
7. **NOTE: For Sensor Signal and Pump Motor faults, the ABM must sense all 4 wheels at 25 km/h (15 mph) before it will extinguish the ABS Indicator.**
8. If there are no DTC's present after turning ignition on, road test the vehicle for at least 5 minutes. Perform several anti-lock braking stops.
9. **Caution: Ensure braking capability is available before road testing.**
10. Again, with the DRBIII® read DTC's. If any DTC's are present, return to Symptom list.
11. If there are no Diagnostic Trouble Codes (DTC's) present, and the customer's concern can no longer be duplicated, the repair is complete.
Are any DTC's present or is the original concern still present?

Yes → Repair is not complete, refer to appropriate symptom.

No → Repair is complete.

BODY VERIFICATION TEST - VER 1

1. Disconnect all jumper wires and reconnect all previously disconnected components and connectors.
2. **NOTE: If the SKIM or PCM/ECM was replaced, refer to the service information for proper programming procedures.**
3. **NOTE: PT27 ONLY: If a Window Regulator Module was replaced, close both doors, raise both door windows fully up and hold the switch in the up position for 2 additional seconds then use the DRBIII to "Initialize Module".**
4. Program all RKE transmitters and other options as necessary.
5. Ensure that all accessories are turned off and the battery is fully charged.
6. With the DRBIII®, record and erase all DTC's from ALL modules. Start and run the engine for 2 minutes. Operate all functions of the system that caused the original concern.
7. Turn the ignition off and wait 5 seconds. Turn the ignition on and using the DRBIII®, read DTC's from ALL modules.
Are any DTC's present or is the original condition still present?

Yes → Repair is not complete, refer to the appropriate symptom.

No → Repair is complete.

CR4020002044000X

Fig. 42 Verification Tests

Dakota

NOTE: On Air Bag Equipped Models, Refer To "Air Bag System Precautions" Located In The Front Of This Manual For System Disarming & Arming Procedures.

NOTE: Refer To "Computer Relearn Procedures" Located In The Front Of This Manual When Battery Power To The Computer Has Been Interrupted.

NOTE: "Electrical Symbol & Wire Color Code Identification" Located In The Front Of This Manual May Be Used As An Aid When Using Wiring Circuits Found In This Section.

INDEX

	Page No.
Description	5-44
Diagnosis & Testing	5-44
Accessing Diagnostic Trouble Codes	5-44
Clearing Diagnostic Trouble Codes	5-45
Connector Pin Identification	5-44
Diagnostic Tests	5-44
Diagnostic Trouble Code Interpretation	5-44
Intermittents & Poor	

	Page No.
Connections	5-45
Symptom Tests	5-45
Wiring Diagrams	5-44
Diagnostic Chart Index	5-47
Precautions	5-44
Air Bag Systems	5-44
Battery Ground Cable	5-44
General Service Precautions	5-44
System Service	5-45
Brake System Bleed	5-45
Component Replacement	5-45

	Page No.
Controller Anit-Lock Brake (CAB) Module, Replace	5-45
Front Wheel Speed Sensor, Replace	5-45
Hydraulic Control Unit (HCU), Replace	5-45
RWAL Valve, Replace	5-45
Rear Wheel Speed Sensor, Replace	5-45

PRECAUTIONS

Air Bag Systems

Refer to "Air Bag System Precautions" in the front of this manual for system disarming and arming procedures.

Battery Ground Cable

Prior to service disconnect battery ground cable and isolate as required.

General Service Precautions

Certain components of the anti-lock brake system are not intended to be serviced individually. Attempting to remove or disconnect components of this type may result in personal injury and/or improper system operation. Only the components with removal and installation procedures should be serviced.

Observe the following general precautions when servicing the anti-lock brake system:
1. If any welding work is to be performed using an arc welder, Controller Anti-Lock Brake (CAB) should be disconnected.
2. When ignition switch is in On position, CAB electrical connector should not be disconnected or connected.
3. Some components of ABS system are not serviced separately and must be serviced as complete assemblies. Do not disassemble any component which is designated as non-serviceable.

DESCRIPTION

When wheel slip is detected during a brake application, the ABS enters anti-lock mode. During anti-lock braking, hydraulic pressure in the individual wheel circuits is controlled to prevent any wheel from slipping. A separate hydraulic line and specific solenoid valves are provided for each wheel. The ABS can decrease, hold, or increase hydraulic pressure to each wheel brake. The ABS cannot, however, increase hydraulic pressure above the amount which is transmitted by the master cylinder during braking.

During anti-lock braking, a series of rapid pulsations is felt in the brake pedal. These pulsations are caused by the rapid changes in position of the individual solenoid valves as the EBCM responds to wheel speed sensor inputs and attempts to prevent wheel slip. These pedal pulsations are present only during anti-lock braking and stop when normal braking is resumed or when the vehicle comes to a stop. A ticking or popping noise may also be heard as the solenoid valves cycle rapidly. During anti-lock braking on dry pavement, intermittent chirping noises may be heard as the tires approach slipping. These noises and pedal pulsations are considered normal during anti-lock operation.

Vehicles equipped with ABS may be stopped by applying normal force to the brake pedal. Brake pedal operation during normal braking is no different than that of previous non-ABS systems. Maintaining a constant force on the brake pedal provides the shortest stopping distance while maintaining vehicle stability.

DIAGNOSIS & TESTING

Accessing Diagnostic Trouble Codes

Connect a suitably programmed scan tool to Data Link Connector (DLC) and follow manufacturer's instructions.

Diagnostic Trouble Code Interpretation

Refer to "Diagnostic Chart Index" for diagnostic trouble code interpretation.

Connector Pin Identification

Refer to **Figs. 1 and 2** for pin connector and terminal identification.

Wiring Diagrams

Refer to **Figs. 3 through 5** for wiring diagrams.

Diagnostic Tests

Refer to "Durango" "Diagnostics Tests" for test procedures.

Symptom Tests

Refer to **Figs. 6 through 27** for diagnostic tests.

Clearing Diagnostic Trouble Codes

Connect a suitably programmed scan tool to Data Link Connector (DLC) and follow manufacturer's instructions.

Intermittents & Poor Connections

Most Intermittents are caused by faulty electrical connections or wiring, although a sticking relay or solenoid can also cause an intermittent condition. Inspect wiring and connectors for the following:

1. Poor mating of connector halves, or terminals not fully seated in connector body.
2. Dirt or corrosion on terminals.
3. Damaged connector body.
4. Improperly formed or damaged terminals.
5. Poor terminal to wire connection.
6. Rubbed through wiring insulation.
7. Wiring broken inside insulation.

SYSTEM SERVICE

Brake System Bleed

The base brake system must be bled anytime air is permitted to enter the hydraulic system. However, anti-lock brake system components should only be bled if the hydraulic control unit has been removed or if there is reason to believe that air has entered the unit. **The ABS portion of the braking system must be bled separately.** Under most circumstances, only the base brake system will require bleeding, refer to the "Hydraulic Brake Systems" chapter for procedure. If the anti-lock brake system must be bled, proceed as follows:

1. Ensure all brake system components are installed and all hydraulic lines are connected securely.
2. Connect DRB diagnostic scan tool to diagnostic connector, then ensure CAB has no stored diagnostic trouble codes.
3. Bleed base brake system as outlined in "Hydraulic Brake Systems" chapter, then select "Anti-Lock Brakes" followed by "Miscellaneous" then "Bleed Brakes" routine on diagnostic scan tool.
4. Bleed base brake system once again, then repeat ABS bleed cycle and base brake system bleed until brake fluid flow (as established in "Hydraulic Brake Systems" bleed procedure) is free of bubbles. **Ensure all bleeder valves are closed tightly after bleed sequence is completed.**
5. Road test vehicle to ensure base hydraulic system and anti-lock brake system operate properly.

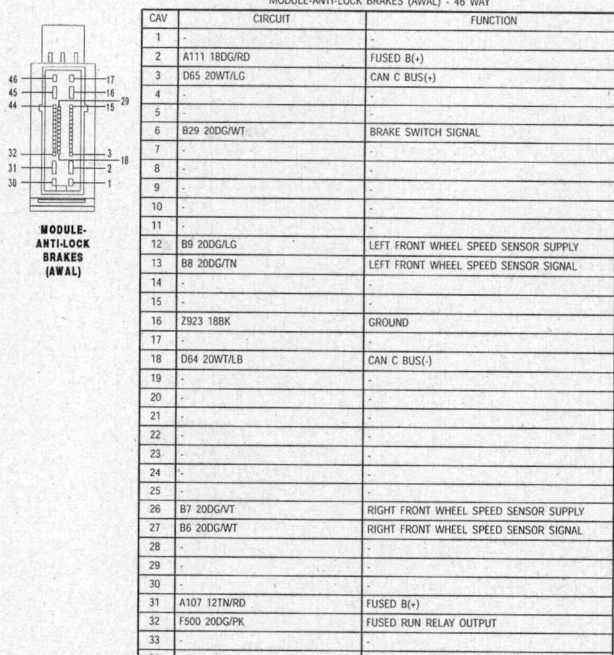

MODULE-ANTI-LOCK BRAKES (AWAL) - 46 WAY

CAV	CIRCUIT	FUNCTION
1	-	-
2	A111 18DG/RD	FUSED B(+)
3	D65 20WT/LG	CAN C BUS(+)
4	-	-
5	-	-
6	B29 20DG/WT	BRAKE SWITCH SIGNAL
7	-	-
8	-	-
9	-	-
10	-	-
11	-	-
12	B9 20DG/LG	LEFT FRONT WHEEL SPEED SENSOR SUPPLY
13	B8 20DG/TN	LEFT FRONT WHEEL SPEED SENSOR SIGNAL
14	-	-
15	-	-
16	Z923 18BK	GROUND
17	-	-
18	D64 20WT/LB	CAN C BUS(-)
19	-	-
20	-	-
21	-	-
22	-	-
23	-	-
24	-	-
25	-	-
26	B7 20DG/VT	RIGHT FRONT WHEEL SPEED SENSOR SUPPLY
27	B6 20DG/WT	RIGHT FRONT WHEEL SPEED SENSOR SIGNAL
28	-	-
29	-	-
30	-	-
31	A107 12TN/RD	FUSED B(+)
32	F500 20DG/PK	FUSED RUN RELAY OUTPUT
33	-	-
34	-	-
35	-	-
36	-	-
37	-	-
38	-	-
39	-	-
40	-	-
41	B22 20DG/YL	REAR WHEEL SPEED SENSOR SIGNAL
42	B222 20DG/WT	REAR WHEEL SPEED SENSOR SUPPLY
43	-	-
44	-	-
45	Z107 12BK/DG	GROUND
46	-	-

LTV0500000005595

Fig. 1 Controller Anti-Lock Brake (CAB) connector & terminal identification.

Component Replacement

CONTROLLER ANIT-LOCK BRAKE (CAB) MODULE, REPLACE

1. Remove HCU as outlined in this section.
2. Disconnect CAB electrical connectors, **Fig. 28.**
3. Disconnect pump motor connector.
4. Remove CAB to HCU mounting screws.
5. Remove CAB.
6. Reverse procedure to install.

FRONT WHEEL SPEED SENSOR, REPLACE

1. Raise and support vehicle.
2. Remove front rotor and caliper adapter.
3. Remove wheel speed sensor mounting bolt.
4. Remove wheel speed sensor from hub.
5. Reverse procedure to install.

HYDRAULIC CONTROL UNIT (HCU), REPLACE

1. Disconnect brake lines to HCU.

2. Disconnect electrical connections.
3. Remove HCU assembly mounting bolts.
4. Raise and support vehicle.
5. Lift HCU assembly off battery tray and remove from vehicle.
6. Reverse procedure to install.

RWAL VALVE, REPLACE

1. Disconnect RWAL electrical connector.
2. Disconnect brake lines from RWAL assembly.
3. Remove RWAL mounting bolt, then RWAL valve.
4. Reverse procedure to install.

REAR WHEEL SPEED SENSOR, REPLACE

1. Raise and support vehicle.
2. Remove brake line mounting nut, then remove brake line from sensor stud.
3. Remove park brake cable and bracket from sensor stud.
4. Disconnect electrical connector.
5. Remove sensor mounting stud, then sensor.
6. Reverse procedure to install.

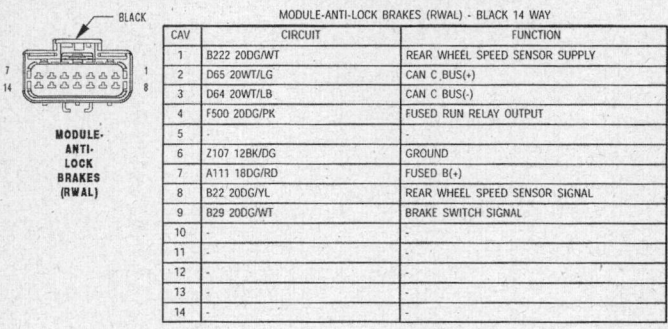

CAV	CIRCUIT	FUNCTION
1	B222 20DG/WT	REAR WHEEL SPEED SENSOR SUPPLY
2	D65 20WT/LG	CAN C BUS(+)
3	D64 20WT/LB	CAN C BUS(-)
4	F500 20DG/PK	FUSED RUN RELAY OUTPUT
5	-	-
6	Z107 12BK/DG	GROUND
7	A111 18DG/RD	FUSED B(+)
8	B22 20DG/YL	REAR WHEEL SPEED SENSOR SIGNAL
9	B29 20DG/WT	BRAKE SWITCH SIGNAL
10	-	-
11	-	-
12	-	-
13	-	-
14	-	-

MODULE-ANTI-LOCK BRAKES (RWAL) - BLACK 14 WAY

CAV	CIRCUIT	FUNCTION
1	A400 14TN/RD	FUSED B(+)
2	B400 12DG	TRAILER TOW ELECTRIC BRAKE OUTPUT
3	L50 18WT/LB	BRAKE LAMP SWITCH OUTPUT
4	Z910 18BK	GROUND

MODULE-BRAKE PROVISION - BLUE 4 WAY

LTV0500000005596

Fig. 2   Controller Anti-Lock Brake (CAB) connector & terminal identification.

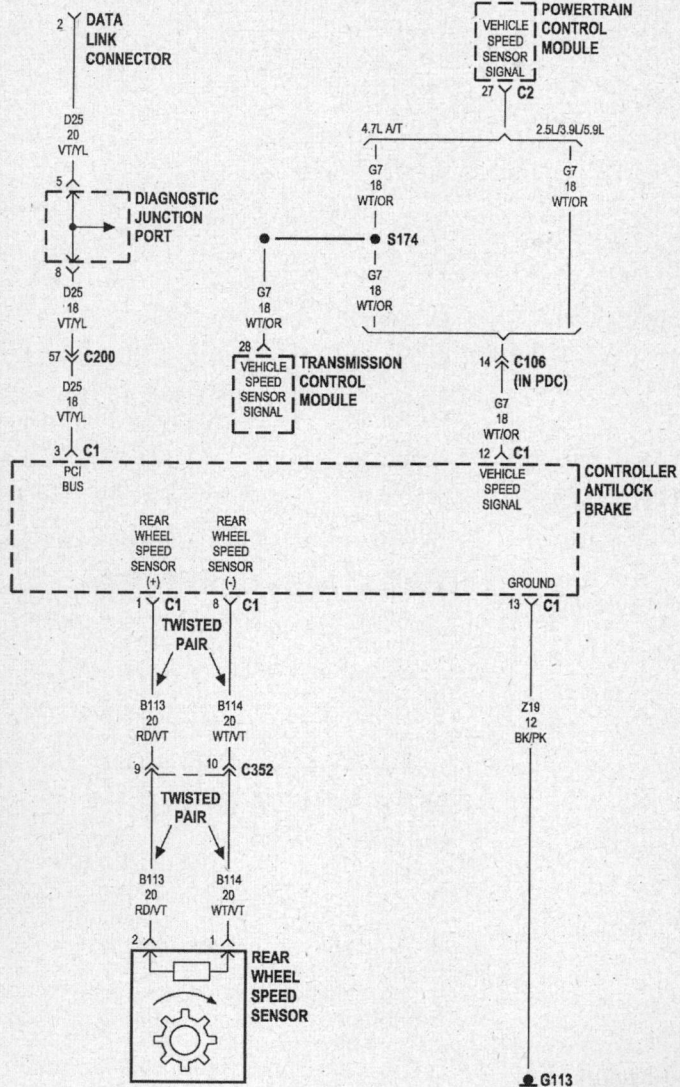

Fig. 3   Wiring diagram (Part 2 of 2). 2002–04 w/RWAL

LTV0500000005598

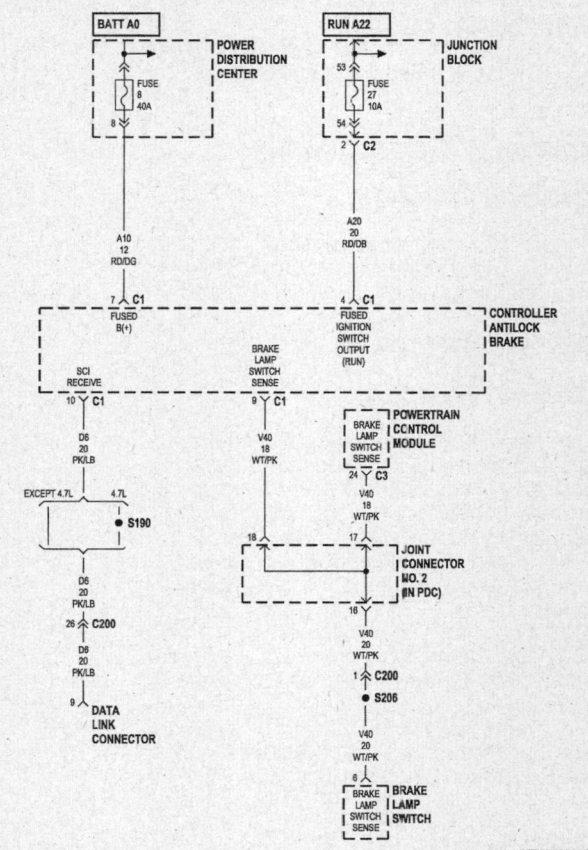

Fig. 3   Wiring diagram (Part 1 of 2). 2002–04 w/RWAL

LTV0500000005597

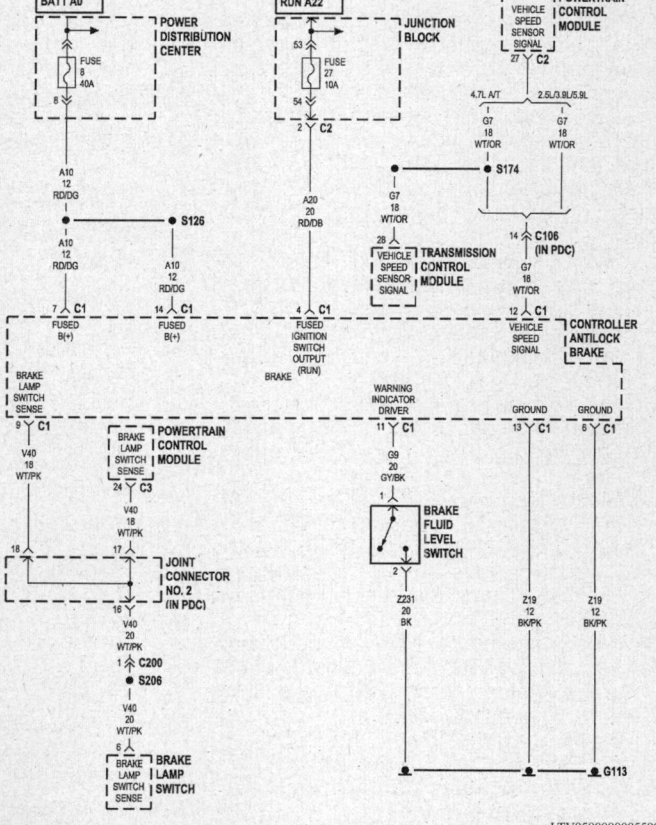

Fig. 4   Wiring diagram (Part 1 of 2). 2002–04 w/4 WABS

LTV0500000005599

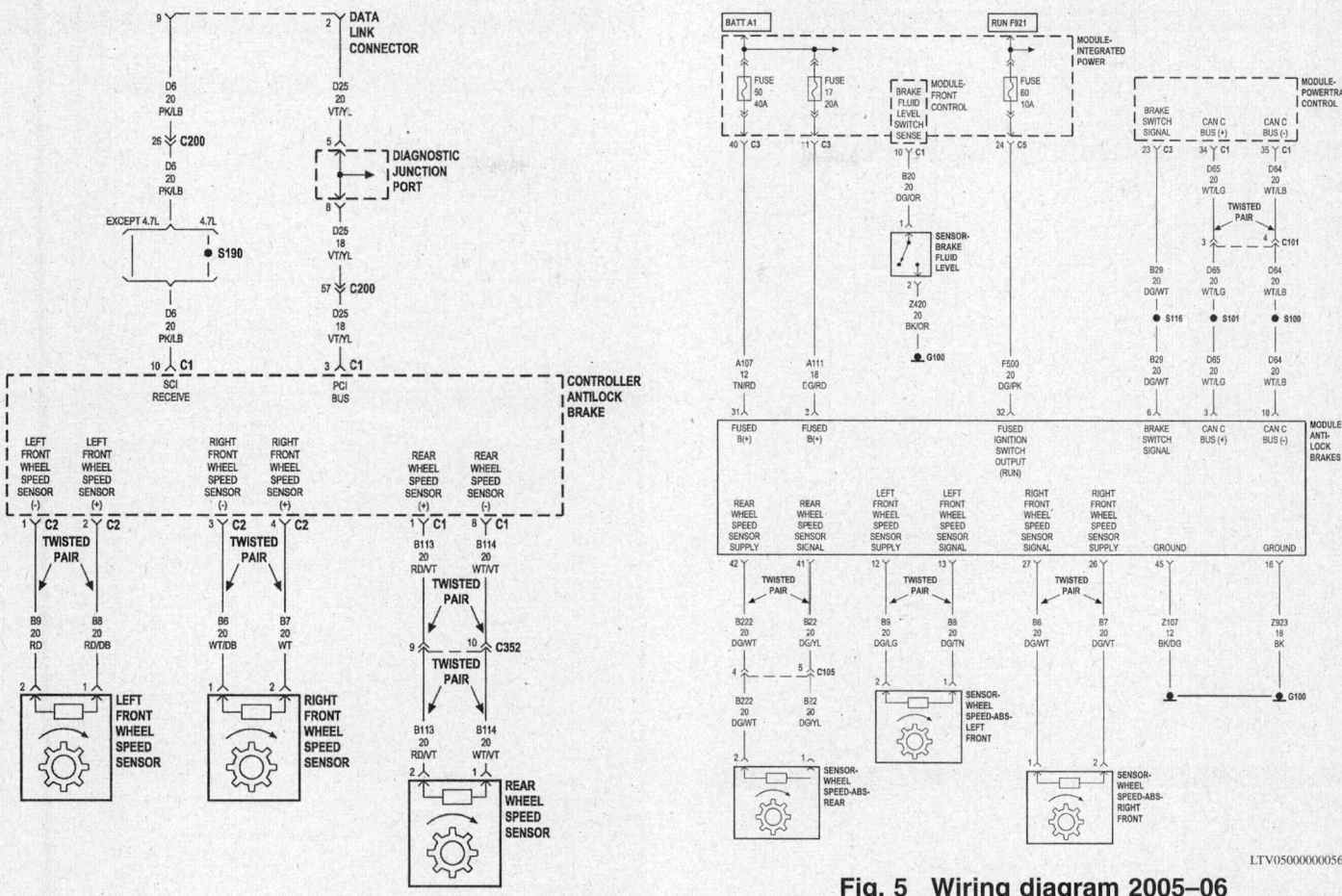

Fig. 4   Wiring diagram (Part 2 of 2). 2002–04 w/4 WABS

Fig. 5   Wiring diagram 2005–06

DIAGNOSTIC CHART INDEX

	Description	Page No.	Fig No.
—	ABS Warning Indicator	5-48	6
—	Body Style Mismatch	5-48	7
—	Brake Switch Circuit	5-48	8
—	DRBIII No Response Message	5-48	9
—	Excessive Dump Time	5-49	10
—	Foundation Brake	5-49	11
—	Internal Main Relay Open/Shorted	5-51	13
—	Mismatched Vin	5-52	15
—	Number Of Tone Ring Teeth Out Of Range	5-53	16
—	Pump Motor Fault	5-53	17
—	Dump Solenoid Fault	5-52	14
—	RAM Read/Write	5-54	18
—	Rear Reset Switch Closed	5-54	19
—	ROM Checksum	5-54	20
—	System Control Mode Timout	5-54	21
—	System Over/Under Voltage	5-55	22
—	Tire Revolutions Per Mile Out Of Range	5-55	23
—	Vehicle Speed Signal Output	5-55	24
—	Verification Tests	5-56	25
—	Watchdog	5-56	26
—	Wheel Sensor Fault	5-50	12
—	Wheel Speed Mismatch	5-56	27

POSSIBLE CAUSES
CLUSTER DTC PRESENT
INSTRUMENT CLUSTER BULB CONCERN
CAB DTC PRESENT
INSTRUMENT CLUSTER INTERNAL CONCERN

TEST	ACTION
1	Turn the ignition on. With the DRBIII®, read DTCs. Are there any Instrument Cluster DTCs present? Yes → Refer to the INSTRUMENT CLUSTER category for the related symptom(s). Perform ABS VERIFICATION TEST - VER 1. No → Go To 2
2	Turn the ignition off. Observe the instrument cluster indicators. Turn the ignition on. Did the ABS Indicator illuminate for several seconds? Yes → Go To 3 No → Replace the Instrument Cluster Perform ABS VERIFICATION TEST - VER 1.
3	Turn the ignition on. NOTE: The DRBIII® communication with the CAB must be operational for the result of this test to be valid. Perform the Key-on Bulb Check. Are there any CAB DTCs present? Yes → Refer to BRAKES category for the related symptom(s). Perform ABS VERIFICATION TEST - VER 1. No → Go To 4
4	If there are no possible causes remaining, view repair. Repair Replace the Instrument Cluster Perform ABS VERIFICATION TEST - VER 1.

LTV0500000005693

Fig. 6   ABS Warning Indicator. 2002–04

POSSIBLE CAUSES
VERIFY THE CONCERN
CAB BRAKE STATUS
BRAKE SWITCH OPEN
BRAKE SWITCH SENSE CIRCUIT OPEN
BRAKE SWITCH GROUND CIRCUIT OPEN
CAB -- INTERNAL CONCERN

TEST	ACTION
1	NOTE: IF DRIVER "RIDES" THE BRAKES, A BRAKE CIRCUIT DIAGNOSTIC CODE MAYBE SET. Turn the ignition off. Ensure all accessories are turned off and the battery is fully charged. Turn the ignition on. With the DRBIII®, erase DTCs. CAUTION: Ensure braking capability is available before road testing. Road test the vehicle for at least 5 minutes over 40 MPH. Perform several antilock braking stops. Monitor the Input/Output status of the brake switch while driving. With the DRBIII®, read DTCs. Does the original DTC recur and/or intermittent brake switch operation occur? Yes → Go To 2 No → Brake Switch circuit is operating correctly at this time. Check for "two footed" driver. Inspect for intermittent condition using the wiring diagram/schematic as a guide, inspect the wiring and connectors for damage. Perform ABS VERIFICATION TEST - VER 1.
2	Turn ignition on. With the DRBIII® in Inputs/Outputs, read the Brake Switch status. Press and release the brake pedal. Does the Brake Switch status match that of the Brake Switch? Yes → Using the wiring diagram/schematic as a guide, inspect the wiring and connectors for damage. Perform ABS VERIFICATION TEST - VER 1. No → Go To 3

LTV0500000005658

Fig. 8   Brake Switch Circuit (Part 1 of 2). 2002–04

POSSIBLE CAUSES
BODY STYLE MISMATCH DTC CONDITION PRESENT

TEST	ACTION
1	Turn the ignition on. With the DRBIII®, erase DTC's. Turn the ignition off. Turn the ignition on. With the DRBIII®, read DTC's. Is the BODY STYLE MISMATCH DTC present? Yes → Replace the Controller Antilock Brake Perform ABS VERIFICATION TEST - VER 1. No → Test Complete.

LTV0500000005657

Fig. 7   Body Style Mismatch. 2002–04

TEST	ACTION
3	Disconnect the Brake Lamp Switch harness connector. With the DRBIII in Inputs/Outputs, read the Brake Switch state. Connect and disconnect a jumper wire between the Brake Switch Ground and Sense circuits. Does the DRBIII display OPEN and CLOSED (jumper connected)? Yes → Replace the Brake Lamp Switch Perform ABS VERIFICATION TEST - VER 1. No → Go To 4
4	Turn the ignition off. Disconnect the CAB harness connector. Disconnect the Brake Lamp Switch harness connector. Measure the resistance of the Brake Switch Sense circuit between the CAB connector and the Brake Lamp Switch connector. Is the Brake Switch Sense circuit open? Yes → Repair the Brake Switch Sense circuit for an open circuit. Perform ABS VERIFICATION TEST - VER 1. No → Go To 5
5	Turn the ignition off. Disconnect the Brake Lamp Switch harness connector. Using a 12-volt test light connected to 12-volts, check the Brake Switch Ground circuit. Does the test light illuminate brightly? Yes → Replace the Controller Antilock Brake Perform ABS VERIFICATION TEST - VER 1. No → Repair the Brake Switch Ground circuit for an open circuit. Perform ABS VERIFICATION TEST - VER 1.

LTV0500000005659

Fig. 8   Brake Switch Circuit (Part 2 of 2). 2002–04

POSSIBLE CAUSES
CHECK COMMUNICATION TO MIC
CAB-- INTERNAL FAULT

TEST	ACTION
1	Turn the ignition on. With the DRBIII®, attempt to communicate with the MIC Was the DRB able to I/D or communicate with the MIC? Yes → Go To 2 No → Refer to the Communication category and perform the symptom Bus +/- Signals Open from the Controller Anti-Lock Brake. Perform ABS VERIFICATION TEST - VER 1.
2	With the DRB, erase DTC's. Turn the ignition on and wait approximately 1 minute. With the DRB, read DTC's. Did this DTC reappear? Yes → Replace the Controller Antilock Brake Perform ABS VERIFICATION TEST - VER 1. No → Test Complete.

LTV0500000005694

Fig. 9   DRBIII No Response Message. 2002–04

POSSIBLE CAUSES
BRAKE SYSTEM MECHANICAL CONCERN
TONE WHEEL CONCERN
WHEEL SPEED WIRING HARNESS CONCERN
HCU INTERNAL CONCERN

TEST	ACTION
1	Inspect the front and rear brakes for anything that would cause the wheel(s) to lock during braking. Is there anything mechanically wrong with the Braking System? Yes → Repair the mechanical braking system as necessary. Perform ABS VERIFICATION TEST - VER 1. No → Go To 2
2	Turn the ignition off. Inspect the Tone Wheel for damaged, missing teeth or looseness. **Note: The Tone Wheel Teeth should be perfectly square, not bent or nicked.** Is the Tone Wheel OK? Yes → Go To 3 No → Replace the Tone Wheel Perform ABS VERIFICATION TEST - VER 1.

LTV0500000005660

Fig. 10 Excessive Dump Time (Part 1 of 2). 2002–04

TEST	ACTION
3	Engine Running. Raise and support the vehicle. With the DRBIII® in Sensors, read the Wheel Speed Sensor signals. **WARNING: BE SURE TO KEEP HANDS, FEET AND CLOTHING CLEAR OF ROTATING COMPONENTS.** Allow the drive wheels to rotate. Rotate the non-driven wheels by hand. Wiggle Wheel Speed wiring harnesses. With the DRBIII® in Sensors, read the Wheel Speed Sensor outputs. Is there a wheel speed dropout when a wiring harness is wiggled? Yes → Repair the Wheel Speed wiring harness as necessary. Perform ABS VERIFICATION TEST - VER 1. No → Go To 4
4	If there are no possible causes remaining, replace the HCU. View repair options. Repair Replace the Hydraulic Control Unit Perform ABS VERIFICATION TEST - VER 1.

LTV0500000005661

Fig. 10 Excessive Dump Time (Part 2 of 2). 2002–04

POSSIBLE CAUSES
LOW BRAKE FLUID LEVEL
BRAKE FLUID LEVEL SWITCH SENSE CIRCUIT SHORTED TO GROUND
BRAKE FLUID LEVEL SWITCH OPEN
BRAKE FLUID LEVEL SWITCH GROUND CIRCUIT OPEN
CAB - INTERNAL CONCERN
FOUNDATION BRAKE INTERMITTENT DTC

TEST	ACTION
1	Release the Parking Brake. Turn the ignition off. Turn the ignition on. Watch the Instrument Cluster. Does the Red Brake Warning Indicator come on and then stay on? Yes → Go To 2 No → Go To 7
2	Turn the ignition off. Inspect the Brake Fluid Level in the Master Cylinder Reservoir. Is the Brake Fluid Level Low? Yes → Repair as necessary. Perform ABS VERIFICATION TEST - VER 1. No → Go To 3

LTV0500000005662

Fig. 11 Foundation Brake (Part 1 of 3). 2002–04

TEST	ACTION
3	Turn the ignition off. Disconnect the Brake Fluid Level Switch connector **Note: Check connector - Clean/repair as necessary.** Disconnect the CAB connector. **Note: Check connector - Clean/repair as necessary.** Turn the ignition on. Using a test light connected to 12 volts, probe the Brake Fluid Level Switch Sense circuit. Does the test light illuminate brightly? Yes → Repair the Brake Fluid Level Switch Sense circuit for a short to ground. Perform ABS VERIFICATION TEST - VER 1. No → Go To 4
4	Turn the ignition off. Disconnect the Brake Fluid Level Switch connector. **Note: Check connector - Clean/repair as necessary.** On the switch, measure the resistance between both of the Brake Fluid Level Switch terminals. **NOTE: Resistance should be 10,000 ohms with a full Master Cylinder Reservoir.** Is the resistance over 10,500 ohms? Yes → Replace the Master Cylinder/Reservoir as necessary. Perform ABS VERIFICATION TEST - VER 1. No → Go To 5
5	Turn the ignition off. Disconnect the Brake Fluid Level Switch connector. **Note: Check connector - Clean/repair as necessary.** Using a 12-volt test light connected to 12-volts, probe the Brake Fluid Level Switch ground circuit. Does the test light illuminate brightly? Yes → Go To 6 No → Repair the Brake Fluid Level Switch ground circuit for an open. Perform ABS VERIFICATION TEST - VER 1.
6	If there are no potential causes remaining, replace the CAB. View repair options. Repair Replace the Controller Antilock Brake Perform ABS VERIFICATION TEST - VER 1.

LTV0500000005663

Fig. 11 Foundation Brake (Part 2 of 3). 2002–04

TEST	ACTION
7	Turn the ignition off. Visually inspect the related wiring harness. Look for any chafed, pierced, pinched, or partially broken wires. Visually inspect the related wire harness connectors. Look for broken, bent, pushed out, or corroded terminals. Refer to any Hotline letters or Technical Service Bulletins that may apply. Were any problems found? Yes → Repair wiring harness/connectors as necessary. Perform ABS VERIFICATION TEST - VER 1. No → Test Complete.

LTV0500000005664

Fig. 11 Foundation Brake (Part 3 of 3). 2002–04

When Monitored and Set Condition:

INTERMITTENT SIGNAL FROM LEFT FRONT SENSOR

When Monitored: Ignition turned on for at least 3.5 seconds. Average filtered speed for the two front wheels above 6 km/h (4 mph). Speed for each suspect sensor above 32 km/h (20 mph) (brake applied or ABS active) or 19 km/h (12 mph) (brake released or ABS inactive).

Set Condition: There is no output signal from the sensor for 15 milliseconds (ms).

INTERMITTENT SIGNAL FROM REAR SENSOR

When Monitored: Ignition turned on for at least 3.5 seconds. Average filtered speed for the wheels above 19 km/h (12 mph) (brake released or ABS inactive) or 32 km/h (20 mph) (brake applied or ABS active).

Set Condition: There is no output signal from the sensor for 15 milliseconds (ms).

INTERMITTENT SIGNAL FROM RIGHT FRONT SENSOR

When Monitored: Ignition turned on for at least 3.5 seconds. Average filtered speed for the two front wheels above 6 km/h (4 mph). Speed for each suspect sensor above 32 km/h (20 mph) (brake applied or ABS active) or 19 km/h (12 mph) (brake released or ABS inactive).

Set Condition: There is no output signal from the sensor for 15 milliseconds (ms).

LEFT FRONT SENSOR OPEN

When Monitored: Ignition on.

Set Condition: If the CAB detects an open wheel speed sensor circuit, the Diagnostic Trouble Code (DTC) will set.

LTV0500000005665

Fig. 12   Wheel Sensor Fault (Part 1 of 6). 2002–04

POSSIBLE CAUSES
WHEEL SPEED SENSOR OR CONNECTOR DAMAGE, LOOSENESS OR METAL CHIPS
INTERMITTENT DTC
WHEEL SPEED SENSOR (+) CIRCUIT SHORTED TO GROUND
WHEEL SPEED SENSOR (-) CIRCUIT SHORTED TO GROUND
WHEEL SPEED SENSOR SHORTED TO GROUND
CAB - INTERNAL SHORT OR OPEN
WHEEL SPEED SENSOR (+) CIRCUIT OPEN
WHEEL SPEED SENSOR (-) CIRCUIT OPEN
WHEEL SPEED SENSOR (+) CIRCUIT SHORTED TO VOLTAGE
WHEEL SPEED SENSOR (-) CIRCUIT SHORTED TO VOLTAGE
WHEEL SPEED SENSOR CIRCUITS SHORT TOGETHER
WHEEL SPEED SENSOR RESISTANCE OUT OF SPECIFICATION
TONE WHEEL/RING DAMAGED

TEST	ACTION
1	Turn the ignition on. With the DRBIII®, read DTC's. With the DRBIII®, erase DTC's. Turn the ignition off. Turn the ignition on. With the DRBIII®, read DTC's. Does the DRBIII® display the appropriate Wheel Speed Sensor circuit failure DTC right now? Yes → Go To 2 No → Go To 15
2	Turn the ignition off. Inspect the appropriate Wheel Speed Sensor for looseness. Inspect the appropriate Wheel Speed Sensor harness connector. Check connectors - Clean/repair as necessary. Inspect the appropriate Wheel Speed Sensor for metal chips on sensor. Is the Sensor or Connector damaged, loose, or metal chips on sensor present? Yes → Repair as necessary. Perform ABS VERIFICATION TEST - VER 1. No → Go To 3

LTV0500000005667

Fig. 12   Wheel Sensor Fault (Part 3 of 6). 2002–04

LEFT FRONT SENSOR SHORTED

When Monitored: Ignition on.

Set Condition: When no output signal from any sensor for one second and continuously excessive sensor resistance for one second is detected.

NO SIGNAL FROM LEFT FRONT SENSOR

When Monitored: Ignition on.

Set Condition: When one sensors signal is prevented above 4 mph while one or more other sensors are indiacating that the vehicle is moving above 8 mph.

NO SIGNAL FROM REAR SENSOR

When Monitored: Ignition on.

Set Condition: When one sensors signal is prevented above 4 mph while one or more other sensors are indiacating that the vehicle is moving above 8 mph.

NO SIGNAL FROM RIGHT FRONT SENSOR

When Monitored: Ignition on.

Set Condition: When one sensors signal is prevented above 4 mph while one or more other sensors are indiacating that the vehicle is moving above 8 mph.

REAR SENSOR OPEN

When Monitored: Ignition on.

Set Condition: If the CAB detects an open wheel speed sensor circuit, the Diagnostic Trouble Code (DTC) will set.

REAR SENSOR SHORTED

When Monitored: Ignition on.

Set Condition: When no output signal from any sensor for one second and continuously excessive sensor resistance for one second is detected.

RIGHT FRONT SENSOR OPEN

When Monitored: Ignition on.

Set Condition: If the CAB detects an open wheel speed sensor circuit, the Diagnostic Trouble Code (DTC) will set.

RIGHT FRONT SENSOR SHORTED

When Monitored: Ignition on.

Set Condition: When no output signal from any sensor for one second and continuously excessive sensor resistance for one second is detected.

LTV0500000005666

Fig. 12   Wheel Sensor Fault (Part 2 of 6). 2002–04

TEST	ACTION
3	Turn the ignition off. Disconnect the appropriate CAB harness connector for the effected Wheel Speed Sensor. **Note: Check connector - Clean/repair as necessary.** Measure the resistance across the appropriate Wheel Speed Sensor (+) and (-) circuits at the CAB connector at 77°F. Is the resistance 1800 - 2200(Front) OR 1600 - 2300(Rear) ohms? Yes → Go To 4 No → Go To 8
4	Turn the ignition off. Disconnect the appropriate Wheel Speed Sensor connector. Disconnect the appropriate CAB harness connector for the effected Wheel Speed Sensor. Measure the resistance between the appropriate Wheel Speed Sensor (+) Circuit and ground. Is the resistance below 20,000 ohms? Yes → Repair the appropriate Wheel Speed Sensor (+) Circuit Short to Ground. Perform ABS VERIFICATION TEST - VER 1. No → Go To 5
5	Turn the ignition off. Disconnect the appropriate Wheel Speed Sensor connector. **Note: Check connector - Clean/repair as necessary.** Disconnect the appropriate CAB harness connector for the effected Wheel Speed Sensor. **Note: Check connector - Clean/repair as necessary.** Measure the resistance between the appropriate Wheel Speed Sensor (-) circuit and ground. Is the resistance below 20,000 ohms? Yes → Repair the appropriate Wheel Speed Sensor (-) Circuit Short to Ground. Perform ABS VERIFICATION TEST - VER 1. No → Go To 6
6	Turn the ignition off. Disconnect the appropriate Wheel Speed Sensor connector. **Note: Check connector - Clean/repair as necessary.** On the component, measure the resistance between both of the appropriate Wheel Speed Sensor terminals and ground. Is the resistance below 20,000 ohms? Yes → Replace the appropriate Wheel Speed Sensor Perform ABS VERIFICATION TEST - VER 1. No → Go To 7
7	If there are no possible causes remaining, view repair. Repair Replace the Controller Antilock Brake Perform ABS VERIFICATION TEST - VER 1.

LTV0500000005668

Fig. 12   Wheel Sensor Fault (Part 4 of 6). 2002–04

TEST	ACTION
8	Turn the ignition off. Disconnect the appropriate Wheel Speed Sensor connector. **Note: Check connector - Clean/repair as necessary.** Disconnect the appropriate CAB harness connector for the effected Wheel Speed Sensor. **Note: Check connector - Clean/repair as necessary.** Measure the resistance of the appropriate Wheel Speed Sensor (+) circuit. Is the resistance below 5 ohms? Yes → Go To 9 No → Repair the appropriate Wheel Speed Sensor (+) Circuit Open. Perform ABS VERIFICATION TEST - VER 1.
9	Turn the ignition off. Disconnect the appropriate Wheel Speed Sensor connector. **Note: Check connector - Clean/repair as necessary.** Disconnect the appropriate CAB harness connector for the effected Wheel Speed Sensor. **Note: Check connector - Clean/repair as necessary.** Measure the resistance of the appropriate Wheel Speed Sensor (-) circuit. Is the resistance below 5 ohms? Yes → Go To 10 No → Repair the appropriate Wheel Speed Sensor (-) Circuit Open. Perform ABS VERIFICATION TEST - VER 1.
10	Turn the ignition off. Disconnect the appropriate Wheel Speed Sensor harness connector. **Note: Check connector - Clean/repair as necessary.** Disconnect the appropriate CAB harness connector for the effected Wheel Speed Sensor. **Note: Check connector - Clean/repair as necessary.** Turn the ignition on. Measure the voltage of the appropriate Wheel Speed Sensor (+) Circuit. Is the voltage above 1 volt? Yes → Repair appropriate Wheel Speed Sensor (+) Circuit Shorted to Voltage. Perform ABS VERIFICATION TEST - VER 1. No → Go To 11
11	Turn the ignition off. Disconnect the appropriate Wheel Speed Sensor connector. **Note: Check connector - Clean/repair as necessary.** Disconnect the appropriate CAB harness connector for the effected Wheel Speed Sensor. **Note: Check connector - Clean/repair as necessary.** Turn the ignition on. Measure the voltage of the appropriate Wheel Speed Sensor (-) Circuit. Is the voltage above 1 volt? Yes → Repair the appropriate Wheel Speed Sensor (-) Circuit Short to Voltage. Perform ABS VERIFICATION TEST - VER 1. No → Go To 12

LTV0500000005669

Fig. 12 Wheel Sensor Fault (Part 5 of 6). 2002–04

POSSIBLE CAUSES
INTERMITTENT DTC
OPEN FUSED B(+) AND FUSED IGNITION SWITCH OUTPUT (RUN)
OPEN GROUND CIRCUITS
CAB - INTERNAL CONCERN

TEST	ACTION
1	**NOTE: Ensure the battery is fully charged.** Turn the ignition on. With the DRBIII®, erase DTC's. Turn the ignition off. Turn the ignition on. With the DRBIII®, read DTC's. Is the INTERNAL MAIN RELAY OPEN DTC present? Yes → Go To 2 No → Go To 4
2	**NOTE: CHECK FOR OPEN FUSES.** Turn the ignition off. Disconnect the CAB harness connector. Check connectors - Clean/repair as necessary. Turn the ignition on. Using a 12-volt test light connected to ground, back probe the Fused B(+) and Fused Ignition Switch Output (RUN) circuits. Does the test light illuminate brightly? Yes → Go To 3 No → Repair the appropriate circuit(s) for an open. Perform ABS VERIFICATION TEST - VER 1.

LTV0500000005671

**Fig. 13 Internal Main Relay Open/Shorted
 (Part 1 of 2). 2002–04**

TEST	ACTION
12	Turn the ignition off. Disconnect the appropriate CAB harness connector for the effected Wheel Speed Sensor. Disconnect the appropriate Wheel Speed Sensor harness connector. Measure the resistance through the appropriate Wheel Speed Sensor (+) and (-) circuits at the CAB harness connector. Is the resistance below 200 ohms? Yes → Repair the appropriate Wheel Speed Sensor Circuits Shorted together. Perform ABS VERIFICATION TEST - VER 1. No → Go To 13
13	Turn the ignition off. Inspect the appropriate Tone Wheel/Ring for damage. **NOTE: The Tone Wheel Teeth should be perfectly square, not bent or nicked.** Is the appropriate Tone Wheel/Ring ok? Yes → Go To 14 No → Replace the appropriate Tone Wheel(s)/Ring in accordance with the Service Information. Perform ABS VERIFICATION TEST - VER 1.
14	If there are no possible causes remaining, view repair. Repair Replace the appropriate Wheel Speed Sensor Perform ABS VERIFICATION TEST - VER 1.
15	Turn the ignition off. Visually inspect the related wiring harness. Look for any chafed, pierced, pinched, or partially broken wires. Visually inspect the related wire harness connectors. Look for broken, bent, pushed out, or corroded terminals. Refer to any Hotline letters or Technical Service Bulletins that may apply. Were any problems found? Yes → Repair as necessary. Perform ABS VERIFICATION TEST - VER 1. No → Test Complete.

LTV0500000005670

Fig. 12 Wheel Sensor Fault (Part 6 of 6). 2002–04

TEST	ACTION
3	Turn the ignition off. Disconnect the CAB harness connector. Check connectors - Clean/repair as necessary. Using a 12-volt test light connected to 12-volts, back probe the Ground circuits. Does the test light illuminate brightly? Yes → Replace and program the CAB Module Perform ABS VERIFICATION TEST - VER 1. No → Repair the Ground circuit(s) for an open. Perform ABS VERIFICATION TEST - VER 1.
4	Turn the ignition off. Visually inspect the related wiring harness. Look for any chafed, pierced, pinched, or partially broken wires. Visually inspect the related wire harness connectors. Look for broken, bent, pushed out, or corroded terminals. Refer to any Hotline letters or Technical Service Bulletins that may apply. Were any problems found? Yes → Repair as necessary. Perform ABS VERIFICATION TEST - VER 1. No → Test Complete.

LTV0500000005672

**Fig. 13 Internal Main Relay Open/Shorted
 (Part 2 of 2). 2002–04**

When Monitored and Set Condition:

LEFT FRONT DUMP SOLENOID OPEN

When Monitored: Ignition on.

Set Condition: When there is low logic feedback voltage from the solenoid when it is expected to be high (solenoid not energized).

LEFT FRONT DUMP SOLENOID SHORTED

When Monitored: Ignition on.

Set Condition: When there is high logic feedback voltage from the solenoid when it is supposed to be low (solenoid energized).

LEFT FRONT ISOLATION SOLENOID OPEN

When Monitored: Ignition on.

Set Condition: When there is low logic feedback voltage from the solenoid when it is expected to be high (solenoid not energized).

LEFT FRONT ISOLATION SOLENOID SHORTED

When Monitored: Ignition on.

Set Condition: When there is high logic feedback voltage from the solenoid when it is supposed to be low (solenoid energized).

LTV0500000005673

Fig. 14   Dump Solenoid Fault (Part 1 of 4). 2002–04

POSSIBLE CAUSES
INTERMITTENT DTC
OPEN FUSED B(+) AND FUSED IGNITION SWITCH OUTPUT (RUN)
OPEN GROUND CIRCUITS
CAB - INTERNAL CONCERN

TEST	ACTION
1	Turn the ignition on. With the DRBIII®, erase DTC's. Turn the ignition off. Turn the ignition on. With the DRBIII®, read DTC's. Is there a OPEN SOLENOID or SHORTED SOLENOID DTC present? Yes → Go To 2 No → Go To 4
2	NOTE: CHECK FOR OPEN FUSES. Turn the ignition off. Disconnect the CAB harness connector. Check connectors - Clean/repair as necessary. Turn the ignition on. Using a 12-volt test light connected to ground, back probe the Fused B(+) and Fused Ignition Switch Output (RUN) circuits. Does the test light illuminate brightly? Yes → Go To 3 No → Repair the appropriate circuit(s) for an open. Perform ABS VERIFICATION TEST - VER 1.
3	Turn the ignition off. Disconnect the CAB harness connector. Check connectors - Clean/repair as necessary. Using a 12-volt test light connected to 12-volts, back probe the Ground circuits. Does the test light illuminate brightly? Yes → Replace and program the CAB Module Perform ABS VERIFICATION TEST - VER 1. No → Repair the Ground circuit(s) for an open. Perform ABS VERIFICATION TEST - VER 1.

LTV0500000005675

Fig. 14   Dump Solenoid Fault (Part 3 of 4). 2002–04

TEST	ACTION
4	Turn the ignition off. Visually inspect the related wiring harness. Look for any chafed, pierced, pinched, or partially broken wires. Visually inspect the related wire harness connectors. Look for broken, bent, pushed out, or corroded terminals. Refer to any Hotline letters or Technical Service Bulletins that may apply. Were any problems found? Yes → Repair as necessary. Perform ABS VERIFICATION TEST - VER 1. No → Test Complete.

LTV0500000005676

Fig. 14   Dump Solenoid Fault (Part 4 of 4). 2002–04

REAR DUMP SOLENOID OPEN

When Monitored: Ignition on.

Set Condition: When there is low logic feedback voltage from the solenoid when it is expected to be high (solenoid not energized).

REAR DUMP SOLENOID SHORTED

When Monitored: Ignition on.

Set Condition: When there is high logic feedback voltage from the solenoid when it is supposed to be low (solenoid energized).

REAR ISOLATION SOLENOID OPEN

When Monitored: Ignition on.

Set Condition: When there is low logic feedback voltage from the solenoid when it is expected to be high (solenoid not energized).

REAR ISOLATION SOLENOID SHORTED

When Monitored: Ignition on.

Set Condition: When there is high logic feedback voltage from the solenoid when it is supposed to be low (solenoid energized).

RIGHT FRONT DUMP SOLENOID OPEN

When Monitored: Ignition on.

Set Condition: When there is low logic feedback voltage from the solenoid when it is expected to be high (solenoid not energized).

RIGHT FRONT DUMP SOLENOID SHORTED

When Monitored: Ignition on.

Set Condition: When there is high logic feedback voltage from the solenoid when it is supposed to be low (solenoid energized).

RIGHT FRONT ISOLATION SOLENOID OPEN

When Monitored: Ignition on.

Set Condition: When there is low logic feedback voltage from the solenoid when it is expected to be high (solenoid not energized).

RIGHT FRONT ISOLATION SOLENOID SHORTED

When Monitored: Ignition on.

Set Condition: When there is high logic feedback voltage from the solenoid when it is supposed to be low (solenoid energized).

LTV0500000005674

Fig. 14   Dump Solenoid Fault (Part 2 of 4). 2002–04

POSSIBLE CAUSES
WRONG VIN PROGRAMMED IN PCM/ WRONG PCM
INTERMITTENT DTC
INCORRECT CAB FOR VEHICLE

TEST	ACTION
1	Turn the ignition on. With the DRBIII®, erase DTC's. Turn the ignition off. Turn the ignition on. Wait ten seconds. Did the ABS Warning Indicator come on after ten seconds? Yes → Go To 2 No → Go To 3
2	Turn the ignition on. With the DRBIII®, read the VIN status. Compare programmed VIN with vehicle VIN. Is the correct VIN programmed in the correct PCM for the vehicle line? Yes → Replace the Controller Antilock Brake Perform ABS VERIFICATION TEST - VER 1. No → Program the correct VIN into the correct PCM for the vehicle line. Perform ABS VERIFICATION TEST - VER 1.
3	Turn the ignition off. Visually inspect the related wiring harness. Look for any chafed, pierced, pinched, or partially broken wires. Visually inspect the related wire harness connectors. Look for broken, bent, pushed out, or corroded terminals. Refer to any Hotline letters or Technical Service Bulletins that may apply. Were any problems found? Yes → Repair as necessary. Perform ABS VERIFICATION TEST - VER 1. No → Test Complete.

LTV0500000005677

Fig. 15   Mismatched Vin. 2002–04

POSSIBLE CAUSES
CAB - SETTING FALSE CODE
TONE RING/AXLE SIZE MISMATCH

TEST	ACTION
1	Turn the ignition on. With the DRBIII®, read the axle size programmed into the CAB. Inspect and identify the vehicle axle size. Compare the axle size programmed into the CAB, and the actual axle size installed into the vehicle. Does the programmed axle size match the installed axle? Yes → Replace the Controller Antilock Brake Perform ABS VERIFICATION TEST - VER 1. No → Using the DRBIII®, reprogram the CAB for the correct axle. Perform ABS VERIFICATION TEST - VER 1.

LTV0500000005678

Fig. 16 Number Of Tone Ring Teeth Out Of Range. 2002–04

TEST	ACTION
1	Turn the ignition on. With the DRBIII®, read DTC's. With the DRBIII®, erase DTC's. Turn the ignition off. Turn the ignition off. With the DRBIII®, actuate the ABS pump motor. Did the Pump Motor operate when actuated? No → Go To 2 Yes → Go To 13
2	Turn the ignition off. Remove and inspect the ABS Pump fuse. Is the Fuse blown? Yes → Go To 3 No → Go To 7
3	Turn the ignition off. Make sure the Pump Motor connector is secure. Visually inspect the Fused B(+) Circuit in the wiring harness from the ABS PUMP fuse to the CAB. Look for any sign of an Intermittent Short to Ground. Is the wiring harness OK? Yes → Go To 4 No → Repair the Fused B(+) Circuit shorted to ground. Perform ABS VERIFICATION TEST - VER 1.
4	Turn the ignition off. Remove the ABS PUMP Fuse. Disconnect the CAB connector. Make sure the Pump Motor connector is secure. **Note: Check connector - Clean/repair as necessary.** Using a test light connected to 12 volts, probe the Fused B (+) Circuit. Is the test light on? Yes → Repair the Fused B(+) circuit short to ground. Perform ABS VERIFICATION TEST - VER 1. No → Go To 5
5	Turn the ignition off. Make sure the Pump Motor connector is secure. Remove the ABS PUMP Fuse. The CAB must be connected for the results of this test to be valid. Using a test light connected to 12 volts, probe the Fused B (+) circuit at the ABS FUSE terminal. Is the test light on? Yes → Replace the Controller Antilock Brake Perform ABS VERIFICATION TEST - VER 1. No → Go To 6

LTV0500000005680

Fig. 17 Pump Motor Fault (Part 2 of 4). 2002–04

When Monitored and Set Condition:

PUMP MOTOR CIRCUIT OPEN

When Monitored: Ignition on.

Set Condition: Igntion on for at least 3.5 seconds. ABS pump motor command never given during the current ABS command. Low feedback voltage from the low side of the motor. All criteria must be seen for 150 ms.

PUMP MOTOR STALLED

When Monitored: Ignition on.

Set Condition: When vehicle speed is above 15 mph without ABS active. Vehicle speed above 4 mph with a fault from the previous igntion cycle. ABS pump motor command given and then turned off. High feedback voltage from the low side of the motor continuously for 5 ms.

POSSIBLE CAUSES
ABS PUMP MOTOR INTERMITTENT DTC
FUSED B(+) CIRCUIT INTERMITTENTLY SHORTED TO GROUND
FUSED B(+) CIRCUIT SHORTED TO GROUND
CAB - FUSED B(+) CIRCUIT SHORTED TO GROUND
FUSE BLOWN - PUMP MOTOR CIRCUIT
NO B+ SUPPLY TO FUSE
ABS PUMP MOTOR INOPERATIVE
FUSED B(+) CIRCUIT OPEN
GROUND CIRCUIT OPEN
GROUND CIRCUIT HIGH RESISTANCE
CAB - INTERNAL FAULT

LTV0500000005679

Fig. 17 Pump Motor Fault (Part 1 of 4). 2002–04

TEST	ACTION
6	Turn the ignition off. Make sure the Pump Motor connector is secure If there are no potential causes remaining, replace the Fuse. If there are no possible causes remaining, view repair. Repair Replace the ABS Pump Motor Fuse. Perform ABS VERIFICATION TEST - VER 1.
7	Turn the ignition off. Remove the ABS PUMP Fuse. Disconnect the CAB connector. **Note: Check connector - Clean/repair as necessary.** Measure the resistance of the Fused B (+) circuit between the ABS PUMP Fuse Terminal and the CAB connector. Is the resistance below 10 ohms? Yes → Go To 8 No → Repair the Fused B(+) circuit for an open. Perform ABS VERIFICATION TEST - VER 1.
8	Turn the ignition on. Using a 12-volt test light connected to ground, check the B+ supply to ABS PUMP Fuse. Is the B+ supply OK? Yes → Go To 9 No → Repair the B+ supply for an open. Perform ABS VERIFICATION TEST - VER 1.
9	Turn the ignition off. Disconnect Pump Motor Connector. Connect a 10 gauge jumper wire between pump motor Fused B (+) circuit and a 40 Amp Fused B (+) circuit. Connect a 10 gauge jumper wire between pump motor ground circuit and a known good body ground. Monitor Pump Motor operation. Is the pump motor running? Yes → Go To 10 No → Replace the ABS Pump Motor/Hydraulic Control Unit assembly. Perform ABS VERIFICATION TEST - VER 1.
10	Turn the ignition off. Disconnect CAB Connector. **Note: Check connector - Clean/repair as necessary.** Measure the resistance of the CAB ground circuits. Is the resistance below 1.0 ohm? Yes → Go To 11 No → Repair the ground circuit for an open. Perform ABS VERIFICATION TEST - VER 1.

LTV0500000005681

Fig. 17 Pump Motor Fault (Part 3 of 4). 2002–04

TEST	ACTION
11	Make sure the Pump Motor connector is secure. Turn the ignition on. With the DRBIII®, enable pump motor actuation. **NOTE: Pump motor will not operate, but voltage will be applied.** Measure the voltage drop across the ABS ground circuit connection, with pump motor actuation enabled. Is the voltage below 0.1 volt? Yes → Go To 12 No → Repair the Ground circuit for an open. Perform ABS VERIFICATION TEST - VER 1.
12	If there are no possible causes remaining, view repair. Repair Replace the Controller Anti-Lock Brake Perform ABS VERIFICATION TEST - VER 1.
13	Turn the ignition off. Visually inspect the related wiring harness. Look for any chafed, pierced, pinched, or partially broken wires. Make sure the Pump Motor connecter is secure. Visually inspect the related wire harness connectors. Look for broken, bent, pushed out, or corroded terminals. Refer to any Hotline letters or Technical Service Bulletins that may apply. Were any problems found? Yes → Repair as necessary. Perform ABS VERIFICATION TEST - VER 1. No → Test Complete.

LTV0500000005682

Fig. 17   Pump Motor Fault (Part 4 of 4). 2002–04

POSSIBLE CAUSES
REAR RESET SWITCH CLOSED DTC CONDITION PRESENT

TEST	ACTION
1	Turn the ignition on. With the DRBIII®, erase DTC's. Turn the ignition off. Turn the ignition on. With the DRBIII®, read DTC's. Is the REAR RESET SWITCH CLOSED DTC present? Yes → Replace the Hydraulic Control Unit Perform ABS VERIFICATION TEST - VER 1. No → Test Complete.

LTV0500000005684

Fig. 19   Rear Reset Switch Closed. 2002–04

POSSIBLE CAUSES
WHEEL SPEED SENSOR CONCERN
CAB - NO RESPONSE TO INPUT
BRAKE LAMP SWITCH
BRAKE SWITCH SENSE CIRCUIT
CAB - INTERNAL FAULT

TEST	ACTION
1	Turn the ignition on. With the DRBIII®, erase DTCs. Turn the ignition off. Turn the ignition on. With the DRBIII®, read DTCs. Does the DRBIII® display any Wheel Speed Sensor circuit failure DTC's right now? Yes → Repair as necessary. Perform ABS VERIFICATION TEST - VER 1. No → Go To 2
2	**NOTE: IF THE DRIVER "RIDES" THE BRAKES A "SYSTEM CONTROL MODE TIMEOUT" DTC MAYBE SET.** **NOTE: DTC must be "active"** With the DRBIII® in Inputs/Outputs, read the Brake Switch state. Apply and release the brake pedal. Does the DRBIII® follow the pedal position? Yes → Using the wiring diagram/schematic as a guide, inspect the wiring and connectors for damage. Inform driver that DTC was set by riding the brakes OR when they had a very long braking maneuver down a grade. Perform ABS VERIFICATION TEST - VER 1. No → Go To 3

LTV0500000005686

Fig. 21   System Control Mode Timeout (Part 1 of 2). 2002–04

POSSIBLE CAUSES
RAM READ/WRITE DTC CONDITION PRESENT
INTERMITTENT DTC

TEST	ACTION
1	Turn the ignition on. With the DRBIII®, erase DTC's. Turn the ignition off. Turn the ignition on. With the DRBIII®, read DTC's. Is the RAM READ/WRITE DTC present? Yes → Replace the Controller Antilock Brake Perform ABS VERIFICATION TEST - VER 1. No → Go To 2
2	Turn the ignition off. Visually inspect the related wiring harness. Look for any chafed, pierced, pinched, or partially broken wires. Visually inspect the related wire harness connectors. Look for broken, bent, pushed out, or corroded terminals. Refer to any Hotline letters or Technical Service Bulletins that may apply. Were any problems found? Yes → Repair as necessary. Perform ABS VERIFICATION TEST - VER 1. No → Test Complete.

LTV0500000005683

Fig. 18   RAM Read/Write. 2002–04

POSSIBLE CAUSES
ROM CHECKSUM DTC CONDITION PRESENT
INTERMITTENT DTC

TEST	ACTION
1	Turn the ignition on. With the DRBIII®, erase DTC's. Turn the ignition off. Turn the ignition on. With the DRBIII®, read DTC's. Is the ROM CHECKSUM DTC set? Yes → Replace the Controller Antilock Brake Perform ABS VERIFICATION TEST - VER 1. No → Go To 2
2	Turn the ignition off. Visually inspect the related wiring harness. Look for any chafed, pierced, pinched, or partially broken wires. Visually inspect the related wire harness connectors. Look for broken, bent, pushed out, or corroded terminals. Refer to any Hotline letters or Technical Service Bulletins that may apply. Were any problems found? Yes → Repair as necessary. Perform ABS VERIFICATION TEST - VER 1. No → Test Complete.

LTV0500000005685

Fig. 20   ROM Checksum. 2002–04

TEST	ACTION
3	Turn the ignition off. Apply and release the brake pedal. Observe the brake lamps. Do the brake lamps operate OK? Yes → Go To 4 No → Repair as necessary. Perform ABS VERIFICATION TEST - VER 1.
4	**NOTE: DTC must be "active"** Turn the ignition off. Disconnect the CAB connector. **Note: Check connector - Clean/repair as necessary.** Turn the ignition on. Apply and release the brake pedal. Check Brake Switch Sense for ground with pedal released and open with pedal applied. Does the Brake Switch Sense circuit change state as specified? Yes → Replace the Controller Antilock Brake Perform ABS VERIFICATION TEST - VER 1. No → Repair the Brake Switch Sense circuit for a short to battery, ground or for an open. Perform ABS VERIFICATION TEST - VER 1.

LTV0500000005687

Fig. 21   System Control Mode Timeout (Part 2 of 2). 2002–04

POSSIBLE CAUSES
CAB VOLTAGE CHECK
INTERMITTENT DTC

TEST	ACTION
1	**NOTE: Ensure the battery is fully charged.** Turn the ignition on. With the DRBIII®, record and erase DTC's. Turn the ignition off. Start the engine. Measure the voltage of the Fused B+ and Fused Ignition Switch Output (RUN) circuits in the CAB connector. Is the voltage between 10 volts and 16.5 volts? Yes → Replace the Contoller Antilock Brake Perform ABS VERIFICATION TEST - VER 1. No → Go To 2
2	Turn the ignition off. Using the wiring diagram/schematic as a guide, inspect the wiring and connectors. Check connectors - Clean/repair as necessary. Inspect the vehicle for aftermarket accessories that may exceed the Generator System output. Refer to any Hotline letters or Technical Service Bulletins that may apply. Were any problems found? Yes → Repair as necessary. Perform ABS VERIFICATION TEST - VER 1. No → Test Complete.

LTV0500000005688

Fig. 22 System Over/Under Voltage. 2002–04

POSSIBLE CAUSES
CONTROLLER ANTILOCK BRAKE DTC'S PRESENT
INTERMITTENT VEHICLE SPEED SIGNAL
VEHICLE SPEED SIGNAL CIRCUIT SHORTED OR OPEN
CAB- NO SPEED SIGNAL OUTPUT
PCM- CAN'T READ VEHICLE SPEED SIGNAL

TEST	ACTION
1	Turn the ignition on. With the DRB III read DTC's. Is the Good Trip Counter for P-0500 displayed and Equal to 0? Yes → Go To 2 No → Go To 6
2	Turn the ignition on. With the DRBIII®, read DTCs. Check for Controller Antilock Brake DTC's. Are any CAB DTC's present? Yes → Repair all Controller Antilock Brake DTC's before proceeding. Perform ABS VERIFICATION TEST - VER 1. No → Go To 3
3	Turn the ignition off. Disconnect the Powertrain Control Module harness connectors. Disconnect the CAB connector. Ignition on, engine not running. Check the Vehicle Speed Signal circuit for a short to B+, short to ground and for an open. Is the Vehicle Speed Signal circuit OK? Yes → Go To 4 No → Repair the open Vehicle Speed Signal circuit for a short or an open. Perform ABS VERIFICATION TEST - VER 1.

LTV0500000005695

Fig. 24 Vehicle Speed Signal Output (Part 1 of 2). 2002–04

POSSIBLE CAUSES
INCORRECT TIRES PROGRAMMED INTO CAB
INTERMITTENT DTC
CAB INTERNAL FAULT

TEST	ACTION
1	Turn the ignition on. Observe the ABS Warning Indicator. Is the ABS Warning Indicator Flashing? Yes → Go To 2 No → Go To 3
2	Inspect all four of the tire sizes on the vehicle. **NOTE: Non-production size tire cannot be programmed into the CAB. The production Powertrain, with the production size tires is the only emissions certified configuration that is available for reprogramming.** Turn the ignition on. With the DRBIII®, read the tire size that is programmed into the CAB. Does the DRBIII® displayed tire size match the actual tire size on the vehicle? Yes → Replace the Controller Antilock Brake Perform ABS VERIFICATION TEST - VER 1. No → Reprogram the tire size. Make sure that the ignition is on throughout the entire reprogramming procedure. Perform ABS VERIFICATION TEST - VER 1.
3	Turn the ignition off. Visually inspect the related wiring harness. Look for any chafed, pierced, pinched, or partially broken wires. Visually inspect the related wire harness connectors. Look for broken, bent, pushed out, or corroded terminals. Refer to any Hotline letters or Technical Service Bulletins that may apply. Were any problems found? Yes → Repair as necessary. Perform ABS VERIFICATION TEST - VER 1. No → Test Complete.

LTV0500000005689

Fig. 23 Tire Revolutions Per Mile Out Of Range. 2002–04

TEST	ACTION
4	Turn ignition off. Disconnect the CAB connector. Connect a jumper wire to the Vehicle Speed Signal circuit in the CAB harness connector. Turn ignition on. Quickly and repeatedly tap the jumper wire to ground. With the DRBIII® read the Vehicle Speed Signal display. Is the DRBIII® reading Vehicle Speed above 0 MPH? Yes → Replace the Controller Antilock Brake Perform ABS VERIFICATION TEST - VER 1. No → Go To 5
5	If there are no possible causes remaining, view repair. Repair Replace the Powertrain Control Module in accordance with the Service Information. Perform POWERTRAIN VERIFICATION TEST VER - 5.
6	At this time, the conditions required to set the DTC are not present. **NOTE: Use the Freeze Frame Data to help duplicate the conditions that set the DTC. Pay particular attention to the DTC set conditions, such as, VSS, MAP, ECT, and Load.** **Note: Visually inspect the related wiring harness. Look for any chafed, pierced, pinched, or partially broken wires.** **Note: Visually inspect the related wire harness connectors. Look for broken, bent, pushed out, or corroded terminals.** **Note: Refer to any technical service bulletins that may apply.** Were any problems found? Yes → Repair as necessary. Perform ABS VERIFICATION TEST - VER 1. No → Test Complete.

LTV0500000005696

Fig. 24 Vehicle Speed Signal Output (Part 2 of 2). 2002–04

ABS VERIFICATION TEST - VER 1

1. Turn the ignition off.
2. Connect all previously disconnected components and connectors.
3. Ensure all accessories are turned off and the battery is fully charged.
4. Ensure that the Ignition is on, and with the DRBIII®, erase all Diagnostic Trouble Codes from ALL modules. Start the engine and allow it to run for 2 minutes and fully operate the system that was malfunctioning.
5. Turn the ignition off and wait 5 seconds. Turn the ignition on and using the DRBIII, read DTC's from ALL modules.
6. If any Diagnostic Trouble Codes are present, return to Symptom list and troubleshoot new or recurring symptom.
7. If there are no DTC's present after turning ignition on, road test the vehicle for at least 5 minutes. Perform several antilock braking stops.
8. **Caution: Ensure braking capability is available before road testing.**
9. Again, with the DRBIII® read DTC's. If any DTC's are present, return to Symptom list.
10. If there are no Diagnostic Trouble Codes (DTC's) present, and the customer's concern can no longer be duplicated, the repair is complete.
Are any DTC's present or is the original concern still present?

    Yes → Repair is not complete, refer to appropriate symptom.

    No → Repair is complete.

LTV0500000005697

Fig. 25 Verification Tests (Part 1 of 2). 2002–04

POSSIBLE CAUSES

INTERMITTENT DTC

OPEN FUSED B(+) AND FUSED IGNITION SWITCH OUTPUT (RUN)

OPEN GROUND CIRCUITS

CAB - INTERNAL CONCERN

TEST	ACTION
1	Turn the ignition on. With the DRBIII®, erase DTC's. Turn the ignition off. Turn the ignition on. With the DRBIII®, read DTC's. Is the WATCHDOG DTC present? Yes → Go To 2 No → Go To 4
2	NOTE: CHECK FOR OPEN FUSES. Turn the ignition off. Disconnect the CAB harness connector. Check connectors - Clean/repair as necessary. Turn the ignition on. Using a 12-volt test light connected to ground, back probe the Fused B(+) and Fused Ignition Switch Output (RUN) circuits. Does the test light illuminate brightly? Yes → Go To 3 No → Repair the appropriate circuit(s) for an open. Perform ABS VERIFICATION TEST - VER 1.

LTV0500000005690

Fig. 26 Watchdog (Part 1 of 2). 2002–04

POSSIBLE CAUSES

WHEEL SPEED MISMATCH DTC CONDITION PRESENT

INCORRECT TONE WHEEL

CAB INTERNAL FAULT

TEST	ACTION
1	Turn the ignition off. Inspect all four tire sizes and measure tire circumferences on vehicle. Are any of the tires/wheels/tire circumferences significantly different in size? Yes → Correct as necessary. All of the tires and wheels must be of uniform size and circumference.. Perform ABS VERIFICATION TEST - VER 1. No → Go To 2
2	Turn the ignition off. Count number of teeth on the suspect Tone Wheel. Does the suspect Tone Wheel match the non-suspect Tone Wheels? Yes → Replace the Controller Antilock Brake Perform ABS VERIFICATION TEST - VER 1. No → Replace the Tone Wheel Perform ABS VERIFICATION TEST - VER 1.

LTV0500000005692

Fig. 27 Wheel Speed Mismatch. 2002–04

POWERTRAIN VERIFICATION TEST VER - 5

1. Inspect the vehicle to ensure that all engine components are properly installed and connected. Reassemble and reconnect components as necessary.
2. If any existing diagnostic trouble codes have not been repaired, go to Symptom List and follow path specified.
3. Connect the DRBIII® to the data link connector.
4. Ensure the fuel tank has at least a quarter tank of fuel. Turn off all accessories.
5. Perform steps 6 through 8 if the PCM has been replaced. Then proceed with the verification. If the PCM has not been replaced skip those steps and continue verification.
6. If PCM has been changed and correct VIN and mileage have not been programmed, a DTC will be set in ABS and Air bag modules. In addition, if vehicle is equipped with a Sentry Key Immobilizer Module (SKIM), Secret Key data must be updated to enable start.
7. For ABS and Air Bag systems: Enter correct VIN and Mileage in PCM. Erase codes in ABS and Air Bag modules.
8. For SKIM theft alarm: Connect DRBIII® to data link conn. Go to Theft Alarm, SKIM, Misc. and place SKIM in secured access mode, by using the appropriate PIN code for this vehicle. Select Update Secret Key data. Data will be transferred from SKIM to PCM.
9. If a Comprehensive Component DTC was repaired, perform steps 10-13. If a Major OBDII Monitor DTC was repaired skip those steps and continue verification.
10. After the ignition has been off for at least 10 seconds, restart the vehicle and run 2 minutes.
11. If the Good Trip counter changed to one or more and there are no new DTC's, the repair was successful and is now complete. Erase DTC's and disconnect the DRBIII®.
12. If the repaired DTC has reset, the repair is not complete. Check for any related TSB's or flash updates and return to the Symptom list.
13. If another DTC has set, return to the Symptom List and follow the path specified for that DTC.
14. With the DRBIII®, monitor the appropriate pre-test enabling conditions until all conditions have been met. Once the conditions have been met, switch screen to the appropriate OBDII monitor, (Audible beeps when the monitor is running).
15. If the monitor ran, and the Good Trip counter changed to one or more, the repair was successful and is now complete. Erase DTC's and disconnect the DRBIII®.
16. If the repaired OBDII trouble code has reset or was seen in the monitor while on the road test, the repair is not complete. Check for any related technical service bulletins or flash updates and return to Symptom List.
17. If another DTC has set, return to the Symptom List and follow the path specified for that DTC.
Press Continue when preceding steps have been performed.

    Continue
    Repair is not complete, refer to appropriate symptom.

LTV0500000005698

Fig. 25 Verification Tests (Part 2 of 2). 2002–04

TEST	ACTION
3	Turn the ignition off. Disconnect the CAB harness connector. Check connectors - Clean/repair as necessary. Using a 12-volt test light connected to 12-volts, back probe the Ground circuits. Does the test light illuminate brightly? Yes → Replace and program the CAB Module Perform ABS VERIFICATION TEST - VER 1. No → Repair the Ground circuit(s) for an open. Perform ABS VERIFICATION TEST - VER 1.
4	Turn the ignition off. Visually inspect the related wiring harness. Look for any chafed, pierced, pinched, or partially broken wires. Visually inspect the related wire harness connectors. Look for broken, bent, pushed out, or corroded terminals. Refer to any Hotline letters or Technical Service Bulletins that may apply. Were any problems found? Yes → Repair as necessary. Perform ABS VERIFICATION TEST - VER 1. No → Test Complete.

LTV0500000005691

Fig. 26 Watchdog (Part 2 of 2). 2002–04

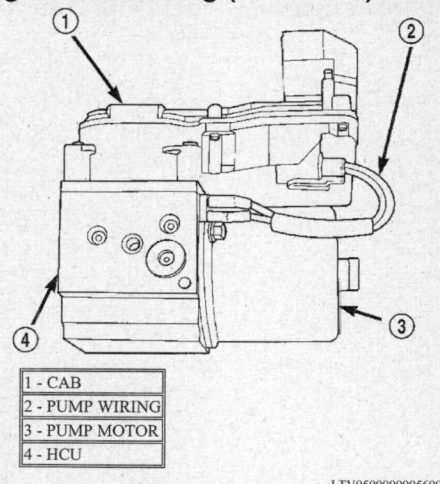

| 1 - CAB |
| 2 - PUMP WIRING |
| 3 - PUMP MOTOR |
| 4 - HCU |

LTV0500000005699

Fig. 28 CAB module replace.

Durango

NOTE: On Air Bag Equipped Models, Refer To "Air Bag System Precautions" Located In The Front Of This Manual For System Disarming & Arming Procedures.

NOTE: Refer To "Computer Relearn Procedures" Located In The Front Of This Manual When Battery Power To The Computer Has Been Interrupted.

NOTE: "Electrical Symbol & Wire Color Code Identification" Located In The Front Of This Manual May Be Used As An Aid When Using Wiring Circuits Found In This Section.

NOTE: For 2002-03 Models Refer To 2002-04 In The "Dakota" Section For Test Procedures.

INDEX

	Page No.		Page No.		Page No.
Description	5-57	Intermittents & Poor		Brake System Bleed	5-58
Diagnosis & Testing	5-57	Connections	5-58	Component Replacement	5-58
Accessing Diagnostic Trouble		Symptom Tests	5-58	Anti-Lock Brake Module,	
Codes	5-57	Wiring Diagrams	5-57	Replace	5-58
Clearing Diagnostic Trouble		**Diagnostic Chart Index**	5-61	Front Wheel Speed Sensor,	
Codes	5-58	**Precautions**	5-57	Replace	5-58
Connector Pin Identification	5-57	Air Bag Systems	5-57	Hydraulic Control Unit (HCU),	
Diagnostic Tests	5-58	Battery Ground Cable	5-57	Replace	5-58
Diagnostic Trouble Code		General Service Precautions	5-57	Rear Wheel Speed Sensor,	
Interpretation	5-57	**System Service**	5-58	Replace	5-58

PRECAUTIONS

Air Bag Systems

Refer to "Air Bag System Precautions" in the front of this manual for system disarming and arming procedures.

Battery Ground Cable

Prior to service disconnect battery ground cable and isolate as required.

General Service Precautions

Certain components of the anti-lock brake system are not intended to be serviced individually. Attempting to remove or disconnect components of this type may result in personal injury and/or improper system operation. Only the components with removal and installation procedures should be serviced.

Observe the following general precautions when servicing the anti-lock brake system:

1. If any welding work is to be performed using an arc welder, Controller Anti-Lock Brake (CAB) should be disconnected.
2. When ignition switch is in On position, CAB electrical connector should not be disconnected or connected.
3. Some components of ABS system are not serviced separately and must be serviced as complete assemblies. Do not disassemble any component which is designated as non-serviceable.

DESCRIPTION

When wheel slip is detected during a brake application, the ABS enters anti-lock mode. During anti-lock braking, hydraulic pressure in the individual wheel circuits is controlled to prevent any wheel from slipping. A separate hydraulic line and specific solenoid valves are provided for each wheel. The ABS can decrease, hold, or increase hydraulic pressure to each wheel brake. The ABS cannot, however, increase hydraulic pressure above the amount which is transmitted by the master cylinder during braking.

During anti-lock braking, a series of rapid pulsations is felt in the brake pedal. These pulsations are caused by the rapid changes in position of the individual solenoid valves as the EBCM responds to wheel speed sensor inputs and attempts to prevent wheel slip. These pedal pulsations are present only during anti-lock braking and stop when normal braking is resumed or when the vehicle comes to a stop. A ticking or popping noise may also be heard as the solenoid valves cycle rapidly. During anti-lock braking on dry pavement, intermittent chirping noises may be heard as the tires approach slipping. These noises and pedal pulsations are considered normal during anti-lock operation.

Vehicles equipped with ABS may be stopped by applying normal force to the brake pedal. Brake pedal operation during normal braking is no different than that of previous non-ABS systems. Maintaining a constant force on the brake pedal provides the shortest stopping distance while maintaining vehicle stability.

DIAGNOSIS & TESTING

Accessing Diagnostic Trouble Codes

Connect a suitably programmed scan tool to Data Link Connector (DLC) and follow manufacturer's instructions.

Diagnostic Trouble Code Interpretation

Refer to "Diagnostic Chart Index" for diagnostic trouble code interpretation.

Connector Pin Identification

Refer to **Fig. 1** for pin connector and terminal identification.

Wiring Diagrams

Refer to **Figs. 2 through 4** for wiring diagrams.

Diagnostic Tests

2002-03

Refer to the "Dakota" sector for diagnostic tests.

2004-06

Refer to **Figs. 5 through 25** for diagnostic tests.

Symptom Tests

Refer to "Dakota" "Symptom Tests" for test procedures.

Clearing Diagnostic Trouble Codes

Connect a suitably programmed scan tool to Data Link Connector (DLC) and follow manufacturer's instructions.

Intermittents & Poor Connections

Most Intermittents are caused by faulty electrical connections or wiring, although a sticking relay or solenoid can also cause an intermittent condition. Inspect wiring and connectors for the following:

1. Poor mating of connector halves, or terminals not fully seated in connector body.
2. Dirt or corrosion on terminals.
3. Damaged connector body.
4. Improperly formed or damaged terminals.
5. Poor terminal to wire connection.
6. Rubbed through wiring insulation.
7. Wiring broken inside insulation.

SYSTEM SERVICE

Brake System Bleed

The base brake system must be bled anytime air is permitted to enter the hydraulic system. However, anti-lock brake system components should only be bled if the hydraulic control unit has been removed or if there is reason to believe that air has entered the unit. **The ABS portion of the braking system must be bled separately.** Under most circumstances, only the base brake system will require bleeding, refer to the "Hydraulic Brake Systems" chapter for procedure. If the anti-lock brake system must be bled, proceed as follows:

1. Ensure all brake system components are installed and all hydraulic lines are connected securely.
2. Connect DRB diagnostic scan tool to diagnostic connector, then ensure CAB has no stored diagnostic trouble codes.
3. Bleed base brake system as outlined in "Hydraulic Brake Systems" chapter, then select "Anti-Lock Brakes" followed by "Miscellaneous" then "Bleed Brakes" routine on diagnostic scan tool.
4. Bleed base brake system once again, then repeat ABS bleed cycle and base brake system bleed until brake fluid flow (as established in "Hydraulic Brake Systems" bleed procedure) is free of bubbles. **Ensure all bleeder valves are closed tightly after bleed sequence is completed.**
5. Road test vehicle to ensure base hydraulic system and anti-lock brake system operate properly.

Component Replacement

ANTI-LOCK BRAKE MODULE, REPLACE

1. Raise and support vehicle.
2. Remove left front tire and wheel assembly.
3. Disconnect ABM module electrical connector.
4. Remove ABM module mounting bolt, then module.
5. Reverse procedure to install.

HYDRAULIC CONTROL UNIT (HCU), REPLACE

1. Install brake pedal prop rod.
2. Siphon master cylinder.
3. Disconnect master cylinder to HCU brake lines.
4. Disconnect chassis lines to HCU.
5. Disconnect wire harness electrical connector.
6. Remove HCU assembly mounting nuts.
7. Raise and support vehicle.
8. Remove left front tire.
9. Lift HCU assembly off mounting bracket and remove from vehicle.
10. Reverse procedure to install.

FRONT WHEEL SPEED SENSOR, REPLACE

1. Raise and support vehicle.
2. Remove wheel and tire assembly.
3. Remove brake rotor.
4. Remove speed sensor mounting bolt, then speed sensor.
5. Reverse procedure to install.

REAR WHEEL SPEED SENSOR, REPLACE

1. Raise and support vehicle.
2. Disconnect speed sensor electrical connector.
3. Remove speed sensor mounting bolt, then sensor.
4. Reverse procedure to install.

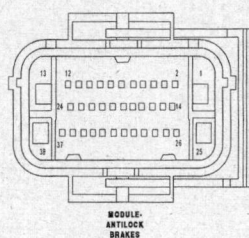

MODULE-ANTILOCK BRAKES

MODULE-ANTILOCK BRAKES - 3E WAY		
CAV	CIRCUIT	FUNCTION
1	A107 12TN/RD	FUSED B(+) (PUMP)
2		
3	B132 20DG/LB (ESP)	ACTIVE BRAKE BOOSTER (-)
4		
5		
6	B6 20DG/WT	RIGHT FRONT WHEEL SPEED SENSOR (-)
7		
8		
9	B31 20DG (ESP)	VACUUM PRESSURE SENSOR SUPPLY
10	B32 20DG/BK (ESP)	VACUUM PRESSURE SENSOR SIGNAL
11		
12		
13	Z107 12BK/DG	GROUND
14	D64 20WT/LB	CAN C BUS (-)
15		
16	B131 20DG/YL (ESP)	ACTIVE BRAKE BOOSTER (+)
17		
18	B7 20DG/VT	RIGHT FRONT WHEEL SPEED SENSOR (+)
19	B2 20DG/LB	RIGHT REAR WHEEL SPEED SENSOR (+)
20	B3 20DG/YL	LEFT REAR WHEEL SPEED SENSOR (-)
21	B9 20DG/LG	LEFT FRONT WHEEL SPEED SENSOR (+)
22		
23		
24	D264 20WT (ESP)	DYNAMICS SENSOR-LOW DATA LINK
25	A111 18DG/RD	FUSED B(+) (VALVE)
26	D65 20YL/RD	CAN C BUS (+
27		
28	B33 20DG/BR (ESP)	VACUUM PRESSURE SENSOR RETURN
29		
30	B29 20DG/WT	BRAKE SWITCH NO. 1 SIGNAL
31	B1 20DG/DB	RIGHT REAR WHEEL SPEED SENSOR (-)
32	F500 20DG/PK	FUSED IGNITION SWITCH OUTPUT (RUN)
33	B4 20LG/GY	LEFT REAR WHEEL SPEED SENSOR (+)
34	B8 20DG/TN	LEFT FRONT WHEEL SPEED SENSOR (-)
35		
36	B45 20DG/LB (ESP)	STOP LAMP INHIBIT RELAY CONTROL
37	D265 20WT/BK (ESP)	DYNAMICS SENSOR HIGH DATA LINK
38	Z923 12BK	GROUND

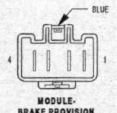

BLUE

MODULE-BRAKE PROVISION

MODULE-BRAKE PROVISION - BLUE 4 WAY		
CAV	CIRCUIT	FUNCTION
1	A400 12TN/RD	FUSED B(+)
2	B400 14DG	TRAILER TOW ELECTRIC BRAKE OUTPUT
3	L50 20WT/TN	BRAKE LAMP SWITCH OUTPUT
4	Z910 12BK	GROUND

LTV0500000005602

Fig. 1 Controller Anti-Lock Brake (CAB) connector & terminal identification.

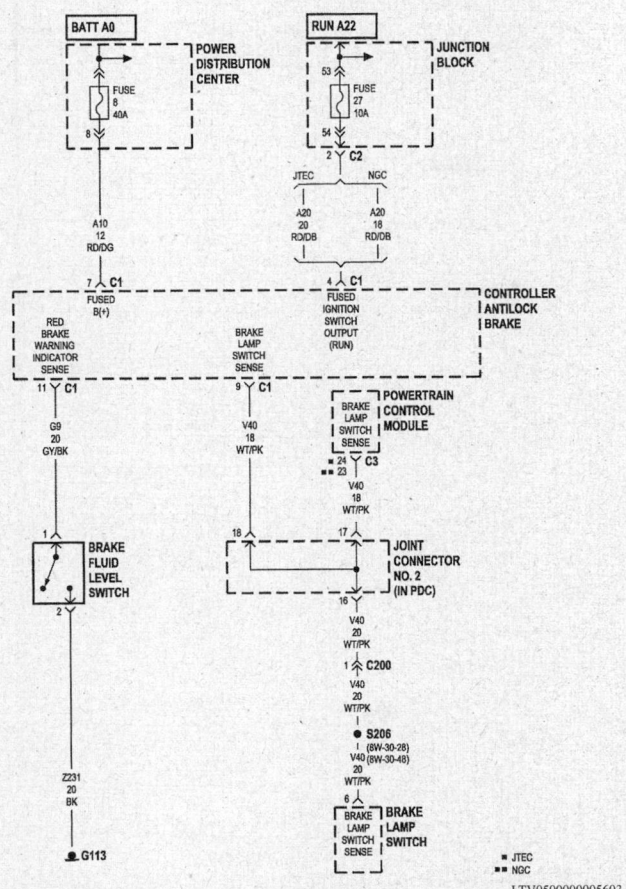

Fig. 2   Wiring diagram (Part 1 of 2). 2002–03 w/RWAL

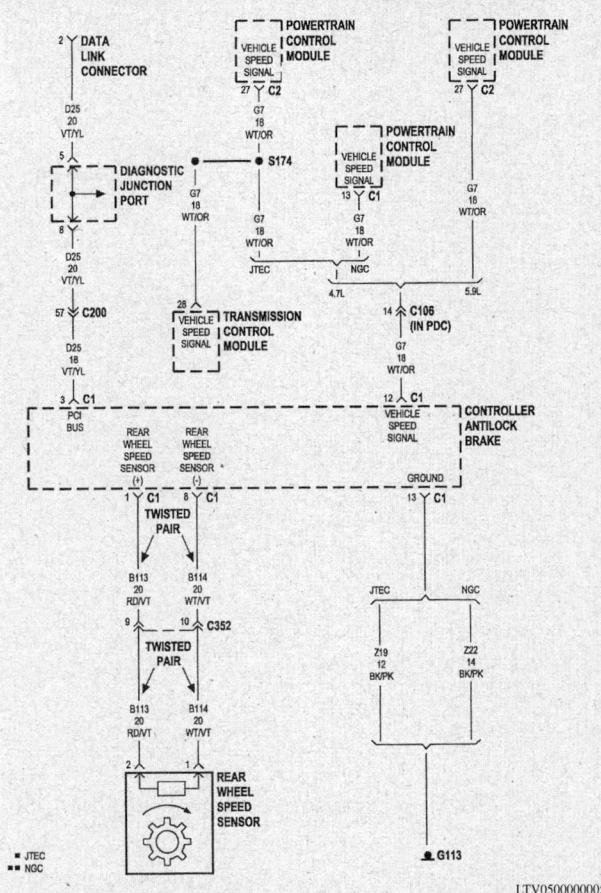

Fig. 2   Wiring diagram (Part 2 of 2). 2002–03 w/RWAL

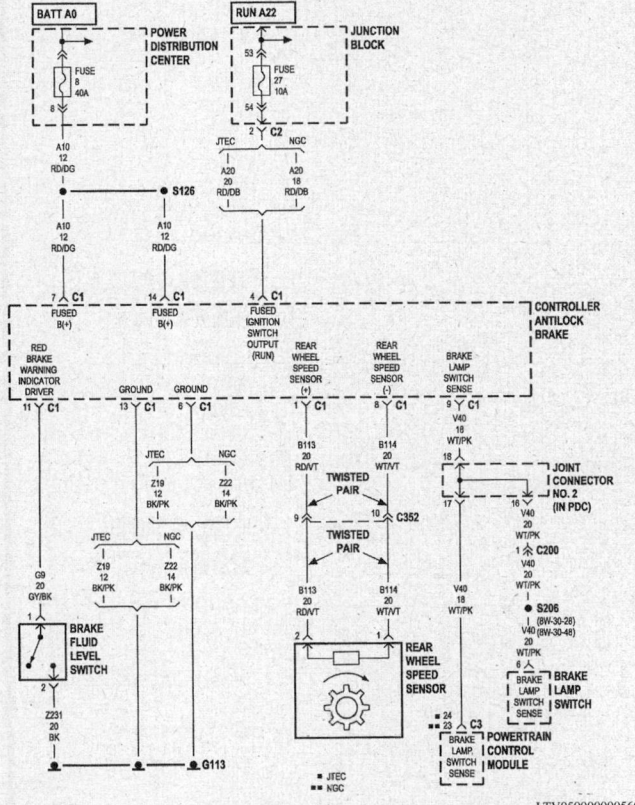

Fig. 3   Wiring diagram (Part 1 of 2). 2002–03 w/4 WABS

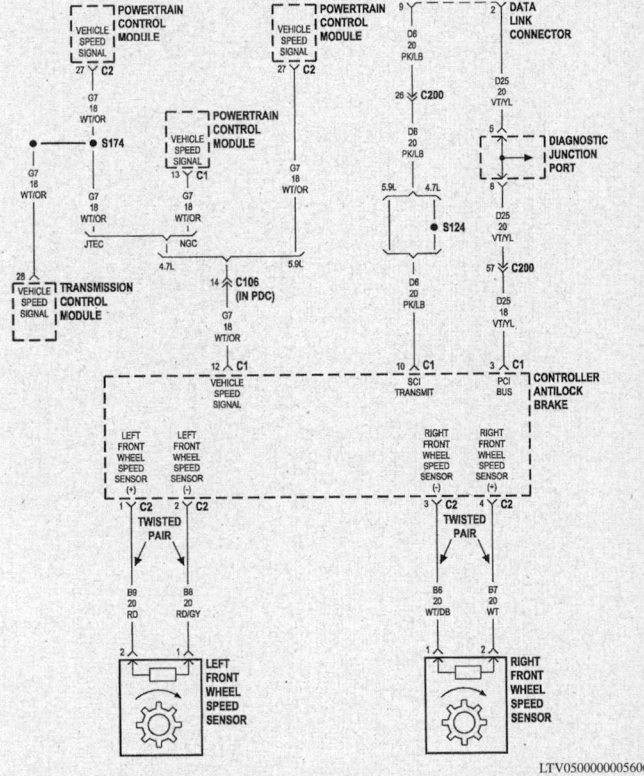

Fig. 3   Wiring diagram (Part 2 of 2). 2002–03 w/4 WABS

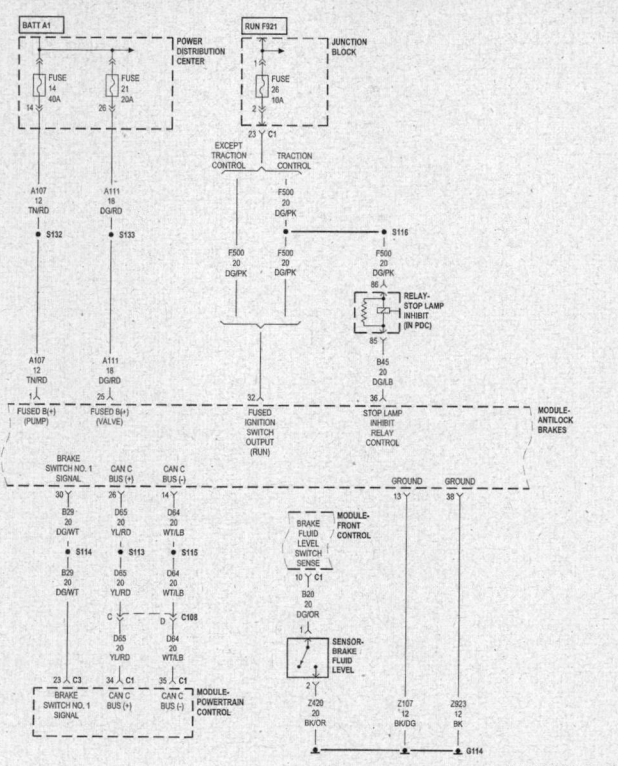

Fig. 4   Wiring diagram (Part 1 of 4). 2004–06

LTV0500000005607

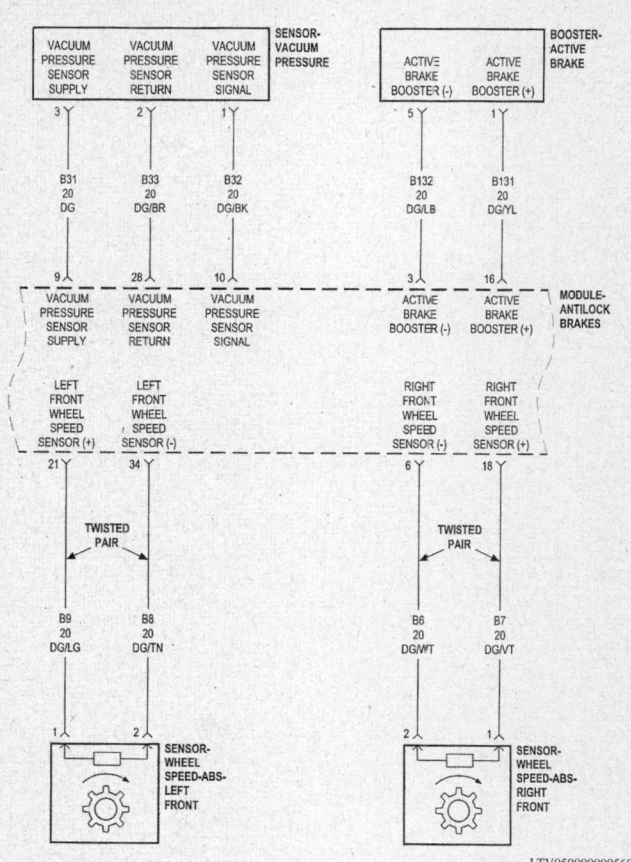

Fig. 4   Wiring diagram (Part 2 of 4). 2004–06

LTV0500000005608

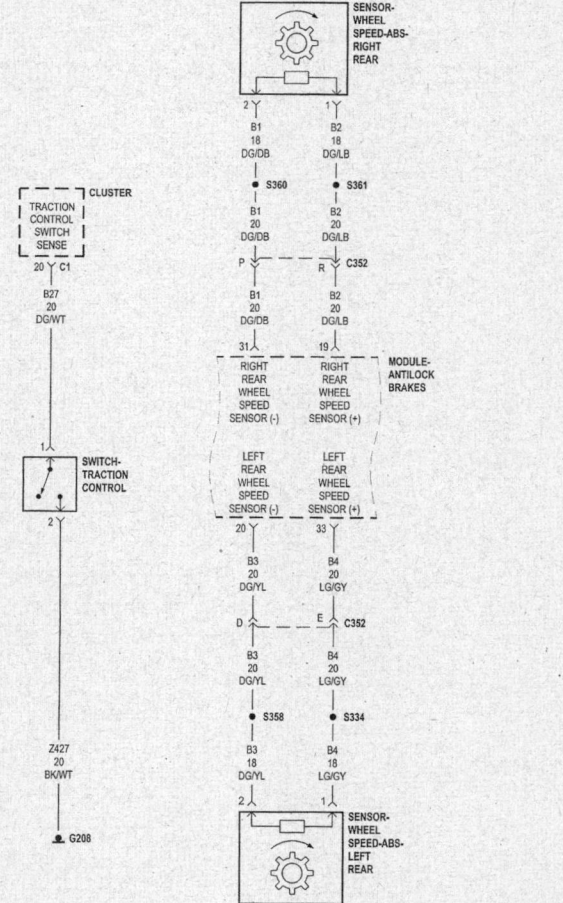

Fig. 4   Wiring diagram (Part 3 of 4). 2004–06

LTV0500000005609

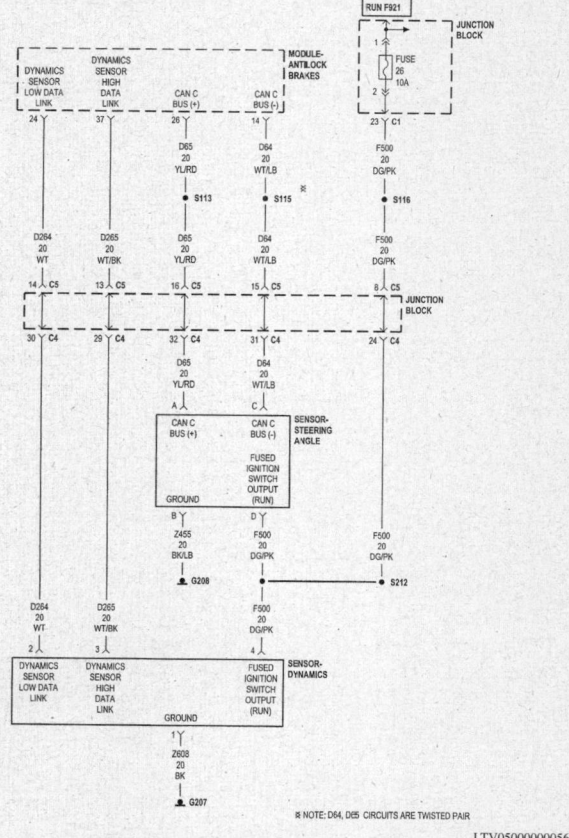

Fig. 4   Wiring diagram (Part 4 of 4). 2004–06

LTV0500000005610

DIAGNOSTIC CHART INDEX

Code	Description	Page No.	Fig No.
—	ABS Verification Test #1	5-62	5
—	Intermittent Condition	5-62	6
B1D56	Adjustable Pedal Sensor Circuit Low	5-62	7
B1D57	Adjustable Pedal Sensor Circuit High	5-63	8
B1D5B	Adjustable Pedal Switch Circuit Performance	5-64	9
B1D5C	Adjustable Pedal Switch Circuit Stuck Forward	5-65	10
B1D5D	Adjustable Pedal Switch Circuit Stuck Rearward	5-66	11
B1D67	Adjustable Pedal Switch Control Circuit Performance	5-66	12
C1008	Brake Fluid Level Input Circuit High	5-67	13
C1009	Brake Fluid Low	5-68	14
C100A	Wheel Speed Sensor Circuit	5-68	15
C1015	Wheel Speed Sensor Circuit	5-68	15
C1020	Wheel Speed Sensor Circuit	5-68	15
C102B	Wheel Speed Sensor Circuit	5-68	15
C1036	Wheel Speed Sensor Circuit	5-68	15
C1011	Wheel Speed Sensor Input Signal Erratic Performance	5-70	16
C101C	Wheel Speed Sensor Input Signal Erratic Performance	5-70	16
C1027	Wheel Speed Sensor Input Signal Erratic Performance	5-70	16
C1032	Wheel Speed Sensor Input Signal Erratic Performance	5-70	16
C103D	Wheel Speed Sensor Input Signal Erratic Performance	5-70	16
C1014	Wheel Speed Comparative Performance	5-72	17
C101F	Wheel Speed Comparative Performance	5-72	17
C102A	Wheel Speed Comparative Performance	5-72	17
C1035	Wheel Speed Comparative Performance	5-72	17
C1040	Wheel Speed Comparative Performance	5-72	17
C1050	Inlet Valve Control Circuit Low	5-73	18
C1054	Inlet Valve Control Circuit Low	5-73	18
C1058	Inlet Valve Control Circuit Low	5-73	18
C105C	Inlet Valve Control Circuit Low	5-73	18
C1060	Inlet Valve Control Circuit Low	5-73	18
C1064	Inlet Valve Control Circuit Low	5-73	18
C1068	Inlet Valve Control Circuit Low	5-73	18
C106C	Inlet Valve Control Circuit Low	5-73	18
C1070	Inlet Valve Control Circuit Low	5-73	18
C1074	Inlet Valve Control Circuit Low	5-73	18
C1078	Tire Revolutions Range Performance	5-73	19
C1079	Tone Wheel Teeth Count Range Performance	5-73	20
C107B	Wheel Speed Comparative Performance	5-73	21
C1201	Traction Control Inlet Valve Circuit Fault	5-74	22
C1205	Traction Control Inlet Valve Circuit Fault	5-74	22
C1209	Traction Control Inlet Valve Circuit Fault	5-74	22
C120D	Traction Control Inlet Valve Circuit Fault	5-74	22
C1210	G Sensor Fault	5-74	23
C1213	G Sensor Fault	5-74	23
C2105	ABS Valve Low Circuit	5-75	24
C2200	ABS Module Internal	5-75	25

Diagnostic Test

1. ABS VERIFICATION TEST — VER 1

1. Turn the ignition off.
2. Connect all previously disconnected components and connectors.
3. Ensure all accessories are turned off and the battery is fully charged.
4. Ensure that the ignition is on, and with the scan tool, erase all Diagnostic Trouble Codes from All modules. Start the engine and allow it to run for 2 minutes and fully operate the system that was malfunctioning.
5. Turn the ignition off and wait 5 seconds. Turn the ignition on and using the scan tool, read DTC's from all modules.
6. If any Diagnostic Trouble Codes are present, return to symptom list and trouble shoot new or recurring symptom.
7. **NOTE: For Sensor Signal and Pump Motor faults, the ABM must sense all 4 wheels at 12 km/h (7.5 mph) before it will extinguish the ABS indicator.**
8. If there are no DTC's present after turning ignition on, road test the vehicle for at least 5 minutes. Perform several anti-lock braking stops.
9. **Caution: Ensure braking capability is available before road testing.**
10. Again, with the scan tool read DTC's . If any DTC's are present, return to Symptom list.
11. If there are no Diagnostic Trouble Codes (DTC's) present, and the customer's concern can no longer be duplicated, the repair is complete.

Are any DTC's present or is the original concern still present?

Yes

- Repair is not complete, refer to appropriate symptom.

No

- Repair is complete.

LTV0500000005700

Fig. 5   ABS Verification Test #1. 2004–06

Diagnostic Test

1. CHECK FOR DTC B1D56–ADJUSTABLE PEDAL SENSOR CIRCUIT LOW

NOTE: This DTC must be active for the results of this test to be valid.

Turn the ignition on.
With the scan tool, record and erase DTC's.
Cycle the ignition switch from off to on.
Cycle the Adjustable Pedals Switch forward and rearward.
With the scan tool, read DTC's

Does the scan tool display: B1D56–ADJUSTABLE PEDAL SENSOR CIRCUIT LOW?

Yes

- Go To 2

No

- Refer to the INTERMITTENT CONDITIONS
- Perform APS VERIFICATION TEST - VER 1.

2. CHECK CONNECTOR/TERMINAL FOR DAMAGE

NOTE: Check all terminals for broken, bent, pushed out, or corroded terminals.

Turn the ignition off.
Inspect the Seat Memory Module harness connector, Adjustable Pedals Sensor, and Adjustable Pedals Sensor harness connector.

Is the Adjustable Pedals Sensor or any of the connectors/terminals damaged?

Yes

- Repair as necessary.
- Perform APS VERIFICATION TEST - VER 1.

No

- Go To 3

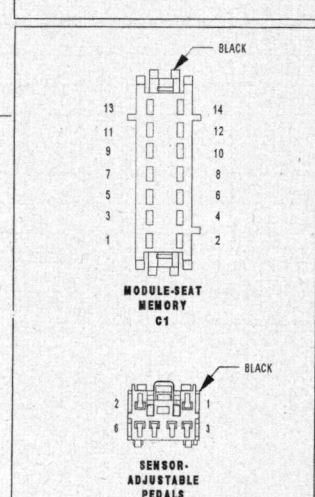

Fig. 7   Code B1D56: Adjustable Pedal Sensor Circuit Low (Part 1 of 4). 2004–06

LTV0500000005701

Diagnostic Test

1. INTERMITTENT CONDITION

NOTE: The conditions that set the DTC are not present at this time. The following list may help in identifying the intermittent condition.

WARNING: When the engine is operating, do not stand in direct line with the fan. Do not put your hands near the pulleys, belts, or fan. Do not wear loose clothing. Failure to follow these instructions can result in personal injury or death.

Refer to any Technical Service Bulletins (TSBs) that may apply.
Review the scan tool Freeze Frame information. If possible, try to duplicate the conditions under which the DTC set.
Turn the ignition off.
Visually inspect the related wire harness. Wiggle the related wire harness and look for an interrupted signal on the affected circuit. Disconnect all the related harness connectors. Look for any chafed, pierced, pinched, partially broken wires and broken, bent, pushed out, or corroded terminals.
Perform a voltage drop test on the related circuits between the suspected faulty component and the Anti-Lock Brake Module.
Inspect and clean all PCM, ABS, engine, and chassis grounds that are related to the most current DTC. If numerous trouble codes were set, use a wire schematic and look for any common ground or supply circuits
For any Relay DTCs, actuate the Relay with the scan tool and wiggle the related wire harness to try to interrupt the actuation.
Use the scan tool to perform a System Test if one applies to failing component.
A co-pilot, data recorder, and/or lab scope should be used to help diagnose intermittent conditions.

Were any problems found during the above inspections?

Yes

- Perform the necessary repairs.
- Perform ABS VERIFICATION TEST VER - 1.

No

- Test Complete.

LTV0500000005751

Fig. 6   Intermittent Condition. 2004–06

3. CHECK (G11) ADJUSTABLE PEDALS SENSOR SUPPLY CIRCUIT FOR A SHORT TO GROUND

Turn the ignition off.
Disconnect the Seat Memory Module harness connector.
Disconnect the Adjustable Pedals Sensor harness connector.
Using a 12-volt test light connected to 12-volts, probe the (G11) Adjustable Pedals Sensor Supply circuit.

Does the test light illuminate brightly?

Yes

- Repair the (G11) Adjustable Pedals Sensor Supply circuit for a short to ground.
- Perform APS VERIFICATION TEST - VER 1.

No

- Go To 4

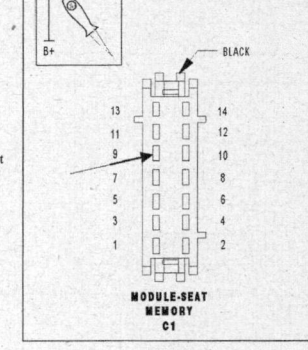

4. CHECK (G11) ADJUSTABLE PEDALS SENSOR SUPPLY CIRCUIT FOR AN OPEN

Turn the ignition off.
Disconnect the Seat Memory Module harness connector.
Disconnect the Adjustable Pedals Sensor harness connector.
Connect a jumper wire between the (G11) Adjustable Pedals Sensor Supply circuit and ground.
Using a 12-volt test light connected to 12-volts, probe the (G11) Adjustable Pedals Sensor Supply circuit.

Does the test light illuminate brightly

Yes

- Go To 5

No

- Repair the (G11) Adjustable Pedals Sensor Supply circuit for an open.
- Perform APS VERIFICATION TEST - VER 1.

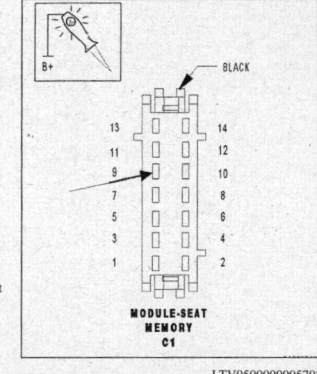

LTV0500000005702

Fig. 7   Code B1D56: Adjustable Pedal Sensor Circuit Low (Part 2 of 4). 2004–06

5. CHECK (G12) ADJUSTABLE PEDALS SENSOR SIGNAL CIRCUIT FOR A SHORT TO GROUND

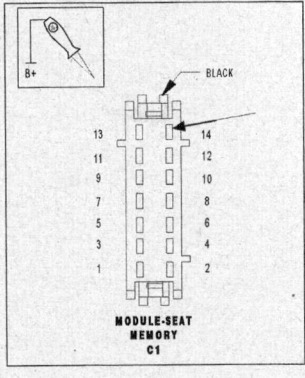

Turn the ignition off.
Disconnect the Seat Memory Module harness connector.
Disconnect the Adjustable Pedals Sensor harness connector.
Using a 12-volt test light connected to 12-volts, probe the (G12) Adjustable Pedals Sensor Signal circuit.

Does the test light illuminate brightly?

Yes

- Repair the (G12) Adjustable Pedals Sensor Signal circuit for a short to ground.
- Perform APS VERIFICATION TEST - VER 1.

No

- Go To 6

6. CHECK (G12) ADJUSTABLE PEDALS SENSOR SIGNAL CIRCUIT FOR AN OPEN

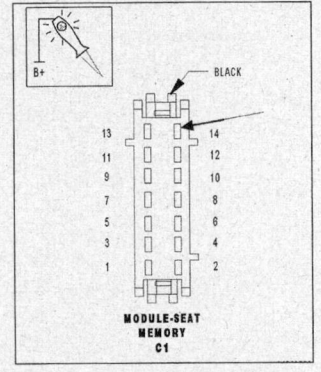

Turn the ignition off.
Disconnect the Seat Memory Module harness connector.
Disconnect the Adjustable Pedals Sensor harness connector.
Connect a jumper wire between the (G12) Adjustable Pedals Sensor Signal circuit and ground.
Using a 12-volt test light connected to 12-volts, probe the (G12) Adjustable Pedals Sensor Signal circuit.

Does the test light illuminate brightly?

Yes

- Go To 7

No

- Repair the (G12) Adjustable Pedals Sensor Signal circuit for an open.
- Perform APS VERIFICATION TEST - VER 1.

LTV0500000005703

Fig. 7   Code B1D56: Adjustable Pedal Sensor Circuit Low (Part 3 of 4). 2004–06

Diagnostic Test

1. CHECK FOR DTC B1D57–ADJUSTABLE PEDAL SENSOR CIRCUIT HIGH

NOTE: This DTC must be active for the results of this test to be valid.

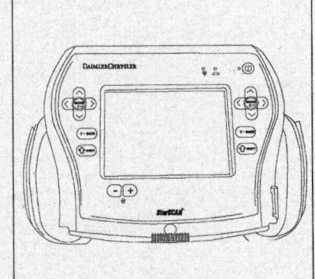

Turn the ignition on.
With the scan tool, record and erase DTC's.
Cycle the ignition switch from off to on.
Cycle the Adjustable Pedals Switch forward and rearward.
With the scan tool, read DTC's

Does the scan tool display: B1D57–ADJUSTABLE PEDAL SENSOR CIRCUIT HIGH?

Yes

- Go To 2

No

- Refer to the INTERMITTENT CONDITIONS
- Perform APS VERIFICATION TEST - VER 1.

LTV0500000005705

Fig. 8   Code B1D57: Adjustable Pedal Sensor Circuit High (Part 1 of 4). 2004–06

7. CHECK (G11) ADJUSTABLE PEDALS SENSOR SUPPLY CIRCUIT VOLTAGE

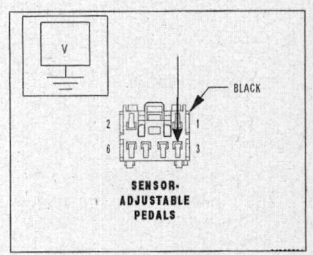

Turn the ignition off.
Disconnect the Adjustable Pedals Sensor harness connector.
Measure the voltage between the (G11) Adjustable Pedals Sensor Supply circuit and ground.

Is the voltage between 4.0 and 5.0 volts?

Yes

- Go To 8

No

- Replace and reprogram the Seat Memory Module
- Perform APS VERIFICATION TEST - VER 1.

8. CHECK (G12) ADJUSTABLE PEDALS SENSOR SIGNAL CIRCUIT VOLTAGE

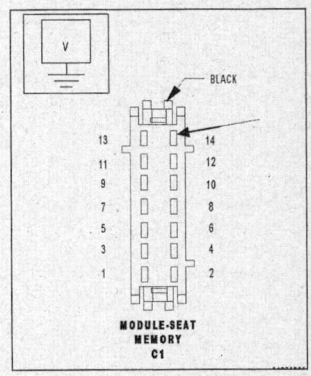

Turn the ignition off.
Reconnect all connectors.
Measure the voltage of the (G12) Adjustable Pedals Sensor Signal circuit in the Seat Memory Module harness connector.

Is the voltage above 0.5 volts?

Yes

- Replace and reprogram the Seat Memory Module
- Perform APS VERIFICATION TEST - VER 1.

No

- Replace the Adjustable Pedals Sensor in accordance with the Service Information.
- Perform APS VERIFICATION TEST - VER 1.

LTV0500000005704

Fig. 7   Code B1D56: Adjustable Pedal Sensor Circuit Low (Part 4 of 4). 2004–06

2. CHECK CONNECTOR/TERMINAL FOR DAMAGE

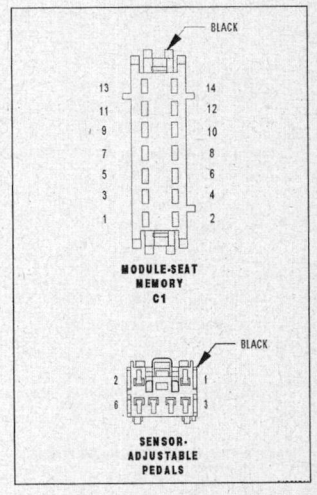

NOTE: Check all terminals for broken, bent, pushed out, or corroded terminals.

Turn the ignition off.
Inspect the Seat Memory Module harness connector, Adjustable Pedals Sensor, and Adjustable Pedals Sensor harness connector.

Is the Adjustable Pedals Sensor or any of the connectors/terminals damaged?

Yes

- Repair as necessary.
- Perform APS VERIFICATION TEST - VER 1.

No

- Go To 3

LTV0500000005706

Fig. 8   Code B1D57: Adjustable Pedal Sensor Circuit High (Part 2 of 4). 2004–06

3. CHECK (G11) ADJUSTABLE PEDALS SENSOR SUPPLY CIRCUIT FOR A SHORT TO VOLTAGE

Turn the ignition off.
Disconnect the Seat Memory Module harness connector.
Turn the ignition on.
Measure the voltage between the (G11) Adjustable Pedals Sensor Supply circuit and ground.

Is the voltage above 5.0 volts?

Yes

- Repair the (G11) Adjustable Pedals Sensor Supply circuit for a short to voltage.
- Perform APS VERIFICATION TEST - VER 1.

No

- Go To 4

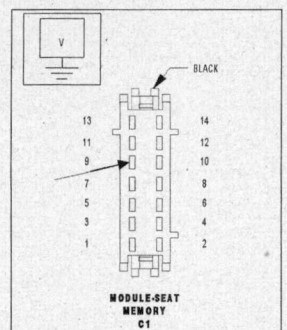

4. CHECK (G12) ADJUSTABLE PEDALS SENSOR SIGNAL CIRCUIT FOR A SHORT TO VOLTAGE

Turn the ignition off.
Disconnect the Seat Memory Module harness connector.
Turn the ignition on.
Measure the voltage between the (G12) Adjustable Pedals Sensor Signal circuit and ground.

Is the voltage above 5.0 volts?

Yes

- Repair the (G12) Adjustable Pedals Sensor Signal circuit for a short to voltage.
- Perform APS VERIFICATION TEST - VER 1.

No

- Go To 5

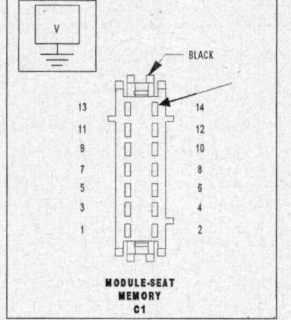

LTV0500000005707

Fig. 8 Code B1D57: Adjustable Pedal Sensor Circuit High (Part 3 of 4). 2004–06

Diagnostic Test

1. CHECK FOR DTC B1D5B–ADJUSTABLE PEDAL SWITCH CIRCUIT PERFORMANCE

NOTE: This DTC must be active for the results of this test to be valid.

Turn the ignition on.
With the scan tool, record and erase DTC's.
Cycle the ignition switch from off to on.
Cycle the Adjustable Pedals Switch forward and rearward.
With the scan tool, read DTC's

Does the scan tool display: B1D5B–ADJUSTABLE PEDAL SWITCH CIRCUIT PERFORMANCE?

Yes

- Go To 2

No

- Refer to the INTERMITTENT CONDITIONS
- Perform APS VERIFICATION TEST - VER 1.

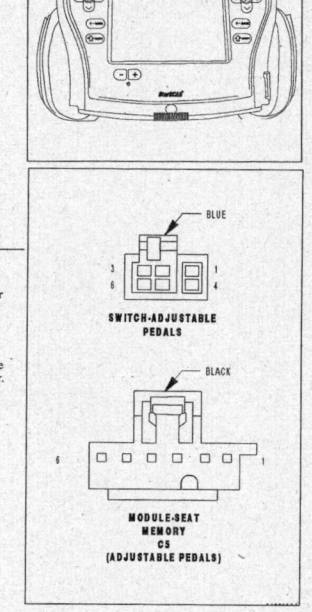

2. CHECK CONNECTOR/TERMINAL FOR DAMAGE

NOTE: Check all terminals for broken, bent, pushed out, or corroded terminals.

Turn the ignition off.
Inspect the Seat Memory Module harness connector, Adjustable Pedals Switch, and Adjustable Pedals Switch harness connector.

Is the Adjustable Pedals Switch or any of the connectors/terminals damaged?

Yes

- Repair as necessary.
- Perform APS VERIFICATION TEST - VER 1.

No

- Go To 3

LTV0500000005709

Fig. 9 Code B1D5B: Adjustable Pedal Switch Circuit Performance (Part 1 of 3). 2004–06

5. CHECK (G12) ADJUSTABLE PEDALS SENSOR SIGNAL CIRCUIT VOLTAGE

Turn the ignition off.
Reconnect all connectors.
Measure the voltage of the (G12) Adjustable Pedals Sensor Signal circuit in the Seat Memory Module harness connector.

Is the voltage below 4.0 volts?

Yes

- Replace and reprogram the Seat Memory Module
- Perform APS VERIFICATION TEST - VER 1.

No

- Replace the Adjustable Pedals Sensor
- Perform APS VERIFICATION TEST - VER 1.

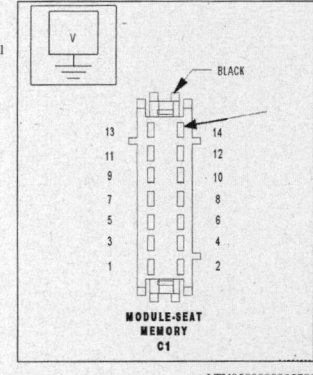

LTV0500000005708

Fig. 8 Code B1D57: Adjustable Pedal Sensor Circuit High (Part 4 of 4). 2004–06

3. CHECK (Q100) ADJUSTABLE PEDALS SWITCH REARWARD CIRCUIT FOR A SHORT TO GROUND

Turn the ignition off.
Disconnect the Seat Memory Module harness connector.
Disconnect the Adjustable Pedals Switch harness connector.
Using a 12-volt test light connected to 12-volts, probe the (Q100) Adjustable Pedals Switch Rearward circuit.

Does the test light illuminate brightly?

Yes

- Repair the (Q100) Adjustable Pedals Switch Rearward circuit for a short to ground.
- Perform APS VERIFICATION TEST - VER 1.

No

- Go To 4

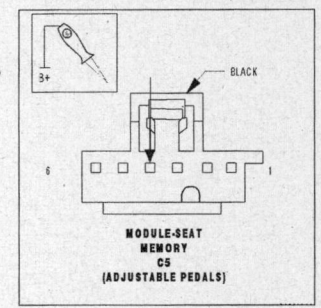

4. CHECK (Q900) ADJUSTABLE PEDALS SWITCH FORWARD CIRCUIT FOR A SHORT TO GROUND

Turn the ignition off.
Disconnect the Seat Memory Module harness connector.
Disconnect the Adjustable Pedals Switch harness connector.
Using a 12-volt test light connected to 12-volts, probe the (Q900) Adjustable Pedals Switch Forward circuit.

Does the test light illuminate brightly?

Yes

- Repair the (Q900) Adjustable Pedals Switch Forward circuit for a short to ground.
- Perform APS VERIFICATION TEST - VER 1.

No

- Go To 5

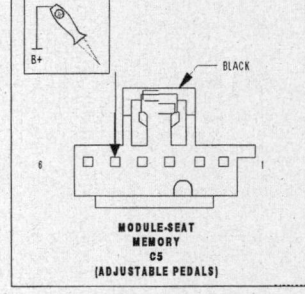

LTV0500000005710

Fig. 9 Code B1D5B: Adjustable Pedal Switch Circuit Performance (Part 2 of 3). 2004–06

5. CHECK (Q100) ADJUSTABLE PEDALS SWITCH REARWARD CIRCUIT AND (Q900) ADJUSTABLE PEDALS SWITCH FORWARD CIRCUIT FOR A SHORT TOGETHER

Turn the ignition off.
Disconnect the Seat Memory Module harness connector.
Disconnect the Adjustable Pedals Switch harness connector.
Measure the resistance between the (Q100) Adjustable Pedals Switch Rearward circuit and (Q900) Adjustable Pedals Switch Forward circuit.

Is the resistance above 5.0 ohms?

Yes

- Go To 6

No

- Repair the (Q100) Adjustable Pedals Switch Rearward circuit and (Q900) Adjustable Pedals Switch Forward circuit for a short together.
- Perform APS VERIFICATION TEST - VER 1.

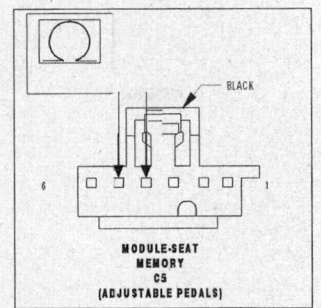

6. CHECK ADJUSTABLE PEDALS SWITCH SHORTED

Turn the ignition off.
Disconnect the Adjustable Pedals Switch harness connector.
Measure the resistance between the (Q100) Adjustable Pedals Switch Rearward and (Q900) Adjustable Pedals Switch Forward terminals at the Adjustable Pedals Switch.

Is the resistance below 5.0 ohms?

Yes

- Replace and reprogram the Seat Memory Module
- Perform APS VERIFICATION TEST - VER 1.

No

- Replace the Adjustable Pedals Switch
- Perform APS VERIFICATION TEST - VER 1.

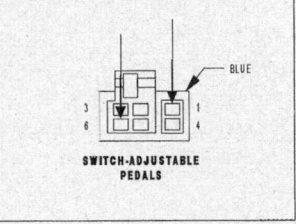

LTV0500000005711

Fig. 9   Code B1D5B: Adjustable Pedal Switch Circuit Performance (Part 3 of 3). 2004–06

2. CHECK CONNECTOR/TERMINAL FOR DAMAGE

NOTE: Check all terminals for broken, bent, pushed out, or corroded terminals.

Turn the ignition off.
Inspect the Seat Memory Module harness connector, Adjustable Pedals Switch, and Adjustable Pedals Switch harness connector.

Is the Adjustable Pedals Switch or any of the connectors/terminals damaged?

Yes

- Repair as necessary.
- Perform APS VERIFICATION TEST - VER 1.

No

- Go To 3

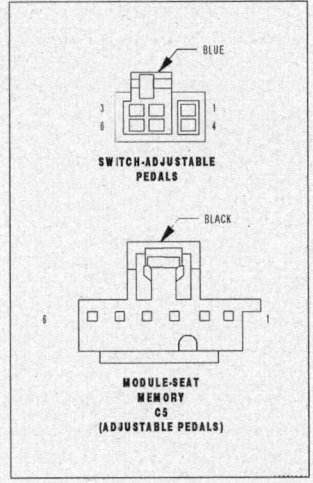

LTV0500000005713

Fig. 10   Code B1D5C: Adjustable Pedal Switch Circuit Stuck Forward (Part 2 of 3). 2004–06

Diagnostic Test

1. CHECK FOR DTC B1D5C–ADJUSTABLE PEDAL SWITCH CIRCUIT STUCK FORWARD

NOTE: This DTC must be active for the results of this test to be valid.

Turn the ignition on.
With the scan tool, record and erase DTC's.
Cycle the ignition switch from off to on.
Cycle the Adjustable Pedals Switch forward and rearward.
With the scan tool, read DTC's

Does the scan tool display: B1D5C–ADJUSTABLE PEDAL SWITCH CIRCUIT STUCK FORWARD?

Yes

- Go To 2

No

- Refer to the INTERMITTENT CONDITIONS
- Perform APS VERIFICATION TEST - VER 1.

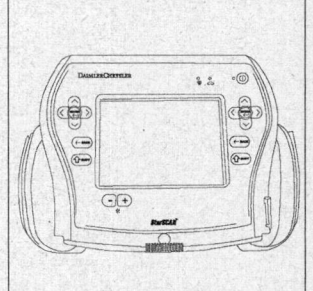

LTV0500000005712

Fig. 10   Code B1D5C: Adjustable Pedal Switch Circuit Stuck Forward (Part 1 of 3). 2004–06

3. CHECK (Q900) ADJUSTABLE PEDALS SWITCH FORWARD CIRCUIT FOR A SHORT TO GROUND

Turn the ignition off.
Disconnect the Seat Memory Module harness connector.
Disconnect the Adjustable Pedals Switch harness connector.
Using a 12-volt test light connected to 12-volts, probe the (Q900) Adjustable Pedals Switch Forward circuit.

Does the test light illuminate brightly?

Yes

- Repair the (Q900) Adjustable Pedals Switch Forward circuit for a short to ground.
- Perform APS VERIFICATION TEST - VER 1.

No

- Go To 4

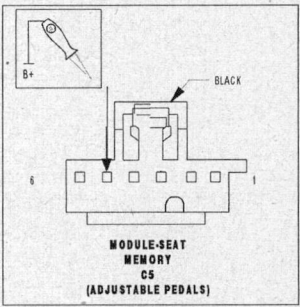

4. CHECK ADJUSTABLE PEDALS SWITCH SHORTED

Turn the ignition off.
Disconnect the Adjustable Pedals Switch harness connector.
Measure the resistance between the (Q100) Adjustable Pedals Switch Rearward and (Q900) Adjustable Pedals Switch Forward terminals at the Adjustable Pedals Switch.

Is the resistance below 5.0 ohms?

Yes

- Replace and reprogram the Seat Memory Module
- Perform APS VERIFICATION TEST - VER 1.

No

- Replace the Adjustable Pedals Switch
- Perform APS VERIFICATION TEST - VER 1.

LTV0500000005714

Fig. 10   Code B1D5C: Adjustable Pedal Switch Circuit Stuck Forward (Part 3 of 3). 2004–06

Diagnostic Test

NOTE: This DTC must be active for the results of this test to be valid.

1. CHECK FOR DTC B1D5D–ADJUSTABLE PEDAL SWITCH CIRCUIT STUCK REARWARD

Turn the ignition on.
With the scan tool, record and erase DTC's.
Cycle the ignition switch from off to on.
Cycle the Adjustable Pedals Switch forward and rearward.
With the scan tool, read DTC's

Does the scan tool display: B1D5D–ADJUSTABLE PEDAL SWITCH CIRCUIT STUCK REARWARD?

Yes

- Go To 2

No

- Refer to the INTERMITTENT CONDITIONS
- Perform APS VERIFICATION TEST - VER 1.

2. CHECK CONNECTOR/TERMINAL FOR DAMAGE

NOTE: Check all terminals for broken, bent, pushed out, or corroded terminals.

Turn the ignition off.
Inspect the Seat Memory Module harness connector, Adjustable Pedals Switch, and Adjustable Pedals Switch harness connector.

Is the Adjustable Pedals Switch or any of the connectors/terminals damaged?

Yes

- Repair as necessary.
- Perform APS VERIFICATION TEST - VER 1.

No

- Go To 3

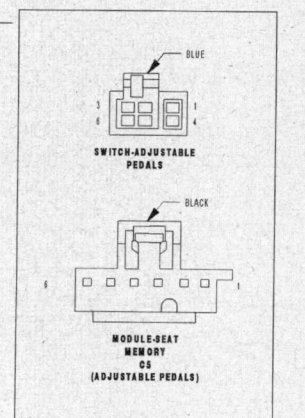

LTV0500000005715

Fig. 11 Code B1D5D: Adjustable Pedal Switch Circuit Stuck Rearward (Part 1 of 2). 2004–06

Diagnostic Test

1. CHECK FOR DTC B1D67–ADJUSTABLE PEDAL CONTROL CIRCUIT PERFORMANCE

NOTE: This DTC must be active for the results of this test to be valid.

Turn the ignition on.
With the scan tool, record and erase DTC's.
Cycle the ignition switch from off to on.
Cycle and hold the Adjustable Pedals Switch forward, rearward, and forward at two second intervals.
With the scan tool, read DTC's

Does the scan tool display: B1D67–ADJUSTABLE PEDAL CONTROL CIRCUIT PERFORMANCE?

Yes

- Go To 2

No

- Refer to the INTERMITTENT CONDITIONS
- Perform APS VERIFICATION TEST - VER 1.

2. CHECK CONNECTOR/TERMINAL FOR DAMAGE

NOTE: Check all terminals for broken, bent, pushed out, or corroded terminals.

Turn the ignition off.
Inspect the Seat Memory Module harness connector, Adjustable Pedals Motor, and Adjustable Pedals Motor harness connector.

Is the Adjustable Pedals Motor or any of the connectors/terminals damaged?

Yes

- Repair as necessary.
- Perform APS VERIFICATION TEST - VER 1.

No

- Go To 3

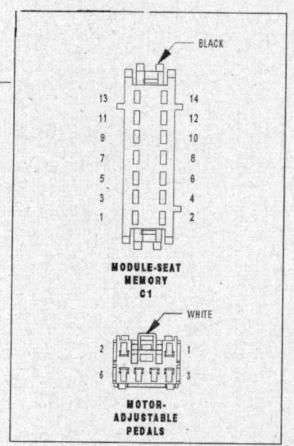

LTV0500000005717

Fig. 12 Code B1D67: Adjustable Pedal Switch Control Circuit Performance (Part 1 of 4). 2004–06

3. CHECK (Q100) ADJUSTABLE PEDALS SWITCH REARWARD CIRCUIT FOR A SHORT TO GROUND

Turn the ignition off.
Disconnect the Seat Memory Module harness connector.
Disconnect the Adjustable Pedals Switch harness connector.
Using a 12-volt test light connected to 12-volts, probe the (Q100) Adjustable Pedals Switch Rearward circuit.

Does the test light illuminate brightly?

Yes

- Repair the (Q100) Adjustable Pedals Switch Rearward circuit for a short to ground.
- Perform APS VERIFICATION TEST - VER 1.

No

- Go To 4

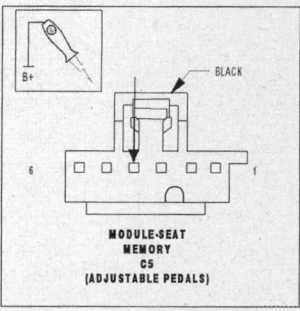

4. CHECK ADJUSTABLE PEDALS SWITCH SHORTED

Turn the ignition off.
Disconnect the Adjustable Pedals Switch harness connector.
Measure the resistance between the (Q100) Adjustable Pedals Switch Rearward and (Q900) Adjustable Pedals Switch Forward terminals at the Adjustable Pedals Switch.

Is the resistance below 5.0 ohms?

Yes

- Replace and reprogram the Seat Memory Module
- Perform APS VERIFICATION TEST - VER 1.

No

- Replace the Adjustable Pedals Switch
- Perform APS VERIFICATION TEST - VER 1.

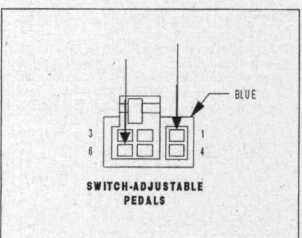

LTV0500000005716

Fig. 11 Code B1D5D: Adjustable Pedal Switch Circuit Stuck Rearward (Part 2 of 2). 2004–06

3. CHECK ADJUSTABLE PEDALS ASSEMBLY FOR MECHANICAL DAMAGE

Turn the ignition off.
Inspect the Adjustable Pedals Assembly for any physical damage.

NOTE: Check for any conditions that would cause the motor to stall or be stuck.

Is the Adjustable Pedals Assembly damaged or broken?

Yes

- Replace the Adjustable Pedals Assembly
- Perform APS VERIFICATION TEST - VER 1.

No

- Go To 4

4. CHECK (P205) ADJUSTABLE PEDALS MOTOR FORWARD CIRCUIT FOR AN OPEN

Turn the ignition off.
Disconnect the Seat Memory Module harness connector.
Disconnect the Adjustable Pedals Motor harness connector.
Connect a jumper wire between the (P205) Adjustable Pedals Motor Forward circuit and ground.
Using a 12-volt test light connected to 12-volts, probe the (P205) Adjustable Pedals Motor Forward circuit.

Does the test light illuminate brightly?

Yes

- Go To 5

No

- Repair the (P205) Adjustable Pedals Motor Forward circuit for an open.
- Perform APS VERIFICATION TEST - VER 1.

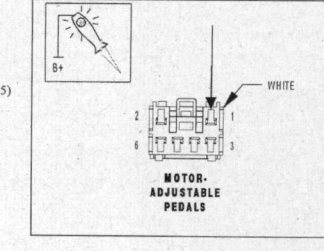

LTV0500000005718

Fig. 12 Code B1D67: Adjustable Pedal Switch Control Circuit Performance (Part 2 of 4). 2004–06

5. CHECK (P206) ADJUSTABLE PEDALS MOTOR REARWARD CIRCUIT FOR AN OPEN

Turn the ignition off.
Disconnect the Seat Memory Module harness connector.
Disconnect the Adjustable Pedals Motor harness connector
Connect a jumper wire between the (P206) Adjustable Pedals
Motor Rearward circuit and ground.
Using a 12-volt test light connected to 12-volts, probe the (P206)
Adjustable Pedals Motor Rearward circuit.

Does the test light illuminate brightly?

Yes

- Go To 6

No

- Repair the (P206) Adjustable Pedals Motor Rearward circuit for an open.
- Perform APS VERIFICATION TEST - VER 1.

6. CHECK (G912) ADJUSTABLE PEDALS SENSOR RETURN CIRCUIT FOR AN OPEN

Turn the ignition off.
Disconnect the Seat Memory Module harness connector.
Disconnect the Adjustable Pedals Sensor harness connector
Connect a jumper wire between the (G912) Adjustable Pedals
Sensor Return circuit and ground.
Using a 12-volt test light connected to 12-volts, probe the (G912)
Adjustable Pedals Sensor Return circuit.

Does the test light illuminate brightly?

Yes

- Go To

No

- Repair the (G912) Adjustable Pedals Sensor Return circuit for an open.
- Perform APS VERIFICATION TEST - VER 1.

LTV0500000005719

**Fig. 12   Code B1D67: Adjustable Pedal Switch
Control Circuit Performance (Part 3 of 4). 2004–06**

Diagnostic Test

1. CHECK FOR DTC C1008–BRAKE FLUID LEVEL
INPUT CIRCUIT HIGH

**NOTE: This DTC must be active for the results of this test to
be valid.**

Turn the ignition on.
With the scan tool, record and erase DTC's.
Cycle the ignition switch from off to on.
With the scan tool, read DTC's

**Does the scan tool display: C1008–BRAKE FLUID LEVEL
INPUT CIRCUIT HIGH?**

Yes

- Go To 2

No

- Refer to the INTERMITTENT CONDITIONS

- Perform APS VERIFICATION TEST - VER 1.

LTV0500000005721

**Fig. 13   Code C1008: Brake Fluid Level Input
Circuit High (Part 1 of 4). 2004–06**

7. CHECK ADJUSTABLE PEDALS MOTOR

Turn the ignition off.
Disconnect the Adjustable Pedals Motor harness connector.
Measure the resistance between the (P205) Adjustable Pedals
Motor Forward and (P206) Adjustable Pedals Motor Rearward
terminals at the Adjustable Pedals Motor.

Is the resistance below 100.0 ohms?

Yes

- Replace and reprogram the Seat Memory Module
- Perform APS VERIFICATION TEST - VER 1.

No

- Replace the Adjustable Pedals Motor
- Perform APS VERIFICATION TEST - VER 1.

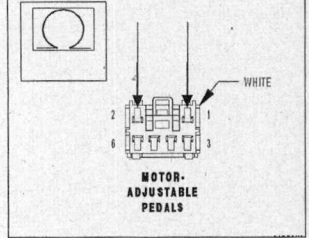

LTV0500000005720

**Fig. 12   Code B1D67: Adjustable Pedal Switch
Control Circuit Performance (Part 4 of 4). 2004–06**

2. CHECK BRAKE FLUID LEVEL SENSOR CONNECTION

Turn the ignition off.
Inspect the connection of the Brake Fluid Level Sensor harness
connector.

**NOTE: Check all terminals for broken, bent, pushed out, or
corroded terminals.**

Is there any damage?

Yes

- Repair as necessary.
- Perform ABS VERIFICATION TEST - VER 1.

No

- Go To 3

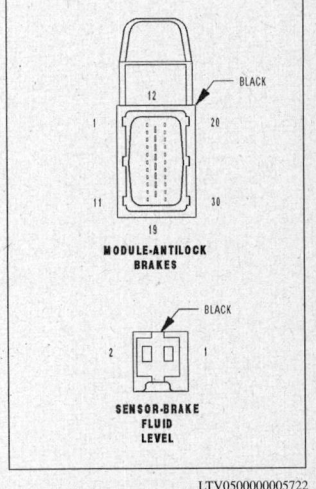

LTV0500000005722

**Fig. 13   Code C1008: Brake Fluid Level Input
Circuit High (Part 2 of 4). 2004–06**

3. CHECK (B20) BRAKE FLUID LEVEL SWITCH SENSE CIRCUIT FOR A SHORT TO VOLTAGE

Turn the ignition off.
Disconnect the Anti-Lock Brake Module harness connector.
Disconnect the Brake Fluid Level Sensor harness connector.
Turn the ignition on.
Measure the voltage between (B20) Brake Fluid Level Switch
Sense circuit and ground.

Is there any voltage present?

Yes

- Repair the (B20) Brake Fluid Level Switch Sense circuit for a short to voltage.
- Perform ABS VERIFICATION TEST - VER 1.

No

- Go To 4

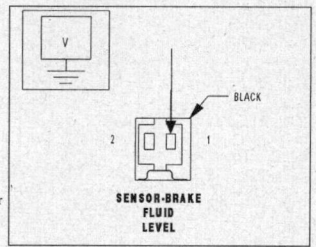

4. CHECK (B20) BRAKE FLUID LEVEL SWITCH SENSE CIRCUIT FOR AN OPEN

Turn the ignition off.
Disconnect the Anti-Lock Brake Module harness connector.
Disconnect the Brake Fluid Level Sensor harness connector.
Connect a jumper wire between the (B20) Brake Fluid Level
Switch Sense and ground.
Using a 12-volt test light connected to 12-volts, probe the (B20)
Brake Fluid Level Switch Sense circuit.

Does the test light illuminate brightly?

Yes

- Go To 5

No

- Repair the (B20) Brake Fluid Level Switch Sense circuit for an open.
- Perform ABS VERIFICATION TEST - VER 1.

LTV0500000005723

Fig. 13   Code C1008: Brake Fluid Level Input Circuit High (Part 3 of 4). 2004–06

Diagnostic Test

1. LOW BRAKE FLUID

Check the Brake fluid level.

Is the brake fluid full?

Yes

- Go To 2

No

- Fill the Brake fluid to proper level.
- Perform ABS VERIFICATION TEST — VER 1.

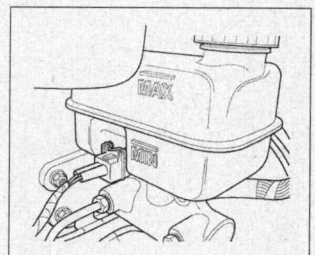

2. (B20) BRAKE FLUID LEVEL SWITCH SENSE CIRCUIT SHORTED TO GROUND

Disconnect the Anti-lock brake module (ABM)
Disconnect the Brake fluid level sensor harness connector.

NOTE: Check connector - Clean/repair as necessary.

Measure the resistance of the Brake fluid level sensor switch sense
circuit at the ABM harness connector to ground.

Is the resistance below 5 ohms?

Yes

- Repair the (B20) Brake fluid level switch sense circuit for a short to ground.
- Perform ABS VERIFICATION TEST — VER 1.

No

- Replace the Brake fluid level sensor.
- Perform ABS VERIFICATION TEST — VER 1.

LTV0500000005725

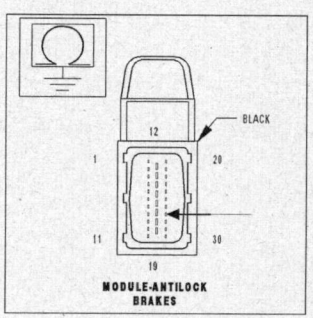

Fig. 14   Code C1009: Brake Fluid Low. 2004–06

5. CHECK (Z420) GROUND CIRCUIT FOR AN OPEN

Turn the ignition off.
Disconnect the Brake Fluid Level Sensor harness connector.
Using a 12-volt test light connected to 12-volts, probe the (Z420)
Ground circuit.

Does the test light illuminate brightly?

Yes

- Go To 6

No

- Repair the (Z420) Ground circuit for an open.
- Perform ABS VERIFICATION TEST - VER 1.

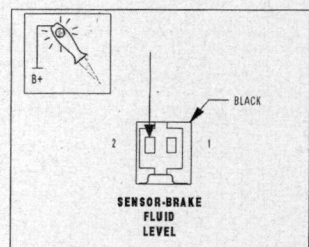

6. CHECK BRAKE FLUID LEVEL SENSOR FOR AN OPEN

Turn the ignition off.
Disconnect the Brake Fluid Level Sensor harness connector.
Measure the resistance between the Brake Fluid Level Sensor terminals.

Is the resistance above 11.0k ohms?

Yes

- Replace the Brake Fluid Level Sensor
- Perform ABS VERIFICATION TEST - VER 1.

No

- Replace the Anti-Lock Brake Module
- Perform ABS VERIFICATION TEST - VER 1.

LTV0500000005724

Fig. 13   Code C1008: Brake Fluid Level Input Circuit High (Part 4 of 4). 2004–06

Diagnostic Test

1. CHECK FOR DTC C100A–LEFT FRONT WHEEL SPEED SENSOR CIRCUIT

NOTE: This DTC must be active for the results of this test to be valid.

Turn the ignition on.
With the scan tool, record and erase DTC's.
Cycle the ignition switch from off to on.
With the scan tool, read DTC's

Does the scan tool display: C100A–LEFT FRONT WHEEL SPEED SENSOR CIRCUIT?

Yes

- Go To 2

No

- Refer to the INTERMITTENT CONDITIONS
- Perform APS VERIFICATION TEST - VER 1.

LTV0500000005726

Fig. 15   Code C100A, C1015, C1020, C102B & C1036: Wheel Speed Sensor Circuit (Part 1 of 8). 2004–06

2. CHECK CONNECTOR/TERMINAL FOR DAMAGE

NOTE: Check all terminals for broken, bent, pushed out, or corroded terminals.

Turn the ignition off.
Inspect the Anti-Lock Brake Module harness connector, Left Front WSS, and Left Front WSS harness connector.

Is the Left Front WSS or any of the connectors/terminals damaged?

Yes

- Repair as necessary.
- Perform ABS VERIFICATION TEST - VER 1.

No

- Go To 3

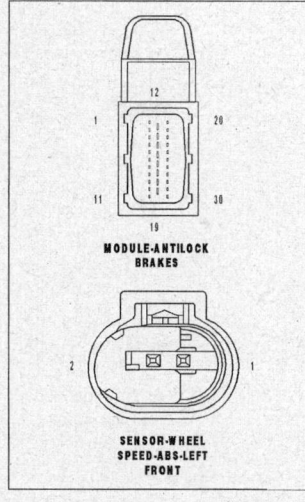

Fig. 15   Code C100A, C1015, C1020, C102B & C1036: Wheel Speed Sensor Circuit (Part 2 of 8). 2004–06

5. CHECK (B9) LEFT FRONT WSS SUPPLY CIRCUIT OPEN

Turn the ignition off.
Disconnect the Anti-Lock Brake Module harness connector.
Disconnect the Left Front WSS harness connector.
Connect a jumper wire between the (B9) Left Front WSS Supply circuit and ground.
Using a 12-volt test light connected to 12-volts, probe the (B9) Left Front WSS Supply circuit.

Does the test light illuminate brightly

Yes

- Go To 6

No

- Repair the (B9) Left Front WSS Supply circuit for an open.
- Perform ABS VERIFICATION TEST - VER 1.

6. CHECK (B8) LEFT FRONT WSS SIGNAL CIRCUIT SHORT TO VOLTAGE

Turn the ignition off.
Disconnect the Left Front WSS harness connector.
Turn the ignition on.
Measure the voltage between the (B8) Left Front WSS Signal circuit and ground.

Is the voltage above one volt?

Yes

- Repair the (B8) Left Front WSS Signal circuit for a short to voltage.
- Perform ABS VERIFICATION TEST - VER 1.

No

- Go To 7

Fig. 15   Code C100A, C1015, C1020, C102B & C1036: Wheel Speed Sensor Circuit (Part 4 of 8). 2004–06

3. CHECK (B9) LEFT FRONT WSS SUPPLY CIRCUIT VOLTAGE

Turn the ignition off.
Disconnect the Left Front WSS harness connector.
Turn the ignition on.
Measure the voltage between the (B9) Left Front WSS Supply circuit and ground.

Is the voltage above 10 volts?

Yes

- Go To 6

No

- Go To 4

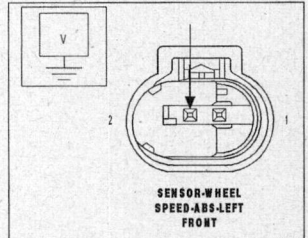

4. CHECK (B9) LEFT FRONT WSS SUPPLY CIRCUIT SHORT TO GROUND

Turn the ignition off.
Disconnect the Anti-Lock Brake Module harness connector.
Disconnect the Left Front WSS harness connector.
Using a 12-volt test light connected to 12-volts, probe the (B9) Left Front WSS Supply circuit.

Does the test light illuminate brightly?

Yes

- Repair the (B9) Left Front WSS Supply circuit for a short to ground.
- Perform ABS VERIFICATION TEST - VER 1.

No

- Go To 5

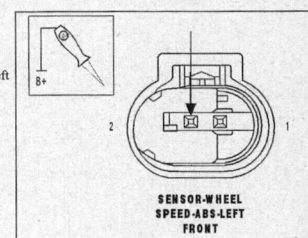

Fig. 15   Code C100A, C1015, C1020, C102B & C1036: Wheel Speed Sensor Circuit (Part 3 of 8). 2004–06

7. CHECK (B8) LEFT FRONT WSS SIGNAL CIRCUIT SHORT TO GROUND

Turn the ignition off.
Disconnect the Anti-Lock Brake Module harness connector.
Disconnect the Left Front WSS harness connector.
Using a 12-volt test light connected to 12-volts, probe the (B8) Left Front WSS Signal circuit.

Does the test light illuminate brightly?

Yes

- Repair the (B8) Left Front WSS Signal circuit for a short to ground.
- Perform ABS VERIFICATION TEST - VER 1.

No

- Go To 8

8. CHECK (B8) LEFT FRONT WSS SIGNAL CIRCUIT OPEN

Turn the ignition off.
Disconnect the Anti-Lock Brake Module harness connector.
Disconnect the Left Front WSS harness connector.
Connect a jumper wire between the (B8) Left Front WSS Signal circuit and ground.
Using a 12-volt test light connected to 12-volts, probe the (B8) Left Front WSS Signal circuit.

Does the test light illuminate brightly?

Yes

- Go To 9

No

- Repair the (B8) Left Front WSS Signal circuit for an open.
- Perform ABS VERIFICATION TEST - VER 1.

Fig. 15   Code C100A, C1015, C1020, C102B & C1036: Wheel Speed Sensor Circuit (Part 5 of 8). 2004–06

9. CHECK (B8) LEFT FRONT WSS SIGNAL CIRCUIT AND (B9) LEFT FRONT WSS SUPPLY CIRCUIT SHORT TOGETHER

Turn the ignition off.
Disconnect the Anti-Lock Brake Module harness connector.
Disconnect the Left Front WSS harness connector.
Measure the resistance between the (B8) Left Front WSS Signal circuit and the (B9) Left Front WSS Supply circuit.

Is the resistance above 5.0 ohms?

Yes

- Go To 10

No

- Repair the (B8) Left Front WSS Signal circuit and the (B9) Left Front WSS Supply circuit for a short together.
- Perform ABS VERIFICATION TEST - VER 1.

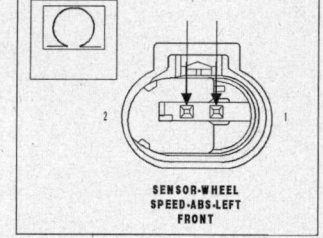

SENSOR-WHEEL
SPEED-ABS-LEFT
FRONT

10. CHECK LEFT FRONT WSS

Turn the ignition off.
Reconnect all connectors.
Disconnect the Left Front WSS harness connector.
Turn the ignition on.
Measure the voltage of the (B9) Left Front WSS Supply circuit while reconnecting the Left Front WSS harness connector.

Did the (B9) Left Front WSS Supply circuit drop voltage to 0 volts?

Yes

- Replace the Left Front WSS

- Perform ABS VERIFICATION TEST - VER 1.

No

- Go To 11

SENSOR-WHEEL
SPEED-ABS-LEFT
FRONT

LTV0500000005731

Fig. 15   Code C100A, C1015, C1020, C102B & C1036: Wheel Speed Sensor Circuit (Part 6 of 8). 2004–06

13. ANTI-LOCK BRAKE MODULE INTERNAL FAULT - (B8) LEFT FRONT WSS SIGNAL CIRCUIT

Turn the ignition off.
Remove the Anti-Lock Brake Module harness connector strain relief to access wires.
Reconnect the Anti-Lock Brake Module harness connector.
Turn the ignition on.
Measure the voltage between the (B9) Left Front WSS Supply circuit and the (B8) Left Front WSS Signal circuit.

Is the voltage above 10 volts?

Yes

- Refer to the INTERMITTENT CONDITIONS

- Perform APS VERIFICATION TEST - VER 1.

No

- Replace the Anti-Lock Brake Module
- Perform ABS VERIFICATION TEST - VER 1.

MODULE-ANTILOCK
BRAKES

LTV0500000005733

Fig. 15   Code C100A, C1015, C1020, C102B & C1036: Wheel Speed Sensor Circuit (Part 8 of 8). 2004–06

11. CHECK LEFT FRONT WSS OUTPUT

Turn the ignition off.
Reconnect all connectors.
Turn the ignition on.
Measure the amperage of the (B8) Left Front WSS Signal circuit in the Left Front WSS harness connector.
Slowly rotate the Left Front wheel.

Does the amperage toggle between 7 mA to 14 mA?

Yes

- Go To 12

No

- Replace the Left Front WSS
- Perform ABS VERIFICATION TEST - VER 1.

SENSOR-WHEEL
SPEED-ABS-LEFT
FRONT

12. ANTI-LOCK BRAKE MODULE INTERNAL FAULT - (B9) LEFT FRONT WSS SUPPLY CIRCUIT

Turn the ignition off.
Remove the Anti-Lock Brake Module harness connector strain relief to access wires.
Reconnect the Anti-Lock Brake Module harness connector.
Turn the ignition on.
Measure the voltage between the (B9) Left Front WSS Supply circuit and ground.

Is the voltage above 10 volts?

Yes

- Go To 13

No

- Replace the Anti-Lock Brake Module
- Perform ABS VERIFICATION TEST - VER 1.

MODULE-ANTILOCK
BRAKES

LTV0500000005732

Fig. 15   Code C100A, C1015, C1020, C102B & C1036: Wheel Speed Sensor Circuit (Part 7 of 8). 2004–06

Diagnostic Test

1. CHECK FOR DTC C1011–LEFT FRONT WHEEL SPEED SENSOR INPUT SIGNAL ERRATIC PERFORMANCE

NOTE: This DTC must be active for the results of this test to be valid.

Turn the ignition on.
With the scan tool, record and erase DTC's.
Cycle the ignition switch from off to on.
With the scan tool, read DTC's

NOTE: The Anti-Lock Brake Module must sense ALL 4 wheels at 12 km/h (7.5 mph) before it will extinguish the ABS indicators.

Does the scan tool display: C1011–LEFT FRONT WHEEL SPEED SENSOR INPUT SIGNAL ERRATIC PERFORMANCE and C100A–LEFT FRONT WHEEL SPEED SENSOR CIRCUIT?

Yes

- Refer to C100A–Left Front Wheel Speed Sensor Circuit for the related symptom(s).
- Perform ABS VERIFICATION TEST - VER 1.

No

- Go To 2

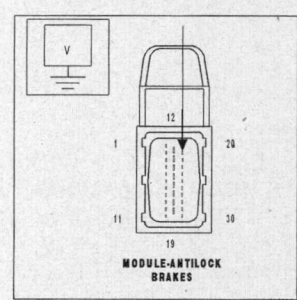

2. CHECK WHEEL SPEED SENSOR SIGNALS

Turn the ignition on.
With the scan tool, monitor ALL the WSS speeds while an assistant drives the vehicle.
Slowly accelerate as straight as possible from a stop to 40 km/h (25 m.p.h.).

Is the Left Front WSS speed showing 0 km/h (0 m.p.h.) or not matching other wheel speeds?

Yes   No

- Go To 3   - Refer to the INTERMITTENT CONDITIONS

                   - Perform APS VERIFICATION TEST - VER 1.

LTV0500000005734

Fig. 16   Code C1011, C101C, C1027, C1032 & C103D: Wheel Speed Sensor Input Signal Erratic Performance (Part 1 of 5). 2004–06

3. CHECK LEFT FRONT WSS LOOSENESS, INSPECT B8,B9 CIRCUITS/CONNECTORS/TERMINALS FOR DAMAGE

NOTE: Check all terminals for broken, bent, pushed out, or corroded terminals.

Turn the ignition off.
Inspect the Anti-Lock Brake Module harness connector, Left Front WSS, and Left Front WSS harness connector.
Inspect the Left Front WSS for looseness and not properly fastened.
Inspect the (B8) Left Front WSS Signal and (B9) Left Front WSS Supply circuits between the Left Front WSS and Anti-Lock Brake Module for damage.

Is the Left Front WSS loose or any of the wiring/connectors/terminals damaged?

Yes

- Repair as necessary.
- Perform ABS VERIFICATION TEST - VER 1.

No

- Go To 4

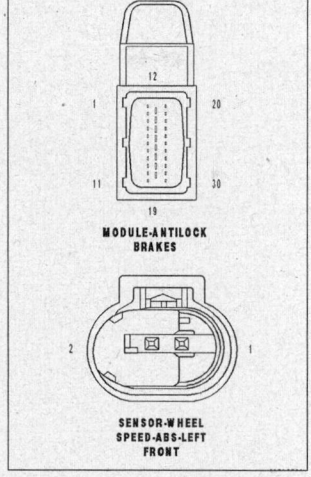

LTV0500000005735

Fig. 16 Code C1011, C101C, C1027, C1032 & C103D: Wheel Speed Sensor Input Signal Erratic Performance (Part 2 of 5). 2004–06

6. CHECK LEFT FRONT WHEEL BEARING DAMAGE

Turn the ignition off.
Inspect the Left Front wheel bearing for excessive runout or clearance.

NOTE: Refer to the appropriate service information, if necessary, for procedures or specifications.

Is the Left Front Wheel Bearing damaged?

Yes

- Repair as necessary.
- Perform ABS VERIFICATION TEST - VER 1.

No

- Go To 7

7. CHECK LEFT FRONT BRAKE HARDWARE DAMAGE

Turn the ignition off.
Visually inspect the Left Front brake linings for contamination or overheating. Check for dragging, bent, or seized components/hardware.

Is any brake lining, component, or hardware damaged?

Yes

- Repair as necessary.
- Perform ABS VERIFICATION TEST - VER 1.

No

- Go To 8

LTV0500000005737

Fig. 16 Code C1011, C101C, C1027, C1032 & C103D: Wheel Speed Sensor Input Signal Erratic Performance (Part 4 of 5). 2004–06

4. CHECK LEFT FRONT TONE WHEEL FOR DAMAGE

Turn the ignition off.
Inspect the Left Front Tone Wheel for damage, missing teeth, cracks, or looseness.

NOTE: The Tone Wheel teeth should be perfectly square, not bent, or nicked.

Is the Left Front Tone Wheel damaged?

Yes

- Repair as necessary.
- Perform ABS VERIFICATION TEST - VER 1.

No

- Go To 5

5. CHECK LEFT FRONT WSS AIR GAP

Turn the ignition off.
Using a feeler gauge, measure the Left Front WSS air gap.

NOTE: Refer to the appropriate service information, if necessary, for procedures or specifications.

Is the Left Front WSS air gap within specifications?

Yes

- Go To 6

No

- Repair as necessary.
- Perform ABS VERIFICATION TEST - VER 1.

LTV0500000005736

Fig. 16 Code C1011, C101C, C1027, C1032 & C103D: Wheel Speed Sensor Input Signal Erratic Performance (Part 3 of 5). 2004–06

8. ANTI-LOCK BRAKE MODULE – INTERNAL FAULT

Turn the ignition off.
Replace the Left Front WSS.
With the scan tool, erase DTC's.
Road test the vehicle over 40 km/h (25 m.p.h.).
Turn the ignition on.
With the scan tool, read DTC's

Did the DTC C1011–LEFT FRONT WHEEL SPEED SENSOR INPUT SIGNAL ERRATIC PERFORMANCE reset?

Yes

- Replace the Anti-Lock Brake Module
- Perform ABS VERIFICATION TEST - VER 1.

No

- Test Complete.

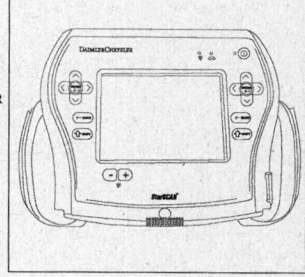

LTV0500000005738

Fig. 16 Code C1011, C101C, C1027, C1032 & C103D: Wheel Speed Sensor Input Signal Erratic Performance (Part 5 of 5). 2004–06

Diagnostic Test

1. CHECK FOR DTC C1014–LEFT FRONT WHEEL SPEED COMPARATIVE PERFORMANCE

NOTE: This DTC must be active for the results of this test to be valid.

Turn the ignition on.
With the scan tool, record and erase DTC's.
Cycle the ignition switch from off to on.
With the scan tool, read DTC's

NOTE: The Anti-Lock Brake Module must sense ALL 4 wheels at 12 km/h (7.5 m.p.h.) before it will extinguish the ABS indicators.

Does the scan tool display: C1014–LEFT FRONT WHEEL SPEED COMPARATIVE PERFORMANCE and C100A–LEFT FRONT WHEEL SPEED SENSOR CIRCUIT?

Yes

- Refer to C100A–Left Front Wheel Speed Sensor Circuit for the related symptom(s).
- Perform ABS VERIFICATION TEST - VER 1.

No

- Go To 2
-

2. CHECK WHEEL SPEED SENSOR SIGNALS

Turn the ignition on.
With the scan tool, monitor ALL the WSS speeds while an assistant drives the vehicle.
Slowly accelerate as straight as possible from a stop to 40 km/h (25 m.p.h.).

Is the Left Front WSS speed showing 0 km/h (0 m.p.h.) or not matching other wheel speeds?

Yes

- Go To 3

No

- Refer to the INTERMITTENT CONDITIONS
- Perform APS VERIFICATION TEST - VER 1.

LTV0500000005739

Fig. 17   Code C1014, C101F, C102A, C1035 & C1040: Wheel Speed Comparative Performance (Part 1 of 4). 2004–06

4. CHECK LEFT FRONT TIRE PRESSURE/INSPECT ALL TIRES

Turn the ignition off.
Check and adjust the Left Front Tire pressure.
Check and adjust all other tire pressures.
Inspect for mismatched tires on vehicle.

Is the Left Front Tire improperly inflated or mismatched tires on vehicle?

Yes

- Repair as necessary.
- Perform ABS VERIFICATION TEST - VER 1.

No

- Go To 5

5. CHECK LEFT FRONT TONE WHEEL FOR DAMAGE

Turn the ignition off.
Inspect the Left Front Tone Wheel for damage, missing teeth, cracks, or looseness.

NOTE: The Tone Wheel teeth should be perfectly square, not bent, or nicked.

Is the Left Front Tone Wheel damaged?

Yes

- Repair as necessary.
- Perform ABS VERIFICATION TEST - VER 1.

No

- Go To 6

LTV0500000005741

Fig. 17   Code C1014, C101F, C102A, C1035 & C1040: Wheel Speed Comparative Performance (Part 3 of 4). 2004–06

3. CHECK LEFT FRONT WSS LOOSENESS, INSPECT B8,B9 CIRCUITS/CONNECTORS/TERMINALS FOR DAMAGE

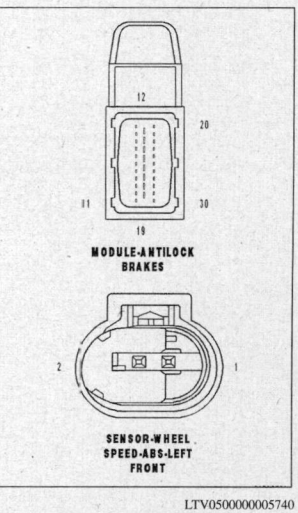

NOTE: Check all terminals for broken, bent, pushed out, or corroded terminals.

Turn the ignition off.
Inspect the Anti-Lock Brake Module harness connector, Left Front WSS, and Left Front WSS harness connector.
Inspect the Left Front WSS for looseness and not properly fastened.
Inspect the (B8) Left Front WSS Signal and (B9) Left Front WSS Supply circuits between the Left Front WSS and Anti-Lock Brake Module for damage.

Is the Left Front WSS loose or any of the wiring/connectors/terminals damaged?

Yes

- Repair as necessary.
- Perform ABS VERIFICATION TEST - VER 1.

No

- Go To 4

LTV0500000005740

Fig. 17   Code C1014, C101F, C102A, C1035 & C1040: Wheel Speed Comparative Performance (Part 2 of 4). 2004–06

6. CHECK LEFT FRONT BRAKE HARDWARE DAMAGE

Turn the ignition off.
Visually inspect the Left Front brake linings for contamination or overheating. Check for dragging, bent, or seized components/hardware.

Is any brake lining, component, or hardware damaged?

Yes

- Repair as necessary.
- Perform ABS VERIFICATION TEST - VER 1.

No

- Go To 7

7. ANTI-LOCK BRAKE MODULE – INTERNAL FAULT

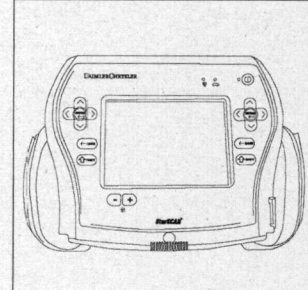

Turn the ignition off.
Replace the Left Front WSS.
With the scan tool, erase DTC's.
Road test the vehicle over 40 km/h (25 m.p.h.).
Turn the ignition on.
With the scan tool, read DTC's

Did the DTC C1014–LEFT FRONT WHEEL SPEED COMPARATIVE PERFORMANCE reset?

Yes

- Replace the Anti-Lock Brake Module
- Perform ABS VERIFICATION TEST - VER 1.

No

- Test Complete.

LTV0500000005742

Fig. 17   Code C1014, C101F, C102A, C1035 & C1040: Wheel Speed Comparative Performance (Part 4 of 4). 2004–06

Diagnostic Test

1. HIGH RESISTANCE IN B+ CIRCUITS

Turn key off.
Disconnect the ABM harness connector.

NOTE: Check connector - Clean/repair as necessary.

Turn key on, engine off.
With a test light connected to ground check (A107) Fused B+,
(A111) Fused B+ and (F500) Fused ignition switch output.

Is the test light bright like when connected to the battery?

Yes

- Go to 2

No

- Repair the high resistance in the circuits.
- Perform ABS VERIFICATION TEST — VER 1.

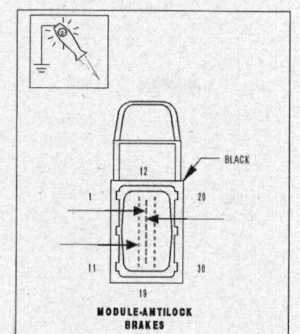

2. HIGH RESISTANCE IN GROUND CIRCUITS

With a test light Connected to B+ check (Z923) Ground and (Z107) Ground.

Is the test light bright like when connected to the battery?

Yes

- Replace the ABM per service information.
- Perform ABS VERIFICATION TEST — VER 1.

No

- Repair the high resistance in the circuits.
- Perform ABS VERIFICATION TEST — VER 1.

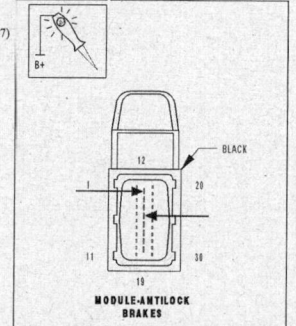

LTV0500000005743

Fig. 18   Code C1050, C1054, C1058, C105C, C1060, C1064, C1068, C106C, C1070 & C1074: Inlet Valve Control Circuit Low. 2004–06

1. CHECK FOR DTC C107B–WHEEL SPEED COMPARATIVE PERFORMANCE

Turn the ignition on.
With the scan tool, record and erase DTC's.
Cycle the ignition switch from off to on.
With the scan tool, read DTC's

NOTE: The Anti-Lock Brake Module must sense ALL 4 wheels at 12 km/h (7.5 m.p.h.) before it will extinguish the ABS indicators.

Does the scan tool display: C107B–WHEEL SPEED COMPARATIVE PERFORMANCE?

Yes

- Go To 2

No

- Refer to the INTERMITTENT CONDITIONS
- Perform APS VERIFICATION TEST - VER 1.

2. CHECK WHEEL SPEED SENSOR SIGNALS

Turn the ignition on.
With the scan tool, monitor ALL the WSS speeds while an assistant drives the vehicle.
Slowly accelerate as straight as possible from a stop to 40 km/h (25 m.p.h.)

Is one or more WSS speeds showing 0 km/h (0 m.p.h.) or not matching other wheel speeds?

Yes

- Go To 3

No

- Refer to the INTERMITTENT CONDITIONS
- Perform APS VERIFICATION TEST - VER 1.

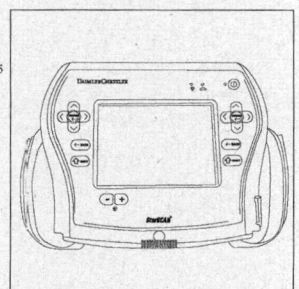

LTV0500000005746

Fig. 21   Code C107B: Wheel Speed Comparative Performance (Part 1 of 4). 2004–06

Possible Causes
INCORRECT VALUE PROGRAMED INTO ABM

Diagnostic Test

1. INCORRECT VALUE PROGRAMED INTO ABM

Verify the correct Tire/wheel information is programed in the ABM.

Is the correct value programed is the ABM acording to the chart?

Yes

- Test complete.
- Perform ABS VERIFICATION TEST — VER 1.

No

- Program the correct Tire/Wheel information in the ABM.
- Perform ABS VERIFICATION TEST — VER 1.

LTV0500000005744

Fig. 19   Code C1078: Tire Revolutions Range Performance. 2004–06

Possible Causes
WRONG TONE WHEEL PROGRAMED INTO THE ABM

Diagnostic Test

1. WRONG TONE WHEEL PROGRAMED INTO THE ABM

Compair the programed tone wheel value in the ABM to the actual tone wheels on the vehicle.

Is the ABM programed correctly?

Yes

- Test Complete.
- Perform ABS VERIFICATION TEST VER — 1.

No

- Reprogram the ABM with the correct values.
- Perform ABS VERIFICATION TEST VER — 1.

LTV0500000005745

Fig. 20   Code C1079: Tone Wheel Teeth Count Range Performance. 2004–06

3. CHECK WSS LOOSENESS, INSPECT SIGNAL,SUPPLY CIRCUITS/CONNECTORS/TERMINALS FOR DAMAGE

NOTE: Check all terminals for broken, bent, pushed out, or corroded terminals.

Turn the ignition off.
Inspect the Anti-Lock Brake Module harness connector, each WSS, and each WSS harness connector.
Inspect each WSS for looseness and not properly fastened.
Inspect each WSS Signal and WSS Supply circuits between each WSS and Anti-Lock Brake Module for damage.

Is any WSS loose or any of the wiring/connectors/terminals damaged?

Yes

- Repair as necessary.
- Perform ABS VERIFICATION TEST - VER 1.

No

- Go To 4

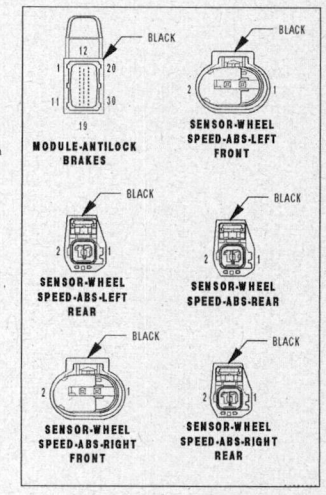

LTV0500000005747

Fig. 21   Code C107B: Wheel Speed Comparative Performance (Part 2 of 4). 2004–06

4. CHECK BRAKE SYSTEM

Turn the ignition off.
Check the brake fluid level.
Check for trapped air in brake lines.
Inspect for brake fluid leakage on vehicle.
Inspect for loose mounted brake hardware.

Is any of the above conditions present?

Yes

- Repair as necessary.
- Perform ABS VERIFICATION TEST - VER 1.

No

- Go To 5

5. CHECK EACH TONE WHEEL FOR DAMAGE

Turn the ignition off.
Inspect each Tone Wheel for damage, missing teeth, cracks, or looseness.

NOTE: The Tone Wheel teeth should be perfectly square, not bent, or nicked.

Is the Tone Wheels damaged?

Yes

- Repair as necessary.
- Perform ABS VERIFICATION TEST - VER 1.

No

- Go To 6

LTV0500000005748

Fig. 21   Code C107B: Wheel Speed Comparative Performance (Part 3 of 4). 2004–06

1. HIGH RESISTANCE IN B+ CIRCUITS

Turn key off.
Disconnect the ABM harness connector.

NOTE: Check connector - Clean/repair as necessary.

Turn key on, engine off.
With a test light connected to ground check (A107) Fused B+, (A111) Fused B+ and (F500) Fused ignition switch output.

Is the test light bright like when connected to the battery?

Yes

- Go to 2

No

- Repair the high resistance in the circuits.
- Perform ABS VERIFICATION TEST — VER 1.

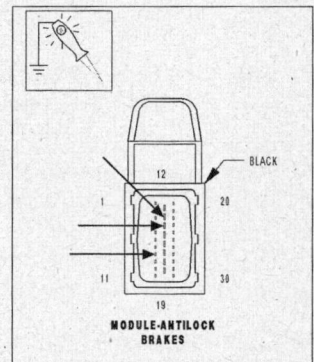

2. HIGH RESISTANCE IN GROUND CIRCUITS

With a test light Connected to B+ check (Z923) Ground and (Z107) Ground.

Is the test light bright like when connected to the battery?

Yes

- Replace the ABM
- Perform ABS VERIFICATION TEST — VER 1.

No

- Repair the high resistance in the circuits.
- Perform ABS VERIFICATION TEST — VER 1.

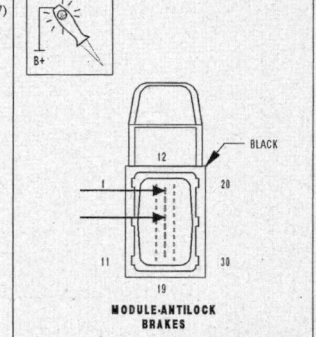

LTV0500000005750

Fig. 22   Code C1201, C1205, C1209 & C120D: Traction Control Inlet Valve Circuit Fault. 2004–06

6. ANTI-LOCK BRAKE MODULE – INTERNAL FAULT

Turn the ignition off.
Replace all WSS's.
With the scan tool, erase DTC's.
Road test the vehicle over 40 km/h (25 m.p.h.).
Turn the ignition on.
With the scan tool, read DTC's

Did the DTC C107B–WHEEL SPEED COMPARATIVE PERFORMANCE reset?

Yes

- Replace the Anti-Lock Brake Module
- Perform ABS VERIFICATION TEST - VER 1.

No

- Test Complete.

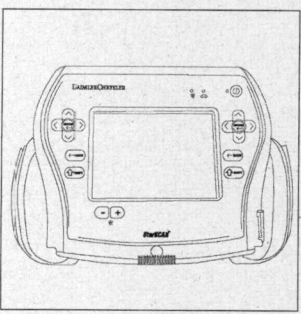

LTV0500000005749

Fig. 21   Code C107B: Wheel Speed Comparative Performance (Part 4 of 4). 2004–06

1. (B24) G-SENSOR SUPPLY CIRCUIT OPEN

Turn the ignition off.
Disconnect the Anti-Lock Brake Module harness connector.
Disconnect the G-Sensor harness connector.

NOTE: Check connector - Clean/repair as necessary.

Measure the resistance of the (B24) G-Sensor Supply circuit from the G-Sensor harness connector to the Anti-Lock Brake Module.

Is the resistance above 5 ohms?

Yes

- Repair the open (B24) G-Sensor Supply circuit.
- Perform ABS VERIFICATION TEST - VER 1.

No

- Go to 2
-

2. (B24) G-SENSOR SUPPLY CIRCUIT SHORTED TO GROUND

Measure the resistance of the (B24) G-Sensor Supply circuit from the G-Sensor harness connector to ground.

Is the resistance below 5 ohms?

Yes

- Repair the (B24) G-Sensor Supply circuit shorted to ground.
- Perform ABS VERIFICATION TEST - VER 1.

No

- Go to 3

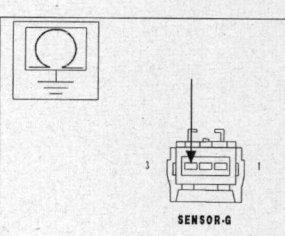

LTV0500000005752

Fig. 23   Code C1210 & C1213: G Sensor Fault (Part 1 of 3). 2004–06

3. (B23) G-SENSOR SIGNAL CIRCUIT OPEN

Measure the resistance of the (B23) G-Sensor Signal circuit from the G-Sensor harness connector to the Anti-Lock Brake Module.

Is the resistance above 5 ohms?

Yes

- Repair the open (B23) G-Sensor Signal circuit.
- Perform ABS VERIFICATION TEST - VER 1.

No

- Go to 4

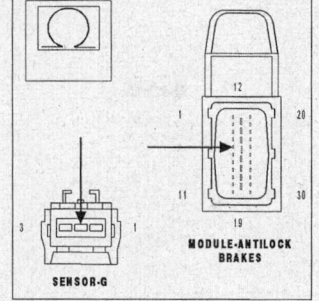

4. (B23) G-SENSOR SIGNAL CIRCUIT SHORTED TO GROUND

Measure the resistance of the (B23) G-Sensor Signal circuit from the G-Sensor harness connector to ground.

Is the resistance below 5 ohms?

Yes

- Repair the (B23) G-Sensor Signal circuit shorted to ground.
- Perform ABS VERIFICATION TEST - VER 1.

No

- Go to 5

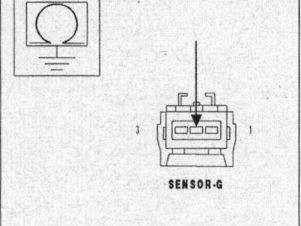

LTV0500000005753

Fig. 23   Code C1210 & C1213: G Sensor Fault (Part 2 of 3). 2004–06

1. LOW VOLTAGE AT THE ABM

With the scan tool read battery voltage and ignition voltage in the ABM and compare the two reading to actual battery voltage from a voltmeter.

NOTE: Battery must be fully charged.

Are all readings within a half of volt?

Yes

- Replace the ABM
- Perform ABS VERIFICATION TEST — VER 1.

No

- Go To 2

2. ABM INTERNAL

Turn key off.
Disconnect the ABM harness connector.

NOTE: Check connector - Clean/repair as necessary.

Turn key on, engine off.
With a test light check (A107) Fused B+, (A111) Fused B+ and (F500) Fused ignition switch output.

Is test light bright like when connected to the battery?

Yes

- Replace the ABM
- Perform ABS VERIFICATION TEST — VER 1.

No

- Repair the high resistance in the circuits.
- Perform ABS VERIFICATION TEST — VER 1.

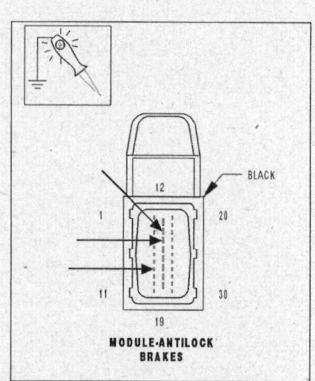

LTV0500000005755

Fig. 24   Code C2105: ABS Valve Low Circuit. 2004–06

5. (B924) G-SENSOR RETURN CIRCUIT OPEN

Measure the resistance of the (B924) G-Sensor Return circuit from the G-Sensor harness connector to the Anti-Lock Brake Module.

Is the resistance above 5 ohms?

Yes

- Repair the open (B924) G-Sensor Return circuit.
- Perform ABS VERIFICATION TEST - VER 1.

No

- Go to 6

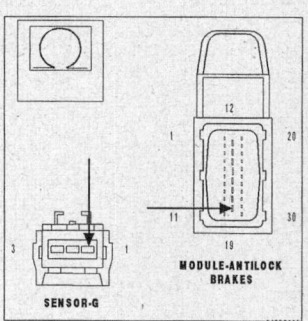

6. (B924) G-SENSOR RETURN CIRCUIT SHORTED TO GROUND

Measure the resistance of the (B924) G-Sensor Return circuit from the G-Sensor harness connector to ground.

Is the resistance below 5 ohms?

Yes

- Repair the (B924) G-Sensor Return circuit shorted to ground.
- Perform ABS VERIFICATION TEST - VER 1.

No

- Replace the G-Sensor.
- Perform ABS VERIFICATION TEST - VER 1.

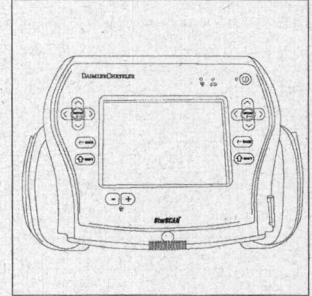

LTV0500000005754

Fig. 23   Code C1210 & C1213: G Sensor Fault (Part 3 of 3). 2004–06

1. ABM INTERNAL FAILURE DTC PRESENT

Turn the ignition on.
With the scan tool, read DTCs.
With the scan tool, erase DTCs.
Turn the ignition off.
Turn the ignition on.
With the scan tool, read DTCs.

Does the scan tool display ANTI—LOCK BRAKE MODULE INTERNAL FAILURE?

Yes

- Go To 2

No

- Refer to the INTERMITTENT CONDITIONS

2. CAB - GROUND CIRCUIT OPEN

Turn the ignition off.
Disconnect the ABM harness connector.
Note: Check clean connectors and terminals,.
Using a 12-volt test light connected to 12-volts, probe the ABM harness connector ground circuits.

Did the test light illuminate?

Yes

- Go To 3

No

- Repair the ABM Ground circuit for an open.
- Perform ABS VERIFICATION TEST - VER 1.

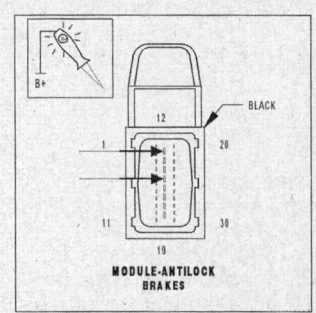

LTV0500000005756

Fig. 25   Code C2200: ABS Module Internal (Part 1 of 2). 2004–06

3. ABS FUSED B(+) CIRCUIT OPEN

Turn the ignition on.
Using a 12-volt test light connected to ground, probe the ABS
Fused B(+) circuit at the ABM harness connector.

Did the test light illuminate?

Yes

- Go To 4

No

- Repair the ABS Valve Fused B(+) circuit for an open.
- Perform ABS VERIFICATION TEST - VER 1.

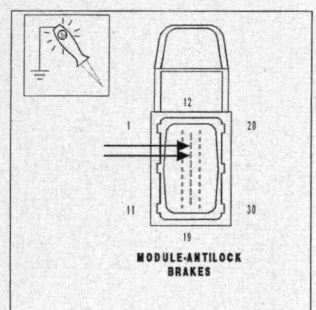

MODULE-ANTILOCK
BRAKES

4. ABS PUMP FUSED B(+) CIRCUIT OPEN

Using a 12-volt test light connected to ground, probe the ABS
Pump Fused B(+) circuit at the ABM harness connector.

Did the test light illuminate?

Yes

- Replace the Anti—lock brake module
- Perform ABS VERIFICATION TEST - VER 1.

No

- Repair the ABS Pump Fused B(+) circuit for an open.
- Perform ABS VERIFICATION TEST - VER 1.

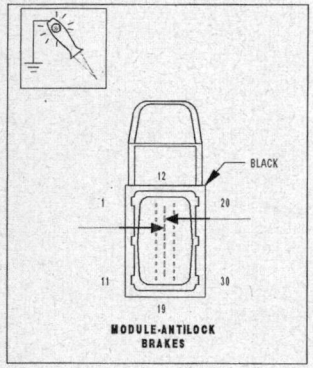

BLACK

MODULE-ANTILOCK
BRAKES

LTV0500000005757

**Fig. 25   Code C2200: ABS Module Internal
(Part 2 of 2). 2004–06**

Full Size Pickup

NOTE: On Air Bag Equipped Models, Refer To "Air Bag System Precautions" Located In The Front Of This Manual For System Disarming & Arming Procedures.

NOTE: Refer To "Computer Relearn Procedures" Located In The Front Of This Manual When Battery Power To The Computer Has Been Interrupted.

NOTE: Electrical Symbol & Wire Color Code Identification Located In The Front Of This Manual May Be Used As An Aid When Using Wiring Circuits Found In This Section.

INDEX

	Page No.		Page No.		Page No.
Description	5-77	Connector Pin Identification	5-77	(CAB) Module, Replace	5-77
Four Wheel Anti-Lock Brake (4 WABS) System	5-77	Diagnostic Tests	5-77	Front Wheel Speed Sensor, Replace	5-77
RWAL System	5-77	Diagnostic Trouble Code Interpretation	5-77	Hydraulic Control Unit (HCU), Replace	5-77
Diagnosis & Testing	5-77	Wiring Diagrams	5-77	Rear Wheel Speed Sensor, Replace	5-77
Accessing Diagnostic Trouble Codes	5-77	System Service	5-77		
Clearing Diagnostic Trouble Codes	5-77	Brake System Bleed	5-77		
		Component Replacement	5-77		
		Controller Anti-Lock Brake			

DESCRIPTION

RWAL SYSTEM

The rear-wheel Anti-Lock Brake System (ABS) is standard equipment on all models. This system prevents rear wheel lock-up by monitoring wheel speed and altering pressure to the rear wheels. Rear brake fluid application is controlled according to wheel speed, degree of wheel slip and rate of deceleration. The main components of the system are an electronic brake control module, a hydraulic pressure control valve, a speed sensor and a sensor exciter ring, **Fig. 1.** A standard master cylinder and power booster are used.

FOUR WHEEL ANTI-LOCK BRAKE (4 WABS) SYSTEM

The 4 WABS System (ABS), is optional equipment for Full Size Van models. This system prevents wheel lock-up by monitoring wheel speed and altering pressure to each wheel. The main components of the system are a rear brake anti-lock valve, rear wheel speed sensor and exciter ring, front wheel speed sensors and tone rings, front brake anti-lock valve assembly, ABS control module and a combination valve. Refer to for electrical component locations.

DIAGNOSIS & TESTING

Accessing Diagnostic Trouble Codes

Connect a suitably programmed scan tool to Data Link Connector (DLC) and follow manufacturer's instructions.

Diagnostic Trouble Code Interpretation

Refer to "Diagnostic Chart Index" for diagnostic trouble code interpretation.

Connector Pin Identification

Refer to **Figs. 2 and 3** for pin connector and terminal identification.

Wiring Diagrams

Refer to **Figs. 4 through 6** for wiring diagrams.

Diagnostic Tests

For 2006 Full Size Pickups refer to "Durango" "Diagnostic tests" for test procedures. For 2002–05 Full Size Pickups refer to "Dakota" "Symptom Tests" for test procedures.

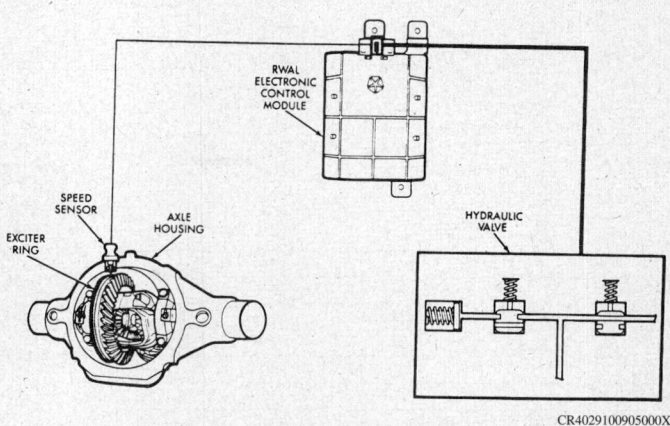

Fig. 1 RWAL brake system main components

Clearing Diagnostic Trouble Codes

Connect a suitably programmed scan tool to Data Link Connector (DLC) and follow manufacturer's instructions.

SYSTEM SERVICE

Brake System Bleed

The anti-lock brake system must be bled any time air enters the hydraulic system. It is important to note that excessive air in the brake system may set a primary pressure diagnostic trouble code in the control module.

Pressure or manual bleeding procedures can be used when bleeding the ABS system after hoses or brake lines have been disconnected. Bleeding the ABS hydraulic system is also necessary after replacement of the hydraulic assembly or wheel brakes. During bleeding procedures, ensure the brake fluid level remains close to the Full mark on the reservoir.

The brake lines may be pressure bled using a standard diaphragm type pressure bleeder. Only diaphragm type pressure bleeding equipment should be used in order to prevent air, moisture and other contaminants from entering the system. In addition, only DOT 3 brake fluid should be used.

Component Replacement

CONTROLLER ANTI-LOCK BRAKE (CAB) MODULE, REPLACE

1. Disconnect CAB electrical connector.
2. Remove CAB mounting bolts.
3. Disconnect pump electrical connector.
4. Remove ABM from HCU.

5. Reverse procedure to install.

HYDRAULIC CONTROL UNIT (HCU), REPLACE

1. Remove battery.
2. Disconnect HCU electrical connectors.
3. Remove brake lines from HCU.
4. Remove HCU mounting bolts, then HCU.
5. Reverse procedure to install.

FRONT WHEEL SPEED SENSOR, REPLACE

1. Raise and support vehicle.
2. Remove front tire and wheel assembly.
3. Remove brake rotor.
4. Remove sensor mounting bolt, then sensor.
5. Reverse procedure to install.

REAR WHEEL SPEED SENSOR, REPLACE

1. Raise and support vehicle.
2. Remove brake line from mounting stud.
3. Remove mounting stud from sensor and shield.
4. Remove sensor and shield from differential housing.
5. Disconnect sensor electrical connector.
6. Reverse procedure to install.

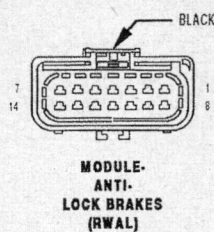

MODULE-
ANTI-
LOCK BRAKES
(RWAL)

CAV	CIRCUIT	FUNCTION
1	B222 18DG/WT	REAR WHEEL SPEED SENSOR (+)
2	D65 18WT/LG	CAN C BUS (+)
3	D64 18WT/LB	CAN C BUS (-)
4	F202 18PK/GY	FUSED IGNITION SWITCH OUTPUT (RUN)
5	B9 18DG/LG (5.7L)	LEFT FRONT WHEEL SPEED SENSOR (+)
6	Z107 14BK/DG	GROUND
7	A111 14DG/RD	FUSED B(+)
8	B22 18DG/YL	REAR WHEEL SPEED SENSOR (-)
9	B29 18DG/WT	BRAKE SWITCH NO. 1 SIGNAL
10	B8 18DG/TN (5.7L)	LEFT FRONT WHEEL SPEED SENSOR (-)
11	-	
12	-	
13	-	
14	-	

LTV0500000005611

Fig. 2   Controller Anti-Lock Brake (CAB) connector & terminal identification.

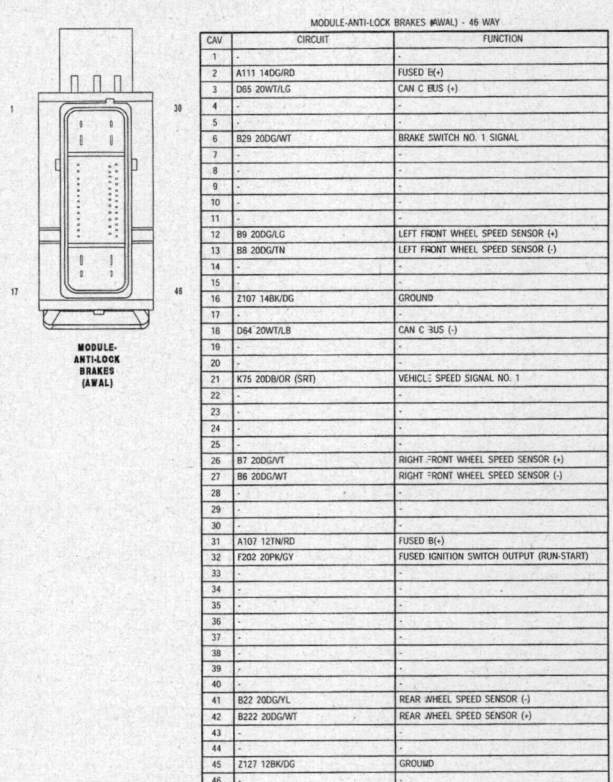

MODULE-ANTI-LOCK BRAKES (AWAL) - 46 WAY

CAV	CIRCUIT	FUNCTION
2	A111 14DG/RD	FUSED B(+)
3	D65 20WT/LG	CAN C BUS (+)
4	-	
5	-	
6	B29 20DG/WT	BRAKE SWITCH NO. 1 SIGNAL
7	-	
8	-	
9	-	
10	-	
11	-	
12	B9 20DG/LG	LEFT FRONT WHEEL SPEED SENSOR (+)
13	B8 20DG/TN	LEFT FRONT WHEEL SPEED SENSOR (-)
14	-	
15	-	
16	Z107 14BK/DG	GROUND
17	-	
18	D64 20WT/LB	CAN C BUS (-)
19	-	
20	-	
21	K75 20DB/OR (SRT)	VEHICLE SPEED SIGNAL NO. 1
22	-	
23	-	
24	-	
25	-	
26	B7 20DG/VT	RIGHT FRONT WHEEL SPEED SENSOR (+)
27	B6 20DG/WT	RIGHT FRONT WHEEL SPEED SENSOR (-)
28	-	
29	-	
30	-	
31	A107 12TN/RD	FUSED B(+)
32	F202 20PK/GY	FUSED IGNITION SWITCH OUTPUT (RUN-START)
33	-	
34	-	
35	-	
36	-	
37	-	
38	-	
39	-	
40	-	
41	B22 20DG/YL	REAR WHEEL SPEED SENSOR (-)
42	B222 20DG/WT	REAR WHEEL SPEED SENSOR (+)
43	-	
44	-	
45	Z127 12BK/DG	GROUND
46	-	

LTV0500000005612

Fig. 3   Controller Anti-Lock Brake (CAB) connector & terminal identification.

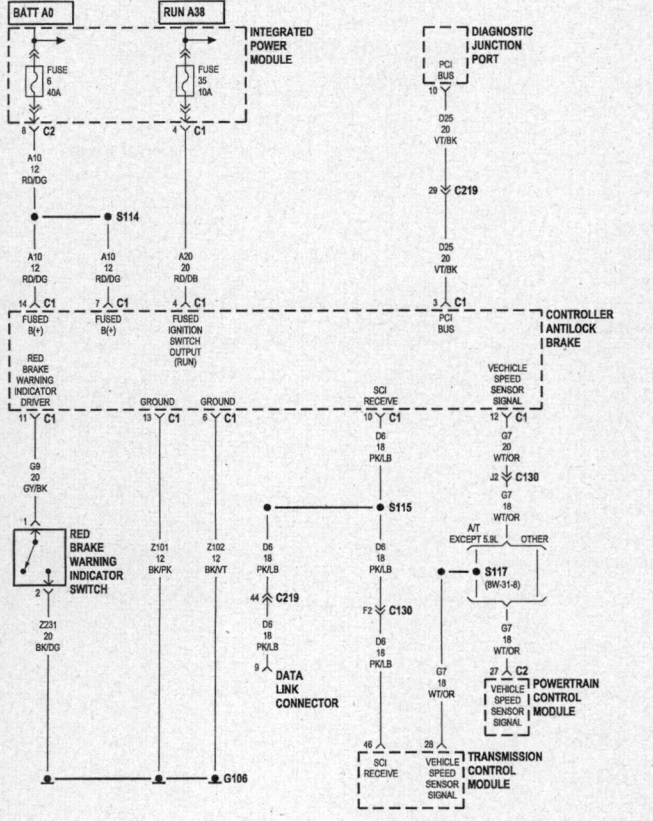

LTV0500000005613

Fig. 4   Wiring diagram (Part 1 of 2). 2002–04 w/RWAL

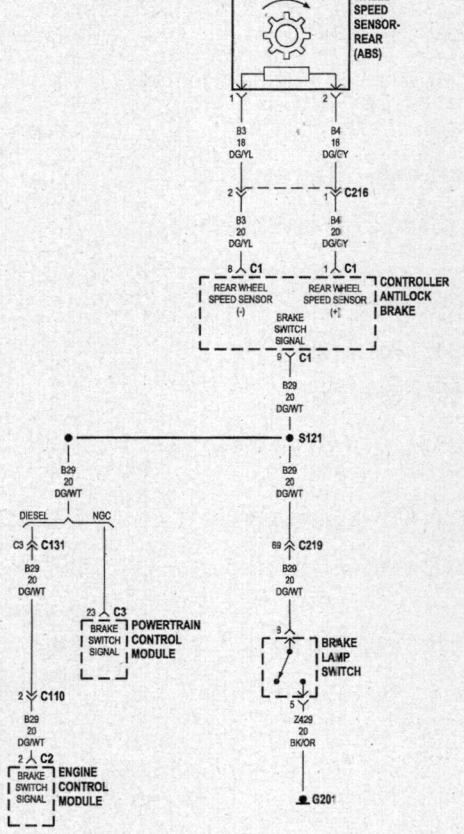

LTV0500000005614

Fig. 4   Wiring diagram (Part 2 of 2). 2002–04 w/RWAL

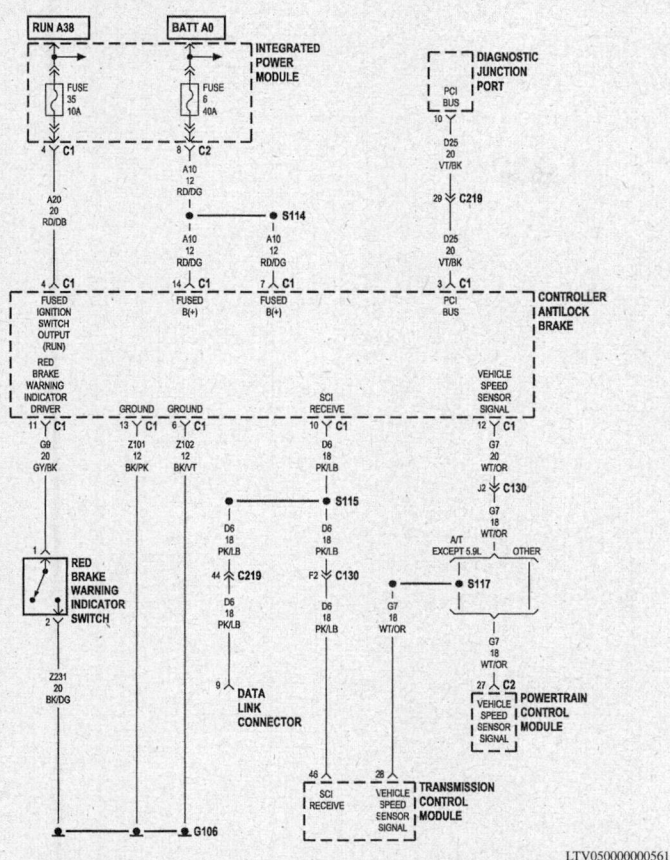

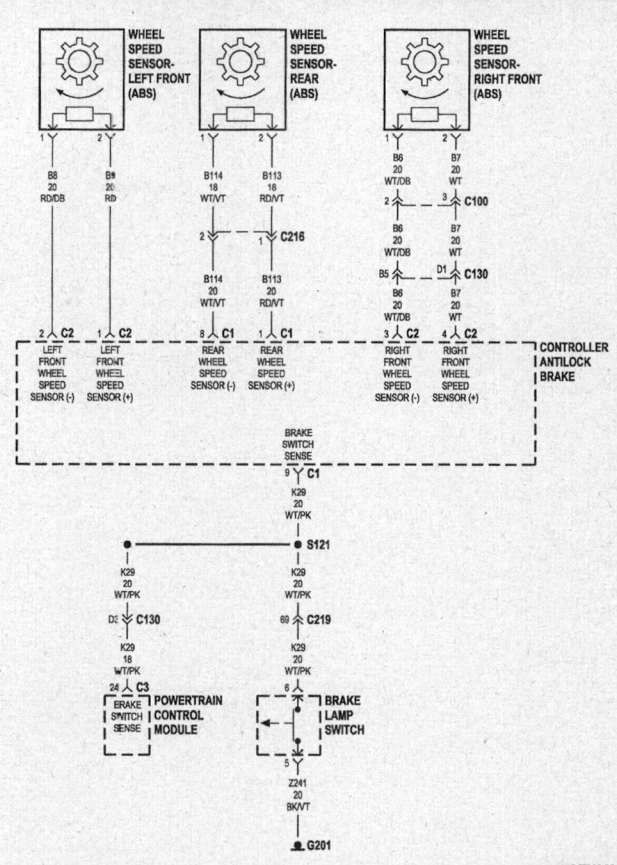

Fig. 5   Wiring diagram (Part 1 of 2). 2002–04 w/4 WABS

Fig. 5   Wiring diagram (Part 2 of 2). 2002–04 w/4 WABS

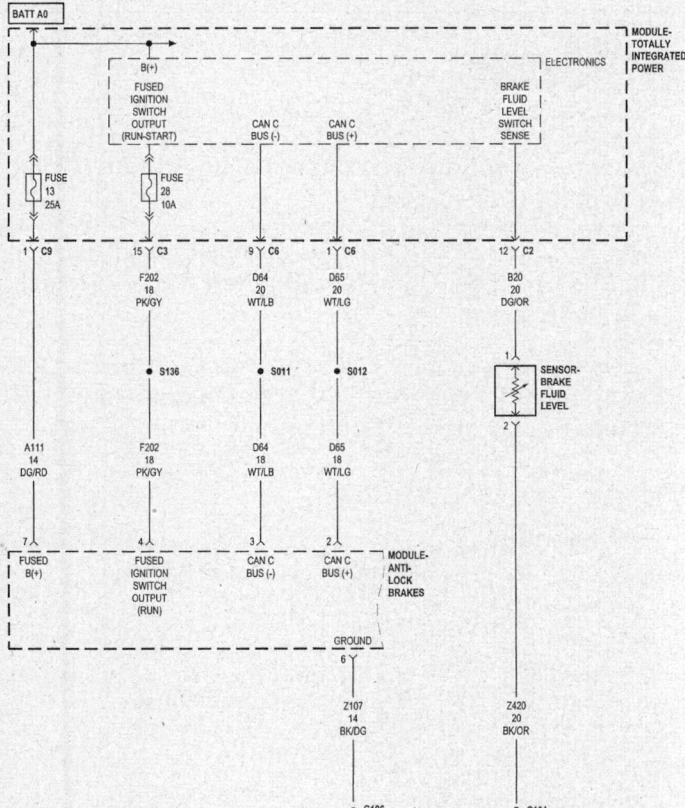

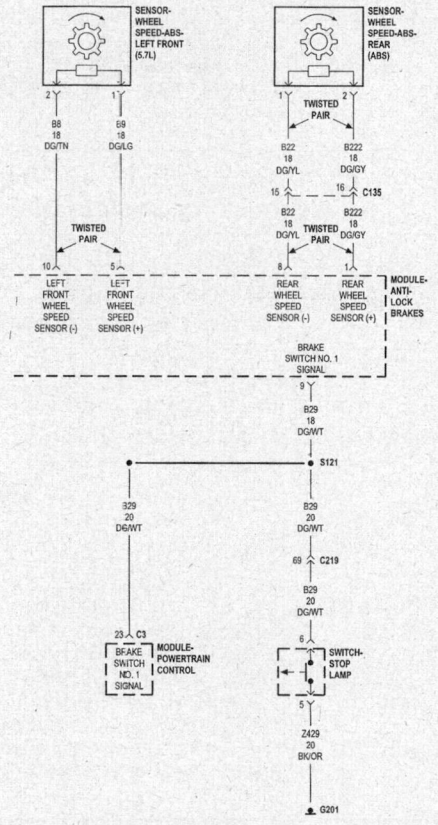

Fig. 6   Wiring diagram (Part 1 of 4). 2005–06

Fig. 6   Wiring diagram (Part 2 of 4). 2005–06

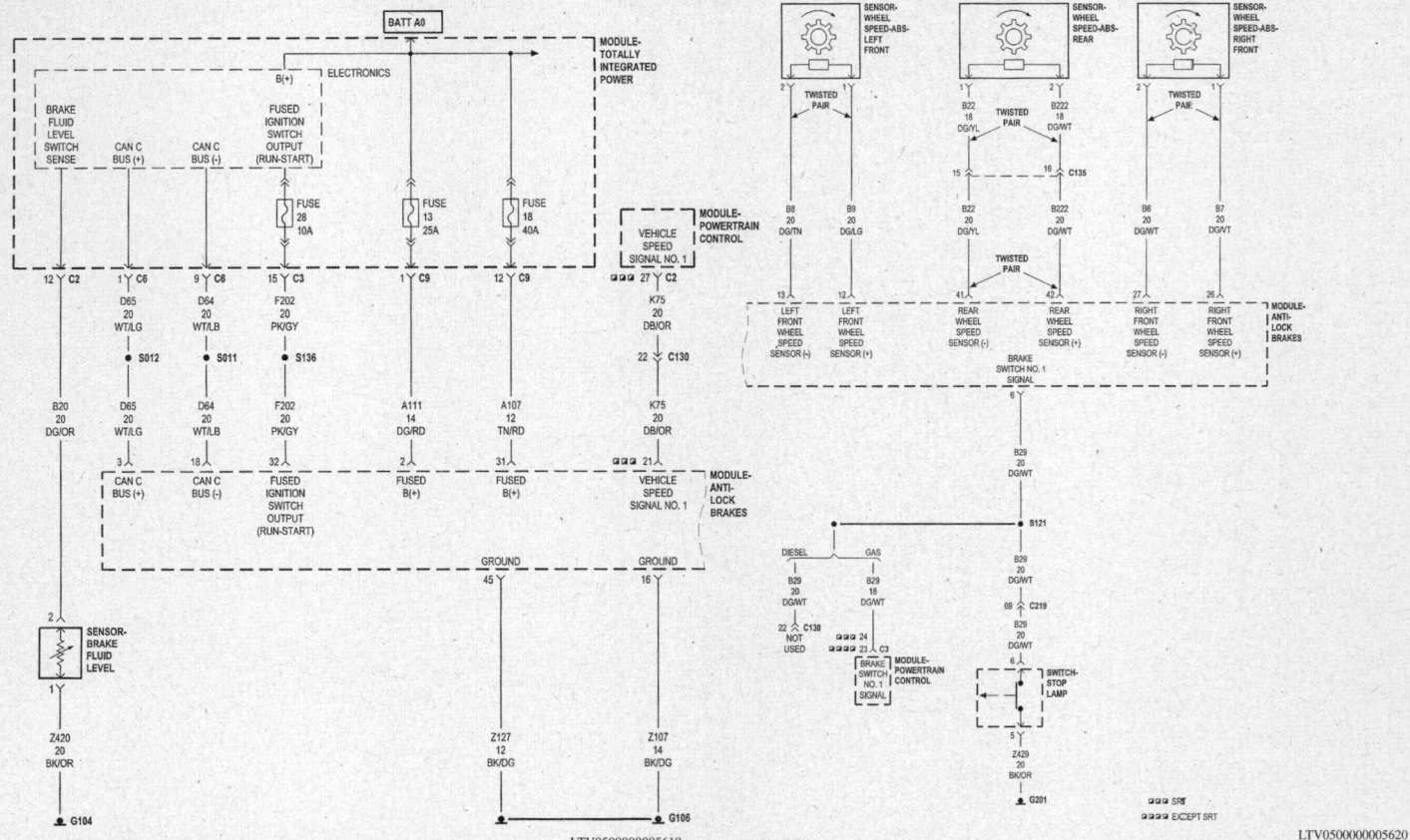

Fig. 6   Wiring diagram (Part 3 of 4). 2005–06

LTV0500000005619

Fig. 6   Wiring diagram (Part 4 of 4). 2005–06

LTV0500000005620

Full Size Van

NOTE: On Air Bag Equipped Models, Refer To "Air Bag System Precautions" Located In The Front Of This Manual For System Disarming & Arming Procedures.

NOTE: Refer To "Computer Relearn Procedures" Located In The Front Of This Manual When Battery Power To The Computer Has Been Interrupted.

NOTE: Electrical Symbol & Wire Color Code Identification Located In The Front Of This Manual May Be Used As An Aid When Using Wiring Circuits Found In This Section.

INDEX

	Page No.		Page No.		Page No.
Description	5-81	Diagnostic Trouble Code Interpretation	5-81	Front Wheel Speed Sensor, Replace	5-81
Four Wheel Anti-Lock Brake (4 WABS) System	5-81	Symptom Tests	5-81	Hydraulic Control Unit (HCU), Replace	5-81
RWAL System	5-81	Wiring Diagrams	5-81	RWAL Valve, Replace	5-81
Diagnosis & Testing	5-81	System Service	5-81	Rear Wheel Speed Sensor, Replace	5-81
Accessing Diagnostic Trouble Codes	5-81	Brake System Bleed	5-81		
Clearing Diagnostic Trouble Codes	5-81	Component Replacement	5-81		
		Controller Anti-Lock Brake (CAB) Module, Replace	5-81		

DESCRIPTION

RWAL SYSTEM

The rear-wheel Anti-Lock Brake System (ABS) is standard equipment on all models. This system prevents rear wheel lock-up by monitoring wheel speed and altering pressure to the rear wheels. Rear brake fluid application is controlled according to wheel speed, degree of wheel slip and rate of deceleration. The main components of the system are an electronic brake control module, a hydraulic pressure control valve, a speed sensor and a sensor exciter ring. A standard master cylinder and power booster are used.

FOUR WHEEL ANTI-LOCK BRAKE (4 WABS) SYSTEM

The 4 WABS System (ABS), is optional equipment for Full Size Van models. This system prevents wheel lock-up by monitoring wheel speed and altering pressure to each wheel. The main components of the system are a rear brake anti-lock valve, rear wheel speed sensor and exciter ring, front wheel speed sensors and tone rings, front brake anti-lock valve assembly, ABS control module and a combination valve.

DIAGNOSIS & TESTING

Accessing Diagnostic Trouble Codes

Connect a suitably programmed scan tool to Data Link Connector (DLC) and follow manufacturer's instructions.

Diagnostic Trouble Code Interpretation

Refer to "Diagnostic Chart Index" for diagnostic trouble code interpretation.

Wiring Diagrams

Refer to **Fig. 1** for wiring diagrams.

Symptom Tests

Refer to "Dakota" "Symptom Tests" for test procedures.

Clearing Diagnostic Trouble Codes

Connect a suitably programmed scan tool to Data Link Connector (DLC) and follow manufacturer's instructions.

SYSTEM SERVICE

Brake System Bleed

ABS system bleeding requires conventional bleeding methods plus use of the DRB scan tool. The procedure involves performing a base brake bleeding, followed by use of the scan tool to cycle and bleed the HCU pump and solenoids. A second base brake bleeding procedure is then required to remove any air remaining in the system.

Component Replacement

CONTROLLER ANTI-LOCK BRAKE (CAB) MODULE, REPLACE

1. Remove battery.
2. Remove power distribution center.
3. Remove battery and power distribution center mount.
4. Remove washer reservoir mounting screws.
5. Lift up reservoir and disconnect pump motor connector and hose.
6. Remove reservoir from engine compartment.
7. Disconnect CAB electrical connectors.
8. Disconnect pump motor electrical connector.
9. Remove CAB to HCU mounting screws, then remove CAB.
10. Reverse procedure to install.

FRONT WHEEL SPEED SENSOR, REPLACE

1. Raise and support vehicle.
2. Disconnect speed sensor electrical connector.
3. Remove speed sensor mounting bolt, then sensor.
4. Reverse procedure to install.

HYDRAULIC CONTROL UNIT (HCU), REPLACE

1. Remove left turn signal housing.
2. Remove extension panel under left turn signal housing opening.
3. Disconnect horn connector and remove access cover.
4. Remove washer reservoir mounting screws.
5. Lift up reservoir and disconnect pump motor connector and hose.
6. Remove reservoir from engine compartment.
7. Remove battery.
8. Remove power distribution center.
9. Remove battery and power distribution center mount.
10. Disconnect CAB electrical connectors.
11. Disconnect brake lines from HCU.
12. Remove front mounting bolt through access opening.
13. Remove rear mounting bolt from engine compartment.
14. Tilt assembly upward where brake lines attach and remove assembly from mounting bracket.
15. Reverse procedure to install.

RWAL VALVE, REPLACE

1. Remove left turn signal housing.
2. Remove extension panel under left turn signal housing opening.
3. Disconnect horn connector and remove access cover.
4. Remove one brake line from rear antilock valve through access cover opening.
5. Disconnect antilock valve electrical connector from controller.
6. Remove remaining brake line and mounting bolt from antilock valve.
7. Remove rear antilock valve.
8. Reverse procedure to install.

REAR WHEEL SPEED SENSOR, REPLACE

1. Raise and support vehicle
2. Disconnect sensor electrical connector.
3. Remove sensor and bracket mounting bolt.
4. Remove sensor and bracket.
5. Reverse procedure to install.

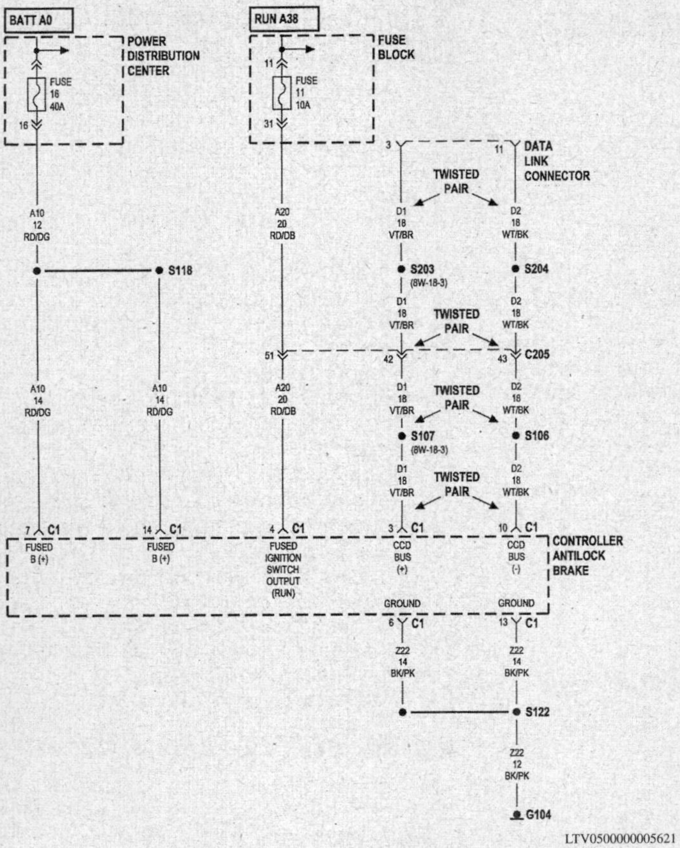

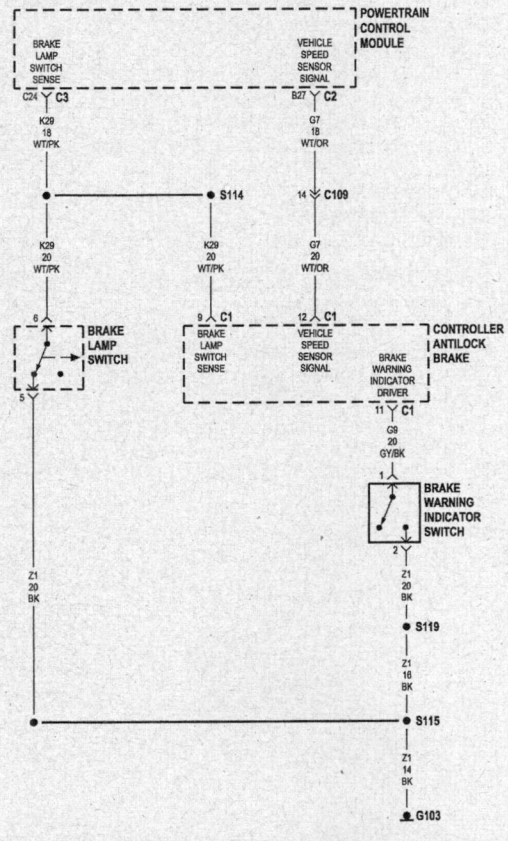

Fig. 1   Wiring diagram (Part 1 of 3)

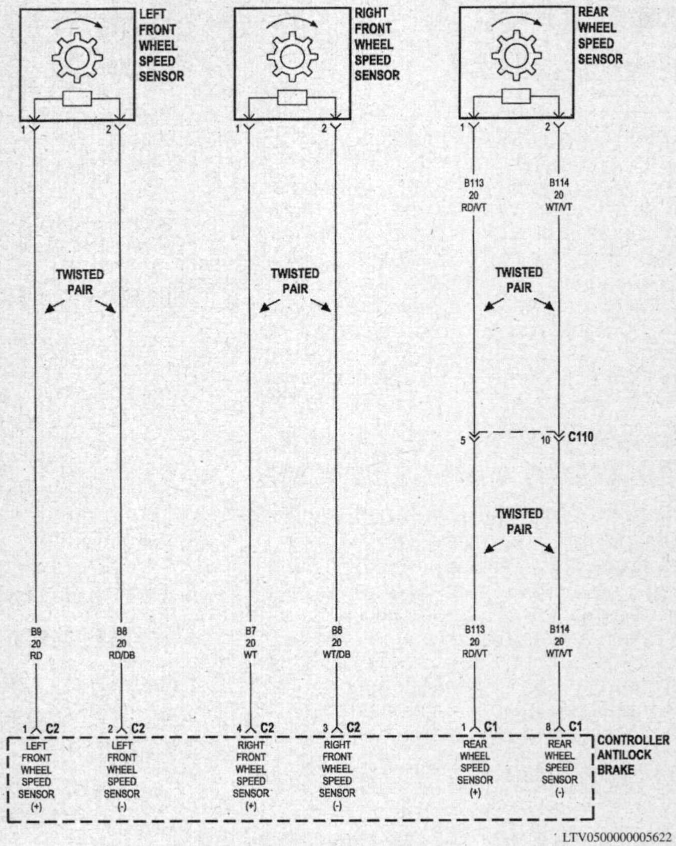

Fig. 1   Wiring diagram (Part 2 of 3)

LTV0500000005621

LTV0500000005622

LTV0500000005623

Fig. 1   Wiring diagram (Part 3 of 3)

Pacifica

NOTE: On Air Bag Equipped Models, Refer To "Air Bag System Precautions" Located In The Front Of This Manual For System Disarming & Arming Procedures.

NOTE: Refer To "Computer Relearn Procedures" Located In The Front Of This Manual When Battery Power To The Computer Has Been Interrupted.

NOTE: Electrical Symbol & Wire Color Code Identification Located In The Front Of This Manual May Be Used As An Aid When Using Wiring Circuits Found In This Section.

INDEX

	Page No.		Page No.		Page No.
Description	5-83	Intermittents & Poor		Component Replacement	5-84
Diagnosis & Testing	5-83	Connections	5-84	Controller Anti-Lock Brake	
Accessing Diagnostic Trouble		Symptom Tests	5-84	Module (CAB), Replace	5-84
Codes	5-83	Wiring Diagrams	5-83	Front Wheel Speed Sensor,	
Clearing Diagnostic Trouble		Precautions	5-83	Replace	5-84
Codes	5-84	Air Bag Systems	5-83	Integrated Control Unit (ICU),	
Connector Pin Identification	5-83	Battery Ground Cable	5-83	Replace	5-84
Diagnostic Tests	5-83	General Service Precautions	5-83	Rear Wheel Speed Sensor,	
Diagnostic Trouble Code		System Service	5-84	Replace	5-84
Interpretation	5-83	Brake System Bleed	5-84		

PRECAUTIONS

Air Bag Systems

Refer to "Air Bag System Precautions" in the front of this manual for system disarming and arming procedures.

Battery Ground Cable

Prior to service disconnect battery ground cable and isolate as required.

General Service Precautions

Certain components of the anti-lock brake system are not intended to be serviced individually. Attempting to remove or disconnect components of this type may result in personal injury and/or improper system operation. Only the components with removal and installation procedures should be serviced.

Observe the following general precautions when servicing the anti-lock brake system:
1. If any welding work is to be performed using an arc welder, Controller Anti-Lock Brake (CAB) should be disconnected.
2. When ignition switch is in On position, CAB electrical connector should not be disconnected or connected.
3. Some components of ABS system are not serviced separately and must be serviced as complete assemblies. Do not disassemble any component

which is designated as non-serviceable.

DESCRIPTION

When wheel slip is detected during a brake application, the ABS enters anti-lock mode. During anti-lock braking, hydraulic pressure in the individual wheel circuits is controlled to prevent any wheel from slipping. A separate hydraulic line and specific solenoid valves are provided for each wheel. The ABS can decrease, hold, or increase hydraulic pressure to each wheel brake. The ABS cannot, however, increase hydraulic pressure above the amount which is transmitted by the master cylinder during braking.

During anti-lock braking, a series of rapid pulsations is felt in the brake pedal. These pulsations are caused by the rapid changes in position of the individual solenoid valves as the EBCM responds to wheel speed sensor inputs and attempts to prevent wheel slip. These pedal pulsations are present only during anti-lock braking and stop when normal braking is resumed or when the vehicle comes to a stop. A ticking or popping noise may also be heard as the solenoid valves cycle rapidly. During anti-lock braking on dry pavement, intermittent chirping noises may be heard as the tires approach slipping. These noises and pedal pulsations are considered normal during anti-lock operation.

Vehicles equipped with ABS may be stopped by applying normal force to the brake pedal. Brake pedal operation during normal braking is no different than that of previous non-ABS systems. Maintaining a

constant force on the brake pedal provides the shortest stopping distance while maintaining vehicle stability.

DIAGNOSIS & TESTING

Accessing Diagnostic Trouble Codes

Connect a suitably programmed scan tool to Data Link Connector (DLC) and follow manufacturer's instructions.

Diagnostic Trouble Code Interpretation

Refer to "Diagnostic Chart Index" for diagnostic trouble code interpretation.

Connector Pin Identification

Refer to **Fig. 1** for connector terminal identification.

Wiring Diagrams

Refer to **Fig. 2** for wiring diagrams.

Diagnostic Tests

Refer to "Caravan, Town & Country & Voyager" "Diagnostic Tests" section for test procedures.

ANTI-LOCK BRAKES

Symptom Tests

Refer to "Caravan, Town & Country & Voyager" "Symptom Tests" section for test procedures.

Clearing Diagnostic Trouble Codes

Connect a suitably programmed scan tool to Data Link Connector (DLC) and follow manufacturer's instructions.

Intermittents & Poor Connections

Most Intermittents are caused by faulty electrical connections or wiring, although a sticking relay or solenoid can also cause an intermittent condition. Inspect wiring and connectors for the following:

1. Poor mating of connector halves, or terminals not fully seated in connector body.
2. Dirt or corrosion on terminals.
3. Damaged connector body.
4. Improperly formed or damaged terminals.
5. Poor terminal to wire connection.
6. Rubbed through wiring insulation.
7. Wiring broken inside insulation.

SYSTEM SERVICE

Brake System Bleed

The base brake system must be bled anytime air is permitted to enter the hydraulic system. However, anti-lock brake system components should only be bled if the hydraulic control unit has been removed or if there is reason to believe that air has entered the unit. **The ABS portion of the braking system must be bled separately.** Under most circumstances, only the base brake system will require bleeding, refer to the "Hydraulic Brake Systems" chapter for procedure. If the anti-lock brake system must be bled, proceed as follows:

1. Ensure all brake system components are installed and all hydraulic lines are connected securely.
2. Connect DRB diagnostic scan tool to diagnostic connector, then ensure Controller Anti-Lock Brake (CAB) has no stored diagnostic trouble codes.
3. Bleed base brake system as outlined in "Hydraulic Brake Systems" chapter, then select "Bleed ABS" routine on diagnostic scan tool.
4. Apply firm pressure to brake pedal and initiate ABS bleed cycle one time, then release pedal.
5. Bleed base brake system once again, then repeat ABS bleed cycle and base brake system bleed until brake fluid flow (as established in "Hydraulic Brake Systems" bleed procedure) is free of bubbles. **Ensure all bleeder valves are closed tightly after bleed sequence is completed.**
6. Road test vehicle to ensure base hydraulic system and anti-lock brake system operate properly.

Component Replacement

CONTROLLER ANTI-LOCK BRAKE MODULE (CAB), REPLACE

1. Raise and support vehicle.
2. Remove CAB to HCU mounting screws.
3. Slide CAB off HCU.
4. Disconnect 47-way electrical connector from CAB.
5. Remove CAB from vehicle.
6. Reverse procedure to install.

FRONT WHEEL SPEED SENSOR, REPLACE

1. Raise and support vehicle.
2. Remove front wheel and tire assembly, then front rotor.
3. Disconnect wheel speed sensor connector from frame rail.
4. Remove wheel speed sensor routing bracket to strut assembly mounting screw.
5. Open routing clip at knuckle and remove wheel speed sensor cable.
6. Remove speed sensor mounting screws, then sensor
7. Reverse procedure to install.

INTEGRATED CONTROL UNIT (ICU), REPLACE

1. With engine not running, pump brake pedal until a firm pedal is achieved.
2. Disconnect coolant recovery bottle and position aside.
3. Thoroughly clean all surfaces of brake fluid reservoir and master cylinder.
4. Disconnect brake fluid level switch electrical connector.
5. Disconnect primary and secondary brake tubes coming from master cylinder.
6. Remove master cylinder to power brake booster retaining nuts.
7. Slide master cylinder straight out of power brake booster.
8. Disconnect chassis brake tubes at ABS ICU.
9. Disconnect 47-way connector from antilock brake module.
10. Loosen bolts fastening ABS ICU bracket to frame rail.
11. Lift ICU off frame rail bolts and remove from vehicle.
12. Reverse procedure to install.

REAR WHEEL SPEED SENSOR, REPLACE

1. Raise and support vehicle.
2. Remove wheel and tire assembly.
3. Remove rear hub and bearing from vehicle.
4. Remove speed sensor mounting screw, then sensor.
5. Reverse procedure to install.

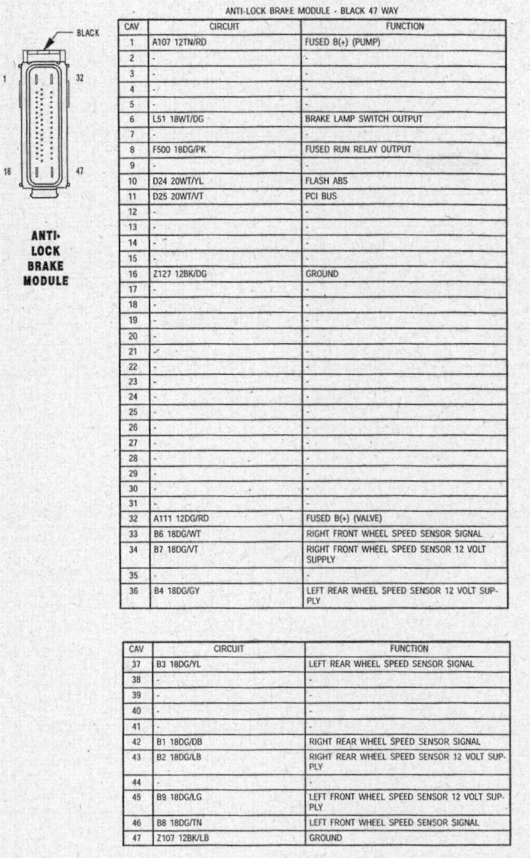

ANTI-LOCK BRAKE MODULE - BLACK 47 WAY

CAV	CIRCUIT	FUNCTION
1	A107 12TN/RD	FUSED B(+) (PUMP)
2	-	-
3	-	-
4	-	-
5	-	-
6	L51 18WT/DG	BRAKE LAMP SWITCH OUTPUT
7	-	-
8	F500 18DG/PK	FUSED RUN RELAY OUTPUT
9	-	-
10	D24 20WT/YL	FLASH ABS
11	D25 20WT/VT	PCI BUS
12	-	-
13	-	-
14	-	-
15	-	-
16	Z127 12BK/DG	GROUND
17	-	-
18	-	-
19	-	-
20	-	-
21	✓	-
22	-	-
23	-	-
24	-	-
25	-	-
26	-	-
27	-	-
28	-	-
29	-	-
30	-	-
31	-	-
32	A111 12DG/RD	FUSED B(+) (VALVE)
33	B6 18DG/WT	RIGHT FRONT WHEEL SPEED SENSOR SIGNAL
34	B7 18DG/VT	RIGHT FRONT WHEEL SPEED SENSOR 12 VOLT SUPPLY
35	-	-
36	B4 18DG/GY	LEFT REAR WHEEL SPEED SENSOR 12 VOLT SUPPLY

CAV	CIRCUIT	FUNCTION
37	B3 18DG/YL	LEFT REAR WHEEL SPEED SENSOR SIGNAL
38	-	-
39	-	-
40	-	-
41	-	-
42	B1 18DG/DB	RIGHT REAR WHEEL SPEED SENSOR SIGNAL
43	B2 18DG/LB	RIGHT REAR WHEEL SPEED SENSOR 12 VOLT SUPPLY
44	-	-
45	B9 18DG/LG	LEFT FRONT WHEEL SPEED SENSOR 12 VOLT SUPPLY
46	B8 18DG/TN	LEFT FRONT WHEEL SPEED SENSOR SIGNAL
47	Z107 12BK/LB	GROUND

LTV0500000005624

Fig. 1 Controller Anti-Lock Brake (CAB) connector terminal identification

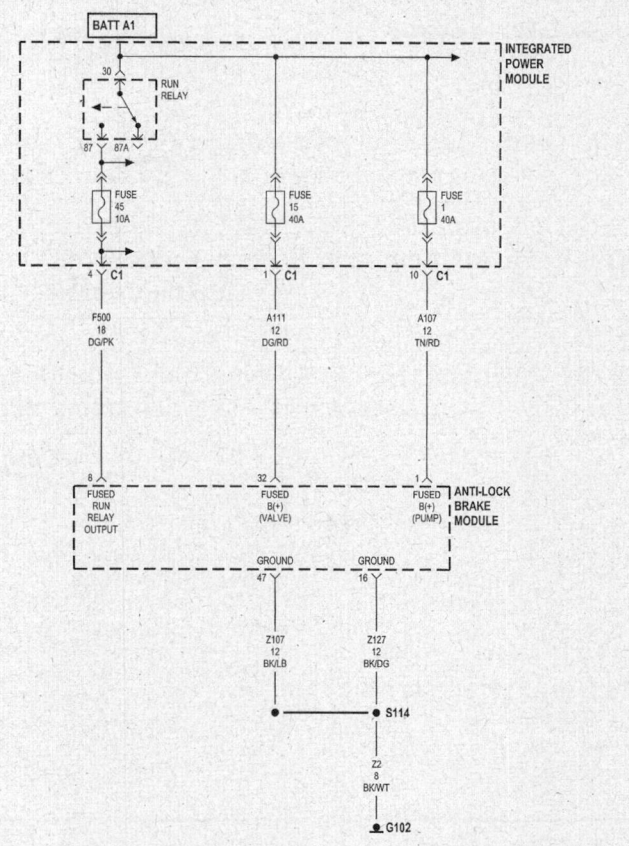

LTV0500000005625

Fig. 2 Wiring diagram (Part 1 of 3)

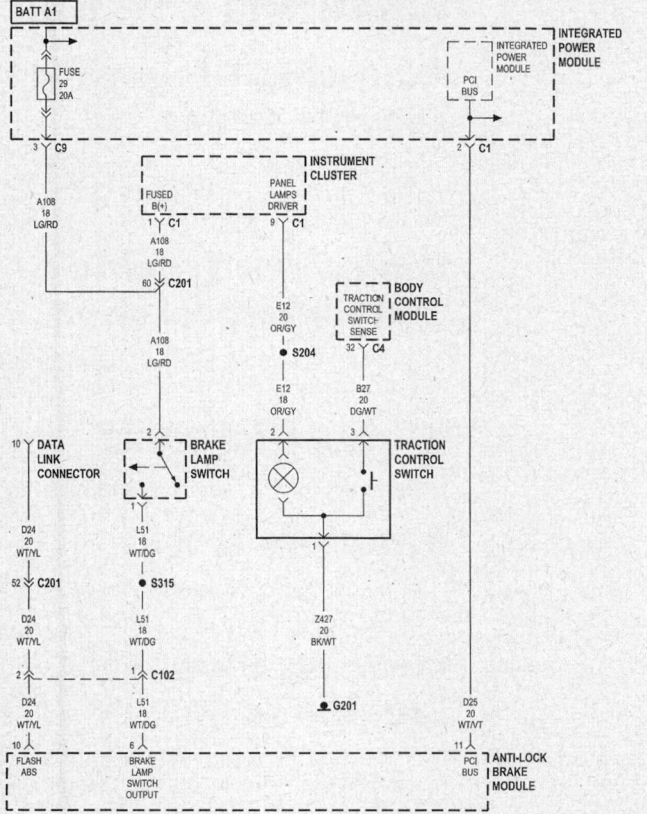

LTV0500000005626

Fig. 2 Wiring diagram (Part 2 of 3)

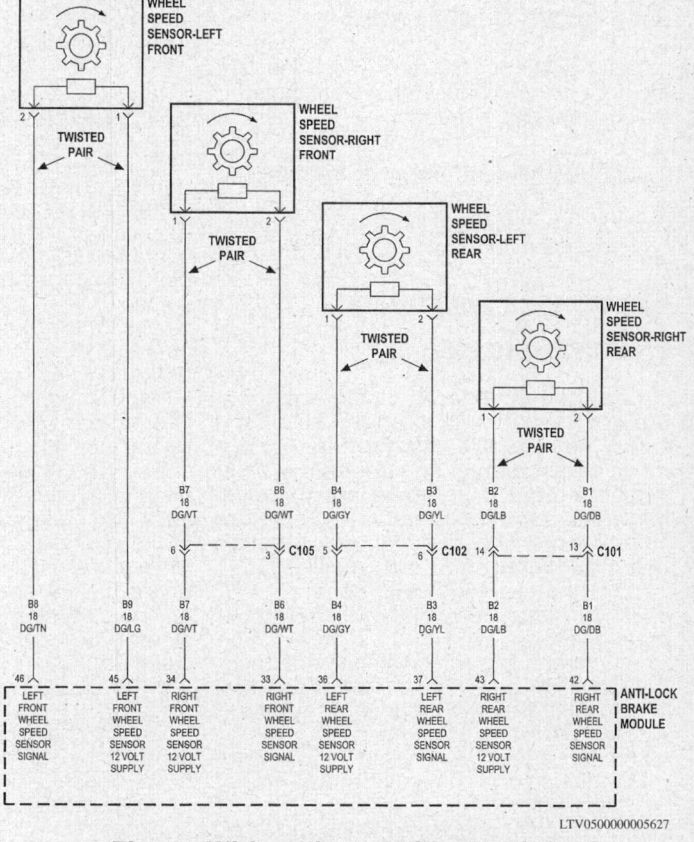

LTV0500000005627

Fig. 2 Wiring diagram (Part 3 of 3)

Sprinter

NOTE: On Air Bag Equipped Models, Refer To "Air Bag System Precautions" Located In The Front Of This Manual For System Disarming & Arming Procedures.

NOTE: Refer To "Computer Relearn Procedures" Located In The Front Of This Manual When Battery Power To The Computer Has Been Interrupted.

NOTE: Electrical Symbol & Wire Color Code Identification Located In The Front Of This Manual May Be Used As An Aid When Using Wiring Circuits Found In This Section.

INDEX

	Page No.		Page No.		Page No.
Description	5-86	Diagnostic Chart Index	5-89	(ALB), Replace	5-87
Diagnosis & Testing	5-86	Precautions	5-86	Controller Anti-Lock Brake	
Accessing Diagnostic Trouble		Air Bag Systems	5-86	(CAB) Module, Replace	5-87
Codes	5-86	Battery Ground Cable	5-86	Front Wheel Speed Sensor,	
Clearing Diagnostic Trouble		General Service Precautions	5-86	Replace	5-87
Codes	5-86	System Service	5-87	Hydraulic Control Unit (HCU),	
Diagnostic Trouble Code		Brake System Bleed	5-87	Replace	5-87
Interpretation	5-86	Component Replacement	5-87	Rear Wheel Speed Sensor,	
Symptom Tests	5-86	Automatic Load-Dependant		Replace	5-87
Wiring Diagrams	5-86	Brake Pressure Controller			

PRECAUTIONS

Air Bag Systems

Refer to "Air Bag System Precautions" in the front of this manual for system disarming and arming procedures.

Battery Ground Cable

Prior to service disconnect battery ground cable and isolate as required.

General Service Precautions

Certain components of the anti-lock brake system are not intended to be serviced individually. Attempting to remove or disconnect components of this type may result in personal injury and/or improper system operation. Only the components with removal and installation procedures should be serviced.

Observe the following general precautions when servicing the anti-lock brake system:
1. If any welding work is to be performed using an arc welder, Controller Anti-Lock Brake (CAB) should be disconnected.
2. When ignition switch is in On position, CAB electrical connector should not be disconnected or connected.
3. Some components of ABS system are not serviced separately and must be serviced as complete assemblies. Do not disassemble any component which is designated as non-serviceable.

DESCRIPTION

When wheel slip is detected during a brake application, the ABS enters anti-lock mode. During anti-lock braking, hydraulic pressure in the individual wheel circuits is controlled to prevent any wheel from slipping. A separate hydraulic line and specific solenoid valves are provided for each wheel. The ABS can decrease, hold, or increase hydraulic pressure to each wheel brake. The ABS cannot, however, increase hydraulic pressure above the amount which is transmitted by the master cylinder during braking.

The Controller Antilock Brake (CAB) is used to monitor wheel speeds and modulates (controls) hydraulic pressure in each brake channel. The modulated hydraulic pressure is used to prevent wheel lock up during braking and maintain vehicle stability. The CAB also provides a vehicle speed signal (VSS) to the Electronic Control Module (ECM). During a non-ABS stop, the system functions as a standard braking system.

Vehicles equipped with ABS may be stopped by applying normal force to the brake pedal. Brake pedal operation during normal braking is no different than that of previous non-ABS systems. Maintaining a constant force on the brake pedal provides the shortest stopping distance while maintaining vehicle stability.

DIAGNOSIS & TESTING

Accessing Diagnostic Trouble Codes

Connect a suitably programmed scan tool to Data Link Connector (DLC) and follow manufacturer's instructions.

Diagnostic Trouble Code Interpretation

Refer to "Diagnostic Chart Index" for diagnostic trouble code interpretation.

Wiring Diagrams

Refer to **Fig. 1** for wiring diagrams.

Symptom Tests

Refer to **Figs. 2 through 23** for diagnostic tests.

Clearing Diagnostic Trouble Codes

Connect a suitably programmed scan tool to Data Link Connector (DLC) and follow manufacturer's instructions.

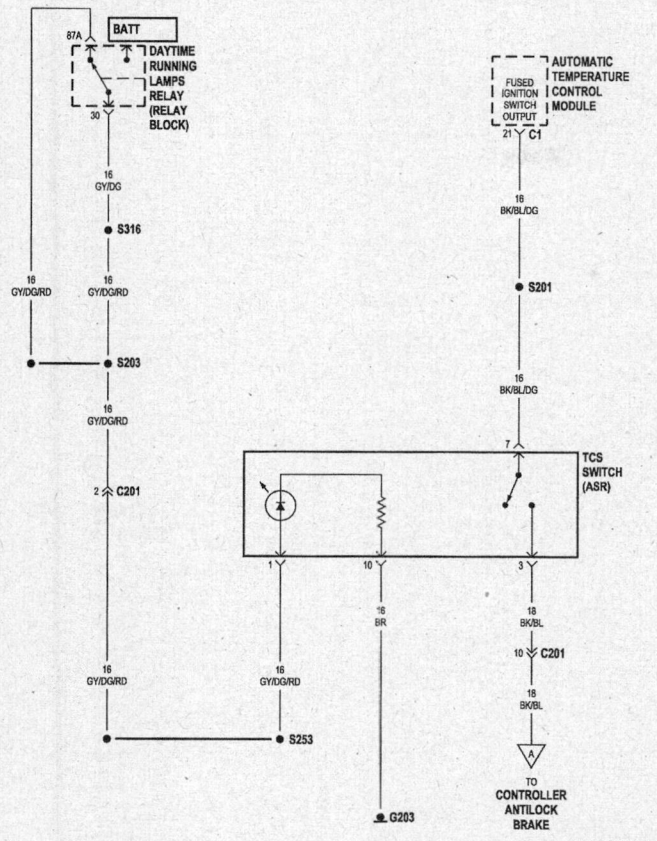

Fig. 1   Wiring diagram (Part 1 of 5)

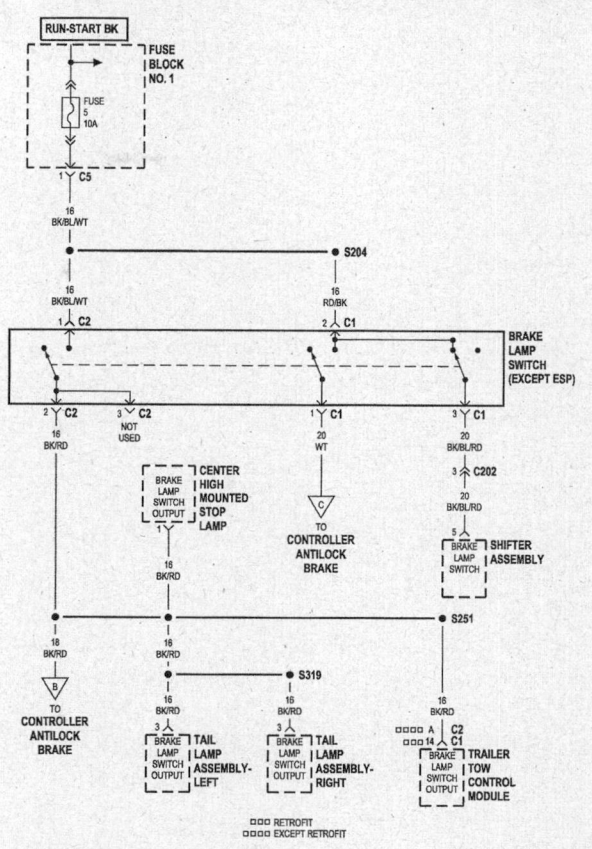

Fig. 1   Wiring diagram (Part 2 of 5)

SYSTEM SERVICE

Brake System Bleed

The anti-lock brake system must be bled any time air enters the hydraulic system. It is important to note that excessive air in the brake system may set a primary pressure diagnostic trouble code in the control module.

Pressure or manual bleeding procedures can be used when bleeding the ABS system after hoses or brake lines have been disconnected. Bleeding the ABS hydraulic system is also necessary after replacement of the hydraulic assembly or wheel brakes. During bleeding procedures, ensure the brake fluid level remains close to the Full mark on the reservoir.

The brake lines may be pressure bled using a standard diaphragm type pressure bleeder. Only diaphragm type pressure bleeding equipment should be used in order to prevent air, moisture and other contaminants from entering the system. In addition, only DOT 3 brake fluid should be used.

Component Replacement

AUTOMATIC LOAD-DEPENDANT BRAKE PRESSURE CONTROLLER (ALB), REPLACE

1. Install brake pedal rod to hold brake pressure.
2. Raise and support vehicle.
3. Remove brake lines to ALB controller.
4. Remove adjusting nut and spring from ALB controller.
5. Remove mounting bolts, then controller.
6. Reverse procedure to install.

CONTROLLER ANTI-LOCK BRAKE (CAB) MODULE, REPLACE

1. Disconnect CAB harness electrical connector.
2. Remove CAB mounting bolts.
3. Remove CAB from HCU.
4. Reverse procedure to install.

FRONT WHEEL SPEED SENSOR, REPLACE

1. Raise and support vehicle.
2. Remove front wheels.
3. Remove wheel speed sensor from front wheel hub.
4. Cut wheel speed sensor cable.
5. Reverse procedure to install.

HYDRAULIC CONTROL UNIT (HCU), REPLACE

1. Disconnect multiplug from control module.
2. Disconnect brake lines from hydraulic control unit.
3. Remove hydraulic control unit from bracket.
4. Reverse procedure to install.

REAR WHEEL SPEED SENSOR, REPLACE

1. Raise and support vehicle.
2. Remove rear wheels.
3. Remove wheel speed sensor from mounting hole in axle supporting tube.
4. Cut wheel speed sensor cable.
5. Reverse procedure to install.

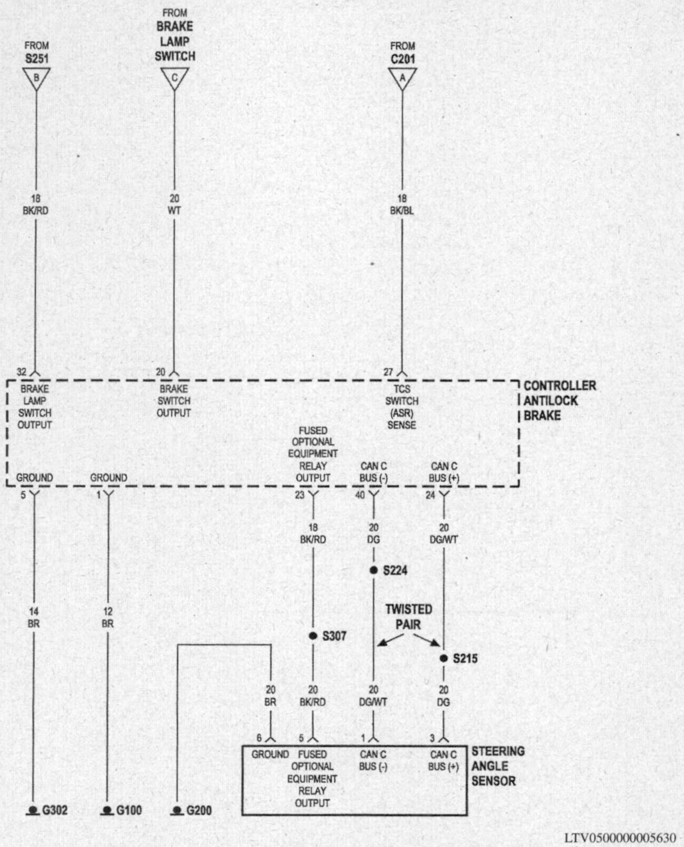

Fig. 1 Wiring diagram (Part 3 of 5)

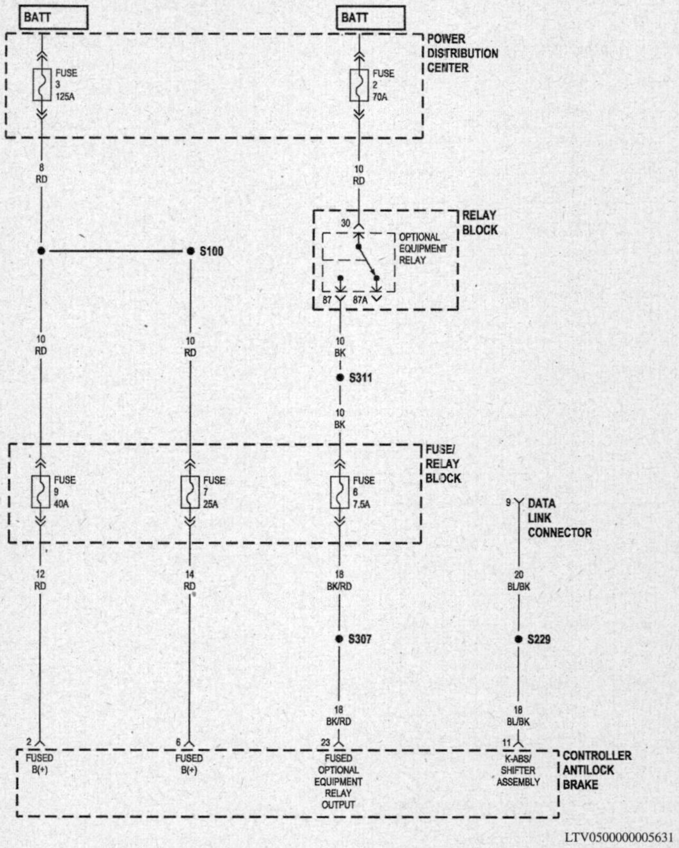

LTV0500000005630

Fig. 1 Wiring diagram (Part 4 of 5)

LTV0500000005631

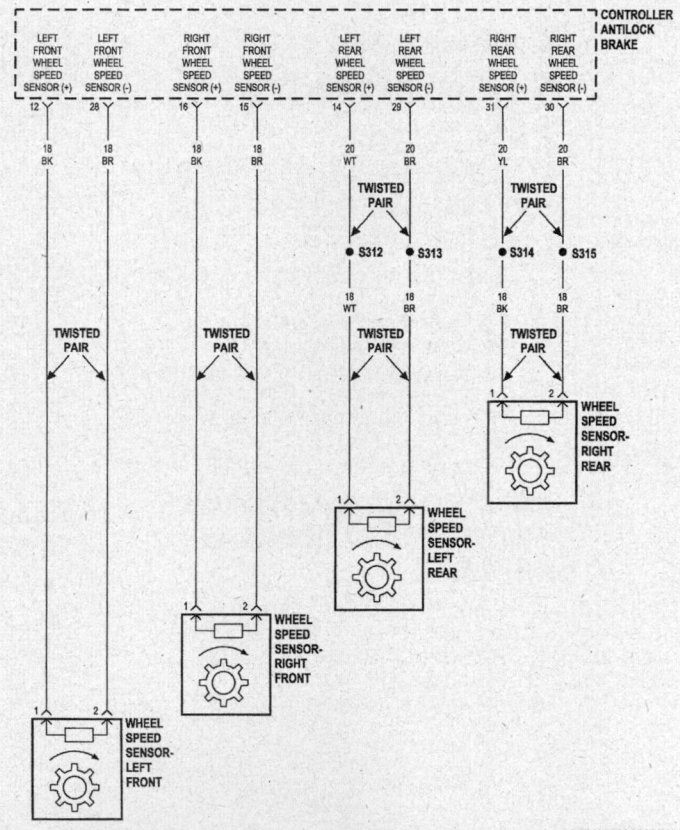

Fig. 1 Wiring diagram (Part 5 of 5)

LTV0500000005632

DIAGNOSTIC CHART INDEX

Description	Page No.	Fig No.
Anti-Lock Brake Module Internal/CAB Internal	5-89	2
Brake Fluid Level	5-90	3
Brake Pressure Sensor Circuit	5-90	4
Brake Switch Circuit	5-91	5
CAB Check Sum	5-91	6
CAB Option	5-92	7
CAN Communication Error	5-92	8
Incorrect Tone Wheel	5-93	9
Lateral Acceleration Sensor Circuit	5-94	10
Lateral Acceleration Sensor Internal Fault	5-95	11
Inlet/Outlet Solenoid Fault	5-95	12
Wheel Speed Sensor Circuit Fault	5-95	13
Wheel Speed Sensor Signal Fault	5-96	14
No Communication With BUS	5-97	15
No Communication With IC	5-97	16
No Communication With ECM	5-98	17
Pump Motor	5-98	18
Relay Output Voltage	5-99	19
Solenoid Relay	5-100	20
System Overvoltage	5-100	21
System Undervoltage	5-100	22
Verification Test	5-101	23

POSSIBLE CAUSES
INTERMITTENT CAB INTERNAL DTC
DAMAGED CAB/CAB HARNESS CONNECTOR
FUSED OPTIONAL EQUIPMENT RELAY OUTPUT CIRCUIT OPEN
FUSED B(+) CIRCUIT OPEN
GROUND CIRCUIT OPEN
ANTI-LOCK BRAKE CONTROLLER

TEST	ACTION
1	Turn the ignition on. With the DRBIII®, read DTCs. With the DRBIII®, erase DTCs. Turn the ignition off. Turn the ignition on. With the DRBIII®, read DTCs. Does this DTC reset? Yes → Go To 2 No → Go To 6

LTV0500000005758

Fig. 2 Anti-Lock Brake Module Internal/CAB Internal (Part 1 of 3)

TEST	ACTION
2	Turn the ignition off. Disconnect the CAB harness connector. Inspect the CAB/CAB harness connector for damage. Is there any broken, bent, pushed out, corroded or spread terminals? Yes → Repair as necessary. Perform ABS VERIFICATION TEST - VER 1. No → Go To 3
3	Turn the ignition off. Disconnect the CAB harness connector. Turn the ignition on. Using a 12-volt test light connected to ground, check the Fused Optional Equipment Relay Output circuit at the CAB harness connector. **NOTE: The test light must illuminate brightly. Compare the brightness to that of a direct connection to the battery.** Does the test light illuminate brightly? Yes → Go To 4 No → Repair the Fused Optional Equipment Relay Output circuit for an open. Perform ABS VERIFICATION TEST - VER 1.
4	Turn the ignition off. Disconnect the CAB harness connector. Using a 12-volt test light connected to ground, check both Fused B(+) circuits at the CAB harness connector. **NOTE: The test light must illuminate brightly. Compare the brightness to that of a direct connection to the battery.** Does the test light illuminate brightly? Yes → Go To 5 No → Repair the Fused B(+) circuit for an open. Perform ABS VERIFICATION TEST - VER 1.
5	Turn the ignition off. Disconnect the CAB harness connector. Using a 12-volt test light connected to 12-volts, check the CAB harness connector Ground circuits. **NOTE: The test light must illuminate brightly. Compare the brightness to that of a direct connection to the battery.** Does the test light illuminate brightly? Yes → Replace the Controller Antilock Brake Perform ABS VERIFICATION TEST - VER 1. No → Repair the Ground circuit for an open. Perform ABS VERIFICATION TEST - VER 1.

LTV0500000005759

Fig. 2 Anti-Lock Brake Module Internal/CAB Internal (Part 2 of 3)

TEST	ACTION

6	Turn the ignition off.
	Visually inspect the related wiring harness.
	Look for any chafed, pierced, pinched, or partially broken wires.
	Look for broken, bent, pushed out, or corroded terminals.
	Were any problems found?
	
	    Yes → Repair as necessary.
	             Perform ABS VERIFICATION TEST - VER 1.
	
	    No → Test Complete.

LTV0500000005760

Fig. 2   Anti-Lock Brake Module Internal/CAB Internal (Part 3 of 3)

TEST	ACTION

4	Turn the ignition off.
	Visually inspect the related wiring harness.
	Look for any chafed, pierced, pinched, or partially broken wires.
	Look for broken, bent, pushed out, or corroded terminals.
	Were any problems found?
	
	    Yes → Repair as necessary.
	
	    No → Test Complete.

LTV0500000006003

Fig. 3   Brake Fluid Level (Part 2 of 2)

POSSIBLE CAUSES
BRAKE PRESSURE SENSOR CIRCUIT INTERMITTENT DTC
BRAKE PRESSURE SENSOR CIRCUIT SHORT TO VOLTAGE
BRAKE PRESSURE SENSOR CIRCUIT SHORT TO GROUND
BRAKE PRESSURE SENSOR CIRCUIT OPEN
BRAKE PRESSURE SENSOR
ANTI-LOCK BRAKE CONTROLLER

TEST	ACTION

1	Turn the ignition off.
	Turn the ignition on.
	With the DRBIII®, read DTCs. Record DTC information.
	NOTE: If a system undervoltage or overvoltage DTC is set along with this DTC, diagnose the system voltage DTC first.
	NOTE: Before continuing, make sure that the Brake Lamp switch is adjusted correctly and functioning properly. Adjust or replace the switch as necessary
	With the DRBIII®, erase DTCs.
	Road test the vehicle and perform several braking maneuvers.
	With the DRBIII®, read DTCs.
	Does this DTC reset?
	
	    Yes → Go To 2
	
	    No → Go To 6

2	Turn the ignition off.
	Disconnect the Brake Pressure Sensor harness connector.
	Disconnect the CAB harness connector.
	Turn the ignition on.
	Measure the voltage of the Brake Pressure Sensor signal circuit.
	Measure the voltage of the Brake Pressure Sensor ground circuit.
	Measure the voltage of the Brake Pressure Sensor 5 volt supply circuit.
	Is there voltage present on any of the circuits?
	
	    Yes → Repair the Brake Pressure Sensor circuit(s) for a short to voltage.
	
	    No → Go To 3

3	Turn the ignition off.
	Disconnect the Brake Pressure Sensor harness connector.
	Disconnect the CAB harness connector.
	Measure the resistance between ground and the Brake Pressure Sensor signal circuit.
	Measure the resistance between ground and the Brake Pressure Sensor 5 volt supply circuit.
	Is the resistance below 5.0 ohms for either circuit?
	
	    Yes → Repair the Brake Pressure Sensor circuit(s) for a short to ground.
	
	    No → Go To 4

LTV0500000006004

Fig. 4   Brake Pressure Sensor Circuit (Part 1 of 2)

POSSIBLE CAUSES
INTERMITTENT DTC
BRAKE FLUID LEVEL SWITCH SIGNAL CIRCUIT SHORT TO GROUND
BRAKE FLUID LEVEL SWITCH
ANTI-LOCK BRAKE MODULE

TEST	ACTION

1	**NOTE: Before proceeding, verify that the brake fluid is at the proper level**
	
	Turn the ignition on.
	With the DRBIII®, read DTCs.
	With the DRBIII®, erase DTCs.
	Turn the ignition off.
	Turn the ignition on.
	With the DRBIII®, read DTCs.
	Does the DRBIII® display BRAKE FLUID LEVEL?
	
	    Yes → Go To 2
	
	    No → Go To 4

2	**NOTE: The brake fluid must be at the proper level. Verify that the brake fluid is at the proper level**
	Turn the ignition off.
	Disconnect the Brake Fluid Level Switch harness connector.
	Measure the resistance between the terminals of the Brake Fluid Level Switch.
	Is the resistance below 5.0 ohms?
	
	    Yes → Replace the Brake Fluid Level Switch
	
	    No → Go To 3

3	Turn the ignition off.
	Disconnect the Brake Fluid Level Switch harness connector.
	Disconnect the Instrument Cluster C2 harness connector.
	Measure the resistance between ground and the Brake Fluid Level Switch signal circuit.
	Is the resistance below 5.0 ohms?
	
	    Yes → Repair the Brake Fluid Level Switch signal circuit for a short to ground.
	
	    No → Replace the Antilock Brake Module

LTV0500000006002

Fig. 3   Brake Fluid Level (Part 1 of 2)

TEST	ACTION

4	Turn the ignition off.
	Disconnect the Brake Pressure Sensor harness connector.
	Disconnect the CAB harness connector.
	Measure the resistance of the Brake Pressure Sensor signal circuit.
	Measure the resistance of the Brake Pressure Sensor ground circuit.
	Measure the resistance of the Brake Pressure Sensor 5 volt supply circuit.
	Is the resistance above 5.0 ohms for any of the circuits?
	
	    Yes → Repair the Brake Pressure Sensor circuit(s) for an open
	
	    No → Go To 5

5	Turn the ignition off.
	Disconnect the Brake Pressure Sensor harness connector.
	Inspect the harness and connectors related to this circuit. If any problems are found, repair as necessary.
	If no problems are found, replace the Brake Pressure Sensor in accordance with the Service Information.
	With the DRBIII®, clear DTCs.
	Road test the vehicle and perform several braking maneuvers.
	With the DRBIII®, read DTCs.
	Does this DTC reset?
	
	    Yes → Replace the CAB
	
	    No → Test Complete.

6	The condition that set this DTC is not present at this time.
	Monitor the DRBIII® while wiggle testing the related harness and connectors. Look for any related parameters to change or for the DTC to reset.
	Inspect the related harness and connectors.
	Look for any chafed, pierced, pinched, or partially broken wires.
	Look for broken, bent, pushed out, or corroded terminals.
	Were any problems found?
	
	    Yes → Repair as necessary.
	
	    No → Test Complete.

LTV0500000006005

Fig. 4   Brake Pressure Sensor Circuit (Part 2 of 2)

POSSIBLE CAUSES

INTERMITTENT BRAKE SWITCH CIRCUIT DTC

BRAKE LAMP SWITCH STATUS

BRAKE SWITCH STATUS

FUSED IGNITION SWITCH OUTPUT CIRCUIT OPEN

OUTPUT CIRCUIT SHORT TO VOLTAGE

OUTPUT CIRCUIT SHORT TO GROUND

OUTPUT CIRCUIT OPEN

BRAKE SWITCH OUTPUT CIRCUIT SHORT TO BRAKE LAMP SWITCH OUTPUT CIRCUIT

BRAKE LAMP SWITCH

BRAKE SWITCH

ANTI-LOCK BRAKE CONTROLLER

TEST	ACTION
1	NOTE: This DTC will set if the Brake Switch, the Brake Lamp Switch, or both switches are inoperative. It will be necessary to verify the functionality of each switch. NOTE: If the Brake Switch and the Brake Lamp Switch are inoperative, it will be necessary to diagnose BOTH circuits. Turn the ignition off. Turn the ignition on. With the DRBIII® in Inputs/Outputs, monitor the Brake Lamp Switch state while pressing and releasing the brake pedal. Does the DRBIII® display change from OPEN to CLOSED as the brake pedal is pressed and released? Yes → Go To 2 No → Go To 5

LTV0500000006006

Fig. 5   Brake Switch Circuit (Part 1 of 4)

TEST	ACTION
6	Turn the ignition off. Disconnect the appropriate brake switch harness connector. Turn the ignition on. Using a 12-volt test light connected to ground, check the Fused Ignition Switch Output circuit at the harness connector. NOTE: The test light must illuminate brightly. Compare the brightness to that of a direct connection to the battery. Is the test light illuminated and bright? Yes → Go To 7 No → Repair the Fused Ignition Switch Output circuit for an open. Perform ABS VERIFICATION TEST - VER 1.
7	Turn the ignition off. Disconnect the CAB harness connector. Disconnect the appropriate brake switch harness connector. Turn the ignition on. Measure the voltage of the output circuit at the brake switch harness connector. NOTE: Measurement is taken at the Brake Switch Output circuit or the Brake Lamp Output circuit as determined by the previously performed switch test. Is there any voltage present? Yes → Repair the affected circuit for a short to voltage. Perform ABS VERIFICATION TEST - VER 1. No → Go To 8
8	Turn the ignition off. Disconnect the CAB harness connector. Disconnect the appropriate brake switch harness connector. Measure the resistance between ground and switch output circuit at the switch connector. NOTE: Measurement is taken at the Brake Switch Output circuit or the Brake Lamp Output circuit as determined by the previously performed switch test. Is the resistance below 5.0 ohms? Yes → Repair the affected circuit for a short to ground. Perform ABS VERIFICATION TEST - VER 1. No → Go To 9
9	Turn the ignition off. Disconnect the CAB harness connector. Disconnect the appropriate brake switch harness connector. Measure the resistance of the output circuit between the switch harness connector and the CAB harness connector. NOTE: Measurement is taken at the Brake Switch Output circuit or the Brake Lamp Output circuit as determined by the previously performed switch test. Is the resistance above 5.0 ohms? Yes → Repair the affected circuit for an open. Perform ABS VERIFICATION TEST - VER 1. No → Go To 10

LTV0500000006008

Fig. 5   Brake Switch Circuit (Part 3 of 4)

TEST	ACTION
2	NOTE: This DTC will set if the Brake Switch, the Brake Lamp Switch, or both switches are inoperative. It will be necessary to verify the functionality of each switch. NOTE: If the Brake Switch and the Brake Lamp Switch are inoperative, it will be necessary to diagnose BOTH circuits. Turn the ignition off. Turn the ignition on. With the DRBIII® in Inputs/Outputs, monitor the Brake Switch state while pressing and releasing the brake pedal. Does the DRBIII® display change from CLOSED to OPEN as the brake pedal is pressed and released? Yes → Go To 3 No → Go To 4
3	Turn the ignition off. Visually inspect the related wiring harness. Look for any chafed, pierced, pinched, or partially broken wires. Look for broken, bent, pushed out, or corroded terminals. Were any problems found? Yes → Repair as necessary. Perform ABS VERIFICATION TEST - VER 1. No → Test Complete.
4	Turn the ignition off. Disconnect the C1 Brake Switch harness connector. Turn the ignition on. With the DRBIII® in Inputs/Outputs, monitor the Brake Switch state. Connect a jumper wire between the Fused Ignition Switch Output circuit and Brake Switch Output circuit in the C1 Brake Switch harness connector. Does the DRBIII® display a change from OPEN to CLOSED? Yes → Replace the Brake Switch Perform ABS VERIFICATION TEST - VER 1. No → Go To 6
5	Turn the ignition off. Disconnect the C2 Brake Lamp Switch harness connector. Turn the ignition on. With the DRBIII® in Inputs/Outputs, monitor the Brake Lamp Switch state. Connect a jumper wire between the Fused Ignition Switch Output circuit and Brake Lamp Switch Output circuit in the C2 Brake Lamp Switch harness connector. Does the DRBIII® display a change from OPEN to CLOSED? Yes → Replace the Brake Lamp Switch Perform ABS VERIFICATION TEST - VER 1. No → Go To 6

LTV0500000006007

Fig. 5   Brake Switch Circuit (Part 2 of 4)

TEST	ACTION
10	Turn the ignition off. Disconnect the CAB harness connector. Disconnect the C1 Brake Switch and C2 Brake Lamp Switch harness connectors. Measure the resistance between the Brake Switch Output circuit and Brake Lamp Switch Output circuit in the C1 and C2 connectors. Is the resistance below 5.0 ohms? Yes → Repair the Brake Switch Output circuit for a short to the Brake Lamp Switch Output circuit. Perform ABS VERIFICATION TEST - VER 1. No → Replace the Controller Antilock Brake Perform ABS VERIFICATION TEST - VER 1.

LTV0500000006009

Fig. 5   Brake Switch Circuit (Part 4 of 4)

POSSIBLE CAUSES

INTERMITTENT CAB CHECK SUM DTC

DAMAGED CAB/CAB HARNESS CONNECTOR

FUSED OPTIONAL EQUIPMENT RELAY OUTPUT CIRCUIT OPEN

FUSED B(+) CIRCUIT OPEN

GROUND CIRCUIT OPEN

ANTI-LOCK ERAKE CONTROLLER

TEST	ACTION
1	Turn the ignition on. With the DRBIII®, read DTCs. With the DRBIII®, erase DTCs. Turn the ignition off. Turn the ignition on. With the DRBIII®, read DTCs. Does the DRBIII® display CAB CHECK SUM? Yes → Go To 2 No → Go To 6
2	Turn the ignition off. Disconnect the CAB harness connector. Inspect the CAB/CAB harness connector for damage. Is there any broken, bent, pushed out, corroded or spread terminals? Yes → Repair as necessary. Perform ABS VERIFICATION TEST - VER 1. No → Go To 3

LTV0500000006010

Fig. 6   CAB Check Sum (Part 1 of 2)

TEST	ACTION
3	Turn the ignition off. Disconnect the CAB harness connector. Turn the ignition on. Using a 12-volt test light connected to ground, check the Fused Optional Equipment Relay Output circuit at the CAB harness connector. **NOTE: The test light must illuminate brightly. Compare the brightness to that of a direct connection to the battery.** Does the test light illuminate brightly? Yes → Go To 4 No → Repair the Fused Optional Equipment Relay Output circuit for an open. Perform ABS VERIFICATION TEST - VER 1.
4	Turn the ignition off. Disconnect the CAB harness connector. Using a 12-volt test light connected to ground, check both Fused B(+) circuits at the CAB harness connector. **NOTE: The test light must illuminate brightly. Compare the brightness to that of a direct connection to the battery.** Does the test light illuminate brightly? Yes → Go To 5 No → Repair the Fused B(+) circuit for an open. Perform ABS VERIFICATION TEST - VER 1.
5	Turn the ignition off. Disconnect the CAB harness connector. Using a 12-volt test light connected to 12-volts, check the CAB harness connector Ground circuits. **NOTE: The test light must illuminate brightly. Compare the brightness to that of a direct connection to the battery.** Does the test light illuminate brightly? Yes → Replace the Controller Antilock Brake Perform ABS VERIFICATION TEST - VER 1. No → Repair the Ground circuit for an open. Perform ABS VERIFICATION TEST - VER 1.
6	Turn the ignition off. Visually inspect the related wiring harness. Look for any chafed, pierced, pinched, or partially broken wires. Look for broken, bent, pushed out, or corroded terminals. Were any problems found? Yes → Repair as necessary. Perform ABS VERIFICATION TEST - VER 1. No → Test Complete.

LTV0500000006011

Fig. 6   CAB Check Sum (Part 2 of 2)

TEST	ACTION
3	Turn the ignition off. Disconnect the CAB harness connector. Turn the ignition on. Using a 12-volt test light connected to ground, check the Fused Optional Equipment Relay Output circuit at the CAB harness connector. **NOTE: The test light must illuminate brightly. Compare the brightness to that of a direct connection to the battery.** Does the test light illuminate brightly? Yes → Go To 4 No → Repair the Fused Optional Equipment Relay Output circuit for an open. Perform ABS VERIFICATION TEST - VER 1.
4	Turn the ignition off. Disconnect the CAB harness connector. Using a 12-volt test light connected to ground, check both Fused B(+) circuits at the CAB harness connector. **NOTE: The test light must illuminate brightly. Compare the brightness to that of a direct connection to the battery.** Does the test light illuminate brightly? Yes → Go To 5 No → Repair the Fused B(+) circuit for an open. Perform ABS VERIFICATION TEST - VER 1.
5	Turn the ignition off. Disconnect the CAB harness connector. Using a 12-volt test light connected to 12-volts, check the CAB harness connector Ground circuits. **NOTE: The test light must illuminate brightly. Compare the brightness to that of a direct connection to the battery.** Does the test light illuminate brightly? Yes → Replace the Controller Antilock Brake Perform ABS VERIFICATION TEST - VER 1. No → Repair the Ground circuit for an open. Perform ABS VERIFICATION TEST - VER 1.
6	Turn the ignition off. Visually inspect the related wiring harness. Look for any chafed, pierced, pinched, or partially broken wires. Look for broken, bent, pushed out, or corroded terminals. Were any problems found? Yes → Repair as necessary. Perform ABS VERIFICATION TEST - VER 1. No → Test Complete.

LTV0500000006013

Fig. 7   CAB Option (Part 2 of 2)

POSSIBLE CAUSES
INTERMITTENT CAB OPTION DTC
DAMAGED CAB/CAB HARNESS CONNECTOR
FUSED OPTIONAL EQUIPMENT RELAY OUTPUT CIRCUIT OPEN
FUSED B(+) CIRCUIT OPEN
GROUND CIRCUIT OPEN
ANTI-LOCK BRAKE CONTROLLER

TEST	ACTION
1	Turn the ignition on. With the DRBIII®, read DTCs. With the DRBIII®, erase DTCs. Turn the ignition off. Turn the ignition on. With the DRBIII®, read DTCs. Does the DRBIII® display CAB OPTION? Yes → Go To 2 No → Go To 6
2	Turn the ignition off. Disconnect the CAB harness connector. Inspect the CAB/CAB harness connector for damage. Is there any broken, bent, pushed out, corroded or spread terminals? Yes → Repair as necessary. Perform ABS VERIFICATION TEST - VER 1. No → Go To 3

LTV0500000006012

Fig. 7   CAB Option (Part 1 of 2)

POSSIBLE CAUSES
CAN DTCS PRESENT IN OTHER MODULES
INTERMITTENT CAN COMMUNICATION ERROR DTC
DAMAGED CAB/CAB HARNESS CONNECTOR
CAN CIRCUIT(S) SHORT TO VOLTAGE
CAN CIRCUIT(S) SHORTED TOGETHER
CAN CIRCUIT(S) SHORT TO GROUND
CAN CIRCUIT(S) OPEN
FUSED OPTIONAL EQUIPMENT RELAY OUTPUT CIRCUIT OPEN
FUSED B(+) CIRCUIT OPEN
GROUND CIRCUIT OPEN
ANTI-LOCK BRAKE CONTROLLER

TEST	ACTION
1	Turn the ignition on. **NOTE: Diagnose any Steering Angle Sensor DTCs that are present in this module before continuing.** With the DRBIII®, read DTCs in the Engine Control Module, Transmission Control Module, and Instrument Cluster. Are there any CAN communication DTCs present in any of these modules? Yes → Refer to the diagnostic procedures for any CAN DTCs in ECM, TCM and Cluster before proceeding with this test. Perform ABS VERIFICATION TEST - VER 1. No → Go To 2
2	**NOTE: If a system undervoltage or overvoltage DTC is set along with this DTC, diagnose the system voltage DTC first.** Turn the ignition on. With the DRBIII®, erase DTCs. Turn the ignition off. Start the engine. With the DRBIII®, read DTCs. Does this DTC reset? Yes → Go To 3 No → Go To 11
3	Turn the ignition off. Disconnect the CAB harness connector. Inspect the CAB/CAB harness connector for damage. Is there any broken, bent, pushed out, corroded or spread terminals? Yes → Repair as necessary. Perform ABS VERIFICATION TEST - VER 1. No → Go To 4

LTV0500000006014

Fig. 8   CAN Communication Error (Part 1 of 3)

TEST	ACTION
4	Turn the ignition off. Disconnect the CAB harness connector. Turn the ignition on. Measure the voltage of the CAN(+) circuit. Measure the voltage of the CAN(-) circuit. Is the voltage above 3.0 volts for either circuit? Yes → Repair the CAN circuit(s) for a short to voltage. Perform ABS VERIFICATION TEST - VER 1. No → Go To 5
5	Turn the ignition off. Disconnect the CAB harness connector. Measure the resistance between ground and the CAN(+) circuit. Measure the resistance between ground and the CAN(-) circuit. Is the resistance below 5.0 ohms for either circuit? Yes → Repair the CAN circuit(s) for a short to ground. Perform ABS VERIFICATION TEST - VER 1. No → Go To 6
6	Turn the ignition off. Disconnect the CAB harness connector. Measure the resistance between the CAN(+) circuit and the CAN(-) circuit. Is the resistance below 5.0 ohms between the circuits? Yes → Repair the shorted CAN circuit(s). Perform ABS VERIFICATION TEST - VER 1. No → Go To 7
7	Turn the ignition off. Disconnect the Engine Control Module harness connector. Disconnect the CAB harness connector. Measure the resistance of the CAN(+) circuit. Measure the resistance of the CAN(-) circuit. Is the resistance above 5.0 ohms for either circuit? Yes → Repair the CAN circuit(s) for an open Perform ABS VERIFICATION TEST - VER 1. No → Go To 8
8	Turn the ignition off. Disconnect the CAB harness connector. Turn the ignition on. Using a 12-volt test light connected to ground, check the Fused Optional Equipment Relay Output circuit at the CAB harness connector. **NOTE: The test light must illuminate brightly. Compare the brightness to that of a direct connection to the battery.** Does the test light illuminate brightly? Yes → Go To 9 No → Repair the Fused Optional Equipment Relay Output circuit for an open. Perform ABS VERIFICATION TEST - VER 1.

LTV0500000006015

Fig. 8   CAN Communication Error (Part 2 of 3)

TEST	ACTION
9	Turn the ignition off. Disconnect the CAB harness connector. Using a 12-volt test light connected to ground, check both Fused B(+) circuits at the CAB harness connector. **NOTE: The test light must illuminate brightly. Compare the brightness to that of a direct connection to the battery.** Does the test light illuminate brightly? Yes → Go To 10 No → Repair the Fused B(+) circuit for an open. Perform ABS VERIFICATION TEST - VER 1.
10	Turn the ignition off. Disconnect the CAB harness connector. Using a 12-volt test light connected to 12-volts, check the CAB harness connector Ground circuits. **NOTE: The test light must illuminate brightly. Compare the brightness to that of a direct connection to the battery.** Does the test light illuminate brightly? Yes → Replace the Controller Antilock Brake Perform ABS VERIFICATION TEST - VER 1. No → Repair the Ground circuit for an open. Perform ABS VERIFICATION TEST - VER 1.
11	Turn the ignition off. Visually inspect the related wiring harness. Look for any chafed, pierced, pinched, or partially broken wires. Look for broken, bent, pushed out, or corroded terminals. Were any problems found? Yes → Repair as necessary. Perform ABS VERIFICATION TEST - VER 1. No → Test Complete.

LTV0500000006016

Fig. 8   CAN Communication Error (Part 3 of 3)

TEST	ACTION
2	Turn the ignition off. Inspect the tire sizes on the vehicle. Is a smaller than production tire or spare tire being used? Yes → Repair as necessary. Perform ABS VERIFICATION TEST - VER 1. No → Go To 3
3	Turn the ignition off. Measure all the tire circumferences. Do all the tire circumferences match? Yes → Go To 4 No → Repair as necessary. Perform ABS VERIFICATION TEST - VER 1.
4	Turn the ignition off. Inspect the tone wheel(s) for damage, missing teeth, cracks, or looseness. **NOTE: Refer to the service manual information, if necessary, for procedures or specifications.** Are one or more tone wheel(s) loose or damaged? Yes → Repair as necessary. Perform ABS VERIFICATION TEST - VER 1. No → Go To 5
5	Turn the ignition off. Inspect the wheel bearings for excessive runout or clearance. **NOTE: Refer to the service information, if necessary, for procedures or specifications.** Is the wheel bearing clearance within specifications? Yes → Go To 6 No → Repair as necessary. Perform ABS VERIFICATION TEST - VER 1.
6	Turn the ignition off. Visually inspect the brakes for locking up due to lining contamination or overheating. Inspect all brake components for any condition that would cause a variation in wheel speed. Is any component damaged? Yes → Repair as necessary. Perform ABS VERIFICATION TEST - VER 1. No → Go To 7
7	Turn the ignition on. With the DRBIII® in Sensors, monitor ALL the Wheel Speed Sensor signals while an assistant drives the vehicle. Slowly accelerate from a stop to 65 km/h (40 mph). **NOTE: Wheel Speed should not vary by more than 10% from wheel to wheel when driving in a straight line.** Do any of the Wheel Speed Sensor signals vary by greater than 10% while driving in a straight line? Yes → Go To 8 No → Go To 13

LTV0500000006018

Fig. 9   Incorrect Tone Wheel (Part 2 of 4)

POSSIBLE CAUSES
INTERMITTENT INCORRECT TONE WHEEL DTC
INCORRECT TIRES ON VEHICLE
TIRE CIRCUMFERENCES NOT MATCHING
WHEEL SPEED SENSOR CIRCUIT SHORT TO VOLTAGE
INCORRECT TONE WHEEL
WHEEL SPEED SENSOR CIRCUIT SHORT TO GROUND
DAMAGED WHEEL BEARING
WHEEL SPEED SENSOR CIRCUIT OPEN
DAMAGED BRAKE LININGS/COMPONENTS
WHEEL SPEED SENSOR CIRCUITS SHORTED TOGETHER
WHEEL SPEED SENSOR

TEST	ACTION
1	Turn the ignition on. With the DRBIII®, read DTCs. With the DRBIII®, erase DTCs. Turn the ignition off. Turn the ignition on. Road test the vehicle. During the road test, drive the vehicle above 100 km/h (62 mph) for at least 3 minutes and perform several stops and Antilock stops. Stop the vehicle. With the DRBIII®, read DTCs. Does the DRBIII® display INCORRECT TONE WHEEL? Yes → Go To 2 No → Go To 13

LTV0500000006017

Fig. 9   Incorrect Tone Wheel (Part 1 of 4)

TEST	ACTION
8	Turn the ignition off. Disconnect the CAB harness connector. Turn the ignition on. Measure the voltage of both affected Wheel Speed Sensor circuits in the CAB harness connector. Is there any voltage present? Yes → Repair the affected Wheel Speed Sensor circuit for a short to voltage. Perform ABS VERIFICATION TEST - VER 1. No → Go To 9
9	Turn the ignition off. Disconnect the CAB harness connector. Measure the resistance between ground and both affected Wheel Speed Sensor circuits in the CAB harness connector. Is the resistance below 5.0 ohms? Yes → Repair the affected Wheel Speed Sensor circuit for a short to ground. Perform ABS VERIFICATION TEST - VER 1. No → Go To 10
10	Turn the ignition off. Disconnect the CAB harness connector. Measure the resistance between the affected Wheel Speed Sensor circuits in the CAB harness connector. Is the resistance over 1,800 ohms? Yes → Repair the affected Wheel Speed Sensor circuit for an open. Perform ABS VERIFICATION TEST - VER 1. No → Go To 11
11	Turn the ignition off. Disconnect the CAB harness connector. Measure the resistance between the affected Wheel Speed Sensor circuits in the CAB harness connector. Is the resistance under 1,100 ohms? Yes → Repair the affected Wheel Speed Sensor circuits for a short to each other. Perform ABS VERIFICATION TEST - VER 1. No → Go To 12
12	Turn the ignition off. Disconnect the CAB harness connector. Measure the resistance between the affected Wheel Speed Sensor circuits in the CAB harness connector. Is the resistance between 1,100 and 1,800 ohms? Yes → Go To 13 No → Replace the Wheel Speed Sensor Perform ABS VERIFICATION TEST - VER 1.

LTV0500000006019

Fig. 9 Incorrect Tone Wheel (Part 3 of 4)

POSSIBLE CAUSES
LATERAL ACCELERATION SENSOR CIRCUIT INTERMITTENT DTC
STEERING COMPONENT INSPECTION
LATERAL ACCELERATION SENSOR CIRCUIT SHORT TO VOLTAGE
LATERAL ACCELERATION SENSOR CIRCUIT SHORT TO GROUND
LATERAL ACCELERATION SENSOR CIRCUIT OPEN
LATERAL ACCELERATION SENSOR
ANTI-LOCK BRAKE CONTROLLER

TEST	ACTION
1	Turn the ignition off. Turn the ignition on. With the DRBIII®, read DTCs. Record DTC information. **NOTE: If a system undervoltage or overvoltage DTC is set along with this DTC, diagnose the system voltage DTC first.** **NOTE: Electromagnetic (radio) interference can cause an intermittent system malfunction by interrupting communication between the sensor and the CAB.** With the DRBIII®, erase DTCs. Road test the vehicle and perform several braking maneuvers. With the DRBIII®, perform the road test procedure. With the DRBIII®, read DTCs. Does this DTC reset? Yes → Go To 2 No → Go To 7
2	**NOTE: When the vehicle is in a turn, the ESP compares the Steering Angle Sensor value and the speed of the inner and outer wheels to determine if the values are plausible.** Inspect the front end and steering components for damage or misalignment. Inspect the Lateral Acceleration Sensor for correct mounting and installation. Inspect the tires and wheels to make sure that they are the correct size. All tires must be the same size. Were any problems found? Yes → Repair or replace components as necessary No → Go To 3

LTV0500000006021

**Fig. 10 Lateral Acceleration Sensor Circuit
(Part 1 of 3)**

TEST	ACTION
13	The condition necessary to set this DTC is not present at this time. Turn the ignition off. Visually inspect the related wiring harness. Look for any chafed, pierced, pinched, or partially broken wires. Visually inspect the related wire harness connectors. Look for broken, bent, pushed out, or corroded terminals. Were any problems found? Yes → Repair as necessary. Perform ABS VERIFICATION TEST - VER 1. No → Test Complete.

LTV0500000006020

Fig. 9 Incorrect Tone Wheel (Part 4 of 4)

TEST	ACTION
3	Turn the ignition off. Disconnect the Lateral Acceleration Sensor harness connector. Disconnect the CAB harness connector. Turn the ignition on. Measure the voltage on all 4 of the Lateral Acceleration Sensor signal circuits. Measure the voltage of the Lateral Acceleration Sensor ground circuit. There should be no voltage present on any of the circuits. Measure the resistance between the Lateral Acceleration supply circuit and all 4 of the Lateral Acceleration Sensor signal circuits. The resistance between the circuits should be above 5.0 ohms. Were there any problems found? Yes → Repair the Lateral Acceleration Sensor circuit(s) for a short to voltage. No → Go To 4
4	Turn the ignition off. Disconnect the Lateral Acceleration Sensor harness connector. Disconnect the CAB harness connector. Measure the resistance between the Lateral Acceleration Sensor ground and the 4 Lateral Acceleration Sensor signal circuits. Measure the resistance between ground and the 4 Lateral Acceleration Sensor signal circuits. Measure the resistance between ground and the Lateral Acceleration Sensor supply circuit. Is the resistance below 5.0 ohms for any of the circuits? Yes → Repair the Lateral Acceleration Sensor circuit(s) for a short to ground. No → Go To 5
5	Turn the ignition off. Disconnect the Lateral Acceleration Sensor harness connector. Disconnect the CAB harness connector. Measure the resistance of the Lateral Acceleration Sensor supply circuit. Measure the resistance of the Lateral Acceleration Sensor ground circuit. Measure the resistance of the 4 Lateral Acceleration Sensor signal circuits. Is the resistance above 5.0 ohms for any of the circuits? Yes → Repair the Lateral Acceleration Sensor circuit(s) for an open No → Go To 6
6	Turn the ignition off. Disconnect the Lateral Acceleration Sensor harness connector. Inspect the harness and connectors related to this circuit. If any problems are found, repair as necessary. If no problems are found, replace the Lateral Acceleration Sensor With the DRBIII®, clear DTCs. With the DRBIII®, perform the road test procedure. With the DRBIII®, read DTCs. Does this DTC reset? Yes → Replace the CAB No → Test Complete.

LTV0500000006022

**Fig. 10 Lateral Acceleration Sensor Circuit
(Part 2 of 3)**

TEST	ACTION
7	The condition that set this DTC is not present at this time. Monitor the DRBIII® while wiggle testing the related harness and connectors. Look for any related parameters to change or for the DTC to reset. Inspect the related harness and connectors. Look for any chafed, pierced, pinched, or partially broken wires. Look for broken, bent, pushed out, or corroded terminals. Were any problems found? Yes → Repair as necessary. No → Test Complete.

LTV0500000006023

Fig. 10   Lateral Acceleration Sensor Circuit (Part 3 of 3)

TEST	ACTION
1	**NOTE: If a system undervoltage or overvoltage DTC is set along with this DTC, diagnose the system voltage DTC first.** Turn the ignition on. With the DRBIII®, read DTCs. With the DRBIII®, erase DTCs. Turn the ignition off. Turn the ignition on. Start the engine. Drive the vehicle over 15 km/h (10 mph) to test solenoid and pump circuits. Stop the vehicle. With the DRBIII®, read DTCs. Does the DRBIII® display any SOLENOID DTCs? Yes → Go To 2 No → Go To 6
2	Turn the ignition off. Disconnect the CAB harness connector. Inspect the CAB/CAB harness connector for damage. Is there any broken, bent, pushed out, corroded or spread terminals? Yes → Repair as necessary. Perform ABS VERIFICATION TEST - VER 1. No → Go To 3
3	Turn the ignition off. Disconnect the CAB harness connector. Turn the ignition on. Using a 12-volt test light connected to ground, check the Fused Optional Equipment Relay Output circuit at the CAB harness connector. **NOTE: The test light must illuminate brightly. Compare the brightness to that of a direct connection to the battery.** Does the test light illuminate brightly? Yes → Go To 4 No → Repair the Fused Optional Equipment Relay Output circuit for an open. Perform ABS VERIFICATION TEST - VER 1.
4	Turn the ignition off. Disconnect the CAB harness connector. Using a 12-volt test light connected to ground, check both Fused B(+) circuits at the CAB harness connector. **NOTE: The test light must illuminate brightly. Compare the brightness to that of a direct connection to the battery.** Does the test light illuminate brightly? Yes → Go To 5 No → Repair the Fused B(+) circuit for an open. Perform ABS VERIFICATION TEST - VER 1.

LTV0500000006025

Fig. 12   Inlet/Outlet Solenoid Fault (Part 1 of 2)

POSSIBLE CAUSES
LATERAL ACCELERATION SENSOR CIRCUIT INTERMITTENT DTC
LATERAL ACCELERATION SENSOR

TEST	ACTION
1	Turn the ignition off. Turn the ignition on. With the DRBIII®, read DTCs. Record DTC information. **NOTE: If a system undervoltage or overvoltage DTC is set along with this DTC, diagnose the system voltage DTC first.** **NOTE: Electromagnetic (radio) interference can cause an intermittent system malfunction by interrupting communication between the sensor and the CAB.** With the DRBIII®, erase DTCs. Road test the vehicle and perform several steering and braking maneuvers. With the DRBIII®, perform the road test procedure. With the DRBIII®, read DTCs. Does this DTC reset? Yes → Replace the Lateral Acceleration Sensor No → Go To 2
2	The condition that set this DTC is not present at this time. Monitor the DRBIII® while wiggle testing the related harness and connectors. Look for any related parameters to change or for the DTC to reset. Inspect the related harness and connectors. Look for any chafed, pierced, pinched, or partially broken wires. Look for broken, bent, pushed out, or corroded terminals. Were any problems found? Yes → Repair as necessary. No → Test Complete.

LTV0500000006024

Fig. 11   Lateral Acceleration Sensor Internal Fault

TEST	ACTION
5	Turn the ignition off. Disconnect the CAB harness connector. Using a 12-volt test light connected to 12-volts, check the CAB harness connector Ground circuits. **NOTE: The test light must illuminate brightly. Compare the brightness to that of a direct connection to the battery.** Does the test light illuminate brightly? Yes → Replace the Controller Antilock Brake Perform ABS VERIFICATION TEST - VER 1. No → Repair the Ground circuit for an open. Perform ABS VERIFICATION TEST - VER 1.
6	Turn the ignition off. Visually inspect the related wiring harness. Look for any chafed, pierced, pinched, or partially broken wires. Look for broken, bent, pushed out, or corroded terminals. Were any problems found? Yes → Repair as necessary. Perform ABS VERIFICATION TEST - VER 1. No → Test Complete.

LTV0500000006026

Fig. 12   Inlet/Outlet Solenoid Fault (Part 2 of 2)

POSSIBLE CAUSES
INTERMITTENT WHEEL SPEED SENSOR CIRCUIT DTC
DAMAGED CAB/CAB HARNESS CONNECTOR
WHEEL SPEED SENSOR CIRCUIT SHORT TO VOLTAGE
WHEEL SPEED SENSOR CIRCUIT SHORT TO GROUND
WHEEL SPEED SENSOR CIRCUIT OPEN
WHEEL SPEED SENSOR CIRCUITS SHORTED TOGETHER
ANTI-LOCK BRAKE CONTROLLER

TEST	ACTION
1	**NOTE: If a system undervoltage or overvoltage DTC is set along with this DTC, diagnose the system voltage DTC first.** Turn the ignition on. With the DRBIII®, read DTCs. With the DRBIII®, erase DTCs. Turn the ignition off. Turn the ignition on. With the DRBIII®, read DTCs. Does the DRBIII® display any WHEEL SPEED SENSOR CIRCUIT DTCs? Yes → Go To 2 No → Go To 7

LTV0500000006027

Fig. 13   Wheel Speed Sensor Circuit Fault (Part 1 of 3)

TEST	ACTION
2	Turn the ignition off. Disconnect the CAB harness connector. Inspect the CAB/CAB harness connector for damage. Is there any broken, bent, pushed out, corroded or spread terminals? Yes → Repair as necessary. Perform ABS VERIFICATION TEST - VER 1. No → Go To 3
3	Turn the ignition off. Disconnect the CAB harness connector. Turn the ignition on. Measure the voltage of both affected Wheel Speed Sensor circuits in the CAB harness connector. **NOTE: If the wheel is rotating, voltage will be present.** Is there any voltage present? Yes → Repair the affected Wheel Speed Sensor circuit for a short to voltage. Perform ABS VERIFICATION TEST - VER 1. No → Go To 4
4	Turn the ignition off. Disconnect the CAB harness connector. Measure the resistance between ground and both affected Wheel Speed Sensor circuits in the CAB harness connector. Is the resistance below 5.0 ohms? Yes → Repair the affected Wheel Speed Sensor circuit for a short to ground. Perform ABS VERIFICATION TEST - VER 1. No → Go To 5
5	Turn the ignition off. Disconnect the CAB harness connector. Measure the resistance between the affected Wheel Speed Sensor circuits in the CAB harness connector. Is the resistance over 1,800 ohms? Yes → Repair the affected Wheel Speed Sensor circuit for an open. Perform ABS VERIFICATION TEST - VER 1. No → Go To 6
6	Turn the ignition off. Disconnect the CAB harness connector. Measure the resistance between the affected Wheel Speed Sensor circuits in the CAB harness connector. Is the resistance under 1,100 ohms? Yes → Repair the affected Wheel Speed Sensor circuits for a short to each other. Perform ABS VERIFICATION TEST - VER 1. No → Replace the Controller Antilock Brake Perform ABS VERIFICATION TEST - VER 1.

LTV0500000006028

Fig. 13   Wheel Speed Sensor Circuit Fault
(Part 2 of 3)

POSSIBLE CAUSES
INTERMITTENT WHEEL SPEED SENSOR SIGNAL DTC
DAMAGED SENSOR/CAB HARNESS CONNECTOR
DAMAGED WHEEL SPEED SENSOR TONE WHEEL
EXCESSIVE WHEEL SPEED SENSOR AIR GAP
DAMAGED WHEEL BEARING
DAMAGED BRAKE LININGS/COMPONENTS
WHEEL SPEED SENSOR FAILURE
ANTI-LOCK BRAKE CONTROLLER

TEST	ACTION
1	**NOTE: Refer to the symptom list and repair any WHEEL SPEED SENSOR CIRCUIT DTCs before continuing.** Turn the ignition on. With the DRBIII® in Sensors, monitor ALL the Wheel Speed Sensor signals while an assistant drives the vehicle. Slowly accelerate from a stop to 65 km/h (40 mph). **NOTE: Wheel Speed should not vary by more than 10% from wheel to wheel when driving in a straight line.** Do any of the Wheel Speed Sensor signals vary by greater than 10% while driving in a straight line? Yes → Go To 2 No → Go To 8

LTV0500000006030

Fig. 14   Wheel Speed Sensor Signal Fault
(Part 1 of 3)

TEST	ACTION
7	Turn the ignition off. Visually inspect the related wiring harness. Look for any chafed, pierced, pinched, or partially broken wires. Look for broken, bent, pushed out, or corroded terminals. Were any problems found? Yes → Repair as necessary. Perform ABS VERIFICATION TEST - VER 1. No → Test Complete.

LTV0500000006029

Fig. 13   Wheel Speed Sensor Circuit Fault
(Part 3 of 3)

TEST	ACTION
2	Turn the ignition off. Inspect the CAB harness connector and affected Wheel Speed Sensor. Inspect for looseness. Inspect wiring harness. Inspect for metal chips on sensor. Is the Wheel Speed Sensor or CAB harness connector damaged? Yes → Repair as necessary. Perform ABS VERIFICATION TEST - VER 1. No → Go To 3
3	Turn the ignition off. Inspect the affected Wheel Speed Sensor(s) tone wheel for damage, looseness, or missing. **NOTE: Refer to the appropriate Service information, if necessary, for procedures or specifications.** Is the affected tone wheel OK? Yes → Go To 4 No → Replace the tone wheel Perform ABS VERIFICATION TEST - VER 1.
4	Turn the ignition off. Inspect the affected Wheel Speed Sensor air gap. **NOTE: Refer to the appropriate Service information, if necessary, for procedures or specifications.** Is the affected air gap OK? Yes → Go To 5 No → Repair as necessary. Perform ABS VERIFICATION TEST - VER 1.
5	Turn the ignition off. Inspect the affected Wheel Speed Sensor(s) wheel bearing. **NOTE: Refer to the appropriate Service information, if necessary, for procedures or specifications.** Is the affected wheel bearing clearance OK? Yes → Go To 6 No → Repair as necessary. Perform ABS VERIFICATION TEST - VER 1.
6	Turn the ignition off. Visually inspect the brakes for locking up due to lining contamination or overheating. Inspect all brake components for defects which would cause a speed difference. Were any problems found? Yes → Repair as necessary. Perform ABS VERIFICATION TEST - VER 1. No → Go To 7

LTV0500000006031

Fig. 14   Wheel Speed Sensor Signal Fault
(Part 2 of 3)

TEST	ACTION
7	Turn the ignition off. Disconnect the Anti-Lock Brake module harness connector. Connect a voltmeter to the Wheel Speed Sensor (+) and (-) circuits at the Antilock Brake module harness connector. Rotate the wheel at a speed of at least one revolution per second while monitoring the voltage. Is the AC voltage fluctuating above 120 mV? Yes → Replace the Controller Antilock Brake Perform ABS VERIFICATION TEST - VER 1. No → Replace the affected Wheel Speed Sensor Perform ABS VERIFICATION TEST - VER 1.
8	Turn the ignition off. Visually inspect the related wiring harness. Look for any chafed, pierced, pinched, or partially broken wires. Look for broken, bent, pushed out, or corroded terminals. Look for any wiring conditions that may cause electromagnetic interference with the Wheel Speed Sensor circuits. Inspect Wheel Speed sensors, Tone Wheels, Brake Rotors, Wheel Bearings, etc, for conditions that may cause speed variations from wheel to wheel. Were any problems found? Yes → Repair as necessary. Perform ABS VERIFICATION TEST - VER 1. No → Test Complete.

LTV0500000006032

Fig. 14 Wheel Speed Sensor Signal Fault (Part 3 of 3)

TEST	ACTION
2	Turn the ignition off. Using a voltmeter, connect one end to the CAN circuit that previously measured above 3.0 volts, and the other end to ground. NOTE: Refer to the wiring diagrams in the service information to help determine which modules are connected to the CAN Bus. NOTE: Wait one minute, after turning the ignition off, before disconnecting the module. Disconnect a module that is connected to the CAN bus. Turn the ignition on. Monitor and note the voltmeter reading. Repeat this procedure until either the voltage reading drops below 3.0 volts or all modules that are connected to the CAN Bus are disconnected and the voltage reading remains above 3.0 volts. Then, proceed to the conclusion question. What is the outcome? > 3.0 volts w/all modules disconnected Repair the CAN C Bus (+) circuit or the CAN C Bus (-) circuit for a short to voltage. Perform BODY VERIFICATION TEST - VER 1. < 3.0 volts after disconnecting a module Replace the module that caused the voltage reading to drop after disconnecting it. Perform BODY VERIFICATION TEST - VER 1.
3	Turn the ignition off. Disconnect the Instrument Cluster harness connectors. Disconnect the negative battery cable. Measure the resistance between ground and the CAN C Bus (+) circuit. Measure the resistance between ground and the CAN C Bus (-) circuit. Is the resistance below 50.0 ohms on either circuit? Yes → Go To 4 No → Go To 5
4	Turn the ignition off. Disconnect the negative battery cable. Using an ohmmeter, connect one end to the CAN Bus circuit that previously measured below 50.0 ohms and the other end to ground. NOTE: Refer to the wiring diagrams in the service information to help determine which modules are connected to the CAN Bus. Disconnect a module that is connected to the CAN Bus. Monitor and note the ohmmeter reading. Repeat this procedure until either the resistance reading goes above 50.0 ohms or all modules that are connected to the CAN Bus are disconnected and the resistance reading remains below 50.0 ohms. Then, proceed to the conclusion question. What is the outcome? < 50.0 ohms w/all modules disconnected Repair the CAN C Bus (+) circuit or the CAN C Bus (-) circuit for a short to ground. Perform BODY VERIFICATION TEST - VER 1. >50.0 ohms after disconnecting a module Replace the module that caused the resistance reading to increase after disconnecting it. Perform BODY VERIFICATION TEST - VER 1.

LTV0500000006034

Fig. 15 No Communication With BUS (Part 2 of 3)

POSSIBLE CAUSES
CAN CIRCUITS SHORTED TO VOLTAGE
MODULE SHORT TO VOLTAGE
CAN CIRCUITS SHORTED TO GROUND
MODULE SHORT TO GROUND
CAN CIRCUITS SHORTED TOGETHER
ENGINE CONTROL MODULE
SENTRY KEY REMOTE ENTRY MODULE

TEST	ACTION
1	Turn the ignition off. Disconnect the Instrument Cluster harness connectors. Turn the ignition on. Measure the voltage between CAN C Bus (+) circuit and ground. Measure the voltage between CAN C Bus (-) circuit and ground. Is the voltage above 3.0 volts on either circuit? Yes → Go To 2 No → Go To 3

LTV0500000006033

Fig. 15 No Communication With BUS (Part 1 of 3)

TEST	ACTION
5	Turn the ignition off. Disconnect the negative battery cable. NOTE: Refer to the wiring diagrams in the service information to help determine which modules are connected to the CAN Bus. Disconnect all of the modules that are connected to the CAN Bus. Measure the resistance between the CAN C Bus (+) circuit and the CAN C Bus (-) circuit at any disconnected module's harness connector. Is the resistance below 10k ohms? Yes → Repair the CAN C Bus (+) circuit for a short to the CAN C Bus (-) circuit. Perform BODY VERIFICATION TEST - VER 1. No → Go To 6
6	Turn the ignition off. Reconnect the Engine Control Module harness connectors. While back probing, measure the resistance of the CAN C Bus (+) circuit and the CAN C Bus (-) circuit at the ECM harness connector. Is the resistance 120.0 ± 2.0 ohms? Yes → Replace the Sentry Key Remote Entry Module Perform BODY VERIFICATION TEST - VER 1. No → Replace the Engine Control Module Perform BODY VERIFICATION TEST - VER 1.

LTV0500000006035

Fig. 15 No Communication With BUS (Part 3 of 3)

POSSIBLE CAUSES
NO COMMUNICATION WITH BUS DTC PRESENT
INSTRUMENT CLUSTER DTC(S) PRESENT
INSTRUMENT CLUSTER'S POWER/GROUND CIRCUIT(S) SHORTED OR OPEN
CAN C BUS (+)/CAN C BUS (-) CIRCUIT(S) OPEN TO INSTRUMENT CLUSTER
CAN C BUS (+)/CAN C BUS (-) CIRCUIT(S) OPEN TO CAB
INSTRUMENT CLUSTER
ANTI-LOCK BRAKE CONTROLLER

TEST	ACTION
1	Turn the ignition on. With the DRBIII®, read CAB DTCs. Does the DRBIII® display: NO COMMUNICATION WITH BUS? Yes → Refer to the symptom list for the appropriate diagnostic procedure. Perform ABS VERIFICATION TEST - VER 1. No → Go To 2
2	Turn the ignition on. With the DRBIII®, read IC DTCs. Does the DRBIII® display any DTCs? Yes → Refer to Instrument Cluster category for the related symptom(s). Perform ABS VERIFICATION TEST - VER 1. No → Go To 3
3	Turn the ignition on. With the DRBIII®, check the TCM and ATC module for the same or similar No Communication with IC DTC. Does the DRBIII® display same or similar DTC in TCM & ATC module? Yes → Go To 4 No → Go To 6

LTV0500000006036

Fig. 16 No Communication With IC (Part 1 of 2)

TEST	ACTION
4	Turn the ignition off. Disconnect the IC harness connectors. Check all of the IC's power circuits for a short or open condition. Check all of the IC's ground circuits for an open condition. Were any problems found? Yes → Repair the power/ground circuit(s) as necessary. Perform ABS VERIFICATION TEST - VER 1. No → Go To 5
5	Turn the ignition off. Disconnect the IC harness connectors. Measure the resistance between the CAN C Bus (+) circuit and the CAN C Bus (-) circuit in the IC harness connector. Is the resistance 57 to 63 ohms? Yes → Replace the Instrument Cluster Perform ABS VERIFICATION TEST - VER 1. No → Repair the CAN C Bus (+)/CAN C Bus (-) circuit(s) for an open. Perform ABS VERIFICATION TEST - VER 1.
6	Turn the ignition off. Disconnect the CAB harness connector. Measure the resistance between the CAN C Bus (+) circuit and the CAN C Bus (-) circuit in the CAB harness connector. Is the resistance 57 to 63 ohms? Yes → Replace the Controller Antilock Brake Perform ABS VERIFICATION TEST - VER 1. No → Repair the CAN C Bus (+)/CAN C Bus (-) circuit(s) for an open. Perform ABS VERIFICATION TEST - VER 1.

LTV0500000006037

Fig. 16   No Communication With IC (Part 2 of 2)

TEST	ACTION
4	Turn the ignition off. Disconnect the ECM harness connectors. Check all of the ECM's power circuits for a short or open condition. Check all of the ECM's ground circuits for an open condition. Were any problems found? Yes → Repair the power/ground circuit(s) as necessary. Perform ABS VERIFICATION TEST - VER 1. No → Go To 5
5	Turn the ignition off. Disconnect the ECM harness connectors. Measure the resistance between the CAN C Bus (+) circuit and the CAN C Bus (-) circuit in the ECM harness connector. Is the resistance 57 to 63 ohms? Yes → Replace the Engine Control Module Perform ABS VERIFICATION TEST - VER 1. No → Repair the CAN C Bus (+)/CAN C Bus (-) circuit(s) for an open. Perform ABS VERIFICATION TEST - VER 1.
6	Turn the ignition off. Disconnect the CAB harness connector. Measure the resistance between the CAN C Bus (+) circuit and the CAN C Bus (-) circuit in the CAB harness connector. Is the resistance 57 to 63 ohms? Yes → Replace the Controller Antilock Brake Perform ABS VERIFICATION TEST - VER 1. No → Repair the CAN C Bus (+)/CAN C Bus (-) circuit(s) for an open. Perform ABS VERIFICATION TEST - VER 1.

LTV0500000006039

Fig. 17   No Communication With ECM (Part 2 of 2)

POSSIBLE CAUSES
NO COMMUNICATION WITH BUS
ENGINE CONTROL MODULE DTC(S) PRESENT
ENGINE CONTROL MODULE'S POWER/GROUND CIRCUIT(S) SHORTED OR OPEN
CAN C BUS (+)/CAN C BUS (-) CIRCUIT(S) OPEN TO ENGINE CONTROL MODULE
CAN C BUS (+)/CAN C BUS (-) CIRCUIT(S) OPEN TO CAB
ANTI-LOCK BRAKE CONTROLLER
ENGINE CONTROL MODULE

TEST	ACTION
1	Turn the ignition on. With the DRBIII®, read CAB DTCs. Does the DRBIII® display: NO COMMUNICATION WITH BUS? Yes → Refer to the symptom list for the appropriate diagnostic procedure. Perform ABS VERIFICATION TEST - VER 1. No → Go To 2
2	Turn the ignition on. With the DRBIII®, read ECM DTCs. Does the DRBIII® display any DTCs? Yes → Refer to Powertrain Diagnostic information for the related symptom(s). Perform ABS VERIFICATION TEST - VER 1. No → Go To 3
3	Turn the ignition on. With the DRBIII®, check the TCM, IC, and ATC module for the same or similar No Communication with Engine Control Module DTC. Does the DRBIII® display same or similar DTC in TCM, IC, & ATC module? Yes → Go To 4 No → Go To 6

LTV0500000006038

Fig. 17   No Communication With ECM (Part 1 of 2)

POSSIBLE CAUSES
INTERMITTENT PUMP MOTOR DTC
DAMAGED CAB/CAB HARNESS CONNECTOR
FUSED OPTIONAL EQUIPMENT RELAY OUTPUT CIRCUIT OPEN
FUSED B(+) CIRCUIT OPEN
GROUND CIRCUIT OPEN
PUMP MOTOR

TEST	ACTION
1	NOTE: If a system undervoltage or overvoltage DTC is set along with this DTC, diagnose the system voltage DTC first. Turn the ignition on. With the DRBIII®, read DTCs. With the DRBIII®, erase DTCs. Turn the ignition off. Turn the ignition on. With the DRBIII®, read DTCs. Does the DRBIII® display PUMP MOTOR? Yes → Go To 4 No → Go To 2
2	Turn the ignition off. Turn the ignition on. With the DRBIII®, actuate the Pump Motor. Is the Pump Motor running? Yes → Go To 3 No → Go To 4

LTV0500000006040

Fig. 18   Pump Motor (Part 1 of 3)

TEST	ACTION

3	The conditions necessary to set this DTC are not present at this time.
	Monitor DRBIII® parameters while wiggle testing the related wiring harness and connectors.
	Turn the ignition off.
	Visually inspect the related wiring harness and connectors.
	Look for any chafed, pierced, pinched, or partially broken wires.
	Look for broken, bent, pushed out, or corroded terminals.
	Were any problems found?
	
	    Yes → Repair as necessary.
	        Perform ABS VERIFICATION TEST - VER 1.
	
	    No → Test Complete.

4	Turn the ignition off.
	Disconnect the CAB harness connector.
	Inspect the CAB/CAB harness connector for damage.
	Is there any broken, bent, pushed out, corroded or spread terminals?
	
	    Yes → Repair as necessary.
	        Perform ABS VERIFICATION TEST - VER 1.
	
	    No → Go To 5

5	Turn the ignition off.
	Disconnect the CAB harness connector.
	Turn the ignition on.
	Using a 12-volt test light connected to ground, check the Fused Optional Equipment Relay Output circuit at the CAB harness connector.
	NOTE: The test light must illuminate brightly. Compare the brightness to that of a direct connection to the battery.
	Does the test light illuminate brightly?
	
	    Yes → Go To 6
	
	    No → Repair the Fused Optional Equipment Relay Output circuit for an open.
	        Perform ABS VERIFICATION TEST - VER 1.

6	Turn the ignition off.
	Disconnect the CAB harness connector.
	Using a 12-volt test light connected to ground, check both Fused B(+) circuits at the CAB harness connector.
	NOTE: The test light must illuminate brightly. Compare the brightness to that of a direct connection to the battery.
	Does the test light illuminate brightly?
	
	    Yes → Go To 7
	
	    No → Repair the Fused B(+) circuit for an open.
	        Perform ABS VERIFICATION TEST - VER 1.

LTV0500000006041

Fig. 18   Pump Motor (Part 2 of 3)

TEST	ACTION

3	Turn the ignition off.
	Disconnect the CAB harness connector.
	Inspect the CAB/CAB harness connector for damage.
	Is there any broken, bent, pushed out, corroded or spread terminals?
	
	    Yes → Repair as necessary.
	        Perform ABS VERIFICATION TEST - VER 1.
	
	    No → Go To 4

4	Turn the ignition off.
	Turn the ignition on.
	With the DRBIII® in Sensors, read the Relay Output voltage.
	Start the engine.
	With the DRBIII® in Sensors, read the Relay Output voltage.
	Select the Relay Output voltage that was displayed on the DRBIII®.
	
	    Voltage below 9.4 volts.
	        Go To 5
	
	    Voltage above 17.4 volts.
	        Go To 7
	
	    Voltage between 9.4 and 17.4 volts.
	        Go To 8

5	Turn the ignition off.
	Disconnect the CAB harness connector.
	Start the engine.
	Allow the engine to idle.
	WARNING: WHEN THE ENGINE IS OPERATING, DO NOT STAND IN A DIRECT LINE WITH THE FAN. DO NOT PUT YOUR HANDS NEAR THE PULLEYS, BELTS OR FAN. DO NOT WEAR LOOSE CLOTHING.
	Measure the voltage of the Fused Optional Equipment Relay Output circuit in the CAB harness connector.
	Raise the engine speed above 2,000 RPM's.
	Measure the voltage of the Fused Optional Equipment Relay Output circuit in the CAB harness connector.
	Is the voltage less than 9.4 volts?
	
	    Yes → Repair the Fused Optional Equipment Relay Output circuit for an open.
	        Perform ABS VERIFICATION TEST - VER 1.
	
	    No → Go To 6

LTV0500000006044

Fig. 19   Relay Output Voltage (Part 2 of 3)

TEST	ACTION

7	Turn the ignition off.
	Disconnect the CAB harness connector.
	Using a 12-volt test light connected to 12-volts, check the CAB harness connector Ground circuits.
	NOTE: The test light must illuminate brightly. Compare the brightness to that of a direct connection to the battery.
	Does the test light illuminate brightly?
	
	    Yes → Replace the Pump Motor
	        Perform ABS VERIFICATION TEST - VER 1.
	
	    No → Repair the Ground circuit for an open.
	        Perform ABS VERIFICATION TEST - VER 1.

LTV0500000006042

Fig. 18   Pump Motor (Part 3 of 3)

POSSIBLE CAUSES
INTERMITTENT RELAY OUTPUT VOLTAGE DTC
BATTERY/CHARGING SYSTEM FAILURE
DAMAGED CAB/CAB HARNESS CONNECTOR
FUSED OPTIONAL EQUIPMENT RELAY OUTPUT CIRCUIT OPEN
FUSED B(+) CIRCUIT OPEN
GROUND CIRCUIT OPEN
ANTI-LOCK BRAKE CONTROLLER

TEST	ACTION

1	Turn the ignition on.
	With the DRBIII®, read DTCs.
	With the DRBIII®, erase DTCs.
	Turn the ignition off.
	Turn the ignition on.
	Start the engine.
	Drive the vehicle above 6 km/h (4 mph) for at least 30 seconds.
	Stop the vehicle.
	With the DRBIII®, read DTCs.
	Does the DRBIII® display RELAY OUTPUT VOLTAGE?
	
	    Yes → Go To 2
	
	    No → Go To 8

2	Turn the ignition off.
	Perform a battery and charging system test in accordance with the Service Information.
	NOTE: Refer to symptom list for any problems related to the battery or charging system.
	Were any problems found?
	
	    Yes → Repair any charging system or battery related symptom(s)
	
	        Perform ABS VERIFICATION TEST - VER 1.
	
	    No → Go To 3

LTV0500000006043

Fig. 19   Relay Output Voltage (Part 1 of 3)

TEST	ACTION

6	Turn the ignition off.
	Disconnect the CAB harness connector.
	Start the engine.
	Allow the engine to idle.
	WARNING: WHEN THE ENGINE IS OPERATING, DO NOT STAND IN A DIRECT LINE WITH THE FAN. DO NOT PUT YOUR HANDS NEAR THE PULLEYS, BELTS OR FAN. DO NOT WEAR LOOSE CLOTHING.
	Measure the voltage of both Fused B(+) circuits in the CAB harness connector.
	Raise the engine speed above 2,000 RPM's.
	Measure the voltage of both Fused B(+) circuits in the CAB harness connector.
	Is the voltage below 9.4 volts?
	
	    Yes → Repair the Fused B(+) circuit for an open.
	        Perform ABS VERIFICATION TEST - VER 1.
	
	    No → Go To 7

7	Turn the ignition off.
	Disconnect the CAB harness connector.
	Measure the voltage between the Fused B(+) circuit and both Ground circuits in the CAB harness connector.
	Is the voltage above 9.4 volts?
	
	    Yes → Repair any charging system related DTCs before continuing. If no charging system or system voltage DTCs are present in any module, replace the Controller Antilock Brake
	
	        Perform ABS VERIFICATION TEST - VER 1.
	
	    No → Repair the Ground circuit for an open.
	        Perform ABS VERIFICATION TEST - VER 1.

8	Turn the ignition off.
	Visually inspect the related wiring harness.
	Look for any chafed, pierced, pinched, or partially broken wires.
	Look for broken, bent, pushed out, or corroded terminals.
	Ensure the battery is fully charged.
	Inspect the vehicle for aftermarket accessories that may exceed the Generator System output.
	Were any problems found?
	
	    Yes → Repair as necessary.
	        Perform ABS VERIFICATION TEST - VER 1.
	
	    No → Test Complete.

LTV0500000006045

Fig. 19   Relay Output Voltage (Part 3 of 3)

POSSIBLE CAUSES
INTERMITTENT SOLENOID RELAY DTC
DAMAGED CAB/CAB HARNESS CONNECTOR
FUSED OPTIONAL EQUIPMENT RELAY OUTPUT CIRCUIT OPEN
FUSED B(+) CIRCUIT OPEN
GROUND CIRCUIT OPEN
ANTI-LOCK BRAKE CONTROLLER

TEST	ACTION
1	Turn the ignition on. With the DRBIII®, read DTCs. With the DRBIII®, erase DTCs. Turn the ignition off. Turn the ignition on. With the DRBIII®, read DTCs. Does the DRBIII® display SOLENOID RELAY? Yes → Go To 2 No → Go To 6
2	Turn the ignition off. Disconnect the CAB harness connector. Inspect the CAB/CAB harness connector for damage. Is there any broken, bent, pushed out, corroded or spread terminals? Yes → Repair as necessary. 　　　　Perform ABS VERIFICATION TEST - VER 1. No → Go To 3

LTV0500000006046

Fig. 20　Solenoid Relay (Part 1 of 2)

POSSIBLE CAUSES
INTERMITTENT DTC
DAMAGED CAB/CAB HARNESS CONNECTOR
GROUND CIRCUIT OPEN
ANTI-LOCK BRAKE CONTROLLER

TEST	ACTION
1	NOTE: Repair any Powertrain charging system DTCs before continuing. Turn the ignition on. With the DRBIII®, read DTCs. With the DRBIII®, erase DTCs. Turn the ignition off. Turn the ignition on. Start the engine. With the DRBIII®, read DTCs. Does this DTC reset? Yes → Go To 2 No → Go To 4
2	Turn the ignition off. Disconnect the CAB harness connector. Inspect the CAB/CAB harness connector for damage. Is there any broken, bent, pushed out, corroded or spread terminals? Yes → Repair as necessary. 　　　　Perform ABS VERIFICATION TEST - VER 1. No → Go To 3
3	Turn the ignition off. Disconnect the CAB harness connector. Using a 12-volt test light connected to 12-volts, check the CAB harness connector Ground circuits. NOTE: The test light must illuminate brightly. Compare the brightness to that of a direct connection to the battery. Does the test light illuminate brightly? Yes → Replace the Controller Antilock Brake 　　　　Perform ABS VERIFICATION TEST - VER 1. No → Repair the Ground circuit for an open. 　　　Perform ABS VERIFICATION TEST - VER 1.

LTV0500000006048

Fig. 21　System Overvoltage (Part 1 of 2)

TEST	ACTION
4	Turn the ignition off. Visually inspect the related wiring harness. Look for any chafed, pierced, pinched, or partially broken wires. Look for broken, bent, pushed out, or corroded terminals. Were any problems found? Yes → Repair as necessary. 　　　　Perform ABS VERIFICATION TEST - VER 1. No → Test Complete.

LTV0500000006049

Fig. 21　System Overvoltage (Part 2 of 2)

TEST	ACTION
3	Turn the ignition off. Disconnect the CAB harness connector. Turn the ignition on. Using a 12-volt test light connected to ground, check the Fused Optional Equipment Relay Output circuit at the CAB harness connector. NOTE: The test light must illuminate brightly. Compare the brightness to that of a direct connection to the battery. Does the test light illuminate brightly? Yes → Go To 4 No → Repair the Fused Optional Equipment Relay Output circuit for an open. 　　　Perform ABS VERIFICATION TEST - VER 1.
4	Turn the ignition off. Disconnect the CAB harness connector. Using a 12-volt test light connected to ground, check both Fused B(+) circuits at the CAB harness connector. NOTE: The test light must illuminate brightly. Compare the brightness to that of a direct connection to the battery. Does the test light illuminate brightly? Yes → Go To 5 No → Repair the Fused B(+) circuit for an open. 　　　Perform ABS VERIFICATION TEST - VER 1.
5	Turn the ignition off. Disconnect the CAB harness connector. Using a 12-volt test light connected to 12-volts, check the CAB harness connector Ground circuits. NOTE: The test light must illuminate brightly. Compare the brightness to that of a direct connection to the battery. Does the test light illuminate brightly? Yes → Replace the Controller Antilock Brake 　　　　Perform ABS VERIFICATION TEST - VER 1. No → Repair the Ground circuit for an open. 　　　Perform ABS VERIFICATION TEST - VER 1.
6	Turn the ignition off. Visually inspect the related wiring harness. Look for any chafed, pierced, pinched, or partially broken wires. Look for broken, bent, pushed out, or corroded terminals. Were any problems found? Yes → Repair as necessary. 　　　　Perform ABS VERIFICATION TEST - VER 1. No → Test Complete.

LTV0500000006047

Fig. 20　Solenoid Relay (Part 2 of 2)

POSSIBLE CAUSES
INTERMITTENT DTC
DAMAGED CAB/CAB HARNESS CONNECTOR
FUSED OPTIONAL EQUIPMENT RELAY OUTPUT CIRCUIT HIGH RESISTANCE
FUSED B(+) CIRCUIT HIGH RESISTANCE
GROUND CIRCUIT HIGH RESISTANCE
ANTI-LOCK BRAKE CONTROLLER

TEST	ACTION
1	NOTE: An undercharged battery may cause this DTC to set. Repair any Powertrain charging system DTCs before continuing. Turn the ignition on. With the DRBIII®, read DTCs. With the DRBIII®, erase DTCs. Turn the ignition off. Turn the ignition on. Start the engine. With the DRBIII®, read DTCs. Does this DTC reset? Yes → Go To 2 No → Go To 6
2	Turn the ignition off. Disconnect the CAB harness connector. Inspect the CAB/CAB harness connector for damage. Is there any broken, bent, pushed out, corroded or spread terminals? Yes → Repair as necessary. 　　　　Perform ABS VERIFICATION TEST - VER 1. No → Go To 3
3	Turn the ignition off. Disconnect the CAB harness connector. Turn the ignition on. Using a 12-volt test light connected to ground, check the Fused Optional Equipment Relay Output circuit at the CAB harness connector. NOTE: The test light must illuminate brightly. Compare the brightness to that of a direct connection to the battery. Does the test light illuminate brightly? Yes → Go To 4 No → Repair the Fused Optional Equipment Relay Output circuit for high resistance. 　　　Perform ABS VERIFICATION TEST - VER 1.

LTV0500000006050

Fig. 22　System Undervoltage (Part 1 of 2)

TEST	ACTION
4	Turn the ignition off. Disconnect the CAB harness connector. Using a 12-volt test light connected to ground, check both Fused B(+) circuits at the CAB harness connector. **NOTE: The test light must illuminate brightly. Compare the brightness to that of a direct connection to the battery.** Does the test light illuminate brightly? Yes → Go To 5 No → Repair the Fused B(+) circuit for high resistance. Perform ABS VERIFICATION TEST - VER 1.
5	Turn the ignition off. Disconnect the CAB harness connector. Using a 12-volt test light connected to 12-volts, check the CAB harness connector Ground circuits. **NOTE: The test light must illuminate brightly. Compare the brightness to that of a direct connection to the battery.** Does the test light illuminate brightly? Yes → Replace the Controller Antilock Brake Perform ABS VERIFICATION TEST - VER 1. No → Repair the Ground circuit for high resistance. Perform ABS VERIFICATION TEST - VER 1.
6	Turn the ignition off. Visually inspect the related wiring harness. Look for any chafed, pierced, pinched, or partially broken wires. Look for broken, bent, pushed out, or corroded terminals. Were any problems found? Yes → Repair as necessary. Perform ABS VERIFICATION TEST - VER 1. No → Test Complete.

LTV0500000006051

Fig. 22 System Undervoltage (Part 2 of 2)

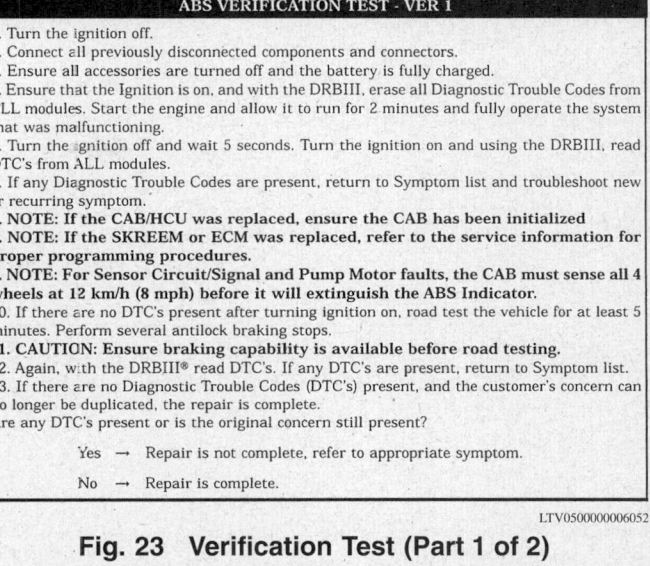

ABS VERIFICATION TEST - VER 1

1. Turn the ignition off.
2. Connect all previously disconnected components and connectors.
3. Ensure all accessories are turned off and the battery is fully charged.
4. Ensure that the Ignition is on, and with the DRBIII, erase all Diagnostic Trouble Codes from ALL modules. Start the engine and allow it to run for 2 minutes and fully operate the system that was malfunctioning.
5. Turn the ignition off and wait 5 seconds. Turn the ignition on and using the DRBIII, read DTC's from ALL modules.
6. If any Diagnostic Trouble Codes are present, return to Symptom list and troubleshoot new or recurring symptom.
7. **NOTE: If the CAB/HCU was replaced, ensure the CAB has been initialized**
8. **NOTE: If the SKREEM or ECM was replaced, refer to the service information for proper programming procedures.**
9. **NOTE: For Sensor Circuit/Signal and Pump Motor faults, the CAB must sense all 4 wheels at 12 km/h (8 mph) before it will extinguish the ABS Indicator.**
10. If there are no DTC's present after turning ignition on, road test the vehicle for at least 5 minutes. Perform several antilock braking stops.
11. **CAUTION: Ensure braking capability is available before road testing.**
12. Again, with the DRBIII® read DTC's. If any DTC's are present, return to Symptom list.
13. If there are no Diagnostic Trouble Codes (DTC's) present, and the customer's concern can no longer be duplicated, the repair is complete.
Are any DTC's present or is the original concern still present?

Yes → Repair is not complete, refer to appropriate symptom.

No → Repair is complete.

LTV0500000006052

Fig. 23 Verification Test (Part 1 of 2)

BODY VERIFICATION TEST - VER 1

1. Disconnect all jumper wires and reconnect all previously disconnected components and connectors.
2. Ensure that all accessories are turned off and the battery is fully charged.
3. **NOTE: Refer to the service information for proper programming procedures if the ABM; ACM; ATC; CTM; ECM; IC; SKREEM; SLA; or SSM was replaced.**
4. If the SKREEM was replaced, program all RKE transmitters used with this vehicle.
5. **NOTE: Perform the next 8 steps of this procedure if either diagnosing the Automatic Temperature Control (ATC) system or if repairs were made to the ATC system. All of the following criteria must be met in order to successfully run the ATC Function Test.**
6. With DRBIII®, record and erase ATC DTCs.
7. Place the shift lever in Park.
8. Start the engine. Allow the engine to reach normal operating temperature.
9. Set the blower to high speed.
10. Press the Air Conditioning switch On.
11. With the DRBIII®, verify that the ambient temperature is above 59°F (15°C), the refrigerant pressure is between 29 and 348 PSI (2 and 24 bar), the evaporator temperature is above 36.5°F (2.5°C), and the coolant temperature is above 158°F (70°C).
12. With the DRBIII® in ATC, select System Tests and select ATC Function Test. When the ATC Function Test is complete, proceed to the next step of this procedure.
13. With the DRBIII®, read active ATC DTCs. If any DTC is active or if the original condition is still present, proceed to the conclusion question and answer Yes.
14. With the DRBIII®, record and erase all DTCs from ALL modules. Start and run the engine for 2 minutes. Operate all functions of the system that caused the original concern.
15. Turn the ignition off and wait 5 seconds. Turn the ignition on and using the DRBIII®, read DTCs from ALL modules.
Are any DTC's present or is the original condition still present?

Yes → Repair is not complete, refer to the appropriate symptom.

No → Repair is complete.

LTV0500000006053

Fig. 23 Verification Test (Part 2 of 2)

Jeep

NOTE: On Air Bag Equipped Models, Refer To "Air Bag System Precautions" Located In The Front Of This Manual For System Disarming & Arming Procedures.

NOTE: Refer To "Computer Relearn Procedures" Located In The Front Of This Manual When Battery Power To The Computer Has Been Interrupted.

NOTE: Electrical Symbol & Wire Color Code Identification Located In The Front Of This Manual May Be Used As An Aid When Using Wiring Circuits Found In This Section.

INDEX

	Page No.		Page No.		Page No.
Description	5-102	Commander, Grand Cherokee & Liberty	5-103	Precautions	5-102
Diagnosis & Testing	5-102	Diagnostic Trouble Code		Air Bag Systems	5-102
Accessing Diagnostic Trouble Codes	5-102	Interpretation	5-102	Battery Ground Cable	5-102
Clearing Diagnostic Trouble		Symptom Test	5-103	General Service Precautions	5-102
Codes	5-103	Wiring Diagrams	5-103	System Service	5-103
Connector Pin Identification	5-102	2002–04 Grand Cherokee	5-103	Brake System Bleed	5-103
Commander & 2005–06		Commander & 2005–06		Component Replacement	5-103
Grand Cherokee	5-102	Grand Cherokee	5-103	Controller Anti-Lock Brake
Liberty	5-102	Liberty	5-103	(CAB) Module, Replace	5-103
Wrangler	5-102	Wrangler	5-103	Front Wheel Sensor	5-103
Diagnostic Tests	5-103	Diagnostic Chart Index	5-110	Hydraulic Control Unit (HCU)	5-104
				Rear Wheel Sensor	5-104

PRECAUTIONS

Air Bag Systems

Refer to "Air Bag System Precautions" in the front of this manual for system disarming and arming procedures.

Battery Ground Cable

Prior to service disconnect battery ground cable and isolate as required.

General Service Precautions

Certain components of the anti-lock brake system are not intended to be serviced individually. Attempting to remove or disconnect components of this type may result in personal injury and/or improper system operation. Only the components with removal and installation procedures should be serviced.

Observe the following general precautions when servicing the anti-lock brake system:

1. If any welding work is to be performed using an arc welder, Controller Anti-Lock Brake (CAB) should be disconnected.
2. When ignition switch is in On position, CAB electrical connector should not be disconnected or connected.
3. Some components of ABS system are not serviced separately and must be serviced as complete assemblies. Do not disassemble any component which is designated as non-serviceable.

DESCRIPTION

The Anti-Lock Brake System (ABS) prevents wheel lock-up by monitoring wheel speed and altering pressure to the wheels. This is accomplished using an anti-lock brake module, power brake hydraulic booster, electric pump, accumulator, three channel modulator and wheel speed sensors.

In the event of emergency braking, monitors will read individual wheel speed so that maximum braking effectiveness can be maintained at all times. As wheel speed deceleration occurs, brake pressure is relieved at slowest wheels, providing stability and steering control to the system.

The anti-lock brake system will detect faults within the system. When a fault is detected, an instrument panel ABS warning lamp will illuminate and a diagnostic trouble code will be stored in the control unit memory. Basic brake system malfunctions will be indicated by a red Brake warning lamp, but these warnings are not stored.

DIAGNOSIS & TESTING

Accessing Diagnostic Trouble Codes

Connect a suitably programmed scan tool to Data Link Connector (DLC) and follow manufacturer's instructions.

Diagnostic Trouble Code Interpretation

Refer to "Diagnostic Chart Index" for diagnostic trouble code interpretation.

Connector Pin Identification

COMMANDER & 2005-06 GRAND CHEROKEE

Refer to **Fig. 1** for connector terminal identification.

LIBERTY

Refer to **Fig. 2** for connector terminal identification.

WRANGLER

Refer to **Fig. 3** for connector terminal identification.

Wiring Diagrams

COMMANDER & 2005-06 GRAND CHEROKEE

Refer to anti-lock brake system wiring diagrams, **Fig. 4** when troubleshooting the system.

2002-04 GRAND CHEROKEE

Refer to anti-lock brake system wiring diagrams, **Fig. 5** when troubleshooting the system.

LIBERTY

Refer to anti-lock brake system wiring diagrams, **Figs. 6 and 7** when troubleshooting the system.

WRANGLER

Refer to anti-lock brake system wiring diagrams, **Figs. 8 and 9** when troubleshooting the system.

Diagnostic Tests

COMMANDER, GRAND CHEROKEE & LIBERTY

2005-06

For diagnostic trouble codes not found here, refer to "Durango" "Diagnostic Tests" section for test procedures.

Refer to **Figs. 10 through 26** for diagnostic tests.

Symptom Test

Refer to "Caravan, Town & Country & Voyager"and "PT Cruiser" "Symptom Tests" sections for test procedures.

Clearing Diagnostic Trouble Codes

Connect a suitably programmed scan tool to Data Link Connector (DLC) and follow manufacturer's instructions.

SYSTEM SERVICE

Brake System Bleed

ABS system bleeding requires conventional bleeding methods plus use of the scan tool. The procedure involves performing a base brake bleeding, followed by use of the scan tool to cycle and bleed the HCU pump and solenoids. A second base brake bleeding procedure is then required to remove any air remaining in the system.

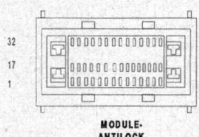

C/A/V	CIRCUIT	FUNCTION
	MODULE-ANTILOCK BRAKES - 47 WAY	
1	A107 12TN/RD	FUSED B(+) (PUMP)
2	-	
3	-	
4	B46 18LB/DB	ESP/TCS ON/OFF SWITCH SENSE
5	-	
6	B15 18DG/WT	BRAKE SWITCH NO. 1 SIGNAL
7	-	
8	F943 18PK/LG	FUSED IGNITION SWITCH OUTPUT (RUN-START)
9	-	
10	D223 18WT/VT	SCI TRANSMIT (PCM)
11	-	
12	D65 18WT/LG	CAN C BUS (+)
13	D64 18WT/LB	CAN C BUS (-)
14	-	
15	-	
16	Z127 12BK/DG	GROUND
17	-	
18	D52 18WT/LB	DYNAMICS SENSOR HIGH DATA LINK
19	D51 18WT/BR	DYNAMICS SENSOR LOW DATA LINK
20	-	
21	-	
22	G4 18VT/LB	DYNAMICS SENSOR SUPPLY
23	-	
24	-	
25	-	
26	-	
27	-	
28	-	
29	G94 18VT/DB	DYNAMICS SENSOR GROUND
30	-	
31	-	
32	A200 12RD/DG	FUSED B(+) (VALVE)
33	B6 18DG/TN	RIGHT FRONT WHEEL SPEED SENSOR SIGNAL
34	B7 18DG/VT	RIGHT FRONT WHEEL SPEED SENSOR SUPPLY
35	-	
36	B4 18LG/YL	LEFT REAR WHEEL SPEED SENSOR SUPPLY
37	B3 18DG/YL	LEFT REAR WHEEL SPEED SENSOR SIGNAL
38	-	
39	-	
40	-	
41	-	
42	B1 18DG/DB	RIGHT REAR WHEEL SPEED SENSOR SIGNAL
43	B2 18DB/WT	RIGHT REAR WHEEL SPEED SENSOR SUPPLY
44	-	
45	B9 18DG/LG	LEFT FRONT WHEEL SPEED SENSOR SUPPLY
46	B8 18DG/TN	LEFT FRONT WHEEL SPEED SENSOR SIGNAL
47	Z107 12BK/DG	GROUND

LTV0500000005633

Fig. 1   Controller Anti-Lock Brake (CAB) connector terminal identification. Commander & 2005–06 Grand Cherokee

Component Replacement

CONTROLLER ANTI-LOCK BRAKE (CAB) MODULE, REPLACE

COMMANDER & 2005-06 GRAND CHEROKEE

1. Install brake pedal prop rod.
2. Siphon master cylinder.
3. Disconnect HCU electrical connectors.
4. Remove primary and secondary brake lines at master cylinder, then HCU.
5. Remove chassis lines at HCU.
6. Remove HCU bracket mounting nuts.
7. Remove HCU with bracket from vehicle.
8. Reverse procedure to install.

GRAND CHEROKEE

2002-04

1. Remove air cleaner housing.
2. Disconnect CAB harness electrical connector.
3. Disconnect pump electrical connector.
4. Remove CAB mounting bolts, then remove CAB from HCU.
5. Reverse procedure to install.

LIBERTY

1. Disconnect CAB electrical connector.
2. Disconnect pump electrical connector from CAB.
3. Disconnect brake lines from CAB.
4. Remove CAB mounting nuts, then CAB.
5. Reverse procedure to install.

WRANGLER

1. Disconnect CAB electrical connector.
2. Disconnect pump electrical connector from CAB.
3. Remove CAB mounting bolts.
4. Remove CAB from HCU.
5. Reverse procedure to install.

FRONT WHEEL SENSOR

COMMANDER, 2005-06 GRAND CHEROKEE & LIBERTY

1. Raise and support vehicle.
2. Remove tire and wheel assembly.
3. Remove caliper adaptor bolts, then brake rotor.
4. Remove wheel sensor mounting nut.
5. Remove speed sensor from hub.
6. Reverse procedure to install.

GRAND CHEROKEE

2002-04

1. Raise and support vehicle and remove tire and wheel assemblies.
2. Remove bolt attaching front sensor to

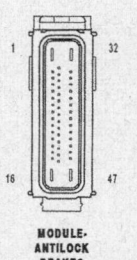

MODULE-ANTILOCK BRAKES - 47 WAY

CAV	CIRCUIT	FUNCTION
1	A107 12TN/RD	FUSED B(+)(PUMP)
2	-	-
3	-	-
4	B46 18DG/WT	ESP ON/OFF SENSE
5	-	-
6	B15 18DG/WT (DIESEL)	SECONDARY BRAKE SWITCH SIGNAL
6	B15 18DG/WT (GAS)	BRAKE SWITCH NO. 1 SIGNAL
7	-	-
8	F1 18PK/WT	FUSED IGNITION SWITCH OUTPUT (RUN-START)
9	-	-
10	D21 18WT/GY (DIESEL)	SCI TRANSMIT (ECM)
10	D21 18WT/GY (GAS)	SCI TRANSMIT (PCM)
11	-	-
12	D65 18WT/LG	CAN C BUS (+)
13	D64 18WT/LB	CAN C BUS (-)
14	-	-
15	-	-
16	Z127 12BK/DG	GROUND
17	-	-
18	D52 18WT/LB	DYNAMICS SENSOR HIGH DATA LINK
19	D51 18PK/RD	DYNAMICS SENSOR LOW DATA LINK
20	-	-
21	-	-
22	G4 18VT/LB	DYNAMICS SENSOR SUPPLY
23	-	-
24	-	-
25	-	-
26	-	-
27	-	-
28	-	-

LTV050000005641

Fig. 2 Controller Anti-Lock Brake (CAB) connector terminal identification. Liberty

CONTROLLER ANTILOCK BRAKE - 25 WAY

CAV	CIRCUIT	FUNCTION
1	B1 18DG/OR	RIGHT REAR WHEEL SPEED SENSOR (-)
2	B3 18DG/YL	LEFT REAR WHEEL SPEED SENSOR (-)
3	B7 18DG/VT	RIGHT FRONT WHEEL SPEED SENSOR (+)
4	B9 18DG/LG	LEFT FRONT WHEEL SPEED SENSOR (+)
5	-	-
6	G117 18VT/LG	G-SWITCH NO. 1 SENSE
7	G118 18VT/YL	G-SWITCH NO. 2 SENSE
8	Z127 12BK/DG	GROUND
9	A111 12DG/RD	FUSED B(+)
10	B4 18DG/GY	LEFT REAR WHEEL SPEED SENSOR (+)
11	B8 18DG/TN	LEFT FRONT WHEEL SPEED SENSOR (-)
12	L50 18WT/TN	BRAKE LAMP SWITCH OUTPUT
13	G119 18VT	G-SWITCH TEST SIGNAL
14	-	-
15	-	-
16	G83 18VT/WT	ABS RELAY CONTROL
17	B2 18DG/LB	RIGHT REAR WHEEL SPEED SENSOR (+)
18	B6 18DG/WT	RIGHT FRONT WHEEL SPEED SENSOR (-)
19	-	-
20	D21 18WT/BR	SCI TRANSMIT
21	-	-
22	-	-
23	F102 18PK/DB	FUSED IGNITION SWITCH OUTPUT (RUN)
24	Z107 12BK/DG	GROUND
25	A107 12TN/RD	FUSED B(+)

LTV0500000005650

Fig. 3 Controller Anti-Lock Brake (CAB) connector terminal identification. Wrangler

steering knuckle.
3. Disengage sensor wire from brackets on steering knuckle and frame.
4. Unseat grommet that secures sensor wire in fender panel.
5. Disconnect sensor wire connector at harness plug in engine compartment, then remove sensor and wires.
6. Reverse procedure to install.

WRANGLER

1. Raise and support vehicle, then turn wheel outward for sensor access.
2. Remove sensor wire from mounting brackets.
3. Clean sensor and surrounding area, then remove sensor securing bolt.
4. Remove sensor, then unseat grommet retaining sensor wire in wheelhouse panel.
5. Disconnect sensor wire connector then remove sensor and wire.
6. Reverse procedure to install.

HYDRAULIC CONTROL UNIT (HCU)

COMMANDER & 2005–06 GRAND CHEROKEE

Refer to "Controller Anti-Lock Brake (CAB) Module, Replace" in this section.

2002–04 GRAND CHEROKEE, LIBERTY & WRANGLER

1. **On Liberty & Wrangler models,** install prop rod on brake pedal.
2. **On all models,** remove air cleaner housing and disconnect CAB harness connector from CAB.
3. Remove brake lines from HCU.
4. Remove CAB/HCU assembly side and two rear mounting bolts.
5. Remove CAB/HCU assembly from vehicle.
6. Reverse procedure to install. Bleed system as outlined under "Brake System Bleed."

REAR WHEEL SENSOR

COMMANDER & 2005–06 GRAND CHEROKEE

1. Raise and support vehicle.
2. Remove wheel speed sensor mounting bolt.
3. Remove wheel speed sensor from support plate.
4. Disconnect wheel speed sensor electrical connector.
5. Reverse procedure to install.

2002–04 GRAND CHEROKEE

1. Raise and fold rear seat forward, then

move carpeting aside for access to rear sensor connectors.
2. Disconnect rear sensor electrical connectors.
3. Push sensor wires and grommets through floorpan holes.
4. Raise and support vehicle.
5. Disconnect sensor wire from axle and chassis brackets, then from brake line retainers.
6. Remove sensor mounting bolt from rear brake backing plate.
7. Remove sensor from backing plate.
8. Reverse procedure to install.

LIBERTY

1. Raise and support vehicle.
2. Disconnect sensor electrical connector.
3. Remove sensor mounting stud, then sensor.
4. Reverse procedure to install.

WRANGLER

1. Raise and support vehicle.
2. Disconnect sensor wires at rear axle connectors.
3. Remove wheel and brake drum.
4. Remove clips securing sensor wire to brake and hoses lines or rear axle.
5. Unseat sensor support plate grommet and remove sensor bolt, bracket and sensor assembly.
6. Reverse procedure to install.

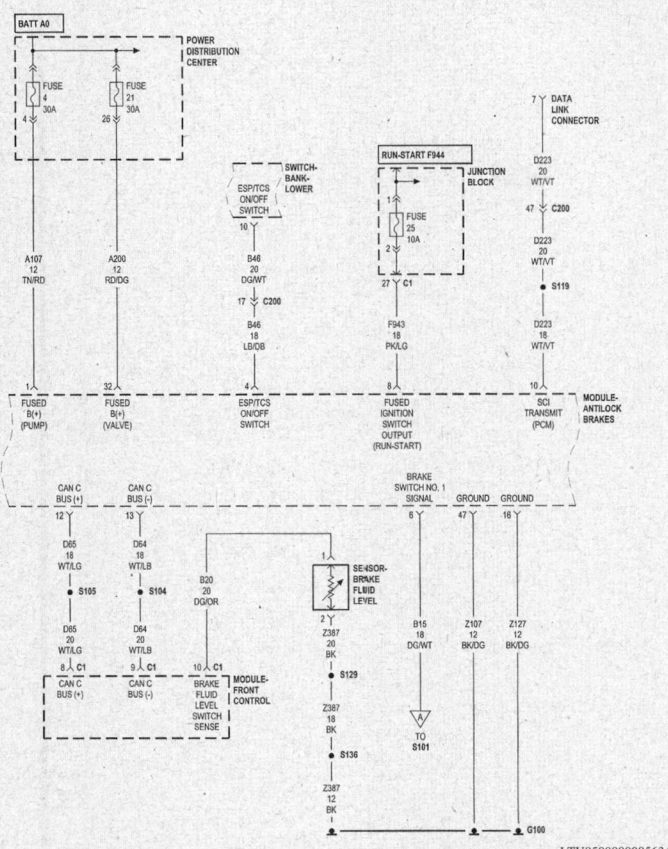

Fig. 4 Wiring diagram (Part 1 of 3). Commander & 2005–06 Grand Cherokee

LTV0500000005634

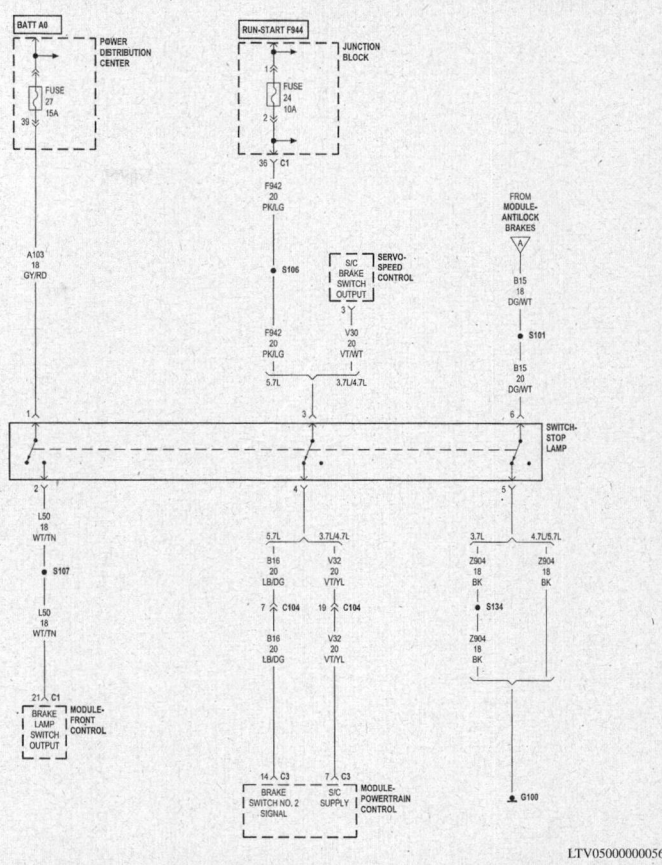

Fig. 4 Wiring diagram (Part 2 of 3). Commander & 2005–06 Grand Cherokee

LTV0500000005635

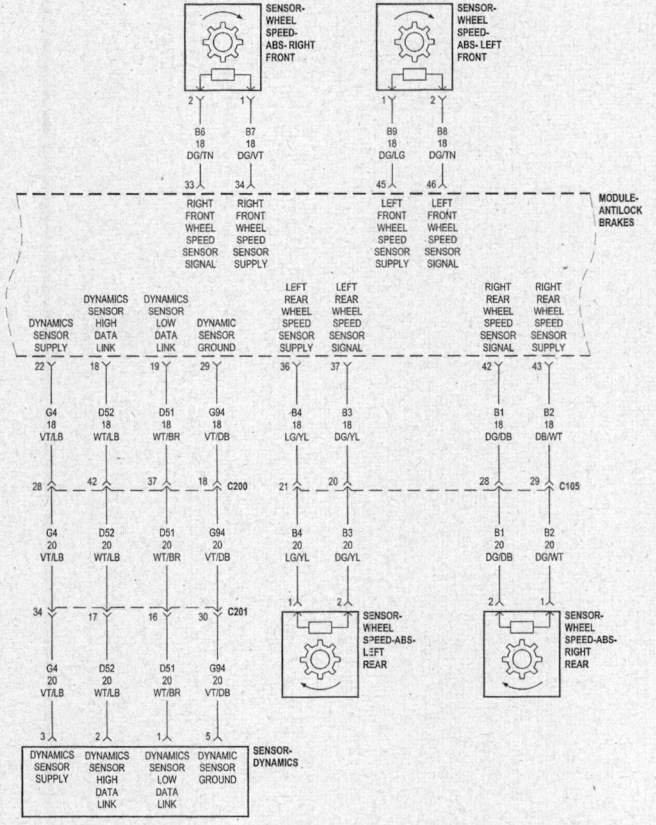

Fig. 4 Wiring diagram (Part 3 of 3). Commander & 2005–06 Grand Cherokee

LTV0500000005636

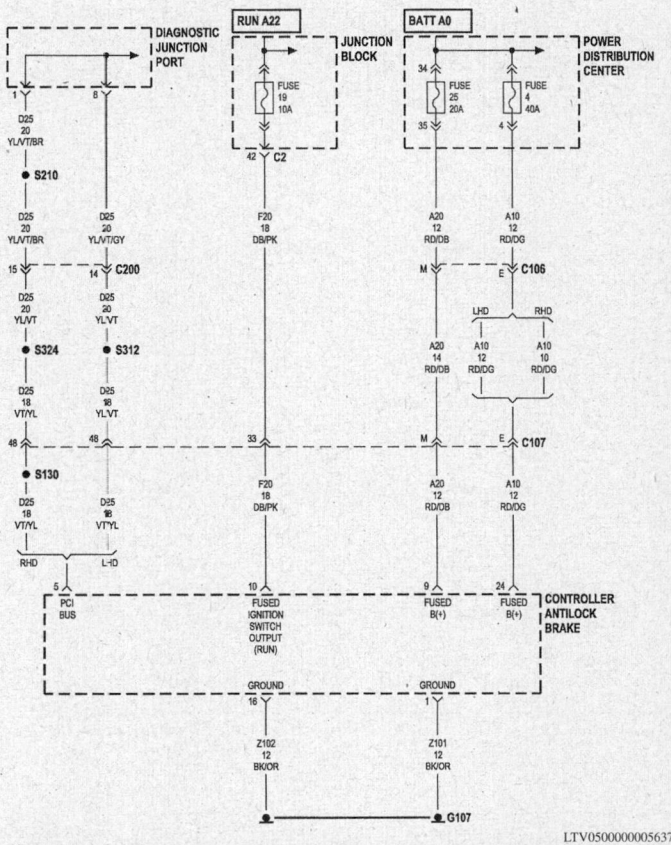

Fig. 5 Wiring diagram (Part 1 of 4). 2002–04 Grand Cherokee

LTV0500000005637

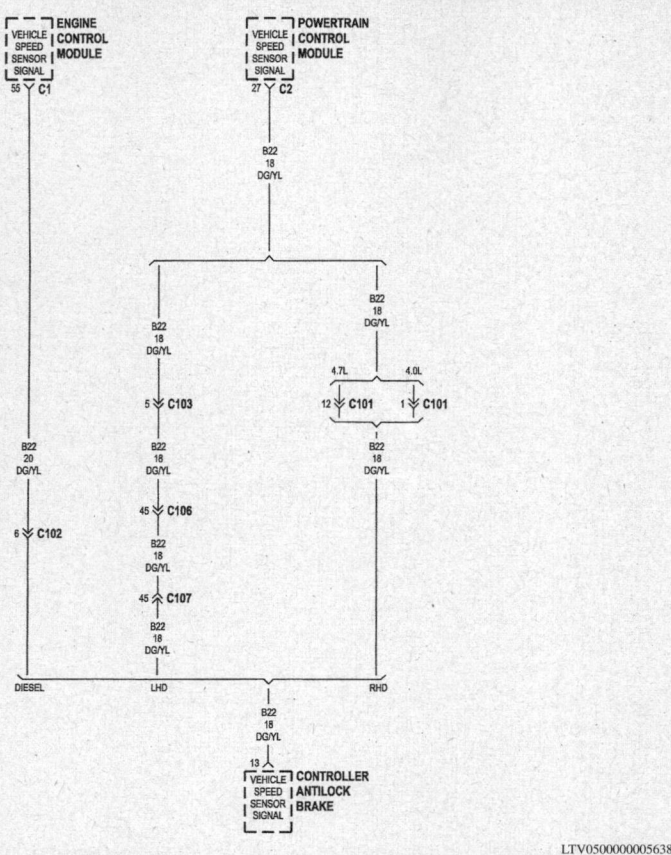

Fig. 5 Wiring diagram (Part 2 of 4). 2002–04 Grand Cherokee

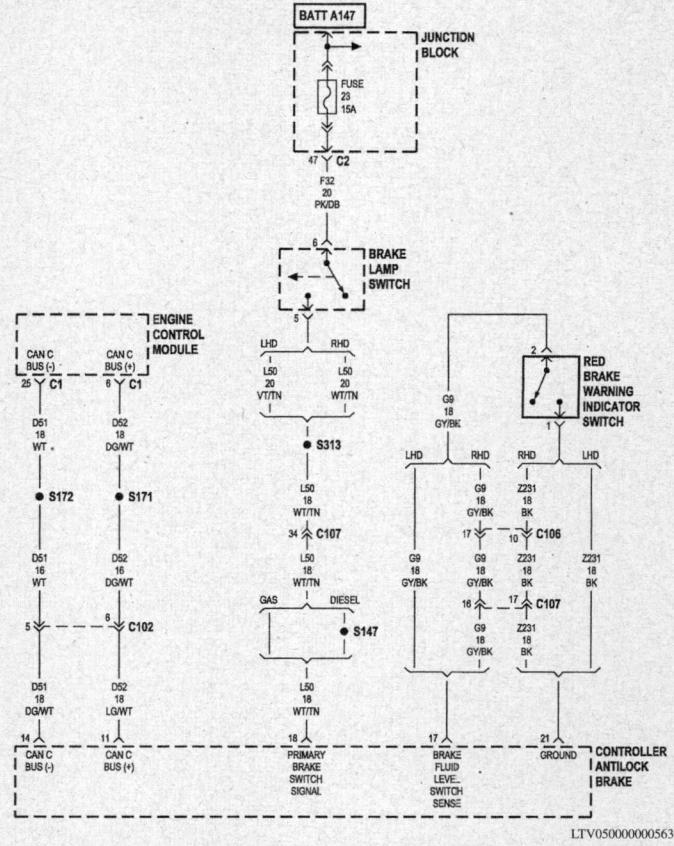

Fig. 5 Wiring diagram (Part 3 of 4). 2002–04 Grand Cherokee

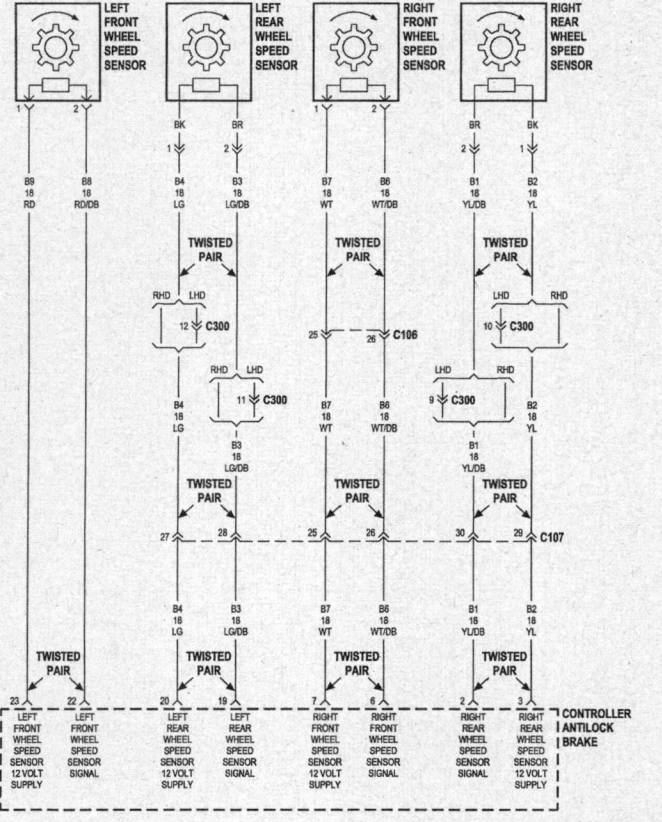

Fig. 5 Wiring diagram (Part 4 of 4). 2002–04 Grand Cherokee

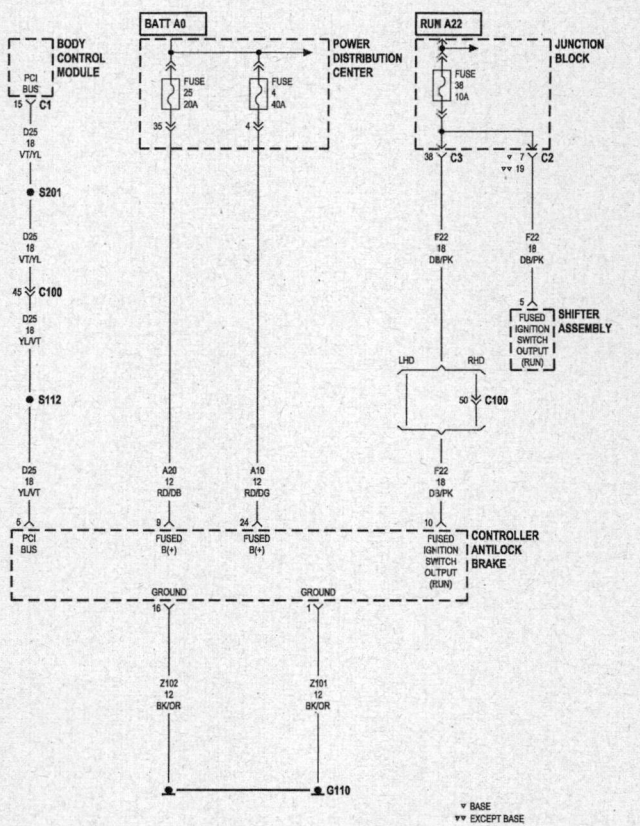

Fig. 6 Wiring diagram (Part 1 of 3). 2002–04 Liberty

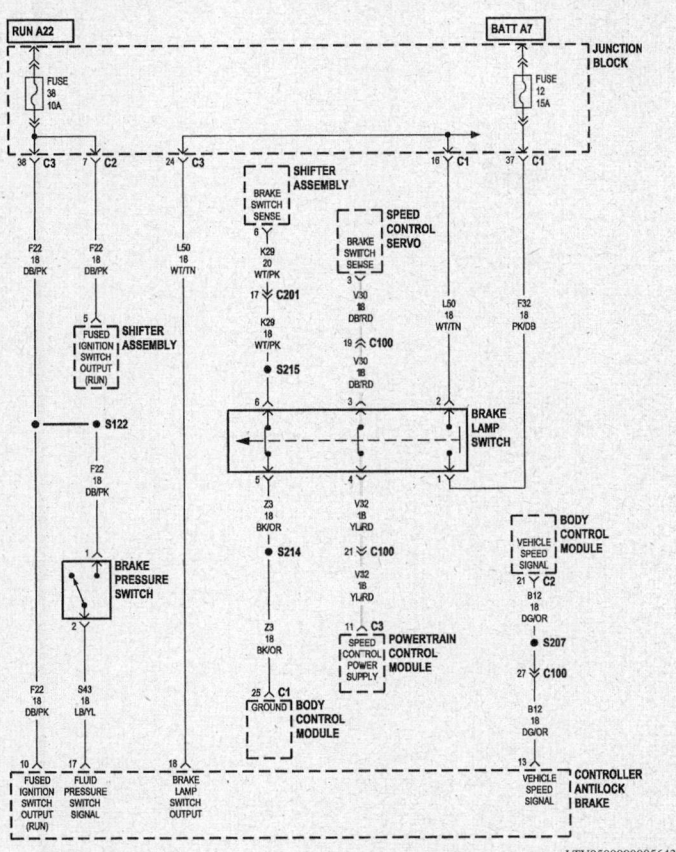

Fig. 6   Wiring diagram (Part 2 of 3). 2002–04 Liberty

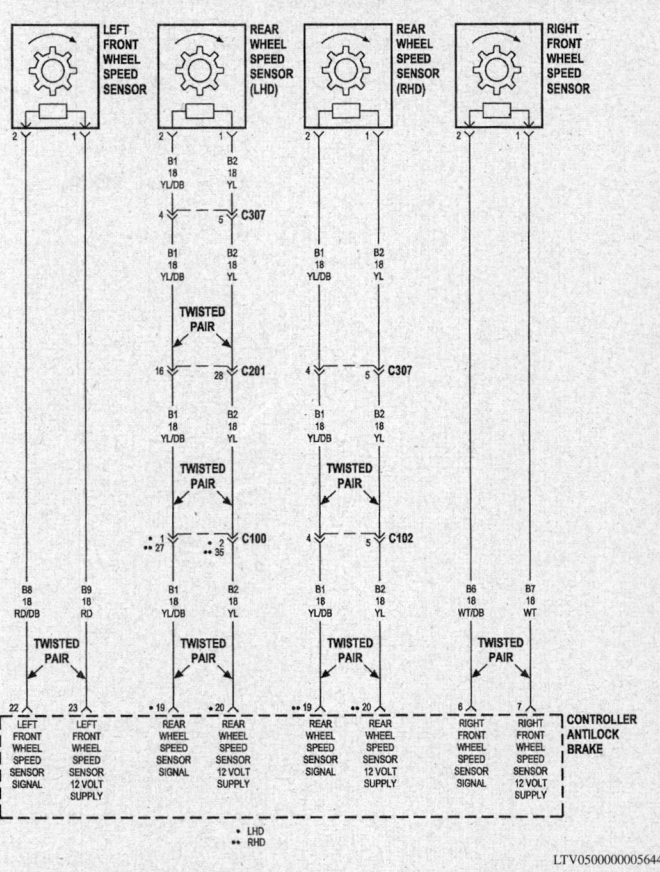

Fig. 6   Wiring diagram (Part 3 of 3). 2002–04 Liberty

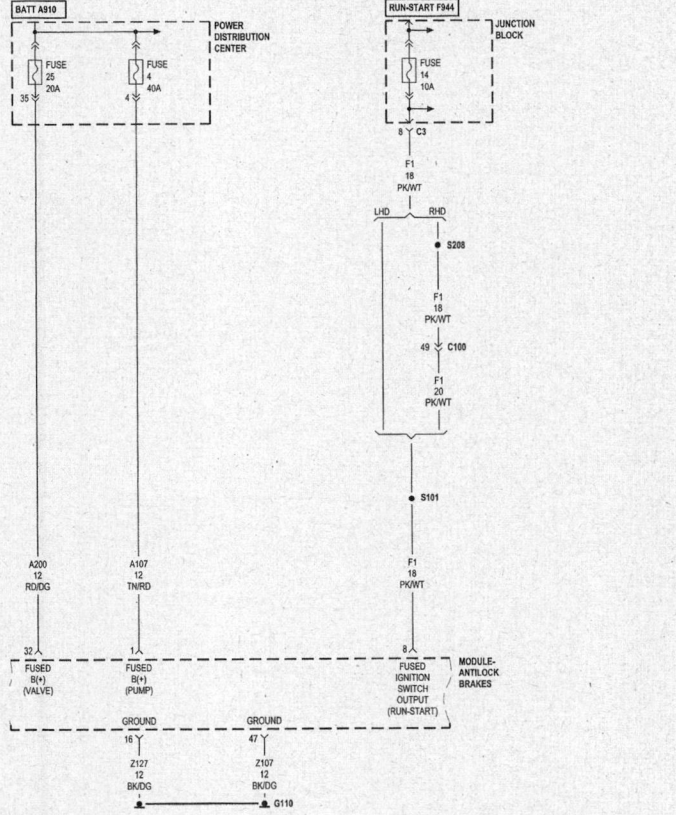

Fig. 7   Wiring diagram (Part 1 of 5). 2005–06 Liberty

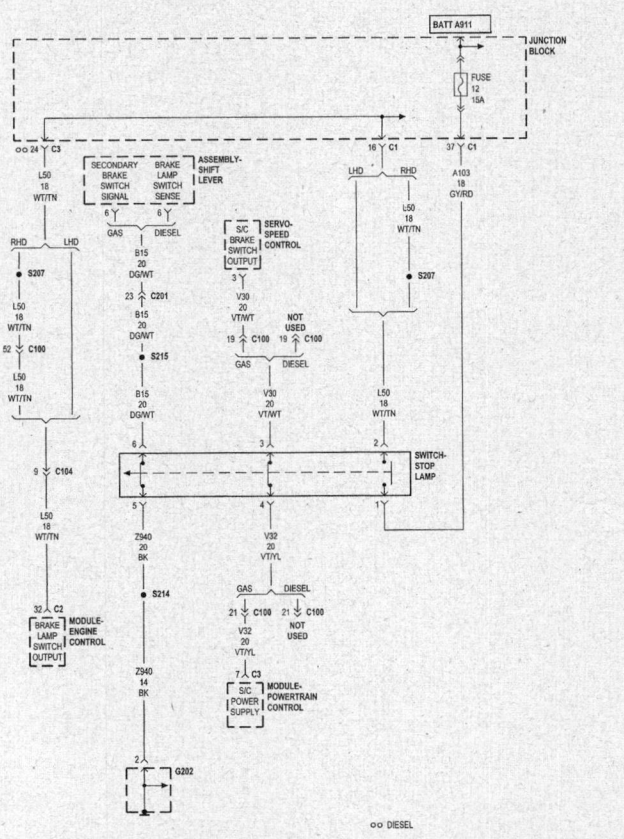

Fig. 7   Wiring diagram (Part 2 of 5). 2005–06 Liberty

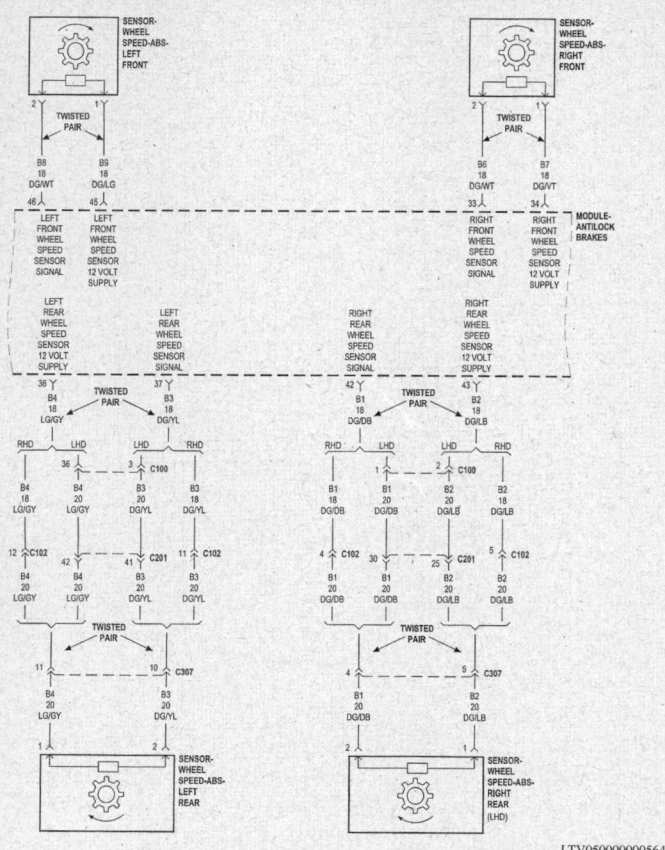

Fig. 7 Wiring diagram (Part 3 of 5). 2005–06 Liberty

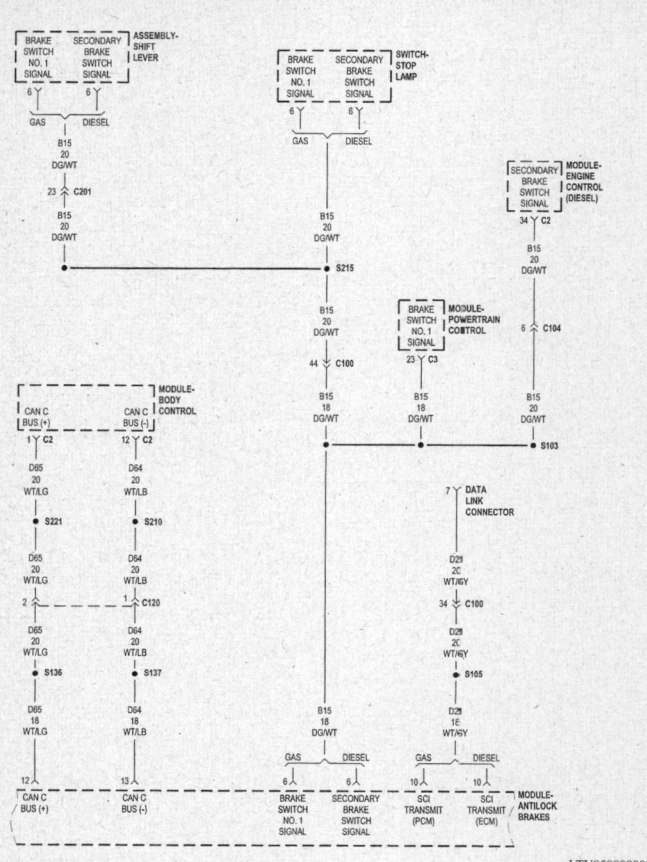

Fig. 7 Wiring diagram (Part 4 of 5). 2005–06 Liberty

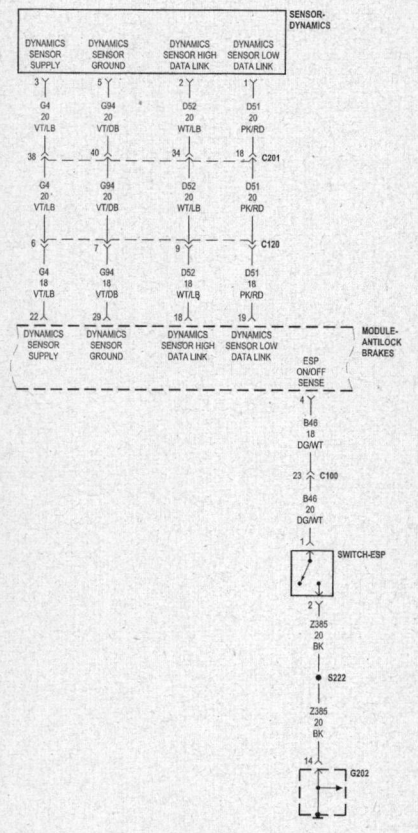

Fig. 7 Wiring diagram (Part 5 of 5). 2005–06 Liberty

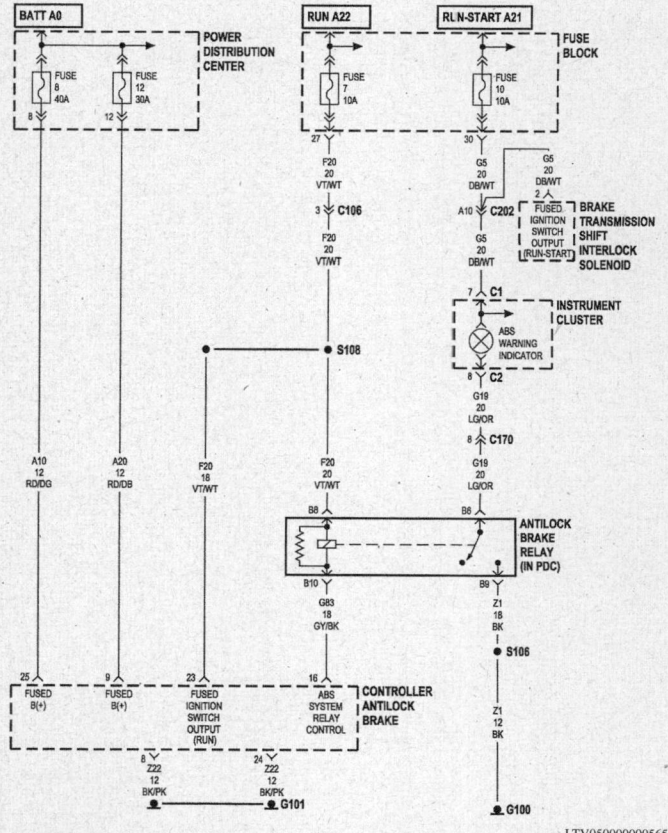

Fig. 8 Wiring diagram (Part 1 of 3). 2002–04 Wrangler

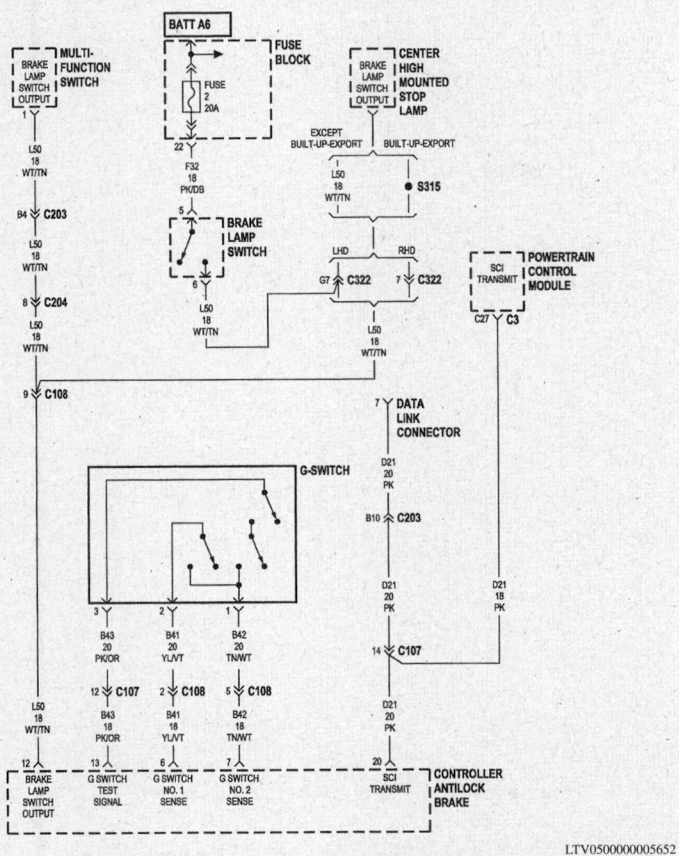

Fig. 8 Wiring diagram (Part 2 of 3). 2002–04 Wrangler

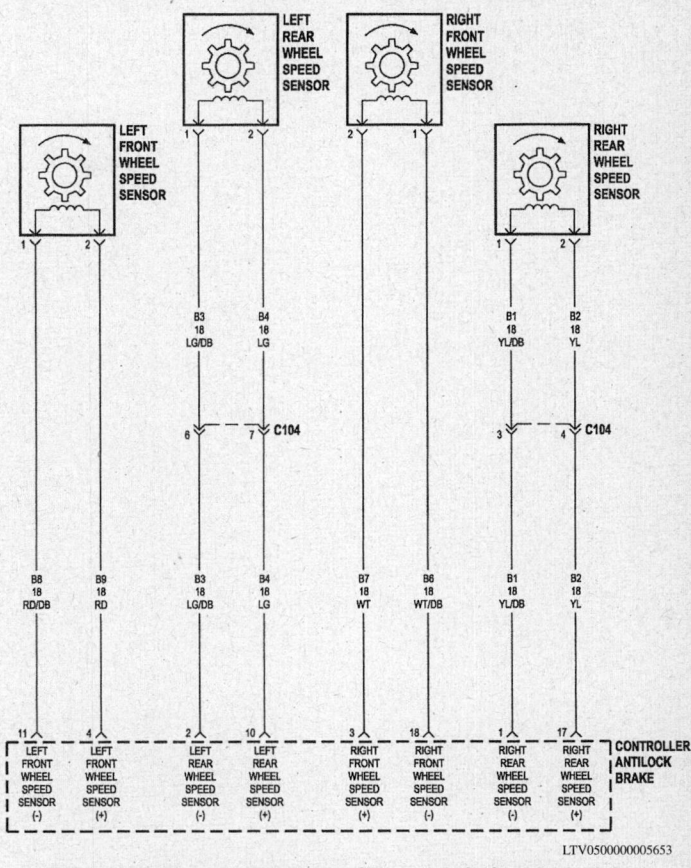

Fig. 8 Wiring diagram (Part 3 of 3). 2002–04 Wrangler

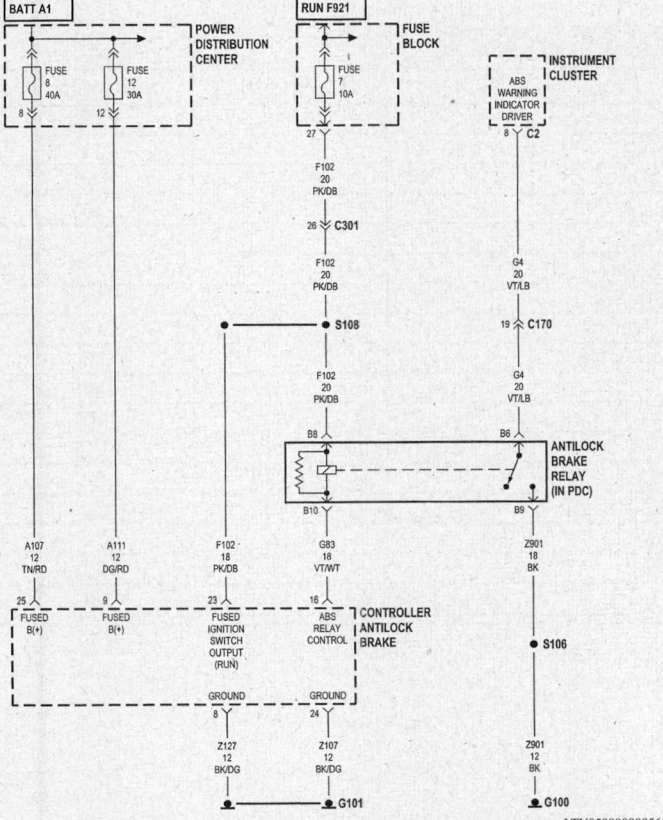

Fig. 9 Wiring diagram (Part 1 of 3). 2005–06 Wrangler

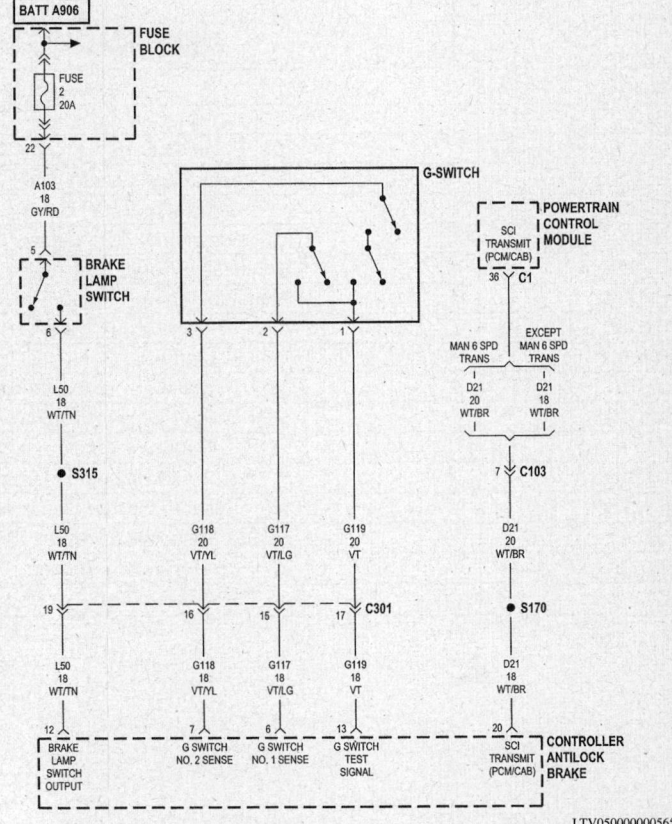

Fig. 9 Wiring diagram (Part 2 of 3). 2005–06 Wrangler

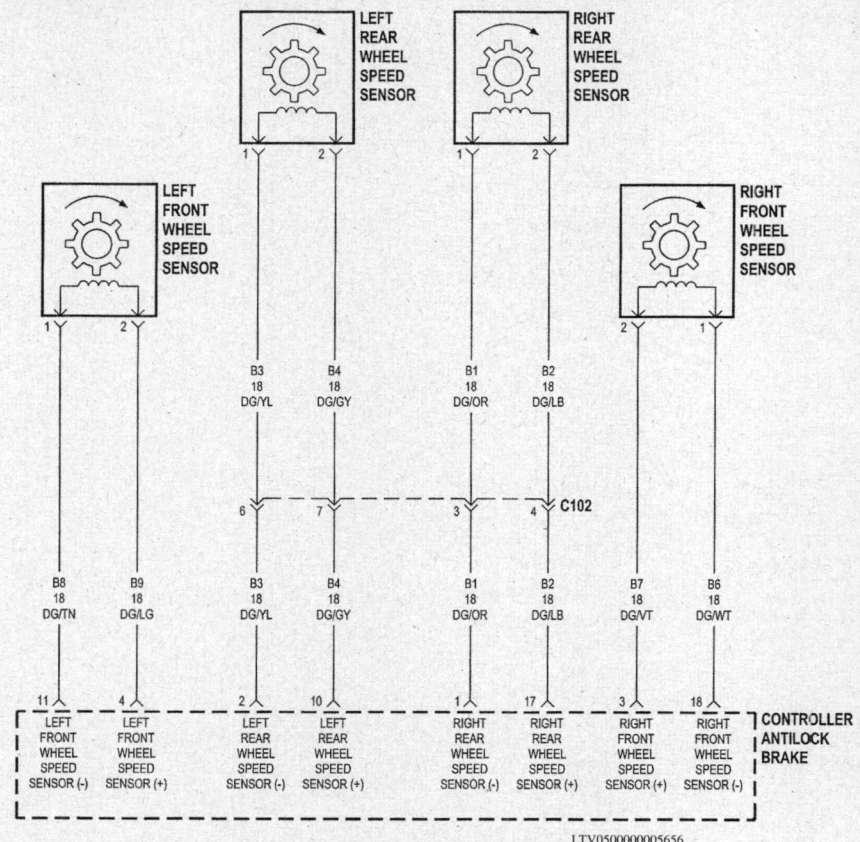

Fig. 9   Wiring diagram (Part 3 of 3). 2005–06 Wrangler

DIAGNOSTIC CHART INDEX

Code	Description	Page No.	Fig No.
B1D4F	Adjustable Pedal Inhibit Circuit Low	5-111	10
B1D450	Adjustable Pedal Inhibit Circuit High	5-111	11
B1D51	Adjustable Pedal Inhibit Circuit Open	5-112	12
B1D56	Adjustable Pedal Sensor Circuit Low	5-113	13
B1D57	Adjustable Pedal Sensor Circuit High	5-114	14
B1D5B	Adjustable Pedal Switch Circuit Performance	5-115	15
B1D5C	Adjustable Pedal Switch Circuit Stuck Forward	5-117	16
B1D5D	Adjustable Pedal Switch Circuit Stuck Rearward	5-118	17
B1D67	Adjustable Pedal Control Circuit Performance	5-119	18
C107C	Brake Pedal Switch Half Stuck	5-121	19
C107D	Brake Pedal Switch Half Correlation	5-122	20
C121C	Torque Request Signal Denied	5-124	21
C121D	Brake Pressure Sensor Circuit	5-124	22
C121E	Brake Pressure Sensor Comparative Performance	5-125	23
C1221	Brake Pressure Sensor/Accel Pedal Position Sensor Correlation	5-126	24
C123A	ESP System Sensors Calibration	5-127	25
C123B	ESP System Sensors Control Too Long	5-128	26

1. CHECK FOR A DTC B1D4F-ADJUSTABLE PEDAL INHIBIT CIRCUIT LOW

NOTE: This DTC must be active for the results of this test to be valid.

Turn the ignition on.
With the scan tool, read and record DTCs.
With the scan tool, read and record Freeze Frame information.
With the scan tool, erase DTCs.
Cycle the ignition switch from off to on.

WARNING: Apply the parking brake. The vehicle may roll when the Transmission is shifted out of Park.

Shift into Reverse for at least 5 seconds, then move the shifter back into Park.
With the scan tool, read and record DTCs.

Does the scan tool display: B1D4F-ADJUSTABLE PEDAL INHIBIT CIRCUIT LOW?

Yes

- Go To 2

No

- Refer to the Adjustable Pedal System intermittent condition test.

2. CHECK THE TERMINALS/CONNECTORS FOR DAMAGE

NOTE: Check all related wiring for bruised, chafed, pierced, or partially broken wires.

NOTE: Check all related connectors for broken, bent, pushed out, or corroded terminals.

Turn the ignition off.
Visually inspect the wiring for damage.

Were any problems found?

Yes

- Repair as necessary.
- Perform APS VERIFICATION TEST.

No

- Go To 3

LTV0500000006054

Fig. 10 Code B1D4F: Adjustable Pedal Inhibit Circuit Low (Part 1 of 3). 2005–06 Commander, Grand Cherokee & Liberty

5. CHECK THE ADJUSTABLE PEDALS RELAY CONTROL CIRCUIT FOR VOLTAGE

Turn the ignition on.
Using a 12-volt test light connected to ground, disconnect the Front Control Module harness connector and check the Adjustable Pedals Relay Control circuit at the Front Control Module connector.

Does the test light illuminate?

Yes

- Go To 6

No

- Repair the Adjustable Pedals Relay Control circuit for an open or high resistance.
- Perform APS VERIFICATION TEST

6. FRONT CONTROL MODULE

Reconnect all components.
Turn the ignition on.
With the scan tool, actuate the Adjustable Pedals Relay.
Measure the voltage of the Adjustable Pedals Relay Control circuit at the Front Control Module connector of the IPM.

NOTE: With the Relay actuated ON, the circuit voltage should be 0 volts.

NOTE: With the Relay actuated OFF, the circuit voltage should be approximately 2.5 volts.

Does the circuit voltage display as described during the actuation test?

Yes

- Replace the Adjustable Pedals Relay
- Perform APS VERIFICATION TEST

No

- Replace the Front Control Module
- Perform APS VERIFICATION TEST

LTV0500000006056

Fig. 10 Code B1D4F: Adjustable Pedal Inhibit Circuit Low (Part 3 of 3). 2005–06 Commander, Grand Cherokee & Liberty

3. FUSED B+ CIRCUIT OPEN OR HIGH RESISTANCE (IPM)

Using a 12-volt test light connect to ground, check the internal Fused B(+) circuits at the Adjustable Pedals Relay connector of the IPM.

NOTE: The test light should be illuminated and bright. Compare the brightness to that of a direct connection to the battery.

Is the test light illuminated and bright for both circuits?

Yes

- Go To 4

No

- Remove and inspect Fuse in the IPM. If the fuse is open, test the circuit for a short to ground. Repair as necessary. If the fuse is OK, replace the Integrated Power Module
- Perform APS VERIFICATION TEST

4. CHECK THE ADJUSTABLE PEDALS RELAY OUTPUT VOLTAGE

Turn the ignition on.
Using a 12-volt test light connected to ground, check the Adjustable Pedals Relay Control circuit.

Does the test light illuminate brightly?

Yes

- Go To 5

No

- Replace the Adjustable Pedals Relay
- Perform APS VERIFICATION TEST

LTV0500000006055

Fig. 10 Code B1D4F: Adjustable Pedal Inhibit Circuit Low (Part 2 of 3). 2005–06 Commander, Grand Cherokee & Liberty

1. CHECK FOR A DTC B1D50-ADJUSTABLE PEDAL INHIBIT CIRCUIT HIGH

NOTE: This DTC must be active for the results of this test to be valid.

Turn the ignition on.
With the scan tool, read and record DTCs.
With the scan tool, read and record Freeze Frame information.
With the scan tool, erase DTCs.
Cycle the ignition switch from off to on.
With the scan tool, read and record DTCs.

Does the scan tool display: B1D50-ADJUSTABLE PEDAL INHIBIT CIRCUIT HIGH?

Yes

- Go To 2

No

- The condition that caused the symptom is currently not present. Inspect the related wiring for a possible intermittent condition. Look for any chafed, pierced, pinched, or partially broken wires.
- Refer to the APS-INTERMITTENT CONDITION TEST.

2. CHECK THE TERMINALS/CONNECTORS FOR DAMAGE

NOTE: Check all related wiring for bruised, chafed, pierced, or partially broken wires.

NOTE: Check all related connectors for broken, bent, pushed out, or corroded terminals.

Turn the ignition off.
Visually inspect the wiring for damage.

Were any problems found?

Yes

- Repair as necessary.
- Perform APS VERIFICATION TEST

No

- Go To 3

LTV0500000006057

Fig. 11 Code B1D450: Adjustable Pedal Inhibit Circuit High (Part 1 of 4). 2005–06 Commander, Grand Cherokee & Liberty

3. SWAP OUT THE ADJUSTABLE PEDALS RELAY

Install a known good relay in place of the Adjustable Pedals Relay.
Turn the ignition on.
With the scan tool, erase DTC's.
Cycle the ignition switch from off to on.
With the scan tool, read and record DTC's

Does the scan tool display: B1D4F-ADJUSTABLE PEDAL INHIBIT CIRCUIT LOW?

Yes

- Go To 4

No

- Replace the Adjustable Pedals Relay
- Perform APS VERIFICATION TEST.

4. CHECK THE VOLTAGE ON THE FUSED B(+) CIRCUIT FOR THE ADJUSTABLE PEDALS RELAY

Turn the ignition off.
Remove the Adjustable Pedals Relay from the IPM.
Measure the voltage of the internal Fused B(+) circuit at the IPM.

Is the voltage above 10 volts?

Yes

- Go To 5

No

- Replace the IPM
- Perform APS VERIFICATION TEST.

LTV0500000006058

Fig. 11   Code B1D50: Adjustable Pedal Inhibit Circuit High (Part 2 of 4). 2005–06 Commander, Grand Cherokee & Liberty

7. CHECK THE ADJUSTABLE PEDALS RELAY CONTROL CIRCUIT FOR AN OPEN

Turn the ignition off.
Connect a jumper wire between the Adjustable Pedals Relay Control circuit and ground.
Using a 12-volt test light connected to 12-volts, check the Adjustable Pedals Relay Control circuit.

Does the test light illuminate brightly

Yes

- Replace the Front Control Module
- Perform APS VERIFICATION TEST.

No

- Repair the Adjustable Pedals Relay Control circuit for an open.
- Perform APS VERIFICATION TEST.

LTV0500000006060

Fig. 11   Code B1D50: Adjustable Pedal Inhibit Circuit High (Part 4 of 4). 2005–06 Commander, Grand Cherokee & Liberty

5. CHECK THE ADJUSTABLE PEDALS RELAY CONTROL CIRCUIT FOR A SHORT TO GROUND

Disconnect the Front Control Module harness connector.
Using a 12-volt test light connected to 12-volts, check the Adjustable Pedals Relay Control circuit.

Does the test light illuminate brightly?

Yes

- Repair the Adjustable Pedals Relay Control circuit for a short to ground.
- Perform APS VERIFICATION TEST.

No

- Go To 6

6. CHECK THE ADJUSTABLE PEDALS RELAY CONTROL CIRCUIT FOR A SHORT TO VOLTAGE

Turn the ignition on.
Using a 12-volt test light connected to ground, check the Adjustable Pedals Relay Control circuit.

Does the test light illuminate brightly?

Yes

- Repair the Adjustable Pedals Relay Control circuit for a short to voltage.
- Perform APS VERIFICATION TEST.

No

- Go To 7

LTV0500000006059

Fig. 11   Code B1D50: Adjustable Pedal Inhibit Circuit High (Part 3 of 4). 2005–06 Commander, Grand Cherokee & Liberty

1. CHECK FOR A DTC B1D51-ADJUSTABLE PEDAL INHIBIT CIRCUIT OPEN

NOTE: This DTC must be active for the results of this test to be valid.

Turn the ignition on.
With the scan tool, read and record DTCs.
With the scan tool, read and record Freeze Frame information.
With the scan tool, erase DTCs.
Cycle the ignition switch from off to on.
With the scan tool, read and record DTCs.

Does the scan tool display:B1D51-ADJUSTABLE PEDAL INHIBIT CIRCUIT OPEN?

Yes

- Go To 2

No

- The condition that caused the symptom is currently not present. Inspect the related wiring for a possible intermittent condition. Look for any chafed, pierced, pinched, or partially broken wires.
- Refer to the APS-INTERMITTENT CONDITIONS

2. CHECK THE TERMINALS/CONNECTORS FOR DAMAGE

NOTE: Check all related wiring for bruised, chafed, pierced, or partially broken wires.

NOTE: Check all related connectors for broken, bent, pushed out, or corroded terminals.

Turn the ignition off.
Visually inspect the wiring for damage.

Were any problems found?

Yes

- Repair as necessary.
- Perform APS VERIFICATION TEST.

No

- Go To 3

LTV0500000006061

Fig. 12   Code B1D51: Adjustable Pedal Inhibit Circuit Open (Part 1 of 4). 2005–06 Commander, Grand Cherokee & Liberty

3. SWAP OUT THE ADJUSTABLE PEDALS RELAY

Install a known good relay in place of the Adjustable Pedals Relay.
Turn the ignition on.
With the scan tool, erase DTC's.
Cycle the ignition switch from off to on.
With the scan tool, read and record DTC's

Does the scan tool display: B1D4F-ADJUSTABLE PEDAL INHIBIT CIRCUIT LOW?

Yes

- Go To 4

No

- Replace the Adjustable Pedals Relay
- Perform APS VERIFICATION TEST.

4. CHECK THE VOLTAGE ON THE FUSED B(+) CIRCUIT FOR THE ADJUSTABLE PEDALS RELAY

Turn the ignition off.
Remove the Adjustable Pedals Relay from the IPM.
Measure the voltage of the internal Fused B(+) circuit at the IPM.

Is the voltage above 10 volts?

Yes

- Go To 5

No

- Replace the IPM
- Perform APS VERIFICATION TEST.

LTV0500000006062

Fig. 12 Code B1D51: Adjustable Pedal Inhibit Circuit Open (Part 2 of 4). 2005–06 Commander, Grand Cherokee & Liberty

7. CHECK THE ADJUSTABLE PEDALS RELAY CONTROL CIRCUIT FOR AN OPEN

Turn the ignition off.
Connect a jumper wire between the Adjustable Pedals Relay Control circuit and ground.
Using a 12-volt test light connected to 12-volts, check the Adjustable Pedals Relay Control circuit.

Does the test light illuminate brightly

Yes

- Replace the Front Control Module
- Perform APS VERIFICATION TEST.

No

- Repair the (P201) Adjustable Pedals Relay Control circuit for an open.
- Perform APS VERIFICATION TEST.

LTV0500000006064

Fig. 12 Code B1D51: Adjustable Pedal Inhibit Circuit Open (Part 4 of 4). 2005–06 Commander, Grand Cherokee & Liberty

5. CHECK THE ADJUSTABLE PEDALS RELAY CONTROL CIRCUIT FOR A SHORT TO GROUND

Disconnect the Front Control Module harness connector.
Using a 12-volt test light connected to 12-volts, check the Adjustable Pedals Relay Control circuit.

Does the test light illuminate brightly?

Yes

- Repair the Adjustable Pedals Relay Control circuit for a short to ground.
- Perform APS VERIFICATION TEST.

No

- Go To 6

6. CHECK THE ADJUSTABLE PEDALS RELAY CONTROL CIRCUIT FOR A SHORT TO VOLTAGE

Turn the ignition on.
Using a 12-volt test light connected to ground, check the Adjustable Pedals Relay Control circuit.

Does the test light illuminate brightly?

Yes

- Repair the Adjustable Pedals Relay Control circuit for a short to voltage.
- Perform APS VERIFICATION TEST.

No

- Go To 7

LTV0500000006063

Fig. 12 Code B1D51: Adjustable Pedal Inhibit Circuit Open (Part 3 of 4). 2005–06 Commander, Grand Cherokee & Liberty

1. CHECK FOR DTC B1D56–ADJUSTABLE PEDAL SENSOR CIRCUIT LOW

NOTE: This DTC must be active for the results of this test to be valid.

Turn the ignition on.
With the scan tool, record and erase DTCs.
Cycle the ignition switch from off to on.
Cycle the Adjustable Pedals Switch forward and rearward.
With the scan tool, read DTCs.

Does the scan tool display: B1D56–ADJUSTABLE PEDAL SENSOR CIRCUIT LOW?

Yes

- Go To 2

No

- The condition that caused the symptom is currently not present. Inspect the related wiring for a possible intermittent condition. Look for any chafed, pierced, pinched, or partially broken wires.
- Refer to the APS-INTERMITTENT CONDITIONS

2. CHECK CONNECTOR/TERMINAL FOR DAMAGE

NOTE: Check all terminals for broken, bent, pushed out, or corroded terminals.

Turn the ignition off.
Inspect the Memory Seat Module harness connector and Adjustable Pedals Motor harness connector.

Is there any connector or terminal damaged?

Yes

- Repair as necessary.
- Perform APS VERIFICATION TEST.

No

- Go To 3

LTV0500000006065

Fig. 13 Code B1D56: Adjustable Pedal Sensor Circuit Low (Part 1 of 4). 2005–06 Commander, Grand Cherokee & Liberty

3. CHECK (G11) ADJUSTABLE PEDALS SENSOR SUPPLY CIRCUIT FOR A SHORT TO GROUND

Disconnect the Memory Seat Module harness connector.
Disconnect the Adjustable Pedals Motor harness connector.
Using a 12-volt test light connected to 12-volts, probe the (G11) Adjustable Pedals Sensor Supply circuit.

Does the test light illuminate brightly?

Yes

- Repair the (G11) Adjustable Pedals Sensor Supply circuit for a short to ground.
- Perform APS VERIFICATION TEST.

No

- Go To 4

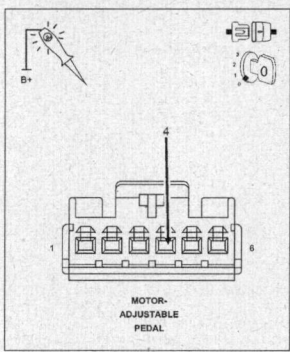

LTV0500000006066

5. CHECK (G12) ADJUSTABLE PEDALS SENSOR SIGNAL CIRCUIT FOR A SHORT TO GROUND

Using a 12-volt test light connected to 12-volts, probe the (G12) Adjustable Pedals Sensor Signal circuit.

Does the test light illuminate brightly?

Yes

- Repair the (G12) Adjustable Pedals Sensor Signal circuit for a short to ground.
- Perform APS VERIFICATION TEST. (Refer to 5 - BRAKES - STANDARD PROCEDURE).

No

- Go To 6

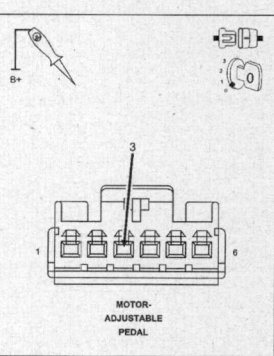

LTV0500000006067

4. CHECK (G11) ADJUSTABLE PEDALS SENSOR SUPPLY CIRCUIT FOR AN OPEN

Connect a jumper wire between the (G11) Adjustable Pedals Sensor Supply circuit and ground at the Memory Seat Module harness connector.
Using a 12-volt test light connected to 12-volts, probe the (G11) Adjustable Pedals Sensor Supply circuit.

Does the test light illuminate brightly

Yes

- Go To 5

No

- Repair the (G11) Adjustable Pedals Sensor Supply circuit for an open.
- Perform APS VERIFICATION TEST.

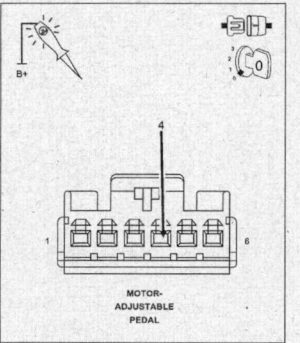

Fig. 13 Code B1D56: Adjustable Pedal Sensor Circuit Low (Part 2 of 4). 2005–06 Commander, Grand Cherokee & Liberty

6. CHECK (G12) ADJUSTABLE PEDALS SENSOR SIGNAL CIRCUIT FOR AN OPEN

Connect a jumper wire between the (G12) Adjustable Pedals Sensor Signal circuit and ground at the Memory Seat Module harness connector.
Using a 12-volt test light connected to 12-volts, probe the (G12) Adjustable Pedals Sensor Signal circuit.

Does the test light illuminate brightly?

Yes

- Go To 7

No

- Repair the (G12) Adjustable Pedals Sensor Signal circuit for an open.
- Perform APS VERIFICATION TEST.

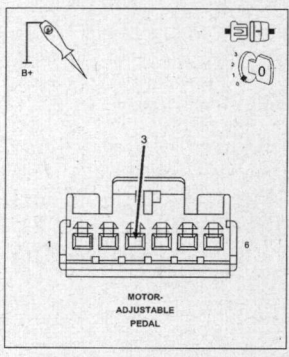

Fig. 13 Code B1D56: Adjustable Pedal Sensor Circuit Low (Part 3 of 4). 2005–06 Commander, Grand Cherokee & Liberty

7. CHECK (G11) ADJUSTABLE PEDALS SENSOR SUPPLY CIRCUIT VOLTAGE

Connect the Memory Seat Module harness connector.
Turn the ignition on.
Measure the voltage between the (G11) Adjustable Pedals Sensor Supply circuit and ground at the Adjustable Pedal Motor harness connector.

Is the voltage between 4.0 and 5.2 volts?

Yes

- Go To 8

No

- Replace and reprogram the Memory Seat Module
- Perform APS VERIFICATION TEST.

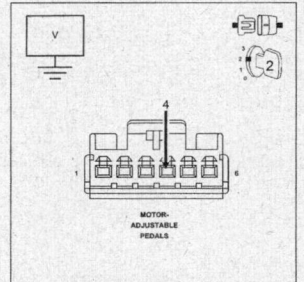

1. CHECK FOR DTC B1D57–ADJUSTABLE PEDAL SENSOR CIRCUIT HIGH

NOTE: This DTC must be active for the results of this test to be valid.

Turn the ignition on.
With the scan tool, record and erase DTCs.
Cycle the ignition switch from off to on.
Cycle the Adjustable Pedals Switch forward and rearward.
With the scan tool, read DTCs.

Does the scan tool display: B1D57–ADJUSTABLE PEDAL SENSOR CIRCUIT HIGH?

Yes

- Go To 2

No

- The condition that caused the symptom is currently not present. Inspect the related wiring for a possible intermittent condition. Look for any chafed, pierced, pinched, or partially broken wires.
- Refer to the APS-INTERMITTENT CONDITIONS

8. CHECK (G12) ADJUSTABLE PEDALS SENSOR SIGNAL CIRCUIT VOLTAGE

Measure the voltage of the (G12) Adjustable Pedals Sensor Signal circuit in the Memory Seat Module harness connector.

Is the voltage above 0.5 volts?

Yes

- Replace and reprogram the Memory Seat Module in
- Perform APS VERIFICATION TEST.

No

- Replace the Adjustable Pedals Sensor
- Perform APS VERIFICATION TEST.

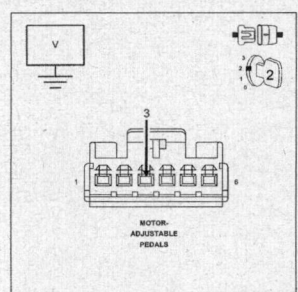

LTV0500000006068

Fig. 13 Code B1D56: Adjustable Pedal Sensor Circuit Low (Part 4 of 4). 2005–06 Commander, Grand Cherokee & Liberty

2. CHECK CONNECTOR/TERMINAL FOR DAMAGE

NOTE: Check all terminals for broken, bent, pushed out, or corroded terminals.

Turn the ignition off.
Inspect the Memory Seat Module harness connector and the Adjustable Pedal Motor harness connector.

Is there any connector or terminal damaged?

Yes

- Repair as necessary.
- Perform APS VERIFICATION TEST.

No

- Go To 3

LTV0500000006069

Fig. 14 Code B1D57: Adjustable Pedal Sensor Circuit High (Part 1 of 4). 2005–06 Commander, Grand Cherokee & Liberty

3. CHECK (G11) ADJUSTABLE PEDALS SENSOR SUPPLY CIRCUIT FOR A SHORT TO VOLTAGE

Disconnect the Memory Seat Module harness connector.
Disconnect the Adjustable Pedal Motor harness connector.
Turn the ignition on.
Measure the voltage between the (G11) Adjustable Pedals Sensor
Supply circuit and ground.

Is voltage present?

Yes

- Repair the (G11) Adjustable Pedals Sensor Supply circuit
  for a short to voltage.
- Perform APS VERIFICATION TEST.

No

- Go To 4

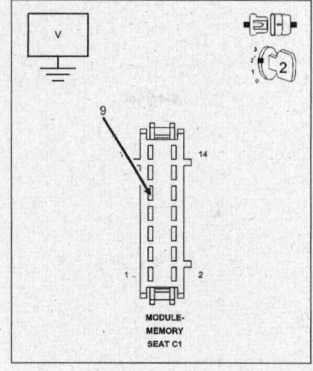

4. CHECK (G12) ADJUSTABLE PEDALS SENSOR SIGNAL CIRCUIT FOR A SHORT TO VOLTAGE

Measure the voltage between the (G12) Adjustable Pedals Sensor
Signal circuit and ground.

Is voltage present?

Yes

- Repair the (G12) Adjustable Pedals Sensor Signal circuit
  for a short to voltage.
- Perform APS VERIFICATION TEST.

No

- Go To 5

LTV0500000006070

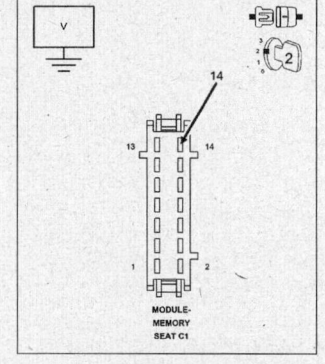

LTV0500000006070

Fig. 14   Code B1D57: Adjustable Pedal Sensor Circuit High (Part 2 of 4). 2005–06 Commander, Grand Cherokee & Liberty

7. CHECK (G12) ADJUSTABLE PEDALS SENSOR SIGNAL CIRCUIT VOLTAGE

Turn the ignition off.
Reconnect the Adjustable Pedal Motor harness connector.
Turn the ignition on.
Measure the voltage of the (G12) Adjustable Pedals Sensor Signal
circuit in the Memory Seat Module harness connector.

Is the voltage below 4.0 volts?

Yes

- Replace and reprogram the Memory Seat Module
- Perform APS VERIFICATION TEST.

No

- Replace the Adjustable Pedals Sensor
- Perform APS VERIFICATION TEST.

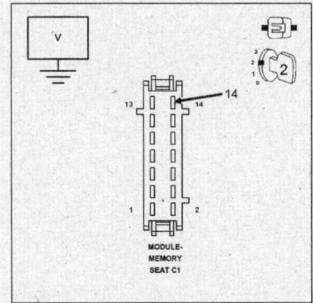

LTV0500000006072

Fig. 14   Code B1D57: Adjustable Pedal Sensor Circuit High (Part 4 of 4). 2005–06 Commander, Grand Cherokee & Liberty

5. (G12) ADJUSTABLE PEDAL SENSOR SIGNAL SHORTED TO SENSOR SUPPLY

Turn ignition off.
Measure the resistance between the (G12) Adjustable Pedals
Sensor Signal circuit and the Sensor Supply circuit.

Is the resistance below 100 ohms?

Yes

- Repair the (G12) Adjustable Pedals Sensor Signal circuit
  for a short to the Sensor Supply circuit.
- Perform APS VERIFICATION TEST.

No

- Go To 6

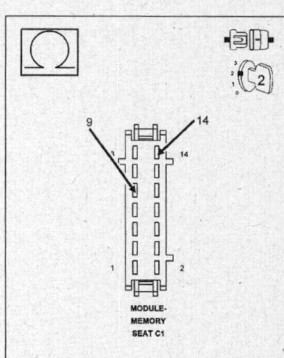

6. (G912) ADJUSTABLE PEDALS SENSOR RETURN CIRCUIT OPEN

Measure the resistance of the (G912) Adjustable Pedals Sensor
Return circuit between the Memory Seat Module harness connector
and the Adjustable Pedal Motor harness connector.

Is the resistance below 5 ohms?

Yes

- Go To 7

No

- Repair the (G912) Adjustable Pedals Sensor Return circuit
  for an open.
- Perform APS VERIFICATION TEST.

LTV0500000006071

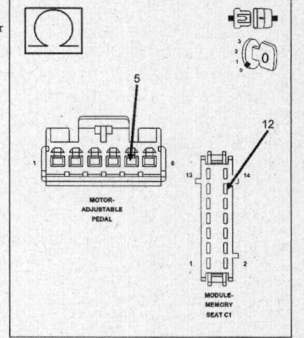

LTV0500000006071

Fig. 14   Code B1D57: Adjustable Pedal Sensor Circuit High (Part 3 of 4). 2005–06 Commander, Grand Cherokee & Liberty

1. CHECK FOR DTC B1D5B–ADJUSTABLE PEDAL SWITCH CIRCUIT PERFORMANCE

NOTE: This DTC must be active for the results of this test to be valid.

Turn the ignition on.
With the scan tool, record and erase DTC's.
Cycle the ignition switch from off to on.
Cycle the Adjustable Pedals Switch forward and rearward.
With the scan tool, read DTC's

Does the scan tool display: B1D5B–ADJUSTABLE PEDAL SWITCH CIRCUIT PERFORMANCE?

Yes

- Go To 2

No

- Refer to the INTERMITTENT CONDITIONS

- Perform APS VERIFICATION TEST - VER 1.

2. CHECK CONNECTOR/TERMINAL FOR DAMAGE

NOTE: Check all terminals for broken, bent, pushed out, or corroded terminals.

Turn the ignition off.
Inspect the Memory Seat Module harness connector and Lower Switch Bank harness connector.

Is the Lower Switch Bank or any of the connectors/terminals damaged?

Yes

- Repair as necessary.
- Perform APS VERIFICATION TEST - VER 1.

No

- Go To 3

LTV0500000006073

Fig. 15   Code B1D5B: Adjustable Pedal Switch Circuit Performance (Part 1 of 3). 2005–06 Commander, Grand Cherokee & Liberty

3. CHECK (Q103) ADJUSTABLE PEDALS SWITCH REARWARD CIRCUIT FOR A SHORT TO GROUND

Disconnect the Memory Seat Module harness connector.
Disconnect the Lower Switch Bank harness connector.
Using a 12-volt test light connected to 12-volts, probe the (Q103)
Adjustable Pedals Switch Rearward circuit.

Does the test light illuminate brightly?

Yes

- Repair the (Q103) Adjustable Pedals Switch Rearward
  circuit for a short to ground.
- Perform APS VERIFICATION TEST - VER 1.

No

- Go To 4

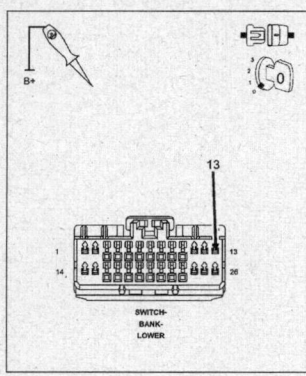

4. CHECK (Q102) ADJUSTABLE PEDALS SWITCH FORWARD CIRCUIT FOR A SHORT TO GROUND

Using a 12-volt test light connected to 12-volts, probe the (Q102) Adjustable Pedals Switch Forward circuit.

Does the test light illuminate brightly?

Yes

- Repair the (Q102) Adjustable Pedals Switch Forward circuit for a short to ground.
- Perform APS VERIFICATION TEST - VER 1.

No

- Go To 5

LTV0500000006074

Fig. 15   Code B1D5B: Adjustable Pedal Switch Circuit Performance (Part 2 of 3). 2005–06 Commander, Grand Cherokee & Liberty

5. CHECK (Q103) ADJUSTABLE PEDALS SWITCH REARWARD CIRCUIT AND ADJUSTABLE PEDALS SWITCH FORWARD CIRCUIT FOR A SHORT TOGETHER

Measure the resistance between the (Q103) Adjustable Pedals
Switch Rearward circuit and (Q102) Adjustable Pedals Switch
Forward circuit.

Is the resistance above 5.0 ohms?

Yes

- Go To 6

No

- Repair the (Q103) Adjustable Pedals Switch Rearward
  circuit and (Q102) Adjustable Pedals Switch Forward
  circuit for a short together.
- Perform APS VERIFICATION TEST - VER 1.

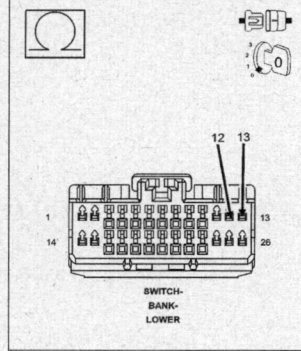

6. CHECK LOWER SWITCH BANK SHORTED

Measure the resistance between the (Q103) Adjustable Pedals
Switch Rearward and (Q102) Adjustable Pedals Switch Forward
terminals at the Lower Switch Bank.

Is the resistance below 5.0 ohms?

Yes

- Replace and reprogram the Memory Seat Module
- Perform APS VERIFICATION TEST - VER 1.

No

- Replace the Lower Switch Bank
- Perform APS VERIFICATION TEST - VER 1.

LTV0500000006075

Fig. 15   Code B1D5B: Adjustable Pedal Switch Circuit Performance (Part 3 of 3). 2005–06 Commander, Grand Cherokee & Liberty

1. CHECK FOR DTC B1D5C–ADJUSTABLE PEDAL SWITCH CIRCUIT STUCK FORWARD

NOTE: This DTC must be active for the results of this test to be valid.

Turn the ignition on.
With the scan tool, record and erase DTCs.
Cycle the ignition switch from off to on.
Cycle the Adjustable Pedals Switch forward and rearward.
With the scan tool, read DTCs.

Does the scan tool display: B1D5C–ADJUSTABLE PEDAL SWITCH CIRCUIT STUCK FORWARD?

Yes

- Go To 2

No

- The condition that caused the symptom is currently not present. Inspect the related wiring for a possible intermittent condition. Look for any chafed, pierced, pinched, or partially broken wires.
- Refer to the APS–INTERMITTENT CONDITION TEST.

2. CHECK CONNECTOR/TERMINAL FOR DAMAGE

NOTE: Check all terminals for broken, bent, pushed out, or corroded terminals.

Turn the ignition off.
Inspect the Memory Seat Module harness connector and Lower Switch Bank Switch harness connector.

Is the Adjustable Pedals Switch or any of the connectors/terminals damaged?

Yes

- Repair as necessary.
- Perform APS VERIFICATION TEST - VER 1.

No

- Go To 3

LTV0500000006076

Fig. 16   Code B1D5C: Adjustable Pedal Switch Circuit Stuck Forward (Part 1 of 2). 2005–06 Commander, Grand Cherokee & Liberty

3. CHECK (Q102) ADJUSTABLE PEDALS SWITCH FORWARD CIRCUIT FOR A SHORT TO GROUND

Disconnect the Memory Seat Module harness connector.
Disconnect the Lower Switch Bank harness connector.
Using a 12-volt test light connected to 12-volts, probe the (Q102) Adjustable Pedals Switch Forward circuit.

Does the test light illuminate brightly?

Yes

- Repair the (Q102) Adjustable Pedals Switch Forward circuit for a short to ground.
- Perform APS VERIFICATION TEST.

No

- Go To 4

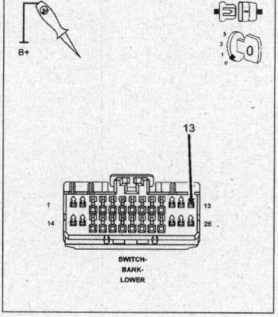

4. CHECK LOWER SWITCH BANK SHORTED

Measure the resistance between the (Q103) Adjustable Pedals Switch Rearward and (Q102) Adjustable Pedals Switch Forward terminals at the Lower Switch Bank.

Is the resistance below 5.0 ohms?

Yes

- Replace and reprogram the Memory Seat Module in accordance with the Service Information.
- Perform APS VERIFICATION TEST.

No

- Replace the Lower Switch Bank
- Perform APS VERIFICATION TEST.

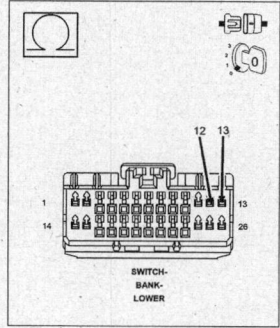

LTV0500000006077

Fig. 16   Code B1D5C: Adjustable Pedal Switch Circuit Stuck Forward (Part 2 of 2). 2005–06 Commander, Grand Cherokee & Liberty

1. CHECK FOR DTC B1D5D–ADJUSTABLE PEDAL SWITCH CIRCUIT STUCK REARWARD

NOTE: This DTC must be active for the results of this test to be valid.

Turn the ignition on.
With the scan tool, record and erase DTCs.
Cycle the ignition switch from off to on.
Cycle the Adjustable Pedals Switch forward and rearward.
With the scan tool, read DTCs.

Does the scan tool display: B1D5D–ADJUSTABLE PEDAL SWITCH CIRCUIT STUCK REARWARD?

Yes

- Go To 2

No

- The condition that caused the symptom is currently not present. Inspect the related wiring for a possible intermittent condition. Look for any chafed, pierced, pinched, or partially broken wires.
- Refer to the APS–INTERMITTENT CONDITION TEST.

2. CHECK CONNECTOR/TERMINAL FOR DAMAGE

NOTE: Check all terminals for broken, bent, pushed out, or corroded terminals.

Turn the ignition off.
Inspect the Memory Seat Module harness connector, and the Lower Switch Bank harness connector.

Is the connectors/terminals damaged?

Yes

- Repair as necessary.
- Perform APS VERIFICATION TEST.

No

- Go To 3

LTV0500000006078

Fig. 17   Code B1D5D: Adjustable Pedal Switch Circuit Stuck Rearward (Part 1 of 2). 2005–06 Commander, Grand Cherokee & Liberty

3. CHECK (Q103) ADJUSTABLE PEDALS SWITCH REARWARD CIRCUIT FOR A SHORT TO GROUND

Disconnect the Memory Seat Module harness connector.
Disconnect the Lower Switch Bank harness connector.
Using a 12-volt test light connected to 12-volts, probe the (Q103) Adjustable Pedals Switch Rearward circuit.

Does the test light illuminate brightly?

Yes

- Repair the (Q103) Adjustable Pedals Switch Rearward circuit for a short to ground.
- Perform APS VERIFICATION TEST.

No

- Go To 4

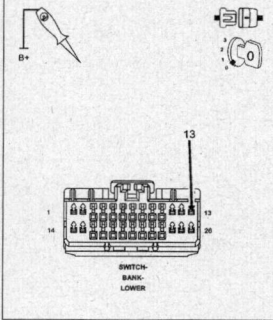

4. CHECK ADJUSTABLE PEDALS SWITCH SHORTED

Measure the resistance between the (Q103) Adjustable Pedals Switch Rearward and (Q102) Adjustable Pedals Switch Forward terminals at the Lower Switch Bank.

Is the resistance below 5.0 ohms?

Yes

- Replace and reprogram the Memory Seat Module
- Perform APS VERIFICATION TEST.

No

- Replace the Lower Switch Band
- Perform APS VERIFICATION TEST.

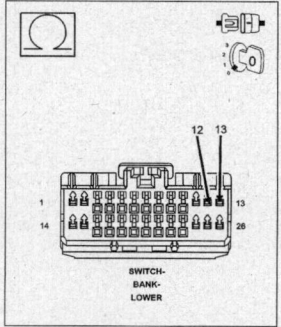

LTV0500000006079

Fig. 17   Code B1D5D: Adjustable Pedal Switch Circuit Stuck Rearward (Part 2 of 2). 2005–06 Commander, Grand Cherokee & Liberty

1. CHECK FOR DTC B1D67–ADJUSTABLE PEDAL CONTROL CIRCUIT PERFORMANCE

NOTE: This DTC must be active for the results of this test to be valid.

Turn the ignition on.
With the scan tool, record and erase DTC's.
Cycle the ignition switch from off to on.
Cycle and hold the Adjustable Pedals Switch forward, rearward, and forward at two second intervals.
With the scan tool, read DTC's

Does the scan tool display: B1D67–ADJUSTABLE PEDAL CONTROL CIRCUIT PERFORMANCE?

Yes

- Go To 2

No

- Refer to the INTERMITTENT CONDITIONS

- Perform APS VERIFICATION TEST - VER 1.

2. CHECK CONNECTOR/TERMINAL FOR DAMAGE

NOTE: Check all terminals for broken, bent, pushed out, or corroded terminals.

Turn the ignition off.
Inspect the Memory Seat Module harness connector, Adjustable Pedals Motor, and Adjustable Pedals Motor harness connector.

Is the Adjustable Pedals Motor or any of the connectors/terminals damaged?

Yes

- Repair as necessary.
- Perform APS VERIFICATION TEST - VER 1

No

- Go To 3

LTV0500000006080

Fig. 18   Code B1D67: Adjustable Pedal Control Circuit Performance (Part 1 of 4). 2005–06 Commander, Grand Cherokee & Liberty

3. CHECK ADJUSTABLE PEDALS ASSEMBLY FOR MECHANICAL DAMAGE

Inspect the Adjustable Pedals Assembly for any physical damage.

NOTE: Check for any conditions that would cause the motor to stall or be stuck.

Is the Adjustable Pedals Assembly damaged or broken?

Yes

- Replace the Adjustable Pedals Assembly
- Perform APS VERIFICATION TEST - VER 1.

No

- Go To 4

4. CHECK (P205) ADJUSTABLE PEDALS MOTOR FORWARD CIRCUIT FOR AN OPEN

Disconnect the Memory Seat Module harness connector.
Disconnect the Adjustable Pedals Motor harness connector
Connect a jumper wire between the (P205) Adjustable Pedals Motor Forward circuit and ground in the Adjustable Pedal Motor harness connector.
Using a 12-volt test light connected to 12-volts, probe the (P205) Adjustable Pedals Motor Forward circuit in the Memory Seat Module harness connector.

Does the test light illuminate brightly?

Yes

- Go To 5

No

- Repair the Adjustable Pedals Motor Forward circuit for an open.
- Perform APS VERIFICATION TEST - VER 1.

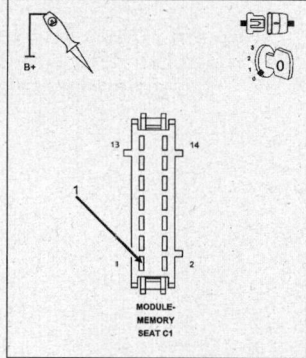

LTV0500000006081

Fig. 18   Code B1D67: Adjustable Pedal Control Circuit Performance (Part 2 of 4). 2005–06 Commander, Grand Cherokee & Liberty

5. CHECK (P206) ADJUSTABLE PEDALS MOTOR REARWARD CIRCUIT FOR AN OPEN

Connect a jumper wire between the Adjustable Pedals Motor Rearward circuit and ground in the Adjustable Pedal Motor harness connector.
Using a 12-volt test light connected to 12-volts, probe the (P206) Adjustable Pedals Motor Rearward circuit in the Memory Seat Module harness connector.

Does the test light illuminate brightly?

Yes

- Go To 6

No

- Repair the (P206) Adjustable Pedals Motor Rearward circuit for an open.
- Perform APS VERIFICATION TEST - VER 1.

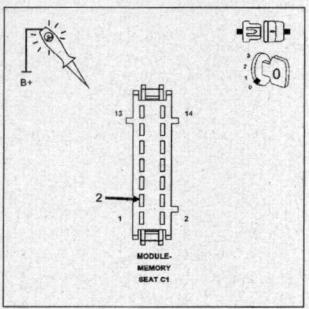

6. CHECK (G912) SENSOR RETURN CIRCUIT FOR AN OPEN

Connect a jumper wire between the (G912) Sensor Return circuit and ground in the Adjustable Pedal Motor harness connector.
Using a 12-volt test light connected to 12-volts, probe the (G912) Sensor Return circuit.

Does the test light illuminate brightly?

Yes

- Go To 7

No

- Repair the (G912) Sensor Return circuit for an open.
- Perform APS VERIFICATION TEST - VER 1.

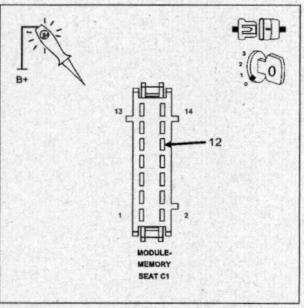

LTV0500000006082

Fig. 18   Code B1D67: Adjustable Pedal Control Circuit Performance (Part 3 of 4). 2005–06 Commander, Grand Cherokee & Liberty

7. CHECK ADJUSTABLE PEDALS MOTOR

Measure the resistance between the (P205) Adjustable Pedals Motor Forward and (P206) Adjustable Pedals Motor Rearward terminals at the Adjustable Pedals Motor.

Is the resistance below 100.0 ohms?

Yes

- Replace and reprogram the Memory Seat Module
- Perform APS VERIFICATION TEST - VER 1.

No

- Replace the Adjustable Pedals Motor
- Perform APS VERIFICATION TEST - VER 1.

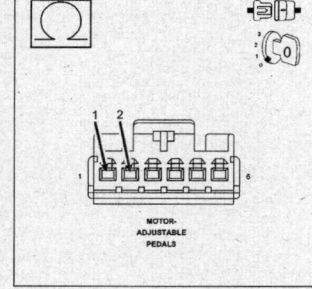

LTV0500000006083

Fig. 18   Code B1D67: Adjustable Pedal Control Circuit Performance (Part 4 of 4). 2005–06 Commander, Grand Cherokee & Liberty

1. CHECK FOR A DTC C107C-BRAKE PEDAL SWITCH 1/2 STUCK

NOTE: This DTC must be active for the results of this test to be valid.

Turn the ignition on.
With the scan tool, read and record DTCs.
With the scan tool, read and record Freeze Frame information.
With the scan tool, erase DTCs.
Cycle the ignition switch from off to on.
With the scan tool, read and record DTCs.

Does the scan tool display: C107C-BRAKE PEDAL SWITCH 1/2 STUCK?

Yes

- Go To 2

No

- Refer to the INTERMITTENT CONDITION diagnostic procedure.
- The condition that caused the symptom is currently not present. Inspect the related wiring for a possible intermittent condition. Look for any chafed, pierced, pinched, or partially broken wires.
- Refer to the ABS-INTERMITTENT CONDITIONS

2. CHECK THE TERMINALS/CONNECTORS/WIRING HARNESS FOR DAMAGE

Check all related wiring for bruised, chafed, pierced, or partially broken wires.
Check all related connectors for broken, bent, pushed out, or corroded terminals.

Were any problems found?

Yes

- Repair as necessary.
- Perform ABS VERIFICATION TEST.

No

- Go To 3

LTV0500000006084

Fig. 19   Code C107C: Brake Pedal Switch Half Stuck (Part 1 of 2). 2005–06 Commander, Grand Cherokee & Liberty

3. CHECK THE (B15) BRAKE SWITCH NO. 1 SIGNAL CIRCUIT WHILE DEPRESSING AND RELEASING BRAKE PEDAL

Turn the ignition off.
Disconnect the Anti-Lock Brake Module harness connector.
Turn the ignition on.
Using a 12-volt test light connected to 12-volts, check the (B15) Brake Switch No. 1 Signal circuit.
Depress and release the brake pedal.

Does the test light illumination toggle from off to on?

Yes

- Replace the Anti-lock Bake Module
- Perform ABS VERIFICATION TEST.

No

- Go To 4

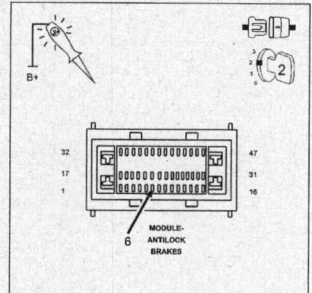

4. CHECK THE (B15) BRAKE SWITCH NO. 1 SIGNAL CIRCUIT FOR AN OPEN

Turn the ignition off.
Disconnect the Stop Lamp Switch harness connector.
Measure the resistance of the (B15) Brake Switch No. 1 Signal circuit.

Is the resistance below 5.0 ohms?

Yes

- Replace the Stop Lamp Switch
- Perform ABS VERIFICATION TEST.

No

- Repair the (B15) Brake Switch No. 1 Signal circuit for an open.
- Perform ABS VERIFICATION TEST.

LTV0500000006085

Fig. 19   Code C107C: Brake Pedal Switch Half Stuck (Part 2 of 2). 2005–06 Commander, Grand Cherokee & Liberty

1. VERIFY DTC IS ACTIVE

NOTE: Diagnose and repair all Pressure Sensor and Voltage related DTCs and all Stop Lamp related DTCs and symptoms before diagnosing this DTC.

Turn the ignition on.
With the scan tool, read ABS DTCs.
With the scan tool, read and record Environmental Data (EV Data).
With the scan tool, erase DTCs.
Cycle the ignition switch.

WARNING: Ensure brake capability is available before road testing.

Test drive the vehicle as follows: Drive for more than 6 minutes at a speed greater than 40 km/h (25 m.p.h.) and accelerate to a speed greater than 40 km/h (25 m.p.h.) and then decelerate to a speed lower than 3 km/h (2 m.p.h.) five consecutive times.
Park the vehicle.
With the scan tool, read ABS DTCs.

Does this DTC reset?

Yes

- Go To 2

No

- The condition that caused the symptom is currently not present. Inspect the related wiring for a possible intermittent condition. Look for any chafed, pierced, pinched, or partially broken wires.
- Refer to the ABS-INTERMITTENT CONDITION TEST.

2. INSPECT RELATED WIRING HARNESS, TERMINALS, & CONNECTORS

Turn the ignition off.
Visually inspect the related wiring harness. Look for any pinched, chafed, pierced, and partially broken wires.
Visually inspect the related wiring harness connectors. Look for broken, bent, pushed out, and corroded terminals.

Were any problems found?

Yes

- Repair as necessary.
- Perform ABS VERIFICATION TEST.

No

- Go To 3

LTV0500000006086

Fig. 20   Code C107D: Brake Pedal Switch Half Correlation (Part 1 of 4). 2005–06 Commander, Grand Cherokee & Liberty

3. CHECK (B15) SECONDARY BRAKE SWITCH SIGNAL CIRCUIT (DIESEL) OR (B15) BRAKE SWITCH NO. 1 SIGNAL CIRCUIT (GAS) FUNCTION WHILE DEPRESSING & RELEASING THE BRAKE PEDAL

Disconnect the Anti-Lock Brakes Module harness connector.
Turn the ignition on.
Using a 12-volt test light connected to 12 volts, backprobe the (B15) Secondary Brake Switch Signal circuit (Diesel) or the (B15) Brake Switch No. 1 Signal circuit (Gas) in the Anti-Lock Brakes Module harness connector.
Depress and release the brake pedal.

Does the test light illumination toggle from off to on?

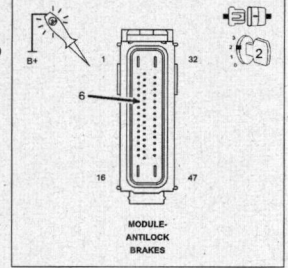

Yes

- Go To 7

No

- Go To 4

4. CHECK (B15) SECONDARY BRAKE SWITCH SIGNAL CIRCUIT (DIESEL) OR (B15) BRAKE SWITCH NO. 1 SIGNAL CIRCUIT (GAS) FOR A SHORT TO GROUND

Turn the ignition off.
Disconnect the Stop Lamp Switch harness connector.
Measure the resistance of the (B15) Secondary Brake Switch Signal circuit (Diesel) or the (B15) Brake Switch No. 1 Signal circuit (Gas) between ground and the Anti-Lock Brakes Module harness connector.

Is the resistance below 5.0 ohms?

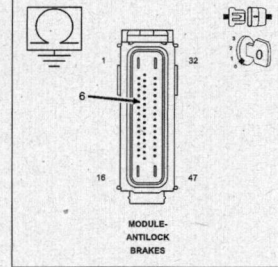

Yes

- Repair the (B15) Secondary Brake Switch Signal circuit (Diesel) or the (B15) Brake Switch No. 1 Signal circuit (Gas) for a short to ground.
- Perform ABS VERIFICATION TEST.

No

- Go To 5

LTV0500000006087

Fig. 20   Code C107D: Brake Pedal Switch Half Correlation (Part 2 of 4). 2005–06 Commander, Grand Cherokee & Liberty

5. CHECK (B15) SECONDARY BRAKE SWITCH SIGNAL CIRCUIT (DIESEL) OR (B15) BRAKE SWITCH NO. 1 SIGNAL CIRCUIT (GAS) FOR AN OPEN

Measure the resistance of the (B15) Secondary Brake Switch Signal circuit (Diesel) or the (B15) Brake Switch No. 1 Signal circuit (Gas) between the Anti-Lock Brakes Module harness connector and the Stop Lamp Switch harness connector.

Is the resistance below 5.0 ohms?

Yes

- Go To 6

No

- Repair the (B15) Secondary Brake Switch Signal circuit (Diesel) or the (B15) Brake Switch No. 1 Signal circuit (Gas) for an open.
- Perform ABS VERIFICATION TEST.

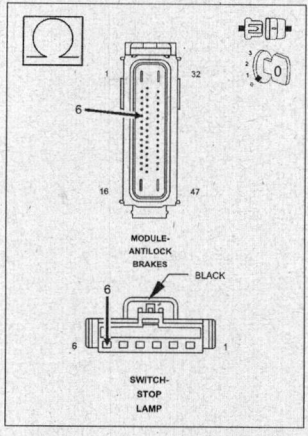

LTV0500000006088

Fig. 20   Code C107D: Brake Pedal Switch Half Correlation (Part 3 of 4). 2005–06 Commander, Grand Cherokee & Liberty

6. CHECK (B15) SECONDARY BRAKE SWITCH SIGNAL CIRCUIT (DIESEL) OR (B15) BRAKE SWITCH NO. 1 SIGNAL CIRCUIT (GAS) FOR A OPEN GROUND

Measure the resistance on the (Z940) Ground circuit and ground in the Stop Lamp Switch harness connector.

Is the resistance below 5 ohms?

Yes

- Replace the Stop Lamp Switch
- Perform ABS VERIFICATION TEST.

No

- Repair the open in the (Z940) Ground circuit.

7. CHECK BRAKE PEDAL ADJUSTMENT

- Reconnect the Stop Lamp Switch harness connector.

Using a 12-volt test light connected to 12 volts, backprobe the (B15) Secondary Brake Switch Signal circuit (Diesel) or the (B15) Brake Switch No. 1 Signal circuit (Gas) in the Stop Lamp Switch harness connector.
Depress and release the brake pedal.

Does the test light illumination toggle from off to on within 4–5 mm of brake pedal travel?

Yes

- Replace the Anti-Lock Bakes Module
- Perform ABS VERIFICATION TEST.

No

- Replace the Stop Lamp Switch
- Perform ABS VERIFICATION TEST.

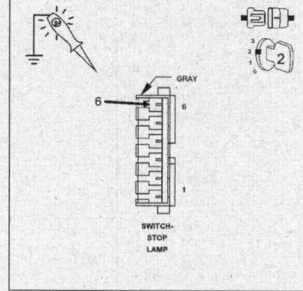

LTV0500000006089

Fig. 20   Code C107D: Brake Pedal Switch Half Correlation (Part 4 of 4). 2005–06 Commander, Grand Cherokee & Liberty

1. CHECK FOR A DTC C121C-TORQUE REQUEST SIGNAL DENIED

NOTE: This DTC must be active for the results of this test to be valid.

NOTE: This DTC may set while driving under severe load conditions.

Turn the ignition on.
With the scan tool, read and record DTCs.
With the scan tool, read and record Freeze Frame information.
With the scan tool, erase DTCs.
Cycle the ignition switch from off to on.
Start Engine.
With the scan tool, read and record DTCs.

Does the scan tool display: C121C-TORQUE REQUEST SIGNAL DENIED?

Yes

- Go To 2

No

- Refer to the INTERMITTENT CONDITIONS

- Perform APS VERIFICATION TEST - VER 1.

2. CHECK THE POWERTRAIN DTCS

With the scan tool, read and record Powertrain DTCs.

Were any Powertrain ESP related DTCs found?

Yes

- Replace the Powertrain Module
- Perform the POWERTRAIN VERIFICATION TEST.

No

- Replace the Anti-Lock Brake Module
- Perform ABS VERIFICATION TEST.

LTV0500000006090

Fig. 21 Code C121C: Torque Request Signal Denied. 2005–06 Commander, Grand Cherokee & Liberty

1. CHECK FOR A DTC C121D-BRAKE PRESSURE SENSOR CIRCUIT

NOTE: This DTC must be active for the results of this test to be valid.

Turn the ignition on.
With the scan tool, read and record DTCs.
With the scan tool, read and record Freeze Fame information.
With the scan tool, erase DTCs.
Start the engine.
Depress and release the brake pedal.
With the scan tool, read and record DTCs.

Does the scan tool display: C121D-BRAKE PRESSURE SENSOR CIRCUIT?

Yes

- Go To 2

No

- Refer to the INTERMITTENT CONDITIONS
- Perform ABS VERIFICATION TEST - VER

2. RECHECK FOR A DTC C121D-BRAKE PRESSURE SENSOR CIRCUIT

Turn the ignition on.
With the scan tool, read and record DTCs.
With the scan tool, read and record Freeze Frame information.
With the scan tool, erase DTCs.
Start the engine.
Depress and release the brake pedal.
With the scan tool, read and record DTCs.

Does the scan tool display: C121D-BRAKE PRESSURE SENSOR CIRCUIT?

Yes

- Replace the ICU
- Perform ABS VERIFICATION TEST - VER 1.

No

- Test complete

LTV0500000006091

Fig. 22 Code C121D: Brake Pressure Sensor Circuit. 2005–06 Commander, Grand Cherokee & Liberty

1. CHECK FOR A DTC C121E-BRAKE PRESSURE SENSOR COMPARATIVE PERFORMANCE

Turn the ignition on.
With the scan tool, read and record DTCs.
With the scan tool, read and record Freeze Frame information.
With the scan tool, erase DTCs.
Start the engine.
Depress and release the brake pedal.
With the scan tool, read and record DTCs.

Does the scan tool display: C121E-BRAKE PRESSURE SENSOR COMPARATIVE PERFORMANCE?

Yes

- Go To 2

No

- Refer to the INTERMITTENT CONDITIONS
- Perform ABS VERIFICATION TEST.

2. CHECK BRAKE SWITCH

With the scan tool look at the Brake Switch Signal.
Apply the brakes on and off while checking for a Brake Switch Signal change.

Did the Brake Switch Signal change?

Yes

- Go To 3

No

- Repair as needed.

LTV0500000006092

Fig. 23   Code C121E: Brake Pressure Sensor Comparative Performance (Part 1 of 2). 2005–06 Commander, Grand Cherokee & Liberty

3. CHECK BRAKE PRESSURE SENSOR

With the scan tool look at Pressure Sensor Signal and the Brake Switch Signal.
With the brakes not applied the Pressure Sensor should read ± 15 bar.
Apply the brakes the Pressure Sensor should read above 15 bar.

Did Brake Pressure Sensor increase above 15 bar?

Yes

- Replace the Integrated Control Unit
- Perform ABS VERIFICATION TEST.

No

- Go To 4

4. CHECK FOR AIR IN BRAKE SYSTEM

NOTE: Before continuing the brake system must be bled to verify there is no air in the brake system.

Turn ignition off.
Bleed brake system.

Was there any air in the brake system?

Yes

- Repair as needed.
- Perform ABS VERIFICATION TEST.

No

- Replace the Integrated Control Unit
- Perform ABS VERIFICATION TEST.

LTV0500000006093

Fig. 23   Code C121E: Brake Pressure Sensor Comparative Performance (Part 2 of 2). 2005–06 Commander, Grand Cherokee & Liberty

1. CHECK FOR A DTC C1221-BRAKE PRESSURE SENSOR/ACCEL PEDAL POSITION SENSOR
CORRELATION

Turn the ignition on.
With the scan tool, read and record DTCs.
With the scan tool, read and record Freeze Frame information.
With the scan tool, erase DTCs.
Start the engine.
Depress and release the brake pedal.
With the scan tool, read and record DTCs.

**Does the scan tool display: C1221-BRAKE PRESSURE SENSOR/ACCEL PEDAL POSITION SENSOR
CORRELATION?**

Yes

- Go To 2

No

- Refer to the INTERMITTENT CONDITIONS
- Perform ABS VERIFICATION TEST.

2. CHECK BRAKE SWITCH

With the scan tool look at the Brake Switch Signal.
Apply the brakes on and off while checking for a Brake Switch Signal change.

Did the Brake Switch Signal change?

Yes

- Go To 3

No

- Repair as needed.

LTV0500000006094

**Fig. 24   Code C1221: Brake Pressure Sensor/Accel
Pedal Position Sensor Correlation (Part 1 of 2).
2005–06 Commander, Grand Cherokee & Liberty**

3. CHECK BRAKE PRESSURE SENSOR

With the scan tool look at Pressure Sensor Signal and the Brake Switch Signal.
With the brakes not applied the Pressure Sensor should read ± 15 bar.
Apply the brakes the Pressure Sensor should read above 15 bar.

Did Brake Pressure Sensor increase above 15 bar?

Yes

- Replace the Integrated Control Unit
- Perform ABS VERIFICATION TEST.

No

- Go To 4

4. CHECK FOR AIR IN BRAKE SYSTEM

NOTE: Before continuing the brake system must be bled to verify there is no air in the brake system.

Turn ignition off.
Bleed brake system.
Check worn mechanical components.

Was there any air in the brake system or worn mechanical components?

Yes

- Repair as needed.
- Perform ABS VERIFICATION TEST.

No

- Replace the Integrated Control Unit
- Perform ABS VERIFICATION TEST.

LTV0500000006095

**Fig. 24   Code C1221: Brake Pressure Sensor/Accel
Pedal Position Sensor Correlation (Part 2 of 2).
2005–06 Commander, Grand Cherokee & Liberty**

1. CHECK FOR A DTC C123A-ESP SYSTEM SENSORS CALIBRATION

NOTE: This DTC must be active for the results of this test to be valid.

Turn the ignition on.
With the scan tool, read and record DTCs.
With the scan tool, read and record Freeze Frame information.
With the scan tool, erase DTCs.
Cycle the ignition switch from off to on.
With the scan tool, read and record DTCs

Does the scan tool display: C123A-ESP SYSTEM SENSORS CALIBRATION?

Yes

- Go To 2

No

- Refer to the INTERMITTENT CONDITIONS
- Refer to the ABS-INTERMITTENT CONDITION TEST.

2. CHECK THE WIRING HARNESS, TERMINALS, AND CONNECTORS

Visually inspect the related wiring harness. Look for any bruised, chafed, pierced, or partially broken wires.
Visually inspect the related wiring harness connectors. Look for broken, bent, pushed out, or corroded terminals.

Were any problems found?

Yes

- Repair as necessary.
- Perform ABS VERIFICATION TEST.

No

- Go To 3

LTV0500000006096

Fig. 25 Code C123A: ESP System Sensors Calibration (Part 1 of 2). 2005–06 Commander, Grand Cherokee & Liberty

3. CHECK THE DYNAMICS SENSOR OUTPUT

CAUTION: Ensure brake capability is available before road testing.

Have an assistant test drive the vehicle while monitoring the Dynamics Sensor operation.

Was the Lateral Sensor output between 0.02 G to 0.16 G and the Yaw Sensor between 1.30° to 5.70°?

Yes

- Replace the Anti-Lock Brake Module
- Perform ABS VERIFICATION TEST.

No

- Replace the Dynamics Sensor
- Perform ABS VERIFICATION TEST.

LTV0500000006097

Fig. 25 Code C123A: ESP System Sensors Calibration (Part 2 of 2). 2005–06 Commander, Grand Cherokee & Liberty

1. CHECK FOR A DTC C123B-ESP SYSTEM CONTROL TOO LONG

NOTE: If other DTCs are set they must be repaired before continuing.

NOTE: This DTC must be active for the results of this test to be valid.

NOTE: This DTC may set while driving under excessive driving conditions.

Turn the ignition on.
With the scan tool, read and record DTCs.
With the scan tool, read and record Freeze Frame information.
Perform ECU initialization with drive test.

NOTE: Drive test must be performed correctly for ECU to initialize.

Cycle the ignition switch from off to on.
With the scan tool, read and record DTCs.

Does the scan tool display: C123B-ESP SYSTEM CONTROL TOO LONG?

Yes

- Go To 2

No

- Refer to the INTERMITTENT CONDITIONS
- Refer to the ABS-INTERMITTENT CONDITIONS

2. CHECK HYDRAULIC SYSTEM & BRAKE SYSTEM COMPONENT INSTALLATION & FUNCTION

Turn ignition off.
Verify that the Anti-Lock Brakes Module and Hydraulic Control Unit are properly installed.
Verify that the hydraulic system is properly filled and bled.
Verify that the brake system components are installed and functioning properly.

Were any problems found?

Yes

- Repair as necessary.
- Perform ABS VERIFICATION TEST.

No

- Replace the Integrated Control Module
- Perform ABS VERIFICATION TEST.

LTV0500000006098

Fig. 26 Code C123B: ESP System Sensors Control Too Long. 2005–06 Commander, Grand Cherokee & Liberty

TIRE PRESSURE MONITORING SYSTEM

INDEX

	Page No.		Page No.		Page No.
Component Replacement	6-1	**Diagnosis & Testing**	6-1	Air Bag Systems	6-1
Tire Pressure Sensor	6-1	Tire Pressure Sensor	6-1	Battery Ground Cable	6-1
Description	6-1	**Precautions**	6-1	Tire Pressure Sensor	6-1

PRECAUTIONS

Air Bag Systems

Refer to "Air Bag System Precautions" in the front of this manual for system disarming and arming procedures.

Battery Ground Cable

Prior to service disconnect battery ground cable and isolate as required.

Tire Pressure Sensor

The use of tire sealants is strictly prohibited for vehicles equipped with Tire Pressure Monitoring system. Tire sealants can clog tire pressure sensors.

Tire pressure sensor valve stem caps and cores are specially designed for the sensors. Due to risk of corrosion, do not use a standard valve stem cap or core in a tire pressure sensor in place of the original equipment style sensor cap and core.

Do not attempt to install a tire pressure sensor in an aftermarket wheel. Use tire pressure sensors in original style factory wheels only. If aftermarket wheels are installed and therefore do not contain tire pressure sensors, the system will not function properly and driver will be continuously notified of a system fault.

Any time a sensor is to be installed in a wheel, a new seal and washer must be installed on the stem to ensure air tight seal. TPM thresholds have been established for original tire size equipped on the vehicle. Use original size tires only to maintain system accuracy.

DESCRIPTION

The Tire Pressure Monitoring (TPM) system monitors air pressure in the four road tires. Pressure in spare tire is not monitored. TPM alerts the driver when tire pressure falls below predetermined thresholds.

The TPM system is controlled by the Wireless Control Module (WCM), commonly referred to as the Sentry Key Remote Entry Module (SKEEM). There is a sensor/transmitter in each of the vehicles four road wheels that operates on a 315 MHz radio frequency.

An indicator lamp located in the instrument cluster and, if equipped, the Electronic Vehicle Information Center (EVIC) are used to communicate system information.

DIAGNOSIS & TESTING

Tire Pressure Sensor

Tire pressure may increase from 2–6 psi during normal driving conditions. Do not reduce this normal pressure build-up.

When diagnosing a tire pressure issue, always inspect air pressure in the tires first with suitable tire air gauge. Adjust air pressure as required to specifications listed on the Tire Inflation Pressure Label card, usually applied within driver side B-pillar. After adjusting air pressure in tire on vehicle, allow approximately two minutes for the message or indicator lamp to go out.

Inspect tire pressure indicator lamp in the instrument cluster. If the lamp is illuminating continuously, proceed as follows; If the indicator is flashing on/off for 60 seconds, once every 10 minutes, there is a system fault detected. Refer to appropriate diagnostic information.

If air pressure in any tire is low, inspect all the tires for leaks. A water tank or other water test may be used to inspect for a leak around the sensor as long as any water at the valve core is removed once the procedure is completed. The water can be easily expelled from the core area by pushing in on the core for several seconds, allowing escaping air to drive out any moisture. Inflate the tire as required. Always ensure the original valve stem cap is securely installed to keep moisture out of the sensor.

If the gauge read pressure in the tires does not indicate a tire pressure issue, refer to appropriate diagnostic information.

COMPONENT REPLACEMENT

Tire Pressure Sensor

1. Remove tire and wheel assembly.
2. Dismount tire from wheel, noting the following:
   a. When breaking tire bead loose from wheel rim, avoid using bead braker in area of sensor. That includes both front and rear beads of tire.
   b. Carefully insert mounting/dismounting tool at valve stem +/-10°, **Fig. 1,** then proceed to dismount tire.
3. Remove sensor nut retaining sensor to wheel, **Fig. 2.** When removing nut, hold pressure against rear of metal valve stem to keep valve stem from pushing rearward.
4. Remove sensor from wheel, **Fig. 2.**
5. Reverse procedure to install, noting the following:
   a. Replace seal and metal washer at base of valve stem, **Fig. 3.**
   b. To avoid damaging sensor antenna strap, **Fig. 4,** hold pressure against rear metal valve stem, **Fig. 5,** while sensor is inserted through wheel mounting hole and nut is installed.
   c. Before tightening sensor nut, push downward on sensor housing in an attempt to make it flush with interior contour of wheel, **Fig. 6.**
   d. **Torque** sensor in position to 58 inch lbs.
   e. If using rotating wheel tire changers, once wheel is mounted to changer, position sensor valve stem approximately 210° from head of changer in a clockwise direction before rotating wheel.

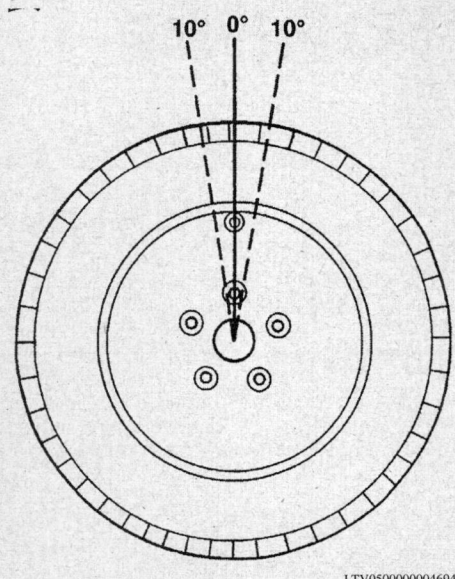

Fig. 1   Tire pressure sensor
removal

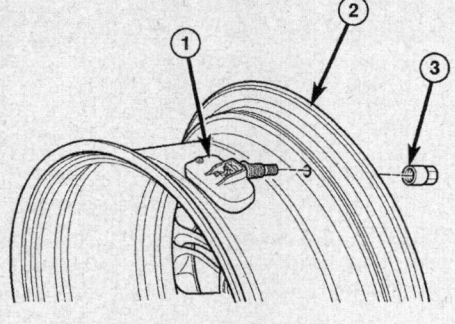

1 - TIRE PRESSURE SENSOR
2 - WHEEL
3 - NUT (WITH PRESSED-IN WASHER)

LTV0500000004695

Fig. 2   Sensor mounting to wheel
removal

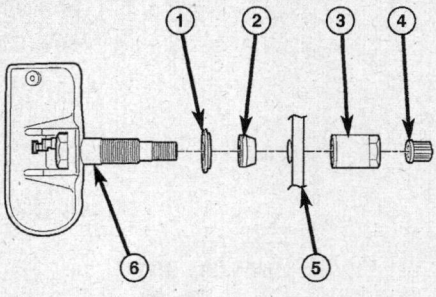

1 - METAL WASHER
2 - SEAL
3 - NUT (WITH PRESSED-IN WASHER)
4 - CAP (WITH SEAL)
5 - SECTIONAL CUTAWAY OF WHEEL
6 - TPM SENSOR

LTV0500000004696

Fig. 3   Exploded view of sensor
mounting

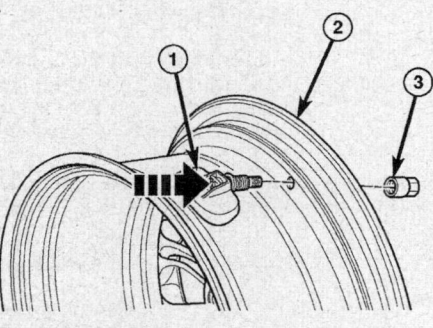

1 - TIRE PRESSURE SENSOR
2 - WHEEL
3 - NUT (WITH WASHER)

LTV0500000004698

Fig. 5   Sensor installation to
wheel

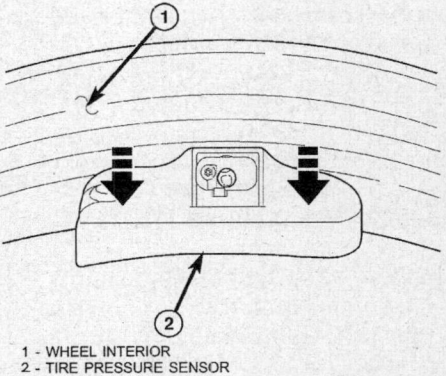

1 - WHEEL INTERIOR
2 - TIRE PRESSURE SENSOR

LTV0500000004699

Fig. 6   Seat sensor against wheel
interior

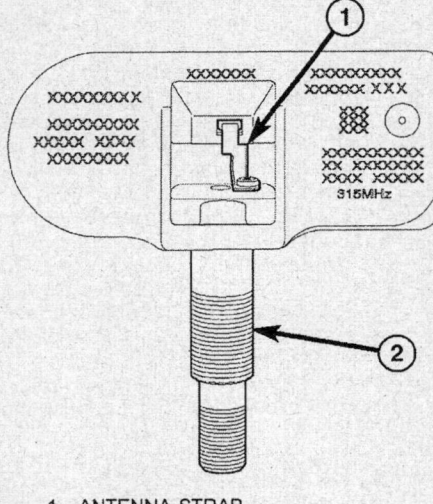

1 - ANTENNA STRAP
2 - VALVE STEM

LTV0500000004697

Fig. 4   Tire pressure sensor

FORD MOTOR COMPANY

Page No.

FORD

Econoline (Volume 1) 1-1
Escape incl. hybrid model (Volume 1) 2-1
E-Super Duty (Volume 1) 1-1
Excursion (Volume 1) 1-1
Expedition (Volume 1) 1-1
Explorer (Volume 1) 3-1
Explorer Sport/Sport Trac (Volume 1). 3-1
E150–550 Vans (Volume 1). 1-1
Freestar (Volume 1) 4-1
Full-Size Pickup Trucks (Volume 1). 1-1
Full-Size Vans (Volume 1) 1-1
F-Super Duty (Volume 1) 1-1
F150–550 (Volume 1). 1-1
Ranger (Volume 1) 3-1
Windstar (Volume 1). 6-1

LINCOLN

Aviator (Volume 1) 3-1
Blackwood (Volume 1) 1-1
Mark LT (Volume 1). 1-1
Navigator (Volume 1) 1-1

MERCURY

Mariner incl. hybrid model (Volume 1) 2-1
Monterey (Volume 1) 4-1
Mountaineer (Volume 1). 3-1
Villager (Volume 1) 5-1

GENERAL SERVICE

Active Suspension System 6-1
Air Bag Systems. 4-1
Air Conditioning (Volume 1) 7-1
All Wheel Drive (Volume 1) 21-1
Alternators (Volume 1). 10-1
Anti-Lock Brake Systems 5-1

Page No.

Axles, Drive (Volume 1) 22-1
Axles, Front Wheel Drive (Volume 1) 20-1
Brakes
   Anti-Lock Brake Systems. 5-1
   Disc Brakes (Volume 1) 14-1
   Drum Brakes (Volume 1) 15-1
   Hydraulic Brake Systems (Volume 1) 16-1
   Power Brake Units (Volume 1). 17-1
Cooling Fans (Volume 1) 8-1
Cruise Control Systems 2-1
Dash Gauges. 1-1
Dash Panel Service (Volume 1). 11-1
Disc Brakes (Volume 1) 14-1
Drive Axles (Volume 1). 22-1
Drum Brakes (Volume 1) 15-1
Electronic Level Control 6-1
Engine Cooling Fans (Volume 1) 8-1
Engine Rebuilding Specifications (Volume 1) . . . 24-1
Fans, Variable Speed (Volume 1). 8-1
Front Wheel Drive Axles (Volume 1). 20-1
Hydraulic Brake Systems (Volume 1). 16-1
Machine Shop Specifications (Volume 1) 24-1
Passive Restraint System 4-1
Power Brake Units (Volume 1). 17-1
Power Steering (Volume 1) 13-1
Speed Control Systems. 2-1
Starter Motors (Volume 1) 9-1
Steering
   Power Steering (Volume 1). 13-1
   Steering Columns (Volume 1) 12-1
Steering Columns (Volume 1) 12-1
Tire Pressure Monitoring Systems. 7-1
Transfer Cases (Volume 1). 19-1
Universal Joints (Volume 1). 23-1
Vacuum Pumps (Volume 1) 18-1
Variable Speed Fans (Volume 1) 8-1
Warning Indicators 1-1
Wiper Systems 3-1

FORD MOTOR COMPANY

Page No.

FORD

Econoline (Volume 1) 1-1
Escape incl. hybrid model (Volume 1) 2-1
E-Super Duty (Volume 1) 1-1
Excursion (Volume 1) 1-1
Expedition (Volume 1) 1-1
Explorer (Volume 1) 3-1
Explorer Sport/Sport Trac (Volume 1) 3-1
E150–550 Vans (Volume 1) 1-1
Freestar (Volume 1) 4-1
Full-Size Pickup Trucks (Volume 1) 1-1
Full-Size Vans (Volume 1) 1-1
F-Super Duty (Volume 1) 1-1
F150–550 (Volume 1) 1-1
Ranger (Volume 1) 3-1
Windstar (Volume 1) 6-1

LINCOLN

Aviator (Volume 1) 3-1
Blackwood (Volume 1) 1-1
Mark LT (Volume 1) 1-1
Navigator (Volume 1) 1-1

MERCURY

Mariner incl. hybrid model (Volume 1) 2-1
Monterey (Volume 1) 4-1
Mountaineer (Volume 1) 3-1
Villager (Volume 1) 5-1

GENERAL SERVICE

Active Suspension System 6-1
Air Bag Systems 4-1
Air Conditioning (Volume 1) 7-1
All Wheel Drive (Volume 1) 21-1
Alternators (Volume 1) 10-1
Anti-Lock Brake Systems 5-1

Page No.

Axles, Drive (Volume 1) 22-1
Axles, Front Wheel Drive (Volume 1) 20-1
Brakes
   Anti-Lock Brake Systems 5-1
   Disc Brakes (Volume 1) 14-1
   Drum Brakes (Volume 1) 15-1
   Hydraulic Brake Systems (Volume 1) 16-1
   Power Brake Units (Volume 1) 17-1
Cooling Fans (Volume 1) 8-1
Cruise Control Systems 2-1
Dash Gauges 1-1
Dash Panel Service (Volume 1) 11-1
Disc Brakes (Volume 1) 14-1
Drive Axles (Volume 1) 22-1
Drum Brakes (Volume 1) 15-1
Electronic Level Control 6-1
Engine Cooling Fans (Volume 1) 8-1
Engine Rebuilding Specifications (Volume 1) . . . 24-1
Fans, Variable Speed (Volume 1) 8-1
Front Wheel Drive Axles (Volume 1) 20-1
Hydraulic Brake Systems (Volume 1) 16-1
Machine Shop Specifications (Volume 1) 24-1
Passive Restraint System 4-1
Power Brake Units (Volume 1) 17-1
Power Steering (Volume 1) 13-1
Speed Control Systems 2-1
Starter Motors (Volume 1) 9-1
Steering
   Power Steering (Volume 1) 13-1
   Steering Columns (Volume 1) 12-1
Steering Columns (Volume 1) 12-1
Tire Pressure Monitoring Systems 7-1
Transfer Cases (Volume 1) 19-1
Universal Joints (Volume 1) 23-1
Vacuum Pumps (Volume 1) 18-1
Variable Speed Fans (Volume 1) 8-1
Warning Indicators 1-1
Wiper Systems 3-1

DASH GAUGES & WARNING INDICATORS

NOTE: On Air Bag Equipped Models, Refer To "Air Bag System Precautions" Located In The Front Of This Manual For System Disarming & Arming Procedures.

NOTE: Refer To The "Dash Panel Service" Section For Dash Panel Removal Procedures.

NOTE: Refer To The "Electronic Instrumentation" Section In MOTOR's "Domestic Truck Engine Performance & Driveability Manual" For Information Related To Electronic Instrumentation.

NOTE: Refer To "Computer Relearn Procedures" Located In The Front Of This Manual When Battery Power To The Computer Has Been Interrupted.

INDEX

	Page No.		Page No.		Page No.
Diagnosis & Testing	1-1	Excursion & F-Super Duty	1-1	Ranger	1-1
Symptom Diagnosis	1-1	Expedition & Navigator	1-1	Villager	1-1
Wiring Diagrams	1-1	Explorer & Mountaineer	1-1	Windstar	1-1
Aviator	1-1	Explorer Sport & Sport Trac	1-1	Precautions	1-1
E-Series	1-1	F-150 & Mark LT	1-1	Air Bag Systems	1-1
Escape & Mariner	1-1	Freestar & Monterey	1-1	Battery Ground Cable	1-1

PRECAUTIONS

Air Bag Systems

Refer to "Air Bag System Precautions" in the front of this manual for system disarming and arming procedures.

Battery Ground Cable

Prior to service, disconnect battery ground cable and isolate as required.

DIAGNOSIS & TESTING

Wiring Diagrams

AVIATOR

Refer to **Fig. 1** for instrument cluster wiring diagrams.

E-SERIES

Refer to **Figs. 2 and 3** for instrument cluster wiring diagrams.

ESCAPE & MARINER

Refer to **Figs. 4 and 5,** for instrument cluster wiring diagram.

EXCURSION & F-SUPER DUTY

Refer to **Figs. 6 and 7** for instrument cluster wiring diagram.

EXPEDITION & NAVIGATOR

Refer to **Figs. 8 and 9** for instrument cluster wiring diagrams.

EXPLORER & MOUNTAINEER

Refer to **Figs. 10 and 11** for instrument cluster wiring diagrams.

EXPLORER SPORT & SPORT TRAC

Refer to **Figs. 12 and 13** for instrument cluster wiring diagrams.

FREESTAR & MONTEREY

Refer to **Fig. 14** for instrument cluster wiring diagrams.

F-150 & MARK LT

Refer to **Figs. 15 and 16** for instrument cluster wiring diagrams.

RANGER

Refer to **Figs. 17 and 18** for instrument cluster wiring diagrams.

VILLAGER

Refer to **Figs. 19 and 20** for instrument cluster wiring diagrams.

WINDSTAR

Refer to **Fig. 21** for instrument cluster wiring diagrams.

Symptom Diagnosis

Refer to **Figs. 22 through 24** and "Wiring Diagrams" for symptom diagnosis.

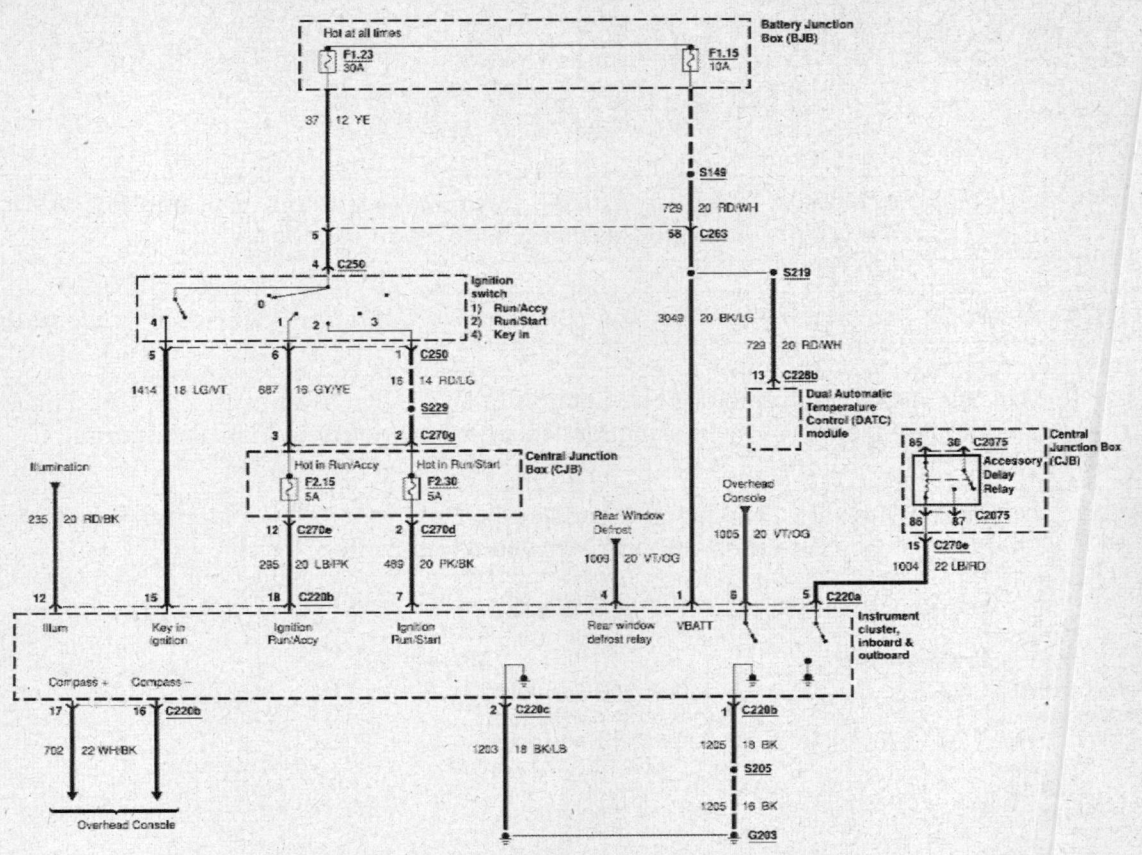

Fig. 1 Instrument cluster wiring diagram (Part 1 of 2). Aviator

LTV0500000001010

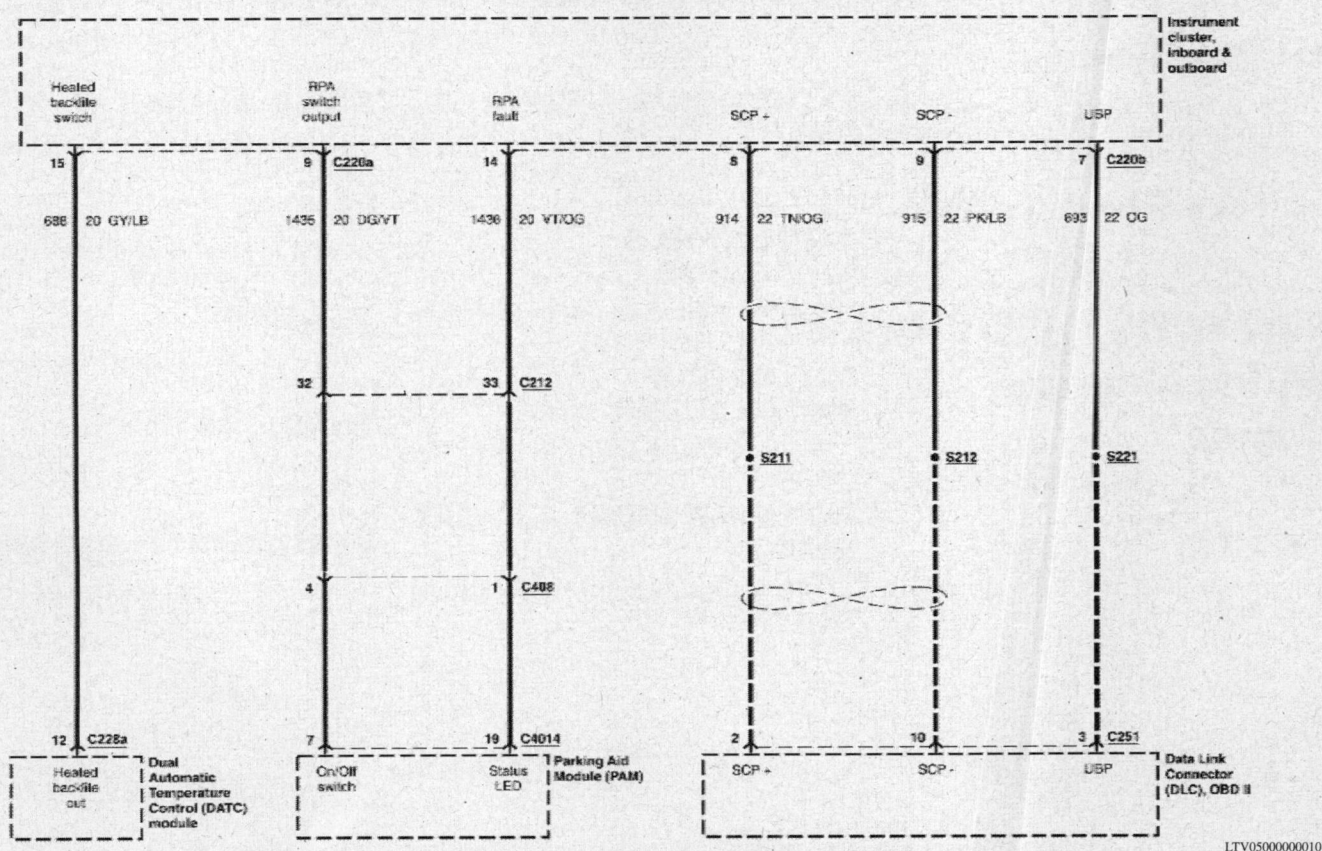

Fig. 1 Instrument cluster wiring diagram (Part 2 of 2). Aviator

LTV0500000001011

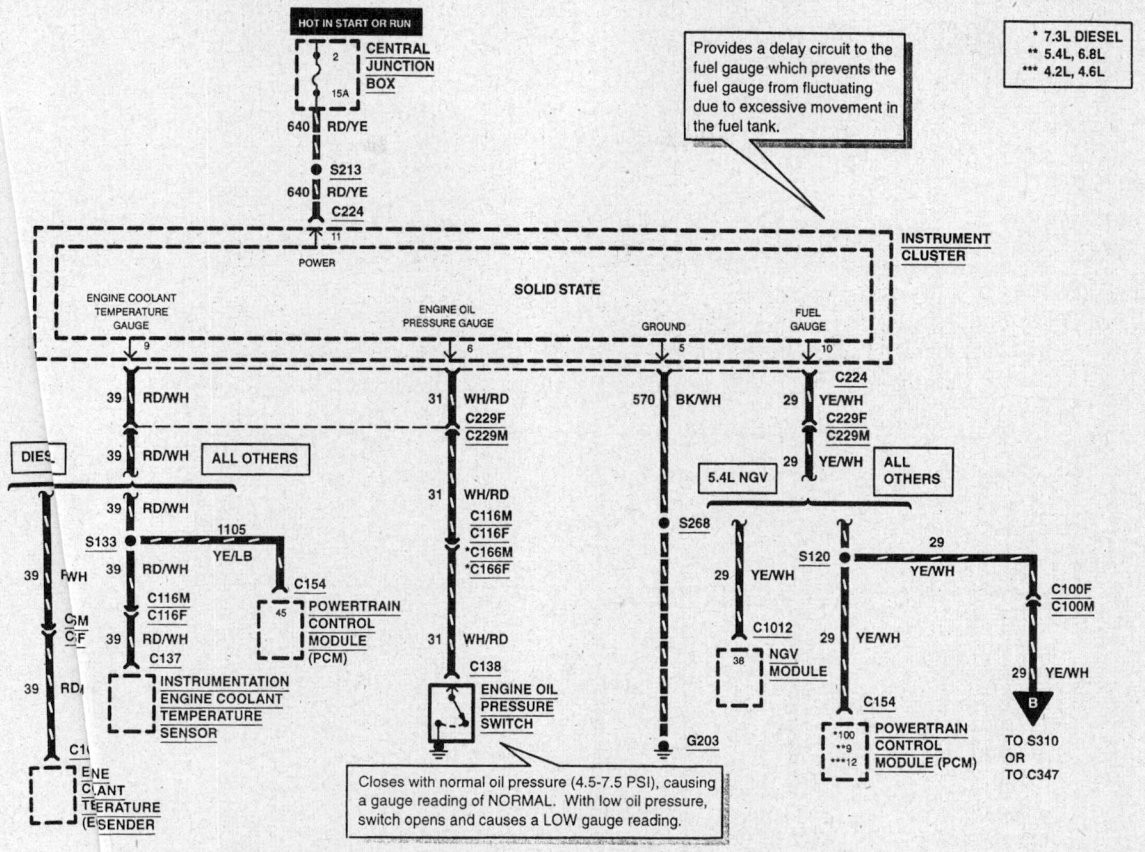

Fig. 2 Instrument cluster wiring diagram (Part 1 of 5). 2002–03 E-Series

FM9040000661010X

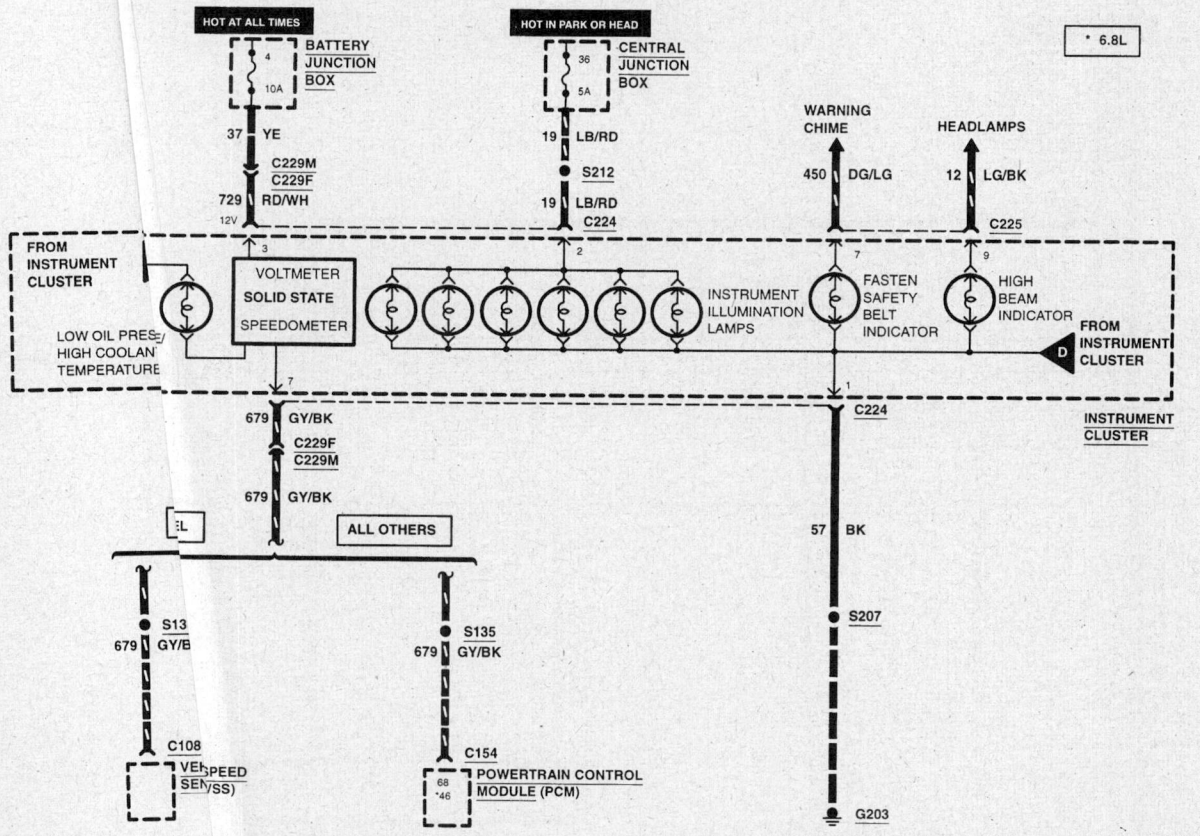

Fig. nstrument cluster wiring diagram (Part 2 of 5). 2002–03 E-Series

FM9040000661020X

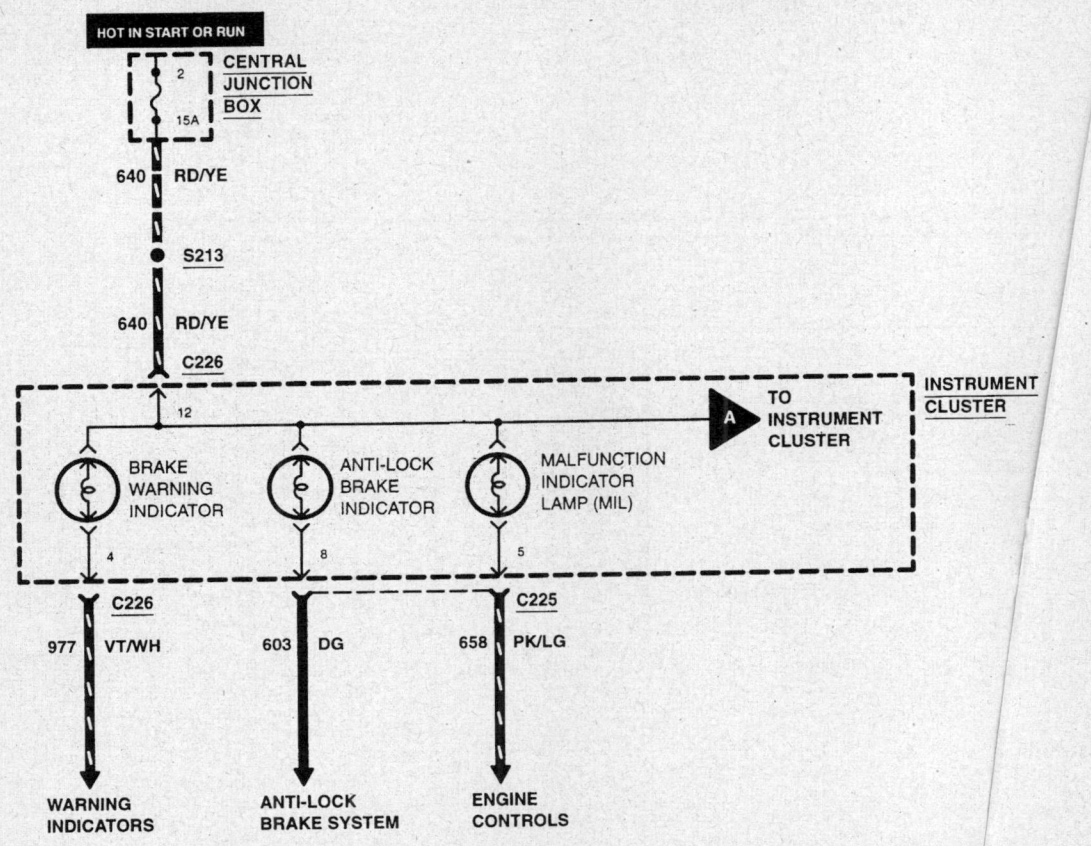

Fig. 2   Instrument cluster wiring diagram (Part 3 of 5). 2002–03 E-Series except 7L engine

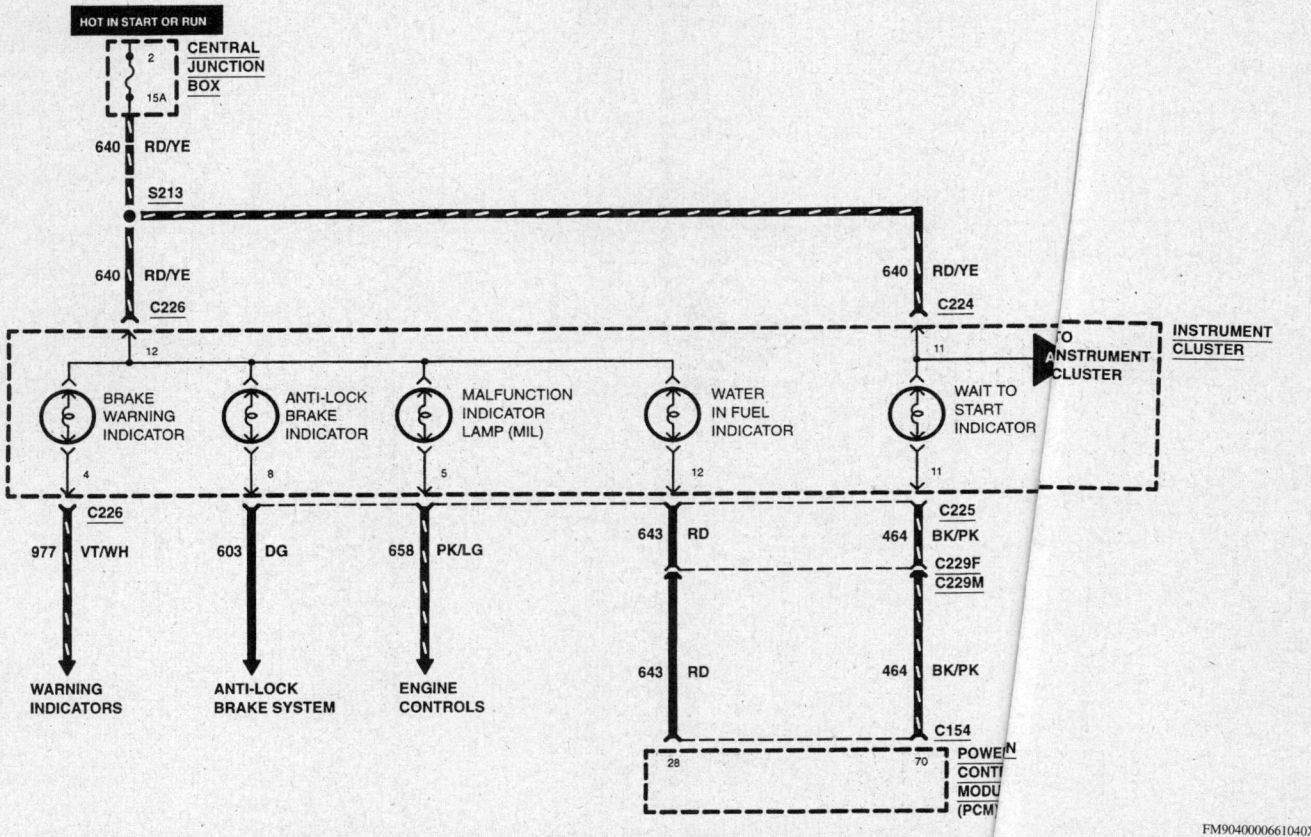

Fig. 2   Instrument cluster wiring diagram (Part 3 of 5). 2002–03 E-Ser w/7.3L engine

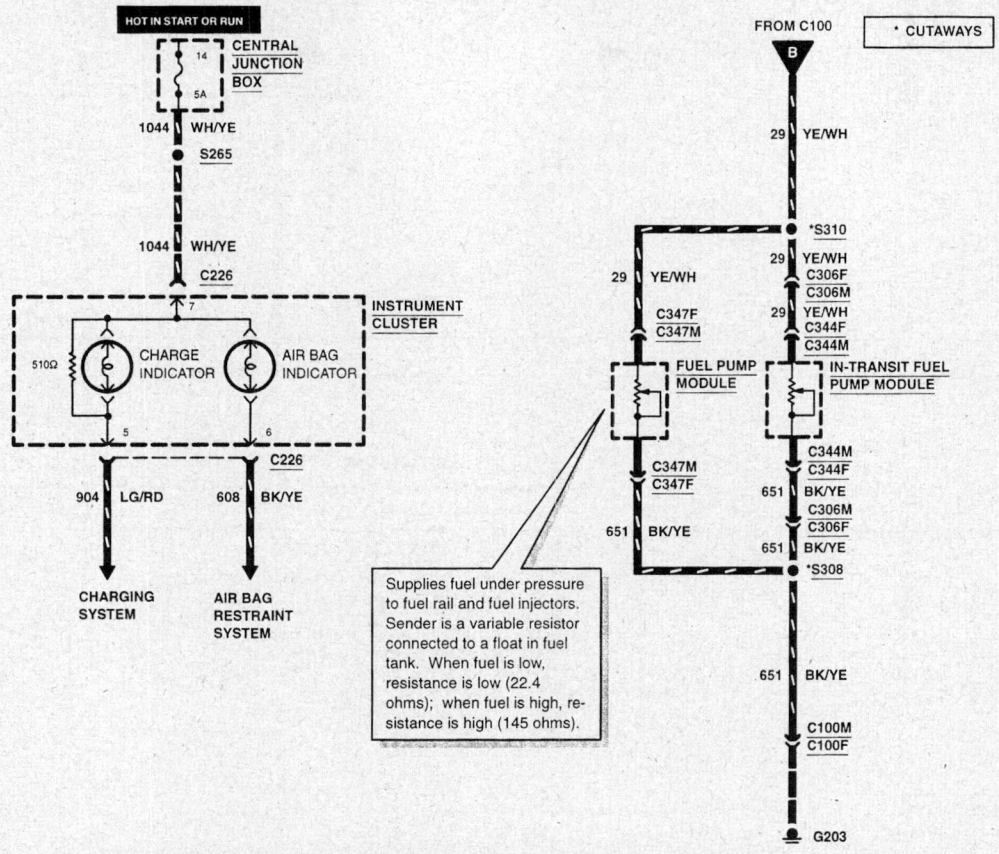

Fig. 2   Instrument cluster wiring diagram (Part 4 of 5). 2002–03 E-Series

FM9040000661050X

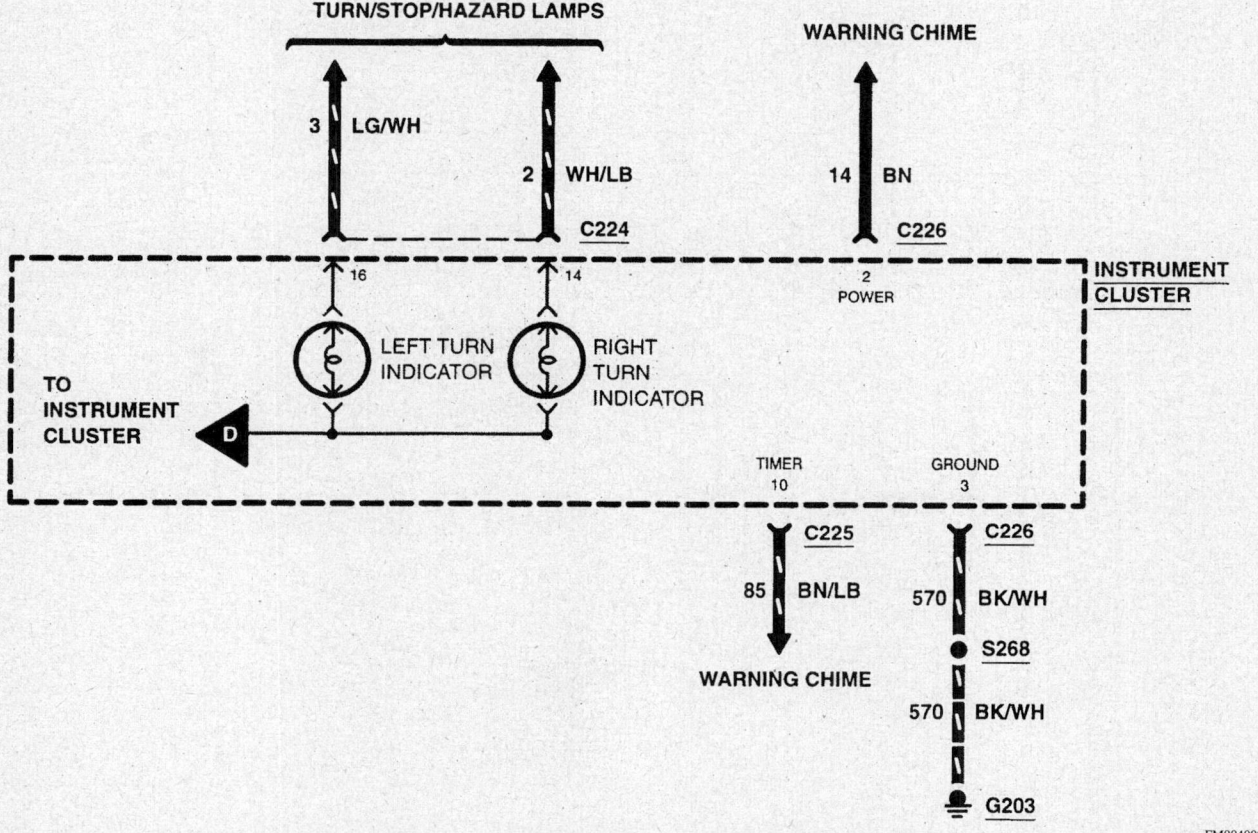

Fig. 2   Instrument cluster wiring diagram (Part 5 of 5). 2002–03 E-Series

FM9040000661060X

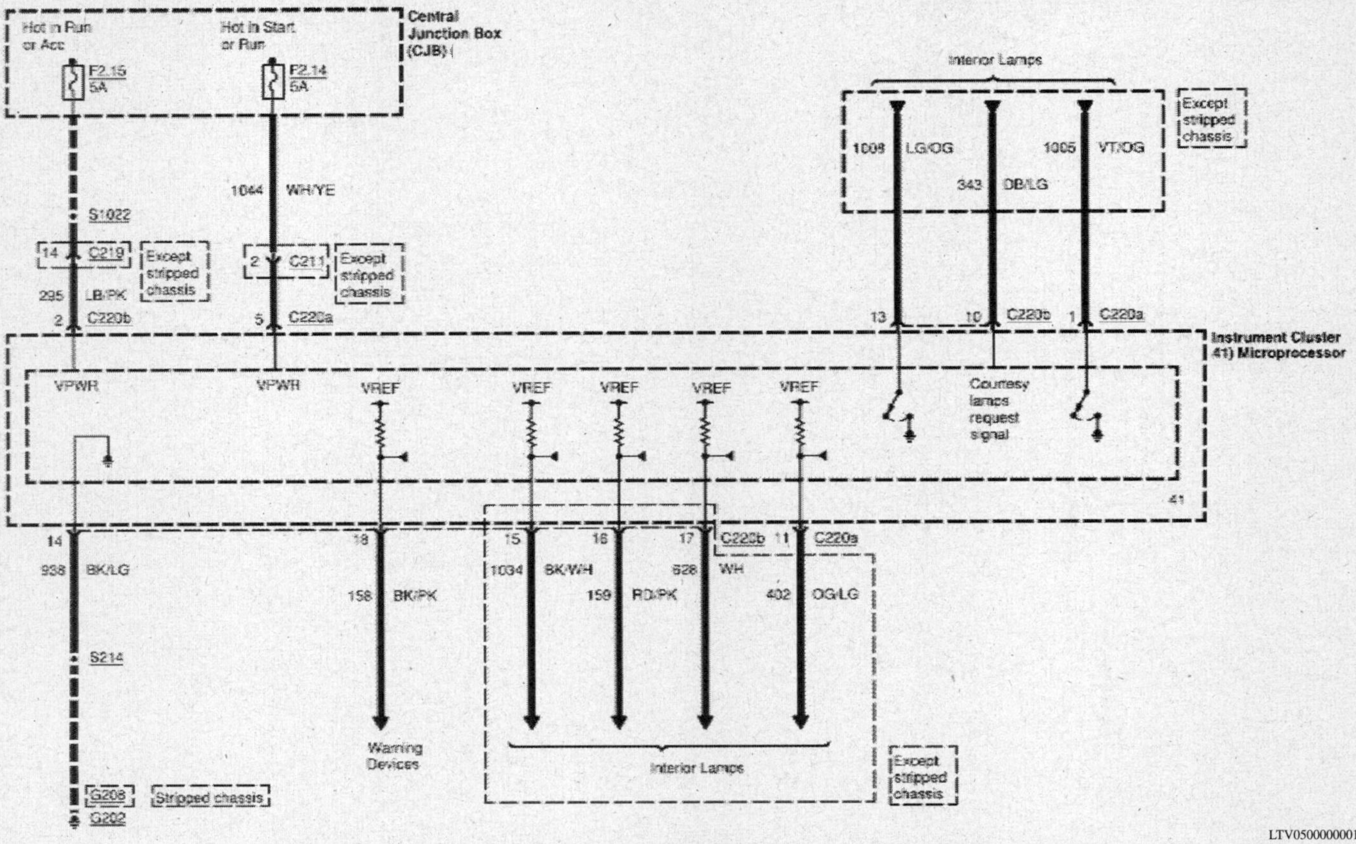

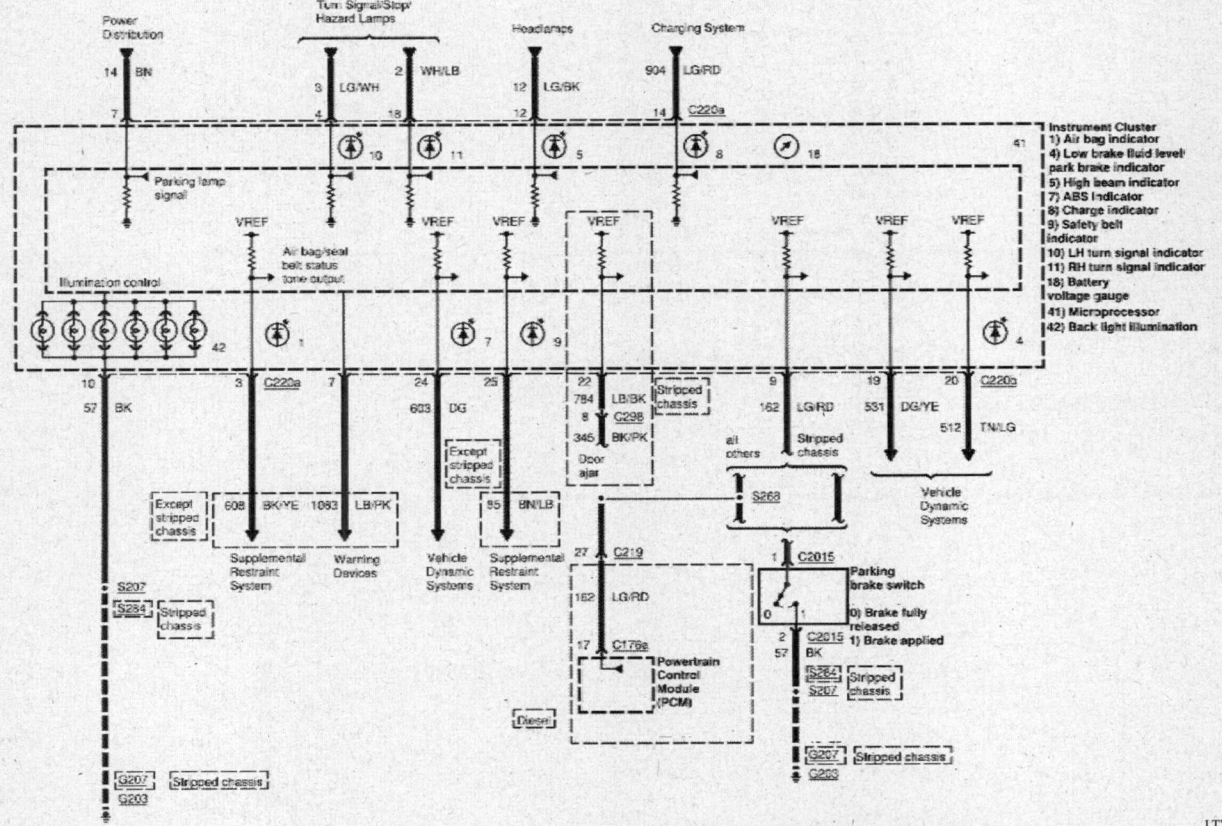

Fig. 3   Instrument cluster wiring diagram (Part 1 of 5). 2004–06 E-Series

LTV0500000001012

Fig. 3   Instrument cluster wiring diagram (Part 2 of 5). 2004–06 E-Series

LTV0500000001013

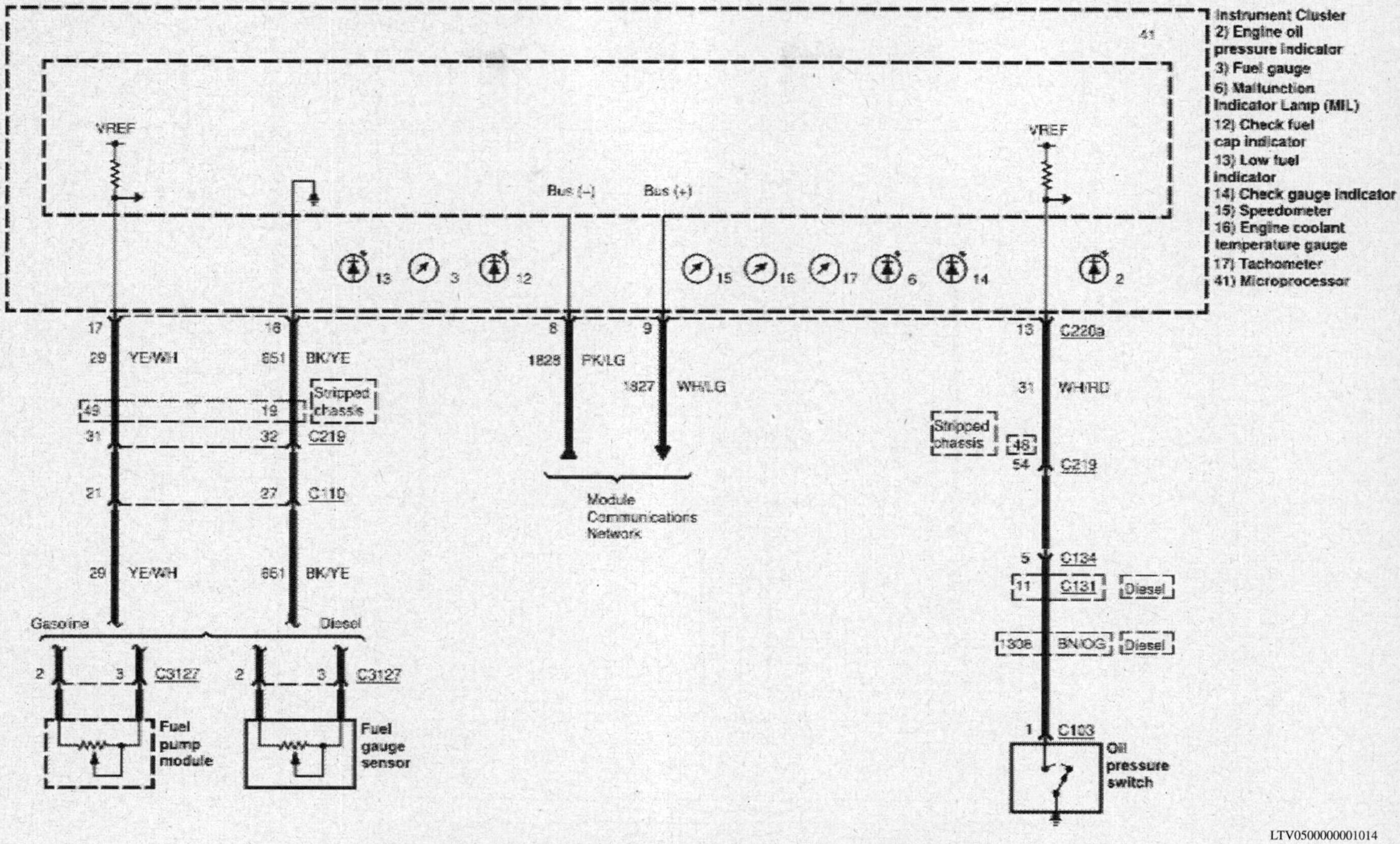

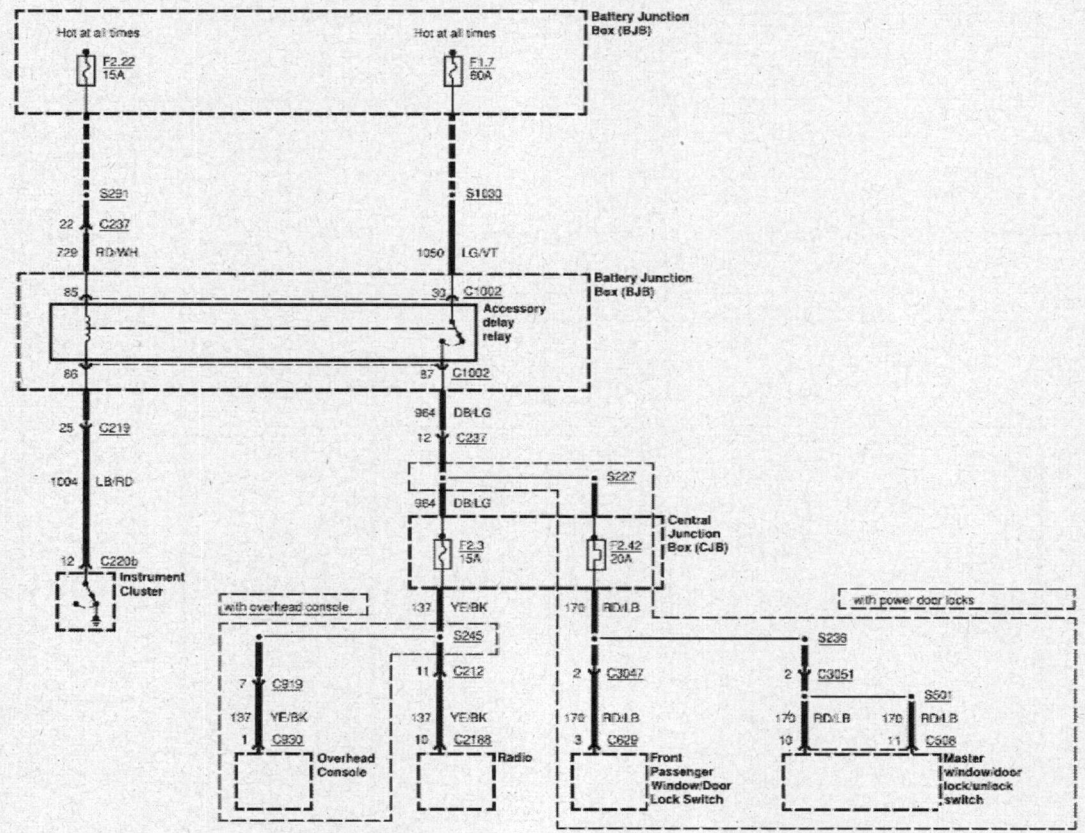

Fig. 3   Instrument cluster wiring diagram (Part 3 of 5). 2004–06 E-Series

LTV0500000001014

Fig. 3   Instrument cluster wiring diagram (Part 4 of 5). 2004–06 E-Series

LTV0500000001015

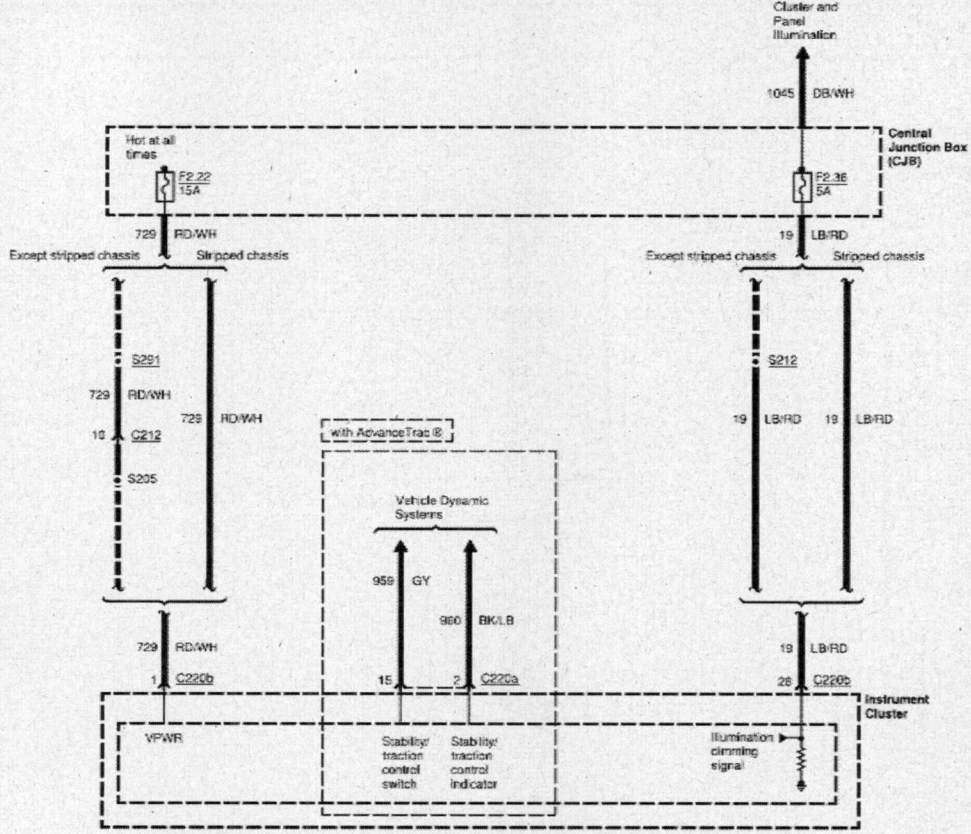

Fig. 3 Instrument cluster wiring diagram (Part 5 of 5). 2004–06 E-Series

LTV0500000001016

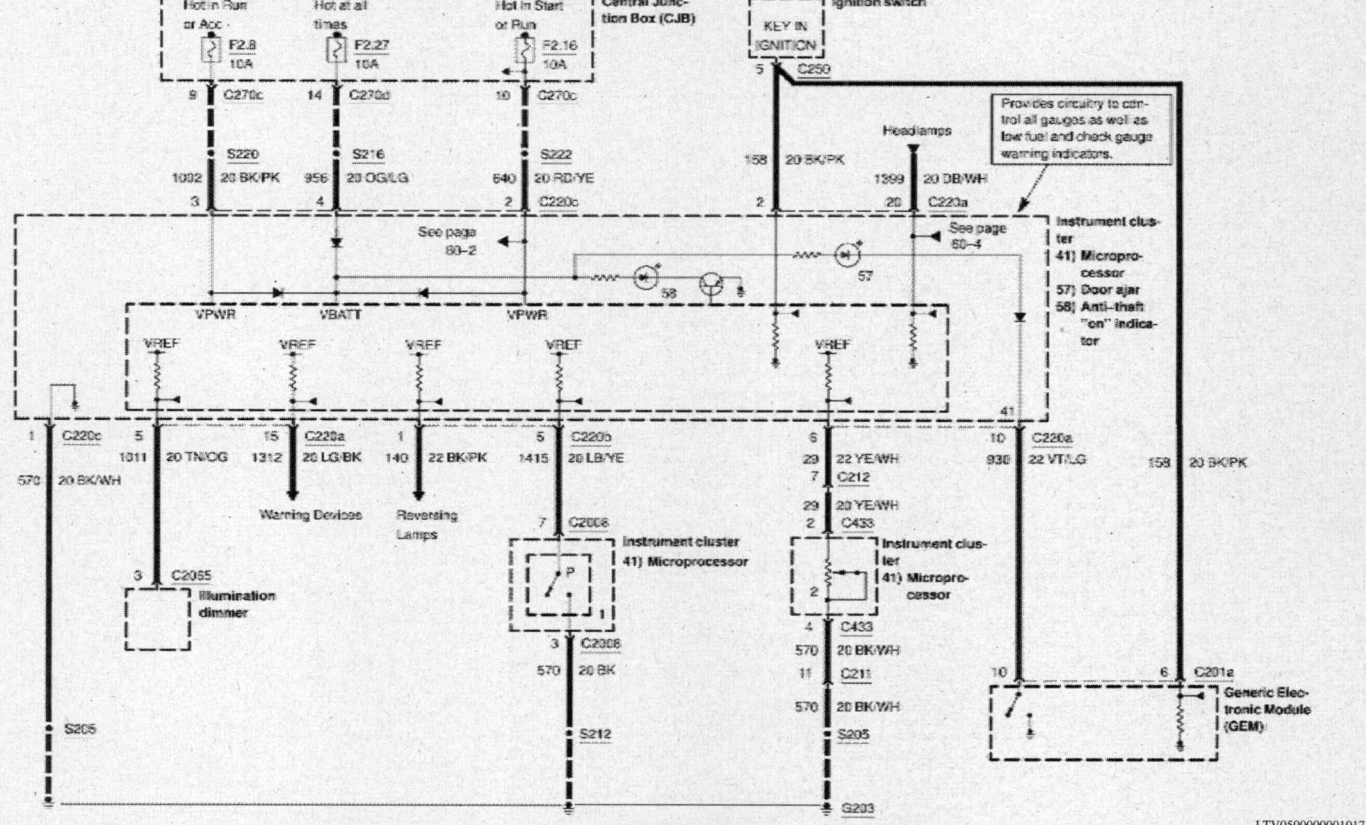

Fig. 4 Instrument cluster wiring diagram (Part 1 of 4). 2002–04 Escape

LTV0500000001017

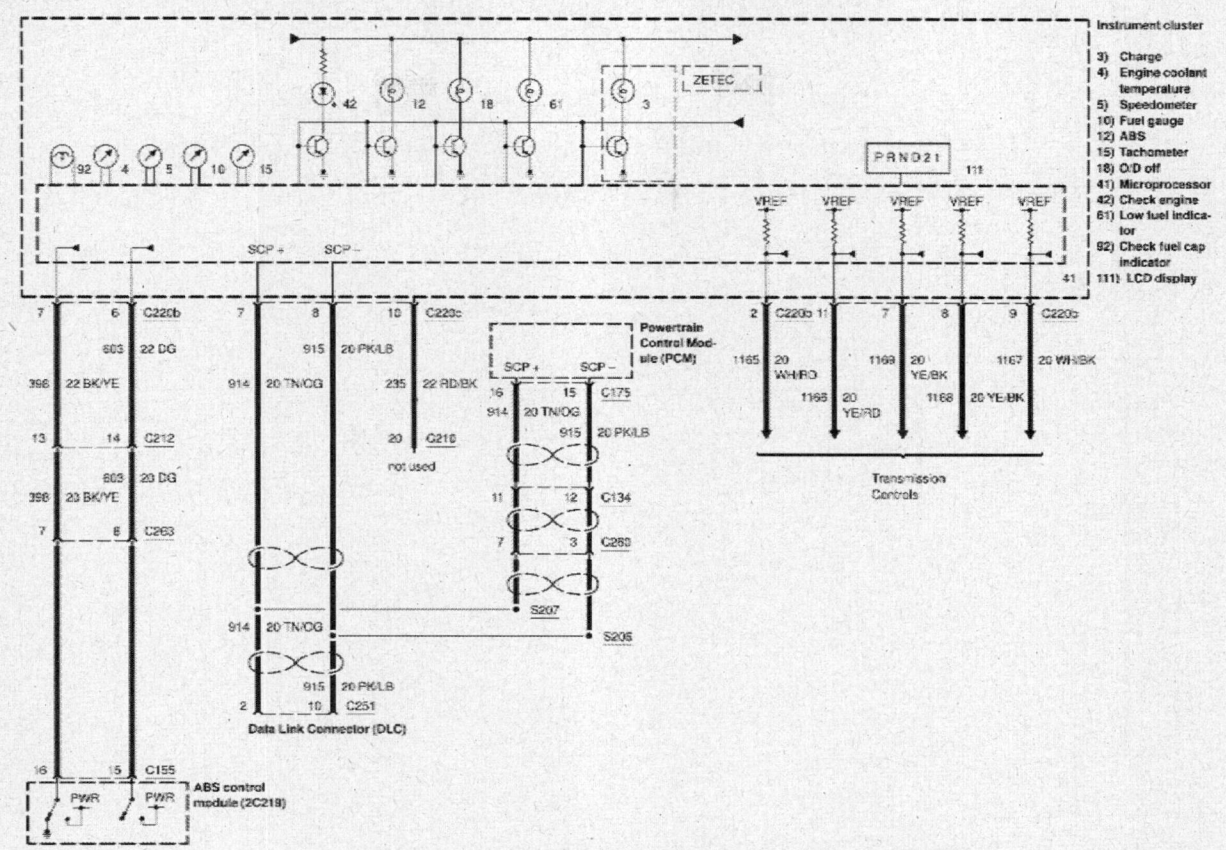

Fig. 4   Instrument cluster wiring diagram (Part 2 of 4). 2002–04 Escape

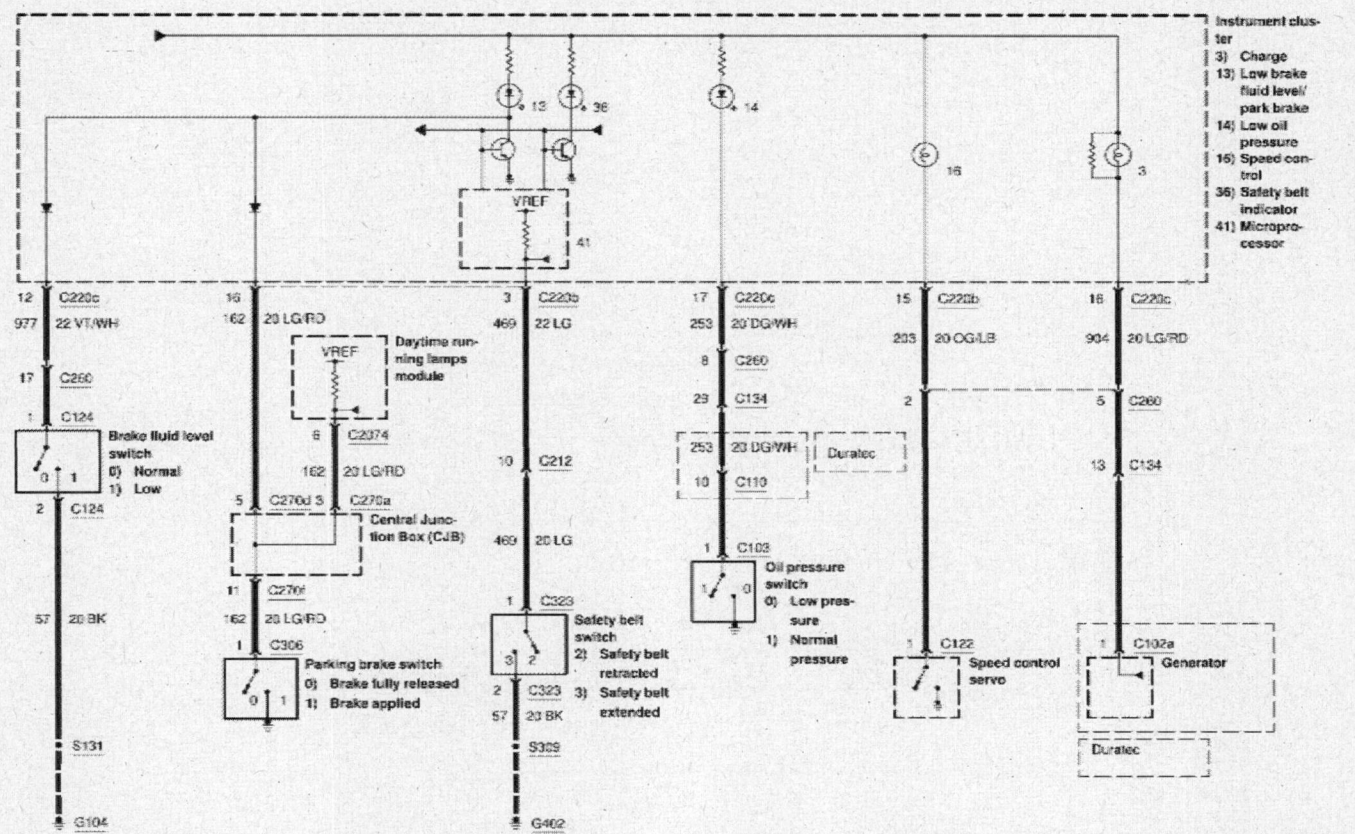

Fig. 4   Instrument cluster wiring diagram (Part 3 of 4). 2002–04 Escape

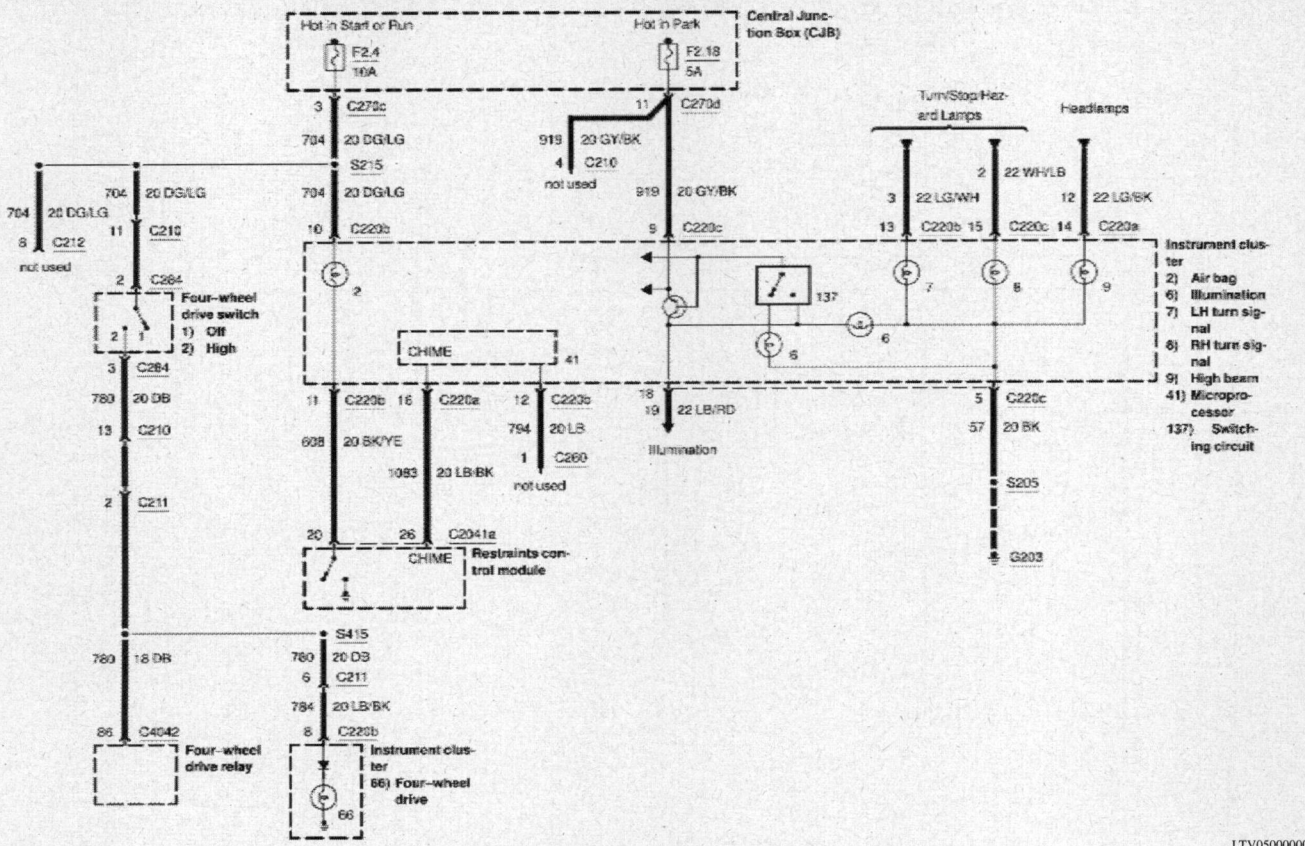

Fig. 4   Instrument cluster wiring diagram (Part 4 of 4). 2002–04 Escape

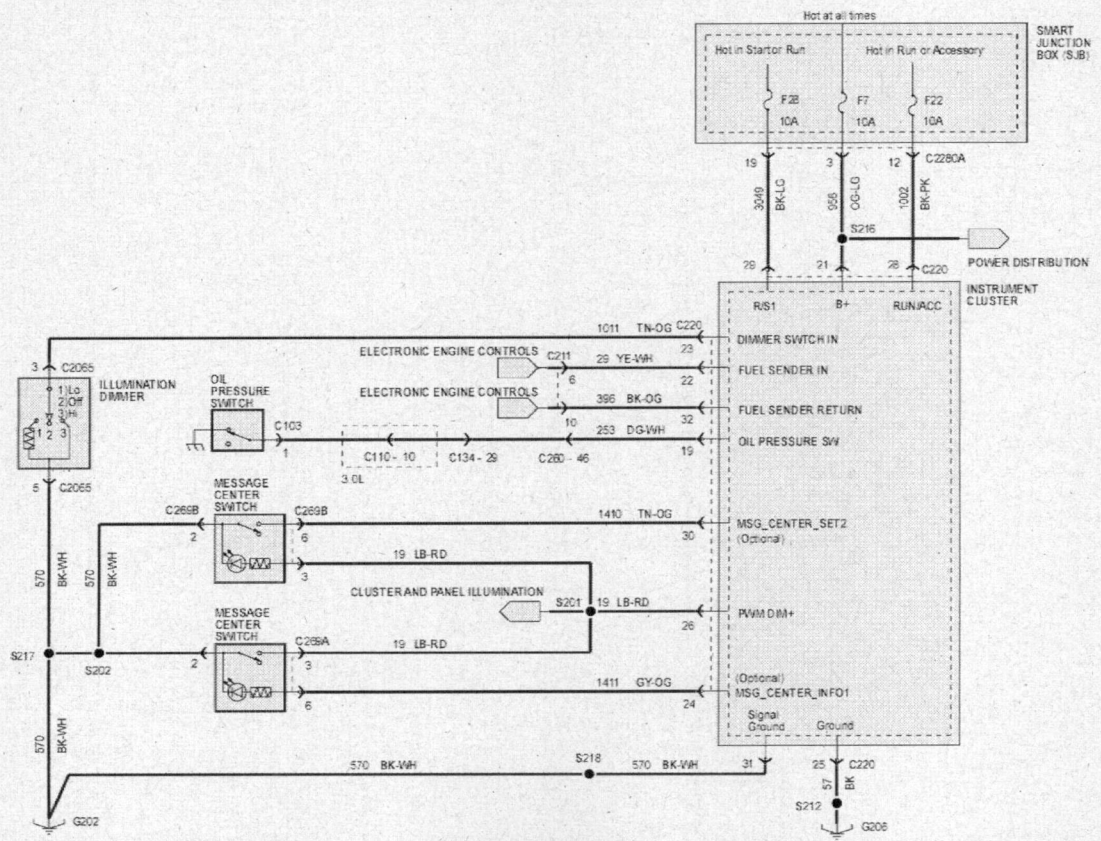

Fig. 5   Instrument cluster wiring diagram (Part 1 of 2). 2005–06 Escape & Mariner

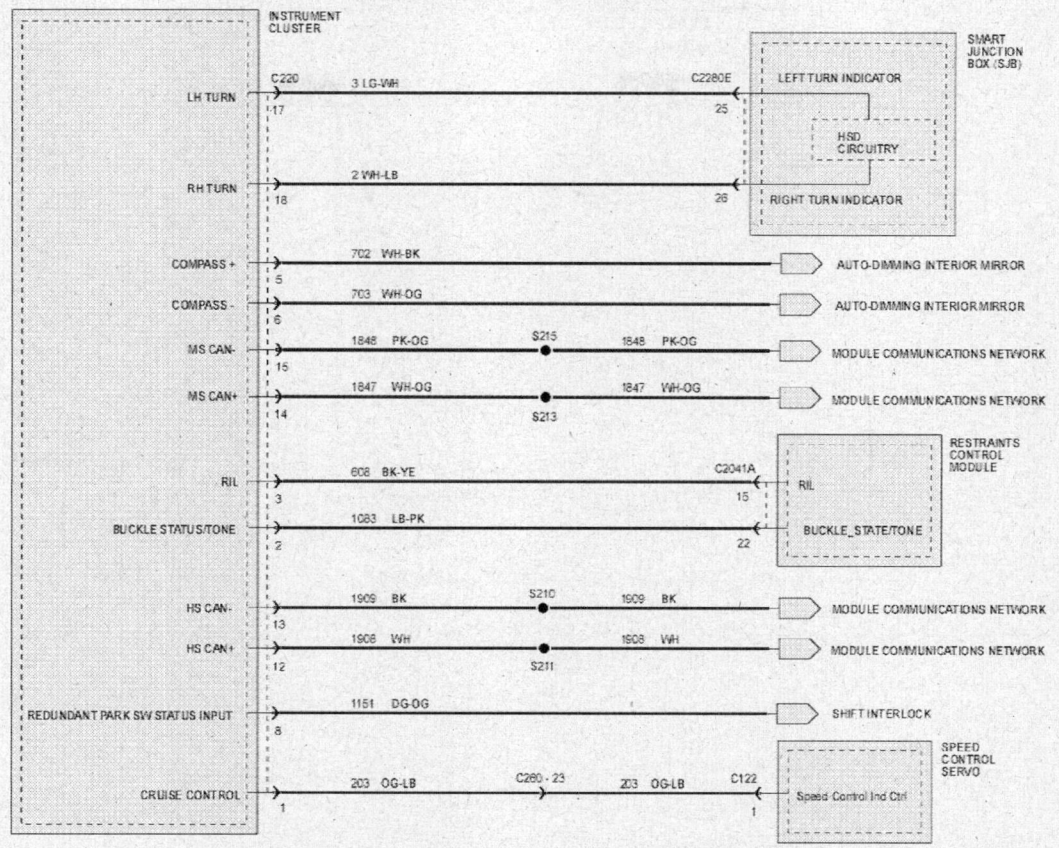

Fig. 5 Instrument cluster wiring diagram (Part 2 of 2). 2005–06 Escape & Mariner

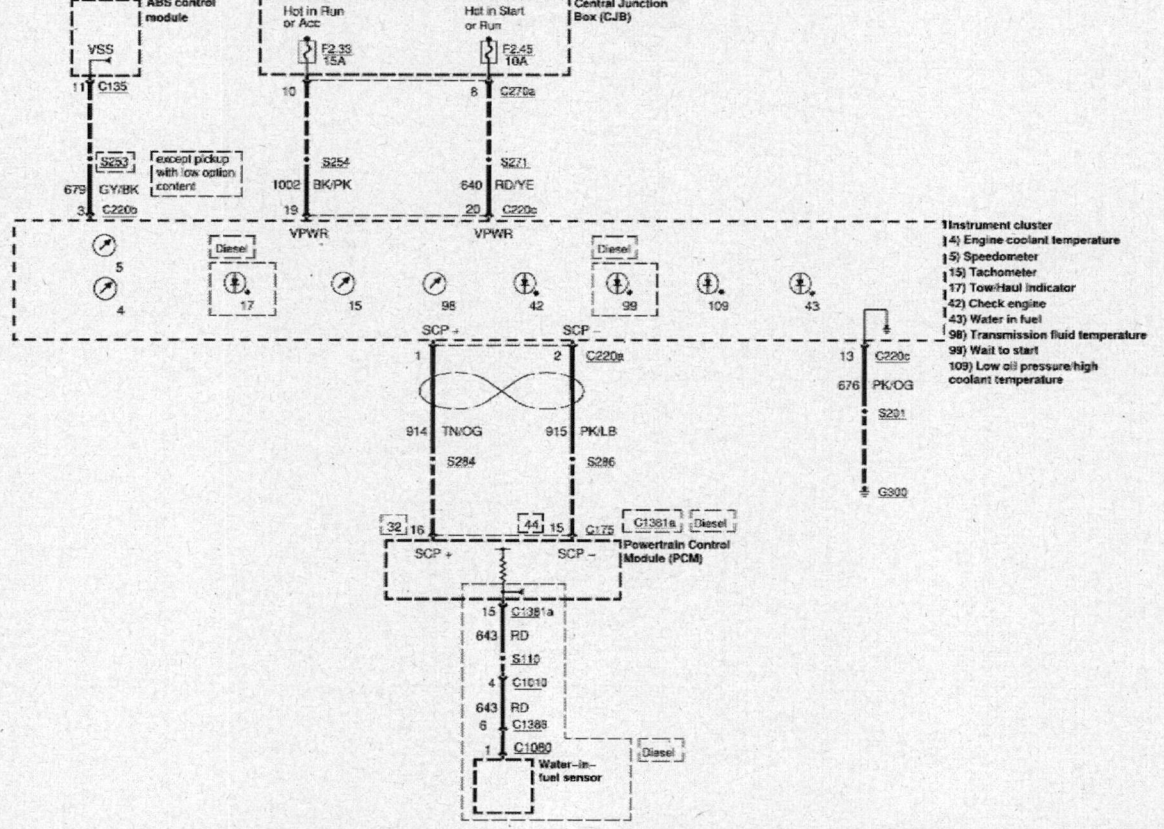

Fig. 6 Instrument cluster wiring diagram (Part 1 of 6). 2002–04 Excursion & F-Super Duty

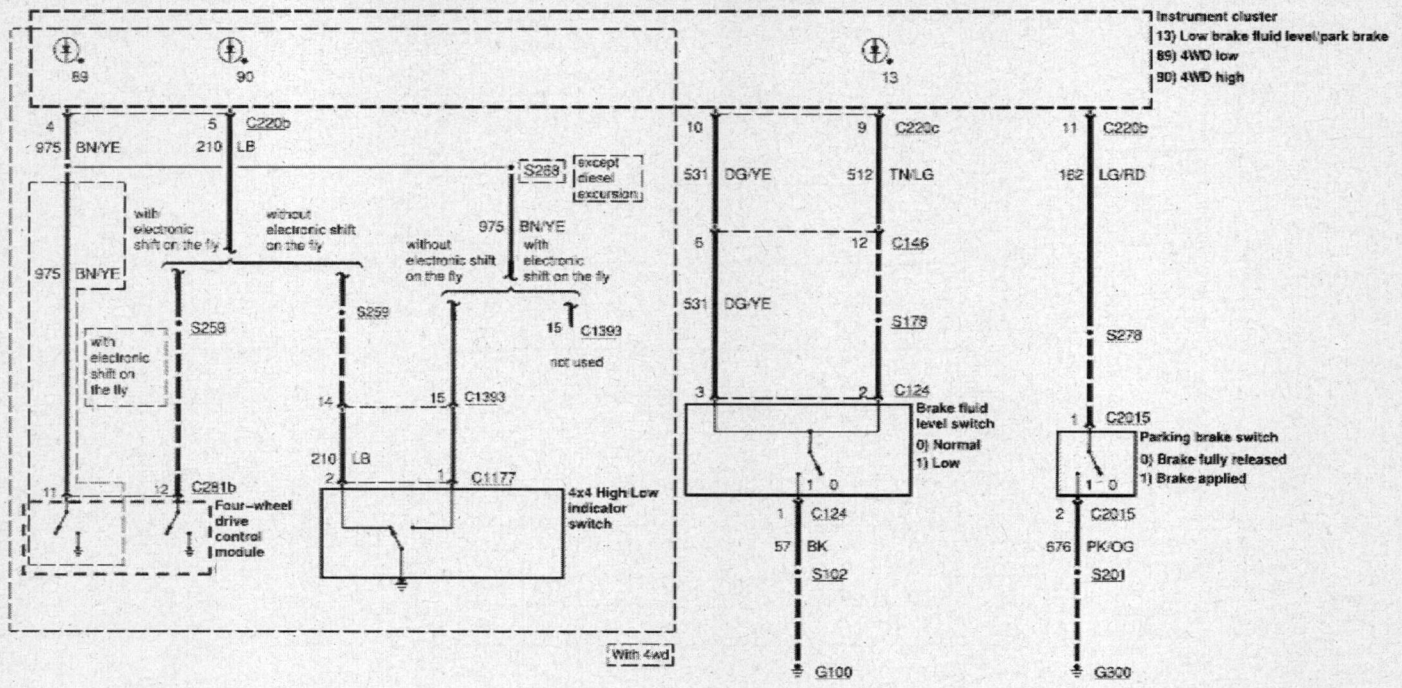

Fig. 6   Instrument cluster wiring diagram (Part 2 of 6). 2002–04 Excursion & F-Super Duty

LTV0500000001024

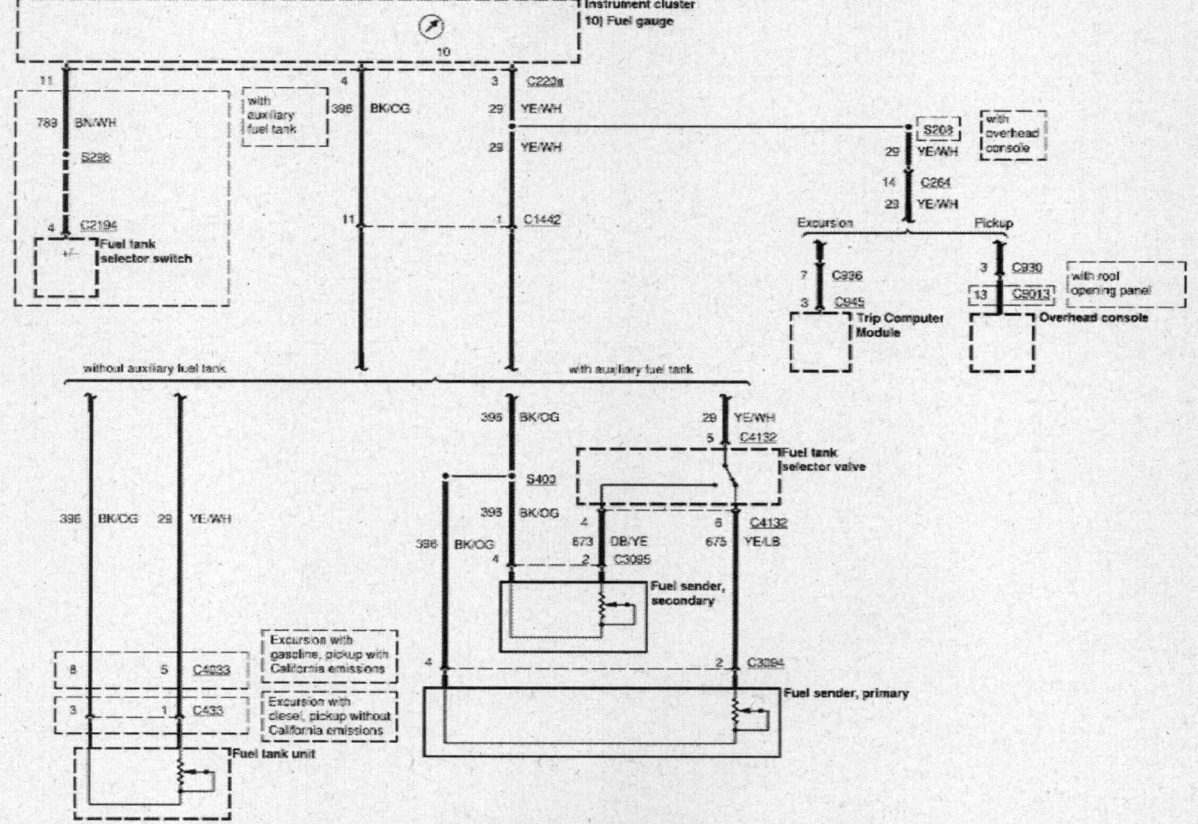

Fig. 6   Instrument cluster wiring diagram (Part 3 of 6). 2002–04 Excursion & F-Super Duty

LTV0500000001025

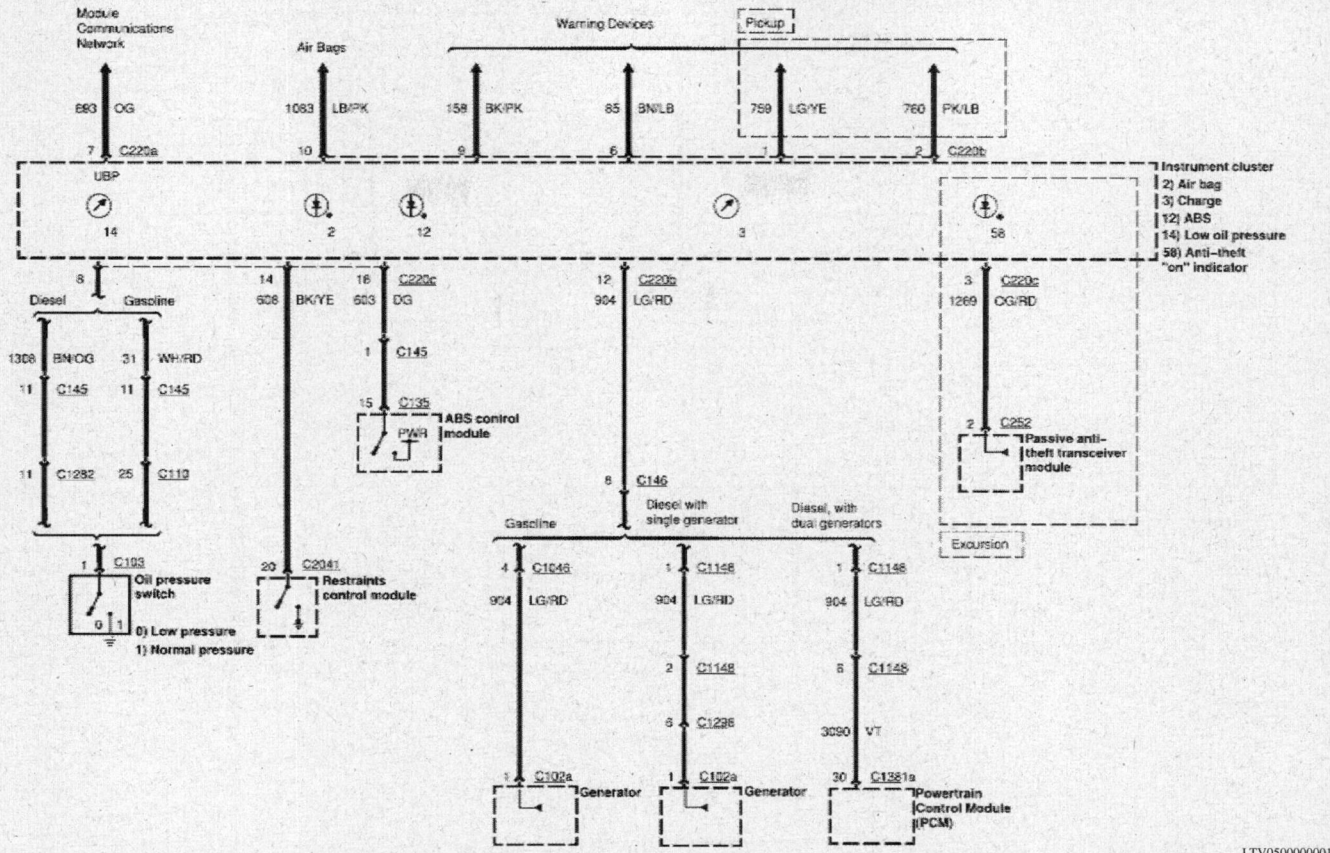

Fig. 6 Instrument cluster wiring diagram (Part 4 of 6). 2002–04 Excursion & F-Super Duty

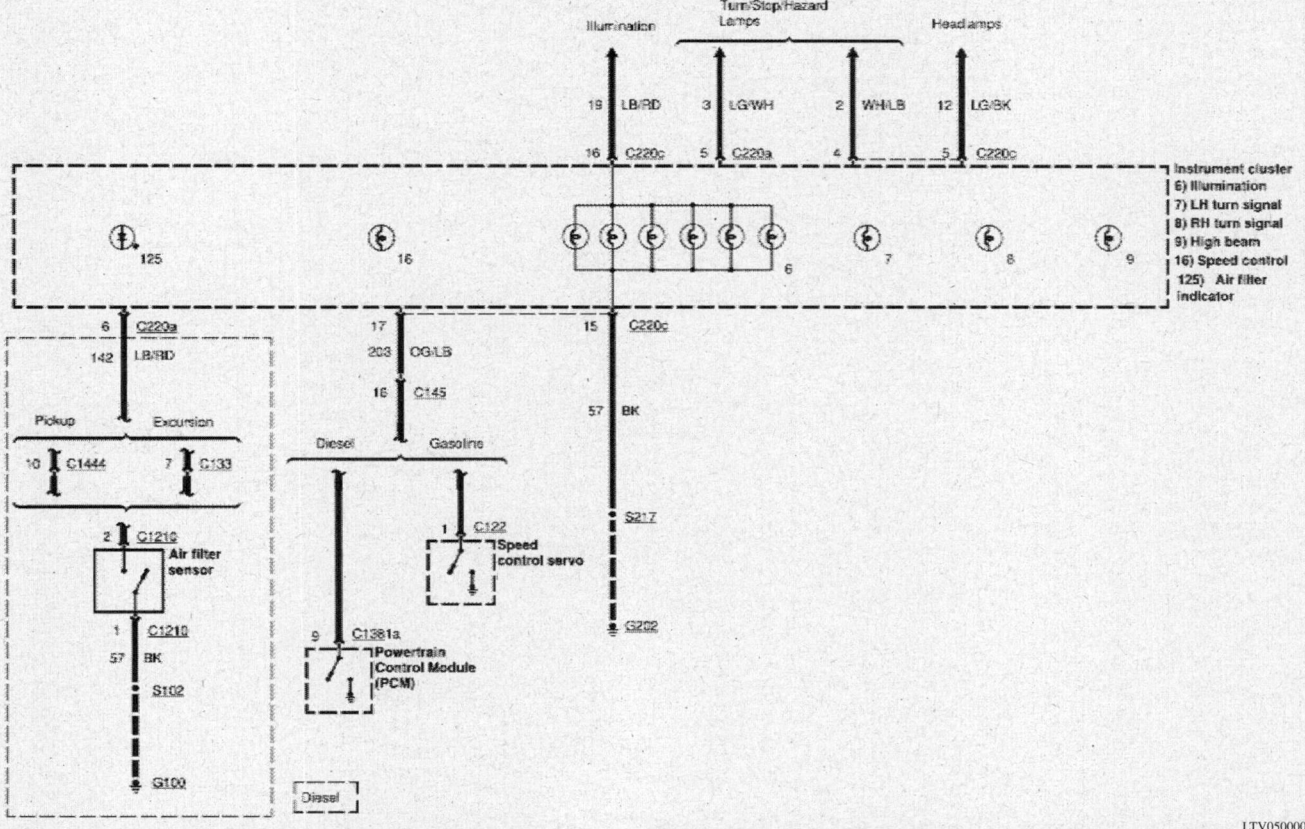

Fig. 6 Instrument cluster wiring diagram (Part 5 of 6). 2002–04 Excursion & F-Super Duty

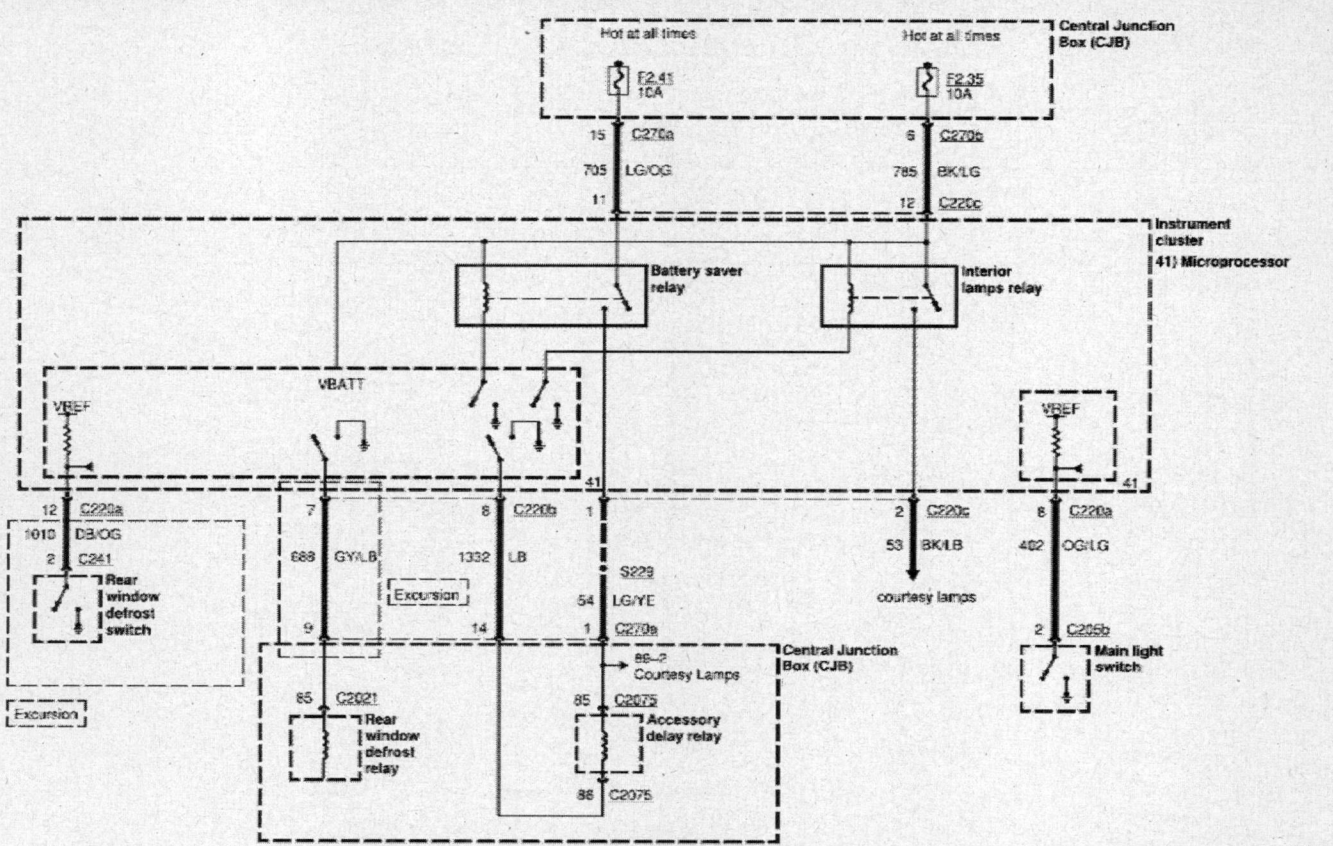

Fig. 6 Instrument cluster wiring diagram (Part 6 of 6). 2002–04 Excursion & F-Super Duty

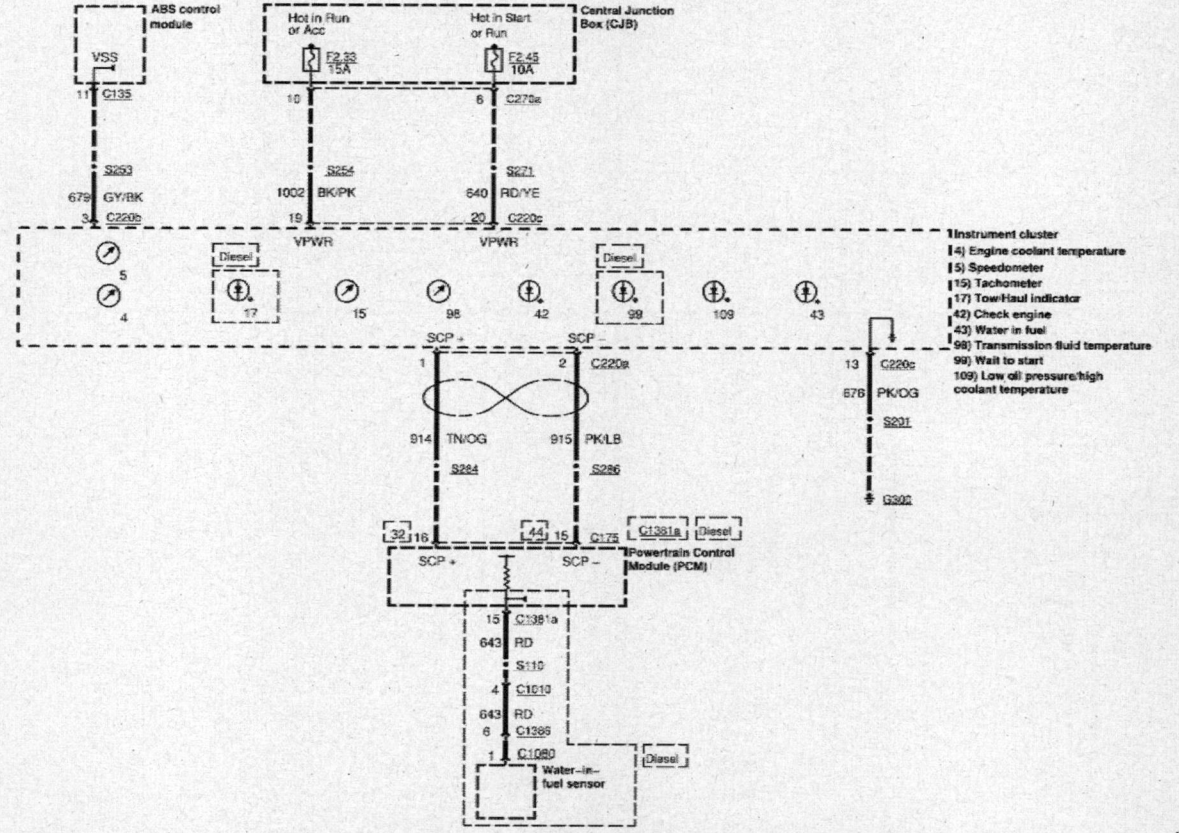

Fig. 7 Instrument cluster wiring diagram (Part 1 of 6). 2005–06 Excursion & F-Super Duty

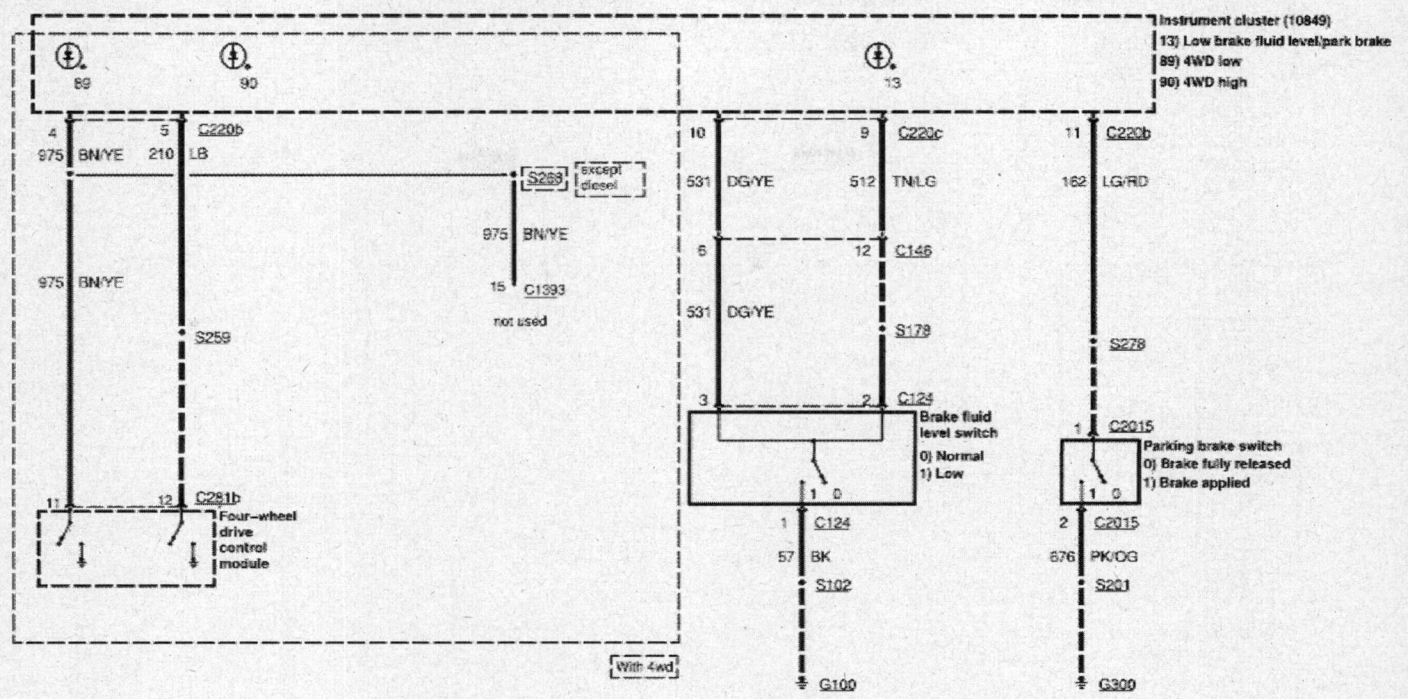

Fig. 7   Instrument cluster wiring diagram (Part 2 of 6). 2005–06 Excursion & F-Super Duty

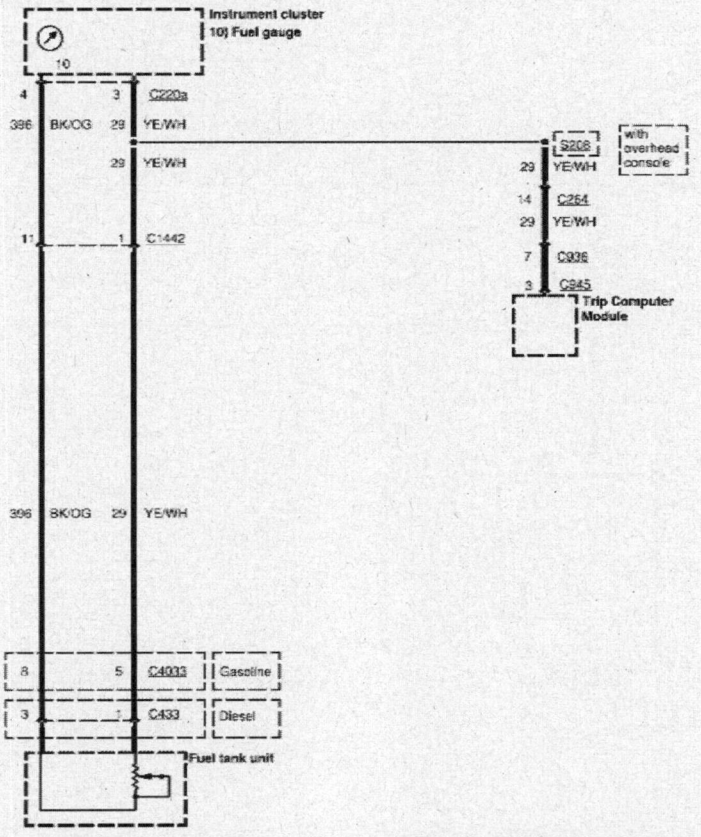

Fig. 7   Instrument cluster wiring diagram (Part 3 of 6). 2005–06 Excursion & F-Super Duty

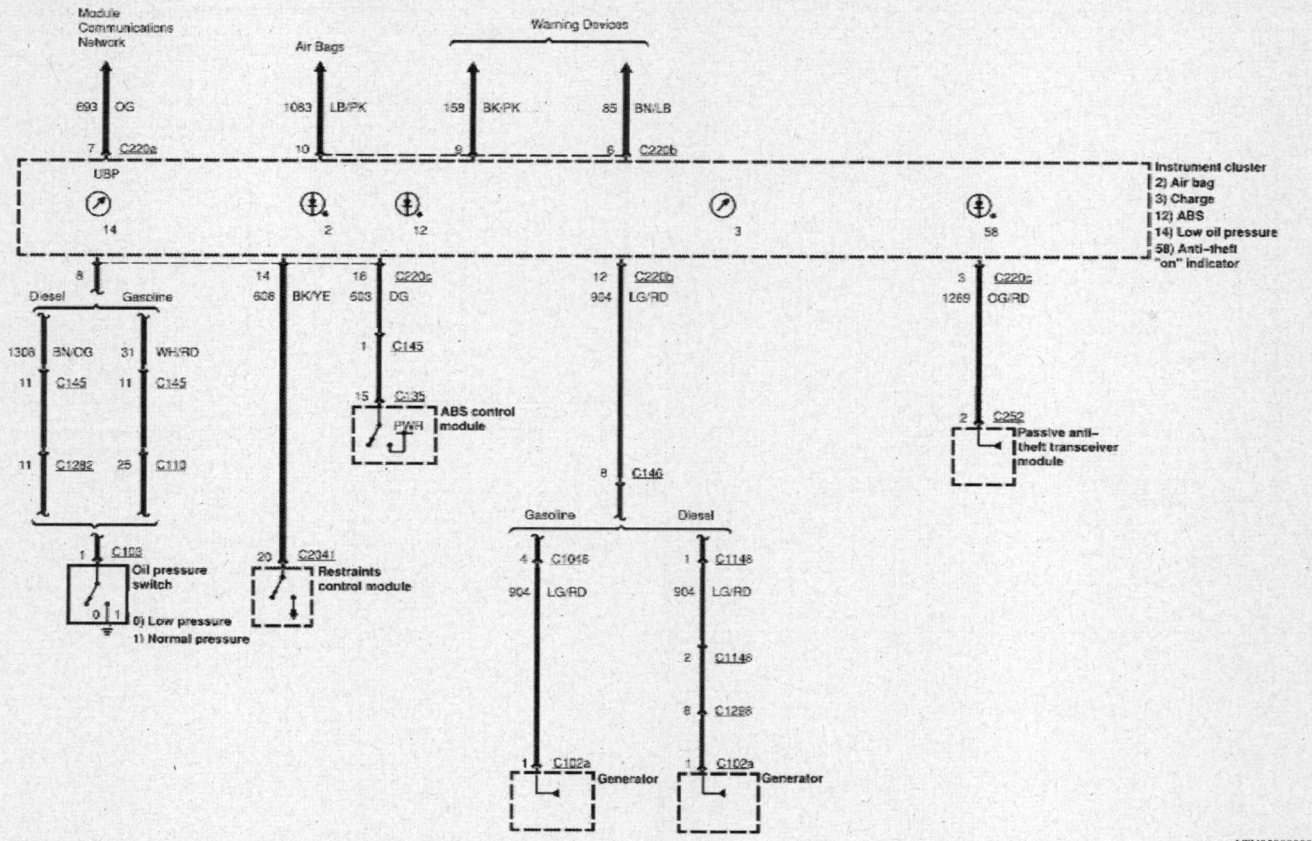

Fig. 7   Instrument cluster wiring diagram (Part 4 of 6). 2005–06 Excursion & F-Super Duty

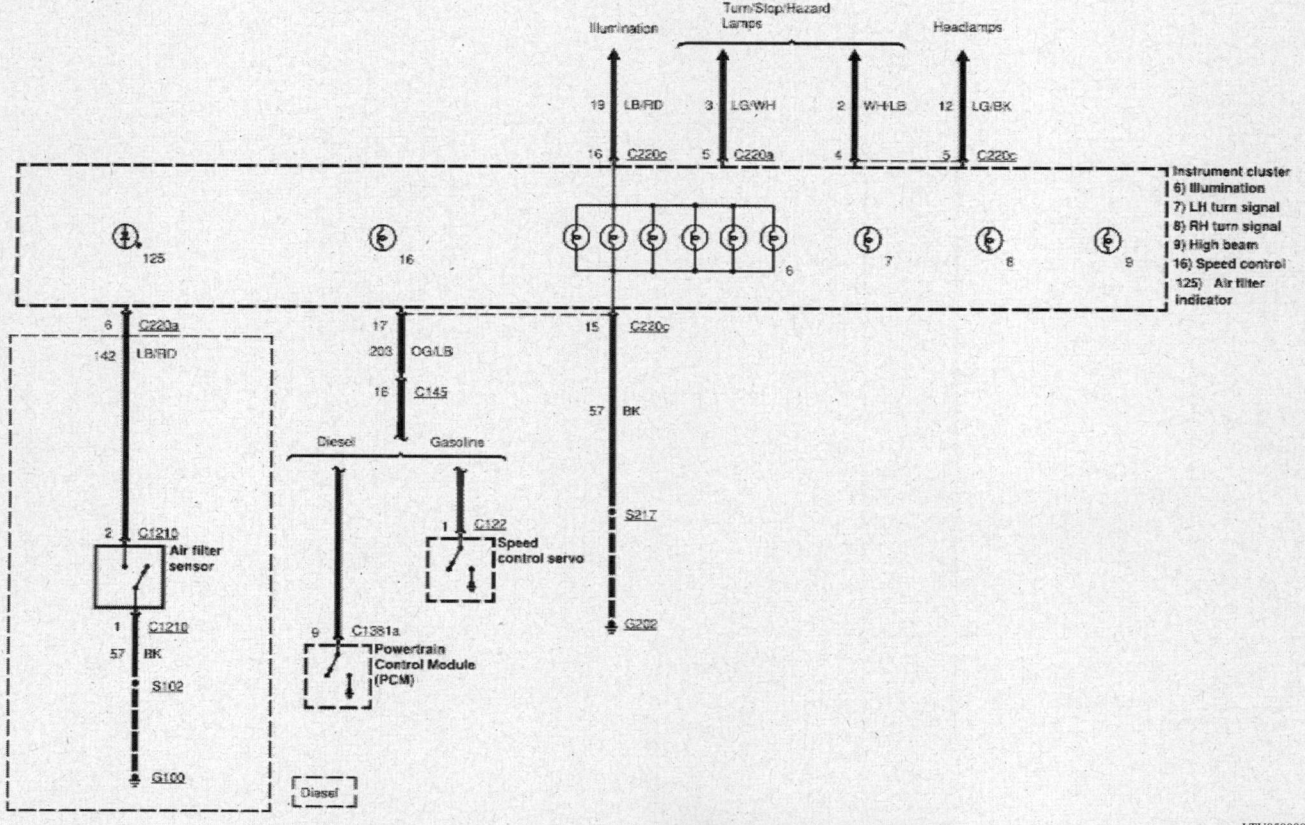

Fig. 7   Instrument cluster wiring diagram (Part 5 of 6). 2005–06 Excursion & F-Super Duty

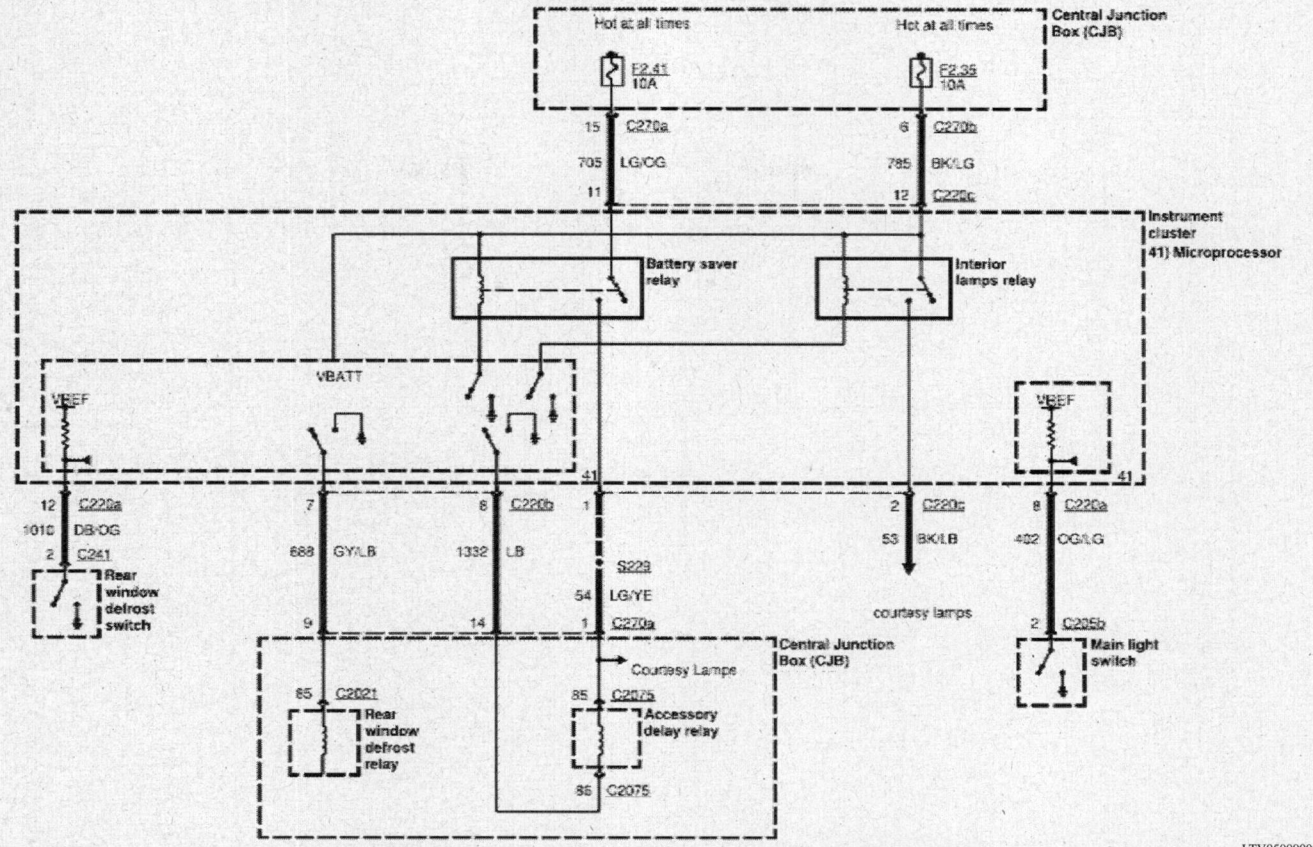

Fig. 7 Instrument cluster wiring diagram (Part 6 of 6). 2005–06 Excursion & F-Super Duty

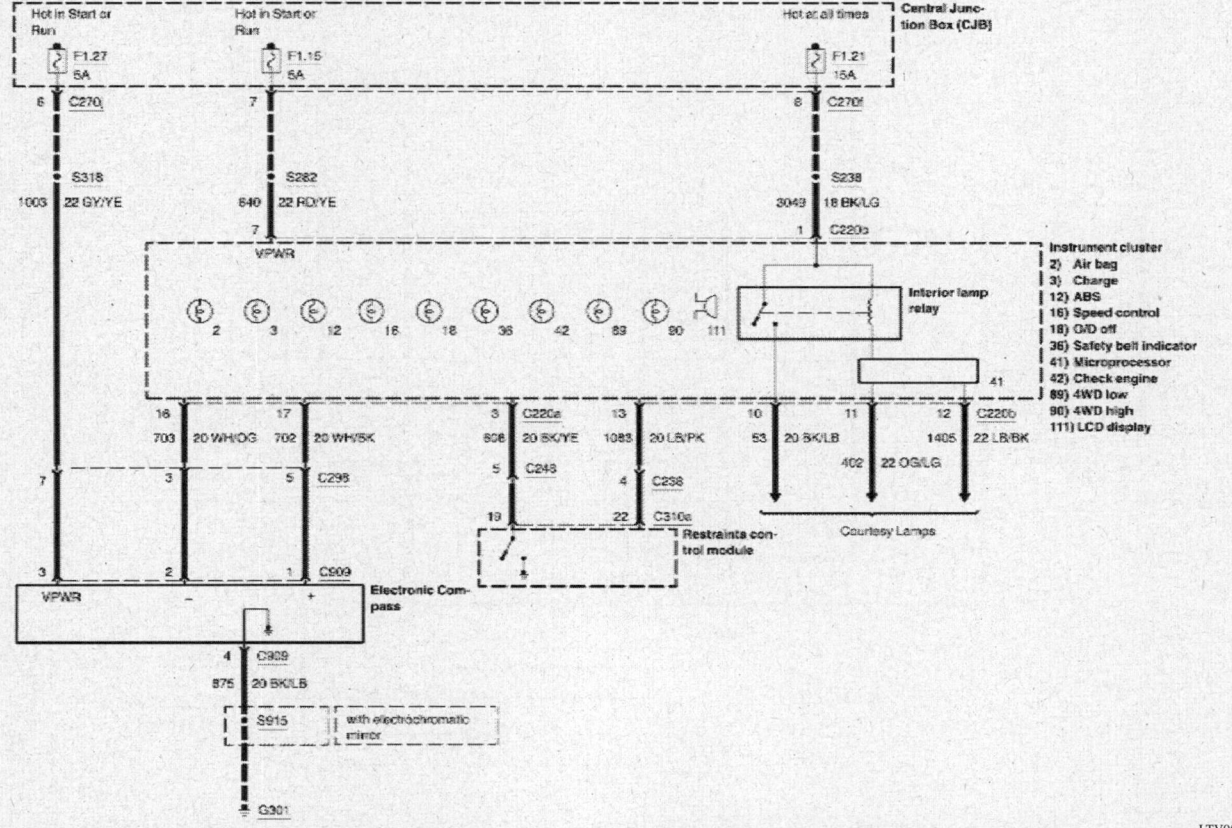

Fig. 8 Instrument cluster wiring diagram (Part 1 of 4). 2002–04 Expedition & Navigator

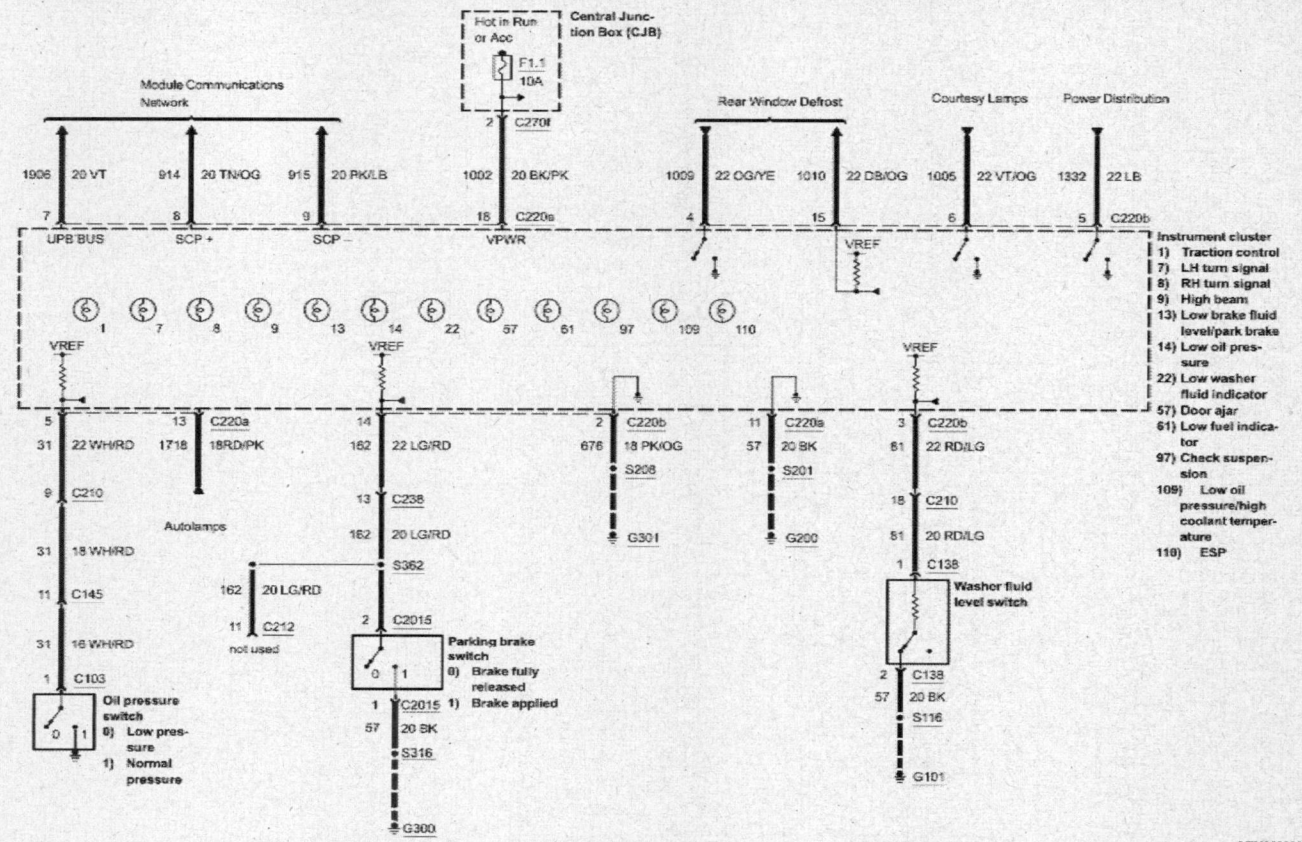

Fig. 8   Instrument cluster wiring diagram (Part 2 of 4). 2002–04 Expedition & Navigator

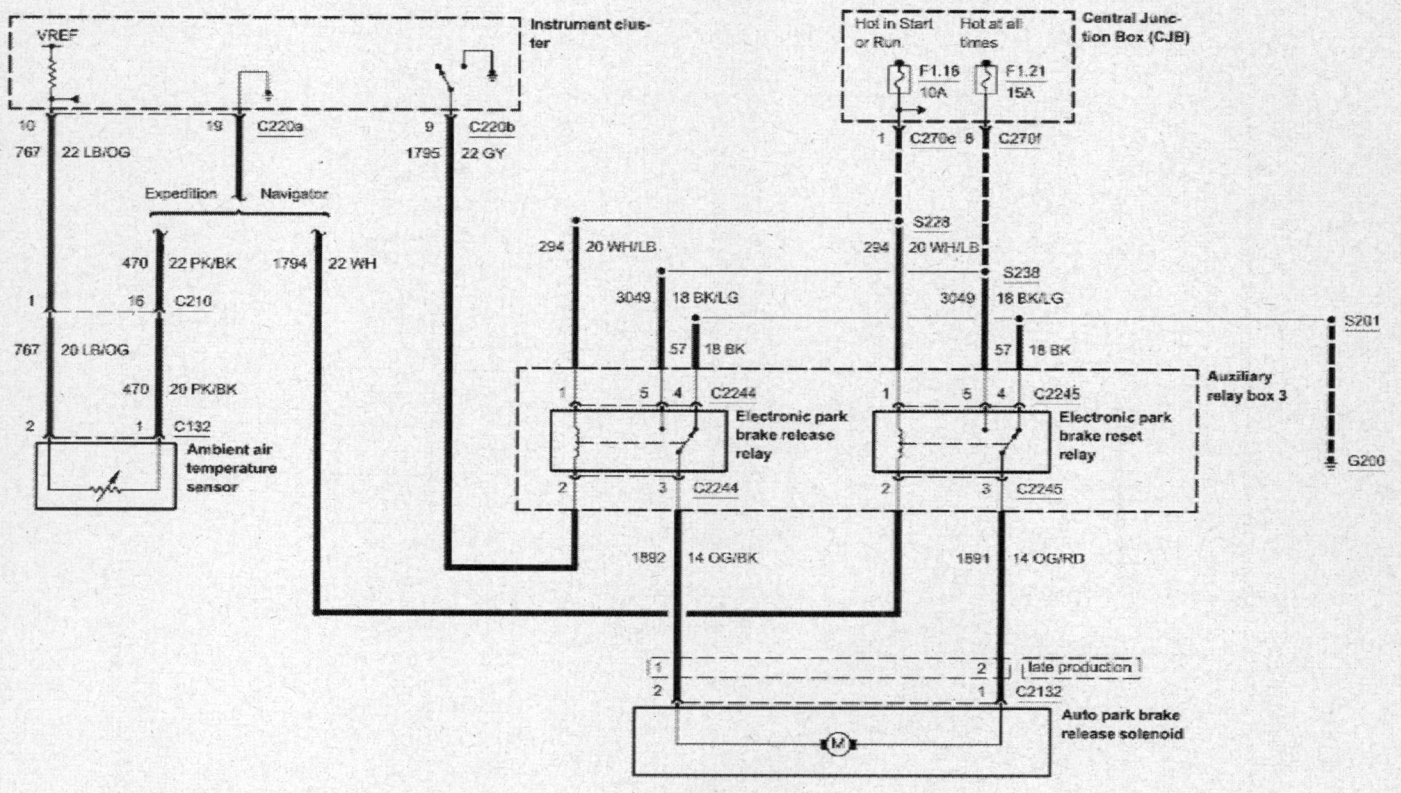

Fig. 8   Instrument cluster wiring diagram (Part 3 of 4). 2002–04 Expedition & Navigator

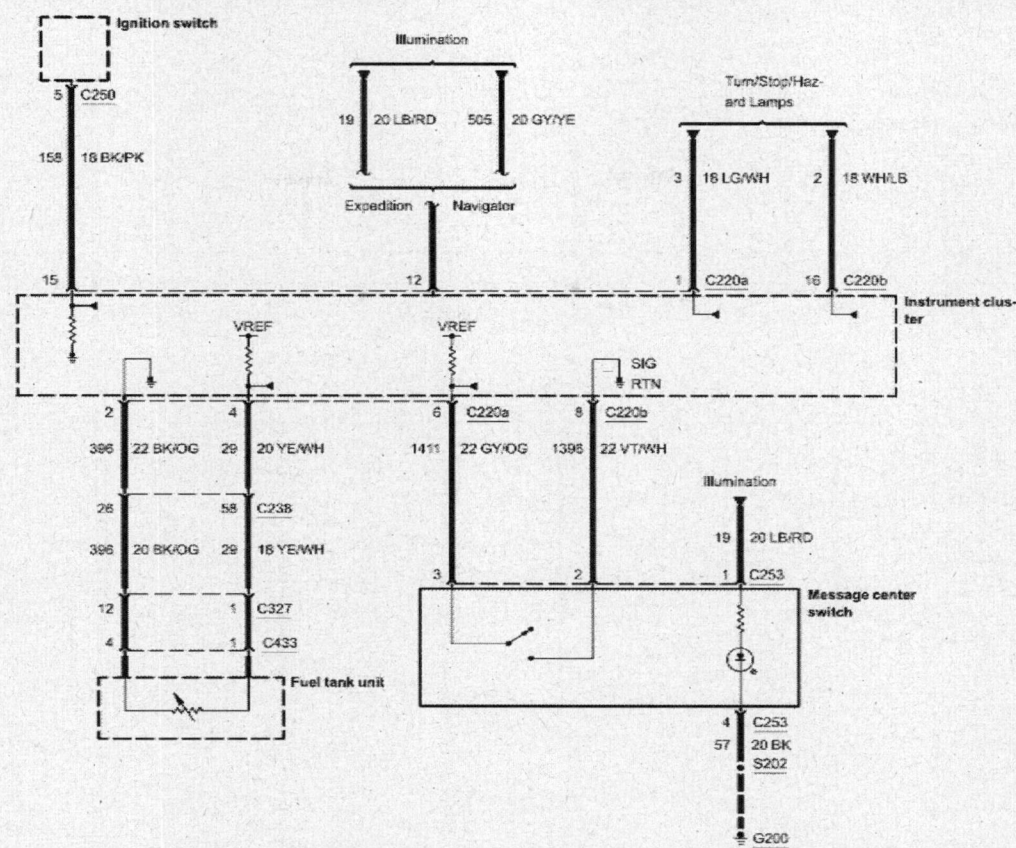

Fig. 8 Instrument cluster wiring diagram (Part 4 of 4). 2002–04 Expedition & Navigator

LTV0500000001038

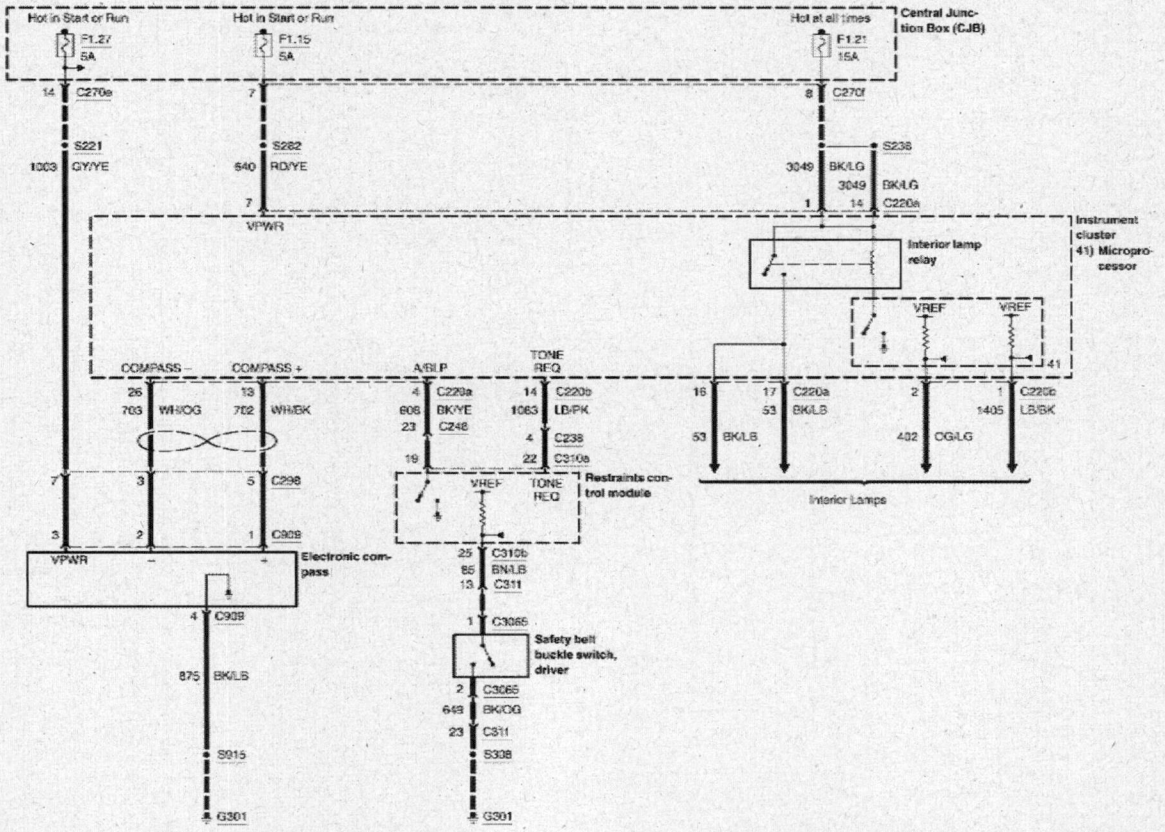

Fig. 9 Instrument cluster wiring diagram (Part 1 of 5). 2005–06 Expedition & Navigator

LTV0500000001039

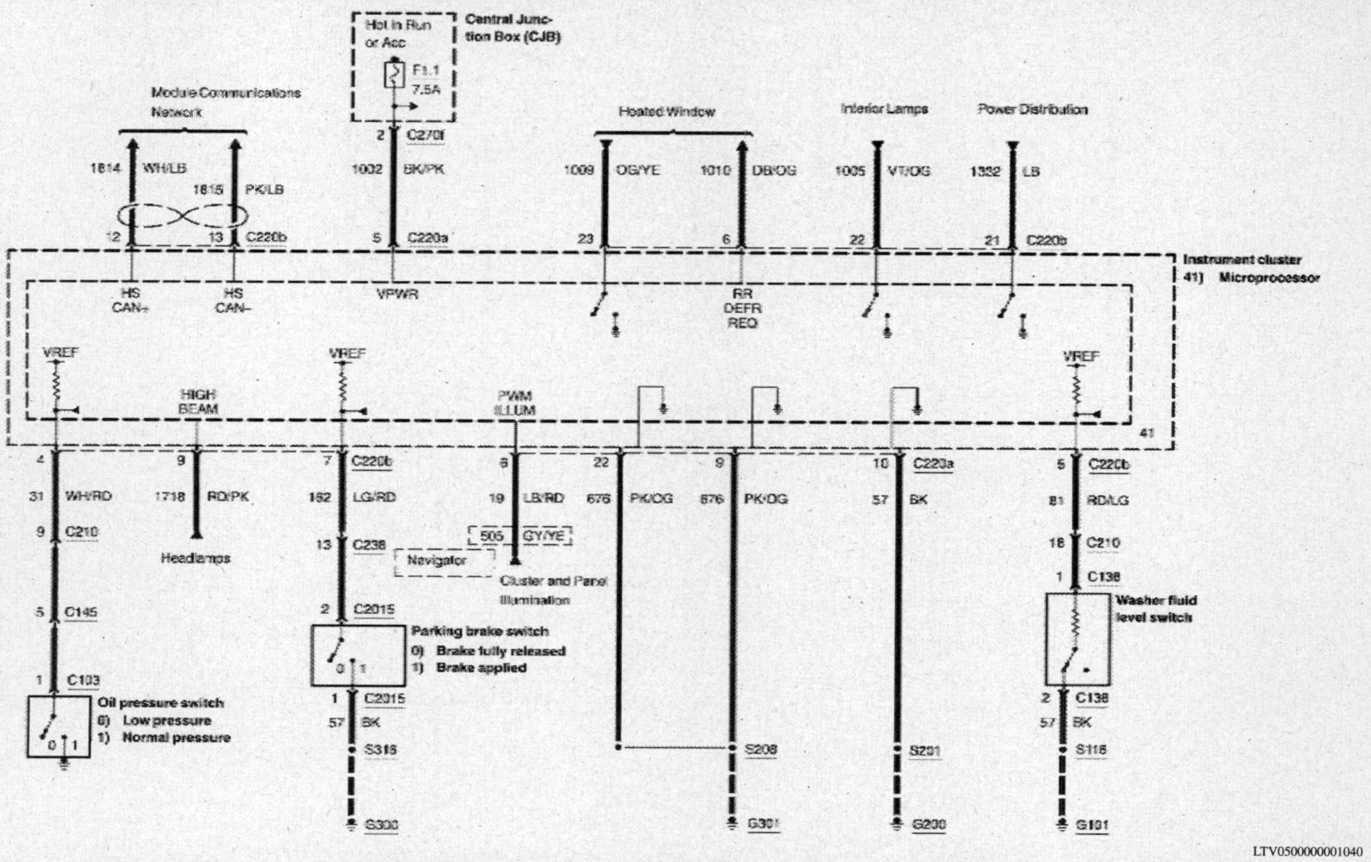

Fig. 9 Instrument cluster wiring diagram (Part 2 of 5). 2005–06 Expedition & Navigator

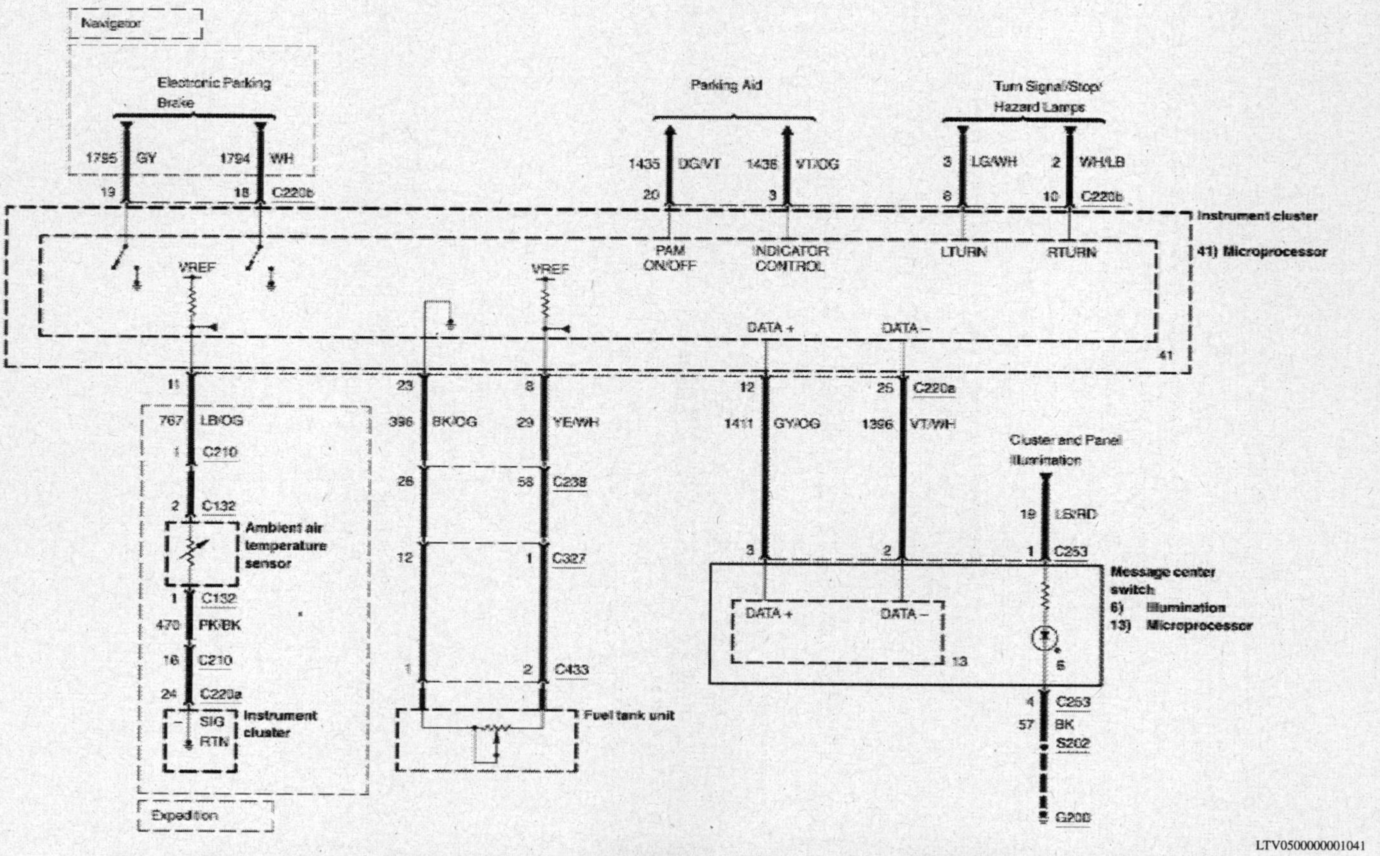

LTV0500000001040

Fig. 9 Instrument cluster wiring diagram (Part 3 of 5). 2005–06 Expedition & Navigator

LTV0500000001041

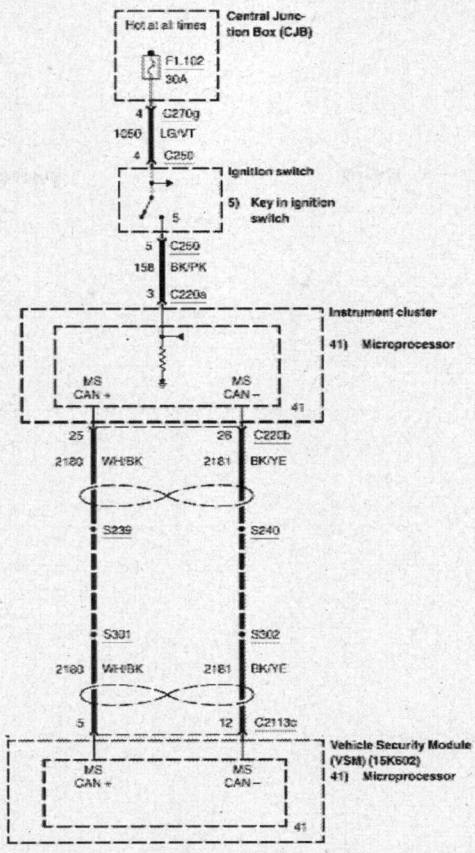

LTV0500000001282

Fig. 9   Instrument cluster wiring diagram (Part 4 of 5). 2005–06 Expedition & Navigator

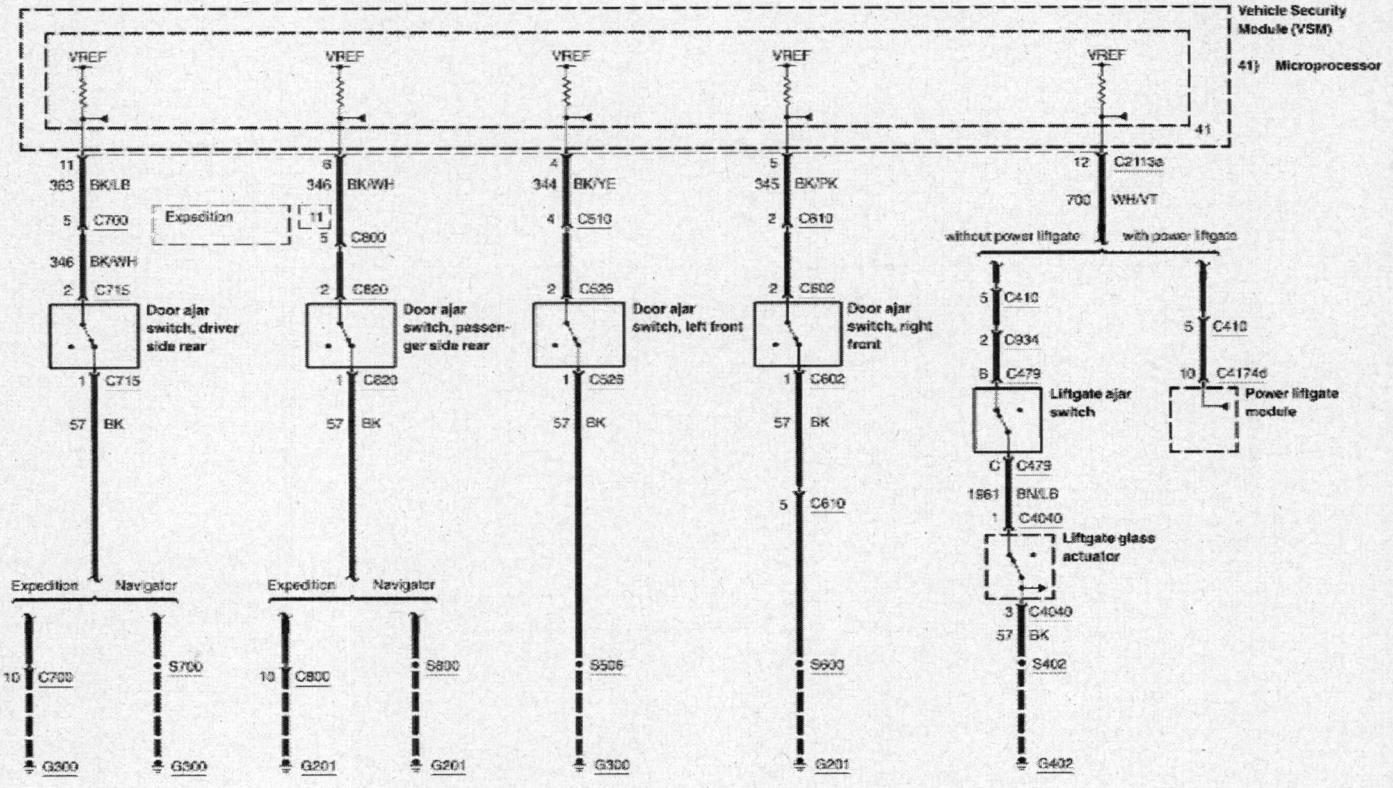

LTV0500000001283

Fig. 9   Instrument cluster wiring diagram (Part 5 of 5). 2005–06 Expedition & Navigator

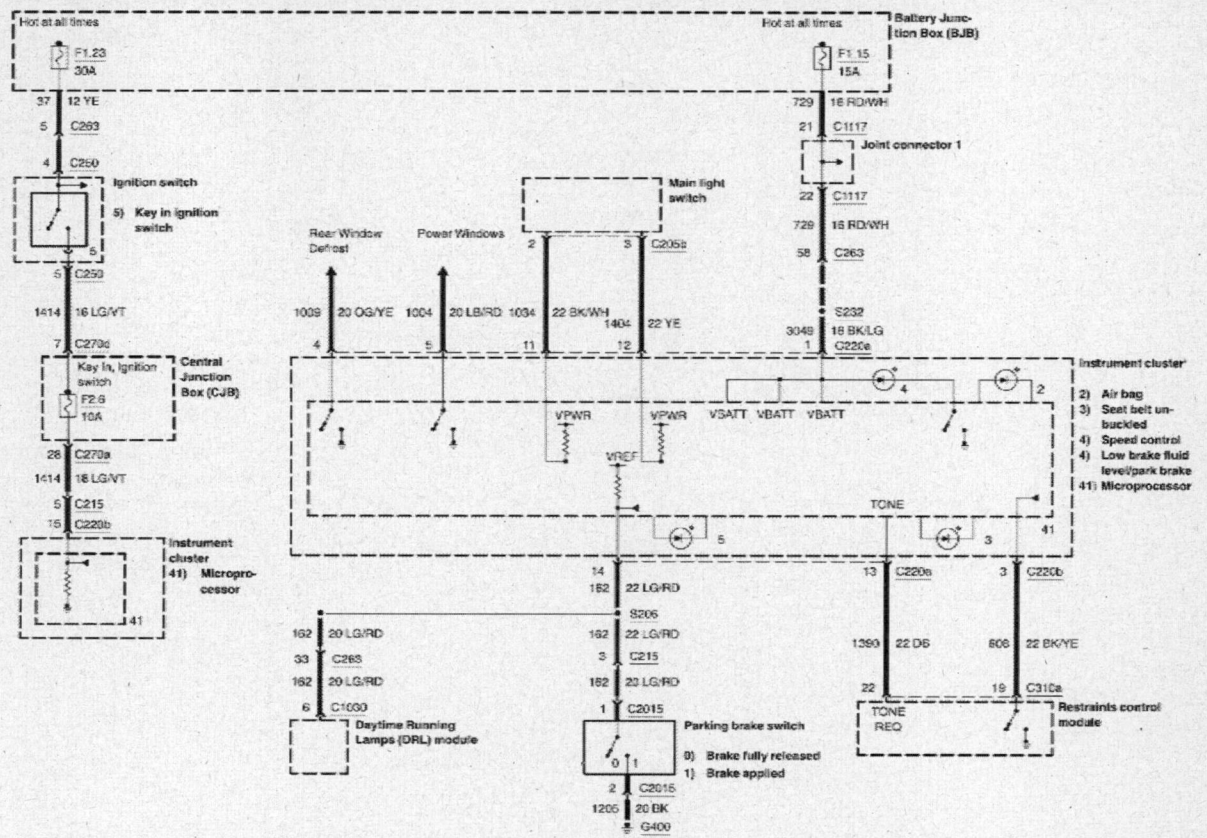

Fig. 10 Instrument cluster wiring diagram (Part 1 of 4). 2002–04 Explorer & Mountaineer

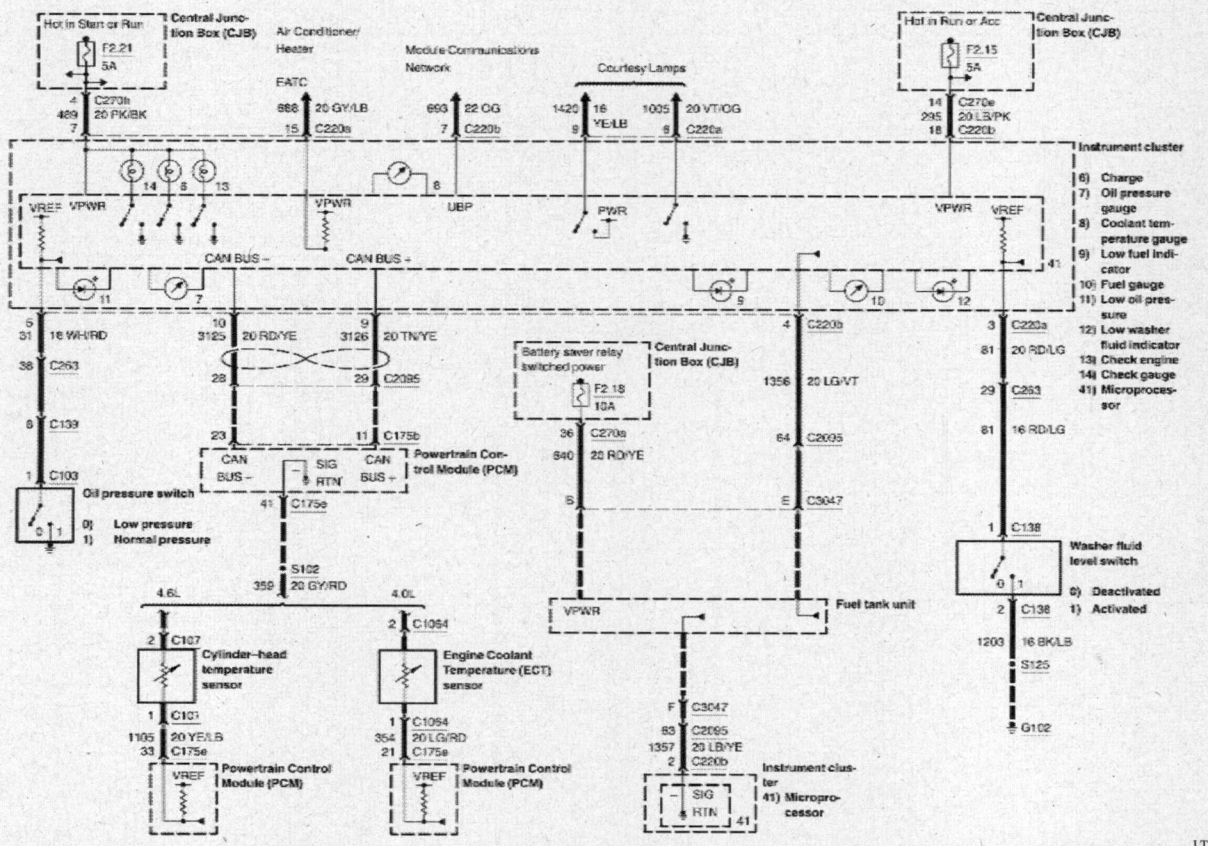

Fig. 10 Instrument cluster wiring diagram (Part 2 of 4). 2002–04 Explorer & Mountaineer

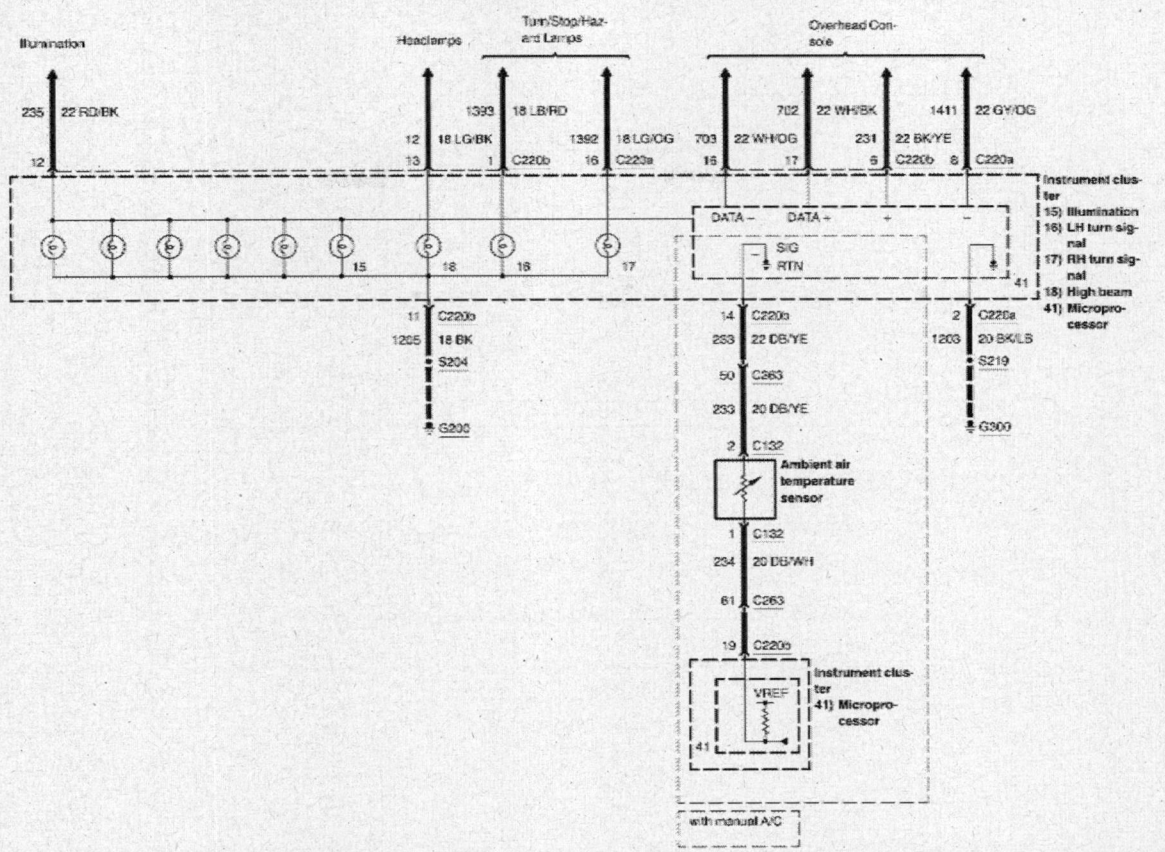

Fig. 10 Instrument cluster wiring diagram (Part 3 of 4). 2002–04 Explorer & Mountaineer

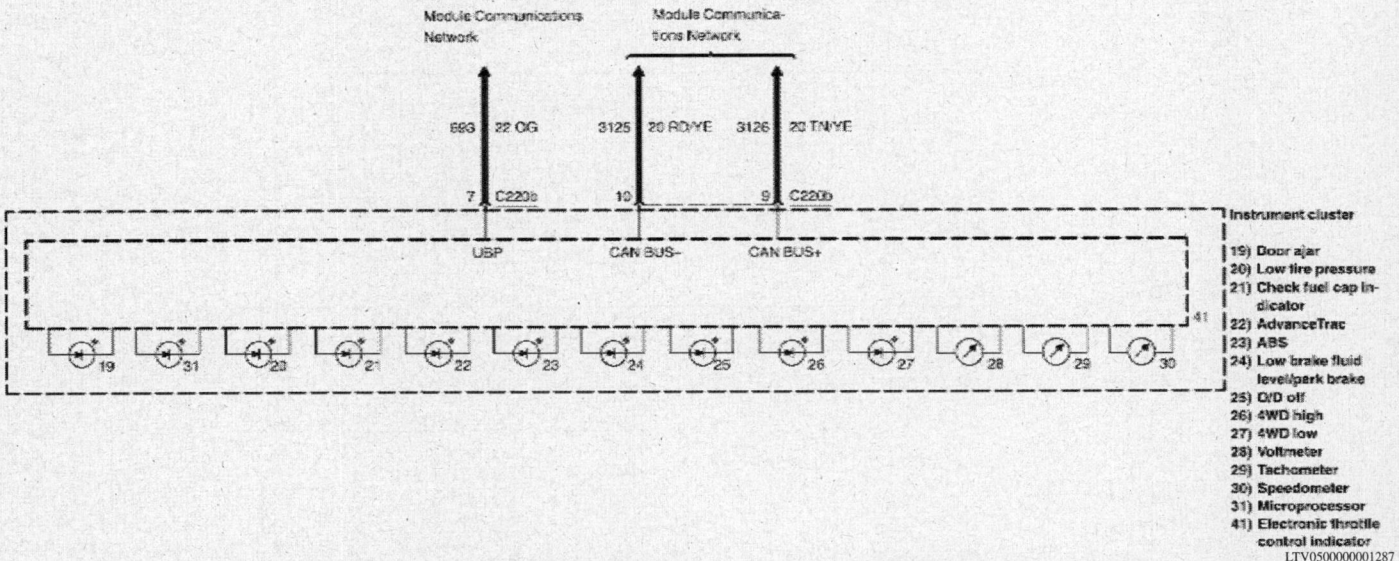

Fig. 10 Instrument cluster wiring diagram (Part 4 of 4). 2002–04 Explorer & Mountaineer

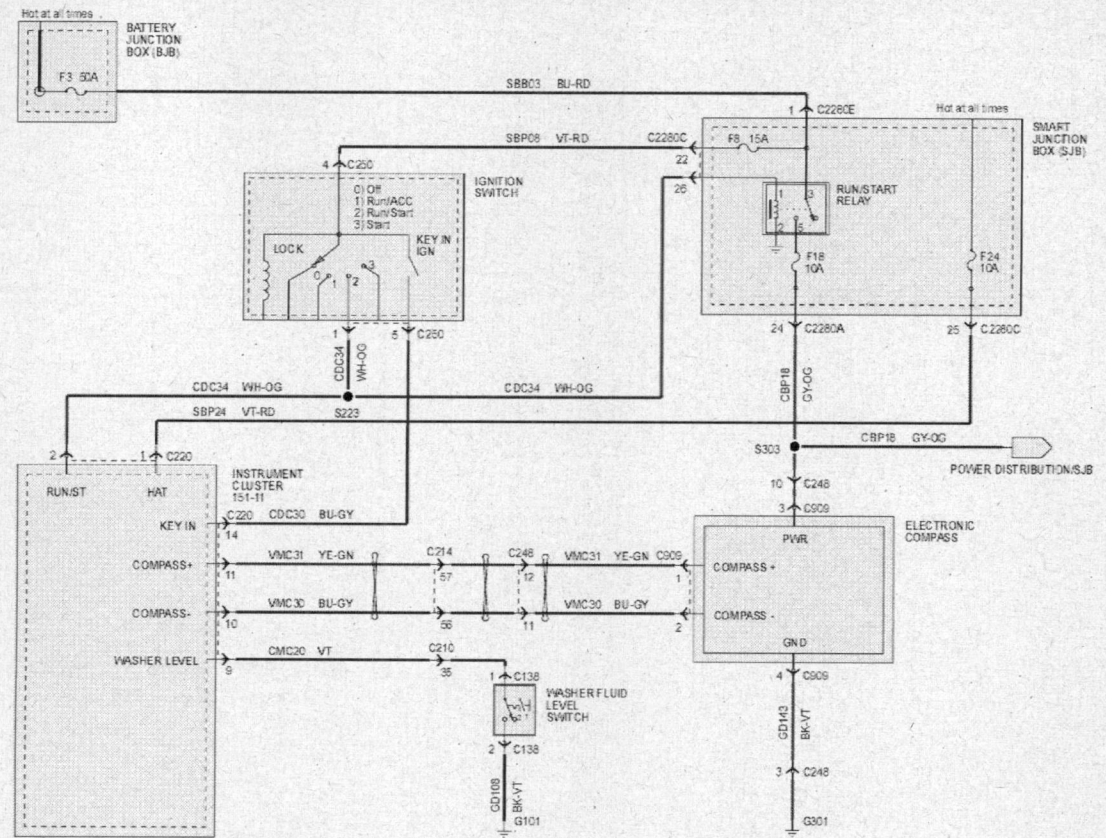

Fig. 11 Instrument cluster wiring diagram (Part 1 of 3). 2005–06 Explorer & Mountaineer

LTV0500000001288

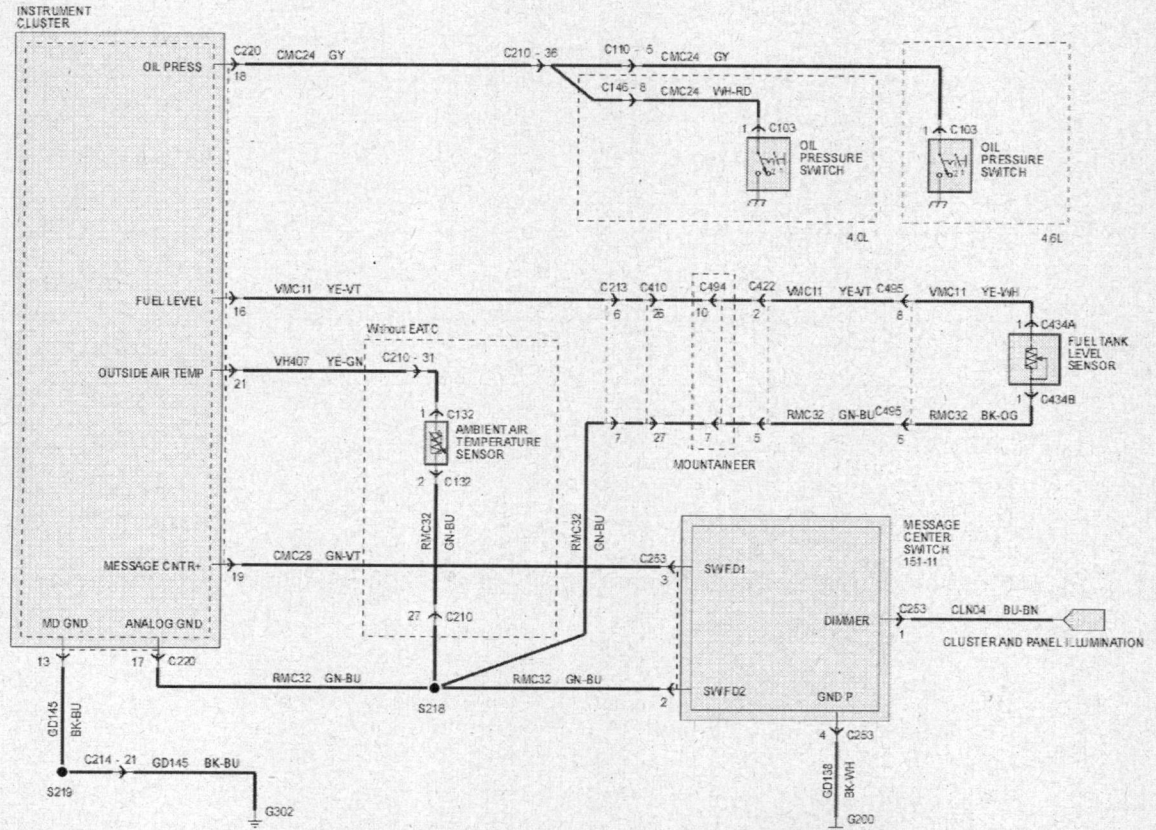

Fig. 11 Instrument cluster wiring diagram (Part 2 of 3). 2005–06 Explorer & Mountaineer

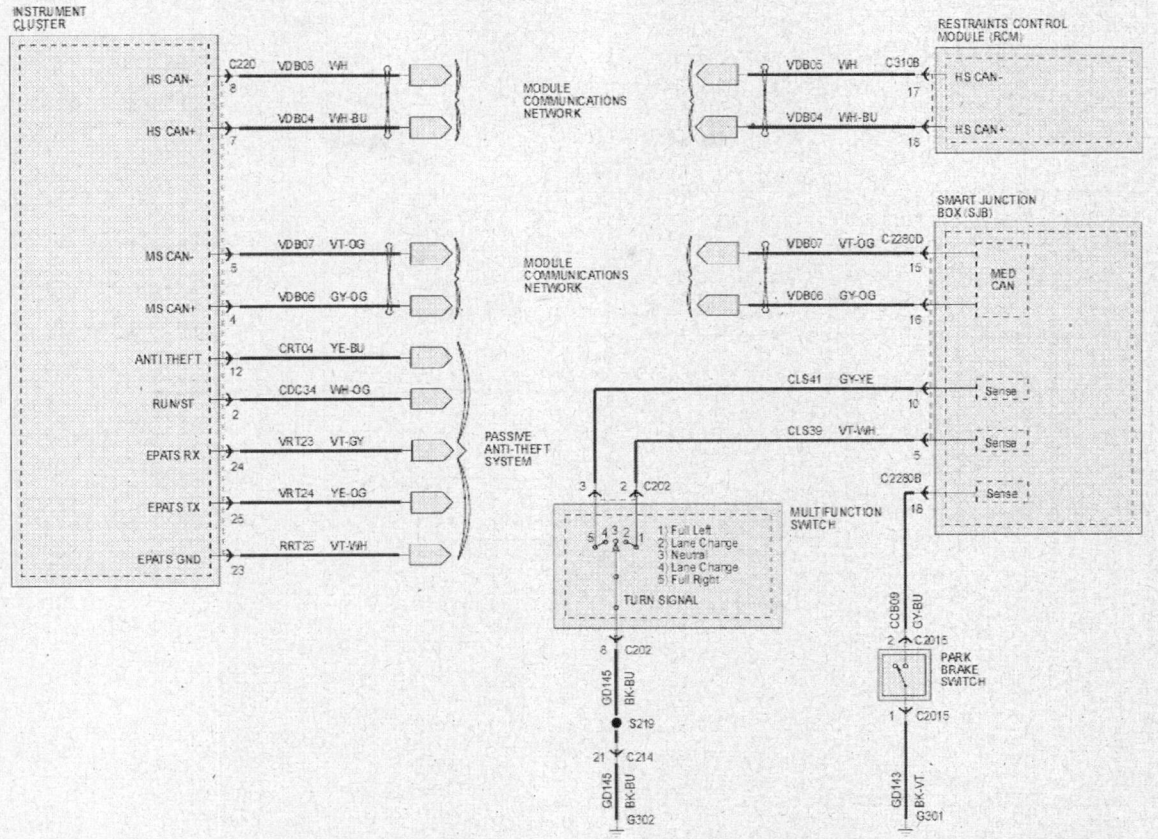

Fig. 11 Instrument cluster wiring diagram (Part 3 of 3). 2005–06 Explorer & Mountaineer

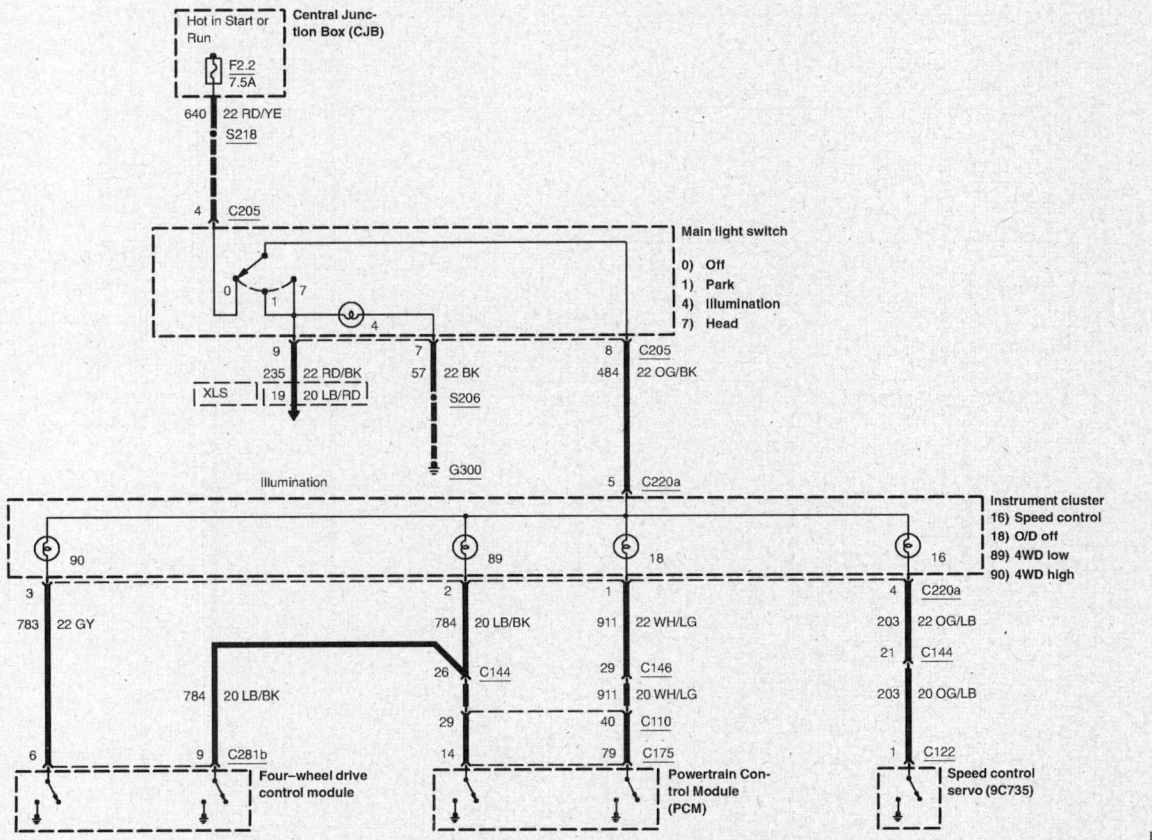

Fig. 12 Instrument cluster wiring diagram (Part 1 of 6). 2002–03 Explorer Sport & Sport Trac

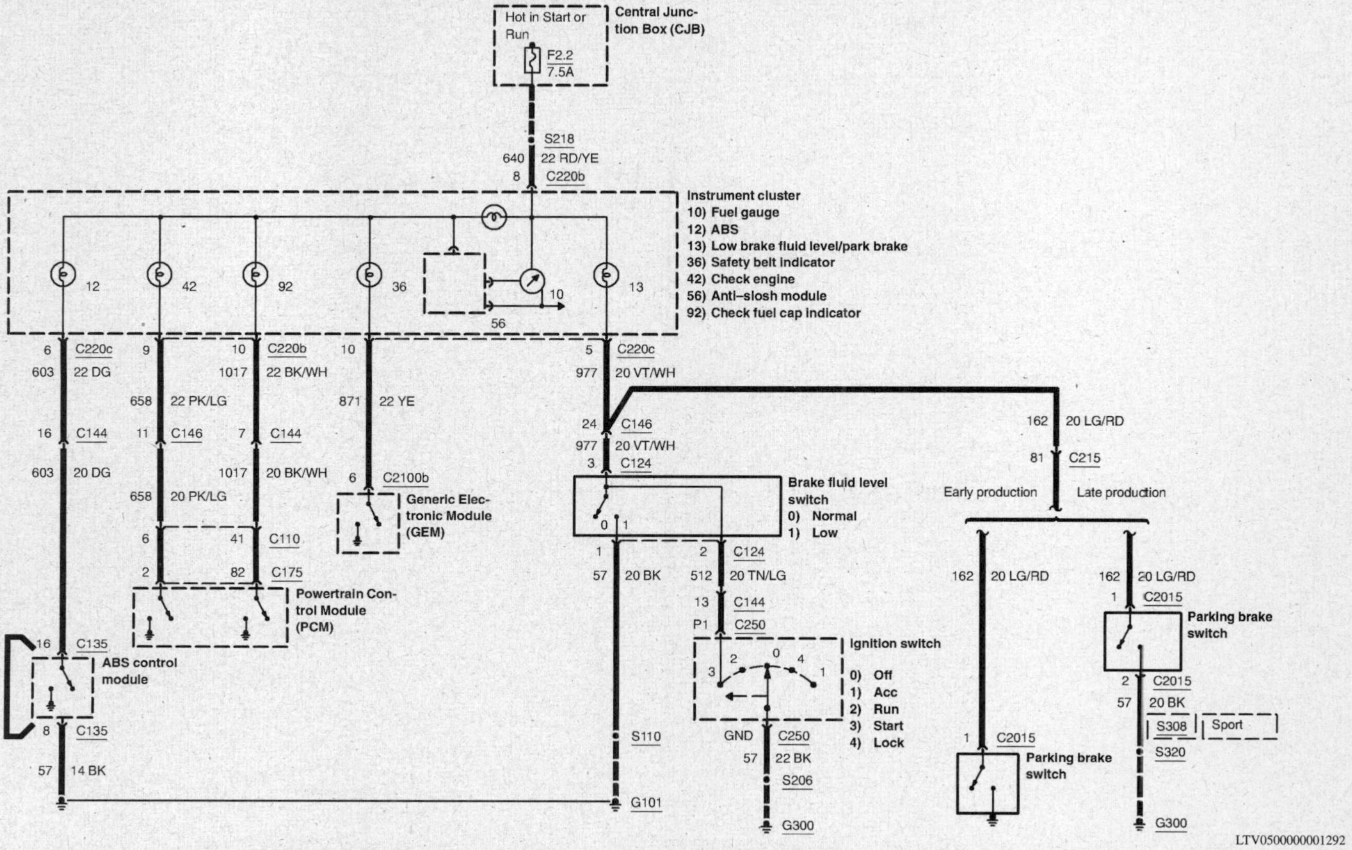

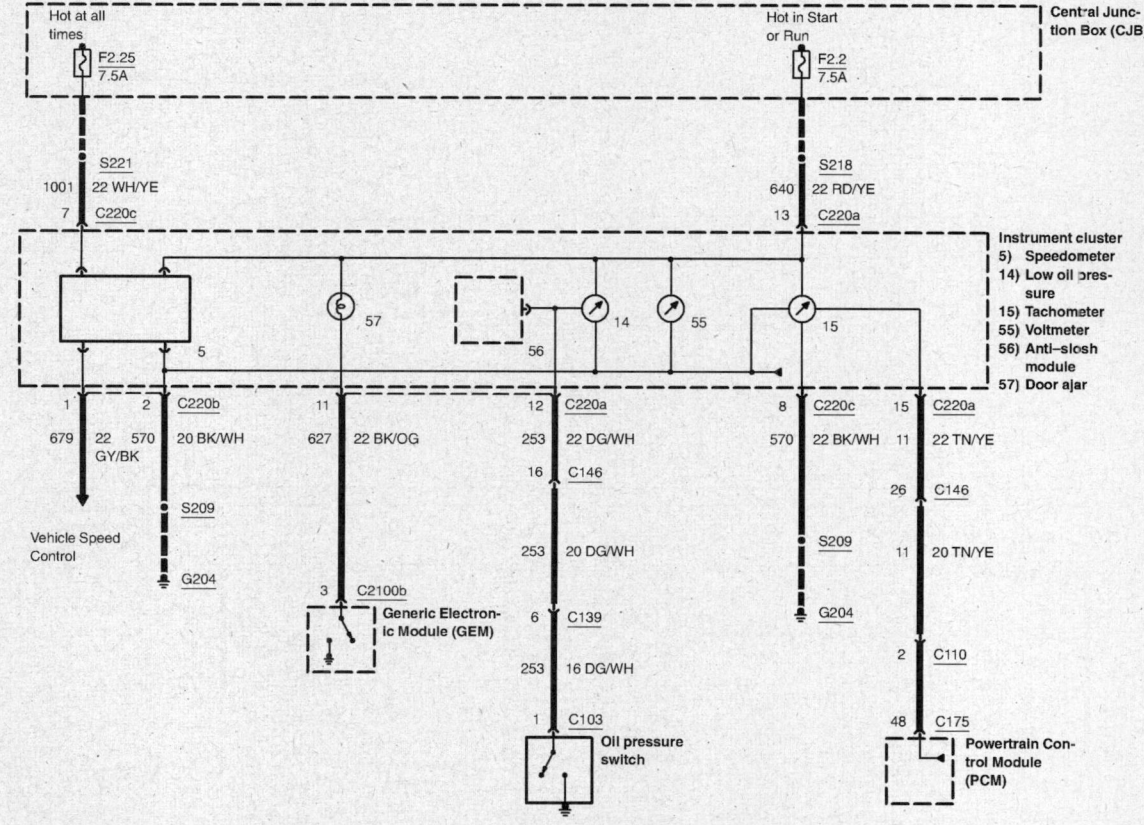

Fig. 12 Instrument cluster wiring diagram (Part 2 of 6). 2002–03 Explorer Sport & Sport Trac

Fig. 12 Instrument cluster wiring diagram (Part 3 of 6). 2002–03 Explorer Sport & Sport Trac

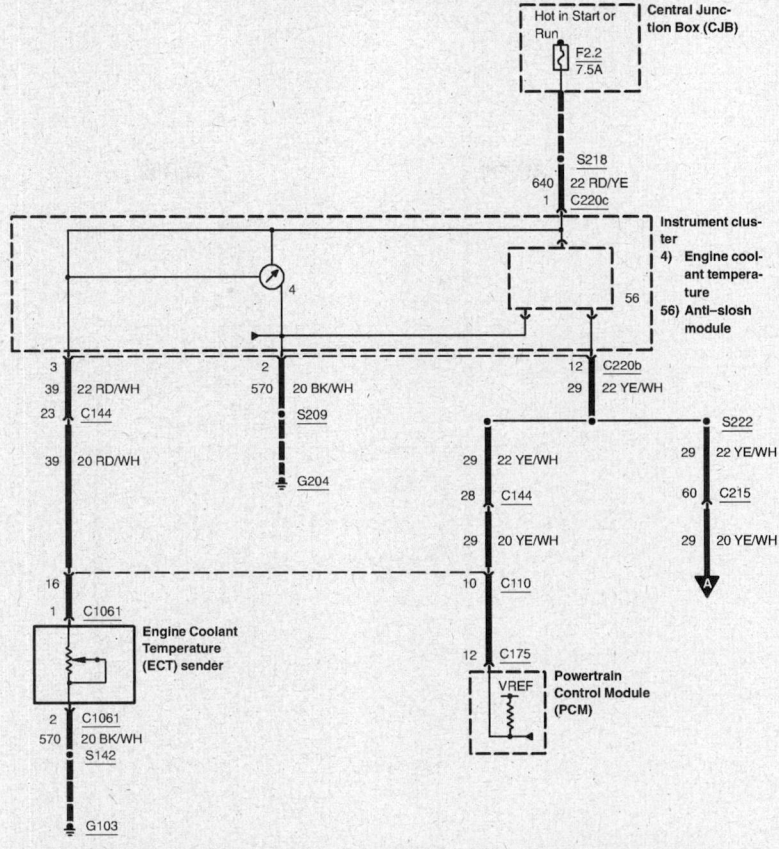

Fig. 12   Instrument cluster wiring diagram (Part 4 of 6). 2002–03 Explorer Sport & Sport Trac

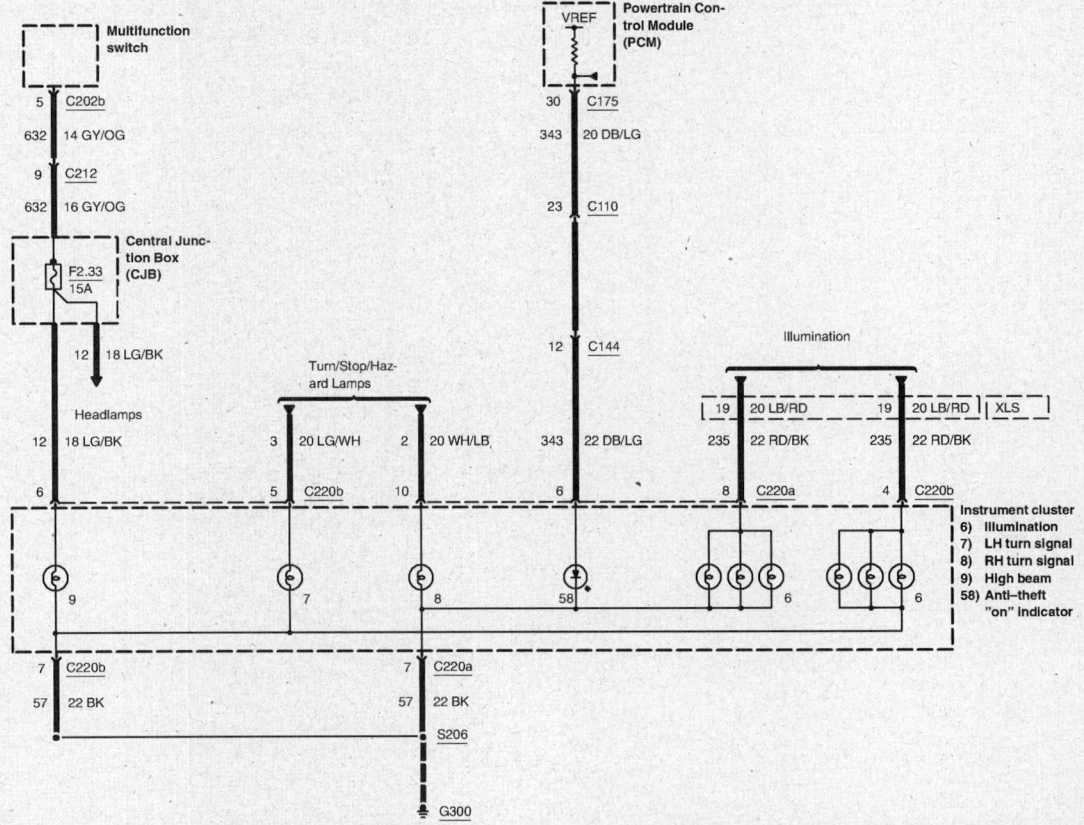

Fig. 12   Instrument cluster wiring diagram (Part 5 of 6). 2002–03 Explorer Sport & Sport Trac

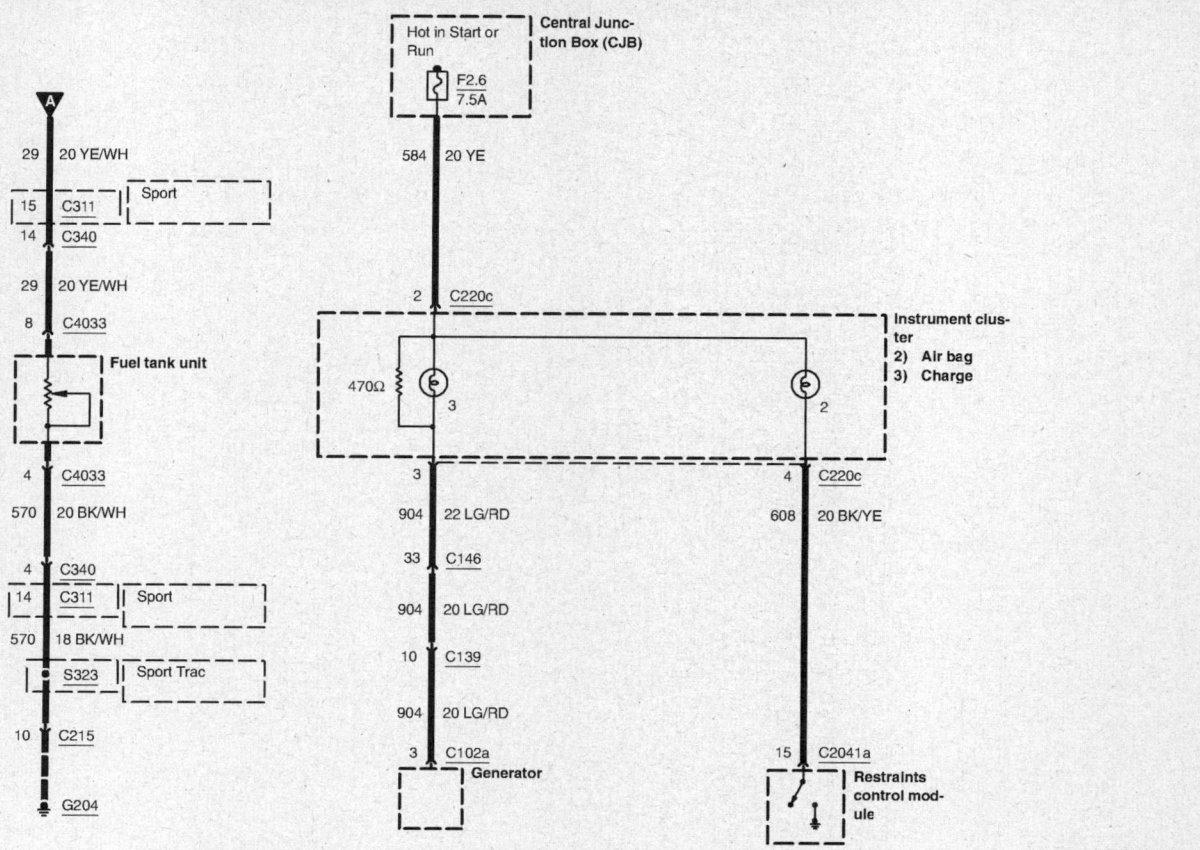

Fig. 12 Instrument cluster wiring diagram (Part 6 of 6). 2002–03 Explorer Sport & Sport Trac

LTV0500000001296

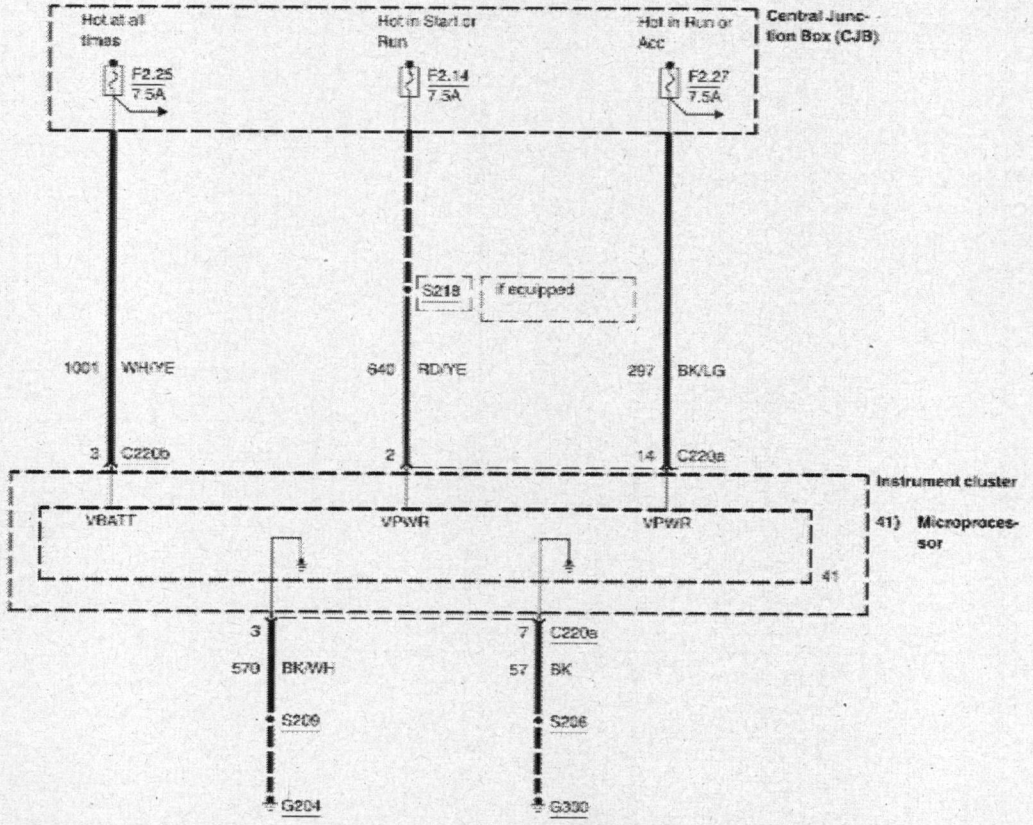

Fig. 13 Instrument cluster wiring diagram (Part 1 of 7). 2004–05 Explorer Sport Trac

LTV0500000001297

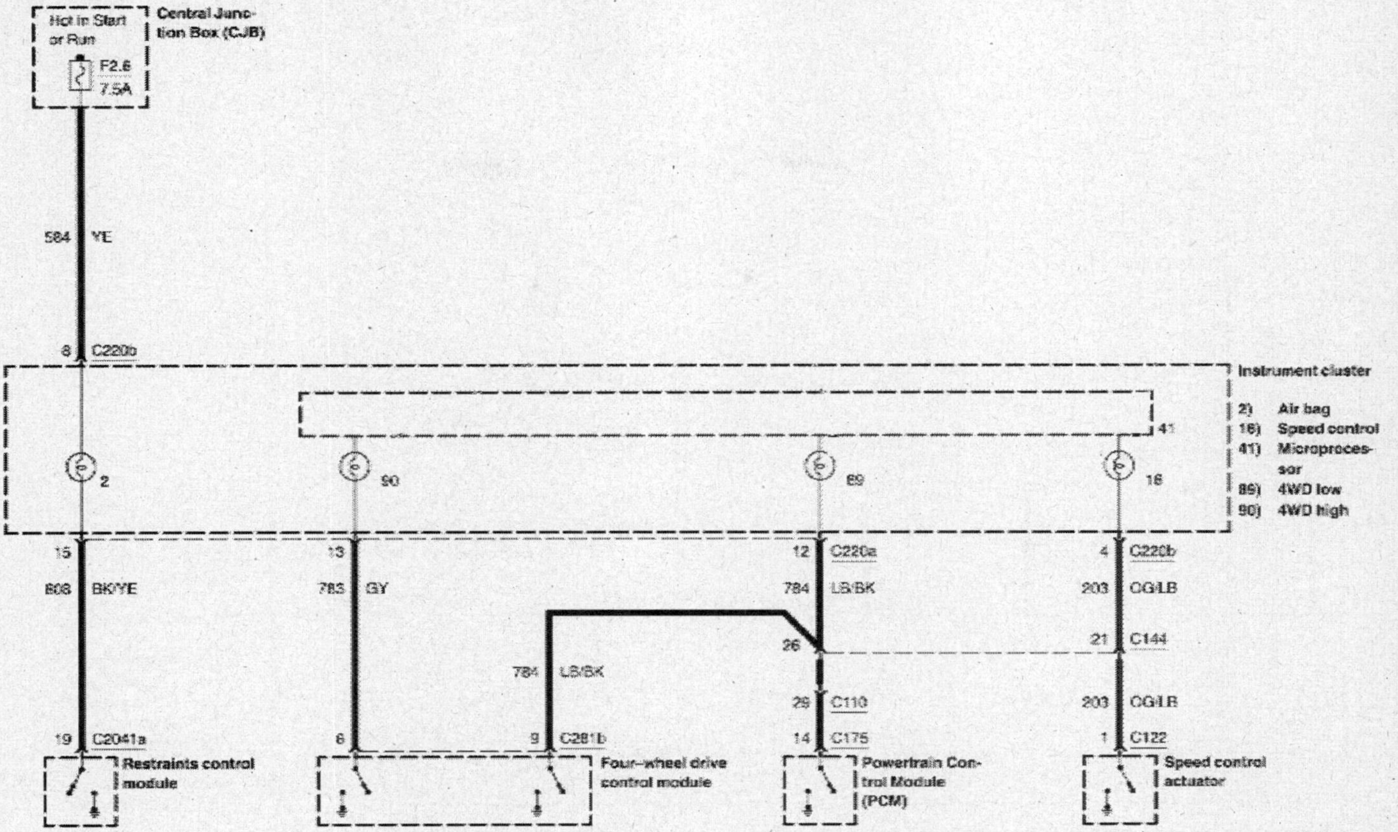

Fig. 13 Instrument cluster wiring diagram (Part 2 of 7). 2004–05 Explorer Sport Trac

Central Junction Box (CJB)

Hot in Start or Run

F2.6 7.5A

584 YE

8 C220b

Instrument cluster
2) Air bag
16) Speed control
41) Microprocessor
89) 4WD low
90) 4WD high

2
90
89
16
41

15
808 BK/YE
13
783 GY
12 C220a
784 LB/BK
4 C220b
203 OG/LB

26
21 C144

784 LB/BK
29 C110
203 OG/LB

19 C2041a
6
9 C281b
14 C175
1 C122

Restraints control module
Four-wheel drive control module
Powertrain Control Module (PCM)
Speed control actuator

LTV050000001298

Fig. 13 Instrument cluster wiring diagram (Part 3 of 7). 2004–05 Explorer Sport Trac

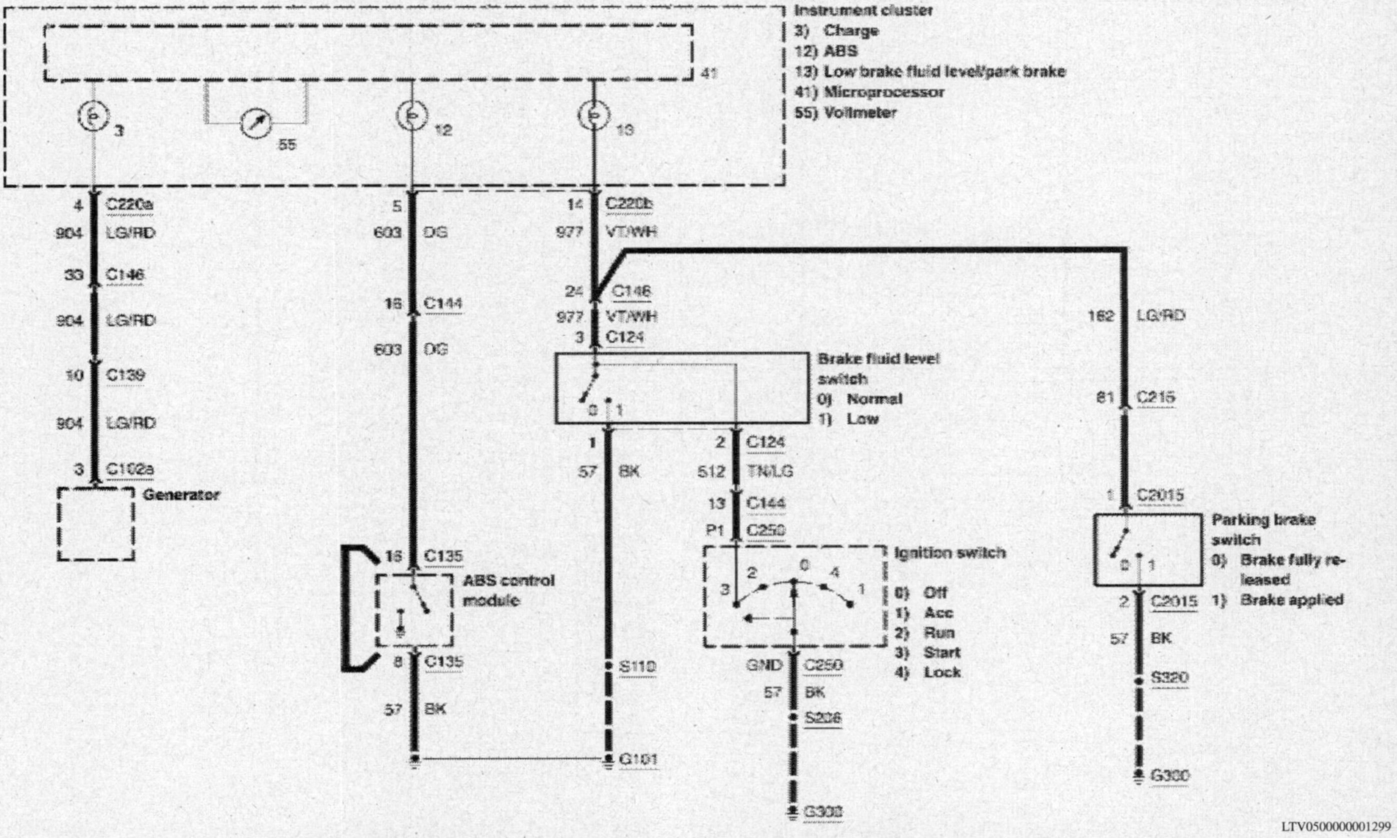

Instrument cluster
3) Charge
12) ABS
13) Low brake fluid level/park brake
41) Microprocessor
55) Voltmeter

3
55
12
13
41

4 C220a
904 LG/RD
5
603 DG
14 C220b
977 VT/WH

33 C146
24 C146

904 LG/RD
16 C144
977 VT/WH
162 LG/RD

10 C139
603 DG
3 C124

904 LG/RD
81 C215

3 C102a

Brake fluid level switch
0) Normal
1) Low

1
57 BK
2 C124
512 TN/LG

Generator

13 C144
P1 C250

1 C2015

16 C135
Ignition switch
2) Off
1) Acc
2) Run
3) Start
4) Lock

Parking brake switch
0) Brake fully released
1) Brake applied

ABS control module

2 C2015
57 BK

8 C135
GND C250

57 BK
57 BK

S110
S206
S320

G101
G308
G300

LTV050000001299

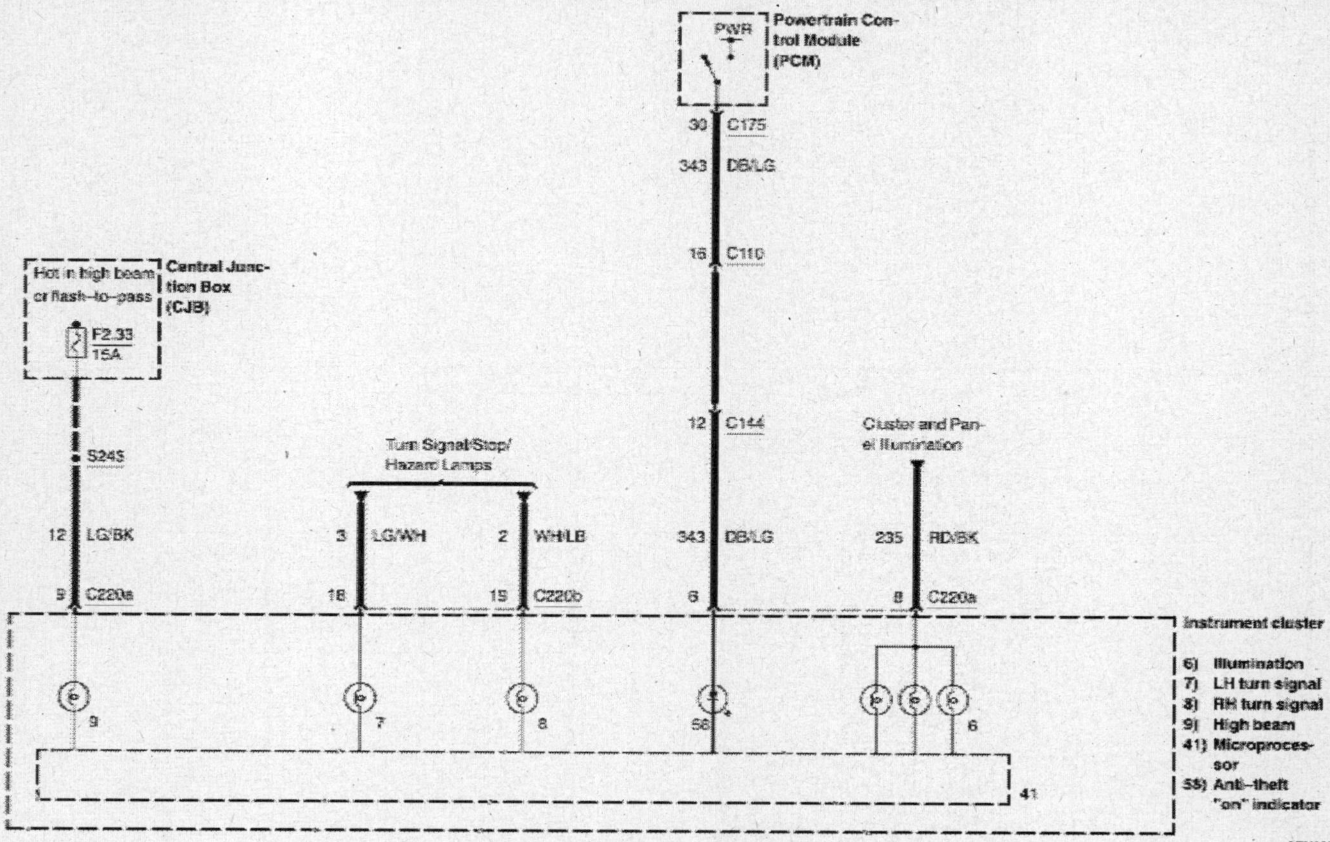

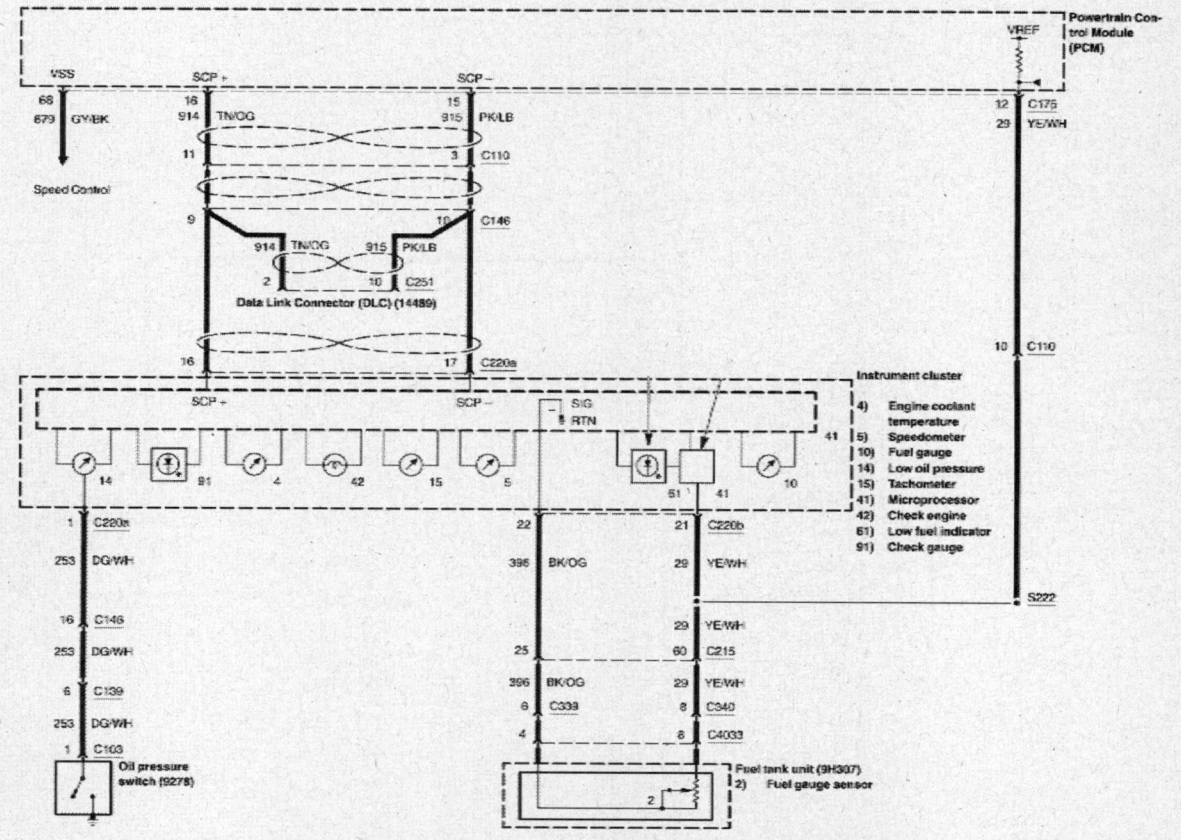

Fig. 13 Instrument cluster wiring diagram (Part 4 of 7). 2004–05 Explorer Sport Trac

LTV0500000001300

Fig. 13 Instrument cluster wiring diagram (Part 5 of 7). 2004–05 Explorer Sport Trac

LTV0500000001301

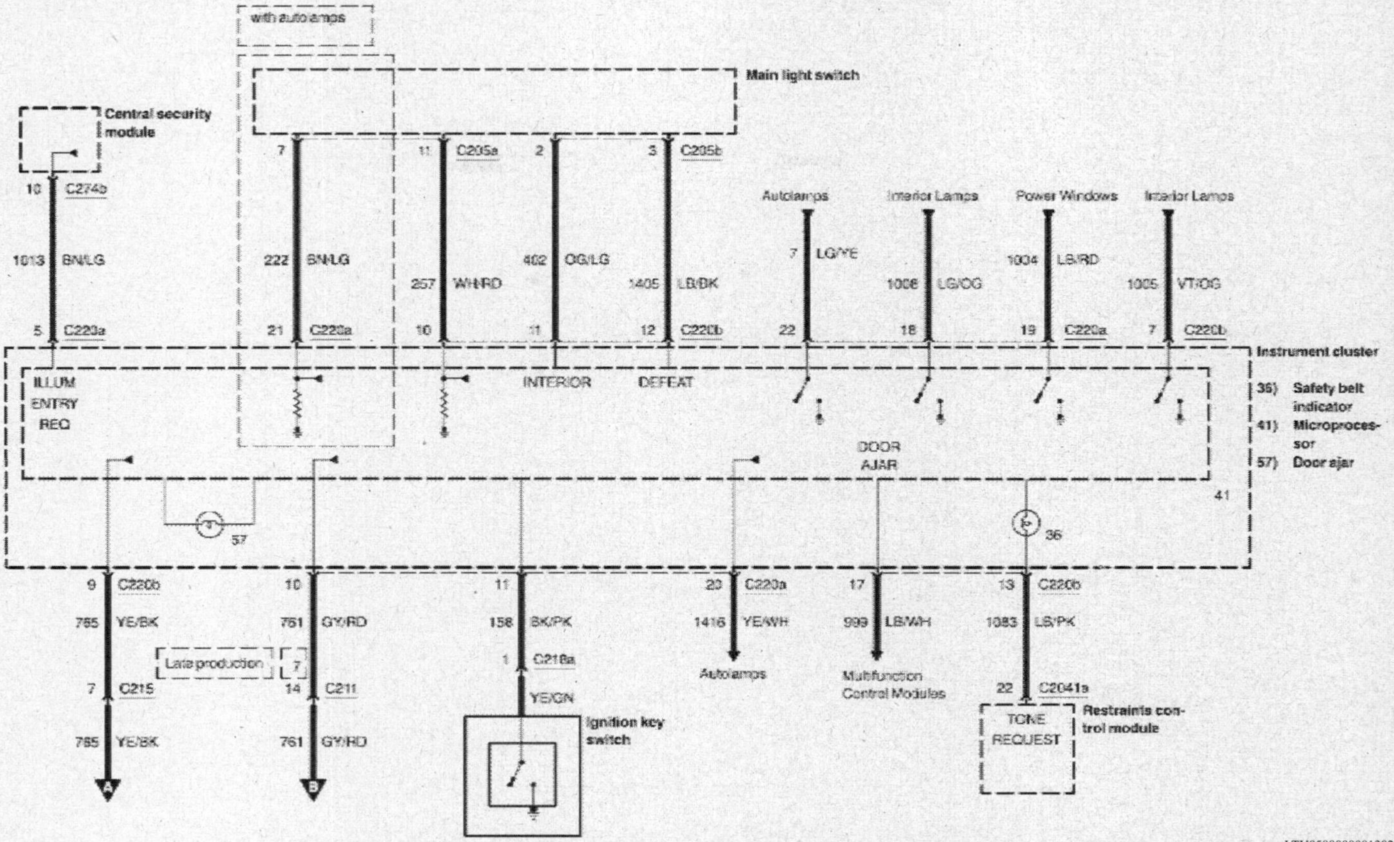

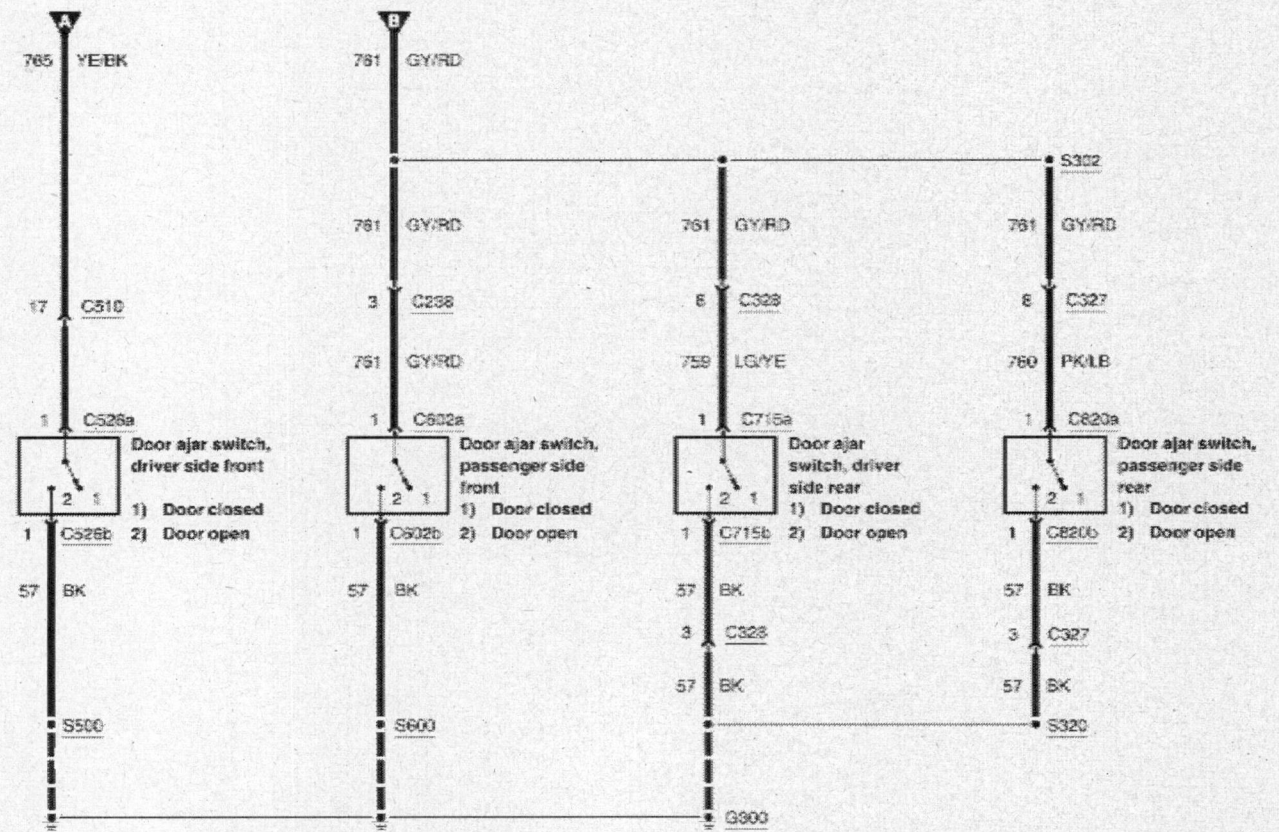

Fig. 13   Instrument cluster wiring diagram (Part 6 of 7). 2004–05 Explorer Sport Trac

LTV0500000001302

Fig. 13   Instrument cluster wiring diagram (Part 7 of 7). 2004–05 Explorer Sport Trac

LTV0500000001303

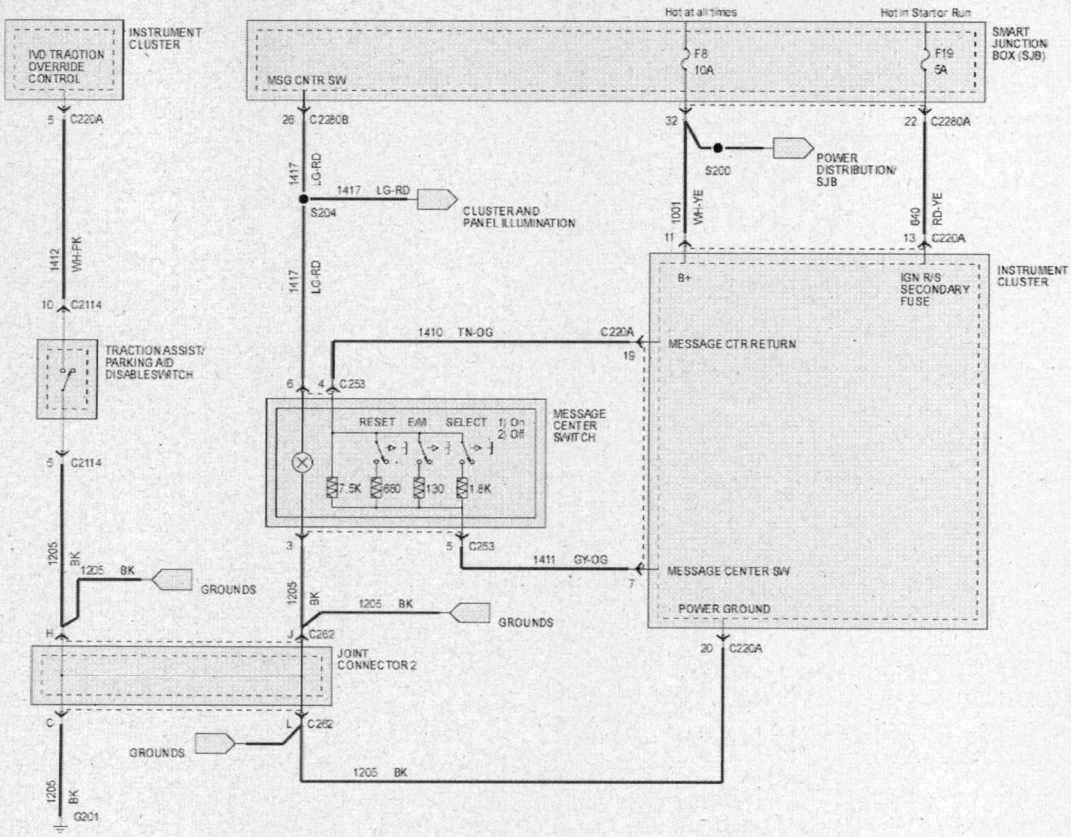

Fig. 14   Instrument cluster wiring diagram (Part 1 of 3). Freestar & Monterey

LTV0500000001304

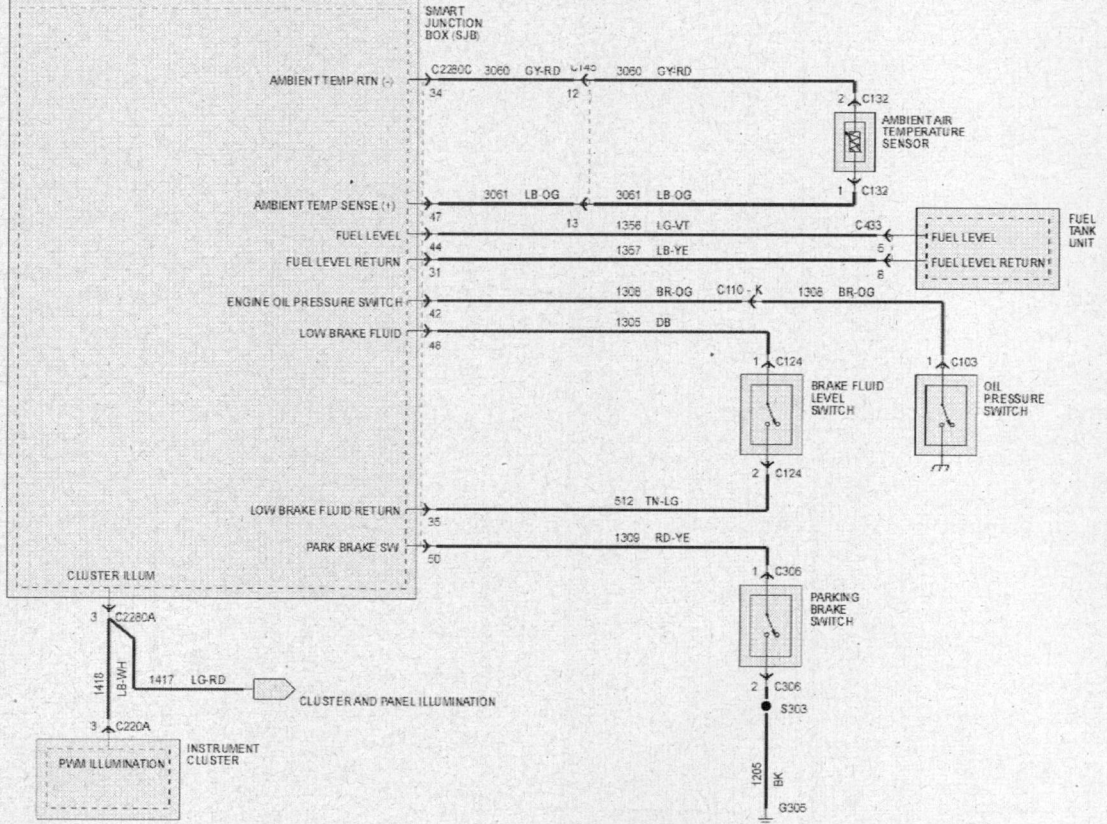

Fig. 14   Instrument cluster wiring diagram (Part 2 of 3). Freestar & Monterey

LTV0500000001305

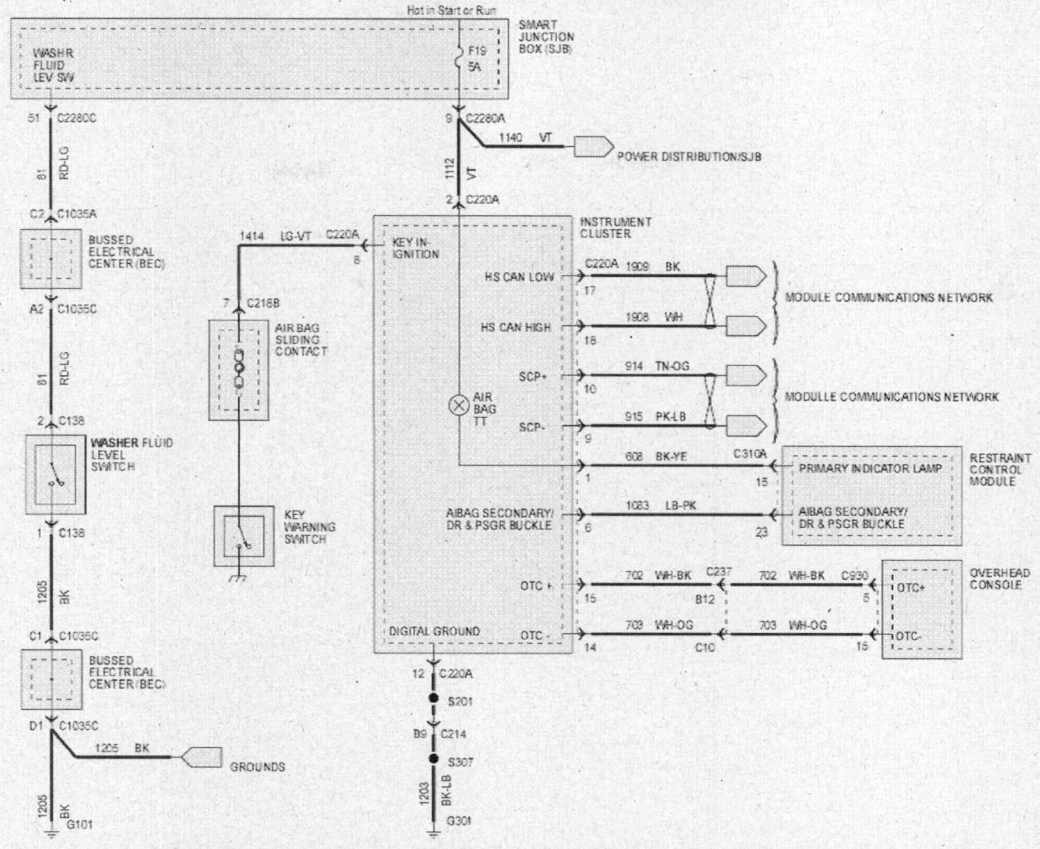

Fig. 14 Instrument cluster wiring diagram (Part 3 of 3). Freestar & Monterey

LTV0500000001306

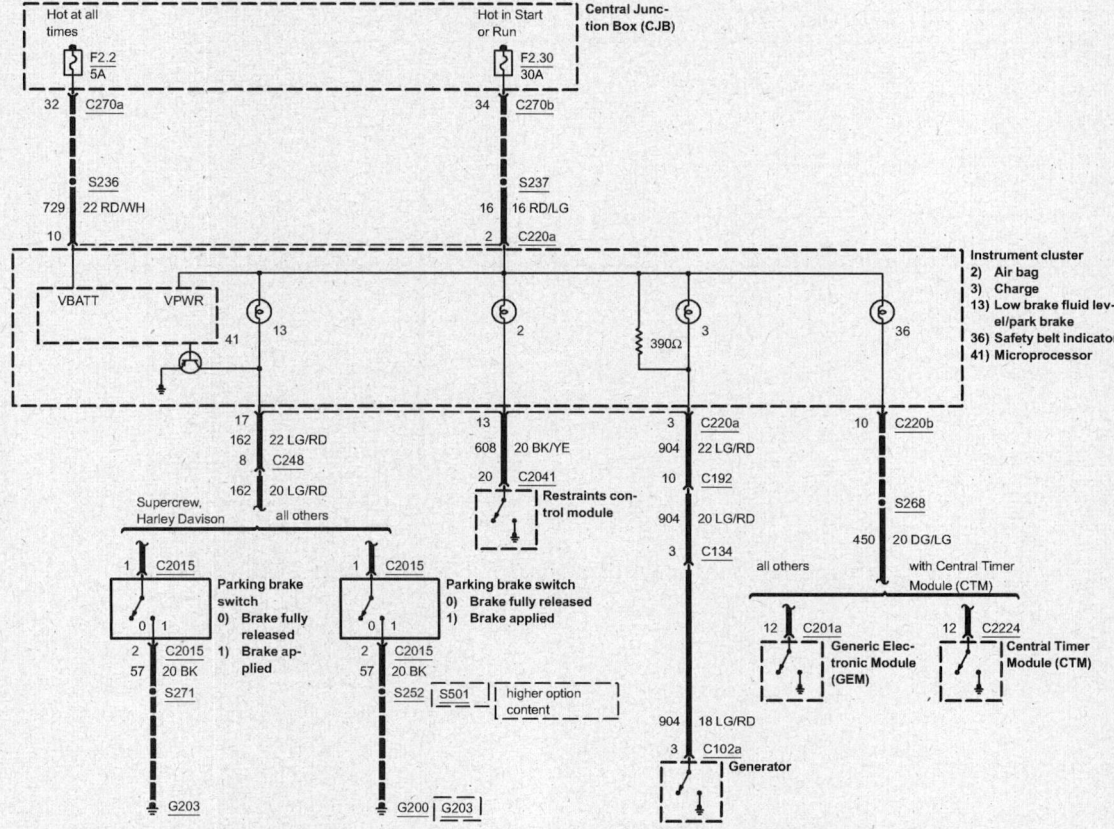

Fig. 15 Instrument cluster wiring diagram (Part 1 of 5). 2002–04 F-150

LTV0500000001307

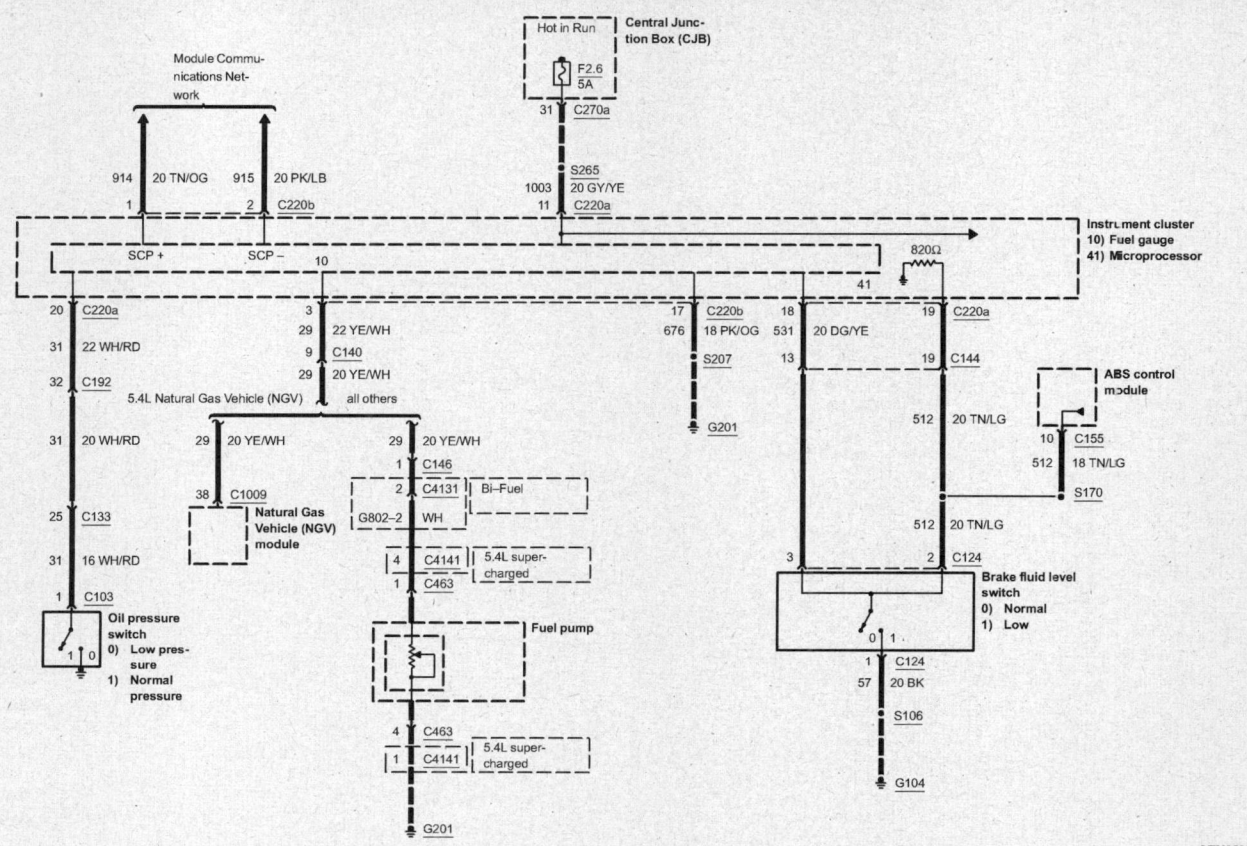

Fig. 15   Instrument cluster wiring diagram (Part 2 of 5). 2002–04 F-150

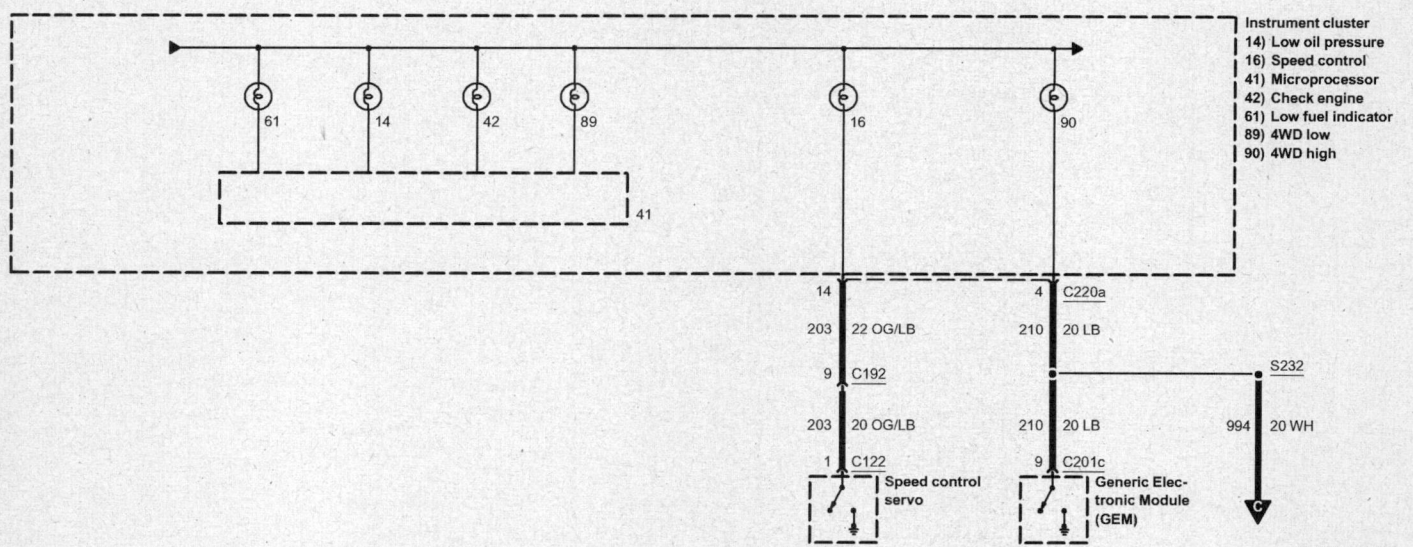

Fig. 15   Instrument cluster wiring diagram (Part 3 of 5). 2002–04 F-150

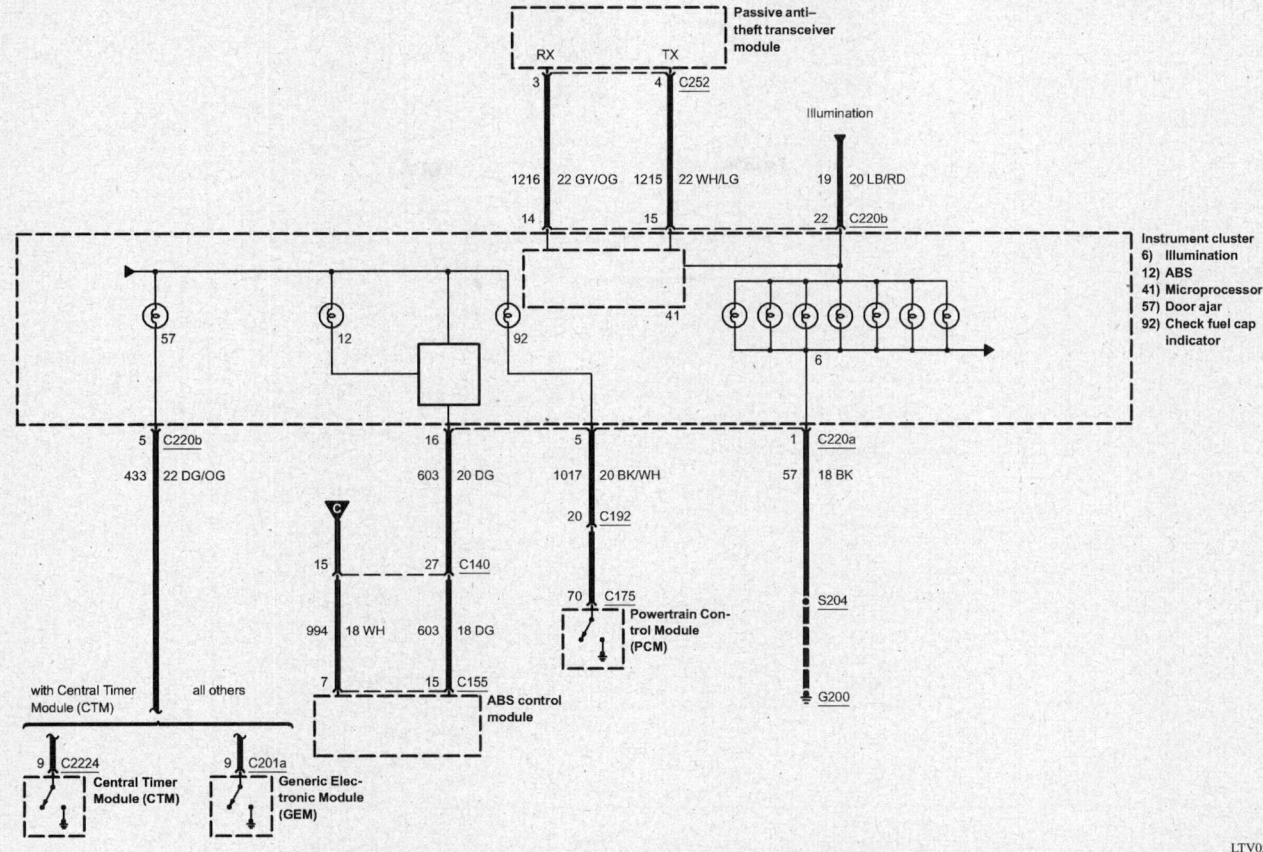

Fig. 15   Instrument cluster wiring diagram (Part 4 of 5). 2002–04 F-150

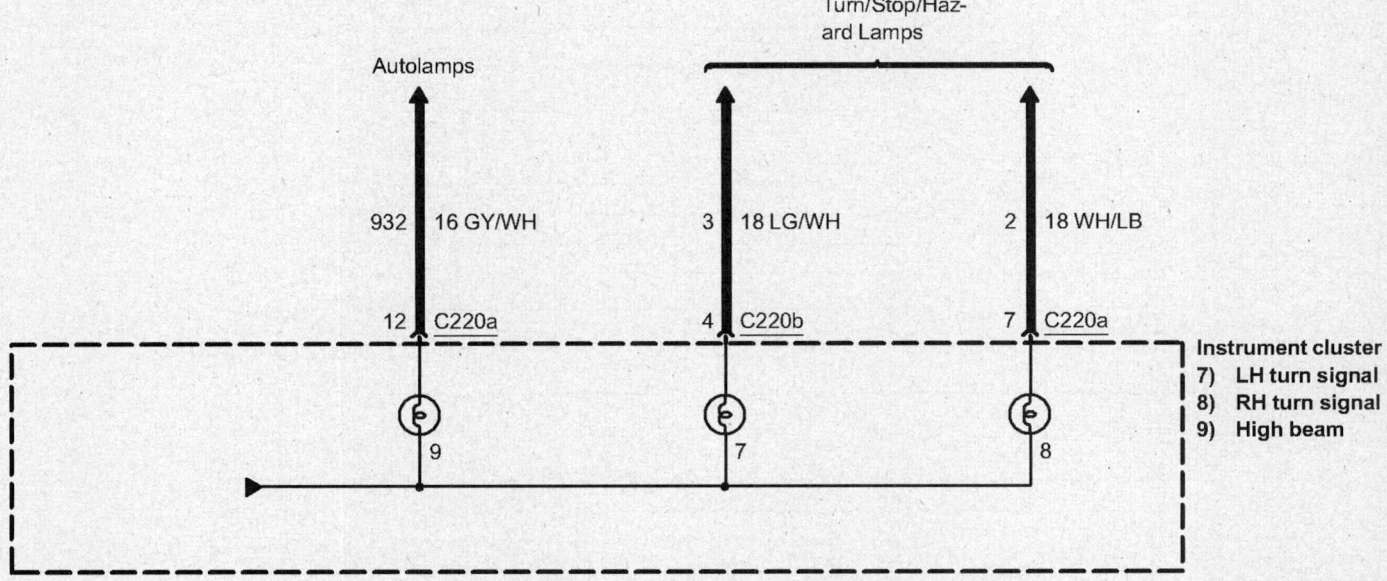

Fig. 15   Instrument cluster wiring diagram (Part 5 of 5). 2002–04 F-150

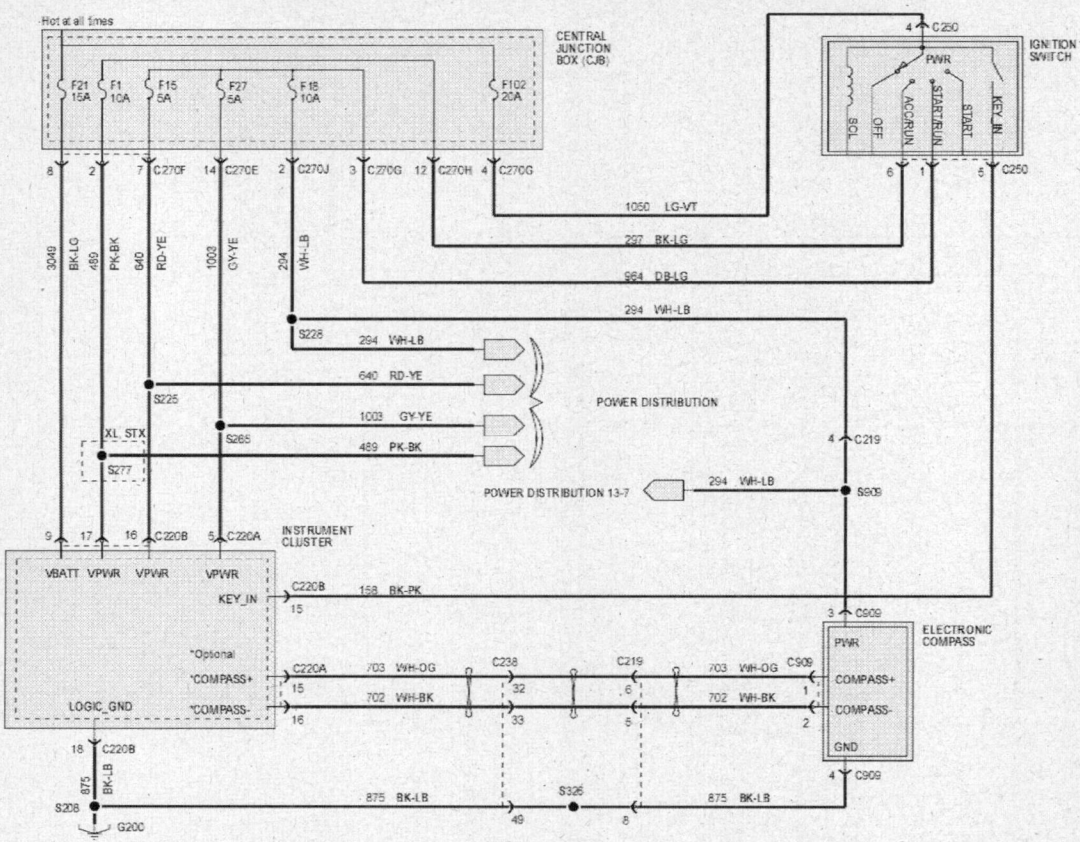

Fig. 16 Instrument cluster wiring diagram (Part 1 of 4). 2005–06 F-150 & Mark LT

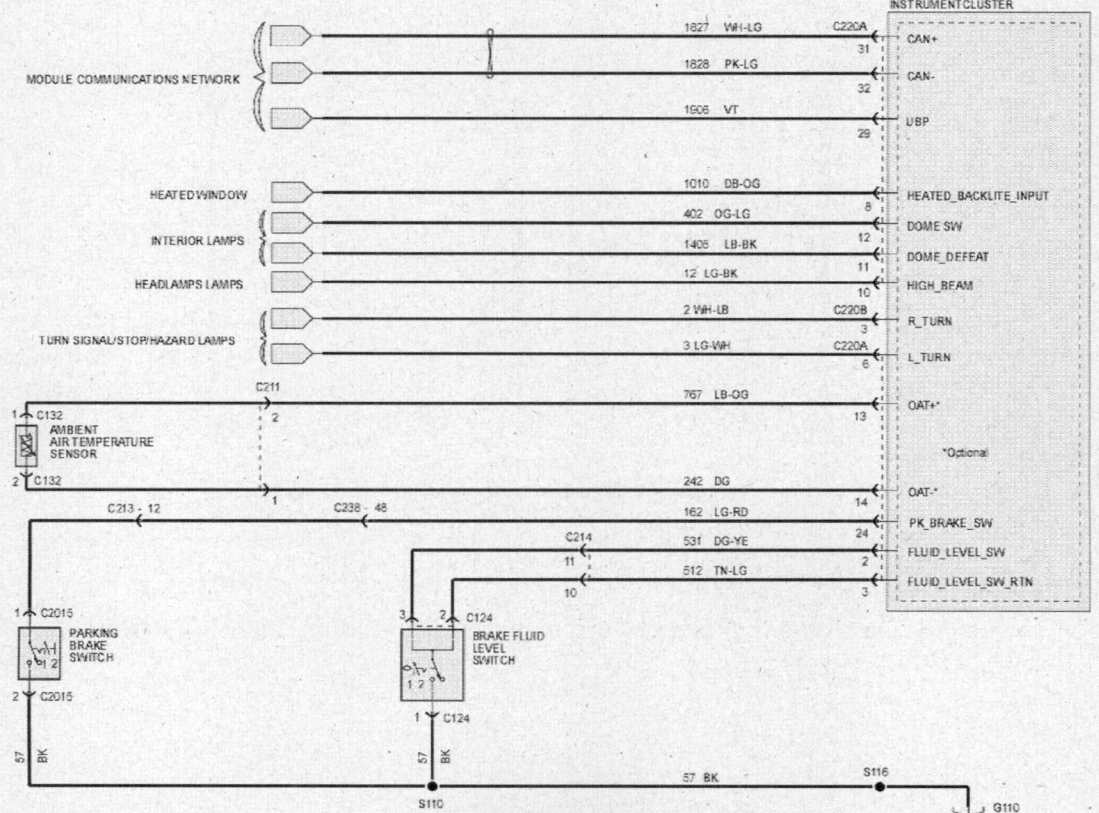

Fig. 16 Instrument cluster wiring diagram (Part 2 of 4). 2005–06 F-150 & Mark LT

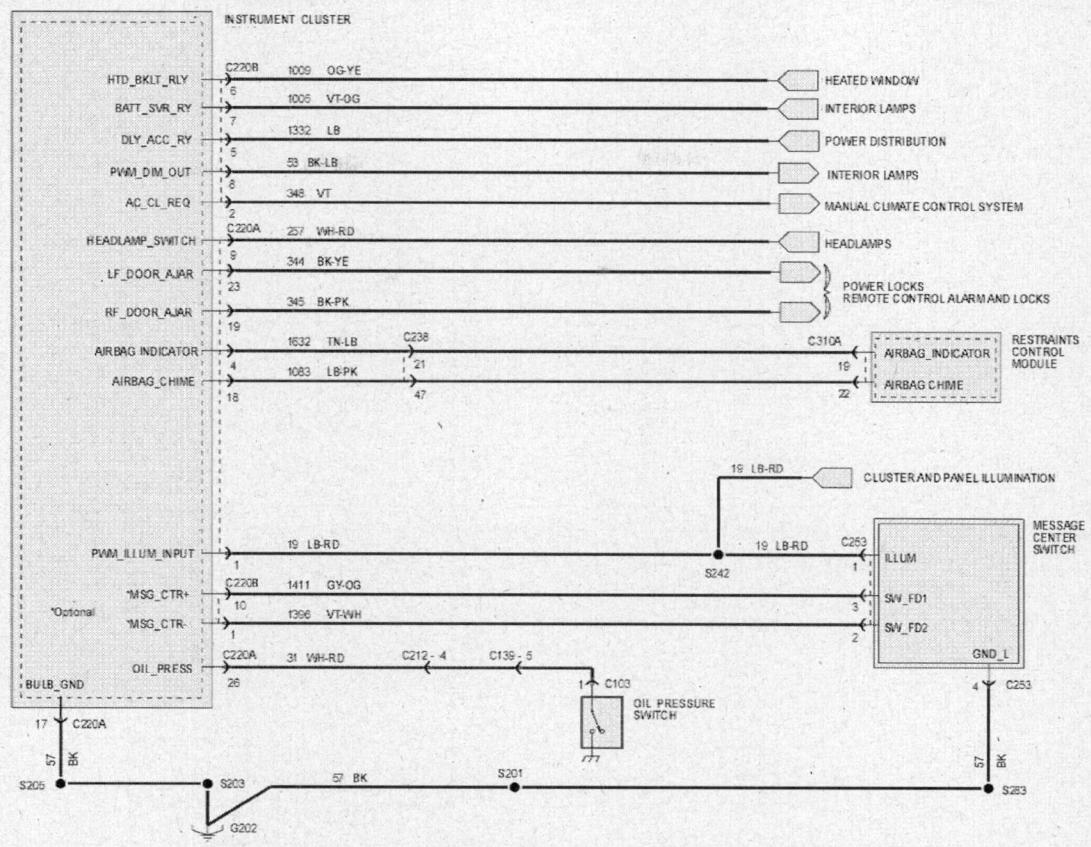

Fig. 16 Instrument cluster wiring diagram (Part 3 of 4). 2005–06 F-150 & Mark LT

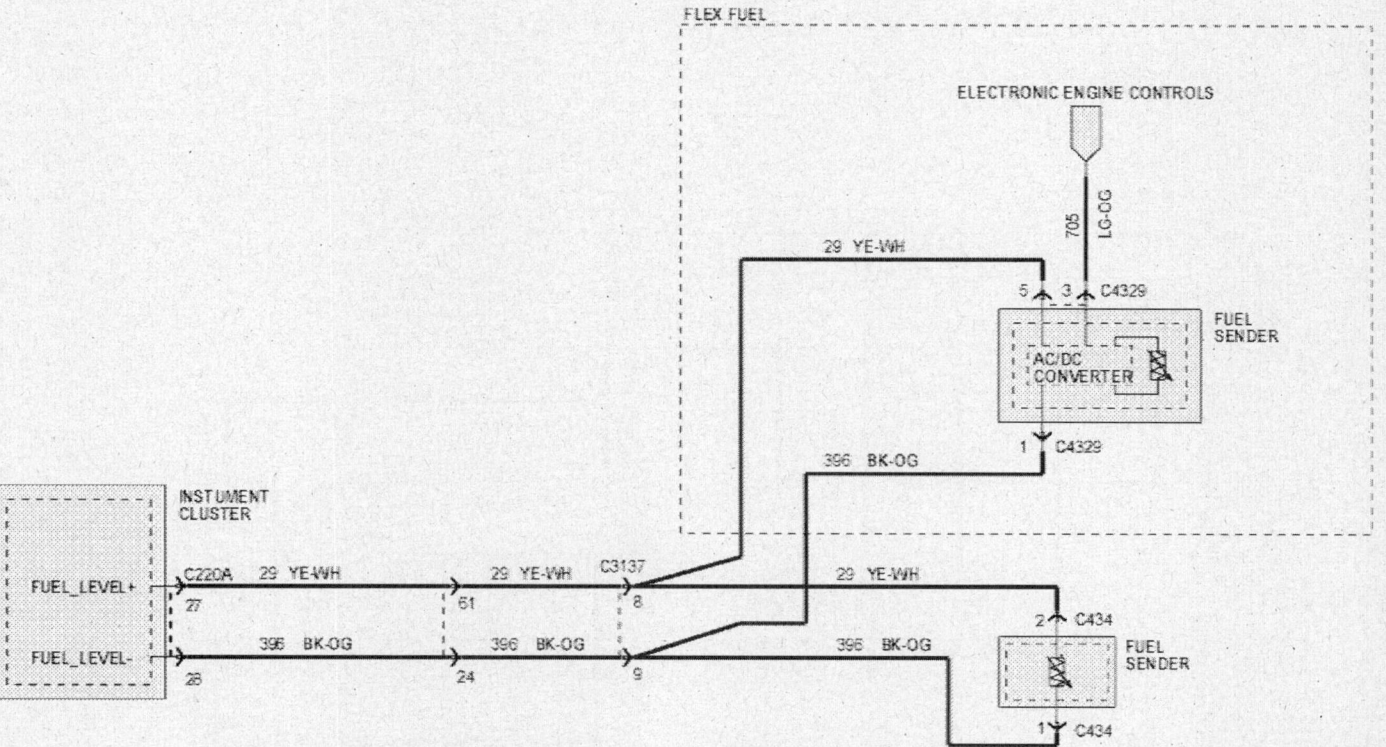

Fig. 16 Instrument cluster wiring diagram (Part 4 of 4). 2005–06 F-150 & Mark LT

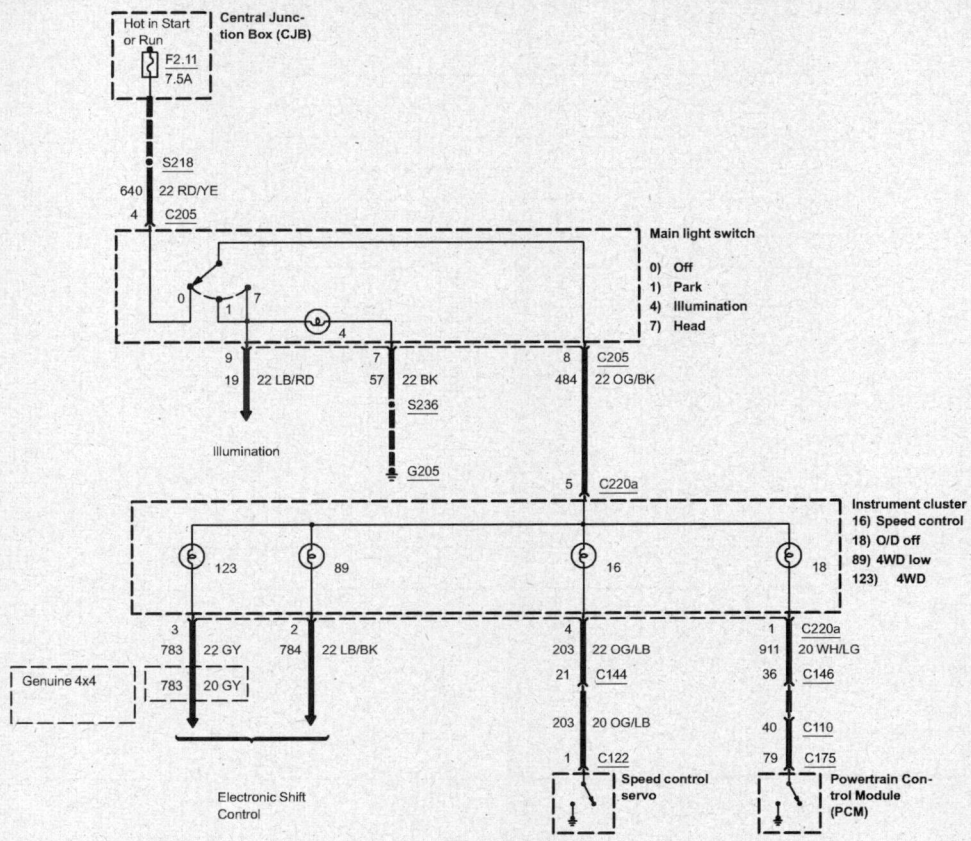

Fig. 17 Instrument cluster wiring diagram (Part 1 of 6). 2002–04 Ranger

LTV0500000001316

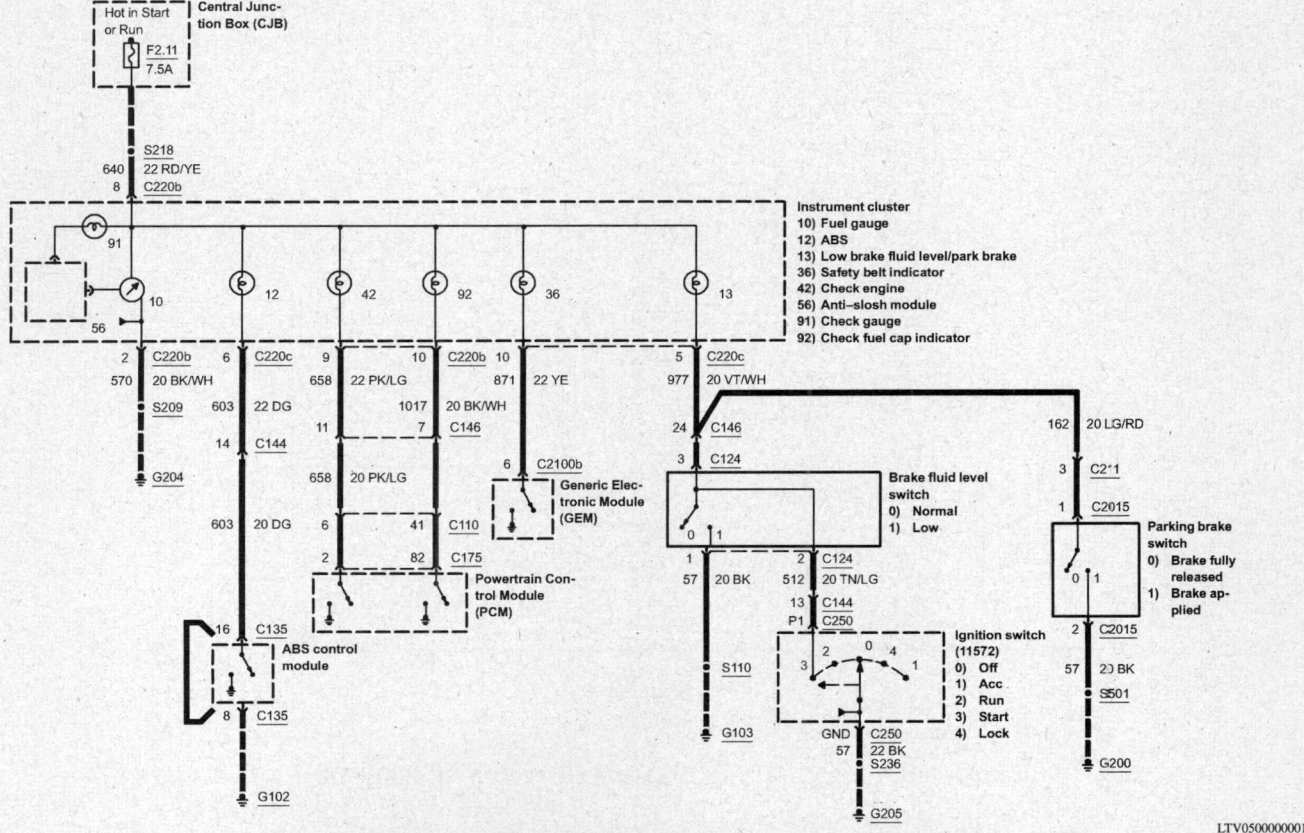

Fig. 17 Instrument cluster wiring diagram (Part 2 of 6). 2002–04 Ranger

LTV0500000001317

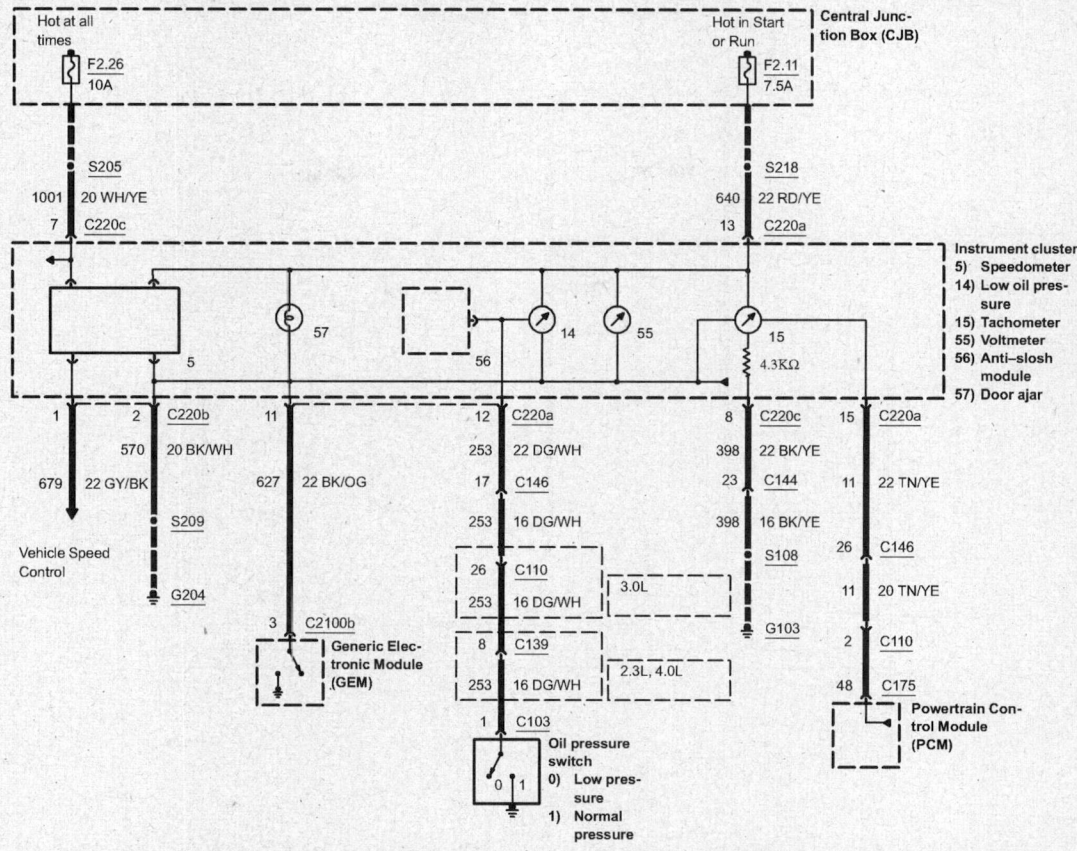

Fig. 17 Instrument cluster wiring diagram (Part 3 of 6). 2002–04 Ranger

LTV0500000001318

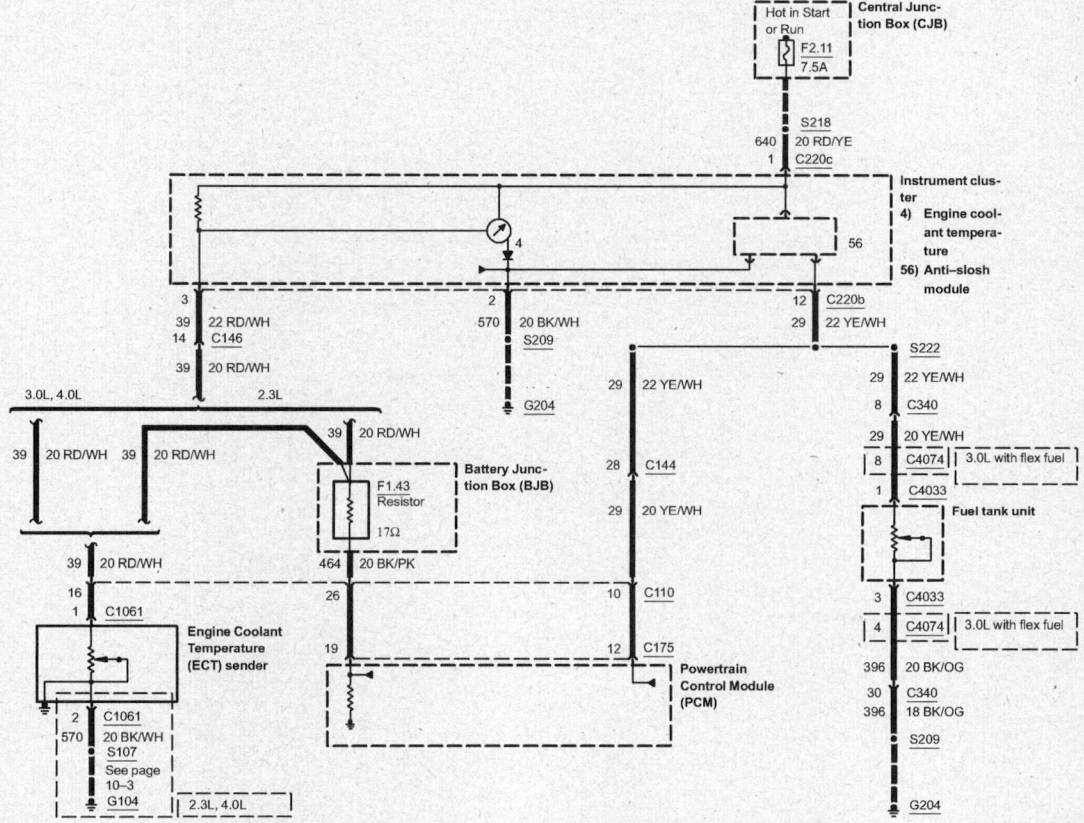

Fig. 17 Instrument cluster wiring diagram (Part 4 of 6). 2002–04 Ranger

LTV0500000001319

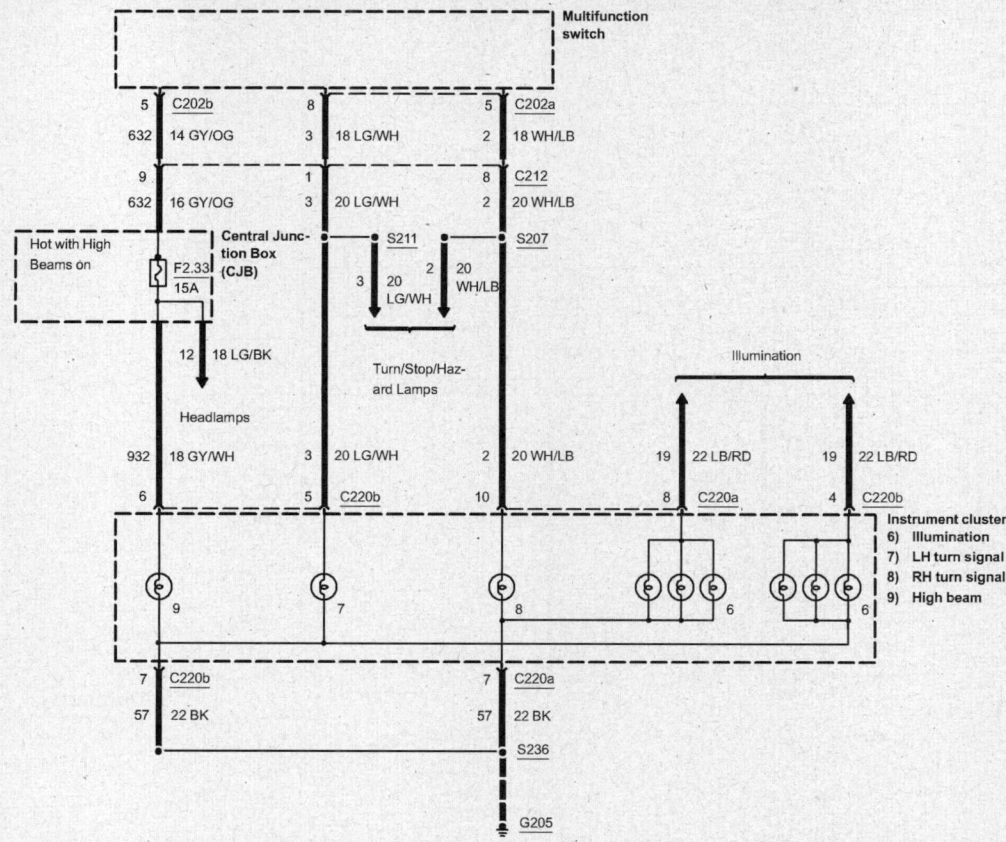

Fig. 17 Instrument cluster wiring diagram (Part 5 of 6). 2002–04 Ranger

LTV0500000001320

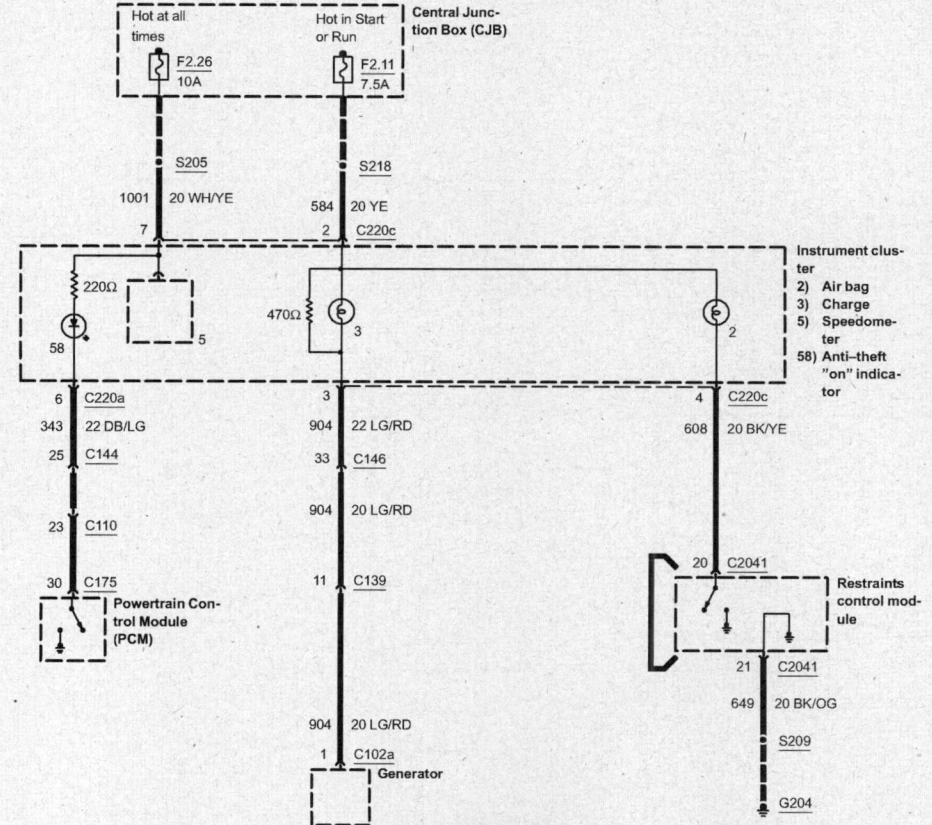

Fig. 17 Instrument cluster wiring diagram (Part 6 of 6). 2002–04 Ranger

LTV0500000001321

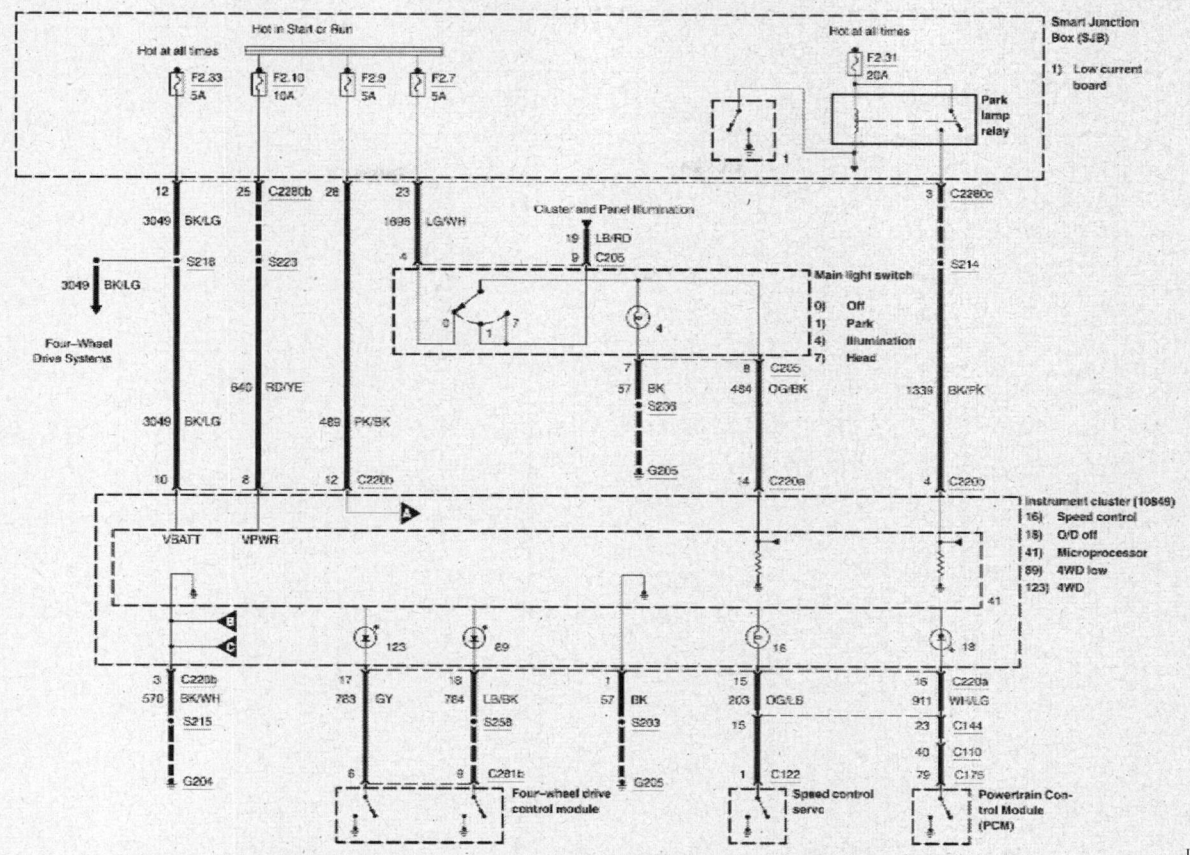

Fig. 18   Instrument cluster wiring diagram (Part 1 of 6). 2005–06 Ranger

LTV0500000001322

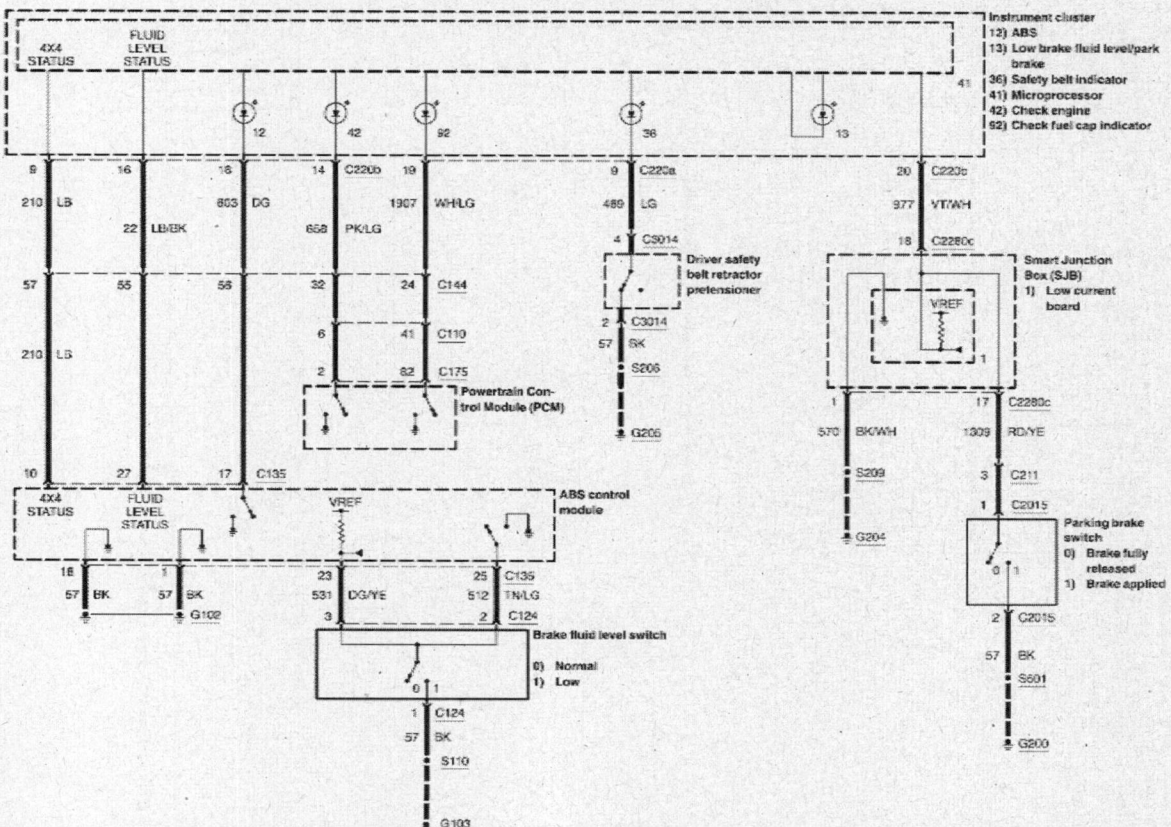

Fig. 18   Instrument cluster wiring diagram (Part 2 of 6). 2005–06 Ranger

LTV0500000001323

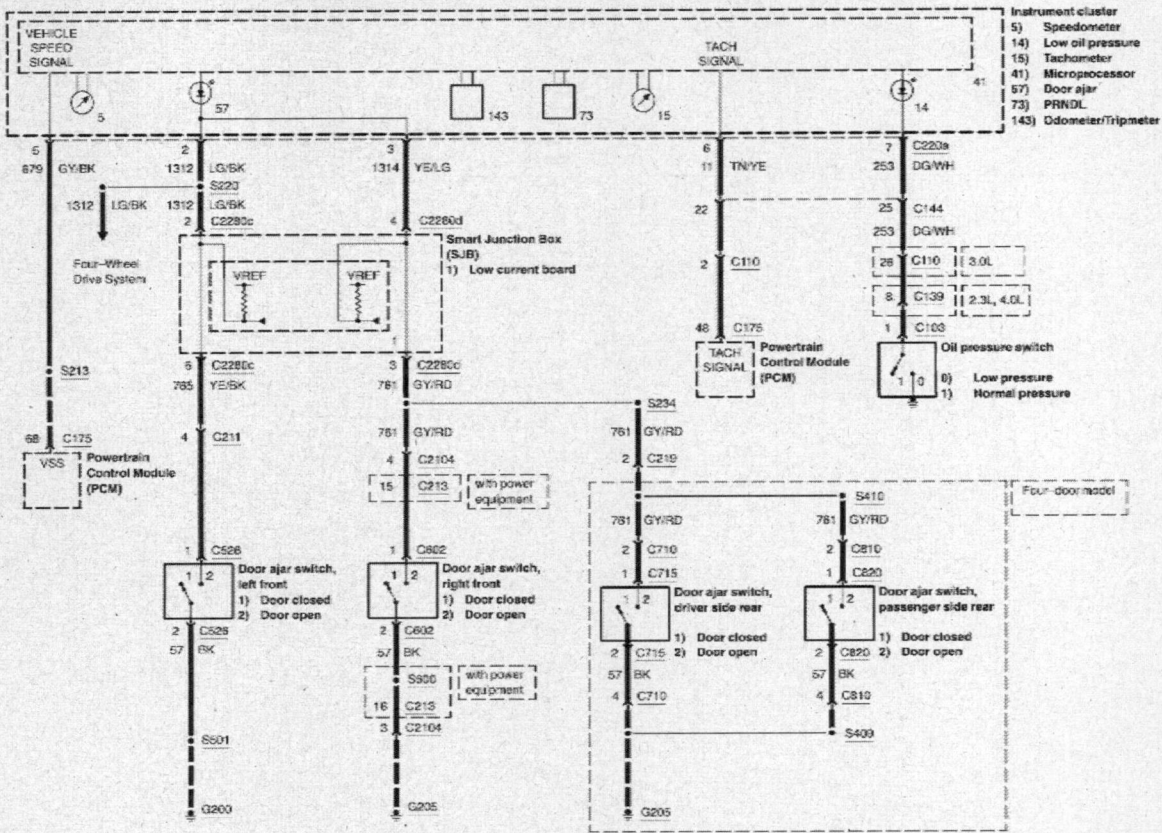

Fig. 18   Instrument cluster wiring diagram (Part 3 of 6). 2005–06 Ranger

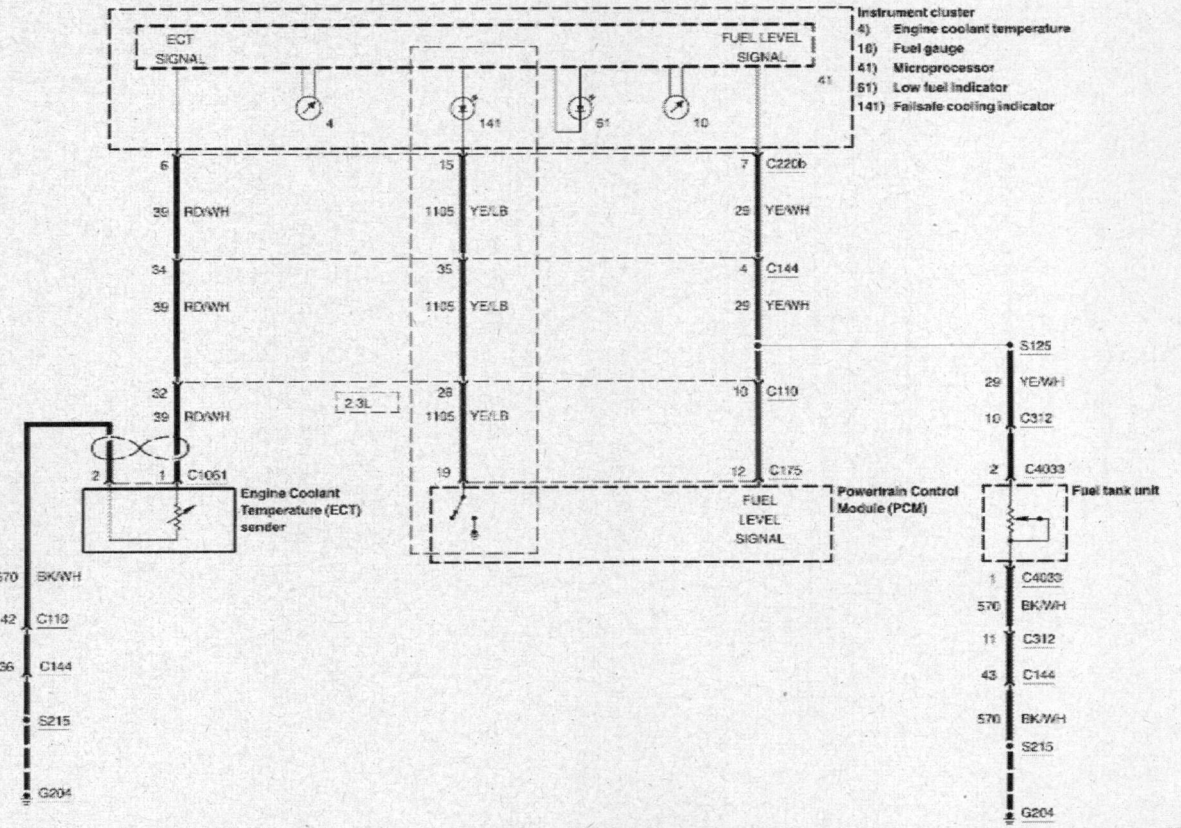

Fig. 18   Instrument cluster wiring diagram (Part 4 of 6). 2005–06 Ranger

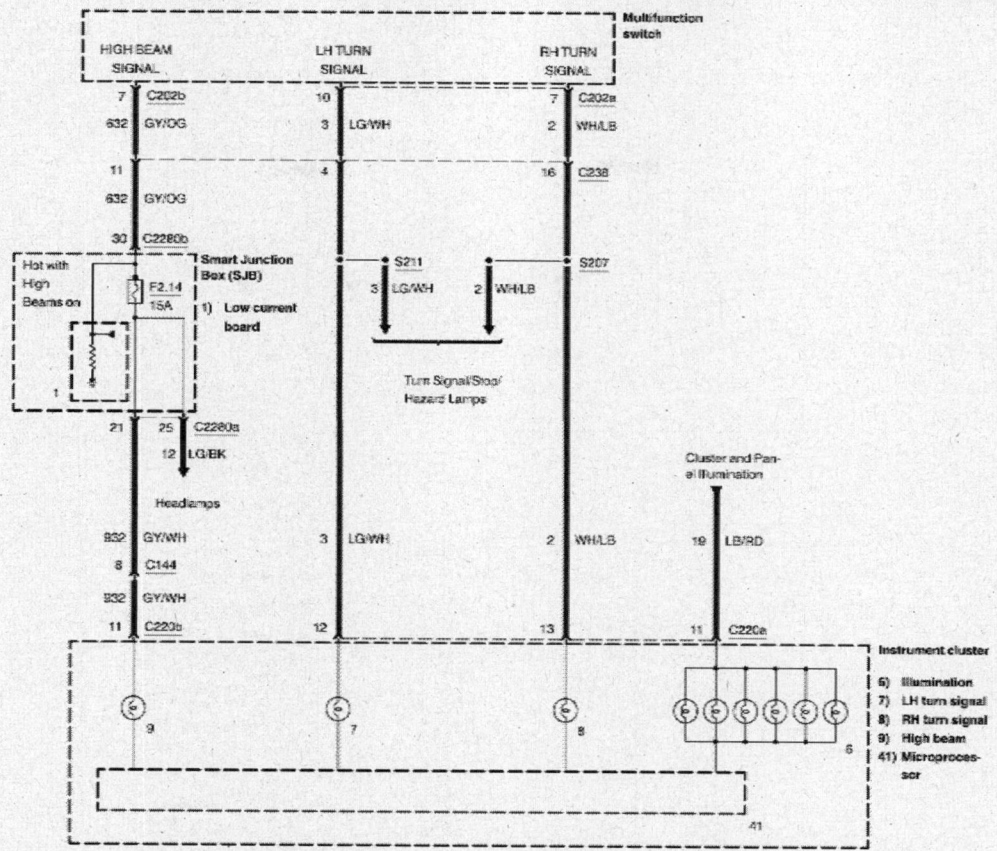

Fig. 18 Instrument cluster wiring diagram (Part 5 of 6). 2005–06 Ranger

LTV0500000001326

Fig. 18 Instrument cluster wiring diagram (Part 6 of 6). 2005–06 Ranger

LTV0500000001327

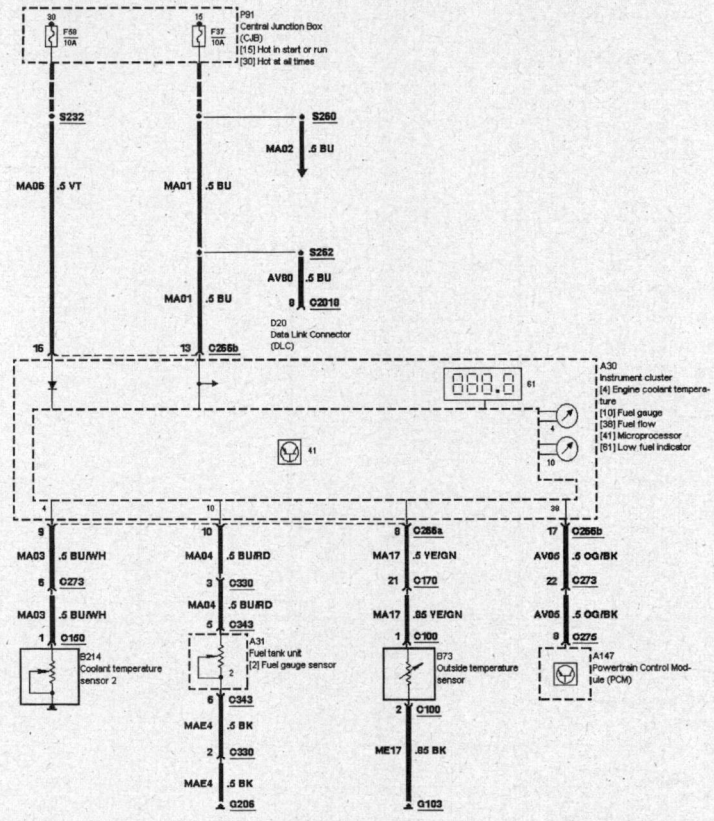

FM1040001660010X

Fig. 19 Conventional instrument wiring diagram (Part 1 of 7). Villager

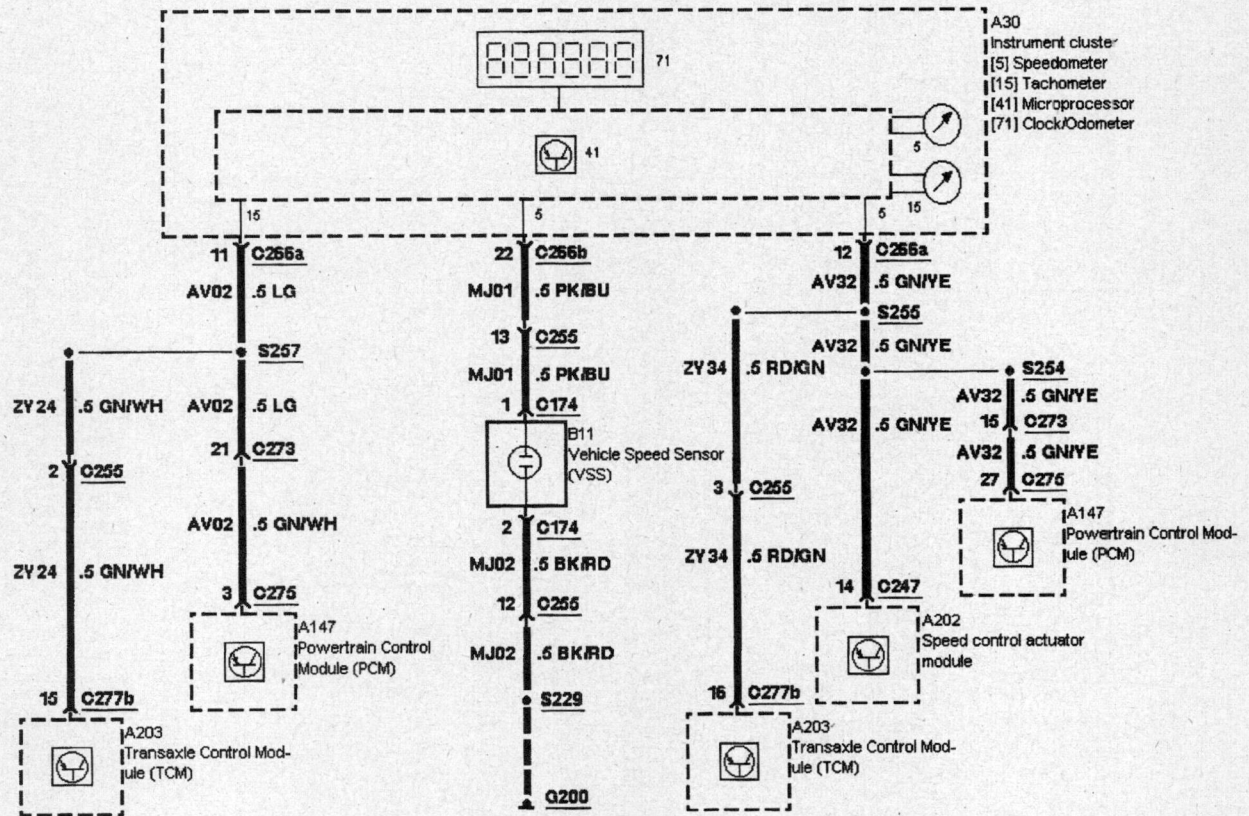

FM1040001660020X

Fig. 19 Conventional instrument wiring diagram (Part 2 of 7). Villager

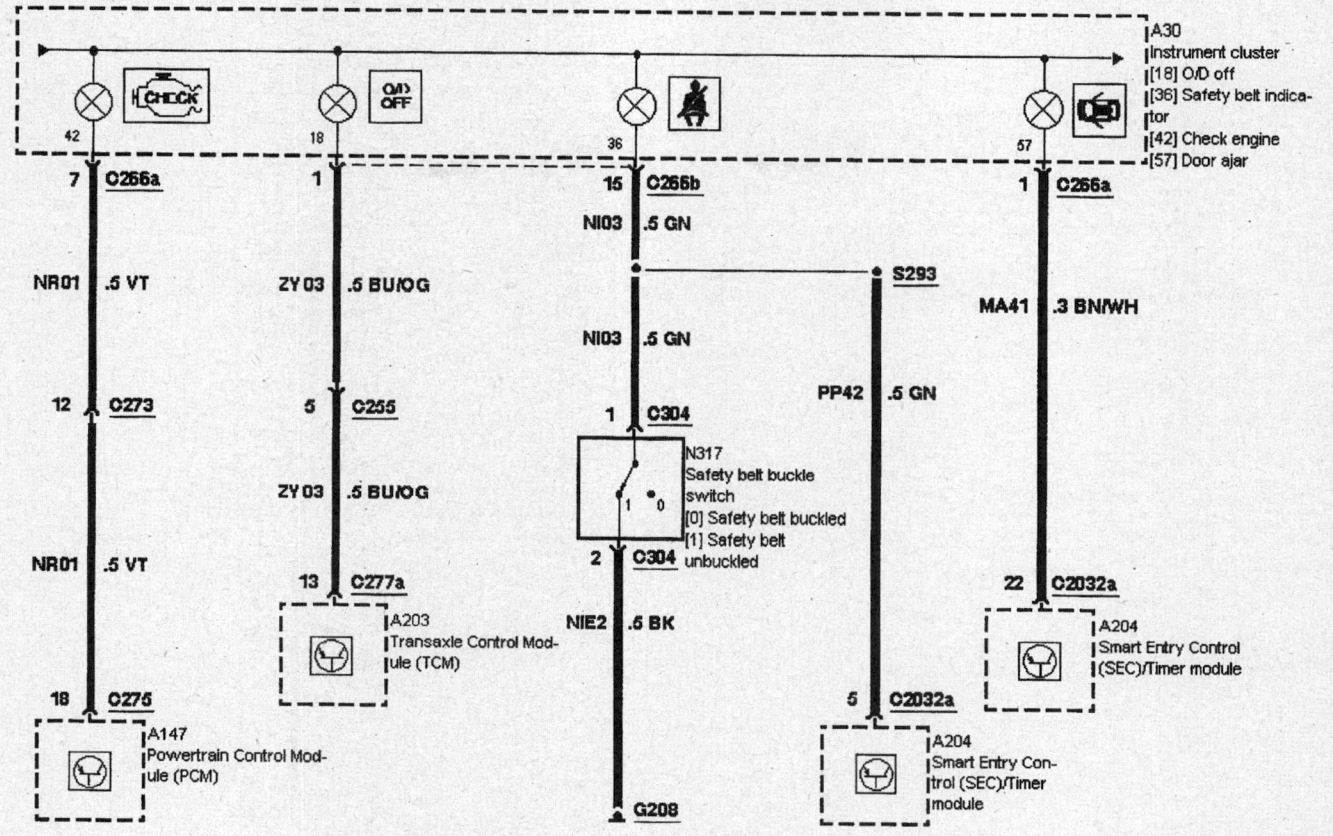

Fig. 19 Conventional instrument wiring diagram (Part 3 of 7). Villager

FM1040001660030X

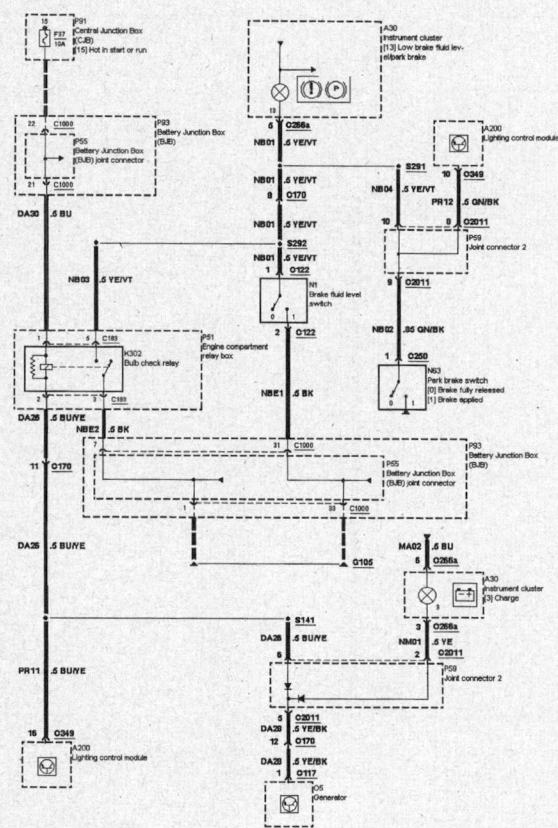

Fig. 19 Conventional instrument wiring diagram (Part 4 of 7). Villager

FM1040001660040X

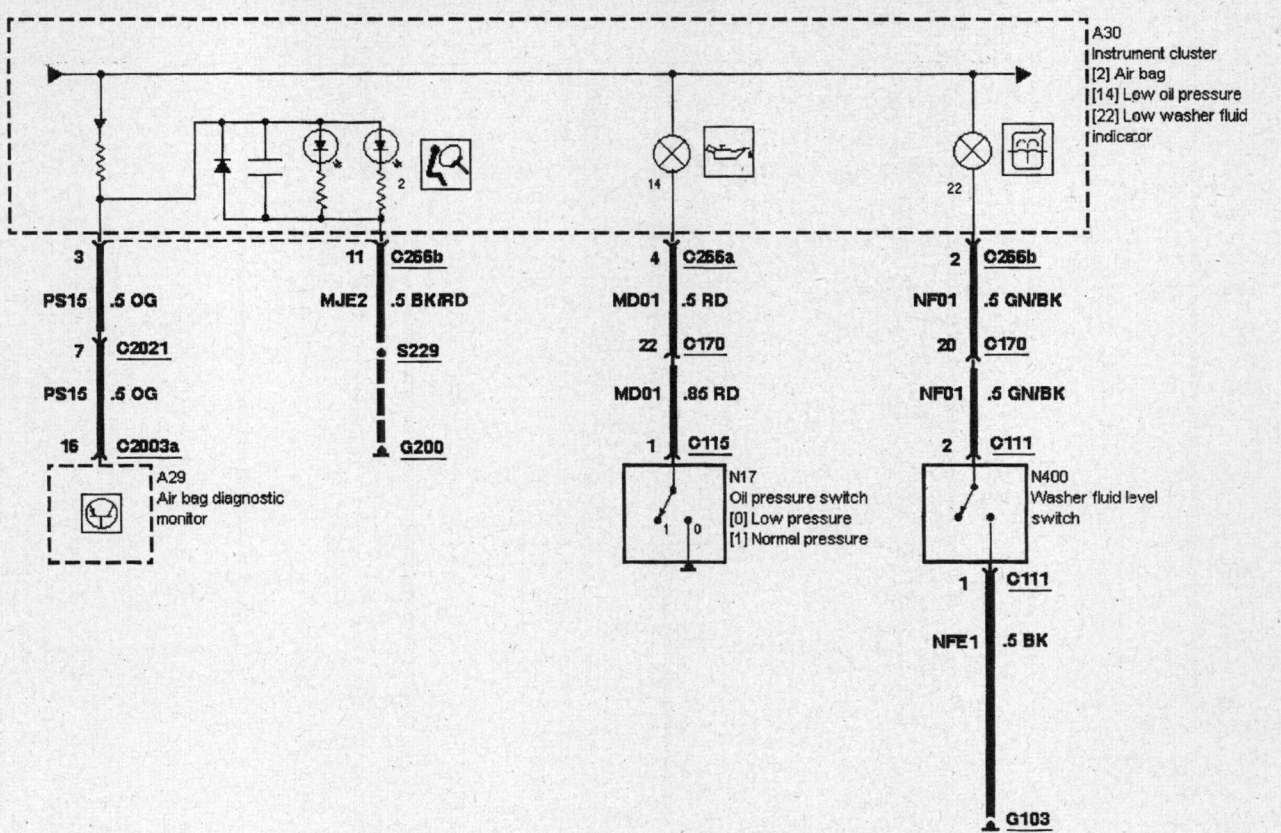

Fig. 19 Conventional instrument wiring diagram (Part 5 of 7). Villager

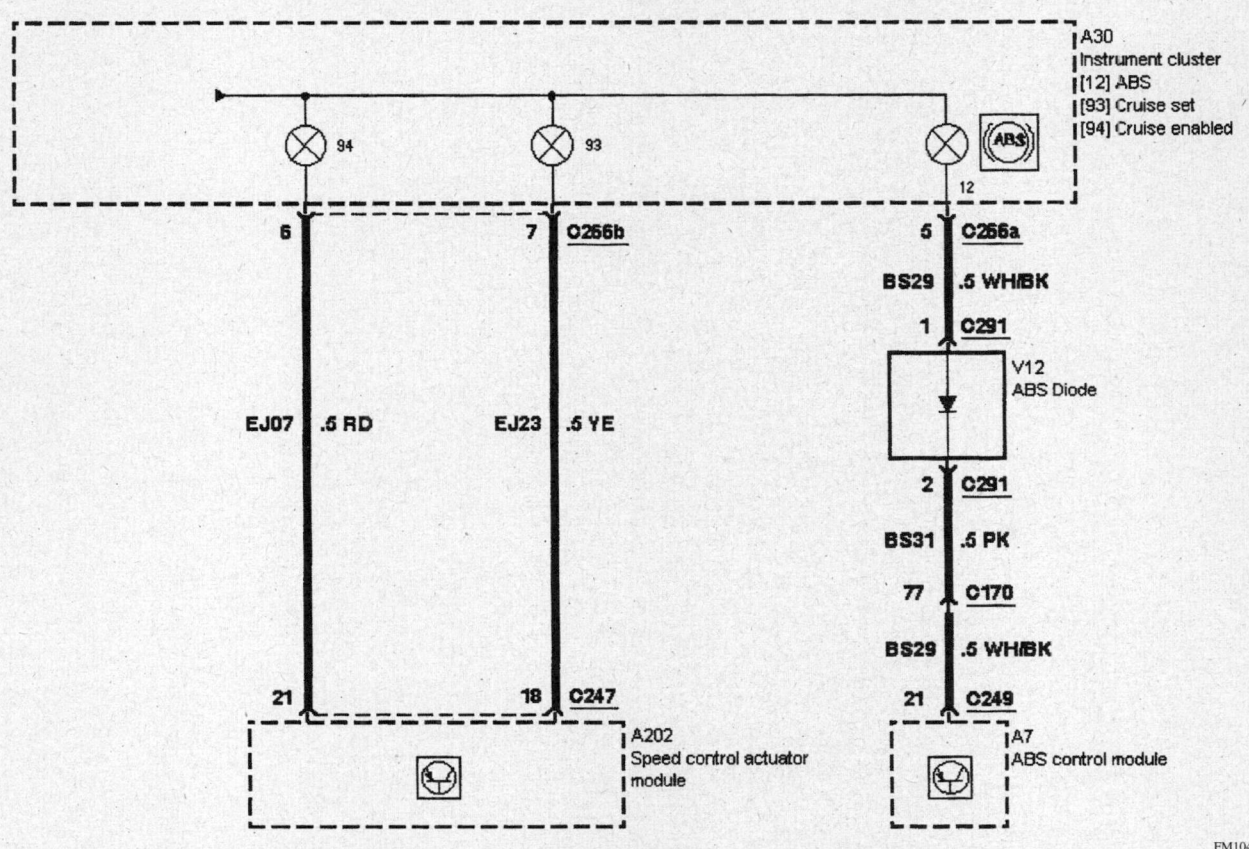

Fig. 19 Conventional instrument wiring diagram (Part 6 of 7). Villager

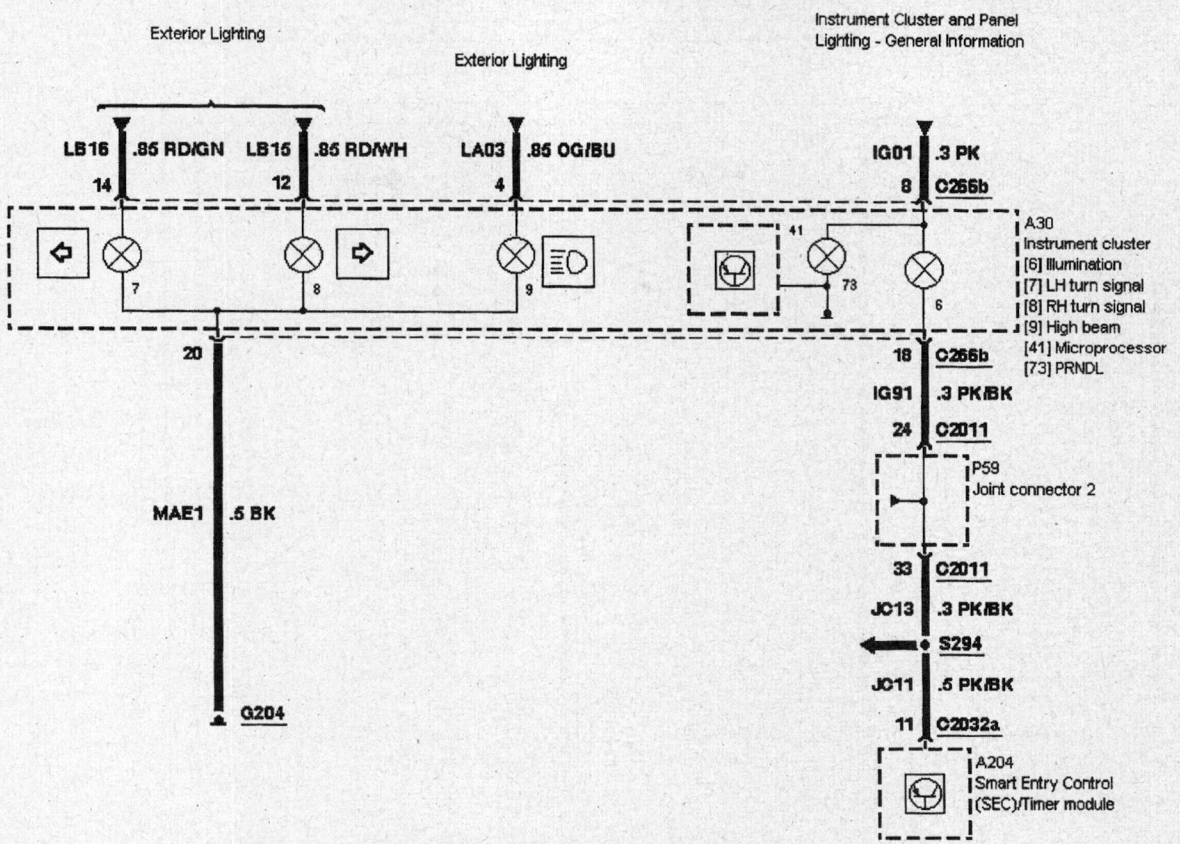

Fig. 19 Conventional instrument wiring diagram (Part 7 of 7). Villager

FM1040001660070X

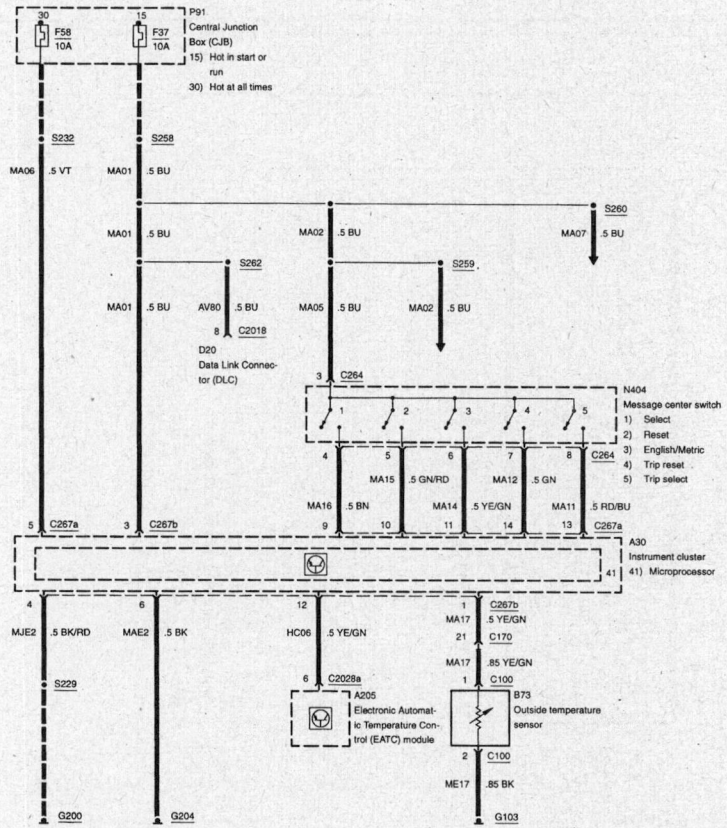

Fig. 20 Electronic instrument wiring diagram (Part 1 of 9). Villager

FM1040001463010X

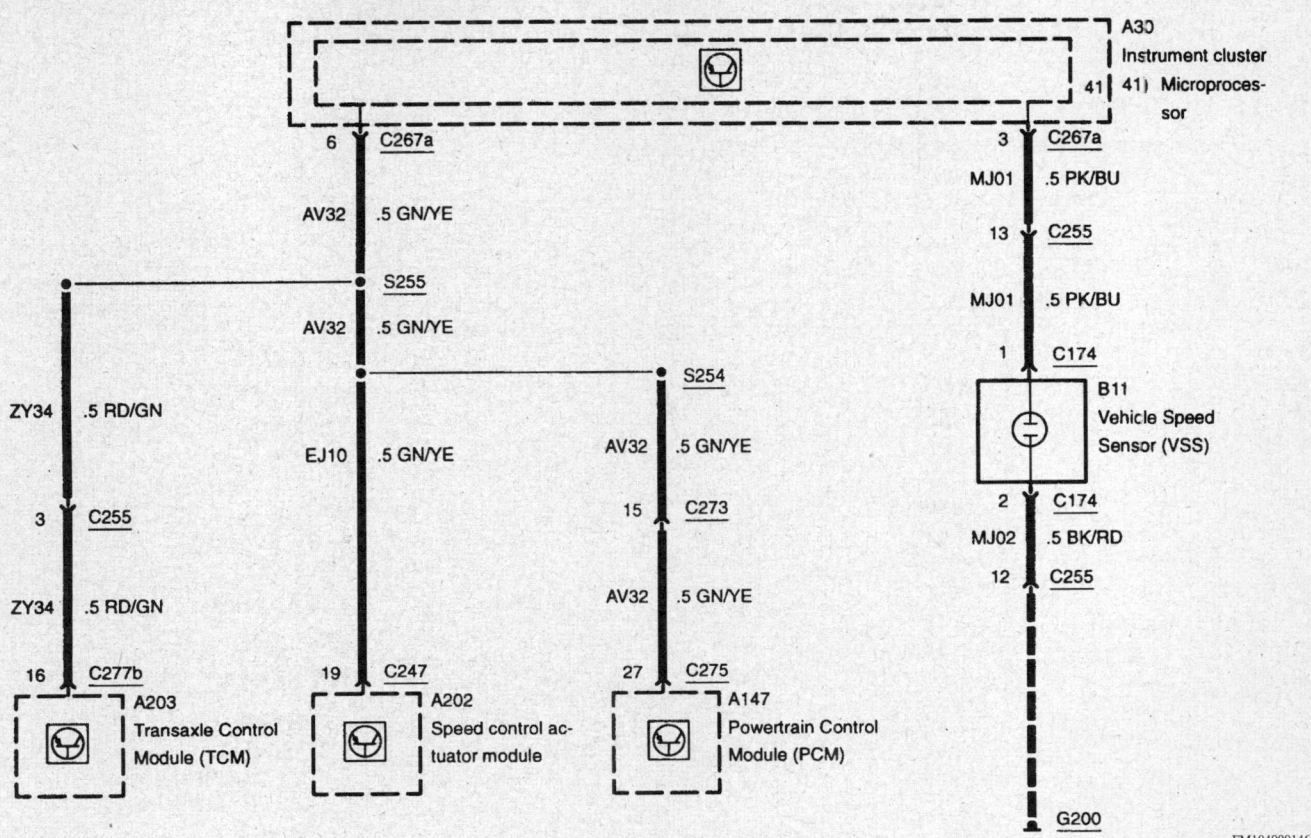

Fig. 20 Electronic instrument wiring diagram (Part 2 of 9). Villager

FM1040001463020X

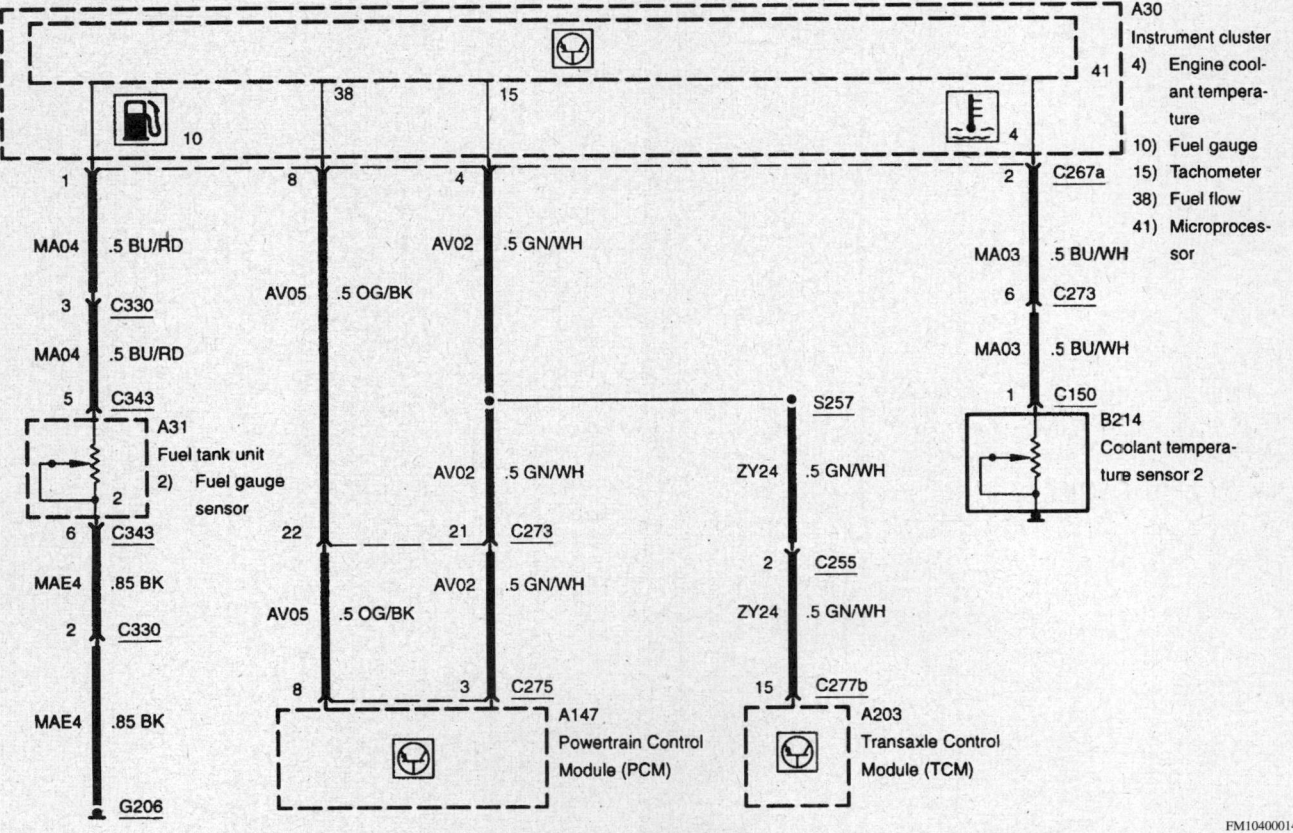

Fig. 20 Electronic instrument wiring diagram (Part 3 of 9). Villager

FM1040001463030X

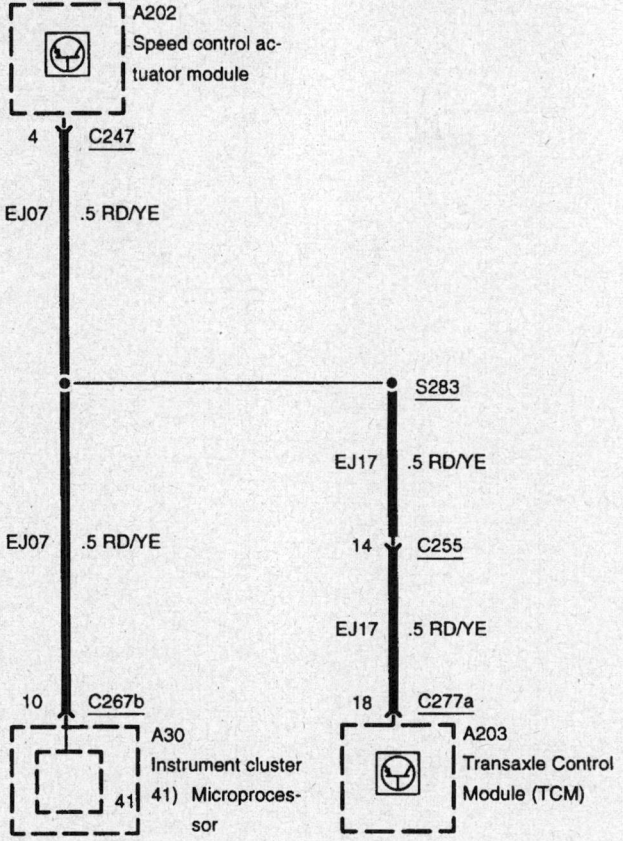

Fig. 20   Electronic instrument wiring diagram (Part 4 of 9). Villager

FM1040001463040X

A202
Speed control ac-
tuator module

4   C247

EJ07   .5 RD/YE

S283

EJ07   .5 RD/YE

EJ17   .5 RD/YE

14   C255

EJ17   .5 RD/YE

10   C267b

18   C277a

A30
Instrument cluster
41) Microproces-
sor

A203
Transaxle Control
Module (TCM)

P91
Central Junction
Box (CJB)

F59
7.5A

22   C2011

P59
Joint connector 2

13   C2011
IG01   .3 PK
12   C267c

73

A30
Instrument cluster
6) Illumination
73) PRNDL

6

5   C267b
IG91   .3 PK/BK
24

11   C267c
IG92   .3 PK/BK
30   C2011

P59
Joint connector 2

33   C2011
JC13   .3 PK/BK

S294

JC11   .3 PK/BK

11   C2032a

A204
Smart Entry Con-
trol (SEC)/Timer
module

Fig. 20   Electronic instrument wiring diagram (Part 5 of 9). Villager

FM1040001463050X

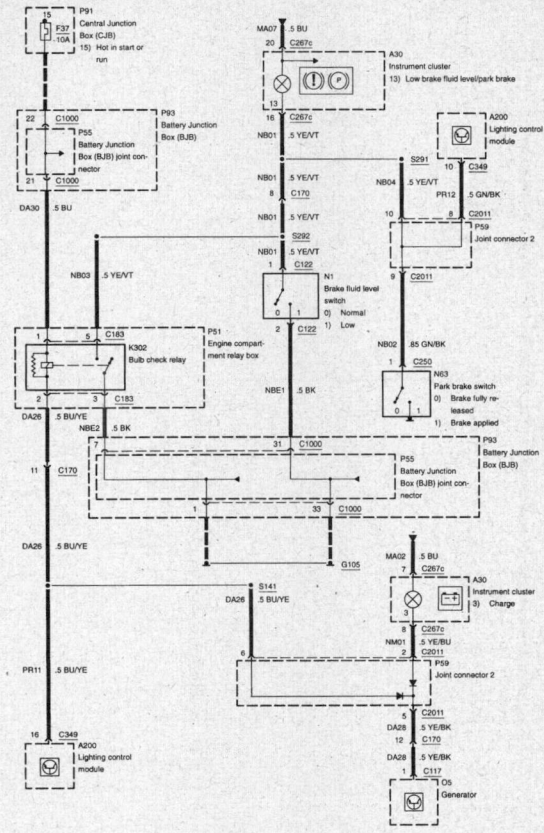

Fig. 20   Electronic instrument wiring diagram (Part 6 of 9). Villager

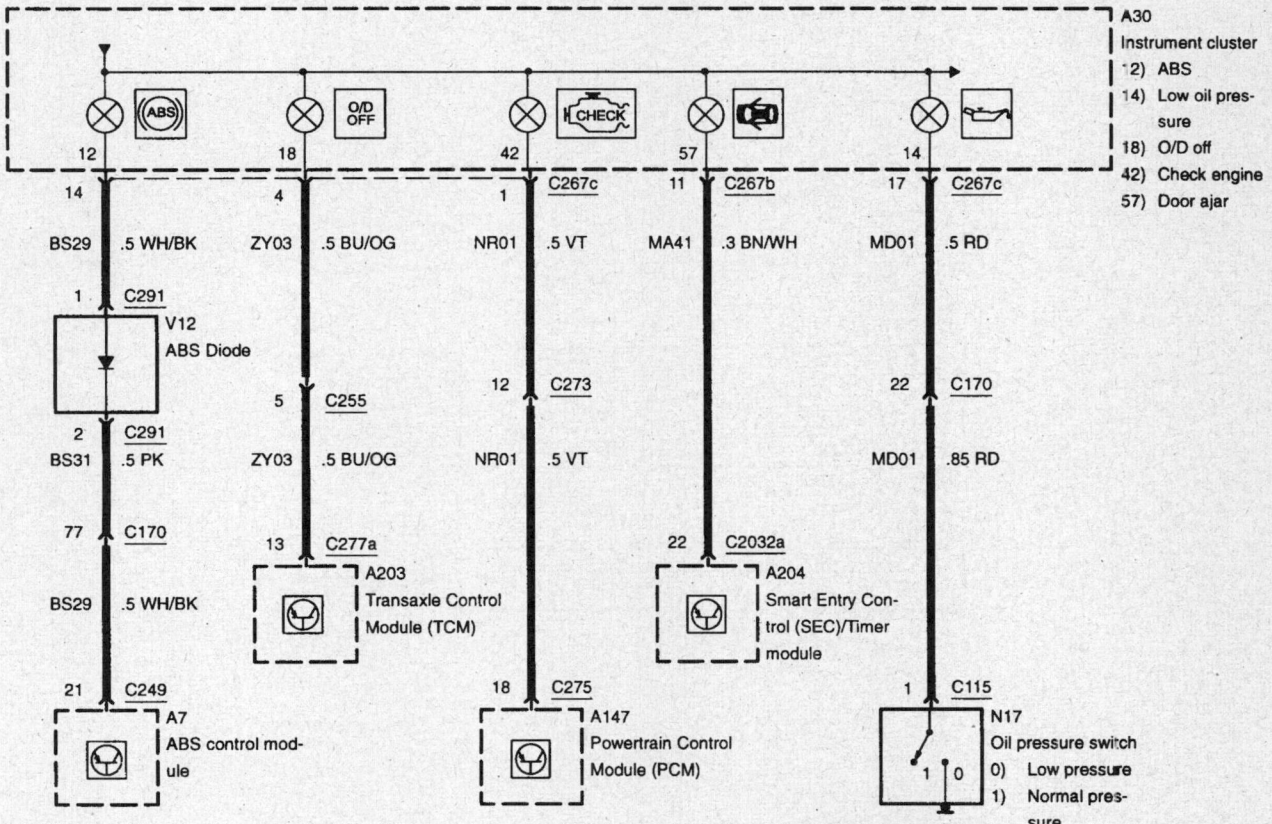

Fig. 20   Electronic instrument wiring diagram (Part 7 of 9). Villager

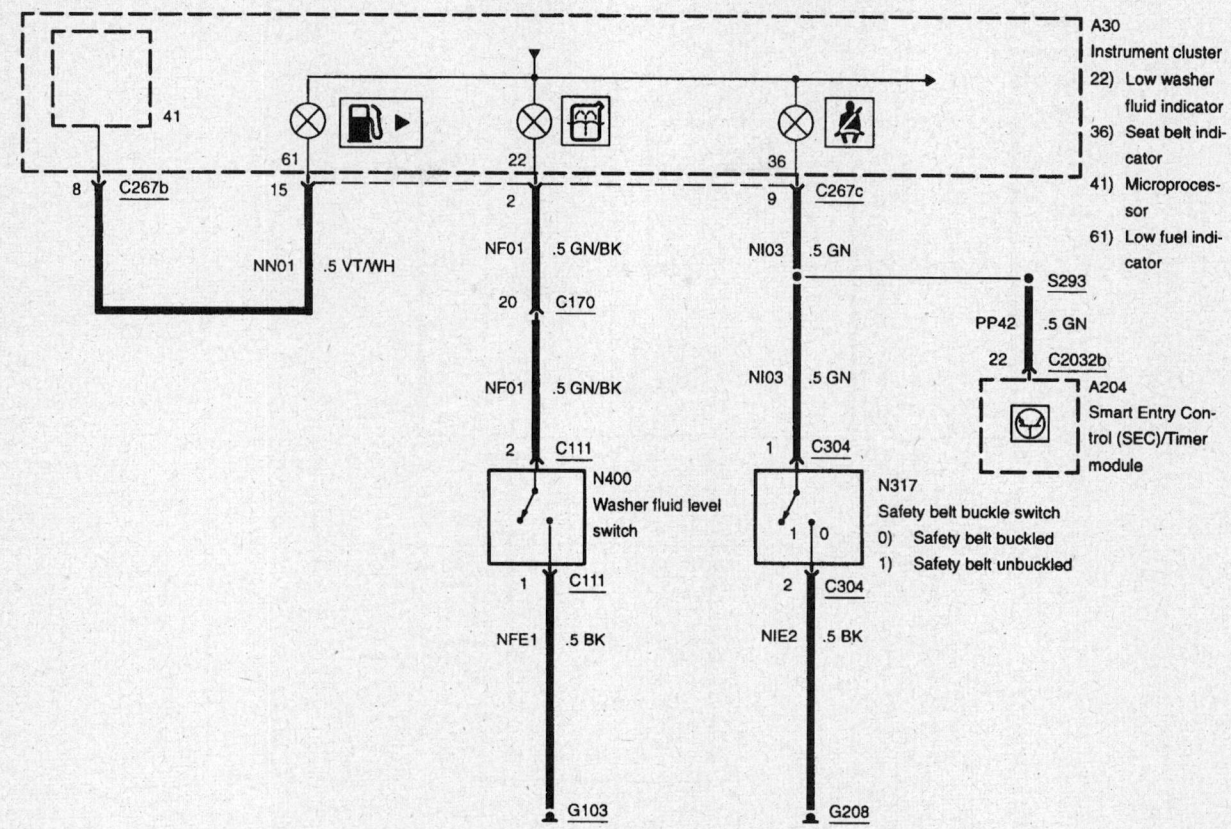

Fig. 20 Electronic instrument wiring diagram (Part 8 of 9). Villager

FM1040001463080X

Fig. 20 Electronic instrument wiring diagram (Part 9 of 9). Villager

FM1040001463090X

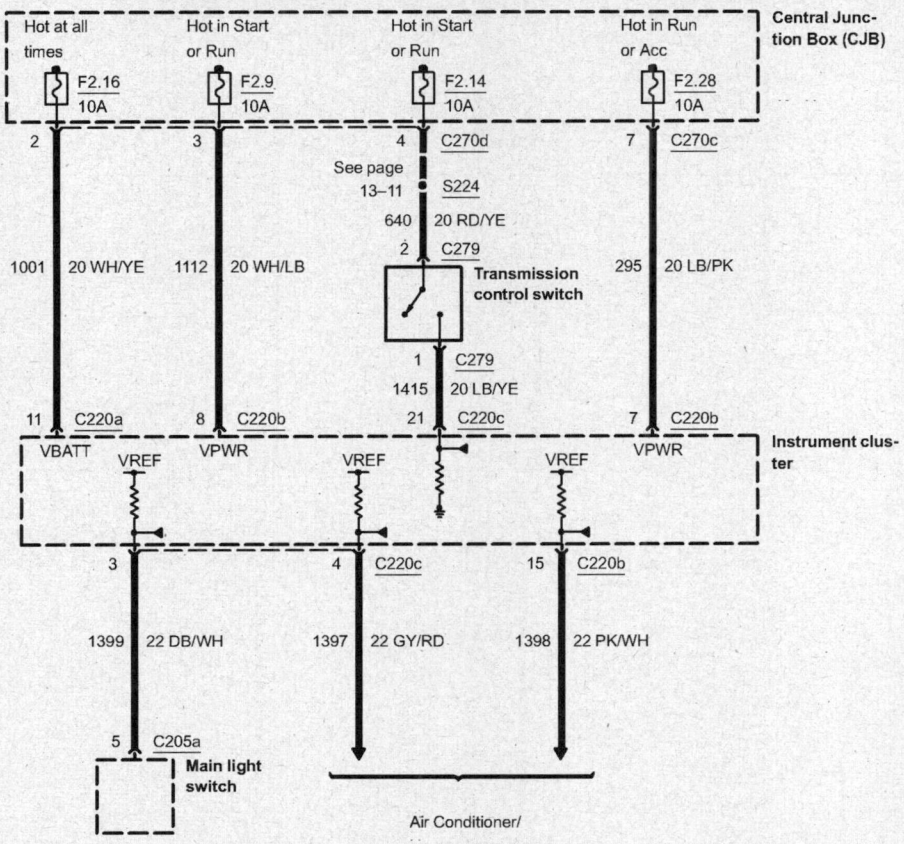

Fig. 21 Instrument cluster wiring diagram (Part 1 of 4). Windstar

LTV0500000001328

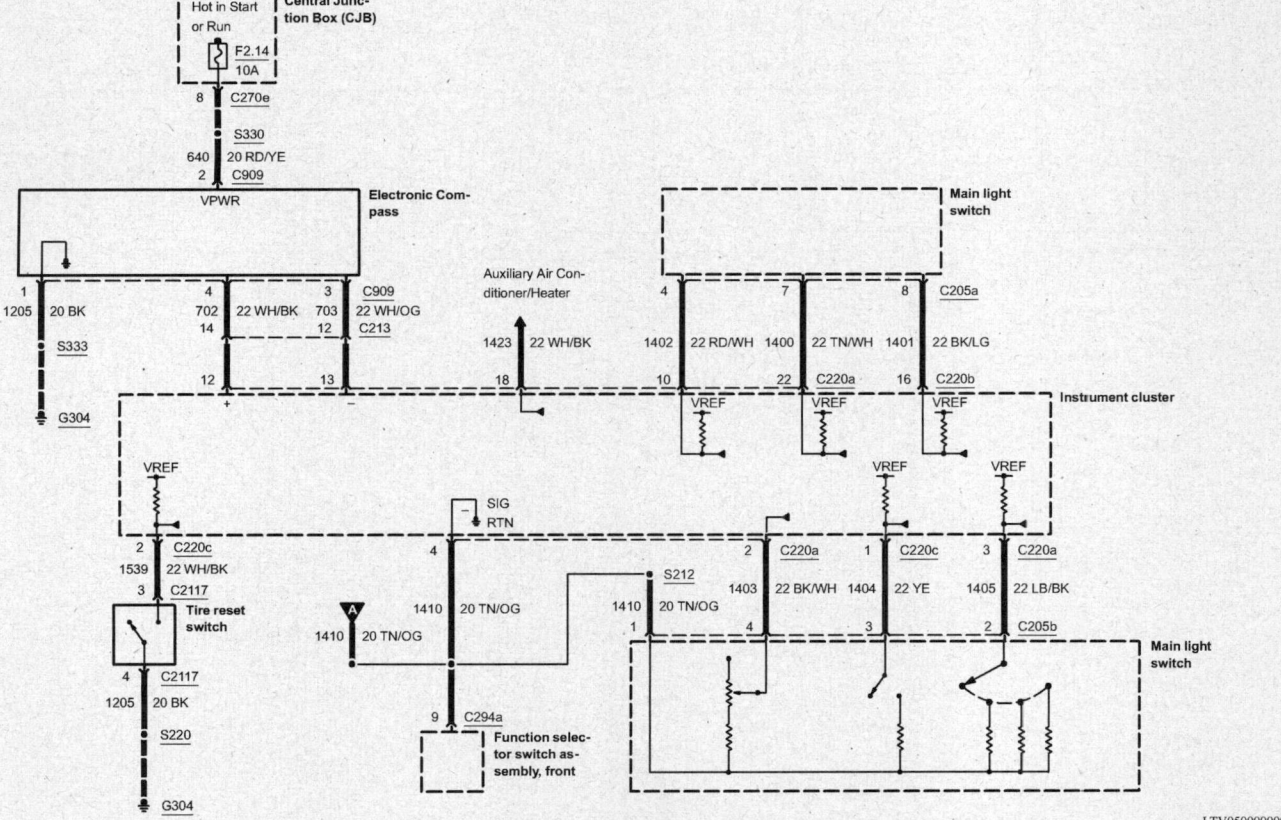

Fig. 21 Instrument cluster wiring diagram (Part 2 of 4). Windstar

LTV0500000001329

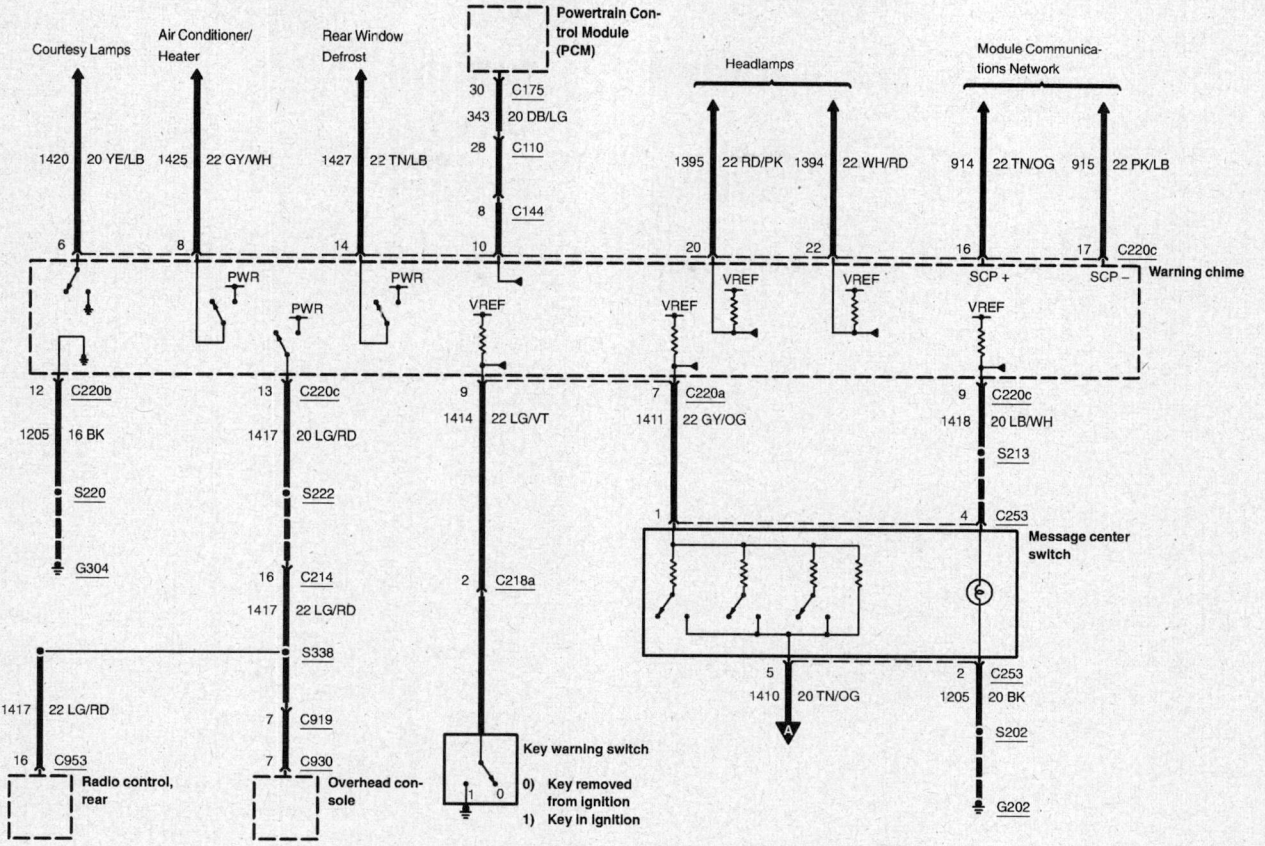

Fig. 21 Instrument cluster wiring diagram (Part 3 of 4). Windstar

LTV0500000001330

Fig. 21 Instrument cluster wiring diagram (Part 4 of 4). Windstar

LTV0500000001331

Condition	Possible Sources
• No communication with the instrument cluster	• Circuitry. • Standard corporate protocol (SCP) communication network. • Universal asynchronous receiver-transmitter (UART) based protocol (UBP) communication network. • Instrument cluster.
• One or more module-controlled illumination source(s) is inoperative	• Circuitry. • Illumination LEDs (part of illumination source component). • Dimmer module.
• The control illumination is inoperative/always on	• Circuitry. • Headlamp switch.
• The instrument cluster illumination is inoperative	• Circuitry. • Illumination LEDs. • Instrument cluster.
• The climate control illumination is inoperative	• Circuitry. • Dual automatic temperature control (DATC) unit.
• The steering wheel control switch is inoperative	• Circuitry. • Clockspring. • Steering wheel control switches. • Steering wheel control harness.
• The instrument panel illumination does not dim	• Circuitry. • Dimmer switch. • Dimmer module.

LTV0500000001332

Fig. 22 Instrument cluster illumination symptom diagnosis

Condition	Possible Sources
• The all-wheel drive (AWD) LOCKED indicator is never/always on	• Circuitry. • AWD control module. • Instrument cluster.
• The speed control indicator is never/always on	• Circuitry. • Speed control servo. • Powertrain control module (PCM). • Instrument cluster.
• The oil pressure warning indicator is never/always on	• Circuitry. • Oil pressure switch. • Powertrain control module (PCM). • Instrument cluster.
• The temperature warning indicator is never/always on	• Circuitry. • Cylinder head temperature sensor. • Powertrain control module (PCM). • Instrument cluster.
• The overdrive off indicator is never/always on	• Circuitry. • Powertrain control module (PCM). • Instrument cluster.
• The traction control indicator is never/always on	• Anti-lock brake system (ABS) module. • Instrument cluster.
• The low tire warning indicator is never on	• Circuitry. • Instrument cluster.
• The instrument cluster is inoperative	• Circuitry. • Instrument cluster.

LTV0500000001335

Fig. 23 Instrument cluster gauges symptom diagnosis (Part 3 of 3)

Condition	Possible Sources
• No communication with the instrument cluster	• Circuitry. • Standard corporate protocol (SCP) communication network. • Universal asynchronous receiver-transmitter (UART) based protocol (UBP) communication network. • Instrument cluster.
• Incorrect fuel gauge indication	• Circuitry. • Fuel pump module. • Fuel level sensor. • Fuel tank. • Instrument cluster.
• Incorrect engine coolant temperature gauge indication	• Circuitry. • Engine coolant temperature sensor. • Powertrain control module (PCM). • Instrument cluster.
• The speedometer/odometer is inoperative	• Circuitry. • Powertrain control module (PCM). • Instrument cluster.
• The tachometer is inoperative	• Circuitry. • Powertrain control module (PCM). • Instrument cluster.
• The safety belt warning indicator is inoperative (chime is operative)/does not operate correctly	• Circuitry. • Restraint control module (RCM). • Safety belt switch (part of the driver belt buckle). • Instrument cluster.
• Inaccurate speedometer reading	• Instrument cluster. • Anti-lock brake system (ABS) module. • Tires.

LTV0500000001333

Fig. 23 Instrument cluster gauges symptom diagnosis (Part 1 of 3)

Condition	Possible Sources
• The key-in-ignition warning chime is inoperative	• Key-in-ignition warning switch. • Door ajar switch. • Circuitry. • Instrument cluster. • Vehicle security module.
• The headlamps on reminder chime is inoperative	• Instrument cluster. • Vehicle security module. • Door ajar switch.
• The door ajar warning chime is inoperative	• Instrument cluster. • Vehicle security module. • Door ajar switch.
• The safety belt warning chime does not operate correctly	• Circuitry. • Instrument cluster. • Safety belt switch(es). • Restraint control module (RCM).
• All the chimes are inoperative	• Instrument cluster. • Circuitry.
• The chime sounds when the driver door is ajar (no key in ignition and headlamps OFF)	• Key-in-ignition warning switch. • Circuitry. • Instrument cluster.
• The belt minder feature does not operate correctly	• Circuitry. • Instrument cluster. • Safety belt switch(es). • Restraint control module (RCM).

LTV0500000001336

Fig. 24 Warning devices symptom diagnosis (Part 1 of 2)

Condition	Possible Sources
• The anti-lock brake system (ABS) warning indicator is never on	• Circuitry. • Instrument cluster. • ABS module.
• The anti-lock brake system (ABS) warning indicator is always on	• Instrument cluster. • ABS module.
• The brake warning indicator is never/always on	• Circuitry. • Brake fluid level switch. • Parking brake switch. • Anti-lock brake system (ABS) module. • Instrument cluster.
• The malfunction indicator lamp (MIL) is never on	• Powertrain control module (PCM). • Instrument cluster.
• The malfunction indicator lamp (MIL) is always on	• Diagnostic trouble code (DTC) related concern(s).
• The charging system warning indicator is never on	• Charging system. • Circuitry. • Powertrain control module (PCM). • Instrument cluster.
• The charging system warning indicator is always on	• Circuitry. • Generator (charging system). • Powertrain control module (PCM). • Instrument cluster.
• The air bag indicator warning is never/always on	• Circuitry. • Restraint control module (RCM). • Instrument cluster.
• The high beam indicator is never on	• Circuitry. • Instrument cluster.
• The LH turn indicator is never on	• Circuitry. • Instrument cluster.
• The RH turn indicator is never on	• Circuitry. • Instrument cluster.

LTV0500000001334

Fig. 23 Instrument cluster gauges symptom diagnosis (Part 2 of 3)

Condition	Possible Sources
• No communication with the parking aid module	• Circuitry. • Parking aid module.
• Parking aid is inoperative	• Circuitry. • Parking aid sensor. • Parking aid speaker. • Parking aid module.
• Continuous or intermittent tone when no obstacles are present (Certain obstacles may appear "stealthy" to the system, depending on geometric shape, size and material.)	• Dirty or iced over parking aid sensor(s).
	• Parking aid sensor painted incorrectly.
	• Parking aid sensor bezel(s) or parking aid sensor(s) locked into the rear bumper incorrectly.
	• Parking aid sensors are not aligned correctly.

LTV0500000001337

Fig. 24 Warning devices symptom diagnosis (Part 2 of 2)

SPEED CONTROL SYSTEMS

NOTE: "Electrical Symbol & Wire Color Code Identification" Located In The Front Of This Manual May Be Used As An Aid When Using Wiring Diagrams Found In This Section.

NOTE: On Air Bag Equipped Models, Refer To "Air Bag System Precautions" Located In The Front Of This Manual For System Disarming & Arming Procedures.

NOTE: Refer To "Computer Relearn Procedures" Located In The Front Of This Manual When Battery Power To The Computer Has Been Interrupted.

INDEX

	Page No.
Application Chart	2-1
Component Diagnosis & Testing	2-4
Component Replacement	2-124
Actuator Cable	2-125
E-Series	2-126
Escape & Mariner	2-125
Excursion & F-Super Duty	2-125
Expedition, F-150 & Navigator	2-125
Explorer, Mountaineer & Ranger	2-125
Villager	2-126
Windstar	2-126
Brake Deactivator Switch	2-127
Control Switch	2-126
Aviator, Excursion, Expedition, E-Series, F-Super Duty, F-150, Mark LT & Navigator	2-126
Escape & Mariner	2-126
Explorer & Mountaineer	2-126
Ranger	2-126
Villager	2-126
Servo (Throttle Actuator) Assembly	2-124
Excursion & F-Super Duty	2-124
Aviator, Expedition, F-150 & Navigator	2-124
E-Series	2-124
Escape & Mariner	2-124
Explorer, Mountaineer & Ranger	2-124

	Page No.
Freestar & Monterey	2-124
Villager	2-124
Windstar	2-125
Speed Control Module/Amplifier	2-127
Vehicle Speed Sensor (VSS)	2-127
Aviator, Excursion, E-Series, Expedition, F-Super Duty, F-150 & Mark LT	2-127
Explorer, Mountaineer & Ranger	2-127
Villager	2-127
Windstar	2-127
Description	2-2
Actuator & Cable Controlled Throttle	2-2
Electronically Controlled Throttle	2-2
Diagnostic Chart Index	2-22
Precautions	2-2
Air Bag Systems	2-2
Battery Ground Cable	2-2
High-Voltage Traction Battery Systems Depowering	2-2
System Diagnosis & Testing	2-3
Accessing Diagnostic Trouble Codes	2-3
Less Scan Tool	2-3
With Scan Tool	2-3
Diagnostic Trouble Code Interpretation	2-3

	Page No.
Pinpoint Tests	2-4
Aviator	2-4
E-Series	2-4
Escape & Mariner	2-4
Excursion & F-Super Duty	2-4
Expedition & Navigator	2-4
Explorer & Mountaineer	2-4
Explorer Sport/Sport Trac	2-4
F-150 & Mark LT	2-4
Freestar & Monterey	2-4
Ranger	2-4
Villager	2-4
Windstar	2-4
Symptom Tests	2-4
Visual Inspection	2-3
Wiring Diagrams	2-3
Aviator	2-3
E-Series	2-3
Escape & Mariner	2-4
Excursion & F-Super Duty	2-4
Expedition & Navigator	2-4
Explorer & Mountaineer	2-4
Explorer Sport & Sport Trac	2-4
F-150 & Mark LT	2-4
Freestar & Monterey	2-4
Ranger	2-4
Villager	2-4
Windstar	2-4

APPLICATION CHART

Model	Year	Transfer Case
Aviator	2003–05	Actuator & Cable Controlled Throttle
Escape	2002–06	Actuator & Cable Controlled Throttle
Escape Hybrid	2005–06	Electronically Controlled Throttle
E-Series	2002–03	Actuator & Cable Controlled Throttle
	2004–06	Electronically Controlled Throttle
Excursion	2002–05	Actuator & Cable Controlled Throttle
Expedition	2002–03	Actuator & Cable Controlled Throttle
	2004–06	Electronically Controlled Throttle
Explorer	2002–03	Actuator & Cable Controlled Throttle
	2004–06	Electronically Controlled Throttle
Explorer Sport	2002–03	Actuator & Cable Controlled Throttle
Explorer Sport Trac	2002–05	Actuator & Cable Controlled Throttle
Freestar	2004–06	Actuator & Cable Controlled Throttle

Continued

APPLICATION CHART—Continued

Model	Year	Transfer Case
F-Super Duty	2002–03	Actuator & Cable Controlled Throttle
	2004–06	Electronically Controlled Throttle
F-150	2002–03	Actuator & Cable Controlled Throttle
	2004–06	Electronically Controlled Throttle
Mariner	2005–06	Actuator & Cable Controlled Throttle
Mariner Hybrid	2005–06	Electronically Controlled Throttle
Mark LT	2006	Electronically Controlled Throttle
Monterey	2004–05	Actuator & Cable Controlled Throttle
Mountaineer	2002–03	Actuator & Cable Controlled Throttle
	2004–06	Electronically Controlled Throttle
Navigator	2002–03	Actuator & Cable Controlled Throttle
	2004–06	Electronically Controlled Throttle
Ranger	2002–06	Actuator & Cable Controlled Throttle

DESCRIPTION

Actuator & Cable Controlled Throttle

The speed control system is designed to automatically maintain vehicle speed at any driver-selected speed above approximately 30 mph. The inputs to the speed control actuator for the speed control system consist of the speed control deactivator switch, smart junction box (SJB), speed control switches, vehicle speed from the anti-lock brake system (ABS) module over the SCP communication network, throttle position status over the SCP communication network, brake pedal position (BPP) switch status over the SCP communication network, PRNDL status over the SCP communications network and a clutch switch for models equipped with manual transmissions. A redundant brake deactivator, the speed control deactivator switch, is provided as an additional safety feature. The speed signal is generated by the Vehicle Speed Sensor (VSS). The electronic actuator is mounted in the engine compartment and is connected to the throttle linkage with an actuator cable. The VSS is mounted on the transaxle/transmission.

To operate the speed control system, the engine must be running and the vehicle speed must exceed 30 mph. When the On–Off switch is actuated, the system is ready to accept a set speed signal. With the On switch engaged and vehicle speed at least 30 mph and stable, depress the Set-Acc button. This speed will be maintained until the brake pedal is depressed, the system is turned off or a new speed has been set.

Electronically Controlled Throttle

The speed control system is controlled by the powertrain control module (PCM). The speed control system is designed to maintain a selected vehicle speed between 30-124 mph. The speed control system is controlled by the steering wheel mounted switches (ON, OFF, SET+, SET- and RE-SUME), the stop lamp switch, the clutch pedal speed control deactivator switch (manual transaxle), and the speed control deactivator switch (part of the stop lamp switch). The steering wheel mounted switches are hard-wired to the PCM through the clockspring.

Tapping the SET+ or the SET- switch while in the set mode respectively, increases or decreases the maintained vehicle speed by 1 mph per tap. If the respective button is pressed and held, the vehicle speed continues to accelerate or decelerate until the button is released. Pressing and releasing the OFF switch, or switching the ignition switch to the OFF position, turns the speed control system off. Applying the brake pedal puts the speed control system into the STANDBY mode. Pressing the RESUME button, when the speed control system is in the STANDBY mode causes the vehicle to accelerate to the last set speed.

Whenever the speed control system is engaged and active, a speed control icon on the instrument cluster is illuminated. The speed control system throttle position is completely controlled by the PCM through the electronically controlled throttle body. Speed control electronics are contained entirely within the PCM.

When the speed control system is active, the PCM corrects for deviations in the actual vehicle speed by proportionally moving the electronically controlled throttle plate. The PCM modulates the throttle to minimize error between the actual vehicle speed and the desired speed.

PRECAUTIONS

Air Bag Systems

Refer to "Air Bag System Precautions" in the front of this manual for system disarming and arming procedures.

Battery Ground Cable

Prior to service, disconnect battery ground cable and isolate as required.

High-Voltage Traction Battery Systems Depowering

The nominal high voltage traction battery (HVTB) voltage is 330 volts DC. The buffer zone must be set up. The high voltage traction battery and charging system contains high voltage components and wiring. High voltage cables and wiring are orange in color. High voltage insulated safety gloves and a face shield must be worn when carrying out any diagnostics on this vehicle. Failure to follow these instructions may result in severe personal injury or death.

Before carrying out any removal and installation procedures of the high voltage traction battery system, the high voltage traction battery must be depowered. The high voltage insulated safety gloves that are to be worn while working on the high voltage system should be of the appropriate safety and protection rating for use on the high voltage system. They must be inspected before use and must always be worn in conjunction with the leather outer glove. Any hole in the rubber insulating glove is a potential entry point for high voltage. Failure to follow these instructions may result in severe personal injury or death.

High voltage insulated safety gloves and a face shield must be worn when working with high voltage cables. The ignition switch must be OFF for a minimum of 5 minutes before removing high voltage cables. The buffer zone is required only when working with the high voltage system. Failure to follow these instructions may result in severe personal injury or death.

1. **Buffer zone is required only when working with high voltage system.** Set up buffer zone around vehicle as follows:
   a. Position vehicle in repair bay.
   b. Position four orange cones around corners of vehicle to mark off a 3 foot perimeter around vehicle, **Fig. 1.**

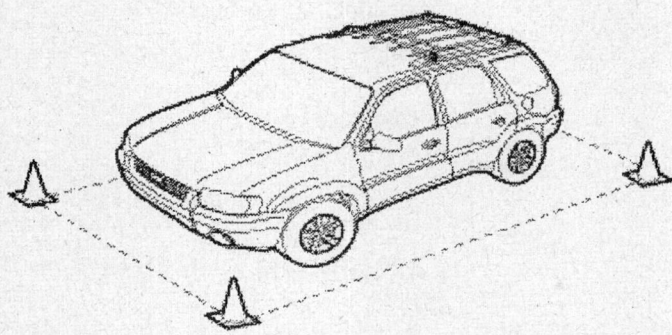

LTV0500000000262

Fig. 1 Setting up a buffer zone

   c. Do not allow any unauthorized personnel into buffer zone during repairs involving high voltage system.
   d. Only personnel trained for repair on high voltage system are to be permitted in buffer zone.
2. Rotate service disconnect plug from lock position to unlock position.
3. Remove service disconnect plug, then place in servicing shipping position. **If service disconnect plug is left out and placed on bench or toolbox, dirt or other contaminants may enter HVTB which can cause damage.**
4. Insert service disconnect plug into servicing shipping position, this will disconnects HVTB.
5. Reverse procedure to connect.

SYSTEM DIAGNOSIS & TESTING

Visual Inspection

Visual inspection is an important part of diagnosis. The inspection is performed to locate obvious fault conditions. During the visual inspection, inspect items for abnormal conditions. Inspect for bare, broken or disconnected wires. Inspect the servo throttle actuator function and free operation of throttle linkage.

If the amber "Check Anti-Lock Brake" indicator remains lit when the ignition is in the Run position, service the rear anti-lock brakes as outlined under "Anti-Lock Brakes" before continuing the speed control diagnosis.

Accessing Diagnostic Trouble Codes

WITH SCAN TOOL

Connect a suitably programmed scan tool and Vehicle Communication Module (VCM) with appropriate adapters, or equivalents, to the Data Link Connector (DCL) located in the passenger compartment beneath the instrument panel. Follow tool manufacturer's instructions for accessing speed control Diagnostic Trouble Codes (DTC).

LESS SCAN TOOL

This test is a Key On Engine Off (KOEO) test. This test should only be performed

Code	Description
B1318	Low Ignition Voltage During Speed Control Operation
B1342	ECU Faulty
C1109	Throttle Did Not Return To Idle After Self-Test
C1126	Command Switch Stuck For 2 Minutes Or Longer
C1127	Deactivator Switch Stuck Open
C1179	Excessive Cable Slack In Speed Control Cable
P0500	Vehicle Speed Error
P0579	Cruise Control Multi-Function Input A Circuit Range/Performance
P0581	Cruise Control Multi-Function Circuit High
P0703	Brake Switch Input Fault
P0720	Output Shaft Speed Sensor
P0721	Output Shaft Speed Sensor Range Performance
P0722	Output Shaft Speed Sensor No Signal
P0833	Clutch Pedal Switch B Circuit
P1500	Vehicle Speed Sensor (VSS) Intermittent
P1501	Vehicle Speed Sensor (VSS) Out Of Self-Test Range
P1565	Speed Control Command Switches High/Out Of Range
P1566	Speed Control Command Switches Low/Out Of Range
P1567	NGSC Drive Fault Output Circuit
P1568	NGSC Actuator Self-Test Failure Unable To Hold Speed
P1572	Brake On/Off Failure
P1703	Brake On/Off Failure
U1027	Missing Or Invalid Throttle Message
U1041	Missing Or Invalid Vehicle Speed Message
U1051	Missing Or Invalid Brake Message
U1059	Missing Or Invalid PRNDL Message

Fig. 2 Diagnostic trouble code interpretation

with vehicle in Park position and parking brake fully applied.
1. Enter self test diagnostics by pressing speed control off switch while turning ignition to On position without starting engine. **If On switch is not pressed within five seconds after entering diagnostic mode, module times out and procedure must be started over.**
2. Speed control indicator lamp will flash once to indicate speed control module entered diagnostic mode.
3. Five additional flashes indicate a faulty speed control servo.
4. Press remaining switches in order from On, RESUME (RSM), COAST (CST) and SET/ACCEL, noting the following:
   a. Speed control indicator lamp will flash as each switch is pressed.
   b. Press each switch in sequence after light goes out of previous switch.
5. Indicator lamp will flash to indicate a pass or fail after all five speed control switches complete sequence:
   a. One flash, test passed.
   b. Two flashes, Brake Pedal Position (BPP), Clutch Pedal Position (CPP), or Brake On/Off (BOO) switch is faulty, circuit is faulty, clutch pedal is applied or brake pedal is applied.
   c. Three flashes, brake deactivation

switch is open or circuit is faulty.
   d. Four flashes, vehicle speed sensor is out of range or disconnected.
6. After static test has passed, speed control servo will perform a dynamic test as follows:
   a. Speed control servo will automatically actuate throttle lever from 1 MM to 10 MM of travel from idle position.
   b. Inspect throttle movement for any binding or sticking of actuator.
   c. Ensure actuator cable and throttle lever are connected properly.
   d. Ensure throttle returns back to idle position.

Diagnostic Trouble Code Interpretation

Refer to **Fig. 2** for diagnostic trouble code interpretation.

Wiring Diagrams

AVIATOR

Refer to **Figs. 3** for wiring diagram.

E-SERIES

Refer to **Figs. 4 through 6** for wiring diagrams.

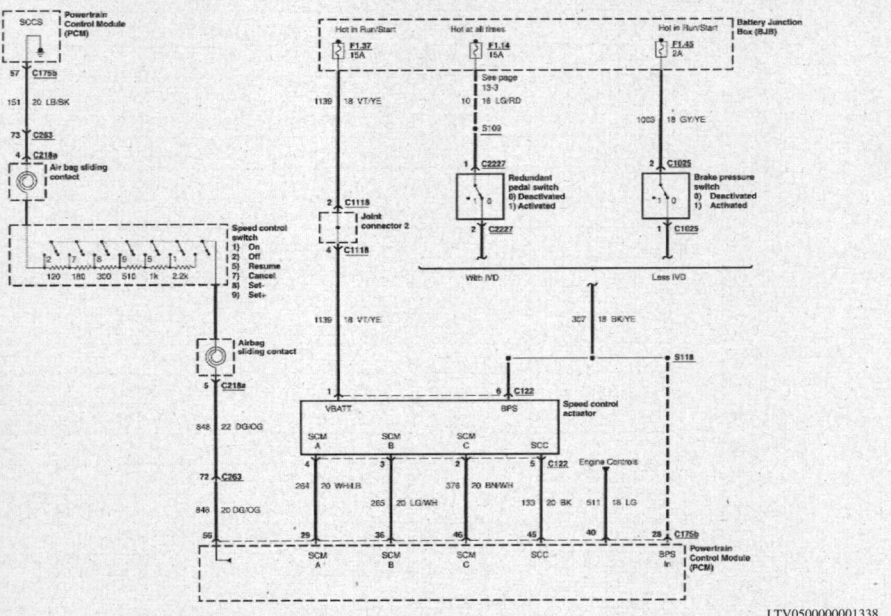

Fig. 3 Speed control wiring diagram. Aviator

ESCAPE & MARINER

Refer to **Figs. 7 through 9** for wiring diagrams.

EXCURSION & F-SUPER DUTY

Refer to **Figs. 10 through 15** for wiring diagrams.

EXPEDITION & NAVIGATOR

Refer to **Figs. 16 through 19** for wiring diagrams.

EXPLORER & MOUNTAINEER

Refer to **Figs. 20 and 21** for wiring diagrams.

EXPLORER SPORT & SPORT TRAC

Refer to **Figs. 22 and 23** for wiring diagrams.

FREESTAR & MONTEREY

Refer to **Figs. 24** for wiring diagram.

F-150 & MARK LT

Refer to **Figs. 25 and 26** for wiring diagrams.

RANGER

Refer to **Figs. 27 and 28** for wiring diagrams.

VILLAGER

Refer to **Figs. 29** for wiring diagram.

WINDSTAR

Refer to **Figs. 30** for wiring diagram.

Symptom Tests

Refer to **Figs. 31 through 49** for symptom tests.

Pinpoint Tests

AVIATOR

Refer to **Figs. 50 through 56** for diagnostic tests.

E-SERIES

Refer to **Figs. 57 through 66** for diagnostic tests.

ESCAPE & MARINER

Refer to **Figs. 67 through 85** for diagnostic tests.

EXPEDITION & NAVIGATOR

Refer to **Figs. 86 through 95** for diagnostic tests.

EXCURSION & F-SUPER DUTY

Refer to **Figs. 96 through 113** for diagnostic tests.

EXPLORER & MOUNTAINEER

Refer to **Figs. 114 through 117** for diagnostic tests.

EXPLORER SPORT/SPORT TRAC

Refer to **Figs. 118 through 134** for diagnostic tests.

FREESTAR & MONTEREY

Refer to **Figs. 135 through 147** for diagnostic tests.

F-150 & MARK LT

Refer to **Figs. 148 through 155** for diagnostic tests.

RANGER

Refer to **Figs. 156 through 173** for diagnostic tests.

VILLAGER

Refer to **Figs. 174 through 178** for diagnostic tests.

WINDSTAR

Refer to **Figs. 179 through 190** for diagnostic tests.

COMPONENT DIAGNOSIS & TESTING

Refer to "System Diagnosis & Testing" for component testing procedures.

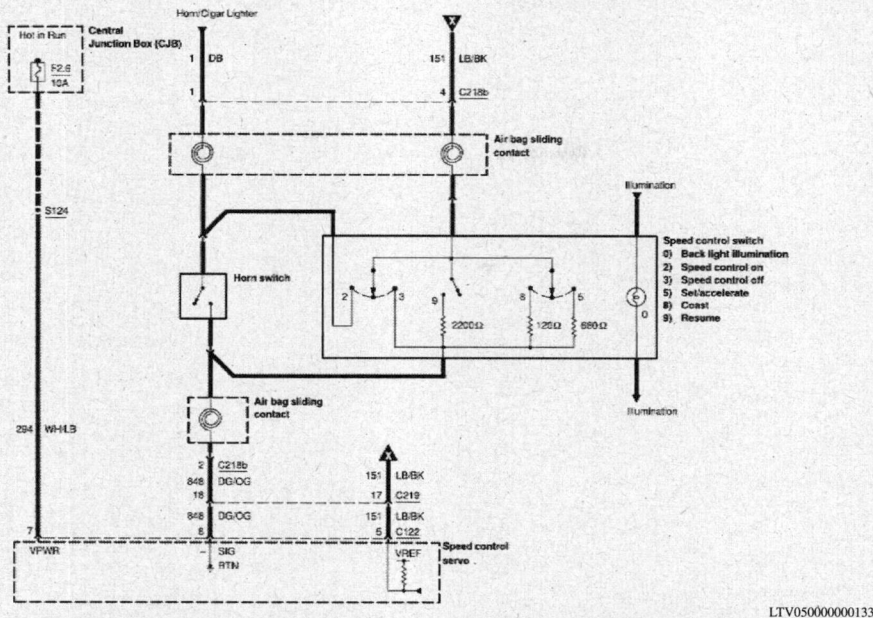

Fig. 4   Speed control wiring diagram (Part 1 of 2). 2002–04 E-Series w/gasoline engine

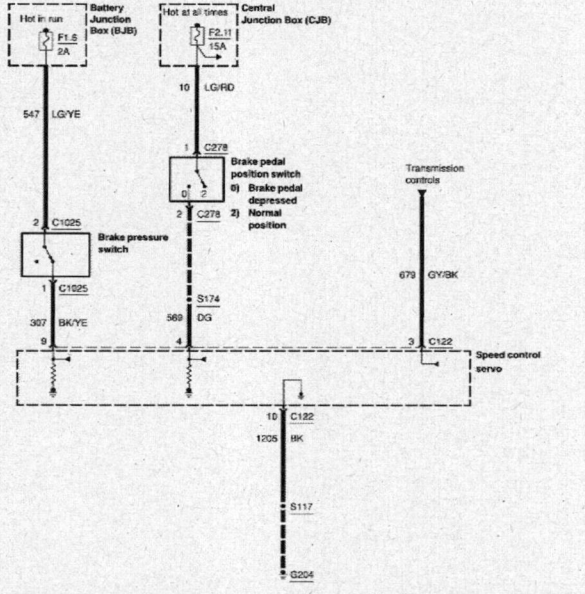

Fig. 4   Speed control wiring diagram (Part 2 of 2). 2002–04 E-Series w/gasoline engine

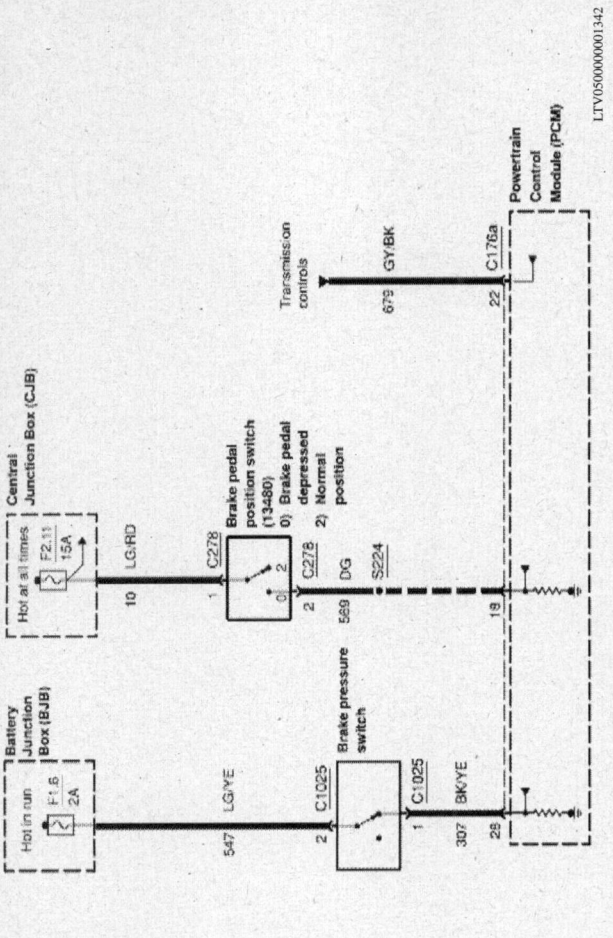

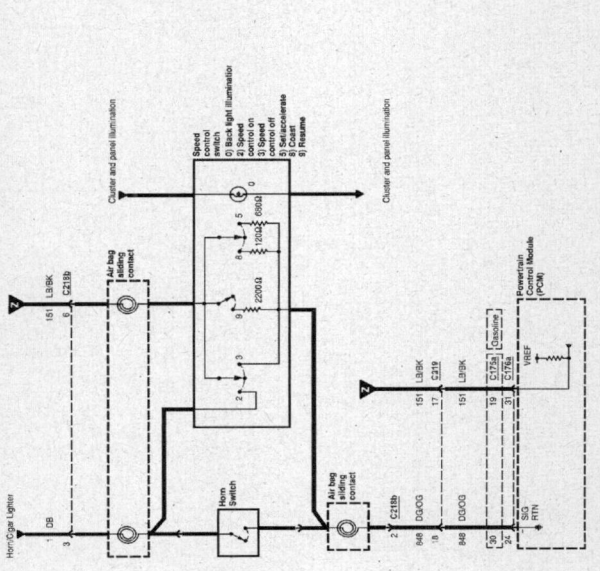

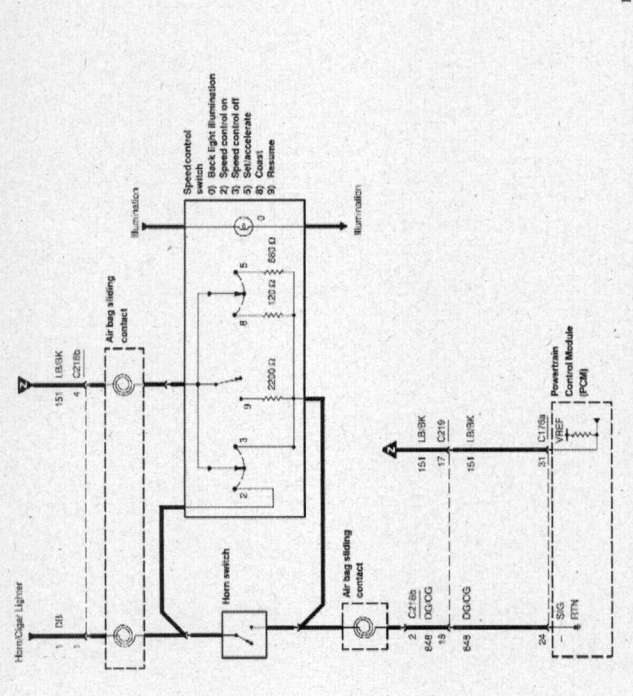

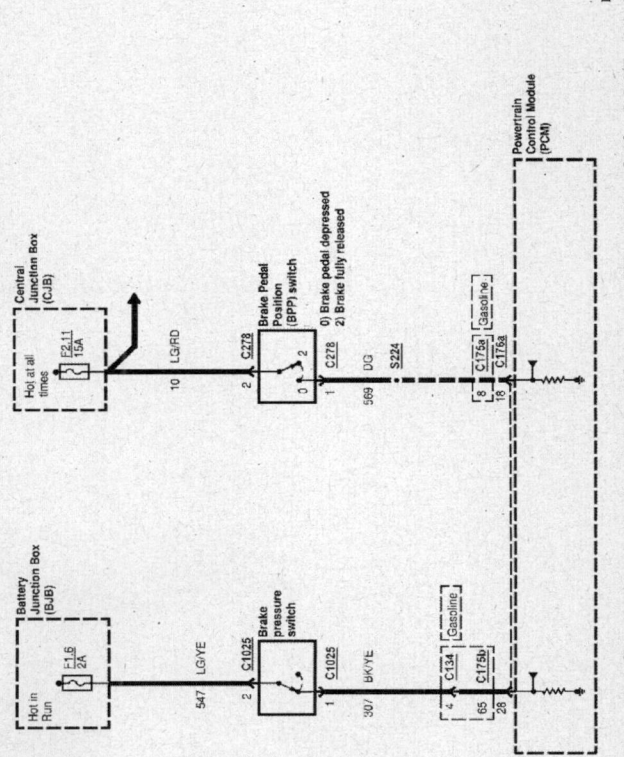

Fig. 5 Speed control wiring diagram (Part 2 of 2). 2002–04 E-Series w/diesel engine

Fig. 6 Speed control wiring diagram (Part 2 of 2). 2005–06 E-Series

Fig. 5 Speed control wiring diagram (Part 1 of 2). 2002–04 E-Series w/diesel engine

Fig. 6 Speed control wiring diagram (Part 1 of 2). 2005–06 E-Series

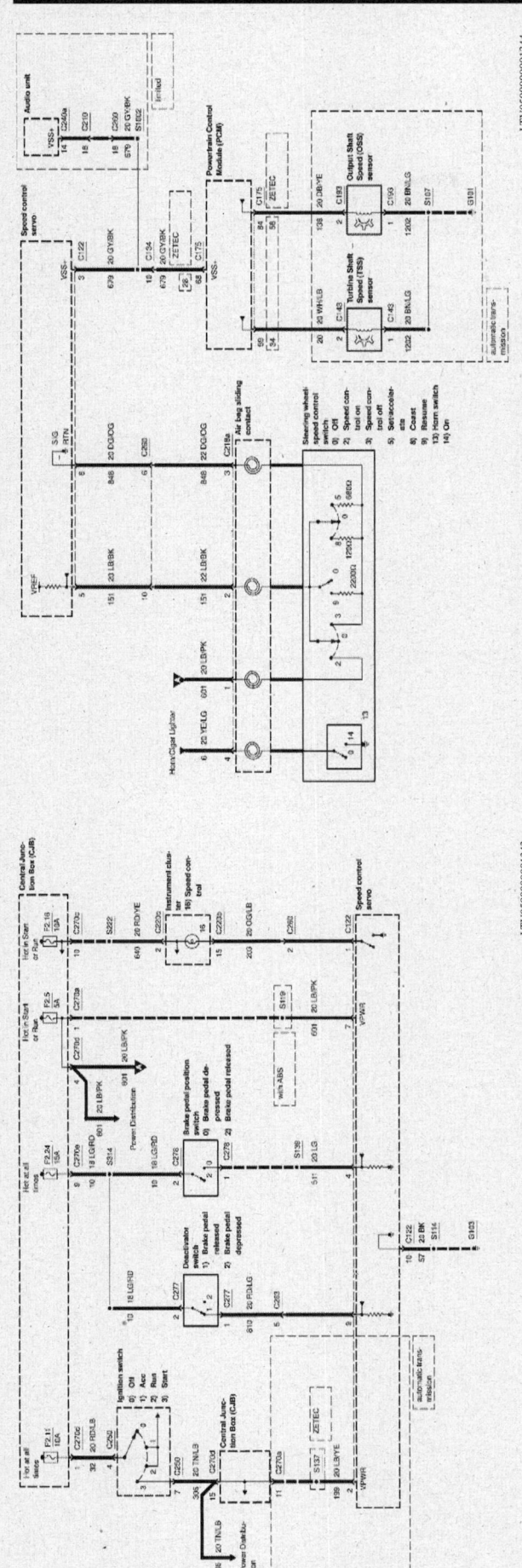

Fig. 7 Speed control wiring diagram (Part 2 of 3). 2002–04 Escape

Fig. 7 Speed control wiring diagram (Part 1 of 3). 2002–04 Escape

Fig. 8 Speed control wiring diagram (Part 1 of 3). 2005–06 Escape & Mariner

Fig. 7 Speed control wiring diagram (Part 3 of 3). 2002–04 Escape

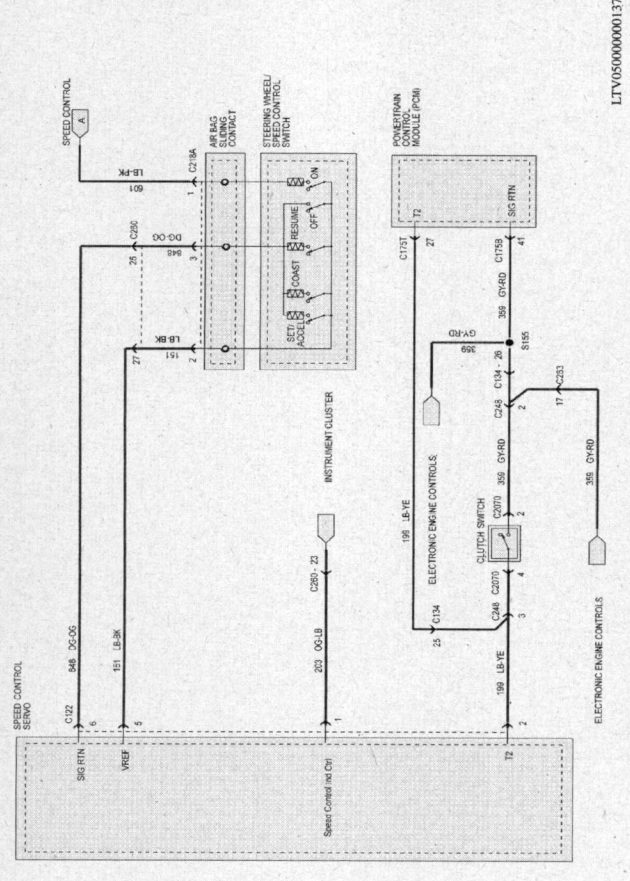

Fig. 8   Speed control wiring diagram (Part 3 of 3). 2005–06 Escape & Mariner

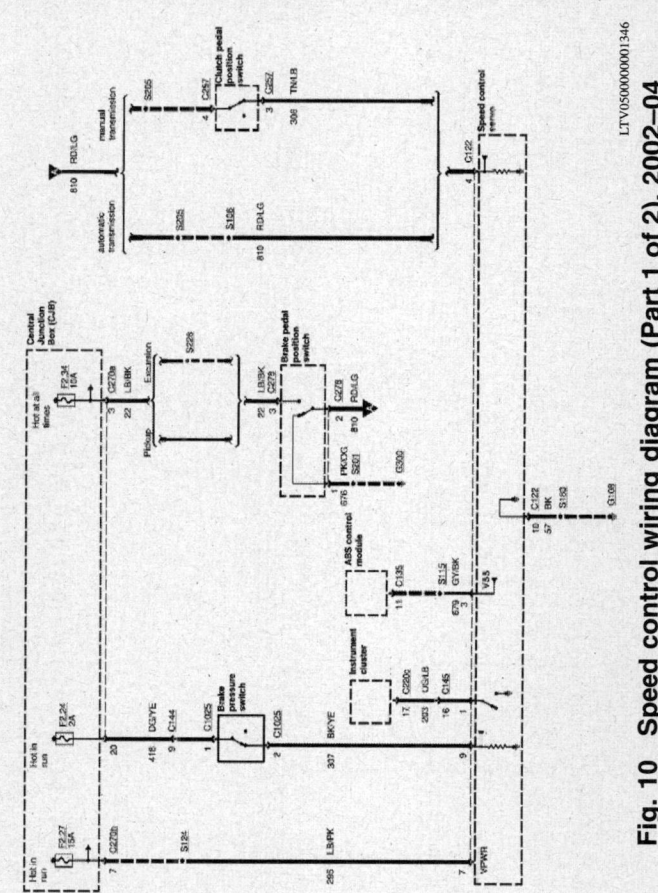

Fig. 10   Speed control wiring diagram (Part 1 of 2). 2002–04 Excursion & F-Super Duty w/gasoline engine

Fig. 8   Speed control wiring diagram (Part 2 of 3). 2005–06 Escape & Mariner

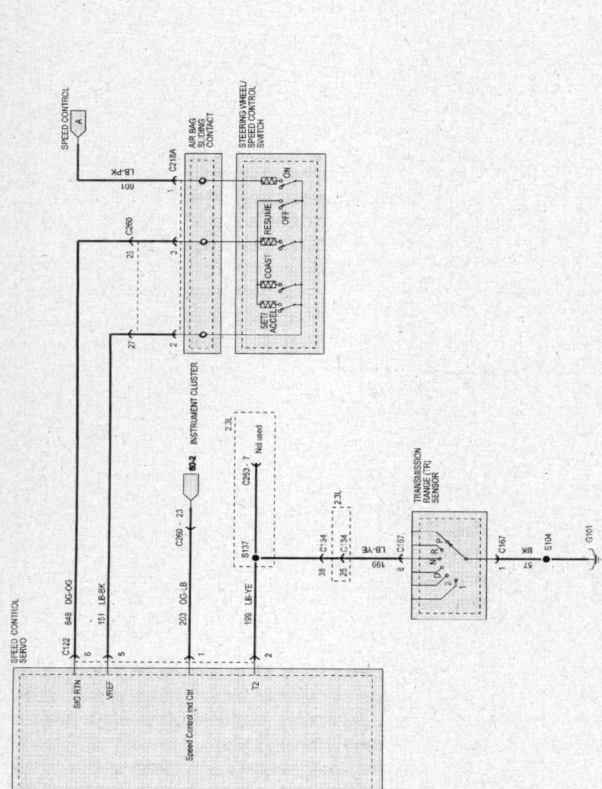

Fig. 9   Speed control wiring diagram. Escape & Mariner Hybrid

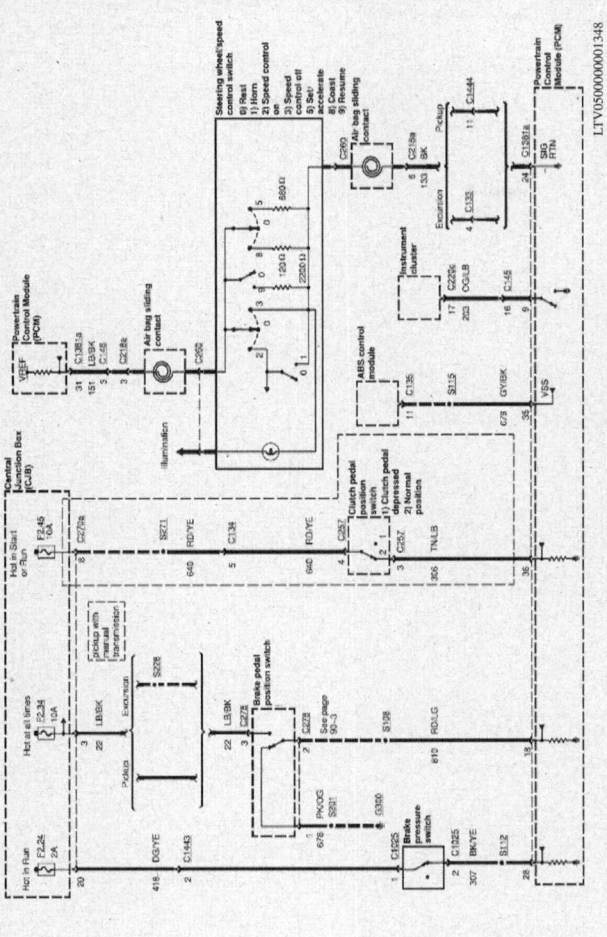

Fig. 11 Speed control wiring diagram. 2002–04 Excursion & Super Duty w/diesel engine

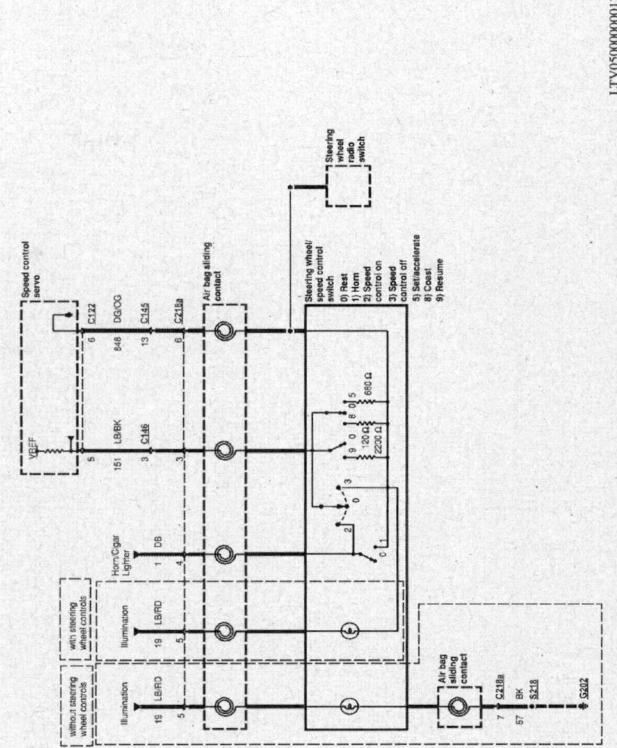

Fig. 12 Speed control wiring diagram (Part 2 of 2). 2005 Excursion w/gasoline engine

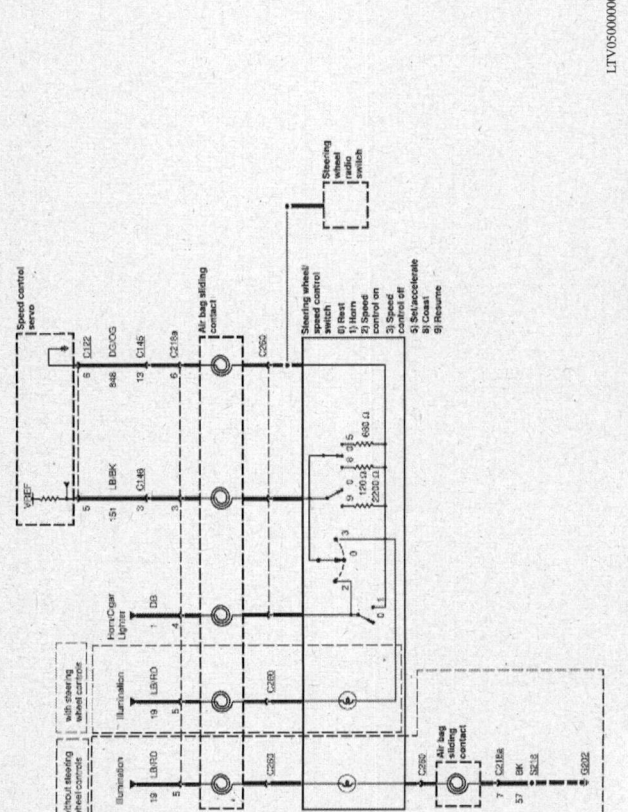

Fig. 10 Speed control wiring diagram (Part 2 of 2). 2002–04 Excursion & Super Duty w/gasoline engine

Fig. 12 Speed control wiring diagram (Part 1 of 2). 2005 Excursion w/gasoline engine

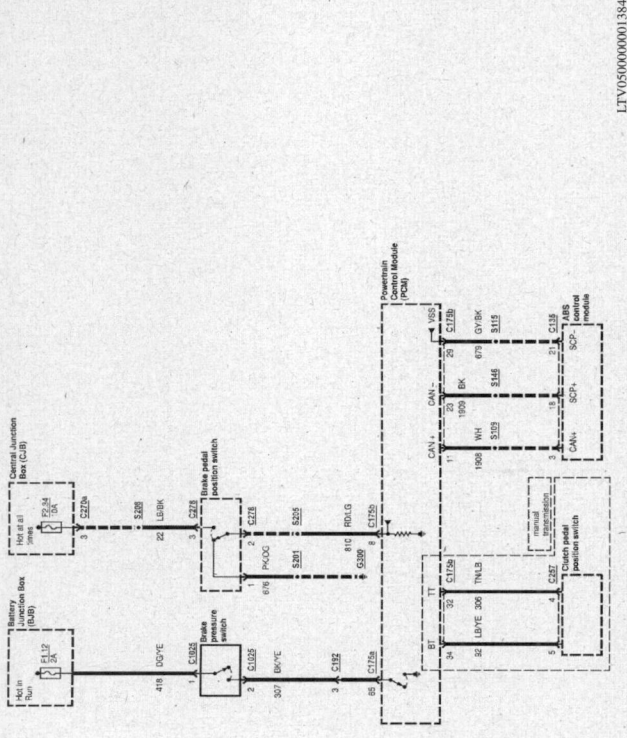

Fig. 14 Speed control wiring diagram (Part 1 of 2). 2005–06 F-Super Duty w/gasoline engine

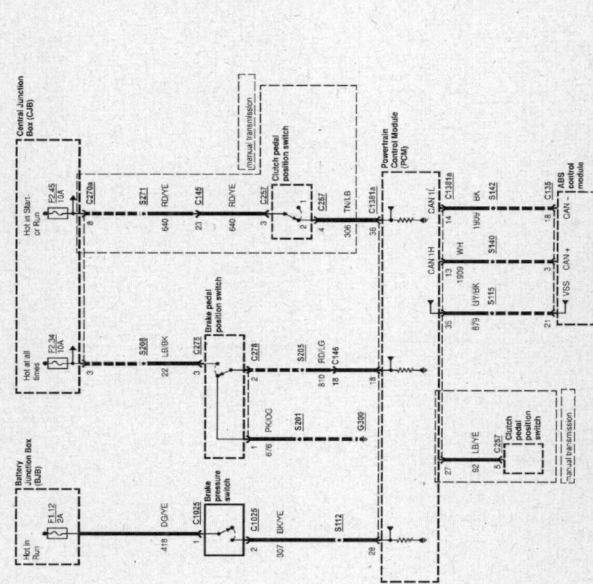

Fig. 15 Speed control wiring diagram (Part 1 of 2). 2005–06 F-Super Duty w/diesel engine

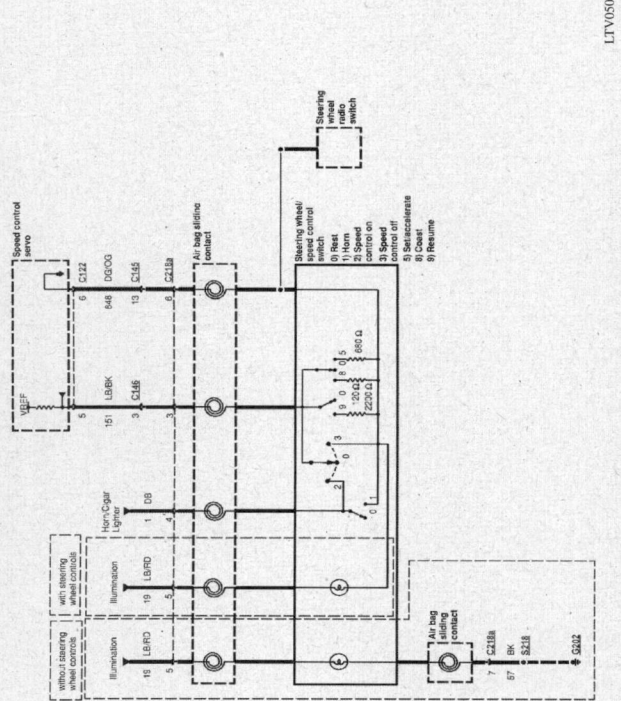

Fig. 13 Speed control wiring diagram. 2005 Excursion w/diesel engine

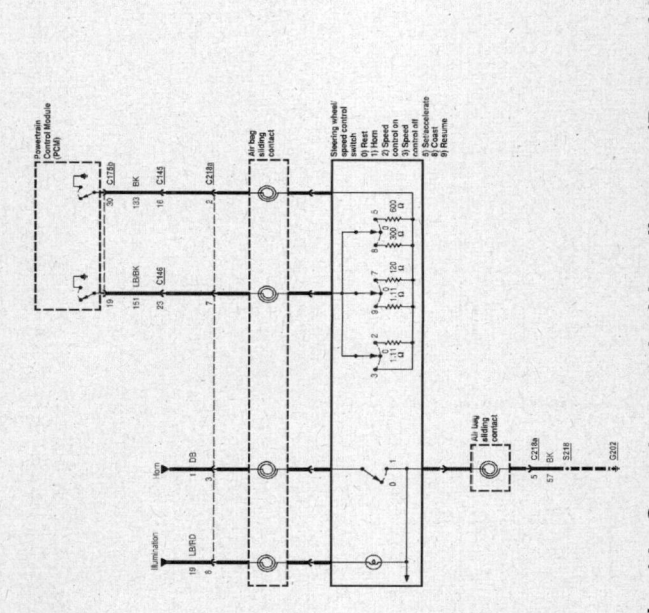

Fig. 14 Speed control wiring diagram (Part 2 of 2). 2005–06 F-Super Duty w/gasoline engine

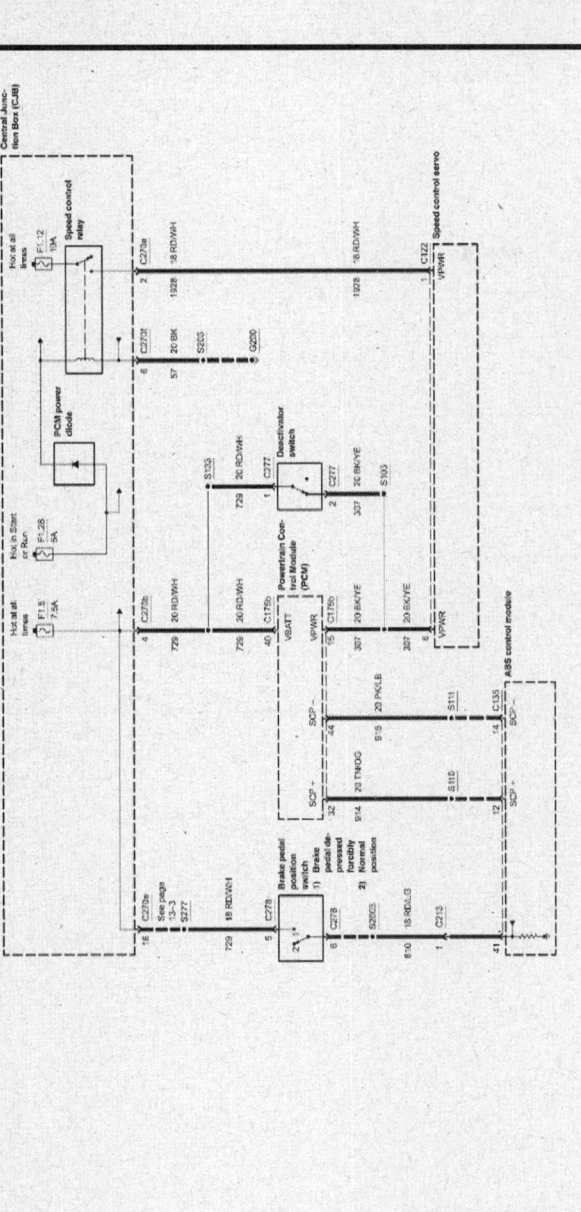

Fig. 16 Speed control wiring diagram (Part 1 of 2).
2002–04 Expedition & Navigator except Eddie Baurer edition

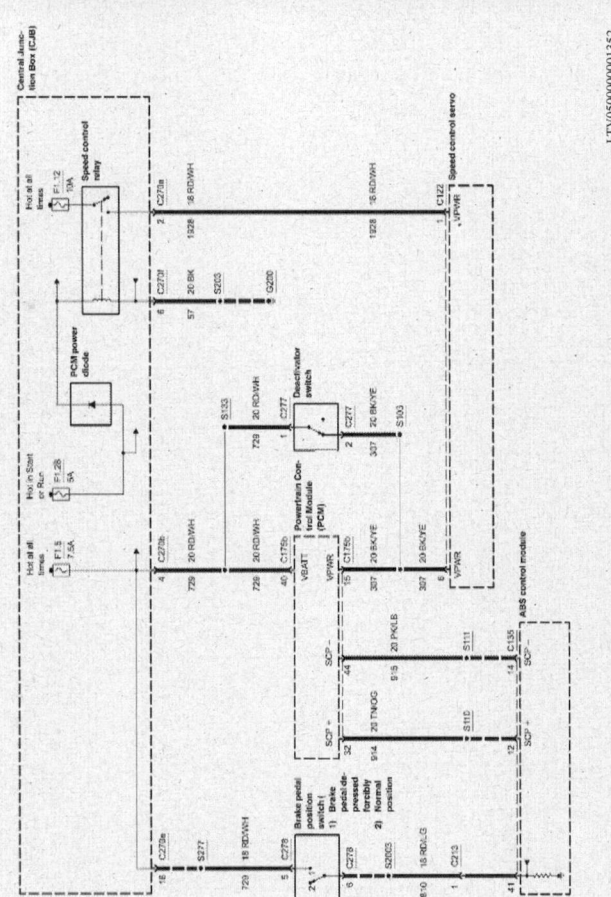

Fig. 17 Speed control wiring diagram (Part 1 of 2).
2002–04 Expedition & Navigator Eddie Baurer edition

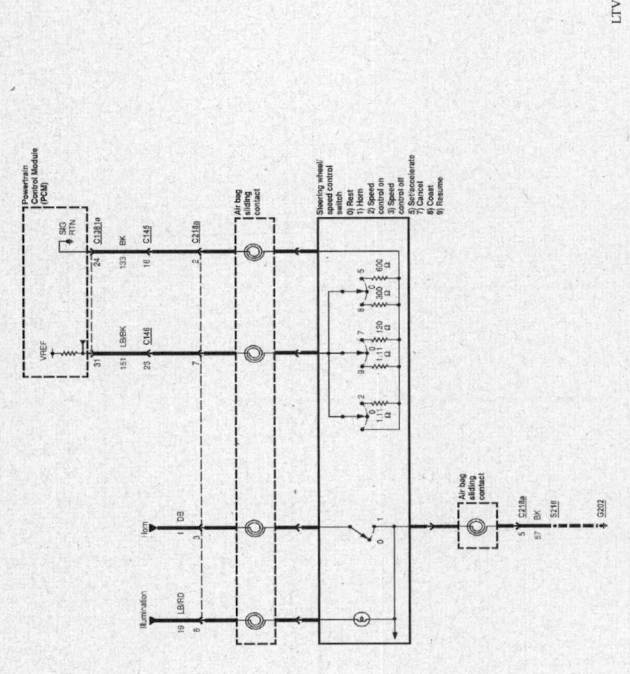

Fig. 15 Speed control wiring diagram (Part 2 of 2).
2005–06 F-Super Duty w/diesel engine

Fig. 16 Speed control wiring diagram (Part 2 of 2).
2002–04 Expedition & Navigator except Eddie Baurer edition

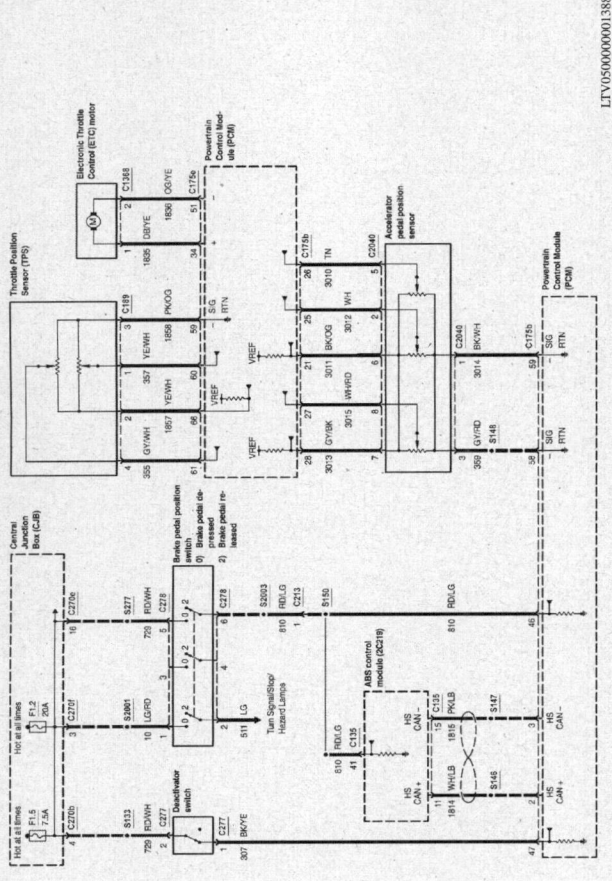

Fig. 18 Speed control wiring diagram (Part 1 of 2). 2005–06 Expedition & Navigator except Eddie Baurer edition

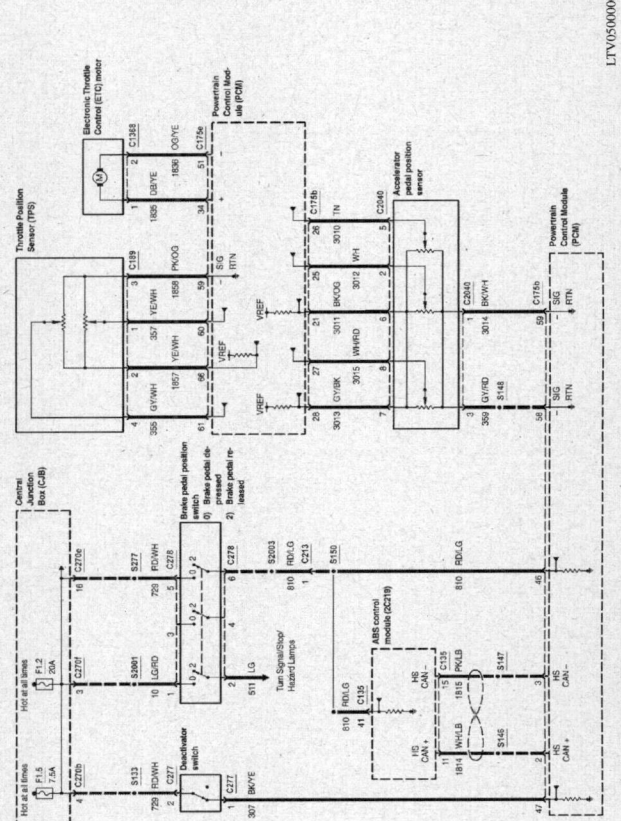

Fig. 19 Speed control wiring diagram (Part 1 of 2). 2005–06 Expedition & Navigator Eddie Baurer edition

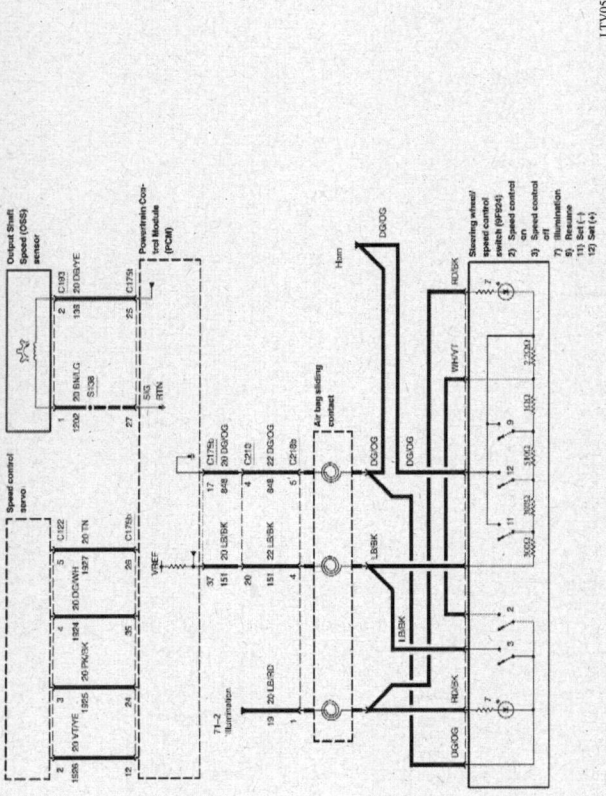

Fig. 17 Speed control wiring diagram (Part 2 of 2). 2002–04 Expedition & Navigator Eddie Baurer edition

Fig. 18 Speed control wiring diagram (Part 2 of 2). 2005–06 Expedition & Navigator except Eddie Baurer edition

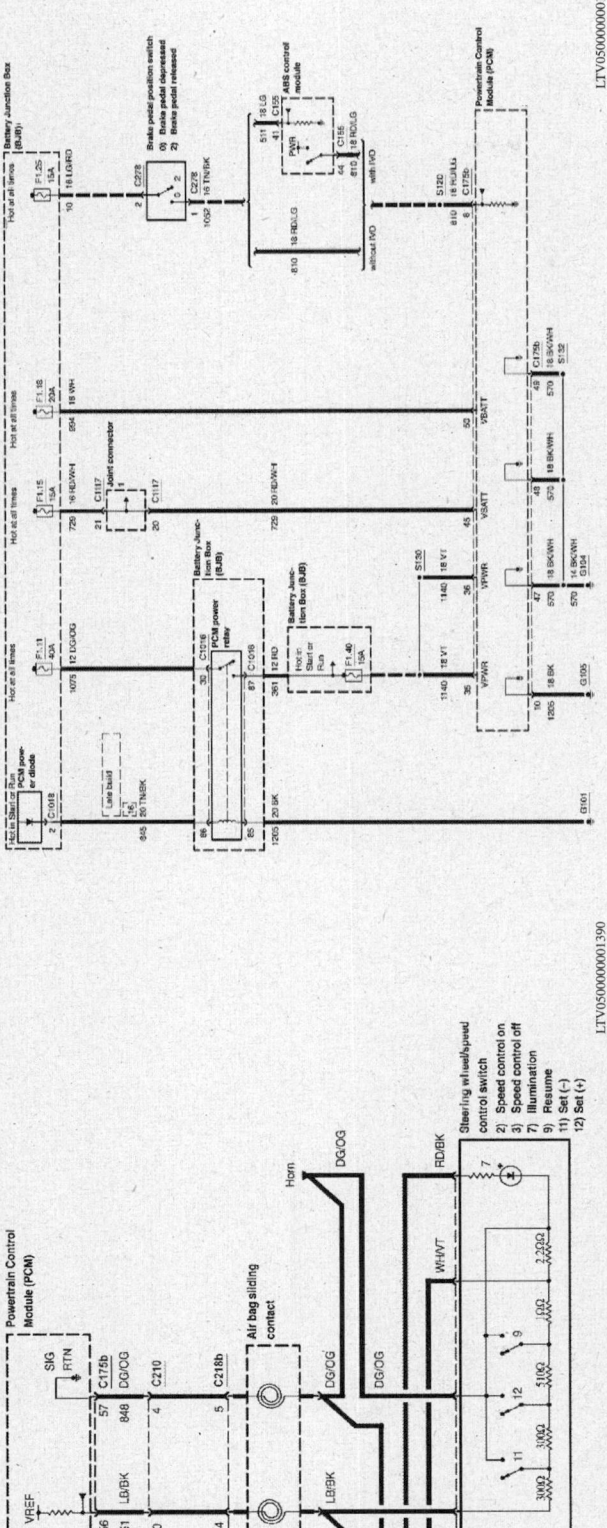

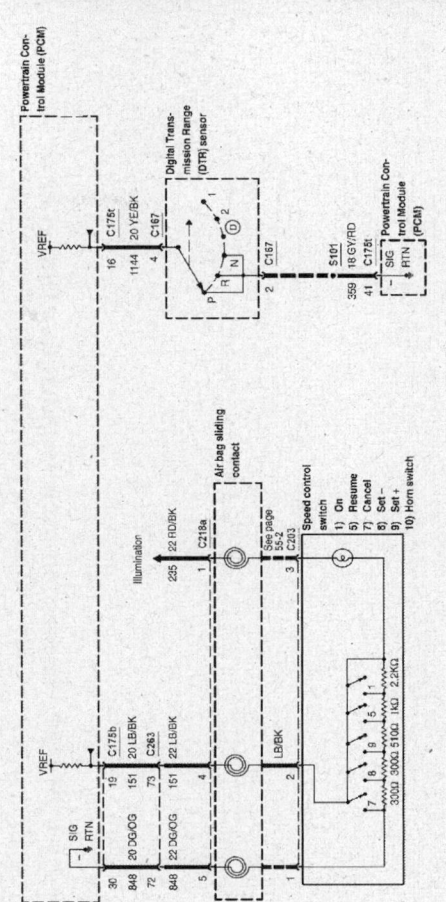

Fig. 20   Speed control wiring diagram (Part 1 of 4).
2002–04 Explorer & Mountaineer

Fig. 20   Speed control wiring diagram (Part 3 of 4).
2002–04 Explorer & Mountaineer

Fig. 19   Speed control wiring diagram (Part 2 of 2).
2005–06 Expedition & Navigator Eddie Bauer edition

Fig. 20   Speed control wiring diagram (Part 2 of 4).
2002–04 Explorer & Mountaineer

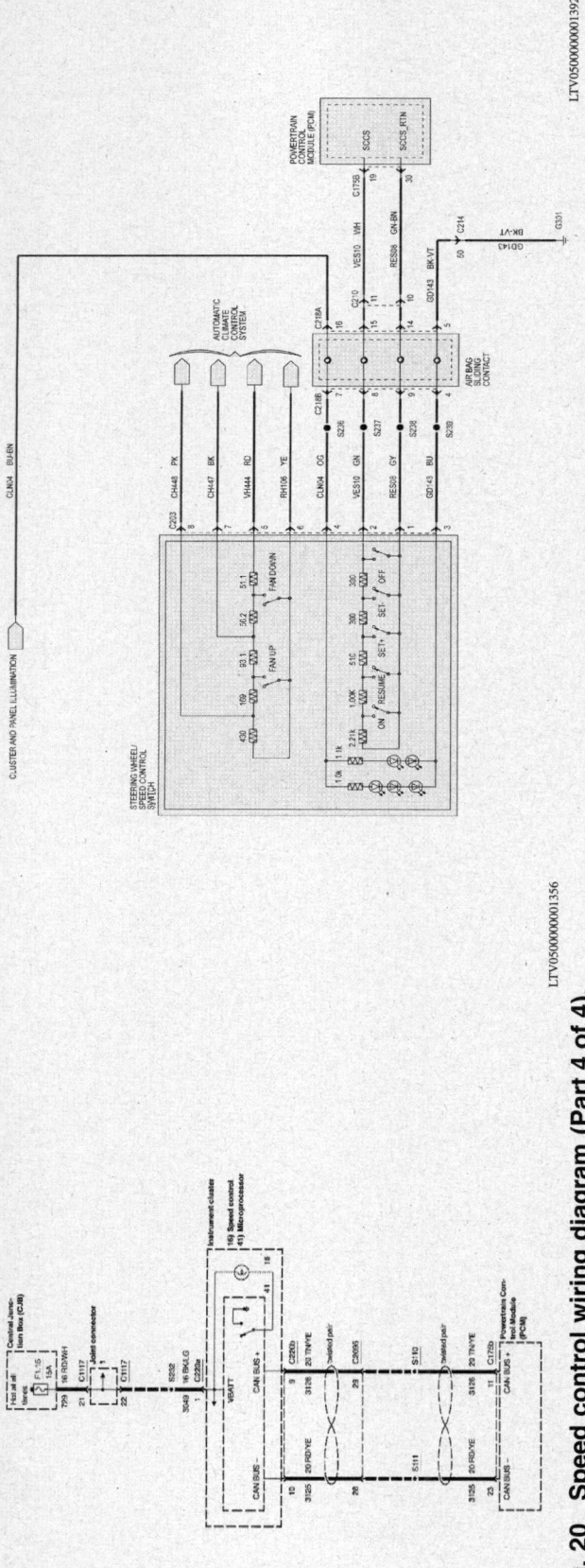

Fig. 21 Speed control wiring diagram (Part 1 of 3). 2005–06 Explorer & Mountaineer

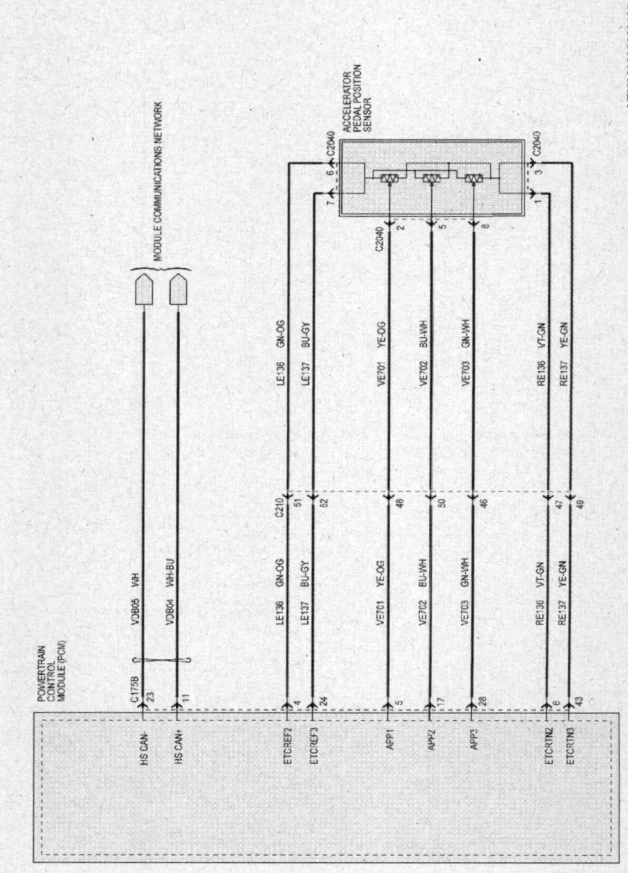

Fig. 21 Speed control wiring diagram (Part 3 of 3). 2005–06 Explorer & Mountaineer

Fig. 20 Speed control wiring diagram (Part 4 of 4). 2002–04 Explorer & Mountaineer

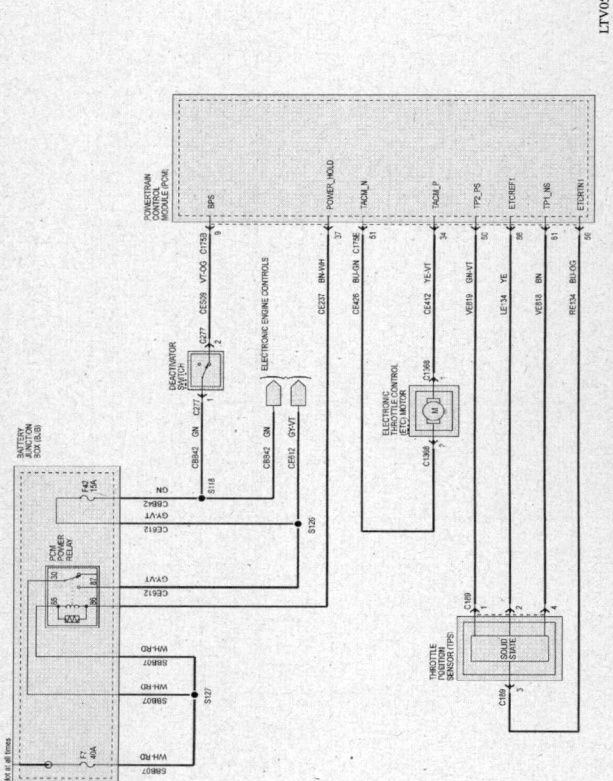

Fig. 21 Speed control wiring diagram (Part 2 of 3). 2005–06 Explorer & Mountaineer

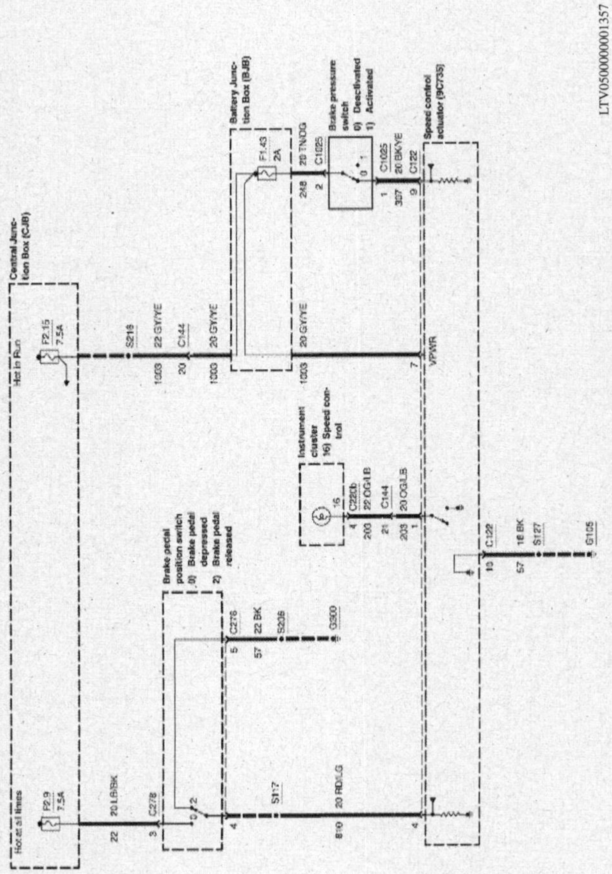

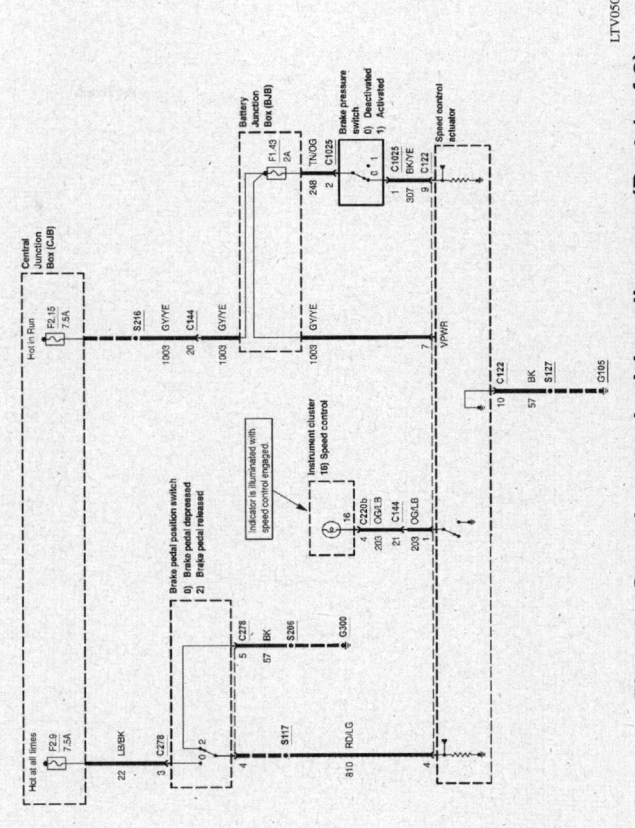

LTV0500000001357

Fig. 22 Speed control wiring diagram (Part 1 of 3). 2002–03 Explorer Sport & Sport Trac

LTV0500000001358

Fig. 22 Speed control wiring diagram (Part 2 of 3). 2002–03 Explorer Sport & Sport Trac

LTV0500000001359

Fig. 22 Speed control wiring diagram (Part 3 of 3). 2002–03 Explorer Sport & Sport Trac

LTV0500000001395

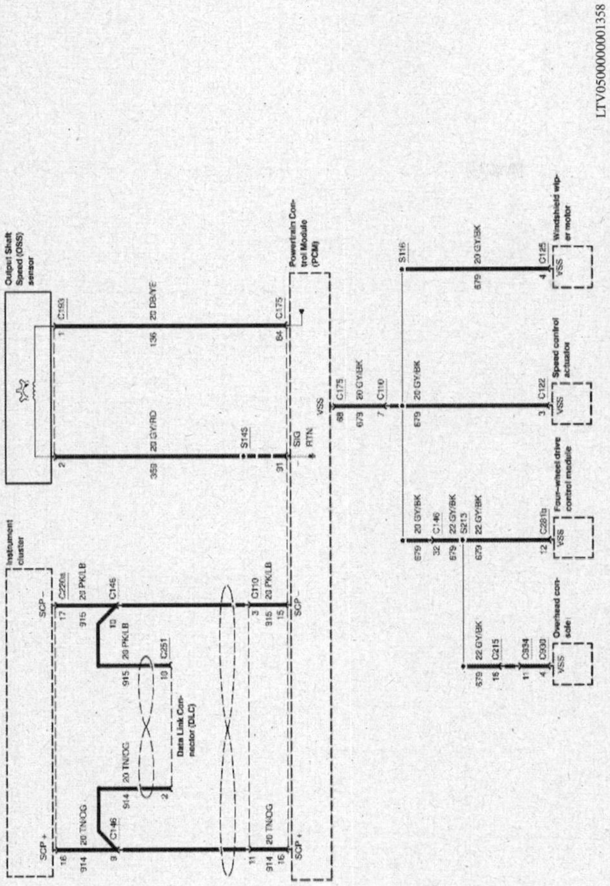

Fig. 23 Speed control wiring diagram (Part 1 of 3). 2004–05 Explorer Sport Trac

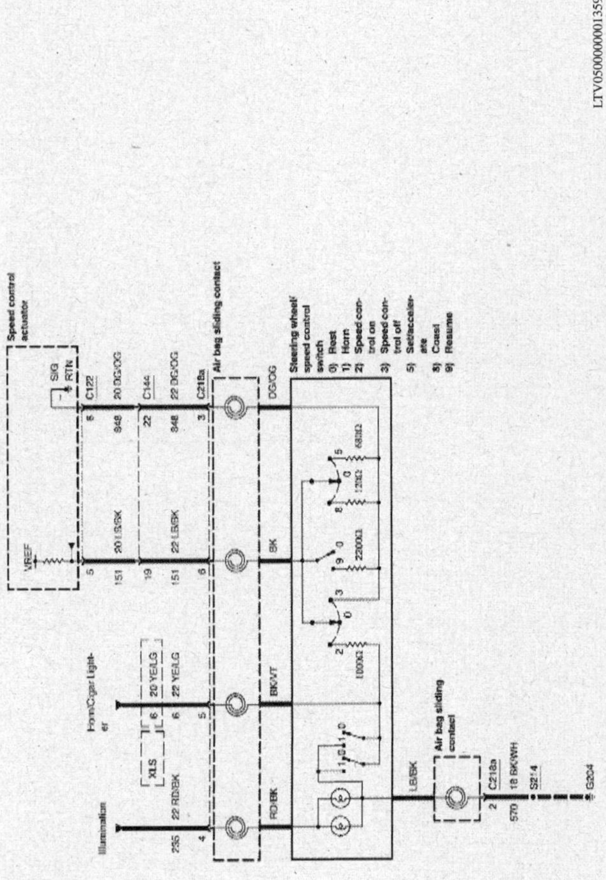

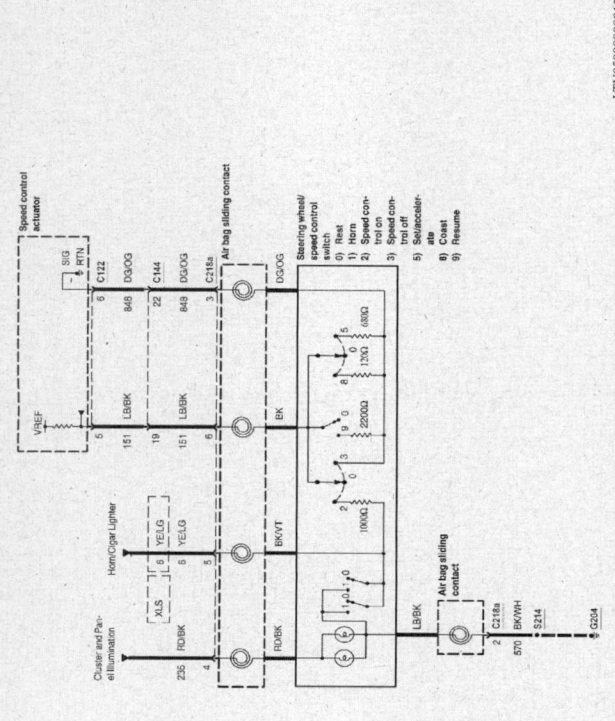

Fig. 23 Speed control wiring diagram (Part 3 of 3). 2004–05 Explorer Sport Trac

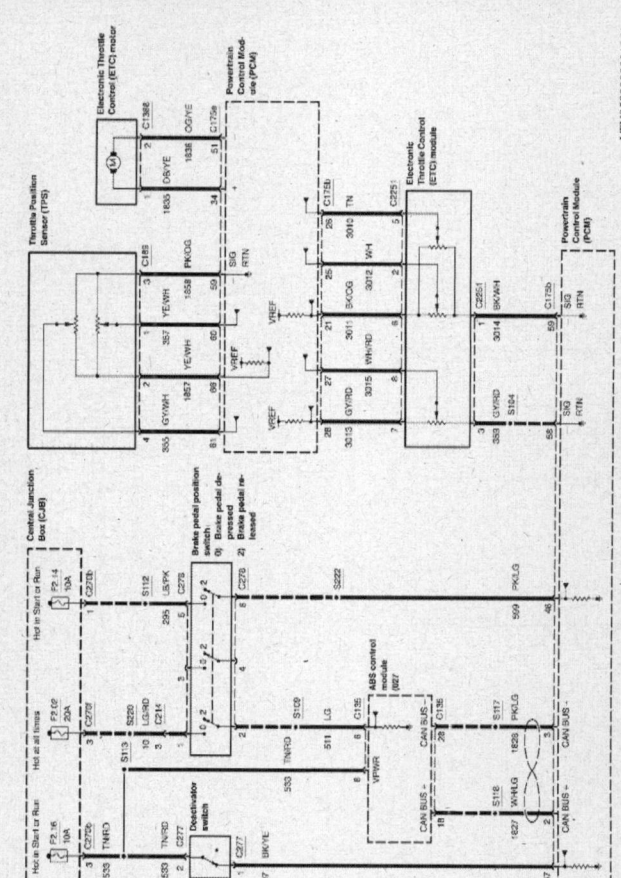

Fig. 25 Speed control wiring diagram (Part 1 of 3). 2002–04 F-150

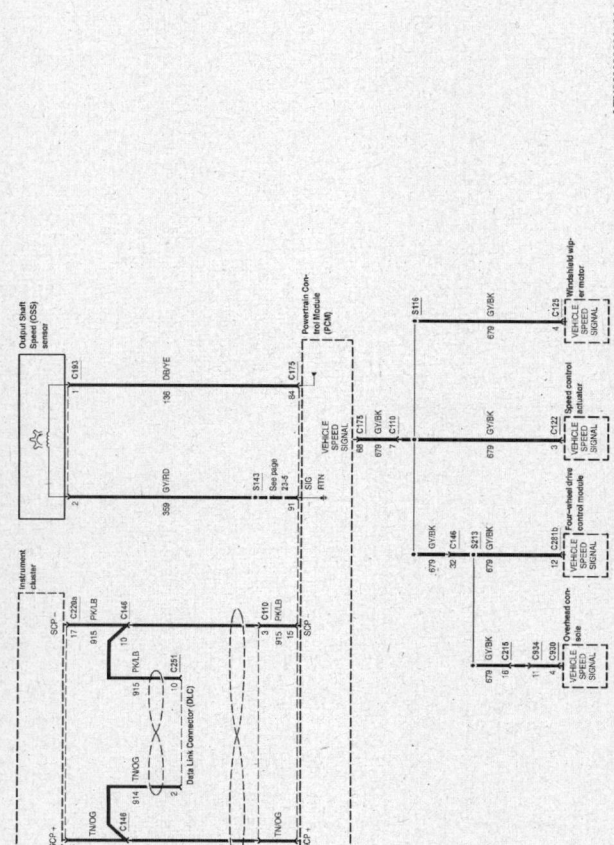

Fig. 23 Speed control wiring diagram (Part 2 of 3). 2004–05 Explorer Sport Trac

Fig. 24 Speed control wiring diagram. Freestar & Monterey

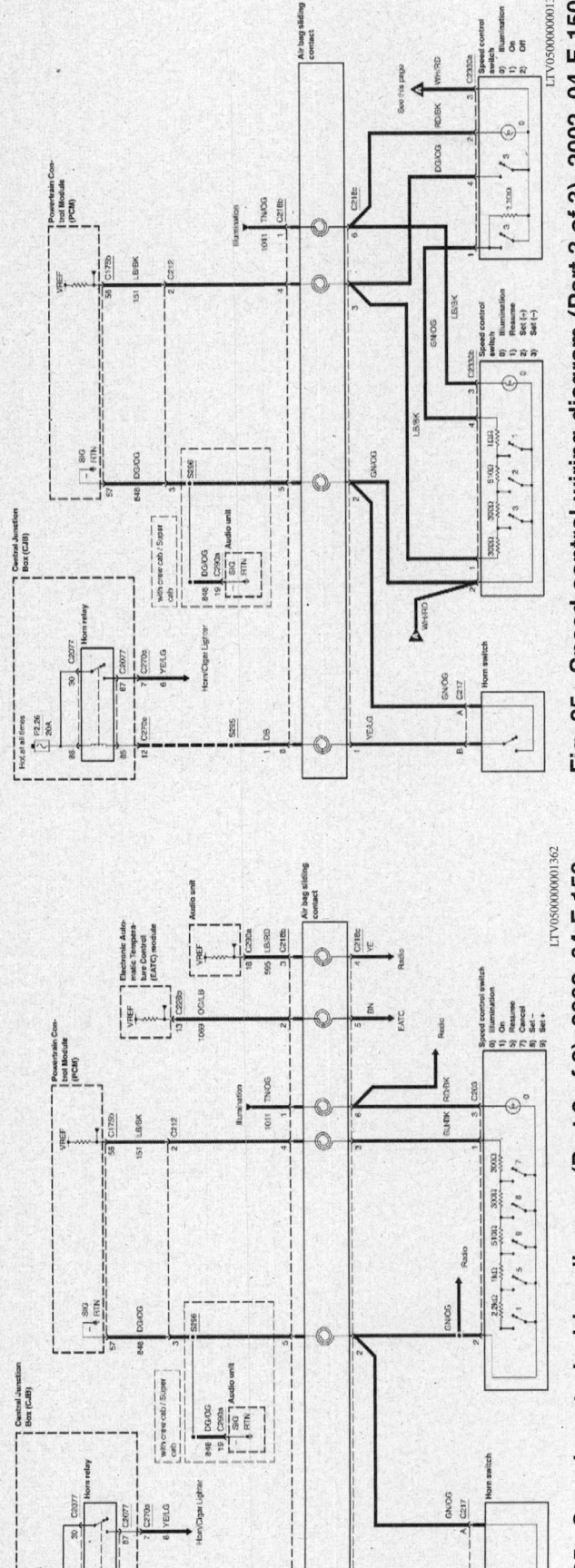

Fig. 25 Speed control wiring diagram (Part 3 of 3). 2002–04 F-150

Fig. 25 Speed control wiring diagram (Part 2 of 3). 2002–04 F-150

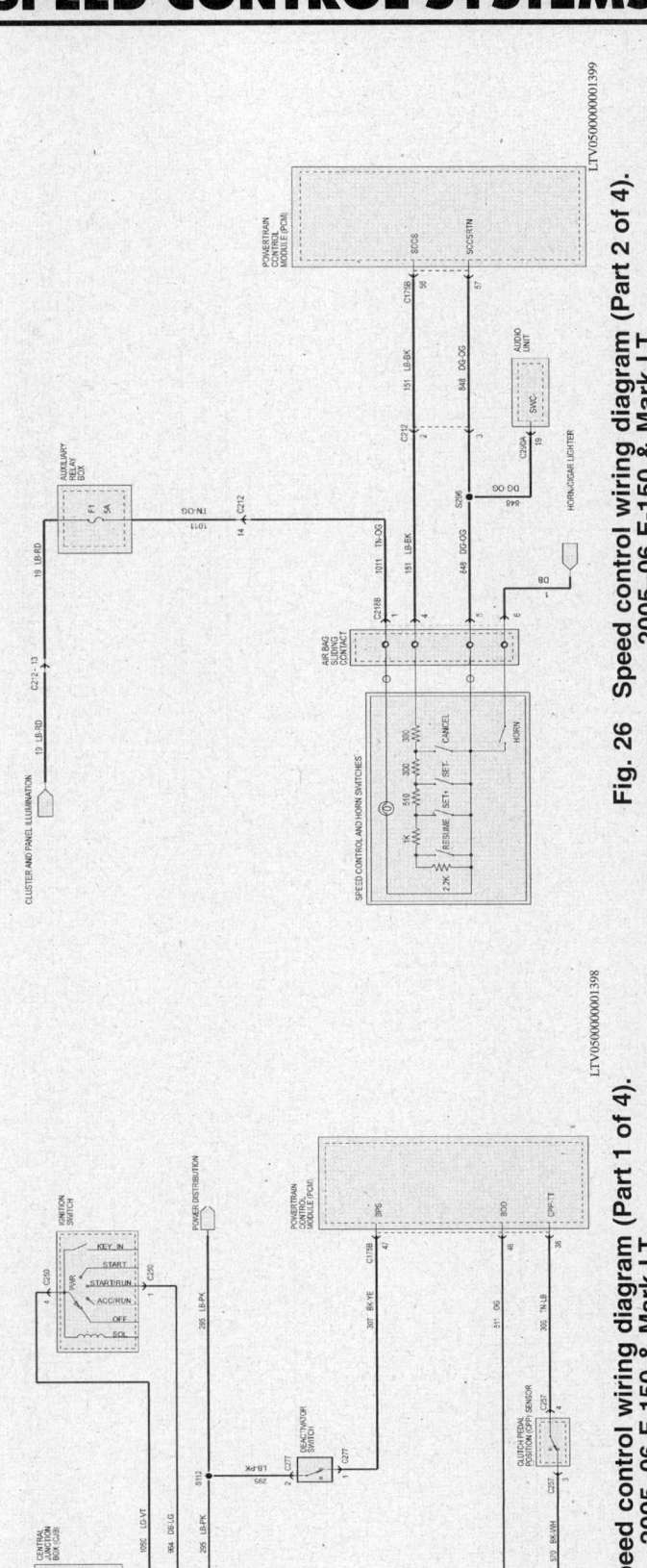

Fig. 26 Speed control wiring diagram (Part 2 of 4). 2005–06 F-150 & Mark LT

Fig. 26 Speed control wiring diagram (Part 1 of 4). 2005–06 F-150 & Mark LT

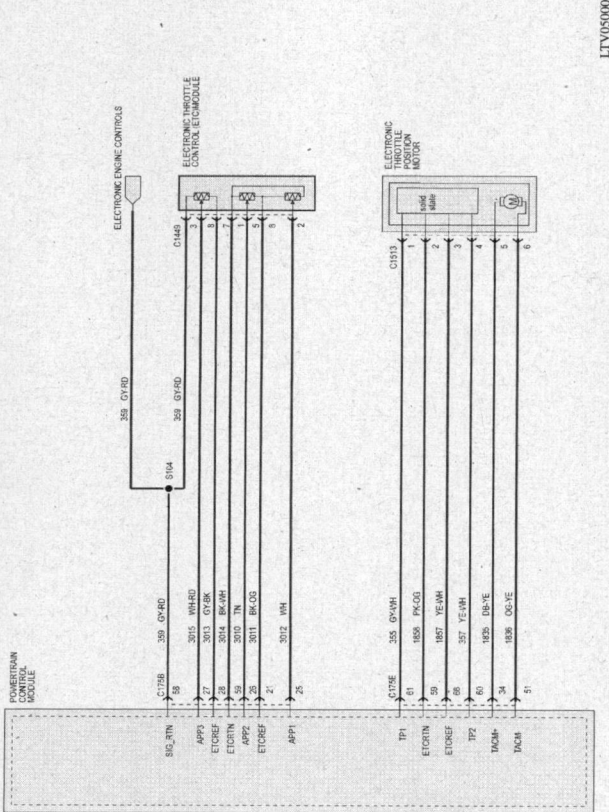

Fig. 26 Speed control wiring diagram (Part 4 of 4). 2005–06 F-150 & Mark LT

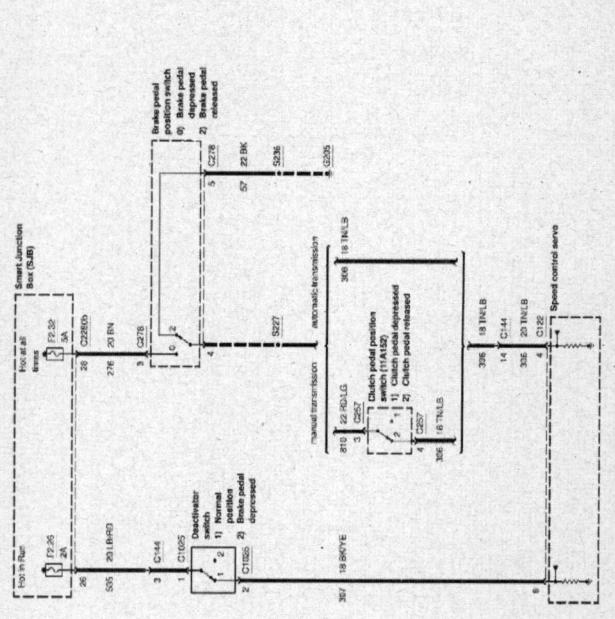

Fig. 27 Speed control wiring (Part 2 of 4). 2002–04 Ranger

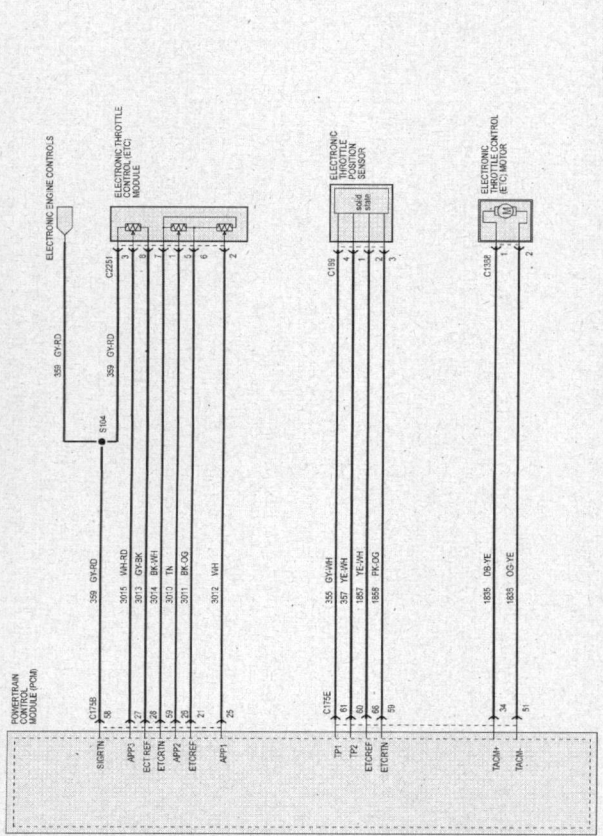

Fig. 26 Speed control wiring diagram (Part 3 of 4). 2005–06 F-150 & Mark LT

Fig. 27 Speed control wiring (Part 1 of 4). 2002–04 Ranger

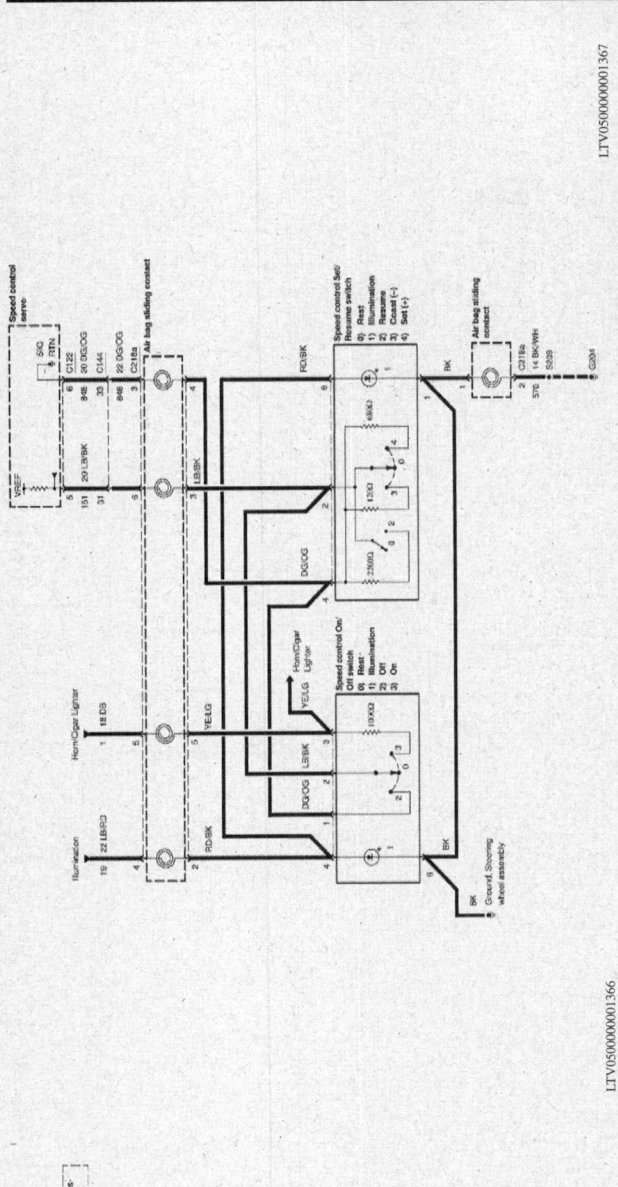

Fig. 27 Speed control wiring (Part 4 of 4). 2002–04 Ranger

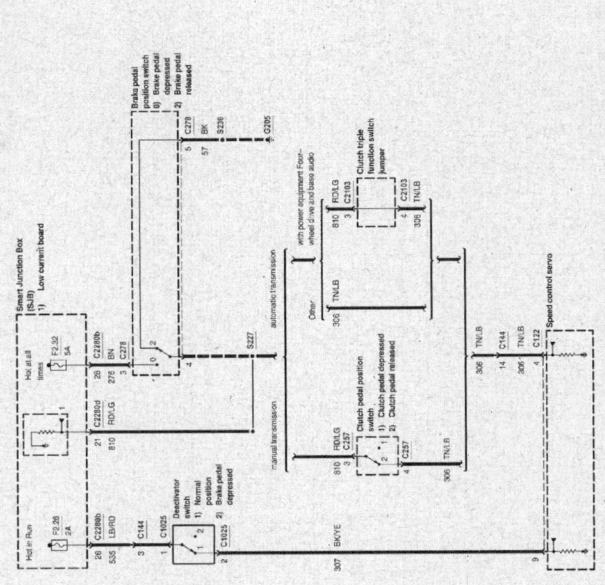

Fig. 28 Speed control wiring diagram (Part 2 of 4). 2005–06 Ranger

Fig. 27 Speed control wiring (Part 3 of 4). 2002–04 Ranger

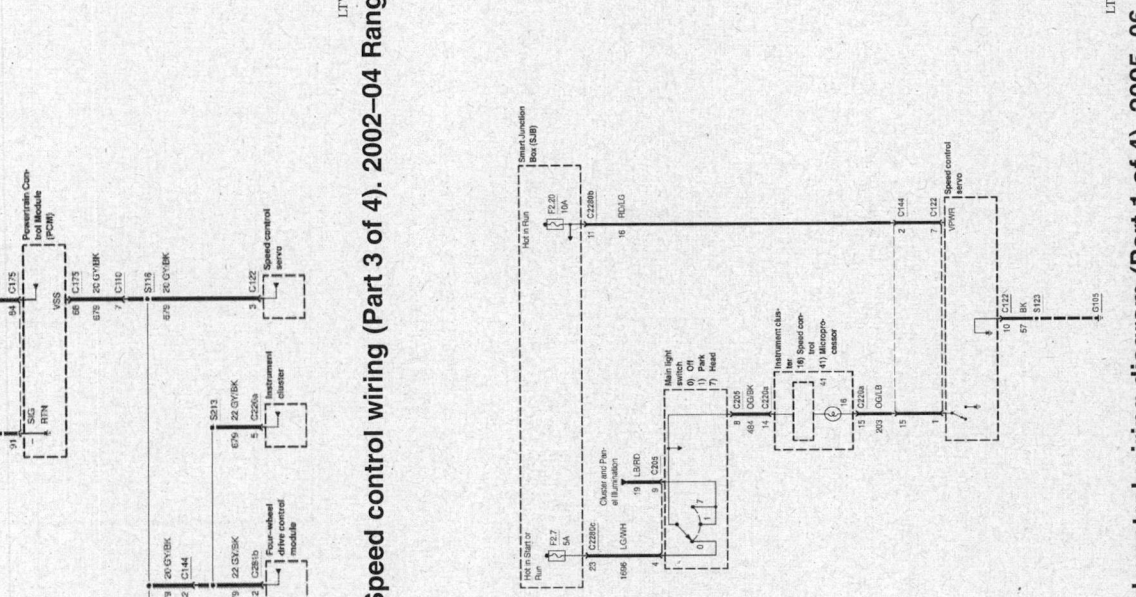

Fig. 28 Speed control wiring diagram (Part 1 of 4). 2005–06 Ranger

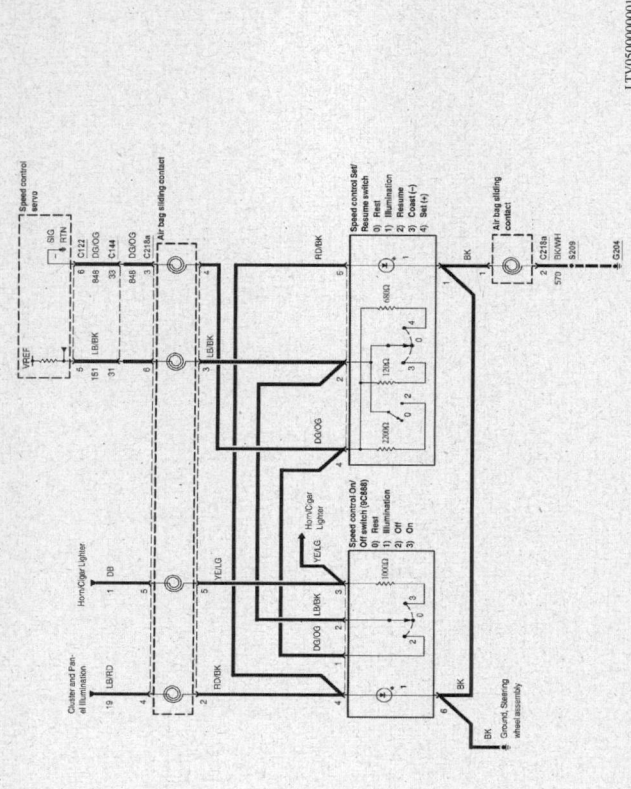

Fig. 28 Speed control wiring diagram (Part 4 of 4). 2005–06 Ranger

LTV050000001405

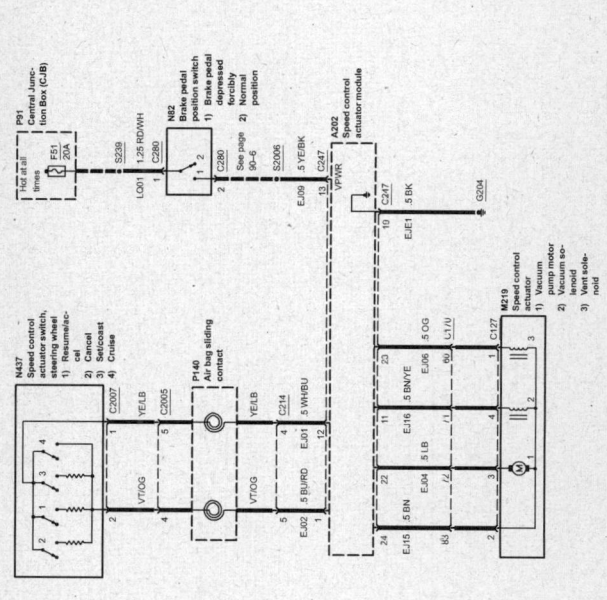

Fig. 29 Speed control wiring diagram (Part 2 of 4). Villager

LTV050000001369

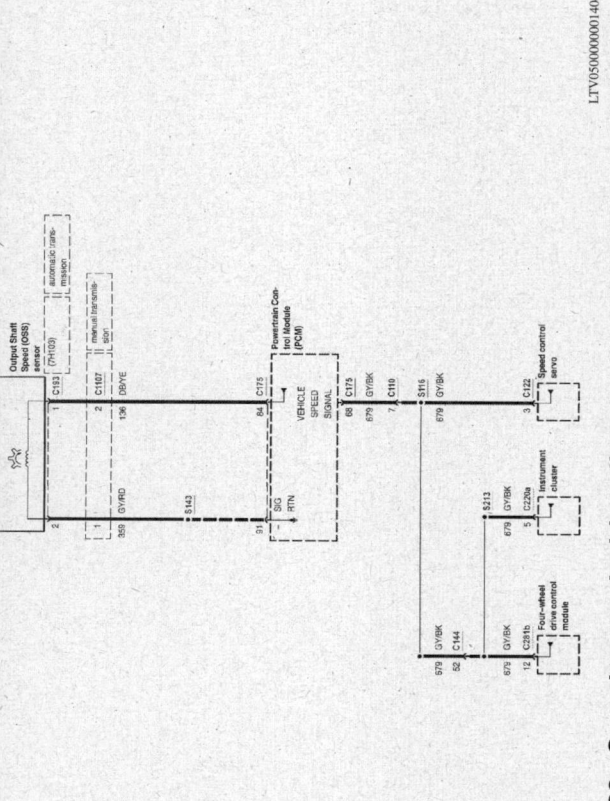

Fig. 28 Speed control wiring diagram (Part 3 of 4). 2005–06 Ranger

LTV050000001404

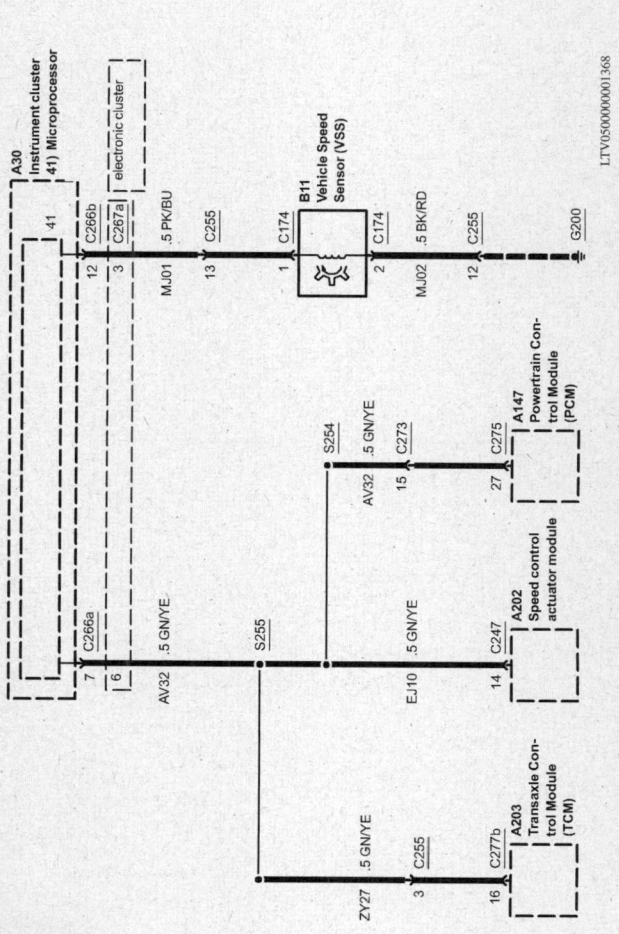

Fig. 29 Speed control wiring diagram (Part 1 of 4). Villager

LTV050000001368

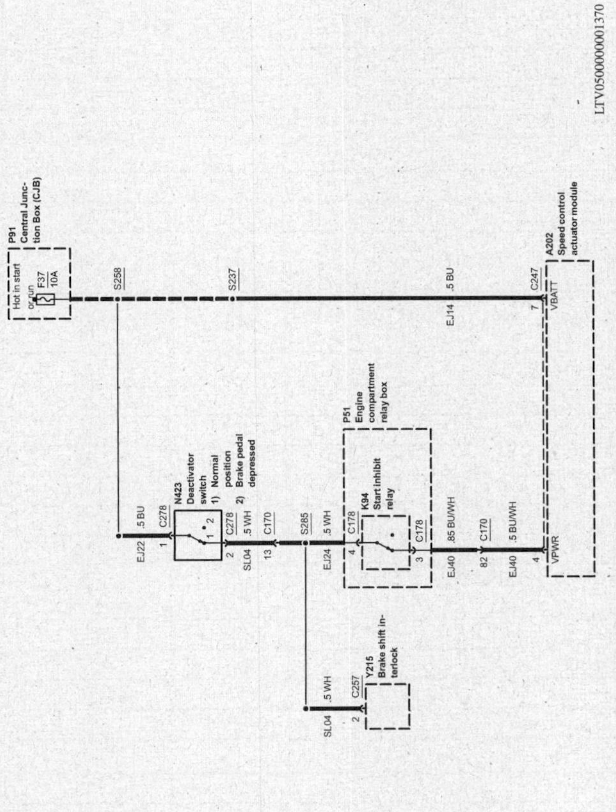

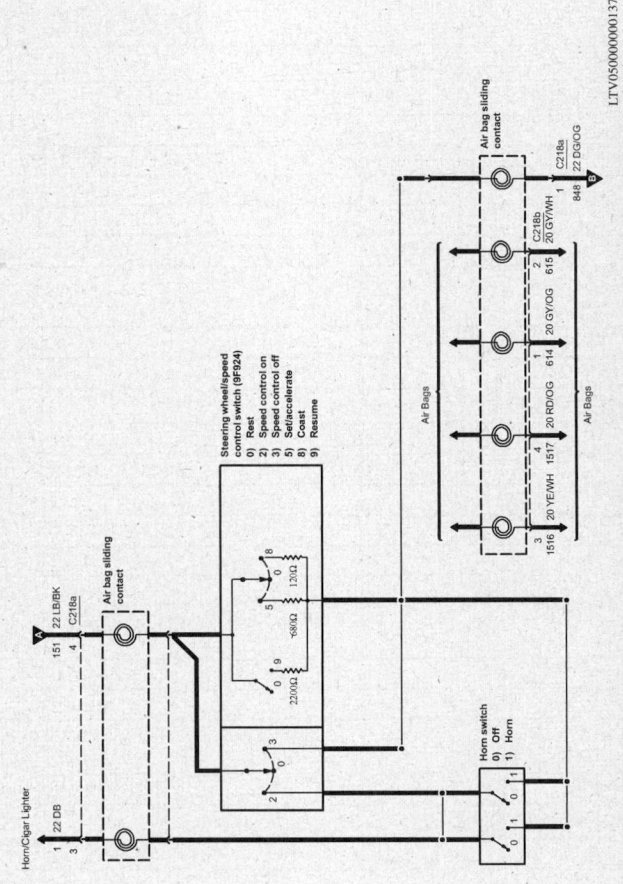

Fig. 30 Speed control wiring diagram (Part 2 of 2). Windstar

Fig. 29 Speed control wiring diagram (Part 4 of 4). Villager

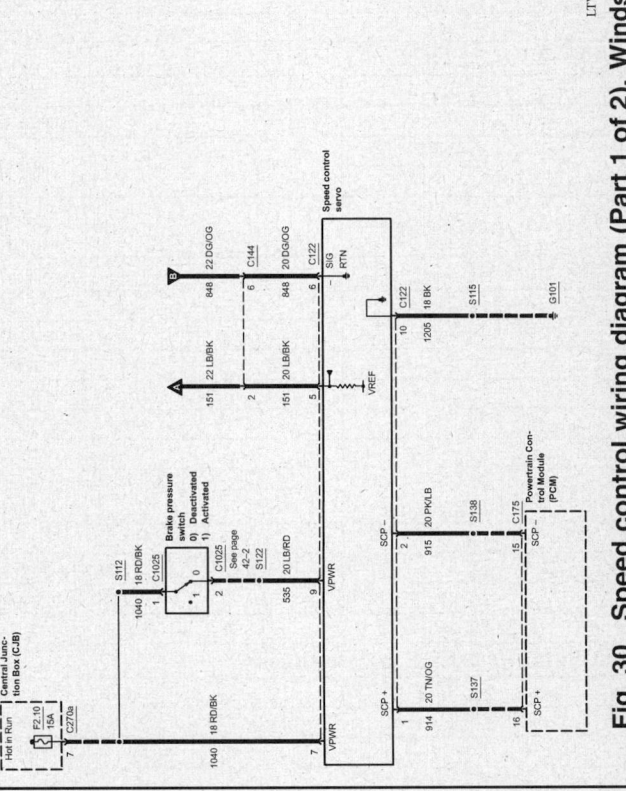

Fig. 30 Speed control wiring diagram (Part 1 of 2). Windstar

Fig. 29 Speed control wiring diagram (Part 3 of 4). Villager

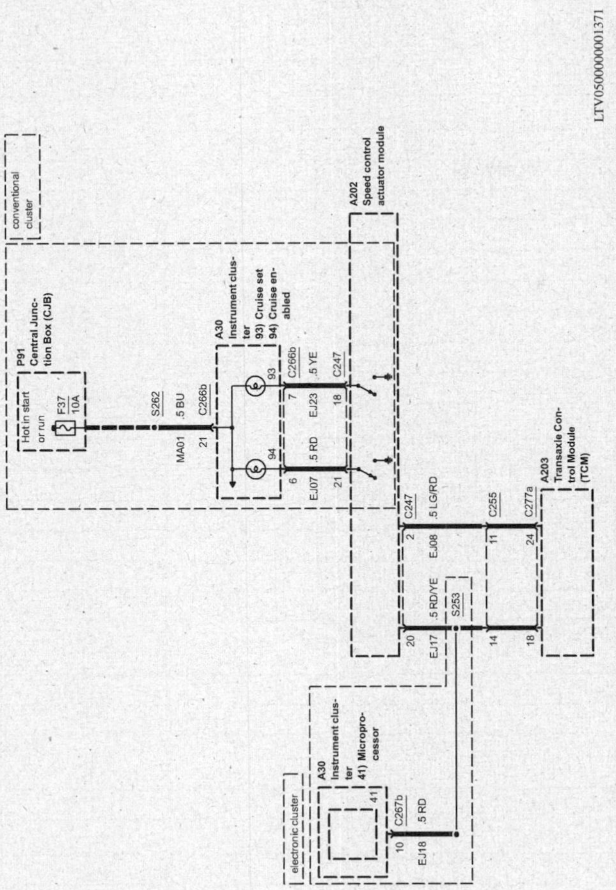

DIAGNOSTIC CHART INDEX

Test	Code	Description	Page No.	Fig. No.
AVIATOR				
—	—	Symptom Tests	2-26	31
A	P1565	Speed Control Command Switches High Out Of Range	2-35	50
B	P1566	Speed Control Command Switches Low Out Of Range	2-36	51
C	P1567	NGSC Driver Fault	2-37	52
D	P1568	NGSC Actuator Self-Test Failure	2-38	53
E	P0703 P1572	Brake On/Off Failure & Brake Switch Input Fault	2-39	54
F	—	Speed Control Is Inoperative w/No DTC	2-40	55
G	—	Speed Control Indicator Lamp Is Always On	2-40	56
EXCURSION				
—	—	Symptom Tests	2-28	36
A	—	Speed Control Is Inoperative	2-67	96
B	—	Set Speed Fluctuates	2-69	97
C	—	Speed Control Does Not Disengage When Brakes Are Applied	2-69	98
D	—	Speed Control Does Not Disengage When Clutch Is Applied	2-70	99
E	—	Speed Control Switch Is Inoperative	2-71	100
F	—	Flash w/Last Switch Pressed, But No Dynamic Pull Occurs At Throttle & Speed Control Is Inoperative	2-71	101
G	—	Brake Pedal Position Switch Circuit Failure	2-71	102
H	—	Deactivator Switch Circuit Failure	2-72	103
I	—	Flash w/Last Switch Pressed, But No Dynamic Pull At Throttle & Speed Control Is Inoperative	2-72	104
J	—	Speed Control Indicator Lamp Is Always On	2-73	105
2002–04 E-SERIES				
—	—	Symptom Tests	2-26	32
A	—	Speed Control Is Inoperative	2-41	57
B	—	Set Speed Fluctuates	2-42	58
C	—	Speed Control Does Not Disengage When Brakes Are Applied	2-42	59
D	—	Speed Control Switch Is Inoperative (SET −)	2-43	60
E	—	Speed Control Switch Is Inoperative (SET +)	2-43	61
F	—	Speed Control Switch Is Inoperative (RESUME)	2-43	62
G	—	Speed Control Switch Is Inoperative (CANCEL)	2-43	63
2005–06 E-SERIES				
—	—	Symptom Tests	2-26	33
A	—	Speed Control Is Inoperative	2-43	64
B	P1703 P1572	Brake On/Off Circuit Failure	2-44	65
C	P0579 P0581	Speed Control Switch Circuit Failure	2-45	66
2002–04 ESCAPE				
—	—	Symptom Tests	2-26	34
A	—	Speed Control Is Inoperative	2-47	67
B	—	Set Speed Fluctuates	2-49	68
C	—	Speed Control Does Not Disengage When Brakes Are Applied	2-49	69
D	—	Speed Control Does Not Disengage When Clutch Is Applied	2-49	70
E	—	Speed Control Switch Is Inoperative	2-50	71
F	—	Flash w/Last Switch Pressed, But No Dynamic Pull Occurs At Throttle & Speed Control Is Inoperative	2-50	72
G	—	Brake Pedal Position Switch Circuit Failure	2-50	73
H	—	Deactivator Switch Circuit Failure	2-50	74
I	—	Clutch/Neutral Switch Circuit Failure	2-51	75
J	—	Speed Control Indicator Lamp Is Always On	2-51	76
2005–06 ESCAPE & MARINER				
—	—	Symptom Tests	2-27	35
A	—	Speed Control Is Inoperative	2-51	77
B	—	Set Speed Fluctuates	2-55	78

Continued

DIAGNOSTIC CHART INDEX—Continued

Test	Code	Description	Page No.	Fig. No.
2005–06 ESCAPE & MARINER				
C	—	Speed Control Does Not Disengage When Brakes Are Applied	2-56	79
D	—	Speed Control Does Not Disengage When Clutch Is Applied	2-56	80
E	—	Single Speed Control Button Is Inoperative	2-57	81
F	—	Flash w/Last Switch Pressed, But No Dynamic Pull Occurs At Throttle & Speed Control Is Inoperative	2-57	82
G	—	Stoplamp Switch Circuit Failure	2-57	83
H	—	Speed Control Deactivator Switch Circuit Failure	2-57	84
I	—	Clutch/Neutral Switch Circuit Failure	2-58	85
2002–04 EXPEDITION & NAVIGATOR				
—	—	Symptom Tests	2-29	38
Test A	—	No Communication w/Powertrain Control Module	2-59	86
Test B	—	Speed Control Is Inoperative	2-59	87
Test C	—	Speed Control Does Not Disengage When Brakes Are Applied	2-61	88
Test D	—	Speed Control Switches Are Inoperative	2-61	89
Test E	—	Speed Control Is Inoperative, Flash w/Last Switch Pressed & No Dynamic Pull Occurs At Throttle	2-62	90
Test F	—	Brake Pedal Position (BPP) Switch Circuit Failure	2-63	91
Test G	—	Deactivator Switch Circuit Failure	2-63	92
2005–06 EXPEDITION & NAVIGATOR				
—	—	Symptom Tests	2-29	39
A	—	Speed Control Is Inoperative	2-64	93
B	P1572	Brake On/Off Circuit Failure	2-64	94
	P1703			
C	P0579	Speed Control Switch Circuit Failure	2-65	95
	P0581			
2002–04 EXPLORER & MOUNTAINEER				
—	—	Symptom Test	2-30	40
A	—	Speed Control Inoperative	2-80	114
2005–06 EXPLORER & MOUNTAINEER				
—	—	Symptom Test	2-30	40
A	—	Speed Control Is Inoperative	2-81	115
B	P1572	Brake On/Off Circuit Failure	2-81	116
	P1703			
C	P0579	Speed Control Switch Circuit Failure	2-82	117
	P0581			
2002–03 EXPLORER SPORT & SPORT TRAC				
—	—	Symptom Tests	2-30	41
A	—	Speed Control Is Inoperative	2-83	118
B	—	Set Speed Fluctuates	2-85	119
C	—	Speed Control Does Not Disengage When Brakes Are Applied	2-85	120
D	—	Speed Control Does Not Disengage When Clutch Is Applied	2-86	121
E	—	Speed Control Switch Is Inoperative	2-86	122
F	—	Flash w/Last Switch Pressed, But No Dynamic Pull Occurs At Throttle & Speed Control Is Inoperative	2-87	123
G	—	Brake Pedal Position Switch Circuit Failure	2-87	124
H	—	Deactivator Switch Circuit Failure	2-88	125
I	—	Speed Control Indicator Lamp Is Always On	2-88	126
2004–05 EXPLORER SPORT TRAC				
—	—	Symptom Tests	2-31	42
A	—	Speed Control Is Inoperative	2-88	127
B	—	Set Speed Fluctuates	2-90	128
C	—	Speed Control Does Not Disengage When Brakes Are Applied	2-90	129
D	—	Speed Control Does Not Disengage When Clutch Is Applied	2-91	130
E	—	Flash w/Last Switch Pressed, But No Dynamic Pull Occurs At Throttle & Speed Control Is Inoperative	2-91	131
F	—	Brake Pedal Position Switch Circuit Failure	2-91	132

Continued

DIAGNOSTIC CHART INDEX—Continued

Test	Code	Description	Page No.	Fig. No.
2004–05 EXPLORER SPORT TRAC				
G	—	Deactivator Switch Circuit Failure	2-92	133
H	—	Speed Control Indicator Lamp Is Always On	2-92	134
FREESTAR & MONTEREY				
—	—	Symptom Tests	2-31	43
A	—	No Communication w/Speed Control Actuator	2-92	135
B	—	Speed Control Is Inoperative & Unable To Enter Self-Test	2-92	136
C	—	Speed Control Is Inoperative	2-93	137
D	—	Set Speed Fluctuates	2-93	138
E	—	Speed Control Does Not Disengage When Brakes Are Applied	2-93	139
F	—	Speed Control Switch Is Inoperative	2-94	140
G	—	Speed Control Indicator Lamp Is Always On	2-95	141
H	C1126	Command Switch Stuck For 2 Minutes Or Longer	2-95	142
I	C1127	Deactivator Switch Stuck Open (Vehicles w/Stability Assist)	2-96	143
J	C1127	Deactivator Switch Stuck Open (Vehicles Less Stability Assist)	2-96	144
K	C1179	Excessive Slack In Speed Control Cable Or Throttle Did Not Return To Idle After Self-Test	2-96	145
L	B1318	Low Ignition Voltage During Speed Control Operation	2-96	146
M	U1027	Missing Or Invalid Message From Throttle Sensor	2-97	147
	U1041	Missing Or Invalid Message From Vehicle Speed Sensor	2-97	147
	U1051	Missing Or Invalid Message From Brake Sensor	2-97	147
	U1059	Missing Or Invalid Message From PRNDL	2-97	147
2002–04 F-SUPER DUTY				
—	—	Symptom Tests	2-28	36
A	—	Speed Control Is Inoperative	2-67	96
B	—	Set Speed Fluctuates	2-69	97
C	—	Speed Control Does Not Disengage When Brakes Are Applied	2-69	98
D	—	Speed Control Does Not Disengage When Clutch Is Applied	2-70	99
E	—	Speed Control Switch Is Inoperative	2-71	100
F	—	Flash w/Last Switch Pressed, But No Dynamic Pull Occurs At Throttle & Speed Control Is Inoperative	2-71	101
G	—	Brake Pedal Position Switch Circuit Failure	2-71	102
H	—	Deactivator Switch Circuit Failure	2-72	103
I	—	Flash w/Last Switch Pressed, But No Dynamic Pull At Throttle & Speed Control Is Inoperative	2-72	104
J	—	Speed Control Indicator Lamp Is Always On	2-73	105
2005–06 F-SUPER DUTY				
—	—	Symptom Tests	2-29	37
A	—	Speed Control Is Inoperative	2-73	106
B	—	Speed Control Inoperative	2-74	107
C	P1572	Brake On/Off Circuit Failure	2-74	108
	P1703			
D	P0579	Speed Control Switch Circuit Failure	2-76	109
	P0581			
E	—	Speed Control Does Not Disengage When Clutch Is Applied (Gasoline Engine)	2-78	110
F	—	Speed Control Does Not Disengage When Clutch Is Applied (Diesel Engine)	2-79	111
G	P0833	Clutch Pedal Switch B Circuit (Gasoline Engine)	2-79	112
H	P0833	Clutch Pedal Switch B Circuit (Diesel Engine)	2-79	113
2002–04 F-150				
—	—	Symptom Tests	2-32	44
A	—	Speed Control Is Inoperative	2-97	148
B	P1572	Brake On/Off Circuit Failure	2-97	149
	P1703			
C	P0579	Speed Control Switch Circuit Failure	2-98	150
	P0581			
2005–06 F-150 & MARK LT				
—	—	Symptom Tests	2-32	45

Continued

DIAGNOSTIC CHART INDEX—Continued

Test	Code	Description	Page No.	Fig. No.
2005–06 F-150 & MARK LT				
A	—	Speed Control Is Inoperative	2-100	151
B	P1572	Brake Circuit On/Off Circuit Failure	2-100	152
	P1703			
C	P0579	Speed Control Switch Circuit Failure	2-101	153
	P0581			
D	—	Speed Control Does Not Disengage When Clutch Is Applied	2-102	154
E	P0833	Clutch Pedal Switch Circuit B	2-103	155
2002–04 RANGER				
—	—	Symptom Tests	2-32	46
A	—	Speed Control Is Inoperative	2-103	156
B	—	Set Speed Fluctuates	2-105	157
C	—	Speed Control Does Not Disengage When Brakes Are Applied	2-105	158
D	—	Speed Control Does Not Disengage When Clutch Is Applied	2-106	159
E	—	Speed Control Switch Is Inoperative	2-107	160
F	—	Flash w/Last Switch Pressed, But No Dynamic Pull Occurs At Throttle & Speed Control Is Inoperative	2-107	161
G	—	Brake Pedal Position (BPP) Switch Circuit Failure	2-107	162
H	—	Deactivator Switch Circuit Failure	2-108	163
I	—	Speed Control Indicator Lamp Is Always On	2-108	164
J	—	Speed Signal Circuit Failure	2-108	165
2005–06 RANGER				
—	—	Symptom Test	2-33	47
A	—	Speed Control Is Inoperative	2-109	166
B	—	Set Speed Fluctuates	2-111	167
C	—	Speed Control Does Not Disengage When Brakes Are Applied	2-112	168
D	—	Stoplamp Switch Circuit Failure	2-112	169
E	—	Speed Control Deactivator Switch Circuit Failure	2-113	170
F	—	Vehicle Speed Signal Circuit Failure	2-114	171
G	—	Speed Control Indicator Lamp Is Always On	2-114	172
H	—	A Single Speed Control Button Is Inoperative	2-114	173
VILLAGER				
—	—	Symptom Tests	2-34	48
A	—	Speed Control Inoperative	2-114	174
B	—	Set Speed Fluctuates	2-119	175
C	—	Speed Control Switch Inoperative	2-120	176
D	—	Speed Control Cruise Indicator Lamp Always On	2-120	177
E	—	Speed Control Set Indicator Lamp Always On	2-120	178
WINDSTAR				
—	—	Symptom Tests	2-35	49
A	—	No Communication w/Module, Speed Control Servo	2-121	179
B	—	Unable To Enter Self Test. Windstar	2-121	180
C	B1318	Battery Voltage Low	2-121	181
D	C1126	Speed Actuator Stuck For Two Minutes Or Longer	2-121	182
E	C1127	Deactivator Switch Circuit Failure	2-122	183
F	C1109	Speed Control Cable Slack Failure/Throttle Position Did Not Return To Idle After Self Test. Windstar	2-122	184
	C1179			
G	—	Speed Control Inoperative	2-122	185
H	—	Set Speed Fluctuates	2-123	186
J	—	Coast Switch Inoperative	2-123	187
K	—	Set/Accel Switch Inoperative	2-123	188
L	—	Resume Switch Inoperative	2-124	189
M	—	Off Switch Inoperative	2-124	190

Condition	Possible Sources	Action
• No communication with the powertrain control module (PCM)	• Circuitry • PCM	• Refer to MOTOR's "Domestic Engine Performance & Drivability Manual".
• The speed control switch is inoperative — no DTCs	• Speed control switch	• INSTALL a new speed control switch TEST the system for normal operation.
• The speed control is inoperative — no DTCs	• Circuitry • Speed control switch • Speed control deactivator switch • Digital transmission range (TR) sensor • Charging system. • Powertrain control module (PCM).	• Go To Pinpoint Test F.
• The speed control indicator lamp is always on	• Instrument cluster • Powertrain control module (PCM)	• Go To Pinpoint Test G.

LTV0500000001411

Fig. 31 Symptom Tests. Aviator

Condition	Possible Sources	Action
• The speed control is inoperative	• Powertrain control module (PCM) not configured for speed control	• CONFIGURE the PCM for speed control.
	• Circuitry • Clockspring • Speed control switches • Digital transmission range (TR) sensor • PCM	• If DTC P0579 or P0581 is retrieved, Go To Pinpoint Test C. Otherwise, Go To Pinpoint Test A.

LTV0500000001465

Fig. 33 Symptom Tests. 2005–06 E-Series

Condition	Possible Sources	Action
• The speed control is inoperative	• Speed control cable not attached to throttle body cam. • Central junction box (CJB) fuse 6 (10A). • Circuitry. • Brake pedal position (BPP) switch. • Speed control switch. • Output shaft speed (OSS) sensor. • Speed control actuator. • Deactivator switch.	• Go To Pinpoint Test A.
• The set speed fluctuates	• Speed control actuator. • Circuitry. • Loose fit or binding between speed control cable and throttle body. • Output shaft speed (OSS) sensor or gear.	• Go To Pinpoint Test B.
• The speed control does not disengage when the brakes are applied	• Brake pedal position (BPP) switch. • Speed control actuator. • Central junction box (CJB) fuse 11 (15A) • Circuitry. • Binding speed control cable.	• Go To Pinpoint Test C.
• The speed control switch is inoperative — SET -	• Speed control switch. • Speed control actuator.	• Go To Pinpoint Test D.
• The speed control switch is inoperative — SET+	• Speed control switch. • Speed control actuator.	• Go To Pinpoint Test E.
• The speed control switch is inoperative — RESUME	• Speed control switch. • Speed control actuator.	• Go To Pinpoint Test F.
• The speed control switch is inoperative — CANCEL	• Speed control switch. • Speed control actuator.	• Go To Pinpoint Test G.

LTV0500000001452

Fig. 32 Symptom Tests. 2002–04 E-Series

Condition	Possible Sources	Action
• The speed control is inoperative — no flash codes	• Central junction box (CJB) fuse(s): ▪ 5 (5A). ▪ 24 (15A). • Circuitry. • Air bag sliding contact. • Brake pedal position (BPP) switch. • Clutch pedal position (CPP) switch (manual transmission). • Speed control deactivator switch. • Speed control switch. • Transmission range (TR) sensor (automatic transmission). • Powertrain control module (PCM). • Speed control actuator.	• Go To Pinpoint Test A
• The set speed fluctuates	• Circuitry. • Speed control actuator. • PCM. • Base engine problem. • Loose or binding speed control cable between the speed control actuator and the throttle body.	• Go To Pinpoint Test B
• The speed control does not disengage when the brakes are applied	• Circuitry. • Speed control deactivator switch. • Brake pedal position (BPP) switch.	• Go To Pinpoint Test C
• The speed control does not disengage when the clutch is applied	• Circuitry. • Clutch pedal position (CPP) switch.	• Go To Pinpoint Test D
• The speed control switch is inoperative	• Speed control switch. • Speed control actuator.	• Go To Pinpoint Test E

LTV0500000001479

Fig. 34 Symptom Tests (Part 1 of 2). 2002–04 Escape

• Flash with last switch pressed and dynamic pull occurs at throttle	• —	• Test passed.
• Flash with last switch pressed, but no dynamic pull occurs at throttle and the speed control is inoperative	• Speed control cable. • Speed control actuator.	• Go To Pinpoint Test F
• Flash with last switch pressed, dynamic pull occurs at throttle and the speed control is inoperative	• Central junction box (CJB) fuse(s): ▪ 5 (5A). ▪ 24 (15A). • Circuitry. • Air bag sliding contact. • Brake pedal position (BPP) switch. • Clutch pedal position (CPP) switch. • Speed control deactivator switch. • Speed control switch. • Powertrain control module (PCM). • Speed control actuator.	• Go To Pinpoint Test A
• Flash Code 2 — BPP switch circuit failure	• Circuitry. • BPP switch. • Speed control actuator.	• Go To Pinpoint Test G.
• Flash Code 3 — deactivator switch circuit failure	• CJB fuse 24 (15A). • Circuitry. • Deactivator switch. • Speed control actuator.	• Go To Pinpoint Test H
• Flash Code 4 — clutch/neutral switch circuit failure	• CPP switch. • PCM.	• Go To Pinpoint Test I
• The speed control indicator lamp is always on	• Circuitry. • Speed control actuator. • Instrument cluster.	• Go To Pinpoint Test J

LTV0500000001480

Fig. 34 Symptom Tests (Part 2 of 2). 2002–04 Escape

Condition	Possible Sources	Action
• The speed control is inoperative — no flash codes	• Speed control switches • Circuitry • Clockspring • Throttle body linkage • Speed control cable • Stoplamp switch • Speed control deactivator switch • Stoplamp bulbs • Transmission range (TR) sensor (automatic transaxle) • Clutch pedal position (CPP) switch (manual transaxle) • Speed control actuator • Smart junction box (SJB) • Anti-lock brake system (ABS) module	• Go To Pinpoint Test A .
• The set speed fluctuates	• Accelerator cable • Base engine concern • Speed control cable • Speed control actuator • ABS speed control • ABS module	• Go To Pinpoint Test B .
• The speed control does not disengage when the brakes are applied	• Circuitry • Stoplamp switch • Speed control deactivator switch • Speed control cable	• Go To Pinpoint Test C .

LTV0500000001499

Fig. 35 Symptom Tests Part 1 of 4). 2005–06 Escape & Mariner

	• Accelerator cable • Speed control actuator	
• The speed control does not disengage when the clutch is applied	• Circuitry • CPP switch • Speed control cable • Speed control actuator • Accelerator cable • Powertrain control module (PCM)	• Go To Pinpoint Test D .
• A single speed control button is inoperative	• Speed control switch • Speed control actuator	• Go To Pinpoint Test E .
• Self-test will not start or complete after multiple attempts	• Circuitry • Speed control switch • Speed control actuator	• Go To Pinpoint Test A .
• Flash Code 0 — no flash after last switch pressed	• Circuitry • Speed control switch	• Go To Pinpoint Test E .
• Flash Code 1 — flash with last switch pressed, but no dynamic pull occurs at the throttle and the speed control is inoperative	• Speed control cable • Speed control actuator	• Go To Pinpoint Test F .
• Flash Code 1 — flash with last switch pressed, dynamic pull occurs at throttle and the speed control is inoperative	• Fuse • Speed control switches • Circuitry • Clockspring • Throttle body linkage • Speed control	• Go To Pinpoint Test A .

LTV0500000001500

Fig. 35 Symptom Tests Part 2 of 4). 2005–06 Escape & Mariner

	• cable • Stoplamp switch • Speed control deactivator switch • Stoplamp bulbs • TR sensor (automatic transaxle) • CPP switch (manual transaxle) • Speed control actuator • SJB • ABS module	
• Flash Code 2 — stoplamp switch circuit failure	• Fuse • Circuitry • Stoplamp switch • Stoplamp bulbs • Speed control actuator	• Go To Pinpoint Test G .
• Flash Code 3 — speed control deactivator switch circuit failure	• Circuitry • Speed control deactivator switch • Speed control actuator • SJB	• Go To Pinpoint Test H .
• Flash Code 4 — clutch/neutral switch circuit failure	• Circuitry • CPP switch (manual transaxle) • TR sensor (automatic transaxle) • Speed control actuator • PCM	• Go To Pinpoint Test I .
• Flash Code 5 — speed control actuator internal failure	• Speed control actuator	• INSTALL a new speed control actuator. TEST the system for normal operation.
• The speed control drops out	• Circuitry • Speed control	• Go To Pinpoint Test E .

LTV0500000001501

Fig. 35 Symptom Tests Part 3 of 4). 2005–06 Escape & Mariner

when pressing buttons	switch	
• The speed control drops out when pressing 2 or more buttons simultaneously	• Normal condition	• ADVISE the customer that when 2 buttons are pressed simultaneously, the speed control system enters a stand-by mode. Pressing the RESUME returns the vehicle to the memory speed.
• The speed control is hard to set	• ON switch and SET switch operation	• ADVISE the customer that the ON switch must be pressed and released before the SET/ACCEL switch is pressed.
• The vehicle does not slow down after deactivating the speed control	• Base engine operation	• CHECK for service bulletins related to engine calibration and REPAIR if required. • The speed control system does not control the vehicle speed when deactivated. ADVISE the customer the brakes must be applied to slow the vehicle.
• The speed control is inoperative when towing a trailer	• Aftermarket trailer tow wiring harness	• ADVISE the customer that the factory trailer tow wiring harness must be used.
• The speed control indicator lamp is never/always on	• Circuitry • Speed control actuator • Instrument cluster	• Continue diagnosis of the speed control indicator lamp.

LTV0500000001502

Fig. 35   Symptom Tests Part 4 of 4). 2005–06 Escape Mariner

	• Deactivator switch. • Speed control servo. • Binding speed control cable. • Clutch pedal position (CPP) switch or jumper.	
• The speed control does not disengage when the clutch is applied (Super Duty only)	• Circuitry. • Clutch pedal position (CPP) switch. • Speed control servo.	• Go To Pinpoint Test D.
• The speed control switch is inoperative	• Speed control switch. • Speed control servo.	• Go To Pinpoint Test E.
• Flash with last switch pressed and dynamic pull occurs at throttle	• —	• Test passed.
• Flash with last switch pressed, but no dynamic pull occurs at throttle and speed control inoperative	• Speed control cable. • Speed control servo.	• Go To Pinpoint Test F.
• Flash code 2 — brake pedal position switch circuit failure	• Circuitry. • Brake pedal position (BPP) switch. • Clutch pedal position (CPP) switch or jumper (Super Duty only). • Speed control servo.	• Go To Pinpoint Test G.
• Flash code 3 — deactivator switch circuit failure	• Central junction box (CJB) fuse 34 (10A). • Circuitry. • Deactivator switch. • Speed control	• Go To Pinpoint Test H.

LTV0500000001702

Fig. 36   Symptom Tests (Part 2 of 3). 2002–05 Excursion & 2002–04 F-Super Duty

Condition	Possible Sources	Action

• The speed control is inoperative — no flash codes	• Speed control cable not attached to throttle.
	• Central junction box (CJB) fuse(s):
	  ▪ 34 (10A).
	  ▪ 27 (15A).
	• Circuitry.
	• Brake pedal position (BPP) switch.
	• Deactivator switch.
	• Speed control switch.
	• Anti-lock brake control module.
	• Powertrain control module (PCM).
	• Speed control servo.
		• Go To Pinpoint Test A.

• The set speed fluctuates	• Speed control servo. • Anti-lock brake control module. • Powertrain control module (PCM). • Circuitry. • Loose fit or binding between speed control cable and throttle body. • Engine controls.	• Go To Pinpoint Test B. Refer to **MOTOR's** "Domestic Engine Performance & Driveability Manual" • REPAIR engine as necessary.
• The speed control does not disengage when the brakes are applied	• Central junction box (CJB) fuse 34 (10A). • Circuitry. • Brake pedal position (BPP) switch.	• Go To Pinpoint Test C.

LTV0500000001701

Fig. 36   Symptom Tests (Part 1 of 3). 2002–05 Excursion & 2002–04 F-Super Duty

	servo.	
• Flash with last switch pressed, dynamic pull occurs at throttle and speed control inoperative	• Circuitry. • Anti-lock brake control module. • Powertrain control module (PCM). • Speed control servo.	• Go To Pinpoint Test I.
• The speed control indicator lamp is always on	• Circuitry. • Bulb. • Instrument cluster. • Speed control servo.	• Go To Pinpoint Test J.
• Flash code 4 — speed signal circuit failure	• Circuitry. • Speed control servo. • Anti-lock brake control module.	• Go To Pinpoint Test I.

LTV0500000001703

Fig. 36   Symptom Tests (Part 3 of 3). 2002–05 Excursion & 2002–04 F-Super Duty

Condition	Possible Sources	Action
• The speed control is inoperative	• Fuse (diesel) • Circuitry • Clockspring • Speed control switches • Digital transmission range (TR) sensor • Powertrain control module (PCM)	• Go To Pinpoint Test A (Gasoline) or Go To Pinpoint Test B (Diesel).
	• PCM not configured for speed control	• CONFIGURE the PCM for speed control..
• The speed control does not disengage when the clutch is applied	• Circuitry • CPP • PCM	• Go To Pinpoint Test E (Gasoline) or Go To Pinpoint Test F (Diesel).
• The speed control indicator lamp is always on	• Circuitry • Instrument cluster • PCM	• REFER to: "Dash Gauges & Warning Indicators" section to continue diagnosis.

LTV0500000001731

Fig. 37   Symptom Tests. 2005–06 F-Super Duty

pressed and no dynamic pull occurs at throttle	actuator. • Circuitry.	
• Flash code 2 — brake pedal position (BPP) switch circuit failure.	• Circuitry. • BPP switch. • Speed control servo.	• Go To Pinpoint Test F .
• Flash code 3 — deactivator switch circuit failure.	• Central junction box (CJB) fuse 34 (10A). • Circuitry. • Deactivator switch. • Speed control servo.	• Go To Pinpoint Test G .
• The speed control is inoperative—no DTCs	• Circuitry. • Deactivator switch. • Digital transmission range (TR) sensor. • Low battery voltage.	• Go To Pinpoint Test B .

LTV0500000001616

Fig. 38   Symptom Tests (Part 2 of 2). 2002–04 Expedition & Navigator

Condition	Possible Sources	Action
• No communication with the powertrain control module (PCM)	• Central junction box (CJB) fuse(s): 　▪ 5 (7.5A) 　▪ 34 (20A) • Circuitry. • PCM.	• Go To Pinpoint Test A .
• The speed control does not disengage when the brake are applied	• Speed control actuator. • Brake pedal position (BPP) switch. • Speed control switch. • Deactivator switch.	• Go To Pinpoint Test C .
• The speed control switches are inoperative—no DTCs	• Speed control switch.	• Go To Pinpoint Test D .
• The speed control indicator lamp is always on	• Instrument cluster.	• REFER to: "Dash Gauges & Warning Indicators" section to continue diagnosis.
• The speed control is inoperative — flash with last switch	• Speed control cable. • Speed control	• Go To Pinpoint Test E .

LTV0500000001615

Fig. 38   Symptom Tests (Part 1 of 2). 2002–04 Expedition & Navigator

Condition	Possible Sources	Action
• The speed control is inoperative	• Speed control switches • Digital transmission range (TR) sensor • Powertrain control module (PCM)	• Go To Pinpoint Test A
• The speed control switch is inoperative	• PCM not configured for speed control	• CONFIGURE the PCM for speed control.
	• Speed control switches • Digital transmission range (TR) sensor • PCM	• Go To Pinpoint Test A

LTV0500000001638

Fig. 39   Symptom Tests. 2005–06 Expedition & Navigator

Condition	Possible Sources	Action
• No communication with the powertrain control module (PCM)	• Battery junction box (BJB) fuse(s): ▪ 18 (20A). ▪ 38 (15A). • Circuitry. • PCM.	• Diagnosis Communications Area Network (CAN)
• The speed control is inoperative	• Clockspring. • Circuitry. • Powertrain control module (PCM). • Speed control switch.	• Go To Pinpoint Test A .
• The speed control switch is inoperative	• Powertrain control module (PCM). • Speed control switch.	• Go To Pinpoint Test A .
• The speed control indicator lamp is always on	• Circuitry. • Instrument cluster. • Powertrain control module (PCM).	• REFER to: "Dash Gauges & Warning Indicators" section to continue diagnosis.

LTV0500000001435

Fig. 40   Symptom Test. Explorer & Mountaineer

	control cable. • Speed control servo.	
• The speed control does not disengage when the clutch is applied	• CPP switch. • Circuitry.	• GO to Pinpoint Test D .
• The speed control switch is inoperative	• Circuitry. • Speed control switch. • Speed control servo.	• GO to Pinpoint Test E .
• Flash with last switch pressed and dynamic pull occurs at the throttle.	• —	• Test passed.
• Flash with last switch pressed, but no dynamic pull occurs at the throttle and the speed control is inoperative	• Speed control cable. • Speed control servo.	• GO to Pinpoint Test F .
• Flash with last switch pressed, dynamic pull occurs at the throttle and the speed control is inoperative	• Circuitry. • Speed control servo. • GEM.	• GO to Pinpoint Test A .
• Flash Code 2 — brake pedal position switch circuit failure	• Circuitry. • BPP switch. • CPP switch. • Speed control servo.	• GO to Pinpoint Test G .
• Flash Code 3 — deactivator switch circuit failure	• CJB fuse 13 (20A). • Circuitry. • Deactivator switch. • Speed control servo.	• GO to Pinpoint Test H .
• Flash Code 4 — speed signal circuit	• Circuitry. • Speed control	• GO to Pinpoint

LTV0500000001653

Fig. 41   Symptom Tests (Part 2 of 3). 2002–03 Explorer Sport & Sport Trac

Condition	Possible Sources	Action
• The speed control is inoperative — no flash codes	• Central junction box (CJB) fuse 10 (7.5A). • Speed control cable not attached to the throttle. • Circuitry. • Brake pedal position (BPP) switch. • Clutch pedal position (CPP) switch (manual transmission only). • Speed control cable. • Speed control switches. • Speed control servo. • Anti-lock brake control module. • Generic electronic module (GEM).	• GO to Pinpoint Test A .
• The set speed fluctuates	• Speed control switch. • Circuitry. • Speed control cable. • Speed control servo. • Anti-lock brake control module.	• GO to Pinpoint Test B .
	• Engine.	Refer to MOTOR's "Domestic Engine Performance & Driveability Manual". • REPAIR the engine as necessary.
• The speed control does not disengage when the brakes are applied	• CJB fuse 9 (7.5A). • BPP switch. • Circuitry. • Deactivator switch. • Binding speed	• GO to Pinpoint Test C .

LTV0500000001652

Fig. 41   Symptom Tests (Part 1 of 3). 2002–03 Explorer Sport & Sport Trac

failure	servo. • Anti-lock brake control module.	Test D .
• Flash Code 5	• Speed control servo.	• INSTALL a new speed control servo. CARRY OUT the self-test diagnostics.
• The speed control indicator lamp is always on	• Circuitry. • Instrument cluster. • Speed control servo.	• GO to Pinpoint Test I .
• The speed control indicator is inoperative	• Circuitry. • Instrument cluster. • Speed control servo.	• REFER to: "Dash Gauges & Warning Indicators" section to continue diagnosis.

LTV0500000001654

Fig. 41   Symptom Tests (Part 3 of 3). 2002–03 Explorer Sport & Sport Trac

Condition	Possible Sources	Action
• The speed control is inoperative — no flash codes	• Speed control cable not attached to the throttle • Circuitry • Brake pedal position (BPP) switch • Speed control cable • Speed control switches • Speed control servo • Anti-lock brake control module	• Go To Pinpoint Test A.
• The set speed fluctuates	• Speed control switch • Circuitry • Speed control cable • Speed control servo • Anti-lock brake control module • Engine	• Go To Pinpoint Test B. Refer to **MOTOR's** "Domestic Engine Performance & Driveability Manual" • REPAIR the engine as necessary.

LTV0500000001679

Fig. 42 Symptom Tests (Part 1 of 3). 2004–05 Explorer Sport Trac

	control module	
• Flash Code 5	• Speed control servo	• INSTALL a new speed control servo. CARRY OUT the self-test diagnostics.
• The speed control indicator lamp is always on	• Circuitry • Instrument cluster • Speed control servo	• Go To Pinpoint Test H.
• The speed control indicator is inoperative	• Circuitry • Instrument cluster • Speed control servo	• REFER to: "Dash Gauges & Warning Indicators" section to continue diagnosis.

LTV0500000001681

Fig. 42 Symptom Tests (Part 3 of 3). 2004–05 Explorer Sport Trac

• The speed control does not disengage when the brakes are applied	• BPP switch • Circuitry • Deactivator switch • Binding speed control cable • Speed control servo	• Go To Pinpoint Test C.
• The speed control switch is inoperative	• Circuitry • Speed control switch • Speed control servo	• Go To Pinpoint Test D.
• Flash with last switch pressed and dynamic pull occurs at the throttle	• —	• Test passed.
• Flash with last switch pressed, but no dynamic pull occurs at the throttle and the speed control is inoperative	• Speed control cable • Speed control servo	• Go To Pinpoint Test E.
• Flash with last switch pressed, dynamic pull occurs at the throttle and the speed control is inoperative	• Circuitry • Speed control servo	• Go To Pinpoint Test A.
• Flash Code 2 — brake pedal position (BPP) switch circuit failure	• Circuitry • BPP switch • Speed control servo	• Go To Pinpoint Test F.
• Flash Code 3 — deactivator switch circuit failure	• Circuitry • Deactivator switch • Speed control servo	• Go To Pinpoint Test G.
• Flash Code 4 — speed signal circuit failure	• Circuitry • Speed control servo • Anti-lock brake	• Go To Pinpoint Test A.

LTV0500000001680

Fig. 42 Symptom Tests (Part 2 of 3). 2004–05 Explorer Sport Trac

Condition	Possible Sources	Action
• No communication with the speed control actuator	• Circuitry • Speed control actuator	• Go To Pinpoint Test A.
• The speed control is inoperative — unable to enter self-test	• Speed control actuator	• Go To Pinpoint Test B.
• The speed control is inoperative — no DTCs	• Circuitry • Speed control cable • Speed control deactivator switch • Clockspring • Horn switch harness • Speed control switch • Speed control actuator • SJB	• Go To Pinpoint Test C.
• The set speed fluctuates	• Throttle lever • Speed control cable • Speed control actuator • Anti-lock brake system (ABS) module	• Go To Pinpoint Test D.

LTV0500000001762

Fig. 43 Symptom Tests (Part 1 of 2). Freestar & Monterey

	Condition		Possible Sources		Action
•	The speed control does not disengage when the brakes are applied	• • • • •	Circuitry Stoplamp switch Speed control deactivator switch Speed control actuator Bussed electrical center (BEC)	•	Go To Pinpoint Test E.
•	The speed control switch is inoperative	• • • •	Circuitry Horn switch wiring harness Speed control switch Clockspring Speed control actuator	•	Go To Pinpoint Test F.
•	The speed control indicator lamp is always on	• •	Speed control actuator Instrument cluster	•	Go To Pinpoint Test G.
•	The speed control indicator lamp is inoperative	• • •	Circuitry Speed control actuator Instrument cluster	•	Diagnosis the speed control indicator lamp.

LTV0500000001763

Fig. 43   Symptom Tests (Part 2 of 2). Freestar & Monterey

	Condition		Possible Sources		Action
•	The speed control is inoperative	• • •	Speed control switch Digital transmission range (TR) sensor Powertrain control module (PCM)	•	Go To Pinpoint Test A.
•	The speed control switch is inoperative (no DTCs)	•	PCM not configured for speed control	•	CONFIGURE the PCM for speed control
		•	Speed control switch(es)	•	INSTALL a new speed control switch.
•	The speed control indicator lamp is always on	• • •	Circuitry Instrument cluster PCM	•	REFER to: "Dash Gauges & Warning Indicators" section to continue diagnosis.
•	The speed control does not disengage when the clutch is applied	• • •	Circuitry Clutch pedal position (CPP) switch PCM	•	Go To Pinpoint Test D.

LTV0500000001848

Fig. 45   Symptom Tests. 2005–06 F-150 & Mark LT

	Condition		Possible Sources		Action
•	The speed control is inoperative	• • • • •	Circuitry. Clockspring. Speed control switch(es). Digital transmission range (TR) sensor. Powertrain control module (PCM).	•	Go To Pinpoint Test A.
•	The speed control switch is inoperative (no DTCs)	•	Powertrain control module (PCM) not configured for speed control.	•	Configure the PCM for speed control.
		•	Speed control switch(es).	•	INSTALL a new speed control switch.
•	The speed control indicator lamp is always on	• • •	Circuitry. Instrument cluster. Powertrain control module (PCM).	•	REFER to: "Dash Gauges & Warning Indicators" section to continue diagnosis.

LTV0500000001847

Fig. 44   Symptom Tests. 2002–04 F-150

	Condition		Possible Sources		Action

•	The speed control is inoperative — no flash codes	•
		
		 •
		
		 •
		
		 •
		 •
		 •
		
		 •
		 •
		
		 •
		
		 •
		
		 •
			Speed control cable not attached to the throttle.
			 Battery junction box (BJB) fuse(s):
			  ▪ 1 (50A)
			  ▪ 3 (50A)
			  ▪ 9 (40A)
			 Smart junction box (SJB) fuse(s):
			  ▪ 7 (5A)
			  ▪ 20 (10A)
			  ▪ 26 (2A)
			  ▪ 32 (5A)
			 SJB.
			 Circuitry.
			 Brake pedal position (BPP) switch.
			 Speed control cable.
			 Speed control switches.
			 Powertrain control module (PCM).
			 Speed control actuator.
			 Speed control connector C122 not connected.
				•	Go To Pinpoint Test A.

•	The set speed fluctuates	• • • • •	Powertrain control module (PCM). Speed control actuator. Speed control switch. Circuitry. Speed control cable.	•	Go To Pinpoint Test B.
		•	Engine.		Refer to **MOTOR's** "Domestic Engine Performance & Driveability Manual"
				•	REPAIR the engine

LTV0500000001786

Fig. 46   Symptom Tests (Part 1 of 3). 2002–04 Ranger

		as necessary.

• The speed control does not disengage when the brakes are applied	• Battery junction box (BJB) fuse(s):
	  ▪ 1 (50A)
	  ▪ 3 (50A)
	  ▪ 9 (40A)
	• Brake pedal position (BPP) switch.
	• Circuitry.
	• Deactivator switch.
	• Binding speed control cable.
	• Speed control actuator.
		• Go To Pinpoint Test C

• The speed control does not disengage when the clutch is applied	• Clutch pedal position (CPP) switch. • Circuitry.	• Go To Pinpoint Test D
• The speed control switch is inoperative	• Speed control switch. • Speed control actuator.	• Go To Pinpoint Test E .
• Flash with last switch pressed and dynamic pull occurs at the throttle	• —	• Test passed.
• The speed control switch is inoperative—flash with last switch pressed, but no dynamic pull occurs at the throttle	• Speed control cable. • Speed control actuator.	• Go To Pinpoint Test F .
• The speed control switch is inoperative—flash with last switch pressed, dynamic pull occurs at the throttle	• Circuitry. • Speed control actuator.	• Go To Pinpoint Test A .
• Flash Code 2 — brake pedal position (BPP) switch circuit failure	• Circuitry. • BPP switch. • Clutch pedal position (CPP) switch. • Speed control actuator.	• Go To Pinpoint Test G

LTV0500000001787

Fig. 46   Symptom Tests (Part 2 of 3). 2002–04 Ranger

Condition	Possible Sources	Action
• The speed control is inoperative — no flash codes	• Fuse • Speed control switch • Circuitry • Clockspring • Throttle body linkage • Speed control cable • Stoplamp switch • Speed control deactivator switch • Clutch pedal position (CPP) switch (manual transmission) • Speed control actuator • Smart junction box (SJB) • Powertrain control module (PCM)	• Go Tc Pinpoint Test A .
• The set speed fluctuates	• Accelerator cable • Base engine concern • Speed control cable • Speed control actuator • PCM	• Go To Pinpoint Test B .
• The speed control does not disengage when the brakes are applied	• Circuitry • Obstructions to the accelerator pedal or linkage • Stoplamp switch • Speed control deactivator switch • Speed control cable • Accelerator cable	• Go To Pinpoint Test C .

LTV0500000001819

Fig. 47   Symptom Test (Part 1 of 4). 2005–06 Ranger

• Flash Code 3 — deactivator switch circuit failure	• Battery junction box (BJB) fuse(s):
	  ▪ 1 (50A)
	  ▪ 3 (50A)
	  ▪ 9 (40A)
	• Circuitry.
	• Deactivator switch.
	• Speed control actuator.
		• Go To Pinpoint Test H

• Flash Code 4 — speed signal circuit failure	• Circuitry. • Speed control actuator. • Powertrain control module (PCM).	• Go To Pinpoint Test J .
• Flash Code 5	• Speed control actuator.	• INSTALL a new speed control actuator CARRY OUT the self-test diagnostics.
• The speed control indicator lamp is always on	• Circuitry. • Instrument cluster. • Speed control actuator.	• Go To Pinpoint Test I .
• The speed control indicator is inoperative	• Circuitry. • Instrument cluster. • Speed control actuator.	• REFER to: "Dash Gauges & Warning Indicators" section to continue diagnosis.

LTV0500000001788

Fig. 46   Symptom Tests (Part 3 of 3). 2002–04 Ranger

	• Speed control actuator	
• The speed control does not disengage when the clutch is applied — no flash codes present	• CPP switch	• INSTALL a new CPP switch (or jumper plug). TEST the system for normal operation.
• The speed control indicator lamp is always on	• Circuitry • Speed control actuator • Instrument cluster	• Go To Pinpoint Test G .
• Self-test will not start or complete after multiple attempts	• Circuitry • Speed control switch • Speed control actuator	• Go To Pinpoint Test A .
• A single speed control button is inoperative	• Speed control switch • Speed control actuator	• Go To Pinpoint Test H .
• Flash Code 0 — no flash after last switch pressed	• Speed control switch • Speed control actuator	• Go To Pinpoint Test H .

• Flash Code 1 — flash with last switch pressed, but no dynamic pull occurs at the throttle and the speed control is inoperative	• Speed control cable
	• Speed control actuator
		• CHECK the speed control cable for attachment and sticking or binding.
		  ▪ If there is a concern with the speed control cable, REPAIR or INSTALL a new speed control cable. TEST the system for normal operation.
		  ▪ Otherwise, INSTALL a new speed control actuator TEST the system for normal

LTV0500000001820

Fig. 47   Symptom Test (Part 2 of 4). 2005–06 Ranger

SPEED CONTROL SYSTEMS

Condition	Possible Sources	Action
		operation.
Flash Code 1 — flash with last switch pressed, dynamic pull occurs at throttle and the speed control is inoperative	Fuse; Speed control switch; Circuitry; Clockspring; Throttle body linkage; Speed control cable; Stoplamp switch; Speed control deactivator switch; CPP switch (manual transmission); Speed control actuator; SJB; PCM	Go To Pinpoint Test A.
Flash Code 2 — stoplamp switch circuit failure	Circuitry; Stoplamp switch; CPP switch (manual transmission); Speed control actuator	Go To Pinpoint Test D.
Flash Code 3 — speed control deactivator switch circuit failure	Fuse; Circuitry; Speed control deactivator switch; Speed control actuator	Go To Pinpoint Test E.
Flash Code 4 — vehicle speed signal circuit failure	Circuitry; Speed control actuator	Go To Pinpoint Test F.
Flash Code 5 — speed control actuator	Speed control actuator	INSTALL a new speed control actuator. TEST the system for normal operation.

LTV0500000001821

Fig. 47 Symptom Test (Part 3 of 4). 2005–06 Ranger

Condition	Possible Sources	Action
	internal failure	
The speed control drops out when pressing buttons	Speed control switch; Speed control actuator	Go To Pinpoint Test H.
The vehicle does not slow down after deactivating the speed control	Base engine operation	CHECK for service bulletins related to engine calibration and REPAIR if required. The speed control system does not control the vehicle speed when deactivated. ADVISE the customer the brakes must be applied to slow the vehicle.
The speed control is inoperative when towing a trailer	Aftermarket trailer tow wiring harness	ADVISE the customer that the factory trailer tow wiring harness must be used.
The speed control indicator lamp is never/always on	Circuitry; Speed control actuator; Instrument cluster	Continue diagnosis of the speed control indicator lamp.

LTV0500000001822

Fig. 47 Symptom Test (Part 4 of 4). 2005–06 Ranger

Condition	Possible Sources	Action
The speed control switch is inoperative	Speed control switch; Speed control module.	Go To Pinpoint Test C.
The speed control indicator lamp is always on — cruise indicator	Circuitry; Instrument cluster; Speed control module.	Go To Pinpoint Test D.
The speed control indicator lamp is always on — set indicator	Circuitry; Instrument cluster; Speed control module.	Go To Pinpoint Test E.

LTV0500000001790

Fig. 48 Symptom Tests (Part 2 of 2). Villager

Condition	Possible Sources	Action
The speed control is inoperative	Central junction box (CJB) fuses. 37 (10A). 51 (20A). Circuitry. Speed control module. Speed control actuator servo. Brake pedal position (BPP) switch. Deactivator switch. Speed control switch. Steering wheel clockspring. Horn relay. Inhibit relay. Vehicle speed sensor (VSS).	Go To Pinpoint Test A.
The set speed fluctuates	VSS. Speed control module. Vacuum leak. Speed control cable. Circuitry. Engine.	Go To Pinpoint Test B. Refer to **MOTOR's** "Domestic Engine Performance & Driveability Manual"
The speed control does not disengage when brakes are applied	Speed control module.	INSTALL a new speed control module; TEST the system for normal operation.

LTV0500000001789

Fig. 48 Symptom Tests (Part 1 of 2). Villager

Condition	Possible Sources	Action
• No communication with the speed control servo	• Central junction box fuse (CJB) 10 (15A). • Circuitry. • Speed control servo.	• Go To Pinpoint Test A .
• The speed control is inoperative — unable to enter self-test	• CJB fuse 10 (15A). • Circuitry. • Speed control servo.	• Go To Pinpoint Test B .
• The speed control is inoperative — no DTCs	• Circuitry. • Speed control switch. • Speed control servo.	• Go To Pinpoint Test G .
• The set speed fluctuates	• Anti-lock brake control module. • Speed control cable. • Throttle lever. • Speed control servo.	• Go To Pinpoint Test H .
• The coast switch is inoperative	• Speed control switch. • Speed control servo.	• Go To Pinpoint Test J .
• The SET/ACCEL switch is inoperative	• Speed control switch. • Speed control servo.	• Go To Pinpoint Test K .
• The RESUME switch is inoperative	• Speed control switch. • Speed control servo.	• Go To Pinpoint Test L .

LTV0500000001791

Fig. 49   Symptom Tests (Part 1 of 2). Windstar

Condition	Possible Sources	Action
• The OFF switch is inoperative	• Speed control switch. • Speed control servo.	• Go To Pinpoint Test M
• The speed control indicator lamp is always on	• Speed control servo. • Instrument cluster.	• Go To Pinpoint Test O .
• The speed control indicator lamp is inoperative	• Speed control servo. • Instrument cluster. • Circuitry.	• REFER to: "Dash Gauges & Warning Indicators" section to continue diagnosis.

LTV0500000001792

Fig. 49   Symptom Tests (Part 2 of 2). Windstar

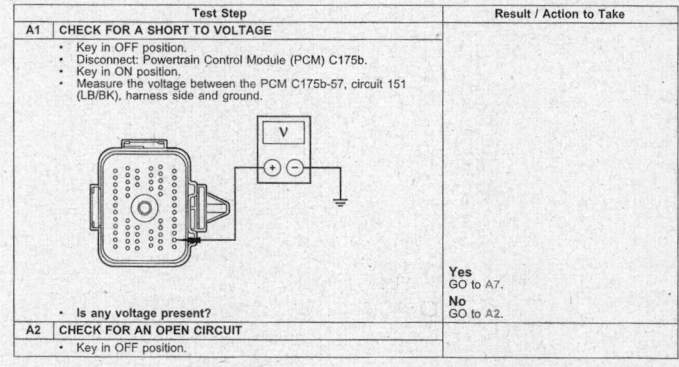

Test Step	Result / Action to Take
A1 CHECK FOR A SHORT TO VOLTAGE • Key in OFF position. • Disconnect: Powertrain Control Module (PCM) C175b. • Key in ON position. • Measure the voltage between the PCM C175b-57, circuit 151 (LB/BK), harness side and ground. • Is any voltage present?	**Yes** GO to A7. **No** GO to A2.
A2 CHECK FOR AN OPEN CIRCUIT • Key in OFF position.	

LTV0500000001407

Fig. 50   Test A, Code P1565: Speed Control Command Switches High Out Of Range (Part 1 of 4). Aviator

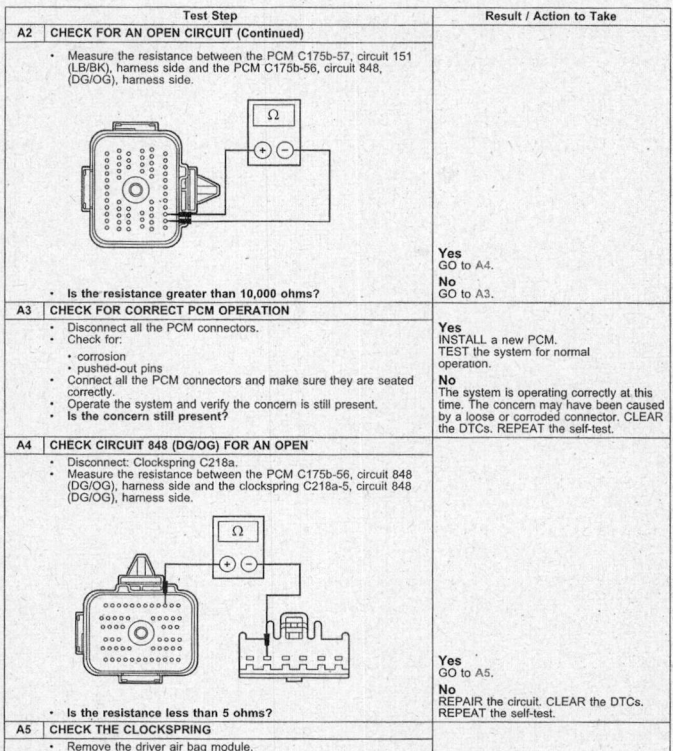

Test Step	Result / Action to Take
A2 CHECK FOR AN OPEN CIRCUIT (Continued) • Measure the resistance between the PCM C175b-57, circuit 151 (LB/BK), harness side and the PCM C175b-56, circuit 848, (DG/OG), harness side. • Is the resistance greater than 10,000 ohms?	**Yes** GO to A4. **No** GO to A3.

A3 CHECK FOR CORRECT PCM OPERATION
• Disconnect all the PCM connectors.
• Check for:
  - corrosion
  - pushed-out pins
• Connect all the PCM connectors and make sure they are seated correctly.
• Operate the system and verify the concern is still present.
• Is the concern still present?
	Yes
	INSTALL a new PCM. TEST the system for normal operation.
	No
	The system is operating correctly at this time. The concern may have been caused by a loose or corroded connector. CLEAR the DTCs. REPEAT the self-test.

A4 CHECK CIRCUIT 848 (DG/OG) FOR AN OPEN • Disconnect: Clockspring C218a. • Measure the resistance between the PCM C175b-56, circuit 848 (DG/OG), harness side and the clockspring C218a-5, circuit 848 (DG/OG), harness side. • Is the resistance less than 5 ohms?	**Yes** GO to A5. **No** REPAIR the circuit. CLEAR the DTCs. REPEAT the self-test.
A5 CHECK THE CLOCKSPRING • Remove the driver air bag module.	

LTV0500000001408

Fig. 50   Test A, Code P1565: Speed Control Command Switches High Out Of Range (Part 2 of 4). Aviator

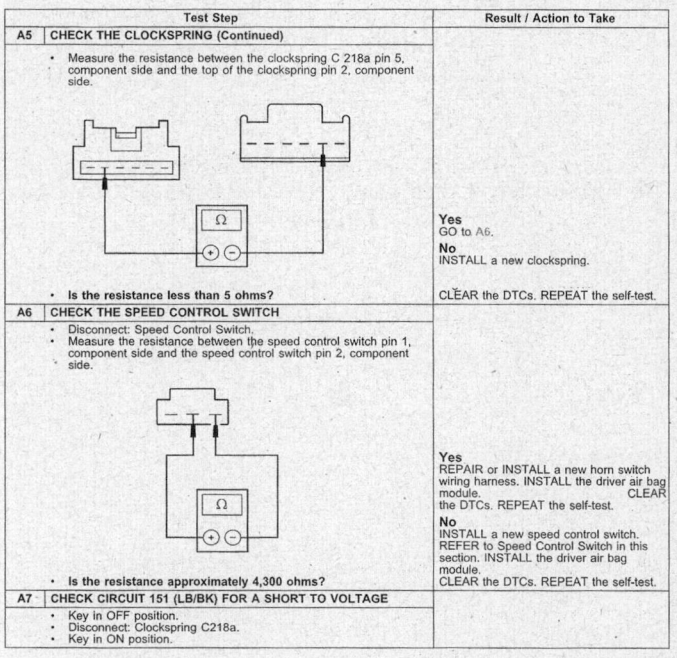

Test Step	Result / Action to Take
A5 CHECK THE CLOCKSPRING (Continued) • Measure the resistance between the clockspring C 218a pin 5, component side and the top of the clockspring pin 2, component side. • Is the resistance less than 5 ohms?	**Yes** GO to A6. **No** INSTALL a new clockspring. CLEAR the DTCs. REPEAT the self-test.
A6 CHECK THE SPEED CONTROL SWITCH • Disconnect: Speed Control Switch. • Measure the resistance between the speed control switch pin 1, component side and the speed control switch pin 2, component side. • Is the resistance approximately 4,300 ohms?	**Yes** REPAIR or INSTALL a new horn switch wiring harness. INSTALL the driver air bag module. CLEAR the DTCs. REPEAT the self-test. **No** INSTALL a new speed control switch. REFER to Speed Control Switch in this section. INSTALL the driver air bag module. CLEAR the DTCs. REPEAT the self-test.
A7 CHECK CIRCUIT 151 (LB/BK) FOR A SHORT TO VOLTAGE • Key in OFF position. • Disconnect: Clockspring C218a. • Key in ON position.	

LTV0500000001409

Fig. 50   Test A, Code P1565: Speed Control Command Switches High Out Of Range (Part 3 of 4). Aviator

Test Step	Result / Action to Take
A7 CHECK CIRCUIT 151 (LB/BK) FOR A SHORT TO VOLTAGE (Continued) • Measure the voltage between the PCM C175b-57, circuit 151 (LB/BK), harness side and ground. • Is any voltage present?	**Yes** REPAIR the circuit. CLEAR the DTCs. REPEAT the self-test. **No** INSTALL a new clockspring. CLEAR the DTCs. REPEAT the self-test.

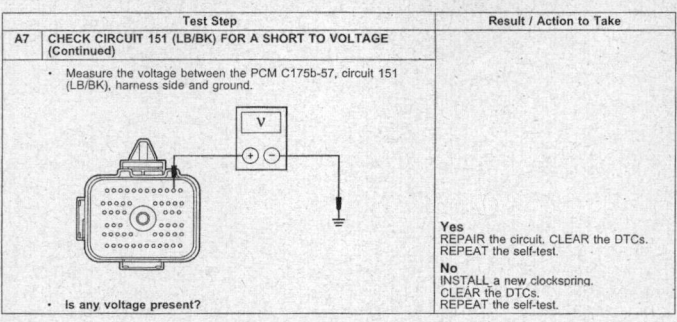

LTV0500000001410

Fig. 50 Test A, Code P1565: Speed Control Command Switches High Out Of Range (Part 4 of 4). Aviator

Test Step	Result / Action to Take
B2 CHECK CIRCUITS 151 (LB/BK) AND 848 (DG/OG) (Continued) • Measure the resistance between the PCM C175b-57, circuit 151 (LB/BK), harness side and ground; and between the PCM C175b-56, circuit 848 (DG/OG), harness side and ground. • Are the resistances greater than 10,000 ohms?	**Yes** GO to B5. **No** GO to B3.
B3 CHECK THE HORN SWITCH WIRING HARNESS FOR A SHORT TO GROUND • Remove the driver air bag module. Refer to Section 501-20B. • Disconnect: Horn Switch Wiring Harness Connector. • Measure the resistance between the PCM C175b-57, circuit 151 (LB/BK), harness side and ground; and between the PCM C175b-56, circuit 848 (DG/OG), harness side and ground. • Are the resistances greater than 10,000 ohms?	**Yes** REPAIR or INSTALL a new horn switch wiring harness. INSTALL the driver air bag module. CLEAR the DTCs. REPEAT the self-test. **No** GO to B4.
B4 CHECK THE CLOCKSPRING • Disconnect: Clockspring C218a.	

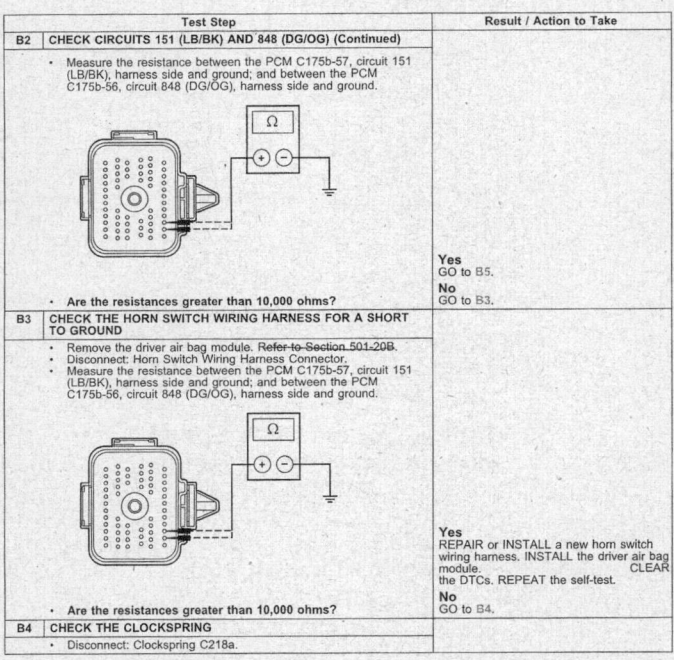

LTV0500000001413

Fig. 51 Test B, Code P1566: Speed Control Command Switches Low Out Of Range (Part 2 of 5). Aviator

Test Step	Result / Action to Take
B1 CHECK FOR A SHORT TO GROUND OR A STUCK SWITCH • Key in ON position. • Monitor the PCM speed control switch PIDs without pressing any speed control switch. • Do any of the PCM PIDs indicate YES?	**Yes** INSTALL a new speed control switch. CLEAR the DTCs. REPEAT the self-test. **No** GO to B2.
B2 CHECK CIRCUITS 151 (LB/BK) AND 848 (DG/OG) • Key in OFF position. • Disconnect: PCM C175b.	

LTV0500000001412

Fig. 51 Test B, Code P1566: Speed Control Command Switches Low Out Of Range (Part 1 of 5). Aviator

Test Step	Result / Action to Take
B4 CHECK THE CLOCKSPRING (Continued) • Measure the resistance between the PCM C175b-57, circuit 151 (LB/BK), harness side and ground; and between the PCM C175b-56, circuit 848 (DG/OG), harness side and ground. • Are the resistances greater than 10,000 ohms?	**Yes** INSTALL a new clockspring. INSTALL the driver air bag module. CLEAR the DTCs. REPEAT the self-test. **No** REPAIR the circuit(s) in question. INSTALL the driver air bag module. CLEAR the DTCs. REPEAT the self-test.
B5 CHECK FOR A SHORT CIRCUIT • Measure the resistance between the PCM C175b-57, circuit 151 (LB/BK), harness side and the PCM C175b-56, circuit 848 (DG/OG), harness side. • Is the resistance greater than 10,000 ohms?	**Yes** GO to B9. **No** GO to B6.
B6 CHECK THE SPEED CONTROL SWITCH • Remove the driver air bag module. Refer to Section 501-20B. • Disconnect: Speed Control Switch.	

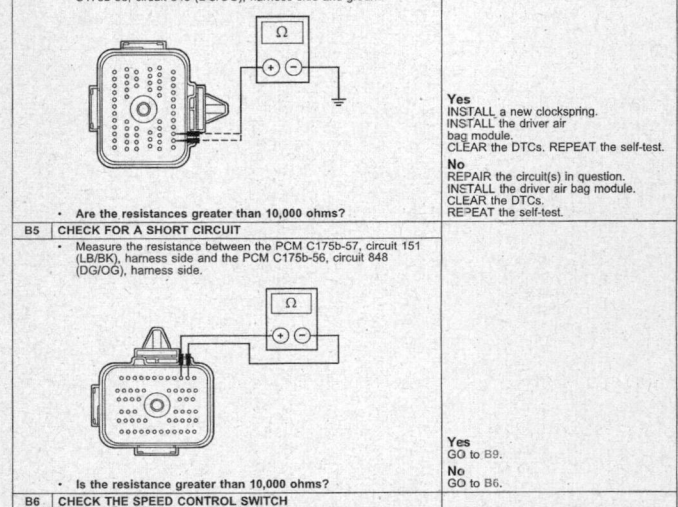

LTV0500000001414

Fig. 51 Test B, Code P1566: Speed Control Command Switches Low Out Of Range (Part 3 of 5). Aviator

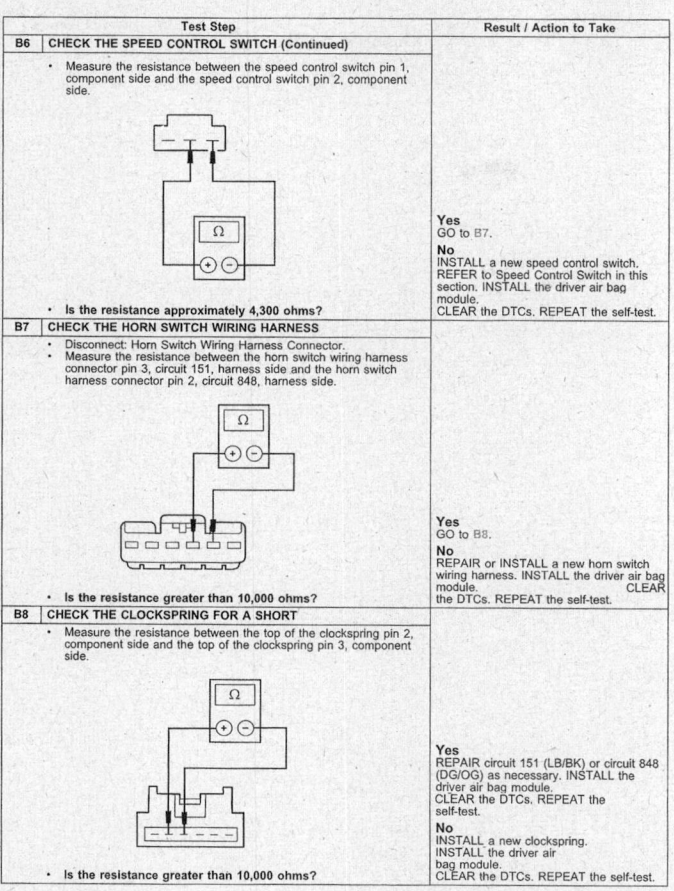

Test Step		Result / Action to Take
B6	CHECK THE SPEED CONTROL SWITCH (Continued)	
	• Measure the resistance between the speed control switch pin 1, component side and the speed control switch pin 2, component side.	
	• Is the resistance approximately 4,300 ohms?	**Yes** GO to B7. **No** INSTALL a new speed control switch. REFER to Speed Control Switch in this section. INSTALL the driver air bag module. CLEAR the DTCs. REPEAT the self-test.
B7	CHECK THE HORN SWITCH WIRING HARNESS	
	• Disconnect: Horn Switch Wiring Harness Connector. • Measure the resistance between the horn switch wiring harness connector pin 3, circuit 151, harness side and the horn switch harness connector pin 2, circuit 848, harness side.	
	• Is the resistance greater than 10,000 ohms?	**Yes** GO to B8. **No** REPAIR or INSTALL a new horn switch wiring harness. INSTALL the driver air bag module. CLEAR the DTCs. REPEAT the self-test.
B8	CHECK THE CLOCKSPRING FOR A SHORT	
	• Measure the resistance between the top of the clockspring pin 2, component side and the top of the clockspring pin 3, component side.	
	• Is the resistance greater than 10,000 ohms?	**Yes** REPAIR circuit 151 (LB/BK) or circuit 848 (DG/OG) as necessary. INSTALL the driver air bag module. CLEAR the DTCs. REPEAT the self-test. **No** INSTALL a new clockspring. INSTALL the driver air bag module. CLEAR the DTCs. REPEAT the self-test.

LTV0500000001415

Fig. 51 Test B, Code P1566: Speed Control Command Switches Low Out Of Range (Part 4 of 5). Aviator

Test Step		Result / Action to Take
C2	CHECK CIRCUIT 1139 (VT/YE) FOR AN OPEN (Continued)	
	• Measure the voltage between the speed control actuator C122-1, circuit 1139 (VT/YE), harness side and ground.	
	• Is the voltage greater than 10 volts?	**Yes** GO to C3. **No** REPAIR the circuit. CLEAR the DTCs. REPEAT the self-test.
C3	CHECK THE SPEED CONTROL ACTUATOR	
	• Key in OFF position. • Measure the resistance between the speed control actuator pins, component side as follows:	

Speed Control Actuator	Speed Control Actuator
C122 pin 1	C122 pin 2
C122 pin 1	C122 pin 3
C122 pin 1	C122 pin 4

	• Are the resistances between 2 and 3 ohms?	**Yes** GO to C4. **No** INSTALL a new speed control actuator. CLEAR the DTCs. REPEAT the self-test.
C4	CHECK THE SPEED CONTROL ACTUATOR CIRCUITRY FOR A SHORT TO VOLTAGE	
	• Disconnect: Powertrain Control Module (PCM) C175b. • Key in ON position. • Measure the voltage between the PCM C175b, harness side and ground as follows:	

LTV0500000001418

Fig. 52 Test C, Code P1567: NGSC Driver Fault (Part 2 of 6). Aviator

Test Step		Result / Action to Take
B9	CHECK FOR CORRECT PCM OPERATION	
	• Disconnect all the PCM connectors. • Check for: • corrosion • pushed-out pins • Connect all the PCM connectors and make sure they are seated correctly. • Operate the system and verify the concern is still present. • Is the concern still present?	**Yes** INSTALL a new PCM. CLEAR the DTCs. REPEAT the self-test. **No** The system is operating correctly at this time. The concern may have been caused by a loose or corroded connector. CLEAR the DTCs. REPEAT the self-test.

LTV0500000001416

Fig. 51 Test B, Code P1566: Speed Control Command Switches Low Out Of Range (Part 5 of 5). Aviator

Test Step		Result / Action to Take
C1	CHECK THE POWERTRAIN CONTROL MODULE (PCM) PIDS	
	• Test drive the vehicle at greater than 40 km/h (25 mph) with and without the speed control engaged, while monitoring the PCM PID SCINT_F and SC_HW_F. • Does either PCM PID SCINT_F or SC_HW_F indicate YES?	**Yes** If the PCM PID SCINT_F indicates YES, GO to C12. If the PCM PID SC_HW_F indicates YES, GO to C2. **No** GO to C7.
C2	CHECK CIRCUIT 1139 (VT/YE) FOR AN OPEN	
	• Key in OFF position. • Disconnect: Speed Control Actuator C122. • Key in ON position.	

LTV0500000001417

Fig. 52 Test C, Code P1567: NGSC Driver Fault (Part 1 of 6). Aviator

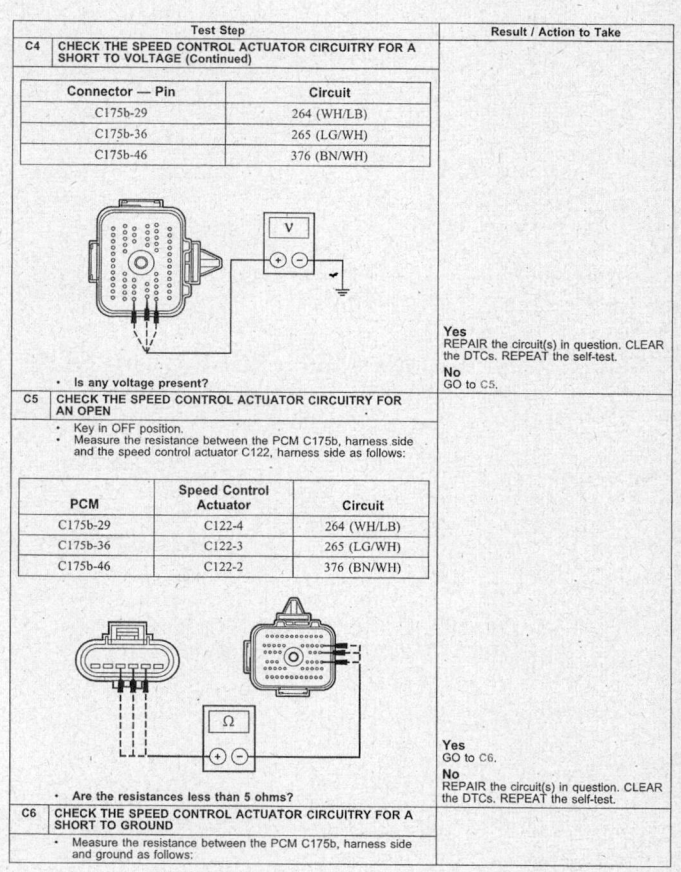

Test Step		Result / Action to Take
C4	CHECK THE SPEED CONTROL ACTUATOR CIRCUITRY FOR A SHORT TO VOLTAGE (Continued)	

Connector — Pin	Circuit
C175b-29	264 (WH/LB)
C175b-36	265 (LG/WH)
C175b-46	376 (BN/WH)

	• Is any voltage present?	**Yes** REPAIR the circuit(s) in question. CLEAR the DTCs. REPEAT the self-test. **No** GO to C5.
C5	CHECK THE SPEED CONTROL ACTUATOR CIRCUITRY FOR AN OPEN	
	• Key in OFF position. • Measure the resistance between the PCM C175b, harness side and the speed control actuator C122, harness side as follows:	

PCM	Speed Control Actuator	Circuit
C175b-29	C122-4	264 (WH/LB)
C175b-36	C122-3	265 (LG/WH)
C175b-46	C122-2	376 (BN/WH)

	• Are the resistances less than 5 ohms?	**Yes** GO to C6. **No** REPAIR the circuit(s) in question. CLEAR the DTCs. REPEAT the self-test.
C6	CHECK THE SPEED CONTROL ACTUATOR CIRCUITRY FOR A SHORT TO GROUND	
	• Measure the resistance between the PCM C175b, harness side and ground as follows:	

LTV0500000001419

Fig. 52 Test C, Code P1567: NGSC Driver Fault (Part 3 of 6). Aviator

Test Step	Result / Action to Take
C6 CHECK THE SPEED CONTROL ACTUATOR CIRCUITRY FOR A SHORT TO GROUND (Continued)	

PCM	Circuit
C175b-29	264 (WH/LB)
C175b-36	265 (LG/WH)
C175b-46	376 (BN/WH)

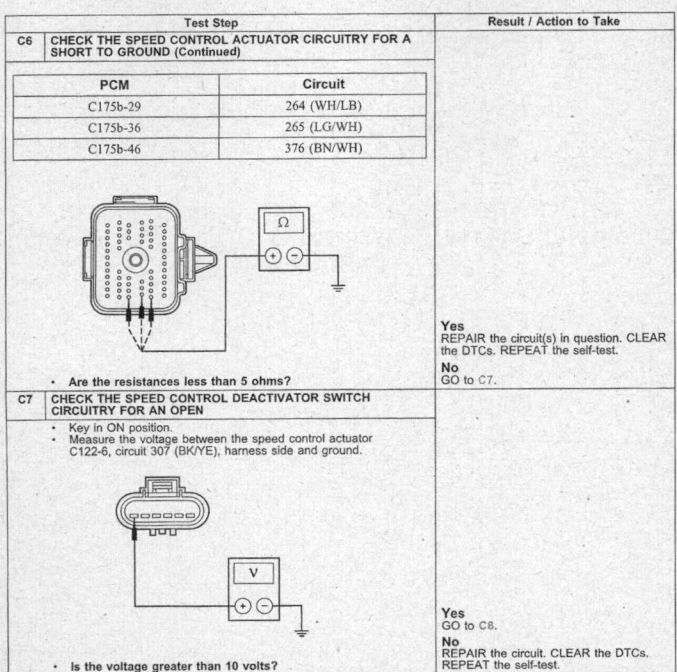

• **Are the resistances less than 5 ohms?**	**Yes** REPAIR the circuit(s) in question. CLEAR the DTCs. REPEAT the self-test. **No** GO to C7.
C7 CHECK THE SPEED CONTROL DEACTIVATOR SWITCH CIRCUITRY FOR AN OPEN	
• Key in ON position. • Measure the voltage between the speed control actuator C122-6, circuit 307 (BK/YE), harness side and ground.	
• **Is the voltage greater than 10 volts?**	**Yes** GO to C8. **No** REPAIR the circuit. CLEAR the DTCs. REPEAT the self-test.

LTV0500000001420

Fig. 52 Test C, Code P1567: NGSC Driver Fault (Part 4 of 6). Aviator

Test Step	Result / Action to Take
C11 CHECK CIRCUIT 133 (BK) FOR A SHORT TO GROUND	
• Measure the resistance between the speed control actuator C122-5, circuit 133 (BK), harness side and ground.	
• **Is the resistance greater than 10,000 ohms?**	**Yes** GO to C12. **No** REPAIR the circuit. CLEAR the DTCs. REPEAT the self-test.
C12 CHECK FOR CORRECT PCM OPERATION	
• Disconnect all the PCM connectors. • Check for: • corrosion • pushed-out pins • Connect all the PCM connectors and make sure they are seated correctly. • Operate the system and verify the concern is still present. • **Is the concern still present?**	**Yes** INSTALL a new PCM. **No** The system is operating correctly at this time. The concern may have been caused by a loose or corroded connector. CLEAR the DTCs. REPEAT the self-test.

LTV0500000001422

Fig. 52 Test C, Code P1567: NGSC Driver Fault (Part 6 of 6). Aviator

Test Step	Result / Action to Take
D1 CHECK THE SPEED CONTROL CABLE	
• Disconnect the speed control cable at the throttle body. • Check the speed control cable slack by pulling the speed control cable end taut from within the speed control cable housing. • **Is the speed control cable slack greater than 0 mm (0 in) and less than 6 mm (0.24 in) ?**	**Yes** GO to D2. **No** INSTALL a new speed control cable. CLEAR the DTCs. REPEAT the self-test.

LTV0500000001423

Fig. 53 Test D, Code P1568: NGSC Actuator Self-Test Failure (Part 1 of 5). Aviator

Test Step	Result / Action to Take
C8 CHECK THE SPEED CONTROL ACTUATOR FOR A SHORT OR AN OPEN	
• Measure the resistance between the speed control actuator pin 5 component side and the speed control actuator pin 6 component side.	
• **Is the resistance between 20 and 30 ohms?**	**Yes** GO to C9. **No** INSTALL a new speed control actuator. CLEAR the DTCs. REPEAT the self-test.
C9 CHECK CIRCUIT 133 (BK) FOR A SHORT TO VOLTAGE	
• Key in ON position. • Measure the voltage between the speed control actuator C122-5, circuit 133 (BK), harness side and ground.	
• **Is any voltage present?**	**Yes** REPAIR the circuit. CLEAR the DTCs. REPEAT the self-test. **No** GO to C10.
C10 CHECK CIRCUIT 133 (BK) FOR AN OPEN	
• Key in OFF position. • Measure the resistance between the speed control actuator C122-5, circuit 133 (BK), harness side and the PCM C175b-45, circuit 133 (BK), harness side.	
• **Is the resistance less than 5 ohms?**	**Yes** GO to C11. **No** REPAIR the circuit. CLEAR the DTCs. REPEAT the self-test.

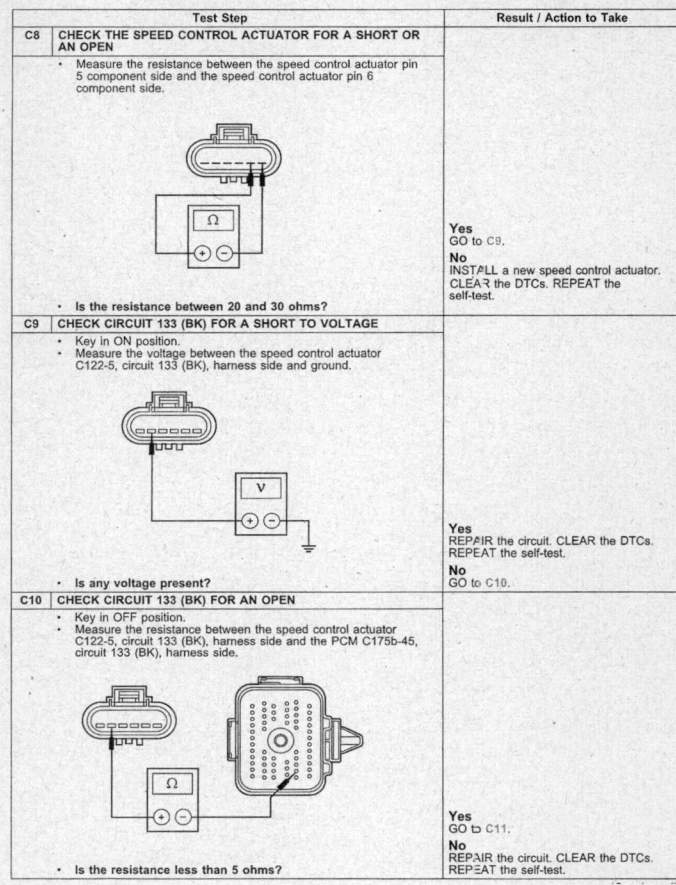

LTV0500000001421

Fig. 52 Test C, Code P1567: NGSC Driver Fault (Part 5 of 6). Aviator

Test Step	Result / Action to Take
D2 CHECK FOR A DAMAGED, STICKING, OR BINDING SPEED CONTROL CABLE	
• Disconnect the speed control cable from the speed control actuator. • Check the speed control cable for damage, sticking, or binding. • **Is the speed control cable OK?**	**Yes** GO to D3. **No** INSTALL a new speed control cable. CLEAR the DTCs. REPEAT the self-test.
D3 CHECK THE SPEED CONTROL ACTUATOR OUTPUT	
• Key in ON position. • Check the speed control actuator pulley for movement while triggering the on-demand self-test. • **Does the speed control actuator pulley move?**	**Yes** GO to D10. **No** GO to D4.
D4 CHECK THE SPEED CONTROL ACTUATOR	
• Key in OFF position. • Disconnect: Speed Control Actuator C122. • Measure the resistance between the speed control actuator pins, component side as follows:	

Speed Control Actuator	Speed Control Actuator	Expected Value
C122 pin 1	C122 pin 2	2 – 3 ohms
C122 pin 1	C122 pin 3	2 – 3 ohms
C122 pin 1	C122 pin 4	2 – 3 ohms
C122 pin 5	C122 pin 6	20 – 30 ohms

• **Are the resistances OK?**	**Yes** GO to D5. **No** INSTALL a new speed control actuator. CLEAR the DTCs. REPEAT the self-test.
D5 CHECK THE SPEED CONTROL ACTUATOR CIRCUITRY FOR A SHORT TO VOLTAGE	
• Disconnect: Powertrain Control Module (PCM) C175b. • Key in ON position. • Measure the voltage between the speed control actuator, harness side and ground as follows:	

LTV0500000001424

Fig. 53 Test D, Code P1568: NGSC Actuator Self-Test Failure (Part 2 of 5). Aviator

Test Step			Result / Action to Take
D5	CHECK THE SPEED CONTROL ACTUATOR CIRCUITRY FOR A SHORT TO VOLTAGE (Continued)		

Speed Control Actuator Connector — Pin	Circuit
C122-5	133 (BK)
C122-4	264 (WH/LB)
C122-3	265 (LG/WH)
C122-2	376 (BN/WH)

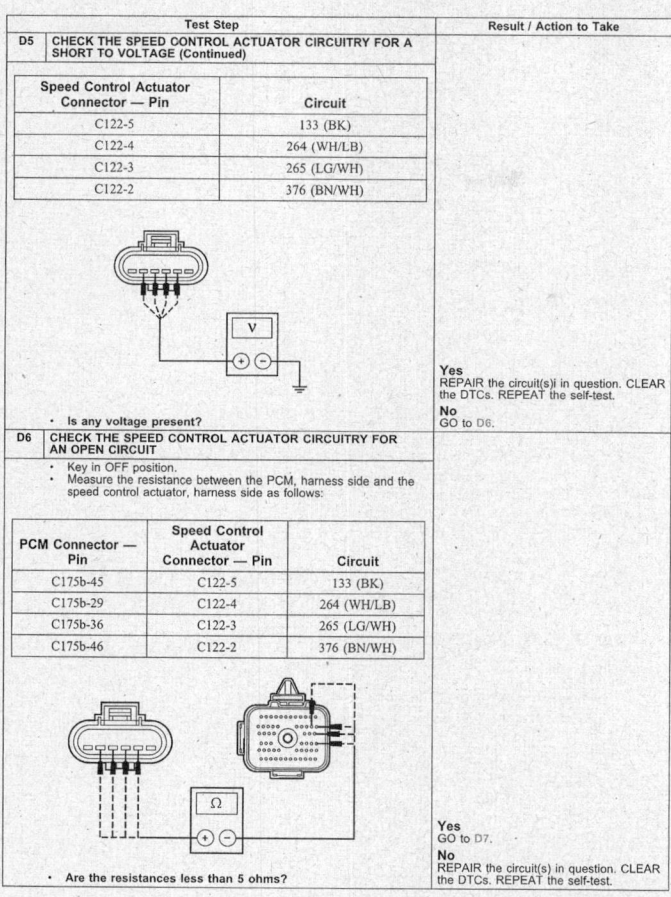

- **Is any voltage present?**

Yes
REPAIR the circuit(s) in question. CLEAR the DTCs. REPEAT the self-test.
No
GO to D6.

Test Step	Result / Action to Take
D6 CHECK THE SPEED CONTROL ACTUATOR CIRCUITRY FOR AN OPEN CIRCUIT	

- Key in OFF position.
- Measure the resistance between the PCM, harness side and the speed control actuator, harness side as follows:

PCM Connector — Pin	Speed Control Actuator Connector — Pin	Circuit
C175b-45	C122-5	133 (BK)
C175b-29	C122-4	264 (WH/LB)
C175b-36	C122-3	265 (LG/WH)
C175b-46	C122-2	376 (BN/WH)

- **Are the resistances less than 5 ohms?**

Yes
GO to D7.
No
REPAIR the circuit(s) in question. CLEAR the DTCs. REPEAT the self-test.

LTV050000001425

Fig. 53   Test D, Code P1568: NGSC Actuator Self-Test Failure (Part 3 of 5). Aviator

Test Step	Result / Action to Take
D9 CHECK THE SPEED CONTROL DEACTIVATOR SWITCH CIRCUITRY FOR AN OPEN (Continued)	

- Measure the voltage between the speed control actuator C122-6, circuit 307 (BK/YE), harness side and ground.

- **Is the voltage greater than 10 volts?**

Yes
INSTALL a new speed control actuator. CLEAR the DTCs. REPEAT the self-test.
No
REPAIR the circuit. CLEAR the DTCs. REPEAT the self-test.

D10 CHECK FOR CORRECT PCM OPERATION	

- Disconnect all the PCM connectors.
- Check for:
  - corrosion
  - pushed-out pins
- Connect all the PCM connectors and make sure they are seated correctly.
- Operate the system and verify the concern is still present.
- **Is the concern still present?**

Yes
INSTALL a new PCM. CLEAR the DTCs. REPEAT the self-test.
No
The system is operating correctly at this time. The concern may have been caused by a loose or corroded connector. CLEAR the DTCs. REPEAT the self-test.

LTV050000001427

Fig. 53   Test D, Code P1568: NGSC Actuator Self-Test Failure (Part 5 of 5). Aviator

Test Step	Result / Action to Take
E1 MONITOR THE POWERTRAIN CONTROL MODULE (PCM) PID BPA__SW	

- Key in ON position.
- Monitor the PCM PID BPA__SW without applying the brake pedal.
- **Does the PCM BPA__SW PID indicate ON?**

Yes
GO to E2.
No
GO to E5.

E2 CHECK FOR AN OPEN CIRCUIT	

- Key in OFF position.
- Disconnect: Powertrain Control Module (PCM) C175b.
- Key in ON position.

LTV050000001428

Fig. 54   Test E, Codes P0703 & P1572: Brake On/Off Failure & Brake Switch Input Fault (Part 1 of 3). Aviator

Test Step	Result / Action to Take
D7 CHECK THE SPEED CONTROL ACTUATOR CIRCUITRY FOR A SHORT TO GROUND	

- Measure the resistance between the PCM, harness side and ground as follows:

Powertrain Control Module (PCM)	Circuit
C175b-45	133 (BK)
C175b-29	264 (LB/WH)
C175b-36	265 (LG/WH)
C175b-46	376 (BN/WH)

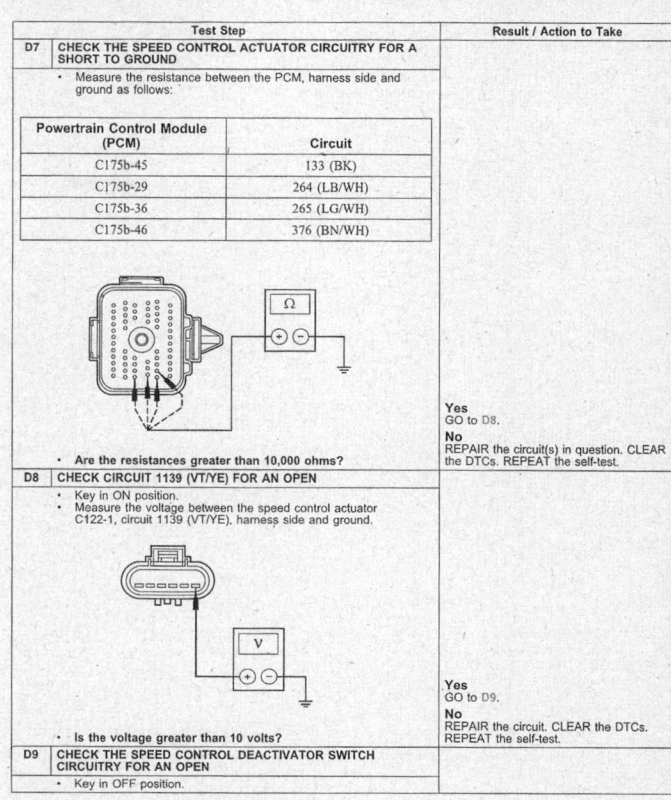

- **Are the resistances greater than 10,000 ohms?**

Yes
GO to D8.
No
REPAIR the circuit(s) in question. CLEAR the DTCs. REPEAT the self-test.

D8 CHECK CIRCUIT 1139 (VT/YE) FOR AN OPEN	

- Key in ON position.
- Measure the voltage between the speed control actuator C122-1, circuit 1139 (VT/YE), harness side and ground.

- **Is the voltage greater than 10 volts?**

Yes
GO to D9.
No
REPAIR the circuit. CLEAR the DTCs. REPEAT the self-test.

D9 CHECK THE SPEED CONTROL DEACTIVATOR SWITCH CIRCUITRY FOR AN OPEN	

- Key in OFF position.

LTV050000001426

Fig. 53   Test D, Code P1568: NGSC Actuator Self-Test Failure (Part 4 of 5). Aviator

Test Step	Result / Action to Take
E2 CHECK FOR AN OPEN CIRCUIT (Continued)	

- Measure the voltage between the PCM C175b-28, circuit 307 (BK/YE), harness side and ground.

- **Is the voltage greater than 10 volts?**

Yes
GO to E6.
No
GO to E3.

E3 CHECK THE SPEED CONTROL DEACTIVATOR SWITCH	

- Key in OFF position.
- Disconnect: Speed Control Deactivator Switch C2227.
- Connect a fused (5A) jumper wire between the speed control deactivator switch C2227-1, circuit 307 (BK/YE), harness side and the speed control deactivator switch C2227-2, circuit 10 (LG/RD), harness side.

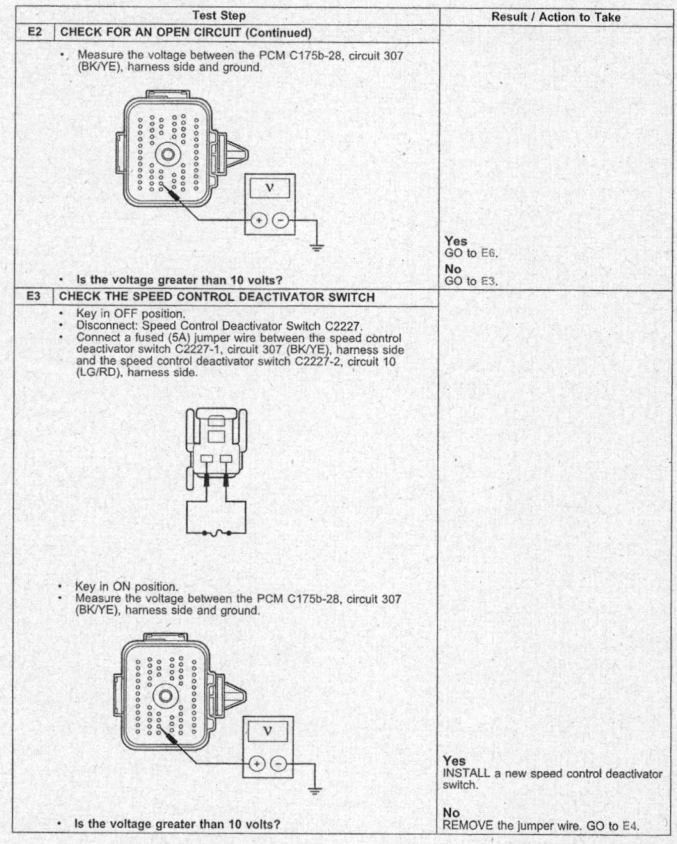

- Key in ON position.
- Measure the voltage between the PCM C175b-28, circuit 307 (BK/YE), harness side and ground.

- **Is the voltage greater than 10 volts?**

Yes
INSTALL a new speed control deactivator switch.
No
REMOVE the jumper wire. GO to E4.

LTV050000001429

Fig. 54   Test E, Codes P0703 & P1572: Brake On/Off Failure & Brake Switch Input Fault (Part 2 of 3). Aviator

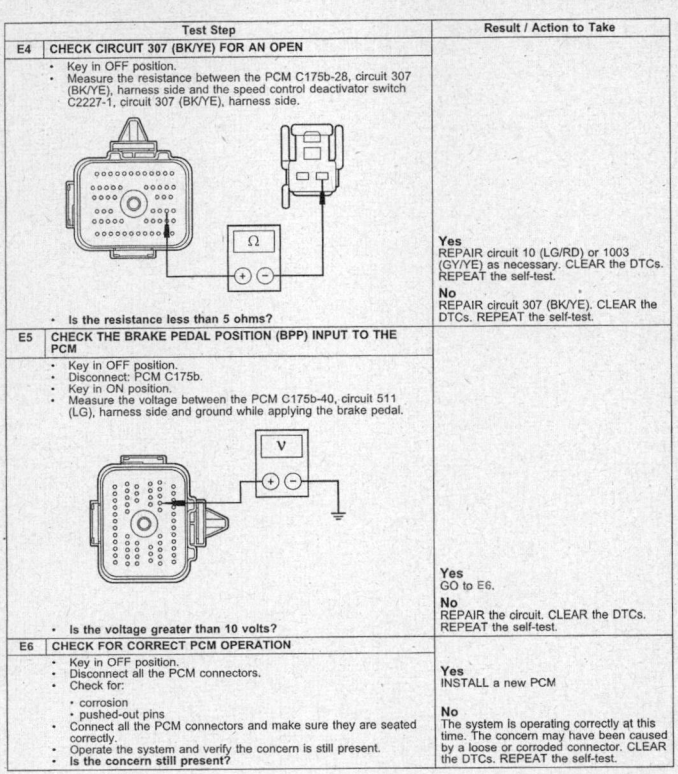

Test Step		Result / Action to Take
E4	CHECK CIRCUIT 307 (BK/YE) FOR AN OPEN • Key in OFF position. • Measure the resistance between the PCM C175b-28, circuit 307 (BK/YE), harness side and the speed control deactivator switch C2227-1, circuit 307 (BK/YE), harness side. • Is the resistance less than 5 ohms?	**Yes** REPAIR circuit 10 (LG/RD) or 1003 (GY/YE) as necessary. CLEAR the DTCs. REPEAT the self-test. **No** REPAIR circuit 307 (BK/YE). CLEAR the DTCs. REPEAT the self-test.
E5	CHECK THE BRAKE PEDAL POSITION (BPP) INPUT TO THE PCM • Key in OFF position. • Disconnect: PCM C175b. • Key in ON position. • Measure the voltage between the PCM C175b-40, circuit 511 (LG), harness side and ground while applying the brake pedal. • Is the voltage greater than 10 volts?	**Yes** GO to E6. **No** REPAIR the circuit. CLEAR the DTCs. REPEAT the self-test.
E6	CHECK FOR CORRECT PCM OPERATION • Key in OFF position. • Disconnect all the PCM connectors. • Check for: • corrosion • pushed-out pins • Connect all the PCM connectors and make sure they are seated correctly. • Operate the system and verify the concern is still present. • Is the concern still present?	**Yes** INSTALL a new PCM **No** The system is operating correctly at this time. The concern may have been caused by a loose or corroded connector. CLEAR the DTCs. REPEAT the self-test.

LTV0500000001430

Fig. 54   Test E, Codes P0703 & P1572: Brake On/Off Failure & Brake Switch Input Fault (Part 3 of 3). Aviator

Test Step		Result / Action to Take
F4	CHECK THE DIGITAL TRANSMISSION RANGE (TR) SENSOR (Continued) • Measure the resistance between the digital TR sensor C167 pin 2 component side, and the digital TR sensor C167 pin 4 component side while placing the transmission range selector lever in PARK and DRIVE. • Is the resistance less than 5 ohms when the selector is in PARK and greater than 10,000 ohms when the selector is in DRIVE ?	**Yes** GO to F5. **No** INSTALL a new digital TR sensor. TEST the system for normal operation.
F5	CHECK CIRCUIT 1144 (YE/BK) FOR A SHORT TO GROUND • Disconnect: Powertrain Control Module (PCM) C175t. • Measure the resistance between the digital TR sensor C167-4, circuit 1144 (YE/BK), harness side and the PCM C175t-22, circuit 1144 (YE/BK), harness side; and between the digital TR sensor C167-4, circuit 1144 (YE/BK), harness side and ground. • Is the resistance less than 5 ohms between the digital TR sensor and the PCM, and greater than 10,000 ohms between the digital TR sensor and ground?	**Yes** GO to F6. **No** REPAIR the circuit. REPEAT the self-test.

LTV0500000001432

Fig. 55   Test F: Speed Control Is Inoperative w/No DTC (Part 2 of 3). Aviator

Test Step		Result / Action to Take
F1	CHECK THE POWERTRAIN CONTROL MODULE (PCM) PID IDBRKSW • Key in ON position. • Monitor the PCM PID IDBRKSW. • Does the PCM PID IDBRKSW indicate OFF?	**Yes** GO to F3. **No** GO to F2.
F2	CHECK THE STOPLAMP SWITCH INPUT TO THE PCM • Key in OFF position. • Disconnect: PCM C175b. • Measure the voltage between the PCM C175b-40, circuit 511 (LG), harness side and ground. • Is any voltage present?	**Yes** Continue diagnosis of stoplamps. **No** GO to F8.
F3	CHECK THE PCM PID BPA__SW • Monitor the PCM PID BPA__SW while firmly applying the brake pedal. • Does the PCM PID BPA__SW indicate ON with the brake pedal firmly applied?	**Yes** GO to F4. **No** INSTALL a new speed control deactivator switch.
F4	CHECK THE DIGITAL TRANSMISSION RANGE (TR) SENSOR • Key in OFF position. • Disconnect: Digital TR Sensor C167.	

LTV0500000001431

Fig. 55   Test F: Speed Control Is Inoperative w/No DTC (Part 1 of 3). Aviator

Test Step		Result / Action to Take
F6	CHECK CIRCUIT 359 (GY/RD) FOR AN OPEN AND A SHORT TO GROUND • Measure the resistance between the digital TR sensor C167-2, circuit 359 (GY/RD), harness side and the PCM C175t-17, circuit 359 (GY/RD), harness side; and between the digital TR sensor C167-2, circuit 359 (GY/RD), harness side and ground. • Is the resistance less than 5 ohms between the digital TR sensor and the PCM, and greater than 10,000 ohms between the digital TR sensor and ground?	**Yes** GO to F7. **No** REPAIR the circuit. REPEAT the self-test.
F7	CHECK THE PCM SPEED CONTROL SWITCH PID • Key in ON position. • Monitor the PCM speed control switch PID while pressing and releasing the speed control switches. • Does the speed control switch match the PCM PID?	**Yes** GO to F8. **No** INSTALL a new speed control switch. CLEAR the DTCs. REPEAT the self-test.
F8	CHECK THE PCM PID VBAT • Monitor the PCM PID VBAT. • Does the PCM PID VBAT indicate greater than 10 volts with the engine running?	**Yes** GO to F9. **No** Continue diagnosis of charging system.
F9	CHECK FOR CORRECT PCM OPERATION • Disconnect all the PCM connectors. • Check for: • corrosion • pushed-out pins • Connect all the PCM connectors and make sure they are seated correctly. • Operate the system and verify the concern is still present. • Is the concern still present?	**Yes** INSTALL a new PCM. CLEAR the DTCs. REPEAT the self-test. **No** The system is operating correctly at this time. The concern may have been caused by a loose or corroded connector. CLEAR the DTCs. REPEAT the self-test.

LTV0500000001433

Fig. 55   Test F: Speed Control Is Inoperative w/No DTC (Part 3 of 3). Aviator

Test Step		Result / Action to Take
G1	CHECK THE POWERTRAIN CONTROL MODULE (PCM) • Key in OFF position. • Disconnect all the PCM connectors. • Key in ON position. • Is the concern still present?	**Yes** GO to G2. **No** GO to G3.
G2	CHECK FOR CORRECT INSTRUMENT CLUSTER OPERATION • Key in OFF position. • Disconnect all the instrument cluster connectors. • Check for: • corrosion • pushed-out pins • Connect all the instrument cluster connectors and make sure they are seated correctly. • Operate the system and verify the concern is still present. • Is the concern still present?	**Yes** INSTALL a new instrument cluster. **No** The system is operating correctly at this time. The concern may have been caused by a loose or corroded connector.
G3	CHECK FOR CORRECT PCM OPERATION • Key in OFF position. • Disconnect all the PCM connectors. • Check for: • corrosion • pushed-out pins • Connect all the PCM connectors and make sure they are seated correctly. • Operate the system and verify the concern is still present. • Is the concern still present?	**Yes** INSTALL a new TEST the system for normal operation. **No** The system is operating correctly at this time. The concern may have been caused by a loose or corroded connector.

LTV0500000001434

Fig. 56   Test G: Speed Control Indicator Lamp Is Always On. Aviator

Test Step	Result / Action to Take
A1 CHECK THE POWER TO THE SPEED CONTROL ACTUATOR • Key in OFF position. • Disconnect: Speed Control Actuator C122. • Key in ON position. • Measure the voltage between the speed control actuator C122 pin 7, circuit 294 (WH/LB), harness side and the speed control actuator C122 pin 10, circuit 1205 (OG/YE), harness side. 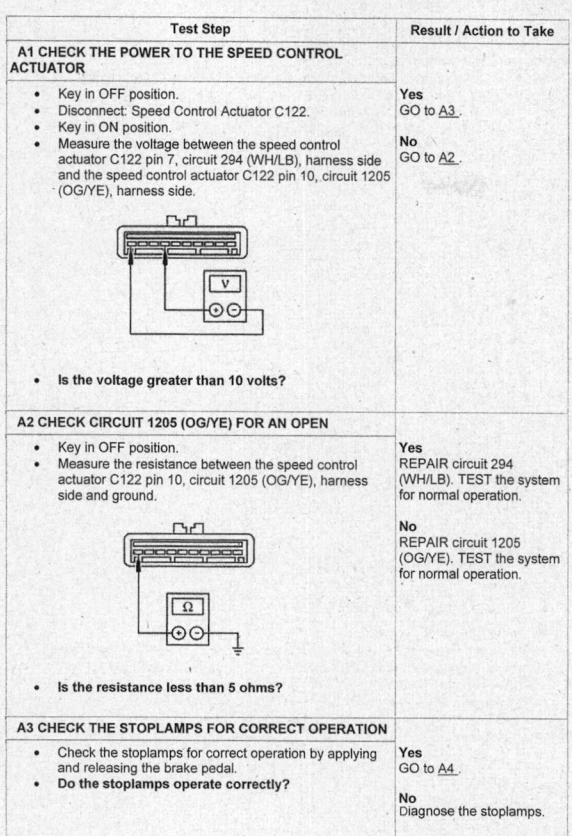 • Is the voltage greater than 10 volts?	**Yes** GO to <u>A3</u> . **No** GO to <u>A2</u> .
A2 CHECK CIRCUIT 1205 (OG/YE) FOR AN OPEN • Key in OFF position. • Measure the resistance between the speed control actuator C122 pin 10, circuit 1205 (OG/YE), harness side and ground. • Is the resistance less than 5 ohms?	**Yes** REPAIR circuit 294 (WH/LB). TEST the system for normal operation. **No** REPAIR circuit 1205 (OG/YE). TEST the system for normal operation.
A3 CHECK THE STOPLAMPS FOR CORRECT OPERATION • Check the stoplamps for correct operation by applying and releasing the brake pedal. • **Do the stoplamps operate correctly?**	**Yes** GO to <u>A4</u> . **No** Diagnose the stoplamps.

LTV0500000001453

Fig. 57 Test A: Speed Control Is Inoperative (Part 1 of 6). 2002–04 E-Series

Test Step	Result / Action to Take
A4 CHECK THE DEACTIVATOR SWITCH INPUT TO THE SPEED CONTROL ACTUATOR • Measure the voltage between the speed control actuator C122 pin 9, circuit 307 (BK/YE), harness side and the speed control actuator C122 pin 10, circuit 1205 (OG/YE), harness side. 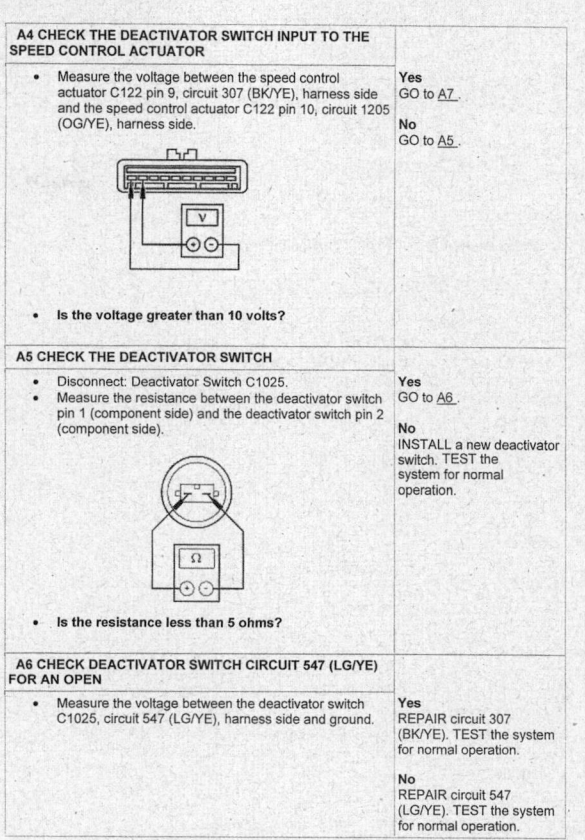 • Is the voltage greater than 10 volts?	**Yes** GO to <u>A7</u> . **No** GO to <u>A5</u> .
A5 CHECK THE DEACTIVATOR SWITCH • Disconnect: Deactivator Switch C1025. • Measure the resistance between the deactivator switch pin 1 (component side) and the deactivator switch pin 2 (component side). • Is the resistance less than 5 ohms?	**Yes** GO to <u>A6</u> . **No** INSTALL a new deactivator switch. TEST the system for normal operation.
A6 CHECK DEACTIVATOR SWITCH CIRCUIT 547 (LG/YE) FOR AN OPEN • Measure the voltage between the deactivator switch C1025, circuit 547 (LG/YE), harness side and ground.	**Yes** REPAIR circuit 307 (BK/YE). TEST the system for normal operation. **No** REPAIR circuit 547 (LG/YE). TEST the system for normal operation.

LTV0500000001454

Fig. 57 Test A: Speed Control Is Inoperative (Part 2 of 6). 2002–04 E-Series

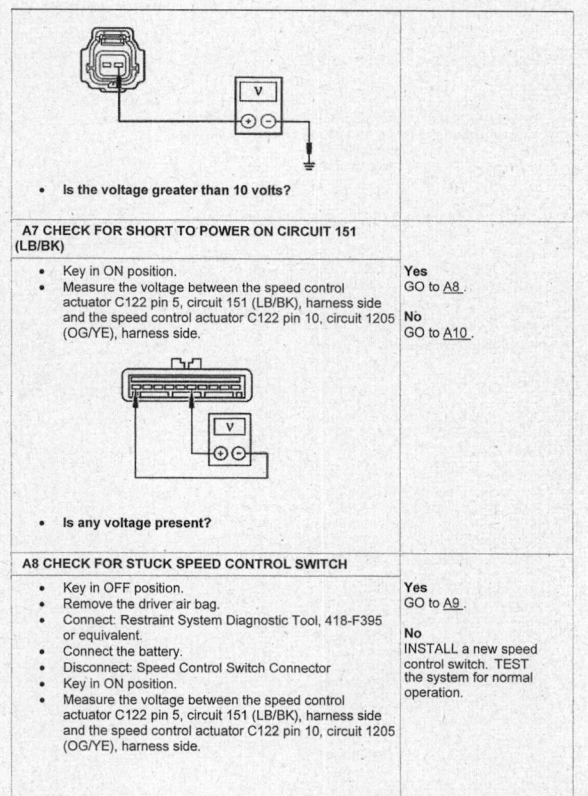

Test Step	Result / Action to Take
• Is the voltage greater than 10 volts?	
A7 CHECK FOR SHORT TO POWER ON CIRCUIT 151 (LB/BK) • Key in ON position. • Measure the voltage between the speed control actuator C122 pin 5, circuit 151 (LB/BK), harness side and the speed control actuator C122 pin 10, circuit 1205 (OG/YE), harness side. • Is any voltage present?	**Yes** GO to <u>A8</u> . **No** GO to <u>A10</u> .
A8 CHECK FOR STUCK SPEED CONTROL SWITCH • Key in OFF position. • Remove the driver air bag. • Connect: Restraint System Diagnostic Tool, 418-F395 or equivalent. • Connect the battery. • Disconnect: Speed Control Switch Connector • Key in ON position. • Measure the voltage between the speed control actuator C122 pin 5, circuit 151 (LB/BK), harness side and the speed control actuator C122 pin 10, circuit 1205 (OG/YE), harness side.	**Yes** GO to <u>A9</u> . **No** INSTALL a new speed control switch. TEST the system for normal operation.

LTV0500000001455

Fig. 57 Test A: Speed Control Is Inoperative (Part 3 of 6). 2002–04 E-Series

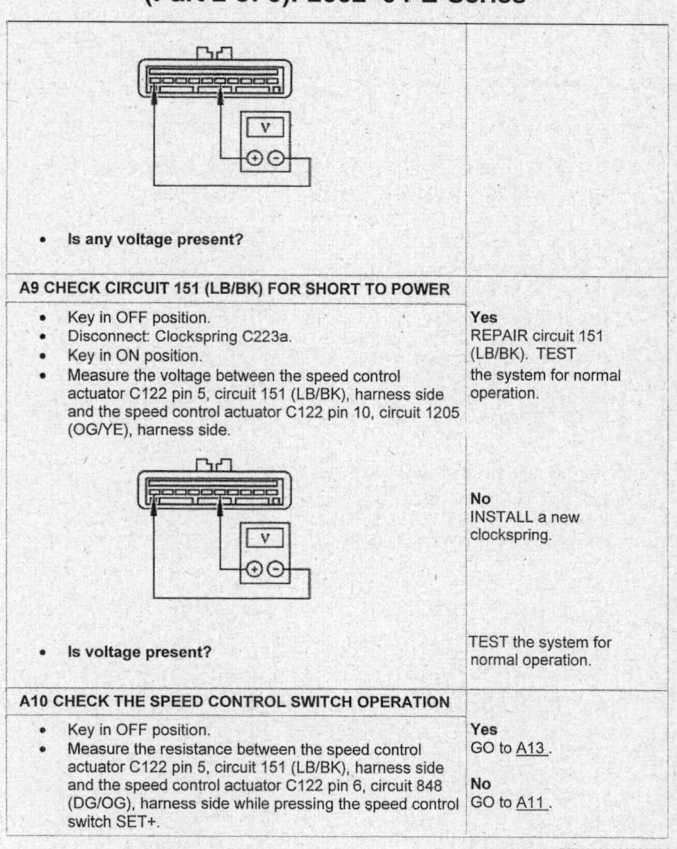

Test Step	Result / Action to Take
• Is any voltage present?	
A9 CHECK CIRCUIT 151 (LB/BK) FOR SHORT TO POWER • Key in OFF position. • Disconnect: Clockspring C223a. • Key in ON position. • Measure the voltage between the speed control actuator C122 pin 5, circuit 151 (LB/BK), harness side and the speed control actuator C122 pin 10, circuit 1205 (OG/YE), harness side. • Is voltage present?	**Yes** REPAIR circuit 151 (LB/BK). TEST the system for normal operation. **No** INSTALL a new clockspring. TEST the system for normal operation.
A10 CHECK THE SPEED CONTROL SWITCH OPERATION • Key in OFF position. • Measure the resistance between the speed control actuator C122 pin 5, circuit 151 (LB/BK), harness side and the speed control actuator C122 pin 6, circuit 848 (DG/OG), harness side while pressing the speed control switch SET+.	**Yes** GO to <u>A13</u> . **No** GO to <u>A11</u> .

LTV0500000001456

Fig. 57 Test A: Speed Control Is Inoperative (Part 4 of 6). 2002–04 E-Series

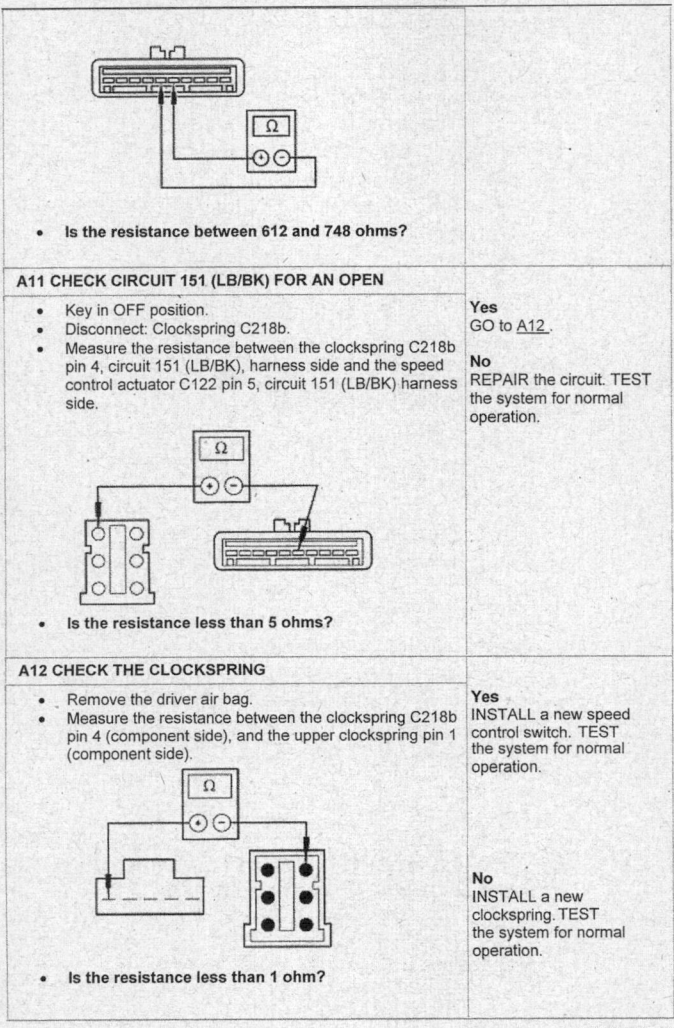

- **Is the resistance between 612 and 748 ohms?**

A11 CHECK CIRCUIT 151 (LB/BK) FOR AN OPEN

• Key in OFF position. • Disconnect: Clockspring C218b. • Measure the resistance between the clockspring C218b pin 4, circuit 151 (LB/BK), harness side and the speed control actuator C122 pin 5, circuit 151 (LB/BK) harness side.	**Yes** GO to A12. **No** REPAIR the circuit. TEST the system for normal operation.

- **Is the resistance less than 5 ohms?**

A12 CHECK THE CLOCKSPRING

• Remove the driver air bag. • Measure the resistance between the clockspring C218b pin 4 (component side), and the upper clockspring pin 1 (component side).	**Yes** INSTALL a new speed control switch. TEST the system for normal operation. **No** INSTALL a new clockspring. TEST the system for normal operation.

- **Is the resistance less than 1 ohm?**

LTV0500000001457

Fig. 57   Test A: Speed Control Is Inoperative (Part 5 of 6). 2002–04 E-Series

Test Step	Result / Action to Take
B1 CHECK THE SPEED CONTROL CABLE/THROTTLE BODY LINKAGE • Key in OFF position. • Remove the speed control cable from the speed control actuator. Visually inspect the core wire and check the speed control cable by pulling on it and noting the throttle movement. • **Is the speed control cable OK?**	**Yes** GO to B2. **No** INSTALL a new speed control cable or repair the throttle body linkage. TEST the system for normal operation.
B2 CHECK THE SPEEDOMETER OPERATION • Drive the vehicle and observe the speedometer operation without using the speed control. • **Does the speedometer needle fluctuate?**	**Yes** REFER to: "Dash Gauges & Warning Indicators" section to continue diagnosis. **No** INSTALL a new speed control actuator. TEST the system for normal operation.

LTV0500000001459

Fig. 58   Test B: Set Speed Fluctuates. 2002–04 E-Series

A13 CHECK CIRCUIT 679 (GY/BK) FOR AN OPEN

• Disconnect: Powertrain Control Module C175. • Measure the resistance between the speed control actuator C122 pin 3, circuit 679 (GY/BK), harness side and the powertrain control module (PCM) C175 pin 68 (4.6L and 5.4L), or pin 46 (6.8L), circuit 679 (GY/BK), harness side.	**Yes** GO to A14. **No** REPAIR the circuit. TEST the system for normal operation.

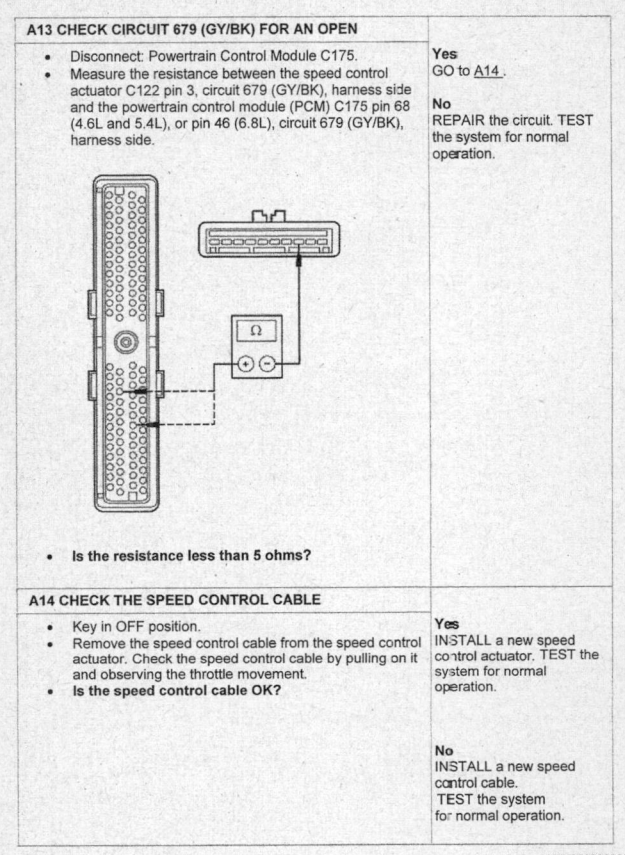

- **Is the resistance less than 5 ohms?**

A14 CHECK THE SPEED CONTROL CABLE

• Key in OFF position. • Remove the speed control cable from the speed control actuator. Check the speed control cable by pulling on it and observing the throttle movement. • **Is the speed control cable OK?**	**Yes** INSTALL a new speed control actuator. TEST the system for normal operation. **No** INSTALL a new speed control cable. TEST the system for normal operation.

LTV0500000001458

Fig. 57   Test A: Speed Control Is Inoperative (Part 6 of 6). 2002–04 E-Series

Test Step	Result / Action to Take
C1 CHECK THE SPEED CONTROL CABLE/THROTTLE BODY LINKAGE • Key in OFF position. • Remove the speed control cable from the speed control actuator. Check the speed control cable by pulling on it and observing the throttle movement. • **Is the speed control cable OK?**	**Yes** GO to C2. **No** INSTALL a new speed control cable or repair of the throttle body linkage. TEST the system for normal operation.
C2 CHECK THE STOPLAMP OPERATION • Check the stoplamps for correct operation by applying and releasing the brake pedal. • **Do the stoplamps operate correctly?**	**Yes** GO to C3. **No** Diagnose stoplamps.
C3 CHECK THE BRAKE PEDAL POSITION (BPP) SWITCH CIRCUIT 569 (DG) • Key in OFF position. • Disconnect: Speed Control Actuator C122. • Measure the voltage between the speed control actuator C122 pin 4, circuit 569 (DG), harness side and the speed control actuator C122 pin 10, circuit 1205 (OG/YE), harness side, while applying the brake pedal. DL0031-A • **Is the voltage greater than 10 volts?**	**Yes** INSTALL a new speed control actuator. TEST the system for normal operation. **No** REPAIR circuit 569 (DG). TEST the system for normal operation.

LTV0500000001460

Fig. 59   Test C: Speed Control Does Not Disengage When Brakes Are Applied. 2002–04 E-Series

Test Step	Result / Action to Take
D1 CHECK SET- SWITCH OPERATION • Key in OFF position. • Disconnect: Speed Control Actuator C122. • With the speed control switch SET- pressed, turn the steering wheel from stop to stop, measuring the resistance between the speed control actuator C122 pin 5, circuit 151 (LB/BK), harness side and the speed control actuator C122 pin 6, circuit 848 (DG/OG), harness side. • Is the resistance between 108 and 132 ohms?	**Yes** INSTALL a new speed control actuator. TEST the system for normal operation. **No** INSTALL a new speed control switch. TEST the system for normal operation.

LTV0500000001461

Fig. 60   Test D: Speed Control Switch Is Inoperative (SET –). 2002–04 E-Series

Test Step	Result / Action to Take
E1 CHECK SET+ SWITCH OPERATION • Key in OFF position. • Disconnect: Speed Control Actuator C122. • With the speed control switch SET+ pressed and while turning the steering wheel from stop to stop, measure the resistance between the speed control actuator C122 pin 5, circuit 151 (LB/BK), harness side and the speed control actuator C122 pin 6, circuit 848 (DG/OG), harness side. • Is the resistance between 612 and 748 ohms?	**Yes** INSTALL a new speed control actuator. TEST the system for normal operation. **No** INSTALL a new speed control switch. TEST the system for normal operation.

LTV0500000001462

Fig. 61   Test E: Speed Control Switch Is Inoperative (SET +). 2002–04 E-Series

Test Step	Result / Action to Take
F1 CHECK THE RESUME SWITCH OPERATION • Key in OFF position. • Disconnect: Speed Control Actuator C122. • With the speed control switch RESUME pressed, turn the steering wheel from stop to stop, measuring the resistance between the speed control actuator C122 pin 5, circuit 151 (LB/BK), harness side and the speed control actuator C122 pin 6, circuit 848 (DG/OG), harness side. • Is the resistance between 1,980 and 2,420 ohms?	**Yes** INSTALL a new speed control actuator. TEST the system for normal operation. **No** INSTALL a new speed control switch. TEST the system for normal operation.

LTV0500000001463

Fig. 62   Test F: Speed Control Switch Is Inoperative (RESUME). 2002–04 E-Series

Test Step	Result / Action to Take
G1 CHECK CANCEL SWITCH OPERATION • Key in OFF position. • Disconnect: Speed Control Actuator C122. • With the speed control switch CANCEL pressed, turn the steering wheel from stop to stop, measure the resistance between the speed control actuator C122 pin 5, circuit 151 (LB/BK), harness side and the speed control actuator C122 pin 6, circuit 848 (DG/OG), harness side. • Is the resistance less than 5 ohms?	**Yes** INSTALL a new speed control actuator. TEST the system for normal operation. **No** INSTALL a new speed control switch. TEST the system for normal operation.

LTV0500000001464

Fig. 63   Test G: Speed Control Switch Is Inoperative (CANCEL). 2002–04 E-Series

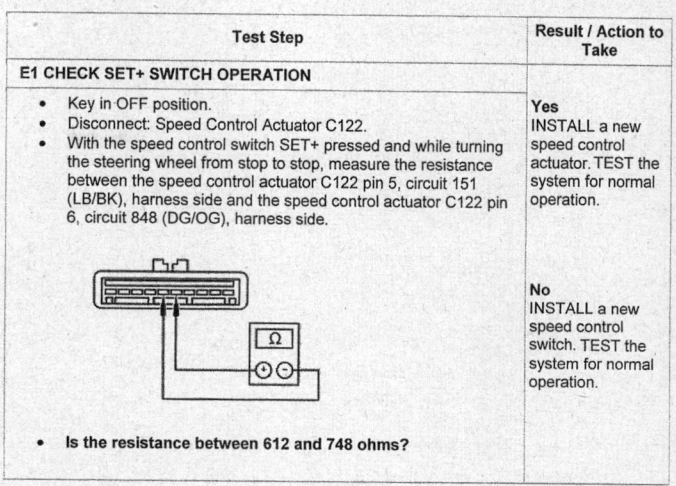

Test Step	Result / Action to Take
A1 RETRIEVE THE RECORDED PCM DTCs FROM BOTH THE CONTINUOUS AND ON-DEMAND SELF-TESTS • Check for recorded PCM DTCs from the continuous and on-demand self-tests. • Are any DTCs recorded?	**Yes** REFER to the Powertrain Control Module (PCM) Diagnostic Trouble Code (DTC) Index to continue diagnosis. **No** GO to A2.
A2 CHECK THE SPEED CONTROL SWITCH • Key in OFF position. • Disconnect: PCM C175a (Gasoline) or C176a (Diesel). • For gasoline vehicles, measure the resistance between the PCM C175a-19, circuit 151 (LB/BK), harness side and the PCM C175a-30, circuit 848 (DG/OG), harness side while pressing the speed control buttons as follows:	

Speed Control Switch	Resistance Value
OFF	Less than 5 ohms
COAST	276 - 324 ohms
SET/ACCEL	552 - 648 ohms
RESUME	1,021 - 1,199 ohms
ON	1,941 - 2,278 ohms
No switch pressed	3,965 - 4,655 ohms

• For diesel vehicles, measure the resistance between the PCM C176a-31, circuit 151 (LB/BK), harness side and the PCM C176a-24, circuit 848 (DG/OG), harness side while pressing the speed control buttons as follows:

Speed Control Switch	Resistance Value
OFF	Less than 5 ohms
COAST	276 - 324 ohms
SET/ACCEL	552 - 648 ohms
RESUME	1,021 - 1,199 ohms
ON	1,941 - 2,278 ohms
No switch pressed	3,965 - 4,655 ohms

LTV0500000001466

Fig. 64   Test A: Speed Control Is Inoperative (Part 1 of 2). 2005–06 E-Series

Test Step	Result / Action to Take
A2 CHECK THE SPEED CONTROL SWITCH (Continued)	
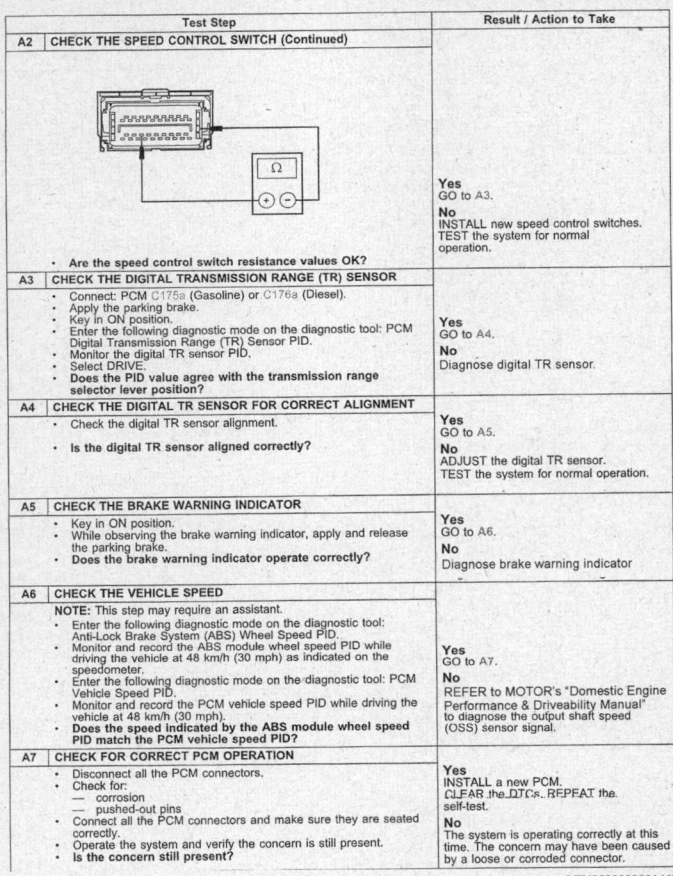 • Are the speed control switch resistance values OK?	**Yes** GO to A3. **No** INSTALL new speed control switches. TEST the system for normal operation.
A3 CHECK THE DIGITAL TRANSMISSION RANGE (TR) SENSOR • Connect: PCM C175a (Gasoline) or C176a (Diesel). • Apply the parking brake. • Key in ON position. • Enter the following diagnostic mode on the diagnostic tool: PCM Digital Transmission Range (TR) Sensor PID. • Monitor the digital TR sensor PID. • Select DRIVE. • **Does the PID value agree with the transmission range selector lever position?**	**Yes** GO to A4. **No** Diagnose digital TR sensor.
A4 CHECK THE DIGITAL TR SENSOR FOR CORRECT ALIGNMENT • Check the digital TR sensor alignment. • **Is the digital TR sensor aligned correctly?**	**Yes** GO to A5. **No** ADJUST the digital TR sensor. TEST the system for normal operation.
A5 CHECK THE BRAKE WARNING INDICATOR • Key in ON position. • While observing the brake warning indicator, apply and release the parking brake. • **Does the brake warning indicator operate correctly?**	**Yes** GO to A6. **No** Diagnose brake warning indicator
A6 CHECK THE VEHICLE SPEED NOTE: This step may require an assistant. • Enter the following diagnostic mode on the diagnostic tool: Anti-Lock Brake System (ABS) Wheel Speed PID. • Monitor and record the ABS module wheel speed PID while driving the vehicle at 48 km/h (30 mph) as indicated on the speedometer. • Enter the following diagnostic mode on the diagnostic tool: PCM Vehicle Speed PID. • Monitor and record the PCM vehicle speed PID while driving the vehicle at 48 km/h (30 mph). • **Does the speed indicated by the ABS module wheel speed PID match the PCM vehicle speed PID?**	**Yes** GO to A7. **No** REFER to MOTOR's "Domestic Engine Performance & Driveability Manual" to diagnose the output shaft speed (OSS) sensor signal.
A7 CHECK FOR CORRECT PCM OPERATION • Disconnect all the PCM connectors. • Check for: — corrosion — pushed-out pins • Connect all the PCM connectors and make sure they are seated correctly. • Operate the system and verify the concern is still present. • **Is the concern still present?**	**Yes** INSTALL a new PCM. CLEAR the DTCs. REPEAT the self-test. **No** The system is operating correctly at this time. The concern may have been caused by a loose or corroded connector.

LTV0500000001467

Fig. 64   Test A: Speed Control Is Inoperative (Part 2 of 2). 2005–06 E-Series

Test Step	Result / Action to Take
B3 CHECK THE SPEED CONTROL DEACTIVATOR SWITCH FOR CORRECT OPERATION • Disconnect: PCM C175b (Gasoline) or C176a (Diesel). • Key in ON position. • For gasoline vehicles, while firmly applying and releasing the brake pedal, measure the voltage between the PCM C175b-65, circuit 307 (BK/YE), harness side and ground.	
• For diesel vehicles, while firmly applying and releasing the brake pedal, measure the voltage between the PCM C176a-28, circuit 307 (BK/YE), harness side and ground. • **Is the voltage greater than 10 volts with the brake pedal released and 0 volts with the brake pedal firmly applied?**	**Yes** GO to B7. **No** GO to B4.
B4 CHECK CIRCUIT 547 (LG/YE) FOR AN OPEN • Key in OFF position. • Disconnect: Speed Control Deactivator Switch C1025. • Key in ON position.	

LTV0500000001469

Fig. 65   Test B, Codes P1703 & P1572: Brake On/Off Circuit Failure (Part 2 of 4). 2005–06 E-Series

Test Step	Result / Action to Take
B1 CHECK THE STOPLAMP OPERATION • Apply and release the brake pedal while observing the stoplamps. • **Do the stoplamps operate correctly?**	**Yes** GO to B2. **No** Diagnose stoplamps.
B2 CHECK CIRCUIT 569 (DG) FOR AN OPEN • Key in OFF position. • Disconnect: PCM C175a (Gasoline) or C176a (Diesel). • For gasoline vehicles, measure the voltage between the PCM C175a-8, circuit 569 (DG), harness side and ground while applying the brake pedal. 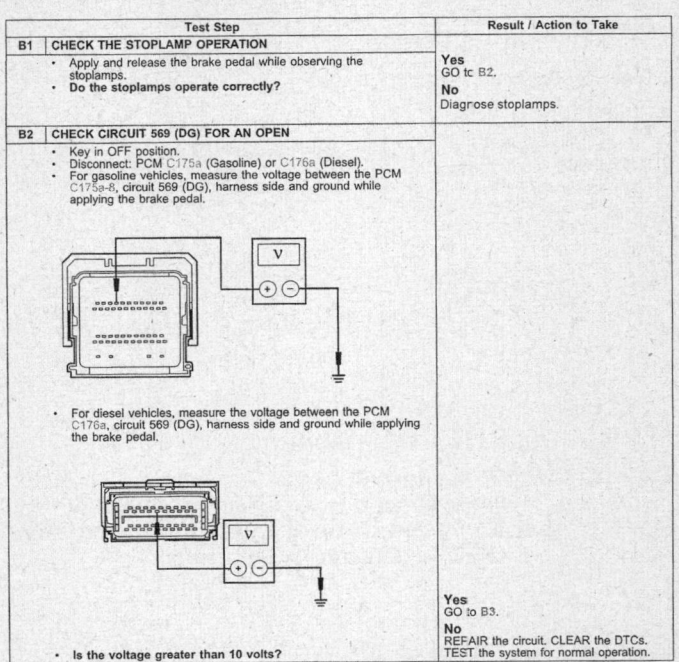 • For diesel vehicles, measure the voltage between the PCM C176a, circuit 569 (DG), harness side and ground while applying the brake pedal. • **Is the voltage greater than 10 volts?**	**Yes** GO to B3. **No** REPAIR the circuit. CLEAR the DTCs. TEST the system for normal operation.

LTV0500000001468

Fig. 65   Test B, Codes P1703 & P1572: Brake On/Off Circuit Failure (Part 1 of 4). 2005–06 E-Series

Test Step	Result / Action to Take
B4 CHECK CIRCUIT 547 (LG/YE) FOR AN OPEN (Continued) • Measure the voltage between the speed control deactivator switch C1025-2, circuit 547 (LG/YE), harness side and ground. • **Is the voltage greater than 10 volts?**	**Yes** GO to B5. **No** VERIFY the battery junction box (BJB) fuse 6 (2A) is OK. If OK, REPAIR the circuit. CLEAR the DTCs. REPEAT the self-test.
B5 CHECK CIRCUIT 307 (BK/YE) FOR A SHORT TO VOLTAGE • Measure the voltage between the speed control deactivator switch C1025-1, circuit 307 (BK/YE), harness side and ground. • **Is any voltage present?**	**Yes** REPAIR the circuit. CLEAR the DTCs. REPEAT the self-test. **No** GO to B6.
B6 CHECK CIRCUIT 307 (BK/YE) FOR AN OPEN • Key in OFF position. • For gasoline vehicles, measure the resistance between the PCM C175b-65, circuit 307 (BK/YE), harness side, and the speed control deactivator switch C1025-1, circuit 307 (BK/YE), harness side.	

LTV0500000001470

Fig. 65   Test B, Codes P1703 & P1572: Brake On/Off Circuit Failure (Part 3 of 4). 2005–06 E-Series

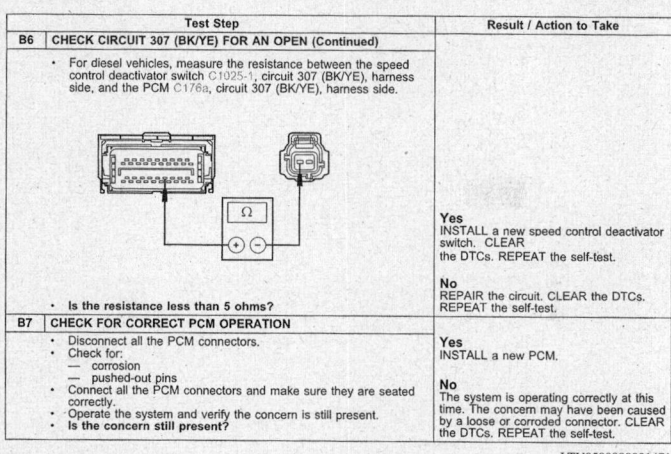

Test Step	Result / Action to Take
B6 CHECK CIRCUIT 307 (BK/YE) FOR AN OPEN (Continued) • For diesel vehicles, measure the resistance between the speed control deactivator switch C1025-1, circuit 307 (BK/YE), harness side, and the PCM C176a, circuit 307 (BK/YE), harness side. • Is the resistance less than 5 ohms?	**Yes** INSTALL a new speed control deactivator switch. CLEAR the DTCs. REPEAT the self-test. **No** REPAIR the circuit. CLEAR the DTCs. REPEAT the self-test.
B7 CHECK FOR CORRECT PCM OPERATION • Disconnect all the PCM connectors. • Check for: — corrosion — pushed-out pins • Connect all the PCM connectors and make sure they are seated correctly. • Operate the system and verify the concern is still present. • Is the concern still present?	**Yes** INSTALL a new PCM. **No** The system is operating correctly at this time. The concern may have been caused by a loose or corroded connector. CLEAR the DTCs. REPEAT the self-test.

LTV0500000001471

Fig. 65   Test B, Codes P1703 & P1572: Brake On/Off Circuit Failure (Part 4 of 4). 2005–06 E-Series

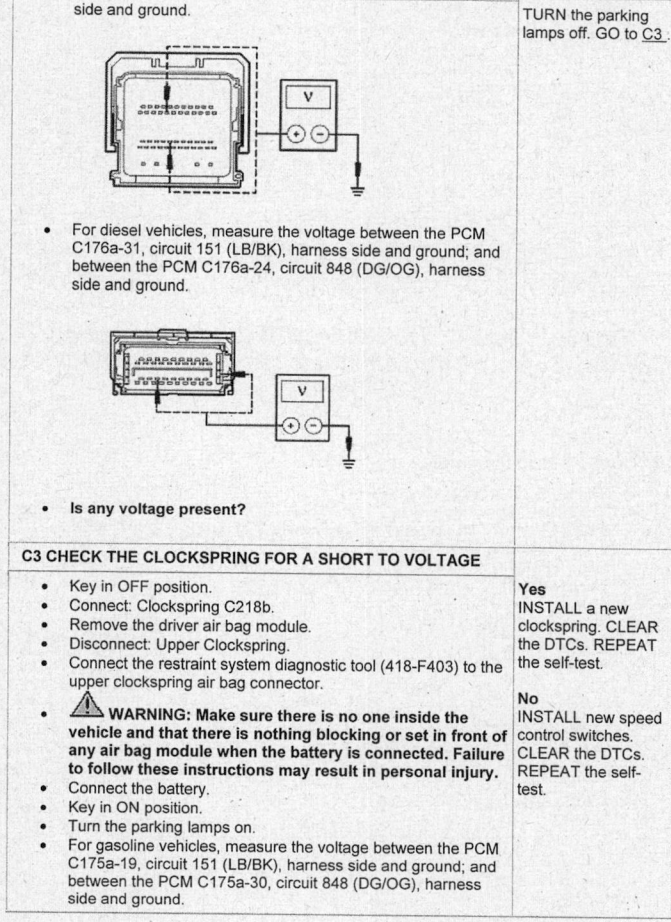

Test Step	Result / Action to Take
side and ground. • For diesel vehicles, measure the voltage between the PCM C176a-31, circuit 151 (LB/BK), harness side and ground; and between the PCM C176a-24, circuit 848 (DG/OG), harness side and ground. • Is any voltage present?	TURN the parking lamps off. GO to C3.
C3 CHECK THE CLOCKSPRING FOR A SHORT TO VOLTAGE • Key in OFF position. • Connect: Clockspring C218b. • Remove the driver air bag module. • Disconnect: Upper Clockspring. • Connect the restraint system diagnostic tool (418-F403) to the upper clockspring air bag connector. • ⚠ **WARNING:** Make sure there is no one inside the vehicle and that there is nothing blocking or set in front of any air bag module when the battery is connected. Failure to follow these instructions may result in personal injury. • Connect the battery. • Key in ON position. • Turn the parking lamps on. • For gasoline vehicles, measure the voltage between the PCM C175a-19, circuit 151 (LB/BK), harness side and ground; and between the PCM C175a-30, circuit 848 (DG/OG), harness side and ground.	**Yes** INSTALL a new clockspring. CLEAR the DTCs. REPEAT the self-test. **No** INSTALL new speed control switches. CLEAR the DTCs. REPEAT the self-test.

LTV0500000001473

Fig. 66   Test C, Codes P0579 & P0581: Speed Control Switch Circuit Failure (Part 2 of 7). 2005–06 E-Series

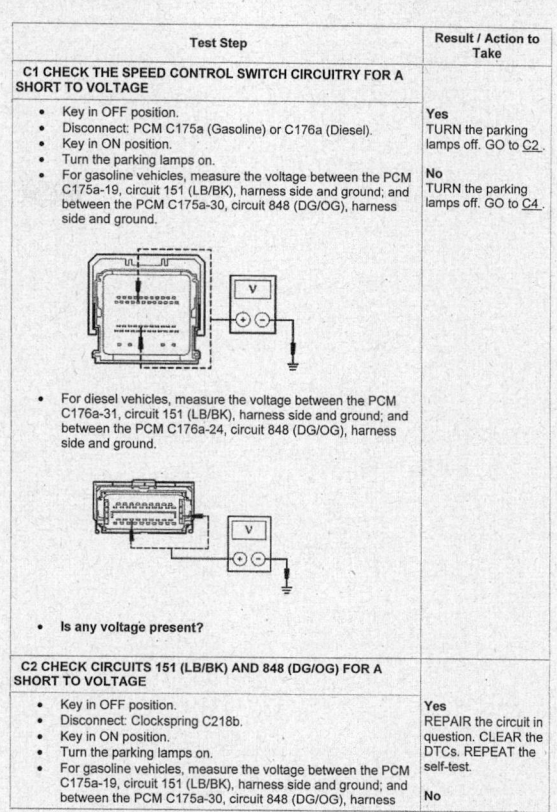

Test Step	Result / Action to Take
C1 CHECK THE SPEED CONTROL SWITCH CIRCUITRY FOR A SHORT TO VOLTAGE • Key in OFF position. • Disconnect: PCM C175a (Gasoline) or C176a (Diesel). • Key in ON position. • Turn the parking lamps on. • For gasoline vehicles, measure the voltage between the PCM C175a-19, circuit 151 (LB/BK), harness side and ground; and between the PCM C175a-30, circuit 848 (DG/OG), harness side and ground. • For diesel vehicles, measure the voltage between the PCM C176a-31, circuit 151 (LB/BK), harness side and ground; and between the PCM C176a-24, circuit 848 (DG/OG), harness side and ground. • Is any voltage present?	**Yes** TURN the parking lamps off. GO to C2. **No** TURN the parking lamps off. GO to C4.
C2 CHECK CIRCUITS 151 (LB/BK) AND 848 (DG/OG) FOR A SHORT TO VOLTAGE • Key in OFF position. • Disconnect: Clockspring C218b. • Key in ON position. • Turn the parking lamps on. • For gasoline vehicles, measure the voltage between the PCM C175a-19, circuit 151 (LB/BK), harness side and ground; and between the PCM C175a-30, circuit 848 (DG/OG), harness	**Yes** REPAIR the circuit in question. CLEAR the DTCs. REPEAT the self-test. **No**

LTV0500000001472

Fig. 66   Test C, Codes P0579 & P0581: Speed Control Switch Circuit Failure (Part 1 of 7). 2005–06 E-Series

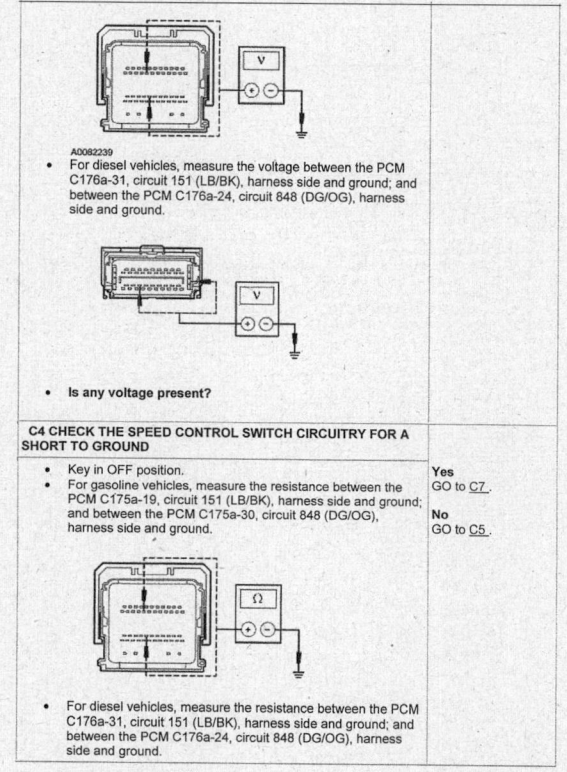

Test Step	Result / Action to Take
A0082239 • For diesel vehicles, measure the voltage between the PCM C176a-31, circuit 151 (LB/BK), harness side and ground; and between the PCM C176a-24, circuit 848 (DG/OG), harness side and ground. • Is any voltage present?	
C4 CHECK THE SPEED CONTROL SWITCH CIRCUITRY FOR A SHORT TO GROUND • Key in OFF position. • For gasoline vehicles, measure the resistance between the PCM C175a-19, circuit 151 (LB/BK), harness side and ground; and between the PCM C175a-30, circuit 848 (DG/OG), harness side and ground. • For diesel vehicles, measure the resistance between the PCM C176a-31, circuit 151 (LB/BK), harness side and ground; and between the PCM C176a-24, circuit 848 (DG/OG), harness side and ground.	**Yes** GO to C7. **No** GO to C5.

LTV0500000001474

Fig. 66   Test C, Codes P0579 & P0581: Speed Control Switch Circuit Failure (Part 3 of 7). 2005–06 E-Series

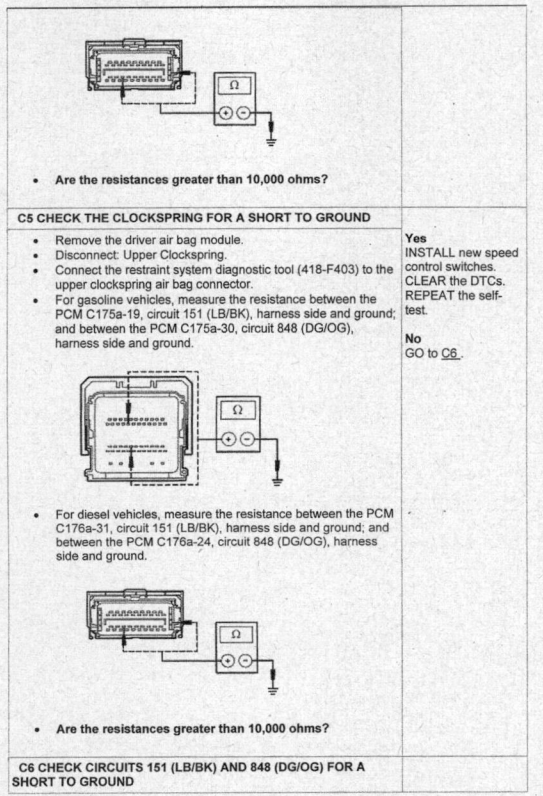

- Are the resistances greater than 10,000 ohms?

C5 CHECK THE CLOCKSPRING FOR A SHORT TO GROUND

- Remove the driver air bag module.
- Disconnect: Upper Clockspring.
- Connect the restraint system diagnostic tool (418-F403) to the upper clockspring air bag connector.
- For gasoline vehicles, measure the resistance between the PCM C175a-19, circuit 151 (LB/BK), harness side and ground; and between the PCM C175a-30, circuit 848 (DG/OG), harness side and ground.

Yes
INSTALL new speed control switches. CLEAR the DTCs. REPEAT the self-test.

No
GO to C6.

- For diesel vehicles, measure the resistance between the PCM C176a-31, circuit 151 (LB/BK), harness side and ground; and between the PCM C176a-24, circuit 848 (DG/OG), harness side and ground.

- Are the resistances greater than 10,000 ohms?

C6 CHECK CIRCUITS 151 (LB/BK) AND 848 (DG/OG) FOR A SHORT TO GROUND

LTV0500000001475

Fig. 66 Test C, Codes P0579 & P0581: Speed Control Switch Circuit Failure (Part 4 of 7). 2005–06 E-Series

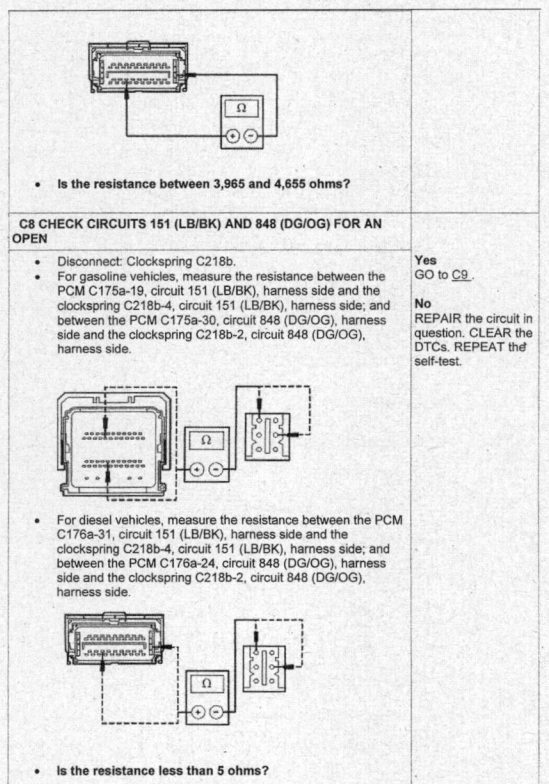

- Is the resistance between 3,965 and 4,655 ohms?

C8 CHECK CIRCUITS 151 (LB/BK) AND 848 (DG/OG) FOR AN OPEN

- Disconnect: Clockspring C218b.
- For gasoline vehicles, measure the resistance between the PCM C175a-19, circuit 151 (LB/BK), harness side and the clockspring C218b-4, circuit 151 (LB/BK), harness side; and between the PCM C175a-30, circuit 848 (DG/OG), harness side and the clockspring C218b-2, circuit 848 (DG/OG), harness side.

Yes
GO to C9.

No
REPAIR the circuit in question. CLEAR the DTCs. REPEAT the self-test.

- For diesel vehicles, measure the resistance between the PCM C176a-31, circuit 151 (LB/BK), harness side and the clockspring C218b-4, circuit 151 (LB/BK), harness side; and between the PCM C176a-24, circuit 848 (DG/OG), harness side and the clockspring C218b-2, circuit 848 (DG/OG), harness side.

- Is the resistance less than 5 ohms?

LTV0500000001477

Fig. 66 Test C, Codes P0579 & P0581: Speed Control Switch Circuit Failure (Part 6 of 7). 2005–06 E-Series

- Disconnect: Clockspring C218b.
- For gasoline vehicles, measure the resistance between the PCM C175a-19, circuit 151 (LB/BK), harness side and ground; and between the PCM C175a-30, circuit 848 (DG/OG), harness side and ground.

Yes
INSTALL a new clockspring. CLEAR the DTCs. REPEAT the self-test.

No
REPAIR the circuit in question. CLEAR the DTCs. REPEAT the self-test.

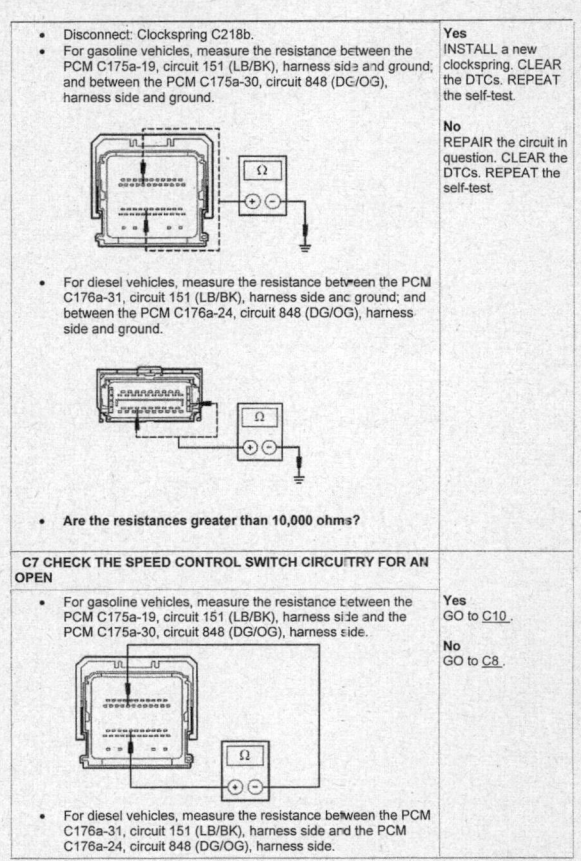

- For diesel vehicles, measure the resistance between the PCM C176a-31, circuit 151 (LB/BK), harness side and ground; and between the PCM C176a-24, circuit 848 (DG/OG), harness side and ground.

- Are the resistances greater than 10,000 ohms?

C7 CHECK THE SPEED CONTROL SWITCH CIRCUITRY FOR AN OPEN

- For gasoline vehicles, measure the resistance between the PCM C175a-19, circuit 151 (LB/BK), harness side and the PCM C175a-30, circuit 848 (DG/OG), harness side.

Yes
GO to C10.

No
GO to C8.

- For diesel vehicles, measure the resistance between the PCM C176a-31, circuit 151 (LB/BK), harness side and the PCM C176a-24, circuit 848 (DG/OG), harness side.

LTV0500000001476

Fig. 66 Test C, Codes P0579 & P0581: Speed Control Switch Circuit Failure (Part 5 of 7). 2005–06 E-Series

C9 CHECK THE CLOCKSPRING

- Remove the driver air bag module.
- Disconnect: Upper Clockspring.
- Measure the resistance between the clockspring C218b pin 4, component side and the upper clockspring pin 1, component side; and between the clockspring C218b pin 2, component side and the upper clockspring pin 2, component side.

Yes
INSTALL new speed control switches. TEST the system for normal operation.

No
INSTALL a new clockspring. CLEAR the DTCs. REPEAT the self-test.

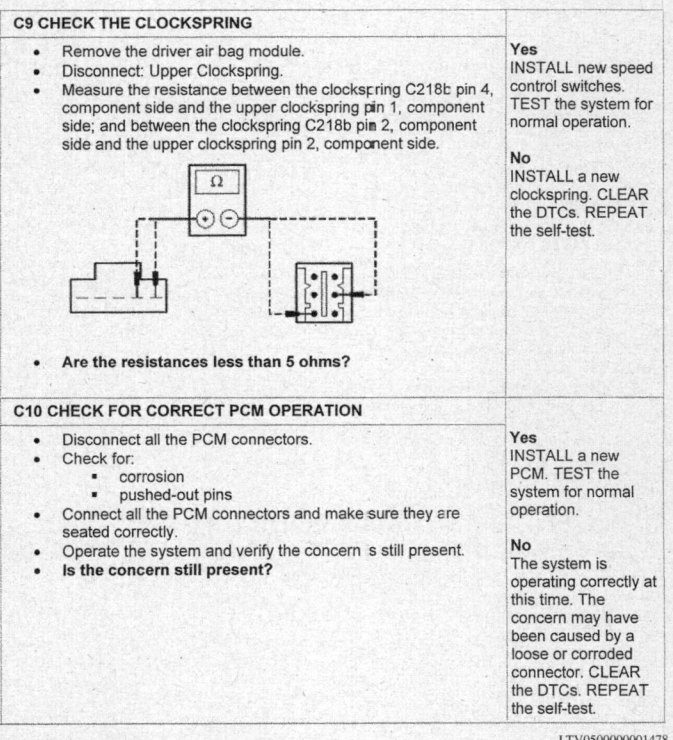

- Are the resistances less than 5 ohms?

C10 CHECK FOR CORRECT PCM OPERATION

- Disconnect all the PCM connectors.
- Check for:
    - corrosion
    - pushed-out pins
- Connect all the PCM connectors and make sure they are seated correctly.
- Operate the system and verify the concern is still present.
- Is the concern still present?

Yes
INSTALL a new PCM. TEST the system for normal operation.

No
The system is operating correctly at this time. The concern may have been caused by a loose or corroded connector. CLEAR the DTCs. REPEAT the self-test.

LTV0500000001478

Fig. 66 Test C, Codes P0579 & P0581: Speed Control Switch Circuit Failure (Part 7 of 7). 2005–06 E-Series

Test Step	Result / Action to Take
A1 CHECK POWER AND GROUND TO THE SPEED CONTROL ACTUATOR • Key in OFF position. • Disconnect: Speed Control Actuator C122. • Key in ON position. • Measure the voltage between the speed control actuator C122 pin 7, circuit 601 (LB/PK), harness side and the speed control actuator C122 pin 10, circuit 57 (BK), harness side. 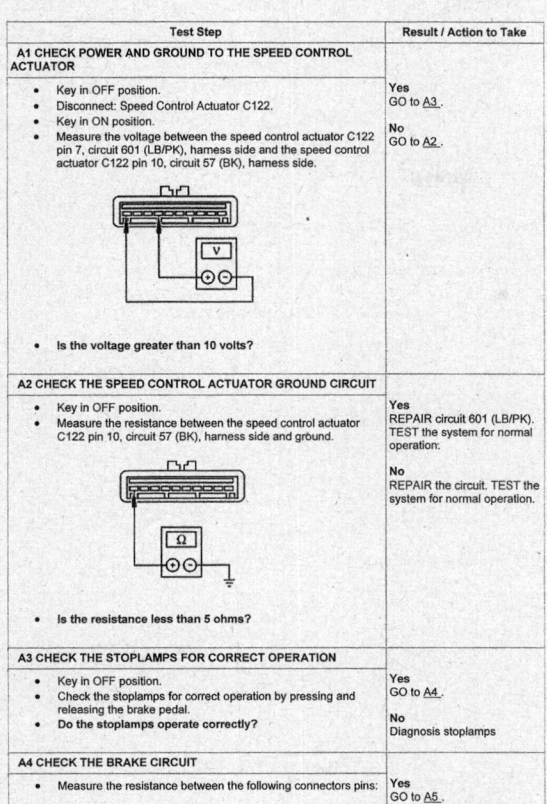 • Is the voltage greater than 10 volts?	**Yes** GO to A3. **No** GO to A2.
A2 CHECK THE SPEED CONTROL ACTUATOR GROUND CIRCUIT • Key in OFF position. • Measure the resistance between the speed control actuator C122 pin 10, circuit 57 (BK), harness side and ground. • Is the resistance less than 5 ohms?	**Yes** REPAIR circuit 601 (LB/PK). TEST the system for normal operation. **No** REPAIR the circuit. TEST the system for normal operation.
A3 CHECK THE STOPLAMPS FOR CORRECT OPERATION • Key in OFF position. • Check the stoplamps for correct operation by pressing and releasing the brake pedal. • Do the stoplamps operate correctly?	**Yes** GO to A4. **No** Diagnosis stoplamps
A4 CHECK THE BRAKE CIRCUIT • Measure the resistance between the following connectors pins:	**Yes** GO to A5.

LTV0500000001481

Fig. 67   Test A: Speed Control Is Inoperative (Part 1 of 8). 2002–04 Escape

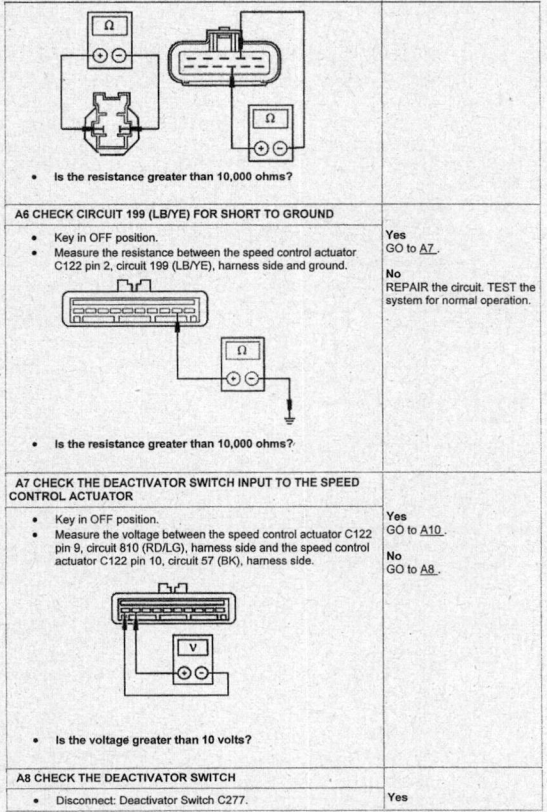

Test Step	Result / Action to Take
• Is the resistance greater than 10,000 ohms?	
A6 CHECK CIRCUIT 199 (LB/YE) FOR SHORT TO GROUND • Key in OFF position. • Measure the resistance between the speed control actuator C122 pin 2, circuit 199 (LB/YE), harness side and ground. • Is the resistance greater than 10,000 ohms?	**Yes** GO to A7. **No** REPAIR the circuit. TEST the system for normal operation.
A7 CHECK THE DEACTIVATOR SWITCH INPUT TO THE SPEED CONTROL ACTUATOR • Key in OFF position. • Measure the voltage between the speed control actuator C122 pin 9, circuit 810 (RD/LG), harness side and the speed control actuator C122 pin 10, circuit 57 (BK), harness side. • Is the voltage greater than 10 volts?	**Yes** GO to A10. **No** GO to A8.
A8 CHECK THE DEACTIVATOR SWITCH • Disconnect: Deactivator Switch C277.	**Yes**

LTV0500000001483

Fig. 67   Test A: Speed Control Is Inoperative (Part 3 of 8). 2002–04 Escape

Speed Control Actuator C122	PCM C175	Anti-lock Brake Control Module C155	BPP Switch C278	Circuit
4	92	—	—	511 (LG)
4	—	2	—	511 (LG)
4	—	—	1	511 (LG)

No
REPAIR the circuit. TEST the system for normal operation.

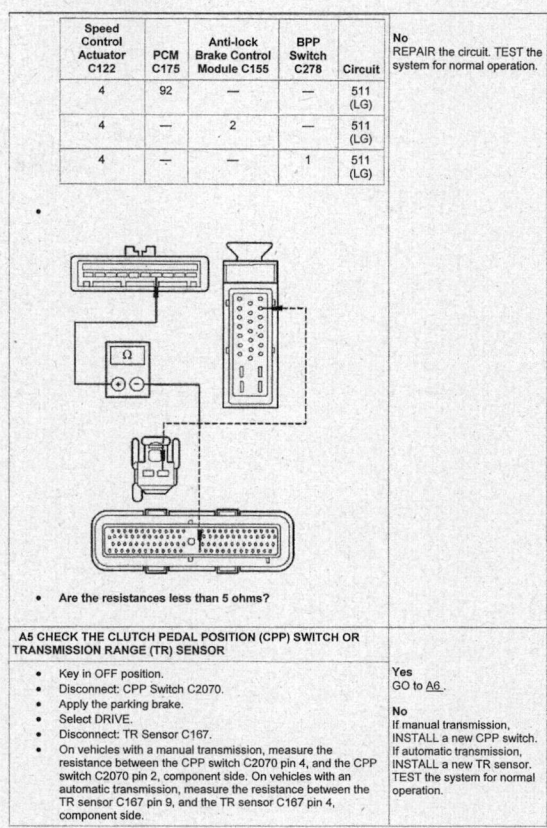

Test Step	Result / Action to Take
• Are the resistances less than 5 ohms?	
A5 CHECK THE CLUTCH PEDAL POSITION (CPP) SWITCH OR TRANSMISSION RANGE (TR) SENSOR • Key in OFF position. • Disconnect: CPP Switch C2070. • Apply the parking brake. • Select DRIVE. • Disconnect: TR Sensor C167. • On vehicles with a manual transmission, measure the resistance between the CPP switch C2070 pin 4, and the CPP switch C2070 pin 2, component side. On vehicles with an automatic transmission, measure the resistance between the TR sensor C167 pin 9, and the TR sensor C167 pin 4, component side.	**Yes** GO to A6. **No** If manual transmission, INSTALL a new CPP switch. If automatic transmission, INSTALL a new TR sensor. TEST the system for normal operation.

LTV0500000001482

Fig. 67   Test A: Speed Control Is Inoperative (Part 2 of 8). 2002–04 Escape

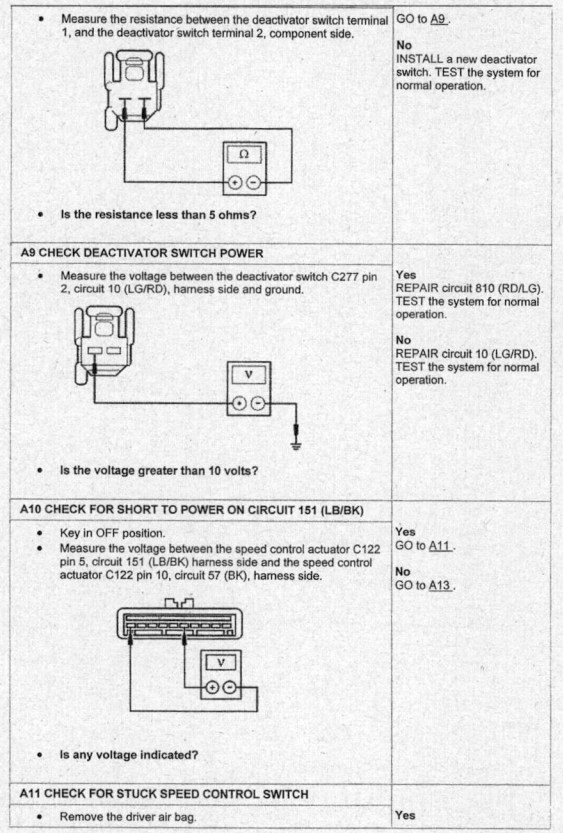

Test Step	Result / Action to Take
• Measure the resistance between the deactivator switch terminal 1, and the deactivator switch terminal 2, component side. • Is the resistance less than 5 ohms?	GO to A9. **No** INSTALL a new deactivator switch. TEST the system for normal operation.
A9 CHECK DEACTIVATOR SWITCH POWER • Measure the voltage between the deactivator switch C277 pin 2, circuit 10 (LG/RD), harness side and ground. • Is the voltage greater than 10 volts?	**Yes** REPAIR circuit 810 (RD/LG). TEST the system for normal operation. **No** REPAIR circuit 10 (LG/RD). TEST the system for normal operation.
A10 CHECK FOR SHORT TO POWER ON CIRCUIT 151 (LB/BK) • Key in OFF position. • Measure the voltage between the speed control actuator C122 pin 5, circuit 151 (LB/BK) harness side and the speed control actuator C122 pin 10, circuit 57 (BK), harness side. • Is any voltage indicated?	**Yes** GO to A11. **No** GO to A13.
A11 CHECK FOR STUCK SPEED CONTROL SWITCH • Remove the driver air bag.	**Yes**

LTV0500000001484

Fig. 67   Test A: Speed Control Is Inoperative (Part 4 of 8). 2002–04 Escape

- Connect: Restraint System Diagnostic Tool 418-F468 or Equivalent.
- Connect the battery.
- Disconnect: Speed Control Switch.
- Key in ON position.
- Measure the voltage between the speed control actuator C122 pin 5, circuit 151 (LB/BK), harness side and the speed control actuator C122 pin 10, circuit 57 (BK), harness side.

GO to A12.
No INSTALL a new speed control switch. TEST the system for normal operation.

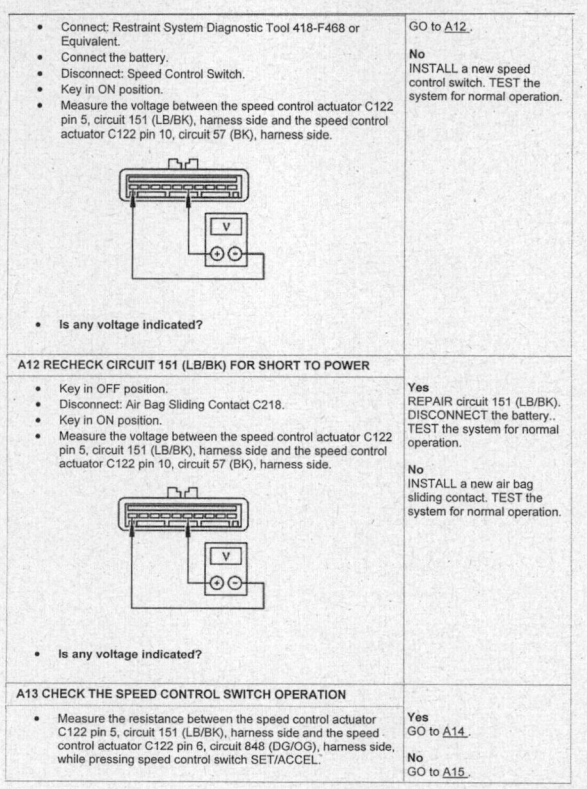

- Is any voltage indicated?

A12 RECHECK CIRCUIT 151 (LB/BK) FOR SHORT TO POWER

- Key in OFF position.
- Disconnect: Air Bag Sliding Contact C218.
- Key in ON position.
- Measure the voltage between the speed control actuator C122 pin 5, circuit 151 (LB/BK), harness side and the speed control actuator C122 pin 10, circuit 57 (BK), harness side.

Yes REPAIR circuit 151 (LB/BK). DISCONNECT the battery. TEST the system for normal operation.
No INSTALL a new air bag sliding contact. TEST the system for normal operation.

- Is any voltage indicated?

A13 CHECK THE SPEED CONTROL SWITCH OPERATION

- Measure the resistance between the speed control actuator C122 pin 5, circuit 151 (LB/BK), harness side and the speed control actuator C122 pin 6, circuit 848 (DG/OG), harness side, while pressing speed control switch SET/ACCEL.

Yes GO to A14.
No GO to A15.

LTV0500000001485

Fig. 67   Test A: Speed Control Is Inoperative (Part 5 of 8). 2002–04 Escape

---

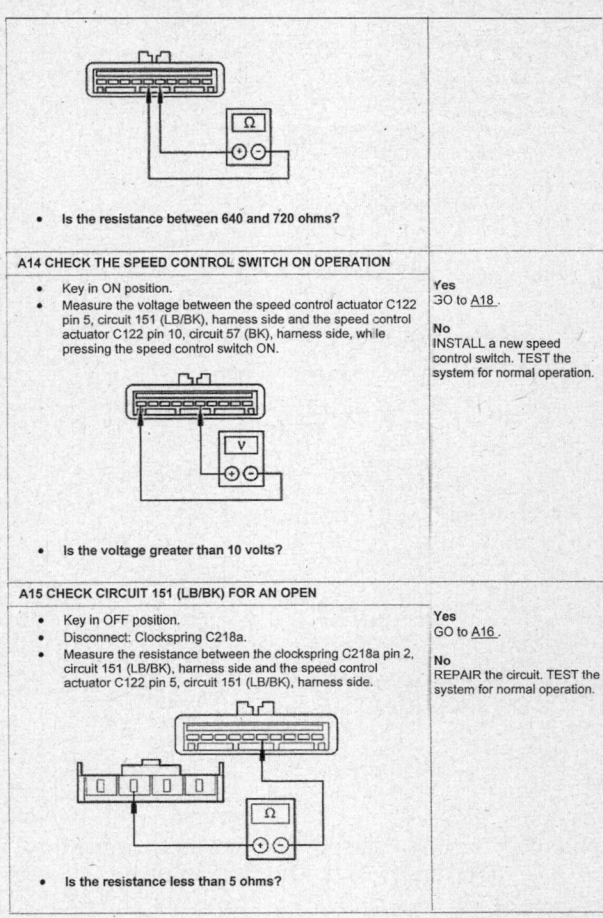

- Is the resistance between 640 and 720 ohms?

A14 CHECK THE SPEED CONTROL SWITCH ON OPERATION

- Key in ON position.
- Measure the voltage between the speed control actuator C122 pin 5, circuit 151 (LB/BK), harness side and the speed control actuator C122 pin 10, circuit 57 (BK), harness side, while pressing the speed control switch ON.

Yes GO to A18.
No INSTALL a new speed control switch. TEST the system for normal operation.

- Is the voltage greater than 10 volts?

A15 CHECK CIRCUIT 151 (LB/BK) FOR AN OPEN

- Key in OFF position.
- Disconnect: Clockspring C218a.
- Measure the resistance between the clockspring C218a pin 2, circuit 151 (LB/BK), harness side and the speed control actuator C122 pin 5, circuit 151 (LB/BK), harness side.

Yes GO to A16.
No REPAIR the circuit. TEST the system for normal operation.

- Is the resistance less than 5 ohms?

LTV0500000001486

Fig. 67   Test A: Speed Control Is Inoperative (Part 6 of 8). 2002–04 Escape

---

A16 CHECK CIRCUIT 848 (DG/OG) FOR AN OPEN

- Measure the resistance between the clockspring C218a pin 3, circuit 848 (DG/OG), harness side and the speed control actuator C122 pin 6, circuit 848 (DG/OG), harness side.

Yes GO to A17.
No REPAIR the circuit. TEST the system for normal operation.

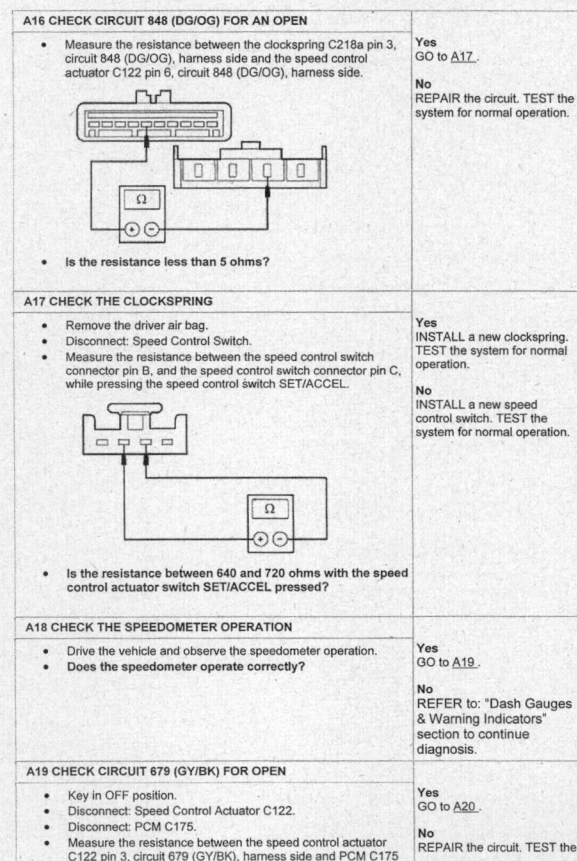

- Is the resistance less than 5 ohms?

A17 CHECK THE CLOCKSPRING

- Remove the driver air bag.
- Disconnect: Speed Control Switch.
- Measure the resistance between the speed control switch connector pin B, and the speed control switch connector pin C, while pressing the speed control switch SET/ACCEL.

Yes INSTALL a new clockspring. TEST the system for normal operation.
No INSTALL a new speed control switch. TEST the system for normal operation.

- Is the resistance between 640 and 720 ohms with the speed control actuator switch SET/ACCEL pressed?

A18 CHECK THE SPEEDOMETER OPERATION

- Drive the vehicle and observe the speedometer operation.
- Does the speedometer operate correctly?

Yes GO to A19.
No REFER to: "Dash Gauges & Warning Indicators" section to continue diagnosis.

A19 CHECK CIRCUIT 679 (GY/BK) FOR OPEN

- Key in OFF position.
- Disconnect: Speed Control Actuator C122.
- Disconnect: PCM C175.
- Measure the resistance between the speed control actuator C122 pin 3, circuit 679 (GY/BK), harness side and PCM C175

Yes GO to A20.
No REPAIR the circuit. TEST the

LTV0500000001487

Fig. 67   Test A: Speed Control Is Inoperative (Part 7 of 8). 2002–04 Escape

---

pin 28 (2.0L Zetec) or pin 68 (3.0L 4V), circuit 679 (GY/BK), harness side.	system for normal operation.

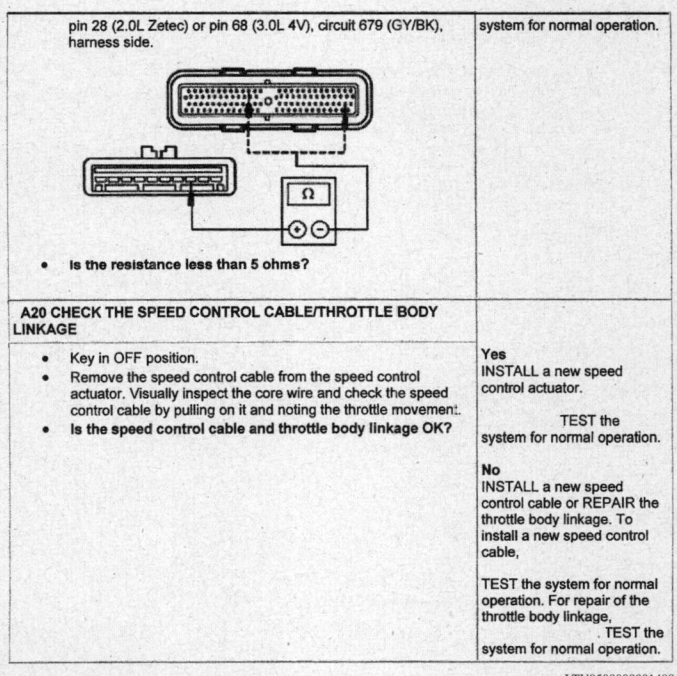

- **Is the resistance less than 5 ohms?**

A20 CHECK THE SPEED CONTROL CABLE/THROTTLE BODY LINKAGE

- Key in OFF position.
- Remove the speed control cable from the speed control actuator. Visually inspect the core wire and check the speed control cable by pulling on it and noting the throttle movement.
- **Is the speed control cable and throttle body linkage OK?**

Yes INSTALL a new speed control actuator. TEST the system for normal operation.
No INSTALL a new speed control cable or REPAIR the throttle body linkage. To install a new speed control cable, TEST the system for normal operation. For repair of the throttle body linkage, TEST the system for normal operation.

LTV0500000001488

Fig. 67   Test A: Speed Control Is Inoperative (Part 8 of 8). 2002–04 Escape

Test Step	Result / Action to Take
B1 CHECK THE SPEED CONTROL CABLE/THROTTLE BODY LINKAGE	
• Key in OFF position. • Remove the speed control cable from the speed control actuator. Visually inspect the core wire and check the speed control cable by pulling on it and noting the throttle movement. • **Is the speed control cable and throttle body linkage OK?**	**Yes** GO to <u>B2</u>. **No** INSTALL a new speed control cable or REPAIR the throttle body linkage. TEST the system for normal operation.
B2 CHECK THE SPEEDOMETER OPERATION	
• Drive the vehicle and observe the speedometer operation. • **Does the speedometer needle fluctuate?**	**Yes** REFER to: "Dash Gauges & Warning Indicators" section to continue diagnosis. **No** INSTALL a new speed control actuator. TEST the system for normal operation.

LTV0500000001489

Fig. 68   Test B: Set Speed Fluctuates. 2002–04 Escape

Test Step	Result / Action to Take
D1 CHECK THE CLUTCH PEDAL POSITION (CPP) SWITCH	
• Key in OFF position. • Disconnect: CPP Switch C2070. • Clutch is applied. • Measure the resistance between the clutch pedal position (CPP) switch terminal A, and the CPP switch terminal B (component side). • **Is the resistance less than 5 ohms?**	**Yes** GO to <u>D2</u>. **No** INSTALL a new CPP switch. TEST the system for normal operation.
D2 CHECK CIRCUIT 199 (LB/YE) FOR AN OPEN	
• Key in OFF position. • Disconnect: Speed Control Actuator C122. • Measure the resistance between the speed control actuator C122 pin 2, circuit 199 (LB/YE), harness side and the CPP switch C2070, circuit 199 (LB/YE), harness side. • **Is the resistance less than 5 ohms?**	**Yes** GO to <u>D3</u>. **No** REPAIR the circuit. TEST the system for normal operation.
D3 CHECK CIRCUIT 89 (OG) FOR AN OPEN	
• Measure the resistance between the CPP switch C2070, circuit 89 (OG), harness side and ground.	**Yes** INSTALL a new speed control actuator. Test system for normal operation.

LTV0500000001491

Fig. 70   Test D: Speed Control Does Not Disengage When Clutch Is Applied (Part 1 of 2). 2002–04 Escape

Test Step	Result / Action to Take
C1 CHECK THE STOPLAMPS FOR CORRECT OPERATION	
• Check the stoplamps for correct operation by pressing and releasing the brake pedal. • **Do the stoplamps operate correctly?**	**Yes** GO to <u>C2</u>. **No** Check stoplamp operation.
C2 CHECK THE BRAKE CIRCUIT	
• Disconnect: Speed Control Actuator C122. 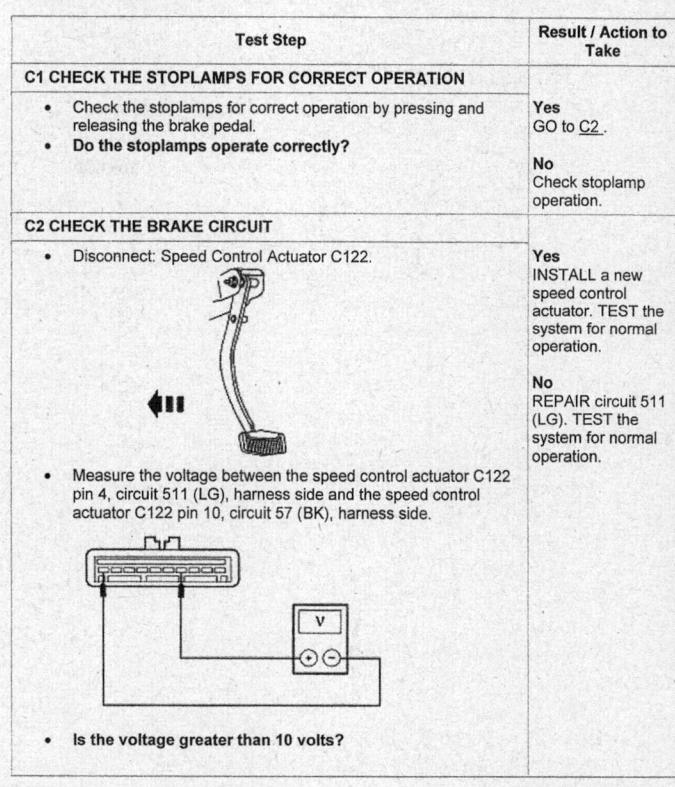 • Measure the voltage between the speed control actuator C122 pin 4, circuit 511 (LG), harness side and the speed control actuator C122 pin 10, circuit 57 (BK), harness side. • **Is the voltage greater than 10 volts?**	**Yes** INSTALL a new speed control actuator. TEST the system for normal operation. **No** REPAIR circuit 511 (LG). TEST the system for normal operation.

LTV0500000001490

Fig. 69   Test C: Speed Control Does Not Disengage When Brakes Are Applied. 2002–04 Escape

	Result / Action to Take
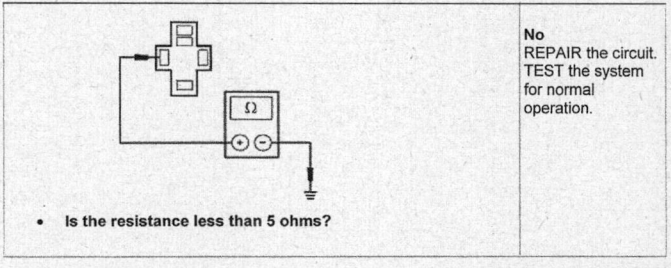 • **Is the resistance less than 5 ohms?**	**No** REPAIR the circuit. TEST the system for normal operation.

LTV0500000001492

Fig. 70   Test D: Speed Control Does Not Disengage When Clutch Is Applied (Part 2 of 2). 2002–04 Escape

Test Step	Result / Action to Take
E1 CHECK THE SPEED CONTROL SWITCH	
• Key in OFF position. • Disconnect: Speed Control Actuator C122. • Measure the resistance between the speed control actuator C122 pin 5, circuit 151 (LB/BK), harness side and the speed control actuator C122 pin 6, circuit 848 (DG/OG), harness side while pressing the speed control switch as follows:	**Yes** INSTALL a new speed control actuator. TEST the system for normal operation.

Speed Control Switch	Resistance Value
Coast	Between 114 and 126 ohms
SET/ACCEL	Between 646 and 714 ohms
Resume	Between 2,090 and 2,310 ohms
Off	Less than 5 ohms

No
INSTALL a new speed control switch. TEST the system for normal operation.

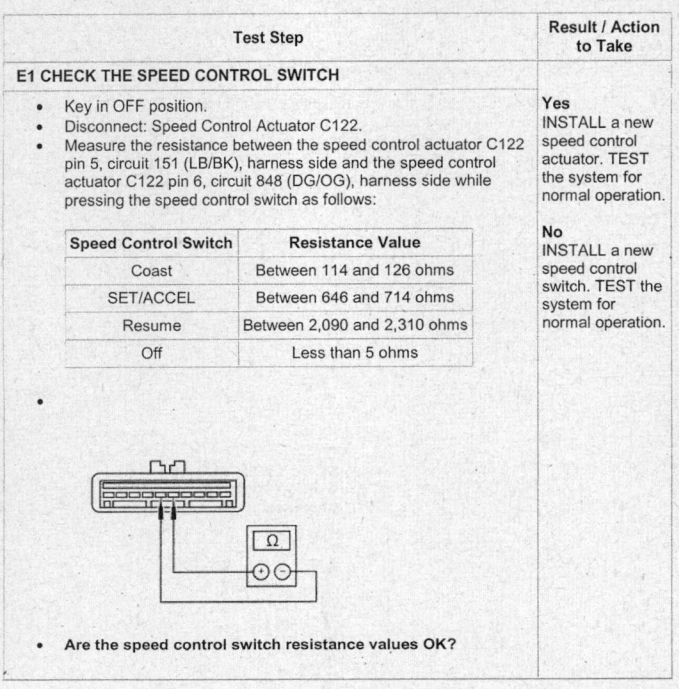

• Are the speed control switch resistance values OK?

LTV0500000001493

Fig. 71   Test E: Speed Control Switch Is Inoperative. 2002–04 Escape

Test Step	Result / Action to Take
F1 CHECK THE SPEED CONTROL CABLE	
• Check the speed control cable for correct attachment at the speed control actuator and throttle body. • **Is the speed control cable attached correctly?**	**Yes** GO to F2. **No** RECONNECT the speed control cable. REPEAT the self-test.
F2 CHECK FOR A STICKING OR BINDING SPEED CONTROL CABLE	
• Check the speed control cable for sticking or binding. • **Is the speed control cable OK?**	**Yes** INSTALL a new speed control actuator. TEST the system for normal operation. **No** REPAIR or INSTALL a new speed control cable. REPEAT the self-test.

LTV0500000001494

Fig. 72   Test F: Flash w/Last Switch Pressed, But No Dynamic Pull Occurs At Throttle & Speed Control Is Inoperative. 2002–04 Escape

Test Step	Result / Action to Take
G1 CHECK THE STOPLAMP OPERATION	
• Press and release the brake pedal while observing the stoplamps. • **Do the stoplamps operate correctly?**	**Yes** GO to G2. **No** Diagnose stoplamps.
G2 CHECK THE BRAKE CIRCUIT	
• Key in OFF position. • Disconnect: Speed Control Actuator C122. • Disconnect: PCM C175. • Disconnect: Anti-lock Brake Control Module C155. • Disconnect: BPP Switch C278. • Measure the resistance between the following connectors pins:	

Speed Control Actuator C122	PCM C175	Anti-lock Brake Control Module C155	BPP Switch C278	Circuit
4	92	—	—	511 (LG)
4	—	2	—	511 (LG)
4	—	—	1	511 (LG)

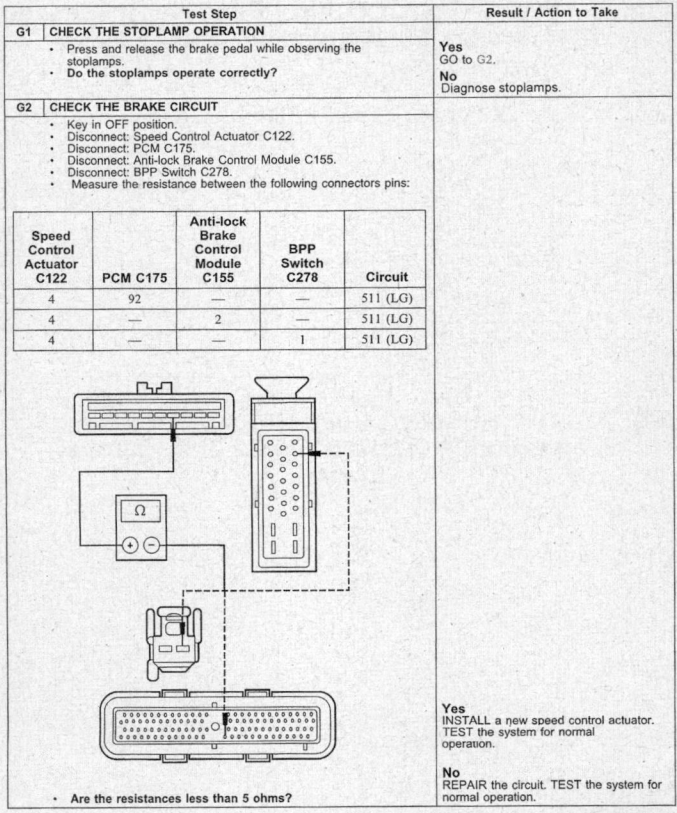

Yes
INSTALL a new speed control actuator. TEST the system for normal operation.

No
REPAIR the circuit. TEST the system for normal operation.

• Are the resistances less than 5 ohms?

LTV0500000001495

Fig. 73   Test G: Brake Pedal Position Switch Circuit Failure. 2002–04 Escape

Test Step	Result / Action to Take
H1 CHECK THE DEACTIVATOR SWITCH INPUT TO THE SPEED CONTROL ACTUATOR	
• Disconnect: Speed Control Actuator C122. • Measure the voltage between the speed control actuator C122 pin 9, circuit 810 (RD/LG), harness side and the speed control actuator C122 pin 10, circuit 57 (BK), harness side.	**Yes** INSTALL a new speed control actuator. REPEAT the self-test. **No** GO to H2.
• Is the voltage greater than 10 volts?	
H2 CHECK THE DEACTIVATOR SWITCH	
• Disconnect: Deactivator Switch C277. • Measure the resistance between the deactivator switch terminal 1, and the deactivator switch terminal 2, component side.	**Yes** GO to H3. **No** INSTALL a new deactivator switch. REPEAT the self-test.
• Is the resistance less than 5 ohms?	
H3 CHECK DEACTIVATOR SWITCH POWER	
• Measure the voltage between the deactivator switch C277 pin 2, circuit 10 (LG/RD), harness side and ground.	**Yes** REPAIR circuit 810 (RD/LG). REPEAT the self-test. **No** REPAIR circuit 10 (LG/RD). TEST the system for normal operation.
• Is the voltage greater than 10 volts?	

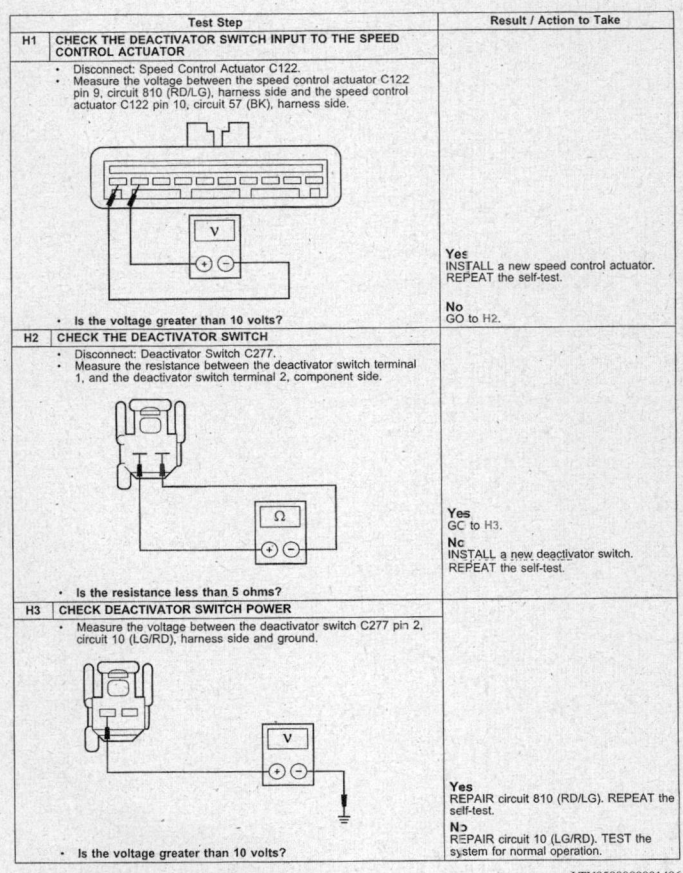

LTV0500000001496

Fig. 74   Test H: Deactivator Switch Circuit Failure. 2002–04 Escape

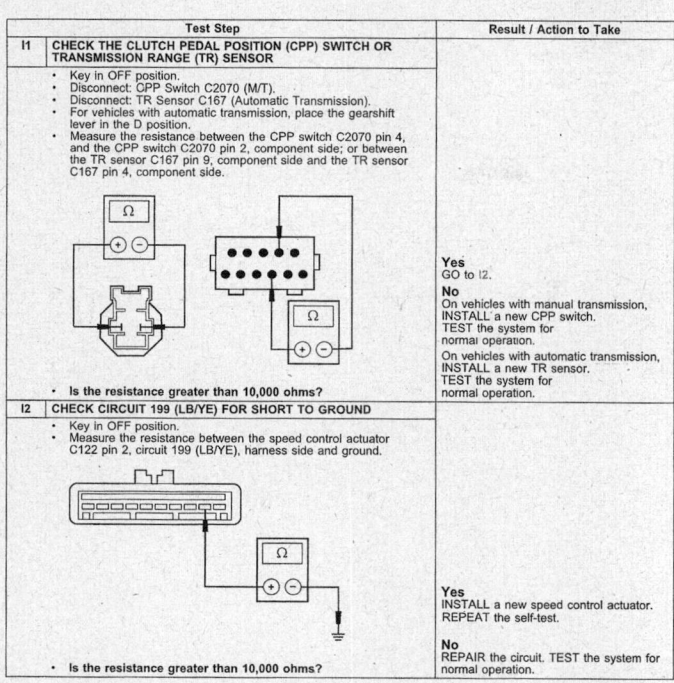

Test Step	Result / Action to Take
I1 CHECK THE CLUTCH PEDAL POSITION (CPP) SWITCH OR TRANSMISSION RANGE (TR) SENSOR • Key in OFF position. • Disconnect: CPP Switch C2070 (M/T). • Disconnect: TR Sensor C167 (Automatic Transmission). • For vehicles with automatic transmission, place the gearshift lever in the D position. • Measure the resistance between the CPP switch C2070 pin 4, and the CPP switch C2070 pin 2, component side; or between the TR sensor C167 pin 9, component side and the TR sensor C167 pin 4, component side. • Is the resistance greater than 10,000 ohms?	**Yes** GO to I2. **No** On vehicles with manual transmission, INSTALL a new CPP switch. TEST the system for normal operation. On vehicles with automatic transmission, INSTALL a new TR sensor. TEST the system for normal operation.
I2 CHECK CIRCUIT 199 (LB/YE) FOR SHORT TO GROUND • Key in OFF position. • Measure the resistance between the speed control actuator C122 pin 2, circuit 199 (LB/YE), harness side and ground. • Is the resistance greater than 10,000 ohms?	**Yes** INSTALL a new speed control actuator. REPEAT the self-test. **No** REPAIR the circuit. TEST the system for normal operation.

LTV0500000001497

Fig. 75   Test I: Clutch/Neutral Switch Circuit Failure. 2002–04 Escape

Test Step	Result / Action to Take
A1 CHECK THE SPEED CONTROL CABLE/THROTTLE BODY LINKAGE • Key in OFF position. • Visually inspect the speed control cable connections, the throttle body linkage, and the speed control actuator pulley cover. • Are the speed control cable connections, the throttle body linkage, and the speed control actuator pulley cover OK?	**Yes** GO to A2. **No** INSTALL a new speed control cable or REPAIR the throttle body linkage. TEST the system for normal operation.
A2 CHECK CIRCUIT 151 (LB/BK) FOR A SHORT TO GROUND • Disconnect: Speed Control Actuator C122.	

LTV0500000001503

Fig. 77   Test A: Speed Control Is Inoperative (Part 1 of 16). 2005–06 Escape & Mariner

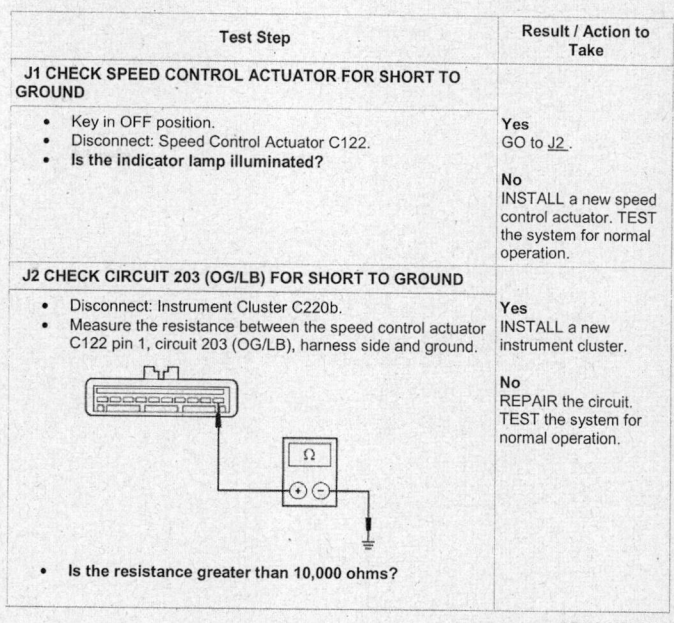

Test Step	Result / Action to Take
J1 CHECK SPEED CONTROL ACTUATOR FOR SHORT TO GROUND • Key in OFF position. • Disconnect: Speed Control Actuator C122. • **Is the indicator lamp illuminated?**	**Yes** GO to J2. **No** INSTALL a new speed control actuator. TEST the system for normal operation.
J2 CHECK CIRCUIT 203 (OG/LB) FOR SHORT TO GROUND • Disconnect: Instrument Cluster C220b. • Measure the resistance between the speed control actuator C122 pin 1, circuit 203 (OG/LB), harness side and ground. • Is the resistance greater than 10,000 ohms?	**Yes** INSTALL a new instrument cluster. **No** REPAIR the circuit. TEST the system for normal operation.

LTV0500000001498

Fig. 76   Test J: Speed Control Indicator Lamp Is Always On. 2002–04 Escape

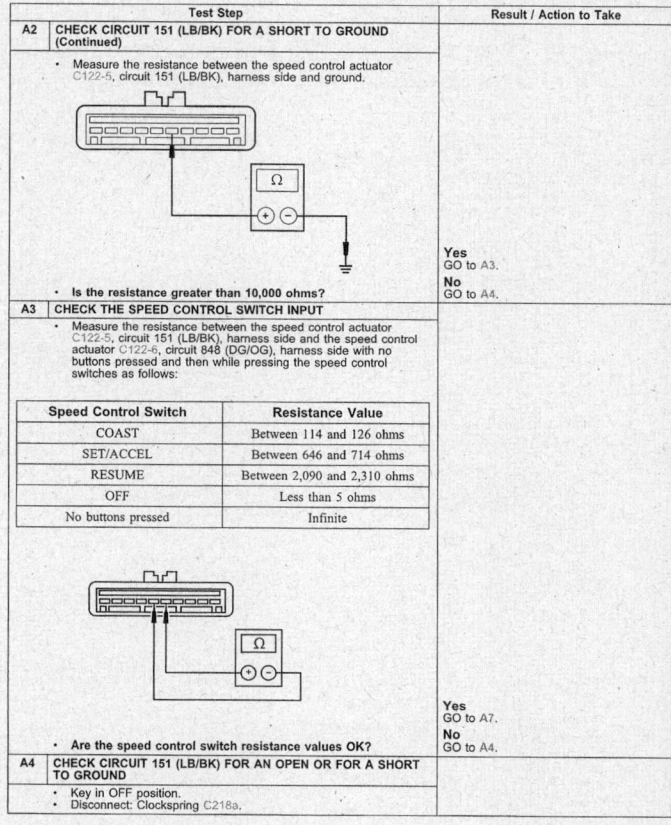

Test Step	Result / Action to Take
A2 CHECK CIRCUIT 151 (LB/BK) FOR A SHORT TO GROUND (Continued) • Measure the resistance between the speed control actuator C122-5, circuit 151 (LB/BK), harness side and ground. • Is the resistance greater than 10,000 ohms?	**Yes** GO to A3. **No** GO to A4.
A3 CHECK THE SPEED CONTROL SWITCH INPUT • Measure the resistance between the speed control actuator C122-5, circuit 151 (LB/BK), harness side and the speed control actuator C122-6, circuit 848 (DG/OG), harness side with no buttons pressed and then while pressing the speed control switches as follows: • Are the speed control switch resistance values OK?	**Yes** GO to A7. **No** GO to A4.
A4 CHECK CIRCUIT 151 (LB/BK) FOR AN OPEN OR FOR A SHORT TO GROUND • Key in OFF position. • Disconnect: Clockspring C218a.	

Speed Control Switch	Resistance Value
COAST	Between 114 and 126 ohms
SET/ACCEL	Between 646 and 714 ohms
RESUME	Between 2,090 and 2,310 ohms
OFF	Less than 5 ohms
No buttons pressed	Infinite

LTV0500000001504

Fig. 77   Test A: Speed Control Is Inoperative (Part 2 of 16). 2005–06 Escape & Mariner

Test Step	Result / Action to Take
A4 CHECK CIRCUIT 151 (LB/BK) FOR AN OPEN OR FOR A SHORT TO GROUND (Continued)	
• Measure the resistance between the speed control actuator C122-5, circuit 151 (LB/BK), harness side and the clockspring C218a-2, circuit 151 (LB/BK), harness side; and between the speed control actuator C122-5, circuit 151 (LB/BK), harness side and ground. 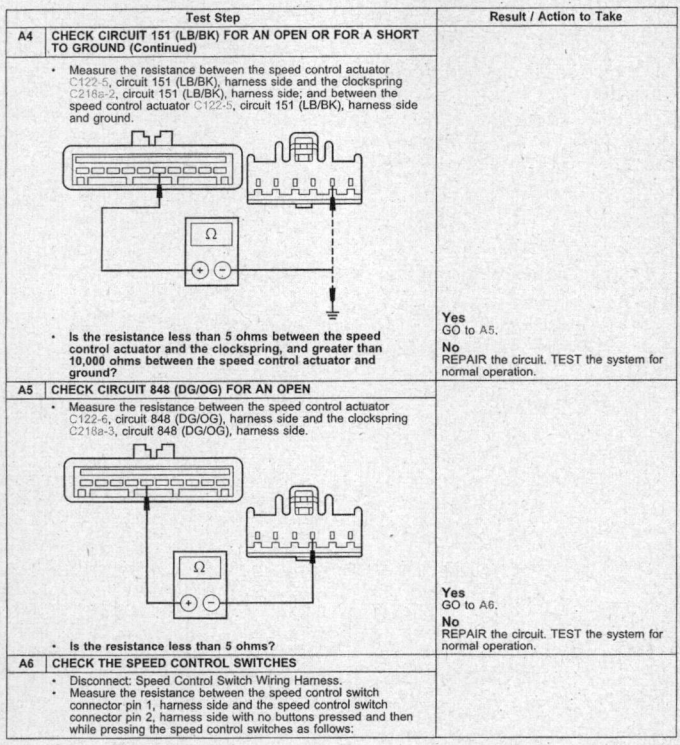 • Is the resistance less than 5 ohms between the speed control actuator and the clockspring, and greater than 10,000 ohms between the speed control actuator and ground?	**Yes** GO to A5. **No** REPAIR the circuit. TEST the system for normal operation.
A5 CHECK CIRCUIT 848 (DG/OG) FOR AN OPEN	
• Measure the resistance between the speed control actuator C122-6, circuit 848 (DG/OG), harness side and the clockspring C218a-3, circuit 848 (DG/OG), harness side. • Is the resistance less than 5 ohms?	**Yes** GO to A6. **No** REPAIR the circuit. TEST the system for normal operation.
A6 CHECK THE SPEED CONTROL SWITCHES	
• Disconnect: Speed Control Switch Wiring Harness. • Measure the resistance between the speed control switch connector pin 1, harness side and the speed control switch connector pin 2, harness side with no buttons pressed and then while pressing the speed control switches as follows:	

LTV0500000001505

Fig. 77   Test A: Speed Control Is Inoperative (Part 3 of 16). 2005–06 Escape & Mariner

Test Step	Result / Action to Take
A6 CHECK THE SPEED CONTROL SWITCHES (Continued)	

Speed Control Switch	Resistance Value
COAST	Between 114 and 126 ohms
SET/ACCEL	Between 646 and 714 ohms
RESUME	Between 2,090 and 2,310 ohms
OFF	Less than 5 ohms
No buttons pressed	Infinite

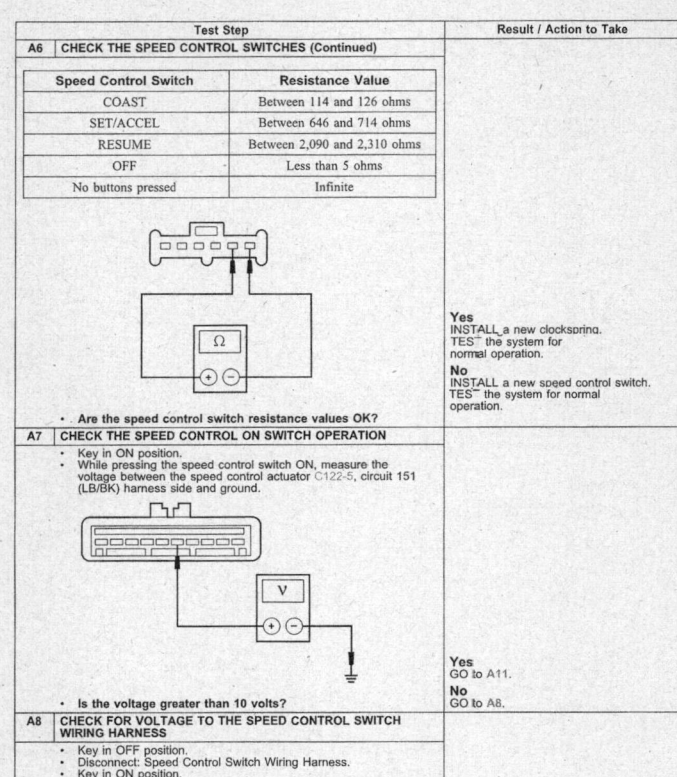

Test Step	Result / Action to Take
• Are the speed control switch resistance values OK?	**Yes** INSTALL a new clockspring. TEST the system for normal operation. **No** INSTALL a new speed control switch. TEST the system for normal operation.
A7 CHECK THE SPEED CONTROL ON SWITCH OPERATION	
• Key in ON position. • While pressing the speed control switch ON, measure the voltage between the speed control actuator C122-5, circuit 151 (LB/BK) harness side and ground. • Is the voltage greater than 10 volts?	**Yes** GO to A11. **No** GO to A8.
A8 CHECK FOR VOLTAGE TO THE SPEED CONTROL SWITCH WIRING HARNESS	
• Key in OFF position. • Disconnect: Speed Control Switch Wiring Harness. • Key in ON position.	

LTV0500000001506

Fig. 77   Test A: Speed Control Is Inoperative (Part 4 of 16). 2005–06 Escape & Mariner

Test Step	Result / Action to Take
A8 CHECK FOR VOLTAGE TO THE SPEED CONTROL SWITCH WIRING HARNESS (Continued)	
• Measure the voltage between the top of the clockspring pin 3, harness side and ground. 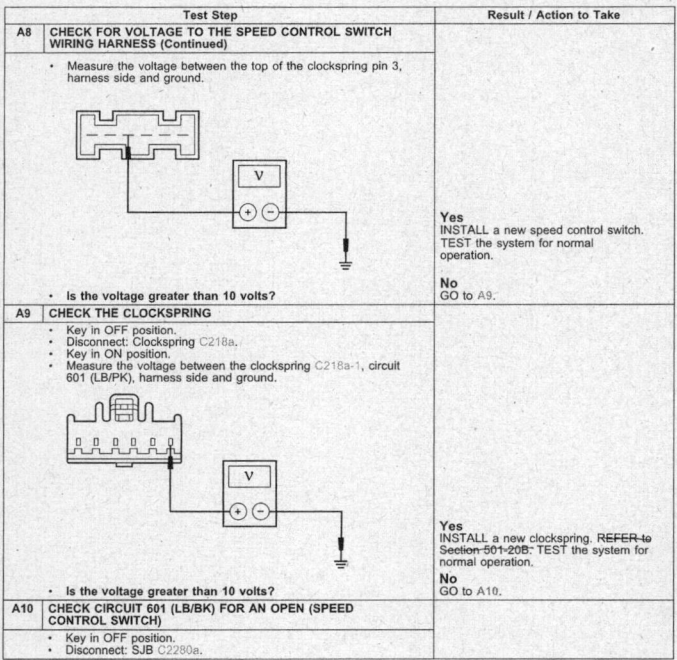 • Is the voltage greater than 10 volts?	**Yes** INSTALL a new speed control switch. TEST the system for normal operation. **No** GO to A9.
A9 CHECK THE CLOCKSPRING	
• Key in OFF position. • Disconnect: Clockspring C218a. • Key in ON position. • Measure the voltage between the clockspring C218a-1, circuit 601 (LB/PK), harness side and ground. • Is the voltage greater than 10 volts?	**Yes** INSTALL a new clockspring. REFER to Section 501-20B. TEST the system for normal operation. **No** GO to A10.
A10 CHECK CIRCUIT 601 (LB/BK) FOR AN OPEN (SPEED CONTROL SWITCH)	
• Key in OFF position. • Disconnect: SJB C2280a.	

LTV0500000001507

Fig. 77   Test A: Speed Control Is Inoperative (Part 5 of 16). 2005–06 Escape & Mariner

Test Step	Result / Action to Take
A10 CHECK CIRCUIT 601 (LB/BK) FOR AN OPEN (SPEED CONTROL SWITCH) (Continued)	
• Measure the resistance between the clockspring C218a-1, circuit 601 (LB/PK), harness side and the SJB C2280a-28, circuit 601 (LB/PK), harness side. 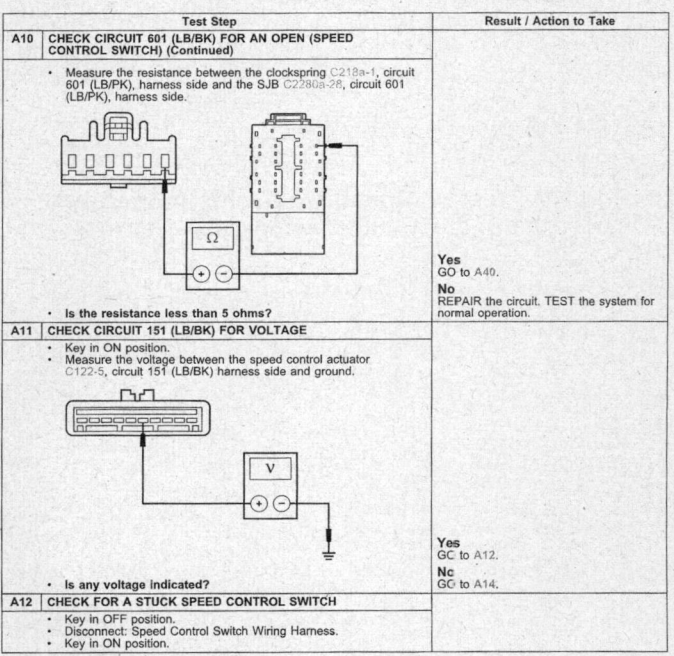 • Is the resistance less than 5 ohms?	**Yes** GO to A40. **No** REPAIR the circuit. TEST the system for normal operation.
A11 CHECK CIRCUIT 151 (LB/BK) FOR VOLTAGE	
• Key in ON position. • Measure the voltage between the speed control actuator C122-5, circuit 151 (LB/BK) harness side and ground. • Is any voltage indicated?	**Yes** GO to A12. **No** GO to A14.
A12 CHECK FOR A STUCK SPEED CONTROL SWITCH	
• Key in OFF position. • Disconnect: Speed Control Switch Wiring Harness. • Key in ON position.	

LTV0500000001508

Fig. 77   Test A: Speed Control Is Inoperative (Part 6 of 16). 2005–06 Escape & Mariner

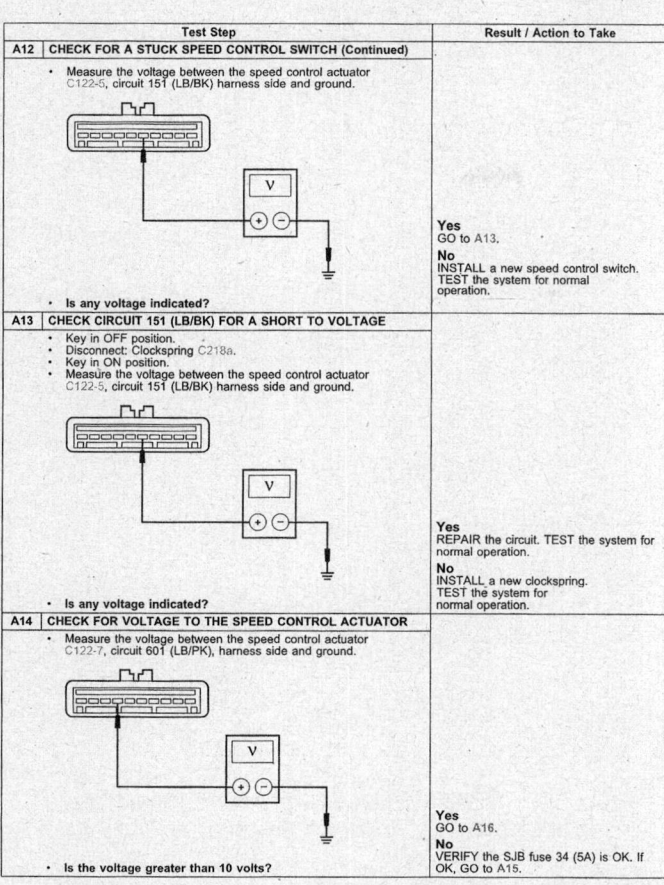

Test Step	Result / Action to Take
A12 CHECK FOR A STUCK SPEED CONTROL SWITCH (Continued)	
• Measure the voltage between the speed control actuator C122-5, circuit 151 (LB/BK) harness side and ground. • Is any voltage indicated?	**Yes** GO to A13. **No** INSTALL a new speed control switch. TEST the system for normal operation.
A13 CHECK CIRCUIT 151 (LB/BK) FOR A SHORT TO VOLTAGE	
• Key in OFF position. • Disconnect: Clockspring C218a. • Key in ON position. • Measure the voltage between the speed control actuator C122-5, circuit 151 (LB/BK) harness side and ground. • Is any voltage indicated?	**Yes** REPAIR the circuit. TEST the system for normal operation. **No** INSTALL a new clockspring. TEST the system for normal operation.
A14 CHECK FOR VOLTAGE TO THE SPEED CONTROL ACTUATOR	
• Measure the voltage between the speed control actuator C122-7, circuit 601 (LB/PK), harness side and ground. • Is the voltage greater than 10 volts?	**Yes** GO to A16. **No** VERIFY the SJB fuse 34 (5A) is OK. If OK, GO to A15.

LTV0500000001509

Fig. 77 Test A: Speed Control Is Inoperative (Part 7 of 16). 2005–06 Escape & Mariner

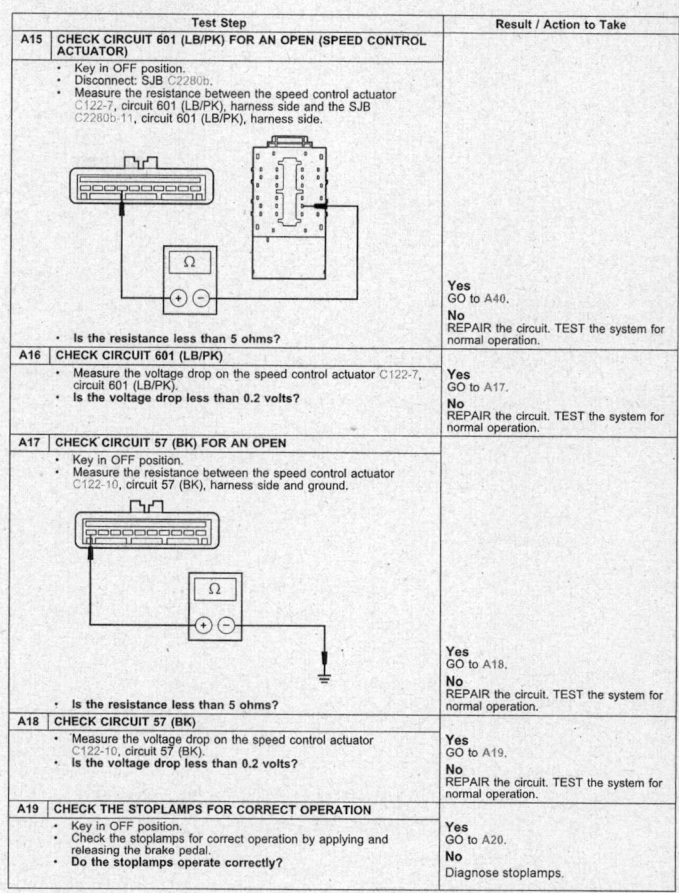

Test Step	Result / Action to Take
A15 CHECK CIRCUIT 601 (LB/PK) FOR AN OPEN (SPEED CONTROL ACTUATOR)	
• Key in OFF position. • Disconnect: SJB C2280b. • Measure the resistance between the speed control actuator C122-7, circuit 601 (LB/PK), harness side and the SJB C2280b-11, circuit 601 (LB/PK), harness side. • Is the resistance less than 5 ohms?	**Yes** GO to A40. **No** REPAIR the circuit. TEST the system for normal operation.
A16 CHECK CIRCUIT 601 (LB/PK)	
• Measure the voltage drop on the speed control actuator C122-7, circuit 601 (LB/PK). • Is the voltage drop less than 0.2 volts?	**Yes** GO to A17. **No** REPAIR the circuit. TEST the system for normal operation.
A17 CHECK CIRCUIT 57 (BK) FOR AN OPEN	
• Key in OFF position. • Measure the resistance between the speed control actuator C122-10, circuit 57 (BK), harness side and ground. • Is the resistance less than 5 ohms?	**Yes** GO to A18. **No** REPAIR the circuit. TEST the system for normal operation.
A18 CHECK CIRCUIT 57 (BK)	
• Measure the voltage drop on the speed control actuator C122-10, circuit 57 (BK). • Is the voltage drop less than 0.2 volts?	**Yes** GO to A19. **No** REPAIR the circuit. TEST the system for normal operation.
A19 CHECK THE STOPLAMPS FOR CORRECT OPERATION	
• Key in OFF position. • Check the stoplamps for correct operation by applying and releasing the brake pedal. • Do the stoplamps operate correctly?	**Yes** GO to A20. **No** Diagnose stoplamps.

LTV0500000001510

Fig. 77 Test A: Speed Control Is Inoperative (Part 8 of 16). 2005–06 Escape & Mariner

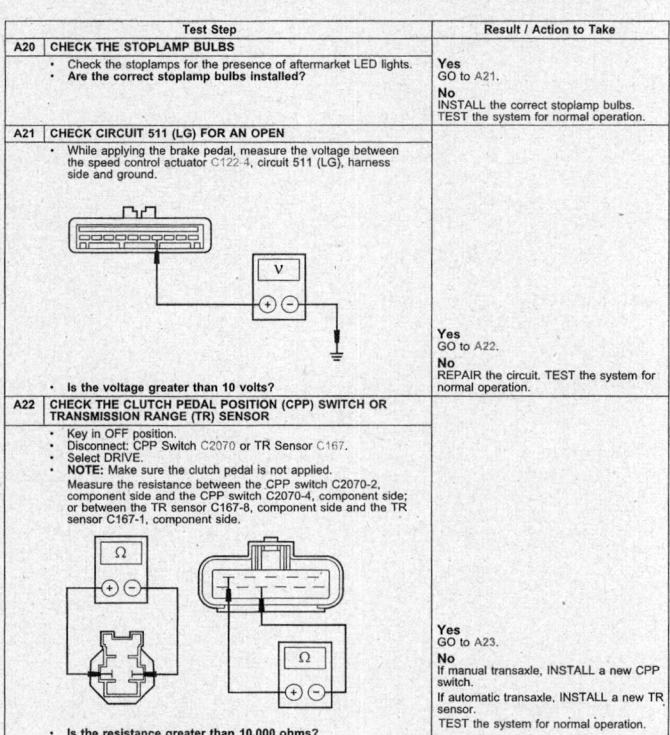

Test Step	Result / Action to Take
A20 CHECK THE STOPLAMP BULBS	
• Check the stoplamps for the presence of aftermarket LED lights. • Are the correct stoplamp bulbs installed?	**Yes** GO to A21. **No** INSTALL the correct stoplamp bulbs. TEST the system for normal operation.
A21 CHECK CIRCUIT 511 (LG) FOR AN OPEN	
• While applying the brake pedal, measure the voltage between the speed control actuator C122-4, circuit 511 (LG), harness side and ground. • Is the voltage greater than 10 volts?	**Yes** GO to A22. **No** REPAIR the circuit. TEST the system for normal operation.
A22 CHECK THE CLUTCH PEDAL POSITION (CPP) SWITCH OR TRANSMISSION RANGE (TR) SENSOR	
• Key in OFF position. • Disconnect: CPP Switch C2070 or TR Sensor C167. • Select DRIVE. • NOTE: Make sure the clutch pedal is not applied. Measure the resistance between the CPP switch C2070-2, component side and the CPP switch C2070-4, component side; or between the TR sensor C167-8, component side and the TR sensor C167-1, component side. • Is the resistance greater than 10,000 ohms?	**Yes** GO to A23. **No** If manual transaxle, INSTALL a new CPP switch. If automatic transaxle, INSTALL a new TR sensor. TEST the system for normal operation.

LTV0500000001511

Fig. 77 Test A: Speed Control Is Inoperative (Part 9 of 16). 2005–06 Escape & Mariner

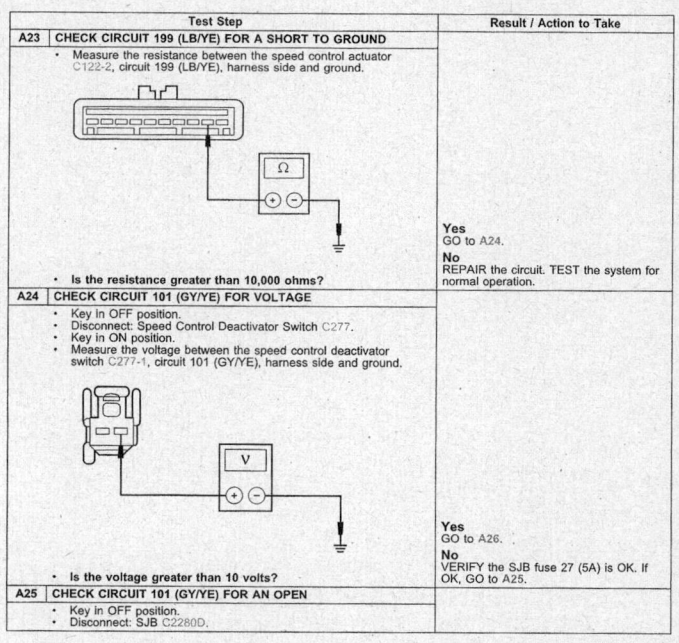

Test Step	Result / Action to Take
A23 CHECK CIRCUIT 199 (LB/YE) FOR A SHORT TO GROUND	
• Measure the resistance between the speed control actuator C122-2, circuit 199 (LB/YE), harness side and ground. • Is the resistance greater than 10,000 ohms?	**Yes** GO to A24. **No** REPAIR the circuit. TEST the system for normal operation.
A24 CHECK CIRCUIT 101 (GY/YE) FOR VOLTAGE	
• Key in OFF position. • Disconnect: Speed Control Deactivator Switch C277. • Key in ON position. • Measure the voltage between the speed control deactivator switch C277-1, circuit 101 (GY/YE), harness side and ground. • Is the voltage greater than 10 volts?	**Yes** GO to A26. **No** VERIFY the SJB fuse 27 (5A) is OK. If OK, GO to A25.
A25 CHECK CIRCUIT 101 (GY/YE) FOR AN OPEN	
• Key in OFF position. • Disconnect: SJB C2280D.	

LTV0500000001512

Fig. 77 Test A: Speed Control Is Inoperative (Part 10 of 16). 2005–06 Escape & Mariner

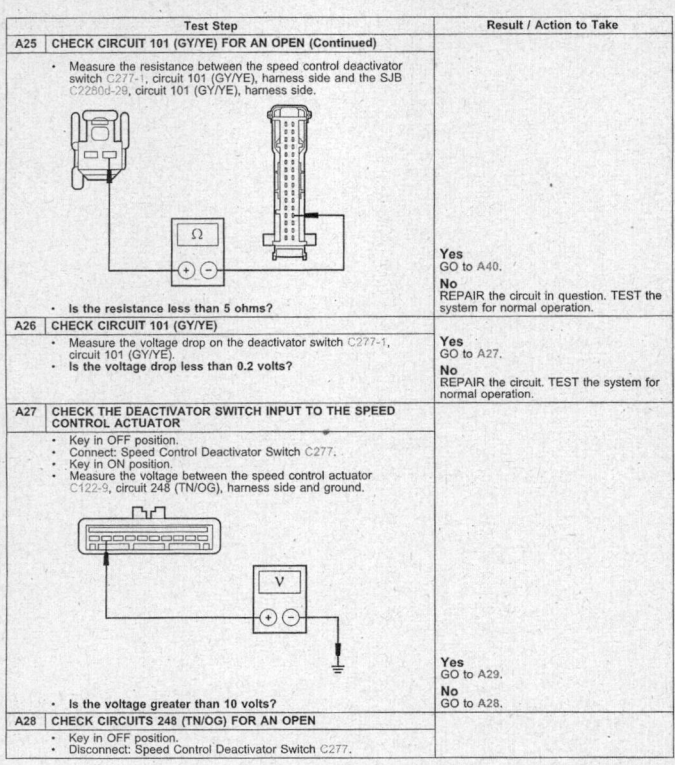

Test Step	Result / Action to Take
A25 CHECK CIRCUIT 101 (GY/YE) FOR AN OPEN (Continued) • Measure the resistance between the speed control deactivator switch C277-1, circuit 101 (GY/YE), harness side and the SJB C2280d-29, circuit 101 (GY/YE), harness side. • Is the resistance less than 5 ohms?	**Yes** GO to A40. **No** REPAIR the circuit in question. TEST the system for normal operation.
A26 CHECK CIRCUIT 101 (GY/YE) • Measure the voltage drop on the deactivator switch C277-1, circuit 101 (GY/YE). • Is the voltage drop less than 0.2 volts?	**Yes** GO to A27. **No** REPAIR the circuit. TEST the system for normal operation.
A27 CHECK THE DEACTIVATOR SWITCH INPUT TO THE SPEED CONTROL ACTUATOR • Key in OFF position. • Connect: Speed Control Deactivator Switch C277. • Key in ON position. • Measure the voltage between the speed control actuator C122-9, circuit 248 (TN/OG), harness side and ground. • Is the voltage greater than 10 volts?	**Yes** GO to A29. **No** GO to A28.
A28 CHECK CIRCUITS 248 (TN/OG) FOR AN OPEN • Key in OFF position. • Disconnect: Speed Control Deactivator Switch C277.	

LTV0500000001513

Fig. 77 Test A: Speed Control Is Inoperative (Part 11 of 16). 2005–06 Escape & Mariner

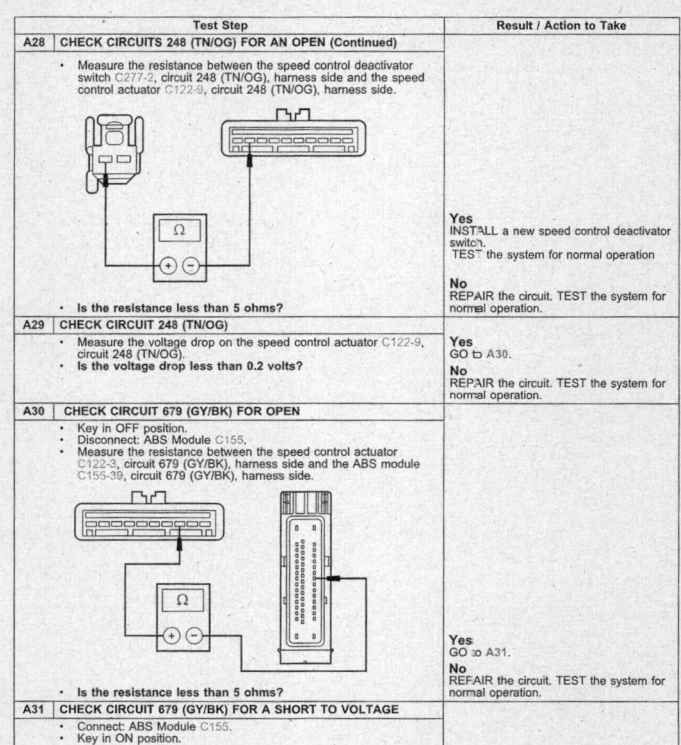

Test Step	Result / Action to Take
A28 CHECK CIRCUITS 248 (TN/OG) FOR AN OPEN (Continued) • Measure the resistance between the speed control deactivator switch C277-2, circuit 248 (TN/OG), harness side and the speed control actuator C122-9, circuit 248 (TN/OG), harness side. • Is the resistance less than 5 ohms?	**Yes** INSTALL a new speed control deactivator switch. TEST the system for normal operation **No** REPAIR the circuit. TEST the system for normal operation.
A29 CHECK CIRCUIT 248 (TN/OG) • Measure the voltage drop on the speed control actuator C122-9, circuit 248 (TN/OG). • Is the voltage drop less than 0.2 volts?	**Yes** GO to A30. **No** REPAIR the circuit. TEST the system for normal operation.
A30 CHECK CIRCUIT 679 (GY/BK) FOR OPEN • Key in OFF position. • Disconnect: ABS Module C155. • Measure the resistance between the speed control actuator C122-3, circuit 679 (GY/BK), harness side and the ABS module C155-39, circuit 679 (GY/BK), harness side. • Is the resistance less than 5 ohms?	**Yes** GO to A31. **No** REPAIR the circuit. TEST the system for normal operation.
A31 CHECK CIRCUIT 679 (GY/BK) FOR A SHORT TO VOLTAGE • Connect: ABS Module C155. • Key in ON position.	

LTV0500000001514

Fig. 77 Test A: Speed Control Is Inoperative (Part 12 of 16). 2005–06 Escape & Mariner

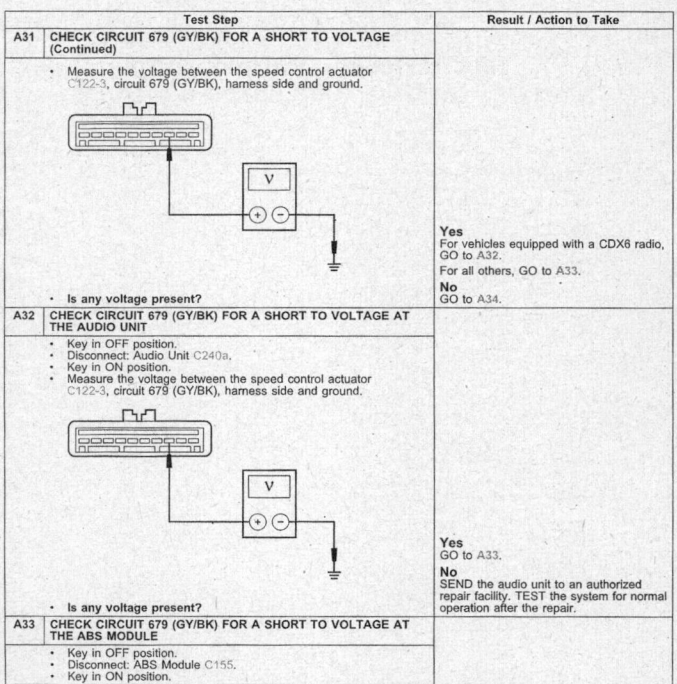

Test Step	Result / Action to Take
A31 CHECK CIRCUIT 679 (GY/BK) FOR A SHORT TO VOLTAGE (Continued) • Measure the voltage between the speed control actuator C122-3, circuit 679 (GY/BK), harness side and ground. • Is any voltage present?	**Yes** For vehicles equipped with a CDX6 radio, GO to A32. For all others, GO to A33. **No** GO to A34.
A32 CHECK CIRCUIT 679 (GY/BK) FOR A SHORT TO VOLTAGE AT THE AUDIO UNIT • Key in OFF position. • Disconnect: Audio Unit C240a. • Key in ON position. • Measure the voltage between the speed control actuator C122-3, circuit 679 (GY/BK), harness side and ground. • Is any voltage present?	**Yes** GO to A33. **No** SEND the audio unit to an authorized repair facility. TEST the system for normal operation after the repair.
A33 CHECK CIRCUIT 679 (GY/BK) FOR A SHORT TO VOLTAGE AT THE ABS MODULE • Key in OFF position. • Disconnect: ABS Module C155. • Key in ON position.	

LTV0500000001515

Fig. 77 Test A: Speed Control Is Inoperative (Part 13 of 16). 2005–06 Escape & Mariner

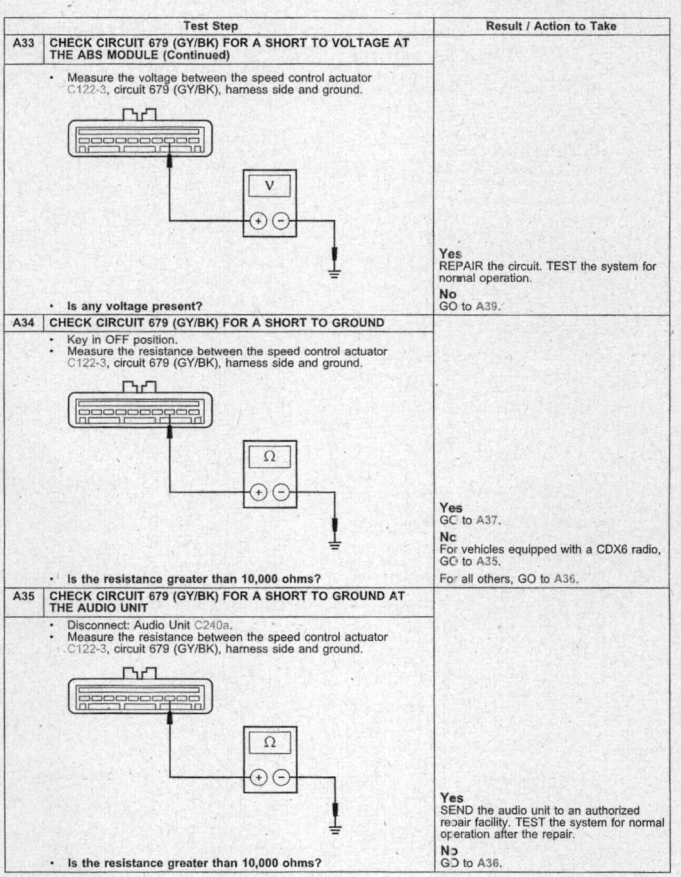

Test Step	Result / Action to Take
A33 CHECK CIRCUIT 679 (GY/BK) FOR A SHORT TO VOLTAGE AT THE ABS MODULE (Continued) • Measure the voltage between the speed control actuator C122-3, circuit 679 (GY/BK), harness side and ground. • Is any voltage present?	**Yes** REPAIR the circuit. TEST the system for normal operation. **No** GO to A39.
A34 CHECK CIRCUIT 679 (GY/BK) FOR A SHORT TO GROUND • Key in OFF position. • Measure the resistance between the speed control actuator C122-3, circuit 679 (GY/BK), harness side and ground. • Is the resistance greater than 10,000 ohms?	**Yes** GO to A37. **No** For vehicles equipped with a CDX6 radio, GO to A35. For all others, GO to A36.
A35 CHECK CIRCUIT 679 (GY/BK) FOR A SHORT TO GROUND AT THE AUDIO UNIT • Disconnect: Audio Unit C240a. • Measure the resistance between the speed control actuator C122-3, circuit 679 (GY/BK), harness side and ground. • Is the resistance greater than 10,000 ohms?	**Yes** SEND the audio unit to an authorized repair facility. TEST the system for normal operation after the repair. **No** GO to A36.

LTV0500000001516

Fig. 77 Test A: Speed Control Is Inoperative (Part 14 of 16). 2005–06 Escape & Mariner

Test Step	Result / Action to Take
A36 CHECK CIRCUIT 679 (GY/BK) FOR A SHORT TO GROUND AT THE ABS MODULE • Disconnect: ABS Module C155. • Measure the resistance between the speed control actuator C122-3, circuit 679 (GY/BK), harness side and ground. 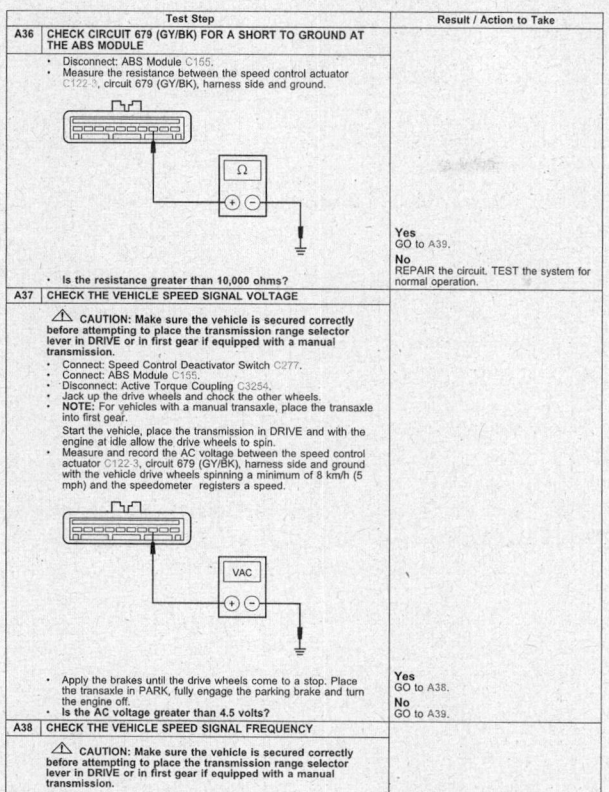 • Is the resistance greater than 10,000 ohms?	**Yes** GO to A39. **No** REPAIR the circuit. TEST the system for normal operation.
A37 CHECK THE VEHICLE SPEED SIGNAL VOLTAGE ⚠ CAUTION: Make sure the vehicle is secured correctly before attempting to place the transmission range selector lever in DRIVE or in first gear if equipped with a manual transmission. • Connect: Speed Control Deactivator Switch C277. • Connect: ABS Module C155. • Disconnect: Active Torque Coupling C3254. • Jack up the drive wheels and chock the other wheels. • NOTE: For vehicles with a manual transaxle, place the transaxle into first gear. Start the vehicle, place the transmission in DRIVE and with the engine at idle allow the drive wheels to spin. • Measure and record the AC voltage between the speed control actuator C122-3, circuit 679 (GY/BK), harness side and ground with the vehicle drive wheels spinning a minimum of 8 km/h (5 mph) and the speedometer registers a speed. • Apply the brakes until the drive wheels come to a stop. Place the transaxle in PARK, fully engage the parking brake and turn the engine off. • Is the AC voltage greater than 4.5 volts?	**Yes** GO to A38. **No** GO to A39.
A38 CHECK THE VEHICLE SPEED SIGNAL FREQUENCY ⚠ CAUTION: Make sure the vehicle is secured correctly before attempting to place the transmission range selector lever in DRIVE or in first gear if equipped with a manual transmission.	

LTV0500000001517

Fig. 77 Test A: Speed Control Is Inoperative (Part 15 of 16). 2005–06 Escape & Mariner

Test Step	Result / Action to Take
A38 CHECK THE VEHICLE SPEED SIGNAL FREQUENCY (Continued) • NOTE: For vehicles with a manual transaxle, place the transaxle into first gear. Start the vehicle, place the transmission in DRIVE and with the engine at idle allow the drive wheels to spin. • Measure and record the frequency between the speed control actuator C122-3, circuit 679 (GY/BK), harness side and ground with the vehicle drive wheels spinning a minimum of 8 km/h (5 mph) and the speedometer registers a speed. Record the speedometer reading. 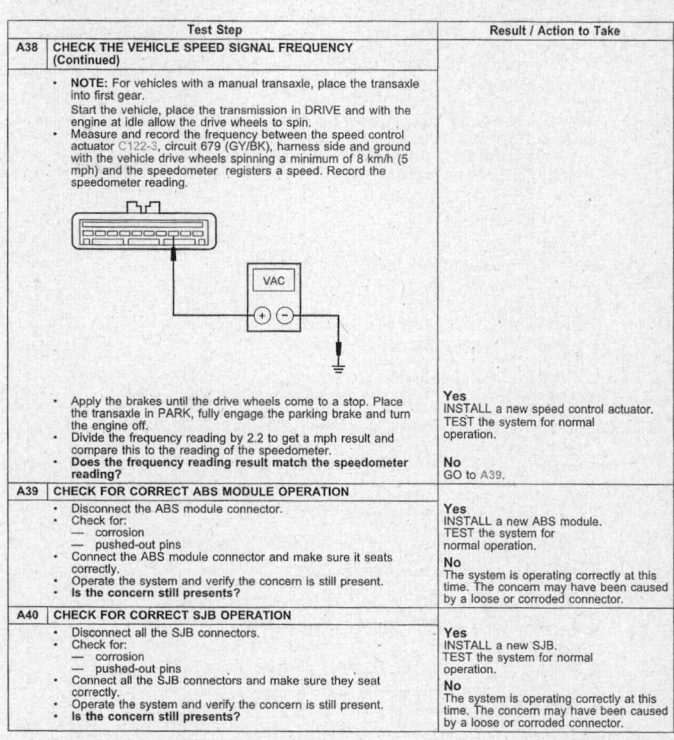 • Apply the brakes until the drive wheels come to a stop. Place the transaxle in PARK, fully engage the parking brake and turn the engine off. • Divide the frequency reading by 2.2 to get a mph result and compare this to the reading of the speedometer. • **Does the frequency reading result match the speedometer reading?**	**Yes** INSTALL a new speed control actuator. TEST the system for normal operation. **No** GO to A39.
A39 CHECK FOR CORRECT ABS MODULE OPERATION • Disconnect the ABS module connector. • Check for: — corrosion — pushed-out pins • Connect the ABS module connector and make sure it seats correctly. • Operate the system and verify the concern is still present. • **Is the concern still presents?**	**Yes** INSTALL a new ABS module. TEST the system for normal operation. **No** The system is operating correctly at this time. The concern may have been caused by a loose or corroded connector.
A40 CHECK FOR CORRECT SJB OPERATION • Disconnect all the SJB connectors. • Check for: — corrosion — pushed-out pins • Connect all the SJB connectors and make sure they seat correctly. • Operate the system and verify the concern is still present. • **Is the concern still presents?**	**Yes** INSTALL a new SJB. TEST the system for normal operation. **No** The system is operating correctly at this time. The concern may have been caused by a loose or corroded connector.

LTV0500000001518

Fig. 77 Test A: Speed Control Is Inoperative (Part 16 of 16). 2005–06 Escape & Mariner

Test Step	Result / Action to Take
B1 CHECK THE SPEED CONTROL CABLE/THROTTLE BODY LINKAGE • Key in OFF position. • Visually inspect the speed control cable connections, the throttle body linkage, and the speed control actuator pulley cover. • **Are the speed control cable connections, the throttle body linkage, and the speed control actuator pulley cover OK?**	**Yes** GO to B2. **No** INSTALL a new speed control cable or REPAIR the throttle body linkage. INSTALL the cover correctly. TEST the system for normal operation.
B2 CHECK THE SPEEDOMETER OPERATION • Drive the vehicle and observe the speedometer operation. • **Does the speedometer needle fluctuate?**	**Yes** Continue to diagnosis the speedometer. **No** GO to B3.
B3 CHECK FOR A BASE ENGINE CONCERN • Drive the vehicle and determine if there is a base engine concern. • **Is a base engine concern present?**	**Yes** Refer to **MOTOR's** "Domestic Engine Performance & Driveability Manual" to continue diagnosis of the base engine concern. **No** GO to B4.
B4 CHECK THE VEHICLE SPEED SIGNAL VOLTAGE ⚠ CAUTION: Make sure the vehicle is secured correctly before attempting to place the transmission range selector lever in DRIVE or in first gear if equipped with a manual transmission. • Disconnect: Speed Control Actuator C122. • Connect: ABS Module C155. • Disconnect: Active Torque Coupling C3254. • Jack up the drive wheels and chock the other wheels.	**Yes** GO to B5. **No** GO to B6.

LTV0500000001519

Fig. 78 Test B: Set Speed Fluctuates (Part 1 of 2). 2005–06 Escape & Mariner

• NOTE: For vehicles with a manual transaxle, place the transaxle into first gear.
• Start the vehicle, place the transmission in DRIVE and with the engine at idle allow the drive wheels to spin.
• Measure and record the AC voltage between the speed control actuator C122-3, circuit 679 (GY/BK), harness side and ground with the vehicle drive wheels spinning a minimum of 8 km/h (5 mph) and the speedometer registers a speed.

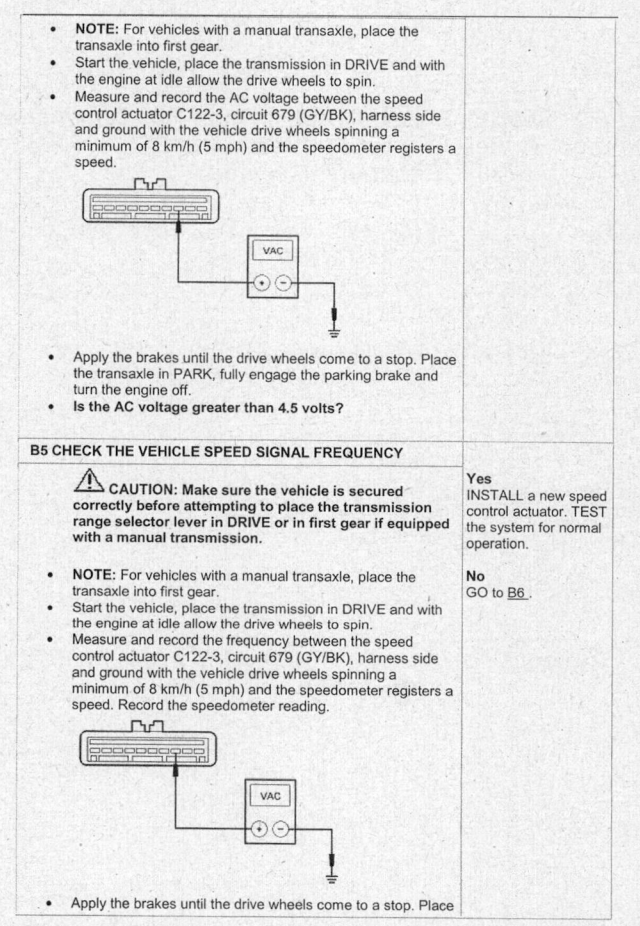

• Apply the brakes until the drive wheels come to a stop. Place the transaxle in PARK, fully engage the parking brake and turn the engine off.
• Is the AC voltage greater than 4.5 volts?

B5 CHECK THE VEHICLE SPEED SIGNAL FREQUENCY	
⚠ CAUTION: Make sure the vehicle is secured correctly before attempting to place the transmission range selector lever in DRIVE or in first gear if equipped with a manual transmission. • NOTE: For vehicles with a manual transaxle, place the transaxle into first gear. • Start the vehicle, place the transmission in DRIVE and with the engine at idle allow the drive wheels to spin. • Measure and record the frequency between the speed control actuator C122-3, circuit 679 (GY/BK), harness side and ground with the vehicle drive wheels spinning a minimum of 8 km/h (5 mph) and the speedometer registers a speed. Record the speedometer reading. • Apply the brakes until the drive wheels come to a stop. Place	**Yes** INSTALL a new speed control actuator. TEST the system for normal operation. **No** GO to B6.

LTV0500000001520

Fig. 78 Test B: Set Speed Fluctuates (Part 2 of 2). 2005–06 Escape & Mariner

Test Step	Result / Action to Take
C1 VERIFY SPEED CONTROL DEACTIVATION	
• Enter the following diagnostic mode on the diagnostic tool: PCM Throttle Position Sensor (TPS) PID. • Drive the vehicle and engage the speed control. • Monitor the PCM TPS PID voltage while tapping the brake pedal to disengage the speed control. • **Does the PID display a return to base TPS voltage?**	**Yes** INFORM the customer that tapping the brake pedal only disengages the speed control and the brakes must be used to slow the vehicle down. **No** GO to <u>C2</u>.
C2 CHECK THE SPEED CONTROL CABLE/ACCELERATOR CABLE	
• Key in OFF position. • **NOTE:** Make sure the floor mat, insulation, wiring harnesses location, and other item do not interfere with the accelerator pedal and linkage. • Visually inspect the speed control cable connections, the throttle body linkage, and the speed control actuator pulley cover. • **Are the speed control cable connections, the throttle body linkage, and the speed control actuator pulley cover OK?**	**Yes** GO to <u>C3</u>. **No** INSTALL a new speed control cable or accelerator cable. To INSTALL a new speed control cable. TEST the system for normal operation.
C3 CHECK THE STOPLAMPS FOR CORRECT OPERATION	
• Check the stoplamps for correct operation by firmly applying and releasing the brake pedal. • **Do the stoplamps operate correctly?**	**Yes** GO to <u>C4</u>. **No** Diagnosis the stoplamps.
C4 CHECK THE SPEED CONTROL DEACTIVATOR CIRCUIT	
• Key in ON position. • Measure the voltage between the speed control actuator C122-9, circuit 248 (TN/OG), harness side and ground while firmly applying the brake pedal. 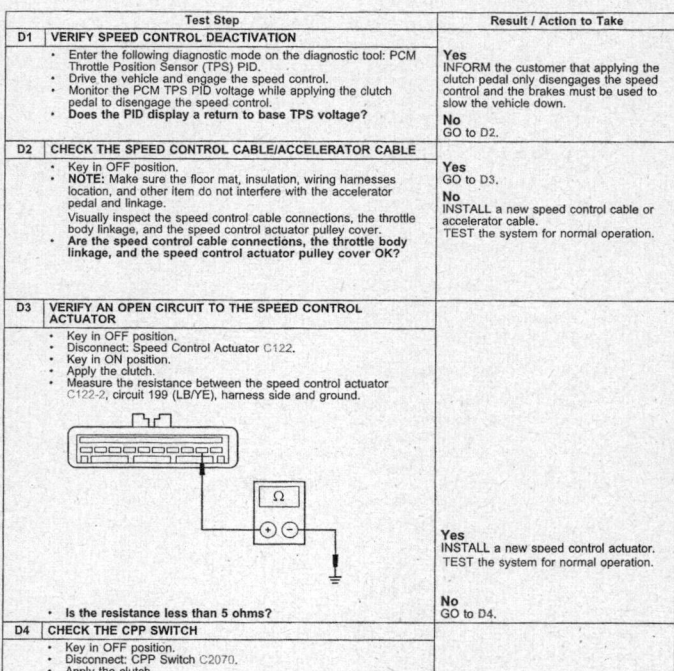	**Yes** GO to <u>C5</u>. **No** INSTALL a new speed control actuator TEST the system for normal operation.

LTV0500000001602

Fig. 79 Test C: Speed Control Does Not Disengage When Brakes Are Applied (Part 1 of 2). 2005–06 Escape & Mariner

Test Step	Result / Action to Take
D1 VERIFY SPEED CONTROL DEACTIVATION	
• Enter the following diagnostic mode on the diagnostic tool: PCM Throttle Position Sensor (TPS) PID. • Drive the vehicle and engage the speed control. • Monitor the PCM TPS PID voltage while applying the clutch pedal to disengage the speed control. • **Does the PID display a return to base TPS voltage?**	**Yes** INFORM the customer that applying the clutch pedal only disengages the speed control and the brakes must be used to slow the vehicle down. **No** GO to D2.
D2 CHECK THE SPEED CONTROL CABLE/ACCELERATOR CABLE	
• Key in OFF position. • **NOTE:** Make sure the floor mat, insulation, wiring harnesses location, and other item do not interfere with the accelerator pedal and linkage. • Visually inspect the speed control cable connections, the throttle body linkage, and the speed control actuator pulley cover. • **Are the speed control cable connections, the throttle body linkage, and the speed control actuator pulley cover OK?**	**Yes** GO to D3. **No** INSTALL a new speed control cable or accelerator cable. TEST the system for normal operation.
D3 VERIFY AN OPEN CIRCUIT TO THE SPEED CONTROL ACTUATOR	
• Key in OFF position. • Disconnect: Speed Control Actuator C122. • Key in ON position. • Apply the clutch. • Measure the resistance between the speed control actuator C122-2, circuit 199 (LB/YE), harness side and ground. • Is the resistance less than 5 ohms?	**Yes** INSTALL a new speed control actuator. TEST the system for normal operation. **No** GO to D4.
D4 CHECK THE CPP SWITCH	
• Key in OFF position. • Disconnect: CPP Switch C2070. • Apply the clutch.	

LTV0500000001604

Fig. 80 Test D: Speed Control Does Not Disengage When Clutch Is Applied (Part 1 of 3). 2005–06 Escape & Mariner

• Is any voltage present?

Test Step	Result / Action to Take
C5 CHECK CIRCUIT 248 (TN/OG) FOR A SHORT TO VOLTAGE	
• Key in OFF position. • Disconnect: Speed Control Deactivator Switch C277. • Key in ON position. • Measure the voltage between the speed control actuator C122-9, circuit 248 (TN/OG), harness side and ground. 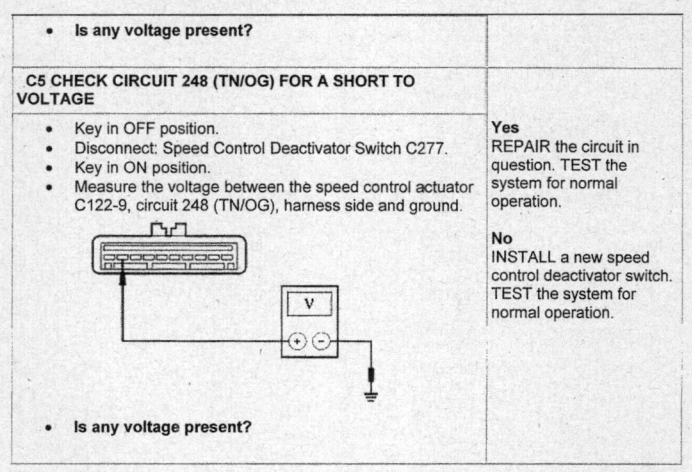 • Is any voltage present?	**Yes** REPAIR the circuit in question. TEST the system for normal operation. **No** INSTALL a new speed control deactivator switch. TEST the system for normal operation.

LTV0500000001603

Fig. 79 Test C: Speed Control Does Not Disengage When Brakes Are Applied (Part 2 of 2). 2005–06 Escape & Mariner

Test Step	Result / Action to Take
D4 CHECK THE CPP SWITCH (Continued)	
• Measure the resistance between the CPP switch pin 2, and the CPP switch pin 4, component side. 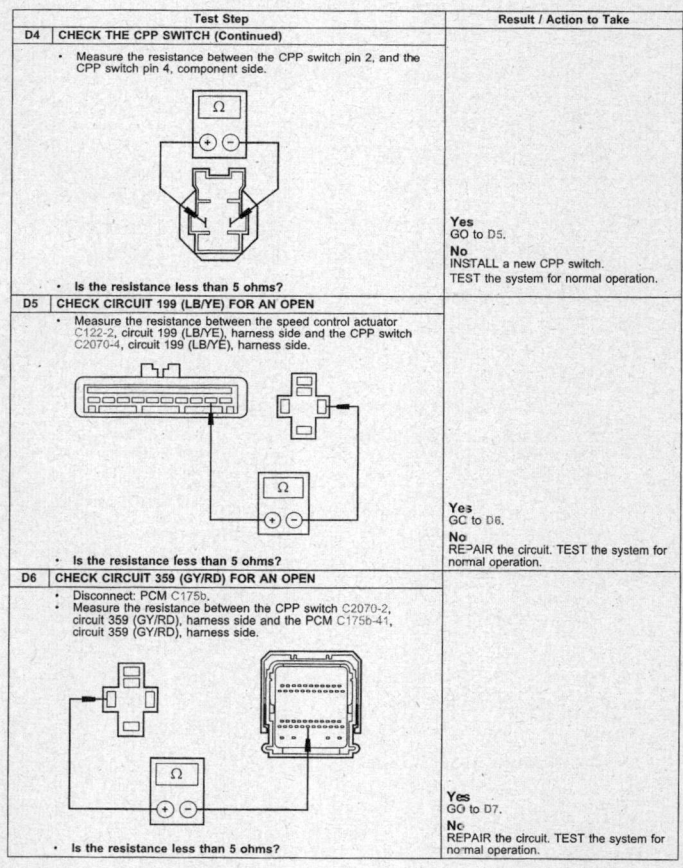 • Is the resistance less than 5 ohms?	**Yes** GO to D5. **No** INSTALL a new CPP switch. TEST the system for normal operation.
D5 CHECK CIRCUIT 199 (LB/YE) FOR AN OPEN	
• Measure the resistance between the speed control actuator C122-2, circuit 199 (LB/YE), harness side and the CPP switch C2070-4, circuit 199 (LB/YE), harness side. • Is the resistance less than 5 ohms?	**Yes** GC to D6. **No** REPAIR the circuit. TEST the system for normal operation.
D6 CHECK CIRCUIT 359 (GY/RD) FOR AN OPEN	
• Disconnect: PCM C175b. • Measure the resistance between the CPP switch C2070-2, circuit 359 (GY/RD), harness side and the PCM C175b-41, circuit 359 (GY/RD), harness side. • Is the resistance less than 5 ohms?	**Yes** GO to D7. **No** REPAIR the circuit. TEST the system for normal operation.

LTV0500000001605

Fig. 80 Test D: Speed Control Does Not Disengage When Clutch Is Applied (Part 2 of 3). 2005–06 Escape & Mariner

Test Step	Result / Action to Take
D7 CHECK FOR CORRECT PCM MODULE OPERATION	

• Disconnect the PCM connectors.
• Check for:
  — corrosion
  — pushed-out pins
• Connect the PCM connectors and make sure they seat correctly.
• Operate the system and verify the concern is still present.
• **Is the concern still presents?**
	Yes
	INSTALL a new PCM
	TEST the system for normal operation.
	
	No
	The system is operating correctly at this time. The concern may have been caused by a loose or corroded connector.

LTV0500000001606

Fig. 80   Test D: Speed Control Does Not Disengage When Clutch Is Applied (Part 3 of 3). 2005–06 Escape & Mariner

Test Step	Result / Action to Take
F1 CHECK THE SPEED CONTROL CABLE	
• Check the speed control cable for correct attachment at the speed control actuator and throttle body. • **Is the speed control cable attached correctly?**	**Yes** GO to F2. **No** CONNECT the speed control cable. TEST the system for normal operation.
F2 CHECK FOR A STICKING OR BINDING SPEED CONTROL CABLE	
• Check the speed control cable for sticking or binding. • **Is the speed control cable OK?**	**Yes** INSTALL a new speed control actuator. TEST the system for normal operation. **No** REPAIR or INSTALL a new speed control cable. TEST the system for normal operation.

LTV0500000001608

Fig. 82   Test F: Flash w/Last Switch Pressed, But No Dynamic Pull Occurs At Throttle & Speed Control Is Inoperative. 2005–06 Escape & Mariner

Test Step	Result / Action to Take
G1 CHECK THE STOPLAMP OPERATION	
• Apply and release the brake pedal while observing the stoplamps. • **Do the stoplamps operate correctly?**	**Yes** GO to G2. **No** Continue diagnosis the stoplamps.
G2 CHECK THE STOPLAMP BULBS	
• Check the stoplamps for the presence of aftermarket LED lights. • **Are the correct stoplamp bulbs installed?**	**Yes** GO to G3. **No** INSTALL the correct stoplamp bulbs. TEST the system for normal operation.
G3 CHECK CIRCUIT 511 (LG) FOR AN OPEN	
• Disconnect: Speed Control Actuator C122. • While applying the brake pedal, measure the voltage between the speed control actuator C122-4, circuit 511 (LG), harness side and ground. • **Is the voltage greater than 10 volts?**	**Yes** INSTALL a new speed control actuator. REPEAT the self-test. **No** REPAIR the circuit. REPEAT the self-test.

LTV0500000001609

Fig. 83   Test G: Stoplamp Switch Circuit Failure. 2005–06 Escape & Mariner

Test Step	Result / Action to Take
E1 CHECK THE SPEED CONTROL SWITCH	
• Key in OFF position. • Disconnect: Speed Control Actuator C122. • Measure the resistance between the speed control actuator C122-5, circuit 151 (LB/BK), harness side and the speed control actuator C122-6, circuit 848 (DG/OG), harness side while pressing the speed control switch as follows:	

Speed Control Switch	Resistance Value
COAST	Between 114 and 126 ohms
SET/ACCEL	Between 646 and 714 ohms
RESUME	Between 2,090 and 2,310 ohms
OFF	Less than 5 ohms
No buttons pressed	Infinite

• **Are the speed control switch resistance values OK?**

Yes
INSTALL a new speed control actuator. TEST the system for normal operation.

No
INSTALL a new speed control switch. TEST the system for normal operation.

LTV0500000001607

Fig. 81   Test E: Single Speed Control Button Is Inoperative. 2005–06 Escape & Mariner

Test Step	Result / Action to Take
H1 CHECK THE SPEED CONTROL DEACTIVATOR SWITCH INPUT TO THE SPEED CONTROL ACTUATOR	
• Disconnect: Speed Control Actuator C122. • Key in ON position. • Measure the voltage between the speed control actuator C122-9, circuit 248 (TN/OG), harness side and ground. • **Is the voltage greater than 10 volts?**	**Yes** INSTALL a new speed control actuator. REPEAT the self-test. **No** GO to H2.
H2 CHECK THE SPEED CONTROL DEACTIVATOR SWITCH	
• Key in OFF position. • Disconnect: Speed Control Deactivator Switch C277. • Measure the resistance between the speed control deactivator switch terminal 1, and the speed control deactivator switch terminal 2, component side. • **Is the resistance less than 5 ohms?**	**Yes** GO to H3. **No** INSTALL a new speed control deactivator switch. REPEAT the self-test.
H3 CHECK THE SPEED CONTROL DEACTIVATOR SWITCH VOLTAGE	
• Key in ON position. • Measure the voltage between the speed control deactivator switch C277-1, circuit 101 (GY/YE), harness side and ground.	**Yes** REPAIR circuit 248 (TN/OG) as necessary. REPEAT the self-test. **No**

LTV0500000001610

Fig. 84   Test H: Speed Control Deactivator Switch Circuit Failure (Part 1 of 2). 2005–06 Escape & Mariner

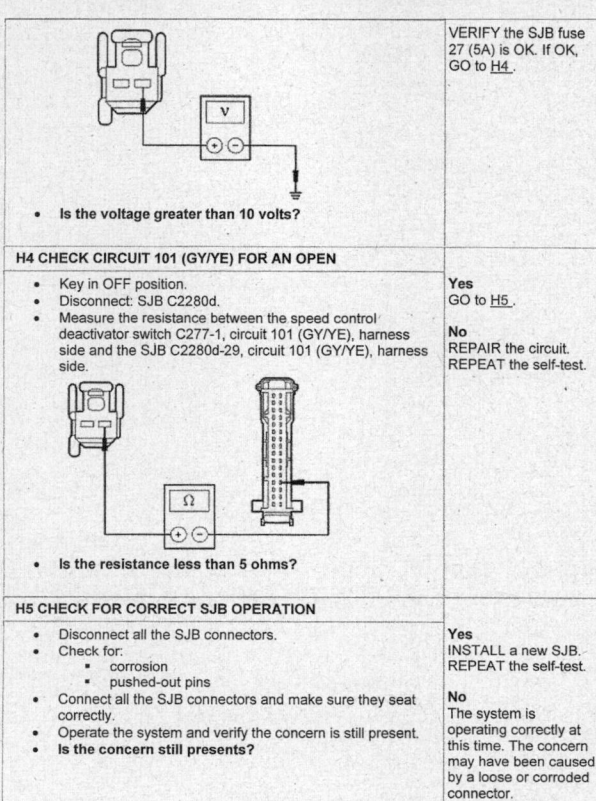

	VERIFY the SJB fuse 27 (5A) is OK. If OK, GO to H4 .
• Is the voltage greater than 10 volts?	

H4 CHECK CIRCUIT 101 (GY/YE) FOR AN OPEN	
• Key in OFF position. • Disconnect: SJB C2280d. • Measure the resistance between the speed control deactivator switch C277-1, circuit 101 (GY/YE), harness side and the SJB C2280d-29, circuit 101 (GY/YE), harness side.	**Yes** GO to H5 . **No** REPAIR the circuit. REPEAT the self-test.
• Is the resistance less than 5 ohms?	

H5 CHECK FOR CORRECT SJB OPERATION	

• Disconnect all the SJB connectors.
• Check for:
  ▪ corrosion
  ▪ pushed-out pins
• Connect all the SJB connectors and make sure they seat correctly.
• Operate the system and verify the concern is still present.
• **Is the concern still presents?**
	Yes
	INSTALL a new SJB. REPEAT the self-test.
	
	No
	The system is operating correctly at this time. The concern may have been caused by a loose or corroded connector.

LTV0500000001611

Fig. 84   Test H: Speed Control Deactivator Switch Circuit Failure (Part 2 of 2). 2005–06 Escape & Mariner

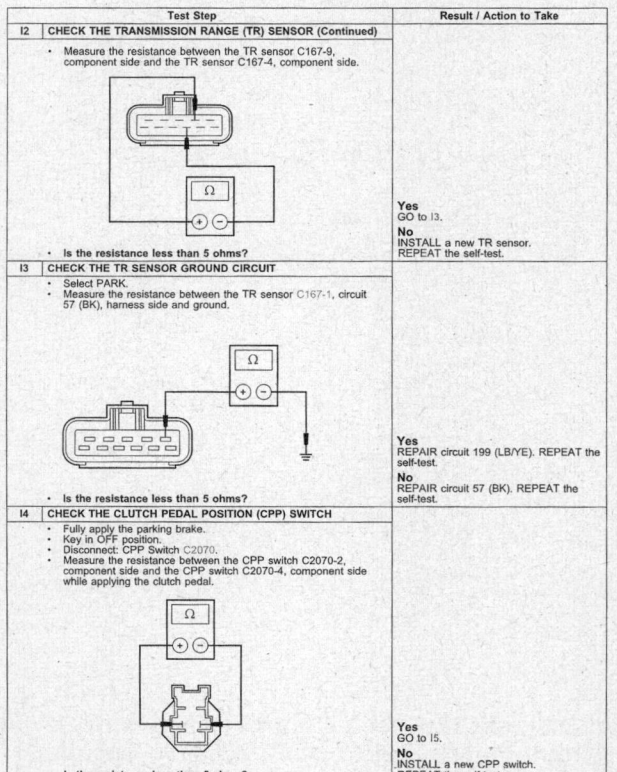

Test Step	**Result / Action to Take**
I2 CHECK THE TRANSMISSION RANGE (TR) SENSOR (Continued)	
• Measure the resistance between the TR sensor C167-9, component side and the TR sensor C167-4, component side.	**Yes** GO to I3. **No** INSTALL a new TR sensor. REPEAT the self-test.
• Is the resistance less than 5 ohms?	
I3 CHECK THE TR SENSOR GROUND CIRCUIT	
• Select PARK. • Measure the resistance between the TR sensor C167-1, circuit 57 (BK), harness side and ground.	**Yes** REPAIR circuit 199 (LB/YE). REPEAT the self-test. **No** REPAIR circuit 57 (BK). REPEAT the self-test.
• Is the resistance less than 5 ohms?	
I4 CHECK THE CLUTCH PEDAL POSITION (CPP) SWITCH	
• Fully apply the parking brake. • Key in OFF position. • Disconnect: CPP Switch C2070. • Measure the resistance between the CPP switch C2070-2, component side and the CPP switch C2070-4, component side while applying the clutch pedal.	**Yes** GO to I5. **No** INSTALL a new CPP switch. REPEAT the self-test.
• Is the resistance less than 5 ohms?	

LTV0500000001613

Fig. 85   Test I: Clutch/Neutral Switch Circuit Failure (Part 2 of 3). 2005–06 Escape & Mariner

Test Step	**Result / Action to Take**
I1 VERIFY FLASH CODE 4	
• Key in OFF position. • Disconnect: Speed Control Actuator C122. • Key in ON position. • Select NEUTRAL. • Apply the clutch. • Measure the resistance between the speed control actuator C122-2, circuit 199 (LB/YE), harness side and ground.	**Yes** INSTALL a new speed control actuator. TEST the system for normal operation. **No** If automatic transaxle, GO to I2. If manual transaxle, GO to I4.
• Is the resistance less than 5 ohms?	
I2 CHECK THE TRANSMISSION RANGE (TR) SENSOR	
• Fully apply the parking brake. • Key in OFF position. • Disconnect: TR Sensor C167. • Select NEUTRAL.	

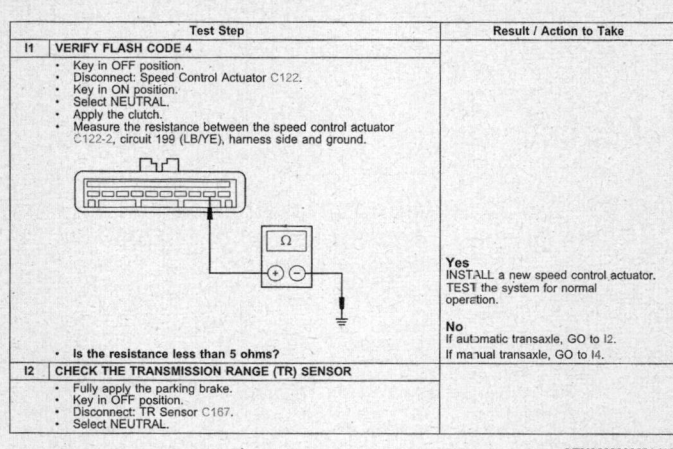

LTV0500000001612

Fig. 85   Test I: Clutch/Neutral Switch Circuit Failure (Part 1 of 3). 2005–06 Escape & Mariner

Test Step	**Result / Action to Take**
I5 CHECK CIRCUIT 199 (LB/YE) FOR AN OPEN	
• Measure the resistance between the speed control actuator C122-2, circuit 199 (LB/YE), harness side and the CPP switch C2070-4, circuit 199 (LB/YE), harness side.	**Yes** GO to I6. **No** REPAIR the circuit. REPEAT the self-test.
• Is the resistance less than 5 ohms?	
I6 CHECK CIRCUIT 359 (GY/RD) FOR AN OPEN	
• Disconnect PCM C175b. • Measure the resistance between the CPP switch C2070-2, circuit 359 (GY/RD), harness side and the PCM C175b-41, circuit 359 (GY/RD), harness side.	**Yes** GO to I7. **No** REPAIR the circuit. TEST the system for normal operation.
• Is the resistance less than 5 ohms?	
I7 CHECK FOR CORRECT PCM MODULE OPERATION	

• Disconnect the PCM connectors.
• Check for:
  — corrosion
  — pushed-out pins
• Connect the PCM connectors and make sure they seat correctly.
• Operate the system and verify the concern is still present.
• **Is the concern still presents?**
	Yes
	INSTALL a new PCM. TEST the system for normal operation.
	
	No
	The system is operating correctly at this time. The concern may have been caused by a loose or corroded connector.

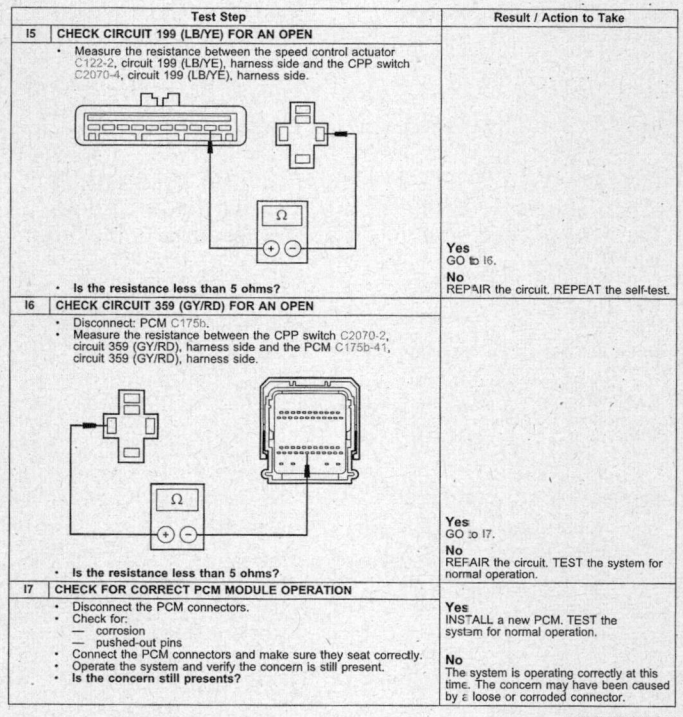

LTV0500000001614

Fig. 85   Test I: Clutch/Neutral Switch Circuit Failure (Part 3 of 3). 2005–06 Escape & Mariner

Test Step	Result / Action to Take
A1 CHECK THE PCM POWER CIRCUITS	
• Key in OFF position. • Disconnect: PCM C175b. • Key in ON position. • Measure the voltage between the PCM C175b and ground as follows:	**Yes** GO to A2 . **No** REPAIR the circuit. CLEAR the DTCs. REPEAT the self-test.

Pin	Circuit
34	361 (RD)
40	729 (RD/WH)
46	361 (RD)

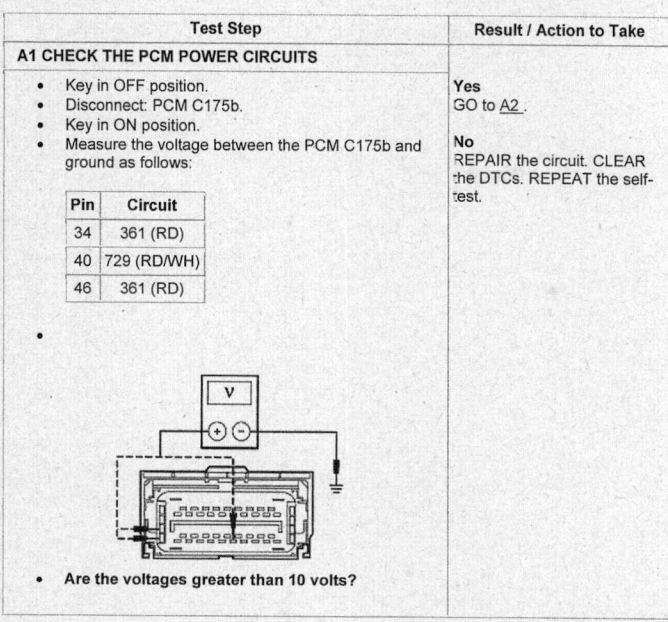

• Are the voltages greater than 10 volts?

LTV0500000001617

Fig. 86 Test A: No Communication w/Powertrain Control Module (Part 1 of 2). 2002–04 Expedition & Navigator

Test Step	Result / Action to Take
A2 CHECK THE PCM GROUND CIRCUITS	
• Key in OFF position. • Measure the resistance between the PCM C175b and ground as follows:	**Yes** Diagnosis Communications Area Network (CAN) **No** REPAIR the circuit. CLEAR the DTCs. REPEAT the self-test.

Pin	Circuit
1	570 (BK/WH)
10	567 (LB/YE)
11	570 (BK/WH)
23	570 (BK/WH)

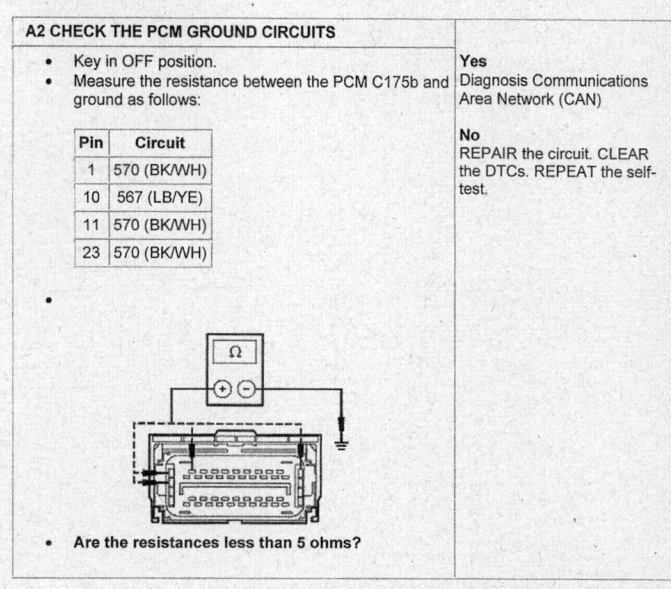

• Are the resistances less than 5 ohms?

LTV0500000001618

Fig. 86 Test A: No Communication w/Powertrain Control Module (Part 2 of 2). 2002–04 Expedition & Navigator

Test Step	Result / Action to Take
B1 CHECK THE PCM POWER CIRCUITS	
NOTE: Carry out the speed control self-test diagnostics before entering the pinpoint test. • Key in OFF position. • Disconnect: PCM C175b. • Key in ON position. • Measure the voltage between the PCM C175b and ground as follows:	

Pin	Circuit
34	361 (RD)
40	729 (RD/WH)
46	361 (RD)

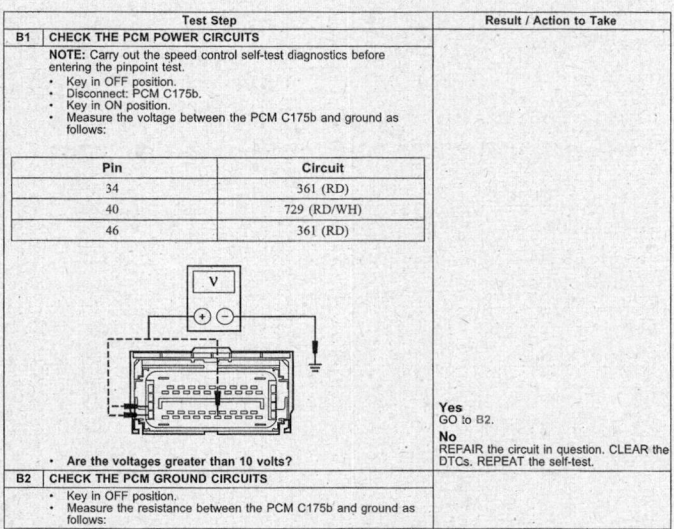

• Are the voltages greater than 10 volts?	**Yes** GO to B2. **No** REPAIR the circuit in question. CLEAR the DTCs. REPEAT the self-test.
B2 CHECK THE PCM GROUND CIRCUITS • Key in OFF position. • Measure the resistance between the PCM C175b and ground as follows:	

LTV0500000001619

Fig. 87 Test B: Speed Control Is Inoperative (Part 1 of 8). 2002–04 Expedition & Navigator

Test Step	Result / Action to Take
B2 CHECK THE PCM GROUND CIRCUITS (Continued)	

Pin	Circuit
1	570 (BK/WH)
10	567 (LB/YE)
11	570 (BK/WH)
23	570 (BK/WH)

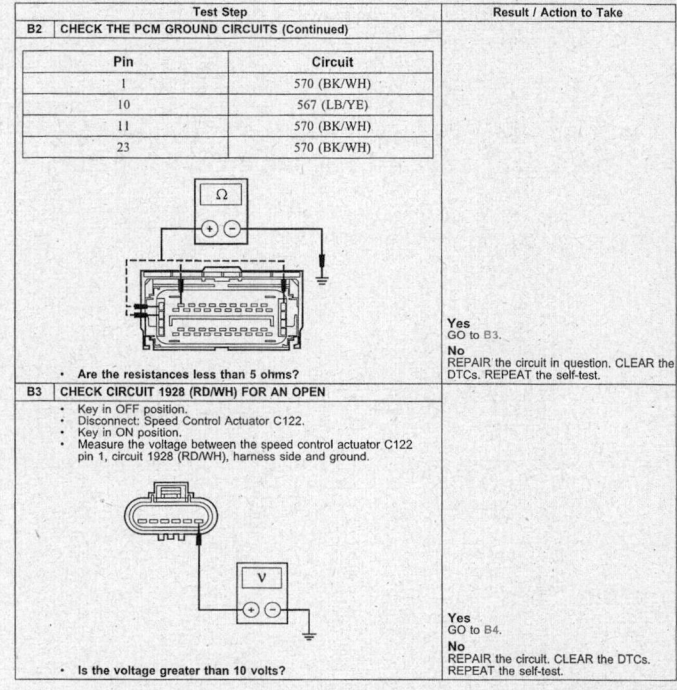

• Are the resistances less than 5 ohms?	**Yes** GO to B3. **No** REPAIR the circuit in question. CLEAR the DTCs. REPEAT the self-test.
B3 CHECK CIRCUIT 1928 (RD/WH) FOR AN OPEN • Key in OFF position. • Disconnect: Speed Control Actuator C122. • Key in ON position. • Measure the voltage between the speed control actuator C122 pin 1, circuit 1928 (RD/WH), harness side and ground.	
• Is the voltage greater than 10 volts?	**Yes** GO to B4. **No** REPAIR the circuit. CLEAR the DTCs. REPEAT the self-test.

LTV0500000001620

Fig. 87 Test B: Speed Control Is Inoperative (Part 2 of 8). 2002–04 Expedition & Navigator

Test Step	Result / Action to Take
B4 CHECK THE DEACTIVATOR SWITCH CIRCUITRY FOR AN OPEN • Measure the voltage between the speed control actuator C122 pin 6, circuit 307 (BK/YE), harness side and ground. 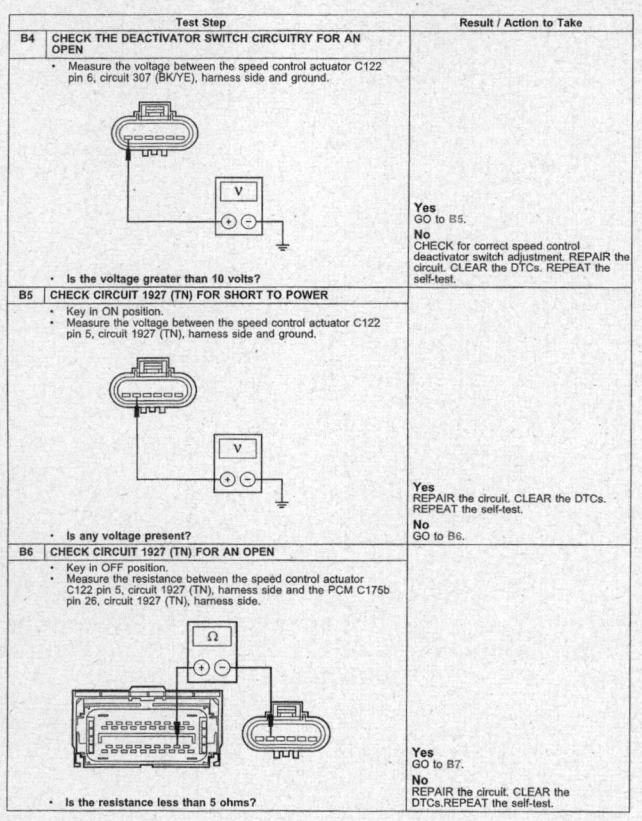 • Is the voltage greater than 10 volts?	**Yes** GO to B5. **No** CHECK for correct speed control deactivator switch adjustment. REPAIR the circuit. CLEAR the DTCs. REPEAT the self-test.
B5 CHECK CIRCUIT 1927 (TN) FOR SHORT TO POWER • Key in ON position. • Measure the voltage between the speed control actuator C122 pin 5, circuit 1927 (TN), harness side and ground. • Is any voltage present?	**Yes** REPAIR the circuit. CLEAR the DTCs. REPEAT the self-test. **No** GO to B6.
B6 CHECK CIRCUIT 1927 (TN) FOR AN OPEN • Key in OFF position. • Measure the resistance between the speed control actuator C122 pin 5, circuit 1927 (TN), harness side and the PCM C175b pin 26, circuit 1927 (TN), harness side. • Is the resistance less than 5 ohms?	**Yes** GO to B7. **No** REPAIR the circuit. CLEAR the DTCs.REPEAT the self-test.

LTV0500000001621

Fig. 87 Test B: Speed Control Is Inoperative (Part 3 of 8). 2002–04 Expedition & Navigator

Test Step	Result / Action to Take
B7 CHECK CIRCUIT 1927 (TN) FOR SHORT TO GROUND • Measure the resistance between the speed control actuator C122 pin 5, circuit 1927 (TN), harness side and ground. 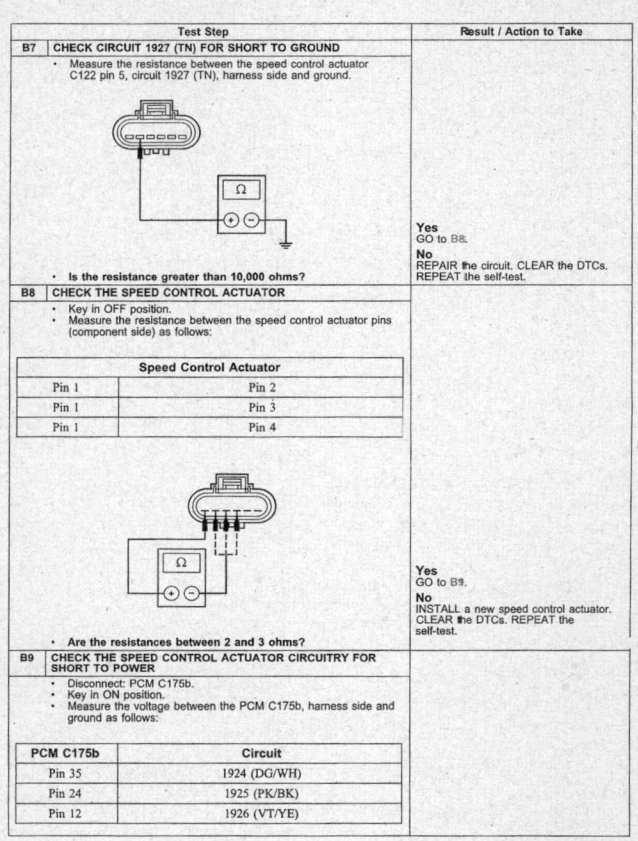 • Is the resistance greater than 10,000 ohms?	**Yes** GO to B8. **No** REPAIR the circuit. CLEAR the DTCs. REPEAT the self-test.
B8 CHECK THE SPEED CONTROL ACTUATOR • Key in OFF position. • Measure the resistance between the speed control actuator pins (component side) as follows:	

Speed Control Actuator

Pin 1	Pin 2
Pin 1	Pin 3
Pin 1	Pin 4

Test Step	Result / Action to Take
• Are the resistances between 2 and 3 ohms?	**Yes** GO to B9. **No** INSTALL a new speed control actuator. CLEAR the DTCs. REPEAT the self-test.
B9 CHECK THE SPEED CONTROL ACTUATOR CIRCUITRY FOR SHORT TO POWER • Disconnect: PCM C175b. • Key in ON position. • Measure the voltage between the PCM C175b, harness side and ground as follows:	

PCM C175b	Circuit
Pin 35	1924 (DG/WH)
Pin 24	1925 (PK/BK)
Pin 12	1926 (VT/YE)

LTV0500000001622

Fig. 87 Test B: Speed Control Is Inoperative (Part 4 of 8). 2002–04 Expedition & Navigator

Test Step	Result / Action to Take
B9 CHECK THE SPEED CONTROL ACTUATOR CIRCUITRY FOR SHORT TO POWER (Continued) 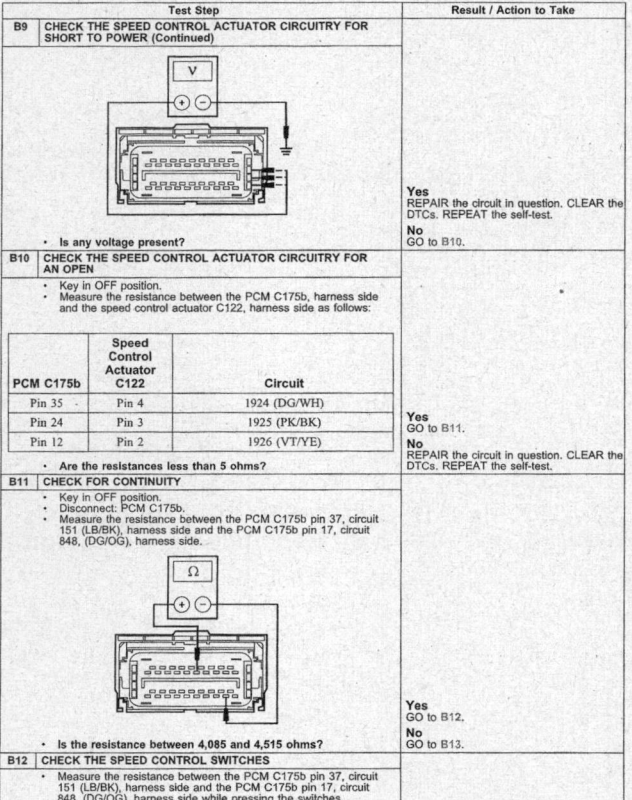 • Is any voltage present?	**Yes** REPAIR the circuit in question. CLEAR the DTCs. REPEAT the self-test. **No** GO to B10.
B10 CHECK THE SPEED CONTROL ACTUATOR CIRCUITRY FOR AN OPEN • Key in OFF position. • Measure the resistance between the PCM C175b, harness side and the speed control actuator C122, harness side as follows:	

PCM C175b	Speed Control Actuator C122	Circuit
Pin 35	Pin 4	1924 (DG/WH)
Pin 24	Pin 3	1925 (PK/BK)
Pin 12	Pin 2	1926 (VT/YE)

Test Step	Result / Action to Take
• Are the resistances less than 5 ohms?	**Yes** GO to B11. **No** REPAIR the circuit in question. CLEAR the DTCs. REPEAT the self-test.
B11 CHECK FOR CONTINUITY • Key in OFF position. • Disconnect: PCM C175b. • Measure the resistance between the PCM C175b pin 37, circuit 151 (LB/BK), harness side and the PCM C175b pin 17, circuit 848, (DG/OG), harness side. • Is the resistance between 4,085 and 4,515 ohms?	**Yes** GO to B12. **No** GO to B13.
B12 CHECK THE SPEED CONTROL SWITCHES • Measure the resistance between the PCM C175b pin 37, circuit 151 (LB/BK), harness side and the PCM C175b pin 17, circuit 848, (DG/OG), harness side while pressing the switches.	

LTV0500000001623

Fig. 87 Test B: Speed Control Is Inoperative (Part 5 of 8). 2002–04 Expedition & Navigator

Test Step	Result / Action to Take
B12 CHECK THE SPEED CONTROL SWITCHES (Continued)	

Speed Control Switch with remote audio/climate control

Speed Control Actuator Switch	Resistance Value
SETt -	Between 285 and 315 ohms
SET +	Between 570 and 630 ohms
Resume	Between 1,055 and 1,165 ohms
On	Between 1,995 and 2,205 ohms
Off	Less than 5 ohms

Test Step	Result / Action to Take
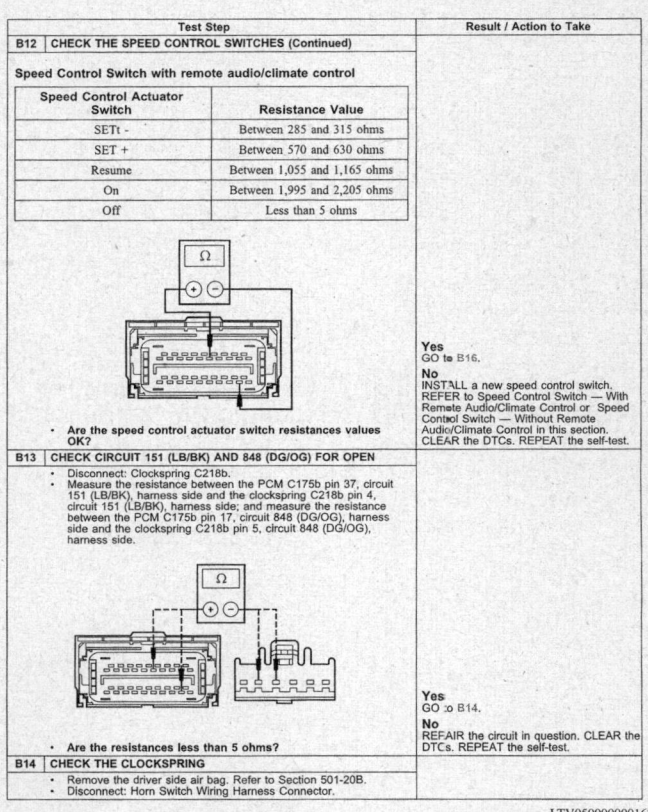 • Are the speed control actuator switch resistances values OK?	**Yes** GO to B16. **No** INSTALL a new speed control switch. REFER to Speed Control Switch — With Remote Audio/Climate Control or Speed Control Switch — Without Remote Audio/Climate Control in this section. CLEAR the DTCs. REPEAT the self-test.
B13 CHECK CIRCUIT 151 (LB/BK) AND 848 (DG/OG) FOR OPEN • Disconnect: Clockspring C218b. • Measure the resistance between the PCM C175b pin 37, circuit 151 (LB/BK), harness side and the clockspring C218b pin 4, circuit 151 (LB/BK), harness side; and measure the resistance between the PCM C175b pin 17, circuit 848 (DG/OG), harness side and the clockspring C218b pin 5, circuit 848 (DG/OG), harness side. • Are the resistances less than 5 ohms?	**Yes** GO to B14. **No** REPAIR the circuit in question. CLEAR the DTCs. REPEAT the self-test.
B14 CHECK THE CLOCKSPRING • Remove the driver side air bag. Refer to Section 501-20B. • Disconnect: Horn Switch Wiring Harness Connector.	

LTV0500000001624

Fig. 87 Test B: Speed Control Is Inoperative (Part 6 of 8). 2002–04 Expedition & Navigator

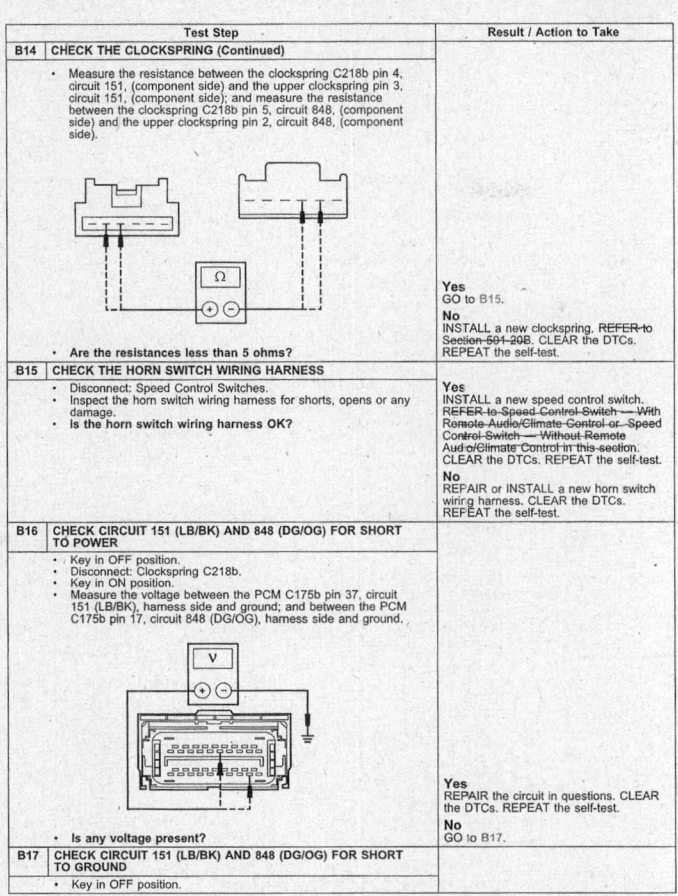

Test Step	Result / Action to Take
B14 CHECK THE CLOCKSPRING (Continued)	
• Measure the resistance between the clockspring C218b pin 4, circuit 151, (component side) and the upper clockspring pin 3, circuit 151, (component side); and measure the resistance between the clockspring C218b pin 5, circuit 848, (component side) and the upper clockspring pin 2, circuit 848, (component side).	**Yes** GO to B15. **No** INSTALL a new clockspring. REFER to Section 501-20B. CLEAR the DTCs. REPEAT the self-test.
• Are the resistances less than 5 ohms?	
B15 CHECK THE HORN SWITCH WIRING HARNESS	
• Disconnect: Speed Control Switches.	**Yes** INSTALL a new speed control switch. REFER to Speed Control Switch — With Remote Audio/Climate Control or Speed Control Switch — Without Remote Aud o/Climate Control in this section. CLEAR the DTCs. REPEAT the self-test. **No** REPAIR or INSTALL a new horn switch wiring harness. CLEAR the DTCs. REPEAT the self-test.
• Inspect the horn switch wiring harness for shorts, opens or any damage.	
• Is the horn switch wiring harness OK?	
B16 CHECK CIRCUIT 151 (LB/BK) AND 848 (DG/OG) FOR SHORT TO POWER	
• Key in OFF position.	
• Disconnect: Clockspring C218b.	
• Key in ON position.	
• Measure the voltage between the PCM C175b pin 37, circuit 151 (LB/BK), harness side and ground; and between the PCM C175b pin 17, circuit 848 (DG/OG), harness side and ground.	**Yes** REPAIR the circuit in questions. CLEAR the DTCs. REPEAT the self-test. **No** GO to B17.
• Is any voltage present?	
B17 CHECK CIRCUIT 151 (LB/BK) AND 848 (DG/OG) FOR SHORT TO GROUND	
• Key in OFF position.	

LTV0500000001625

Fig. 87 Test B: Speed Control Is Inoperative (Part 7 of 8). 2002–04 Expedition & Navigator

Test Step	Result / Action to Take
C1 CHECK THE BRAKE PEDAL POSITION (BPP) INPUT TO PCM	
• Key in OFF position.	**Yes** GO to C2. **No** GO to Pinpoint Test F.
• Monitor the PCM PID BPP__SW while applying and releasing the brake pedal.	
• Do the PIDs agree with the brake pedal position?	
C2 CHECK FOR CORRECT PCM OPERATION	
• Key in OFF position.	**Yes** INSTALL a new PCM. REFER to Section 303-14. CLEAR the DTCs. REPEAT the self-test. **No** The system is operating correctly at this time. Concern may have been caused by a loose or corroded connector. CLEAR the DTCs. REPEAT the self-test.
• Disconnect all the PCM connectors.	
• Check for:	
• corrosion	
• pushed-out pins	
• Connect all PCM connectors and make sure they are seated correctly.	
• Operate the system and verify the concern is still present.	
• Is the concern still present?	

LTV0500000001627

Fig. 88 Test C: Speed Control Does Not Disengage When Brakes Are Applied. 2002–04 Expedition & Navigator

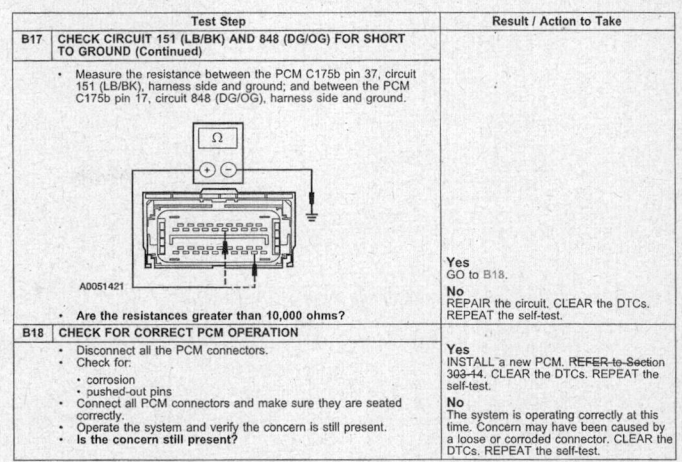

Test Step	Result / Action to Take
B17 CHECK CIRCUIT 151 (LB/BK) AND 848 (DG/OG) FOR SHORT TO GROUND (Continued)	
• Measure the resistance between the PCM C175b pin 37, circuit 151 (LB/BK), harness side and ground; and between the PCM C175b pin 17, circuit 848 (DG/OG), harness side and ground.	**Yes** GO to B18. **No** REPAIR the circuit. CLEAR the DTCs. REPEAT the self-test.
• Are the resistances greater than 10,000 ohms?	
B18 CHECK FOR CORRECT PCM OPERATION	
• Disconnect all the PCM connectors.	**Yes** INSTALL a new PCM. REFER to Section 303-14. CLEAR the DTCs. REPEAT the self-test. **No** The system is operating correctly at this time. Concern may have been caused by a loose or corroded connector. CLEAR the DTCs. REPEAT the self-test.
• Check for:	
• corrosion	
• pushed-out pins	
• Connect all PCM connectors and make sure they are seated correctly.	
• Operate the system and verify the concern is still present.	
• Is the concern still present?	

A0051421

LTV0500000001626

Fig. 87 Test B: Speed Control Is Inoperative (Part 8 of 8). 2002–04 Expedition & Navigator

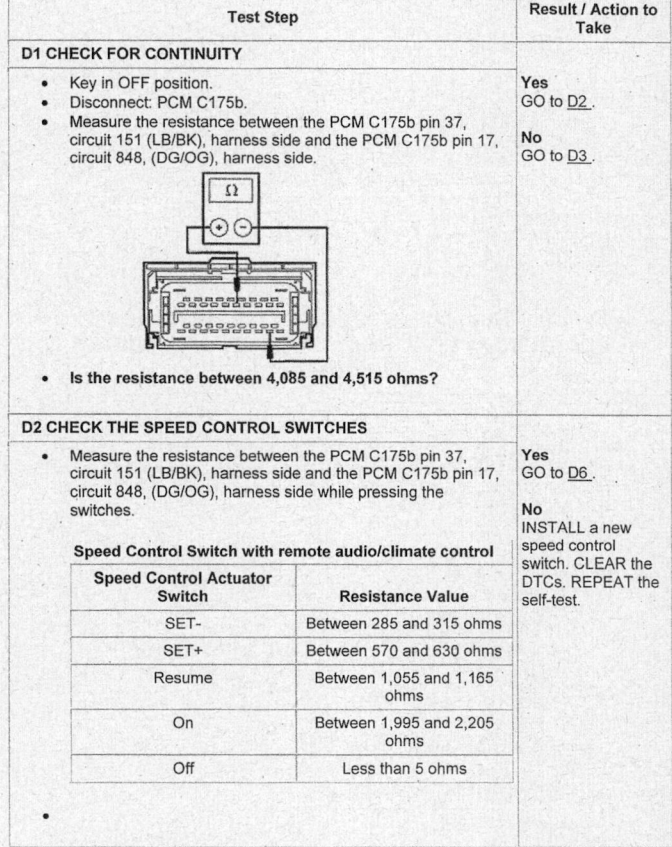

Test Step	Result / Action to Take
D1 CHECK FOR CONTINUITY	
• Key in OFF position.	**Yes** GO to D2. **No** GO to D3.
• Disconnect: PCM C175b.	
• Measure the resistance between the PCM C175b pin 37, circuit 151 (LB/BK), harness side and the PCM C175b pin 17, circuit 848, (DG/OG), harness side.	
• Is the resistance between 4,085 and 4,515 ohms?	
D2 CHECK THE SPEED CONTROL SWITCHES	
• Measure the resistance between the PCM C175b pin 37, circuit 151 (LB/BK), harness side and the PCM C175b pin 17, circuit 848, (DG/OG), harness side while pressing the switches.	**Yes** GO to D6. **No** INSTALL a new speed control switch. CLEAR the DTCs. REPEAT the self-test.

Speed Control Switch with remote audio/climate control

Speed Control Actuator Switch	Resistance Value
SET-	Between 285 and 315 ohms
SET+	Between 570 and 630 ohms
Resume	Between 1,055 and 1,165 ohms
On	Between 1,995 and 2,205 ohms
Off	Less than 5 ohms

LTV0500000001628

Fig. 89 Test D: Speed Control Switches Are Inoperative (Part 1 of 4). 2002–04 Expedition & Navigator

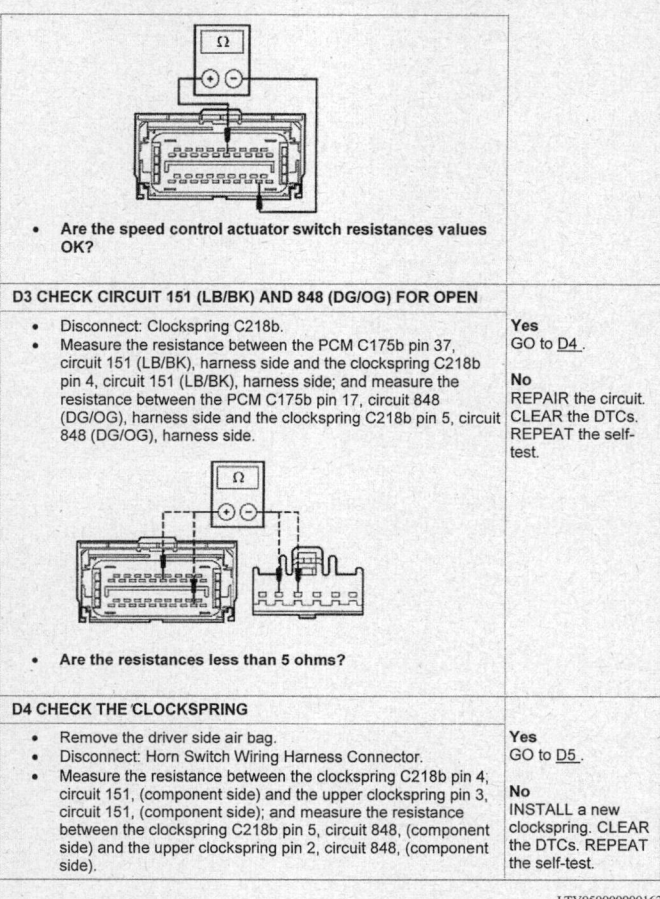

- **Are the speed control actuator switch resistances values OK?**

D3 CHECK CIRCUIT 151 (LB/BK) AND 848 (DG/OG) FOR OPEN	
• Disconnect: Clockspring C218b. • Measure the resistance between the PCM C175b pin 37, circuit 151 (LB/BK), harness side and the clockspring C218b pin 4, circuit 151 (LB/BK), harness side; and measure the resistance between the PCM C175b pin 17, circuit 848 (DG/OG), harness side and the clockspring C218b pin 5, circuit 848 (DG/OG), harness side. • **Are the resistances less than 5 ohms?**	**Yes** GO to D4 . **No** REPAIR the circuit. CLEAR the DTCs. REPEAT the self-test.

D4 CHECK THE CLOCKSPRING	
• Remove the driver side air bag. • Disconnect: Horn Switch Wiring Harness Connector. • Measure the resistance between the clockspring C218b pin 4, circuit 151, (component side) and the upper clockspring pin 3, circuit 151, (component side); and measure the resistance between the clockspring C218b pin 5, circuit 848, (component side) and the upper clockspring pin 2, circuit 848, (component side).	**Yes** GO to D5 . **No** INSTALL a new clockspring. CLEAR the DTCs. REPEAT the self-test.

LTV0500000001629

Fig. 89   Test D: Speed Control Switches Are Inoperative (Part 2 of 4). 2002–04 Expedition & Navigator

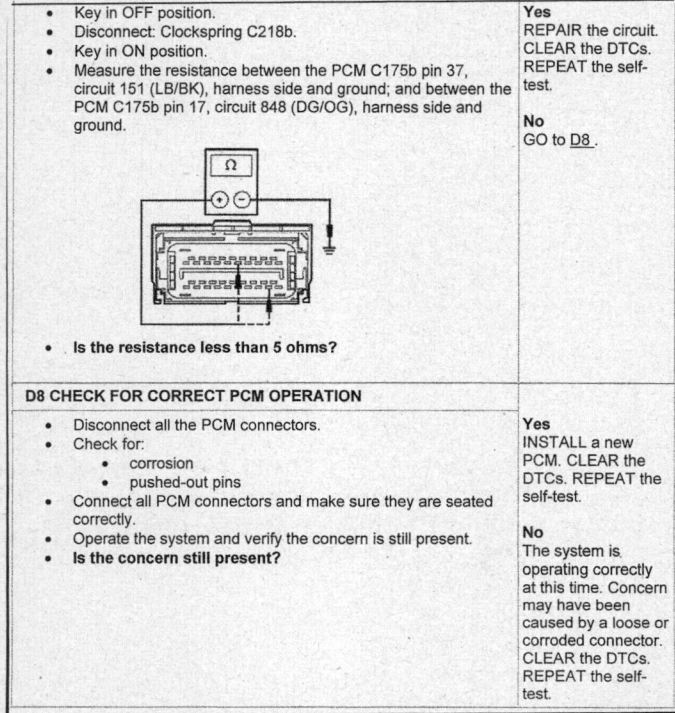

• Key in OFF position. • Disconnect: Clockspring C218b. • Key in ON position. • Measure the resistance between the PCM C175b pin 37, circuit 151 (LB/BK), harness side and ground; and between the PCM C175b pin 17, circuit 848 (DG/OG), harness side and ground. • **Is the resistance less than 5 ohms?**	**Yes** REPAIR the circuit. CLEAR the DTCs. REPEAT the self-test. **No** GO to D8 .

D8 CHECK FOR CORRECT PCM OPERATION	

• Disconnect all the PCM connectors.
• Check for:
   • corrosion
   • pushed-out pins
• Connect all PCM connectors and make sure they are seated correctly.
• Operate the system and verify the concern is still present.
• **Is the concern still present?**
	Yes
	INSTALL a new PCM. CLEAR the DTCs. REPEAT the self-test.
	
	No
	The system is operating correctly at this time. Concern may have been caused by a loose or corroded connector. CLEAR the DTCs. REPEAT the self-test.

LTV0500000001631

Fig. 89   Test D: Speed Control Switches Are Inoperative (Part 4 of 4). 2002–04 Expedition & Navigator

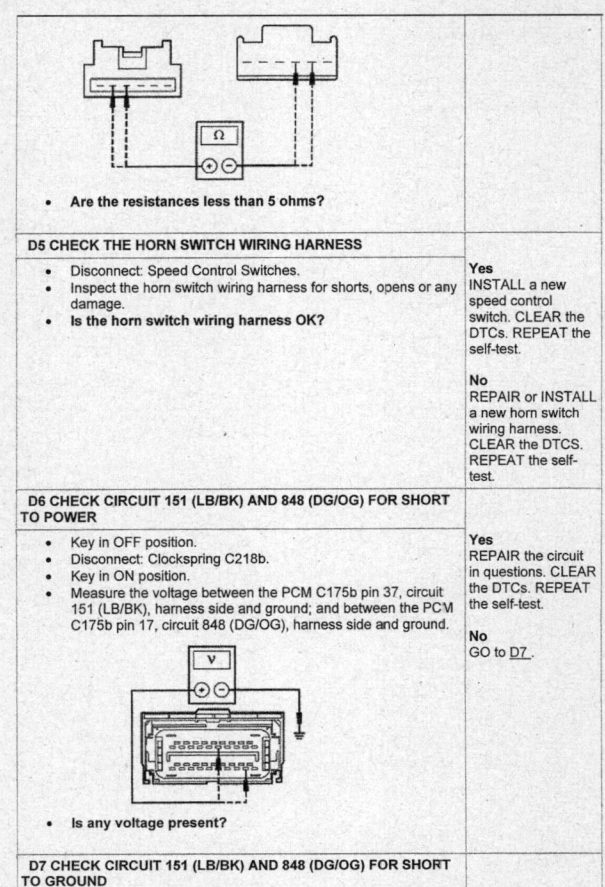

- **Are the resistances less than 5 ohms?**

D5 CHECK THE HORN SWITCH WIRING HARNESS	
• Disconnect: Speed Control Switches. • Inspect the horn switch wiring harness for shorts, opens or any damage. • **Is the horn switch wiring harness OK?**	**Yes** INSTALL a new speed control switch. CLEAR the DTCs. REPEAT the self-test. **No** REPAIR or INSTALL a new horn switch wiring harness. CLEAR the DTCs. REPEAT the self-test.

D6 CHECK CIRCUIT 151 (LB/BK) AND 848 (DG/OG) FOR SHORT TO POWER	
• Key in OFF position. • Disconnect: Clockspring C218b. • Key in ON position. • Measure the voltage between the PCM C175b pin 37, circuit 151 (LB/BK), harness side and ground; and between the PCM C175b pin 17, circuit 848 (DG/OG), harness side and ground. • **Is any voltage present?**	**Yes** REPAIR the circuit in questions. CLEAR the DTCs. REPEAT the self-test. **No** GO to D7 .

D7 CHECK CIRCUIT 151 (LB/BK) AND 848 (DG/OG) FOR SHORT TO GROUND	

LTV0500000001630

Fig. 89   Test D: Speed Control Switches Are Inoperative (Part 3 of 4). 2002–04 Expedition & Navigator

Test Step	**Result / Action to Take**
E1 CHECK THE SPEED CONTROL CABLE • Disconnect the speed control cable at the throttle body. • Check the speed control cable slack by pulling the speed control cable end taut from within the speed control cable housing. • **Is the speed control cable slack greater than 0 mm (0 in) and less than 0.24 in (6 mm) ?**	**Yes** GO to E2. **No** INSTALL a new speed control cable. CLEAR the self-test.
E2 CHECK FOR DAMAGE, STICKING OR BINDING SPEED CONTROL CABLE • Disconnect the speed control cable from the speed control actuator. • Check the speed control cable for damage, sticking or binding. • **Is the speed control cable OK?**	**Yes** GO to E3. **No** INSTALL a new speed control cable. REFER to Speed Control Cable in this section. CLEAR the DTCs. REPEAT the self-test.
E3 CHECK THE SPEED CONTROL ACTUATOR OUTPUT • Key in ON position. • Check the speed control actuator pulley for movement while triggering the on-demand self-test. • **Does the speed control actuator pulley move?**	**Yes** REFER to the Powertrain Control/Emissions Diagnosis (PC/ED) manual. **No** GO to E4.
E4 CHECK THE SPEED CONTROL ACTUATOR • Key in OFF position. • Disconnect: Speed Control Actuator C122. • Measure the resistance between the speed control actuator pins (component side) as follows:	

Speed Control Actuator	Speed Control Actuator	Expected Value
Pin 1	Pin 2	Between 2 and 3 ohms
Pin 1	Pin 3	Between 2 and 3 ohms
Pin 1	Pin 4	Between 2 and 3 ohms
Pin 5	Pin 6	Between 20 and 30 ohms

• **Are the resistances OK?**	**Yes** GO to E5. **No** INSTALL a new speed control actuator. CLEAR the DTCs. REPEAT the self-test.
E5 CHECK THE SPEED CONTROL ACTUATOR CIRCUITRY FOR SHORT TO POWER • Disconnect: PCM C175b. • Key in ON position. • Measure the voltage between the speed control actuator C122, harness side and ground as follows:	

LTV0500000001632

Fig. 90   Test E: Speed Control Is Inoperative, Flash w/Last Switch Pressed & No Dynamic Pull Occurs At Throttle (Part 1 of 3). 2002–04 Expedition & Navigator

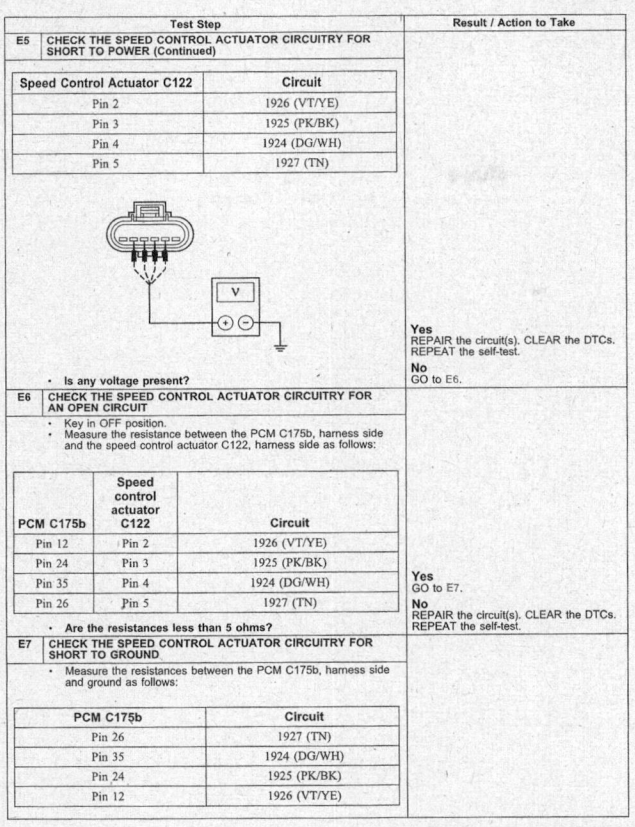

Test Step		Result / Action to Take
E5 CHECK THE SPEED CONTROL ACTUATOR CIRCUITRY FOR SHORT TO POWER (Continued)		

Speed Control Actuator C122	Circuit
Pin 2	1926 (VT/YE)
Pin 3	1925 (PK/BK)
Pin 4	1924 (DG/WH)
Pin 5	1927 (TN)

Test Step	Result / Action to Take
• Is any voltage present?	**Yes** REPAIR the circuit(s). CLEAR the DTCs. REPEAT the self-test. **No** GO to E6.
E6 CHECK THE SPEED CONTROL ACTUATOR CIRCUITRY FOR AN OPEN CIRCUIT	
• Key in OFF position. • Measure the resistance between the PCM C175b, harness side and the speed control actuator C122, harness side as follows:	

PCM C175b	Speed control actuator C122	Circuit
Pin 12	Pin 2	1926 (VT/YE)
Pin 24	Pin 3	1925 (PK/BK)
Pin 35	Pin 4	1924 (DG/WH)
Pin 26	Pin 5	1927 (TN)

Test Step	Result / Action to Take
• Are the resistances less than 5 ohms?	**Yes** GO to E7. **No** REPAIR the circuit(s). CLEAR the DTCs. REPEAT the self-test.
E7 CHECK THE SPEED CONTROL ACTUATOR CIRCUITRY FOR SHORT TO GROUND	
• Measure the resistances between the PCM C175b, harness side and ground as follows:	

PCM C175b	Circuit
Pin 26	1927 (TN)
Pin 35	1924 (DG/WH)
Pin 24	1925 (PK/BK)
Pin 12	1926 (VT/YE)

LTV0500000001633

Fig. 90   Test E: Speed Control Is Inoperative, Flash w/Last Switch Pressed & No Dynamic Pull Occurs At Throttle (Part 2 of 3). 2002–04 Expedition & Navigator

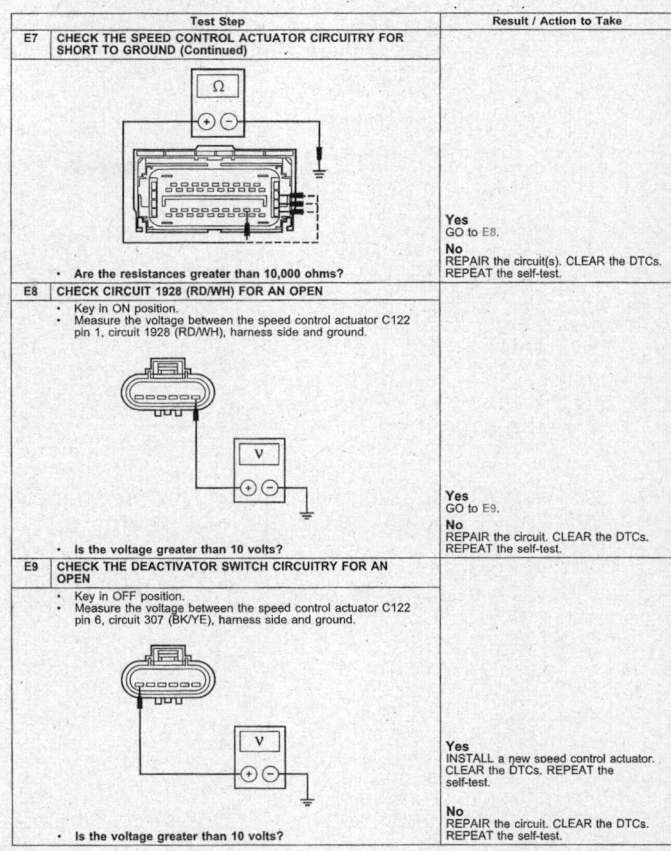

Test Step	Result / Action to Take
E7 CHECK THE SPEED CONTROL ACTUATOR CIRCUITRY FOR SHORT TO GROUND (Continued)	
• Are the resistances greater than 10,000 ohms?	**Yes** GO to E8. **No** REPAIR the circuit(s). CLEAR the DTCs. REPEAT the self-test.
E8 CHECK CIRCUIT 1928 (RD/WH) FOR AN OPEN	
• Key in ON position. • Measure the voltage between the speed control actuator C122 pin 1, circuit 1928 (RD/WH), harness side and ground.	
• Is the voltage greater than 10 volts?	**Yes** GO to E9. **No** REPAIR the circuit. CLEAR the DTCs. REPEAT the self-test.
E9 CHECK THE DEACTIVATOR SWITCH CIRCUITRY FOR AN OPEN	
• Key in OFF position. • Measure the voltage between the speed control actuator C122 pin 6, circuit 307 (BK/YE), harness side and ground.	
• Is the voltage greater than 10 volts?	**Yes** INSTALL a new speed control actuator. CLEAR the DTCs. REPEAT the self-test. **No** REPAIR the circuit. CLEAR the DTCs. REPEAT the self-test.

LTV0500000001634

Fig. 90   Test E: Speed Control Is Inoperative, Flash w/Last Switch Pressed & No Dynamic Pull Occurs At Throttle (Part 3 of 3). 2002–04 Expedition & Navigator

Test Step	Result / Action to Take
F1 MONITOR THE PCM PID BPP__SW	
• Key in ON position. • Monitor the PCM BPP PID while applying and releasing the brake pedal. • Does the PCM BPP PID agree with the brake pedal position	**Yes** GO to F4. **No** GO to F2.
F2 CHECK CIRCUIT 729 (RD/WH)	
• Key in OFF position. • Disconnect: BPP Switch C278. • Measure the voltage between the BPP C278 pin 5, circuit 729 (RD/WH), harness side and ground.	
• Is the voltage greater than 10 volts?	**Yes** GO to F3. **No** REPAIR the circuit. CLEAR the DTCs. REPEAT the self-test.
F3 CHECK CIRCUIT 810 (RD/LG)	
• Key in OFF position. • Disconnect: ABS Module C135. • Measure the resistance between the BPP C278 pin 6, circuit 810 (RD/LG), harness side and ABS C135 pin 41, circuit 810 (RD/LG), harness side.	
• Is the resistance less than 5 ohms?	**Yes** INSTALL a new BPP switch. REFER to CLEAR the DTCs. REPEAT the self-test. **No** REPAIR the circuit. CLEAR the DTCs. REPEAT the self-test.
F4 CHECK FOR CORRECT PCM OPERATION	
• Disconnect all the PCM connectors. • Check for: - corrosion - pushed-out pins • Connect all the PCM connectors and make sure they seat correctly. • Operate the system and verify the concern is still present. • Is the concern still present?	**Yes** INSTALL a new PCM. 303-14. CLEAR the DTCs. REPEAT the self-test. **No** The system is operating correctly at this time. Concern may have been caused by a loose or corroded connector. CLEAR the DTCs. REPEAT the self-test.

LTV0500000001635

Fig. 91   Test F: Brake Pedal Position (BPP) Switch Circuit Failure. 2002–04 Expedition & Navigator

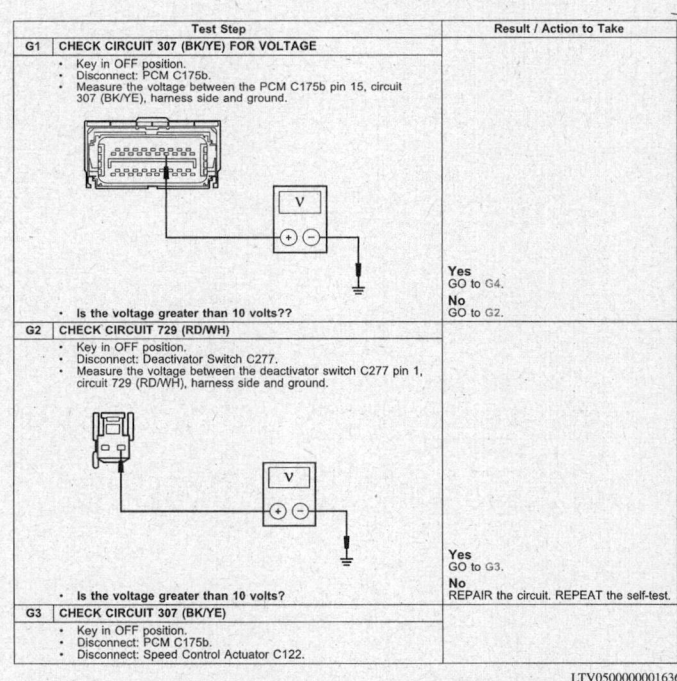

Test Step	Result / Action to Take
G1 CHECK CIRCUIT 307 (BK/YE) FOR VOLTAGE	
• Key in OFF position. • Disconnect: PCM C175b. • Measure the voltage between the PCM C175b pin 15, circuit 307 (BK/YE), harness side and ground.	
• Is the voltage greater than 10 volts??	**Yes** GO to G4. **No** GO to G2.
G2 CHECK CIRCUIT 729 (RD/WH)	
• Key in OFF position. • Disconnect: Deactivator Switch C277. • Measure the voltage between the deactivator switch C277 pin 1, circuit 729 (RD/WH), harness side and ground.	
• Is the voltage greater than 10 volts?	**Yes** GO to G3. **No** REPAIR the circuit. REPEAT the self-test.
G3 CHECK CIRCUIT 307 (BK/YE)	
• Key in OFF position. • Disconnect: PCM C175b. • Disconnect: Speed Control Actuator C122.	

LTV0500000001636

Fig. 92   Test G: Deactivator Switch Circuit Failure (Part 1 of 2). 2002–04 Expedition & Navigator

G3	CHECK CIRCUIT 307 (BK/YE) (Continued)	Result / Action to Take
	• Measure the resistance between the deactivator switch C277 pin 2, circuit 307 (BK/YE), harness side and the PCM C175b pin 15, circuit 307 (BK/YE), harness side; and between the deactivator switch C277 pin 2, circuit 307 (BK/YE), harness side. 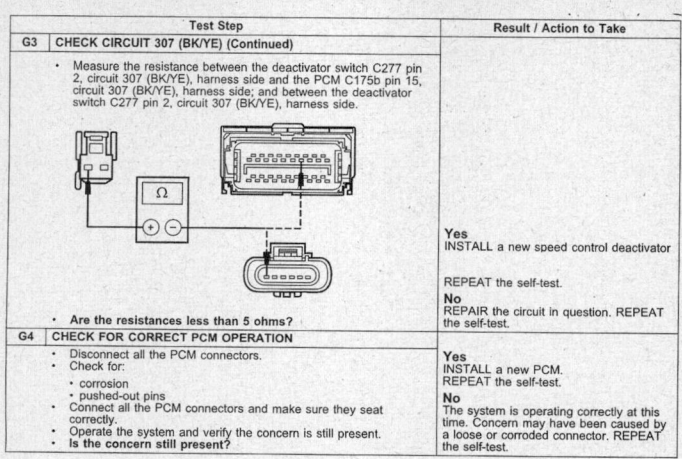 • Are the resistances less than 5 ohms?	**Yes** INSTALL a new speed control deactivator REPEAT the self-test. **No** REPAIR the circuit in question. REPEAT the self-test.
G4	CHECK FOR CORRECT PCM OPERATION	

	• Disconnect all the PCM connectors.
	• Check for:
	  - corrosion
	  - pushed-out pins
	• Connect all the PCM connectors and make sure they seat correctly.
	• Operate the system and verify the concern is still present.
	• **Is the concern still present?**
		Yes
		INSTALL a new PCM. REPEAT the self-test.
		No
		The system is operating correctly at this time. Concern may have been caused by a loose or corroded connector. REPEAT the self-test.

LTV0500000001637

Fig. 92 Test G: Deactivator Switch Circuit Failure (Part 2 of 2). 2002–04 Expedition & Navigator

A2	CHECK THE SPEED CONTROL SWITCH (Continued)	Result / Action to Take
	 • Are the speed control switch resistance values OK?	**Yes** GO to A3. **No** GO to Pinpoint Test C.
A3	CHECK THE DIGITAL TR SENSOR	
	• Connect: PCM C175b. • Apply the parking brake. • Key in ON position. • Enter the following diagnostic mode on the diagnostic tool: PCM Digital TR Sensor PID. • Monitor the digital TR sensor PID. • Select DRIVE. • **Does the PID value agree with the transmission range selector lever position?**	**Yes** GO to A4. **No** Diagnose digital TR sensor.
A4	CHECK THE DIGITAL TR SENSOR FOR CORRECT ALIGNMENT	
	• Check the digital TR sensor alignment. • **Is the digital TR sensor aligned correctly?**	**Yes** GO to A5. **No** ADJUST the digital TR sensor. TEST the system for normal operation.
A5	CHECK THE BRAKE WARNING INDICATOR	
	• Key in ON position. • While observing the brake warning indicator, apply and release the parking brake. • **Does the brake warning indicator operate correctly?**	**Yes** GO to A6. **No** Diagnose brake warning indicator.
A6	CHECK THE VEHICLE SPEED	
	NOTE: This step may require an assistant. • Enter the following diagnostic mode on the diagnostic tool: Anti-lock Brake System (ABS) Wheel Speed PID. • Monitor and record the ABS module wheel speed PID while driving the vehicle at 48 km/h (30 mph) as indicated on the speedometer. • Enter the following diagnostic mode on the diagnostic tool: PCM Vehicle Speed PID. • Monitor and record the PCM vehicle speed PID while driving the vehicle at 48 km/h (30 mph). • **Does the speed indicated by the ABS module wheel speed PID match the PCM vehicle speed PID?**	**Yes** GO to A7. **No** REFER to MOTOR's "Domestic Engine Performance & Driveability Manual" to diagnose output shaft speed (OSS) sensor signal.
A7	CHECK FOR CORRECT PCM OPERATION	

	• Disconnect all the PCM connectors.
	• Check for:
	  — corrosion
	  — pushed-out pins
	• Connect all the PCM connectors and make sure they are seated correctly.
	• Operate the system and verify the concern is still present.
	• **Is the concern still present?**
		Yes
		INSTALL a new PCM. CLEAR the DTCs. REPEAT the self-test.
		No
		The system is operating correctly at this time. The concern may have been caused by a loose or corroded connector.

LTV0500000001640

Fig. 93 Test A: Speed Control Is Inoperative (Part 2 of 2). 2005–06 Expedition & Navigator

A1	RETRIEVE THE RECORDED PCM DTCs FROM BOTH THE CONTINUOUS AND ON-DEMAND SELF-TESTS	Result / Action to Take
	• Check for recorded PCM DTCs from the continuous and on-demand self-tests. • **Are any DTCs recorded?**	**Yes** REFER to the Powertrain Control Module (PCM) Diagnostic Trouble Code (DTC) Index. **No** GO to A2.
A2	CHECK THE SPEED CONTROL SWITCH	
	• Key in OFF position. • Disconnect: PCM C175b. • Measure the resistance between the PCM C175b-56, circuit 151 (LB/BK), harness side and the PCM C175b-57, circuit 848 (DG/OG), harness side while pressing the speed control buttons as follows:	

Speed Control Switch	Resistance Value
OFF	Less than 5 ohms
SET –	285 – 315 ohms
SET +	570 – 630 ohms
RESUME	1,055 – 1,165 ohms
ON	2,004 – 2,216 ohms
No switch pressed	4,094 – 4,526 ohms

LTV0500000001639

Fig. 93 Test A: Speed Control Is Inoperative (Part 1 of 2). 2005–06 Expedition & Navigator

B1	CHECK CIRCUIT 810 (RD/LG) FOR VOLTAGE	Result / Action to Take
	• Key in OFF position. • Disconnect: PCM C175b. • Key in ON position. • Measure the voltage between the PCM C175b-46, circuit 810 (RD/LG), harness side and ground. 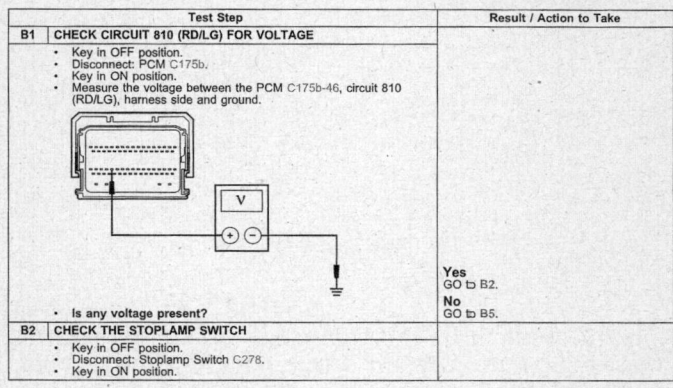 • **Is any voltage present?**	**Yes** GO to B2. **No** GO to B5.
B2	CHECK THE STOPLAMP SWITCH	
	• Key in OFF position. • Disconnect: Stoplamp Switch C278. • Key in ON position.	

LTV0500000001641

Fig. 94 Test B, Codes P1572 & P1703: Brake On/Off Circuit Failure (Part 1 of 6). 2005–06 Expedition & Navigator

B2	CHECK THE STOPLAMP SWITCH (Continued)	Result / Action to Take
	• Measure the voltage between the PCM C175b-46, circuit 810 (RD/LG), harness side and ground. 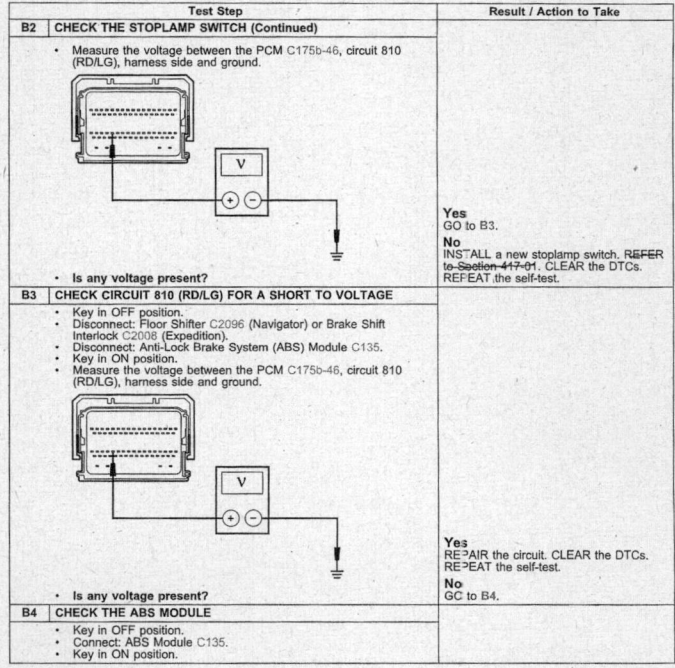 • **Is any voltage present?**	**Yes** GO to B3. **No** INSTALL a new stoplamp switch. REFER to Section 417-01. CLEAR the DTCs. REPEAT the self-test.
B3	CHECK CIRCUIT 810 (RD/LG) FOR A SHORT TO VOLTAGE	
	• Key in OFF position. • Disconnect: Floor Shifter C2096 (Navigator) or Brake Shift Interlock C2008 (Expedition). • Disconnect: Anti-Lock Brake System (ABS) Module C135. • Key in ON position. • Measure the voltage between the PCM C175b-46, circuit 810 (RD/LG), harness side and ground. • **Is any voltage present?**	**Yes** REPAIR the circuit. CLEAR the DTCs. REPEAT the self-test. **No** GO to B4.
B4	CHECK THE ABS MODULE	
	• Key in OFF position. • Connect: ABS Module C135. • Key in ON position.	

LTV0500000001642

Fig. 94 Test B, Codes P1572 & P1703: Brake On/Off Circuit Failure (Part 2 of 6). 2005–06 Expedition & Navigator

Test Step	Result / Action to Take
B4 CHECK THE ABS MODULE (Continued)	
• Measure the voltage between the PCM C175b-46, circuit 810 (RD/LG), harness side and ground. 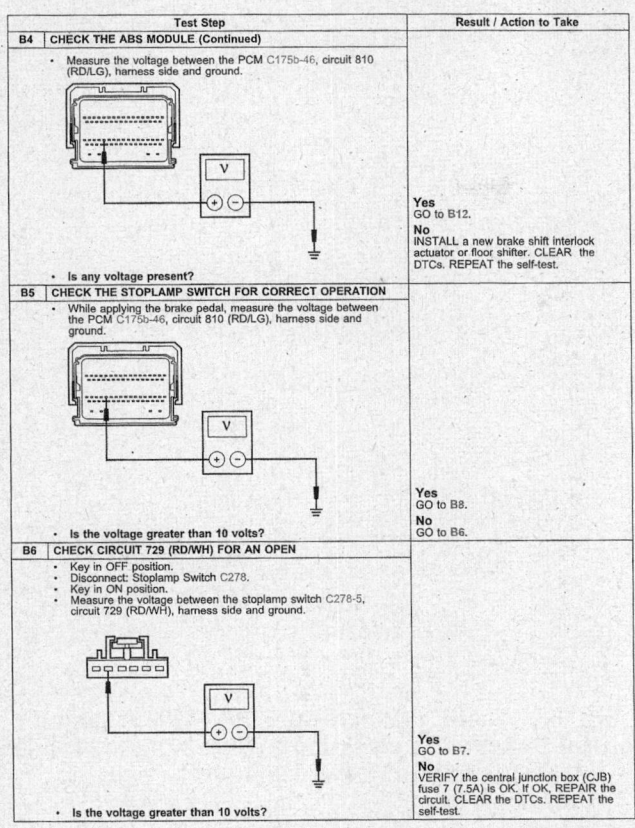	**Yes** GO to B12. **No** INSTALL a new brake shift interlock actuator or floor shifter. CLEAR the DTCs. REPEAT the self-test.
• Is any voltage present?	
B5 CHECK THE STOPLAMP SWITCH FOR CORRECT OPERATION	
• While applying the brake pedal, measure the voltage between the PCM C175b-46, circuit 810 (RD/LG), harness side and ground.	**Yes** GO to B8. **No** GO to B6.
• Is the voltage greater than 10 volts?	
B6 CHECK CIRCUIT 729 (RD/WH) FOR AN OPEN	
• Key in OFF position. • Disconnect: Stoplamp Switch C278. • Key in ON position. • Measure the voltage between the stoplamp switch C278-5, circuit 729 (RD/WH), harness side and ground.	**Yes** GO to B7. **No** VERIFY the central junction box (CJB) fuse 7 (7.5A) is OK. If OK, REPAIR the circuit. CLEAR the DTCs. REPEAT the self-test.
• Is the voltage greater than 10 volts?	

LTV0500000001643

Fig. 94 Test B, Codes P1572 & P1703: Brake On/Off Circuit Failure (Part 3 of 6). 2005–06 Expedition & Navigator

Test Step	Result / Action to Take
B9 CHECK CIRCUIT 729 (RD/WH) FOR AN OPEN (Continued)	
• Measure the voltage between the speed control deactivator switch C277-2, circuit 729 (RD/WH), harness side and ground. 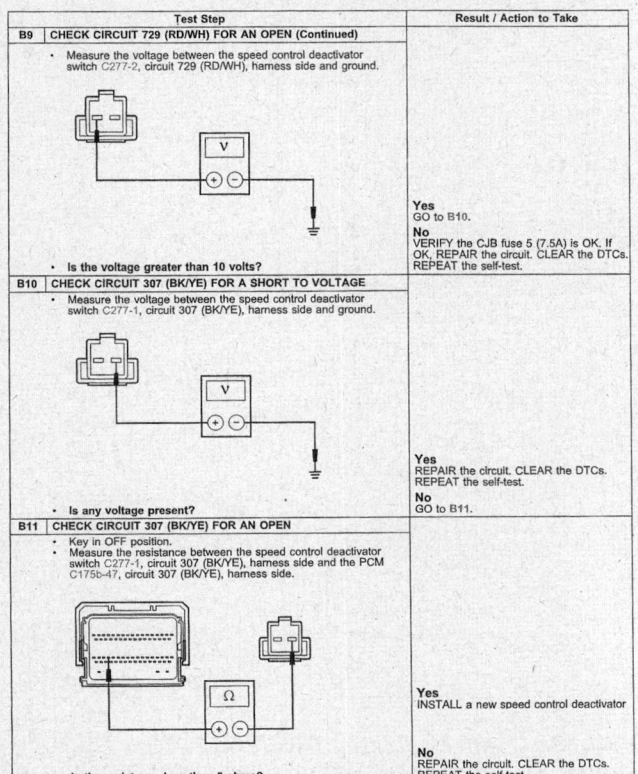	**Yes** GO to B10. **No** VERIFY the CJB fuse 5 (7.5A) is OK. If OK, REPAIR the circuit. CLEAR the DTCs. REPEAT the self-test.
• Is the voltage greater than 10 volts?	
B10 CHECK CIRCUIT 307 (BK/YE) FOR A SHORT TO VOLTAGE	
• Measure the voltage between the speed control deactivator switch C277-1, circuit 307 (BK/YE), harness side and ground.	**Yes** REPAIR the circuit. CLEAR the DTCs. REPEAT the self-test. **No** GO to B11.
• Is any voltage present?	
B11 CHECK CIRCUIT 307 (BK/YE) FOR AN OPEN	
• Key in OFF position. • Measure the resistance between the speed control deactivator switch C277-1, circuit 307 (BK/YE), harness side and the PCM C175b-47, circuit 307 (BK/YE), harness side.	**Yes** INSTALL a new speed control deactivator **No** REPAIR the circuit. CLEAR the DTCs. REPEAT the self-test.
• Is the resistance less than 5 ohms?	

LTV0500000001651

Fig. 94 Test B, Codes P1572 & P1703: Brake On/Off Circuit Failure (Part 5 of 6). 2005–06 Expedition & Navigator

Test Step	Result / Action to Take
B7 CHECK CIRCUIT 810 (RD/LG) FOR AN OPEN	
• Key in OFF position. • Measure the resistance between the stoplamp switch C278-6, circuit 810 (RD/LG), harness side and the PCM C175b-46, circuit 810 (RD/LG), harness side. 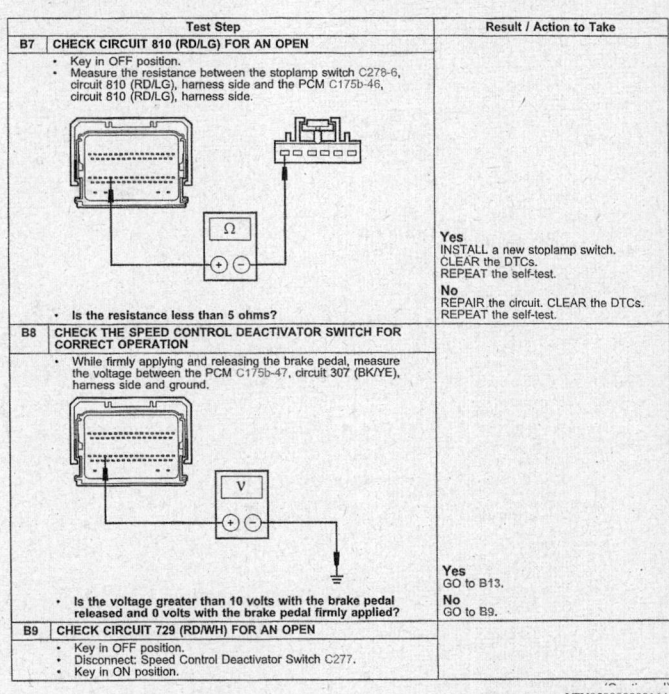	**Yes** INSTALL a new stoplamp switch. CLEAR the DTCs. REPEAT the self-test. **No** REPAIR the circuit. CLEAR the DTCs. REPEAT the self-test.
• Is the resistance less than 5 ohms?	
B8 CHECK THE SPEED CONTROL DEACTIVATOR SWITCH FOR CORRECT OPERATION	
• While firmly applying and releasing the brake pedal, measure the voltage between the PCM C175b-47, circuit 307 (BK/YE), harness side and ground.	**Yes** GO to B13. **No** GO to B9.
• Is the voltage greater than 10 volts with the brake pedal released and 0 volts with the brake pedal firmly applied?	
B9 CHECK CIRCUIT 729 (RD/WH) FOR AN OPEN	
• Key in OFF position. • Disconnect: Speed Control Deactivator Switch C277. • Key in ON position.	

LTV0500000001644

Fig. 94 Test B, Codes P1572 & P1703: Brake On/Off Circuit Failure (Part 4 of 6). 2005–06 Expedition & Navigator

Test Step	Result / Action to Take
B12 CHECK FOR CORRECT ABS MODULE OPERATION	
• Disconnect the ABS module connector. • Check for: — corrosion — pushed-out pins • Connect the ABS module connector and make sure it is seated correctly. • Operate the system and verify the concern is still present. • Is the concern still present?	**Yes** INSTALL a new ABS module. **No** The system is operating correctly at this time. The concern may have been caused by a loose or corroded connector. CLEAR the DTCs. REPEAT the self-test.
B13 CHECK FOR CORRECT PCM OPERATION	
• Disconnect all the PCM connectors. • Check for: — corrosion — pushed-out pins • Connect all the PCM connectors and make sure they are seated correctly. • Operate the system and verify the concern is still present. • Is the concern still present?	**Yes** INSTALL a new PCM. **No** The system is operating correctly at this time. The concern may have been caused by a loose or corroded connector. CLEAR the DTCs. REPEAT the self-test.

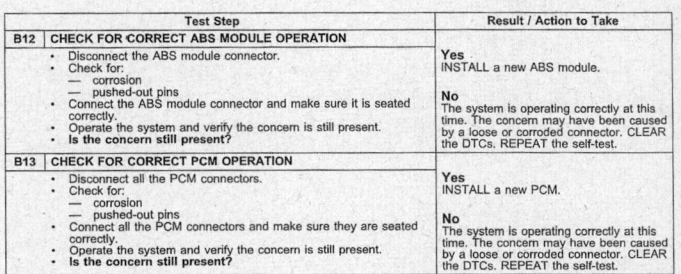

LTV0500000001645

Fig. 94 Test B, Codes P1572 & P1703: Brake On/Off Circuit Failure (Part 6 of 6). 2005–06 Expedition & Navigator

Test Step	Result / Action to Take
C1 CHECK THE SPEED CONTROL SWITCH CIRCUITRY FOR A SHORT TO VOLTAGE	
• Key in OFF position. • Disconnect: PCM C175b. • Key in ON position. • Turn the parking lamps on. • Measure the voltage between the PCM C175b-56, circuit 151 (LB/BK), harness side and ground; and between the PCM C175b-57, circuit 848 (DG/OG), harness side and ground. 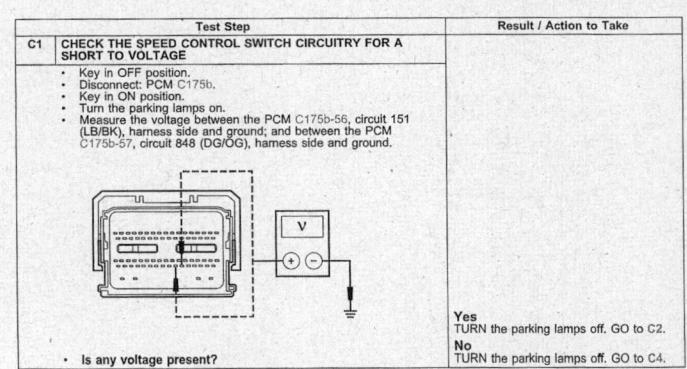	**Yes** TURN the parking lamps off. GO to C2. **No** TURN the parking lamps off. GO to C4.
• Is any voltage present?	

LTV0500000001646

Fig. 95 Test C, Codes P0579 & P0581: Speed Control Switch Circuit Failure (Part 1 of 5). 2005–06 Expedition & Navigator

Test Step	Result / Action to Take
C2 CHECK CIRCUITS 151 (LB/BK) AND 848 (DG/OG) FOR A SHORT TO VOLTAGE • Key in OFF position. • Disconnect: Clockspring C218b. • Key in ON position. • Turn the parking lamps on. • Measure the voltage between the PCM C175b-56, circuit 151 (LB/BK), harness side and ground; and between the PCM C175b-57, circuit 848 (DG/OG), harness side and ground. 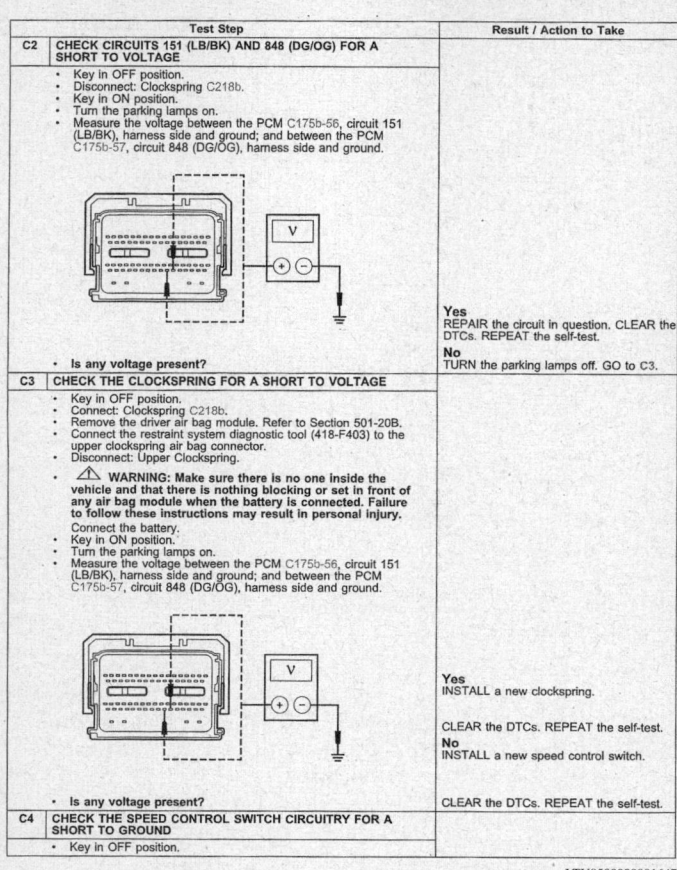 • Is any voltage present?	**Yes** REPAIR the circuit in question. CLEAR the DTCs. REPEAT the self-test. **No** TURN the parking lamps off. GO to C3.
C3 CHECK THE CLOCKSPRING FOR A SHORT TO VOLTAGE • Key in OFF position. • Connect: Clockspring C218b. • Remove the driver air bag module. Refer to Section 501-20B. • Connect the restraint system diagnostic tool (418-F403) to the upper clockspring air bag connector. • Disconnect: Upper Clockspring. • ⚠ **WARNING:** Make sure there is no one inside the vehicle and that there is nothing blocking or set in front of any air bag module when the battery is connected. Failure to follow these instructions may result in personal injury. • Connect the battery. • Key in ON position. • Turn the parking lamps on. • Measure the voltage between the PCM C175b-56, circuit 151 (LB/BK), harness side and ground; and between the PCM C175b-57, circuit 848 (DG/OG), harness side and ground. • Is any voltage present?	**Yes** INSTALL a new clockspring. CLEAR the DTCs. REPEAT the self-test. **No** INSTALL a new speed control switch. CLEAR the DTCs. REPEAT the self-test.
C4 CHECK THE SPEED CONTROL SWITCH CIRCUITRY FOR A SHORT TO GROUND • Key in OFF position.	

Fig. 95 Test C, Codes P0579 & P0581: Speed Control Switch Circuit Failure (Part 2 of 5). 2005–06 Expedition & Navigator

LTV0500000001647

Test Step	Result / Action to Take
C4 CHECK THE SPEED CONTROL SWITCH CIRCUITRY FOR A SHORT TO GROUND (Continued) • Measure the resistance between the PCM C175b-56, circuit 151 (LB/BK), harness side and ground; and between the PCM C175b-57, circuit 848 (DG/OG), harness side and ground. 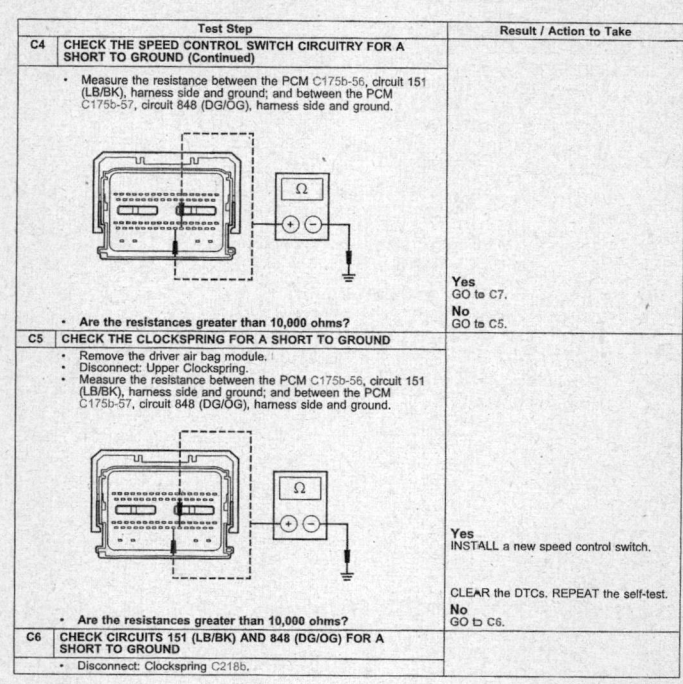 • Are the resistances greater than 10,000 ohms?	**Yes** GO to C7. **No** GO to C5.
C5 CHECK THE CLOCKSPRING FOR A SHORT TO GROUND • Remove the driver air bag module. • Disconnect: Upper Clockspring. • Measure the resistance between the PCM C175b-56, circuit 151 (LB/BK), harness side and ground; and between the PCM C175b-57, circuit 848 (DG/OG), harness side and ground. • Are the resistances greater than 10,000 ohms?	**Yes** INSTALL a new speed control switch. CLEAR the DTCs. REPEAT the self-test. **No** GO to C6.
C6 CHECK CIRCUITS 151 (LB/BK) AND 848 (DG/OG) FOR A SHORT TO GROUND • Disconnect: Clockspring C218b.	

Fig. 95 Test C, Codes P0579 & P0581: Speed Control Switch Circuit Failure (Part 3 of 5). 2005–06 Expedition & Navigator

LTV0500000001648

Test Step	Result / Action to Take
C6 CHECK CIRCUITS 151 (LB/BK) AND 848 (DG/OG) FOR A SHORT TO GROUND (Continued) • Measure the resistance between the PCM C175b-56, circuit 151 (LB/BK), harness side and ground; and between the PCM C175b-57, circuit 848 (DG/OG), harness side and ground. 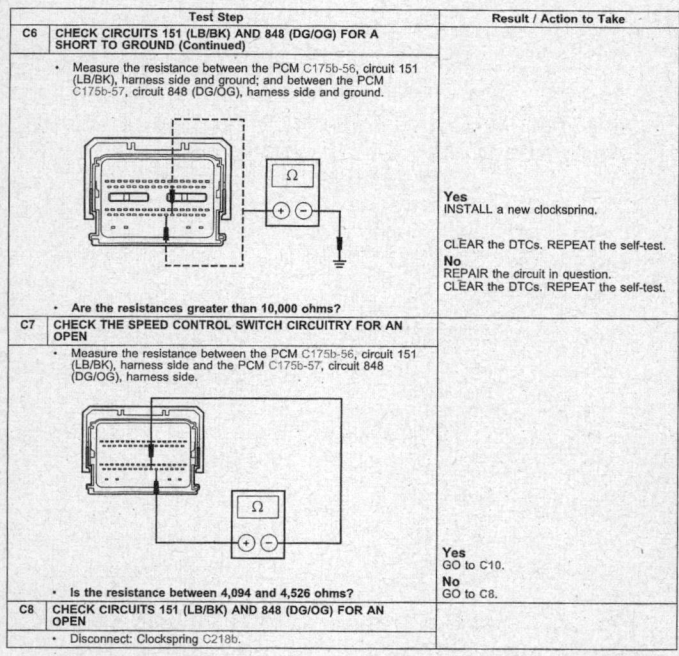 • Are the resistances greater than 10,000 ohms?	**Yes** INSTALL a new clockspring. CLEAR the DTCs. REPEAT the self-test. **No** REPAIR the circuit in question. CLEAR the DTCs. REPEAT the self-test.
C7 CHECK THE SPEED CONTROL SWITCH CIRCUITRY FOR AN OPEN • Measure the resistance between the PCM C175b-56, circuit 151 (LB/BK), harness side and the PCM C175b-57, circuit 848 (DG/OG), harness side. • Is the resistance between 4,094 and 4,526 ohms?	**Yes** GO to C10. **No** GO to C8.
C8 CHECK CIRCUITS 151 (LB/BK) AND 848 (DG/OG) FOR AN OPEN • Disconnect: Clockspring C218b.	

Fig. 95 Test C, Codes P0579 & P0581: Speed Control Switch Circuit Failure (Part 4 of 5). 2005–06 Expedition & Navigator

LTV0500000001649

Test Step	Result / Action to Take
C8 CHECK CIRCUITS 151 (LB/BK) AND 848 (DG/OG) FOR AN OPEN (Continued) • Measure the resistance between the PCM C175b-56, circuit 151 (LB/BK), harness side and the clockspring C218b-4, circuit 151 (LB/BK), harness side; and between the PCM C175b-57, circuit 848 (DG/OG), harness side and the clockspring C218a-5, circuit 848 (DG/OG), harness side. 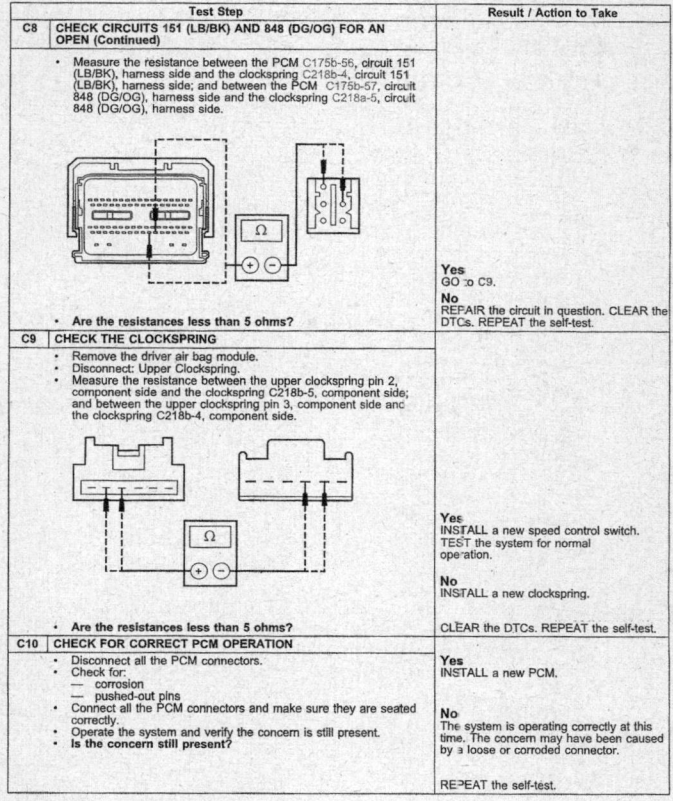 • Are the resistances less than 5 ohms?	**Yes** GO to C9. **No** REPAIR the circuit in question. CLEAR the DTCs. REPEAT the self-test.
C9 CHECK THE CLOCKSPRING • Remove the driver air bag module. • Disconnect: Upper Clockspring. • Measure the resistance between the upper clockspring pin 2, component side and the clockspring C218b-5, component side; and between the upper clockspring pin 3, component side and the clockspring C218b-4, component side. • Are the resistances less than 5 ohms?	**Yes** INSTALL a new speed control switch. TEST the system for normal operation. **No** INSTALL a new clockspring. CLEAR the DTCs. REPEAT the self-test.
C10 CHECK FOR CORRECT PCM OPERATION • Disconnect all the PCM connectors. • Check for: — corrosion — pushed-out pins • Connect all the PCM connectors and make sure they are seated correctly. • Operate the system and verify the concern is still present. • Is the concern still present?	**Yes** INSTALL a new PCM. **No** The system is operating correctly at this time. The concern may have been caused by a loose or corroded connector. REPEAT the self-test.

Fig. 95 Test C, Codes P0579 & P0581: Speed Control Switch Circuit Failure (Part 5 of 5). 2005–06 Expedition & Navigator

LTV0500000001650

Test Step		Result / Action to Take
A1	CHECK THE SPEED CONTROL CABLE ATTACHMENT TO THE THROTTLE	
	• Key in OFF position. • Remove the accelerator control splash shield. Inspect the speed control cable attachment. Check the speed control cable by pulling on the cable and noting the throttle movement. • **Is the speed control cable OK?**	**Yes** GO to A2. **No** REPAIR/RE-ATTACH the speed control cable. TEST the system for normal operation.
A2	CHECK THE VOLTAGE TO THE SPEED CONTROL SERVO	
	• Disconnect: Speed Control Servo C122. • Key in ON position.	

Fig. 96   Test A: Speed Control Is Inoperative (Part 1 of 11). 2002–05 Excursion & 2002–04 F-Super Duty

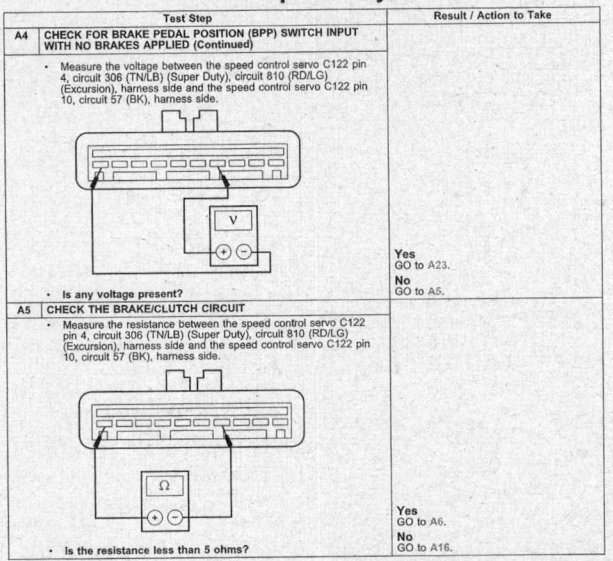

Test Step		Result / Action to Take
A4	CHECK FOR BRAKE PEDAL POSITION (BPP) SWITCH INPUT WITH NO BRAKES APPLIED (Continued)	
	• Measure the voltage between the speed control servo C122 pin 4, circuit 306 (TN/LB) (Super Duty), circuit 810 (RD/LG) (Excursion), harness side and the speed control servo C122 pin 10, circuit 57 (BK), harness side.	**Yes** GO to A23. **No** GO to A5.
	• **Is any voltage present?**	
A5	CHECK THE BRAKE/CLUTCH CIRCUIT	
	• Measure the resistance between the speed control servo C122 pin 4, circuit 306 (TN/LB) (Super Duty), circuit 810 (RD/LG) (Excursion), harness side and the speed control servo C122 pin 10, circuit 57 (BK), harness side.	**Yes** GO to A6. **No** GO to A16.
	• **Is the resistance less than 5 ohms?**	

Fig. 96   Test A: Speed Control Is Inoperative (Part 3 of 11). 2002–05 Excursion & 2002–04 F-Super Duty

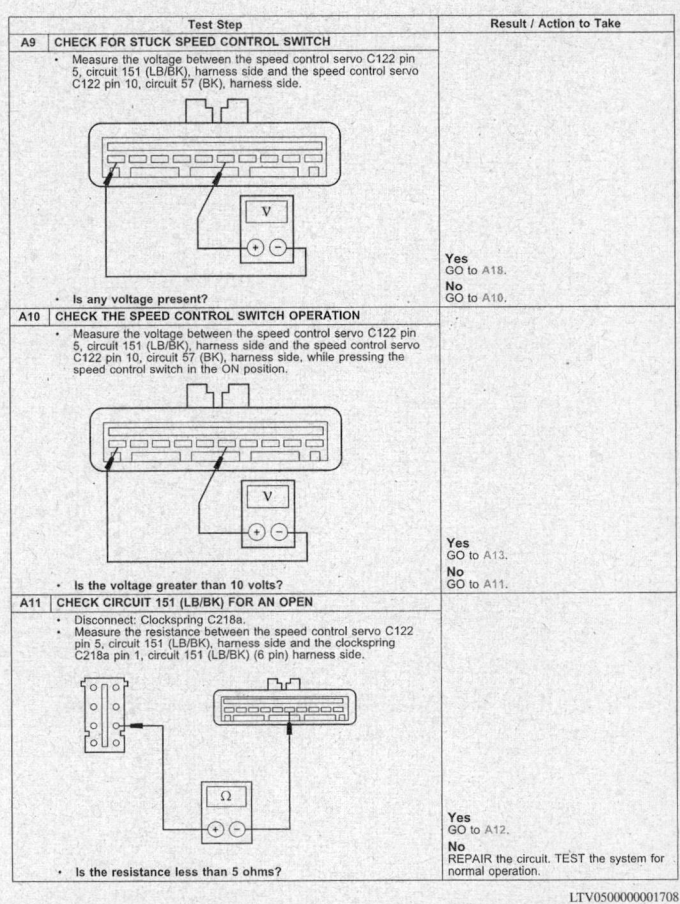

Test Step		Result / Action to Take
A6	CHECK THE DEACTIVATOR SWITCH INPUT TO SPEED CONTROL SERVO	
	• Measure the voltage between the speed control servo C122 pin 9, circuit 307 (BK/YE), harness side and the speed control servo C122 pin 10, circuit 57 (BK), harness side.	**Yes** GO to A9. **No** GO to A7.
	• **Is the voltage greater than 10 volts?**	
A7	CHECK THE DEACTIVATOR SWITCH	
	• Disconnect: Deactivator Switch C1025. • Measure the resistance between the deactivator switch pins (component side).	**Yes** GO to A8. **No** INSTALL a new deactivator switch. TEST the system for normal operation.
	• **Is the resistance less than 5 ohms?**	
A8	CHECK DEACTIVATOR SWITCH POWER	
	• Measure the voltage between the deactivator switch, harness side and ground.	**Yes** REPAIR circuit 307 (BK/YE). TEST the system for normal operation. **No** REPAIR circuit 10 (LG/RD) or circuit 22 (LB/BK). TEST the system for normal operation.
	• **Is the voltage greater than 10 volts?**	

Fig. 96   Test A: Speed Control Is Inoperative (Part 4 of 11). 2002–05 Excursion & 2002–04 F-Super Duty

Test Step		Result / Action to Take
A2	CHECK THE VOLTAGE TO THE SPEED CONTROL SERVO (Continued)	
	• Measure the voltage between the speed control servo C122 pin 7, circuit 295 (LB/PK), harness side and the speed control servo C122 pin 10, circuit 57 (BK), harness side.	**Yes** GO to A4. **No** GO to A3.
	• **Is the voltage greater than 10 volts?**	
A3	CHECK THE SPEED CONTROL SERVO GROUND CIRCUIT 57 (BK)	
	• Measure the resistance between the speed control servo C122 pin 10, circuit 57 (BK), harness side and ground.	**Yes** REPAIR circuit 295 (LB/PK). TEST the system for normal operation. **No** REPAIR circuit 57 (BK). TEST the system for normal operation.
	• **Is the resistance less than 5 ohms?**	
A4	CHECK FOR BRAKE PEDAL POSITION (BPP) SWITCH INPUT WITH NO BRAKES APPLIED	
	• Key in OFF position.	

Fig. 96   Test A: Speed Control Is Inoperative (Part 2 of 11). 2002–05 Excursion & 2002–04 F-Super Duty

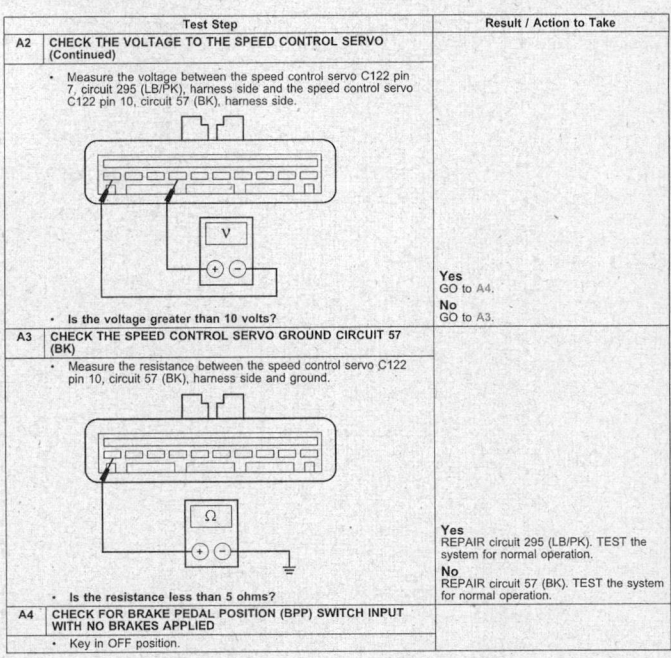

Test Step		Result / Action to Take
A9	CHECK FOR STUCK SPEED CONTROL SWITCH	
	• Measure the voltage between the speed control servo C122 pin 5, circuit 151 (LB/BK), harness side and the speed control servo C122 pin 10, circuit 57 (BK), harness side.	**Yes** GO to A18. **No** GO to A10.
	• **Is any voltage present?**	
A10	CHECK THE SPEED CONTROL SWITCH OPERATION	
	• Measure the voltage between the speed control servo C122 pin 5, circuit 151 (LB/BK), harness side and the speed control servo C122 pin 10, circuit 57 (BK), harness side, while pressing the speed control switch in the ON position.	**Yes** GO to A13. **No** GO to A11.
	• **Is the voltage greater than 10 volts?**	
A11	CHECK CIRCUIT 151 (LB/BK) FOR AN OPEN	
	• Disconnect: Clockspring C218a. • Measure the resistance between the speed control servo C122 pin 5, circuit 151 (LB/BK), harness side and the clockspring C218a pin 1, circuit 151 (LB/BK) (6 pin) harness side.	**Yes** GO to A12. **No** REPAIR the circuit. TEST the system for normal operation.
	• **Is the resistance less than 5 ohms?**	

Fig. 96   Test A: Speed Control Is Inoperative (Part 5 of 11). 2002–05 Excursion & 2002–04 F-Super Duty

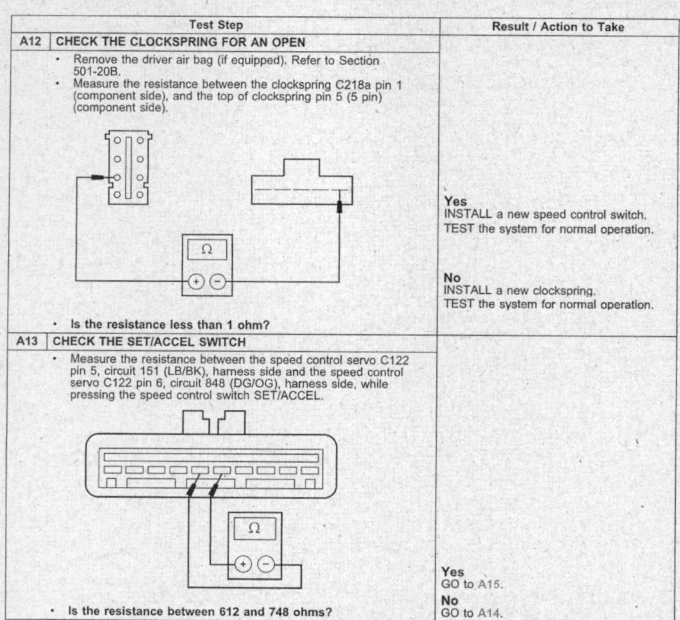

Test Step	Result / Action to Take
A12 CHECK THE CLOCKSPRING FOR AN OPEN • Remove the driver air bag (if equipped). Refer to Section 501-20B. • Measure the resistance between the clockspring C218a pin 1 (component side), and the top of clockspring pin 5 (5 pin) (component side).	**Yes** INSTALL a new speed control switch. TEST the system for normal operation. **No** INSTALL a new clockspring. TEST the system for normal operation.
• Is the resistance less than 1 ohm?	
A13 CHECK THE SET/ACCEL SWITCH • Measure the resistance between the speed control servo C122 pin 5, circuit 151 (LB/BK), harness side and the speed control servo C122 pin 6, circuit 848 (DG/OG), harness side, while pressing the speed control switch SET/ACCEL.	**Yes** GO to A15. **No** GO to A14.
• Is the resistance between 612 and 748 ohms?	

LTV0500000001709

Fig. 96   Test A: Speed Control Is Inoperative (Part 6 of 11). 2002–05 Excursion & 2002–04 F-Super Duty

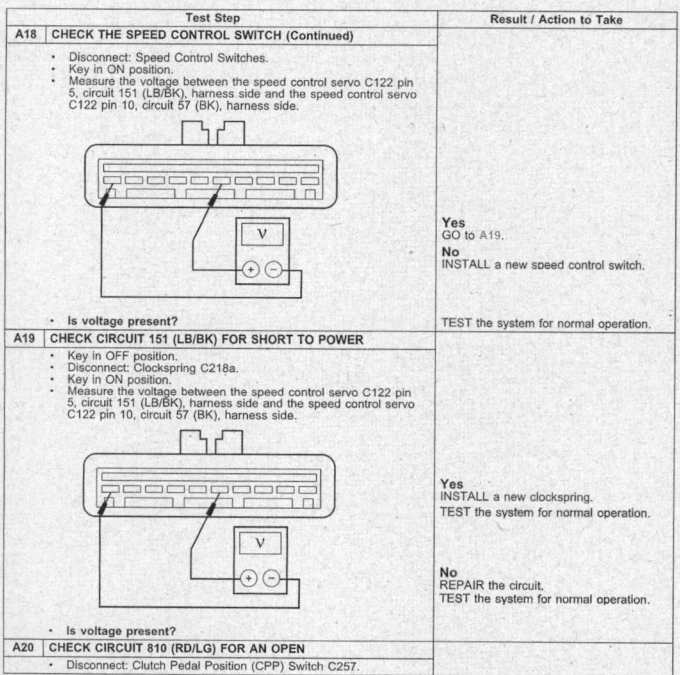

Test Step	Result / Action to Take
A18 CHECK THE SPEED CONTROL SWITCH (Continued) • Disconnect: Speed Control Switches. • Key in ON position. • Measure the voltage between the speed control servo C122 pin 5, circuit 151 (LB/BK), harness side and the speed control servo C122 pin 10, circuit 57 (BK), harness side.	**Yes** GO to A19. **No** INSTALL a new speed control switch. TEST the system for normal operation.
• Is voltage present?	
A19 CHECK CIRCUIT 151 (LB/BK) FOR SHORT TO POWER • Key in OFF position. • Disconnect: Clockspring C218a. • Key in ON position. • Measure the voltage between the speed control servo C122 pin 5, circuit 151 (LB/BK), harness side and the speed control servo C122 pin 10, circuit 57 (BK), harness side.	**Yes** INSTALL a new clockspring. TEST the system for normal operation. **No** REPAIR the circuit. TEST the system for normal operation.
• Is voltage present?	
A20 CHECK CIRCUIT 810 (RD/LG) FOR AN OPEN • Disconnect: Clutch Pedal Position (CPP) Switch C257.	

LTV0500000001711

Fig. 96   Test A: Speed Control Is Inoperative (Part 8 of 11). 2002–05 Excursion & 2002–04 F-Super Duty

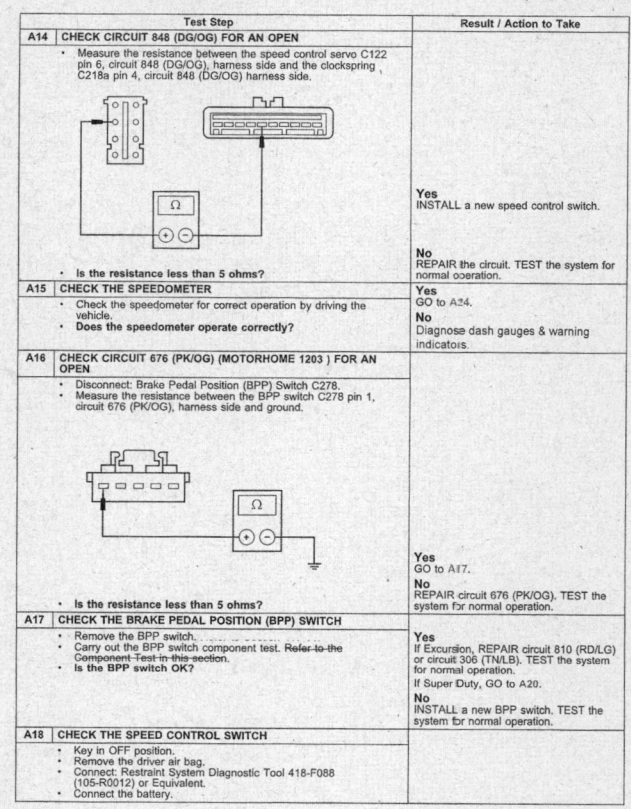

Test Step	Result / Action to Take
A14 CHECK CIRCUIT 848 (DG/OG) FOR AN OPEN • Measure the resistance between the speed control servo C122 pin 6, circuit 848 (DG/OG), harness side and the clockspring C218a pin 4, circuit 848 (DG/OG) harness side.	**Yes** INSTALL a new speed control switch. **No** REPAIR the circuit. TEST the system for normal operation.
• Is the resistance less than 5 ohms?	
A15 CHECK THE SPEEDOMETER • Check the speedometer for correct operation by driving the vehicle. • Does the speedometer operate correctly?	**Yes** GO to A24. **No** Diagnose dash gauges & warning indicators.
A16 CHECK CIRCUIT 676 (PK/OG) (MOTORHOME 1203) FOR AN OPEN • Disconnect: Brake Pedal Position (BPP) Switch C278. • Measure the resistance between the BPP switch C278 pin 1, circuit 676 (PK/OG), harness side and ground.	**Yes** GO to A17. **No** REPAIR circuit 676 (PK/OG). TEST the system for normal operation.
• Is the resistance less than 5 ohms?	
A17 CHECK THE BRAKE PEDAL POSITION (BPP) SWITCH • Remove the BPP switch. • Carry out the BPP switch component test. Refer to the Component Test in this section. • Is the BPP switch OK?	**Yes** If Excursion, REPAIR circuit 810 (RD/LG) or circuit 306 (TN/LB). TEST the system for normal operation. If Super Duty, GO to A20. **No** INSTALL a new BPP switch. TEST the system for normal operation.
A18 CHECK THE SPEED CONTROL SWITCH • Key in OFF position. • Remove the driver air bag. • Connect: Restraint System Diagnostic Tool 418-F088 (105-R0012) or Equivalent. • Connect the battery.	

LTV0500000001710

Fig. 96   Test A: Speed Control Is Inoperative (Part 7 of 11). 2002–05 Excursion & 2002–04 F-Super Duty

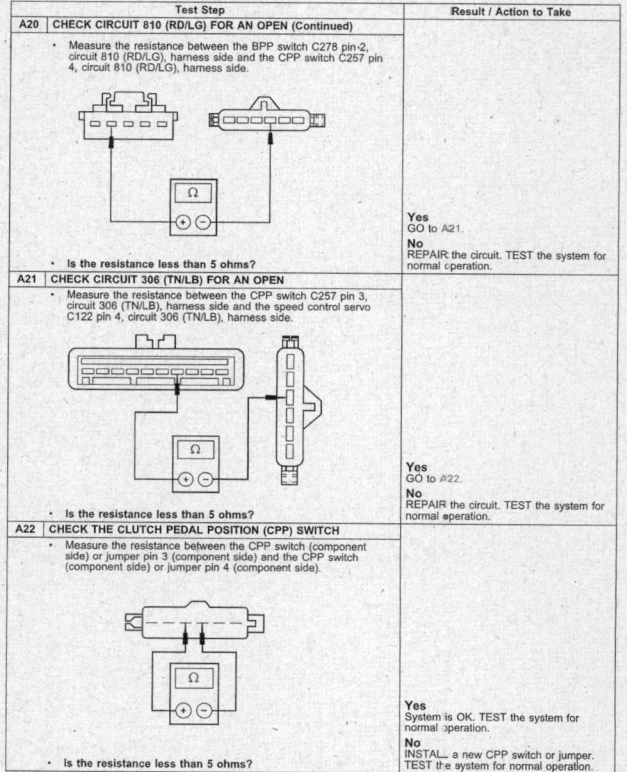

Test Step	Result / Action to Take
A20 CHECK CIRCUIT 810 (RD/LG) FOR AN OPEN (Continued) • Measure the resistance between the BPP switch C278 pin 2, circuit 810 (RD/LG), harness side and the CPP switch C257 pin 4, circuit 810 (RD/LG), harness side.	**Yes** GO to A21. **No** REPAIR the circuit. TEST the system for normal operation.
• Is the resistance less than 5 ohms?	
A21 CHECK CIRCUIT 306 (TN/LB) FOR AN OPEN • Measure the resistance between the CPP switch C257 pin 3, circuit 306 (TN/LB), harness side and the speed control servo C122 pin 4, circuit 306 (TN/LB), harness side.	**Yes** GO to A22. **No** REPAIR the circuit. TEST the system for normal operation.
• Is the resistance less than 5 ohms?	
A22 CHECK THE CLUTCH PEDAL POSITION (CPP) SWITCH • Measure the resistance between the CPP switch (component side) or jumper pin 3 (component side) and the CPP switch (component side) or jumper pin 4 (component side).	**Yes** System is OK. TEST the system for normal operation. **No** INSTALL a new CPP switch or jumper. TEST the system for normal operation.
• Is the resistance less than 5 ohms?	

LTV0500000001712

Fig. 96   Test A: Speed Control Is Inoperative (Part 9 of 11). 2002–05 Excursion & 2002–04 F-Super Duty

Test Step	Result / Action to Take
A23 CHECK BRAKE PEDAL POSITION (BPP) SWITCH INPUT CIRCUITRY FOR SHORT TO POWER • Key in OFF position. • Disconnect: BPP Switch C278. • Measure the voltage between the speed control servo C122 pin 4, circuit 306 (TN/LB) (Super Duty), circuit 810 (RD/LG) (Excursion), harness side and the speed control servo C122 pin 10, circuit 57 (BK), harness side. 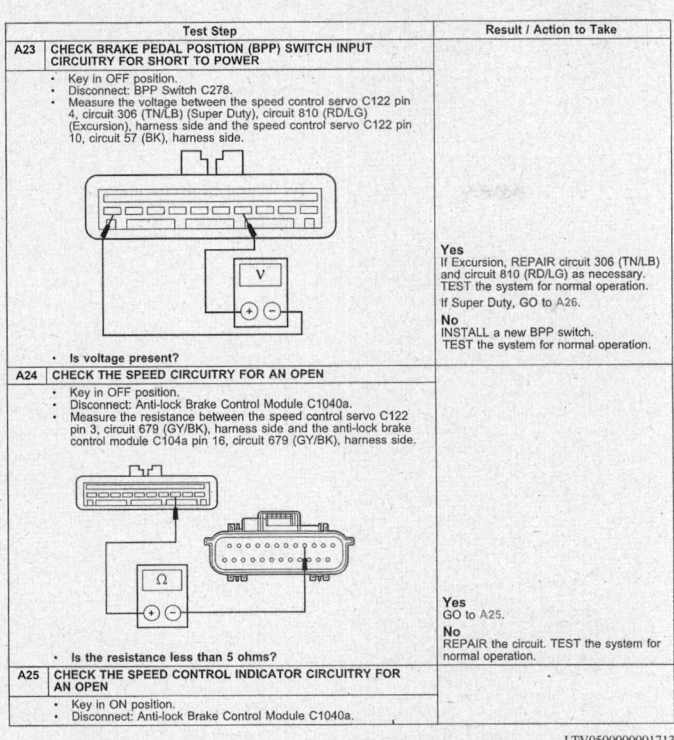 • **Is voltage present?**	**Yes** If Excursion, REPAIR circuit 306 (TN/LB) and circuit 810 (RD/LG) as necessary. TEST the system for normal operation. If Super Duty, GO to A26. **No** INSTALL a new BPP switch. TEST the system for normal operation.
A24 CHECK THE SPEED CIRCUITRY FOR AN OPEN • Key in OFF position. • Disconnect: Anti-lock Brake Control Module C1040a. • Measure the resistance between the speed control servo C122 pin 3, circuit 679 (GY/BK), harness side and the anti-lock brake control module C104a pin 16, circuit 679 (GY/BK), harness side. • **Is the resistance less than 5 ohms?**	**Yes** GO to A25. **No** REPAIR the circuit. TEST the system for normal operation.
A25 CHECK THE SPEED CONTROL INDICATOR CIRCUITRY FOR AN OPEN • Key in ON position. • Disconnect: Anti-lock Brake Control Module C1040a.	

LTV0500000001713

Fig. 96 Test A: Speed Control Is Inoperative (Part 10 of 11). 2002–05 Excursion & 2002–04 F-Super Duty

Test Step	Result / Action to Take
B1 CHECK SPEED CONTROL CABLE/THROTTLE BODY LINKAGE • Key in OFF position. • Remove the speed control cable from the speed control servo. Visually inspect the core wire and check the speed control cable by pulling on the cable and noting the throttle movement. • **Is the speed control cable OK?**	**Yes** GO to B2. **No** INSTALL a new speed control cable or REPAIR the throttle body linkage.
B2 CHECK THE SPEEDOMETER • Check the speedometer for correct operation by driving the vehicle. • **Does the speedometer fluctuate?**	**Yes** Diagnose dash gauges & warning indicators. **No** INSTALL a new speed control servo. TEST the system for normal operation.

LTV0500000001715

Fig. 97 Test B: Set Speed Fluctuates. 2002–05 Excursion & 2002–04 F-Super Duty

Test Step	Result / Action to Take
C1 CHECK THE BRAKE PEDAL POSITION (BPP) SWITCH OPERATION • Disconnect: Speed Control Servo C122. • Measure the voltage between the speed control servo C122 pin 4, circuit 306 (TN/LB) (Super Duty), circuit 810 (RD/LG) (Excursion), harness side and the speed control servo C122 pin 10, circuit 57 (BK), harness side, while pressing and releasing the brake pedal. 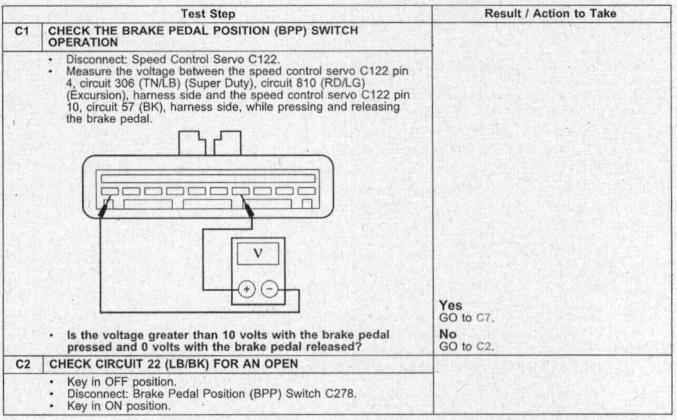 • **Is the voltage greater than 10 volts with the brake pedal pressed and 0 volts with the brake pedal released?**	**Yes** GO to C7. **No** GO to C2.
C2 CHECK CIRCUIT 22 (LB/BK) FOR AN OPEN • Key in OFF position. • Disconnect: Brake Pedal Position (BPP) Switch C278. • Key in ON position.	

LTV0500000001716

Fig. 98 Test C: Speed Control Does Not Disengage When Brakes Are Applied (Part 1 of 5). 2002–05 Excursion & 2002–04 F-Super Duty

Test Step	Result / Action to Take
A25 CHECK THE SPEED CONTROL INDICATOR CIRCUITRY FOR AN OPEN (Continued) • Connect a fused (10A) jumper wire between the speed control servo C122 pin 1, circuit 203 (OG/LB), harness side and ground, while observing the speed control indicator. 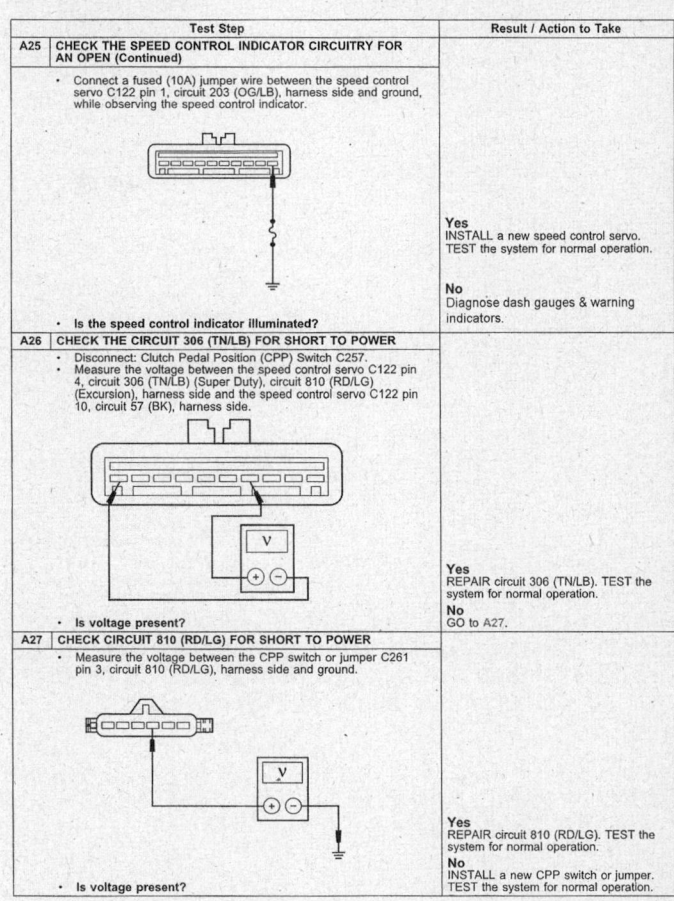 • **Is the speed control indicator illuminated?**	**Yes** INSTALL a new speed control servo. TEST the system for normal operation. **No** Diagnose dash gauges & warning indicators.
A26 CHECK THE CIRCUIT 306 (TN/LB) FOR SHORT TO POWER • Disconnect: Clutch Pedal Position (CPP) Switch C257. • Measure the voltage between the speed control servo C122 pin 4, circuit 306 (TN/LB) (Super Duty), circuit 810 (RD/LG) (Excursion), harness side and the speed control servo C122 pin 10, circuit 57 (BK), harness side. • **Is voltage present?**	**Yes** REPAIR circuit 306 (TN/LB). TEST the system for normal operation. **No** GO to A27.
A27 CHECK CIRCUIT 810 (RD/LG) FOR SHORT TO POWER • Measure the voltage between the CPP switch or jumper C261 pin 3, circuit 810 (RD/LG), harness side and ground. • **Is voltage present?**	**Yes** REPAIR circuit 810 (RD/LG). TEST the system for normal operation. **No** INSTALL a new CPP switch or jumper. TEST the system for normal operation.

LTV0500000001714

Fig. 96 Test A: Speed Control Is Inoperative (Part 11 of 11). 2002–05 Excursion & 2002–04 F-Super Duty

Test Step	Result / Action to Take
C2 CHECK CIRCUIT 22 (LB/BK) FOR AN OPEN (Continued) • Measure the voltage between the BPP switch C278 pin 3, circuit 22 (LB/BK), harness side and ground. 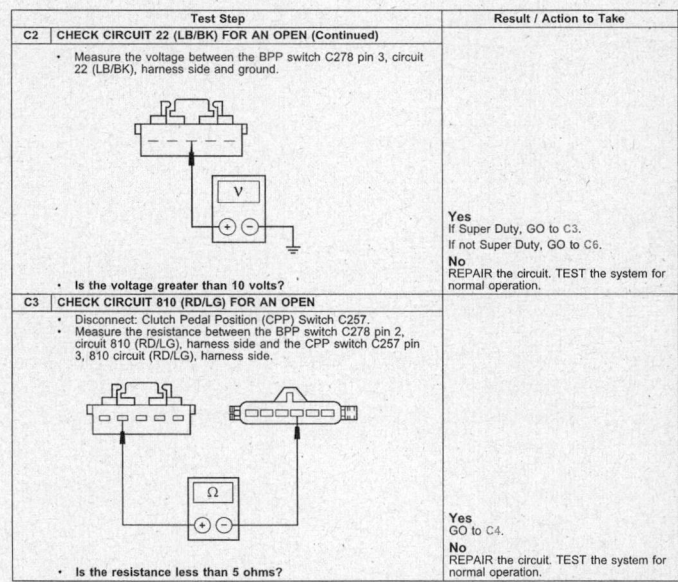 • **Is the voltage greater than 10 volts?**	**Yes** If Super Duty, GO to C3. If not Super Duty, GO to C6. **No** REPAIR the circuit. TEST the system for normal operation.
C3 CHECK CIRCUIT 810 (RD/LG) FOR AN OPEN • Disconnect: Clutch Pedal Position (CPP) Switch C257. • Measure the resistance between the BPP switch C278 pin 2, circuit 810 (RD/LG), harness side and the CPP switch C257 pin 3, 810 circuit (RD/LG), harness side. • **Is the resistance less than 5 ohms?**	**Yes** GO to C4. **No** REPAIR the circuit. TEST the system for normal operation.

LTV0500000001717

Fig. 98 Test C: Speed Control Does Not Disengage When Brakes Are Applied (Part 2 of 5). 2002–05 Excursion & 2002–04 F-Super Duty

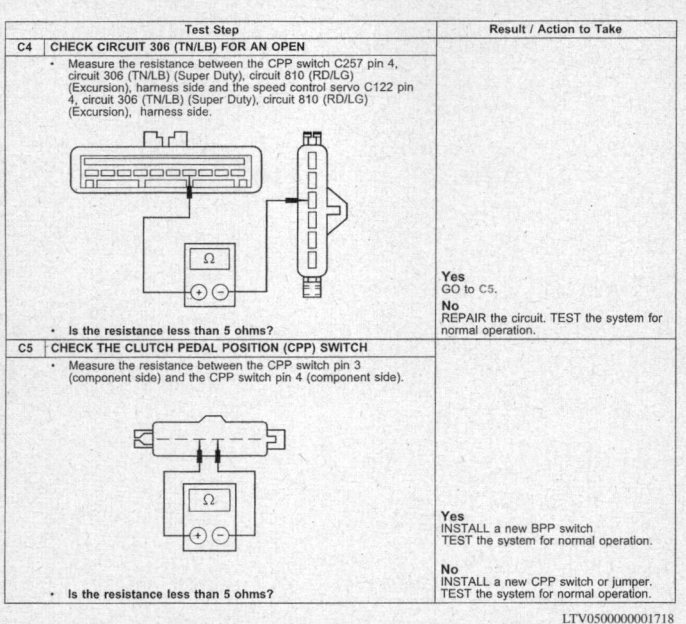

Test Step	Result / Action to Take
C4 CHECK CIRCUIT 306 (TN/LB) FOR AN OPEN • Measure the resistance between the CPP switch C257 pin 4, circuit 306 (TN/LB) (Super Duty), circuit 810 (RD/LG) (Excursion), harness side and the speed control servo C122 pin 4, circuit 306 (TN/LB) (Super Duty), circuit 810 (RD/LG) (Excursion), harness side. • Is the resistance less than 5 ohms?	**Yes** GO to C5. **No** REPAIR the circuit. TEST the system for normal operation.
C5 CHECK THE CLUTCH PEDAL POSITION (CPP) SWITCH • Measure the resistance between the CPP switch pin 3 (component side) and the CPP switch pin 4 (component side). • Is the resistance less than 5 ohms?	**Yes** INSTALL a new BPP switch TEST the system for normal operation. **No** INSTALL a new CPP switch or jumper. TEST the system for normal operation.

LTV0500000001718

Fig. 98 Test C: Speed Control Does Not Disengage When Brakes Are Applied (Part 3 of 5). 2002–05 Excursion & 2002–04 F-Super Duty

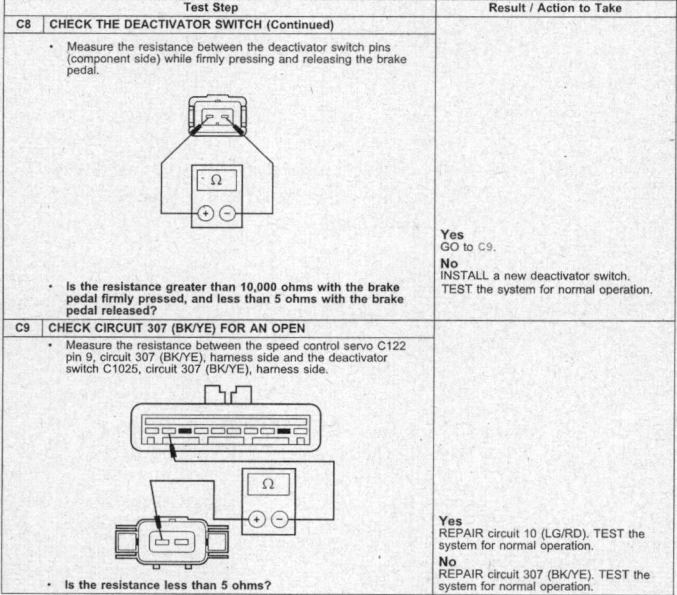

Test Step	Result / Action to Take
C8 CHECK THE DEACTIVATOR SWITCH (Continued) • Measure the resistance between the deactivator switch pins (component side) while firmly pressing and releasing the brake pedal. • Is the resistance greater than 10,000 ohms with the brake pedal firmly pressed, and less than 5 ohms with the brake pedal released?	**Yes** GO to C9. **No** INSTALL a new deactivator switch. TEST the system for normal operation.
C9 CHECK CIRCUIT 307 (BK/YE) FOR AN OPEN • Measure the resistance between the speed control servo C122 pin 9, circuit 307 (BK/YE), harness side and the deactivator switch C1025, circuit 307 (BK/YE), harness side. • Is the resistance less than 5 ohms?	**Yes** REPAIR circuit 10 (LG/RD). TEST the system for normal operation. **No** REPAIR circuit 307 (BK/YE). TEST the system for normal operation.

LTV0500000001720

Fig. 98 Test C: Speed Control Does Not Disengage When Brakes Are Applied (Part 5 of 5). 2002–05 Excursion & 2002–04 F-Super Duty

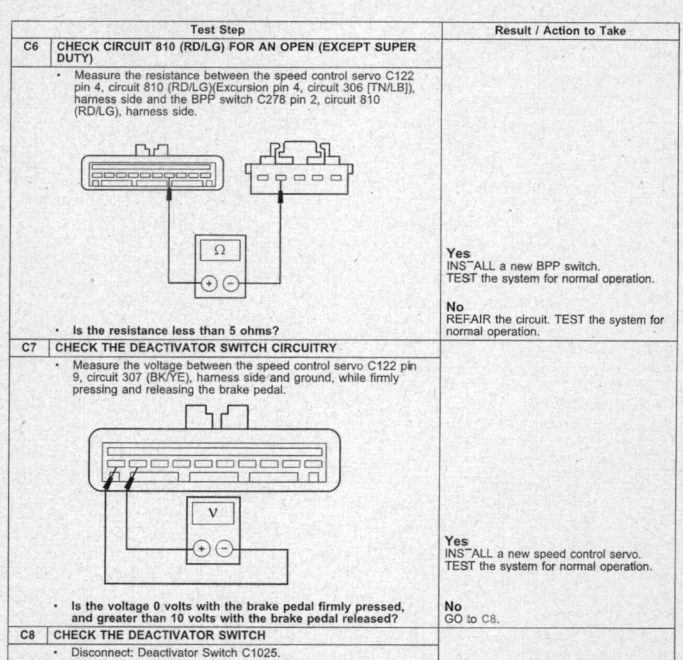

Test Step	Result / Action to Take
C6 CHECK CIRCUIT 810 (RD/LG) FOR AN OPEN (EXCEPT SUPER DUTY) • Measure the resistance between the speed control servo C122 pin 4, circuit 810 (RD/LG) (Excursion pin 4, circuit 306 (TN/LB)), harness side and the BPP switch C278 pin 2, circuit 810 (RD/LG), harness side. • Is the resistance less than 5 ohms?	**Yes** INSTALL a new BPP switch. TEST the system for normal operation. **No** REPAIR the circuit. TEST the system for normal operation.
C7 CHECK THE DEACTIVATOR SWITCH CIRCUITRY • Measure the voltage between the speed control servo C122 pin 9, circuit 307 (BK/YE), harness side and ground, while firmly pressing and releasing the brake pedal. • Is the voltage 0 volts with the brake pedal firmly pressed, and greater than 10 volts with the brake pedal released?	**Yes** INSTALL a new speed control servo. TEST the system for normal operation. **No** GO to C8.
C8 CHECK THE DEACTIVATOR SWITCH • Disconnect: Deactivator Switch C1025.	

LTV0500000001719

Fig. 98 Test C: Speed Control Does Not Disengage When Brakes Are Applied (Part 4 of 5). 2002–05 Excursion & 2002–04 F-Super Duty

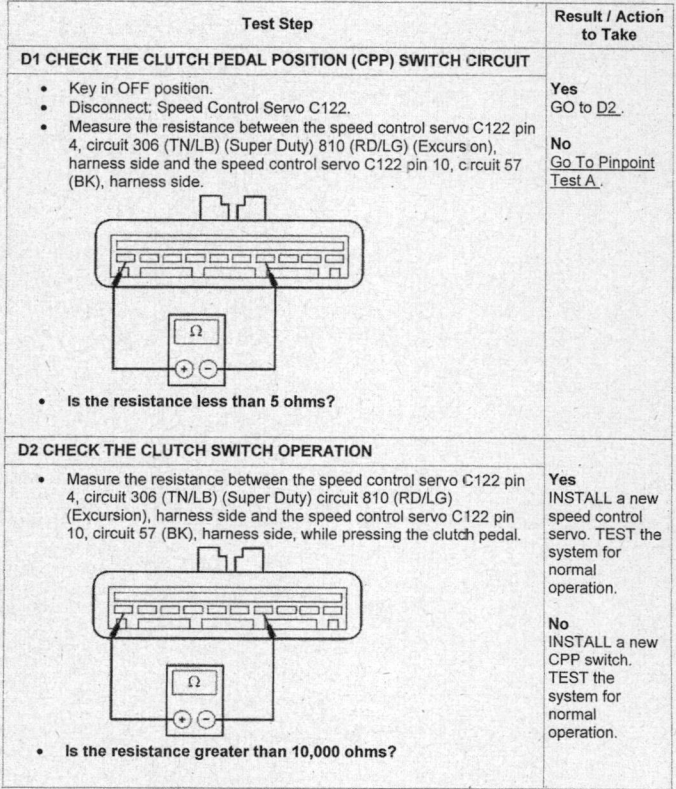

Test Step	Result / Action to Take
D1 CHECK THE CLUTCH PEDAL POSITION (CPP) SWITCH CIRCUIT • Key in OFF position. • Disconnect: Speed Control Servo C122. • Measure the resistance between the speed control servo C122 pin 4, circuit 306 (TN/LB) (Super Duty) 810 (RD/LG) (Excursion), harness side and the speed control servo C122 pin 10, circuit 57 (BK), harness side. • Is the resistance less than 5 ohms?	**Yes** GO to D2. **No** Go To Pinpoint Test A.
D2 CHECK THE CLUTCH SWITCH OPERATION • Masure the resistance between the speed control servo C122 pin 4, circuit 306 (TN/LB) (Super Duty) circuit 810 (RD/LG) (Excursion), harness side and the speed control servo C122 pin 10, circuit 57 (BK), harness side, while pressing the clutch pedal. • Is the resistance greater than 10,000 ohms?	**Yes** INSTALL a new speed control servo. TEST the system for normal operation. **No** INSTALL a new CPP switch. TEST the system for normal operation.

LTV0500000001721

Fig. 99 Test D: Speed Control Does Not Disengage When Clutch Is Applied. 2002–05 Excursion & 2002–04 F-Super Duty

Test Step	Result / Action to Take
E1 CHECK THE SPEED CONTROL SWITCH OPERATION	**Yes** INSTALL a new speed control servo. TEST the system for normal operation. **No** INSTALL a new speed control switch. TEST the system for normal operation.
• Key in OFF position. • Disconnect: Speed Control Servo C122. • Measure the resistance between the speed control servo C122 pin 5, circuit 151 (LB/BK), harness side and the speed control servo C122 pin 6, circuit 848 (DG/OG), harness side, while pressing the speed control switch as follows:	

Speed Control Switch	Resistance Value
Coast	Between 114 and 126 ohms
SET/ACCEL	Between 612 and 748 ohms
Resume	Between 2,090 and 2,310 ohms
Off	Less than 5 ohms

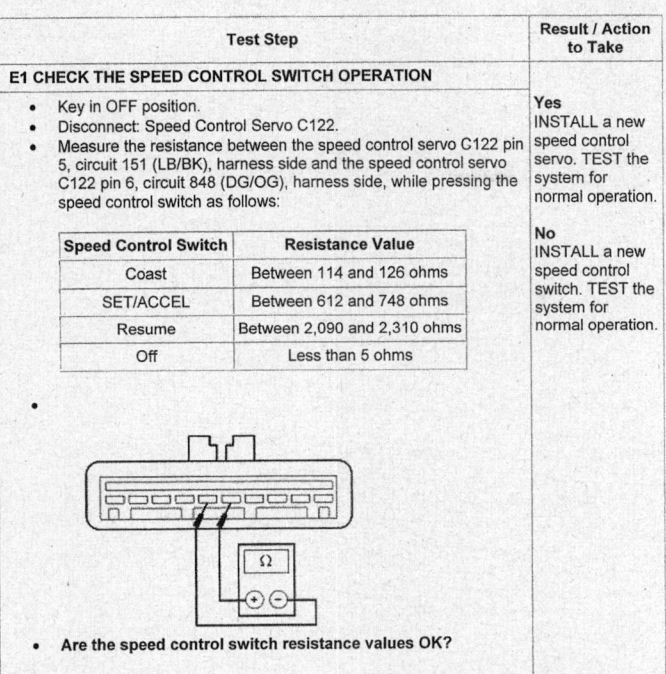

• **Are the speed control switch resistance values OK?**

LTV0500000001722

Fig. 100   Test E: Speed Control Switch Is Inoperative. 2002–05 Excursion & 2002–04 F-Super Duty

Test Step	Result / Action to Take
G1 CHECK STOPLAMP OPERATION	
• Press and release the brake pedal while observing the stoplamps. • **Do the stoplamps operate correctly?**	**Yes** GO to G2. **No** Diagnosis stoplamps.
G2 CHECK CIRCUIT 810 (RD/LG) FOR AN OPEN	
• Key in OFF position. • Disconnect: Speed Control Servo C122. • Measure the voltage between the speed control servo C122 pin 4, circuit 810 (RD/LG), (circuit 306 [TN/LB] Super Duty), harness side and the speed control servo C122 pin 10, circuit 57 (BK), harness side; while pressing the brake pedal.	**Yes** GO to G3. **No** GO to G5.

• **Is the voltage greater than 10 volts?**

Test Step	Result / Action to Take
G3 CHECK THE BRAKE CIRCUIT	
• Measure the resistance between the speed control servo C122 pin 4, circuit 306 (TN/LB) (Super Duty), circuit 810 (RD/LG) (Excursion), harness side and the speed control servo C122 pin 10, circuit 57 (BK) harness side.	**Yes** INSTALL a new speed control servo REPEAT the self-test. **No** GO to G4.

• **Is the resistance less than 5 ohms?**

LTV0500000001724

Fig. 102   Test G: Brake Pedal Position Switch Circuit Failure (Part 1 of 3). 2002–05 Excursion & 2002–04 F-Super Duty

Test Step	Result / Action to Take
F1 CHECK THE SPEED CONTROL CABLE	
• Check the speed control cable for correct attachment at the speed control servo and throttle body. • **Is the speed control cable attached correctly?**	**Yes** GO to F2. **No** RECONNECT the speed control cable. REPEAT the self-test.
F2 CHECK FOR A STICKING OR BINDING SPEED CONTROL CABLE	
• Check the speed control cable for sticking or binding. • **Is the speed control cable OK?**	**Yes** INSTALL a new speed control servo. REPEAT the self-test. **No** REPAIR or INSTALL a new speed control cable. REPEAT the self-test.

LTV0500000001723

Fig. 101   Test F: Flash w/Last Switch Pressed, But No Dynamic Pull Occurs At Throttle & Speed Control Is Inoperative. 2002–05 Excursion & 2002–04 F-Super Duty

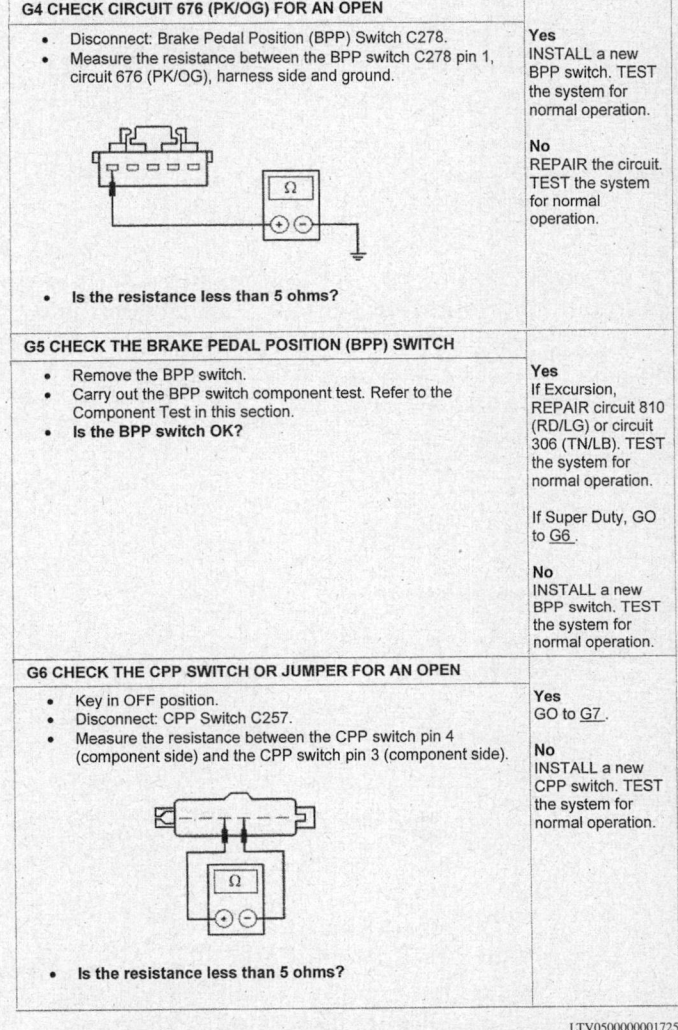

G4 CHECK CIRCUIT 676 (PK/OG) FOR AN OPEN	**Yes** INSTALL a new BPP switch. TEST the system for normal operation. **No** REPAIR the circuit. TEST the system for normal operation.
• Disconnect: Brake Pedal Position (BPP) Switch C278. • Measure the resistance between the BPP switch C278 pin 1, circuit 676 (PK/OG), harness side and ground.	
• **Is the resistance less than 5 ohms?**	
G5 CHECK THE BRAKE PEDAL POSITION (BPP) SWITCH	**Yes** If Excursion, REPAIR circuit 810 (RD/LG) or circuit 306 (TN/LB). TEST the system for normal operation. If Super Duty, GO to G6. **No** INSTALL a new BPP switch. TEST the system for normal operation.
• Remove the BPP switch. • Carry out the BPP switch component test. Refer to the Component Test in this section. • **Is the BPP switch OK?**	
G6 CHECK THE CPP SWITCH OR JUMPER FOR AN OPEN	**Yes** GO to G7. **No** INSTALL a new CPP switch. TEST the system for normal operation.
• Key in OFF position. • Disconnect: CPP Switch C257. • Measure the resistance between the CPP switch pin 4 (component side) and the CPP switch pin 3 (component side).	
• **Is the resistance less than 5 ohms?**	

LTV0500000001725

Fig. 102   Test G: Brake Pedal Position Switch Circuit Failure (Part 2 of 3). 2002–05 Excursion & 2002–04 F-Super Duty

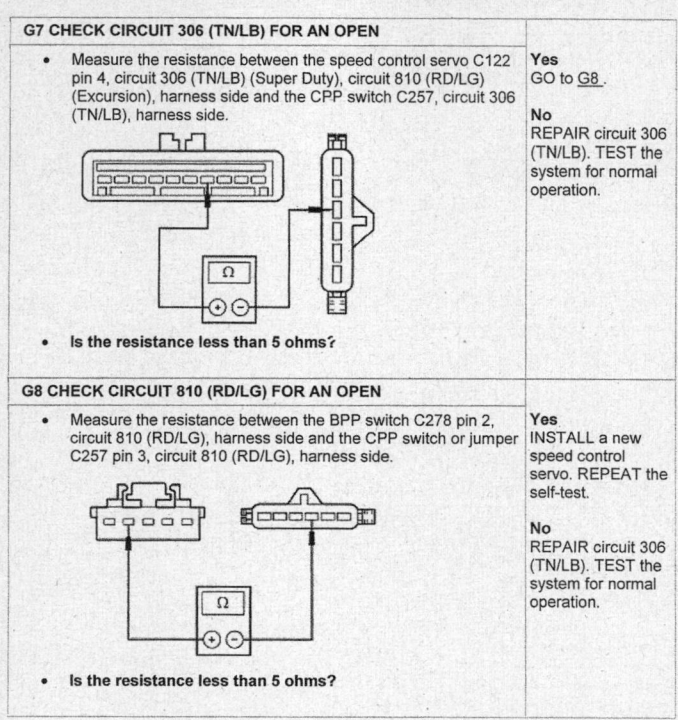

G7 CHECK CIRCUIT 306 (TN/LB) FOR AN OPEN

- Measure the resistance between the speed control servo C122 pin 4, circuit 306 (TN/LB) (Super Duty), circuit 810 (RD/LG) (Excursion), harness side and the CPP switch C257, circuit 306 (TN/LB), harness side.

- Is the resistance less than 5 ohms?

Yes
GO to G8.

No
REPAIR circuit 306 (TN/LB). TEST the system for normal operation.

G8 CHECK CIRCUIT 810 (RD/LG) FOR AN OPEN

- Measure the resistance between the BPP switch C278 pin 2, circuit 810 (RD/LG), harness side and the CPP switch or jumper C257 pin 3, circuit 810 (RD/LG), harness side.

- Is the resistance less than 5 ohms?

Yes
INSTALL a new speed control servo. REPEAT the self-test.

No
REPAIR circuit 306 (TN/LB). TEST the system for normal operation.

LTV0500000001726

Fig. 102   Test G: Brake Pedal Position Switch Circuit Failure (Part 3 of 3). 2002–05 Excursion & 2002–04 F-Super Duty

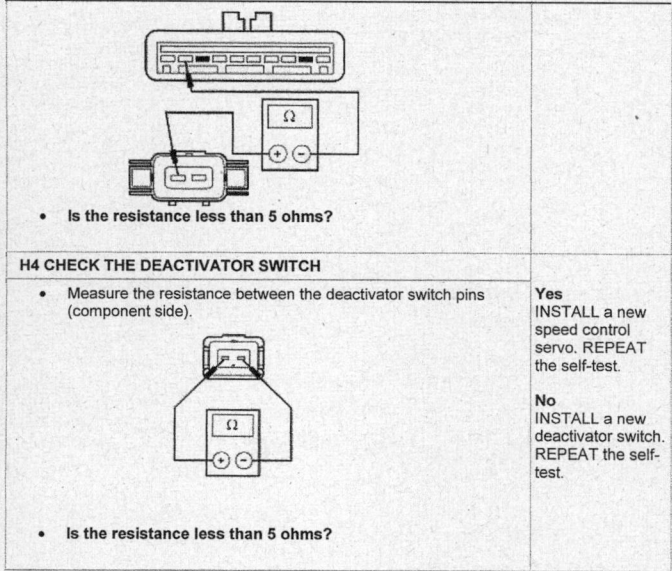

- Is the resistance less than 5 ohms?

H4 CHECK THE DEACTIVATOR SWITCH

- Measure the resistance between the deactivator switch pins (component side).

- Is the resistance less than 5 ohms?

Yes
INSTALL a new speed control servo. REPEAT the self-test.

No
INSTALL a new deactivator switch. REPEAT the self-test.

LTV0500000001728

Fig. 103   Test H: Deactivator Switch Circuit Failure (Part 2 of 2). 2002–05 Excursion & 2002–04 F-Super Duty

Test Step	Result / Action to Take
H1 CHECK THE DEACTIVATOR SWITCH CIRCUITRY • Key in OFF position. • Disconnect: Speed Control Servo C122. • Measure the voltage between the speed control servo C122 pin 9, circuit 307 (BK/YE), harness side and the speed control servo C122 pin 10, circuit 57 (BK), harness side. • Is the voltage greater than 10 volts?	**Yes** INSTALL a new speed control servo REPEAT the self-test. **No** GO to H2.
H2 CHECK DEACTIVATOR SWITCH POWER • Disconnect: Deactivator Switch C1025. • Measure the voltage between the deactivator switch C1025, circuit 10 (LG/RD), harness side and ground. • Is the voltage greater than 10 volts?	**Yes** GO to H3. **No** REPAIR the circuit. REPEAT the self-test.
H3 CHECK CIRCUIT 307 (BK/YE) FOR AN OPEN • Measure the resistance between the speed control servo C122 pin 9, circuit 307 (BK/YE), harness side and the deactivator switch C1025, circuit 307 (BK/YE), harness side.	**Yes** GO to H4. **No** REPAIR the circuit. REPEAT the self-test.

LTV0500000001727

Fig. 103   Test H: Deactivator Switch Circuit Failure (Part 1 of 2). 2002–05 Excursion & 2002–04 F-Super Duty

Test Step	Result / Action to Take
I1 CHECK THE SPEEDOMETER OPERATION • Check the speedometer for correct operation by driving the vehicle. • **Does the speedometer operate correctly?**	**Yes** GO to I2. **No** Diagnose dash gauges & warning indicators
I2 CHECK CIRCUIT 679 (GY/BK) FOR AN OPEN • Key in OFF position. • Disconnect: Speed Control Servo C122. • Disconnect: Anti-lock Brake Control Module C1040a. • Measure the resistance between the speed control servo C122 pin 3, circuit 679 (GY/BK), harness side and the anti-lock brake control module C104a, circuit 679 (GY/BK), harness side. 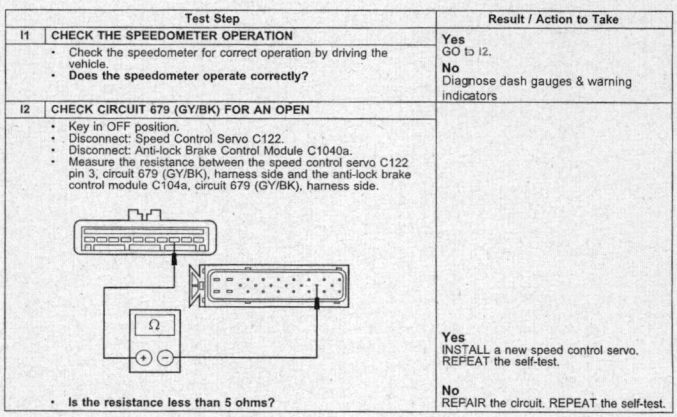 • Is the resistance less than 5 ohms?	**Yes** INSTALL a new speed control servo. REPEAT the self-test. **No** REPAIR the circuit. REPEAT the self-test.

LTV0500000001729

Fig. 104   Test I: Flash w/Last Switch Pressed, But No Dynamic Pull At Throttle & Speed Control Is Inoperative. 2002–05 Excursion & 2002–04 F-Super Duty

Test Step		Result / Action to Take
J1	CHECK THE SPEED CONTROL SERVO	**Yes** GO to J2. **No** INSTALL a new speed control servo. TEST the system for normal operation.
	• Key in OFF position. • Disconnect: Speed Control Servo C122. • Key in ON position. • Check the speed control indicator lamp. • **Is the speed control indicator lamp always on?**	
J2	CHECK CIRCUIT 203 (OG/LB) FOR A SHORT TO GROUND	
	• Key in OFF position. • Disconnect: Instrument Cluster C220b. • Measure the resistance between the speed control servo C122 pin 1, circuit 203 (OG/LB), harness side and ground.	

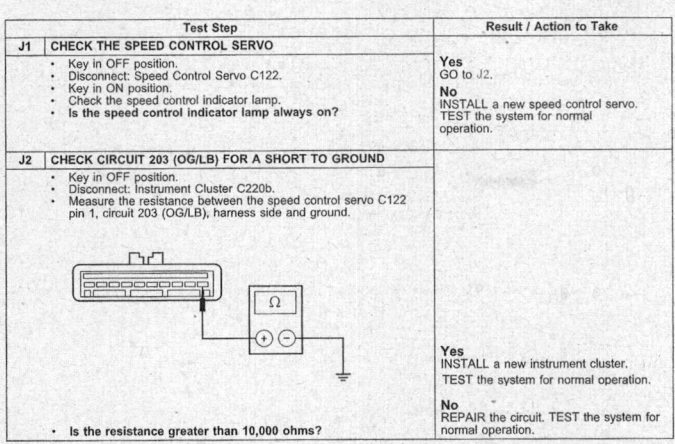

		Yes INSTALL a new instrument cluster. TEST the system for normal operation. **No** REPAIR the circuit. TEST the system for normal operation.
	• **Is the resistance greater than 10,000 ohms?**	

LTV0500000001730

Fig. 105   Test J: Speed Control Indicator Lamp Is Always On. 2002–05 Excursion & 2002–04 F-Super Duty

Test Step		Result / Action to Take
A2	CHECK THE SPEED CONTROL SWITCH (Continued)	

Speed Control Switch	Resistance Value
OFF	Less than 5 ohms
SET -	285 - 315 ohms
SET +	570 - 630 ohms
RESUME	1,055 - 1,165 ohms
ON	2,004 - 2,216 ohms
No switch pressed	4,094 - 4,526 ohms

		Yes If equipped with an automatic transmission, GO to A3. If equipped with a manual transmission, GO to A5. **No** INSTALL a new speed control switch. CLEAR the DTCs. REPEAT the self-test.
	• **Are the speed control switch resistance values OK?**	
A3	CHECK THE DIGITAL TR SENSOR	
	• Connect: PCM C175b. • Key in ON position. • Enter the following diagnostic mode on the diagnostic tool: PCM PID Data Monitor and Record. • Monitor the PCM TR sensor PID. • Select DRIVE. • **Does the PID value agree with the transmission range selector lever position?**	**Yes** GO to A4. **No** Diagnose digital TR sensor.
A4	CHECK THE DIGITAL TR SENSOR FOR CORRECT ALIGNMENT	
	• Check the digital TR sensor alignment. Refer to Section 307-01. • **Is the digital TR sensor aligned correctly?**	**Yes** GO to A8. **No** ADJUST the digital TR sensor.

LTV0500000001733

Fig. 106   Test A: Speed Control Is Inoperative (Part 2 of 4). 2005–06 F-Super Duty w/gasoline engine

Test Step		Result / Action to Take
A1	CHECK FOR DTCs	**Yes** REFER to the Powertrain Control Module (PCM) Diagnostic Trouble Code (DTC) Index. **No** GO to A2.
	• Review the recorded DTCs from the PCM self-test. • **Are any DTCs recorded?**	
A2	CHECK THE SPEED CONTROL SWITCH	
	• Disconnect: PCM C175b. • Measure the resistance between the PCM C175b-19, circuit 151 (LB/BK), harness side and the PCM C175b-30, circuit 133 (BK), harness side.	

LTV0500000001732

Fig. 106   Test A: Speed Control Is Inoperative (Part 1 of 4). 2005–06 F-Super Duty w/gasoline engine

Test Step		Result / Action to Take
A5	CHECK THE CPP SWITCH	
	• While pressing and releasing the clutch pedal, measure the resistance between the PCM C175b-32, circuit 306 (TN/LB), harness side and ground.	

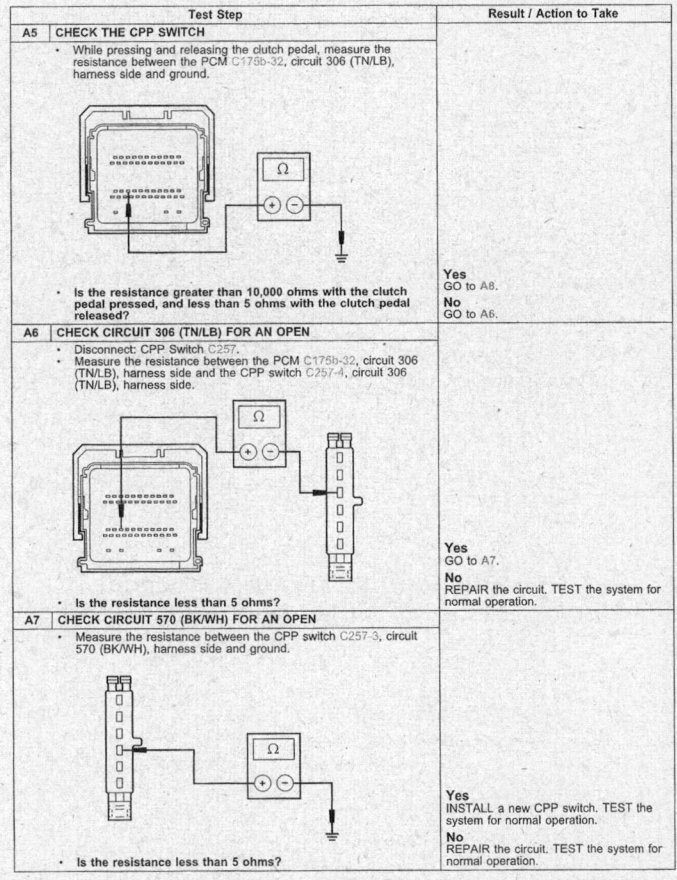

		Yes GO to A8. **No** GO to A6.
	• **Is the resistance greater than 10,000 ohms with the clutch pedal pressed, and less than 5 ohms with the clutch pedal released?**	
A6	CHECK CIRCUIT 306 (TN/LB) FOR AN OPEN	
	• Disconnect: CPP Switch C257. • Measure the resistance between the PCM C175b-32, circuit 306 (TN/LB), harness side and the CPP switch C257-4, circuit 306 (TN/LB), harness side.	**Yes** GO to A7. **No** REPAIR the circuit. TEST the system for normal operation.
	• **Is the resistance less than 5 ohms?**	
A7	CHECK CIRCUIT 570 (BK/WH) FOR AN OPEN	
	• Measure the resistance between the CPP switch C257-3, circuit 570 (BK/WH), harness side and ground.	**Yes** INSTALL a new CPP switch. TEST the system for normal operation. **No** REPAIR the circuit. TEST the system for normal operation.
	• **Is the resistance less than 5 ohms?**	

LTV0500000001734

Fig. 106   Test A: Speed Control Is Inoperative (Part 3 of 4). 2005–06 F-Super Duty w/gasoline engine

Test Step		Result / Action to Take
A8	CHECK THE PARKING BRAKE WARNING INDICATOR	
	• Key in ON position. • While observing the parking brake warning indicator, apply and release the parking brake. • **Does the parking brake warning indicator operate correctly?**	**Yes** GO to A9. **No** Diagnose parking brake warning indicator.
A9	CHECK THE VEHICLE SPEED	
	NOTE: This step may require an assistant. • Enter the following diagnostic mode on the diagnostic tool: Anti-lock Brake System (ABS) Wheel Speed PID. • Monitor and record the ABS module wheel speed PID while driving the vehicle at 48 km/h (30 mph) as indicated on the speedometer. • Enter the following diagnostic mode on the diagnostic tool: PCM Vehicle Speed PID. • Monitor and record the PCM vehicle speed PID while driving the vehicle at 48 km/h (30 mph). • **Does the speed indicated by the ABS module wheel speed PID match the PCM vehicle speed PID?**	**Yes** GO to A10. **No** REFER to MOTOR's "Domestic Engine Performance & Driveability Manual" to diagnose output shaft speed (OSS) sensor signal.
A10	CHECK FOR CORRECT PCM OPERATION	

	• Disconnect all the PCM connectors.
	• Check for:
	  — corrosion
	  — pushed-out pins
	• Connect all the PCM connectors and make sure they are seated correctly.
	• Operate the system and verify the concern is still present.
	• **Is the concern still present?**
		Yes
		INSTALL a new PCM. CLEAR the DTCs, REPEAT the self-test.
		No
		The system is operating correctly at this time. The concern may have been caused by a loose or corroded connector.

LTV0500000001735

Fig. 106   Test A: Speed Control Is Inoperative (Part 4 of 4). 2005–06 F-Super Duty w/gasoline engine

Test Step		Result / Action to Take
B1	**CHECK FOR DTCs**	**Yes** REFER to the Powertrain Control Module (PCM) Diagnostic Trouble Code (DTC) Index. **No** GO to B2.
	• Review the recorded DTCs from the PCM self-test. • **Are any DTCs recorded?**	
B2	**CHECK THE SPEED CONTROL SWITCH**	
	• Disconnect: PCM C1381a. • Measure the resistance between the PCM C1381a-31, circuit 151 (LB/BK), harness side and the PCM C1381a-24, circuit 133 (BK), harness side.	

Speed Control Switch	Resistance Value
OFF	Less than 5 ohms
SET -	285 - 315 ohms
SET +	570 - 630 ohms
RESUME	1,055 - 1,165 ohms
ON	2,004 - 2,216 ohms
No switch pressed	4,094 - 4,526 ohms

Test Step		Result / Action to Take
	• **Are the speed control switch resistance values OK?**	**Yes** If equipped with an automatic transmission, GO to B3. If equipped with a manual transmission, GO to B5. **No** INSTALL a new speed control switch. CLEAR the DTCs. REPEAT the self-test.
B3	**CHECK THE DIGITAL TR SENSOR**	**Yes** GO to B4. **No** Diagnose digital TR sensor.
	• Connect: PCM C1381a. • Key in ON position. • Enter the following diagnostic mode on the diagnostic tool: PCM PID Data Monitor and Record. • Monitor the PCM TR sensor PID. • Select DRIVE. • **Does the PID value agree with the transmission range selector lever position?**	
B4	**CHECK THE DIGITAL TR SENSOR FOR CORRECT ALIGNMENT**	**Yes** GO to B8. **No** ADJUST the digital TR sensor.
	• Check the digital TR sensor alignment. • **Is the digital TR sensor aligned correctly?**	
B5	**CHECK THE CPP SWITCH**	
	• Key in OFF position. • Disconnect: PCM C1381a. • Key in ON position.	

LTV0500000001736

Fig. 107 Test B: Speed Control Inoperative (Part 1 of 3). 2005–06 F-Super Duty w/diesel engine

Test Step		Result / Action to Take
B5	**CHECK THE CPP SWITCH (Continued)**	
	• While pressing and releasing the clutch pedal, measure the voltage between the PCM C1381a-36, circuit 306 (TN/LB), harness side and ground.	

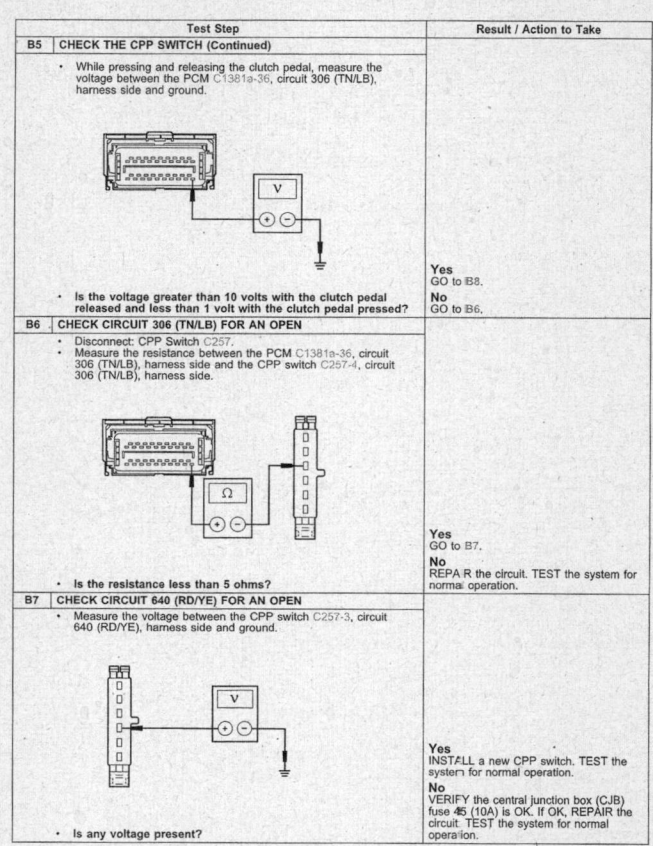

Test Step		Result / Action to Take
	• **Is the voltage greater than 10 volts with the clutch pedal released and less than 1 volt with the clutch pedal pressed?**	**Yes** GO to B8. **No** GO to B6.
B6	**CHECK CIRCUIT 306 (TN/LB) FOR AN OPEN**	
	• Disconnect: CPP Switch C257. • Measure the resistance between the PCM C1381a-36, circuit 306 (TN/LB), harness side and the CPP switch C257-4, circuit 306 (TN/LB), harness side.	
	• **Is the resistance less than 5 ohms?**	**Yes** GO to B7. **No** REPAIR the circuit. TEST the system for normal operation.
B7	**CHECK CIRCUIT 640 (RD/YE) FOR AN OPEN**	
	• Measure the voltage between the CPP switch C257-3, circuit 640 (RD/YE), harness side and ground.	
	• **Is any voltage present?**	**Yes** INSTALL a new CPP switch. TEST the system for normal operation. **No** VERIFY the central junction box (CJB) fuse 45 (10A) is OK. If OK, REPAIR the circuit. TEST the system for normal operation.

LTV0500000001737

Fig. 107 Test B: Speed Control Inoperative (Part 2 of 3). 2005–06 F-Super Duty w/diesel engine

Test Step		Result / Action to Take
B8	**CHECK THE PARKING BRAKE WARNING INDICATOR**	**Yes** GO to B9. **No** Diagnose parking brake warning indicator.
	• Key in ON position. • While observing the parking brake warning indicator, apply and release the parking brake. • **Does the parking brake warning indicator operate correctly?**	
B9	**CHECK THE VEHICLE SPEED**	
	NOTE: This step may require an assistant. • Enter the following diagnostic mode on the diagnostic tool: Anti-lock Brake System (ABS) Wheel Speed PID. • Monitor and record the ABS module wheel speed PID while driving the vehicle at 48 km/h (30 mph) as indicated on the speedometer. • Enter the following diagnostic mode on the diagnostic tool: PCM Vehicle Speed PID. • Monitor and record the PCM vehicle speed PID while driving the vehicle at 48 km/h (30 mph). • **Does the speed indicated by the ABS module wheel speed PID match the PCM vehicle speed PID?**	**Yes** GO to B10. **No** REFER to MOTOR's "Domestic Engine Performance & Driveability Manual" to diagnose output shaft speed (OSS) sensor signal.
B10	**CHECK FOR CORRECT PCM OPERATION**	**Yes** INSTALL a new PCM. CLEAR the DTCs. REPEAT the self-test. **No** The system is operating correctly at this time. The concern may have been caused by a loose or corroded connector.
	• Disconnect all the PCM connectors. • Check for: — corrosion — pushed-out pins • Connect all the PCM connectors and make sure they are seated correctly. • Operate the system and verify the concern is still present. • **Is the concern still present?**	

LTV0500000001738

Fig. 107 Test B: Speed Control Inoperative (Part 3 of 3). 2005–06 F-Super Duty w/diesel engine

Test Step		Result / Action to Take
C1	**CHECK CIRCUIT 810 (RD/LG) FOR VOLTAGE (Continued)**	
	• For gasoline vehicles, measure the voltage between the PCM C175b-8, circuit 810 (RD/LG), harness side and ground.	
	• For diesel vehicles, measure the voltage between the PCM C1381a-18, circuit 810 (RD/LG), harness side and ground.	

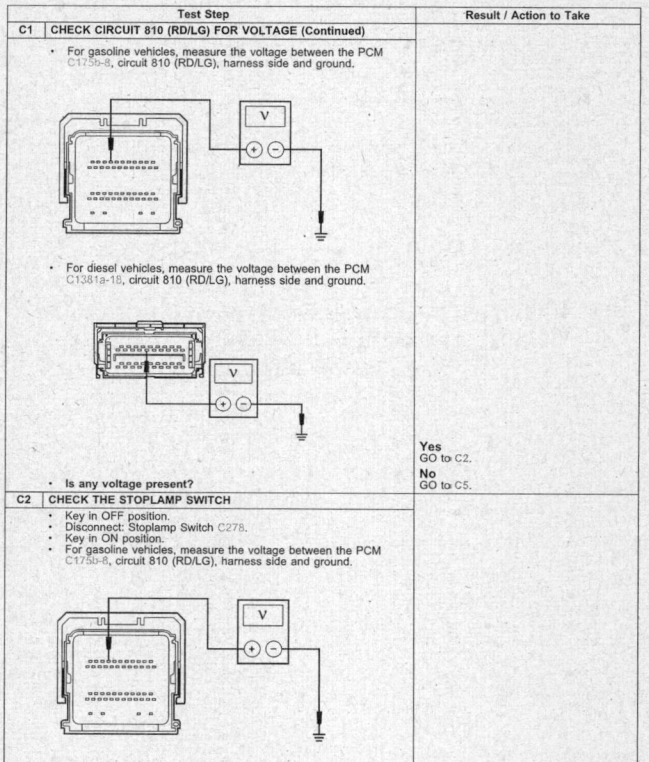

Test Step		Result / Action to Take
	• **Is any voltage present?**	**Yes** GO to C2. **No** GO to C5.
C2	**CHECK THE STOPLAMP SWITCH**	
	• Key in OFF position. • Disconnect: Stoplamp Switch C278. • Key in ON position. • For gasoline vehicles, measure the voltage between the PCM C175b-8, circuit 810 (RD/LG), harness side and ground.	

LTV0500000001739

Fig. 108 Test C, Codes P1572 & P1703: Brake On/Off Circuit Failure (Part 1 of 8). 2005–06 F-Super Duty

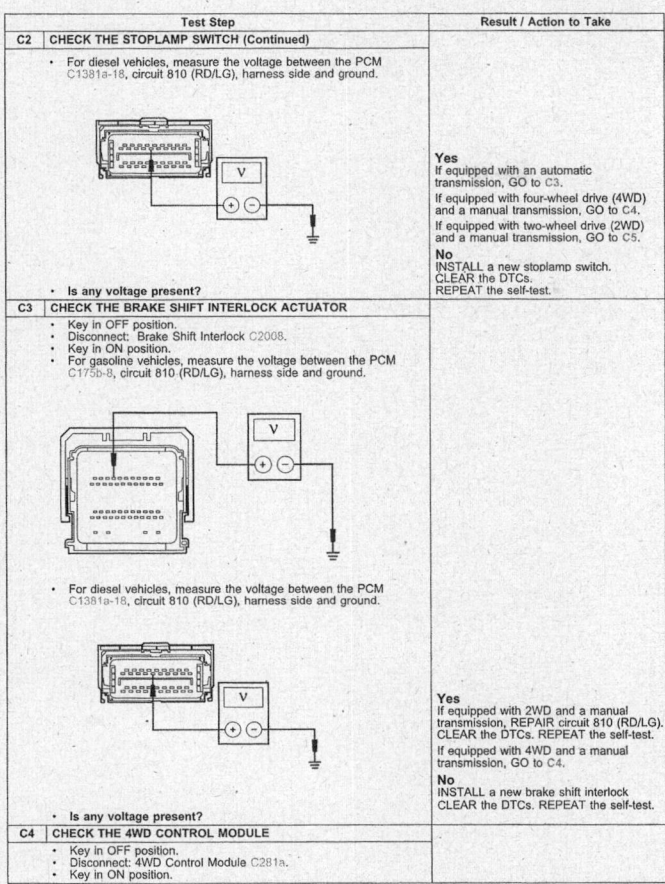

Test Step	Result / Action to Take
C2 CHECK THE STOPLAMP SWITCH (Continued)	
• For diesel vehicles, measure the voltage between the PCM C1381a-18, circuit 810 (RD/LG), harness side and ground.	**Yes** If equipped with an automatic transmission, GO to C3. If equipped with four-wheel drive (4WD) and a manual transmission, GO to C4. If equipped with two-wheel drive (2WD) and a manual transmission, GO to C5. **No** INSTALL a new stoplamp switch. CLEAR the DTCs. REPEAT the self-test.
• Is any voltage present?	
C3 CHECK THE BRAKE SHIFT INTERLOCK ACTUATOR	
• Key in OFF position. • Disconnect: Brake Shift Interlock C2008. • Key in ON position. • For gasoline vehicles, measure the voltage between the PCM C175b-8, circuit 810 (RD/LG), harness side and ground.	
• For diesel vehicles, measure the voltage between the PCM C1381a-18, circuit 810 (RD/LG), harness side and ground.	**Yes** If equipped with 2WD and a manual transmission, REPAIR circuit 810 (RD/LG). CLEAR the DTCs. REPEAT the self-test. If equipped with 4WD and a manual transmission, GO to C4. **No** INSTALL a new brake shift interlock CLEAR the DTCs. REPEAT the self-test.
• Is any voltage present?	
C4 CHECK THE 4WD CONTROL MODULE	
• Key in OFF position. • Disconnect: 4WD Control Module C281a. • Key in ON position.	

LTV0500000001740

Fig. 108 Test C, Codes P1572 & P1703: Brake On/Off Circuit Failure (Part 2 of 8). 2005–06 F-Super Duty

Test Step	Result / Action to Take
C5 CHECK THE STOPLAMP SWITCH FOR CORRECT OPERATION (Continued)	
• For diesel vehicles, while applying the brake pedal, measure the voltage between the PCM C1381a-18, circuit 810 (RD/LG), harness side and ground.	
	Yes GO to C8. **No** GO to C6.
• Is the voltage greater than 10 volts?	
C6 CHECK CIRCUIT 22 (LB/BK) FOR AN OPEN	
• Key in OFF position. • Disconnect: Stoplamp Switch C278. • Key in ON position. • Measure the voltage between the stoplamp switch C278-3, circuit 22 (LB/BK), harness side and ground.	
	Yes GO to C7. **No** REPAIR the circuit. CLEAR the DTCs. REPEAT the self-test.
• Is the voltage greater than 10 volts?	
C7 CHECK CIRCUIT 810 (RD/LG) FOR AN OPEN	
• Key in OFF position.	

LTV0500000001742

Fig. 108 Test C, Codes P1572 & P1703: Brake On/Off Circuit Failure (Part 4 of 8). 2005–06 F-Super Duty

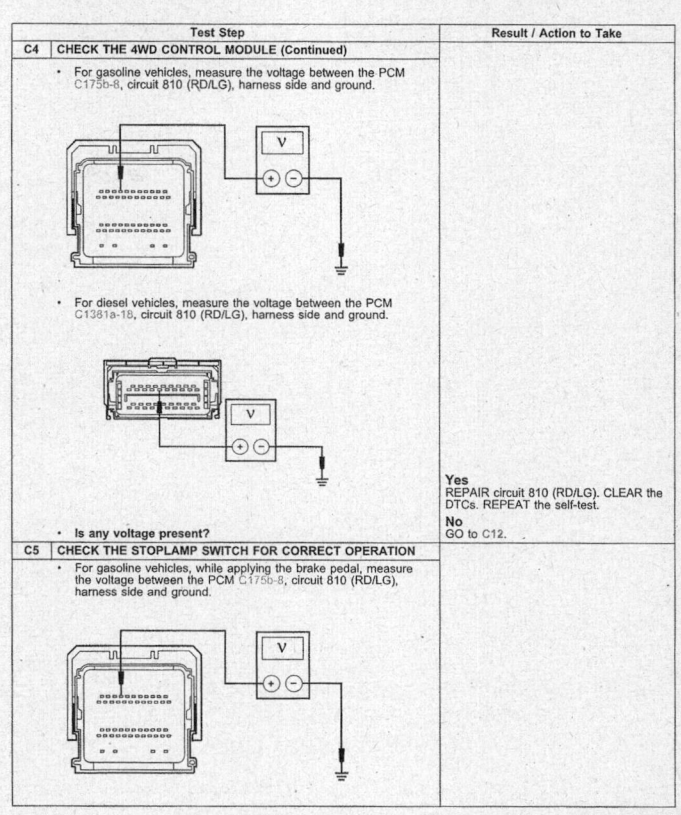

Test Step	Result / Action to Take
C4 CHECK THE 4WD CONTROL MODULE (Continued)	
• For gasoline vehicles, measure the voltage between the PCM C175b-8, circuit 810 (RD/LG), harness side and ground.	
• For diesel vehicles, measure the voltage between the PCM C1381a-18, circuit 810 (RD/LG), harness side and ground.	**Yes** REPAIR circuit 810 (RD/LG). CLEAR the DTCs. REPEAT the self-test. **No** GO to C12.
• Is any voltage present?	
C5 CHECK THE STOPLAMP SWITCH FOR CORRECT OPERATION	
• For gasoline vehicles, while applying the brake pedal, measure the voltage between the PCM C175b-8, circuit 810 (RD/LG), harness side and ground.	

LTV0500000001741

Fig. 108 Test C, Codes P1572 & P1703: Brake On/Off Circuit Failure (Part 3 of 8). 2005–06 F-Super Duty

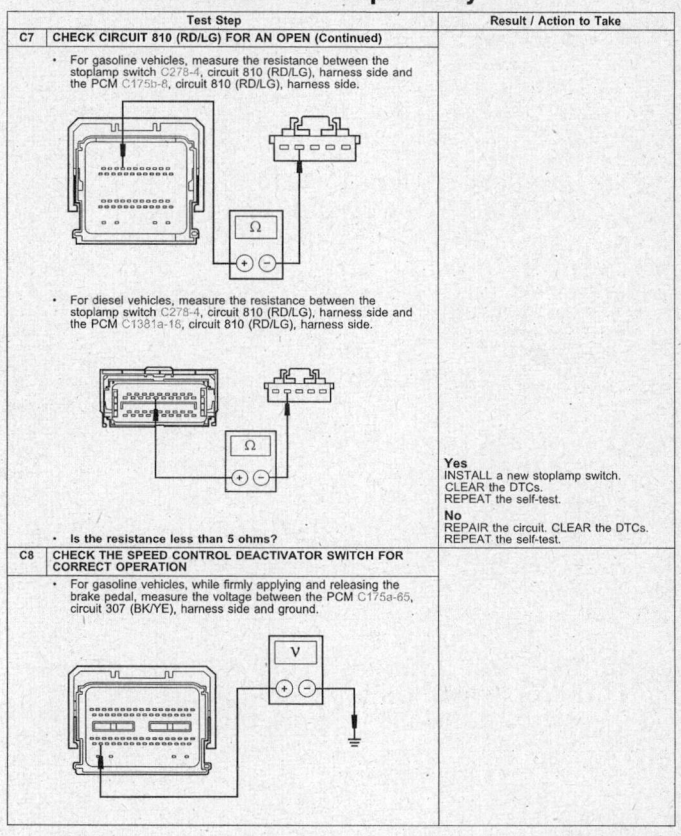

Test Step	Result / Action to Take
C7 CHECK CIRCUIT 810 (RD/LG) FOR AN OPEN (Continued)	
• For gasoline vehicles, measure the resistance between the stoplamp switch C278-4, circuit 810 (RD/LG), harness side and the PCM C175b-8, circuit 810 (RD/LG), harness side.	
• For diesel vehicles, measure the resistance between the stoplamp switch C278-4, circuit 810 (RD/LG), harness side and the PCM C1381a-18, circuit 810 (RD/LG), harness side.	**Yes** INSTALL a new stoplamp switch. CLEAR the DTCs. REPEAT the self-test. **No** REPAIR the circuit. CLEAR the DTCs. REPEAT the self-test.
• Is the resistance less than 5 ohms?	
C8 CHECK THE SPEED CONTROL DEACTIVATOR SWITCH FOR CORRECT OPERATION	
• For gasoline vehicles, while firmly applying and releasing the brake pedal, measure the voltage between the PCM C175a-65, circuit 307 (BK/YE), harness side and ground.	

LTV0500000001743

Fig. 108 Test C, Codes P1572 & P1703: Brake On/Off Circuit Failure (Part 5 of 8). 2005–06 F-Super Duty

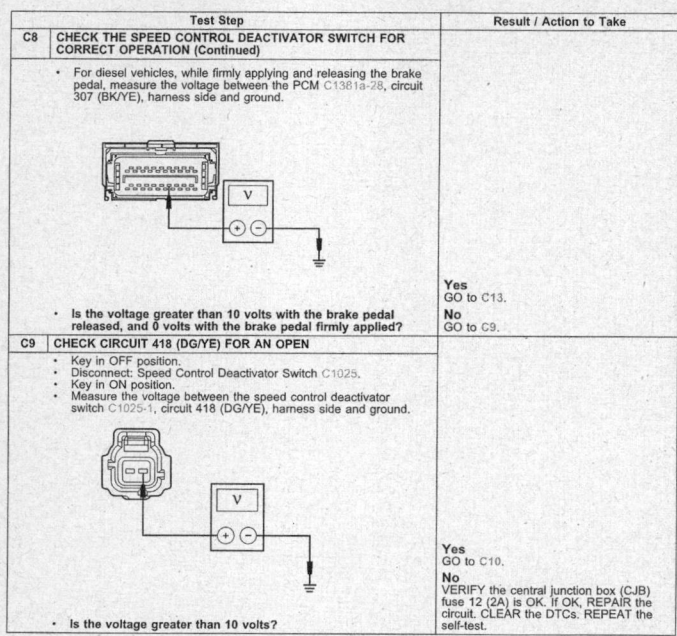

Test Step	Result / Action to Take
C8 CHECK THE SPEED CONTROL DEACTIVATOR SWITCH FOR CORRECT OPERATION (Continued)	
• For diesel vehicles, while firmly applying and releasing the brake pedal, measure the voltage between the PCM C1381a-28, circuit 307 (BK/YE), harness side and ground.	
• Is the voltage greater than 10 volts with the brake pedal released, and 0 volts with the brake pedal firmly applied?	**Yes** GO to C13. **No** GO to C9.
C9 CHECK CIRCUIT 418 (DG/YE) FOR AN OPEN	
• Key in OFF position. • Disconnect: Speed Control Deactivator Switch C1025. • Key in ON position. • Measure the voltage between the speed control deactivator switch C1025-1, circuit 418 (DG/YE), harness side and ground.	
• Is the voltage greater than 10 volts?	**Yes** GO to C10. **No** VERIFY the central junction box (CJB) fuse 12 (2A) is OK. If OK, REPAIR the circuit. CLEAR the DTCs. REPEAT the self-test.

LTV0500000001744

Fig. 108   Test C, Codes P1572 & P1703: Brake On/Off Circuit Failure (Part 6 of 8). 2005–06 F-Super Duty

Test Step	Result / Action to Take
C12 CHECK FOR CORRECT 4WD CONTROL MODULE OPERATION	
• Disconnect all the 4WD control module connectors. • Check for: — corrosion — pushed-out pins • Connect all the 4WD control module connectors and make sure they are seated correctly. • Operate the system and verify the concern is still present. • **Is the concern still present?**	**Yes** INSTALL a new 4WD control module. **No** The system is operating correctly at this time. The concern may have been caused by a loose or corroded connector. CLEAR the DTCs. REPEAT the self-test.
C13 CHECK FOR CORRECT PCM OPERATION	
• Disconnect all the PCM connectors. • Check for: — corrosion — pushed-out pins • Connect all the PCM connectors and make sure they are seated correctly. • Operate the system and verify the concern is still present. • **Is the concern still present?**	**Yes** INSTALL a new PCM. **No** The system is operating correctly at this time. The concern may have been caused by a loose or corroded connector. CLEAR the DTCs. REPEAT the self-test.

LTV0500000001746

Fig. 108   Test C, Codes P1572 & P1703: Brake On/Off Circuit Failure (Part 8 of 8). 2005–06 F-Super Duty

Test Step	Result / Action to Take
D1 CHECK THE SPEED CONTROL SWITCH CIRCUITRY FOR A SHORT TO VOLTAGE	
• Key in ON position. • Turn the parking lamps on. • For gasoline vehicles, measure the voltage between the PCM C175b-19, circuit 151 (LB/BK), harness side and ground; and between the PCM C175b-30, circuit 133 (BK), harness side and ground.	

LTV0500000001747

Fig. 109   Test D, Codes P0579 & P0581: Speed Control Switch Circuit Failure (Part 1 of 9). 2005–06 F-Super Duty

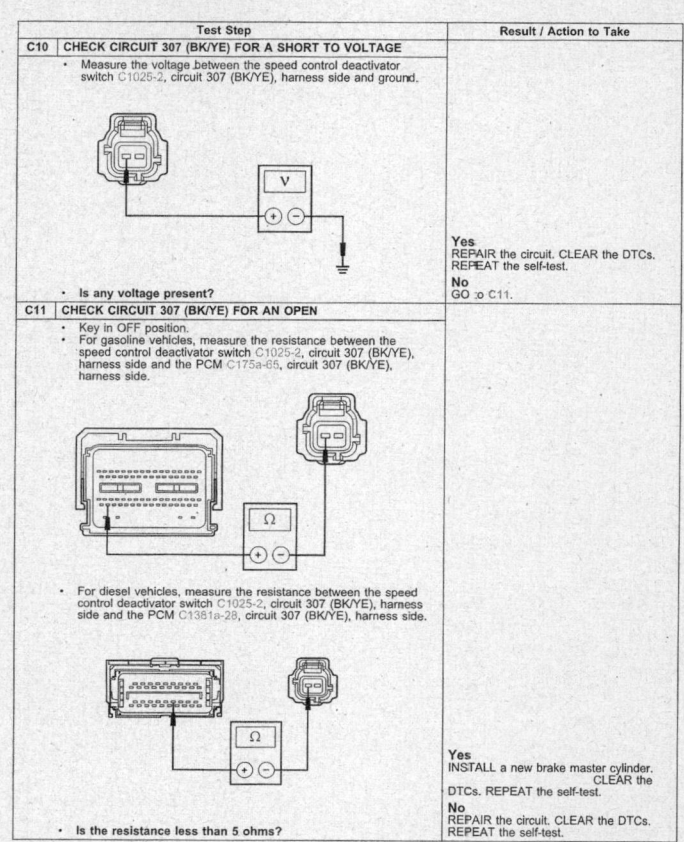

Test Step	Result / Action to Take
C10 CHECK CIRCUIT 307 (BK/YE) FOR A SHORT TO VOLTAGE	
• Measure the voltage between the speed control deactivator switch C1025-2, circuit 307 (BK/YE), harness side and ground.	
• Is any voltage present?	**Yes** REPAIR the circuit. CLEAR the DTCs. REPEAT the self-test. **No** GO to C11.
C11 CHECK CIRCUIT 307 (BK/YE) FOR AN OPEN	
• Key in OFF position. • For gasoline vehicles, measure the resistance between the speed control deactivator switch C1025-2, circuit 307 (BK/YE), harness side and the PCM C175a-65, circuit 307 (BK/YE), harness side.	
• For diesel vehicles, measure the resistance between the speed control deactivator switch C1025-2, circuit 307 (BK/YE), harness side and the PCM C1381a-28, circuit 307 (BK/YE), harness side.	
• Is the resistance less than 5 ohms?	**Yes** INSTALL a new brake master cylinder. CLEAR the DTCs. REPEAT the self-test. **No** REPAIR the circuit. CLEAR the DTCs. REPEAT the self-test.

LTV0500000001745

Fig. 108   Test C, Codes P1572 & P1703: Brake On/Off Circuit Failure (Part 7 of 8). 2005–06 F-Super Duty

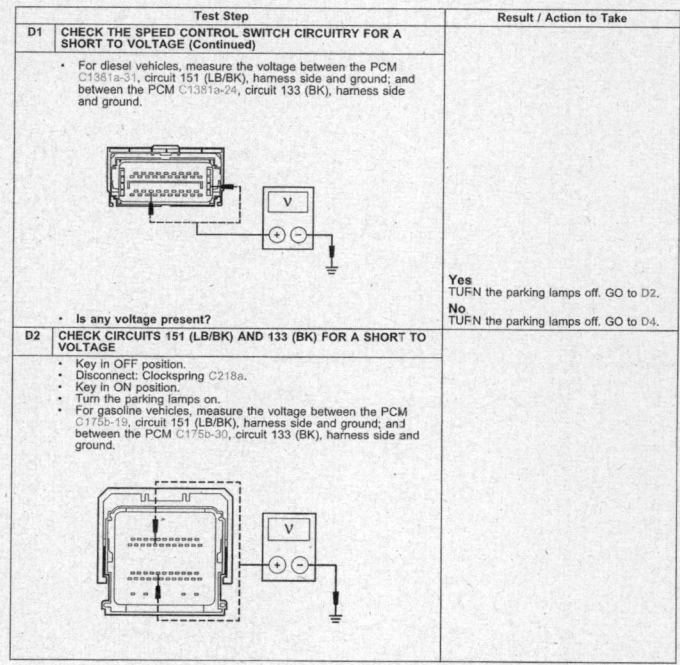

Test Step	Result / Action to Take
D1 CHECK THE SPEED CONTROL SWITCH CIRCUITRY FOR A SHORT TO VOLTAGE (Continued)	
• For diesel vehicles, measure the voltage between the PCM C1381a-31, circuit 151 (LB/BK), harness side and ground; and between the PCM C1381a-24, circuit 133 (BK), harness side and ground.	
• Is any voltage present?	**Yes** TURN the parking lamps off. GO to D2. **No** TURN the parking lamps off. GO to D4.
D2 CHECK CIRCUITS 151 (LB/BK) AND 133 (BK) FOR A SHORT TO VOLTAGE	
• Key in OFF position. • Disconnect: Clockspring C218a. • Key in ON position. • Turn the parking lamps on. • For gasoline vehicles, measure the voltage between the PCM C175b-19, circuit 151 (LB/BK), harness side and ground; and between the PCM C175b-30, circuit 133 (BK), harness side and ground.	

LTV0500000001748

Fig. 109   Test D, Codes P0579 & P0581: Speed Control Switch Circuit Failure (Part 2 of 9). 2005–06 F-Super Duty

Test Step		Result / Action to Take
D2	**CHECK CIRCUITS 151 (LB/BK) AND 133 (BK) FOR A SHORT TO VOLTAGE (Continued)** • For diesel vehicles, measure the voltage between the PCM C1381a-31, circuit 151 (LB/BK), harness side and ground; and between the PCM C1381a-24, circuit 133 (BK), harness side and ground.	
		Yes REPAIR the circuit in question. CLEAR the DTCs. REPEAT the self-test. **No** TURN the parking lamps off. GO to D3.
	• Is any voltage present?	
D3	**CHECK THE CLOCKSPRING FOR A SHORT TO VOLTAGE** • Key in OFF position. • Connect: Clockspring C218a. • Remove the driver air bag module. • Connect the restraint system diagnostic tool (418-F403) to the upper clockspring air bag connector. • Disconnect: Upper Clockspring. ⚠ **WARNING: Make sure there is no one inside the vehicle and that there is nothing blocking or set in front of any air bag module when the battery is connected. Failure to follow these instructions may result in personal injury.** Connect the battery. • Key in ON position. • Turn the parking lamps on. • For gasoline vehicles, measure the voltage between the PCM C175b-19, circuit 151 (LB/BK), harness side and ground; and between the PCM C175b-30, circuit 133 (BK), harness side and ground.	

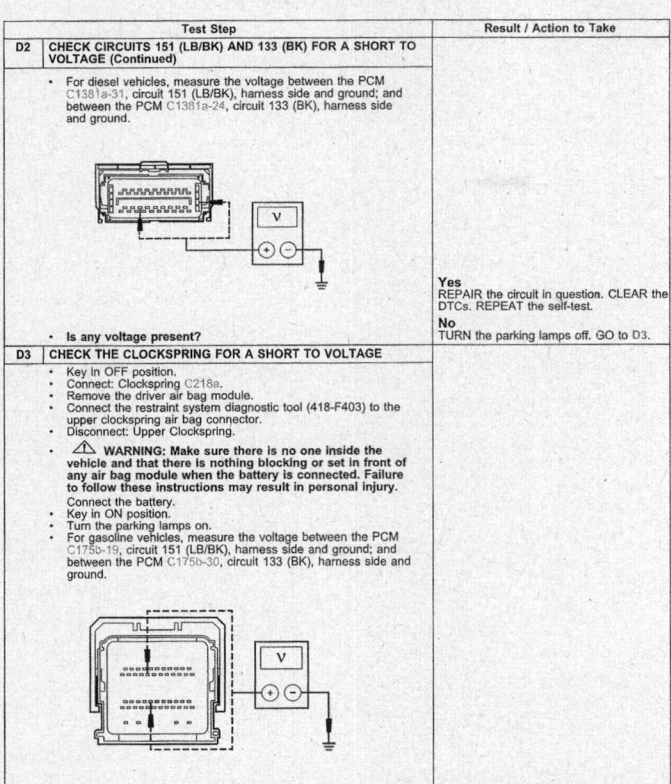

LTV0500000001749

Fig. 109   Test D, Codes P0579 & P0581: Speed Control Switch Circuit Failure (Part 3 of 9). 2005–06 F-Super Duty

Test Step		Result / Action to Take
D4	**CHECK THE SPEED CONTROL SWITCH CIRCUITRY FOR A SHORT TO GROUND (Continued)** • For diesel vehicles, measure the resistance between the PCM C1381a-31, circuit 151 (LB/BK), harness side and ground; and between the PCM C1381a-24, circuit 133 (BK), harness side and ground.	
		Yes GO to D7. **No** GO to D5.
	• Are the resistances greater than 10,000 ohms?	
D5	**CHECK THE CLOCKSPRING FOR A SHORT TO GROUND** • Remove the driver air bag module. • Disconnect: Upper Clockspring. • For gasoline vehicles, measure the resistance between the PCM C175b-19, circuit 151 (LB/BK), harness side and ground; and between the PCM C175b-30, circuit 133 (BK), harness side and ground.	

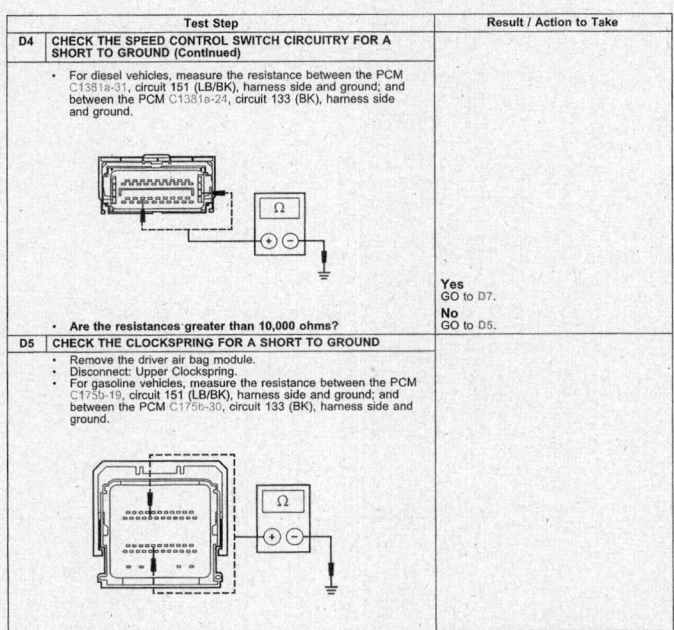

LTV0500000001751

Fig. 109   Test D, Codes P0579 & P0581: Speed Control Switch Circuit Failure (Part 5 of 9). 2005–06 F-Super Duty

Test Step		Result / Action to Take
D3	**CHECK THE CLOCKSPRING FOR A SHORT TO VOLTAGE (Continued)** • For diesel vehicles, measure the voltage between the PCM C1381a-31, circuit 151 (LB/BK), harness side and ground; and between the PCM C1381a-24, circuit 133 (BK), harness side and ground.	
		Yes INSTALL a new clockspring. CLEAR the DTCs. REPEAT the self-test. **No** INSTALL a new speed control switch(es) harness. CLEAR the DTCs. REPEAT the self-test.
	• Is any voltage present?	
D4	**CHECK THE SPEED CONTROL SWITCH CIRCUITRY FOR A SHORT TO GROUND** • Key in OFF position. • For gasoline vehicles, measure the resistance between the PCM C175b-19, circuit 151 (LB/BK), harness side and ground; and between the PCM C175b-30, circuit 133 (BK), harness side and ground.	

LTV0500000001750

Fig. 109   Test D, Codes P0579 & P0581: Speed Control Switch Circuit Failure (Part 4 of 9). 2005–06 F-Super Duty

Test Step		Result / Action to Take
D5	**CHECK THE CLOCKSPRING FOR A SHORT TO GROUND (Continued)** • Measure the resistance between the PCM C1381a-31, circuit 151 (LB/BK), harness side and ground; and between the PCM C1381a-24, circuit 133 (BK), harness side and ground.	
		Yes INSTALL a new speed control switch(es) harness. CLEAR the DTCs. REPEAT the self-test. **No** GO to D6.
	• Are the resistances greater than 10,000 ohms?	
D6	**CHECK CIRCUITS 151 (LB/BK) AND 133 (BK) FOR A SHORT TO GROUND** • Disconnect: Clockspring C218a. • For gasoline vehicles, measure the resistance between the PCM C175b-19, harness side and ground; and between the PCM C175b-30, circuit 133 (BK), harness side and ground.	
	• For diesel vehicles, measure the resistance between the PCM C1381a-31, harness side and ground; and between the PCM C1381a-24, circuit 133 (BK), harness side and ground.	
		Yes INSTALL a new clockspring. CLEAR the DTCs. REPEAT the self-test. **No** REPAIR the circuit in question. CLEAR the DTCs. REPEAT the self-test.
	• Are the resistances greater than 10,000 ohms?	

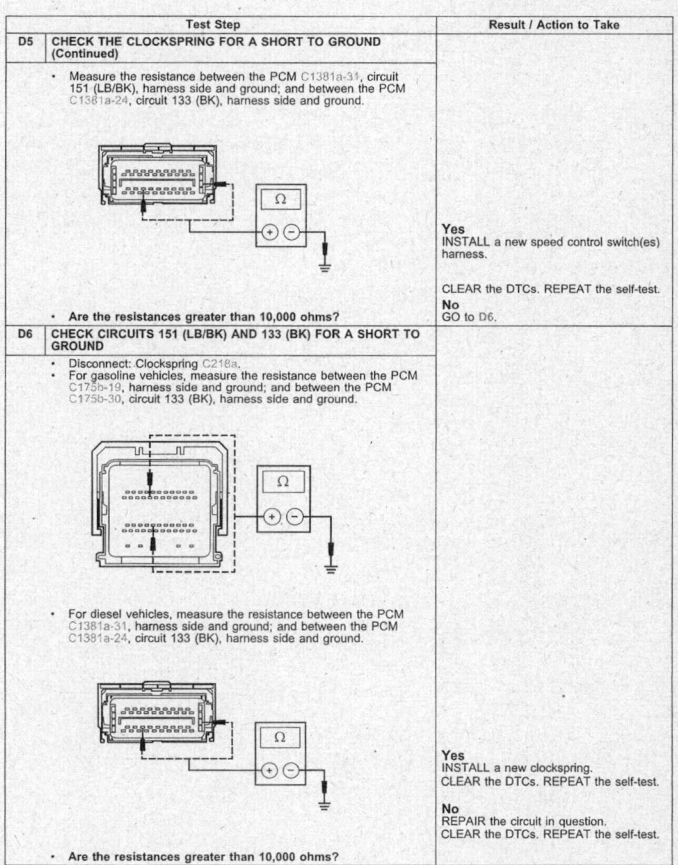

LTV0500000001752

Fig. 109   Test D, Codes P0579 & P0581: Speed Control Switch Circuit Failure (Part 6 of 9). 2005–06 F-Super Duty

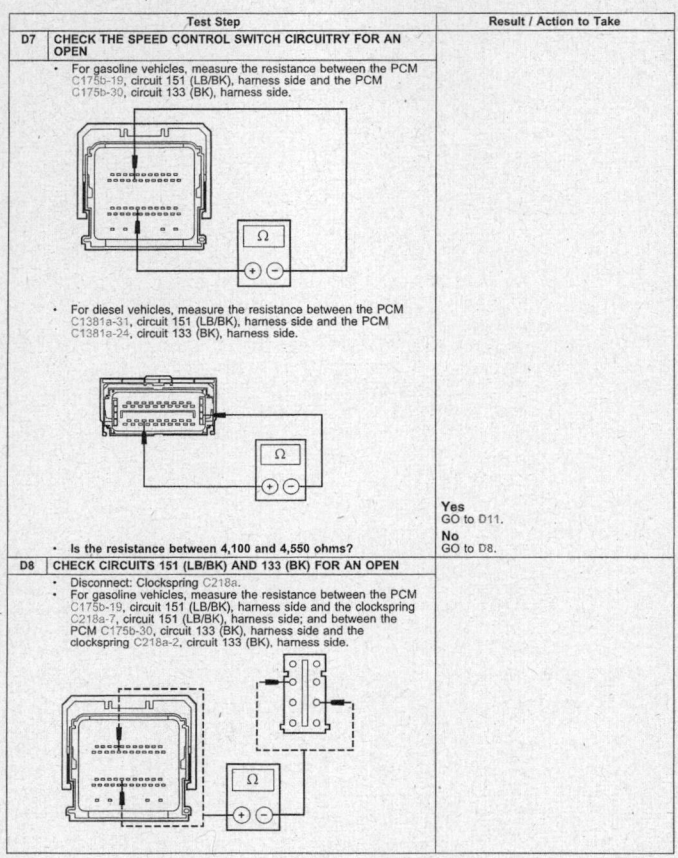

Test Step	Result / Action to Take
D7 CHECK THE SPEED CONTROL SWITCH CIRCUITRY FOR AN OPEN • For gasoline vehicles, measure the resistance between the PCM C175b-19, circuit 151 (LB/BK), harness side and the PCM C175b-30, circuit 133 (BK), harness side.	
• For diesel vehicles, measure the resistance between the PCM C1381a-31, circuit 151 (LB/BK), harness side and the PCM C1381a-24, circuit 133 (BK), harness side.	**Yes** GO to D11. **No** GO to D8.
• **Is the resistance between 4,100 and 4,550 ohms?**	
D8 CHECK CIRCUITS 151 (LB/BK) AND 133 (BK) FOR AN OPEN • Disconnect: Clockspring C218a. • For gasoline vehicles, measure the resistance between the PCM C175b-19, circuit 151 (LB/BK), harness side and the clockspring C218a-7, circuit 151 (LB/BK), harness side; and between the PCM C175b-30, circuit 133 (BK), harness side and the clockspring C218a-2, circuit 133 (BK), harness side.	

LTV0500000001753

Fig. 109   Test D, Codes P0579 & P0581: Speed Control Switch Circuit Failure (Part 7 of 9). 2005–06 F-Super Duty

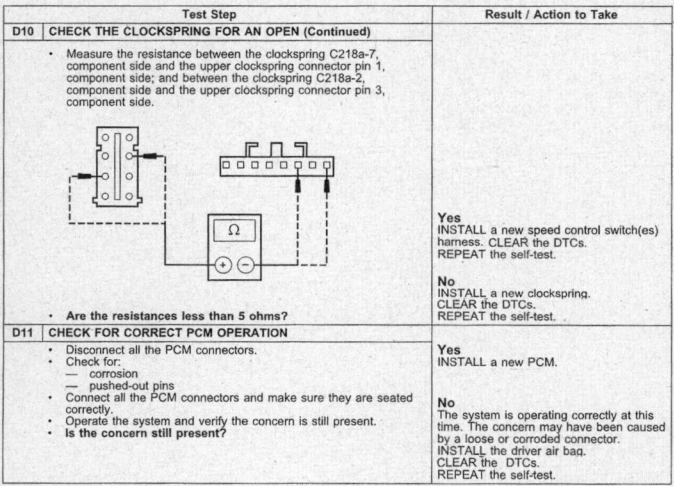

Test Step	Result / Action to Take
D10 CHECK THE CLOCKSPRING FOR AN OPEN (Continued) • Measure the resistance between the clockspring C218a-7, component side and the upper clockspring connector pin 1, component side; and between the clockspring C218a-2, component side and the upper clockspring connector pin 3, component side.	
• **Are the resistances less than 5 ohms?**	**Yes** INSTALL a new speed control switch(es) harness. CLEAR the DTCs. REPEAT the self-test. **No** INSTALL a new clockspring. CLEAR the DTCs. REPEAT the self-test.
D11 CHECK FOR CORRECT PCM OPERATION • Disconnect all the PCM connectors. • Check for: — corrosion — pushed-out pins • Connect all the PCM connectors and make sure they are seated correctly. • Operate the system and verify the concern is still present. • **Is the concern still present?**	**Yes** INSTALL a new PCM. **No** The system is operating correctly at this time. The concern may have been caused by a loose or corroded connector. INSTALL the driver air bag. CLEAR the DTCs. REPEAT the self-test.

LTV0500000001755

Fig. 109   Test D, Codes P0579 & P0581: Speed Control Switch Circuit Failure (Part 9 of 9). 2005–06 F-Super Duty

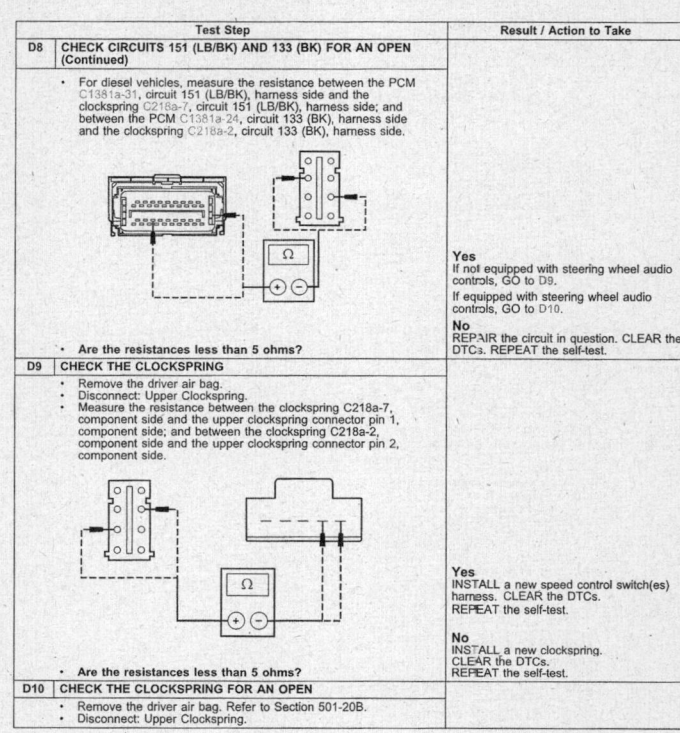

Test Step	Result / Action to Take
D8 CHECK CIRCUITS 151 (LB/BK) AND 133 (BK) FOR AN OPEN (Continued) • For diesel vehicles, measure the resistance between the PCM C1381a-31, circuit 151 (LB/BK), harness side and the clockspring C218a-7, circuit 151 (LB/BK), harness side; and between the PCM C1381a-24, circuit 133 (BK), harness side and the clockspring C218a-2, circuit 133 (BK), harness side.	
• **Are the resistances less than 5 ohms?**	**Yes** If not equipped with steering wheel audio controls, GO to D9. If equipped with steering wheel audio controls, GO to D10. **No** REPAIR the circuit in question. CLEAR the DTCs.
D9 CHECK THE CLOCKSPRING • Remove the driver air bag. • Disconnect: Upper Clockspring. • Measure the resistance between the clockspring C218a-7, component side and the upper clockspring connector pin 1, component side; and between the clockspring C218a-2, component side and the upper clockspring connector pin 2, component side.	
• **Are the resistances less than 5 ohms?**	**Yes** INSTALL a new speed control switch(es) harness. CLEAR the DTCs. REPEAT the self-test. **No** INSTALL a new clockspring. CLEAR the DTCs. REPEAT the self-test.
D10 CHECK THE CLOCKSPRING FOR AN OPEN • Remove the driver air bag. Refer to Section 501-20B. • Disconnect: Upper Clockspring.	

LTV0500000001754

Fig. 109   Test D, Codes P0579 & P0581: Speed Control Switch Circuit Failure (Part 8 of 9). 2005–06 F-Super Duty

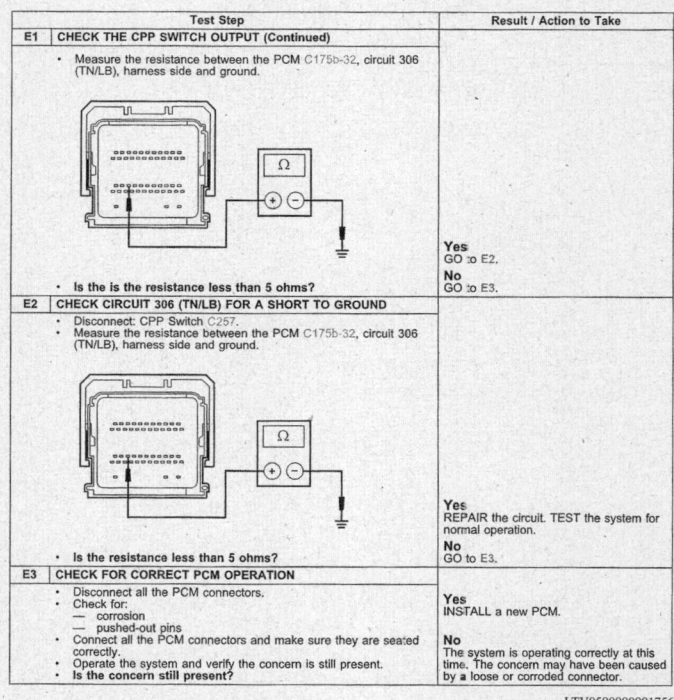

Test Step	Result / Action to Take
E1 CHECK THE CPP SWITCH OUTPUT (Continued) • Measure the resistance between the PCM C175b-32, circuit 306 (TN/LB), harness side and ground.	
• **Is the is the resistance less than 5 ohms?**	**Yes** GO to E2. **No** GO to E3.
E2 CHECK CIRCUIT 306 (TN/LB) FOR A SHORT TO GROUND • Disconnect: CPP Switch C257. • Measure the resistance between the PCM C175b-32, circuit 306 (TN/LB), harness side and ground.	
• **Is the resistance less than 5 ohms?**	**Yes** REPAIR the circuit. TEST the system for normal operation. **No** GO to E3.
E3 CHECK FOR CORRECT PCM OPERATION • Disconnect all the PCM connectors. • Check for: — corrosion — pushed-out pins • Connect all the PCM connectors and make sure they are seated correctly. • Operate the system and verify the concern is still present. • **Is the concern still present?**	**Yes** INSTALL a new PCM. **No** The system is operating correctly at this time. The concern may have been caused by a loose or corroded connector.

LTV0500000001756

Fig. 110   Test E: Speed Control Does Not Disengage When Clutch Is Applied. 2005–06 F-Super Duty w/gasoline engine

Test Step	Result / Action to Take
F1 CHECK THE CPP SWITCH OUTPUT	
• Disconnect: PCM C1381a. • Measure the voltage between the PCM C1318a-36, circuit 306 (TN/LB), harness side and ground. 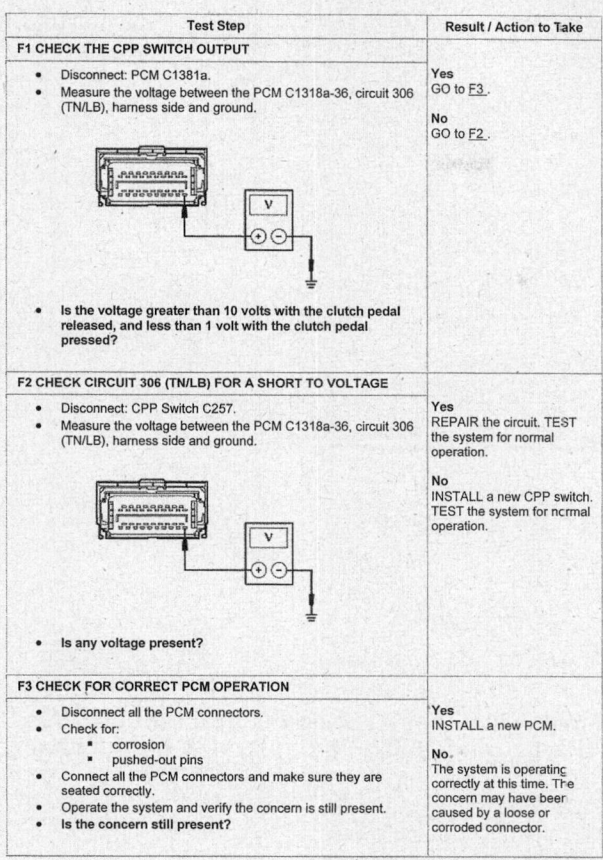 • Is the voltage greater than 10 volts with the clutch pedal released, and less than 1 volt with the clutch pedal pressed?	**Yes** GO to F3. **No** GO to F2.
F2 CHECK CIRCUIT 306 (TN/LB) FOR A SHORT TO VOLTAGE	
• Disconnect: CPP Switch C257. • Measure the voltage between the PCM C1318a-36, circuit 306 (TN/LB), harness side and ground. • Is any voltage present?	**Yes** REPAIR the circuit. TEST the system for normal operation. **No** INSTALL a new CPP switch. TEST the system for normal operation.
F3 CHECK FOR CORRECT PCM OPERATION	

• Disconnect all the PCM connectors.
• Check for:
  ▪ corrosion
  ▪ pushed-out pins
• Connect all the PCM connectors and make sure they are seated correctly.
• Operate the system and verify the concern is still present.
• **Is the concern still present?**
	Yes
	INSTALL a new PCM.
	
	No.
	The system is operating correctly at this time. The concern may have been caused by a loose or corroded connector.

LTV0500000001757

Fig. 111   Test F: Speed Control Does Not Disengage When Clutch Is Applied. 2005–06 F-Super Duty w/diesel engine

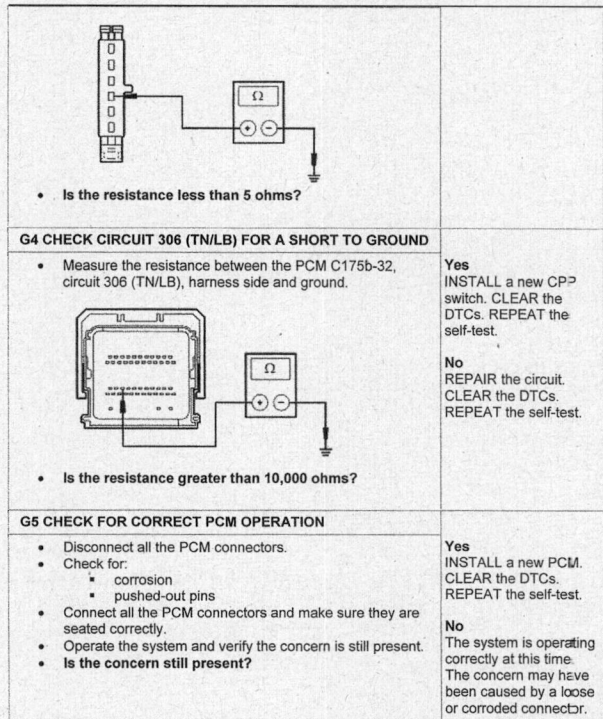

Test Step	Result / Action to Take
• Is the resistance less than 5 ohms?	
G4 CHECK CIRCUIT 306 (TN/LB) FOR A SHORT TO GROUND	
• Measure the resistance between the PCM C175b-32, circuit 306 (TN/LB), harness side and ground. • Is the resistance greater than 10,000 ohms?	**Yes** INSTALL a new CPP switch. CLEAR the DTCs. REPEAT the self-test. **No** REPAIR the circuit. CLEAR the DTCs. REPEAT the self-test.
G5 CHECK FOR CORRECT PCM OPERATION	

• Disconnect all the PCM connectors.
• Check for:
  ▪ corrosion
  ▪ pushed-out pins
• Connect all the PCM connectors and make sure they are seated correctly.
• Operate the system and verify the concern is still present.
• **Is the concern still present?**
	Yes
	INSTALL a new PCM. CLEAR the DTCs. REPEAT the self-test.
	
	No
	The system is operating correctly at this time. The concern may have been caused by a loose or corroded connector.

LTV0500000001759

Fig. 112   Test G, Code P0833: Clutch Pedal Switch B Circuit (Part 2 of 2). 2005–06 F-Super Duty w/gasoline engine

Test Step	Result / Action to Take
G1 CHECK THE CPP SWITCH	
• Key in OFF position. • Disconnect: PCM C175b. • While pressing and releasing the clutch pedal, measure the resistance between the PCM C175b-32, circuit 306 (TN/LB), harness side and ground. 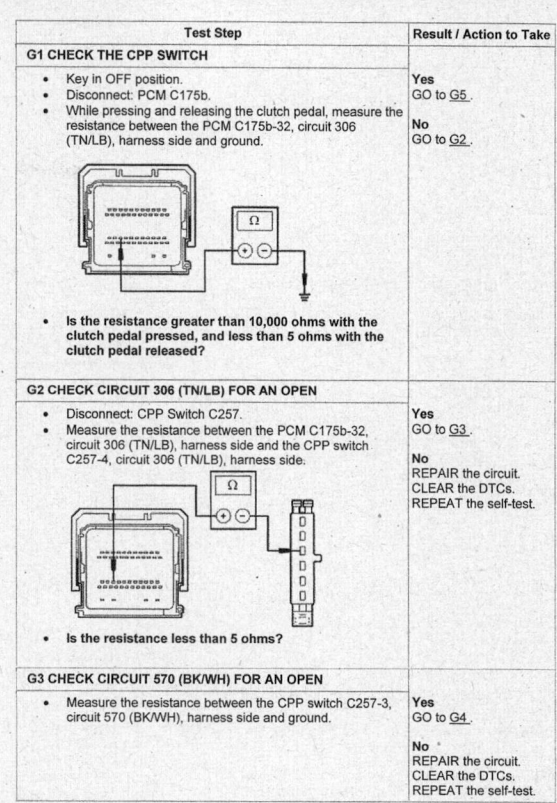 • Is the resistance greater than 10,000 ohms with the clutch pedal pressed, and less than 5 ohms with the clutch pedal released?	**Yes** GO to G5. **No** GO to G2.
G2 CHECK CIRCUIT 306 (TN/LB) FOR AN OPEN	
• Disconnect: CPP Switch C257. • Measure the resistance between the PCM C175b-32, circuit 306 (TN/LB), harness side and the CPP switch C257-4, circuit 306 (TN/LB), harness side. • Is the resistance less than 5 ohms?	**Yes** GO to G3. **No** REPAIR the circuit. CLEAR the DTCs. REPEAT the self-test.
G3 CHECK CIRCUIT 570 (BK/WH) FOR AN OPEN	
• Measure the resistance between the CPP switch C257-3, circuit 570 (BK/WH), harness side and ground.	**Yes** GO to G4. **No** REPAIR the circuit. CLEAR the DTCs. REPEAT the self-test.

LTV0500000001758

Fig. 112   Test G, Code P0833: Clutch Pedal Switch B Circuit (Part 1 of 2). 2005–06 F-Super Duty w/gasoline engine

Test Step	Result / Action to Take
H1 CHECK THE CPP SWITCH	
• Key in OFF position. • Disconnect: PCM C1381a. • While pressing and releasing the clutch pedal, measure the voltage between the PCM C1381a-36, circuit 306 (TN/LB), harness side and ground. • Is the voltage greater than 10 volts with the clutch pedal released, and less than 1 volt with the clutch pedal pressed?	**Yes** GO to H5. **No** GO to H2.
H2 CHECK CIRCUIT 306 (TN/LB) FOR A SHORT TO VOLTAGE	
• Disconnect: CPP Switch C257. • Measure the voltage between the PCM C1318a-36, circuit 306 (TN/LB), harness side and ground. • Is any voltage present?	**Yes** REPAIR the circuit. TEST the system for normal operation. **No** GO to H3.
H3 CHECK CIRCUIT 306 (TN/LB) FOR AN OPEN	
• Disconnect: CPP Switch C257. • Measure the resistance between the PCM C1381a-36, circuit 306 (TN/LB), harness side and the CPP switch C257-4, circuit 306 (TN/LB), harness side.	**Yes** GO to H4. **No** REPAIR the circuit. TEST the system for normal operation.

LTV0500000001760

Fig. 113   Test H, Code P0833: Clutch Pedal Switch B Circuit (Part 1 of 2). 2005–06 F-Super Duty w/diesel engine

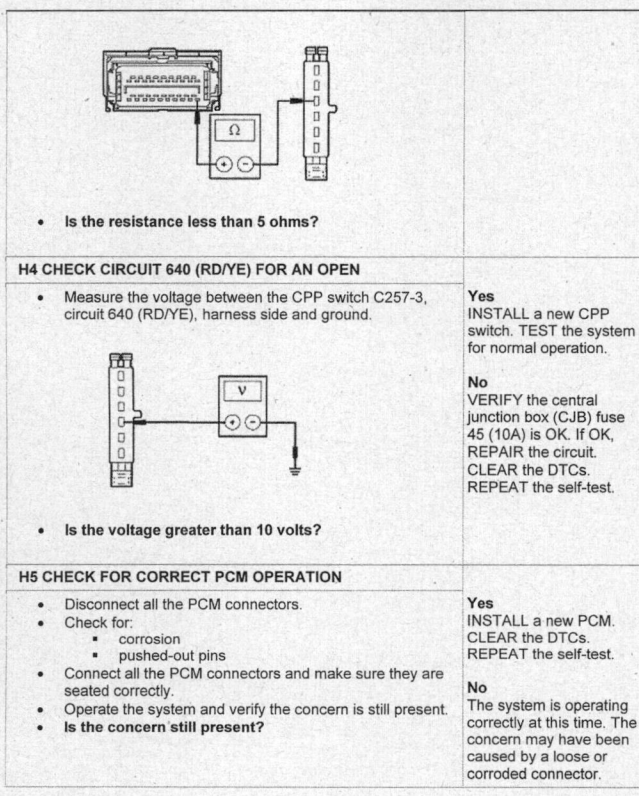

- **Is the resistance less than 5 ohms?**

H4 CHECK CIRCUIT 640 (RD/YE) FOR AN OPEN

• Measure the voltage between the CPP switch C257-3, circuit 640 (RD/YE), harness side and ground.	**Yes** INSTALL a new CPP switch. TEST the system for normal operation. **No** VERIFY the central junction box (CJB) fuse 45 (10A) is OK. If OK, REPAIR the circuit. CLEAR the DTCs. REPEAT the self-test.
• **Is the voltage greater than 10 volts?**	

H5 CHECK FOR CORRECT PCM OPERATION

• Disconnect all the PCM connectors. • Check for: ▪ corrosion ▪ pushed-out pins • Connect all the PCM connectors and make sure they are seated correctly. • Operate the system and verify the concern is still present. • **Is the concern still present?**	**Yes** INSTALL a new PCM. CLEAR the DTCs. REPEAT the self-test. **No** The system is operating correctly at this time. The concern may have been caused by a loose or corroded connector.

LTV0500000001761

Fig. 113 Test H, Code P0833: Clutch Pedal Switch B Circuit (Part 2 of 2). 2005–06 F-Super Duty w/diesel engine

Test Step	Result / Action to Take
A3 CHECK CIRCUITS 151 (LB/BK) AND 848 (DG/OG) FOR AN OPEN • Measure the resistance between the PCM C175b-19, circuit 151 (LB/BK), harness side and the clockspring C218a-4, circuit 151 (LB/BK), harness side; and between the PCM C175b-30, circuit 848 (DG/OG), harness side and the clockspring C218a-5, circuit 848 (DG/OG), harness side. • **Are the resistances less than 5 ohms?**	**Yes** GO to A4. **No** REPAIR the circuit in question. CLEAR the DTCs. REPEAT the self-test.
A4 CHECK THE CLOCKSPRING • Remove the driver air bag module. • Disconnect: Upper Clockspring. • Measure the resistance between the clockspring C218a-4, circuit 151 (LB/BK), (component side) and the upper clockspring pin 4, (component side); and measure the resistance between the clockspring C218a-5, circuit 848 (DG/OG), (component side) and the upper clockspring pin 5, (component side). • **Are the resistances less than 5 ohms?**	**Yes** GO to A5. **No** INSTALL a new clockspring. CLEAR the DTCs. REPEAT the self-test.
A5 CHECK THE HORN SWITCH WIRING HARNESS • Disconnect: Horn Switch Wiring Harness Connector. • Inspect the horn switch wiring harness for shorts, opens or any damage. • **Is the horn switch wiring harness OK?**	**Yes** GO to A6. **No** REPAIR or INSTALL a new horn switch wiring harness. CLEAR the DTCs. REPEAT the self-test.
A6 CHECK THE SPEED CONTROL SWITCH • Connect: Horn Switch Wiring Harness Connector. • Measure the resistance between the horn switch harness connector pin 4, harness side and the horn switch harness connector pin 5, harness side while pressing the following switches:	

LTV0500000001437

Fig. 114 Test A: Speed Control Inoperative (Part 2 of 5). 2002–04 Explorer & Mountaineer

Test Step	Result / Action to Take
A1 CHECK CIRCUITS 151 (LB/BK) AND 848 (DG/OG) FOR SHORT TO BATTERY • Key in OFF position • Disconnect: PCM C175b. • Disconnect: Clockspring C218a. • Key in ON position. • Measure the voltage between the PCM C175b-19, circuit 151 (LB/BK), harness side and ground; and between the PCM C175b-30, circuit 848 (DG/OG), harness side and ground. • **Is any voltage present?**	**Yes** REPAIR the circuit in question. CLEAR the DTCs. REPEAT the self-test. **No** GO to A2.
A2 CHECK CIRCUITS 151 (LB/BK) AND 848 (DG/OG) FOR SHORT TO GROUND • Key in OFF position • Measure the resistance between the PCM C175b-19, circuit 151 (LB/BK), harness side and ground; and between the PCM C175b-30, circuit 848 (DG/OG), harness side and ground. • **Are the resistances greater than 10,000 ohms?**	**Yes** GO to A3. **No** REPAIR the circuit in question. CLEAR the DTCs. REPEAT the self-test.

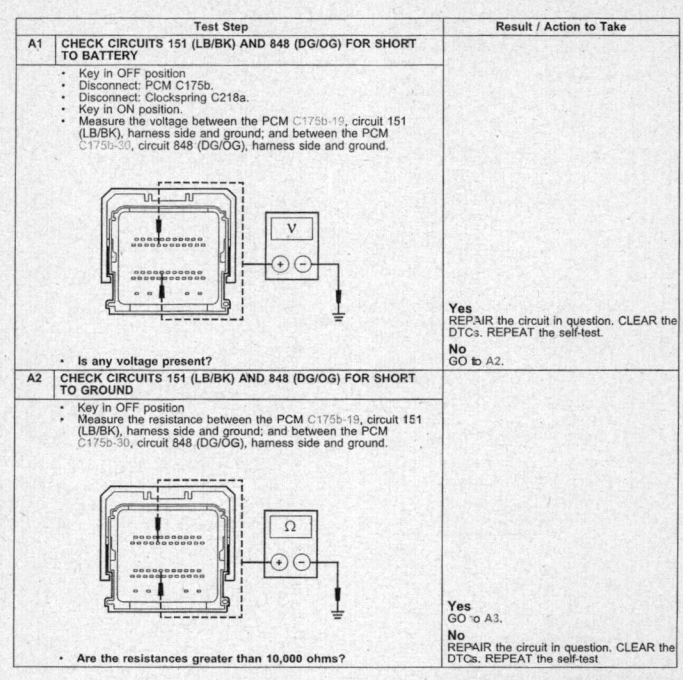

LTV0500000001436

Fig. 114 Test A: Speed Control Inoperative (Part 1 of 5). 2002–04 Explorer & Mountaineer

Test Step	Result / Action to Take
A6 CHECK THE SPEED CONTROL SWITCH (Continued)	

Speed Control Switch

Speed Control Switch	Resistance Value
SET-	Between 285 and 315 ohms
SET+	Between 570 and 630 ohms
RESUME	Between 1,055 and 1,165 ohms
ON	Between 1,995 and 2,205 ohms
OFF	Less than 5 ohms

• **Are the speed control switch resistance values OK?**	**Yes** INSTALL the driver air bag. GO to A7. **No** INSTALL a new speed control switch. CLEAR the DTCs. REPEAT the self-test.
A7 CHECK THE DEACTIVATOR SWITCH CIRCUITRY • Measure the voltage between the PCM C175b-7, circuit 307 (BK/YE), harness side and ground, while firmly pressing and releasing the brake pedal. • **Is the voltage 0 volts with the brake pedal firmly pressed, and greater than 10 volts with the brake pedal released?**	**Yes** GO to A11. **No** GO to A8.

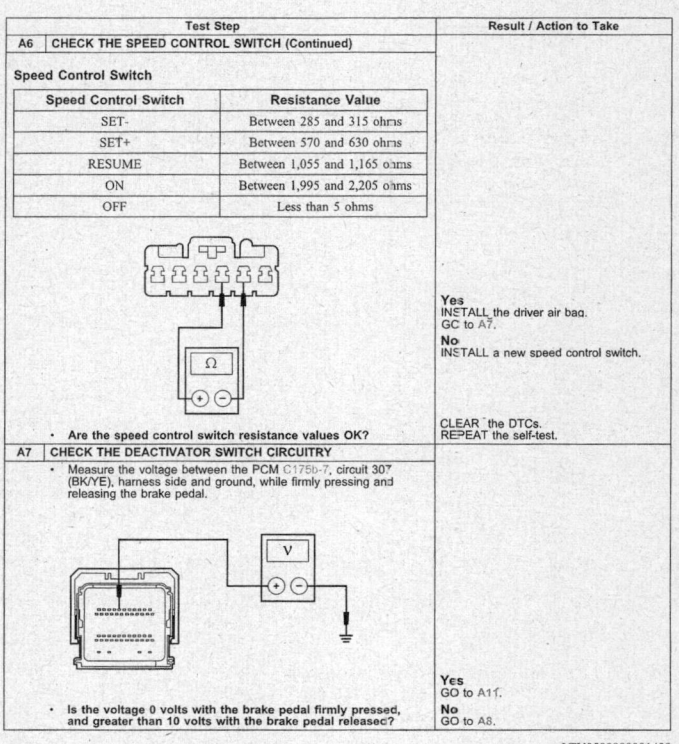

LTV0500000001438

Fig. 114 Test A: Speed Control Inoperative (Part 3 of 5). 2002–04 Explorer & Mountaineer

Test Step	Result / Action to Take
A8	**CHECK THE DEACTIVATOR SWITCH**
• Disconnect: Deactivator Switch C1025.	
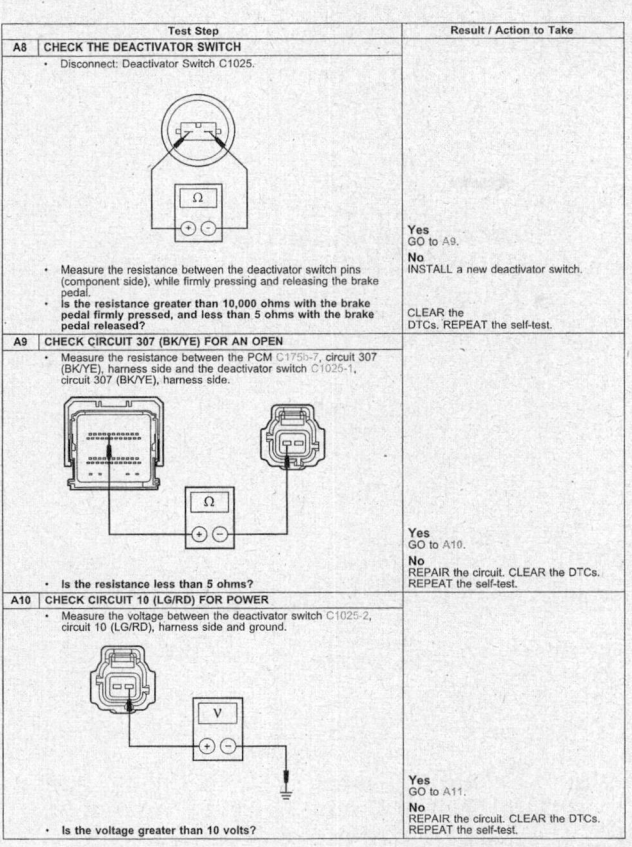	
• Measure the resistance between the deactivator switch pins (component side), while firmly pressing and releasing the brake pedal.	**Yes** GO to A9.
• Is the resistance greater than 10,000 ohms with the brake pedal firmly pressed, and less than 5 ohms with the brake pedal released?	**No** INSTALL a new deactivator switch. CLEAR the DTCs. REPEAT the self-test.
A9	**CHECK CIRCUIT 307 (BK/YE) FOR AN OPEN**
• Measure the resistance between the PCM C175b-7, circuit 307 (BK/YE), harness side and the deactivator switch C1025-1, circuit 307 (BK/YE), harness side.	
• Is the resistance less than 5 ohms?	**Yes** GO to A10. **No** REPAIR the circuit. CLEAR the DTCs. REPEAT the self-test.
A10	**CHECK CIRCUIT 10 (LG/RD) FOR POWER**
• Measure the voltage between the deactivator switch C1025-2, circuit 10 (LG/RD), harness side and ground.	
• Is the voltage greater than 10 volts?	**Yes** GO to A11. **No** REPAIR the circuit. CLEAR the DTCs. REPEAT the self-test.

LTV0500000001439

Fig. 114 Test A: Speed Control Inoperative (Part 4 of 5). 2002–04 Explorer & Mountaineer

Test Step	Result / Action to Take
A1	**CHECK FOR DIAGNOSTIC TROUBLE CODES (DTCs)**
• Review the recorded DTCs from the PCM self-test.	**Yes** REFER to the Powertrain Control Module (PCM) Diagnostic Trouble Code (DTC) Index for correct diagnosis.
• Are any DTCs recorded?	**No** GO to A2.
A2	**CHECK THE STOPLAMP SWITCH**
• Key in ON position.	
• Enter the following diagnostic mode on the diagnostic tool: PCM Stoplamp Switch PID.	**Yes** GO to A3.
• Monitor the PCM stoplamp switch PID.	
• Apply and release the brake pedal.	**No**
• Does the PID value agree with the brake pedal position?	GO to Pinpoint Test B.
A3	**CHECK THE SPEED CONTROL SWITCH**
• Key in OFF position.	
• Disconnect: PCM C175b.	
• Measure the resistance between the PCM C175b-19, circuit VES10 (WH), harness side and the PCM C175b-30, circuit RES08 (GN/BN), harness side while pressing the speed control switches as follows:	

Speed Control Switch	Resistance Value
OFF	Less than 5 ohms
SET -	285 - 315 ohms
SET +	570 - 630 ohms
RESUME	1,055 - 1,166 ohms
ON	2,005 - 2,216 ohms
No switch pressed	4,103 - 4,535 ohms

Test Step	Result / Action to Take
• Are the speed control switch resistance values OK?	**Yes** GO to A4. **No** INSTALL a new speed control switch. TEST the system for normal operation.
A4	**CHECK THE DIGITAL TR SENSOR**
• Connect: PCM C175b.	
• Apply the parking brake.	
• Key in ON position.	
• Enter the following diagnostic mode on the diagnostic tool: PCM TR Sensor PID.	**Yes** GO to A5.
• Monitor the PCM TR sensor PID.	
• Select DRIVE.	**No**
• Does the PID value agree with the transmission range selector lever position?	Diagnose the digital TR sensor.

LTV0500000001441

Fig. 115 Test A: Speed Control Is Inoperative (Part 1 of 2). 2005–06 Explorer & Mountaineer

Test Step	Result / Action to Take
A11	**CHECK FOR CORRECT PCM OPERATION**
• Disconnect all the PCM connectors.	**Yes** INSTALL a new PCM. CLEAR the DTCs. REPEAT the self-test.
• Check for:	
• corrosion	**No**
• pushed-out pins	The system is operating correctly at this time. Concern may have been caused by a loose or corroded connector. CLEAR the DTCs. REPEAT the self-test.
• Connect all PCM connectors and make sure they are seated correctly.	
• Operate the system and verify the concern is still present.	
• **Is the concern still present?**	

LTV0500000001440

Fig. 114 Test A: Speed Control Inoperative (Part 5 of 5). 2002–04 Explorer & Mountaineer

Test Step	Result / Action to Take
A5	**CHECK THE DIGITAL TR SENSOR FOR CORRECT ALIGNMENT**
• Check the digital TR sensor alignment	**Yes** GO to A6.
• **Is the digital TR sensor aligned correctly?**	**No** ADJUST the digital TR sensor. TEST the system for normal operation.
A6	**CHECK THE VEHICLE SPEED**
NOTE: This step may require an assistant.	
• Enter the following diagnostic mode on the diagnostic tool: Anti-lock Brake System (ABS) Module Wheel Speed PID.	
• Monitor and record the ABS module wheel speed PID while driving the vehicle at 48 km/h (30 mph) as indicated on the speedometer.	**Yes** GO to A7.
• Enter the following diagnostic mode on the diagnostic tool: PCM Vehicle Speed PID.	**No** REFER to MOTOR's "Domestic Engine Performance & Driveability Manual" to diagnose the output shaft speed (OSS) sensor signal.
• Monitor and record the PCM vehicle speed PID while driving the vehicle at 48 km/h (30 mph).	
• **Does the speed indicated by the ABS module wheel speed PID match the PCM vehicle speed PID?**	
A7	**CHECK FOR CORRECT PCM OPERATION**
• Disconnect all the PCM connectors.	**Yes** INSTALL a new PCM. TEST the system for normal operation.
• Check for:	
— corrosion	**No**
— pushed-out pins	The system is operating correctly at this time. The concern may have been caused by a loose or corroded connector.
• Connect all PCM connectors and make sure they seat correctly.	
• Operate the system and verify the concern is still present.	
• **Is the concern still present?**	

LTV0500000001442

Fig. 115 Test A: Speed Control Is Inoperative (Part 2 of 2). 2005–06 Explorer & Mountaineer

Test Step	Result / Action to Take
B1	**CHECK THE OPERATION OF THE STOPLAMPS**
• Key in ON position.	**Yes** GO to B2.
• Operate the stoplamps.	**No** Diagnose stoplamps.
• **Do the stoplamps operate correctly?**	
B2	**CHECK CIRCUIT A__CCB08 (VT/WH) FOR VOLTAGE**
• Key in OFF position.	
• Disconnect: PCM C175b.	
• Key in ON position.	

LTV0500000001443

Fig. 116 Test B, Codes P1572 & P1703: Brake On/Off Circuit Failure (Part 1 of 4). 2005–06 Explorer & Mountaineer

Test Step	Result / Action to Take
B2	**CHECK CIRCUIT A__CCB08 (VT/WH) FOR VOLTAGE (Continued)**
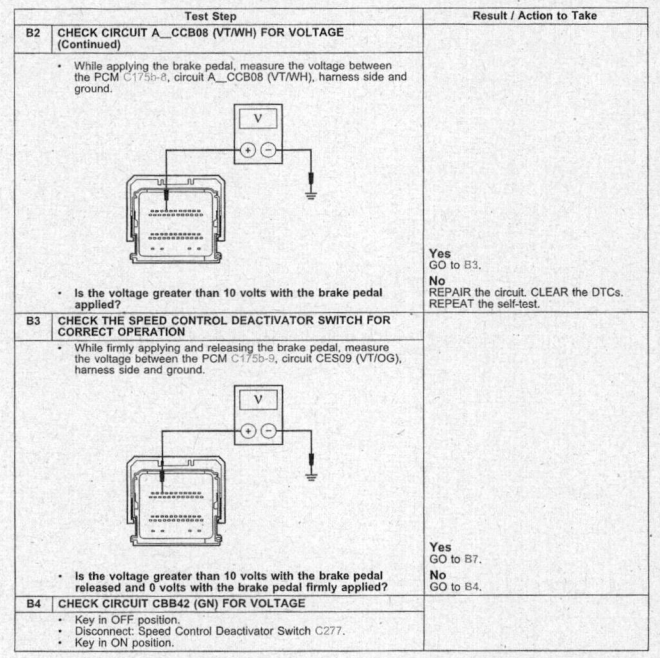	
• While applying the brake pedal, measure the voltage between the PCM C175b-8, circuit A__CCB08 (VT/WH), harness side and ground.	**Yes** GO to B3.
• Is the voltage greater than 10 volts with the brake pedal applied?	**No** REPAIR the circuit. CLEAR the DTCs. REPEAT the self-test.
B3	**CHECK THE SPEED CONTROL DEACTIVATOR SWITCH FOR CORRECT OPERATION**
• While firmly applying and releasing the brake pedal, measure the voltage between the PCM C175b-9, circuit CES09 (VT/OG), harness side and ground.	**Yes** GO to B7.
• Is the voltage greater than 10 volts with the brake pedal released and 0 volts with the brake pedal firmly applied?	**No** GO to B4.
B4	**CHECK CIRCUIT CBB42 (GN) FOR VOLTAGE**
• Key in OFF position.	
• Disconnect: Speed Control Deactivator Switch C277.	
• Key in ON position.	

LTV0500000001444

Fig. 116 Test B, Codes P1572 & P1703: Brake On/Off Circuit Failure (Part 2 of 4). 2005–06 Explorer & Mountaineer

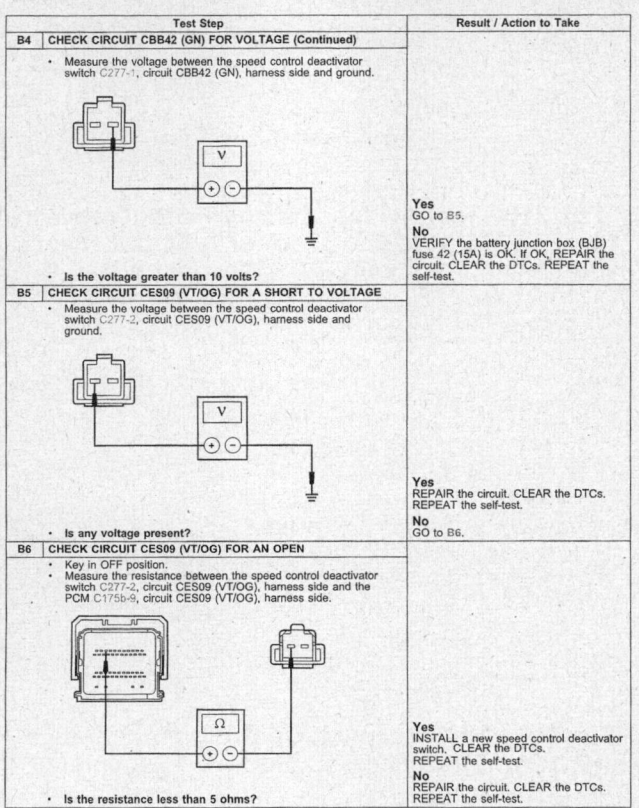

Test Step	Result / Action to Take
B4 CHECK CIRCUIT CBB42 (GN) FOR VOLTAGE (Continued)	
• Measure the voltage between the speed control deactivator switch C277-1, circuit CBB42 (GN), harness side and ground.	**Yes** GO to B5. **No** VERIFY the battery junction box (BJB) fuse 42 (15A) is OK. If OK, REPAIR the circuit. CLEAR the DTCs. REPEAT the self-test.
• Is the voltage greater than 10 volts?	
B5 CHECK CIRCUIT CES09 (VT/OG) FOR A SHORT TO VOLTAGE	
• Measure the voltage between the speed control deactivator switch C277-2, circuit CES09 (VT/OG), harness side and ground.	**Yes** REPAIR the circuit. CLEAR the DTCs. REPEAT the self-test. **No** GO to B6.
• Is any voltage present?	
B6 CHECK CIRCUIT CES09 (VT/OG) FOR AN OPEN	
• Key in OFF position. • Measure the resistance between the speed control deactivator switch C277-2, circuit CES09 (VT/OG), harness side and the PCM C175b-9, circuit CES09 (VT/OG), harness side.	**Yes** INSTALL a new speed control deactivator switch. CLEAR the DTCs. REPEAT the self-test. **No** REPAIR the circuit. CLEAR the DTCs. REPEAT the self-test.
• Is the resistance less than 5 ohms?	

LTV0500000001445

Fig. 116   Test B, Codes P1572 & P1703: Brake On/Off Circuit Failure (Part 3 of 4). 2005–06 Explorer & Mountaineer

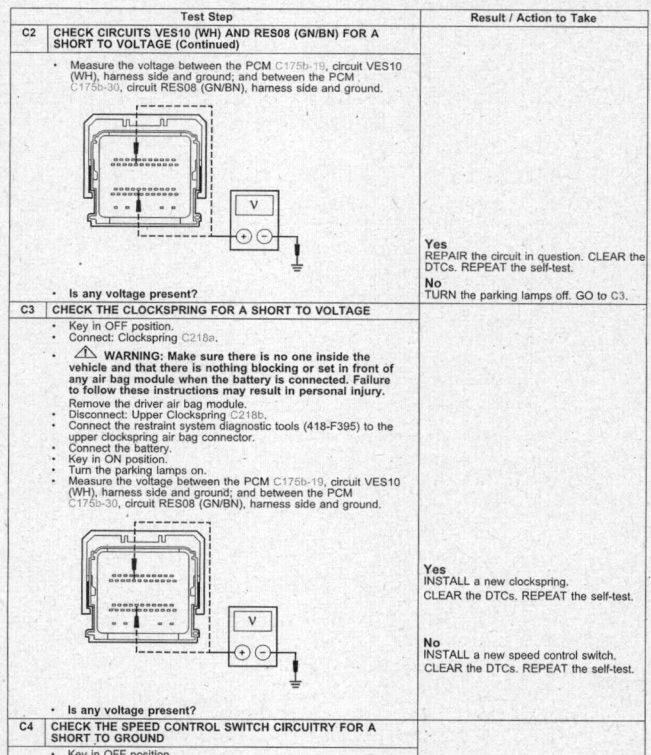

Test Step	Result / Action to Take
C2 CHECK CIRCUITS VES10 (WH) AND RES08 (GN/BN) FOR A SHORT TO VOLTAGE (Continued)	
• Measure the voltage between the PCM C175b-19, circuit VES10 (WH), harness side and ground; and between the PCM C175b-30, circuit RES08 (GN/BN), harness side and ground.	**Yes** REPAIR the circuit in question. CLEAR the DTCs. REPEAT the self-test. **No** TURN the parking lamps off. GO to C3.
• Is any voltage present?	
C3 CHECK THE CLOCKSPRING FOR A SHORT TO VOLTAGE	
• Key in OFF position. • Connect: Clockspring C218a. **⚠ WARNING: Make sure there is no one inside the vehicle and that there is nothing blocking or set in front of any air bag module when the battery is connected. Failure to follow these instructions may result in personal injury.** Remove the driver air bag module. • Disconnect: Upper Clockspring C218b. • Connect the restraint system diagnostic tools (418-F395) to the upper clockspring air bag connector. • Connect the battery. • Key in ON position. • Turn the parking lamps on. • Measure the voltage between the PCM C175b-19, circuit VES10 (WH), harness side and ground; and between the PCM C175b-30, circuit RES08 (GN/BN), harness side and ground.	**Yes** INSTALL a new clockspring. CLEAR the DTCs. REPEAT the self-test. **No** INSTALL a new speed control switch. CLEAR the DTCs. REPEAT the self-test.
• Is any voltage present?	
C4 CHECK THE SPEED CONTROL SWITCH CIRCUITRY FOR A SHORT TO GROUND	
• Key in OFF position.	

LTV0500000001448

Fig. 117   Test C, Codes P0579 & P0581: Speed Control Switch Circuit Failure (Part 2 of 5). 2005–06 Explorer & Mountaineer

Test Step	Result / Action to Take
B7 CHECK FOR CORRECT PCM OPERATION	
• Disconnect all the PCM connectors. • Check for: — corrosion — pushed-out pins • Connect all the PCM connectors and make sure they seat correctly. • Operate the system and verify the concern is still present. • Is the concern still present?	**Yes** INSTALL a new PCM. TEST the system for normal operation. **No** The system is operating correctly at this time. The concern may have been caused by a loose or corroded connector.

LTV0500000001446

Fig. 116   Test B, Codes P1572 & P1703: Brake On/Off Circuit Failure (Part 4 of 4). 2005–06 Explorer & Mountaineer

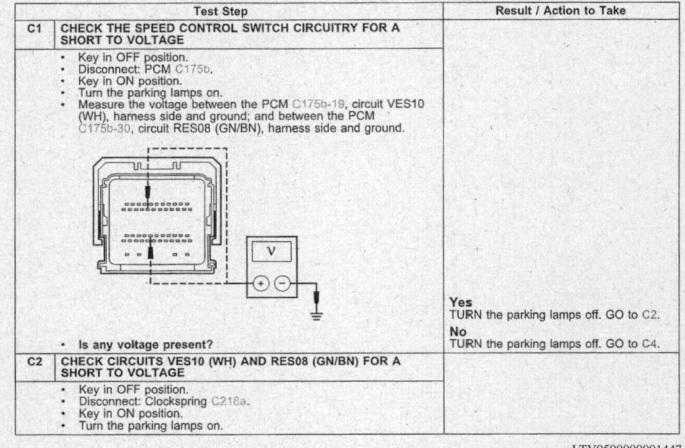

Test Step	Result / Action to Take
C1 CHECK THE SPEED CONTROL SWITCH CIRCUITRY FOR A SHORT TO VOLTAGE	
• Key in OFF position. • Disconnect: PCM C175b. • Key in ON position. • Turn the parking lamps on. • Measure the voltage between the PCM C175b-19, circuit VES10 (WH), harness side and ground; and between the PCM C175b-30, circuit RES08 (GN/BN), harness side and ground.	**Yes** TURN the parking lamps off. GO to C2. **No** TURN the parking lamps off. GO to C4.
• Is any voltage present?	
C2 CHECK CIRCUITS VES10 (WH) AND RES08 (GN/BN) FOR A SHORT TO VOLTAGE	
• Key in OFF position. • Disconnect: Clockspring C218a. • Key in ON position. • Turn the parking lamps on.	

LTV0500000001447

Fig. 117   Test C, Codes P0579 & P0581: Speed Control Switch Circuit Failure (Part 1 of 5). 2005–06 Explorer & Mountaineer

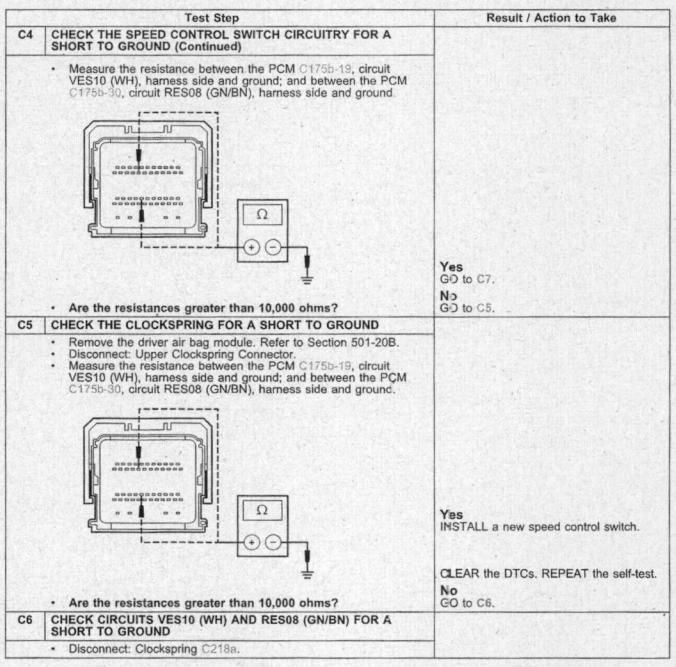

Test Step	Result / Action to Take
C4 CHECK THE SPEED CONTROL SWITCH CIRCUITRY FOR A SHORT TO GROUND (Continued)	
• Measure the resistance between the PCM C175b-19, circuit VES10 (WH), harness side and ground; and between the PCM C175b-30, circuit RES08 (GN/BN), harness side and ground.	**Yes** GO to C7. **No** GO to C5.
• Are the resistances greater than 10,000 ohms?	
C5 CHECK THE CLOCKSPRING FOR A SHORT TO GROUND	
• Remove the driver air bag module. Refer to Section 501-20B. • Disconnect: Upper Clockspring Connector. • Measure the resistance between the PCM C175b-19, circuit VES10 (WH), harness side and ground; and between the PCM C175b-30, circuit RES08 (GN/BN), harness side and ground.	**Yes** INSTALL a new speed control switch. CLEAR the DTCs. REPEAT the self-test. **No** GO to C6.
• Are the resistances greater than 10,000 ohms?	
C6 CHECK CIRCUITS VES10 (WH) AND RES08 (GN/BN) FOR A SHORT TO GROUND	
• Disconnect: Clockspring C218a.	

LTV0500000001449

Fig. 117   Test C, Codes P0579 & P0581: Speed Control Switch Circuit Failure (Part 3 of 5). 2005–06 Explorer & Mountaineer

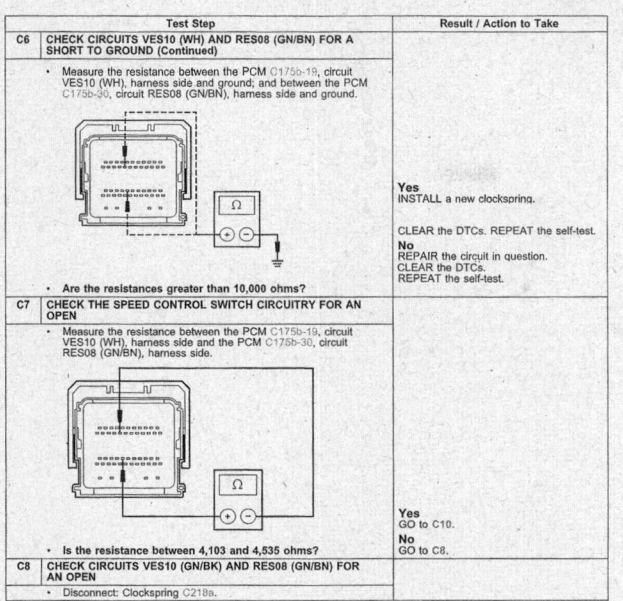

Test Step	Result / Action to Take
C6 CHECK CIRCUITS VES10 (WH) AND RES08 (GN/BN) FOR A SHORT TO GROUND (Continued)	
• Measure the resistance between the PCM C175b-19, circuit VES10 (WH), harness side and ground; and between the PCM C175b-30, circuit RES08 (GN/BN), harness side and ground.	**Yes** INSTALL a new clockspring. CLEAR the DTCs. REPEAT the self-test. **No** REPAIR the circuit in question. CLEAR the DTCs. REPEAT the self-test.
• Are the resistances greater than 10,000 ohms?	
C7 CHECK THE SPEED CONTROL SWITCH CIRCUITRY FOR AN OPEN	
• Measure the resistance between the PCM C175b-19, circuit VES10 (WH), harness side and the PCM C175b-30, circuit RES08 (GN/BN), harness side.	**Yes** GO to C10. **No** GO to C8.
• Is the resistance between 4,103 and 4,535 ohms?	
C8 CHECK CIRCUITS VES10 (GN/BK) AND RES08 (GN/BN) FOR AN OPEN	
• Disconnect: Clockspring C218a.	

LTV0500000001450

Fig. 117 Test C, Codes P0579 & P0581: Speed Control Switch Circuit Failure (Part 4 of 5). 2005–06 Explorer & Mountaineer

Test Step	Result / Action to Take
A1 CHECK THE SPEED CONTROL CABLE ATTACHMENT TO THE THROTTLE	
• Key in OFF position. • Remove the accelerator control splash shield. Inspect the speed control cable attachment. Check the speed control cable by pulling on the speed control cable and noting the throttle movement. • Is the speed control cable snapped onto the throttle body and is the speed control cable movement OK?	**Yes** GO to A2. **No** REATTACH or INSTALL a new speed control cable. TEST the system for normal operation.
A2 CHECK THE VOLTAGE TO THE SPEED CONTROL SERVO	
• Disconnect: Speed Control Servo C122. • Key in ON position.	

LTV0500000001655

Fig. 118 Test A: Speed Control Is Inoperative (Part 1 of 10). 2002–03 Explorer Sport & Sport Trac

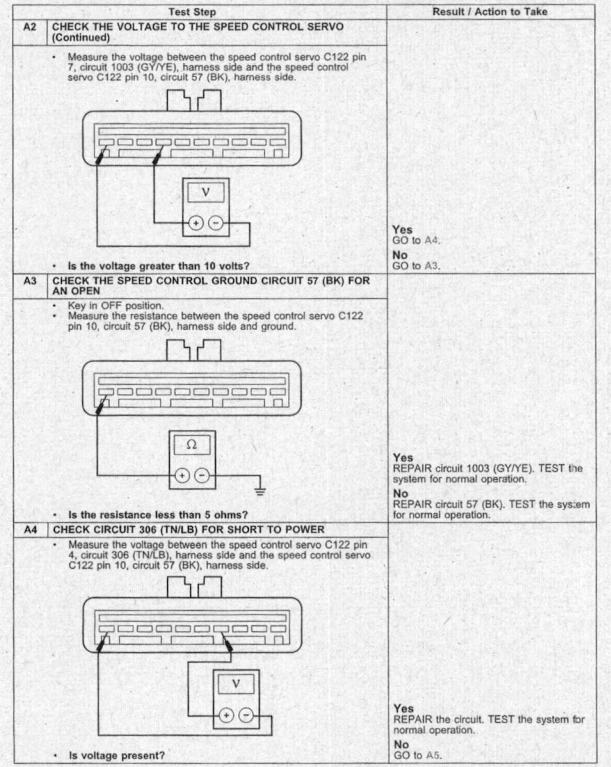

Test Step	Result / Action to Take
A2 CHECK THE VOLTAGE TO THE SPEED CONTROL SERVO (Continued)	
• Measure the voltage between the speed control servo C122 pin 7, circuit 1003 (GY/YE), harness side and the speed control servo C122 pin 10, circuit 57 (BK), harness side.	**Yes** GO to A4. **No** GO to A3.
• Is the voltage greater than 10 volts?	
A3 CHECK THE SPEED CONTROL GROUND CIRCUIT 57 (BK) FOR AN OPEN	
• Key in OFF position. • Measure the resistance between the speed control servo C122 pin 10, circuit 57 (BK), harness side and ground.	**Yes** REPAIR circuit 1003 (GY/YE). TEST the system for normal operation. **No** REPAIR circuit 57 (BK). TEST the system for normal operation.
• Is the resistance less than 5 ohms?	
A4 CHECK CIRCUIT 306 (TN/LB) FOR SHORT TO POWER	
• Measure the voltage between the speed control servo C122 pin 4, circuit 306 (TN/LB), harness side and the speed control servo C122 pin 10, circuit 57 (BK), harness side.	**Yes** REPAIR the circuit. TEST the system for normal operation. **No** GO to A5.
• Is voltage present?	

LTV0500000001656

Fig. 118 Test A: Speed Control Is Inoperative (Part 2 of 10). 2002–03 Explorer Sport & Sport Trac

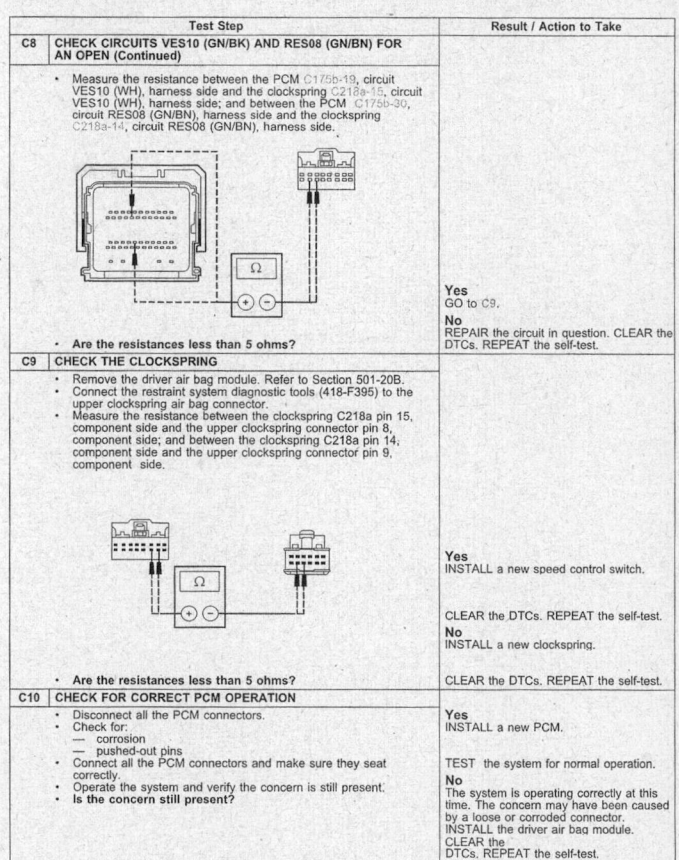

Test Step	Result / Action to Take
C8 CHECK CIRCUITS VES10 (GN/BK) AND RES08 (GN/BN) FOR AN OPEN (Continued)	
• Measure the resistance between the PCM C175b-19, circuit VES10 (WH), harness side and the clockspring C218a-15, circuit VES10 (WH), harness side; and between the PCM C175b-30, circuit RES08 (GN/BN), harness side and the clockspring C218a-14, circuit RES08 (GN/BN), harness side.	**Yes** GO to C9. **No** REPAIR the circuit in question. CLEAR the DTCs. REPEAT the self-test.
• Are the resistances less than 5 ohms?	
C9 CHECK THE CLOCKSPRING	
• Remove the driver air bag module. Refer to Section 501-20B. • Connect the restraint system diagnostic tools (418-F395) to the upper clockspring air bag connector. • Measure the resistance between the clockspring C218a pin 15, component side and the upper clockspring connector pin 8, component side; and between the clockspring C218a pin 14, component side and the upper clockspring connector pin 9, component side.	**Yes** INSTALL a new speed control switch. CLEAR the DTCs. REPEAT the self-test. **No** INSTALL a new clockspring. CLEAR the DTCs. REPEAT the self-test.
• Are the resistances less than 5 ohms?	
C10 CHECK FOR CORRECT PCM OPERATION	
• Disconnect all the PCM connectors. • Check for: — corrosion — pushed-out pins • Connect all the PCM connectors and make sure they seat correctly. • Operate the system and verify the concern is still present. • Is the concern still present?	**Yes** INSTALL a new PCM. TEST the system for normal operation. **No** The system is operating correctly at this time. The concern may have been caused by a loose or corroded connector. INSTALL the driver air bag module. CLEAR the DTCs. REPEAT the self-test.

LTV0500000001451

Fig. 117 Test C, Codes P0579 & P0581: Speed Control Switch Circuit Failure (Part 5 of 5). 2005–06 Explorer & Mountaineer

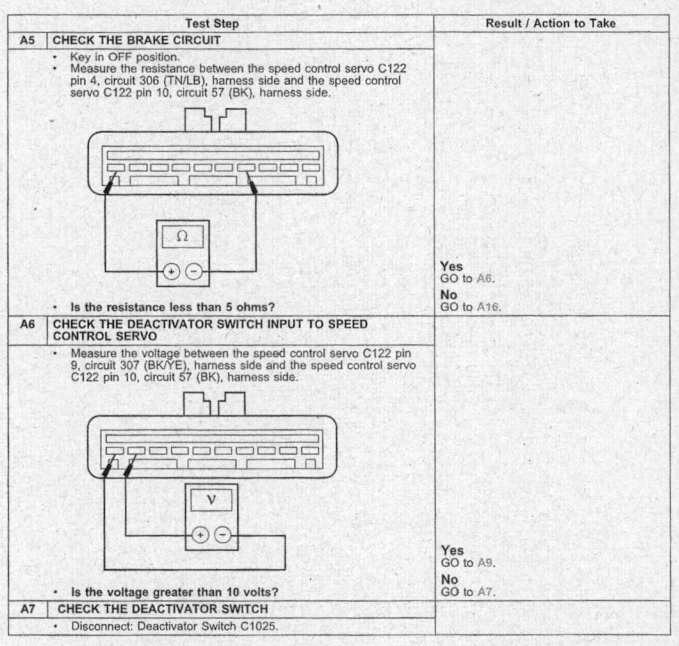

Test Step	Result / Action to Take
A5 CHECK THE BRAKE CIRCUIT	
• Key in OFF position. • Measure the resistance between the speed control servo C122 pin 4, circuit 306 (TN/LB), harness side and the speed control servo C122 pin 10, circuit 57 (BK), harness side.	**Yes** GO to A6. **No** GO to A16.
• Is the resistance less than 5 ohms?	
A6 CHECK THE DEACTIVATOR SWITCH INPUT TO SPEED CONTROL SERVO	
• Measure the voltage between the speed control servo C122 pin 9, circuit 307 (BK/YE), harness side and the speed control servo C122 pin 10, circuit 57 (BK), harness side.	**Yes** GO to A9. **No** GO to A7.
• Is the voltage greater than 10 volts?	
A7 CHECK THE DEACTIVATOR SWITCH	
• Disconnect: Deactivator Switch C1025.	

LTV0500000001657

Fig. 118 Test A: Speed Control Is Inoperative (Part 3 of 10). 2002–03 Explorer Sport & Sport Trac

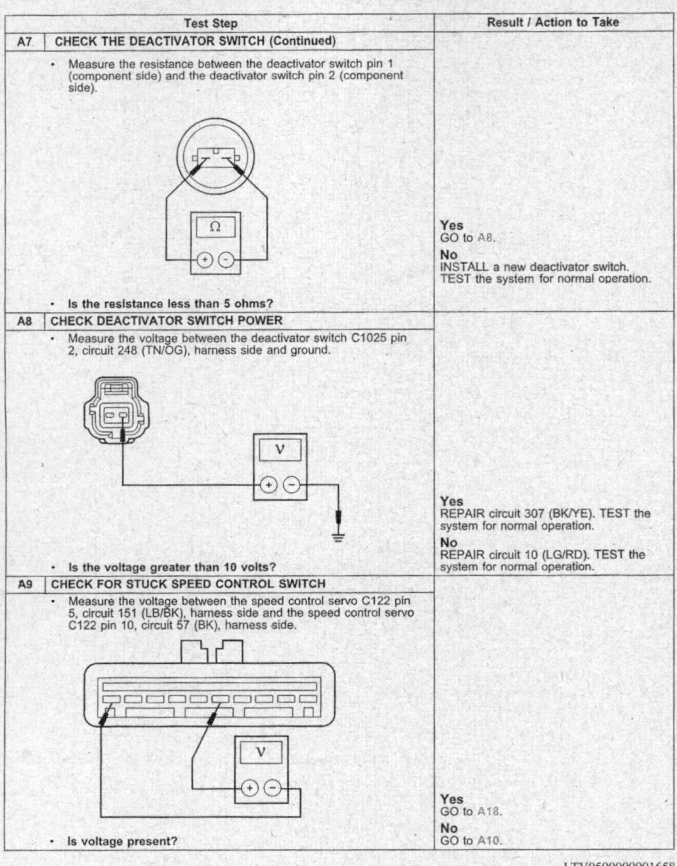

Test Step	Result / Action to Take
A7 CHECK THE DEACTIVATOR SWITCH (Continued)	
• Measure the resistance between the deactivator switch pin 1 (component side) and the deactivator switch pin 2 (component side).	**Yes** GO to A8. **No** INSTALL a new deactivator switch. TEST the system for normal operation.
• Is the resistance less than 5 ohms?	
A8 CHECK DEACTIVATOR SWITCH POWER	
• Measure the voltage between the deactivator switch C1025 pin 2, circuit 248 (TN/OG), harness side and ground.	**Yes** REPAIR circuit 307 (BK/YE). TEST the system for normal operation. **No** REPAIR circuit 10 (LG/RD). TEST the system for normal operation.
• Is the voltage greater than 10 volts?	
A9 CHECK FOR STUCK SPEED CONTROL SWITCH	
• Measure the voltage between the speed control servo C122 pin 5, circuit 151 (LB/BK), harness side and the speed control servo C122 pin 10, circuit 57 (BK), harness side.	**Yes** GO to A18. **No** GO to A10.
• Is voltage present?	

LTV0500000001658

Fig. 118 Test A: Speed Control Is Inoperative (Part 4 of 10). 2002–03 Explorer Sport & Sport Trac

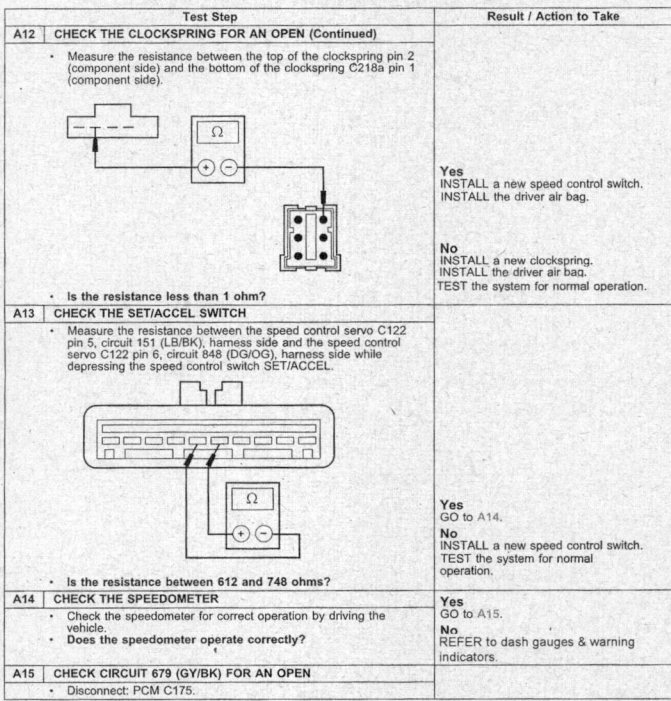

Test Step	Result / Action to Take
A12 CHECK THE CLOCKSPRING FOR AN OPEN (Continued)	
• Measure the resistance between the top of the clockspring pin 2 (component side) and the bottom of the clockspring C218a pin 1 (component side).	**Yes** INSTALL a new speed control switch. INSTALL the driver air bag. **No** INSTALL a new clockspring. INSTALL the driver air bag. TEST the system for normal operation.
• Is the resistance less than 1 ohm?	
A13 CHECK THE SET/ACCEL SWITCH	
• Measure the resistance between the speed control servo C122 pin 5, circuit 151 (LB/BK), harness side and the speed control servo C122 pin 6, circuit 848 (DG/OG), harness side while depressing the speed control switch SET/ACCEL.	**Yes** GO to A14. **No** INSTALL a new speed control switch. TEST the system for normal operation.
• Is the resistance between 612 and 748 ohms?	
A14 CHECK THE SPEEDOMETER	
• Check the speedometer for correct operation by driving the vehicle. • **Does the speedometer operate correctly?**	**Yes** GO to A15. **No** REFER to dash gauges & warning indicators.
A15 CHECK CIRCUIT 679 (GY/BK) FOR AN OPEN	
• Disconnect: PCM C175.	

LTV0500000001660

Fig. 118 Test A: Speed Control Is Inoperative (Part 6 of 10). 2002–03 Explorer Sport & Sport Trac

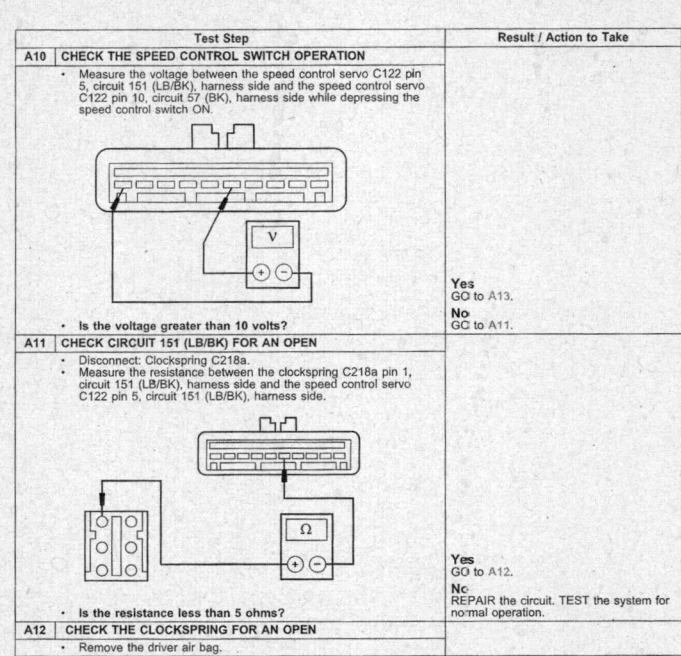

Test Step	Result / Action to Take
A10 CHECK THE SPEED CONTROL SWITCH OPERATION	
• Measure the voltage between the speed control servo C122 pin 5, circuit 151 (LB/BK), harness side and the speed control servo C122 pin 10, circuit 57 (BK), harness side while depressing the speed control switch ON.	**Yes** GO to A13. **No** GO to A11.
• Is the voltage greater than 10 volts?	
A11 CHECK CIRCUIT 151 (LB/BK) FOR AN OPEN	
• Disconnect: Clockspring C218a. • Measure the resistance between the clockspring C218a pin 1, circuit 151 (LB/BK), harness side and the speed control servo C122 pin 5, circuit 151 (LB/BK), harness side.	**Yes** GO to A12. **No** REPAIR the circuit. TEST the system for normal operation.
• Is the resistance less than 5 ohms?	
A12 CHECK THE CLOCKSPRING FOR AN OPEN	
• Remove the driver air bag.	

LTV0500000001659

Fig. 118 Test A: Speed Control Is Inoperative (Part 5 of 10). 2002–03 Explorer Sport & Sport Trac

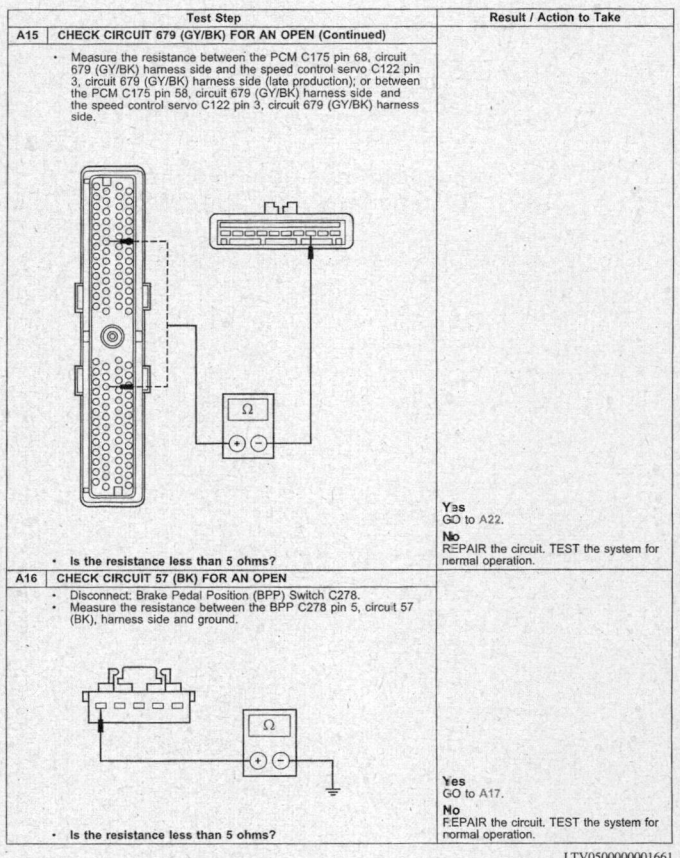

Test Step	Result / Action to Take
A15 CHECK CIRCUIT 679 (GY/BK) FOR AN OPEN (Continued)	
• Measure the resistance between the PCM C175 pin 68, circuit 679 (GY/BK) harness side and the speed control servo C122 pin 3, circuit 679 (GY/BK) harness side (late production); or between the PCM C175 pin 58, circuit 679 (GY/BK) harness side and the speed control servo C122 pin 3, circuit 679 (GY/BK) harness side.	**Yes** GO to A22. **No** REPAIR the circuit. TEST the system for normal operation.
• Is the resistance less than 5 ohms?	
A16 CHECK CIRCUIT 57 (BK) FOR AN OPEN	
• Disconnect: Brake Pedal Position (BPP) Switch C278. • Measure the resistance between the BPP C278 pin 5, circuit 57 (BK), harness side and ground.	**Yes** GO to A17. **No** REPAIR the circuit. TEST the system for normal operation.
• Is the resistance less than 5 ohms?	

LTV0500000001661

Fig. 118 Test A: Speed Control Is Inoperative (Part 7 of 10). 2002–03 Explorer Sport & Sport Trac

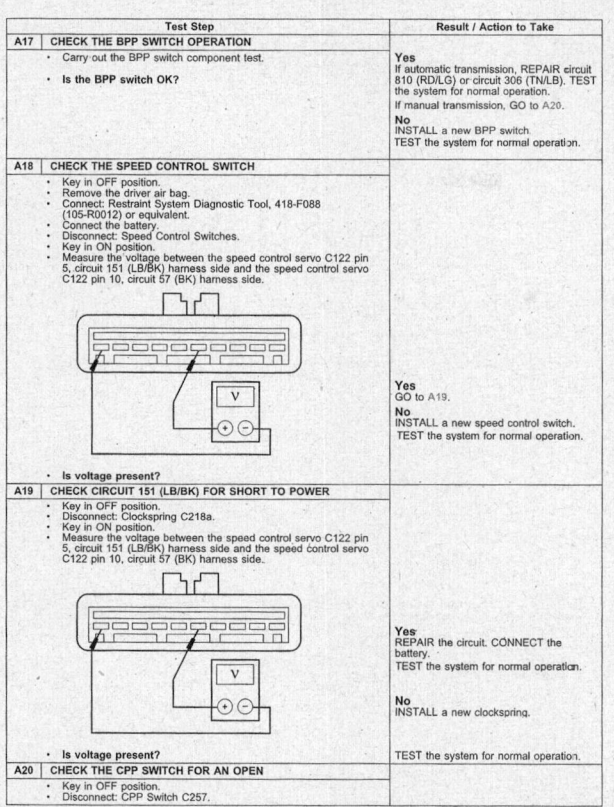

Test Step	Result / Action to Take
A17 CHECK THE BPP SWITCH OPERATION	
• Carry out the BPP switch component test. • **Is the BPP switch OK?**	**Yes** If automatic transmission, REPAIR circuit 810 (RD/LG) or circuit 306 (TN/LB). TEST the system for normal operation. If manual transmission, GO to A20. **No** INSTALL a new BPP switch. TEST the system for normal operation.
A18 CHECK THE SPEED CONTROL SWITCH	
• Key in OFF position. • Remove the driver air bag. • Connect: Restraint System Diagnostic Tool, 418-F088 (105-R0012) or equivalent. • Connect the battery. • Disconnect: Speed Control Switches. • Key in ON position. • Measure the voltage between the speed control servo C122 pin 5, circuit 151 (LB/BK) harness side and the speed control servo C122 pin 10, circuit 57 (BK) harness side. • **Is voltage present?**	**Yes** GO to A19. **No** INSTALL a new speed control switch. TEST the system for normal operation.
A19 CHECK CIRCUIT 151 (LB/BK) FOR SHORT TO POWER	
• Key in OFF position. • Disconnect: Clockspring C218a. • Key in ON position. • Measure the voltage between the speed control servo C122 pin 5, circuit 151 (LB/BK) harness side and the speed control servo C122 pin 10, circuit 57 (BK) harness side. • **Is voltage present?**	**Yes** REPAIR the circuit. CONNECT the battery. TEST the system for normal operation. **No** INSTALL a new clockspring. TEST the system for normal operation.
A20 CHECK THE CPP SWITCH FOR AN OPEN	
• Key in OFF position. • Disconnect: CPP Switch C257.	

LTV050000001662

Fig. 118 Test A: Speed Control Is Inoperative (Part 8 of 10). 2002–03 Explorer Sport & Sport Trac

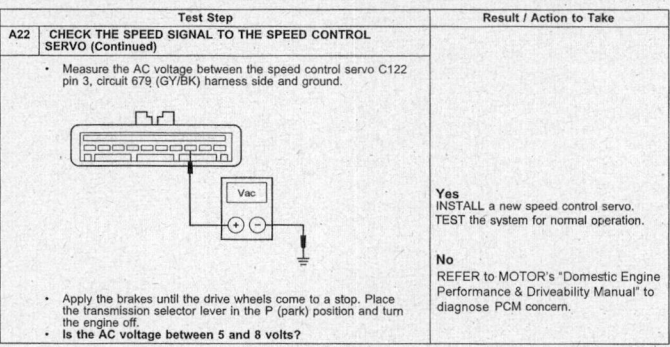

Test Step	Result / Action to Take
A22 CHECK THE SPEED CONTROL SIGNAL TO THE SPEED CONTROL SERVO (Continued)	
• Measure the AC voltage between the speed control servo C122 pin 3, circuit 679 (GY/BK) harness side and ground. • Apply the brakes until the drive wheels come to a stop. Place the transmission selector lever in the P (park) position and turn the engine off. • **Is the AC voltage between 5 and 8 volts?**	**Yes** INSTALL a new speed control servo. TEST the system for normal operation. **No** REFER to MOTOR's "Domestic Engine Performance & Driveability Manual" to diagnose PCM concern.

LTV050000001664

Fig. 118 Test A: Speed Control Is Inoperative (Part 10 of 10). 2002–03 Explorer Sport & Sport Trac

Test Step	Result / Action to Take
B1 CHECK SPEED CONTROL CABLE/THROTTLE BODY LINKAGE	
• Key in OFF position. • Hold the throttle open and remove the speed control cable from the speed control servo. Visually inspect the core wire and check the speed control cable by pulling on the cable and noting the throttle movement. • **Is the speed control cable OK?**	**Yes** If early production vehicle, GO to B2. If late production vehicle, GO to B3. **No** INSTALL a new speed control cable or REPAIR the throttle body linkage. TEST the system for normal operation.
B2 CHECK FOR CORRECT AMOUNT OF SLACK IN SPEED CABLE	
• Remove the speed control cable from the throttle. • Check for correct amount of slack in the speed control cable. • **Is there approximately 3 mm (0.12 in) of slack in the cable?**	**Yes** GO to B3. **No** ADJUST the speed control cable slack to approximately 3 mm (0.12 in). TEST the system for normal operation.
B3 CHECK THE SPEEDOMETER	
• Check the speedometer for correct operation by driving the vehicle. • **Does the speedometer fluctuate?**	**Yes** Diagnose speedometer. **No** INSTALL a new speed control servo. TEST the system for normal operation.

LTV050000001665

Fig. 119 Test B: Set Speed Fluctuates. 2002–03 Explorer Sport & Sport Trac

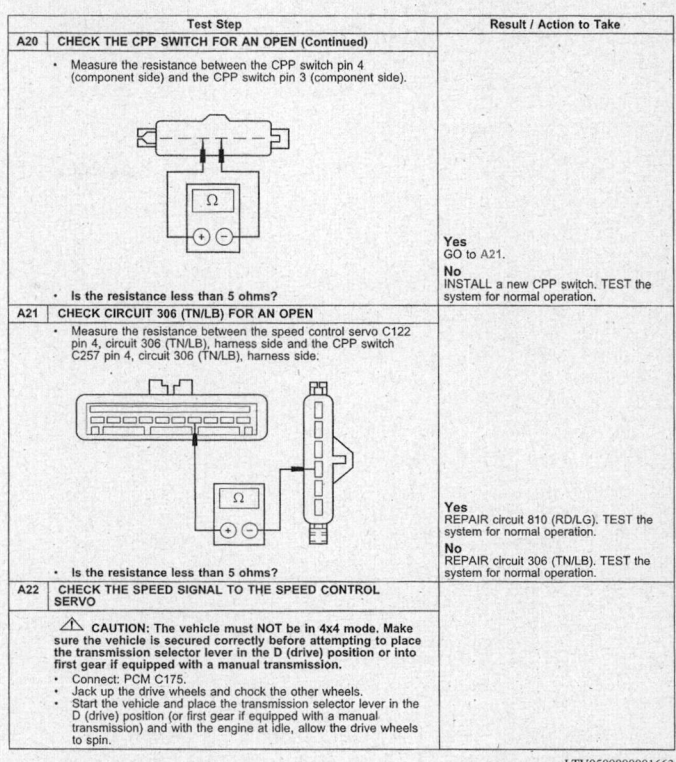

Test Step	Result / Action to Take
A20 CHECK THE CPP SWITCH FOR AN OPEN (Continued)	
• Measure the resistance between the CPP switch pin 4 (component side) and the CPP switch pin 3 (component side). • **Is the resistance less than 5 ohms?**	**Yes** GO to A21. **No** INSTALL a new CPP switch. TEST the system for normal operation.
A21 CHECK CIRCUIT 306 (TN/LB) FOR AN OPEN	
• Measure the resistance between the speed control servo C122 pin 4, circuit 306 (TN/LB), harness side and the CPP switch C257 pin 4, circuit 306 (TN/LB), harness side. • **Is the resistance less than 5 ohms?**	**Yes** REPAIR circuit 810 (RD/LG). TEST the system for normal operation. **No** REPAIR circuit 306 (TN/LB). TEST the system for normal operation.
A22 CHECK THE SPEED SIGNAL TO THE SPEED CONTROL SERVO	
⚠ **CAUTION:** The vehicle must NOT be in 4x4 mode. Make sure the vehicle is secured correctly before attempting to place the transmission selector lever in the D (drive) position or into first gear if equipped with a manual transmission. • Connect: PCM C175. • Jack up the drive wheels and chock the other wheels. • Start the vehicle and place the transmission selector lever in the D (drive) position (or first gear if equipped with a manual transmission) and with the engine at idle, allow the drive wheels to spin.	

LTV050000001663

Fig. 118 Test A: Speed Control Is Inoperative (Part 9 of 10). 2002–03 Explorer Sport & Sport Trac

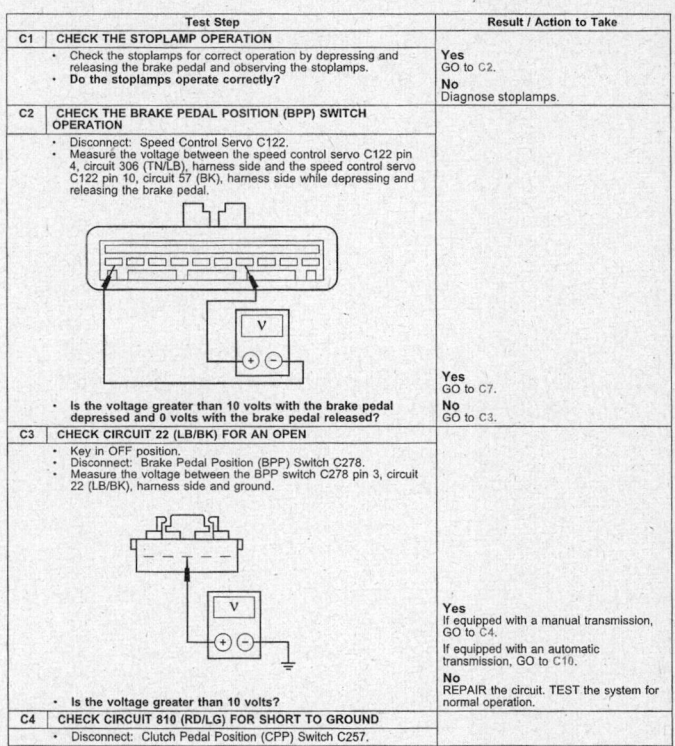

Test Step	Result / Action to Take
C1 CHECK THE STOPLAMP OPERATION	
• Check the stoplamps for correct operation by depressing and releasing the brake pedal and observing the stoplamps. • **Do the stoplamps operate correctly?**	**Yes** GO to C2. **No** Diagnose stoplamps.
C2 CHECK THE BRAKE PEDAL POSITION (BPP) SWITCH OPERATION	
• Disconnect: Speed Control Servo C122. • Measure the voltage between the speed control servo C122 pin 4, circuit 306 (TN/LB), harness side and the speed control servo C122 pin 10, circuit 57 (BK), harness side while depressing and releasing the brake pedal. • **Is the voltage greater than 10 volts with the brake pedal depressed and 0 volts with the brake pedal released?**	**Yes** GO to C7. **No** GO to C3.
C3 CHECK CIRCUIT 22 (LB/BK) FOR AN OPEN	
• Key in OFF position. • Disconnect: Brake Pedal Position (BPP) Switch C278. • Measure the voltage between the BPP switch C278 pin 3, circuit 22 (LB/BK), harness side and ground. • **Is the voltage greater than 10 volts?**	**Yes** If equipped with a manual transmission, GO to C4. If equipped with an automatic transmission, GO to C10. **No** REPAIR the circuit. TEST the system for normal operation.
C4 CHECK CIRCUIT 810 (RD/LG) FOR SHORT TO GROUND	
• Disconnect: Clutch Pedal Position (CPP) Switch C257.	

LTV050000001666

Fig. 120 Test C: Speed Control Does Not Disengage When Brakes Are Applied (Part 1 of 4). 2002–03 Explorer Sport & Sport Trac

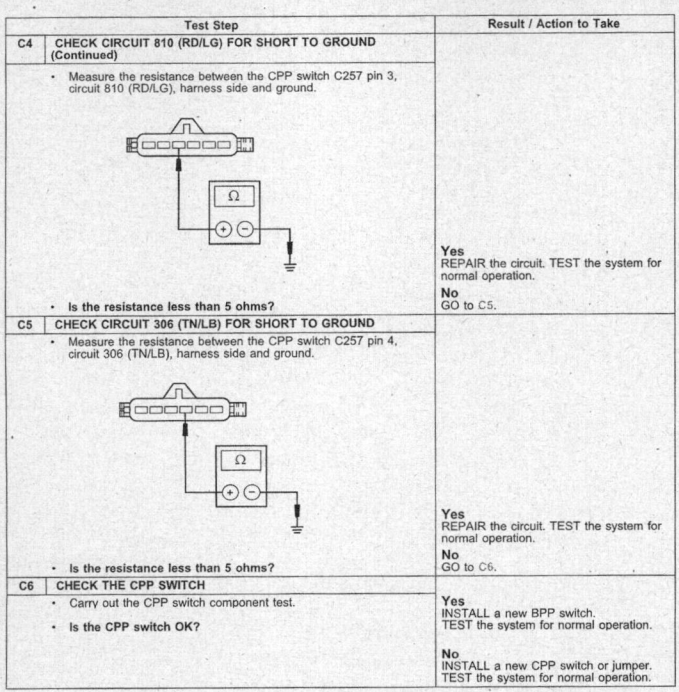

Test Step	Result / Action to Take
C4 **CHECK CIRCUIT 810 (RD/LG) FOR SHORT TO GROUND** (Continued) • Measure the resistance between the CPP switch C257 pin 3, circuit 810 (RD/LG), harness side and ground. • Is the resistance less than 5 ohms?	**Yes** REPAIR the circuit. TEST the system for normal operation. **No** GO to C5.
C5 **CHECK CIRCUIT 306 (TN/LB) FOR SHORT TO GROUND** • Measure the resistance between the CPP switch C257 pin 4, circuit 306 (TN/LB), harness side and ground. • Is the resistance less than 5 ohms?	**Yes** REPAIR the circuit. TEST the system for normal operation. **No** GO to C6.
C6 **CHECK THE CPP SWITCH** • Carry out the CPP switch component test. • Is the CPP switch OK?	**Yes** INSTALL a new BPP switch. TEST the system for normal operation. **No** INSTALL a new CPP switch or jumper. TEST the system for normal operation.

LTV0500000001667

Fig. 120 Test C: Speed Control Does Not Disengage When Brakes Are Applied (Part 2 of 4). 2002–03 Explorer Sport & Sport Trac

Test Step	Result / Action to Take
C10 **CHECK CIRCUITS 306 (TN/LB) AND 810 (RD/LG) FOR TO GROUND** • Measure the resistance between the BPP switch C278 pin 4, circuit 810 (RD/LG), harness side and ground. • Is the resistance less than 5 ohms?	**Yes** REPAIR circuits 306 (TN/LB) or 810 (RD/LG) as necessary. TEST the system for normal operation. **No** INSTALL a new BPP switch. TEST the system for normal operation.

LTV0500000001669

Fig. 120 Test C: Speed Control Does Not Disengage When Brakes Are Applied (Part 4 of 4). 2002–03 Explorer Sport & Sport Trac

Test Step	Result / Action to Take
D1 **CHECK THE CLUTCH PEDAL POSITION (CPP) SWITCH** • Key in OFF position. • Disconnect: CPP Switch C257. • Measure the resistance between the CPP switch pin 3 (component side) and the CPP switch pin 4 (component side), while depressing and releasing the clutch pedal. • Is the resistance less than 5 ohms with the clutch pedal released and greater than 10,000 ohms with the clutch pedal depressed?	**Yes** INSTALL a new speed control servo. TEST the system for normal operation. **No** INSTALL a new CPP switch. TEST the system for normal operation.

LTV0500000001670

Fig. 121 Test D: Speed Control Does Not Disengage When Clutch Is Applied. 2002–03 Explorer Sport & Sport Trac

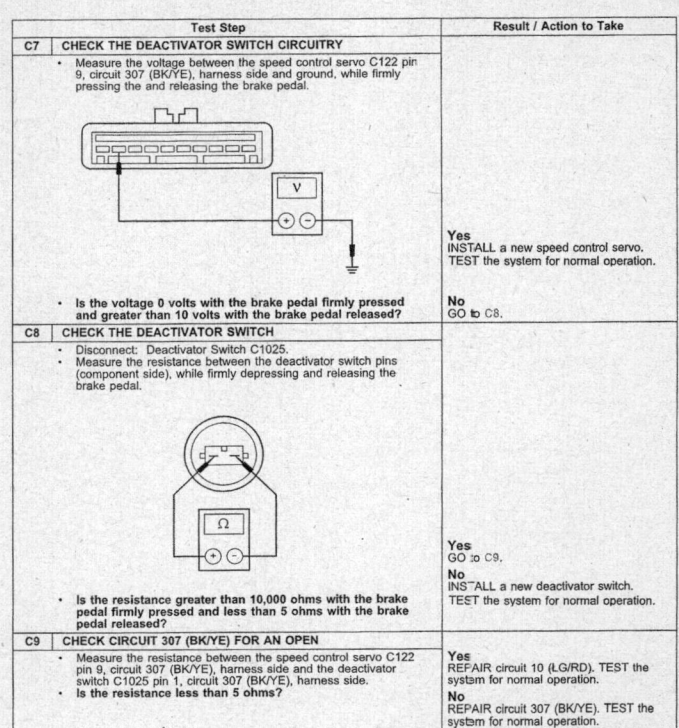

Test Step	Result / Action to Take
C7 **CHECK THE DEACTIVATOR SWITCH CIRCUITRY** • Measure the voltage between the speed control servo C122 pin 9, circuit 307 (BK/YE), harness side and ground, while firmly pressing the and releasing the brake pedal. • Is the voltage 0 volts with the brake pedal firmly pressed and greater than 10 volts with the brake pedal released?	**Yes** INSTALL a new speed control servo. TEST the system for normal operation. **No** GO to C8.
C8 **CHECK THE DEACTIVATOR SWITCH** • Disconnect: Deactivator Switch C1025. • Measure the resistance between the deactivator switch pins (component side), while firmly depressing and releasing the brake pedal. • Is the resistance greater than 10,000 ohms with the brake pedal firmly pressed and less than 5 ohms with the brake pedal released?	**Yes** GO to C9. **No** INSTALL a new deactivator switch. TEST the system for normal operation.
C9 **CHECK CIRCUIT 307 (BK/YE) FOR AN OPEN** • Measure the resistance between the speed control servo C122 pin 9, circuit 307 (BK/YE), harness side and the deactivator switch C1025 pin 1, circuit 307 (BK/YE), harness side. • Is the resistance less than 5 ohms?	**Yes** REPAIR circuit 10 (LG/RD). TEST the system for normal operation. **No** REPAIR circuit 307 (BK/YE). TEST the system for normal operation.

LTV0500000001668

Fig. 120 Test C: Speed Control Does Not Disengage When Brakes Are Applied (Part 3 of 4). 2002–03 Explorer Sport & Sport Trac

Test Step	Result / Action to Take
E1 CHECK THE SPEED CONTROL SWITCH • Key in OFF position. • Disconnect: Speed Control Servo C122. • Measure the resistance between the speed control servo C122 pin 5, circuit 151 (LB/BK), harness side and the speed control servo C122 pin 6, circuit 848 (DG/OG), harness side while depressing the speed control switch as follows: | Speed Control Switch	Resistance Value
Coast	Between 114 and 126 ohms
SET/ACCEL	Between 612 and 748 ohms
Resume	Between 2,090 and 2,310 ohms
Off	Less than 5 ohms | • Are the speed control switch resistance values OK?	**Yes** INSTALL a new speed control servo. TEST the system for normal operation. **No** INSTALL a new speed control switch. TEST the system for normal operation.

LTV0500000001671

Fig. 122 Test E: Speed Control Switch Is Inoperative. 2002–03 Explorer Sport & Sport Trac

Test Step	Result / Action to Take
F1 CHECK THE SPEED CONTROL CABLE	
• Check the speed control cable for correct attachment at the speed control servo and throttle body. • **Is the speed control cable attached correctly?**	**Yes** If early production vehicle, GO to F2. If late production vehicle, GO to F3. **No** RECONNECT the speed control cable. REPEAT the self-test.
F2 CHECK FOR CORRECT AMOUNT OF SLACK IN SPEED CONTROL CABLE	
• Remove the speed control cable from the throttle. • Check for correct amount of slack in the speed control cable. • **Is there approximately 3 mm (0.12 in) of slack in the cable?**	**Yes** GO to F3. **No** ADJUST the speed control cable slack to approximately 3 mm (0.12 in). TEST the system for normal operation.
F3 CHECK FOR A STICKING OR BINDING SPEED CONTROL CABLE	
• Check the speed control cable for sticking or binding. • **Is the speed control cable OK?**	**Yes** INSTALL a new speed control servo. REPEAT the self-test. **No** REPAIR or INSTALL a new speed control cable. REPEAT the self-test.

LTV0500000001672

Fig. 123 Test F: Flash w/Last Switch Pressed, But No Dynamic Pull Occurs At Throttle & Speed Control Is Inoperative. 2002–03 Explorer Sport & Sport Trac

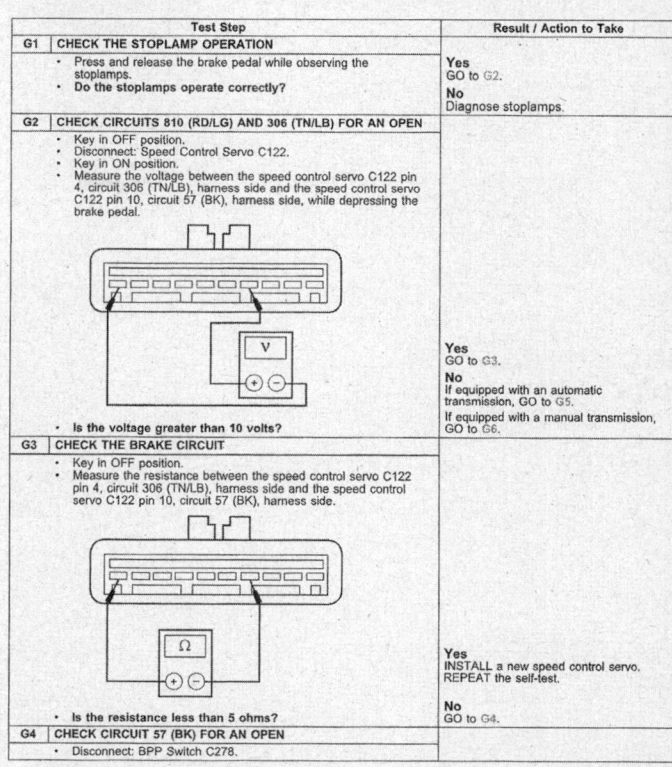

Fig. 124 Test G: Brake Pedal Position Switch Circuit Failure (Part 1 of 3). 2002–03 Explorer Sport & Sport Trac

Test Step	Result / Action to Take
G4 CHECK CIRCUIT 57 (BK) FOR AN OPEN (Continued)	
• Measure the resistance between the BPP switch C278 pin 5, circuit 57 (BK), harness side and ground. • **Is the resistance less than 5 ohms?**	**Yes** INSTALL a new BPP switch. TEST the system for normal operation. **No** REPAIR the circuit. TEST the system for normal operation.
G5 CHECK THE BPP SWITCH	
• Key in OFF position. • Disconnect: BPP Switch C278. • Measure the resistance between the speed control servo C122 pin 4, circuit 306 (TN/LB), harness side and the BPP switch C278 pin 4, circuit 810 (RD/LG), harness side. • **Is the resistance less than 5 ohms?**	**Yes** INSTALL a new BPP switch. TEST the system for normal operation. **No** REPAIR circuits 306 (TN/LB) or 810 (RD/LG) as necessary. TEST the system for normal operation.
G6 CHECK CIRCUIT 306 (TN/LB) FOR AN OPEN	
• Key in OFF position. • Disconnect: CPP Switch C257.	

LTV0500000001674

Fig. 124 Test G: Brake Pedal Position Switch Circuit Failure (Part 2 of 3). 2002–03 Explorer Sport & Sport Trac

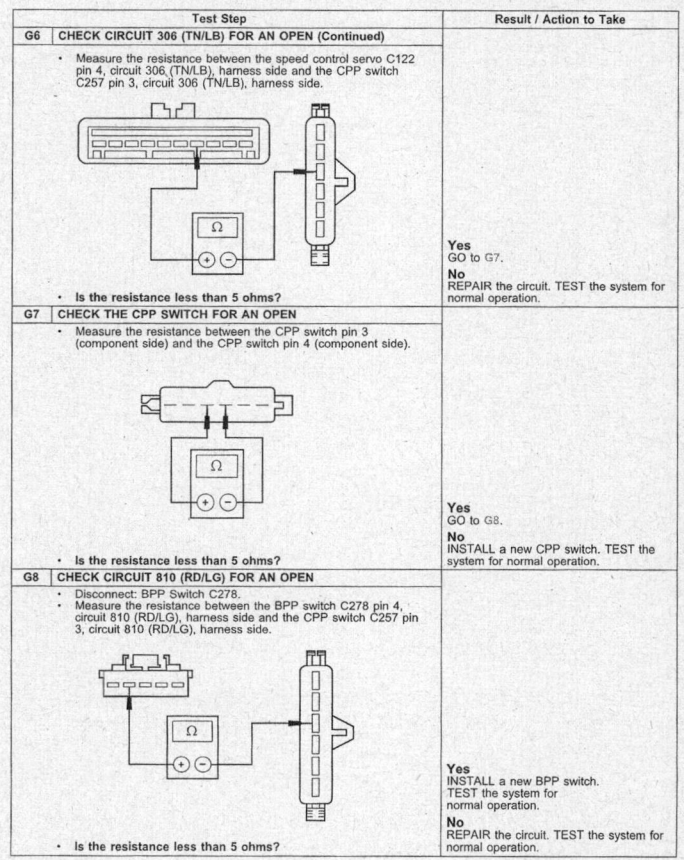

Fig. 124 Test G: Brake Pedal Position Switch Circuit Failure (Part 3 of 3). 2002–03 Explorer Sport & Sport Trac

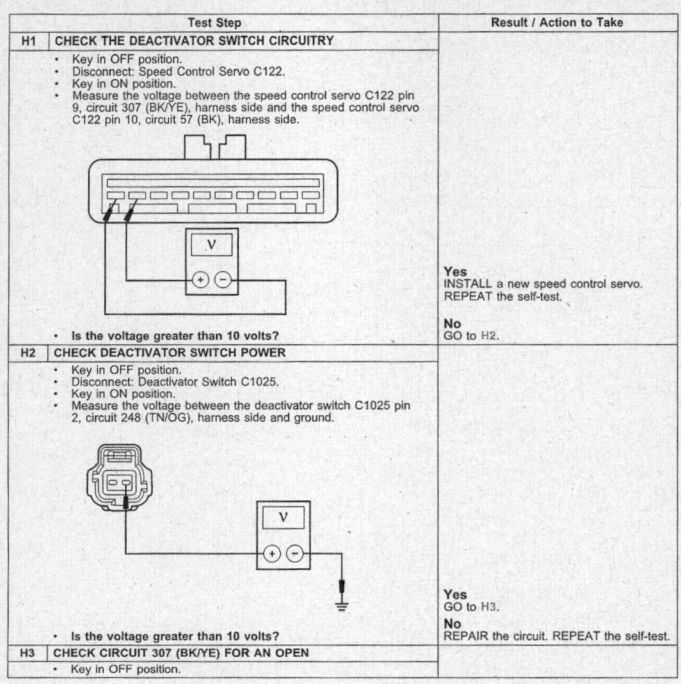

Test Step	Result / Action to Take
H1 CHECK THE DEACTIVATOR SWITCH CIRCUITRY	
• Key in OFF position. • Disconnect: Speed Control Servo C122. • Key in ON position. • Measure the voltage between the speed control servo C122 pin 9, circuit 307 (BK/YE), harness side and the speed control servo C122 pin 10, circuit 57 (BK), harness side.	**Yes** INSTALL a new speed control servo. REPEAT the self-test. **No** GO to H2.
• Is the voltage greater than 10 volts?	
H2 CHECK DEACTIVATOR SWITCH POWER	
• Key in OFF position. • Disconnect: Deactivator Switch C1025. • Key in ON position. • Measure the voltage between the deactivator switch C1025 pin 2, circuit 248 (TN/OG), harness side and ground.	**Yes** GO to H3. **No** REPAIR the circuit. REPEAT the self-test.
• Is the voltage greater than 10 volts?	
H3 CHECK CIRCUIT 307 (BK/YE) FOR AN OPEN	
• Key in OFF position.	LTV0500000001676

Fig. 125   Test H: Deactivator Switch Circuit Failure (Part 1 of 2). 2002–03 Explorer Sport & Sport Trac

Test Step	Result / Action to Take
A1 CHECK THE SPEED CONTROL CABLE ATTACHMENT TO THE THROTTLE	
• Key in OFF position. • Remove the accelerator control splash shield. Inspect the speed control cable attachment. Check the speed control cable by pulling on the speed control cable and noting the throttle movement. • Is the speed control cable snapped onto the throttle body and is the speed control cable movement OK?	**Yes** GO to A2. **No** REATTACH or INSTALL a new speed control cable. TEST the system for normal operation.
A2 CHECK THE VOLTAGE TO THE SPEED CONTROL SERVO	
• Disconnect: Speed Control Servo C122. • Key in ON position. • Measure the voltage between the speed control servo C122 pin 7, circuit 1003 (GY/YE), harness side and the speed control servo C122 pin 10, circuit 57 (BK), harness side.	**Yes** GO to A4. **No** GO to A3.
• Is the voltage greater than 10 volts?	
A3 CHECK THE SPEED CONTROL GROUND CIRCUIT 57 (BK) FOR AN OPEN	
• Key in OFF position. • Measure the resistance between the speed control servo C122 pin 10, circuit 57 (BK), harness side and ground.	**Yes** REPAIR circuit 1003 (GY/YE). TEST the system for normal operation. **No** REPAIR circuit 57 (BK). TEST the system for normal operation.
• Is the resistance less than 5 ohms?	
	LTV0500000001682

Fig. 127   Test A: Speed Control Is Inoperative (Part 1 of 8). 2004–05 Explorer Sport Trac

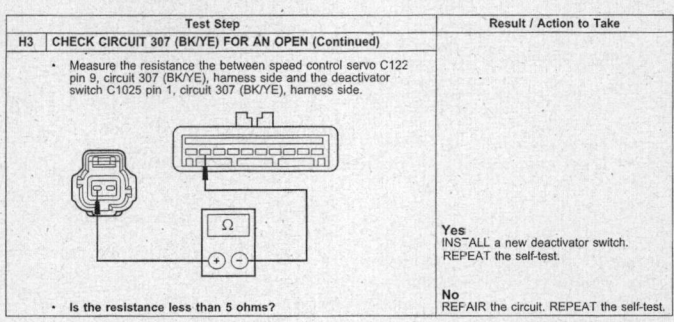

Test Step	Result / Action to Take
H3 CHECK CIRCUIT 307 (BK/YE) FOR AN OPEN (Continued)	
• Measure the resistance the between speed control servo C122 pin 9, circuit 307 (BK/YE), harness side and the deactivator switch C1025 pin 1, circuit 307 (BK/YE), harness side.	
• Is the resistance less than 5 ohms?	**Yes** INSTALL a new deactivator switch. REPEAT the self-test. **No** REPAIR the circuit. REPEAT the self-test.
	LTV0500000001677

Fig. 125   Test H: Deactivator Switch Circuit Failure (Part 2 of 2). 2002–03 Explorer Sport & Sport Trac

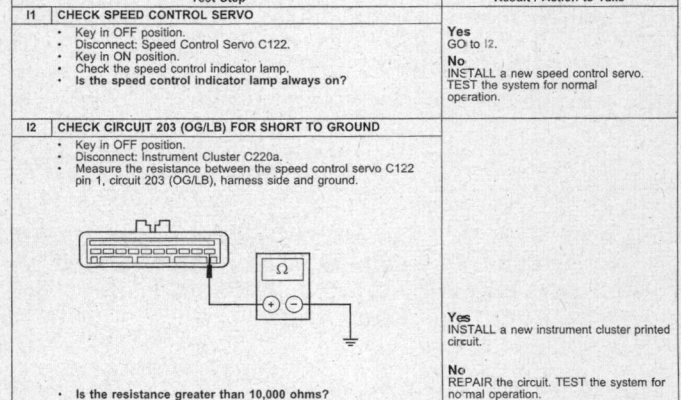

Test Step	Result / Action to Take
I1 CHECK SPEED CONTROL SERVO	
• Key in OFF position. • Disconnect: Speed Control Servo C122. • Key in ON position. • Check the speed control indicator lamp. • Is the speed control indicator lamp always on?	**Yes** GO to I2. **No** INSTALL a new speed control servo. TEST the system for normal operation.
I2 CHECK CIRCUIT 203 (OG/LB) FOR SHORT TO GROUND	
• Key in OFF position. • Disconnect: Instrument Cluster C220a. • Measure the resistance between the speed control servo C122 pin 1, circuit 203 (OG/LB), harness side and ground.	
• Is the resistance greater than 10,000 ohms?	**Yes** INSTALL a new instrument cluster printed circuit. **No** REPAIR the circuit. TEST the system for normal operation.
	LTV0500000001678

Fig. 126   Test I: Speed Control Indicator Lamp Is Always On. 2002–03 Explorer Sport & Sport Trac

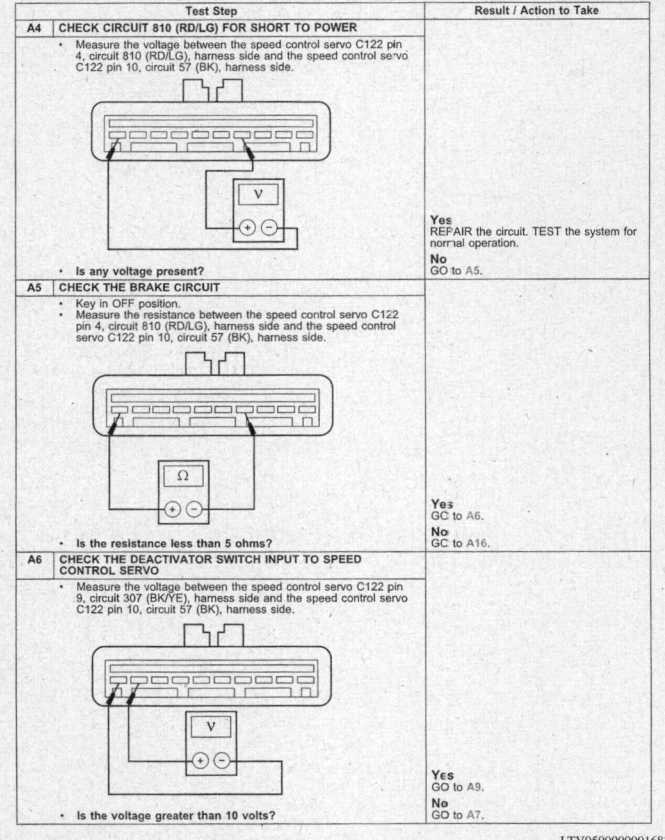

Test Step	Result / Action to Take
A4 CHECK CIRCUIT 810 (RD/LG) FOR SHORT TO POWER	
• Measure the voltage between the speed control servo C122 pin 4, circuit 810 (RD/LG), harness side and the speed control servo C122 pin 10, circuit 57 (BK), harness side.	
• Is any voltage present?	**Yes** REPAIR the circuit. TEST the system for normal operation. **No** GO to A5.
A5 CHECK THE BRAKE CIRCUIT	
• Key in OFF position. • Measure the resistance between the speed control servo C122 pin 4, circuit 810 (RD/LG), harness side and the speed control servo C122 pin 10, circuit 57 (BK), harness side.	
• Is the resistance less than 5 ohms?	**Yes** GO to A6. **No** GO to A16.
A6 CHECK THE DEACTIVATOR SWITCH INPUT TO SPEED CONTROL SERVO	
• Measure the voltage between the speed control servo C122 pin 9, circuit 307 (BK/YE), harness side and the speed control servo C122 pin 10, circuit 57 (BK), harness side.	
• Is the voltage greater than 10 volts?	**Yes** GO to A9. **No** GO to A7.
	LTV0500000001683

Fig. 127   Test A: Speed Control Is Inoperative (Part 2 of 8). 2004–05 Explorer Sport Trac

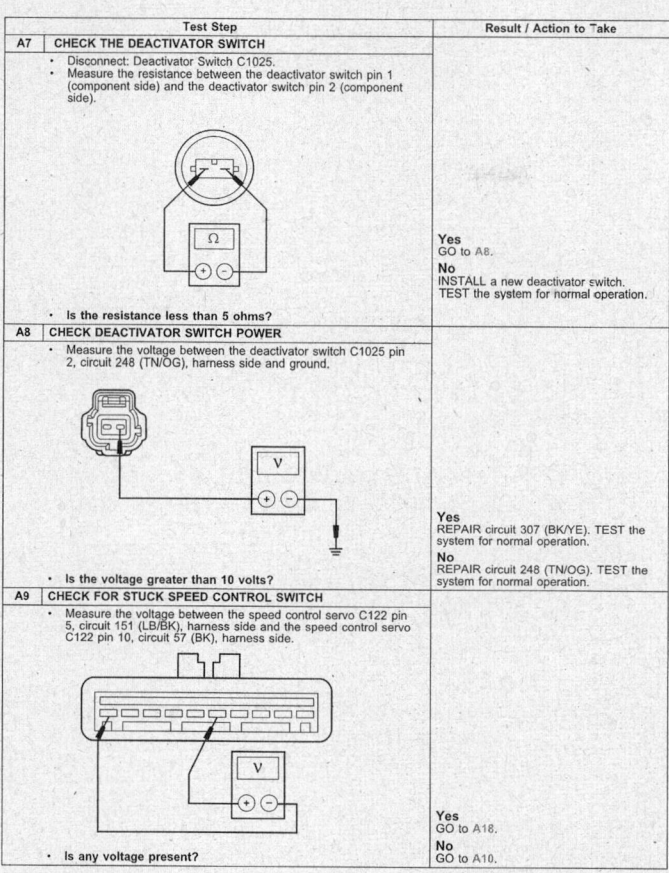

Test Step	Result / Action to Take
A7 CHECK THE DEACTIVATOR SWITCH	
• Disconnect: Deactivator Switch C1025. • Measure the resistance between the deactivator switch pin 1 (component side) and the deactivator switch pin 2 (component side).	**Yes** GO to A8. **No** INSTALL a new deactivator switch. TEST the system for normal operation.
• Is the resistance less than 5 ohms?	
A8 CHECK DEACTIVATOR SWITCH POWER	
• Measure the voltage between the deactivator switch C1025 pin 2, circuit 248 (TN/OG), harness side and ground.	**Yes** REPAIR circuit 307 (BK/YE). TEST the system for normal operation. **No** REPAIR circuit 248 (TN/OG). TEST the system for normal operation.
• Is the voltage greater than 10 volts?	
A9 CHECK FOR STUCK SPEED CONTROL SWITCH	
• Measure the voltage between the speed control servo C122 pin 5, circuit 151 (LB/BK), harness side and the speed control servo C122 pin 10, circuit 57 (BK), harness side.	**Yes** GO to A18. **No** GO to A10.
• Is any voltage present?	

LTV0500000001684

Fig. 127 Test A: Speed Control Is Inoperative (Part 3 of 8). 2004–05 Explorer Sport Trac

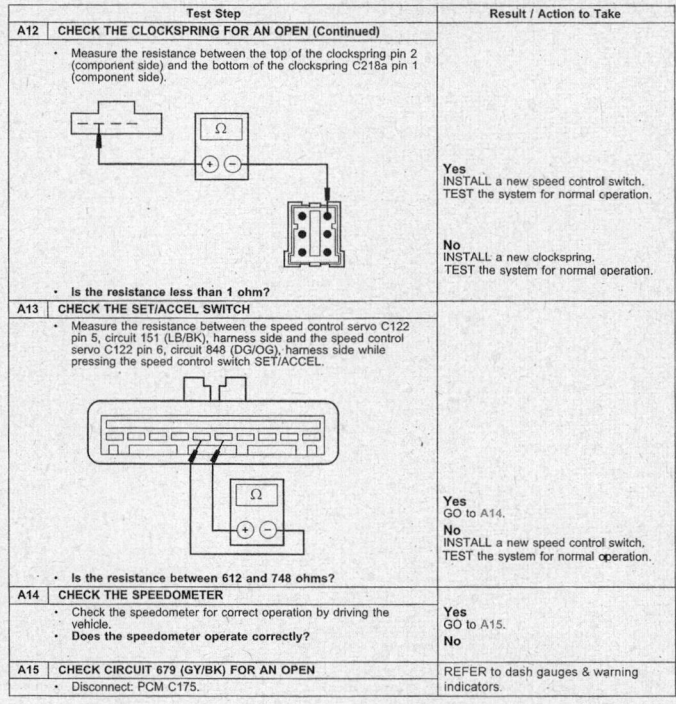

Test Step	Result / Action to Take
A12 CHECK THE CLOCKSPRING FOR AN OPEN (Continued)	
• Measure the resistance between the top of the clockspring pin 2 (component side) and the bottom of the clockspring C218a pin 1 (component side).	**Yes** INSTALL a new speed control switch. TEST the system for normal operation. **No** INSTALL a new clockspring. TEST the system for normal operation.
• Is the resistance less than 1 ohm?	
A13 CHECK THE SET/ACCEL SWITCH	
• Measure the resistance between the speed control servo C122 pin 5, circuit 151 (LB/BK), harness side and the speed control servo C122 pin 6, circuit 848 (DG/OG), harness side while pressing the speed control switch SET/ACCEL.	**Yes** GO to A14. **No** INSTALL a new speed control switch. TEST the system for normal operation.
• Is the resistance between 612 and 748 ohms?	
A14 CHECK THE SPEEDOMETER	
• Check the speedometer for correct operation by driving the vehicle. • **Does the speedometer operate correctly?**	**Yes** GO to A15. **No**
A15 CHECK CIRCUIT 679 (GY/BK) FOR AN OPEN	
• Disconnect: PCM C175.	REFER to dash gauges & warning indicators.

LTV0500000001686

Fig. 127 Test A: Speed Control Is Inoperative (Part 5 of 8). 2004–05 Explorer Sport Trac

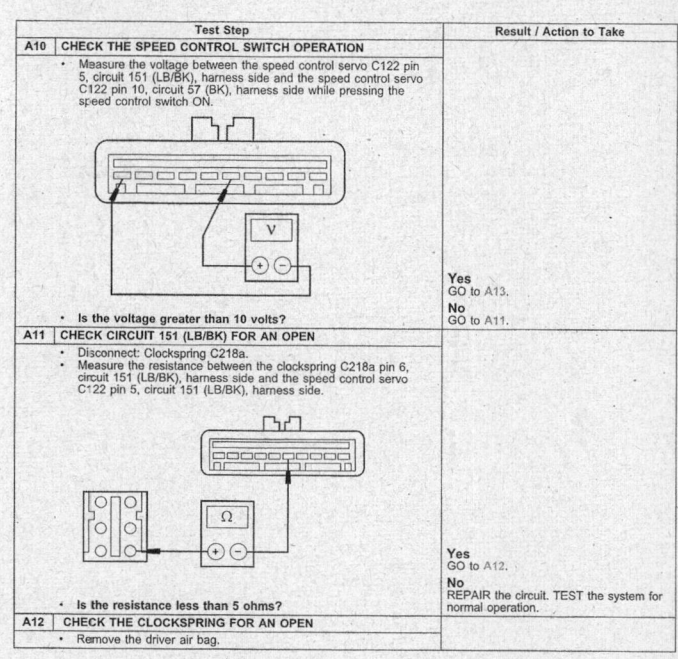

Test Step	Result / Action to Take
A10 CHECK THE SPEED CONTROL SWITCH OPERATION	
• Measure the voltage between the speed control servo C122 pin 5, circuit 151 (LB/BK), harness side and the speed control servo C122 pin 10, circuit 57 (BK), harness side while pressing the speed control switch ON.	**Yes** GO to A13. **No** GO to A11.
• Is the voltage greater than 10 volts?	
A11 CHECK CIRCUIT 151 (LB/BK) FOR AN OPEN	
• Disconnect: Clockspring C218a. • Measure the resistance between the clockspring C218a pin 6, circuit 151 (LB/BK), harness side and the speed control servo C122 pin 5, circuit 151 (LB/BK), harness side.	**Yes** GO to A12. **No** REPAIR the circuit. TEST the system for normal operation.
• Is the resistance less than 5 ohms?	
A12 CHECK THE CLOCKSPRING FOR AN OPEN	
• Remove the driver air bag.	

LTV0500000001685

Fig. 127 Test A: Speed Control Is Inoperative (Part 4 of 8). 2004–05 Explorer Sport Trac

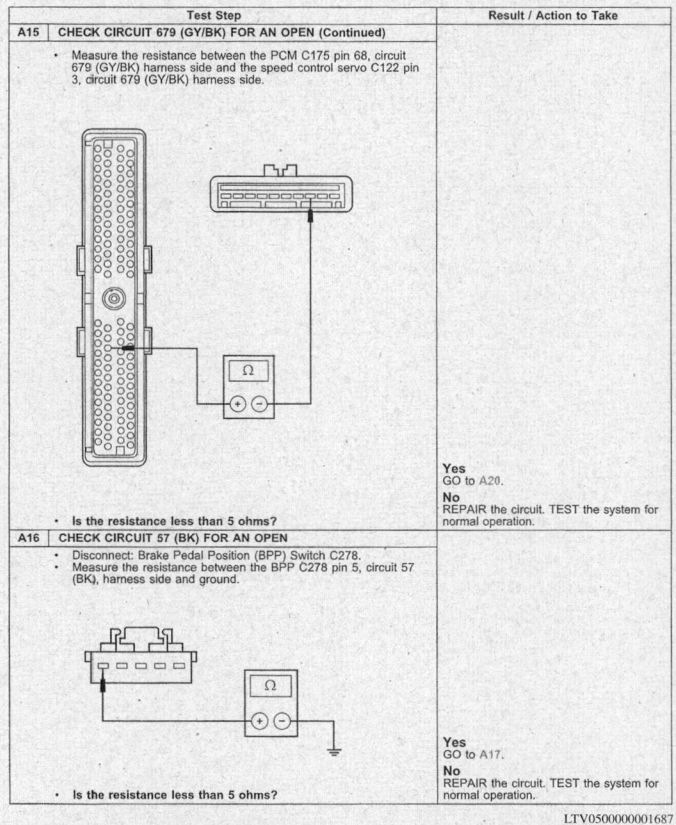

Test Step	Result / Action to Take
A15 CHECK CIRCUIT 679 (GY/BK) FOR AN OPEN (Continued)	
• Measure the resistance between the PCM C175 pin 68, circuit 679 (GY/BK) harness side and the speed control servo C122 pin 3, circuit 679 (GY/BK) harness side.	**Yes** GO to A20. **No** REPAIR the circuit. TEST the system for normal operation.
• Is the resistance less than 5 ohms?	
A16 CHECK CIRCUIT 57 (BK) FOR AN OPEN	
• Disconnect: Brake Pedal Position (BPP) Switch C278. • Measure the resistance between the BPP C278 pin 5, circuit 57 (BK), harness side and ground.	**Yes** GO to A17. **No** REPAIR the circuit. TEST the system for normal operation.
• Is the resistance less than 5 ohms?	

LTV0500000001687

Fig. 127 Test A: Speed Control Is Inoperative (Part 6 of 8). 2004–05 Explorer Sport Trac

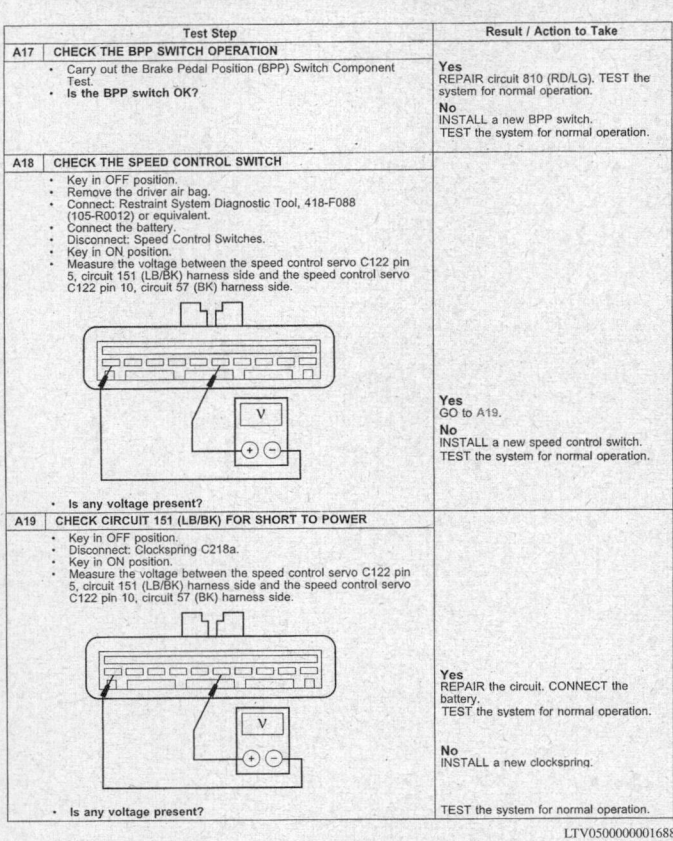

Test Step	Result / Action to Take
A17 CHECK THE BPP SWITCH OPERATION	
• Carry out the Brake Pedal Position (BPP) Switch Component Test. • **Is the BPP switch OK?**	**Yes** REPAIR circuit 810 (RD/LG). TEST the system for normal operation. **No** INSTALL a new BPP switch. TEST the system for normal operation.
A18 CHECK THE SPEED CONTROL SWITCH	
• Key in OFF position. • Remove the driver air bag. • Connect: Restraint System Diagnostic Tool, 418-F088 (105-R0012) or equivalent. • Connect the battery. • Disconnect: Speed Control Switches. • Key in ON position. • Measure the voltage between the speed control servo C122 pin 5, circuit 151 (LB/BK) harness side and the speed control servo C122 pin 10, circuit 57 (BK) harness side.	
• **Is any voltage present?**	**Yes** GO to A19. **No** INSTALL a new speed control switch. TEST the system for normal operation.
A19 CHECK CIRCUIT 151 (LB/BK) FOR SHORT TO POWER	
• Key in OFF position. • Disconnect: Clockspring C218a. • Key in ON position. • Measure the voltage between the speed control servo C122 pin 5, circuit 151 (LB/BK) harness side and the speed control servo C122 pin 10, circuit 57 (BK) harness side.	
• **Is any voltage present?**	**Yes** REPAIR the circuit. CONNECT the battery. TEST the system for normal operation. **No** INSTALL a new clockspring. TEST the system for normal operation.

LTV0500000001688

Fig. 127   Test A: Speed Control Is Inoperative (Part 7 of 8). 2004–05 Explorer Sport Trac

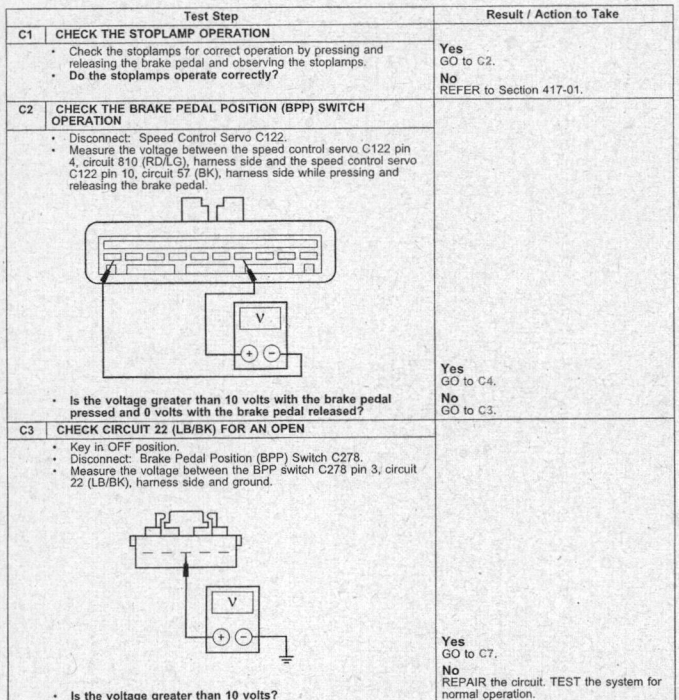

Test Step	Result / Action to Take
C1 CHECK THE STOPLAMP OPERATION	
• Check the stoplamps for correct operation by pressing and releasing the brake pedal and observing the stoplamps. • **Do the stoplamps operate correctly?**	**Yes** GO to C2. **No** REFER to Section 417-01.
C2 CHECK THE BRAKE PEDAL POSITION (BPP) SWITCH OPERATION	
• Disconnect: Speed Control Servo C122. • Measure the voltage between the speed control servo C122 pin 4, circuit 810 (RD/LG), harness side and the speed control servo C122 pin 10, circuit 57 (BK), harness side while pressing and releasing the brake pedal.	
• **Is the voltage greater than 10 volts with the brake pedal pressed and 0 volts with the brake pedal released?**	**Yes** GO to C4. **No** GO to C3.
C3 CHECK CIRCUIT 22 (LB/BK) FOR AN OPEN	
• Key in OFF position. • Disconnect: Brake Pedal Position (BPP) Switch C278. • Measure the voltage between the BPP switch C278 pin 3, circuit 22 (LB/BK), harness side and ground.	
• **Is the voltage greater than 10 volts?**	**Yes** GO to C7. **No** REPAIR the circuit. TEST the system for normal operation.

LTV0500000001691

Fig. 129   Test C: Speed Control Does Not Disengage When Brakes Are Applied (Part 1 of 3). 2004–05 Explorer Sport Trac

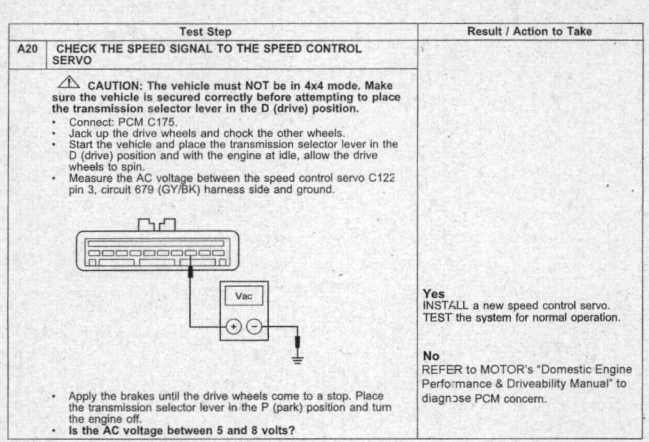

Test Step	Result / Action to Take
A20 CHECK THE SPEED SIGNAL TO THE SPEED CONTROL SERVO	
⚠ CAUTION: The vehicle must NOT be in 4x4 mode. Make sure the vehicle is secured correctly before attempting to place the transmission selector lever in the D (drive) position. • Connect: PCM C175. • Jack up the drive wheels and chock the other wheels. • Start the vehicle and place the transmission selector lever in the D (drive) position and with the engine at idle, allow the drive wheels to spin. • Measure the AC voltage between the speed control servo C122 pin 3, circuit 679 (GY/BK) harness side and ground.	
	Yes INSTALL a new speed control servo. TEST the system for normal operation. **No** REFER to MOTOR's "Domestic Engine Performance & Driveability Manual" to diagnose PCM concern.
• Apply the brakes until the drive wheels come to a stop. Place the transmission selector lever in the P (park) position and turn the engine off. • **Is the AC voltage between 5 and 8 volts?**	

LTV0500000001689

Fig. 127   Test A: Speed Control Is Inoperative (Part 8 of 8). 2004–05 Explorer Sport Trac

Test Step	Result / Action to Take
B1 CHECK SPEED CONTROL CABLE/THROTTLE BODY LINKAGE	
• Key in OFF position. • Hold the throttle open and remove the speed control cable from the speed control servo. Visually inspect the core wire and check the speed control cable by pulling on the cable and noting the throttle movement. • **Is the speed control cable OK?**	**Yes** GO to B2. **No** INSTALL a new speed control cable or REPAIR the throttle body linkage. TEST the system for normal operation.
B2 CHECK FOR CORRECT AMOUNT OF SLACK IN SPEED CONTROL CABLE	
• Remove the speed control cable from the throttle. • Check for correct amount of slack in the speed control cable. • **Is there approximately 3 mm (0.12 in) of slack in the cable?**	**Yes** GO to B3. **No** ADJUST the speed control cable slack to approximately 3 mm (0.12 in). TEST the system for normal operation.
B3 CHECK THE SPEEDOMETER	
• Check the speedometer for correct operation by driving the vehicle. • **Does the speedometer fluctuate?**	**Yes** Diagnose dash gauges & warning indicators. **No** INSTALL a new speed control servo. TEST the system for normal operation.

LTV0500000001690

Fig. 128   Test B: Set Speed Fluctuates. 2004–05 Explorer Sport Trac

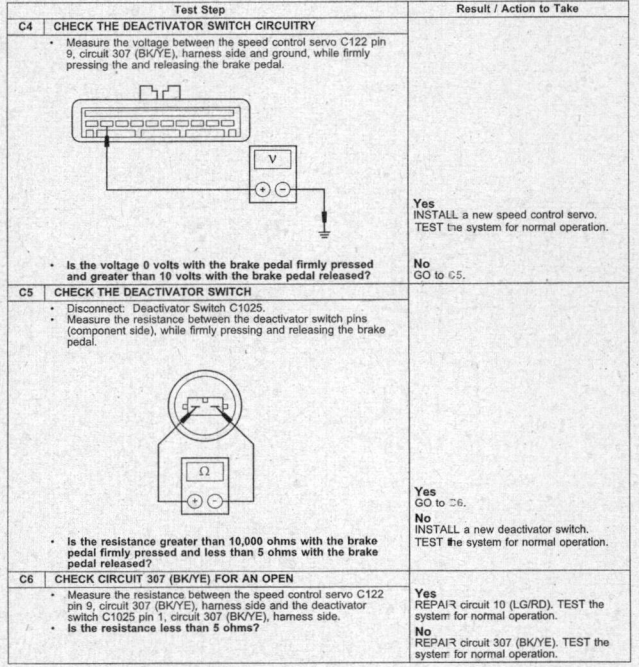

Test Step	Result / Action to Take
C4 CHECK THE DEACTIVATOR SWITCH CIRCUITRY	
• Measure the voltage between the speed control servo C122 pin 9, circuit 307 (BK/YE), harness side and ground, while firmly pressing the and releasing the brake pedal.	
	Yes INSTALL a new speed control servo. TEST the system for normal operation.
• **Is the voltage 0 volts with the brake pedal firmly pressed and greater than 10 volts with the brake pedal released?**	**No** GO to C5.
C5 CHECK THE DEACTIVATOR SWITCH	
• Disconnect: Deactivator Switch C1025. • Measure the resistance between the deactivator switch pins (component side), while firmly pressing and releasing the brake pedal.	
• **Is the resistance greater than 10,000 ohms with the brake pedal firmly pressed and less than 5 ohms with the brake pedal released?**	**Yes** GO to C6. **No** INSTALL a new deactivator switch. TEST the system for normal operation.
C6 CHECK CIRCUIT 307 (BK/YE) FOR AN OPEN	
• Measure the resistance between the speed control servo C122 pin 9, circuit 307 (BK/YE), harness side and the deactivator switch C1025 pin 1, circuit 307 (BK/YE), harness side. • **Is the resistance less than 5 ohms?**	**Yes** REPAIR circuit 10 (LG/RD). TEST the system for normal operation. **No** REPAIR circuit 307 (BK/YE). TEST the system for normal operation.

LTV0500000001692

Fig. 129   Test C: Speed Control Does Not Disengage When Brakes Are Applied (Part 2 of 3). 2004–05 Explorer Sport Trac

Test Step	Result / Action to Take
C7 CHECK CIRCUIT 810 (RD/LG) FOR GROUND	
• Measure the resistance between the BPP switch C278 pin 4, circuit 810 (RD/LG), harness side and ground. 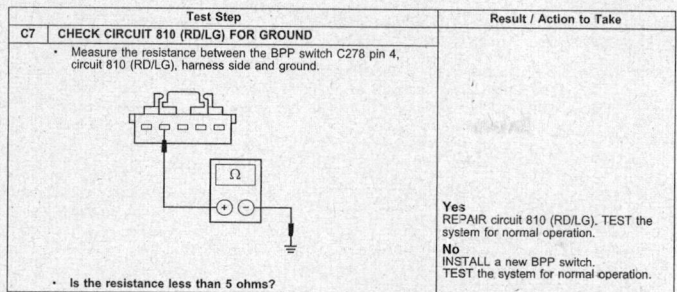 • Is the resistance less than 5 ohms?	**Yes** REPAIR circuit 810 (RD/LG). TEST the system for normal operation. **No** INSTALL a new BPP switch. TEST the system for normal operation.

LTV0500000001693

Fig. 129 Test C: Speed Control Does Not Disengage When Brakes Are Applied (Part 3 of 3). 2004–05 Explorer Sport Trac

Test Step	Result / Action to Take
E1 CHECK THE SPEED CONTROL CABLE	
• Check the speed control cable for correct attachment at the speed control servo and throttle body. • Is the speed control cable attached correctly?	**Yes** GO to E2. **No** RECONNECT the speed control cable. REPEAT the self-test.
E2 CHECK FOR CORRECT AMOUNT OF SLACK IN SPEED CONTROL CABLE	
• Remove the speed control cable from the throttle. • Check for correct amount of slack in the speed control cable. • Is there approximately 3 mm (0.12 in) of slack in the cable?	**Yes** GO to E3. **No** ADJUST the speed control cable slack to approximately 3 mm (0.12 in). TEST the system for normal operation.
E3 CHECK FOR A STICKING OR BINDING SPEED CONTROL CABLE	
• Check the speed control cable for sticking or binding. • Is the speed control cable OK?	**Yes** INSTALL a new speed control servo. REPEAT the self-test. **No** REPAIR or INSTALL a new speed control cable. REPEAT the self-test.

LTV0500000001695

Fig. 131 Test E: Flash w/Last Switch Pressed, But No Dynamic Pull Occurs At Throttle & Speed Control Is Inoperative. 2004–05 Explorer Sport Trac

Test Step	Result / Action to Take
F1 CHECK THE STOPLAMP OPERATION	
• Press and release the brake pedal while observing the stoplamps. • Do the stoplamps operate correctly?	**Yes** GO to F2. **No** Diagnose stoplamps.
F2 CHECK CIRCUIT 810 (RD/LG) FOR AN OPEN	
• Key in OFF position. • Disconnect: Speed Control Servo C122. • Key in ON position. • Measure the voltage between the speed control servo C122 pin 4, circuit 810 (RD/LG), harness side and the speed control servo C122 pin 10, circuit 57 (BK), harness side, while pressing the brake pedal. • Is the voltage greater than 10 volts?	**Yes** GO to F3. **No** GO to F5.
F3 CHECK THE BRAKE CIRCUIT	
• Key in OFF position.	

LTV0500000001696

Fig. 132 Test F: Brake Pedal Position Switch Circuit Failure (Part 1 of 2). 2004–05 Explorer Sport Trac

Test Step	Result / Action to Take
D1 CHECK THE SPEED CONTROL SWITCH	
• Key in OFF position. • Disconnect: Speed Control Servo C122. • Measure the resistance between the speed control servo C122 pin 5, circuit 151 (LB/BK), harness side and the speed control servo C122 pin 6, circuit 848 (DG/OG), harness side while pressing the speed control switch as follows: 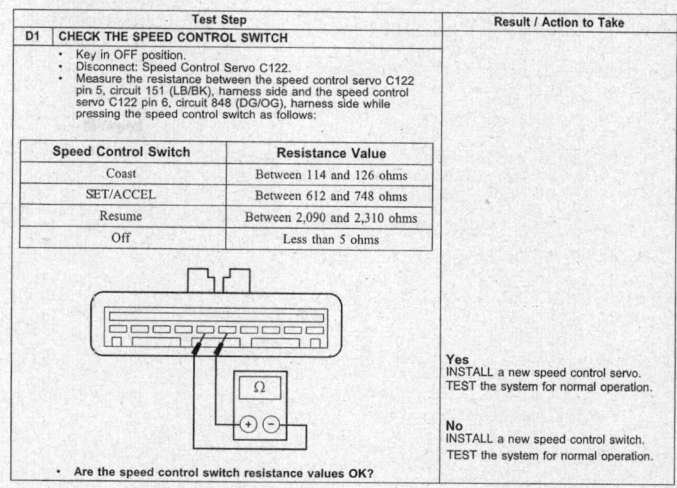	**Yes** INSTALL a new speed control servo. TEST the system for normal operation. **No** INSTALL a new speed control switch. TEST the system for normal operation.

Speed Control Switch	Resistance Value
Coast	Between 114 and 126 ohms
SET/ACCEL	Between 612 and 748 ohms
Resume	Between 2,090 and 2,310 ohms
Off	Less than 5 ohms

• Are the speed control switch resistance values OK?

LTV0500000001694

Fig. 130 Test D: Speed Control Does Not Disengage When Clutch Is Applied. 2004–05 Explorer Sport Trac

Test Step	Result / Action to Take
F3 CHECK THE BRAKE CIRCUIT (Continued)	
• Measure the resistance between the speed control servo C122 pin 4, circuit 810 (RD/LG), harness side and the speed control servo C122 pin 10, circuit 57 (BK), harness side. • Is the resistance less than 5 ohms?	**Yes** INSTALL a new speed control servo. TEST the system for normal operation. **No** GO to F4.
F4 CHECK CIRCUIT 57 (BK) FOR AN OPEN	
• Disconnect: BPP Switch C278. • Measure the resistance between the BPP switch C278 pin 5, circuit 57 (BK), harness side and ground. • Is the resistance less than 5 ohms?	**Yes** INSTALL a new BPP switch. TEST the system for normal operation. **No** REPAIR the circuit. TEST the system for normal operation.
F5 CHECK THE BPP SWITCH	
• Key in OFF position. • Disconnect: BPP Switch C278. • Measure the resistance between the speed control servo C122 pin 4, circuit 810 (RD/LG), harness side and the BPP switch C278 pin 4, circuit 810 (RD/LG), harness side. • Is the resistance less than 5 ohms?	**Yes** INSTALL a new BPP switch. TEST the system for normal operation. **No** REPAIR circuit 810 (RD/LG). TEST the system for normal operation.

LTV0500000001697

Fig. 132 Test F: Brake Pedal Position Switch Circuit Failure (Part 2 of 2). 2004–05 Explorer Sport Trac

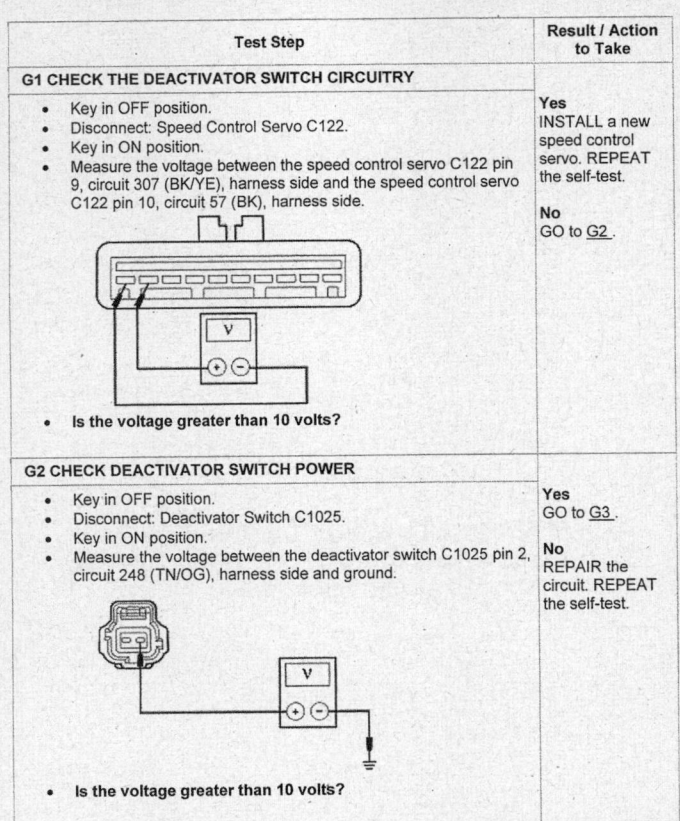

Test Step	Result / Action to Take
G1 CHECK THE DEACTIVATOR SWITCH CIRCUITRY	
• Key in OFF position. • Disconnect: Speed Control Servo C122. • Key in ON position. • Measure the voltage between the speed control servo C122 pin 9, circuit 307 (BK/YE), harness side and the speed control servo C122 pin 10, circuit 57 (BK), harness side.	**Yes** INSTALL a new speed control servo. REPEAT the self-test. **No** GO to G2.
• Is the voltage greater than 10 volts?	
G2 CHECK DEACTIVATOR SWITCH POWER	
• Key in OFF position. • Disconnect: Deactivator Switch C1025. • Key in ON position. • Measure the voltage between the deactivator switch C1025 pin 2, circuit 248 (TN/OG), harness side and ground.	**Yes** GO to G3. **No** REPAIR the circuit. REPEAT the self-test.
• Is the voltage greater than 10 volts?	

Fig. 133 Test G: Deactivator Switch Circuit Failure (Part 1 of 2). 2004–05 Explorer Sport Trac

Test Step	Result / Action to Take
H1 CHECK SPEED CONTROL SERVO	
• Key in OFF position. • Disconnect: Speed Control Servo C122. • Key in ON position. • Check the speed control indicator lamp always on? **• Is the speed control indicator lamp always on?**	**Yes** GO to H2. **No** INSTALL a new speed control servo. TEST the system for normal operation.
H2 CHECK CIRCUIT 203 (OG/LB) FOR SHORT TO GROUND	
• Key in OFF position. • Disconnect: Instrument Cluster C220a. • Measure the resistance between the speed control servo C122 pin 1, circuit 203 (OG/LB), harness side and ground.	**Yes** INSTALL a new instrument cluster. TEST the system for normal operation. **No** REPAIR the circuit. TEST the system for normal operation.
• Is the resistance greater than 10,000 ohms?	

Fig. 134 Test H: Speed Control Indicator Lamp Is Always On. 2004–05 Explorer Sport Trac

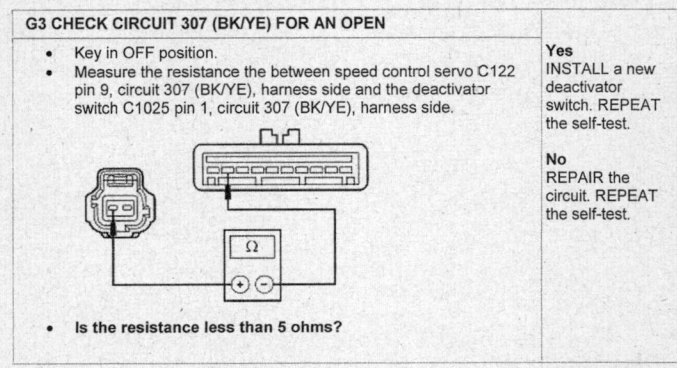

Test Step	Result / Action to Take
G3 CHECK CIRCUIT 307 (BK/YE) FOR AN OPEN	
• Key in OFF position. • Measure the resistance the between speed control servo C122 pin 9, circuit 307 (BK/YE), harness side and the deactivator switch C1025 pin 1, circuit 307 (BK/YE), harness side.	**Yes** INSTALL a new deactivator switch. REPEAT the self-test. **No** REPAIR the circuit. REPEAT the self-test.
• Is the resistance less than 5 ohms?	

Fig. 133 Test G: Deactivator Switch Circuit Failure (Part 2 of 2). 2004–05 Explorer Sport Trac

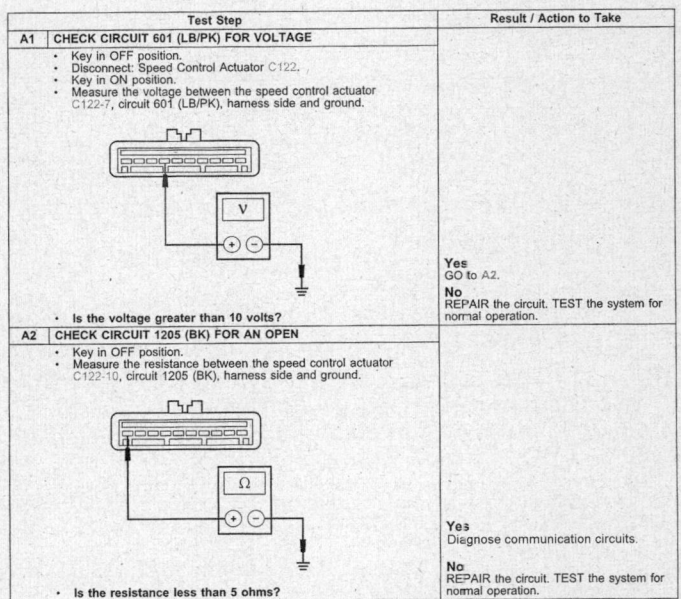

Test Step	Result / Action to Take
A1 CHECK CIRCUIT 601 (LB/PK) FOR VOLTAGE	
• Key in OFF position. • Disconnect: Speed Control Actuator C122. • Key in ON position. • Measure the voltage between the speed control actuator C122-7, circuit 601 (LB/PK), harness side and ground.	**Yes** GO to A2. **No** REPAIR the circuit. TEST the system for normal operation.
• Is the voltage greater than 10 volts?	
A2 CHECK CIRCUIT 1205 (BK) FOR AN OPEN	
• Key in OFF position. • Measure the resistance between the speed control actuator C122-10, circuit 1205 (BK), harness side and ground.	**Yes** Diagnose communication circuits. **No** REPAIR the circuit. TEST the system for normal operation.
• Is the resistance less than 5 ohms?	

Fig. 135 Test A: No Communication w/Speed Control Actuator. Freestar & Monterey

Test Step	Result / Action to Take
B1 CHECK THE COMMUNICATION TO THE SPEED CONTROL MODULE	
• Check the communication to the speed control module. **• Does the diagnostic tool communicate with the speed control actuator?**	**Yes** INSTALL a new speed control actuator. TEST the system for normal operation. **No** GO to Pinpoint Test A.

Fig. 136 Test B: Speed Control Is Inoperative & Unable To Enter Self-Test. Freestar & Monterey

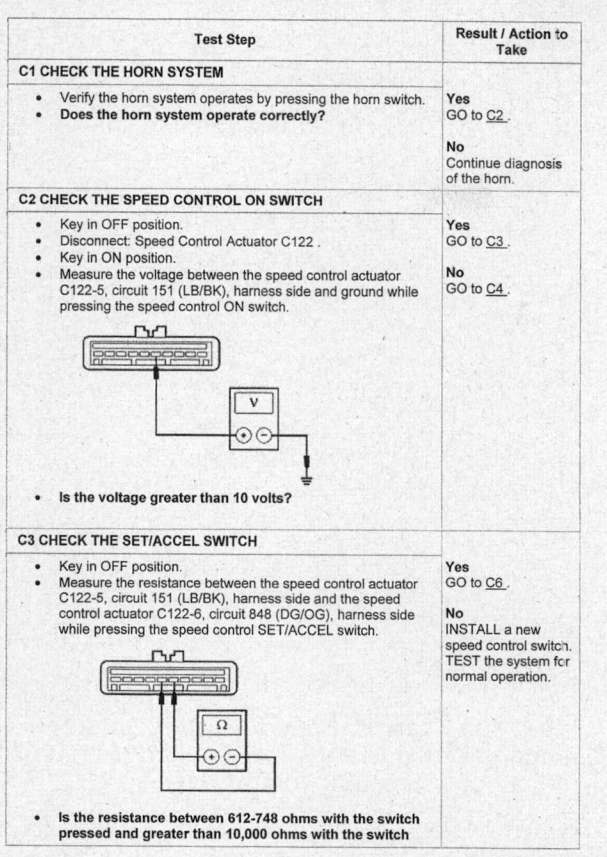

Test Step	Result / Action to Take
C1 CHECK THE HORN SYSTEM	
• Verify the horn system operates by pressing the horn switch. • **Does the horn system operate correctly?**	**Yes** GO to C2. **No** Continue diagnosis of the horn.
C2 CHECK THE SPEED CONTROL ON SWITCH	
• Key in OFF position. • Disconnect: Speed Control Actuator C122. • Key in ON position. • Measure the voltage between the speed control actuator C122-5, circuit 151 (LB/BK), harness side and ground while pressing the speed control ON switch. • **Is the voltage greater than 10 volts?**	**Yes** GO to C3. **No** GO to C4.
C3 CHECK THE SET/ACCEL SWITCH	
• Key in OFF position. • Measure the resistance between the speed control actuator C122-5, circuit 151 (LB/BK), harness side and the speed control actuator C122-6, circuit 848 (DG/OG), harness side while pressing the speed control SET/ACCEL switch. • **Is the resistance between 612-748 ohms with the switch pressed and greater than 10,000 ohms with the switch**	**Yes** GO to C6. **No** INSTALL a new speed control switch. TEST the system for normal operation.

LTV0500000001766

Fig. 137 Test C: Speed Control Is Inoperative (Part 1 of 3). Freestar & Monterey

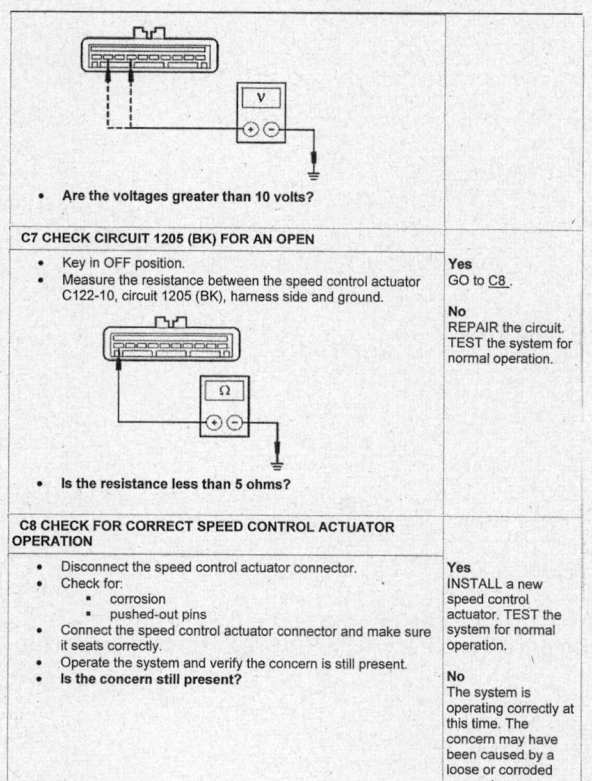

Test Step	Result / Action to Take
• **Are the voltages greater than 10 volts?**	
C7 CHECK CIRCUIT 1205 (BK) FOR AN OPEN	
• Key in OFF position. • Measure the resistance between the speed control actuator C122-10, circuit 1205 (BK), harness side and ground. • **Is the resistance less than 5 ohms?**	**Yes** GO to C8. **No** REPAIR the circuit. TEST the system for normal operation.
C8 CHECK FOR CORRECT SPEED CONTROL ACTUATOR OPERATION	

• Disconnect the speed control actuator connector.
• Check for:
  ▪ corrosion
  ▪ pushed-out pins
• Connect the speed control actuator connector and make sure it seats correctly.
• Operate the system and verify the concern is still present.
• **Is the concern still present?**
	Yes
	INSTALL a new speed control actuator. TEST the system for normal operation.
	
	No
	The system is operating correctly at this time. The concern may have been caused by a loose or corroded connector.

LTV0500000001768

Fig. 137 Test C: Speed Control Is Inoperative (Part 3 of 3). Freestar & Monterey

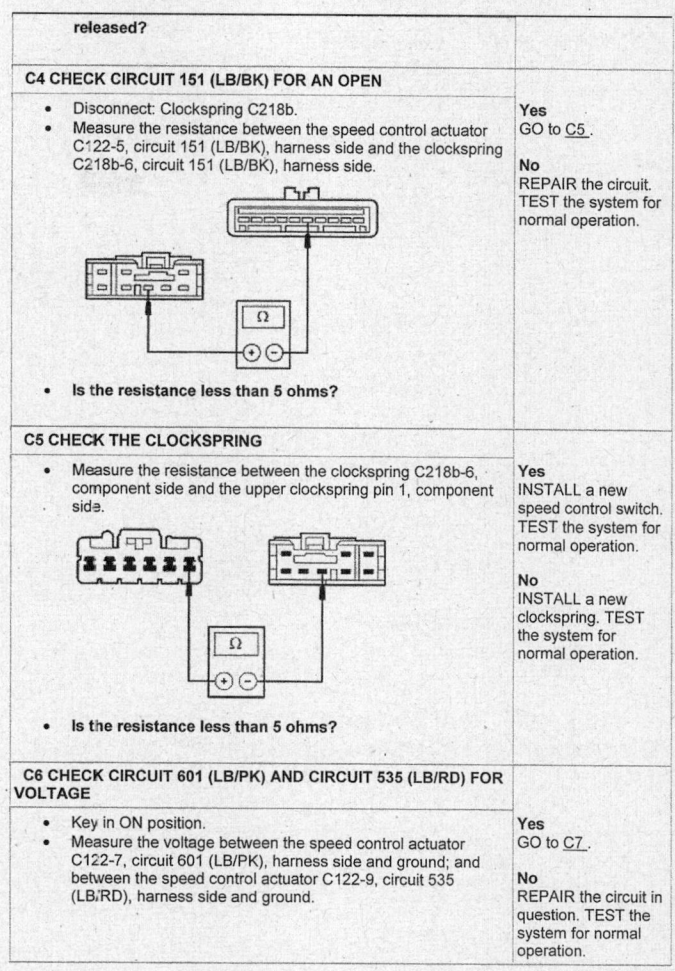

Test Step	Result / Action to Take
released?	
C4 CHECK CIRCUIT 151 (LB/BK) FOR AN OPEN	
• Disconnect: Clockspring C218b. • Measure the resistance between the speed control actuator C122-5, circuit 151 (LB/BK), harness side and the clockspring C218b-6, circuit 151 (LB/BK), harness side. • **Is the resistance less than 5 ohms?**	**Yes** GO to C5. **No** REPAIR the circuit. TEST the system for normal operation.
C5 CHECK THE CLOCKSPRING	
• Measure the resistance between the clockspring C218b-6, component side and the upper clockspring pin 1, component side. • **Is the resistance less than 5 ohms?**	**Yes** INSTALL a new speed control switch. TEST the system for normal operation. **No** INSTALL a new clockspring. TEST the system for normal operation.
C6 CHECK CIRCUIT 601 (LB/PK) AND CIRCUIT 535 (LB/RD) FOR VOLTAGE	
• Key in ON position. • Measure the voltage between the speed control actuator C122-7, circuit 601 (LB/PK), harness side and ground; and between the speed control actuator C122-9, circuit 535 (LB/RD), harness side and ground.	**Yes** GO to C7. **No** REPAIR the circuit in question. TEST the system for normal operation.

LTV0500000001767

Fig. 137 Test C: Speed Control Is Inoperative (Part 2 of 3). Freestar & Monterey

Test Step		Result / Action to Take
D1	**CHECK THE SPEED CONTROL THROTTLE ATTACHMENT**	
	NOTE: There must not be any loose components when carrying out the speed control actuator slack test. • Check the throttle lever, speed control cable, and accelerator cable bracket for correct operation while carrying out the speed control actuator slack test on the diagnostic tool. • **Do the throttle lever components operate correctly?**	**Yes** The system is operating correctly at this time. **No** GO to D2.
D2	**CHECK FOR CORRECT SPEED CONTROL ACTUATOR OPERATION**	

	• Disconnect the speed control actuator connector.
	• Check for:
	  — corrosion
	  — pushed-out pins
	• Connect the speed control actuator connector and make sure it seats correctly.
	• Operate the system and verify the concern is still present.
	• **Is the concern still present?**
		Yes
		INSTALL a new speed control actuator. TEST the system for normal operation.
		
		No
		The system is operating correctly at this time. The concern may have been caused by a loose or corroded connector.

LTV0500000001769

Fig. 138 Test D: Set Speed Fluctuates. Freestar & Monterey

Test Step		Result / Action to Take
E1	**MONITOR THE STOPLAMP SWITCH PID**	
	• Monitor the smart junction box (SJB) stoplamp switch PID while applying and releasing the brake pedal. • **Do the PID values agree with the application and release of the brake pedal?**	**Yes** GO to E2. **No** Diagnose stoplamps.
E2	**CHECK CIRCUIT 535 (LB/RD) FOR VOLTAGE**	
	• Disconnect: Speed Control Actuator C122. • Key in ON position.	

LTV0500000001770

Fig. 139 Test E: Speed Control Does Not Disengage When Brakes Are Applied (Part 1 of 4). Freestar & Monterey

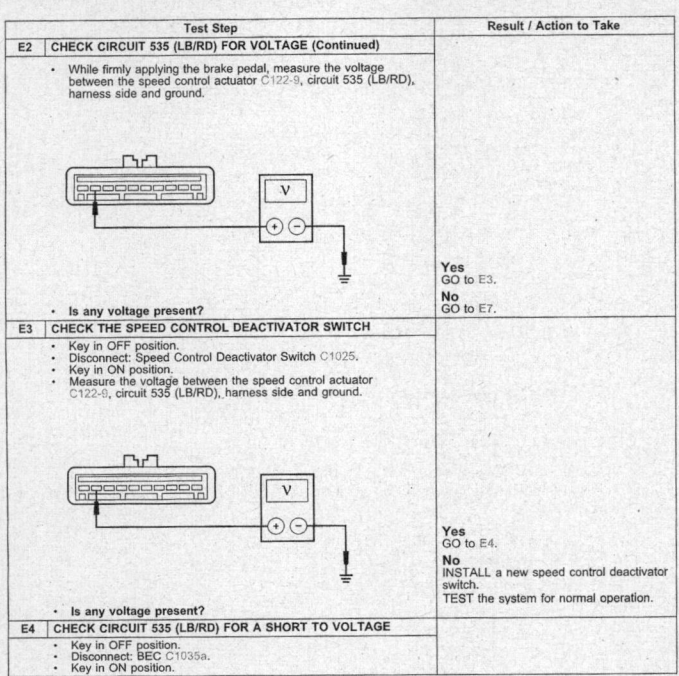

Test Step		Result / Action to Take
E2	CHECK CIRCUIT 535 (LB/RD) FOR VOLTAGE (Continued)	
	• While firmly applying the brake pedal, measure the voltage between the speed control actuator C122-9, circuit 535 (LB/RD), harness side and ground.	
	• Is any voltage present?	**Yes** GO to E3. **No** GO to E7.
E3	CHECK THE SPEED CONTROL DEACTIVATOR SWITCH	
	• Key in OFF position. • Disconnect: Speed Control Deactivator Switch C1025. • Key in ON position. • Measure the voltage between the speed control actuator C122-9, circuit 535 (LB/RD), harness side and ground.	
	• Is any voltage present?	**Yes** GO to E4. **No** INSTALL a new speed control deactivator switch. TEST the system for normal operation.
E4	CHECK CIRCUIT 535 (LB/RD) FOR A SHORT TO VOLTAGE	
	• Key in OFF position. • Disconnect: BEC C1035a. • Key in ON position.	

LTV0500000001771

Fig. 139   Test E: Speed Control Does Not Disengage When Brakes Are Applied (Part 2 of 4). Freestar & Monterey

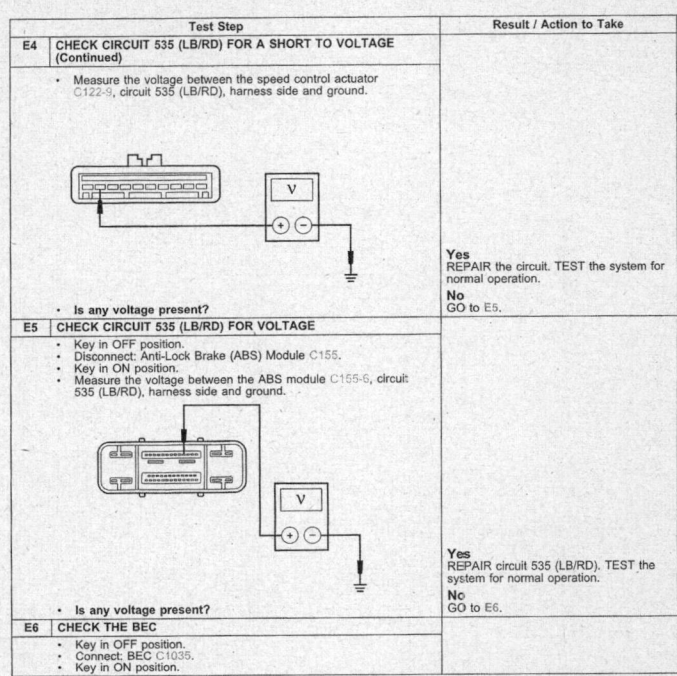

Test Step		Result / Action to Take
E4	CHECK CIRCUIT 535 (LB/RD) FOR A SHORT TO VOLTAGE (Continued)	
	• Measure the voltage between the speed control actuator C122-9, circuit 535 (LB/RD), harness side and ground.	
	• Is any voltage present?	**Yes** REPAIR the circuit. TEST the system for normal operation. **No** GO to E5.
E5	CHECK CIRCUIT 535 (LB/RD) FOR VOLTAGE	
	• Key in OFF position. • Disconnect: Anti-Lock Brake (ABS) Module C155. • Key in ON position. • Measure the voltage between the ABS module C155-6, circuit 535 (LB/RD), harness side and ground.	
	• Is any voltage present?	**Yes** REPAIR circuit 535 (LB/RD). TEST the system for normal operation. **No** GO to E6.
E6	CHECK THE BEC	
	• Key in OFF position. • Connect: BEC C1035. • Key in ON position.	

LTV0500000001772

Fig. 139   Test E: Speed Control Does Not Disengage When Brakes Are Applied (Part 3 of 4). Freestar & Monterey

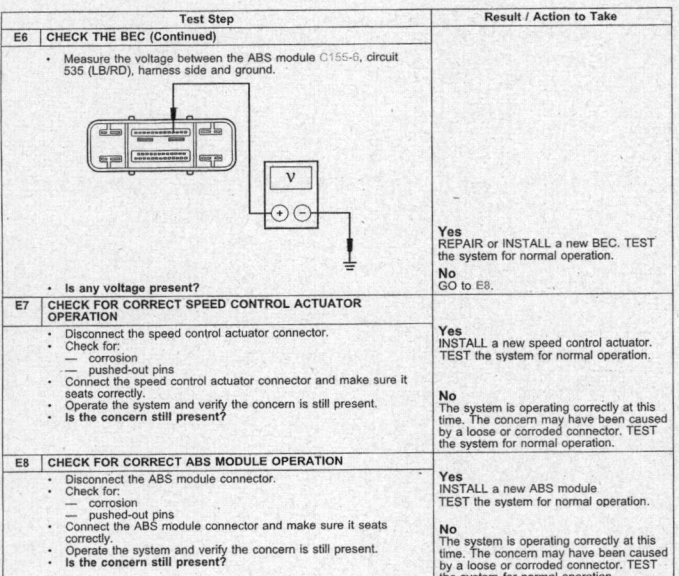

Test Step		Result / Action to Take
E6	CHECK THE BEC (Continued)	
	• Measure the voltage between the ABS module C155-6, circuit 535 (LB/RD), harness side and ground.	
	• Is any voltage present?	**Yes** REPAIR or INSTALL a new BEC. TEST the system for normal operation. **No** GO to E8.
E7	CHECK FOR CORRECT SPEED CONTROL ACTUATOR OPERATION	
	• Disconnect the speed control actuator connector. • Check for: — corrosion — pushed-out pins • Connect the speed control actuator connector and make sure it seats correctly. • Operate the system and verify the concern is still present. • Is the concern still present?	**Yes** INSTALL a new speed control actuator. TEST the system for normal operation. **No** The system is operating correctly at this time. The concern may have been caused by a loose or corroded connector. TEST the system for normal operation.
E8	CHECK FOR CORRECT ABS MODULE OPERATION	
	• Disconnect the ABS module connector. • Check for: — corrosion — pushed-out pins • Connect the ABS module connector and make sure it seats correctly. • Operate the system and verify the concern is still present. • Is the concern still present?	**Yes** INSTALL a new ABS module TEST the system for normal operation. **No** The system is operating correctly at this time. The concern may have been caused by a loose or corroded connector. TEST the system for normal operation.

LTV0500000001773

Fig. 139   Test E: Speed Control Does Not Disengage When Brakes Are Applied (Part 4 of 4). Freestar & Monterey

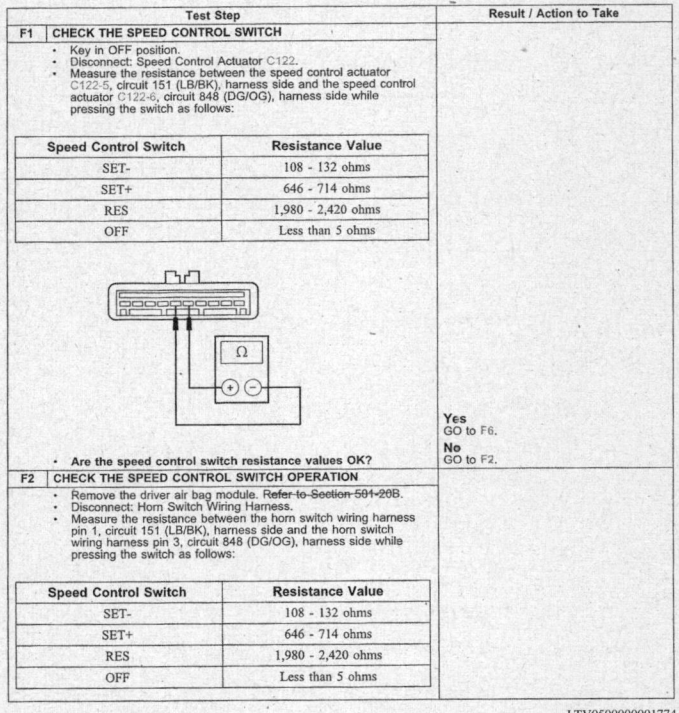

Test Step		Result / Action to Take
F1	CHECK THE SPEED CONTROL SWITCH	
	• Key in OFF position. • Disconnect: Speed Control Actuator C122. • Measure the resistance between the speed control actuator C122-5, circuit 151 (LB/BK), harness side and the speed control actuator C122-6, circuit 848 (DG/OG), harness side while pressing the switch as follows:	

Speed Control Switch	Resistance Value
SET-	108 - 132 ohms
SET+	646 - 714 ohms
RES	1,980 - 2,420 ohms
OFF	Less than 5 ohms

Test Step		Result / Action to Take
	• Are the speed control switch resistance values OK?	**Yes** GO to F6. **No** GO to F2.
F2	CHECK THE SPEED CONTROL SWITCH OPERATION	
	• Remove the driver air bag module. Refer to Section 501-20B. • Disconnect: Horn Switch Wiring Harness. • Measure the resistance between the horn switch wiring harness pin 1, circuit 151 (LB/BK), harness side and the horn switch wiring harness pin 3, circuit 848 (DG/OG), harness side while pressing the switch as follows:	

Speed Control Switch	Resistance Value
SET-	108 - 132 ohms
SET+	646 - 714 ohms
RES	1,980 - 2,420 ohms
OFF	Less than 5 ohms

LTV0500000001774

Fig. 140   Test F: Speed Control Switch Is Inoperative (Part 1 of 3). Freestar & Monterey

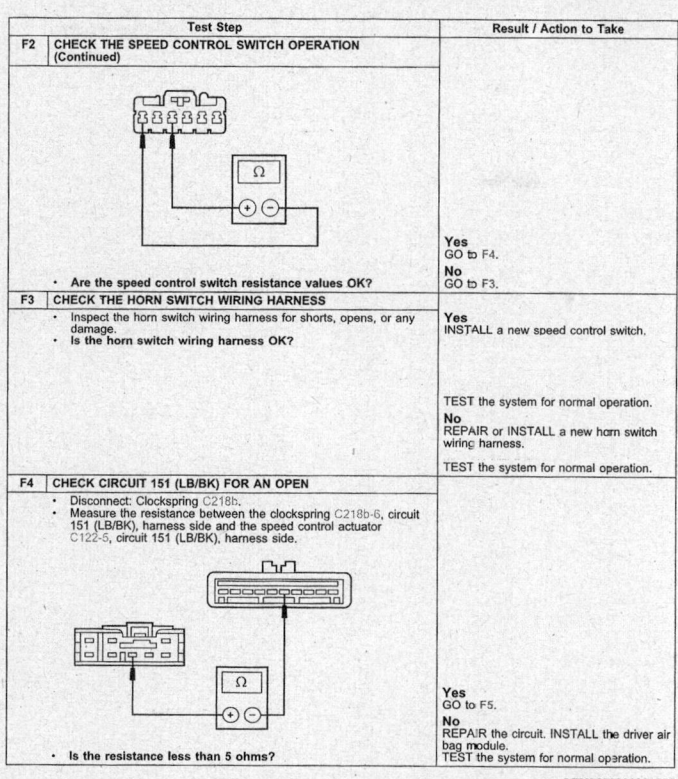

Test Step	Result / Action to Take
F2 CHECK THE SPEED CONTROL SWITCH OPERATION (Continued)	
• Are the speed control switch resistance values OK?	**Yes** GO to F4. **No** GO to F3.
F3 CHECK THE HORN SWITCH WIRING HARNESS	
• Inspect the horn switch wiring harness for shorts, opens, or any damage. • Is the horn switch wiring harness OK?	**Yes** INSTALL a new speed control switch. TEST the system for normal operation. **No** REPAIR or INSTALL a new horn switch wiring harness. TEST the system for normal operation.
F4 CHECK CIRCUIT 151 (LB/BK) FOR AN OPEN	
• Disconnect: Clockspring C218b. • Measure the resistance between the clockspring C218b-6, circuit 151 (LB/BK), harness side and the speed control actuator C122-5, circuit 151 (LB/BK), harness side. • Is the resistance less than 5 ohms?	**Yes** GO to F5. **No** REPAIR the circuit. INSTALL the driver air bag module. TEST the system for normal operation.

LTV0500000001775

Fig. 140   Test F: Speed Control Switch Is Inoperative (Part 2 of 3). Freestar & Monterey

Test Step	Result / Action to Take
G1 CHECK THE SPEED CONTROL ACTUATOR	
• Key in OFF position. • Disconnect: Speed Control Actuator C122. • Key in ON position. • **Does the speed control indicator lamp remain on?**	**Yes** GO to G2. **No** GO to G3.
G2 CHECK FOR CORRECT INSTRUMENT CLUSTER OPERATION	
• Disconnect the instrument cluster connector. • Check for: ▪ corrosion ▪ pushed-out pins • Connect the instrument cluster connector and make sure it seats correctly. • Operate the system and verify the concern is still present. • **Is the concern still present?**	**Yes** INSTALL a new instrument cluster. TEST the system for normal operation. **No** The system is operating correctly at this time. The concern may have been caused by a loose or corroded connector.
G3 CHECK FOR CORRECT SPEED CONTROL ACTUATOR OPERATION	
• Disconnect the speed control actuator connector. • Check for: ▪ corrosion ▪ pushed-out pins • Connect the speed control actuator connector and make sure it seats correctly. • Operate the system and verify the concern is still present. • **Is the concern still present?**	**Yes** INSTALL a new speed control actuator. TEST the system for normal operation. **No** The system is operating correctly at this time. The concern may have been caused by a loose or corroded connector.

LTV0500000001777

Fig. 141   Test G: Speed Control Indicator Lamp Is Always On. Freestar & Monterey

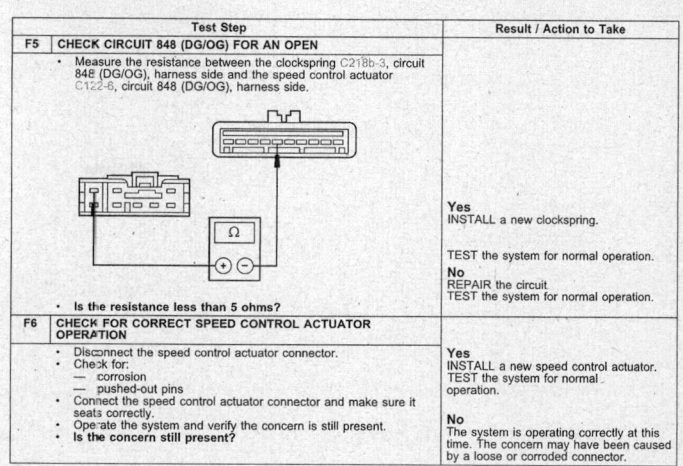

Test Step	Result / Action to Take
F5 CHECK CIRCUIT 848 (DG/OG) FOR AN OPEN	
• Measure the resistance between the clockspring C218b-3, circuit 848 (DG/OG), harness side and the speed control actuator C122-6, circuit 848 (DG/OG), harness side. • Is the resistance less than 5 ohms?	**Yes** INSTALL a new clockspring. TEST the system for normal operation. **No** REPAIR the circuit. TEST the system for normal operation.
F6 CHECK FOR CORRECT SPEED CONTROL ACTUATOR OPERATION	
• Disconnect the speed control actuator connector. • Check for: — corrosion — pushed-out pins • Connect the speed control actuator connector and make sure it seats correctly. • Operate the system and verify the concern is still present. • **Is the concern still present?**	**Yes** INSTALL a new speed control actuator. TEST the system for normal operation. **No** The system is operating correctly at this time. The concern may have been caused by a loose or corroded connector.

LTV0500000001776

Fig. 140   Test F: Speed Control Switch Is Inoperative (Part 3 of 3). Freestar & Monterey

Test Step	Result / Action to Take
H1 CHECK THE SPEED CONTROL ACTUATOR PID	
• Monitor the speed control actuator steering wheel switch PIDs. • Press and release all the speed control switches. • **Does the PID indicate ACTIVE with each speed control switch pressed and NOT ACTIVE with each speed control switch released?**	**Yes** The system is operating correctly at this time. CLEAR the DTCs. REPEAT the self-test. **No** GO to H2.
H2 CHECK THE SPEED CONTROL SWITCH	
• Key in OFF position. • Remove the driver air bag module. Connect the restraint system diagnostic tool (418-F403) to the driver air bag module electrical connector. • ⚠ **WARNING: Make sure there is no one inside the vehicle and that there is nothing blocking or set in front of any air bag module when the battery is connected.** • Connect the battery. • Disconnect: Speed Control Switch. • Key in ON position. • Enter the following diagnostic mode on the diagnostic tool: Clear Continuous DTCs. • Wait 3 minutes. • Retrieve and document the continuous DTCs. • **Is DTC C1126 retrieved?**	**Yes** GO to H3. **No** INSTALL a new speed control switch. CLEAR the DTCs. REPEAT the self-test.
H3 CHECK CIRCUIT 151 (LB/BK) FOR A SHORT TO GROUND	
• Key in OFF position. • Disconnect: Speed Control Actuator C122. • Measure the resistance between the speed control actuator C122-5, circuit 151 (LB/BK), harness side and ground.	**Yes** GO to H5. **No** GO to H4.

LTV0500000001778

Fig. 142   Test H, Code C1126: Command Switch Stuck For 2 Minutes Or Longer (Part 1 of 2). Freestar & Monterey

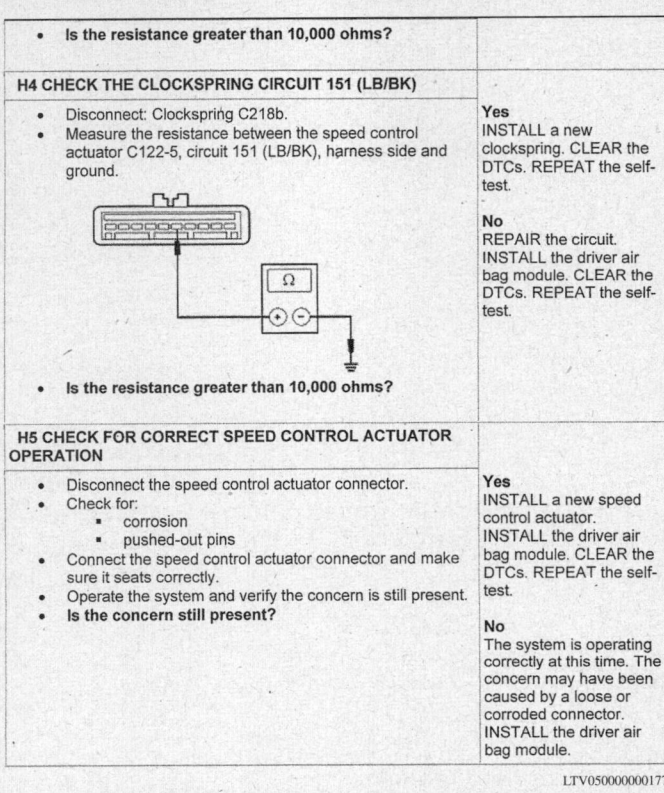

- Is the resistance greater than 10,000 ohms?

Test Step	Result / Action to Take
H4 CHECK THE CLOCKSPRING CIRCUIT 151 (LB/BK)	
• Disconnect: Clockspring C218b. • Measure the resistance between the speed control actuator C122-5, circuit 151 (LB/BK), harness side and ground. • Is the resistance greater than 10,000 ohms?	**Yes** INSTALL a new clockspring. CLEAR the DTCs. REPEAT the self-test. **No** REPAIR the circuit. INSTALL the driver air bag module. CLEAR the DTCs. REPEAT the self-test.
H5 CHECK FOR CORRECT SPEED CONTROL ACTUATOR OPERATION	

• Disconnect the speed control actuator connector.
• Check for:
  ▪ corrosion
  ▪ pushed-out pins
• Connect the speed control actuator connector and make sure it seats correctly.
• Operate the system and verify the concern is still present.
• **Is the concern still present?**
	Yes
	INSTALL a new speed control actuator. INSTALL the driver air bag module. CLEAR the DTCs. REPEAT the self-test.
	
	No
	The system is operating correctly at this time. The concern may have been caused by a loose or corroded connector. INSTALL the driver air bag module.

LTV0500000001779

Fig. 142 Test H, Code C1126: Command Switch Stuck For 2 Minutes Or Longer (Part 2 of 2). Freestar & Monterey

Test Step	Result / Action to Take
J1 CHECK CIRCUIT 601 (LB/PK) FOR VOLTAGE	
• Key in OFF position. • Disconnect: Speed Control Deactivator Switch C1025. • Key in ON position. • Measure the voltage between the speed control deactivator switch C1025-2, circuit 601 (LB/PK), harness side and ground. • Is the voltage greater than 10 volts?	**Yes** GO to J3. **No** VERIFY the smart junction box (SJB) fuse 18 (10A) is OK. If OK, GO to J2.
J2 CHECK CIRCUIT 601 (LB/PK) FOR AN OPEN	
• Key in OFF position. • Disconnect: SJB C2280h. • Measure the resistance between the SJB C2280h-24, circuit 601 (LB/PK), harness side and the speed control deactivator switch C1025-2, circuit 601 (LB/PK), harness side. • Is the resistance less than 5 ohms?	**Yes** GO to J4. **No** REPAIR the circuit. CLEAR the DTCs. REPEAT the self-test.
J3 CHECK THE DEACTIVATOR SWITCH	
• Key in OFF position. • Disconnect: Speed Control Actuator C122. • Key in ON position.	

LTV0500000001781

Fig. 144 Test J, Code C1127: Deactivator Switch Stuck Open (Vehicles Less Stability Assist, (Part 1 of 2). Freestar & Monterey

Test Step	Result / Action to Take
I1 CHECK FOR VALID DTC C1127	
• Clear all DTCs from the speed control system. • NOTE: Make sure the vehicle is driven so that a stability assist event does not occur. • Road test the vehicle with the speed control engaged. Apply the brake pedal lightly and resume speed control. Apply the brake pedal hard and resume speed control. • Carry out the speed control system self-test. • **Does DTC C1127 still exist?**	**Yes** GO to Pinpoint Test J. **No** The system is operating correctly at this time. CLEAR the DTCs. REPEAT the self-test.

LTV0500000001780

Fig. 143 Test I, Code C1127: Deactivator Switch Stuck Open (Vehicles w/Stability Assist). Freestar & Monterey

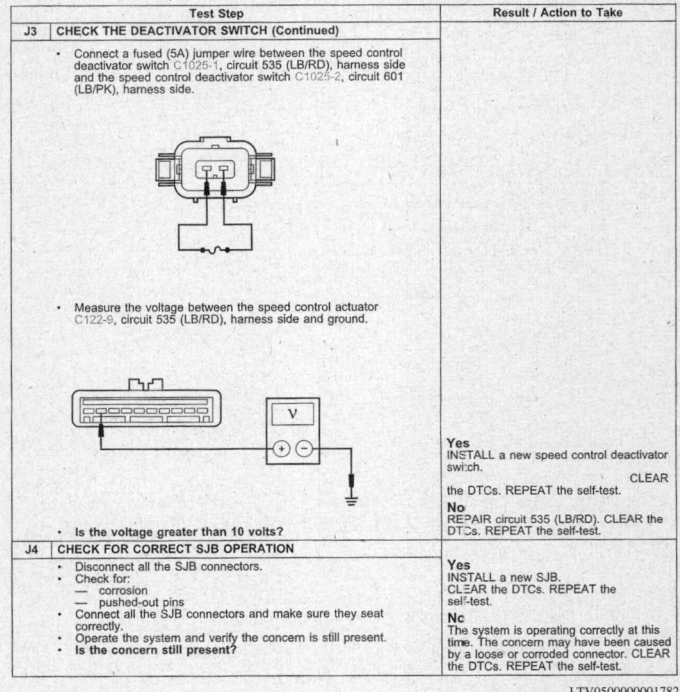

Test Step	Result / Action to Take
J3 CHECK THE DEACTIVATOR SWITCH (Continued)	
• Connect a fused (5A) jumper wire between the speed control deactivator switch C1025-1, circuit 535 (LB/RD), harness side and the speed control deactivator switch C1025-2, circuit 601 (LB/PK), harness side. • Measure the voltage between the speed control actuator C122-9, circuit 535 (LB/RD), harness side and ground. • Is the voltage greater than 10 volts?	**Yes** INSTALL a new speed control deactivator switch. CLEAR the DTCs. REPEAT the self-test. **No** REPAIR circuit 535 (LB/RD). CLEAR the DTCs. REPEAT the self-test.
J4 CHECK FOR CORRECT SJB OPERATION	

• Disconnect all the SJB connectors.
• Check for:
  — corrosion
  — pushed-out pins
• Connect all the SJB connectors and make sure they seat correctly.
• Operate the system and verify the concern is still present.
• **Is the concern still present?**
	Yes
	INSTALL a new SJB. CLEAR the DTCs. REPEAT the self-test.
	No
	The system is operating correctly at this time. The concern may have been caused by a loose or corroded connector. CLEAR the DTCs. REPEAT the self-test.

LTV0500000001782

Fig. 144 Test J, Code C1127: Deactivator Switch Stuck Open (Vehicles Less Stability Assist, (Part 2 of 2). Freestar & Monterey

Test Step	Result / Action to Take
K1 CHECK THE SPEED CONTROL THROTTLE ATTACHMENT	
• Measure the speed control cable slack to make sure it is within specification 0-6 mm (0-0.24 inch). • Check the throttle lever and the speed control cable for correct operation while carrying out the speed control actuator slack test on the diagnostic tool. • **Does the cable slack measure within specification and does the throttle lever operate correctly?**	**Yes** INSTALL a new speed control actuator. CLEAR the DTCs. REPEAT the self-test. **No** INSTALL a new speed control cable. CLEAR the DTCs. REPEAT the self-test.

LTV0500000001783

Fig. 145 Test K, Codes C1179 & C1109: Excessive Slack In Speed Control Cable Or Throttle Did Not Return To Idle After Self-Test. Freestar & Monterey

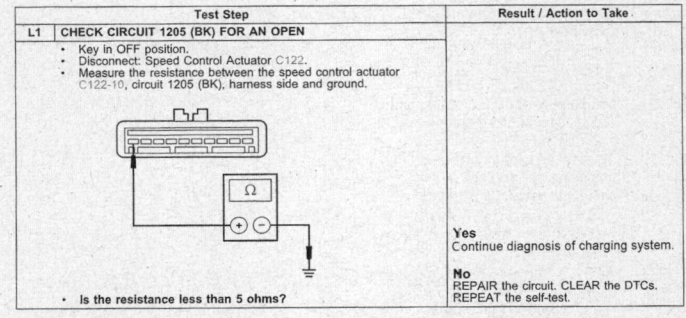

Test Step	Result / Action to Take
L1 CHECK CIRCUIT 1205 (BK) FOR AN OPEN	
• Key in OFF position. • Disconnect: Speed Control Actuator C122. • Measure the resistance between the speed control actuator C122-10, circuit 1205 (BK), harness side and ground. • Is the resistance less than 5 ohms?	**Yes** Continue diagnosis of charging system. **No** REPAIR the circuit. CLEAR the DTCs. REPEAT the self-test.

LTV0500000001784

Fig. 146 Test L, Code B1318: Low Ignition Voltage During Speed Control Operation. Freestar & Monterey

Test Step	Result / Action to Take
M1 RETRIEVE THE RECORDED DTCs FROM BOTH THE CONTINUOUS AND ON-DEMAND SELF-TESTS — SPEED CONTROL ACTUATOR • Check for recorded speed control actuator DTCs from the continuous and on-demand self-test. • **Are any DTCs recorded?**	**Yes** For DTC U1027, GO to M2. For DTC U1041, GO to M3. For DTC U1051, GO to M4. For DTC U1059, GO to M5. **No** GO to Symptom Chart.
M2 MONITOR THE THROTTLE POSITION SENSOR (TPS) • Key in ON position. • Enter the following diagnostic mode on the diagnostic tool: PCM PID. • Monitor the powertrain control module (PCM) TPS signal PID. • **Do the PID values agree with the throttle position?**	**Yes** GO to M6. **No** REFER to MOTOR's "Domestic Engine Performance & Driveability Manual" to continue diagnosis of the TPS.
M3 MONITOR THE VEHICLE SPEED SENSOR (VSS) SIGNAL • Key in ON position. • Enter the following diagnostic mode on the diagnostic tool: ABS PID. • Monitor the ABS module VSS signal PID. • **Do the PID values agree with the speed signal?**	**Yes** GO to M6. **No** Continue diagnosis of VSS signal.
M4 MONITOR THE SJB STOPLAMP SWITCH • Key in ON position. • Enter the following diagnostic mode on the diagnostic tool: SJB PID. • Check the speed control actuator for correct operation by monitoring the SJB stoplamp switch signal PID. • **Do the PID values agree with the stoplamp switch signal?**	**Yes** GO to M6. **No** Continue diagnosis of stoplamps.
M5 MONITOR THE PRNDL • Key in ON position. • Enter the following diagnostic mode on the diagnostic tool: PCM PID. • Monitor the PCM digital transmission range (TR) sensor PID while selecting different gear positions. • **Do the PID values agree with the PRNDL display?**	**Yes** GO to M6. **No** Continue diagnosis of digital TR sensor.

M6 CHECK FOR CORRECT SPEED CONTROL ACTUATOR OPERATION
 	
• Disconnect the speed control actuator connector.
• Check for:
  — corrosion
  — pushed-out pins
• Connect the speed control actuator connector and make sure it seats correctly.
• Operate the system and verify the concern is still present.
• **Is the concern still present?**
	Yes
	INSTALL a new speed control actuator. CLEAR the DTCs. REPEAT the self-test.
	No
	The system is operating correctly at this time. The concern may have been caused by a loose or corroded connector. CLEAR the DTCs. REPEAT the self-test.

LTV0500000001785

Fig. 147 Test M, Codes U1027, U1041, U1051 & U1059: Missing Or Invalid Message From, Throttle, Vehicle Speed, Brake Sensors Or PRNDL. Freestar & Monterey

ALIGNMENT • Check the digital TR sensor alignment. • **Is the digital TR sensor aligned correctly?**	**Yes** GO to A5. **No** ADJUST the digital TR sensor.. TEST the system for normal operation.
A5 CHECK THE PARKING BRAKE WARNING INDICATOR • Key in ON position. • While observing the parking brake warning indicator, apply and release the parking brake. • **Does the parking brake warning indicator operate correctly?**	**Yes** GO to A6. **No** Diagnose the parking brake warning indicator.
A6 CHECK THE VEHICLE SPEED NOTE: This step may require an assistant. • Enter the following diagnostic mode on the diagnostic tool: Anti-lock Brake System (ABS) Wheel Speed PID. • Monitor and record the ABS module wheel speed PID while driving the vehicle at 48 km/h (30 mph) as indicated on the speedometer. • Enter the following diagnostic mode on the diagnostic tool: PCM Vehicle Speed PID. • Monitor and record the PCM vehicle speed PID while driving the vehicle at 48 km/h (30 mph). • **Does the speed indicated by the ABS module wheel speed PID match the PCM vehicle speed PID?**	**Yes** GO to A7. **No** Diagnose the output shaft sensor (OSS) signal.

A7 CHECK FOR CORRECT PCM OPERATION
 	
• Disconnect all the PCM connectors.
• Check for:
  • corrosion
  • pushed-out pins
• Connect all the PCM connectors and make sure they are seated correctly.
• Operate the system and verify the concern is still present.
• **Is the concern still present?**
	Yes
	INSTALL a new PCM.. CLEAR the DTCs. REPEAT the self-test.
	
	No
	The system is operating correctly at this time. The concern may have been caused by a loose or corroded connector. CLEAR the DTCs. REPEAT the self-test.

LTV0500000001850

Fig. 148 Test A: Speed Control Is Inoperative (Part 2 of 2). 2004–04 F-150.

Test Step	Result / Action to Take
A1 CHECK FOR DTCS • Review the recorded DTCs from the powertrain control module (PCM) self-test. • **Are any DTCs recorded?**	**Yes** REFER to Diagnostic Trouble Code (DTC) Index. **No** GO to A2.
A2 CHECK THE SPEED CONTROL SWITCH • Disconnect: PCM C175b. • Measure the resistance between the PCM C175b-56, circuit 151 (LB/BK), harness side and the PCM C175b-57, circuit 848 (DG/OG), harness side.	**Yes** GO to A3. **No** INSTALL a new speed control switch. CLEAR the DTCs. REPEAT the self-test.

Speed Control Switch	Resistance Value
OFF	Less than 5 ohms
COAST	285 - 315 ohms
SET	570 - 630 ohms
RESUME	1,055 - 1,165 ohms
ON	2,005 - 2,216 ohms
No switch pressed	4,094 - 4,526 ohms

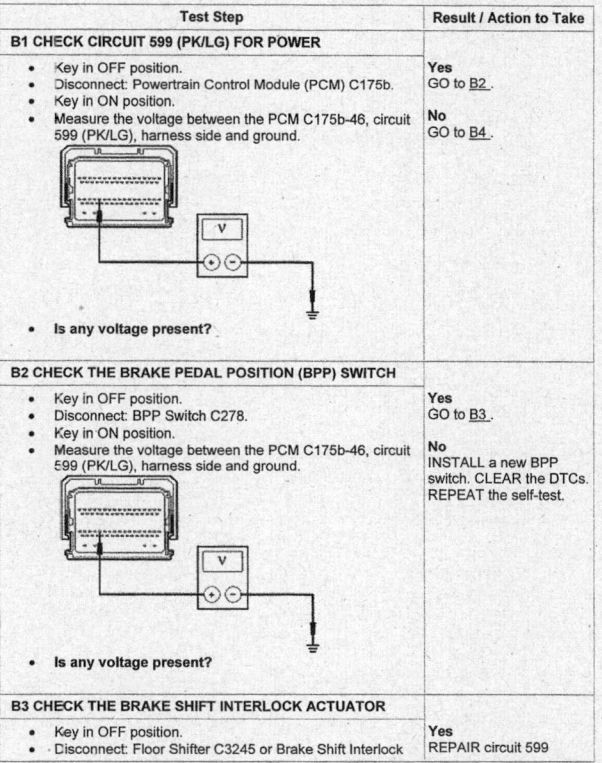

• **Are the speed control switch resistance values OK?**	
A3 CHECK THE DIGITAL TRANSMISSION RANGE (TR) SENSOR • Connect: PCM C175b. • Key in ON position. • Enter the following diagnostic mode on the diagnostic tool: PID Data Monitor and Record. • Monitor the TR sensor PID. • Select DRIVE. • **Does the PID value agree with the transmission range selector lever position?**	**Yes** GO to A4. **No** Diagnose the TR sensor.
A4 CHECK THE DIGITAL TR SENSOR FOR CORRECT	

LTV0500000001849

Fig. 148 Test A: Speed Control Is Inoperative (Part 1 of 2). 2004–04 F-150

Test Step	Result / Action to Take
B1 CHECK CIRCUIT 599 (PK/LG) FOR POWER • Key in OFF position. • Disconnect: Powertrain Control Module (PCM) C175b. • Key in ON position. • Measure the voltage between the PCM C175b-46, circuit 599 (PK/LG), harness side and ground. • **Is any voltage present?**	**Yes** GO to B2. **No** GO to B4.
B2 CHECK THE BRAKE PEDAL POSITION (BPP) SWITCH • Key in OFF position. • Disconnect: BPP Switch C278. • Key in ON position. • Measure the voltage between the PCM C175b-46, circuit 599 (PK/LG), harness side and ground. • **Is any voltage present?**	**Yes** GO to B3. **No** INSTALL a new BPP switch. CLEAR the DTCs. REPEAT the self-test.
B3 CHECK THE BRAKE SHIFT INTERLOCK ACTUATOR • Key in OFF position. • Disconnect: Floor Shifter C3245 or Brake Shift Interlock	**Yes** REPAIR circuit 599

LTV0500000001851

Fig. 149 Test B, Codes P1572 & P1703: Brake On/Off Circuit Failure (Part 1 of 5). 2002–04 F-150

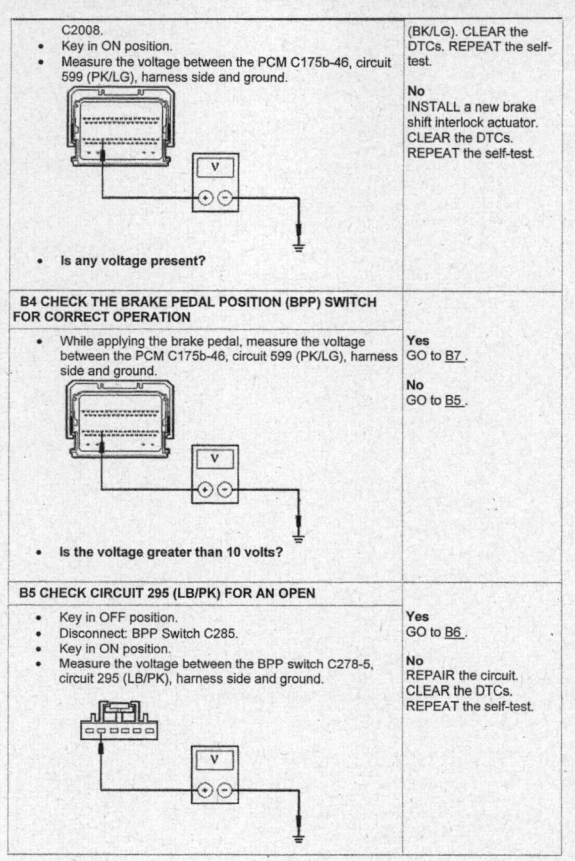

C2008.
- Key in ON position.
- Measure the voltage between the PCM C175b-46, circuit 599 (PK/LG), harness side and ground.

- Is any voltage present?

(BK/LG). CLEAR the DTCs. REPEAT the self-test.

No
INSTALL a new brake shift interlock actuator. CLEAR the DTCs. REPEAT the self-test.

B4 CHECK THE BRAKE PEDAL POSITION (BPP) SWITCH FOR CORRECT OPERATION

- While applying the brake pedal, measure the voltage between the PCM C175b-46, circuit 599 (PK/LG), harness side and ground.

Yes
GO to B7.

No
GO to B5.

- Is the voltage greater than 10 volts?

B5 CHECK CIRCUIT 295 (LB/PK) FOR AN OPEN

- Key in OFF position.
- Disconnect: BPP Switch C285.
- Key in ON position.
- Measure the voltage between the BPP switch C278-5, circuit 295 (LB/PK), harness side and ground.

Yes
GO to B6.

No
REPAIR the circuit. CLEAR the DTCs. REPEAT the self-test.

- Is the voltage greater than 10 volts?

B6 CHECK CIRCUIT 599 (PK/LG) FOR AN OPEN

- Key in OFF position.
- Measure the resistance between the BPP switch C278-6, circuit 599 (PK/LG), harness side and the PCM C175b-46, circuit 599 (PK/LG), harness side.

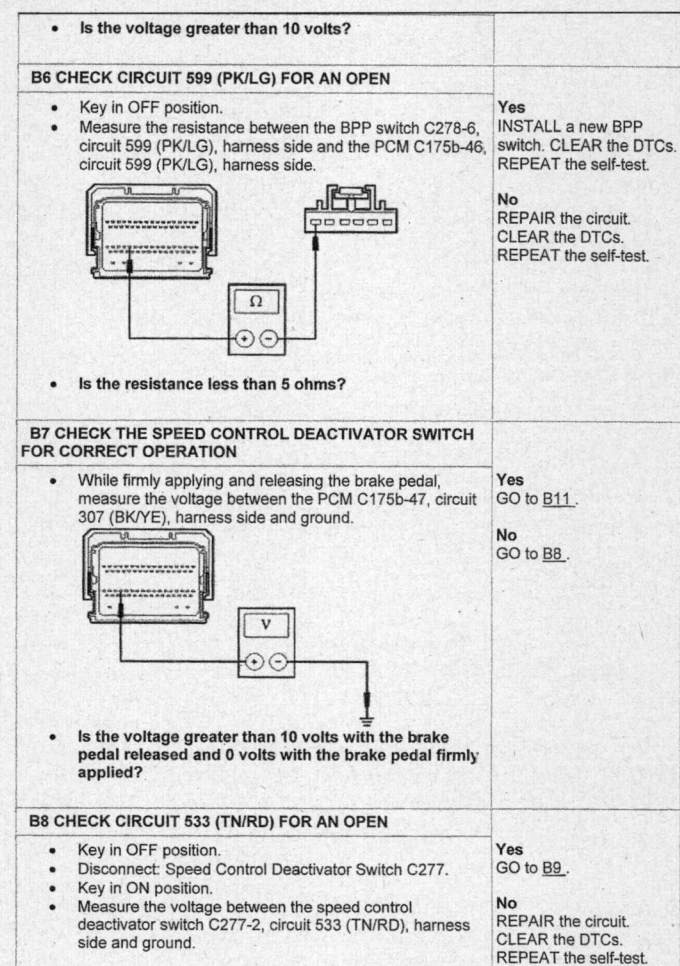

Yes
INSTALL a new BPP switch. CLEAR the DTCs. REPEAT the self-test.

No
REPAIR the circuit. CLEAR the DTCs. REPEAT the self-test.

- Is the resistance less than 5 ohms?

B7 CHECK THE SPEED CONTROL DEACTIVATOR SWITCH FOR CORRECT OPERATION

- While firmly applying and releasing the brake pedal, measure the voltage between the PCM C175b-47, circuit 307 (BK/YE), harness side and ground.

Yes
GO to B11.

No
GO to B8.

- Is the voltage greater than 10 volts with the brake pedal released and 0 volts with the brake pedal firmly applied?

B8 CHECK CIRCUIT 533 (TN/RD) FOR AN OPEN

- Key in OFF position.
- Disconnect: Speed Control Deactivator Switch C277.
- Key in ON position.
- Measure the voltage between the speed control deactivator switch C277-2, circuit 533 (TN/RD), harness side and ground.

Yes
GO to B9.

No
REPAIR the circuit. CLEAR the DTCs. REPEAT the self-test.

LTV0500000001853

Fig. 149 Test B, Codes P1572 & P1703: Brake On/Off Circuit Failure (Part 3 of 5). 2002–04 F-150

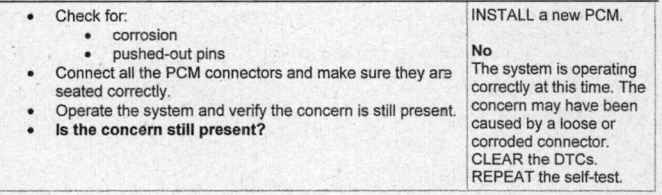

- Check for:
  - corrosion
  - pushed-out pins
- Connect all the PCM connectors and make sure they are seated correctly.
- Operate the system and verify the concern is still present.
- **Is the concern still present?**

INSTALL a new PCM.

No
The system is operating correctly at this time. The concern may have been caused by a loose or corroded connector. CLEAR the DTCs. REPEAT the self-test.

LTV0500000001855

Fig. 149 Test B, Codes P1572 & P1703: Brake On/Off Circuit Failure (Part 5 of 5). 2002–04 F-150

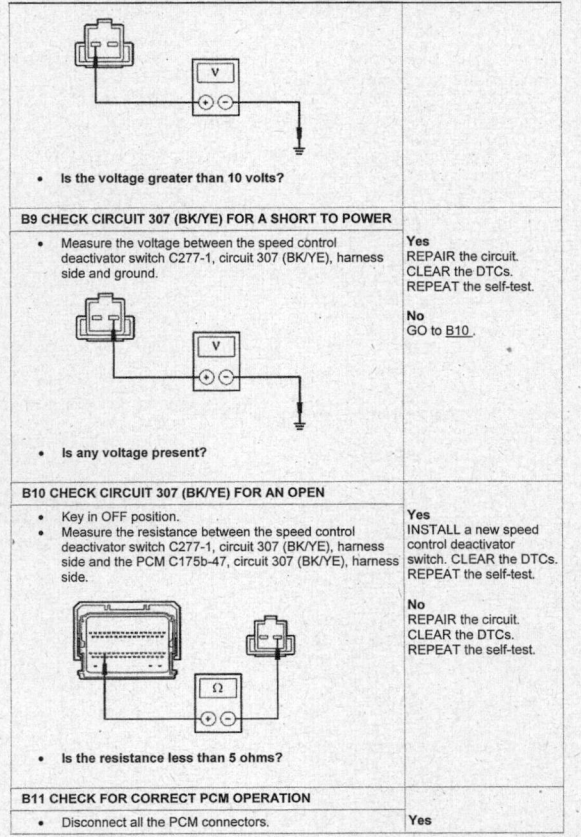

- Is the voltage greater than 10 volts?

B9 CHECK CIRCUIT 307 (BK/YE) FOR A SHORT TO POWER

- Measure the voltage between the speed control deactivator switch C277-1, circuit 307 (BK/YE), harness side and ground.

Yes
REPAIR the circuit. CLEAR the DTCs. REPEAT the self-test.

No
GO to B10.

- Is any voltage present?

B10 CHECK CIRCUIT 307 (BK/YE) FOR AN OPEN

- Key in OFF position.
- Measure the resistance between the speed control deactivator switch C277-1, circuit 307 (BK/YE), harness side and the PCM C175b-47, circuit 307 (BK/YE), harness side.

Yes
INSTALL a new speed control deactivator switch. CLEAR the DTCs. REPEAT the self-test.

No
REPAIR the circuit. CLEAR the DTCs. REPEAT the self-test.

- Is the resistance less than 5 ohms?

B11 CHECK FOR CORRECT PCM OPERATION

- Disconnect all the PCM connectors.

Yes

LTV0500000001854

Fig. 149 Test B, Codes P1572 & P1703: Brake On/Off Circuit Failure (Part 4 of 5). 2002–04 F-150

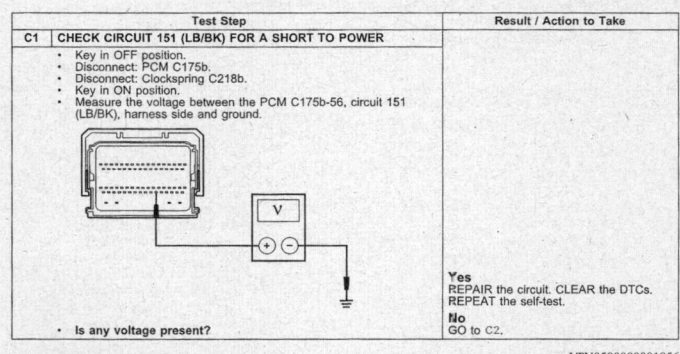

Test Step	Result / Action to Take
C1 CHECK CIRCUIT 151 (LB/BK) FOR A SHORT TO POWER	
- Key in OFF position. - Disconnect: PCM C175b. - Disconnect: Clockspring C218b. - Key in ON position. - Measure the voltage between the PCM C175b-56, circuit 151 (LB/BK), harness side and ground.	

- Is any voltage present?

Yes
REPAIR the circuit. CLEAR the DTCs. REPEAT the self-test.
No
GO to C2.

LTV0500000001856

Fig. 150 Test C, Codes P0579 & P0581: Speed Control Switch Circuit Failure (Part 1 of 6). 2002–04 F-150

Test Step	Result / Action to Take
C2 CHECK CIRCUIT 848 (DG/OG) FOR A SHORT TO POWER • Measure the voltage between the PCM C175b-57, circuit 848 (DG/OG), harness side and ground. 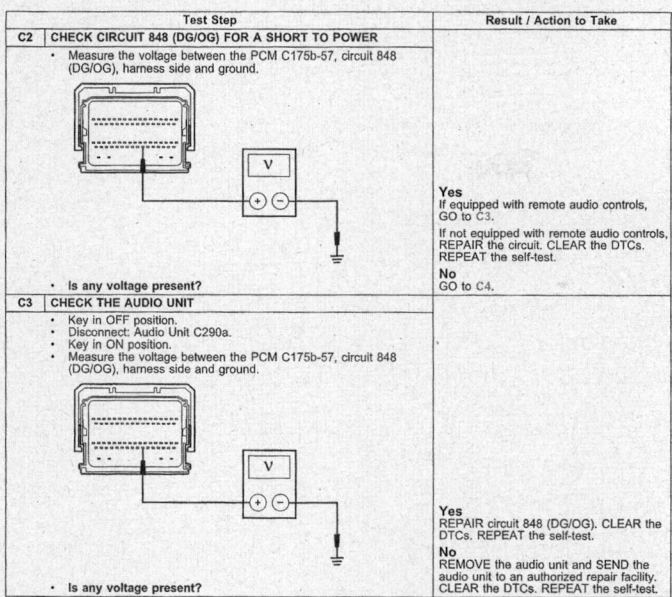 • Is any voltage present?	**Yes** If equipped with remote audio controls, GO to C3. If not equipped with remote audio controls, REPAIR the circuit. CLEAR the DTCs. REPEAT the self-test. **No** GO to C4.
C3 CHECK THE AUDIO UNIT • Key in OFF position. • Disconnect: Audio Unit C290a. • Key in ON position. • Measure the voltage between the PCM C175b-57, circuit 848 (DG/OG), harness side and ground. • Is any voltage present?	**Yes** REPAIR circuit 848 (DG/OG). CLEAR the DTCs. REPEAT the self-test. **No** REMOVE the audio unit and SEND the audio unit to an authorized repair facility. CLEAR the DTCs. REPEAT the self-test.

LTV0500000001857

Fig. 150   Test C, Codes P0579 & P0581: Speed Control Switch Circuit Failure (Part 2 of 6). 2002–04 F-150

Test Step	Result / Action to Take
C4 CHECK THE CLOCKSPRING FOR A SHORT TO POWER • Turn the headlamp switch to PARK position and measure the voltage between the PCM C175b-56, circuit 151 (LB/BK), harness side and ground; and between the C175b-57, circuit 848 (DG/OG), harness side and ground. 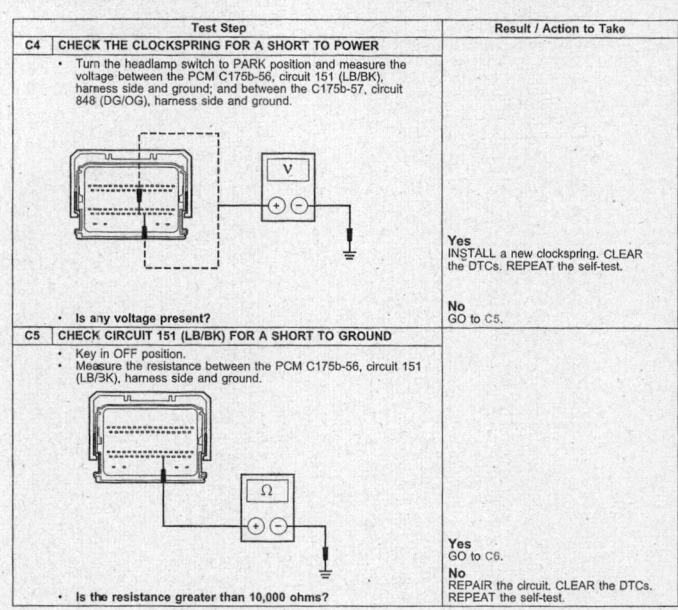 • Is any voltage present?	**Yes** INSTALL a new clockspring. CLEAR the DTCs. REPEAT the self-test. **No** GO to C5.
C5 CHECK CIRCUIT 151 (LB/BK) FOR A SHORT TO GROUND • Key in OFF position. • Measure the resistance between the PCM C175b-56, circuit 151 (LB/BK), harness side and ground. • Is the resistance greater than 10,000 ohms?	**Yes** GO to C6. **No** REPAIR the circuit. CLEAR the DTCs. REPEAT the self-test.

LTV0500000001858

Fig. 150   Test C, Codes P0579 & P0581: Speed Control Switch Circuit Failure (Part 3 of 6). 2002–04 F-150

Test Step	Result / Action to Take
C6 CHECK CIRCUITS 151 (LB/BK) AND 848 (DG/OG) FOR AN OPEN • Measure the resistance between the PCM C175b-56, circuit 151 (LB/BK), harness side and the clockspring C218b-4, circuit 151 (LB/BK), harness side; and between the PCM C175b-57 circuit 848 (DG/OG), harness side and the clockspring C218b-5, circuit 848 (DG/OG), harness side. 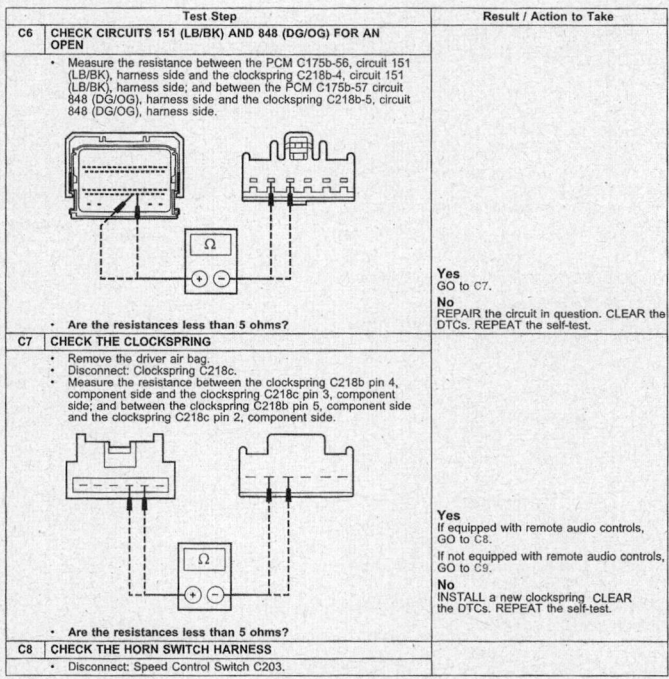 • Are the resistances less than 5 ohms?	**Yes** GO to C7. **No** REPAIR the circuit in question. CLEAR the DTCs. REPEAT the self-test.
C7 CHECK THE CLOCKSPRING • Remove the driver air bag. • Disconnect: Clockspring C218c. • Measure the resistance between the clockspring C218b pin 4, component side and the clockspring C218c pin 3, component side; and between the clockspring C218b pin 5, component side and the clockspring C218c pin 2, component side. • Are the resistances less than 5 ohms?	**Yes** If equipped with remote audio controls, GO to C8. If not equipped with remote audio controls, GO to C9. **No** INSTALL a new clockspring. CLEAR the DTCs. REPEAT the self-test.
C8 CHECK THE HORN SWITCH HARNESS • Disconnect: Speed Control Switch C203.	

LTV0500000001859

Fig. 150   Test C, Codes P0579 & P0581: Speed Control Switch Circuit Failure (Part 4 of 6). 2002–04 F-150

Test Step	Result / Action to Take
C8 CHECK THE HORN SWITCH HARNESS (Continued) • Measure the resistance between the clockspring C218c-3, harness side and the speed control switch C203-1, harness side; and between the clockspring C218c-2, harness side and the speed control switch C203-2, harness side. 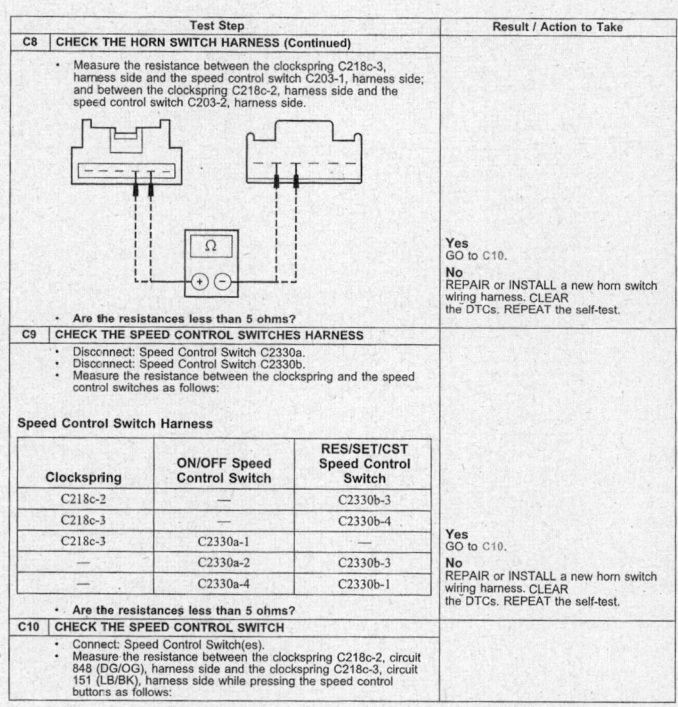 • Are the resistances less than 5 ohms?	**Yes** GO to C10. **No** REPAIR or INSTALL a new horn switch wiring harness. CLEAR the DTCs. REPEAT the self-test.
C9 CHECK THE SPEED CONTROL SWITCHES HARNESS • Disconnect: Speed Control Switch C2330a. • Disconnect: Speed Control Switch C2330b. • Measure the resistance between the clockspring and the speed control switches as follows:	

Speed Control Switch Harness

Clockspring	ON/OFF Speed Control Switch	RES/SET/CST Speed Control Switch
C218c-2	—	C2330b-3
C218c-3	—	C2330b-4
C218c-3	C2330a-1	—
—	C2330a-2	C2330b-3
—	C2330a-4	C2330b-1

Test Step	Result / Action to Take
• Are the resistances less than 5 ohms?	**Yes** GO to C10. **No** REPAIR or INSTALL a new horn switch wiring harness. CLEAR the DTCs. REPEAT the self-test.
C10 CHECK THE SPEED CONTROL SWITCH • Connect: Speed Control Switch(es). • Measure the resistance between the clockspring C218c-2, circuit 848 (DG/OG), harness side and the clockspring C218c-3, circuit 151 (LB/BK), harness side while pressing the speed control buttons as follows:	

LTV0500000001860

Fig. 150   Test C, Codes P0579 & P0581: Speed Control Switch Circuit Failure (Part 5 of 6). 2002–04 F-150

Test Step	Result / Action to Take
C10 CHECK THE SPEED CONTROL SWITCH (Continued)	

Speed Control Switch

Speed Control Switch	Resistance Value
OFF	Less than 5 ohms
COAST	285 - 315 ohms
SET	570 - 630 ohms
RESUME	1,055 - 1,165 ohms
ON	2,005 - 2,216 ohms
No switch pressed	4,094 - 4,526 ohms

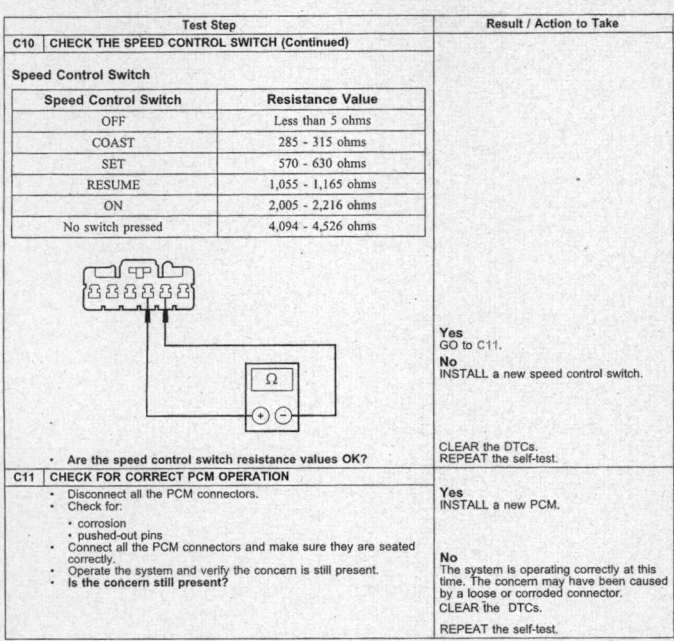

Test Step	Result / Action to Take
• Are the speed control switch resistance values OK?	**Yes** GO to C11. **No** INSTALL a new speed control switch. CLEAR the DTCs. REPEAT the self-test.
C11 CHECK FOR CORRECT PCM OPERATION	
• Disconnect all the PCM connectors. • Check for: — corrosion — pushed-out pins • Connect all the PCM connectors and make sure they are seated correctly. • Operate the system and verify the concern is still present. • **Is the concern still present?**	**Yes** INSTALL a new PCM. **No** The system is operating correctly at this time. The concern may have been caused by a loose or corroded connector. CLEAR the DTCs. REPEAT the self-test.

LTV0500000001861

Fig. 150 Test C, Codes P0579 & P0581: Speed Control Switch Circuit Failure (Part 6 of 6). 2002–04 F-150

Test Step	Result / Action to Take
A5 CHECK THE DIGITAL TR SENSOR FOR CORRECT ALIGNMENT	
• Check the digital TR sensor alignment. • **Is the digital TR sensor aligned correctly?**	**Yes** GO to A6. **No** ADJUST the digital TR sensor. TEST the system for normal operation.
A6 CHECK THE VEHICLE SPEED	
NOTE: This step may require an assistant. • Enter the following diagnostic mode on the diagnostic tool: Anti-lock Brake System (ABS) Module Wheel Speed PID. • Monitor and record the ABS module wheel speed PID while driving the vehicle at 48 km/h (30 mph) as indicated on the speedometer. • Enter the following diagnostic mode on the diagnostic tool: PCM Vehicle Speed PID. • Monitor and record the PCM vehicle speed PID while driving the vehicle at 48 km/h (30 mph). • **Does the speed indicated by the ABS module wheel speed PID match the PCM vehicle speed PID?**	**Yes** GO to A7. **No** REFER to MOTOR's "Domestic Engine Performance & Driveability Manual" to diagnose output shaft speed (OSS) sensor signal.
A7 CHECK FOR CORRECT PCM OPERATION	
• Disconnect all the PCM connectors. • Check for: — corrosion — pushed-out pins • Connect all the PCM connectors and make sure they seat correctly. • Operate the system and verify the concern is still present. • **Is the concern still present?**	**Yes** INSTALL a new PCM. TEST the system for normal operation. **No** The system is operating correctly at this time. The concern may have been caused by a loose or corroded connector.

LTV0500000001863

Fig. 151 Test A: Speed Control Is Inoperative (Part 2 of 2). 2005–06 F-150 & Mark LT

Test Step	Result / Action to Take
A1 CHECK FOR DTCs	
• Review the recorded DTCs from the powertrain control module (PCM) self-test. • **Are any DTCs recorded?**	**Yes** Diagnostic Trouble Code (DTC) Module Index. **No** GO to A2.
A2 CHECK THE PARKING BRAKE WARNING INDICATOR	
• Key in ON position. • While observing the parking brake warning indicator, apply and release the parking brake. • **Does the parking brake warning indicator operate correctly?**	**Yes** GO to A3. **No** Diagnose brake warning indicator.
A3 CHECK THE SPEED CONTROL SWITCH	
• Key in OFF position. • Disconnect: PCM C175b. • Measure the resistance between the PCM C175b-56, circuit 151 (LB/BK), harness side and the PCM C175b-57, circuit 848 (DG/OG), harness side.	

Speed Control Switch	Resistance Value
OFF	Less than 5 ohms
COAST	276 - 324 ohms
SET/ACCEL	552 - 648 ohms
RESUME	1,021 - 1,199 ohms
ON	1,941 - 2,278 ohms
No switch pressed	3,965 - 4,655 ohms

Test Step	Result / Action to Take
• Are the speed control switch resistance values OK?	**Yes** If equipped with an automatic transmission, GO to A4. If equipped with a manual transmission, GO to A6. **No** INSTALL a new speed control switch. TEST the system for normal operation.
A4 CHECK THE DIGITAL TRANSMISSION RANGE (TR) SENSOR	
• Connect: PCM C175b. • Key in ON position. • Enter the following diagnostic mode on the diagnostic tool: PCM TR Sensor PID. • Monitor the PCM TR sensor PID. • Select DRIVE. • **Does the PID value agree with the transmission range selector lever position?**	**Yes** GO to A5. **No** Diagnose digital TR sensor.

LTV0500000001862

Fig. 151 Test A: Speed Control Is Inoperative (Part 1 of 2). 2005–06 F-150 & Mark LT

Test Step	Result / Action to Take
B1 CHECK THE OPERATION OF THE STOPLAMPS	
• Apply and release the brake pedal while observing the stoplamps. • **Do the stoplamps operate correctly?**	**Yes** GO to B2. **No** Continue diagnosis of the stoplamps.
B2 CHECK CIRCUIT 511 (LG) FOR AN OPEN	
• Key in OFF position. • Disconnect: Powertrain Control Module (PCM) C175b. • While applying the brake pedal, measure the voltage between the PCM C175b-46, circuit 511 (LG), harness side and ground. • **Is the voltage greater than 10 volts?**	**Yes** GO to B3. **No** REPAIR the circuit. CLEAR the DTCs. REPEAT the self test.
B3 CHECK THE SPEED CONTROL DEACTIVATOR SWITCH FOR CORRECT OPERATION	
• Key in ON position. • While firmly applying and releasing the brake pedal, measure the voltage between the PCM C175b-47, circuit 307 (BK/YE), harness side and ground. • **Is the voltage greater than 10 volts with the brake pedal released, and 0 volts with the brake pedal firmly applied?**	**Yes** GO to B7. **No** GO to B4.

LTV0500000001864

Fig. 152 Test B, Codes P1572 & P1703: Brake Circuit On/Off Circuit Failure (Part 1 of 3). 2005–06 F-150 & Mark LT

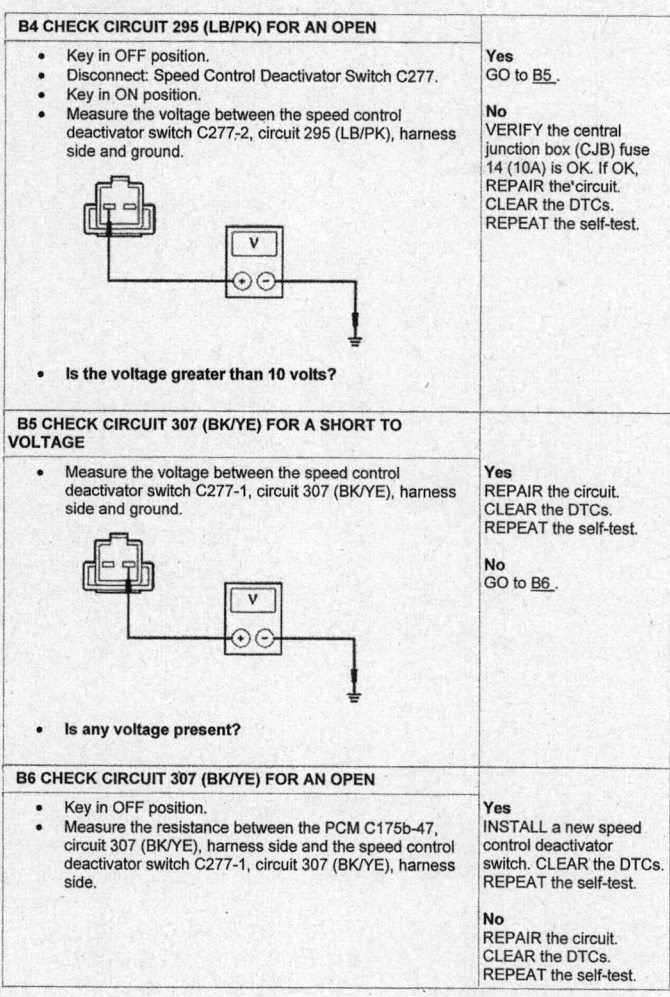

B4 CHECK CIRCUIT 295 (LB/PK) FOR AN OPEN

- Key in OFF position.
- Disconnect: Speed Control Deactivator Switch C277.
- Key in ON position.
- Measure the voltage between the speed control deactivator switch C277-2, circuit 295 (LB/PK), harness side and ground.

- **Is the voltage greater than 10 volts?**

Yes
GO to B5.

No
VERIFY the central junction box (CJB) fuse 14 (10A) is OK. If OK, REPAIR the circuit. CLEAR the DTCs. REPEAT the self-test.

B5 CHECK CIRCUIT 307 (BK/YE) FOR A SHORT TO VOLTAGE

- Measure the voltage between the speed control deactivator switch C277-1, circuit 307 (BK/YE), harness side and ground.

- **Is any voltage present?**

Yes
REPAIR the circuit. CLEAR the DTCs. REPEAT the self-test.

No
GO to B6.

B6 CHECK CIRCUIT 307 (BK/YE) FOR AN OPEN

- Key in OFF position.
- Measure the resistance between the PCM C175b-47, circuit 307 (BK/YE), harness side and the speed control deactivator switch C277-1, circuit 307 (BK/YE), harness side.

Yes
INSTALL a new speed control deactivator switch. CLEAR the DTCs. REPEAT the self-test.

No
REPAIR the circuit. CLEAR the DTCs. REPEAT the self-test.

LTV0500000001865

Fig. 152 Test B, Codes P1572 & P1703 : Brake Circuit On/Off Circuit Failure (Part 2 of 3). 2005–06 F-150 & Mark LT

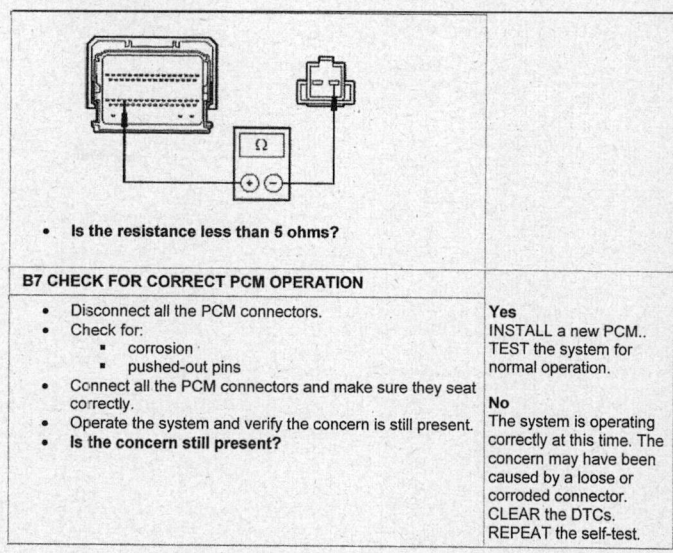

- **Is the resistance less than 5 ohms?**

B7 CHECK FOR CORRECT PCM OPERATION

- Disconnect all the PCM connectors.
- Check for:
  - corrosion
  - pushed-out pins
- Connect all the PCM connectors and make sure they seat correctly.
- Operate the system and verify the concern is still present.
- **Is the concern still present?**

Yes
INSTALL a new PCM. TEST the system for normal operation.

No
The system is operating correctly at this time. The concern may have been caused by a loose or corroded connector. CLEAR the DTCs. REPEAT the self-test.

LTV0500000001866

Fig. 152 Test B, Codes P1572 & P1703 : Brake Circuit On/Off Circuit Failure (Part 3 of 3). 2005–06 F-150 & Mark LT

Test Step	Result / Action to Take
C1 CHECK THE SPEED CONTROL SWITCH CIRCUITRY FOR A SHORT TO VOLTAGE	
• Key in OFF position. • Disconnect: PCM C175b. • Key in ON position. • Turn the parking lamps on. • Measure the voltage between the PCM C175b-56, circuit 151 (LB/BK), harness side and ground; and between the C175b-57, circuit 848 (DG/OG), harness side and ground.	

- **Is any voltage present?**

Yes
TURN the parking lamps off. GO to C2.
No
TURN the parking lamps off. GO to C5.

C2 CHECK THE AUDIO UNIT
- Key in OFF position.
- Disconnect: Audio Unit C290a.
- Key in ON position.
- Turn the parking lamps on.

LTV0500000001867

Fig. 153 Test C, Codes P0579 & P0581: Speed Control Switch Circuit Failure (Part 1 of 5). 2005–06 F-150 Mark LT

Test Step	Result / Action to Take
C2 CHECK THE AUDIO UNIT (Continued)	
• Measure the voltage between the PCM C175b-57, circuit 848 (DG/OG), harness side and ground.	

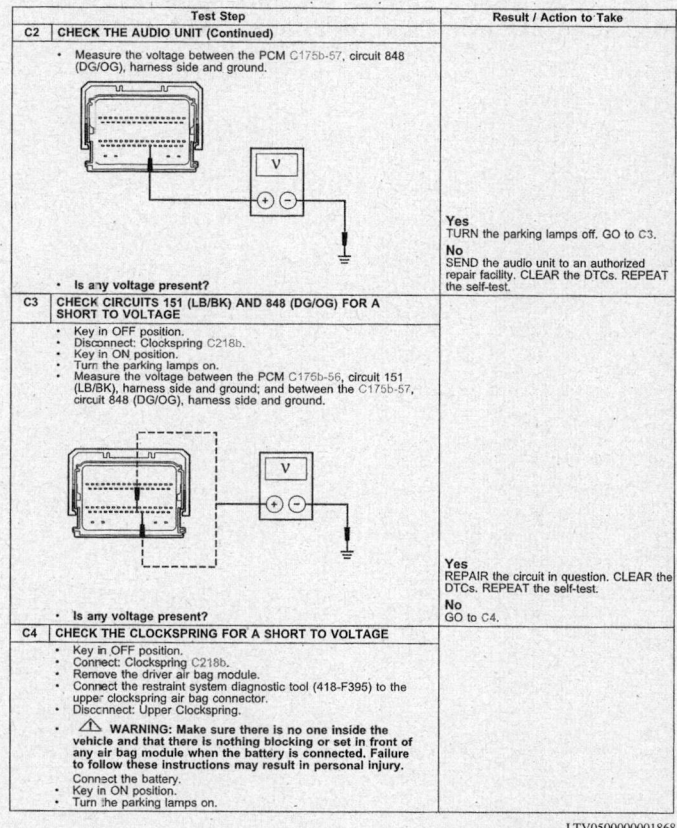

- **Is any voltage present?**

Yes
TURN the parking lamps off. GO to C3.
No
SEND the audio unit to an authorized repair facility. CLEAR the DTCs. REPEAT the self-test.

C3 CHECK CIRCUITS 151 (LB/BK) AND 848 (DG/OG) FOR A SHORT TO VOLTAGE
- Key in OFF position.
- Disconnect: Clockspring C218b.
- Key in ON position.
- Turn the parking lamps on.
- Measure the voltage between the PCM C175b-56, circuit 151 (LB/BK), harness side and ground; and between the C175b-57, circuit 848 (DG/OG), harness side and ground.

- **Is any voltage present?**

Yes
REPAIR the circuit in question. CLEAR the DTCs. REPEAT the self-test.
No
GO to C4.

C4 CHECK THE CLOCKSPRING FOR A SHORT TO VOLTAGE
- Key in OFF position.
- Connect: Clockspring C218b.
- Remove the driver air bag module.
- Connect the restraint system diagnostic tool (418-F395) to the upper clockspring air bag connector.
- Disconnect: Upper Clockspring.
- ⚠ **WARNING: Make sure there is no one inside the vehicle and that there is nothing blocking or set in front of any air bag module when the battery is connected. Failure to follow these instructions may result in personal injury.**
- Connect the battery.
- Key in ON position.
- Turn the parking lamps on.

LTV0500000001868

Fig. 153 Test C, Codes P0579 & P0581: Speed Control Switch Circuit Failure (Part 2 of 5). 2005–06 F-150 Mark LT

Test Step	Result / Action to Take
C4 CHECK THE CLOCKSPRING FOR A SHORT TO VOLTAGE (Continued) • Measure the voltage between the PCM C175b-56, circuit 151 (LB/BK), harness side and ground; and between the C175b-57, circuit 848 (DG/OG), harness side and ground. 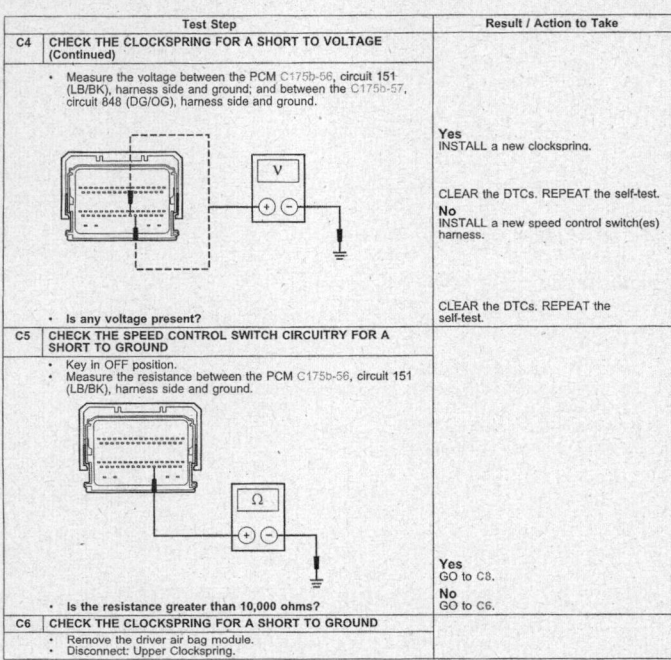 • Is any voltage present?	**Yes** INSTALL a new clockspring. CLEAR the DTCs. REPEAT the self-test. **No** INSTALL a new speed control switch(es) harness. CLEAR the DTCs. REPEAT the self-test.
C5 CHECK THE SPEED CONTROL SWITCH CIRCUITRY FOR A SHORT TO GROUND • Key in OFF position. • Measure the resistance between the PCM C175b-56, circuit 151 (LB/BK), harness side and ground. 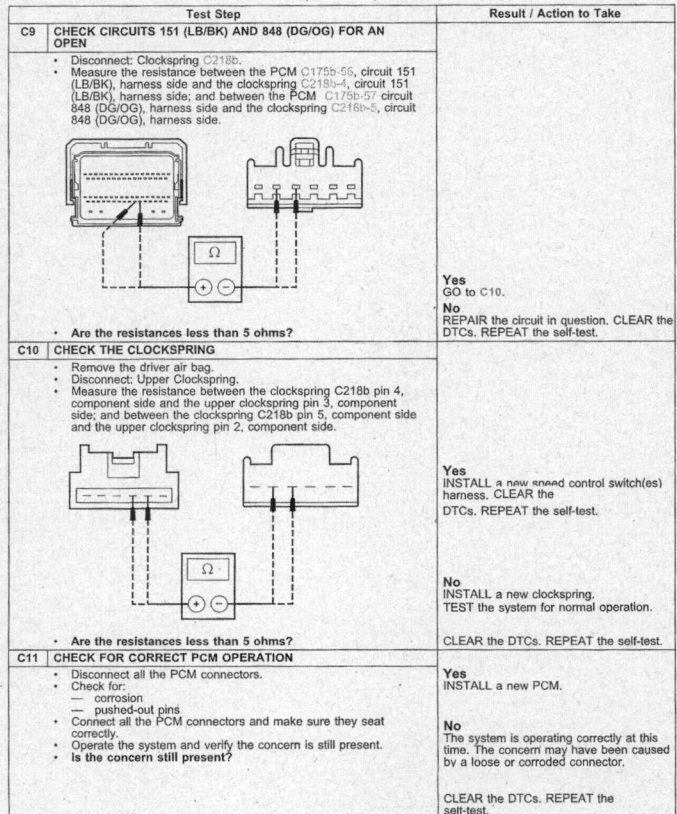 • Is the resistance greater than 10,000 ohms?	**Yes** GO to C8. **No** GO to C6.
C6 CHECK THE CLOCKSPRING FOR A SHORT TO GROUND • Remove the driver air bag module. • Disconnect: Upper Clockspring.	

LTV0500000001869

Fig. 153   Test C, Codes P0579 & P0581: Speed Control Switch Circuit Failure (Part 3 of 5). 2005–06 F-150 Mark LT

Test Step	Result / Action to Take
C9 CHECK CIRCUITS 151 (LB/BK) AND 848 (DG/OG) FOR AN OPEN • Disconnect: Clockspring C218b. • Measure the resistance between the PCM C175b-56, circuit 151 (LB/BK), harness side and the clockspring C218b-4, circuit 151 (LB/BK), harness side; and between the PCM C175b-57 circuit 848 (DG/OG), harness side and the clockspring C218b-5, circuit 848 (DG/OG), harness side. 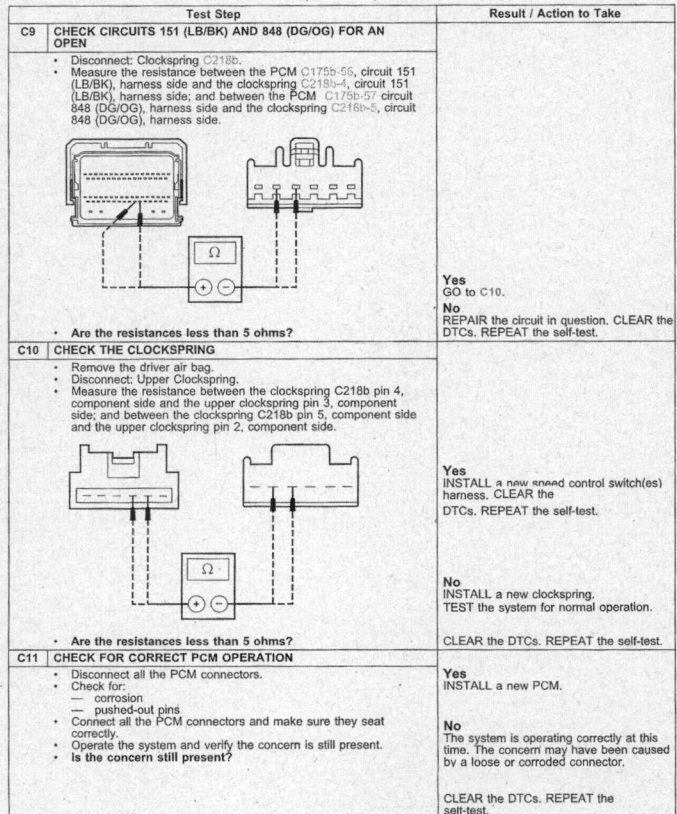 • Are the resistances less than 5 ohms?	**Yes** GO to C10. **No** REPAIR the circuit in question. CLEAR the DTCs. REPEAT the self-test.
C10 CHECK THE CLOCKSPRING • Remove the driver air bag. • Disconnect: Upper Clockspring. • Measure the resistance between the clockspring C218b pin 4, component side and the upper clockspring pin 3, component side; and between the clockspring C218b pin 5, component side and the upper clockspring pin 2, component side. • Are the resistances less than 5 ohms?	**Yes** INSTALL a new speed control switch(es) harness. CLEAR the DTCs. REPEAT the self-test. **No** INSTALL a new clockspring. TEST the system for normal operation. CLEAR the DTCs. REPEAT the self-test.

C11 CHECK FOR CORRECT PCM OPERATION
 • Disconnect all the PCM connectors.
 • Check for:
   — corrosion
   — pushed-out pins
 • Connect all the PCM connectors and make sure they seat correctly.
 • Operate the system and verify the concern is still present.
 • Is the concern still present?
	Yes
	 INSTALL a new PCM.
	
	 No
	 The system is operating correctly at this time. The concern may have been caused by a loose or corroded connector.
	
	 CLEAR the DTCs. REPEAT the self-test.

LTV0500000001871

Fig. 153   Test C, Codes P0579 & P0581: Speed Control Switch Circuit Failure (Part 5 of 5). 2005–06 F-150 Mark LT

Test Step	Result / Action to Take
C6 CHECK THE CLOCKSPRING FOR A SHORT TO GROUND (Continued) • Measure the resistance between the PCM C175b-56, circuit 151 (LB/BK), harness side and ground. 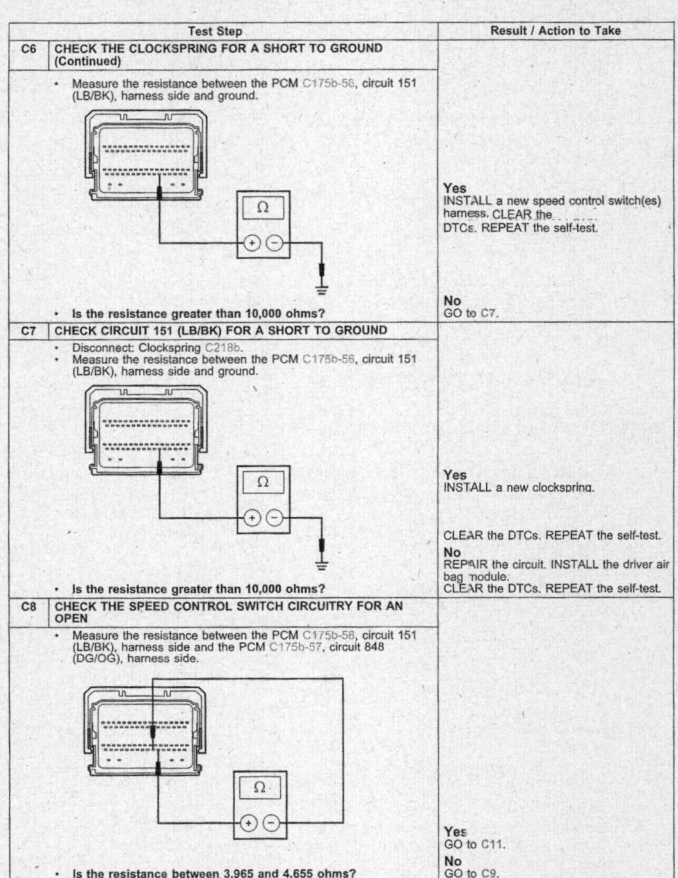 • Is the resistance greater than 10,000 ohms?	**Yes** INSTALL a new speed control switch(es) harness. CLEAR the DTCs. REPEAT the self-test. **No** GO to C7.
C7 CHECK CIRCUIT 151 (LB/BK) FOR A SHORT TO GROUND • Disconnect: Clockspring C218b. • Measure the resistance between the PCM C175b-56, circuit 151 (LB/BK), harness side and ground. • Is the resistance greater than 10,000 ohms?	**Yes** INSTALL a new clockspring. CLEAR the DTCs. REPEAT the self-test. **No** REPAIR the circuit. INSTALL the driver air bag module. CLEAR the DTCs. REPEAT the self-test.
C8 CHECK THE SPEED CONTROL SWITCH CIRCUITRY FOR AN OPEN • Measure the resistance between the PCM C175b-56, circuit 151 (LB/BK), harness side and the PCM C175b-57, circuit 848 (DG/OG), harness side. • Is the resistance between 3,965 and 4,655 ohms?	**Yes** GO to C11. **No** GO to C9.

LTV0500000001870

Fig. 153   Test C, Codes P0579 & P0581: Speed Control Switch Circuit Failure (Part 4 of 5). 2005–06 F-150 Mark LT

Test Step	Result / Action to Take
D1 CHECK THE PCM CPP SWITCH PID • Key in ON position. • Enter the following diagnostic mode on the diagnostic tool: PCM CPP Switch PID. • Monitor the PCM CPP switch PID while pressing and releasing the clutch pedal. • Does the CPP switch PID agree with the clutch pedal position?	**Yes** GO to D3. **No** GO to D2.
D2 CHECK CIRCUIT 306 (TN/LB) FOR A SHORT TO GROUND • Key in OFF position. • Disconnect: PCM C175b. • Disconnect: CPP Switch C257. • Measure the resistance between the PCM C175b-38, circuit 306 (TN/LB), harness side and ground. 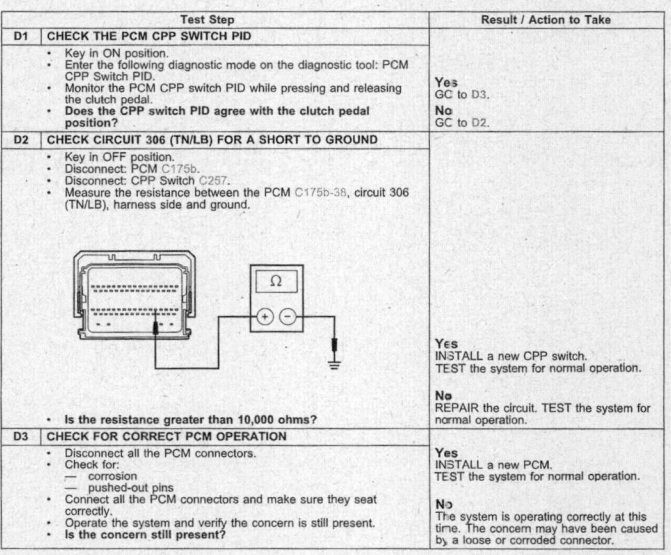 • Is the resistance greater than 10,000 ohms?	**Yes** INSTALL a new CPP switch. TEST the system for normal operation. **No** REPAIR the circuit. TEST the system for normal operation.

D3 CHECK FOR CORRECT PCM OPERATION
 • Disconnect all the PCM connectors.
 • Check for:
   — corrosion
   — pushed-out pins
 • Connect all the PCM connectors and make sure they seat correctly.
 • Operate the system and verify the concern is still present.
 • Is the concern still present?
	Yes
	 INSTALL a new PCM. TEST the system for normal operation.
	
	 No
	 The system is operating correctly at this time. The concern may have been caused by a loose or corroded connector.

LTV0500000001872

Fig. 154   Test D: Speed Control Does Not Disengage When Clutch Is Applied. 2005–06 F-150 & Mark LT

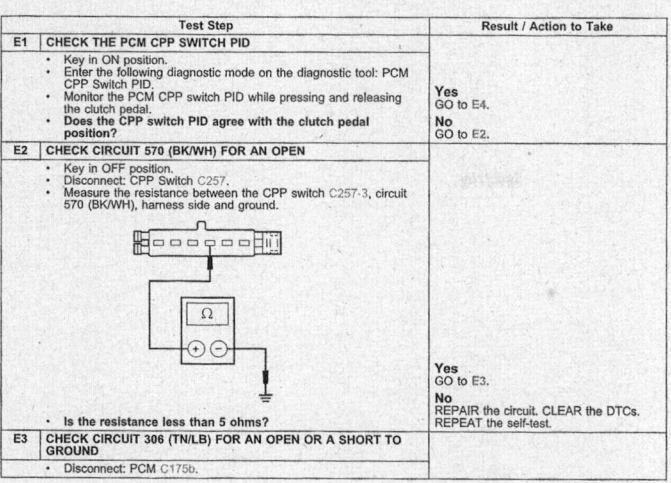

Test Step	Result / Action to Take
E1 CHECK THE PCM CPP SWITCH PID • Key in ON position. • Enter the following diagnostic mode on the diagnostic tool: PCM CPP Switch PID. • Monitor the PCM CPP switch PID while pressing and releasing the clutch pedal. • **Does the CPP switch PID agree with the clutch pedal position?**	**Yes** GO to E4. **No** GO to E2.
E2 CHECK CIRCUIT 570 (BK/WH) FOR AN OPEN • Key in OFF position. • Disconnect: CPP Switch C257. • Measure the resistance between the CPP switch C257-3, circuit 570 (BK/WH), harness side and ground. • **Is the resistance less than 5 ohms?**	**Yes** GO to E3. **No** REPAIR the circuit. CLEAR the DTCs. REPEAT the self-test.
E3 CHECK CIRCUIT 306 (TN/LB) FOR AN OPEN OR A SHORT TO GROUND • Disconnect: PCM C175b.	

LTV050000001873

Fig. 155   Test E, Code P0833: Clutch Pedal Switch Circuit B (Part 1 of 2). 2005–06 F-150 & Mark LT

Test Step	Result / Action to Take
A1 CHECK THE SPEED CONTROL CABLE ATTACHMENT TO THE THROTTLE • Key in OFF position. • Remove the accelerator control splash shield (if equipped). • Inspect the speed control cable attachment. Check the speed control cable by pulling on the speed control cable and noting the throttle movement. • **Is the speed control cable snapped onto the throttle body and is the speed control cable movement OK?**	**Yes** GO to A2. **No** CONNECT the speed control cable. TEST the system for normal operation.

LTV050000001793

Fig. 156   Test A: Speed Control Is Inoperative (Part 1 of 10). 2002–04 Ranger

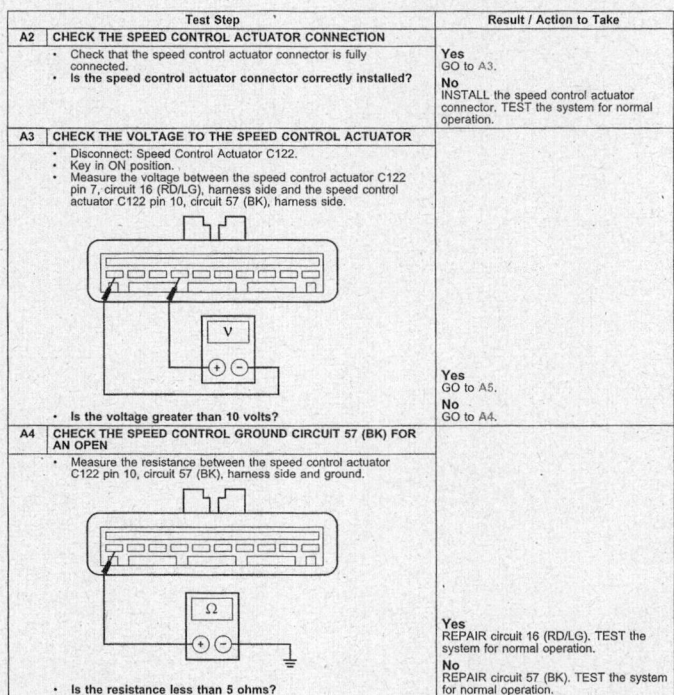

Test Step	Result / Action to Take
A2 CHECK THE SPEED CONTROL ACTUATOR CONNECTION • Check that the speed control actuator connector is fully connected. • **Is the speed control actuator connector correctly installed?**	**Yes** GO to A3. **No** INSTALL the speed control actuator connector. TEST the system for normal operation.
A3 CHECK THE VOLTAGE TO THE SPEED CONTROL ACTUATOR • Disconnect: Speed Control Actuator C122. • Key in ON position. • Measure the voltage between the speed control actuator C122 pin 7, circuit 16 (RD/LG), harness side and the speed control actuator C122 pin 10, circuit 57 (BK), harness side. • **Is the voltage greater than 10 volts?**	**Yes** GO to A5. **No** GO to A4.
A4 CHECK THE SPEED CONTROL GROUND CIRCUIT 57 (BK) FOR AN OPEN • Measure the resistance between the speed control actuator C122 pin 10, circuit 57 (BK), harness side and ground. • **Is the resistance less than 5 ohms?**	**Yes** REPAIR circuit 16 (RD/LG). TEST the system for normal operation. **No** REPAIR circuit 57 (BK). TEST the system for normal operation.

LTV050000001794

Fig. 156   Test A: Speed Control Is Inoperative (Part 2 of 10). 2002–04 Ranger

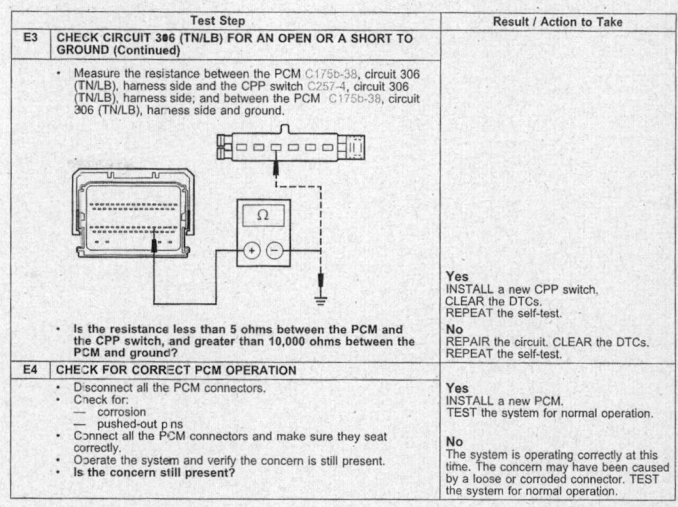

Test Step	Result / Action to Take
E3 CHECK CIRCUIT 306 (TN/LB) FOR AN OPEN OR A SHORT TO GROUND (Continued) • Measure the resistance between the PCM C175b-38, circuit 306 (TN/LB), harness side and the CPP switch C257-4, circuit 306 (TN/LB), harness side; and between the PCM C175b-38, circuit 306 (TN/LB), harness side and ground. • **Is the resistance less than 5 ohms between the PCM and the CPP switch, and greater than 10,000 ohms between the PCM and ground?**	**Yes** INSTALL a new CPP switch. CLEAR the DTCs. REPEAT the self-test. **No** REPAIR the circuit. CLEAR the DTCs. REPEAT the self-test.
E4 CHECK FOR CORRECT PCM OPERATION • Disconnect all the PCM connectors. • Check for: — corrosion — pushed-out pins • Connect all the PCM connectors and make sure they seat correctly. • Operate the system and verify the concern is still present. • **Is the concern still present?**	**Yes** INSTALL a new PCM. TEST the system for normal operation. **No** The system is operating correctly at this time. The concern may have been caused by a loose or corroded connector. TEST the system for normal operation.

LTV050000001874

Fig. 155   Test E, Code P0833: Clutch Pedal Switch Circuit B (Part 2 of 2). 2005–06 F-150 & Mark LT

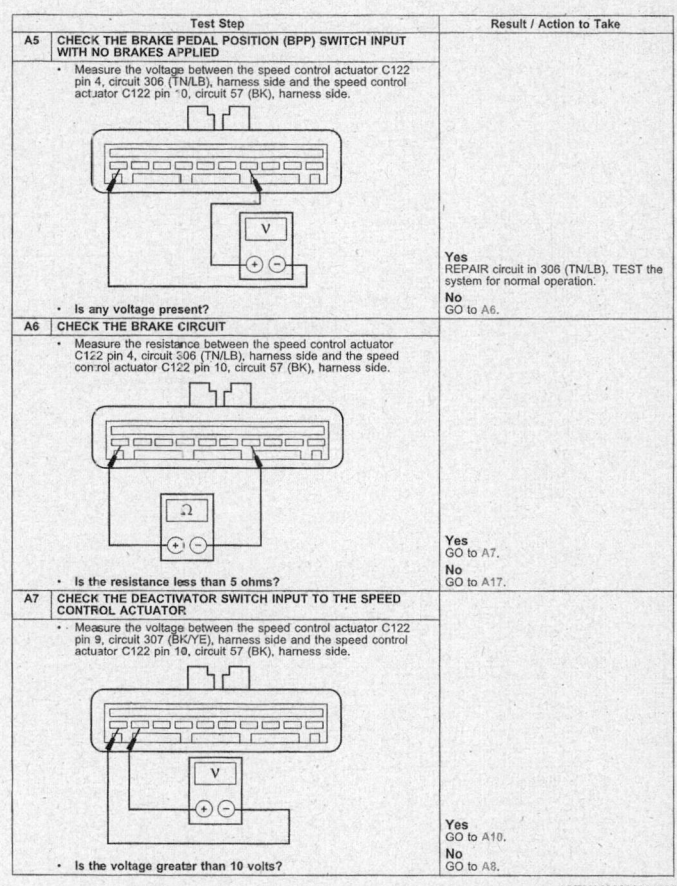

Test Step	Result / Action to Take
A5 CHECK THE BRAKE PEDAL POSITION (BPP) SWITCH INPUT WITH NO BRAKES APPLIED • Measure the voltage between the speed control actuator C122 pin 4, circuit 306 (TN/LB), harness side and the speed control actuator C122 pin 10, circuit 57 (BK), harness side. • **Is any voltage present?**	**Yes** REPAIR circuit in 306 (TN/LB). TEST the system for normal operation. **No** GO to A6.
A6 CHECK THE BRAKE CIRCUIT • Measure the resistance between the speed control actuator C122 pin 4, circuit 306 (TN/LB), harness side and the speed control actuator C122 pin 10, circuit 57 (BK), harness side. • **Is the resistance less than 5 ohms?**	**Yes** GO to A7. **No** GO to A17.
A7 CHECK THE DEACTIVATOR SWITCH INPUT TO THE SPEED CONTROL ACTUATOR • Measure the voltage between the speed control actuator C122 pin 9, circuit 307 (BK/YE), harness side and the speed control actuator C122 pin 10, circuit 57 (BK), harness side. • **Is the voltage greater than 10 volts?**	**Yes** GO to A10. **No** GO to A8.

LTV050000001795

Fig. 156   Test A: Speed Control Is Inoperative (Part 3 of 10). 2002–04 Ranger

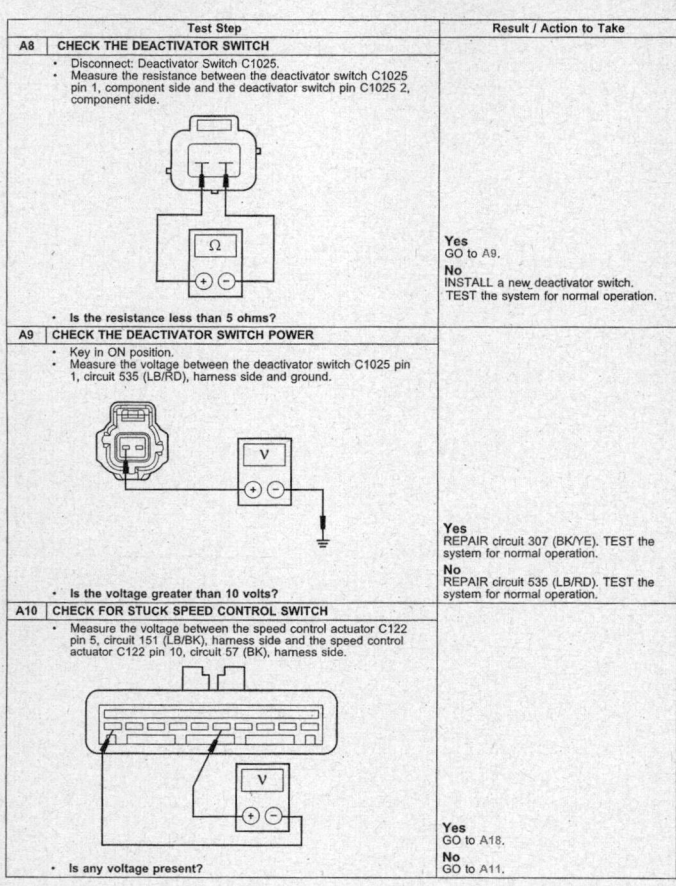

Test Step	Result / Action to Take
A8 CHECK THE DEACTIVATOR SWITCH • Disconnect: Deactivator Switch C1025. • Measure the resistance between the deactivator switch C1025 pin 1, component side and the deactivator switch pin C1025 2, component side. • Is the resistance less than 5 ohms?	**Yes** GO to A9. **No** INSTALL a new deactivator switch. TEST the system for normal operation.
A9 CHECK THE DEACTIVATOR SWITCH POWER • Key in ON position. • Measure the voltage between the deactivator switch C1025 pin 1, circuit 535 (LB/RD), harness side and ground. • Is the voltage greater than 10 volts?	**Yes** REPAIR circuit 307 (BK/YE). TEST the system for normal operation. **No** REPAIR circuit 535 (LB/RD). TEST the system for normal operation.
A10 CHECK FOR STUCK SPEED CONTROL SWITCH • Measure the voltage between the speed control actuator C122 pin 5, circuit 151 (LB/BK), harness side and the speed control actuator C122 pin 10, circuit 57 (BK), harness side. • Is any voltage present?	**Yes** GO to A18. **No** GO to A11.

LTV0500000001796

Fig. 156   Test A: Speed Control Is Inoperative (Part 4 of 10). 2002–04 Ranger

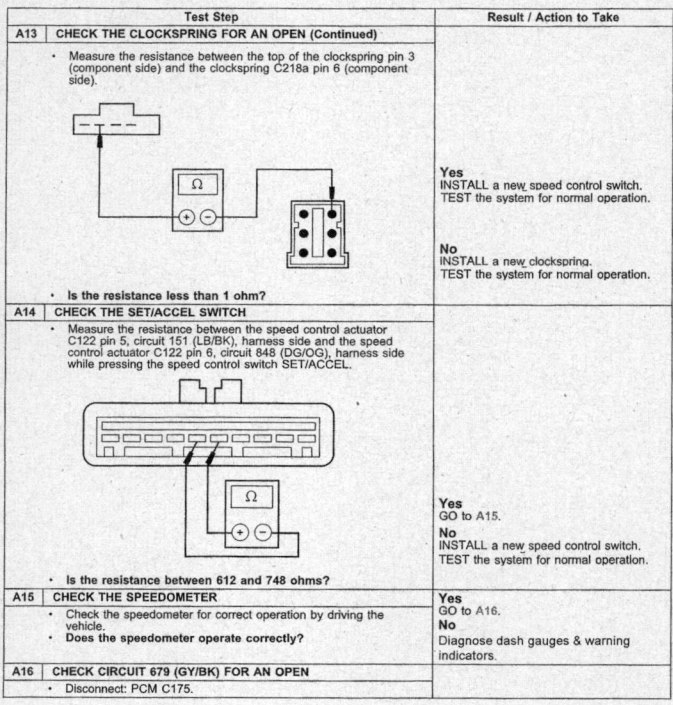

Test Step	Result / Action to Take
A13 CHECK THE CLOCKSPRING FOR AN OPEN (Continued) • Measure the resistance between the top of the clockspring pin 3 (component side) and the clockspring C218a pin 6 (component side). • Is the resistance less than 1 ohm?	**Yes** INSTALL a new speed control switch. TEST the system for normal operation. **No** INSTALL a new clockspring. TEST the system for normal operation.
A14 CHECK THE SET/ACCEL SWITCH • Measure the resistance between the speed control actuator C122 pin 5, circuit 151 (LB/BK), harness side and the speed control actuator C122 pin 6, circuit 848 (DG/OG), harness side while pressing the speed control switch SET/ACCEL. • Is the resistance between 612 and 748 ohms?	**Yes** GO to A15. **No** INSTALL a new speed control switch. TEST the system for normal operation.
A15 CHECK THE SPEEDOMETER • Check the speedometer for correct operation by driving the vehicle. • Does the speedometer operate correctly?	**Yes** GO to A16. **No** Diagnose dash gauges & warning indicators.
A16 CHECK CIRCUIT 679 (GY/BK) FOR AN OPEN • Disconnect: PCM C175.	

LTV0500000001798

Fig. 156   Test A: Speed Control Is Inoperative (Part 6 of 10). 2002–04 Ranger

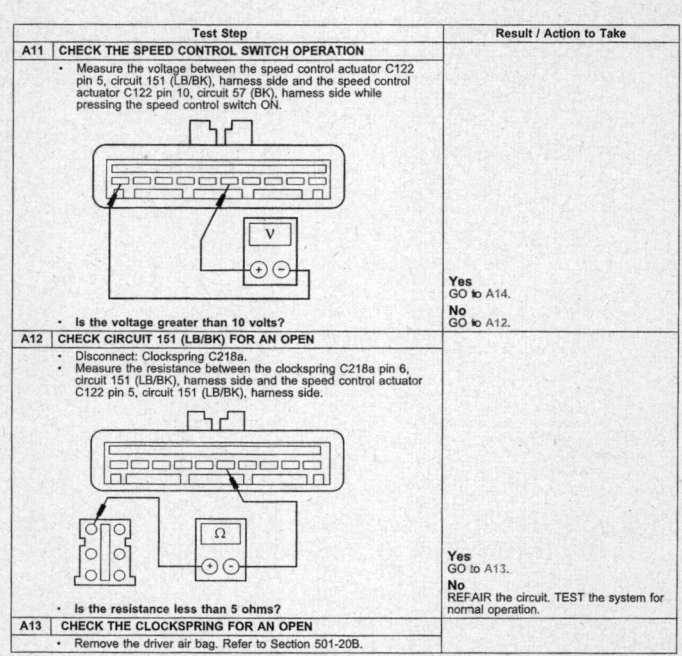

Test Step	Result / Action to Take
A11 CHECK THE SPEED CONTROL SWITCH OPERATION • Measure the voltage between the speed control actuator C122 pin 5, circuit 151 (LB/BK), harness side and the speed control actuator C122 pin 10, circuit 57 (BK), harness side while pressing the speed control switch ON. • Is the voltage greater than 10 volts?	**Yes** GO to A14. **No** GO to A12.
A12 CHECK CIRCUIT 151 (LB/BK) FOR AN OPEN • Disconnect: Clockspring C218a. • Measure the resistance between the clockspring C218a pin 6, circuit 151 (LB/BK), harness side and the speed control actuator C122 pin 5, circuit 151 (LB/BK), harness side. • Is the resistance less than 5 ohms?	**Yes** GO to A13. **No** REPAIR the circuit. TEST the system for normal operation.
A13 CHECK THE CLOCKSPRING FOR AN OPEN • Remove the driver air bag. Refer to Section 501-20B.	

LTV0500000001797

Fig. 156   Test A: Speed Control Is Inoperative (Part 5 of 10). 2002–04 Ranger

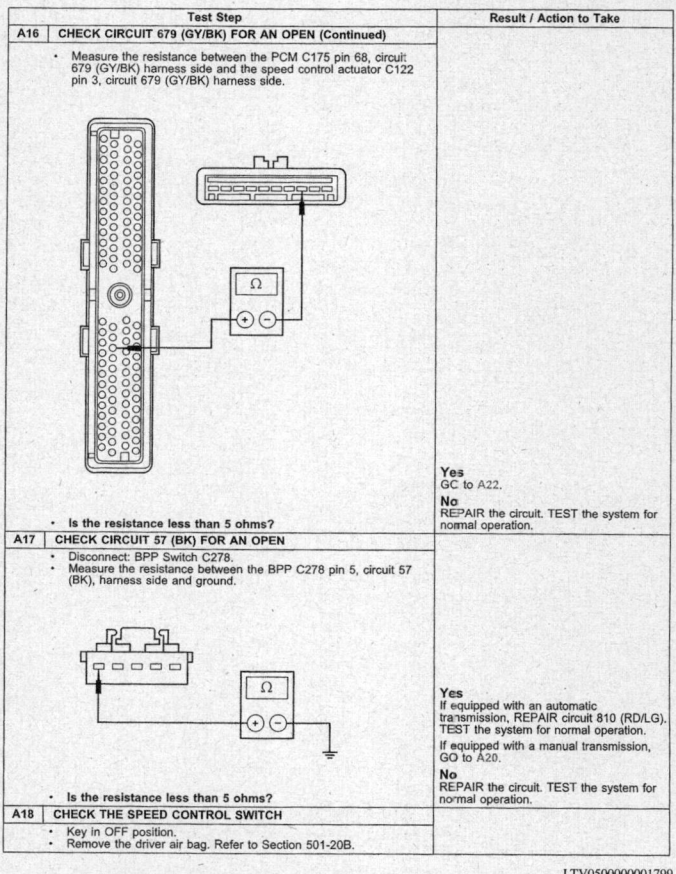

Test Step	Result / Action to Take
A16 CHECK CIRCUIT 679 (GY/BK) FOR AN OPEN (Continued) • Measure the resistance between the PCM C175 pin 68, circuit 679 (GY/BK) harness side and the speed control actuator C122 pin 3, circuit 679 (GY/BK) harness side. • Is the resistance less than 5 ohms?	**Yes** GC to A22. **No** REPAIR the circuit. TEST the system for normal operation.
A17 CHECK CIRCUIT 57 (BK) FOR AN OPEN • Disconnect: BPP Switch C278. • Measure the resistance between the BPP C278 pin 5, circuit 57 (BK), harness side and ground. • Is the resistance less than 5 ohms?	**Yes** If equipped with an automatic transmission, REPAIR circuit 810 (RD/LG). TEST the system for normal operation. If equipped with a manual transmission, GO to A20. **No** REPAIR the circuit. TEST the system for normal operation.
A18 CHECK THE SPEED CONTROL SWITCH • Key in OFF position. • Remove the driver air bag. Refer to Section 501-20B.	

LTV0500000001799

Fig. 156   Test A: Speed Control Is Inoperative (Part 7 of 10). 2002–04 Ranger

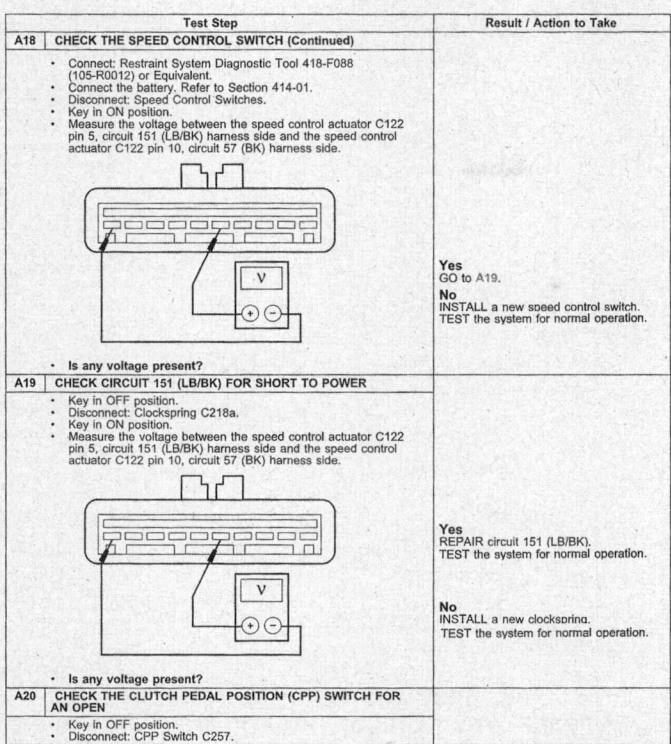

Test Step	Result / Action to Take
A18 CHECK THE SPEED CONTROL SWITCH (Continued)	
• Connect: Restraint System Diagnostic Tool 418-F088 (105-R0012) or Equivalent. • Connect the battery. Refer to Section 414-01. • Disconnect: Speed Control Switches. • Key in ON position. • Measure the voltage between the speed control actuator C122 pin 5, circuit 151 (LB/BK) harness side and the speed control actuator C122 pin 10, circuit 57 (BK) harness side. • Is any voltage present?	**Yes** GO to A19. **No** INSTALL a new speed control switch. TEST the system for normal operation.
A19 CHECK CIRCUIT 151 (LB/BK) FOR SHORT TO POWER	
• Key in OFF position. • Disconnect: Clockspring C218a. • Key in ON position. • Measure the voltage between the speed control actuator C122 pin 5, circuit 151 (LB/BK) harness side and the speed control actuator C122 pin 10, circuit 57 (BK) harness side. • Is any voltage present?	**Yes** REPAIR circuit 151 (LB/BK). TEST the system for normal operation. **No** INSTALL a new clockspring. TEST the system for normal operation.
A20 CHECK THE CLUTCH PEDAL POSITION (CPP) SWITCH FOR AN OPEN	
• Key in OFF position. • Disconnect: CPP Switch C257.	

LTV0500000001800

Fig. 156 Test A: Speed Control Is Inoperative (Part 8 of 10). 2002–04 Ranger

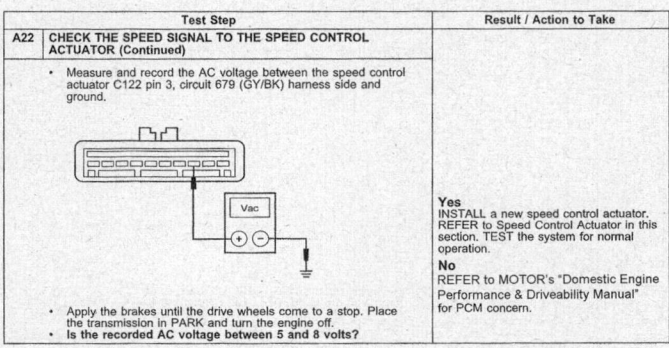

Test Step	Result / Action to Take
A22 CHECK THE SPEED SIGNAL TO THE SPEED CONTROL ACTUATOR (Continued)	
• Measure and record the AC voltage between the speed control actuator C122 pin 3, circuit 679 (GY/BK) harness side and ground. • Apply the brakes until the drive wheels come to a stop. Place the transmission in PARK and turn the engine off. • Is the recorded AC voltage between 5 and 8 volts?	**Yes** INSTALL a new speed control actuator. REFER to Speed Control Actuator in this section. TEST the system for normal operation. **No** REFER to MOTOR's "Domestic Engine Performance & Driveability Manual" for PCM concern.

LTV0500000001802

Fig. 156 Test A: Speed Control Is Inoperative (Part 10 of 10). 2002–04 Ranger

Test Step	Result / Action to Take
B1 CHECK SPEED CONTROL CABLE/THROTTLE BODY LINKAGE	
NOTE: It is normal for the engine rpm to increase slightly and then drop off slowly when the clutch pedal is applied during operation. • Key in OFF position. • Remove the speed control cable from the speed control actuator. Visually inspect the core wire and check the speed control cable by pulling on the cable and noting the throttle movement. • Is the speed control cable OK?	**Yes** GO to B2. **No** INSTALL a new speed control cable or REPAIR the throttle body linkage.
B2 CHECK THE SPEEDOMETER	
• Check the speedometer for correct operation by driving the vehicle. • Does the speedometer fluctuate?	**Yes** REPAIR the speedometer. **No** INSTALL a new speed control actuator. TEST the system for normal operation.

LTV0500000001803

Fig. 157 Test B: Set Speed Fluctuates. 2002–04 Ranger

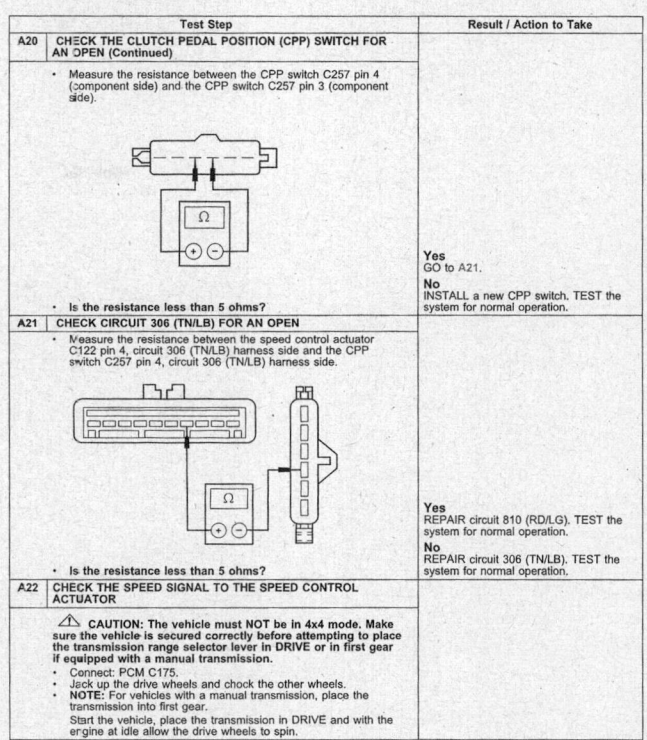

Test Step	Result / Action to Take
A20 CHECK THE CLUTCH PEDAL POSITION (CPP) SWITCH FOR AN OPEN (Continued)	
• Measure the resistance between the CPP switch C257 pin 4 (component side) and the CPP switch C257 pin 3 (component side). • Is the resistance less than 5 ohms?	**Yes** GO to A21. **No** INSTALL a new CPP switch. TEST the system for normal operation.
A21 CHECK CIRCUIT 306 (TN/LB) FOR AN OPEN	
Measure the resistance between the speed control actuator C122 pin 4, circuit 306 (TN/LB) harness side and the CPP switch C257 pin 4, circuit 306 (TN/LB) harness side. • Is the resistance less than 5 ohms?	**Yes** REPAIR circuit 810 (RD/LG). TEST the system for normal operation. **No** REPAIR circuit 306 (TN/LB). TEST the system for normal operation.
A22 CHECK THE SPEED SIGNAL TO THE SPEED CONTROL ACTUATOR	
⚠ **CAUTION:** The vehicle must NOT be in 4x4 mode. Make sure the vehicle is secured correctly before attempting to place the transmission range selector lever in DRIVE or in first gear if equipped with a manual transmission. • Connect: PCM C175. • Jack up the drive wheels and chock the other wheels. • **NOTE:** For vehicles with a manual transmission, place the transmission into first gear. Start the vehicle, place the transmission in DRIVE and with the engine at idle allow the drive wheels to spin.	

LTV0500000001801

Fig. 156 Test A: Speed Control Is Inoperative (Part 9 of 10). 2002–04 Ranger

Test Step	Result / Action to Take
C1 CHECK THE STOPLAMP OPERATION	
• Check the stoplamps for correct operation by applying and releasing the brake pedal and observing the stoplamps. • **Do the stoplamps operate correctly?**	**Yes** GO to C2. **No** Continue diagnosis of the stoplamps.
C2 CHECK THE BRAKE PEDAL POSITION (BPP) SWITCH OPERATION	
• Disconnect: Speed Control Actuator C122. • Measure the voltage between the speed control actuator C122 pin 4, circuit 306 (TN/LB), harness side and the speed control actuator C122 pin 10, circuit 57 (BK), harness side while applying and releasing the brake pedal. • Is the voltage greater than 10 volts with the brake pedal applied and 0 volts with the brake pedal released?	**Yes** GO to C7. **No** GO to C3.
C3 CHECK CIRCUIT 307 (BN) FOR AN OPEN	
• Key in OFF position. • Disconnect: BPP Switch C278. • Measure the voltage between the BPP switch C278 pin 3, circuit 276 (BN), harness side and ground. • Is the voltage greater than 10 volts?	**Yes** GO to C4. **No** REPAIR the circuit. TEST the system for normal operation.
C4 CHECK CIRCUIT 810 (RD/LG) FOR AN OPEN	
• Disconnect: CPP Switch C257.	**Yes**

LTV0500000001804

Fig. 158 Test C: Speed Control Does Not Disengage When Brakes Are Applied (Part 1 of 4). 2002–04 Ranger

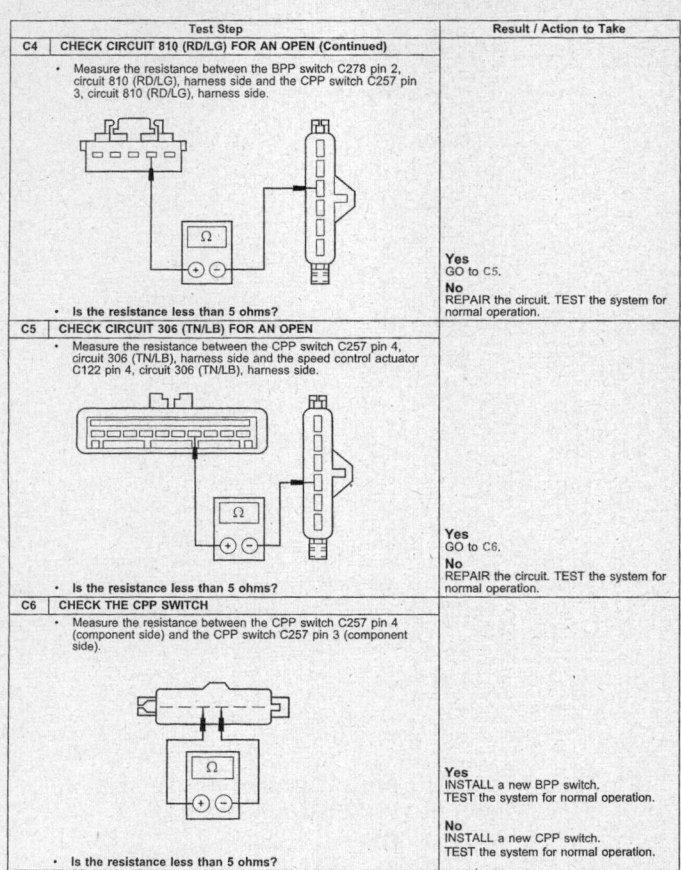

Test Step	Result / Action to Take
C4 CHECK CIRCUIT 810 (RD/LG) FOR AN OPEN (Continued)	
• Measure the resistance between the BPP switch C278 pin 2, circuit 810 (RD/LG), harness side and the CPP switch C257 pin 3, circuit 810 (RD/LG), harness side.	**Yes** GO to C5. **No** REPAIR the circuit. TEST the system for normal operation.
• Is the resistance less than 5 ohms?	
C5 CHECK CIRCUIT 306 (TN/LB) FOR AN OPEN	
• Measure the resistance between the CPP switch C257 pin 4, circuit 306 (TN/LB), harness side and the speed control actuator C122 pin 4, circuit 306 (TN/LB), harness side.	**Yes** GO to C6. **No** REPAIR the circuit. TEST the system for normal operation.
• Is the resistance less than 5 ohms?	
C6 CHECK THE CPP SWITCH	
• Measure the resistance between the CPP switch C257 pin 4 (component side) and the CPP switch C257 pin 3 (component side).	**Yes** INSTALL a new BPP switch. TEST the system for normal operation. **No** INSTALL a new CPP switch. TEST the system for normal operation.
• Is the resistance less than 5 ohms?	

LTV0500000001805

Fig. 158 Test C: Speed Control Does Not Disengage When Brakes Are Applied (Part 2 of 4). 2002–04 Ranger

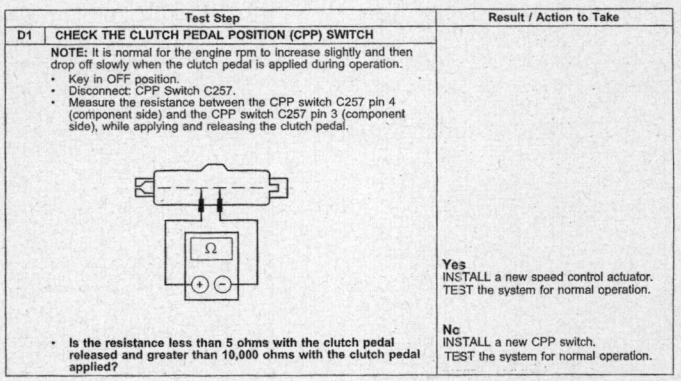

pedal released?	
C9 CHECK CIRCUIT 307 (BK/YE) FOR AN OPEN	
• Measure the resistance between the speed control actuator C122 pin 9, circuit 307 (BK/YE), harness side and the deactivator switch C1025 pin 2, circuit 307 (BK/YE) harness side.	**Yes** REPAIR circuit 535 (LB/RD). TEST the system for normal operation. **No** REPAIR circuit 307 (BK/YE). TEST the system for normal operation.
A0078916	
• Is the resistance less than 5 ohms?	

LTV0500000001807

Fig. 158 Test C: Speed Control Does Not Disengage When Brakes Are Applied (Part 4 of 4). 2002–04 Ranger

Test Step	Result / Action to Take
C7 CHECK THE DEACTIVATOR SWITCH CIRCUITRY	
• Key in ON position.	
• Measure the voltage between the speed control actuator C122 pin 9, circuit 307 (BK/YE), harness side and ground, while firmly applying and releasing the brake pedal.	**Yes** INSTALL a new speed control actuator. TEST the system for normal operation. **No** GO to C8.
• Is the voltage 0 volts with the brake pedal firmly applied and greater than 10 volts with the brake pedal released?	
C8 CHECK THE DEACTIVATOR SWITCH	
• Key in OFF position.	
• Disconnect: Deactivator Switch C1025.	
• Measure the resistance between the deactivator switch pins (component side), while firmly pressing and releasing the brake pedal.	**Yes** GO to C9. **No** INSTALL a new deactivator switch. TEST the system for normal operation.
• Is the resistance greater than 10,000 ohms with the brake pedal firmly applied and less than 5 ohms with the brake pedal released?	

LTV0500000001806

Fig. 158 Test C: Speed Control Does Not Disengage When Brakes Are Applied (Part 3 of 4). 2002–04 Ranger

Test Step	Result / Action to Take
D1 CHECK THE CLUTCH PEDAL POSITION (CPP) SWITCH	
NOTE: It is normal for the engine rpm to increase slightly and then drop off slowly when the clutch pedal is applied during operation.	
• Key in OFF position.	
• Disconnect: CPP Switch C257.	
• Measure the resistance between the CPP switch C257 pin 4 (component side) and the CPP switch C257 pin 3 (component side), while applying and releasing the clutch pedal.	**Yes** INSTALL a new speed control actuator. TEST the system for normal operation. **No** INSTALL a new CPP switch. TEST the system for normal operation.
• Is the resistance less than 5 ohms with the clutch pedal released and greater than 10,000 ohms with the clutch pedal applied?	

LTV0500000001808

Fig. 159 Test D: Speed Control Does Not Disengage When Clutch Is Applied. 2002–04 Ranger

Test Step	Result / Action to Take
E1 CHECK THE SPEED CONTROL SWITCH	
• Key in OFF position. • Disconnect: Speed Control Actuator C122. • Measure the resistance between the speed control actuator C122 pin 5, circuit 151 (LB/BK), harness side and the speed control actuator C122 pin 6, circuit 848 (DG/OG), harness side while pressing the speed control switch as follows: <table><tr><th>Speed Control Switch</th><th>Resistance Value</th></tr><tr><td>COAST</td><td>Between 114 and 126 ohms</td></tr><tr><td>SET/ACCEL</td><td>Between 612 and 748 ohms</td></tr><tr><td>RESUME</td><td>Between 2,090 and 2,310 ohms</td></tr><tr><td>OFF</td><td>Less than 5 ohms</td></tr></table>	**Yes** INSTALL a new speed control actuator. TEST the system for normal operation. **No** INSTALL a new speed control switch TEST the system for normal operation.
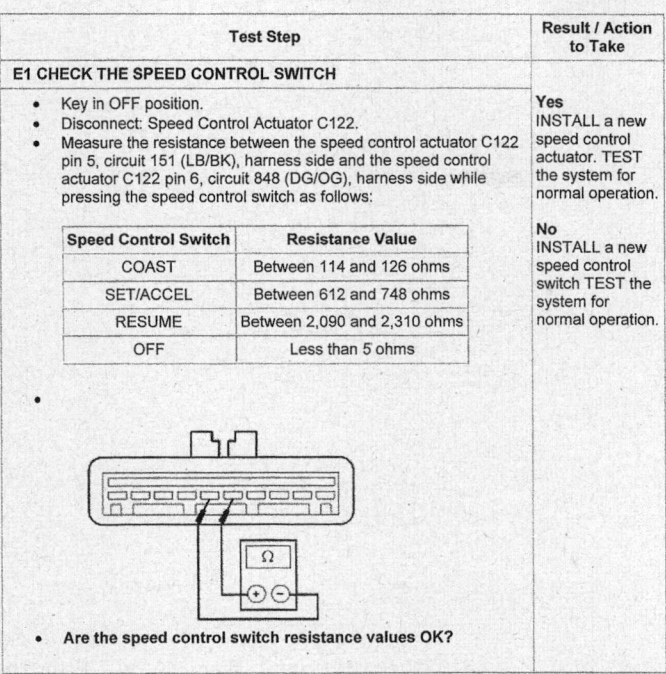 • **Are the speed control switch resistance values OK?**	

LTV0500000001809

Fig. 160 Test E: Speed Control Switch Is Inoperative. 2002–04 Ranger

Test Step	Result / Action to Take
G1 CHECK THE STOPLAMP OPERATION	
• Apply and release the brake pedal while observing the stoplamps. • **Do the stoplamps operate correctly?**	**Yes** GO to G2. **No** Continue diagnosis of the stoplamps.
G2 CHECK CIRCUIT 810 FOR AN OPEN	
• Key in OFF position. • Disconnect: Speed Control Actuator C122. • Key in ON position. • Measure the voltage between the speed control actuator C122 pin 4, circuit 306 (TN/LB), harness side and the speed control actuator C122 pin 10, circuit 57 (BK), harness side.	**Yes** GO to G3. **No** GO to G5.
• **Is the voltage greater than 10 volts?**	
G3 CHECK THE BRAKE CIRCUIT	
• Key in OFF position. • Measure the resistance between the speed control actuator C122 pin 4, circuit 306 (TN/LB), harness side and the speed	**Yes** INSTALL a new speed control TEST

LTV0500000001811

Fig. 162 Test G: Brake Pedal Position (BPP) Switch Circuit Failure (Part 1 of 3). 2002–04 Ranger

Test Step	Result / Action to Take
F1 CHECK THE SPEED CONTROL CABLE	
• Check the speed control cable for correct attachment at the speed control actuator and throttle body. • **Is the speed control cable attached correctly?**	**Yes** GO to F2. **No** CONNECT the speed control cable. REPEAT the self-test.
F2 CHECK FOR A STICKING OR BINDING SPEED CONTROL CABLE	
• Check the speed control cable from sticking or binding. • **Is the speed control cable OK?**	**Yes** INSTALL a new speed control actuator. REPEAT the self-test. **No** REPAIR or INSTALL a new speed control cable. REPEAT the self-test.

LTV0500000001810

Fig. 161 Test F: Flash w/Last Switch Pressed, But No Dynamic Pull Occurs At Throttle & Speed Control Is Inoperative. 2002–04 Ranger

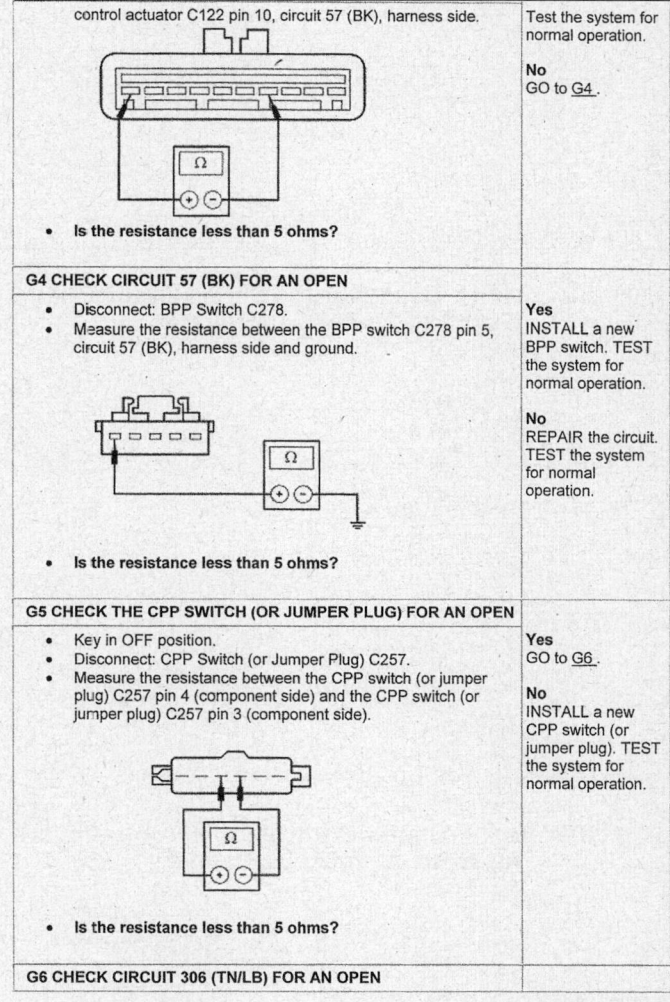

Test Step	Result / Action to Take
control actuator C122 pin 10, circuit 57 (BK), harness side. • **Is the resistance less than 5 ohms?**	Test the system for normal operation. **No** GO to G4.
G4 CHECK CIRCUIT 57 (BK) FOR AN OPEN	
• Disconnect: BPP Switch C278. • Measure the resistance between the BPP switch C278 pin 5, circuit 57 (BK), harness side and ground. • **Is the resistance less than 5 ohms?**	**Yes** INSTALL a new BPP switch. TEST the system for normal operation. **No** REPAIR the circuit. TEST the system for normal operation.
G5 CHECK THE CPP SWITCH (OR JUMPER PLUG) FOR AN OPEN	
• Key in OFF position. • Disconnect: CPP Switch (or Jumper Plug) C257. • Measure the resistance between the CPP switch (or jumper plug) C257 pin 4 (component side) and the CPP switch (or jumper plug) C257 pin 3 (component side). • **Is the resistance less than 5 ohms?**	**Yes** GO to G6. **No** INSTALL a new CPP switch (or jumper plug). TEST the system for normal operation.
G6 CHECK CIRCUIT 306 (TN/LB) FOR AN OPEN	

LTV0500000001812

Fig. 162 Test G: Brake Pedal Position (BPP) Switch Circuit Failure (Part 2 of 3). 2002–04 Ranger

- Measure the resistance between the speed control actuator C122 pin 4, circuit 306 (TN/LB), harness side and the CPP switch (or jumper plug) C257 pin 4, circuit 306 (TN/LB), harness side.

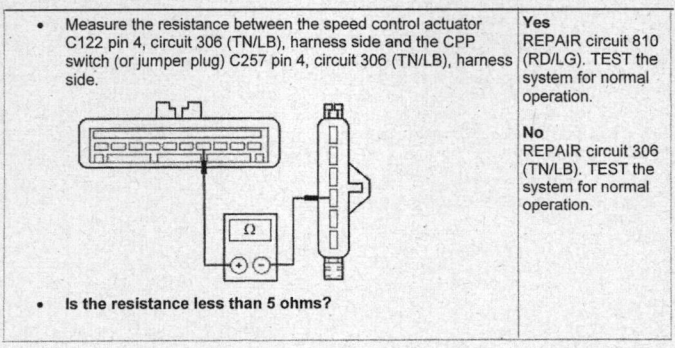

- **Is the resistance less than 5 ohms?**

Yes
REPAIR circuit 810 (RD/LG). TEST the system for normal operation.

No
REPAIR circuit 306 (TN/LB). TEST the system for normal operation.

LTV0500000001813

Fig. 162   Test G: Brake Pedal Position (BPP) Switch Circuit Failure (Part 3 of 3). 2002–04 Ranger

Test Step	Result / Action to Take
H3 CHECK CIRCUIT 307 (BK/YE) FOR AN OPEN (Continued)	
• Measure the resistance between the speed control actuator C122 pin 9, circuit 307 (BK/YE), harness side and the deactivator switch C1025 pin 2, circuit 307 (BK/YE), harness side. 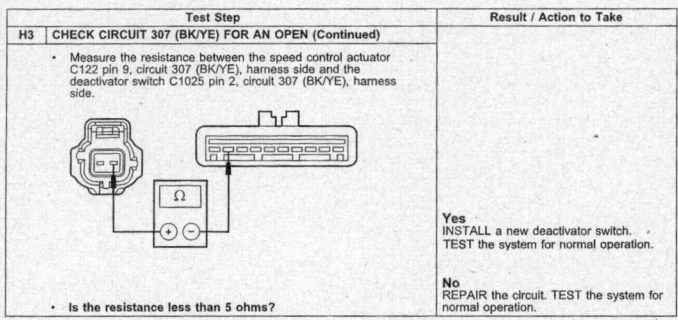 • **Is the resistance less than 5 ohms?**	**Yes** INSTALL a new deactivator switch. TEST the system for normal operation. **No** REPAIR the circuit. TEST the system for normal operation.

LTV0500000001815

Fig. 163   Test H: Deactivator Switch Circuit Failure (Part 2 of 2). 2002–04 Ranger

Test Step	Result / Action to Take
I1 CHECK SPEED CONTROL ACTUATOR	
• Key in OFF position. • Disconnect: Speed Control Actuator C122. • Key in ON position. • Check the speed control indicator lamp. • **Does the speed control indicator lamp remain on?**	**Yes** GO to I2. **No** INSTALL a new speed control actuator. TEST the system for normal operation.
I2 CHECK CIRCUIT 203 (OG/LB) FOR SHORT TO GROUND	
• Key in OFF position. • Disconnect: Instrument Cluster C220a. • Measure the resistance between the speed control actuator C122 pin 1, circuit 203 (OG/LB), harness side and ground. 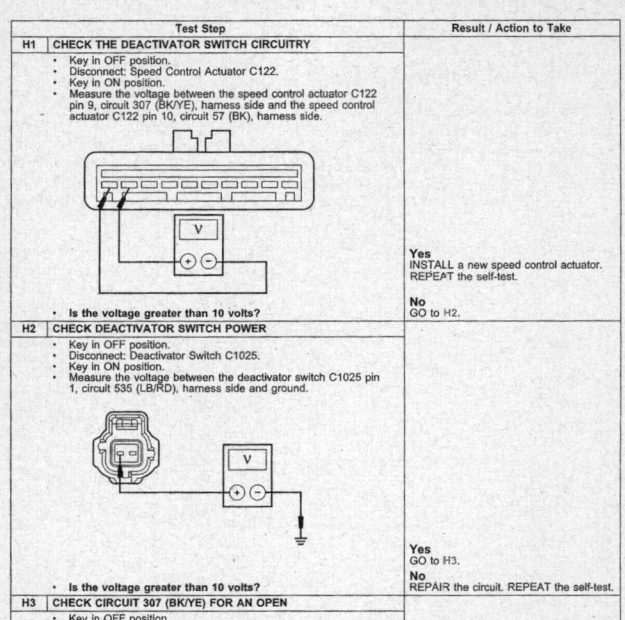 • **Is the resistance greater than 10,000 ohms?**	**Yes** INSTALL a new instrument cluster. TEST the system for normal operation. **No** REPAIR the circuit. TEST the system for normal operation.

LTV0500000001816

Fig. 164   Test I: Speed Control Indicator Lamp Is Always On. 2002–04 Ranger

Test Step	Result / Action to Take
H1 CHECK THE DEACTIVATOR SWITCH CIRCUITRY	
• Key in OFF position. • Disconnect: Speed Control Actuator C122. • Key in ON position. • Measure the voltage between the speed control actuator C122 pin 9, circuit 307 (BK/YE), harness side and the speed control actuator C122 pin 10, circuit 57 (BK), harness side. • **Is the voltage greater than 10 volts?**	**Yes** INSTALL a new speed control actuator. REPEAT the self-test. **No** GO to H2.
H2 CHECK DEACTIVATOR SWITCH POWER	
• Key in OFF position. • Disconnect: Deactivator Switch C1025. • Key in ON position. • Measure the voltage between the deactivator switch C1025 pin 1, circuit 535 (LB/RD), harness side and ground. • **Is the voltage greater than 10 volts?**	**Yes** GO to H3. **No** REPAIR the circuit. REPEAT the self-test.
H3 CHECK CIRCUIT 307 (BK/YE) FOR AN OPEN	
• Key in OFF position.	

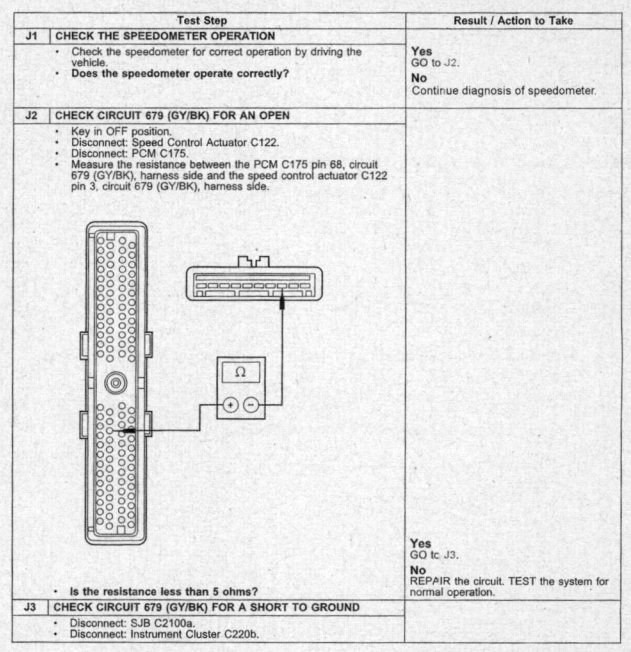

LTV0500000001814

Fig. 163   Test H: Deactivator Switch Circuit Failure (Part 1 of 2). 2002–04 Ranger

Test Step	Result / Action to Take
J1 CHECK THE SPEEDOMETER OPERATION	
• Check the speedometer for correct operation by driving the vehicle. • **Does the speedometer operate correctly?**	**Yes** GO to J2. **No** Continue diagnosis of speedometer.
J2 CHECK CIRCUIT 679 (GY/BK) FOR AN OPEN	
• Key in OFF position. • Disconnect: Speed Control Actuator C122. • Disconnect: PCM C175. • Measure the resistance between the PCM C175 pin 68, circuit 679 (GY/BK), harness side and the speed control actuator C122 pin 3, circuit 679 (GY/BK), harness side. • **Is the resistance less than 5 ohms?**	**Yes** GO to J3. **No** REPAIR the circuit. TEST the system for normal operation.
J3 CHECK CIRCUIT 679 (GY/BK) FOR A SHORT TO GROUND	
• Disconnect: SJB C2100a. • Disconnect: Instrument Cluster C220b.	

LTV0500000001817

Fig. 165   Test J: Speed Signal Circuit Failure (Part 1 of 2). 2002–04 Ranger

Test Step	Result / Action to Take
J3 CHECK CIRCUIT 679 (GY/BK) FOR A SHORT TO GROUND (Continued)	
• Measure the resistance between the speed control actuator C122 pin 3, circuit 679 (GY/BK), harness side and ground. 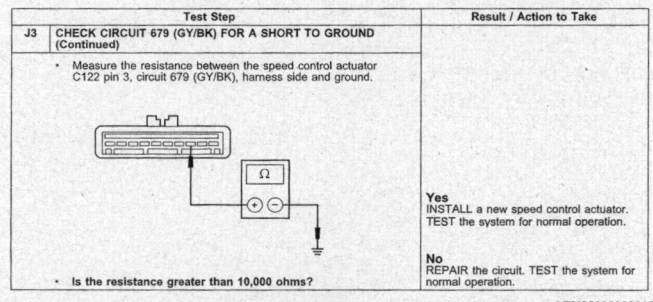 • **Is the resistance greater than 10,000 ohms?**	**Yes** INSTALL a new speed control actuator. TEST the system for normal operation. **No** REPAIR the circuit. TEST the system for normal operation.

LTV0500000001818

Fig. 165   Test J: Speed Signal Circuit Failure (Part 2 of 2). 2002–04 Ranger

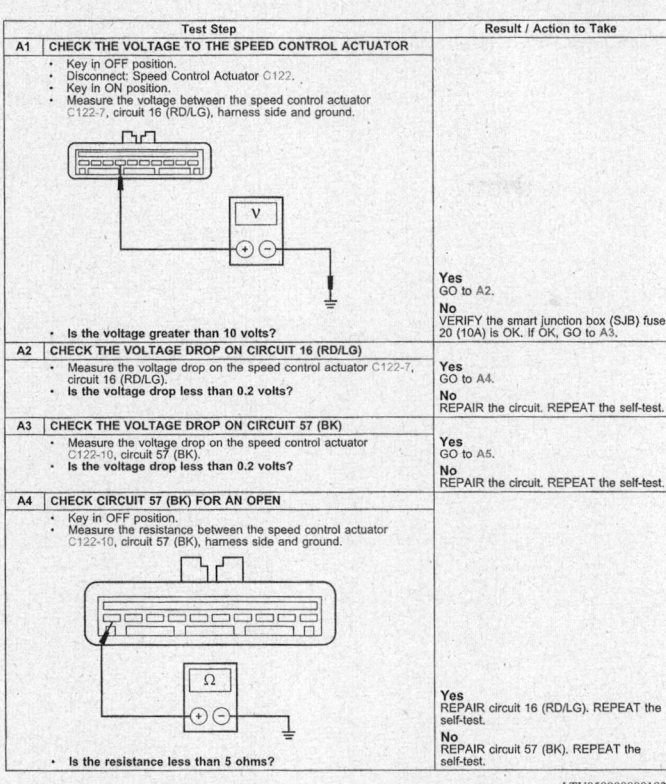

Test Step		Result / Action to Take
A1	**CHECK THE VOLTAGE TO THE SPEED CONTROL ACTUATOR**	
	• Key in OFF position. • Disconnect: Speed Control Actuator C122. • Key in ON position. • Measure the voltage between the speed control actuator C122-7, circuit 16 (RD/LG), harness side and ground.	
	• Is the voltage greater than 10 volts?	**Yes** GO to A2. **No** VERIFY the smart junction box (SJB) fuse 20 (10A) is OK. If OK, GO to A3.
A2	**CHECK THE VOLTAGE DROP ON CIRCUIT 16 (RD/LG)**	
	• Measure the voltage drop on the speed control actuator C122-7, circuit 16 (RD/LG). • Is the voltage drop less than 0.2 volts?	**Yes** GO to A4. **No** REPAIR the circuit. REPEAT the self-test.
A3	**CHECK THE VOLTAGE DROP ON CIRCUIT 57 (BK)**	
	• Measure the voltage drop on the speed control actuator C122-10, circuit 57 (BK). • Is the voltage drop less than 0.2 volts?	**Yes** GO to A5. **No** REPAIR the circuit. REPEAT the self-test.
A4	**CHECK CIRCUIT 57 (BK) FOR AN OPEN**	
	• Key in OFF position. • Measure the resistance between the speed control actuator C122-10, circuit 57 (BK), harness side and ground.	
	• Is the resistance less than 5 ohms?	**Yes** REPAIR circuit 16 (RD/LG). REPEAT the self-test. **No** REPAIR circuit 57 (BK). REPEAT the self-test.

LTV0500000001823

Fig. 166   Test A: Speed Control Is Inoperative (Part 1 of 11). 2005–06 Ranger

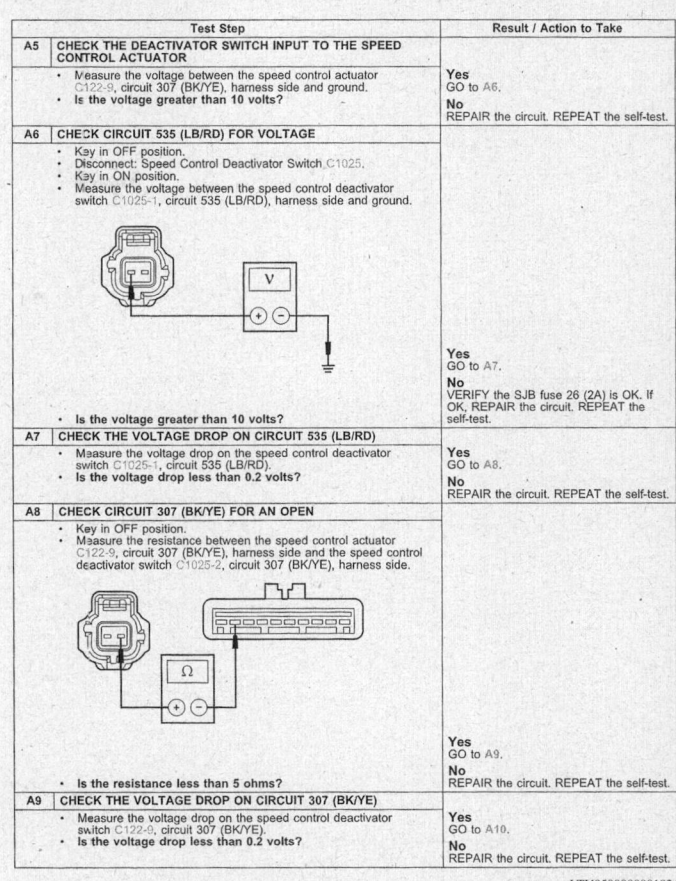

Test Step		Result / Action to Take
A5	**CHECK THE DEACTIVATOR SWITCH INPUT TO THE SPEED CONTROL ACTUATOR**	
	• Measure the voltage between the speed control actuator C122-9, circuit 307 (BK/YE), harness side and ground. • Is the voltage greater than 10 volts?	**Yes** GO to A6. **No** REPAIR the circuit. REPEAT the self-test.
A6	**CHECK CIRCUIT 535 (LB/RD) FOR VOLTAGE**	
	• Key in OFF position. • Disconnect: Speed Control Deactivator Switch C1025. • Key in ON position. • Measure the voltage between the speed control deactivator switch C1025-1, circuit 535 (LB/RD), harness side and ground.	
	• Is the voltage greater than 10 volts?	**Yes** GO to A7. **No** VERIFY the SJB fuse 26 (2A) is OK. If OK, REPAIR the circuit. REPEAT the self-test.
A7	**CHECK THE VOLTAGE DROP ON CIRCUIT 535 (LB/RD)**	
	• Measure the voltage drop on the speed control deactivator switch C1025-1, circuit 535 (LB/RD). • Is the voltage drop less than 0.2 volts?	**Yes** GO to A8. **No** REPAIR the circuit. REPEAT the self-test.
A8	**CHECK CIRCUIT 307 (BK/YE) FOR AN OPEN**	
	• Key in OFF position. • Measure the resistance between the speed control actuator C122-9, circuit 307 (BK/YE), harness side and the speed control deactivator switch C1025-2, circuit 307 (BK/YE), harness side.	
	• Is the resistance less than 5 ohms?	**Yes** GO to A9. **No** REPAIR the circuit. REPEAT the self-test.
A9	**CHECK THE VOLTAGE DROP ON CIRCUIT 307 (BK/YE)**	
	• Measure the voltage drop on the speed control deactivator switch C122-9, circuit 307 (BK/YE). • Is the voltage drop less than 0.2 volts?	**Yes** GO to A10. **No** REPAIR the circuit. REPEAT the self-test.

LTV0500000001824

Fig. 166   Test A: Speed Control Is Inoperative (Part 2 of 11). 2005–06 Ranger

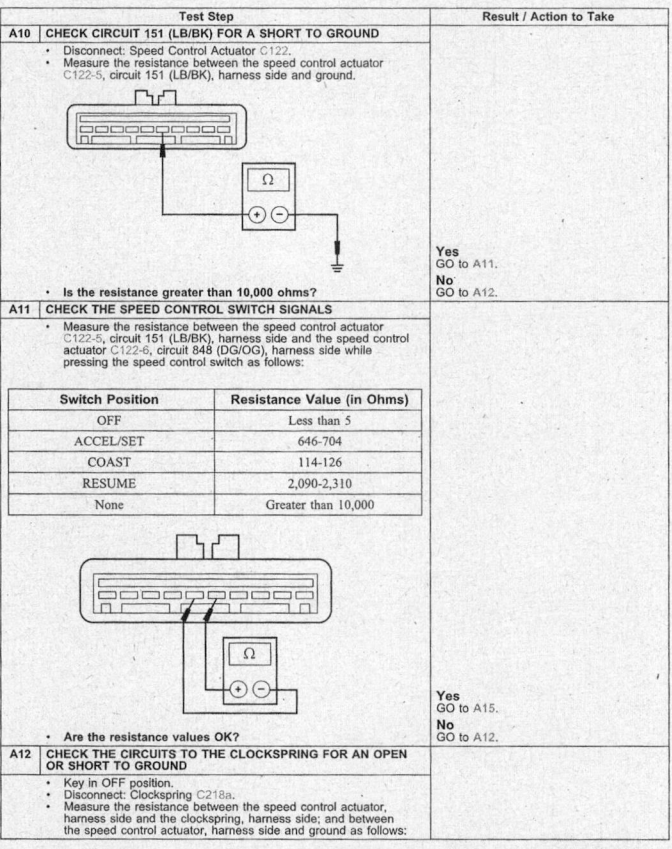

Test Step		Result / Action to Take
A10	**CHECK CIRCUIT 151 (LB/BK) FOR A SHORT TO GROUND**	
	• Disconnect: Speed Control Actuator C122. • Measure the resistance between the speed control actuator C122-5, circuit 151 (LB/BK), harness side and ground.	
	• Is the resistance greater than 10,000 ohms?	**Yes** GO to A11. **No** GO to A12.
A11	**CHECK THE SPEED CONTROL SWITCH SIGNALS**	
	• Measure the resistance between the speed control actuator C122-5, circuit 151 (LB/BK), harness side and speed control actuator C122-6, circuit 848 (DG/OG), harness side while pressing the speed control switch as follows:	

Switch Position	Resistance Value (in Ohms)
OFF	Less than 5
ACCEL/SET	646-704
COAST	114-126
RESUME	2,090-2,310
None	Greater than 10,000

Test Step		Result / Action to Take
	• Are the resistance values OK?	**Yes** GO to A15. **No** GO to A12.
A12	**CHECK THE CIRCUITS TO THE CLOCKSPRING FOR AN OPEN OR SHORT TO GROUND**	
	• Key in OFF position. • Disconnect: Clockspring C218a. • Measure the resistance between the speed control actuator, harness side and the clockspring, harness side; and between the speed control actuator, harness side and ground as follows:	

LTV0500000001825

Fig. 166   Test A: Speed Control Is Inoperative (Part 3 of 11). 2005–06 Ranger

Test Step		Result / Action to Take
A12	**CHECK THE CIRCUITS TO THE CLOCKSPRING FOR AN OPEN OR SHORT TO GROUND (Continued)**	

Speed Control Actuator Connector-Pin	Clockspring Connector-Pin or Ground	Circuit	
C122-5	C218a-6	151 (LB/BK)	
C122-5	Ground	151 (LB/BK)	
C122-6	C218a-3	848 (DG/OG)	

Test Step		Result / Action to Take
	• Is the resistance less than 5 ohms between the speed control actuator and the clockspring, and greater than 10,000 ohms between the speed control actuator and ground?	**Yes** GO to A13. **No** REPAIR the circuit. TEST the system for normal operation.
A13	**CHECK THE CIRCUITS TO THE CLOCKSPRING FOR AN OPEN OR SHORT TO GROUND**	
	• Disconnect: Clockspring C218a. • Measure the resistance between the speed control actuator, harness side and the clockspring, harness side; and between the speed control actuator, harness side and ground as follows:	

Speed Control Actuator Connector-Pin	Clockspring Connector-Pin	Circuit
C122-5	C218a-6	151 (LB/BK)
C122-6	C218a-3	848 (DG/OG)

Test Step		Result / Action to Take
	• Are the resistances less than 5 ohms between the speed control actuator and the clockspring, and greater than 10,000 ohms between the speed control actuator and ground?	**Yes** GO to A14. **No** REPAIR the circuit in question. TEST the system for normal operation.
A14	**CHECK THE SPEED CONTROL SWITCHES**	
	• Disconnect: Speed Control Switch Wiring Harness. • Measure the resistance between the speed control switch connector pin 2, harness side and the speed control switch connector pin 4, harness side with no buttons pressed and then while pressing the speed control switches as follows:	

Switch Position	Resistance Value (in Ohms)
OFF	Less than 5
ACCEL/SET	646-704
COAST	114-126
RESUME	2,090-2,310
None	Greater than 10,000

Test Step		Result / Action to Take
	• Are the speed control switch resistance values OK?	**Yes** INSTALL a new clockspring. TEST the system for normal operation. **No** INSTALL a new speed control switch. TEST the system for normal operation.
A15	**CHECK THE SPEED CONTROL ON SWITCH OPERATION**	
	• Key in ON position.	

LTV0500000001826

Fig. 166   Test A: Speed Control Is Inoperative (Part 4 of 11). 2005–06 Ranger

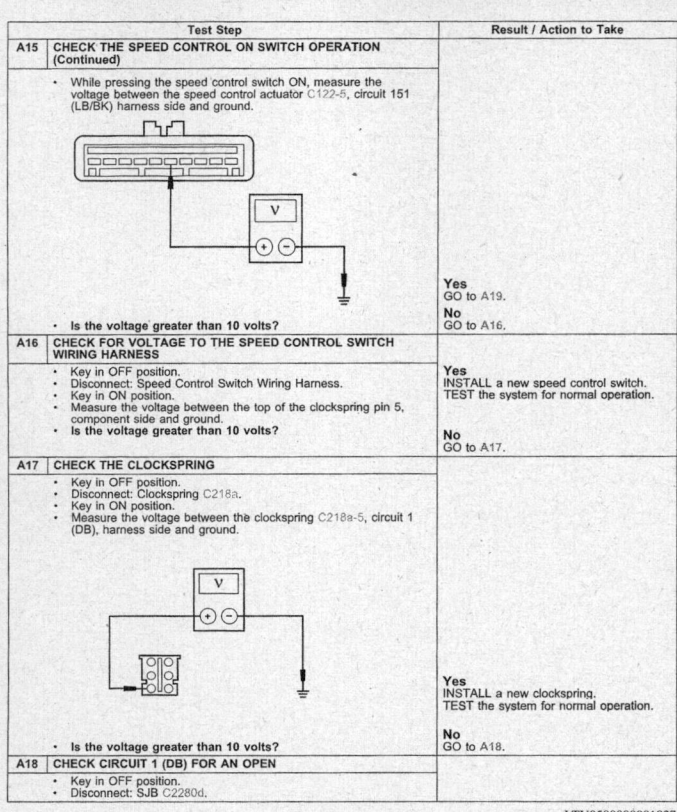

Test Step	Result / Action to Take
A15 CHECK THE SPEED CONTROL ON SWITCH OPERATION (Continued)	
• While pressing the speed control switch ON, measure the voltage between the speed control actuator C122-5, circuit 151 (LB/BK) harness side and ground.	**Yes** GO to A19. **No** GO to A16.
• Is the voltage greater than 10 volts?	
A16 CHECK FOR VOLTAGE TO THE SPEED CONTROL SWITCH WIRING HARNESS	
• Key in OFF position. • Disconnect: Speed Control Switch Wiring Harness. • Key in ON position. • Measure the voltage between the top of the clockspring pin 5, component side and ground. • Is the voltage greater than 10 volts?	**Yes** INSTALL a new speed control switch. TEST the system for normal operation. **No** GO to A17.
A17 CHECK THE CLOCKSPRING	
• Key in OFF position. • Disconnect: Clockspring C218a. • Key in ON position. • Measure the voltage between the clockspring C218a-5, circuit 1 (DB), harness side and ground.	**Yes** INSTALL a new clockspring. TEST the system for normal operation. **No** GO to A18.
• Is the voltage greater than 10 volts?	
A18 CHECK CIRCUIT 1 (DB) FOR AN OPEN	
• Key in OFF position. • Disconnect: SJB C2280d.	

LTV0500000001827

Fig. 166 Test A: Speed Control Is Inoperative (Part 5 of 11). 2005–06 Ranger

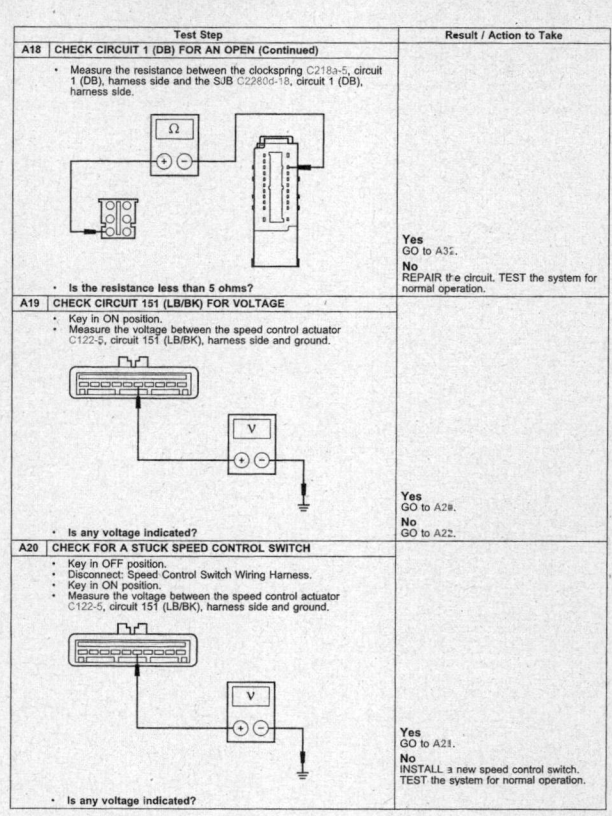

Test Step	Result / Action to Take
A18 CHECK CIRCUIT 1 (DB) FOR AN OPEN (Continued)	
• Measure the resistance between the clockspring C218a-5, circuit 1 (DB), harness side and the SJB C2280d-18, circuit 1 (DB), harness side.	**Yes** GO to A32. **No** REPAIR the circuit. TEST the system for normal operation.
• Is the resistance less than 5 ohms?	
A19 CHECK CIRCUIT 151 (LB/BK) FOR VOLTAGE	
• Key in ON position. • Measure the voltage between the speed control actuator C122-5, circuit 151 (LB/BK) harness side and ground.	**Yes** GO to A20. **No** GO to A22.
• Is any voltage indicated?	
A20 CHECK FOR A STUCK SPEED CONTROL SWITCH	
• Key in OFF position. • Disconnect: Speed Control Switch Wiring Harness. • Key in ON position. • Measure the voltage between the speed control actuator C122-5, circuit 151 (LB/BK), harness side and ground.	**Yes** GO to A21. **No** INSTALL a new speed control switch. TEST the system for normal operation.
• Is any voltage indicated?	

LTV0500000001828

Fig. 166 Test A: Speed Control Is Inoperative (Part 6 of 11). 2005–06 Ranger

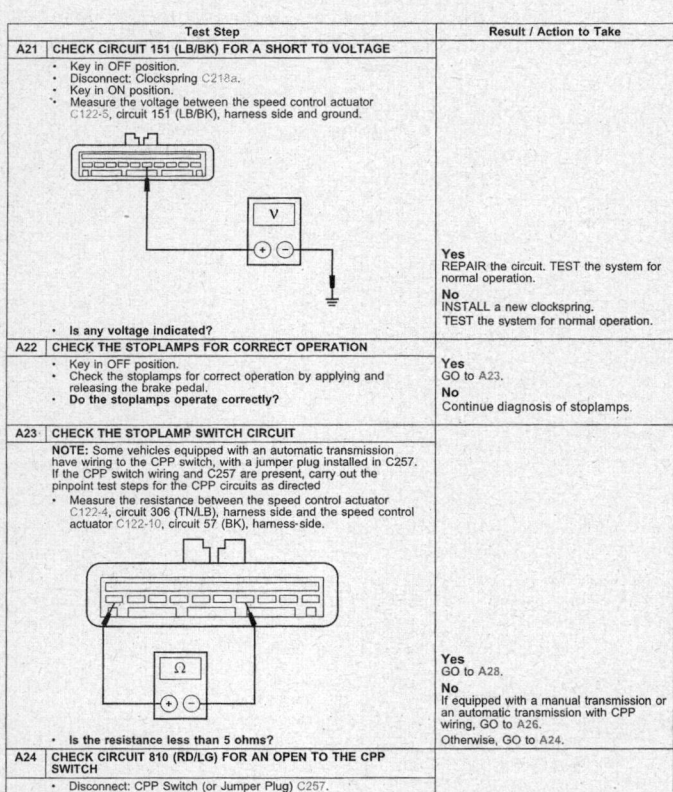

Test Step	Result / Action to Take
A21 CHECK CIRCUIT 151 (LB/BK) FOR A SHORT TO VOLTAGE	
• Key in OFF position. • Disconnect: Clockspring C218a. • Key in ON position. • Measure the voltage between the speed control actuator C122-5, circuit 151 (LB/BK), harness side and ground.	**Yes** REPAIR the circuit. TEST the system for normal operation. **No** INSTALL a new clockspring. TEST the system for normal operation.
• Is any voltage indicated?	
A22 CHECK THE STOPLAMPS FOR CORRECT OPERATION	
• Key in OFF position. • Check the stoplamps for correct operation by applying and releasing the brake pedal. • Do the stoplamps operate correctly?	**Yes** GO to A23. **No** Continue diagnosis of stoplamps.
A23 CHECK THE STOPLAMP SWITCH CIRCUIT	
NOTE: Some vehicles equipped with an automatic transmission have wiring to the CPP switch, with a jumper plug installed in C257. If the CPP switch wiring and C257 are present, carry out the pinpoint test steps for the CPP circuits as directed. • Measure the resistance between the speed control actuator C122-4, circuit 306 (TN/LB), harness side and the speed control actuator C122-10, circuit 57 (BK), harness-side.	**Yes** GO to A28. **No** If equipped with a manual transmission or an automatic transmission with CPP wiring, GO to A26. Otherwise, GO to A24.
• Is the resistance less than 5 ohms?	
A24 CHECK CIRCUIT 810 (RD/LG) FOR AN OPEN TO THE CPP SWITCH	
• Disconnect: CPP Switch (or Jumper Plug) C257.	

LTV0500000001829

Fig. 166 Test A: Speed Control Is Inoperative (Part 7 of 11). 2005–06 Ranger

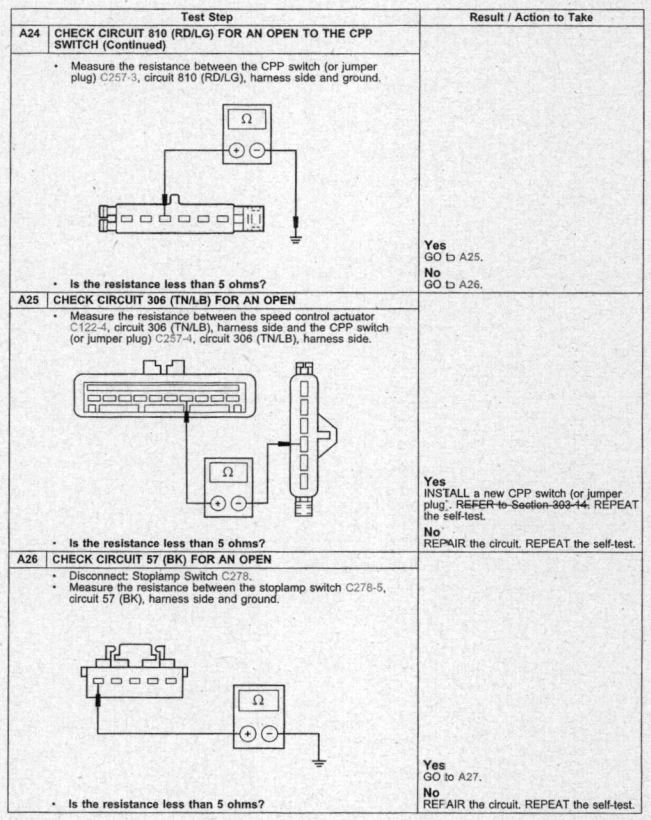

Test Step	Result / Action to Take
A24 CHECK CIRCUIT 810 (RD/LG) FOR AN OPEN TO THE CPP SWITCH (Continued)	
• Measure the resistance between the CPP switch (or jumper plug) C257-3, circuit 810 (RD/LG), harness side and ground.	**Yes** GO to A25. **No** GO to A26.
• Is the resistance less than 5 ohms?	
A25 CHECK CIRCUIT 306 (TN/LB) FOR AN OPEN	
• Measure the resistance between the speed control actuator C122-4, circuit 306 (TN/LB), harness side and the CPP switch (or jumper plug) C257-4, circuit 306 (TN/LB), harness side.	**Yes** INSTALL a new CPP switch (or jumper plug). REFER to Section 303-14. REPEAT the self-test. **No** REPAIR the circuit. REPEAT the self-test.
• Is the resistance less than 5 ohms?	
A26 CHECK CIRCUIT 57 (BK) FOR AN OPEN	
• Disconnect: Stoplamp Switch C278. • Measure the resistance between the stoplamp switch C278-5, circuit 57 (BK), harness side and ground.	**Yes** GO to A27. **No** REPAIR the circuit. REPEAT the self-test.
• Is the resistance less than 5 ohms?	

LTV0500000001830

Fig. 166 Test A: Speed Control Is Inoperative (Part 8 of 11). 2005–06 Ranger

Test Step	Result / Action to Take
A27 CHECK THE STOPLAMP SWITCH • Disconnect: Stoplamp Switch C278. • Install a fused (5A) jumper wire between the stoplamp switch C278-4, circuit 810 (RD/LG), harness side and the stoplamp switch C278-5, circuit 57 (BK), harness side. • Measure the resistance between the speed control actuator C122-4, circuit 306 (TN/LB), harness side and the speed control actuator C122-10, circuit 57 (BK), harness side. • **Is the resistance less than 5 ohms?**	**Yes** INSTALL a new stoplamp switch. REPEAT the self-test. **No** REPAIR the circuit. REPEAT the self-test.
A28 CHECK CIRCUIT 679 (GY/BK) FOR AN OPEN • Key in OFF position. • Disconnect: PCM C175. • Measure the resistance between the speed control actuator C122-3, circuit 679 (GY/BK), harness side and the PCM C175-68, circuit 679 (GY/BK), harness side. • **Is the resistance less than 5 ohms?**	**Yes** GO to A29. **No** REPAIR the circuit. REPEAT the self-test.

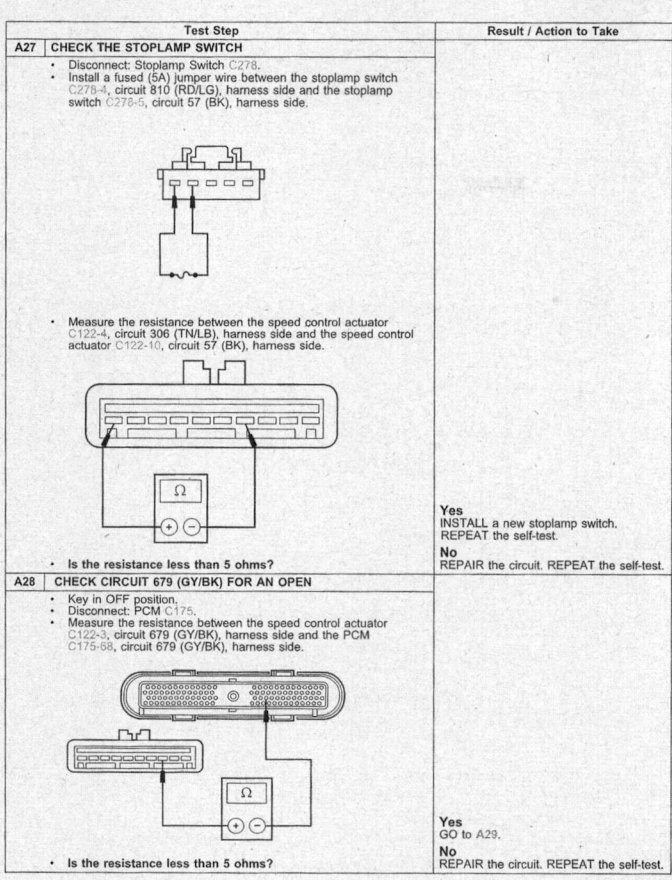

LTV0500000001831

Fig. 166   Test A: Speed Control Is Inoperative (Part 9 of 11). 2005–06 Ranger

Test Step	Result / Action to Take
A30 CHECK THE VEHICLE SPEED SIGNAL FREQUENCY (Continued) • Measure and record the frequency between the speed control actuator C122-3, circuit 679 (GY/BK), harness side and ground with the vehicle drive wheels spinning a minimum of 8 km/h (5 mph) and the speedometer registers a speed. Record the speedometer reading. • Apply the brakes until the drive wheels come to a stop. Place the transmission in PARK, fully engage the parking brake and turn the engine off. • Divide the frequency reading by 2.2 to get a mph result and compare this to the reading of the speedometer. • **Does the frequency reading result match the speedometer reading?**	**Yes** INSTALL a new speed control actuator. REPEAT the self-test. **No** GO to A31.
A31 CHECK FOR CORRECT PCM OPERATION • Disconnect the PCM connector. • Check for: — corrosion — pushed-out pins • Connect the PCM connector and make sure it seats correctly. • Operate the system and verify the concern is still present. • **Is the concern still presents?**	**Yes** INSTALL a new PCM. REPEAT the self-test. **No** The system is operating correctly at this time. The concern may have been caused by a loose or corroded connector.
A32 CHECK FOR CORRECT SJB OPERATION • Disconnect all the SJB connectors. • Check for: — corrosion — pushed-out pins • Connect all the SJB connectors and make sure they seat correctly. • Operate the system and verify the concern is still present. • **Is the concern still presents?**	**Yes** INSTALL a new SJB. TEST the system for normal operation. **No** The system is operating correctly at this time. The concern may have been caused by a loose or corroded connector.

LTV0500000001833

Fig. 166   Test A: Speed Control Is Inoperative (Part 11 of 11). 2005–06 Ranger

Test Step	Result / Action to Take
A29 CHECK THE VEHICLE SPEED SIGNAL VOLTAGE ⚠ **CAUTION: Make sure the vehicle is secured correctly before attempting to place the transmission range selector lever in DRIVE or in first gear if equipped with a manual transmission.** • Connect: Speed Control Deactivator Switch C277. • Connect: PCM C175. • Jack up the drive wheels and chock the other wheels. • **NOTE:** For vehicles with a manual transmission, place the transmission into first gear. Start the vehicle, place the transmission in DRIVE, and with the engine at idle, allow the drive wheels to spin. • Measure and record the AC voltage between the speed control actuator C122-3, circuit 679 (GY/BK), harness side and ground with the vehicle drive wheels spinning a minimum of 8 km/h (5 mph) and the speedometer registers a speed.	
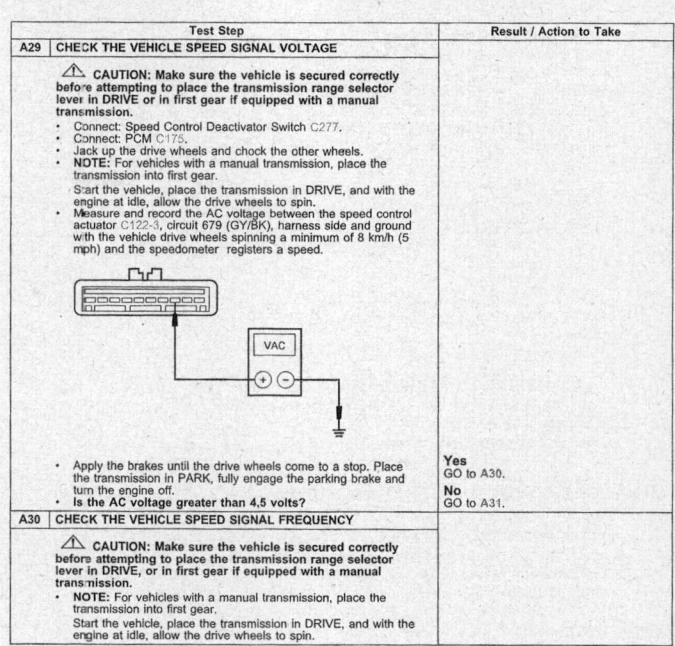	
• Apply the brakes until the drive wheels come to a stop. Place the transmission in PARK, fully engage the parking brake and turn the engine off. • **Is the AC voltage greater than 4.5 volts?**	**Yes** GO to A30. **No** GO to A31.
A30 CHECK THE VEHICLE SPEED SIGNAL FREQUENCY ⚠ **CAUTION: Make sure the vehicle is secured correctly before attempting to place the transmission range selector lever in DRIVE, or in first gear if equipped with a manual transmission.** • **NOTE:** For vehicles with a manual transmission, place the transmission into first gear. Start the vehicle, place the transmission in DRIVE, and with the engine at idle, allow the drive wheels to spin.	

LTV0500000001832

Fig. 166   Test A: Speed Control Is Inoperative (Part 10 of 11). 2005–06 Ranger

Test Step	Result / Action to Take
B1 CHECK THE SPEED CONTROL CABLE/THROTTLE BODY LINKAGE • Key in OFF position. • Visually inspect the speed control cable connections, the throttle body linkage, and the speed control actuator pulley cover. • **Are the speed control cable connections, the throttle body linkage, and the speed control actuator pulley cover OK?**	**Yes** GO to B2. **No** INSTALL a new speed control cable or REPAIR the throttle body linkage. TEST the system for normal operation. INSTALL the cover correctly. TEST the system for normal operation.
B2 CHECK THE SPEEDOMETER OPERATION • Drive the vehicle and observe the speedometer operation. • **Does the speedometer needle fluctuate?**	**Yes** Continue diagnosis of the speedometer. **No** GO to B3.
B3 CHECK FOR A BASE ENGINE CONCERN • Drive the vehicle and determine if there is a base engine concern. • **Is a base engine concern present?**	**Yes** Refer to **MOTOR's** "Domestic Engine Performance & Driveability Manual" to continue diagnosis of the base engine concern. **No** GO to B4.
B4 CHECK THE VEHICLE SPEED SIGNAL VOLTAGE ⚠ **CAUTION: Make sure the vehicle is secured correctly before attempting to place the transmission range selector lever in DRIVE, or in first gear if equipped with a manual transmission.** • Disconnect: Speed Control Actuator C122. • Jack up the drive wheels and chock the other wheels. • **NOTE:** For vehicles with a manual transmission, place the	**Yes** GO to B5. **No** GO to B6.

LTV0500000001834

Fig. 167   Test B: Set Speed Fluctuates (Part 1 of 3). 2005–06 Ranger

transmission into first gear.

- Start the vehicle, place the transmission in DRIVE, and with the engine at idle, allow the drive wheels to spin.
- Measure and record the AC voltage between the speed control actuator C122-3, circuit 679 (GY/BK), harness side and ground with the vehicle drive wheels spinning a minimum of 8 km/h (5 mph) and the speedometer registers a speed.

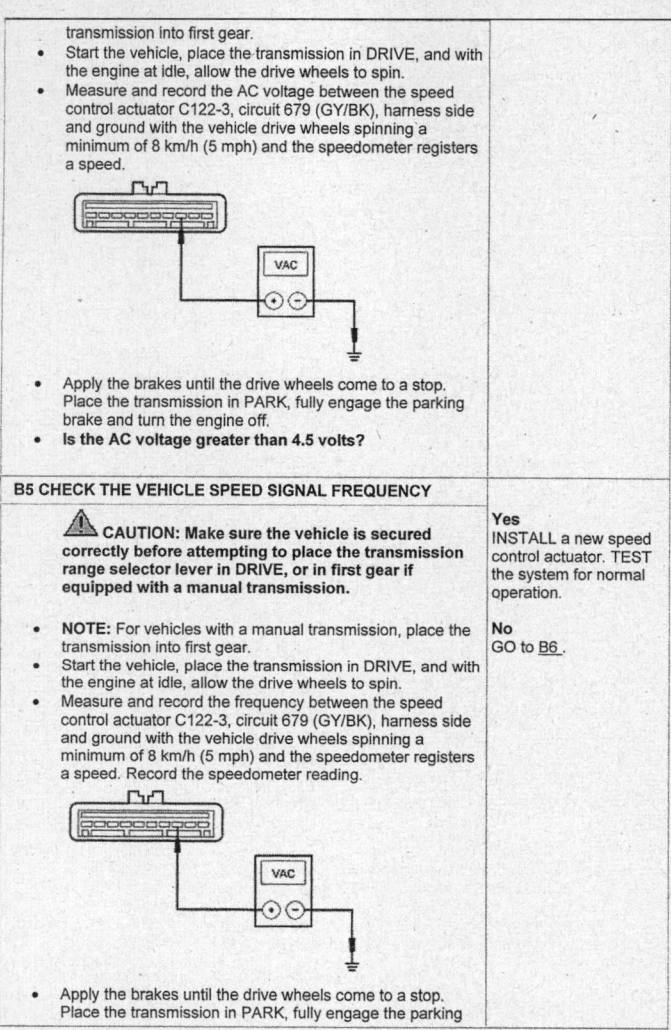

- Apply the brakes until the drive wheels come to a stop. Place the transmission in PARK, fully engage the parking brake and turn the engine off.
- **Is the AC voltage greater than 4.5 volts?**

B5 CHECK THE VEHICLE SPEED SIGNAL FREQUENCY	
⚠ **CAUTION: Make sure the vehicle is secured correctly before attempting to place the transmission range selector lever in DRIVE, or in first gear if equipped with a manual transmission.** • **NOTE:** For vehicles with a manual transmission, place the transmission into first gear. • Start the vehicle, place the transmission in DRIVE, and with the engine at idle, allow the drive wheels to spin. • Measure and record the frequency between the speed control actuator C122-3, circuit 679 (GY/BK), harness side and ground with the vehicle drive wheels spinning a minimum of 8 km/h (5 mph) and the speedometer registers a speed. Record the speedometer reading. 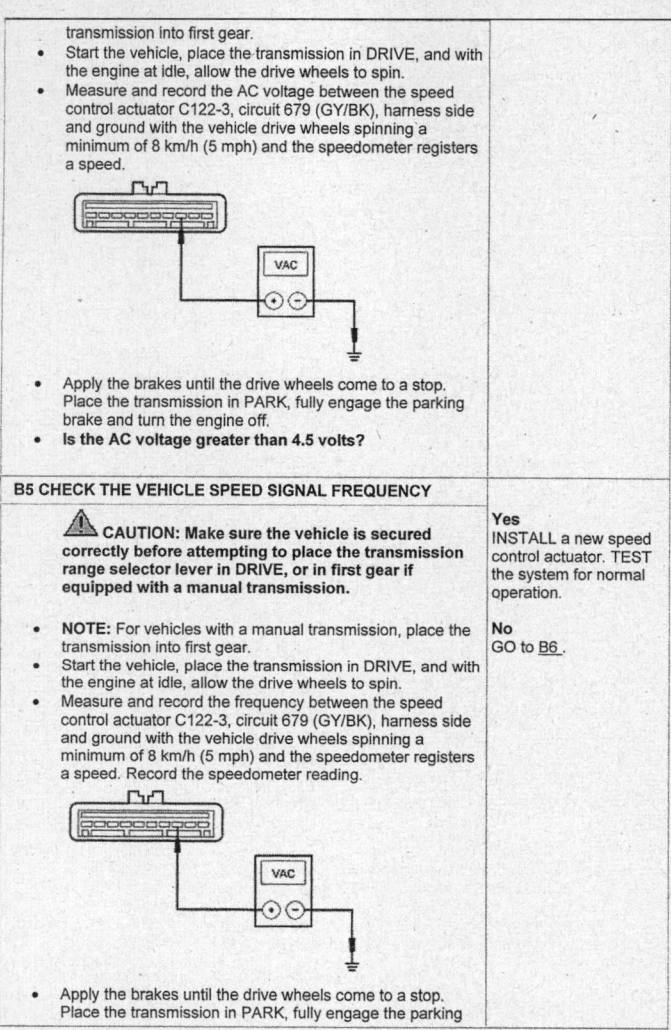 • Apply the brakes until the drive wheels come to a stop. Place the transmission in PARK, fully engage the parking	**Yes** INSTALL a new speed control actuator. TEST the system for normal operation. **No** GO to B6.

LTV0500000001835

Fig. 167   Test B: Set Speed Fluctuates (Part 2 of 3). 2005–06 Ranger

---

brake and turn the engine off.

- Divide the frequency reading by 2.2 to get a mph result and compare this to the reading of the speedometer.
- **Does the frequency reading result match the speedometer reading?**

B6 CHECK FOR CORRECT PCM OPERATION	

• Disconnect the PCM connector.
• Check for:
  ▪ corrosion
  ▪ pushed-out pins
• Connect the PCM connector and make sure it seats correctly.
• Operate the system and verify the concern is still present.
• **Is the concern still presents?**
	Yes
	INSTALL a new PCM. TEST the system for normal operation.
	
	No
	The system is operating correctly at this time. The concern may have been caused by a loose or corroded connector.

LTV0500000001836

Fig. 167   Test B: Set Speed Fluctuates (Part 3 of 3). 2005–06 Ranger

Test Step	Result / Action to Take
C1 CHECK THE SPEED CONTROL CABLE/ACCELERATOR CABLE	
• Key in OFF position. • **NOTE:** Make sure the floor mat, insulation, wiring harnesses location, and other item do not interfere with the accelerator pedal and linkage. • Visually inspect the speed control cable connections, the throttle body linkage, and the speed control actuator pulley cover. • **Are the speed control cable connections, the throttle body linkage, and the speed control actuator pulley cover OK?**	**Yes** GO to C2. **No** INSTALL a new speed control cable or accelerator cable. TEST the system for normal operation.
C2 CHECK THE STOPLAMPS FOR CORRECT OPERATION	
• Check the stoplamps for correct operation by firmly applying and releasing the brake pedal. • **Do the stoplamps operate correctly?**	**Yes** GO to C3. **No** Continue diagnosis of stoplamps.
C3 CHECK THE SPEED CONTROL DEACTIVATOR CIRCUIT	
• Key in ON position.	

LTV0500000001837

Fig. 168   Test C: Speed Control Does Not Disengage When Brakes Are Applied (Part 1 of 2). 2005–06 Ranger

---

Test Step	Result / Action to Take
C3 CHECK THE SPEED CONTROL DEACTIVATOR CIRCUIT (Continued)	
• Measure the voltage between the speed control actuator C122-9, circuit 307 (BK/YE), harness side and ground while firmly applying the brake pedal. 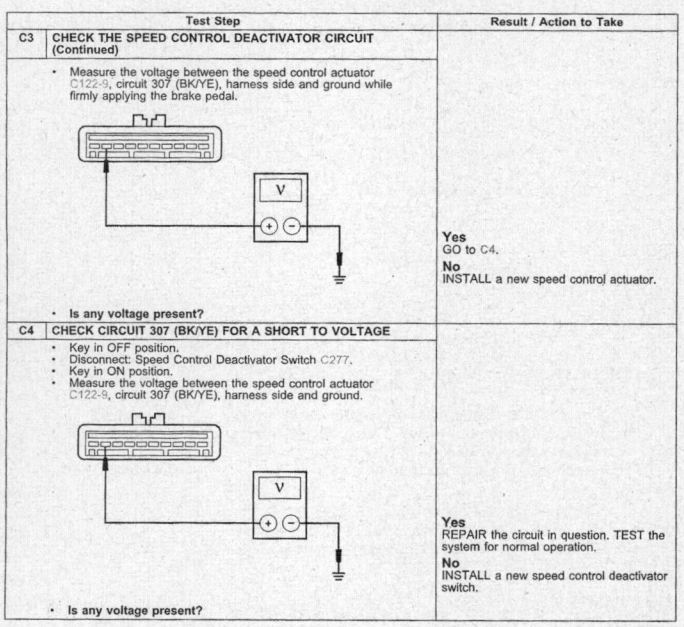 • **Is any voltage present?**	**Yes** GO to C4. **No** INSTALL a new speed control actuator.
C4 CHECK CIRCUIT 307 (BK/YE) FOR A SHORT TO VOLTAGE	
• Key in OFF position. • Disconnect: Speed Control Deactivator Switch C277. • Key in ON position. • Measure the voltage between the speed control actuator C122-9, circuit 307 (BK/YE), harness side and ground. 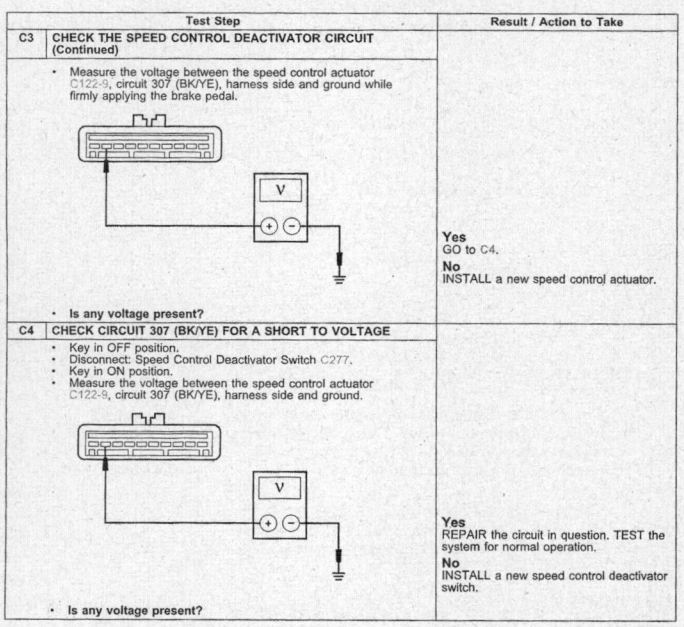 • **Is any voltage present?**	**Yes** REPAIR the circuit in question. TEST the system for normal operation. **No** INSTALL a new speed control deactivator switch.

LTV0500000001838

Fig. 168   Test C: Speed Control Does Not Disengage When Brakes Are Applied (Part 2 of 2). 2005–06 Ranger

Test Step	Result / Action to Take
D1 CHECK THE STOPLAMP OPERATION	
• Apply and release the brake pedal while observing the stoplamps. • **Do the stoplamps operate correctly?**	**Yes** GO to D2. **No** Continue diagnosis of stoplamps.
D2 CHECK THE STOPLAMP SWITCH CIRCUIT	
• Key in OFF position. • Disconnect: Speed Control Actuator C122. • Measure the resistance between the speed control actuator C122-4, circuit 306 (TN/LB), harness side and the speed control actuator C122-10, circuit 57 (BK), harness side. 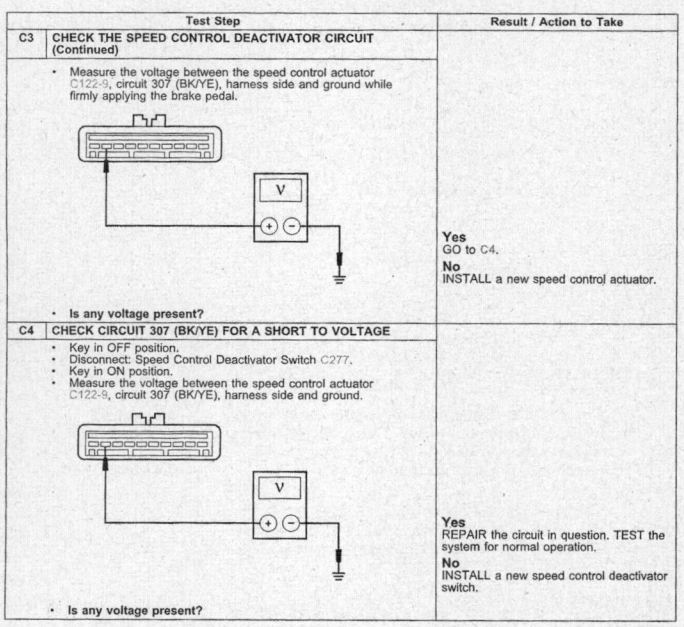 • **Is the resistance less than 5 ohms?**	**Yes** INSTALL a new speed control actuator. REPEAT the self-test. **No** If equipped with a manual transmission or an automatic transmission with CPP wiring, GO to D3. Otherwise, GO to D5.
D3 CHECK CIRCUIT 810 (RD/LG) FOR AN OPEN TO THE CPP SWITCH	
• Disconnect: CPP Switch (or Jumper Plug) C257.	

LTV0500000001839

Fig. 169   Test D: Stoplamp Switch Circuit Failure (Part 1 of 3). 2005–06 Ranger

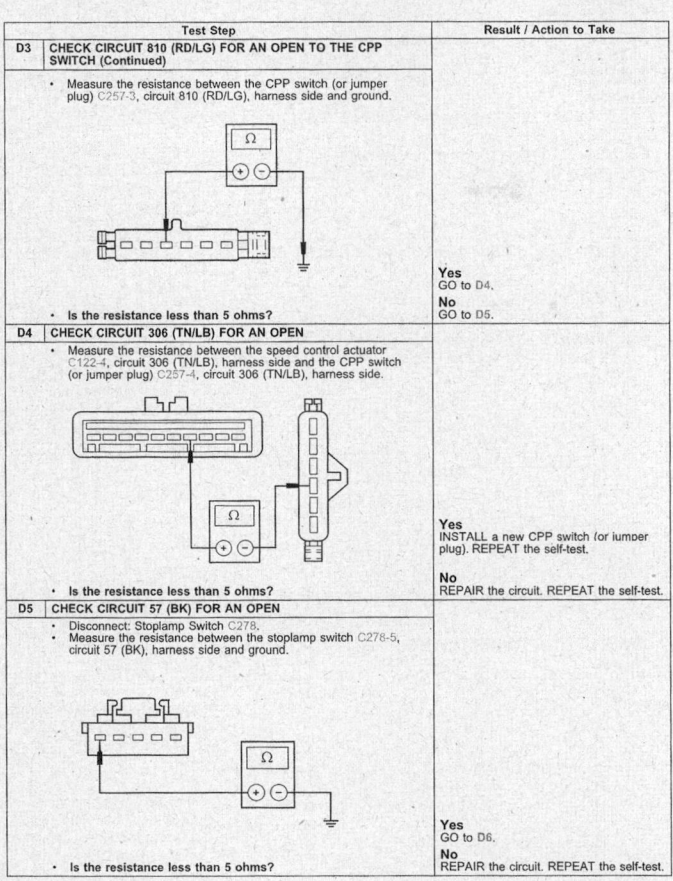

Test Step	Result / Action to Take
D3 CHECK CIRCUIT 810 (RD/LG) FOR AN OPEN TO THE CPP SWITCH (Continued) • Measure the resistance between the CPP switch (or jumper plug) C257-3, circuit 810 (RD/LG), harness side and ground. • Is the resistance less than 5 ohms?	**Yes** GO to D4. **No** GO to D5.
D4 CHECK CIRCUIT 306 (TN/LB) FOR AN OPEN • Measure the resistance between the speed control actuator C122-4, circuit 306 (TN/LB), harness side and the CPP switch (or jumper plug) C257-4, circuit 306 (TN/LB), harness side. • Is the resistance less than 5 ohms?	**Yes** INSTALL a new CPP switch (or jumper plug). REPEAT the self-test. **No** REPAIR the circuit. REPEAT the self-test.
D5 CHECK CIRCUIT 57 (BK) FOR AN OPEN • Disconnect: Stoplamp Switch C278. • Measure the resistance between the stoplamp switch C278-5, circuit 57 (BK), harness side and ground. • Is the resistance less than 5 ohms?	**Yes** GO to D6. **No** REPAIR the circuit. REPEAT the self-test.

LTV0500000001840

Fig. 169 Test D: Stoplamp Switch Circuit Failure (Part 2 of 3). 2005–06 Ranger

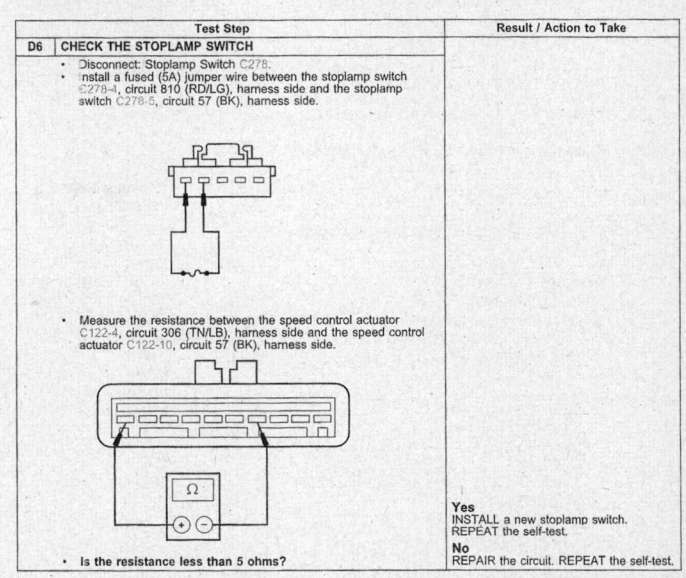

Test Step	Result / Action to Take
D6 CHECK THE STOPLAMP SWITCH • Disconnect: Stoplamp Switch C278. • Install a fused (5A) jumper wire between the stoplamp switch C278-4, circuit 810 (RD/LG), harness side and the stoplamp switch C278-5, circuit 57 (BK), harness side. • Measure the resistance between the speed control actuator C122-4, circuit 306 (TN/LB), harness side and the speed control actuator C122-10, circuit 57 (BK), harness side. • Is the resistance less than 5 ohms?	**Yes** INSTALL a new stoplamp switch. REPEAT the self-test. **No** REPAIR the circuit. REPEAT the self-test.

LTV0500000001841

Fig. 169 Test D: Stoplamp Switch Circuit Failure (Part 3 of 3). 2005–06 Ranger

Test Step	Result / Action to Take
E1 CHECK THE SPEED CONTROL DEACTIVATOR SWITCH SIGNAL • Key in OFF position. • Disconnect: Speed Control Actuator C122. • Key in ON position. • Measure the voltage between the speed control actuator C122-9, circuit 307 (BK/YE), harness side and the speed control actuator C122-10, circuit 57 (BK), harness side. • Is the voltage greater than 10 volts?	**Yes** INSTALL a new speed Control actuator. REPEAT the self-test. **No** GO to E2.
E2 CHECK CIRCUIT 535 (LB/RD) FOR VOLTAGE • Key in OFF position. • Disconnect: Speed Control Deactivator Switch C1025. • Key in ON position. • Measure the voltage between the speed control deactivator switch C1025-1, circuit 535 (LB/RD), harness side and ground.	**Yes** GO to E3. **No** VERIFY the smart junction box (SJB) fuse 26 (2A) is OK. If OK, REPAIR the circuit. REPEAT the self-test.

LTV0500000001842

Fig. 170 Test E: Speed Control Deactivator Switch Circuit Failure (Part 1 of 2). 2005–06 Ranger

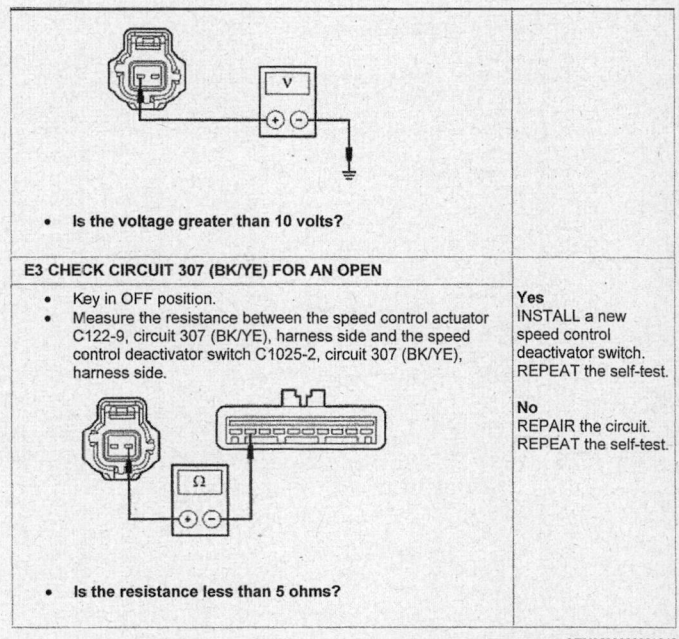

Test Step	Result / Action to Take
• Is the voltage greater than 10 volts?	
E3 CHECK CIRCUIT 307 (BK/YE) FOR AN OPEN • Key in OFF position. • Measure the resistance between the speed control actuator C122-9, circuit 307 (BK/YE), harness side and the speed control deactivator switch C1025-2, circuit 307 (BK/YE), harness side. • Is the resistance less than 5 ohms?	**Yes** INSTALL a new speed control deactivator switch. REPEAT the self-test. **No** REPAIR the circuit. REPEAT the self-test.

LTV0500000001843

Fig. 170 Test E: Speed Control Deactivator Switch Circuit Failure (Part 2 of 2). 2005–06 Ranger

Test Step	Result / Action to Take
F1 CHECK THE SPEEDOMETER OPERATION	
• Check the speedometer for correct operation by driving the vehicle. • **Does the speedometer operate correctly?**	**Yes** GO to F2 . **No** Continue diagnosis of the speedometer.
F2 CHECK CIRCUIT 679 (GY/BK) FOR AN OPEN	
• Key in OFF position. • Disconnect: Speed Control Actuator C122. • Disconnect: PCM C175. • Measure the resistance between the PCM C175-68, circuit 679 (GY/BK), harness side and the speed control actuator C122-3, circuit 679 (GY/BK), harness side.	**Yes** INSTALL a new speed control actuatorREPEAT the self-test. **No** REPAIR the circuit. REPEAT the self-test.
GV1325-A	
• **Is the resistance less than 5 ohms?**	

LTV0500000001844

Fig. 171   Test F: Vehicle Speed Signal Circuit Failure. 2005–06 Ranger

Test Step	Result / Action to Take
G1 CHECK THE SPEED CONTROL ACTUATOR	
• Key in OFF position. • Disconnect: Speed Control Actuator C122. • Key in ON position. • Check the speed control indicator lamp. • **Does the speed control indicator lamp remain on?**	**Yes** GO to G2 . **No** INSTALL a new speed control actuator. TEST the system for normal operation.
G2 CHECK CIRCUIT 203 (OG/LB) FOR A SHORT TO GROUND	
• Key in OFF position. • Disconnect: Instrument Cluster C220a. • Measure the resistance between the speed control actuator C122-1, circuit 203 (OG/LB), harness side and ground.	**Yes** GO to G3 . **No** REPAIR the circuit. TEST the system for normal operation.
• **Is the resistance greater than 10,000 ohms?**	
G3 CHECK FOR CORRECT INSTRUMENT CLUSTER OPERATION	

• Disconnect all the instrument cluster connectors.
• Check for:
  ▪ corrosion
  ▪ pushed-out pins
• Connect all the instrument cluster connectors and make sure they seat correctly.
• Operate the system and verify the concern is still present.
• **Is the concern still present?**
	Yes
	INSTALL a new instrument cluster. TEST the system normal operation.
	
	No
	The system is operating correctly at this time. The concern may have been caused by a loose or corroded connector.

LTV0500000001845

Fig. 172   Test G: Speed Control Indicator Lamp Is Always On. 2005–06 Ranger

Test Step	Result / Action to Take
H1 CHECK THE SPEED CONTROL SWITCHES	
• Disconnect: Speed Control Actuator C122. • Measure the resistance between the speed control actuator C122-5, circuit 151 (LB/BK), harness side and the speed control actuator C122-6, circuit 848 (DG/OG), harness side while pressing the speed control switches as follows:	**Yes** INSTALL a new speed control actuator. TEST the system for normal operation. **No** INSTALL a new speed control switch. TEST the system for normal operation.

Switch Position	Resistance Value (in Ohms)
OFF	Less than 5
ACCEL/SET	646-704
COAST	114-126
RESUME	2,090-2,310
None	Greater than 10,000

• **Are the speed control switch resistance values OK?**

LTV0500000001846

Fig. 173   Test H: A Single Speed Control Button Is Inoperative. 2005–06 Ranger

A1	CHECK THE VOLTAGE TO THE SPEED CONTROL MODULE

1

2   *Speed Control Module C247*

3

4   Depress the speed control switch ON.

FM1100100826010X

Fig. 174   Test A: Speed Control Inoperative (Part 1 of 18). Villager

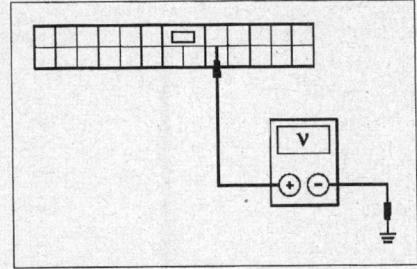

5

Measure the voltage between the speed control module C247 pin 7, circuit EJ14 (BU), harness side and ground.

- Is the voltage greater than 10 volts?

→ Yes

Go to «A2».

→ No

REPAIR the circuit. TEST the system for normal operation.

FM1100100826020X

Fig. 174   Test A: Speed Control Inoperative (Part 2 of 18). Villager

---

A3	CHECK THE INHIBIT RELAY

1

2   *Inhibit Relay C178*

3   Carry out the inhibit relay component test.

- Is the inhibit relay OK?

→ Yes

Go to «A4».

→ No

INSTALL a new relay. TEST the system for normal operation.

FM1100100826040X

Fig. 174   Test A: Speed Control Inoperative (Part 4 of 18). Villager

---

A4	CHECK CIRCUIT EJ40 (BU/WH) FOR AN OPEN

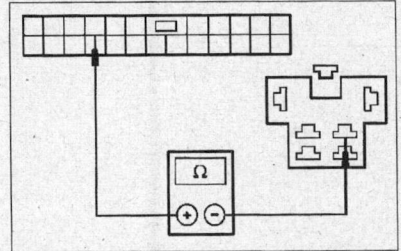

1

Measure the resistance between the inhibit relay C178 pin 3, circuit EJ40 (BU/WH), harness side and the sped control module C247 pin 4 circuit EJ40 (BU/WH), harness side.

- Is the resistance less than 5 ohms?

→ Yes

Go to «A5».

→ No

REPAIR the circuit. TEST the system for normal operation.

FM1100100826050X

Fig. 174   Test A: Speed Control Inoperative (Part 5 of 18). Villager

---

A2	CHECK THE DEACTIVATOR SWITCH INPUT TO THE SPEED CONTROL MODULE

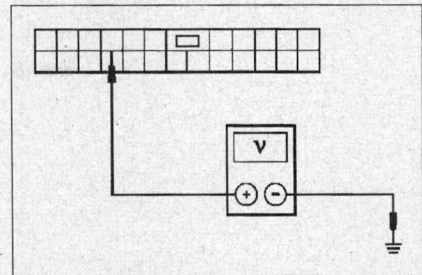

1

Measure the voltage between the speed control module C247 pin 4, circuit EJ40 (BU/WH), harness side and ground.

- Is the voltage greater than 10 volts?

→ Yes

Go to «A7».

→ No

Go to «A3».

FM1100100826030X

Fig. 174   Test A: Speed Control Inoperative (Part 3 of 18). Villager

---

A5	CHECK CIRCUITS SL04 (WH) AND EJ24 (WH) FOR AN OPEN

1   *Deactivator Switch C278*

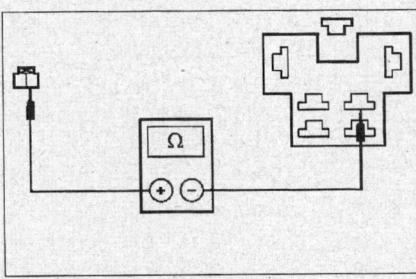

2

Measure the resistance between the deactivator switch C278 pin 2, circuit SL04 (WH), harness side and the inhibit relay C178 pin 4, circuit EJ24 (WH), harness side.

- Is the resistance less than 5 ohms?

→ Yes

Go to «A6».

→ No

REPAIR the circuit. TEST the system for normal operation.

FM1100100826060X

Fig. 174   Test A: Speed Control Inoperative (Part 6 of 18). Villager

A6   CHECK CIRCUIT EJ22 (BU) FOR OPEN

Measure the voltage between the deactivator switch C278 pin 1, circuit EJ22 (BU), harness side and ground.

● **Is the voltage greater than 10 volts?**

→ Yes

INSTALL a new deactivator switch. TEST the system for normal operation.

→ No

REPAIR the circuit. TEST the system for normal operation.

FM1100100826070X

Fig. 174   Test A: Speed Control Inoperative (Part 7 of 18). Villager

A8   CHECK SPEED CONTROL ACTUATOR CIRCUITS FOR OPEN

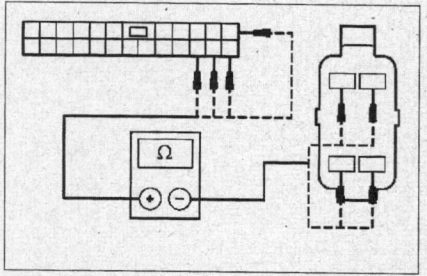

Speed Control Actuator C127

Measure the resistance between the speed control module pins and the speed control actuator pins as follows:

Speed Control Module	Speed Control Actuator	Circuit
C247 pin 24	C127 pin 2	circuit EJ15 (BN)
C247 pin 22	C127 pin 3	circuit EJ04 (LB)
C247 pin 11	C127 pin 4	circuit EJ16 (BN/YE)
C247 pin 23	C127 pin 1	circuit EJ06 (OG)

● **Are the resistances less than 5 ohms?**

→ Yes

Go to «A9».

→ No

REPAIR the circuit. TEST the system for normal operation.

FM1100100826090X

Fig. 174   Test A: Speed Control Inoperative (Part 9 of 18). Villager

A7   CHECK CIRCUITS EJ10 (GN/YE) AND AV32 (GN/YE) FOR OPEN

Instrument Cluster C266b (conventional) or C267a (electronic)

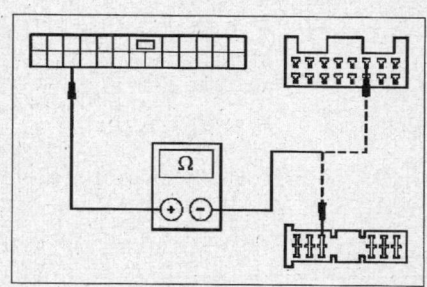

Measure the resistance between the speed control module C247 pin 14, circuit EJ10 (GN/YE), harness side and the instrument cluster C266b pin 4 (conventional) or C267a pin 6 (electronic), circuit AV32 (GN/YE), harness side.

● **Is the resistance less than 5 ohms?**

→ Yes

Go to «A8».

→ No

REPAIR the circuit. TEST the system for normal operation.

FM1100100826080X

Fig. 174   Test A: Speed Control Inoperative (Part 8 of 18). Villager

A9   CHECK THE SPEED CONTROL ACTUATOR CIRCUITS FOR SHORT TO GROUND

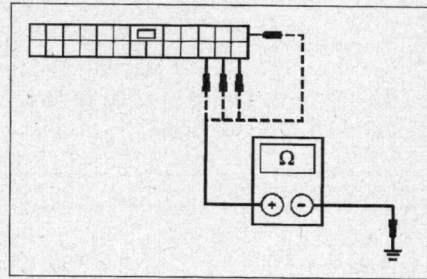

Measure the resistance between the speed control module pins and ground as follows:

Speed Control Actuator Module	Circuit
C247 pin 24	Circuit EJ15 (BN)
C247 pin 22	Circuit EJ04 (LB)
C247 pin 11	Circuit EJ16 (BN/YE)
C247 pin 23	Circuit EJ06 (OG)

● **Are the resistances greater than 10,000 ohms?**

→ Yes

Go to «A10».

→ No

REPAIR the circuit. TEST the system for normal operation.

FM1100100826100X

Fig. 174   Test A: Speed Control Inoperative (Part 10 of 18). Villager

A10   CHECK THE SPEED CONTROL ACTUATOR FOR CORRECT OPERATION

1   Pull a vacuum at the speed control vacuum canister inlet port (located underneath the vacuum canister).

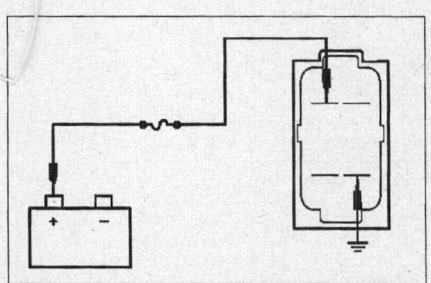

2

Connect a fused (10A) jumper wire between the speed control actuator pin 2 (component side), and the positive battery post and connect a jumper wire between the speed control actuator pin 3 (component side), and ground.

●   **Does the speed control actuator motor operate?**

→   **Yes**

Go to «A11».

→   **No**

INSTALL a new speed control actuator.
TEST the system for normal operation.

FM1100100826110X

**Fig. 174   Test A: Speed Control Inoperative
(Part 11 of 18). Villager**

A12   CHECK THAT THE SPEED CONTROL ACTUATOR STAYS PULLED IN

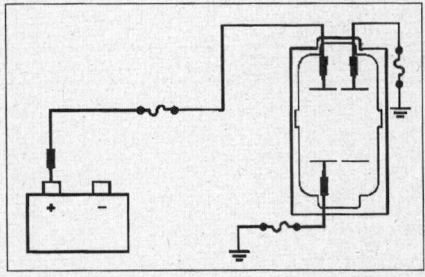

1

With the fused (10A) jumper wire still connected between the positive battery post and the speed control actuator pin 2 (component side), and with the ground jumper wire still connected to the speed control actuator pin 1 and pin 4 (component side), remove the jumper wire between the speed control actuator pin 3 (component side), and ground.

●   **Does the speed control actuator remain pulled in?**

→   **Yes**

Go to «A13».

→   **No**

INSTALL a new speed control actuator.
TEST the system for normal operation.

FM1100100826130X

**Fig. 174   Test A: Speed Control Inoperative
(Part 13 of 18). Villager**

A11   CHECK THE SPEED CONTROL ACTUATOR FOR PULLING SPEED CONTROL CABLE IN

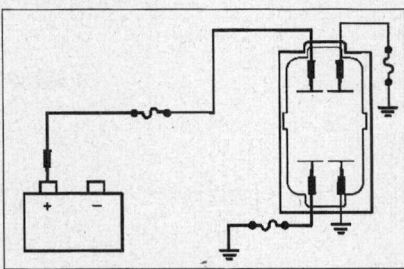

1

With the fused (10A) jumper wire still connected between the positive battery post and the speed control actuator pin 2 (component side), connect jumper wires between the speed control actuator pin 1, pin 3, and pin 4 (component side) and ground.

●   **Does the speed control actuator pull the speed control cable inward?**

→   **Yes**

Go to «A12».

→   **No**

INSTALL a new speed control actuator.
TEST the system for normal operation.

FM1100100826120X

**Fig. 174   Test A: Speed Control Inoperative
(Part 12 of 18). Villager**

A13   CHECK THE SPEED CONTROL ACTUATOR FOR RETURNABILITY

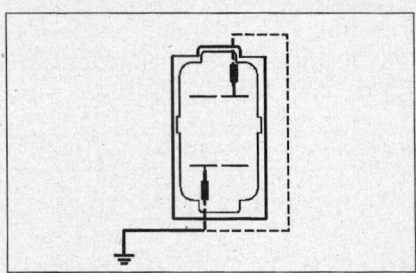

1

With the ground jumper wire still connected to the speed control actuator pin 1 and pin 4 (component side), remove the jumper wire from the speed control actuator pin 2 (component side) and the positive battery post.

●   **Does the speed control actuator release immediately?**

→   **Yes**

Go to «A14».

→   **No**

INSTALL a new speed control actuator.
TEST the system for normal operation.

FM1100100826140X

**Fig. 174   Test A: Speed Control Inoperative
(Part 14 of 18). Villager**

SPEED CONTROL SYSTEMS

1   Remove the speed control switch.

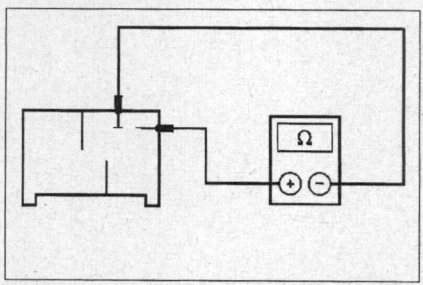

2

Measure the resistance between the speed control switch pin 1 (component side) and the speed control switch pin 2 (component side) while depressing the speed control switch as follows:

Speed Control Switch	Resistance Value
ON/OFF	Less than 5 ohms
COAST/SET	Between 1,094 and 1,204 ohms
CANCEL	Between 4,845 and 5,355 ohms
RES/ACCEL	Between 3,135 ohms and 3,465 ohms

- **Are the speed control switch resistance values OK?**

➔ **Yes**

   Go to «A15».

➔ **No**

   INSTALL a new speed control switch.
   TEST the system for normal operation.

FM1100100826150X

Fig. 174   Test A: Speed Control Inoperative (Part 15 of 18). Villager

---

1   Remove the driver side air bag to access the horn switch harness connector.

2   **Horn Switch Harness**

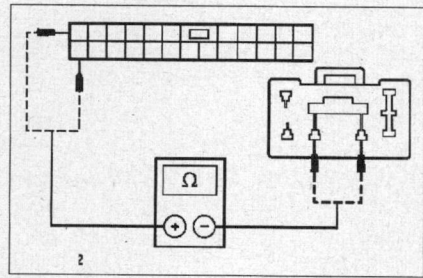

3

Measure the resistance between the speed control module C247 pin 12, circuit EJ01 (WH/BU), harness side and the top of the clockspring pin 4, circuit EJ01 (YE/LB) component side; and between the speed control module C247 pin 1, circuit EJ02 (BU/RD), harness side and the top of the clockspring pin 5, circuit EJ02 (VT/OG) harness side.

- **Is the resistance less than 5 ohms?**

➔ **Yes**

   Go to «A17».

➔ **No**

   REPAIR or INSTALL a new horn switch harness. TEST the system for normal operation.

FM1100100826170X

Fig. 174   Test A: Speed Control Inoperative (Part 17 of 18). Villager

---

1   **Speed Control Switch**

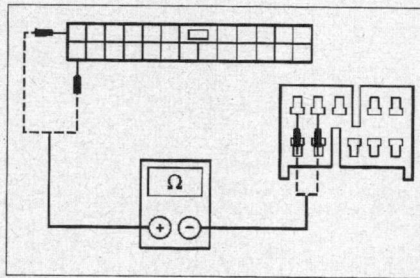

2

Measure the resistance between the speed control module C247 pin 12, circuit EJ01 (WH/BU), harness side and the speed control switch pin 1, circuit EJ01 (YE/LB) harness side; and between the speed control module C247 pin 1, circuit EJ02 (BU/RD), harness sice and the speed control switch pin 2, circuit EJ02 (VT/OG) harness side.

- **Is the resistance less than 5 ohms?**

➔ **Yes**

   INSTALL a new speed control module.
   TEST the system for normal operation.

➔ **No**

   Go to «A16».

FM1100100826160X

Fig. 174   Test A: Speed Control Inoperative (Part 16 of 18). Villager

---

1   **Clockspring C214**

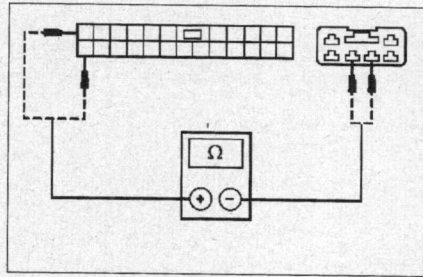

2

Measure the resistance between the speed control module C247 pin 12, circuit EJ01 (WH/BU), harness side and the clockspring C214 pin 4, circuit EJ01 (WH/BU) harness side; and between the speed control module C247 pin 1 circuit EJ02 (BU/RD), harness sice and the clockspring C214 pin 5, circuit EJ02 (BU/RD) harness side.

- **Is the resistance less than 5 ohms?**

➔ **Yes**

   INSTALL a new clockspring. TEST the system for normal operation.

➔ **No**

   REPAIR circuit EJ01 (WH/BU) or EJ02 (BU/RD) as necessary. TEST the system for normal operation.

FM1100100826180X

Fig. 174   Test A: Speed Control Inoperative (Part 18 of 18). Villager

---

B1   CHECK THE SPEEDOMETER

1   Check the speedometer for fluctuation without the speed control engaged by test driving the vehicle.

- ● **Does the speedometer fluctuate?**

- → **Yes**

   Diagnose Instrument Cluster Fault Condition. TEST the system for normal operation.

- → **No**

   Go to «B2».

FM1100100827010X

Fig. 175   Test B: Set Speed Fluctuates (Part 1 of 5). Villager

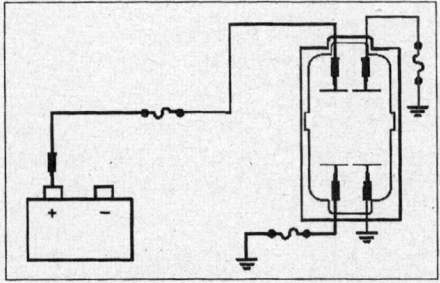

4

Connect a fused (10A) jumper wire between the positive battery post and the speed control actuator pin 2 (component side); connect jumper wires between the speed control actuator pin 1, pin 3, and pin 4 (component side) and ground.

- ● **Does the speed control actuator pull the speed control cable inward?**

- → **Yes**

   Go to «B3».

- → **No**

   INSTALL a new speed control actuator. TEST the system for normal operation.

FM1100100827030X

Fig. 175   Test B: Set Speed Fluctuates (Part 3 of 5). Villager

B2   CHECK THE SPEED CONTROL ACTUATOR FOR PULLING SPEED CONTROL CABLE IN

1

2   *Speed Control Actuator C127*

3   Pull a vacuum at the speed control vacuum canister inlet port (located underneath the vacuum canister).

FM1100100827020X

Fig. 175   Test B: Set Speed Fluctuates (Part 2 of 5). Villager

B3   CHECK THE SPEED CONTROL ACTUATOR FOR VACUUM LEAKS

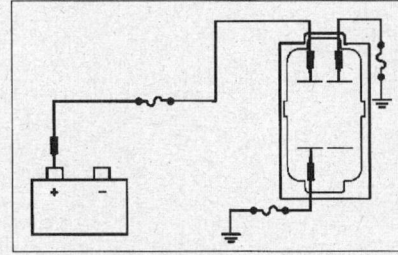

1

With the positive battery post still connected to the speed control actuator pin 2 (component side), remove the jumper wire between the speed control actuator pin 3 (component side), and ground.

- ● **Does the speed control cable remain pulled in?**

- → **Yes**

   Go to «B4».

- → **No**

   INSTALL a new speed control actuator. TEST the system for normal operation.

FM1100100827040X

Fig. 175   Test B: Set Speed Fluctuates (Part 4 of 5). Villager

B4   CHECK THE SPEED CONTROL ACTUATOR FOR RETURNABILITY

1

With the ground jumper wire still connected to the speed control actuator pin 1 and pin 4 (component side), remove the jumper wire from the speed control actuator pin 2 (component side), and the positive battery post.

- ● **Does the speed control actuator release immediately?**

- → **Yes**

   INSTALL a new speed control module. TEST the system for normal operation.

- → **No**

   INSTALL a new speed control actuator. TEST the system for normal operation.

FM1100100827050X

Fig. 175   Test B: Set Speed Fluctuates (Part 5 of 5). Villager

C1   CHECK THE SPEED CONTROL SWITCH

1   Remove the speed control switch.

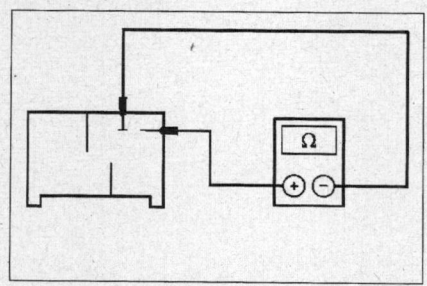

2

Measure the resistance between the speed control switch pin 1 (component side) and the speed control switch pin 2 (component side) while depressing the speed control switch as follows:

Speed Control Switch	Resistance Value
ON/OFF	Less than 5 ohms
COAST/SET	Between 1,094 and 1,204 ohms
CANCEL	Between 4,845 and 5,355 ohms
RES/ACCEL	Between 3,135 ohms and 3,465 ohms

● **Are the speed control switch resistance values OK?**

➔ **Yes**

INSTALL a new speed control module.
TEST the system for normal operation.

➔ **No**

INSTALL a new speed control switch.

FM1100100828000X

Fig. 176   Test C: Speed Control Switch Inoperative. Villager

D2   CHECK CIRCUIT EJ07 (RD/YE) FOR SHORT TO GROUND

1   *Instrument Cluster C266b (conventional) or C267a (electronic)*

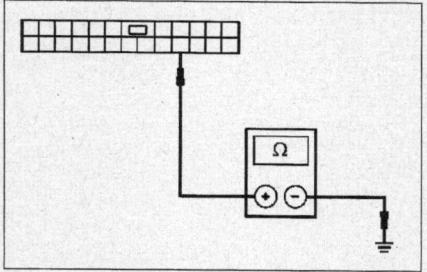

2

Measure the resistance between the speed control module C247 pin 21, circuit EJ07 (RD), harness side and ground.

● **Is the resistance less than 5 ohms?**

➔ **Yes**

REPAIR the circuit. TEST the system for normal operation.

➔ **No**

INSTALL a new instrument cluster.

FM1100100829020X

Fig. 177   Test D: Speed Control Cruise Indicator Lamp Always On (Part 2 of 2). Villager

D1   CHECK THE SPEED CONTROL MODULE

1   *Speed Control Module C247*

2

● **Is the speed control indicator illuminated?**

➔ **Yes**

Go to «D2».

➔ **No**

INSTALL a new speed control module.
TEST the system for normal operation.

FM1100100829010X

Fig. 177   Test D: Speed Control Cruise Indicator Lamp Always On (Part 1 of 2). Villager

E1   CHECK THE SPEED CONTROL INDICATOR IN THE INSTRUMENT PANEL

1

2   *Speed Control Module C247*

3

4   Check the speed control indicator in the instrument panel.

● **Is the speed control indicator always ON?**

➔ **Yes**

Go to «E2».

➔ **No**

INSTALL a new speed control module.
TEST the system for normal operation.

FM1100100830010X

Fig. 178   Test E: Speed Control Set Indicator Lamp Always On (Part 1 of 2). Villager

E2   CHECK CIRCUIT EJ23 (YE) FOR SHORT TO GROUND

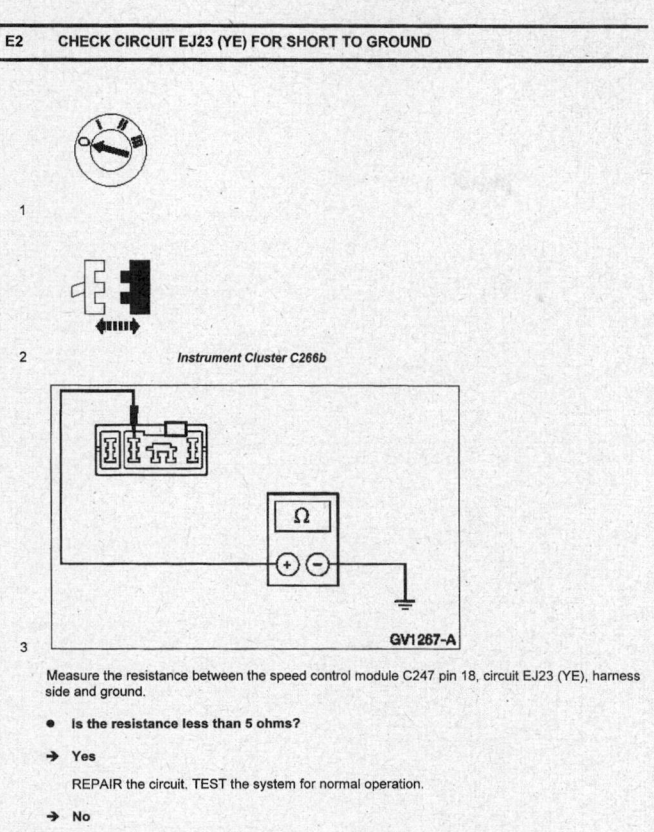

Instrument Cluster C266b

GV1267-A

Measure the resistance between the speed control module C247 pin 18, circuit EJ23 (YE), harness side and ground.

- ● Is the resistance less than 5 ohms?
- → Yes

  REPAIR the circuit. TEST the system for normal operation.

- → No

  INSTALL a new instrument cluster.

FM1100100830020X

Fig. 178   Test E: Speed Control Set Indicator Lamp Always On (Part 2 of 2). Villager

TEST CONDITIONS	TESTDETAILS/RESULTS/ACTIONS
B1 CHECK THE COMMUNICATIONS TO THE SPEED CONTROL MODULE	

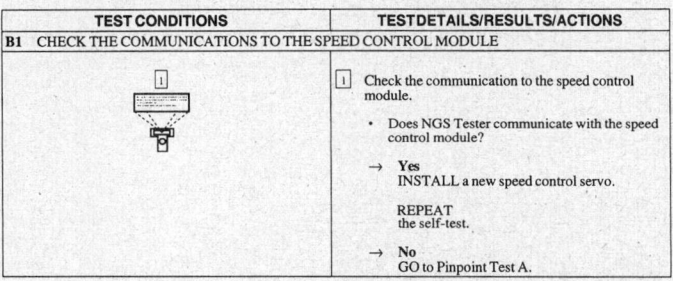	1 Check the communication to the speed control module.
	
	  • Does NGS Tester communicate with the speed control module?
	
	  → **Yes**
	  INSTALL a new speed control servo.
	
	  REPEAT the self-test.
	
	  → **No**
	  GO to Pinpoint Test A.

FM1109900649000X

Fig. 180   Test B: Unable To Enter Self Test. Windstar

TEST CONDITIONS	TESTDETAILS/RESULTS/ACTIONS
C1 CHECK CIRCUIT 1205 (BK) FOR AN OPEN	

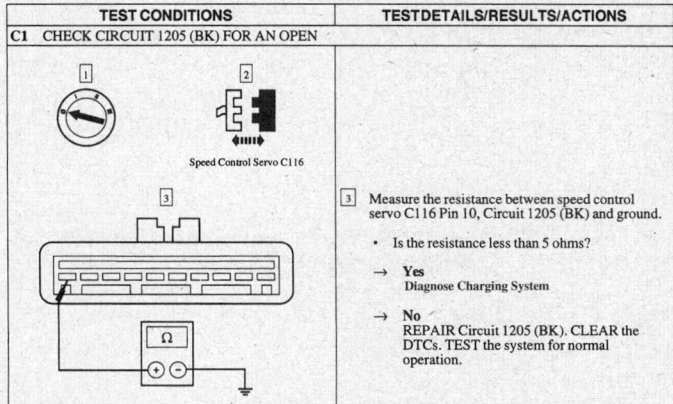	3 Measure the resistance between speed control servo C116 Pin 10, Circuit 1205 (BK) and ground.
	
	  • Is the resistance less than 5 ohms?
	
	  → **Yes**
	  Diagnose Charging System
	
	  → **No**
	  REPAIR Circuit 1205 (BK). CLEAR the DTCs. TEST the system for normal operation.

FM1109900650000X

Fig. 181   Test C, Code B1318: Battery Voltage Low. Windstar

TEST CONDITIONS	TESTDETAILS/RESULTS/ACTIONS
A1 CHECK CIRCUIT 1040 (RD/BK) FOR AN OPEN	

Speed Control Servo C116	4 Measure the voltage between speed control servo C116 Pin 7, Circuit 1040 (RD/BK) and ground.
	
	  • Is the voltage greater than 10 volts?
	
	  → **Yes**
	  GO to A2.
	
	  → **No**
	  REPAIR Circuit 1040 (RD/BK). TEST the system for normal operation.

A2 CHECK CIRCUIT 1205 (BK) FOR AN OPEN	

	2 Measure the resistance between speed control servo C116 Pin 10, Circuit 1205 (BK) and ground.
	
	  • Is the resistance less than 5 ohms?
	
	  → **Yes**
	  Diagnose Modular Communications Network
	
	  → **No**
	  REPAIR Circuit 1205 (BK). TEST the system for normal operation.

FM1109900648000X

Fig. 179   Test A: No Communication w/Module, Speed Control Servo. Windstar

TEST CONDITIONS	TESTDETAILS/RESULTS/ACTIONS
D1 CHECK THE SPEED CONTROL SERVO PIDS	

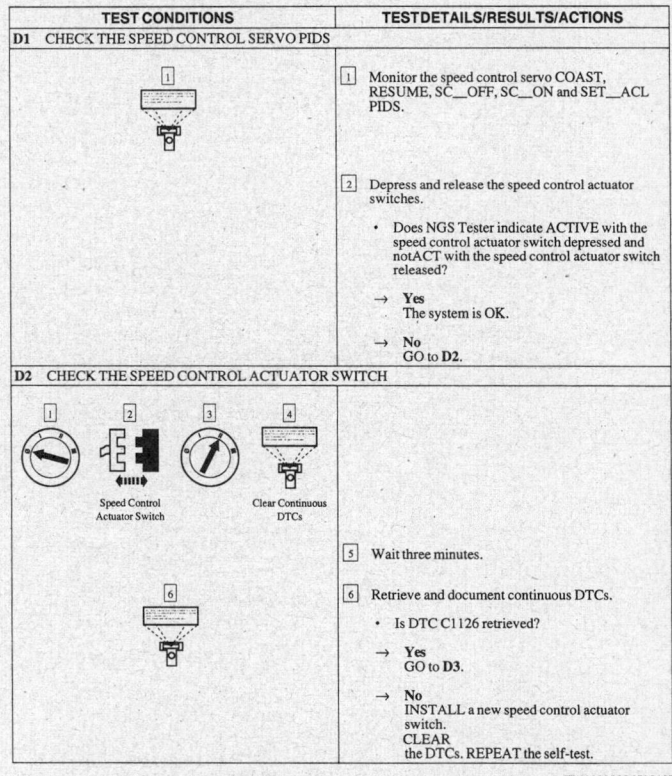	1 Monitor the speed control servo COAST, RESUME, SC__OFF, SC__ON and SET__ACL PIDS.
	
	2 Depress and release the speed control actuator switches.
	
	  • Does NGS Tester indicate ACTIVE with the speed control actuator switch depressed and notACT with the speed control actuator switch released?
	
	  → **Yes**
	  The system is OK.
	
	  → **No**
	  GO to D2.

D2 CHECK THE SPEED CONTROL ACTUATOR SWITCH	

Speed Control Actuator Switch Clear Continuous DTCs	5 Wait three minutes.
	
	6 Retrieve and document continuous DTCs.
	
	  • Is DTC C1126 retrieved?
	
	  → **Yes**
	  GO to D3.
	
	  → **No**
	  INSTALL a new speed control actuator switch.
	  CLEAR the DTCs. REPEAT the self-test.

FM1109900651010X

Fig. 182   Test D, Code C1126: Speed Actuator Stuck For Two Minutes Or Longer (Part 1 of 2). Windstar

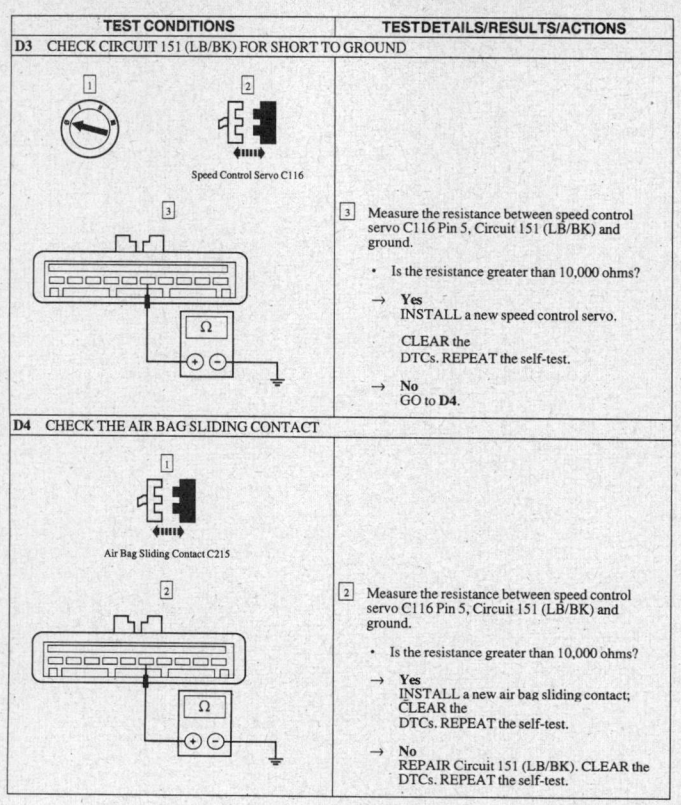

TEST CONDITIONS	TEST DETAILS/RESULTS/ACTIONS
D3 CHECK CIRCUIT 151 (LB/BK) FOR SHORT TO GROUND	

Speed Control Servo C116

③ Measure the resistance between speed control servo C116 Pin 5, Circuit 151 (LB/BK) and ground.

- Is the resistance greater than 10,000 ohms?

→ **Yes**
INSTALL a new speed control servo.

CLEAR the DTCs. REPEAT the self-test.

→ **No**
GO to **D4**.

TEST CONDITIONS	TEST DETAILS/RESULTS/ACTIONS
D4 CHECK THE AIR BAG SLIDING CONTACT	

Air Bag Sliding Contact C215

② Measure the resistance between speed control servo C116 Pin 5, Circuit 151 (LB/BK) and ground.

- Is the resistance greater than 10,000 ohms?

→ **Yes**
INSTALL a new air bag sliding contact; CLEAR the DTCs. REPEAT the self-test.

→ **No**
REPAIR Circuit 151 (LB/BK). CLEAR the DTCs. REPEAT the self-test.

FM1109900651020X

Fig. 182 Test D, Code C1126: Speed Actuator Stuck For Two Minutes Or Longer (Part 2 of 2). Windstar

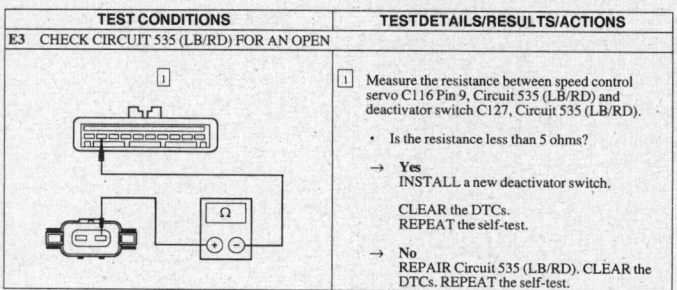

TEST CONDITIONS	TEST DETAILS/RESULTS/ACTIONS
E3 CHECK CIRCUIT 535 (LB/RD) FOR AN OPEN	

① Measure the resistance between speed control servo C116 Pin 9, Circuit 535 (LB/RD) and deactivator switch C127, Circuit 535 (LB/RD).

- Is the resistance less than 5 ohms?

→ **Yes**
INSTALL a new deactivator switch.

CLEAR the DTCs. REPEAT the self-test.

→ **No**
REPAIR Circuit 535 (LB/RD). CLEAR the DTCs. REPEAT the self-test.

FM1109900652020X

Fig. 183 Test E, Code C1127: Deactivator Switch Circuit Failure (Part 2 of 2). Windstar

TEST CONDITIONS	TEST DETAILS/RESULTS/ACTIONS
F1 CHECK THE SPEED CONTROL THROTTLE ATTACHMENT	

① Measure the speed control actuator cable slack to make sure it is within specification (0-6 mm).

② Check the throttle lever and speed control actuator cable for correct operation while carrying out the speed control servo slack test on NGS Tester.

- Does the cable slack measure within specification and the throttle lever operate correctly?

→ **Yes**
INSTALL a new speed control servo.

CLEAR the DTCs. REPEAT the self-test.

→ **No**
INSTALL a new component. CLEAR the DTCs. REPEAT the self-test.

FM1109900653000X

Fig. 184 Test F, Codes C1179, C1109: Speed Control Cable Slack Failure/Throttle Position Did Not Return To Idle After Self Test. Windstar

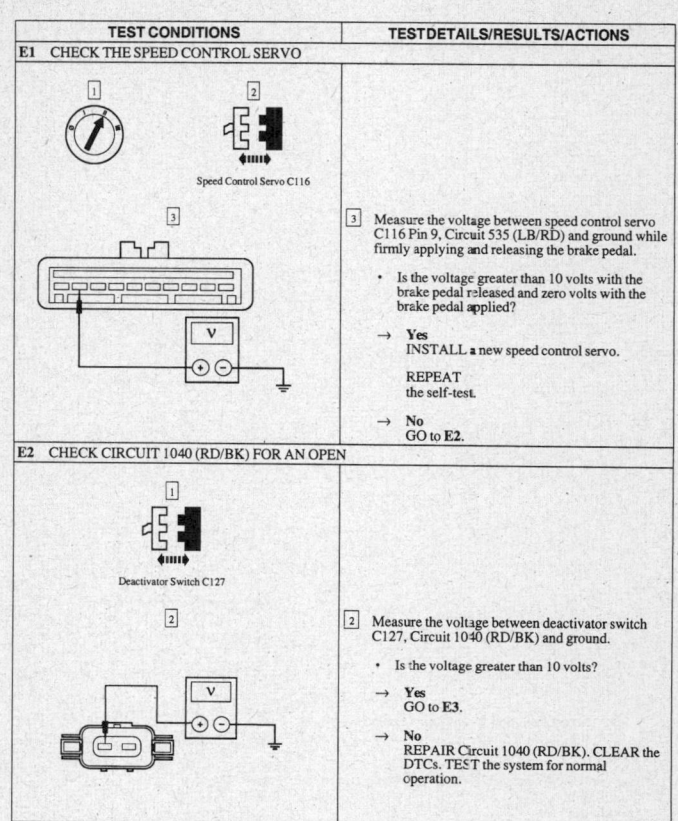

TEST CONDITIONS	TEST DETAILS/RESULTS/ACTIONS
E1 CHECK THE SPEED CONTROL SERVO	

Speed Control Servo C116

③ Measure the voltage between speed control servo C116 Pin 9, Circuit 535 (LB/RD) and ground while firmly applying and releasing the brake pedal.

- Is the voltage greater than 10 volts with the brake pedal released and zero volts with the brake pedal applied?

→ **Yes**
INSTALL a new speed control servo.

REPEAT the self-test.

→ **No**
GO to **E2**.

TEST CONDITIONS	TEST DETAILS/RESULTS/ACTIONS
E2 CHECK CIRCUIT 1040 (RD/BK) FOR AN OPEN	

Deactivator Switch C127

② Measure the voltage between deactivator switch C127, Circuit 1040 (RD/BK) and ground.

- Is the voltage greater than 10 volts?

→ **Yes**
GO to **E3**.

→ **No**
REPAIR Circuit 1040 (RD/BK). CLEAR the DTCs. TEST the system for normal operation.

FM1109900652010X

Fig. 183 Test E, Code C1127: Deactivator Switch Circuit Failure (Part 1 of 2). Windstar

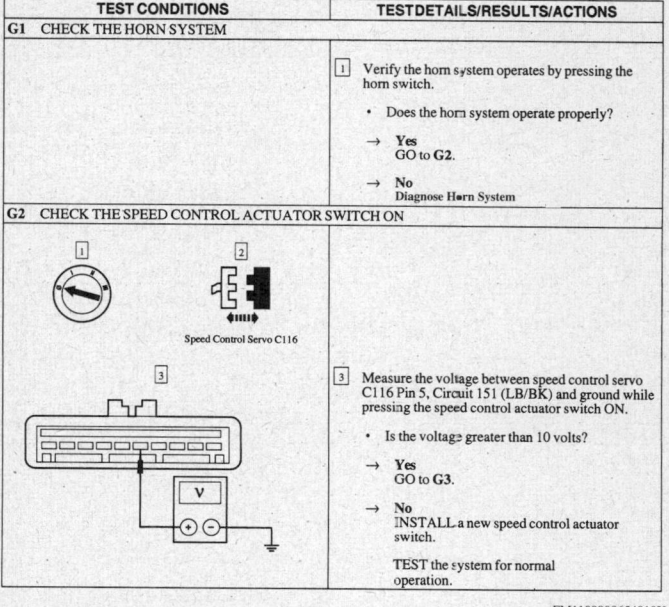

TEST CONDITIONS	TEST DETAILS/RESULTS/ACTIONS
G1 CHECK THE HORN SYSTEM	

① Verify the horn system operates by pressing the horn switch.

- Does the horn system operate properly?

→ **Yes**
GO to **G2**.

→ **No**
Diagnose Horn System

TEST CONDITIONS	TEST DETAILS/RESULTS/ACTIONS
G2 CHECK THE SPEED CONTROL ACTUATOR SWITCH ON	

Speed Control Servo C116

③ Measure the voltage between speed control servo C116 Pin 5, Circuit 151 (LB/BK) and ground while pressing the speed control actuator switch ON.

- Is the voltage greater than 10 volts?

→ **Yes**
GO to **G3**.

→ **No**
INSTALL a new speed control actuator switch.

TEST the system for normal operation.

FM1109900654010X

Fig. 185 Test G: Speed Control Inoperative (Part 1 of 2). Windstar

TEST CONDITIONS	TESTDETAILS/RESULTS/ACTIONS
G3 CHECK THE SET/ACCEL SWITCH	
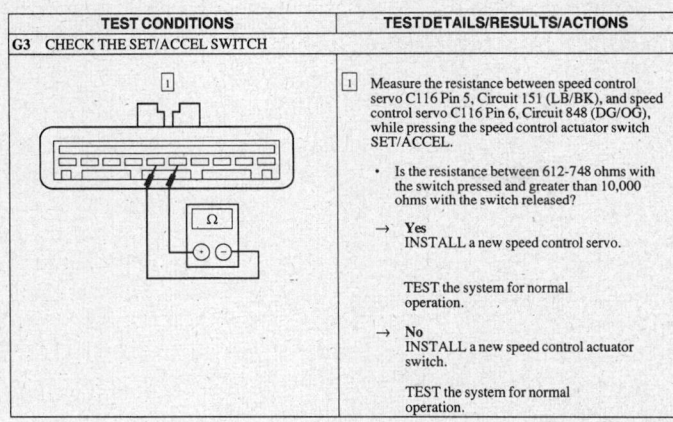	☐ Measure the resistance between speed control servo C116 Pin 5, Circuit 151 (LB/BK), and speed control servo C116 Pin 6, Circuit 848 (DG/OG), while pressing the speed control actuator switch SET/ACCEL. • Is the resistance between 612-748 ohms with the switch pressed and greater than 10,000 ohms with the switch released? → **Yes** INSTALL a new speed control servo. TEST the system for normal operation. → **No** INSTALL a new speed control actuator switch. TEST the system for normal operation.

FM1109900654020X

Fig. 185   Test G: Speed Control Inoperative (Part 2 of 2). Windstar

TEST CONDITIONS	TESTDETAILS/RESULTS/ACTIONS
J1 CHECK THE SPEED CONTROL ACTUATOR SWITCH COAST PID	
☐	☐ Monitor the speed control servo COAST PID. Depress and release the speed control actuator switch COAST button while slightly turning the steering wheel from side to side. • Does NGS Tester indicate ACTIVE with the speed control actuator switch depressed and notACT with the speed control actuator switch released? → **Yes** The system is OK. → **No** GO to **J2**.
J2 CHECK THE SPEED CONTROL ACTUATOR SWITCH COAST	
Speed Control Servo C116	☐ Measure the resistance between speed control servo C116 Pin 5, Circuit 151 (LB/BK) and speed control servo C116 Pin 6, Circuit 848 (DG/OG) while pressing the speed control actuator switch COAST and slightly turning the steering wheel from side to side. • Is the resistance between 108-132 ohms with COAST pressed and greater than 10,000 ohms with COAST released? → **Yes** INSTALL a new speed control servo. TEST the system for normal operation. → **No** INSTALL a new speed control actuator switch. TEST the system for normal operation.

FM1109900656000X

Fig. 187   Test J: Coast Switch Inoperative. Windstar

TEST CONDITIONS	TESTDETAILS/RESULTS/ACTIONS
H1 CHECK THE SPEED CONTROL THROTTLE ATTACHMENT	
Note: There must not be any loose components when carrying out the speed control servo slack test.	
	☐ Check the throttle lever, speed control actuator cable, and accelerator cable bracket for correct operation while carrying out the speed control servo slack test on NGS Tester. • Do the throttle lever components operate correctly? → **Yes** The system is OK. TEST the system for normal operation. → **No** INSTALL a new component. TEST the system for normal operation.

FM1109900655000X

Fig. 186   Test H: Set Speed Fluctuates. Windstar

TEST CONDITIONS	TESTDETAILS/RESULTS/ACTIONS
K1 CHECK THE SPEED CONTROL ACTUATOR SWITCH SET__ACL PID	
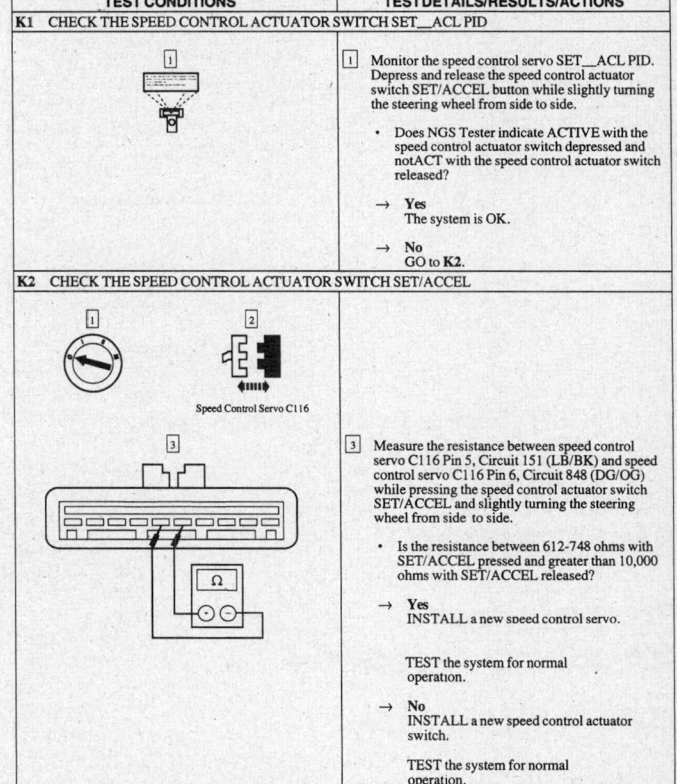	☐ Monitor the speed control servo SET__ACL PID. Depress and release the speed control actuator switch SET/ACCEL button while slightly turning the steering wheel from side to side. • Does NGS Tester indicate ACTIVE with the speed control actuator switch depressed and notACT with the speed control actuator switch released? → **Yes** The system is OK. → **No** GO to **K2**.
K2 CHECK THE SPEED CONTROL ACTUATOR SWITCH SET/ACCEL	
	☐ Measure the resistance between speed control servo C116 Pin 5, Circuit 151 (LB/BK) and speed control servo C116 Pin 6, Circuit 848 (DG/OG) while pressing the speed control actuator switch SET/ACCEL and slightly turning the steering wheel from side to side. • Is the resistance between 612-748 ohms with SET/ACCEL pressed and greater than 10,000 ohms with SET/ACCEL released? → **Yes** INSTALL a new speed control servo. TEST the system for normal operation. → **No** INSTALL a new speed control actuator switch. TEST the system for normal operation.

FM1109900657000X

Fig. 188   Test K: Set/Accel Switch Inoperative. Windstar

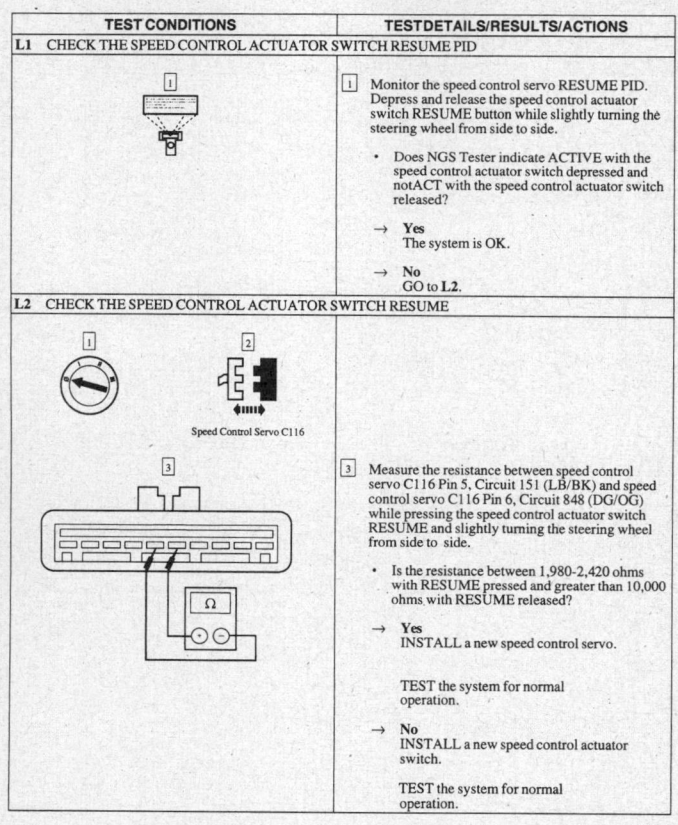

Fig. 189 Test L: Resume Switch Inoperative. Windstar

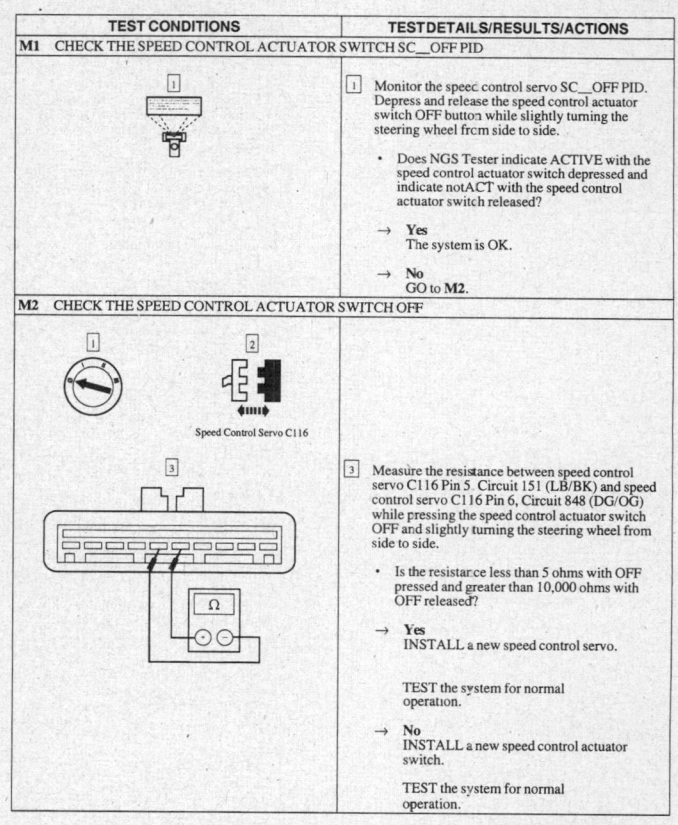

Fig. 190 Test M: Off Switch Inoperative. Windstar

COMPONENT REPLACEMENT

Servo (Throttle Actuator) Assembly

ESCAPE & MARINER

1. Press locking tab and rotate speed control cable cap to remove, **Fig. 191.**
2. Gently push retaining spring, **Fig. 192.**
3. Disconnect speed control cable lug from speed control actuator pulley.
4. Reverse procedure to install. **Torque** actuator mounting nuts to 80 inch lbs.

EXCURSION & F-SUPER DUTY

1. Disconnect speed control servo electrical connector, **Fig. 193.**
2. Remove speed control actuator servo mounting bolts and bracket.
3. Remove speed control actuator cable cap from control servo.
4. Slide core wire end out of speed control servo pulley.
5. Remove speed control actuator.
6. Reverse procedure to install. **Torque** mounting bolts to 80 inch lbs.

E-SERIES

1. Remove air cleaner assembly and throttle body cover.

2. Remove radiator coolant recovery reservoir retaining bolts, then position reservoir aside.
3. Disconnect speed control throttle actuator cable from servo cable as follows:
   a. Hold throttle actuator cable and twist outer cover clockwise until outer cover unlocks.
   b. Twist outer cover counterclockwise until white tab is in unlock position.
   c. Slide cover towards servo, then disconnect core wire from connector.
4. Disconnect electrical connector from speed control servo.
5. Remove retaining screws and speed control servo from vehicle.
6. Reverse procedure to install, noting the following:
   a. **Torque** servo retaining screws to 84–108 inch lbs.
   b. Vehicle may need to be driven 10 or more miles to relearn strategy.

EXPLORER, MOUNTAINEER & RANGER

1. Disconnect speed control servo electrical connector, **Fig. 194.**
2. Remove speed control actuator cable from speed control servo by depressing actuator cable cap tab inward and twisting cap counterclockwise.
3. Remove speed control servo bracket bolt, then the servo.
4. Reverse procedure to install. **Torque** speed control servo bracket bolt to 108 inch lbs.

AVIATOR, EXPEDITION, F-150 & NAVIGATOR

1. Press locking tab and rotate speed control cable cap to remove, **Fig. 195.**
2. Gently push retaining spring, **Fig. 196.**
3. Disconnect speed control cable lug from speed control actuator pulley.
4. Reverse procedure to install. **Torque** actuator mounting nuts to 80 inch lbs.

FREESTAR & MONTEREY

1. Disconnect actuator electrical connector, **Fig. 197.**
2. Disconnect speed control actuator cable from throttle body.
3. Press locking tab on speed control cable cap, rotate speed control cable cap counterclockwise.
4. Remove speed control actuator bolts to battery tray, then the actuator.
5. Reverse procedure to install. **Torque** mounting bolts to 89 inch lbs.

VILLAGER

1. Loosen speed control actuator locknut.
2. Remove actuator from throttle lever, then disconnect speed control servo motor electrical connector.
3. Remove three servo bracket bolts from servo bracket, then the servo from vehicle.
4. Reverse procedure to install. **Torque** actuator locknut to 72–96 inch lbs.

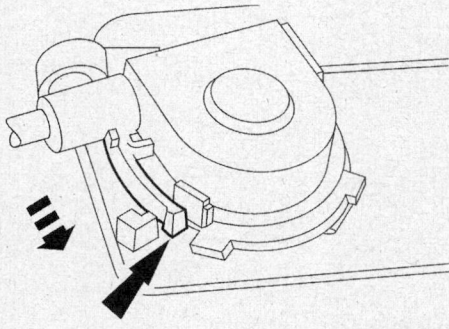

Fig. 191 Actuator cable locking cap removal. Escape & Mariner

WINDSTAR

3.0L ENGINE

1. Remove battery and harness main wiring "Christmas tree" connector.
2. Remove speed control servo to vehicle lefthand apron screws and disconnect speed control actuator from lefthand apron clips. Do not remove clips from apron.
3. Disconnect electrical connector, then remove speed control module from lefthand apron.
4. Disconnect actuator at throttle body, depress actuator cap locking arm and rotate counterclockwise while lifting upward.
5. Insert suitable small screwdriver in locking spring, gently pry spring back and remove cable slug from servo pulley.
6. Remove mounting screws and bracket from servo.
7. Reverse procedure to install, noting the following:
   a. **Torque** servo bracket screws to 72–96 inch lbs.
   b. Ensure rubber seal is fully seated on actuator cable cap.
   c. **Torque** servo screws to 48–60 inch lbs.
   d. When battery has been disconnected and connected, some abnormal drive symptoms may occur while Powertrain Control Module (PCM) relearns its adaptive strategy. Vehicle may need to be driven ten miles or more to learn strategy.
   e. Adjust speed control actuator as outlined under "Adjustments."

3.8L ENGINE

1. Disconnect conical air inlet tube by loosening clamp at throttle body and releasing snap ring at air cleaner, then position tube up and out of the way to access servo.
2. Remove two screws that mount servo to battery tray, then disconnect servo by pressing down on connector locking tabs.
3. Lift and remove servo and bracket from battery tray, then disconnect actuator cable at throttle lever by snapping off nailhead.
4. Depress locking arm on speed control actuator cap and rotate counterclockwise while lifting upward.

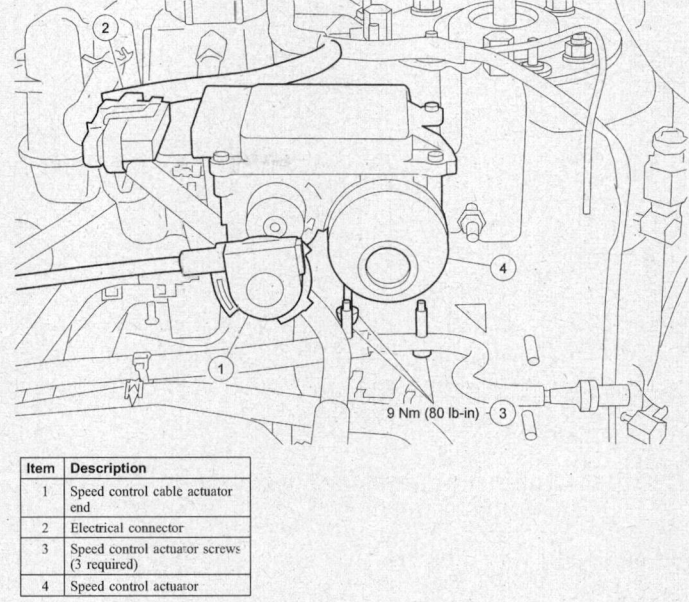

Item	Description
1	Speed control cable actuator end
2	Electrical connector
3	Speed control actuator screws (3 required)
4	Speed control actuator

Fig. 192 Speed control servo replacement. Escape & Mariner

5. Insert a small screwdriver in locking spring, then gently pry spring back and remove cable slug from servo pulley.
6. Reverse procedure to install, noting the following:
   a. **Torque** servo bracket to speed control servo screws to 72–84 inch lbs.
   b. Ensure rubber seal is fully seated on actuator cable cap.
   c. **Torque** bracket to battery tray to 96–120 inch lbs.
   d. Adjust speed control actuator as outlined under "Adjustments."

Actuator Cable

ESCAPE & MARINER

1. **On models equipped with 2.0L engine,** disconnect speed control cable from throttle control linkage and bracket.
2. **On models equipped with 3.0L engine,** proceed as follows:
   a. Disconnect cable from throttle control linkage.
   b. Squeeze tabs and disconnect speed control cable from bracket.
3. **On all models,** depress speed control cable cap retaining tab, then rotate and release cap.
4. Depress spring retainer.
5. Slide core wire end out of servo pulley and remove speed control cable.
6. Reverse procedure to install.

EXCURSION & F-SUPER DUTY

1. Remove air cleaner outlet tube.
2. Remove accelerator control splash shield.
3. Remove speed control actuator cable from throttle nail head as follows:
   a. Lift speed control actuator cable upward.
   b. Squeeze speed control actuator cable tabs and remove from throttle nail head.
4. Remove speed control actuator cable cap from speed control servo as follows:
   a. Push in locking arm on speed control actuator cable cap.
   b. Rotate speed control actuator cable cap counterclockwise and remove from control servo.
5. Depress spring retainer and remove speed control actuator cable.
6. Reverse procedure to install.

EXPEDITION, F-150 & NAVIGATOR

1. Remove air cleaner outlet tube.
2. Remove accelerator control splash shield.
3. Remove speed control actuator cable from throttle nail head as follows:
   a. Lift speed control actuator cable upward.
   b. Squeeze speed control actuator cable tabs and remove from throttle nail head.
4. Remove speed control actuator cable cap from speed control servo as follows:
   a. Push in locking arm on speed control actuator cable cap.
   b. Rotate speed control actuator cable cap counterclockwise and remove from control servo.
5. Depress spring retainer and remove speed control actuator cable.
6. Reverse procedure to install.

EXPLORER, MOUNTAINEER & RANGER

1. Remove accelerator control splash shield.
2. **On models equipped with 3.0L engine,** remove speed control actuator bolt.

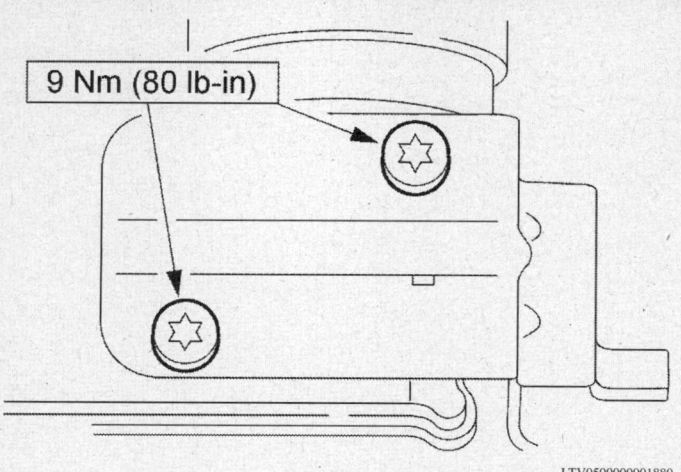

Fig. 193 Throttle actuator replacement. Excursion & F-Super Duty

3. **On models equipped with 4.0L engine,** remove speed control actuator clip.
4. **On all models,** disconnect speed control actuator cable from throttle body linkage.
5. Remove speed control actuator cable from speed control servo by pressing actuator locking clip inward and twisting actuator counterclockwise.
6. Reverse procedure to install, noting the following:
   a. Ensure seal is pressed into position.
   b. Ensure white indicator mark is visible on speed control actuator cable for proper routing.
   c. **On models equipped with 2.5L and 3.0L engines, torque** mounting bolt 27–38 inch lbs.

E-SERIES

Refer to "Servo (Throttle Actuator) Assembly" for removal and installation of the actuator cable.

VILLAGER

1. Loosen locknut, then disconnect cable from bracket and throttle lever.
2. Use screwdriver to pry cable end from actuator, then use needle nose pliers to remove snap ring from actuator.
3. Disconnect cable from actuator, then remove cable from vehicle.
4. Reverse procedure to install. Adjust cable after installation as outlined under "Actuator Cable, Adjust."

WINDSTAR

1. Remove speed control actuator from speed control servo as outlined under "Servo (Throttle Actuator) Assembly."
2. Remove speed control actuator from throttle bracket, then the actuator from accelerator cable.
3. Reverse procedure to install. Adjust cable after installation as outlined under "Actuator Cable, Adjust."

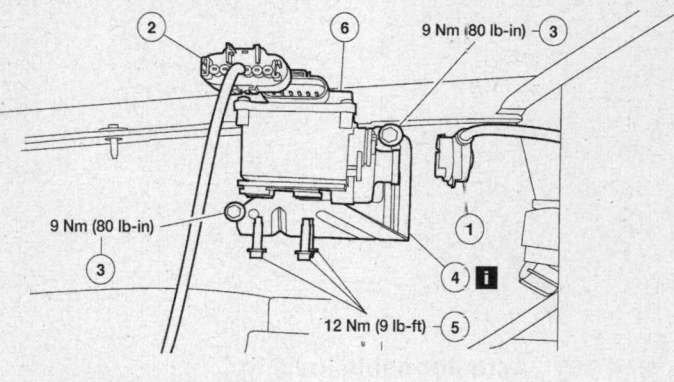

Item	Description
1	Speed control cable actuator end
2	Electrical connector
3	Speed control actuator bracket bolts to body
4	Speed control actuator and bracket
5	Speed control actuator bolts to bracket
6	Speed control actuator

Fig. 194 Throttle actuator replacement. Explorer, Mountaineer & Ranger

Control Switch

ESCAPE & MARINER

1. Remove steering wheel as outlined in "Electrical" section of chassis chapter.
2. Remove steering wheel cover.
3. Disconnect ground wire.
4. Remove steering wheel frame mounting nuts, then the frame.
5. Disconnect speed control switches electrical connector.
6. Remove control switch mounting screws, then the switch.
7. Reverse procedure to install. **Torque** frame mounting nuts to 80 inch lbs.

AVIATOR, EXCURSION, EXPEDITION, E-SERIES, F-SUPER DUTY, F-150, MARK LT & NAVIGATOR

1. Remove two driver air bag module screws, then disconnect air bag sliding contact electrical connector and horn electrical connector.
2. Release four speed control switch clips, disconnect electrical connector and remove switches from vehicle.
3. Reverse procedure to install.

EXPLORER & MOUNTAINEER

LESS REMOTE AUDIO/CLIMATE CONTROL

1. Disconnect wiring connectors at side of switches.
2. Remove two screws per switch and switch from steering wheel.

3. Reverse procedure to install.

WITH AUDIO/CLIMATE CONTROL

1. Separate speed control actuator switch from steering wheel.
2. Remove speed control actuator switch, then disconnect actuator switch connector.
3. Remove actuator switch.
4. Reverse procedure to install.

RANGER

1. Remove steering wheel as outlined in "Electrical" section of chassis chapter.
2. Remove steering wheel rear cover.
3. Remove ribbon harness from clips.
4. Remove horn contact electrical connectors.
5. Remove righthand side horn contact.
6. Remove speed control actuator switch assembly retaining bolts, then the switch assembly.
7. Reverse procedure to install.

VILLAGER

1. Remove air bag module bolt access cover from righthand side of steering wheel, **Fig. 198,** then the two speed control switch assembly screws.
2. Disconnect speed control switch assembly electrical connector by gently moving switch assembly up and down while pulling it away from side of steering wheel.
3. Remove speed control switch assembly.
4. Reverse procedure to install.

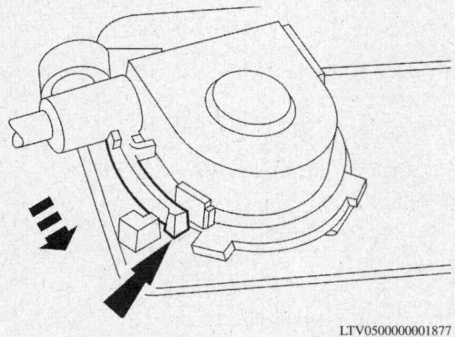

Fig. 195 Actuator cable locking cap removal. Aviator, Expedition, F-150 & Navigator

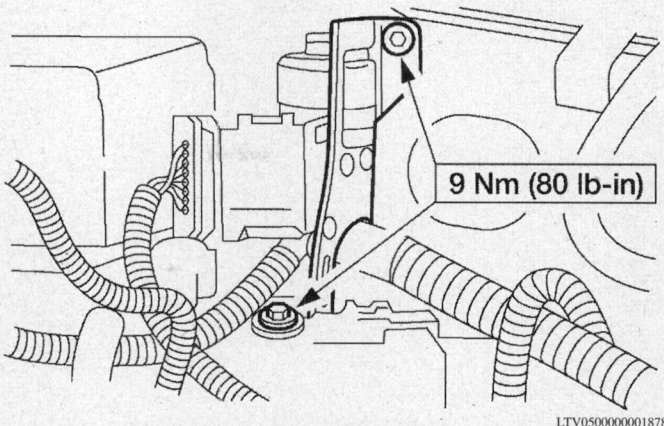

9 Nm (80 lb-in)

Fig. 196 Speed control servo replacement. Expedition, F-150 & Navigator

Speed Control Module/Amplifier

VILLAGER

Electronic modules are sensitive to static electrical charges. Damage may result if exposed to these charges.

1. Remove storage bin screws and storage bin from control console.
2. Remove lefthand and righthand inner lower instrument panels, then disconnect speed control module electrical connector.
3. Remove module nuts from module, then the module from vehicle.
4. Reverse procedure to install.

Vehicle Speed Sensor (VSS)

EXPLORER, MOUNTAINEER & RANGER

1. Separate electrical connector to speed sensor.
2. Remove sensor mounting bolt or nut, then the sensor.
3. Remove drive gear.
4. Reverse procedure to install. Ensure drive gear is installed on sensor before installing sensor into transmission.

AVIATOR, EXCURSION, E-SERIES, EXPEDITION, F-SUPER DUTY, F-150 & MARK LT

1. Separate electrical connector to speed sensor on transfer case or rear axle, as equipped.
2. Remove sensor attaching bolt, then the sensor.
3. Reverse procedure to install.

VILLAGER

The Vehicle Speed Sensor (VSS) is located on the upper rear portion of the transaxle housing.

1. Raise and support vehicle.
2. Disconnect VSS electrical connector, then remove VSS hold-down bracket bolt and bracket.
3. Remove VSS from transaxle and inspect O-rings for nicks or cuts. Replace if required.
4. Reverse procedure to install. **Torque** VSS hold-down bracket bolt to 45–61 inch lbs.

WINDSTAR

1. Raise and support vehicle, then remove dual converter Y-pipe from exhaust system.
2. Remove heat shield from transaxle, then disconnect VSS electrical connector.
3. Remove VSS retaining bolt and VSS from transaxle.
4. Reverse procedure to install. **Torque** VSS retaining bolt to 48–72 inch lbs.

Brake Deactivator Switch

1. Disconnect deactivator switch electrical connector.
2. Rotate switch as required to remove.
3. Reverse procedure to install, noting the following:
   a. **On Escape & Mariner models,** initial installation of a deactivator switch allows for one adjustment. If additional adjustments are required, install a new switch as follows:
      1. Rotate lock knob counterclockwise until first click is felt.
      2. Depress brake pedal.
      3. Position deactivator switch in bracket and rotate clockwise 45°.
      4. Connect electrical connector.
      5. Slowly release brake pedal and tug moderately once pedal reaches rest position. An extra click should be heard when tugging on pedal.

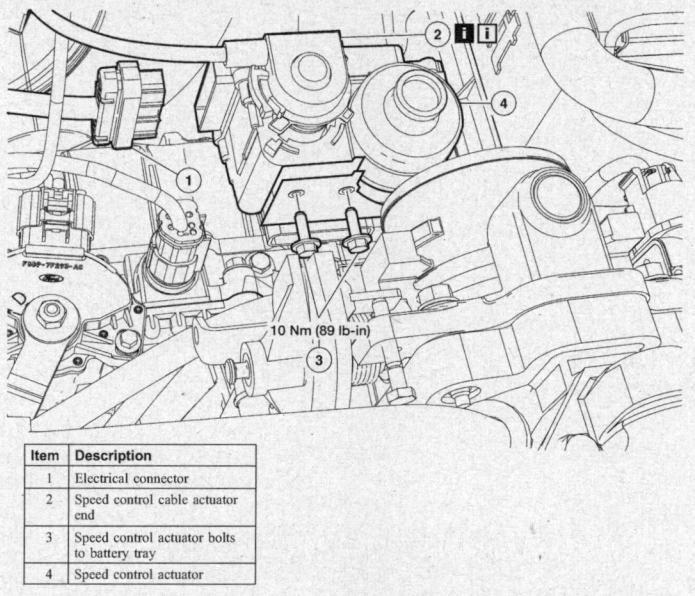

Item	Description
1	Electrical connector
2	Speed control cable actuator end
3	Speed control actuator bolts to battery tray
4	Speed control actuator

LTV0500000001879

**Fig. 197 Throttle actuator assembly replacement.
Freestar & Monterey**

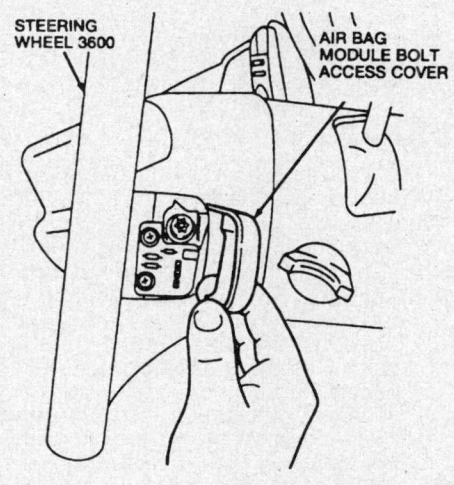

FM1109400094000X

**Fig. 198 Air bag module bolt
access cover removal. Villager**

WIPER SYSTEMS

TABLE OF CONTENTS

	Page No.		Page No.
AVIATOR	3-1	EXPLORER SPORT & SPORT	
ESCAPE & MARINER	3-11	TRAC	3-132
E-SERIES	3-27	F-150 & MARK LT	3-147
EXCURSION & F-SUPER DUTY	3-39	FREESTAR & MONTEREY	3-138
EXPEDITION & NAVIGATOR	3-68	RANGER	3-154
EXPLORER & MOUNTAINEER	3-96	VILLAGER	3-180
		WINDSTAR	3-165

Aviator

NOTE: On Air Bag E____ped Models, Refer To "Air Bag System Precautions" Located In The Front Of This ____ Manual For System Disarming & Arming Procedures.

NOTE: "Electrical Sy____ ____ire Color Code Identification" Located In The Front Of This Manual Ma____ Us____ ____id When Using Wiring Diagrams Found In This Section.

NOTE: Refer To "Co____ ____Procedures" Located In The Front Of This Manual When Batte____ The Computer Has Been Interrupted.

INDEX

	Page No.		P____
Component Diagnosis & Testing		Front	3-10	Accessing Diagnostic Trouble Codes	
Washer Pump Relay (Inte____		Rear	3-10	Clearing Diagnostic Trouble Codes	
Front		Diagnostic Chart Index	3-3	Diagnostic Tests	
Rear		Precautions	3-1	Wiring Diagrams	
Windshield Wiper Motor		Battery Ground Cable	3-1		
		System Diagnosis & Testing	3-1		

PRECAUTIONS

Battery Groun____ ____le

Prior to service, disc____ ____attery ground cable and isolate as ____ ____.

SYSTEM DIAGN____IS & TESTING

Accessing Diagnostic Trouble Codes

Connect a suitably programmed scan tool and Vehicle Communication Module (VCM) with appropriate adapters, or equivalents, to the Data Link Connector (DCL) located in the passenger compartment beneath the instrument panel. Follow tool manufacturer's instructions for accessing speed control Diagnostic Trouble Codes (DTC).

Wiring Diagrams

Refer to **Fig. 1** for wiring diagrams.

Diagnostic Tests

Refer to **Figs. 2 through 13** for diagnostic tests.

Clearing Diagnostic Trouble Codes

Connect a suitably programmed scan tool and Vehicle Communication Module (VCM) with appropriate adapters, or equivalents, to the Data Link Connector (DCL) located in the passenger compartment beneath the instrument panel. Follow tool manufacturer's instructions for accessing speed control Diagnostic Trouble Codes (DTC).

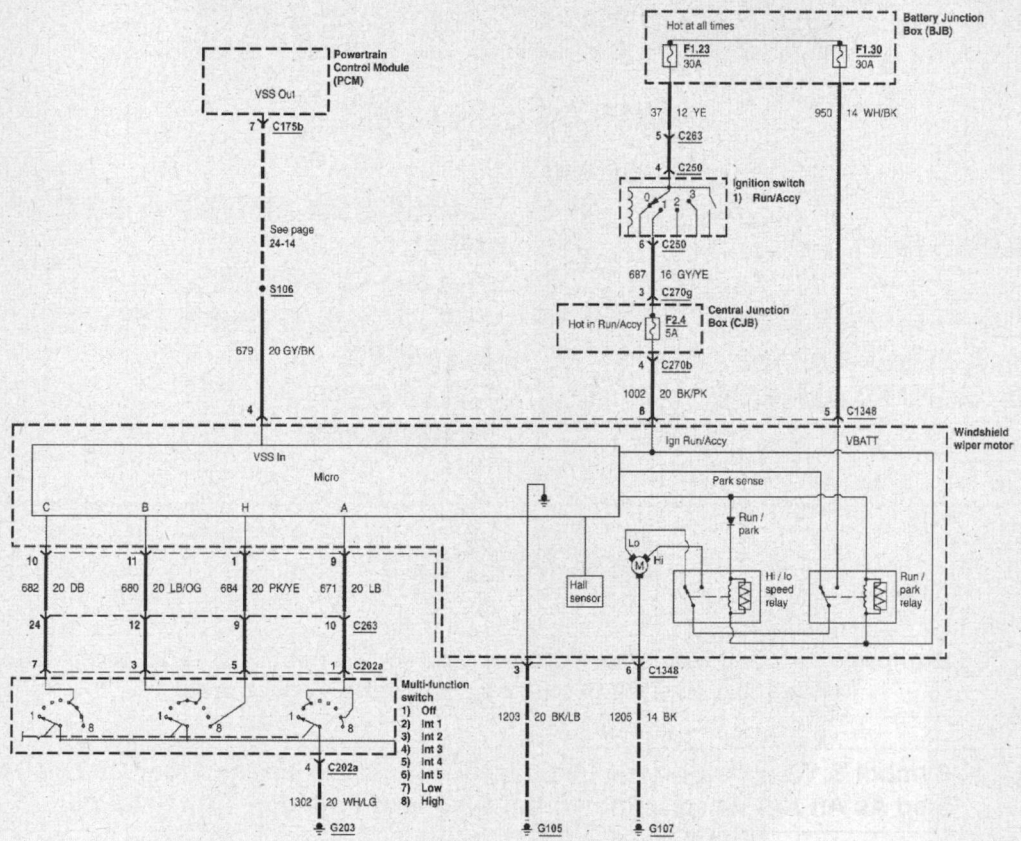

Fig. 1 Wiring diagram (Part 1 of 2)

LTV0500000002383

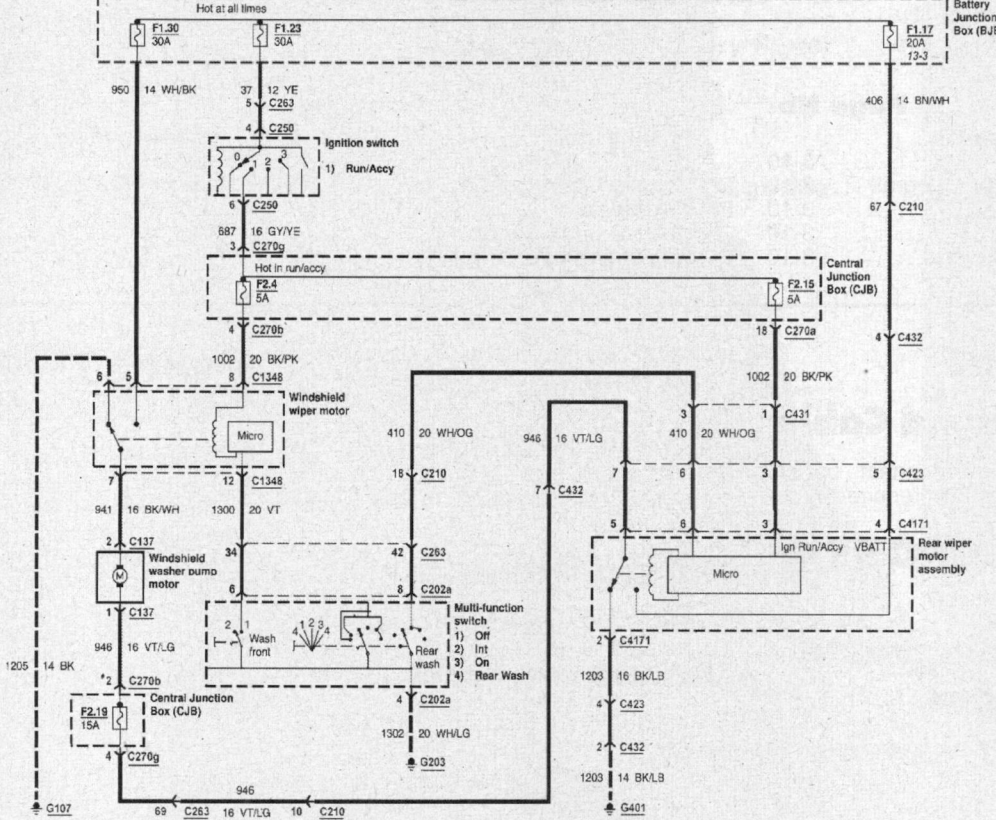

Fig. 1 Wiring diagram (Part 2 of 2)

LTV0500000002384

DIAGNOSTIC CHART INDEX

Test	Code	Description	Page No.	Fig. No.
—	—	Symptom Tests	3-3	2
A	—	Front Wipers Are Inoperative	3-4	3
B	—	Rear Wipers Are Inoperative	3-4	4
C	—	Front Wipers Stay On Continuously	3-5	5
D	—	Rear Wipers Stay On Continuously	3-6	6
E	—	High/Low Wiper Speeds Do Not Operate Correctly, Intermittent Mode OK	3-6	7
F	—	Low Rear Wiper Speed Does Not Operate Correctly	3-7	8
G	—	Intermittent Wiper Speed Does Not Operate Correctly, High/Low Speeds OK	3-7	9
H	—	Intermittent Rear Wiper Speed Does Not Operate Correctly	3-8	10
J	—	Rear Wipe & Wash Function Does Not Operate	3-8	11
K	—	Washer Pump Is Inoperative	3-8	12
L	—	Speed Dependent Interval Mode Does Not Operate Correctly	3-9	13

Condition	Possible Sources	Action
• The wipers are inoperative	• Multifunction switch. • Circuitry. • Ignition switch. • Windshield wiper motor.	• Go To Pinpoint Test A.
• The rear wiper is inoperative	• Multifunction switch. • Circuitry. • Ignition switch. • Rear window wiper motor.	• Go To Pinpoint Test B.
• The wipers stay on continuously	• Windshield wiper motor. • Multifunction switch. • Circuitry.	• Go To Pinpoint Test C.
• The rear wiper stays on continuously	• Rear window wiper motor. • Multifunction switch. • Circuitry.	• Go To Pinpoint Test D.
• The high/low wiper speeds do not operate correctly (intermittent wiper mode OK)	• Multifunction switch. • Circuitry. • Windshield wiper motor.	• Go To Pinpoint Test E.
• The low rear wiper speed does not operate correctly	• Multifunction switch. • Circuitry. • Rear window wiper motor.	• Go To Pinpoint Test F.
• The intermittent wiper speed does not operate correctly (high/low speeds OK)	• Multifunction switch. • Circuitry. • Windshield wiper motor.	• Go To Pinpoint Test G.
• The intermittent rear wiper speed does not operate	• Multifunction switch.	• Go To Pinpoint

LTV0500000002391

Fig. 2 Symptom Tests (Part 1 of 2)

correctly	• Circuitry. • Rear window wiper motor.	Test H.
• The wipers do not operate correctly in the MIST position	• Multifunction switch. • Circuitry. • Washer pump. • Windshield wiper motor.	• Go To Pinpoint Test I.
• The rear wiper wash and wipe function does not operate	• Multifunction switch. • Circuitry. • Washer pump. • Rear window wiper motor.	• Go To Pinpoint Test J.
• The washer pump is inoperative	• Washer pump. • Multifunction switch. • Windshield wiper motor. • Rear window wiper motor. • Circuitry.	• Go To Pinpoint Test K.
• The speed dependent interval mode does not operate correctly	• Windshield wiper motor. • Circuitry. • Powertrain control module (PCM).	• Go To Pinpoint Test L.

LTV0500000002392

Fig. 2 Symptom Tests (Part 2 of 2)

Test Step	Result / Action to Take
A1 CHECK CIRCUITS 950 (WH/BK) AND 1002 (BK/PK) FOR VOLTAGE • Key in OFF position. • Disconnect: Windshield Wiper Motor C1348. • Key in ON position. • Measure the voltage between windshield wiper C1348-5, circuit 950 (WH/BK), harness side and ground; and between windshield wiper motor C1348-8, circuit 1002 (BK/PK), harness side and ground. • Are the voltages greater than 10 volts?	**Yes** GO to A2. **No** REPAIR the circuit(s) in question. TEST the system for normal operation.
A2 CHECK CIRCUITS 1205 (BK) AND 1203 (BK/LB) FOR OPENS • Key in OFF position. • Measure the resistance between windshield wiper C1348-6, circuit 1205 (BK), harness side and ground; and between windshield wiper motor C1348-3, circuit 1203 (BK/LB), harness side and ground. • Are the resistances less than 5 ohms?	**Yes** GO to A3. **No** REPAIR the circuit(s) in question. TEST the system for normal operation.
A3 CHECK THE MULTIFUNCTION SWITCH • Disconnect: Multifunction Switch C202a. • Carry out the multifunction switch component test.	**Yes** GO to A4. **No**

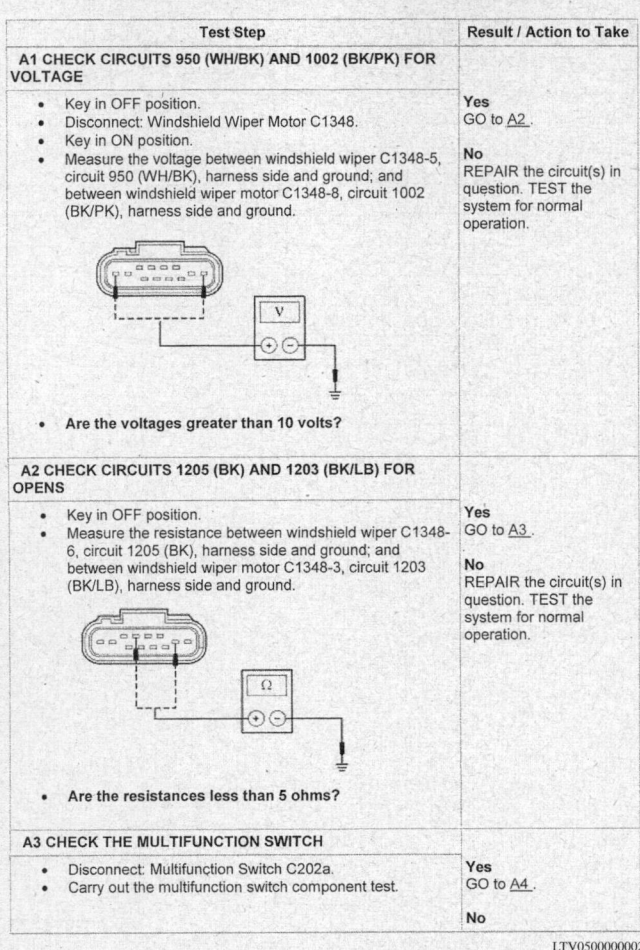

LTV0500000002393

Fig. 3 Test A: Front Wipers Are Inoperative
(Part 1 of 3)

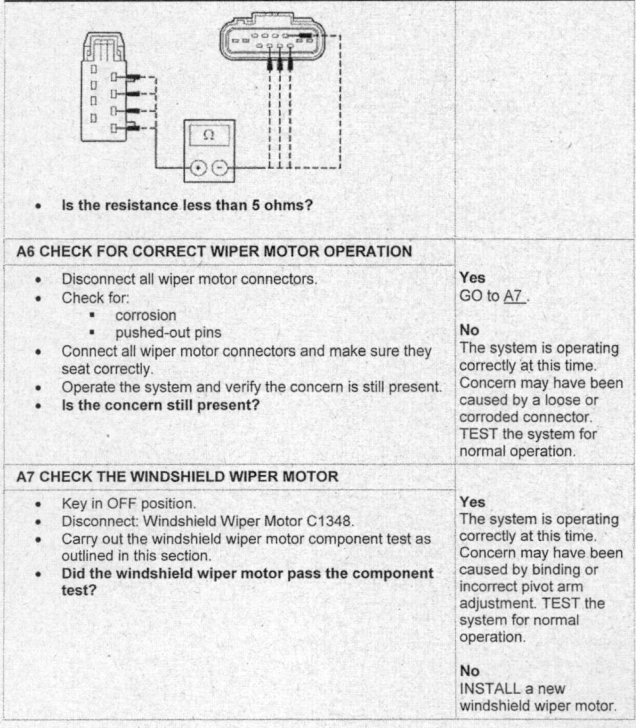

• Is the resistance less than 5 ohms?	

A6 CHECK FOR CORRECT WIPER MOTOR OPERATION
• Disconnect all wiper motor connectors.
• Check for:
  ▪ corrosion
  ▪ pushed-out pins
• Connect all wiper motor connectors and make sure they seat correctly.
• Operate the system and verify the concern is still present.
• **Is the concern still present?**
	Yes
	GO to A7.
	
	No
	The system is operating correctly at this time. Concern may have been caused by a loose or corroded connector. TEST the system for normal operation.

A7 CHECK THE WINDSHIELD WIPER MOTOR • Key in OFF position. • Disconnect: Windshield Wiper Motor C1348. • Carry out the windshield wiper motor component test as outlined in this section. • **Did the windshield wiper motor pass the component test?**	**Yes** The system is operating correctly at this time. Concern may have been caused by binding or incorrect pivot arm adjustment. TEST the system for normal operation. **No** INSTALL a new windshield wiper motor.

LTV0500000002395

Fig. 3 Test A: Front Wipers Are Inoperative
(Part 3 of 3)

	INSTALL a new multifunction switch.
Refer to "Wiring Diagrams" • **Did the multifunction switch pass the component test?**	
A4 CHECK CIRCUIT 1302 (WH/LG) FOR AN OPEN • Measure the resistance between C202a-4, circuit 1302 (WH/LG), harness side and ground. • Is the resistance less than 5 ohms?	**Yes** GO to A5. **No** REPAIR the circuit. TEST the system for normal operation.
A5 CHECK CIRCUITS 682 (DB), 680 (LB/OG), 684 (PK/YE), AND 671 (LB) FOR OPENS • Using the following table, measure the resistance between the multifunction switch C202a harness side and the windshield wiper motor C1348 harness side:	**Yes** GO to A6. **No** REPAIR the circuit(s) in question. TEST the system for normal operation.

Multifunction Switch C202a	Windshield Wiper Motor C1348
C202a-7, circuit 682 (DB)	C1348-10, circuit 682 (DB)
C202a-3, circuit 680 (LB/OG)	C1348-11, circuit 680 (LB/OG)
C202a-5, circuit 684 (PK/YE)	C1348-1, circuit 684 (PK/YE)
C202a-1, circuit 671 (LB)	C1348-9, circuit 671 (LB)

LTV0500000002394

Fig. 3 Test A: Front Wipers Are Inoperative
(Part 2 of 3)

Test Step	Result / Action to Take
B1 CHECK CIRCUITS 1002 (BK/PK) AND 406 (BN/WH) FOR VOLTAGE • Key in OFF position. • Disconnect: Rear Wiper Motor C4171. • Key in ON position. • Measure the voltage between rear wiper motor C4171-3, circuit 1002 (BK/PK), harness side and ground; and between rear wiper motor C4171-4, circuit 406 (BN/WH), harness side and ground. • Are the voltages greater than 10 volts?	**Yes** GO to B2. **No** REPAIR the circuit(s) in question. TEST the system for normal operation.
B2 CHECK CIRCUIT 1205 (BK) FOR OPEN • Key in OFF position. • Measure the resistance between rear wiper C4171-1, circuit 1205 (BK), harness side and ground. • Is the resistance less than 5 ohms?	**Yes** GO to B3. **No** REPAIR the circuit(s) in question. TEST the system for normal operation.
B3 CHECK THE MULTIFUNCTION SWITCH • Key in OFF position. • Disconnect: Multifunction Switch C202a. • Carry out the multifunction switch component test. Refer to "Wiring Diagrams"	**Yes** GO to B4. **No** INSTALL a new multifunction switch.

LTV0500000002396

Fig. 4 Test B: Rear Wipers Are Inoperative
(Part 1 of 3)

- Did the multifunction switch pass the component test?

Test Step	Result / Action to Take
B4 CHECK CIRCUIT 1302 (WH/LG) FOR AN OPEN • Measure the resistance between multifunction switch C202a-4, circuit 1302 (WH/LG), harness side and ground. 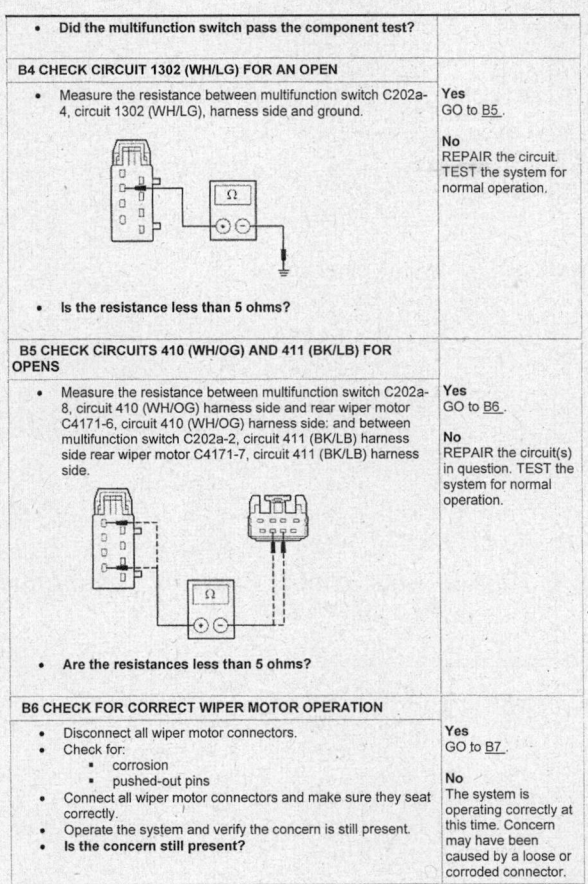 • Is the resistance less than 5 ohms?	**Yes** GO to B5 . **No** REPAIR the circuit. TEST the system for normal operation.
B5 CHECK CIRCUITS 410 (WH/OG) AND 411 (BK/LB) FOR OPENS • Measure the resistance between multifunction switch C202a-8, circuit 410 (WH/OG) harness side and rear wiper motor C4171-6, circuit 410 (WH/OG) harness side; and between multifunction switch C202a-2, circuit 411 (BK/LB) harness side rear wiper motor C4171-7, circuit 411 (BK/LB) harness side. • Are the resistances less than 5 ohms?	**Yes** GO to B6 . **No** REPAIR the circuit(s) in question. TEST the system for normal operation.

B6 CHECK FOR CORRECT WIPER MOTOR OPERATION
 	
• Disconnect all wiper motor connectors.
• Check for:
   • corrosion
   • pushed-out pins
• Connect all wiper motor connectors and make sure they seat correctly.
• Operate the system and verify the concern is still present.
• **Is the concern still present?**
	Yes
	GO to B7 .
	
	No
	The system is operating correctly at this time. Concern may have been caused by a loose or corroded connector.

LTV0500000002397

Fig. 4 Test B: Rear Wipers Are Inoperative (Part 2 of 3)

Test Step	Result / Action to Take
C1 CHECK THE MULTIFUNCTION SWITCH • Key in OFF position. • Disconnect: Multifunction Switch C202a. • Carry out the multifunction switch component test. Refer to "Wiring Diagrams" • **Did the multifunction switch pass the component test?**	**Yes** GO to C2 . **No** INSTALL a new multifunction switch.
C2 CHECK CIRCUIT 1302 (WH/LG) FOR AN OPEN • Measure the resistance between multifunction switch C202a-4, circuit 1302 (WH/LG), harness side and ground. • Is the resistance less than 5 ohms?	**Yes** GO to B3 . **No** REPAIR the circuit. TEST the system for normal operation.
C3 CHECK CIRCUITS 682 (DB), 680 (LB/OG), 684 (PK/YE), AND 671 (LB) FOR SHORTS • Disconnect: Windshield Wiper Motor C1348. • Using the following table, measure the resistance between the windshield wiper motor C1348 harness side and ground: | Windshield Wiper Motor C1348	Ground
C1348-10, circuit 682 (DB)	ground
C1348-11, circuit 680 (LB/OG)	ground
C1348-1, circuit 684 (PK/YE)	ground
C1348-9, circuit 671 (LB)	ground		**Yes** GO to C4 . **No** REPAIR the circuit(s) in question. TEST the system for normal operation.

LTV0500000002399

Fig. 5 Test C: Front Wipers Stay On Continuously (Part 1 of 2)

Test Step	Result / Action to Take
B7 CHECK THE REAR WINDOW WIPER MOTOR • Carry out the rear widow wiper motor component test as outlined in this section. • **Did the rear window wiper motor pass the component test?**	TEST the system for normal operation. **Yes** The system is operating correctly at this time. Concern may have been caused by binding or incorrect pivot arm adjustment. TEST the system for normal operation. **No** INSTALL a new rear window wiper motor.

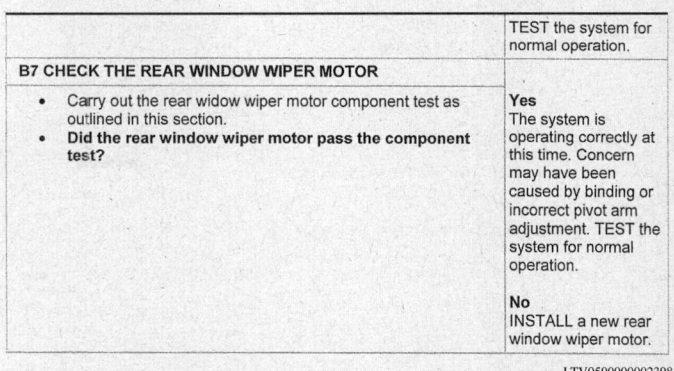

LTV0500000002398

Fig. 4 Test B: Rear Wipers Are Inoperative (Part 3 of 3)

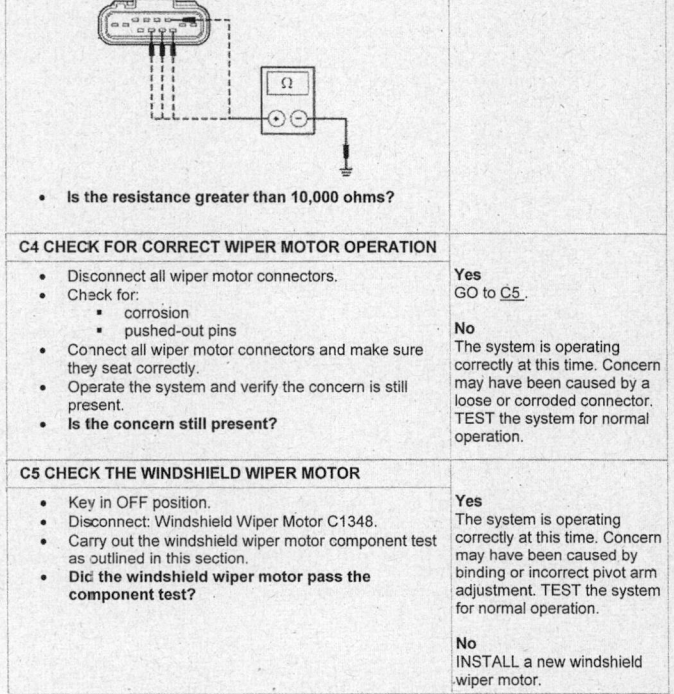

Test Step	Result / Action to Take
• Is the resistance greater than 10,000 ohms?	

C4 CHECK FOR CORRECT WIPER MOTOR OPERATION
 	
• Disconnect all wiper motor connectors.
• Check for:
   • corrosion
   • pushed-out pins
• Connect all wiper motor connectors and make sure they seat correctly.
• Operate the system and verify the concern is still present.
• **Is the concern still present?**
	Yes
	GO to C5 .
	
	No
	The system is operating correctly at this time. Concern may have been caused by a loose or corroded connector. TEST the system for normal operation.

C5 CHECK THE WINDSHIELD WIPER MOTOR • Key in OFF position. • Disconnect: Windshield Wiper Motor C1348. • Carry out the windshield wiper motor component test as outlined in this section. • **Did the windshield wiper motor pass the component test?**	**Yes** The system is operating correctly at this time. Concern may have been caused by binding or incorrect pivot arm adjustment. TEST the system for normal operation. **No** INSTALL a new windshield wiper motor.

LTV0500000002400

Fig. 5 Test C: Front Wipers Stay On Continuously (Part 2 of 2)

Test Step	Result / Action to Take
D1 CHECK THE MULTIFUNCTION SWITCH • Key in OFF position. • Disconnect: Multifunction Switch C202a. • Carry out the multifunction switch component test. Refer to "Wiring Diagrams" • **Did the multifunction switch pass the component test?**	**Yes** GO to <u>D2</u>. **No** INSTALL a new multifunction switch.
D2 CHECK CIRCUIT 1302 (WH/LG) FOR AN OPEN • Measure the resistance between multifunction switch C202a-4, circuit 1302 (WH/LG), harness side and ground. • **Is the resistance less than 5 ohms?**	**Yes** GO to <u>D3</u>. **No** REPAIR the circuit. TEST the system for normal operation.
D3 CHECK CIRCUITS 410 (WH/OG) AND 411 (BK/LB) FOR SHORTS • Disconnect: Rear Window Wiper Motor C4171. • Measure the resistance between rear window wiper motor C4171-6, circuit 410 (WH/OG), harness side and ground; and between rear wiper motor C4171-7, circuit 411 (BK/LB), harness side and ground. • **Are the resistances greater than 10,000 ohms?**	**Yes** GO to <u>D4</u>. **No** REPAIR the circuit(s) in question. TEST the system for normal operation.

LTV0500000002401

Fig. 6   Test D: Rear Wipers Stay On Continuously (Part 1 of 2)

Test Step	Result / Action to Take
E1 CHECK THE MULTIFUNCTION SWITCH • Key in OFF position. • Disconnect: Multifunction Switch C202a. • Carry out the multifunction switch component test. Refer to "Wiring Diagrams" • **Did the multifunction switch pass the component test?**	**Yes** GO to <u>E2</u>. **No** INSTALL a new multifunction switch. TEST the system for normal operation.
E2 CHECK CIRCUIT 1302 (WH/LG) FOR AN OPEN • Measure the resistance between multifunction switch C202a-4, circuit 1302 (WH/LG), harness side and ground. • **Is the resistance less than 5 ohms?**	**Yes** GO to <u>E3</u>. **No** REPAIR the circuit. TEST the system for normal operation.
E3 CHECK CIRCUITS 682 (DB), 684 (PK/YE), AND 671 (LB) FOR OPENS • Disconnect: Windshield Wiper Motor C1348. • Using the following table, measure the resistance between multifunction switch C202a harness side and windshield wiper motor C1348 harness side: | Multifunction Switch C202a	Windshield Wiper Motor C1348	 |---|---| | C202a-7, circuit 682 (DB)	C1348-10, circuit 682 (DB)	 | C202a-5, circuit 684 (PK/YE)	C1348-1, circuit 684 (PK/YE)	 | C202a-1, circuit 671 (LB)	C1348-9, circuit 671 (LB)		**Yes** GO to <u>E4</u>. **No** REPAIR the circuit(s) in question. TEST the system for normal operation.

LTV0500000002563

Fig. 7   Test E: High/Low Wiper Speeds Do Not Operate Correctly, Intermittent Mode OK (Part 1 of 2)

Test Step	Result / Action to Take

D4 CHECK FOR CORRECT WIPER MOTOR OPERATION
• Disconnect all wiper motor connectors.
• Check for:
  ▪ corrosion
  ▪ pushed-out pins
• Connect all wiper motor connectors and make sure they seat correctly.
• Operate the system and verify the concern is still present
• **Is the concern still present?**
	Yes
	GO to <u>D5</u>.
	
	No
	The system is operating correctly at this time. Concern may have been caused by a loose or corroded connector. TEST the system for normal operation.

D5 CHECK THE REAR WINDOW WIPER MOTOR • Carry out the rear window wiper motor component test as outlined in this section. • **Did the rear window wiper motor pass the component test?**	**Yes** The system is operating correctly at this time. Concern may have been caused by binding or incorrect pivot arm adjustment. TEST the system for normal operation. **No** INSTALL a new rear window wiper motor.

LTV0500000002562

Fig. 6   Test D: Rear Wipers Stay On Continuously (Part 2 of 2)

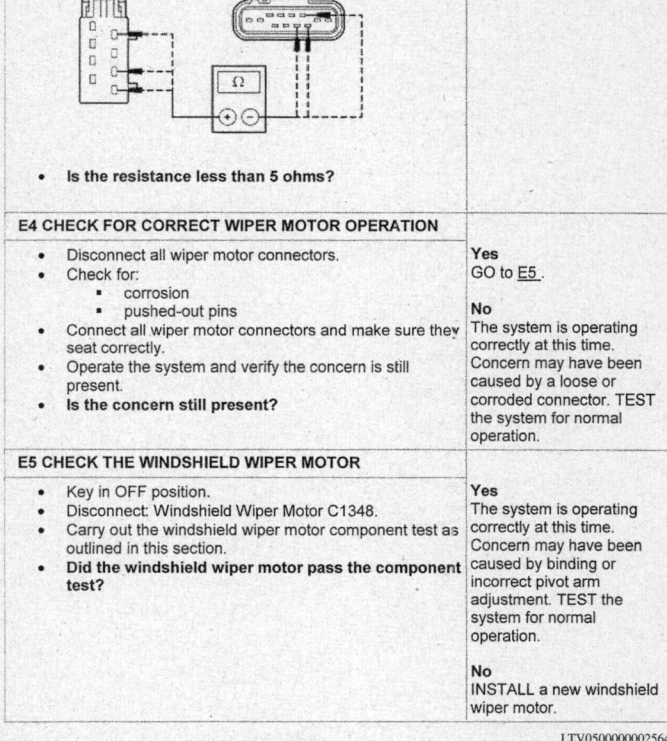

Test Step	Result / Action to Take
• **Is the resistance less than 5 ohms?**	

E4 CHECK FOR CORRECT WIPER MOTOR OPERATION
• Disconnect all wiper motor connectors.
• Check for:
  ▪ corrosion
  ▪ pushed-out pins
• Connect all wiper motor connectors and make sure they seat correctly.
• Operate the system and verify the concern is still present.
• **Is the concern still present?**
	Yes
	GO to <u>E5</u>.
	
	No
	The system is operating correctly at this time. Concern may have been caused by a loose or corroded connector. TEST the system for normal operation.

E5 CHECK THE WINDSHIELD WIPER MOTOR • Key in OFF position. • Disconnect: Windshield Wiper Motor C1348. • Carry out the windshield wiper motor component test as outlined in this section. • **Did the windshield wiper motor pass the component test?**	**Yes** The system is operating correctly at this time. Concern may have been caused by binding or incorrect pivot arm adjustment. TEST the system for normal operation. **No** INSTALL a new windshield wiper motor.

LTV0500000002564

Fig. 7   Test E: High/Low Wiper Speeds Do Not Operate Correctly, Intermittent Mode OK (Part 2 of 2)

Test Step	Result / Action to Take
F1 CHECK THE MULTIFUNCTION SWITCH	
• Key in OFF position. • Disconnect: Multifunction Switch C202a. • Carry out the multifunction switch component test. Refer to "Wiring Diagrams" • **Did the multifunction switch pass the component test?**	**Yes** GO to F2. **No** INSTALL a new multifunction switch.
F2 CHECK CIRCUIT 1302 (WH/LG) FOR AN OPEN	
• Measure the resistance between multifunction switch C202a-4, circuit 1302 (WH/LG), harness side and ground. 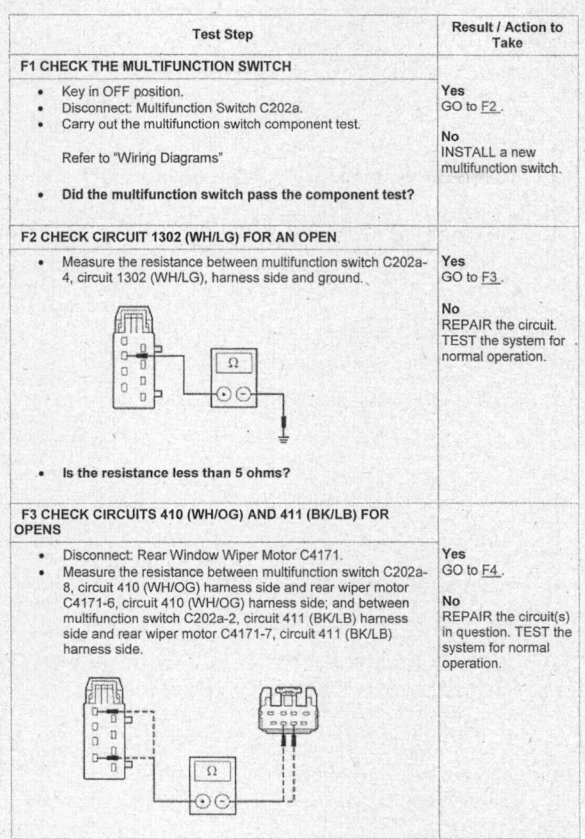 • **Is the resistance less than 5 ohms?**	**Yes** GO to F3. **No** REPAIR the circuit. TEST the system for normal operation.
F3 CHECK CIRCUITS 410 (WH/OG) AND 411 (BK/LB) FOR OPENS	
• Disconnect: Rear Window Wiper Motor C4171. • Measure the resistance between multifunction switch C202a-8, circuit 410 (WH/OG) harness side and rear wiper motor C4171-6, circuit 410 (WH/OG) harness side; and between multifunction switch C202a-2, circuit 411 (BK/LB) harness side and rear wiper motor C4171-7, circuit 411 (BK/LB) harness side.	**Yes** GO to F4. **No** REPAIR the circuit(s) in question. TEST the system for normal operation.

LTV0500000002565

Fig. 8   Test F: Low Rear Wiper Speed Does Not Operate Correctly (Part 1 of 2)

Test Step	Result / Action to Take
G1 CHECK THE MULTIFUNCTION SWITCH	
• Key in OFF position. • Disconnect: Multifunction Switch C202a. • Carry out the multifunction switch component test. Refer to "Wiring Diagrams" • **Did the multifunction switch pass the component test?**	**Yes** GO to G2. **No** INSTALL a new multifunction switch. TEST the system for normal operation.
G2 CHECK CIRCUIT 1302 (WH/LG) FOR AN OPEN	
• Measure the resistance between mulitfunction switch C202a pin 4, circuit 1302 (WH/LG), harness side and ground. • **Is the resistance less than 5 ohms?**	**Yes** GO to G3. **No** REPAIR the circuit. TEST the system for normal operation.
G3 CHECK CIRCUITS 682 (DB), 684 (PK/YE), AND 671 (LB) FOR OPENS	
• Disconnect: Windshield Wiper Motor C1348. • Using the following table, measure the resistance between multifunction switch C202a harness side and windshield wiper motor C1348 harness side:	**Yes** GO to G4. **No** REPAIR the circuit(s) in question. TEST the system for normal operation.

Multifunction Switch C202a	Windshield Wiper Motor C1348
C202a-7, circuit 682 (DB)	C1348-10, circuit 682 (DB)
C202a-5, circuit 684 (PK/YE)	C1348-1, circuit 684 (PK/YE)
C202a-1, circuit 671 (LB)	C1348-9, circuit 671 (LB)
C202a-3, circuit 680 (LB/OG)	C1348-11, circuit 680 (LB/OG)

LTV0500000002567

Fig. 9   Test G: Intermittent Wiper Speed Does Not Operate Correctly, High/Low Speeds OK (Part 1 of 2)

Test Step	Result / Action to Take
• Are the resistances less than 5 ohms?	
F4 CHECK FOR CORRECT WIPER MOTOR OPERATION	

• Disconnect all wiper motor connectors.
• Check for:
   ▪ corrosion
   ▪ pushed-out pins
• Connect all wiper motor connectors and make sure they seat correctly.
• Operate the system and verify the concern is still present.
• **Is the concern still present?**
	Yes
	GO to F5.
	
	No
	The system is operating correctly at this time. Concern may have been caused by a loose or corroded connector. TEST the system for normal operation.

F5 CHECK THE REAR WINDOW WIPER MOTOR	
• Carry out the rear window wiper motor component test as outlined • **Did the rear window wiper motor pass the component test?**	**Yes** The system is operating correctly at this time. Concern may have been caused by binding or incorrect pivot arm adjustment. TEST the system for normal operation. **No** INSTALL a new rear window wiper motor.

LTV0500000002566

Fig. 8   Test F: Low Rear Wiper Speed Does Not Operate Correctly (Part 2 of 2)

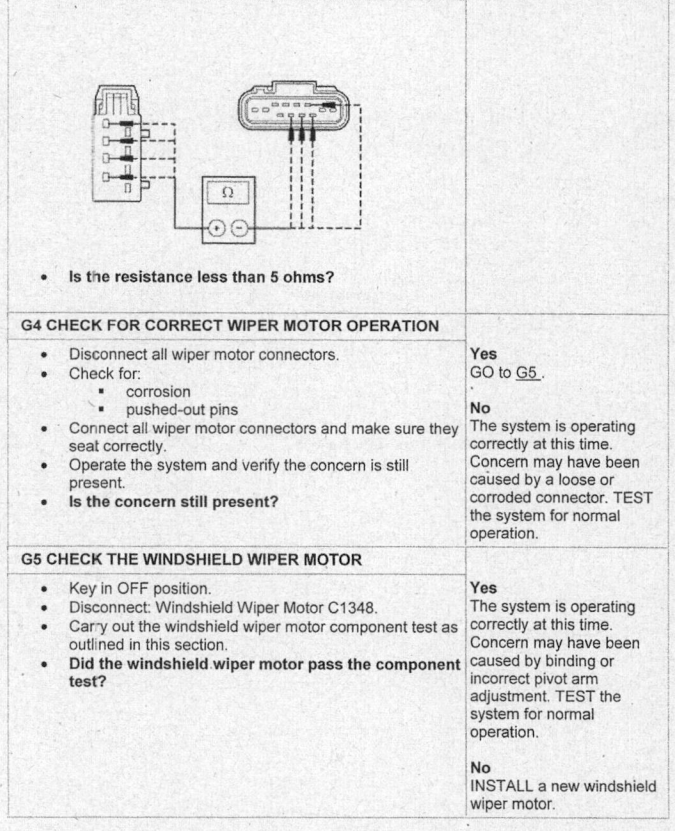

Test Step	Result / Action to Take
• **Is the resistance less than 5 ohms?**	
G4 CHECK FOR CORRECT WIPER MOTOR OPERATION	

• Disconnect all wiper motor connectors.
• Check for:
   ▪ corrosion
   ▪ pushed-out pins
• Connect all wiper motor connectors and make sure they seat correctly.
• Operate the system and verify the concern is still present.
• **Is the concern still present?**
	Yes
	GO to G5.
	
	No
	The system is operating correctly at this time. Concern may have been caused by a loose or corroded connector. TEST the system for normal operation.

G5 CHECK THE WINDSHIELD WIPER MOTOR	
• Key in OFF position. • Disconnect: Windshield Wiper Motor C1348. • Carry out the windshield wiper motor component test as outlined in this section. • **Did the windshield wiper motor pass the component test?**	**Yes** The system is operating correctly at this time. Concern may have been caused by binding or incorrect pivot arm adjustment. TEST the system for normal operation. **No** INSTALL a new windshield wiper motor.

LTV0500000002568

Fig. 9   Test G: Intermittent Wiper Speed Does Not Operate Correctly, High/Low Speeds OK (Part 2 of 2)

Test Step	Result / Action to Take
H1 CHECK THE MULTIFUNCTION SWITCH	
• Key in OFF position. • Disconnect: Multifunction Switch C202a. • Carry out the multifunction switch component test. Refer to "Wiring Diagrams" • **Did the multifunction switch pass the component test?**	**Yes** GO to <u>H2</u>. **No** INSTALL a new multifunction switch.
H2 CHECK CIRCUIT 1302 (WH/LG) FOR OPEN	
• Measure the resistance between multifunction switch C202a-4, circuit 1302 (WH/LG), harness side and ground. • Is the resistance less than 5 ohms?	**Yes** GO to <u>H3</u>. **No** REPAIR the circuit. TEST the system for normal operation.
H3 CHECK CIRCUITS 410 (WH/OG) AND 411 (BK/LB) FOR OPENS	
• Disconnect: Rear Window Wiper Motor C4171. • Measure the resistance between multifunction switch C202a-8, circuit 410 (WH/OG) harness side and rear wiper motor C4171-6, circuit 410 (WH/OG) harness side; and between multifunction switch C202a-2, circuit 411 (BK/LB) harness side and rear wiper motor C4171-7, circuit 411 (BK/LB) harness side.	**Yes** GO to <u>H4</u>. **No** REPAIR the circuit(s) in question. TEST the system for normal operation.

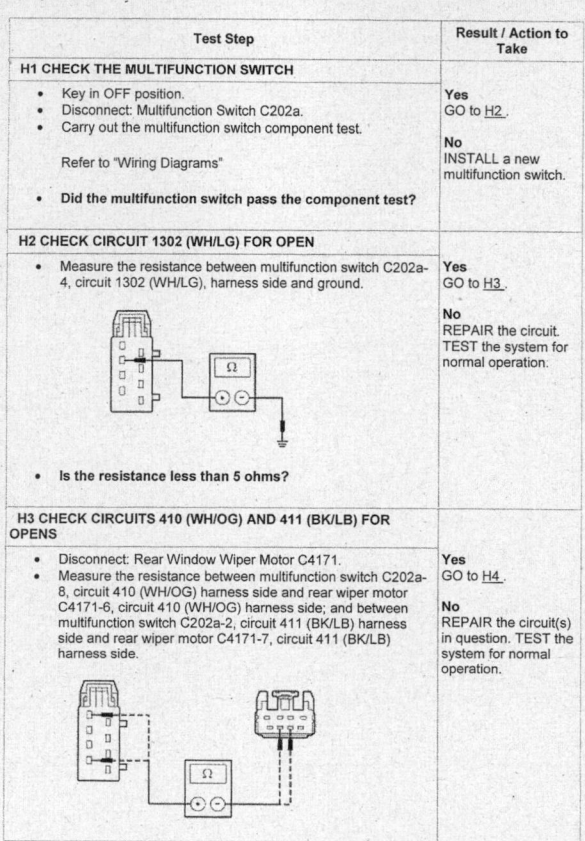

LTV0500000002569

Fig. 10   Test H: Intermittent Rear Wiper Speed Does Not Operate Correctly (Part 1 of 2)

Test Step	Result / Action to Take
J1 CHECK THE MULTIFUNCTION SWITCH	
• Key in OFF position. • Disconnect: Multifunction Switch C202a. • Carry out the multifunction switch component test. Refer to "Wiring Diagrams" • **Did the multifunction switch pass the component test?**	**Yes** GO to <u>J2</u>. **No** INSTALL a new multifunction switch.
J2 CHECK CIRCUIT 1302 (WH/LG) FOR AN OPEN	
• Measure the resistance between multifunction switch C202a-4, circuit 1302 (WH/LG), harness side and ground. • Is the resistance less than 5 ohms?	**Yes** GO to <u>J3</u>. **No** REPAIR the circuit. TEST the system for normal operation.
J3 CHECK CIRCUIT 410 (WH/OG) FOR AN OPEN	
• Key in OFF position. • Disconnect: Rear Window Wiper Motor C4171. • Measure the resistance between multifunction switch C202a-8, circuit 410 (WH/OG), harness side and rear window wiper motor C4171-6, circuit 410 (WH/OG), harness side. • Is the resistance less than 5 ohms?	**Yes** Go To Pinpoint Test K to diagnose the washer circuits. **No** REPAIR the circuit. TEST the system for normal operation.

LTV0500000002571

Fig. 11   Test J: Rear Wipe & Wash Function Does Not Operate

Test Step	Result / Action to Take
• Are the resistances less than 5 ohms?	
H4 CHECK FOR CORRECT WIPER MOTOR OPERATION	

• Disconnect all wiper motor connectors.
• Check for:
  ▪ corrosion
  ▪ pushed-out pins
• Connect all wiper motor connectors and make sure they seat correctly.
• Operate the system and verify the concern is still present.
• **Is the concern still present?**
	Yes
	GO to <u>H5</u>.
	
	No
	The system is operating correctly at this time. Concern may have been caused by a loose or corroded connector. TEST the system for normal operation.

H5 CHECK THE REAR WINDOW WIPER MOTOR	
• Carry out the rear window wiper motor component test as outlined • **Did the rear window wiper motor pass the component test?**	**Yes** The system is operating correctly at this time. Concern may have been caused or binding or incorrect pivot arm adjustment. TEST the system for normal operation. **No** INSTALL a new rear window wiper motor.

LTV0500000002570

Fig. 10   Test H: Intermittent Rear Wiper Speed Does Not Operate Correctly (Part 2 of 2)

Test Step	Result / Action to Take
K1 CHECK CIRCUIT 1300 (VT) FOR GROUND	
• Disconnect: Windshield Wiper Motor C1348. • Key in ON position. • Measure the resistance between windshield wiper motor C1348-12, circuit 1300 (VT), harness side and ground while depressing the multifunction switch to the windshield wiper WASH position. • Is the resistance less than 5 ohms?	**Yes** GO to <u>K3</u>. **No** GO to <u>K2</u>.
K2 CHECK THE MULTIFUNCTION SWITCH	
• Key in OFF position. • Disconnect: Multifunction Switch C202a. • Carry out the multifunction switch component test. Refer to "Wiring Diagrams" • **Did the multifunction switch pass the component test?**	**Yes** REPAIR circuit 1300 (VT) for an open. TEST the system for normal operation. **No** INSTALL a new multifunction switch..
K3 CHECK CIRCUIT 941 (BK/WH) FOR GROUND	
• Key in OFF position. • Connect: Windshield Wiper Motor C1348. • Disconnect: Washer Pump Motor C137. • Measure the resistance between washer pump motor C137-2, circuit 941 (BK/WH) harness side and ground.	**Yes** GO to <u>K4</u>. **No** GO to <u>K8</u>.

LTV0500000002572

Fig. 12   Test K: Washer Pump Is Inoperative (Part 1 of 4)

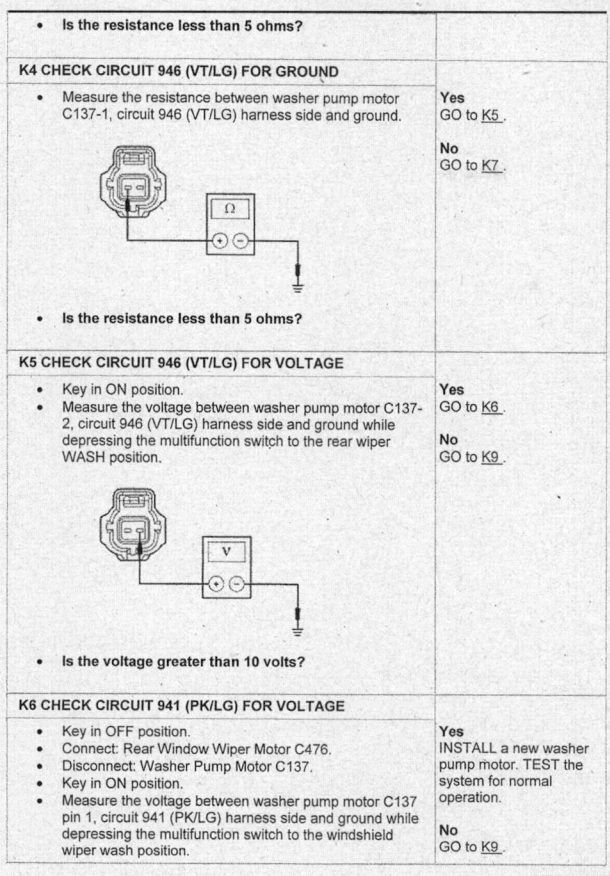

Test Step	Result / Action to Take
• Is the resistance less than 5 ohms?	
K4 CHECK CIRCUIT 946 (VT/LG) FOR GROUND	
• Measure the resistance between washer pump motor C137-1, circuit 946 (VT/LG) harness side and ground. • Is the resistance less than 5 ohms?	**Yes** GO to K5. **No** GO to K7.
K5 CHECK CIRCUIT 946 (VT/LG) FOR VOLTAGE	
• Key in ON position. • Measure the voltage between washer pump motor C137-2, circuit 946 (VT/LG) harness side and ground while depressing the multifunction switch to the rear wiper WASH position. • Is the voltage greater than 10 volts?	**Yes** GO to K6. **No** GO to K9.
K6 CHECK CIRCUIT 941 (PK/LG) FOR VOLTAGE	
• Key in OFF position. • Connect: Rear Window Wiper Motor C476. • Disconnect: Washer Pump Motor C137. • Key in ON position. • Measure the voltage between washer pump motor C137 pin 1, circuit 941 (PK/LG) harness side and ground while depressing the multifunction switch to the windshield wiper wash position.	**Yes** INSTALL a new washer pump motor. TEST the system for normal operation. **No** GO to K9.

Fig. 12   Test K: Washer Pump Is Inoperative (Part 2 of 4)

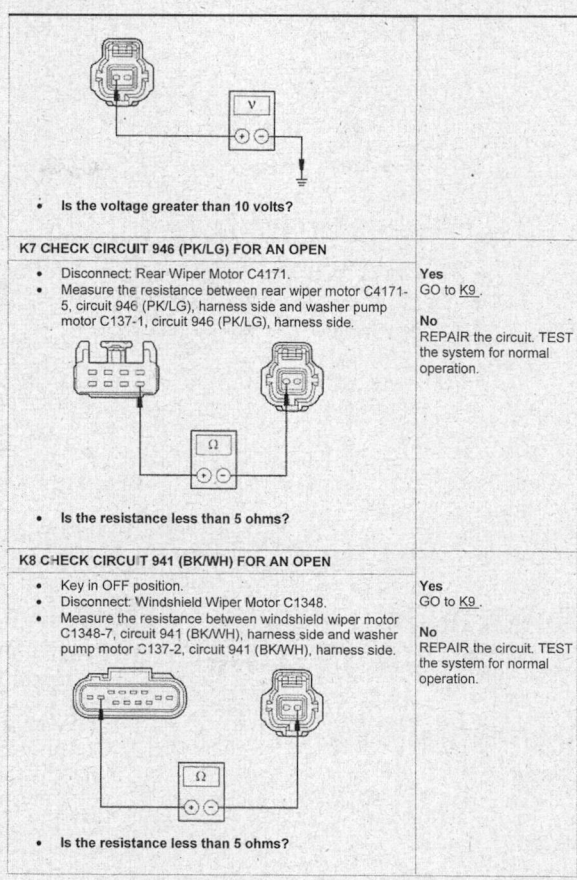

Test Step	Result / Action to Take
• Is the voltage greater than 10 volts?	
K7 CHECK CIRCUIT 946 (PK/LG) FOR AN OPEN	
• Disconnect: Rear Wiper Motor C4171. • Measure the resistance between rear wiper motor C4171-5, circuit 946 (PK/LG), harness side and washer pump motor C137-1, circuit 946 (PK/LG), harness side. • Is the resistance less than 5 ohms?	**Yes** GO to K9. **No** REPAIR the circuit. TEST the system for normal operation.
K8 CHECK CIRCUIT 941 (BK/WH) FOR AN OPEN	
• Key in OFF position. • Disconnect: Windshield Wiper Motor C1348. • Measure the resistance between windshield wiper motor C1348-7, circuit 941 (BK/WH), harness side and washer pump motor C137-2, circuit 941 (BK/WH), harness side. • Is the resistance less than 5 ohms?	**Yes** GO to K9. **No** REPAIR the circuit. TEST the system for normal operation.

Fig. 12   Test K: Washer Pump Is Inoperative (Part 3 of 4)

Test Step	Result / Action to Take
K9 CHECK FOR CORRECT WIPER MOTOR OPERATION	

• Disconnect all wiper motor connectors.
 • Check for:
   ▪ corrosion
   ▪ pushed-out pins
 • Connect all wiper motor connectors and make sure they seat correctly.
 • Operate the system and verify the concern is still present.
 • **Is the concern still present?**
	Yes
	 For the windshield wiper motor, GO to K10. For the rear window wiper motor, GO to K11.
	
	 No
	 The system is operating correctly at this time. Concern may have been caused by a loose or corroded connector. TEST the system for normal operation.

K10 CHECK THE WINDSHIELD WIPER MOTOR	
• Key in OFF position. • Disconnect: Windshield Wiper Motor C1348. • Carry out the windshield wiper motor component test as outlined • **Did the windshield wiper motor pass the component test?**	**Yes** The system is operating correctly at this time. Concern may have been caused by binding or incorrect pivot arm adjustment. TEST the system for normal operation. **No** INSTALL a new windshield wiper motor.
K11 CHECK THE REAR WINDOW WIPER MOTOR	
• Carry out the rear window wiper motor component test as outlined • **Did the rear window wiper motor pass the component test?**	**Yes** The system is operating correctly at this time. Concern may have been caused by binding or incorrect pivot arm adjustment. TEST the system for normal operation. **No** INSTALL a new rear window wiper motor.

Fig. 12   Test K: Washer Pump Is Inoperative (Part 4 of 4)

Test Step	Result / Action to Take
L1 CHECK THE PCM — MONITOR THE VSS	
• Monitor the VSS while driving the vehicle from 0 to 88.5 kph (55 mph). • **Does the VSS agree with the PCM PIDs?**	**Yes** GO to L2. **No** Check Vehicle Speed Sensor VSS and circuit.
L2 CHECK CIRCUIT 679 (GY/BK) FOR AN OPEN	
• Disconnect: PCM C175a. • Disconnect: Windshield Wiper Motor C1348. • Measure the resistance between PCM C175a-7, circuit 679 (GY/BK), harness side and windshield wiper motor C1348-4, circuit 679 (GY/BK), harness side. • Is the resistance less than 5 ohms?	**Yes** GO to L3. **No** REPAIR the circuit. CLEAR the DTCs. REPEAT the self-test.
L3 CHECK CIRCUIT 679 (GY/BK) FOR A SHORT TO GROUND	
• Measure the resistance between PCM C175a-7, circuit 679 (GY/BK), harness side and ground. • Is the resistance greater than 10,000 ohms?	**Yes** GO to L4. **No** REPAIR the circuit. CLEAR the DTCs. REPEAT the self-test.
L4 CHECK FOR CORRECT WIPER MOTOR OPERATION	
• Disconnect all wiper motor connectors.	**Yes**

Fig. 13   Test L: Speed Dependent Interval Mode Does Not Operate Correctly (Part 1 of 2)

• Check for: ▪ corrosion ▪ pushed-out pins • Connect all wiper motor connectors and make sure they seat correctly. • Operate the system and verify the concern is still present. • **Is the concern still present?**	GO to L5. **No** The system is operating correctly at this time. Concern may have been caused by a loose or corroded connector. TEST the system for normal operation.
L5 CHECK THE WINDSHIELD WIPER MOTOR • Key in OFF position. • Disconnect: Windshield Wiper Motor C1348. • Carry out the windshield wiper motor component test as outlined in this section. • **Did the windshield wiper motor pass the component test?**	**Yes** The system is operating correctly at this time. Concern may have been caused by binding or incorrect pivot arm adjustment. TEST the system for normal operation. **No** INSTALL a new windshield wiper motor.

LTV0500000002577

Fig. 13 Test L: Speed Dependent Interval Mode Does Not Operate Correctly (Part 2 of 2)

COMPONENT DIAGNOSIS & TESTING

Windshield Wiper Motor

FRONT

When connecting the power and ground test leads to the windshield wiper motor terminals, care must be taken to not short terminals between power and ground, as well as making sure the logic ground, pin 3, **Fig. 14**, is always securely connected to prevent permanent windshield wiper motor module damage.

1. Disconnect wiper motor electrical connector, then connect No.1 green lead from No. 2 SABRE tester or equivalent, battery ground (-) post.
2. Connect red lead No. 3 from SABRE tester or equivalent to wiper motor, component side connector ground and logic ground pins No. 6 and No. 3.
3. Connect battery positive cable to windshield wiper motor battery and logic positive pins No. 5 and No. 8.
4. Test low speed mode by connecting a separate set of test leads from battery ground (-) post to windshield wiper motor component side pins, No. 9 and 10. When these pins are grounded, windshield wiper motor operation should now be in low speed mode.
5. Test high speed mode by connecting a separate set of test leads from battery ground (-) post to windshield wiper motor component side pins No. 1, 9, and 10. When these pins are grounded, windshield wiper motor operation should now be in high speed mode.

REAR

1. Disconnect wiper motor electrical connector, then connect No.1 green lead, **Fig. 15**, from No. 2 SABRE tester or equivalent, battery ground (-) post.
2. Connect red lead No. 3 from SABRE tester or equivalent to wiper motor, component side connector ground pins No. 1 and No. 2.
3. Connect battery positive cable to windshield wiper motor battery and logic positive pins No. 3 and No. 4.
4. Test ON mode by connecting a separate set of test leads from battery ground (-) post to windshield wiper motor pins 6 and 7. When these pins are grounded, the rear window wiper motor operation should now be in ON mode.

Washer Pump Relay (Integral)

FRONT

Test the windshield wiper motor internal washer relay function by measuring the voltage between the windshield wiper motor component side pin No. 7, **Fig. 14**, and ground while grounding the windshield wiper motor component side pin No. 12. When wash command input pin No. 12 is grounded, measured voltage should read 10 volts or greater.

REAR

Test the rear wiper motor internal washer relay function by measuring the voltage between the rear wiper motor component side pin No. 5, **Fig. 15**, and ground. When wash command input pin No. 6 is grounded, measured voltage should read 10 volts or greater.

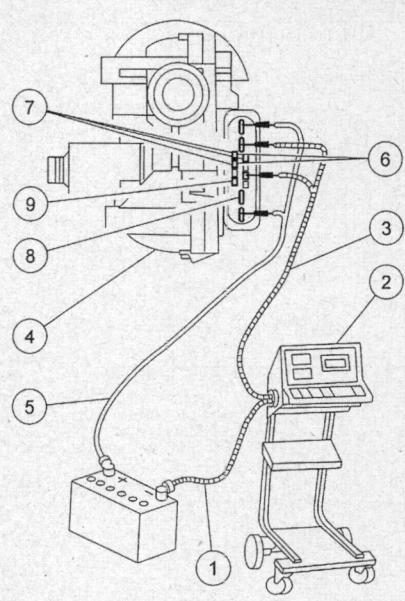

1. Green lead
2. SABRE battery & electrical tester
3. Red lead
4. Wiper Motor
5. Battery positive lead
6. Logic ground pins
7. Pins No. 1, 9 & 10
8. Pin No. 7

LTV0500000001882

Fig. 14 Front wiper motor terminal locations & tester connections

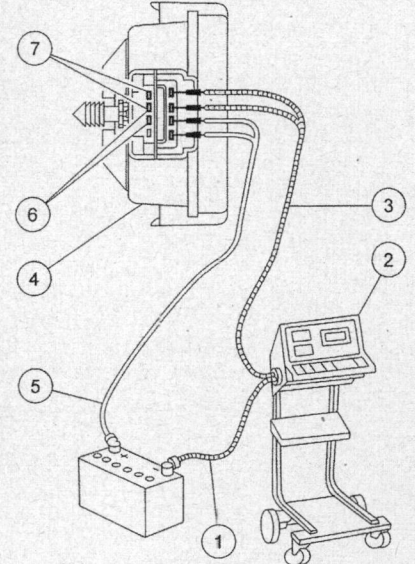

1. Green lead
2. SABRE battery & electrical tester
3. Red lead
4. Wiper Motor
5. Battery positive cable
6. Pins No. 6 & 7
7. Pin No. 5

LTV0500000002382

Fig. 15 Rear wiper motor terminal locations & tester connections

Escape & Mariner

NOTE: On Air Bag Equipped Models, Refer To "Air Bag System Precautions" Located In The Front Of This Manual For System Disarming & Arming Procedures.

NOTE: "Electrical Symbol & Wire Color Code Identification" Located In The Front Of This Manual May Be Used As An Aid When Using Wiring Diagrams Found In This Section.

NOTE: Refer To "Computer Relearn Procedures" Located In The Front Of This Manual When Battery Power To The Computer Has Been Interrupted.

INDEX

	Page No.		Page No.		Page No.
Component Diagnosis &		Accessing Diagnostic Trouble		2005–06	3-11
Testing	3-26	Codes	3-11	Diagnostic Trouble Code	
Diagnostic Chart Index	3-14	Clearing Diagnostic Trouble		Interpretation	3-11
Precautions	3-11	Codes	3-11	Wiring Diagrams	3-11
Battery Ground Cable	3-11	Diagnostic Tests	3-11		
System Diagnosis & Testing	3-11	2002–04	3-11		

PRECAUTIONS

Battery Ground Cable

Prior to service, disconnect battery ground cable and isolate as required.

SYSTEM DIAGNOSIS & TESTING

Accessing Diagnostic Trouble Codes

Connect a suitably programmed scan tool and Vehicle Communication Module (VCM) with appropriate adapters, or equivalents, to the Data Link Connector (DCL) located in the passenger compartment beneath the instrument panel. Follow tool manufacturer's instructions for accessing speed control Diagnostic Trouble Codes (DTC).

Code	Description
B1244	Wiper Rear Motor Run Relay Coil Circuit Failure
B1245	Wiper Rear Motor Run Relay Coil Circuit Short to Battery
B1614	Wiper Rear Mode Select Switch Circuit Short To Ground

Fig. 1 Diagnostic trouble code interpretation

Diagnostic Trouble Code Interpretation

Refer to **Fig. 1** for diagnostic trouble code interpretation.

Wiring Diagrams

Refer to **Figs. 2 through 4** for wiring diagrams.

Diagnostic Tests

2002–04

Refer to **Figs. 5 through 15** for diagnostic tests.

2005–06

Refer to **Figs. 16 through 26** for diagnostic tests.

Clearing Diagnostic Trouble Codes

Connect a suitably programmed scan tool and Vehicle Communication Module (VCM) with appropriate adapters, or equivalents, to the Data Link Connector (DCL) located in the passenger compartment beneath the instrument panel. Follow tool manufacturer's instructions for accessing speed control Diagnostic Trouble Codes (DTC).

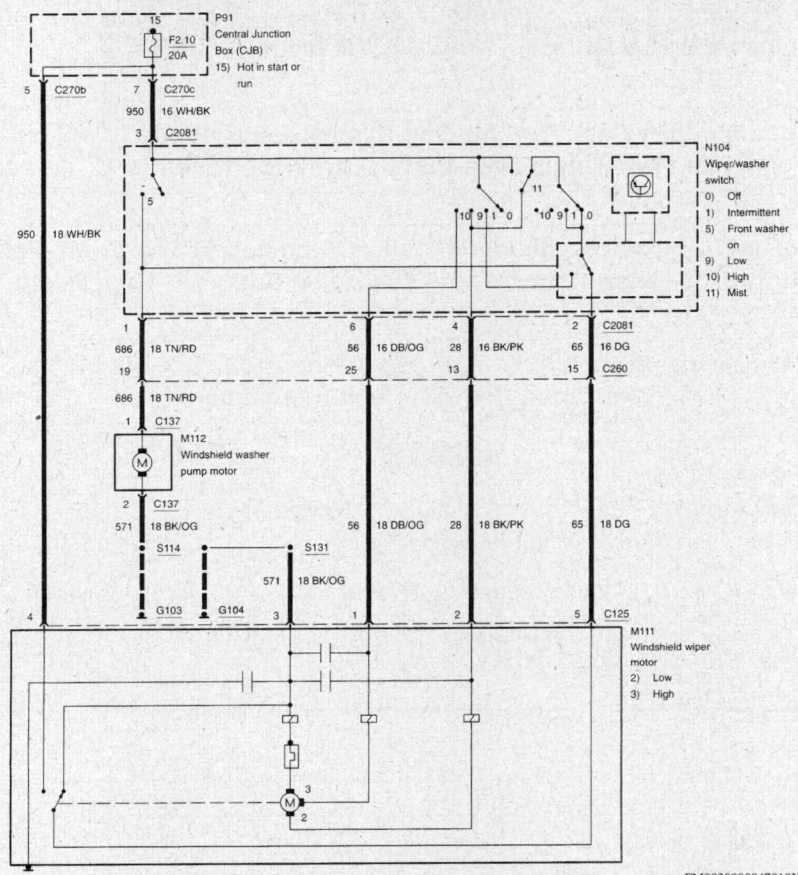

Fig. 2 Wiring diagram (Part 1 of 2). 2002–04

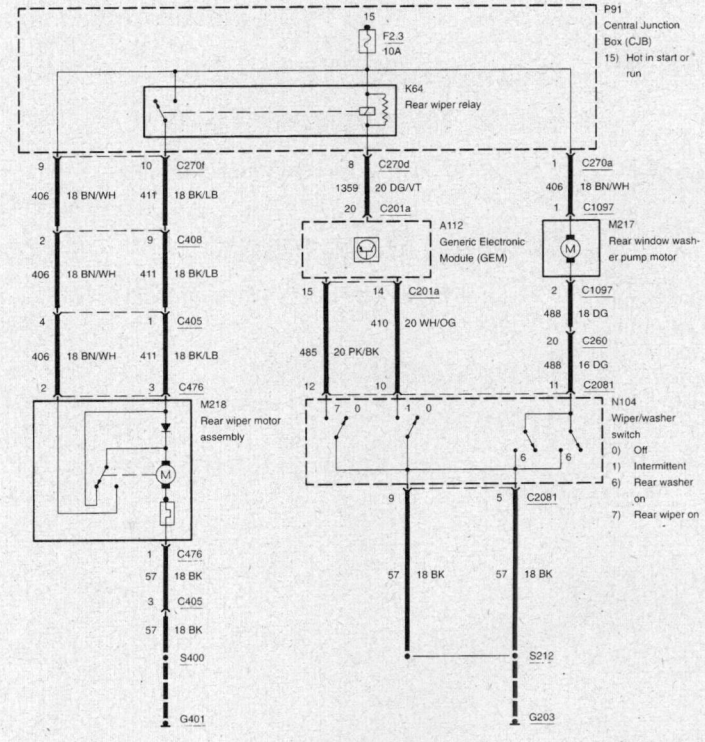

Fig. 2 Wiring diagram (Part 2 of 2). 2002–04

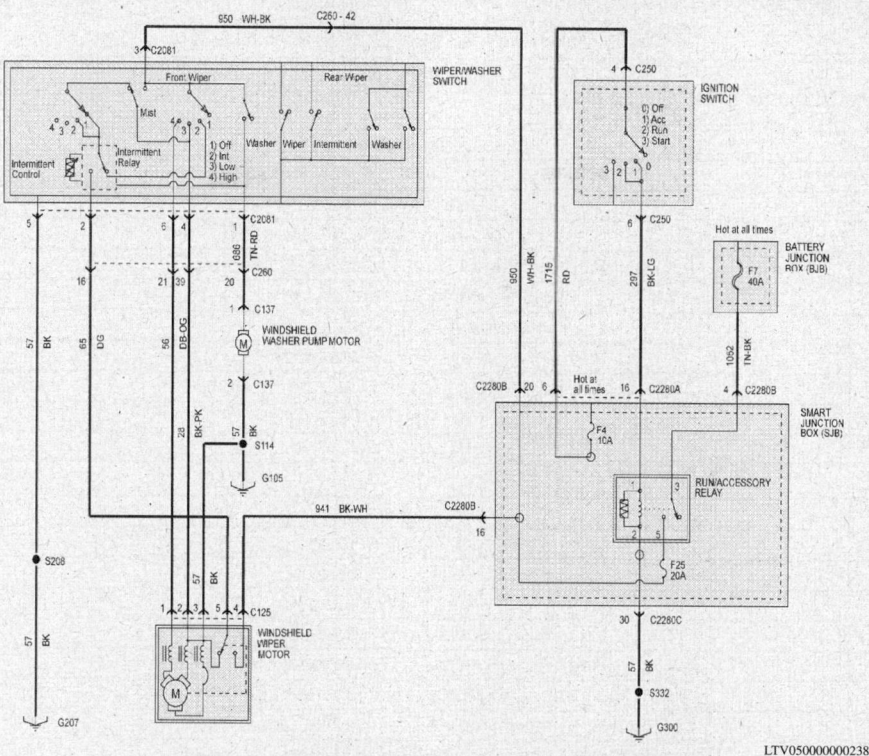

Fig. 3 Wiring diagram (Front). 2005–06

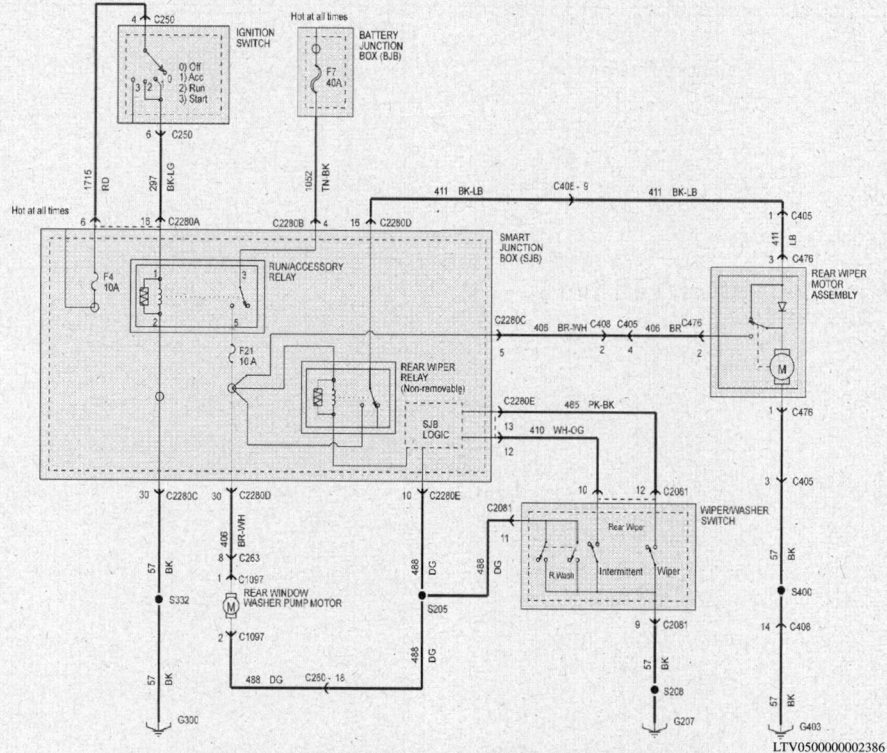

Fig. 4 Wiring diagram (Rear). 2005–06

DIAGNOSTIC CHART INDEX

Test	Code	Description	Page No.	Fig. No.
2002–04				
A	—	Wipers Inoperative	3-14	5
B	—	Wipers Stay On Continuously	3-15	6
C	—	High Speed Wipers Do Not Operate Properly	3-15	7
D	—	Low Speed Wipers Do Not Operate Properly	3-15	8
E	—	Intermittent Wiper Mode Does Not Operate Properly	3-16	9
F	—	Washer Pump Inoperative	3-16	10
G	—	Rear Wipers Inoperative	3-16	11
H	—	Rear Wiper Stays On Continuously	3-18	12
I	—	Intermittent Rear Wipers Do Not Operate Properly	3-19	13
J	—	Rear Wipers Do Not Park	3-20	14
K	—	Rear Washer Pump Inoperative	3-20	15
2005–06				
—	—	Symptom Tests	3-21	16
A	—	Front Wipers Are Inoperative	3-21	17
B	B1245	Rear Wiper Is Inoperative	3-22	18
C	—	Front Wipers Stay On Continuously	3-23	19
D	B1245	Rear Wiper Stays On Continuously	3-23	20
	B1614	Rear Wiper Stays On Continuously	3-23	20
E	—	Front High Speed Wipers Do Not Operate Correctly	3-24	21
F	—	Front Low Speed & Intermittent Wipers Do Not Operate Correctly	3-24	22
G	—	Rear Intermittent Wiper Speed Does Not Operate Correctly	3-24	23
H	—	Front Washer Pump Is Inoperative	3-25	24
I	—	Rear Wash & Wipe Function Does Not Operate	3-25	25
J	—	Front Wipers Do Not Park In Correct Position	3-26	26

CONDITIONS	DETAILS/RESULTS/ACTIONS
A1 CHECK THE WIPER/WASHER SWITCH CIRCUIT 950 (WH/BK) FOR VOLTAGE	

Wiper/Washer Switch
C2081

FM9020000836010X

Fig. 5   Test A: Wipers Inoperative (Part 1 of 3).
2002–04

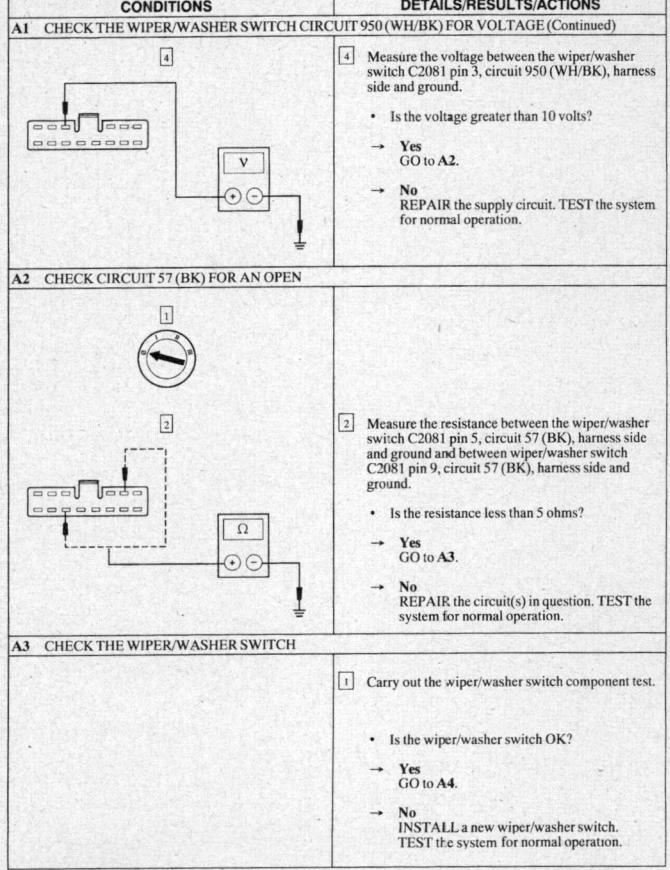

Fig. 5   Test A: Wipers Inoperative (Part 2 of 3).
2002–04

FM9020000836020X

CONDITIONS	DETAILS/RESULTS/ACTIONS
A4 CHECK CIRCUIT 571 (BK/OG) FOR AN OPEN	

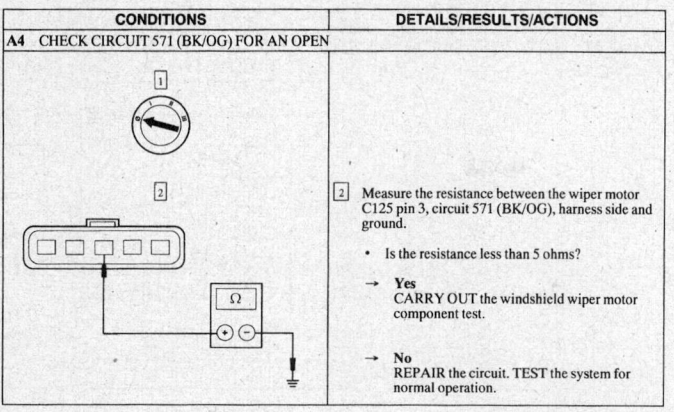

[2] Measure the resistance between the wiper motor C125 pin 3, circuit 571 (BK/OG), harness side and ground.

- Is the resistance less than 5 ohms?

→ **Yes**
CARRY OUT the windshield wiper motor component test.

→ **No**
REPAIR the circuit. TEST the system for normal operation.

FM9020000836030X

Fig. 5 Test A: Wipers Inoperative (Part 3 of 3). 2002–04

CONDITIONS	DETAILS/RESULTS/ACTIONS
B2 CHECK CIRCUIT 56 (DB/OG) FOR A SHORT TO VOLTAGE	

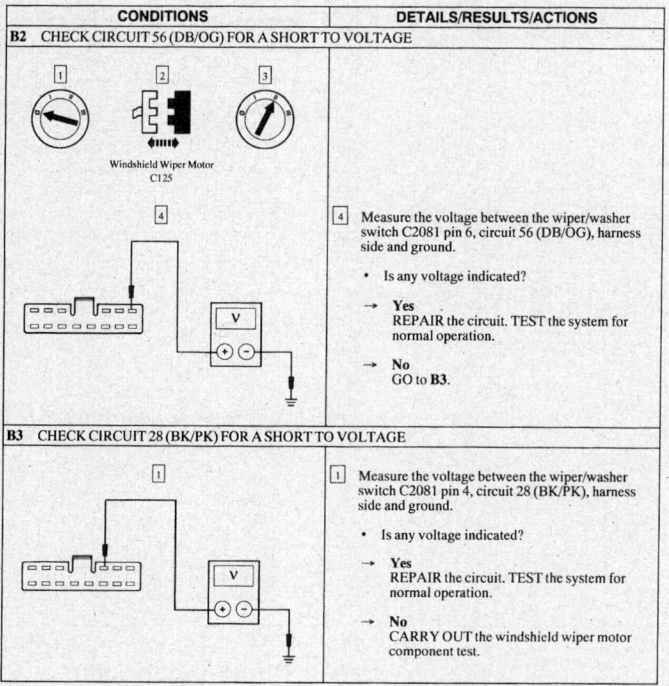

[4] Measure the voltage between the wiper/washer switch C2081 pin 6, circuit 56 (DB/OG), harness side and ground.

- Is any voltage indicated?

→ **Yes**
REPAIR the circuit. TEST the system for normal operation.

→ **No**
GO to **B3**.

CONDITIONS	DETAILS/RESULTS/ACTIONS
B3 CHECK CIRCUIT 28 (BK/PK) FOR A SHORT TO VOLTAGE	

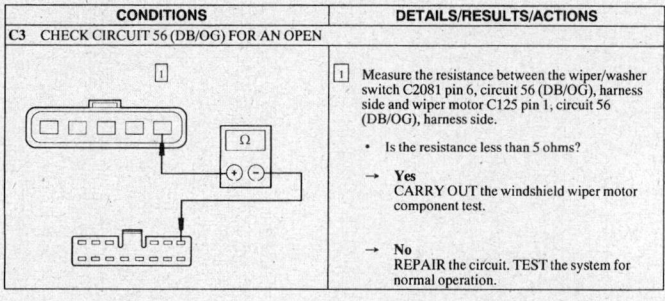

[1] Measure the voltage between the wiper/washer switch C2081 pin 4, circuit 28 (BK/PK), harness side and ground.

- Is any voltage indicated?

→ **Yes**
REPAIR the circuit. TEST the system for normal operation.

→ **No**
CARRY OUT the windshield wiper motor component test.

FM9020000837020X

Fig. 6 Test B: Wipers Stay On Continuously (Part 2 of 2). 2002–04

CONDITIONS	DETAILS/RESULTS/ACTIONS
C3 CHECK CIRCUIT 56 (DB/OG) FOR AN OPEN	

[1] Measure the resistance between the wiper/washer switch C2081 pin 6, circuit 56 (DB/OG), harness side and wiper motor C125 pin 1, circuit 56 (DB/OG), harness side.

- Is the resistance less than 5 ohms?

→ **Yes**
CARRY OUT the windshield wiper motor component test.

→ **No**
REPAIR the circuit. TEST the system for normal operation.

FM9020000838020X

Fig. 7 Test C: High Speed Wipers Do Not Operate Properly (Part 2 of 2). 2002–04

CONDITIONS	DETAILS/RESULTS/ACTIONS
B1	

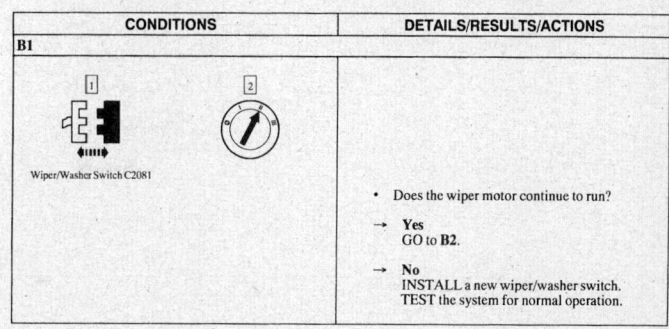

Wiper/Washer Switch C2081

- Does the wiper motor continue to run?

→ **Yes**
GO to **B2**.

→ **No**
INSTALL a new wiper/washer switch. TEST the system for normal operation.

FM9020000837010X

Fig. 6 Test B: Wipers Stay On Continuously (Part 1 of 2). 2002–04

CONDITIONS	DETAILS/RESULTS/ACTIONS
C1 CHECK THE WIPER/WASHER SWITCH	

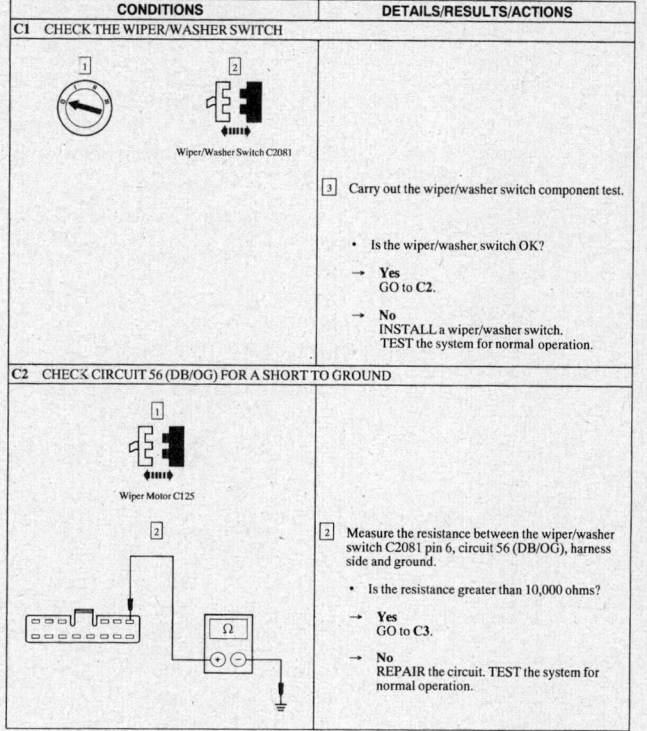

Wiper/Washer Switch C2081

[3] Carry out the wiper/washer switch component test.

- Is the wiper/washer switch OK?

→ **Yes**
GO to **C2**.

→ **No**
INSTALL a wiper/washer switch. TEST the system for normal operation.

CONDITIONS	DETAILS/RESULTS/ACTIONS
C2 CHECK CIRCUIT 56 (DB/OG) FOR A SHORT TO GROUND	

Wiper Motor C125

[2] Measure the resistance between the wiper/washer switch C2081 pin 6, circuit 56 (DB/OG), harness side and ground.

- Is the resistance greater than 10,000 ohms?

→ **Yes**
GO to **C3**.

→ **No**
REPAIR the circuit. TEST the system for normal operation.

FM9020000838010X

Fig. 7 Test C: High Speed Wipers Do Not Operate Properly (Part 1 of 2). 2002–04

CONDITIONS	DETAILS/RESULTS/ACTIONS
D1 CHECK THE WIPER/WASHER SWITCH	

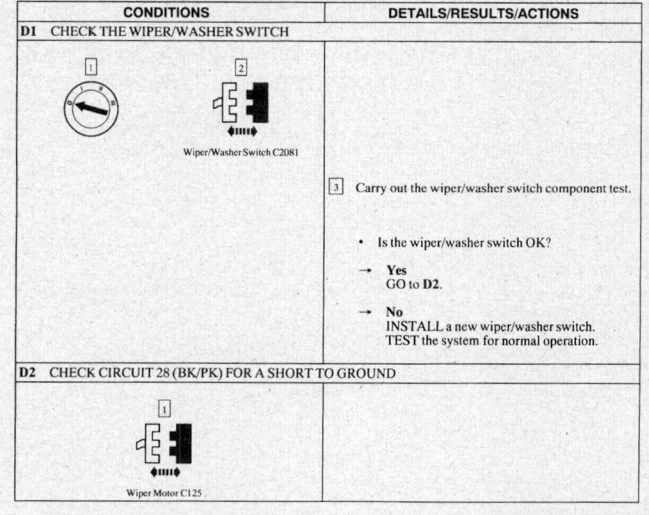

Wiper/Washer Switch C2081

[3] Carry out the wiper/washer switch component test.

- Is the wiper/washer switch OK?

→ **Yes**
GO to **D2**.

→ **No**
INSTALL a new wiper/washer switch. TEST the system for normal operation.

CONDITIONS	DETAILS/RESULTS/ACTIONS
D2 CHECK CIRCUIT 28 (BK/PK) FOR A SHORT TO GROUND	

Wiper Motor C125

FM9020000839010X

Fig. 8 Test D: Low Speed Wipers Do Not Operate Properly (Part 1 of 2). 2002–04

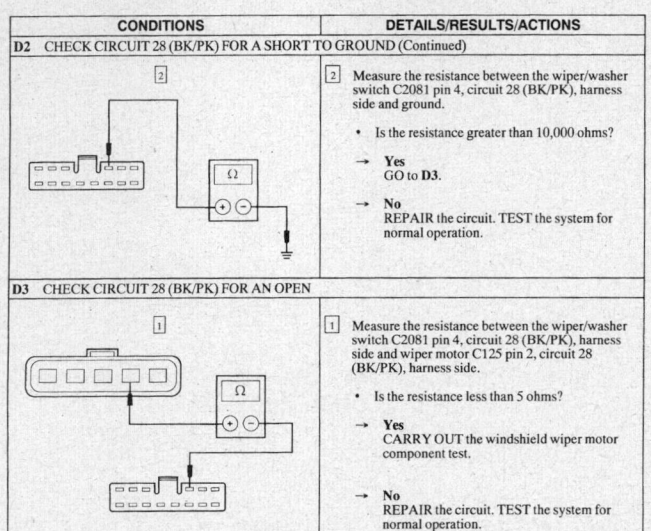

CONDITIONS	DETAILS/RESULTS/ACTIONS
D2 CHECK CIRCUIT 28 (BK/PK) FOR A SHORT TO GROUND (Continued)	**2** Measure the resistance between the wiper/washer switch C2081 pin 4, circuit 28 (BK/PK), harness side and ground. • Is the resistance greater than 10,000 ohms? → **Yes** GO to **D3**. → **No** REPAIR the circuit. TEST the system for normal operation.
D3 CHECK CIRCUIT 28 (BK/PK) FOR AN OPEN	**1** Measure the resistance between the wiper/washer switch C2081 pin 4, circuit 28 (BK/PK), harness side and wiper motor C125 pin 2, circuit 28 (BK/PK), harness side. • Is the resistance less than 5 ohms? → **Yes** CARRY OUT the windshield wiper motor component test. → **No** REPAIR the circuit. TEST the system for normal operation.

FM9020000839020X

Fig. 8 Test D: Low Speed Wipers Do Not Operate Properly (Part 2 of 2). 2002–04

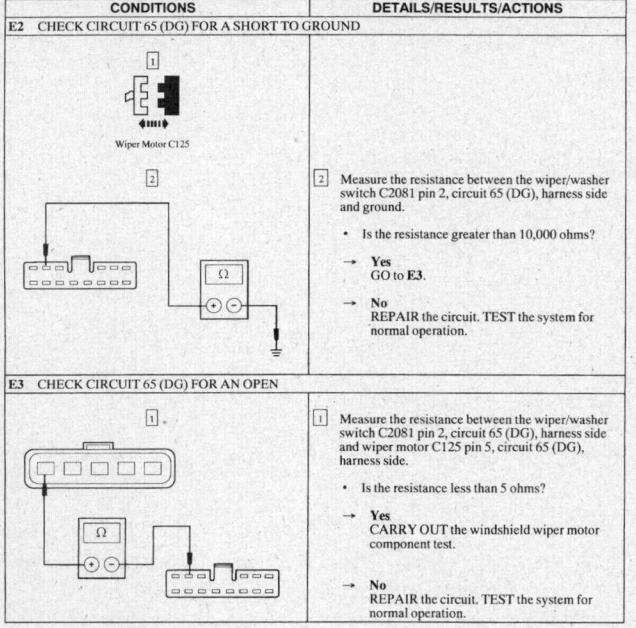

CONDITIONS	DETAILS/RESULTS/ACTIONS
E2 CHECK CIRCUIT 65 (DG) FOR A SHORT TO GROUND	**2** Measure the resistance between the wiper/washer switch C2081 pin 2, circuit 65 (DG), harness side and ground. • Is the resistance greater than 10,000 ohms? → **Yes** GO to **E3**. → **No** REPAIR the circuit. TEST the system for normal operation.
E3 CHECK CIRCUIT 65 (DG) FOR AN OPEN	**1** Measure the resistance between the wiper/washer switch C2081 pin 2, circuit 65 (DG), harness side and wiper motor C125 pin 5, circuit 65 (DG), harness side. • Is the resistance less than 5 ohms? → **Yes** CARRY OUT the windshield wiper motor component test. → **No** REPAIR the circuit. TEST the system for normal operation.

FM9020000840020X

Fig. 9 Test E: Intermittent Wiper Mode Does Not Operate Properly (Part 2 of 2). 2002–04

CONDITIONS	DETAILS/RESULTS/ACTIONS
F3 CHECK CIRCUIT 571E (BK/OG) FOR AN OPEN	**2** Measure the resistance between the washer pump C137 pin 2, circuit 571E (BK/OG) harness side and ground. • Is the resistance less than 5 ohms? → **Yes** INSTALL a new washer pump. TEST the system for normal operation. → **No** REPAIR the circuit. TEST the system for normal operation.

FM9020000841020X

Fig. 10 Test F: Washer Pump Inoperative (Part 2 of 2). 2002–04

CONDITIONS	DETAILS/RESULTS/ACTIONS
E1 CHECK THE OPERATION OF THE LOW-SPEED WIPERS	**1** Check the operation of the low-speed wipers. • Do the low-speed wipers operate correctly? → **Yes** GO to **E2**. → **No** GO to Pinpoint Test D.

FM9020000840010X

Fig. 9 Test E: Intermittent Wiper Mode Does Not Operate Properly (Part 1 of 2). 2002–04

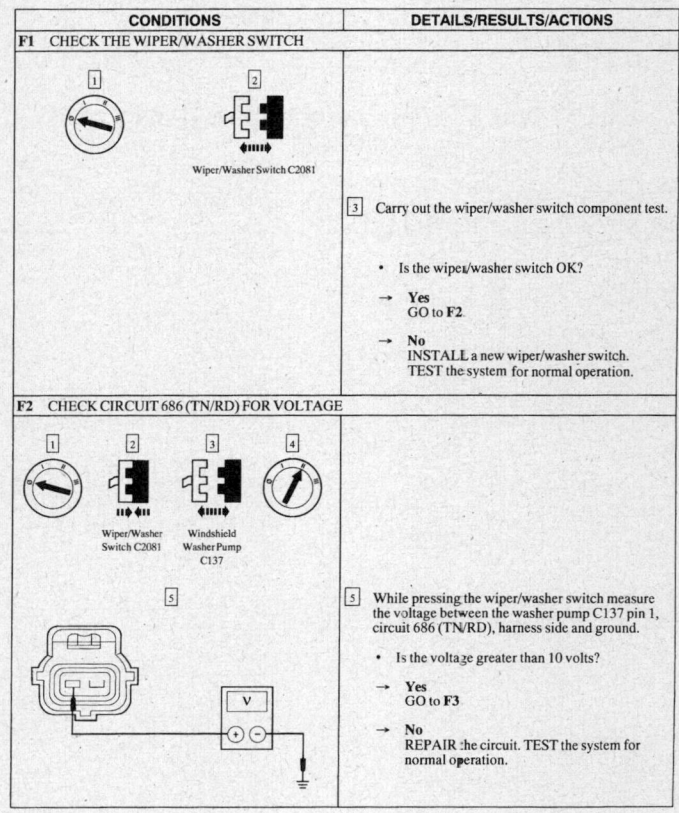

CONDITIONS	DETAILS/RESULTS/ACTIONS
F1 CHECK THE WIPER/WASHER SWITCH	**3** Carry out the wiper/washer switch component test. • Is the wiper/washer switch OK? → **Yes** GO to **F2**. → **No** INSTALL a new wiper/washer switch. TEST the system for normal operation.
F2 CHECK CIRCUIT 686 (TN/RD) FOR VOLTAGE	**5** While pressing the wiper/washer switch measure the voltage between the washer pump C137 pin 1, circuit 686 (TN/RD), harness side and ground. • Is the voltage greater than 10 volts? → **Yes** GO to **F3**. → **No** REPAIR the circuit. TEST the system for normal operation.

FM9020000841010X

Fig. 10 Test F: Washer Pump Inoperative (Part 1 of 2). 2002–04

CONDITIONS	DETAILS/RESULTS/ACTIONS
G1 CHECK THE GENERIC ELECTRONIC MODULE (GEM) DIAGNOSTIC TROUBLE CODES (DTCs)	**1** Use the recorded results from the GEM continuous and on-demand self-test. • Are any DTCs recorded? → **Yes** If DTC B1244, GO to **G5**. If DTC B1245, GO to **G8**. → **No** GO to **G2**.
G2 CHECK THE WIPER/WASHER SWITCH	**2** Place the wiper/washer switch in the ON position.

FM9020000842010X

Fig. 11 Test G: Rear Wipers Inoperative (Part 1 of 8). 2002–04

CONDITIONS	DETAILS/RESULTS/ACTIONS
G2 CHECK THE WIPER/WASHER SWITCH (Continued)	
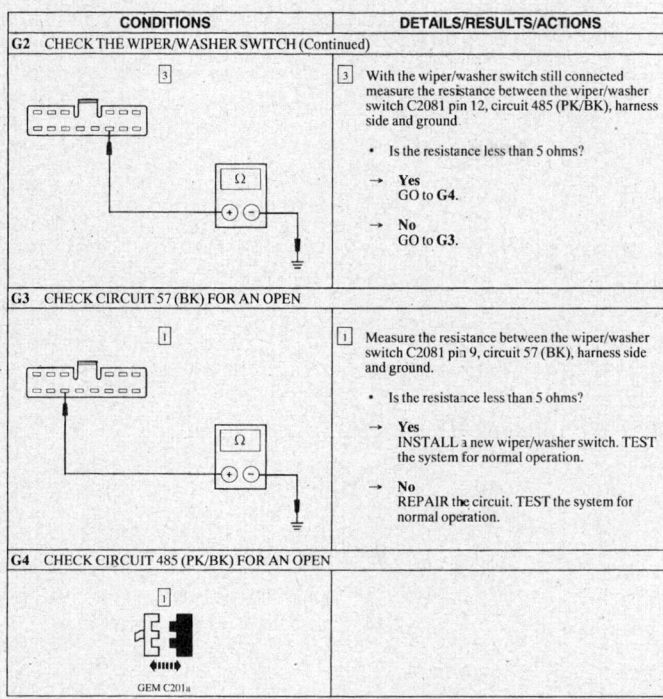	3 With the wiper/washer switch still connected measure the resistance between the wiper/washer switch C2081 pin 12, circuit 485 (PK/BK), harness side and ground. • Is the resistance less than 5 ohms? → **Yes** GO to **G4**. → **No** GO to **G3**.
G3 CHECK CIRCUIT 57 (BK) FOR AN OPEN	
	1 Measure the resistance between the wiper/washer switch C2081 pin 9, circuit 57 (BK), harness side and ground. • Is the resistance less than 5 ohms? → **Yes** INSTALL a new wiper/washer switch. TEST the system for normal operation. → **No** REPAIR the circuit. TEST the system for normal operation.
G4 CHECK CIRCUIT 485 (PK/BK) FOR AN OPEN	

FM9020000842020X

Fig. 11 Test G: Rear Wipers Inoperative (Part 2 of 8). 2002–04

CONDITIONS	DETAILS/RESULTS/ACTIONS
G6 CHECK CIRCUIT 1359 (DG/VT) FOR A SHORT TO GROUND (Continued)	
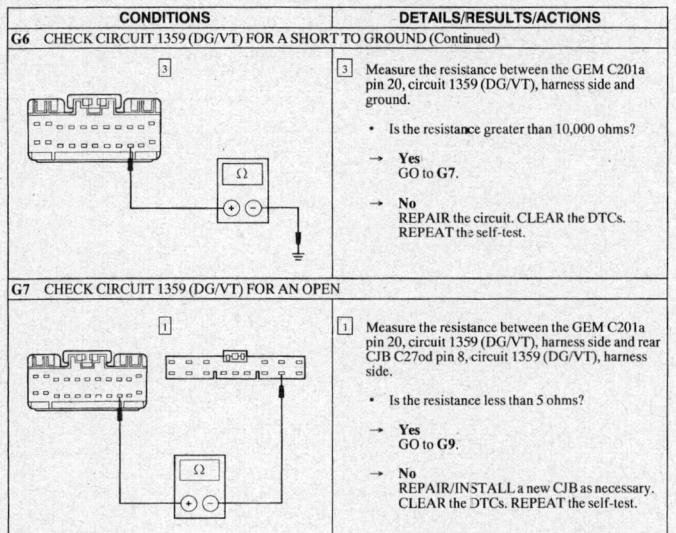	3 Measure the resistance between the GEM C201a pin 20, circuit 1359 (DG/VT), harness side and ground. • Is the resistance greater than 10,000 ohms? → **Yes** GO to **G7**. → **No** REPAIR the circuit. CLEAR the DTCs. REPEAT the self-test.
G7 CHECK CIRCUIT 1359 (DG/VT) FOR AN OPEN	
	1 Measure the resistance between the GEM C201a pin 20, circuit 1359 (DG/VT), harness side and rear CJB C27od pin 8, circuit 1359 (DG/VT), harness side. • Is the resistance less than 5 ohms? → **Yes** GO to **G9**. → **No** REPAIR/INSTALL a new CJB as necessary. CLEAR the DTCs. REPEAT the self-test.

FM9020000842040X

Fig. 11 Test G: Rear Wipers Inoperative (Part 4 of 8). 2002–04

CONDITIONS	DETAILS/RESULTS/ACTIONS
G4 CHECK CIRCUIT 485 (PK/BK) FOR AN OPEN (Continued)	
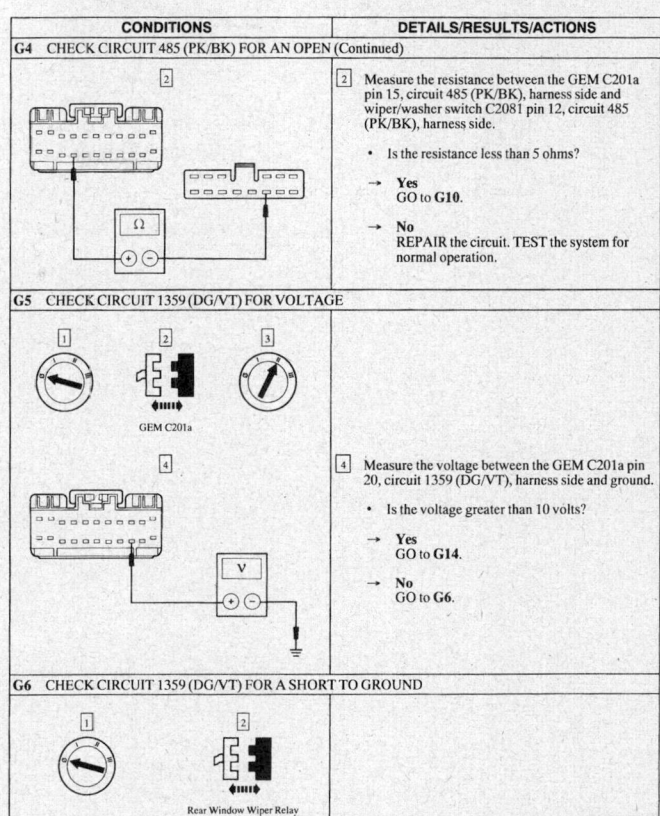	2 Measure the resistance between the GEM C201a pin 15, circuit 485 (PK/BK), harness side and wiper/washer switch C2081 pin 12, circuit 485 (PK/BK), harness side. • Is the resistance less than 5 ohms? → **Yes** GO to **G10**. → **No** REPAIR the circuit. TEST the system for normal operation.
G5 CHECK CIRCUIT 1359 (DG/VT) FOR VOLTAGE	
	4 Measure the voltage between the GEM C201a pin 20, circuit 1359 (DG/VT), harness side and ground. • Is the voltage greater than 10 volts? → **Yes** GO to **G14**. → **No** GO to **G6**.
G6 CHECK CIRCUIT 1359 (DG/VT) FOR A SHORT TO GROUND	

FM9020000842030X

Fig. 11 Test G: Rear Wipers Inoperative (Part 3 of 8). 2002–04

CONDITIONS	DETAILS/RESULTS/ACTIONS
G8 CHECK CIRCUIT 1359 (DG/VT) FOR A SHORT TO VOLTAGE	
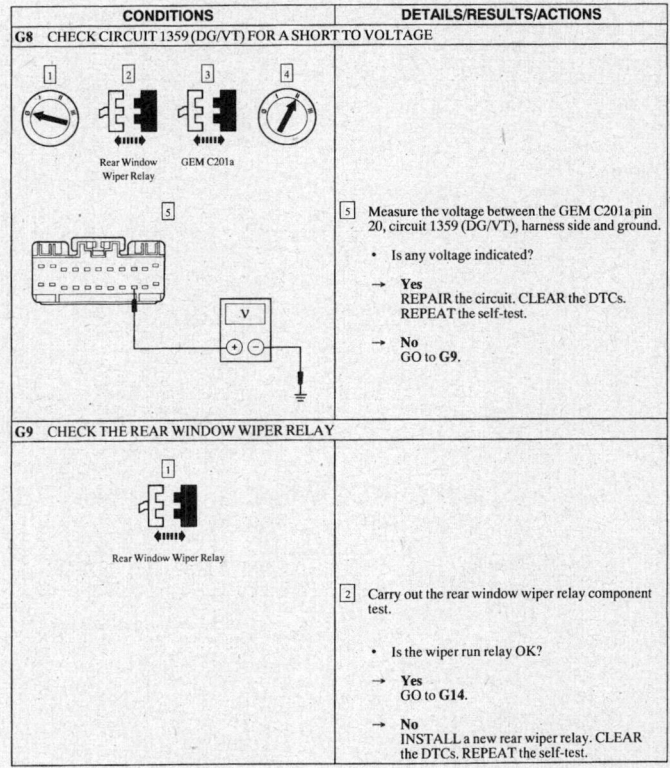	5 Measure the voltage between the GEM C201a pin 20, circuit 1359 (DG/VT), harness side and ground. • Is any voltage indicated? → **Yes** REPAIR the circuit. CLEAR the DTCs. REPEAT the self-test. → **No** GO to **G9**.
G9 CHECK THE REAR WINDOW WIPER RELAY	
	2 Carry out the rear window wiper relay component test. • Is the wiper run relay OK? → **Yes** GO to **G14**. → **No** INSTALL a new rear wiper relay. CLEAR the DTCs. REPEAT the self-test.

FM9020000842050X

Fig. 11 Test G: Rear Wipers Inoperative (Part 5 of 8). 2002–04

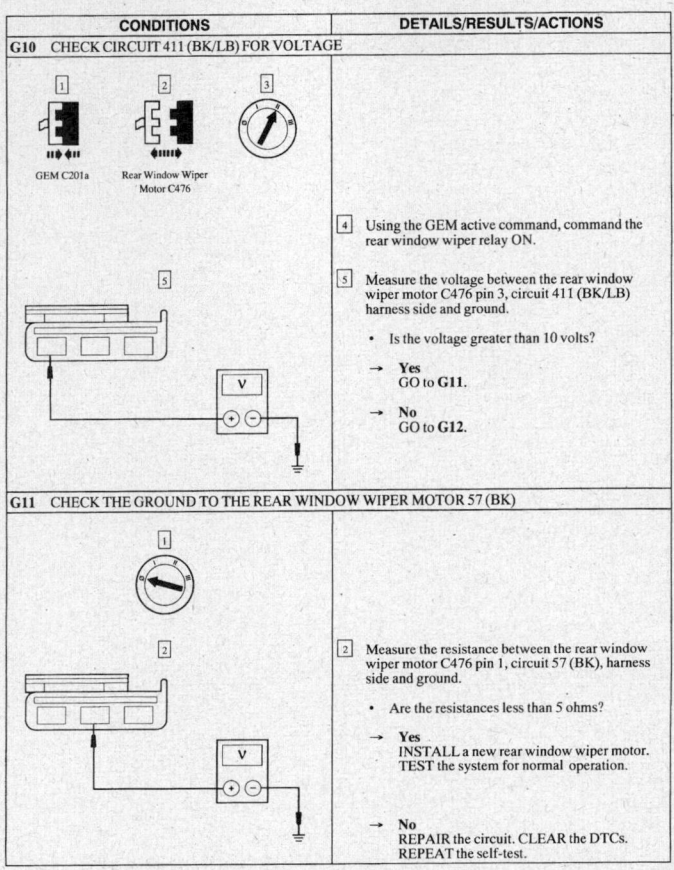

CONDITIONS	DETAILS/RESULTS/ACTIONS
G10 CHECK CIRCUIT 411 (BK/LB) FOR VOLTAGE	
	4 Using the GEM active command, command the rear window wiper relay ON.
	5 Measure the voltage between the rear window wiper motor C476 pin 3, circuit 411 (BK/LB) harness side and ground.
	• Is the voltage greater than 10 volts?
	→ **Yes** GO to **G11**.
	→ **No** GO to **G12**.
G11 CHECK THE GROUND TO THE REAR WINDOW WIPER MOTOR 57 (BK)	
	2 Measure the resistance between the rear window wiper motor C476 pin 1, circuit 57 (BK), harness side and ground.
	• Are the resistances less than 5 ohms?
	→ **Yes** INSTALL a new rear window wiper motor. TEST the system for normal operation.
	→ **No** REPAIR the circuit. CLEAR the DTCs. REPEAT the self-test.

FM9020000842060X

Fig. 11 Test G: Rear Wipers Inoperative (Part 6 of 8). 2002–04

CONDITIONS	DETAILS/RESULTS/ACTIONS
G14 CHECK FOR CORRECT GEM OPERATION (Continued)	
	2 Check for: • corrosion • pushed-out pins
	3 Connect all GEM connectors and make sure they seat correctly.
	4 Operate the system and verify the concern is still present.
	• Is the concern still present?
	→ **Yes** INSTALL a new GEM. CLEAR the DTCs. REPEAT the GEM self-test.
	→ **No** The system is operating correctly at this time. Concern may have been caused by a loose or corroded connector. CLEAR the DTCs. REPEAT the self-test.

FM9020000842080X

Fig. 11 Test G: Rear Wipers Inoperative (Part 8 of 8). 2002–04

CONDITIONS	DETAILS/RESULTS/ACTIONS
H1 CHECK THE GENERIC ELECTRONIC MODULE DIAGNOSTIC TROUBLE CODES (DTCS)	
	1 Use the recorded results from the GEM continuous and on-demand self-test.
	• Are any DTCs recorded?
	→ **Yes** If DTC B1611, GO to **H2**. If DTC B1244, GO to **H4**.
	→ **No** GO to **H6**.

FM9020000843010X

Fig. 12 Test H: Rear Wiper Stays On Continuously (Part 1 of 5). 2002–04

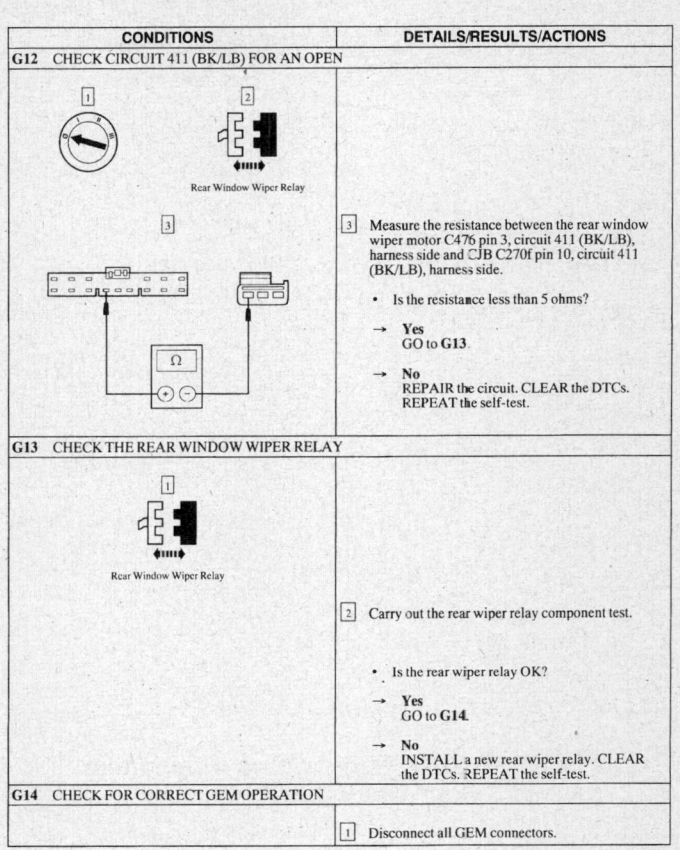

CONDITIONS	DETAILS/RESULTS/ACTIONS
G12 CHECK CIRCUIT 411 (BK/LB) FOR AN OPEN	
	3 Measure the resistance between the rear window wiper motor C476 pin 3, circuit 411 (BK/LB), harness side and CJB C270f pin 10, circuit 411 (BK/LB), harness side.
	• Is the resistance less than 5 ohms?
	→ **Yes** GO to **G13**.
	→ **No** REPAIR the circuit. CLEAR the DTCs. REPEAT the self-test.
G13 CHECK THE REAR WINDOW WIPER RELAY	
	2 Carry out the rear wiper relay component test.
	• Is the rear wiper relay OK?
	→ **Yes** GO to **G14**.
	→ **No** INSTALL a new rear wiper relay. CLEAR the DTCs. REPEAT the self-test.
G14 CHECK FOR CORRECT GEM OPERATION	
	1 Disconnect all GEM connectors.

FM9020000842070X

Fig. 11 Test G: Rear Wipers Inoperative (Part 7 of 8). 2002–04

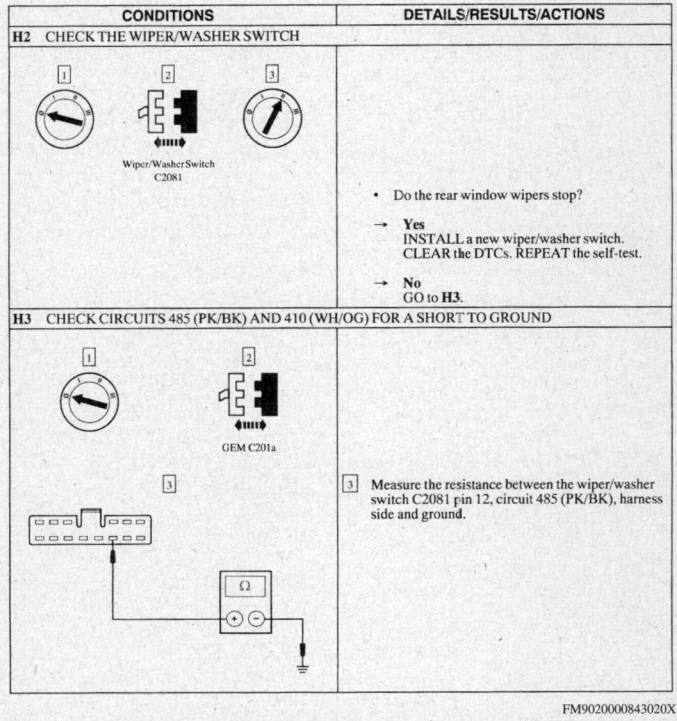

CONDITIONS	DETAILS/RESULTS/ACTIONS
H2 CHECK THE WIPER/WASHER SWITCH	
	• Do the rear window wipers stop?
	→ **Yes** INSTALL a new wiper/washer switch. CLEAR the DTCs. REPEAT the self-test.
	→ **No** GO to **H3**.
H3 CHECK CIRCUITS 485 (PK/BK) AND 410 (WH/OG) FOR A SHORT TO GROUND	
	3 Measure the resistance between the wiper/washer switch C2081 pin 12, circuit 485 (PK/BK), harness side and ground.

FM9020000843020X

Fig. 12 Test H: Rear Wiper Stays On Continuously (Part 2 of 5). 2002–04

CONDITIONS	DETAILS/RESULTS/ACTIONS
H3 CHECK CIRCUITS 485 (PK/BK) AND 410 (WH/OG) FOR A SHORT TO GROUND (Continued)	
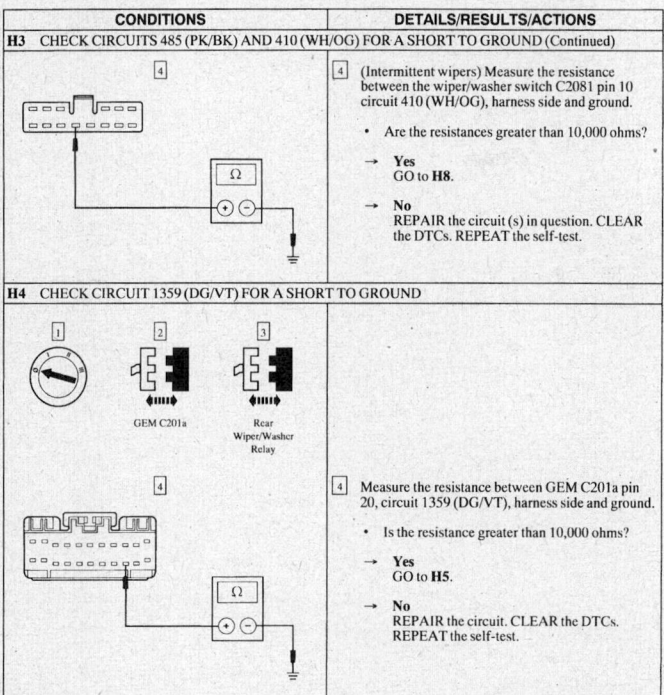	[4] (Intermittent wipers) Measure the resistance between the wiper/washer switch C2081 pin 10 circuit 410 (WH/OG), harness side and ground. • Are the resistances greater than 10,000 ohms? → **Yes** GO to **H8**. → **No** REPAIR the circuit (s) in question. CLEAR the DTCs. REPEAT the self-test.
H4 CHECK CIRCUIT 1359 (DG/VT) FOR A SHORT TO GROUND	
	[4] Measure the resistance between GEM C201a pin 20, circuit 1359 (DG/VT), harness side and ground. • Is the resistance greater than 10,000 ohms? → **Yes** GO to **H5**. → **No** REPAIR the circuit. CLEAR the DTCs. REPEAT the self-test.

FM9020000843030X

Fig. 12 Test H: Rear Wiper Stays On Continuously (Part 3 of 5). 2002–04

CONDITIONS	DETAILS/RESULTS/ACTIONS
H5 CHECK THE REAR WINDOW WIPER RELAY	
	[1] Carry out the rear wiper relay component test. • Is the rear wiper relay OK? → **Yes** GO to **H8**. → **No** INSTALL a new rear wiper relay. CLEAR the DTCs. REPEAT the self-test.
H6 CHECK CIRCUIT 411 (BK/LB) FOR A SHORT TO VOLTAGE	
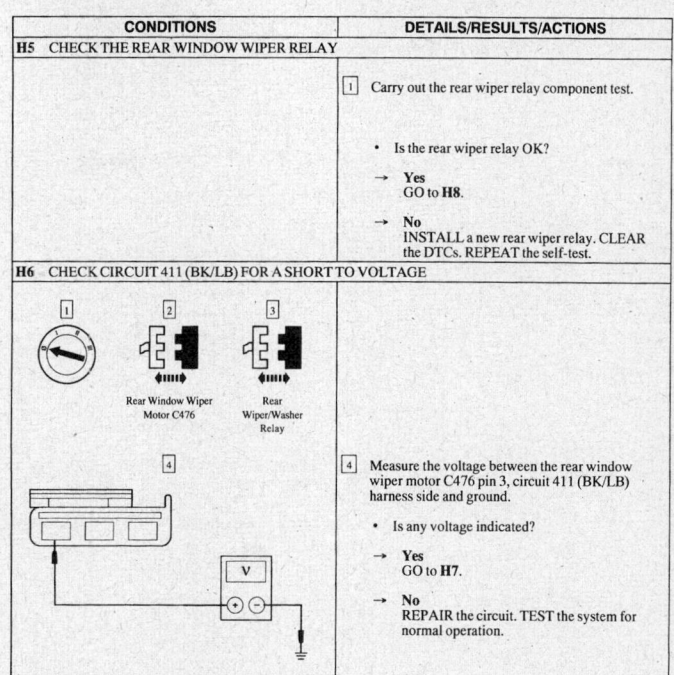	[4] Measure the voltage between the rear window wiper motor C476 pin 3, circuit 411 (BK/LB) harness side and ground. • Is any voltage indicated? → **Yes** GO to **H7**. → **No** REPAIR the circuit. TEST the system for normal operation.

FM9020000843040X

Fig. 12 Test H: Rear Wiper Stays On Continuously (Part 4 of 5). 2002–04

CONDITIONS	DETAILS/RESULTS/ACTIONS
H7 CHECK THE REAR WINDOW WIPER RELAY	
	[1] Carry out the rear wiper relay component test. • Is the wiper run relay OK? → **Yes** INSTALL a new rear window wiper motor. → **No** INSTALL a new rear wiper relay. CLEAR the DTCs. REPEAT the self-test.
H8 CHECK FOR CORRECT GEM OPERATION	
	[1] Disconnect all GEM connectors. [2] Check for: • corrosion • pushed-out pins [3] Connect all GEM connectors and make sure they seat correctly. [4] Operate the system and verify the concern is still present. • Is the concern still present? → **Yes** INSTALL a new GEM. REPEAT the GEM self-test. → **No** The system is operating correctly at this time. Concern may have been caused by a loose or corroded connector. CLEAR the DTCs. REPEAT the self-test.

FM9020000843050X

Fig. 12 Test H: Rear Wiper Stays On Continuously (Part 5 of 5). 2002–04

CONDITIONS	DETAILS/RESULTS/ACTIONS
I1 CHECK THE OPERATION OF THE REAR WINDOW WIPERS	
	[1] Check the operation of the rear window wipers in the ON mode. • Do the rear window wipers operate correctly? → **Yes** GO to **I2**. → **No** GO to Pinpoint Test G.
I2 CHECK THE WIPER/WASHER SWITCH	
	[3] Place the wiper/washer switch in the INT position. [4] Measure the resistance between the GEM C201a pin 14, circuit 410 (WH/OG), harness side and ground. • Is the resistance less than 5 ohms or less? → **Yes** GO to **I4**. → **No** GO to **I3**.
I3 CHECK CIRCUIT 410 (WH/OG) FOR AN OPEN	

FM9020000844010X

Fig. 13 Test I: Intermittent Rear Wipers Do Not Operate Properly (Part 1 of 2). 2002–04

CONDITIONS	DETAILS/RESULTS/ACTIONS
I3 CHECK CIRCUIT 410 (WH/OG) FOR AN OPEN (Continued)	
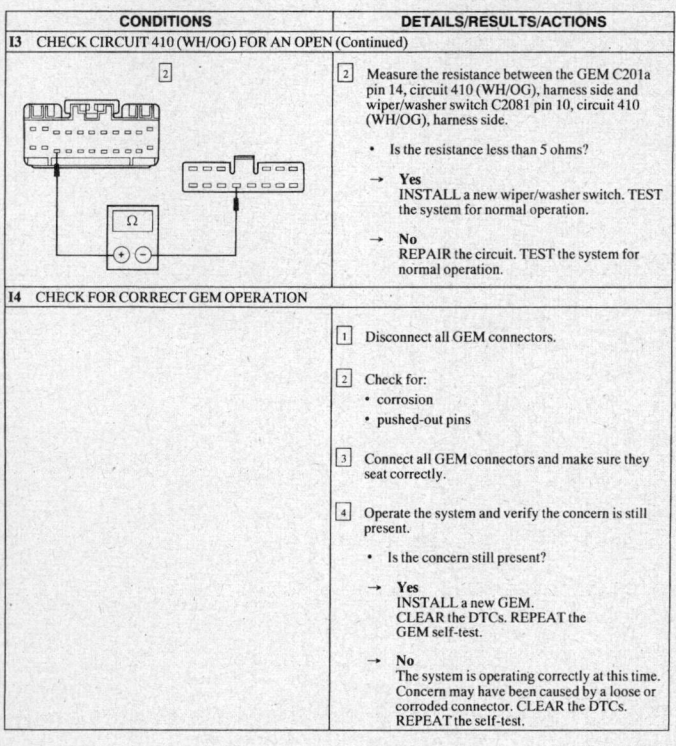	[2] Measure the resistance between the GEM C201a pin 14, circuit 410 (WH/OG), harness side and wiper/washer switch C2081 pin 10, circuit 410 (WH/OG), harness side. • Is the resistance less than 5 ohms? → **Yes** INSTALL a new wiper/washer switch. TEST the system for normal operation. → **No** REPAIR the circuit. TEST the system for normal operation.
I4 CHECK FOR CORRECT GEM OPERATION	
	[1] Disconnect all GEM connectors. [2] Check for: • corrosion • pushed-out pins [3] Connect all GEM connectors and make sure they seat correctly. [4] Operate the system and verify the concern is still present. • Is the concern still present? → **Yes** INSTALL a new GEM. CLEAR the DTCs. REPEAT the GEM self-test. → **No** The system is operating correctly at this time. Concern may have been caused by a loose or corroded connector. CLEAR the DTCs. REPEAT the self-test.

FM9020000844020X

Fig. 13   Test I: Intermittent Rear Wipers Do Not Operate Properly (Part 2 of 2). 2002–04

CONDITIONS	DETAILS/RESULTS/ACTIONS
J1 CHECK CIRCUIT 406 (BN/YE) FOR VOLTAGE	
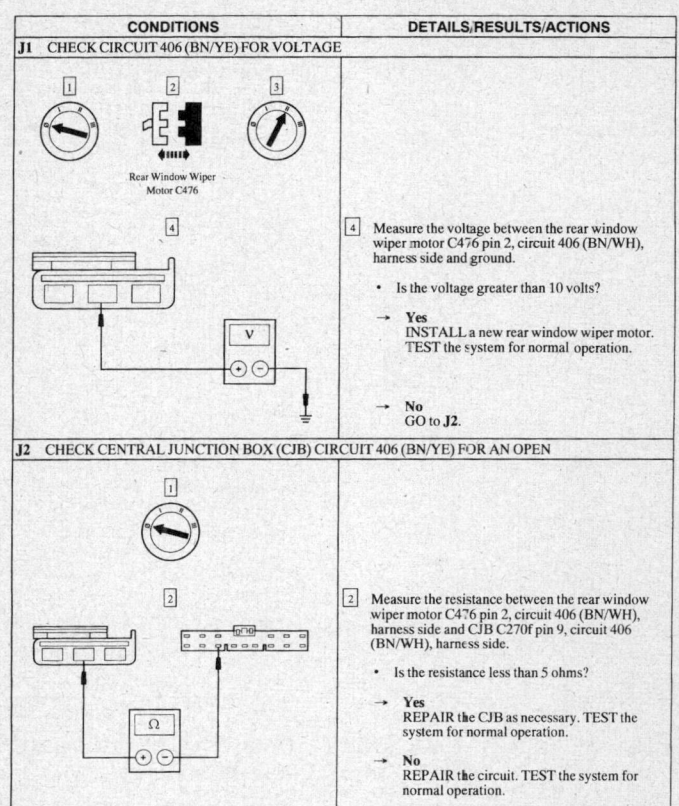	[4] Measure the voltage between the rear window wiper motor C476 pin 2, circuit 406 (BN/WH), harness side and ground. • Is the voltage greater than 10 volts? → **Yes** INSTALL a new rear window wiper motor. TEST the system for normal operation. → **No** GO to **J2**.
J2 CHECK CENTRAL JUNCTION BOX (CJB) CIRCUIT 406 (BN/YE) FOR AN OPEN	
	[2] Measure the resistance between the rear window wiper motor C476 pin 2, circuit 406 (BN/WH), harness side and CJB C270f pin 9, circuit 406 (BN/WH), harness side. • Is the resistance less than 5 ohms? → **Yes** REPAIR the CJB as necessary. TEST the system for normal operation. → **No** REPAIR the circuit. TEST the system for normal operation.

FM9020000845000X

Fig. 14   Test J: Rear Wipers Do Not Park. 2002–04

CONDITIONS	DETAILS/RESULTS/ACTIONS
K1 CHECK THE WIPER/WASHER SWITCH GROUND	
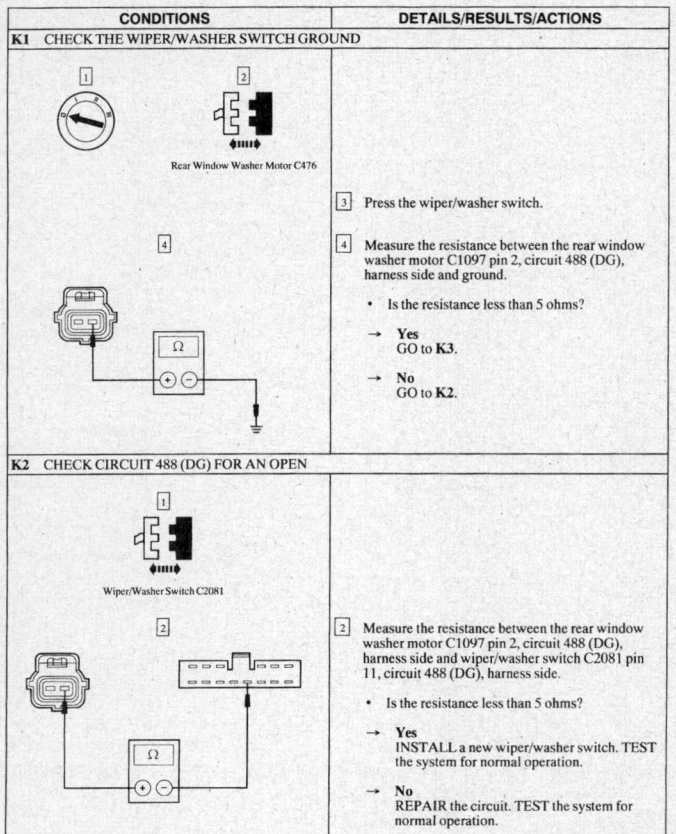	[3] Press the wiper/washer switch. [4] Measure the resistance between the rear window washer motor C1097 pin 2, circuit 488 (DG), harness side and ground. • Is the resistance less than 5 ohms? → **Yes** GO to **K3**. → **No** GO to **K2**.
K2 CHECK CIRCUIT 488 (DG) FOR AN OPEN	
	[2] Measure the resistance between the rear window washer motor C1097 pin 2, circuit 488 (DG), harness side and wiper/washer switch C2081 pin 11, circuit 488 (DG), harness side. • Is the resistance less than 5 ohms? → **Yes** INSTALL a new wiper/washer switch. TEST the system for normal operation. → **No** REPAIR the circuit. TEST the system for normal operation.

FM9020000846010X

Fig. 15   Test K: Rear Washer Pump Inoperative (Part 1 of 2). 2002–04

CONDITIONS	DETAILS/RESULTS/ACTIONS
K3 CHECK CIRCUIT 406 (BN/YE) FOR VOLTAGE	
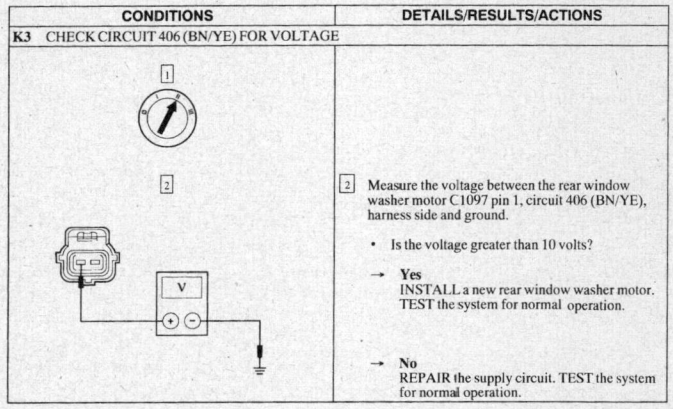	[2] Measure the voltage between the rear window washer motor C1097 pin 1, circuit 406 (BN/YE), harness side and ground. • Is the voltage greater than 10 volts? → **Yes** INSTALL a new rear window washer motor. TEST the system for normal operation. → **No** REPAIR the supply circuit. TEST the system for normal operation.

FM9020000846020X

Fig. 15   Test K: Rear Washer Pump Inoperative (Part 2 of 2). 2002–04

Condition	Possible Sources	Action
• The wipers are inoperative — front	• Fuse. • Circuitry. • Multifunction switch. • Windshield wiper motor. • Smart junction box (SJB).	• Go To Pinpoint Test A.
• The wiper is inoperative — rear	• Fuse. • Circuitry. • Multifunction switch. • Rear wiper motor. • Smart junction box (SJB).	• Go To Pinpoint Test B.
• The wipers stay on continuously — front	• Circuitry. • Windshield wiper motor. • Multifunction switch.	• Go To Pinpoint Test C.
• The wiper stays on continuously — rear	• Circuitry. • Rear wiper motor. • Multifunction switch. • Smart junction box (SJB).	• Go To Pinpoint Test D.
• The high speed wipers do not operate correctly	• Circuitry. • Multifunction switch. • Windshield wiper motor.	• Go To Pinpoint Test E.
• The low speed and intermittent wipers	• Circuitry. • Multifunction switch. • Windshield	• Go To Pinpoint Test F.

LTV0500000002578

Fig. 16 Symptom Tests (Part 1 of 3). 2005–06

	• Windshield wiper motor.	
• The wipers will not park at the correct position — rear	• Pivot arm adjustment.	• ADJUST/REPAIR as necessary.
	• Rear wiper motor.	• INSTALL a new rear wiper motor. TEST the system for normal operation.

LTV0500000002580

Fig. 16 Symptom Tests (Part 3 of 3). 2005–06

• do not operate correctly — front	• wiper motor.	
• The intermittent wiper speed does not operate correctly — rear	• Circuitry. • Multifunction switch. • Smart junction box (SJB).	• Go To Pinpoint Test G.
• The washer pump is inoperative — front	• Circuitry. • Windshield washer pump. • Multifunction switch.	• Go To Pinpoint Test H.
• The wash and wipe function does not operate correctly — front	• Multifunction switch.	• If the LOW speed wiper is inoperative, Go To Pinpoint Test F. If the front washer is inoperative, Go To Pinpoint Test H. If the front wiper does not sweep when the front washer is in the ON position, INSTALL a new multifunction switch.
• The wash and wipe function does not operate correctly — rear	• Circuitry. • Multifunction switch. • Rear washer pump. • Smart junction box (SJB).	• Go To Pinpoint Test I.
• The wipers do not park at the correct position — front	• Pivot arm adjustment. • Linkage.	• ADJUST/REPAIR as necessary.
	• Circuitry. • Multifunction switch.	• Go To Pinpoint Test J.

LTV0500000002579

Fig. 16 Symptom Tests (Part 2 of 3). 2005–06

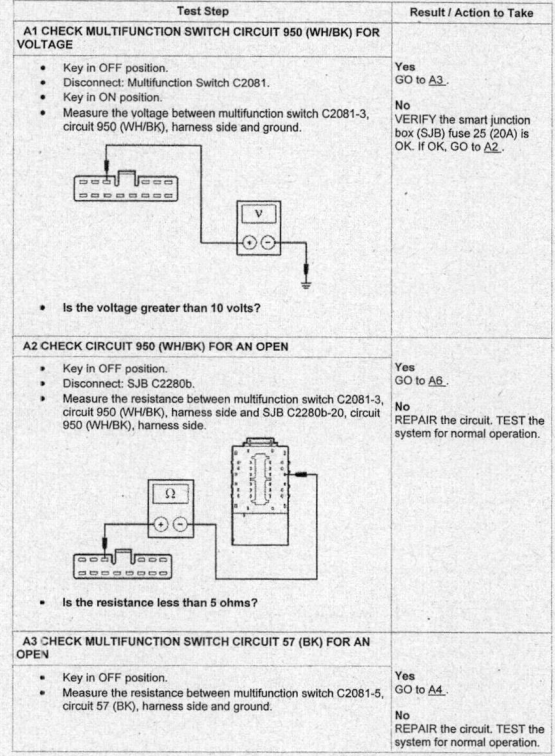

LTV0500000002581

Fig. 17 Test A: Front Wipers Are Inoperative (Part 1 of 2). 2005–06

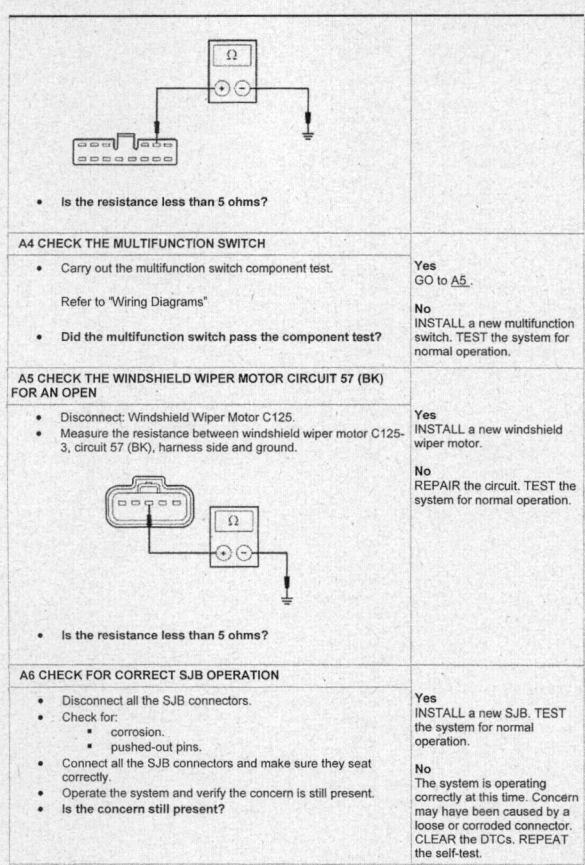

* Is the resistance less than 5 ohms?

A4 CHECK THE MULTIFUNCTION SWITCH	
• Carry out the multifunction switch component test. Refer to "Wiring Diagrams" • Did the multifunction switch pass the component test?	**Yes** GO to A5 . **No** INSTALL a new multifunction switch. TEST the system for normal operation.
A5 CHECK THE WINDSHIELD WIPER MOTOR CIRCUIT 57 (BK) FOR AN OPEN	
• Disconnect: Windshield Wiper Motor C125. • Measure the resistance between windshield wiper motor C125-3, circuit 57 (BK), harness side and ground.	**Yes** INSTALL a new windshield wiper motor. **No** REPAIR the circuit. TEST the system for normal operation.
• Is the resistance less than 5 ohms?	
A6 CHECK FOR CORRECT SJB OPERATION	

• Disconnect all the SJB connectors.
• Check for:
    ▪ corrosion.
    ▪ pushed-out pins.
• Connect all the SJB connectors and make sure they seat correctly.
• Operate the system and verify the concern is still present.
• Is the concern still present?
	Yes
	INSTALL a new SJB. TEST the system for normal operation.
	
	No
	The system is operating correctly at this time. Concern may have been caused by a loose or corroded connector. CLEAR the DTCs. REPEAT the self-test.

LTV0500000002582

Fig. 17 Test A: Front Wipers Are Inoperative (Part 2 of 2). 2005–06

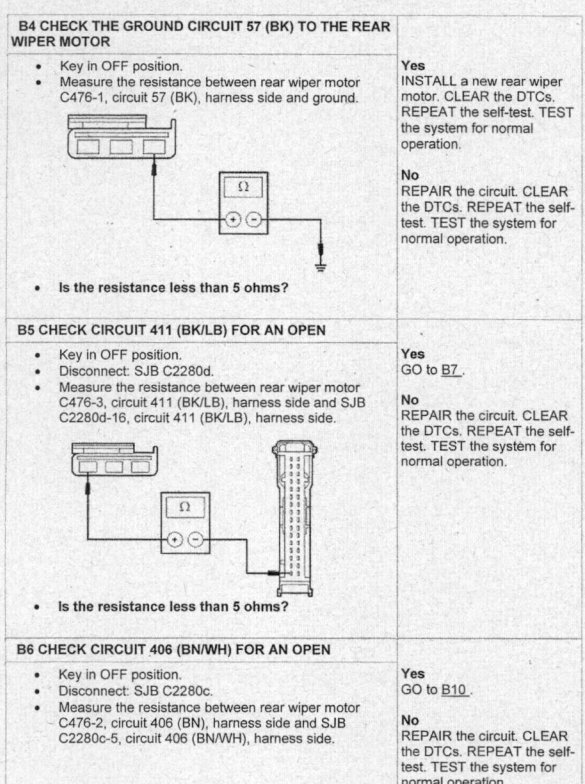

B4 CHECK THE GROUND CIRCUIT 57 (BK) TO THE REAR WIPER MOTOR	
• Key in OFF position. • Measure the resistance between rear wiper motor C476-1, circuit 57 (BK), harness side and ground.	**Yes** INSTALL a new rear wiper motor. CLEAR the DTCs. REPEAT the self-test. TEST the system for normal operation. **No** REPAIR the circuit. CLEAR the DTCs. REPEAT the self-test. TEST the system for normal operation.
• Is the resistance less than 5 ohms?	
B5 CHECK CIRCUIT 411 (BK/LB) FOR AN OPEN	
• Key in OFF position. • Disconnect: SJB C2280d. • Measure the resistance between rear wiper motor C476-3, circuit 411 (BK/LB), harness side and SJB C2280d-16, circuit 411 (BK/LB), harness side.	**Yes** GO to B7 . **No** REPAIR the circuit. CLEAR the DTCs. REPEAT the self-test. TEST the system for normal operation.
• Is the resistance less than 5 ohms?	
B6 CHECK CIRCUIT 406 (BN/WH) FOR AN OPEN	
• Key in OFF position. • Disconnect: SJB C2280c. • Measure the resistance between rear wiper motor C476-2, circuit 406 (BN), harness side and SJB C2280c-5, circuit 406 (BN/WH), harness side.	**Yes** GO to B10 . **No** REPAIR the circuit. CLEAR the DTCs. REPEAT the self-test. TEST the system for normal operation.

LTV0500000002584

Fig. 18   Test B: Rear Wiper Is Inoperative (Part 2 of 4). 2005–06

Test Step	Result / Action to Take
B1 CHECK THE LIFTGATE GLASS AJAR SWITCH AND THE LIFTGATE AJAR SWITCH	
• Key in ON position. • Open and close the liftgate glass and the liftgate. • **Does the warning chime sound when the liftgate and the liftgate glass are in the OPEN position?**	**Yes** GO to B2 . **No** Diagnose liftgate glass or liftgate warning chime concern.
B2 CHECK CIRCUIT 411 (BK/LB) FOR VOLTAGE	
• Key in OFF position. • Disconnect: Rear Wiper Motor C476. • Key in ON position. • Turn the multifunction switch for the rear window wiper to the ON position. • **NOTE:** Make sure the liftgate glass and liftgate are fully closed. • Measure the voltage between rear wiper motor C476-3, circuit 411 (BK/LB), harness side and ground.	**Yes** GO to B3 . **No** GO to B5 .
• Is the voltage greater than 10 volts?	
B3 CHECK CIRCUIT 406 (BN) FOR VOLTAGE	
• Measure the voltage between rear wiper motor C476-2, circuit 406 (BN), harness side and ground.	**Yes** GO to B4 . **No** VERIFY the smart junction box (SJB) fuse 21 (10A) is OK. If OK, GO to B6 .
• Is the voltage greater than 10 volts?	

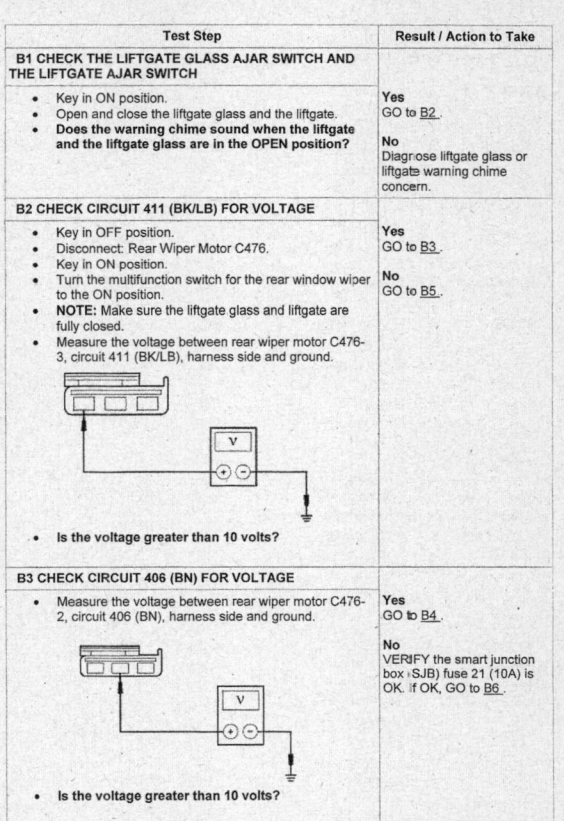

LTV0500000002583

Fig. 18   Test B: Rear Wiper Is Inoperative (Part 1 of 4). 2005–06

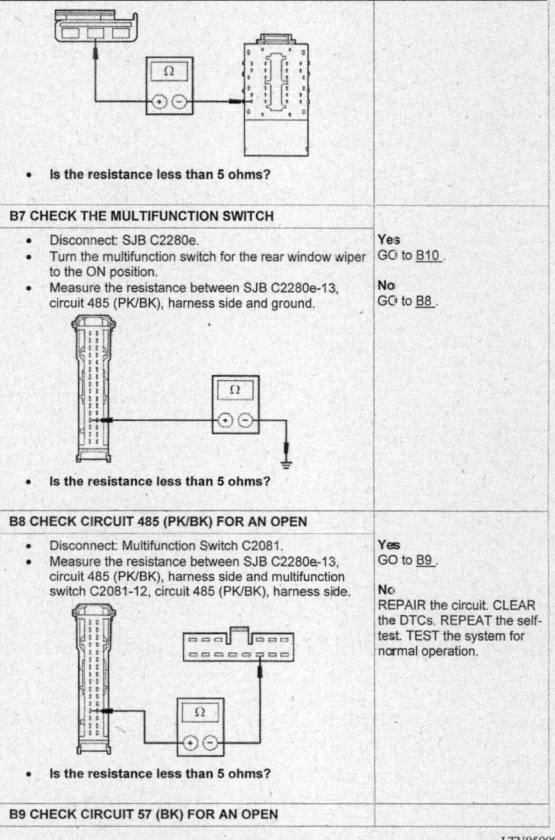

* Is the resistance less than 5 ohms?

B7 CHECK THE MULTIFUNCTION SWITCH	
• Disconnect: SJB C2280e. • Turn the multifunction switch for the rear window wiper to the ON position. • Measure the resistance between SJB C2280e-13, circuit 485 (PK/BK), harness side and ground.	**Yes** GO to B10 . **No** GO to B8 .
• Is the resistance less than 5 ohms?	
B8 CHECK CIRCUIT 485 (PK/BK) FOR AN OPEN	
• Disconnect: Multifunction Switch C2081. • Measure the resistance between SJB C2280e-13, circuit 485 (PK/BK), harness side and multifunction switch C2081-12, circuit 485 (PK/BK), harness side.	**Yes** GO to B9 . **No** REPAIR the circuit. CLEAR the DTCs. REPEAT the self-test. TEST the system for normal operation.
• Is the resistance less than 5 ohms?	
B9 CHECK CIRCUIT 57 (BK) FOR AN OPEN	

LTV0500000002585

Fig. 18   Test B: Rear Wiper Is Inoperative (Part 3 of 4). 2005–06

Test Step	Result / Action to Take
• Measure the resistance between multifunction switch C2081-9, circuit 57 (BK), harness side and ground. 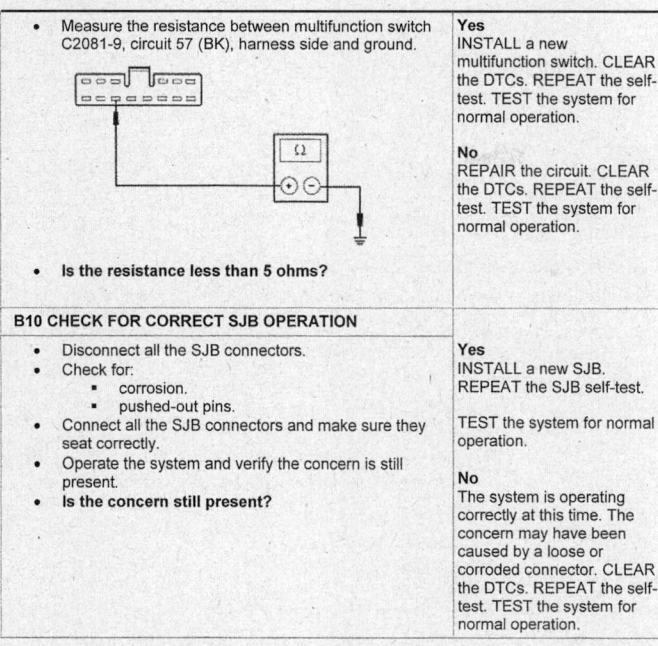 • **Is the resistance less than 5 ohms?**	**Yes** INSTALL a new multifunction switch. CLEAR the DTCs. REPEAT the self-test. TEST the system for normal operation. **No** REPAIR the circuit. CLEAR the DTCs. REPEAT the self-test. TEST the system for normal operation.

B10 CHECK FOR CORRECT SJB OPERATION
• Disconnect all the SJB connectors.
• Check for:
  ▪ corrosion.
  ▪ pushed-out pins.
• Connect all the SJB connectors and make sure they seat correctly.
• Operate the system and verify the concern is still present.
• **Is the concern still present?**
	Yes
	INSTALL a new SJB. REPEAT the SJB self-test.
	
	TEST the system for normal operation.
	
	No
	The system is operating correctly at this time. The concern may have been caused by a loose or corroded connector. CLEAR the DTCs. REPEAT the self-test. TEST the system for normal operation.

LTV0500000002586

Fig. 18   Test B: Rear Wiper Is Inoperative (Part 4 of 4). 2005–06

Test Step	Result / Action to Take
D1 CHECK THE SJB DIAGNOSTIC TROUBLE CODES (DTCS) • Use the recorded results from the SJB continuous and on-demand self-test. • **Are any DTCs recorded?**	**Yes** If DTC B1614, GO to D2 . If DTC B1244, GO to D6 . **No** GO to D2 .
D2 CHECK THE MULTIFUNCTION SWITCH • Key in OFF position. • Disconnect: Multifunction Switch C2081. • Key in ON position. • **Does the rear window wiper continue to run?**	**Yes** GO to D3 . **No** INSTALL a new multifunction switch. CLEAR the DTCs. REPEAT the self-test. TEST the system for normal operation.
D3 CHECK CIRCUITS 485 (PK/BK) AND 410 (WH/OG) FOR A SHORT TO GROUND • Key in OFF position. • Disconnect: SJB C2280e. • For the low speed wiper, measure the resistance between multifunction switch C2081-12, circuit 485 (PK/BK), harness side and ground. 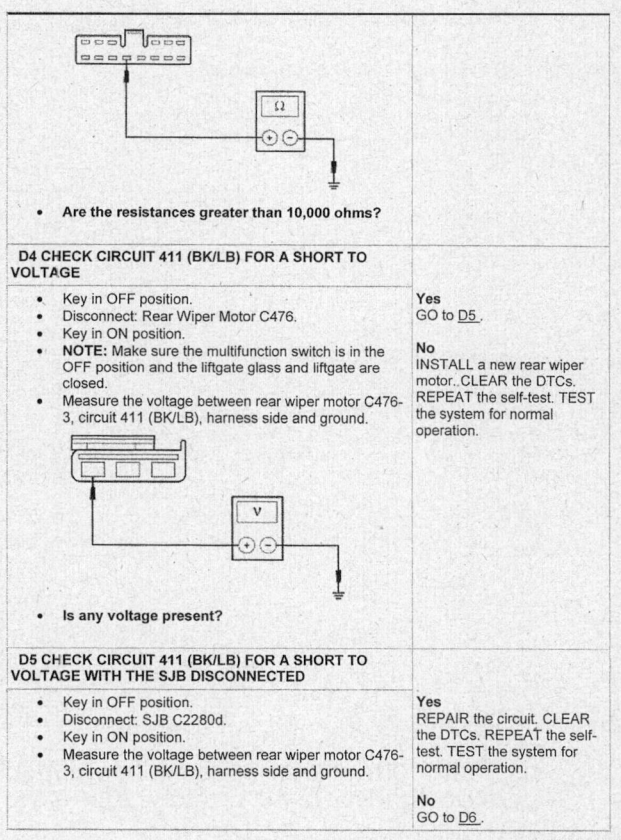 • For the intermittent wiper, measure the resistance between multifunction switch C2081-10, circuit 410 (WH/OG), harness side and ground.	**Yes** GO to D4 . **No** REPAIR the circuit in question. CLEAR the DTCs. REPEAT the self-test. TEST the system for normal operation.

LTV0500000002588

Fig. 20   Test D: Rear Wiper Stays On Continuously (Part 1 of 3). 2005–06

Test Step	Result / Action to Take
C1 CHECK THE MULTIFUNCTION SWITCH • Key in OFF position. • Disconnect: Multifunction Switch C2081. • Key in ON position. • **Does the wiper motor continue to run?**	**Yes** GO to C2 . **No** INSTALL a new multifunction switch. TEST the system for normal operation.
C2 CHECK CIRCUIT 56 (DB/OG) FOR A SHORT TO VOLTAGE • Key in OFF position. • Disconnect: Windshield Wiper Motor C125. • Key in ON position. • Measure the voltage between multifunction switch C2081-6, circuit 56 (DB/OG), harness side and ground. 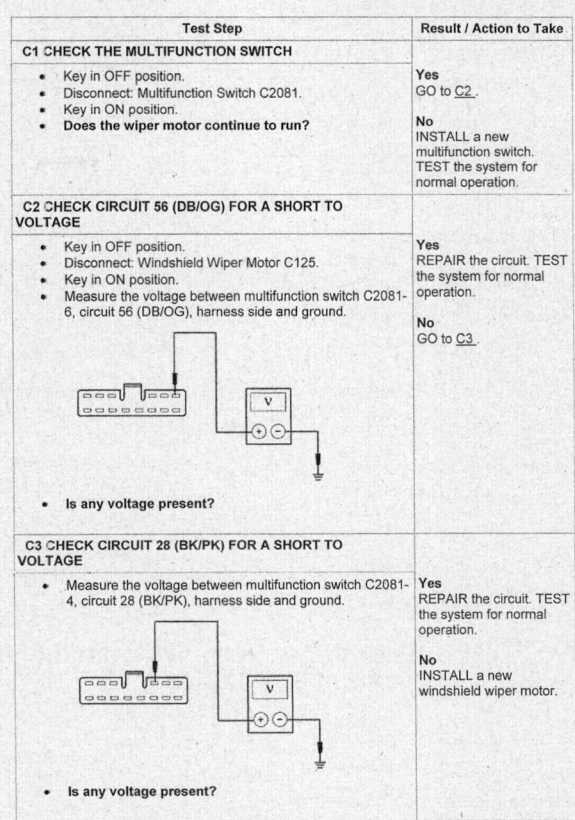 • **Is any voltage present?**	**Yes** REPAIR the circuit. TEST the system for normal operation. **No** GO to C3 .
C3 CHECK CIRCUIT 28 (BK/PK) FOR A SHORT TO VOLTAGE • Measure the voltage between multifunction switch C2081-4, circuit 28 (BK/PK), harness side and ground. • **Is any voltage present?**	**Yes** REPAIR the circuit. TEST the system for normal operation. **No** INSTALL a new windshield wiper motor.

LTV0500000002587

Fig. 19   Test C: Front Wipers Stay On Continuously. 2005–06

Test Step	Result / Action to Take
• Are the resistances greater than 10,000 ohms?	
D4 CHECK CIRCUIT 411 (BK/LB) FOR A SHORT TO VOLTAGE • Key in OFF position. • Disconnect: Rear Wiper Motor C476. • Key in ON position. • **NOTE:** Make sure the multifunction switch is in the OFF position and the liftgate glass and liftgate are closed. • Measure the voltage between rear wiper motor C476-3, circuit 411 (BK/LB), harness side and ground. • **Is any voltage present?**	**Yes** GO to D5 . **No** INSTALL a new rear wiper motor..CLEAR the DTCs. REPEAT the self-test. TEST the system for normal operation.
D5 CHECK CIRCUIT 411 (BK/LB) FOR A SHORT TO VOLTAGE WITH THE SJB DISCONNECTED • Key in OFF position. • Disconnect: SJB C2280d. • Key in ON position. • Measure the voltage between rear wiper motor C476-3, circuit 411 (BK/LB), harness side and ground.	**Yes** REPAIR the circuit. CLEAR the DTCs. REPEAT the self-test. TEST the system for normal operation. **No** GO to D6 .

LTV0500000002589

Fig. 20   Test D: Rear Wiper Stays On Continuously (Part 2 of 3). 2005–06

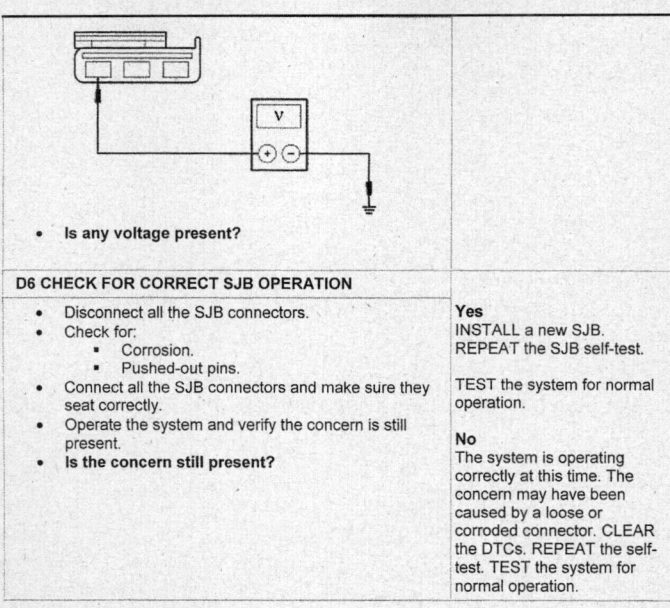

Test Step	Result / Action to Take
• **Is any voltage present?**	
D6 CHECK FOR CORRECT SJB OPERATION	

• Disconnect all the SJB connectors.
• Check for:
  ▪ Corrosion.
  ▪ Pushed-out pins.
• Connect all the SJB connectors and make sure they seat correctly.
• Operate the system and verify the concern is still present.
• **Is the concern still present?**
	Yes
	INSTALL a new SJB. REPEAT the SJB self-test.
	
	TEST the system for normal operation.
	
	No
	The system is operating correctly at this time. The concern may have been caused by a loose or corroded connector. CLEAR the DTCs. REPEAT the self-test. TEST the system for normal operation.

LTV0500000002590

Fig. 20   Test D: Rear Wiper Stays On Continuously (Part 3 of 3). 2005–06

Test Step	Result / Action to Take
E1 CHECK THE MULTIFUNCTION SWITCH	
• Key in OFF position. • Disconnect: Multifunction Switch C2081. • Carry out the multifunction switch component test. Refer to "Wiring Diagrams" • **Did the multifunction switch pass the component test?**	**Yes** GO to E2. **No** INSTALL a new multifunction switch. TEST the system for normal operation.
E2 CHECK CIRCUIT 56 (DB/OG) FOR AN OPEN	
• Disconnect: Windshield Wiper Motor C125. • Measure the resistance between windshield wiper motor C125-1, circuit 56 (DB/OG), harness side and multifunction switch C2081-6, circuit 56 (DB/OG), harness side. • **Is the resistance less than 5 ohms?**	**Yes** INSTALL a new windshield wiper motor. **No** REPAIR the circuit. TEST the system for normal operation.

LTV0500000002591

Fig. 21   Test E: Front High Speed Wipers Do Not Operate Correctly. 2005–06

Test Step	Result / Action to Take
F1 CHECK THE MULTIFUNCTION SWITCH	
• Key in OFF position. • Disconnect: Multifunction Switch C2081. • Carry out the multifunction switch component test. Refer to "Wiring Diagrams" • **Did the multifunction switch pass the component test?**	**Yes** GO to F2. **No** INSTALL a new multifunction switch. TEST the system for normal operation.
F2 CHECK CIRCUIT 28 (BK/PK) FOR A SHORT TO GROUND	
• Disconnect: Wiper Motor C125. • Measure the resistance between multifunction switch C2081-4, circuit 28 (BK/PK), harness side and ground. • **Is the resistance greater than 10,000 ohms?**	**Yes** GO to F3. **No** REPAIR the circuit. TEST the system for normal operation.
F3 CHECK CIRCUIT 28 (BK/PK) FOR AN OPEN	
• Measure the resistance between wiper motor C125-2, circuit 28 (BK/PK), harness side and multifunction switch C2081-4, circuit 28 (BK/PK), harness side. • **Is the resistance less than 5 ohms?**	**Yes** INSTALL a new windshield wiper motor. **No** REPAIR the circuit. TEST the system for normal operation.

LTV0500000002592

Fig. 22   Test F: Front Low Speed & Intermittent Wipers Do Not Operate Correctly. 2005–06

Test Step	Result / Action to Take
G1 CHECK REAR WIPER OPERATION	
• Key in ON position. • Turn the multifunction switch for the rear window wiper to the ON position. • **Does the rear wiper operate at low speed?**	**Yes** GO to G2. **No** Go To Pinpoint Test B.
G2 CHECK CIRCUIT 410 (WH/OG) FOR GROUND	
• Key in OFF position. • Disconnect: SJB C2280e. • Turn the multifunction switch for the rear wiper to the INTERMITTENT position. • Measure the resistance between SJB C2280e-12, circuit 410 (WH/OG), harness side and ground. • **Is the resistance less than 5 ohms?**	**Yes** GO to G4. **No** GO to G3.
G3 CHECK CIRCUIT 410 (WH/OG) FOR AN OPEN	
• Disconnect: Multifunction Switch C2081. • Measure the resistance between multifunction switch C2081-10, circuit 410 (WH/OG), harness side and SJE C2280e-12, circuit 410 (WH/OG), harness side. • **Is the resistance less than 5 ohms?**	**Yes** INSTALL a new multifunction switch. TEST the system for normal operation. **No** REPAIR the circuit. TEST the system for normal operation.

LTV0500000002593

Fig. 23   Test G: Rear Intermittent Wiper Speed Does Not Operate Correctly (Part 1 of 2). 2005–06

G4 CHECK FOR CORRECT SJB OPERATION

Test Step	Result / Action to Take
• Disconnect all the SJB connectors. • Check for: 　▪ corrosion. 　▪ pushed-out pins. • Connect all the SJB connectors and make sure they seat correctly. • Operate the system and verify the concern is still present. • **Is the concern still present?**	**Yes** INSTALL a new SJB.. REPEAT the SJB self-test. TEST the system for normal operation. **No** The system is operating correctly at this time. The concern may have been caused by a loose or corroded connector. CLEAR the DTCs. REPEAT the self-test.

LTV0500000002594

Fig. 23 Test G: Rear Intermittent Wiper Speed Does Not Operate Correctly (Part 2 of 2). 2005–06

Test Step	Result / Action to Take
I1 CHECK THE MULTIFUNCTION SWITCH	
• Key in OFF position. • Disconnect: Multifunction Switch C2081. • Carry out the multifunction switch component test. 　Refer to "Wiring Diagrams" • **Did the multifunction switch pass the component test?**	**Yes** GO to I2 . **No** INSTALL a new multifunction switch.. TEST the system for normal operation.
I2 CHECK THE REAR WIPER OPERATION	
• Connect: Multifunction Switch C2081. • Key in ON position. • Operate the rear washer pump. • **Does the rear wiper operate?**	**Yes** GO to I3 . **No** GO to I6 .
I3 CHECK CIRCUIT 406 (BN/WH) FOR VOLTAGE	
• Key in OFF position. • Disconnect: Rear Washer Pump C1097. • Key in ON position. • Measure the voltage between rear washer pump C1097-1, circuit 406 (BN/WH), harness side and ground. • **Is the voltage greater than 10 volts?**	**Yes** GO to I5 . **No** GO to I4 .
I4 CHECK CIRCUIT 406 (BN/WH) FOR AN OPEN	
• Key in OFF position. • Disconnect: SJB C2280d. • Measure the resistance between rear washer pump C1097-1, circuit 406 (BN/WH), harness side and SJB C2280d-30, circuit 406 (BN/WH), harness side.	**Yes** GO to I7 . **No** REPAIR the circuit. TEST the system for normal operation.

LTV0500000002596

Fig. 25 Test I: Rear Wash & Wipe Function Does Not Operate (Part 1 of 3). 2005–06

Test Step	Result / Action to Take
H1 CHECK THE MULTIFUNCTION SWITCH	
• Key in OFF position. • Disconnect: Multifunction Switch C2081. • Carry out the multifunction switch component test. 　Refer to "Wiring Diagrams" • **Did the multifunction switch pass the component test?**	**Yes** GO to H2 . **No** INSTALL a new multifunction switch. TEST the system for normal operation
H2 CHECK CIRCUIT 686 (TN/RD) FOR VOLTAGE	
• Connect: Multifunction Switch C2081. • Disconnect: Windshield Washer Pump C137. • Key in ON position. • While activating the front washer pump using the multifunction switch, measure the voltage between windshield washer pump C137-1, circuit 686 (TN/RD), harness side and ground. • Is the voltage greater than 10 volts?	**Yes** GO to H3 . **No** REPAIR the circuit. TEST the system for normal operation.
H3 CHECK CIRCUIT 57 (BK) FOR AN OPEN	
• Key in OFF position. • Measure the resistance between windshield washer pump C137-2, circuit 57 (BK), harness side and ground. • Is the resistance less than 5 ohms?	**Yes** INSTALL a new windshield washer pump. TEST the system for normal operation. **No** REPAIR the circuit. TEST the system for normal operation.

LTV0500000002595

Fig. 24 Test H: Front Washer Pump Is Inoperative. 2005–06

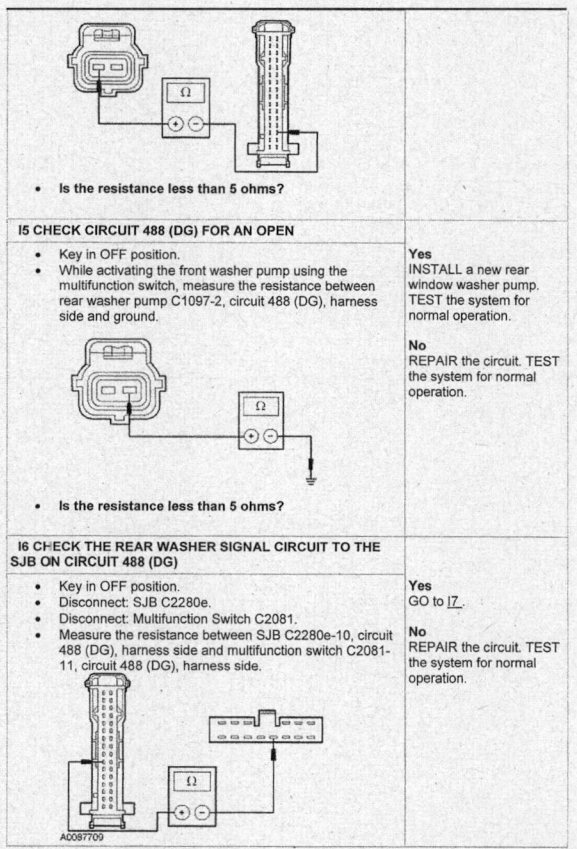

Test Step	Result / Action to Take
• Is the resistance less than 5 ohms?	
I5 CHECK CIRCUIT 488 (DG) FOR AN OPEN	
• Key in OFF position. • While activating the front washer pump using the multifunction switch, measure the resistance between rear washer pump C1097-2, circuit 488 (DG), harness side and ground. • Is the resistance less than 5 ohms?	**Yes** INSTALL a new rear window washer pump. TEST the system for normal operation. **No** REPAIR the circuit. TEST the system for normal operation.
I6 CHECK THE REAR WASHER SIGNAL CIRCUIT TO THE SJB ON CIRCUIT 488 (DG)	
• Key in OFF position. • Disconnect: SJB C2280e. • Disconnect: Multifunction Switch C2081. • Measure the resistance between SJB C2280e-10, circuit 488 (DG), harness side and multifunction switch C2081-11, circuit 488 (DG), harness side.	**Yes** GO to I7 . **No** REPAIR the circuit. TEST the system for normal operation.

A0087709

LTV0500000002597

Fig. 25 Test I: Rear Wash & Wipe Function Does Not Operate (Part 2 of 3). 2005–06

• Is the resistance less than 5 ohms?	
I7 CHECK FOR CORRECT SJB OPERATION	

• Disconnect all the SJB connectors.
• Check for:
  ▪ Corrosion.
  ▪ Pushed-out pins.
• Connect all the SJB connectors and make sure they seat correctly.
• Operate the system and verify the concern is still present.
• **Is the concern still present?**
	Yes
	INSTALL a new SJB.. REPEAT the SJB self-test.
	
	TEST the system for normal operation.
	
	No
	The system is operating correctly at this time. The concern may have been caused by a loose or corroded connector. CLEAR the DTCs. REPEAT the self-test.

LTV0500000002598

Fig. 25   Test I: Rear Wash & Wipe Function Does Not Operate (Part 3 of 3). 2005–06

COMPONENT DIAGNOSIS & TESTING

Refer to "Aviator" for component diagnosis and testing.

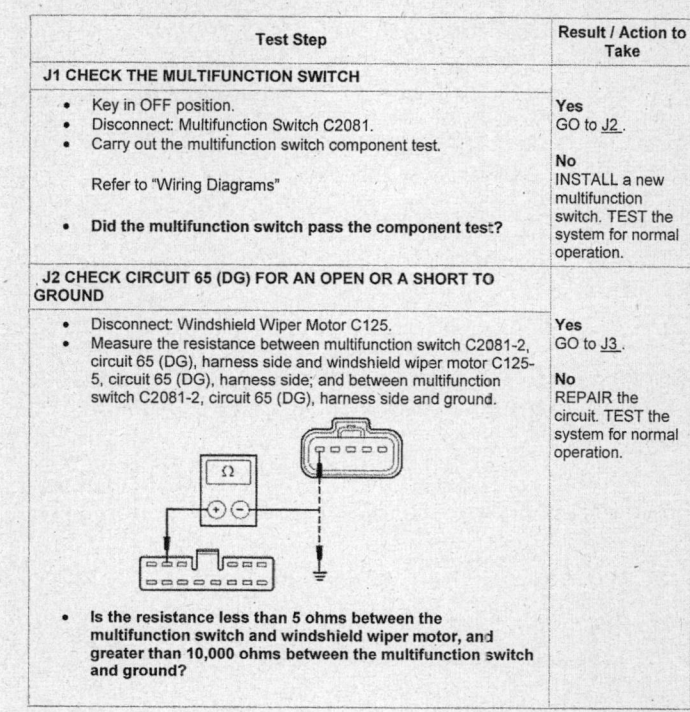

Test Step	Result / Action to Take
J1 CHECK THE MULTIFUNCTION SWITCH	
• Key in OFF position. • Disconnect: Multifunction Switch C2081. • Carry out the multifunction switch component test. Refer to "Wiring Diagrams" • **Did the multifunction switch pass the component test?**	**Yes** GO to <u>J2</u>. **No** INSTALL a new multifunction switch. TEST the system for normal operation.
J2 CHECK CIRCUIT 65 (DG) FOR AN OPEN OR A SHORT TO GROUND	
• Disconnect: Windshield Wiper Motor C125. • Measure the resistance between multifunction switch C2081-2, circuit 65 (DG), harness side and windshield wiper motor C125-5, circuit 65 (DG), harness side; and between multifunction switch C2081-2, circuit 65 (DG), harness side and ground. • **Is the resistance less than 5 ohms between the multifunction switch and windshield wiper motor, and greater than 10,000 ohms between the multifunction switch and ground?**	**Yes** GO to <u>J3</u>. **No** REPAIR the circuit. TEST the system for normal operation.

LTV0500000002599

Fig. 26   Test J: Front Wipers Do Not Park In Correct Position (Part 1 of 2). 2005–06

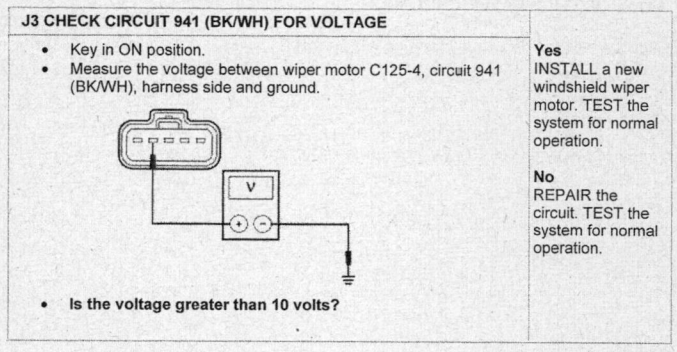

J3 CHECK CIRCUIT 941 (BK/WH) FOR VOLTAGE	
• Key in ON position. • Measure the voltage between wiper motor C125-4, circuit 941 (BK/WH), harness side and ground. • **Is the voltage greater than 10 volts?**	**Yes** INSTALL a new windshield wiper motor. TEST the system for normal operation. **No** REPAIR the circuit. TEST the system for normal operation.

LTV0500000002600

Fig. 26   Test J: Front Wipers Do Not Park In Correct Position (Part 2 of 2). 2005–06

E-Series

NOTE: On Air Bag Equipped Models, Refer To "Air Bag System Precautions" Located In The Front Of This Manual For System Disarming & Arming Procedures.

NOTE: "Electrical Symbol & Wire Color Code Identification" Located In The Front Of This Manual May Be Used As An Aid When Using Wiring Diagrams Found In This Section.

NOTE: Refer To "Computer Relearn Procedures" Located In The Front Of This Manual When Battery Power To The Computer Has Been Interrupted.

INDEX

	Page No.
Component Diagnosis & Testing	3-39
Diagnostic Chart Index	3-30
Precautions	3-27
Battery Ground Cable	3-27
System Diagnosis & Testing	3-27
Accessing Diagnostic Trouble Codes	3-27
Clearing Diagnostic Trouble Codes	3-27
Diagnostic Tests	3-27
2002–04	3-27
2005–06	3-27
Wiring Diagrams	3-27

PRECAUTIONS

Battery Ground Cable

Prior to service, disconnect battery ground cable and isolate as required.

SYSTEM DIAGNOSIS & TESTING

Accessing Diagnostic Trouble Codes

Connect a suitably programmed scan tool and Vehicle Communication Module (VCM) with appropriate adapters, or equivalents, to the Data Link Connector (DCL) located in the passenger compartment beneath the instrument panel. Follow tool manufacturer's instructions for accessing speed control Diagnostic Trouble Codes (DTC).

Wiring Diagrams

Refer to **Figs. 1 and 2** for wiring diagrams.

Diagnostic Tests

2002–04

Refer to **Figs. 3 through 9** for diagnostic tests.

2005–06

Refer to **Figs. 10 through 16** for diagnostic tests.

Clearing Diagnostic Trouble Codes

Connect a suitably programmed scan tool and Vehicle Communication Module (VCM) with appropriate adapters, or equivalents, to the Data Link Connector (DCL) located in the passenger compartment beneath the instrument panel. Follow tool manufacturer's instructions for accessing speed control Diagnostic Trouble Codes (DTC).

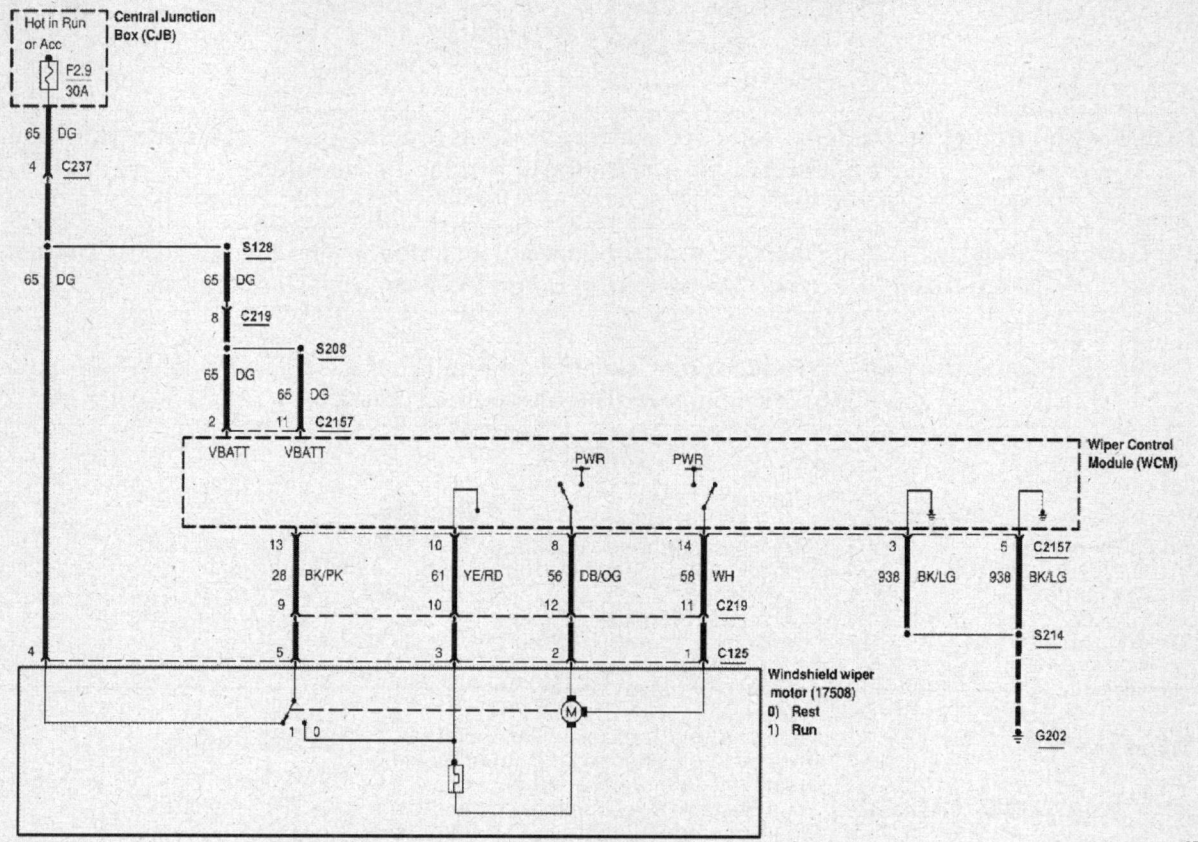

Fig. 1   Wiring diagram (Part 1 of 2). 2002–04

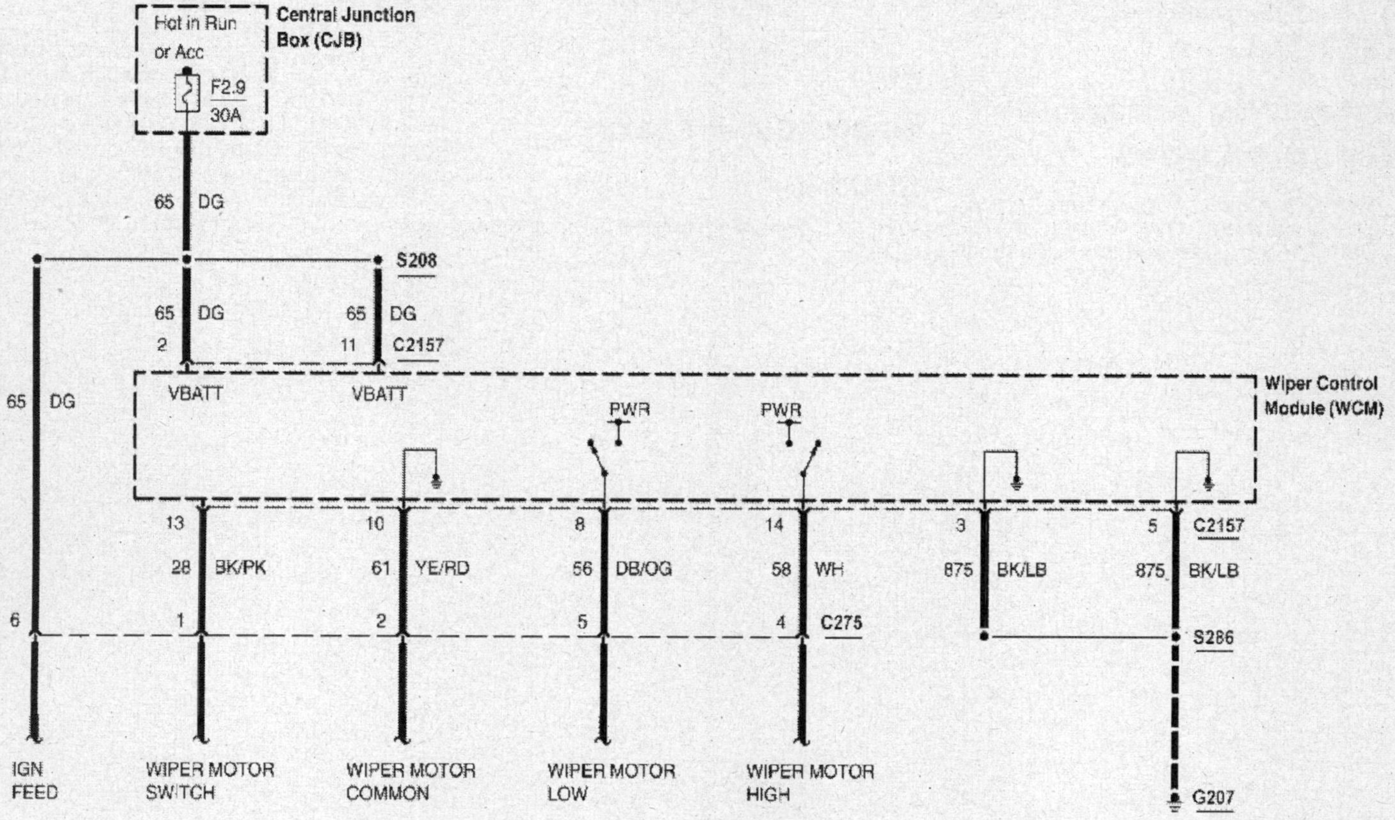

LTV0500000001884

Fig. 1   Wiring diagram (Part 2 of 2). 2002–04

LTV0500000001885

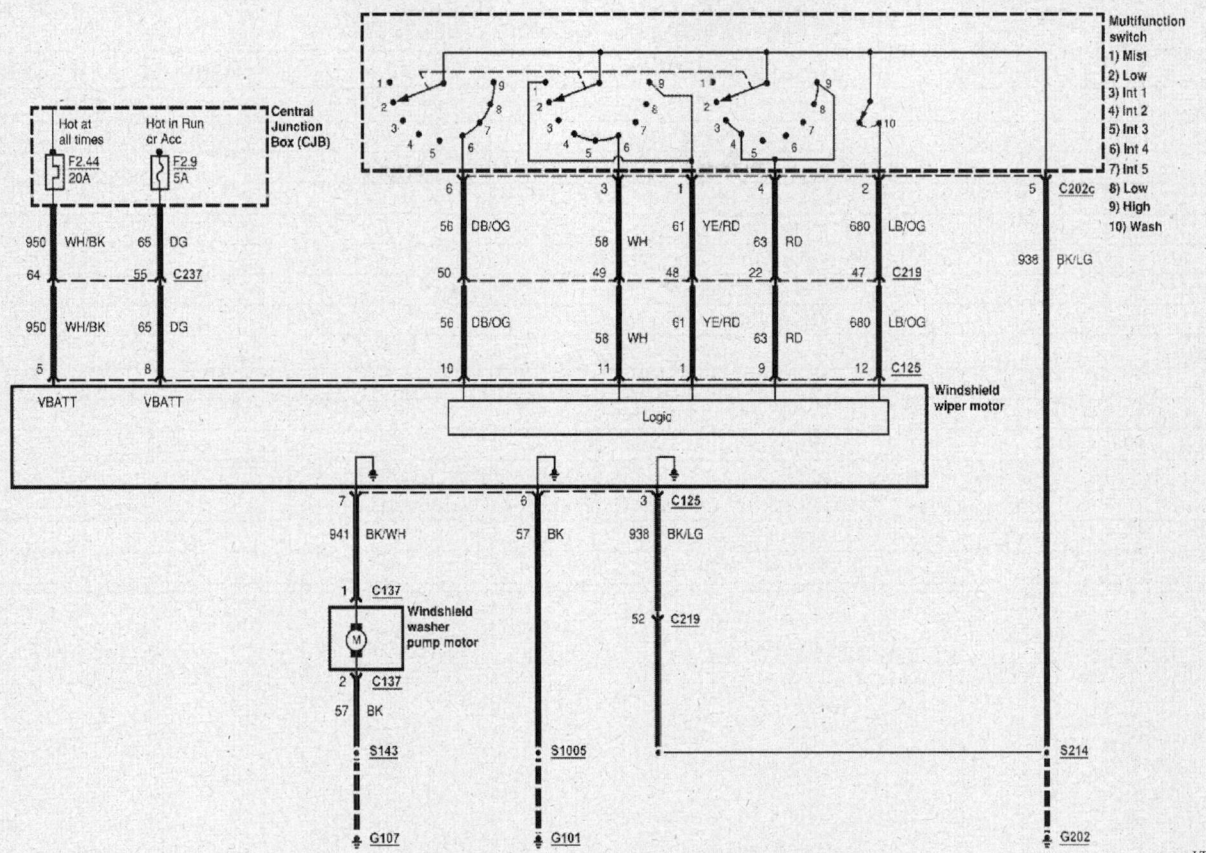

Fig. 2   Wiring diagram (Part 1 of 2). 2005–06

LTV0500000001894

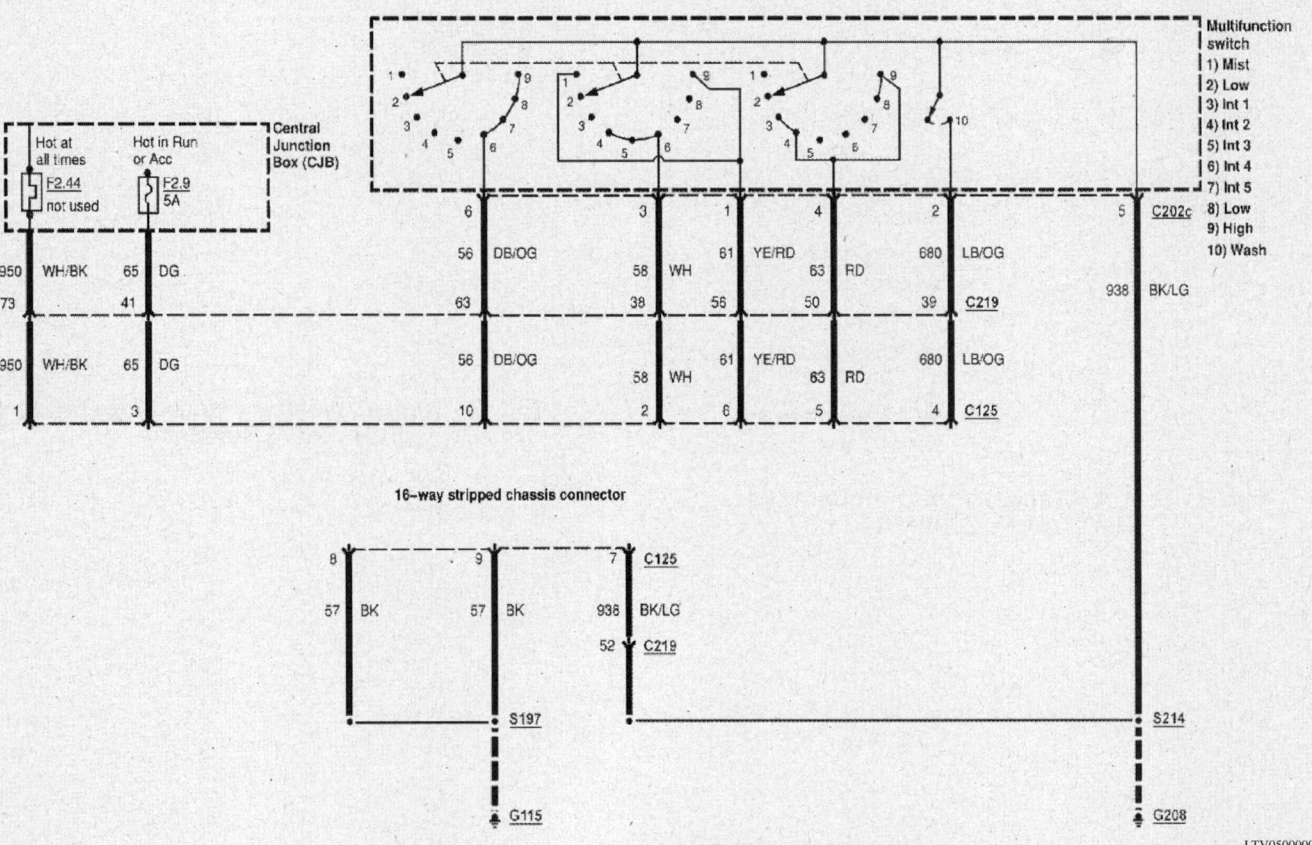

Fig. 2   Wiring diagram (Part 2 of 2). 2005–06

LTV0500000001895

WIPER SYSTEMS

DIAGNOSTIC CHART INDEX

Test	Description	Page No.	Fig. No.
2002–04			
A	Washer Pump Inoperative	3-30	3
B	Wipers Inoperative	3-31	4
C	Low Wiper Speed Does Not Operate Properly	3-32	5
D	High Speed Does Not Operate Properly	3-33	6
E	Intermittent Wiper Speed Does Not Operate Properly	3-34	7
F	Wipers Will Not Park At Proper Position	3-34	8
G	Wipers Stay On Continuously	3-35	9
2005–06			
—	Symptom Tests	3-35	10
A	Wipers Are Inoperative	3-36	11
B	Wipers Stay On Continuously	3-36	12
C	High/Low Wiper Speed Does Not Operate Correctly, Intermittent Mode OK	3-37	13
D	Intermittent Wiper Speed Does Not Operate Correctly, High/Low Speeds OK	3-37	14
E	Wipers Do Not Operate Correctly In Mist Position	3-38	15
F	Washer Pump Is Inoperative	3-38	16

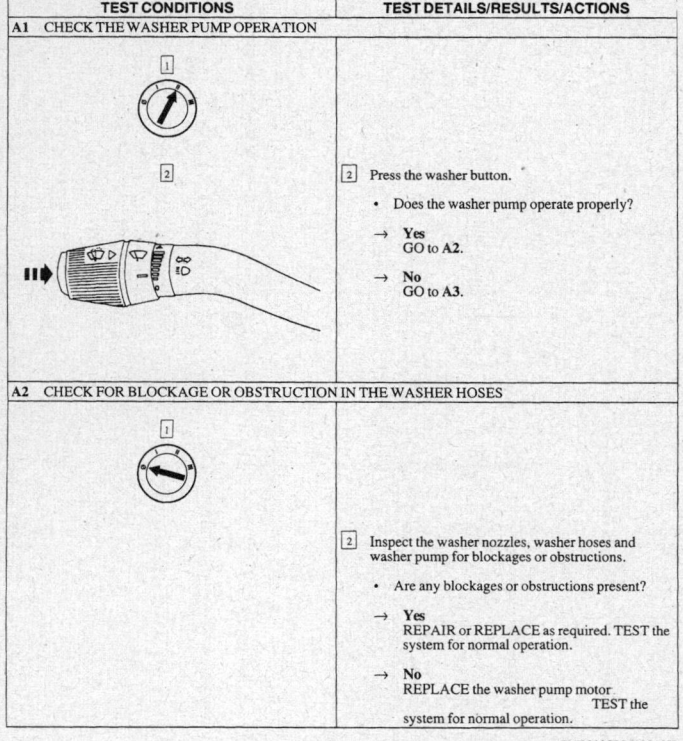

FM9029800610010X

**Fig. 3   Test A: Washer Pump Inoperative
(Part 1 of 4). 2002–04**

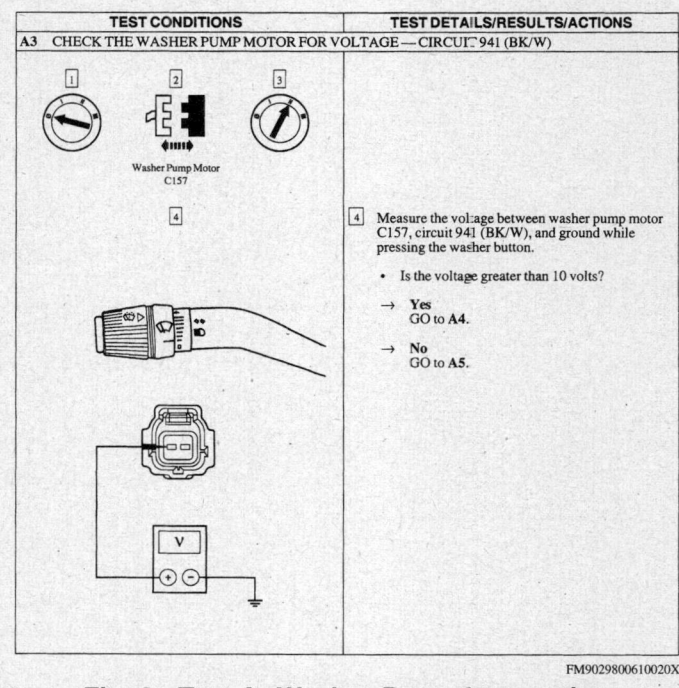

FM9029800610020X

**Fig. 3   Test A: Washer Pump Inoperative
(Part 2 of 4). 2002–04**

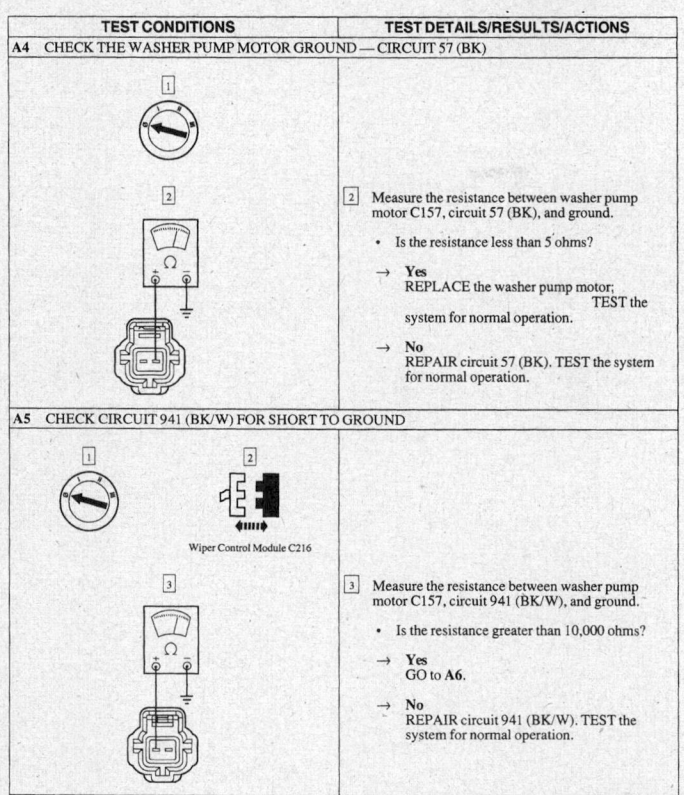

TEST CONDITIONS	TEST DETAILS/RESULTS/ACTIONS
A4 CHECK THE WASHER PUMP MOTOR GROUND — CIRCUIT 57 (BK)	

2 Measure the resistance between washer pump motor C157, circuit 57 (BK), and ground.

- Is the resistance less than 5 ohms?

→ **Yes**
REPLACE the washer pump motor; TEST the system for normal operation.

→ **No**
REPAIR circuit 57 (BK). TEST the system for normal operation.

TEST CONDITIONS	TEST DETAILS/RESULTS/ACTIONS
A5 CHECK CIRCUIT 941 (BK/W) FOR SHORT TO GROUND	

Wiper Control Module C216

3 Measure the resistance between washer pump motor C157, circuit 941 (BK/W), and ground.

- Is the resistance greater than 10,000 ohms?

→ **Yes**
GO to **A6**.

→ **No**
REPAIR circuit 941 (BK/W). TEST the system for normal operation.

FM9029800610030X

**Fig. 3   Test A: Washer Pump Inoperative
(Part 3 of 4). 2002–04**

TEST CONDITIONS	TEST DETAILS/RESULTS/ACTIONS
B1 CHECK FUSE JUNCTION PANEL FUSE 9 (30A)	

Fuse 9 (30A)

- Is fuse junction panel 9 (30A) OK?

→ **Yes**
GO to **B2**.

→ **No**
REPLACE fuse junction panel fuse 9 (30A). TEST the system for normal operation. If the fuse fails again, CHECK for a short to ground. REPAIR as necessary.

TEST CONDITIONS	TEST DETAILS/RESULTS/ACTIONS
B2 CHECK FOR VOLTAGE TO THE WIPER CONTROL MODULE — CIRCUIT 65 (DG)	

Wiper Control Module C216

3 Measure the voltage between wiper control module C216-2, circuit 65 (DG), and ground; and between wiper control module C216-11, circuit 65 (DG), and ground.

- Is the voltage greater than 10 volts?

→ **Yes**
GO to **B3**.

→ **No**
REPAIR circuit 65 (DG). TEST the system for normal operation.

FM9029800611010X

**Fig. 4   Test B: Wipers Inoperative (Part 1 of 5).
2002–04**

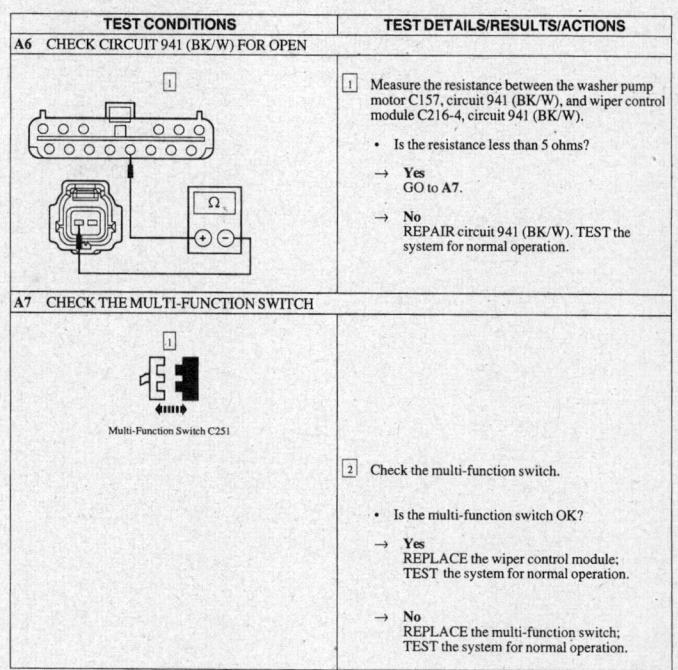

TEST CONDITIONS	TEST DETAILS/RESULTS/ACTIONS
A6 CHECK CIRCUIT 941 (BK/W) FOR OPEN	

1 Measure the resistance between the washer pump motor C157, circuit 941 (BK/W), and wiper control module C216-4, circuit 941 (BK/W).

- Is the resistance less than 5 ohms?

→ **Yes**
GO to **A7**.

→ **No**
REPAIR circuit 941 (BK/W). TEST the system for normal operation.

TEST CONDITIONS	TEST DETAILS/RESULTS/ACTIONS
A7 CHECK THE MULTI-FUNCTION SWITCH	

Multi-Function Switch C251

2 Check the multi-function switch.

- Is the multi-function switch OK?

→ **Yes**
REPLACE the wiper control module; TEST the system for normal operation.

→ **No**
REPLACE the multi-function switch; TEST the system for normal operation.

FM9029800610040X

**Fig. 3   Test A: Washer Pump Inoperative
(Part 4 of 4). 2002–04**

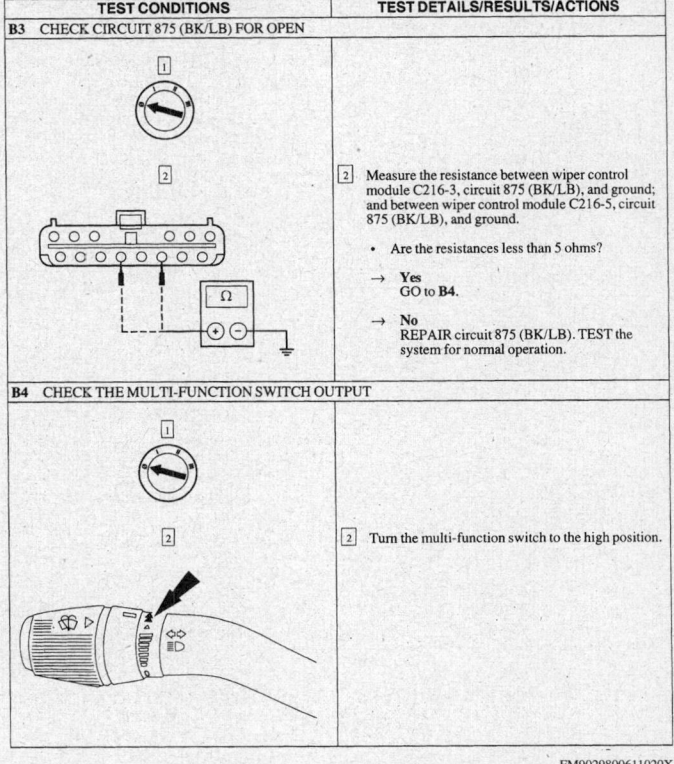

TEST CONDITIONS	TEST DETAILS/RESULTS/ACTIONS
B3 CHECK CIRCUIT 875 (BK/LB) FOR OPEN	

2 Measure the resistance between wiper control module C216-3, circuit 875 (BK/LB), and ground; and between wiper control module C216-5, circuit 875 (BK/LB), and ground.

- Are the resistances less than 5 ohms?

→ **Yes**
GO to **B4**.

→ **No**
REPAIR circuit 875 (BK/LB). TEST the system for normal operation.

TEST CONDITIONS	TEST DETAILS/RESULTS/ACTIONS
B4 CHECK THE MULTI-FUNCTION SWITCH OUTPUT	

2 Turn the multi-function switch to the high position.

FM9029800611020X

**Fig. 4   Test B: Wipers Inoperative (Part 2 of 5).
2002–04**

TEST CONDITIONS	TEST DETAILS/RESULTS/ACTIONS
B4 CHECK THE MULTI-FUNCTION SWITCH OUTPUT (Continued)	

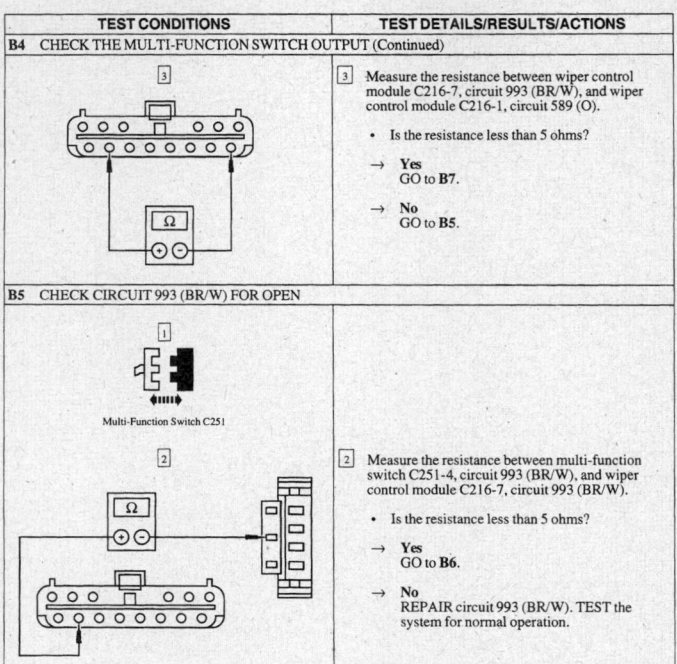

[3] Measure the resistance between wiper control module C216-7, circuit 993 (BR/W), and wiper control module C216-1, circuit 589 (O).

- Is the resistance less than 5 ohms?

→ **Yes**
GO to **B7**.

→ **No**
GO to **B5**.

TEST CONDITIONS	TEST DETAILS/RESULTS/ACTIONS
B5 CHECK CIRCUIT 993 (BR/W) FOR OPEN	

Multi-Function Switch C251

[2] Measure the resistance between multi-function switch C251-4, circuit 993 (BR/W), and wiper control module C216-7, circuit 993 (BR/W).

- Is the resistance less than 5 ohms?

→ **Yes**
GO to **B6**.

→ **No**
REPAIR circuit 993 (BR/W). TEST the system for normal operation.

FM9029800611030X

Fig. 4 Test B: Wipers Inoperative (Part 3 of 5). 2002–04

TEST CONDITIONS	TEST DETAILS/RESULTS/ACTIONS
B7 CHECK THE WIPER CONTROL MODULE OUTPUT FOR VOLTAGE (Continued)	

[5] Measure the voltage between wiper motor C147-3, circuit 61 (Y/R), and wiper motor C197-5, circuit 58 (W).

- Is the voltage greater than 10 volts?

→ **Yes**
REPLACE the wiper motor. TEST the system for normal operation.

→ **No**
GO to **B8**.

TEST CONDITIONS	TEST DETAILS/RESULTS/ACTIONS
B8 CHECK CIRCUIT 61 (Y/R) FOR OPEN	

Wiper Control Module C216

[3] Measure the resistance between wiper control module C216-10, circuit 61 (Y/R), and wiper motor C147-3, circuit 61 (Y/R).

- Is the resistance less than 5 ohms?

→ **Yes**
REPLACE the wiper control module. TEST the system for normal operation.

→ **No**
REPAIR circuit 61 (Y/R). TEST the system for normal operation.

FM9029800611050X

Fig. 4 Test B: Wipers Inoperative (Part 5 of 5). 2002–04

TEST CONDITIONS	TEST DETAILS/RESULTS/ACTIONS
B6 CHECK CIRCUIT 589 (O) FOR OPEN	

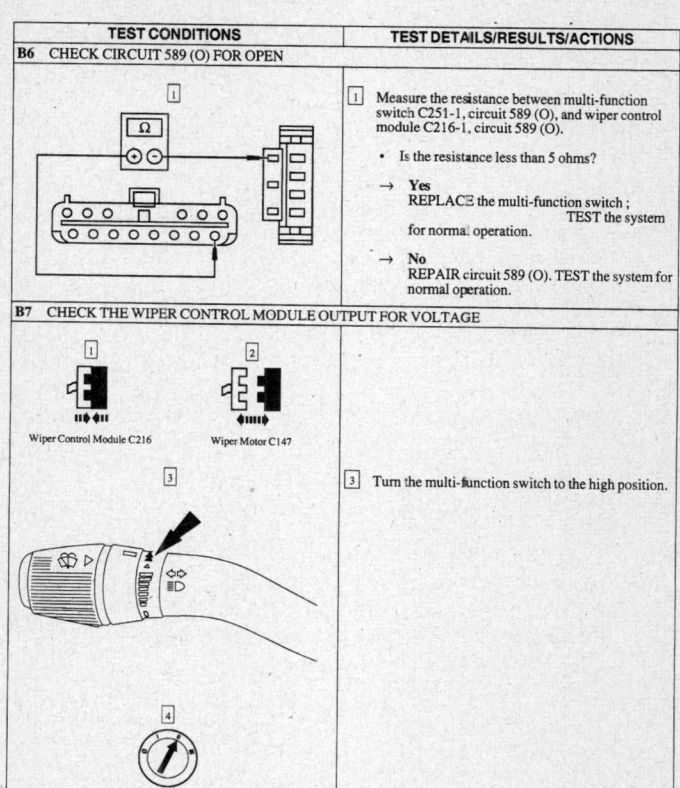

[1] Measure the resistance between multi-function switch C251-1, circuit 589 (O), and wiper control module C216-1, circuit 589 (O).

- Is the resistance less than 5 ohms?

→ **Yes**
REPLACE the multi-function switch ; TEST the system for normal operation.

→ **No**
REPAIR circuit 589 (O). TEST the system for normal operation.

TEST CONDITIONS	TEST DETAILS/RESULTS/ACTIONS
B7 CHECK THE WIPER CONTROL MODULE OUTPUT FOR VOLTAGE	

Wiper Control Module C216   Wiper Motor C147

[3] Turn the multi-function switch to the high position.

FM9029800611040X

Fig. 4 Test B: Wipers Inoperative (Part 4 of 5). 2002–04

TEST CONDITIONS	TEST DETAILS/RESULTS/ACTIONS
C1 CHECK THE VOLTAGE TO THE WIPER MOTOR LOW POSITION — CIRCUIT 56 (DB/O)	

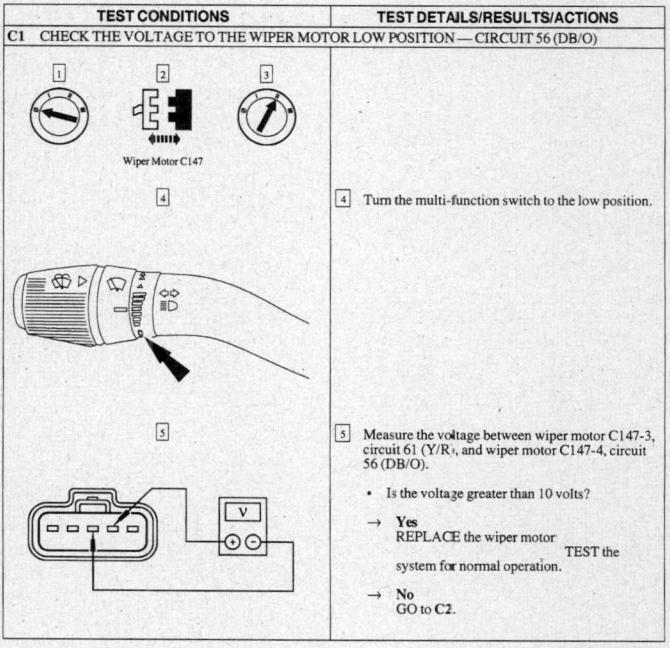

Wiper Motor C147

[4] Turn the multi-function switch to the low position.

[5] Measure the voltage between wiper motor C147-3, circuit 61 (Y/R), and wiper motor C147-4, circuit 56 (DB/O).

- Is the voltage greater than 10 volts?

→ **Yes**
REPLACE the wiper motor TEST the system for normal operation.

→ **No**
GO to **C2**.

FM9029800612010X

Fig. 5 Test C: Low Wiper Speed Does Not Operate Properly (Part 1 of 3). 2002–04

TEST CONDITIONS	TEST DETAILS/RESULTS/ACTIONS
C2 CHECK CIRCUIT 56 (DB/O) FOR SHORT TO GROUND	

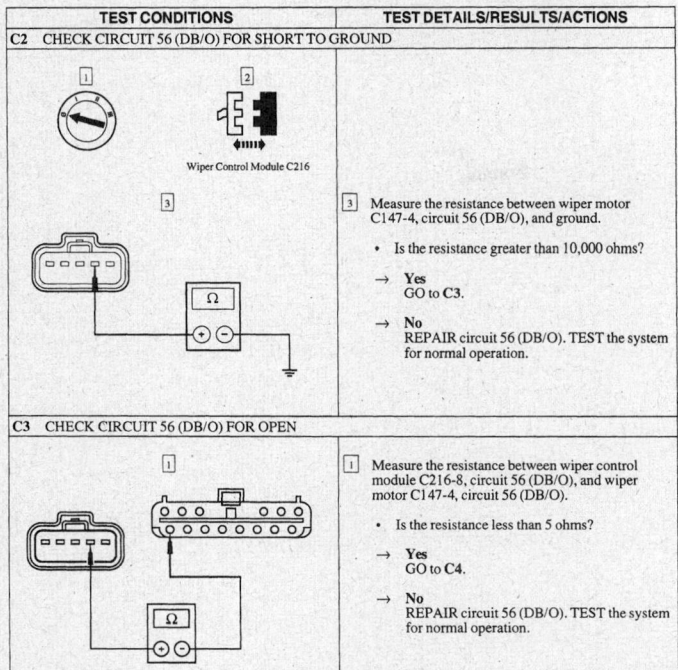

	③ Measure the resistance between wiper motor C147-4, circuit 56 (DB/O), and ground. • Is the resistance greater than 10,000 ohms? → **Yes** GO to **C3**. → **No** REPAIR circuit 56 (DB/O). TEST the system for normal operation.

TEST CONDITIONS	TEST DETAILS/RESULTS/ACTIONS
C3 CHECK CIRCUIT 56 (DB/O) FOR OPEN	

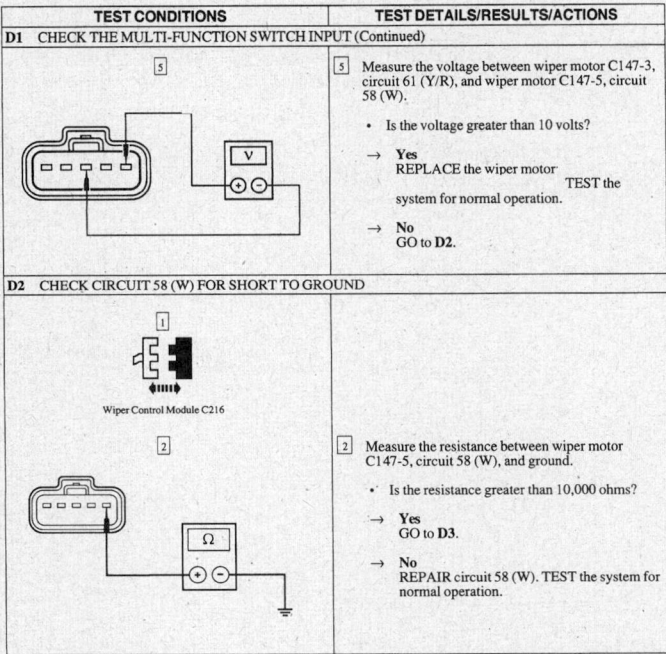

	① Measure the resistance between wiper control module C216-8, circuit 56 (DB/O), and wiper motor C147-4, circuit 56 (DB/O). • Is the resistance less than 5 ohms? → **Yes** GO to **C4**. → **No** REPAIR circuit 56 (DB/O). TEST the system for normal operation.

FM9029800612020X

Fig. 5   Test C: Low Wiper Speed Does Not Operate Properly (Part 2 of 3). 2002–04

TEST CONDITIONS	TEST DETAILS/RESULTS/ACTIONS
D1 CHECK THE MULTI-FUNCTION SWITCH INPUT (Continued)	

| ⑤ | ⑤ Measure the voltage between wiper motor C147-3, circuit 61 (Y/R), and wiper motor C147-5, circuit 58 (W).

 • Is the voltage greater than 10 volts?

 → **Yes**
 REPLACE the wiper motor. TEST the system for normal operation.

 → **No**
 GO to **D2**. |

TEST CONDITIONS	
D2 CHECK CIRCUIT 58 (W) FOR SHORT TO GROUND	

Wiper Control Module C216

	② Measure the resistance between wiper motor C147-5, circuit 58 (W), and ground. • Is the resistance greater than 10,000 ohms? → **Yes** GO to **D3**. → **No** REPAIR circuit 58 (W). TEST the system for normal operation.

FM9029800613020X

Fig. 6   Test D: High Speed Does Not Operate Properly (Part 2 of 3). 2002–04

TEST CONDITIONS	TEST DETAILS/RESULTS/ACTIONS
C4 CHECK THE MULTI-FUNCTION SWITCH INPUT	

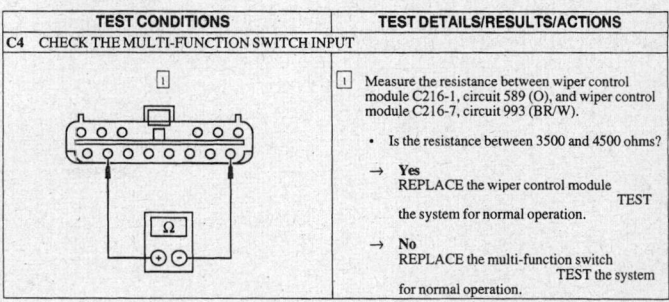

	① Measure the resistance between wiper control module C216-1, circuit 589 (O), and wiper control module C216-7, circuit 993 (BR/W). • Is the resistance between 3500 and 4500 ohms? → **Yes** REPLACE the wiper control module. TEST the system for normal operation. → **No** REPLACE the multi-function switch. TEST the system for normal operation.

FM9029800612030X

Fig. 5   Test C: Low Wiper Speed Does Not Operate Properly (Part 3 of 3). 2002–04

TEST CONDITIONS	TEST DETAILS/RESULTS/ACTIONS
D1 CHECK THE MULTI-FUNCTION SWITCH INPUT	

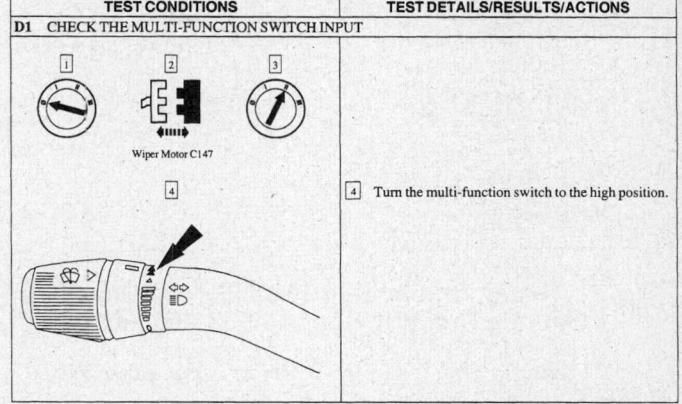

Wiper Motor C147

	④ Turn the multi-function switch to the high position.

FM9029800613010X

Fig. 6   Test D: High Speed Does Not Operate Properly (Part 1 of 3). 2002–04

TEST CONDITIONS	TEST DETAILS/RESULTS/ACTIONS
D3 CHECK CIRCUIT 58 (W) FOR OPEN	

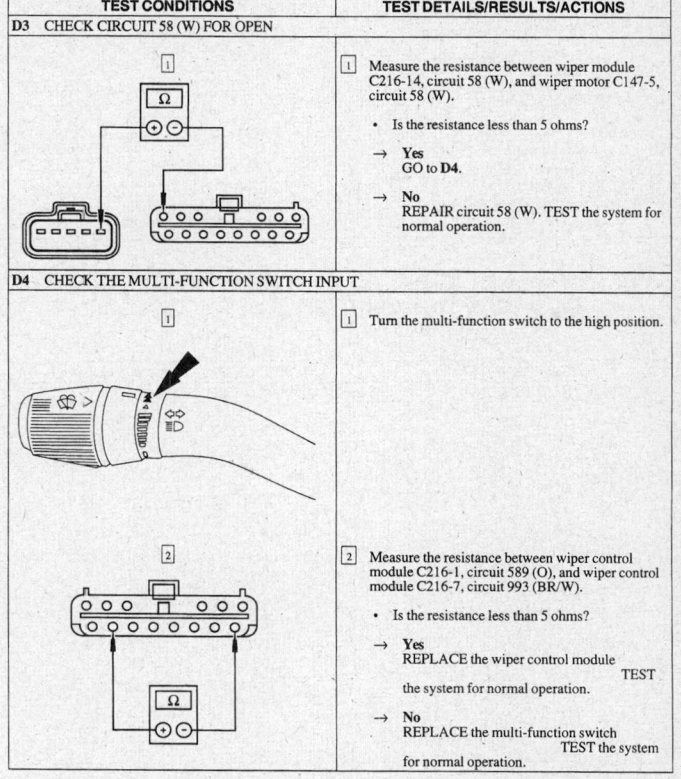

	① Measure the resistance between wiper module C216-14, circuit 58 (W), and wiper motor C147-5, circuit 58 (W). • Is the resistance less than 5 ohms? → **Yes** GO to **D4**. → **No** REPAIR circuit 58 (W). TEST the system for normal operation.

TEST CONDITIONS	
D4 CHECK THE MULTI-FUNCTION SWITCH INPUT	

| ① | ① Turn the multi-function switch to the high position. |

| | ② Measure the resistance between wiper control module C216-1, circuit 589 (O), and wiper control module C216-7, circuit 993 (BR/W).

 • Is the resistance less than 5 ohms?

 → **Yes**
 REPLACE the wiper control module. TEST the system for normal operation.

 → **No**
 REPLACE the multi-function switch. TEST the system for normal operation. |

FM9029800613030X

Fig. 6   Test D: High Speed Does Not Operate Properly (Part 3 of 3). 2002–04

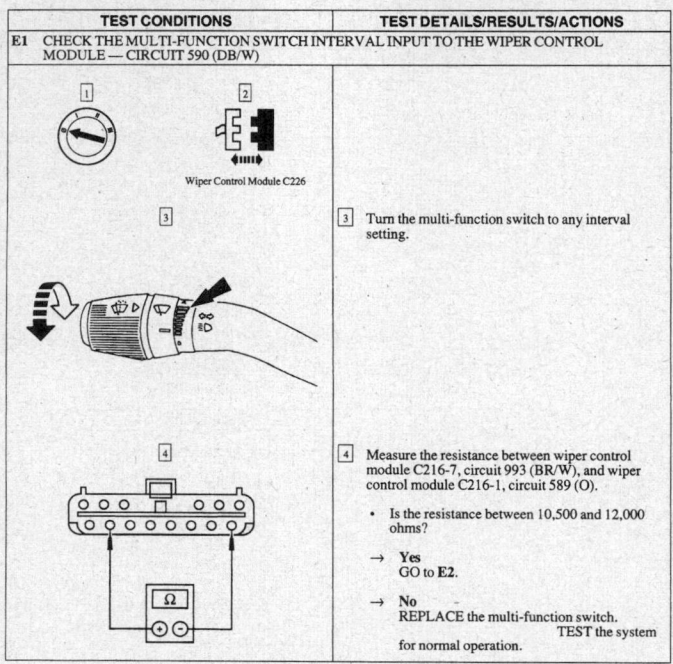

TEST CONDITIONS	TEST DETAILS/RESULTS/ACTIONS
E1 CHECK THE MULTI-FUNCTION SWITCH INTERVAL INPUT TO THE WIPER CONTROL MODULE — CIRCUIT 590 (DB/W)	

Wiper Control Module C226

3 Turn the multi-function switch to any interval setting.

4 Measure the resistance between wiper control module C216-7, circuit 993 (BR/W), and wiper control module C216-1, circuit 589 (O).

- Is the resistance between 10,500 and 12,000 ohms?
  - → **Yes** GO to **E2**.
  - → **No** REPLACE the multi-function switch. TEST the system for normal operation.

FM9029800614010X

Fig. 7   Test E: Intermittent Wiper Speed Does Not Operate Properly (Part 1 of 3). 2002–04

TEST CONDITIONS	TEST DETAILS/RESULTS/ACTIONS
E4 CHECK CIRCUIT 590 (DB/W) FOR OPEN	

Multi-Function Switch C251

2 Measure the resistance between wiper control module C216-9, circuit 590 (DB/W), and multi-function switch C251-6, circuit 590 (DB/W).

- Is the resistance less than 5 ohms?
  - → **Yes** REPLACE the multi-function switch TEST the system for normal operation.
  - → **No** REPAIR circuit 590 (DB/W). TEST the system for normal operation.

FM9029800614030X

Fig. 7   Test E: Intermittent Wiper Speed Does Not Operate Properly (Part 3 of 3). 2002–04

TEST CONDITIONS	TEST DETAILS/RESULTS/ACTIONS
F1 CHECK THE WINDSHIELD WIPER MOTOR FOR VOLTAGE CIRCUIT 65 (DG)	

Wiper Motor C147

4 Measure the voltage between wiper motor C147-2, circuit 65 (DG), and ground.

- Is the voltage greater than 10 volts?
  - → **Yes** GO to **F2**.
  - → **No** REPAIR circuit 65 (DG). TEST the system for normal operation.

FM9029800615010X

Fig. 8   Test F: Wipers Will Not Park At Proper Position (Part 1 of 3). 2002–04

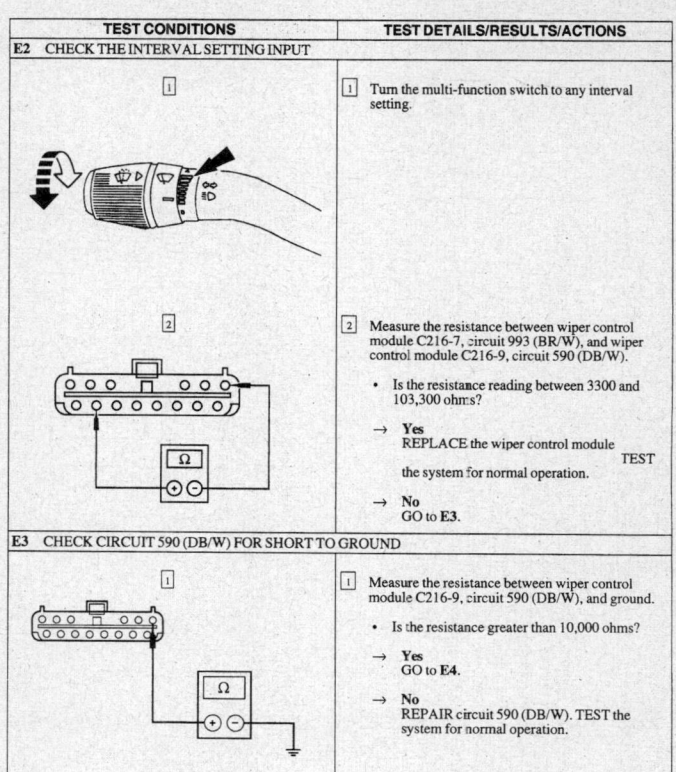

TEST CONDITIONS	TEST DETAILS/RESULTS/ACTIONS
E2 CHECK THE INTERVAL SETTING INPUT	

1 Turn the multi-function switch to any interval setting.

2 Measure the resistance between wiper control module C216-7, circuit 993 (BR/W), and wiper control module C216-9, circuit 590 (DB/W).

- Is the resistance reading between 3300 and 103,300 ohms?
  - → **Yes** REPLACE the wiper control module TEST the system for normal operation.
  - → **No** GO to **E3**.

TEST CONDITIONS	TEST DETAILS/RESULTS/ACTIONS
E3 CHECK CIRCUIT 590 (DB/W) FOR SHORT TO GROUND	

1 Measure the resistance between wiper control module C216-9, circuit 590 (DB/W), and ground.

- Is the resistance greater than 10,000 ohms?
  - → **Yes** GO to **E4**.
  - → **No** REPAIR circuit 590 (DB/W). TEST the system for normal operation.

FM9029800614020X

Fig. 7   Test E: Intermittent Wiper Speed Does Not Operate Properly (Part 2 of 3). 2002–04

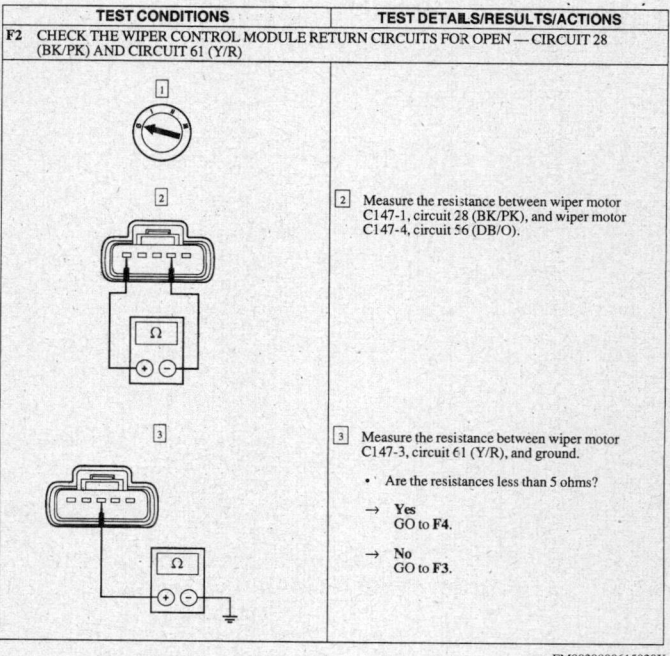

TEST CONDITIONS	TEST DETAILS/RESULTS/ACTIONS
F2 CHECK THE WIPER CONTROL MODULE RETURN CIRCUITS FOR OPEN — CIRCUIT 28 (BK/PK) AND CIRCUIT 61 (Y/R)	

2 Measure the resistance between wiper motor C147-1, circuit 28 (BK/PK), and wiper motor C147-4, circuit 56 (DB/O).

3 Measure the resistance between wiper motor C147-3, circuit 61 (Y/R), and ground.

- Are the resistances less than 5 ohms?
  - → **Yes** GO to **F4**.
  - → **No** GO to **F3**.

FM9029800615020X

Fig. 8   Test F: Wipers Will Not Park At Proper Position (Part 2 of 3). 2002–04

TEST CONDITIONS	TEST DETAILS/RESULTS/ACTIONS

F3   CHECK THE WIPER CONTROL MODULE/WIPER MOTOR CIRCUITS FOR OPEN

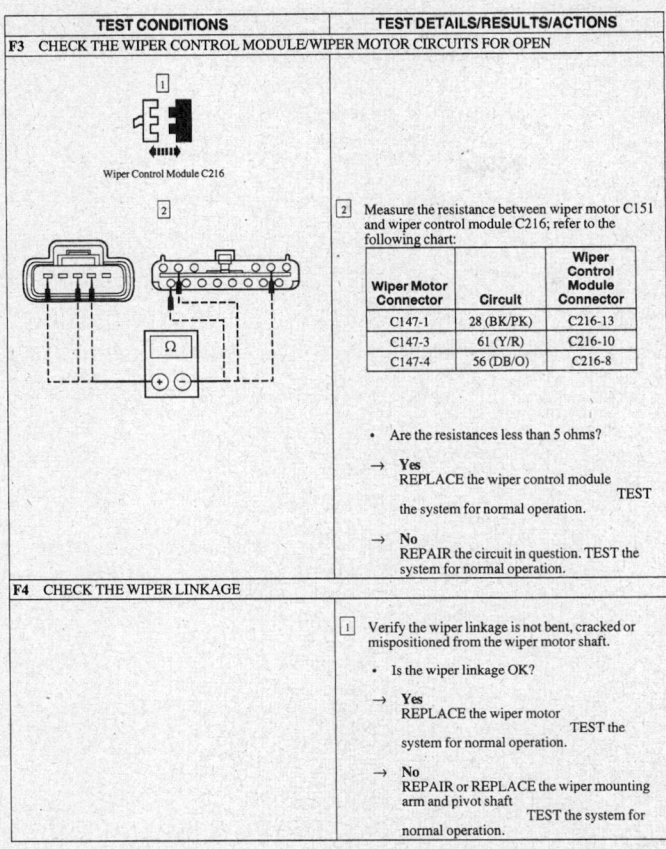

Wiper Control Module C216

2 Measure the resistance between wiper motor C151 and wiper control module C216; refer to the following chart:

Wiper Motor Connector	Circuit	Wiper Control Module Connector
C147-1	28 (BK/PK)	C216-13
C147-3	61 (Y/R)	C216-10
C147-4	56 (DB/O)	C216-8

- Are the resistances less than 5 ohms?

→ **Yes**
  REPLACE the wiper control module TEST the system for normal operation.

→ **No**
  REPAIR the circuit in question. TEST the system for normal operation.

F4   CHECK THE WIPER LINKAGE

1 Verify the wiper linkage is not bent, cracked or mispositioned from the wiper motor shaft.

- Is the wiper linkage OK?

→ **Yes**
  REPLACE the wiper motor TEST the system for normal operation.

→ **No**
  REPAIR or REPLACE the wiper mounting arm and pivot shaft TEST the system for normal operation.

FM9029800615030X

Fig. 8   Test F: Wipers Will Not Park At Proper Position (Part 3 of 3). 2002–04

TEST CONDITIONS	TEST DETAILS/RESULTS/ACTIONS

G3   CHECK CIRCUIT 589 (O) FOR SHORT TO GROUND

1 Measure the resistance between wiper control module C216-1, circuit 589 (O), and ground.

- Is the resistance greater than 10,000 ohms?

→ **Yes**
  GO to **G4.**

→ **No**
  REPAIR circuit 589 (O). TEST the system for normal operation.

G4   CHECK CIRCUIT 993 (BR/W) FOR SHORT TO GROUND

1 Measure the resistance between wiper control module C216-7, circuit 993 (BR/W), and ground.

- Is the resistance greater than 10,000 ohms?

→ **Yes**
  REPLACE the wiper control module TEST the system for normal operation.

→ **No**
  REPAIR circuit 993 (BR/W). TEST the system for normal operation.

FM9029800616020X

Fig. 9   Test G: Wipers Stay On Continuously (Part 2 of 2). 2002–04

TEST CONDITIONS	TEST DETAILS/RESULTS/ACTIONS

G1   CHECK THE MULTI-FUNCTION SWITCH

1 Check the multi-function switch.

- Is the multi-function switch OK?

→ **Yes**
  GO to **G2.**

→ **No**
  REPLACE the multi-function switch TEST the system for normal operation.

G2   CHECK CIRCUIT 590 (DB/W) FOR SHORT TO GROUND

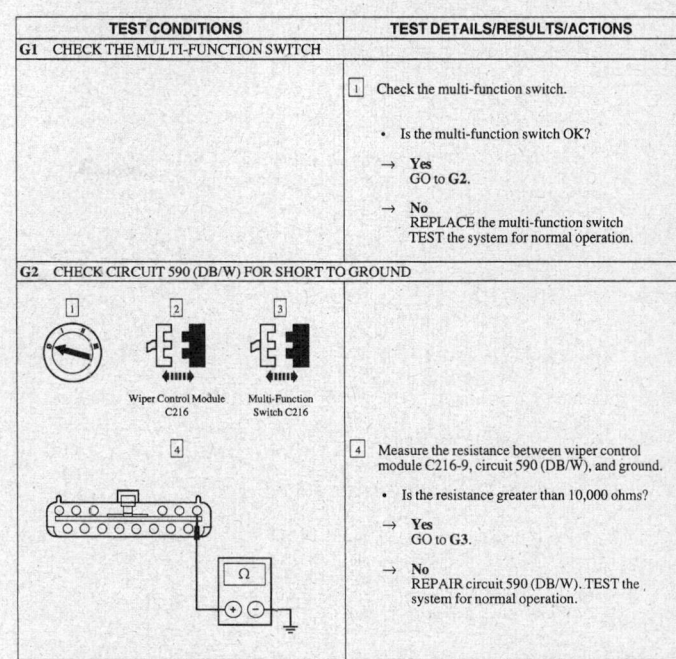

Wiper Control Module C216   Multi-Function Switch C216

4 Measure the resistance between wiper control module C216-9, circuit 590 (DB/W), and ground.

- Is the resistance greater than 10,000 ohms?

→ **Yes**
  GO to **G3.**

→ **No**
  REPAIR circuit 590 (DB/W). TEST the system for normal operation.

FM9029800616010X

Fig. 9   Test G: Wipers Stay On Continuously (Part 1 of 2). 2002–04

Condition	Possible Sources	Action
- The wipers are inoperative	- Fuse. - Multifunction switch. - Circuitry. - Ignition switch. - Windshield wiper motor.	- Go To Pinpoint Test A.
- The wipers stay on continuously	- Windshield wiper motor. - Multifunction switch. - Circuitry.	- Go To Pinpoint Test B.
- The high/low wiper speeds do not operate correctly (intermittent wiper mode OK)	- Multifunction switch. - Circuitry. - Windshield wiper motor.	- Go To Pinpoint Test C.
- The intermittent wiper speed does not operate correctly (high/low speeds OK)	- Multifunction switch. - Circuitry. - Windshield wiper motor.	- Go To Pinpoint Test D.
- The wipers will not park at the correct position	- Wiper motor. - Pivot arm adjustment. - Linkage.	- Repair or adjust wiper blade or pivot arm adjustment.
- The wipers do not operate correctly in the MIST position	- Multifunction switch. - Circuitry. - Washer pump. - Windshield wiper motor.	- Go To Pinpoint Test E.
- The washer pump is inoperative	- Washer pump. - Multifunction switch. - Wiper motor. - Circuitry.	- Go To Pinpoint Test F.

LTV0500000001904

Fig. 10   Symptom Tests. 2005–06

Test Step	Result / Action to Take
A1 CHECK CIRCUITS 65 (DG) AND 950 (WH/BK) FOR VOLTAGE • Key in OFF position. • Disconnect: Windshield Wiper Motor C125. • Key in ON position. • Measure the voltage between windshield wiper motor C125 pin 8, circuit 65 (DG), harness side and ground; and between windshield wiper motor C125 pin 5, circuit 950 (WH/BK), harness side and ground. • **Are the voltages greater than 10 volts?**	**Yes** GO to A2 . **No** VERIFY the central junction box (CJB) fuse 9 (5A) and 44 (20A) are OK. If OK, REPAIR the circuit(s) in question. TEST the system for normal operation.
A2 CHECK CIRCUITS 57 (BK) AND 938 (BK/LG) FOR OPENS • Key in OFF position. • Measure the resistance between windshield wiper motor C125 pin 6, circuit 57 (BK), harness side and ground; and between windshield wiper motor C125 pin 3, circuit 938 (BK/LG), harness side and ground. • **Are the resistances less than 5 ohms?**	**Yes** GO to A3 . **No** REPAIR the circuit(s) in question. TEST the system for normal operation.
A3 CHECK THE MULTIFUNCTION SWITCH • Disconnect: Multifunction Switch C202c. • Carry out the multifunction switch component test.	**Yes** GO to A4 . **No**

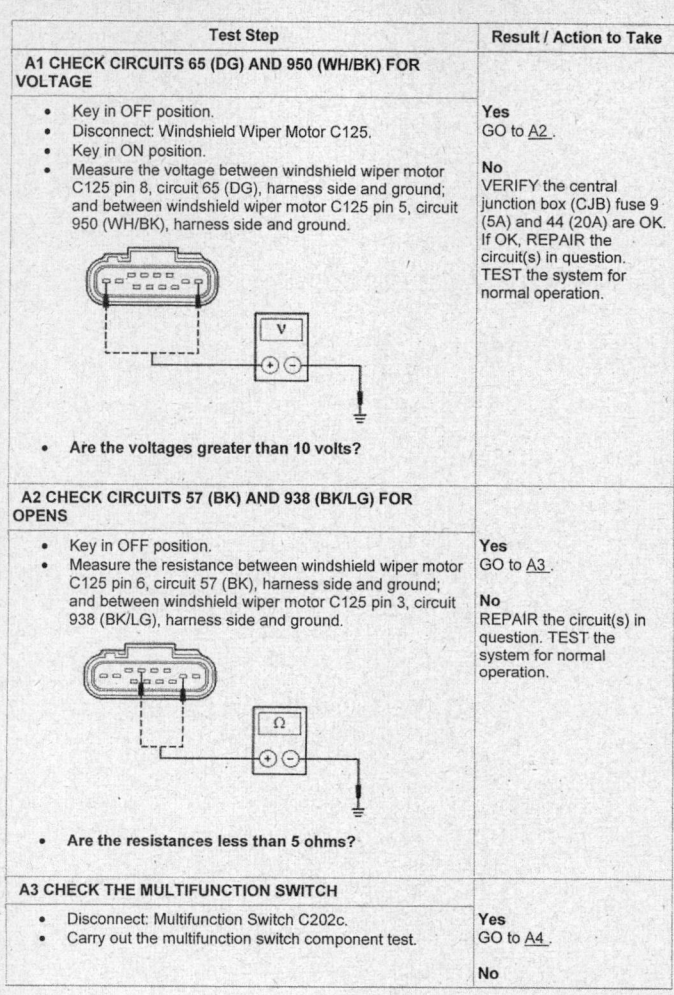

LTV0500000001905

**Fig. 11   Test A: Wipers Are Inoperative (Part 1 of 3).
2005–06**

• **Is the resistance less than 5 ohms?**	

A6 CHECK FOR CORRECT WIPER MOTOR OPERATION
• Disconnect all wiper motor connectors.
• Check for:
  ▪ corrosion.
  ▪ pushed-out pins.
• Connect all wiper motor connectors and make sure they seat correctly.
• Operate the system and verify the concern is still present.
• **Is the concern still present?**
	Yes
	GO to A7 .
	
	No
	The system is operating correctly at this time. Concern may have been caused by a loose or corroded connector. TEST the system for normal operation.

A7 CHECK THE WINDSHIELD WIPER MOTOR • Key in OFF position. • Disconnect: Windshield Wiper Motor C125. • Carry out the windshield wiper motor component test as outlined in this section. • **Did the windshield wiper motor pass the component test?**	**Yes** The system is operating correctly at this time. Concern may have been caused by binding or incorrect pivot arm adjustment. Repair or adjust wiper arm and/or pivot arm. TEST the system for normal operation. **No** INSTALL a new windshield wiper motor.

LTV0500000001907

**Fig. 11   Test A: Wipers Are Inoperative (Part 3 of 3).
2005–06**

	INSTALL a new multifunction switch.
• **Did the multifunction switch pass the component test?**	
A4 CHECK CIRCUIT 938 (BK/LG) FOR AN OPEN • Measure the resistance between multifunction switch C202c pin 5, circuit 938 (BK/LG), harness side and ground. • **Is the resistance less than 5 ohms?**	**Yes** GO to A5 . **No** REPAIR the circuit. TEST the system for normal operation.
A5 CHECK CIRCUITS 56 (DB/OG), 58 (WH), 61 (YE/RD) AND 63 (RD) FOR OPENS • Using the following table, measure the resistance between multifunction switch C202c harness side and windshield wiper motor C125 harness side:	**Yes** GO to A6 . **No** REPAIR the circuit(s) in question. TEST the system for normal operation.

Multifunction Switch C202c	Windshield Wiper Motor C125
Pin 6, circuit 56 (DB/OG)	Pin 10, circuit 56 (DB/OG)
Pin 3, circuit 58 (WH)	Pin 11, circuit 58 (WH)
Pin 1, circuit 61 (YE/RD)	Pin 1, circuit 61 (YE/RD)
Pin 4, circuit 63 (RD)	Pin 9, circuit 63 (RD)

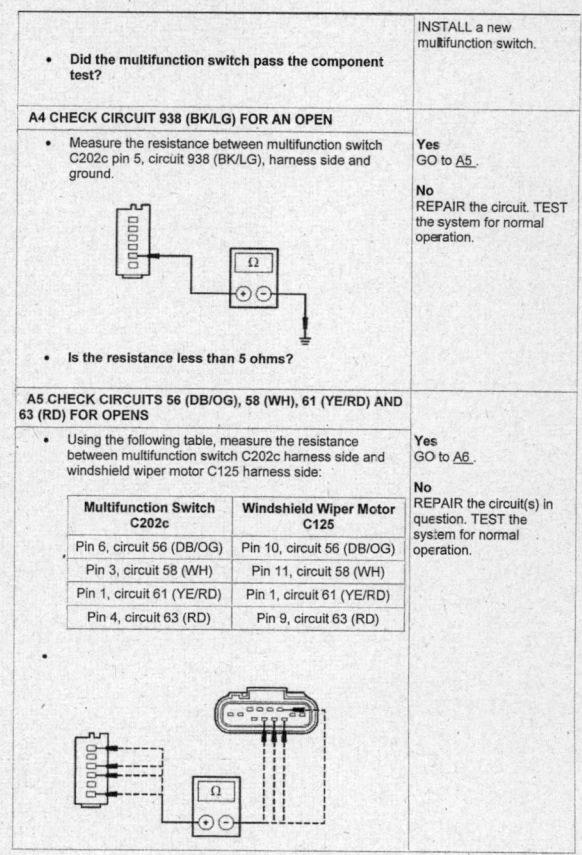

LTV0500000001906

**Fig. 11   Test A: Wipers Are Inoperative (Part 2 of 3).
2005–06**

Test Step	Result / Action to Take
B1 CHECK THE MULTIFUNCTION SWITCH • Key in OFF position. • Disconnect: Multifunction Switch C202c. • Carry out the multifunction switch component test. • **Did the multifunction switch pass the component test?**	**Yes** GO to B2 . **No** INSTALL a new multifunction switch.
B2 CHECK CIRCUIT 938 (BK/LG) FOR AN OPEN • Measure the resistance between multifunction switch C202c pin 5, circuit 938 (BK/LG), harness side and ground. A0079581 • **Is the resistance less than 5 ohms?**	**Yes** GO to B3 . **No** REPAIR the circuit. TEST the system for normal operation.
B3 CHECK CIRCUITS 56 (DB/OG), 58 (WH), 61 (YE/RD) AND 63 (RD) FOR SHORTS • Disconnect: Windshield Wiper Motor C125. • Using the following table, measure the resistance between windshield wiper motor C125 harness side and ground:	**Yes** GO to B4 . **No** REPAIR the circuit(s) in question. TEST the system for normal operation.

Windshield Wiper Motor C125	Ground
Pin 10, circuit 56 (DB/OG)	ground
Pin 11, circuit 58 (WH)	ground
Pin 1, circuit 61 (YE/RD)	ground
Pin 9, circuit 63 (RD)	ground

LTV0500000001908

**Fig. 12   Test B: Wipers Stay On Continuously
(Part 1 of 2). 2005–06**

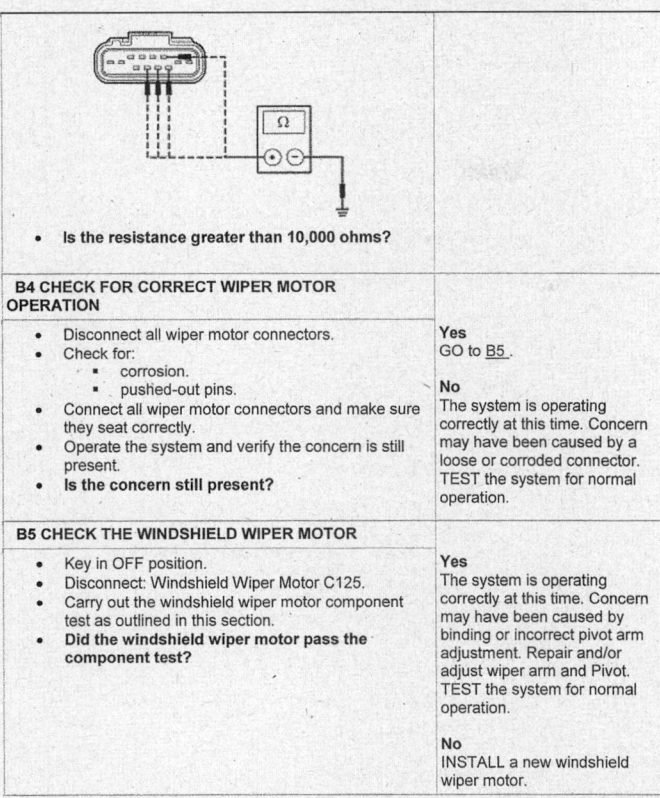

- **Is the resistance greater than 10,000 ohms?**

B4 CHECK FOR CORRECT WIPER MOTOR OPERATION	

• Disconnect all wiper motor connectors.
• Check for:
  ▪ corrosion.
  ▪ pushed-out pins.
• Connect all wiper motor connectors and make sure they seat correctly.
• Operate the system and verify the concern is still present.
• **Is the concern still present?**
	Yes
	GO to B5 .
	
	No
	The system is operating correctly at this time. Concern may have been caused by a loose or corroded connector. TEST the system for normal operation.

B5 CHECK THE WINDSHIELD WIPER MOTOR	
• Key in OFF position. • Disconnect: Windshield Wiper Motor C125. • Carry out the windshield wiper motor component test as outlined in this section. • **Did the windshield wiper motor pass the component test?**	**Yes** The system is operating correctly at this time. Concern may have been caused by binding or incorrect pivot arm adjustment. Repair and/or adjust wiper arm and Pivot. TEST the system for normal operation. **No** INSTALL a new windshield wiper motor.

LTV0500000001909

Fig. 12   Test B: Wipers Stay On Continuously (Part 2 of 2). 2005–06

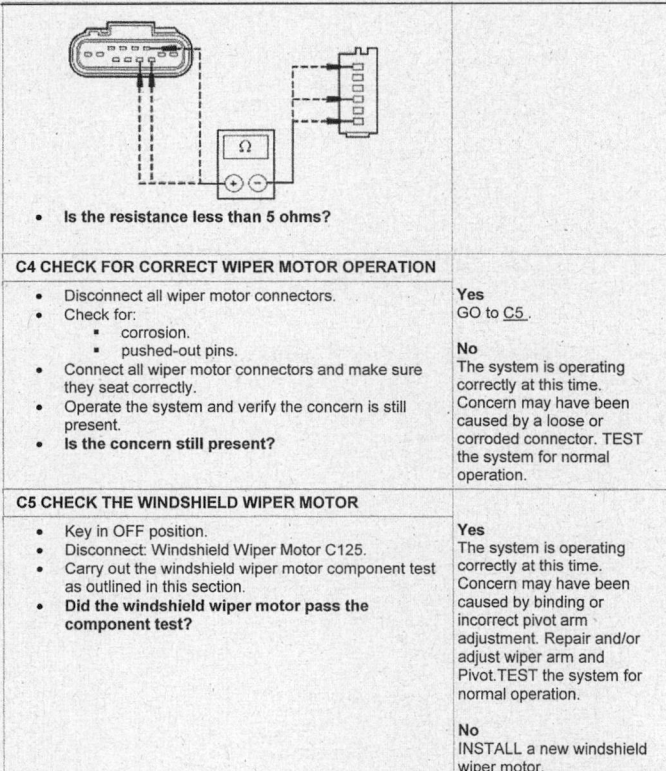

- **Is the resistance less than 5 ohms?**

C4 CHECK FOR CORRECT WIPER MOTOR OPERATION	

• Disconnect all wiper motor connectors.
• Check for:
  ▪ corrosion.
  ▪ pushed-out pins.
• Connect all wiper motor connectors and make sure they seat correctly.
• Operate the system and verify the concern is still present.
• **Is the concern still present?**
	Yes
	GO to C5 .
	
	No
	The system is operating correctly at this time. Concern may have been caused by a loose or corroded connector. TEST the system for normal operation.

C5 CHECK THE WINDSHIELD WIPER MOTOR	
• Key in OFF position. • Disconnect: Windshield Wiper Motor C125. • Carry out the windshield wiper motor component test as outlined in this section. • **Did the windshield wiper motor pass the component test?**	**Yes** The system is operating correctly at this time. Concern may have been caused by binding or incorrect pivot arm adjustment. Repair and/or adjust wiper arm and Pivot. TEST the system for normal operation. **No** INSTALL a new windshield wiper motor.

LTV0500000001911

Fig. 13   Test C: High/Low Wiper Speed Does Not Operate Correctly, Intermittent Mode OK (Part 2 of 2). 2005–06

Test Step	Result / Action to Take
C1 CHECK THE MULTIFUNCTION SWITCH	
• Key in OFF position. • Disconnect: Multifunction Switch C202c. • Carry out the multifunction switch component test. • **Did the multifunction switch pass the component test?**	**Yes** GO to C2 . **No** INSTALL a new multifunction switch.
C2 CHECK CIRCUIT 938 (BK/LG) FOR AN OPEN	
• Measure the resistance between multifunction switch C202c pin 5, circuit 938 (BK/LG), harness side and ground. • **Is the resistance less than 5 ohms?**	**Yes** GO to C3 . **No** REPAIR the circuit. TEST the system for normal operation.
C3 CHECK CIRCUITS 56 (DB/OG), 61 (YE/RD) AND 63 (RD) FOR OPENS	
• Disconnect: Windshield Wiper Motor C125. • Using the following table, measure the resistance between multifunction switch C202c harness side and windshield wiper motor C125 harness side:	**Yes** GO to C4 . **No** REPAIR the circuit(s) in question. TEST the system for normal operation.

Multifunction Switch C202c	Windshield Wiper Motor C125
Pin 6, circuit 56 (DB/OG)	Pin 10, circuit 56 (DB/OG)
Pin 1, circuit 61 (YE/RD)	Pin 1, circuit 61 (YE/RD)
Pin 4, circuit 63 (RD)	Pin 9, circuit 63 (RD)

LTV0500000001910

Fig. 13   Test C: High/Low Wiper Speed Does Not Operate Correctly, Intermittent Mode OK (Part 1 of 2). 2005–06

Test Step	Result / Action to Take
D1 CHECK THE MULTIFUNCTION SWITCH	
• Key in OFF position. • Disconnect: Multifunction Switch C202c. • Carry out the multifunction switch component test. • **Did the multifunction switch pass the component test?**	**Yes** GO to D2 . **No** INSTALL a new multifunction switch..
D2 CHECK CIRCUIT 938 (BK/LG) FOR AN OPEN	
• Measure the resistance between multifunction switch C202c pin 5, circuit 938 (BK/LG), harness side and ground. • **Is the resistance less than 5 ohms?**	**Yes** GO to D3 . **No** REPAIR the circuit. TEST the system for normal operation.
D3 CHECK CIRCUITS 56 (DB/OG), 61 (YE/RD) AND 63 (RD) FOR OPENS	
• Disconnect: Windshield Wiper Motor C125. • Using the following table, measure the resistance between multifunction switch C202c harness side and windshield wiper motor C125 harness side:	**Yes** GO to D4 . **No** REPAIR the circuit(s) in question. TEST the system for normal operation.

Multifunction Switch C202c	Windshield Wiper Motor C125
Pin 6, circuit 56 (DB/OG)	Pin 10, circuit 56 (DB/OG)
Pin 1, circuit 61 (YE/RD)	Pin 1, circuit 61 (YE/RD)
Pin 4, circuit 63 (RD)	Pin 9, circuit 63 (RD)

LTV0500000001912

Fig. 14   Test D: Intermittent Wiper Speed Does Not Operate Correctly, High/Low Speeds OK (Part 1 of 2). 2005–06

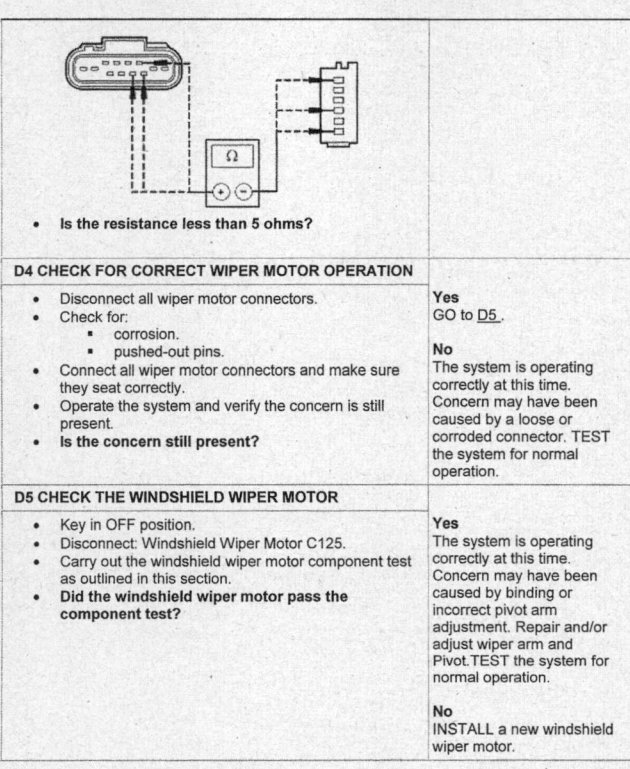

- Is the resistance less than 5 ohms?

Test Step	Result / Action to Take
D4 CHECK FOR CORRECT WIPER MOTOR OPERATION	

• Disconnect all wiper motor connectors.
• Check for:
  ▪ corrosion.
  ▪ pushed-out pins.
• Connect all wiper motor connectors and make sure they seat correctly.
• Operate the system and verify the concern is still present.
• **Is the concern still present?**
	Yes
	GO to D5 .
	
	No
	The system is operating correctly at this time. Concern may have been caused by a loose or corroded connector. TEST the system for normal operation.

D5 CHECK THE WINDSHIELD WIPER MOTOR	
• Key in OFF position. • Disconnect: Windshield Wiper Motor C125. • Carry out the windshield wiper motor component test as outlined in this section. • **Did the windshield wiper motor pass the component test?**	**Yes** The system is operating correctly at this time. Concern may have been caused by binding or incorrect pivot arm adjustment. Repair and/or adjust wiper arm and Pivot. TEST the system for normal operation. **No** INSTALL a new windshield wiper motor.

LTV0500000001913

Fig. 14 Test D: Intermittent Wiper Speed Does Not Operate Correctly, High/Low Speeds OK (Part 2 of 2). 2005–06

Test Step	Result / Action to Take
F1 CHECK THE WASHER PUMP MOTOR FOR VOLTAGE	
• Key in OFF position. • Disconnect: Washer Pump Motor C137. • Key in ON position. • Measure the voltage between washer pump motor C137 pin 1, circuit 941 (BK/WH) harness side and ground while depressing the multifunction switch to the wash position. • Is the voltage greater than 10 volts?	**Yes** GO to F2 . **No** GO to F3 .
F2 CHECK CIRCUIT 57 (BK) FOR GROUND	
• Measure the resistance between washer pump motor C137 pin 2, circuit 57 (BK) harness side and ground. • Is the resistance less than 5 ohms?	**Yes** INSTALL a new washer pump. **No** REPAIR the circuit. TEST the system for normal operation.
F3 CHECK CIRCUIT 941 (BK/WH) FOR AN OPEN	
• Key in OFF position. • Disconnect: Windshield Wiper Motor C125. • Measure the resistance between windshield wiper motor C125 pin 7, circuit 941 (BK/WH), harness side and washer pump motor C137 pin 1, circuit 941 (BK/WH), harness side.	**Yes** GO to F4 . **No** REPAIR the circuit. TEST the system for normal operation.

LTV0500000001915

Fig. 16 Test F: Washer Pump Is Inoperative (Part 1 of 3). 2005–06

Test Step	Result / Action to Take
E1 CHECK THE MULTIFUNCTION SWITCH	
• Key in OFF position. • Disconnect: Multifunction Switch C202c. • Carry out the multifunction switch component test. • **Did the multifunction switch pass the component test?**	**Yes** GO to E2 . **No** INSTALL a new multifunction switch
E2 CHECK CIRCUIT 938 (BK/LG) FOR AN OPEN	
• Measure the resistance between multifunction switch C202c pin 5, circuit 938 (BK/LG), harness side and ground. • Is the resistance less than 5 ohms?	**Yes** GO to E3 . **No** REPAIR the circuit. TEST the system for normal operation.
E3 CHECK CIRCUIT 680 (LB/OG) FOR AN OPEN	
• Disconnect: Windshield Wiper Motor C125. • Measure the resistance between multifunction switch C202c pin 2, circuit 680 (LB/OG), harness side and windshield wiper motor C125 pin 12, circuit 680 (LB/OG), harness side. • Is the resistance less than 5 ohms?	**Yes** Go To Pinpoint Test F . **No** REPAIR the circuit. TEST the system for normal operation.

LTV0500000001914

Fig. 15 Test E: Wipers Do Not Operate Correctly In Mist Position. 2005-06

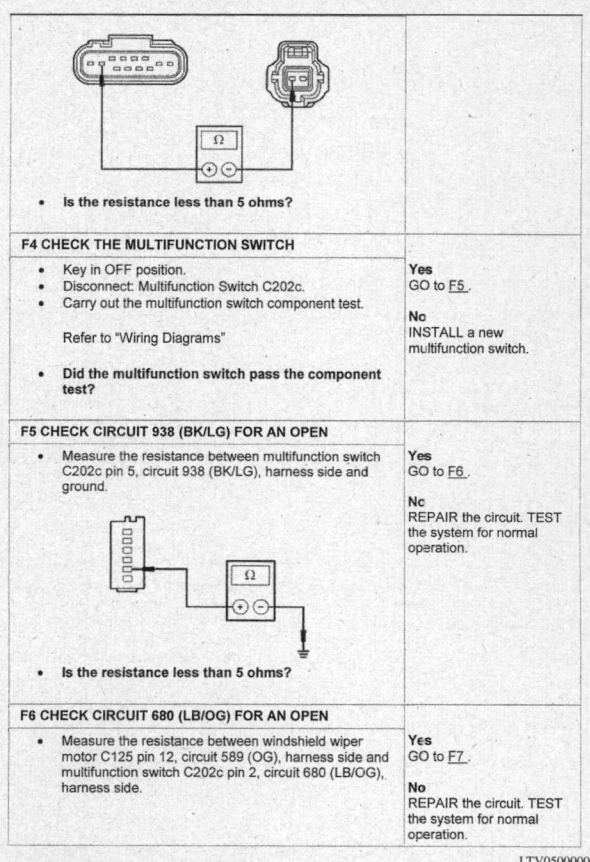

- is the resistance less than 5 ohms?

Test Step	Result / Action to Take
F4 CHECK THE MULTIFUNCTION SWITCH	
• Key in OFF position. • Disconnect: Multifunction Switch C202c. • Carry out the multifunction switch component test. Refer to "Wiring Diagrams" • **Did the multifunction switch pass the component test?**	**Yes** GO to F5 . **No** INSTALL a new multifunction switch.
F5 CHECK CIRCUIT 938 (BK/LG) FOR AN OPEN	
• Measure the resistance between multifunction switch C202c pin 5, circuit 938 (BK/LG), harness side and ground. • Is the resistance less than 5 ohms?	**Yes** GO to F6 . **No** REPAIR the circuit. TEST the system for normal operation.
F6 CHECK CIRCUIT 680 (LB/OG) FOR AN OPEN	
• Measure the resistance between windshield wiper motor C125 pin 12, circuit 589 (OG), harness side and multifunction switch C202c pin 2, circuit 680 (LB/OG), harness side.	**Yes** GO to F7 . **No** REPAIR the circuit. TEST the system for normal operation.

LTV0500000001916

Fig. 16 Test F: Washer Pump Is Inoperative (Part 2 of 3). 2005–06

COMPONENT DIAGNOSIS & TESTING

Refer to "Aviator" for component diagnosis and testing procedures.

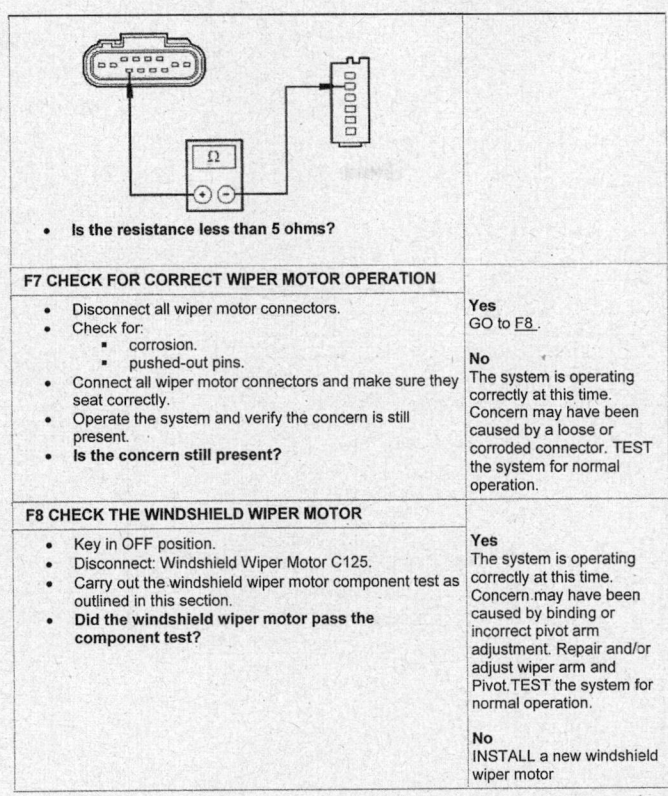

- **Is the resistance less than 5 ohms?**

F7 CHECK FOR CORRECT WIPER MOTOR OPERATION	

• Disconnect all wiper motor connectors.
• Check for:
    ▪ corrosion.
    ▪ pushed-out pins.
• Connect all wiper motor connectors and make sure they seat correctly.
• Operate the system and verify the concern is still present.
• **Is the concern still present?**
	Yes
	GO to F8.
	
	No
	The system is operating correctly at this time. Concern may have been caused by a loose or corroded connector. TEST the system for normal operation.

F8 CHECK THE WINDSHIELD WIPER MOTOR	
• Key in OFF position. • Disconnect: Windshield Wiper Motor C125. • Carry out the windshield wiper motor component test as outlined in this section. • **Did the windshield wiper motor pass the component test?**	**Yes** The system is operating correctly at this time. Concern may have been caused by binding or incorrect pivot arm adjustment. Repair and/or adjust wiper arm and Pivot.TEST the system for normal operation. **No** INSTALL a new windshield wiper motor

LTV0500000001917

Fig. 16   Test F: Washer Pump Is Inoperative (Part 3 of 3). 2005–06

Excursion & F-Super Duty

NOTE: On Air Bag Equipped Models, Refer To "Air Bag System Precautions" Located In The Front Of This Manual For System Disarming & Arming Procedures.

NOTE: "Electrical Symbol & Wire Color Code Identification" Located In The Front Of This Manual May Be Used As An Aid When Using Wiring Diagrams Found In This Section.

NOTE: Refer To "Computer Relearn Procedures" Located In The Front Of This Manual When Battery Power To The Computer Has Been Interrupted.

INDEX

	Page No.		Page No.		Page No.
Component Diagnosis & Testing	3-67	**System Diagnosis & Testing**	3-40	Diagnostic Tests	3-40
Diagnostic Chart Index	3-43	Accessing Diagnostic Trouble Codes	3-40	2005–06 F-Super Duty	3-40
Precautions	3-40	Clearing Diagnostic Trouble Codes	3-40	Excursion & 2002–04 F-Super Duty	3-40
Battery Ground Cable	3-40			Wiring Diagrams	3-40

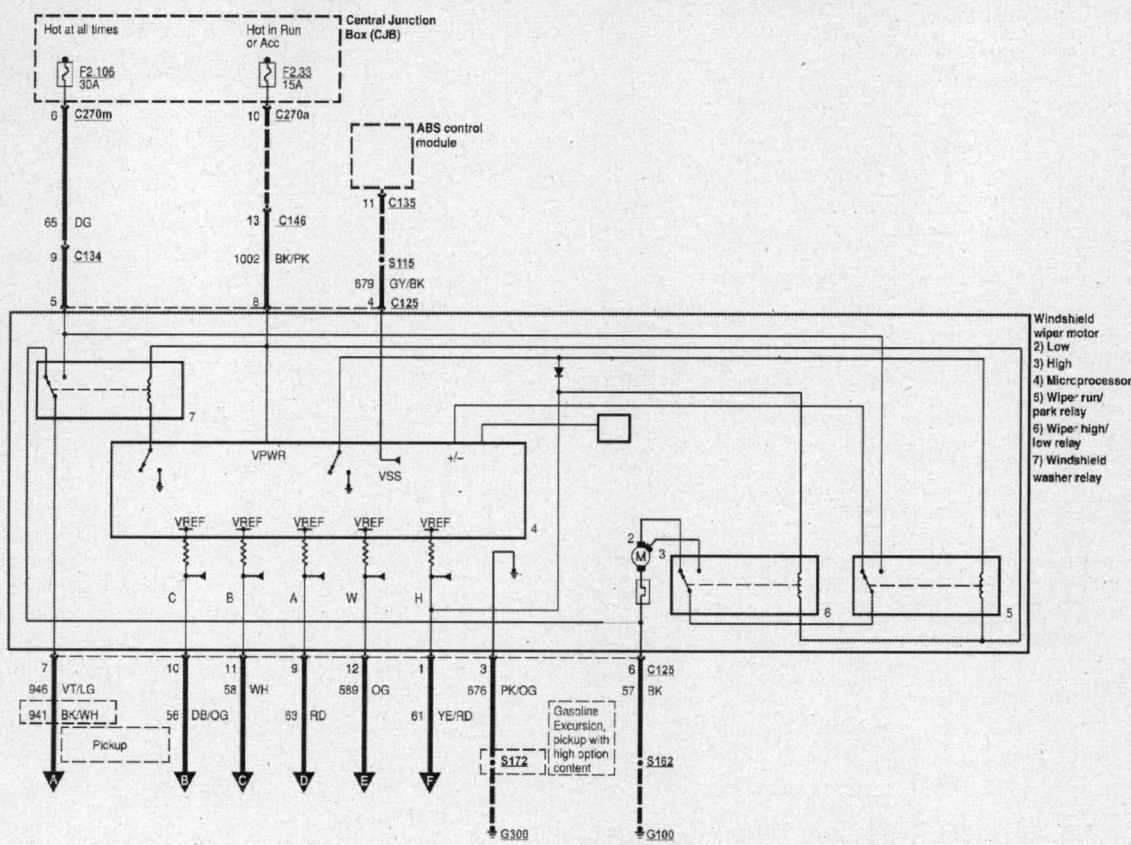

Fig. 1   Wiring diagram (Part 1 of 3). Excursion & 2002–05 F-Super Duty

PRECAUTIONS

Battery Ground Cable

Prior to service, disconnect battery ground cable and isolate as required.

SYSTEM DIAGNOSIS & TESTING

Accessing Diagnostic Trouble Codes

Connect a suitably programmed scan tool and Vehicle Communication Module (VCM) with appropriate adapters, or equivalents, to the Data Link Connector (DCL) located in the passenger compartment beneath the instrument panel. Follow tool manufacturer's instructions for accessing speed control Diagnostic Trouble Codes (DTC).

Wiring Diagrams

Refer to **Figs. 1 and 2** for wiring diagrams.

Diagnostic Tests

EXCURSION & 2002–04 F-SUPER DUTY

Refer to **Figs. 3 through 15** for diagnostic tests.

2005–06 F-SUPER DUTY

Refer to **Figs. 16 through 23** for diagnostic tests.

Clearing Diagnostic Trouble Codes

Connect a suitably programmed scan tool and Vehicle Communication Module (VCM) with appropriate adapters, or equivalents, to the Data Link Connector (DCL) located in the passenger compartment beneath the instrument panel. Follow tool manufacturer's instructions for accessing speed control Diagnostic Trouble Codes (DTC).

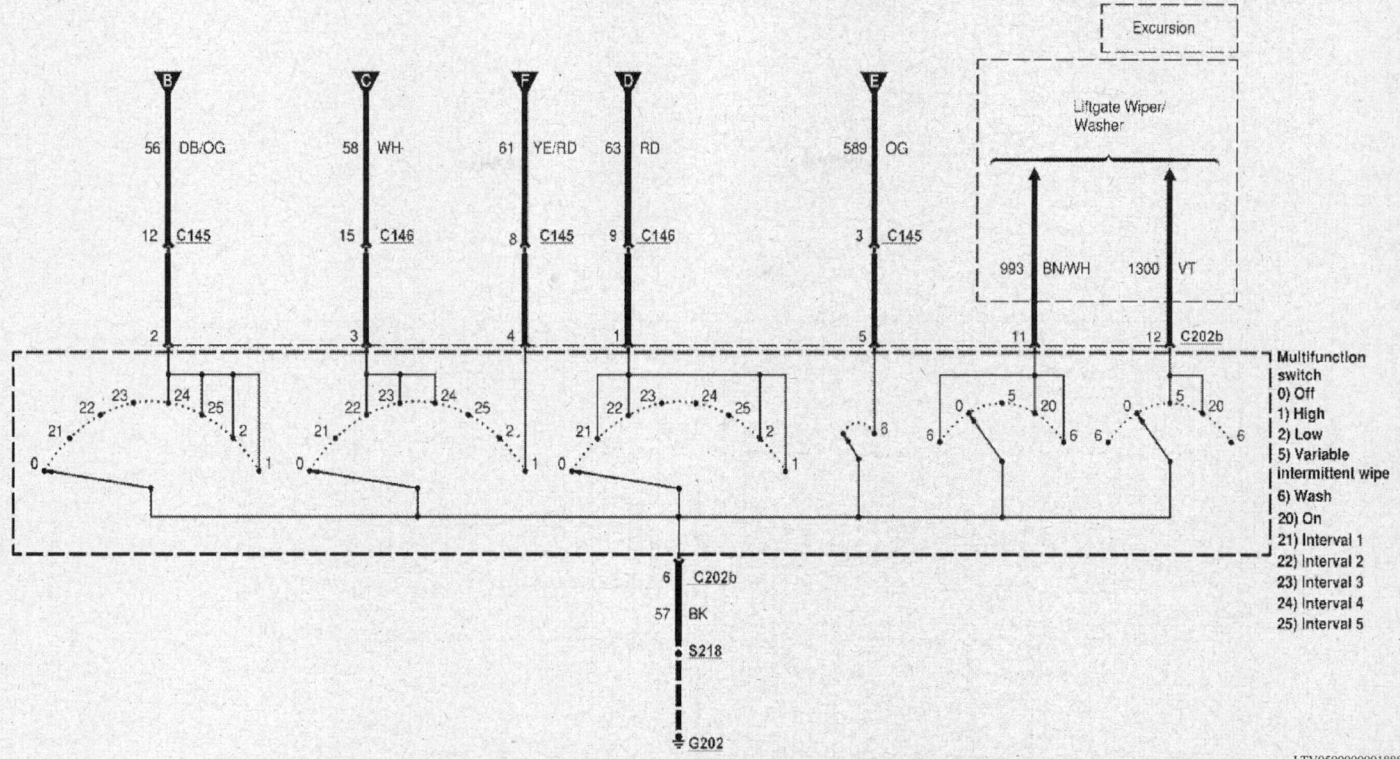

Fig. 1   Wiring diagram (Part 2 of 3). Excursion & 2002–05 F-Super Duty

LTV0500000001888

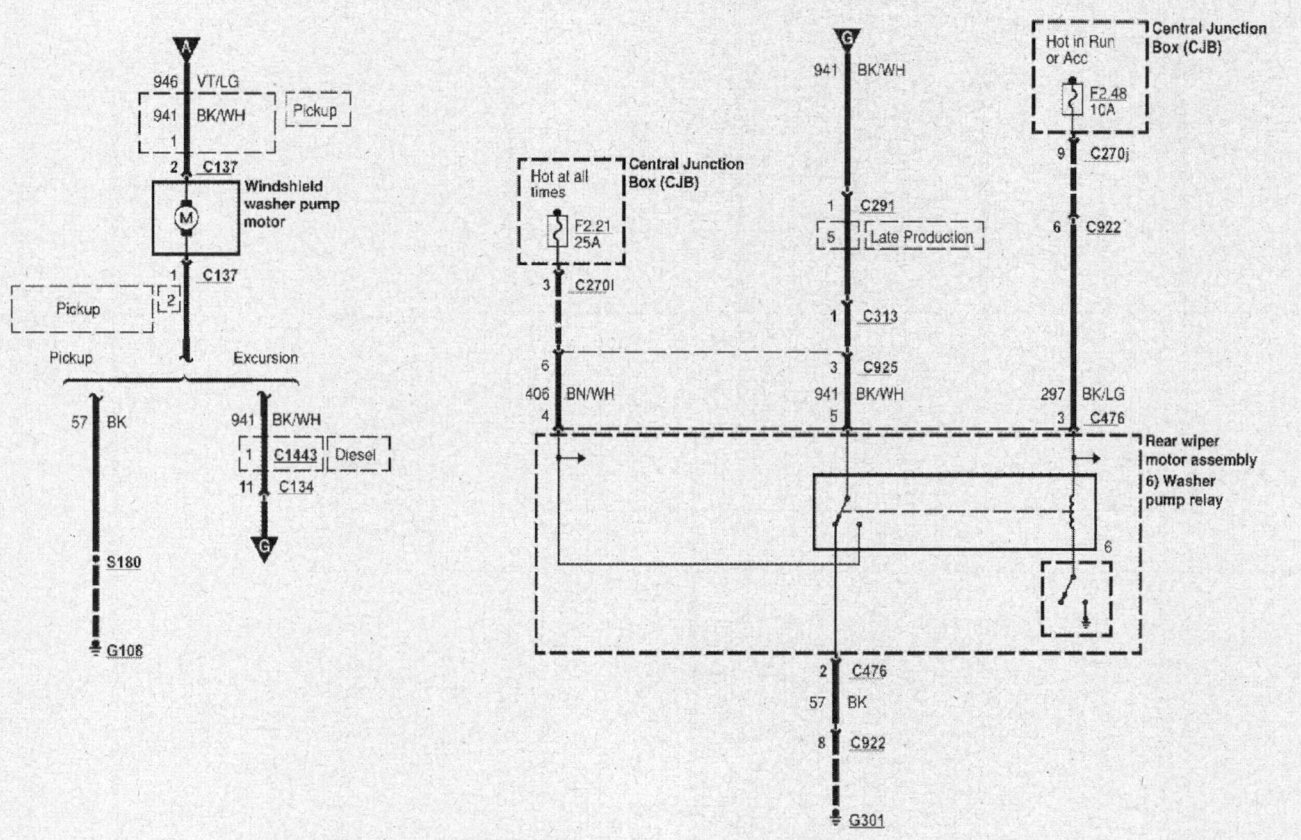

Fig. 1   Wiring diagram (Part 3 of 3). Excursion & 2002–05 F-Super Duty

LTV0500000001889

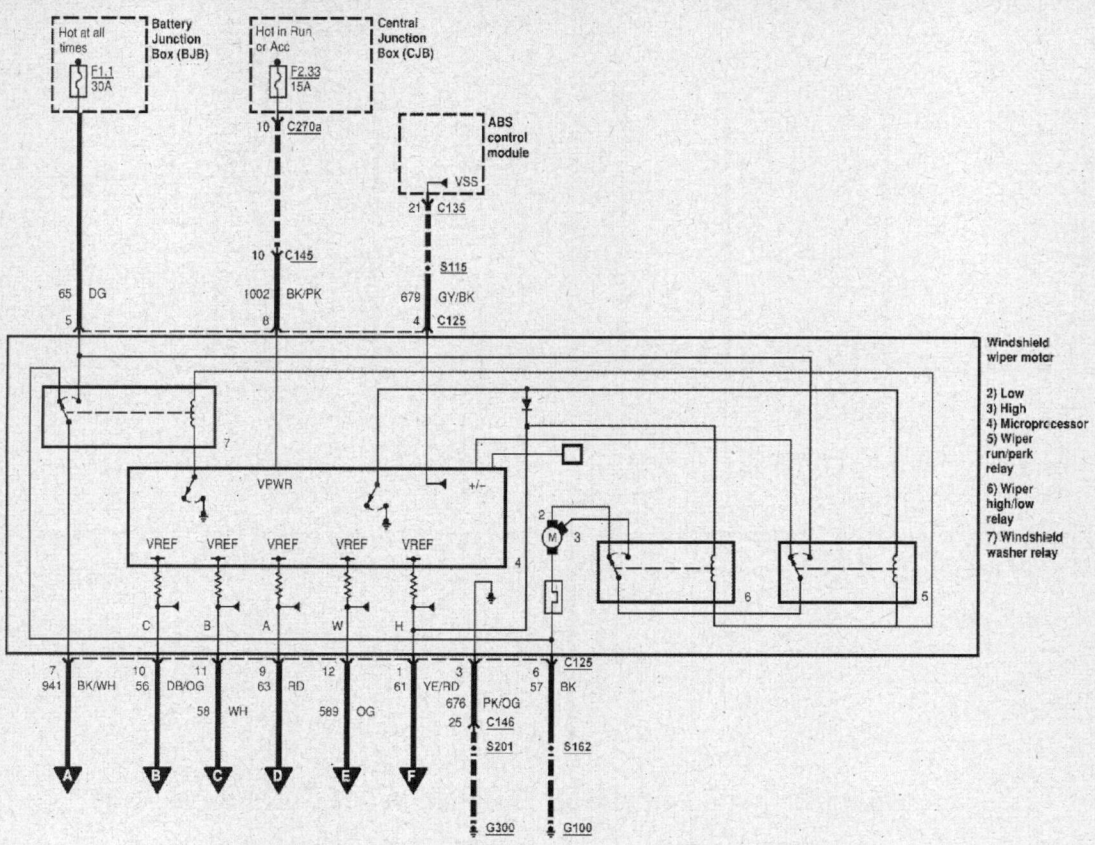

Fig. 2   Wiring diagram (Part 1 of 2). 2006 F-Super Duty

LTV0500000001896

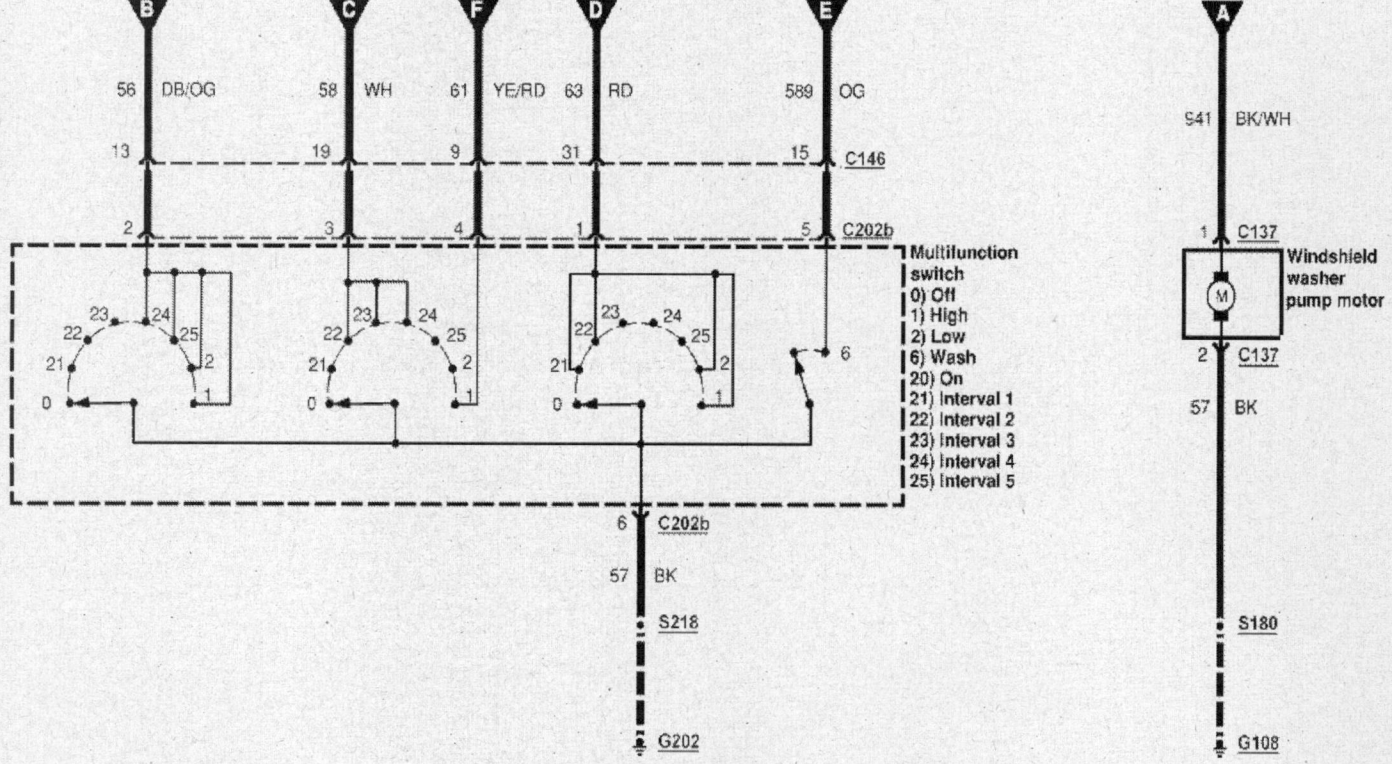

Fig. 2   Wiring diagram (Part 2 of 2). 2006 F-Super Duty

LTV0500000001897

DIAGNOSTIC CHART INDEX

Test	Description	Page No.	Fig. No.
EXCURSION & 2002–04 F–SUPER DUTY			
A	No Communication w/GEM/CTM	3-43	3
B	Wipers Inoperative	3-43	4
C	Wipers Stay On Continuously	3-45	5
D	Hi/Low Wiper Speed Do Not Operate Properly	3-47	6
E	Intermittent Wiper Speed Does Not Operate Properly	3-49	7
F	Wash & Wipe Function Does Not Operate Properly	3-50	8
G	Speed Dependent Interval Mode Does Not Operate Properly	3-52	9
H	Rear Wipers Inoperative	3-53	10
I	Rear Wipers Stay On Continuously	3-55	11
J	Intermittent Rear Wiper Speed Does Not Operate Properly	3-56	12
K	Rear Wash & Wipe Function Does Not Operate	3-57	13
L	Wipers Inoperative	3-59	14
M	Wash & Wipe Function Inoperative	3-61	15
2005–06 F-SUPER DUTY			
—	Symptom Tests	3-62	16
A	Windshield Wipers Are Inoperative	3-63	17
B	Windshield Wipers Stay On Continuously	3-64	18
C	High/Low Wiper Speeds Do Not Operate Correctly	3-64	19
D	Intermittent Wiper Speed Does Not Operate Correctly	3-65	20
E	Wipers Do Not Operate In Mist Position	3-65	21
F	Washer Pump Is Inoperative	3-65	22
G	Wiper Speed Dependent Mode Does Not Operate Correctly	3-66	23

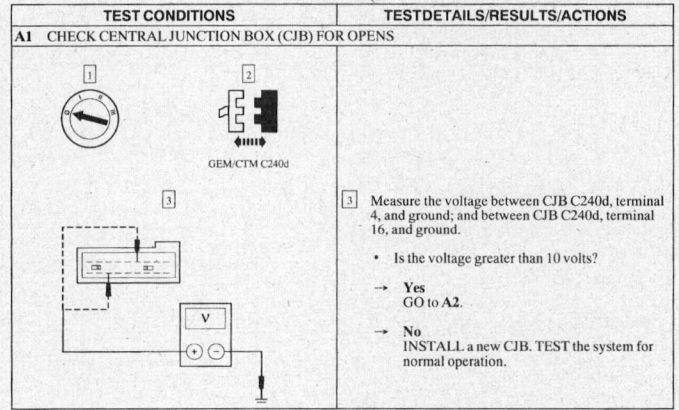

Fig. 3   Test A: No Communication w/GEM/CTM (Part 1 of 2). Excursion & 2002–04 F-Super Duty

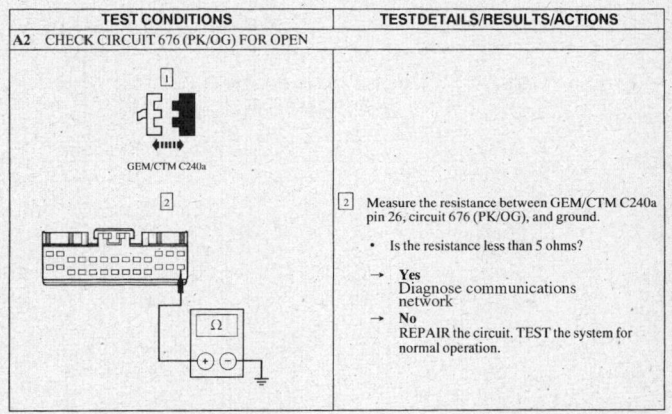

Fig. 3   Test A: No Communication w/GEM/CTM (Part 2 of 2). Excursion & 2002–04 F-Super Duty

TEST CONDITIONS	TESTDETAILS/RESULTS/ACTIONS
B1 CHECK THE REAR WINDOW WIPER OPERATION	

2   Activate the rear window wiper ON and OFF.

- Does the rear window wiper operate correctly?

→ **Yes**
GO to **B2**.

→ **No**
GO to Pinpoint Test L.

FM9020000824010X

Fig. 4   Test B: Wipers Inoperative (Part 1 of 9). Excursion & 2002–04 F-Super Duty

TEST CONDITIONS	TESTDETAILS/RESULTS/ACTIONS
B2 RETRIEVE RECORDED GEM DIAGNOSTIC TROUBLE CODES (DTCs)	
	1 Using the recorded results from the generic electronic module (GEM) front wiper self-test. • Are any DTCs recorded? → **Yes** If DTC B1431 and windshield wipers are inoperative, GO to **B4**. If DTC B1432, B1458, B1840, B1473, and B1476 are recorded together, GO to **B4**. If DTC B1438, GO to **B5**. If DTC B1446, GO to Pinpoint Test L. If DTCs B1473, and B1476 are recorded and the wipers operate in high speed only, or in low speed only, GO to Pinpoint Test D. → **No** GO to **B3**.
B3 MONITOR THE GEM PIDs WPMODE, WPHISP, AND WPRUN	
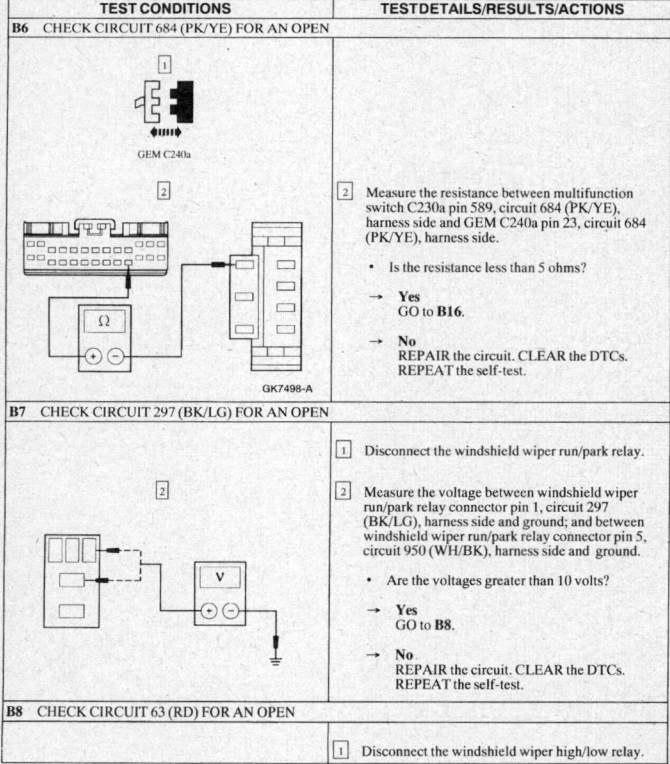	2 Monitor GEM PIDs WPMODE, WPHISP, and WPRUN while selecting each of the windshield wiper multifunction switch positions and depressing the windshield washer switch.

	WPHISP	WPRUN	WPMOD
INTER-MITTENT	OFF	ON	INTV 1-7
LOW	OFF	ON	LOW
HIGH	ON	ON	HIGH
WASH			WASH

• Do the GEM PID values agree with the multifunction switch positions?

→ **Yes**
GO to **B4**.

→ **No**
GO to **B5**.

FM9020000824020X

**Fig. 4 Test B: Wipers Inoperative (Part 2 of 9).
Excursion & 2002–04 F-Super Duty**

TEST CONDITIONS	TESTDETAILS/RESULTS/ACTIONS
B6 CHECK CIRCUIT 684 (PK/YE) FOR AN OPEN	
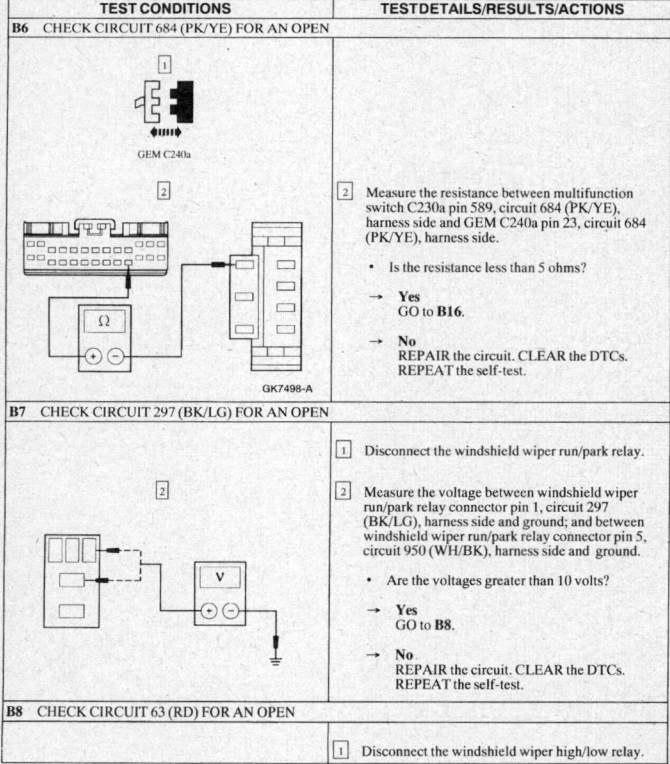 GEM C240a GK7498-A	2 Measure the resistance between multifunction switch C230a pin 589, circuit 684 (PK/YE), harness side and GEM C240a pin 23, circuit 684 (PK/YE), harness side. • Is the resistance less than 5 ohms? → **Yes** GO to **B16**. → **No** REPAIR the circuit. CLEAR the DTCs. REPEAT the self-test.
B7 CHECK CIRCUIT 297 (BK/LG) FOR AN OPEN	
	1 Disconnect the windshield wiper run/park relay. 2 Measure the voltage between windshield wiper run/park relay connector pin 1, circuit 297 (BK/LG), harness side and ground; and between windshield wiper run/park relay connector pin 5, circuit 950 (WH/BK), harness side and ground. • Are the voltages greater than 10 volts? → **Yes** GO to **B8**. → **No** REPAIR the circuit. CLEAR the DTCs. REPEAT the self-test.
B8 CHECK CIRCUIT 63 (RD) FOR AN OPEN	
	1 Disconnect the windshield wiper high/low relay.

FM9020000824040X

**Fig. 4 Test B: Wipers Inoperative (Part 4 of 9).
Excursion & 2002–04 F-Super Duty**

TEST CONDITIONS	TESTDETAILS/RESULTS/ACTIONS
B4 CHECK THE WINDSHIELD WIPER MOTOR OPERATION	
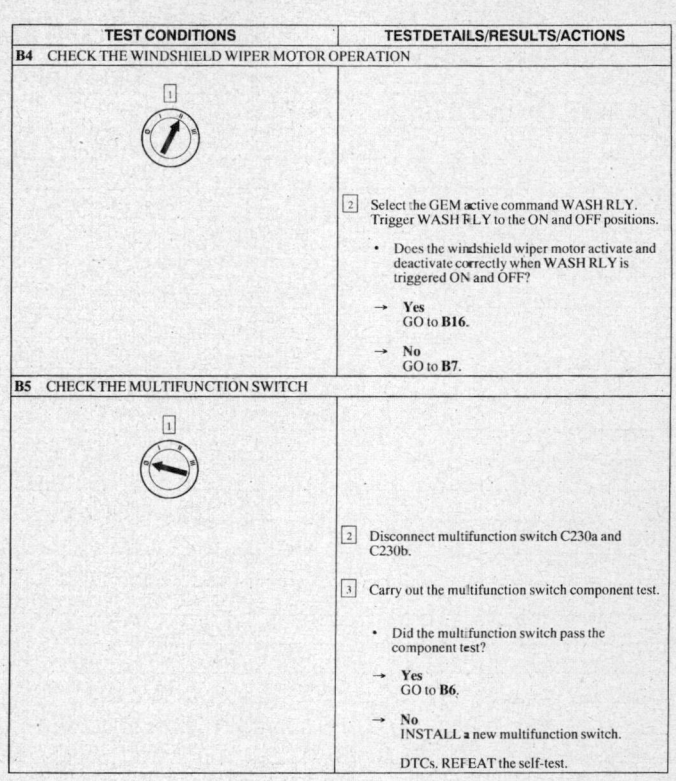	2 Select the GEM active command WASH RLY. Trigger WASH RLY to the ON and OFF positions. • Does the windshield wiper motor activate and deactivate correctly when WASH RLY is triggered ON and OFF? → **Yes** GO to **B16**. → **No** GO to **B7**.
B5 CHECK THE MULTIFUNCTION SWITCH	
	2 Disconnect multifunction switch C230a and C230b. 3 Carry out the multifunction switch component test. • Did the multifunction switch pass the component test? → **Yes** GO to **B6**. → **No** INSTALL a new multifunction switch. DTCs. REPEAT the self-test.

FM9020000824030X

**Fig. 4 Test B: Wipers Inoperative (Part 3 of 9).
Excursion & 2002–04 F-Super Duty**

TEST CONDITIONS	TESTDETAILS/RESULTS/ACTIONS
B8 CHECK CIRCUIT 63 (RD) FOR AN OPEN (Continued)	
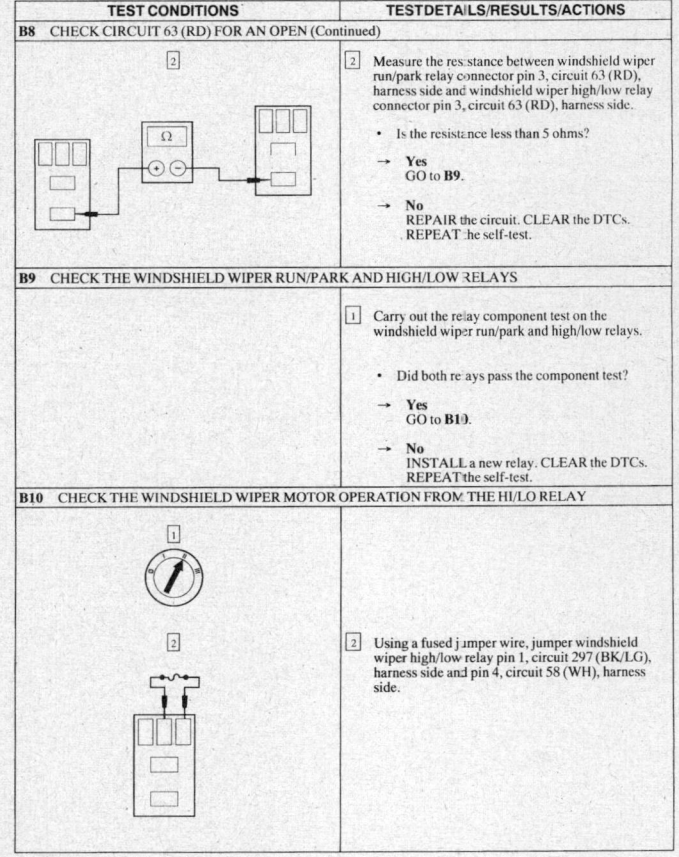	2 Measure the resistance between windshield wiper run/park relay connector pin 3, circuit 63 (RD), harness side and windshield wiper high/low relay connector pin 3, circuit 63 (RD), harness side. • Is the resistance less than 5 ohms? → **Yes** GO to **B9**. → **No** REPAIR the circuit. CLEAR the DTCs. REPEAT the self-test.
B9 CHECK THE WINDSHIELD WIPER RUN/PARK AND HIGH/LOW RELAYS	
	1 Carry out the relay component test on the windshield wiper run/park and high/low relays. • Did both relays pass the component test? → **Yes** GO to **B10**. → **No** INSTALL a new relay. CLEAR the DTCs. REPEAT the self-test.
B10 CHECK THE WINDSHIELD WIPER MOTOR OPERATION FROM THE HI/LO RELAY	
	2 Using a fused jumper wire, jumper windshield wiper high/low relay pin 1, circuit 297 (BK/LG), harness side and pin 4, circuit 58 (WH), harness side.

FM9020000824050X

**Fig. 4 Test B: Wipers Inoperative (Part 5 of 9).
Excursion & 2002–04 F-Super Duty**

TEST CONDITIONS	TEST DETAILS/RESULTS/ACTIONS
B10 CHECK THE WINDSHIELD WIPER MOTOR OPERATION FROM THE HI/LO RELAY (Continued)	

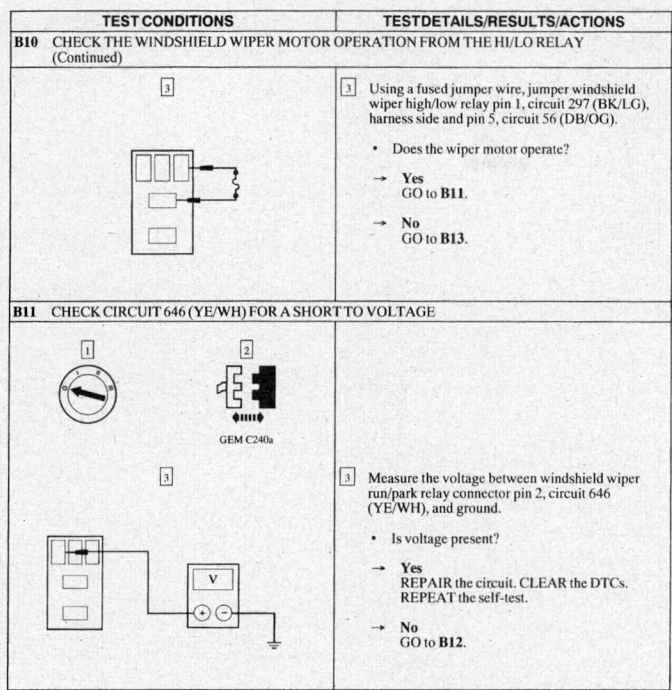

③	③ Using a fused jumper wire, jumper windshield wiper high/low relay pin 1, circuit 297 (BK/LG), harness side and pin 5, circuit 56 (DB/OG). • Does the wiper motor operate? → **Yes** GO to **B11**. → **No** GO to **B13**.

TEST CONDITIONS	TEST DETAILS/RESULTS/ACTIONS
B11 CHECK CIRCUIT 646 (YE/WH) FOR A SHORT TO VOLTAGE	

③	③ Measure the voltage between windshield wiper run/park relay connector pin 2, circuit 646 (YE/WH), and ground. • Is voltage present? → **Yes** REPAIR the circuit. CLEAR the DTCs. REPEAT the self-test. → **No** GO to **B12**.

FM9020000824060X

Fig. 4   Test B: Wipers Inoperative (Part 6 of 9). Excursion & 2002–04 F-Super Duty

TEST CONDITIONS	TEST DETAILS/RESULTS/ACTIONS
B14 CHECK CIRCUIT 57 (BK) FOR AN OPEN	

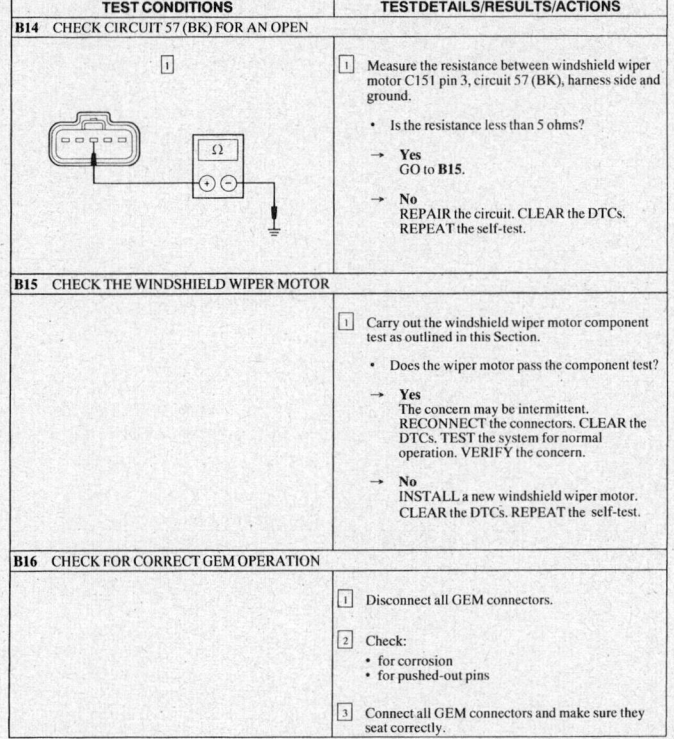

①	① Measure the resistance between windshield wiper motor C151 pin 3, circuit 57 (BK), harness side and ground. • Is the resistance less than 5 ohms? → **Yes** GO to **B15**. → **No** REPAIR the circuit. CLEAR the DTCs. REPEAT the self-test.

TEST CONDITIONS	TEST DETAILS/RESULTS/ACTIONS
B15 CHECK THE WINDSHIELD WIPER MOTOR	

	① Carry out the windshield wiper motor component test as outlined in this Section. • Does the wiper motor pass the component test? → **Yes** The concern may be intermittent. RECONNECT the connectors. CLEAR the DTCs. TEST the system for normal operation. VERIFY the concern. → **No** INSTALL a new windshield wiper motor. CLEAR the DTCs. REPEAT the self-test.

TEST CONDITIONS	TEST DETAILS/RESULTS/ACTIONS
B16 CHECK FOR CORRECT GEM OPERATION	

	① Disconnect all GEM connectors. ② Check: • for corrosion • for pushed-out pins ③ Connect all GEM connectors and make sure they seat correctly.

FM9020000824080X

Fig. 4   Test B: Wipers Inoperative (Part 8 of 9). Excursion & 2002–04 F-Super Duty

TEST CONDITIONS	TEST DETAILS/RESULTS/ACTIONS
B12 CHECK CIRCUIT 646 (YE/WH) FOR AN OPEN	

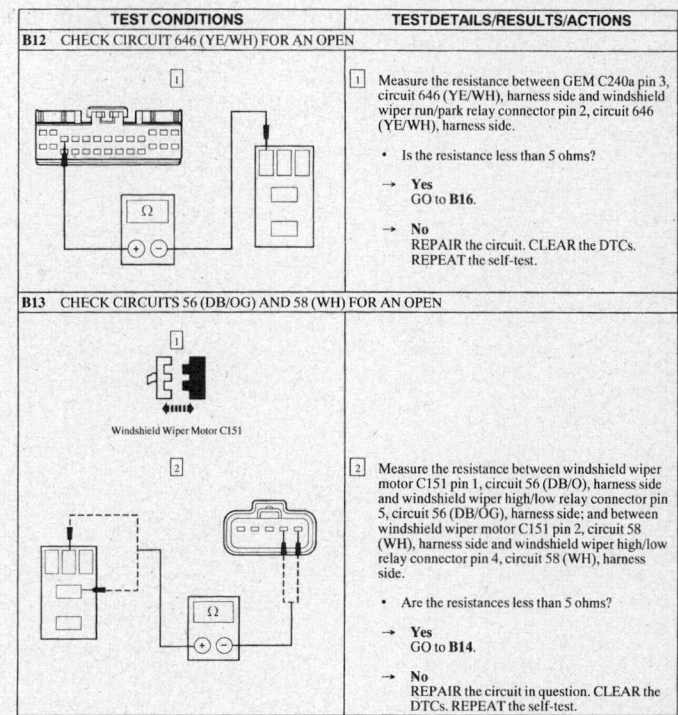

①	① Measure the resistance between GEM C240a pin 3, circuit 646 (YE/WH), harness side and windshield wiper run/park relay connector pin 2, circuit 646 (YE/WH), harness side. • Is the resistance less than 5 ohms? → **Yes** GO to **B16**. → **No** REPAIR the circuit. CLEAR the DTCs. REPEAT the self-test.

TEST CONDITIONS	TEST DETAILS/RESULTS/ACTIONS
B13 CHECK CIRCUITS 56 (DB/OG) AND 58 (WH) FOR AN OPEN	

Windshield Wiper Motor C151

②	② Measure the resistance between windshield wiper motor C151 pin 1, circuit 56 (DB/O), harness side and windshield wiper high/low relay connector pin 5, circuit 56 (DB/OG), harness side; and between windshield wiper motor C151 pin 2, circuit 58 (WH), harness side and windshield wiper high/low relay connector pin 4, circuit 58 (WH), harness side. • Are the resistances less than 5 ohms? → **Yes** GO to **B14**. → **No** REPAIR the circuit in question. CLEAR the DTCs. REPEAT the self-test.

FM9020000824070X

Fig. 4   Test B: Wipers Inoperative (Part 7 of 9). Excursion & 2002–04 F-Super Duty

TEST CONDITIONS	TEST DETAILS/RESULTS/ACTIONS
B16 CHECK FOR CORRECT GEM OPERATION (Continued)	

	④ Operate the system and verify the concern is still present. • Is the concern still present? → **Yes** INSTALL a new GEM. REPEAT the self-test. → **No** The system is operating correctly at this time. Concern may have been caused by a loose or corroded connector. CLEAR the DTCs. REPEAT the self-test.

FM9020000824090X

Fig. 4   Test B: Wipers Inoperative (Part 9 of 9). Excursion & 2002–04 F-Super Duty

TEST CONDITIONS	TEST DETAILS/RESULTS/ACTIONS
C1 CHECK THE REAR WINDOW WIPER OPERATION	

	② Activate the rear window wiper on and off. • Does the rear window wiper operate correctly? → **Yes** GO to **C2**. → **No** GO to Pinpoint Test L.

FM9020000825010X

Fig. 5   Test C: Wipers Stay On Continuously (Part 1 of 6). Excursion & 2002–04 F-Super Duty

TEST CONDITIONS	TESTDETAILS/RESULTS/ACTIONS
C2 RETRIEVE THE RECORDED GENERIC ELECTRONIC MODULE (GEM) DIAGNOSTIC TROUBLE CODES (DTCs)	
	1 Using the recorded results from the GEM front wiper self-test: • Are any DTCs retrieved? → **Yes** If DTC B1431, GO to **C4**. If DTC B1441, GO to **C5**. If DTC B1453, GO to **C5**. → **No** GO to **C3**.
C3 MONITOR THE GEM PIDs WPMODE AND WASH__SW	
1 **2**	**2** Monitor GEM PIDs WPMODE and WASHSW while selecting each of the windshield wiper multifunction switch positions and depressing the windshield washer switch. • Do the GEM PID values agree with the multifunction switch positions? → **Yes** GO to **C4**. → **No** GO to **C5**.
C4 CHECK THE WINDSHIELD WIPER MOTOR OPERATION USING GEM ACTIVE COMMAND WIPER RLY	
1 **2**	**2** Select GEM active command WIPER RLY. Trigger WIPER RLY to the ON and OFF positions. • Does the windshield wiper motor activate and deactivate correctly when WIPER RLY is triggered ON and OFF? → **Yes** GO to **C13**. → **No** GO to **C7**.

FM9020000825020X

Fig. 5   Test C: Wipers Stay On Continuously (Part 2 of 6). Excursion & 2002–04 F-Super Duty

TEST CONDITIONS	TESTDETAILS/RESULTS/ACTIONS
C7 ISOLATE SHORT TO GROUND AT THE WINDSHIELD WIPER RUN/PARK RELAY	
	1 Disconnect the windshield wiper run/park relay. • Do the wipers stop operating? → **Yes** GO to **C8**. → **No** GO to **C10**.
C8 CHECK THE WINDSHIELD WIPER RUN/PARK RELAY	
1	**2** Disconnect the windshield wiper run/park relay. **3** Carry out the component test on the windshield wiper run/park relay. • Did the windshield wiper run/park relay pass the component test? → **Yes** GO to **C9**. → **No** INSTALL a new windshield wiper run/park relay. CLEAR the DTCs. REPEAT the self-test.
C9 CHECK CIRCUIT 646 (YE/WH) FOR A SHORT TO GROUND	
1 GEM C240a	

FM9020000825040X

Fig. 5   Test C: Wipers Stay On Continuously (Part 4 of 6). Excursion & 2002–04 F-Super Duty

TEST CONDITIONS	TESTDETAILS/RESULTS/ACTIONS
C5 CHECK THE MULTIFUNCTION SWITCH	
1	**2** Disconnect multifunction switch C230a and C230b. **3** Carry out the multifunction switch component test. • Did the multifunction switch pass the component test? → **Yes** GO to **C6**. → **No** INSTALL a new multifunction switch. DTCs. REPEAT the self-test.
C6 CHECK CIRCUITS 680 (LB/OG) AND 684 (PK/YE) FOR A SHORT TO GROUND	

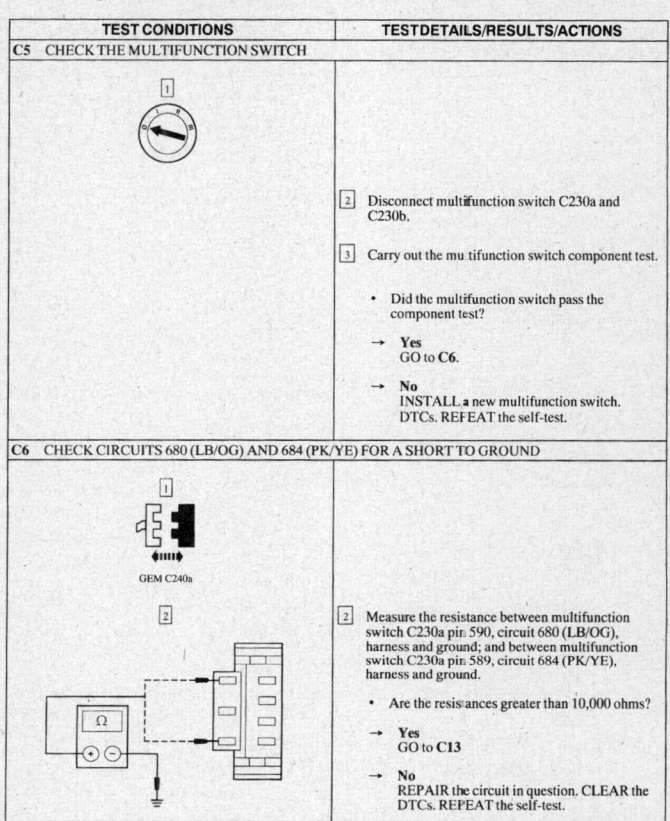

1 GEM C240a **2**	**2** Measure the resistance between multifunction switch C230a pin 590, circuit 680 (LB/OG), harness and ground; and between multifunction switch C230a pin 589, circuit 684 (PK/YE), harness and ground. • Are the resistances greater than 10,000 ohms? → **Yes** GO to **C13**. → **No** REPAIR the circuit in question. CLEAR the DTCs. REPEAT the self-test.

FM9020000825030X

Fig. 5   Test C: Wipers Stay On Continuously (Part 3 of 6). Excursion & 2002–04 F-Super Duty

TEST CONDITIONS	TESTDETAILS/RESULTS/ACTIONS
C9 CHECK CIRCUIT 646 (YE/WH) FOR A SHORT TO GROUND (Continued)	
2	**2** Measure the resistance between GEM C240a pin 3, circuit 646 (YE/WH), harness side and ground. • Is the resistance greater than 10,000 ohms? → **Yes** GO to **C13**. → **No** REPAIR the circuit. CLEAR the DTCs. REPEAT the self-test.
C10 ISOLATE SHORT TO GROUND AT THE WINDSHIELD WIPER HIGH/LOW RELAY	
	1 Disconnect the windshield wiper high/low relay. • Do the wipers stop operating? → **Yes** GO to **C11**. → **No** GO to **C12**
C11 CHECK CIRCUIT 63 (RD) FOR A SHORT TO VOLTAGE	
1 GN1456-A	**1** Measure the voltage between windshield wiper high/low relay connector pin 3, circuit 63 (RD), harness side and ground. • Is the voltage greater than 10 volts? → **Yes** REPAIR the circuit. CLEAR the DTCs. REPEAT the self-test. → **No** INSTALL a new windshield wiper high/low relay. CLEAR the DTCs. REPEAT the self-test.
C12 CHECK CIRCUITS 56 (DB/OG) AND 58 (WH) FOR A SHORT TO VOLTAGE	
1 Windshield Wiper Motor C151	

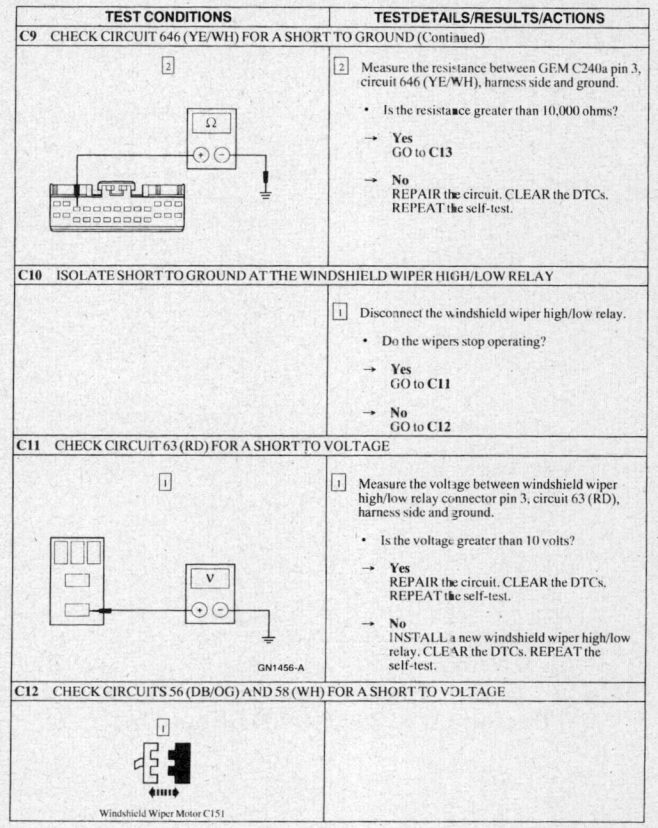

FM9020000825050X

Fig. 5   Test C: Wipers Stay On Continuously (Part 5 of 6). Excursion & 2002–04 F-Super Duty

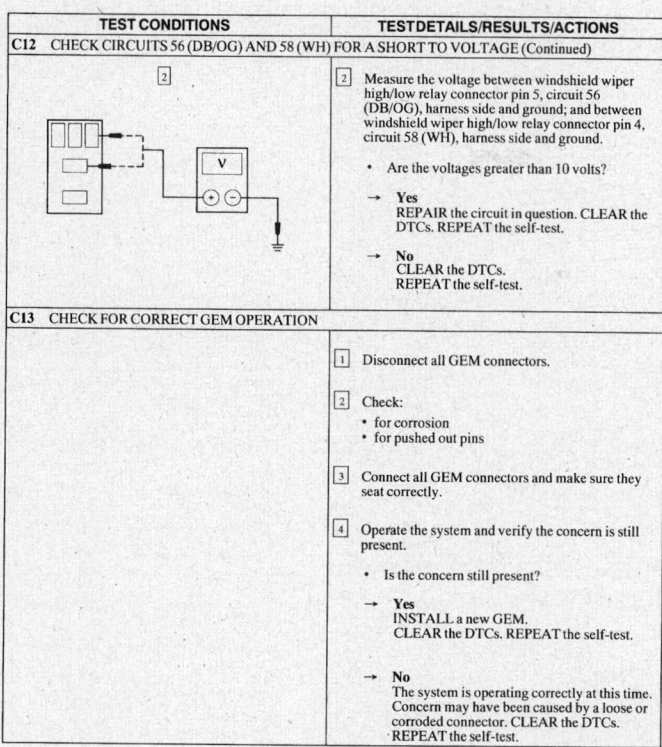

TEST CONDITIONS	TESTDETAILS/RESULTS/ACTIONS
C12 CHECK CIRCUITS 56 (DB/OG) AND 58 (WH) FOR A SHORT TO VOLTAGE (Continued)	
[2]	[2] Measure the voltage between windshield wiper high/low relay connector pin 5, circuit 56 (DB/OG), harness side and ground; and between windshield wiper high/low relay connector pin 4, circuit 58 (WH), harness side and ground. • Are the voltages greater than 10 volts? → **Yes** REPAIR the circuit in question. CLEAR the DTCs. REPEAT the self-test. → **No** CLEAR the DTCs. REPEAT the self-test.
C13 CHECK FOR CORRECT GEM OPERATION	
	[1] Disconnect all GEM connectors. [2] Check: • for corrosion • for pushed out pins [3] Connect all GEM connectors and make sure they seat correctly. [4] Operate the system and verify the concern is still present. • Is the concern still present? → **Yes** INSTALL a new GEM. CLEAR the DTCs. REPEAT the self-test. → **No** The system is operating correctly at this time. Concern may have been caused by a loose or corroded connector. CLEAR the DTCs. REPEAT the self-test.

FM9020000825060X

Fig. 5   Test C: Wipers Stay On Continuously (Part 6 of 6). Excursion & 2002–04 F-Super Duty

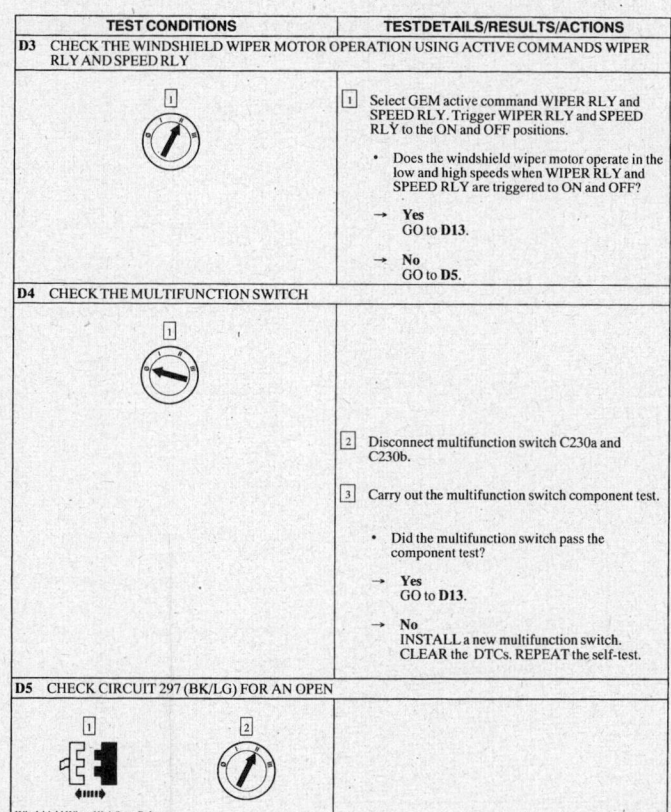

TEST CONDITIONS	TESTDETAILS/RESULTS/ACTIONS
D3 CHECK THE WINDSHIELD WIPER MOTOR OPERATION USING ACTIVE COMMANDS WIPER RLY AND SPEED RLY	
[1]	[1] Select GEM active command WIPER RLY and SPEED RLY. Trigger WIPER RLY and SPEED RLY to the ON and OFF positions. • Does the windshield wiper motor operate in the low and high speeds when WIPER RLY and SPEED RLY are triggered to ON and OFF? → **Yes** GO to **D13**. → **No** GO to **D5**.
D4 CHECK THE MULTIFUNCTION SWITCH	
[1]	[2] Disconnect multifunction switch C230a and C230b. [3] Carry out the multifunction switch component test. • Did the multifunction switch pass the component test? → **Yes** GO to **D13**. → **No** INSTALL a new multifunction switch. CLEAR the DTCs. REPEAT the self-test.
D5 CHECK CIRCUIT 297 (BK/LG) FOR AN OPEN	
[1] Windshield Wiper High/Low Relay [2]	

FM9020000826020X

Fig. 6   Test D: Hi/Low Wiper Speed Do Not Operate Properly (Part 2 of 7). Excursion & 2002–04 F-Super Duty

TEST CONDITIONS	TESTDETAILS/RESULTS/ACTIONS
D1 RETRIEVE THE RECORDED GENERIC ELECTRONIC MODULE (GEM) DIAGNOSTIC TROUBLE CODES (DTCs)	
	[1] Using the recorded results from the GEM front wiper self-test: • Are any DTCs recorded? → **Yes** If DTC B1434, GO to **D5**. If DTC B1436, GO to **D6**. If DTC B1473, GO to **D6**. If DTC B1476, GO to **D6**. → **No** GO to **D2**.
D2 MONITOR THE GEM PIDs WPMODE AND WASHSW	
[1] [2]	[3] Monitor GEM PIDs WPMODE and WASHSW while selecting each of the windshield wiper multifunction switch positions and depressing the windshield washer switch. • Do the GEM PID values agree with the multifunction switch positions? → **Yes** GO to **D3**. → **No** GO to **D4**.

FM9020000826010X

Fig. 6   Test D: Hi/Low Wiper Speed Do Not Operate Properly (Part 1 of 7). Excursion & 2002–04 F-Super Duty

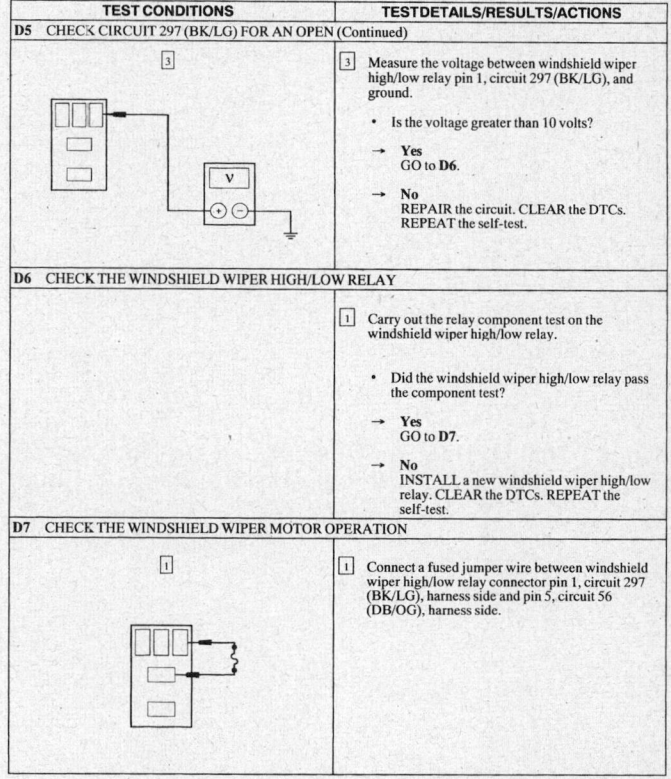

TEST CONDITIONS	TESTDETAILS/RESULTS/ACTIONS
D5 CHECK CIRCUIT 297 (BK/LG) FOR AN OPEN (Continued)	
[3]	[3] Measure the voltage between windshield wiper high/low relay pin 1, circuit 297 (BK/LG), and ground. • Is the voltage greater than 10 volts? → **Yes** GO to **D6**. → **No** REPAIR the circuit. CLEAR the DTCs. REPEAT the self-test.
D6 CHECK THE WINDSHIELD WIPER HIGH/LOW RELAY	
	[1] Carry out the relay component test on the windshield wiper high/low relay. • Did the windshield wiper high/low relay pass the component test? → **Yes** GO to **D7**. → **No** INSTALL a new windshield wiper high/low relay. CLEAR the DTCs. REPEAT the self-test.
D7 CHECK THE WINDSHIELD WIPER MOTOR OPERATION	
[1]	[1] Connect a fused jumper wire between windshield wiper high/low relay connector pin 1, circuit 297 (BK/LG), harness side and pin 5, circuit 56 (DB/OG), harness side.

FM9020000826030X

Fig. 6   Test D: Hi/Low Wiper Speed Do Not Operate Properly (Part 3 of 7). Excursion & 2002–04 F-Super Duty

TEST CONDITIONS	TESTDETAILS/RESULTS/ACTIONS
D7 CHECK THE WINDSHIELD WIPER MOTOR OPERATION (Continued)	
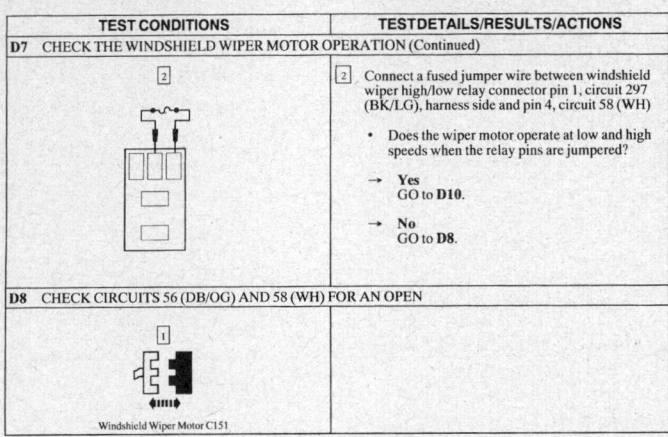	☑ Connect a fused jumper wire between windshield wiper high/low relay connector pin 1, circuit 297 (BK/LG), harness side and pin 4, circuit 58 (WH). • Does the wiper motor operate at low and high speeds when the relay pins are jumpered? → **Yes** GO to **D10**. → **No** GO to **D8**.
D8 CHECK CIRCUITS 56 (DB/OG) AND 58 (WH) FOR AN OPEN	
Windshield Wiper Motor C151	

Fig. 6 Test D: Hi/Low Wiper Speed Do Not Operate Properly (Part 4 of 7). Excursion & 2002–04 F-Super Duty

TEST CONDITIONS	TESTDETAILS/RESULTS/ACTIONS
D10 CHECK CIRCUIT 647 (GY/LB) FOR A SHORT TO VOLTAGE	
GEM C240a	
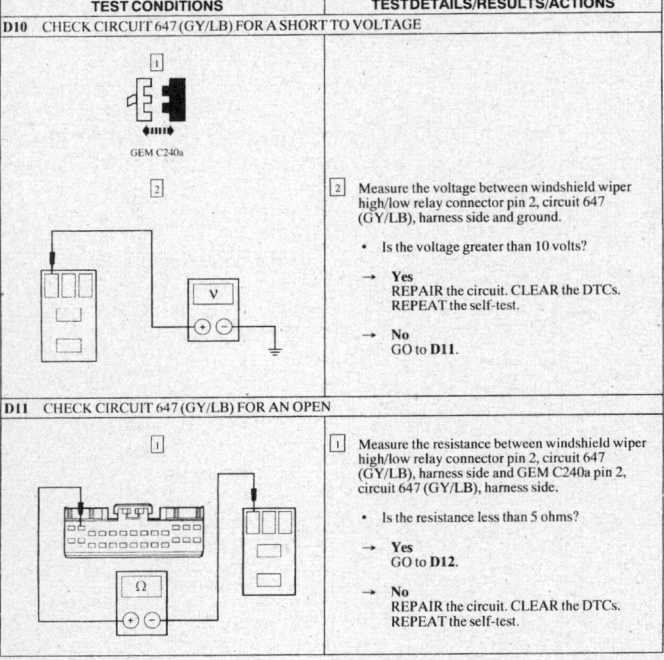	☑ Measure the voltage between windshield wiper high/low relay connector pin 2, circuit 647 (GY/LB), harness side and ground. • Is the voltage greater than 10 volts? → **Yes** REPAIR the circuit. CLEAR the DTCs. REPEAT the self-test. → **No** GO to **D11**.
D11 CHECK CIRCUIT 647 (GY/LB) FOR AN OPEN	
	☑ Measure the resistance between windshield wiper high/low relay connector pin 2, circuit 647 (GY/LB), harness side and GEM C240a pin 2, circuit 647 (GY/LB), harness side. • Is the resistance less than 5 ohms? → **Yes** GO to **D12**. → **No** REPAIR the circuit. CLEAR the DTCs. REPEAT the self-test.

FM9020000826060X

Fig. 6 Test D: Hi/Low Wiper Speed Do Not Operate Properly (Part 6 of 7). Excursion & 2002–04 F-Super Duty

TEST CONDITIONS	TESTDETAILS/RESULTS/ACTIONS
D8 CHECK CIRCUITS 56 (DB/OG) AND 58 (WH) FOR AN OPEN (Continued)	
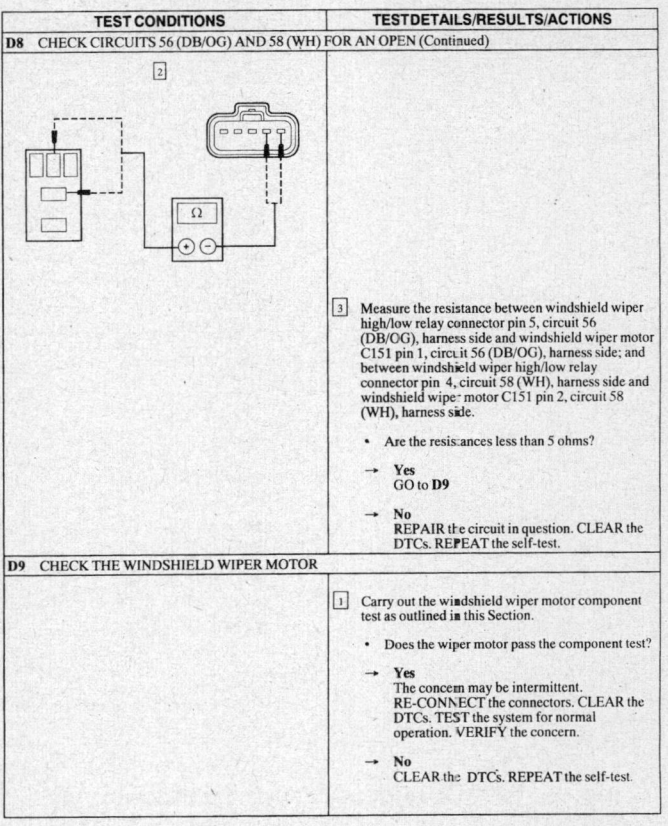	☑ Measure the resistance between windshield wiper high/low relay connector pin 5, circuit 56 (DB/OG), harness side and windshield wiper motor C151 pin 1, circuit 56 (DB/OG), harness side; and between windshield wiper high/low relay connector pin 4, circuit 58 (WH), harness side and windshield wiper motor C151 pin 2, circuit 58 (WH), harness side. • Are the resistances less than 5 ohms? → **Yes** GO to **D9** → **No** REPAIR the circuit in question. CLEAR the DTCs. REPEAT the self-test.
D9 CHECK THE WINDSHIELD WIPER MOTOR	
	☑ Carry out the windshield wiper motor component test as outlined in this Section. • Does the wiper motor pass the component test? → **Yes** The concern may be intermittent. RE-CONNECT the connectors. CLEAR the DTCs. TEST the system for normal operation. VERIFY the concern. → **No** CLEAR the DTCs. REPEAT the self-test.

FM9020000826050X

Fig. 6 Test D: Hi/Low Wiper Speed Do Not Operate Properly (Part 5 of 7). Excursion & 2002–04 F-Super Duty

TEST CONDITIONS	TESTDETAILS/RESULTS/ACTIONS
D12 CHECK CIRCUIT 647 (GY/LB) FOR A SHORT TO GROUND	
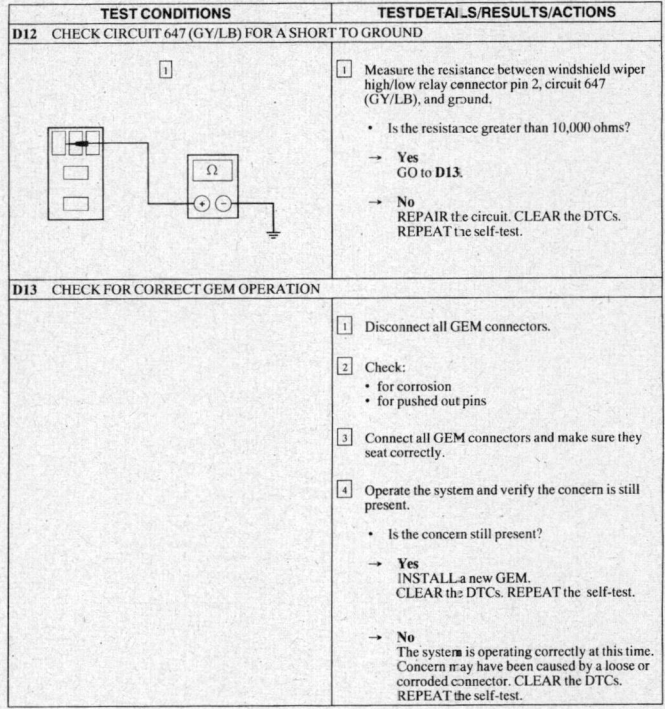	☑ Measure the resistance between windshield wiper high/low relay connector pin 2, circuit 647 (GY/LB), and ground. • Is the resistance greater than 10,000 ohms? → **Yes** GO to **D13**. → **No** REPAIR the circuit. CLEAR the DTCs. REPEAT the self-test.
D13 CHECK FOR CORRECT GEM OPERATION	
	☑ Disconnect all GEM connectors. ☑ Check: • for corrosion • for pushed out pins ☑ Connect all GEM connectors and make sure they seat correctly. ☑ Operate the system and verify the concern is still present. • Is the concern still present? → **Yes** INSTALL a new GEM. CLEAR the DTCs. REPEAT the self-test. → **No** The system is operating correctly at this time. Concern may have been caused by a loose or corroded connector. CLEAR the DTCs. REPEAT the self-test.

FM9020000826070X

Fig. 6 Test D: Hi/Low Wiper Speed Do Not Operate Properly (Part 7 of 7). Excursion & 2002–04 F-Super Duty

TEST CONDITIONS	TESTDETAILS/RESULTS/ACTIONS
E1 RETRIEVE THE GENERIC ELECTRONIC MODULE (GEM) DIAGNOSTIC TROUBLE CODES (DTCs)	
	1 Using the recorded results from the GEM front wiper self-test: • Are any DTCs recorded? → **Yes** If DTC B1450, GO to **E3**. If DTCs B1446, B1473, and B1476 are all recorded, GO to **E6**. → **No** GO to **E2**.
E2 MONITOR THE GEM PID WPMODE	
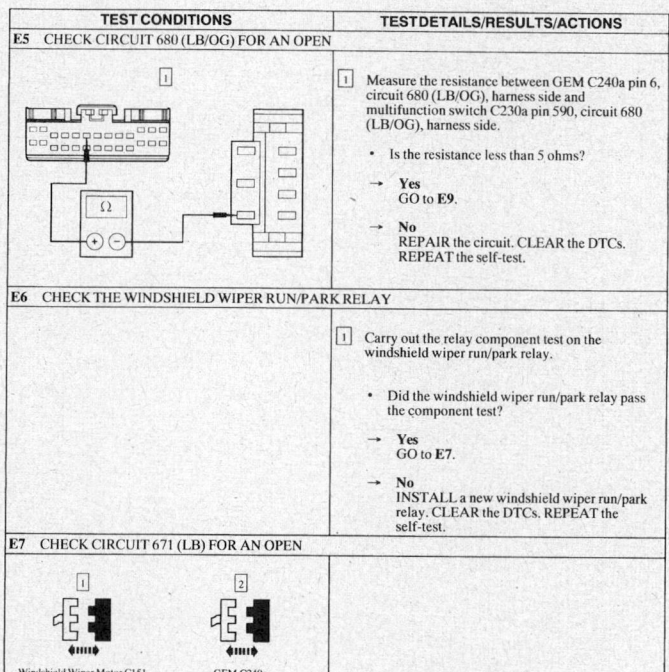	**2** Monitor GEM PID WPMODE while selecting each of the windshield wiper multifunction switch positions. • Do the GEM PID values agree with the multifunction switch positions? → **Yes** GO to **E6**. → **No** GO to **E3**.
E3 CHECK THE MULTIFUNCTION SWITCH	
	2 Disconnect multifunction switch C230a and C230b.

FM9020000827010X

Fig. 7   Test E: Intermittent Wiper Speed Does Not Operate Properly (Part 1 of 5). Excursion & 2002–04 F-Super Duty

TEST CONDITIONS	TESTDETAILS/RESULTS/ACTIONS
E3 CHECK THE MULTIFUNCTION SWITCH (Continued)	
	3 Carry out the multifunction switch component test. • Did the multifunction switch pass the component test? → **Yes** GO to **E4**. → **No** INSTALL a new multifunction switch. CLEAR the DTCs. REPEAT the self-test.
E4 CHECK CIRCUIT 680 (LB/OG) FOR A SHORT TO VOLTAGE	
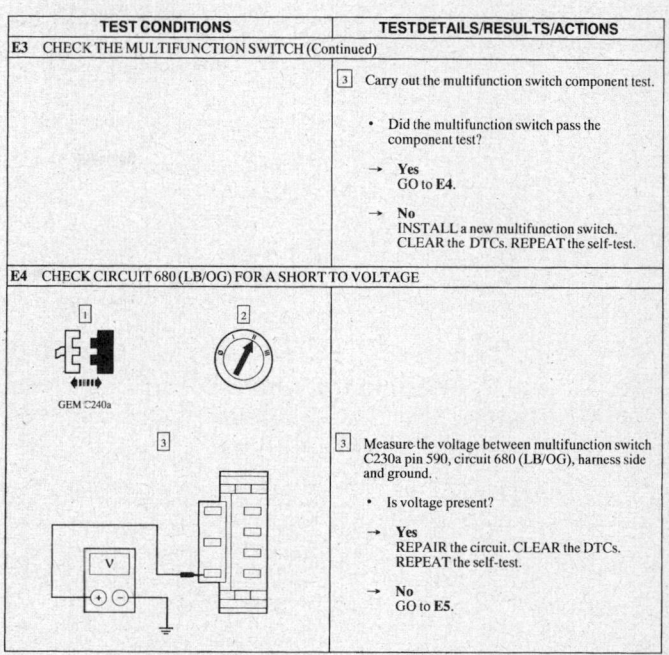	**3** Measure the voltage between multifunction switch C230a pin 590, circuit 680 (LB/OG), harness side and ground. • Is voltage present? → **Yes** REPAIR the circuit. CLEAR the DTCs. REPEAT the self-test. → **No** GO to **E5**.

FM9020000827020X

Fig. 7   Test E: Intermittent Wiper Speed Does Not Operate Properly (Part 2 of 5). Excursion & 2002–04 F-Super Duty

TEST CONDITIONS	TESTDETAILS/RESULTS/ACTIONS
E5 CHECK CIRCUIT 680 (LB/OG) FOR AN OPEN	
	1 Measure the resistance between GEM C240a pin 6, circuit 680 (LB/OG), harness side and multifunction switch C230a pin 590, circuit 680 (LB/OG), harness side. • Is the resistance less than 5 ohms? → **Yes** GO to **E9**. → **No** REPAIR the circuit. CLEAR the DTCs. REPEAT the self-test.
E6 CHECK THE WINDSHIELD WIPER RUN/PARK RELAY	
	1 Carry out the relay component test on the windshield wiper run/park relay. • Did the windshield wiper run/park relay pass the component test? → **Yes** GO to **E7**. → **No** INSTALL a new windshield wiper run/park relay. CLEAR the DTCs. REPEAT the self-test.
E7 CHECK CIRCUIT 671 (LB) FOR AN OPEN	
Windshield Wiper Motor C151 GEM C240a	

FM9020000827030X

Fig. 7   Test E: Intermittent Wiper Speed Does Not Operate Properly (Part 3 of 5). Excursion & 2002–04 F-Super Duty

TEST CONDITIONS	TESTDETAILS/RESULTS/ACTIONS
E7 CHECK CIRCUIT 671 (LB) FOR AN OPEN (Continued)	
	3 Measure the resistance between windshield wiper run/park relay connector pin 4, circuit 671 (LB), harness side and GEM C240a pin 14, circuit 671 (LB), harness side; and between windshield wiper motor C151 pin 5, circuit 671 (LB), harness side and GEM C240a pin 14, circuit 671 (LB) harness side. • Are the resistances less than 5 ohms? → **Yes** GO to **E8**. → **No** REPAIR the circuit. CLEAR the DTCs. REPEAT the self-test.
E8 CHECK THE WINDSHIELD WIPER MOTOR PARK POSITION STATUS— MONITOR THE GEM PID WPPRKSW	
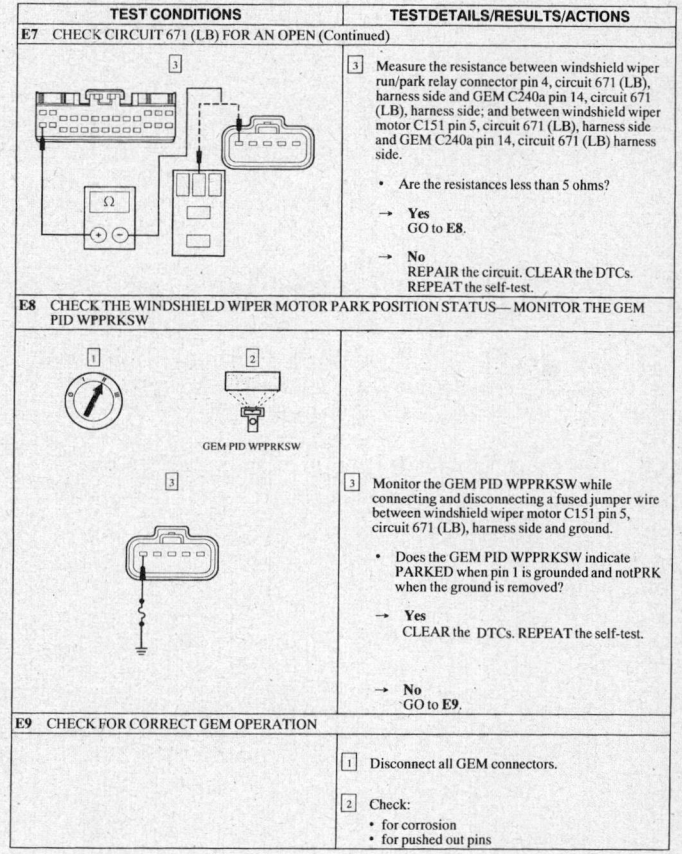	**3** Monitor the GEM PID WPPRKSW while connecting and disconnecting a fused jumper wire between windshield wiper motor C151 pin 5, circuit 671 (LB), harness side and ground. • Does the GEM PID WPPRKSW indicate PARKED when pin 1 is grounded and notPRK when the ground is removed? → **Yes** CLEAR the DTCs. REPEAT the self-test. → **No** GO to **E9**.
E9 CHECK FOR CORRECT GEM OPERATION	
	1 Disconnect all GEM connectors. **2** Check: • for corrosion • for pushed out pins

FM9020000827040X

Fig. 7   Test E: Intermittent Wiper Speed Does Not Operate Properly (Part 4 of 5). Excursion & 2002–04 F-Super Duty

TEST CONDITIONS	TESTDETAILS/RESULTS/ACTIONS
E9 CHECK FOR CORRECT GEM OPERATION (Continued)	
	☐3 Connect all GEM connectors and make sure they seat correctly.
	☐4 Operate the system and verify the concern is still present.
	• Is the concern still present?
	→ **Yes** INSTALL a new GEM. REPEAT the self-test.
	→ **No** The system is operating correctly at this time. Concern may have been caused by a loose or corroded connector. CLEAR the DTCs. REPEAT the self-test.

FM9020000827050X

Fig. 7   Test E: Intermittent Wiper Speed Does Not Operate Properly (Part 5 of 5). Excursion & 2002–04 F-Super Duty

TEST CONDITIONS	TESTDETAILS/RESULTS/ACTIONS
F1 RETRIEVE THE RECORDED GENERIC ELECTRONIC MODULE (GEM) DIAGNOSTIC TROUBLE CODES (DTCs)	
	☐1 Using the recorded results from the GEM front wiper self-test:
	• Are any DTCs recorded?
	→ **Yes** If DTC B1450, GO to **F4**. If DTC B1453, GO to **F4**. If DTC 1458, GO to **F8**. If DTC B1460, GO to **F8**.
	→ **No** GO to **F2**.

FM9020000828010X

Fig. 8   Test F: Wash & Wipe Function Does Not Operate Properly (Part 1 of 10). Excursion & 2002–04 F-Super Duty

TEST CONDITIONS	TESTDETAILS/RESULTS/ACTIONS
F2 MONITOR THE GEM PIDs WPMODE AND WASHSW	
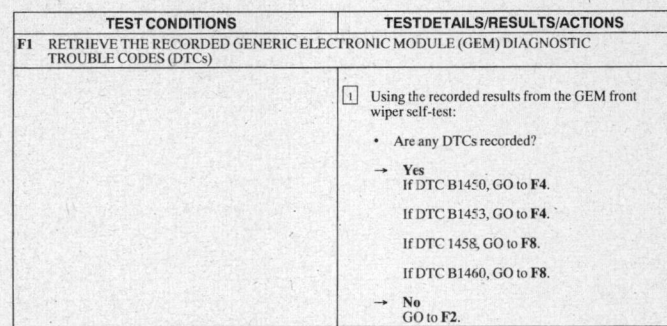	☐2 Monitor GEM PIDs WPMODE AND WASHSW while selecting each of the windshield wiper multifunction switch positions and depressing the windshield washer switch.
	• Do the GEM PID values agree with the multifunction switch positions?
	→ **Yes** GO to **F3**.
	→ **No** GO to **F4**.
F3 CHECK THE WASHER PUMP OPERATION USING ACTIVE COMMAND WASH RLY	
	☐2 Select GEM active command WASH RLY. Trigger WASH RLY to the ON and OFF positions.
	• Does the windshield washer activate and deactivate correctly when WASH RLY is triggered ON and OFF?
	→ **Yes** GO to **F15**.
	→ **No** GO to **F7**.
F4 CHECK THE MULTIFUNCTION SWITCH	
	☐2 Disconnect multifunction switch C230a and C230b.

FM9020000828020X

Fig. 8   Test F: Wash & Wipe Function Does Not Operate Properly (Part 2 of 10). Excursion & 2002–04 F-Super Duty

TEST CONDITIONS	TESTDETAILS/RESULTS/ACTIONS
F4 CHECK THE MULTIFUNCTION SWITCH (Continued)	
	☐3 Carry out the multifunction switch component test.
	• Did the multifunction switch pass the component test?
	→ **Yes** GO to **F5**.
	→ **No** INSTALL a new multifunction switch. CLEAR the DTCs. REPEAT the self-test.
F5 CHECK CIRCUIT 680 (LB/OG) FOR AN OPEN	
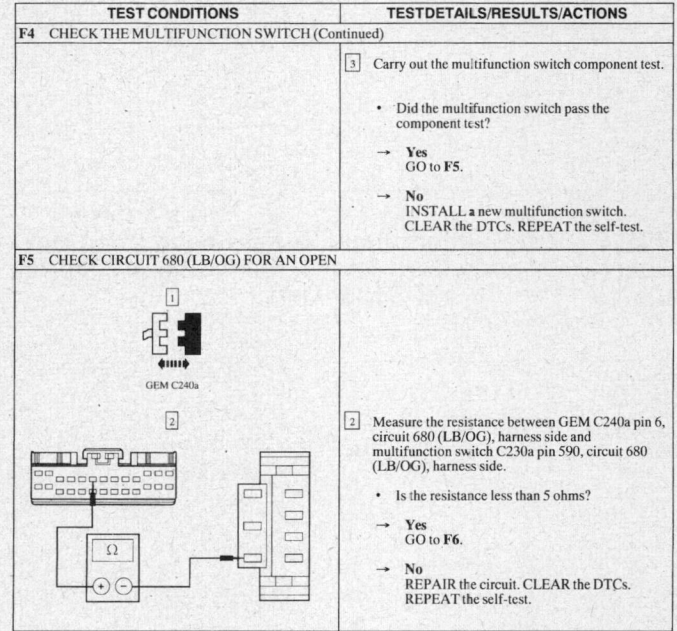 GEM C240a	☐2 Measure the resistance between GEM C240a pin 6, circuit 680 (LB/OG), harness side and multifunction switch C230a pin 590, circuit 680 (LB/OG), harness side.
	• Is the resistance less than 5 ohms?
	→ **Yes** GO to **F6**.
	→ **No** REPAIR the circuit. CLEAR the DTCs. REPEAT the self-test.

FM9020000828030X

Fig. 8   Test F: Wash & Wipe Function Does Not Operate Properly (Part 3 of 10). Excursion & 2002–04 F-Super Duty

TEST CONDITIONS	TESTDETAILS/RESULTS/ACTIONS
F6 CHECK CIRCUIT 680 (LB/OG) FOR A SHORT TO GROUND	
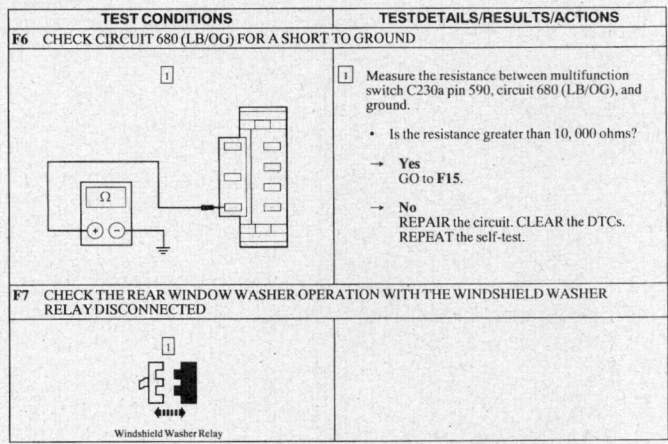	☐1 Measure the resistance between multifunction switch C230a pin 590, circuit 680 (LB/OG), and ground.
	• Is the resistance greater than 10, 000 ohms?
	→ **Yes** GO to **F15**.
	→ **No** REPAIR the circuit. CLEAR the DTCs. REPEAT the self-test.
F7 CHECK THE REAR WINDOW WASHER OPERATION WITH THE WINDSHIELD WASHER RELAY DISCONNECTED	
Windshield Washer Relay	

FM9020000828040X

Fig. 8   Test F: Wash & Wipe Function Does Not Operate Properly (Part 4 of 10). Excursion & 2002–04 F-Super Duty

TEST CONDITIONS	TESTDETAILS/RESULTS/ACTIONS
F7 CHECK THE REAR WINDOW WASHER OPERATION WITH THE WINDSHIELD WASHER RELAY DISCONNECTED (Continued)	
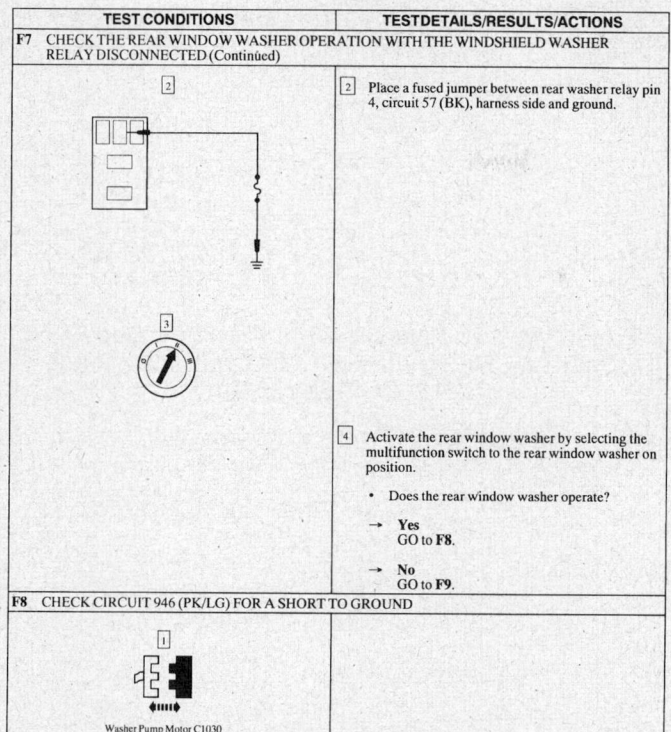	☐2 Place a fused jumper between rear washer relay pin 4, circuit 57 (BK), harness side and ground. ☐4 Activate the rear window washer by selecting the multifunction switch to the rear window washer on position. • Does the rear window washer operate? → **Yes** GO to **F8**. → **No** GO to **F9**.
F8 CHECK CIRCUIT 946 (PK/LG) FOR A SHORT TO GROUND	

FM9020000828050X

Fig. 8 Test F: Wash & Wipe Function Does Not Operate Properly (Part 5 of 10). Excursion & 2002–04 F-Super Duty

TEST CONDITIONS	TESTDETAILS/RESULTS/ACTIONS
F8 CHECK CIRCUIT 946 (PK/LG) FOR A SHORT TO GROUND (Continued)	
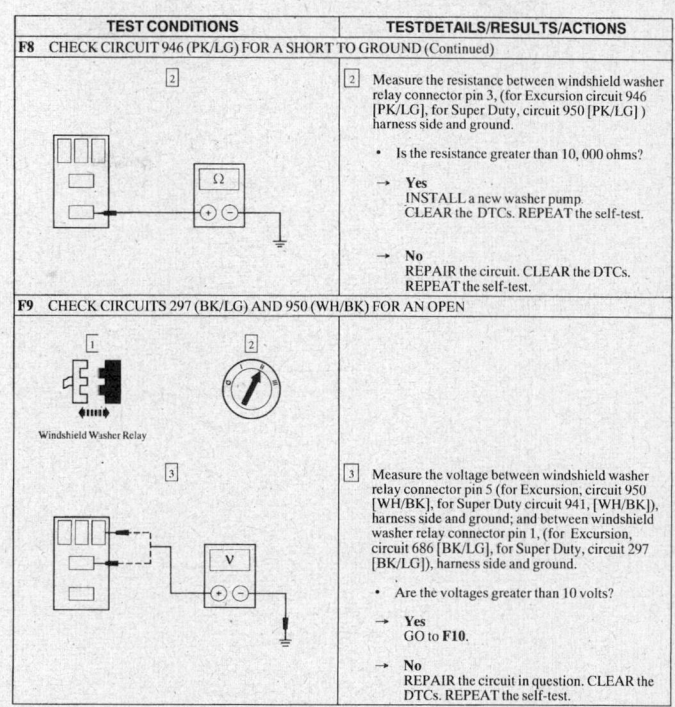	☐2 Measure the resistance between windshield washer relay connector pin 3, (for Excursion circuit 946 [PK/LG], for Super Duty, circuit 950 [PK/LG]) harness side and ground. • Is the resistance greater than 10, 000 ohms? → **Yes** INSTALL a new washer pump. CLEAR the DTCs. REPEAT the self-test. → **No** REPAIR the circuit. CLEAR the DTCs. REPEAT the self-test.
F9 CHECK CIRCUITS 297 (BK/LG) AND 950 (WH/BK) FOR AN OPEN	
Windshield Washer Relay	☐3 Measure the voltage between windshield washer relay connector pin 5 (for Excursion, circuit 950 [WH/BK], for Super Duty circuit 941, [WH/BK]), harness side and ground; and between windshield washer relay connector pin 1, (for Excursion, circuit 686 [BK/LG], for Super Duty, circuit 297 [BK/LG]), harness side and ground. • Are the voltages greater than 10 volts? → **Yes** GO to **F10**. → **No** REPAIR the circuit in question. CLEAR the DTCs. REPEAT the self-test.

FM9020000828060X

Fig. 8 Test F: Wash & Wipe Function Does Not Operate Properly (Part 6 of 10). Excursion & 2002–04 F-Super Duty

TEST CONDITIONS	TESTDETAILS/RESULTS/ACTIONS
F10 CHECK THE WINDSHIELD AND REAR WINDOW WASHER RELAYS	
	☐1 Carry out the relay component test on the windshield washer and rear window washer relay. • Did the washer relays pass the component test? → **Yes** For Excursion, GO to **F11**. For Super Duty, GO to **F12**. → **No** INSTALL a new relay. CLEAR the DTCs. REPEAT the self-test.
F11 CHECK CIRCUIT 57 (BK) FOR AN OPEN	
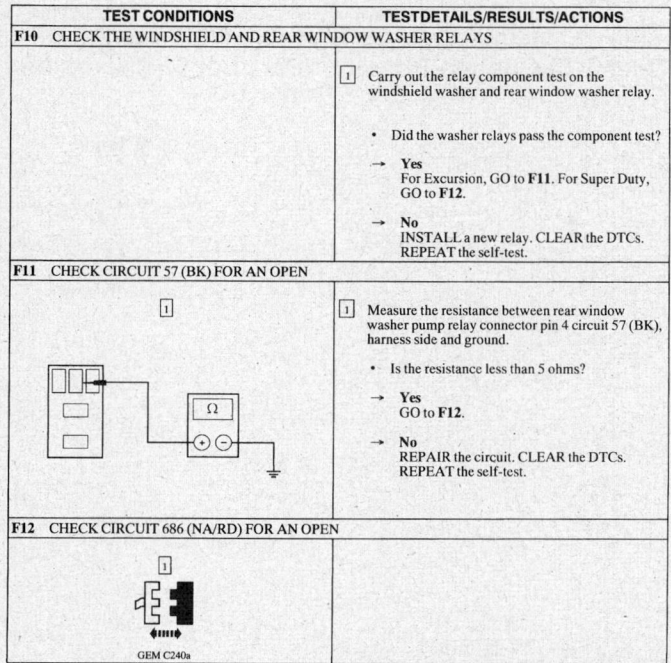	☐1 Measure the resistance between rear window washer pump relay connector pin 4 circuit 57 (BK), harness side and ground. • Is the resistance less than 5 ohms? → **Yes** GO to **F12**. → **No** REPAIR the circuit. CLEAR the DTCs. REPEAT the self-test.
F12 CHECK CIRCUIT 686 (NA/RD) FOR AN OPEN	
GEM C240a	

FM9020000828080X

Fig. 8 Test F: Wash & Wipe Function Does Not Operate Properly (Part 7 of 10). Excursion & 2002–04 F-Super Duty

TEST CONDITIONS	TESTDETAILS/RESULTS/ACTIONS
F12 CHECK CIRCUIT 686 (NA/RD) FOR AN OPEN (Continued)	
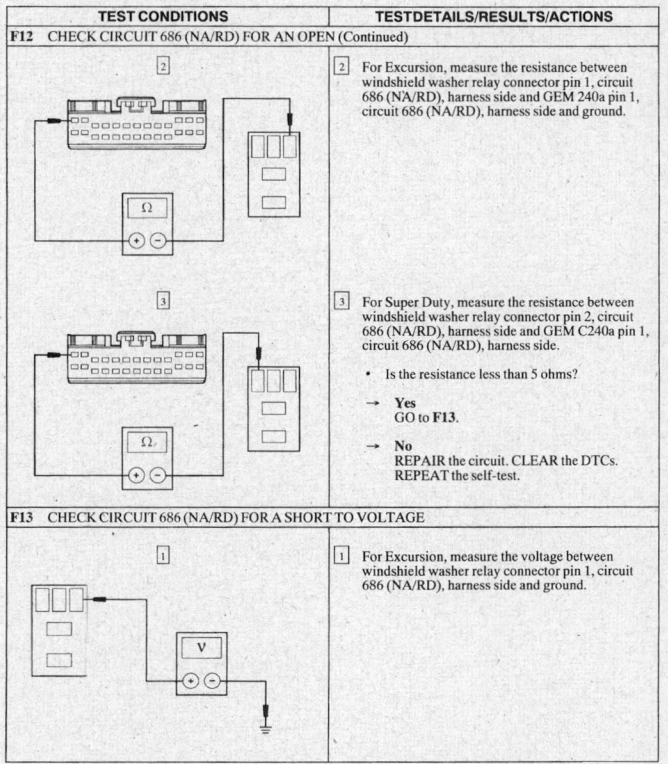	☐2 For Excursion, measure the resistance between windshield washer relay connector pin 1, circuit 686 (NA/RD), harness side and GEM 240a pin 1, circuit 686 (NA/RD), harness side and ground. ☐3 For Super Duty, measure the resistance between windshield washer relay connector pin 2, circuit 686 (NA/RD), harness side and GEM C240a pin 1, circuit 686 (NA/RD), harness side. • Is the resistance less than 5 ohms? → **Yes** GO to **F13**. → **No** REPAIR the circuit. CLEAR the DTCs. REPEAT the self-test.
F13 CHECK CIRCUIT 686 (NA/RD) FOR A SHORT TO VOLTAGE	
	☐1 For Excursion, measure the voltage between windshield washer relay connector pin 1, circuit 686 (NA/RD), harness side and ground.

FM9020000828090X

Fig. 8 Test F: Wash & Wipe Function Does Not Operate Properly (Part 8 of 10). Excursion & 2002–04 F-Super Duty

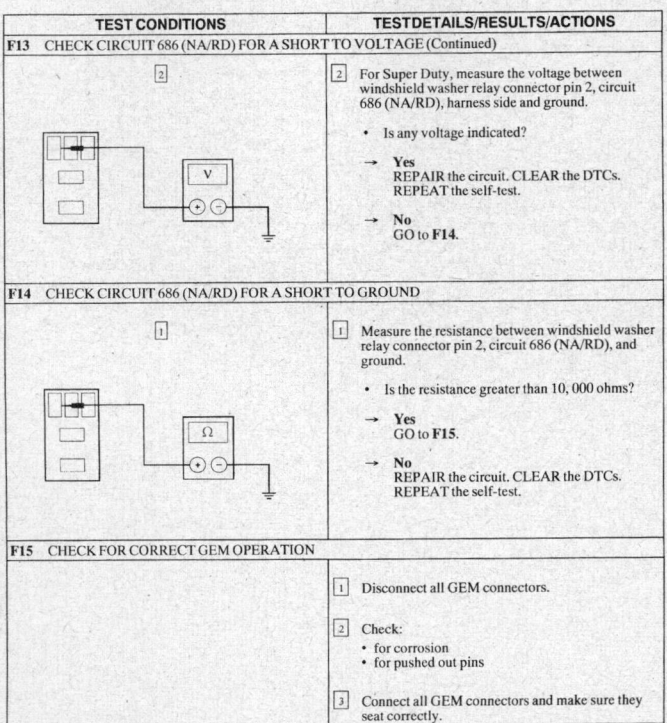

TEST CONDITIONS	TESTDETAILS/RESULTS/ACTIONS
F13 CHECK CIRCUIT 686 (NA/RD) FOR A SHORT TO VOLTAGE (Continued)	
2	2 For Super Duty, measure the voltage between windshield washer relay connector pin 2, circuit 686 (NA/RD), harness side and ground. • Is any voltage indicated? → **Yes** REPAIR the circuit. CLEAR the DTCs. REPEAT the self-test. → **No** GO to **F14**.
F14 CHECK CIRCUIT 686 (NA/RD) FOR A SHORT TO GROUND	
1	1 Measure the resistance between windshield washer relay connector pin 2, circuit 686 (NA/RD), and ground. • Is the resistance greater than 10,000 ohms? → **Yes** GO to **F15**. → **No** REPAIR the circuit. CLEAR the DTCs. REPEAT the self-test.
F15 CHECK FOR CORRECT GEM OPERATION	
	1 Disconnect all GEM connectors.
	2 Check: • for corrosion • for pushed out pins
	3 Connect all GEM connectors and make sure they seat correctly.

FM9020000828100X

Fig. 8   Test F: Wash & Wipe Function Does Not Operate Properly (Part 9 of 10). Excursion & 2002–04 F-Super Duty

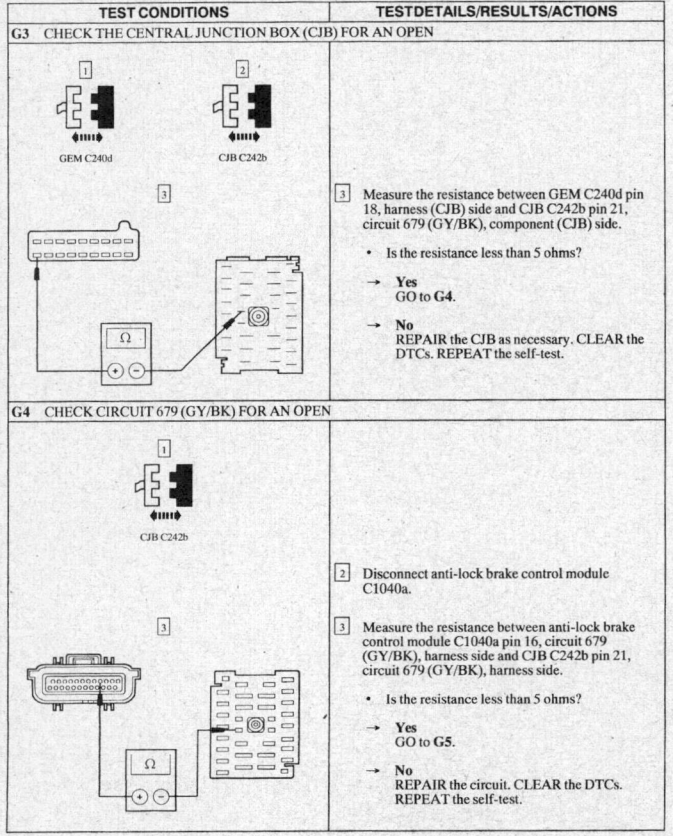

TEST CONDITIONS	TESTDETAILS/RESULTS/ACTIONS
G3 CHECK THE CENTRAL JUNCTION BOX (CJB) FOR AN OPEN	
GEM C240d CJB C242b	3 Measure the resistance between GEM C240d pin 18, harness side and CJB C242b pin 21, circuit 679 (GY/BK), component (CJB) side. • Is the resistance less than 5 ohms? → **Yes** GO to **G4**. → **No** REPAIR the CJB as necessary. CLEAR the DTCs. REPEAT the self-test.
G4 CHECK CIRCUIT 679 (GY/BK) FOR AN OPEN	
CJB C242b	2 Disconnect anti-lock brake control module C1040a.
	3 Measure the resistance between anti-lock brake control module C1040a pin 16, circuit 679 (GY/BK), harness side and CJB C242b pin 21, circuit 679 (GY/BK), harness side. • Is the resistance less than 5 ohms? → **Yes** GO to **G5**. → **No** REPAIR the circuit. CLEAR the DTCs. REPEAT the self-test.

FM9020000829020X

Fig. 9   Test G: Speed Dependent Interval Mode Does Not Operate Properly (Part 2 of 5). Excursion & 2002–04 F-Super Duty

TEST CONDITIONS	TESTDETAILS/RESULTS/ACTIONS
F15 CHECK FOR CORRECT GEM OPERATION (Continued)	
	4 Operate the system and verify the concern is still present. • Is the concern still present? → **Yes** INSTALL a new GEM. REPEAT the self-test. → **No** The system is operating correctly at this time. Concern may have been caused by a loose or corroded connector. CLEAR the DTCs. REPEAT the self-test.

FM9020000828110X

Fig. 8   Test F: Wash & Wipe Function Does Not Operate Properly (Part 10 of 10). Excursion & 2002–04 F-Super Duty

TEST CONDITIONS	TESTDETAILS/RESULTS/ACTIONS
G1 RETRIEVE RECORDED GENERIC ELECTRONIC MODULE (GEM) DIAGNOSTIC TROUBLE CODES (DTCs)	
	1 Using the recorded results from the GEM front wiper self-test: • Are any DTCs recorded? → **Yes** If DTC B1446, GO to **G6**. → **No** GO to **G2**.
G2 CHECK THE VSS — MONITOR THE GEM PID VSS	
1	1 Monitor ABS PIDs LF_WSPD, RF_WSPD, R_WSSP and GEM PID VSS while driving the vehicle from 0 to 88.5 kph (55 mph). • Does the GEM PID VSS agree with the ABS PIDs LF_WSPD, RF_WSPD, R_WSSP and GEM PID VSS? → **Yes** GO to **G9**. → **No** GO to **G3**.

FM9020000829010X

Fig. 9   Test G: Speed Dependent Interval Mode Does Not Operate Properly (Part 1 of 5). Excursion & 2002–04 F-Super Duty

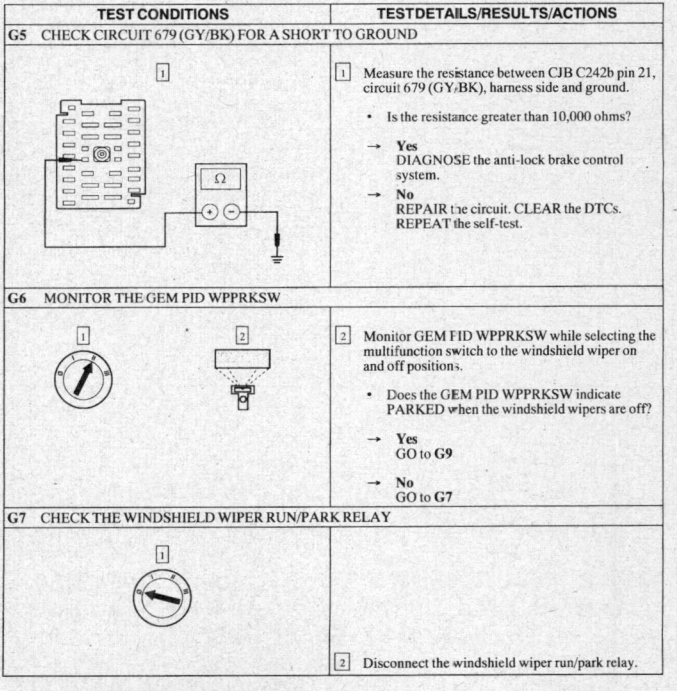

TEST CONDITIONS	TESTDETAILS/RESULTS/ACTIONS
G5 CHECK CIRCUIT 679 (GY/BK) FOR A SHORT TO GROUND	
1	1 Measure the resistance between CJB C242b pin 21, circuit 679 (GY/BK), harness side and ground. • Is the resistance greater than 10,000 ohms? → **Yes** DIAGNOSE the anti-lock brake control system. → **No** REPAIR the circuit. CLEAR the DTCs. REPEAT the self-test.
G6 MONITOR THE GEM PID WPPRKSW	
1 2	2 Monitor GEM PID WPPRKSW while selecting the multifunction switch to the windshield wiper on and off positions. • Does the GEM PID WPPRKSW indicate PARKED when the windshield wipers are off? → **Yes** GO to **G9**. → **No** GO to **G7**
G7 CHECK THE WINDSHIELD WIPER RUN/PARK RELAY	
1	
	2 Disconnect the windshield wiper run/park relay.

FM9020000829030X

Fig. 9   Test G: Speed Dependent Interval Mode Does Not Operate Properly (Part 3 of 5). Excursion & 2002–04 F-Super Duty

TEST CONDITIONS	TESTDETAILS/RESULTS/ACTIONS
G7 CHECK THE WINDSHIELD WIPER RUN/PARK RELAY (Continued)	
	3 Carry out the relay component test on the windshield wiper run/park relay. • Did the windshield wiper run/park relay pass the component test? → **Yes** GO to **G8**. → **No** INSTALL a new windshield wiper run/park relay. CLEAR the DTCs. REPEAT the self-test.
G8 CHECK CIRCUIT 671 (LB) FOR AN OPEN	
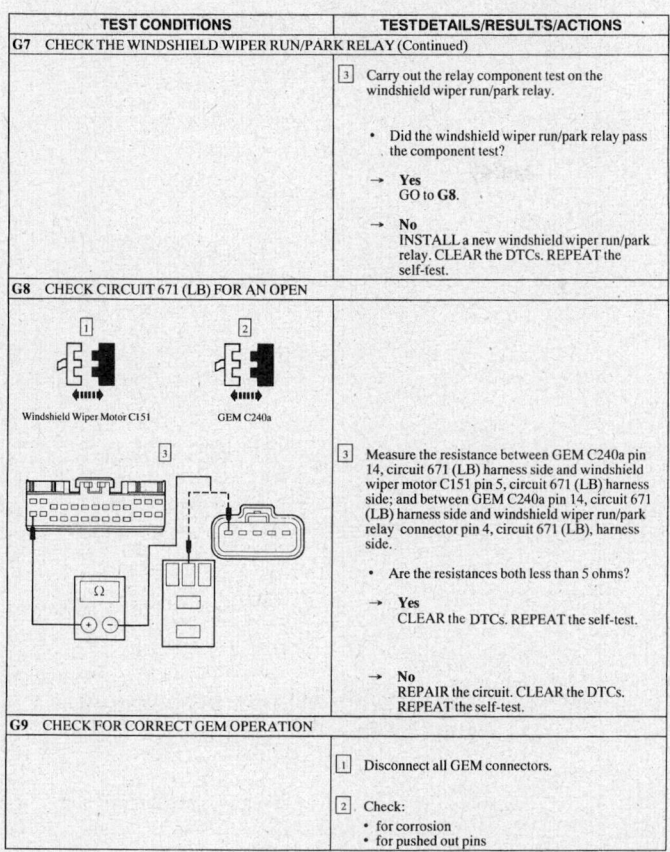	3 Measure the resistance between GEM C240a pin 14, circuit 671 (LB) harness side and windshield wiper motor C151 pin 5, circuit 671 (LB) harness side; and between GEM C240a pin 14, circuit 671 (LB) harness side and windshield wiper run/park relay connector pin 4, circuit 671 (LB), harness side. • Are the resistances both less than 5 ohms? → **Yes** CLEAR the DTCs. REPEAT the self-test. → **No** REPAIR the circuit. CLEAR the DTCs. REPEAT the self-test.
G9 CHECK FOR CORRECT GEM OPERATION	
	1 Disconnect all GEM connectors.
	2 Check: • for corrosion • for pushed out pins

FM9020000829040X

Fig. 9 Test G: Speed Dependent Interval Mode Does Not Operate Properly (Part 4 of 5). Excursion & 2002–04 F-Super Duty

TEST CONDITIONS	TESTDETAILS/RESULTS/ACTIONS
H2 RETRIEVE RECORDED GENERIC ELECTRONIC MODULE (GEM) DIAGNOSTIC TROUBLE CODES (DTCs)	
	2 Using the recorded results from the GEM rear wiper self-test: • Are any DTCs recorded? → **Yes** If DTC B1240, GO to Pinpoint Test **K**. If DTC B1241, GO to Pinpoint Test **K**. If DTC B1611, GO to **H5**. If DTC B1614, GO to Pinpoint Test **I**. If DTC B1820, GO to **H10**. If DTC B1839, GO to **H7**. → **No** GO to **H3**.
H3 MONITOR THE GEM PID R__WP__MD	
	2 Monitor GEM PID R__WP__MD while selecting each of the multifunction switch windshield wiper positions. • Do the GEM PID values agree with the multifunction switch positions? → **Yes** GO to **H4**. → **No** GO to **H5**.

FM9020000830020X

Fig. 10 Test H: Rear Wipers Inoperative (Part 2 of 9). Excursion

TEST CONDITIONS	TESTDETAILS/RESULTS/ACTIONS
G9 CHECK FOR CORRECT GEM OPERATION (Continued)	
	3 Connect all GEM connectors and make sure they seat correctly. 4 Operate the system and verify the concern is still present. • Is the concern still present? → **Yes** INSTALL a new GEM. REPEAT the self-test. → **No** The system is operating correctly at this time. Concern may have been caused by a loose or corroded connector. CLEAR the DTCs. REPEAT the self-test.

FM9020000829050X

Fig. 9 Test G: Speed Dependent Interval Mode Does Not Operate Properly (Part 5 of 5). Excursion & 2002–04 F-Super Duty

TEST CONDITIONS	TESTDETAILS/RESULTS/ACTIONS
H1 CHECK THE FRONT WINDSHIELD WIPER OPERATION	
	2 Using the multifunction switch, activate the front windshield wipers on and off. • Do the front windshield wipers operate correctly? → **Yes** GO to **H2**. → **No** GO to Pinpoint Test **L**.

FM9020000830010X

Fig. 10 Test H: Rear Wipers Inoperative (Part 1 of 9). Excursion

TEST CONDITIONS	TESTDETAILS/RESULTS/ACTIONS
H4 CHECK THE REAR WINDOW WIPER MOTOR OPERATION USING ACTIVE COMMAND UP RELAY	
	1 Select GEM active command UP RELAY. Trigger UP RELAY to the ON and OFF positions. • Does the rear window wiper motor activate and deactivate correctly when UP RELAY is triggered ON and OFF? → **Yes** GO to **H16**. → **No** GO to **H7**.
H5 CHECK THE MULTIFUNCTION SWITCH	
	2 Disconnect multifunction switch C230a and C230b. 3 Carry out the multifunction switch component test. • Did the multifunction switch pass the component test? → **Yes** GO to **H6**. → **No** INSTALL a new multifunction switch. CLEAR the DTCs. REPEAT the self-test.
H6 CHECK CIRCUIT 485 (PK/BK) FOR AN OPEN	

FM9020000830030X

Fig. 10 Test H: Rear Wipers Inoperative (Part 3 of 9). Excursion

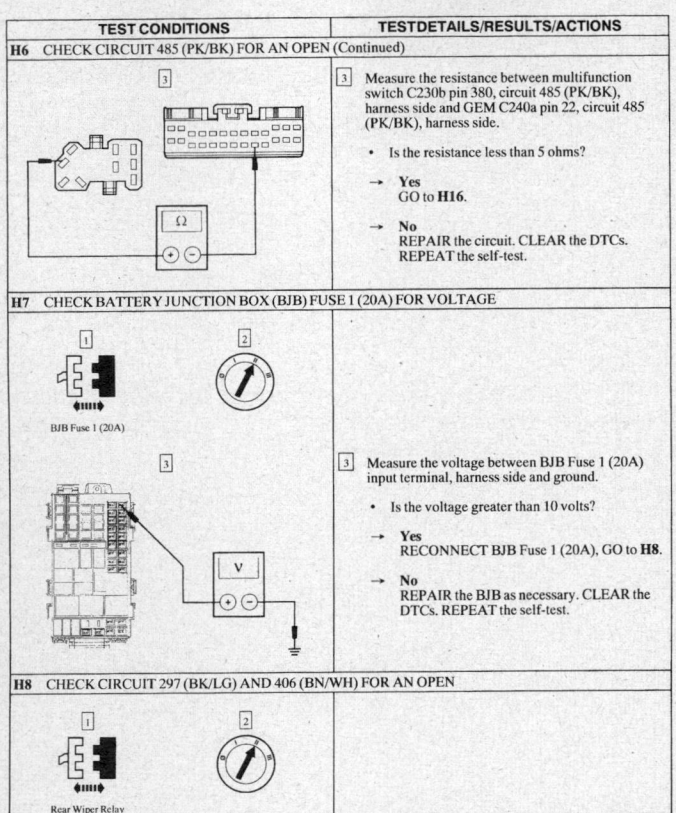

TEST CONDITIONS	TESTDETAILS/RESULTS/ACTIONS
H6 CHECK CIRCUIT 485 (PK/BK) FOR AN OPEN (Continued)	
③	③ Measure the resistance between multifunction switch C230b pin 380, circuit 485 (PK/BK), harness side and GEM C240a pin 22, circuit 485 (PK/BK), harness side. • Is the resistance less than 5 ohms? → **Yes** GO to **H16**. → **No** REPAIR the circuit. CLEAR the DTCs. REPEAT the self-test.
H7 CHECK BATTERY JUNCTION BOX (BJB) FUSE 1 (20A) FOR VOLTAGE	
① ② BJB Fuse 1 (20A) ③	③ Measure the voltage between BJB Fuse 1 (20A) input terminal, harness side and ground. • Is the voltage greater than 10 volts? → **Yes** RECONNECT BJB Fuse 1 (20A), GO to **H8**. → **No** REPAIR the BJB as necessary. CLEAR the DTCs. REPEAT the self-test.
H8 CHECK CIRCUIT 297 (BK/LG) AND 406 (BN/WH) FOR AN OPEN	
① ② Rear Wiper Relay	

Fig. 10 Test H: Rear Wipers Inoperative (Part 4 of 9). Excursion

FM9020000830040X

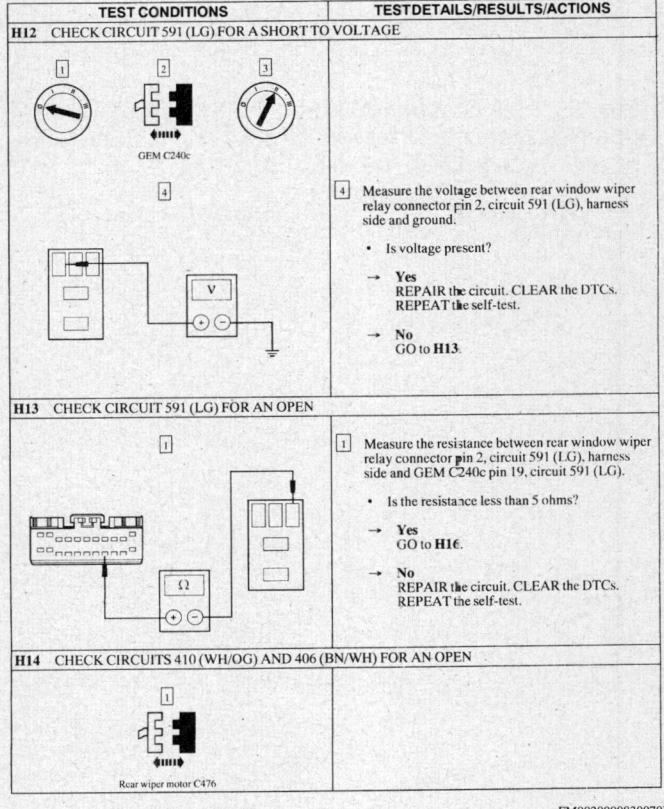

TEST CONDITIONS	TESTDETAILS/RESULTS/ACTIONS
H8 CHECK CIRCUIT 297 (BK/LG) AND 406 (BN/WH) FOR AN OPEN (Continued)	
③	③ Measure the voltage between rear window wiper relay pin 1, circuit 297 (BK/LG), harness side and ground; and between rear window wiper relay pin 5, circuit 406 (BN/WH), harness side and ground. • Is voltage present? → **Yes** GO to **H9**. → **No** REPAIR the circuit in question. CLEAR the DTCs. REPEAT the self-test.
H9 CHECK CIRCUIT 57 (BK) FOR AN OPEN	
① ②	② Measure the resistance between rear window wiper relay connector pin 4, circuit 57 (BK), harness side and ground. • Is the resistance less than 5 ohms? → **Yes** GO to **H10** → **No** REPAIR circuit 56 (DB/O) and/or circuit 58 (WH). CLEAR the DTCs. TEST the system for normal operation.

FM9020000830050X

Fig. 10 Test H: Rear Wipers Inoperative (Part 5 of 9). Excursion

TEST CONDITIONS	TESTDETAILS/RESULTS/ACTIONS
H10 CHECK THE REAR WINDOW WIPER RELAY	
①	② Carry out the relay component test on the rear window wiper relay. • Did the rear window wiper relay pass the component test? → **Yes** GO to **H11**. → **No** INSTALL a new relay. CLEAR the DTCs. REPEAT the self-test.
H11 CHECK THE REAR WINDOW WIPER MOTOR FUNCTION	
① ②	② Connect a fused jumper wire between rear window wiper relay connector pin 5, circuit 406 (BN/WH), harness side and rear window wiper relay connector pin 3, circuit 410 (WH/OG), harness side. • Does the rear window wiper motor operate? → **Yes** GO to **H12**. → **No** GO to **H14**.

FM9020000830060X

Fig. 10 Test H: Rear Wipers Inoperative (Part 6 of 9). Excursion

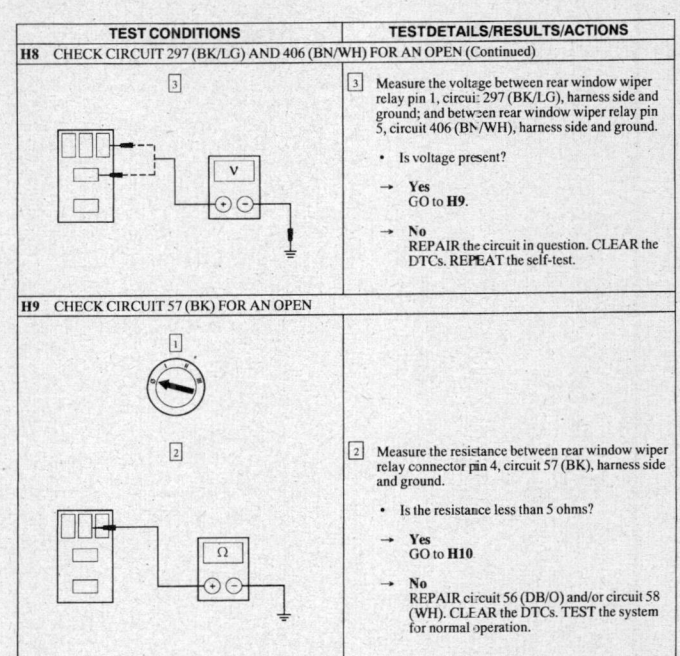

TEST CONDITIONS	TESTDETAILS/RESULTS/ACTIONS
H12 CHECK CIRCUIT 591 (LG) FOR A SHORT TO VOLTAGE	
① ② ③ GEM C240c ④	④ Measure the voltage between rear window wiper relay connector pin 2, circuit 591 (LG), harness side and ground. • Is voltage present? → **Yes** REPAIR the circuit. CLEAR the DTCs. REPEAT the self-test. → **No** GO to **H13**.
H13 CHECK CIRCUIT 591 (LG) FOR AN OPEN	
①	① Measure the resistance between rear window wiper relay connector pin 2, circuit 591 (LG), harness side and GEM C240c pin 19, circuit 591 (LG). • Is the resistance less than 5 ohms? → **Yes** GO to **H16**. → **No** REPAIR the circuit. CLEAR the DTCs. REPEAT the self-test.
H14 CHECK CIRCUITS 410 (WH/OG) AND 406 (BN/WH) FOR AN OPEN	
① Rear wiper motor C476	

FM9020000830070X

Fig. 10 Test H: Rear Wipers Inoperative (Part 7 of 9). Excursion

TEST CONDITIONS	TESTDETAILS/RESULTS/ACTIONS
H14 CHECK CIRCUITS 410 (WH/OG) AND 406 (BN/WH) FOR AN OPEN (Continued)	
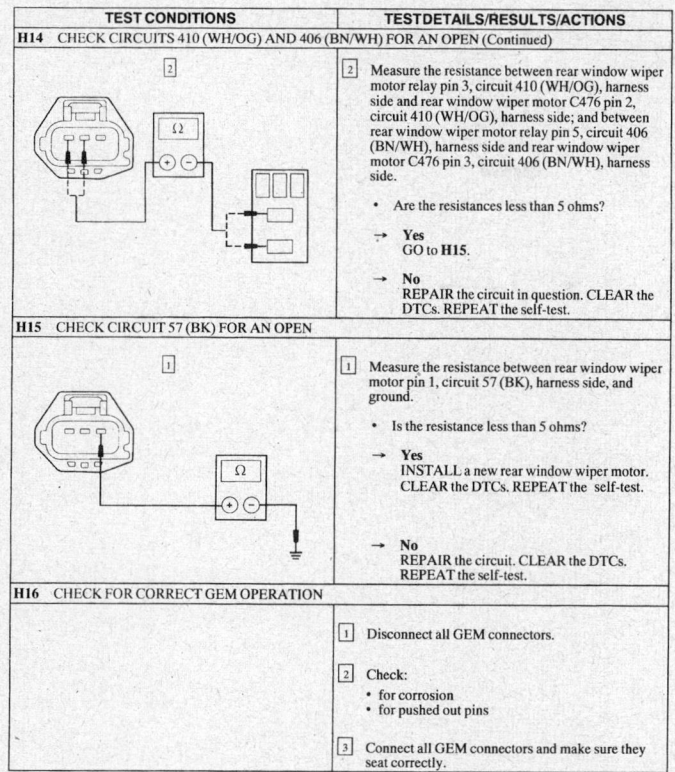	**2** Measure the resistance between rear window wiper motor relay pin 3, circuit 410 (WH/OG), harness side and rear window wiper motor C476 pin 2, circuit 410 (WH/OG), harness side; and between rear window wiper motor relay pin 5, circuit 406 (BN/WH), harness side and rear window wiper motor C476 pin 3, circuit 406 (BN/WH), harness side. • Are the resistances less than 5 ohms? → **Yes** GO to **H15**. → **No** REPAIR the circuit in question. CLEAR the DTCs. REPEAT the self-test.
H15 CHECK CIRCUIT 57 (BK) FOR AN OPEN	
	1 Measure the resistance between rear window wiper motor pin 1, circuit 57 (BK), harness side, and ground. • Is the resistance less than 5 ohms? → **Yes** INSTALL a new rear window wiper motor. CLEAR the DTCs. REPEAT the self-test. → **No** REPAIR the circuit. CLEAR the DTCs. REPEAT the self-test.
H16 CHECK FOR CORRECT GEM OPERATION	
	1 Disconnect all GEM connectors. **2** Check: • for corrosion • for pushed out pins **3** Connect all GEM connectors and make sure they seat correctly.

FM9020000830080X

Fig. 10 Test H: Rear Wipers Inoperative (Part 8 of 9). Excursion

TEST CONDITIONS	TESTDETAILS/RESULTS/ACTIONS
I2 RETRIEVE THE RECORDED GENERIC ELECTRONIC MODULE (GEM) DIAGNOSTIC TROUBLE CODES (DTCs)	
	1 Using the recorded results from the GEM rear wiper self-test. • Are any DTCs retrieved? → **Yes** If DTC B1240, GO to Pinpoint Test K. If DTC B1241, GO to Pinpoint Test K. If DTC B1611, GO to Pinpoint Test H. If DTC B1614, GO to **I5**. If DTC B1820, GO to Pinpoint Test H. → **No** GO to **I3**.
I3 MONITOR THE GEM PID R__WP__MD	
	3 Monitor GEM PID R__WP__MD while selecting each of the multifunction switch rear window wiper positions. • Do the GEM PID values agree with the multifunction switch positions? → **Yes** GO to **I4**. → **No** GO to **I5**.

FM9020000831020X

Fig. 11 Test I: Rear Wipers Stay On Continuously (Part 2 of 6). Excursion

TEST CONDITIONS	TESTDETAILS/RESULTS/ACTIONS
H16 CHECK FOR CORRECT GEM OPERATION (Continued)	
	4 Operate the system and verify the concern is still present. • Is the concern still present? → **Yes** INSTALL a new GEM. CLEAR the DTCs. REPEAT the self-test. → **No** The system is operating correctly at this time. Concern may have been caused by a loose or corroded connector. CLEAR the DTCs. REPEAT the self-test.

FM9020000830090X

Fig. 10 Test H: Rear Wipers Inoperative (Part 9 of 9). Excursion

TEST CONDITIONS	TESTDETAILS/RESULTS/ACTIONS
I1 CHECK THE WINDSHIELD WIPER OPERATION	
	2 Using the multifunction switch, activate the windshield wiper motor on and off. • Does the windshield wiper motor operate correctly? → **Yes** GO to **I2**. → **No** GO to Pinpoint Test L.

FM9020000831010X

Fig. 11 Test I: Rear Wipers Stay On Continuously (Part 1 of 6). Excursion

TEST CONDITIONS	TESTDETAILS/RESULTS/ACTIONS
I4 CHECK THE REAR WINDOW WIPER MOTOR OPERATION USING ACTIVE COMMAND UP RELAY	
	1 Select the GEM active command UP RELAY. Trigger UP RELAY to the ON and OFF positions. • Does the rear window wiper motor activate and deactivate correctly when UP RELAY is triggered ON and OFF? → **Yes** GO to **I11**. → **No** GO to **I7**.
I5 CHECK THE MULTIFUNCTION SWITCH	
	2 Disconnect multifunction switch C230a and C230b. **3** Carry out the multifunction switch component test. • Did the multifunction switch pass the component test? → **Yes** GO to **I6**. → **No** INSTALL a new multifunction switch. CLEAR the DTCs. REPEAT the self-test.
I6 CHECK CIRCUIT 485 (PK/BK) FOR A SHORT TO GROUND	
GEM C240a	

FM9020000831030X

Fig. 11 Test I: Rear Wipers Stay On Continuously (Part 3 of 6). Excursion

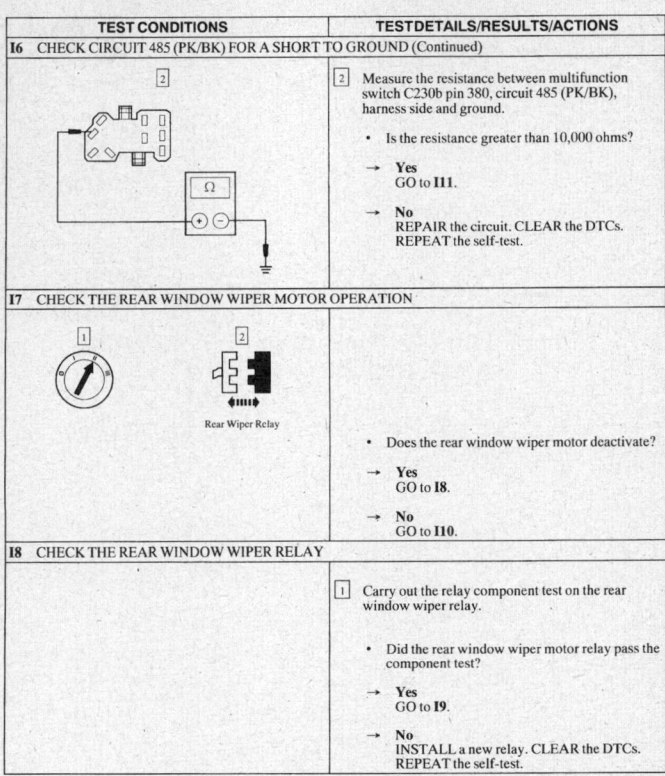

TEST CONDITIONS	TEST DETAILS/RESULTS/ACTIONS
I6 CHECK CIRCUIT 485 (PK/BK) FOR A SHORT TO GROUND (Continued)	
	[2] Measure the resistance between multifunction switch C230b pin 380, circuit 485 (PK/BK), harness side and ground. • Is the resistance greater than 10,000 ohms? → **Yes** GO to **I11**. → **No** REPAIR the circuit. CLEAR the DTCs. REPEAT the self-test.
I7 CHECK THE REAR WINDOW WIPER MOTOR OPERATION	
	• Does the rear window wiper motor deactivate? → **Yes** GO to **I8**. → **No** GO to **I10**.
I8 CHECK THE REAR WINDOW WIPER RELAY	
	[1] Carry out the relay component test on the rear window wiper relay. • Did the rear window wiper motor relay pass the component test? → **Yes** GO to **I9**. → **No** INSTALL a new relay. CLEAR the DTCs. REPEAT the self-test.

FM9020000831040X

Fig. 11 Test I: Rear Wipers Stay On Continuously (Part 4 of 6). Excursion

TEST CONDITIONS	TEST DETAILS/RESULTS/ACTIONS
I11 CHECK FOR CORRECT GEM OPERATION (Continued)	
	[2] Check: • for corrosion • for pushed out pins [3] Connect all GEM connectors and make sure they seat correctly. [4] Operate the system and verify the concern is still present. • Is the concern still present? → **Yes** INSTALL a new GEM. CLEAR the DTCs. REPEAT the self-test. → **No** The system is operating correctly at this time. Concern may have been caused by a loose or corroded connector. CLEAR the DTCs. REPEAT the self-test.

FM9020000831060X

Fig. 11 Test I: Rear Wipers Stay On Continuously (Part 6 of 6). Excursion

TEST CONDITIONS	TEST DETAILS/RESULTS/ACTIONS
J1 RETRIEVE THE RECORDED GENERIC ELECTRONIC MODULE (GEM) DIAGNOSTIC TROUBLE CODES (DTCs)	
	[1] Using the recorded results from the GEM rear wiper self-test: • Are any DTCs retrieved? → **Yes** If DTC B1240, or B1241, GO to Pinpoint Test K. If DTC B1611, B1820, or B1839, GO to Pinpoint Test H. If DTC B1614, GO to Pinpoint Test I. → **No** GO to **J2**.

FM9020000832010X

Fig. 12 Test J: Intermittent Rear Wiper Speed Does Not Operate Properly (Part 1 of 3). Excursion

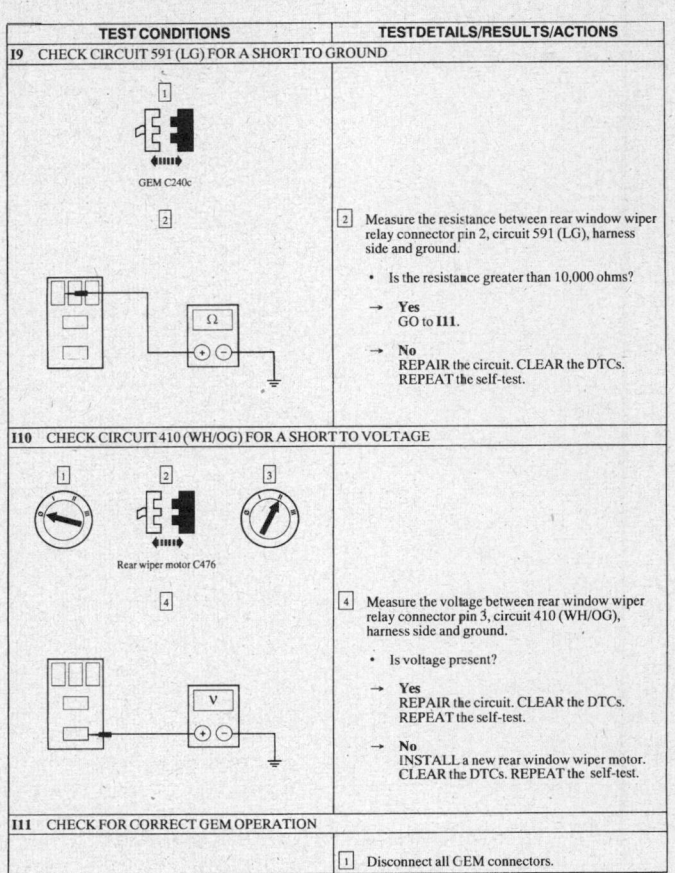

TEST CONDITIONS	TEST DETAILS/RESULTS/ACTIONS
I9 CHECK CIRCUIT 591 (LG) FOR A SHORT TO GROUND	
	[2] Measure the resistance between rear window wiper relay connector pin 2, circuit 591 (LG), harness side and ground. • Is the resistance greater than 10,000 ohms? → **Yes** GO to **I11**. → **No** REPAIR the circuit. CLEAR the DTCs. REPEAT the self-test.
I10 CHECK CIRCUIT 410 (WH/OG) FOR A SHORT TO VOLTAGE	
	[4] Measure the voltage between rear window wiper relay connector pin 3, circuit 410 (WH/OG), harness side and ground. • Is voltage present? → **Yes** REPAIR the circuit. CLEAR the DTCs. REPEAT the self-test. → **No** INSTALL a new rear window wiper motor. CLEAR the DTCs. REPEAT the self-test.
I11 CHECK FOR CORRECT GEM OPERATION	
	[1] Disconnect all GEM connectors.

FM9020000831050X

Fig. 11 Test I: Rear Wipers Stay On Continuously (Part 5 of 6). Excursion

TEST CONDITIONS	TEST DETAILS/RESULTS/ACTIONS
J2 MONITOR THE GEM PID R__WP__MD	
	[3] Monitor GEM PID R__WP__MD while selecting each of the rear window wiper positions on the multifunction switch. • Do the GEM PID values agree with the multifunction switch positions? → **Yes** GO to **J3**. → **No** GO to **J4**.
J3 CHECK THE REAR WINDOW WIPER MOTOR OPERATION USING ACTIVE COMMAND UP RELAY	
	[1] Select GEM active command UP RELAY. Trigger UP RELAY to the ON and OFF positions. • Does the rear window wiper motor activate and deactivate correctly when UP RELAY is triggered ON and OFF? → **Yes** GO to **J5**. → **No** GO to Pinpoint Test H.
J4 CHECK THE MULTIFUNCTION SWITCH	
	[2] Disconnect multifunction switch C230a and C230b.

FM9020000832020X

Fig. 12 Test J: Intermittent Rear Wiper Speed Does Not Operate Properly (Part 2 of 3). Excursion

TEST CONDITIONS	TESTDETAILS/RESULTS/ACTIONS
J4 CHECK THE MULTIFUNCTION SWITCH (Continued)	
	3 Carry out the multifunction switch component test. • Did the multifunction switch pass the component test? → **Yes** GO to **J5**. → **No** INSTALL a new multifunction switch. CLEAR the DTCs. REPEAT the self-test.
J5 CHECK FOR CORRECT GEM OPERATION	
	1 Disconnect all GEM connectors. 2 Check: • for corrosion • for pushed out pins 3 Connect all GEM connectors and make sure they seat correctly. 4 Operate the system and verify the concern is still present. • Is the concern still present? → **Yes** INSTALL a new GEM. REPEAT the self-test. → **No** The system is operating correctly at this time. Concern may have been caused by a loose or corroded connector. CLEAR the DTCs. REPEAT the self-test.

FM9020000832030X

Fig. 12　Test J: Intermittent Rear Wiper Speed Does Not Operate Properly (Part 3 of 3). Excursion

TEST CONDITIONS	TESTDETAILS/RESULTS/ACTIONS
K3 CHECK THE WASHER PUMP OPERATION USING ACTIVE COMMAND WASH RLY	
	1 Select GEM active command WASH RLY. Trigger GEM active command WASH RLY ON and OFF. • Does the rear window washer activate and deactivate correctly when WASH RLY is triggered ON and OFF? → **Yes** GO to **K13**. → **No** GO to **K5**.
K4 CHECK THE MULTIFUNCTION SWITCH	
	2 Disconnect multifunction switch C230a and C230b. 3 Carry out the multifunction switch component test. • Did the multifunction switch pass the component test? → **Yes** GO to **K13**. → **No** INSTALL a new multifunction switch. CLEAR the DTCs. REPEAT the self-test.
K5 CHECK THE WINDSHIELD WASHER OPERATION WITH THE REAR WINDOW WASHER RELAY DISCONNECTED	
  Rear Washer Relay	

FM9020000833020X

Fig. 13　Test K: Rear Wash & Wipe Function Does Not Operate (Part 2 of 7). Excursion

TEST CONDITIONS	TESTDETAILS/RESULTS/ACTIONS
K1 RETRIEVE THE RECORDED GENERIC ELECTRONIC MODULE (GEM) DIAGNOSTIC TROUBLE CODES (DTCs)	
	1 Using the recorded results from the GEM rear wiper self-test: • Are any DTCs retrieved? → **Yes** If DTC B1240, GO to **K7**. If DTC B1241, GO to **K8**. If DTC B1611, GO to Pinpoint Test H. If DTC B1614, GO to Pinpoint Test I. If DTC B1820, GO to Pinpoint Test H. If DTC 1839, GO to Pinpoint Test H. → **No** GO to **K2**.
K2 MONITOR THE GEM PID R__WP__MD	
	3 Monitor GEM PID R__WP__MD while selecting each of the rear window wiper positions on the multifunction switch and depressing the rear window washer switch. • Do the GEM PID values agree with the multifunction switch positions? → **Yes** GO to **K3**. → **No** If no GEM PID values agree, GO to Pinpoint Test H. If GEM PID value WASH does not agree, GO to **K4**.

FM9020000833010X

Fig. 13　Test K: Rear Wash & Wipe Function Does Not Operate (Part 1 of 7). Excursion

TEST CONDITIONS	TESTDETAILS/RESULTS/ACTIONS
K5 CHECK THE WINDSHIELD WASHER OPERATION WITH THE REAR WINDOW WASHER RELAY DISCONNECTED (Continued)	
	2 Connect a jumper between rear windshield washer relay pin 4, harness side and ground. 4 Jump ground across relay. 5 Activate the windshield washer from the multifunction switch. • Does the windshield washer operate? → **Yes** GO to **K6**. → **No** GO to **K7**.
K6 CHECK CIRCUIT 941 (BK/WH) FOR A SHORT TO GROUND	
  Washer Pump Motor C1030	

FM9020000833030X

Fig. 13　Test K: Rear Wash & Wipe Function Does Not Operate (Part 3 of 7). Excursion

TEST CONDITIONS	TESTDETAILS/RESULTS/ACTIONS
K6 CHECK CIRCUIT 941 (BK/WH) FOR A SHORT TO GROUND (Continued)	
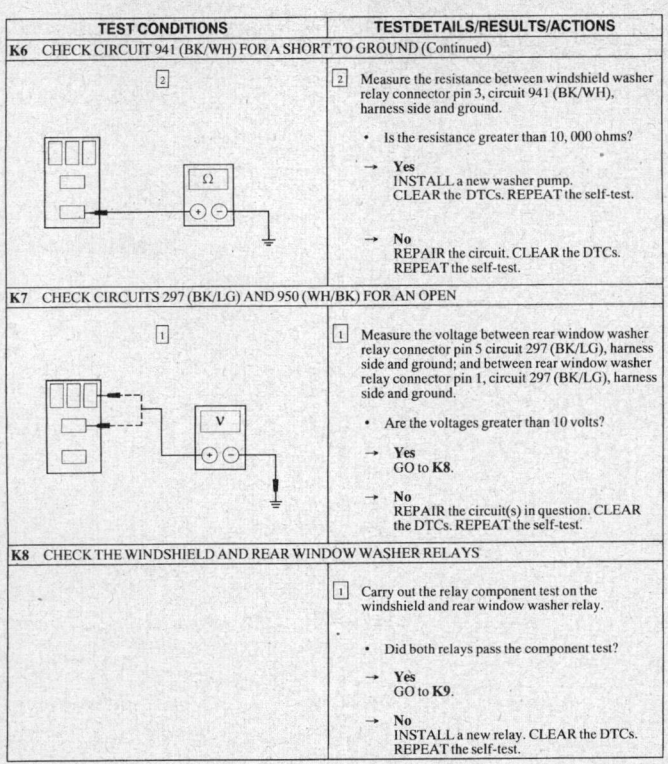	**2** Measure the resistance between windshield washer relay connector pin 3, circuit 941 (BK/WH), harness side and ground. • Is the resistance greater than 10,000 ohms? → **Yes** INSTALL a new washer pump. CLEAR the DTCs. REPEAT the self-test. → **No** REPAIR the circuit. CLEAR the DTCs. REPEAT the self-test.
K7 CHECK CIRCUITS 297 (BK/LG) AND 950 (WH/BK) FOR AN OPEN	
	1 Measure the voltage between rear window washer relay connector pin 5 circuit 297 (BK/LG), harness side and ground; and between rear window washer relay connector pin 1, circuit 297 (BK/LG), harness side and ground. • Are the voltages greater than 10 volts? → **Yes** GO to **K8**. → **No** REPAIR the circuit(s) in question. CLEAR the DTCs. REPEAT the self-test.
K8 CHECK THE WINDSHIELD AND REAR WINDOW WASHER RELAYS	
	1 Carry out the relay component test on the windshield and rear window washer relay. • Did both relays pass the component test? → **Yes** GO to **K9**. → **No** INSTALL a new relay. CLEAR the DTCs. REPEAT the self-test.

FM9020000833040X

Fig. 13 Test K: Rear Wash & Wipe Function Does Not Operate (Part 4 of 7). Excursion

TEST CONDITIONS	TESTDETAILS/RESULTS/ACTIONS
K11 CHECK CIRCUIT 488 (DG) FOR A SHORT TO VOLTAGE (Continued)	
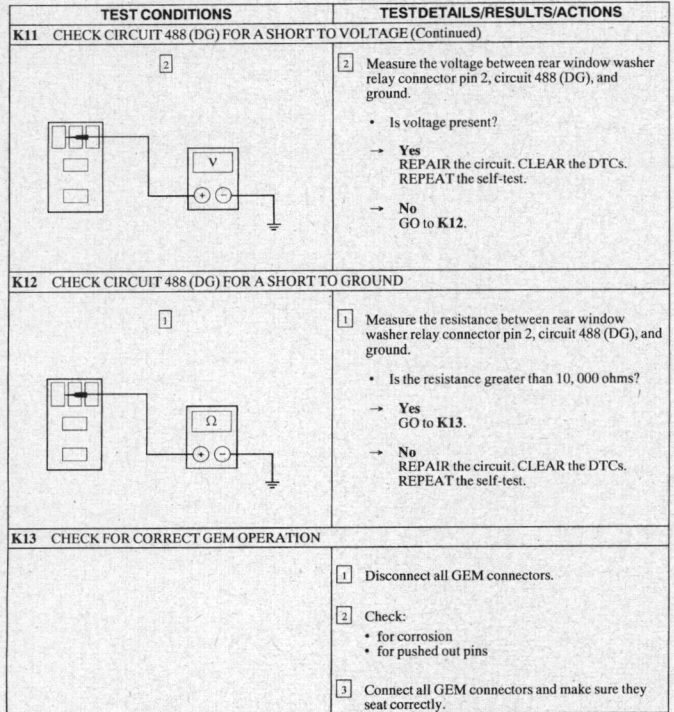	**2** Measure the voltage between rear window washer relay connector pin 2, circuit 488 (DG), and ground. • Is voltage present? → **Yes** REPAIR the circuit. CLEAR the DTCs. REPEAT the self-test. → **No** GO to **K12**.
K12 CHECK CIRCUIT 488 (DG) FOR A SHORT TO GROUND	
	1 Measure the resistance between rear window washer relay connector pin 2, circuit 488 (DG), and ground. • Is the resistance greater than 10,000 ohms? → **Yes** GO to **K13**. → **No** REPAIR the circuit. CLEAR the DTCs. REPEAT the self-test.
K13 CHECK FOR CORRECT GEM OPERATION	
	1 Disconnect all GEM connectors. **2** Check: • for corrosion • for pushed out pins **3** Connect all GEM connectors and make sure they seat correctly.

FM9020000833060X

Fig. 13 Test K: Rear Wash & Wipe Function Does Not Operate (Part 6 of 7). Excursion

TEST CONDITIONS	TESTDETAILS/RESULTS/ACTIONS
K9 CHECK CIRCUIT 57 (BK) FOR AN OPEN	
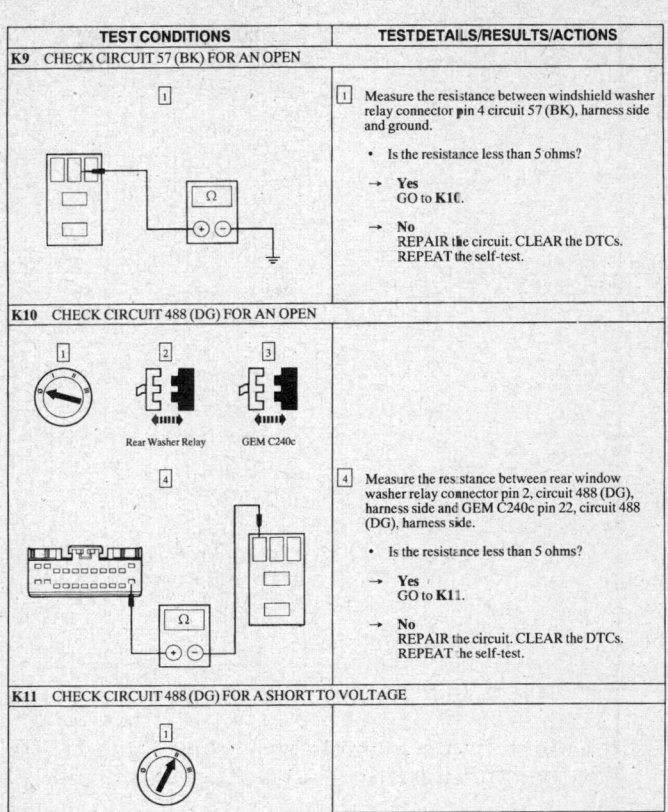	**1** Measure the resistance between windshield washer relay connector pin 4 circuit 57 (BK), harness side and ground. • Is the resistance less than 5 ohms? → **Yes** GO to **K10**. → **No** REPAIR the circuit. CLEAR the DTCs. REPEAT the self-test.
K10 CHECK CIRCUIT 488 (DG) FOR AN OPEN	
Rear Washer Relay GEM C240c	**4** Measure the resistance between rear window washer relay connector pin 2, circuit 488 (DG), harness side and GEM C240c pin 22, circuit 488 (DG), harness side. • Is the resistance less than 5 ohms? → **Yes** GO to **K11**. → **No** REPAIR the circuit. CLEAR the DTCs. REPEAT the self-test.
K11 CHECK CIRCUIT 488 (DG) FOR A SHORT TO VOLTAGE	

FM9020000833050X

Fig. 13 Test K: Rear Wash & Wipe Function Does Not Operate (Part 5 of 7). Excursion

TEST CONDITIONS	TESTDETAILS/RESULTS/ACTIONS
K13 CHECK FOR CORRECT GEM OPERATION (Continued)	
	4 Operate the system and verify the concern is still present. • Is the concern still present? → **Yes** INSTALL a new GEM. CLEAR the DTCs. REPEAT the self-test. → **No** The system is operating correctly at this time. Concern may have been caused by a loose or corroded connector. CLEAR the DTCs. REPEAT the self-test.

FM9020000833070X

Fig. 13 Test K: Rear Wash & Wipe Function Does Not Operate (Part 7 of 7). Excursion

TEST CONDITIONS	TEST DETAILS/RESULTS/ACTIONS
L1 RETRIEVE RECORDED GENERIC ELECTRONIC MODULE (GEM) DIAGNOSTIC TROUBLE CODES (DTCs)	
	① Using the recorded results from the GEM front wiper self-test: • Are any DTCs recorded? → **Yes** If DTC B1450, and B1438, GO to **L4**. For all other DTCs, GO to **L2**. → **No** GO to **L2**.
L2 MONITOR THE GEM PIDs	
① ②	② Monitor the following GEM PIDs while selecting each of the washer/wiper switch positions on the multifunction switch: • R_WP_MD • WASH_SW • WPMODE • Do the GEM PID values agree with the multifunction switch positions? → **Yes** GO to **L3**. → **No** GO to **L4**.

FM9020000834010X

Fig. 14   Test L: Wipers Inoperative-Front & Rear (Part 1 of 9). Excursion

TEST CONDITIONS	TEST DETAILS/RESULTS/ACTIONS
L5 CHECK CIRCUIT 682 (DB) FOR AN OPEN	
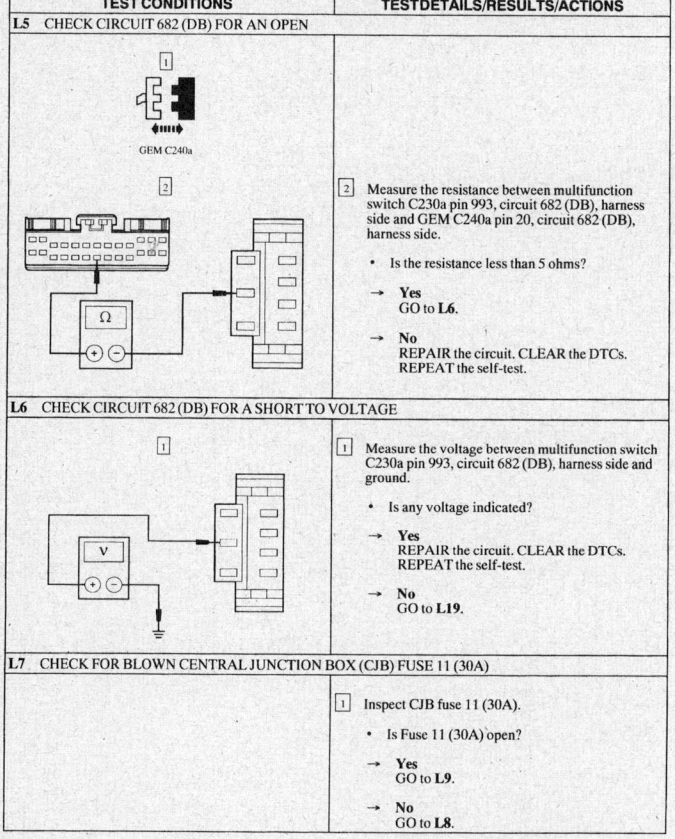 GEM C240a ②	② Measure the resistance between multifunction switch C230a pin 993, circuit 682 (DB), harness side and GEM C240a pin 20, circuit 682 (DB), harness side. • Is the resistance less than 5 ohms? → **Yes** GO to **L6**. → **No** REPAIR the circuit. CLEAR the DTCs. REPEAT the self-test.
L6 CHECK CIRCUIT 682 (DB) FOR A SHORT TO VOLTAGE	
①	① Measure the voltage between multifunction switch C230a pin 993, circuit 682 (DB), harness side and ground. • Is any voltage indicated? → **Yes** REPAIR the circuit. CLEAR the DTCs. REPEAT the self-test. → **No** GO to **L19**.
L7 CHECK FOR BLOWN CENTRAL JUNCTION BOX (CJB) FUSE 11 (30A)	
	① Inspect CJB fuse 11 (30A). • Is Fuse 11 (30A) open? → **Yes** GO to **L9**. → **No** GO to **L8**.

FM9020000834030X

Fig. 14   Test L: Wipers Inoperative-Front & Rear (Part 3 of 9). Excursion

TEST CONDITIONS	TEST DETAILS/RESULTS/ACTIONS
L3 CHECK THE WINDSHIELD WIPER, REAR WINDOW WIPER, WINDSHIELD WASHER, AND REAR WINDOW WASHER OPERATION	
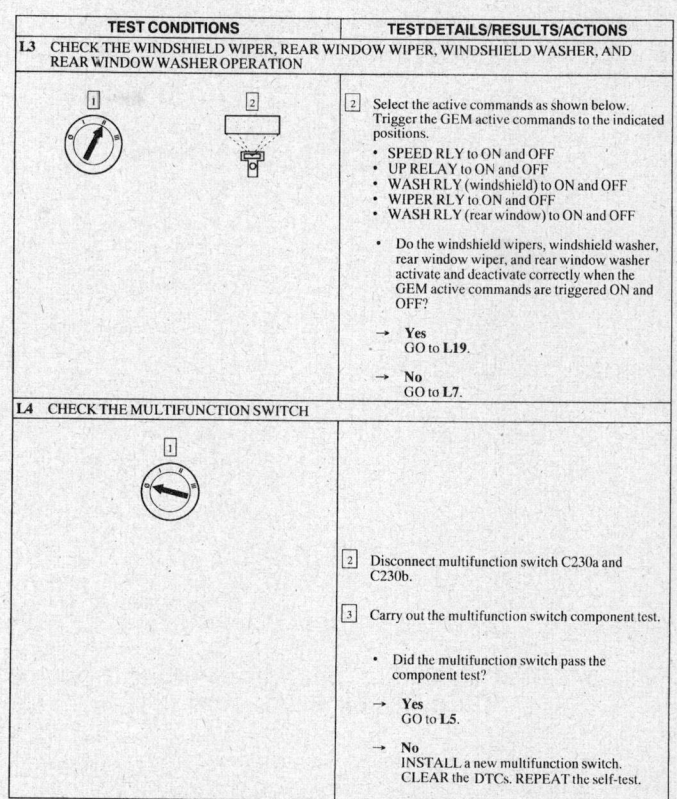 ① ②	② Select the active commands as shown below. Trigger the GEM active commands to the indicated positions. • SPEED RLY to ON and OFF • UP RELAY to ON and OFF • WASH RLY (windshield) to ON and OFF • WIPER RLY to ON and OFF • WASH RLY (rear window) to ON and OFF • Do the windshield wipers, windshield washer, rear window wiper, and rear window washer activate and deactivate correctly when the GEM active commands are triggered ON and OFF? → **Yes** GO to **L19**. → **No** GO to **L7**.
L4 CHECK THE MULTIFUNCTION SWITCH	
①	② Disconnect multifunction switch C230a and C230b. ③ Carry out the multifunction switch component test. • Did the multifunction switch pass the component test? → **Yes** GO to **L5**. → **No** INSTALL a new multifunction switch. CLEAR the DTCs. REPEAT the self-test.

FM9020000834020X

Fig. 14   Test L: Wipers Inoperative-Front & Rear (Part 2 of 9). Excursion

TEST CONDITIONS	TEST DETAILS/RESULTS/ACTIONS
L8 CHECK CJB FUSE 11 (30A) FOR VOLTAGE	
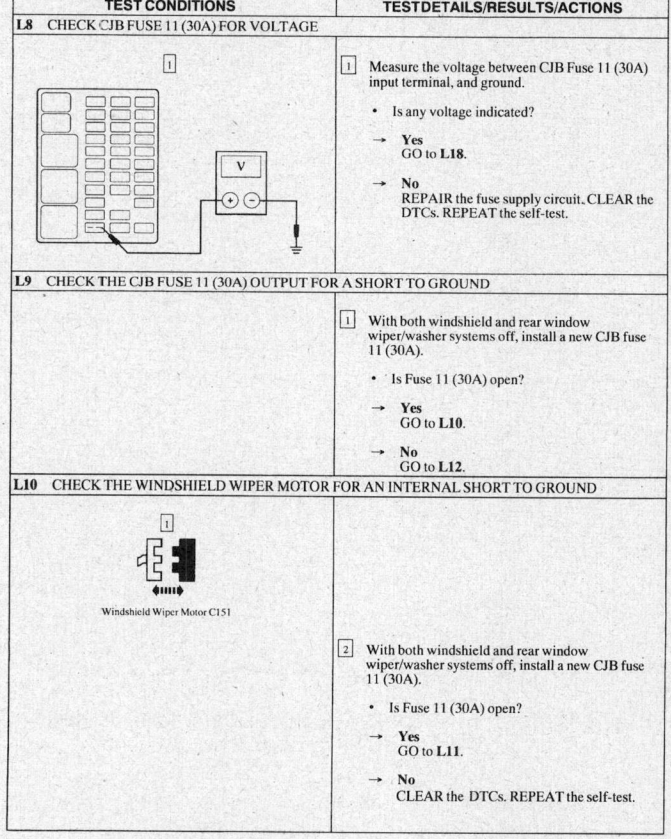 ①	① Measure the voltage between CJB Fuse 11 (30A) input terminal, and ground. • Is any voltage indicated? → **Yes** GO to **L18**. → **No** REPAIR the fuse supply circuit. CLEAR the DTCs. REPEAT the self-test.
L9 CHECK THE CJB FUSE 11 (30A) OUTPUT FOR A SHORT TO GROUND	
	① With both windshield and rear window wiper/washer systems off, install a new CJB fuse 11 (30A). • Is Fuse 11 (30A) open? → **Yes** GO to **L10**. → **No** GO to **L12**.
L10 CHECK THE WINDSHIELD WIPER MOTOR FOR AN INTERNAL SHORT TO GROUND	
① Windshield Wiper Motor C151	② With both windshield and rear window wiper/washer systems off, install a new CJB fuse 11 (30A). • Is Fuse 11 (30A) open? → **Yes** GO to **L11**. → **No** CLEAR the DTCs. REPEAT the self-test.

FM9020000834040X

Fig. 14   Test L: Wipers Inoperative-Front & Rear (Part 4 of 9). Excursion

TEST CONDITIONS	TESTDETAILS/RESULTS/ACTIONS
L11 CHECK THE WIPER/WASHER SYSTEM RELAYS	
	☐1 Disconnect and carry out the relay component test on all of the following wiper/washer system relays. • windshield wiper run/park relay • windshield wiper high/low relay • windshield washer relay • rear window wiper relay • rear window washer relay • Did all of the relays pass the component test? → **Yes** REPAIR circuit 297 for a short to ground. CLEAR the DTCs. REPEAT the self-test. → **No** INSTALL a new relay in question. CLEAR the DTCs. REPEAT the self-test.
L12 CHECK THE WINDSHIELD WIPER RUN/PARK AND HIGH/LOW RELAYS	
	☐1 Disconnect the windshield wiper high/low and run/park relays. ☐2 Carry out the relay component test on the windshield wiper high/low and run/park relays. • Did both relays pass the component test? → **Yes** GO to **L13**. → **No** INSTALL a new relay in question. CLEAR the DTCs. REPEAT the self-test.

FM9020000834050X

Fig. 14 Test L: Wipers Inoperative-Front & Rear (Part 5 of 9). Excursion

TEST CONDITIONS	TESTDETAILS/RESULTS/ACTIONS
L15 CHECK CIRCUITS 56 (DB/OG) AND 58 (WH) FOR A SHORT TO GROUND (Continued)	
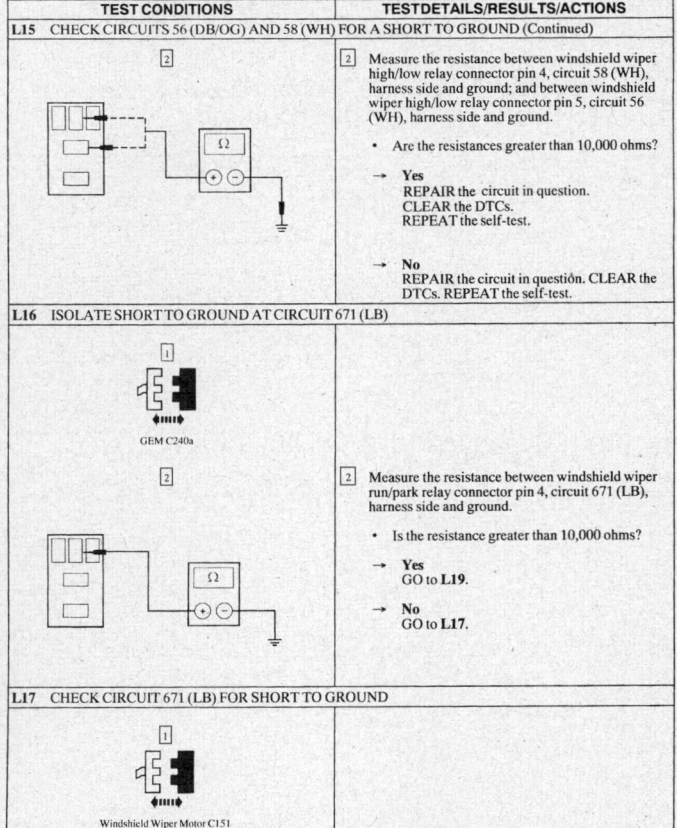	☐2 Measure the resistance between windshield wiper high/low relay connector pin 4, circuit 58 (WH), harness side and ground; and between windshield wiper high/low relay connector pin 5, circuit 56 (WH), harness side and ground. • Are the resistances greater than 10,000 ohms? → **Yes** REPAIR the circuit in question. CLEAR the DTCs. REPEAT the self-test. → **No** REPAIR the circuit in question. CLEAR the DTCs. REPEAT the self-test.
L16 ISOLATE SHORT TO GROUND AT CIRCUIT 671 (LB)	
GEM C240a 	☐2 Measure the resistance between windshield wiper run/park relay connector pin 4, circuit 671 (LB), harness side and ground. • Is the resistance greater than 10,000 ohms? → **Yes** GO to **L19**. → **No** GO to **L17**.
L17 CHECK CIRCUIT 671 (LB) FOR SHORT TO GROUND	
Windshield Wiper Motor C151	

FM9020000834070X

Fig. 14 Test L: Wipers Inoperative-Front & Rear (Part 7 of 9). Excursion

TEST CONDITIONS	TESTDETAILS/RESULTS/ACTIONS
L13 CHECK CIRCUIT 63 (RD) FOR A SHORT TO GROUND	
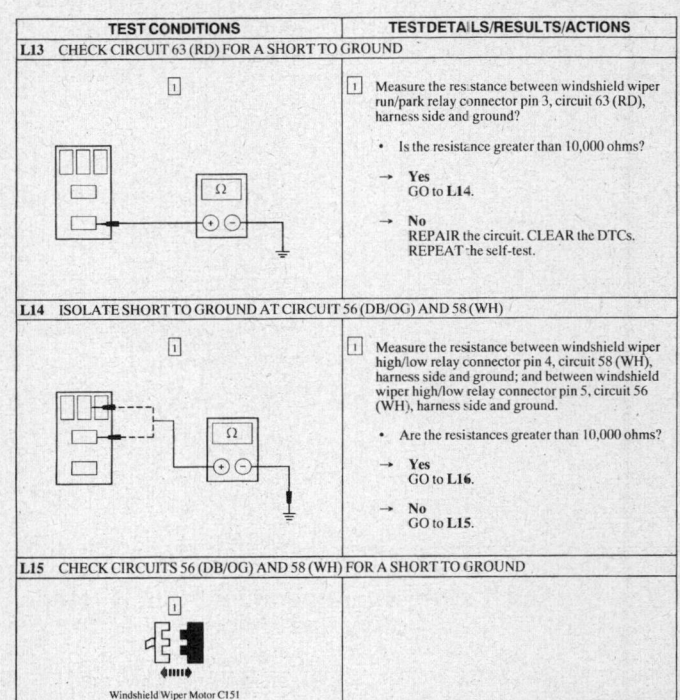	☐1 Measure the resistance between windshield wiper run/park relay connector pin 3, circuit 63 (RD), harness side and ground? • Is the resistance greater than 10,000 ohms? → **Yes** GO to **L14**. → **No** REPAIR the circuit. CLEAR the DTCs. REPEAT the self-test.
L14 ISOLATE SHORT TO GROUND AT CIRCUIT 56 (DB/OG) AND 58 (WH)	
	☐1 Measure the resistance between windshield wiper high/low relay connector pin 4, circuit 58 (WH), harness side and ground; and between windshield wiper high/low relay connector pin 5, circuit 56 (WH), harness side and ground. • Are the resistances greater than 10,000 ohms? → **Yes** GO to **L16**. → **No** GO to **L15**.
L15 CHECK CIRCUITS 56 (DB/OG) AND 58 (WH) FOR A SHORT TO GROUND	
Windshield Wiper Motor C151	

FM9020000834060X

Fig. 14 Test L: Wipers Inoperative-Front & Rear (Part 6 of 9). Excursion

TEST CONDITIONS	TESTDETAILS/RESULTS/ACTIONS
L17 CHECK CIRCUIT 671 (LB) FOR SHORT TO GROUND (Continued)	
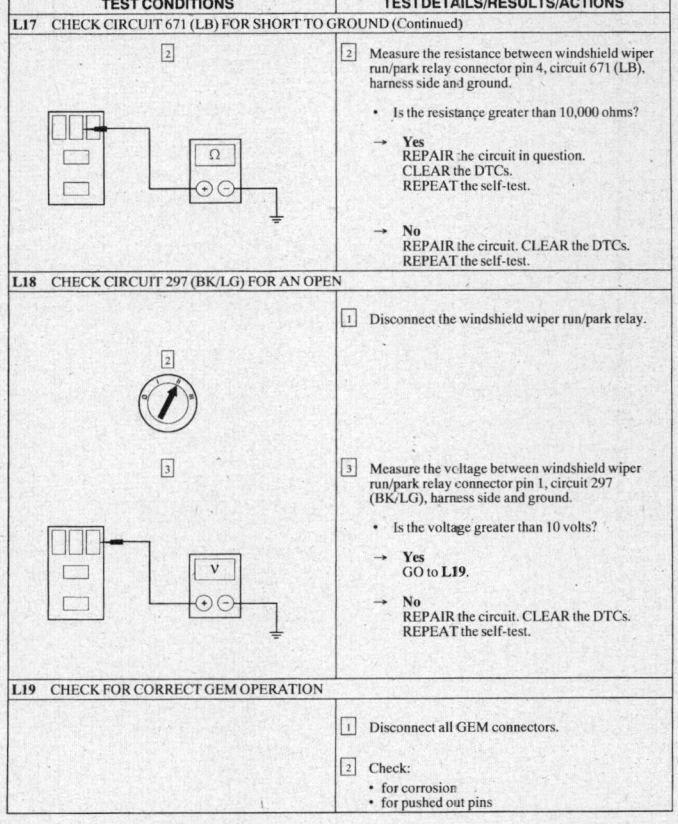	☐2 Measure the resistance between windshield wiper run/park relay connector pin 4, circuit 671 (LB), harness side and ground. • Is the resistance greater than 10,000 ohms? → **Yes** REPAIR the circuit in question. CLEAR the DTCs. REPEAT the self-test. → **No** REPAIR the circuit in question. CLEAR the DTCs. REPEAT the self-test.
L18 CHECK CIRCUIT 297 (BK/LG) FOR AN OPEN	
	☐1 Disconnect the windshield wiper run/park relay. ☐3 Measure the voltage between windshield wiper run/park relay connector pin 1, circuit 297 (BK/LG), harness side and ground. • Is the voltage greater than 10 volts? → **Yes** GO to **L19**. → **No** REPAIR the circuit. CLEAR the DTCs. REPEAT the self-test.
L19 CHECK FOR CORRECT GEM OPERATION	
	☐1 Disconnect all GEM connectors. ☐2 Check: • for corrosion • for pushed out pins

FM9020000834080X

Fig. 14 Test L: Wipers Inoperative-Front & Rear (Part 8 of 9). Excursion

TEST CONDITIONS	TESTDETAILS/RESULTS/ACTIONS
L19 CHECK FOR CORRECT GEM OPERATION (Continued)	
	3 Connect all GEM connectors and make sure they seat correctly.
	4 Operate the system and verify the concern is still present.
	• Is the concern still present?
	→ **Yes** INSTALL a new GEM. REPEAT the self-test.
	→ **No** The system is operating correctly at this time. Concern may have been caused by a loose or corroded connector. CLEAR the DTCs. REPEAT the self-test.

FM9020000834090X

Fig. 14   Test L: Wipers Inoperative-Front & Rear (Part 9 of 9). Excursion

TEST CONDITIONS	TESTDETAILS/RESULTS/ACTIONS
M2 CHECK THE WINDSHIELD AND REAR WINDOW WIPER/WASHER OPERATION	
1	**1** Select GEM active command WASH RLY. Trigger GEM active command WASH RLY to the ON and OFF positions.
	• Does the wiper/washer system operate correctly when WASH RLY is triggered ON and OFF?
	→ **Yes** GO to **M11**.
	→ **No** GO to **M3**.
M3 CHECK BATTERY JUNCTION BOX (BJB) FUSE 13 (10A) FOR VOLTAGE	
1 **2** BJB Fuse 13 (10A)	
3	**3** Measure the voltage between BJB Fuse 13 (10A) input terminal and ground.
	• Is the voltage greater than 10 volts?
	→ **Yes** RECONNECT BJB Fuse 13 (10A). GO to **M4**.
	→ **No** REPAIR the BJB as necessary. CLEAR the DTCs. REPEAT the self-test.
M4 CHECK CIRCUIT 950 (WH/BK) FOR AN OPEN	
1 **2** Rear Washer Relay	

FM9020000835020X

Fig. 15   Test M: Wash & Wipe Function Inoperative-Front & Rear (Part 2 of 6). Excursion

TEST CONDITIONS	TESTDETAILS/RESULTS/ACTIONS
M1 MONITOR THE GENERIC ELECTRONIC MODULE (GEM) PID WPMODE	
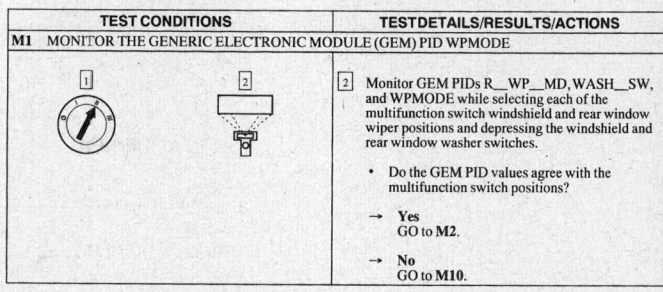	**2** Monitor GEM PIDs R__WP__MD, WASH__SW, and WPMODE while selecting each of the multifunction switch windshield and rear window wiper positions and depressing the windshield and rear window washer switches.
	• Do the GEM PID values agree with the multifunction switch positions?
	→ **Yes** GO to **M2**.
	→ **No** GO to **M10**.

FM9020000835010X

Fig. 15   Test M: Wash & Wipe Function Inoperative-Front & Rear (Part 1 of 6). Excursion

TEST CONDITIONS	TESTDETAILS/RESULTS/ACTIONS
M4 CHECK CIRCUIT 950 (WH/BK) FOR AN OPEN (Continued)	
3	**3** Measure the voltage between rear window washer relay connector pin 5, circuit 297 (BK/LG), harness side and ground.
	• Is the voltage greater than 10 volts?
	→ **Yes** GO to **M5**.
	→ **No** REPAIR the circuit. CLEAR the DTCs. REPEAT the self-test.
M5 CHECK CIRCUIT 57 (BK) FOR AN OPEN	
1 Windshield Washer Relay	
2	**2** Measure the resistance between windshield washer relay connector pin 4, circuit 57 (BK), harness side and ground; and between rear window washer relay connector pin 4, circuit 57 (BK), harness side and ground.
	• Is the resistance less than 5 ohms?
	→ **Yes** GO to **M6**.
	→ **No** REPAIR the circuit. CLEAR the DTCs. REPEAT the self-test.

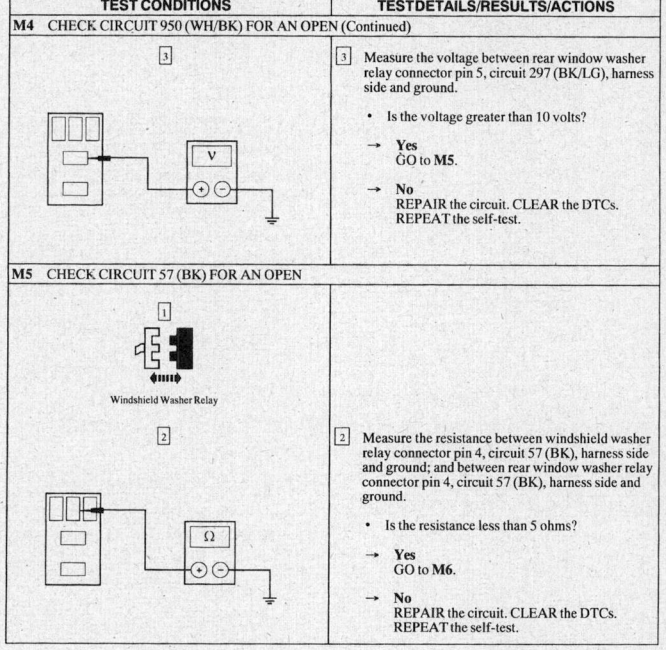

FM9020000835030X

Fig. 15   Test M: Wash & Wipe Function Inoperative-Front & Rear (Part 3 of 6). Excursion

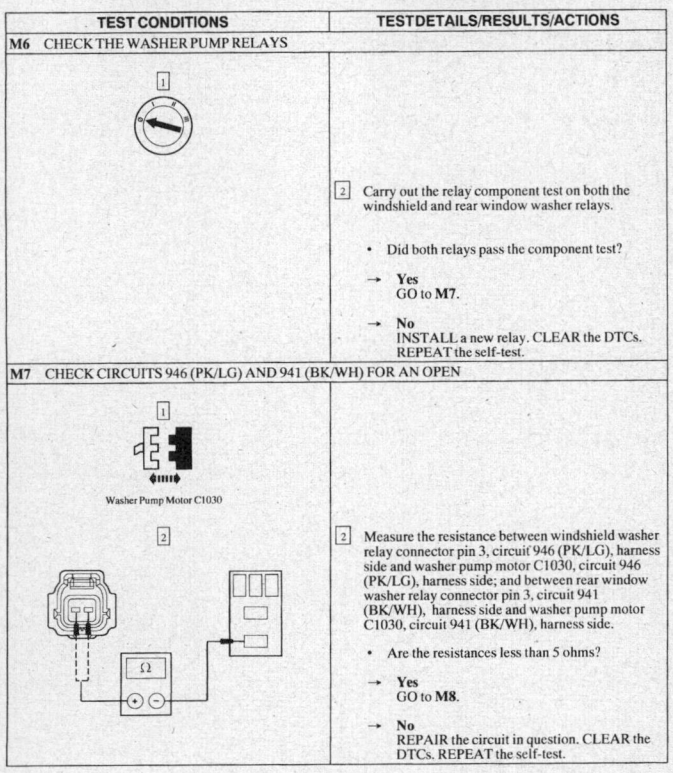

TEST CONDITIONS	TESTDETAILS/RESULTS/ACTIONS
M6 CHECK THE WASHER PUMP RELAYS	
	2 Carry out the relay component test on both the windshield and rear window washer relays.
	• Did both relays pass the component test?
	→ **Yes** GO to **M7**.
	→ **No** INSTALL a new relay. CLEAR the DTCs. REPEAT the self-test.
M7 CHECK CIRCUITS 946 (PK/LG) AND 941 (BK/WH) FOR AN OPEN	
Washer Pump Motor C1030	2 Measure the resistance between windshield washer relay connector pin 3, circuit 946 (PK/LG), harness side and washer pump motor C1030, circuit 946 (PK/LG), harness side; and between rear window washer relay connector pin 3, circuit 941 (BK/WH), harness side and washer pump motor C1030, circuit 941 (BK/WH), harness side.
	• Are the resistances less than 5 ohms?
	→ **Yes** GO to **M8**.
	→ **No** REPAIR the circuit in question. CLEAR the DTCs. REPEAT the self-test.

FM9020000835040X

Fig. 15   Test M: Wash & Wipe Function Inoperative-Front & Rear (Part 4 of 6). Excursion

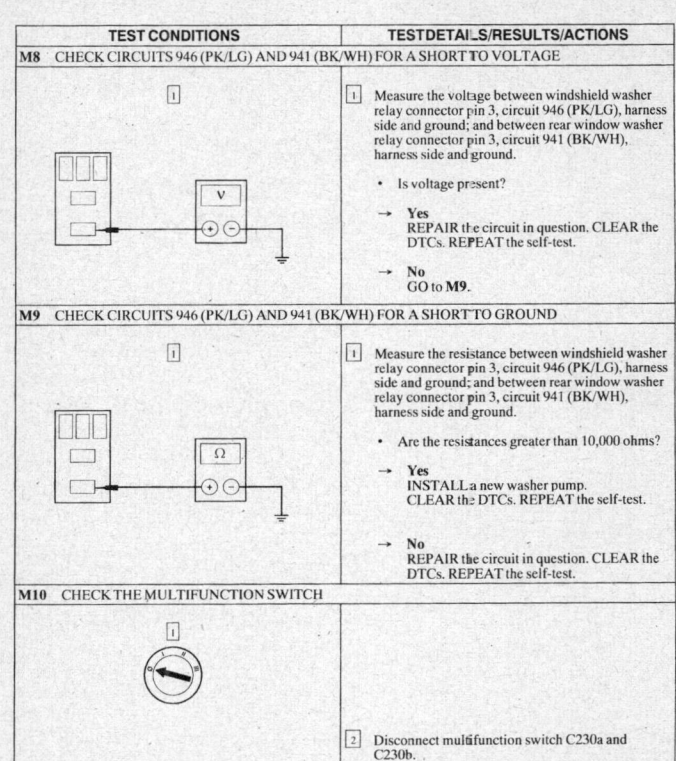

TEST CONDITIONS	TESTDETAILS/RESULTS/ACTIONS
M8 CHECK CIRCUITS 946 (PK/LG) AND 941 (BK/WH) FOR A SHORT TO VOLTAGE	
	1 Measure the voltage between windshield washer relay connector pin 3, circuit 946 (PK/LG), harness side and ground; and between rear window washer relay connector pin 3, circuit 941 (BK/WH), harness side and ground.
	• Is voltage present?
	→ **Yes** REPAIR the circuit in question. CLEAR the DTCs. REPEAT the self-test.
	→ **No** GO to **M9**.
M9 CHECK CIRCUITS 946 (PK/LG) AND 941 (BK/WH) FOR A SHORT TO GROUND	
	1 Measure the resistance between windshield washer relay connector pin 3, circuit 946 (PK/LG), harness side and ground; and between rear window washer relay connector pin 3, circuit 941 (BK/WH), harness side and ground.
	• Are the resistances greater than 10,000 ohms?
	→ **Yes** INSTALL a new washer pump. CLEAR the DTCs. REPEAT the self-test.
	→ **No** REPAIR the circuit in question. CLEAR the DTCs. REPEAT the self-test.
M10 CHECK THE MULTIFUNCTION SWITCH	
	2 Disconnect multifunction switch C230a and C230b.

FM9020000835050X

Fig. 15   Test M: Wash & Wipe Function Inoperative-Front & Rear (Part 5 of 6). Excursion

TEST CONDITIONS	TESTDETAILS/RESULTS/ACTIONS
M10 CHECK THE MULTIFUNCTION SWITCH (Continued)	
	3 Carry out the multifunction switch component test.
	• Did the multifunction switch pass the component test?
	→ **Yes** GO to **M11**.
	→ **No** INSTALL a new multifunction switch. CLEAR the DTCs. REPEAT the self-test.
M11 CHECK FOR CORRECT GEM OPERATION	
	1 Disconnect all GEM connectors.
	2 Check: • for corrosion • for pushed out pins
	3 Connect all GEM connectors and make sure they seat correctly.
	4 Operate the system and verify the concern is still present.
	• Is the concern still present?
	→ **Yes** INSTALL a new GEM. REPEAT the self-test.
	→ **No** The system is operating correctly at this time. Concern may have been caused by a loose or corroded connector. CLEAR the DTCs. REPEAT the self-test.

FM9020000835060X

Fig. 15   Test M: Wash & Wipe Function Inoperative-Front & Rear (Part 6 of 6). Excursion

Condition	Possible Sources	Action
• The windshield wipers are inoperative	• Fuse(s). • Multifunction switch. • Circuitry. • Ignition switch. • Windshield wiper motor.	• Go To Pinpoint Test A .
• The windshield wipers stay on continuously	• Windshield wiper motor. • Multifunction switch. • Circuitry.	• Go To Pinpoint Test B .
• The high/low windshield wiper speeds do not operate correctly	• Multifunction switch. • Circuitry. • Windshield wiper motor.	• Go To Pinpoint Test C .
• The intermittent windshield wiper speed does not operate correctly	• Multifunction switch. • Circuitry. • Windshield wiper motor.	• Go To Pinpoint Test D .
• The windshield wipers do not operate correctly in the MIST position	• Multifunction switch. • Circuitry. • Washer pump. • Windshield wiper motor.	• Go To Pinpoint Test E .

LTV0500000001918

Fig. 16   Symptom Tests (Part 1 of 2). 2005–06 F-Super Duty

• The washer pump is inoperative	• Fuse. • Washer pump. • Multifunction switch. • Windshield wiper motor. • Circuitry.	• Go To Pinpoint Test F .
• The windshield wiper speed dependent interval mode does not operate correctly	• Windshield wiper motor. • Circuitry. • Anti-lock brake system (ABS) module.	• Go To Pinpoint Test G .
• The wipers will not park at correct position	• Windshield wiper motor. • Pivot arm adjustment. • Linkage.	• Repair and/or adjust wiper arm and Pivot.

LTV0500000001919

Fig. 16   Symptom Tests (Part 2 of 2). 2005–06 F-Super Duty

• **Did the multifunction switch pass the component test?**	INSTALL a new multifunction switch.
A4 CHECK CIRCUIT 57 (BK) FOR AN OPEN	
• Measure the resistance between C202b-6, circuit 57 (BK), harness side and ground. • **Is the resistance less than 5 ohms?**	**Yes** GO to A5 . **No** REPAIR the circuit. TEST the system for normal operation.
A5 CHECK CIRCUITS 56 (DB/OG), 58 (WH), 61 (YE/RD) AND 63 (RD) FOR OPENS	
• Using the following table, measure the resistance between multifunction switch C202b harness side and windshield wiper motor C125 harness side:	**Yes** GO to A6 . **No** REPAIR the circuit(s) in question. TEST the system for normal operation.

Multifunction Switch C202b	Windshield Wiper Motor C125
Pin 2, circuit 56 (DB/OG)	Pin 10, circuit 56 (DB/OG)
Pin 3, circuit 58 (WH)	Pin 11, circuit 58 (WH)
Pin 4, circuit 61 (YE/RD)	Pin 1, circuit 61 (YE/RD)
Pin 1, circuit 63 (RD)	Pin 9, circuit 63 (RD)

LTV0500000001921

Fig. 17   Test A: Windshield Wipers Are Inoperative (Part 2 of 3). 2005–06 F-Super Duty

Test Step	Result / Action to Take
A1 CHECK CIRCUITS 65 (DG) AND 1002 (BK/PK) FOR VOLTAGE	
• Key in OFF position. • Disconnect: Windshield Wiper Motor C125. • Key in ON position. • Measure the voltage between windshield wiper C125-5, circuit 65 (DG), harness side and ground; and between windshield wiper motor C125-8, circuit 1002 (BK/PK), harness side and ground. • **Are the voltages greater than 10 volts?**	**Yes** GO to A2 . **No** VERIFY central junction box (CJB) fuse 33 (15A) and battery junction box (BJB) fuse 1 (30A) are OK. If OK, REPAIR the circuit(s) in question. TEST the system for normal operation.
A2 CHECK CIRCUITS 57 (BK) AND 676 (PK/OG) FOR OPENS	
• Key in OFF position. • Measure the resistance between windshield wiper C125-6, circuit 57 (BK), harness side and ground; and between windshield wiper motor C125-3, circuit 676 (PK/OG), harness side and ground. • **Are the resistances less than 5 ohms?**	**Yes** GO to A3 . **No** REPAIR the circuit(s) in question. TEST the system for normal operation.
A3 CHECK THE MULTIFUNCTION SWITCH	
• Disconnect: Multifunction Switch C202b. • Carry out the multifunction switch component test.	**Yes** GO to A4 . **No**

LTV0500000001920

Fig. 17   Test A: Windshield Wipers Are Inoperative (Part 1 of 3). 2005–06 F-Super Duty

• **Is the resistance less than 5 ohms?**	
A6 CHECK FOR CORRECT WIPER MOTOR OPERATION	

• Disconnect all wiper motor connectors.
• Check for:
  ▪ corrosion.
  ▪ pushed-out pins.
• Connect all wiper motor connectors and make sure they seat correctly.
• Operate the system and verify the concern is still present.
• **Is the concern still present?**
	Yes
	GO to A7 .
	
	No
	The system is operating correctly at this time. Concern may have been caused by a loose or corroded connector. TEST the system for normal operation.

A7 CHECK THE WINDSHIELD WIPER MOTOR	
• Key in OFF position. • Disconnect: Windshield Wiper Motor C125. • Carry out the windshield wiper motor component test as outlined in this section. • **Did the windshield wiper motor pass the component test?**	**Yes** The system is operating correctly at this time. Concern may have been caused by incorrect binding pivot arm adjustment. Repair and/or adjust wiper arm and Pivot. TEST the system for normal operation. **No** INSTALL a new windshield wiper motor.

LTV0500000002322

Fig. 17   Test A: Windshield Wipers Are Inoperative (Part 3 of 3). 2005–06 F-Super Duty

Test Step	Result / Action to Take
B1 CHECK THE MULTIFUNCTION SWITCH	
• Key in OFF position. • Disconnect: Multifunction Switch C202b. • Carry out the multifunction switch component test. Refer to "Wiring Diagrams" • **Did the multifunction switch pass the component test?**	**Yes** GO to B2 . **No** INSTALL a new multifunction switch.
B2 CHECK CIRCUIT 57 (BK) FOR AN OPEN	
• Measure the resistance between multifunction switch C202b-6, circuit 57 (BK), harness side and ground. • **Is the resistance less than 5 ohms?**	**Yes** GO to B3 . **No** REPAIR the circuit. TEST the system for normal operation.
B3 CHECK CIRCUITS 56 (DB/OG), 58 (WH), 61 (YE/RD) AND 63 (RD) FOR SHORTS	
• Disconnect: Windshield Wiper Motor C125. • Using the following table, measure the resistance between windshield wiper motor C125 harness side and ground. | Windshield Wiper Motor C125	Ground
Pin 10, circuit 56 (DB/OG)	Ground
Pin 11, circuit 58 (WH)	Ground
Pin 1, circuit 61 (YE/RD)	Ground
Pin 9, circuit 63 (RD)	Ground		**Yes** GO to B4 . **No** REPAIR the circuit(s) in question. TEST the system for normal operation.

LTV0500000002323

Fig. 18 Test B: Windshield Wipers Stay On Continuously (Part 1 of 2). 2005–06 F-Super Duty

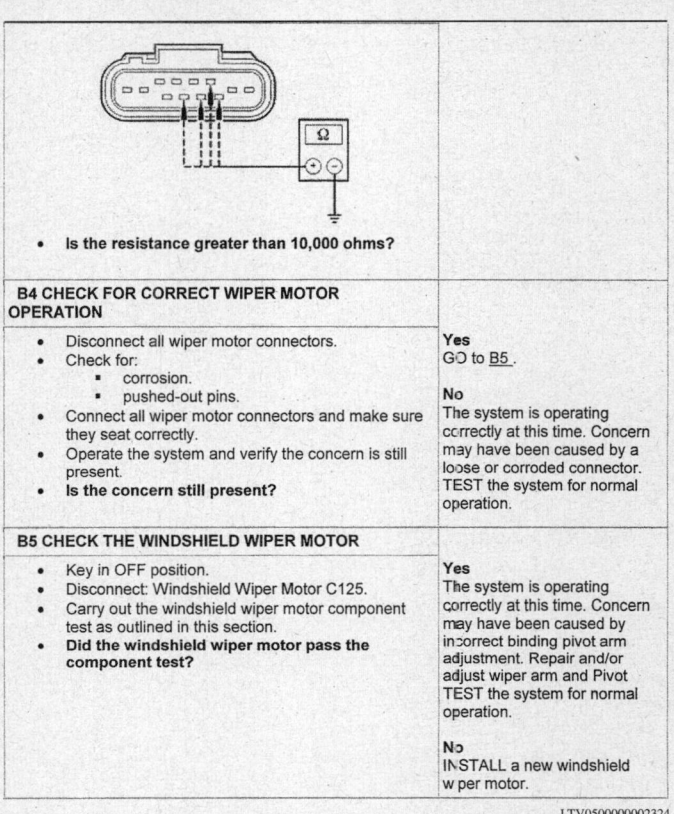

• **Is the resistance greater than 10,000 ohms?**	
B4 CHECK FOR CORRECT WIPER MOTOR OPERATION	
• Disconnect all wiper motor connectors. • Check for: ▪ corrosion. ▪ pushed-out pins. • Connect all wiper motor connectors and make sure they seat correctly. • Operate the system and verify the concern is still present. • **Is the concern still present?**	**Yes** GO to B5 . **No** The system is operating correctly at this time. Concern may have been caused by a loose or corroded connector. TEST the system for normal operation.
B5 CHECK THE WINDSHIELD WIPER MOTOR	
• Key in OFF position. • Disconnect: Windshield Wiper Motor C125. • Carry out the windshield wiper motor component test as outlined in this section. • **Did the windshield wiper motor pass the component test?**	**Yes** The system is operating correctly at this time. Concern may have been caused by incorrect binding pivot arm adjustment. Repair and/or adjust wiper arm and Pivot TEST the system for normal operation. **No** INSTALL a new windshield wiper motor.

LTV0500000002324

Fig. 18 Test B: Windshield Wipers Stay On Continuously (Part 2 of 2). 2005–06 F-Super Duty

Test Step	Result / Action to Take
C1 CHECK THE MULTIFUNCTION SWITCH	
• Key in OFF position. • Disconnect: Multifunction Switch C202b. • Carry out the multifunction switch component test. • **Did the multifunction switch pass the component test?**	**Yes** GO to C2 . **No** INSTALL a new multifunction switch.
C2 CHECK CIRCUIT 57 (BK) FOR AN OPEN	
• Measure the resistance between multifunction switch C202b-6, circuit 57 (BK), harness side and ground. • **Is the resistance less than 5 ohms?**	**Yes** GO to C3 . **No** REPAIR the circuit. TEST the system for normal operation.
C3 CHECK CIRCUITS 56 (DB/OG), 61 (YE/RD) AND 63 (RD) FOR OPENS	
• Disconnect: Windshield Wiper Motor C125. • Using the following table, measure the resistance between multifunction switch C202b harness side and windshield wiper motor C125 harness side: | Multifunction Switch C202b	Windshield Wiper Motor C125
Pin 2, circuit 56 (DB/OG)	Pin 10, circuit 56 (DB/OG)
Pin 4, circuit 61 (YE/RD)	Pin 1, circuit 61 (YE/RD)
Pin 1, circuit 63 (RD)	Pin 9, circuit 63 (RD)		**Yes** GO to C4 . **No** REPAIR the circuit(s) in question. TEST the system for normal operation.

LTV0500000002325

Fig. 19 Test C: High/Low Wiper Speeds Do Not Operate Correctly (Part 1 of 2). 2005–06 F-Super Duty

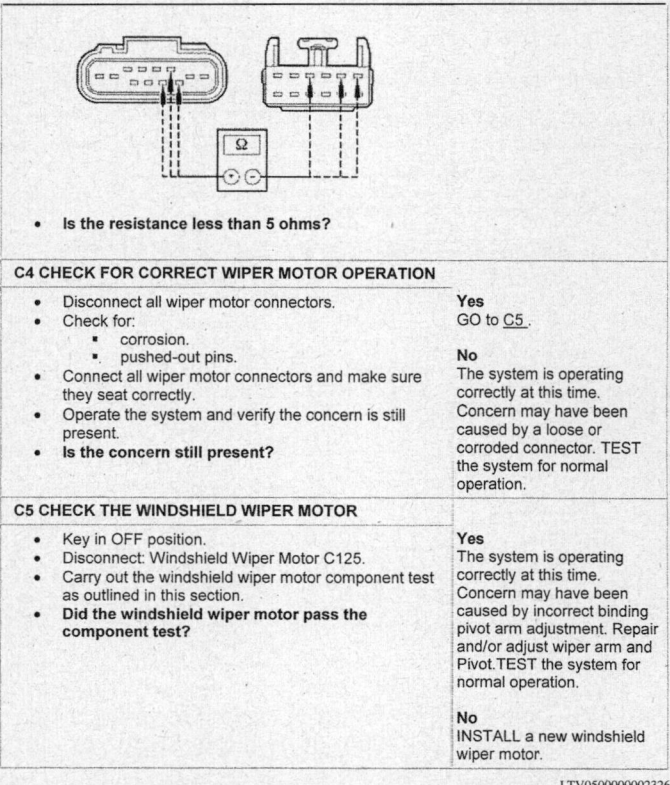

• **Is the resistance less than 5 ohms?**	
C4 CHECK FOR CORRECT WIPER MOTOR OPERATION	
• Disconnect all wiper motor connectors. • Check for: ▪ corrosion. ▪ pushed-out pins. • Connect all wiper motor connectors and make sure they seat correctly. • Operate the system and verify the concern is still present. • **Is the concern still present?**	**Yes** GO to C5 . **No** The system is operating correctly at this time. Concern may have been caused by a loose or corroded connector. TEST the system for normal operation.
C5 CHECK THE WINDSHIELD WIPER MOTOR	
• Key in OFF position. • Disconnect: Windshield Wiper Motor C125. • Carry out the windshield wiper motor component test as outlined in this section. • **Did the windshield wiper motor pass the component test?**	**Yes** The system is operating correctly at this time. Concern may have been caused by incorrect binding pivot arm adjustment. Repair and/or adjust wiper arm and Pivot. TEST the system for normal operation. **No** INSTALL a new windshield wiper motor.

LTV0500000002326

Fig. 19 Test C: High/Low Wiper Speeds Do Not Operate Correctly (Part 2 of 2). 2005–06 F-Super Duty

Test Step	Result / Action to Take
D1 CHECK THE MULTIFUNCTION SWITCH • Key in OFF position. • Disconnect: Multifunction Switch C202b. • Carry out the multifunction switch component test. Refer to "Wiring Diagrams" • **Did the multifunction switch pass the component test?**	**Yes** GO to D2. **No** INSTALL a new multifunction switch.
D2 CHECK CIRCUIT 57 (BK) FOR OPEN • Measure the resistance between multifunction switch C202b-6, circuit 57 (BK), harness side and ground. 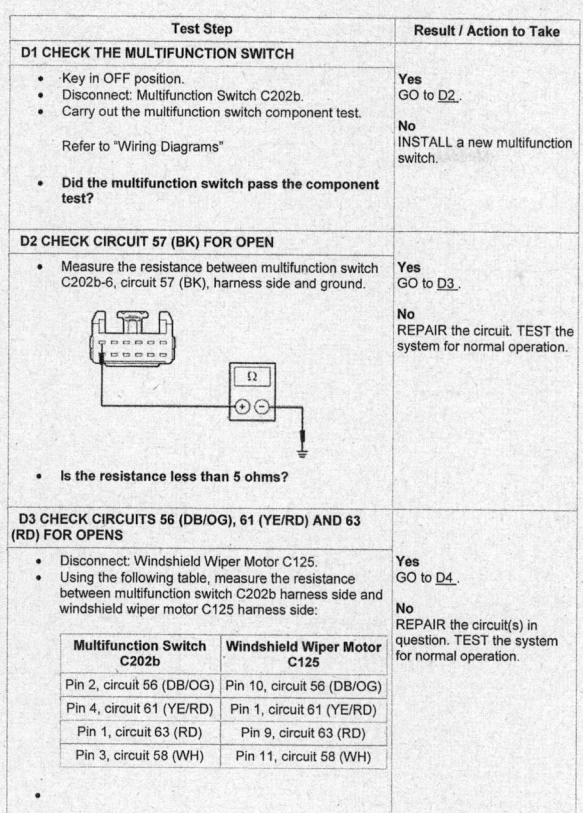 • **Is the resistance less than 5 ohms?**	**Yes** GO to D3. **No** REPAIR the circuit. TEST the system for normal operation.
D3 CHECK CIRCUITS 56 (DB/OG), 61 (YE/RD) AND 63 (RD) FOR OPENS • Disconnect: Windshield Wiper Motor C125. • Using the following table, measure the resistance between multifunction switch C202b harness side and windshield wiper motor C125 harness side:	**Yes** GO to D4. **No** REPAIR the circuit(s) in question. TEST the system for normal operation.

Multifunction Switch C202b	Windshield Wiper Motor C125
Pin 2, circuit 56 (DB/OG)	Pin 10, circuit 56 (DB/OG)
Pin 4, circuit 61 (YE/RD)	Pin 1, circuit 61 (YE/RD)
Pin 1, circuit 63 (RD)	Pin 9, circuit 63 (RD)
Pin 3, circuit 58 (WH)	Pin 11, circuit 58 (WH)

LTV0500000002327

Fig. 20 Test D: Intermittent Wiper Speed Does Not Operate Correctly (Part 1 of 2). 2005–06 F-Super Duty

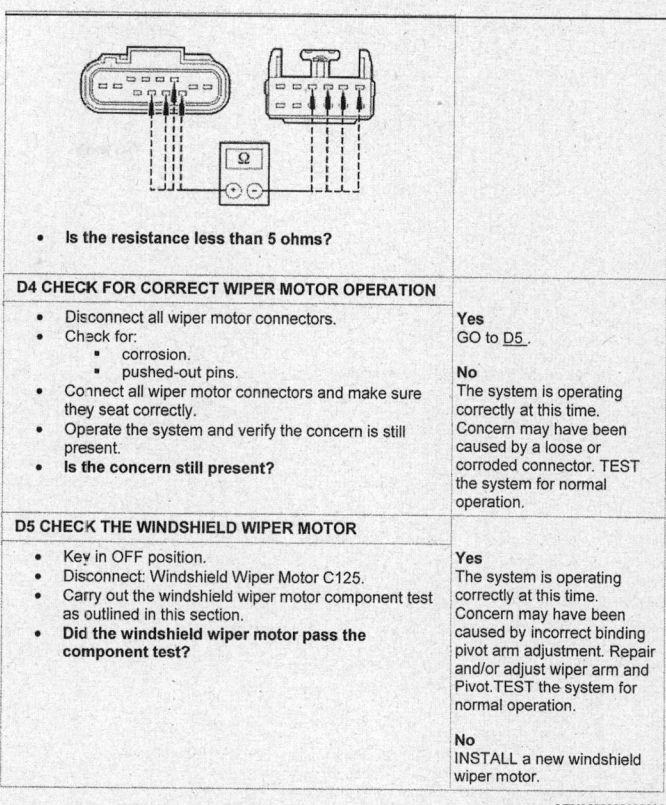

Test Step	Result / Action to Take
• **Is the resistance less than 5 ohms?**	

D4 CHECK FOR CORRECT WIPER MOTOR OPERATION
• Disconnect all wiper motor connectors.
• Check for:
  ▪ corrosion.
  ▪ pushed-out pins.
• Connect all wiper motor connectors and make sure they seat correctly.
• Operate the system and verify the concern is still present.
• **Is the concern still present?**
	Yes
	GO to D5.
	
	No
	The system is operating correctly at this time. Concern may have been caused by a loose or corroded connector. TEST the system for normal operation.

D5 CHECK THE WINDSHIELD WIPER MOTOR • Key in OFF position. • Disconnect: Windshield Wiper Motor C125. • Carry out the windshield wiper motor component test as outlined in this section. • **Did the windshield wiper motor pass the component test?**	**Yes** The system is operating correctly at this time. Concern may have been caused by incorrect binding pivot arm adjustment. Repair and/or adjust wiper arm and Pivot.TEST the system for normal operation. **No** INSTALL a new windshield wiper motor.

LTV0500000002328

Fig. 20 Test D: Intermittent Wiper Speed Does Not Operate Correctly (Part 2 of 2). 2005–06 F-Super Duty

Test Step	Result / Action to Take
E1 CHECK THE MULTIFUNCTION SWITCH • Key in OFF position. • Disconnect: Multifunction Switch C202b. • Carry out the multifunction switch component test. "Refer to Wiring Diagrams" • **Did the multifunction switch pass the component test?**	**Yes** GO to E2. **No** INSTALL a new multifunction switch.
E2 CHECK CIRCUIT 57 (BK) FOR AN OPEN • Measure the resistance between multifunction switch C202b-6, circuit 57 (BK), harness side and ground. • **Is the resistance less than 5 ohms?**	**Yes** GO to E3. **No** REPAIR the circuit. TEST the system for normal operation.
E3 CHECK CIRCUIT 589 (OG) FOR AN OPEN • Disconnect: Windshield Wiper Motor C125. • Measure the resistance between multifunction switch C202b-5, circuit 589 (OG), harness side and windshield wiper motor C125-12, circuit 589 (OG), harness side. • **Is the resistance less than 5 ohms?**	**Yes** Go To Pinpoint Test F. **No** REPAIR the circuit. TEST the system for normal operation.

LTV0500000002329

Fig. 21 Test E: Wipers Do Not Operate In Mist Position. 2005–06 F-Super Duty

Test Step	Result / Action to Take
F1 CHECK THE MULTIFUNCTION SWITCH • Key in OFF position. • Disconnect: Multifunction Switch C202b. • Carry out the multifunction switch component test. Refer to "Wiring Diagrams" • **Did the multifunction switch pass the component test?**	**Yes** GO to F2. **No** INSTALL a new multifunction switch.
F2 CHECK CIRCUIT 57 (BK) FOR AN OPEN • Measure the resistance between multifunction switch C202b-6, circuit 57 (BK), harness side and ground. • **Is the resistance less than 5 ohms?**	**Yes** GO to F3. **No** REPAIR the circuit. TEST the system for normal operation.
F3 CHECK CIRCUIT 589 (OG) FOR AN OPEN • Key in OFF position. • Disconnect: Windshield Wiper Motor C125. • Disconnect: Multifunction Switch C202b. • Measure the resistance between windshield wiper motor C125-12, circuit 589 (OG), harness side and	**Yes** GO to F4. **No** REPAIR the circuit. TEST

LTV0500000002330

Fig. 22 Test F: Washer Pump Is Inoperative (Part 1 of 4). 2005–06 F-Super Duty

multifunction switch C202b-5, circuit 589 (OG), harness side.

the system for normal operation.

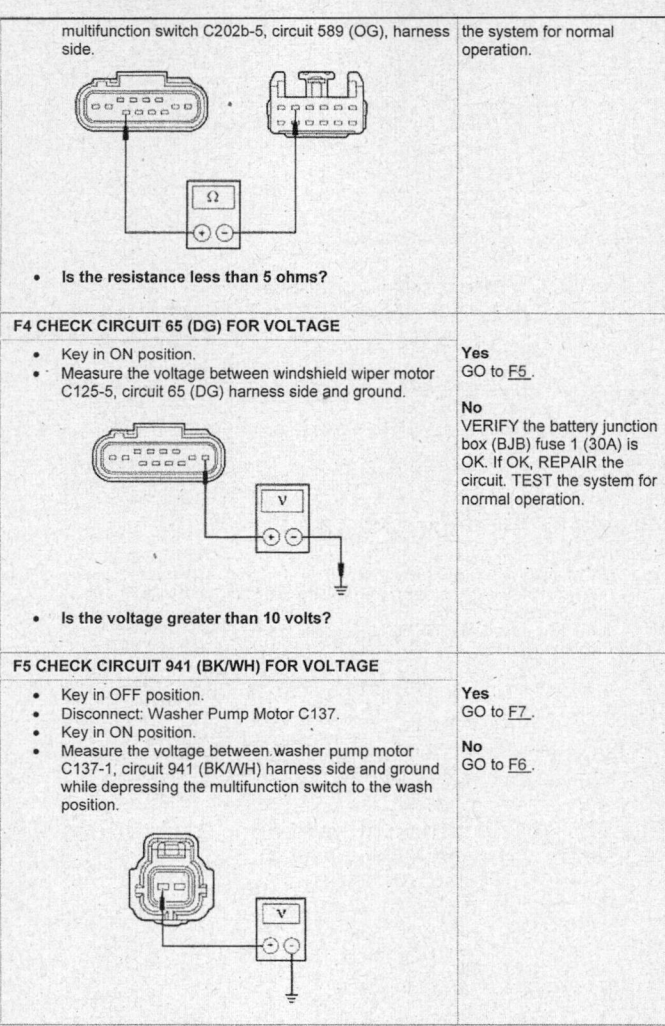

- **Is the resistance less than 5 ohms?**

F4 CHECK CIRCUIT 65 (DG) FOR VOLTAGE

- Key in ON position.
- Measure the voltage between windshield wiper motor C125-5, circuit 65 (DG) harness side and ground.

Yes
GO to F5 .

No
VERIFY the battery junction box (BJB) fuse 1 (30A) is OK. If OK, REPAIR the circuit. TEST the system for normal operation.

- **Is the voltage greater than 10 volts?**

F5 CHECK CIRCUIT 941 (BK/WH) FOR VOLTAGE

- Key in OFF position.
- Disconnect: Washer Pump Motor C137.
- Key in ON position.
- Measure the voltage between washer pump motor C137-1, circuit 941 (BK/WH) harness side and ground while depressing the multifunction switch to the wash position.

Yes
GO to F7 .

No
GO to F6 .

LTV0500000002331

Fig. 22   Test F: Washer Pump Is Inoperative (Part 2 of 4). 2005–06 F-Super Duty

F9 CHECK THE WINDSHIELD WIPER MOTOR

- Key in OFF position.
- Disconnect: Windshield Wiper Motor C125.
- Carry out the windshield wiper motor component test as outlined in this section.
- **Did the windshield wiper motor pass the component test?**

Yes
The system is operating correctly at this time. Concern may have been caused by incorrect binding pivot arm adjustment. Repair and/or adjust wiper arm and Pivot. TEST the system for normal operation.

No
INSTALL a new windshield wiper motor.

LTV0500000002333

Fig. 22   Test F: Washer Pump Is Inoperative (Part 4 of 4). 2005–06 F-Super Duty

- Is the voltage greater than 10 volts?

F6 CHECK CIRCUIT 941 (BK/WH) FOR AN OPEN

- Key in OFF position.
- Disconnect: Windshield Wiper Motor C125.
- Measure the resistance between windshield wiper motor C125-7, circuit 941 (BK/WH), harness side and washer pump motor C137-1, circuit 941 (BK/WH) harness side.

Yes
GO to F8 .

No
REPAIR the circuit. TEST the system for normal operation.

- Is the resistance less than 5 ohms?

F7 CHECK CIRCUIT 57 (BK) FOR AN OPEN

- Measure the resistance between washer pump motor C137-2, circuit 57 (BK) harness side and ground.

Yes
INSTALL a new washer pump.

No
REPAIR the circuit. TEST the system for normal operation.

- Is the resistance less than 5 ohms?

F8 CHECK FOR CORRECT WIPER MOTOR OPERATION

- Disconnect all wiper motor connectors.
- Check for:
    - corrosion.
    - pushed-out pins.
- Connect all wiper motor connectors and make sure they seat correctly.
- Operate the system and verify the concern is still present.
- **Is the concern still present?**

Yes
GO to F9 .

No
The system is operating correctly at this time. Concern may have been caused by a loose or corroded connector. TEST the system for normal operation.

LTV0500000002332

Fig. 22   Test F: Washer Pump Is Inoperative (Part 3 of 4). 2005–06 F-Super Duty

Test Step	Result / Action to Take
G1 CHECK THE ABS — MONITOR THE VSS	
• Monitor VSS while driving the vehicle from 0 to 88.5 kph (55 mph). • **Does the VSS agree with the ABS PIDs?**	**Yes** GO to G2 . **No** Check ABS system.
G2 CHECK CIRCUIT 679 (GY/BK) FOR AN OPEN	
• Disconnect: ABS C135. • Disconnect: Windshield Wiper Motor C125. • Measure the resistance between anti-lock brake control module C135-21, circuit 679 (GY/BK), harness side and windshield wiper motor C125-4, circuit 679 (GY/BK), harness side. • Is the resistance less than 5 ohms?	**Yes** GO to G3 . **No** REPAIR the circuit. CLEAR the DTCs. REPEAT the self-test.
G3 CHECK CIRCUIT 679 (GY/BK) FOR A SHORT TO GROUND	
• Measure the resistance between ABS C135-21, circuit 679 (GY/BK), harness side and ground. • Is the resistance greater than 10,000 ohms?	**Yes** GO to G4 . **No** REPAIR the circuit. CLEAR the DTCs. REPEAT the self-test.
G4 CHECK FOR CORRECT WIPER MOTOR OPERATION	
• Disconnect all wiper motor connectors.	**Yes**

LTV0500000002334

Fig. 23   Test G: Wiper Speed Dependent Mode Does Not Operate Correctly (Part 1 of 2). 2005–06 F-Super Duty

• Check for:
   ■ corrosion.
   ■ pushed-out pins.
• Connect all wiper motor connectors and make sure they seat correctly.
• Operate the system and verify the concern is still present.
• **Is the concern still present?**
	GO to <u>G5</u> .
	
	No
	The system is operating correctly at this time. Concern may have been caused by a loose or corroded connector. TEST the system for normal operation.

G5 CHECK THE WINDSHIELD WIPER MOTOR	
• Key in OFF position. • Disconnect: Windshield Wiper Motor C125. • Carry out the windshield wiper motor component test as outlined in this section. • **Did the windshield wiper motor pass the component test?**	**Yes** The system is operating correctly at this time. Concern may have been caused by incorrect binding pivot arm adjustment. Repair and/or adjust wiper arm and Pivot.TEST the system for normal operation. **No** INSTALL a new windshield wiper motor.

LTV0500000002335

Fig. 23   Test G: Wiper Speed Dependent Mode Does Not Operate Correctly (Part 2 of 2). 2005–06 F-Super Duty

COMPONENT DIAGNOSIS & TESTING

Refer to "Aviator" for component diagnosis and testing procedures.

Expedition & Navigator

NOTE: On Air Bag Equipped Models, Refer To "Air Bag System Precautions" Located In The Front Of This Manual For System Disarming & Arming Procedures.

NOTE: "Electrical Symbol & Wire Color Code Identification" Located In The Front Of This Manual May Be Used As An Aid When Using Wiring Diagrams Found In This Section.

NOTE: Refer To "Computer Relearn Procedures" Located In The Front Of This Manual When Battery Power To The Computer Has Been Interrupted.

INDEX

	Page No.		Page No.		Page No.
Component Diagnosis & Testing	3-95	Accessing Diagnostic Trouble Codes	3-68	2005–06	3-68
Diagnostic Chart Index	3-72	Clearing Diagnostic Trouble Codes	3-68	Diagnostic Trouble Code Interpretation	3-68
Precautions	3-68	Diagnostic Tests	3-68	Wiring Diagrams	3-68
Battery Ground Cable	3-68	2002–04	3-68		
System Diagnosis & Testing	3-68				

PRECAUTIONS

Battery Ground Cable

Prior to service, disconnect battery ground cable and isolate as required.

SYSTEM DIAGNOSIS & TESTING

Accessing Diagnostic Trouble Codes

Connect a suitably programmed scan tool and Vehicle Communication Module (VCM) with appropriate adapters, or equivalents, to the Data Link Connector (DCL) located in the passenger compartment beneath the instrument panel. Follow tool manufacturer's instructions for accessing speed control Diagnostic Trouble Codes (DTC).

Diagnostic Trouble Code Interpretation

Refer to **Fig. 1** for diagnostic trouble code interpretation.

Code	Description
B1432	Wiper Run Relay Short To Battery
B1436	Wiper Hi/Lo Speed Relay Circuit Short To Battery
B1446	Wiper Park Sense Circuit Failure
B1450	Wiper/Washer Interval Delay Switch Input Circuit Failure
B1458	Wiper/Washer Pump Motor Relay Coil Circuit Failure
B1460	Wiper/Washer Pump Motor Relay Coil Short To Battery
B1466	Wiper Speed Not Switching
B1467	Wiper Hi/Lo Speed Circuit Motor Short To Battery
B1840	Wiper Front Power Circuit Failure

Fig. 1 Diagnostic trouble code interpretation

Wiring Diagrams

Refer to **Figs. 2 through 4** for wiring diagrams.

Diagnostic Tests

2002–04

Refer to **Figs. 5 through 17** for diagnostic tests.

2005–06

Refer to **Figs. 18 through 29** for diagnostic tests.

Clearing Diagnostic Trouble Codes

Connect a suitably programmed scan tool and Vehicle Communication Module (VCM) with appropriate adapters, or equivalents, to the Data Link Connector (DCL) located in the passenger compartment beneath the instrument panel. Follow tool manufacturer's instructions for accessing speed control Diagnostic Trouble Codes (DTC).

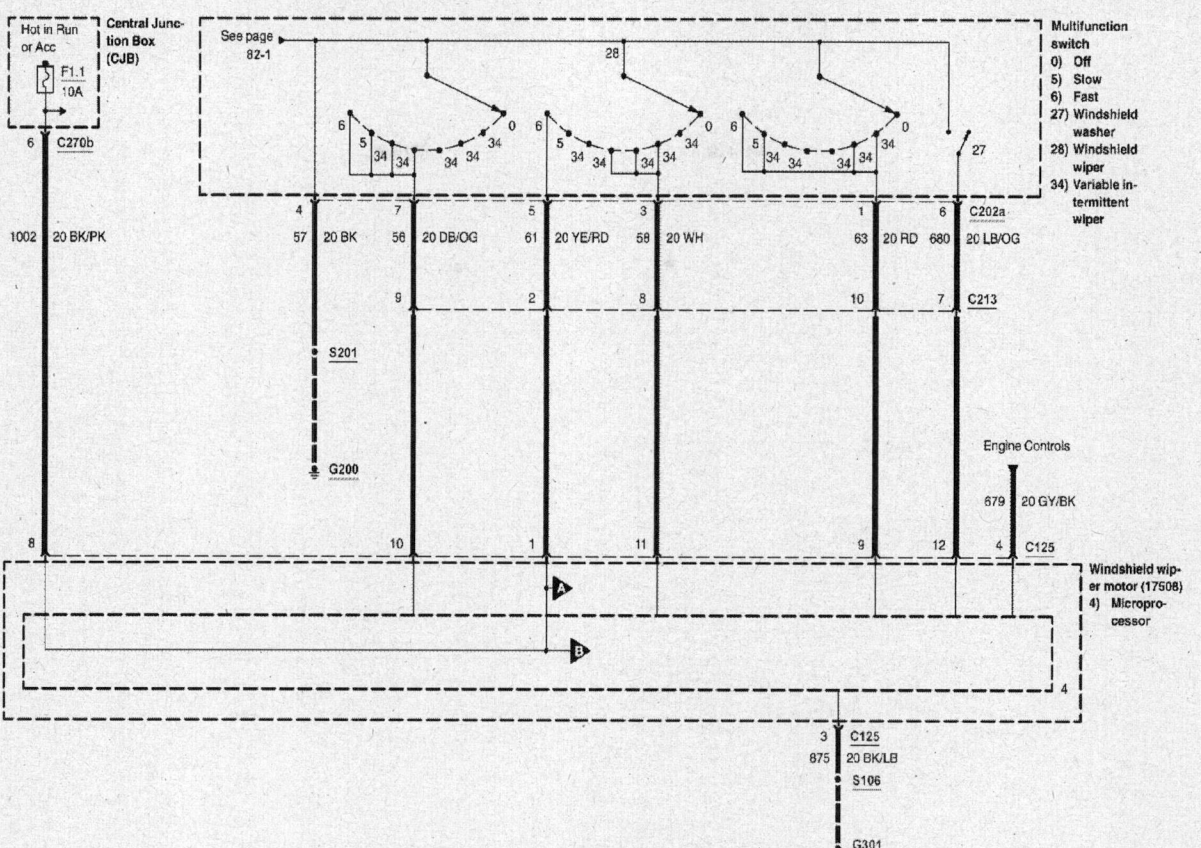

Fig. 2 Wiring diagram (Part 1 of 2). 2002–04

LTV0500000001890

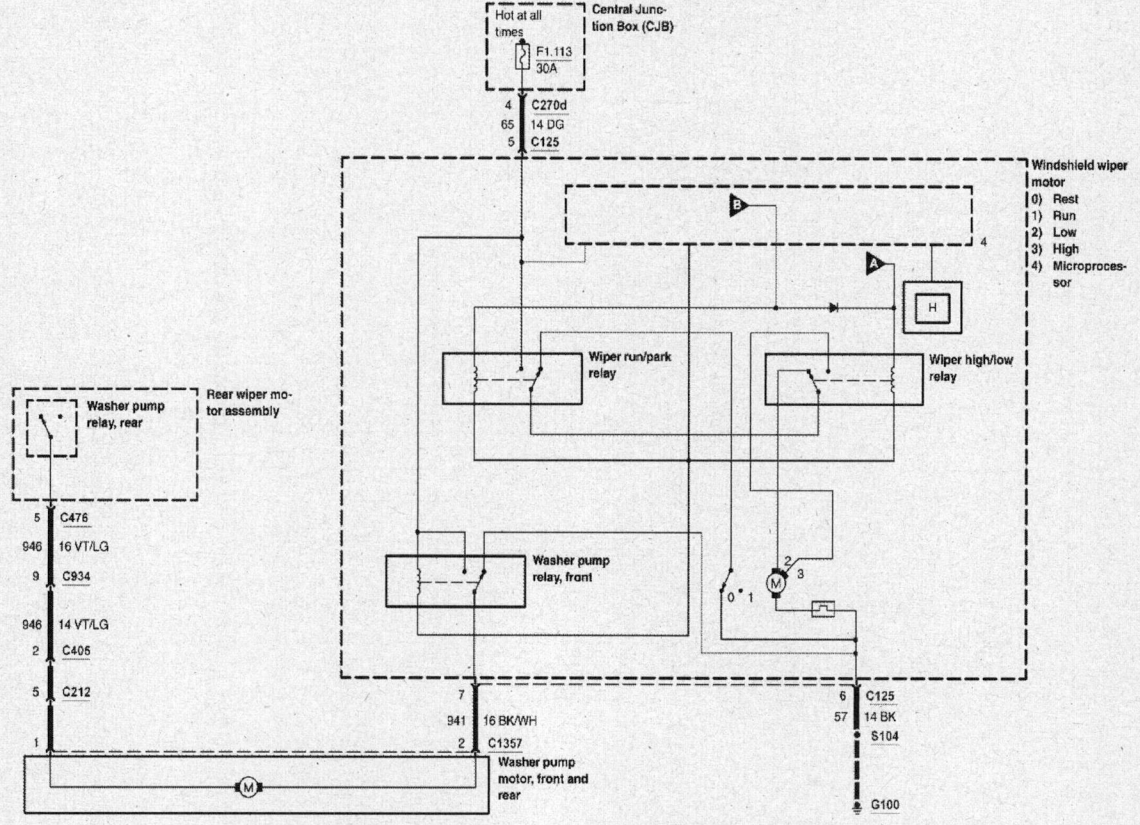

Fig. 2 Wiring diagram (Part 2 of 2). 2002–04

LTV0500000001891

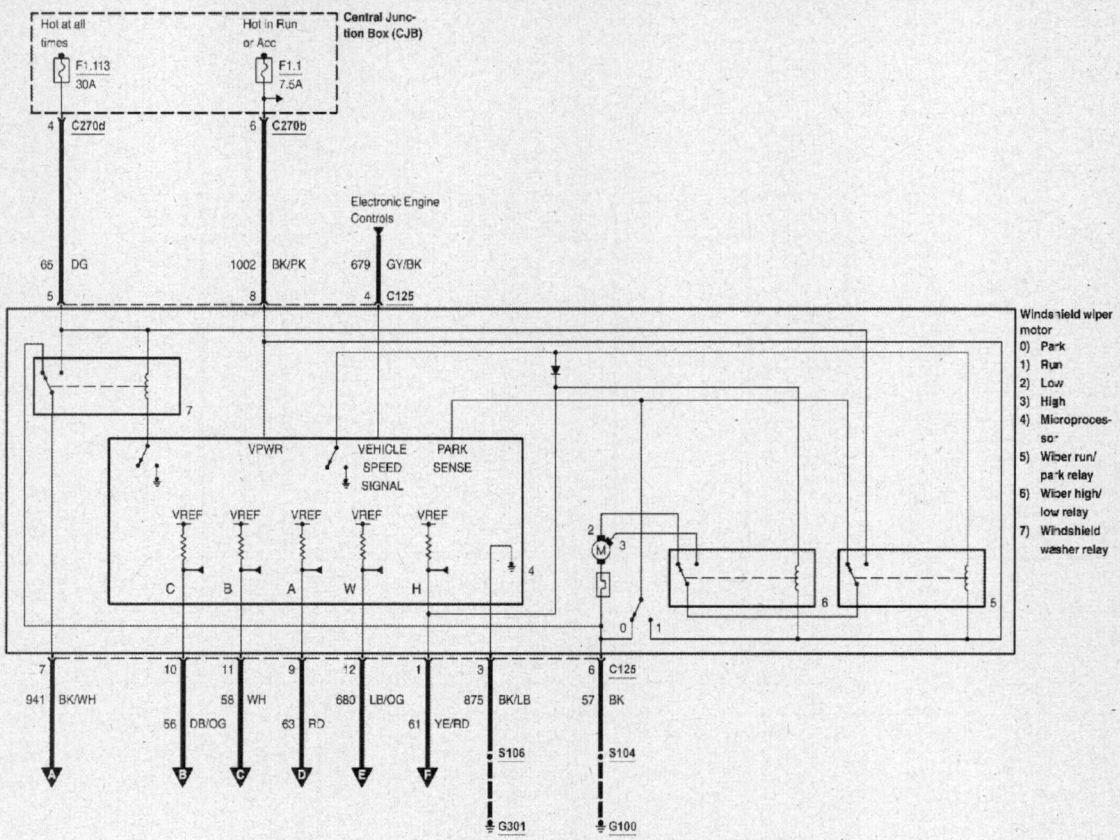

Fig. 3   Front wiring diagram (Part 1 of 3). 2005–06

LTV0500000001898

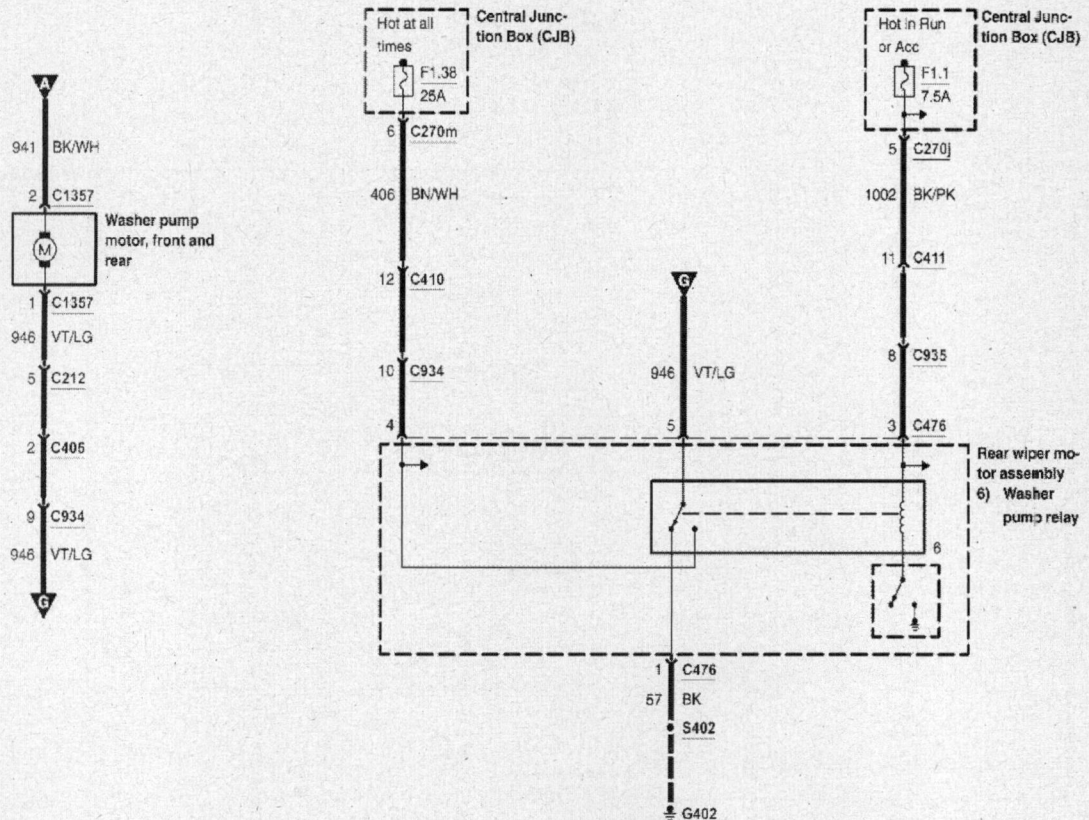

Fig. 3   Front wiring diagram (Part 2 of 3). 2005–06

LTV0500000001899

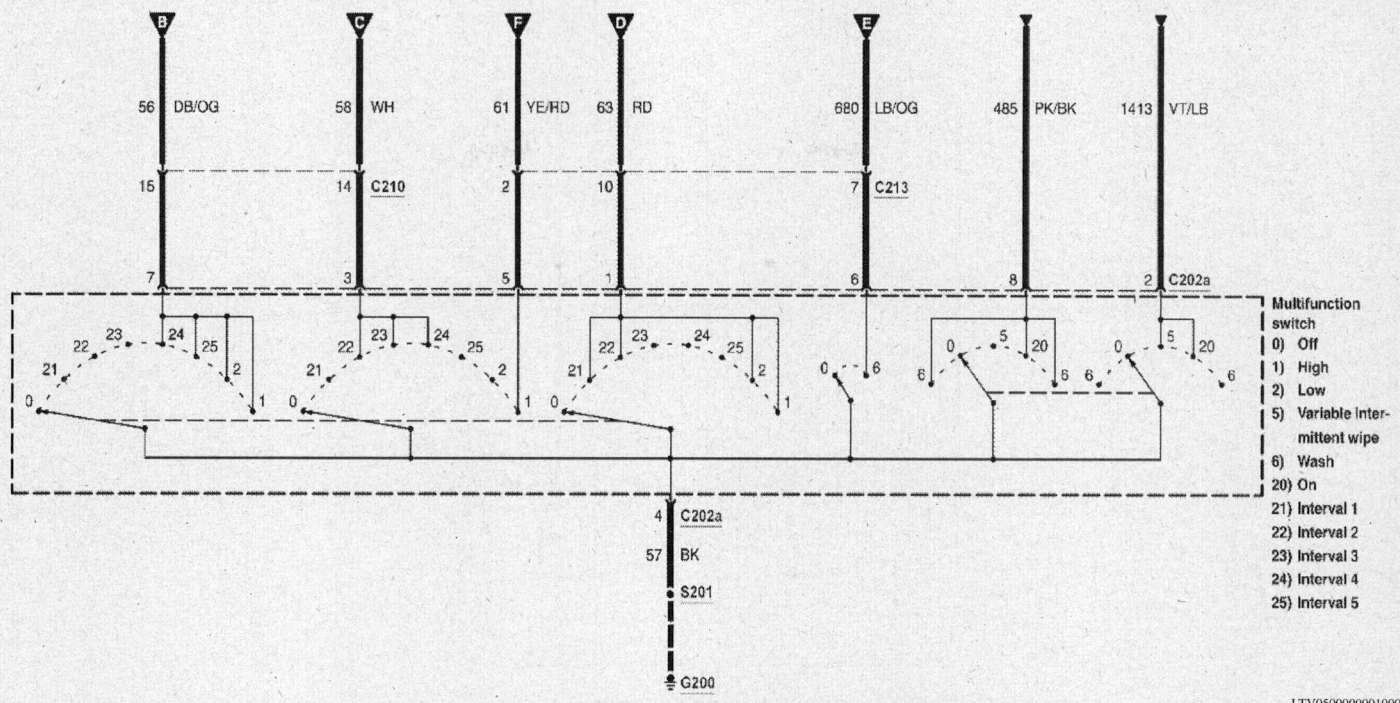

Fig. 3   Front wiring diagram (Part 3 of 3). 2005–06

LTV0500000001900

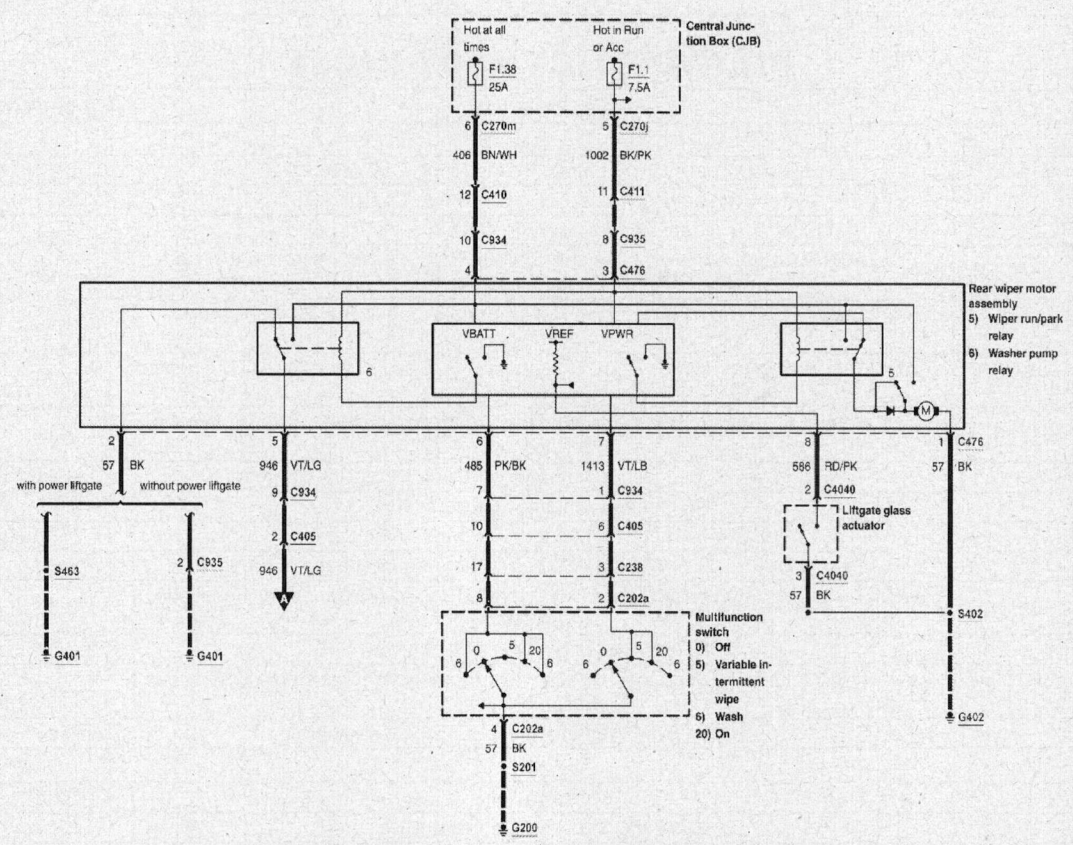

Fig. 4   Rear wiring diagram (Part 1 of 2). 2005–06

LTV0500000001901

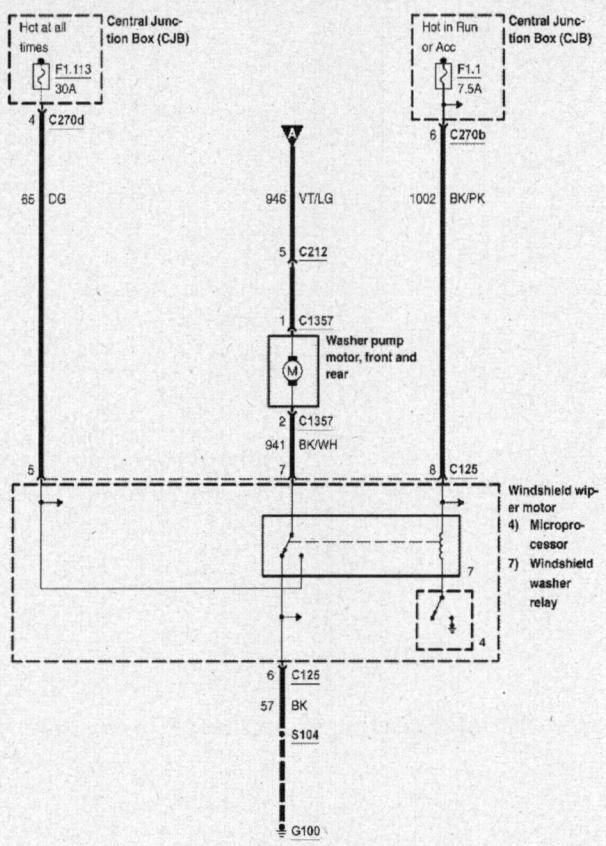

Fig. 4   Rear wiring diagram (Part 2 of 2). 2005–06

LTV0500000001902

DIAGNOSTIC CHART INDEX

Test	Code	Description	Page No.	Fig. No.
2002–04				
A	B1432	Front Wipers Do Not Move In Any Mode Of Operation	3-73	5
	B1840	Front Wipers Do Not Move In Any Mode Of Operation	3-73	5
B	B1467	Front Wipers Stay On Continuously	3-75	6
C	B1436	Front High/Low Wiper Speeds Do Not Operate Properly But Intermittent Wiper Mode Does	3-76	7
D	B1446	Front Intermittent Wiper Mode Does Not Operate Properly But High/Low Wiper Speeds Do	3-78	8
E	B1458	Front Washer Pump Function Does Not Operate Properly, Other Wiper Functions Do Operate	3-79	9
	B1460	Front Washer Pump Function Does Not Operate Properly, Other Wiper Functions Do Operate	3-79	9
F	—	Front Wiper Speed Dependent Interval Mode Does Not Operate	3-81	10
G	—	No Communication w/GEM Module	3-81	11
	—	Rear Wiper Does Not Move In Any Mode Of Operation	3-83	12
H	—	Rear Wiper Parks Off Glass Between Wipes When In Interval Mode	3-85	13
J	—	Rear Washer Pump Function Does Not Operate Properly, Other Wiper Functions Do Operate	3-85	14
K	—	Rear Wiper Stays On Continuously	3-87	15
L	—	Low Washer Fluid Warning Does Not Operate Properly, Washer Pump Operation Satisfactory	3-87	16
M	—	Low Washer Fluid Warning Indicator Does Not Operate	3-88	17
2005–06				
—	—	Symptom Tests	3-88	18
A	—	Windshield Wipers Are Inoperative	3-89	19
B	—	Rear Wiper Is Inoperative	3-90	20
C	—	Windshield Wipers Stay On Continuously	3-90	21

Continued

DIAGNOSTIC CHART INDEX—Continued

Test	Code	Description	Page No.	Fig. No.
2005–06				
D	—	Rear Wiper Stays On Continuously	3-91	22
E	—	High/Low Windshield Wiper Speeds Do Not Operate Correctly	3-91	23
F	—	Intermittent Windshield Wiper Speed Does Not Work Correctly	3-92	24
G	—	Intermittent Rear Wiper Speed Does Not Operate	3-92	25
H	—	Windshield Wipers Do Not Operate Correctly In Mist Position	3-93	26
I	—	Rear Wiper & Wash Function Does Not Operate	3-93	27
J	—	Washer Pump Is Inoperative	3-94	28
K	—	Windshield Wiper Speed Dependent Interval Mode Does Not Operate Correctly	3-95	29

A1 CHECK THE VOLTAGE OUTPUT FROM FUSES 11 (30A) AND 15 (5A)

2 Measure the voltage between fuse 11 (30A) pin 2 and ground, fuse 15 (5A) pin 1 and ground.

- Are the voltages greater than 10 volts?

→ **Yes**
  GO to **A2**.

→ **No**
  REPLACE the fuse(s) in question or REPAIR circuit 1052 (T/BK) or 297 (BK/LG). CLEAR the DTCs. TEST system for normal operation. If the fuse fails again, CHECK for a short to ground. REPAIR as necessary.

A2 CHECK THE IGNITION STATES

3 Monitor the PID IGN__GEM while turning the ignition switch through the START, RUN, OFF, and ACC positions.

- Do the PID values agree with the ignition switch positions?

→ **Yes**
  GO to **A3**.

→ **No**
  REPAIR the ignition circuit (RUN/ACC: circuit 297 [BK/LG], RUN: circuit 1040 [R/LB], START: circuit 32 [R/LB] or circuit 481 [GY/Y]) in question. CLEAR the DTCs. TEST the system for normal operation.

FM9029700510010X

Fig. 5   Test A: Front Wipers Do Not Move In Any Mode Of Operation (Part 1 of 13). 2002–04

A3 RETRIEVE THE DIAGNOSTIC TROUBLE CODES (DTCS)

- Are DTCs retrieved?

→ **Yes**
  If DTC B1431, GO to **A12**.

  If DTC B1432, GO to **A12**.

  If DTC B1438, GO to **A5**.

  If DTC B1441, GO to **A5**.

  If DTC B1450, GO to **A5**.

  If DTC B1453, GO to **A5**.

  If DTC B1840, GO to **A4**.

  If DTC B1342, REPLACE the GEM. CLEAR the DTCs. TEST the system for normal operation.

→ **No**
  GO to **A5**.

FM9029700510020X

Fig. 5   Test A: Front Wipers Do Not Move In Any Mode Of Operation (Part 2 of 13). 2002–04

A4 CHECK THE VOLTAGE TO THE WIPER/WASHER SYSTEM RELAYS

5 Measure the voltage between windshield wiper HI/LO relay connector pin 1, circuit 950 (W/BK), and ground, and between windshield wiper run/park relay connector pin 1, circuit 950 (W/BK), and ground.

- Are the voltages greater than 10 volts?
→ **Yes**
  RECONNECT the relays. GO to **A5**.

→ **No**
  REPAIR circuit 950 (W/BK). CLEAR the DTCs. TEST the system for normal operation.

A5 CHECK THE WIPER SWITCH OUTPUTS BY MONITORING THE PID WPMODE

2 Monitor the PID WPMODE while turning the wiper switch through all switch positions.

- Does the PID WPMODE values agree with all the wiper switch positions?

→ **Yes**
  GO to **A12**.

→ **No**
  GO to **A6**.

FM9029700510030X

Fig. 5   Test A: Front Wipers Do Not Move In Any Mode Of Operation (Part 3 of 13). 2002–04

A6 CHECK THE WIPER/WASHER SWITCH

3 Check the wiper/washer switch (multi-function switch) for proper operation. Refer to Pinpoint Test F.

- Is the multi-function switch OK?

→ **Yes**
GO to **A7**.

→ **No**
REPLACE the multi-function switch. CLEAR the DTCs. TEST the system for normal operation.

A7 CHECK CIRCUIT 680 (LB/O) FOR OPEN

2 Measure the resistance between GEM C239-13, circuit 680 (LB/O), and multi-function switch C259-680, circuit 680 (LB/O).

- Is the resistance less than 5 ohms?

→ **Yes**
GO to **A8**.

→ **No**
REPAIR circuit 680 (LB/O). CLEAR the DTCs. TEST the system for normal operation.

FM9029700510040X

Fig. 5 Test A: Front Wipers Do Not Move In Any Mode Of Operation (Part 4 of 13). 2002–04

A8 CHECK CIRCUIT 682 (DB) FOR OPEN

1 Measure the resistance between GEM C239-21, circuit 682 (DB), and multi-function switch C259-682, circuit 682 (DB).

- Is the resistance less than 5 ohms?

→ **Yes**
GO to **A9**.

→ **No**
REPAIR circuit 682 (DB). CLEAR the DTCs. TEST the system for normal operation.

A9 CHECK CIRCUIT 684 (PK/Y) FOR OPEN

1 Measure the resistance between GEM C239-22, circuit 684 (PK/Y), and multi-function switch C259-684, circuit 684 (PK/Y).

- Is the resistance less than 5 ohms?

→ **Yes**
GO to **A10**.

→ **No**
REPAIR circuit 684 (PK/Y). CLEAR the DTCs. TEST the system for normal operation.

FM9029700510050X

Fig. 5 Test A: Front Wipers Do Not Move In Any Mode Of Operation (Part 5 of 13). 2002–04

A10 CHECK CIRCUIT 680 (LB/O) FOR SHORT TO POWER

2 Measure the voltage between GEM C239-13, circuit 680 (LB/O) and ground.

- Is any voltage indicated?

→ **Yes**
REPAIR circuit 680 (LB/O). CLEAR the DTCs. TEST the system for normal operation.

→ **No**
GO to **A11**.

A11 CHECK CIRCUIT 684 (PK/Y) FOR SHORT TO POWER

1 Measure the voltage between GEM C239-22, circuit 684 (PK/Y), and ground.

- Is any voltage indicated?

→ **Yes**
REPAIR circuit 684 (PK/Y). CLEAR the DTCs. TEST the system for normal operation.

→ **No**
REPLACE the GEM. CLEAR the DTCs. TEST the system for normal operation.

FM9029700510060X

Fig. 5 Test A: Front Wipers Do Not Move In Any Mode Of Operation (Part 6 of 13). 2002–04

A12 CHECK THE FRONT WIPER RUN/PARK RELAY COIL CIRCUIT

2 Monitor the PID WPRUN while toggling the active command WIPER RLY ON and OFF.

- Does the PID WPRUN agree with the command mode?

→ **Yes**
If the PID WPRUN displays ON--- and OFF---, GO to **A18**.

→ **No**
If the PID WPRUN displays OFF O-G, GO to **A13**. If the PID WPRUN displays ON-B-, GO to **A16**.

A13 CHECK THE VOLTAGE TO THE WIND-SHIELD WIPER RUN/PARK RELAY COIL

4 Measure the voltage between windshield wiper run/park relay connector pin 1, circuit 950 (W/BK) and ground.

- Is the voltage greater than 10 volts?

→ **Yes**
GO to **A14**.

→ **No**
REPAIR circuit 950 (W/BK). CLEAR the DTCs. TEST the system for normal operation.

FM9029700510070X

Fig. 5 Test A: Front Wipers Do Not Move In Any Mode Of Operation (Part 7 of 13). 2002–04

A14 CHECK THE WINDSHIELD WIPER RUN/PARK RELAY

2 Check the windshield wiper run/park relay.

- Is the windshield wiper run/park relay OK?

→ **Yes**
GO to **A15**.

→ **No**
REPLACE the windshield wiper run/park relay. CLEAR the DTCs. TEST the system for normal operation.

A15 CHECK CIRCUIT 646 (Y/W) FOR OPEN

2 Measure the resistance between GEM C239-19, circuit 646 (Y/W), and windshield wiper run/park relay connector pin 2, circuit 646 (Y/W).

- Is the resistance less than 5 ohms?

→ **Yes**
REPLACE the GEM. CLEAR the DTCs. TEST the system for normal operation.

→ **No**
REPAIR circuit 646 (Y/W). CLEAR the DTCs. TEST the system for normal operation.

FM9029700510080X

Fig. 5 Test A: Front Wipers Do Not Move In Any Mode Of Operation (Part 8 of 13). 2002–04

A16 CHECK CIRCUIT 646 (Y/W) FOR A SHORT TO POWER

5 Measure the voltage between windshield wiper run/park relay connector pin 2, circuit 646 (Y/W), and ground.

- Is any voltage indicated?

→ **Yes**
REPAIR circuit 646 (Y/W). CLEAR the DTCs. TEST the system for normal operation.

→ **No**
GO to **A17**.

A17 CHECK THE WINDSHIELD WIPER RUN/PARK RELAY

2 Check the windshield wiper run/park relay.

- Is the windshield wiper run/park relay OK?

→ **Yes**
REPLACE the GEM. CLEAR the DTCs. TEST the system for normal operation.

→ **No**
REPLACE the front wiper run/park relay. CLEAR the DTCs. TEST the system for normal operation.

FM9029700510090X

Fig. 5 Test A: Front Wipers Do Not Move In Any Mode Of Operation (Part 9 of 13). 2002–04

A18 CHECK THE WINDSHIELD WIPER RUN/PARK RELAY SWITCH CIRCUIT

4 Set the active command mode WIPER RLY to ON.

5 Measure the voltage between windshield wiper HI/LO relay connector pin 3, circuit 63 (R), and ground.

- Is the voltage greater than 10 volts?
- → **Yes**
  GO to **A21**.
- → **No**
  GO to **A19**.

A19 CHECK CIRCUIT 63 (R) FOR OPEN

3 Measure the resistance between front wiper HI/LO relay connector pin 3, circuit 63 (R), and front wiper run/park relay connector pin 3, circuit 63 (R).

- Is the resistance less than 5 ohms?
- → **Yes**
  GO to **A20**.
- → **No**
  REPAIR circuit 63 (R). CLEAR the DTCs. TEST the system for normal operation.

FM9029700510100X

Fig. 5 Test A: Front Wipers Do Not Move In Any Mode Of Operation (Part 10 of 13). 2002–04

A20 CHECK THE VOLTAGE TO THE FRONT WIPER RUN/PARK RELAY SWITCH

2 Measure the voltage between front wiper run/park relay connector pin 5, circuit 950 (W/BK), and ground.

- Is the voltage greater than 10 volts?
- → **Yes**
  REPLACE the windshield wiper run/park relay. CLEAR the DTCs. TEST the system for normal operation.
- → **No**
  REPAIR circuit 950 (W/BK). CLEAR the DTCs. TEST the system for normal operation.

A21 CHECK THE WINDSHIELD WIPER HI/LO RELAY SWITCH CIRCUIT

2 Set the active command WIPER RLY to ON.

3 Connect a jumper wire between front wiper HI/LO relay connector pin 3, circuit 63 (R), and pin 5, circuit 56 (DB/O), or pin 4, circuit 58 (W).

- Do the wipers operate?
- → **Yes**
  REPLACE the windshield wiper hi/lo relay. CLEAR the DTCs. TEST the system for normal operation.
- → **No**
  GO to **A22**.

FM9029700510110X

Fig. 5 Test A: Front Wipers Do Not Move In Any Mode Of Operation (Part 11 of 13). 2002–04

A22 CHECK THE GROUND TO THE WINDSHIELD WIPER MOTOR FOR OPEN

3 Measure the resistance between windshield wiper motor C165-3, circuit 57 (BK), and ground.

- Is the resistance less than 5 ohms?
- → **Yes**
  GO to **A23**.
- → **No**
  REPAIR circuit 57 (BK). CLEAR the DTCs. TEST the system for normal operation.

A23 CHECK CIRCUIT 56 (DB/O) FOR OPEN

1 Measure the resistance between windshield wiper motor C165-5, circuit 56 (DB/O), and windshield wiper HI/LO relay connector pin 5, circuit 56 (DB/O).

- Is the resistance less than 5 ohms?
- → **Yes**
  GO to **A24**.
- → **No**
  REPAIR circuit 56 (DB/O). CLEAR the DTCs. TEST the system for normal operation.

FM9029700510120X

Fig. 5 Test A: Front Wipers Do Not Move In Any Mode Of Operation (Part 12 of 13). 2002–04

A24 CHECK CIRCUIT 58 (W) FOR OPEN

1 Measure the resistance between windshield wiper motor C165-4, circuit 58 (W), and windshield wiper HI/LO relay connector pin 4, circuit 58 (W).

- Is the resistance less than 5 ohms?
- → **Yes**
  GO to **A25**.
- → **No**
  REPAIR circuit 58 (W). CLEAR the DTCs. TEST the system for normal operation.

A25 CHECK THE WIPER MECHANISM

1 Remove the linkage from the front wiper motor.
- Are the wipers free?
- → **Yes**
  CHECK the windshield wiper motor by performing the Windshield Wiper Motor Current Draw Test. REPLACE the front wiper motor if it does not pass the test. CLEAR the DTCs. TEST the system for normal operation.
- → **No**
  REPAIR the windshield wiper mechanism. CLEAR the DTCs. TEST the system for normal operation.

FM9029700510130X

Fig. 5 Test A: Front Wipers Do Not Move In Any Mode Of Operation (Part 13 of 13). 2002–04

B1 CHECK THE IGNITION STATES

3 Monitor the PID IGN__GEM while turning the ignition switch through the START, RUN, OFF, and ACC positions.
- Do the PID values agree with the ignition switch positions?
- → **Yes**
  GO to **B2**.
- → **No**
  REPAIR the ignition circuit (RUN/ACC: circuit 297 [BK/LG], RUN: circuit 1040 [R/LB], START: circuit 32 [R/LB] or circuit 481 [GY/Y]) in question. CLEAR the DTCs. TEST the system for normal operation.

B2 RETRIEVE THE DIAGNOSTIC TROUBLE CODES (DTCS)

- Are any DTCs retrieved?
- → **Yes**
  If DTC B1431, GO to **B7**.
  If DTC B1441, GO to **B3**.
  If DTC B1453, GO to **B3**.
  If DTC B1342, REPLACE the GEM. CLEAR the DTCs. TEST the system for normal operation.
- → **No**
  GO to **B3**.

FM9029700511010X

Fig. 6 Test B: Front Wipers Stay On Continuously (Part 1 of 7). 2002–04

B3 CHECK THE WIPER SWITCH OUTPUTS

2 Monitor the PID WPMODE while turning the wiper switch through all switch positions.
- Does the PID WPMODE value agree with all the wiper switch positions?
- → **Yes**
  GO to **B7**.
- → **No**
  GO to **B4**.

B4 CHECK THE WIPER/WASHER SWITCH

3 Check the wiper/washer switch (multi-function switch) for proper operation. Pinpoint Test F.
- Is the multi-function switch OK?
- → **Yes**
  GO to **B5**.
- → **No**
  REPLACE the multi-function switch. CLEAR the DTCs. TEST the system for normal operation.

FM9029700511020X

Fig. 6 Test B: Front Wipers Stay On Continuously (Part 2 of 7). 2002–04

B5 CHECK CIRCUIT 680 (LB/O) FOR SHORT TO GROUND

2 Measure the resistance between multi-function switch C259-680, circuit 680 (LB/O), and ground.

- Is the resistance greater than 10,000 ohms?

→ **Yes**
GO to **B6**.

→ **No**
REPAIR circuit 680 (LB/O). CLEAR the DTCs. TEST the system for normal operation.

B6 CHECK CIRCUIT 684 (PK/Y) FOR SHORT TO GROUND

1 Measure the resistance between multi-function switch C259-684, circuit 684 (PK/Y), and ground.

- Is the resistance greater than 10,000 ohms?

→ **Yes**
REPLACE the GEM. CLEAR the DTCs. TEST the system for normal operation.

→ **No**
REPAIR circuit 684 (PK/Y). CLEAR the DTCs. TEST the system for normal operation.

FM9029700511030X

Fig. 6 Test B: Front Wipers Stay On Continuously (Part 3 of 7). 2002–04

B11 CHECK CIRCUIT 56 (DB/O) FOR SHORT TO POWER

5 Measure the voltage between front wiper HI/LO relay connector pin 5, circuit 56 (DB/O), and ground.

- Is any voltage indicated?

→ **Yes**
REPAIR circuit 56 (DB/O). CLEAR the DTCs. TEST the system for normal operation.

→ **No**
GO to **B12**.

B12 CHECK CIRCUIT 58 (W) FOR SHORT TO POWER

1 Measure the voltage between front wiper HI/LO relay connector pin 4, circuit 58 (W), and ground.

- Is any voltage indicated?

→ **Yes**
REPAIR circuit 58 (W). CLEAR the DTCs. TEST the system for normal operation.

→ **No**
REPLACE the front wiper motor. CLEAR the DTCs. TEST the system for normal operation.

B13 CHECK CIRCUIT 671 (BK) FOR VOLTAGE— WIPER/WASHER SWITCH IN THE PARK POSITION

2 Turn the wiper/washer switch to park position.

FM9029700511060X

Fig. 6 Test B: Front Wipers Stay On Continuously (Part 6 of 7). 2002–04

B7 CHECK THE FRONT WIPER RUN/PARK RELAY COIL CIRCUIT

2 Monitor the PID WPRUN while toggling the active command WIPER RLY ON and OFF.

- Does the PID WPRUN agree with the command mode?

→ **Yes**
If the PID WRPRUN displays ON--- and OFF---, GO to **B10**.

→ **No**
IF the PID WPRUN displays OFF O-G, GO to **B8**.

B8 CHECK THE FRONT WIPER RUN/PARK RELAY

3 Check the windshield wiper run/park relay.

- Is the front wiper run/park relay OK?

→ **Yes**
GO to **B9**.

→ **No**
REPLACE the front wiper run/park relay. CLEAR the DTCs. TEST the system for normal operation.

FM9029700511040X

Fig. 6 Test B: Front Wipers Stay On Continuously (Part 4 of 7). 2002–04

B13 CHECK CIRCUIT 671 (BK) FOR VOLTAGE— WIPER/WASHER SWITCH IN THE PARK POSITION (Continued)

3 Measure the voltage between windshield wiper run/park relay connector pin 4, circuit 671 (BK), and ground.

- Is the voltage greater than 10 volts?

→ **Yes**
GO to **B14**.

→ **No**
REPLACE the windshield wiper run/park relay. CLEAR the DTCs. TEST the system for normal operation.

B14 CHECK CIRCUIT 671 (BK) FOR SHORT TO POWER

4 Measure the voltage between windshield wiper run/park relay connector pin 4, circuit 671 (BK), and ground.

- Is any voltage indicated?

→ **Yes**
REPAIR circuit 671 (BK). CLEAR the DTCs. TEST the system for normal operation.

→ **No**
REPLACE the wiper motor. CLEAR the DTCs. TEST the system for normal operation.

FM9029700511070X

Fig. 6 Test B: Front Wipers Stay On Continuously (Part 7 of 7). 2002–04

B9 CHECK CIRCUIT 646 (Y/W) FOR SHORT TO GROUND

2 Measure the resistance between windshield wiper run/park relay connector pin 2, circuit 646 (Y/W), and ground.

- Is the resistance greater than 10,000 ohms?

→ **Yes**
REPLACE the GEM. CLEAR the DTCs. TEST the system for normal operation.

→ **No**
REPAIR circuit 646 (Y/W). CLEAR the DTCs. TEST the system for normal operation.

B10 CHECK THE FRONT WIPER RUN/PARK RELAY SWITCH CIRCUIT

- Do the wipers stop operating?

→ **Yes**
GO to **B13**.

→ **No**
RECONNECT the windshield wiper run/park relay. GO to **B11**.

FM9029700511050X

Fig. 6 Test B: Front Wipers Stay On Continuously (Part 5 of 7). 2002–04

C1 RETRIEVE THE DIAGNOSTIC TROUBLE CODES (DTCS)

- Are DTCs recorded?

→ **Yes**
If DTC B1434, GO to **C8**.

If DTC B1436, GO to **C8**.

If DTC B1438, GO to **C2**.

If DTC B1450, GO to **C2**.

If DTC B1466, GO to **C2**.

If DTC B1342, REPLACE the GEM. CLEAR the DTCs. TEST the system for normal operation.

→ **No**
GO to **C2**.

C2 CHECK THE WIPER SWITCH OUTPUTS

2 Monitor the PID WPMODE while turning the wiper switch through all switch positions.

- Does the PID WPMODE value agree with all the wiper switch positions?

→ **Yes**
GO to **C8**.

→ **No**
GO to **C3**.

FM9029700512010X

Fig. 7 Test C: Front High/Low Wiper Speeds Do Not Operate Properly But Intermittent Wiper Mode Does (Part 1 of 10). 2002–04

C3	CHECK THE WIPER/WASHER SWITCH

☒3 Check the wiper/washer switch (multi-function switch) for proper operation. Refer to Pinpoint Test F.

- Is the multi-function switch OK?

→ **Yes**
GO to **C4**.

→ **No**
REPLACE the multi-function switch. CLEAR the DTCs. TEST the system for normal operation.

C4	CHECK CIRCUIT 680 (LB/O) FOR SHORT TO POWER

☒3 Measure the voltage between multi-function switch C259-680, circuit 680 (LB/O), and ground.

- Is any voltage indicated?

→ **Yes**
REPAIR circuit 680 (LB/O). CLEAR the DTCs. TEST the system for normal operation.

→ **No**
GO to **C6**.

FM9029700512020X

Fig. 7 Test C: Front High/Low Wiper Speeds Do Not Operate Properly But Intermittent Wiper Mode Does (Part 2 of 10). 2002–04

C5	CHECK CIRCUIT 684 (PK/Y) FOR SHORT TO POWER

☒1 Measure the voltage between multi-function switch C259-684, circuit 684 (PK/Y), and ground.

- Is any voltage indicated?

→ **Yes**
REPAIR circuit 684 (PK/Y). CLEAR the DTCs. TEST the system for normal operation.

→ **No**
GO to **C6**.

C6	CHECK CIRCUIT 680 (LB/O) FOR OPEN

☒2 Measure the resistance between GEM C239-13, circuit 680 (LB/O), and multi-function switch C259-680, circuit 680 (LB/O).

- Is the resistance less than 5 ohms?

→ **Yes**
GO to **C7**.

→ **No**
REPAIR circuit 680 (LB/O). CLEAR the DTCs. TEST the system for normal operation.

FM9029700512030X

Fig. 7 Test C: Front High/Low Wiper Speeds Do Not Operate Properly But Intermittent Wiper Mode Does (Part 3 of 10). 2002–04

C7	CHECK CIRCUIT 684 (PK/Y) FOR OPEN

☒1 Measure the resistance between GEM C239-22, circuit 684 (PK/Y), and multi-function switch C259-684, circuit 684 (PK/Y).

- Is the resistance less than 5 ohms?

→ **Yes**
REPLACE the GEM. CLEAR the DTCs. TEST the system for normal operation.

→ **No**
REPAIR circuit 684 (PK/Y). CLEAR the DTCs. TEST the system for normal operation.

C8	CHECK THE WINDSHIELD WIPER HI/LO RELAY COIL CIRCUIT

☒2 Monitor the PID WPHISP while toggling the active command SPEED RLY ON and OFF.
- Does the PID WPHISP agree with the command mode?
→ **Yes**
If the PID WPHISP displays ON--- and OFF---, GO to **C15**.
→ **No**
If the PID WPHISP displays OFF O-G, GO to **C11**.

If the PID WPHISP displays ON-B-, GO to **C9**.

FM9029700512040X

Fig. 7 Test C: Front High/Low Wiper Speeds Do Not Operate Properly But Intermittent Wiper Mode Does (Part 4 of 10). 2002–04

C9	CHECK CIRCUIT 647 (GY/LB) FOR SHORT TO POWER

☒5 Measure the voltage between windshield wiper HI/LO relay connector pin 2, circuit 647 (GY/LB), and ground.

- Is any voltage indicated?

→ **Yes**
REPAIR circuit 647 (GY/LB). CLEAR the DTCs. TEST the system for normal operation.

→ **No**
GO to **C10**.

C10	CHECK THE WINDSHIELD WIPER HI/LO RELAY

☒2 Check the windshield wiper HI/LO relay.

- Is the windshield wiper HI/LO relay OK?
→ **Yes**
REPLACE the GEM. CLEAR the DTCs. TEST the system for normal operation.

→ **No**
REPLACE the windshield wiper HI/LO relay. CLEAR the DTCs. TEST the system for normal operation.

FM9029700512050X

Fig. 7 Test C: Front High/Low Wiper Speeds Do Not Operate Properly But Intermittent Wiper Mode Does (Part 5 of 10). 2002–04

C11	CHECK THE WINDSHIELD WIPER HI/LO RELAY

☒3 Check the windshield wiper HI/LO relay.

- Is the windshield wiper HI/LO relay OK?

→ **Yes**
GO to **C12**.

→ **No**
REPLACE the windshield wiper HI/LO relay. CLEAR the DTCs. TEST the system for normal operation.

C12	CHECK CIRCUIT 950 (W/BK) FOR VOLTAGE

☒2 Measure the voltage between HI/LO wiper relay pin 1, circuit 950 (W/BK), and ground.

- Is the voltage greater than 10 volts?

→ **Yes**
GO to **C13**.

→ **No**
REPAIR circuit 950 (W/BK). CLEAR the DTCs. TEST the system for normal operation.

FM9029700512060X

Fig. 7 Test C: Front High/Low Wiper Speeds Do Not Operate Properly But Intermittent Wiper Mode Does (Part 6 of 10). 2002–04

C13	CHECK CIRCUIT 647 (GY/LB) FOR SHORT TO GROUND

☒2 Measure the resistance between windshield wiper HI/LO relay connector pin 2, circuit 647 (GY/LB), and ground.

- Is the resistance greater than 10,000 ohms?

→ **Yes**
GO to **C14**.

→ **No**
REPAIR circuit 647 (GY/LB). CLEAR the DTCs. TEST the system for normal operation.

C14	CHECK CIRCUIT 647 (GY/LB) FOR OPEN

☒1 Measure the resistance between windshield wiper HI/LO relay connector pin 2, circuit 647 (GY/LB), and GEM C239-18, circuit 647 (GY/LB).

- Is the resistance less than 5 ohms?

→ **Yes**
REPLACE the GEM. CLEAR the DTCs. TEST the system for normal operation.

→ **No**
REPAIR circuit 647 (GY/LB). CLEAR the DTCs. TEST the system for normal operation.

FM9029700512070X

Fig. 7 Test C: Front High/Low Wiper Speeds Do Not Operate Properly But Intermittent Wiper Mode Does (Part 7 of 10). 2002–04

C15	CHECK THE WINDSHIELD WIPER HI/LO RELAY SWITCH CIRCUIT

4 Turn the wiper/washer switch to the high wiper speed position.

5 Connect a jumper wire between windshield wiper HI/LO relay connector pin 3, circuit 63 (R), and pin 5, circuit 56 (DB/O). The wipers should move at high speed.

FM9029700512080X

Fig. 7   Test C: Front High/Low Wiper Speeds Do Not Operate Properly But Intermittent Wiper Mode Does (Part 8 of 10). 2002–04

D1	RETRIEVE THE DIAGNOSTIC TROUBLE CODES (DTCS)

• Are any DTCs recorded?

→ **Yes**
If DTC B1438, GO to **D2**.

If DTC B1441, GO to **D2**.

If DTC B1446, GO to **D8**.

If DTC B1450, GO to **D2**.

If DTC B1453, GO to **D2**.

If DTC B1342, REPLACE the GEM. CLEAR the DTCs. TEST the system for normal operation.

→ **No**
GO to **D2**.

D2	CHECK THE WIPER SWITCH OUTPUTS

2 Monitor the PID WPMODE while turning the wiper switch through all switch positions.

• Does the PID WPMODE value agree with all the wiper switch positions?

→ **Yes**
GO to **D8**.

→ **No**
GO to **D3**.

FM9029700513010X

Fig. 8   Test D: Front Intermittent Wiper Mode Does Not Operate Properly But High/Low Wiper Speeds Do (Part 1 of 7). 2002–04

C15	CHECK THE WINDSHIELD WIPER HI/LO RELAY SWITCH CIRCUIT (Continued)

6 Turn the wiper/washer switch to the low wiper speed position.

7 Connect a jumper wire between windshield wiper HI/LO relay connector pin 3, circuit 63 (R), and pin 4, circuit 58 (W). The wipers should move at low speed.

• Do the wipers operate at the correct speeds?

→ **Yes**
REPLACE the windshield wiper HI/LO relay. CLEAR the DTCs. TEST the system for normal operation.

→ **No**
REMOVE the jumper wire. GO to **C16**.

FM9029700512090X

Fig. 7   Test C: Front High/Low Wiper Speeds Do Not Operate Properly But Intermittent Wiper Mode Does (Part 9 of 10). 2002–04

D3	CHECK THE WIPER/WASHER SWITCH

3 Check the wiper/washer switch (multi-function switch) for proper operation. Pinpoint Test F.
• Is the multi-function switch OK?

→ **Yes**
GO to **D4**.

→ **No**
REPLACE the multi-function switch. CLEAR the DTCs. TEST the system for normal operation.

D4	CHECK CIRCUIT 680 (LB/O) FOR SHORT TO POWER

3 Measure the voltage between the multi-function switch C259-680, circuit 680 (LB/O), and ground.

• Is any voltage indicated?

→ **Yes**
REPAIR circuit 680 (LB/O). CLEAR the DTCs. TEST the system for normal operation.

→ **No**
GO to **D5**.

FM9029700513020X

Fig. 8   Test D: Front Intermittent Wiper Mode Does Not Operate Properly But High/Low Wiper Speeds Do (Part 2 of 7). 2002–04

C16	CHECK CIRCUITS 56 (DB/O) FOR OPEN

3 Measure the resistance between windshield wiper motor C165-5, circuit 56 (DB/O), and windshield wiper HI/LO relay connector pin 5, circuit 56 (DB/O).

• Is the resistance less than 5 ohms?

→ **Yes**
GO to **C17**.

→ **No**
REPAIR circuit 56 (DB/O). CLEAR the DTCs. TEST the system for normal operation.

C17	CHECK CIRCUIT 58 (W) FOR OPEN

1 Measure the resistance between windshield wiper motor C165-4, circuit 58 (W), and windshield wiper HI/LO relay connector pin 4, circuit 58 (W).

• Is the resistance less than 5 ohms?

→ **Yes**
CHECK the windshield wiper motor. REPLACE the windshield wiper motor if it does not pass the test. CLEAR the DTCs. TEST the system for normal operation.

→ **No**
REPAIR circuit 58 (W). CLEAR the DTCs. TEST the system for normal operation.

FM9029700512100X

Fig. 7   Test C: Front High/Low Wiper Speeds Do Not Operate Properly But Intermittent Wiper Mode Does (Part 10 of 10). 2002–04

D5	CHECK CIRCUIT 684 (PK/Y) FOR SHORT TO POWER

1 Measure the voltage between the multi-function switch C259-684, circuit 684 (PK/Y), and ground.

• Is any voltage indicated?

→ **Yes**
REPAIR circuit 684 (PK/Y). CLEAR the DTCs. TEST the system for normal operation.

→ **No**
GO to **D6**.

D6	CHECK CIRCUIT 680 (LB/O) FOR OPEN

2 Measure the resistance between GEM C239-13, circuit 680 (LB/O), and multi-function switch C259-680, circuit 680 (LB/O).

• Is the resistance less than 5 ohms?

→ **Yes**
GO to **D7**.

→ **No**
REPAIR circuit 680 (LB/O). CLEAR the DTCs. TEST the system for normal operation.

FM9029700513030X

Fig. 8   Test D: Front Intermittent Wiper Mode Does Not Operate Properly But High/Low Wiper Speeds Do (Part 3 of 7). 2002–04

D7 CHECK CIRCUIT 684 (PK/Y) FOR OPEN

1 Measure the resistance between GEM C239-22, circuit 684 (PK/Y), and multi-function switch C259-684, circuit 684 (PK/Y).

- Is the resistance less than 5 ohms?

→ **Yes**
REPLACE the GEM. CLEAR the DTCs. TEST the system for normal operation.

→ **No**
REPAIR circuit 684 (PK/Y). CLEAR the DTCs. TEST the system for normal operation.

D8 CHECK THE WINDSHIELD WIPER MOTOR PARK SWITCH STATUS PID WPPRKSW

2 Turn the wiper/washer switch to the low wiper speed position.

3 **NOTE:** The record function of the NGS must be used to perform this test.
Monitor and record the PID WPPRKSW while the wipers are operating.

FM9029700513040X

Fig. 8 Test D: Front Intermittent Wiper Mode Does Not Operate Properly But High/Low Wiper Speeds Do (Part 4 of 7). 2002–04

D12 CHECK THE PARK FUNCTION OF THE WINDSHIELD WIPER MOTOR

2 Monitor the PID WPPRKSW.

3 Connect a jumper wire between windshield wiper motor C165-1, circuit 671 (BK), and ground.

4 Remove the jumper wire from windshield wiper motor C165.

5 Connect a jumper wire between windshield wiper motor C165-1, circuit 671 (BK), and the positive battery terminal.

- Does the PID WPPRKSW indicate PARKED when C165-1 is grounded and not PRK when 12 volts is applied?

→ **Yes**
REPLACE the windshield wiper motor. CLEAR the DTCs. TEST the system for normal operation.

→ **No**
REPLACE the GEM. CLEAR the DTCs. TEST the system for normal operation.

FM9029700513070X

Fig. 8 Test D: Front Intermittent Wiper Mode Does Not Operate Properly But High/Low Wiper Speeds Do (Part 7 of 7). 2002–04

D8 CHECK THE WINDSHIELD WIPER MOTOR PARK SWITCH STATUS PID WPPRKSW

4 Use the NGS tester View Recorder Areas to view the stored WPPRKSW graph.

- Does the PID WPPRKSW indicate PARK when the wipers are at the park position and not PARK when the wipers are out of the park position?

→ **Yes**
REPLACE the GEM. CLEAR the DTCs. TEST the system for normal operation.

→ **No**
GO to **D9.**

D9 CHECK THE GROUND TO THE WINDSHIELD WIPER MOTOR

3 Measure the resistance between windshield wiper motor C165-3, circuit 57 (BK), and ground.

- Is the resistance less than 5 ohms?

→ **Yes**
GO to **D10.**

→ **No**
REPAIR circuit 57 (BK). CLEAR the DTCs. TEST the system for normal operation.

FM9029700513050X

Fig. 8 Test D: Front Intermittent Wiper Mode Does Not Operate Properly But High/Low Wiper Speeds Do (Part 5 of 7). 2002–04

E1 RETRIEVE THE DIAGNOSTIC TROUBLE CODES (DTCs)

- Are DTCs retrieved?

→ **Yes**
If DTC B1450, GO to **E2.**
If DTC B1458, GO to **E5.**
If DTC B1460, GO to **E5.**

→ **No**
GO to **E12.**

E2 CHECK THE WASHER SWITCH BY MONITORING THE PID WPMODE

2 Monitor the PID WPMODE while turning the wiper switch through all positions and depressing the washer switch.

- Does the PID WPMODE agree with all of the switch positions?

→ **Yes**
GO to **E5.**

→ **No**
GO to **E3.**

FM9029700514010X

Fig. 9 Test E: Front Washer Pump Function Does Not Operate Properly, Other Wiper Functions Do Operate (Part 1 of 8). 2002–04

D10 CHECK THE VOLTAGE TO THE WINDSHIELD WIPER MOTOR

2 Measure the voltage between windshield wiper motor C165-2, circuit 950 (W/BK), and ground.

- Is the voltage greater than 10 volts?

→ **Yes**
GO to **D11.**

→ **No**
REPAIR circuit 950 (W/BK). CLEAR the DTCs. TEST the system for normal operation.

D11 CHECK CIRCUIT 671 (BK) FOR OPEN

3 Measure the resistance between windshield wiper motor C165-1, circuit 671 (BK), and GEM C239-15, circuit 671 (BK).

- Is the resistance less than 5 ohms?

→ **Yes**
RECONNECT GEM C239. GO to **D12.**

→ **No**
REPAIR circuit 671 (BK). CLEAR the DTCs. TEST the system for normal operation.

FM9029700513060X

Fig. 8 Test D: Front Intermittent Wiper Mode Does Not Operate Properly But High/Low Wiper Speeds Do (Part 6 of 7). 2002–04

E3 CHECK THE WASHER SWITCH

3 Measure the resistance between multi-function switch terminals 590 and 993 while depressing and releasing the washer switch.

- Is the resistance less than 5 ohms with washer switch depressed and greater than 10,000 ohms with the washer switch released?

→ **Yes**
GO to **E4.**

→ **No**
REPLACE the multi-function switch. CLEAR the DTCs. TEST the system for normal operation.

E4 CHECK CIRCUIT 680 (LB/O) FOR OPEN

2 Measure the resistance between GEM C239-13, circuit 680 (LB/O), and multi-function switch C259-680, circuit 680 (LB/O).

- Is resistance less than 5 ohms?

→ **Yes**
REPLACE the GEM. CLEAR the DTCs. TEST the system for normal operation.

→ **No**
REPAIR circuit 680 (LB/O). CLEAR the DTCs. TEST the system for normal operation.

FM9029700514020X

Fig. 9 Test E: Front Washer Pump Function Does Not Operate Properly, Other Wiper Functions Do Operate (Part 2 of 8). 2002–04

E5   CHECK THE FRONT WASHER PUMP RELAY COIL CIRCUIT

2 Monitor the PID WASHRLY while toggling the active command WSHRLY ON and OFF.

- Does the PID WASHRLY agree with the active command?

→ **Yes**
If the PID WASHRLY displays ON--, OFF--, GO to E12.

→ **No**
If the PID WASHRLY displays OFF O-G, GO to E6.

If the PID WASHRLY displays ON-B-, GO to E10.

E6   CHECK FRONT WASHER PUMP RELAY

3 Check the front washer pump relay; refer to the Relay Component Test in this section.

- Is the front washer pump relay OK?

→ **Yes**
GO to E7.

→ **No**
REPLACE the front washer pump relay. CLEAR the DTCs. TEST the system for normal operation.

FM9029700514030X

Fig. 9   Test E: Front Washer Pump Function Does Not Operate Properly, Other Wiper Functions Do Operate (Part 3 of 8). 2002–04

E7   CHECK CIRCUIT 950 (W/BK) FOR VOLTAGE

2 Measure the voltage between front washer pump relay connector pin 1, circuit 950 (W/BK), and ground.

- Is the voltage greater than 10 volts?

→ **Yes**
GO to E8.

→ **No**
REPLACE fuse 11 (30A) or REPAIR circuit 950 (W/BK). CLEAR the DTCs. TEST the system for normal operation. If the fuse fails again, CHECK for a short to ground. REPAIR as necessary.

E8   CHECK CIRCUIT 686 (T/R) FOR OPEN

3 Measure the resistance between GEM C239-24, circuit 686 (T/R), and front washer pump relay connector pin 2, circuit 686 (T/R).

- Is the resistance less than 5 ohms?

→ **Yes**
GO to E9.

→ **No**
REPAIR circuit 686 (T/R). CLEAR the DTCs. TEST the system for normal operation.

FM9029700514040X

Fig. 9   Test E: Front Washer Pump Function Does Not Operate Properly, Other Wiper Functions Do Operate (Part 4 of 8). 2002–04

E9   CHECK CIRCUIT 686 (T/R) FOR SHORT TO GROUND

1 Measure the resistance between front washer pump relay connector pin 2, circuit 686 (T/R), and ground.

- Is the resistance greater than 10,000 ohms?

→ **Yes**
REPLACE the GEM. CLEAR the DTCs. TEST the system for normal operation.

→ **No**
REPAIR circuit 686 (T/R). CLEAR the DTCs. TEST the system for normal operation.

E10   CHECK FRONT WASHER PUMP RELAY

1 Check the front washer pump relay.

- Is the front washer pump relay OK?

→ **Yes**
GO to E11.

→ **No**
REPLACE the front washer pump relay. CLEAR the DTCs. TEST the system for normal operation.

FM9029700514050X

Fig. 9   Test E: Front Washer Pump Function Does Not Operate Properly, Other Wiper Functions Do Operate (Part 5 of 8). 2002–04

E11   CHECK CIRCUIT 686 (T/R) FOR SHORT TO POWER

3 Measure the voltage between front washer pump relay connector pin 2, circuit 686 (T/R), and ground.

- Is any voltage indicated?

→ **Yes**
REPAIR circuit 686 (T/R). CLEAR the DTCs. TEST the system for normal operation.

→ **No**
REPLACE the GEM. CLEAR the DTCs. TEST the system for normal operation.

E12   CHECK CIRCUIT 57 (BK) FOR OPEN

3 Measure the resistance between rear washer pump relay connector pin 4, circuit 57 (BK), and ground.

- Is the resistance less than 5 ohms?

→ **Yes**
GO to E13.

→ **No**
REPAIR circuit 57 (BK). CLEAR the DTCs. TEST the system for normal operation.

FM9029700514060X

Fig. 9   Test E: Front Washer Pump Function Does Not Operate Properly, Other Wiper Functions Do Operate (Part 6 of 8). 2002–04

E13   CHECK CIRCUIT 950 (W/BK) FOR VOLTAGE

2 Measure the voltage between front washer pump relay connector pin 5, circuit 950 (W/BK), and ground.

- Is the voltage greater than 10 volts?

→ **Yes**
GO to E14.

→ **No**
REPAIR circuit 950 (W/BK). CLEAR the DTCs. TEST the system for normal operation.

E14   CHECK THE FRONT AND REAR WASHER PUMP RELAYS

3 Check the front and rear washer pump relays.

- Are the front and rear washer pump relays OK?

→ **Yes**
GO to E15.

→ **No**
REPLACE the relay in question. CLEAR the DTCs. TEST the system for normal operation.

FM9029700514070X

Fig. 9   Test E: Front Washer Pump Function Does Not Operate Properly, Other Wiper Functions Do Operate (Part 7 of 8). 2002–04

E15   CHECK CIRCUIT 941 (BK/W) FOR OPEN

2 Measure the resistance between front washer pump relay connector pin 3, circuit 941 (BK/W), and washer pump motor C138, circuit 941 (BK/W).

- Is the resistance less than 5 ohms?

→ **Yes**
GO to E16.

→ **No**
REPAIR circuit 941 (BK/W). CLEAR the DTCs. TEST the system for normal operation.

E16   CHECK CIRCUIT 946 (P/LG) FOR OPEN

1 Measure the resistance between rear washer pump relay connector pin 3, circuit 946 (P/LG), and washer pump motor C138, circuit 946 (P/LG).

- Is the resistance less than 5 ohms?

→ **Yes**
REPLACE the washer pump motor. CLEAR the DTCs. TEST the system for normal operation.

→ **No**
REPAIR circuit 946 (P/LG). CLEAR the DTCs. TEST the system for normal operation.

FM9029700514080X

Fig. 9   Test E: Front Washer Pump Function Does Not Operate Properly, Other Wiper Functions Do Operate (Part 8 of 8). 2002–04

F1 RETRIEVE THE DIAGNOSTIC TROUBLE CODES (DTCS)

- Are any DTCs recorded?

→ **Yes**
If DTC P0500, GO to **F3**.

If DTC B1342, REPLACE the GEM. CLEAR the DTCs. TEST the system for normal operation.

→ **No**
GO to **F2**.

F2 CHECK THE PID SPEEDWP

2 Monitor the PID SPEEDWP.

- Does the PID SPEEDWP indicate ACTIVE?

→ **Yes**
GO to **F3**.

→ **No**
SET the active command SPD WIPER to ON. CLEAR the DTCs. TEST the system for normal operation.

F3 CHECK THE VEHICLE SPEED SENSOR

2 Monitor the PID VSS__GEM while driving the vehicle 0 to 55 mph.

- Do the PID VSS__GEM values agree with the vehicle speed?

→ **Yes**
REPLACE the GEM. CLEAR the DTCs. TEST the system for normal operation.

→ **No**
GO to **F4**.

FM9029700515010X

Fig. 10   Test F: Front Wiper Speed Dependent Interval Mode Does Not Operate (Part 1 of 4). 2002–04

F8 CHECK THE FUSE JUNCTION PANEL CIRCUIT – RETURN FROM VEHICLE SPEED SENSOR

2 Measure the resistance between fuse junction panel terminal 9 and fuse junction panel terminal 10.

- Is the resistance less than 5 ohms?

→ **Yes**
GO to **F9**.

→ **No**
REPAIR the fuse junction panel. CLEAR the DTCs. TEST the system for normal operation.

F9 CHECK THE FUSE JUNCTION PANEL CIRCUIT – FEED TO THE VEHICLE SPEED SENSOR

1 Measure the resistance between fuse junction panel terminal 21 and fuse junction panel terminal 18.

- Is the resistance less than 5 ohms?

→ **Yes**
REPLACE the vehicle speed sensor. CLEAR the DTCs. TEST the system for normal operation.

→ **No**
REPAIR the fuse junction panel. CLEAR the DTCs. TEST the system for normal operation.

FM9029700515040X

Fig. 10   Test F: Front Wiper Speed Dependent Interval Mode Does Not Operate (Part 4 of 4). 2002–04

F4 CHECK CIRCUIT 676 (PK/O) FOR OPEN

4 Measure the resistance between fuse junction panel C242-9, circuit 676 (PK/O), and vehicle speed sensor C186, circuit 676 (PK/O).

- Is the resistance less than 5 ohms?

→ **Yes**
GO to **F5**.

→ **No**
REPAIR circuit 676 (PK/O). CLEAR the DTCs. TEST the system for normal operation.

F5 CHECK CIRCUIT 679 (GY/BK) FOR OPEN

2 Measure the resistance between fuse junction panel C243-21, circuit 679 (GY/BK), and vehicle speed sensor C186, circuit 679 (GY/BK).

- Is the resistance less than 5 ohms?

→ **Yes**
GO to **F6**.

→ **No**
REPAIR circuit 679 (GY/BK). CLEAR the DTCs. TEST the system for normal operation.

FM9029700515020X

Fig. 10   Test F: Front Wiper Speed Dependent Interval Mode Does Not Operate (Part 2 of 4). 2002–04

F6 CHECK CIRCUIT 676 (PK/O) FOR CONTINUITY TO GROUND

1 Measure the resistance between fuse junction panel C242-9, circuit 676 (PK/O), and ground.

- Is the resistance less than 5 ohms?

→ **Yes**
GO to **F7**.

→ **No**
REPAIR circuit 676 (PK/O). CLEAR the DTCs. TEST the system for normal operation.

F7 CHECK CIRCUIT 679 (GY/BK) FOR SHORT TO GROUND

1 Measure the resistance between fuse junction panel C243-21, circuit 679 (GY/BK), and ground.

- Is the resistance greater than 10,000 ohms?

→ **Yes**
GO to **F8**.

→ **No**
REPAIR circuit 679 (GY/BK). CLEAR the DTCs. TEST the system for normal operation.

FM9029700515030X

Fig. 10   Test F: Front Wiper Speed Dependent Interval Mode Does Not Operate (Part 3 of 4). 2002–04

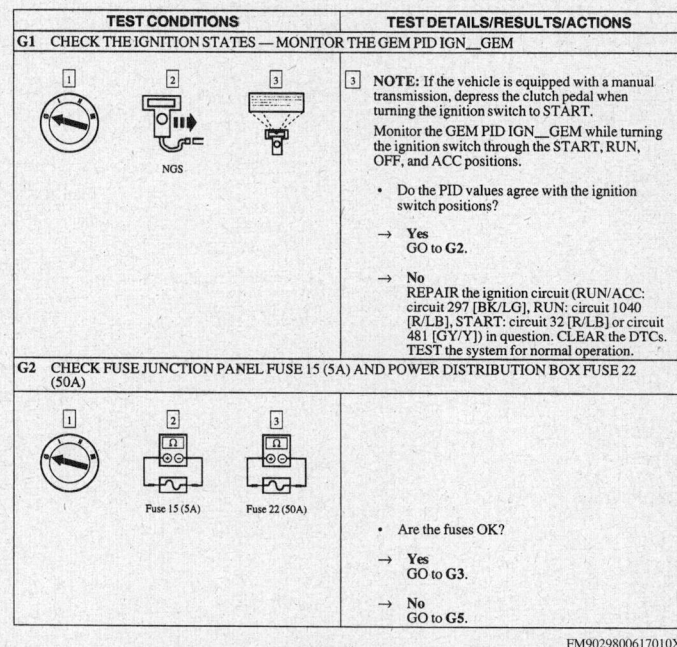

TEST CONDITIONS	TEST DETAILS/RESULTS/ACTIONS
G1 CHECK THE IGNITION STATES — MONITOR THE GEM PID IGN__GEM	
	3 **NOTE:** If the vehicle is equipped with a manual transmission, depress the clutch pedal when turning the ignition switch to START. Monitor the GEM PID IGN__GEM while turning the ignition switch through the START, RUN, OFF, and ACC positions. • Do the PID values agree with the ignition switch positions? → **Yes** GO to **G2**. → **No** REPAIR the ignition circuit (RUN/ACC: circuit 297 [BK/LG], RUN: circuit 1040 [R/LB], START: circuit 32 [R/LB] or circuit 481 [GY/Y]) in question. CLEAR the DTCs. TEST the system for normal operation.
G2 CHECK FUSE JUNCTION PANEL FUSE 15 (5A) AND POWER DISTRIBUTION BOX FUSE 22 (50A)	
	• Are the fuses OK? → **Yes** GO to **G3**. → **No** GO to **G5**.

FM9029800617010X

Fig. 11   Test G: No Communication w/GEM Module (Part 1 of 5). 2002–04 w/GEM

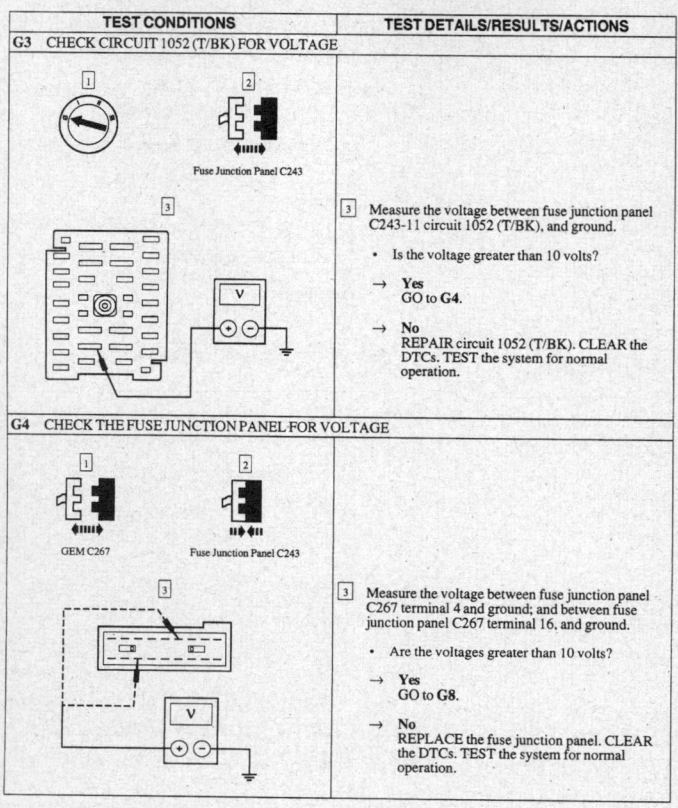

TEST CONDITIONS	TEST DETAILS/RESULTS/ACTIONS
G3 CHECK CIRCUIT 1052 (T/BK) FOR VOLTAGE	
Fuse Junction Panel C243	3 Measure the voltage between fuse junction panel C243-11 circuit 1052 (T/BK), and ground. • Is the voltage greater than 10 volts? → **Yes** GO to **G4**. → **No** REPAIR circuit 1052 (T/BK). CLEAR the DTCs. TEST the system for normal operation.
G4 CHECK THE FUSE JUNCTION PANEL FOR VOLTAGE	
GEM C267 Fuse Junction Panel C243	3 Measure the voltage between fuse junction panel C267 terminal 4 and ground; and between fuse junction panel C267 terminal 16, and ground. • Are the voltages greater than 10 volts? → **Yes** GO to **G8**. → **No** REPLACE the fuse junction panel. CLEAR the DTCs. TEST the system for normal operation.

FM9029800617020X

**Fig. 11   Test G: No Communication w/GEM Module
(Part 2 of 5). 2002–04 w/GEM**

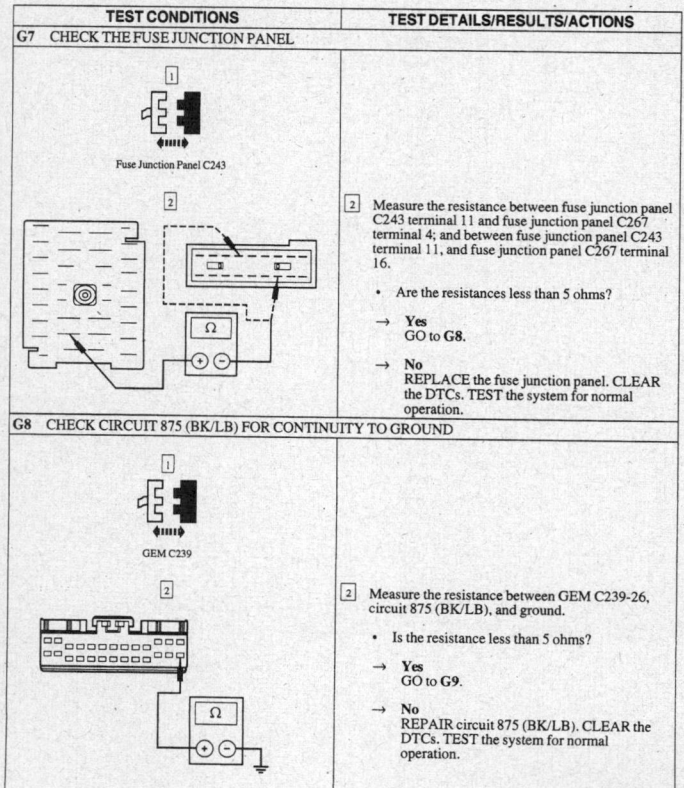

TEST CONDITIONS	TEST DETAILS/RESULTS/ACTIONS
G7 CHECK THE FUSE JUNCTION PANEL	
Fuse Junction Panel C243	2 Measure the resistance between fuse junction panel C243 terminal 11 and fuse junction panel C267 terminal 4; and between fuse junction panel C243 terminal 11, and fuse junction panel C267 terminal 16. • Are the resistances less than 5 ohms? → **Yes** GO to **G8**. → **No** REPLACE the fuse junction panel. CLEAR the DTCs. TEST the system for normal operation.
G8 CHECK CIRCUIT 875 (BK/LB) FOR CONTINUITY TO GROUND	
GEM C239	2 Measure the resistance between GEM C239-26, circuit 875 (BK/LB), and ground. • Is the resistance less than 5 ohms? → **Yes** GO to **G9**. → **No** REPAIR circuit 875 (BK/LB). CLEAR the DTCs. TEST the system for normal operation.

FM9029800617040X

**Fig. 11   Test G: No Communication w/GEM Module
(Part 4 of 5). 2002–04 w/GEM**

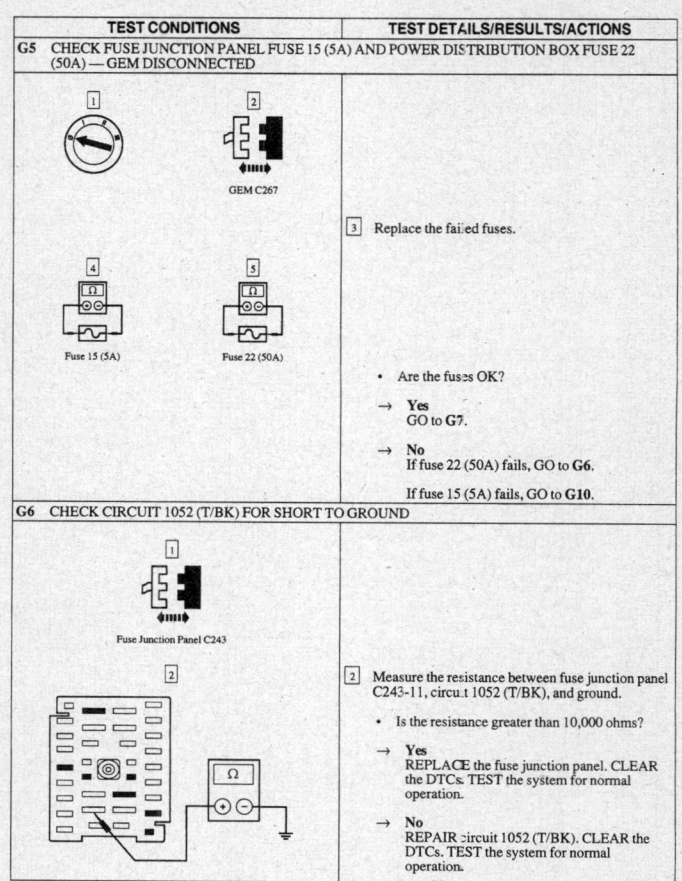

TEST CONDITIONS	TEST DETAILS/RESULTS/ACTIONS
G5 CHECK FUSE JUNCTION PANEL FUSE 15 (5A) AND POWER DISTRIBUTION BOX FUSE 22 (50A) — GEM DISCONNECTED	
GEM C267 Fuse 15 (5A) Fuse 22 (50A)	3 Replace the failed fuses. • Are the fuses OK? → **Yes** GO to **G7**. → **No** If fuse 22 (50A) fails, GO to **G6**. If fuse 15 (5A) fails, GO to **G10**.
G6 CHECK CIRCUIT 1052 (T/BK) FOR SHORT TO GROUND	
Fuse Junction Panel C243	2 Measure the resistance between fuse junction panel C243-11, circuit 1052 (T/BK), and ground. • Is the resistance greater than 10,000 ohms? → **Yes** REPLACE the fuse junction panel. CLEAR the DTCs. TEST the system for normal operation. → **No** REPAIR circuit 1052 (T/BK). CLEAR the DTCs. TEST the system for normal operation.

FM9029800617030X

**Fig. 11   Test G: No Communication w/GEM Module
(Part 3 of 5). 2002–04 w/GEM**

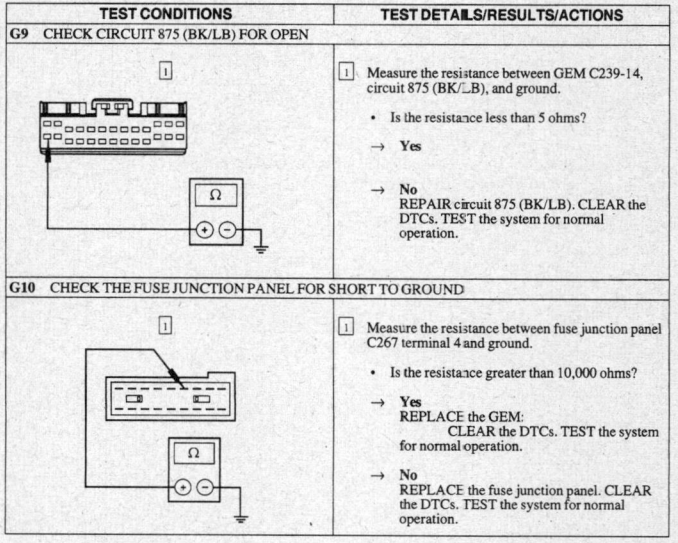

TEST CONDITIONS	TEST DETAILS/RESULTS/ACTIONS
G9 CHECK CIRCUIT 875 (BK/LB) FOR OPEN	
	1 Measure the resistance between GEM C239-14, circuit 875 (BK/LB), and ground. • Is the resistance less than 5 ohms? → **Yes** → **No** REPAIR circuit 875 (BK/LB). CLEAR the DTCs. TEST the system for normal operation.
G10 CHECK THE FUSE JUNCTION PANEL FOR SHORT TO GROUND	
	1 Measure the resistance between fuse junction panel C267 terminal 4 and ground. • Is the resistance greater than 10,000 ohms? → **Yes** REPLACE the GEM: CLEAR the DTCs. TEST the system for normal operation. → **No** REPLACE the fuse junction panel. CLEAR the DTCs. TEST the system for normal operation.

FM9029800617050X

**Fig. 11   Test G: No Communication w/GEM Module
(Part 5 of 5). 2002–04 w/GEM**

G1   CHECK THE VOLTAGE FROM FUSES 12 (20A) AND 15 (5A)

2   Measure the voltage between fuse 12 (20A), pin 1 of the power distribution box, fuse 15 (5A), pin 1 of the fuse junction panel and ground.

- Are the voltages greater than 10 volts?
- →   **Yes**
       GO to **G2**.
- →   **No**
       REPLACE the fuse(s) in question or REPAIR circuit(s) 1052 (T/BK) and/or circuit 406 (BR/W). CLEAR the DTCs. TEST the system for normal operation. If the fuse(s) fail again, CHECK for a short to ground. REPAIR as necessary.

G2   CHECK THE IGNITION STATES

2   Monitor the PID IGN__GEM while turning the ignition switch through the START, RUN, OFF, and ACC positions.

- Do the PID values agree with the ignition switch positions?
- →   **Yes**
       GO to **G3**.
- →   **No**
       REPAIR the ignition circuit (RUN/ACC: circuit 297 [BK/LG], RUN: circuit 1040 [R/LB], START: circuit 32 [R/LB or circuit 481 [GY/Y]) in question. CLEAR the DTCs. TEST the system for normal operation.

FM9029700516010X

Fig. 12   Test G: Rear Wiper Does Not Move In Any Mode Of Operation (Part 1 of 13). 2002–04

G7   CHECK THE REAR WIPER SWITCH OUTPUTS

1   Monitor the PID R__WP__MD while turning the rear wiper switch through all positions.

- Does the PID R__WP__MD value agree with all the rear wiper switch positions?
- →   **Yes**
       GO to **G14**.
- →   **No**
       GO to **G8**.

G8   CHECK THE REAR WIPER/WASHER SWITCH

2   Measure the resistance between multi-function switch C258 terminal 380 and C259 terminal 993 (refer to Pinpoint Test F) while turning the rear wiper switch through all positions. The resistance should be as follows:

Switch Position	Expected Value
OFF	2850-3150 ohms
INTERVAL 1	950-1050 ohms
INTERVAL 2	310-350 ohms
WASH	0-40 ohms

- Do the measured values agree with values above?
- →   **Yes**
       GO to **G9**.
- →   **No**
       REPLACE the multi-function switch. CLEAR the DTCs. TEST the system for normal operation.

FM9029700516040X

Fig. 12   Test G: Rear Wiper Does Not Move In Any Mode Of Operation (Part 4 of 13). 2002–04

G3   RETRIEVE DIAGNOSTIC TROUBLE CODES

- Are any DTCs recorded?
- →   **Yes**
       If DTC B1334, GO to **G4**.
       If DTC B1611, GO to **G7**.
       If DTC B1814, GO to **G13**.
       If DTC B1816, GO to **G13**.
       If DTC B1818, GO to **G13**.
       If DTC B1820, GO to **G13**.
       If DTC B1342, REPLACE the GEM. CLEAR the DTCs. TEST the system for normal operation.
- →   **No**
       GO to **G4**.

G4   CHECK THE LIFTGATE AJAR STATES

1   Monitor the PID LGATE__SW.
2   Open and close the liftgate.
3   Open and close the liftgate glass.

- Does the PID LGATE__SW indicate CLOSED when both are closed?
- →   **Yes**
       GO to **G7**.
- →   **No**
       GO to **G5**.

FM9029700516020X

Fig. 12   Test G: Rear Wiper Does Not Move In Any Mode Of Operation (Part 2 of 13). 2002–04

G9   CHECK CIRCUIT 485 (PK/BK) FOR OPEN

3   Measure the resistance between GEM C240-12, circuit 485 (PK/BK), and multi-function switch C258-485, circuit 485 (PK/BK).

- Is the resistance less than 5 ohms?
- →   **Yes**
       GO to **G10**.
- →   **No**
       REPAIR circuit 485 (PK/BK). CLEAR the DTCs. TEST the system for normal operation.

G10   CHECK CIRCUIT 485 (PK/BK) FOR SHORT TO POWER

2   Measure the voltage between GEM C240-12, circuit 485 (PK/BK), and ground.

- Is any voltage indicated?
- →   **Yes**
       REPAIR circuit 485(PK/BK). CLEAR the DTCs. TEST the system for normal operation.
- →   **No**
       GO to **G11**.

FM9029700516050X

Fig. 12   Test G: Rear Wiper Does Not Move In Any Mode Of Operation (Part 5 of 13). 2002–04

G5   CHECK THE LIFTGATE AJAR SWITCHES

3   Monitor the PID LGATE__SW.

- Does the PID LGATE__SW indicate CLOSED when both switches are removed?
- →   **Yes**
       REPLACE the switch in question. CLEAR the DTCs. TEST the system for normal operation.
- →   **No**
       GO to **G6**.

G6   CHECK CIRCUIT 700 (W/P) FOR SHORT TO GROUND

4   Measure the resistance between GEM C239-4, circuit 700 (W/P), and ground.

- Is the resistance greater than 10,000 ohms?
- →   **Yes**
       REPLACE the GEM. CLEAR the DTCs. TEST the system for normal operation.
- →   **No**
       REPAIR circuit 700 (W/P). CLEAR the DTCs. TEST the system for normal operation.

FM9029700516030X

Fig. 12   Test G: Rear Wiper Does Not Move In Any Mode Of Operation (Part 3 of 13). 2002–04

G11   CHECK CIRCUIT 485 (PK/BK) FOR SHORT TO GROUND

1   Measure the resistance between GEM C240-12, circuit 485 (PK/BK), and ground.

- Is the resistance greater than 10,000 ohms?
- →   **Yes**
       GO to **G12**.
- →   **No**
       REPAIR circuit 485 (PK/BK). CLEAR the DTCs. TEST the system for normal operation.

G12   CHECK CIRCUIT 682 (DB) FOR OPEN

1   Measure the resistance between GEM C239-21, circuit 682 (DB), and multi-function switch C259-682, circuit 682 (DB).

- Is the resistance less than 5 ohms?
- →   **Yes**
       REPLACE the GEM. CLEAR the DTCs. TEST the system for normal operation.
- →   **No**
       REPAIR circuit 682 (DB). CLEAR the DTCs. TEST the system for normal operation.

G13   CHECK THE REAR WIPER UP AND DOWN RELAY COIL CIRCUITS

1   Monitor the PIDs R__WP__UP and R__WP__DN while toggling the active commands UP RELAY and DWN RELAY ON and OFF.

- Do the PIDs R__WP__UP and R__WP__DN agree with the command mode?
- →   **Yes**
       If the PIDs R__WP__UP and R__WP__DN display ON -- and OFF --, GO to **G23**.
- →   **No**
       If the PIDs R__WP__UP and/or R__WP__DN display OFF O-G, GO to **G14**.
       If the PIDs R__WP__UP and/or R__WP__DN display ON-B-, GO to **G20**.

FM9029700516060X

Fig. 12   Test G: Rear Wiper Does Not Move In Any Mode Of Operation (Part 6 of 13). 2002–04

G14   CHECK THE VOLTAGE TO THE REAR WIPER UP AND DOWN RELAY COILS

3   Measure the voltage between rear wiper up relay connector pin 1, circuit 705 (LG/O), and ground, and between rear wiper down relay connector pin 1, circuit 705 (LG/O), and ground.

- Are the voltages greater than 10 volts?

→ **Yes**
GO to **G15**.

→ **No**
REPAIR circuit 705 (LG/O). CLEAR the DTCs. TEST the system for normal operation.

G15   CHECK REAR WIPER UP RELAY AND REAR WIPER DOWN RELAY COILS

1   Check the rear wiper up and down relays.

- Are the rear wiper up and down relays OK?

→ **Yes**
GO to **G16**.

→ **No**
REPLACE the relay in question. CLEAR the DTCs. TEST the system for normal operation.

FM9029700516070X

Fig. 12   Test G: Rear Wiper Does Not Move In Any Mode Of Operation (Part 7 of 13). 2002–04

G16   CHECK CIRCUIT 591 (LG) FOR OPEN

2   Measure the resistance between rear wiper up relay connector pin 2, circuit 591 (LG), and GEM C240-8, circuit 591 (LG).

- Is the resistance less than 5 ohms?

→ **Yes**
GO to **G17**.

→ **No**
REPAIR circuit 591 (LG). CLEAR the DTCs. TEST the system for normal operation.

G17   CHECK CIRCUIT 592 (T) FOR OPEN

1   Measure the resistance between rear wiper down relay connector pin 2, circuit 592 (T), and GEM C240-10, circuit 592 (T).

- Is the resistance less than 5 ohms?

→ **Yes**
GO to **G18**.

→ **No**
REPAIR circuit 592 (T). CLEAR the DTCs. TEST the system for normal operation.

FM9029700516080X

Fig. 12   Test G: Rear Wiper Does Not Move In Any Mode Of Operation (Part 8 of 13). 2002–04

G18   CHECK CIRCUIT 591 (LG) FOR SHORT TO GROUND

1   Measure resistance between rear wiper up relay connector pin 2, circuit 591 (LG) and ground.

- Is the resistance greater than 10,000 ohms?

→ **Yes**
GO to **G19**.

→ **No**
REPAIR circuit 591 (LG). CLEAR the DTCs. TEST the system for normal operation.

G19   CHECK CIRCUIT 592 (T) FOR SHORT TO GROUND

1   Measure the resistance between rear wiper down relay connector pin 2, circuit 592 (T), and ground.

- Is the resistance greater than 10,000 ohms?

→ **Yes**
REPLACE the GEM. CLEAR the DTCs. TEST the system for normal operation.

→ **No**
REPAIR circuit 592 (T). CLEAR the DTCs. TEST the system for normal operation.

G20   CHECK THE REAR WIPER UP RELAY AND REAR WIPER DOWN RELAYS

1   Check the rear wiper up and down relays.

- Are the rear wiper up and down relays OK?

→ **Yes**
GO to **G21**.

→ **No**
REPLACE the relay in question. CLEAR the DTCs. TEST the system for normal operation.

FM9029700516090X

Fig. 12   Test G: Rear Wiper Does Not Move In Any Mode Of Operation (Part 9 of 13). 2002–04

G21   CHECK CIRCUIT 591 (LG) FOR SHORT TO POWER

4   Measure the voltage between rear wiper up relay connector pin 2, circuit 591 (LG), and ground.

- Is any voltage indicated?

→ **Yes**
REPAIR circuit 591 (LG). CLEAR the DTCs. TEST the system for normal operation.

→ **No**
GO to **G22**.

G22   CHECK CIRCUIT 592 (T) FOR SHORT TO POWER

4   Measure the voltage between rear wiper down relay connector pin 2, circuit 592 (T), and ground.

- Is any voltage indicated?

→ **Yes**
REPAIR circuit 592 (T). CLEAR the DTCs. TEST the system for normal operation.

→ **No**
REPLACE the GEM. CLEAR the DTCs. TEST the system for normal operation.

FM9029700516100X

Fig. 12   Test G: Rear Wiper Does Not Move In Any Mode Of Operation (Part 10 of 13). 2002–04

G23   CHECK THE REAR WIPER UP AND REAR WIPER DOWN RELAYS

1   Check the rear wiper up and down relays.

- Are the rear wiper up and down relays OK?

→ **Yes**
GO to **G24**.

→ **No**
REPLACE the relay in question. CLEAR the DTCs. TEST the system for normal operation.

G24   CHECK CIRCUIT 406 (BR/W) FOR VOLTAGE TO THE REAR WIPER DOWN RELAY — SWITCH SIDE

1   Measure the voltage between rear wiper down relay connector pin 5, circuit 406 (BR/W), and ground.

- Is the voltage greater than 10 volts?

→ **Yes**
GO to **G25**.

→ **No**
REPAIR circuit 406 (BR/W). CLEAR the DTCs. TEST the system for normal operation.

G25   CHECK CIRCUIT 406 (BR/W) FOR VOLTAGE TO THE REAR WIPER UP RELAY — SWITCH SIDE

1   Measure the voltage between rear wiper up relay connector pin 5, circuit 406 (BR/W), and ground.

- Is the voltage greater than 10 volts?

→ **Yes**
GO to **G26**.

→ **No**
REPAIR circuit 406 (BR/W). CLEAR the DTCs. TEST the system for normal operation.

FM9029700516110X

Fig. 12   Test G: Rear Wiper Does Not Move In Any Mode Of Operation (Part 11 of 13). 2002–04

G26   CHECK THE GROUND TO THE REAR WIPER DOWN RELAY FOR OPEN

1   Measure the resistance between rear wiper down relay connector pin 4, circuit 57 (BK), and ground.

- Is the resistance less than 5 ohms?

→ **Yes**
GO to **G27**.

→ **No**
REPAIR circuit 57 (BK). CLEAR the DTCs. TEST the system for normal operation.

G27   CHECK THE GROUND TO THE REAR WIPER UP RELAY FOR OPEN

1   Measure the resistance between rear wiper up relay connector pin 4, circuit 57 (BK), and ground.

- Is the resistance less than 5 ohms?

→ **Yes**
GO to **G28**.

→ **No**
REPAIR circuit 57 (BK). CLEAR the DTCs. TEST the system for normal operation.

FM9029700516120X

Fig. 12   Test G: Rear Wiper Does Not Move In Any Mode Of Operation (Part 12 of 13). 2002–04

G28　CHECK CIRCUIT 410 (W/O) FOR OPEN

2 Measure the resistance between rear wiper up relay connector pin 3, circuit 410 (W/O), and rear wiper motor C417, circuit 410 (BK/LB).

- Is the resistance less than 5 ohms?

→ **Yes**
GO to **G29**.

→ **No**
REPAIR circuit 410 (W/O). CLEAR the DTCs. TEST the system for normal operation.

G29　CHECK CIRCUIT 411 (BK/LB) FOR OPEN

1 Measure the resistance between rear wiper down relay connector pin 3, circuit 411 (BK/LB), and rear wiper motor C417-2, circuit 411 (BK/LB).

- Is the resistance less than 5 ohms?

→ **Yes**
REPLACE the rear wiper motor. CLEAR the DTCs. TEST the system for normal operation.

→ **No**
REPAIR circuit 411 (BK/LB). CLEAR the DTCs. TEST the system for normal operation.

FM9029700516130X

Fig. 12　Test G: Rear Wiper Does Not Move In Any Mode Of Operation (Part 13 of 13). 2002–04

H4　CHECK CIRCUIT 587 (PK/Y) FOR SHORT TO GROUND

3 Measure the resistance between rear wiper motor C417-3, circuit 587 (P/Y), and ground.

- Is the resistance greater than 10,000 ohms?

→ **Yes**
REPLACE the GEM. CLEAR the DTCs. TEST the system for normal operation.

→ **No**
REPAIR circuit 587 (P/Y). CLEAR the DTCs. TEST the system for normal operation.

H5　CHECK CIRCUIT 57 (BK) FOR OPEN

3 Measure the resistance between rear wiper motor C417-4, circuit 57 (BK), and ground.

- Is the resistance less than 5 ohms?

→ **Yes**
GO to **H6**.

→ **No**
REPAIR circuit 57 (BK). CLEAR the DTCs. TEST the system for normal operation.

FM9029700517030X

Fig. 13　Test H: Rear Wiper Parks Off Glass Between Wipes When In Interval Mode (Part 3 of 5). 2002–04

H1　RETRIEVE THE DIAGNOSTIC TROUBLE CODES

- Are any DTC recorded?

→ **Yes**
If DTC B1839, GO to **H2**.

If DTC B1342, REPLACE the GEM. CLEAR the DTCs. TEST the system for normal operation.

→ **No**
GO to **H2**.

FM9029700517010X

Fig. 13　Test H: Rear Wiper Parks Off Glass Between Wipes When In Interval Mode (Part 1 of 5). 2002–04

H6　CHECK REAR WIPER MOTOR SWITCH FOR OPEN

2 Connect a jumper wire between rear wiper motor C417-3, circuit 587 (P/Y), and C417-4, circuit 57 (BK).

3 Monitor the PID R__WP__PK.

- Does the PID R__WP__PK indicate PARK?

→ **Yes**
REPLACE the rear wiper motor. CLEAR the DTCs. TEST the system for normal operation.

→ **No**
GO to **H7**.

FM9029700517040X

Fig. 13　Test H: Rear Wiper Parks Off Glass Between Wipes When In Interval Mode (Part 4 of 5). 2002–04

H7　CHECK CIRCUIT 587 (P/Y) FOR OPEN

3 Measure the resistance between rear wiper motor C417-3, circuit 587 (P/Y), and GEM C240-7, circuit 587 (P/Y).

- Is the resistance less than 5 ohms?

→ **Yes**
REPLACE the GEM. CLEAR the DTCs. TEST the system for normal operation.

→ **No**
REPAIR circuit 587 (P/Y). CLEAR the DTCs. TEST the system for normal operation.

FM9029700517050X

Fig. 13　Test H: Rear Wiper Parks Off Glass Between Wipes When In Interval Mode (Part 5 of 5). 2002–04

H2　CHECK THE PID R__WP__PK

1 **NOTE:** The PID R__WP__PK should indicate park when at the high limit of travel and any position between the parked position and low limit of travel (on glass). When the blade is between the high and low limits of travel, the PID R__WP__PK should indicate ''no park.''

Monitor the PID R__WP__PK while the wipers are moving.

- Does the PID R__WP__PK change between PARK and no PARK as expected?

→ **Yes**
CHECK wiper arm to motor shaft for proper alignment.

→ **No**
If the PID R__WP__PK always indicates PARK, GO to **H3**.

If the PID R__WP__PK always indicates no PARK, GO to **H5**.

If the PID R__WP__PK changes values, but does not correspond with the intended operation, CHECK the wiper arm for proper alignment with the motor. If OK, REPLACE the wiper motor. TEST the system for normal operation.

H3　CHECK THE REAR WINDOW MOTOR SWITCH

2 Monitor the PID R__W__PK.

- Does the PID still indicate PARK?

→ **Yes**
GO to **H4**.

→ **No**
REPLACE the rear wiper motor. CLEAR the DTCs. TEST the system for normal operation.

FM9029700517020X

Fig. 13　Test H: Rear Wiper Parks Off Glass Between Wipes When In Interval Mode (Part 2 of 5). 2002–04

CONDITIONS	DETAILS/RESULTS/ACTIONS
J1 VERIFY THE OPERATION OF THE FRONT WASHER PUMP	
	Verify the operation of the front windshield washer pump.
	• Does the front windshield washer operate properly?
	→ Yes GO to J2.
	→ No GO to Pinpoint Test E.
J2 RETRIEVE THE DIAGNOSTIC TROUBLE CODES (DTCS)	
	Diagnostic Tool
	Retrieve and Document Continuous DTCs
	Clear Continuous DTCs

LTV0500000015001

Fig. 14　Test J: Rear Washer Pump Function Does Not Operate Properly, Other Wiper Functions Do Operate (Part 1 of 8). 2002–04

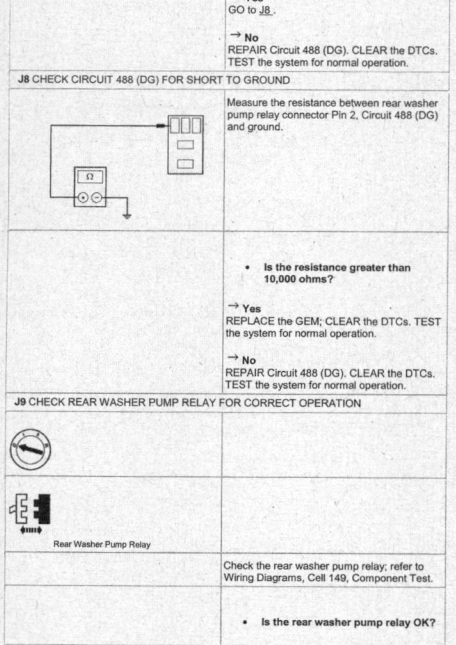

On-Demand Self-Test

Rear Wiper Self-Test

• Are any DTCs retrieved?

→ Yes
If DTC B1240, GO to J4.

If DTC B1241 GO to J4.

If DTC B1342, REPLACE the GEM; CLEAR the DTCs. TEST the system for normal operation.

→ No
GO to J3.

J3 CHECK THE REAR WIPER/WASHER SWITCH — MONITOR THE PID R_WP_MD

Monitor the PID R_WP_MD while activating the rear wash switch.

• Does the PID R_WP_MD indicate WASH when the switch is activated?

→ Yes
GO to J4.

→ No
REPLACE the multifunction switch; CLEAR the DTCs. TEST the system for normal operation.

J4 CHECK THE REAR WASHER PUMP RELAY COIL CIRCUIT — MONITOR THE PID RWASHSW

Monitor the PID RWASHSW while toggling the active command WASHRLY to ON and OFF.

LTV0500000015002

Fig. 14 Test J: Rear Washer Pump Function Does Not Operate Properly, Other Wiper Functions Do Operate (Part 2 of 8). 2002–04

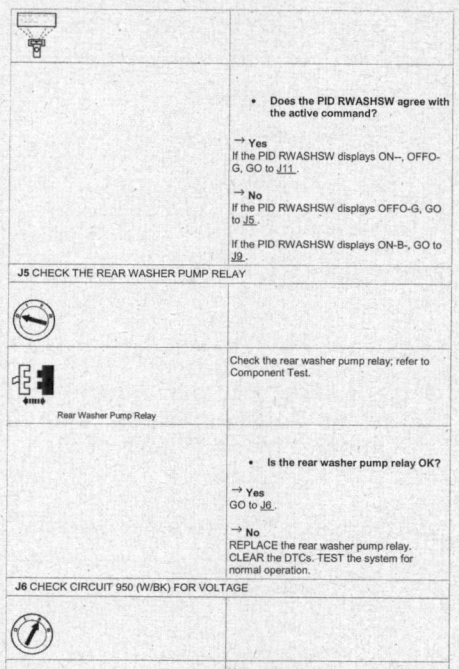

• Does the PID RWASHSW agree with the active command?

→ Yes
If the PID RWASHSW displays ON–, OFFO-G, GO to J11.

→ No
If the PID RWASHSW displays OFFO-G, GO to J5.

If the PID RWASHSW displays ON-B-, GO to J9.

J5 CHECK THE REAR WASHER PUMP RELAY

Rear Washer Pump Relay

Check the rear washer pump relay; refer to Component Test.

• Is the rear washer pump relay OK?

→ Yes
GO to J6.

→ No
REPLACE the rear washer pump relay. CLEAR the DTCs. TEST the system for normal operation.

J6 CHECK CIRCUIT 950 (W/BK) FOR VOLTAGE

Measure the voltage between rear washer

LTV0500000015003

Fig. 14 Test J: Rear Washer Pump Function Does Not Operate Properly, Other Wiper Functions Do Operate (Part 3 of 8). 2002–04

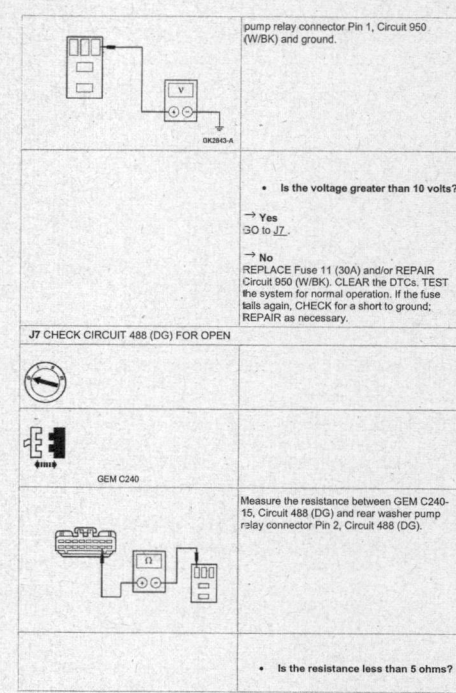

pump relay connector Pin 1, Circuit 950 (W/BK) and ground.

OK2843-A

• Is the voltage greater than 10 volts?

→ Yes
GO to J7.

→ No
REPLACE Fuse 11 (30A) and/or REPAIR Circuit 950 (W/BK). CLEAR the DTCs. TEST the system for normal operation. If the fuse fails again, CHECK for a short to ground; REPAIR as necessary.

J7 CHECK CIRCUIT 488 (DG) FOR OPEN

GEM C240

Measure the resistance between GEM C240-15, Circuit 488 (DG) and rear washer pump relay connector Pin 2, Circuit 488 (DG).

• Is the resistance less than 5 ohms?

LTV0500000015004

Fig. 14 Test J: Rear Washer Pump Function Does Not Operate Properly, Other Wiper Functions Do Operate (Part 4 of 8). 2002–04

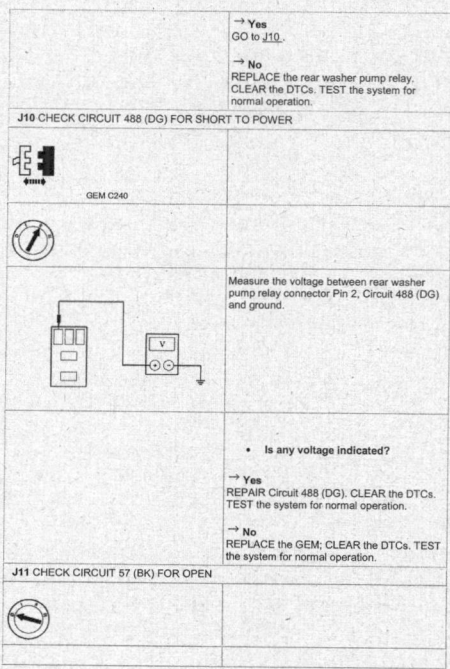

→ Yes
GO to J8.

→ No
REPAIR Circuit 488 (DG). CLEAR the DTCs. TEST the system for normal operation.

J8 CHECK CIRCUIT 488 (DG) FOR SHORT TO GROUND

Measure the resistance between rear washer pump relay connector Pin 2, Circuit 488 (DG) and ground.

• Is the resistance greater than 10,000 ohms?

→ Yes
REPLACE the GEM; CLEAR the DTCs. TEST the system for normal operation.

→ No
REPAIR Circuit 488 (DG). CLEAR the DTCs. TEST the system for normal operation.

J9 CHECK REAR WASHER PUMP RELAY FOR CORRECT OPERATION

Rear Washer Pump Relay

Check the rear washer pump relay; refer to Wiring Diagrams, Cell 149, Component Test.

• Is the rear washer pump relay OK?

LTV0500000015005

Fig. 14 Test J: Rear Washer Pump Function Does Not Operate Properly, Other Wiper Functions Do Operate (Part 5 of 8). 2002–04

→ Yes
GO to J10.

→ No
REPLACE the rear washer pump relay. CLEAR the DTCs. TEST the system for normal operation.

J10 CHECK CIRCUIT 488 (DG) FOR SHORT TO POWER

GEM C240

Measure the voltage between rear washer pump relay connector Pin 2, Circuit 488 (DG) and ground.

• Is any voltage indicated?

→ Yes
REPAIR Circuit 488 (DG). CLEAR the DTCs. TEST the system for normal operation.

→ No
REPLACE the GEM; CLEAR the DTCs. TEST the system for normal operation.

J11 CHECK CIRCUIT 57 (BK) FOR OPEN

LTV0500000015006

Fig. 14 Test J: Rear Washer Pump Function Does Not Operate Properly, Other Wiper Functions Do Operate (Part 6 of 8). 2002–04

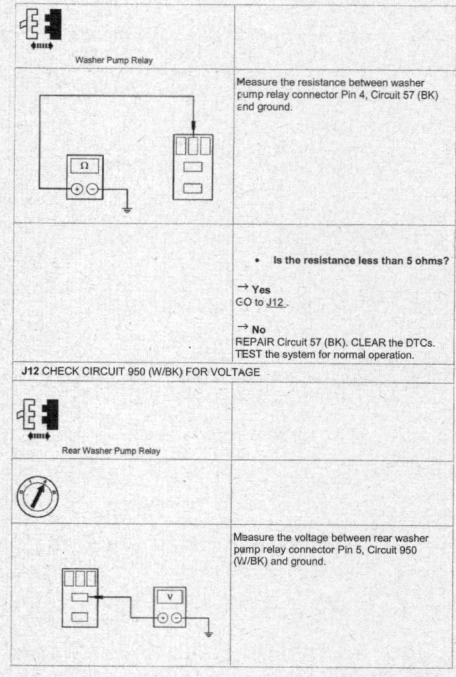

Washer Pump Relay

Measure the resistance between washer pump relay connector Pin 4, Circuit 57 (BK) and ground.

• Is the resistance less than 5 ohms?

→ Yes
GO to J12.

→ No
REPAIR Circuit 57 (BK). CLEAR the DTCs. TEST the system for normal operation.

J12 CHECK CIRCUIT 950 (W/BK) FOR VOLTAGE

Rear Washer Pump Relay

Measure the voltage between rear washer pump relay connector Pin 5, Circuit 950 (W/BK) and ground.

LTV0500000015007

Fig. 14 Test J: Rear Washer Pump Function Does Not Operate Properly, Other Wiper Functions Do Operate (Part 7 of 8). 2002–04

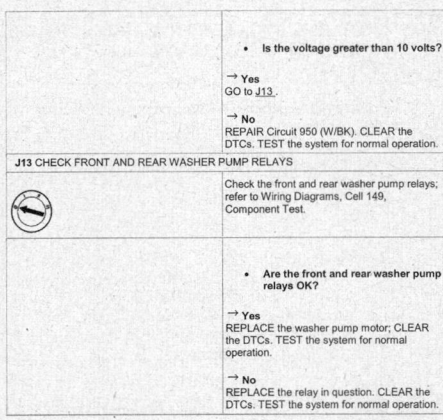

	• Is the voltage greater than 10 volts?
	→ **Yes** GO to J13.
	→ **No** REPAIR Circuit 950 (W/BK). CLEAR the DTCs. TEST the system for normal operation.
J13 CHECK FRONT AND REAR WASHER PUMP RELAYS	
	Check the front and rear washer pump relays; refer to Wiring Diagrams, Cell 149, Component Test.
	• Are the front and rear washer pump relays OK?
	→ **Yes** REPLACE the washer pump motor; CLEAR the DTCs. TEST the system for normal operation.
	→ **No** REPLACE the relay in question. CLEAR the DTCs. TEST the system for normal operation.

LTV0500000015008

Fig. 14 Test J: Rear Washer Pump Function Does Not Operate Properly, Other Wiper Functions Do Operate (Part 8 of 8). 2002–04

L1 CHECK THE IGNITION STATES
1 Monitor the PID IGN__GEM while turning the ignition switch through the START, RUN, OFF, and ACC positions.
• Do the PID values agree with the ignition switch positions?
→ **Yes** GO to L2.
→ **No** REPAIR the ignition circuit (RUN/ACC: circuit 297 [BK/LG], RUN: circuit 1040 [R/LB, START: circuit 32 [R/LB] or circuit 481 [GY/Y]) in question. CLEAR the DTCs. TEST the system for normal operation.
L2 RETRIEVE THE DIAGNOSTIC TROUBLE
• Are any DTCs retrieved?
→ **Yes** If DTC B1454, GO to Pinpoint Test M. If DTC B1456, GO to Pinpoint Test M. If DTC B1342, REPLACE the GEM. CLEAR the DTCs. TEST the system for normal operation.
→ **No** GO to L3.
L3 CHECK THE LOW WASHER FLUID WARNING INDICATOR SWITCH
2 Monitor the PID WFLUID.

FM9029700520010X

Fig. 16 Test L: Low Washer Fluid Warning Does Not Operate Properly, Washer Pump Operation Satisfactory (Part 1 of 3). 2002–04

K1 RETRIEVE THE DIAGNOSTIC TROUBLE CODES (DTCs)
1 Place the rear wiper switch in the OFF position.
• Are DTCs retrieved?
→ **Yes** If DTC B1614, GO to K2. If DTC B1342, REPLACE the GEM. CLEAR the DTCs. TEST the system for normal operation.
→ **No** GO to K2.

FM9029700519010X

Fig. 15 Test K: Rear Wiper Stays On Continuously (Part 1 of 2). 2002–04

L3 CHECK THE LOW WASHER FLUID WARNING INDICATOR SWITCH (Continued)
3 Connect then remove a jumper wire between low washer fluid warning indicator switch C198, circuit 81 (R/LG), and C198, circuit 57 (BK).
• Does the PID WFLUID indicate LOW when connected and OK when disconnected?
→ **Yes** REPLACE the low washer fluid warning indicator switch. CLEAR the DTCs. TEST the system for normal operation.
→ **No** GO to L4.
L4 CHECK CIRCUIT 57 (BK) FOR OPEN
1 Measure the resistance between low washer fluid warning indicator switch C198, circuit 57 (BK), and ground.
• Is the resistance less than 5 ohms?
→ **Yes** GO to L5.
→ **No** REPAIR circuit 57 (BK). CLEAR the DTCs. TEST the system for normal operation.

FM9029700520020X

Fig. 16 Test L: Low Washer Fluid Warning Does Not Operate Properly, Washer Pump Operation Satisfactory (Part 2 of 3). 2002–04

K2 CHECK THE REAR WIPER SWITCH
3 Measure the resistance between multi-function switch terminal 380 and terminal 993.
• Is the resistance approximately 2900 ohms?
→ **Yes** GO to K3.
→ **No** REPLACE the multi-function switch. CLEAR the DTCs. TEST the system for normal operation.
K3 CHECK CIRCUIT 485 (PK/BK) FOR A SHORT TO GROUND
2 Measure the resistance between multi-function switch C258-485, circuit 485 (PK/BK), and ground.
• Is the resistance greater than 10,000 ohms?
→ **Yes** REPLACE the GEM. CLEAR the DTCs. TEST the system for normal operation.
→ **No** REPAIR circuit 485 (PK/BK). CLEAR the DTCs. TEST the system for normal operation.

FM9029700519020X

Fig. 15 Test K: Rear Wiper Stays On Continuously (Part 2 of 2). 2002–04

L5 CHECK CIRCUIT 81 (R/LG) FOR OPEN
3 Measure the resistance between GEM C240-16, circuit 81 (R/LG), and low washer fluid warning indicator switch C198, circuit 81 (R/LG).
• Is the resistance less than 5 ohms?
→ **Yes** GO to L6.
→ **No** REPAIR circuit 81 (R/LG). CLEAR the DTCs. TEST the system for normal operation.
L6 CHECK CIRCUIT 81 (R/LG) FOR SHORT TO GROUND
1 Measure the resistance between GEM C240-16, circuit 81 (R/LG), and ground.
• Is the resistance greater than 10,000 ohms?
→ **Yes** REPLACE the GEM. CLEAR the DTCs. TEST the system for normal operation.
→ **No** REPAIR circuit 81 (R/LG). CLEAR the DTCs. TEST the system for normal operation.

FM9029700520030X

Fig. 16 Test L: Low Washer Fluid Warning Does Not Operate Properly, Washer Pump Operation Satisfactory (Part 3 of 3). 2002–04

M1	CHECK FUSES 15 (5A) AND 29 (5A)

- Are the fuses OK?

→ **Yes**
GO to **M2**.

→ **No**
REPLACE the fuse(s). CLEAR the DTCs.
TEST the system for proper operation. If the
fuse(s) fail again, CHECK for a short to
ground. REPAIR as necessary.

M2	CHECK THE IGNITION STATES

3 Monitor the PID IGN__GEM while turning the
ignition switch through the START, RUN, OFF
and ACC positions.
- Do the PID values agree with the ignition
switch positions?

→ **Yes**
GO to **M3**.

→ **No**
REPAIR the ignition circuit (RUN/ACC:
circuit 297 [BK/LG], RUN: circuit 1040
[R/LB], START: circuit: 32 [R/LB], or circuit
441 [GY/Y]) in question. CLEAR DTCs.
TEST the system for proper operation.

FM9029700521010X

**Fig. 17 Test M: Low Washer Fluid
Warning Indicator Does Not
Operate (Part 1 of 5). 2002–04**

M6	CHECK CIRCUIT 82 (PK/Y) FOR OPEN

2 Measure the resistance between GEM C240-14,
circuit 82 (PK/Y), and instrument cluster C236-2,
circuit 82 (PK/Y).
- Is the resistance less than 5 ohms?

→ **Yes**
GO to **M8**.

→ **No**
REPAIR circuit 82 (PK/Y). CLEAR the
DTCs. TEST the system for normal
operation.

M7	CHECK CIRCUIT 82 (PK/Y) FOR SHORT TO POWER

1 Measure the voltage between GEM C240-14,
circuit 82 (PK/Y), and ground.
- Is any voltage indicated?

→ **Yes**
REPAIR circuit 82 (PK/Y). CLEAR DTCs.
TEST the system for proper operation.

→ **No**
REPLACE the GEM. CLEAR DTCs. TEST
the system for proper operation.

FM9029700521040X

**Fig. 17 Test M: Low Washer Fluid
Warning Indicator Does Not
Operate (Part 4 of 5). 2002–04**

M8	CHECK CIRCUIT 82 (PK/Y) FOR SHORT TO POWER

5 Measure the voltage between GEM C240-14,
circuit 82 (PK/Y), and ground.
- Is any voltage indicated?

→ **Yes**
REPAIR circuit 82 (PK/Y). CLEAR DTCs.
TEST the system for proper operation.

→ **No**
REPLACE the GEM. CLEAR DTCs. TEST
the system for proper operation.

FM9029700521050X

**Fig. 17 Test M: Low Washer Fluid
Warning Indicator Does Not
Operate (Part 5 of 5). 2002–04**

M3	RETRIEVE THE DIAGNOSTIC TROUBLE CODES (DTCS)

- Are DTCs retrieved?

→ **Yes**
If DTC B1454, GO to **M4**.

If DTC B1456, GO to **M8**.

If DTC B1342, REPLACE the GEM.
CLEAR DTCs. TEST the system for proper
operation.

→ **No**
GO to **M4**.

M4	CHECK THE VOLTAGE TO THE LOW WASHER FLUID WARNING INDICATOR

4 Measure the voltage between instrument cluster
C238-12, circuit 640 (R/Y), and ground.
- Is the voltage greater than 10 volts?

→ **Yes**
GO to **M5**.

→ **No**
REPAIR circuit 640 (R/Y). CLEAR the
DTCs. TEST the system for normal
operation.

FM9029700521020X

**Fig. 17 Test M: Low Washer Fluid
Warning Indicator Does Not
Operate (Part 2 of 5). 2002–04**

M5	CHECK THE INSTRUMENT CLUSTER CIRCUIT TO THE LOW WASH FLUID WARNING INDICATOR

3 Measure the resistance between instrument cluster
terminals 2 and 12.
- Is the resistance less than 5 ohms?

→ **Yes**
GO to **M6**.

→ **No**
CHECK the low washer fluid warning
indicator bulb. If the bulb is OK, REPAIR the
instrument cluster. CLEAR the DTCs. TEST
the system for normal operation.

FM9029700521030X

**Fig. 17 Test M: Low Washer Fluid
Warning Indicator Does Not
Operate (Part 3 of 5). 2002–04**

Condition	Possible Sources	Action
• The windshield wipers are inoperative	• Fuse. • Multifunction switch. • Circuitry. • Ignition switch. • Windshield wiper motor.	• Go To Pinpoint Test A.
• The rear window wiper is inoperative	• Fuse. • Multifunction switch. • Circuitry. • Ignition switch. • Rear window wiper motor.	• Go To Pinpoint Test B.
• The windshield wipers stay on continuously	• Windshield wiper motor. • Multifunction switch. • Circuitry.	• Go To Pinpoint Test C.
• The rear window wiper stays on continuously	• Rear window wiper motor. • Multifunction switch. • Circuitry.	• Go To Pinpoint Test D.
• The high/low windshield wiper speeds do not operate correctly (intermittent wiper mode OK)	• Multifunction switch. • Circuitry. • Windshield wiper motor.	• Go To Pinpoint Test E.
• The intermittent windshield wiper speed does not operate correctly (high/low speeds OK)	• Multifunction switch. • Circuitry. • Windshield wiper motor.	• Go To Pinpoint Test F.
• The intermittent rear window wiper speed does not operate correctly	• Multifunction switch. • Circuitry. • Rear window wiper motor.	• Go To Pinpoint Test G.

LTV0500000002336

Fig. 18 Symptom Tests (Part 1 of 2). 2005–06

• The windshield wipers do not operate correctly in the MIST position	• Multifunction switch. • Circuitry. • Washer pump. • Windshield wiper motor. • Rear wiper motor.	• Go To Pinpoint Test H .
• The rear window wiper wash and wipe function does not operate	• Multifunction switch. • Circuitry. • Washer pump. • Rear window wiper motor. • Windshield wiper motor.	• Go To Pinpoint Test I .
• The washer pump is inoperative	• Washer pump. • Multifunction switch. • Windshield wiper motor. • Rear window wiper motor. • Circuitry.	• Go To Pinpoint Test J .
• The windshield wiper speed dependent interval mode does not operate correctly	• Windshield wiper motor. • Circuitry. • Powertrain control module (PCM).	• Go To Pinpoint Test K .
• The wipers will not park at correct position	• Pivot arm adjustment. • Linkage.	• Repair and/or adjust wiper arm and Pivot.

LTV0500000002337

Fig. 18 Symptom Tests (Part 2 of 2). 2005–06

connector information. • **Did the multifunction switch pass the component test?**		INSTALL a new multifunction switch.
A4 CHECK CIRCUIT 57 (BK) FOR OPEN		
• Measure the resistance between C202a-4, circuit 57 (BK), harness side and ground. • **Is the resistance less than 5 ohms?**		**Yes** GO to A5 . **No** REPAIR the circuit. TEST the system for normal operation.
A5 CHECK CIRCUITS 56 (DB/OG), 58 (WH), 61 (YE/RD) AND 63 (RD) FOR OPENS		
• Using the following table, measure the resistance between multifunction switch C202a, harness side and windshield wiper motor C125, harness side:		**Yes** GO to A6 . **No** REPAIR the circuit(s) in question. TEST the system for normal operation.

Multifunction Switch C202a	Windshield Wiper Motor C125
pin 7, circuit 56 (DB/OG)	pin 10, circuit 56 (DB/OG)
pin 3, circuit 58 (WH)	pin 11, circuit 58 (WH)
pin 5, circuit 61 (YE/RD)	pin 1, circuit 61 (YE/RD)
pin 1, circuit 63 (RD)	pin 9, circuit 63 (RD)

LTV0500000002339

Fig. 19 Test A: Windshield Wipers Are Inoperative (Part 2 of 3). 2005–06

Test Step	Result / Action to Take
A1 CHECK CIRCUITS 65 (DG) AND 1002 (BK/PK) FOR VOLTAGE	
• Key in OFF position. • Disconnect: Windshield Wiper Motor C125. • Key in ON position. • Measure the voltage between windshield wiper C125-5, circuit 65 (DG), harness side and ground; and between windshield wiper motor C125-8, circuit 1002 (BK/PK), harness side and ground. 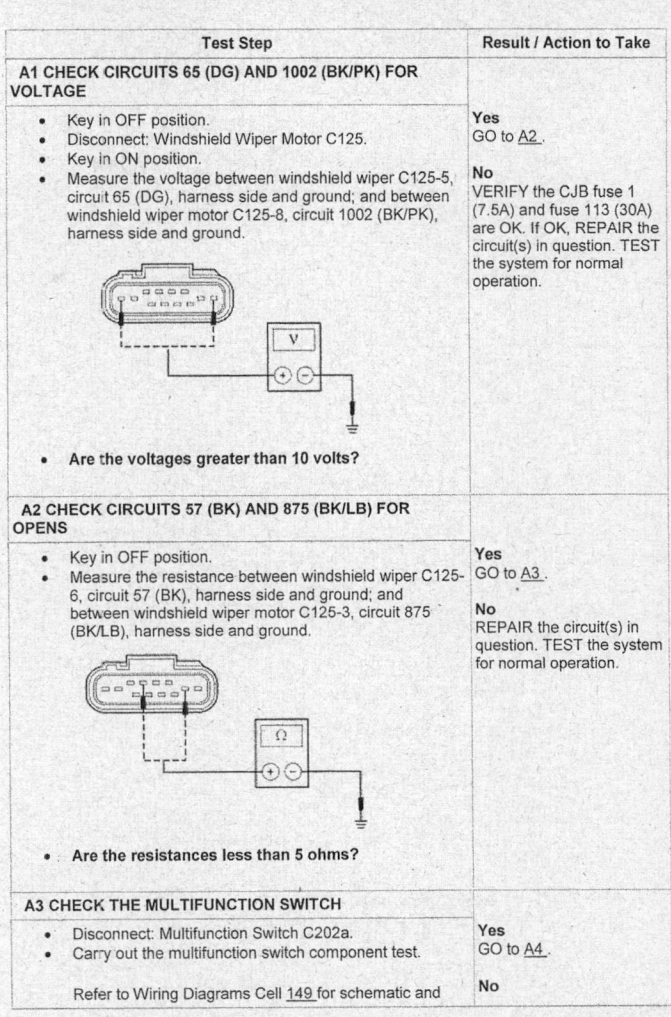 • **Are the voltages greater than 10 volts?**	**Yes** GO to A2 . **No** VERIFY the CJB fuse 1 (7.5A) and fuse 113 (30A) are OK. If OK, REPAIR the circuit(s) in question. TEST the system for normal operation.
A2 CHECK CIRCUITS 57 (BK) AND 875 (BK/LB) FOR OPENS	
• Key in OFF position. • Measure the resistance between windshield wiper C125-6, circuit 57 (BK), harness side and ground; and between windshield wiper motor C125-3, circuit 875 (BK/LB), harness side and ground. • **Are the resistances less than 5 ohms?**	**Yes** GO to A3 . **No** REPAIR the circuit(s) in question. TEST the system for normal operation.
A3 CHECK THE MULTIFUNCTION SWITCH	
• Disconnect: Multifunction Switch C202a. • Carry out the multifunction switch component test. Refer to Wiring Diagrams Cell 149 for schematic and	**Yes** GO to A4 . **No**

LTV0500000002338

Fig. 19 Test A: Windshield Wipers Are Inoperative (Part 1 of 3). 2005–06

• **Is the resistance less than 5 ohms?**	
A6 CHECK FOR CORRECT WIPER MOTOR OPERATION	

• Disconnect all wiper motor connectors.
• Check for:
  ▪ corrosion.
  ▪ pushed-out pins.
• Connect all wiper motor connectors and make sure they seat correctly.
• Operate the system and verify the concern is still present.
• **Is the concern still present?**
	Yes
	GO to A7 .
	
	No
	The system is operating correctly at this time. Concern may have been caused by a loose or corroded connector. TEST the system for normal operation.

A7 CHECK THE WINDSHIELD WIPER MOTOR	
• Key in OFF position. • Disconnect: Windshield Wiper Motor C125. • Carry out the windshield wiper motor component test as described in this section. • **Did the windshield wiper motor pass the component test?**	**Yes** The system is operating correctly at this time. Concern may have been caused by binding or incorrect pivot arm adjustment. Repair and/or adjust wiper arm and Pivot. TEST the system for normal operation. **No** INSTALL a new windshield wiper motor.

LTV0500000002340

Fig. 19 Test A: Windshield Wipers Are Inoperative (Part 3 of 3). 2005–06

Test Step	Result / Action to Take
B1 CHECK CIRCUITS 1002 (BK/PK) AND 406 (BN/WH) FOR VOLTAGE • Key in OFF position. • Disconnect: Rear Wiper Motor C476. • Key in ON position. • Measure the voltage between rear wiper motor C476-3, circuit 1002 (BK/PK), harness side and ground; and between rear wiper motor C476-4, circuit 406 (BN/WH), harness side and ground. 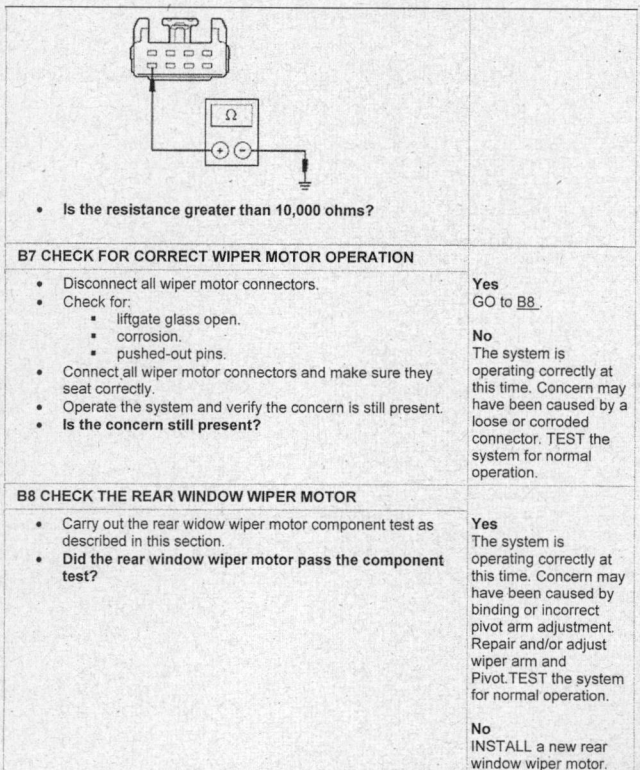 • Are the voltages greater than 10 volts?	**Yes** GO to B2. **No** VERIFY CJB fuse 1 (7.5A) and fuse 38 (25A) are OK. If OK, REPAIR the circuit(s) in question. TEST the system for normal operation.
B2 CHECK CIRCUIT 57 (BK) FOR OPEN • Key in OFF position. • Measure the resistance between rear wiper C476-1, circuit 57 (BK), harness side and ground. • Is the resistance less than 5 ohms?	**Yes** GO to B3. **No** REPAIR the circuit(s) in question. TEST the system for normal operation.
B3 CHECK THE MULTIFUNCTION SWITCH • Key in OFF position. • Disconnect: Multifunction Switch C202a. • Carry out the multifunction switch component test. Refer to "Wiring Diagrams"	**Yes** GO to B4. **No** INSTALL a new multifunction switch.

LTV0500000002341

Fig. 20   Test B: Rear Wiper Is Inoperative (Part 1 of 3). 2005–06

Test Step	Result / Action to Take
• Did the multifunction switch pass the component test?	
B4 CHECK CIRCUIT 57 (BK) FOR OPEN • Measure the resistance between C202a-4, circuit 57 (BK), harness side and ground. 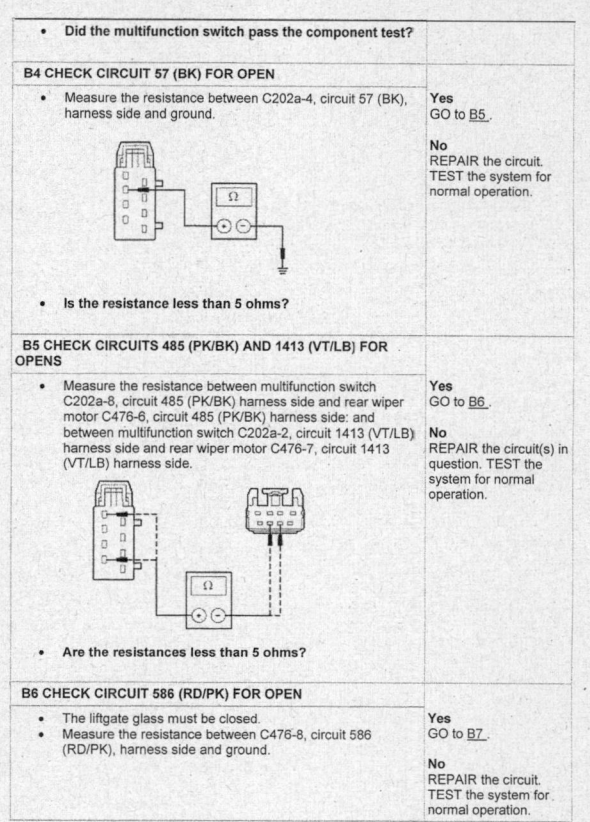 • Is the resistance less than 5 ohms?	**Yes** GO to B5. **No** REPAIR the circuit. TEST the system for normal operation.
B5 CHECK CIRCUITS 485 (PK/BK) AND 1413 (VT/LB) FOR OPENS • Measure the resistance between multifunction switch C202a-8, circuit 485 (PK/BK) harness side and rear wiper motor C476-6, circuit 485 (PK/BK) harness side: and between multifunction switch C202a-2, circuit 1413 (VT/LB) harness side and rear wiper motor C476-7, circuit 1413 (VT/LB) harness side. • Are the resistances less than 5 ohms?	**Yes** GO to B6. **No** REPAIR the circuit(s) in question. TEST the system for normal operation.
B6 CHECK CIRCUIT 586 (RD/PK) FOR OPEN • The liftgate glass must be closed. • Measure the resistance between C476-8, circuit 586 (RD/PK), harness side and ground.	**Yes** GO to B7. **No** REPAIR the circuit. TEST the system for normal operation.

LTV0500000002342

Fig. 20   Test B: Rear Wiper Is Inoperative (Part 2 of 3). 2005–06

• Is the resistance greater than 10,000 ohms?	
B7 CHECK FOR CORRECT WIPER MOTOR OPERATION • Disconnect all wiper motor connectors. • Check for: ▪ liftgate glass open. ▪ corrosion. ▪ pushed-out pins. • Connect all wiper motor connectors and make sure they seat correctly. • Operate the system and verify the concern is still present. • **Is the concern still present?**	**Yes** GO to B8. **No** The system is operating correctly at this time. Concern may have been caused by a loose or corroded connector. TEST the system for normal operation.
B8 CHECK THE REAR WINDOW WIPER MOTOR • Carry out the rear widow wiper motor component test as described in this section. • **Did the rear window wiper motor pass the component test?**	**Yes** The system is operating correctly at this time. Concern may have been caused by binding or incorrect pivot arm adjustment. Repair and/or adjust wiper arm and Pivot.TEST the system for normal operation. **No** INSTALL a new rear window wiper motor.

LTV0500000002343

Fig. 20   Test B: Rear Wiper Is Inoperative (Part 3 of 3). 2005–06

Test Step	Result / Action to Take
C1 CHECK THE MULTIFUNCTION SWITCH • Key in OFF position. • Disconnect: Multifunction Switch C202a. • Carry out the multifunction switch component test. Refer to "Wiring Diagrams" • **Did the multifunction switch pass the component test?**	**Yes** GO to C2. **No** INSTALL a new multifunction switch.
C2 CHECK CIRCUIT 57 (BK) FOR OPEN • Measure the resistance between C202a-4, circuit 57 (BK), harness side and ground. • Is the resistance less than 5 ohms?	**Yes** GO to C3. **No** REPAIR the circuit. TEST the system for normal operation.
C3 CHECK CIRCUITS 56 (DB/OG), 58 (WH), 61 (YE/RD) AND 63 (RD) FOR SHORTS • Disconnect: Windshield Wiper Motor C125. • Using the following table, measure the resistance between the windshield wiper motor C125 harness side and ground: | Windshield Wiper Motor C125	Ground
pin 10, circuit 56 (DB/OG)	ground
pin 11, circuit 58 (WH)	ground
pin 1, circuit 61 (YE/RD)	ground
pin 9, circuit 63 (RD)	ground		**Yes** GO to C4. **No** REPAIR the circuit(s) in question. TEST the system for normal operation.

LTV0500000002344

Fig. 21   Test C: Windshield Wipers Stay On Continuously (Part 1 of 2). 2005–06

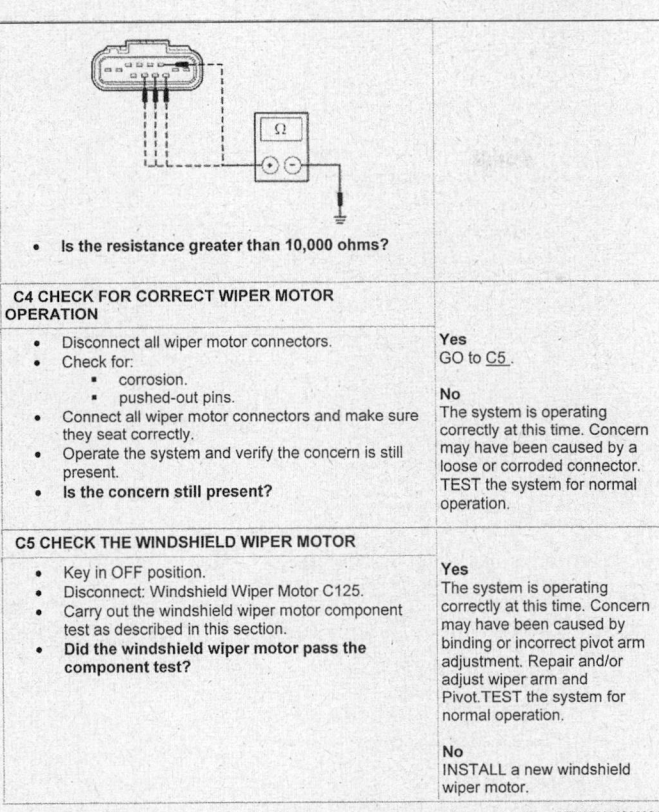

- **Is the resistance greater than 10,000 ohms?**

C4 CHECK FOR CORRECT WIPER MOTOR OPERATION

• Disconnect all wiper motor connectors.
• Check for:
   ■ corrosion.
   ■ pushed-out pins.
• Connect all wiper motor connectors and make sure they seat correctly.
• Operate the system and verify the concern is still present.
• **Is the concern still present?**
	Yes
	GO to <u>C5</u>.
	
	No
	The system is operating correctly at this time. Concern may have been caused by a loose or corroded connector. TEST the system for normal operation.

C5 CHECK THE WINDSHIELD WIPER MOTOR

• Key in OFF position. • Disconnect: Windshield Wiper Motor C125. • Carry out the windshield wiper motor component test as described in this section. • **Did the windshield wiper motor pass the component test?**	**Yes** The system is operating correctly at this time. Concern may have been caused by binding or incorrect pivot arm adjustment. Repair and/or adjust wiper arm and Pivot. TEST the system for normal operation. **No** INSTALL a new windshield wiper motor.

LTV0500000002345

Fig. 21 Test C: Windshield Wipers Stay On Continuously (Part 2 of 2). 2005–06

D4 CHECK FOR CORRECT WIPER MOTOR OPERATION

• Disconnect all wiper motor connectors.
• Check for:
   ■ liftgate glass open.
   ■ corrosion.
   ■ pushed-out pins.
• Connect all wiper motor connectors and make sure they seat correctly.
• Operate the system and verify the concern is still present.
• **Is the concern still present?**
	Yes
	GO to <u>D5</u>.
	
	No
	The system is operating correctly at this time. Concern may have been caused by a loose or corroded connector. TEST the system for normal operation.

D5 CHECK THE REAR WINDOW WIPER MOTOR

• Carry out the rear window wiper motor component test as described in this section. • **Did the rear window wiper motor pass the component test?**	**Yes** The system is operating correctly at this time. Concern may have been caused by binding or incorrect pivot arm adjustment. Repair and/or adjust wiper arm and Pivot. TEST the system for normal operation. **No** INSTALL a new rear window wiper motor.

LTV0500000002347

Fig. 22 Test D: Rear Wiper Stays On Continuously. (Part 2 of 2). 2005–06

Test Step	Result / Action to Take
D1 CHECK THE MULTIFUNCTION SWITCH • Key in OFF position. • Disconnect: Multifunction Switch C202a. • Carry out the multifunction switch component test. Refer to "Wiring Diagrams" • **Did the multifunction switch pass the component test?**	**Yes** GO to <u>D2</u>. **No** INSTALL a new multifunction switch.
D2 CHECK CIRCUIT 57 (BK) FOR OPEN • Measure the resistance between C202a-4, circuit 57 (BK), harness side and ground. • **Is the resistance less than 5 ohms?**	**Yes** GO to <u>D3</u>. **No** REPAIR the circuit. TEST the system for normal operation.
D3 CHECK CIRCUITS 485 (PK/BK) AND 1413 (VT/LB) FOR SHORTS • Disconnect: Rear Window Wiper Motor C476. • Measure the resistance between the rear window wiper motor C476-6, circuit 485 (PK/BK), harness side and ground; and between the rear wiper motor C476-7, circuit 1413 (VT/LB), harness side and ground. • **Are the resistances greater than 10,000 ohms?**	**Yes** GO to <u>D4</u>. **No** REPAIR the circuit(s) in question. TEST the system for normal operation.

LTV0500000002346

Fig. 22 Test D: Rear Wiper Stays On Continuously. (Part 1 of 2). 2005–06

Test Step	Result / Action to Take
E1 CHECK THE MULTIFUNCTION SWITCH • Key in OFF position. • Disconnect: Multifunction Switch C202a. • Carry out the multifunction switch component test. Refer to "Wiring Diagrams" • **Did the multifunction switch pass the component test?**	**Yes** GO to <u>E2</u>. **No** INSTALL a new multifunction switch. TEST the system for normal operation.
E2 CHECK CIRCUIT 57 (BK) FOR OPEN • Measure the resistance between C202a-4, circuit 57 (BK), harness side and ground. • **Is the resistance less than 5 ohms?**	**Yes** GO to <u>E3</u>. **No** REPAIR the circuit. TEST the system for normal operation.
E3 CHECK CIRCUITS 56 (DB/OG), 61 (YE/RD) AND 63 (RD) FOR OPENS • Disconnect: Windshield Wiper Motor C125. • Using the following table, measure the resistance between the multifunction switch C202a harness side and the windshield wiper motor C125 harness side:	**Yes** GO to <u>E4</u>. **No** REPAIR the circuit(s) in question. TEST the system for normal operation.

Multifunction Switch C202a	Windshield Wiper Motor C125
pin 7, circuit 56 (DB/OG)	pin 10, circuit 56 (DB/OG)
pin 5, circuit 61 (YE/RD)	pin 1, circuit 61 (YE/RD)
pin 1, circuit 63 (RD)	pin 9, circuit 63 (RD)

LTV0500000002348

Fig. 23 Test E: High/Low Windshield Wiper Speeds Do Not Operate Correctly (Part 1 of 2). 2005–06

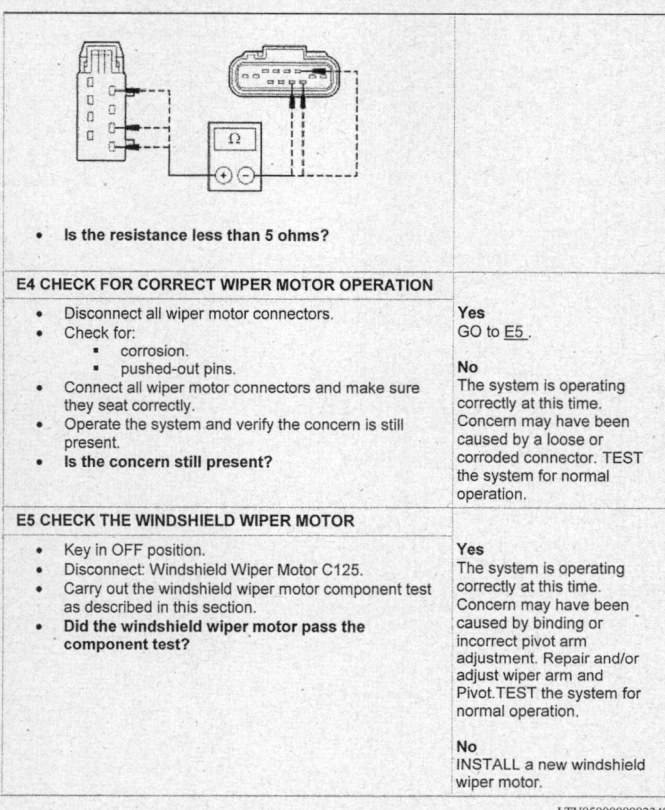

- **Is the resistance less than 5 ohms?**

E4 CHECK FOR CORRECT WIPER MOTOR OPERATION

- Disconnect all wiper motor connectors.
- Check for:
  - corrosion.
  - pushed-out pins.
- Connect all wiper motor connectors and make sure they seat correctly.
- Operate the system and verify the concern is still present.
- **Is the concern still present?**

Yes
GO to E5 .

No
The system is operating correctly at this time. Concern may have been caused by a loose or corroded connector. TEST the system for normal operation.

E5 CHECK THE WINDSHIELD WIPER MOTOR

- Key in OFF position.
- Disconnect: Windshield Wiper Motor C125.
- Carry out the windshield wiper motor component test as described in this section.
- **Did the windshield wiper motor pass the component test?**

Yes
The system is operating correctly at this time. Concern may have been caused by binding or incorrect pivot arm adjustment. Repair and/or adjust wiper arm and Pivot.TEST the system for normal operation.

No
INSTALL a new windshield wiper motor.

LTV0500000002349

Fig. 23   Test E: High/Low Windshield Wiper Speeds Do Not Operate Correctly (Part 2 of 2). 2005–06

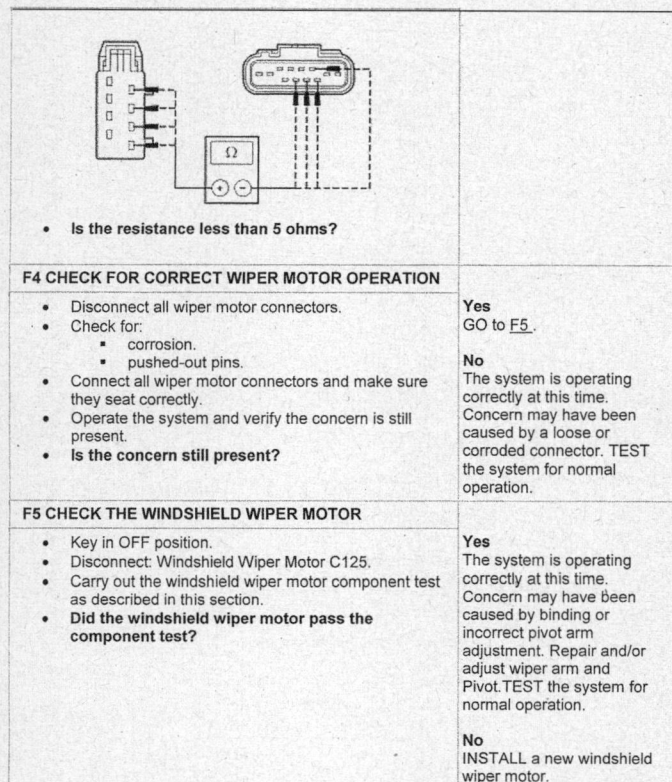

- **Is the resistance less than 5 ohms?**

F4 CHECK FOR CORRECT WIPER MOTOR OPERATION

- Disconnect all wiper motor connectors.
- Check for:
  - corrosion.
  - pushed-out pins.
- Connect all wiper motor connectors and make sure they seat correctly.
- Operate the system and verify the concern is still present.
- **Is the concern still present?**

Yes
GO to F5 .

No
The system is operating correctly at this time. Concern may have been caused by a loose or corroded connector. TEST the system for normal operation.

F5 CHECK THE WINDSHIELD WIPER MOTOR

- Key in OFF position.
- Disconnect: Windshield Wiper Motor C125.
- Carry out the windshield wiper motor component test as described in this section.
- **Did the windshield wiper motor pass the component test?**

Yes
The system is operating correctly at this time. Concern may have been caused by binding or incorrect pivot arm adjustment. Repair and/or adjust wiper arm and Pivot.TEST the system for normal operation.

No
INSTALL a new windshield wiper motor.

LTV0500000002351

Fig. 24   Test F: Intermittent Windshield Wiper Speed Does Not Work Correctly (Part 2 of 2). 2005–06

Test Step	Result / Action to Take
F1 CHECK THE MULTIFUNCTION SWITCH • Key in OFF position. • Disconnect: Multifunction Switch C202a. • Carry out the multifunction switch component test. Refer to "Wiring Diagrams" • **Did the multifunction switch pass the component test?**	**Yes** GO to F2 . **No** INSTALL a new multifunction switch. TEST the system for normal operation.
F2 CHECK CIRCUIT 57 (BK) FOR OPEN • Measure the resistance between C202a-4, circuit 57 (BK), harness side and ground. • **Is the resistance less than 5 ohms?**	**Yes** GC to F3 . **No** REPAIR the circuit. TEST the system for normal operation.
F3 CHECK CIRCUITS 56 (DB/OG), 61 (YE/RD) AND 63 (RD) FOR OPENS • Disconnect: Windshield Wiper Motor C125. • Using the following table, measure the resistance between multifunction switch C202a harness side and windshield wiper motor C125 harness side:	**Yes** GO to F4 . **No** REPAIR the circuit(s) in question. TEST the system for normal operation.

Multifunction Switch C202a	Windshield Wiper Motor C125
pin 7, circuit 56 (DB/OG)	pin 10, circuit 56 (DB/OG)
pin 5, circuit 61 (YE/RD)	pin 1, circuit 61 (YE/RD)
pin 1, circuit 63 (RD)	pin 9, circuit 63 (RD)
pin 3, circuit 58 (WH)	pin 11, circuit 58 (WH)

LTV0500000002350

Fig. 24   Test F: Intermittent Windshield Wiper Speed Does Not Work Correctly (Part 1 of 2). 2005–06

Test Step	Result / Action to Take
G1 CHECK THE MULTIFUNCTION SWITCH • Key in OFF position. • Disconnect: Multifunction Switch C202a. • Carry out the multifunction switch component test. Refer to "Wiring Diagrams" • **Did the multifunction switch pass the component test?**	**Yes** GO to G2 . **No** INSTALL a new multifunction switch.
G2 CHECK CIRCUIT 57 (BK) FOR OPEN • Measure the resistance between C202a-4, circuit 57 (BK), harness side and ground. • **Is the resistance less than 5 ohms?**	**Yes** GO to G3 . **No** REPAIR the circuit. TEST the system for normal operation.
G3 CHECK CIRCUITS 485 (PK/BK) AND 1413 (VT/LB) FOR OPENS • Disconnect: Rear Window Wiper Motor C476. • Measure the resistance between multifunction switch C202a-8, circuit 485 (PK/BK) harness side and rear wiper motor C476-6, circuit 485 (PK/BK) harness side; and between multifunction switch C202a-2, circuit 1413 (VT/LB) harness side and rear wiper motor C476-7, circuit 1413 (VT/LB) harness side.	**Yes** GO to G4 . **No** REPAIR the circuit(s) in question. TEST the system for normal operation.

LTV0500000002352

Fig. 25   Test G: Intermittent Rear Wiper Speed Does Not Operate (Part 1 of 2). 2005–06

Test Step	Result / Action to Take
• Are the resistances less than 5 ohms?	
G4 CHECK FOR CORRECT WIPER MOTOR OPERATION	

• Disconnect all wiper motor connectors.
• Check for:
  ▪ liftgate glass open.
  ▪ corrosion.
  ▪ pushed-out pins.
• Connect all wiper motor connectors and make sure they seat correctly.
• Operate the system and verify the concern is still present.
• **Is the concern still present?**
	Yes
	GO to G5 .
	
	No
	The system is operating correctly at this time. Concern may have been caused by a loose or corroded connector. TEST the system for normal operation.

G5 CHECK THE REAR WINDOW WIPER MOTOR	
• Carry out the rear widow wiper motor component test as described in this section. • **Did the rear window wiper motor pass the component test?**	**Yes** The system is operating correctly at this time. Concern may have been caused by binding or incorrect pivot arm adjustment. Repair and/or adjust wiper arm and Pivot. TEST the system for normal operation. **No** INSTALL a new rear window wiper motor.

LTV0500000002353

Fig. 25   Test G: Intermittent Rear Wiper Speed Does Not Operate (Part 2 of 2). 2005–06

Test Step	Result / Action to Take
I1 CHECK THE MULTIFUNCTION SWITCH	
• Key in OFF position. • Disconnect: Multifunction Switch C202a. • Carry out the multifunction switch component test. Refer to "Wiring Diagrams" • **Did the multifunction switch pass the component test?**	**Yes** GO to I2 . **No** INSTALL a new multifunction switch.
I2 CHECK CIRCUIT 57 (BK) FOR OPEN	
• Measure the resistance between C202a-4, circuit 57 (BK), harness side and ground. • **Is the resistance less than 5 ohms?**	**Yes** GO to I3 . **No** REPAIR the circuit. TEST the system for normal operation.
I3 CHECK CIRCUITS 485 (PK/BK) AND 1413 (VT/LB) FOR OPENS	
• Key in OFF position. • Disconnect: Rear Window Wiper Motor C476. • Measure the resistance between multifunction switch C202a-8, circuit 485 (PK/BK) harness side and rear wiper motor C476-6, circuit 485 (PK/BK) harness side: and between multifunction switch C202a-2, circuit 1413 (VT/LB) harness side and rear wiper motor C476-7, circuit 1413 (VT/LB) harness side.	**Yes** GO to I4 . **No** REPAIR the circuit. TEST the system for normal operation.

LTV0500000002355

Fig. 27   Test I: Rear Wiper & Wash Function Does Not Operate (Part 1 of 2). 2005–06

Test Step	Result / Action to Take
H1 CHECK THE MULTIFUNCTION SWITCH	
• Key in OFF position. • Disconnect: Multifunction Switch C202a. • Carry out the multifunction switch component test. Refer to "Wiring Diagrams" • **Did the multifunction switch pass the component test?**	**Yes** GO to H2 . **No** INSTALL a new multifunction switch.
H2 CHECK CIRCUIT 57 (BK) FOR OPEN	
• Measure the resistance between C202a-4, circuit 57 (BK), harness side and ground. • Is the resistance less than 5 ohms?	**Yes** GO to H3 . **No** REPAIR the circuit. TEST the system for normal operation.
H3 CHECK CIRCUIT 680 (LB/OG) FOR OPEN	
• D sconnect: Windshield Wiper Motor C125. • Measure the resistance between C202a-6, circuit 680 (LB/OG), harness side and C125-12, circuit 680 (LB/OG), harness side. • Is the resistance less than 5 ohms?	**Yes** Go To Pinpoint Test K . **No** REPAIR the circuit. TEST the system for normal operation.

LTV0500000002354

Fig. 26   Test H: Windshield Wipers Do Not Operate Correctly In Mist Position. 2005–06

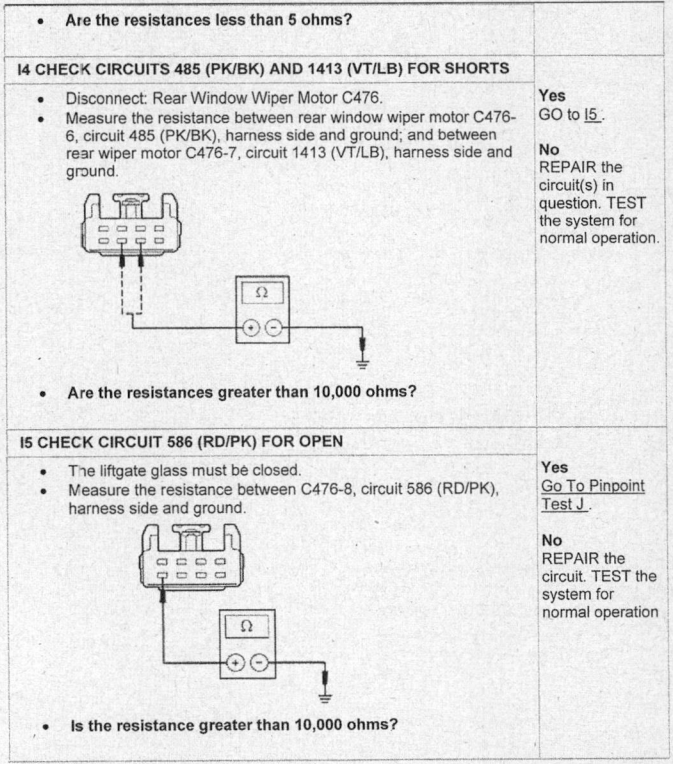

Test Step	Result / Action to Take
• Are the resistances less than 5 ohms?	
I4 CHECK CIRCUITS 485 (PK/BK) AND 1413 (VT/LB) FOR SHORTS	
• Disconnect: Rear Window Wiper Motor C476. • Measure the resistance between rear window wiper motor C476-6, circuit 485 (PK/BK), harness side and ground; and between rear wiper motor C476-7, circuit 1413 (VT/LB), harness side and ground. • Are the resistances greater than 10,000 ohms?	**Yes** GO to I5 . **No** REPAIR the circuit(s) in question. TEST the system for normal operation.
I5 CHECK CIRCUIT 586 (RD/PK) FOR OPEN	
• The liftgate glass must be closed. • Measure the resistance between C476-8, circuit 586 (RD/PK), harness side and ground. • Is the resistance greater than 10,000 ohms?	**Yes** Go To Pinpoint Test J . **No** REPAIR the circuit. TEST the system for normal operation

LTV0500000002356

Fig. 27   Test I: Rear Wiper & Wash Function Does Not Operate (Part 2 of 2). 2005–06

Test Step	Result / Action to Take
J1 CHECK CIRCUIT 941 (BK/WH) FOR GROUND • Key in OFF position. • Disconnect: Washer Pump Motor C1357. • Measure the resistance between C1357-2, circuit 941 (BK/WH) harness side and ground. 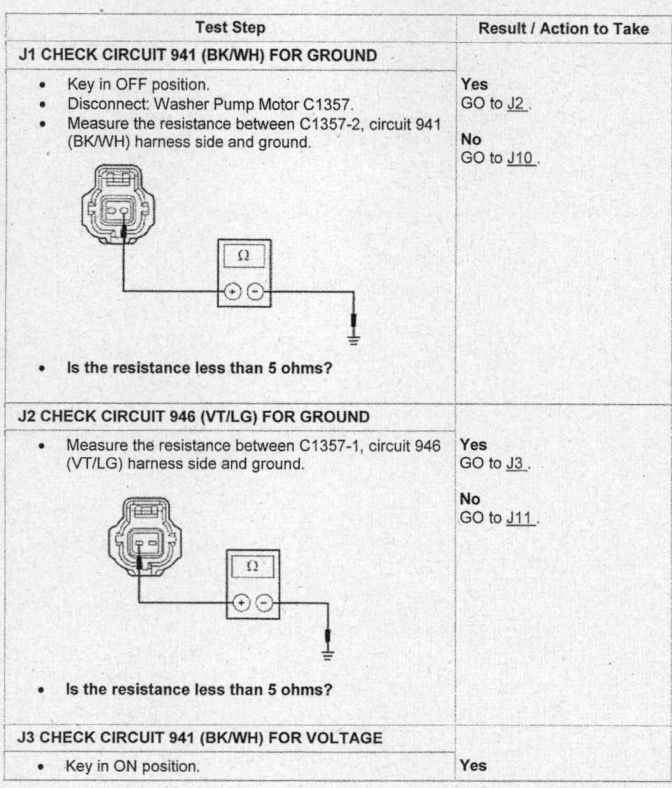 • Is the resistance less than 5 ohms?	**Yes** GO to J2 . **No** GO to J10 .
J2 CHECK CIRCUIT 946 (VT/LG) FOR GROUND • Measure the resistance between C1357-1, circuit 946 (VT/LG) harness side and ground. 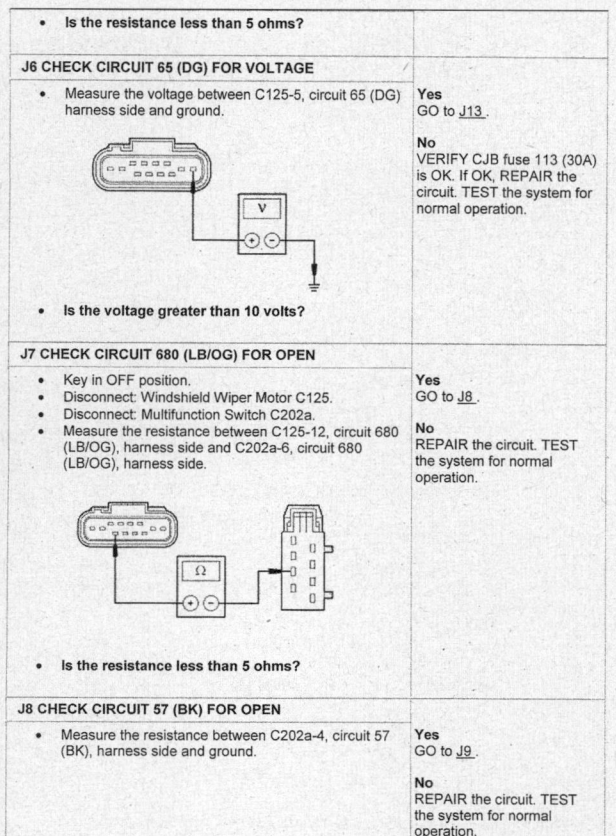 • Is the resistance less than 5 ohms?	**Yes** GO to J3 . **No** GO to J11 .
J3 CHECK CIRCUIT 941 (BK/WH) FOR VOLTAGE • Key in ON position.	**Yes**

LTV0500000002357

Fig. 28   Test J: Washer Pump Is Inoperative (Part 1 of 6). 2005–06

Test Step	Result / Action to Take
• Measure the voltage between C1357-2, circuit 941 (BK/WH) harness side and ground while depressing the multifunction switch to the wash position. 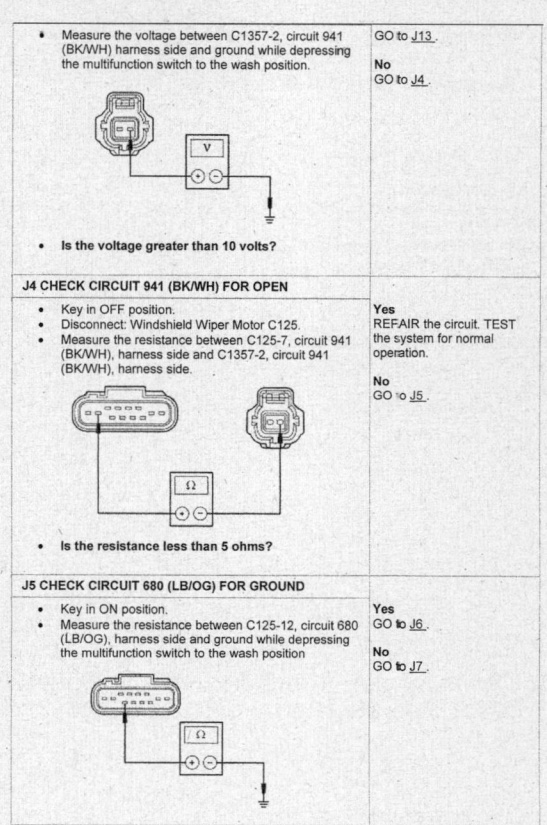 • Is the voltage greater than 10 volts?	GO to J13 . **No** GO to J4 .
J4 CHECK CIRCUIT 941 (BK/WH) FOR OPEN • Key in OFF position. • Disconnect: Windshield Wiper Motor C125. • Measure the resistance between C125-7, circuit 941 (BK/WH) harness side and C1357-2, circuit 941 (BK/WH), harness side. • Is the resistance less than 5 ohms?	**Yes** REFAIR the circuit. TEST the system for normal operation. **No** GO to J5 .
J5 CHECK CIRCUIT 680 (LB/OG) FOR GROUND • Key in ON position. • Measure the resistance between C125-12, circuit 680 (LB/OG), harness side and ground while depressing the multifunction switch to the wash position	**Yes** GO to J6 . **No** GO to J7 .

LTV0500000002358

Fig. 28   Test J: Washer Pump Is Inoperative (Part 2 of 6). 2005–06

Test Step	Result / Action to Take
• Is the resistance less than 5 ohms?	
J6 CHECK CIRCUIT 65 (DG) FOR VOLTAGE • Measure the voltage between C125-5, circuit 65 (DG) harness side and ground. 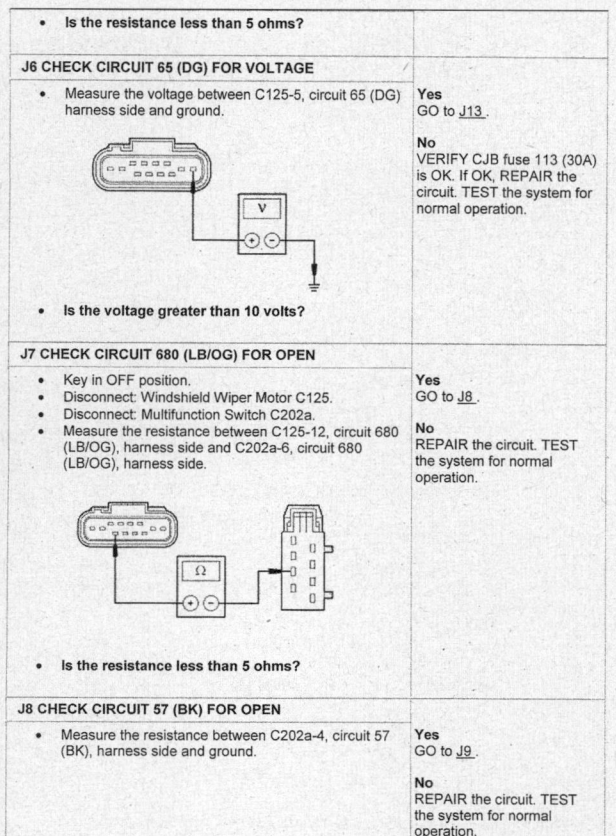 • Is the voltage greater than 10 volts?	**Yes** GO to J13 . **No** VERIFY CJB fuse 113 (30A) is OK. If OK, REPAIR the circuit. TEST the system for normal operation.
J7 CHECK CIRCUIT 680 (LB/OG) FOR OPEN • Key in OFF position. • Disconnect: Windshield Wiper Motor C125. • Disconnect: Multifunction Switch C202a. • Measure the resistance between C125-12, circuit 680 (LB/OG), harness side and C202a-6, circuit 680 (LB/OG), harness side. • Is the resistance less than 5 ohms?	**Yes** GO to J8 . **No** REPAIR the circuit. TEST the system for normal operation.
J8 CHECK CIRCUIT 57 (BK) FOR OPEN • Measure the resistance between C202a-4, circuit 57 (BK), harness side and ground.	**Yes** GO to J9 . **No** REPAIR the circuit. TEST the system for normal operation.

LTV0500000002359

Fig. 28   Test J: Washer Pump Is Inoperative (Part 3 of 6). 2005–06

Test Step	Result / Action to Take
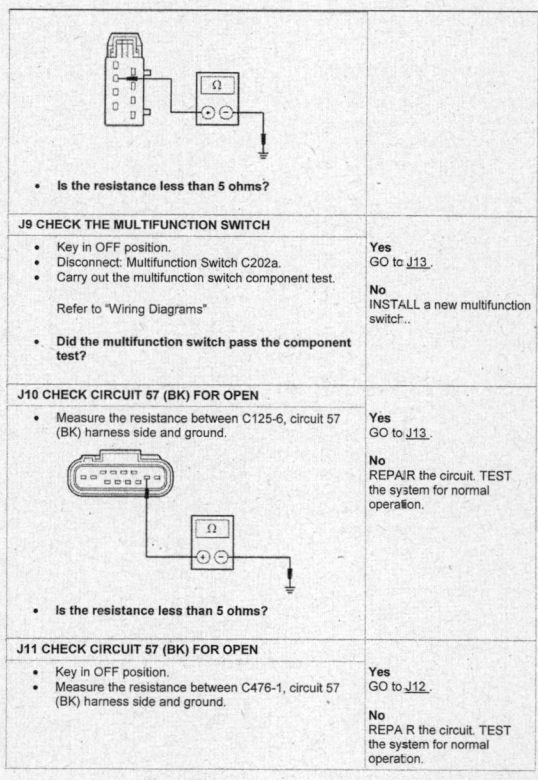 • Is the resistance less than 5 ohms?	
J9 CHECK THE MULTIFUNCTION SWITCH • Key in OFF position. • Disconnect: Multifunction Switch C202a. • Carry out the multifunction switch component test. Refer to "Wiring Diagrams" • Did the multifunction switch pass the component test?	**Yes** GO to J13 . **No** INSTALL a new multifunction switch..
J10 CHECK CIRCUIT 57 (BK) FOR OPEN • Measure the resistance between C125-6, circuit 57 (BK) harness side and ground. • Is the resistance less than 5 ohms?	**Yes** GO to J13 . **No** REPAIR the circuit. TEST the system for normal operation.
J11 CHECK CIRCUIT 57 (BK) FOR OPEN • Key in OFF position. • Measure the resistance between C476-1, circuit 57 (BK) harness side and ground.	**Yes** GO to J12 . **No** REPAR the circuit. TEST the system for normal operation.

LTV0500000002360

Fig. 28   Test J: Washer Pump Is Inoperative (Part 4 of 6). 2005–06

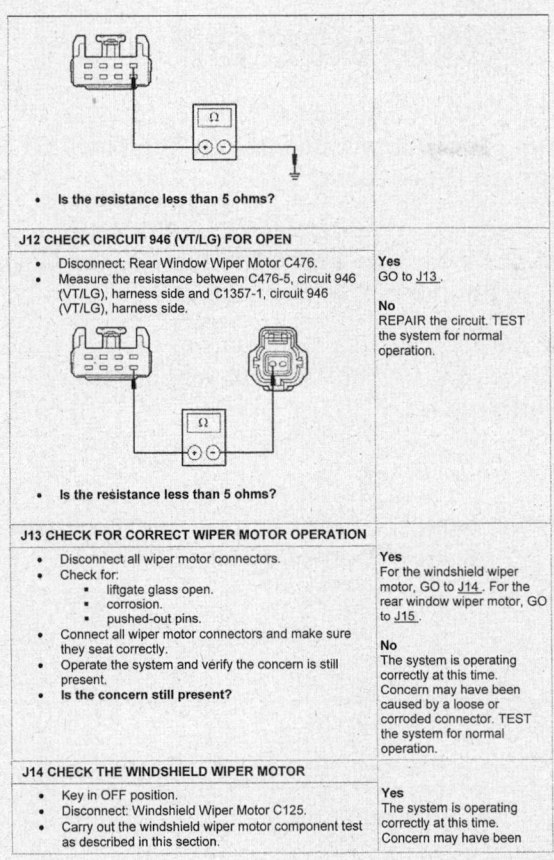

- Is the resistance less than 5 ohms?

J12 CHECK CIRCUIT 946 (VT/LG) FOR OPEN

• Disconnect: Rear Window Wiper Motor C476. • Measure the resistance between C476-5, circuit 946 (VT/LG), harness side and C1357-1, circuit 946 (VT/LG), harness side.	**Yes** GO to J13. **No** REPAIR the circuit. TEST the system for normal operation.

- Is the resistance less than 5 ohms?

J13 CHECK FOR CORRECT WIPER MOTOR OPERATION

• Disconnect all wiper motor connectors.
• Check for:
  ■ liftgate glass open.
  ■ corrosion.
  ■ pushed-out pins.
• Connect all wiper motor connectors and make sure they seat correctly.
• Operate the system and verify the concern is still present.
• **Is the concern still present?**
	Yes
	For the windshield wiper motor, GO to J14. For the rear window wiper motor, GO to J15.
	
	No
	The system is operating correctly at this time. Concern may have been caused by a loose or corroded connector. TEST the system for normal operation.

J14 CHECK THE WINDSHIELD WIPER MOTOR

• Key in OFF position. • Disconnect: Windshield Wiper Motor C125. • Carry out the windshield wiper motor component test as described in this section.	**Yes** The system is operating correctly at this time. Concern may have been

LTV0500000002361

Fig. 28   Test J: Washer Pump Is Inoperative (Part 5 of 6). 2005–06

Test Step	Result / Action to Take
K1 CHECK THE PCM — MONITOR THE VSS	
• Monitor the VSS while driving the vehicle from 0 to 88.5 kph (55 mph). • **Does the VSS agree with the PCM PIDs?**	**Yes** GO to K2. **No** Check ABS system
K2 CHECK CIRCUIT 679 (GY/BK) FOR AN OPEN	
• Disconnect: PCM C175b. • Disconnect: Windshield Wiper Motor C125. • Measure the resistance between PCM C175b-13, circuit 679 (GY/BK), harness side and windshield wiper motor C125-4, circuit 679 (GY/BK), harness side.	**Yes** GO to K3. **No** REPAIR the circuit. CLEAR the DTCs. REPEAT the self-test.
• Is the resistance less than 5 ohms?	
K3 CHECK CIRCUIT 679 (GY/BK) FOR A SHORT TO GROUND	
• Measure the resistance between PCM C175b-13, circuit 679 (GY/BK), harness side and ground.	**Yes** GO to K4. **No** REPAIR the circuit. CLEAR the DTCs. REPEAT the self-test.
• Is the resistance greater than 10,000 ohms?	
K4 CHECK FOR CORRECT WIPER MOTOR OPERATION	
• Disconnect all wiper motor connectors. • Check for:	**Yes** GO to K5.

LTV0500000002363

Fig. 29   Test K: Windshield Wiper Speed Dependent Interval Mode Does Not Operate Correctly (Part 1 of 2). 2005–06

• **Did the windshield wiper motor pass the component test?**	caused by binding or incorrect pivot arm adjustment. Repair and/or adjust wiper arm and Pivot. TEST the system for normal operation. **No** INSTALL a new windshield wiper motor.

J15 CHECK THE REAR WINDOW WIPER MOTOR

• Carry out the rear widow wiper motor component test as described in this section. • **Did the rear window wiper motor pass the component test?**	**Yes** The system is operating correctly at this time. Concern may have been caused by binding or incorrect pivot arm adjustment. Repair and/or adjust wiper arm and Pivot. TEST the system for normal operation. **No** INSTALL a new rear window wiper motor.

LTV0500000002362

Fig. 28   Test J: Washer Pump Is Inoperative (Part 6 of 6). 2005–06

■ corrosion. ■ pushed-out pins. • Connect all wiper motor connectors and make sure they seat correctly. • Operate the system and verify the concern is still present. • **Is the concern still present?**	**No** The system is operating correctly at this time. Concern may have been caused by a loose or corroded connector. TEST the system for normal operation.

K5 CHECK THE WINDSHIELD WIPER MOTOR

• Key in OFF position. • Disconnect: Windshield Wiper Motor C125. • Carry out the windshield wiper motor component test as cescribed in this section. • **Did the windshield wiper motor pass the component test?**	**Yes** The system is operating correctly at this time. Concern may have been caused by binding or incorrect pivot arm adjustment. Repair and/or adjust wiper arm and Pivot. TEST the system for normal operation. **No** INSTALL a new windshield wiper motor.

LTV0500000002364

Fig. 29   Test K: Windshield Wiper Speed Dependent Interval Mode Does Not Operate Correctly (Part 2 of 2). 2005–06

COMPONENT DIAGNOSIS & TESTING

Refer to "Aviator" for component diagnosis and testing procedures.

WIPER SYSTEMS

Explorer & Mountaineer

NOTE: On Air Bag Equipped Models, Refer To "Air Bag System Precautions" Located In The Front Of This Manual For System Disarming & Arming Procedures.

NOTE: "Electrical Symbol & Wire Color Code Identification" Located In The Front Of This Manual May Be Used As An Aid When Using Wiring Diagrams Found In This Section.

NOTE: Refer To "Computer Relearn Procedures" Located In The Front Of This Manual When Battery Power To The Computer Has Been Interrupted.

INDEX

	Page No.		Page No.		Page No.
Component Diagnosis & Testing	3-131	System Diagnosis & Testing	3-96	Diagnostic Tests	3-96
Diagnostic Chart Index	3-100	Accessing Diagnostic Trouble Codes	3-96	2002–04	3-96
Precautions	3-96	Clearing Diagnostic Trouble Codes	3-96	2005–06	3-96
Battery Ground Cable	3-96			Wiring Diagrams	3-96

PRECAUTIONS

Battery Ground Cable

Prior to service, disconnect battery ground cable and isolate as required.

SYSTEM DIAGNOSIS & TESTING

Accessing Diagnostic Trouble Codes

Connect a suitably programmed scan tool and Vehicle Communication Module (VCM) with appropriate adapters, or equivalents, to the Data Link Connector (DCL) located in the passenger compartment beneath the instrument panel. Follow tool manufacturer's instructions for accessing speed control Diagnostic Trouble Codes (DTC).

Wiring Diagrams

Refer to **Figs. 1 through 4** for wiring diagrams.

Diagnostic Tests

2002–04

Refer to **Figs. 5 through 16** for diagnostic tests.

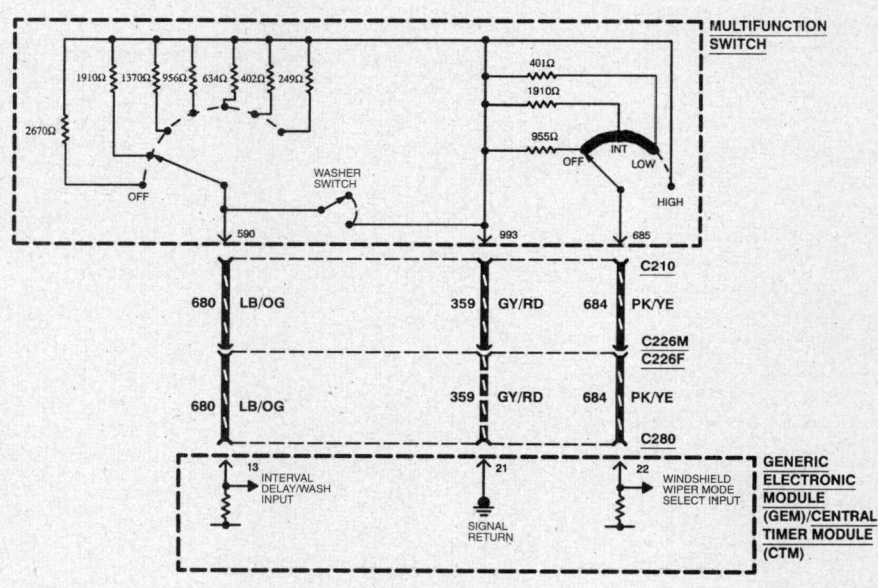

FM9029900735010X

Fig. 1   Front wiper system wiring diagram (Part 1 of 2). 2002–04

2005–06

Refer to **Figs. 17 through 30** for diagnostic tests.

Clearing Diagnostic Trouble Codes

Connect a suitably programmed scan tool and Vehicle Communication Module (VCM) with appropriate adapters, or equivalents, to the Data Link Connector (DCL) located in the passenger compartment beneath the instrument panel. Follow tool manufacturer's instructions for accessing speed control Diagnostic Trouble Codes (DTC).

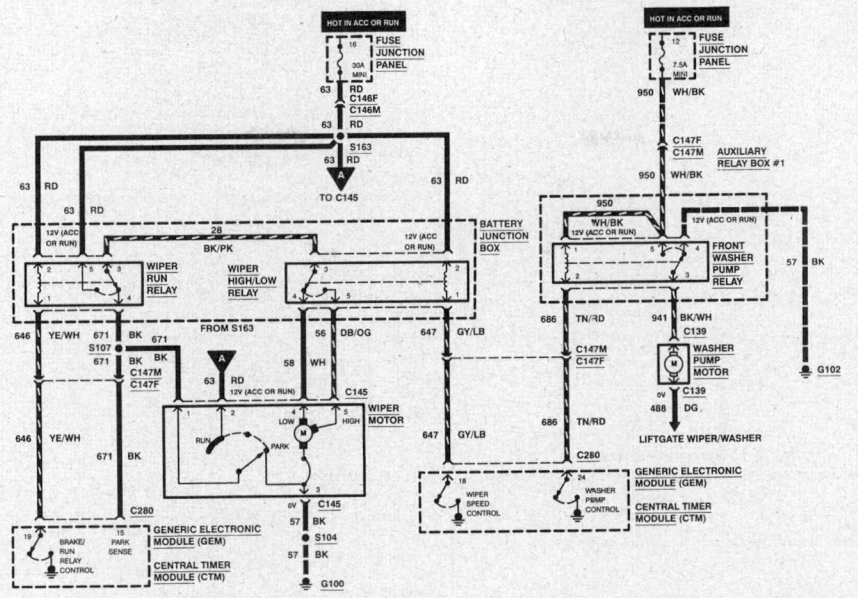

Fig. 1 Front wiper system wiring diagram (Part 2 of 2). 2002–04

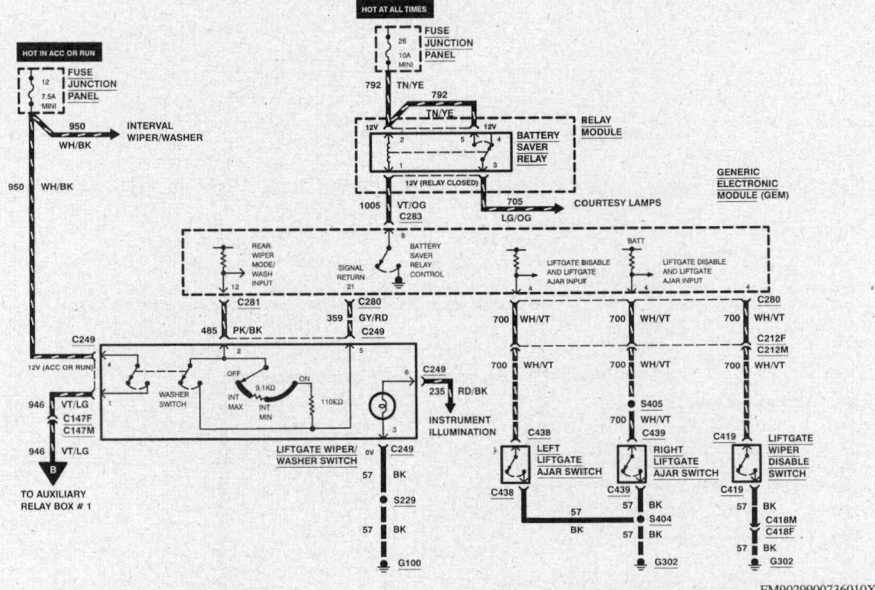

Fig. 2 Rear wiper system wiring diagram (Part 1 of 3). 2002–04

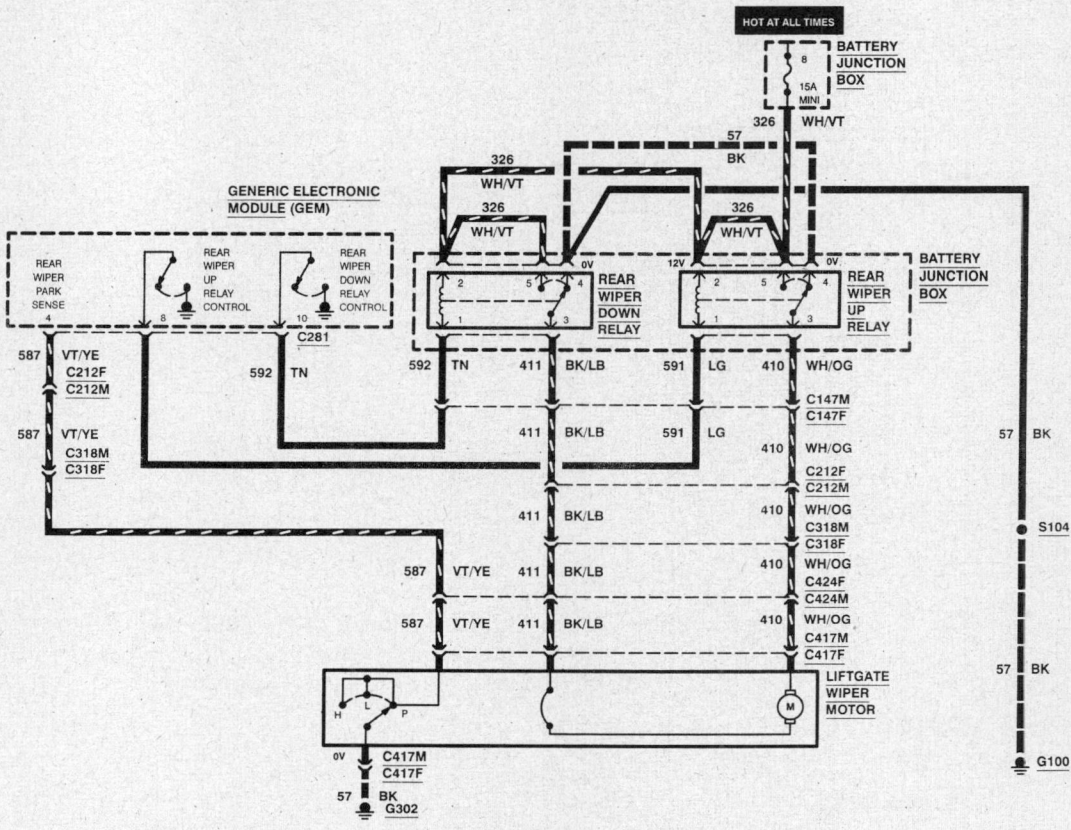

Fig. 2   Rear wiper system wiring diagram (Part 2 of 3). 2002–04

FM9029900736020X

Fig. 2   Rear wiper system wiring diagram (Part 3 of 3). 2002–04

FM9029900736030X

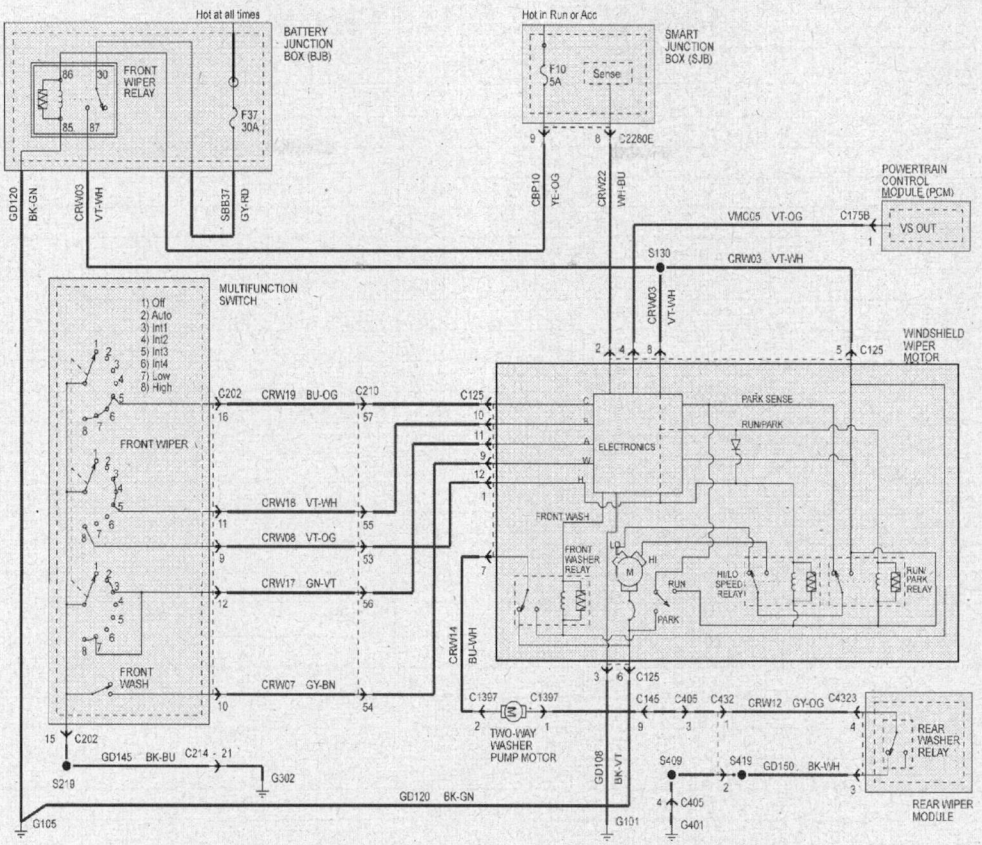

Fig. 3   Front wiper system wiring diagram. 2005–06

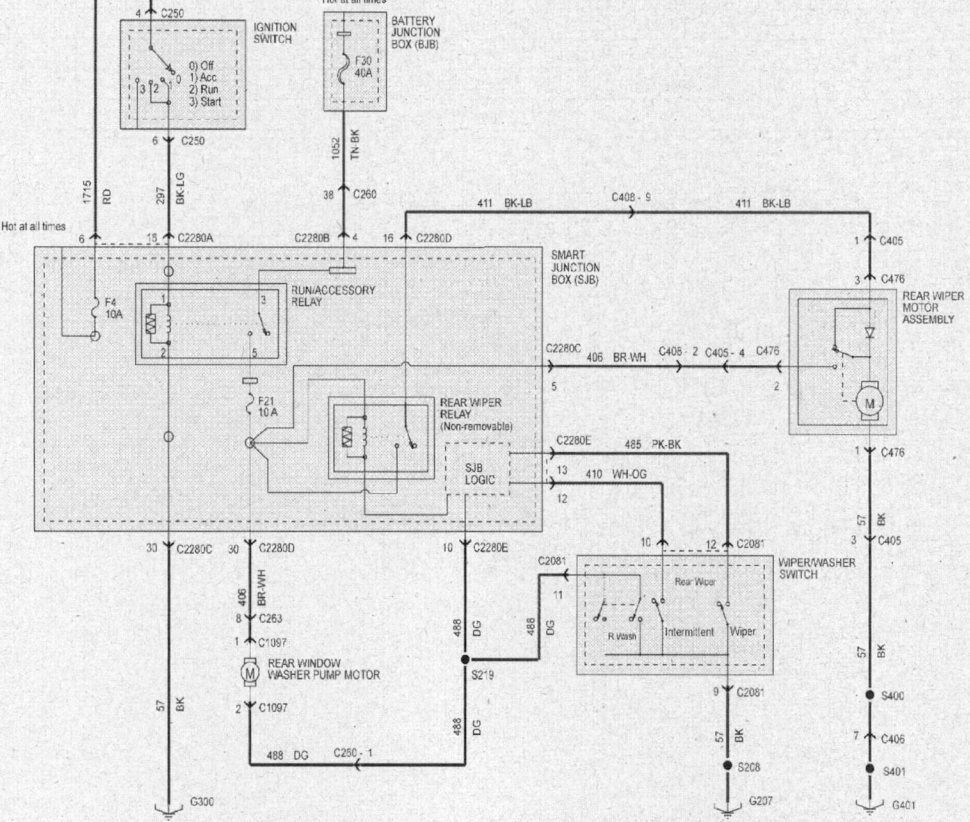

Fig. 4   Rear wiper system wiring diagram. 2005–06

DIAGNOSTIC CHART INDEX

Test	Code	Description	Page No.	Fig. No.
2002–04				
A	B1413	Wipers Are Inoperative	3-100	5
	B1432	Wipers Are Inoperative	3-100	5
	B1840	Wipers Are Inoperative	3-100	5
B	—	Wipers Stay On Continuously	3-103	6
C	B1436	High/Low Wiper Speeds Do Not Operate Properly	3-104	7
	B1466	High/Low Wiper Speeds Do Not Operate Properly	3-104	7
D	B1446	Intermittent Wiper Speed Does Not Operate Properly	3-107	8
E	B1458	Washer Pump Is Inoperative	3-109	9
	B1460	Washer Pump Is Inoperative	3-109	9
F	—	Speed Dependent Interval Mode Does Not Operate Properly	3-112	10
G	—	Wiper Do Not Operate Properly, High Speed Wipers Only Operate	3-113	11
H	—	Rear Wiper Stay On Continuously	3-115	12
J	—	Rear Washer Pump Is Inoperative	3-116	13
K	—	Rear Wiper Inoperative	3-117	14
L	—	Rear Wiper Does Not Operate Properly	3-121	15
M	—	No Communication w/GEM Module	3-123	16
2005–06				
—	—	Symptom Tests	3-123	17
A	—	Front Wipers Are Inoperative	3-124	18
B	—	Rear Wiper Is Inoperative	3-125	19
C	—	Front Wipers Stay On Continuously	3-126	20
D	—	Rear Wipers Stay On Continuously	3-126	21
E	—	Front High/Low Wiper Speeds Do Not Operate Correctly, Intermittent Mode OK	3-127	22
F	—	Rear High/Low Wiper Speeds Do Not Operate Correctly, Intermittent Mode OK	3-127	23
G	—	Front Intermittent Speed Does Not Operate Correctly, High/Low Speeds OK	3-128	24
H	—	Rear Intermittent Speed Does Not Operate Correctly, High/Low Speeds OK	3-128	25
I	—	Wipers Do Not Operate Correctly In Mist Position	3-129	26
J	—	Rear Wash & Wipe Function Is Inoperative	3-129	27
K	—	Washer Pump Is Inoperative	3-129	28
L	—	Speed Dependent Interval Mode Does Not Operate Correctly	3-130	29
M	—	Headlamps Do Not Illuminate When Wipers Are On	3-131	30

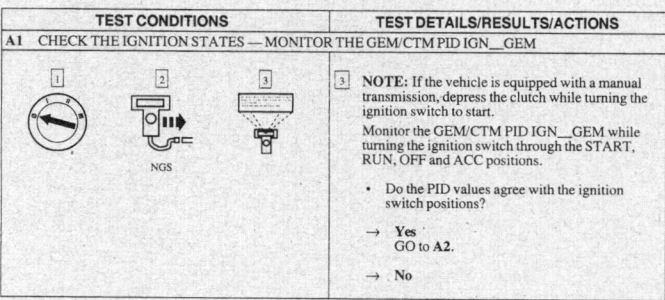

FM9029800622010X

Fig. 5   Test A: Wipers Are Inoperative (Part 1 of 10).
2002–04

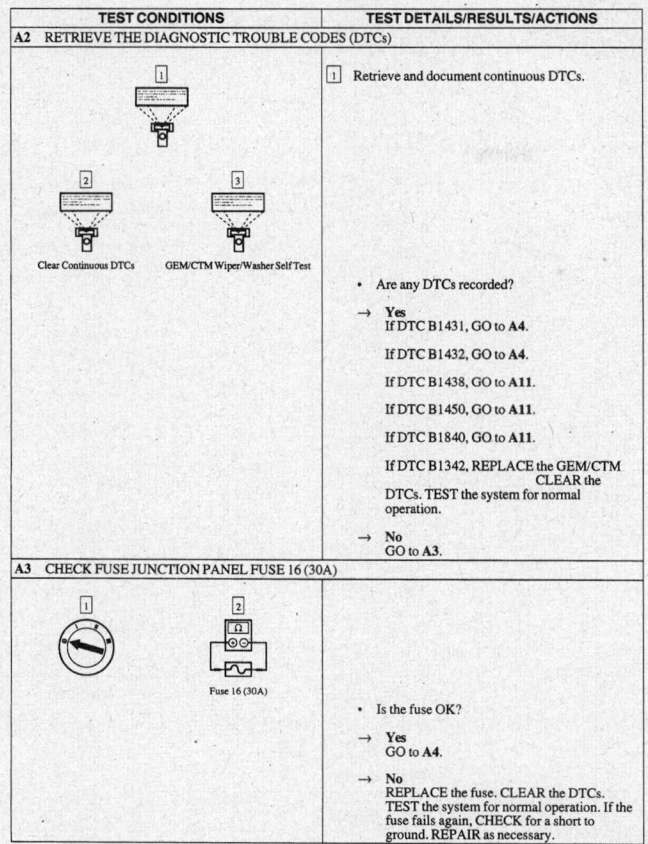

TEST CONDITIONS	TEST DETAILS/RESULTS/ACTIONS
A2 RETRIEVE THE DIAGNOSTIC TROUBLE CODES (DTCs)	

Clear Continuous DTCs   GEM/CTM Wiper/Washer Self Test

1 Retrieve and document continuous DTCs.

- Are any DTCs recorded?
- → Yes
  If DTC B1431, GO to **A4**.
  If DTC B1432, GO to **A4**.
  If DTC B1438, GO to **A11**.
  If DTC B1450, GO to **A11**.
  If DTC B1840, GO to **A11**.
  If DTC B1342, REPLACE the GEM/CTM CLEAR the DTCs. TEST the system for normal operation.
- → No
  GO to **A3**.

| A3   CHECK FUSE JUNCTION PANEL FUSE 16 (30A) | |

Fuse 16 (30A)

- Is the fuse OK?
- → Yes
  GO to **A4**.
- → No
  REPLACE the fuse. CLEAR the DTCs. TEST the system for normal operation. If the fuse fails again, CHECK for a short to ground. REPAIR as necessary.

FM9029800622020X

Fig. 5   Test A: Wipers Are Inoperative (Part 2 of 10). 2002–04

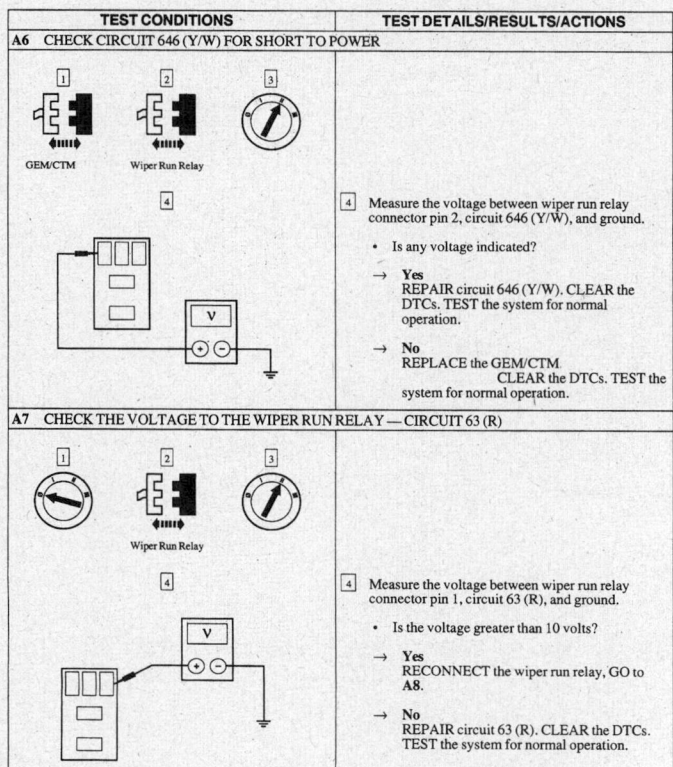

TEST CONDITIONS	TEST DETAILS/RESULTS/ACTIONS
A6 CHECK CIRCUIT 646 (Y/W) FOR SHORT TO POWER	

GEM/CTM   Wiper Run Relay

4 Measure the voltage between wiper run relay connector pin 2, circuit 646 (Y/W), and ground.

- Is any voltage indicated?
- → Yes
  REPAIR circuit 646 (Y/W). CLEAR the DTCs. TEST the system for normal operation.
- → No
  REPLACE the GEM/CTM. CLEAR the DTCs. TEST the system for normal operation.

| A7   CHECK THE VOLTAGE TO THE WIPER RUN RELAY — CIRCUIT 63 (R) | |

Wiper Run Relay

4 Measure the voltage between wiper run relay connector pin 1, circuit 63 (R), and ground.

- Is the voltage greater than 10 volts?
- → Yes
  RECONNECT the wiper run relay, GO to **A8**.
- → No
  REPAIR circuit 63 (R). CLEAR the DTCs. TEST the system for normal operation.

FM9029800622040X

Fig. 5   Test A: Wipers Are Inoperative (Part 4 of 10). 2002–04

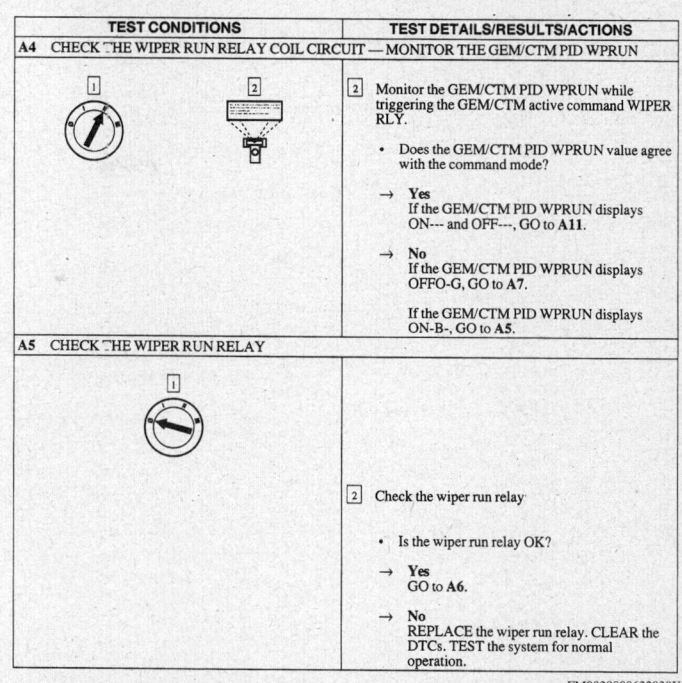

TEST CONDITIONS	TEST DETAILS/RESULTS/ACTIONS
A4 CHECK THE WIPER RUN RELAY COIL CIRCUIT — MONITOR THE GEM/CTM PID WPRUN	

2 Monitor the GEM/CTM PID WPRUN while triggering the GEM/CTM active command WIPER RLY.

- Does the GEM/CTM PID WPRUN value agree with the command mode?
- → Yes
  If the GEM/CTM PID WPRUN displays ON--- and OFF---, GO to **A11**.
- → No
  If the GEM/CTM PID WPRUN displays OFFO-G, GO to **A7**.
  If the GEM/CTM PID WPRUN displays ON-B-, GO to **A5**.

| A5   CHECK THE WIPER RUN RELAY | |

2 Check the wiper run relay

- Is the wiper run relay OK?
- → Yes
  GO to **A6**.
- → No
  REPLACE the wiper run relay. CLEAR the DTCs. TEST the system for normal operation.

FM9029800622030X

Fig. 5   Test A: Wipers Are Inoperative (Part 3 of 10). 2002–04

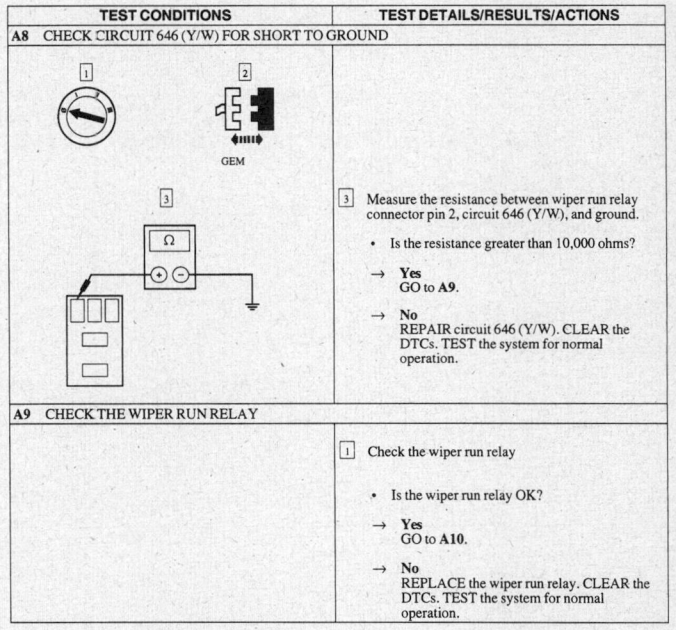

TEST CONDITIONS	TEST DETAILS/RESULTS/ACTIONS
A8 CHECK CIRCUIT 646 (Y/W) FOR SHORT TO GROUND	

GEM

3 Measure the resistance between wiper run relay connector pin 2, circuit 646 (Y/W), and ground.

- Is the resistance greater than 10,000 ohms?
- → Yes
  GO to **A9**.
- → No
  REPAIR circuit 646 (Y/W). CLEAR the DTCs. TEST the system for normal operation.

| A9   CHECK THE WIPER RUN RELAY | |

1 Check the wiper run relay

- Is the wiper run relay OK?
- → Yes
  GO to **A10**.
- → No
  REPLACE the wiper run relay. CLEAR the DTCs. TEST the system for normal operation.

FM9029800622050X

Fig. 5   Test A: Wipers Are Inoperative (Part 5 of 10). 2002–04

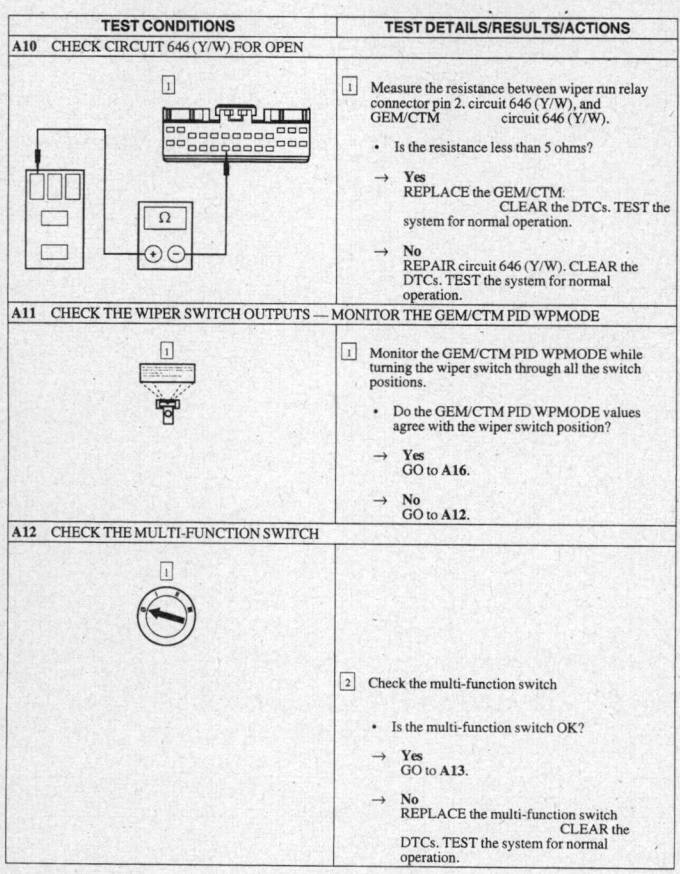

TEST CONDITIONS	TEST DETAILS/RESULTS/ACTIONS
A10 CHECK CIRCUIT 646 (Y/W) FOR OPEN	1 Measure the resistance between wiper run relay connector pin 2, circuit 646 (Y/W), and GEM/CTM circuit 646 (Y/W). • Is the resistance less than 5 ohms? → **Yes** REPLACE the GEM/CTM. CLEAR the DTCs. TEST the system for normal operation. → **No** REPAIR circuit 646 (Y/W). CLEAR the DTCs. TEST the system for normal operation.
A11 CHECK THE WIPER SWITCH OUTPUTS — MONITOR THE GEM/CTM PID WPMODE	1 Monitor the GEM/CTM PID WPMODE while turning the wiper switch through all the switch positions. • Do the GEM/CTM PID WPMODE values agree with the wiper switch position? → **Yes** GO to **A16**. → **No** GO to **A12**.
A12 CHECK THE MULTI-FUNCTION SWITCH	2 Check the multi-function switch • Is the multi-function switch OK? → **Yes** GO to **A13**. → **No** REPLACE the multi-function switch. CLEAR the DTCs. TEST the system for normal operation.

Fig. 5   Test A: Wipers Are Inoperative (Part 6 of 10). 2002–04

FM9029800622060X

TEST CONDITIONS	TEST DETAILS/RESULTS/ACTIONS
A15 CHECK CIRCUIT 684 (PK/Y) FOR OPEN	1 Measure the resistance between multi-function switch circuit 684 (PK/Y), and GEM/CTM circuit 684 (PK/Y). • Is the resistance less than 5 ohms? → **Yes** REPLACE the GEM/CTM CLEAR the DTCs. TEST the system for normal operation. → **No** REPAIR circuit 684 (PK/Y). CLEAR the DTCs. TEST the system for normal operation.
A16 CHECK THE VOLTAGE TO THE SWITCH SIDE OF THE WIPER RUN RELAY — CIRCUIT 63 (R)	4 Measure the voltage between wiper run relay connector pin 5, circuit 63 (R), and ground. • Is the voltage greater than 10 volts? → **Yes** RECONNECT the wiper run relay; GO to **A17**. → **No** REPAIR circuit 63 (R). CLEAR the DTCs. TEST the system for normal operation.

Fig. 5   Test A: Wipers Are Inoperative (Part 8 of 10). 2002–04

FM9029800622080X

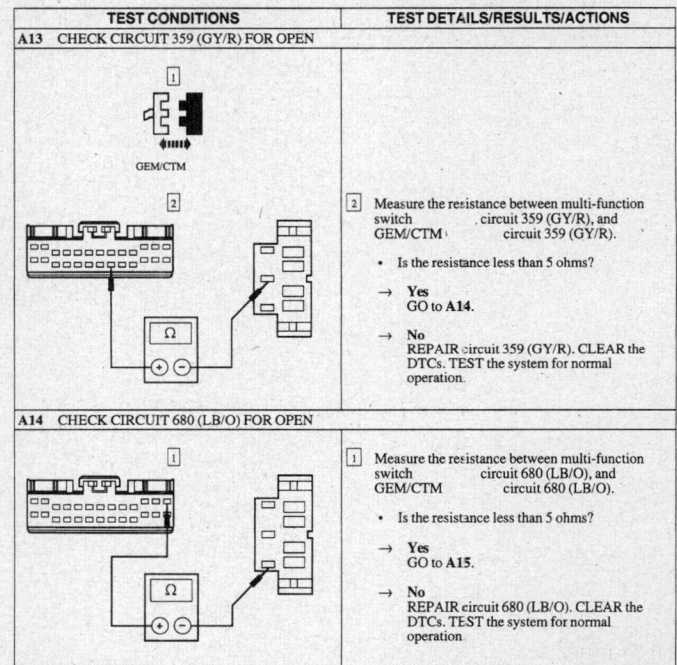

TEST CONDITIONS	TEST DETAILS/RESULTS/ACTIONS
A13 CHECK CIRCUIT 359 (GY/R) FOR OPEN	2 Measure the resistance between multi-function switch circuit 359 (GY/R), and GEM/CTM circuit 359 (GY/R). • Is the resistance less than 5 ohms? → **Yes** GO to **A14**. → **No** REPAIR circuit 359 (GY/R). CLEAR the DTCs. TEST the system for normal operation.
A14 CHECK CIRCUIT 680 (LB/O) FOR OPEN	1 Measure the resistance between multi-function switch circuit 680 (LB/O), and GEM/CTM circuit 680 (LB/O). • Is the resistance less than 5 ohms? → **Yes** GO to **A15**. → **No** REPAIR circuit 680 (LB/O). CLEAR the DTCs. TEST the system for normal operation.

FM9029800622070X

Fig. 5   Test A: Wipers Are Inoperative (Part 7 of 10). 2002–04

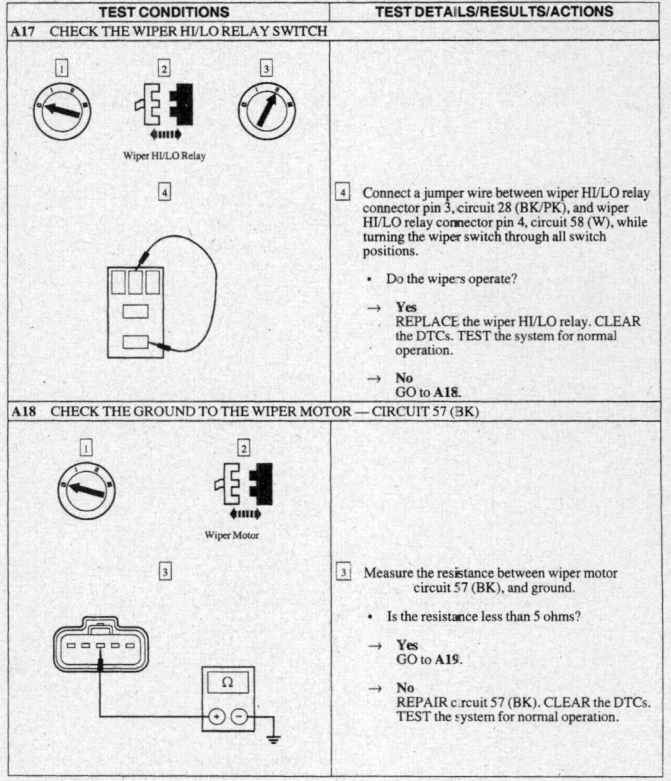

TEST CONDITIONS	TEST DETAILS/RESULTS/ACTIONS
A17 CHECK THE WIPER HI/LO RELAY SWITCH	4 Connect a jumper wire between wiper HI/LO relay connector pin 3, circuit 28 (BK/PK), and wiper HI/LO relay connector pin 4, circuit 58 (W), while turning the wiper switch through all switch positions. • Do the wipers operate? → **Yes** REPLACE the wiper HI/LO relay. CLEAR the DTCs. TEST the system for normal operation. → **No** GO to **A18**.
A18 CHECK THE GROUND TO THE WIPER MOTOR — CIRCUIT 57 (BK)	3 Measure the resistance between wiper motor circuit 57 (BK), and ground. • Is the resistance less than 5 ohms? → **Yes** GO to **A19**. → **No** REPAIR circuit 57 (BK). CLEAR the DTCs. TEST the system for normal operation.

FM9029800622090X

Fig. 5   Test A: Wipers Are Inoperative (Part 9 of 10). 2002–04

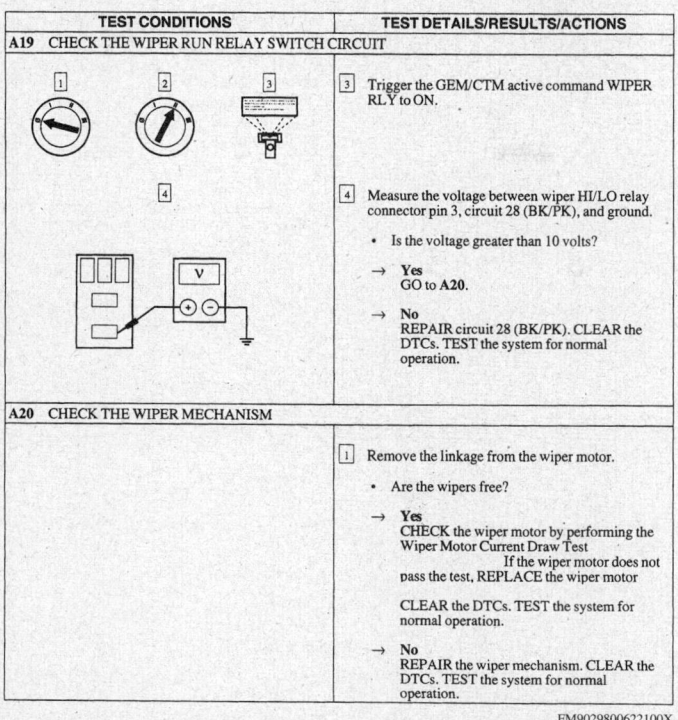

TEST CONDITIONS	TEST DETAILS/RESULTS/ACTIONS
A19 CHECK THE WIPER RUN RELAY SWITCH CIRCUIT	**3** Trigger the GEM/CTM active command WIPER RLY to ON.
	4 Measure the voltage between wiper HI/LO relay connector pin 3, circuit 28 (BK/PK), and ground. • Is the voltage greater than 10 volts? → **Yes** GO to **A20**. → **No** REPAIR circuit 28 (BK/PK). CLEAR the DTCs. TEST the system for normal operation.
A20 CHECK THE WIPER MECHANISM	**1** Remove the linkage from the wiper motor. • Are the wipers free? → **Yes** CHECK the wiper motor by performing the Wiper Motor Current Draw Test If the wiper motor does not pass the test, REPLACE the wiper motor CLEAR the DTCs. TEST the system for normal operation. → **No** REPAIR the wiper mechanism. CLEAR the DTCs. TEST the system for normal operation.

FM9029800622100X

Fig. 5 Test A: Wipers Are Inoperative (Part 10 of 10). 2002–04

TEST CONDITIONS	TEST DETAILS/RESULTS/ACTIONS
B3 CHECK THE WIPER SWITCH OUTPUTS — MONITOR THE GEM/CTM PID WPMODE	**2** Monitor the GEM/CTM PID WPMODE while turning the wiper switch through all the switch positions. • Does the GEM/CTM PID WPMODE agree with the wiper switch positions? → **Yes** GO to **B7**. → **No** GO to **B4**.
B4 CHECK THE WIPER SWITCH Multi-Function Switch C210	**3** Check the multi-function switch • Is the wiper switch OK? → **Yes** GO to **B5**. → **No** REPLACE the multi-function switch CLEAR the DTCs. TEST the system for normal operation.

FM9029800623020X

Fig. 6 Test B: Wipers Stay On Continuously (Part 2 of 7). 2002–04

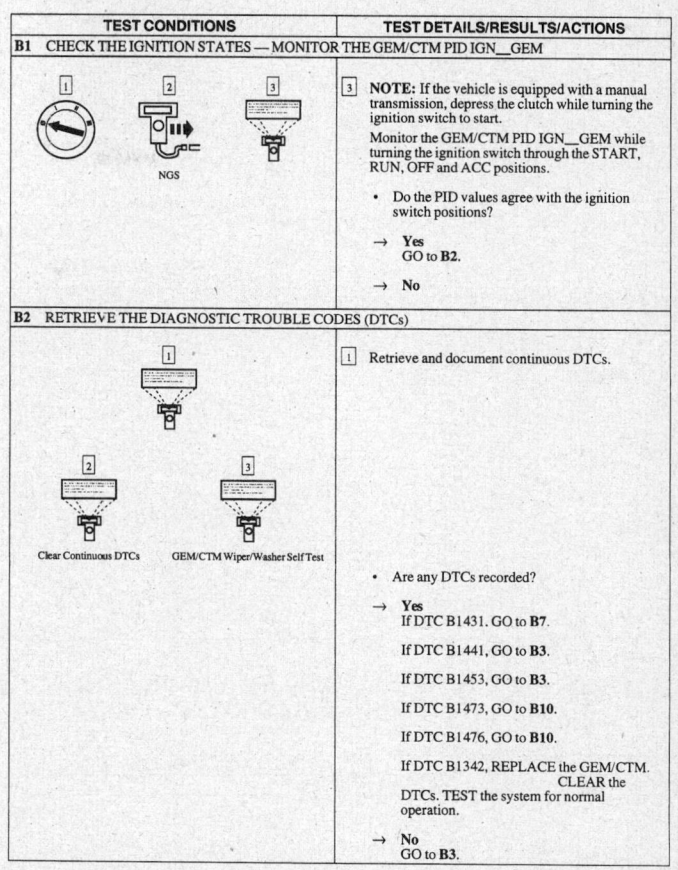

TEST CONDITIONS	TEST DETAILS/RESULTS/ACTIONS
B1 CHECK THE IGNITION STATES — MONITOR THE GEM/CTM PID IGN__GEM NGS	**3** NOTE: If the vehicle is equipped with a manual transmission, depress the clutch while turning the ignition switch to start. Monitor the GEM/CTM PID IGN__GEM while turning the ignition switch through the START, RUN, OFF and ACC positions. • Do the PID values agree with the ignition switch positions? → **Yes** GO to **B2**. → **No**
B2 RETRIEVE THE DIAGNOSTIC TROUBLE CODES (DTCs) Clear Continuous DTCs GEM/CTM Wiper/Washer Self Test	**1** Retrieve and document continuous DTCs. • Are any DTCs recorded? → **Yes** If DTC B1431. GO to **B7**. If DTC B1441, GO to **B3**. If DTC B1453, GO to **B3**. If DTC B1473, GO to **B10**. If DTC B1476, GO to **B10**. If DTC B1342, REPLACE the GEM/CTM. CLEAR the DTCs. TEST the system for normal operation. → **No** GO to **B3**.

FM9029800623010X

Fig. 6 Test B: Wipers Stay On Continuously (Part 1 of 7). 2002–04

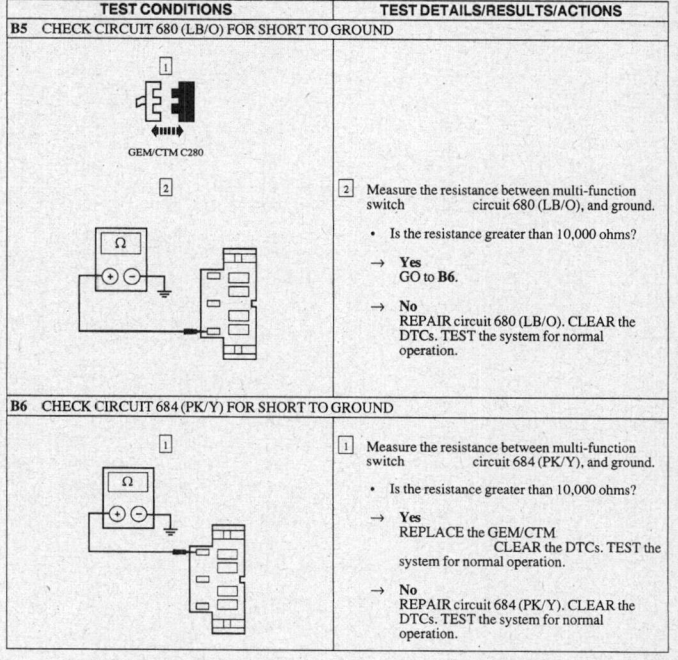

TEST CONDITIONS	TEST DETAILS/RESULTS/ACTIONS
B5 CHECK CIRCUIT 680 (LB/O) FOR SHORT TO GROUND GEM/CTM C280	**2** Measure the resistance between multi-function switch circuit 680 (LB/O), and ground. • Is the resistance greater than 10,000 ohms? → **Yes** GO to **B6**. → **No** REPAIR circuit 680 (LB/O). CLEAR the DTCs. TEST the system for normal operation.
B6 CHECK CIRCUIT 684 (PK/Y) FOR SHORT TO GROUND	**1** Measure the resistance between multi-function switch circuit 684 (PK/Y), and ground. • Is the resistance greater than 10,000 ohms? → **Yes** REPLACE the GEM/CTM CLEAR the DTCs. TEST the system for normal operation. → **No** REPAIR circuit 684 (PK/Y). CLEAR the DTCs. TEST the system for normal operation.

FM9029800623030X

Fig. 6 Test B: Wipers Stay On Continuously (Part 3 of 7). 2002–04

TEST CONDITIONS	TEST DETAILS/RESULTS/ACTIONS
B7 CHECK THE WIPER RUN RELAY COIL CIRCUIT — MONITOR THE GEM/CTM PID WPRUN	
[1] [2]	[2] Monitor the GEM/CTM PID WPRUN while triggering the GEM/CTM active command WIPER RLY. • Does the GEM/CTM PID WPRUN agree with the active command mode? → **Yes** If the GEM/CTM PID WPRUN displays ON--- and OFF---, GO to **B10**. → **No** If the GEM/CTM PID WPRUN displays OFFO-G, GO to **B8**.
B8 CHECK THE WIPER RUN RELAY	
[1] [2] Wiper Run Relay	[3] Check the wiper run relay • Is the wiper run relay OK? → **Yes** GO to **B9**. → **No** REPLACE wiper run relay. CLEAR the DTCs. TEST the system for normal operation.

FM9029800623040X

Fig. 6   Test B: Wipers Stay On Continuously (Part 4 of 7). 2002–04

TEST CONDITIONS	TEST DETAILS/RESULTS/ACTIONS
B11 CHECK CIRCUIT 56 (DB/O) FOR SHORT TO POWER	
[1] [2] [3] [4] Wiper HI/LO Relay Wiper Motor [5]	[5] Measure the voltage between wiper HI/LO relay connector pin 5, circuit 56 (DB/O), and ground. • Is any voltage indicated? → **Yes** REPAIR circuit 56 (DB/O). CLEAR the DTCs. TEST the system for normal operation. → **No** GO to **B12**.
B12 CHECK CIRCUIT 58 (W) FOR SHORT TO POWER	
[1]	[1] Measure the voltage between wiper HI/LO relay connector pin 4, circuit 58 (W), and ground. • Is any voltage indicated? → **Yes** REPAIR circuit 58 (W). CLEAR the DTCs. TEST the system for normal operation. → **No** GO to **B13**.

FM9029800623060X

Fig. 6   Test B: Wipers Stay On Continuously (Part 6 of 7). 2002–04

TEST CONDITIONS	TEST DETAILS/RESULTS/ACTIONS
B9 CHECK CIRCUIT 646 (Y/W) FOR SHORT TO GROUND	
[1] GEM/CTM [2]	[2] Measure the resistance between wiper run relay connector pin 2, circuit 646 (Y/W), and ground. • Is the resistance greater than 10,000 ohms? → **Yes** REPLACE the GEM/CTM CLEAR the DTCs. TEST the system for normal operation. → **No** REPAIR circuit 646 (Y/W). CLEAR the DTCs. TEST the system for normal operation.
B10 CHECK THE WINDSHIELD WIPER RUN RELAY SWITCH CIRCUIT	
[1] [2] Wiper Run Relay	• Do the wipers stop operating? → **Yes** REPLACE the wiper run relay. CLEAR the DTCs. TEST the system for normal operation. → **No** GO to **B11**.

FM9029800623050X

Fig. 6   Test B: Wipers Stay On Continuously (Part 5 of 7). 2002–04

TEST CONDITIONS	TEST DETAILS/RESULTS/ACTIONS
B13 CHECK CIRCUIT 28 (BK/PK) FOR SHORT TO POWER	
[1]	[1] Measure the voltage between wiper HI/LO relay connector pin 3, circuit 28 (BK/PK), and ground. • Is any voltage indicated? → **Yes** REPAIR circuit 28 (BK/PK). CLEAR the DTCs. TEST the system for normal operation. → **No** REPLACE the wiper motor CLEAR the DTCs. TEST the system for normal operation

FM9029800623070X

Fig. 6   Test B: Wipers Stay On Continuously (Part 7 of 7). 2002–04

TEST CONDITIONS	TEST DETAILS/RESULTS/ACTIONS
C1 CHECK THE IGNITION STATES — MONITOR THE GEM/CTM PID IGN__GEM	
[1] [2] [3] NGS	[3] **NOTE:** If the vehicle is equipped with a manual transmission, depress the clutch while turning the ignition switch to start. Monitor the GEM/CTM PID IGN__GEM while turning the ignition switch through the START, RUN, OFF and ACC positions. • Do the PID values agree with the ignition switch positions? → **Yes** GO to **C2** → **No**
C2 RETRIEVE THE DIAGNOSTIC TROUBLE CODES (DTCS)	
[1] [2] [3] Clear Continuous DTCs GEM/CTM Wiper/Washer Self-Test	[1] Retrieve and document continuous DTCs.

FM9029800624010X

Fig. 7   Test C: High/Low Wiper Speeds Do Not Operate Properly (Part 1 of 11). 2002–04

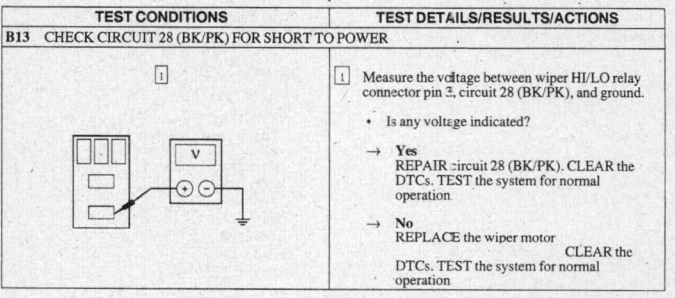

TEST CONDITIONS	TEST DETAILS/RESULTS/ACTIONS
C2 RETRIEVE THE DIAGNOSTIC TROUBLE CODES (DTCS) (Continued)	
	• Are any DTCs recorded?
	→ **Yes** If DTC B1434, GO to **C9**. If DTC B1436, GO to **C9**. If DTC B1438, GO to **C3**. If DTC B1441, GO to **C3**. If DTC B1450, GO to **C3**. If DTC B1466, GO to **C3**. If DTC B1473, GO to **C3**. If DTC B1476, GO to **C3**. If DTC B1342, REPLACE the GEM/CTM CLEAR the DTCs. TEST the system for normal operation. → **No** GO to **C3**.
C3 CHECK THE WIPER SWITCH OUTPUTS — MONITOR THE GEM/CTM PID WPMODE	
☐1	1 Monitor the GEM/CTM PID WPMODE while turning the wiper switch through all switch positions. • Does the GEM/CTM PID WPMODE value agree with the wiper switch position? → **Yes** GO to **C9**. → **No** GO to **C4**.

FM9029800624020X

Fig. 7 Test C: High/Low Wiper Speeds Do Not Operate Properly (Part 2 of 11). 2002–04

TEST CONDITIONS	TEST DETAILS/RESULTS/ACTIONS
C6 CHECK CIRCUIT 684 (PK/Y) FOR SHORT TO POWER	
	1 Measure the voltage between multi-function switch circuit 684 (PK/Y), and ground. • Is any voltage indicated? → **Yes** REPAIR circuit 684 (PK/Y). CLEAR the DTCs. TEST the system for normal operation. → **No** GO to **C7**.
C7 CHECK CIRCUIT 680 (LB/O) FOR OPEN	
	2 Measure the resistance between multi-function switch circuit 680 (LB/O), and GEM circuit 680 (LB/O). • Is the resistance less than 5 ohms? → **Yes** GO to **C8**. → **No** REPAIR circuit 680 (LB/O). CLEAR the DTCs. TEST the system for normal operation.

FM9029800624040X

Fig. 7 Test C: High/Low Wiper Speeds Do Not Operate Properly (Part 4 of 11). 2002–04

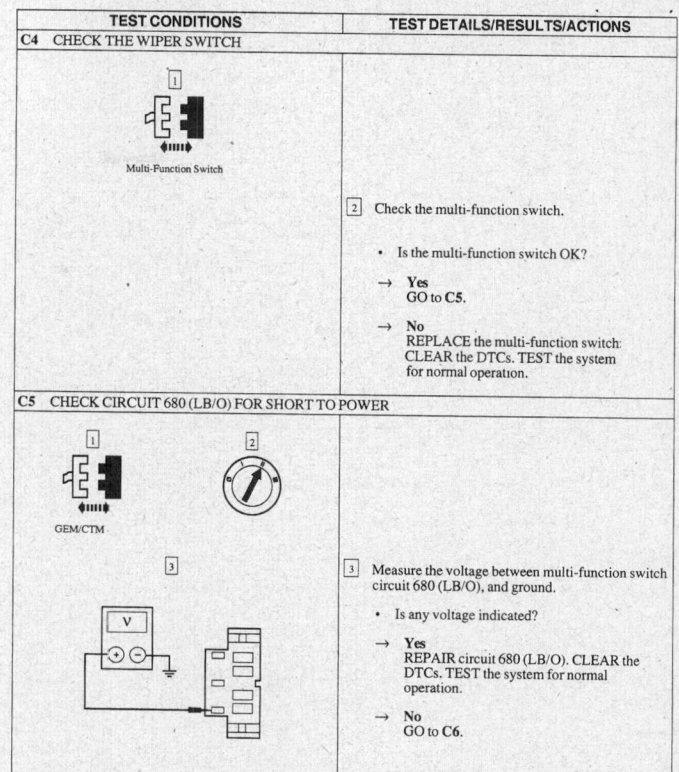

TEST CONDITIONS	TEST DETAILS/RESULTS/ACTIONS
C4 CHECK THE WIPER SWITCH	
Multi-Function Switch	2 Check the multi-function switch. • Is the multi-function switch OK? → **Yes** GO to **C5**. → **No** REPLACE the multi-function switch: CLEAR the DTCs. TEST the system for normal operation.
C5 CHECK CIRCUIT 680 (LB/O) FOR SHORT TO POWER	
GEM/CTM	3 Measure the voltage between multi-function switch circuit 680 (LB/O), and ground. • Is any voltage indicated? → **Yes** REPAIR circuit 680 (LB/O). CLEAR the DTCs. TEST the system for normal operation. → **No** GO to **C6**.

FM9029800624030X

Fig. 7 Test C: High/Low Wiper Speeds Do Not Operate Properly (Part 3 of 11). 2002–04

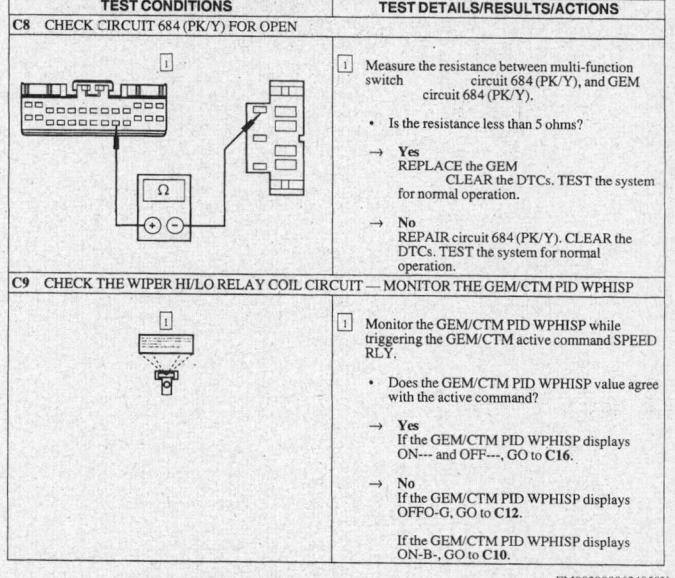

TEST CONDITIONS	TEST DETAILS/RESULTS/ACTIONS
C8 CHECK CIRCUIT 684 (PK/Y) FOR OPEN	
	1 Measure the resistance between multi-function switch circuit 684 (PK/Y), and GEM circuit 684 (PK/Y). • Is the resistance less than 5 ohms? → **Yes** REPLACE the GEM CLEAR the DTCs. TEST the system for normal operation. → **No** REPAIR circuit 684 (PK/Y). CLEAR the DTCs. TEST the system for normal operation.
C9 CHECK THE WIPER HI/LO RELAY COIL CIRCUIT — MONITOR THE GEM/CTM PID WPHISP	
	1 Monitor the GEM/CTM PID WPHISP while triggering the GEM/CTM active command SPEED RLY. • Does the GEM/CTM PID WPHISP value agree with the active command? → **Yes** If the GEM/CTM PID WPHISP displays ON--- and OFF---, GO to **C16**. → **No** If the GEM/CTM PID WPHISP displays OFFO-G, GO to **C12**. If the GEM/CTM PID WPHISP displays ON-B-, GO to **C10**.

FM9029800624050X

Fig. 7 Test C: High/Low Wiper Speeds Do Not Operate Properly (Part 5 of 11). 2002–04

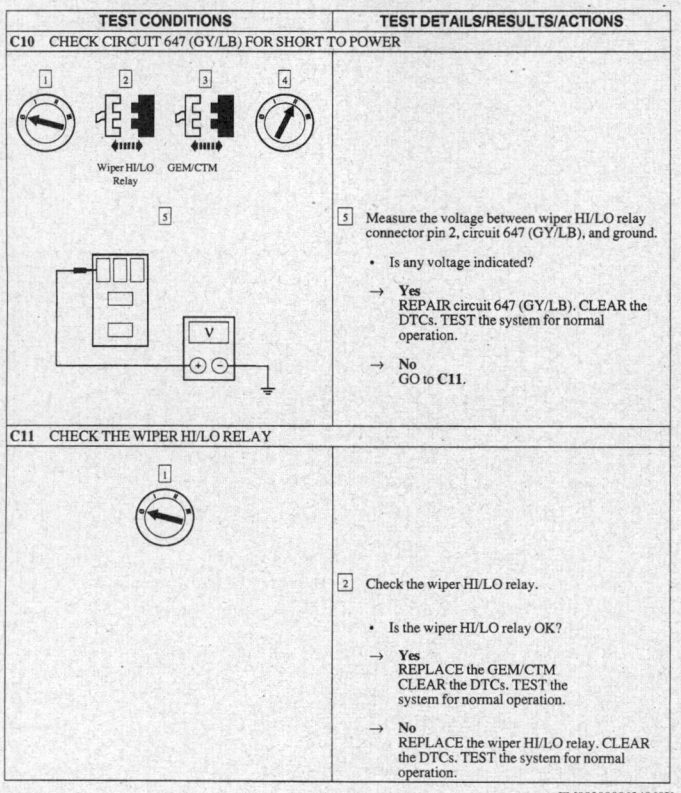

TEST CONDITIONS	TEST DETAILS/RESULTS/ACTIONS
C10 CHECK CIRCUIT 647 (GY/LB) FOR SHORT TO POWER	

5 | Measure the voltage between wiper HI/LO relay connector pin 2, circuit 647 (GY/LB), and ground.

- Is any voltage indicated?

→ **Yes**
REPAIR circuit 647 (GY/LB). CLEAR the DTCs. TEST the system for normal operation.

→ **No**
GO to **C11**.

| **C11   CHECK THE WIPER HI/LO RELAY** | |

2 | Check the wiper HI/LO relay.

- Is the wiper HI/LO relay OK?

→ **Yes**
REPLACE the GEM/CTM CLEAR the DTCs. TEST the system for normal operation.

→ **No**
REPLACE the wiper HI/LO relay. CLEAR the DTCs. TEST the system for normal operation.

FM9029800624060X

Fig. 7   Test C: High/Low Wiper Speeds Do Not Operate Properly (Part 6 of 11). 2002–04

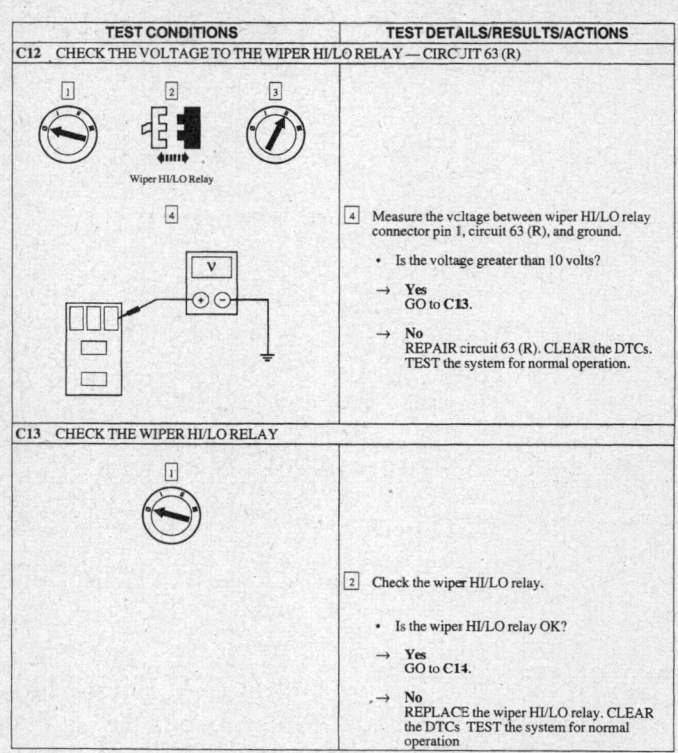

TEST CONDITIONS	TEST DETAILS/RESULTS/ACTIONS
C12 CHECK THE VOLTAGE TO THE WIPER HI/LO RELAY — CIRCUIT 63 (R)	

4 | Measure the voltage between wiper HI/LO relay connector pin 1, circuit 63 (R), and ground.

- Is the voltage greater than 10 volts?

→ **Yes**
GO to **C13**.

→ **No**
REPAIR circuit 63 (R). CLEAR the DTCs. TEST the system for normal operation.

| **C13   CHECK THE WIPER HI/LO RELAY** | |

2 | Check the wiper HI/LO relay.

- Is the wiper HI/LO relay OK?

→ **Yes**
GO to **C14**.

→ **No**
REPLACE the wiper HI/LO relay. CLEAR the DTCs. TEST the system for normal operation

FM9029800624070X

Fig. 7   Test C: High/Low Wiper Speeds Do Not Operate Properly (Part 7 of 11). 2002–04

TEST CONDITIONS	TEST DETAILS/RESULTS/ACTIONS
C14 CHECK CIRCUIT 647 (GY/LB) FOR SHORT TO GROUND	

2 | Measure the resistance between wiper HI/LO relay connector pin 2, circuit 647 (GY/LB), and ground.

- Is the resistance greater than 10,000 ohms?

→ **Yes**
GO to **C15**.

→ **No**
REPAIR circuit 647 (GY/LB). CLEAR the DTCs. TEST the system for normal operation.

| **C15   CHECK CIRCUIT 647 (GY/LB) FOR OPEN** | |

1 | Measure the resistance between GEM/CTM circuit 647 (GY/LB), and wiper HI/LO relay connector pin 2, circuit 647 (GY/LB).

- Is the resistance less than 5 ohms?

→ **Yes**
REPLACE the GEM/CTM CLEAR the DTCs. TEST the system for normal operation.

→ **No**
REPAIR circuit 647 (GY/LB). CLEAR the DTCs. TEST the system for normal operation.

FM9029800624080X

Fig. 7   Test C: High/Low Wiper Speeds Do Not Operate Properly (Part 8 of 11). 2002–04

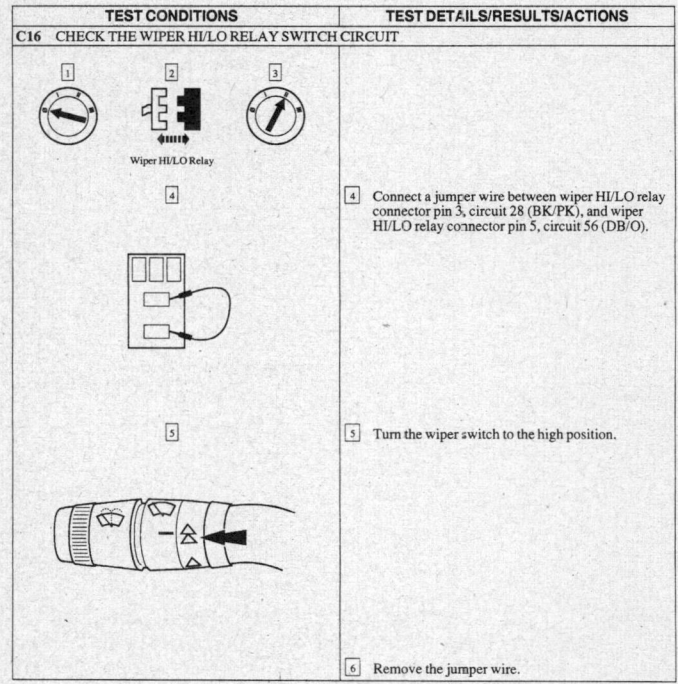

TEST CONDITIONS	TEST DETAILS/RESULTS/ACTIONS
C16 CHECK THE WIPER HI/LO RELAY SWITCH CIRCUIT	

4 | Connect a jumper wire between wiper HI/LO relay connector pin 3, circuit 28 (BK/PK), and wiper HI/LO relay connector pin 5, circuit 56 (DB/O).

5 | Turn the wiper switch to the high position.

6 | Remove the jumper wire.

FM9029800624090X

Fig. 7   Test C: High/Low Wiper Speeds Do Not Operate Properly (Part 9 of 11). 2002–04

TEST CONDITIONS	TEST DETAILS/RESULTS/ACTIONS
C16 CHECK THE WIPER HI/LO RELAY SWITCH CIRCUIT (Continued)	

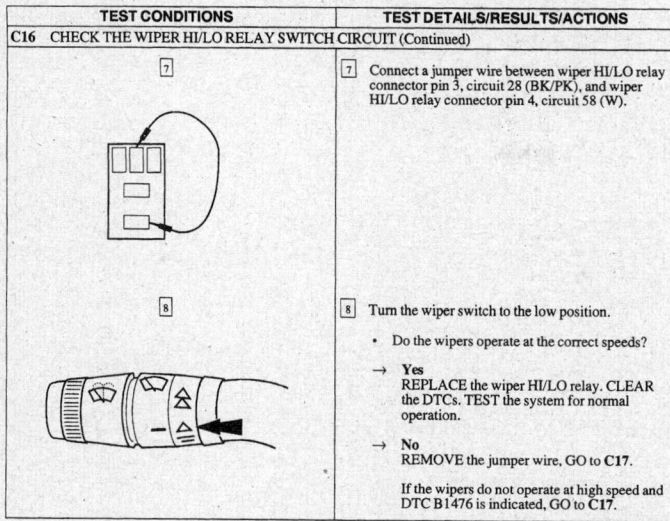

7 Connect a jumper wire between wiper HI/LO relay connector pin 3, circuit 28 (BK/PK), and wiper HI/LO relay connector pin 4, circuit 58 (W).

8 Turn the wiper switch to the low position.

- Do the wipers operate at the correct speeds?

→ **Yes**
REPLACE the wiper HI/LO relay. CLEAR the DTCs. TEST the system for normal operation.

→ **No**
REMOVE the jumper wire, GO to **C17**.

If the wipers do not operate at high speed and DTC B1476 is indicated, GO to **C17**.

FM9029800624100X

Fig. 7   Test C: High/Low Wiper Speeds Do Not Operate Properly (Part 10 of 11). 2002–04

TEST CONDITIONS	TEST DETAILS/RESULTS/ACTIONS
D1 CHECK THE IGNITION STATES — MONITOR THE GEM/CTM PID IGN__GEM	

NGS

3 NOTE: If the vehicle is equipped with a manual transmission, depress the clutch while turning the ignition switch to start.
Monitor the GEM/CTM PID IGN__GEM while turning the ignition switch through the START, RUN, OFF and ACC positions.

- Do the PID values agree with the ignition switch positions?

→ **Yes**
GO to **D2**.

→ **No**

TEST CONDITIONS	TEST DETAILS/RESULTS/ACTIONS
D2 RETRIEVE THE DIAGNOSTIC TROUBLE CODES (DTCS)	

Clear Continuous DTCs   GEM/CTM Wiper/Washer Self-Test

1 Retrieve and document continuous DTCs.

- Are any DTCs recorded?

→ **Yes**
If DTC B1438, GO to **D3**.
If DTC B1446, GO to **D9**.
If DTC B1450, GO to **D3**.
If DTC B1453, GO to **D3**.
If DTC B1342, REPLACE the GEM/CTM. CLEAR the DTCs. TEST the system for normal operation.

→ **No**
GO to **D3**.

FM9029800625010X

Fig. 8   Test D: Intermittent Wiper Speed Does Not Operate Properly (Part 1 of 9). 2002–04

TEST CONDITIONS	TEST DETAILS/RESULTS/ACTIONS
C17 CHECK CIRCUIT 56 (DB/O) FOR OPEN	

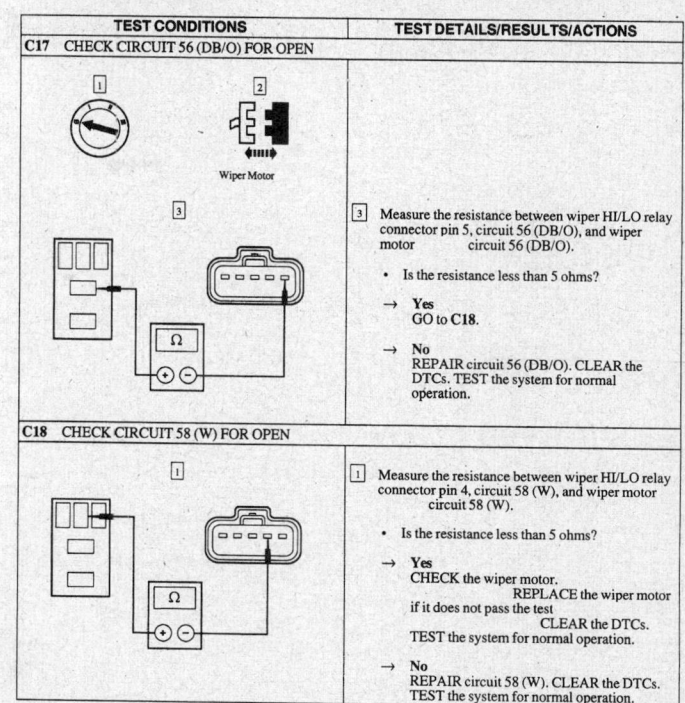

Wiper Motor

3 Measure the resistance between wiper HI/LO relay connector pin 5, circuit 56 (DB/O), and wiper motor   circuit 56 (DB/O).

- Is the resistance less than 5 ohms?

→ **Yes**
GO to **C18**.

→ **No**
REPAIR circuit 56 (DB/O). CLEAR the DTCs. TEST the system for normal operation.

TEST CONDITIONS	TEST DETAILS/RESULTS/ACTIONS
C18 CHECK CIRCUIT 58 (W) FOR OPEN	

1 Measure the resistance between wiper HI/LO relay connector pin 4, circuit 58 (W), and wiper motor circuit 58 (W).

- Is the resistance less than 5 ohms?

→ **Yes**
CHECK the wiper motor.
REPLACE the wiper motor if it does not pass the test
CLEAR the DTCs.
TEST the system for normal operation.

→ **No**
REPAIR circuit 58 (W). CLEAR the DTCs. TEST the system for normal operation.

FM9029800624110X

Fig. 7   Test C: High/Low Wiper Speeds Do Not Operate Properly (Part 11 of 11). 2002–04

TEST CONDITIONS	TEST DETAILS/RESULTS/ACTIONS
D3 CHECK THE WIPER SWITCH OUTPUTS — MONITOR THE GEM/CTM PID WPMODE	

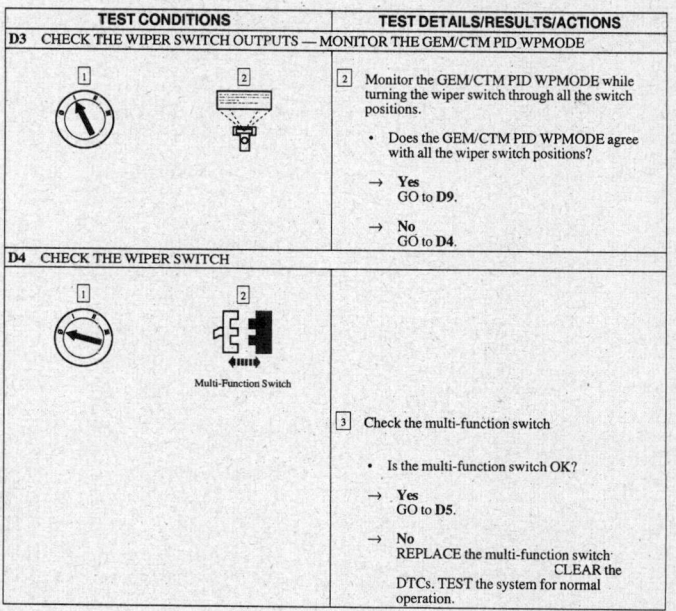

2 Monitor the GEM/CTM PID WPMODE while turning the wiper switch through all the switch positions.

- Does the GEM/CTM PID WPMODE agree with all the wiper switch positions?

→ **Yes**
GO to **D9**.

→ **No**
GO to **D4**.

TEST CONDITIONS	TEST DETAILS/RESULTS/ACTIONS
D4 CHECK THE WIPER SWITCH	

Multi-Function Switch

3 Check the multi-function switch.

- Is the multi-function switch OK?

→ **Yes**
GO to **D5**.

→ **No**
REPLACE the multi-function switch. CLEAR the DTCs. TEST the system for normal operation.

FM9029800625020X

Fig. 8   Test D: Intermittent Wiper Speed Does Not Operate Properly (Part 2 of 9). 2002–04

WIPER SYSTEMS

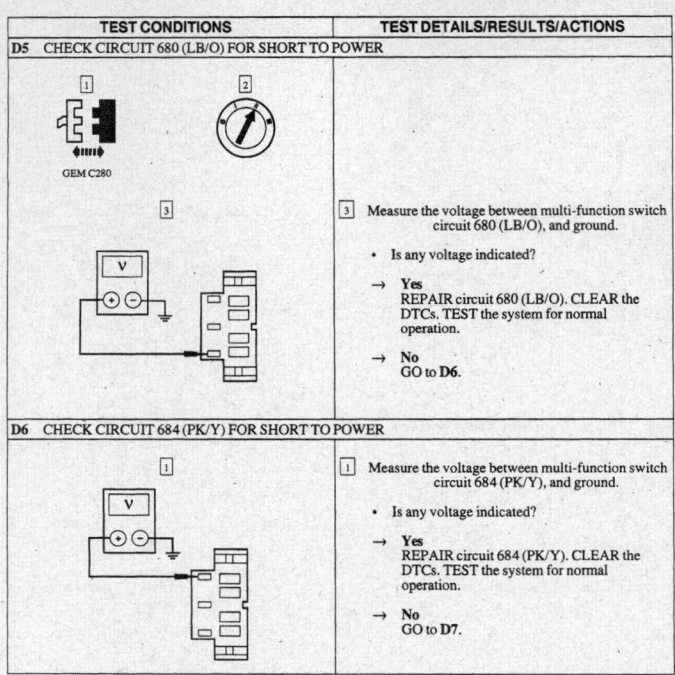

TEST CONDITIONS	TEST DETAILS/RESULTS/ACTIONS
D5 CHECK CIRCUIT 680 (LB/O) FOR SHORT TO POWER	
	3 Measure the voltage between multi-function switch circuit 680 (LB/O), and ground. • Is any voltage indicated? → **Yes** REPAIR circuit 680 (LB/O). CLEAR the DTCs. TEST the system for normal operation. → **No** GO to **D6**.
D6 CHECK CIRCUIT 684 (PK/Y) FOR SHORT TO POWER	
	1 Measure the voltage between multi-function switch circuit 684 (PK/Y), and ground. • Is any voltage indicated? → **Yes** REPAIR circuit 684 (PK/Y). CLEAR the DTCs. TEST the system for normal operation. → **No** GO to **D7**.

FM9029800625030X

Fig. 8 Test D: Intermittent Wiper Speed Does Not Operate Properly (Part 3 of 9). 2002–04

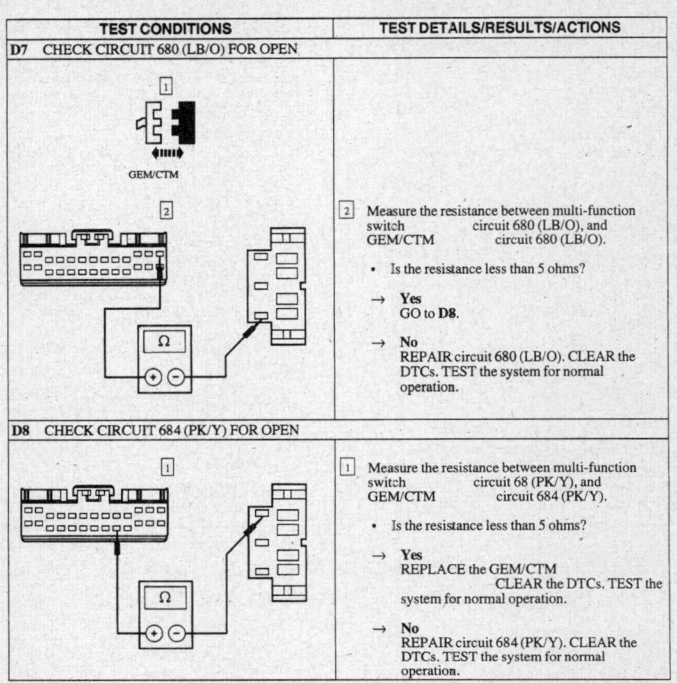

TEST CONDITIONS	TEST DETAILS/RESULTS/ACTIONS
D7 CHECK CIRCUIT 680 (LB/O) FOR OPEN	
	2 Measure the resistance between multi-function switch circuit 680 (LB/O), and GEM/CTM circuit 680 (LB/O). • Is the resistance less than 5 ohms? → **Yes** GO to **D8**. → **No** REPAIR circuit 680 (LB/O). CLEAR the DTCs. TEST the system for normal operation.
D8 CHECK CIRCUIT 684 (PK/Y) FOR OPEN	
	1 Measure the resistance between multi-function switch circuit 68 (PK/Y), and GEM/CTM circuit 684 (PK/Y). • Is the resistance less than 5 ohms? → **Yes** REPLACE the GEM/CTM CLEAR the DTCs. TEST the system for normal operation. → **No** REPAIR circuit 684 (PK/Y). CLEAR the DTCs. TEST the system for normal operation.

FM9029800625040X

Fig. 8 Test D: Intermittent Wiper Speed Does Not Operate Properly (Part 4 of 9). 2002–04

TEST CONDITIONS	TEST DETAILS/RESULTS/ACTIONS
D9 CHECK THE WIPER MOTOR PARK SWITCH STATUS — MONITOR THE GEM/CTM PID WPPRKSW	
	2 Monitor the GEM/CTM PID WPPRKSW while the wipers are operating. • Does the GEM/CTM PID WPPRKSW agree with the status of the wipers? → **Yes** REPLACE the GEM/CTM CLEAR the DTCs. TEST the system for normal operation. → **No** GO to **D10**.
D10 CHECK THE VOLTAGE TO THE WIPER MOTOR PARK SENSE SWITCH — CIRCUIT 63 (R)	
	4 Measure the voltage between wiper motor circuit 63 (R), and ground. • Is the voltage greater than 10 volts? → **Yes** GO to **D11**. → **No** REPAIR circuit 63 (R). CLEAR the DTCs. TEST the system for normal operation.

FM9029800625050X

Fig. 8 Test D: Intermittent Wiper Speed Does Not Operate Properly (Part 5 of 9). 2002–04

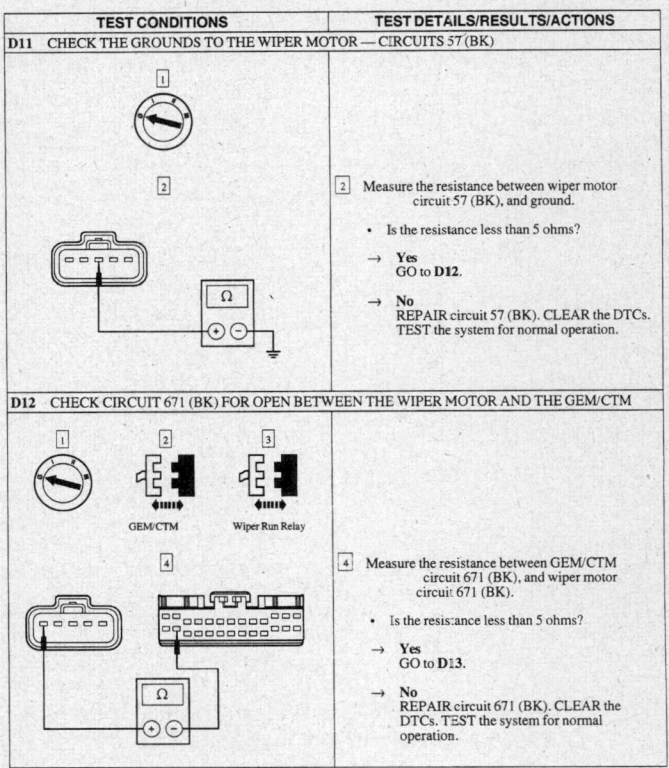

TEST CONDITIONS	TEST DETAILS/RESULTS/ACTIONS
D11 CHECK THE GROUNDS TO THE WIPER MOTOR — CIRCUITS 57 (BK)	
	2 Measure the resistance between wiper motor circuit 57 (BK), and ground. • Is the resistance less than 5 ohms? → **Yes** GO to **D12**. → **No** REPAIR circuit 57 (BK). CLEAR the DTCs. TEST the system for normal operation.
D12 CHECK CIRCUIT 671 (BK) FOR OPEN BETWEEN THE WIPER MOTOR AND THE GEM/CTM	
	4 Measure the resistance between GEM/CTM circuit 671 (BK), and wiper motor circuit 671 (BK). • Is the resistance less than 5 ohms? → **Yes** GO to **D13**. → **No** REPAIR circuit 671 (BK). CLEAR the DTCs. TEST the system for normal operation.

FM9029800625060X

Fig. 8 Test D: Intermittent Wiper Speed Does Not Operate Properly (Part 6 of 9). 2002–04

TEST CONDITIONS	TEST DETAILS/RESULTS/ACTIONS
D13 CHECK CIRCUIT 671 (BK) FOR OPEN BETWEEN THE WIPER RUN RELAY AND THE WIPER MOTOR	

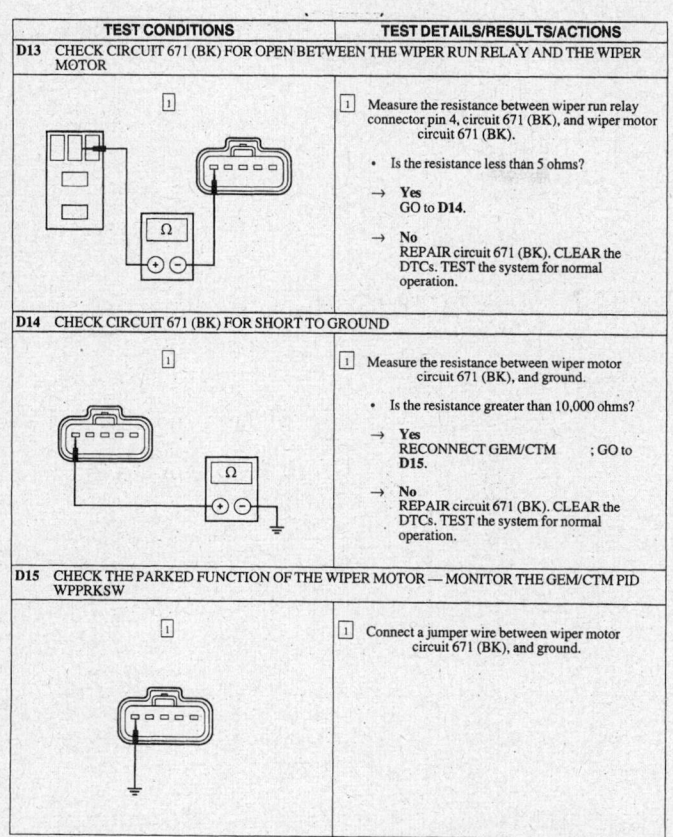

1	1 Measure the resistance between wiper run relay connector pin 4, circuit 671 (BK), and wiper motor circuit 671 (BK). • Is the resistance less than 5 ohms? → **Yes** GO to **D14**. → **No** REPAIR circuit 671 (BK). CLEAR the DTCs. TEST the system for normal operation.
D14 CHECK CIRCUIT 671 (BK) FOR SHORT TO GROUND	
1	1 Measure the resistance between wiper motor circuit 671 (BK), and ground. • Is the resistance greater than 10,000 ohms? → **Yes** RECONNECT GEM/CTM ; GO to **D15**. → **No** REPAIR circuit 671 (BK). CLEAR the DTCs. TEST the system for normal operation.
D15 CHECK THE PARKED FUNCTION OF THE WIPER MOTOR — MONITOR THE GEM/CTM PID WPPRKSW	
1	1 Connect a jumper wire between wiper motor circuit 671 (BK), and ground.

FM9029800625070X

Fig. 8   Test D: Intermittent Wiper Speed Does Not Operate Properly (Part 7 of 9). 2002–04

TEST CONDITIONS	TEST DETAILS/RESULTS/ACTIONS
D16 CHECK THE NOT PARKED FUNCTION OF THE WIPER MOTOR — MONITOR THE GEM/CTM PID WPPRKSW (Continued)	
	• Does the GEM/CTM PID WPPRKSW indicate notPRK? → **Yes** REPLACE the wiper motor. CLEAR the DTCs. TEST the system for normal operation. → **No** REPLACE the GEM/CTM CLEAR the DTCs. TEST the system for normal operation.

FM9029800625090X

Fig. 8   Test D: Intermittent Wiper Speed Does Not Operate Properly (Part 9 of 9). 2002–04

TEST CONDITIONS	TEST DETAILS/RESULTS/ACTIONS
D15 CHECK THE PARKED FUNCTION OF THE WIPER MOTOR — MONITOR THE GEM/CTM PID WPPRKSW (Continued)	

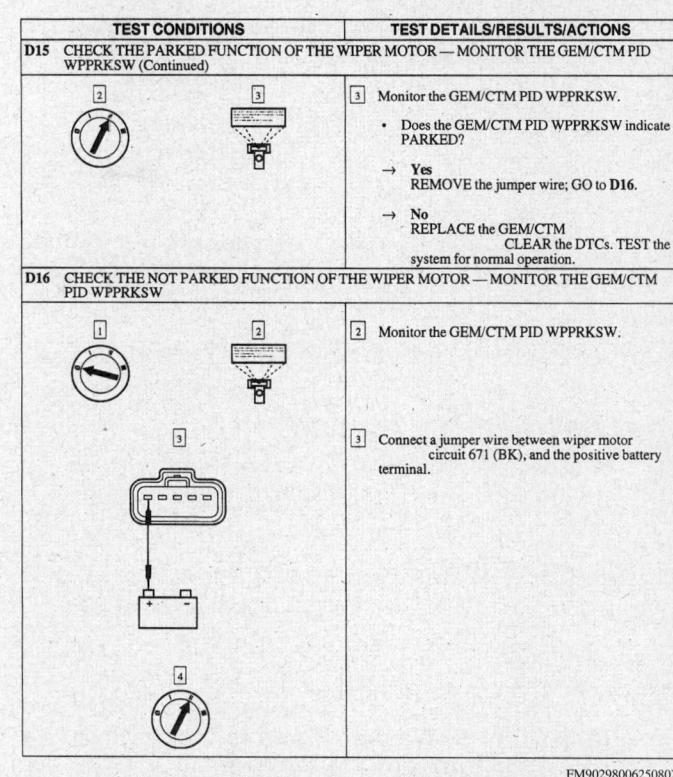

2 3	3 Monitor the GEM/CTM PID WPPRKSW. • Does the GEM/CTM PID WPPRKSW indicate PARKED? → **Yes** REMOVE the jumper wire; GO to **D16**. → **No** REPLACE the GEM/CTM CLEAR the DTCs. TEST the system for normal operation.
D16 CHECK THE NOT PARKED FUNCTION OF THE WIPER MOTOR — MONITOR THE GEM/CTM PID WPPRKSW	
1 2 3 4	2 Monitor the GEM/CTM PID WPPRKSW. 3 Connect a jumper wire between wiper motor circuit 671 (BK), and the positive battery terminal.

FM9029800625080X

Fig. 8   Test D: Intermittent Wiper Speed Does Not Operate Properly (Part 8 of 9). 2002–04

TEST CONDITIONS	TEST DETAILS/RESULTS/ACTIONS
E1 CHECK THE IGNITION STATES — MONITOR THE GEM/CTM PID IGN__GEM	

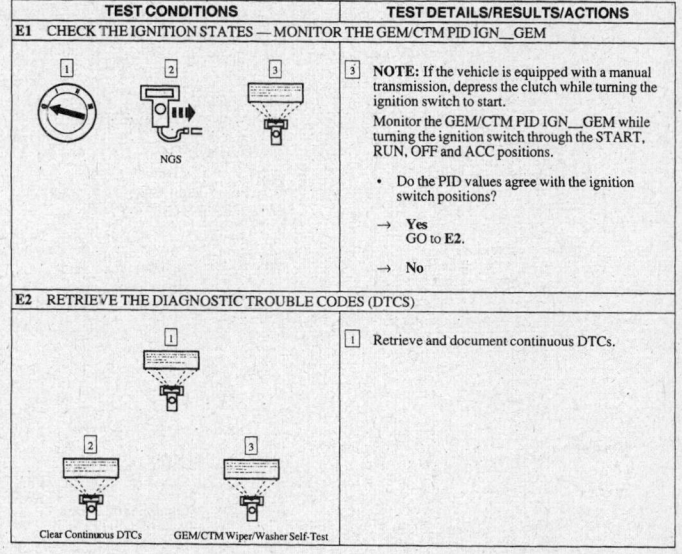

1 2 3 NGS	3 **NOTE:** If the vehicle is equipped with a manual transmission, depress the clutch while turning the ignition switch to start. Monitor the GEM/CTM PID IGN__GEM while turning the ignition switch through the START, RUN, OFF and ACC positions. • Do the PID values agree with the ignition switch positions? → **Yes** GO to **E2**. → **No**
E2 RETRIEVE THE DIAGNOSTIC TROUBLE CODES (DTCS)	
1 2 3 Clear Continuous DTCs GEM/CTM Wiper/Washer Self-Test	1 Retrieve and document continuous DTCs.

FM9029800626010X

Fig. 9   Test E: Washer Pump Is Inoperative (Part 1 of 11). 2002–04

TEST CONDITIONS	TEST DETAILS/RESULTS/ACTIONS
E2 RETRIEVE THE DIAGNOSTIC TROUBLE CODES (DTCS) (Continued)	
	• Are any DTCs recorded? → **Yes** If DTC B1450, GO to **E3**. If DTC B1453, GO to **E3**. If DTC B1458, GO to **E9**. If DTC B1460, GO to **E9**. If DTC B1342, REPLACE the GEM/CTM. CLEAR the DTCs. TEST the system for normal operation. → **No** GO to **E3**.
E3 CHECK THE WASHER SWITCH OUTPUTS — MONITOR THE GEM/CTM PID WPMODE	
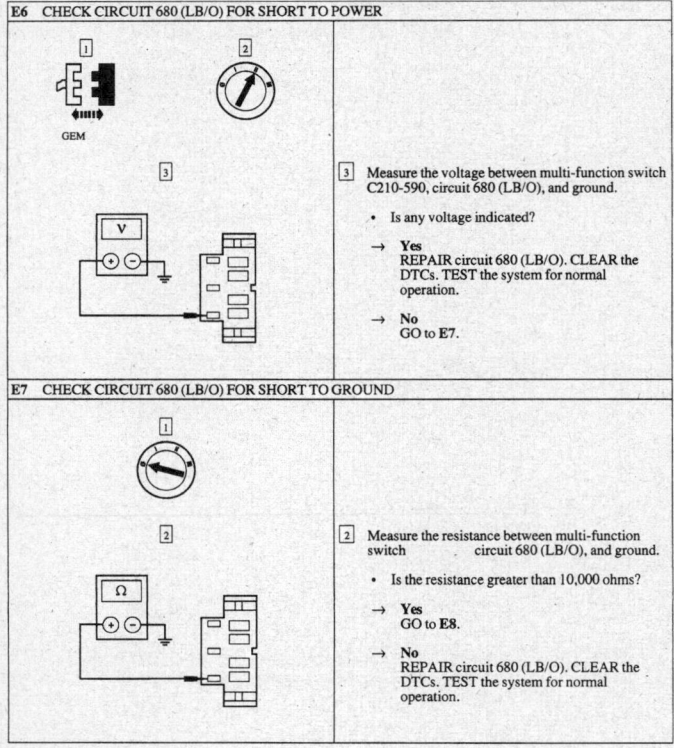	3 Monitor the GEM/CTM PID WPMODE while turning the wiper switch through all the switch positions. • Does the GEM/CTM PID WPMODE agree with all the wiper switch positions? → **Yes** GO to **E4**. → **No** GO to **E6**.
E4 CHECK THE WASHER SWITCH — MONITOR THE GEM/CTM PID WASH__SW	
	1 Monitor the GEM/CTM PID WASH__SW.

FM9029800626020X

Fig. 9   Test E: Washer Pump Is Inoperative (Part 2 of 11). 2002–04

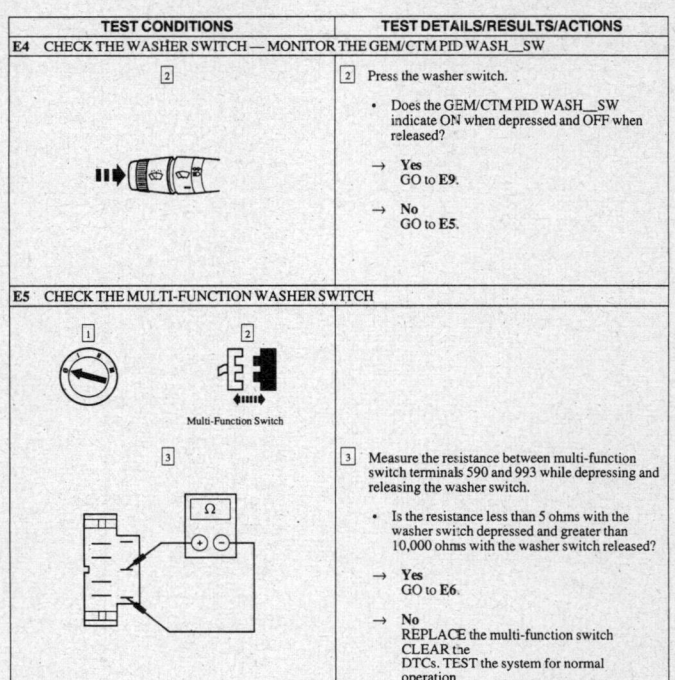

TEST CONDITIONS	TEST DETAILS/RESULTS/ACTIONS
E4 CHECK THE WASHER SWITCH — MONITOR THE GEM/CTM PID WASH__SW	
	2 Press the washer switch. • Does the GEM/CTM PID WASH__SW indicate ON when depressed and OFF when released? → **Yes** GO to **E9**. → **No** GO to **E5**.
E5 CHECK THE MULTI-FUNCTION WASHER SWITCH	
	3 Measure the resistance between multi-function switch terminals 590 and 993 while depressing and releasing the washer switch. • Is the resistance less than 5 ohms with the washer switch depressed and greater than 10,000 ohms with the washer switch released? → **Yes** GO to **E6**. → **No** REPLACE the multi-function switch CLEAR the DTCs. TEST the system for normal operation.

FM9029800626030X

Fig. 9   Test E: Washer Pump Is Inoperative (Part 3 of 11). 2002–04

E6 CHECK CIRCUIT 680 (LB/O) FOR SHORT TO POWER	
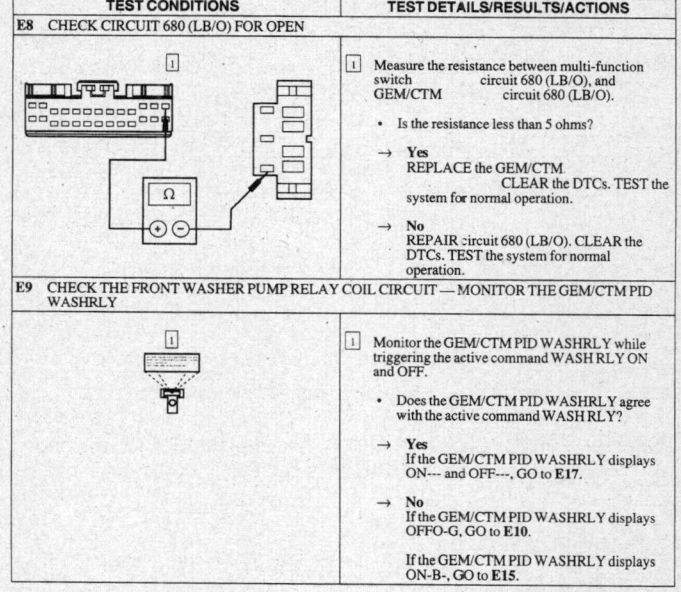	3 Measure the voltage between multi-function switch C210-590, circuit 680 (LB/O), and ground. • Is any voltage indicated? → **Yes** REPAIR circuit 680 (LB/O). CLEAR the DTCs. TEST the system for normal operation. → **No** GO to **E7**.
E7 CHECK CIRCUIT 680 (LB/O) FOR SHORT TO GROUND	
	2 Measure the resistance between multi-function switch circuit 680 (LB/O), and ground. • Is the resistance greater than 10,000 ohms? → **Yes** GO to **E8**. → **No** REPAIR circuit 680 (LB/O). CLEAR the DTCs. TEST the system for normal operation.

FM9029800626040X

Fig. 9   Test E: Washer Pump Is Inoperative (Part 4 of 11). 2002–04

TEST CONDITIONS	TEST DETAILS/RESULTS/ACTIONS
E8 CHECK CIRCUIT 680 (LB/O) FOR OPEN	
	1 Measure the resistance between multi-function switch circuit 680 (LB/O), and GEM/CTM circuit 680 (LB/O). • Is the resistance less than 5 ohms? → **Yes** REPLACE the GEM/CTM. CLEAR the DTCs. TEST the system for normal operation. → **No** REPAIR circuit 680 (LB/O). CLEAR the DTCs. TEST the system for normal operation.
E9 CHECK THE FRONT WASHER PUMP RELAY COIL CIRCUIT — MONITOR THE GEM/CTM PID WASHRLY	
	1 Monitor the GEM/CTM PID WASHRLY while triggering the active command WASH RLY ON and OFF. • Does the GEM/CTM PID WASHRLY agree with the active command WASH RLY? → **Yes** If the GEM/CTM PID WASHRLY displays ON--- and OFF---, GO to **E17**. → **No** If the GEM/CTM PID WASHRLY displays OFFO-G, GO to **E10**. If the GEM/CTM PID WASHRLY displays ON-B-, GO to **E15**.

FM9029800626050X

Fig. 9   Test E: Washer Pump Is Inoperative (Part 5 of 11). 2002–04

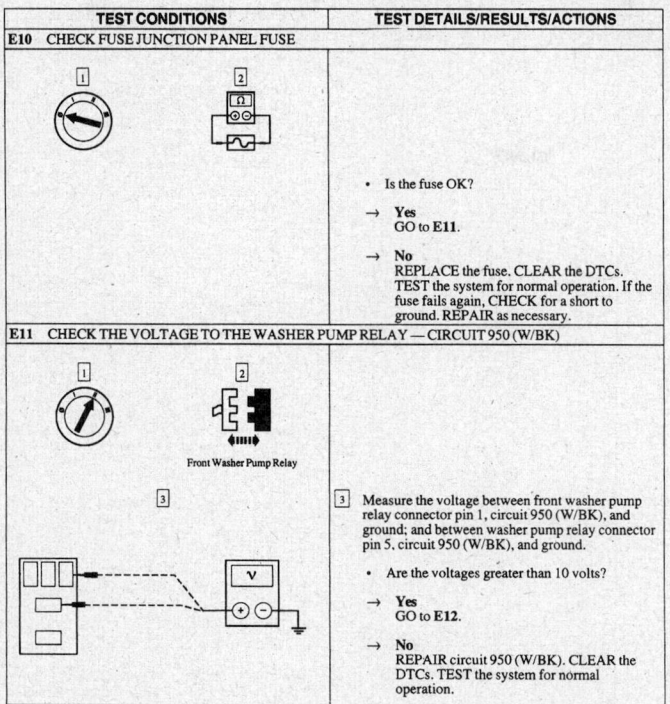

TEST CONDITIONS	TEST DETAILS/RESULTS/ACTIONS
E10 CHECK FUSE JUNCTION PANEL FUSE	
	• Is the fuse OK?
	→ **Yes** GO to **E11**.
	→ **No** REPLACE the fuse. CLEAR the DTCs. TEST the system for normal operation. If the fuse fails again, CHECK for a short to ground. REPAIR as necessary.
E11 CHECK THE VOLTAGE TO THE WASHER PUMP RELAY — CIRCUIT 950 (W/BK)	
	Measure the voltage between front washer pump relay connector pin 1, circuit 950 (W/BK), and ground; and between washer pump relay connector pin 5, circuit 950 (W/BK), and ground.
	• Are the voltages greater than 10 volts?
	→ **Yes** GO to **E12**.
	→ **No** REPAIR circuit 950 (W/BK). CLEAR the DTCs. TEST the system for normal operation.

FM9029800626060X

Fig. 9 Test E: Washer Pump Is Inoperative (Part 6 of 11). 2002–04

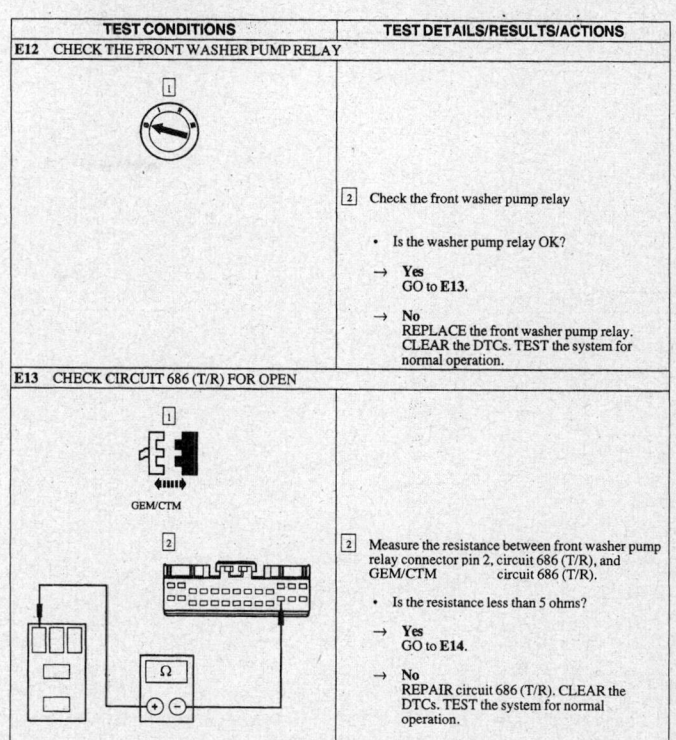

TEST CONDITIONS	TEST DETAILS/RESULTS/ACTIONS
E12 CHECK THE FRONT WASHER PUMP RELAY	
	Check the front washer pump relay
	• Is the washer pump relay OK?
	→ **Yes** GO to **E13**.
	→ **No** REPLACE the front washer pump relay. CLEAR the DTCs. TEST the system for normal operation.
E13 CHECK CIRCUIT 686 (T/R) FOR OPEN	
	Measure the resistance between front washer pump relay connector pin 2, circuit 686 (T/R), and GEM/CTM, circuit 686 (T/R).
	• Is the resistance less than 5 ohms?
	→ **Yes** GO to **E14**.
	→ **No** REPAIR circuit 686 (T/R). CLEAR the DTCs. TEST the system for normal operation.

FM9029800626070X

Fig. 9 Test E: Washer Pump Is Inoperative (Part 7 of 11). 2002–04

TEST CONDITIONS	TEST DETAILS/RESULTS/ACTIONS
E14 CHECK CIRCUIT 686 (T/R) FOR SHORT TO GROUND	
	Measure the resistance between front washer pump relay connector pin 2, circuit 686 (T/R), and ground.
	• Is the resistance greater than 10,000 ohms?
	→ **Yes** REPLACE the GEM/CTM CLEAR the DTCs. TEST the system for normal operation.
	→ **No** REPAIR circuit 686 (T/R). CLEAR the DTCs. TEST the system for normal operation.
E15 CHECK THE FRONT WASHER PUMP RELAY	
	Check the front washer pump relay; refer to Component Test.
	• Is the washer pump relay OK?
	→ **Yes** GO to **E16**.
	→ **No** REPLACE the front washer pump relay. CLEAR the DTCs. TEST the system for normal operation.

FM9029800626080X

Fig. 9 Test E: Washer Pump Is Inoperative (Part 8 of 11). 2002–04

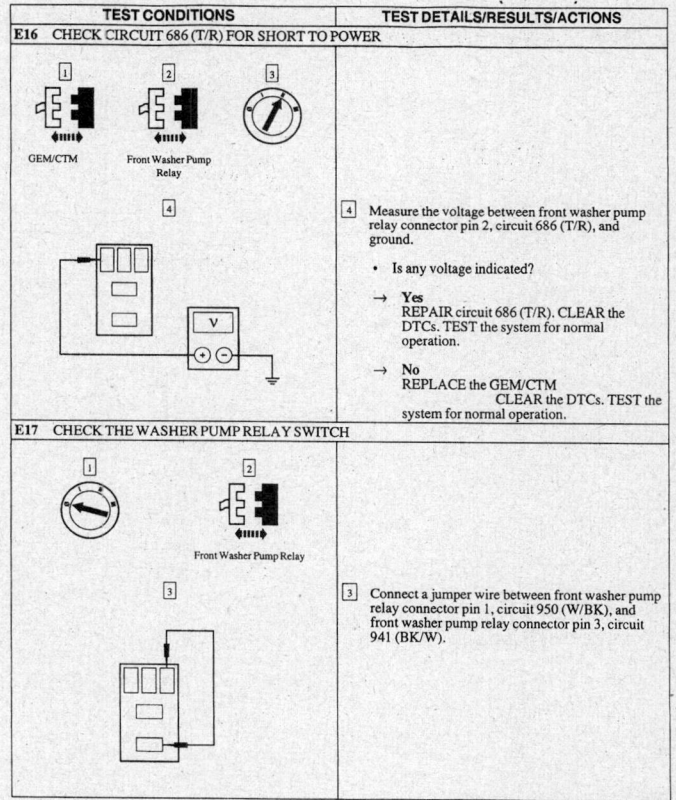

TEST CONDITIONS	TEST DETAILS/RESULTS/ACTIONS
E16 CHECK CIRCUIT 686 (T/R) FOR SHORT TO POWER	
	Measure the voltage between front washer pump relay connector pin 2, circuit 686 (T/R), and ground.
	• Is any voltage indicated?
	→ **Yes** REPAIR circuit 686 (T/R). CLEAR the DTCs. TEST the system for normal operation.
	→ **No** REPLACE the GEM/CTM CLEAR the DTCs. TEST the system for normal operation.
E17 CHECK THE WASHER PUMP RELAY SWITCH	
	Connect a jumper wire between front washer pump relay connector pin 1, circuit 950 (W/BK), and front washer pump relay connector pin 3, circuit 941 (BK/W).

FM9029800626090X

Fig. 9 Test E: Washer Pump Is Inoperative (Part 9 of 11). 2002–04

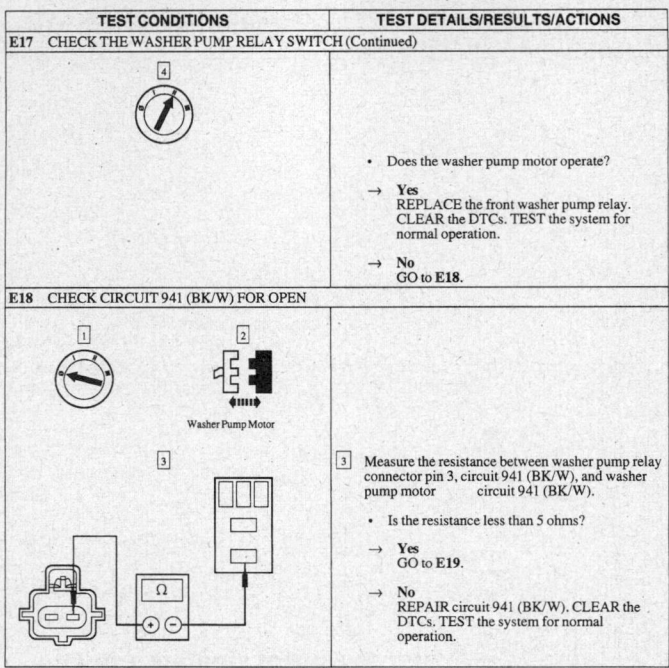

TEST CONDITIONS	TEST DETAILS/RESULTS/ACTIONS
E17 CHECK THE WASHER PUMP RELAY SWITCH (Continued)	• Does the washer pump motor operate? → **Yes** REPLACE the front washer pump relay. CLEAR the DTCs. TEST the system for normal operation. → **No** GO to **E18**.
E18 CHECK CIRCUIT 941 (BK/W) FOR OPEN	3 Measure the resistance between washer pump relay connector pin 3, circuit 941 (BK/W), and washer pump motor circuit 941 (BK/W). • Is the resistance less than 5 ohms? → **Yes** GO to **E19**. → **No** REPAIR circuit 941 (BK/W). CLEAR the DTCs. TEST the system for normal operation.

FM9029800626100X

Fig. 9 Test E: Washer Pump Is Inoperative (Part 10 of 11). 2002–04

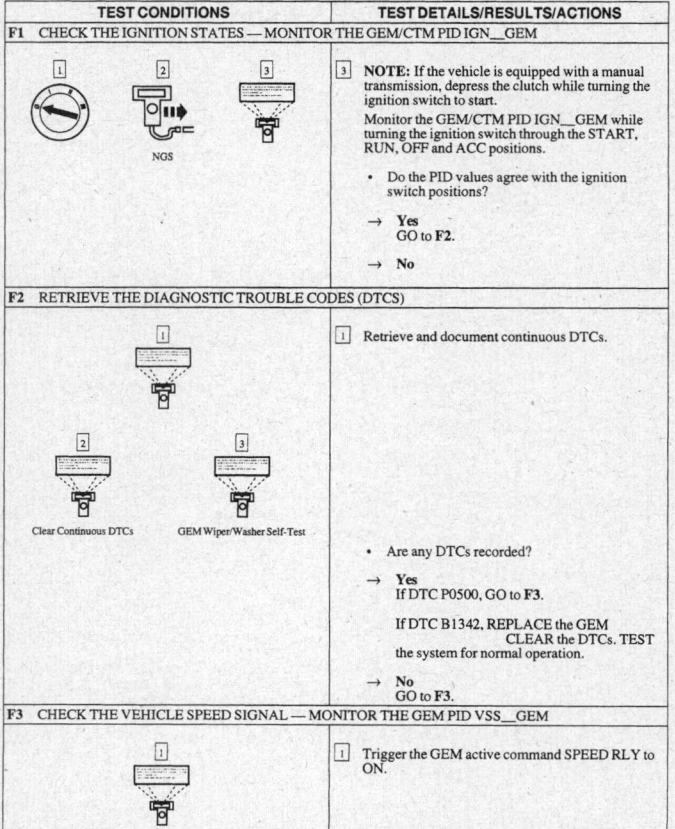

TEST CONDITIONS	TEST DETAILS/RESULTS/ACTIONS
F1 CHECK THE IGNITION STATES — MONITOR THE GEM/CTM PID IGN__GEM	3 **NOTE:** If the vehicle is equipped with a manual transmission, depress the clutch while turning the ignition switch to start. Monitor the GEM/CTM PID IGN__GEM while turning the ignition switch through the START, RUN, OFF and ACC positions. • Do the PID values agree with the ignition switch positions? → **Yes** GO to **F2**. → **No**
F2 RETRIEVE THE DIAGNOSTIC TROUBLE CODES (DTCS)	1 Retrieve and document continuous DTCs. • Are any DTCs recorded? → **Yes** If DTC P0500, GO to **F3**. If DTC B1342, REPLACE the GEM CLEAR the DTCs. TEST the system for normal operation. → **No** GO to **F3**.
F3 CHECK THE VEHICLE SPEED SIGNAL — MONITOR THE GEM PID VSS__GEM	1 Trigger the GEM active command SPEED RLY to ON.

FM9029800627010X

Fig. 10 Test F: Speed Dependent Interval Mode Does Not Operate Properly (Part 1 of 2). 2002–04

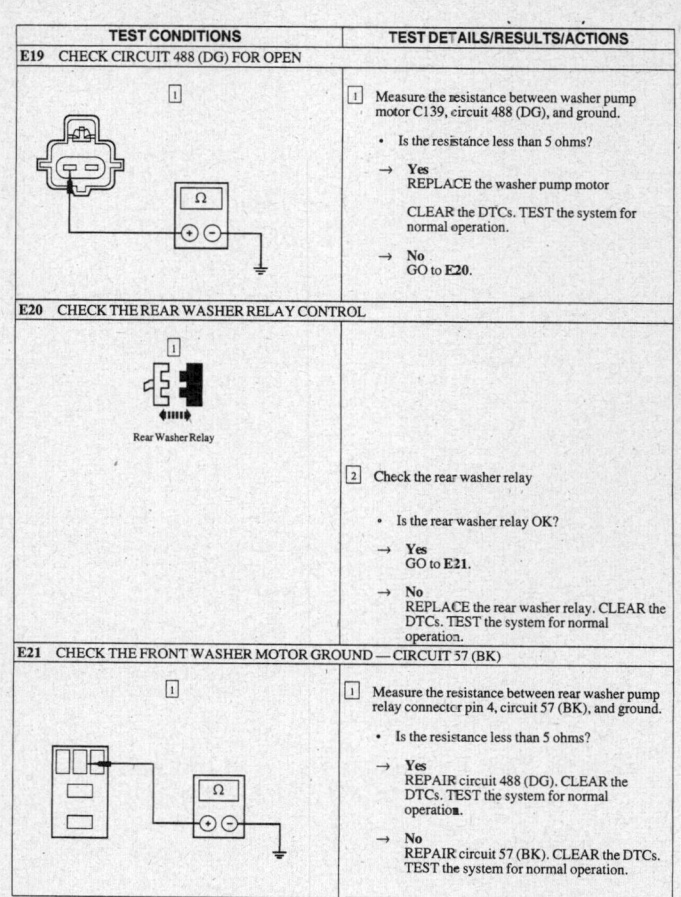

TEST CONDITIONS	TEST DETAILS/RESULTS/ACTIONS
E19 CHECK CIRCUIT 488 (DG) FOR OPEN	1 Measure the resistance between washer pump motor C139, circuit 488 (DG), and ground. • Is the resistance less than 5 ohms? → **Yes** REPLACE the washer pump motor CLEAR the DTCs. TEST the system for normal operation. → **No** GO to **E20**.
E20 CHECK THE REAR WASHER RELAY CONTROL	2 Check the rear washer relay • Is the rear washer relay OK? → **Yes** GO to **E21**. → **No** REPLACE the rear washer relay. CLEAR the DTCs. TEST the system for normal operation.
E21 CHECK THE FRONT WASHER MOTOR GROUND — CIRCUIT 57 (BK)	1 Measure the resistance between rear washer pump relay connector pin 4, circuit 57 (BK), and ground. • Is the resistance less than 5 ohms? → **Yes** REPAIR circuit 488 (DG). CLEAR the DTCs. TEST the system for normal operation. → **No** REPAIR circuit 57 (BK). CLEAR the DTCs. TEST the system for normal operation.

FM9029800626110X

Fig. 9 Test E: Washer Pump Is Inoperative (Part 11 of 11). 2002–04

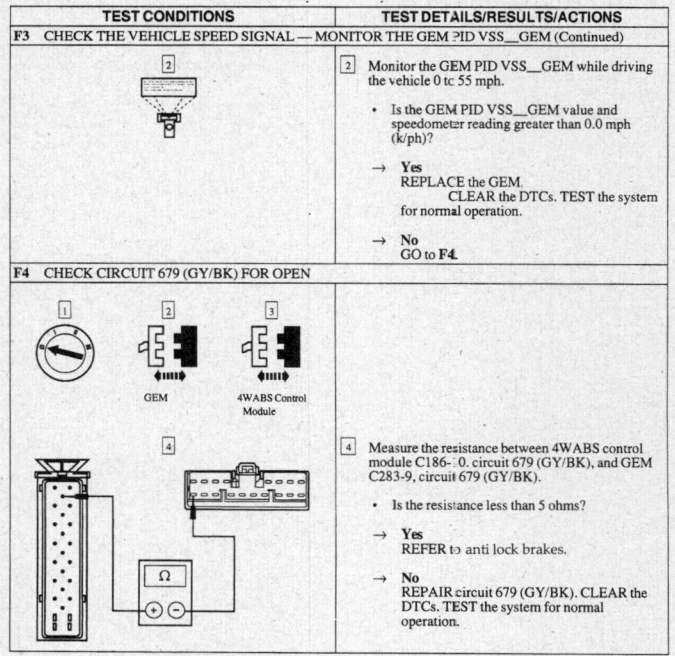

TEST CONDITIONS	TEST DETAILS/RESULTS/ACTIONS
F3 CHECK THE VEHICLE SPEED SIGNAL — MONITOR THE GEM PID VSS__GEM (Continued)	2 Monitor the GEM PID VSS__GEM while driving the vehicle 0 to 55 mph. • Is the GEM PID VSS__GEM value and speedometer reading greater than 0.0 mph (k/ph)? → **Yes** REPLACE the GEM. CLEAR the DTCs. TEST the system for normal operation. → **No** GO to **F4**.
F4 CHECK CIRCUIT 679 (GY/BK) FOR OPEN	4 Measure the resistance between 4WABS control module C186-30, circuit 679 (GY/BK), and GEM C283-9, circuit 679 (GY/BK). • Is the resistance less than 5 ohms? → **Yes** REFER to anti lock brakes. → **No** REPAIR circuit 679 (GY/BK). CLEAR the DTCs. TEST the system for normal operation.

FM9029800627020X

Fig. 10 Test F: Speed Dependent Interval Mode Does Not Operate Properly (Part 2 of 2). 2002–04

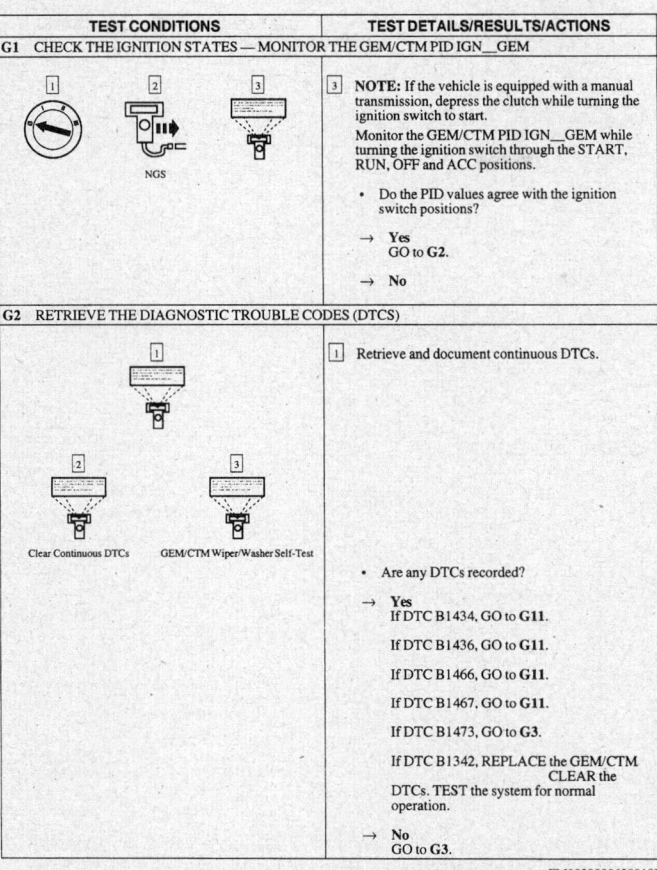

TEST CONDITIONS	TEST DETAILS/RESULTS/ACTIONS
G1 CHECK THE IGNITION STATES — MONITOR THE GEM/CTM PID IGN__GEM	
NGS	**3** **NOTE:** If the vehicle is equipped with a manual transmission, depress the clutch while turning the ignition switch to start. Monitor the GEM/CTM PID IGN__GEM while turning the ignition switch through the START, RUN, OFF and ACC positions. • Do the PID values agree with the ignition switch positions? → **Yes** GO to **G2**. → **No**
G2 RETRIEVE THE DIAGNOSTIC TROUBLE CODES (DTCS)	
Clear Continuous DTCs GEM/CTM Wiper/Washer Self-Test	**1** Retrieve and document continuous DTCs. • Are any DTCs recorded? → **Yes** If DTC B1434, GO to **G11**. If DTC B1436, GO to **G11**. If DTC B1466, GO to **G11**. If DTC B1467, GO to **G11**. If DTC B1473, GO to **G3**. If DTC B1342, REPLACE the GEM/CTM CLEAR the DTCs. TEST the system for normal operation. → **No** GO to **G3**.

FM9029800628010X

Fig. 11 Test G: Wiper Do Not Operate Properly, High Speed Wipers Only Operate (Part 1 of 10). 2002–04

TEST CONDITIONS	TEST DETAILS/RESULTS/ACTIONS
G5 CHECK CIRCUIT 680 (LB/O) FOR SHORT TO POWER	
GEM/CTM	**3** Measure the voltage between multi-function switch circuit 680 (LB/O), and ground. • Is any voltage indicated? → **Yes** REPAIR circuit 680 (LB/O). CLEAR the DTCs. TEST the system for normal operation. → **No** GO to **G6**.
G6 CHECK CIRCUIT 684 (PK/Y) FOR SHORT TO POWER	
	1 Measure the voltage between multi-function switch circuit 684 (PK/Y), and ground. • Is any voltage indicated? → **Yes** REPAIR circuit 684 (PK/Y). CLEAR the DTCs. TEST the system for normal operation. → **No** GO to **G7**.

FM9029800628030X

Fig. 11 Test G: Wiper Do Not Operate Properly, High Speed Wipers Only Operate (Part 3 of 10). 2002–04

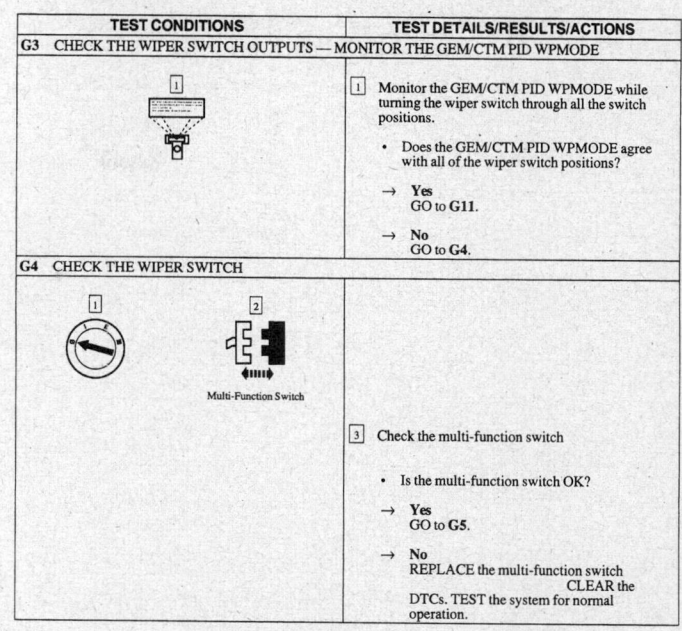

TEST CONDITIONS	TEST DETAILS/RESULTS/ACTIONS
G3 CHECK THE WIPER SWITCH OUTPUTS — MONITOR THE GEM/CTM PID WPMODE	
	1 Monitor the GEM/CTM PID WPMODE while turning the wiper switch through all the switch positions. • Does the GEM/CTM PID WPMODE agree with all of the wiper switch positions? → **Yes** GO to **G11**. → **No** GO to **G4**.
G4 CHECK THE WIPER SWITCH	
Multi-Function Switch	**3** Check the multi-function switch • Is the multi-function switch OK? → **Yes** GO to **G5**. → **No** REPLACE the multi-function switch CLEAR the DTCs. TEST the system for normal operation.

FM9029800628020X

Fig. 11 Test G: Wiper Do Not Operate Properly, High Speed Wipers Only Operate (Part 2 of 10). 2002–04

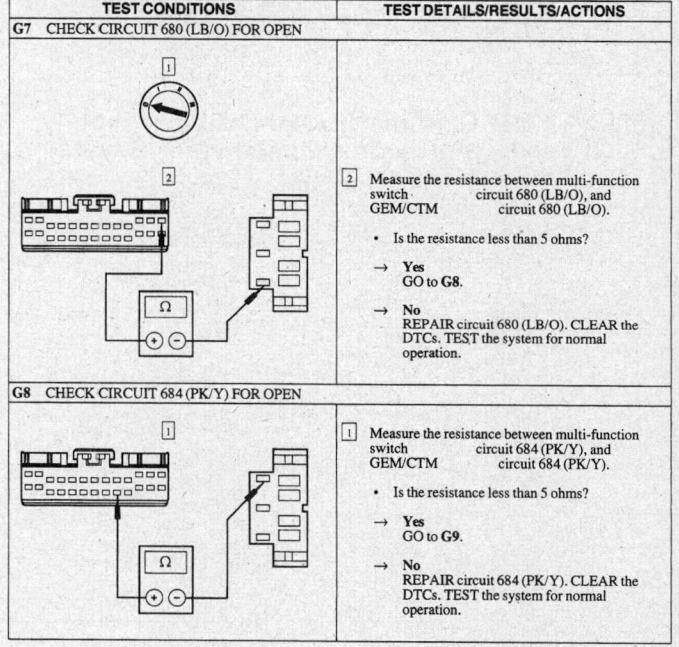

TEST CONDITIONS	TEST DETAILS/RESULTS/ACTIONS
G7 CHECK CIRCUIT 680 (LB/O) FOR OPEN	
	2 Measure the resistance between multi-function switch circuit 680 (LB/O), and GEM/CTM circuit 680 (LB/O). • Is the resistance less than 5 ohms? → **Yes** GO to **G8**. → **No** REPAIR circuit 680 (LB/O). CLEAR the DTCs. TEST the system for normal operation.
G8 CHECK CIRCUIT 684 (PK/Y) FOR OPEN	
	1 Measure the resistance between multi-function switch circuit 684 (PK/Y), and GEM/CTM circuit 684 (PK/Y). • Is the resistance less than 5 ohms? → **Yes** GO to **G9**. → **No** REPAIR circuit 684 (PK/Y). CLEAR the DTCs. TEST the system for normal operation.

FM9029800628040X

Fig. 11 Test G: Wiper Do Not Operate Properly, High Speed Wipers Only Operate (Part 4 of 10). 2002–04

TEST CONDITIONS	TEST DETAILS/RESULTS/ACTIONS
G9 CHECK CIRCUIT 684 (PK/Y) FOR SHORT TO GROUND	

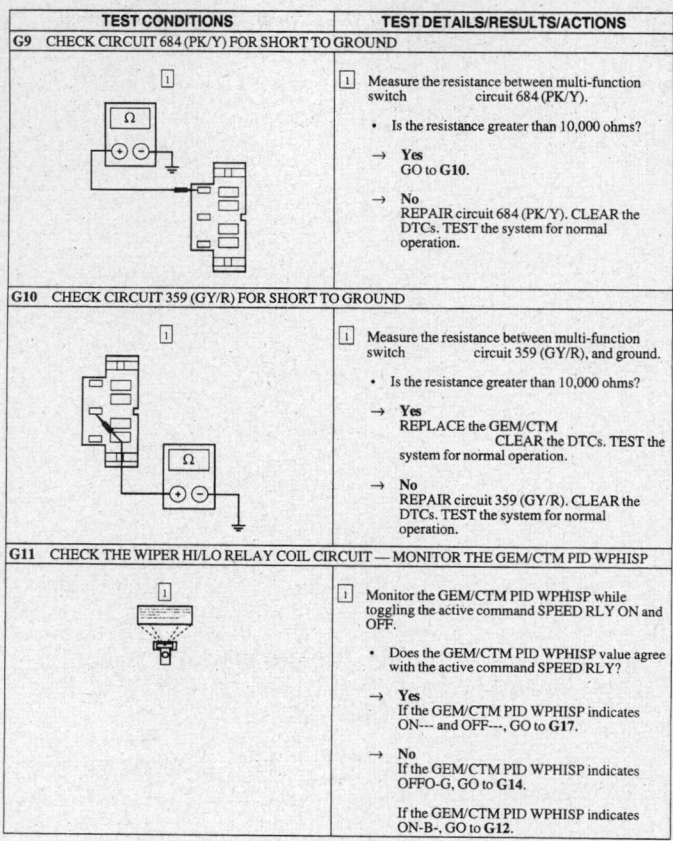

	1 Measure the resistance between multi-function switch ___ circuit 684 (PK/Y). • Is the resistance greater than 10,000 ohms? → **Yes** GO to **G10**. → **No** REPAIR circuit 684 (PK/Y). CLEAR the DTCs. TEST the system for normal operation.
G10 CHECK CIRCUIT 359 (GY/R) FOR SHORT TO GROUND	
	1 Measure the resistance between multi-function switch ___ circuit 359 (GY/R), and ground. • Is the resistance greater than 10,000 ohms? → **Yes** REPLACE the GEM/CTM ___ CLEAR the DTCs. TEST the system for normal operation. → **No** REPAIR circuit 359 (GY/R). CLEAR the DTCs. TEST the system for normal operation.
G11 CHECK THE WIPER HI/LO RELAY COIL CIRCUIT — MONITOR THE GEM/CTM PID WPHISP	
	1 Monitor the GEM/CTM PID WPHISP while toggling the active command SPEED RLY ON and OFF. • Does the GEM/CTM PID WPHISP value agree with the active command SPEED RLY? → **Yes** If the GEM/CTM PID WPHISP indicates ON--- and OFF---, GO to **G17**. → **No** If the GEM/CTM PID WPHISP indicates OFFO-G, GO to **G14**. If the GEM/CTM PID WPHISP indicates ON-B-, GO to **G12**.

FM9029800628050X

Fig. 11 Test G: Wiper Do Not Operate Properly, High Speed Wipers Only Operate (Part 5 of 10). 2002–04

TEST CONDITIONS	TEST DETAILS/RESULTS/ACTIONS
G12 CHECK CIRCUIT 647 (GY/LB) FOR SHORT TO POWER	

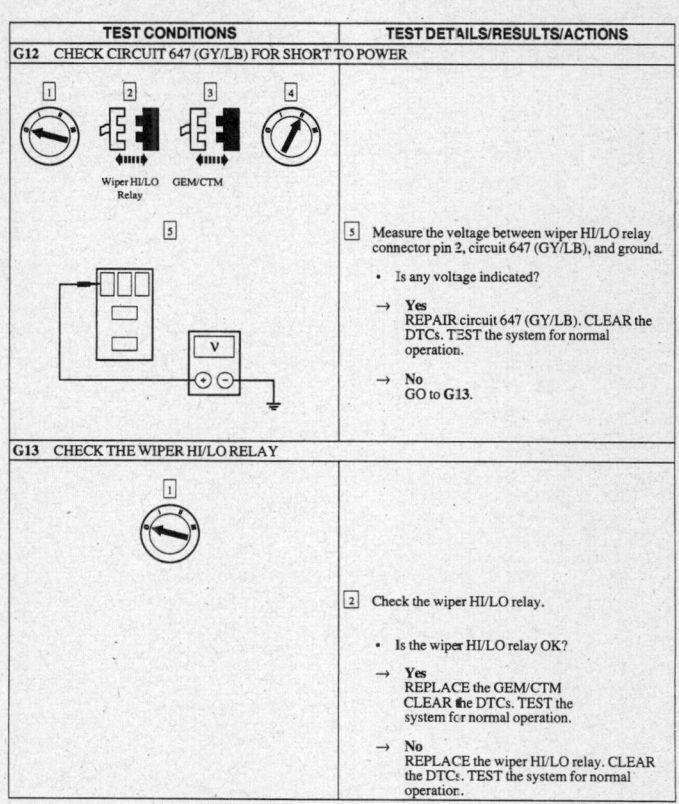

	5 Measure the voltage between wiper HI/LO relay connector pin 2, circuit 647 (GY/LB), and ground. • Is any voltage indicated? → **Yes** REPAIR circuit 647 (GY/LB). CLEAR the DTCs. TEST the system for normal operation. → **No** GO to **G13**.
G13 CHECK THE WIPER HI/LO RELAY	
	2 Check the wiper HI/LO relay. • Is the wiper HI/LO relay OK? → **Yes** REPLACE the GEM/CTM CLEAR the DTCs. TEST the system for normal operation. → **No** REPLACE the wiper HI/LO relay. CLEAR the DTCs. TEST the system for normal operation.

FM9029800628060X

Fig. 11 Test G: Wiper Do Not Operate Properly, High Speed Wipers Only Operate (Part 6 of 10). 2002–04

TEST CONDITIONS	TEST DETAILS/RESULTS/ACTIONS
G14 CHECK CIRCUIT 63 (R) FOR VOLTAGE	

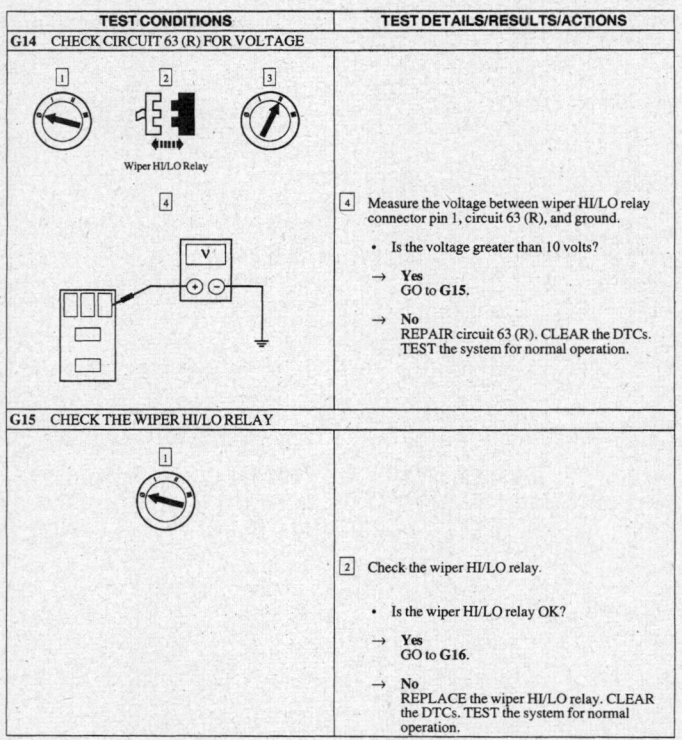

	4 Measure the voltage between wiper HI/LO relay connector pin 1, circuit 63 (R), and ground. • Is the voltage greater than 10 volts? → **Yes** GO to **G15**. → **No** REPAIR circuit 63 (R). CLEAR the DTCs. TEST the system for normal operation.
G15 CHECK THE WIPER HI/LO RELAY	
	2 Check the wiper HI/LO relay. • Is the wiper HI/LO relay OK? → **Yes** GO to **G16**. → **No** REPLACE the wiper HI/LO relay. CLEAR the DTCs. TEST the system for normal operation.

FM9029800628070X

Fig. 11 Test G: Wiper Do Not Operate Properly, High Speed Wipers Only Operate (Part 7 of 10). 2002–04

TEST CONDITIONS	TEST DETAILS/RESULTS/ACTIONS
G16 CHECK CIRCUIT 647 (GY/LB) FOR SHORT TO GROUND	

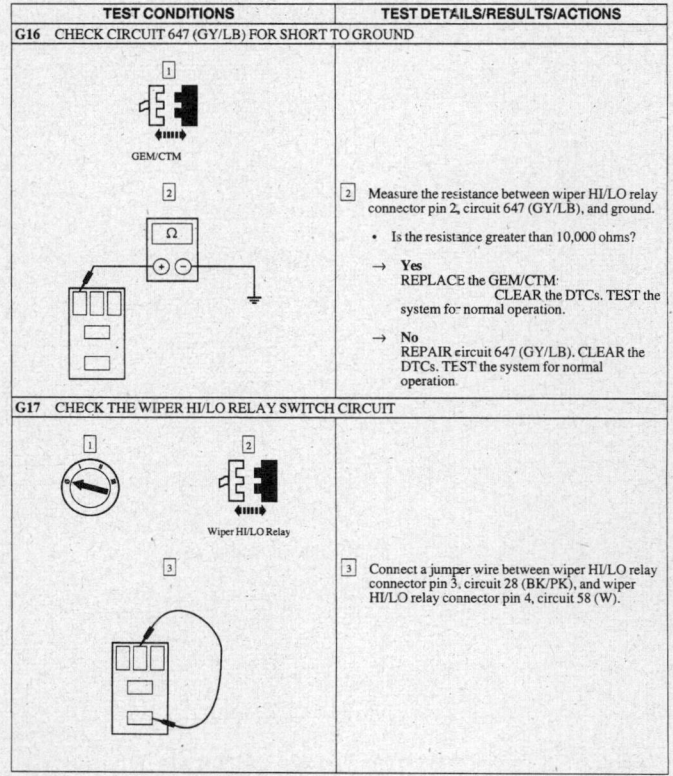

	2 Measure the resistance between wiper HI/LO relay connector pin 2, circuit 647 (GY/LB), and ground. • Is the resistance greater than 10,000 ohms? → **Yes** REPLACE the GEM/CTM. CLEAR the DTCs. TEST the system for normal operation. → **No** REPAIR circuit 647 (GY/LB). CLEAR the DTCs. TEST the system for normal operation.
G17 CHECK THE WIPER HI/LO RELAY SWITCH CIRCUIT	
	3 Connect a jumper wire between wiper HI/LO relay connector pin 3, circuit 28 (BK/PK), and wiper HI/LO relay connector pin 4, circuit 58 (W).

FM9029800628080X

Fig. 11 Test G: Wiper Do Not Operate Properly, High Speed Wipers Only Operate (Part 8 of 10). 2002–04

TEST CONDITIONS	TEST DETAILS/RESULTS/ACTIONS
G17 CHECK THE WIPER HI/LO RELAY SWITCH CIRCUIT (Continued)	

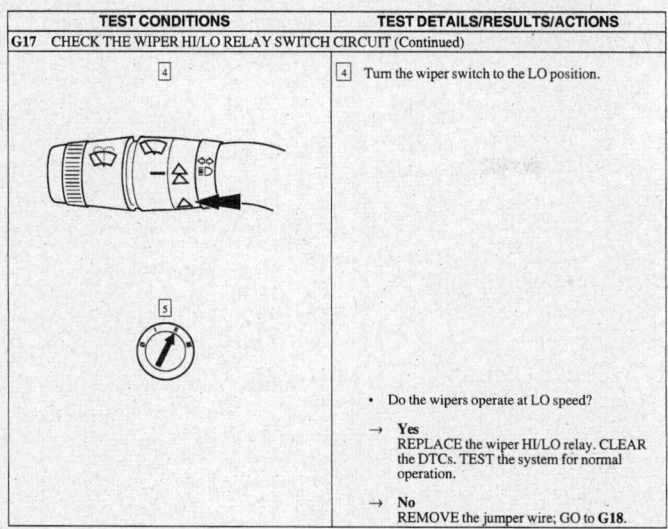

4 Turn the wiper switch to the LO position.

- Do the wipers operate at LO speed?

→ **Yes**
REPLACE the wiper HI/LO relay. CLEAR the DTCs. TEST the system for normal operation.

→ **No**
REMOVE the jumper wire; GO to **G18**.

FM9029800628090X

Fig. 11 Test G: Wiper Do Not Operate Properly, High Speed Wipers Only Operate (Part 9 of 10). 2002–04

TEST CONDITIONS	TEST DETAILS/RESULTS/ACTIONS
G18 CHECK CIRCUIT 58 (W) FOR OPEN	

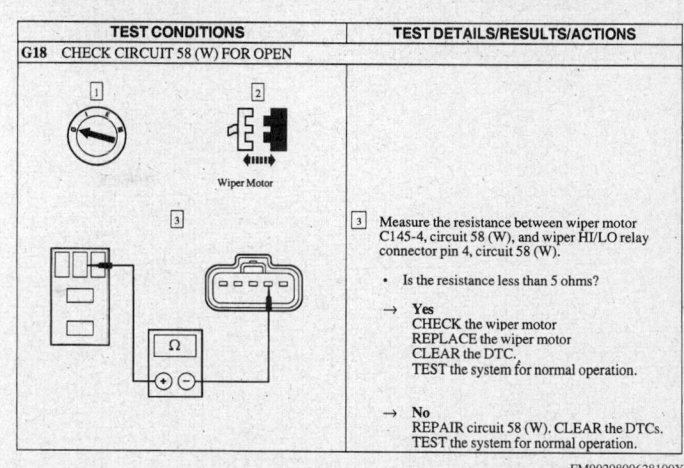

3 Measure the resistance between wiper motor C145-4, circuit 58 (W), and wiper HI/LO relay connector pin 4, circuit 58 (W).

- Is the resistance less than 5 ohms?

→ **Yes**
CHECK the wiper motor
REPLACE the wiper motor
CLEAR the DTC.
TEST the system for normal operation.

→ **No**
REPAIR circuit 58 (W). CLEAR the DTCs. TEST the system for normal operation.

FM9029800628100X

Fig. 11 Test G: Wiper Do Not Operate Properly, High Speed Wipers Only Operate (Part 10 of 10). 2002–04

TEST CONDITIONS	TEST DETAILS/RESULTS/ACTIONS
H1 CHECK THE IGNITION STATES — MONITOR THE GEM/CTM PID __GEM	

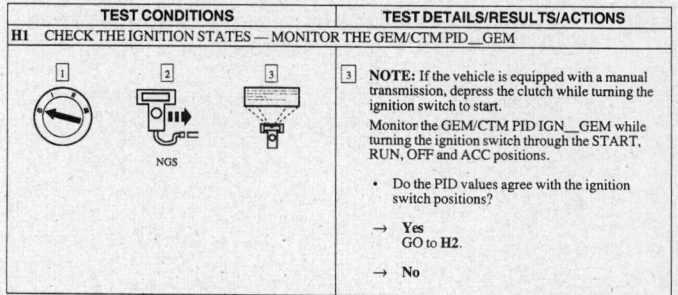

3 **NOTE:** If the vehicle is equipped with a manual transmission, depress the clutch while turning the ignition switch to start.

Monitor the GEM/CTM PID IGN__GEM while turning the ignition switch through the START, RUN, OFF and ACC positions.

- Do the PID values agree with the ignition switch positions?

→ **Yes**
GO to **H2**.

→ **No**

FM9029800629010X

Fig. 12 Test H: Rear Wiper Stay On Continuously (Part 1 of 3). 2002–04

TEST CONDITIONS	TEST DETAILS/RESULTS/ACTIONS
H2 RETRIEVE THE DIAGNOSTIC TROUBLE CODES (DTCS)	

1 Retrieve and document continuous DTCs.

Clear Continuous DTCs

GEM/CTM Wiper/Washer Self Test

- Are any DTCs recorded?

→ **Yes**
If DTC B1614, GO to **H3**.

If DTC B1342, REPLACE the GEM/CTM CLEAR the DTCs. TEST the system for normal operation.

→ **No**
GO to **H3**.

TEST CONDITIONS	TEST DETAILS/RESULTS/ACTIONS
H3 CHECK THE REAR WIPER SWITCH	

Rear Wiper Switch C249

3 Measure the resistance between the following rear wiper switch terminals 2 and 5.

Switch Position	Resistance (Ohms)
OFF	4200-9100
First Interval Delay	1000-2420
Second Interval Delay	220-900
HI	50-230

FM9029800629020X

Fig. 12 Test H: Rear Wiper Stay On Continuously (Part 2 of 3). 2002–04

TEST CONDITIONS	TEST DETAILS/RESULTS/ACTIONS
H3 CHECK THE REAR WIPER SWITCH (Continued)	

- Are the resistances as indicated?

→ **Yes**
GO to **H4**.

→ **No**
REPLACE the rear wiper switch CLEAR the DTCs. TEST the system for normal operation.

H4 CHECK CIRCUIT 485 (PK/LB) FOR SHORT TO GROUND	

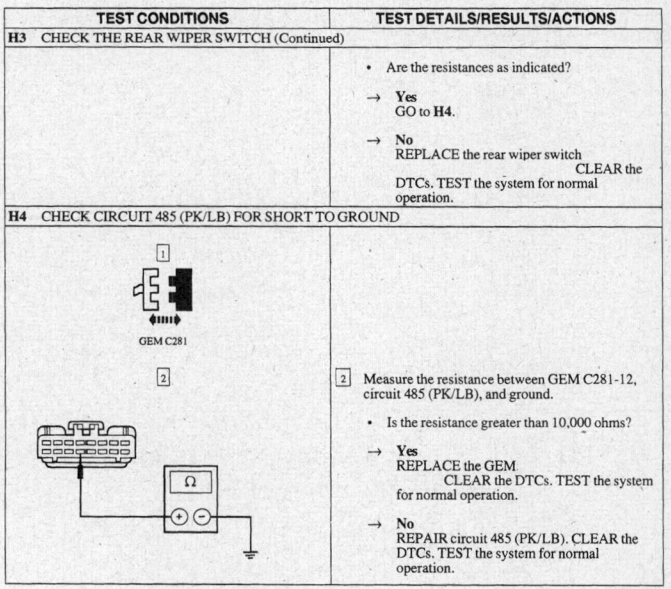

GEM C281

2 Measure the resistance between GEM C281-12, circuit 485 (PK/LB), and ground.

- Is the resistance greater than 10,000 ohms?

→ **Yes**
REPLACE the GEM CLEAR the DTCs. TEST the system for normal operation.

→ **No**
REPAIR circuit 485 (PK/LB). CLEAR the DTCs. TEST the system for normal operation.

FM9029800629030X

Fig. 12 Test H: Rear Wiper Stay On Continuously (Part 3 of 3). 2002–04

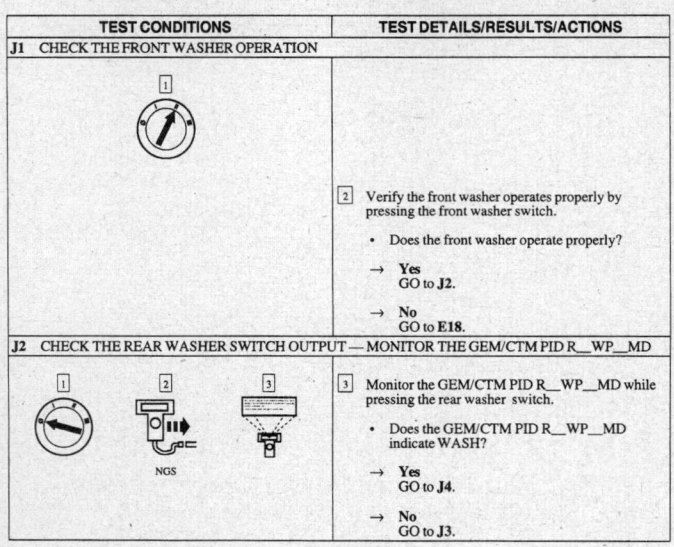

TEST CONDITIONS	TEST DETAILS/RESULTS/ACTIONS
J1 CHECK THE FRONT WASHER OPERATION	

	2 Verify the front washer operates properly by pressing the front washer switch.
	
	 • Does the front washer operate properly?
	
	 → **Yes**
	  GO to **J2**.
	
	 → **No**
	  GO to **E18**.

J2 CHECK THE REAR WASHER SWITCH OUTPUT — MONITOR THE GEM/CTM PID R__WP__MD	

	3 Monitor the GEM/CTM PID R__WP__MD while pressing the rear washer switch.
	
	 • Does the GEM/CTM PID R__WP__MD indicate WASH?
	
	 → **Yes**
	  GO to **J4**.
	
	 → **No**
	  GO to **J3**.

FM9029800630010X

Fig. 13 Test J: Rear Washer Pump Is Inoperative (Part 1 of 4). 2002–04

TEST CONDITIONS	TEST DETAILS/RESULTS/ACTIONS
J5 CHECK THE VOLTAGE TO THE REAR WASHER RELAY — CIRCUIT 946 (P/LG)	

	3 Measure the voltage between rear washer relay connector pin 5, circuit 946 (P/LG), and ground, while pressing the rear washer switch; and between rear washer relay connector pin 1, circuit 946 (P/LG), and ground while pressing the rear washer switch.
	
	 • Are the voltages greater than 10 volts?
	
	 → **Yes**
	  GO to **J8**.
	
	 → **No**
	  GO to **J6**.

J6 CHECK THE VOLTAGE TO THE REAR WIPER/WASHER SWITCH — CIRCUIT 950 (W/BK)	

	4 Measure the voltage between rear wiper/washer switch C249-4, circuit 950 (W/BK), and ground.
	
	 • Is the voltage greater than 10 volts?
	
	 → **Yes**
	  GO to **J7**.
	
	 → **No**
	  REPAIR circuit 950 (W/BK). CLEAR the DTCs. TEST the system for normal operation.

FM9029800630030X

Fig. 13 Test J: Rear Washer Pump Is Inoperative (Part 3 of 4). 2002–04

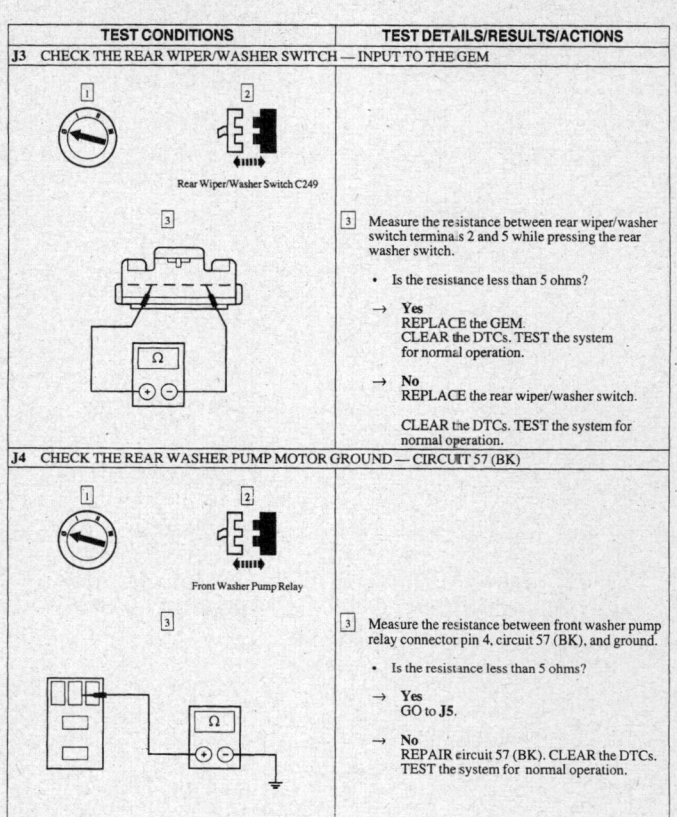

TEST CONDITIONS	TEST DETAILS/RESULTS/ACTIONS
J3 CHECK THE REAR WIPER/WASHER SWITCH — INPUT TO THE GEM	

	3 Measure the resistance between rear wiper/washer switch terminals 2 and 5 while pressing the rear washer switch.
	
	 • Is the resistance less than 5 ohms?
	
	 → **Yes**
	  REPLACE the GEM. CLEAR the DTCs. TEST the system for normal operation.
	
	 → **No**
	  REPLACE the rear wiper/washer switch.
	
	 CLEAR the DTCs. TEST the system for normal operation.

J4 CHECK THE REAR WASHER PUMP MOTOR GROUND — CIRCUIT 57 (BK)	

	3 Measure the resistance between front washer pump relay connector pin 4, circuit 57 (BK), and ground.
	
	 • Is the resistance less than 5 ohms?
	
	 → **Yes**
	  GO to **J5**.
	
	 → **No**
	  REPAIR circuit 57 (BK). CLEAR the DTCs. TEST the system for normal operation.

FM9029800630020X

Fig. 13 Test J: Rear Washer Pump Is Inoperative (Part 2 of 4). 2002–04

TEST CONDITIONS	TEST DETAILS/RESULTS/ACTIONS
J7 CHECK THE REAR WIPER/WASHER SWITCH FOR OPEN TO THE WASHER PUMP	

	2 Measure the resistance between rear wiper/washer switch terminals 1 and 4 while pressing the rear washer switch.
	
	 • Is the resistance less than 5 ohms?
	
	 → **Yes**
	  REPAIR circuit 946 (P/LG). CLEAR the DTCs. TEST the system for normal operation.
	
	 → **No**
	  REPLACE the rear wiper/washer switch
	
	 CLEAR the DTCs. TEST the system for normal operation.

J8 CHECK THE REAR WASHER RELAY SOLENOID GROUND — CIRCUIT 57 (BK)	

	2 Measure the resistance between rear washer relay connector pin 2, circuit 57 (BK), and ground.
	
	 • Is the resistance less than 5 ohms?
	
	 → **Yes**
	  REPLACE the rear washer relay. CLEAR the DTCs. TEST the system for normal operation.
	
	 → **No**
	  REPAIR circuit 57 (BK). CLEAR the DTCs. TEST the system for normal operation.

FM9029800630040X

Fig. 13 Test J: Rear Washer Pump Is Inoperative (Part 4 of 4). 2002–04

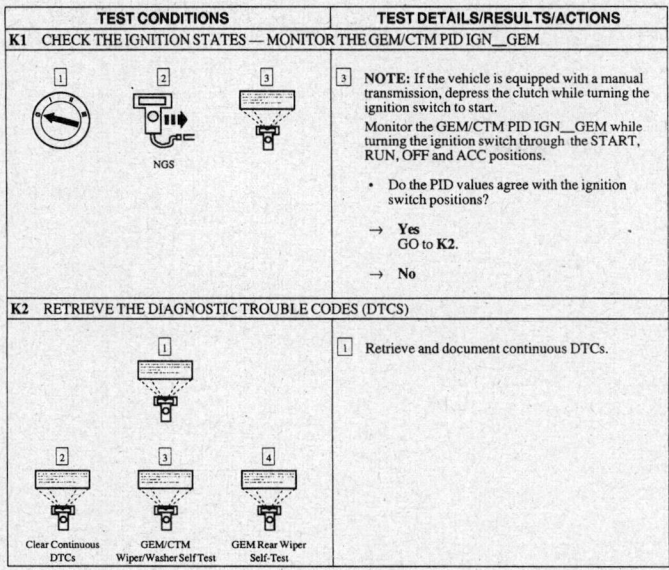

TEST CONDITIONS	TEST DETAILS/RESULTS/ACTIONS
K1 CHECK THE IGNITION STATES — MONITOR THE GEM/CTM PID IGN__GEM	
	3 NOTE: If the vehicle is equipped with a manual transmission, depress the clutch while turning the ignition switch to start. Monitor the GEM/CTM PID IGN__GEM while turning the ignition switch through the START, RUN, OFF and ACC positions.
	• Do the PID values agree with the ignition switch positions?
	→ Yes GO to **K2**.
	→ No
K2 RETRIEVE THE DIAGNOSTIC TROUBLE CODES (DTCS)	
	1 Retrieve and document continuous DTCs.

Fig. 14 Test K: Rear Wiper Inoperative (Part 1 of 18). 2002–04

TEST CONDITIONS	TEST DETAILS/RESULTS/ACTIONS
K4 CHECK THE WIPER DISABLE SWITCH — MONITOR THE GEM PID LGATESW (Continued)	
	5 Monitor the GEM PID LGATESW.
	• Does the GEM PID LGATESW indicate AJAR?
	→ Yes GO to **K5**.
	→ No REPLACE the liftgate wiper disable switch. CLEAR the DTCs. TEST the system for normal operation.
K5 CHECK THE RH LIFTGATE AJAR SWITCH — MONITOR THE GEM PID LGATESW	
	3 Close the liftgate and liftgate glass.
	5 Monitor the GEM PID LGATESW.
	• Does the GEM PID LGATESW indicate AJAR?
	→ Yes GO to **K6**.
	→ No REPLACE the RH liftgate ajar switch. CLEAR the DTCs. TEST the system for normal operation.
K6 CHECK THE LH LIFTGATE AJAR SWITCH — MONITOR THE GEM PID LGATESW	
	3 Close the liftgate and liftgate glass.

Fig. 14 Test K: Rear Wiper Inoperative (Part 3 of 18). 2002–04

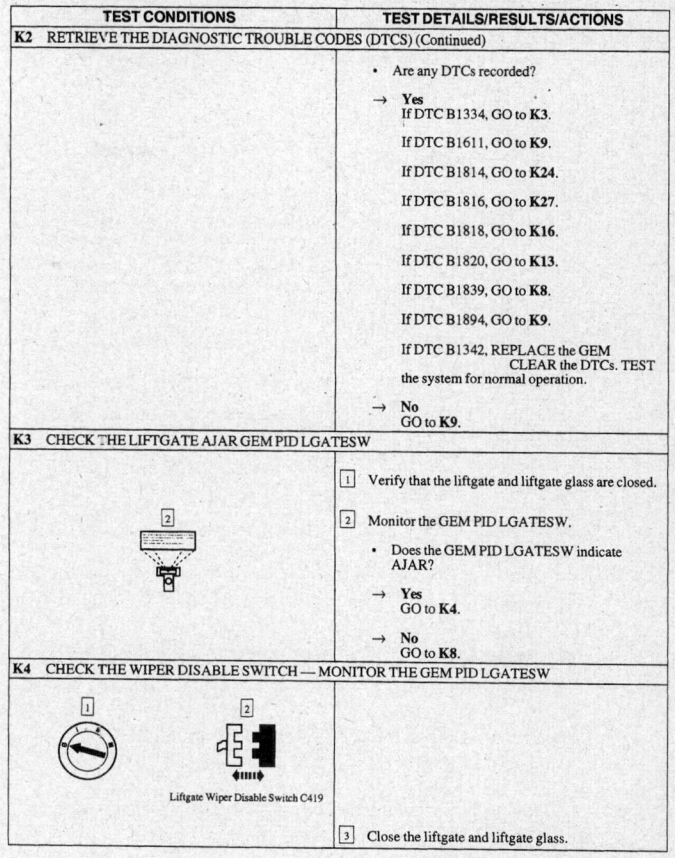

TEST CONDITIONS	TEST DETAILS/RESULTS/ACTIONS
K2 RETRIEVE THE DIAGNOSTIC TROUBLE CODES (DTCS) (Continued)	
	• Are any DTCs recorded?
	→ Yes If DTC B1334, GO to **K3**. If DTC B1611, GO to **K9**. If DTC B1814, GO to **K24**. If DTC B1816, GO to **K27**. If DTC B1818, GO to **K16**. If DTC B1820, GO to **K13**. If DTC B1839, GO to **K8**. If DTC B1894, GO to **K9**. If DTC B1342, REPLACE the GEM CLEAR the DTCs. TEST the system for normal operation.
	→ No GO to **K9**.
K3 CHECK THE LIFTGATE AJAR GEM PID LGATESW	
	1 Verify that the liftgate and liftgate glass are closed.
	2 Monitor the GEM PID LGATESW.
	• Does the GEM PID LGATESW indicate AJAR?
	→ Yes GO to **K4**.
	→ No GO to **K8**.
K4 CHECK THE WIPER DISABLE SWITCH — MONITOR THE GEM PID LGATESW	
	3 Close the liftgate and liftgate glass.

Fig. 14 Test K: Rear Wiper Inoperative (Part 2 of 18). 2002–04

TEST CONDITIONS	TEST DETAILS/RESULTS/ACTIONS
K6 CHECK THE LH LIFTGATE AJAR SWITCH — MONITOR THE GEM PID LGATESW (Continued)	
	5 Monitor the GEM PID LGATESW.
	• Does the GEM PID LGATESW indicate AJAR?
	→ Yes GO to **K7**.
	→ No REPLACE the LH liftgate ajar switch. CLEAR the DTCs. TEST the system for normal operation.
K7 CHECK CIRCUIT 700 (W/P) FOR SHORT TO GROUND	
	3 Measure the resistance between GEM C280-4, circuit 700 (W/P), and ground.
	• Is the resistance greater than 10,000 ohms?
	→ Yes REPLACE the GEM CLEAR the DTCs. TEST the system for normal operation.
	→ No REPAIR circuit 700 (W/P). CLEAR the DTCs. TEST the system for normal operation.

Fig. 14 Test K: Rear Wiper Inoperative (Part 4 of 18). 2002–04

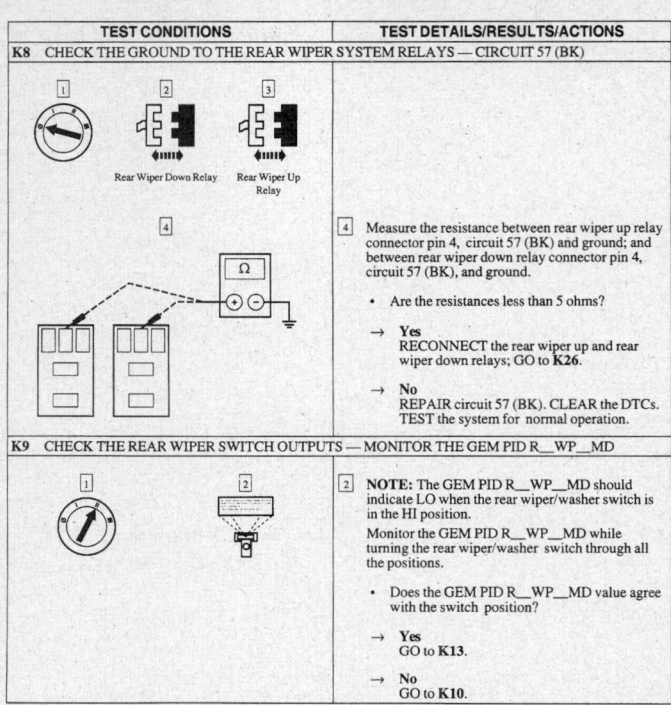

TEST CONDITIONS	TEST DETAILS/RESULTS/ACTIONS
K8 CHECK THE GROUND TO THE REAR WIPER SYSTEM RELAYS — CIRCUIT 57 (BK)	

4 Measure the resistance between rear wiper up relay connector pin 4, circuit 57 (BK) and ground; and between rear wiper down relay connector pin 4, circuit 57 (BK), and ground.

- Are the resistances less than 5 ohms?

→ **Yes**
RECONNECT the rear wiper up and rear wiper down relays; GO to **K26**.

→ **No**
REPAIR circuit 57 (BK). CLEAR the DTCs. TEST the system for normal operation.

TEST CONDITIONS	TEST DETAILS/RESULTS/ACTIONS
K9 CHECK THE REAR WIPER SWITCH OUTPUTS — MONITOR THE GEM PID R__WP__MD	

2 **NOTE:** The GEM PID R__WP__MD should indicate LO when the rear wiper/washer switch is in the HI position.

Monitor the GEM PID R__WP__MD while turning the rear wiper/washer switch through all the positions.

- Does the GEM PID R__WP__MD value agree with the switch position?

→ **Yes**
GO to **K13**.

→ **No**
GO to **K10**.

FM9029800631050X

Fig. 14   Test K: Rear Wiper Inoperative (Part 5 of 18). 2002–04

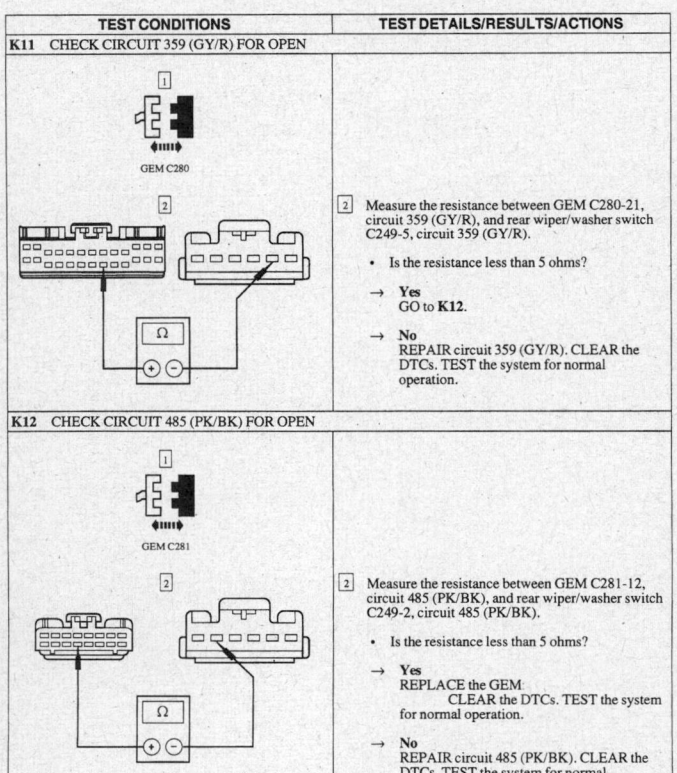

TEST CONDITIONS	TEST DETAILS/RESULTS/ACTIONS
K11 CHECK CIRCUIT 359 (GY/R) FOR OPEN	

2 Measure the resistance between GEM C280-21, circuit 359 (GY/R), and rear wiper/washer switch C249-5, circuit 359 (GY/R).

- Is the resistance less than 5 ohms?

→ **Yes**
GO to **K12**.

→ **No**
REPAIR circuit 359 (GY/R). CLEAR the DTCs. TEST the system for normal operation.

TEST CONDITIONS	TEST DETAILS/RESULTS/ACTIONS
K12 CHECK CIRCUIT 485 (PK/BK) FOR OPEN	

2 Measure the resistance between GEM C281-12, circuit 485 (PK/BK), and rear wiper/washer switch C249-2, circuit 485 (PK/BK).

- Is the resistance less than 5 ohms?

→ **Yes**
REPLACE the GEM. CLEAR the DTCs. TEST the system for normal operation.

→ **No**
REPAIR circuit 485 (PK/BK). CLEAR the DTCs. TEST the system for normal operation.

FM9029800631070X

Fig. 14   Test K: Rear Wiper Inoperative (Part 7 of 18). 2002–04

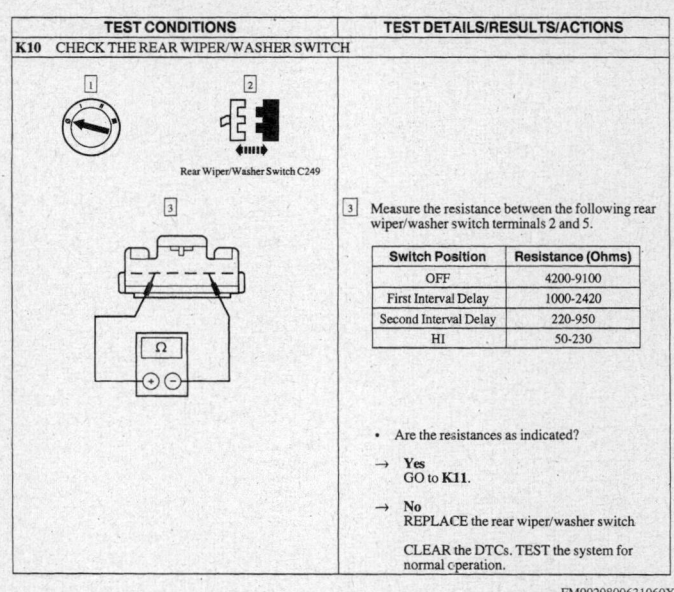

TEST CONDITIONS	TEST DETAILS/RESULTS/ACTIONS
K10 CHECK THE REAR WIPER/WASHER SWITCH	

3 Measure the resistance between the following rear wiper/washer switch terminals 2 and 5.

Switch Position	Resistance (Ohms)
OFF	4200-9100
First Interval Delay	1000-2420
Second Interval Delay	220-950
HI	50-230

- Are the resistances as indicated?

→ **Yes**
GO to **K11**.

→ **No**
REPLACE the rear wiper/washer switch

CLEAR the DTCs. TEST the system for normal operation.

FM9029800631060X

Fig. 14   Test K: Rear Wiper Inoperative (Part 6 of 18). 2002–04

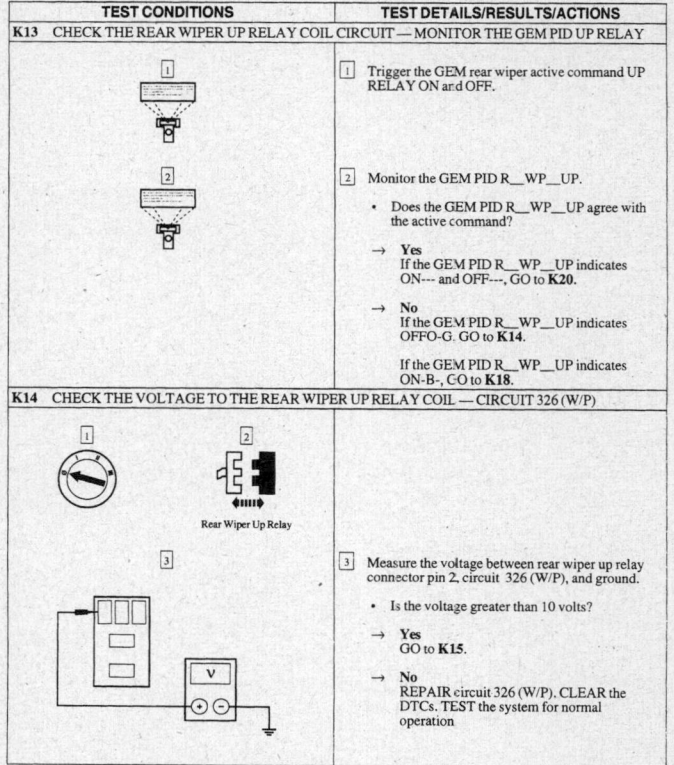

TEST CONDITIONS	TEST DETAILS/RESULTS/ACTIONS
K13 CHECK THE REAR WIPER UP RELAY COIL CIRCUIT — MONITOR THE GEM PID UP RELAY	

1 Trigger the GEM rear wiper active command UP RELAY ON and OFF.

2 Monitor the GEM PID R__WP__UP.

- Does the GEM PID R__WP__UP agree with the active command?

→ **Yes**
If the GEM PID R__WP__UP indicates ON--- and OFF---, GO to **K20**.

→ **No**
If the GEM PID R__WP__UP indicates OFFO-G. GO to **K14**.

If the GEM PID R__WP__UP indicates ON-B-, GO to **K18**.

TEST CONDITIONS	TEST DETAILS/RESULTS/ACTIONS
K14 CHECK THE VOLTAGE TO THE REAR WIPER UP RELAY COIL — CIRCUIT 326 (W/P)	

3 Measure the voltage between rear wiper up relay connector pin 2, circuit 326 (W/P), and ground.

- Is the voltage greater than 10 volts?

→ **Yes**
GO to **K15**.

→ **No**
REPAIR circuit 326 (W/P). CLEAR the DTCs. TEST the system for normal operation

FM9029800631080X

Fig. 14   Test K: Rear Wiper Inoperative (Part 8 of 18). 2002–04

TEST CONDITIONS	TEST DETAILS/RESULTS/ACTIONS
K15 CHECK THE REAR WIPER UP RELAY	

	1 Check the rear wiper up relay
	
	• Is the rear wiper up relay OK?
	
	→ **Yes**
	  GO to **K16**.
	
	→ **No**
	  REPLACE the rear wiper up relay. CLEAR the DTCs. TEST the system for normal operation.

K16 CHECK CIRCUIT 591 (LG) FOR OPEN	

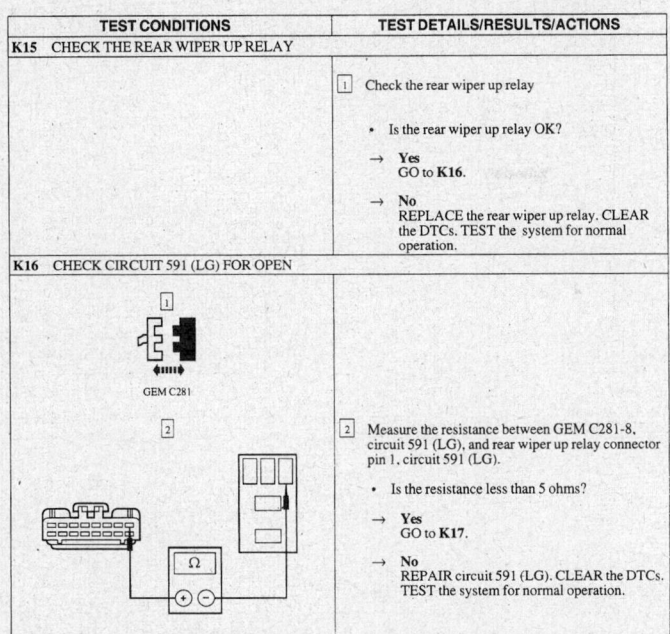

GEM C281

TEST CONDITIONS	TEST DETAILS/RESULTS/ACTIONS

	2 Measure the resistance between GEM C281-8, circuit 591 (LG), and rear wiper up relay connector pin 1, circuit 591 (LG).
	
	• Is the resistance less than 5 ohms?
	
	→ **Yes**
	  GO to **K17**.
	
	→ **No**
	  REPAIR circuit 591 (LG). CLEAR the DTCs. TEST the system for normal operation.

FM9029800631090X

Fig. 14 Test K: Rear Wiper Inoperative (Part 9 of 18). 2002–04

TEST CONDITIONS	TEST DETAILS/RESULTS/ACTIONS
K17 CHECK CIRCUIT 591 (LG) FOR A SHORT TO GROUND	

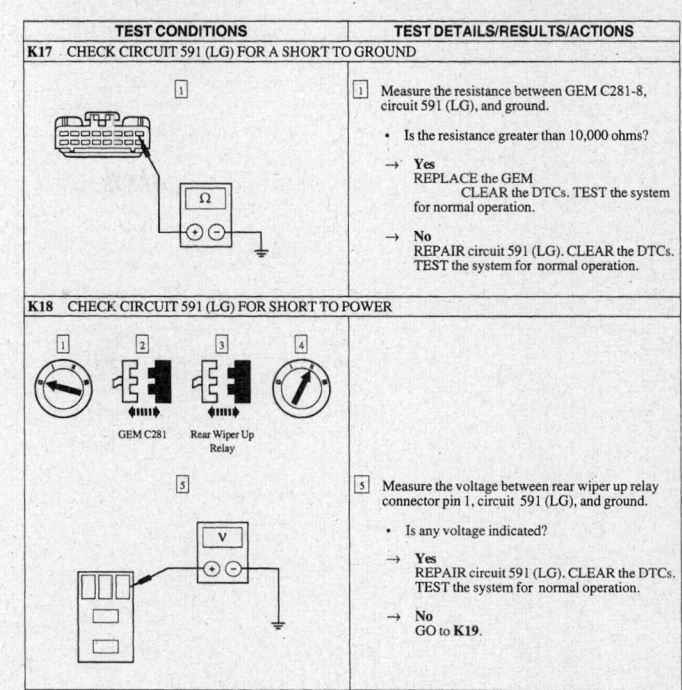

GEM C281

Rear Wiper Up Relay

TEST CONDITIONS	TEST DETAILS/RESULTS/ACTIONS

	1 Measure the resistance between GEM C281-8, circuit 591 (LG), and ground.
	
	• Is the resistance greater than 10,000 ohms?
	
	→ **Yes**
	  REPLACE the GEM CLEAR the DTCs. TEST the system for normal operation.
	
	→ **No**
	  REPAIR circuit 591 (LG). CLEAR the DTCs. TEST the system for normal operation.

K18 CHECK CIRCUIT 591 (LG) FOR SHORT TO POWER	

	5 Measure the voltage between rear wiper up relay connector pin 1, circuit 591 (LG), and ground.
	
	• Is any voltage indicated?
	
	→ **Yes**
	  REPAIR circuit 591 (LG). CLEAR the DTCs. TEST the system for normal operation.
	
	→ **No**
	  GO to **K19**.

FM9029800631100X

Fig. 14 Test K: Rear Wiper Inoperative (Part 10 of 18). 2002–04

TEST CONDITIONS	TEST DETAILS/RESULTS/ACTIONS
K19 CHECK THE REAR WIPER UP RELAY	

	1 Check the rear wiper up relay.
	
	• Is the rear wiper up relay OK?
	
	→ **Yes**
	  REPLACE the GEM CLEAR the DTCs. TEST the system for normal operation.
	
	→ **No**
	  REPLACE the rear wiper up relay. CLEAR the DTCs. TEST the system for normal operation.

K20 CHECK POWER DISTRIBUTION MINI-FUSE 8 (15A)	

Fuse 8 (15A)

TEST CONDITIONS	TEST DETAILS/RESULTS/ACTIONS

	• Is the fuse OK?
	
	→ **Yes**
	  GO to **K21**.
	
	→ **No**
	  REPLACE fuse 8 (15A). CLEAR the DTCs. TEST the system for normal operation. If the fuse fails again, CHECK for a short to ground. REPAIR as necessary.

K21 CHECK THE VOLTAGE TO THE REAR WIPER MOTOR CIRCUIT 410 (W/O)	

Rear Wiper Motor C417

TEST CONDITIONS	TEST DETAILS/RESULTS/ACTIONS
	4 Trigger the GEM active command UP RELAY to ON.

FM9029800631110X

Fig. 14 Test K: Rear Wiper Inoperative (Part 11 of 18). 2002–04

TEST CONDITIONS	TEST DETAILS/RESULTS/ACTIONS
K21 CHECK THE VOLTAGE TO THE REAR WIPER MOTOR CIRCUIT 410 (W/O) (Continued)	

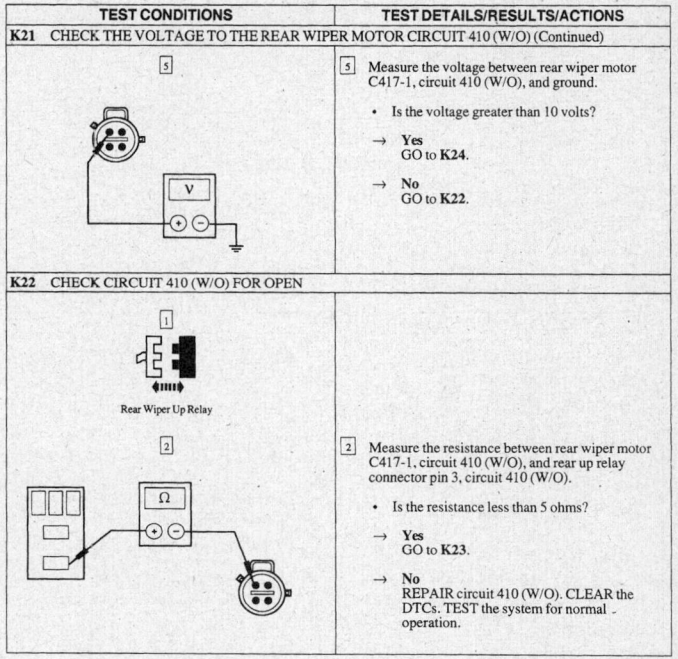

Rear Wiper Up Relay

TEST CONDITIONS	TEST DETAILS/RESULTS/ACTIONS

	5 Measure the voltage between rear wiper motor C417-1, circuit 410 (W/O), and ground.
	
	• Is the voltage greater than 10 volts?
	
	→ **Yes**
	  GO to **K24**.
	
	→ **No**
	  GO to **K22**.

K22 CHECK CIRCUIT 410 (W/O) FOR OPEN	

	2 Measure the resistance between rear wiper motor C417-1, circuit 410 (W/O), and rear up relay connector pin 3, circuit 410 (W/O).
	
	• Is the resistance less than 5 ohms?
	
	→ **Yes**
	  GO to **K23**.
	
	→ **No**
	  REPAIR circuit 410 (W/O). CLEAR the DTCs. TEST the system for normal operation.

FM9029800631120X

Fig. 14 Test K: Rear Wiper Inoperative (Part 12 of 18). 2002–04

WIPER SYSTEMS

TEST CONDITIONS	TEST DETAILS/RESULTS/ACTIONS
K23 CHECK THE VOLTAGE TO THE REAR WIPER UP RELAY — CIRCUIT 326 (W/P)	
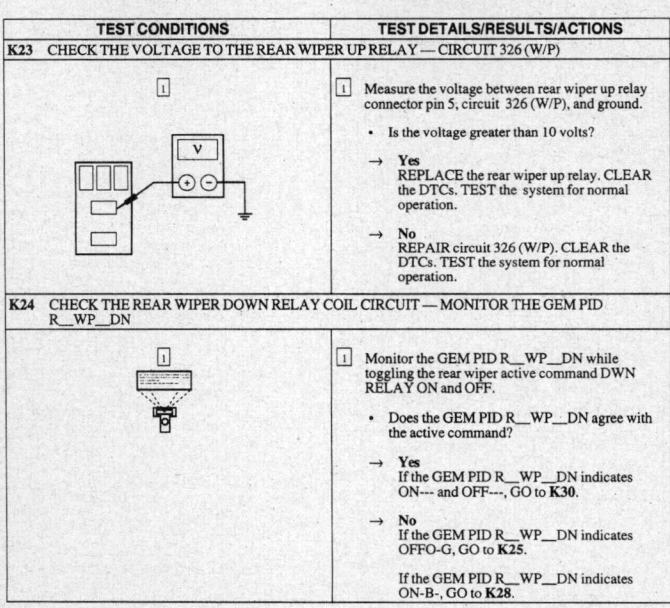	① Measure the voltage between rear wiper up relay connector pin 5, circuit 326 (W/P), and ground. • Is the voltage greater than 10 volts? → **Yes** REPLACE the rear wiper up relay. CLEAR the DTCs. TEST the system for normal operation. → **No** REPAIR circuit 326 (W/P). CLEAR the DTCs. TEST the system for normal operation.
K24 CHECK THE REAR WIPER DOWN RELAY COIL CIRCUIT — MONITOR THE GEM PID R__WP__DN	
	① Monitor the GEM PID R__WP__DN while toggling the rear wiper active command DWN RELAY ON and OFF. • Does the GEM PID R__WP__DN agree with the active command? → **Yes** If the GEM PID R__WP__DN indicates ON--- and OFF---, GO to **K30**. → **No** If the GEM PID R__WP__DN indicates OFFO-G, GO to **K25**. If the GEM PID R__WP__DN indicates ON-B-, GO to **K28**.

FM9029800631130X

Fig. 14   Test K: Rear Wiper Inoperative (Part 13 of 18). 2002–04

TEST CONDITIONS	TEST DETAILS/RESULTS/ACTIONS
K25 CHECK THE VOLTAGE TO THE REAR WIPER DOWN RELAY COIL	
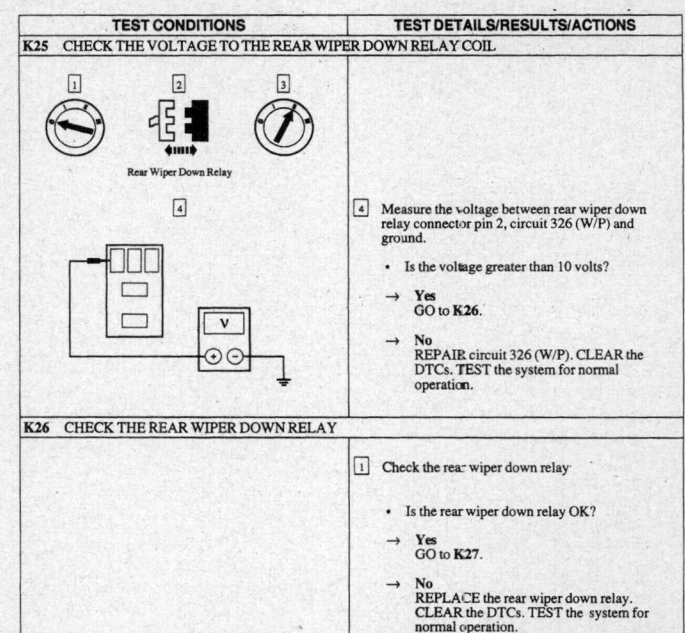	④ Measure the voltage between rear wiper down relay connector pin 2, circuit 326 (W/P) and ground. • Is the voltage greater than 10 volts? → **Yes** GO to **K26**. → **No** REPAIR circuit 326 (W/P). CLEAR the DTCs. TEST the system for normal operation.
K26 CHECK THE REAR WIPER DOWN RELAY	
	① Check the rear wiper down relay • Is the rear wiper down relay OK? → **Yes** GO to **K27**. → **No** REPLACE the rear wiper down relay. CLEAR the DTCs. TEST the system for normal operation.

FM9029800631140X

Fig. 14   Test K: Rear Wiper Inoperative (Part 14 of 18). 2002–04

TEST CONDITIONS	TEST DETAILS/RESULTS/ACTIONS
K27 CHECK CIRCUIT 592 (T) FOR OPEN	
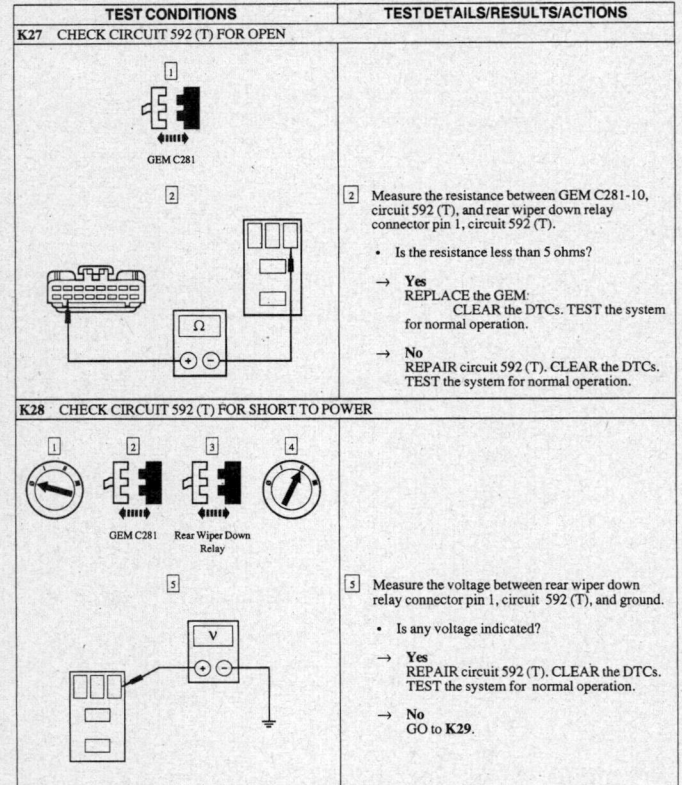	② Measure the resistance between GEM C281-10, circuit 592 (T), and rear wiper down relay connector pin 1, circuit 592 (T). • Is the resistance less than 5 ohms? → **Yes** REPLACE the GEM. CLEAR the DTCs. TEST the system for normal operation. → **No** REPAIR circuit 592 (T). CLEAR the DTCs. TEST the system for normal operation.
K28 CHECK CIRCUIT 592 (T) FOR SHORT TO POWER	
	⑤ Measure the voltage between rear wiper down relay connector pin 1, circuit 592 (T), and ground. • Is any voltage indicated? → **Yes** REPAIR circuit 592 (T). CLEAR the DTCs. TEST the system for normal operation. → **No** GO to **K29**.

FM9029800631150X

Fig. 14   Test K: Rear Wiper Inoperative (Part 15 of 18). 2002–04

TEST CONDITIONS	TEST DETAILS/RESULTS/ACTIONS
K29 CHECK THE REAR WIPER DOWN RELAY	
	① Check the rear wiper down relay • Is the rear wiper down relay OK? → **Yes** REPLACE the GEM CLEAR the DTCs. TEST the system for normal operation. → **No** REPLACE the rear wiper down relay. CLEAR the DTCs. TEST the system for normal operation.
K30 CHECK POWER DISTRIBUTION BOX MINI-FUSE 8 (15A)	
	• Is the fuse OK? → **Yes** GO to **K31**. → **No** REPLACE fuse 8 (15A). CLEAR the DTCs. TEST the system for normal operation. If the fuse fails again, CHECK for a short to ground. REPAIR as necessary.
K31 CHECK CIRCUIT 411 (BK/LB) FOR VOLTAGE	
	④ Trigger the GEM rear wiper active command DWN RELAY to ON.

FM9029800631160X

Fig. 14   Test K: Rear Wiper Inoperative (Part 16 of 18). 2002–04

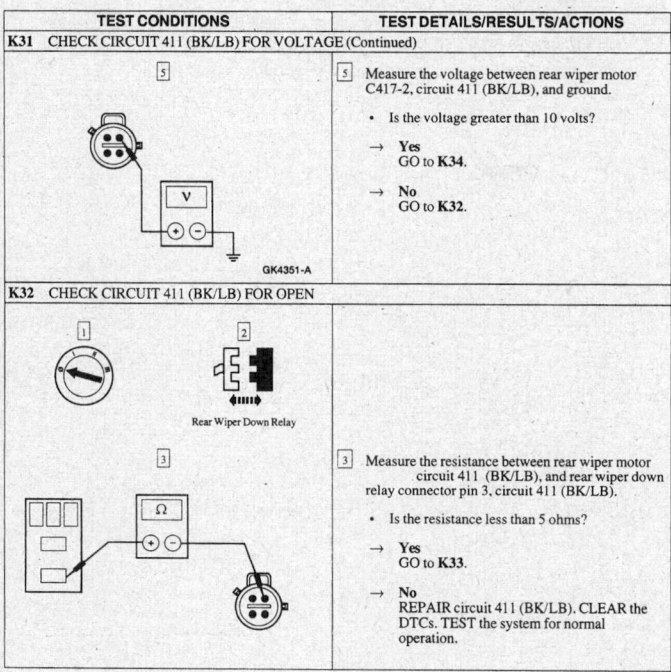

TEST CONDITIONS	TEST DETAILS/RESULTS/ACTIONS
K31 CHECK CIRCUIT 411 (BK/LB) FOR VOLTAGE (Continued)	[5] Measure the voltage between rear wiper motor C417-2, circuit 411 (BK/LB), and ground. • Is the voltage greater than 10 volts? → **Yes** GO to **K34**. → **No** GO to **K32**.
K32 CHECK CIRCUIT 411 (BK/LB) FOR OPEN	[3] Measure the resistance between rear wiper motor circuit 411 (BK/LB), and rear wiper down relay connector pin 3, circuit 411 (BK/LB). • Is the resistance less than 5 ohms? → **Yes** GO to **K33**. → **No** REPAIR circuit 411 (BK/LB). CLEAR the DTCs. TEST the system for normal operation.

FM9029800631170X

Fig. 14   Test K: Rear Wiper Inoperative (Part 17 of 18). 2002–04

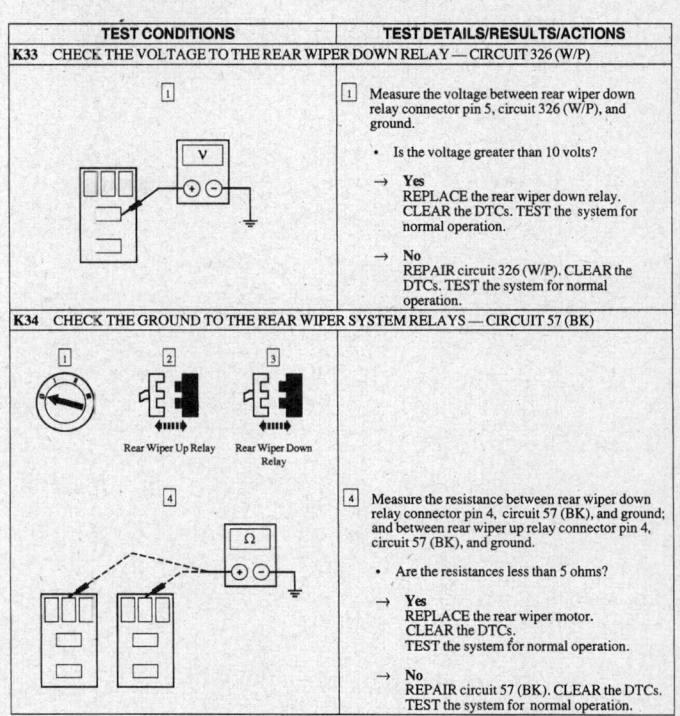

TEST CONDITIONS	TEST DETAILS/RESULTS/ACTIONS
K33 CHECK THE VOLTAGE TO THE REAR WIPER DOWN RELAY — CIRCUIT 326 (W/P)	[1] Measure the voltage between rear wiper down relay connector pin 5, circuit 326 (W/P), and ground. • Is the voltage greater than 10 volts? → **Yes** REPLACE the rear wiper down relay. CLEAR the DTCs. TEST the system for normal operation. → **No** REPAIR circuit 326 (W/P). CLEAR the DTCs. TEST the system for normal operation.
K34 CHECK THE GROUND TO THE REAR WIPER SYSTEM RELAYS — CIRCUIT 57 (BK)	[4] Measure the resistance between rear wiper down relay connector pin 4, circuit 57 (BK), and ground; and between rear wiper up relay connector pin 4, circuit 57 (BK), and ground. • Are the resistances less than 5 ohms? → **Yes** REPLACE the rear wiper motor. CLEAR the DTCs. TEST the system for normal operation. → **No** REPAIR circuit 57 (BK). CLEAR the DTCs. TEST the system for normal operation.

FM9029800631180X

Fig. 14   Test K: Rear Wiper Inoperative (Part 18 of 18). 2002–04

TEST CONDITIONS	TEST DETAILS/RESULTS/ACTIONS
L1 RETRIEVE THE DIAGNOSTIC TROUBLE CODES (DTCs) NGS Clear Continuous DTCs — GEM Wiper/Washer Self Test — GEM Rear Wiper Self Test	[3] Retrieve and document continuous DTCs. • Are any DTCs recorded? → **Yes** If DTC B1611, GO to **L2**. If DTC B1614, GO to **L2**. If DTC B1839, GO to **L6**. If DTC B1894, GO to **L6**. If DTC B1342, REPLACE the GEM CLEAR the DTCs. TEST the system for normal operation. → **No** GO to **L2**.
L2 CHECK THE REAR WIPER/WASHER SWITCH — MONITOR THE GEM PID R__WP__MD	[1] Monitor the GEM PID R__WP__MD.

FM9029800632010X

Fig. 15   Test L: Rear Wiper Does Not Operate Properly (Part 1 of 6). 2002–04

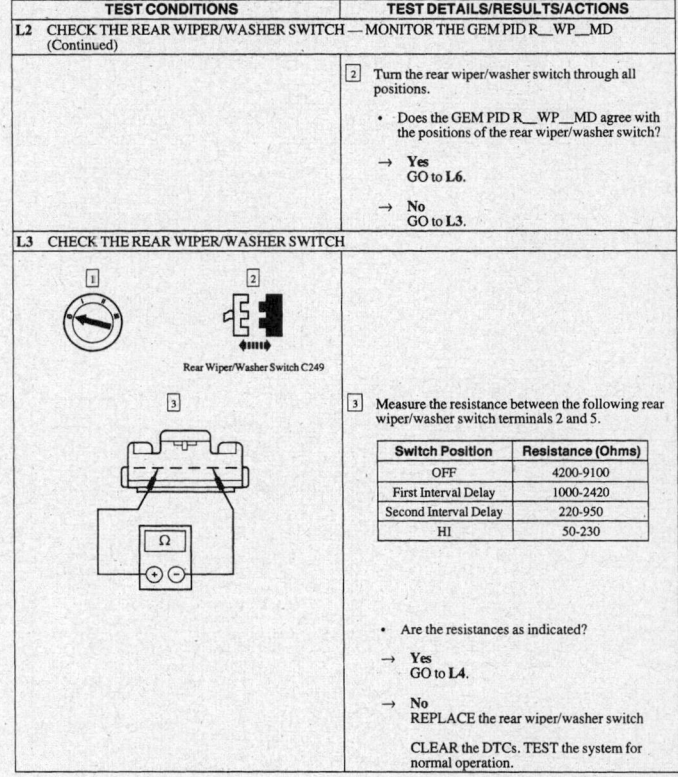

TEST CONDITIONS	TEST DETAILS/RESULTS/ACTIONS
L2 CHECK THE REAR WIPER/WASHER SWITCH — MONITOR THE GEM PID R__WP__MD (Continued)	[2] Turn the rear wiper/washer switch through all positions. • Does the GEM PID R__WP__MD agree with the positions of the rear wiper/washer switch? → **Yes** GO to **L6**. → **No** GO to **L3**.
L3 CHECK THE REAR WIPER/WASHER SWITCH Rear Wiper/Washer Switch C249	[3] Measure the resistance between the following rear wiper/washer switch terminals 2 and 5. <table><tr><td>**Switch Position**</td><td>**Resistance (Ohms)**</td></tr><tr><td>OFF</td><td>4200-9100</td></tr><tr><td>First Interval Delay</td><td>1000-2420</td></tr><tr><td>Second Interval Delay</td><td>220-950</td></tr><tr><td>HI</td><td>50-230</td></tr></table> • Are the resistances as indicated? → **Yes** GO to **L4**. → **No** REPLACE the rear wiper/washer switch. CLEAR the DTCs. TEST the system for normal operation.

FM9029800632020X

Fig. 15   Test L: Rear Wiper Does Not Operate Properly (Part 2 of 6). 2002–04

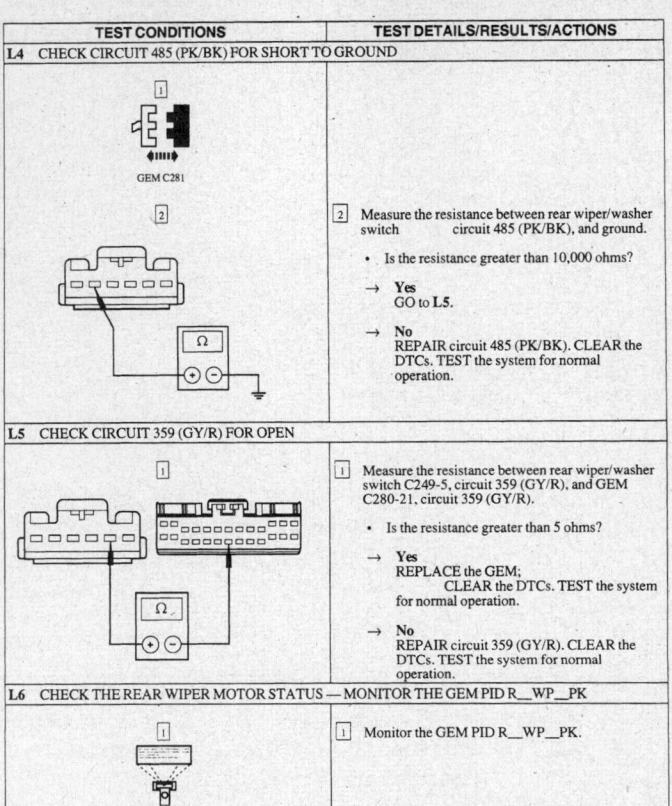

TEST CONDITIONS	TEST DETAILS/RESULTS/ACTIONS
L4 CHECK CIRCUIT 485 (PK/BK) FOR SHORT TO GROUND	

GEM C281	[2] Measure the resistance between rear wiper/washer switch circuit 485 (PK/BK), and ground.
	
	 • Is the resistance greater than 10,000 ohms?
	
	 → Yes
	    GO to L5.
	
	 → No
	    REPAIR circuit 485 (PK/BK). CLEAR the DTCs. TEST the system for normal operation.

L5 CHECK CIRCUIT 359 (GY/R) FOR OPEN	

	[1] Measure the resistance between rear wiper/washer switch C249-5, circuit 359 (GY/R), and GEM C280-21, circuit 359 (GY/R).
	
	 • Is the resistance greater than 5 ohms?
	
	 → Yes
	    REPLACE the GEM;
	      CLEAR the DTCs. TEST the system for normal operation.
	
	 → No
	    REPAIR circuit 359 (GY/R). CLEAR the DTCs. TEST the system for normal operation.

L6 CHECK THE REAR WIPER MOTOR STATUS — MONITOR THE GEM PID R__WP__PK	
	[1] Monitor the GEM PID R__WP__PK.

FM9029800632030X

Fig. 15   Test L: Rear Wiper Does Not Operate Properly (Part 3 of 6). 2002–04

TEST CONDITIONS	TEST DETAILS/RESULTS/ACTIONS
L8 CHECK CIRCUIT 587 (P/Y) FOR SHORT TO GROUND	

	[1] Measure the resistance between GEM C281-4, circuit 587 (P/Y), and ground.
	
	 • Is the resistance greater than 10,000 ohms?
	
	 → Yes
	    GO to L9.
	
	 → No
	    REPAIR circuit 587 (P/Y). CLEAR the DTCs. TEST the system for normal operation.

L9 CHECK THE GROUND TO THE REAR WIPER MOTOR STATUS — CIRCUIT 57 (BK)	

	[1] Measure the resistance between rear wiper motor C417-4, circuit 57 (BK), and ground.
	
	 • Is the resistance less than 5 ohms?
	
	 → Yes
	    GO to L10.
	
	 → No
	    REPAIR circuit 57 (BK). CLEAR the DTCs. TEST the system for normal operation.

L10 CHECK THE WIPER PARK INDICATOR SWITCH — PARKED POSITION	

	[1] Place the rear wiper arm in the PARKED position.
	
	 [2] Measure the resistance between rear wiper motor terminals 3 and 4.
	
	 • Is the resistance less than 5 ohms?
	
	 → Yes
	    GO to L11.
	
	 → No
	    REPLACE the rear wiper motor
	      CLEAR the DTCs. TEST the system for normal operation.

GK6120-A

FM9029800632050X

Fig. 15   Test L: Rear Wiper Does Not Operate Properly (Part 5 of 6). 2002–04

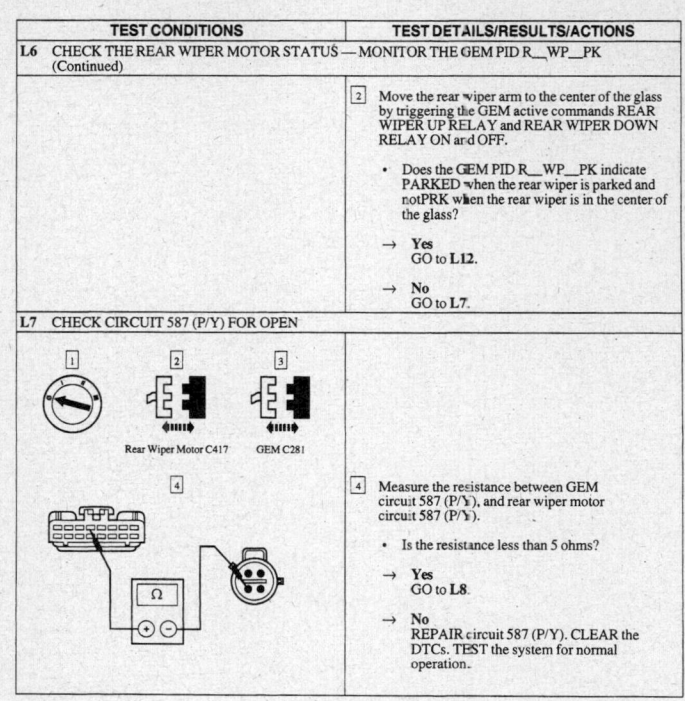

TEST CONDITIONS	TEST DETAILS/RESULTS/ACTIONS
L6 CHECK THE REAR WIPER MOTOR STATUS — MONITOR THE GEM PID R__WP__PK (Continued)	

	[2] Move the rear wiper arm to the center of the glass by triggering the GEM active commands REAR WIPER UP RELAY and REAR WIPER DOWN RELAY ON and OFF.
	
	 • Does the GEM PID R__WP__PK indicate PARKED when the rear wiper is parked and notPRK when the rear wiper is in the center of the glass?
	
	 → Yes
	    GO to L12.
	
	 → No
	    GO to L7.

L7 CHECK CIRCUIT 587 (P/Y) FOR OPEN	

Rear Wiper Motor C417 GEM C281	[4] Measure the resistance between GEM circuit 587 (P/Y), and rear wiper motor circuit 587 (P/Y).
	
	 • Is the resistance less than 5 ohms?
	
	 → Yes
	    GO to L8.
	
	 → No
	    REPAIR circuit 587 (P/Y). CLEAR the DTCs. TEST the system for normal operation.

FM9029800632040X

Fig. 15   Test L: Rear Wiper Does Not Operate Properly (Part 4 of 6). 2002–04

TEST CONDITIONS	TEST DETAILS/RESULTS/ACTIONS
L11 CHECK THE WIPER PARK INDICATOR SWITCH — NOT-PARKED POSITION	

	[1] Place the rear wiper arm in the middle of the glass.
	
	 [2] Measure the resistance between rear wiper motor terminals 3 and 4.
	
	 • Is the resistance greater than 10,000 ohms?
	
	 → Yes
	    REPLACE the GEM
	      CLEAR the DTCs. TEST the system for normal operation.
	
	 → No
	    REPLACE the rear wiper motor
	      CLEAR the DTCs. TEST the system for normal operation.

L12 CHECK THE WIPER MECHANISM	

	[1] Remove the linkage from the wiper motor.
	
	 • Are the wipers free?
	
	 → Yes
	    CHECK the wiper motor
	    If the wiper motor does not pass the test, REPLACE the rear wiper motor. CLEAR the DTCs. TEST the system for normal operation.
	
	 → No
	    REPAIR the wiper mechanism. CLEAR the DTCs. TEST the system for normal operation.

FM9029800632060X

Fig. 15   Test L: Rear Wiper Does Not Operate Properly (Part 6 of 6). 2002–04

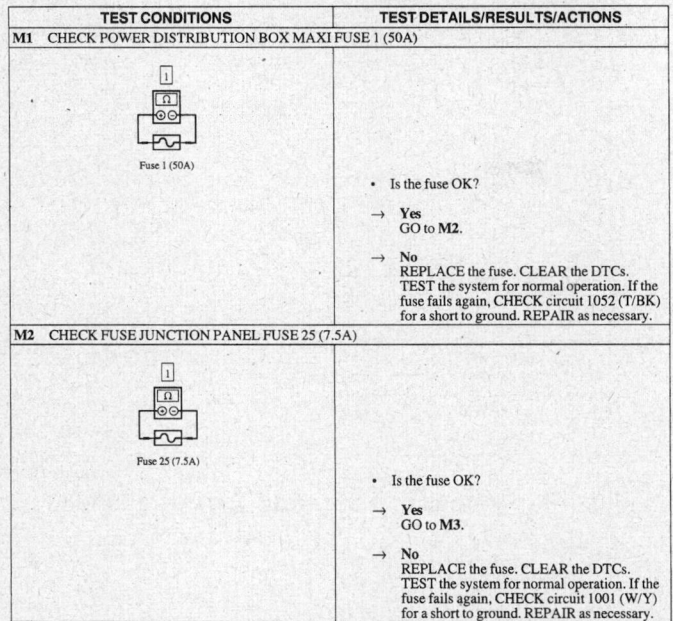

TEST CONDITIONS	TEST DETAILS/RESULTS/ACTIONS
M1 CHECK POWER DISTRIBUTION BOX MAXI FUSE 1 (50A)	
Fuse 1 (50A)	• Is the fuse OK? → **Yes** GO to **M2**. → **No** REPLACE the fuse. CLEAR the DTCs. TEST the system for normal operation. If the fuse fails again, CHECK circuit 1052 (T/BK) for a short to ground. REPAIR as necessary.
M2 CHECK FUSE JUNCTION PANEL FUSE 25 (7.5A)	
Fuse 25 (7.5A)	• Is the fuse OK? → **Yes** GO to **M3**. → **No** REPLACE the fuse. CLEAR the DTCs. TEST the system for normal operation. If the fuse fails again, CHECK circuit 1001 (W/Y) for a short to ground. REPAIR as necessary.

FM9029800633010X

Fig. 16 Test M: No Communication w/GEM Module (Part 1 of 3). 2002–04

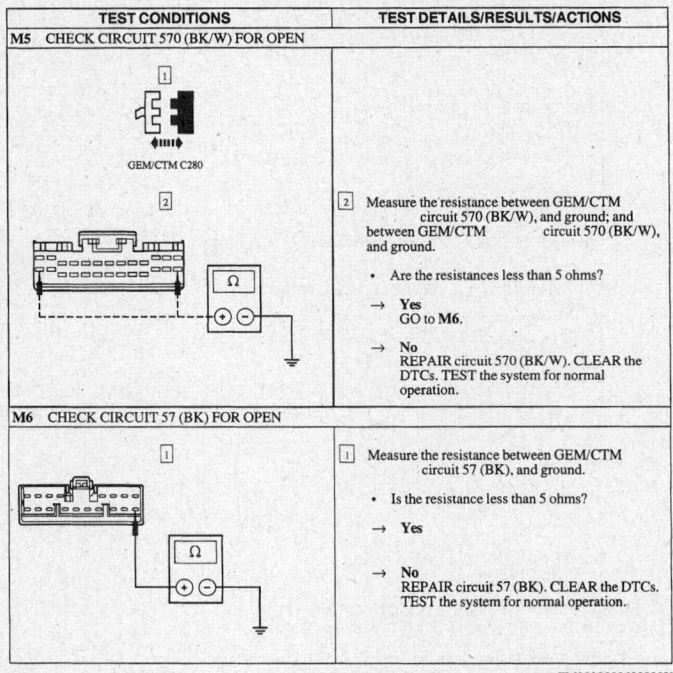

TEST CONDITIONS	TEST DETAILS/RESULTS/ACTIONS
M5 CHECK CIRCUIT 570 (BK/W) FOR OPEN	
GEM/CTM C280	Measure the resistance between GEM/CTM circuit 570 (BK/W), and ground; and between GEM/CTM circuit 570 (BK/W), and ground. • Are the resistances less than 5 ohms? → **Yes** GO to **M6**. → **No** REPAIR circuit 570 (BK/W). CLEAR the DTCs. TEST the system for normal operation.
M6 CHECK CIRCUIT 57 (BK) FOR OPEN	
	Measure the resistance between GEM/CTM circuit 57 (BK), and ground. • Is the resistance less than 5 ohms? → **Yes** → **No** REPAIR circuit 57 (BK). CLEAR the DTCs. TEST the system for normal operation.

FM9029800633030X

Fig. 16 Test M: No Communication w/GEM Module (Part 3 of 3). 2002–04

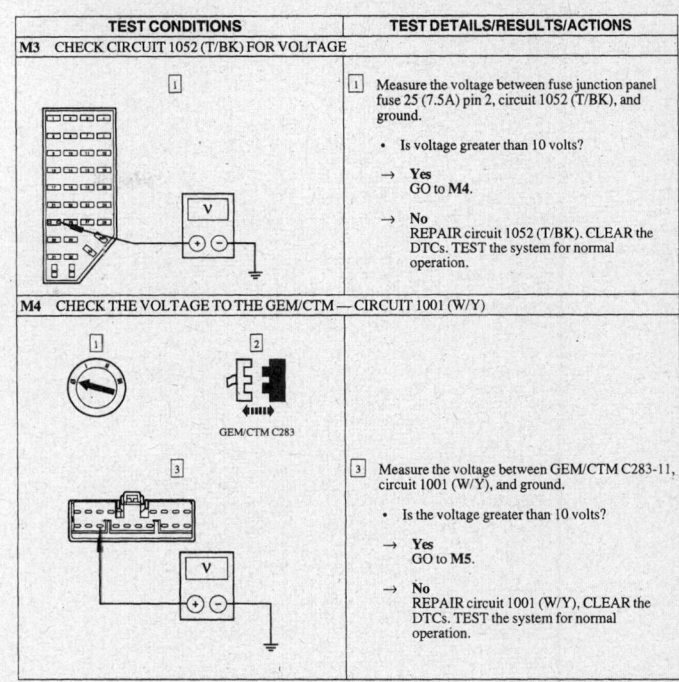

TEST CONDITIONS	TEST DETAILS/RESULTS/ACTIONS
M3 CHECK CIRCUIT 1052 (T/BK) FOR VOLTAGE	
	Measure the voltage between fuse junction panel fuse 25 (7.5A) pin 2, circuit 1052 (T/BK), and ground. • Is voltage greater than 10 volts? → **Yes** GO to **M4**. → **No** REPAIR circuit 1052 (T/BK). CLEAR the DTCs. TEST the system for normal operation.
M4 CHECK THE VOLTAGE TO THE GEM/CTM — CIRCUIT 1001 (W/Y)	
GEM/CTM C283	Measure the voltage between GEM/CTM C283-11, circuit 1001 (W/Y), and ground. • Is the voltage greater than 10 volts? → **Yes** GO to **M5**. → **No** REPAIR circuit 1001 (W/Y), CLEAR the DTCs. TEST the system for normal operation.

FM9029800633020X

Fig. 16 Test M: No Communication w/GEM Module (Part 2 of 3). 2002–04

Condition	Possible Sources	Action
• The wipers are inoperative	• Fuse(s) • Multi-function switch • Circuitry • Ignition switch • Windshield wiper motor	• Go To Pinpoint Test A .
• The rear wiper is inoperative	• Fuse(s) • Multi-function switch • Circuitry • Ignition switch • Rear window wiper motor	• Go To Pinpoint Test B .
• The wipers stay on continuously	• Windshield wiper motor • Multi-function switch • Circuitry	• Go To Pinpoint Test C .
• The rear wiper stays on continuously	• Rear window wiper motor • Multi-function switch • Circuitry	• Go To Pinpoint Test D .

LTV0500000002601

Fig. 17 Symptom Tests (Part 1 of 3). 2005–06

• The high/low wiper speeds do not operate correctly (intermittent wiper mode OK)	• Multi-function switch • Circuitry • Windshield wiper motor	• Go To Pinpoint Test E.
• The low rear wiper speed does not operate correctly	• Multi-function switch • Circuitry • Rear window wiper motor	• Go To Pinpoint Test F.
• The intermittent wiper speed does not operate correctly (high/low speeds OK)	• Multi-function switch • Circuitry • Windshield wiper motor	• Go To Pinpoint Test G.
• The intermittent rear wiper speed does not operate correctly	• Multi-function switch • Circuitry • Rear window wiper motor	• Go To Pinpoint Test H.
• The wipers do not operate correctly in the MIST position	• Multi-function switch • Circuitry • Washer pump • Windshield wiper motor	• Go To Pinpoint Test I.
• The rear wiper wash and wipe function does not operate	• Multi-function switch • Circuitry • Washer pump • Rear window wiper motor	• Go To Pinpoint Test J.
• The washer pump is inoperative	• Windshield washer pump • Multi-function switch • Windshield wiper motor • Rear window wiper motor • Circuitry	• Go To Pinpoint Test K.

LTV0500000002602

Fig. 17 Symptom Tests (Part 2 of 3). 2005–06

• The speed dependent interval mode does not operate correctly	• Windshield wiper motor • Circuitry • Powertrain control module (PCM)	• Go To Pinpoint Test L.
• The wipers will not park at the correct position	• Windshield wiper motor • Rear window wiper motor • Pivot arm adjustment • Linkage	• ADJUST the windshield wiper blade and pivot arm. Repair and/or adjust wiper arm and Pivot.
• The headlamps do not illuminate when the wipers are on	• Circuitry • Windshield wiper motor • SJB	• Go To Pinpoint Test M.

LTV0500000002603

Fig. 17 Symptom Tests (Part 3 of 3). 2005–06

Test Step	Result / Action to Take
A1 CHECK CIRCUIT CRW03 (VT/WH) FOR VOLTAGE • Key in OFF position. • Disconnect: Windshield Wiper Motor C125. • Key in ON position. • Measure the voltage between windshield wiper motor C1348-5, circuit CRW03 (VT/WH), harness side and ground; and between windshield wiper motor C1348-8, circuit CRW03 (VT/WH), harness side and ground. • Are the voltages greater than 10 volts?	**Yes** GO to A2. **No** VERIFY the BJB fuse 37 (30A) is OK. If OK, REPAIR the circuit(s) in question. TEST the system for normal operation.
A2 CHECK CIRCUITS GD120 (BK/GN) AND B_GD108 (BK/VT) FOR AN OPEN • Key in OFF position. • Measure the resistance between windshield wiper motor C1348-6, circuit GD120 (BK/GN), harness side and ground; and between windshield wiper motor C1348-3, circuit B_GD108 (BK/VT), harness side and ground. • Are the resistances less than 5 ohms?	**Yes** GO to A3. **No** REPAIR the circuit(s) in question. TEST the system for normal operation.

LTV0500000002604

Fig. 18 Test A: Front Wipers Are Inoperative (Part 1 of 3). 2005–06

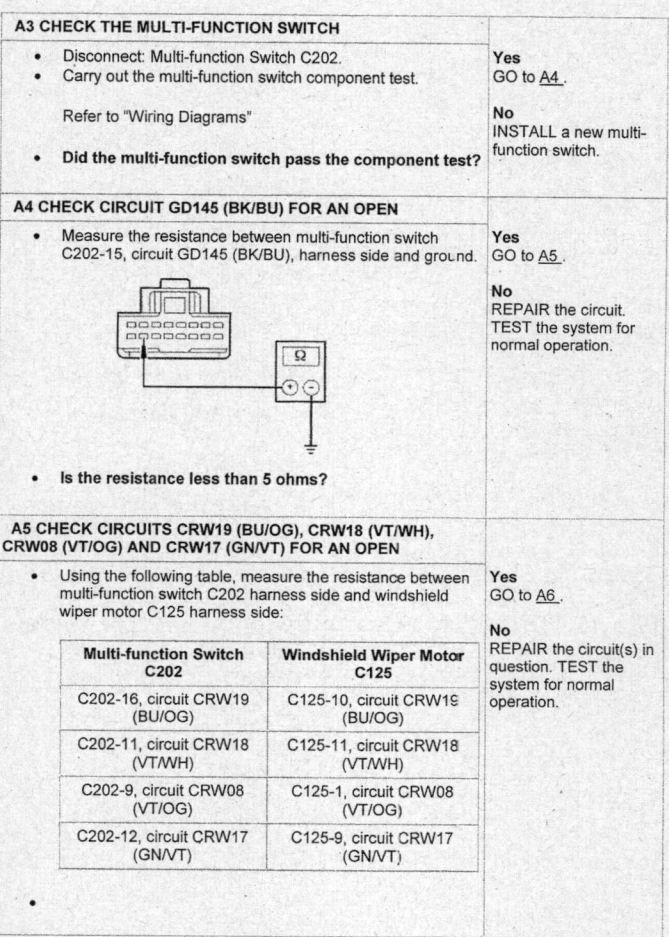

A3 CHECK THE MULTI-FUNCTION SWITCH	
• Disconnect: Multi-function Switch C202. • Carry out the multi-function switch component test. Refer to "Wiring Diagrams" • **Did the multi-function switch pass the component test?**	**Yes** GO to A4. **No** INSTALL a new multi-function switch.
A4 CHECK CIRCUIT GD145 (BK/BU) FOR AN OPEN	
• Measure the resistance between multi-function switch C202-15, circuit GD145 (BK/BU), harness side and ground. • Is the resistance less than 5 ohms?	**Yes** GO to A5. **No** REPAIR the circuit. TEST the system for normal operation.
A5 CHECK CIRCUITS CRW19 (BU/OG), CRW18 (VT/WH), CRW08 (VT/OG) AND CRW17 (GN/VT) FOR AN OPEN	

• Using the following table, measure the resistance between multi-function switch C202 harness side and windshield wiper motor C125 harness side:	**Yes** GO to A6. **No** REPAIR the circuit(s) in question. TEST the system for normal operation.

Multi-function Switch C202	Windshield Wiper Motor C125
C202-16, circuit CRW19 (BU/OG)	C125-10, circuit CRW19 (BU/OG)
C202-11, circuit CRW18 (VT/WH)	C125-11, circuit CRW18 (VT/WH)
C202-9, circuit CRW08 (VT/OG)	C125-1, circuit CRW08 (VT/OG)
C202-12, circuit CRW17 (GN/VT)	C125-9, circuit CRW17 (GN/VT)

LTV0500000002605

Fig. 18 Test A: Front Wipers Are Inoperative (Part 2 of 3). 2005–06

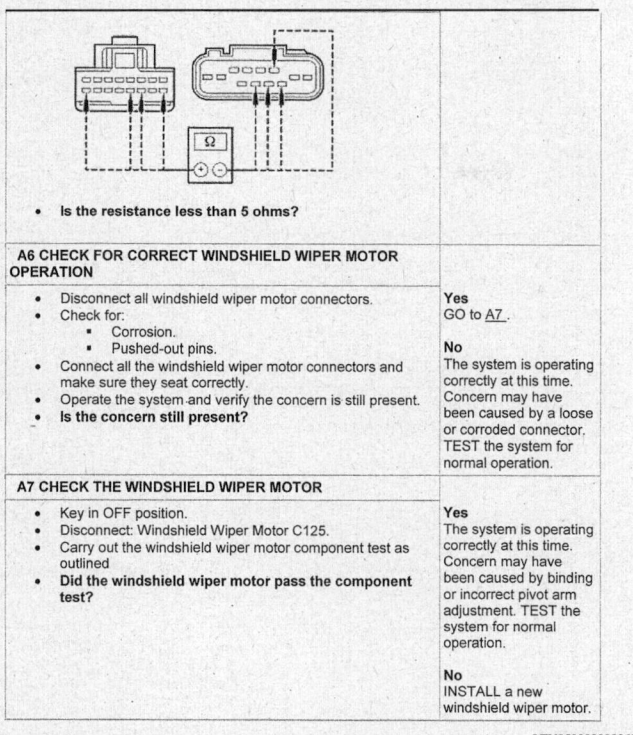

- Is the resistance less than 5 ohms?

A6 CHECK FOR CORRECT WINDSHIELD WIPER MOTOR OPERATION	
• Disconnect all windshield wiper motor connectors. • Check for: ▪ Corrosion. ▪ Pushed-out pins. • Connect all the windshield wiper motor connectors and make sure they seat correctly. • Operate the system and verify the concern is still present. • **Is the concern still present?**	**Yes** GO to A7. **No** The system is operating correctly at this time. Concern may have been caused by a loose or corroded connector. TEST the system for normal operation.
A7 CHECK THE WINDSHIELD WIPER MOTOR	
• Key in OFF position. • Disconnect: Windshield Wiper Motor C125. • Carry out the windshield wiper motor component test as outlined • **Did the windshield wiper motor pass the component test?**	**Yes** The system is operating correctly at this time. Concern may have been caused by binding or incorrect pivot arm adjustment. TEST the system for normal operation. **No** INSTALL a new windshield wiper motor.

LTV0500000002606

Fig. 18   Test A: Front Wipers Are Inoperative (Part 3 of 3). 2005–06

B3 CHECK THE MULTI-FUNCTION SWITCH	
• Key in OFF position. • Disconnect: Multi-function Switch C202. • Carry out the multi-function switch component test. Refer to "Wiring Diagrams" • **Did the multi-function switch pass the component test?**	**Yes** GO to B4. **No** INSTALL a new multi-function switch.
B4 CHECK CIRCUIT GD145 (BK/BU) FOR AN OPEN	
• Measure the resistance between multi-function switch C202-.15, circuit GD145 (BK/BU), harness side and ground. 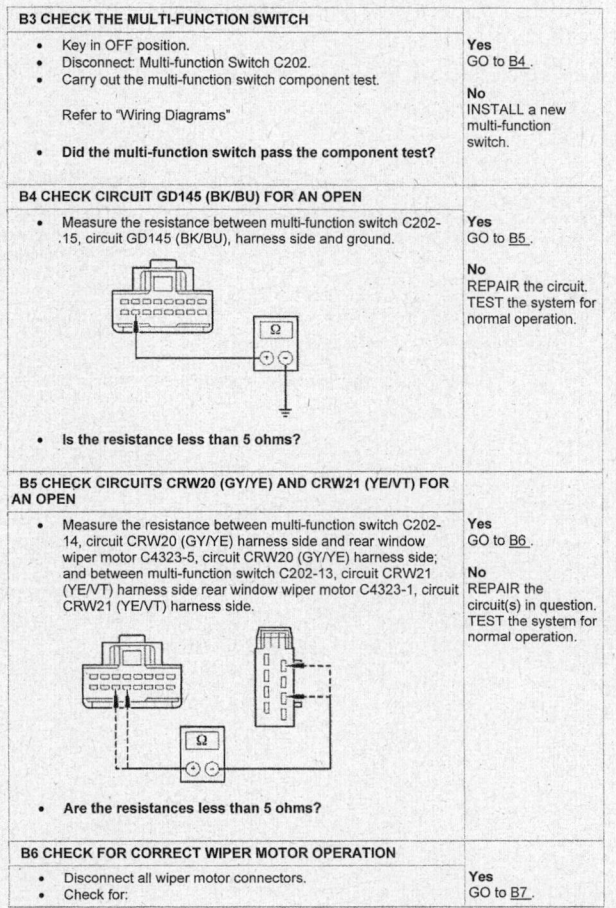 • Is the resistance less than 5 ohms?	**Yes** GO to B5. **No** REPAIR the circuit. TEST the system for normal operation.
B5 CHECK CIRCUITS CRW20 (GY/YE) AND CRW21 (YE/VT) FOR AN OPEN	
• Measure the resistance between multi-function switch C202-14, circuit CRW20 (GY/YE) harness side and rear window wiper motor C4323-5, circuit CRW20 (GY/YE) harness side; and between multi-function switch C202-13, circuit CRW21 (YE/VT) harness side rear window wiper motor C4323-1, circuit CRW21 (YE/VT) harness side. • Are the resistances less than 5 ohms?	**Yes** GO to B6. **No** REPAIR the circuit(s) in question. TEST the system for normal operation.
B6 CHECK FOR CORRECT WIPER MOTOR OPERATION	
• Disconnect all wiper motor connectors. • Check for:	**Yes** GO to B7.

LTV0500000002608

Fig. 19   Test B: Rear Wiper Is Inoperative (Part 2 of 3). 2005–06

Test Step	Result / Action to Take
B1 CHECK CIRCUITS A_CBP12 (GN/WH) AND SBB30 (BN/RD) FOR VOLTAGE	
• Key in OFF position. • Disconnect: Rear Window Wiper Motor C4323. • Key in ON position. • Measure the voltage between rear window wiper motor C4323-7, circuit A_CBP12 (GN/WH), harness side and ground; and between rear window wiper motor C4323-8, circuit SBB30 (BN/RD), harness side and ground. 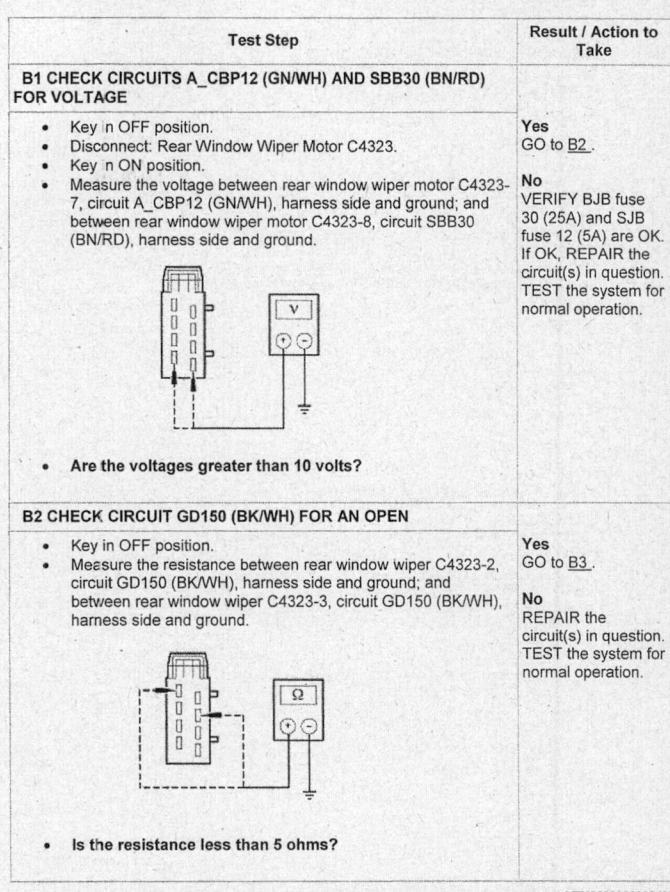 • **Are the voltages greater than 10 volts?**	**Yes** GO to B2. **No** VERIFY BJB fuse 30 (25A) and SJB fuse 12 (5A) are OK. If OK, REPAIR the circuit(s) in question. TEST the system for normal operation.
B2 CHECK CIRCUIT GD150 (BK/WH) FOR AN OPEN	
• Key in OFF position. • Measure the resistance between rear window wiper C4323-2, circuit GD150 (BK/WH), harness side and ground; and between rear window wiper C4323-3, circuit GD150 (BK/WH), harness side and ground. • Is the resistance less than 5 ohms?	**Yes** GO to B3. **No** REPAIR the circuit(s) in question. TEST the system for normal operation.

LTV0500000002607

Fig. 19   Test B: Rear Wiper Is Inoperative (Part 1 of 3). 2005–06

▪ Corrosion. ▪ Pushed-out pins. • Connect all wiper motor connectors and make sure they seat correctly. • Operate the system and verify the concern is still present. • **Is the concern still present?**	**No** The system is operating correctly at this time. Concern may have been caused by a loose or corroded connector. TEST the system for normal operation.
B7 CHECK THE REAR WINDOW WIPER MOTOR	
• Carry out the rear window wiper motor component test as outlined • **Did the rear window wiper motor pass the component test?**	**Yes** The system is operating correctly at this time. Concern may have been caused by binding or incorrect pivot arm adjustment. TEST the system for normal operation. **No** INSTALL a new rear window wiper motor.

LTV0500000002609

Fig. 19   Test B: Rear Wiper Is Inoperative (Part 3 of 3). 2005–06

Test Step	Result / Action to Take
C1 CHECK THE MULTI-FUNCTION SWITCH • Key in OFF position. • Disconnect: Multi-function Switch C202. • Carry out the multi-function switch component test. Refer to "Wiring Diagrams" • **Did the multi-function switch pass the component test?**	**Yes** GO to <u>C2</u>. **No** INSTALL a new multi-function switch.
C2 CHECK CIRCUIT GD145 (BK/BU) FOR AN OPEN • Measure the resistance between multi-function switch C202-15, circuit GD145 (BK/BU), harness side and ground. • **Is the resistance less than 5 ohms?**	**Yes** GO to <u>C3</u>. **No** REPAIR the circuit. TEST the system for normal operation.
C3 CHECK CIRCUITS CRW19 (BU/OG), CRW18 (VT/WH), CRW08 (VT/OG) AND CRW17 (GN/VT) FOR A SHORT TO GROUND • Disconnect: Windshield Wiper Motor C125. • Using the following table, measure the resistance between windshield wiper motor C125 harness side and ground: 	Windshield Wiper Motor C125	Ground	 |---|---| 	C125-10, circuit CRW19 (BU/OG)	ground	 	C125-11, circuit CRW18 (VT/WH)	ground	 	C125-1, circuit CRW08 (VT/OG)	ground	 	C125-9, circuit CRW17 (GN/VT)	ground		**Yes** GO to <u>C4</u>. **No** REPAIR the circuit(s) in question. TEST the system for normal operation.

Fig. 20 Test C: Front Wipers Stay On Continuously (Part 1 of 2). 2005–06

LTV0500000002610

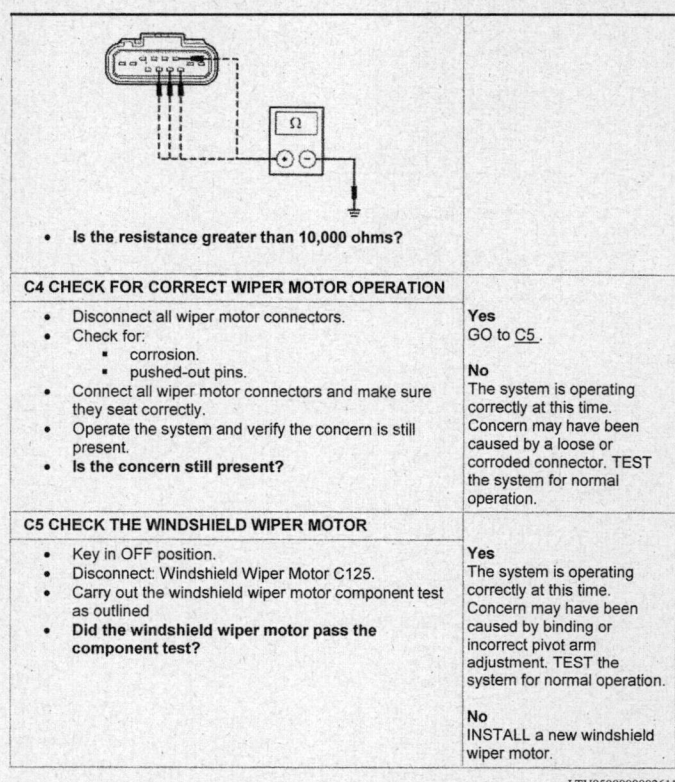

• **Is the resistance greater than 10,000 ohms?**	

C4 CHECK FOR CORRECT WIPER MOTOR OPERATION
 • Disconnect all wiper motor connectors.
 • Check for:
   • corrosion.
   • pushed-out pins.
 • Connect all wiper motor connectors and make sure they seat correctly.
 • Operate the system and verify the concern is still present.
 • **Is the concern still present?**
	Yes
	 GO to <u>C5</u>.
	
	 No
	 The system is operating correctly at this time. Concern may have been caused by a loose or corroded connector. TEST the system for normal operation.

C5 CHECK THE WINDSHIELD WIPER MOTOR • Key in OFF position. • Disconnect: Windshield Wiper Motor C125. • Carry out the windshield wiper motor component test as outlined • **Did the windshield wiper motor pass the component test?**	**Yes** The system is operating correctly at this time. Concern may have been caused by binding or incorrect pivot arm adjustment. TEST the system for normal operation. **No** INSTALL a new windshield wiper motor.

LTV0500000002611

Fig. 20 Test C: Front Wipers Stay On Continuously (Part 2 of 2). 2005–06

Test Step	Result / Action to Take
D1 CHECK THE MULTI-FUNCTION SWITCH • Key in OFF position. • Disconnect: Multi-function Switch C202. • Carry out the multi-function switch component test. Refer to "Wiring Diagrams" • **Did the multi-function switch pass the component test?**	**Yes** GO to <u>D2</u>. **No** INSTALL a new multi-function switch.
D2 CHECK CIRCUIT GD145 (BK/BU) FOR AN OPEN • Measure the resistance between multi-function switch C202-15, circuit GD145 (BK/BU), harness side and ground. • **Is the resistance less than 5 ohms?**	**Yes** GO to <u>D3</u>. **No** REPAIR the circuit. TEST the system for normal operation.
D3 CHECK CIRCUITS CRW20 (GY/YE) AND CRW21 (YE/VT) FOR A SHORT TO GROUND • Disconnect: Rear Window Wiper Motor C4323. • Measure the resistance between rear window wiper motor C4323-5, circuit CRW20 (GY/YE), harness side and ground; and between rear window wiper motor C4323-1, circuit CRW21 (YE/VT), harness side and ground. • **Are the resistances greater than 10,000 ohms?**	**Yes** GO to <u>D4</u>. **No** REPAIR the circuit(s) in question. TEST the system for normal operation.

LTV0500000002612

Fig. 21 Test D: Rear Wipers Stay On Continuously (Part 1 of 2). 2005–06

D4 CHECK FOR CORRECT WIPER MOTOR OPERATION
 • Disconnect all wiper motor connectors.
 • Check for:
   • corrosion.
   • pushed-out pins.
 • Connect all wiper motor connectors and make sure they seat correctly.
 • Operate the system and verify the concern is still present.
 • **Is the concern still present?**
	Yes
	 GO to <u>D5</u>.
	
	 No
	 The system is operating correctly at this time. Concern may have been caused by a loose or corroded connector. TEST the system for normal operation.

D5 CHECK THE REAR WINDOW WIPER MOTOR • Carry out the rear window wiper motor component test as outlined • **Did the rear window wiper motor pass the component test?**	**Yes** The system is operating correctly at this time. Concern may have been caused by binding or incorrect pivot arm adjustment. TEST the system for normal operation. **No** INSTALL a new rear window wiper motor.

LTV0500000002613

Fig. 21 Test D: Rear Wipers Stay On Continuously (Part 2 of 2). 2005–06

Test Step	Result / Action to Take
E1 CHECK THE MULTI-FUNCTION SWITCH	
• Key in OFF position. • Disconnect: Multi-function Switch C202. • Carry out the multi-function switch component test. Refer to "Wiring Diagrams" • **Did the multi-function switch pass the component test?**	**Yes** GO to E2. **No** INSTALL a new multi-function switch. TEST the system for normal operation.
E2 CHECK CIRCUIT GD145 (BK/BU) FOR AN OPEN	
• Measure the resistance between multi-function switch C202-15, circuit GD145 (BK/BU), harness side and ground. 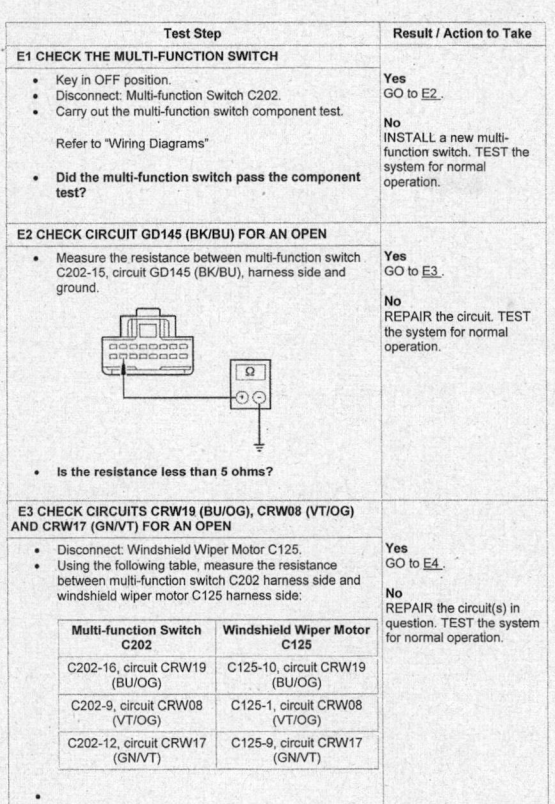 • **Is the resistance less than 5 ohms?**	**Yes** GO to E3. **No** REPAIR the circuit. TEST the system for normal operation.
E3 CHECK CIRCUITS CRW19 (BU/OG), CRW08 (VT/OG) AND CRW17 (GN/VT) FOR AN OPEN	
• Disconnect: Windshield Wiper Motor C125. • Using the following table, measure the resistance between multi-function switch C202 harness side and windshield wiper motor C125 harness side:	**Yes** GO to E4. **No** REPAIR the circuit(s) in question. TEST the system for normal operation.

Multi-function Switch C202	Windshield Wiper Motor C125
C202-16, circuit CRW19 (BU/OG)	C125-10, circuit CRW19 (BU/OG)
C202-9, circuit CRW08 (VT/OG)	C125-1, circuit CRW08 (VT/OG)
C202-12, circuit CRW17 (GN/VT)	C125-9, circuit CRW17 (GN/VT)

LTV0500000002614

Fig. 22   Test E: Front High/Low Wiper Speeds Do Not Operate Correctly, Intermittent Mode OK (Part 1 of 2). 2005–06

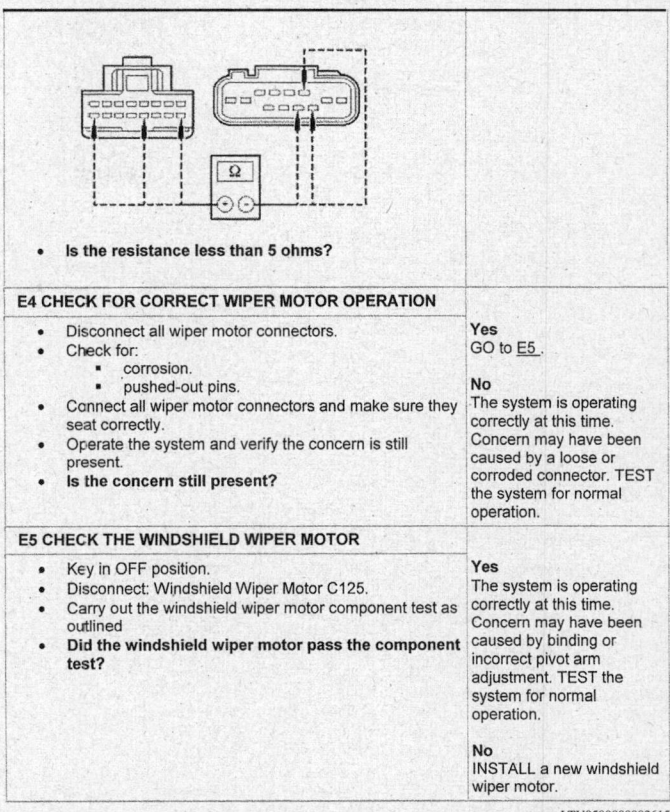

• **Is the resistance less than 5 ohms?**	
E4 CHECK FOR CORRECT WIPER MOTOR OPERATION	
• Disconnect all wiper motor connectors. • Check for: 　▪ corrosion. 　▪ pushed-out pins. • Connect all wiper motor connectors and make sure they seat correctly. • Operate the system and verify the concern is still present. • **Is the concern still present?**	**Yes** GO to E5. **No** The system is operating correctly at this time. Concern may have been caused by a loose or corroded connector. TEST the system for normal operation.
E5 CHECK THE WINDSHIELD WIPER MOTOR	
• Key in OFF position. • Disconnect: Windshield Wiper Motor C125. • Carry out the windshield wiper motor component test as outlined • **Did the windshield wiper motor pass the component test?**	**Yes** The system is operating correctly at this time. Concern may have been caused by binding or incorrect pivot arm adjustment. TEST the system for normal operation. **No** INSTALL a new windshield wiper motor.

LTV0500000002615

Fig. 22   Test E: Front High/Low Wiper Speeds Do Not Operate Correctly, Intermittent Mode OK (Part 2 of 2). 2005–06

Test Step	Result / Action to Take
F1 CHECK THE MULTI-FUNCTION SWITCH	
• Key in OFF position. • Disconnect: Multi-function Switch C202. • Carry out the multi-function switch component test. Refer to "Wiring Diagrams" • **Did the multi-function switch pass the component test?**	**Yes** GO to F2. **No** INSTALL a new multi-function switch.
F2 CHECK CIRCUIT GD145 (BK/BU) FOR AN OPEN	
• Measure the resistance between multi-function switch C202-15, circuit GD145 (BK/BU), harness side and ground. • **Is the resistance less than 5 ohms?**	**Yes** GO to F3. **No** REPAIR the circuit. TEST the system for normal operation.
F3 CHECK CIRCUITS CRW20 (GY/YE) AND CRW21 (YE/VT) FOR AN OPEN	
• Disconnect: Rear Window Wiper Motor C4323. • Measure the resistance between multi-function switch C202-14, circuit CRW20 (GY/YE) harness side and rear window wiper motor C4323-5, circuit CRW20 (GY/YE) harness side; and between multi-function switch C202-13, circuit CRW21 (YE/VT) harness side and rear window wiper motor C4323-1, circuit CRW21 (YE/VT) harness side.	**Yes** GO to F4. **No** REPAIR the circuit(s) in question. TEST the system for normal operation.

LTV0500000002616

Fig. 23   Test F: Rear High/Low Wiper Speeds Do Not Operate Correctly, Intermittent Mode OK (Part 1 of 2). 2005–06

• **Are the resistances less than 5 ohms?**	
F4 CHECK FOR CORRECT WIPER MOTOR OPERATION	
• Disconnect all wiper motor connectors. • Check for: 　▪ corrosion. 　▪ pushed-out pins. • Connect all wiper motor connectors and make sure they seat correctly. • Operate the system and verify the concern is still present. • **Is the concern still present?**	**Yes** GO to F5. **No** The system is operating correctly at this time. Concern may have been caused by a loose or corroded connector. TEST the system for normal operation.
F5 CHECK THE REAR WINDOW WIPER MOTOR	
• Carry out the rear window wiper motor component test as outlined • **Did the rear window wiper motor pass the component test?**	**Yes** The system is operating correctly at this time. Concern may have been caused by binding or incorrect pivot arm adjustment. TEST the system for normal operation. **No** INSTALL a new rear window wiper motor.

LTV0500000002617

Fig. 23   Test F: Rear High/Low Wiper Speeds Do Not Operate Correctly, Intermittent Mode OK (Part 2 of 2). 2005–06

Test Step	Result / Action to Take
G1 CHECK THE MULTI-FUNCTION SWITCH • Key in OFF position. • Disconnect: Multi-function Switch C202. • Carry out the multi-function switch component test. Refer to "Wiring Diagrams" • **Did the multi-function switch pass the component test?**	**Yes** GO to G2. **No** INSTALL a new multi-function switch. TEST the system for normal operation.
G2 CHECK CIRCUIT GD145 (BK/BU) FOR AN OPEN • Measure the resistance between multi-function switch C202-15, circuit GD145 (BK/BU), harness side and ground. 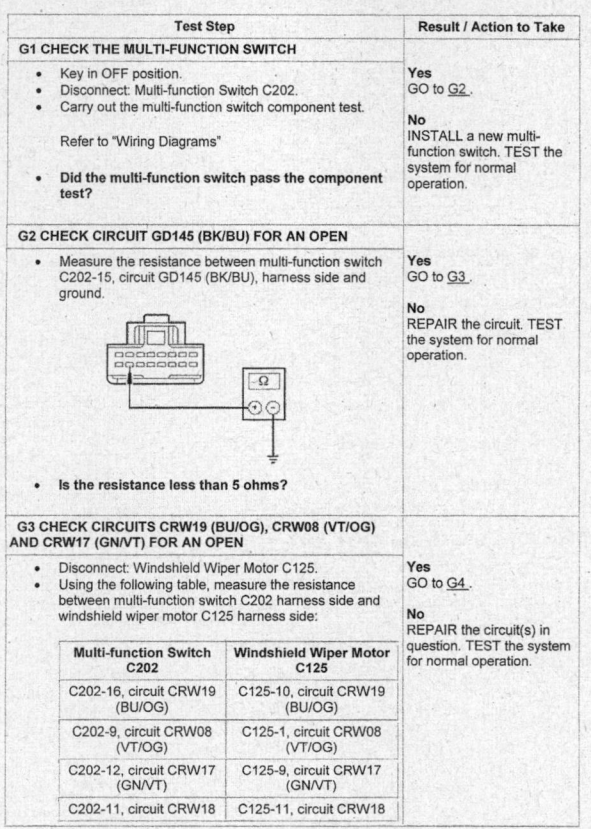 • **Is the resistance less than 5 ohms?**	**Yes** GO to G3. **No** REPAIR the circuit. TEST the system for normal operation.
G3 CHECK CIRCUITS CRW19 (BU/OG), CRW08 (VT/OG) AND CRW17 (GN/VT) FOR AN OPEN • Disconnect: Windshield Wiper Motor C125. • Using the following table, measure the resistance between multi-function switch C202 harness side and windshield wiper motor C125 harness side:	**Yes** GO to G4. **No** REPAIR the circuit(s) in question. TEST the system for normal operation.

Multi-function Switch C202	Windshield Wiper Motor C125
C202-16, circuit CRW19 (BU/OG)	C125-10, circuit CRW19 (BU/OG)
C202-9, circuit CRW08 (VT/OG)	C125-1, circuit CRW08 (VT/OG)
C202-12, circuit CRW17 (GN/VT)	C125-9, circuit CRW17 (GN/VT)
C202-11, circuit CRW18	C125-11, circuit CRW18

LTV0500000002618

Fig. 24 Test G: Front Intermittent Wiper Speed Does Not Operate Correctly, High/Low Speeds OK (Part 1 of 2). 2005–06

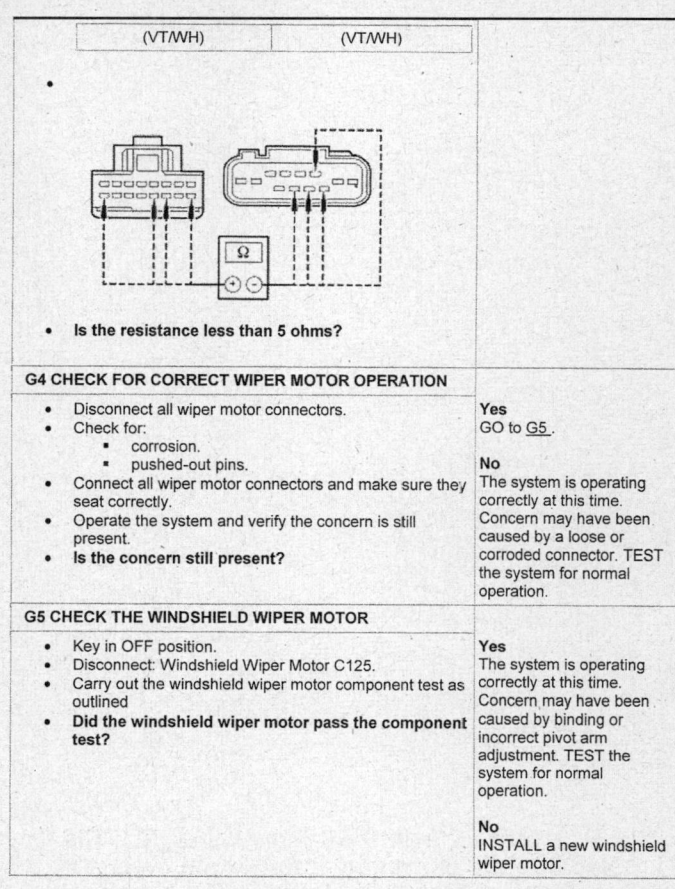

(VT/WH) (VT/WH) • • **Is the resistance less than 5 ohms?**	

G4 CHECK FOR CORRECT WIPER MOTOR OPERATION
• Disconnect all wiper motor connectors.
• Check for:
  ▪ corrosion.
  ▪ pushed-out pins.
• Connect all wiper motor connectors and make sure they seat correctly.
• Operate the system and verify the concern is still present.
• **Is the concern still present?**
	Yes
	GO to G5.
	
	No
	The system is operating correctly at this time. Concern may have been caused by a loose or corroded connector. TEST the system for normal operation.

G5 CHECK THE WINDSHIELD WIPER MOTOR • Key in OFF position. • Disconnect: Windshield Wiper Motor C125. • Carry out the windshield wiper motor component test as outlined • **Did the windshield wiper motor pass the component test?**	**Yes** The system is operating correctly at this time. Concern may have been caused by binding or incorrect pivot arm adjustment. TEST the system for normal operation. **No** INSTALL a new windshield wiper motor.

LTV0500000002619

Fig. 24 Test G: Front Intermittent Wiper Speed Does Not Operate Correctly, High/Low Speeds OK (Part 2 of 2). 2005–06

Test Step	Result / Action to Take
H1 CHECK THE MULTI-FUNCTION SWITCH • Key in OFF position. • Disconnect: Multi-function Switch C202. • Carry out the multi-function switch component test. Refer to "Wiring Diagrams" • **Did the multi-function switch pass the component test?**	**Yes** GO to H2. **No** INSTALL a new multi-function switch.
H2 CHECK CIRCUIT GD145 (BK/BU) FOR AN OPEN • Measure the resistance between multi-function switch C202-15, circuit GD145 (BK/BU), harness side and ground. • **Is the resistance less than 5 ohms?**	**Yes** GO to H3. **No** REPAIR the circuit. TEST the system for normal operation.
H3 CHECK CIRCUITS CRW20 (GY/YE) AND CRW21 (YE/VT) FOR AN OPEN • Disconnect: Rear Window Wiper Motor C4323. • Measure the resistance between multi-function switch C202-14, circuit CRW20 (GY/YE) harness side and rear window wiper motor C4323-5, circuit CRW20 (GY/YE) harness side; and between multi-function switch C202-13, circuit CRW21 (YE/VT) harness side and rear window wiper motor C4323-1, circuit CRW21 (YE/VT) harness side.	**Yes** GO to H4. **No** REPAIR the circuit(s) in question. TEST the system for normal operation.

LTV0500000002620

Fig. 25 Test H: Rear Intermittent Wiper Speed Does Not Operate Correctly, High/Low Speeds OK (Part 1 of 2). 2005–06

• **Are the resistances less than 5 ohms?**	

H4 CHECK FOR CORRECT WIPER MOTOR OPERATION
• Disconnect all wiper motor connectors.
• Check for:
  ▪ corrosion.
  ▪ pushed-out pins.
• Connect all wiper motor connectors and make sure they seat correctly.
• Operate the system and verify the concern is still present.
• **Is the concern still present?**
	Yes
	GO to H5.
	
	No
	The system is operating correctly at this time. Concern may have been caused by a loose or corroded connector. TEST the system for normal operation.

H5 CHECK THE REAR WINDOW WIPER MOTOR • Carry out the rear window wiper motor component test as outlined • **Did the rear window wiper motor pass the component test?**	**Yes** The system is operating correctly at this time. Concern may have been caused by binding or incorrect pivot arm adjustment. TEST the system for normal operation. **No** INSTALL a new rear window wiper motor.

LTV0500000002621

Fig. 25 Test H: Rear Intermittent Wiper Speed Does Not Operate Correctly, High/Low Speeds OK (Part 2 of 2). 2005–06

Test Step	Result / Action to Take
I1 CHECK THE MULTI-FUNCTION SWITCH • Key in OFF position. • Disconnect: Multi-function Switch C202. • Carry out the multi-function switch component test. Refer to "Wiring Diagrams" • **Did the multi-function switch pass the component test?**	**Yes** GO to I2. **No** INSTALL a new multi-function switch.
I2 CHECK CIRCUIT GD145 (BK/BU) FOR AN OPEN • Measure the resistance between multi-function switch C202-15, circuit GD145 (BK/BU), harness side and ground. • **Is the resistance less than 5 ohms?**	**Yes** GO to I3. **No** REPAIR the circuit. TEST the system for normal operation.
I3 CHECK CIRCUIT CRW07 (GY/BN) FOR AN OPEN • Disconnect: Windshield Wiper Motor C125. • Measure the resistance between multi-function switch C202-10, circuit CRW07 (GY/BN), harness side and C125-12, circuit CRW07 (GY/BN), harness side. • **Is the resistance less than 5 ohms?**	**Yes** Go To Pinpoint Test K to diagnose the washer circuits. **No** REPAIR the circuit. TEST the system for normal operation.

LTV0500000002622

Fig. 26 Test I: Wipers Do Not Operate Correctly In Mist Position. 2005–06

Test Step	Result / Action to Take
J1 CHECK THE MULTI-FUNCTION SWITCH • Key in OFF position. • Disconnect: Multi-function Switch C202. • Carry out the multi-function switch component test. Refer to "Wiring Diagrams" • **Did the multi-function switch pass the component test?**	**Yes** GO to J2. **No** INSTALL a new multi-function switch.
J2 CHECK CIRCUIT GD145 (BK/BU) FOR AN OPEN • Measure the resistance between multi-function switch C202-15, circuit GD145 (BK/BU), harness side and ground. • **Is the resistance less than 5 ohms?**	**Yes** GO to J3. **No** REPAIR the circuit. TEST the system for normal operation.
J3 CHECK CIRCUIT CRW20 (GY/YE) FOR AN OPEN • Key in OFF position. • Disconnect: Rear Window Wiper Motor C4323. • Measure the resistance between multi-function switch C202-14, circuit CRW20 (GY/YE), harness side and rear window wiper motor C4323-5, circuit CRW20 (GY/YE), harness side. • **Is the resistance less than 5 ohms?**	**Yes** Go To Pinpoint Test K. **No** REPAIR the circuit. TEST the system for normal operation.

LTV0500000002623

Fig. 27 Test J: Rear Wash & Wipe Function Is Inoperative. 2005–06

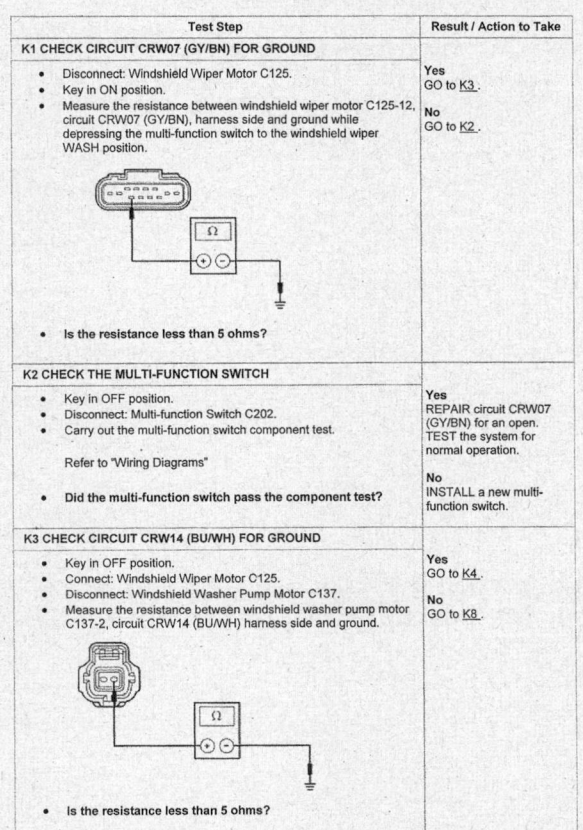

Test Step	Result / Action to Take
K1 CHECK CIRCUIT CRW07 (GY/BN) FOR GROUND • Disconnect: Windshield Wiper Motor C125. • Key in ON position. • Measure the resistance between windshield wiper motor C125-12, circuit CRW07 (GY/BN), harness side and ground while depressing the multi-function switch to the windshield wiper WASH position. • **Is the resistance less than 5 ohms?**	**Yes** GO to K3. **No** GO to K2.
K2 CHECK THE MULTI-FUNCTION SWITCH • Key in OFF position. • Disconnect: Multi-function Switch C202. • Carry out the multi-function switch component test. Refer to "Wiring Diagrams" • **Did the multi-function switch pass the component test?**	**Yes** REPAIR circuit CRW07 (GY/BN) for an open. TEST the system for normal operation. **No** INSTALL a new multi-function switch.
K3 CHECK CIRCUIT CRW14 (BU/WH) FOR GROUND • Key in OFF position. • Connect: Windshield Wiper Motor C125. • Disconnect: Windshield Washer Pump Motor C137. • Measure the resistance between windshield washer pump motor C137-2, circuit CRW14 (BU/WH) harness side and ground. • **Is the resistance less than 5 ohms?**	**Yes** GO to K4. **No** GO to K8.

LTV0500000002624

Fig. 28 Test K: Washer Pump Is Inoperative (Part 1 of 4). 2005–06

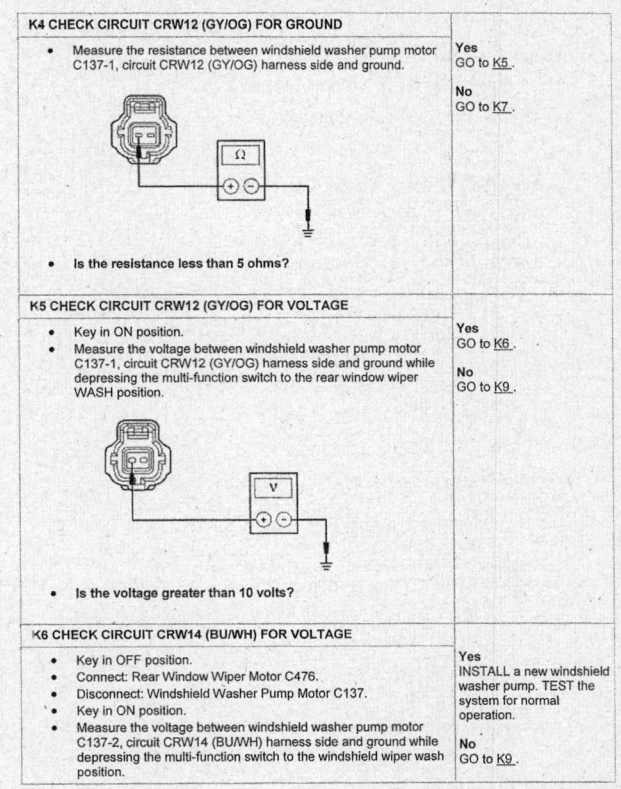

Test Step	Result / Action to Take
K4 CHECK CIRCUIT CRW12 (GY/OG) FOR GROUND • Measure the resistance between windshield washer pump motor C137-1, circuit CRW12 (GY/OG) harness side and ground. • **Is the resistance less than 5 ohms?**	**Yes** GO to K5. **No** GO to K7.
K5 CHECK CIRCUIT CRW12 (GY/OG) FOR VOLTAGE • Key in ON position. • Measure the voltage between windshield washer pump motor C137-1, circuit CRW12 (GY/OG) harness side and ground while depressing the multi-function switch to the rear window wiper WASH position. • **Is the voltage greater than 10 volts?**	**Yes** GO to K6. **No** GO to K9.
K6 CHECK CIRCUIT CRW14 (BU/WH) FOR VOLTAGE • Key in OFF position. • Connect: Rear Window Wiper Motor C476. • Disconnect: Windshield Washer Pump Motor C137. • Key in ON position. • Measure the voltage between windshield washer pump motor C137-2, circuit CRW14 (BU/WH) harness side and ground while depressing the multi-function switch to the windshield wiper wash position.	**Yes** INSTALL a new windshield washer pump. TEST the system for normal operation. **No** GO to K9.

LTV0500000002625

Fig. 28 Test K: Washer Pump Is Inoperative (Part 2 of 4). 2005–06

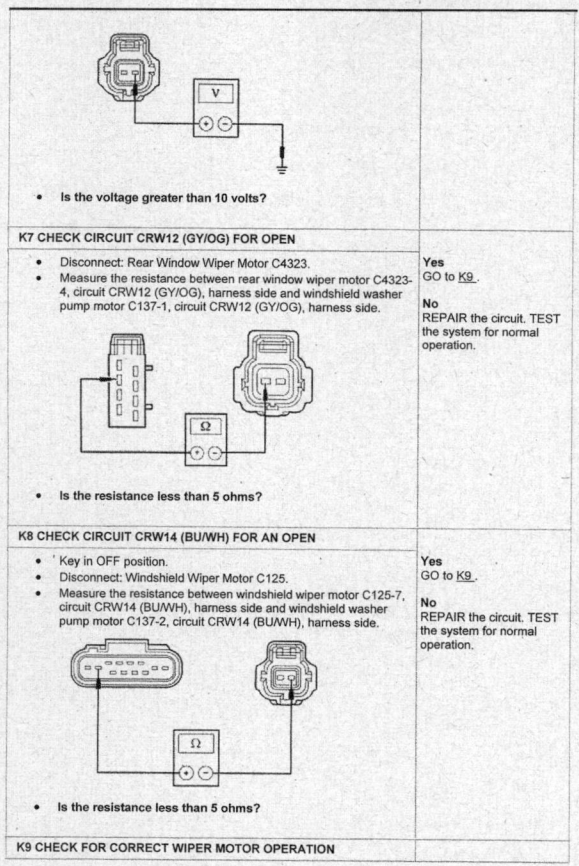

• Is the voltage greater than 10 volts?	
K7 CHECK CIRCUIT CRW12 (GY/OG) FOR OPEN	
• Disconnect: Rear Window Wiper Motor C4323. • Measure the resistance between rear window wiper motor C4323-4, circuit CRW12 (GY/OG), harness side and windshield washer pump motor C137-1, circuit CRW12 (GY/OG), harness side.	**Yes** GO to K9 . **No** REPAIR the circuit. TEST the system for normal operation.
• Is the resistance less than 5 ohms?	
K8 CHECK CIRCUIT CRW14 (BU/WH) FOR AN OPEN	
• Key in OFF position. • Disconnect: Windshield Wiper Motor C125. • Measure the resistance between windshield wiper motor C125-7, circuit CRW14 (BU/WH), harness side and windshield washer pump motor C137-2, circuit CRW14 (BU/WH), harness side.	**Yes** GO to K9 . **No** REPAIR the circuit. TEST the system for normal operation.
• Is the resistance less than 5 ohms?	
K9 CHECK FOR CORRECT WIPER MOTOR OPERATION	

LTV0500000002626

Fig. 28 Test K: Washer Pump Is Inoperative (Part 3 of 4). 2005–06

Test Step	Result / Action to Take
L1 CHECK THE PCM — MONITOR THE VSS	
• Monitor the VSS while driving the vehicle from 0 to 88.5 km/h (55 mph). • **Does the VSS agree with the PCM PIDs?**	**Yes** GO to L2 . **No** Check Vehicle Speed Sensor VSS and circuits.
L2 CHECK CIRCUIT VMC05 (VT/OG) FOR AN OPEN	
• Disconnect: PCM C175b. • Disconnect: Windshield Wiper Motor C125. • Measure the resistance between PCM C175b-1, circuit VMC05 (VT/OG), harness side and windshield wiper motor C125-4, circuit VMC05 (VT/OG), harness side.	**Yes** GO to L3 . **No** REPAIR the circuit. CLEAR the DTCs. REPEAT the self-test.
• Is the resistance less than 5 ohms?	
L3 CHECK CIRCUIT VMC05 (VT/OG) FOR A SHORT TO GROUND	
• Measure the resistance between PCM C175b-1, circuit VMC05 (VT/OG), harness side and ground.	**Yes** GO to L4 . **No** REPAIR the circuit. CLEAR the DTCs. REPEAT the self-test.

LTV0500000002628

Fig. 29 Test L: Speed Dependent Interval Mode Does Not Operate Correctly (Part 1 of 2). 2005–06

• Disconnect all wiper motor connectors.
• Check for:
  ▪ corrosion.
  ▪ pushed-out pins.
• Connect all wiper motor connectors and make sure they seat correctly.
• Operate the system and verify the concern is still present.
• **Is the concern still present?**
	Yes
	For the windshield wiper motor, GO to K10. For the rear window wiper motor, GO to K11.
	
	No
	The system is operating correctly at this time. Concern may have been caused by a loose or corroded connector. TEST the system for normal operation.

K10 CHECK THE WINDSHIELD WIPER MOTOR	
• Key in OFF position. • Disconnect: Windshield Wiper Motor C125. • Carry out the windshield wiper motor component test as outlined. • **Did the windshield wiper motor pass the component test?**	**Yes** The system is operating correctly at this time. Concern may have been caused by binding or incorrect pivot arm adjustment. TEST the system for normal operation. **No** INSTALL a new windshield wiper motor.
K11 CHECK THE REAR WINDOW WIPER MOTOR	
• Carry out the rear window wiper motor component test as outlined. • **Did the rear window wiper motor pass the component test?**	**Yes** The system is operating correctly at this time. Concern may have been caused by binding or incorrect pivot arm adjustment. TEST the system for normal operation. **No** INSTALL a new rear window wiper motor.

LTV0500000002627

Fig. 28 Test K: Washer Pump Is Inoperative (Part 4 of 4). 2005–06

• Is the resistance greater than 10,000 ohms?	
L4 CHECK FOR CORRECT WIPER MOTOR OPERATION	

• Disconnect all wiper motor connectors.
• Check for:
  ▪ corrosion.
  ▪ pushed-out pins.
• Connect all wiper motor connectors and make sure they seat correctly.
• Operate the system and verify the concern is still present.
• **Is the concern still present?**
	Yes
	GO to L5 .
	
	No
	The system is operating correctly at this time. Concern may have been caused by a loose or corroded connector. TEST the system for normal operation.

L5 CHECK THE WINDSHIELD WIPER MOTOR	
• Key in OFF position. • Disconnect: Windshield Wiper Motor C125. • Carry out the windshield wiper motor component test as outlined. • **Did the windshield wiper motor pass the component test?**	**Yes** The system is operating correctly at this time. Concern may have been caused by binding or incorrect pivot arm adjustment. TEST the system for normal operation. **No** INSTALL a new windshield wiper motor.

LTV0500000002629

Fig. 29 Test L: Speed Dependent Interval Mode Does Not Operate Correctly (Part 2 of 2). 2005–06

Test Step	Result / Action to Take
M1 CHECK CIRCUIT CRW22 (WH/BU) FOR VOLTAGE	
• Disconnect: Windshield Wiper Motor C125. • Key in ON position. • Measure the voltage between windshield wiper motor C125-2 circuit CRW22 (WH/BU), harness side and ground. 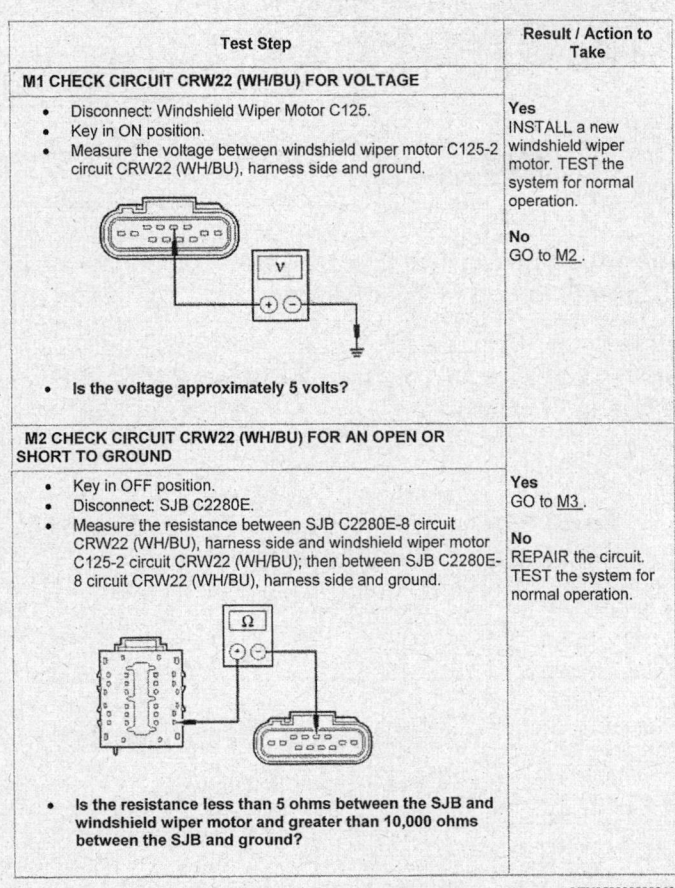 • **Is the voltage approximately 5 volts?**	**Yes** INSTALL a new windshield wiper motor. TEST the system for normal operation. **No** GO to M2.
M2 CHECK CIRCUIT CRW22 (WH/BU) FOR AN OPEN OR SHORT TO GROUND	
• Key in OFF position. • Disconnect: SJB C2280E. • Measure the resistance between SJB C2280E-8 circuit CRW22 (WH/BU), harness side and windshield wiper motor C125-2 circuit CRW22 (WH/BU); then between SJB C2280E-8 circuit CRW22 (WH/BU), harness side and ground. • **Is the resistance less than 5 ohms between the SJB and windshield wiper motor and greater than 10,000 ohms between the SJB and ground?**	**Yes** GO to M3. **No** REPAIR the circuit. TEST the system for normal operation.

LTV0500000002630

Fig. 30   Test M: Headlamps Do Not Illuminate When Wipers Are On (Part 1 of 2). 2005–06

COMPONENT DIAGNOSIS & TESTING

Refer to "Aviator" for component diagnosis and testing.

M3 CHECK FOR CORRECT MODULE OPERATION	

• Disconnect all the SJB connectors.
 • Check for:
     ▪ Corrosion.
     ▪ Pushed-out pins.
 • Connect all the SJB connectors and make sure they are seated correctly.
 • Operate the system and verify the concern is still present.
 • **Is the concern still present?**
	Yes
	 INSTALL a new SJB. CLEAR the DTCs. REPEAT the SJB self-test.
	
	 No
	 The system is operating correctly at this time. Concern may have been caused by a loose or corroded connector. CLEAR the DTCs. REPEAT the self-test.

LTV0500000002631

Fig. 30   Test M: Headlamps Do Not Illuminate When Wipers Are On (Part 2 of 2). 2005–06

Explorer Sport & Sport Trac

NOTE: On Air Bag Equipped Models, Refer To "Air Bag System Precautions" Located In The Front Of This Manual For System Disarming & Arming Procedures.

NOTE: "Electrical Symbol & Wire Color Code Identification" Located In The Front Of This Manual May Be Used As An Aid When Using Wiring Diagrams Found In This Section.

NOTE: Refer To "Computer Relearn Procedures" Located In The Front Of This Manual When Battery Power To The Computer Has Been Interrupted.

INDEX

	Page No.		Page No.		Page No.
Component Diagnosis & Testing	3-138	Battery Ground Cable	3-132	Clearing Diagnostic Trouble Codes	3-132
Diagnostic Chart Index	3-134	**System Diagnosis & Testing**	3-132	Diagnostic Tests	3-132
Precautions	3-132	Accessing Diagnostic Trouble Codes	3-132	Wiring Diagrams	3-132

PRECAUTIONS

Battery Ground Cable

Prior to service, disconnect battery ground cable and isolate as required.

SYSTEM DIAGNOSIS & TESTING

Accessing Diagnostic Trouble Codes

Connect a suitably programmed scan tool and Vehicle Communication Module (VCM) with appropriate adapters, or equivalents, to the Data Link Connector (DCL) located in the passenger compartment beneath the instrument panel. Follow tool manufacturer's instructions for accessing speed control Diagnostic Trouble Codes (DTC).

Wiring Diagrams

Refer to **Fig. 1** for wiring diagrams.

Diagnostic Tests

Refer to **Figs. 2 through 9** for diagnostic tests.

Clearing Diagnostic Trouble Codes

Connect a suitably programmed scan tool and Vehicle Communication Module (VCM) with appropriate adapters, or equivalents, to the Data Link Connector (DCL) located in the passenger compartment beneath the instrument panel. Follow tool manufacturer's instructions for accessing speed control Diagnostic Trouble Codes (DTC).

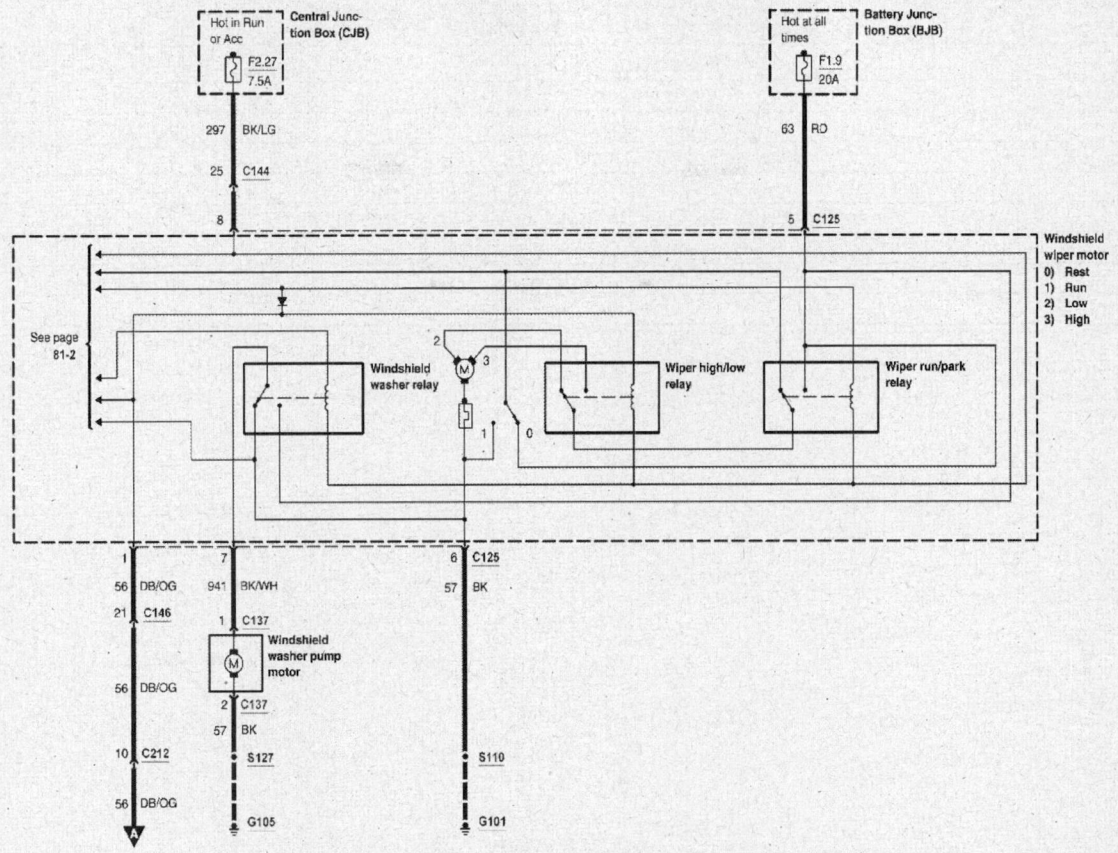

Fig. 1   Wiring diagram (Part 1 of 2)

LTV0500000002690

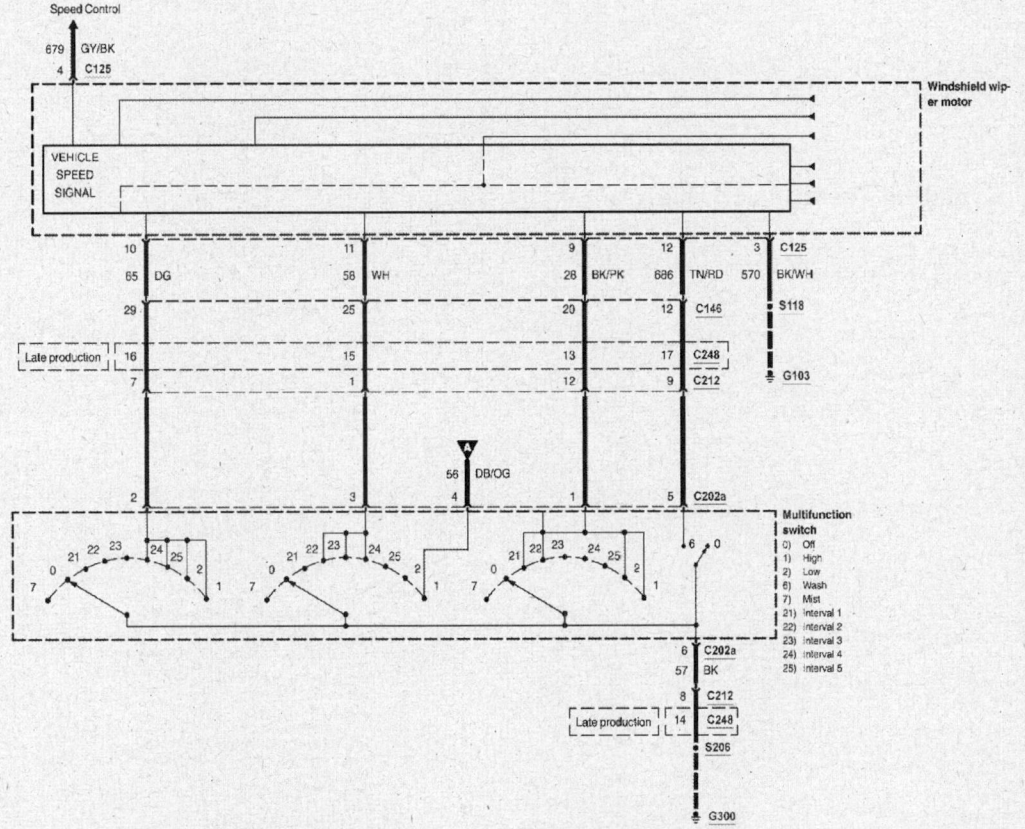

Fig. 1   Wiring diagram (Part 2 of 2)

LTV0500000002691

WIPER SYSTEMS

DIAGNOSTIC CHART INDEX

Test	Description	Page No.	Fig. No.
—	Symptom Tests	3-134	2
A	Wipers Are Inoperative	3-134	3
B	Wipers Stay On Continuously	3-135	4
C	High/Low Wiper Speeds Do Not Operate Correctly. Intermittent Wiper Mode OK	3-135	5
D	Intermittent Wiper Mode Does Not Operate Correctly, High/Low Speeds OK	3-136	6
E	Wipers Do Not Operate Correctly In Mist Position	3-136	7
F	Washer Pump Is Inoperative	3-137	8
G	Speed Dependent Interval Mode Does Not Operate Correctly	3-137	9

Condition	Possible Sources	Action
• The windshield wipers are inoperative	• Battery junction box (BJB) fuse 9 (20A). • Circuitry. • Multifunction switch. • Windshield wiper motor.	• Go To Pinpoint Test A .
• The windshield wipers stay on continuously	• Circuitry. • Multifunction switch. • Windshield wiper motor.	• Go To Pinpoint Test B .
• The high/low wiper speeds do not operate correctly (intermittent wiper mode OK)	• Circuitry. • Multifunction switch. • Windshield wiper motor.	• Go To Pinpoint Test C .
• The intermittent wiper mode does not operate correctly (high/low speeds OK).	• Circuitry. • Multifunction switch. • Windshield wiper motor.	• Go To Pinpoint Test D .
• The wipers do not operate correctly in the MIST position	• Multifunction switch. • Circuitry. • Washer pump. • Windshield wiper motor.	• Go To Pinpoint Test E .

LTV0500000002692

Fig. 2   Symptom Tests (Part 1 of 2)

Condition	Possible Sources	Action
• The windshield washer pump is inoperative	• Central junction box (CJB) fuse 23 (7.5A). • Circuitry. • Multifunction switch. • Windshield wiper motor. • Washer pump.	• Go To Pinpoint Test F .
• The speed dependent interval mode does not operate correctly	• Circuitry. • Powertrain control module (PCM). • Windshield wiper motor.	• Go To Pinpoint Test G .
• The wipers will not park at correct position	• Windshield wiper motor. • Pivot arm adjustment. • Linkage.	• ADJUST the windshield wiper blade and pivot arm.

LTV0500000002693

Fig. 2   Symptom Tests (Part 2 of 2)

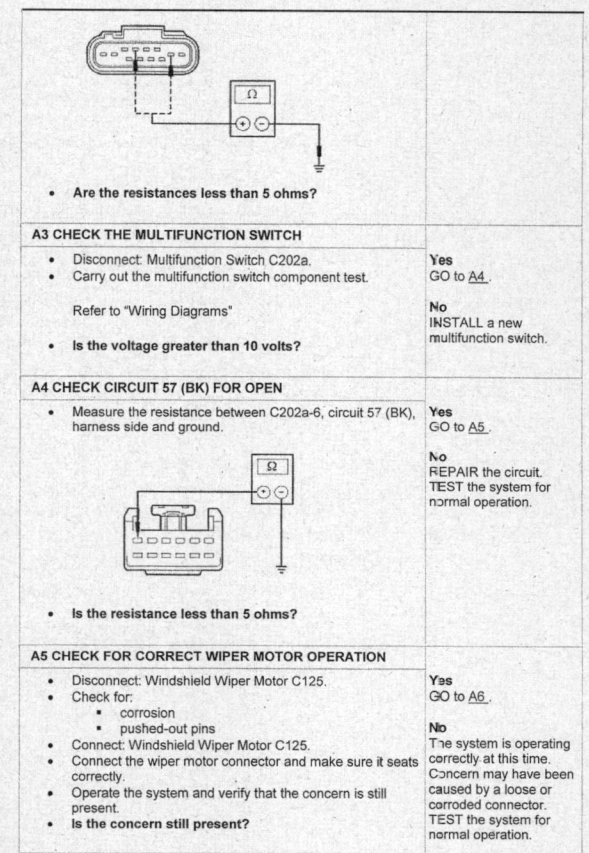

• **Are the resistances less than 5 ohms?**

A3 CHECK THE MULTIFUNCTION SWITCH

Test Step	Result / Action to Take
• Disconnect: Multifunction Switch C202a. • Carry out the multifunction switch component test. Refer to "Wiring Diagrams" • Is the voltage greater than 10 volts?	**Yes** GO to A4 . **No** INSTALL a new multifunction switch.

A4 CHECK CIRCUIT 57 (BK) FOR OPEN

Test Step	Result / Action to Take
• Measure the resistance between C202a-6, circuit 57 (BK), harness side and ground. • Is the resistance less than 5 ohms?	**Yes** GO to A5 . **No** REPAIR the circuit. TEST the system for normal operation.

A5 CHECK FOR CORRECT WIPER MOTOR OPERATION

Test Step	Result / Action to Take
• Disconnect: Windshield Wiper Motor C125. • Check for: • corrosion • pushed-out pins • Connect: Windshield Wiper Motor C125. • Connect the wiper motor connector and make sure it seats correctly. • Operate the system and verify that the concern is still present. • **Is the concern still present?**	**Yes** GO to A6 . **No** The system is operating correctly at this time. Concern may have been caused by a loose or corroded connector. TEST the system for normal operation.

LTV0500000002695

Fig. 3   Test A: Wipers Are Inoperative (Part 2 of 3)

A1 CHECK CIRCUITS 63 (RD) AND 297 (BK/LG) FOR VOLTAGE

Test Step	Result / Action to Take
• Key in OFF position. • Disconnect: Windshield Motor C125. • Key in ON position. • Measure the voltage between windshield wiper C125-5, circuit 63 (RD), harness side and ground; and between windshield wiper motor C125-8, circuit 297 (BK/LG), harness side and ground. • **Are the voltages greater than 10 volts?**	**Yes** GO to A2 . **No** REPAIR the circuit(s) in question. TEST the system for normal operation.

A2 CHECK CIRCUITS 57 (BK) AND 570 (BK/WH) FOR OPENS

Test Step	Result / Action to Take
• Key in OFF position. • Measure the resistance between windshield wiper C125-6, circuit 57 (BK), harness side and ground; and between windshield wiper motor C125-3, circuit 570 (BK/WH), harness side and ground.	**Yes** GO to A3 . **No** REPAIR the circuit(s) in question. TEST the system for normal operation.

LTV0500000002694

Fig. 3   Test A: Wipers Are Inoperative (Part 1 of 3)

A6 CHECK CIRCUITS 65 (DG), 58 (WH), 56 (DB/OG), AND 28 (BK/PK) FOR OPENS

- Disconnect: Windshield Wiper Motor C125.
- Using the following table, measure the resistance between the multifunction switch C202a harness side and the windshield wiper motor C125 harness side:

Multifunction Switch C202a	Windshield Wiper Motor C125
C202a-2, circuit 65 (DG)	C125-10, circuit 65 (DG)
C202a-3, circuit 58 (WH)	C125-11, circuit 58 (WH)
C202a-4, circuit 56 (DB/OG)	C125-1, circuit 56 (DB/OG)
C202a-1, circuit 28 (BK/PK)	C125-9, circuit 28 (BK/PK)

Yes
INSTALL a new windshield wiper motor. TEST the system for normal operation.

No
REPAIR the circuit(s) in question. TEST the system for normal operation.

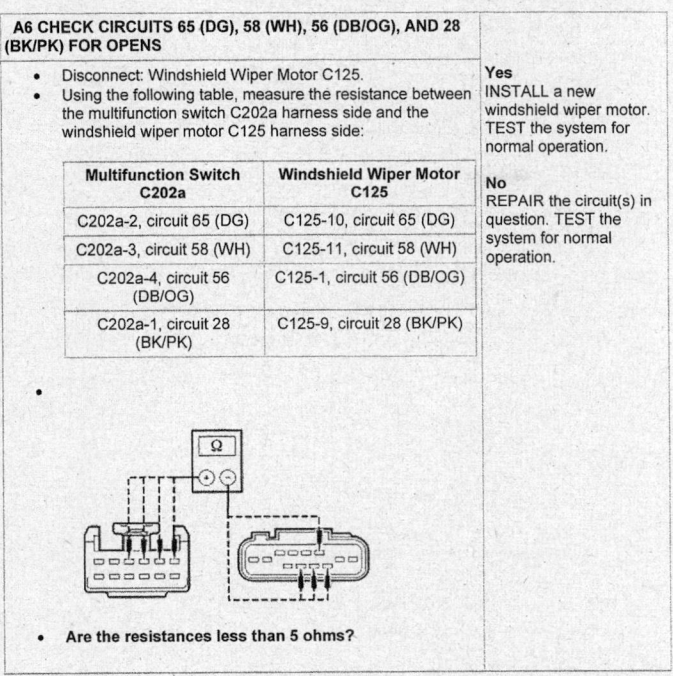

- **Are the resistances less than 5 ohms?**

LTV0500000002696

Fig. 3   Test A: Wipers Are Inoperative (Part 3 of 3)

B4 CHECK CIRCUITS 65 (DG), 58 (WH), 56 (DB/OG), AND 28 (BK/PK) FOR SHORTS

- Disconnect: Windshield Wiper Motor C125.
- Using the following table, measure the resistance between the windshield wiper motor C125 harness side and ground:

Windshield Wiper Motor C125	Ground
C125-10, circuit 65 (DG)	ground
C125-11, circuit 58 (WH)	ground
C125-1, circuit 56 (DB/OG)	ground
C125-9, circuit 28 (BK/PK)	ground

Yes
INSTALL a new windshield wiper motor

No
REPAIR the circuit(s) in question. TEST the system for normal operation.

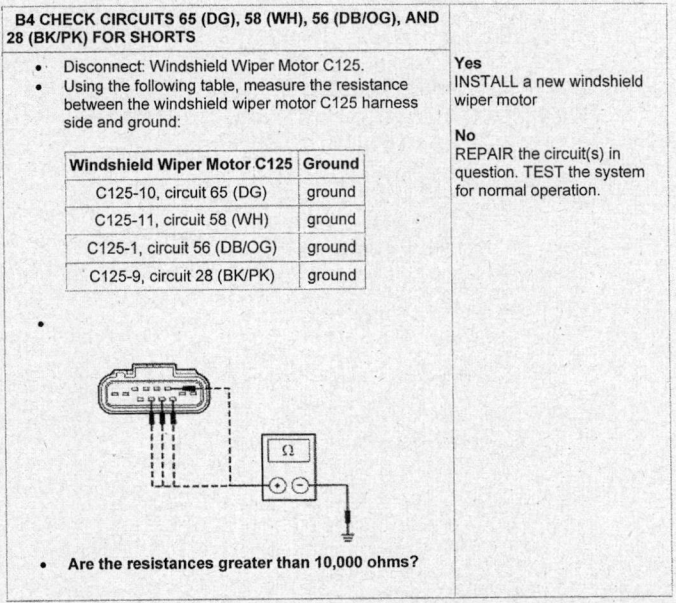

- **Are the resistances greater than 10,000 ohms?**

LTV0500000002698

Fig. 4   Test B: Wipers Stay On Continuously (Part 2 of 2)

Test Step	Result / Action to Take
B1 CHECK THE MULTIFUNCTION SWITCH • Key in OFF position. • Disconnect: Multifunction Switch C202a. • Carry out the multifunction switch component test. Refer to "Wiring Diagrams" • **Did the multifunction switch pass the component test?**	**Yes** GO to B2 . **No** INSTALL a new multifunction switch..
B2 CHECK CIRCUIT 57 (BK) FOR OPEN • Measure the resistance between C202a-6, circuit 57 (BK), harness side and ground. • **Is the resistance less than 5 ohms?**	**Yes** GO to B3 . **No** REPAIR the circuit. TEST the system for normal operation.

B3 CHECK FOR CORRECT WIPER MOTOR OPERATION
• Disconnect: Windshield Wiper Motor C125.
• Check for:
  ▪ corrosion
  ▪ pushed-out pins
• Connect: Windshield Wiper Motor C125.
• Operate the system and verify the concern is still present.
• **Is the concern still present?**
	Yes
	GO to B4
	
	No
	The system is operating correctly at this time. Concern may have been caused by a loose or corroded connector. TEST the system for normal operation.

LTV0500000002697

Fig. 4   Test B: Wipers Stay On Continuously (Part 1 of 2)

Test Step	Result / Action to Take
C1 CHECK THE MULTIFUNCTION SWITCH • Key in OFF position. • Disconnect: Multifunction Switch C202a. • Carry out the multifunction switch component test. Refer to "Wiring Diagrams" • **Did the multifunction switch pass the component test?**	**Yes** GO to C2 . **No** INSTALL a new multifunction switch.
C2 CHECK CIRCUIT 57 (BK) FOR OPEN • Measure the resistance between C202a-6, circuit 57 (BK), harness side and ground. • Is the resistance less than 5 ohms?	**Yes** GO to C3 . **No** REPAIR the circuit. TEST the system for normal operation.

C3 CHECK FOR CORRECT WIPER MOTOR OPERATION
• Disconnect: Windshield Wiper Motor C125.
• Check for:
  ▪ corrosion
  ▪ pushed-out pins
• Connect: Windshield Wiper Motor C125.
• Connect the wiper motor connector and make sure it seats correctly.
• Operate the system and verify the concern is still present.
	Yes
	GO to C4 .
	
	No
	The system is operating correctly at this time. Concern may have been caused by a loose or corroded connector. TEST the system for normal

LTV0500000002699

Fig. 5   Test C: High/Low Wiper Speeds Do Not Operate Correctly. Intermittent Wiper Mode OK (Part 1 of 2)

• Is the concern still present?

operation.

C4 CHECK CIRCUITS 65 (DG), 56 (DB/OG), AND 28 (BK/PK) FOR OPENS

• Disconnect: Windshield Wiper Motor C125.
• Using the following table, measure the resistance between the multifunction switch C202a harness side and the windshield wiper motor C125 harness side:

Multifunction Switch C202a	Windshield Wiper Motor C125
C202a-2, circuit 65 (DG)	C125-10, circuit 65 (DG)
C202a-4, circuit 56 (DB/OG)	C125-1, circuit 56 (DB/OG)
C202a-1, circuit 28 (BK/PK)	C125-9, circuit 28 (BK/PK)

Yes
INSTALL a new windshield wiper motor.

No
REPAIR the circuit(s) in question. TEST the system for normal operation.

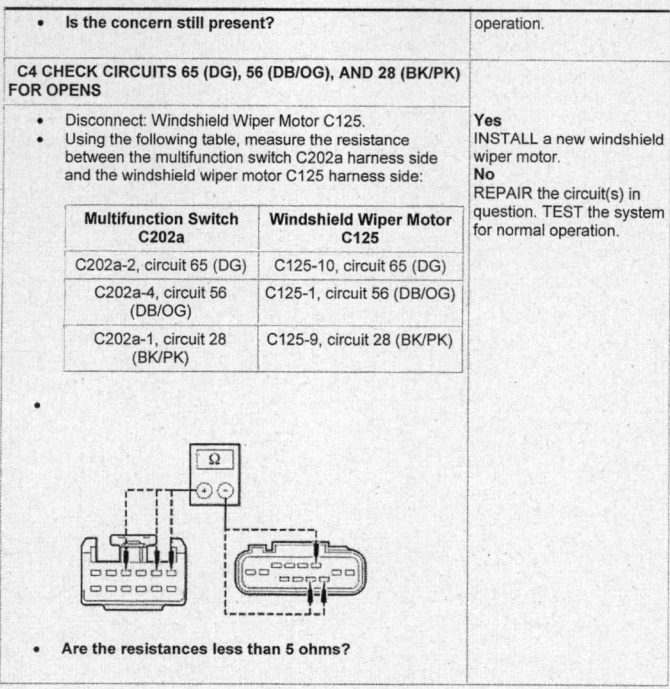

• Are the resistances less than 5 ohms?

LTV0500000002700

Fig. 5   Test C: High/Low Wiper Speeds Do Not Operate Correctly. Intermittent Wiper Mode OK (Part 2 of 2)

operation.

D4 CHECK CIRCUITS 65 (DG), 56 (DB/OG), AND 28 (BK/PK) FOR OPENS

• Disconnect: Windshield Wiper Motor C125.
• Using the following table, measure the resistance between the multifunction switch C202a harness side and the windshield wiper motor C125 harness side:

Multifunction Switch C202a	Windshield Wiper Motor C125
C202a-2, circuit 65 (DG)	C125-10, circuit 65 (DG)
C202a-4, circuit 56 (DB/OG)	C125-1, circuit 56 (DB/OG)
C202a-1, circuit 28 (BK/PK)	C125-9, circuit 28 (BK/PK)
C202a-3, circuit 58 (WH)	C125-11, circuit 58 (WH)

Yes
INSTALL a new windshield wiper motor

No
REPAIR the circuit(s) in question. TEST the system for normal operation.

• Is the resistance less than 5 ohms?

LTV0500000002702

Fig. 6   Test D: Intermittent Wiper Mode Does Not Operate Correctly, High/Low Speeds OK. (Part 2 of 2)

Test Step	Result / Action to Take
D1 CHECK THE MULTIFUNCTION SWITCH • Key in OFF position. • Disconnect: Multifunction Switch C202a. • Carry out the multifunction switch component test. Refer to "Wiring Diagrams" • **Did the multifunction switch pass the component test?**	**Yes** GO to D2 . **No** INSTALL a new multifunction switch.. TEST the system for normal operation.
D2 CHECK CIRCUIT 57 (BK) FOR OPEN • Measure the resistance between C202a-6, circuit 57 (BK), harness side and ground. • Is the resistance less than 5 ohms?	**Yes** GO to D3 **No** REPAIR the circuit. TEST the system for normal operation..

D3 CHECK FOR CORRECT WIPER MOTOR OPERATION
• Disconnect: Windshield Wiper Motor C125.
• Check for:
  ▪ corrosion
  ▪ pushed-out pins
• Connect: Windshield Wiper Motor C125.
• Operate the system and verify the concern is still present.
• **Is the concern still present?**
	Yes
	GO to D4 .
	
	No
	The system is operating correctly at this time. Concern may have been caused by a loose or corroded connector. TEST the system for normal

LTV0500000002701

Fig. 6   Test D: Intermittent Wiper Mode Does Not Operate Correctly, High/Low Speeds OK. (Part 1 of 2).

Test Step	Result / Action to Take
E1 CHECK THE MULTIFUNCTION SWITCH • Key in OFF position. • Disconnect: Multifunction Switch C202a. • Carry out the multifunction switch component test. Refer to "Wiring Diagrams" • **Did the multifunction switch pass the component test?**	**Yes** GO to E2 . **No** INSTALL a new multifunction switch.. TEST the system for normal operation.
E2 CHECK CIRCUIT 57 (BK) FOR OPEN • Measure the resistance between C202a-6, circuit 57 (BK), harness side and ground. • Is the resistance less than 5 ohms?	**Yes** GO to E3 . **No** REPAIR the circuit. TEST the system for normal operation.
E3 CHECK CIRCUIT 686 (TN/RD) FOR OPEN • Disconnect: Windshield Wiper Motor C125. • Measure the resistance between C202a-5, circuit 686 (TN/RD), harness side and C125-12, circuit 686 (TN/RD), harness side. • Is the resistance less than 5 ohms?	**Yes** Go To Pinpoint Test F to diagnose the washer circuit. **No** REPAIR the circuit. TEST the system for normal operation.

LTV0500000002703

Fig. 7   Test E: Wipers Do Not Operate Correctly In Mist Position

Test Step	Result / Action to Take
F1 CHECK CIRCUIT 686 (TN/RD) FOR GROUND	
• Disconnect: Windshield Wiper Motor C125. • Key in ON position. • Measure the resistance between C125-12, circuit 686 (TN/RD), harness side and ground while depressing the multifunction switch to the windshield wiper wash position. 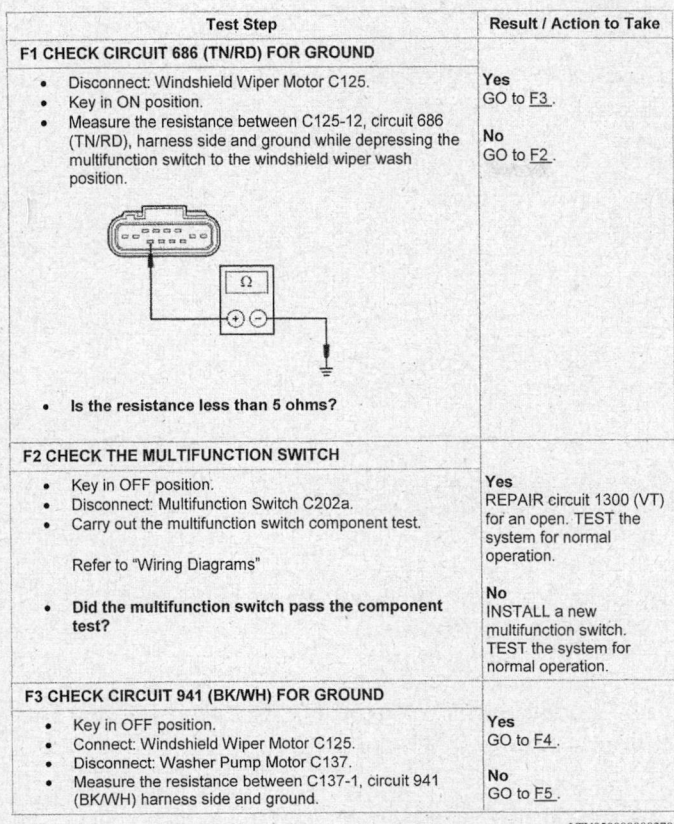 • **Is the resistance less than 5 ohms?**	**Yes** GO to F3 . **No** GO to F2 .
F2 CHECK THE MULTIFUNCTION SWITCH	
• Key in OFF position. • Disconnect: Multifunction Switch C202a. • Carry out the multifunction switch component test. Refer to "Wiring Diagrams" • **Did the multifunction switch pass the component test?**	**Yes** REPAIR circuit 1300 (VT) for an open. TEST the system for normal operation. **No** INSTALL a new multifunction switch. TEST the system for normal operation.
F3 CHECK CIRCUIT 941 (BK/WH) FOR GROUND	
• Key in OFF position. • Connect: Windshield Wiper Motor C125. • Disconnect: Washer Pump Motor C137. • Measure the resistance between C137-1, circuit 941 (BK/WH) harness side and ground.	**Yes** GO to F4 . **No** GO to F5 .

LTV0500000002706

Fig. 8   Test F: Washer Pump Is Inoperative (Part 1 of 3)

(BK/WH), harness side and C137-1, circuit 941 (BK/WH), harness side. 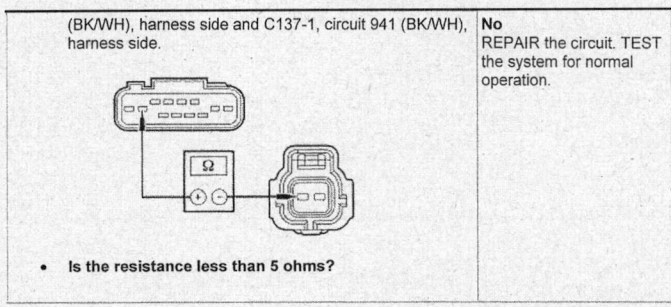 • **Is the resistance less than 5 ohms?**	**No** REPAIR the circuit. TEST the system for normal operation.

LTV0500000002708

Fig. 8   Test F: Washer Pump Is Inoperative (Part 3 of 3)

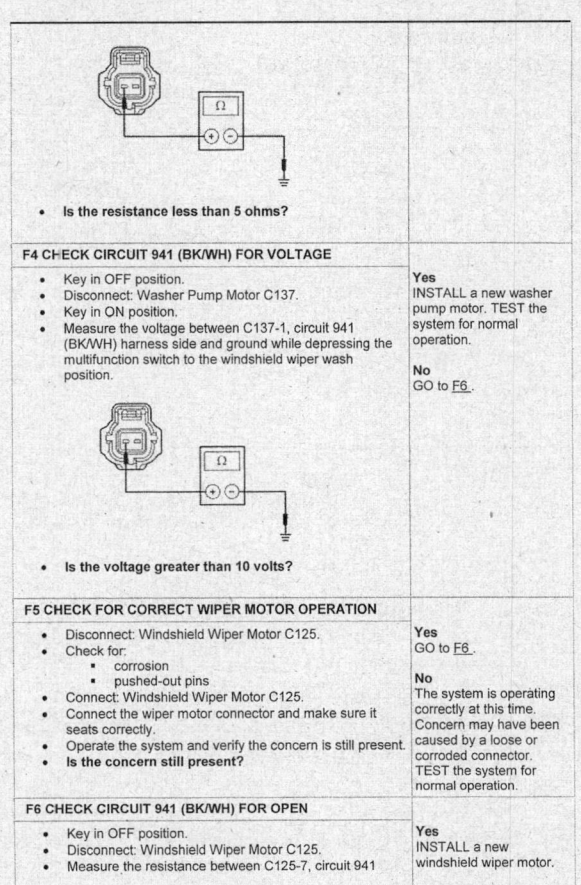 • **Is the resistance less than 5 ohms?**	
F4 CHECK CIRCUIT 941 (BK/WH) FOR VOLTAGE	
• Key in OFF position. • Disconnect: Washer Pump Motor C137. • Key in ON position. • Measure the voltage between C137-1, circuit 941 (BK/WH) harness side and ground while depressing the multifunction switch to the windshield wiper wash position. • **Is the voltage greater than 10 volts?**	**Yes** INSTALL a new washer pump motor. TEST the system for normal operation. **No** GO to F6 .
F5 CHECK FOR CORRECT WIPER MOTOR OPERATION	

• Disconnect: Windshield Wiper Motor C125.
• Check for:
  ■ corrosion
  ■ pushed-out pins
• Connect: Windshield Wiper Motor C125.
• Connect the wiper motor connector and make sure it seats correctly.
• Operate the system and verify the concern is still present.
• **Is the concern still present?**
	Yes
	GO to F6 .
	
	No
	The system is operating correctly at this time. Concern may have been caused by a loose or corroded connector. TEST the system for normal operation.

F6 CHECK CIRCUIT 941 (BK/WH) FOR OPEN	
• Key in OFF position. • Disconnect: Windshield Wiper Motor C125. • Measure the resistance between C125-7, circuit 941	**Yes** INSTALL a new windshield wiper motor.

LTV0500000002707

Fig. 8   Test F: Washer Pump Is Inoperative (Part 2 of 3)

Test Step	Result / Action to Take
G1 CHECK THE PCM — MONITOR THE VSS	
• Monitor the VSS PID while driving the vehicle from 0 to 88.5 kph (55 mph). • **Does the VSS PID agree with the actual vehicle speed?**	**Yes** GO to G2 . **No** Check Vehicle Speed Sensor VSS and circuit.
G2 CHECK CIRCUIT 679 (GY/BK) FOR AN OPEN	
• Disconnect: PCM C175. • Disconnect: Windshield Wiper Motor C125. • Measure the resistance between PCM C175-68, circuit 679 (GY/BK), harness side and windshield wiper motor C125-4, circuit 679 (GY/BK), harness side. • **Is the resistance less than 5 ohms?**	**Yes** GO to G3 . **No** REPAIR the circuit. CLEAR the DTCs. REPEAT the self-test.
G3 CHECK CIRCUIT 679 (GY/BK) FOR A SHORT TO GROUND	
• Measure the resistance between PCM C175-68, circuit 679 (GY/BK), harness side and ground.	**Yes** GO to G4 . **No** REPAIR the circuit. CLEAR the DTCs. REPEAT the self-test.

LTV0500000002704

Fig. 9   Test G: Speed Dependent Interval Mode Does Not Operate Correctly (Part 1 of 2)

COMPONENT DIAGNOSIS & TESTING

Refer to "Aviator" for component diagnosis and testing procedures.

• Is the resistance greater than 10,000 ohms?	
G4 CHECK FOR CORRECT WIPER MOTOR OPERATION	

• Disconnect: Windshield Wiper Motor C125.
• Check for:
  ▪ corrosion
  ▪ pushed-out pins
• Connect: Windshield Wiper Motor C125.
• Operate the system and verify that the concern is still present.
• **Is the concern still present?**
	Yes
	INSTALL a new windshield wiper motor
	
	No
	The system is operating correctly at this time. Concern may have been caused by a loose or corroded connector. TEST the system for normal operation.

LTV0500000002705

Fig. 9   Test G: Speed Dependent Interval Mode Does Not Operate Correctly (Part 2 of 2)

Freestar & Monterey

NOTE: On Air Bag Equipped Models, Refer To "Air Bag System Precautions" Located In The Front Of This Manual For System Disarming & Arming Procedures.

NOTE: "Electrical Symbol & Wire Color Code Identification" Located In The Front Of This Manual May Be Used As An Aid When Using Wiring Diagrams Found In This Section.

NOTE: Refer To "Computer Relearn Procedures" Located In The Front Of This Manual When Battery Power To The Computer Has Been Interrupted.

INDEX

	Page No.		Page No.		Page No.
Component Diagnosis & Testing	3-146	System Diagnosis & Testing	3-138	Diagnostic Tests	3-138
Diagnostic Chart Index	3-140	Accessing Diagnostic Trouble Codes	3-138	Diagnostic Trouble Code Interpretation	3-138
Precautions	3-138	Clearing Diagnostic Trouble Codes	3-138	Wiring Diagrams	3-138
Battery Ground Cable	3-138				

PRECAUTIONS

Battery Ground Cable

Prior to service, disconnect battery ground cable and isolate as required.

SYSTEM DIAGNOSIS & TESTING

Accessing Diagnostic Trouble Codes

Connect a suitably programmed scan tool and Vehicle Communication Module (VCM) with appropriate adapters, or equivalents, to the Data Link Connector (DCL) located in the passenger compartment beneath the instrument panel. Follow tool manufacturer's instructions for accessing speed control Diagnostic Trouble Codes (DTC).

Diagnostic Trouble Code Interpretation

Refer to **Fig. 1** for diagnostic trouble code interpretation.

Wiring Diagrams

Refer to **Figs. 2 and 3** for wiper system wiring diagrams.

Diagnostic Tests

Refer to **Figs. 4 through 11** for diagnostic tests.

Clearing Diagnostic Trouble Codes

Connect a suitably programmed scan tool and Vehicle Communication Module (VCM) with appropriate adapters, or equivalents, to the Data Link Connector (DCL) located in the passenger compartment beneath the instrument panel. Follow tool manufacturer's instructions for accessing speed control Diagnostic Trouble Codes (DTC).

Code	Description
B1482	Wiper Washer Fluid Level Sensor Circuit Short To Ground
B2008	Wipers On Signal Circuit Short to Ground

Fig. 1   Diagnostic trouble code interpretation

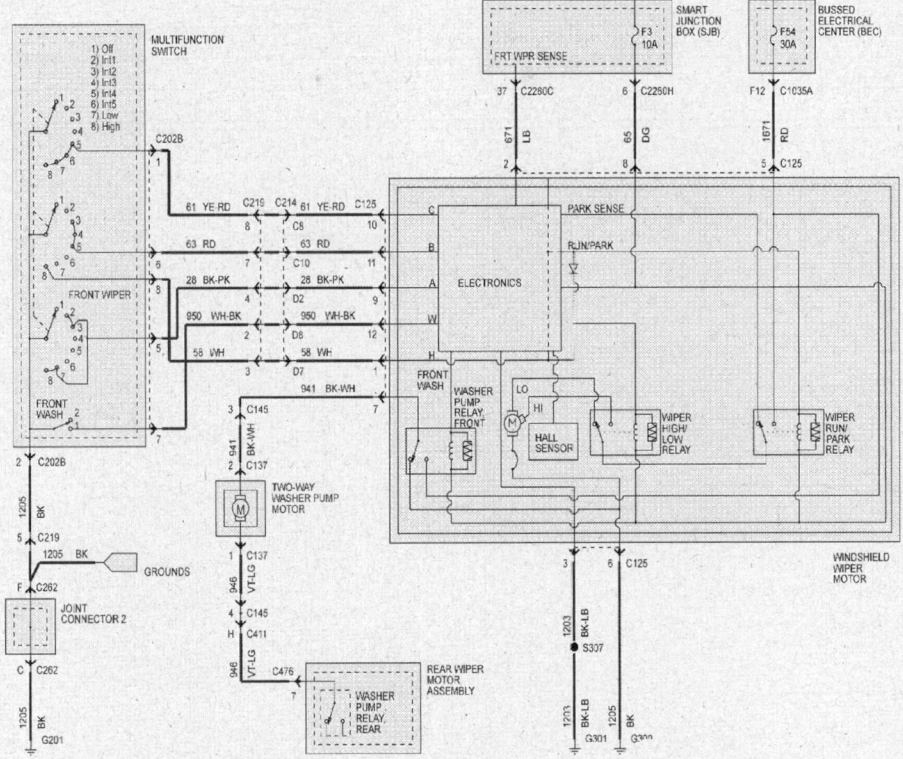

LTV0500000002632

Fig. 2   Front wiring diagram

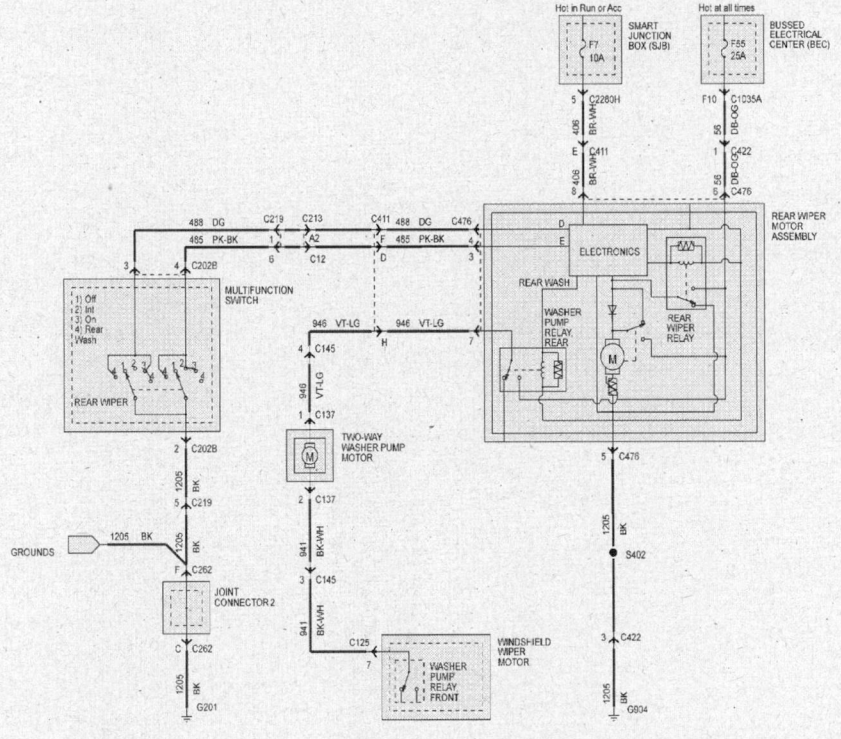

LTV0500000002633

Fig. 3   Rear wiring diagram

DIAGNOSTIC CHART INDEX

Test	Code	Description	Page No.	Fig. No.
—	—	Symptom Tests	3-140	4
A	—	Front Wipers Are Inoperative	3-141	5
B	—	Rear Wipers Are Inoperative	3-142	6
C	—	Front Or Rear Wipers Stay On Continuously	3-143	7
D	—	Intermittent Wiper Speed Does Not Operate Correctly	3-143	8
E	—	Front High/Low Wiper Speeds Do Not Operate Correctly	3-144	9
F	—	Washer Pump Is Inoperative	3-144	10
G	B2008	Headlamps Do Not Illuminate When Wipers Are On	3-145	11

Condition	Possible Sources	Action
• No communication with the smart junction box (SJB)	• Fuse • Circuitry • SJB	• Diagnosis Communications Area Network (CAN)
• The wipers are inoperative — windshield wipers	• Fuse • Circuitry • Multi-function switch • Windshield wiper motor • SJB • BEC	• Go To Pinpoint Test A .
• The wipers are inoperative — rear wipers	• Fuse • Circuitry • Multi-function switch • Rear wiper motor • SJB • BEC	• Go To Pinpoint Test B .
• The wipers are inoperative — front and rear wipers	• Multi-function switch	• CARRY OUT the Multi-function Switch Component Test Refer to" Wiring Diagrams"
	• Circuitry	• If the multi-function switch passed the component test, REPAIR the multi-function switch ground circuit 1205 (BK).
• The wipers stay on continuously — front or rear	• Circuitry • Multi-function switch • Windshield wiper motor • Rear wiper motor	• Go To Pinpoint Test C .

LTV0500000002634

Fig. 4 Symptom Tests (Part 1 of 2)

Condition	Possible Sources	Action
• The intermittent wiper speed does not operate correctly	• Circuitry • Multi-function switch • Windshield wiper motor • Rear wiper motor	• Go To Pinpoint Test D .
• The high/low wiper speeds do not operate correctly — windshield	• Circuitry • Multi-function switch • Windshield wiper motor	• Go To Pinpoint Test E .
• The washer pump is inoperative	• Circuitry • Two-way washer motor pump • Multi-function switch • Windshield wiper motor • Rear wiper motor	• Go To Pinpoint Test F .
• The headlamps do not illuminate when the wipers are on	• Circuitry • Windshield wiper motor • SJB	• Go To Pinpoint Test G .

LTV0500000002635

Fig. 4 Symptom Tests (Part 2 of 2)

Test Step	Result / Action to Take
A1 CHECK THE FRONT WIPER MOTOR GROUND CIRCUITS • Disconnect: Windshield Wiper Motor C125. • Measure the resistance between windshield wiper motor C125-3 circuit 1203 (BK/LB), harness side and ground; then between windshield wiper motor C125-6 circuit 1205 (BK), harness side and ground. 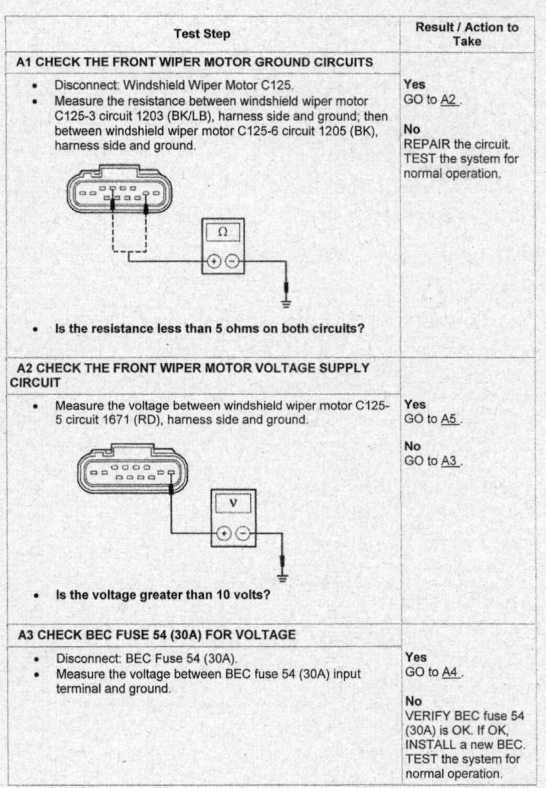 • Is the resistance less than 5 ohms on both circuits?	**Yes** GO to A2. **No** REPAIR the circuit. TEST the system for normal operation.
A2 CHECK THE FRONT WIPER MOTOR VOLTAGE SUPPLY CIRCUIT • Measure the voltage between windshield wiper motor C125-5 circuit 1671 (RD), harness side and ground. • Is the voltage greater than 10 volts?	**Yes** GO to A5. **No** GO to A3.
A3 CHECK BEC FUSE 54 (30A) FOR VOLTAGE • Disconnect: BEC Fuse 54 (30A). • Measure the voltage between BEC fuse 54 (30A) input terminal and ground.	**Yes** GO to A4. **No** VERIFY BEC fuse 54 (30A) is OK. If OK, INSTALL a new BEC. TEST the system for normal operation.

LTV0500000002636

Fig. 5 Test A: Front Wipers Are Inoperative (Part 1 of 4)

Test Step	Result / Action to Take
• Is the voltage greater than 10 volts?	
A6 CHECK THE SJB FUSE 3 (10A) FOR VOLTAGE • Key in OFF position. • Disconnect: SJB Fuse 3 (10A). • Key in ON position. • Measure the voltage between SJB fuse 3 (10A) input terminal and ground. • Is the voltage greater than 10 volts?	**Yes** GO to A7. **No** VERIFY SJB fuse 3 (10A) is OK. If OK, GO to A9.
A7 CHECK CIRCUIT 65 (DG) FOR AN OPEN OR SHORT TO GROUND • Key in OFF position. • Disconnect: SJB C2280h. • Measure the resistance between SJB C2280h-6 circuit 65 (DG), harness side and windshield wiper motor C125-8 circuit 65 (DG), harness side; then between SJB C2280h-6 circuit 65 (DG), harness side and ground. 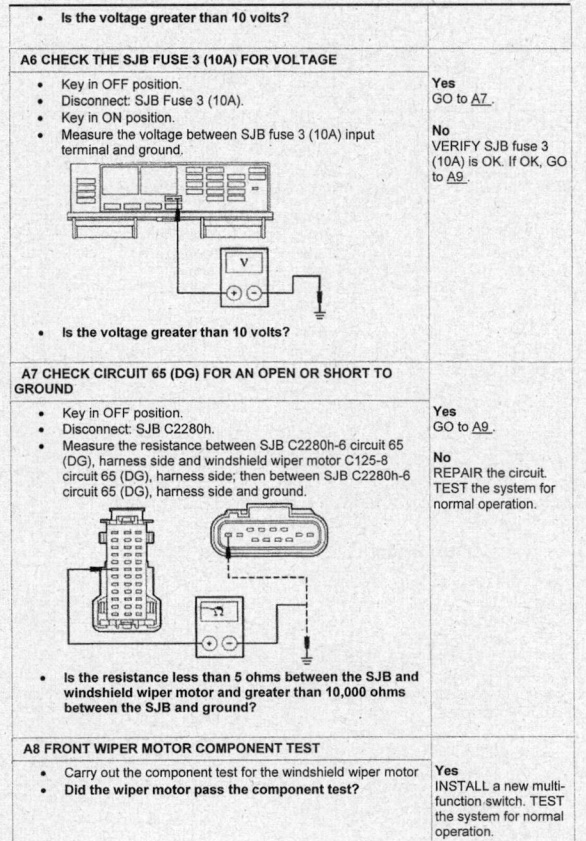 • Is the resistance less than 5 ohms between the SJB and windshield wiper motor and greater than 10,000 ohms between the SJB and ground?	**Yes** GO to A9. **No** REPAIR the circuit. TEST the system for normal operation.
A8 FRONT WIPER MOTOR COMPONENT TEST • Carry out the component test for the windshield wiper motor. • **Did the wiper motor pass the component test?**	**Yes** INSTALL a new multi-function switch. TEST the system for normal operation.

LTV0500000002638

Fig. 5 Test A: Front Wipers Are Inoperative (Part 3 of 4)

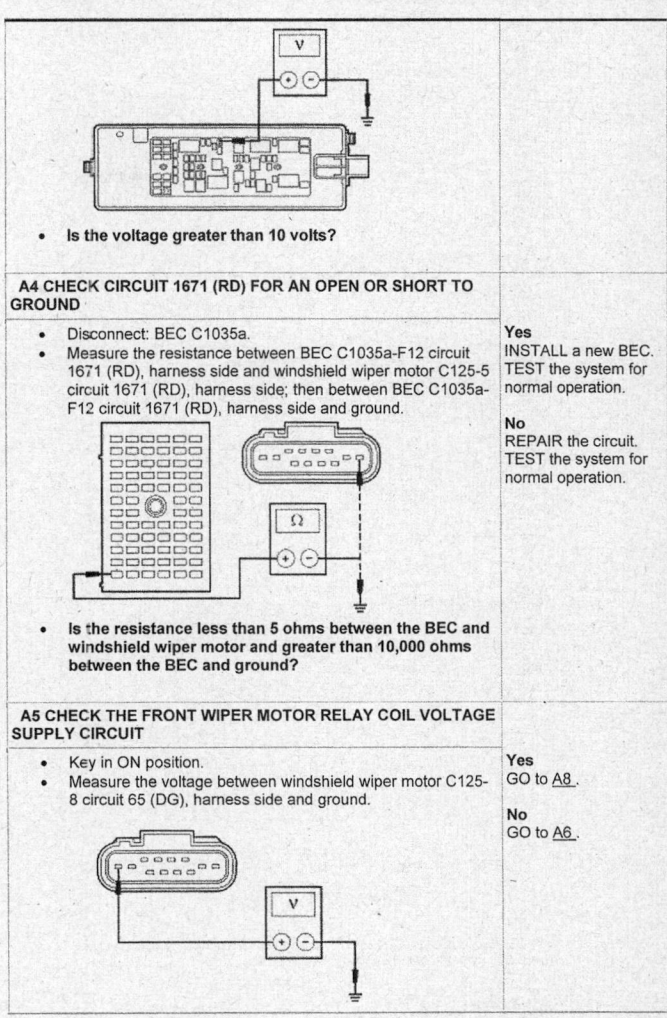

Test Step	Result / Action to Take
• Is the voltage greater than 10 volts?	
A4 CHECK CIRCUIT 1671 (RD) FOR AN OPEN OR SHORT TO GROUND • Disconnect: BEC C1035a. • Measure the resistance between BEC C1035a-F12 circuit 1671 (RD), harness side and windshield wiper motor C125-5 circuit 1671 (RD), harness side; then between BEC C1035a-F12 circuit 1671 (RD), harness side and ground. • Is the resistance less than 5 ohms between the BEC and windshield wiper motor and greater than 10,000 ohms between the BEC and ground?	**Yes** INSTALL a new BEC. TEST the system for normal operation. **No** REPAIR the circuit. TEST the system for normal operation.
A5 CHECK THE FRONT WIPER MOTOR RELAY COIL VOLTAGE SUPPLY CIRCUIT • Key in ON position. • Measure the voltage between windshield wiper motor C125-8 circuit 65 (DG), harness side and ground.	**Yes** GO to A8. **No** GO to A6.

LTV0500000002637

Fig. 5 Test A: Front Wipers Are Inoperative (Part 2 of 4)

Test Step	Result / Action to Take
	No INSTALL a new windshield wiper motor. TEST the system for normal operation.
A9 CHECK FOR CORRECT MODULE OPERATION • Disconnect all the SJB connectors. • Check for: ▪ corrosion. ▪ pushed-out pins. • Connect all the SJB connectors and make sure they are seated correctly. • Operate the system and verify the concern is still present. • **Is the concern still present?**	**Yes** INSTALL a new SJB. CLEAR the DTCs. REPEAT the SJB self-test. **No** The system is operating correctly at this time. Concern may have been caused by a loose or corroded connector. CLEAR the DTCs. REPEAT the self-test.

LTV0500000002639

Fig. 5 Test A: Front Wipers Are Inoperative (Part 4 of 4)

Test Step	Result / Action to Take
B1 CHECK THE REAR WIPER MOTOR GROUND CIRCUIT • Disconnect: Rear Wiper Motor C476. • Measure the resistance between rear wiper motor C476-5 circuit 1205 (BK), harness side and ground. • Is the resistance less than 5 ohms?	**Yes** GO to B2. **No** REPAIR the circuit. TEST the system for normal operation.
B2 CHECK THE REAR WIPER MOTOR VOLTAGE SUPPLY CIRCUIT • Measure the voltage between rear wiper motor C476-6 circuit 56 (DB/OG), harness side and ground. • Is the voltage greater than 10 volts?	**Yes** GO to B5. **No** GO to B3.
B3 CHECK BEC FUSE 55 (25A) FOR VOLTAGE • Disconnect: BEC Fuse 55 (25A). • Measure the voltage between BEC fuse 55 (25A) input terminal and ground.	**Yes** GO to B4. **No** VERIFY BEC fuse 55 (25A) is OK. If OK, INSTALL a new BEC. TEST the system for normal operation.

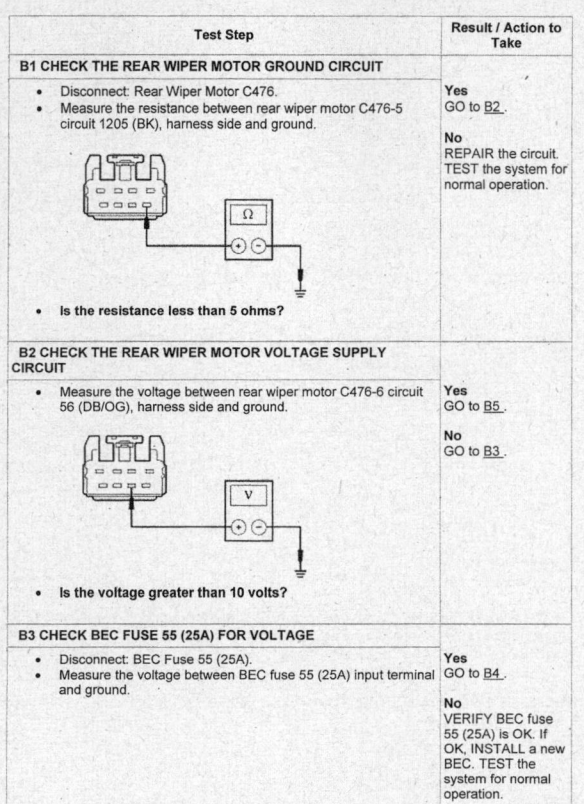

LTV0500000002640

Fig. 6 Test B: Rear Wipers Are Inoperative (Part 1 of 4)

	Result / Action to Take
• Is the voltage greater than 10 volts?	
B4 CHECK CIRCUIT 56 (DB/OG) FOR AN OPEN OR SHORT TO GROUND • Disconnect: BEC C1035a. • Measure the resistance between BEC C1035a-F10 circuit 56 (DB/OG), harness side and rear wiper motor C476-6 circuit 56 (DB/OG), harness side; then between BEC C1035a-F10 circuit 56 (DB/OG), harness side and ground. • Is the resistance less than 5 ohms between the BEC and rear wiper motor and greater than 10,000 ohms between the BEC and ground?	**Yes** INSTALL a new BEC. TEST the system for normal operation. **No** REPAIR the circuit. TEST the system for normal operation.
B5 CHECK THE REAR WIPER MOTOR MODULE (INTERNAL) VOLTAGE SUPPLY CIRCUIT • Key in ON position. • Measure the voltage between rear wiper motor C476-8 circuit 406 (BN/WH), harness side and ground.	**Yes** GO to B8. **No** GO to B6.

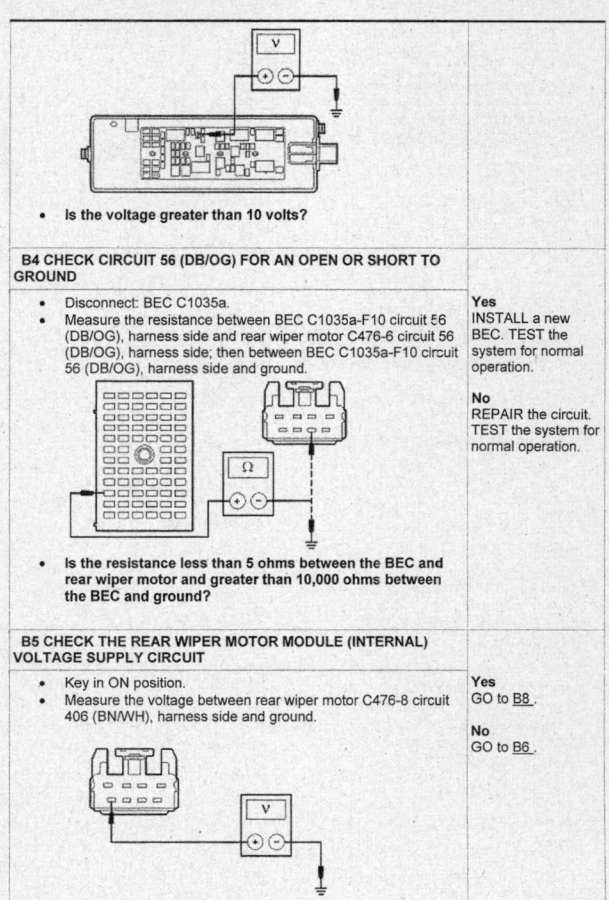

LTV0500000002641

Fig. 6 Test B: Rear Wipers Are Inoperative (Part 2 of 4)

	Result / Action to Take
• Is the voltage greater than 10 volts?	
B6 CHECK SJB FUSE 7 (10A) FOR VOLTAGE • Key in OFF position. • Disconnect: SJB Fuse 7 (10A). • Key in ON position. • Measure the voltage between SJB fuse 7 (10A) input terminal and ground. • Is the voltage greater than 10 volts?	**Yes** GO to B7. **No** VERIFY SJB fuse 7 (10A) is OK. If OK, GO to B10.
B7 CHECK CIRCUIT 406 (BN/WH) FOR AN OPEN OR SHORT TO GROUND • Key in OFF position. • Disconnect: SJB C2280h. • Measure the resistance between SJB C2280h-5 circuit 406 (BN/WH), harness side and rear wiper motor C476-8 circuit 406 (BN/WH), harness side; then between SJB C2280h-5 circuit 406 (BN/WH), harness side and ground. • Is the resistance less than 5 ohms between the SJB and rear wiper motor and greater than 10,000 ohms between the SJB and ground?	**Yes** GO to B10. **No** REPAIR the circuit. TEST the system for normal operation.
B8 MULTI-FUNCTION SWITCH COMPONENT TEST • Carry out the Multi-function Switch Component Test. Refer to "Wiring Diagrams"	**Yes** GO to B9. **No** INSTALL a new multi-function

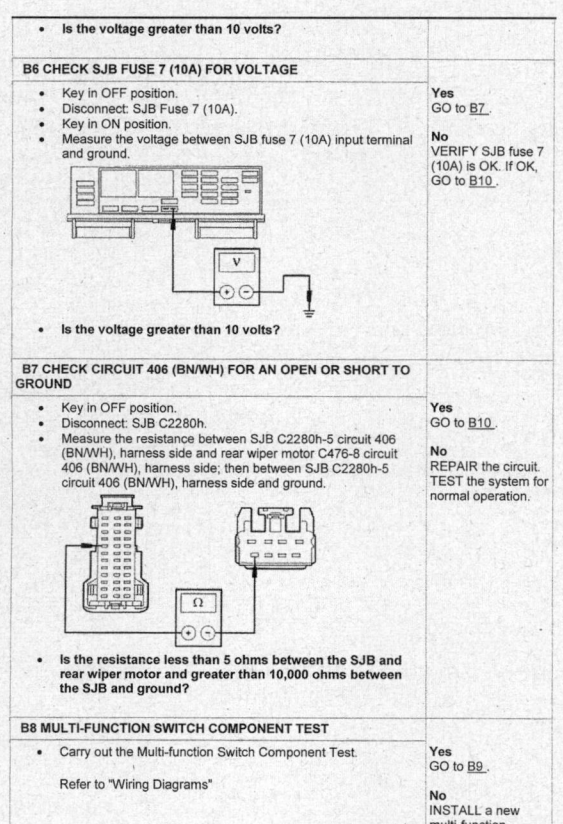

LTV0500000002642

Fig. 6 Test B: Rear Wipers Are Inoperative (Part 3 of 4)

	Result / Action to Take
• Did the multi-function switch pass the component test?	switch. TEST the system for normal operation.
B9 CHECK CIRCUITS 485 (PK/BK) AND 488 (DG) FOR AN OPEN • Measure the resistance between rear wiper motor C476-4, circuit 488 (DG), harness side and multi-function switch C202b-3, circuit 488 (DG), harness side; then between rear wiper motor C476-3 circuit 485 (PK/BK), harness side and multi-function switch C202b-4, circuit 485 (PK/BK), harness side. • Is the resistance less than 5 ohms on both circuits?	**Yes** INSTALL a new rear wiper motor. TEST the system for normal operation. **No** REPAIR the circuit. TEST the system for normal operation.

B10 CHECK FOR CORRECT MODULE OPERATION
• Disconnect all the SJB connectors.
• Check for:
  ▪ corrosion.
  ▪ pushed-out pins.
• Connect all the SJB connectors and make sure they are seated correctly.
• Operate the system and verify the concern is still present.
• **Is the concern still present?**
	Yes
	INSTALL a new SJB. CLEAR the DTCs. REPEAT the SJB self-test.
	
	No
	The system is operating correctly at this time. Concern may have been caused by a loose or corroded connector. CLEAR the DTCs. REPEAT the self-test.

LTV0500000002643

Fig. 6 Test B: Rear Wipers Are Inoperative (Part 4 of 4)

Test Step	Result / Action to Take
C1 DETERMINE IF THE FRONT AND REAR WIPERS STAY ON	
• Turn the front and rear wiper motor switches to the OFF position. • **Are the front and rear wipers still operating?**	**Yes** INSTALL a new multi-function switch. TEST the system for normal operation. **No** GO to C2 .
C2 CHECK THE MULTI-FUNCTION SWITCH	
• Disconnect: Multi-function Switch C202b. • Check the multi-function switch for correct operation. Refer to "Wiring Diagrams" • **Did the multi-function switch pass the component test?**	**Yes** For windshield wiper concerns, GO to C3 . For rear wiper concerns, GO to C4 . **No** INSTALL a new multi-function switch. TEST the system for normal operation.
C3 CHECK CIRCUITS 28 (BK/PK), 63 (RD) and 61 (YE/RD) FOR SHORT TO GROUND	
• Disconnect: Windshield Wiper Motor C125. • Measure the resistance between multi-function switch C202b-1 circuit 61 (YE/RD), harness side and ground; then between multi-function switch C202b-5 circuit 28 (BK/PK), harness side and ground; then between multi-function switch C202b-6 circuit 63 (RD), harness side and ground.	**Yes** INSTALL a new windshield wiper motor.. TEST the system for normal operation.

LTV0500000002644

Fig. 7   Test C: Front Or Rear Wipers Stay On Continuously (Part 1 of 2)

Test Step	Result / Action to Take
D1 CHECK THE MULTI-FUNCTION SWITCH	
• Disconnect: Multi-function Switch C202b. • Check the multi-function switch for correct operation. Refer to "Wiring Diagrams" • **Did the multi-function switch pass the component test?**	**Yes** For windshield wiper concerns, GO to D2 . For rear wiper concerns, GO to D4 . **No** INSTALL a new multi-function switch. TEST the system for normal operation.
D2 CHECK CIRCUITS 28 (BK/PK), 63 (RD) and 61 (YE/RD) FOR AN OPEN	
• Disconnect: Windshield Wiper Motor C125. • Measure the resistance between the multi-function switch and the windshield wiper motor using the following chart:	**Yes** GO to D3 . **No** REPAIR the circuit. TEST the system for normal operation.

Multi-function Switch C202b	Windshield Wiper Motor C125	Circuit
Pin 1	Pin 10	61 (YE/RD)
Pin 6	Pin 11	63 (RD)
Pin 5	Pin 9	28 (BK/PK)

LTV0500000002646

Fig. 8   Test D: Intermittent Wiper Speed Does Not Operate Correctly (Part 1 of 3)

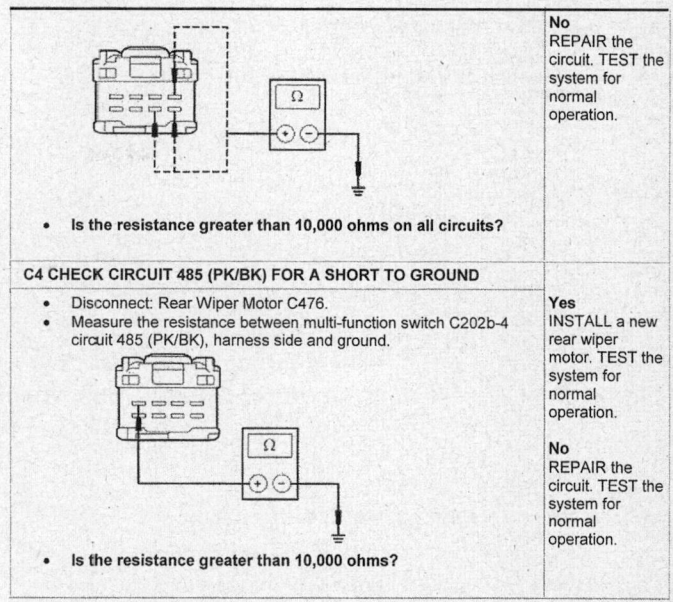

	No REPAIR the circuit. TEST the system for normal operation.
• **Is the resistance greater than 10,000 ohms on all circuits?**	
C4 CHECK CIRCUIT 485 (PK/BK) FOR A SHORT TO GROUND	
• Disconnect: Rear Wiper Motor C476. • Measure the resistance between multi-function switch C202b-4 circuit 485 (PK/BK), harness side and ground. • **Is the resistance greater than 10,000 ohms?**	**Yes** INSTALL a new rear wiper motor. TEST the system for normal operation. **No** REPAIR the circuit. TEST the system for normal operation.

LTV0500000002645

Fig. 7   Test C: Front Or Rear Wipers Stay On Continuously (Part 2 of 2)

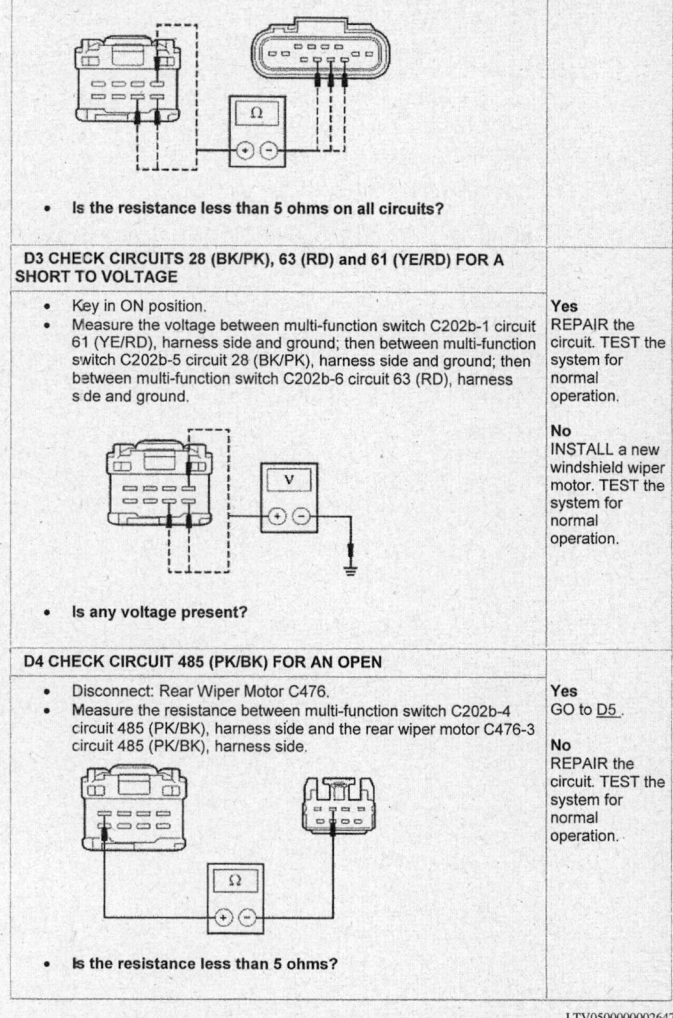

• **Is the resistance less than 5 ohms on all circuits?**	
D3 CHECK CIRCUITS 28 (BK/PK), 63 (RD) and 61 (YE/RD) FOR A SHORT TO VOLTAGE	
• Key in ON position. • Measure the voltage between multi-function switch C202b-1 circuit 61 (YE/RD), harness side and ground; then between multi-function switch C202b-5 circuit 28 (BK/PK), harness side and ground; then between multi-function switch C202b-6 circuit 63 (RD), harness side and ground. • **Is any voltage present?**	**Yes** REPAIR the circuit. TEST the system for normal operation. **No** INSTALL a new windshield wiper motor. TEST the system for normal operation.
D4 CHECK CIRCUIT 485 (PK/BK) FOR AN OPEN	
• Disconnect: Rear Wiper Motor C476. • Measure the resistance between multi-function switch C202b-4 circuit 485 (PK/BK), harness side and the rear wiper motor C476-3 circuit 485 (PK/BK), harness side. • **Is the resistance less than 5 ohms?**	**Yes** GO to D5 . **No** REPAIR the circuit. TEST the system for normal operation.

LTV0500000002647

Fig. 8   Test D: Intermittent Wiper Speed Does Not Operate Correctly (Part 2 of 3)

D5 CHECK CIRCUIT 485 (PK/BK) FOR A SHORT TO VOLTAGE

- Key in ON position.
- Measure the voltage between multi-function switch C202b-4 circuit 485 (PK/BK), harness side and ground.

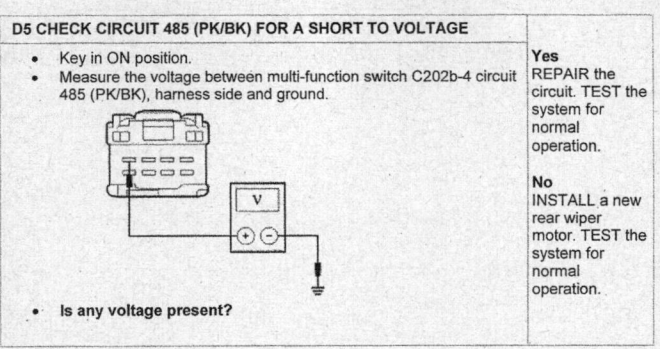

Yes
REPAIR the circuit. TEST the system for normal operation.

No
INSTALL a new rear wiper motor. TEST the system for normal operation.

- **Is any voltage present?**

LTV0500000002648

Fig. 8   Test D: Intermittent Wiper Speed Does Not Operate Correctly (Part 3 of 3)

E3 CHECK CIRCUITS 28 (BK/PK), 58 (WH) and 61 (YE/RD) FOR A SHORT TO VOLTAGE

- Key in ON position.
- Measure the voltage between multi-function switch C202b-5 circuit 28 (BK/PK), harness side and ground; then between multi-function switch C202b-8 circuit 58 (WH), harness side and ground; then between multi-function switch C202b-1 circuit 61 (YE/RD), harness side and ground.

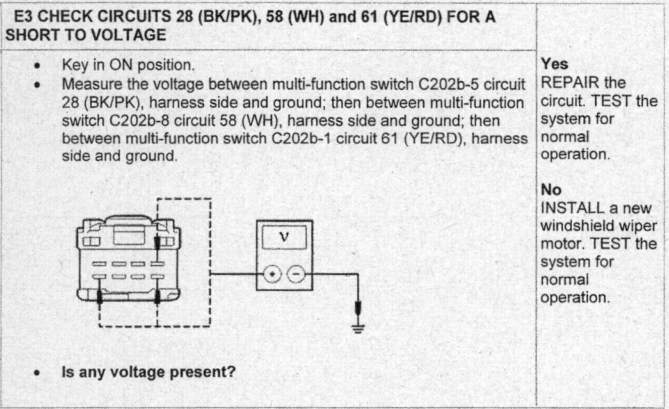

Yes
REPAIR the circuit. TEST the system for normal operation.

No
INSTALL a new windshield wiper motor. TEST the system for normal operation.

- **Is any voltage present?**

LTV0500000002650

Fig. 9   Test E: Front High/Low Wiper Speeds Do Not Operate Correctly (Part 2 of 2)

Test Step	Result / Action to Take
E1 CHECK THE MULTI-FUNCTION SWITCH • Disconnect: Multi-function Switch C202b. • Check the multi-function switch for correct operation. Refer to "Wiring Diagrams" • **Did the multi-function switch pass the component test?**	**Yes** GO to E2. **No** INSTALL a new multi-function switch. TEST the system for normal operation.

E2 CHECK CIRCUITS 28 (BK/PK), 58 (WH) and 61 (YE/RD) FOR AN OPEN

- Disconnect: Windshield Wiper Motor C125.
- Measure the resistance between the multi-function switch and the windshield wiper motor using the following chart:

Multi-function Switch C202b	Windshield Wiper Motor C125	Circuit
Pin 5	Pin 9	28 (BK/PK)
Pin 8	Pin 1	58 (WH)
Pin 1	Pin 10	61 (YE/RD)

Yes
GO to E3.

No
REPAIR the circuit. TEST the system for normal operation.

- **Is the resistance less than 5 ohms on all circuits?**

LTV0500000002649

Fig. 9   Test E: Front High/Low Wiper Speeds Do Not Operate Correctly (Part 1 of 2)

Test Step	Result / Action to Take
F1 CHECK CIRCUIT 941 (BK/WH) FOR GROUND • Disconnect: 2-Way Washer Motor Pump C1397. • Key in ON position. • Measure the resistance between 2-way washer motor pump C1397-2 circuit 941 (BK/WH), harness side and ground. • **Is the resistance less than 5 ohms?**	**Yes** GO to F3. **No** GO to F2.
F2 CHECK CIRCUIT 941 (BK/WH) FOR AN OPEN • Key in OFF position. • Disconnect: Windshield Wiper Motor C125. • Measure the resistance between windshield wiper motor C125-7 circuit 941 (BK/WH), harness side and 2-way washer motor pump C1397-2 circuit 941 (BK/WH), harness side. • **Is the resistance less than 5 ohms between the wiper motor and 2-way washer motor pump?**	**Yes** INSTALL a new windshield wiper motor. TEST the system for normal operation. **No** REPAIR the circuit. TEST the system for normal operation.
F3 CHECK CIRCUIT 946 (VT/LG) FOR GROUND • Measure the resistance between 2-way washer motor pump C1397-1 circuit 946 (VT/LG), harness side and ground.	**Yes** GO to F5. **No** GO to F4.

LTV0500000002651

Fig. 10   Test F: Washer Pump Is Inoperative (Part 1 of 4)

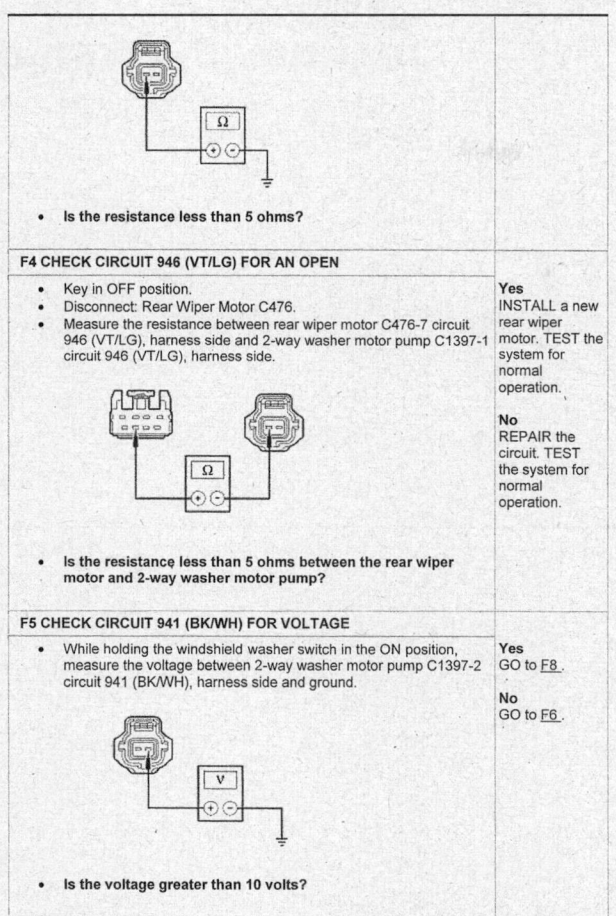

• Is the resistance less than 5 ohms?	
F4 CHECK CIRCUIT 946 (VT/LG) FOR AN OPEN	
• Key in OFF position. • Disconnect: Rear Wiper Motor C476. • Measure the resistance between rear wiper motor C476-7 circuit 946 (VT/LG), harness side and 2-way washer motor pump C1397-1 circuit 946 (VT/LG), harness side.	**Yes** INSTALL a new rear wiper motor. TEST the system for normal operation. **No** REPAIR the circuit. TEST the system for normal operation.
• Is the resistance less than 5 ohms between the rear wiper motor and 2-way washer motor pump?	
F5 CHECK CIRCUIT 941 (BK/WH) FOR VOLTAGE	
• While holding the windshield washer switch in the ON position, measure the voltage between 2-way washer motor pump C1397-2 circuit 941 (BK/WH), harness side and ground.	**Yes** GO to F8. **No** GO to F6.
• Is the voltage greater than 10 volts?	

LTV0500000002652

Fig. 10   Test F: Washer Pump Is Inoperative (Part 2 of 4)

F6 CHECK CIRCUIT 950 (WH/BK) FOR GROUND	
• D sconnect: Windshield Wiper Motor C125. • Key in ON position. • While holding the windshield washer switch in the ON position, measure the resistance between windshield wiper motor C125-12 circuit 950 (WH/BK), harness side and ground.	**Yes** INSTALL a new windshield wiper motor. TEST the system for normal operation. **No** GO to F7.
• Is the resistance between the windshield wiper motor and ground less than 5 ohms?	
F7 CHECK THE MULTI-FUNCTION SWITCH	
• Key in OFF position. • Disconnect: Multi-function Switch C202b. • Check the multi-function switch for correct operation. Refer to "Wiring Diagrams" • **Did the multi-function switch pass the component test?**	**Yes** REPAIR open in circuit 950 (WH/BK). TEST the system for normal operation. **No** INSTALL a new multi-function switch. TEST the system for normal operation.
F8 CHECK CIRCUIT 946 (VT/LG) FOR VOLTAGE	
• While holding the rear washer switch in the ON position, measure the voltage between 2-way washer motor pump C1397-1 circuit 946 (VT/LG), harness side and ground.	**Yes** INSTALL a new 2-way washer pump motor. **No** GO to F9.

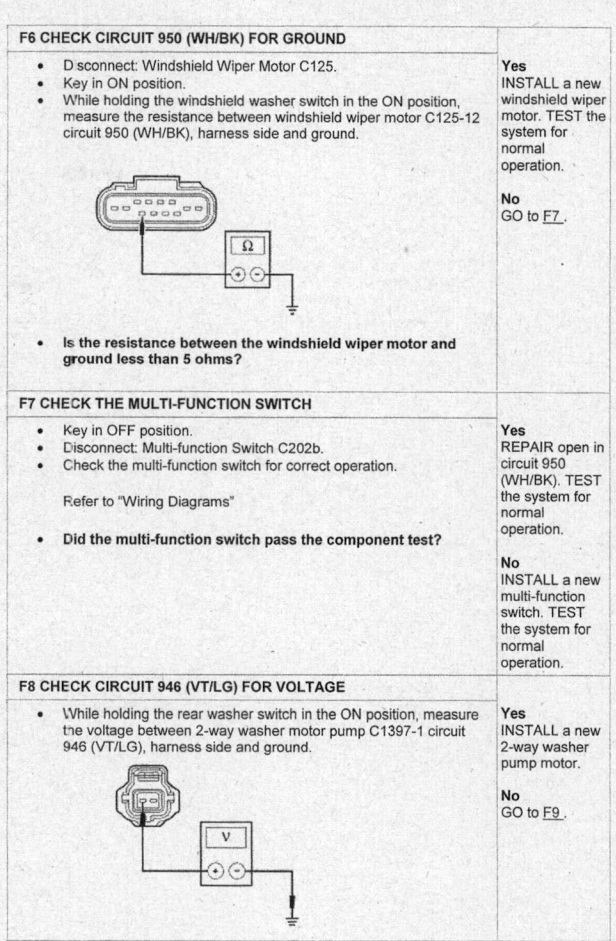

LTV0500000002653

Fig. 10   Test F: Washer Pump Is Inoperative (Part 3 of 4)

• Is the voltage greater than 10 volts?	
F9 CHECK THE MULTI-FUNCTION SWITCH	
• Key in OFF position. • Disconnect: Multi-function Switch C202b. • Check the multi-function switch for correct operation. Refer to "Wiring Diagrams" • **Did the multi-function switch pass the component test?**	**Yes** GO to F10. **No** INSTALL a new multi-function switch. TEST the system for normal operation.
F10 CHECK CIRCUIT 488 (DG) AND 485 (PK/BK) FOR AN OPEN	
• Key in OFF position. • Disconnect: Rear Wiper Motor C476. • Measure the resistance between rear wiper motor C476-4 circuit 488 (DG), harness side and multi-function switch C202b-3 circuit 488 (DG), harness side; then between rear wiper motor C476-3 circuit 485 (PK/BK), harness side and multi-function switch C202b-4 circuit 485 (PK/BK), harness side.	**Yes** INSTALL a new rear wiper motor. TEST the system for normal operation. **No** REPAIR the circuit. TEST the system for normal operation.
• Are both resistance measurements less than 5 ohms between the multi-function switch and rear wiper motor?	

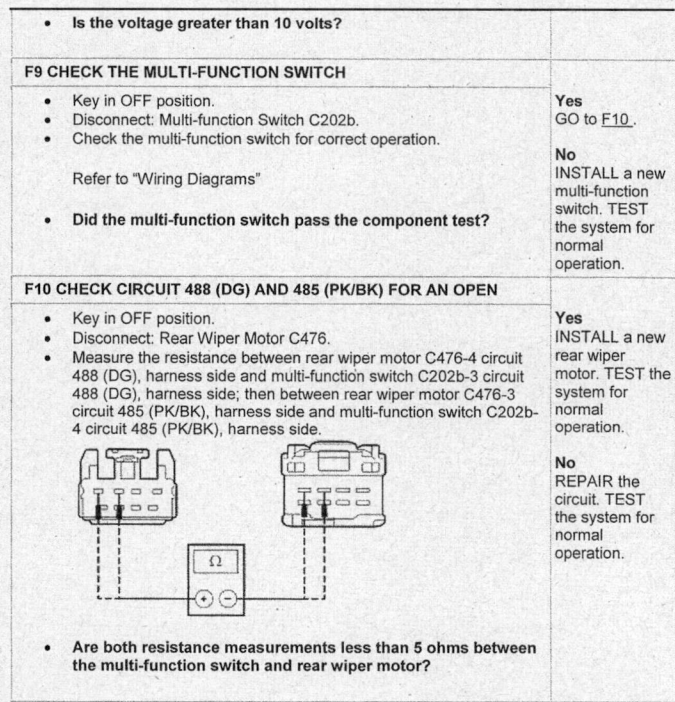

LTV0500000002654

Fig. 10   Test F: Washer Pump Is Inoperative (Part 4 of 4)

Test Step	Result / Action to Take
G1 CHECK CIRCUIT 671 (LB) FOR VOLTAGE	
• Disconnect: Windshield Wiper Motor C125. • Key in ON position. • Measure the voltage between windshield wiper motor C125-2 circuit 671 (LB), harness side and ground.	**Yes** INSTALL a new windshield wiper motor. TEST the system for normal operation. **No** GO to G2.
• Is the voltage approximately 5 volts?	
G2 CHECK CIRCUIT 671 (LB) FOR AN OPEN OR SHORT TO GROUND	
• Key in OFF position. • Disconnect: SJB C2280c. • Measure the resistance between SJB C2280c-37 circuit 671 (LB), harness side and windshield wiper motor C125-2 circuit 671 (LB), harness side; then between SJB C2280c-37 circuit 671 (LB), harness side and ground.	**Yes** GO to G3. **No** REPAIR the circuit. TEST the system for normal operation.

LTV0500000002655

Fig. 11   Test G: Headlamps Do Not Illuminate When Wipers Are On (Part 1 of 2)

• Is the resistance less than 5 ohms between the SJB and windshield wiper motor and greater than 10,000 ohms between the SJB and ground?	
G3 CHECK FOR CORRECT MODULE OPERATION	

• Disconnect all the SJB connectors.
• Check for:
  ▪ corrosion.
  ▪ pushed-out pins.
• Connect all the SJB connectors and make sure they are seated correctly.
• Operate the system and verify the concern is still present.
• **Is the concern still present?**
	Yes
	INSTALL a new SJB. CLEAR the DTCs. REPEAT the SJB self-test.
	
	No
	The system is operating correctly at this time. Concern may have been caused by a loose or corroded connector. CLEAR the DTCs. REPEAT the self-test.

LTV0500000002656

Fig. 11   Test G: Headlamps Do Not Illuminate When Wipers Are On (Part 2 of 2)

COMPONENT DIAGNOSIS & TESTING

Refer to "Aviator" for component diagnosis and testing procedures.

F-150 & Mark LT

NOTE: On Air Bag Equipped Models, Refer To "Air Bag System Precautions" Located In The Front Of This Manual For System Disarming & Arming Procedures.

NOTE: "Electrical Symbol & Wire Color Code Identification" Located In The Front Of This Manual May Be Used As An Aid When Using Wiring Diagrams Found In This Section.

NOTE: Refer To "Computer Relearn Procedures" Located In The Front Of This Manual When Battery Power To The Computer Has Been Interrupted.

INDEX

	Page No.		Page No.		Page No.
Component Diagnosis & Testing	3-153	System Diagnosis & Testing	3-147	Diagnostic Tests	3-147
Diagnostic Chart Index	3-149	Accessing Diagnostic Trouble Codes	3-147	Diagnostic Trouble Code Interpretation	3-147
Precautions	3-147	Clearing Diagnostic Trouble Codes	3-147	Wiring Diagrams	3-147
Battery Ground Cable	3-147				

PRECAUTIONS

Battery Ground Cable

Prior to service, disconnect battery ground cable and isolate as required.

SYSTEM DIAGNOSIS & TESTING

Accessing Diagnostic Trouble Codes

Connect a suitably programmed scan tool and Vehicle Communication Module (VCM) with appropriate adapters, or equivalents, to the Data Link Connector (DCL) located in the passenger compartment beneath the instrument panel. Follow tool manufacturer's instructions for accessing speed control Diagnostic Trouble Codes (DTC).

Diagnostic Trouble Code Interpretation

Refer to **Fig. 1** for diagnostic trouble code interpretation.

Wiring Diagrams

Refer to **Figs. 2 and 3** for wiring diagrams.

Diagnostic Tests

Refer to **Figs. 4 through 11** for diagnostic tests.

Code	Description
B1240	Rear Washer Pump Relay Circuit Failure
B1241	Rear Washer Pump Relay Circuit Short To Battery
B1342	ECU Faulty
B1431	Wiper/Brake Run Relay Circuit Failure
B1432	Wiper Run Relay Short To Battery
B1434	Wiper Hi/Lo Speed Relay Circuit Failure
B1436	Wiper Hi/Lo Speed Relay Circuit Short To Battery
B1438	Wiper Mode Select Switch Circuit Failure
B1441	Wiper Mode Select Switch Input Short To Ground
B1446	Wiper Park Sense Circuit Failure
B1450	Wiper/Washer Interval Delay Switch Input Circuit Failure
B1453	Wiper/Washer Interval Delay Switch Input Short To Ground
B1458	Wiper/Washer Pump Motor Relay Coil Circuit Failure
B1460	Wiper/Washer Pump Motor Relay Coil Short To Battery
B1466	Wiper Speed Not Switching
B1467	Wiper Hi/Lo Speed Circuit Motor Short To Battery
B1473	Wiper Low Speed Circuit Motor Failure
B1476	Wiper High Speed Circuit Motor Failure
B1611	Rear Wiper Mode Circuit Failure
B1614	Rear Wiper Mode Switch Circuit Short To Ground
B1820	Rear Wiper Motor Up Relay Circuit Short To Battery
B1839	Rear Wiper Motor Circuit Failure
B1840	Wiper Front Power Circuit Failure

Fig. 1 Diagnostic trouble code interpretation

Clearing Diagnostic Trouble Codes

Connect a suitably programmed scan tool and Vehicle Communication Module (VCM) with appropriate adapters, or equivalents, to the Data Link Connector (DCL) located in the passenger compartment beneath the instrument panel. Follow tool manufacturer's instructions for accessing speed control Diagnostic Trouble Codes (DTC).

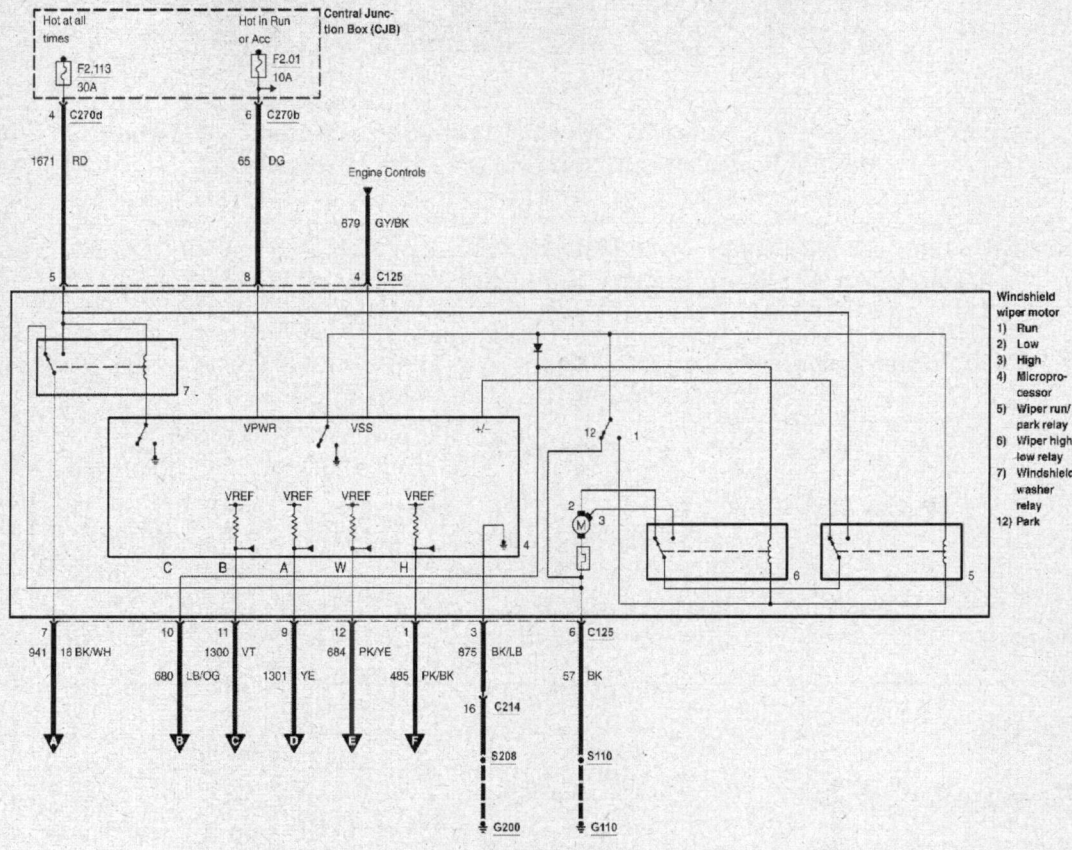

Fig. 2 Wiring diagram (Part 1 of 2). 2002–04 F-150

LTV0500000001892

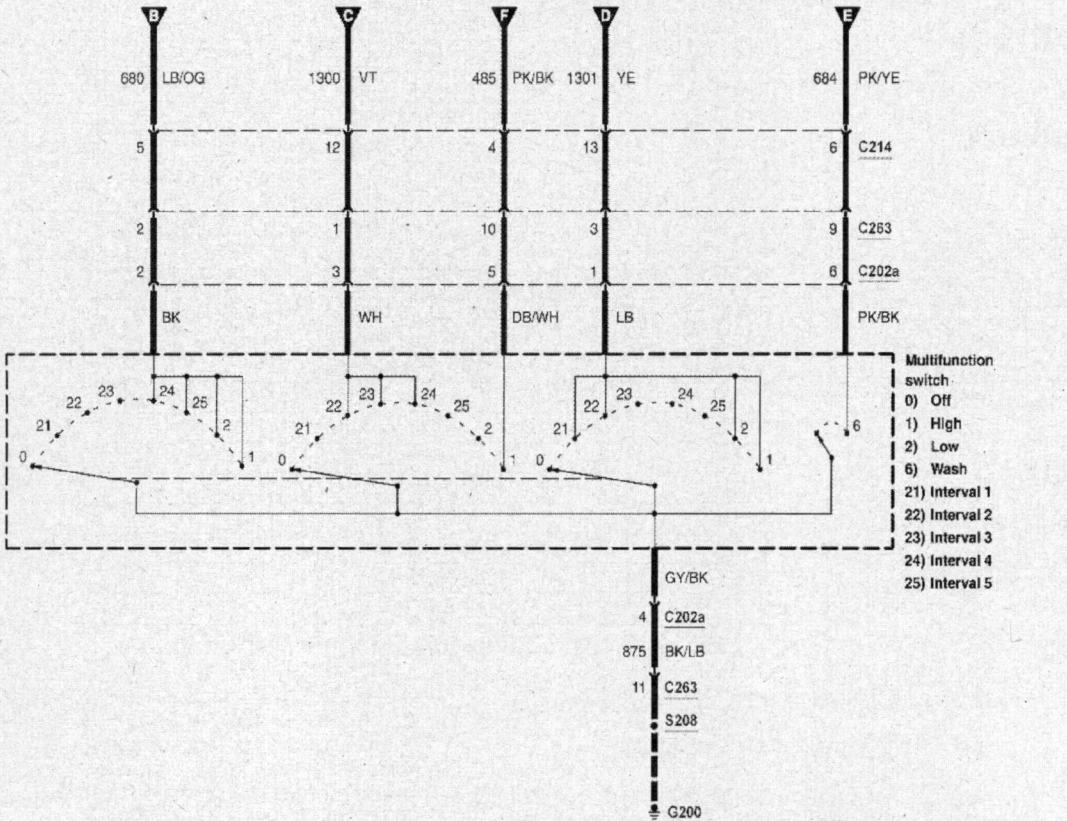

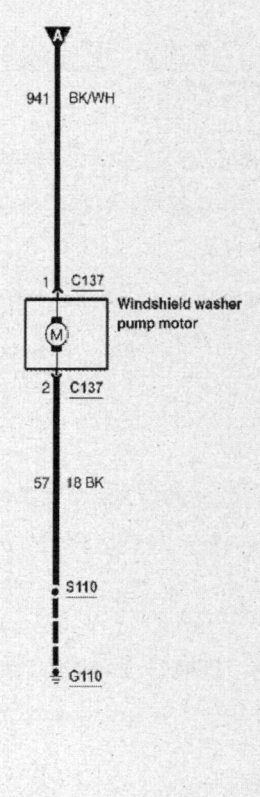

Fig. 2 Wiring diagram (Part 2 of 2). 2002–04 F-150

LTV0500000001893

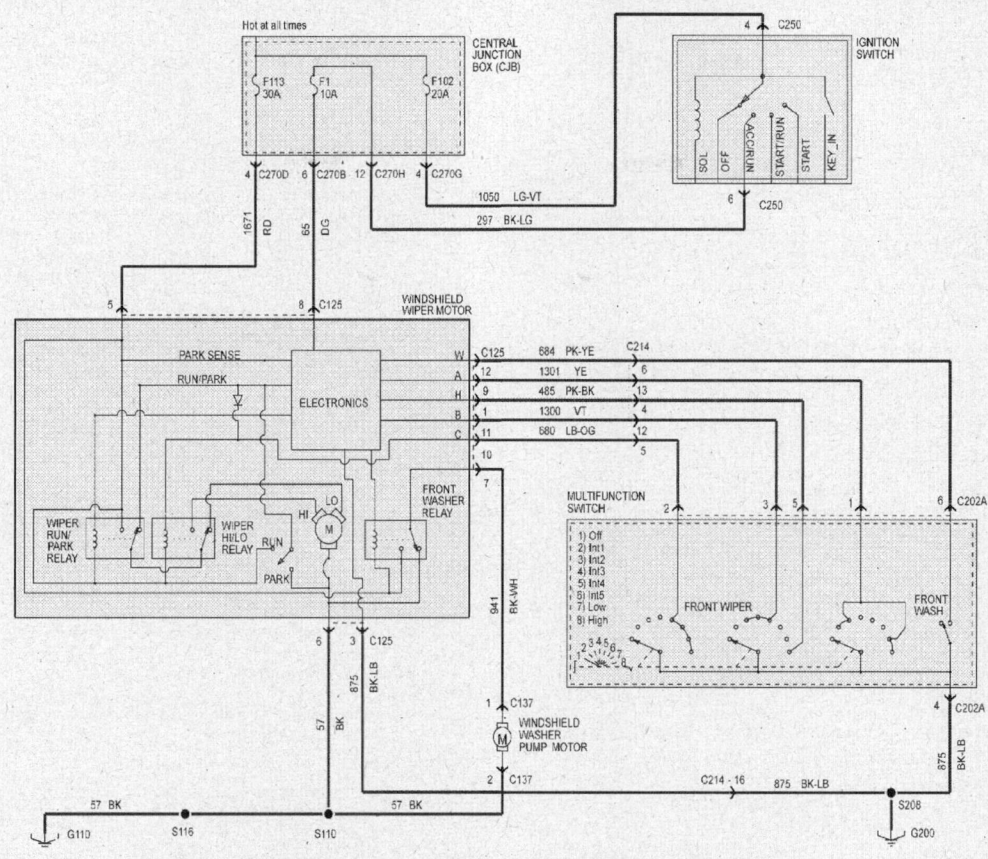

Fig. 3   Wiring diagram. Mark LT & 2005–06 F-150

DIAGNOSTIC CHART INDEX

Test	Description	Page No.	Fig. No.
—	Symptom Tests	3-150	4
A	Wipers Are Inoperative	3-150	5
B	Wipers Stay On Continuously	3-151	6
C	High/Low Wiper Speeds Do Not Operate Correctly, Interval Wiper Mode Is OK	3-151	7
D	Interval Wiper Speed Does Not Operate Correctly, High & Low Speeds OK	3-152	8
E	Wipers Do Not Operate Correctly In Mist Position	3-152	9
F	Washer Pump Is Inoperative	3-152	10
G	Speed Dependent Interval Mode Does Not Operate Correctly	3-153	11

Condition	Possible Sources	Action
• The wipers are inoperative	• Fuse(s) • Multi-function switch • Circuitry • Ignition switch • Windshield wiper motor	• Go To Pinpoint Test A.
• The wipers operate only in HIGH SPEED regardless of the speed selected with the multi-function switch	• Windshield wiper motor	• Go To Pinpoint Test B.
• The wipers stay ON continuously	• Windshield wiper motor • Multi-function switch • Circuitry	• Go To Pinpoint Test B.
• The HIGH/LOW wiper speeds do not operate correctly (INTERVAL wiper mode OK)	• Multi-function switch • Circuitry • Windshield wiper motor	• Go To Pinpoint Test C.
• The INTERVAL wiper speed does not operate correctly (HIGH/LOW speeds OK)	• Multi-function switch • Circuitry • Windshield wiper motor	• Go To Pinpoint Test D.
• The wipers do not operate correctly in the MIST position	• Multi-function switch • Circuitry • Washer pump • Windshield wiper motor	• Go To Pinpoint Test E.

LTV0500000002365

Fig. 4   Symptom Tests (Part 1 of 2)

• The washer pump is inoperative	• Washer pump • Multi-function switch • Windshield wiper motor • Circuitry	• Go To Pinpoint Test F.
• The speed dependent INTERVAL mode does not operate correctly	• Windshield wiper motor • Circuitry • Powertrain control module (PCM)	• Go To Pinpoint Test G.
• The wipers will not park at correct position	• Windshield wiper motor • Pivot arm adjustment • Linkage	• Repair and/or adjust wiper arm and Pivot.

LTV0500000002366

Fig. 4   Symptom Tests (Part 2 of 2)

Test Step	Result / Action to Take
A1 CHECK CIRCUITS 65 (DG) AND 1671 (RD) FOR VOLTAGE	
• Key in OFF position. • Disconnect: Windshield Wiper Motor C125. • Key in ON position. • Measure the voltage between windshield wiper C125-5, circuit 1671 (RD), harness side and ground; and between windshield wiper motor C125-8, circuit 65 (DG), harness side and ground. • Are the voltages greater than 10 volts?	**Yes** GO to A2. **No** VERIFY the central junction box (CJB) fuses 1 (10A) and 113 (30A) are OK. If OK, REPAIR the circuit(s) in question. TEST the system for normal operation.
A2 CHECK CIRCUITS 57 (BK) AND 875 (BK/LB) FOR OPENS	
• Key in OFF position. • Measure the resistance between windshield wiper C125-6, circuit 57 (BK), harness side and ground; and between windshield wiper motor C125-3, circuit 875 (BK/LB), harness side and ground. • Are the resistances less than 5 ohms?	**Yes** GO to A3. **No** REPAIR the circuit(s) in question. TEST the system for normal operation.
A3 CHECK THE MULTI-FUNCTION SWITCH	
• Disconnect: Multi-Function Switch C202a.	**Yes** GO to A4.

LTV0500000002367

Fig. 5   Test A: Wipers Are Inoperative (Part 1 of 3)

• Carry out the multi-function switch component test. Refer to "Wiring Diagrams" • **Did the multi-function switch pass the component test?**	**No** INSTALL a new multi-function switch.
A4 CHECK CIRCUIT 875 (BK/LB) FOR AN OPEN	
• Measure the resistance between C202a-4, circuit 875 (BK/LB), harness side and ground. • Is the resistance less than 5 ohms?	**Yes** GO to A5. **No** REPAIR the circuit. TEST the system for normal operation.
A5 CHECK CIRCUITS 680 (LB/OG), 1300 (PK), 485 (PK/BK) AND 1301 (YE) FOR OPENS	
• Using the following table, measure the resistance between the multi-function switch C202a harness side and the windshield wiper motor C125 harness side:	**Yes** GO to A6. **No** REPAIR the circuit(s) in question. TEST the system for normal operation.

Multi-Function Switch C202a	Windshield Wiper Motor C125
C202a-2, circuit 680 (LB/OG)	C125-10, circuit 680 (LB/OG)
C202a-3, circuit 1300 (PK)	C125-11, circuit 1300 (PK)
C202a-5, 485 (PK/BK)	C125-1, circuit 485 (PK/BK)
C202a-1, circuit 1301 (YE)	C125-9, circuit 1301 (YE)

LTV0500000002368

Fig. 5   Test A: Wipers Are Inoperative (Part 2 of 3)

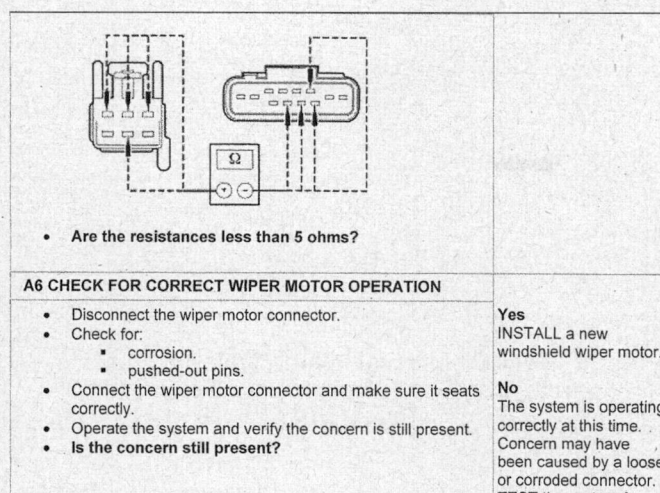

- **Are the resistances less than 5 ohms?**

A6 CHECK FOR CORRECT WIPER MOTOR OPERATION	
• Disconnect the wiper motor connector. • Check for: ▪ corrosion. ▪ pushed-out pins. • Connect the wiper motor connector and make sure it seats correctly. • Operate the system and verify the concern is still present. • **Is the concern still present?**	**Yes** INSTALL a new windshield wiper motor. **No** The system is operating correctly at this time. Concern may have been caused by a loose or corroded connector. TEST the system for normal operation.

LTV0500000002369

Fig. 5   Test A: Wipers Are Inoperative (Part 3 of 3)

B3 CHECK FOR CORRECT WIPER MOTOR OPERATION	
• Disconnect the wiper motor connector. • Check for: ▪ corrosion. ▪ pushed-out pins. • Connect the wiper motor connectors and make sure they seat correctly. • Operate the system and verify the concern is still present. • **Is the concern still present?**	**Yes** INSTALL a new windshield wiper motor. **No** The system is operating correctly at this time. Concern may have been caused by a loose or corroded connector. TEST the system for normal operation.

LTV0500000002371

Fig. 6   Test B: Wipers Stay On Continuously (Part 2 of 2)

Test Step	Result / Action to Take
C1 CHECK THE MULTI-FUNCTION SWITCH	
• Key in OFF position. • Disconnect: Multi-Function Switch C202a. • Carry out the multi-function switch component test. Refer to "Wiring Diagrams" • **Did the multi-function switch pass the component test?**	**Yes** GO to C2. **No** INSTALL a new multi-function switch.
C2 CHECK CIRCUITS 680 (LB/OG), 485 (PK/BK) AND 1301 (YE) FOR OPENS	
• Disconnect: Windshield Wiper Motor C125. • Using the following table, measure the resistance between multi-function switch C202a harness side and windshield wiper motor C125 harness side:	**Yes** GO to C3. **No** REPAIR the circuit(s) in question. TEST the system for normal operation.

Multi-Function Switch C202a	Windshield Wiper Motor C125
C202a-2, circuit 680 (LB/OG)	C125-10, circuit 680 (LB/OG)
C202a-5, circuit 485 (PK/BK)	C125-1, circuit 485 (PK/BK)
C202a-1, circuit 1301 (YE)	C125-9, circuit 1301 (YE)

LTV0500000002372

Fig. 7   Test C: High/Low Wiper Speeds Do Not Operate Correctly, Interval Wiper Mode Is OK (Part 1 of 2)

Test Step	Result / Action to Take
B1 CHECK THE MULTI-FUNCTION SWITCH	
• Key in OFF position. • Disconnect: Multi-Function Switch C202a. • Carry out the multi-function switch component test. Refer to "Wiring Diagrams" • **Did the multi-function switch pass the component test?**	**Yes** GO to B2. **No** INSTALL a new multi-function switch.
B2 CHECK CIRCUITS 680 (LB/OG), 1300 (PK), 485 (PK/BK) AND 1301 (YE) FOR SHORTS	
• Disconnect: Windshield Wiper Motor C125. • Using the following table, measure the resistance between windshield wiper motor C125 harness side and ground:	**Yes** GO to B3. **No** REPAIR the circuit(s) in question. TEST the system for normal operation.

Windshield Wiper Motor C125	Ground
C125-10, circuit 680 (LB/OG)	ground
C125-11, circuit 1300 (PK)	ground
C125-1, circuit 485 (PK/BK)	ground
C125-9, circuit 1301 (YE)	ground

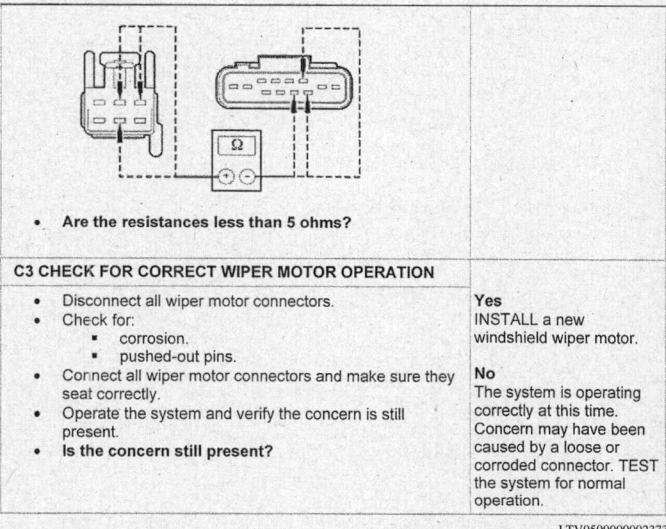

- **Are the resistances greater than 10,000 ohms?**

LTV0500000002370

Fig. 6   Test B: Wipers Stay On Continuously (Part 1 of 2)

• **Are the resistances less than 5 ohms?**	
C3 CHECK FOR CORRECT WIPER MOTOR OPERATION	
• Disconnect all wiper motor connectors. • Check for: ▪ corrosion. ▪ pushed-out pins. • Connect all wiper motor connectors and make sure they seat correctly. • Operate the system and verify the concern is still present. • **Is the concern still present?**	**Yes** INSTALL a new windshield wiper motor. **No** The system is operating correctly at this time. Concern may have been caused by a loose or corroded connector. TEST the system for normal operation.

LTV0500000002373

Fig. 7   Test C: High/Low Wiper Speeds Do Not Operate Correctly, Interval Wiper Mode Is OK (Part 2 of 2)

Test Step	Result / Action to Take
D1 CHECK THE MULTI-FUNCTION SWITCH <ul><li>Key in OFF position.</li><li>Disconnect: Multi-Function Switch C202a.</li><li>Carry out the multi-function switch component test.</li></ul> Refer to "Wiring Diagrams" <ul><li>**Did the multi-function switch pass the component test?**</li></ul>	**Yes** GO to D2. **No** INSTALL a new multi-function switch. TEST the system for normal operation.
D2 CHECK CIRCUITS 680 (LB/OG), 485 (PK/BK) AND 1301 (YE) FOR OPENS <ul><li>Disconnect: Windshield Wiper Motor C125.</li><li>Using the following table, measure the resistance between multi-function switch C202a harness side and windshield wiper motor C125 harness side:</li></ul>	**Yes** GO to D3. **No** REPAIR the circuit(s) in question. TEST the system for normal operation.

Multi-Function Switch C202a	Windshield Wiper Motor C125
C202a-2, circuit 680 (LB/OG)	C125-10, circuit 680 (LB/OG)
C202a-5, circuit 485 (PK/BK)	C125-1, circuit 485 (PK/BK)
C202a-1, circuit 1301 (YE)	C125-9, circuit 1301 (YE)
C202a-3, circuit 1300 (PK)	C125-11, circuit 1300 (PK)

Fig. 8 Test D: Interval Wiper Speed Does Not Operate Correctly, High & Low Speeds OK (Part 1 of 2)

LTV0500000002374

Test Step	Result / Action to Take
E1 CHECK THE MULTI-FUNCTION SWITCH <ul><li>Key in OFF position.</li><li>Disconnect: Multi-Function Switch C202a.</li><li>Carry out the multi-function switch component test.</li></ul> Refer to "Wiring Diagrams" <ul><li>**Did the multi-function switch pass the component test?**</li></ul>	**Yes** GO to E2. **No** INSTALL a new multi-function switch.
E2 CHECK CIRCUIT 875 (BK/LB) FOR AN OPEN <ul><li>Measure the resistance between C202a-4, circuit 875 (BK/LB), harness side and ground.</li></ul> <ul><li>Is the resistance less than 5 ohms?</li></ul>	**Yes** GO to E3. **No** REPAIR the circuit. TEST the system for normal operation.
E3 CHECK CIRCUIT 684 (PK/YE) FOR AN OPEN <ul><li>Disconnect: Windshield Wiper Motor C125.</li><li>Measure the resistance between C202a-6, circuit 684 (PK/YE), harness side and C125-12, circuit 684 (PK/YE), harness side.</li></ul> <ul><li>Is the resistance less than 5 ohms?</li></ul>	**Yes** Go To Pinpoint Test F to diagnose the washer circuit. **No** REPAIR the circuit. TEST the system for normal operation.

LTV0500000002376

Fig. 9 Test E: Wipers Do Not Operate Correctly In Mist Position

<ul><li>Are the resistances less than 5 ohms?</li></ul>	
D3 CHECK FOR CORRECT WIPER MOTOR OPERATION <ul><li>Disconnect all wiper motor connectors.</li><li>Check for:<ul><li>corrosion.</li><li>pushed-out pins.</li></ul></li><li>Connect all wiper motor connectors and make sure they seat correctly.</li><li>Operate the system and verify the concern is still present.</li><li>**Is the concern still present?**</li></ul>	**Yes** INSTALL a new windshield wiper motor. **No** The system is operating correctly at this time. Concern may have been caused by a loose or corroded connector. TEST the system for normal operation.

LTV0500000002375

Fig. 8 Test D: Interval Wiper Speed Does Not Operate Correctly, High & Low Speeds OK (Part 2 of 2)

Test Step	Result / Action to Take
F1 CHECK CIRCUIT 684 (PK/YE) FOR A SHORT TO GROUND <ul><li>Disconnect: Windshield Wiper Motor C125.</li><li>Key in ON position.</li><li>Measure the resistance between C125-12, circuit 684 (PK/YE), harness side and ground while depressing the multi-function switch to the windshield wiper wash position.</li></ul> <ul><li>Is the resistance less than 5 ohms?</li></ul>	**Yes** GO to F3. **No** GO to F2.
F2 CHECK THE MULTI-FUNCTION SWITCH <ul><li>Key in OFF position.</li><li>Disconnect: Multi-Function Switch C202a.</li><li>Carry out the multi-function switch component test.</li></ul> Refer to "Wiring Diagrams" <ul><li>**Did the multi-function switch pass the component test?**</li></ul>	**Yes** REPAIR circuit 685 (PK/YE) for an open. TEST the system for normal operation. **No** INSTALL a new multi-function switch
F3 CHECK CIRCUIT 941 (BK/WH) FOR A SHORT TO GROUND <ul><li>Key in OFF position.</li><li>Connect: Windshield Wiper Motor C125.</li><li>Disconnect: Washer Pump Motor C137.</li><li>Measure the resistance between C137-1, circuit 941 (BK/WH) harness side and ground.</li></ul>	**Yes** GO to F4. **No** GO to F5.

LTV0500000002377

Fig. 10 Test F: Washer Pump Is Inoperative (Part 1 of 3)

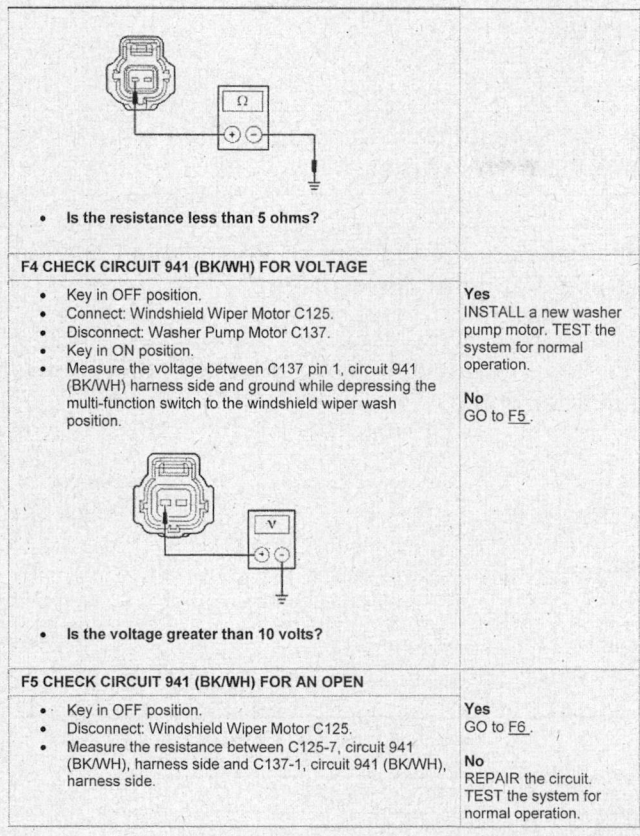

- **Is the resistance less than 5 ohms?**

F4 CHECK CIRCUIT 941 (BK/WH) FOR VOLTAGE	
• Key in OFF position. • Connect: Windshield Wiper Motor C125. • Disconnect: Washer Pump Motor C137. • Key in ON position. • Measure the voltage between C137 pin 1, circuit 941 (BK/WH) harness side and ground while depressing the multi-function switch to the windshield wiper wash position.	**Yes** INSTALL a new washer pump motor. TEST the system for normal operation. **No** GO to F5.

- **Is the voltage greater than 10 volts?**

F5 CHECK CIRCUIT 941 (BK/WH) FOR AN OPEN	
• Key in OFF position. • Disconnect: Windshield Wiper Motor C125. • Measure the resistance between C125-7, circuit 941 (BK/WH), harness side and C137-1, circuit 941 (BK/WH), harness side.	**Yes** GO to F6. **No** REPAIR the circuit. TEST the system for normal operation.

LTV0500000002378

**Fig. 10   Test F: Washer Pump Is Inoperative
(Part 2 of 3)**

Test Step	Result / Action to Take
G1 CHECK THE PCM — MONITOR THE VSS	
• Monitor the VSS while driving the vehicle from 0 to 88.5 kph (55 mph). • **Does the VSS agree with the PCM PIDs?**	**Yes** GO to G2. **No** Check VSS system.
G2 CHECK CIRCUIT 679 (GY/BK) FOR AN OPEN	
• Disconnect: PCM C175a. • Disconnect: Windshield Wiper Motor C125. • Measure the resistance between PCM C175b-63, circuit 679 (GY/BK), harness side and windshield wiper motor C125-4, circuit 679 (GY/BK), harness side.	**Yes** GO to G3. **No** REPAIR the circuit.
• Is the resistance less than 5 ohms?	
G3 CHECK CIRCUIT 679 (GY/BK) FOR A SHORT TO GROUND	
• Measure the resistance between PCM C175b-63, circuit 679 (GY/BK), harness side and ground.	**Yes** GO to G4. **No** REPAIR the circuit.
• Is the resistance greater than 10,000 ohms?	

LTV0500000002380

**Fig. 11   Test G: Speed Dependent Interval
Mode Does Not Operate Correctly (Part 1 of 2)**

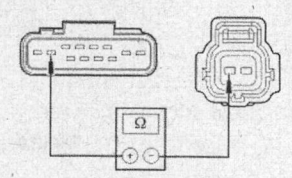

- **Is the resistance less than 5 ohms?**

F6 CHECK FOR CORRECT WIPER MOTOR OPERATION	

• Disconnect the wiper motor connector.
• Check for:
  ▪ corrosion.
  ▪ pushed-out pins.
• Connect the wiper motor connector and make sure it seats correctly.
• Operate the system and verify the concern is still present.
• **Is the concern still present?**
	Yes
	INSTALL a new windshield wiper motor.
	No
	The system is working correctly at this time. The concern might have been caused by a loose or corroded connector. TEST the system for normal operation.

LTV0500000002379

**Fig. 10   Test F: Washer Pump Is Inoperative
(Part 3 of 3)**

G4 CHECK FOR CORRECT WIPER MOTOR OPERATION	

• Disconnect all wiper motor connectors.
• Check for:
  ▪ corrosion.
  ▪ pushed-out pins.
• Connect all wiper motor connectors and make sure they seat correctly.
• Operate the system and verify the concern is still present.
• **Is the concern still present?**
	Yes
	INSTALL a new windshield wiper motor.
	No
	The system is operating correctly at this time. Concern may have been caused by a loose or corroded connector. TEST the system for normal operation.

LTV0500000002381

**Fig. 11   Test G: Speed Dependent Interval Mode
Does Not Operate Correctly (Part 2 of 2)**

COMPONENT DIAGNOSIS & TESTING

Refer to "Aviator" for component diagnosis and testing procedures.

Ranger

NOTE: On Air Bag Equipped Models, Refer To "Air Bag System Precautions" Located In The Front Of This Manual For System Disarming & Arming Procedures.

NOTE: "Electrical Symbol & Wire Color Code Identification" Located In The Front Of This Manual May Be Used As An Aid When Using Wiring Diagrams Found In This Section.

NOTE: Refer To "Computer Relearn Procedures" Located In The Front Of This Manual When Battery Power To The Computer Has Been Interrupted.

INDEX

	Page No.		Page No.		Page No.
Component Diagnosis &		Battery Ground Cable...........	3-154	Diagnostic Tests	3-154
Testing........................	3-165	**System Diagnosis & Testing**	3-154	Diagnostic Trouble Code	
Wiper Motor Current Draw Test .	3-165	Accessing Diagnostic Trouble		Interpretation	3-154
Wiper Switch Continuity Test....	3-165	Codes	3-154	Wiring Diagrams................	3-154
Diagnostic Chart Index..........	3-157	Clearing Diagnostic Trouble			
Precautions......................	3-154	Codes	3-154		

PRECAUTIONS

Battery Ground Cable

Prior to service, disconnect battery ground cable and isolate as required.

SYSTEM DIAGNOSIS & TESTING

Accessing Diagnostic Trouble Codes

Connect a suitably programmed scan tool and Vehicle Communication Module (VCM) with appropriate adapters, or equivalents, to the Data Link Connector (DCL) located in the passenger compartment beneath the instrument panel. Follow tool manufacturer's instructions for accessing speed control Diagnostic Trouble Codes (DTC).

Diagnostic Trouble Code Interpretation

Refer to **Fig. 1** for diagnostic trouble code interpretation.

Code	Description
B1431	Wiper/Brake Run Relay Circuit Failure
B1432	Wiper Run Relay Short To Battery
B1434	Wiper Hi/Lo Speed Relay Circuit Failure
B1436	Wiper Hi/Lo Speed Relay Circuit Short To Battery
B1342	ECU Is Faulty
B1446	Wiper Park Sense Circuit Failure
B1460	Wiper/Washer Pump Motor Relay Coil Short To Battery
B1466	Wiper Speed Not Switching
B1840	Wiper Power Circuit Failure
B2179	Wiper Select Switch A Short to Ground
B2180	Wiper Select Switch B Short to Ground
B2181	Wiper Select Switch C Short to Ground
B2183	Wiper Select Switch H Short to Ground
B2184	Wiper Select Switch W Short to Grounc SJB

Fig. 1 Diagnostic trouble code interpretation

Wiring Diagrams

Refer to **Figs. 2 and 3** for wiring diagrams.

Diagnostic Tests

Refer to **Figs. 4 through 11** for diagnostic tests.

Clearing Diagnostic Trouble Codes

Connect a suitably programmed scan tool and Vehicle Communication Module (VCM) with appropriate adapters, or equivalents, to the Data Link Connector (DCL) located in the passenger compartment beneath the instrument panel. Follow tool manufacturer's instructions for accessing speed control Diagnostic Trouble Codes (DTC).

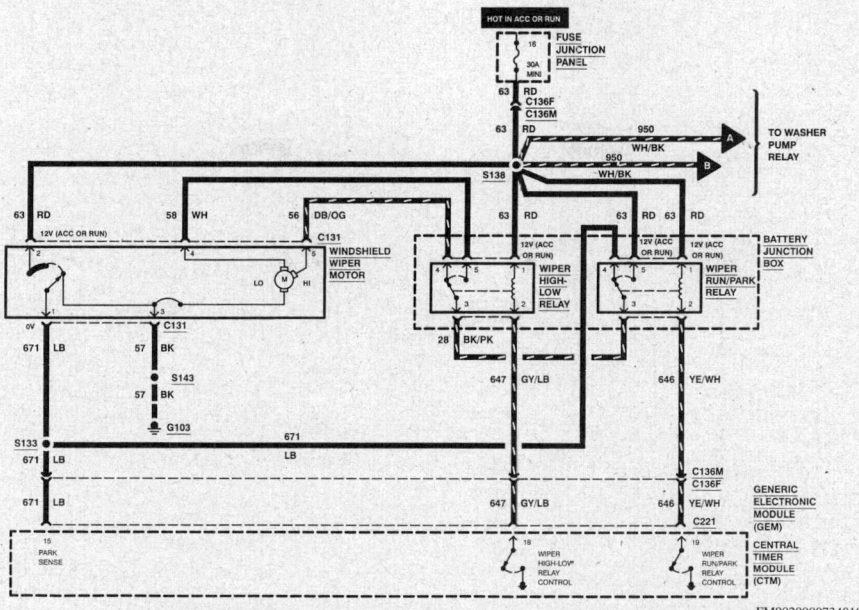

Fig. 2 Front wiring diagram (Part 1 of 2). 2002–04

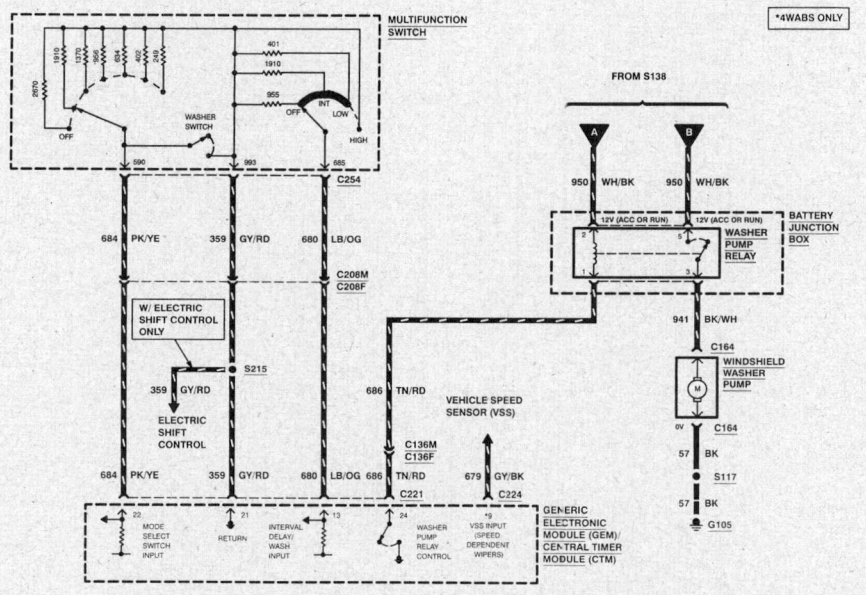

Fig. 2 Front wiring diagram (Part 2 of 2). 2002–04

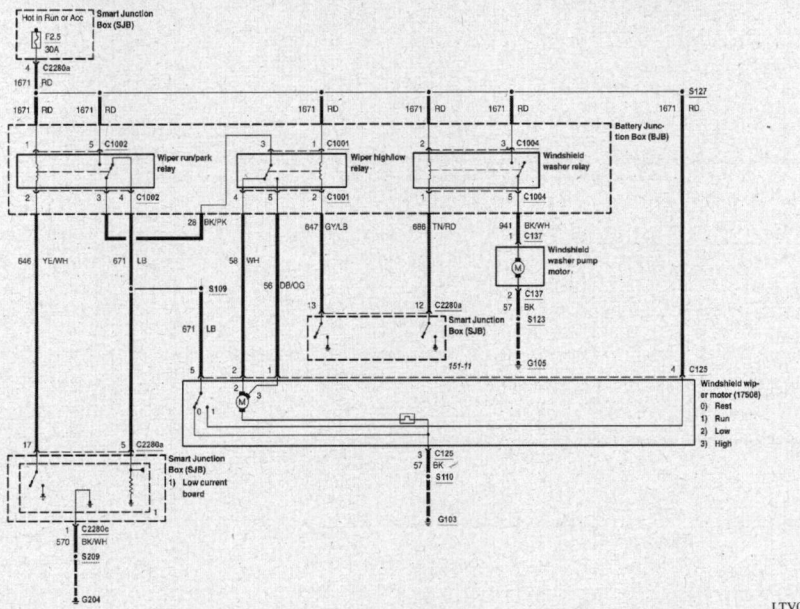

Fig. 3 Wiper diagram (Part 1 of 2). 2005-06

LTV050000002389

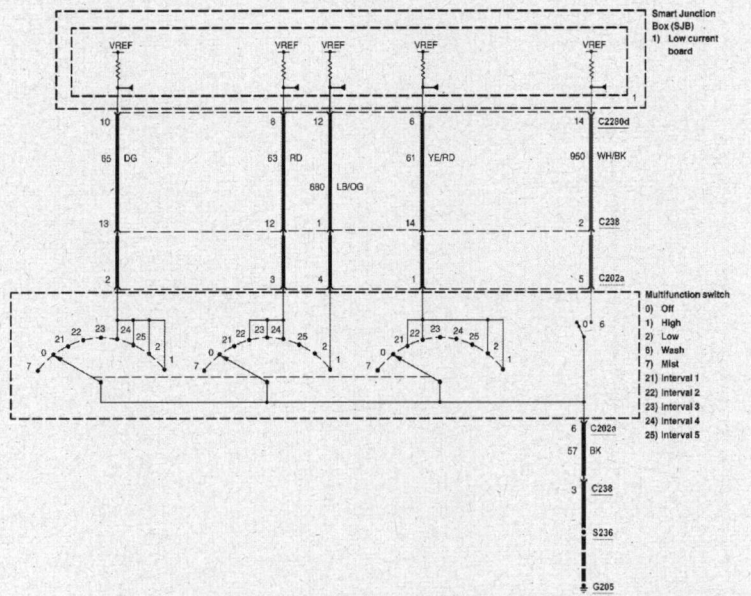

Fig. 3 Wiper diagram (Part 2 of 2). 2005-06

LTV050000002390

DIAGNOSTIC CHART INDEX

Test	Code	Description	Page No.	Fig No.
—	—	Symptom Tests	3-157	4
A	B1431	Wipers Are Inoperative	3-158	5
	B1432	Wipers Are Inoperative	3-158	5
	B1840	Wipers Are Inoperative	3-158	5
B	B1431	Wiper Stay On Continuously	3-159	6
	B2179	Wiper Stay On Continuously	3-159	6
	B2180	Wiper Stay On Continuously	3-159	6
	B2181	Wiper Stay On Continuously	3-159	6
	B2183	Wiper Stay On Continuously	3-159	6
C	B1434	High/Low Wiper Speeds Do Not Operate Correctly	3-160	7
	B1436	High/Low Wiper Speeds Do Not Operate Correctly	3-160	7
	B1466	High/Low Wiper Speeds Do Not Operate Correctly	3-160	7
	B2183	High/Low Wiper Speeds Do Not Operate Correctly	3-160	7
D	B2179	Intermittent Wiper Speed Does Not Operate Correctly	3-161	8
	B2180	Intermittent Wiper Speed Does Not Operate Correctly	3-161	8
	B2181	Intermittent Wiper Speed Does Not Operate Correctly	3-161	8
E	B1446	Wipers Will Not Park At Correct Position	3-162	9
F	B1458	Washer Pump Is Inoperative	3-163	10
	B1460	Washer Pump Is Inoperative	3-163	10
G	B1458	Washer Pump Stays On Continuously	3-164	11
	B2184	Washer Pump Stays On Continuously	3-164	11

Condition	Possible Sources	Action
• The wipers are inoperative	• Fuse • Multi-function switch • Wiper run/park relay • Wiper high/low relay • Wiper motor • Circuitry open/shorted • SJB	• Go To Pinpoint Test a .
• The wipers stay on continuously	• Circuitry shorted • Multi-function switch • Wiper run/park relay • SJB	• Go To Pinpoint Test b .
• The high/low wiper speeds do not operate correctly	• Circuitry open/shorted • Multi-function switch • Wiper high/low relay • Wiper motor • SJB	• Go To Pinpoint Test c .
• The intermittent wiper speed does not operate correctly	• Circuitry open/shorted • Multi-function switch • SJB	• Go To Pinpoint Test d .

LTV0500000002657

Fig. 4   Symptom Tests (Part 1 of 2)

Condition	Possible Sources	Action
• The wipers will not park at the correct position	• Circuitry open/shorted • Wiper run/park relay • Wiper motor • SJB	• Go To Pinpoint Test e .
• The washer pump is inoperative	• Circuitry open/shorted • Multi-function switch • Washer pump relay • Washer pump • SJB	• Go To Pinpoint Test f .
• The washer pump stays on continuously	• Circuitry shorted • Multi-function switch • Washer pump relay • SJB	• Go To Pinpoint Test g .

LTV0500000002658

Fig. 4   Symptom Tests (Part 2 of 2)

Test Step	Result / Action to Take
A1 RETRIEVE THE DIAGNOSTIC TROUBLE CODES (DTCs)	
• Retrieve and document continuous DTCs. • Enter the following diagnostic mode on the diagnostic tool: Clear Continuous DTCs. • Enter the following diagnostic mode on the diagnostic tool: SJB Wiper/Washer Self-Test. • **Are DTCs recorded?**	**Yes** If DTC B1431 only, GO to <u>A2</u>. If DTC B1432 only, GO to <u>A4</u>. If DTC B1431, B1434, B1458 and B1840, VERIFY the smart junction box fuse 5 (30A) is OK. If OK, GO to <u>A5</u> **No** GO to <u>A6</u>.
A2 CHECK THE VOLTAGE TO THE WIPER RUN/PARK RELAY	
• Key in OFF position. • Disconnect: Wiper Run/Park Relay. • Key in ON position. • Measure the voltage between ground and wiper run/park relay pin 1, circuit 1671 (RD).	**Yes** CARRY OUT the run/park relay component test. Refer to "Wiring Diagrams" If the relay tests OK, GO to <u>A3</u>. **No** REPAIR circuit 1671 (RD) for an open. TEST the system for normal operation.
• **Is the voltage greater than 10 volts?**	
A3 CHECK CIRCUIT 646 (YE/WH) FOR AN OPEN	
• Key in OFF position. • Disconnect: C2280a. • Measure the resistance between SJB C2280a-17, circuit 646 (YE/WH) and wiper run/park relay pin 2, circuit 646 (YE/WH).	**Yes** GO to <u>A11</u>. **No** REPAIR circuit 646 (YE/WH) for an open. TEST the system for normal operation.

LTV0500000002659

Fig. 5   Test A: Wipers Are Inoperative (Part 1 of 5)

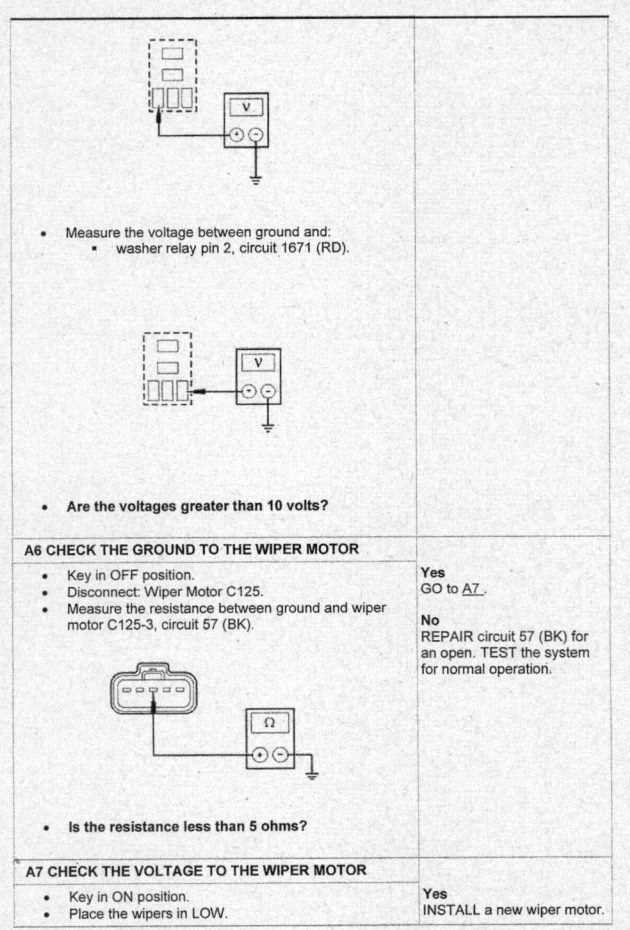

• Measure the voltage between ground and: ▪ washer relay pin 2, circuit 1671 (RD).	
• **Are the voltages greater than 10 volts?**	
A6 CHECK THE GROUND TO THE WIPER MOTOR	
• Key in OFF position. • Disconnect: Wiper Motor C125. • Measure the resistance between ground and wiper motor C125-3, circuit 57 (BK).	**Yes** GO to <u>A7</u>. **No** REPAIR circuit 57 (BK) for an open. TEST the system for normal operation.
• **Is the resistance less than 5 ohms?**	
A7 CHECK THE VOLTAGE TO THE WIPER MOTOR	
• Key in ON position. • Place the wipers in LOW.	**Yes** INSTALL a new wiper motor.

LTV0500000002661

Fig. 5   Test A: Wipers Are Inoperative (Part 3 of 5)

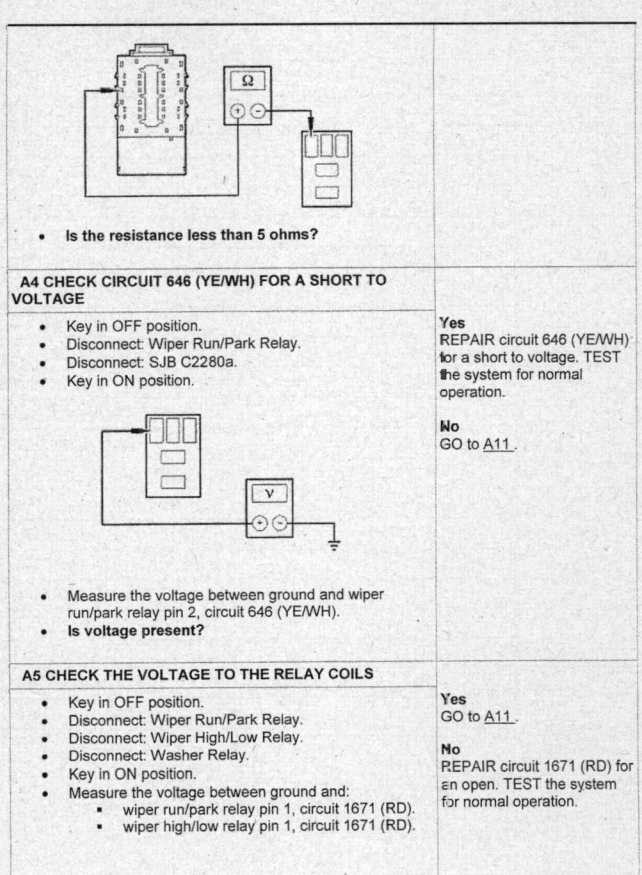

• **Is the resistance less than 5 ohms?**	
A4 CHECK CIRCUIT 646 (YE/WH) FOR A SHORT TO VOLTAGE	
• Key in OFF position. • Disconnect: Wiper Run/Park Relay. • Disconnect: SJB C2280a. • Key in ON position.	**Yes** REPAIR circuit 646 (YE/WH) for a short to voltage. TEST the system for normal operation. **No** GO to <u>A11</u>.
• Measure the voltage between ground and wiper run/park relay pin 2, circuit 646 (YE/WH). • **Is voltage present?**	
A5 CHECK THE VOLTAGE TO THE RELAY COILS	

• Key in OFF position.
• Disconnect: Wiper Run/Park Relay.
• Disconnect: Wiper High/Low Relay.
• Disconnect: Washer Relay.
• Key in ON position.
• Measure the voltage between ground and:
  ▪ wiper run/park relay pin 1, circuit 1671 (RD).
  ▪ wiper high/low relay pin 1, circuit 1671 (RD).
	Yes
	GO to <u>A11</u>.
	
	No
	REPAIR circuit 1671 (RD) for an open. TEST the system for normal operation.

LTV0500000002660

Fig. 5   Test A: Wipers Are Inoperative (Part 2 of 5)

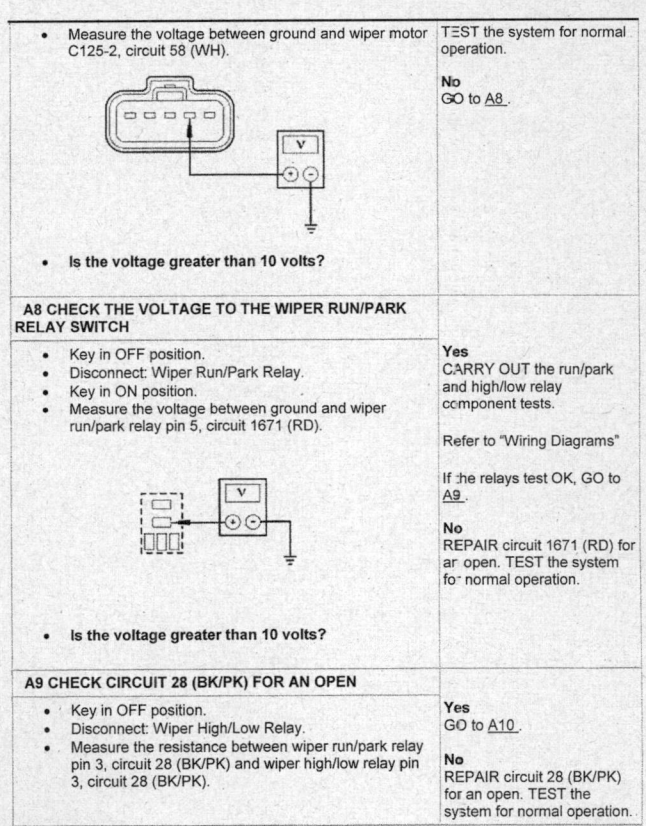

• Measure the voltage between ground and wiper motor C125-2, circuit 58 (WH).	TEST the system for normal operation. **No** GO to <u>A8</u>.
• **Is the voltage greater than 10 volts?**	
A8 CHECK THE VOLTAGE TO THE WIPER RUN/PARK RELAY SWITCH	
• Key in OFF position. • Disconnect: Wiper Run/Park Relay. • Key in ON position. • Measure the voltage between ground and wiper run/park relay pin 5, circuit 1671 (RD).	**Yes** CARRY OUT the run/park and high/low relay component tests. Refer to "Wiring Diagrams" If the relays test OK, GO to <u>A9</u>. **No** REPAIR circuit 1671 (RD) for an open. TEST the system for normal operation.
• **Is the voltage greater than 10 volts?**	
A9 CHECK CIRCUIT 28 (BK/PK) FOR AN OPEN	
• Key in OFF position. • Disconnect: Wiper High/Low Relay. • Measure the resistance between wiper run/park relay pin 3, circuit 28 (BK/PK) and wiper high/low relay pin 3, circuit 28 (BK/PK).	**Yes** GO to <u>A10</u>. **No** REPAIR circuit 28 (BK/PK) for an open. TEST the system for normal operation.

LTV0500000002662

Fig. 5   Test A: Wipers Are Inoperative (Part 4 of 5)

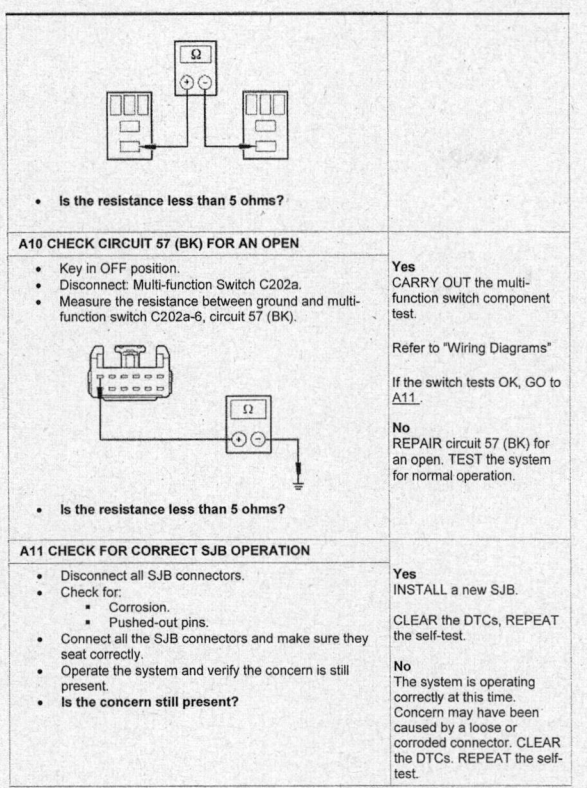

- Is the resistance less than 5 ohms?

A10 CHECK CIRCUIT 57 (BK) FOR AN OPEN	
• Key in OFF position. • Disconnect: Multi-function Switch C202a. • Measure the resistance between ground and multi-function switch C202a-6, circuit 57 (BK).	**Yes** CARRY OUT the multi-function switch component test. Refer to "Wiring Diagrams" If the switch tests OK, GO to A11. **No** REPAIR circuit 57 (BK) for an open. TEST the system for normal operation.

- Is the resistance less than 5 ohms?

A11 CHECK FOR CORRECT SJB OPERATION	

• Disconnect all SJB connectors.
• Check for:
  ▪ Corrosion.
  ▪ Pushed-out pins.
• Connect all the SJB connectors and make sure they seat correctly.
• Operate the system and verify the concern is still present.
• **Is the concern still present?**
	Yes
	INSTALL a new SJB.
	
	CLEAR the DTCs, REPEAT the self-test.
	
	No
	The system is operating correctly at this time. Concern may have been caused by a loose or corroded connector. CLEAR the DTCs. REPEAT the self-test.

LTV0500000002663

Fig. 5   Test A: Wipers Are Inoperative (Part 5 of 5)

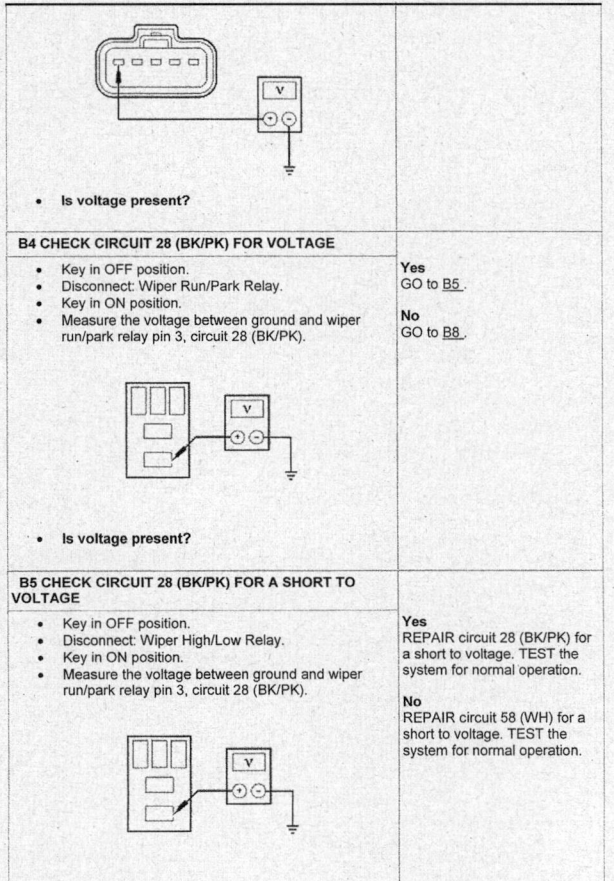

- Is voltage present?

B4 CHECK CIRCUIT 28 (BK/PK) FOR VOLTAGE	
• Key in OFF position. • Disconnect: Wiper Run/Park Relay. • Key in ON position. • Measure the voltage between ground and wiper run/park relay pin 3, circuit 28 (BK/PK).	**Yes** GO to B5. **No** GO to B8.

- Is voltage present?

B5 CHECK CIRCUIT 28 (BK/PK) FOR A SHORT TO VOLTAGE	
• Key in OFF position. • Disconnect: Wiper High/Low Relay. • Key in ON position. • Measure the voltage between ground and wiper run/park relay pin 3, circuit 28 (BK/PK).	**Yes** REPAIR circuit 28 (BK/PK) for a short to voltage. TEST the system for normal operation. **No** REPAIR circuit 58 (WH) for a short to voltage. TEST the system for normal operation.

LTV0500000002665

Fig. 6   TEST B: Wiper Stay On Continuously (Part 2 of 4)

Test Step	Result / Action to Take
B1 RETRIEVE THE DIAGNOSTIC TROUBLE CODES (DTCs) • Retrieve and document continuous DTCs. • Enter the following diagnostic mode on the diagnostic tool: Clear Continuous DTCs. • Enter the following diagnostic mode on the diagnostic tool: SJB Wiper/Washer Self-Test. • **Are DTCs present?**	**Yes** If DTC B1431, GO to B2. If DTC B1446, GO to B3. If DTC B2179, B2180, B2181 or B2183, GO to B6. **No** CARRY OUT the run/park relay component test. Refer to "Wiring Diagrams" If the relay tests OK, GO to B7
B2 CHECK CIRCUIT 646 (YE/WH) FOR A SHORT TO GROUND • Key in OFF position. • Disconnect: Wiper Run/Park Relay. • Disconnect: SJB C2280a. • Measure the resistance between ground and wiper run/park relay pin 2, circuit 646 (YE/WH).	**Yes** GO to B8. **No** REPAIR circuit 646 (YE/WH) for a short to ground. TEST the system for normal operation.
• Is the resistance greater than 10,000 ohms?	
B3 CHECK CIRCUIT 671 (LB) FOR A SHORT TO VOLTAGE • Key in OFF position. • Disconnect: SJB C2280a. • Disconnect: Wiper Motor C125. • Key in ON position. • Measure the voltage between ground and wiper motor C125-5, circuit 671 (LB).	**Yes** REPAIR circuit 671 (LB) for a short to voltage. TEST the system for normal operation. **No** GO to B4.

LTV0500000002664

Fig. 6   TEST B: Wiper Stay On Continuously (Part 1 of 4)

- Is voltage present?

B6 CHECK CIRCUITS 61 (YE/RD), 63 (RD), 65 (DG) AND 680 (LB/OG) FOR A SHORT TO GROUND	

• Key in OFF position.
• Disconnect: SJB C2280d.
• Disconnect: Multi-function Switch C202a.
• Measure the resistance between ground and multi-function switch:
  ▪ (DTC B2179) C202a-1, circuit 61 (YE/RD).
  ▪ (DTC B2180) C202a-2, circuit 65 (DG).
  ▪ (DTC B2181) C202a-3, circuit 63 (RD).
  ▪ (DTC B2183) C202a-4, circuit 680 (LB/OG).
	Yes
	CARRY OUT the multi-function switch component test.
	
	Refer to "Wiring Diagrams"
	
	If the switch tests OK, GO to B8.
	
	No
	REPAIR circuit 61 (YE/RD), 63 (RD), 65 (DG) or 680 (LB/OG) for a short to ground. TEST the system for normal operation.

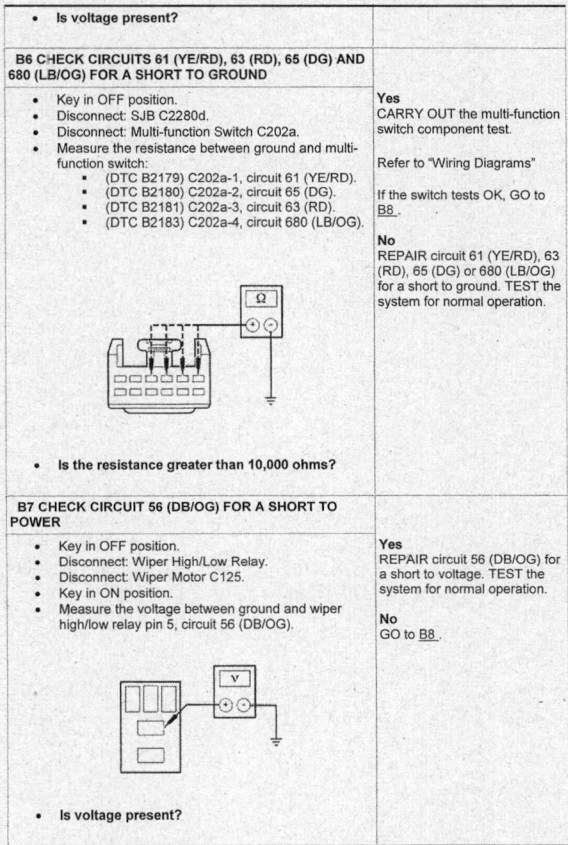

- Is the resistance greater than 10,000 ohms?

B7 CHECK CIRCUIT 56 (DB/OG) FOR A SHORT TO POWER	
• Key in OFF position. • Disconnect: Wiper High/Low Relay. • Disconnect: Wiper Motor C125. • Key in ON position. • Measure the voltage between ground and wiper high/low relay pin 5, circuit 56 (DB/OG).	**Yes** REPAIR circuit 56 (DB/OG) for a short to voltage. TEST the system for normal operation. **No** GO to B8.

- Is voltage present?

LTV0500000002666

Fig. 6   TEST B: Wiper Stay On Continuously (Part 3 of 4)

B8 CHECK FOR CORRECT SJB OPERATION	
• Disconnect all SJB connectors. • Check for: ▪ Corrosion. ▪ Pushed-out pins. • Connect all the SJB connectors and make sure they seat correctly. • Operate the system and verify the concern is still present. • **Is the concern still present?**	**Yes** INSTALL a new SJB. CLEAR the DTCs, REPEAT the self-test. **No** The system is operating correctly at this time. Concern may have been caused by a loose or corroded connector. CLEAR the DTCs. REPEAT the self-test.

LTV0500000002667

Fig. 6   TEST B: Wiper Stay On Continuously (Part 4 of 4)

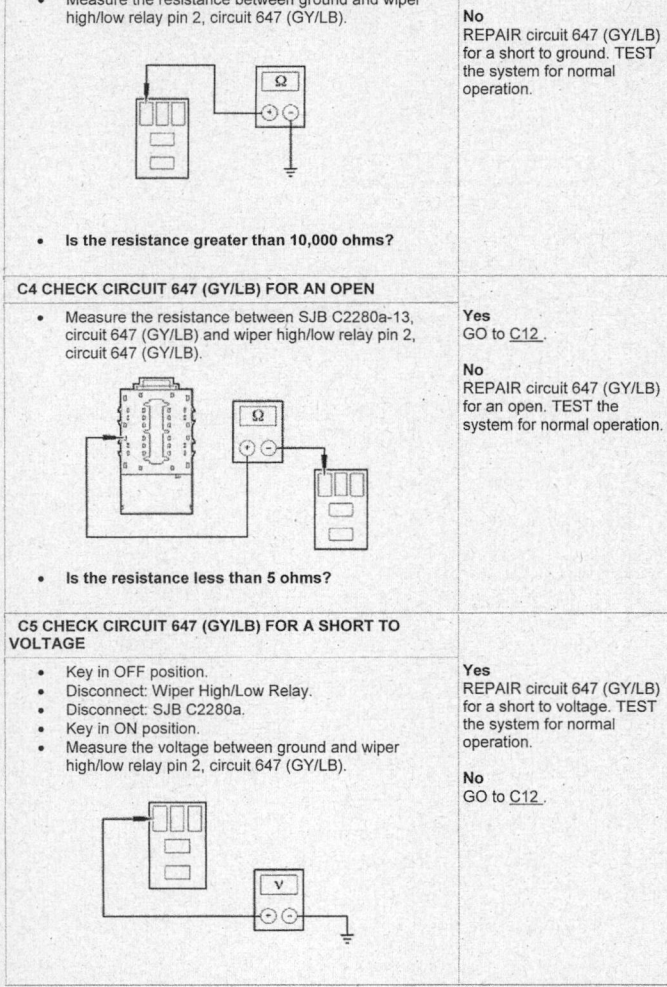

• Measure the resistance between ground and wiper high/low relay pin 2, circuit 647 (GY/LB).	**No** REPAIR circuit 647 (GY/LB) for a short to ground. TEST the system for normal operation.
• **Is the resistance greater than 10,000 ohms?**	
C4 CHECK CIRCUIT 647 (GY/LB) FOR AN OPEN	
• Measure the resistance between SJB C2280a-13, circuit 647 (GY/LB) and wiper high/low relay pin 2, circuit 647 (GY/LB).	**Yes** GO to C12 . **No** REPAIR circuit 647 (GY/LB) for an open. TEST the system for normal operation.
• **Is the resistance less than 5 ohms?**	
C5 CHECK CIRCUIT 647 (GY/LB) FOR A SHORT TO VOLTAGE	
• Key in OFF position. • Disconnect: Wiper High/Low Relay. • Disconnect: SJB C2280a. • Key in ON position. • Measure the voltage between ground and wiper high/low relay pin 2, circuit 647 (GY/LB).	**Yes** REPAIR circuit 647 (GY/LB) for a short to voltage. TEST the system for normal operation. **No** GO to C12 .

LTV0500000002669

Fig. 7   Test C: High/Low Wiper Speeds Do Not Operate Correctly (Part 2 of 6)

Test Step	Result / Action to Take
C1 RETRIEVE THE DIAGNOSTIC TROUBLE CODES (DTCs)	
• Retrieve and document continuous DTCs. • Enter the following diagnostic mode on the diagnostic tool: Clear Continuous DTCs. • Enter the following diagnostic mode on the diagnostic tool: SJB Wiper/Washer Self-Test. • **Are DTCs recorded?**	**Yes** If DTC B1434, CARRY OUT the high/low relay component test. Refer to "Wiring Diagrams" If the relay tests OK, GO to C2 . If DTC B1436, GO to C5 . If DTC B1466, GO to C7 . If DTC B2183, CARRY OUT the multi-function switch component test. Refer to "Wiring Diagrams" If the switch tests OK, GO to C6 . **No** GO to C7 .
C2 CHECK THE VOLTAGE TO THE WIPER HIGH/LOW RELAY	
• Key in OFF position. • Disconnect: Wiper High/Low Relay. • Key in ON position. • Measure the voltage between ground and wiper high/low relay pin 1, circuit 1671 (RD).	**Yes** GO to C3 . **No** REPAIR circuit 1671 (RD) for an open. TEST the system for normal operation.
• **Is the voltage greater than 10 volts?**	
C3 CHECK CIRCUIT 647 (GY/LB) FOR A SHORT TO GROUND	
• Key in OFF position. • Disconnect: SJB C2280a.	**Yes** GO to C4 .

LTV0500000002668

Fig. 7   Test C: High/Low Wiper Speeds Do Not Operate Correctly (Part 1 of 6)

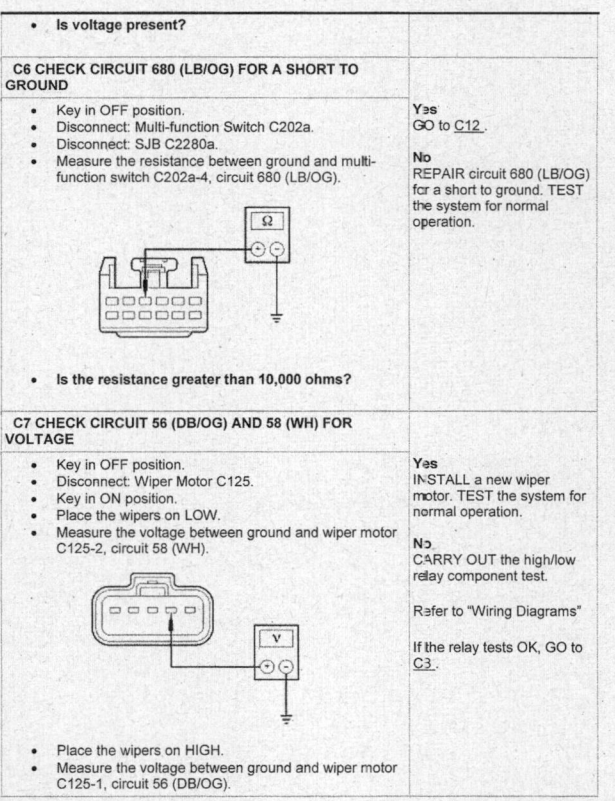

• **Is voltage present?**	
C6 CHECK CIRCUIT 680 (LB/OG) FOR A SHORT TO GROUND	
• Key in OFF position. • Disconnect: Multi-function Switch C202a. • Disconnect: SJB C2280a. • Measure the resistance between ground and multi-function switch C202a-4, circuit 680 (LB/OG).	**Yes** GO to C12 . **No** REPAIR circuit 680 (LB/OG) for a short to ground. TEST the system for normal operation.
• **Is the resistance greater than 10,000 ohms?**	
C7 CHECK CIRCUIT 56 (DB/OG) AND 58 (WH) FOR VOLTAGE	
• Key in OFF position. • Disconnect: Wiper Motor C125. • Key in ON position. • Place the wipers on LOW. • Measure the voltage between ground and wiper motor C125-2, circuit 58 (WH).	**Yes** INSTALL a new wiper motor. TEST the system for normal operation. **No** CARRY OUT the high/low relay component test. Refer to "Wiring Diagrams" If the relay tests OK, GO to C3 .
• Place the wipers on HIGH. • Measure the voltage between ground and wiper motor C125-1, circuit 56 (DB/OG).	

LTV0500000002670

Fig. 7   Test C: High/Low Wiper Speeds Do Not Operate Correctly (Part 3 of 6)

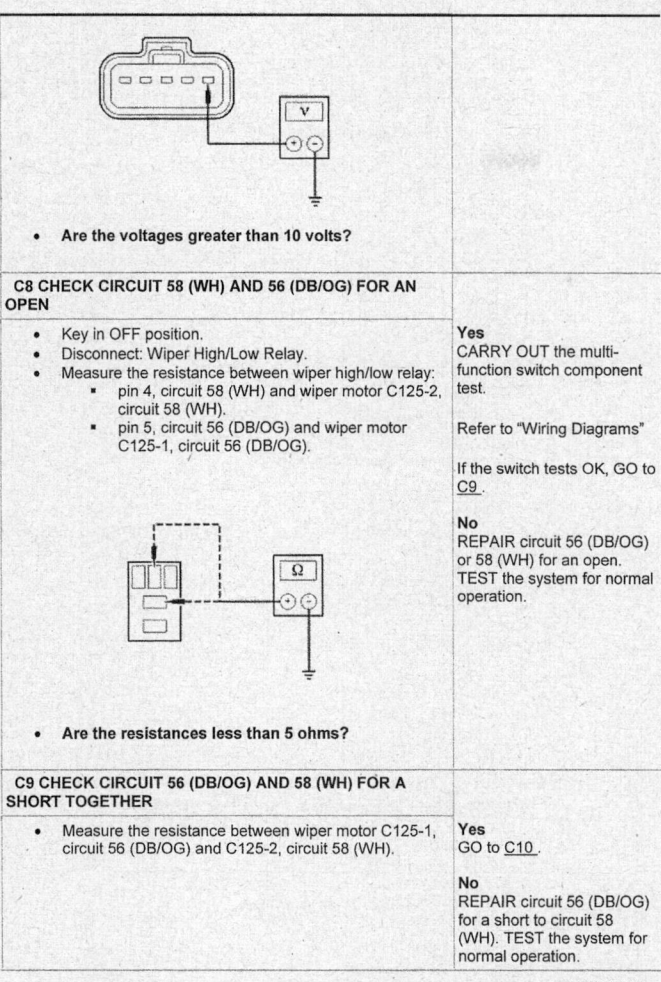

- **Are the voltages greater than 10 volts?**

C8 CHECK CIRCUIT 58 (WH) AND 56 (DB/OG) FOR AN OPEN	
<ul><li>Key in OFF position.</li><li>Disconnect: Wiper High/Low Relay.</li><li>Measure the resistance between wiper high/low relay:<ul><li>pin 4, circuit 58 (WH) and wiper motor C125-2, circuit 58 (WH).</li><li>pin 5, circuit 56 (DB/OG) and wiper motor C125-1, circuit 56 (DB/OG).</li></ul></li></ul>	**Yes** CARRY OUT the multi-function switch component test. Refer to "Wiring Diagrams" If the switch tests OK, GO to C9 . **No** REPAIR circuit 56 (DB/OG) or 58 (WH) for an open. TEST the system for normal operation.
<ul><li>**Are the resistances less than 5 ohms?**</li></ul>	

C9 CHECK CIRCUIT 56 (DB/OG) AND 58 (WH) FOR A SHORT TOGETHER	
<ul><li>Measure the resistance between wiper motor C125-1, circuit 56 (DB/OG) and C125-2, circuit 58 (WH).</li></ul>	**Yes** GO to C10 . **No** REPAIR circuit 56 (DB/OG) for a short to circuit 58 (WH). TEST the system for normal operation.

LTV0500000002671

Fig. 7   Test C: High/Low Wiper Speeds Do Not Operate Correctly (Part 4 of 6)

C12 CHECK FOR CORRECT SJB OPERATION	
<ul><li>Disconnect all SJB connectors.</li><li>Check for:<ul><li>corrosion.</li><li>pushed-out pins.</li></ul></li><li>Connect all the SJB connectors and make sure they seat correctly.</li><li>Operate the system and verify the concern is still present.</li><li>**Is the concern still present?**</li></ul>	**Yes** INSTALL a new SJB. CLEAR the DTCs, REPEAT the self-test. **No** The system is operating correctly at this time. Concern may have been caused by a loose or corroded connector. CLEAR the DTCs. REPEAT the self-test.

LTV0500000002673

Fig. 7   Test C: High/Low Wiper Speeds Do Not Operate Correctly (Part 6 of 6)

- **Is the resistance greater than 10,000 ohms?**

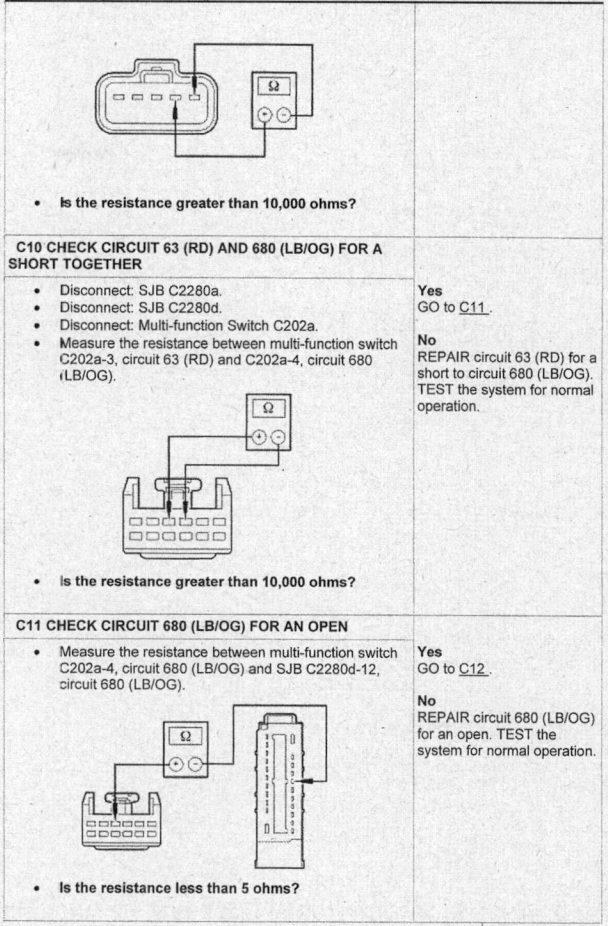

C10 CHECK CIRCUIT 63 (RD) AND 680 (LB/OG) FOR A SHORT TOGETHER	
<ul><li>Disconnect: SJB C2280a.</li><li>Disconnect: SJB C2280d.</li><li>Disconnect: Multi-function Switch C202a.</li><li>Measure the resistance between multi-function switch C202a-3, circuit 63 (RD) and C202a-4, circuit 680 (LB/OG).</li></ul>	**Yes** GO to C11 . **No** REPAIR circuit 63 (RD) for a short to circuit 680 (LB/OG). TEST the system for normal operation.
<ul><li>**Is the resistance greater than 10,000 ohms?**</li></ul>	

C11 CHECK CIRCUIT 680 (LB/OG) FOR AN OPEN	
<ul><li>Measure the resistance between multi-function switch C202a-4, circuit 680 (LB/OG) and SJB C2280d-12, circuit 680 (LB/OG).</li></ul>	**Yes** GO to C12 . **No** REPAIR circuit 680 (LB/OG) for an open. TEST the system for normal operation.
<ul><li>**Is the resistance less than 5 ohms?**</li></ul>	

LTV0500000002672

Fig. 7   Test C: High/Low Wiper Speeds Do Not Operate Correctly (Part 5 of 6)

Test Step	Result / Action to Take
D1 RETRIEVE THE DIAGNOSTIC TROUBLE CODES (DTCs)	
<ul><li>Retrieve and document continuous DTCs.</li><li>Enter the following diagnostic mode on the diagnostic tool: Clear Continuous DTCs.</li><li>Enter the following diagnostic mode on the diagnostic tool: Wiper/Washer SJB On-Demand Self Test.</li><li>**Are DTCs recorded?**</li></ul>	**Yes** If DTC B2179, B2180, B2181, CARRY OUT the multi-function switch component test. Refer to "Wiring Diagrams" If the switch tests OK, GO to D2 . **No** CARRY OUT the multi-function switch component test. Refer to "Wiring Diagrams" If the switch tests OK, GO to D3 .
D2 CHECK CIRCUIT 61 (YE/RD), 63 (RD), 65 (DG) AND 680 (LB/OG) FOR A SHORT TO GROUND	
<ul><li>Key in OFF position.</li><li>Disconnect: Multi-function Switch C202a.</li><li>Disconnect: SJB C2280d.</li><li>Key in ON position.</li><li>Measure the resistance between ground and multi-function switch:<ul><li>C202a-1, circuit 61 (YE/RD).</li><li>C202a-2, circuit 65 (DG).</li><li>C202a-3, circuit 63 (RD).</li><li>C202a-4, circuit 680 (LB/OG).</li></ul></li></ul>	**Yes** GO to D5 . **No** REPAIR circuit 61 (YE/RD), 63 (RD), 65 (DG) or 680 (LB/OG) for a short to ground. TEST the system for normal operation.

LTV0500000002674

Fig. 8   Test D: Intermittent Wiper Speed Does Not Operate Correctly (Part 1 of 3)

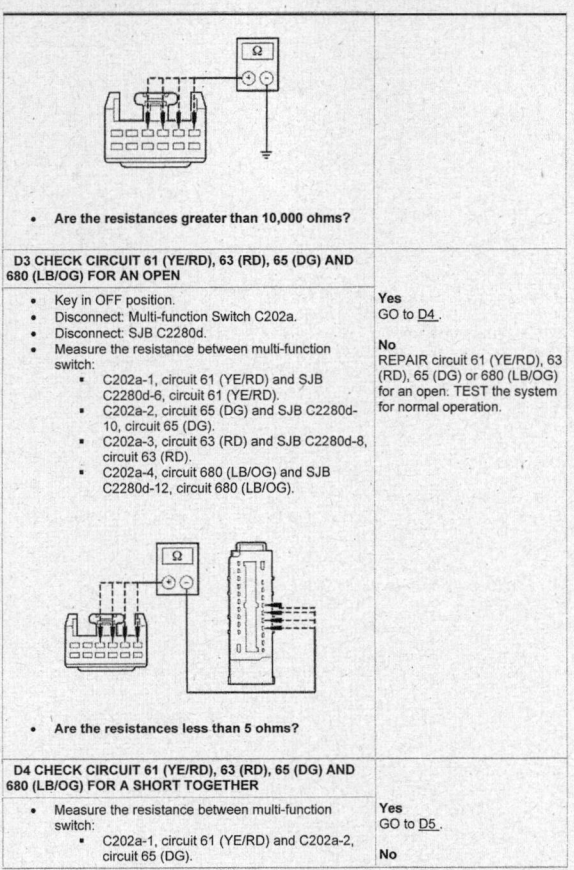

- Are the resistances greater than 10,000 ohms?

D3 CHECK CIRCUIT 61 (YE/RD), 63 (RD), 65 (DG) AND 680 (LB/OG) FOR AN OPEN
 • Key in OFF position.
 • Disconnect: Multi-function Switch C202a.
 • Disconnect: SJB C2280d.
 • Measure the resistance between multi-function switch:
   ▪ C202a-1, circuit 61 (YE/RD) and SJB C2280d-6, circuit 61 (YE/RD).
   ▪ C202a-2, circuit 65 (DG) and SJB C2280d-10, circuit 65 (DG).
   ▪ C202a-3, circuit 63 (RD) and SJB C2280d-8, circuit 63 (RD).
   ▪ C202a-4, circuit 680 (LB/OG) and SJB C2280d-12, circuit 680 (LB/OG).
	Yes
	 GO to D4.
	
	 No
	 REPAIR circuit 61 (YE/RD), 63 (RD), 65 (DG) or 680 (LB/OG) for an open. TEST the system for normal operation.

- Are the resistances less than 5 ohms?

D4 CHECK CIRCUIT 61 (YE/RD), 63 (RD), 65 (DG) AND 680 (LB/OG) FOR A SHORT TOGETHER • Measure the resistance between multi-function switch: ▪ C202a-1, circuit 61 (YE/RD) and C202a-2, circuit 65 (DG).	**Yes** GO to D5. **No**

LTV0500000002675

Fig. 8 Test D: Intermittent Wiper Speed Does Not Operate Correctly (Part 2 of 3)

▪ C202a-1, circuit 61 (YE/RD) and C202a-3, circuit 63 (RD).
   ▪ C202a-1, circuit 61 (YE/RD) and C202a-4, circuit 680 (LB/OG).
   ▪ C202a-2, circuit 65 (DG) and C202a-3, circuit 63 (RD).
   ▪ C202a-2, circuit 65 (DG) and C202a-4, circuit 680 (LB/OG).
   ▪ C202a-3, circuit 63 (RD) and C202a-4, circuit 680 (LB/OG).
	REPAIR circuit 61 (YE/RD), 63 (RD), 65 (DG) or 680 (LB/OG) for a short together. TEST the system for normal operation.

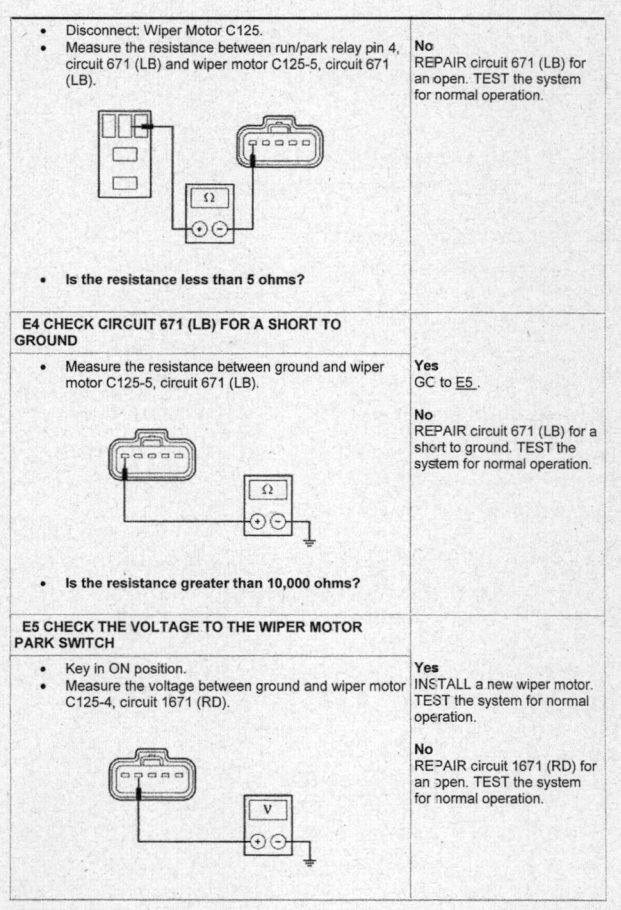

- Are the resistances greater than 10,000 ohms?

D5 CHECK FOR CORRECT SJB OPERATION
 • Disconnect all SJB connectors.
 • Check for:
   ▪ corrosion.
   ▪ pushed-out pins.
 • Connect all the SJB connectors and make sure they seat correctly.
 • Operate the system and verify the concern is still present.
 • **Is the concern still present?**
	Yes
	 INSTALL a new SJB. CLEAR the DTCs, REPEAT the self-test.
	
	 No
	 The system is operating correctly at this time. Concern may have been caused by a loose or corroded connector. CLEAR the DTCs. REPEAT the self-test.

LTV0500000002676

Fig. 8 Test D: Intermittent Wiper Speed Does Not Operate Correctly (Part 3 of 3)

Test Step	Result / Action to Take
E1 RETRIEVE THE DIAGNOSTIC TROUBLE CODES (DTCs) • Retrieve and document continuous DTCs. • Enter the following diagnostic mode on the diagnostic tool: Clear Continuous DTCs. • Enter the following diagnostic mode on the diagnostic tool: Wiper/Washer SJB On-Demand Self Test. • **Are DTCs recorded?**	**Yes** If DTC B1446 and the wipers park correctly, GO to E2. If DTC B1446 and the wipers do not park correctly, GO to E3. **No** CARRY OUT the run/park component test. Refer to "Wiring Diagrams" If the relay tests OK, INSTALL a new wiper motor.
E2 CHECK CIRCUIT 671 (LB) FOR AN OPEN BETWEEN THE SJB AND THE WIPER MOTOR • Key in OFF position. • Disconnect: SJB C2280a. • Disconnect: Wiper Motor C125. • Measure the resistance between SJB C2280a-5, circuit 671 (LB) and wiper motor C125-5, circuit 671 (LB).	**Yes** GO to E6. **No** REPAIR circuit 671 (LB) for an open. TEST the system for normal operation.

- Is the resistance less than 5 ohms?

E3 CHECK CIRCUIT 671 (LB) FOR AN OPEN BETWEEN THE SJB AND THE WIPER MOTOR • Key in OFF position. • Disconnect: Wiper Run/Park Relay.	**Yes** GO to E4.

LTV0500000002677

Fig. 9 Test E: Wipers Will Not Park At Correct Position (Part 1 of 3)

• Disconnect: Wiper Motor C125. • Measure the resistance between run/park relay pin 4, circuit 671 (LB) and wiper motor C125-5, circuit 671 (LB).	**No** REPAIR circuit 671 (LB) for an open. TEST the system for normal operation.

- Is the resistance less than 5 ohms?

E4 CHECK CIRCUIT 671 (LB) FOR A SHORT TO GROUND • Measure the resistance between ground and wiper motor C125-5, circuit 671 (LB).	**Yes** GC to E5. **No** REPAIR circuit 671 (LB) for a short to ground. TEST the system for normal operation.

- Is the resistance greater than 10,000 ohms?

E5 CHECK THE VOLTAGE TO THE WIPER MOTOR PARK SWITCH • Key in ON position. • Measure the voltage between ground and wiper motor C125-4, circuit 1671 (RD).	**Yes** INSTALL a new wiper motor. TEST the system for normal operation. **No** REPAIR circuit 1671 (RD) for an open. TEST the system for normal operation.

LTV0500000002678

Fig. 9 Test E: Wipers Will Not Park At Correct Position (Part 2 of 3)

• Is the voltage greater than 10 volts?	
E6 CHECK FOR CORRECT SJB OPERATION	

• Disconnect all SJB connectors.
• Check for:
  • Corrosion.
  • Pushed-out pins.
• Connect all the SJB connectors and make sure they seat correctly.
• Operate the system and verify the concern is still present.
• **Is the concern still present?**
	Yes
	INSTALL a new SJB.
	
	CLEAR the DTCs, REPEAT the self-test.
	
	No
	The system is operating correctly at this time. Concern may have been caused by a loose or corroded connector. CLEAR the DTCs. REPEAT the self-test.

LTV0500000002679

Fig. 9 Test E: Wipers Will Not Park At Correct Position (Part 3 of 3)

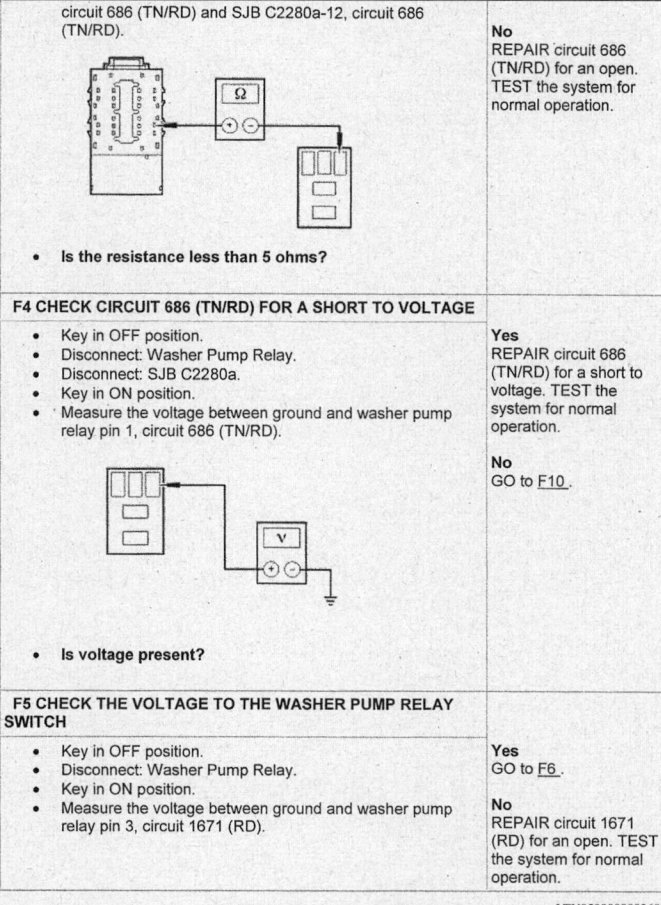

circuit 686 (TN/RD) and SJB C2280a-12, circuit 686 (TN/RD).	**No** REPAIR circuit 686 (TN/RD) for an open. TEST the system for normal operation.
• Is the resistance less than 5 ohms?	
F4 CHECK CIRCUIT 686 (TN/RD) FOR A SHORT TO VOLTAGE	
• Key in OFF position. • Disconnect: Washer Pump Relay. • Disconnect: SJB C2280a. • Key in ON position. • Measure the voltage between ground and washer pump relay pin 1, circuit 686 (TN/RD).	**Yes** REPAIR circuit 686 (TN/RD) for a short to voltage. TEST the system for normal operation. **No** GO to F10 .
• Is voltage present?	
F5 CHECK THE VOLTAGE TO THE WASHER PUMP RELAY SWITCH	
• Key in OFF position. • Disconnect: Washer Pump Relay. • Key in ON position. • Measure the voltage between ground and washer pump relay pin 3, circuit 1671 (RD).	**Yes** GO to F6 . **No** REPAIR circuit 1671 (RD) for an open. TEST the system for normal operation.

LTV0500000002681

Fig. 10 Test F: Washer Pump Is Inoperative (Part 2 of 4)

Test Step	Result / Action to Take
F1 RETRIEVE THE DIAGNOSTIC TROUBLE CODES (DTCs)	
• Retrieve and document continuous DTCs. • Enter the following diagnostic mode on the diagnostic tool: Clear Continuous DTCs. • Enter the following diagnostic mode on the diagnostic tool: SJB Wiper/Washer Self-Test. • **Are DTCs recorded?**	**Yes** If DTC B1458, CARRY OUT the washer relay component test. Refer to "Wiring Diagrams" If the relay tests OK, GO to F2 . If DTC B1460, GO to F4 . **No** CARRY OUT the washer relay component test. Refer to "Wiring Diagrams" If the relay tests OK, GO to F5 .
F2 CHECK THE VOLTAGE TO THE WASHER PUMP RELAY COIL	
• Key in OFF position. • Disconnect: Washer Pump Relay. • Key in ON position. • Measure the voltage between ground and washer pump relay pin 2, circuit 1671 (RD).	**Yes** GO to F3 . **No** REPAIR circuit 1671 (RD) for an open. TEST the system for normal operation.
• Is the voltage greater than 10 volts?	
F3 CHECK CIRCUIT 686 (TN/RD) FOR AN OPEN	
• Disconnect: SJB C2280a. • Measure the resistance between washer pump relay pin 1,	**Yes** GO to F10 .

LTV0500000002680

Fig. 10 Test F: Washer Pump Is Inoperative (Part 1 of 4)

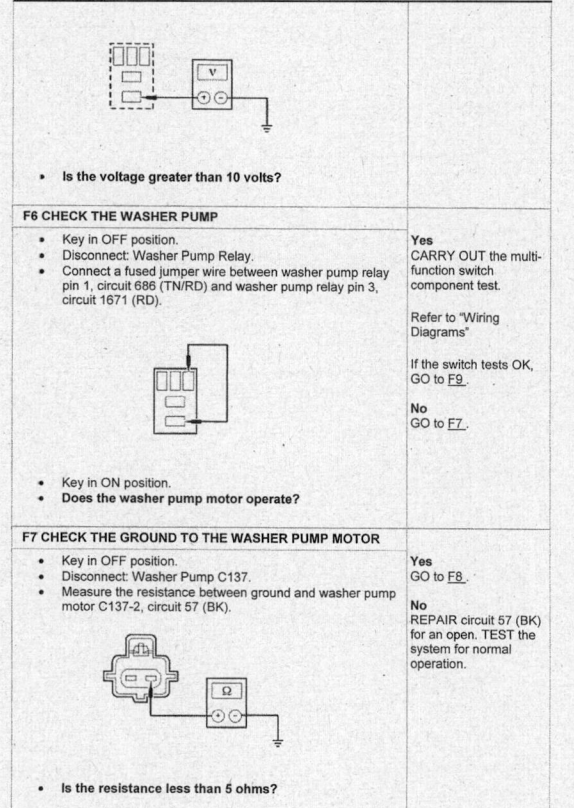

• Is the voltage greater than 10 volts?	
F6 CHECK THE WASHER PUMP	
• Key in OFF position. • Disconnect: Washer Pump Relay. • Connect a fused jumper wire between washer pump relay pin 1, circuit 686 (TN/RD) and washer pump relay pin 3, circuit 1671 (RD).	**Yes** CARRY OUT the multi-function switch component test. Refer to "Wiring Diagrams" If the switch tests OK, GO to F9 . **No** GO to F7 .
• Key in ON position. • **Does the washer pump motor operate?**	
F7 CHECK THE GROUND TO THE WASHER PUMP MOTOR	
• Key in OFF position. • Disconnect: Washer Pump C137. • Measure the resistance between ground and washer pump motor C137-2, circuit 57 (BK).	**Yes** GO to F8 . **No** REPAIR circuit 57 (BK) for an open. TEST the system for normal operation.
• Is the resistance less than 5 ohms?	

LTV0500000002682

Fig. 10 Test F: Washer Pump Is Inoperative (Part 3 of 4)

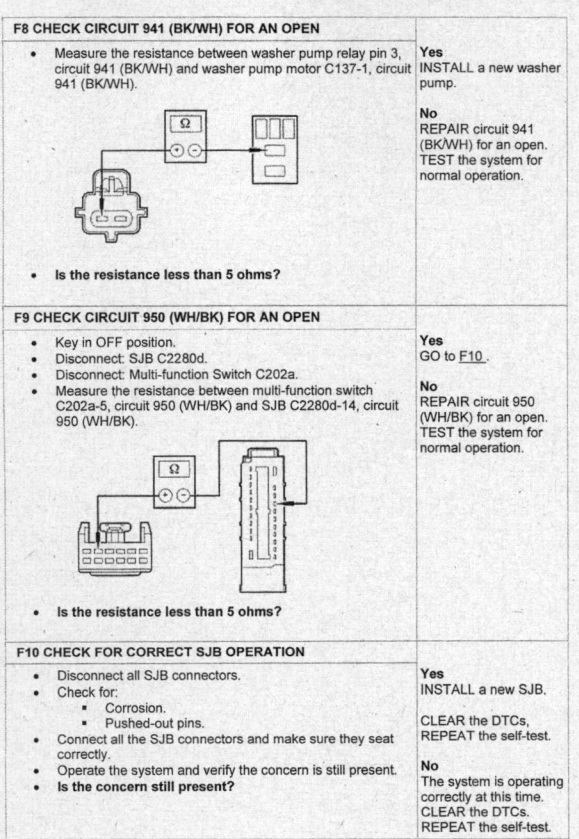

F8 CHECK CIRCUIT 941 (BK/WH) FOR AN OPEN	
• Measure the resistance between washer pump relay pin 3, circuit 941 (BK/WH) and washer pump motor C137-1, circuit 941 (BK/WH).	**Yes** INSTALL a new washer pump.
	No REPAIR circuit 941 (BK/WH) for an open. TEST the system for normal operation.
• **Is the resistance less than 5 ohms?**	
F9 CHECK CIRCUIT 950 (WH/BK) FOR AN OPEN	
• Key in OFF position. • Disconnect: SJB C2280d. • Disconnect: Multi-function Switch C202a. • Measure the resistance between multi-function switch C202a-5, circuit 950 (WH/BK) and SJB C2280d-14, circuit 950 (WH/BK).	**Yes** GO to F10. **No** REPAIR circuit 950 (WH/BK) for an open. TEST the system for normal operation.
• **Is the resistance less than 5 ohms?**	
F10 CHECK FOR CORRECT SJB OPERATION	
• Disconnect all SJB connectors. • Check for: ▪ Corrosion. ▪ Pushed-out pins. • Connect all the SJB connectors and make sure they seat correctly. • Operate the system and verify the concern is still present. • **Is the concern still present?**	**Yes** INSTALL a new SJB. CLEAR the DTCs, REPEAT the self-test. **No** The system is operating correctly at this time. CLEAR the DTCs. REPEAT the self-test.

LTV0500000002683

Fig. 10   Test F: Washer Pump Is Inoperative (Part 4 of 4)

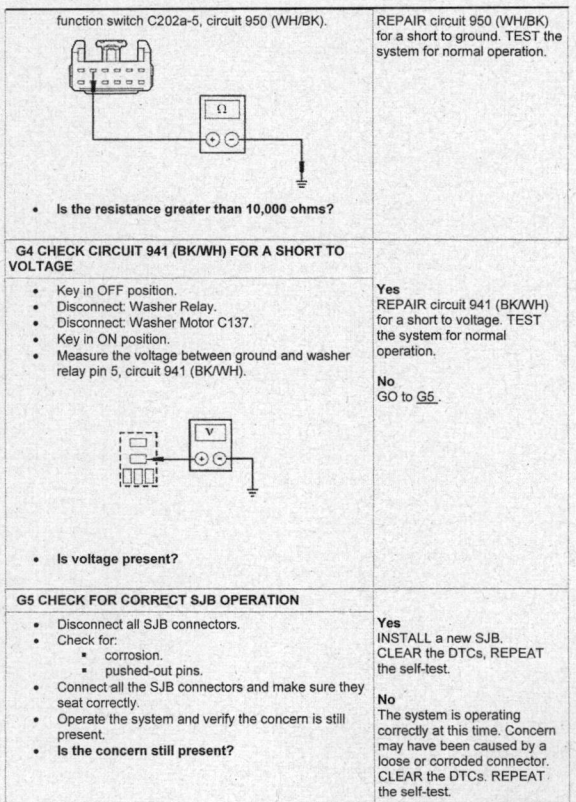

function switch C202a-5, circuit 950 (WH/BK).	REPAIR circuit 950 (WH/BK) for a short to ground. TEST the system for normal operation.
• **Is the resistance greater than 10,000 ohms?**	
G4 CHECK CIRCUIT 941 (BK/WH) FOR A SHORT TO VOLTAGE	
• Key in OFF position. • Disconnect: Washer Relay. • Disconnect: Washer Motor C137. • Key in ON position. • Measure the voltage between ground and washer relay pin 5, circuit 941 (BK/WH).	**Yes** REPAIR circuit 941 (BK/WH) for a short to voltage. TEST the system for normal operation. **No** GO to G5.
• **Is voltage present?**	
G5 CHECK FOR CORRECT SJB OPERATION	
• Disconnect all SJB connectors. • Check for: ▪ corrosion. ▪ pushed-out pins. • Connect all the SJB connectors and make sure they seat correctly. • Operate the system and verify the concern is still present. • **Is the concern still present?**	**Yes** INSTALL a new SJB. CLEAR the DTCs, REPEAT the self-test. **No** The system is operating correctly at this time. Concern may have been caused by a loose or corroded connector. CLEAR the DTCs. REPEAT the self-test.

LTV0500000002685

Fig. 11   Test G: Washer Pump Stays On Continuously (Part 2 of 2)

Test Step	Result / Action to Take
G1 RETRIEVE THE DIAGNOSTIC TROUBLE CODES (DTCs)	
• Retrieve any continuous DTCs. • Enter the following diagnostic mode on the diagnostic tool: Clear Continuous DTCs. • Enter the following diagnostic mode on the diagnostic tool: SJB Wiper/Washer Self-Test. • **Are DTCs present?**	**Yes** If DTC B1458, GO to G2. If DTC B1458, CARRY OUT the multi-function switch component test. Refer to "Wiring Diagrams" If the switch tests OK, GO to G3. **No** CARRY OUT the washer relay component test. Refer to "Wiring Diagrams" If the relay tests OK, GO to G4
G2 CHECK CIRCUIT 686 (TN/RD) FOR A SHORT TO GROUND	
• Key in OFF position. • Disconnect: Washer Relay. • Disconnect: SJB C2280a. • Measure the resistance between ground and washer relay pin 1, circuit 686 (TN/RD).	**Yes** GO to G5. **No** REPAIR circuit 686 (TN/RD) for a short to ground. TEST the system for normal operation.
• **Is the resistance greater than 10,000 ohms?**	
G3 CHECK CIRCUIT 950 (WH/BK) FOR A SHORT TO GROUND	
• Key in OFF position. • Disconnect: Multi-function Switch C202a. • Disconnect: SJB C2280d. • Measure the resistance between ground and multi-	**Yes** GO to G5. **No**

LTV0500000002684

Fig. 11   Test G: Washer Pump Stays On Continuously (Part 1 of 2)

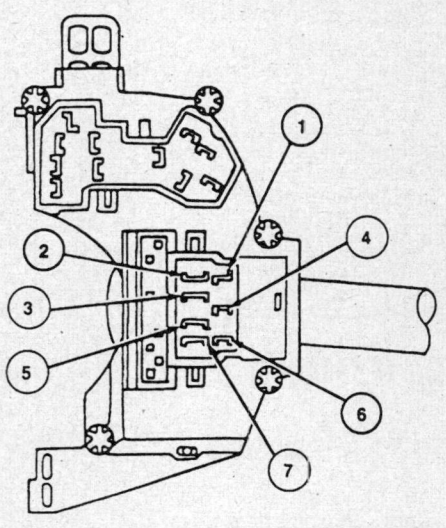

FM9029500306010X

Fig. 12   Wiper switch continuity test (Part 1 of 2)

COMPONENT DIAGNOSIS & TESTING

Wiper Motor Current Draw Test

1. Connect positive (red) lead from Rotunda Battery and Starter Tester tool No. 010-00725, or equivalent, to common (c) terminal of windshield wiper motor.
2. Connect green lead from tester to battery positive post, then jumper wire from battery ground post to low speed terminal of wiper motor and read draw.
3. Move jumper wire from low-speed terminal to high-speed terminal and read high-speed current draw.

Switch Position	Resistance by Pin Number
Interval Wiper/Washer Switching:	
● Wash ON	Closed Pin 4 to Pin 6
● Wiper OFF	Resistance Pin 4 to Pin 6, 103.3 k Ohms
● Wash OFF	Resistance Pin 4 to Pin 1, 47.6 k Ohms
● Wiper Interval at MAX. Delay (Closest Position to OFF) to MIN. Delay (Closest Position to LO)	Resistance Pin 4 to Pin 1, 11.33 k Ohms Resistance Pin 4 to Pin 6 linear decreasing from 103.3 k Ohms to 3.3 k Ohms
● Wiper LO ● Wash OFF	Resistance Pin 4 to Pin 6, 3.3 k Ohms Resistance Pin 4 to Pin 1, 4.08 k Ohms
● Wiper HI ● Wash OFF	Resistance Pin 4 to Pin 6, 3.3 k Ohms Closed Pin 4 to Pin 1

FM9029500306020X

Fig. 12 Wiper switch continuity test (Part 2 of 2)

4. In either case, current draw should not exceed 3.5 amps for low speed and 5.5 amps for high speed. If current draw does exceed 3.5 or 5.5 amps, inspect output arm and windlatch mechanism for binding or damage before replacing motor.

Wiper Switch Continuity Test

1. Inspect continuity between switch terminals, **Fig. 12.**
2. To detect marginal operation of switch, move switch lever while each reading is being taken.
3. If switch does not show continuity or if poor continuity exists at any switch position, replace switch.

Windstar

NOTE: On Air Bag Equipped Models, Refer To "Air Bag System Precautions" Located In The Front Of This Manual For System Disarming & Arming Procedures.

NOTE: "Electrical Symbol & Wire Color Code Identification" Located In The Front Of This Manual May Be Used As An Aid When Using Wiring Diagrams Found In This Section.

NOTE: Refer To "Computer Relearn Procedures" Located In The Front Of This Manual When Battery Power To The Computer Has Been Interrupted.

INDEX

	Page No.
Component Diagnosis & Testing	3-178
Rear Wiper/Washer Switch Continuity Test	3-178
Washer Pump Current Draw Test	3-178
Wiper Motor Current Draw Test	3-178
Wiper Motor	3-178
Windshield Wiper Motor Stops When Turn Signal & Windshield Wiper Switch Are Turned To Off (Does Not Complete Cycle)	3-178
Wipers Stall Or Jam (Windshield Wiper Motor Starts Running In Reverse Direction) While Going From Park To Depressed Park (Below Windshield)	3-178
Wiper Switch Continuity Test	3-178
Description	3-165
Front	3-165
Rear	3-166
Diagnostic Chart Index	3-167
Precautions	3-165
Battery Ground Cable	3-165
System Diagnosis & Testing	3-166
Accessing Diagnostic Trouble Codes	3-166
Clearing Diagnostic Trouble Codes	3-166
Diagnostic Tests	3-166
Diagnostic Trouble Code Interpretation	3-166
Wiring Diagrams	3-166

PRECAUTIONS

Battery Ground Cable

Prior to service, disconnect battery ground cable and isolate as required.

DESCRIPTION

Front

The front wipers and washer are controlled by the Front Electronic Module (FEM). The front washer/wiper portion of the fault switch is hardwired to the FEM. FEM processes information and outputs appropriate command(s) to one of several hardwired relays which control front wiper motor speeds or front washer pump activation.

Intermittent wiper speed control can vary dependent upon vehicle speed. The FEM receives vehicle speed information from the ABS control module and throttle position status from the Powertrain Control Module (PCM). When front wiper/washer switch is in any of the intermittent positions, the FEM will process the information from the PCM and ABS control module and decrease wiper delay time when vehicle is above 10 mph.

WIPER SYSTEMS

Rear

The rear wiper and washer are controlled by the FEM. The rear wiper/washer portion of the fault switch is hardwired to the FEM.

SYSTEM DIAGNOSIS & TESTING

Accessing Diagnostic Trouble Codes

Connect a suitably programmed scan tool and Vehicle Communication Module (VCM) with appropriate adapters, or equivalents, to the Data Link Connector (DCL) located in the passenger compartment beneath the instrument panel. Follow tool manufacturer's instructions for accessing speed control Diagnostic Trouble Codes (DTC).

Diagnostic Trouble Code Interpretation

Refer to **Fig. 1** for diagnostic trouble code interpretation.

Wiring Diagrams

Refer to **Figs. 2 and 3** for wiper system wiring diagrams.

Diagnostic Tests

Refer to **Figs. 4 through 11** for diagnostic tests.

Clearing Diagnostic Trouble Codes

Connect a suitably programmed scan tool and Vehicle Communication Module (VCM) with appropriate adapters, or equivalents, to the Data Link Connector (DCL) located in the passenger compartment beneath the instrument panel. Follow tool manufacturer's instructions for accessing speed control Diagnostic Trouble Codes (DTC).

Code	Description
B1241	Wiper Washer Rear Pump Relay Circuit Short To Battery
B1244	Wiper Rear Motor Run Relay Circuit Failure
B1245	Wiper Rear Motor Run Relay Circuit Short To Battery
B1431	Wiper Brake/Run Relay Circuit Failure
B1432	Wiper Brake/Run Relay Circuit Short To Battery
B1436	Wiper Hi/Low Speed Relay Coil Circuit Short To Battery
B1438	Wiper Mode Select Switch Circuit Failure
B1446	Wiper Park Sense Circuit Failure
B1448	Wiper Park Sense Circuit Short To Battery
B1450	Wiper Wash/Delay Switch Circuit Failure
B1460	Wiper Washer Pump Motor Relay Coil Circuit Short To Battery
B1482	Wiper Washer Fluid Level Sensor Circuit Short To Ground
B1611	Wiper Rear Mode Select Switch Circuit Failure

Fig. 1   Diagnostic trouble code interpretation

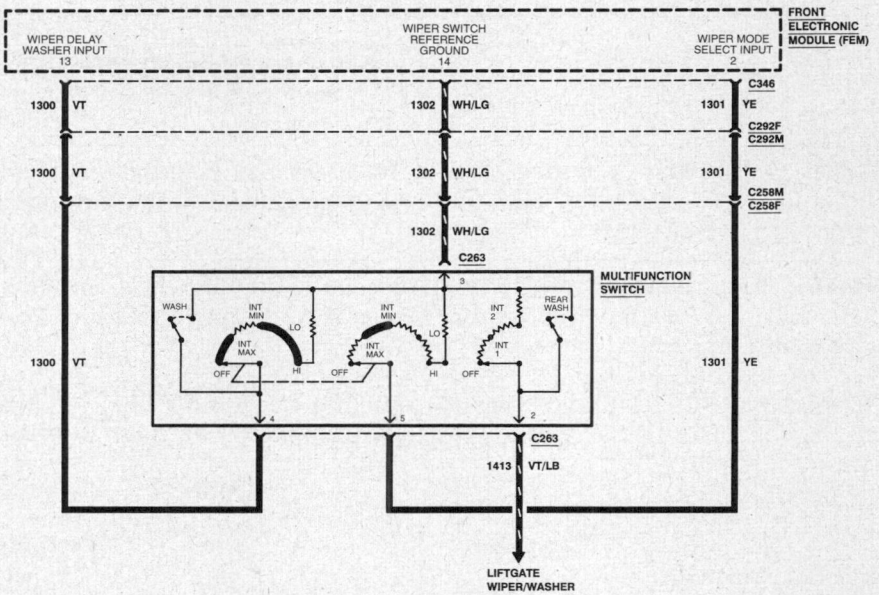

FM9029900708010X

Fig. 2   Front wiring diagram (Part 1 of 2)

Fig. 2   Front wiring diagram (Part 2 of 2)

FM9029900708020X

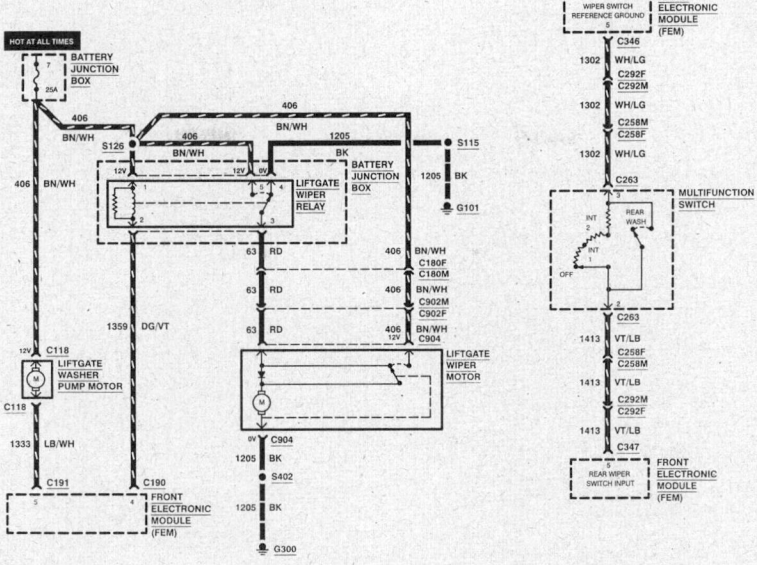

Fig. 3 Rear wiring diagram

FM9029900709000X

DIAGNOSTIC CHART INDEX

Test	Code	Description	Page No.	Fig. No.
A	—	No Communication w/FEM	3-167	4
B	B1431	Front Wipers Are Inoperative	3-168	5
	B1432	Front Wipers Are Inoperative	3-168	5
	B1438	Front Wipers Are Inoperative	3-168	5
	B1450	Front Wipers Are Inoperative	3-168	5
C	B1244	Rear Wipers Inoperative	3-171	6
	B1245	Rear Wipers Inoperative	3-171	6
	B1611	Rear Wipers Inoperative	3-171	6
D	—	Front Or Rear Wipers Stay On Continuously	3-172	7
E	BI446	Intermittent Wiper Speed Does Not Operate Properly	3-173	8
	B1448	Intermittent Wiper Speed Does Not Operate Properly	3-173	8
F	B1241	Front & Rear Washer Pump Inoperative	3-174	9
	B1460	Front & Rear Washer Pump Inoperative	3-174	9
G	—	Washer Pump Inoperative, Front & Rear Washers Stay On Continuously	3-176	10
H	B1436	High/Low Wiper Speeds Do Not Operate Properly	3-176	11

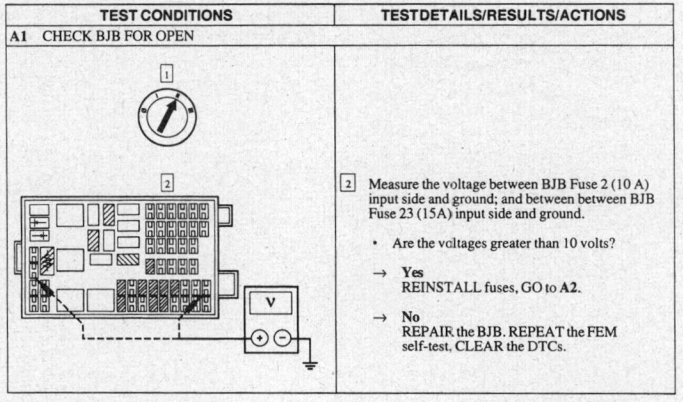

FM9029900710010X

Fig. 4 Test A: No Communication w/FEM
(Part 1 of 3)

WIPER SYSTEMS

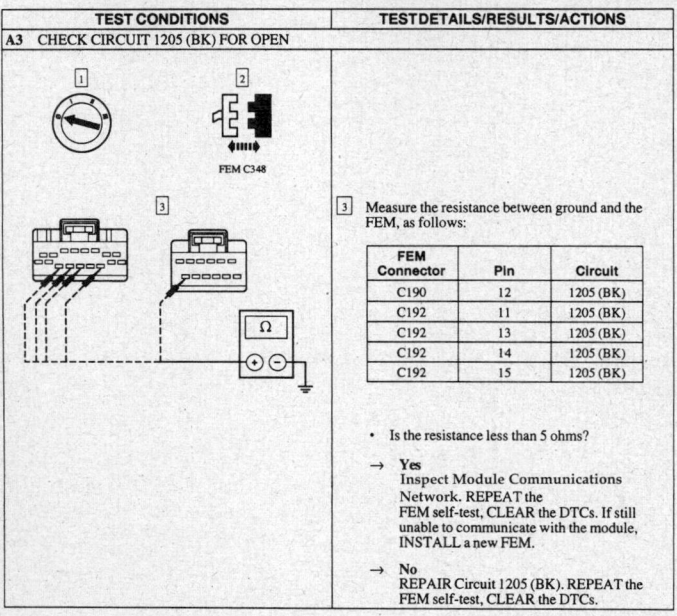

TEST CONDITIONS	TESTDETAILS/RESULTS/ACTIONS
A3 CHECK CIRCUIT 1205 (BK) FOR OPEN	

3 Measure the resistance between ground and the FEM, as follows:

FEM Connector	Pin	Circuit
C190	12	1205 (BK)
C192	11	1205 (BK)
C192	13	1205 (BK)
C192	14	1205 (BK)
C192	15	1205 (BK)

- Is the resistance less than 5 ohms?
→ **Yes**
   Inspect Module Communications Network. REPEAT the FEM self-test, CLEAR the DTCs. If still unable to communicate with the module, INSTALL a new FEM.
→ **No**
   REPAIR Circuit 1205 (BK). REPEAT the FEM self-test, CLEAR the DTCs.

FM9029900710020X

Fig. 4   Test A: No Communication w/FEM (Part 2 of 3)

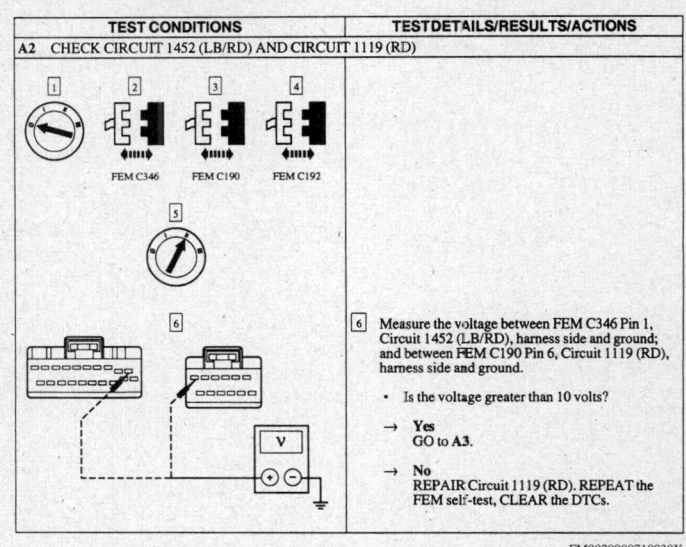

TEST CONDITIONS	TESTDETAILS/RESULTS/ACTIONS
A2 CHECK CIRCUIT 1452 (LB/RD) AND CIRCUIT 1119 (RD)	

6 Measure the voltage between FEM C346 Pin 1, Circuit 1452 (LB/RD), harness side and ground; and between FEM C190 Pin 6, Circuit 1119 (RD), harness side and ground.

- Is the voltage greater than 10 volts?
→ **Yes**
   GO to A3.
→ **No**
   REPAIR Circuit 1119 (RD). REPEAT the FEM self-test, CLEAR the DTCs.

FM9029900710030X

Fig. 4   Test A: No Communication w/FEM (Part 3 of 3)

TEST CONDITIONS	TESTDETAILS/RESULTS/ACTIONS
B1 USE THE RECORDED RESULTS FROM THE FEM SELF-TEST	

1 Use the recorded results from the FEM self-test.

- Are any DTCs recorded?
→ **Yes**
   If DTC B1431, GO to **B2**.
   If DTC B1432, GO to **B4**.
   If DTC B1438, GO to **B6**.
   If DTC B1450, GO to **B9**.
→ **No**
   GO to **B12**.

TEST CONDITIONS	TESTDETAILS/RESULTS/ACTIONS
B2 CHECK THE WIPER ON / OFF RELAY — USE THE FEM ACTIVE COMAND WIPER RLY	

1 Access the FEM active command WIPER RLY.

3 Trigger the FEM active command WIPER RLY to ON.

Windshield Wiper ON / OFF Relay

4 Measure the resistance between windshield wiper ON / OFF relay Pin 2, Circuit 1318 (DG/WH), harness side and ground.

- Is the resistance less than 5 ohms?
→ **Yes**
   INSTALL a new windshield wiper ON / OFF relay. REPEAT the FEM self-test, CLEAR the DTCs.
→ **No**
   GO to **B3**.

FM9029900711010X

Fig. 5   Test B: Front Wipers Are Inoperative (Part 1 of 11)

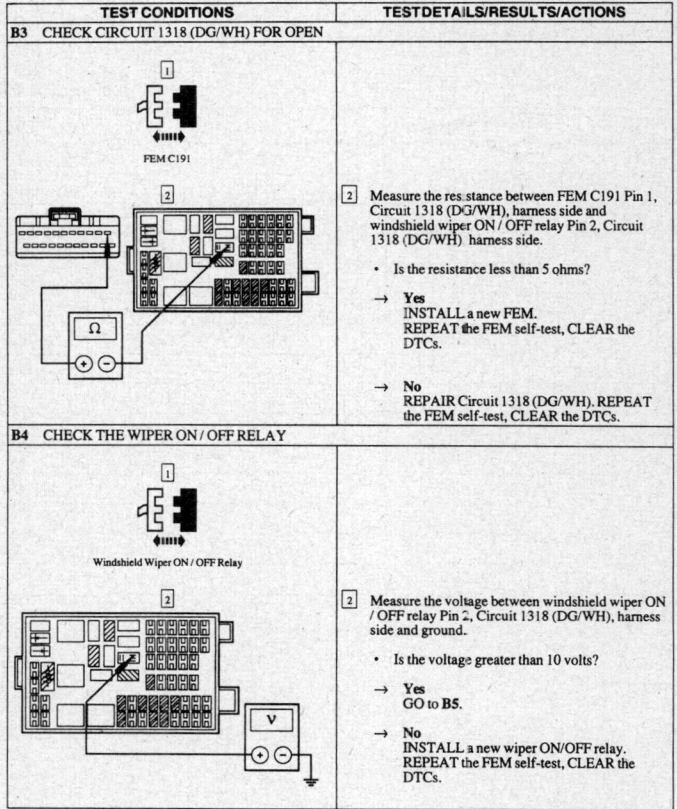

TEST CONDITIONS	TESTDETAILS/RESULTS/ACTIONS
B3 CHECK CIRCUIT 1318 (DG/WH) FOR OPEN	

FEM C191

2 Measure the resistance between FEM C191 Pin 1, Circuit 1318 (DG/WH), harness side and windshield wiper ON / OFF relay Pin 2, Circuit 1318 (DG/WH), harness side.

- Is the resistance less than 5 ohms?
→ **Yes**
   INSTALL a new FEM. REPEAT the FEM self-test, CLEAR the DTCs.
→ **No**
   REPAIR Circuit 1318 (DG/WH). REPEAT the FEM self-test, CLEAR the DTCs.

TEST CONDITIONS	TESTDETAILS/RESULTS/ACTIONS
B4 CHECK THE WIPER ON / OFF RELAY	

Windshield Wiper ON / OFF Relay

2 Measure the voltage between windshield wiper ON / OFF relay Pin 2, Circuit 1318 (DG/WH), harness side and ground.

- Is the voltage greater than 10 volts?
→ **Yes**
   GO to **B5**.
→ **No**
   INSTALL a new wiper ON/OFF relay. REPEAT the FEM self-test, CLEAR the DTCs.

FM9029900711020X

Fig. 5   Test B: Front Wipers Are Inoperative (Part 2 of 11)

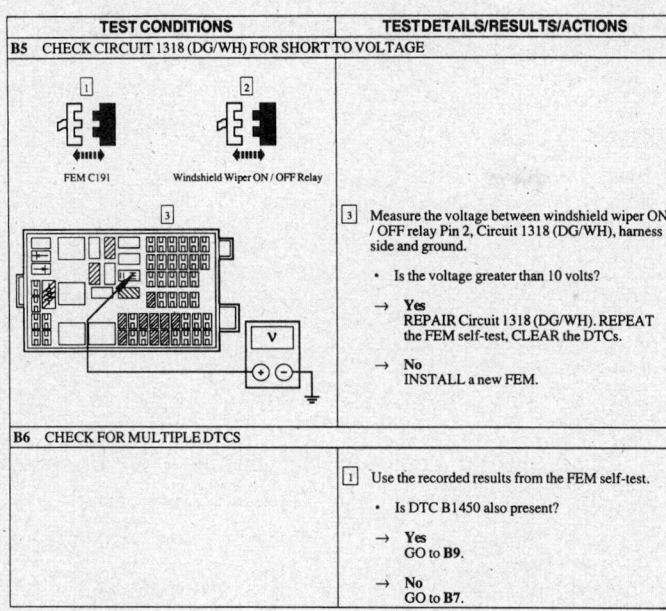

TEST CONDITIONS	TESTDETAILS/RESULTS/ACTIONS
B5 CHECK CIRCUIT 1318 (DG/WH) FOR SHORT TO VOLTAGE	
	3 Measure the voltage between windshield wiper ON / OFF relay Pin 2, Circuit 1318 (DG/WH), harness side and ground.
	• Is the voltage greater than 10 volts?
	→ **Yes** REPAIR Circuit 1318 (DG/WH). REPEAT the FEM self-test, CLEAR the DTCs.
	→ **No** INSTALL a new FEM.
B6 CHECK FOR MULTIPLE DTCS	
	1 Use the recorded results from the FEM self-test.
	• Is DTC B1450 also present?
	→ **Yes** GO to **B9**.
	→ **No** GO to **B7**.

FM9029900711030X

Fig. 5 Test B: Front Wipers Are Inoperative (Part 3 of 11)

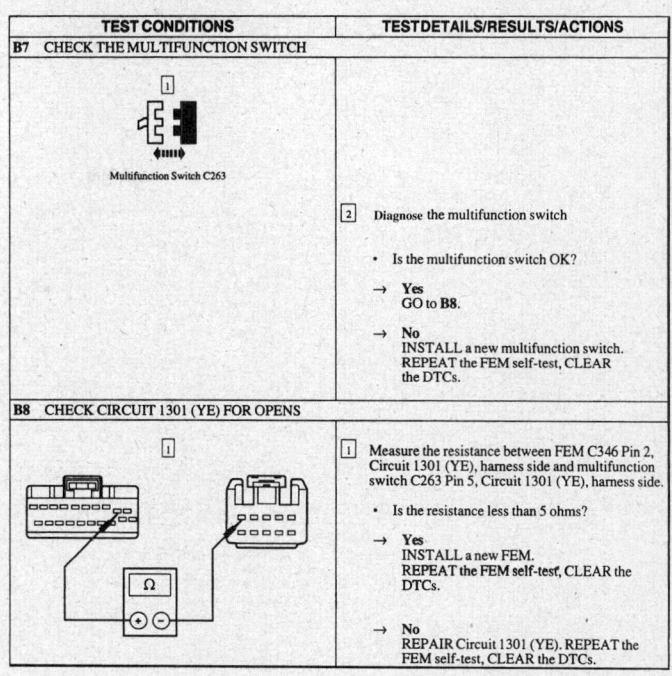

TEST CONDITIONS	TESTDETAILS/RESULTS/ACTIONS
B7 CHECK THE MULTIFUNCTION SWITCH	
	2 Diagnose the multifunction switch
	• Is the multifunction switch OK?
	→ **Yes** GO to **B8**.
	→ **No** INSTALL a new multifunction switch. REPEAT the FEM self-test, CLEAR the DTCs.
B8 CHECK CIRCUIT 1301 (YE) FOR OPENS	
	1 Measure the resistance between FEM C346 Pin 2, Circuit 1301 (YE), harness side and multifunction switch C263 Pin 5, Circuit 1301 (YE), harness side.
	• Is the resistance less than 5 ohms?
	→ **Yes** INSTALL a new FEM. REPEAT the FEM self-test, CLEAR the DTCs.
	→ **No** REPAIR Circuit 1301 (YE). REPEAT the FEM self-test, CLEAR the DTCs.

FM9029900711040X

Fig. 5 Test B: Front Wipers Are Inoperative (Part 4 of 11)

TEST CONDITIONS	TESTDETAILS/RESULTS/ACTIONS
B9 CHECK THE MULTIFUNCTION SWITCH FOR CORRECT OPERATION	
	2 Diagnose multifunction switch.
	• Is the multifunction switch OK?
	→ **Yes** GO to **B10**.
	→ **No** INSTALL a new multifunction switch. REPEAT the FEM self-test, CLEAR the DTCs.
B10 CHECK CIRCUIT 1302 (WH/LG) FOR OPEN	
	2 Measure the resistance between the FEM C346 Pin 14, Circuit 1302 (WH/LG), harness side and multifunction switch C263 Pin 3, Circuit 1302 (WH/LG), harness side.
	• Is the resistance less than 5 ohms?
	→ **Yes** GO to **B11**.
	→ **No** REPAIR Circuit 1302 (WH/LG). REPEAT the FEM self-test, CLEAR the DTCs.

FM9029900711050X

Fig. 5 Test B: Front Wipers Are Inoperative (Part 5 of 11)

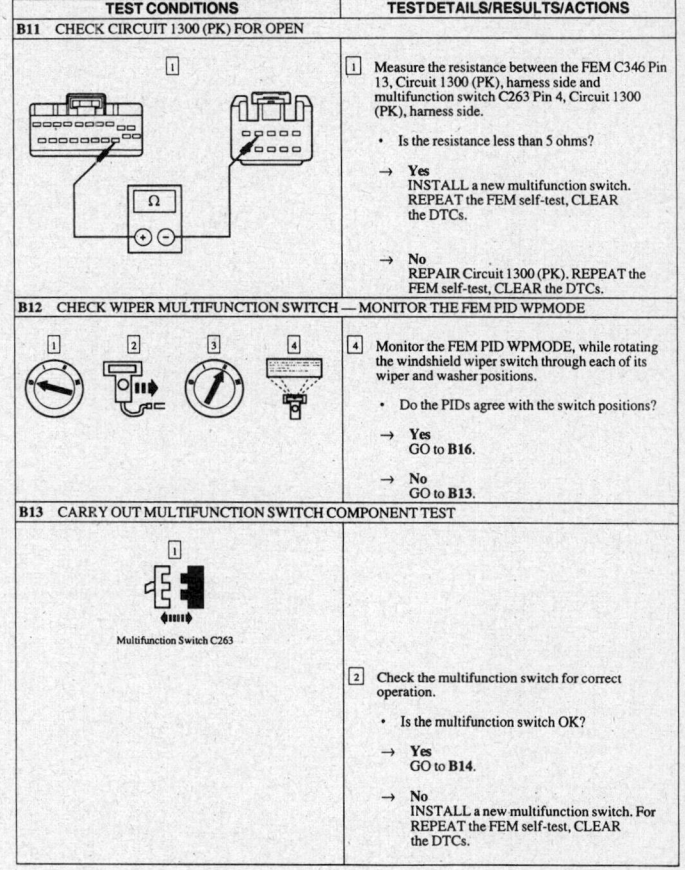

TEST CONDITIONS	TESTDETAILS/RESULTS/ACTIONS
B11 CHECK CIRCUIT 1300 (PK) FOR OPEN	
	1 Measure the resistance between the FEM C346 Pin 13, Circuit 1300 (PK), harness side and multifunction switch C263 Pin 4, Circuit 1300 (PK), harness side.
	• Is the resistance less than 5 ohms?
	→ **Yes** INSTALL a new multifunction switch. REPEAT the FEM self-test, CLEAR the DTCs.
	→ **No** REPAIR Circuit 1300 (PK). REPEAT the FEM self-test, CLEAR the DTCs.
B12 CHECK WIPER MULTIFUNCTION SWITCH — MONITOR THE FEM PID WPMODE	
	4 Monitor the FEM PID WPMODE, while rotating the windshield wiper switch through each of its wiper and washer positions.
	• Do the PIDs agree with the switch positions?
	→ **Yes** GO to **B16**.
	→ **No** GO to **B13**.
B13 CARRY OUT MULTIFUNCTION SWITCH COMPONENT TEST	
	2 Check the multifunction switch for correct operation.
	• Is the multifunction switch OK?
	→ **Yes** GO to **B14**.
	→ **No** INSTALL a new multifunction switch. For REPEAT the FEM self-test, CLEAR the DTCs.

FM9029900711060X

Fig. 5 Test B: Front Wipers Are Inoperative (Part 6 of 11)

TEST CONDITIONS	TESTDETAILS/RESULTS/ACTIONS
B14 CHECK CIRCUITS 1300 (PK), 1301 (YE), AND 1302 (WH/LG) FOR OPENS	

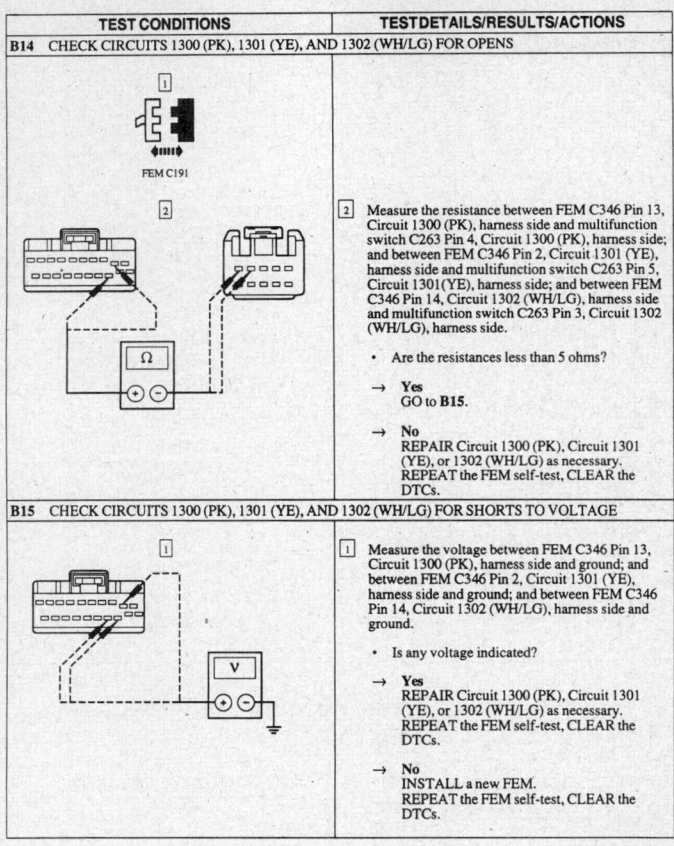

FEM C191

2. Measure the resistance between FEM C346 Pin 13, Circuit 1300 (PK), harness side and multifunction switch C263 Pin 4, Circuit 1300 (PK), harness side; and between FEM C346 Pin 2, Circuit 1301 (YE), harness side and multifunction switch C263 Pin 5, Circuit 1301 (YE), harness side; and between FEM C346 Pin 14, Circuit 1302 (WH/LG), harness side and multifunction switch C263 Pin 3, Circuit 1302 (WH/LG), harness side.

- Are the resistances less than 5 ohms?

→ Yes
GO to **B15**.

→ No
REPAIR Circuit 1300 (PK), Circuit 1301 (YE), or 1302 (WH/LG) as necessary. REPEAT the FEM self-test, CLEAR the DTCs.

B15 CHECK CIRCUITS 1300 (PK), 1301 (YE), AND 1302 (WH/LG) FOR SHORTS TO VOLTAGE	

1. Measure the voltage between FEM C346 Pin 13, Circuit 1300 (PK), harness side and ground; and between FEM C346 Pin 2, Circuit 1301 (YE), harness side and ground; and between FEM C346 Pin 14, Circuit 1302 (WH/LG), harness side and ground.

- Is any voltage indicated?

→ Yes
REPAIR Circuit 1300 (PK), Circuit 1301 (YE), or 1302 (WH/LG) as necessary. REPEAT the FEM self-test, CLEAR the DTCs.

→ No
INSTALL a new FEM. REPEAT the FEM self-test, CLEAR the DTCs.

FM9029900711070X

Fig. 5 Test B: Front Wipers Are Inoperative (Part 7 of 11)

TEST CONDITIONS	TESTDETAILS/RESULTS/ACTIONS
B18 CHECK WIPER ON/OFF RELAY	

Wiper ON/OFF Relay

2. Check the wiper ON/OFF relay for correct operation.

- Is the wiper ON/OFF relay OK?

→ Yes
GO to **B19**.

→ No
INSTALL a new wiper ON/OFF relay. REPEAT the FEM self-test, CLEAR the DTCs.

B19 CHECK CIRCUIT 65 (DG) FOR VOLTAGE	

1. Measure the voltage between the wiper ON/OFF relay Pin 2, Circuit 65 (DG), harness side and ground.

- Is the voltage greater than 10 volts?

→ Yes
GO to **B20**.

→ No
REPAIR Circuit 65 (DG). REPEAT the FEM self-test, CLEAR the DTCs.

FM9029900711090X

Fig. 5 Test B: Front Wipers Are Inoperative (Part 9 of 11)

TEST CONDITIONS	TESTDETAILS/RESULTS/ACTIONS
B16 CHECK FOR CORRECT WIPER OPERATION — USING FEM ACTIVE COMMANDS	

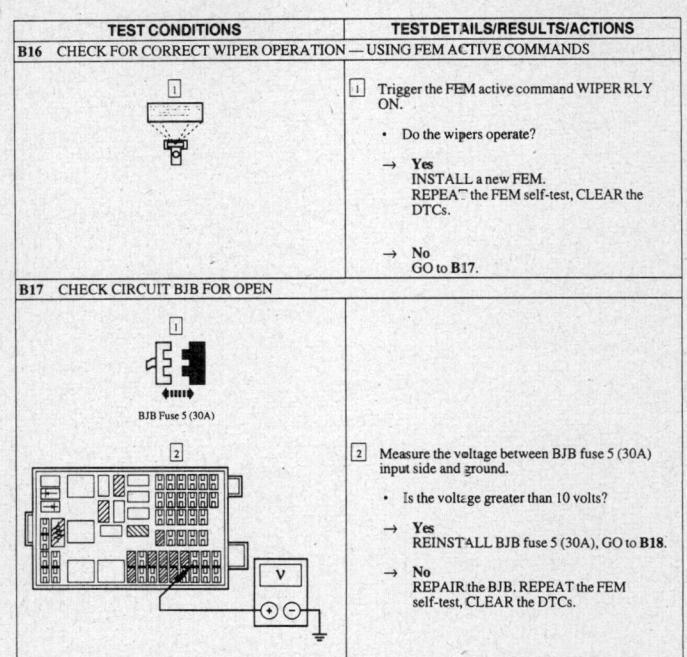

1. Trigger the FEM active command WIPER RLY ON.

- Do the wipers operate?

→ Yes
INSTALL a new FEM. REPEAT the FEM self-test, CLEAR the DTCs.

→ No
GO to **B17**.

B17 CHECK CIRCUIT BJB FOR OPEN	

BJB Fuse 5 (30A)

2. Measure the voltage between BJB fuse 5 (30A) input side and ground.

- Is the voltage greater than 10 volts?

→ Yes
REINSTALL BJB fuse 5 (30A), GO to **B18**.

→ No
REPAIR the BJB. REPEAT the FEM self-test, CLEAR the DTCs.

FM9029900711080X

Fig. 5 Test B: Front Wipers Are Inoperative (Part 8 of 11)

TEST CONDITIONS	TESTDETAILS/RESULTS/ACTIONS
B20 CHECK CIRCUIT 65 (DG) FOR OPEN	

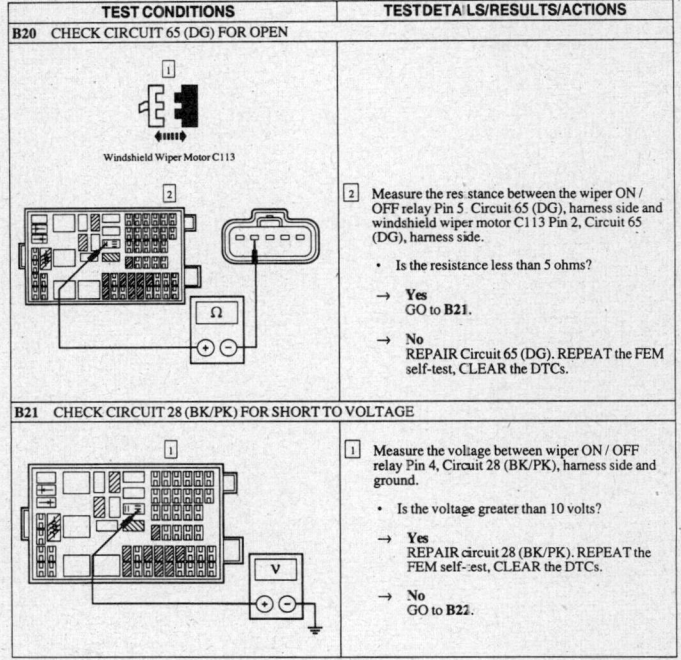

Windshield Wiper Motor C113

2. Measure the resistance between the wiper ON/OFF relay Pin 5, Circuit 65 (DG), harness side and windshield wiper motor C113 Pin 2, Circuit 65 (DG), harness side.

- Is the resistance less than 5 ohms?

→ Yes
GO to **B21**.

→ No
REPAIR Circuit 65 (DG). REPEAT the FEM self-test, CLEAR the DTCs.

B21 CHECK CIRCUIT 28 (BK/PK) FOR SHORT TO VOLTAGE	

1. Measure the voltage between wiper ON/OFF relay Pin 4, Circuit 28 (BK/PK), harness side and ground.

- Is the voltage greater than 10 volts?

→ Yes
REPAIR circuit 28 (BK/PK). REPEAT the FEM self-test, CLEAR the DTCs.

→ No
GO to **B22**.

FM9029900711100X

Fig. 5 Test B: Front Wipers Are Inoperative (Part 10 of 11)

TEST CONDITIONS	TESTDETAILS/RESULTS/ACTIONS
B22 CHECK WIPER MOTOR GROUND CIRCUIT 1205 (BK) FOR OPEN	

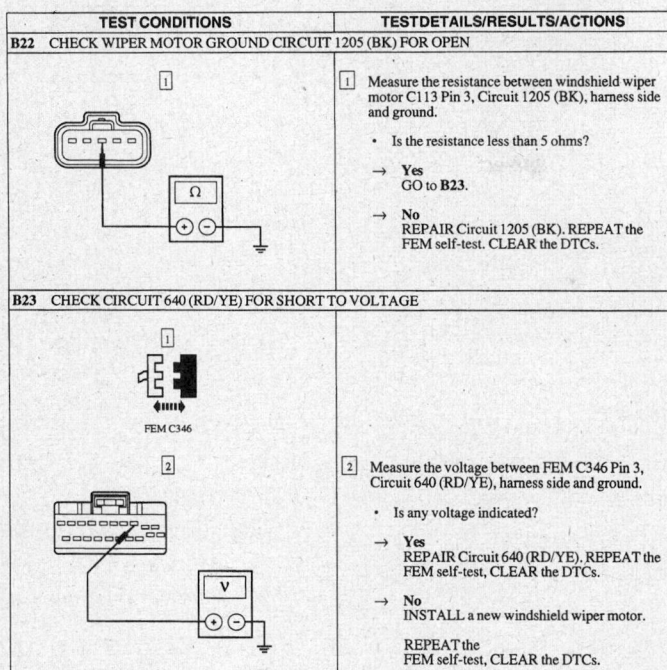

1. Measure the resistance between windshield wiper motor C113 Pin 3, Circuit 1205 (BK), harness side and ground.
   - Is the resistance less than 5 ohms?
   → **Yes**
     GO to **B23**.
   → **No**
     REPAIR Circuit 1205 (BK). REPEAT the FEM self-test. CLEAR the DTCs.

TEST CONDITIONS	TESTDETAILS/RESULTS/ACTIONS
B23 CHECK CIRCUIT 640 (RD/YE) FOR SHORT TO VOLTAGE	

FEM C346

2. Measure the voltage between FEM C346 Pin 3, Circuit 640 (RD/YE), harness side and ground.
   - Is any voltage indicated?
   → **Yes**
     REPAIR Circuit 640 (RD/YE). REPEAT the FEM self-test, CLEAR the DTCs.
   → **No**
     INSTALL a new windshield wiper motor.

     REPEAT the FEM self-test, CLEAR the DTCs.

FM9029900711120X

Fig. 5   Test B: Front Wipers Are Inoperative (Part 11 of 11)

TEST CONDITIONS	TESTDETAILS/RESULTS/ACTIONS
C4 CHECK CIRCUIT 1359 (DG/PK) FOR OPEN	

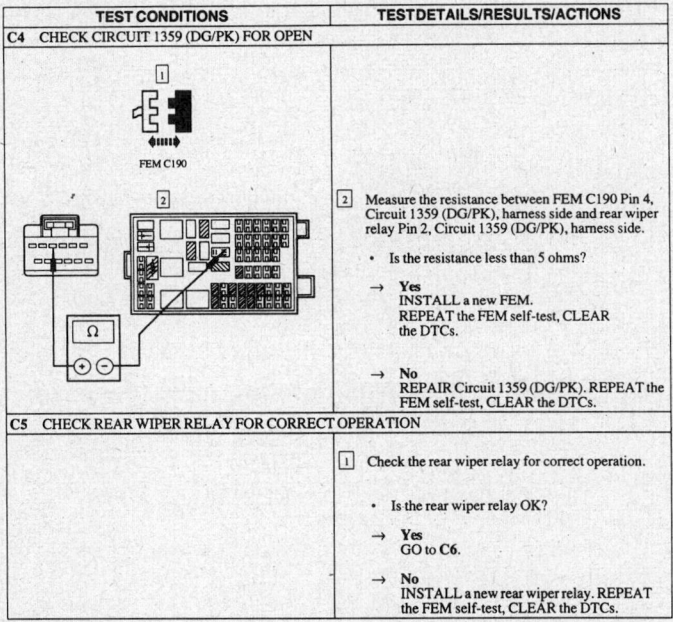

FEM C190

2. Measure the resistance between FEM C190 Pin 4, Circuit 1359 (DG/PK), harness side and rear wiper relay Pin 2, Circuit 1359 (DG/PK), harness side.
   - Is the resistance less than 5 ohms?
   → **Yes**
     INSTALL a new FEM.
     REPEAT the FEM self-test, CLEAR the DTCs.
   → **No**
     REPAIR Circuit 1359 (DG/PK). REPEAT the FEM self-test, CLEAR the DTCs.

TEST CONDITIONS	TESTDETAILS/RESULTS/ACTIONS
C5 CHECK REAR WIPER RELAY FOR CORRECT OPERATION	

1. Check the rear wiper relay for correct operation.
   - Is the rear wiper relay OK?
   → **Yes**
     GO to **C6**.
   → **No**
     INSTALL a new rear wiper relay. REPEAT the FEM self-test, CLEAR the DTCs.

FM9029900712020X

Fig. 6   Test C: Rear Wipers Inoperative (Part 2 of 7)

TEST CONDITIONS	TESTDETAILS/RESULTS/ACTIONS
C1 USE THE RECORDED DTCS FROM THE FEM SELF-TEST	

1. Use the recorded results from FEM self-test.
   - Are any DTCs recorded?
   → **Yes**
     If DTC B1244, GO to **C2**.
     If DTC B1245, GO to **C5**.
     If DTC B1611, GO to **C7**.
   → **No**
     GO to **C9**.

TEST CONDITIONS	TESTDETAILS/RESULTS/ACTIONS
C2 CHECK THE REAR WIPER RELAY	

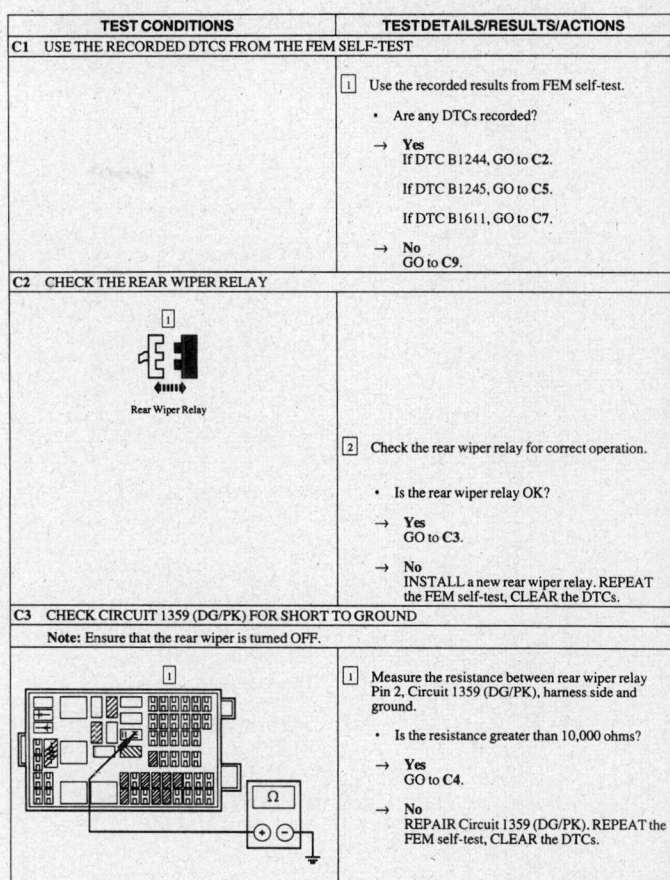

Rear Wiper Relay

2. Check the rear wiper relay for correct operation.
   - Is the rear wiper relay OK?
   → **Yes**
     GO to **C3**.
   → **No**
     INSTALL a new rear wiper relay. REPEAT the FEM self-test, CLEAR the DTCs.

TEST CONDITIONS	TESTDETAILS/RESULTS/ACTIONS
C3 CHECK CIRCUIT 1359 (DG/PK) FOR SHORT TO GROUND	
Note: Ensure that the rear wiper is turned OFF.	

1. Measure the resistance between rear wiper relay Pin 2, Circuit 1359 (DG/PK), harness side and ground.
   - Is the resistance greater than 10,000 ohms?
   → **Yes**
     GO to **C4**.
   → **No**
     REPAIR Circuit 1359 (DG/PK). REPEAT the FEM self-test, CLEAR the DTCs.

FM9029900712010X

Fig. 6   Test C: Rear Wipers Inoperative (Part 1 of 7)

TEST CONDITIONS	TESTDETAILS/RESULTS/ACTIONS
C6 CHECK CIRCUIT 1359 (DG/VT) FOR SHORT TO VOLTAGE	

1. Measure the voltage between FEM C190 Pin 4, Circuit 1359 (DG/PK), harness side and ground.
   - Is the voltage greater than 10 volts?
   → **Yes**
     REPAIR circuit 1359 (DG/VT). REPEAT the FEM self-test. CLEAR the DTCs.
   → **No**
     INSTALL a new FEM.
     REPEAT the FEM self-test, CLEAR the DTCs.

TEST CONDITIONS	TESTDETAILS/RESULTS/ACTIONS
C7 CHECK THE MULTIFUNCTION SWITCH FOR CORRECT OPERATION	

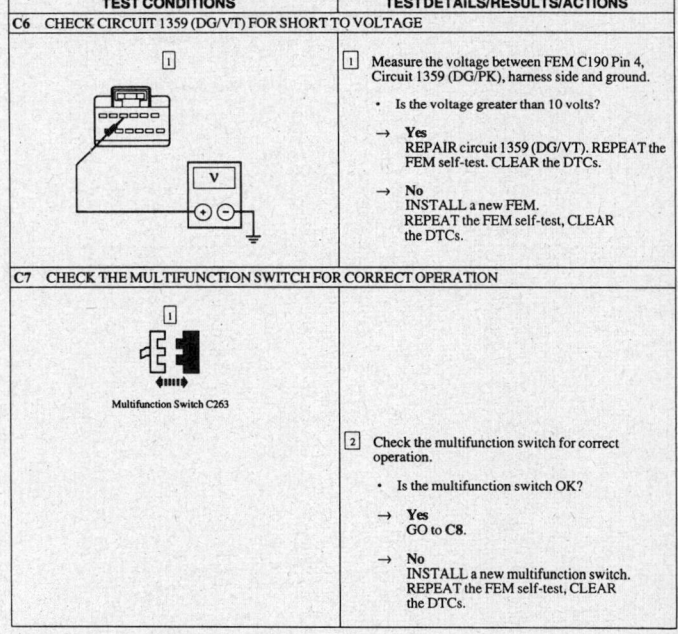

Multifunction Switch C263

2. Check the multifunction switch for correct operation.
   - Is the multifunction switch OK?
   → **Yes**
     GO to **C8**.
   → **No**
     INSTALL a new multifunction switch. REPEAT the FEM self-test, CLEAR the DTCs.

FM9029900712030X

Fig. 6   Test C: Rear Wipers Inoperative (Part 3 of 7)

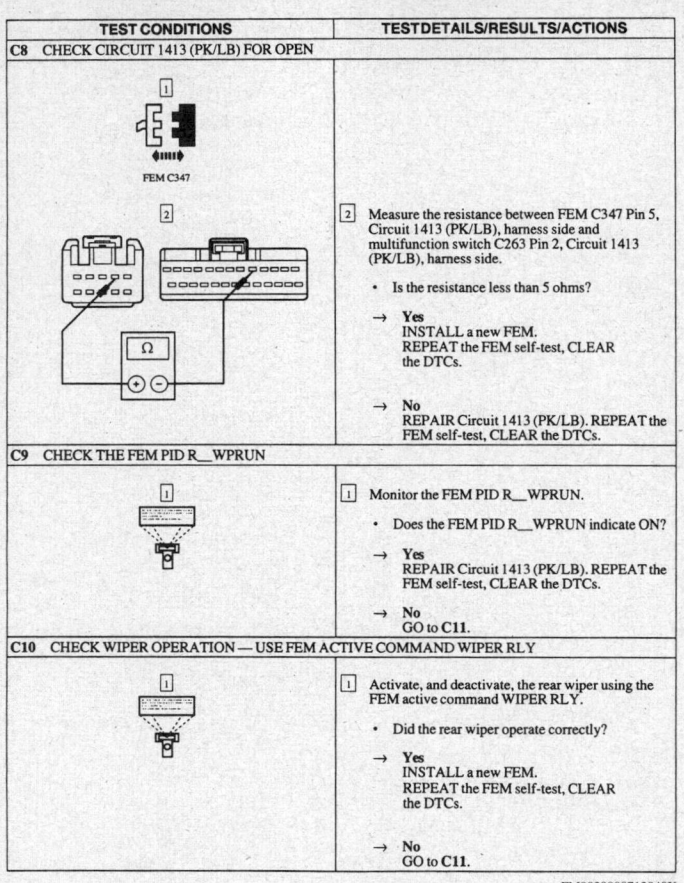

TEST CONDITIONS	TEST DETAILS/RESULTS/ACTIONS
C8 CHECK CIRCUIT 1413 (PK/LB) FOR OPEN	
FEM C347	[2] Measure the resistance between FEM C347 Pin 5, Circuit 1413 (PK/LB), harness side and multifunction switch C263 Pin 2, Circuit 1413 (PK/LB), harness side. • Is the resistance less than 5 ohms? → **Yes** INSTALL a new FEM. REPEAT the FEM self-test, CLEAR the DTCs. → **No** REPAIR Circuit 1413 (PK/LB). REPEAT the FEM self-test, CLEAR the DTCs.
C9 CHECK THE FEM PID R__WPRUN	[1] Monitor the FEM PID R__WPRUN. • Does the FEM PID R__WPRUN indicate ON? → **Yes** REPAIR Circuit 1413 (PK/LB). REPEAT the FEM self-test, CLEAR the DTCs. → **No** GO to C11.
C10 CHECK WIPER OPERATION — USE FEM ACTIVE COMMAND WIPER RLY	[1] Activate, and deactivate, the rear wiper using the FEM active command WIPER RLY. • Did the rear wiper operate correctly? → **Yes** INSTALL a new FEM. REPEAT the FEM self-test, CLEAR the DTCs. → **No** GO to C11.

FM9029900712040X

Fig. 6 Test C: Rear Wipers Inoperative (Part 4 of 7)

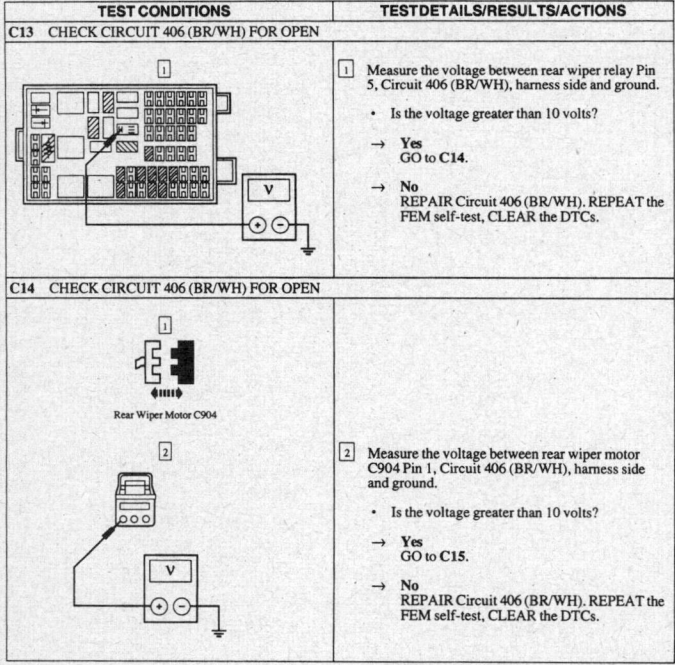

TEST CONDITIONS	TEST DETAILS/RESULTS/ACTIONS
C13 CHECK CIRCUIT 406 (BR/WH) FOR OPEN	[1] Measure the voltage between rear wiper relay Pin 5, Circuit 406 (BR/WH), harness side and ground. • Is the voltage greater than 10 volts? → **Yes** GO to C14. → **No** REPAIR Circuit 406 (BR/WH). REPEAT the FEM self-test, CLEAR the DTCs.
C14 CHECK CIRCUIT 406 (BR/WH) FOR OPEN	
Rear Wiper Motor C904	[2] Measure the voltage between rear wiper motor C904 Pin 1, Circuit 406 (BR/WH), harness side and ground. • Is the voltage greater than 10 volts? → **Yes** GO to C15. → **No** REPAIR Circuit 406 (BR/WH). REPEAT the FEM self-test, CLEAR the DTCs.

FM9029900712060X

Fig. 6 Test C: Rear Wipers Inoperative (Part 6 of 7)

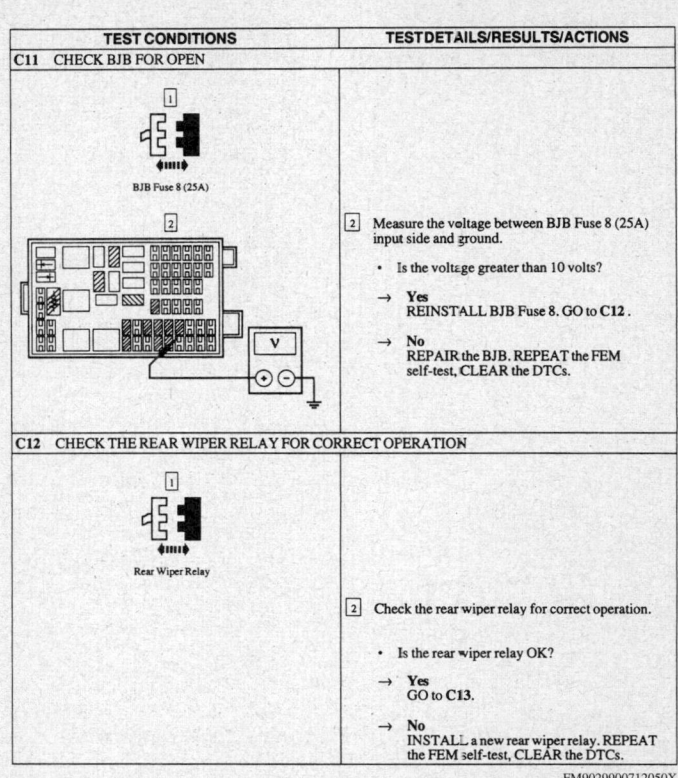

TEST CONDITIONS	TEST DETAILS/RESULTS/ACTIONS
C11 CHECK BJB FOR OPEN	
BJB Fuse 8 (25A)	[2] Measure the voltage between BJB Fuse 8 (25A) input side and ground. • Is the voltage greater than 10 volts? → **Yes** REINSTALL BJB Fuse 8. GO to C12. → **No** REPAIR the BJB. REPEAT the FEM self-test, CLEAR the DTCs.
C12 CHECK THE REAR WIPER RELAY FOR CORRECT OPERATION	
Rear Wiper Relay	[2] Check the rear wiper relay for correct operation. • Is the rear wiper relay OK? → **Yes** GO to C13. → **No** INSTALL a new rear wiper relay. REPEAT the FEM self-test, CLEAR the DTCs.

FM9029900712050X

Fig. 6 Test C: Rear Wipers Inoperative (Part 5 of 7)

TEST CONDITIONS	TEST DETAILS/RESULTS/ACTIONS
C15 CHECK CIRCUIT 63 (RD) FOR OPEN	[1] Measure the resistance between rear wiper relay Pin 5, Circuit 63 (RD), harness side and rear wiper motor C904 Pin 2, Circuit 63 (RD), harness side. • Is the resistance less than 5 ohms? → **Yes** REPAIR the BJB. REPEAT the FEM self-test, CLEAR the DTCs. → **No** REPAIR Circuit 63 (RD). REPEAT the FEM self-test, CLEAR the DTCs.

FM9029900712070X

Fig. 6 Test C: Rear Wipers Inoperative (Part 7 of 7)

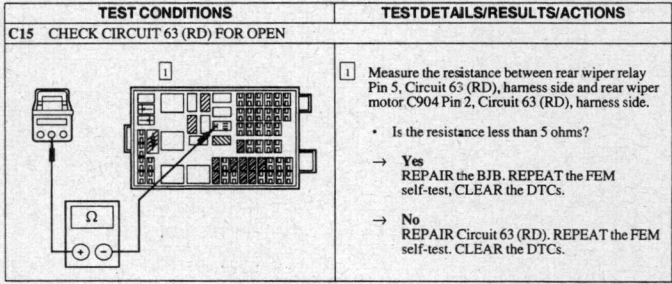

TEST CONDITIONS	TEST DETAILS/RESULTS/ACTIONS
D1 USE THE RESULTS FROM THE FEM SELF-TEST	[1] Use the recorded results from FEM self-test. • Are any DTCs recorded? → **Yes** REFER to Diagnostic Chart Index. → **No** For front wiper concerns, GO to D2. For rear wiper concerns, GO to D6.

FM9029900713010X

Fig. 7 Test D: Front Or Rear Wipers Stay On Continuously (Part 1 of 5)

TEST CONDITIONS	TEST DETAILS/RESULTS/ACTIONS
D2 CHECK WIPER ON / OFF RELAY	
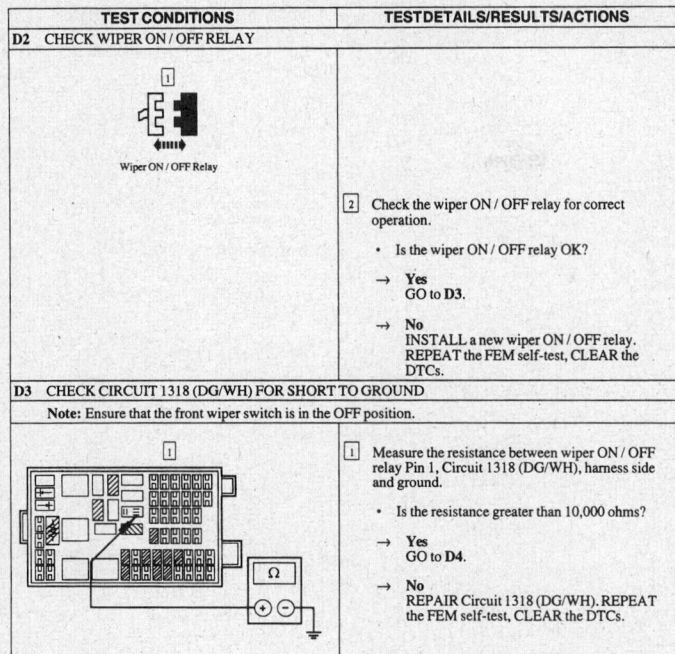 Wiper ON / OFF Relay	2 Check the wiper ON / OFF relay for correct operation. • Is the wiper ON / OFF relay OK? → **Yes** GO to **D3**. → **No** INSTALL a new wiper ON / OFF relay. REPEAT the FEM self-test, CLEAR the DTCs.
D3 CHECK CIRCUIT 1318 (DG/WH) FOR SHORT TO GROUND	
Note: Ensure that the front wiper switch is in the OFF position.	
	1 Measure the resistance between wiper ON / OFF relay Pin 1, Circuit 1318 (DG/WH), harness side and ground. • Is the resistance greater than 10,000 ohms? → **Yes** GO to **D4**. → **No** REPAIR Circuit 1318 (DG/WH). REPEAT the FEM self-test, CLEAR the DTCs.

FM9029900713020X

Fig. 7 Test D: Front Or Rear Wipers Stay On Continuously (Part 2 of 5)

TEST CONDITIONS	TEST DETAILS/RESULTS/ACTIONS
D7 CHECK CIRCUIT 1359 (DG/PK) FOR OPEN	
	1 Measure the resistance between rear wiper relay Pin 2, Circuit 1359 (DG/PK), harness side and ground. • Is the resistance greater than 10,000 ohms? → **Yes** GO to **D8**. → **No** REPAIR Circuit 1359 (DG/PK). REPEAT the FEM self-test, CLEAR the DTCs.
D8 CHECK THE MULTIFUNCTION SWITCH	
Multifunction Switch C263	2 Check the multifunction switch for correct operation. • Is the multifunction switch OK? → **Yes** GO to **D9**. → **No** INSTALL a new multifunction switch. REPEAT the FEM self-test, CLEAR the DTCs.

FM9029900713040X

Fig. 7 Test D: Front Or Rear Wipers Stay On Continuously (Part 4 of 5)

TEST CONDITIONS	TEST DETAILS/RESULTS/ACTIONS
D4 CHECK THE MULTIFUNCTION SWITCH	
Multifunction Switch C263	2 Check the multifunction switch for correct operation. • Is the multifunction switch OK? → **Yes** GO to **D5**. → **No** INSTALL a new multifunction switch. REPEAT the FEM self-test, CLEAR the DTCs.
D5 CHECK CIRCUIT 1301 (YE) FOR SHORT TO GROUND	
	1 Measure the resistance between multifunctuon switch C263 Pin 5, Circuit 1301 (YE), harness side and ground. • Is the resistance greater than 10,000 ohms? → **Yes** INSTALL a new FEM. REPEAT the FEM self-test, CLEAR the DTCs. → **No** REPAIR Circuit 1301 (YE). REPEAT the FEM self-test, CLEAR the DTCs.
D6 CHECK REAR WIPER RELAY FOR CORRECT OPERATION	
	1 Check the rear wiper relay for correct operation. • Is the rear wiper relay OK? → **Yes** GO to **C6**. → **No** INSTALL a new rear wiper switch.

FM9029900713030X

Fig. 7 Test D: Front Or Rear Wipers Stay On Continuously (Part 3 of 5)

TEST CONDITIONS	TEST DETAILS/RESULTS/ACTIONS
D9 CHECK CIRCUIT 1413 (PK/LB) FOR SHORT TO GROUND	
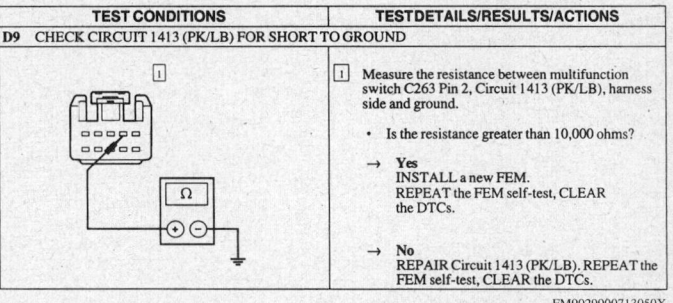	1 Measure the resistance between multifunction switch C263 Pin 2, Circuit 1413 (PK/LB), harness side and ground. • Is the resistance greater than 10,000 ohms? → **Yes** INSTALL a new FEM. REPEAT the FEM self-test, CLEAR the DTCs. → **No** REPAIR Circuit 1413 (PK/LB). REPEAT the FEM self-test, CLEAR the DTCs.

FM9029900713050X

Fig. 7 Test D: Front Or Rear Wipers Stay On Continuously (Part 5 of 5)

TEST CONDITIONS	TEST DETAILS/RESULTS/ACTIONS
E1 USE THE RESULTS FROM THE FEM SELF-TEST	
	1 Use the recorded results from FEM self-test. • Are any DTCs recorded? → **Yes** If DTC B1446, GO to **E2**. If DTC B1448, GO to **E4**. → **No** GO to **E6**.

FM9029900714010X

Fig. 8 Test E: Intermittent Wiper Speed Does Not Operate Properly (Part 1 of 4)

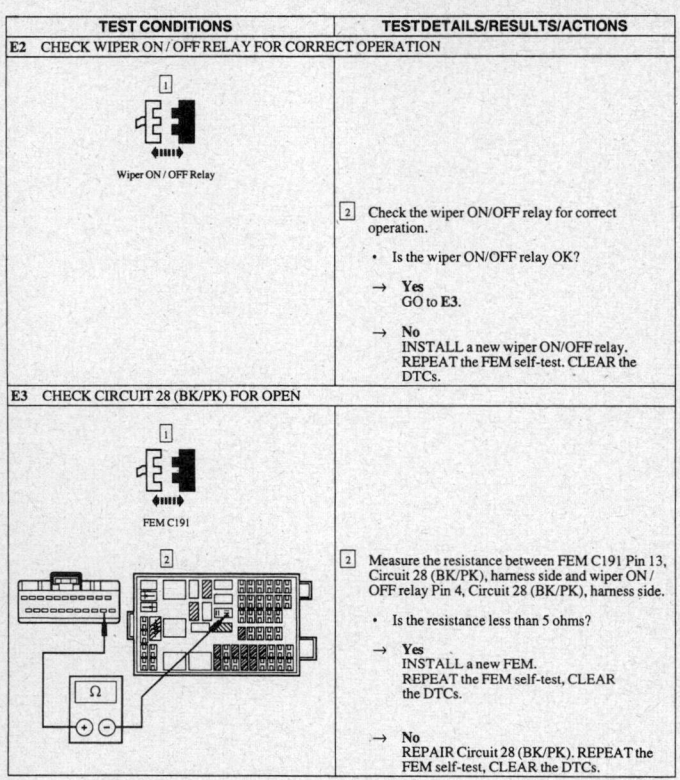

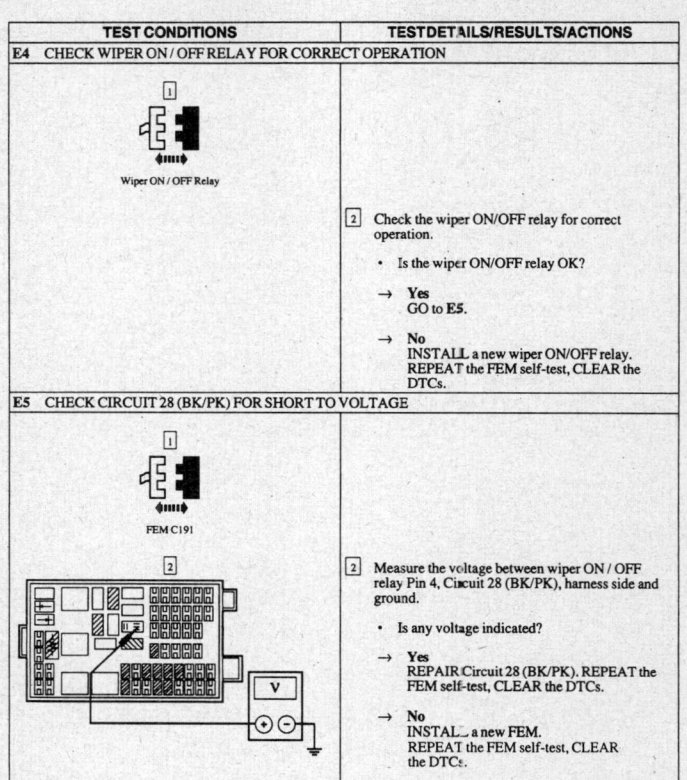

TEST CONDITIONS	TEST DETAILS/RESULTS/ACTIONS
E2 CHECK WIPER ON / OFF RELAY FOR CORRECT OPERATION	
Wiper ON / OFF Relay	2 Check the wiper ON/OFF relay for correct operation. • Is the wiper ON/OFF relay OK? → **Yes** GO to E3. → **No** INSTALL a new wiper ON/OFF relay. REPEAT the FEM self-test. CLEAR the DTCs.
E3 CHECK CIRCUIT 28 (BK/PK) FOR OPEN	
FEM C191	2 Measure the resistance between FEM C191 Pin 13, Circuit 28 (BK/PK), harness side and wiper ON / OFF relay Pin 4, Circuit 28 (BK/PK), harness side. • Is the resistance less than 5 ohms? → **Yes** INSTALL a new FEM. REPEAT the FEM self-test, CLEAR the DTCs. → **No** REPAIR Circuit 28 (BK/PK). REPEAT the FEM self-test, CLEAR the DTCs.

FM9029900714020X

Fig. 8   Test E: Intermittent Wiper Speed Does Not Operate Properly (Part 2 of 4)

TEST CONDITIONS	TEST DETAILS/RESULTS/ACTIONS
E4 CHECK WIPER ON / OFF RELAY FOR CORRECT OPERATION	
Wiper ON / OFF Relay	2 Check the wiper ON/OFF relay for correct operation. • Is the wiper ON/OFF relay OK? → **Yes** GO to E5. → **No** INSTALL a new wiper ON/OFF relay. REPEAT the FEM self-test, CLEAR the DTCs.
E5 CHECK CIRCUIT 28 (BK/PK) FOR SHORT TO VOLTAGE	
FEM C191	2 Measure the voltage between wiper ON / OFF relay Pin 4, Circuit 28 (BK/PK), harness side and ground. • Is any voltage indicated? → **Yes** REPAIR Circuit 28 (BK/PK). REPEAT the FEM self-test, CLEAR the DTCs. → **No** INSTALL a new FEM. REPEAT the FEM self-test, CLEAR the DTCs.

FM9029900714030X

Fig. 8   Test E: Intermittent Wiper Speed Does Not Operate Properly (Part 3 of 4)

TEST CONDITIONS	TEST DETAILS/RESULTS/ACTIONS
E6 CHECK THE MULTIFUNCTION SWITCH	
Multifunction Switch C263	2 Check the multifunction switch for correct operation. • Is the multifunction switch OK? → **Yes** GO to E7. → **No** INSTALL a new multifunction switch. REPEAT the FEM self-test, CLEAR the DTCs.
E7 CHECK CIRCUIT 640 (RD/YE) FOR SHORT TO VOLTAGE	
FEM C346	2 Measure the voltage between FEM C346 Pin 3, Circuit 640 (RD/YE), harness side and ground. • Is any voltage indicated? → **Yes** REPAIR Circuit 640 (RD/YE). REPEAT the FEM self-test, CLEAR the DTCs. → **No** INSTALL a new FEM. REPEAT the FEM self-test, CLEAR the DTCs.

FM9029900714040X

Fig. 8   Test E: Intermittent Wiper Speed Does Not Operate Properly (Part 4 of 4)

TEST CONDITIONS	TEST DETAILS/RESULTS/ACTIONS
F1 USE THE RECORDED RESULTS FROM THE FEM SELF-TEST	
	1 Use the recorded results from the FEM self-test. • Are any DTCs recorded? → **Yes** If B1241, GO to F2. If B1460, GO to F3. → **No** If the front washer is inoperative, GO to F4. If the rear washer is inoperative, GO to F7.
F2 CHECK CIRCUIT 1333 (LB/WH) FOR SHORT TO VOLTAGE	
FEM C191	2 Measure the voltage between FEM C191 Pin 5, Circuit 1333 (LB/WH), harness side and ground. • Is any voltage indicated? → **Yes** REPAIR Circuit 1333 (LB/WH). REPEAT the FEM self-test, CLEAR the DTCs. → **No** INSTALL a new FEM. REPEAT the FEM self-test, CLEAR the DTCs.

FM9029900715010X

Fig. 9   Test F: Front & Rear Washer Pump Inoperative (Part 1 of 6)

TEST CONDITIONS	TEST DETAILS/RESULTS/ACTIONS

F3   CHECK CIRCUIT 1321 (TN/BK) FOR SHORT TO VOLTAGE

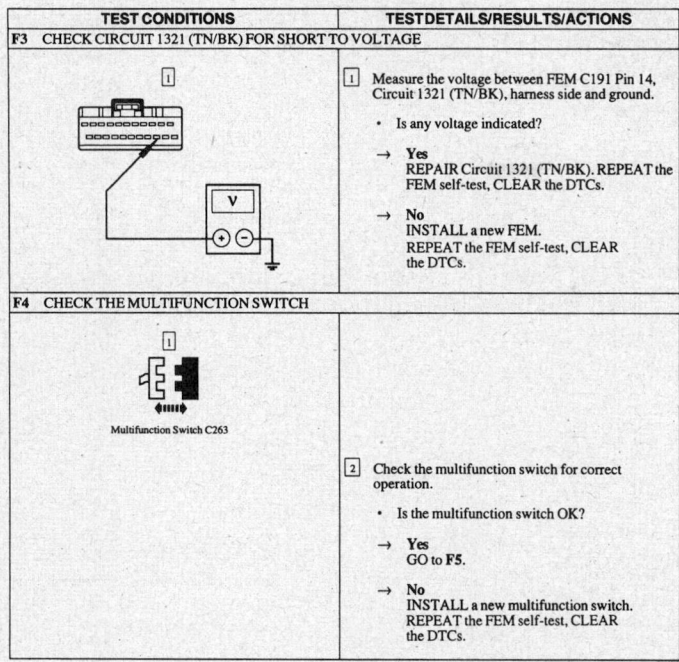

1. Measure the voltage between FEM C191 Pin 14, Circuit 1321 (TN/BK), harness side and ground.

   - Is any voltage indicated?

   → **Yes**
   REPAIR Circuit 1321 (TN/BK). REPEAT the FEM self-test, CLEAR the DTCs.

   → **No**
   INSTALL a new FEM.
   REPEAT the FEM self-test, CLEAR the DTCs.

F4   CHECK THE MULTIFUNCTION SWITCH

Multifunction Switch C263

2. Check the multifunction switch for correct operation.

   - Is the multifunction switch OK?

   → **Yes**
   GO to **F5**.

   → **No**
   INSTALL a new multifunction switch.
   REPEAT the FEM self-test, CLEAR the DTCs.

FM9029900715020X

Fig. 9   Test F: Front & Rear Washer Pump Inoperative (Part 2 of 6)

TEST CONDITIONS	TEST DETAILS/RESULTS/ACTIONS

F7   CHECK THE BJB FOR OPEN

BJB Fuse 8 (25A)

2. Measure the voltage between BJB Fuse 8 (25A) input side and ground.

   - Is the voltage greater than 10 volts?

   → **Yes**
   GO to **F8**.

   → **No**
   REPAIR the BJB. REPEAT the FEM self-test, CLEAR the DTCs.

F8   CHECK CIRCUIT 406 (BR/WH) FOR OPEN

Rear Washer Pump C118

2. Measure the voltage between rear washer C118 Pin 1, Circuit 406 (BR/WH), harness side and ground.

   - Is the voltage greater than 10 volts?

   → **Yes**
   GO to **F9**.

   → **No**
   REPAIR Circuit 406 (BR/WH). REPEAT the FEM self-test, CLEAR the DTCs.

FM9029900715040X

Fig. 9   Test F: Front & Rear Washer Pump Inoperative (Part 4 of 6)

TEST CONDITIONS	TEST DETAILS/RESULTS/ACTIONS

F5   CHECK CIRCUIT 1321 (TN/BK) FOR OPEN

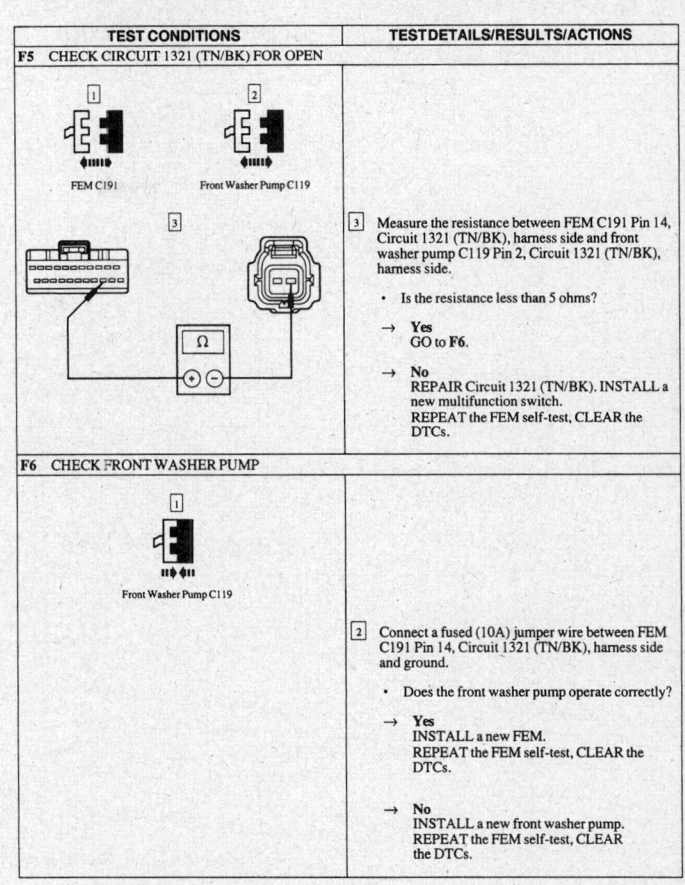

FEM C191   Front Washer Pump C119

3. Measure the resistance between FEM C191 Pin 14, Circuit 1321 (TN/BK), harness side and front washer pump C119 Pin 2, Circuit 1321 (TN/BK), harness side.

   - Is the resistance less than 5 ohms?

   → **Yes**
   GO to **F6**.

   → **No**
   REPAIR Circuit 1321 (TN/BK). INSTALL a new multifunction switch.
   REPEAT the FEM self-test, CLEAR the DTCs.

F6   CHECK FRONT WASHER PUMP

Front Washer Pump C119

2. Connect a fused (10A) jumper wire between FEM C191 Pin 14, Circuit 1321 (TN/BK), harness side and ground.

   - Does the front washer pump operate correctly?

   → **Yes**
   INSTALL a new FEM.
   REPEAT the FEM self-test, CLEAR the DTCs.

   → **No**
   INSTALL a new front washer pump.
   REPEAT the FEM self-test, CLEAR the DTCs.

FM9029900715030X

Fig. 9   Test F: Front & Rear Washer Pump Inoperative (Part 3 of 6)

TEST CONDITIONS	TEST DETAILS/RESULTS/ACTIONS

F9   CHECK REAR WASHER PUMP

Rear Washer Pump C118

2. Connect a fused (10A) jumper wire between FEM C191 Pin 5, Circuit 1333 (LB/WH), harness side and ground.

   - Did the rear washer pump operate correctly?

   → **Yes**
   GO to **F10**.

   → **No**
   INSTALL a new rear washer pump.
   REPEAT the FEM self-test, CLEAR the DTCs.

F10   CHECK CIRCUIT 1333 (LB/WH) FOR OPEN

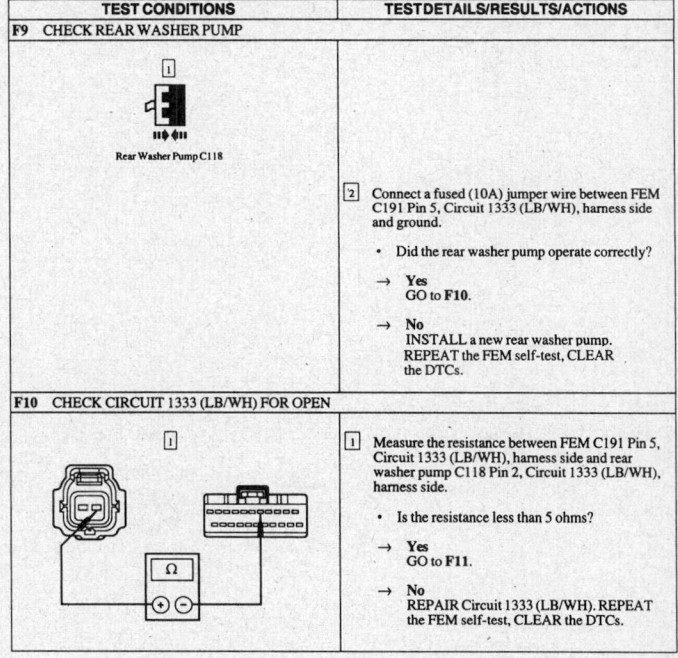

1. Measure the resistance between FEM C191 Pin 5, Circuit 1333 (LB/WH), harness side and rear washer pump C118 Pin 2, Circuit 1333 (LB/WH), harness side.

   - Is the resistance less than 5 ohms?

   → **Yes**
   GO to **F11**.

   → **No**
   REPAIR Circuit 1333 (LB/WH). REPEAT the FEM self-test, CLEAR the DTCs.

FM9029900715050X

Fig. 9   Test F: Front & Rear Washer Pump Inoperative (Part 5 of 6)

TEST CONDITIONS	TEST DETAILS/RESULTS/ACTIONS
F11 CHECK THE MULTIFUNCTION SWITCH	

1
 	
Multifunction Switch C263
	2 Check the multifunction switch for correct operation.
	
	• Is the multifunction switch OK?
	
	→ **Yes**
	   REPAIR Circuit 1333 (LB/WH). REPEAT the FEM self-test, CLEAR the DTCs.
	
	→ **No**
	   INSTALL a new multifunction switch. REPEAT the FEM self-test, CLEAR the DTCs.

FM9029900715060X

Fig. 9   Test F: Front & Rear Washer Pump Inoperative (Part 6 of 6)

TEST CONDITIONS	TEST DETAILS/RESULTS/ACTIONS
G2 CHECK THE MULTIFUNCTION SWITCH	

1
 	
Multifunction Switch C263
	2 Check the multifunction switch for correct operation.
	
	• Is the multifunction switch OK?
	
	→ **Yes**
	   If the front washer pump is ON continuously, GO to **G3**.
	
	   If the rear washer pump is ON continuously, GO to **G4**.
	
	→ **No**
	   INSTALL a new multifunction switch. REPEAT the FEM self-test, CLEAR the DTCs.

G3 CHECK CIRCUIT 1321 (TN/BK) FOR SHORT TO GROUND	

1
 	
FEM C191
 	
2
Ω
	2 Measure the resistance between FEM C191 Pin 14, Circuit 1321 (TN/BK), harness side and ground.
	
	• Is the resistance greater than 10,000 ohms?
	
	→ **Yes**
	   INSTALL a new FEM. REPEAT the FEM self-test, CLEAR the DTCs.
	
	→ **No**
	   REPAIR Circuit 1321 (TN/BK). REPEAT the FEM self-test, CLEAR the DTCs.

FM9029900716020X

Fig. 10   Test G: Washer Pump Inoperative, Front & Rear Washers Stay On Continuously (Part 2 of 3)

TEST CONDITIONS	TEST DETAILS/RESULTS/ACTIONS
G1 USE THE RESULTS FROM FEM SELF-TEST	

	1 Use the recorded results from FEM self-test.
	
	• Are any DTCs recorded?
	
	→ **Yes**
	   REFER to Diagnostic Chart Index.
	
	→ **No**
	   GO to **G2**.

FM9029900716010X

Fig. 10   Test G: Washer Pump Inoperative, Front & Rear Washers Stay On Continuously (Part 1 of 3)

TEST CONDITIONS	TEST DETAILS/RESULTS/ACTIONS
G4 CHECK CIRCUIT 1333 (LB/WH) FOR SHORT TO GROUND	

1
 	
FEM C191
 	
2
Ω
	2 Measure the resistance between FEM C191 Pin 5, Circuit 1333 (LB/WH), harness side and ground.
	
	• Is the resistance greater than 10,000 ohms?
	
	→ **Yes**
	   INSTALL a new FEM. REPEAT the FEM self-test, CLEAR the DTCs.
	
	→ **No**
	   REPAIR Circuit 1333 (LB/WH). REPEAT the FEM self-test, CLEAR the DTCs.

FM9029900716030X

Fig. 10   Test G: Washer Pump Inoperative, Front & Rear Washers Stay On Continuously (Part 3 of 3)

TEST CONDITIONS	TEST DETAILS/RESULTS/ACTIONS
H1 USE THE RESULTS FROM FEM SELF-TEST	

	1 Use the recorded results from FEM self-test.
	
	• Are any DTCs recorded?
	
	→ **Yes**
	   If DTC B1436, GO to **H2**.
	
	→ **No**
	   GO to **H4**.

FM9029900717010X

Fig. 11   Test H: High/Low Wiper Speeds Do Not Operate Properly (Part 1 of 7)

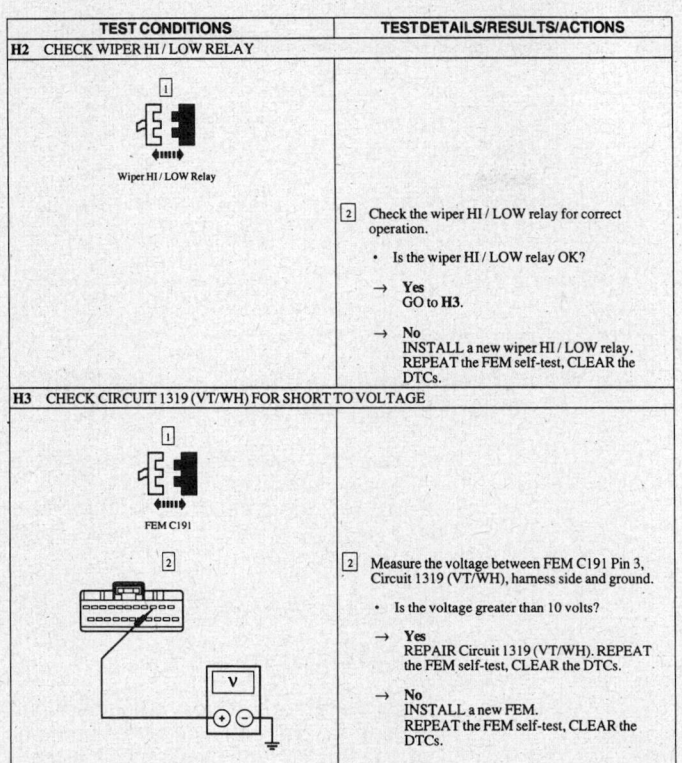

TEST CONDITIONS	TEST DETAILS/RESULTS/ACTIONS
H2 CHECK WIPER HI / LOW RELAY	
Wiper HI / LOW Relay	② Check the wiper HI / LOW relay for correct operation. • Is the wiper HI / LOW relay OK? → **Yes** GO to **H3**. → **No** INSTALL a new wiper HI / LOW relay. REPEAT the FEM self-test, CLEAR the DTCs.
H3 CHECK CIRCUIT 1319 (VT/WH) FOR SHORT TO VOLTAGE	
FEM C191	② Measure the voltage between FEM C191 Pin 3, Circuit 1319 (VT/WH), harness side and ground. • Is the voltage greater than 10 volts? → **Yes** REPAIR Circuit 1319 (VT/WH). REPEAT the FEM self-test, CLEAR the DTCs. → **No** INSTALL a new FEM. REPEAT the FEM self-test, CLEAR the DTCs.

FM9029900717020X

Fig. 11   Test H: High/Low Wiper Speeds Do Not Operate Properly (Part 2 of 7)

TEST CONDITIONS	TEST DETAILS/RESULTS/ACTIONS
H6 CHECK THE CIRCUIT 1319 (PK/WH) FOR SHORT TO GROUND	
FEM C191	② Measure the resistance between FEM C191 Pin 3, Circuit 1319 (PK/WH), harness side and ground. • Is the resistance greater than 10,000 ohms? → **Yes** GO to **H7**. → **No** REPAIR Circuit 1319 (PK/WH). REPEAT the FEM self-test, CLEAR the DTCs.
H7 CHECK THE CIRCUIT 1319 (PK/WH) FOR OPEN	
	② Measure the resistance between FEM C191 Pin 3, Circuit 1319 (PK/WH), harness side and wiper HI/LOW relay Pin 1, Circuit 1319 (PK/WH), harness side. • Is the resistance less than 5 ohms? → **Yes** GO to **H8**. → **No** REPAIR Circuit 1319 (PK/WH). REPEAT the FEM self-test, CLEAR the DTCs.

FM9029900717040X

Fig. 11   Test H: High/Low Wiper Speeds Do Not Operate Properly (Part 4 of 7)

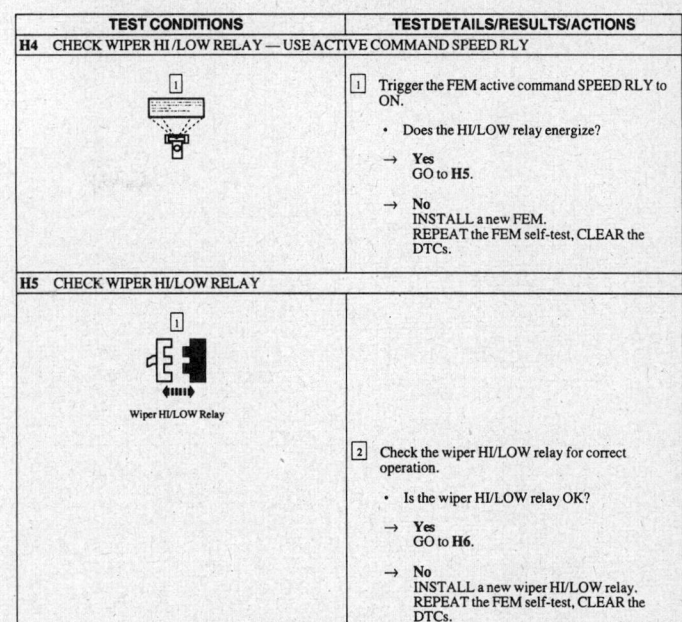

TEST CONDITIONS	TEST DETAILS/RESULTS/ACTIONS
H4 CHECK WIPER HI /LOW RELAY — USE ACTIVE COMMAND SPEED RLY	
	① Trigger the FEM active command SPEED RLY to ON. • Does the HI/LOW relay energize? → **Yes** GO to **H5**. → **No** INSTALL a new FEM. REPEAT the FEM self-test, CLEAR the DTCs.
H5 CHECK WIPER HI/LOW RELAY	
Wiper HI/LOW Relay	② Check the wiper HI/LOW relay for correct operation. • Is the wiper HI/LOW relay OK? → **Yes** GO to **H6**. → **No** INSTALL a new wiper HI/LOW relay. REPEAT the FEM self-test, CLEAR the DTCs.

FM9029900717030X

Fig. 11   Test H: High/Low Wiper Speeds Do Not Operate Properly (Part 3 of 7)

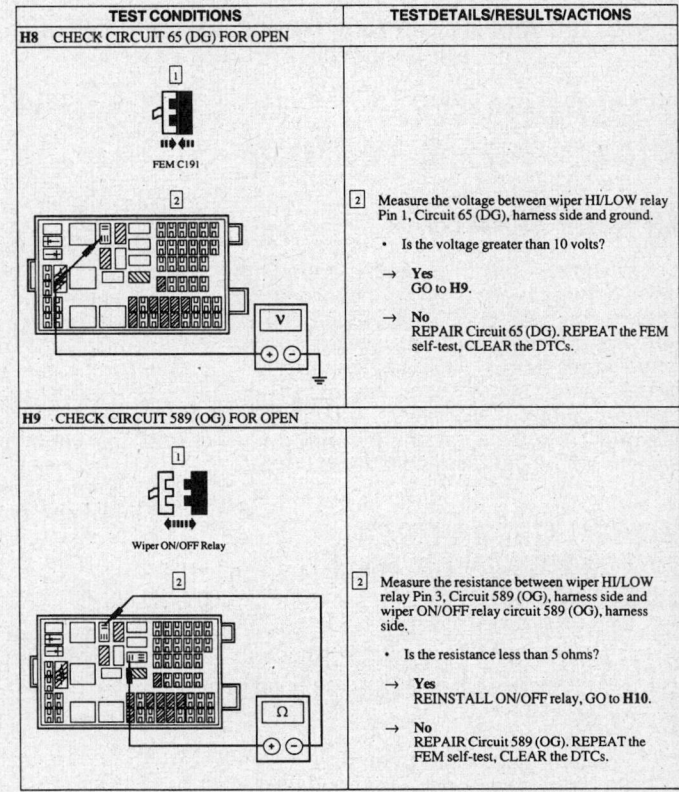

TEST CONDITIONS	TEST DETAILS/RESULTS/ACTIONS
H8 CHECK CIRCUIT 65 (DG) FOR OPEN	
FEM C191	② Measure the voltage between wiper HI/LOW relay Pin 1, Circuit 65 (DG), harness side and ground. • Is the voltage greater than 10 volts? → **Yes** GO to **H9**. → **No** REPAIR Circuit 65 (DG). REPEAT the FEM self-test, CLEAR the DTCs.
H9 CHECK CIRCUIT 589 (OG) FOR OPEN	
Wiper ON/OFF Relay	② Measure the resistance between wiper HI/LOW relay Pin 3, Circuit 589 (OG), harness side and wiper ON/OFF relay circuit 589 (OG), harness side. • Is the resistance less than 5 ohms? → **Yes** REINSTALL ON/OFF relay, GO to **H10**. → **No** REPAIR Circuit 589 (OG). REPEAT the FEM self-test, CLEAR the DTCs.

FM9029900717050X

Fig. 11   Test H: High/Low Wiper Speeds Do Not Operate Properly (Part 5 of 7)

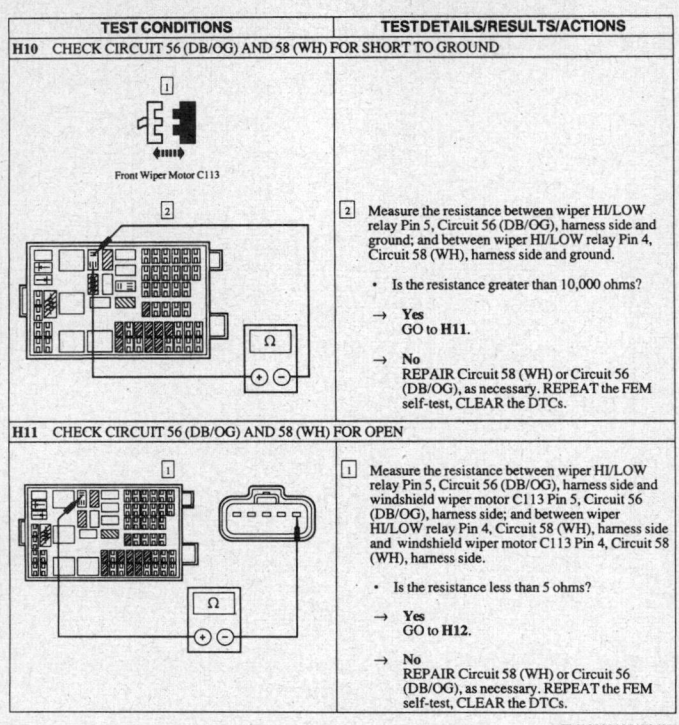

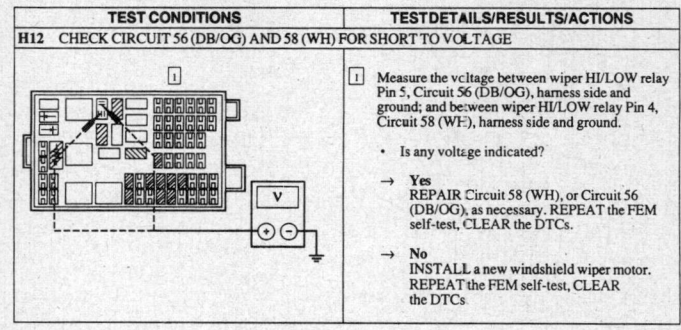

TEST CONDITIONS	TEST DETAILS/RESULTS/ACTIONS
H10 CHECK CIRCUIT 56 (DB/OG) AND 58 (WH) FOR SHORT TO GROUND	② Measure the resistance between wiper HI/LOW relay Pin 5, Circuit 56 (DB/OG), harness side and ground; and between wiper HI/LOW relay Pin 4, Circuit 58 (WH), harness side and ground. • Is the resistance greater than 10,000 ohms? → **Yes** GO to **H11**. → **No** REPAIR Circuit 58 (WH) or Circuit 56 (DB/OG), as necessary. REPEAT the FEM self-test, CLEAR the DTCs.
H11 CHECK CIRCUIT 56 (DB/OG) AND 58 (WH) FOR OPEN	① Measure the resistance between wiper HI/LOW relay Pin 5, Circuit 56 (DB/OG), harness side and windshield wiper motor C113 Pin 5, Circuit 56 (DB/OG), harness side; and between wiper HI/LOW relay Pin 4, Circuit 58 (WH), harness side and windshield wiper motor C113 Pin 4, Circuit 58 (WH), harness side. • Is the resistance less than 5 ohms? → **Yes** GO to **H12**. → **No** REPAIR Circuit 58 (WH) or Circuit 56 (DB/OG), as necessary. REPEAT the FEM self-test, CLEAR the DTCs.

FM9029900717060X

Fig. 11 Test H: High/Low Wiper Speeds Do Not Operate Properly (Part 6 of 7)

TEST CONDITIONS	TEST DETAILS/RESULTS/ACTIONS
H12 CHECK CIRCUIT 56 (DB/OG) AND 58 (WH) FOR SHORT TO VOLTAGE	① Measure the voltage between wiper HI/LOW relay Pin 5, Circuit 56 (DB/OG), harness side and ground; and between wiper HI/LOW relay Pin 4, Circuit 58 (WH), harness side and ground. • Is any voltage indicated? → **Yes** REPAIR Circuit 58 (WH), or Circuit 56 (DB/OG), as necessary. REPEAT the FEM self-test, CLEAR the DTCs. → **No** INSTALL a new windshield wiper motor. REPEAT the FEM self-test, CLEAR the DTCs.

FM9029900717070X

Fig. 11 Test H: High/Low Wiper Speeds Do Not Operate Properly (Part 7 of 7)

COMPONENT DIAGNOSIS & TESTING

Wiper Motor

The ignition switch must be in the Run position for all tests. Verify proper operation of the wiper system at low speed. With system operating in low, turn switch to Off when wiper blades are in vertical position. Wiper blades should complete cycle and park at bottom of windshield. If blades do not park, refer to appropriate condition of system below. Test and service as indicated.

WINDSHIELD WIPER MOTOR STOPS WHEN TURN SIGNAL & WINDSHIELD WIPER SWITCH ARE TURNED TO OFF (DOES NOT COMPLETE CYCLE)

1. Remove wiper motor park switch connector and inspect for battery voltage using suitable ohmmeter. If battery voltage is not present, repair circuit as required. If voltage is present, proceed to following step.
2. Inspect wiper motor ground wiring at turn signal and windshield wiper switch connector.
3. With both wiper motor connectors disconnected, use suitable ohmmeter to verify continuity (less than 1 ohm) between Circuits 28 (BK/PK) and 58 (W) in wiring harness. If continuity is not present, trace and service as required.

If continuity is satisfactory, leave connectors disconnected and proceed to following step.
4. Inspect for continuity to ground terminal on gear cover at circuit terminal 28 (BK/PK) on windshield wiper motor. If open, replace motor. If ground is present, leave connectors disconnected and proceed to following step.
5. Verify continuity between Circuits 61 (Y/R) and 63 (R) in wiring harness, noting the following:
   a. If continuity is not present, trace and service as required. If lack of continuity is traced to GEM, inspect wiper switch for continuity as outlined under "Windshield Wiper Switch Continuity Test."
   b. If continuity is not present in switch, replace switch. If continuity is present in switch and lack of continuity has been traced to GEM, replace GEM.
   c. If continuity between Circuits 61 (Y/R) and 63 (R) is satisfactory, leave connectors disconnected and proceed to following step.
6. Inspect for continuity between Circuits 63 (R) and 65 (DG) on motor. If open, replace motor.

WIPERS STALL OR JAM (WINDSHIELD WIPER MOTOR STARTS RUNNING IN REVERSE DIRECTION) WHILE GOING FROM PARK TO DEPRESSED PARK (BELOW WINDSHIELD)

1. Inspect windshield wiper mounting arm and pivot shaft. Service as re-

quired. If satisfactory, proceed to following step.
2. Inspect wiper motor arm and windlatch assembly. If bent or cracked, replace wiper motor.

Wiper Switch Continuity Test

Test windshield wiper switch continuity between circuits with a suitable ohmmeter. Refer to **Fig. 12** when testing the switch.

Rear Wiper/Washer Switch Continuity Test

Inspect the continuity between the rear wiper/washer switch terminals using either a suitable self-powered test lamp or a suitable ohmmeter. To detect marginal operation of the switch, move the button while each reading is taken. If the switch does not show continuity or if poor continuity exists in any position of the switch, replace the switch.

Washer Pump Current Draw Test

Attach the leads of a suitable ohmmeter, **Fig. 13**. Current draw should not exceed 4 amps or indicate less than 4 amps while the pump motor is pumping fluid.

Wiper Motor Current Draw Test

Use caution when handling wiper motor. Rough handling may damage magnets.
1. Disconnect windshield wiper mounting arm and pivot shaft from wiper motor, then disconnect electrical plug to test motor.
2. Connect green lead from suitable test equipment to battery positive post.
3. Connect positive (red) lead from tester to common brush terminal. Attach ground first to low-speed connection, then to high-speed connection at connector plug, **Fig. 14**. In either case, draw should not exceed 3.5 amperes (amps).

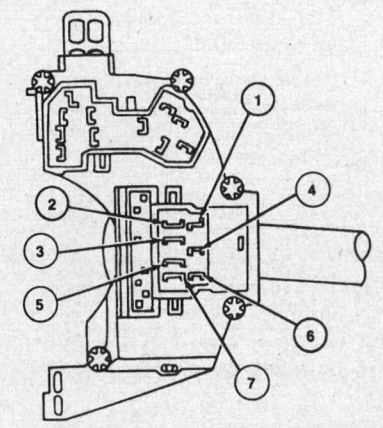

Switch Position	Resistance by Pin Number
Interval Wiper / Washer Switching:	
• Wash ON	Closed Pin 4 to Pin 6
• Wash OFF	Resistance Pin 4 to Pin 6, 103.3 K ohms Resistance Pin 4 to Pin 1, 47.6 K ohms
• Wiper Interval at MAX.	Resistance Pin 4 to Pin 1, 11.33 K ohms
• Delay (Closest Position to OFF) to MIN. Delay (Closest Position to LO)	Resistance Pin 4 to Pin 6 linear decreasing from 103.3 K ohms to 3.3 K ohms
• Wiper LO, Wash OFF	Resistance Pin 4 to Pin 6, 3.3 K ohms Resistance Pin 4 to Pin 1, 4.08 K ohms
• Wiper HI, Wash OFF	Resistance Pin 4 to Pin 6, 3.3 K ohms Closed Pin 4 to Pin 1

FM9029500322000X

Fig. 12   Wiper switch continuity test

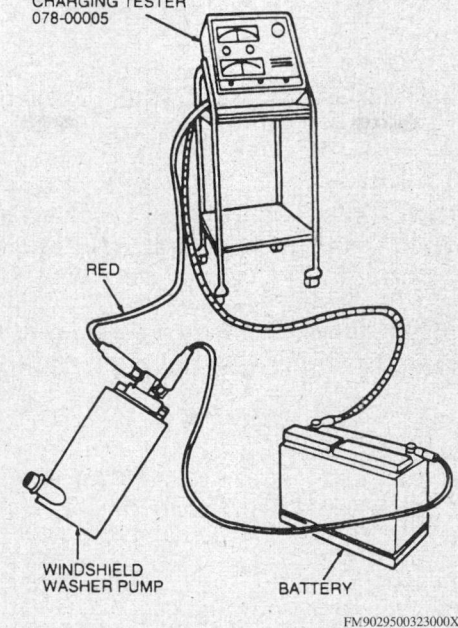

FM9029500323000X

Fig. 13   Washer pump current draw test

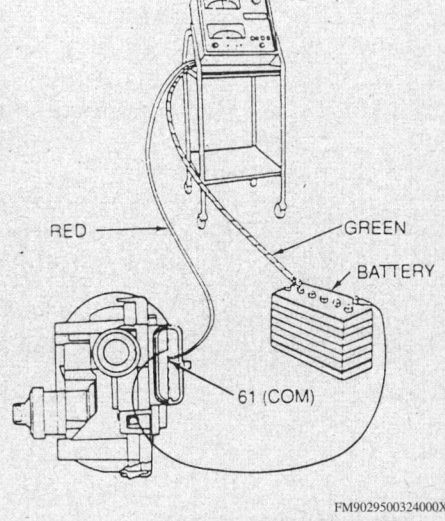

FM9029500324000X

Fig. 14   Wiper motor current draw test

Villager

NOTE: On Air Bag Equipped Models, Refer To "Air Bag System Precautions" Located In The Front Of This Manual For System Disarming & Arming Procedures.

NOTE: "Electrical Symbol & Wire Color Code Identification" Located In The Front Of This Manual May Be Used As An Aid When Using Wiring Diagrams Found In This Section.

NOTE: Refer To "Computer Relearn Procedures" Located In The Front Of This Manual When Battery Power To The Computer Has Been Interrupted.

INDEX

	Page No.		Page No.		Page No.
Component Diagnosis & Testing	3-190	Windshield Wiper/Washer Switch Test	3-190	**Diagnostic Chart Index**	3-181
Rear Window Wiper/Washer Switch Test	3-190	Wiper Motor	3-190	**Precautions**	3-180
Windshield Wiper Motor Current Draw Test	3-190	**Description**	3-180	Battery Ground Cable	3-180
		Front	3-180	**System Diagnosis & Testing**	3-180
		Rear	3-180	Diagnostic Tests	3-180
				Wiring Diagrams	3-180

PRECAUTIONS

Battery Ground Cable

Prior to service, disconnect battery ground cable and isolate as required.

DESCRIPTION

Front

Operation of the windshield wiper and washer is controlled by the front wiper/washer amplifier assembly. The front wiper/washer amplifier input comes from the multi-function switch by means of a voltage divider circuit.

Rear

Operation of the rear wiper and washer is controlled by the rear wiper/washer switch. Voltage is supplied to the rear window wiper motor by the fuse junction panel fuse F44 (10A).

SYSTEM DIAGNOSIS & TESTING

Wiring Diagrams

Refer to **Figs. 1 through 3** for wiring diagrams.

Diagnostic Tests

Refer to **Figs. 4 through 16** diagnostic tests.

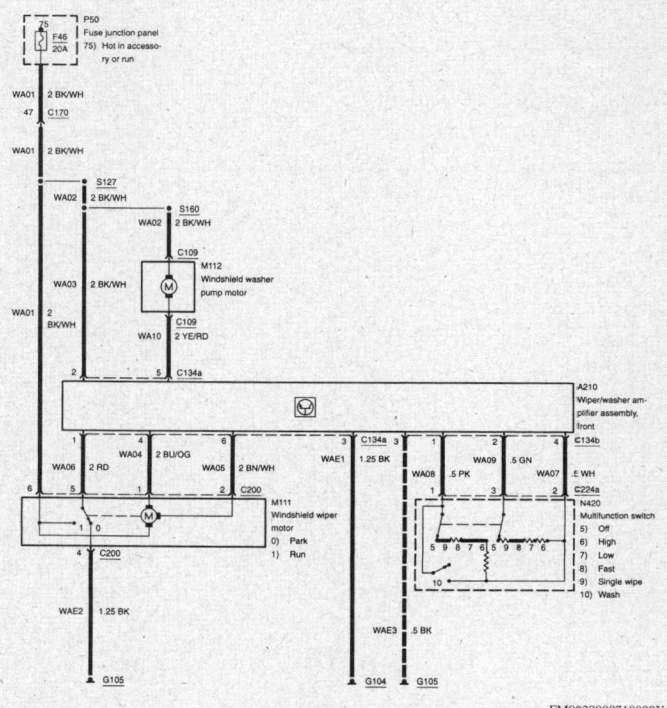

Fig. 1   Front wiring diagram

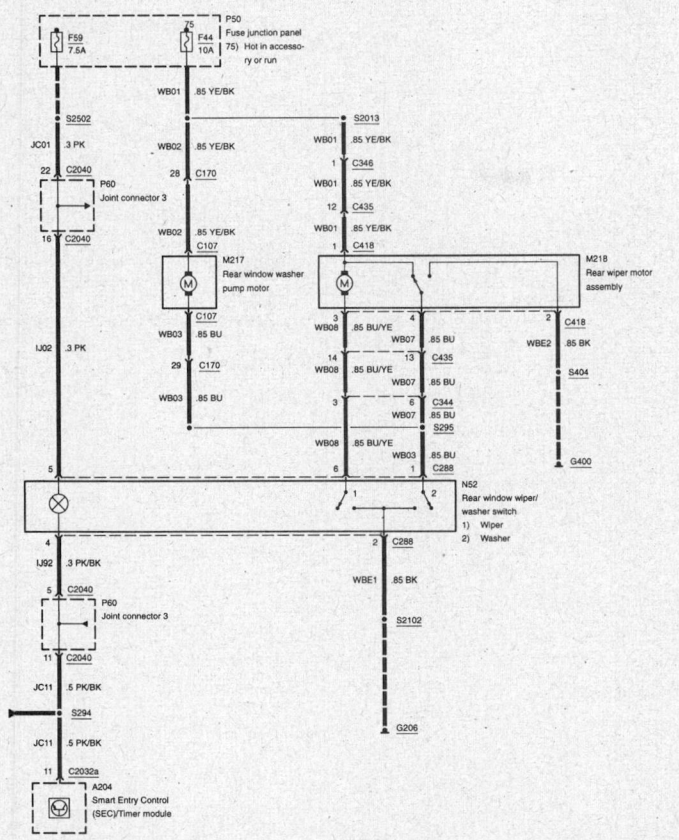

FM9029900719000X

Fig. 2 Rear wiring diagram. Less moveable liftgate glass

FM9029900720000X

Fig. 3 Rear wiring diagram. With moveable liftgate glass

DIAGNOSTIC CHART INDEX

Test	Description	Page No.	Fig. No.
A	Front Washer Pump Is Inoperative	3-182	4
B	All Control Positions Inoperative	3-183	5
C	High Wiper Speed Does Not Operate Properly, Intermittent Mode Operates Properly	3-184	6
D	Low Wiper Speed Does Not Operate Properly, Intermittent Mode Operates Properly	3-184	7
E	Intermittent Wiper Speed Does Not Operate Properly, High/Low Speed Operate Properly	3-184	8
F	Wipers Will Not Park At Correct Position	3-185	9
G	Wipers Stay On Continuously	3-185	10
H	Rear Wiper Washer Pump Inoperative	3-186	11
I	Rear Wipers Are Inoperative	3-186	12
J	Rear Wipers Are Inoperative	3-187	13
K	Rear Wipers Will Not Park At Correct Position	3-188	14
L	Rear Wipers Stay On Continuously	3-188	15
M	Rear Wipers Will Not Park At Correct Position/Rear Wipers Will Not Move Into Liftgate Glass Open Position	3-189	16

WIPER SYSTEMS

TEST CONDITIONS	TEST DETAILS/RESULTS/ACTIONS
A1 CHECK CIRCUIT WA02 (BK/WH) FOR VOLTAGE	

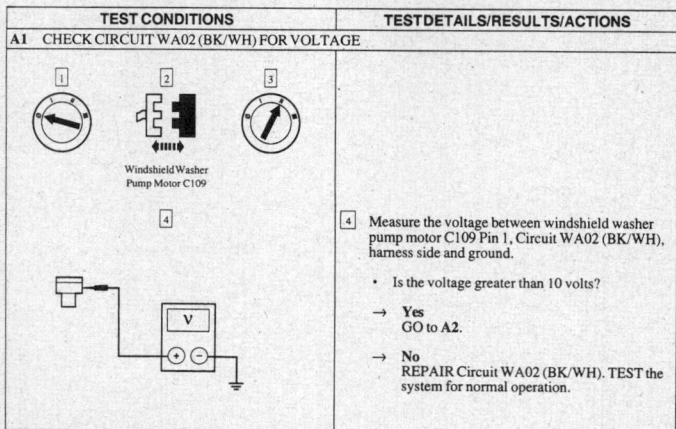

| | 4   Measure the voltage between windshield washer pump motor C109 Pin 1, Circuit WA02 (BK/WH), harness side and ground. • Is the voltage greater than 10 volts? → Yes GO to A2. → No REPAIR Circuit WA02 (BK/WH). TEST the system for normal operation. |

FM9029900721010X

Fig. 4   Test A: Front Washer Pump Is Inoperative (Part 1 of 4)

TEST CONDITIONS	TEST DETAILS/RESULTS/ACTIONS
A4 CHECK THE MULTI-FUNCTION SWITCH	
	1 Carry out the multifunction switch component test. • Is the multifunction switch OK? → Yes GO to A5. → No INSTALL a new multifunction switch. TEST the system for normal operation.
A5 CHECK CIRCUIT WA08 (PK) FOR OPEN AND SHORT TO GROUND	

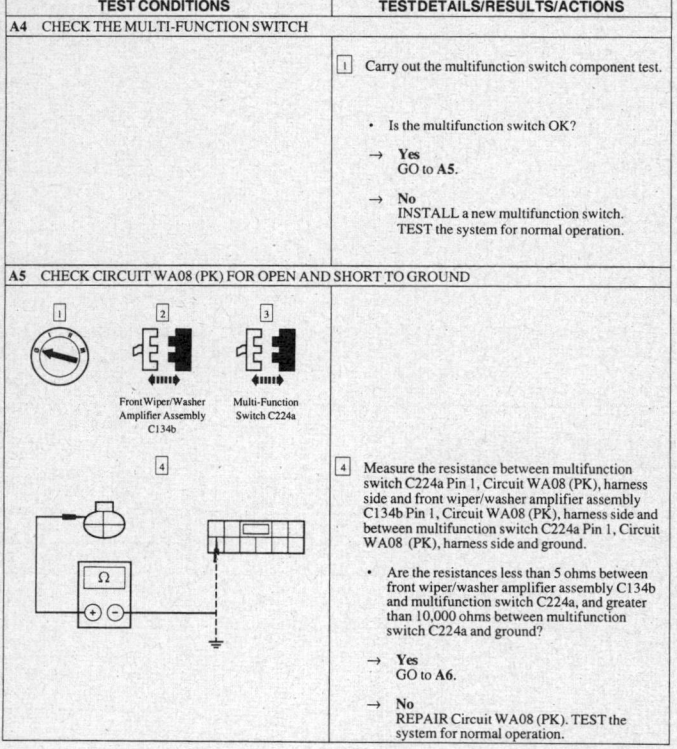

| | 4   Measure the resistance between multifunction switch C224a Pin 1, Circuit WA08 (PK), harness side and front wiper/washer amplifier assembly C134b Pin 1, Circuit WA08 (PK), harness side and between multifunction switch C224a Pin 1, Circuit WA08 (PK), harness side and ground. • Are the resistances less than 5 ohms between front wiper/washer amplifier assembly C134b and multifunction switch C224a, and greater than 10,000 ohms between multifunction switch C224a and ground? → Yes GO to A6. → No REPAIR Circuit WA08 (PK). TEST the system for normal operation. |

FM9029900721030X

Fig. 4   Test A: Front Washer Pump Is Inoperative (Part 3 of 4)

TEST CONDITIONS	TEST DETAILS/RESULTS/ACTIONS
A2 CHECK WINDSHIELD WASHER PUMP MOTOR	

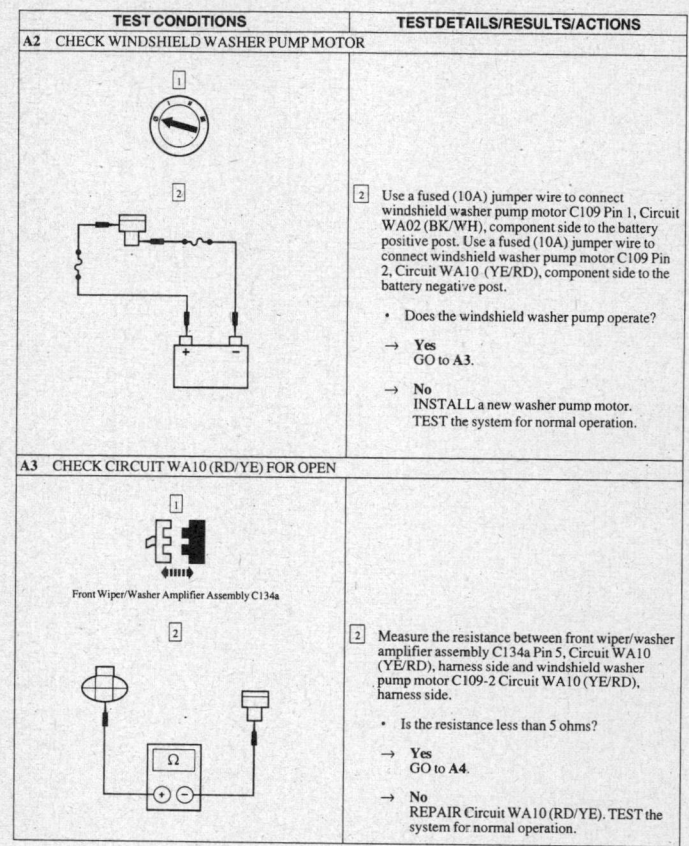

	2 Use a fused (10A) jumper wire to connect windshield washer pump motor C109 Pin 1, Circuit WA02 (BK/WH), component side to the battery positive post. Use a fused (10A) jumper wire to connect windshield washer pump motor C109 Pin 2, Circuit WA10 (YE/RD), component side to the battery negative post. • Does the windshield washer pump operate? → Yes GO to A3. → No INSTALL a new washer pump motor. TEST the system for normal operation.
A3 CHECK CIRCUIT WA10 (RD/YE) FOR OPEN	
	2 Measure the resistance between front wiper/washer amplifier assembly C134a Pin 5, Circuit WA10 (YE/RD), harness side and windshield washer pump motor C109-2 Circuit WA10 (YE/RD), harness side. • Is the resistance less than 5 ohms? → Yes GO to A4. → No REPAIR Circuit WA10 (RD/YE). TEST the system for normal operation.

FM9029900721020X

Fig. 4   Test A: Front Washer Pump Is Inoperative (Part 2 of 4)

TEST CONDITIONS	TEST DETAILS/RESULTS/ACTIONS
A6 CHECK CIRCUIT WA09 (GN) FOR OPEN AND SHORT TO GROUND	
	1 Measure the resistance between multifunction switch C224a Pin 3, Circuit WA09 (GN), harness side and front wiper/washer amplifier assembly C134a Pin 2, Circuit WA09 (GN), harness side and between multifunction switch C224a Pin 3, Circuit WA09 (GN), harness side and ground. • Are the resistances less than 5 ohms between front wiper/washer amplifier assembly C134b and multifunction switch C224a, and greater than 10,000 ohms between multifunction switch C224a and ground? → Yes GO to A7. → No REPAIR Circuit WA09 (GN). TEST the system for normal operation.
A7 CHECK CIRCUITS WAE1 (BK) AND WAE3 (BK) FOR OPEN	

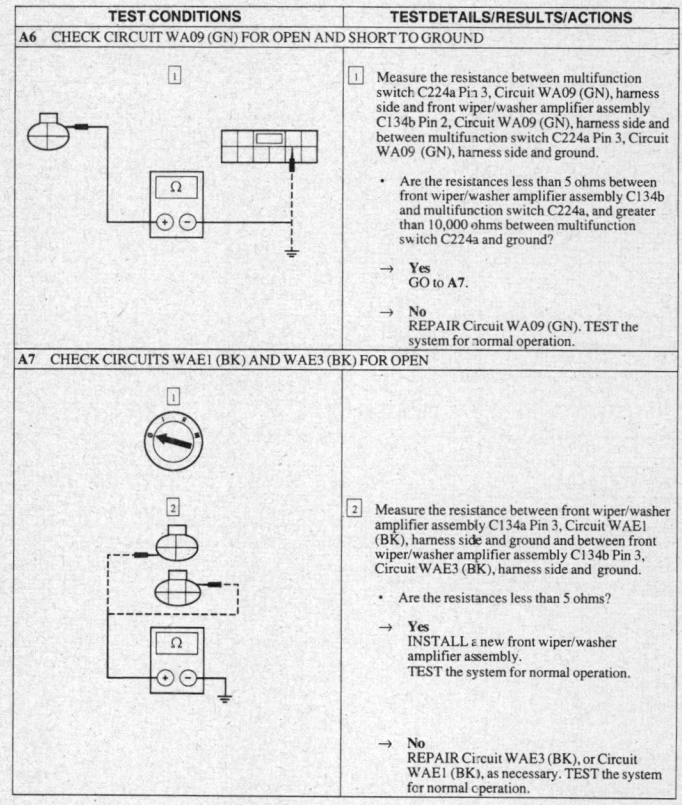

| | 2   Measure the resistance between front wiper/washer amplifier assembly C134a Pin 3, Circuit WAE1 (BK), harness side and ground and between front wiper/washer amplifier assembly C134b Pin 3, Circuit WAE3 (BK), harness side and ground. • Are the resistances less than 5 ohms? → Yes INSTALL a new front wiper/washer amplifier assembly. TEST the system for normal operation. → No REPAIR Circuit WAE3 (BK), or Circuit WAE1 (BK), as necessary. TEST the system for normal operation. |

FM9029900721040X

Fig. 4   Test A: Front Washer Pump Is Inoperative (Part 4 of 4)

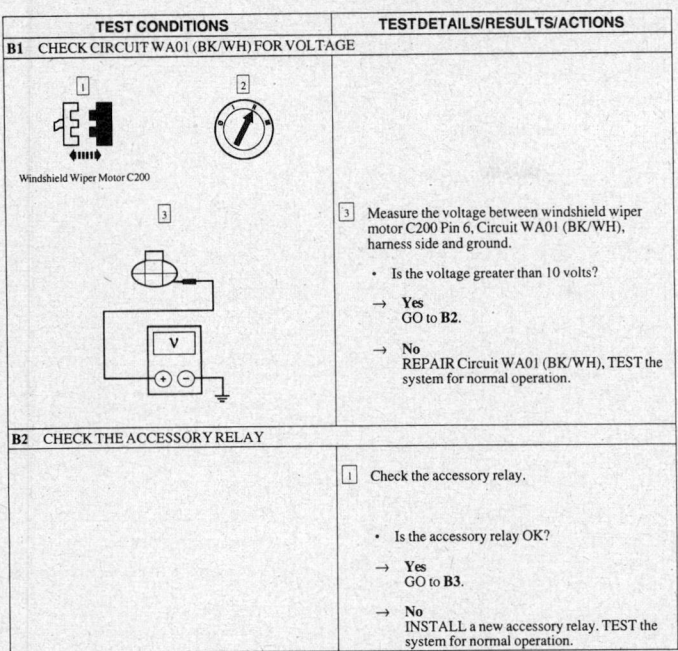

TEST CONDITIONS	TESTDETAILS/RESULTS/ACTIONS
B1 CHECK CIRCUIT WA01 (BK/WH) FOR VOLTAGE	
Windshield Wiper Motor C200	
③	③ Measure the voltage between windshield wiper motor C200 Pin 6, Circuit WA01 (BK/WH), harness side and ground. • Is the voltage greater than 10 volts? → **Yes** GO to **B2**. → **No** REPAIR Circuit WA01 (BK/WH), TEST the system for normal operation.
B2 CHECK THE ACCESSORY RELAY	
	① Check the accessory relay. • Is the accessory relay OK? → **Yes** GO to **B3**. → **No** INSTALL a new accessory relay. TEST the system for normal operation.

FM9029900722010X

Fig. 5   Test B: All Control Positions Inoperative (Part 1 of 5)

TEST CONDITIONS	TESTDETAILS/RESULTS/ACTIONS
B5 CHECK CIRCUITS WAE1 (BK) AND WAE3 (BK) FOR OPEN	
Front Wiper/Washer Amplifier Assembly C134a Front Wiper/Washer Amplifier Assembly C134b	
③	③ Measure the resistance between front wiper/washer amplifier assembly C134b Pin 3, Circuit WAE3 (BK), harness side and ground and between front wiper/washer amplifier assembly C134a Pin 3, Circuit WAE1 (BK), harness side and ground.
④	④ Measure the resistance between windshield wiper motor C200 Pin 4, Circuit WAE2 (BK), harness side and ground. • Are the resistances less than 5 ohms? → **Yes** GO to **B6**. → **No** REPAIR Circuit WAE2 (BK), Circuit WAE2 (BK), or Circuit WAE3 (BK), as necessary. TEST the system for normal operation.

FM9029900722030X

Fig. 5   Test B: All Control Positions Inoperative (Part 3 of 5)

TEST CONDITIONS	TESTDETAILS/RESULTS/ACTIONS
B3 CHECK THE MULTI-FUNCTION SWITCH	
	① Carry out the multifunction switch component test. • Is the multifunction switch OK? → **Yes** GO to **B4**. → **No** INSTALL a new multifunction switch. TEST the system for normal operation.
B4 CHECK WINDSHIELD WIPER MOTOR	
	① Carry out the windshield wiper motor component test. • Is the windshield wiper motor OK? → **Yes** GO to **B5**. → **No** INSTALL a new windshield wiper motor. TEST the system for normal operation.

FM9029900722020X

Fig. 5   Test B: All Control Positions Inoperative (Part 2 of 5)

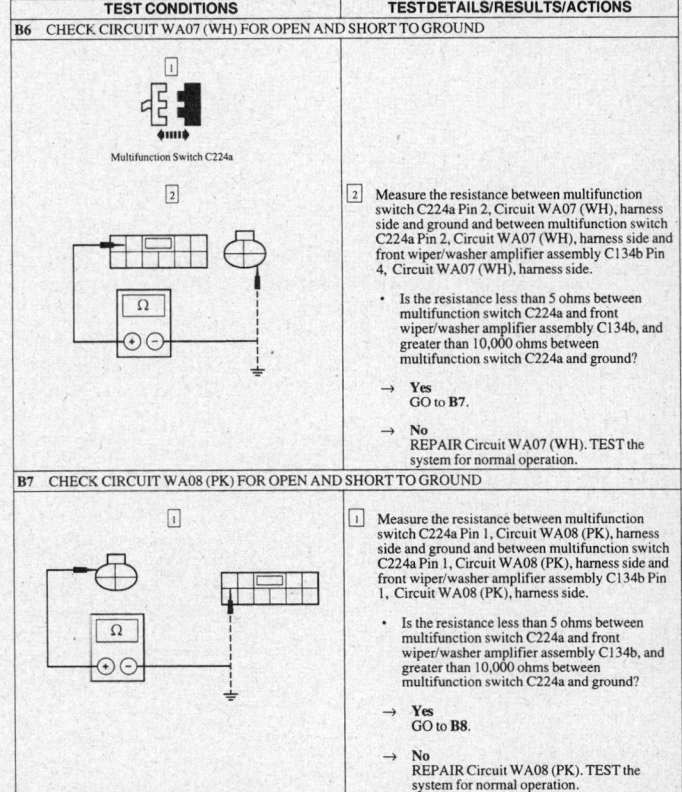

TEST CONDITIONS	TESTDETAILS/RESULTS/ACTIONS
B6 CHECK CIRCUIT WA07 (WH) FOR OPEN AND SHORT TO GROUND	
Multifunction Switch C224a	
②	② Measure the resistance between multifunction switch C224a Pin 2, Circuit WA07 (WH), harness side and ground and between multifunction switch C224a Pin 2, Circuit WA07 (WH), harness side and front wiper/washer amplifier assembly C134b Pin 4, Circuit WA07 (WH), harness side. • Is the resistance less than 5 ohms between multifunction switch C224a and front wiper/washer amplifier assembly C134b, and greater than 10,000 ohms between multifunction switch C224a and ground? → **Yes** GO to **B7**. → **No** REPAIR Circuit WA07 (WH). TEST the system for normal operation.
B7 CHECK CIRCUIT WA08 (PK) FOR OPEN AND SHORT TO GROUND	
①	① Measure the resistance between multifunction switch C224a Pin 1, Circuit WA08 (PK), harness side and ground and between multifunction switch C224a Pin 1, Circuit WA08 (PK), harness side and front wiper/washer amplifier assembly C134b Pin 1, Circuit WA08 (PK), harness side. • Is the resistance less than 5 ohms between multifunction switch C224a and front wiper/washer amplifier assembly C134b, and greater than 10,000 ohms between multifunction switch C224a and ground? → **Yes** GO to **B8**. → **No** REPAIR Circuit WA08 (PK). TEST the system for normal operation.

FM9029900722040X

Fig. 5   Test B: All Control Positions Inoperative (Part 4 of 5)

TEST CONDITIONS	TEST DETAILS/RESULTS/ACTIONS
B8 CHECK CIRCUIT WA09 (GN) FOR OPEN AND SHORT TO GROUND	
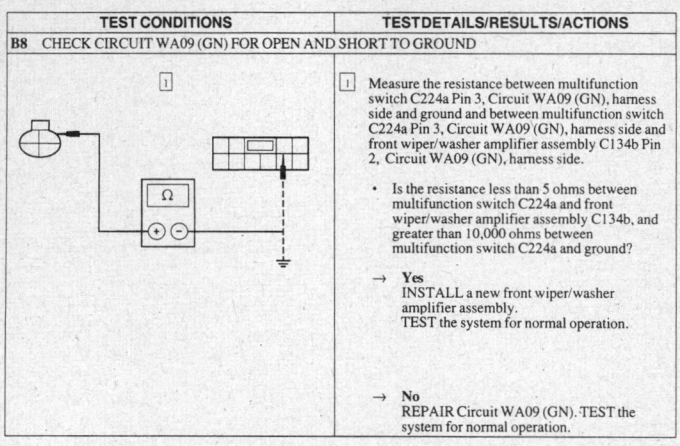	① Measure the resistance between multifunction switch C224a Pin 3, Circuit WA09 (GN), harness side and ground and between multifunction switch C224a Pin 3, Circuit WA09 (GN), harness side and front wiper/washer amplifier assembly C134b Pin 2, Circuit WA09 (GN), harness side. • Is the resistance less than 5 ohms between multifunction switch C224a and front wiper/washer amplifier assembly C134b, and greater than 10,000 ohms between multifunction switch C224a and ground? → **Yes** INSTALL a new front wiper/washer amplifier assembly. TEST the system for normal operation. → **No** REPAIR Circuit WA09 (GN). TEST the system for normal operation.

FM9029900722050X

Fig. 5   Test B: All Control Positions Inoperative (Part 5 of 5)

TEST CONDITIONS	TEST DETAILS/RESULTS/ACTIONS
C3 CHECK THE MULTI-FUNCTION SWITCH	
	① Carry out the multifunction switch component test. • Is the multifunction switch OK? → **Yes** INSTALL a new front wiper/washer amplifier assembly. TEST the system for normal operation. → **No** INSTALL a new multifunction switch. TEST the system for normal operation.

FM9029900723020X

Fig. 6   Test C: High Wiper Speed Does Not Operate Properly, Intermittent Mode Operates Properly (Part 2 of 2)

TEST CONDITIONS	TEST DETAILS/RESULTS/ACTIONS
D1 CHECK CIRCUIT WA05 (BN/WH) FOR OPEN AND SHORT TO GROUND	
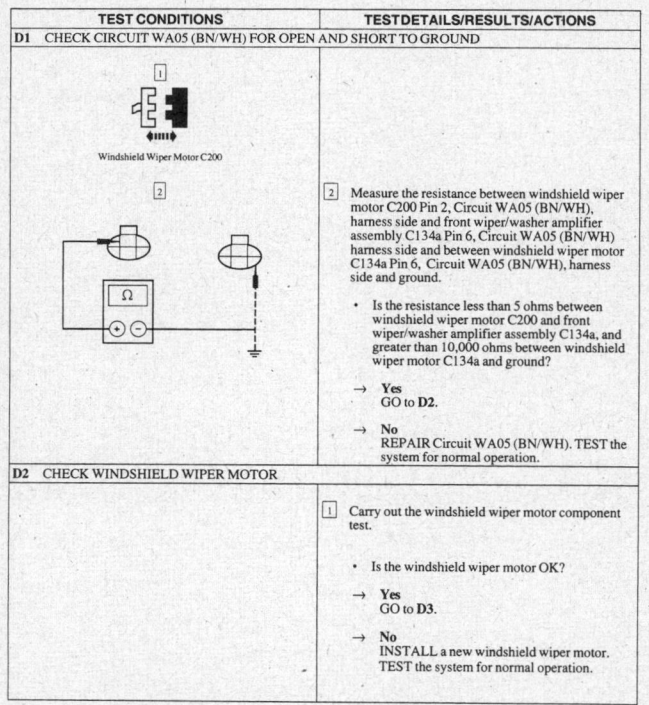 Windshield Wiper Motor C200	② Measure the resistance between windshield wiper motor C200 Pin 2, Circuit WA05 (BN/WH), harness side and front wiper/washer amplifier assembly C134a Pin 6, Circuit WA05 (BN/WH) harness side and between windshield wiper motor C134a Pin 6, Circuit WA05 (BN/WH), harness side and ground. • Is the resistance less than 5 ohms between windshield wiper motor C200 and front wiper/washer amplifier assembly C134a, and greater than 10,000 ohms between windshield wiper motor C134a and ground? → **Yes** GO to D2. → **No** REPAIR Circuit WA05 (BN/WH). TEST the system for normal operation.
D2 CHECK WINDSHIELD WIPER MOTOR	
	① Carry out the windshield wiper motor component test. • Is the windshield wiper motor OK? → **Yes** GO to D3. → **No** INSTALL a new windshield wiper motor. TEST the system for normal operation.

FM9029900724010X

Fig. 7   Test D: Low Wiper Speed Does Not Operate Properly, Intermittent Mode Operates Properly (Part 1 of 2)

TEST CONDITIONS	TEST DETAILS/RESULTS/ACTIONS
C1 CHECK CIRCUIT WA04 (BU/OG) FOR OPEN AND SHORT TO GROUND	
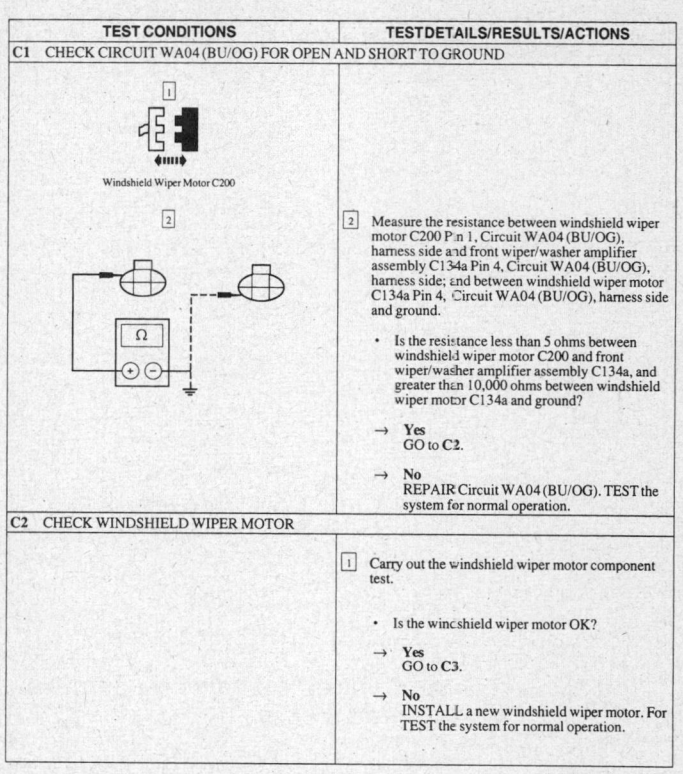 Windshield Wiper Motor C200	② Measure the resistance between windshield wiper motor C200 Pin 1, Circuit WA04 (BU/OG), harness side and front wiper/washer amplifier assembly C134a Pin 4, Circuit WA04 (BU/OG), harness side; and between windshield wiper motor C134a Pin 4, Circuit WA04 (BU/OG), harness side and ground. • Is the resistance less than 5 ohms between windshield wiper motor C200 and front wiper/washer amplifier assembly C134a, and greater than 10,000 ohms between windshield wiper motor C134a and ground? → **Yes** GO to C2. → **No** REPAIR Circuit WA04 (BU/OG). TEST the system for normal operation.
C2 CHECK WINDSHIELD WIPER MOTOR	
	① Carry out the windshield wiper motor component test. • Is the windshield wiper motor OK? → **Yes** GO to C3. → **No** INSTALL a new windshield wiper motor. For TEST the system for normal operation.

FM9029900723010X

Fig. 6   Test C: High Wiper Speed Does Not Operate Properly, Intermittent Mode Operates Properly (Part 1 of 2)

TEST CONDITIONS	TEST DETAILS/RESULTS/ACTIONS
D3 CHECK THE MULTIFUNCTION SWITCH	
	① Carry out the multifunction switch component test. • Is the multifunction switch OK? → **Yes** INSTALL a new front wiper/washer amplifier assembly. TEST the system for normal operation. → **No** INSTALL a new multifunction switch. TEST the system for normal operation.

FM9029900724020X

Fig. 7   Test D: Low Wiper Speed Does Not Operate Properly, Intermittent Mode Operates Properly (Part 2 of 2)

TEST CONDITIONS	TEST DETAILS/RESULTS/ACTIONS
E1 CHECK THE MULTIFUNCTION SWITCH	
	① Carry out the multifunction switch component test. • Is the multi-function switch OK? → **Yes** INSTALL a new front wiper/washer amplifier assembly. TEST the system for normal operation. → **No** INSTALL a new multifunction switch. TEST the system for normal operation.

FM9029900725000X

Fig. 8   Test E: Intermittent Wiper Speed Does Not Operate Properly, High/Low Speed Operate Properly

TEST CONDITIONS	TESTDETAILS/RESULTS/ACTIONS
F1 CHECK WINDSHIELD WIPER MOTOR	

	1 Carry out the windshield wiper motor component test.
	
	• Is the windshield wiper motor OK?
	
	→ **Yes**
	    GO to **F2**.
	
	→ **No**
	    INSTALL a new windshield wiper motor.
	    TEST the system for normal operation.

F2 CHECK CIRCUIT WA06 (RD) FOR OPEN	

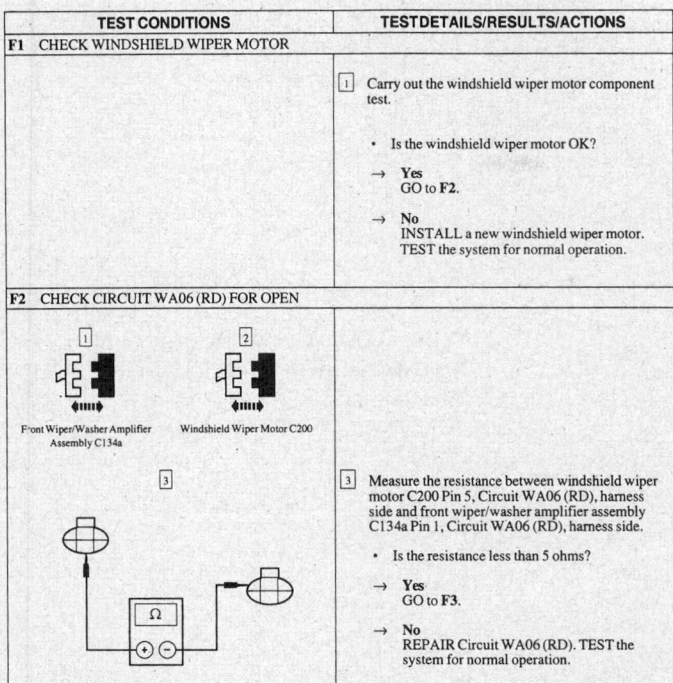	3 Measure the resistance between windshield wiper motor C200 Pin 5, Circuit WA06 (RD), harness side and front wiper/washer amplifier assembly C134a Pin 1, Circuit WA06 (RD), harness side.
	
	• Is the resistance less than 5 ohms?
	
	→ **Yes**
	    GO to **F3**.
	
	→ **No**
	    REPAIR Circuit WA06 (RD). TEST the system for normal operation.

FM9029900726010X

Fig. 9   Test F: Wipers Will Not Park At Correct Position (Part 1 of 2)

TEST CONDITIONS	TESTDETAILS/RESULTS/ACTIONS
G1 CHECK THE MULTIFUNCTION SWITCH	

	1 Carry out the multifunction switch component test.
	
	• Is the multifunction switch OK?
	
	→ **Yes**
	    GO to **G2**.
	
	→ **No**
	    INSTALL a new multifunction switch.
	    TEST the system for normal operation.

FM9029900727010X

Fig. 10   Test G: Wipers Stay On Continuously (Part 1 of 3)

TEST CONDITIONS	TESTDETAILS/RESULTS/ACTIONS
F3 CHECK CIRCUIT WA05 (BN/WH) FOR OPEN	

	1 Measure the resistance between windshield wiper motor C200 Pin 2, Circuit WA05 (BN/WH), harness side and front wiper/washer amplifier assembly C134a Pin 6, Circuit WA05 (BN/WH), harness side.
	
	• Is the resistance less than 5 ohms?
	
	→ **Yes**
	    INSTALL a new front wiper/washer amplifier assembly.
	    TEST the system for normal operation.
	
	→ **No**
	    REPAIR Circuit WA05 (BN/WH). TEST the system for normal operation.

FM9029900726020X

Fig. 9   Test F: Wipers Will Not Park At Correct Position (Part 2 of 2)

TEST CONDITIONS	TESTDETAILS/RESULTS/ACTIONS
G2 CHECK CIRCUIT WA04 (BU/OG) FOR SHORT TO GROUND	

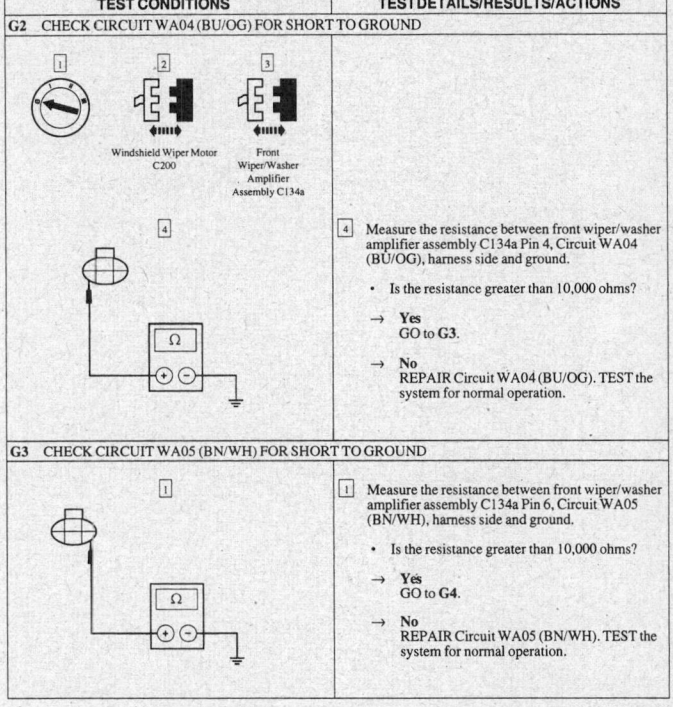	4 Measure the resistance between front wiper/washer amplifier assembly C134a Pin 4, Circuit WA04 (BU/OG), harness side and ground.
	
	• Is the resistance greater than 10,000 ohms?
	
	→ **Yes**
	    GO to **G3**.
	
	→ **No**
	    REPAIR Circuit WA04 (BU/OG). TEST the system for normal operation.

G3 CHECK CIRCUIT WA05 (BN/WH) FOR SHORT TO GROUND	

	1 Measure the resistance between front wiper/washer amplifier assembly C134a Pin 6, Circuit WA05 (BN/WH), harness side and ground.
	
	• Is the resistance greater than 10,000 ohms?
	
	→ **Yes**
	    GO to **G4**.
	
	→ **No**
	    REPAIR Circuit WA05 (BN/WH). TEST the system for normal operation.

FM9029900727020X

Fig. 10   Test G: Wipers Stay On Continuously (Part 2 of 3)

TEST CONDITIONS	TESTDETAILS/RESULTS/ACTIONS
G4 CHECK CIRCUIT WA06 (RD) FOR OPEN AND SHORT TO GROUND	

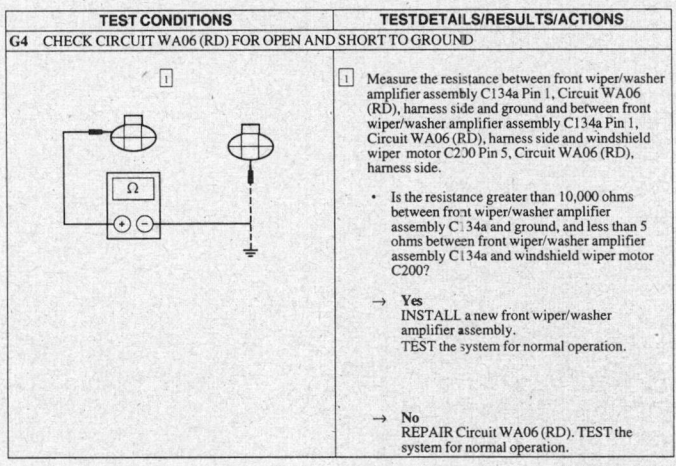	1 Measure the resistance between front wiper/washer amplifier assembly C134a Pin 1, Circuit WA06 (RD), harness side and ground and between front wiper/washer amplifier assembly C134a Pin 1, Circuit WA06 (RD), harness side and windshield wiper motor C200 Pin 5, Circuit WA06 (RD), harness side.
	
	• Is the resistance greater than 10,000 ohms between front wiper/washer amplifier assembly C134a and ground, and less than 5 ohms between front wiper/washer amplifier assembly C134a and windshield wiper motor C200?
	
	→ **Yes**
	    INSTALL a new front wiper/washer amplifier assembly.
	    TEST the system for normal operation.
	
	→ **No**
	    REPAIR Circuit WA06 (RD). TEST the system for normal operation.

FM9029900727030X

Fig. 10   Test G: Wipers Stay On Continuously (Part 3 of 3)

TEST CONDITIONS	TEST DETAILS/RESULTS/ACTIONS
H1 CHECK REAR WINDOW WASHER PUMP MOTOR OPERATION	

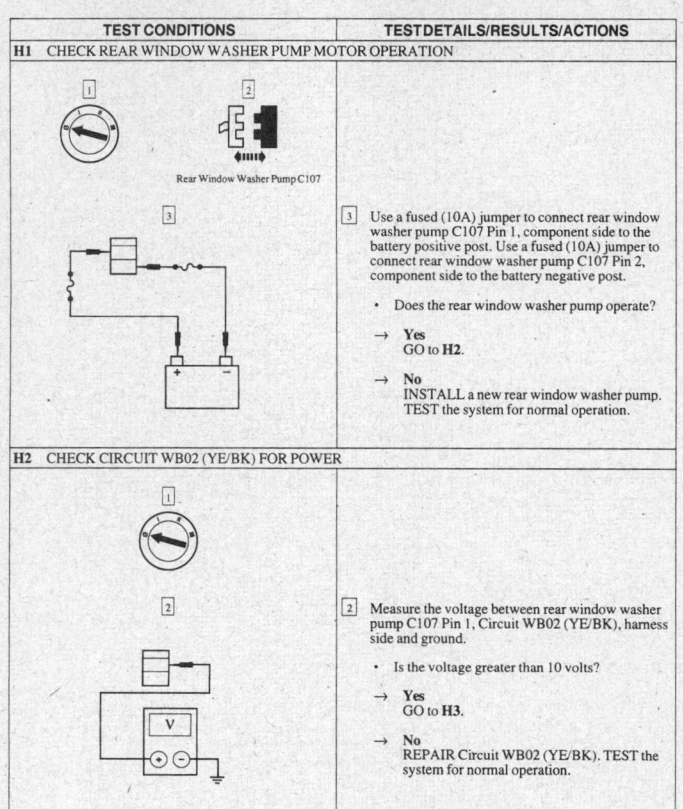

3	③ Use a fused (10A) jumper to connect rear window washer pump C107 Pin 1, component side to the battery positive post. Use a fused (10A) jumper to connect rear window washer pump C107 Pin 2, component side to the battery negative post. • Does the rear window washer pump operate? → **Yes** GO to **H2**. → **No** INSTALL a new rear window washer pump. TEST the system for normal operation.

TEST CONDITIONS	TEST DETAILS/RESULTS/ACTIONS
H2 CHECK CIRCUIT WB02 (YE/BK) FOR POWER	

	② Measure the voltage between rear window washer pump C107 Pin 1, Circuit WB02 (YE/BK), harness side and ground. • Is the voltage greater than 10 volts? → **Yes** GO to **H3**. → **No** REPAIR Circuit WB02 (YE/BK). TEST the system for normal operation.

FM9029900728010X

Fig. 11 Test H: Rear Wiper Washer Pump Inoperative (Part 1 of 2)

TEST CONDITIONS	TEST DETAILS/RESULTS/ACTIONS
I2 CHECK REAR WIPER MOTOR OPERATION	

	③ Use a fused (10A) jumper to connect rear window wiper motor C418 Pin 1, component side to the battery positive post. Use a fused (10A) jumper to connect rear window wiper motor C418 Pin 3, component side to the battery negative post. • Does the rear window wiper motor operate? → **Yes** GO to **I3**. → **No** INSTALL a new rear window wiper motor. TEST the system for normal operation.

TEST CONDITIONS	TEST DETAILS/RESULTS/ACTIONS
I3 CHECK CIRCUIT WB01 (YE/BK) FOR POWER	

	① Measure the voltage between rear window wiper motor C418 Pin 1, Circuit WB01 (YE/BK), harness side and ground • Is the voltage greater than 10 volts? → **Yes** GO to **I4**. → **No** REPAIR Circuit WB01 (YE/BK). TEST the system for normal operation.

FM9029900729020X

Fig. 12 Test I: Rear Wipers Are Inoperative (Part 2 of 3). Less movable liftgate glass

TEST CONDITIONS	TEST DETAILS/RESULTS/ACTIONS
H3 CHECK REAR WIPER/WASHER SWITCH OPERATION	

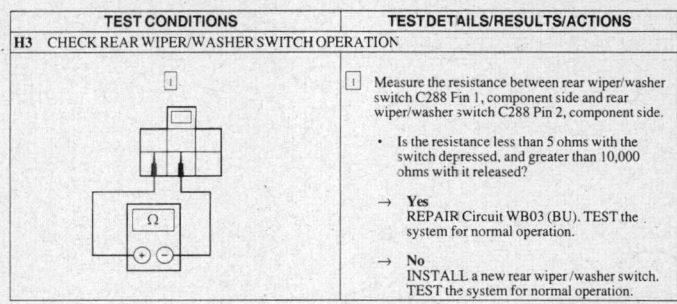

	① Measure the resistance between rear wiper/washer switch C288 Pin 1, component side and rear wiper/washer switch C288 Pin 2, component side. • Is the resistance less than 5 ohms with the switch depressed, and greater than 10,000 ohms with it released? → **Yes** REPAIR Circuit WB03 (BU). TEST the system for normal operation. → **No** INSTALL a new rear wiper/washer switch. TEST the system for normal operation.

FM9029900728020X

Fig. 11 Test H: Rear Wiper Washer Pump Inoperative (Part 2 of 2)

TEST CONDITIONS	TEST DETAILS/RESULTS/ACTIONS
I1 CHECK REAR WIPER/WASHER SWITCH OPERATION	

	① Measure the resistance between rear wiper/washer switch C288 Pin 6, component side and rear wiper/washer switch C288 Pin 2, component side. • Is the resistance less than 5 ohms with the switch depressed, and greater than 10,000 ohms with it released? → **Yes** GO to **I2**. → **No** INSTALL a new rear wiper/washer switch. TEST the system for normal operation.

FM9029900729010X

Fig. 12 Test I: Rear Wipers Are Inoperative (Part 1 of 3). Less movable liftgate glass

TEST CONDITIONS	TEST DETAILS/RESULTS/ACTIONS
I4 CHECK CIRCUIT WBE1 (BK), AND CIRCUIT WBE2 (BK) FOR OPEN	

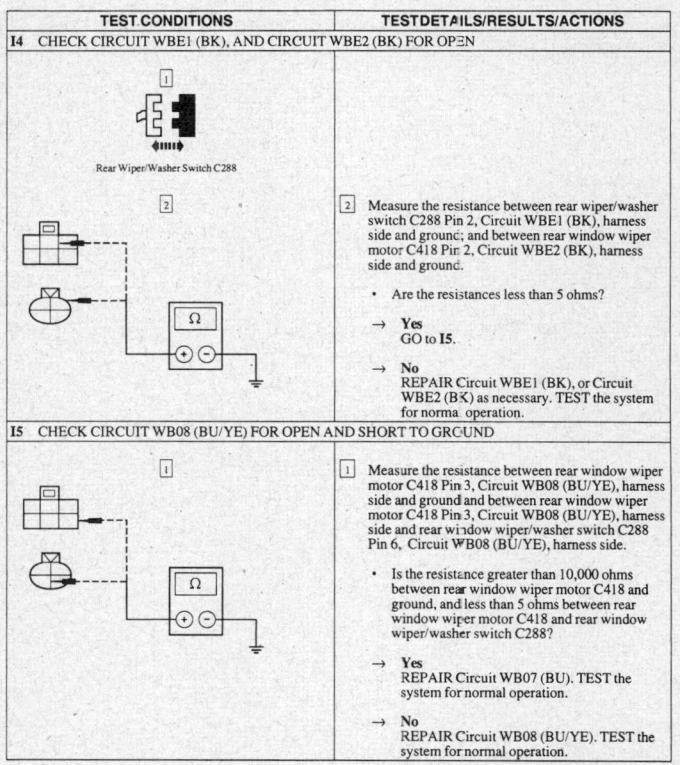

	② Measure the resistance between rear wiper/washer switch C288 Pin 2, Circuit WBE1 (BK), harness side and ground; and between rear window wiper motor C418 Pin 2, Circuit WBE2 (BK), harness side and ground. • Are the resistances less than 5 ohms? → **Yes** GO to **I5**. → **No** REPAIR Circuit WBE1 (BK), or Circuit WBE2 (BK) as necessary. TEST the system for normal operation.

TEST CONDITIONS	TEST DETAILS/RESULTS/ACTIONS
I5 CHECK CIRCUIT WB08 (BU/YE) FOR OPEN AND SHORT TO GROUND	

	① Measure the resistance between rear window wiper motor C418 Pin 3, Circuit WB08 (BU/YE), harness side and ground and between rear window wiper motor C418 Pin 3, Circuit WB08 (BU/YE), harness side and rear window wiper/washer switch C288 Pin 6, Circuit WB08 (BU/YE), harness side. • Is the resistance greater than 10,000 ohms between rear window wiper motor C418 and ground, and less than 5 ohms between rear window wiper motor C418 and rear window wiper/washer switch C288? → **Yes** REPAIR Circuit WB07 (BU). TEST the system for normal operation. → **No** REPAIR Circuit WB08 (BU/YE). TEST the system for normal operation.

FM9029900729030X

Fig. 12 Test I: Rear Wipers Are Inoperative (Part 3 of 3). Less movable liftgate glass

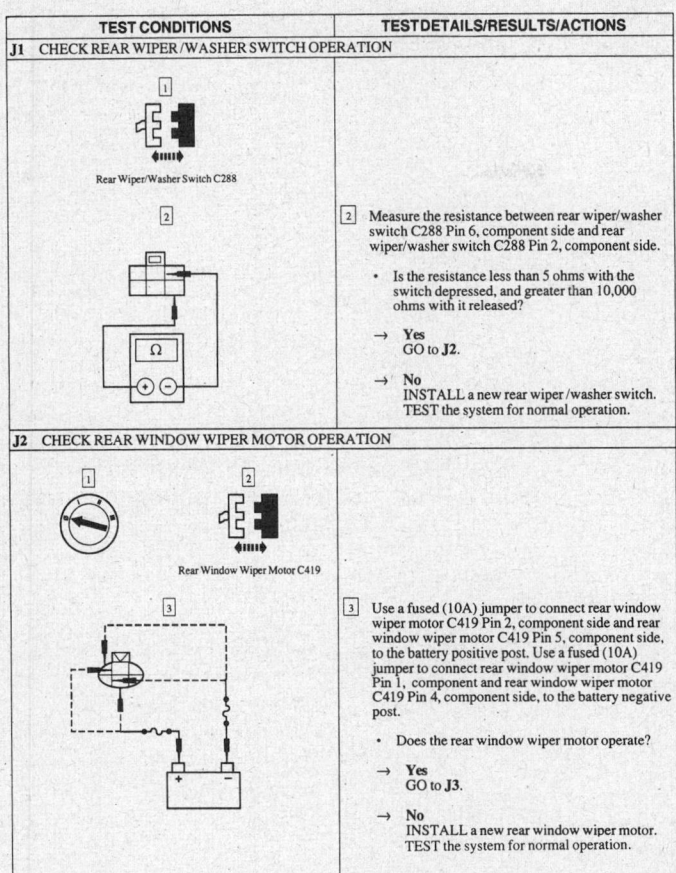

TEST CONDITIONS	TESTDETAILS/RESULTS/ACTIONS
J1 CHECK REAR WIPER/WASHER SWITCH OPERATION	
Rear Wiper/Washer Switch C288	2 Measure the resistance between rear wiper/washer switch C288 Pin 6, component side and rear wiper/washer switch C288 Pin 2, component side. • Is the resistance less than 5 ohms with the switch depressed, and greater than 10,000 ohms with it released? → **Yes** GO to **J2**. → **No** INSTALL a new rear wiper/washer switch. TEST the system for normal operation.
J2 CHECK REAR WINDOW WIPER MOTOR OPERATION	
Rear Window Wiper Motor C419	3 Use a fused (10A) jumper to connect rear window wiper motor C419 Pin 2, component side and rear window wiper motor C419 Pin 5, component side, to the battery positive post. Use a fused (10A) jumper to connect rear window wiper motor C419 Pin 1, component and rear window wiper motor C419 Pin 4, component side, to the battery negative post. • Does the rear window wiper motor operate? → **Yes** GO to **J3**. → **No** INSTALL a new rear window wiper motor. TEST the system for normal operation.

FM9029900730010X

Fig. 13   Test J: Rear Wipers Are Inoperative (Part 1 of 5). With moveable liftgate glass

TEST CONDITIONS	TESTDETAILS/RESULTS/ACTIONS
J5 CHECK CIRCUIT WB21 (BK/YE) FOR OPEN	
1	1 Measure the resistance between liftgate glass switch C421 Pin 1, Circuit WB21 (BK/YE) harness side and rear window wiper motor C419 Pin 1, Circuit WB21 (BK/YE) harness side. • Is the resistance less than 5 ohms? → **Yes** GO to **J6**. → **No** REPAIR Circuit WB21 (BK/YE). TEST the system for normal operation.
J6 CHECK CIRCUIT WBE4 (BK) FOR OPEN	
1	1 Measure the resistance between liftgate glass switch C421 Pin 2, Circuit WBE4 (BK) harness side and ground. • Is the resistance less than 5 ohms? → **Yes** GO to **J7**. → **No** REPAIR Circuit WBE4 (BK). TEST the system for normal operation.

FM9029900730030X

Fig. 13   Test J: Rear Wipers Are Inoperative (Part 3 of 5). With moveable liftgate glass

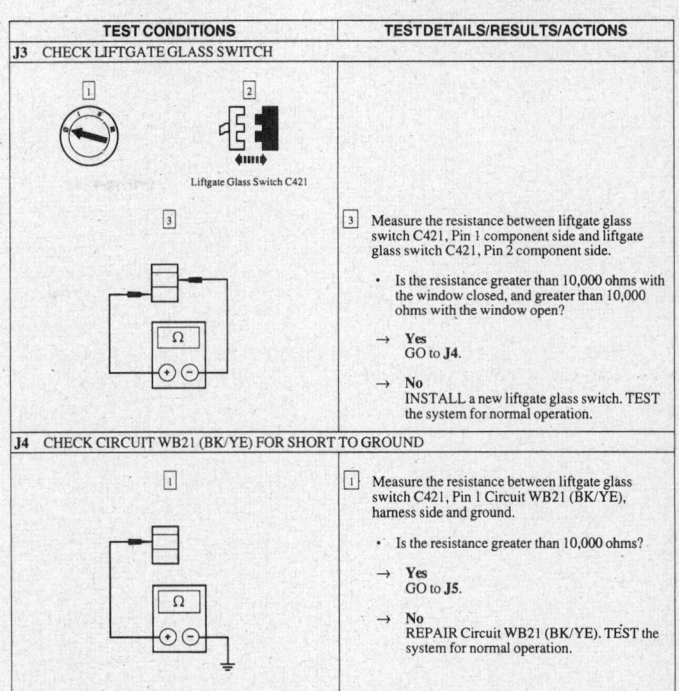

TEST CONDITIONS	TESTDETAILS/RESULTS/ACTIONS
J3 CHECK LIFTGATE GLASS SWITCH	
Liftgate Glass Switch C421	3 Measure the resistance between liftgate glass switch C421, Pin 1 component side and liftgate glass switch C421, Pin 2 component side. • Is the resistance greater than 10,000 ohms with the window closed, and greater than 10,000 ohms with the window open? → **Yes** GO to **J4**. → **No** INSTALL a new liftgate glass switch. TEST the system for normal operation.
J4 CHECK CIRCUIT WB21 (BK/YE) FOR SHORT TO GROUND	
1	1 Measure the resistance between liftgate glass switch C421, Pin 1 Circuit WB21 (BK/YE), harness side and ground. • Is the resistance greater than 10,000 ohms? → **Yes** GO to **J5**. → **No** REPAIR Circuit WB21 (BK/YE). TEST the system for normal operation.

FM9029900730020X

Fig. 13   Test J: Rear Wipers Are Inoperative (Part 2 of 5). With moveable liftgate glass

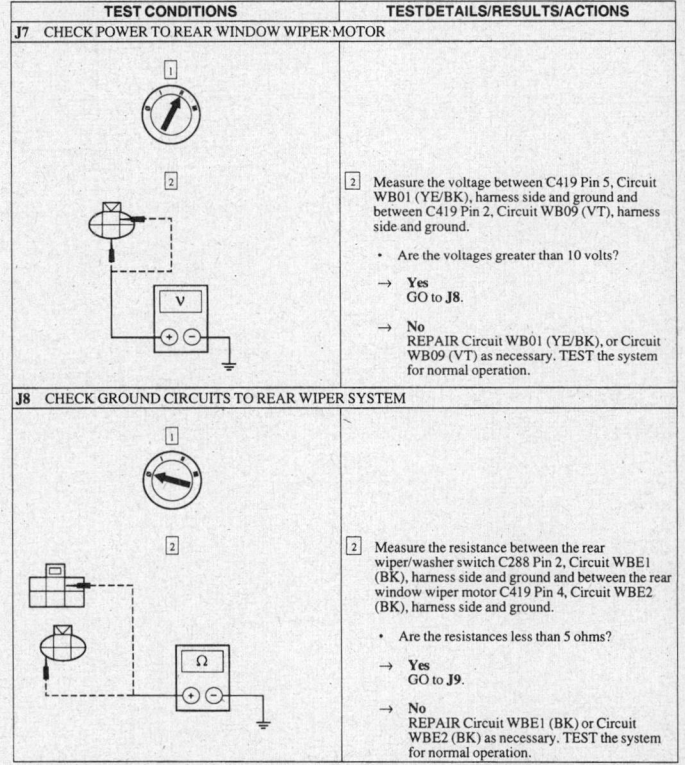

TEST CONDITIONS	TESTDETAILS/RESULTS/ACTIONS
J7 CHECK POWER TO REAR WINDOW WIPER MOTOR	
1 2	2 Measure the voltage between C419 Pin 5, Circuit WB01 (YE/BK), harness side and ground and between C419 Pin 2, Circuit WB09 (VT), harness side and ground. • Are the voltages greater than 10 volts? → **Yes** GO to **J8**. → **No** REPAIR Circuit WB01 (YE/BK), or Circuit WB09 (VT) as necessary. TEST the system for normal operation.
J8 CHECK GROUND CIRCUITS TO REAR WIPER SYSTEM	
1 2	2 Measure the resistance between the rear wiper/washer switch C288 Pin 2, Circuit WBE1 (BK), harness side and ground and between the rear window wiper motor C419 Pin 4, Circuit WBE2 (BK), harness side and ground. • Are the resistances less than 5 ohms? → **Yes** GO to **J9**. → **No** REPAIR Circuit WBE1 (BK) or Circuit WBE2 (BK) as necessary. TEST the system for normal operation.

FM9029900730040X

Fig. 13   Test J: Rear Wipers Are Inoperative (Part 4 of 5). With moveable liftgate glass

TEST CONDITIONS	TEST DETAILS/RESULTS/ACTIONS
J9 CHECK CIRCUITS WB08 (BU/YE) FOR OPEN	

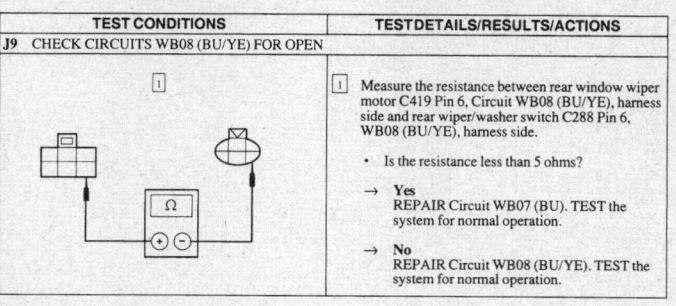

1. Measure the resistance between rear window wiper motor C419 Pin 6, Circuit WB08 (BU/YE), harness side and rear wiper/washer switch C288 Pin 6, WB08 (BU/YE), harness side.

   - Is the resistance less than 5 ohms?

   → **Yes**
   REPAIR Circuit WB07 (BU). TEST the system for normal operation.

   → **No**
   REPAIR Circuit WB08 (BU/YE). TEST the system for normal operation.

FM9029900730050X

Fig. 13   Test J: Rear Wipers Are Inoperative (Part 5 of 5). With moveable liftgate glass

TEST CONDITIONS	TEST DETAILS/RESULTS/ACTIONS
K1 CHECK PARK SWITCH OPERATION (Continued)	

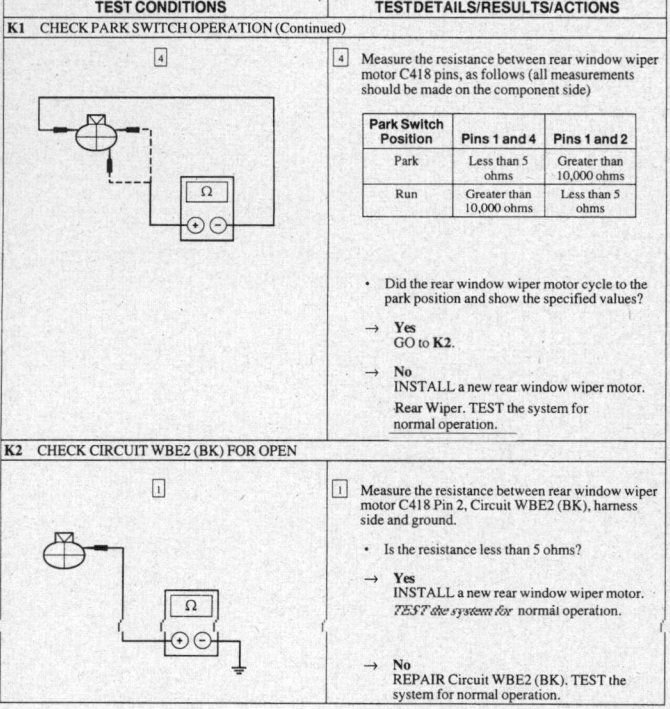

4. Measure the resistance between rear window wiper motor C418 pins, as follows (all measurements should be made on the component side)

Park Switch Position	Pins 1 and 4	Pins 1 and 2
Park	Less than 5 ohms	Greater than 10,000 ohms
Run	Greater than 10,000 ohms	Less than 5 ohms

   - Did the rear window wiper motor cycle to the park position and show the specified values?

   → **Yes**
   GO to **K2**.

   → **No**
   INSTALL a new rear window wiper motor. Rear Wiper. TEST the system for normal operation.

K2 CHECK CIRCUIT WBE2 (BK) FOR OPEN	

1. Measure the resistance between rear window wiper motor C418 Pin 2, Circuit WBE2 (BK), harness side and ground.

   - Is the resistance less than 5 ohms?

   → **Yes**
   INSTALL a new rear window wiper motor. TEST the system for normal operation.

   → **No**
   REPAIR Circuit WBE2 (BK). TEST the system for normal operation.

FM9029900731020X

Fig. 14   Test K: Rear Wipers Will Not Park At Correct Position (Part 2 of 2). Less moveable liftgate glass

TEST CONDITIONS	TEST DETAILS/RESULTS/ACTIONS
K1 CHECK PARK SWITCH OPERATION	

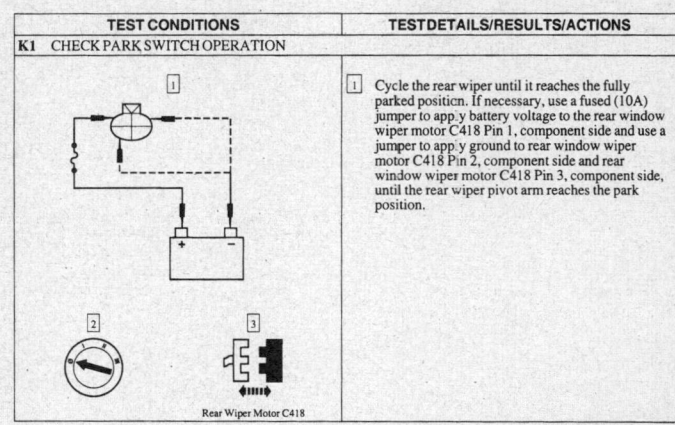

1. Cycle the rear wiper until it reaches the fully parked position. If necessary, use a fused (10A) jumper to apply battery voltage to the rear window wiper motor C418 Pin 1, component side and use a jumper to apply ground to rear window wiper motor C418 Pin 2, component side and rear window wiper motor C418 Pin 3, component side, until the rear wiper pivot arm reaches the park position.

FM9029900731010X

Fig. 14   Test K: Rear Wipers Will Not Park At Correct Position (Part 1 of 2). Less moveable liftgate glass

TEST CONDITIONS	TEST DETAILS/RESULTS/ACTIONS
L1 CHECK REAR WIPER/WASHER SWITCH OPERATION	

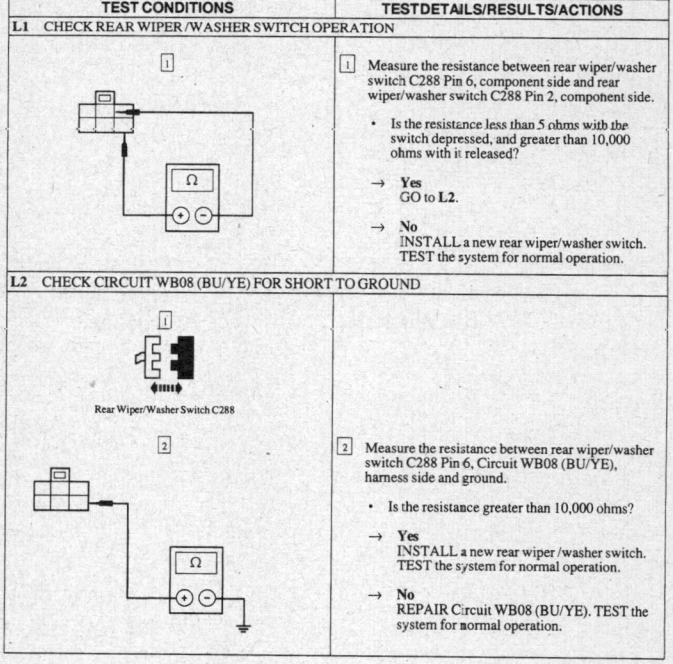

1. Measure the resistance between rear wiper/washer switch C288 Pin 6, component side and rear wiper/washer switch C288 Pin 2, component side.

   - Is the resistance less than 5 ohms with the switch depressed, and greater than 10,000 ohms with it released?

   → **Yes**
   GO to **L2**.

   → **No**
   INSTALL a new rear wiper/washer switch. TEST the system for normal operation.

L2 CHECK CIRCUIT WB08 (BU/YE) FOR SHORT TO GROUND	

2. Measure the resistance between rear wiper/washer switch C288 Pin 6, Circuit WB08 (BU/YE), harness side and ground.

   - Is the resistance greater than 10,000 ohms?

   → **Yes**
   INSTALL a new rear wiper/washer switch. TEST the system for normal operation.

   → **No**
   REPAIR Circuit WB08 (BU/YE). TEST the system for normal operation.

FM9029900732000X

Fig. 15   Test L: Rear Wipers Stay On Continuously

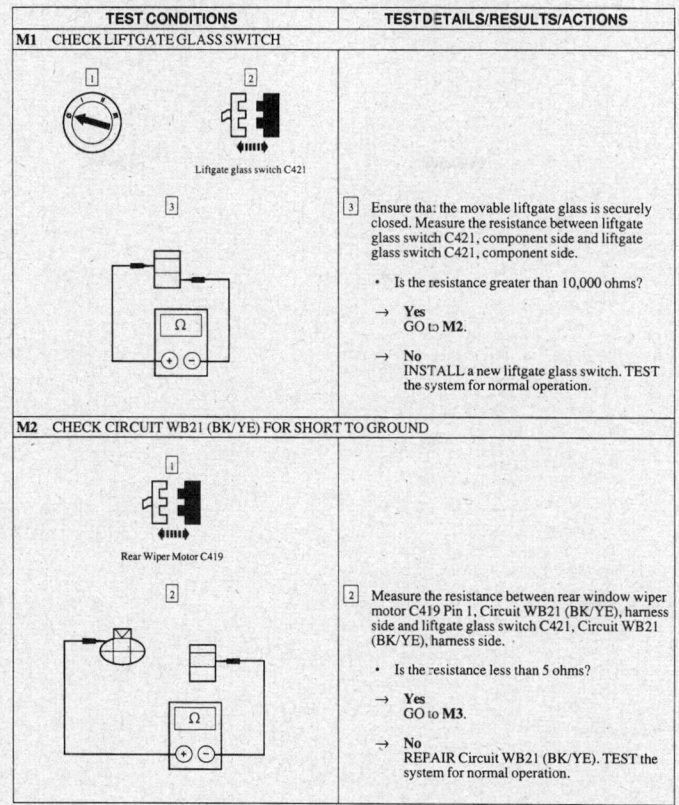

TEST CONDITIONS	TEST DETAILS/RESULTS/ACTIONS
M1 CHECK LIFTGATE GLASS SWITCH	
Liftgate glass switch C421	3 Ensure that the movable liftgate glass is securely closed. Measure the resistance between liftgate glass switch C421, component side and liftgate glass switch C421, component side. • Is the resistance greater than 10,000 ohms? → **Yes** GO to **M2**. → **No** INSTALL a new liftgate glass switch. TEST the system for normal operation.
M2 CHECK CIRCUIT WB21 (BK/YE) FOR SHORT TO GROUND	
Rear Wiper Motor C419	2 Measure the resistance between rear window wiper motor C419 Pin 1, Circuit WB21 (BK/YE), harness side and liftgate glass switch C421, Circuit WB21 (BK/YE), harness side. • Is the resistance less than 5 ohms? → **Yes** GO to **M3**. → **No** REPAIR Circuit WB21 (BK/YE). TEST the system for normal operation.

FM9029900733010X

Fig. 16   Test M: Rear Wipers Will Not Park At Correct Position/Rear Wipers Will Not Move Into Liftgate Glass Open Position (Part 1 of 2)

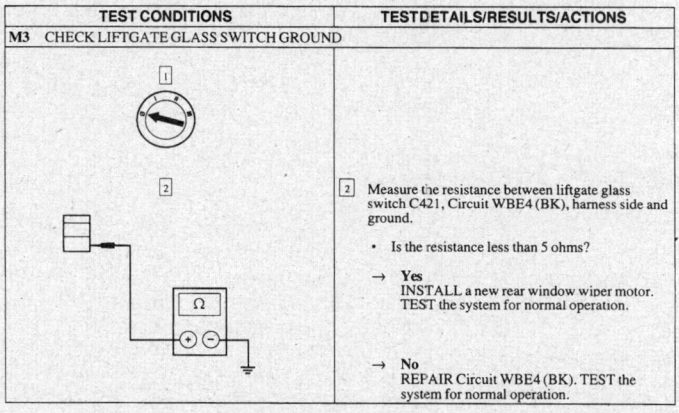

TEST CONDITIONS	TEST DETAILS/RESULTS/ACTIONS
M3 CHECK LIFTGATE GLASS SWITCH GROUND	
	2 Measure the resistance between liftgate glass switch C421, Circuit WBE4 (BK), harness side and ground. • Is the resistance less than 5 ohms? → **Yes** INSTALL a new rear window wiper motor. TEST the system for normal operation. → **No** REPAIR Circuit WBE4 (BK). TEST the system for normal operation.

FM9029900733020X

Fig. 16   Test M: Rear Wipers Will Not Park At Correct Position/Rear Wipers Will Not Move Into Liftgate Glass Open Position (Part 2 of 2)

Windshield Wiper/Washer Switch Position	Resistance Between Wire Terminals (Connector C1)	
	3 to 2	1 to 3
OFF	47,600 ohms	103,300 ohms
MAX DELAY	11,300 ohms	103,300 ohms
MIN DELAY	11,300 ohms	3,300 ohms
LO	4,080 ohms	3,300 ohms
HI	0 ohms	3,300 ohms
WASH	NA	Less than 5 ohms

* Resistance may vary by ± 15%.

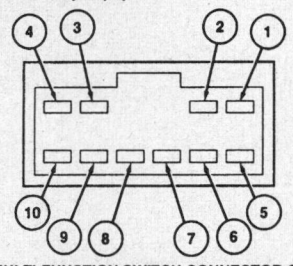

MULTI-FUNCTION SWITCH CONNECTOR C1

FM9029500260000X

Fig. 17 Windshield wiper/washer switch test

COMPONENT DIAGNOSIS & TESTING

Windshield Wiper/Washer Switch Test

1. Turn ignition key to Off position.
2. Disconnect multi-function switch connector C1 located on steering column.
3. Verify resistance between following terminals on turn signal and windshield wiper switch as specified, **Fig. 17**.
4. If windshield wiper/washer switch tests satisfactory, return to diagnostic tests. If not, replace faulty switch.

Rear Window Wiper/Washer Switch Test

1. Turn ignition key to Off position, then remove and disconnect rear window wiper/washer switch located in instrument panel.
2. Verify resistance between wire terminals at rear window wiper/washer switch as specified, **Fig. 18**.
3. If rear window wiper/washer switch tests satisfactory, return to diagnostic tests. If not, replace switch.

Windshield Wiper Motor Current Draw Test

1. Turn ignition key to Off position, then

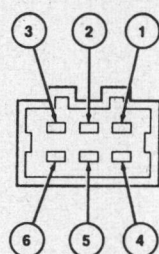

Switch	Resistance	
	Pin 6 and Pin 5	Pin 4 and Pin 5
Rear Window Wiper Switch ON	Less than 5 ohms	NA
Rear Window Wiper Switch OFF	Greater than 10,000 ohms	NA
Rear Window Washer Switch ON	NA	Less than 5 ohms
Rear Window Washer Switch OFF	NA	Greater than 10,000 ohms

FM9029400261000X

Fig. 18 Rear window wiper/washer switch test

disconnect windshield wiper motor connector located behind cowl top vent panel.
2. Using jumper, connect "BK/W" wire terminal at windshield wiper motor connector (component side) to battery positive terminal.
3. Using jumper, connect "BR/W" wire terminal at wiper motor connector (component side) to battery ground terminal. Verify low speed operation of wiper motor.
4. Using jumper, connect "BK/W" wire terminal at wiper motor connector (component side) to battery positive connector.
5. Using jumper, connect "BL/O" wire terminal at wiper motor connector (component side) to battery ground terminal. Verify high speed operation of wiper motor.
6. Connect wiper motor electrical connector, then turn key to On position.
7. Cycle windshield wipers until they reach fully parked position. If required, disconnect wiper motor connector, then, using jumper, connect "BK/W" wire terminal to battery positive terminal and "BR/W" wire terminal to battery ground terminal until wipers reach park position.
8. Turn key to Off position, then disconnect wiper motor electrical connector.
9. Verify resistance between "BK/W" wire terminal and "R" wire terminal, at connect leading to wiper motor as specified, **Fig. 19**.
10. Verify resistance between "R" wire terminal and "BK" wire terminal, at connector leading to wiper motor as specified, **Fig. 19**.

Windshield Wiper Position	Resistance Between Terminals
	6 to 5 "R"
Park	Less than 5 ohms
Run	Greater than 10,000 ohms

Windshield Wiper Position	Resistance Between Terminals
	4 to 5
Park	Greater than 10,000 ohms
Run	Less than 5 ohms

FM9029400262000X

Fig. 19 Windshield wiper motor current draw test

11. If wipers operate properly and park switch resistances are correct, return to diagnostic tests. If not, replace wiper motor.

Wiper Motor

1. Place ignition in Off position.
2. Disconnect windshield wiper motor.
3. Using a fused 20A jumper, connect wiper motor pin No. 6 component side to battery positive terminal.
4. Using a fused 20A jumper, connect wiper motor pin No. 2 component side to battery ground. Ensure low speed operates.
5. Remove jumper from pin No. 2 component side, then connect jumper to pin No. 1 component side at wiper motor. Ensure high speed operates.
6. Connect wiper motor connections.
7. Place ignition in On position.
8. Cycle wipers until they reach fully parked position.
9. Place ignition in Off position.
10. Disconnect wiper motor.
11. Measure resistance between pin Nos. 6 and 5 component side of wiper motor, noting the following:
   a. With wipers in Park position, resistance should be less than five ohms.
   b. With wipers in Run position, resistance should be greater than 10,000 ohms.
12. Measure resistance between pin Nos. 4 and 5 component side of wiper motor, noting the following:
   a. With wipers in Park position, resistance should be greater than 10,000 ohms.
   b. With wipers in Run position, resistance should be less than five ohms.
13. If wipers operate properly, refer to "Diagnostic Tests." If resistance is not as specified, replace wiper motor.

AIR BAG SYSTEM
INDEX

Page No.

**Air Bag System Disarming &
Arming**............................ 4-1
  Arming............................... 4-1
  Disarming........................... 4-1
Collision Inspection.............. 4-2
  Inspection 4-2
  Replacement 4-2
Component Locations........... 4-2
Component Service 4-2
  Clockspring (Sliding Contact) ... 4-2
    Aviator, Excursion, Expedition,
      F-Series, Mark LT, Navigator
      & Econoline 4-2
    Escape, Explorer, Mariner,
      Mountaineer & Ranger 4-3
    Freestar, Monterey &
      Windstar 4-3
    Villager 4-3
  Crash Sensors, Replace 4-3
    Aviator, Escape & Mariner 4-3
    E-Series 4-4
    Excursion, F-150, F-Super
      Duty & Mark LT 4-5
    Expedition & Navigator 4-4
    Explorer & Mountaineer....... 4-5
    Freestar & Monterey 4-6
    Ranger 4-7
    Villager 4-7

Page No.

Windstar....................... 4-7
Diagnostic Monitor, Replace 4-7
  Escape & Mariner.............. 4-7
  Excursion, F-150, F-Super
    Duty & Mark LT 4-7
  Expedition & Navigator 4-7
  Explorer, Mountaineer &
    Ranger...................... 4-7
  Freestar, Monterey &
    Windstar 4-8
  Villager 4-8
Driver Air Bag Module, Replace . 4-8
  Aviator, E-Series, Escape,
    Excursion, Expedition,
    Explorer, F-Series, Mariner,
    Mark LT, Mountaineer,
    Navigator & Ranger 4-8
  Freestar, Monterey &
    Windstar 4-9
  Villager 4-8
Passenger Air Bag Module,
  Replace 4-9
  Aviator, Expedition, F-Series
    & Navigator 4-9
  E-Series & Excursion 4-9
  Escape & Mariner............. 4-9
  Explorer, Mountaineer &
    Ranger...................... 4-9

Page No.

Freestar, Monterey &
  Windstar 4-10
  Villager 4-10
Roof Panel Air Bag Module 4-10
  Aviator......................... 4-10
  Escape & Mariner............. 4-10
  Expedition & Navigator 4-11
  Explorer & Mountaineer....... 4-11
  Explorer Sport & Sport Trac... 4-11
  Freestar & Monterey 4-12
Side Impact Air Bag Module,
  Replace 4-12
  Explorer & Mountaineer....... 4-13
  Aviator, Expedition &
    Navigator................... 4-13
  Escape & Mariner............. 4-12
  Freestar, Monterey &
    Windstar 4-14
Description & Operation........ 4-1
Diagnosis & Testing............ 4-2
Precautions.................... 4-1
  Battery Fuse................... 4-1
  Deployed Air Bags............. 4-1
  General Precautions............ 4-1
  Live Air Bags 4-1
Tightening Specifications 4-20

AIR BAG SYSTEM DISARMING & ARMING

Disarming

Refer to "Air Bag System Precautions" in the front of this manual for air bag system disarming procedures.

Arming

Refer to "Air Bag System Precautions" in the front of this manual for air bag system arming procedures.

DESCRIPTION & OPERATION

The SIR system helps supplement the protection offered by the seat belt by deploying an driver air bag module from the center of the steering wheel, passenger air bag module, side impact air bag module, roof panel air bag module, door panel air bag module, rear side impact air bag module and or a knee blocker air bag module.

PRECAUTIONS

The electrical circuitry required to provide deployment for the air bag is powered directly from the battery and back-up power supply incorporated within the diagnostic monitor. To avoid accidental deployment and possible personal injury, the air bag system must be disarmed prior to servicing or replacing any of the system components.

Safe handling of air bags requires following the procedures outlined below for both live and deployed air bags. **Always wear safety glasses when servicing a vehicle equipped with air bags or when handling an air bag.**

Live Air Bags

When carrying a live air bag, ensure the bag and trim cover are pointing away from your body. In the event of an accidental deployment, this will reduce the chance of personal injury.

When placing a live air bag on a bench or other surface, always face the bag and trim cover up, away from the surface.

Deployed Air Bags

After deployment, the air bag surface may contain deposits of sodium hydroxide, a skin irritant that is a product of the gas generant combustion.

Always wear gloves and safety glasses when handling a deployed air bag. Wash hands with mild soap and water afterward.

General Precautions

Air bag modules with discolored or damaged cover deployment doors must be replaced. **Do not repaint air bag deployment doors (covers) that show discoloration, scratches or tears. Air bag repairs are to be made by replacement only.**

Never attempt to service sensors, clockspring, monitor, back-up power supply or air bag. Service is by replacement only.

If a component is replaced and the new component does not correct the condition, reinstall the original component and perform "Diagnosis & Testing" procedures again.

Never probe connectors on air bags. This may result in air bag deployment and possible personal injury.

All component replacements and wiring service must be performed with air bag system disarmed prior to service or replacement procedures being performed.

Vehicle sensor orientation is critical for proper operation of the system. If the vehicle is involved in an accident where the radiator support, frame or cowls have been damaged, the sensors should be replaced regardless if the air bag was deployed. Also, ensure the body structure in the sensor mounting area is restored to its original condition.

Battery Fuse

Under no circumstances should you substitute another fuse value for the 10A battery fuse. Any fuse other than 10A may cause disarming failure and may result in

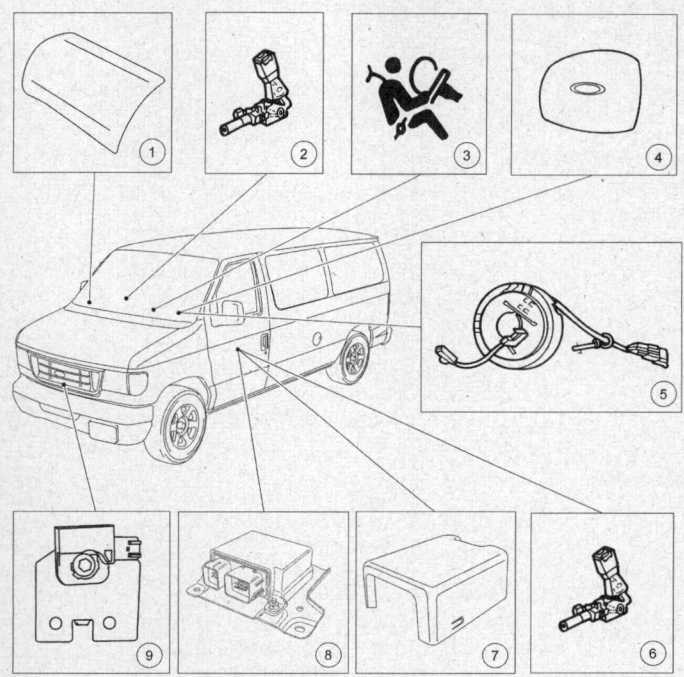

Item	Description	Item	Description
1	Passenger air bag module	6	Driver safety belt buckle and pretensioner
2	Passenger safety belt buckle and pretensioner	7	Restraints control module (RCM) protective cover
3	Air bag indicator	8	RCM
4	Driver air bag module	9	Front impact severity sensor
5	Clockspring		

LTV0500000002709

Fig. 1   SIR component locations. E-Series

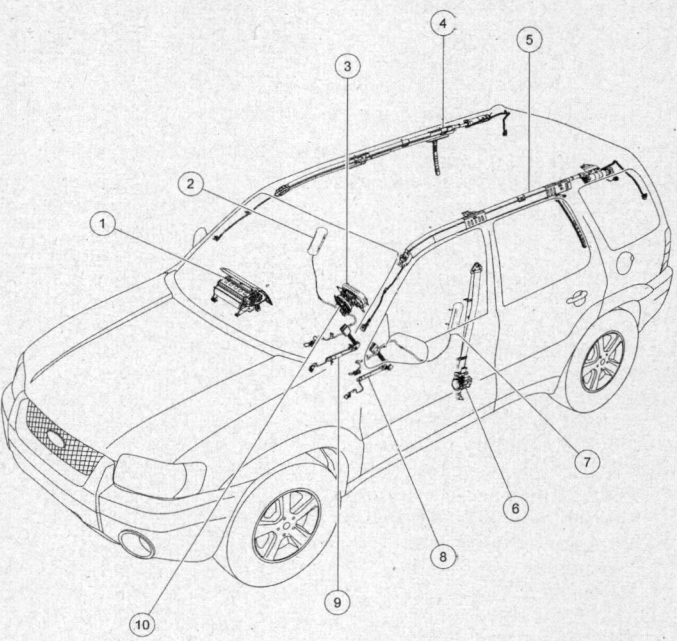

LTV0500000002713

Fig. 2   SIR component locations (Part 1 of 4). Escape & Mariner

danger to occupants of the vehicle. Do not attempt to replace the 10A battery fuse until the air bag system first has been deactivated. Refer to "Air Bag System Disarming & Arming" procedures found in this section.

COMPONENT LOCATIONS

Refer to **Figs. 1 through 14** for component locations.

DIAGNOSIS & TESTING

Refer to **MOTOR's "Air Bag Manual"** or "Air Bag Diagnostics CD" for system diagnosis and testing procedures.

COLLISION INSPECTION

On vehicles that have experienced an air bag system deployment, certain air bag system components must be replaced.

To ensure proper system operation on any vehicle involved in a collision, perform procedures outlined under "Diagnosis & Testing." All system components should be inspected for dents, cracks, exposure to excessive heat and other damage. The air bag sliding contact, steering wheel and steering column should also be inspected. All air bag system wiring should be inspected for chafing and interference with other

vehicle components. If a vehicle has any degree of frontal body damage, the dash sensors should be inspected for dents, cracks, deformation and other damage and replaced with a new unit as required. Dash sensors should also be inspected for secure mounting. When repairing the vehicle, the system should be disarmed as outlined under "Air Bag System Disarming & Arming." Also when performing service procedures, do not expose sensors or wiring or other air bag system components to heat guns, welding or spray guns. If deployment has taking place, the air bag module(s) and clockspring should be replaced. When handling a deployed air bag module, wear gloves and safety glasses. Deployed air bag modules may contain deposits of sodium hydroxide.

Inspection

The following components must be inspected for damage and replaced if required, following a collision.

1. Wiring harness.
2. Terminals.
3. Insulation.
4. Connectors.
5. Steering column.
6. Steering wheel.
7. Clockspring.
8. Diagnostic module.
9. Seat belts.
10. Impact sensors, brackets and housing.

Replacement

The air bag module components are mandatory replacement items following an air bag deployment according to current vehicle manufacturer recommendations.

The seatback pad and trim cover components are mandatory replacement items following an air bag deployment according to current vehicle manufacturer recommendations.

COMPONENT SERVICE

Component orientation is critical in air bag system performance. When replacing these components, ensure that they are installed with the proper orientation.

When replacing air bag system components, ensure proper tightening torque is used to obtain proper system performance.

Clockspring (Sliding Contact)

AVIATOR, EXCURSION, EXPEDITION, F-SERIES, MARK LT, NAVIGATOR & ECONOLINE

1. Disarm air bag system as outlined under "Air Bag System Disarming & Arming."
2. Ensure front wheels aligned straight ahead and steering column shaft alignment mark is at 12 O'clock position.
3. Remove steering wheel as outlined under "Electrical" in appropriate chassis chapter.
4. If equipped, twist tilt wheel handle and shank and remove.

Item	Description
1	Passenger air bag module
2	Passenger seat side air bag module (if equipped)
3	Driver air bag module
4	Passenger safety canopy module (if equipped)
5	Driver safety canopy module (if equipped)
6	Driver safety belt retractor pretensioner (Hybrid only)

Item	Description
7	Driver seat side air bag module (if equipped)
8	Driver safety belt buckle pretensioner (includes safety belt buckle switch)
9	Passenger safety belt buckle pretensioner (includes safety belt buckle switch)
10	Clockspring

LTV0500000002714

Fig. 2   SIR component locations (Part 2 of 4). Escape & Mariner

5. Remove three screws securing lower steering column shroud, then shroud.
6. Remove ignition switch lock cylinder as follows:
   a. Insert ignition key into cylinder and turn to Run position.
   b. Push igniting switch lock cylinder release tab with a punch.
   c. Pull out ignition switch lock cylinder.
7. Carefully pry to release clips and remove steering column opening cover.
8. Remove upper steering column shroud. **Ensure sliding contact has a lock to prevent accidental rotation.**
9. If lock is missing, apply two strips of masking tape across air bag housing to prevent accidental rotation.
10. **On models equipped with Passive Anti-Theft System (PATS),** remove "PATS" retaining screw, then remove transmitter.
11. **On all models,** remove key-in ignition warning indicator switch.
12. Disconnect air bag sliding contact electrical connector and separate air bag electrical connector from bracket.
13. Pry retaining clips loose.
14. Separate wire from two retaining clips holding wire to column.
15. Remove air bag sliding contact and feed wiring harness through instrument panel.
16. Reverse procedure to install.

ESCAPE, EXPLORER, MARINER, MOUNTAINEER & RANGER

1. Disarm air bag system as outlined under "Air Bag System Disarming & Arming."
2. Remove steering wheel as outlined under "Electrical" section of appropriate chassis chapter.
3. Unscrew and remove tilt wheel handle and shank, if equipped.
4. Remove three screws and lower steering column shroud.
5. Remove ignition lock cylinder as outlined under "Ignition Lock, Replace" in appropriate chassis chapter.
6. Remove upper steering column shroud.
7. Remove air bag sliding contact electrical connectors from bend bracket.
8. Disconnect two wire harness clips from steering column.
9. Remove air bag sliding contact by pushing snap back at 6 O'clock posi-

tion, then 3 O'clock position, then 12 O'clock position and remove from steering shaft.
10. Reverse procedure to install, noting the following:
    a. Align air bag sliding contact to column shaft and mounting tabs and slide onto shaft. Push on air bag sliding contact to snap three tabs onto lock cylinder housing.
    b. Install air bag sliding contact connector retainers into holes in steering column.
    c. Install air bag sliding contact retainers into holes in steering column bend bracket.

VILLAGER

1. Disarm air bag system as outlined under "Air Bag System Disarming & Arming."
2. Remove steering wheel as outlined under "Electrical" section of appropriate chassis chapter.
3. Match mark and tape in place inner and outer elements of air bag sliding contact.
4. Remove two steering column shroud screws and lower steering column shroud.
5. Loosen shifter boot and position upper steering column shroud out of way.
6. Remove three air bag sliding contact screws.
7. Disconnect two lower air bag sliding contact electrical connectors.
8. Remove air bag sliding contact from vehicle.
9. Reverse procedure to install.

FREESTAR, MONTEREY & WINDSTAR

1. Disarm air bag system as outlined

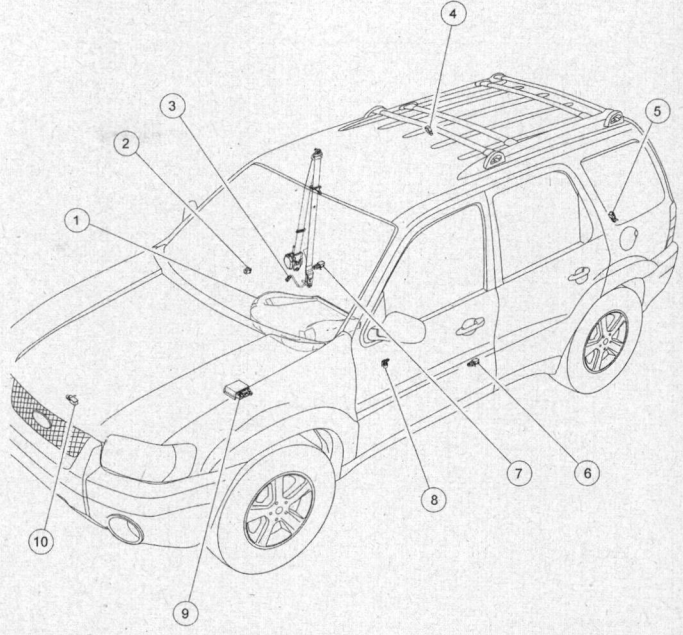

LTV0500000002715

Fig. 2   SIR component locations (Part 3 of 4). Escape & Mariner

under "Air Bag System Disarming & Arming."
2. Remove steering wheel as outlined under "Electrical" section of appropriate chassis chapter.
3. Unscrew and remove tilt wheel handle and shank, if equipped.
4. Remove air bag sliding contact electrical connectors from bend bracket.
5. Disconnect two wire harness clips from steering column.
6. Remove air bag sliding contact by pushing snap back at 6 O'clock position, then 3 O'clock position, then 12 O'clock position and remove from steering shaft.
7. Reverse procedure to install, noting the following:
   a. Align air bag sliding contact to column shaft and mounting tabs and slide onto shaft. Push on air bag sliding contact to snap three tabs onto steering column tube flange.
   b. Install air bag sliding contact connector retainers into holes in steering column.
   c. Install air bag sliding contact retainers into holes in steering column bend bracket.

Crash Sensors, Replace

AVIATOR, ESCAPE & MARINER

FRONT IMPACT SENSOR

1. Disarm air bag system as outlined under "Air Bag System Disarming & Arming."
2. Mark hood latch position, then release cable retaining clamp.
3. Remove latch assembly mounting

Item	Description
1	Occupant classification sensor (OCS) system
2	Passenger air bag deactivation (PAD) indicator
3	Belt tension sensor (part of passenger safety belt and retractor assembly)
4	Passenger second row side impact sensor (if equipped)
5	Driver second row side impact sensor (if equipped)
6	Driver first row side impact sensor (if equipped)
7	Passenger first row side impact sensor (if equipped)
8	Driver seat position sensor
9	Restraints control module
10	Front impact severity sensor

LTV0500000002716

Fig. 2 SIR component locations (Part 4 of 4). Escape & Mariner

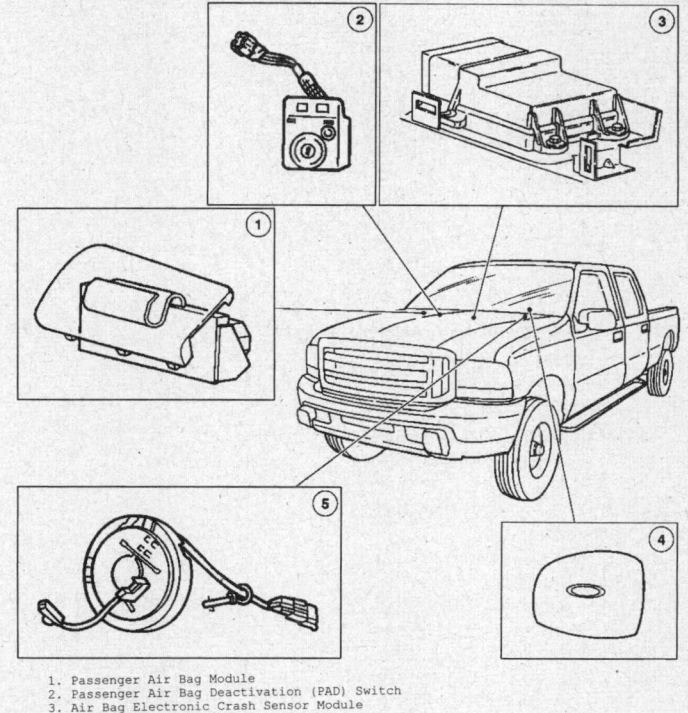

1. Passenger Air Bag Module
2. Passenger Air Bag Deactivation (PAD) Switch
3. Air Bag Electronic Crash Sensor Module
4. Driver Air Bag Module
5. Air Bag Sliding Contact

FM8010002855000X

Fig. 3 SIR component locations. Excursion

bolts and position latch aside.
4. Disconnect impact sensor electrical connector.
5. Remove radiator support bracket bolt.
6. Remove sensor mounting bolts, then the sensor.
7. Reverse procedure to install. Ensure to align locator tabs of front impact sensor to openings in radiator support bracket.

OCCUPANT CLASSIFICATION SENSOR (OCS)

1. Disarm air bag system as outlined under "Air Bag System Disarming & Arming."
2. Remove front passenger seat mounting bolts and electrical connectors, then the seat.
3. Remove four seat cushion bolts retaining seat cushion to seat track, **Fig. 15.**
4. Remove seat cushion and pan assembly. To aid in removal, recline seat.
5. Detach seat cushion trim cover J-clips from seat cushion pan and remove seat cushion trim cover.
6. Remove seat cushion foam pad.
7. Bend retaining tab away from pressure sensor, then slide pressure sensor off bracket.
8. Remove two rivets, then the OCS ECU.
9. Remove two pin-type retainers from OCS bladder and seat cushion pan.
10. Feed OCS hose and pressure sensor

through seat cushion pan opening and remove as an assembly with the bladder.
11. Reverse procedure to install. Ensure pressure sensor hose is not kinked during installation.

SIDE IMPACT SENSORS

1. Disarm air bag system as outlined under "Air Bag System Disarming & Arming."
2. Remove front safety belt retractor anchor bolt and belt.
3. Remove B-pillar or C-pillar trim panels and scuff plates.
4. Disconnect side crash sensor electrical connector.
5. Remove sensor attaching bolts, then the sensor.
6. Reverse procedure to install.

E-SERIES

1. Disarm air bag system as outlined under "Air Bag System Disarming & Arming."
2. Remove radiator grille, **Fig. 16.**
3. Disconnect primary crash sensor electrical connector.
4. Lower front air foil to access front impact sensor bolts.
5. Remove primary crash sensor attaching screw, then the sensor.
6. Reverse procedure to install.

EXPEDITION & NAVIGATOR

FRONT IMPACT SENSOR

1. Disarm air bag system as outlined under "Air Bag System Disarming & Arming."
2. Remove pin-type retainers and lower front lower splash shield to access front impact sensor.
3. Note position of front impact sensor locator tabs to the hood latch support bracket alignment holes for installation.
4. Disconnect sensor electrical connector.
5. Remove impact sensor attaching screws, then the sensor.
6. Reverse procedure to install.

SIDE IMPACT SENSOR (FRONT DOOR)

1. Disarm air bag system as outlined under "Air Bag System Disarming & Arming."
2. Remove front interior door trim panel.
3. Separate weathershield enough to access side impact sensor.
4. Disconnect impact sensor electrical connector.
5. Note position of impact sensor locating tabs for installation.

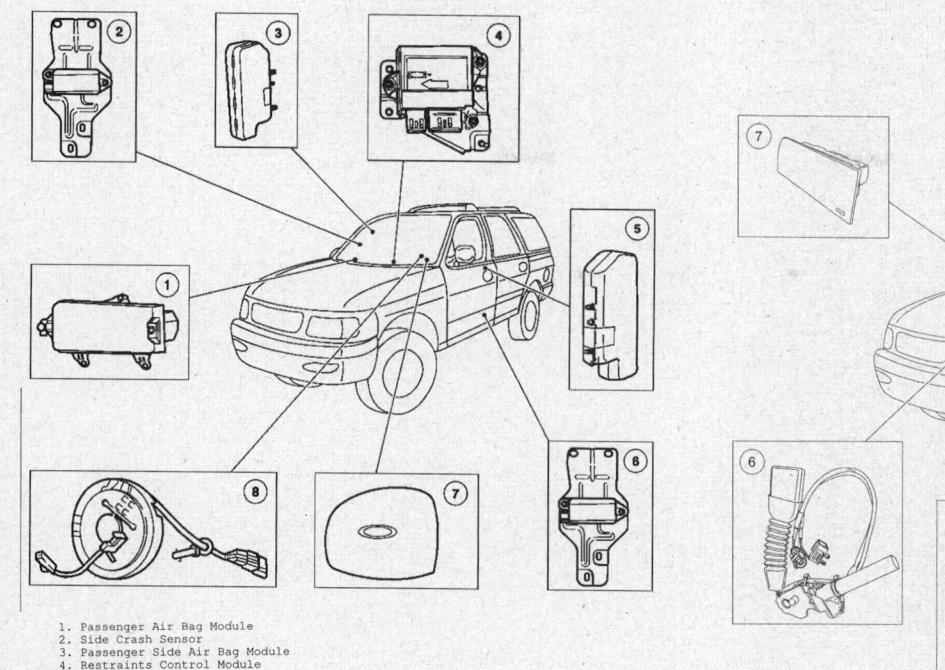

1. Passenger Air Bag Module
2. Side Crash Sensor
3. Passenger Side Air Bag Module
4. Restraints Control Module
5. Driver Side Air Bag Module
6. Side Crash Sensor
7. Driver Air Bag Module
8. Air Bag Sliding Contact

FM8010002852000X

Fig. 4 SIR component locations. 2002–03 Expedition & Navigator

LTV0500000002717

Fig. 5 SIR component locations (Part 1 of 4). 2004–06 Expedition & Navigator

6. Remove sensor mounting bolt, then the sensor.
7. Reverse procedure to install.

SIDE IMPACT SENSOR (C-PILLAR)

1. Disarm air bag system as outlined under "Air Bag System Disarming & Arming."
2. Lift to release and remove rear door scuff plate, **Fig. 17.**
3. Remove safety belt retractor anchor bolt.
4. Pull out at front of rear quarter trim panel, releasing retaining clips and allowing access to impact sensor.
5. Remove side impact sensor retaining bolt.
6. Disconnect impact sensor electrical connector, then remove sensor and bracket.
7. Reverse procedure to install.

EXPLORER & MOUNTAINEER

FRONT IMPACT SENSOR

1. Disarm air bag system as outlined under "Air Bag System Disarming & Arming."
2. Remove four pin-type retainers, then the lower radiator air deflector, **Fig. 18.**
3. Remove front impact sensor bolt.
4. Disconnect sensor electrical connector, then remove sensor. Note position of locator tab on sensor bracket for installation.
5. Reverse procedure to install.

OCCUPANT CLASSIFICATION SENSOR (OCS)

1. Disarm air bag system as outlined under "Air Bag System Disarming & Arming."
2. Remove front passenger seat mounting bolts and electrical connectors, then the seat.
3. Remove four seat cushion bolts retaining seat cushion to seat track, **Fig. 19.**
4. Remove seat cushion and pan assembly. To aid in removal, recline seat.
5. Detach seat cushion trim cover J-clips from seat cushion pan and remove seat cushion trim cover.
6. Remove seat cushion foam pad.
7. Bend retaining tab away from pressure sensor, then slide pressure sensor off bracket.
8. Remove two rivets, then the OCS ECU.
9. Remove two pin-type retainers from OCS bladder and seat cushion pan.
10. Feed OCS hose and pressure sensor through seat cushion pan opening and remove as an assembly with the bladder.
11. Reverse procedure to install. Ensure pressure sensor hose is not kinked during installation.

SEAT POSITION SENSOR

1. Position front seat to rear and upward most position.
2. Disconnect seat position sensor electrical connector.
3. Remove position sensor mounting bolt and sensor. Note position of seat position sensor locating tab for installation.
4. Reverse procedure to install.

SIDE IMPACT SENSOR (FRONT DOOR)

1. Disarm air bag system as outlined under "Air Bag System Disarming & Arming."
2. Remove front interior door trim panel.
3. Separate weathershield enough to access side impact sensor.
4. Disconnect impact sensor electrical connector.
5. Note position of impact sensor locating tabs for installation.
6. Remove sensor mounting bolt, then the sensor.
7. Reverse procedure to install.

SIDE IMPACT SENSOR (C-PILLAR)

1. Disarm air bag system as outlined under "Air Bag System Disarming & Arming."
2. Lift to release and remove rear door scuff plate.
3. Remove safety belt retractor anchor bolt.
4. Pull out at front of rear quarter trim panel, releasing retaining clips and allowing access to impact sensor.
5. Remove side impact sensor retaining bolt.
6. Disconnect impact sensor electrical connector, then remove sensor and bracket.
7. Reverse procedure to install.

EXCURSION, F-SUPER DUTY, F-150 & MARK LT

FRONT IMPACT SENSOR

1. Disarm air bag system as outlined

Item	Description
1	Passenger side safety canopy module (if equipped)
2	Driver side safety canopy module (if equipped)
3	Driver safety belt buckle and pretensioner
4	Driver air bag module

Item	Description
5	Clockspring
6	Passenger safety belt buckle and pretensioner
7	Passenger air bag module

LTV0500000002718

Fig. 5 SIR component locations (Part 2 of 4). 2004–06 Expedition & Navigator

under "Air Bag System Disarming & Arming."
2. Remove front impact sensor bolt from hood release support bracket.
3. Disconnect sensor electrical connector, then remove sensor. Note position of locator tab on sensor bracket for installation.
4. Reverse procedure to install.

OCCUPANT CLASSIFICATION SENSOR (OCS)

1. Disarm air bag system as outlined under "Air Bag System Disarming & Arming."
2. Remove front passenger seat mounting bolts and electrical connectors, then the seat.
3. Remove four seat cushion bolts retaining seat cushion to seat track, **Fig. 20.**
4. Remove seat cushion and pan assembly. To aid in removal, recline seat.
5. Detach seat cushion trim cover J-clips from seat cushion pan and remove seat cushion trim cover.
6. Remove seat cushion foam pad.
7. Bend retaining tab away from pressure sensor, then slide pressure sensor off bracket.
8. Remove two rivets, then the OCS ECU.
9. Remove two pin-type retainers from OCS bladder and seat cushion pan.
10. Feed OCS hose and pressure sensor through seat cushion pan opening and remove as an assembly with the bladder.
11. Reverse procedure to install. Ensure pressure sensor hose is not kinked during installation.

SEAT POSITION SENSOR

1. Position front seat to rear and upward most position.
2. Disconnect seat position sensor electrical connector.
3. Remove position sensor mounting bolt and sensor. Note position of seat position sensor locating tab for installation.
4. Reverse procedure to install.

FREESTAR & MONTEREY

FRONT IMPACT SENSOR

1. Disarm air bag system as outlined under "Air Bag System Disarming & Arming."
2. Remove four pin-type retainers, then the lower radiator air deflector, **Fig. 21.**
3. Remove front impact sensor bolt.
4. Disconnect sensor electrical connector, then remove sensor. Note position

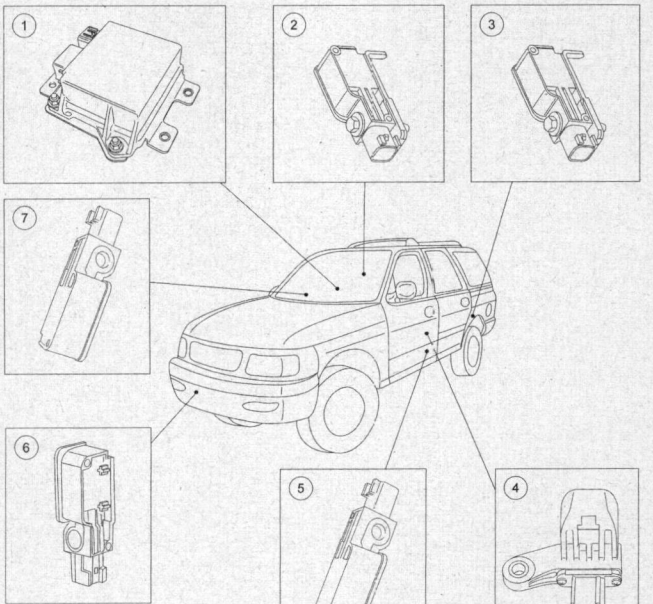

LTV0500000002719

Fig. 5 SIR component locations (Part 3 of 4). 2004–06 Expedition & Navigator

of locator tab on sensor bracket for installation.
5. Reverse procedure to install.

OCCUPANT CLASSIFICATION SENSOR (OCS)

1. Disarm air bag system as outlined under "Air Bag System Disarming & Arming."
2. Remove front passenger seat mounting bolts and electrical connectors, then the seat.
3. Remove four seat cushion bolts retaining seat cushion to seat track, **Fig. 22.**
4. Remove seat cushion and pan assembly. To aid in removal, recline seat.
5. Detach seat cushion trim cover J-clips from seat cushion pan and remove seat cushion trim cover.
6. Remove seat cushion foam pad.
7. Bend retaining tab away from pressure sensor, then slide pressure sensor off bracket.
8. Remove two rivets, then the OCS ECU.
9. Remove two pin-type retainers from OCS bladder and seat cushion pan.
10. Feed OCS hose and pressure sensor through seat cushion pan opening and remove as an assembly with the bladder.
11. Reverse procedure to install. Ensure pressure sensor hose is not kinked during installation.

SEAT POSITION SENSOR

1. Position front seat to rear and upward most position.
2. Disconnect seat position sensor electrical connector.
3. Remove position sensor mounting bolt and sensor. Note position of seat position sensor locating tab for installation.
4. Reverse procedure to install.

SIDE IMPACT SENSOR (FIRST ROW)

1. Disarm air bag system as outlined under "Air Bag System Disarming & Arming."
2. Remove front seat on side with affected sensor.
3. Remove front door scuff plate.
4. Remove kick panel to prevent damaging carpet.
5. Lift carpet to gain access to first row side impact sensor.
6. Disconnect impact sensor electrical connector.
7. Note position of impact sensor locating tabs for installation.
8. Remove sensor mounting bolt, then the sensor.
9. Reverse procedure to install.

SIDE IMPACT SENSOR (SECOND ROW)

1. Disarm air bag system as outlined under "Air Bag System Disarming & Arming."
2. Lift to release and remove rear door scuff plate, **Fig. 23.**
3. Remove safety belt retractor anchor bolt.
4. Pull out on quarter trim panel at C-pillar to release retaining clips and access side impact sensor.
5. Separate weatherstrip at quarter trim panel.
6. Disconnect electrical connector from speaker.
7. Remove speaker mounting bolts, then the speaker.
8. Remove side impact sensor retaining bolt.
9. Disconnect impact sensor electrical

Item	Description
1	Restraints control module (RCM)
2	Second row, C-pillar side impact sensor (if equipped)
3	Second row, C-pillar side impact sensor (if equipped)
4	Driver seat track position sensor
5	Front row, driver door, side impact sensor (if equipped)
6	Front impact severity sensor
7	Front row, passenger door, side impact sensor (if equipped)

LTV0500000002720

Fig. 5 SIR component locations (Part 4 of 4). 2004–06 Expedition & Navigator

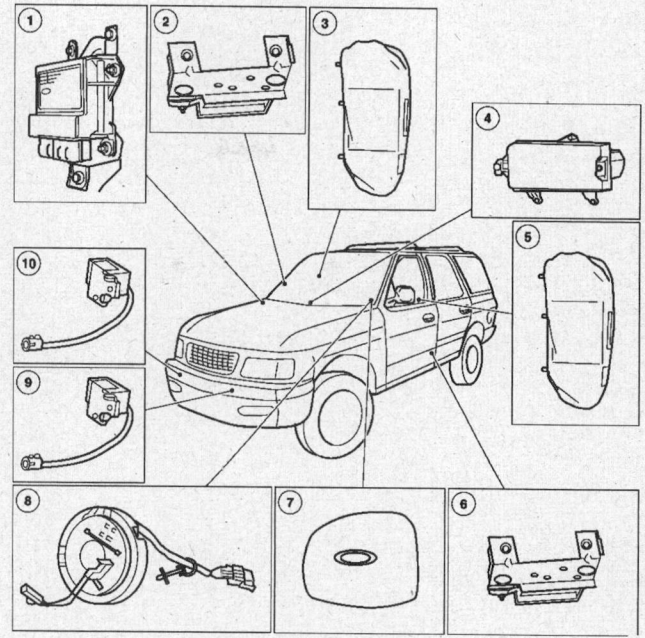

1. Restraints Control Module
2. Side Crash Sensor
3. Passenger Side Air Bag Module
4. Passenger Air Bag Module
5. Driver Side Air Bag Module
6. Side Crash Sensor
7. Driver Air Bag Module
8. Air Bag Sliding Contact
9. Air Bag Sensor and Bracket (LH)
10. Air Bag Sensor and Bracket (RH)

FM8010002853000X

Fig. 6 SIR component locations. 2002–03 Explorer & Mountaineer

connector, then remove sensor and bracket.
10. Reverse procedure to install.

RANGER

FRONT SENSOR & BRACKET

To service stripped sensor retaining screws, replace sensor bracket with part No. 14B190RH, 14B191LH, screw part No. N806327-S190 and nut part No. W620397-S36 or equivalent components. Tighten to specification.
1. Disarm air bag system as outlined under "Air Bag System Disarming & Arming."
2. Remove radiator grille and radiator opening cover.
3. Remove two radiator primary crash front air bag sensor and bracket screws.
4. Remove three righthand crash sensor bracket attaching screws.
5. Disconnect lefthand primary crash sensor and bracket electrical connector and remove radiator primary crash front air bag sensor and bracket.
6. Reverse procedure to install. Tighten bolts to specification.

VILLAGER

CRASH SENSOR & SAFING AIR BAG SENSOR

The primary crash air bag sensor and the safing air bag sensor are incorporated into the air bag diagnostic monitor. The sensors cannot be serviced. The air bag diagnostic monitor, primary crash sensor and the safing air bag sensor are serviced as a complete assembly.

WINDSTAR

On these models, the air bag diagnostic monitor contains a safing sensor that are integral to the unit and cannot be replaced separately. Refer to "Diagnostic Monitor, Replace" for replacement procedure.

Diagnostic Monitor, Replace

ESCAPE & MARINER

1. Disarm air bag system as outlined under "Air Bag System Disarming & Arming."
2. Position carpet back at righthand and lefthand center tunnel area under instrument panel.
3. Slide and disengage two RCM electrical connector locking clips, then push down to disconnect.
4. Remove retaining bolts, then the module.
5. Reverse procedure to install.

EXPLORER, MOUNTAINEER & RANGER

1. Disarm air bag system as outlined under "Air Bag System Disarming & Arming."
2. Remove righthand kick panel. Air bag diagnostic monitor is blue box with two connectors mounted below climate control head.
3. Disconnect air bag diagnostic monitor electrical connectors.
4. Remove screws retaining air bag diag-

nostic monitor and bracket to instrument panel brace.
5. Remove monitor and bracket.
6. Reverse procedure to install.

EXPEDITION & NAVIGATOR

1. Disarm air bag system as outlined under "Air Bag System Disarming & Arming."
2. Remove righthand cowl side trim panel.
3. Disconnect two electrical connectors and four screws to remove diagnostic monitor. If required, access screws through glove compartment opening.
4. Remove diagnostic monitor from vehicle.
5. Reverse procedure to install.

EXCURSION, F-SUPER DUTY, F-150 & MARK LT

1. Disarm air bag system as outlined under "Air Bag System Disarming & Arming."
2. Remove air bag electronic crash sensor module cover.
3. Disconnect diagnostic monitor electrical connector locking clip, then disconnect connector.
4. Remove monitor bracket bolts, then the monitor and bracket.
5. Reverse procedure to install.

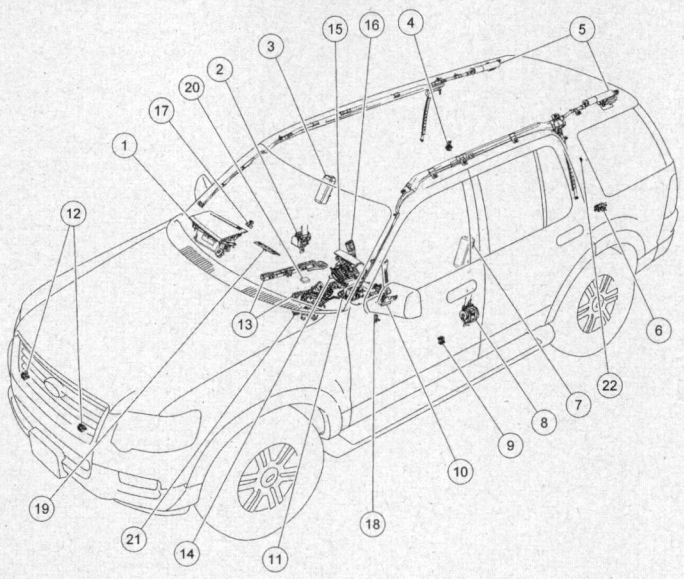

Item	Description
1	Passenger air bag module
2	Passenger adaptive load limiting safety belt retractor
3	Passenger seat side air bag module
4	Second row RH side impact sensor (if equipped)
5	Safety canopy modules (if equipped)

Item	Description
6	Second row LH side impact sensor (if equipped)
7	Driver seat side air bag module
8	Driver adaptive load limiting safety belt retractor
9	Driver first row side impact sensor (in driver front door)

LTV0500000002721

Fig. 7 SIR component locations (Part 1 of 2). 2004–06 Explorer & Mountaineer

Item	Description
10	Driver safety belt buckle pretensioner (includes safety belt buckle switch)
11	Restraints control module (RCM)
12	Front impact severity sensors
13	Occupant classification sensor (OCS) rails (outboard/inboard)
14	Clockspring
15	Driver air bag module
16	Passenger safety belt buckle pretensioner (includes safety belt buckle switch)
17	Passenger first row side impact sensor (in passenger front door)
18	Driver seat track position sensor
19	Passenger air bag deactivation (PAD) indicator
20	Occupant classification sensor (OCS) module
21	Deployable steering column
22	Safety canopy bridge resistor

LTV0500000004082

Fig. 7 SIR component locations (Part 2 of 2). 2004–06 Explorer & Mountaineer

VILLAGER

1. Disarm air bag system as outlined under "Air Bag System Disarming & Arming."
2. Remove four console compartment plastic screws or C/D changer cover plastic screws (if equipped) and console compartment door or C/D changer cover (if equipped).
3. Remove two lefthand inner instrument panel lower cover screws and plastic nut, then the lefthand inner instrument panel lower cover.
4. Disconnect foot lamp electrical connector.
5. Remove two righthand inner instrument panel lower cover screws and plastic nut, then the righthand inner instrument panel lower cover and disconnect foot lamp electrical connector.
6. Remove four air bag diagnostic monitor bolts and air bag diagnostic monitor.
7. Disconnect air bag diagnostic monitor electrical connector.
8. Remove air bag diagnostic monitor from vehicle.
9. Reverse procedure to install.

FREESTAR, MONTEREY & WINDSTAR

1. Disarm air bag system as outlined under "Air Bag System Disarming & Arming."

2. Remove four utility compartment pushpins, then pull straight out to remove compartment.
3. Roll back carpet to access monitor bracket attaching bolts and electrical connectors, **Fig. 24.**
4. Disengage two electrical connector locking tabs, then the electrical connectors from module.
5. Remove module bracket attaching bolts, then the module and bracket.
6. Reverse procedure to install.

Driver Air Bag Module, Replace

AVIATOR, ESCAPE, E-SERIES, EXCURSION, EXPEDITION, EXPLORER, F-SERIES, MARINER, MARK LT, MOUNTAINEER, NAVIGATOR & RANGER

1. Disarm air bag system as outlined under "Air Bag System Disarming & Arming."
2. Ensure wheels are in straight ahead position.
3. Remove two back cover plugs, then air bag module screws.
4. Disconnect horn electrical connector, then air bag sliding contact electrical connector.

5. Remove driver air bag module.
6. Reverse procedure to install, tighten air bag module in two steps as follows:
   a. Step one, **torque** outboard module nut then inboard module nut to 44 inch lbs.
   b. Step two, **torque** outboard module nut then inboard module nut to 80 inch lbs.

VILLAGER

If the air bag did not deploy in an accident, it may not have been needed. In this case, perform "Diagnosis & Testing" prior to replacing air bag module.

1. Disarm air bag system as outlined under "Air Bag System Disarming & Arming."
2. Center front wheels to straight ahead position, then disarm air bag system as outlined under "Air Bag System Disarming & Arming."
3. Remove lefthand and righthand air bag module bolt access covers, **Fig. 25,** then the steering wheel bottom access cover, **Fig. 26.**
4. Disconnect driver air bag module electrical connector.
5. Remove driver air bag module bolts, then the module. **Discard bolts.**

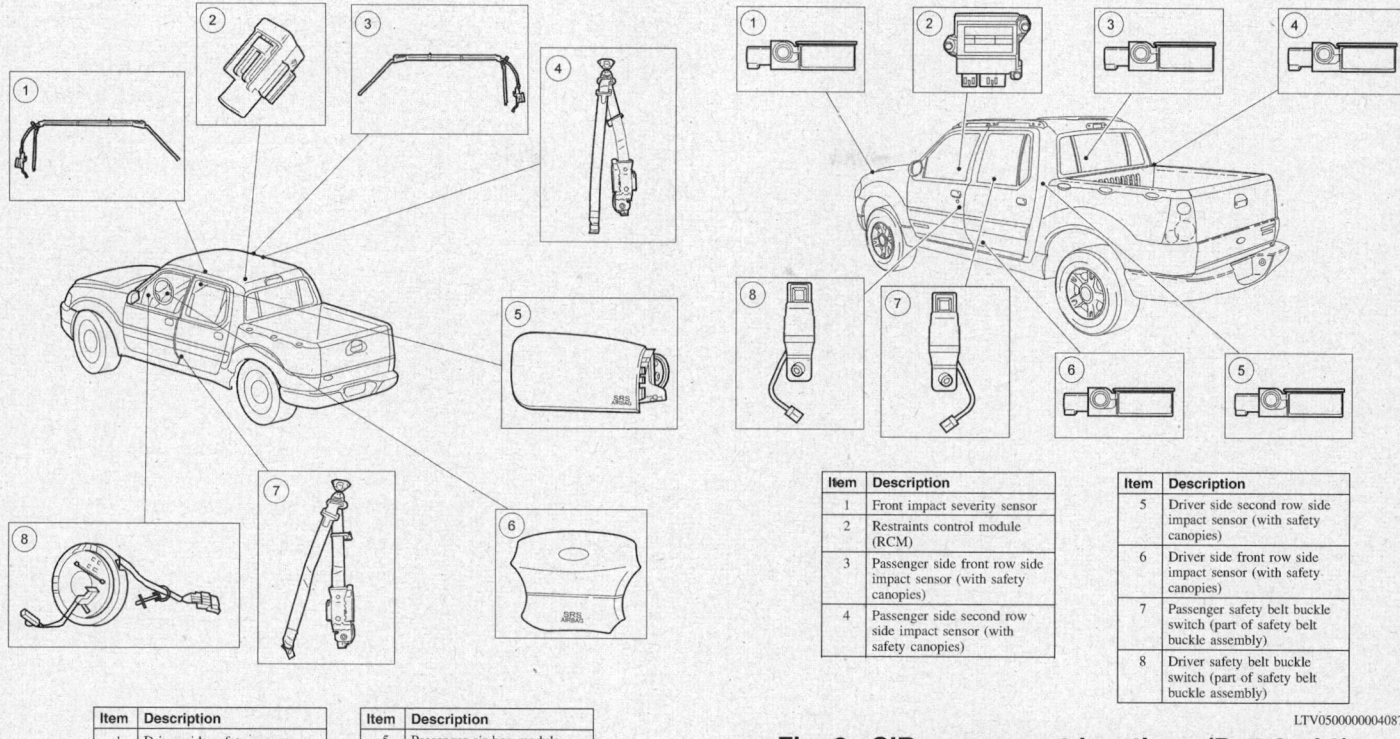

Fig. 8 SIR component locations (Part 2 of 2).
Explorer Sport & Sport Trac

Item	Description
1	Front impact severity sensor
2	Restraints control module (RCM)
3	Passenger side front row side impact sensor (with safety canopies)
4	Passenger side second row side impact sensor (with safety canopies)

Item	Description
5	Driver side second row side impact sensor (with safety canopies)
6	Driver side front row side impact sensor (with safety canopies)
7	Passenger safety belt buckle switch (part of safety belt buckle assembly)
8	Driver safety belt buckle switch (part of safety belt buckle assembly)

LTV0500000004087

Item	Description
1	Driver side safety canopy module (if equipped)
2	Safety canopy bridge resister (if equipped)
3	Passenger side safety canopy module (if equipped)
4	Passenger side safety belt retractor pretensioner

Item	Description
5	Passenger air bag module
6	Driver air bag module
7	Driver side safety belt retractor pretensioner
8	Clockspring

LTV0500000004086

Fig. 8 SIR component locations (Part 1 of 2).
Explorer Sport & Sport Trac

6. Reverse procedure to install, noting the following:
   a. Align splines on module.
   b. **Driver air bag module bolts are coated with a special bonding agent. Always replace old module bolts with new module bolts.** Tighten driver air bag module bolts to specifications.
   c. Verify air bag warning indicator operation.

FREESTAR, MONTEREY & WINDSTAR

If the air bag did not deploy in an accident, it may not have been needed. In this case, perform "Diagnosis & Testing" prior to replacing air bag module.

1. Disarm air bag system as outlined under "Air Bag System Disarming & Arming."
2. Remove two side cover plugs.
3. Remove air bag module to steering wheel retaining screws and washers.
4. Disconnect air bag electrical connector.
5. Remove driver air bag module.
6. Reverse procedure to install. Tighten module retaining screws to specifications.
7. Arm air bag system as outlined under "Air Bag System Disarming & Arming."
8. Verify air bag readiness indicator operation.

Passenger Air Bag Module, Replace
AVIATOR, EXPEDITION, F-SERIES & NAVIGATOR

1. Disarm air bag system as outlined under "Air Bag System Disarming & Arming."
2. Remove instrument panel relay cover.
3. Remove three screws, disconnect electrical connector and remove air bag module.
4. Reverse procedure to install.

E-SERIES & EXCURSION

1. Disarm air bag system as outlined under "Air Bag System Disarming & Arming."
2. Remove instrument panel access hole cover and panel reinforcement.
3. Remove passenger air bag module retaining nuts.
4. Separating door from clip. Separate rest of door from clips by lifting door with your hands.
5. Disconnect passenger air bag module connector, then the air bag module.
6. Remove six offset fasteners used for retaining air bag module door from instrument panel.
7. Reverse procedure to install placing six new offset fasteners onto air bag module door.

ESCAPE & MARINER

1. Disarm air bag system as outlined under "Air Bag System Disarming & Arming."
2. Open the glove box past its stops, then disconnect electrical connector from air bag.
3. Remove four passenger air bag attaching bolts.
4. Remove passenger air bag module from instrument panel, through glove compartment opening.
5. Reverse procedure to install.

EXPLORER, MOUNTAINEER & RANGER

1. Disarm air bag system as outlined under "Air Bag System Disarming & Arming."
2. Open glove compartment, then press side inward and lower glove compartment to floor.
3. Remove two screws that attach air bag module to steel instrument panel reinforcement.
4. Disconnect air bag electrical connector on lefthand lower rear corner of air bag module.
5. Remove air bag connector from steel reinforcement by prying "Christmas tree" out of hole in reinforcement.
6. Pull each corner of air bag cover to disengage cover to instrument panel attachments.
7. Gently push air bag module from behind, out of instrument panel opening in order to pull passenger air bag module out completely with both hands.
8. Reverse procedure to install. Tighten retaining screws to specifications.

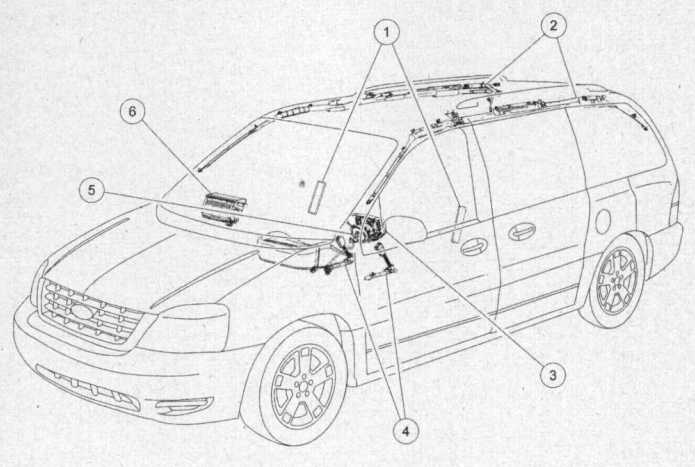

Item	Description		Item	Description
1	Seat side air bag modules (if equipped)		4	Safety belt buckle and pretensioners
2	Safety canopy modules (if equipped)		5	Clockspring
3	Driver air bag module		6	Passenger air bag module

LTV0500000004083

Fig. 9   SIR component locations (Part 1 of 2). Freestar & Monterey

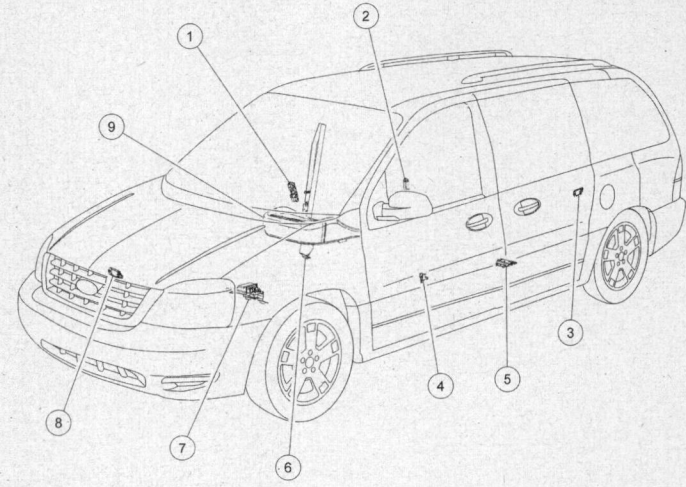

Item	Description		Item	Description
1	Passenger air bag deactivation (PAD) indicator		5	First row side impact sensor
2	Passenger second row side impact sensor (if equipped)		6	Belt tension sensor (part of passenger safety belt and retractor assembly)
3	Driver second row side impact sensor (if equipped)		7	Restraints control module (RCM)
4	Driver seat position sensor		8	Front impact severity sensor

LTV0500000004084

Fig. 9   SIR component locations (Part 2 of 2). Freestar & Monterey

VILLAGER

1. Disarm air bag system as outlined under "Air Bag System Disarming & Arming."
2. Remove four console compartment plastic screws or C/D changer cover plastic screws (if equipped) and console compartment door or C/D changer cover (if equipped).
3. Remove two lefthand and righthand inner instrument panel lower cover screws and plastic nuts.
4. Remove lefthand and righthand inner instrument panel lower covers and disconnect foot lamp electrical connector.
5. Remove plastic screw, two large screws, two center bolts, two upper screws and screw at instrument panel bracket, then separate glove compartment from instrument panel.
6. Disconnect glove compartment striker plate catch electrical connector.
7. Disconnect passenger air bag module electrical connector.
8. Remove four passenger air bag module nuts and passenger air bag.
9. Reverse procedure to install and tighten nuts to specification. Verify that air bag warning indicator is operative.

FREESTAR, MONTEREY & WINDSTAR

1. Disarm air bag system as outlined under "Air Bag System Disarming & Arming."
2. Remove righthand and lefthand finish panel.
3. Remove instrument panel finish panel retaining spear clips.

4. Open glove compartment, then press side inward and lower glove compartment to floor.
5. Remove four passenger air bag module retaining screws from side of air bag cover.
6. Disconnect electrical connector attached to lefthand side of air bag module.
7. Remove passenger air bag module.
8. Reverse procedure to install. Tighten module retaining screws to specifications.

Roof Panel Air Bag Module

AVIATOR

1. Disarm air bag system as outlined under "Air Bag System Disarming & Arming."
2. Remove headliner, **Fig. 27.**
3. Disconnect roof panel air bag module electrical connector.
4. Remove three rearward roof panel air bag bolts located between C-pillar and D-pillar.
5. Remove three pin-type retainers.
6. Remove two C-pillar tether anchor assembly bolts.
7. Slide tether anchor assembly up and out to disengage it from C-pillar.
8. Remove two roof panel air bag bolts located near C-pillar.
9. Remove two roof panel air bag bolts located near B-pillar.

10. Remove one roof panel air bag bolt located near the A-pillar.
11. Remove A-pillar tether bracket bolt, then the bracket.
12. Remove A-pillar tether with pin-type retainer.
13. Push retainers together and separate rear ramp from sheet metal.
14. Push roof panel air bag cover in, releasing it from front ramp lower retainers and rotate bottom of air bag up and out of ramp.
15. Separate roof panel air bag from front ramp upper retainers.
16. Remove roof panel air bag module.
17. Reverse procedure to install, noting the following:
    a. Position ramp upper retainers around air bag module, ensure retainers are in air bag module cover locator cutouts.
    b. Air bag module cover must be located behind ramp tabs.
    c. Angle rear of module toward sheet metal. Insert deployment canister into sheet metal opening.
    d. Push in on front and rear ramps engaging ramp retainers to sheet metal. An audible click should be heard, indicating that retainers have engaged into sheet metal.
    e. Install air bag module bolts in sequence, **Fig. 28.**

ESCAPE & MARINER

1. Disarm air bag system as outlined under "Air Bag System Disarming & Arming."

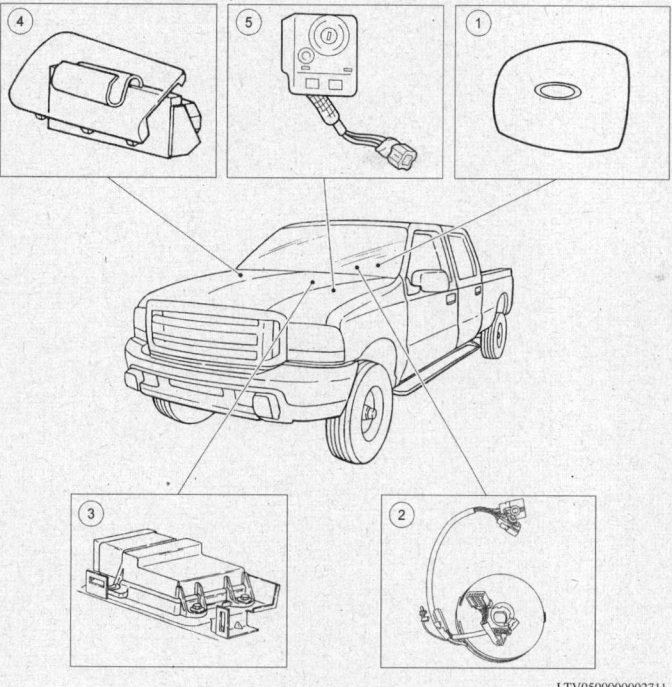

LTV0500000002711

Fig. 10 SIR component locations (Part 1 of 2). F-Super Duty

Item	Description
1	Driver air bag module
2	Clockspring
3	Restraints control module (RCM)
4	Passenger air bag module
5	Passenger air bag deactivation (PAD) switch

LTV0500000002712

Fig. 10 SIR component locations (Part 2 of 2). F-Super Duty

6. **On models equipped with rear with entertainment system,** disconnect two entertainment system wiring retainers, then position wiring aside.
7. **On all models,** remove retaining bolt and front tether anchor bracket. Note locator tab on front tether anchor bracket to A-pillar sheetmetal for installation.
8. Disconnect three air bag module front tether pin type retainers from A-pillar.
9. Remove air bag module front retaining bolts.
10. Remove two bolts and air bag module C-pillar tether bracket.
11. Remove three air bag module retaining bolts near C-pillar.
12. Remove two air bag module rear bracket bolts.
13. Remove air bag module bolt located at B-pillar.
14. Gently lift air bag module up and inward at B-pillar to release bracket hook from sheetmetal.
15. Move air bag module forward to release rear bracket hook from sheetmetal, the remove roof panel air bag module.
16. Reverse procedure to install. Install new J-nuts.

EXPLORER SPORT & SPORT TRAC

1. Disarm air bag system as outlined under "Air Bag System Disarming & Arming."
2. Remove overhead console.
3. **On models equipped with roof opening panel,** remove roof opening panel gimp.
4. **On all models,** remove lefthand and righthand sun visors and retaining brackets.
5. Remove A-pillar assist handles.
6. Remove windshield side garnish mouldings.
7. Open cover and remove front seat safety belt guide nut.
8. Remove upper B-pillar trim panel.
9. Position lower C-pillar trim panel aside.
10. Open cover and remove rear seat safety belt guide nut.
11. Remove upper C-pillar trim panel.
12. Remove interior lamp lens.
13. Remove interior lamp retaining screws, then disconnect electrical connector, then remove lamp assembly.

2. Remove headliner, **Fig. 29.**
3. Disconnect A-pillar tether, pin-type retainer from A-pillar.
4. **On models equipped with moon roof or rear wiper,** note position and routing of moonroof front drain hose and/or rear window washer solvent hose for installation purposes. Disconnect hose or hoses and position aside.
5. **On all models,** remove A-pillar tether bolt.
6. Remove two air bag module bolts located near top of A- and B-pillars.
7. Disconnect air bag module electrical connector, then detach connector from D-pillar.
8. Disconnect air bag module wiring clip from roof panel brace.
9. Remove two air bag module bolts located near ignitor between C- and D-pillars.
10. Remove two bolts from air bag module tether bracket at C-pillar.
11. Remove remaining two air bag module bolts, one near top of C-pillar and one between B- and C-pillars.
12. Move air bag module forward and release rear hook.
13. Reverse procedure to install. Install new roof panel air bag module J-nuts.

EXPEDITION & NAVIGATOR

1. Disarm air bag system as outlined under "Air Bag System Disarming & Arming."
2. Remove headliner, **Fig. 30.**
3. **On models equipped with moonroof,** separate moonroof drain tube and position aside.
4. **On all models,** remove front tether cord bolt and bracket from A-pillar.
5. Remove front tether cord and pin-type

retainer from A-pillar.
6. Remove air bag module retaining bolt located at roof line near A-pillar.
7. Remove two bolts, then slide up and rotate rear tether bracket assembly out from C-pillar.
8. Disconnect air bag module electrical connector.
9. Remove air bag module wire harness and electrical connector pin-type retainers at C-pillar.
10. Remove air bag module rear ramp bolt.
11. Remove three air bag module canister bolts.
12. Remove two air bag module front ramp bolts.
13. Slide front of air bag module up, then rotate hook out of roof line sheet metal and remove module.
14. Reverse procedure to install. Angle rear of air bag module to sheet metal, so that deployment canister can be inserted into sheet metal opening.

EXPLORER & MOUNTAINEER

1. Disarm air bag system as outlined under "Air Bag System Disarming & Arming."
2. Remove headliner, **Fig. 31.**
3. **On models equipped with auxiliary climate control,** remove two retainers and auxiliary climate control headliner duct from C-pillar.
4. **On all models,** disconnect air bag module electrical connector, then detach connector and wiring pin-type retainers from C-pillar.
5. **On models equipped with moonroof,** disconnect rear moonroof drain tube and two rear drain hose routing clips.

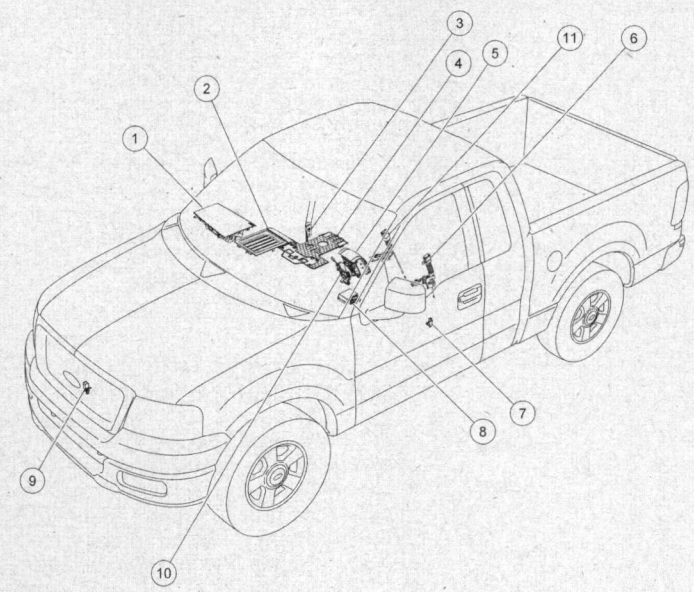

Item	Description
1	Passenger air bag module
2	Passenger air bag deactivation (PAD) indicator
3	Belt tension sensor (BTS) (part of passenger safety belt retractor)
4	Occupant classification sensor (OCS) system
5	Driver air bag module

Item	Description
6	Driver safety belt buckle pretensioner
7	Driver seat track position sensor
8	Restraints control module (RCM)
9	Front impact severity sensor
10	Clockspring
11	Passenger safety belt buckle pretensioner

LTV0500000002710

Fig. 11 SIR component locations. F-150 & Mark LT

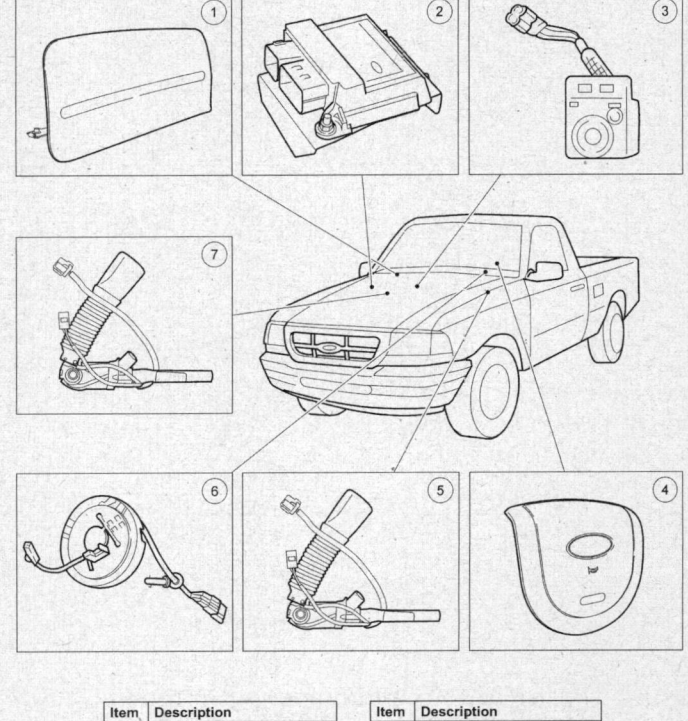

Item	Description
1	Passenger air bag module
2	Restraints control module (RCM)
3	Passenger air bag deactivation (PAD) switch
4	Driver air bag module

Item	Description
5	Driver safety belt buckle and pretensioner
6	Clockspring
7	Passenger safety belt buckle and pretensioner

LTV0500000004085

Fig. 12 SIR component locations. Ranger

14. Remove remaining assist handles, and headliner trim.
15. Remove headliner through righthand rear passenger door opening.
16. Disconnect driver roof panel air bag electrical connector.
17. Remove bolt, bracket and pin-type retainers for tether cord from A-pillar.
18. Remove tether cord retaining screws.
19. Slide tether anchor up, releasing hook, then separate tether anchor from sheet metal. Note position of air bag module wire harness routing for installation.
20. Remove air bag module canister bolts and wire harness pin-type retainers.
21. Remove roof panel air bag module retaining screws.
22. Lift up on air bag module, disengaging canister bracket hook.
23. Rotate air bag module away from roof, then lift canister out of C-pillar sheet metal and remove module.
24. Reverse procedure to install.

FREESTAR & MONTEREY

1. Disarm air bag system as outlined under "Air Bag System Disarming & Arming."
2. Remove headliner, **Fig. 32.**
3. Remove front tether anchor bolt located at A-pillar.
4. Remove front tether anchor pin-type retainer.
5. remove two assist handle bracket bolts.
6. Remove two air bag module bolts lo-

cated above front door.
7. Remove two rear tether anchor bolts located at lower D-pillar.
8. Remove two air bag module bolts located above rear quarter glass.
9. Disconnect air bag module electrical connector located just behind C-pillar.
10. Disconnect driver air bag module harness electrical connector from air bag bracket.
11. Disconnect passenger air bag module electrical connector, then detach it from D-pillar.
12. Remove two air bag bolts located above rear sliding door.
13. Slide rear of air bag module up, then rotate middle retainer out of sheet metal.
14. Remove bolt and air bag module bracket if required, then the roof panel air bag module.
15. Reverse procedure to install. install new J-nuts.

Side Impact Air Bag Module, Replace

Before installing side impact air bag module, inspect it for damage and foreign objects. If module is damaged, replace it. If any foreign objects are found, remove them. Failure to do so may result in personal injury in the event of an air bag deployment.

ESCAPE & MARINER

1. Disarm air bag system as outlined under "Air Bag System Disarming & Arming."
2. Position front seats forward, then remove seat track to floor nuts.
3. Position front seat rearward, then remove seat track to floor bolts.
4. Disconnect power seat electrical connector (if equipped), then remove seat.
5. Remove seat cushion adjusting handle plug, release retaining tabs and adjuster handle.
6. Remove seat back lever cover, then the screw.
7. Pull out to release retaining clips, then remove outboard and inboard seat cushion side shields.
8. Disconnect power seat switch electrical connector. **Note wire harness routing for installation.**
9. Release pin-type retainers, then separate side impact air bag electrical connector and wire harness from seat.
10. Remove seat back pivot nut, then the bolts and slide seat back pivot stud out of seat cushion frame.
11. Remove seat back, then turn manual lumber handle clockwise until it stops releasing all tension on manual support cable.
12. Remove manual lumber support adjusting handle, then separate seat back trim cover J-retainers.
13. Placing a hand between seat back trim cover and pad, carefully separate hook

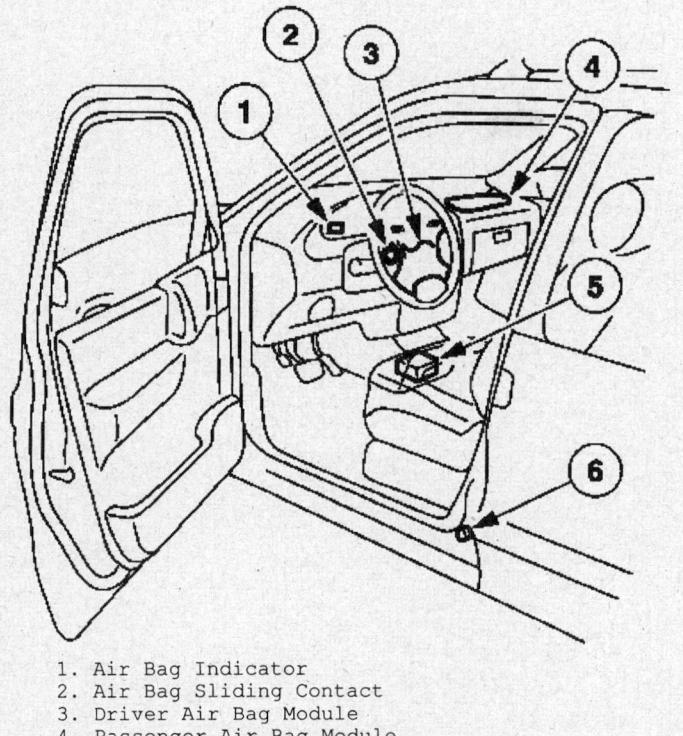

1. Air Bag Indicator
2. Air Bag Sliding Contact
3. Driver Air Bag Module
4. Passenger Air Bag Module
5. Air Bag Diagnostic Monitor
6. Courtesy Lamp Switch

FM8010002856000X

Fig. 13 SIR component locations. Villager

1. Passenger Air Bag Module
2. Passenger Side Air Bag Module
3. Side Crash Sensor (RH)
4. Driver Side Air Bag Module
5. Side Crash Sensor (LH)
6. Driver Air Bag Module
7. Air Bag Sliding Contact
8. Restraints Control Module

FM8010002857000X

Fig. 14 SIR component locations. Windstar

and loop strips.
14. Roll up seat back trim cover in an inside out fashion, then remove seat back trim cover.
15. Remove seat back pad from frame, then separate side impact air bag module wiring harness pin-type retainers from seat back frame.
16. Remove retaining nuts, then the side impact air bag module from seat back.
17. Reverse procedure to install.

AVIATOR, EXPEDITION & NAVIGATOR

1. Disarm air bag system as outlined under "Air Bag System Disarming & Arming."
2. Position front seat rearward, then remove front track covers and bolts.
3. Move front seat forward, then remove rear track covers and bolts.
4. Disconnect electrical connectors, then remove front seat from vehicle.
5. From under trim cover separate hook and loop strip.
6. Separate seat back trim cover lower J-clips.
7. Position seat back trim cover back flap up, then separate side impact air bag wire harness pin-type retainers from seat back frame.
8. Pull any extra wire harness toward air bag to allow for removal.
9. Remove air bag plastic shield, then retaining nuts.
10. Position air bag module and deployment chute away from mounting bracket and seat back frame.
11. Position seat back trim cover and foam pad away from frame.
12. Invert seat back trim cover, then remove module from deployment chute.
13. Disconnect electrical connector, then remove module from vehicle.
14. Reverse procedure to install.

EXPLORER & MOUNTAINEER

1. Disarm air bag system as outlined under "Air Bag System Disarming & Arming."
2. Position seat in full up position.
3. Remove rear bolt covers, then the bolts.
4. Remove slide bar bolt cover plug, then the bolt.
5. Remove front seat track to floor bolts.
6. Disconnect safety belt warning indicator electrical connector.
7. Disconnect side impact air bag electrical connector.
8. Disconnect power seat electrical connectors if equipped.
9. Remove front seat.
10. Disconnect power seat electrical connectors from seat as required.
11. Remove four bolts and seat track from seat bottom.
12. Disconnect power seat switch electrical connector if equipped.
13. Release all tension from manual lumbar support cable. Pull and remove manual lumbar support adjustment handle and remove lower seat trim panel screw.
14. Depress lower seat trim panel tabs, then remove trim panel from lower seat frame.
15. Disconnect heated seat switch if equipped.
16. Remove lumbar support cable push pin holder and separate lumbar support case assembly by sliding apart.
17. Remove cable end ball from cable end retainer and separate.
18. Disconnect heated seat electrical connector from seat bottom frame.
19. Disconnect side impact air bag electrical connector and wiring harness push pins from seat bottom frame.
20. Remove seat back retaining bolts. Ensure seat back pivot, cables and wires are clear when performing this step.
21. Remove seat back from seat bottom.
22. Separate seat back trim cover lower J clip.
23. Remove hog rings from swing rods, then slide rods out of seat back trim cover.
24. Unzip side impact air bag deployment chute.
25. Remove side impact air bag wire harness tie strap retainer.

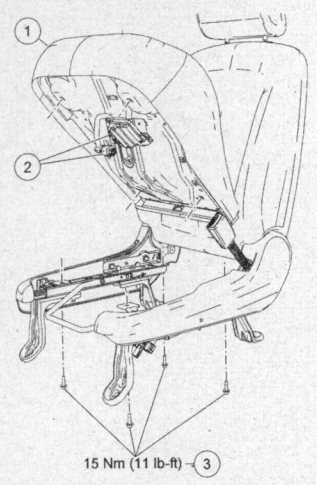

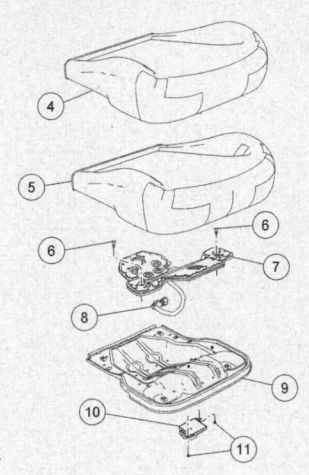

Item	Description
1	Seat cushion assembly
2	Electrical connectors
3	Seat cushion bolts

Item	Description
4	Seat cushion trim cover
5	Seat cushion foam pad
6	Pin-type retainers
7	Occupant classification sensor (OCS) bladder
8	Pressure sensor
9	Seat cushion pan
10	OCS electronic control unit (ECU)
11	OCS ECU rivets

LTV0500000004089

Fig. 15 Occupant classification sensor (OCS) replacement. Aviator, Escape & Mariner

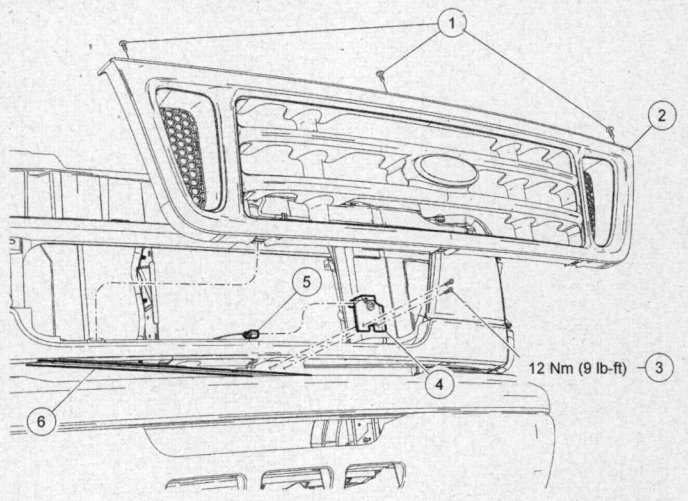

Item	Description
1	Radiator grille screws
2	Radiator grille
3	Front impact severity sensor bolts
4	Front impact severity sensor
5	Front impact severity sensor electrical connector
6	Front air foil

LTV0500000004088

Fig. 16 Front impact sensor replacement. E-Series

26. Remove seat back cover enough to gain access to side impact air bag module.
27. Remove three side impact air bag retaining nuts and discard if new module is being used.
28. Separate air bag module from mounting bracket, then disconnect electrical connector and remove from vehicle.
29. Reverse procedure to install. Inspect all components involved with removal procedure and replace if damaged.

FREESTAR, MONTEREY & WINDSTAR

1. Disarm air bag system as outlined under "Air Bag System Disarming & Arming."
2. Remove seat attaching nuts from bottom of vehicle.
3. Disconnect seat electrical connectors, then remove seat.
4. Remove lower seat trim panel.
5. Depress armrest release tab, then remove armrest.
6. Remove armrest stop and retainer.
7. Remove side impact air bag wiring harness pushpins from seat bottom.
8. Remove seat back attaching bolts.
9. Release seat back cover retaining strips.
10. Remove seat back cover enough to gain access to side impact air bag module. **Do not disconnect wire connector at side impact air bag module. This is a permanent connection. Disconnection may result in air bag deployment.**
11. Remove air bag module wire harness

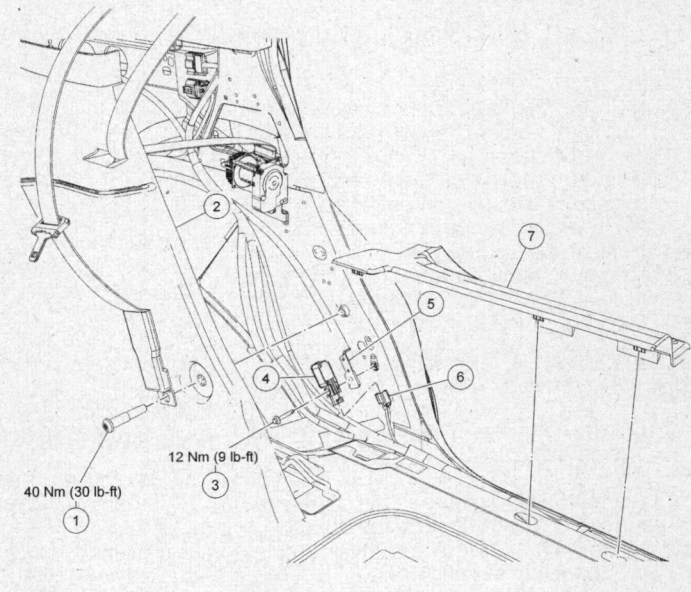

Item	Description
1	Safety belt retractor anchor bolt
2	Rear quarter trim panel
3	Side impact sensor bolt
4	Side impact sensor

Item	Description
5	Side impact sensor bracket
6	Side impact sensor electrical connector
7	Rear door scuff plate

LTV0500000004090

Fig. 17 Side impact sensor (C-Pillar). Expedition & Navigator

to seat frame push pins.
12. Remove air bag module retaining bolts, then the module.
13. Reverse procedure to install. Inspect

all components involved with removal and replace as required.

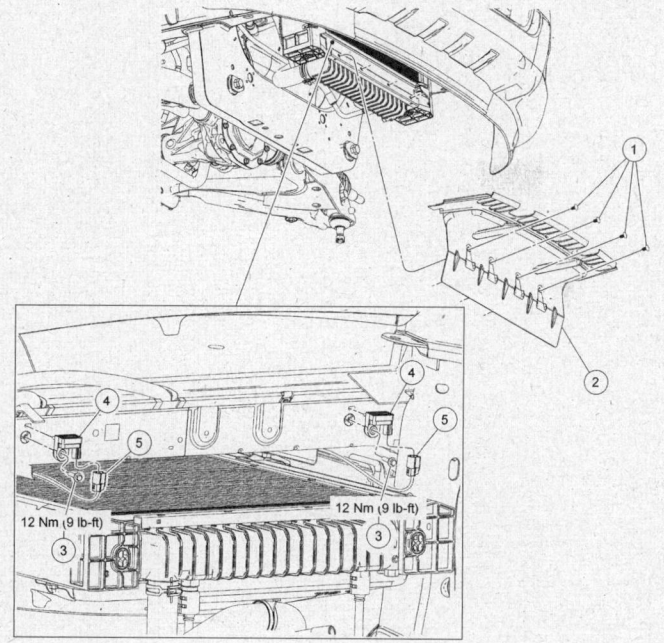

Item	Description		Item	Description
1	Lower radiator air deflector pin-type retainers (4 required)		4	LH and RH front impact severity sensors
2	Lower radiator air deflector		5	LH and RH front impact severity sensor electrical connectors
3	LH and RH front impact severity sensor bolts			

LTV0500000004091

Fig. 18 Front impact sensor replacement. Explorer & Mountaineer

Item	Description		Item	Description
1	Occupant classification sensor (OCS) rail locating pin		3	OCS rail front mounting position front bolt
2	OCS rail front mounting position rear bolt		4	OCS rail shield
			5	OCS rail

LTV0500000004092

Fig. 19 Occupant classification sensor (OCS) replacement (Part 1 of 2). Explorer & Mountaineer

Item	Description
6	OCS rail wiring retainers (2 required)
7	Power seat track motor electrical connector
8	OCS rail electrical connector
9	OCS rail rear bolts (2 required)

LTV0500000004093

Fig. 19 Occupant classification sensor (OCS) replacement (Part 2 of 2). Explorer & Mountaineer

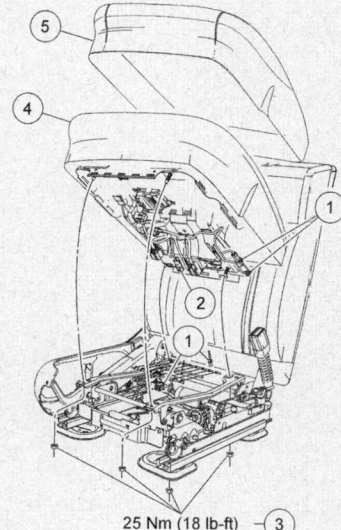

Item	Description
1	Electrical connectors
2	Belt tension sensor (BTS) electrical connector
3	Seat cushion nut (4 required)
4	Occupant classification sensor (OCS) assembly
5	Seat cushion trim cover

LTV0500000004094

Fig. 20 Occupant classification sensor (OCS) replacement. Excursion, F-Super Duty, F-150 & Mark LT

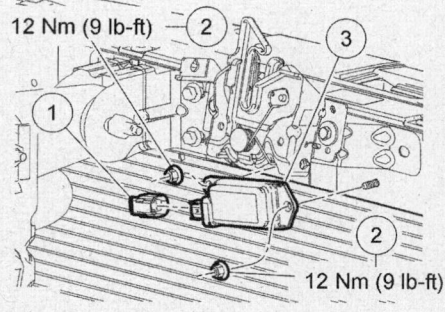

Item	Description
1	Front impact severity sensor electrical connector
2	Front impact severity sensor nuts (2 required)
3	Front impact severity sensor

LTV0500000004095

Fig. 21 Front impact sensor replacement. Freestar & Monterey

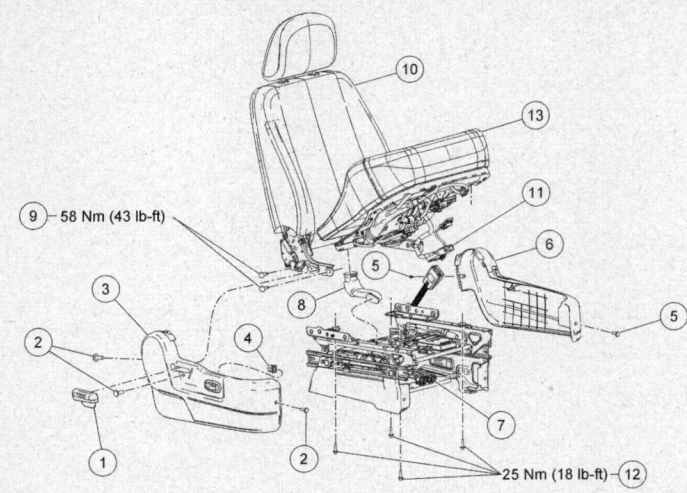

Item	Description	Item	Description
1	Recliner handle cover	6	LH side shield
2	RH side shield screws (3 required)	7	Side air bag module electrical connector (if equipped)
3	RH side shield	8	Climate control seat duct (if equipped)
4	Power seat switch electrical connector (if equipped)	9	Backrest-to-seat track bolts (4 required)
5	LH side shield screws (3 required)	10	Seat backrest assembly

LTV0500000004096

Fig. 22 Occupant classification sensor (OCS) replacement (Part 1 of 2). Freestar & Monterey

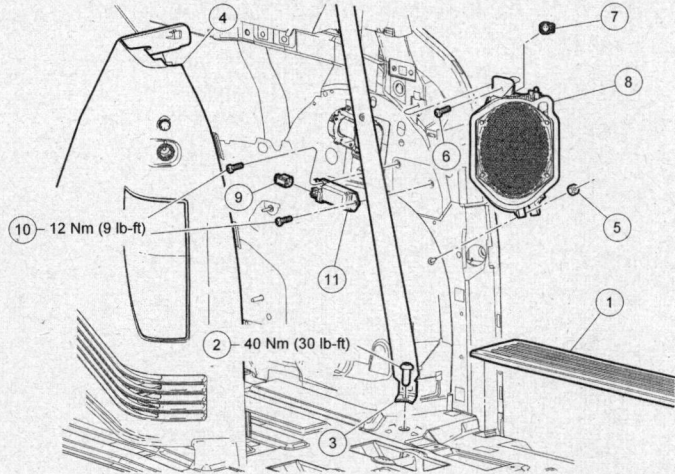

Item	Description
1	Rear door scuff plate
2	Safety belt anchor bolt (if equipped)
3	Safety belt anchor (if equipped)
4	Quarter trim panel
5	Rear speaker nut
6	Rear speaker bolt
7	Rear speaker electrical connector
8	Rear speaker
9	Side impact sensor electrical connector
10	Side impact sensor bolts (2 required)
11	Side impact sensor

LTV0500000004098

Fig. 23 Side impact sensor replacement (Second row). Freestar & Monterey

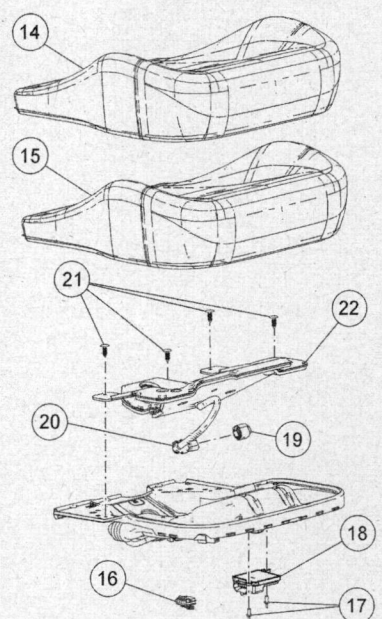

Item	Description
14	Seat cushion trim cover
15	Seat cushion foam pad
16	Electronic control unit (ECU) electrical connector
17	Rivets
18	Electronic control unit (ECU)
19	Pressure sensor electrical connector
20	Pressure sensor
21	Pin-type retainers

LTV0500000004097

Fig. 22 Occupant classification sensor (OCS) replacement (Part 2 of 2). Freestar & Monterey

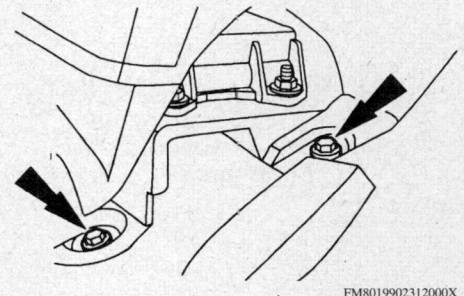

FM8019902312000X

Fig. 24 Air bag diagnostic monitor bolt locations. Freestar, Monterey & Windstar

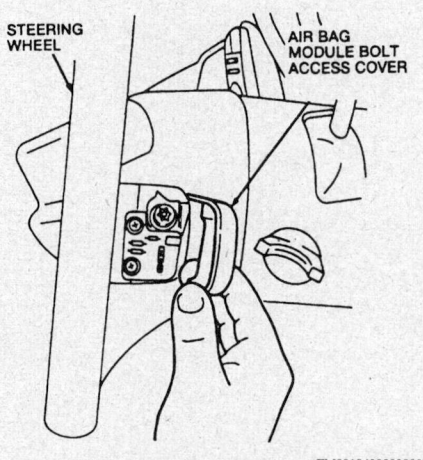

Fig. 25 Air bag module bolt access cover removal. Villager

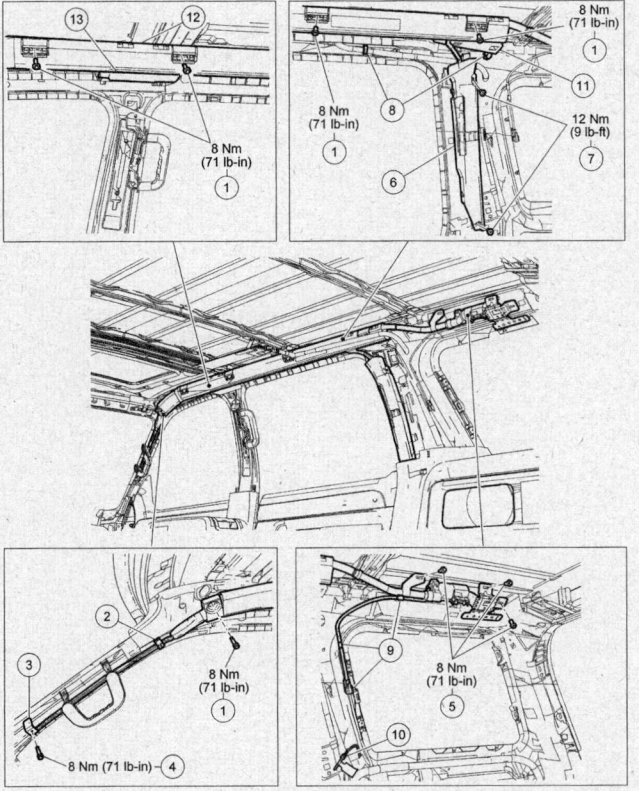

Fig. 27 Roof panel air bag replacement (Part 1 of 2). Aviator

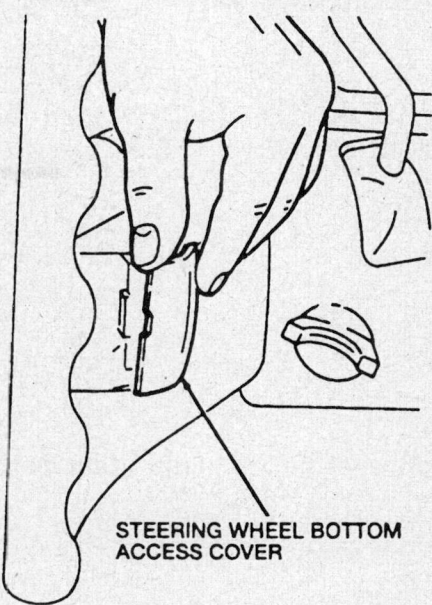

Fig. 26 Steering wheel bottom access cover removal. Villager

Item	Description
1	Safety canopy bolts (5 required)
2	A-pillar tether pin-type retainer
3	A-pillar tether bracket
4	A-pillar tether bracket bolt
5	Rearward safety canopy bolts (3 required)
6	C-pillar tether anchor assembly
7	C-pillar tether anchor assembly bolts (2 required)
8	Pin-type retainers (if equipped) (2 required)
9	Pin-type retainers (3 required)
10	Safety canopy electrical connector
11	Rear ramp
12	Safety canopy
13	Front ramp

Fig. 27 Roof panel air bag replacement (Part 2 of 2). Aviator

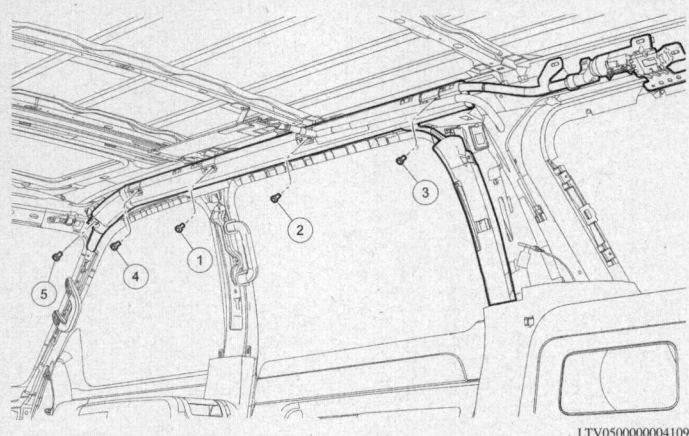

Fig. 28   Roof panel air bag module bolt installation sequence. Aviator

Item	Description
1	Safety canopy module
2	Safety canopy module top of A-Pillar bolt
3	Safety canopy bolts (4 required)
4	Safety canopy module tether bracket upper bolt
5	Safety canopy module bolts near the ignitor (2 required)
6	Safety canopy module electrical connector
7	A-Pillar tether pin-type retainer
8	A-Pillar tether bolt

LTV0500000004102

Fig. 29   Roof panel air bag replacement (Part 2 of 2). Escape & Mariner

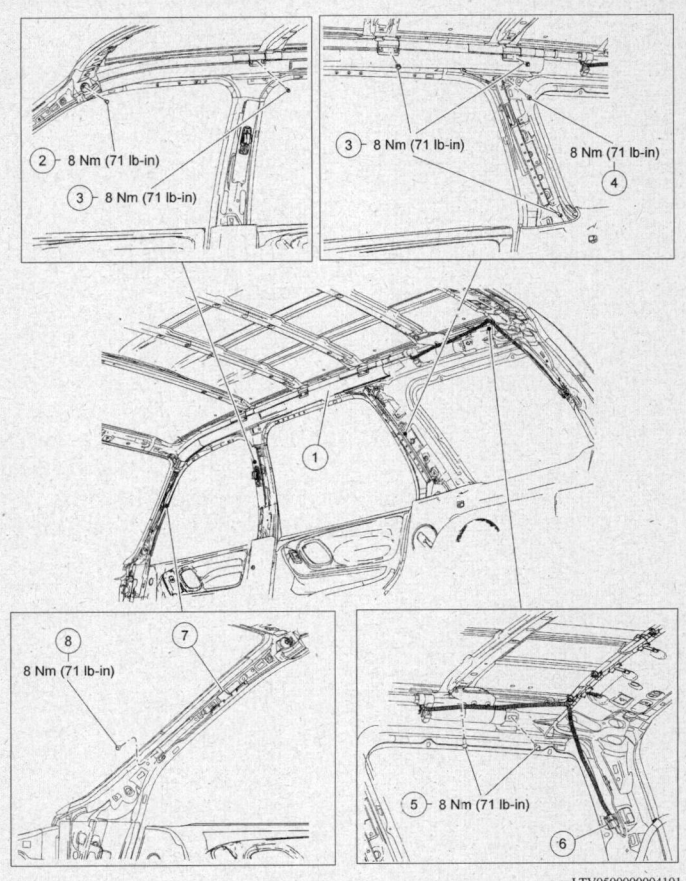

LTV0500000004101

Fig. 29   Roof panel air bag replacement (Part 1 of 2). Escape & Mariner

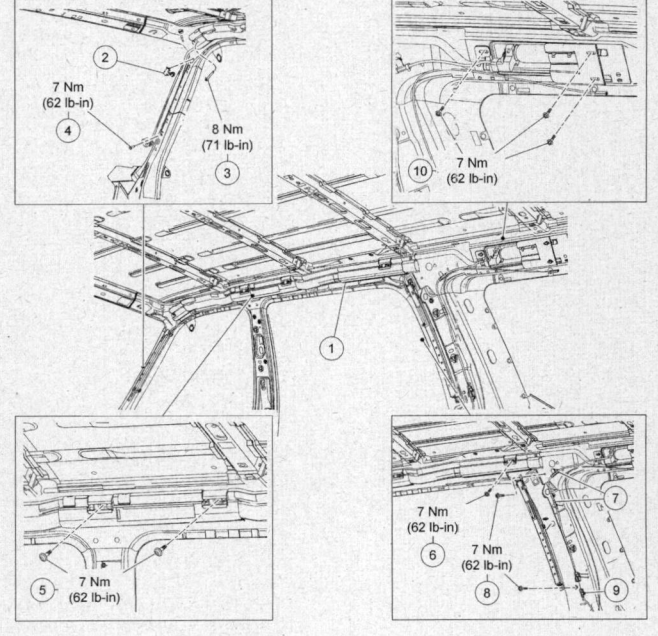

Item	Description		Item	Description
1	Safety canopy module		5	Safety canopy module front ramp bolts (2 required)
2	Front tether cord pin-type retainer		6	Safety canopy module rear ramp bolt
3	Safety canopy module bolt		7	Safety canopy module wire harness retainers
4	Front tether cord bracket bolt			

LTV0500000004103

Fig. 30   Roof panel air bag replacement (Part 1 of 2). Expedition & Navigator

Item	Description
8	Safety canopy module rear tether bracket assembly bolts (2 required)
9	Safety canopy module electrical connector
10	Safety canopy module canister bolts (3 required)

LTV0500000004104

Fig. 30   Roof panel air bag replacement (Part 2 of 2). Expedition & Navigator

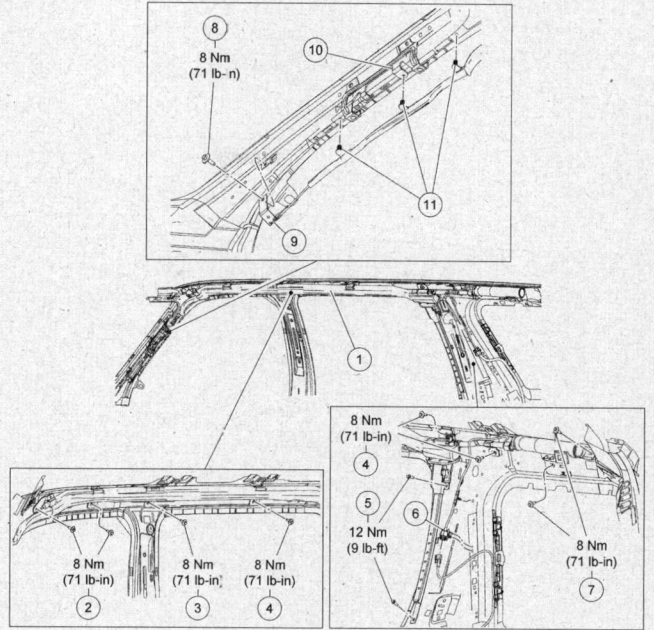

LTV0500000004105

Fig. 31   Roof panel air bag replacement (Part 1 of 2). Explorer & Mountaineer

Item	Description
1	Safety canopy module
2	Safety canopy module front bolts (2 required)
3	Safety canopy module B-pillar bolt
4	Safety canopy module C-pillar bolts (3 required)

Item	Description
5	Safety canopy module C-pillar tether bracket bolts (2 required)
6	Safety canopy module electrical connector

Item	Description
7	Safety canopy module rear bracket bolts (2 required)
8	Safety canopy module front tether bracket bolt
9	Safety canopy module front tether bracket
10	A-pillar trim bracket
11	Front tether pin-type retainers (3 required)

LTV0500000004106

Fig. 31   Roof panel air bag replacement (Part 2 of 2). Explorer & Mountaineer

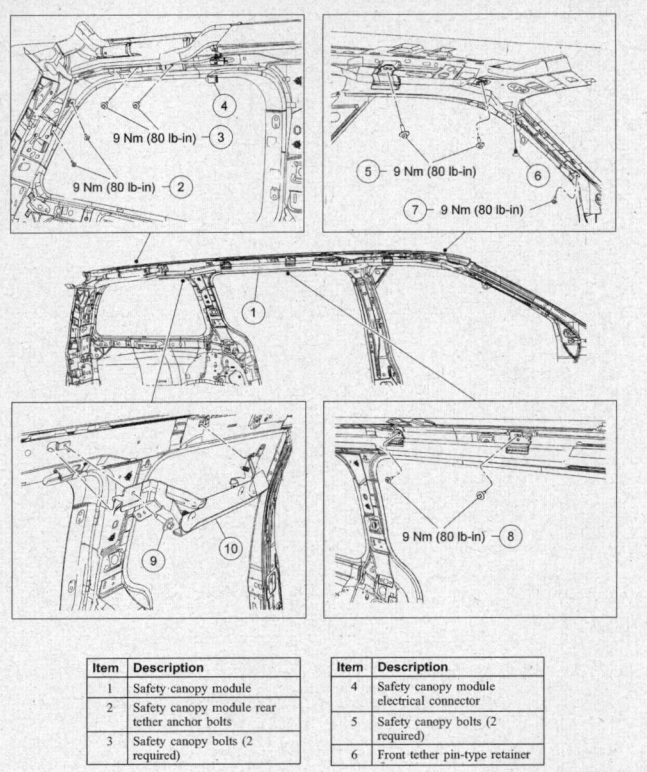

Item	Description
7	Safety canopy module front tether anchor bolt
8	Safety canopy bolts (2 required)
9	Safety canopy bolt (driver side only)
10	Safety canopy module bracket (driver side only)

LTV0500000004108

Fig. 32   Roof panel air bag replacement (Part 2 of 2). Freestar & Monterey

Item	Description
1	Safety canopy module
2	Safety canopy module rear tether anchor bolts
3	Safety canopy bolts (2 required)

Item	Description
4	Safety canopy module electrical connector
5	Safety canopy bolts (2 required)
6	Front tether pin-type retainer

LTV0500000004107

Fig. 32   Roof panel air bag replacement (Part 1 of 2). Freestar & Monterey

TIGHTENING SPECIFICATIONS

Year	Component	Torque Inch Lbs.
AVIATOR		
2003–06	Clockspring	53
	Driver Air Bag Module	80
	Front Impact Sensor	108
	Passenger Air Bag Module	80
	Restraints Control Module	108
	Roof Panel Air Bag Module	71
	Safety Belt Anchor	30①
	Safety Belt Tether	108
	Side Impact Sensor	108
	Steering Wheel	30①
ESCAPE & MARINER		
2002–06	Front Impact Sensor	108
	Passenger Air Bag Module	71
	Restraint Control Module	96
	Roof Panel Air Bag Module	71
	Safety Belt Anchors	35①
	Safety Belt Retractors	35①
	Seat Cushion	11①
	Side Impact Air Bag Module	44
	Side Impact Sensor	80
	Steering Wheel	108

Continued

TIGHTENING
SPECIFICATIONS—Continued

Year	Component	Torque Inch Lbs.
E-SERIES		
2002–06	Driver Air Bag Module	108
	Front Impact Sensor	108
	Front Safety Belt Anchor	33①
	Front Safety Belt Retractor	35①
	Passenger Air Bag Module	96
	Rear Safety Belt Anchor	30①
	Rear Safety Belt Retractor	30①
	Restraints Control Module	108
	Seat Track (Manual)	18①
	Seat Track (Power)	30①
	Steering Column Shroud Screws	84–108
	Steering Wheel	28–32①
	Tilt Wheel Handle & Shank	27–44
EXCURSION		
2002–05	Driver Air Bag Module	98
	Passenger Air Bag Module	80
	Restraints Control Module	108
	Safety Belt Anchor	30①
	Safety Belt Retractor	80
	Steering Wheel	30①
EXPEDITION & NAVIGATOR		
2002–06	Clockspring	53
	Driver Air Bag Module	②
	Front Impact Sensor	108
	Passenger Air Bag Deactivation Switch	18–25
	Passenger Air Bag Module	80
	Restraints Control Module	108
	Roof Panel Air Bag Module (Except Front Upper)	62
	Roof Panel Air Bag Module (Front Upper)	71
	Safety Belt Anchor	30①
	Safety Belt Retractor	30①
	Side Impact Sensor	108
	Steering Wheel Bolt	30①
	Tilt Wheel Handle & Shank	44
EXPLORER & MOUNTAINEER		
2002–06	Driver Air Bag Module	62
	Front Impact Sensor	108
	Occupant Classification Sensor	18①
	Occupant Classification Sensor Module	18
	Passenger Air Bag Module	80
	Restraints Control Module Bracket	108
	Roof Panel Air Bag Module	71
	Safety Belt Anchor	30①
	Safety Belt Retractor	30①
	Side Impact Air Bag Module	89
	Side Crash Sensor	80
	Seat Back Pivot Bolt	21①

Continued

TIGHTENING
SPECIFICATIONS—Continued

Year	Component	Torque Inch Lbs.
EXPLORER & MOUNTAINEER		
2002–06	Seat Back Recliner Bolts	38①
	Steering Column Nuts	11①
	Steering Wheel	30①
	Track To Cushion Frame	15①
EXPLORER SPORT & SPORT TRAC		
2002–06	Driver Air Bag	80
	Front Impact Sensor	108
	Passenger Air Bag Module	80
	Roof Panel Air Bag Module	71
	Safety Belt Anchor	30①
	Safety Belt Retractor (Lower Bolt)	30①
	Safety Belt Retractor (Upper Bolt)	80
	Steering Wheel	30①
FREESTAR & MONTEREY		
2004–06	Backrest To Seat Track	43①
	Cushion To Seat Track	43①
	Front Impact Sensor	108
	Passenger Air Bag Module	80
	Restraints Control Module	108
	Safety Belt Anchor	30①
	Safety Belt Retractor	30①
	Side Impact Air Bag Module	89
	Side Impact Sensor	108
	Steering Wheel Bolt Gear Drive	13①
F-SUPER DUTY		
2002–06	Driver Air Bag Module	96
	Passenger Air Bag Module	80
	Restraints Control Module	108
	Safety Belt Anchor	30①
	Safety Belt Retractor	30①
	Steering Wheel	30①
VILLAGER		
2002	Air Bag Diagnostic Monitor	15①
	Driver Air Bag Module	15①
	Passenger Air Bag Module	18①
WINDSTAR		
2002–03	Armrest Mount	30①
	Driver Air Bag Module	71
	Front Seat Back Pivot Bolt	17①
	Passenger Air Bag Module	108
	Restraints Control Module	108
	Side Crash Sensor	108
	Side Impact Air Bag Module	10①
	Steering Column	12①

① — Ft. lbs.
② — Refer to procedure for tightening specifications.

ANTI-LOCK BRAKES

TABLE OF CONTENTS

	Page No.		Page No.
AVIATOR	5-1	**F-150 & 2002–03 F-SUPER**	
XPLORER & MOUNTAINEER	5-111	DUTY (RABS)	5-153
SCAPE & MARINER	5-21	F-150 & MARK LT (4WABS)	5-145
-SERIES	5-39	FREESTAR & MONTEREY	5-130
XCURSION & 2004–06		RANGER	5-175
-SUPER DUTY	5-73	VILLAGER	5-184
XPEDITION & NAVIGATOR	5-85	WINDSTAR	5-193

Aviator

NOTE: Electrical Symbol & Wire Color Code Identification Located In The Front Of This Manual May Be Used As An Aid When Using Wiring Circuits Found In This Section.

NOTE: Refer To "Computer Relearn Procedures" Located In The Front Of This Manual When Battery Power To The Computer Has Been Interrupted.

INDEX

	Page No.		Page No.		Page No.
Description	5-1	Diagnostic Trouble Code		Component Replacement	5-2
Diagnosis & Testing	5-2	Interpretation	5-2	ABS Control Module	5-2
Accessing Diagnostic Trouble		Wiring Diagrams	5-2	Accelerometer	5-2
Codes	5-2	**Diagnostic Chart Index**	5-6	Brake Pressure Transducer	5-2
Clearing Diagnostic Trouble		**Precautions**	5-1	Hydraulic Control Unit (HCU)	5-2
Codes	5-2	Battery Ground Cable	5-1	Traction Control Switch	5-3
Diagnostic Tests	5-2	Brake Fluid Handling	5-1	Wheel Speed Sensor	5-3
Inspection & Verification	5-2	**System Service**	5-2	**Troubleshooting**	5-2
Pinpoint Tests	5-2	Brake System Bleed	5-2	Symptom Chart	5-2

PRECAUTIONS

BATTERY GROUND CABLE

Prior to service disconnect battery ground cable and isolate as required.

BRAKE FLUID HANDLING

Brake fluid can cause serious injury and vehicle damage if not handled properly. Avoid contact with eyes and do not allow fluid to splash or spill on painted surfaces. Wash hands thoroughly after handling.

DESCRIPTION

The anti-lock brake system (ABS) module, with or without stability assist, simultaneously manages the anti-lock braking, traction control and engine control systems to maintain vehicle control during deceleration and acceleration. The ABS accomplishes this by communicating with the other modules over the high speed controller area network (HS-CAN) bus.

When the ignition switch is in the RUN position, the module carries out a preliminary electrical check and, at approximately 20 km/h (12 mph), the hydraulic pump motor is turned on for approximately one half-second. Any malfunction of the anti-lock brake system disables the traction control and stability assist (if equipped). The ABS module communicates with the instrument cluster over the HS-CAN bus and the cluster illuminates the anti-lock brake warning indicator. However, the power-assist braking system functions normally.

With the ignition switch in the START or RUN positions, the stability assist module functions similarly to a conventional ABS module by monitoring and comparing the rotational speed of each wheel. The wheel speed sensors electrically sense each tooth of the anti-lock sensor ring as they pass through the sensor magnetic field. When the stability assist module detects an impending wheel lock, wheel spin or vehicle motion that is inconsistent with the driver commands, it modulates brake pressure to the appropriate brake caliper(s). The stability assist module triggers the hydraulic control unit (HCU) to open and close the appropriate solenoid valves. Once the affected wheel(s) return to the desired speed, the stability assist module returns the solenoid valves to their normal position, and normal base brake operation is restored.

TROUBLESHOOTING

Symptom Chart

Refer to **Fig. 1** for symptom chart.

DIAGNOSIS & TESTING

Accessing Diagnostic Trouble Codes

Connect a suitably programmed scan tool and Vehicle Communication Module (VCM) with appropriate adapters, or equivalents, to the Data Link Connector (DCL) located in the passenger compartment beneath the instrument panel. Follow tool manufacturer's instructions for accessing Diagnostic Trouble Codes (DTC).

Diagnostic Trouble Code Interpretation

Refer to **Fig. 2** for diagnostic trouble code interpretation.

Wiring Diagrams

Refer to **Fig. 3** for wiring diagram.

Diagnostic Tests

INSPECTION & VERIFICATION

Verify concern by applying brakes under different conditions. Inspect for obvious signs of mechanical and electrical damage such as parking brake cable, tire pressure, tire size or mismatched tires. Check for blown fuse, connectors or connections, harness routing, wire chaffing, circuitry open/shorted and indicator bulb.

PINPOINT TESTS

Refer to **Figs. 4 through 20** for pinpoint tests.

Clearing Diagnostic Trouble Codes

Connect a suitably programmed scan tool and Vehicle Communication Module (VCM) with appropriate adapters, or equivalents, to the Data Link Connector (DCL) located in the passenger compartment beneath the instrument panel. Follow tool manufacturer's instructions for clearing Diagnostic Trouble Codes (DTC).

SYSTEM SERVICE

Brake System Bleed

Refer to "Hydraulic Brake Systems" chapter for bleeding procedure.

Condition	Possible Sources	Action
• No communication with the anti-lock brake system (ABS) module	• Circuitry • ABS module	• Go To Pinpoint Test A .
• The red brake warning indicator stays on when the ignition switch is in RUN	• Circuitry • Instrument cluster • Brake fluid level sensor • Anti-lock brake system (ABS) module	• REFER to "Dash Gauges & Warning Indicators.
• The yellow anti-lock brake system (ABS) warning indicator does not self-check	• Circuitry • Instrument cluster • ABS module	• REFER to "Dash Gauges & Warning Indicators.
• Spongy brake pedal with no warning indicator	• Air in brake hydraulic system	• REFER to "Brake System Bleed".
• The stability assist system cannot be disabled	• Circuitry • Traction control switch • Anti-lock brake system (ABS) module	• Go To Pinpoint Test O .
• The traction control switch indicator is never/always on	• Circuitry • Traction control switch • Anti-lock brake system (ABS) module	• Go To Pinpoint Test Q .

LTV0500000004145

Fig. 1 Symptom Chart

Component Replacement

ACCELEROMETER

1. Remove center floor console, **Fig. 21.**
2. Disconnect accelerometer electrical connector, **Fig. 22.**
3. Remove heater duct.
4. Remove mounting nuts, then the accelerometer.
5. Reverse procedure to install, noting the following:
   a. **Torque** accelerometer mounting nuts to 62 inch lbs.
   b. When installing a new accelerometer, ABS module must be configured using vehicle as-built data and calibrated. Follow diagnostic tool directions for calibration procedures.

BRAKE PRESSURE TRANSDUCER

1. Disconnect brake pressure transducer electrical connector, **Fig. 23.**
2. Remove brake pressure transducer.
3. Reverse procedure to install. **Torque** transducer to 13 ft. lbs.

HYDRAULIC CONTROL UNIT (HCU)

1. Remove battery and battery tray.
2. Raise and support vehicle.
3. Disconnect ABS electrical connector, **Fig. 24.**
4. Remove two brake line to HCU nuts, then position brake lines aside. Note positions of brake lines for installation.
5. Remove four brake line to brake line nuts.
6. Remove three HCU bracket to frame nuts.
7. Remove HCU assembly.
8. Remove brake lines and brackets from HCU as follows:
   a. Remove four brake line to HCU nuts.
   b. Remove two bracket to brake line holder nuts, then the brake line holder assembly.
   c. Remove bracket to HCU bolts, then the HCU bracket.
9. Reverse procedure to install, noting the following:
   a. **Torque** bracket to HCU bolts to 13 ft. lbs.
   b. **Torque** bracket to brake line holder nuts to 80 inch lbs.
   c. **Torque** brake line to HCU nuts to 13 ft. lbs.
   d. **Torque** HCU bracket to frame nuts to 17 ft. lbs.
   e. **Torque** brake line to brake line nuts to 13 ft. lbs.
   f. **Torque** brake line to HCU nuts to 17 ft. lbs.

ABS CONTROL MODULE

1. Remove hydraulic control unit as outlined under "Hydraulic Control Unit (HCU)."
2. Remove three screws, then the ABS control module.
3. Reverse procedure to install. ABS

module must be configured using vehicle as-built data and calibrated. Follow diagnostic tool directions for calibration procedures.

WHEEL SPEED SENSOR

FRONT

1. Raise and support vehicle.
2. Remove tire/wheel assembly.
3. Remove brake caliper mounting bolts, then position caliper aside.
4. Remove disc brake rotor.
5. Disconnect speed sensor electrical connector.
6. Remove three speed sensor harness retainers.
7. Remove two speed sensor harness pin type retainers.
8. Remove wheel speed sensor retaining bolt, then the sensor.
9. Reverse procedure to install. **Torque** wheel speed sensor bolt to 13 ft. lbs.

REAR

1. Raise and support vehicle.
2. Remove tire/wheel assembly.
3. Remove three speed sensor harness pin type retainers.
4. Remove wheel speed sensor retaining bolt, then the sensor.
5. Reverse procedure to install. **Torque** wheel speed sensor bolt to 20 ft. lbs.

TRACTION CONTROL SWITCH

1. Remove center floor console, **Fig. 21.**
2. Disconnect traction control switch electrical connector.
3. Remove traction control switch.
4. Reverse procedure to install.

Code	Description
B1342	ECU is Defective
B1483	Brake Pedal Input Circuit Failure
B1676	Battery Pack Voltage Out Of Range
B2477	Module Configuration Failure
B2734	Pedal Travel Sensor (PTS) Supply Error
B2736	Pedal Travel Sensor (PTS) Circuit Fault
B2737	Pedal Travel Sensor (PTS) Jammed Error
B2738	Pedal Travel Sensor (PTS) Velocity Error
B2740	Pedal Travel Sensor (PTS) Spike Error
B2741	Sensor Cluster Loop End
B2900	VIN Mismatched
C1095	ABS Hydraulic Pump Motor Circuit Failure
C1145	Wheel Speed Sensor RF Input Circuit Failure
C1155	Wheel Speed Sensor LF Input Circuit Failure
C1165	Wheel Speed Sensor RR Input Circuit Failure
C1175	Wheel Speed Sensor LR Input Circuit Failure
C1233	Wheel Speed LF Input Signal Missing
C1234	Wheel Speed RF Input Signal Missing
C1235	Wheel Speed RR Input Signal Missing
C1236	Wheel Speed LR Input Signal Missing
C1277	Steering Wheel Angle 1 and 2 Circuit Failure
C1278	Steering Wheel Angle 1 and 2 Signal Faulted
C1279	Yaw Rate Sensor Circuit Failure
C1280	Yaw Rate Sensor Signal Fault
C1281	Lateral Accelerometer Circuit Failure
C1282	Lateral Accelerometer Signal Fault
C1285	Booster Solenoid Circuit Failure
C1287	Booster Pedal Force Switch Circuit Failure
C1288	Brake Pressure Transducer Input Circuit Failure
C1440	Pressure Transducer Input Circuit Failure
C1516	Roll Rate Signal Fault
C1517	Roll Rate Sensor Circuit Fault
C1730	Reference Voltage Out Of Range (+5 V)
C1805	Mismatched PCM And/Or ABS/TC Module
C1960	Driver Brake Apply Circuit Fault
C1963	Stability Control Inhibit Warning
C1991	Module Calibration Failure
C1996	Active Yaw Control Disabled
C1998	Module Calibration Not Complete
C2769	Longitudinal Acceleration Sensor Circuit Failure
C2770	Longitudinal Acceleration Sensor Signal Fault
C2777	Sensor Cluster Bus Failure
C2778	Sensor Cluster Voltage Supply Failure
U1900	CAN Communication Bus Fault-Receive Error
U1901	CAN Network #2 Communication Bus Fault-Receive Error
U2023	Fault Received From External Node

Fig. 2   Diagnostic trouble code interpretation

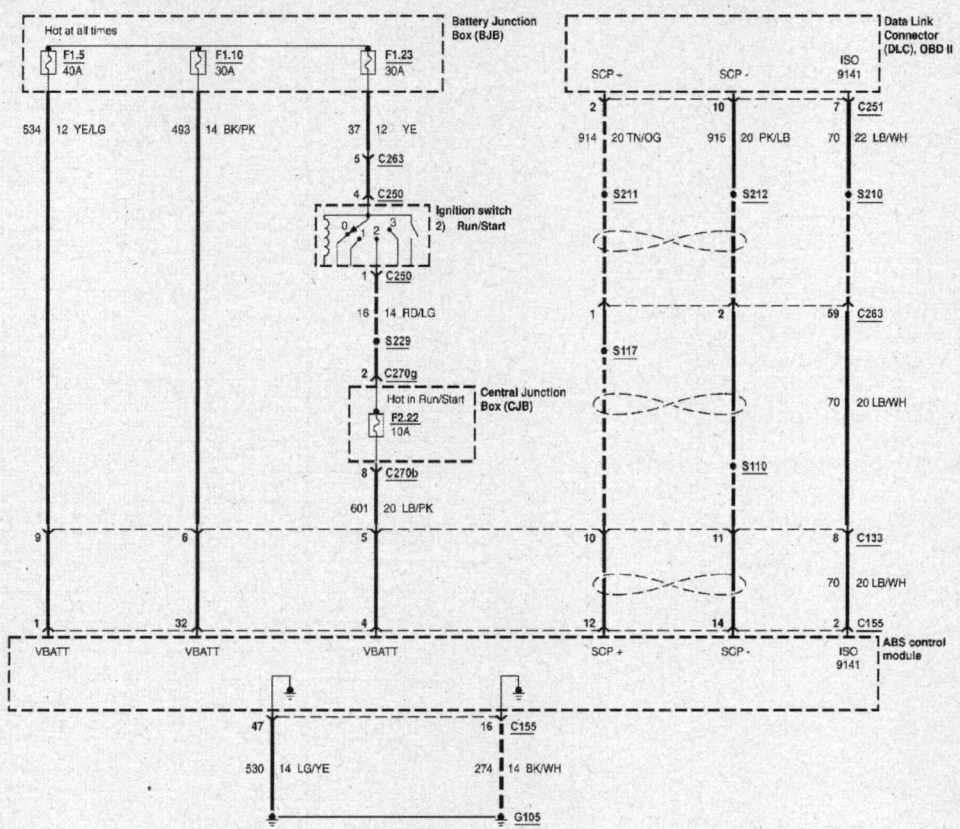

Fig. 3   Wiring diagram (Part 1 of 5)

LTV0500000004146

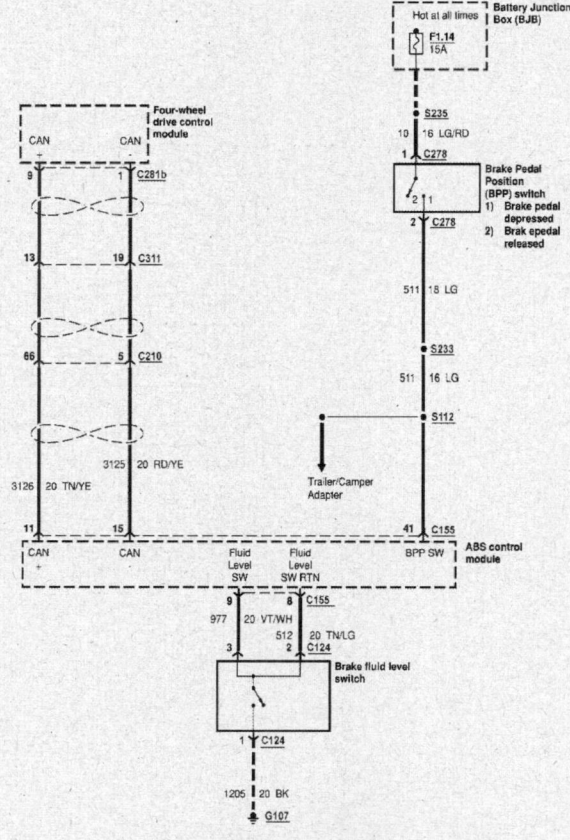

Fig. 3   Wiring diagram (Part 2 of 5)

LTV0500000004147

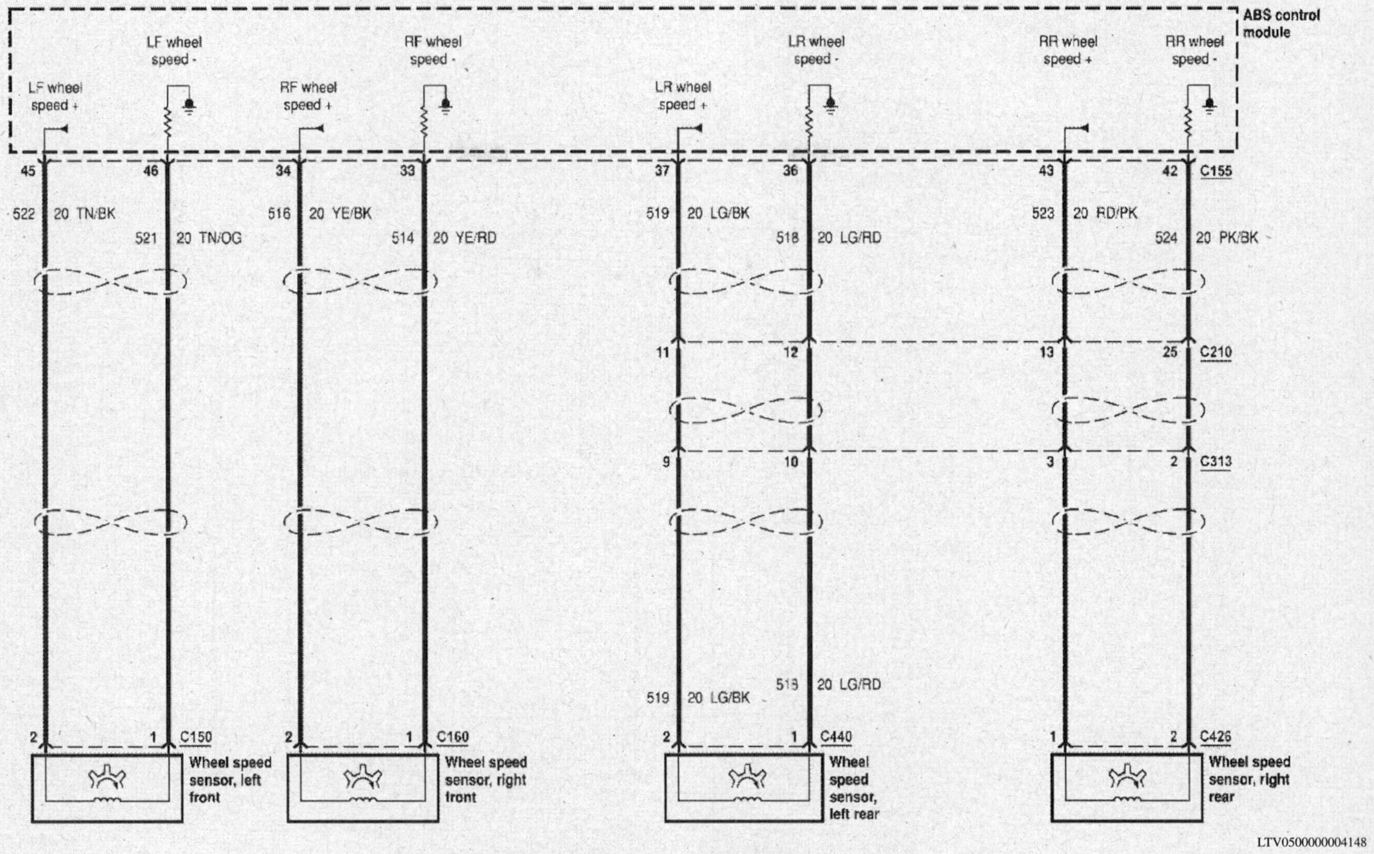

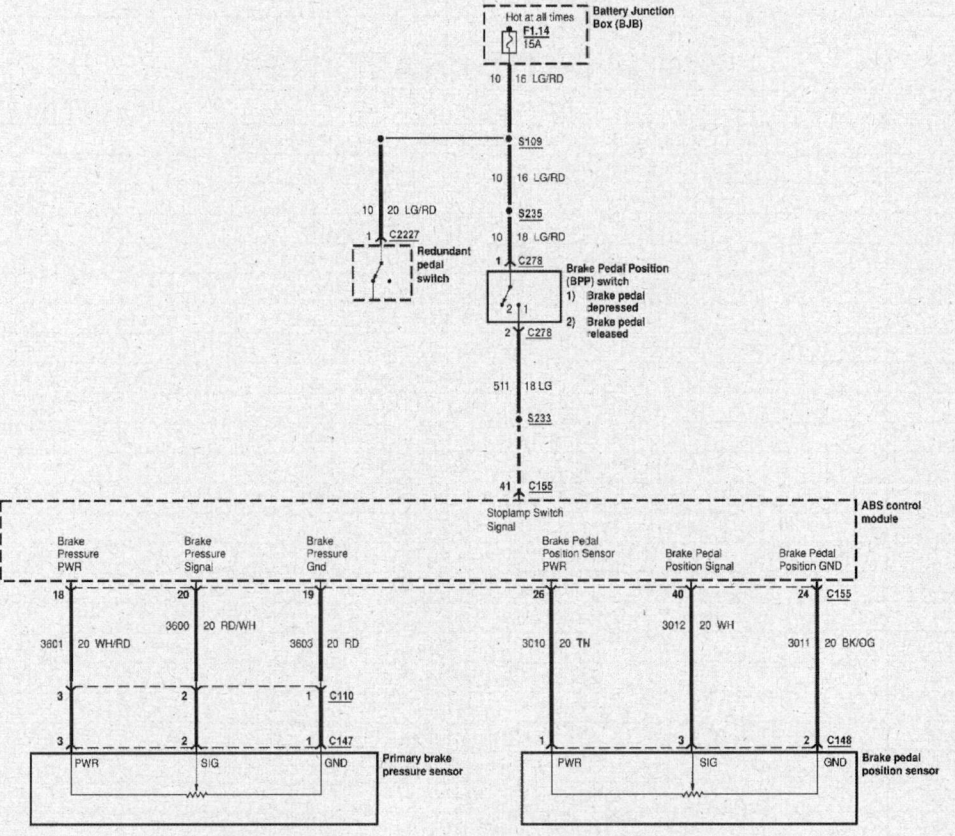

ABS control module

LF wheel speed +
LF wheel speed -
RF wheel speed +
RF wheel speed -
LR wheel speed +
LR wheel speed -
RR wheel speed +
RR wheel speed -

| 45 | 46 | 34 | 33 | 37 | 36 | 43 | 42 | C155 |

522 20 TN/BK
521 20 TN/OG
516 20 YE/BK
514 20 YE/RD
519 20 LG/BK
518 20 LG/RD
523 20 RD/PK
524 20 PK/BK

| 11 | 12 | 13 | 25 | C210 |
| 9 | 10 | 3 | 2 | C313 |

519 20 LG/BK
518 20 LG/RD

| 2 | 1 | C150 | 2 | 1 | C160 | 2 | 1 | C440 | 1 | 2 | C426 |

Wheel speed sensor, left front

Wheel speed sensor, right front

Wheel speed sensor, left rear

Wheel speed sensor, right rear

LTV0500000004148

Fig. 3   Wiring diagram (Part 3 of 5)

Battery Junction Box (BJB)
Hot at all times
F1.14
15A

10 16 LG/RD

S109

10 16 LG/RD

S235

10 18 LG/RD

10 20 LG/RD
1 C2227
Redundant pedal switch

1 C278
Brake Pedal Position (BPP) switch
1) Brake pedal depressed
2) Brake pedal released

2 1

2 C278

511 18 LG

S233

41 C155

ABS control module
Stoplamp Switch Signal

Brake Pressure PWR
Brake Pressure Signal
Brake Pressure Gnd
Brake Pedal Position Sensor PWR
Brake Pedal Position Signal
Brake Pedal Position GND

| 18 | 20 | 19 | 26 | 40 | 24 | C155 |

3601 20 WH/RD
3600 20 RD/WH
3603 20 RD
3010 20 TN
3012 20 WH
3011 20 BK/OG

| 3 | 2 | 1 | C110 |
| 3 | 2 | 1 | C147 | 1 | 3 | 2 | C148 |

PWR SIG GND
Primary brake pressure sensor

PWR SIG GND
Brake pedal position sensor

LTV0500000004149

Fig. 3   Wiring diagram (Part 4 of 5)

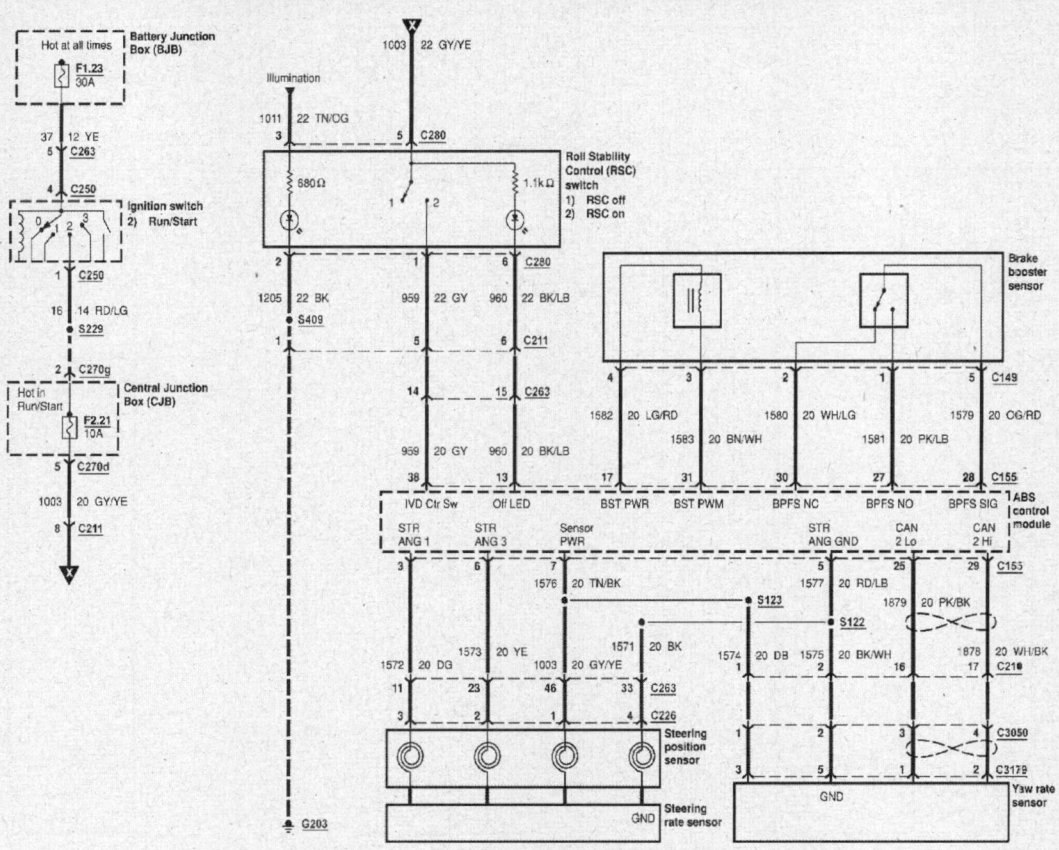

Fig. 3 Wiring diagram (Part 5 of 5)

LTV0500000004150

DIAGNOSTIC CHART INDEX

Test	Code	Description	Page No.	Fig. No.
A	—	No Communications w/Anti-Lock Brake System Module	5-7	4
B	B1483	Brake Pedal Input Signal Failure	5-7	5
C	B1676	Battery Pack Voltage Out Of Range	5-8	6
D	C1095	ABS Hydraulic Pump Motor Circuit Failure	5-8	7
E	C1145	Wheel Speed Sensor Input Circuit Failure	5-9	8
	C1155	Wheel Speed Sensor Input Circuit Failure	5-9	8
	C1165	Wheel Speed Sensor Input Circuit Failure	5-9	8
	C1175	Wheel Speed Sensor Input Circuit Failure	5-9	8
F	C1233	Wheel Speed Sensor Input Signal Missing	5-10	9
	C1234	Wheel Speed Sensor Input Signal Missing	5-10	9
	C1235	Wheel Speed Sensor Input Signal Missing	5-10	9
	C1236	Wheel Speed Sensor Input Signal Missing	5-10	9
G	C1277	Steering Wheel Angle 1 & 2 Circuit Failure	5-10	10
	C1278	Steering Wheel Angle 1 & 2 Circuit Failure	5-10	10
H	C1279	Sensor Cluster Fault	5-11	11
	C1280	Sensor Cluster Fault	5-11	11
	C1281	Sensor Cluster Fault	5-11	11
	C1282	Sensor Cluster Fault	5-11	11
	C1516	Sensor Cluster Fault	5-11	11
	C1517	Sensor Cluster Fault	5-11	11
	C2769	Sensor Cluster Fault	5-11	11
	C2770	Sensor Cluster Fault	5-11	11
	U1900	Sensor Cluster Fault	5-11	11
	U2023	Sensor Cluster Fault	5-11	11
I	C1285	Booster Solenoid Circuit Failure	5-12	12
J	C1287	Brake Booster Pedal Force Switch Circuit Failure	5-13	13

Continued

DIAGNOSTIC CHART INDEX—Continued

K	C1288	Brake Pressure Transducer Input Circuit Failure	5-14	14
	C1440	Brake Pressure Transducer Input Circuit Failure	5-14	14
L	C1730	Reference Voltage Out Of Range	5-15	15
M	C1960	Driver Brake Apply Circuit Fault	5-16	16
N	B2734	Pedal Travel Sensor Fault	5-16	17
	B2736	Pedal Travel Sensor Fault	5-16	17
	B2738	Pedal Travel Sensor Fault	5-16	17
	B2740	Pedal Travel Sensor Fault	5-16	17
O	—	Stability Assist Cannot Be Disabled	5-17	18
P	C1998	Module Calibration Not Complete	5-18	19
Q	—	Traction Control Switch Indicator Is Never/Always ON	5-18	20

Test Step	Result / Action to Take
A1 CHECK CIRCUITS 601 (LB/PK) AND 493 (BK/PK) FOR AN OPEN • Key in OFF position. • Disconnect: ABS Module C155. • Key in ON position. • Measure the voltage between the ABS module C155-4, circuit 601 (LB/PK), harness side and ground; and between the ABS module C155-32, circuit 493 (BK/PK), harness side and ground. • **Are the voltages greater than 10 volts?**	**Yes** GO to A2 . **No** REPAIR the circuit(s) in question. REPEAT the self-test.
A2 CHECK CIRCUIT 274 (BK/WH) FOR AN OPEN • Key in OFF position. • Measure the resistance between the ABS module C155-16, circuit 274 (BK/WH), harness side and ground. • **Is the resistance less than 5 ohms?**	**Yes** CHECK the module communications network. **No** REPAIR the circuit. REPEAT the self-test.

LTV0500000004151

Fig. 4   Test A: No Communications w/Anti-Lock Brake System Module

Test Step	Result / Action to Take
B1 CHECK THE STOPLAMP OPERATION • Key in OFF position. • Observe the stoplamps while pressing and releasing the brake pedal. • **Do the stoplamps operate correctly?**	**Yes** GO to B2 . **No** Diagnose the stoplamps. Clear the DTCs. REPEAT the self-test.
B2 CHECK CIRCUIT 511 (LG) FOR AN OPEN • Disconnect: Anti-lock Brake System (ABS) Module C155. • Measure the voltage between the ABS module C155-41 circuit 511 (LG), harness side and ground while pressing the brake pedal. • **Is the voltage greater than 10 volts?**	**Yes** GO to B3 **No** REPAIR the circuit. CLEAR the DTCs. REPEAT the self-test.

B3 CHECK FOR CORRECT ABS MODULE OPERATION
 	
 • Disconnect all the ABS connectors.
 • Check for:
     • corrosion
     • pushed-out pins
 • Connect all the ABS connectors and make sure they seat correctly.
 • Operate the system and verify the concern is still present.
 • **Is the concern still present?**
	Yes
	 INSTALL a new ABS module. TEST the system for normal operation.
	
	 No
	 The system is operating correctly at this time. The concern may have been caused by a loose or corroded connector. CLEAR the DTCs. REPEAT the self-test.

LTV0500000004152

Fig. 5   Test B, Code B1483: Brake Pedal Input Signal Failure

Test Step	Result / Action to Take
C1 CHECK THE BATTERY VOLTAGE	
• Measure the battery voltage between the positive and negative battery posts with the key ON engine OFF (KOEO), and with the engine running. • **Is the battery voltage between 10 and 13 volts with KOEO, and between 11 and 17 volts with the engine running?**	**Yes** GO to C2. **No** CHECK the charging system. TEST the system for normal operation.
C2 CHECK CIRCUIT 493 (BK/PK) FOR AN OPEN	
• Key in OFF position. • Disconnect: Anti-lock Brake System (ABS) Module C155. • Measure the voltage between the ABS module C155-32, circuit 493 (BK/PK), harness side and ground. • **Is the voltage greater than 10 volts?**	**Yes** GO to C3. **No** REPAIR the circuit. CLEAR the DTCs. REPEAT the self-test.

LTV0500000004153

Fig. 6   Test C, Code B1676: Battery Pack Voltage Out Of Range (Part 1 of 2)

Test Step	Result / Action to Take
C3 CHECK CIRCUIT 274 (BK/WH) FOR AN OPEN	
• Key in OFF position. • Measure the resistance between the ABS module C155-16, circuit 274 (BK/WH), harness side and ground. • **Is the resistance less than 5 ohms?**	**Yes** GO to C4. **No** REPAIR the circuit. CLEAR the DTCs. REPEAT the self-test.
C4 CHECK FOR CORRECT ABS MODULE OPERATION	

• Disconnect all the ABS connectors.
 • Check for:
   • corrosion
   • pushed-out pins
 • Connect all the ABS connectors and make sure they seat correctly.
 • Operate the system and verify the concern is still present.
 • **Is the concern still present?**
	Yes
	 INSTALL a new ABS module. TEST the system for normal operation.
	
	 No
	 The system is operating correctly at this time. The concern may have been caused by a loose or corroded connector. CLEAR the DTCs. REPEAT the self-test.

LTV0500000004154

Fig. 6   Test C, Code B1676: Battery Pack Voltage Out Of Range (Part 2 of 2)

Test Step	Result / Action to Take
D1 CHECK THE ABS PUMP MOTOR	
• Key in ON position. • **Is the ABS pump motor running all the time?**	**Yes** GO to D5. **No** GO to D2.
D2 CHECK THE PUMP MOTOR OPERATION	
• Key in OFF position. • Connect the diagnostic tool. • Key in ON position. • Enter the following diagnostic mode on the diagnostic tool: Active Command. • Trigger the ABS module pump motor ON active command. • **Does the ABS pump motor run for approximately 2 seconds?**	**Yes** CLEAR the DTCs. CHECK the yellow ABS warning indicator while driving the vehicle (brakes must not be applied) above 20 km/h (12 mph). If the yellow ABS warning indicator illuminates, RETRIEVE the DTCs. If DTC C1095 is retrieved, GO to D5. **No** TRIGGER the ABS module pump motor OFF active command. GO to D3.
D3 CHECK CIRCUIT 534 (YE/LG) FOR AN OPEN	
• Disconnect: ABS Module C155. • Measure the voltage between the ABS module C155-1, circuit 534 (YE/LG), harness side and ground. • **Is the voltage greater than 10 volts?**	**Yes** GO to D4. **No** REPAIR the circuit. CLEAR the DTCs. REPEAT the self-test.

LTV0500000004155

Fig. 7   Test D, Code C1095: ABS Hydraulic Pump Motor Circuit Failure (Part 1 of 2)

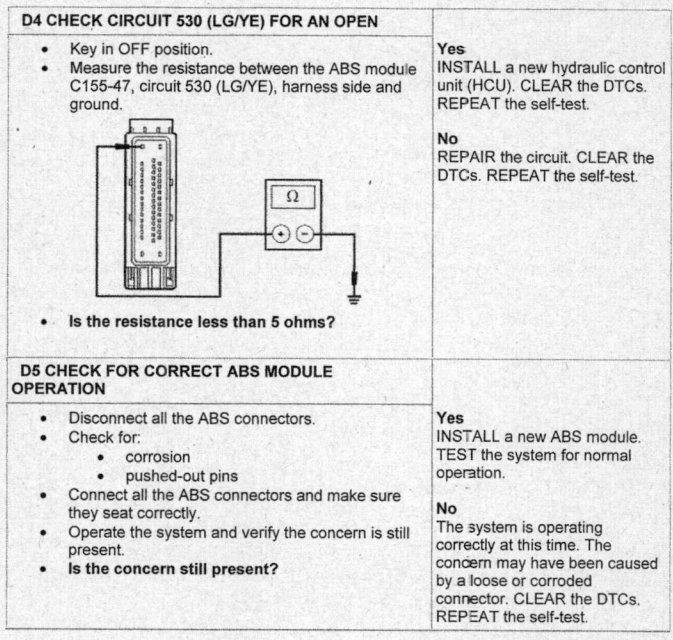

Test Step	Result / Action to Take
D4 CHECK CIRCUIT 530 (LG/YE) FOR AN OPEN	
• Key in OFF position. • Measure the resistance between the ABS module C155-47, circuit 530 (LG/YE), harness side and ground. • **Is the resistance less than 5 ohms?**	**Yes** INSTALL a new hydraulic control unit (HCU). CLEAR the DTCs. REPEAT the self-test. **No** REPAIR the circuit. CLEAR the DTCs. REPEAT the self-test.
D5 CHECK FOR CORRECT ABS MODULE OPERATION	

• Disconnect all the ABS connectors.
 • Check for:
   • corrosion
   • pushed-out pins
 • Connect all the ABS connectors and make sure they seat correctly.
 • Operate the system and verify the concern is still present.
 • **Is the concern still present?**
	Yes
	 INSTALL a new ABS module. TEST the system for normal operation.
	
	 No
	 The system is operating correctly at this time. The concern may have been caused by a loose or corroded connector. CLEAR the DTCs. REPEAT the self-test.

LTV0500000004156

Fig. 7   Test D, Code C1095: ABS Hydraulic Pump Motor Circuit Failure (Part 2 of 2)

Test Step	Result / Action to Take
E1 CHECK THE WHEEL SPEED CIRCUITS FOR A SHORT TO VOLTAGE ⚠️ **CAUTION: No measurements should be taken with the wheel speed sensor connected. Damage to the wheel speed sensor will result. NOTE:** Both circuits must be checked for each DTC. • Key in OFF position. • Disconnect: Anti-lock Brake System (ABS) Module C155. • Disconnect: Suspect Wheel Speed Sensor. • Key in ON position. • Measure the voltage between the ABS module connector, harness side and ground as follows:	**Yes** REPAIR the circuit(s) in question. CLEAR the DTCs. REPEAT the self-test. **No** GO to E2 .

DTC	ABS Module Connector-Pin	Circuit
C1145	C155-33	514 (YE/RD)
C1145	C155-34	516 (YE/BK)
C1155	C155-45	522 (TN/BK)
C1155	C155-46	521 (TN/OG)
C1165	C155-42	524 (PK/BK)
C1165	C155-43	523 (RD/PK)
C1175	C155-36	518 (LG/RD)
C1175	C155-37	519 (LG/BK)

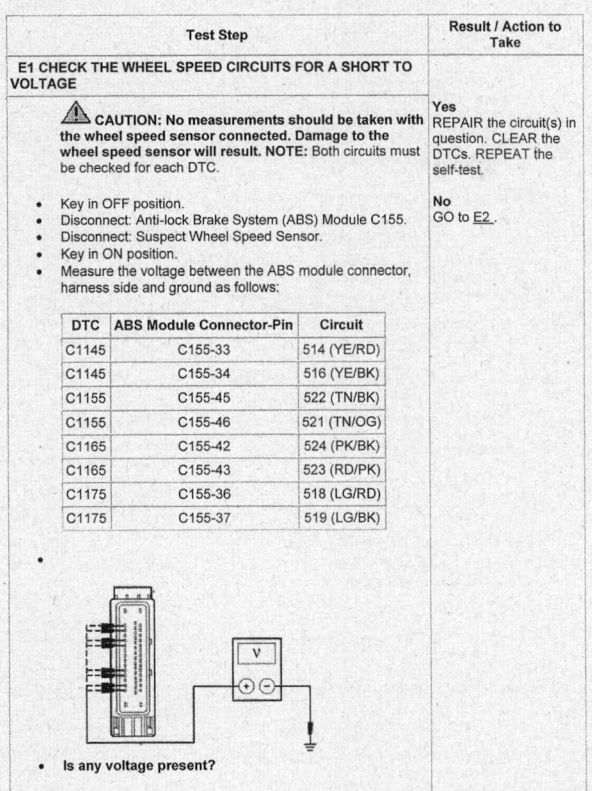

• Is any voltage present?

LTV0500000004157

Fig. 8   Test E, Codes C1145, C1155, C1165 & C1175: Wheel Speed Sensor Input Circuit Failure (Part 1 of 4)

DTC	Circuit	ABS Module Connector-Pin	Wheel Speed Sensor Connector-Pin
C1145	514 (YE/RD)	C155-33	RH front wheel speed sensor C160-1
C1155	522 (TN/BK)	C155-45	LH front wheel speed sensor C150-2
C1155	521 (TN/OG)	C155-46	LH front wheel speed sensor C150-1
C1165	523 (RD/PK)	C155-43	RH rear wheel speed sensor C426-1
C1165	524 (PK/BK)	C155-42	RH rear wheel speed sensor C426-2
C1175	518 (LG/RD)	C155-36	LH rear wheel speed sensor C440-1
C1175	519 (LG/BK)	C155-37	LH rear wheel speed sensor C440-2

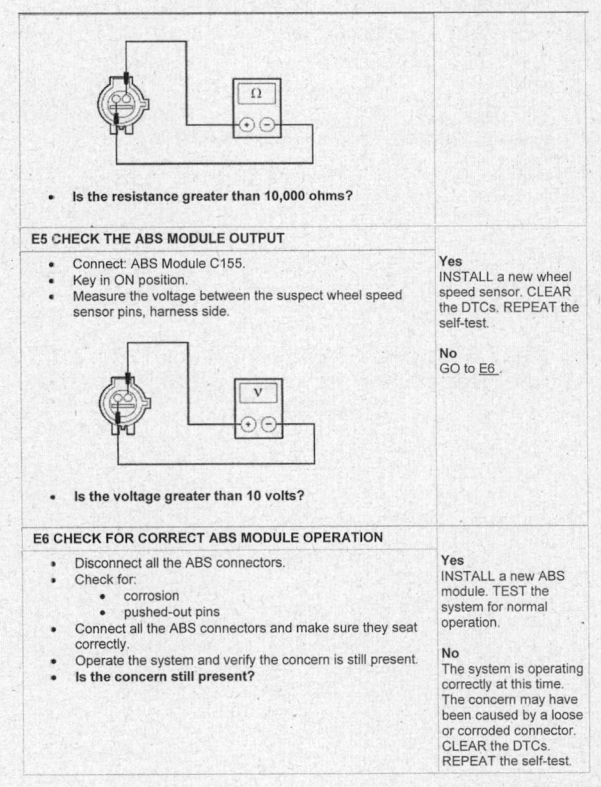

• Are the resistances less than 5 ohms?

E4 CHECK FOR SHORTED WHEEL SPEED SENSOR CIRCUITS	
• Measure the resistance between the suspect wheel speed sensor pins, harness side.	**Yes** GO to E5 . **No** REPAIR the circuit(s) in question. CLEAR the DTCs. REPEAT the self-test.

LTV0500000004803

Fig. 8   Test E, Codes C1145, C1155, C1165 & C1175: Wheel Speed Sensor Input Circuit Failure (Part 3 of 4)

E2 CHECK THE WHEEL SPEED CIRCUITS FOR A SHORT TO GROUND	
NOTE: Both circuits must be checked for each DTC. • Key in OFF position. • REPAIR the resistance between the ABS module connector, harness side and ground as follows:	**Yes** GO to E3 . **No** REPAIR the circuit(s) in question. CLEAR the DTCs. REPEAT the self-test.

DTC	ABS Module Connector-Pin	Circuit
C1145	C155-33	514 (YE/RD)
C1145	C155-34	516 (YE/BK)
C1155	C155-45	522 (TN/BK)
C1155	C155-46	521 (TN/OG)
C1165	C155-42	524 (PK/BK)
C1165	C155-43	523 (RD/PK)
C1175	C155-36	518 (LG/RD)
C1175	C155-37	519 (LG/BK)

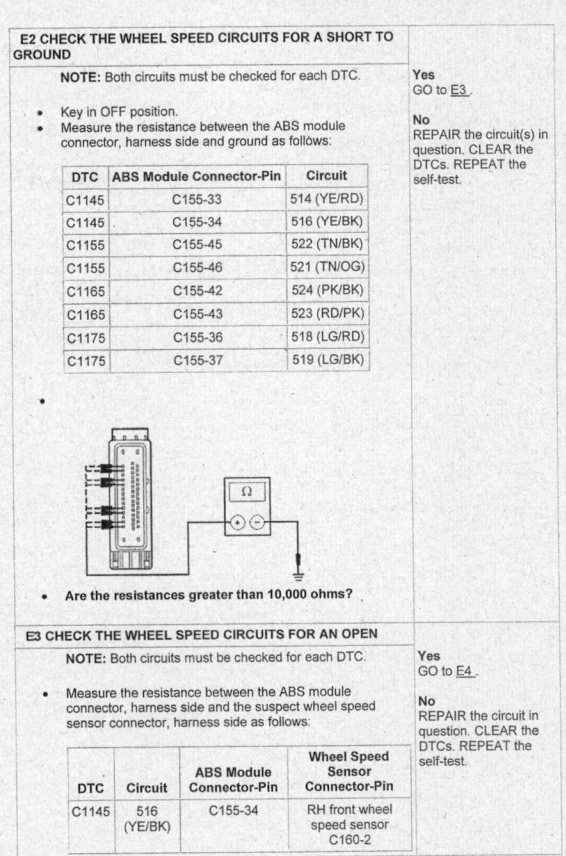

• Are the resistances greater than 10,000 ohms?

E3 CHECK THE WHEEL SPEED CIRCUITS FOR AN OPEN	
NOTE: Both circuits must be checked for each DTC. • Measure the resistance between the ABS module connector, harness side and the suspect wheel speed sensor connector, harness side as follows:	**Yes** GO to E4 . **No** REPAIR the circuit in question. CLEAR the DTCs. REPEAT the self-test.

DTC	Circuit	ABS Module Connector-Pin	Wheel Speed Sensor Connector-Pin
C1145	516 (YE/BK)	C155-34	RH front wheel speed sensor C160-2

LTV0500000004802

Fig. 8   Test E, Codes C1145, C1155, C1165 & C1175: Wheel Speed Sensor Input Circuit Failure (Part 2 of 4)

• Is the resistance greater than 10,000 ohms?

E5 CHECK THE ABS MODULE OUTPUT	
• Connect: ABS Module C155. • Key in ON position. • Measure the voltage between the suspect wheel speed sensor pins, harness side.	**Yes** INSTALL a new wheel speed sensor. CLEAR the DTCs. REPEAT the self-test. **No** GO to E6 .

• Is the voltage greater than 10 volts?

E6 CHECK FOR CORRECT ABS MODULE OPERATION	

• Disconnect all the ABS connectors.
• Check for:
   • corrosion
   • pushed-out pins
• Connect all the ABS connectors and make sure they seat correctly.
• Operate the system and verify the concern is still present.
• **Is the concern still present?**
	Yes
	INSTALL a new ABS module. TEST the system for normal operation.
	
	No
	The system is operating correctly at this time. The concern may have been caused by a loose or corroded connector. CLEAR the DTCs. REPEAT the self-test.

LTV0500000004804

Fig. 8   Test E, Codes C1145, C1155, C1165 & C1175: Wheel Speed Sensor Input Circuit Failure (Part 4 of 4)

Test Step	Result / Action to Take
F1 CHECK THE DTCs FROM THE SELF-TEST	
• Check the recorded results from the anti-lock brake system (ABS) self-test. • **Are DTCs C1145, C1155, C1165, or C1175 present?**	**Yes** Go To Pinpoint Test E . **No** GO to F2 .
F2 MONITOR THE WHEEL SPEED PIDS	
• Connect the diagnostic tool. • Key in ON position. • Enter the following diagnostic mode on the diagnostic tool: ABS Module PIDs. • Use the diagnostic tool to monitor the ABS module wheel speed sensor PIDs while driving the vehicle at a constant speed. • **Are all the wheel speed sensor PID values similar?**	**Yes** CLEAR the DTCs. DRIVE the vehicle. RETRIEVE the DTCs. If DTC C1233, C1234, C1235, or C1236 is present, GO to F9 . **No** GO to F3 .
F3 INSPECT THE WHEEL SPEED SENSOR MOUNTING	
• Key in OFF position. • With the vehicle in NEUTRAL, position it on a hoist. • Inspect the wheel speed sensor for looseness. • **Is the wheel speed sensor loose?**	**Yes** TIGHTEN the wheel speed sensor to specification. CLEAR the DTCs. GO to F4 . **No** GO to F5 .

LTV0500000004805

Fig. 9   Test F, Codes C1233, C1234, C1235 & C1236: Wheel Speed Sensor Input Signal Missing (Part 1 of 3)

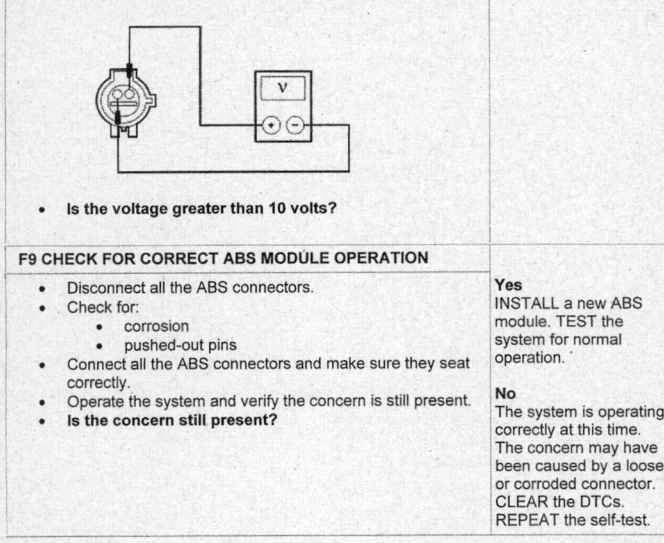

• **Is the voltage greater than 10 volts?**	
F9 CHECK FOR CORRECT ABS MODULE OPERATION	

• Disconnect all the ABS connectors.
• Check for:
  • corrosion
  • pushed-out pins
• Connect all the ABS connectors and make sure they seat correctly.
• Operate the system and verify the concern is still present.
• **Is the concern still present?**
	Yes
	INSTALL a new ABS module. TEST the system for normal operation.
	
	No
	The system is operating correctly at this time. The concern may have been caused by a loose or corroded connector. CLEAR the DTCs. REPEAT the self-test.

LTV0500000004807

Fig. 9   Test F, Codes C1233, C1234, C1235 & C1236: Wheel Speed Sensor Input Signal Missing (Part 3 of 3)

Test Step	Result / Action to Take
F4 RECHECK THE WHEEL SPEED PIDS	
• Connect the diagnostic tool. • Key in ON position. • Enter the following diagnostic mode on the diagnostic tool: ABS Module PIDs. • Use the diagnostic tool to monitor the ABS module wheel speed sensor PIDs while driving the vehicle at a constant speed. • **Are all the wheel speed sensor PID values similar?**	**Yes** The vehicle is OK. The concern may have been caused by a loose wheel speed sensor. **No** GO to F5 .
F5 CHECK THE WHEEL SPEED SENSOR FOR DAMAGE	
• Key in OFF position. • With the vehicle in NEUTRAL, position it on a hoist. • ⚠ **CAUTION: Examine the wheel speed sensor wire carefully with a good light source. Failure to verify damage in the wheel speed sensor wire can lead to unnecessary installation of a new component.** • Inspect the wheel speed sensor for general damage. • **Is the wheel speed sensor OK?**	**Yes** GO to F6 . **No** INSTALL a new wheel speed sensor. CLEAR the DTCs. REPEAT the self-test.
F6 CHECK FOR WHEEL SPEED SENSOR RING DAMAGE	
• Inspect the wheel speed sensor ring for damaged or missing teeth. Rotate the wheel to verify that no teeth are missing. • **Is the wheel speed sensor ring OK?**	**Yes** GO to F7 . **No** INSTALL a new hub and bearing (front wheel) or rear halfshaft. CLEAR the DTCs. REPEAT the self-test.
F7 CHECK FOR BEARING DAMAGE	
• Inspect the wheel bearings for damage. • **Are the wheel bearings OK?**	**Yes** GO to F8 . **No** INSTALL a new wheel bearing as necessary. CLEAR the DTCs. REPEAT the self-test.
F8 CHECK THE ABS MODULE OUTPUT	
• Key in OFF position. • Disconnect: Suspect Wheel Speed Sensor. • Key in ON position. • Measure the voltage between the suspect wheel speed sensor pins, harness side.	**Yes** INSTALL a new wheel speed sensor. CLEAR the DTCs. REPEAT the self-test. **No** GO to F9 .

LTV0500000004806

Fig. 9   Test F, Codes C1233, C1234, C1235 & C1236: Wheel Speed Sensor Input Signal Missing (Part 2 of 3)

Test Step	Result / Action to Take
G1 CARRY OUT THE CALIBRATION PROCEDURE	
• Key in ON position. • Enter the following diagnostic mode on the diagnostic tool: Clear the DTCs. • Carry out the steering position sensor calibration procedure following the diagnostic tool directions. • Enter the following diagnostic mode on the diagnostic tool: Retrieve DTCs. • **Are any DTCs retrieved or does the calibration procedure indicate a fault?**	**Yes** If DTC C1277 or C1278 is retrieved or the calibration procedure indicates a fault, GO to G2 . If any other DTCs are retrieved, GO to the Anti-Lock Brake System (ABS) Module Diagnostic Trouble Code (DTC) Index. If sent here from Pinpoint Test Q , GO to G2 . **No** The ABS system is operating correctly.
G2 MONITOR THE STEERING POSITION SENSOR PIDs	
• Make sure the steering wheel is centered straight forward. • Enter the following diagnostic mode on the diagnostic tool: ABS Module PIDs. • Monitor the ABS module steering position sensor PID while rotating the steering wheel clockwise and counterclockwise. • **Are the 2 PID values similar?**	**Yes** CLEAR the DTCs. DRIVE the vehicle. RETRIEVE the DTCs. If DTC C1277 is present, INSTALL a new ABS module. CALIBRATE the ABS module. FOLLOW the diagnostic tool directions for the calibration procedure. **No** If the value is less than 360, GO to G3 . If the value is greater than 360, Check for alignment concerns, check for a suspension concerns, or steering column concerns. CLEAR the DTCs. REPEAT the self-test.
G3 CHECK CIRCUIT 1003 (GY/YE) FOR AN OPEN	
• Key in OFF position. • Disconnect: Steering Position Sensor C226. • Key in ON position. • Measure the voltage between the steering position sensor C226-1, circuit 1003 (GY/YE), harness side and ground.	**Yes** GO to G4 . **No** REPAIR the circuit. CLEAR the DTCs. CALIBRATE the

LTV0500000004808

Fig. 10   Test G, Codes C1277 & C1278: Steering Wheel Angle 1 & 2 Circuit Failure (Part 1 of 3)

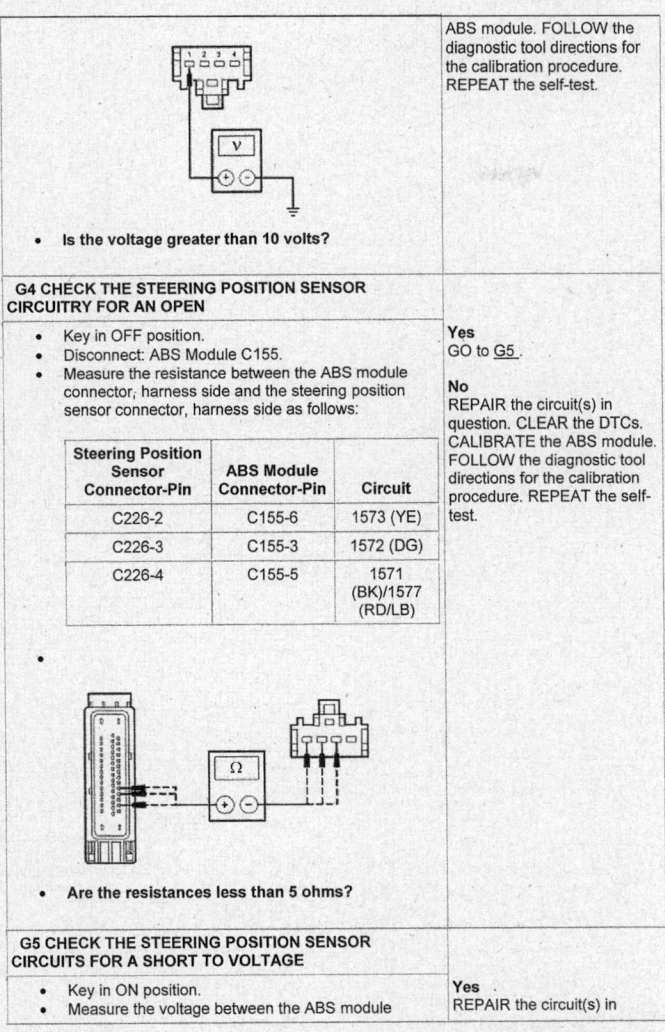

• **Is the voltage greater than 10 volts?**

G4 CHECK THE STEERING POSITION SENSOR CIRCUITRY FOR AN OPEN

Test Step	Result / Action to Take
• Key in OFF position. • Disconnect: ABS Module C155. • Measure the resistance between the ABS module connector, harness side and the steering position sensor connector, harness side as follows:	**Yes** GO to G5. **No** REPAIR the circuit(s) in question. CLEAR the DTCs. CALIBRATE the ABS module. FOLLOW the diagnostic tool directions for the calibration procedure. REPEAT the self-test.

Steering Position Sensor Connector-Pin	ABS Module Connector-Pin	Circuit
C226-2	C155-6	1573 (YE)
C226-3	C155-3	1572 (DG)
C226-4	C155-5	1571 (BK)/1577 (RD/LB)

• **Are the resistances less than 5 ohms?**

G5 CHECK THE STEERING POSITION SENSOR CIRCUITS FOR A SHORT TO VOLTAGE

Test Step	Result / Action to Take
• Key in ON position. • Measure the voltage between the ABS module	**Yes** REPAIR the circuit(s) in

LTV0500000004809

Fig. 10   Test G, Codes C1277 & C1278: Steering Wheel Angle 1 & 2 Circuit Failure (Part 2 of 3)

Test Step	Result / Action to Take
H1 CARRY OUT THE CALIBRATION PROCEDURE	
• Connect the diagnostic tool. • Key in ON position. • Clear the DTCs. • Carry out the yaw rate calibration procedure using the diagnostic tool. • Retrieve the DTCs. • **Are any DTCs retrieved or does the calibration procedure indicate a fault?**	**Yes** GO to H2. **No** The anti-lock brake system (ABS) system is operating correctly. The condition may have been caused by an incomplete or inaccurate calibration.
H2 CHECK THE ABS MODULE YAW RATE PID	
• Enter the following diagnostic mode on the diagnostic tool: ABS Module PID. • Monitor the ABS module yaw rate PID. • **Is the ABS module yaw rate PID value between -0.05 and 0.05?**	**Yes** GO to H3. **No** CHECK the mounting of the sensor cluster. If OK, INSTALL a new sensor cluster. CLEAR the DTCs. CALIBRATE the ABS module. FOLLOW the diagnostic tool directions for

LTV0500000004811

Fig. 11   Test H, Codes C1279, C1280, C1281, C1282, C1516, C1517, C2769, C2770, U1900 & U2023: Sensor Cluster Fault (Part 1 of 5)

---

connector, harness side and ground as follows:

ABS Module Connector-Pin	Circuit
C155-6	1573 (YE)
C155-3	1572 (DG)
C155-5	1577 (RD/LB)

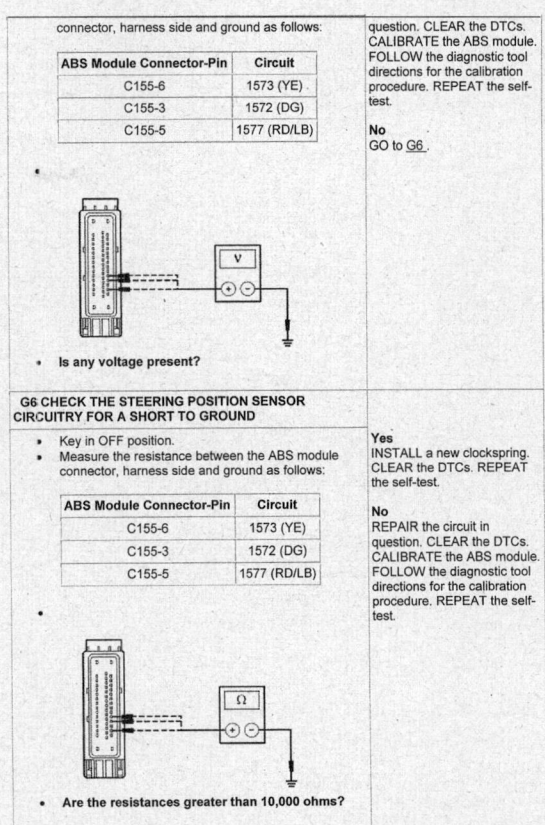

• **Is any voltage present?**

G6 CHECK THE STEERING POSITION SENSOR CIRCUITRY FOR A SHORT TO GROUND

Test Step	Result / Action to Take
• Key in OFF position. • Measure the resistance between the ABS module connector, harness side and ground as follows:	**Yes** INSTALL a new clockspring. CLEAR the DTCs. REPEAT the self-test. **No** REPAIR the circuit in question. CLEAR the DTCs. CALIBRATE the ABS module. FOLLOW the diagnostic tool directions for the calibration procedure. REPEAT the self-test.

ABS Module Connector-Pin	Circuit
C155-6	1573 (YE)
C155-3	1572 (DG)
C155-5	1577 (RD/LB)

• **Are the resistances greater than 10,000 ohms?**

LTV0500000004810

Fig. 10   Test G, Codes C1277 & C1278: Steering Wheel Angle 1 & 2 Circuit Failure (Part 3 of 3)

Test Step	Result / Action to Take
	the calibration procedure. REPEAT the self-test.
H3 CHECK THE ABS MODULE LATERAL ACCELERATION PID	
• Enter the following diagnostic mode on the diagnostic tool: ABS Module PID. • **NOTE:** The vehicle must be on level ground and at a complete standstill. Any vehicle movement will result in false values for this test. • Monitor the ABS module lateral acceleration PID. • **Is the ABS module lateral acceleration PID value between -7 and 7?**	**Yes** If equipped with 4WD, GO to H4. If equipped with 2WD, GO to H5. **No** CHECK the mounting of the sensor cluster. If OK, INSTALL a new sensor cluster. CLEAR the DTCs. CALIBRATE the ABS module. FOLLOW the diagnostic tool directions for the calibration procedure. REPEAT the self-test.
H4 CHECK THE ABS MODULE LONGITUDINAL ACCELERATION PID	
• Enter the following diagnostic mode on the diagnostic tool: ABS Module PID. • Monitor the ABS module longitudinal acceleration PID. • **Is the ABS module longitudinal acceleration PID value between -4 and 4?**	**Yes** GO to H5. **No** CHECK the mounting of the sensor cluster. If OK, INSTALL a new sensor cluster. CLEAR the DTCs. CALIBRATE the ABS module. FOLLOW the diagnostic tool directions for the calibration procedure. REPEAT the self-test.
H5 CHECK THE ABS MODULE ROLL RATE PID	
• Enter the following diagnostic mode on the diagnostic tool: ABS Module PID. • Monitor the ABS module roll rate PID. • **Is the ABS module roll rate PID value between -0.05 and 0.05?**	**Yes** GO to H6. **No** CHECK the mounting of the sensor cluster. If OK, INSTALL a new sensor cluster. CLEAR the DTCs. CALIBRATE the ABS

LTV0500000004812

Fig. 11   Test H, Codes C1279, C1280, C1281, C1282, C1516, C1517, C2769, C2770, U1900 & U2023: Sensor Cluster Fault (Part 2 of 5)

		REPEAT the self-test.
C3179-3	1574 (DB)	
C3179-5	1575 (BK/WH)	**No**
C3179-1	3125 (RD/YE)	GO to H8 .
C3179-2	3126 (TN/YE)	

H6 CHECK THE SENSOR CLUSTER CIRCUITRY FOR AN OPEN

- Key in OFF position.
- Disconnect: Sensor Cluster C3179.
- Disconnect ABS Module C155.
- Measure the resistance between the ABS module connector, harness side and the sensor cluster connector, harness side as follows:

ABS Module Connector-Pin	Circuit	Sensor Cluster Connector-Pin	Circuit
C155-7	1576 (TN/BK)	C3179-3	1574 (DB)
C155-5	1577 (RD/LB)	C3179-5	1575 (BK/WH)
C155-25	1879 (PK/BK)	C3179-1	3125 (RD/YE)
C155-29	1878 (WH/BK)	C3179-2	3126 (TN/YE)

Yes
GO to H7 .

No
REPAIR the circuit(s) in question. CLEAR the DTCs. CALIBRATE the ABS module. FOLLOW the diagnostic tool directions for the calibration procedure. REPEAT the self-test.

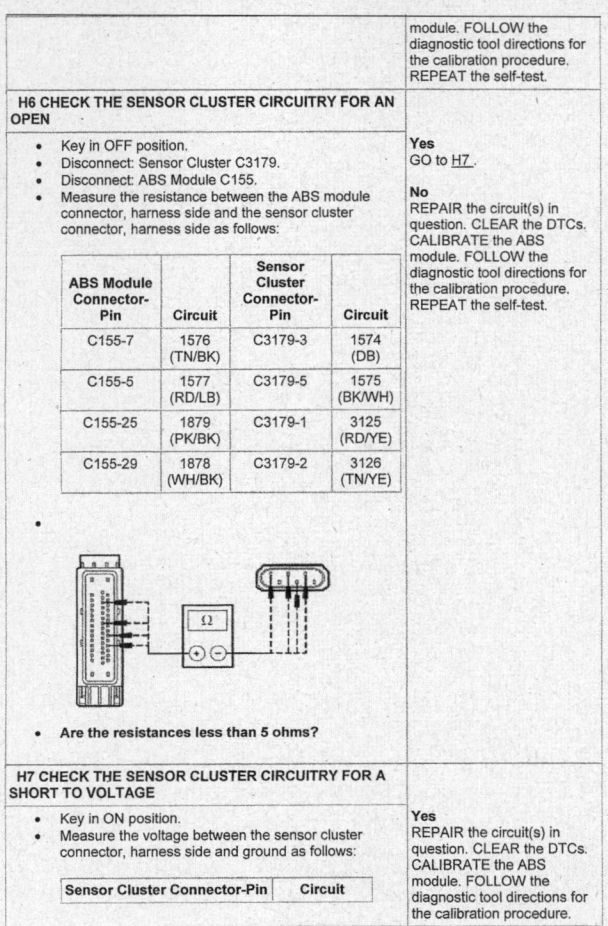

- **Are the resistances less than 5 ohms?**

H7 CHECK THE SENSOR CLUSTER CIRCUITRY FOR A SHORT TO VOLTAGE

- Key in ON position.
- Measure the voltage between the sensor cluster connector, harness side and ground as follows:

Sensor Cluster Connector-Pin	Circuit

Yes
REPAIR the circuit(s) in question. CLEAR the DTCs. CALIBRATE the ABS module. FOLLOW the diagnostic tool directions for the calibration procedure.

LTV0500000004813

Fig. 11   Test H, Codes C1279, C1280, C1281, C1282, C1516, C1517, C2769, C2770, U1900 & U2023: Sensor Cluster Fault (Part 3 of 5)

H9 CHECK THE VOLTAGE FROM THE ABS MODULE

- Connect: ABS Module C155.
- Key in ON position.
- Measure the voltage between the sensor cluster C3179-3, circuit 1574 (DB), harness side and the sensor cluster C3179-5, circuit 1575 (BK/WH), harness side.

Yes
INSTALL a new sensor cluster. CLEAR the DTCs. CALIBRATE the ABS module. FOLLOW the diagnostic tool directions for the calibration procedure. REPEAT the self-test.

No
GO to H10 .

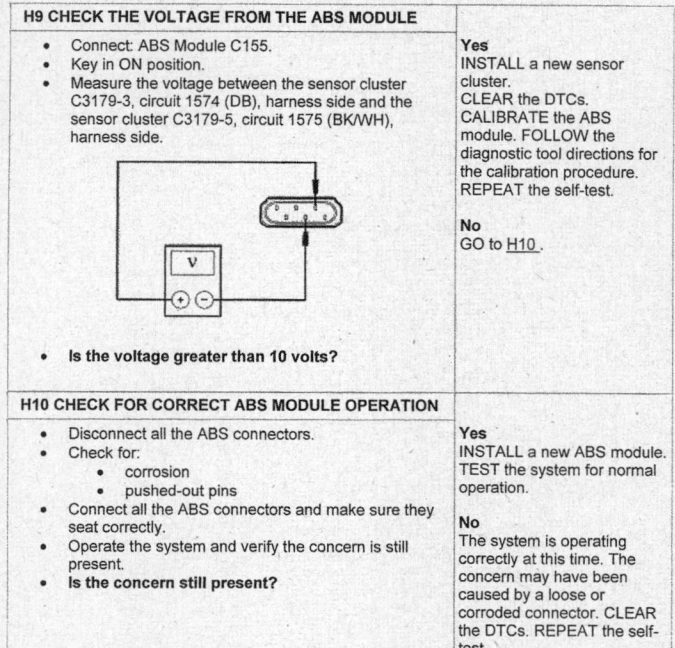

- **Is the voltage greater than 10 volts?**

H10 CHECK FOR CORRECT ABS MODULE OPERATION

- Disconnect all the ABS connectors.
- Check for:
  - corrosion
  - pushed-out pins
- Connect all the ABS connectors and make sure they seat correctly.
- Operate the system and verify the concern is still present.
- **Is the concern still present?**

Yes
INSTALL a new ABS module. TEST the system for normal operation.

No
The system is operating correctly at this time. The concern may have been caused by a loose or corroded connector. CLEAR the DTCs. REPEAT the self-test.

LTV0500000004815

Fig. 11   Test H, Codes C1279, C1280, C1281, C1282, C1516, C1517, C2769, C2770, U1900 & U2023: Sensor Cluster Fault (Part 5 of 5)

- **Is any voltage present?**

H8 CHECK THE SENSOR CLUSTER CIRCUITRY FOR A SHORT TO GROUND

- Key in OFF position.
- Measure the resistance between the sensor cluster connector, harness side and ground as follows:

Sensor Cluster Connector-Pin	Circuit
C3179-3	1574 (DB)
C3179-5	1575 (BK/WH)
C3179-1	3125 (RD/YE)
C3179-2	3126 (TN/YE)

Yes
GO to H9 .

No
REPAIR the circuit(s) in question. CLEAR the DTCs. CALIBRATE the ABS module. FOLLOW the diagnostic tool directions for the calibration procedure. REPEAT the self-test.

- **Are the resistances greater than 10,000 ohms?**

LTV0500000004814

Fig. 11   Test H, Codes C1279, C1280, C1281, C1282, C1516, C1517, C2769, C2770, U1900 & U2023: Sensor Cluster Fault (Part 4 of 5)

Test Step	Result / Action to Take
I1 CARRY OUT THE CALIBRATION PROCEDURE - Key in ON position. - Enter the following diagnostic mode on the diagnostic tool: Clear DTC. - Carry out the active brake booster calibration procedure using the diagnostic tool. - Enter the following diagnostic mode on the diagnostic tool: Retrieve DTCs. - **Are any DTCs retrieved or does the calibration procedure indicate a fault?**	**Yes** If DTC C1285 is retrieved, or the brake booster portion of the calibration procedure indicates a failure, GO to I2 . If any other DTC is retrieved, GO to the Anti-Lock Brake System (ABS) Module Diagnostic Trouble Code (DTC) Index. **No** The ABS system is operating correctly.
I2 CHECK THE BRAKE BOOSTER SOLENOID - Key in OFF position. - Disconnect: Active Brake Booster C149. - Measure the resistance between the active brake booster C149-3, circuit 1583 (BN/WH), component side and the active brake booster C149-4, circuit 1582 (LG/RD), component side. - **Is the resistance between 1 and 2 ohms?**	**Yes** GO to I3 . **No** INSTALL a new active brake booster. CLEAR the DTCs. CALIBRATE the ABS module. FOLLOW the diagnostic tool directions for the calibration procedure. REPEAT the self-test.
I3 CHECK CIRCUIT 1582 (LG/RD) AND CIRCUIT 1583 (BN/WH) FOR AN OPEN - Key in OFF position. - Disconnect: ABS Module C155. - Measure the resistance between the ABS module C155-17, circuit 1582 (LG/RD), harness side and the active brake booster C149-3, circuit 1582 (LG/RD), harness side, and between the ABS module C155-31, circuit 1583 (BN/WH), harness side and the active brake booster C149-4, circuit 1583 (BN/WH).	**Yes** GO to I4 . **No** REPAIR the circuit(s) in question. CLEAR the DTCs. CALIBRATE the ABS module. FOLLOW the diagnostic tool directions for the calibration procedure. REPEAT the self-test.

LTV0500000004816

Fig. 12   Test I, Code C1285: Booster Solenoid Circuit Failure (Part 1 of 3)

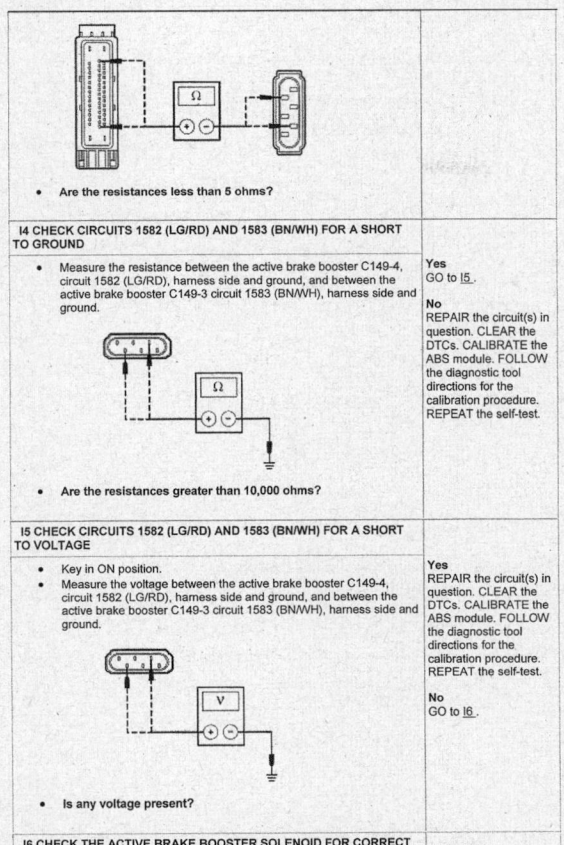

- **Are the resistances less than 5 ohms?**

I4 CHECK CIRCUITS 1582 (LG/RD) AND 1583 (BN/WH) FOR A SHORT TO GROUND	
• Measure the resistance between the active brake booster C149-4, circuit 1582 (LG/RD), harness side and ground, and between the active brake booster C149-3 circuit 1583 (BN/WH), harness side and ground. • **Are the resistances greater than 10,000 ohms?**	**Yes** GO to I5. **No** REPAIR the circuit(s) in question. CLEAR the DTCs. CALIBRATE the ABS module. FOLLOW the diagnostic tool directions for the calibration procedure. REPEAT the self-test.
I5 CHECK CIRCUITS 1582 (LG/RD) AND 1583 (BN/WH) FOR A SHORT TO VOLTAGE	
• Key in ON position. • Measure the voltage between the active brake booster C149-4, circuit 1582 (LG/RD), harness side and ground, and between the active brake booster C149-3 circuit 1583 (BN/WH), harness side and ground. • **Is any voltage present?**	**Yes** REPAIR the circuit(s) in question. CLEAR the DTCs. CALIBRATE the ABS module. FOLLOW the diagnostic tool directions for the calibration procedure. REPEAT the self-test. **No** GO to I6.
I6 CHECK THE ACTIVE BRAKE BOOSTER SOLENOID FOR CORRECT	

LTV0500000004817

Fig. 12   Test I, Code C1285: Booster Solenoid Circuit Failure (Part 2 of 3)

OPERATION	
• Key in OFF position. • Connect: Active Brake Booster C149. • Connect: ABS Module C155. • Key in ON position. • Start the engine and wait approximately 1 minute to create vacuum in the brake booster and then place the ignition switch in the OFF position. • Disconnect: ABS Module C155. • Connect a fused (10A) jumper wire between the ABS module C155-31, circuit 1583 (BN/WH), harness side and ground .	**Yes** GO to I7. **No** INSTALL a new active brake booster. CLEAR the DTCs. CALIBRATE the ABS module. REPEAT the self-test.

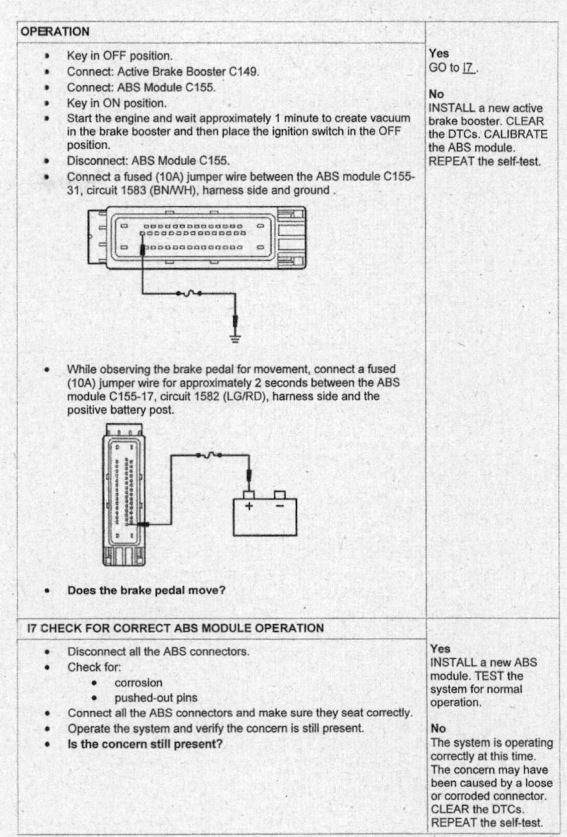

• While observing the brake pedal for movement, connect a fused (10A) jumper wire for approximately 2 seconds between the ABS module C155-17, circuit 1582 (LG/RD), harness side and the positive battery post. • **Does the brake pedal move?**	
I7 CHECK FOR CORRECT ABS MODULE OPERATION	

• Disconnect all the ABS connectors.
• Check for:
   • corrosion
   • pushed-out pins
• Connect all the ABS connectors and make sure they seat correctly.
• Operate the system and verify the concern is still present.
• **Is the concern still present?**
	Yes
	INSTALL a new ABS module. TEST the system for normal operation.
	
	No
	The system is operating correctly at this time. The concern may have been caused by a loose or corroded connector. CLEAR the DTCs. REPEAT the self-test.

LTV0500000004818

Fig. 12   Test I, Code C1285: Booster Solenoid Circuit Failure (Part 3 of 3)

Test Step	Result / Action to Take
J1 CARRY OUT THE CALIBRATION PROCEDURE	
• Key in ON position. • Enter the following diagnostic mode on the diagnostic tool: Clear DTCs. • Carry out the active brake booster calibration procedure using the diagnostic tool. • Enter the following diagnostic mode on the diagnostic tool: Retrieve the DTCs. • **Are any DTCs retrieved or does the calibration procedure indicate a fault?**	**Yes** If DTC C1287 is retrieved or the calibration procedure indicates a fault, GO to J2. If any other DTC, GO to the Anti-Lock Brake System (ABS) Module Diagnostic Trouble Code (DTC) Index. **No** The system is operating correctly.
J2 CHECK THE NORMALLY CLOSED RELEASE SWITCH	
• Key in OFF position. • Disconnect: Active Brake Booster C149. • Measure the resistance between the active brake booster C149-2, circuit 1580 (WH/LG), component side and the active brake booster C149-5, circuit 1579 (OG/RD), component side while pressing and releasing the brake pedal. • **Is the resistance less than 5 ohms with the brake pedal released and greater than 10,000 ohms with the brake pedal applied?**	**Yes** GO to J3. **No** INSTALL a new active brake booster. CLEAR the DTCs. CALIBRATE the ABS module. FOLLOW the diagnostic tool directions for the calibration procedure. REPEAT the self-test.

LTV0500000004819

Fig. 13   Test J, Code C1287: Brake Booster Pedal Force Switch Circuit Failure (Part 1 of 4)

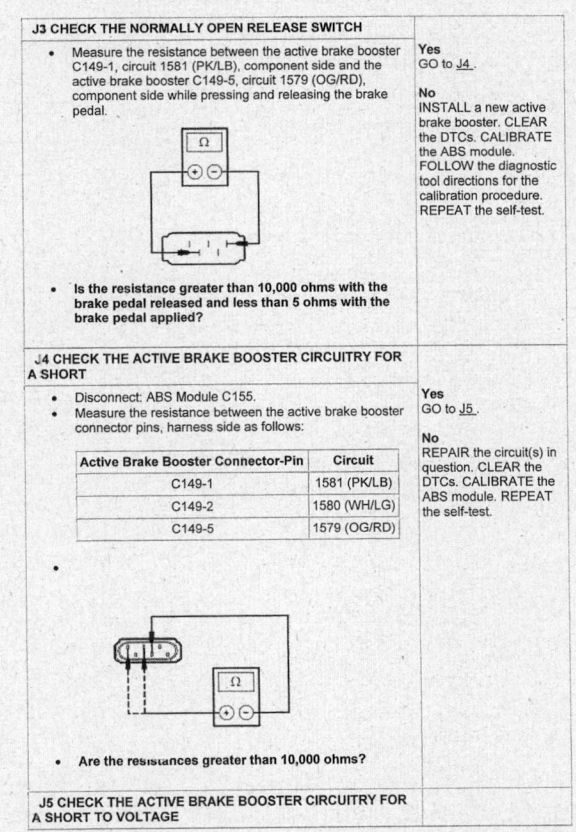

J3 CHECK THE NORMALLY OPEN RELEASE SWITCH	
• Measure the resistance between the active brake booster C149-1, circuit 1581 (PK/LB), component side and the active brake booster C149-5, circuit 1579 (OG/RD), component side while pressing and releasing the brake pedal. • **Is the resistance greater than 10,000 ohms with the brake pedal released and less than 5 ohms with the brake pedal applied?**	**Yes** GO to J4. **No** INSTALL a new active brake booster. CLEAR the DTCs. CALIBRATE the ABS module. FOLLOW the diagnostic tool directions for the calibration procedure. REPEAT the self-test.
J4 CHECK THE ACTIVE BRAKE BOOSTER CIRCUITRY FOR A SHORT	
• Disconnect: ABS Module C155. • Measure the resistance between the active brake booster connector pins, harness side as follows:	**Yes** GO to J5. **No** REPAIR the circuit(s) in question. CLEAR the DTCs. CALIBRATE the ABS module. REPEAT the self-test.

Active Brake Booster Connector-Pin	Circuit
C149-1	1581 (PK/LB)
C149-2	1580 (WH/LG)
C149-5	1579 (OG/RD)

- **Are the resistances greater than 10,000 ohms?**

J5 CHECK THE ACTIVE BRAKE BOOSTER CIRCUITRY FOR A SHORT TO VOLTAGE	

LTV0500000004820

Fig. 13   Test J, Code C1287: Brake Booster Pedal Force Switch Circuit Failure (Part 2 of 4)

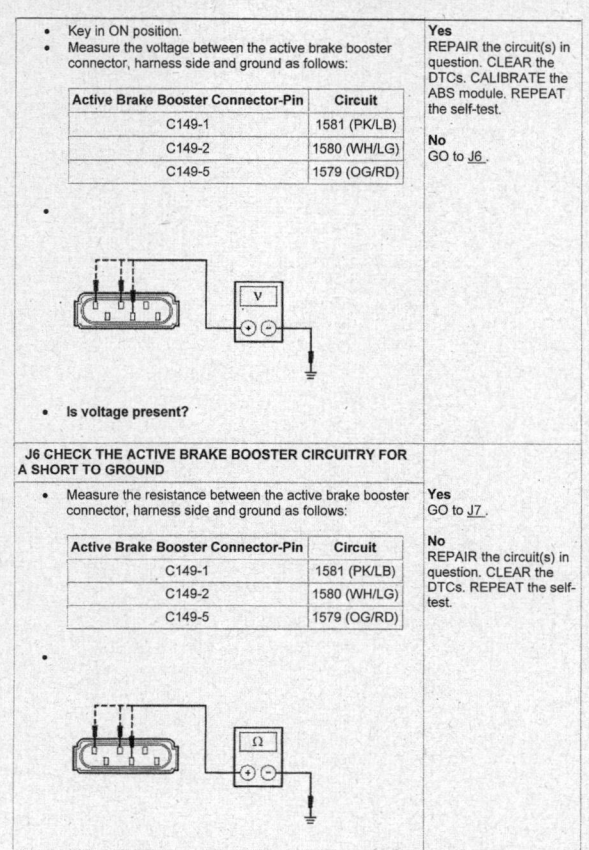

- Key in ON position.
- Measure the voltage between the active brake booster connector, harness side and ground as follows:

Active Brake Booster Connector-Pin	Circuit
C149-1	1581 (PK/LB)
C149-2	1580 (WH/LG)
C149-5	1579 (OG/RD)

Yes
REPAIR the circuit(s) in question. CLEAR the DTCs. CALIBRATE the ABS module. REPEAT the self-test.

No
GO to J6 .

- **Is voltage present?**

J6 CHECK THE ACTIVE BRAKE BOOSTER CIRCUITRY FOR A SHORT TO GROUND

- Measure the resistance between the active brake booster connector, harness side and ground as follows:

Active Brake Booster Connector-Pin	Circuit
C149-1	1581 (PK/LB)
C149-2	1580 (WH/LG)
C149-5	1579 (OG/RD)

Yes
GO to J7 .

No
REPAIR the circuit(s) in question. CLEAR the DTCs. REPEAT the self-test.

Fig. 13   Test J, Code C1287: Brake Booster Pedal Force Switch Circuit Failure (Part 3 of 4)

LTV0500000004821

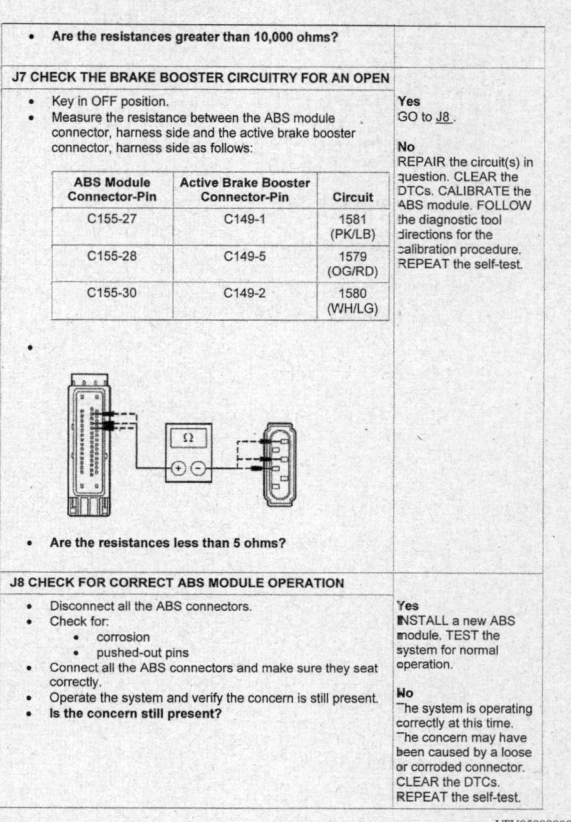

- **Are the resistances greater than 10,000 ohms?**

J7 CHECK THE BRAKE BOOSTER CIRCUITRY FOR AN OPEN

- Key in OFF position.
- Measure the resistance between the ABS module connector, harness side and the active brake booster connector, harness side as follows:

ABS Module Connector-Pin	Active Brake Booster Connector-Pin	Circuit
C155-27	C149-1	1581 (PK/LB)
C155-28	C149-5	1579 (OG/RD)
C155-30	C149-2	1580 (WH/LG)

Yes
GO to J8 .

No
REPAIR the circuit(s) in question. CLEAR the DTCs. CALIBRATE the ABS module. FOLLOW the diagnostic tool directions for the calibration procedure. REPEAT the self-test.

- **Are the resistances less than 5 ohms?**

J8 CHECK FOR CORRECT ABS MODULE OPERATION

- Disconnect all the ABS connectors.
- Check for:
  - corrosion
  - pushed-out pins
- Connect all the ABS connectors and make sure they seat correctly.
- Operate the system and verify the concern is still present.
- **Is the concern still present?**

Yes
INSTALL a new ABS module. TEST the system for normal operation.

No
The system is operating correctly at this time. The concern may have been caused by a loose or corroded connector. CLEAR the DTCs. REPEAT the self-test.

LTV0500000004822

Fig. 13   Test J, Code C1287: Brake Booster Pedal Force Switch Circuit Failure (Part 4 of 4)

Test Step	Result / Action to Take
K1 CHECK FOR DTCS - Key in ON position. - Check the recorded results from the ABS module self-test. - **Is DTC C1287, C1483, B2734, B2736, B2737, B2738, or B2740 present?**	**Yes** REPAIR these DTCs first. REFER to the appropriate pinpoint test for each DTC retrieved. **No** GO to K2 .

K2 CHECK THE PRIMARY BRAKE PRESSURE TRANSDUCER CIRCUITRY FOR A SHORT TO VOLTAGE

- Key in OFF position.
- Disconnect: ABS Module C155.
- Disconnect: Primary Brake Pressure Transducer C147.
- Key in ON position.
- Measure the voltage between the primary brake pressure transducer connector, harness side and ground as follows:

Primary Brake Pressure Transducer Connector-Pin	Circuit
C147-1	3603 (RD)
C147-2	3600 (RD/WH)
C147-3	3601 (WH/RD)

Yes
REPAIR the circuit(s) in question. CLEAR the DTCs. REPEAT the self-test.

No
GO to K3 .

- **Is any voltage present?**

LTV0500000004823

Fig. 14   Test K, Codes C1288 & C1440: Brake Pressure Transducer Input Circuit Failure (Part 1 of 4)

K3 CHECK THE PRIMARY BRAKE PRESSURE TRANSDUCER CIRCUITRY FOR A SHORT TO GROUND

- Key in OFF position.
- Measure the resistance between the primary brake pressure transducer connector, harness side and ground as follows:

Primary Brake Pressure Transducer Connector-Pin	Circuit
C147-1	3603 (RD)
C147-2	3600 (RD/WH)
C147-3	3601 (WH/RD)

Yes
GO to K4 .

No
REPAIR the circuit(s) in question. CLEAR the DTCs. REPEAT the self-test.

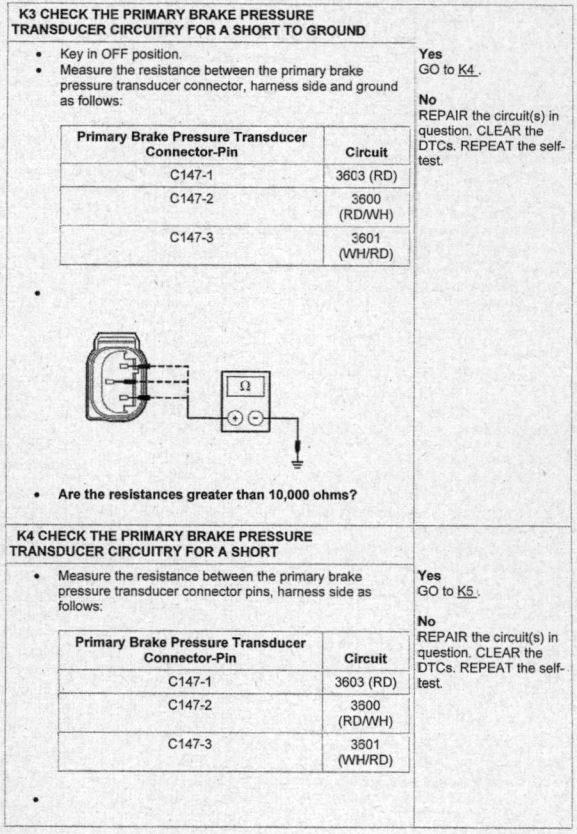

- **Are the resistances greater than 10,000 ohms?**

K4 CHECK THE PRIMARY BRAKE PRESSURE TRANSDUCER CIRCUITRY FOR A SHORT

- Measure the resistance between the primary brake pressure transducer connector pins, harness side as follows:

Primary Brake Pressure Transducer Connector-Pin	Circuit
C147-1	3603 (RD)
C147-2	3600 (RD/WH)
C147-3	3601 (WH/RD)

Yes
GO to K5 .

No
REPAIR the circuit(s) in question. CLEAR the DTCs. REPEAT the self-test.

LTV0500000004824

Fig. 14   Test K, Codes C1288 & C1440: Brake Pressure Transducer Input Circuit Failure (Part 2 of 4)

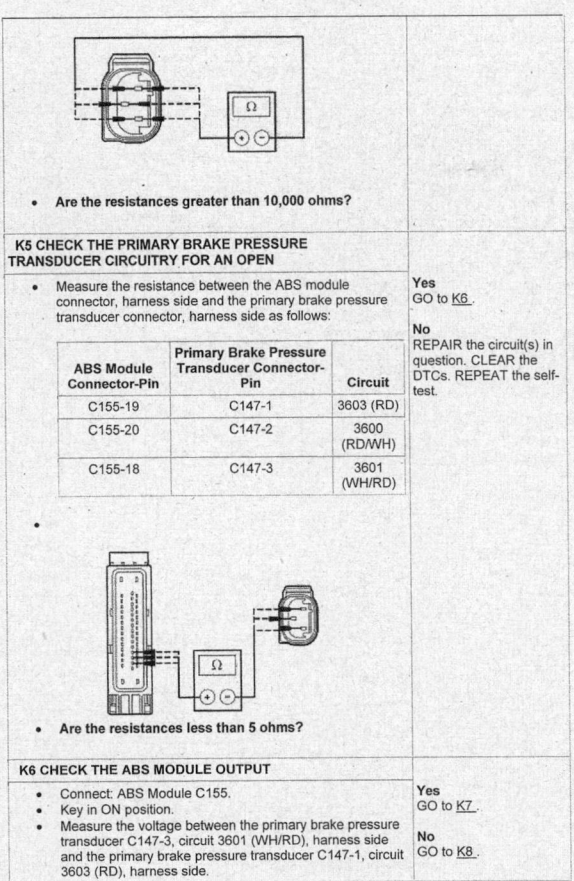

- Are the resistances greater than 10,000 ohms?

K5 CHECK THE PRIMARY BRAKE PRESSURE TRANSDUCER CIRCUITRY FOR AN OPEN	
• Measure the resistance between the ABS module connector, harness side and the primary brake pressure transducer connector, harness side as follows:	**Yes** GO to K6 . **No** REPAIR the circuit(s) in question. CLEAR the DTCs. REPEAT the self-test.

ABS Module Connector-Pin	Primary Brake Pressure Transducer Connector-Pin	Circuit
C155-19	C147-1	3603 (RD)
C155-20	C147-2	3600 (RD/WH)
C155-18	C147-3	3601 (WH/RD)

- Are the resistances less than 5 ohms?

K6 CHECK THE ABS MODULE OUTPUT	
• Connect: ABS Module C155. • Key in ON position. • Measure the voltage between the primary brake pressure transducer C147-3, circuit 3601 (WH/RD), harness side and the primary brake pressure transducer C147-1, circuit 3603 (RD), harness side.	**Yes** GO to K7 . **No** GO to K8 .

LTV0500000004825

Fig. 14   Test K, Codes C1288 & C1440: Brake Pressure Transducer Input Circuit Failure (Part 3 of 4)

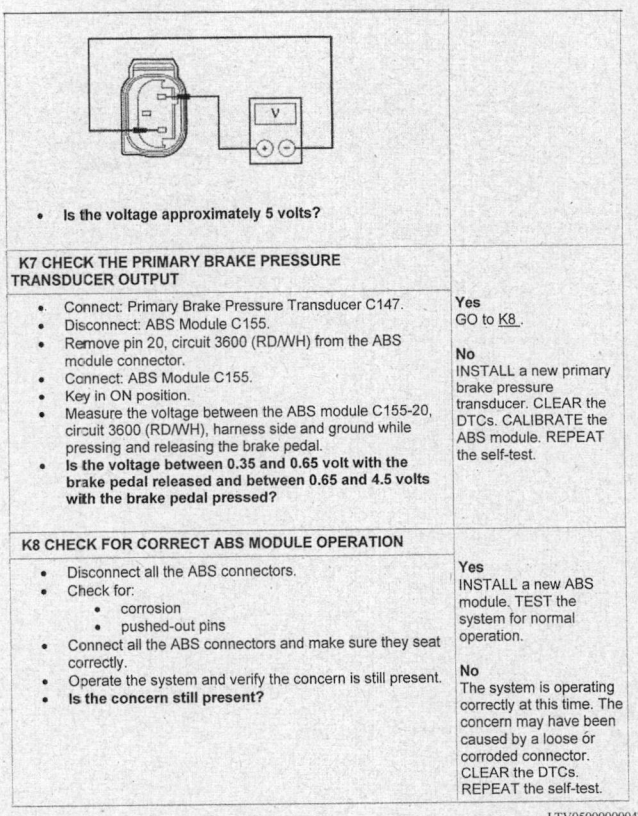

- Is the voltage approximately 5 volts?

K7 CHECK THE PRIMARY BRAKE PRESSURE TRANSDUCER OUTPUT	
• Connect: Primary Brake Pressure Transducer C147. • Disconnect: ABS Module C155. • Remove pin 20, circuit 3600 (RD/WH) from the ABS module connector. • Connect: ABS Module C155. • Key in ON position. • Measure the voltage between the ABS module C155-20, circuit 3600 (RD/WH), harness side and ground while pressing and releasing the brake pedal. • **Is the voltage between 0.35 and 0.65 volt with the brake pedal released and between 0.65 and 4.5 volts with the brake pedal pressed?**	**Yes** GO to K8 . **No** INSTALL a new primary brake pressure transducer. CLEAR the DTCs. CALIBRATE the ABS module. REPEAT the self-test.
K8 CHECK FOR CORRECT ABS MODULE OPERATION	

• Disconnect all the ABS connectors.
• Check for:
    • corrosion
    • pushed-out pins
• Connect all the ABS connectors and make sure they seat correctly.
• Operate the system and verify the concern is still present.
• **Is the concern still present?**
	Yes
	INSTALL a new ABS module. TEST the system for normal operation.
	
	No
	The system is operating correctly at this time. The concern may have been caused by a loose or corroded connector. CLEAR the DTCs. REPEAT the self-test.

LTV0500000004826

Fig. 14   Test K, Codes C1288 & C1440: Brake Pressure Transducer Input Circuit Failure (Part 4 of 4)

Test Step	Result / Action to Take
L1 CHECK CIRCUIT 3601 (WH/RD) AND CIRCUIT 3010 (TN) FOR SHORTS TO VOLTAGE	
• Key in OFF position. • Disconnect: Anti-lock Brake System (ABS) Module C155. • Disconnect: Primary Brake Pressure Transducer C147. • Disconnect: Brake Pedal Travel Sensor C148. • Key in ON position. • Measure the voltage between the ABS module C155-18, circuit 3601 (WH/RD), harness side and ground; and between the ABS module C155-26, circuit 3010 (TN), harness side and ground.	**Yes** REPAIR the circuit in question. CLEAR the DTCs. CALIBRATE the ABS module. FOLLOW the diagnostic tool directions for the calibration procedure. REPEAT the self-test. **No** GO to L2 .

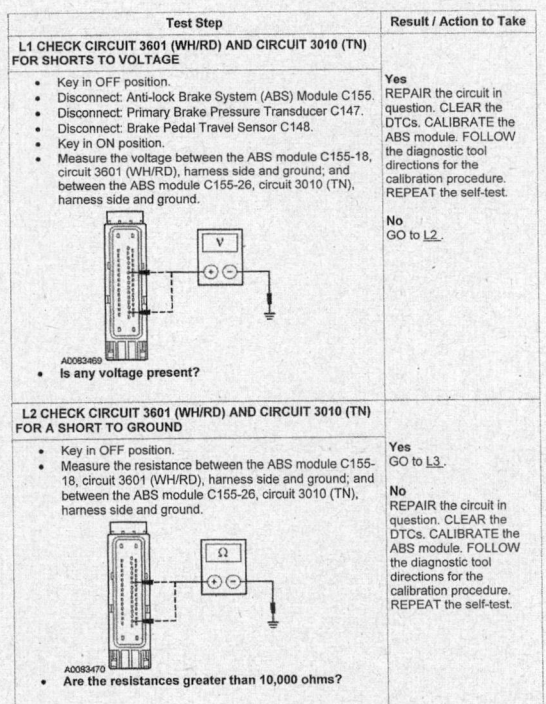

A0093469
- Is any voltage present?

L2 CHECK CIRCUIT 3601 (WH/RD) AND CIRCUIT 3010 (TN) FOR A SHORT TO GROUND	
• Key in OFF position. • Measure the resistance between the ABS module C155-18, circuit 3601 (WH/RD), harness side and ground; and between the ABS module C155-26, circuit 3010 (TN), harness side and ground.	**Yes** GO to L3 . **No** REPAIR the circuit in question. CLEAR the DTCs. CALIBRATE the ABS module. FOLLOW the diagnostic tool directions for the calibration procedure. REPEAT the self-test.

A0093470
- Are the resistances greater than 10,000 ohms?

LTV0500000004827

Fig. 15   Test L, Code C1730: Reference Voltage Out Of Range (Part 1 of 2)

L3 CHECK THE PRIMARY BRAKE PRESSURE TRANSDUCER	
• Disconnect: Primary Brake Pressure Transducer C147. • Measure the resistance between the ABS module C155-18, circuit 3601 (WH/RD), harness side and the ABS module C155-19, circuit 3603 (RD), harness side.	**Yes** GO to L4 . **No** INSTALL a new brake pressure transducer. CLEAR the DTCs. CALIBRATE the ABS module. FOLLOW the diagnostic tool directions for the calibration procedure. REPEAT the self-test.

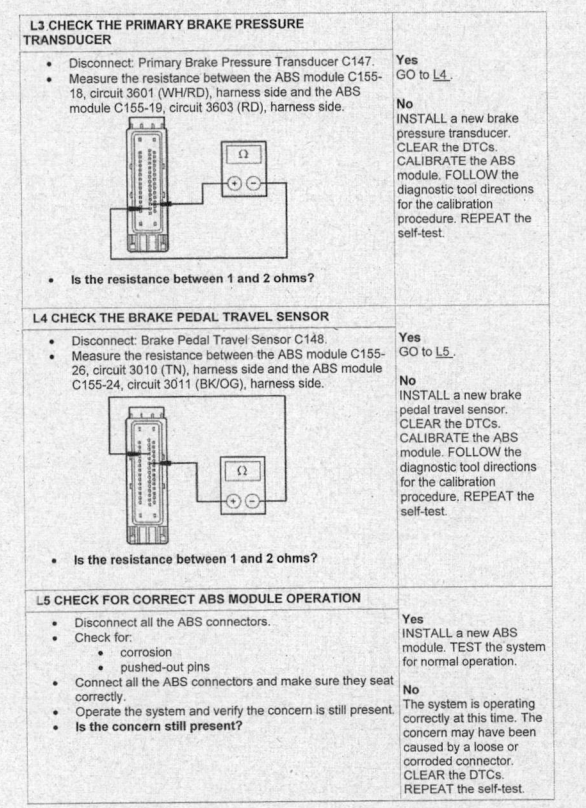

- Is the resistance between 1 and 2 ohms?

L4 CHECK THE BRAKE PEDAL TRAVEL SENSOR	
• Disconnect: Brake Pedal Travel Sensor C148. • Measure the resistance between the ABS module C155-26, circuit 3010 (TN), harness side and the ABS module C155-24, circuit 3011 (BK/OG), harness side.	**Yes** GO to L5 . **No** INSTALL a new brake pedal travel sensor. CLEAR the DTCs. CALIBRATE the ABS module. FOLLOW the diagnostic tool directions for the calibration procedure. REPEAT the self-test.

- Is the resistance between 1 and 2 ohms?

L5 CHECK FOR CORRECT ABS MODULE OPERATION	

• Disconnect all the ABS connectors.
• Check for:
    • corrosion
    • pushed-out pins
• Connect all the ABS connectors and make sure they seat correctly.
• Operate the system and verify the concern is still present.
• **Is the concern still present?**
	Yes
	INSTALL a new ABS module. TEST the system for normal operation.
	
	No
	The system is operating correctly at this time. The concern may have been caused by a loose or corroded connector. CLEAR the DTCs. REPEAT the self-test.

LTV0500000004828

Fig. 15   Test L, Code C1730: Reference Voltage Out Of Range (Part 2 of 2)

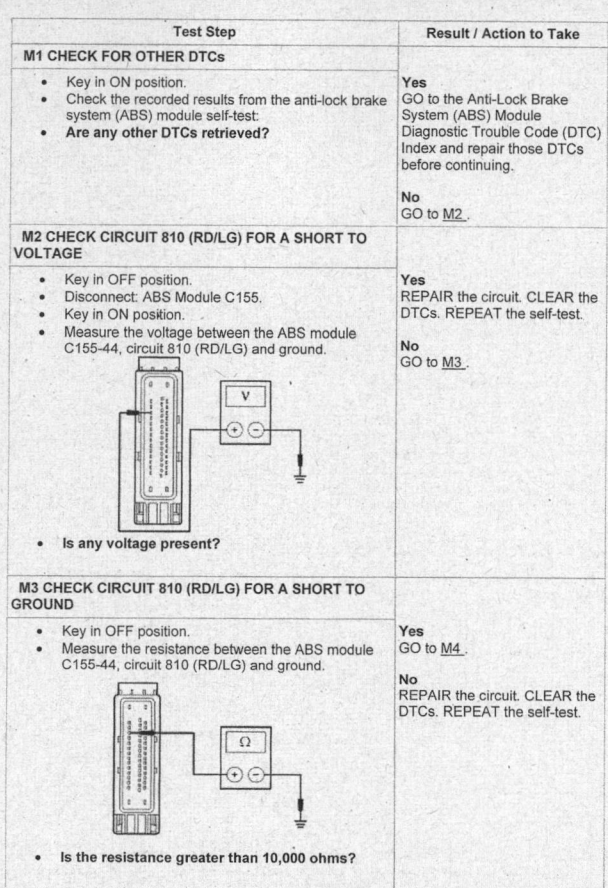

Test Step	Result / Action to Take
M1 CHECK FOR OTHER DTCs	
• Key in ON position. • Check the recorded results from the anti-lock brake system (ABS) module self-test: • **Are any other DTCs retrieved?**	**Yes** GO to the Anti-Lock Brake System (ABS) Module Diagnostic Trouble Code (DTC) Index and repair those DTCs before continuing. **No** GO to <u>M2</u>.
M2 CHECK CIRCUIT 810 (RD/LG) FOR A SHORT TO VOLTAGE	
• Key in OFF position. • Disconnect: ABS Module C155. • Key in ON position. • Measure the voltage between the ABS module C155-44, circuit 810 (RD/LG) and ground. • Is any voltage present?	**Yes** REPAIR the circuit. CLEAR the DTCs. REPEAT the self-test. **No** GO to <u>M3</u>.
M3 CHECK CIRCUIT 810 (RD/LG) FOR A SHORT TO GROUND	
• Key in OFF position. • Measure the resistance between the ABS module C155-44, circuit 810 (RD/LG) and ground. • Is the resistance greater than 10,000 ohms?	**Yes** GO to <u>M4</u>. **No** REPAIR the circuit. CLEAR the DTCs. REPEAT the self-test.

LTV0500000004829

Fig. 16   Test M, Code C1960: Driver Brake Apply Circuit Fault (Part 1 of 2)

Test Step	Result / Action to Take
N1 CHECK THE BRAKE PEDAL TRAVEL SENSOR CIRCUITRY FOR A SHORT TO VOLTAGE	
• Key in OFF position. • Disconnect: Anti-lock Brake System (ABS) Module C155. • Disconnect: Brake Pedal Travel Sensor C148. • Key in ON position. • Measure the voltage between the brake pedal travel sensor connector, harness side and ground as follows:	**Yes** REPAIR the circuit(s) in question. CLEAR the DTCs. REPEAT the self-test. **No** GO to <u>N2</u>.

Brake Pedal Travel Sensor Connector-Pin	Circuit
C148-1	3010 (TN)
C148-2	3011 (BK/OG)
C148-3	3012 (WH)

• Is any voltage present?	
N2 CHECK THE BRAKE PEDAL TRAVEL SENSOR CIRCUITRY FOR A SHORT TO GROUND	
• Key in OFF position. • Measure the resistance between the brake pedal travel sensor connector, harness side and ground as follows:	**Yes** GO to <u>N3</u>. **No**

LTV0500000004831

Fig. 17   Test N, Codes B2734, B2736, B2738 & B2740: Pedal Travel Sensor Fault (Part 1 of 4)

M4 CHECK FOR CORRECT ABS MODULE OPERATION	

• Disconnect all the ABS connectors.
• Check for:
  • corrosion
  • pushed-out pins
• Connect all the ABS connectors and make sure they seat correctly.
• Operate the system and verify the concern is still present.
• **Is the concern still present?**
	Yes
	INSTALL a new ABS module. TEST the system for normal operation.
	
	No
	The system is operating correctly at this time. The concern may have been caused by a loose or corroded connector. CLEAR the DTCs. REPEAT the self-test.

LTV0500000004830

Fig. 16   Test M, Code C1960: Driver Brake Apply Circuit Fault (Part 2 of 2)

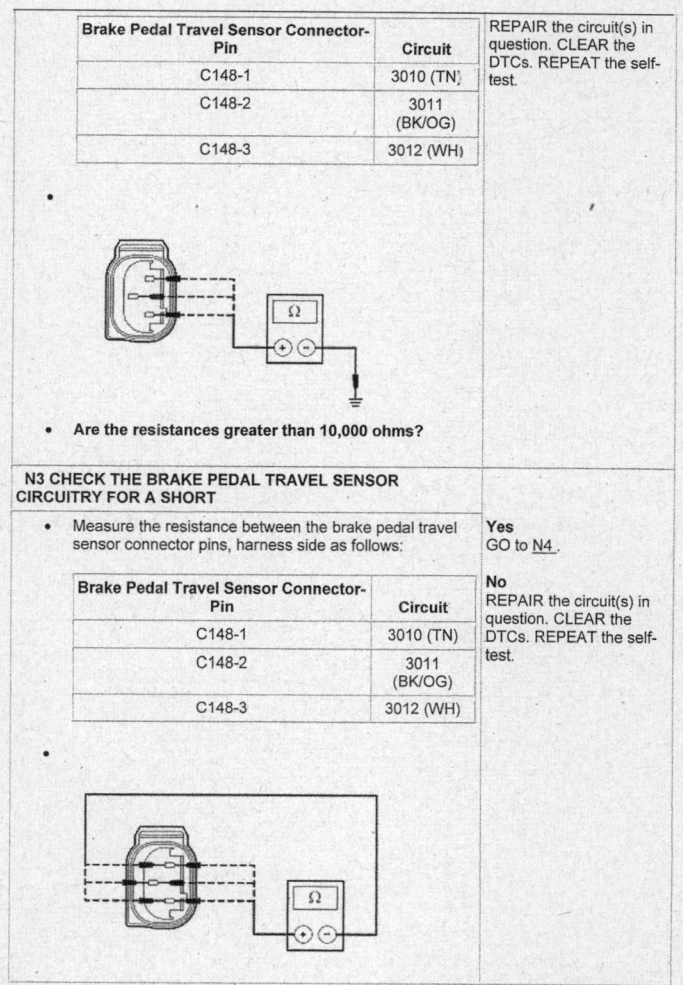

Brake Pedal Travel Sensor Connector-Pin	Circuit	REPAIR the circuit(s) in question. CLEAR the DTCs. REPEAT the self-test.
C148-1	3010 (TN)	
C148-2	3011 (BK/OG)	
C148-3	3012 (WH)	

• Are the resistances greater than 10,000 ohms?

Test Step	Result / Action to Take
N3 CHECK THE BRAKE PEDAL TRAVEL SENSOR CIRCUITRY FOR A SHORT	
• Measure the resistance between the brake pedal travel sensor connector pins, harness side as follows:	**Yes** GO to <u>N4</u>. **No** REPAIR the circuit(s) in question. CLEAR the DTCs. REPEAT the self-test.

Brake Pedal Travel Sensor Connector-Pin	Circuit
C148-1	3010 (TN)
C148-2	3011 (BK/OG)
C148-3	3012 (WH)

LTV0500000004832

Fig. 17   Test N, Codes B2734, B2736, B2738 & B2740: Pedal Travel Sensor Fault (Part 2 of 4)

- Are the resistances greater than 10,000 ohms?

N4 CHECK THE BRAKE PEDAL TRAVEL SENSOR CIRCUITRY FOR AN OPEN	
• Measure the resistance between the ABS module connector, harness side and the brake pedal travel sensor connector, harness side as follows:	**Yes** GO to N5. **No** REPAIR the circuit(s) in question. CLEAR the DTCs, REPEAT the self-test.

ABS Module Connector-Pin	Brake Pedal Travel Sensor Connector-Pin	Circuit
C155-26	C148-1	3010 (TN)
C155-24	C148-2	3011 (BK/OG)
C155-40	C148-3	3012 (WH)

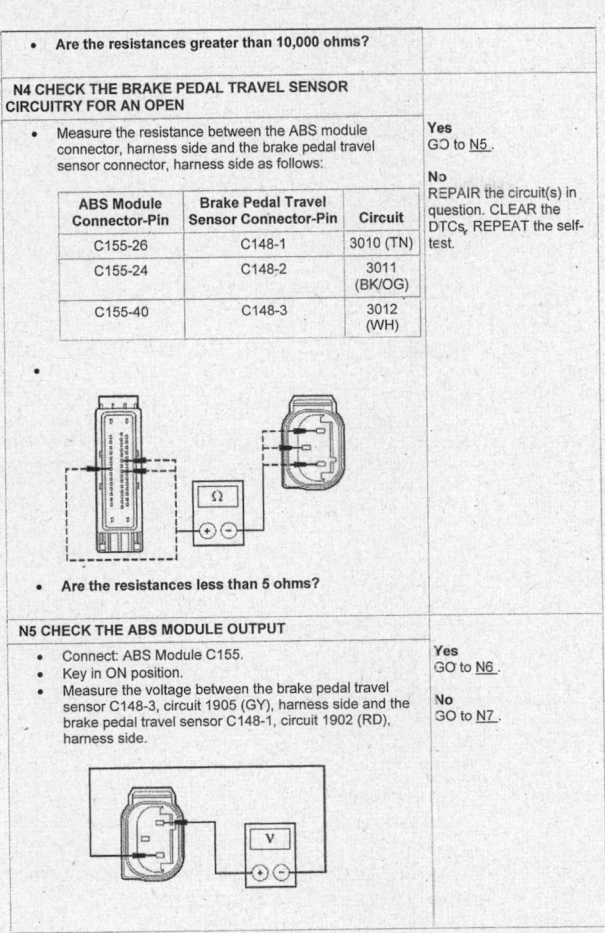

- Are the resistances less than 5 ohms?

N5 CHECK THE ABS MODULE OUTPUT	
• Connect: ABS Module C155. • Key in ON position. • Measure the voltage between the brake pedal travel sensor C148-3, circuit 1905 (GY), harness side and the brake pedal travel sensor C148-1, circuit 1902 (RD), harness side.	**Yes** GO to N6. **No** GO to N7.

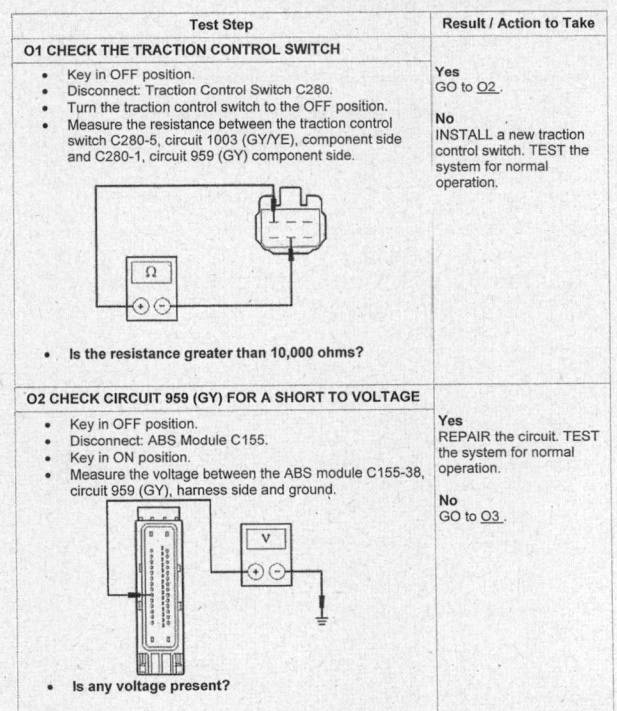

LTV0500000004833

Fig. 17 Test N, Codes B2734, B2736, B2738 & B2740: Pedal Travel Sensor Fault (Part 3 of 4)

Test Step	Result / Action to Take
O1 CHECK THE TRACTION CONTROL SWITCH	
• Key in OFF position. • Disconnect: Traction Control Switch C280. • Turn the traction control switch to the OFF position. • Measure the resistance between the traction control switch C280-5, circuit 1003 (GY/YE), component side and C280-1, circuit 959 (GY) component side.	**Yes** GO to O2. **No** INSTALL a new traction control switch. TEST the system for normal operation.

- Is the resistance greater than 10,000 ohms?

O2 CHECK CIRCUIT 959 (GY) FOR A SHORT TO VOLTAGE	
• Key in OFF position. • Disconnect: ABS Module C155. • Key in ON position. • Measure the voltage between the ABS module C155-38, circuit 959 (GY), harness side and ground.	**Yes** REPAIR the circuit. TEST the system for normal operation. **No** GO to O3.

- Is any voltage present?

LTV0500000004835

Fig. 18 Test O: Stability Assist Cannot Be Disabled (Part 1 of 2)

- Is the voltage approximately 5 volts?

N6 CHECK THE BRAKE PEDAL TRAVEL SENSOR OUTPUT	
• Connect: Brake Pedal Travel Sensor C148. • Disconnect: ABS Module C155. • Remove pin 24, circuit 1904 (GY/BK) from the ABS module connector. • Connect: ABS Module C155. • Key in ON position. • Measure the voltage between the ABS module C155-24, circuit 1904 (GY/BK), harness side and ground while pressing and releasing the brake pedal. • **Is the voltage between 0.35 and 0.65 volt with the brake pedal released and between 0.65 and 4.5 volts with the brake pedal pressed?**	**Yes** GO to N7. **No** INSTALL a new brake pedal travel sensor. CLEAR the DTCs. CALIBRATE the ABS module. REPEAT the self-test.

N7 CHECK FOR CORRECT ABS MODULE OPERATION	

• Disconnect all the ABS connectors.
• Check for:
  • corrosion
  • pushed-out pins
• Connect all the ABS connectors and make sure they seat correctly.
• Operate the system and verify the concern is still present.
• **Is the concern still present?**
	Yes
	INSTALL a new ABS module. TEST the system for normal operation.
	
	No
	The system is operating correctly at this time. The concern may have been caused by a loose or corroded connector. CLEAR the DTCs. REPEAT the self-test.

LTV0500000004834

Fig. 17 Test N, Codes B2734, B2736, B2738 & B2740: Pedal Travel Sensor Fault (Part 4 of 4)

O3 CHECK CIRCUIT 960 (BK/LB) FOR A SHORT TO GROUND	
• Key in OFF position. • Measure the resistance between the ABS module C155-13, circuit 960 (BK/LB), harness side and ground.	**Yes** GO to O4. **No** REPAIR the circuit. TEST the system for normal operation.

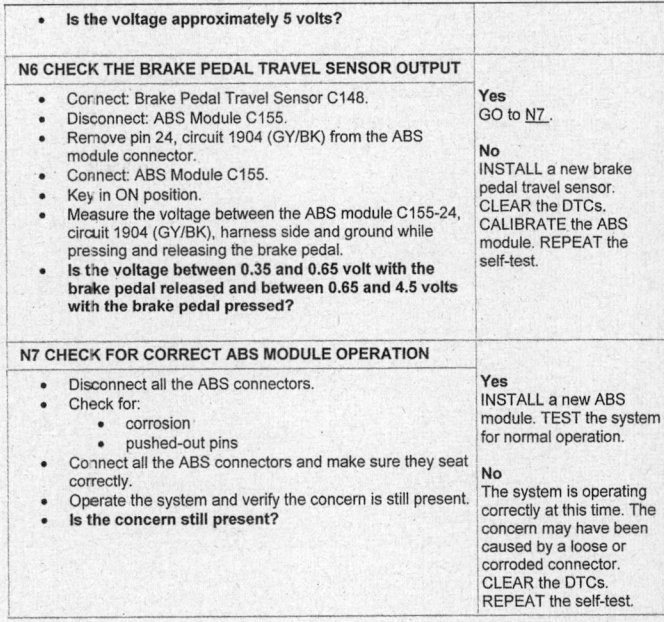

- Is the resistance greater than 10,000 ohms?

O4 CHECK FOR CORRECT ABS MODULE OPERATION	

• Disconnect all the ABS connectors.
• Check for:
  • corrosion
  • pushed-out pins
• Connect all the ABS connectors and make sure they seat correctly.
• Operate the system and verify the concern is still present.
• **Is the concern still present?**
	Yes
	INSTALL a new ABS module. TEST the system for normal operation.
	
	No
	The system is operating correctly at this time. The concern may have been caused by a loose or corroded connector. CLEAR the DTCs. REPEAT the self-test.

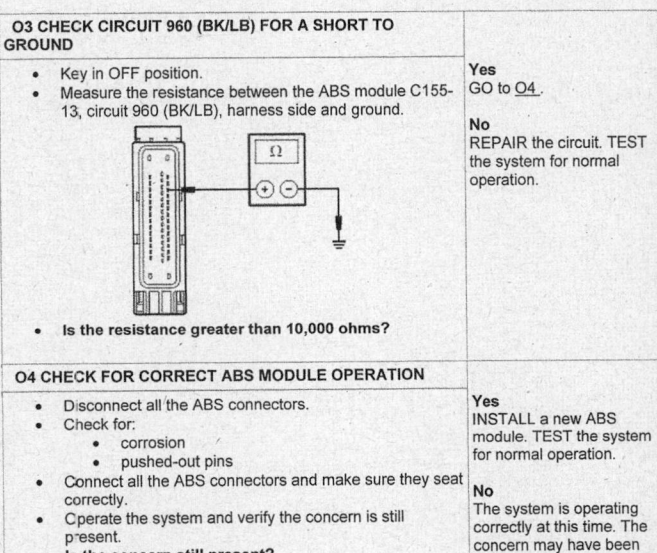

LTV0500000004836

Fig. 18 Test O: Stability Assist Cannot Be Disabled (Part 2 of 2)

Test Step	Result / Action to Take
P1 CHECK FOR DTCs	
• Connect the diagnostic tool. • Key in ON position. • Check the recorded results from the smart junction box (SJB) self-test: • **Is any other DTC retrieved with C1998?**	**Yes** GO to the appropriate pinpoint test for the DTC. Some of the pinpoint tests recommend anti-lock brake system (ABS) module calibration prior to any further diagnostics; in this case, GO to P2. **No** GO to P2.
P2 ABS MODULE CALIBRATION	
• Connect the diagnostic tool. • Start the engine. • **NOTE:** Be sure to rotate the steering wheel lock-to-lock during the calibration of the ABS system. • Carry out the ABS module calibration per the diagnostic tool instructions. • **Did the calibration complete for all of the stability assist sensors and did the stability assist lamp turn off?**	**Yes** GO to P3. **No** GO to P4. Some concerns will cause the calibration to not complete. If sent here from another pinpoint test, RETURN to that pinpoint test for further diagnostics.
P3 CLEAR DTC C1998	
NOTE: Clear DTC C1998 after completing the calibration. • Connect the diagnostic tool. • Key in ON position. • Clear the DTC. • **Did the DTC clear?**	**Yes** TEST DRIVE the vehicle. REPEAT the self-test. If sent here from another pinpoint test, RETURN to that pinpoint test for further diagnostics. **No** GO to P4.
P4 MONITOR THE STEERING POSITION SENSOR PIDS	
• Key in ON position. • Monitor the ABS module steering position sensor PIDS while rotating the steering wheel clockwise and counterclockwise. • **Are the 2 steering position sensor PID values switching as the wheel rotates?**	**Yes** Go To Pinpoint Test H. **No** Go To Pinpoint Test G.

LTV0500000004837

Fig. 19   Test P: Code C1998: Module Calibration Not Complete

Test Step	Result / Action to Take
Q1 DETERMINE THE CONDITION	
• Key in ON position. • Observe the traction control switch indicator. • **Is the OFF indicator on the traction control switch illuminated?**	**Yes** GO to Q2. **No** GO to Q4.
Q2 CHECK THE ABS MODULE	
• Key in OFF position. • Disconnect: ABS Module C155. • Key in ON position. • **Does the OFF indicator on the traction control switch continue to illuminate?**	**Yes** GO to Q3. **No** GO to Q7.
Q3 CHECK CIRCUIT 960 (BK/LB) FOR A SHORT TO GROUND	
• Key in OFF position. • Disconnect: Traction Control Switch C280. • Measure the resistance between the traction control switch C280-6, circuit 960 (BK/LB), harness side and ground. • **Is the resistance greater than 10,000 ohms?**	**Yes** INSTALL a new traction control switchTEST the system for normal operation. **No** REPAIR the circuit. TEST the system for normal operation.
Q4 CHECK CIRCUIT 1003 (GY/YE) FOR AN OPEN	
• Key in OFF position. • Disconnect: Traction Control Switch C280.	**Yes** GO to Q5.

LTV0500000004838

Fig. 20   Test Q: Traction Control Switch Indicator Is Never/Always ON (Part 1 of 3)

Test Step	Result / Action to Take
Q7 CHECK FOR CORRECT ABS MODULE OPERATION	

• Disconnect all the ABS connectors.
 • Check for:
   • corrosion
   • pushed-out pins
 • Connect all the ABS connectors and make sure they seat correctly.
 • Operate the system and verify the concern is still present.
 • **Is the concern still present?**
	Yes
	 INSTALL a new ABS module. TEST the system for normal operation.
	
	 No
	 The system is operating correctly at this time. The concern may have been caused by a loose or corroded connector. CLEAR the DTCs. REPEAT the self-test.

LTV0500000004840

Fig. 20   Test Q: Traction Control Switch Indicator Is Never/Always ON (Part 3 of 3)

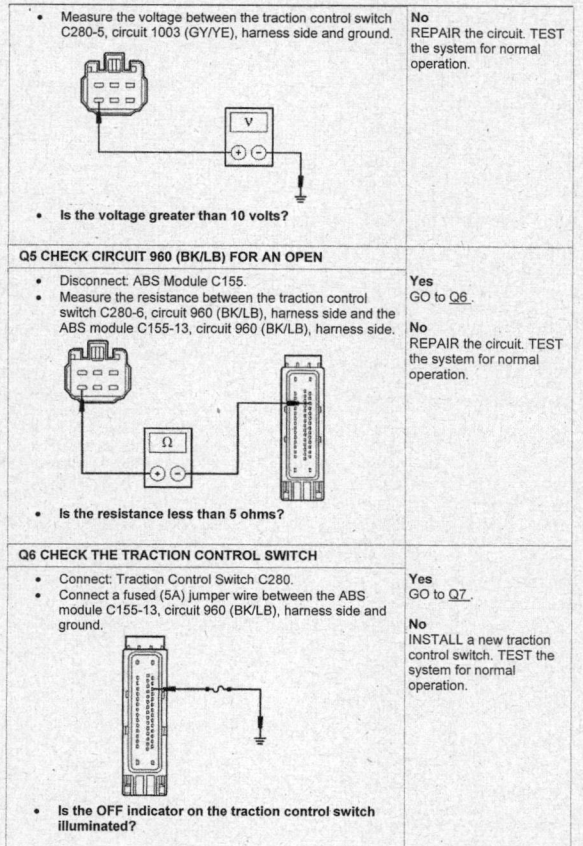

Test Step	Result / Action to Take
• Measure the voltage between the traction control switch C280-5, circuit 1003 (GY/YE), harness side and ground. • **Is the voltage greater than 10 volts?**	**No** REPAIR the circuit. TEST the system for normal operation.
Q5 CHECK CIRCUIT 960 (BK/LB) FOR AN OPEN	
• Disconnect: ABS Module C155. • Measure the resistance between the traction control switch C280-6, circuit 960 (BK/LB), harness side and the ABS module C155-13, circuit 960 (BK/LB), harness side. • **Is the resistance less than 5 ohms?**	**Yes** GO to Q6. **No** REPAIR the circuit. TEST the system for normal operation.
Q6 CHECK THE TRACTION CONTROL SWITCH	
• Connect: Traction Control Switch C280. • Connect a fused (5A) jumper wire between the ABS module C155-13, circuit 960 (BK/LB), harness side and ground. • **Is the OFF indicator on the traction control switch illuminated?**	**Yes** GO to Q7. **No** INSTALL a new traction control switch. TEST the system for normal operation.

LTV0500000004839

Fig. 20   Test Q: Traction Control Switch Indicator Is Never/Always ON (Part 2 of 3)

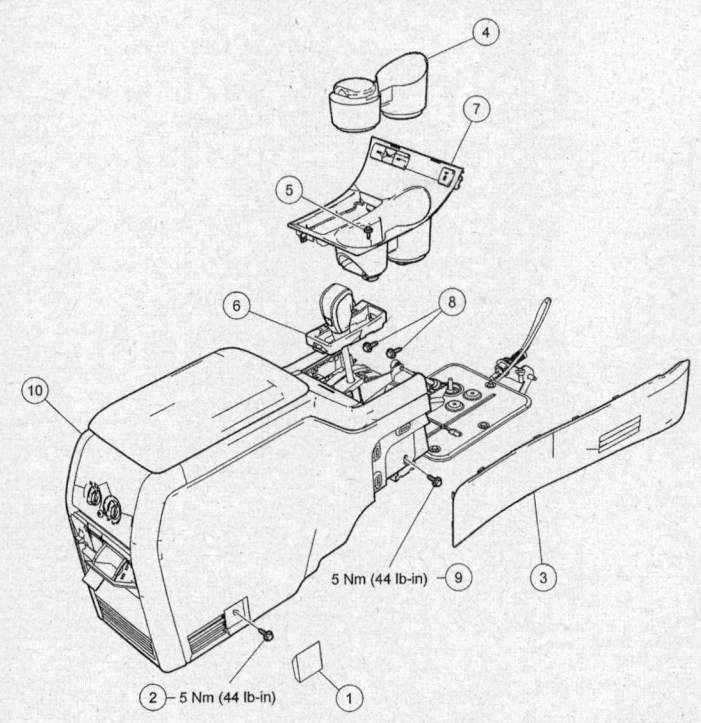

Item	Description
1	Bolt cover (2 required)
2	Floor console bolt (2 required)
3	Floor console side finish trim panel (RH/LH)
4	Cup holder/ash receptacle insert
5	Floor console finish panel screw
6	Shift control bezel
7	Floor console center finish trim panel
8	Floor console screws
9	Floor console bolt (2 required)
10	Floor console

LTV0500000004844

Fig. 21 Floor console replacement (Part 2 of 2)

LTV0500000004843

Fig. 21 Floor console replacement (Part 1 of 2)

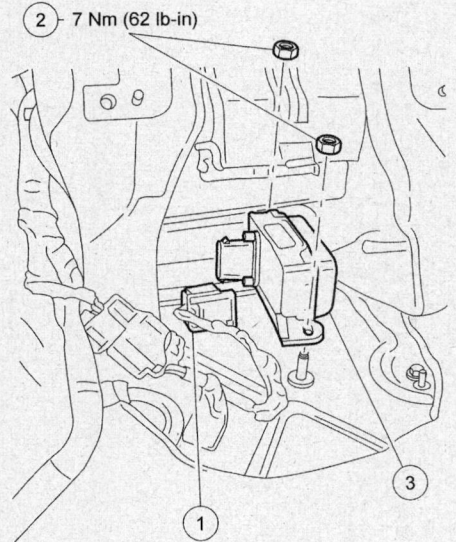

Item	Description
1	Accelerometer electrical connector
2	Accelerometer bracket nuts (2 required)
3	Accelerometer

LTV0500000004845

Fig. 22 Accelerometer replacement

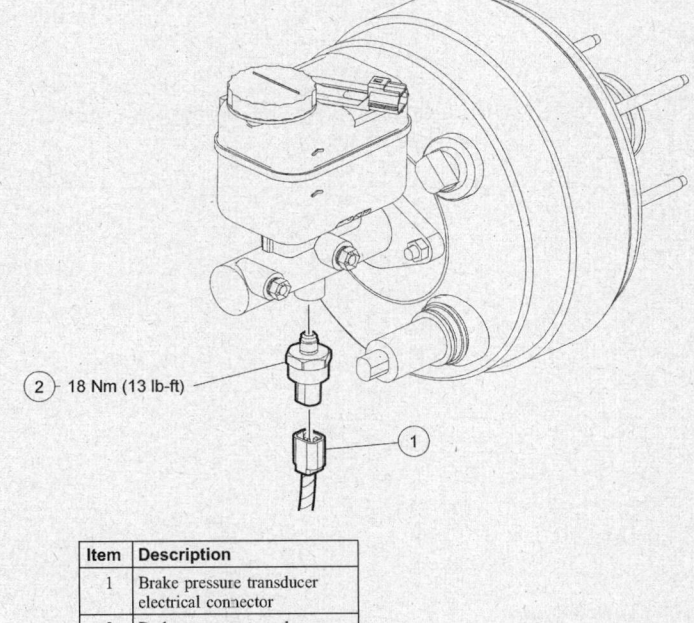

Item	Description
1	Brake pressure transducer electrical connector
2	Brake pressure transducer

LTV0500000004846

Fig. 23 Brake pressure transducer replacement

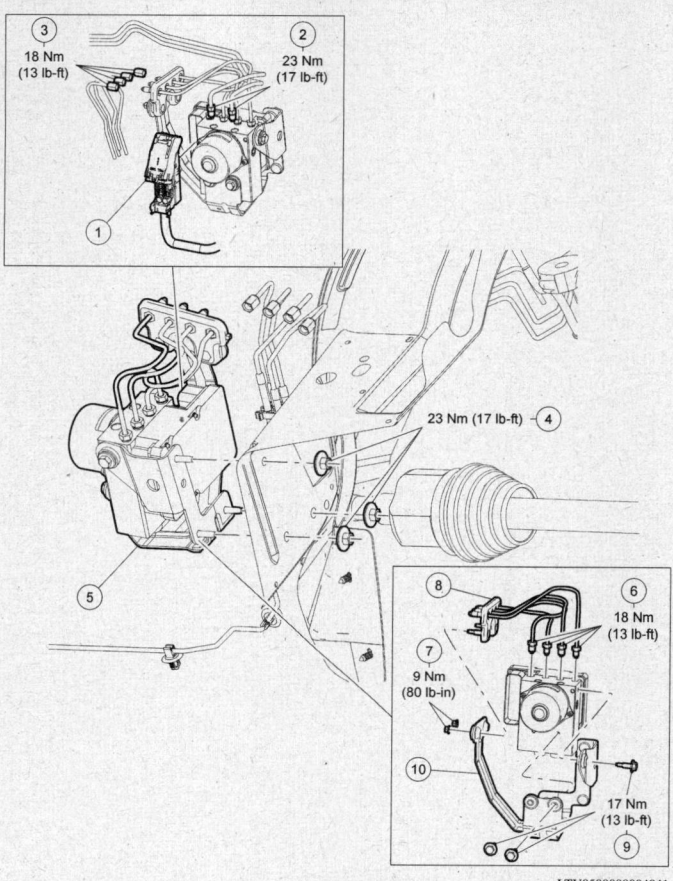

Fig. 24 Hydraulic Control Unit (HCU) replacement (Part 1 of 2)

Item	Description
1	Anti-lock brake system (ABS) module electrical connector
2	Brake line-to-HCU nuts (M12-1)
3	Brake line-to-brake line nuts
4	HCU bracket-to-frame nuts (3 required)
5	HCU assembly
6	Brake line-to-HCU nuts (M10-1)
7	Bracket-to-brake line holder nuts (2 required)
8	Brake line holder assembly
9	Bracket-to-HCU bolts (3 required)
10	HCU Bracket

LTV0500000004842

Fig. 24 Hydraulic Control Unit (HCU) replacement (Part 2 of 2)

Escape & Mariner

NOTE: Electrical Symbol & Wire Color Code Identification Located In The Front Of This Manual May Be Used As An Aid When Using Wiring Circuits Found In This Section.

NOTE: Refer To "Computer Relearn Procedures" Located In The Front Of This Manual When Battery Power To The Computer Has Been Interrupted.

INDEX

	Page No.		Page No.		Page No.
Description	5-21	Diagnostic Trouble Code		Precautions	5-21
Regenerative Braking System	5-22	Interpretation	5-22	Battery Ground Cable	5-21
System Operation	5-21	Wiring Diagrams	5-22	Brake Fluid Handling	5-21
Diagnosis & Testing	5-22	Diagnostic Chart Index	5-28	High-Voltage Traction Battery	
Accessing Diagnostic Trouble		Hydraulic Control Unit (HCU)		Systems Depowering	5-21
Codes	5-22	Depressurization	5-23	System Service	5-22
Clearing Diagnostic Trouble		Component Replacement	5-23	Brake System Bleed	5-22
Codes	5-22	ABS Control Module	5-23	Except Hybrid	5-22
Diagnostic Tests	5-22	Accelerometer	5-23	Hybrid	5-22
Inspection & Verification	5-22	Hydraulic Control Unit (HCU)	5-23	Troubleshooting	5-22
Pinpoint Tests	5-22	Wheel Speed Sensor	5-23	Symptom Chart	5-22

PRECAUTIONS

Battery Ground Cable

Prior to service disconnect battery ground cable and isolate as required.

Brake Fluid Handling

Brake fluid can cause serious injury and vehicle damage if not handled properly. Avoid contact with eyes and do not allow fluid to splash or spill on painted surfaces. Wash hands thoroughly after handling.

High-Voltage Traction Battery Systems Depowering

The nominal high voltage traction battery (HVTB) voltage is 330 volts DC. The buffer zone must be set up. The high voltage traction battery and charging system contains high voltage components and wiring. High voltage cables and wiring are orange in color. High voltage insulated safety gloves and a face shield must be worn when carrying out any diagnostics on this vehicle. Failure to follow these instructions may result in severe personal injury or death.

Before carrying out any removal and installation procedures of the high voltage traction battery system, the high voltage traction battery must be depowered. The high voltage insulated safety gloves that are to be worn while working on the high voltage system should be of the appropriate safety and protection rating for use on the high voltage system. They must be inspected before use and must always be worn in conjunction with the leather outer glove. Any hole in the rubber insulating glove is a potential entry point for high voltage. Failure to follow these instructions may result in severe personal injury or death.

High voltage insulated safety gloves and a face shield must be worn when working with high voltage cables. The ignition switch must be OFF for a minimum of 5 minutes before removing high voltage cables. The buffer zone is required only when working with the high voltage system. Failure to follow these instructions may result in severe personal injury or death.

1. **Buffer zone is required only when working with high voltage system.** Set up buffer zone around vehicle as follows:
   a. Position vehicle in repair bay.
   b. Position four orange cones around corners of vehicle to mark off a 3 foot perimeter around vehicle, **Fig. 1.**
   c. Do not allow any unauthorized personnel into buffer zone during repairs involving high voltage system.
   d. Only personnel trained for repair on high voltage system are to be permitted in buffer zone.
2. Rotate service disconnect plug from lock position to unlock position.
3. Remove service disconnect plug, then place in servicing shipping position. If **service disconnect plug is left out and placed on bench or toolbox, dirt or other contaminants may enter HVTB which can cause damage.**
4. Insert service disconnect plug into servicing shipping position, this will disconnect HVTB.
5. Reverse procedure to connect.

DESCRIPTION

System Operation

The anti-lock brake system (ABS) module, with or without stability assist, simultaneously manages the anti-lock braking, traction control and engine control systems to maintain vehicle control during deceleration and acceleration. The ABS accomplishes this by communicating with the other modules over the high speed controller area network (HS-CAN) bus.

When the ignition switch is in the RUN position, the module carries out a preliminary electrical check and, at approximately 20 km/h (12 mph), the hydraulic pump motor is turned on for approximately one half-second. Any malfunction of the anti-lock brake system disables the traction control and stability assist (if equipped). The ABS module communicates with the instrument cluster over the HS-CAN bus and the cluster illuminates the anti-lock brake warning indicator. However, the power-assist braking system functions normally.

With the ignition switch in the START or RUN positions, the stability assist module functions similarly to a conventional ABS module by monitoring and comparing the rotational speed of each wheel. The wheel speed sensors electrically sense each tooth of the anti-lock sensor ring as they pass through the sensor magnetic field. When the stability assist module detects an impending wheel lock, wheel spin or vehicle motion that is inconsistent with the driver commands, it modulates brake pressure to the appropriate brake caliper(s). The stability assist module triggers the hydraulic control unit (HCU) to open and close the appropriate solenoid valves. Once the affected wheel(s) return to the desired speed,

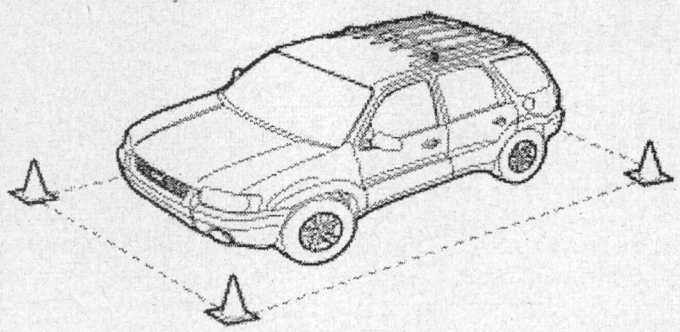

Fig. 1   Setting up a buffer zone

the stability assist module returns the sole-noid valves to their normal position, and normal base brake operation is restored.

Regenerative Braking System

On Hybrid models, instead of just using the brakes to stop the vehicle, the electric motor that drives the hybrid electric vehicle can also slow the vehicle. In this mode, the electric motor acts as a generator and charges the batteries while the vehicle is slowing down. To achieve this, the Anti-Lock Brake System (ABS) module calcu-lates the amount of speed reduction requested by the driver through the accel-erator pedal position and brake pedal travel sensor. The ABS module measures the in-ertia of the vehicle through the longitudinal accelerometer and determines if the re-quired deceleration has been achieved. During deceleration/braking, the Power-train Control Module (PCM) partially en-gages the electronically Controlled Continuously Variable Transmission (eCVT) to be turned by the vehicle's wheels and slow it down. The ABS module re-quests the powertrain more or less depen-dant upon the driver request through the pedals. If the desired deceleration is not achieved through regenerative braking, the ABS module applies the friction brake pads to accommodate the driver request. The driver does not, under normal circumstanc-es, have direct control over the amount of brake pressure that is applied to the rotors. In the event that the ABS module detects a fault which requires the deactivation of this system, the ABS module relinquishes con-trol of braking and the driver will still have the use of manual hydraulic brakes.

Since the regenerative braking uses the electric motor to slow the vehicle's front wheels, front brake pad wear is reduced. The rear brake pads, because of the regen-erative braking, wear at approximately twice the rate of the front brake pads.

TROUBLESHOOTING

Symptom Chart

Refer to **Figs. 2 and 3** for symptom charts.

Condition	Possible Sources	Action
• No communication with the module — anti-lock brake control module	• CJB Fuse 5 (5A). • Circuitry. • Anti-lock brake control module.	• GO to PINPOINT TEST A.
• Loss of sensor signal during vehicle deceleration or sensor signal drops out at low speed	• Anti-lock brake sensor indicator. • Sensor output is weak. • Air gap.	• GO to PINPOINT TEST D.
• Unwarranted ABS activity	• Circuitry. • Anti-lock brake sensor.	• GO to PINPOINT TEST D.
• Maladjusted rear brakes or ''grabby'' brake shoe or pad linings	• Rear brake adjustment. • Linings.	• DIAGNOSE brake system.
• Base brake mechanical concern for wheels lockup	• Rear brake shoe linings. • Wheel cylinder. • Rear brakes. • Parking brake. • Rear axle seal.	• DIAGNOSE brake system. • DIAGNOSE parking brake. • DIAGNOSE brake system.
• Base brake hydraulic concern (soft pedal)	• Brake line or hose, fitting, master cylinder, wheel cylinder or caliper. • Air in brake system.	• DIAGNOSE brake system.
• Base brake mechanical concern (hard pedal)	• Vacuum boost. • Wheel cylinder or caliper. • Brake line or hose.	• DIAGNOSE brake system.
• Base brake hydraulic concern during medium/hard brake application	• Brake line or hose, fitting, master cylinder, wheel cylinder or caliper. • Air in brake system.	• DIAGNOSE brake system.
• Base brake mechanical concern during medium/hard brake application	• Vacuum boost. • Wheel cylinder or caliper. • Brake line or hose. • Brake shoe or pad linings.	• DIAGNOSE brake system.

Fig. 2   Symptom chart (Part 1 of 2). 2002–04

DIAGNOSIS & TESTING

Accessing Diagnostic Trouble Codes

Connect a suitably programmed scan tool and Vehicle Communication Module (VCM) with appropriate adapters, or equiv-alents, to the Data Link Connector (DCL) located in the passenger compartment be-neath the instrument panel. Follow tool manufacturer's instructions for accessing Diagnostic Trouble Codes (DTC).

Diagnostic Trouble Code Interpretation

Refer to **Figs. 4 and 5** for diagnostic trouble code interpretation.

Wiring Diagrams

Refer to **Figs. 6 through 9** for wiring dia-gram.

Diagnostic Tests

INSPECTION & VERIFICATION

Verify concern by applying brakes under different conditions. Inspect for obvious signs of mechanical and electrical damage such as parking brake cable, tire pressure, tire size or mismatched tires. Check for blown fuse, connectors or connections, harness routing, wire chaffing, circuitry open/shorted and indicator bulb.

PINPOINT TESTS

Refer to **Figs. 10 through 22** for pinpoint tests.

Clearing Diagnostic Trouble Codes

Connect a suitably programmed scan tool and Vehicle Communication Module (VCM) with appropriate adapters, or equiv-alents, to the Data Link Connector (DCL) located in the passenger compartment be-neath the instrument panel. Follow tool manufacturer's instructions for clearing Di-agnostic Trouble Codes (DTC).

SYSTEM SERVICE

Brake System Bleed

EXCEPT HYBRID

Refer to "Hydraulic Brake Systems" chapter for bleeding procedure.

HYBRID

1. Connect suitable pressure bleeder to vehicle. **Do not apply pressure to hy-draulic brake system at this time.**
2. Install rubber drain hoses to bleeder screws, then submerge open ends of hoses in clean brake fluid.
3. Connect suitably programed diagnos-tic tool to Data Link Connector (DLC).
4. Using pressure bleeder, apply 2 bars of pressure to brake system.
5. Access service bleed function on diag-nostic tool and follow manufacturers instructions.
6. While following instructions on diag-nostic tool, apply brake pedal one full stroke, then completely release brake pedal. Continue to follow instructions on diagnostic tool to complete service bleed procedure.
7. Diagnostic tool indicates when service bleed procedure is not followed cor-rectly. Refer to service bleed error code chart, **Fig. 23.**

HYDRAULIC CONTROL UNIT (HCU) DEPRESSURIZATION

Mark the level of brake fluid in the master cylinder before starting the depressurization of the system. When the brake fluid level has increased approximately 0.47 inch (12 mm), the system has fully depressurized.

Turn the ignition switch to the OFF position and let the vehicle stand at lest four minutes without opening the doors, pressing the brake pedal, or activating the key fob. **If any of these actions occur the system pressurizes and the procedure must be repeated.**

Component Replacement

ABS CONTROL MODULE

EXCEPT HYBRID

1. **On models equipped with 2.0L & 2.3L engines,** unclip throttle cable from outlet pipe, then loosen screw clamp and disconnect pipe.
2. **On models equipped with 3.0L engine,** disconnect crankcase vent hose, then loosen screw clamps. Air cleaner outlet pipe should be securely sealed to prevent unmetered air from entering engine.
3. **On all models,** disconnect electrical connectors, then remove retaining bolts from module.
4. Raise and support vehicle, then remove screws and control module.
5. Reverse procedure to install, **Torque** control module bolts to 18 inch lbs.

HYBRID

The ABS module is part of the HCU. Do not separate the ABS module from the HCU. Replace HCU and module as a unit.

ACCELEROMETER

1. Depower high-voltage traction battery system as outlined under "Precautions."
2. Remove floor console, **Fig. 24.**
3. Disconnect accelerometer electrical connector, **Fig. 25.**
4. Remove mounting nuts, then the accelerometer.
5. Reverse procedure to install, noting the following:
   a. When installing accelerometer electrical connector must face driver seat.
   b. **Torque** accelerometer mounting nuts to 62 inch lbs.

Condition	Possible Sources	Action
• Base brake mechanical concern for vehicle pulls	• Rear brake. • Caliper. • Brake pad or shoe wear.	• DIAGNOSE brake system.
• Base brake hydraulic concern for vehicle pulls	• Brake line or hose.	• DIAGNOSE brake system.
• One wheel locks up; no DTCs recorded	• Base brake. • Dump valve. • ISO valve.	• DIAGNOSE brake system. • INSTALL a new electronic hydraulic control unit.
• The ABS warning indicator does not self check	• Bulb. • Circuitry. • Instrument cluster. • Anti-lock brake control module.	• GO to PINPOINT TEST F.
• Soft or excessive brake pedal	• Brake line or hose, fitting, master cylinder, wheel cylinder, wheel cylinder or caliper. • Air in brake system. • HCU.	• DIAGNOSE brake system.
• Yellow ABS light always on, no DTC	• Circuitry. • Module.	• GO to PINPOINT TEST G.

FM4020001666020X

Fig. 2   Symptom chart (Part 2 of 2). 2002–04

HYDRAULIC CONTROL UNIT (HCU)

EXCEPT HYBRID

1. **On models equipped with 2.0L & 2.3L engines,** unclip throttle cable from outlet pipe, then loosen screw clamp and disconnect pipe.
2. **On models equipped with 3.0L engine,** disconnect crankcase vent hose, then loosen screw clamps. Air cleaner outlet pipe should be securely sealed to prevent unmetered air from entering engine.
3. **On all models,** disconnect electrical connector, **Fig. 26,** then the brake lines.
4. Remove HCU bracket retaining bolts, then the HCU from bracket.
5. Remove screws, then the control module if necessary.
6. Reverse procedure to install noting, the following:
   a. **Torque** control module retaining bolts to 18 inch lbs.
   b. **Torque** HCU retaining bolts to 80 inch lbs.
   c. **Torque** inlet and outlet brake line nuts to 11 ft. lbs.
   d. **Torque** HCU bracket bolts to 17 ft. lbs.

HYBRID

1. Depressurize HCU as outlined under "Hydraulic Control Unit (HCU) Depressurization."
2. Depower high-voltage traction battery system as outlined under "Precautions."
3. Remove Battery Junction Box (BJB) fuses 24 (50A) and 31 (50A).
4. Remove HCU heat shield pin-type fastener, **Fig. 27.**
5. Remove heat shield retaining screw, then the shield.
6. Disconnect electrical connector by rotating protective cover.
7. Release clamp and remove brake fluid low pressure feed hose.
8. Release clamp and remove brake fluid low pressure return hose.
9. Disconnect 10 mm brake line to HCU fittings. Note order of brake lines.
10. Disconnect 12 mm brake line to HCU fittings. Note order of brake lines.
11. **On early build models,** remove three HCU bracket to frame bolts.
12. **On late build models,** remove three HCU bracket to frame nuts.
13. **On all models,** disconnect brake line from routing clip located at bottom of HCU bracket.
14. Disconnect brake line from routing clip located at bottom of HCU bracket.
15. Remove HCU assembly.
16. Reverse procedure to install, noting the following:
    a. **Torque** brake line fittings to 13 ft. lbs.
    b. **On early build models,** torque HCU bracket to frame bolts to 17 ft. lbs.
    c. **On late build models,** torque HCU bracket to frame nuts 22 ft. lbs.
    d. **Torque** heat shield bolts to 71 inch lbs.

WHEEL SPEED SENSOR

FRONT

1. Raise and support vehicle, then remove wheel and tire.
2. Detach grommet from body, then pull connector through hole and disconnect sensor wiring.
3. Detach retainer, then remove bolts and clean off any dirt around sensor.
4. Remove sensor from vehicle.
5. Reverse procedure to install.

REAR

1. Raise and support vehicle, then remove wheel and tire.
2. Detach grommet from body, then pull connector through hole and disconnect sensor wiring.
3. Detach retainer, then remove bolts and clean off any dirt around sensor.
4. Remove sensor from vehicle.
5. Reverse procedure to install.

ANTI-LOCK BRAKES

Condition	Possible Sources
• No communication with the anti-lock brake system (ABS) module	• Circuitry. • ABS module.
• The red brake warning indicator stays on when the ignition switch is in the RUN position	• Circuitry. • Parking brake. • Instrument cluster. • Anti-lock brake system (ABS) module. • Brake fluid level sensor.
• The yellow anti-lock brake system (ABS) warning indicator does not self-check	• Circuitry. • Instrument cluster. • ABS module.
• Spongy brake pedal with no warning indicator	• Air in brake hydraulic system.

LTV0500000004115

Fig. 3   Symptom chart. 2005-06

Code	Description
B1342	ECU Is Defective
B1676	Battery Pack Voltage Out Of Range
B2477	Module Configuration Failure
B2900	VIN Mismatched
C1095	ABS Hydraulic Pump Motor Circuit Failure
C1145	Wheel Speed Sensor RF Input Circuit Failure
C1155	Wheel Speed Sensor LF Input Circuit Failure
C1165	Wheel Speed Sensor RR Input Circuit Failure
C1175	Wheel Speed Sensor LR Input Circuit Failure
C1233	Wheel Speed Sensor LF Input Signal Missing
C1234	Wheel Speed Sensor RF Input Signal Missing
C1235	Wheel Speed Sensor RR Input Signal Missing
C1236	Wheel Speed Sensor LR Input Signal Missing
U1900	CAN Communication Bus Fault-Receive Error
U2023	Fault Received From External Node

Fig. 4   Diagnostic trouble code interpretation. Except Hybrid

Code	Description
B1317	Battery Voltage High
B1318	Battery Voltage Low
B1342	ECU Is Defective
B2477	Module Configuration Failure
B2741	Sensor Cluster Loop End
B2900	VIN Mismatched
C1095	ABS Hydraulic Pump Motor Circuit Failure
C1141	Wheel Speed Sensor LF Tone Ring Tooth Missing Fault
C1142	Wheel Speed Sensor RF Tone Ring Tooth Missing Fault
C1143	Wheel Speed Sensor LR Tone Ring Tooth Missing Fault
C1143	Wheel Speed Sensor RR Tone Ring Tooth Missing Fault
C1145	Wheel Speed Sensor RF Input Circuit Failure
C1155	Wheel Speed Sensor LF Input Circuit Failure
C1165	Wheel Speed Sensor RR Input Circuit Failure
C1175	Wheel Speed Sensor LR Input Circuit Failure
C1218	Lamp ABS Warning Output Circuit Failure
C1222	Speed Wheel Mismatch
C1233	Wheel Speed LF Input Signal Missing
C1234	Wheel Speed RF Input Signal Missing
C1235	Wheel Speed RR Input Signal Missing
C1236	Wheel Speed LR Input Signal Missing
C1305	Longitudinal Acceleration Sensor Signal Fault
C1998	Module Calibration Not Complete
C2768	Longitudinal Acceleration Sensor Electrical Failure
C2769	Longitudinal Acceleration Sensor Circuit Failure
C2778	Sensor Cluster Power Supply Failure
C2783	Sensor Cluster Incorrect
U1901	CAN Network #2 Communication Bus Fault - Receive Error
U2060	CAN Network #2 Communication Bus Fault - Receive Error
U2062	ECU Redundant Ground Circuit Open
u2527	CAN Network #2 Communication Bus Off - Transmit Error

Fig. 5   Diagnostic trouble code interpretation. Hybrid

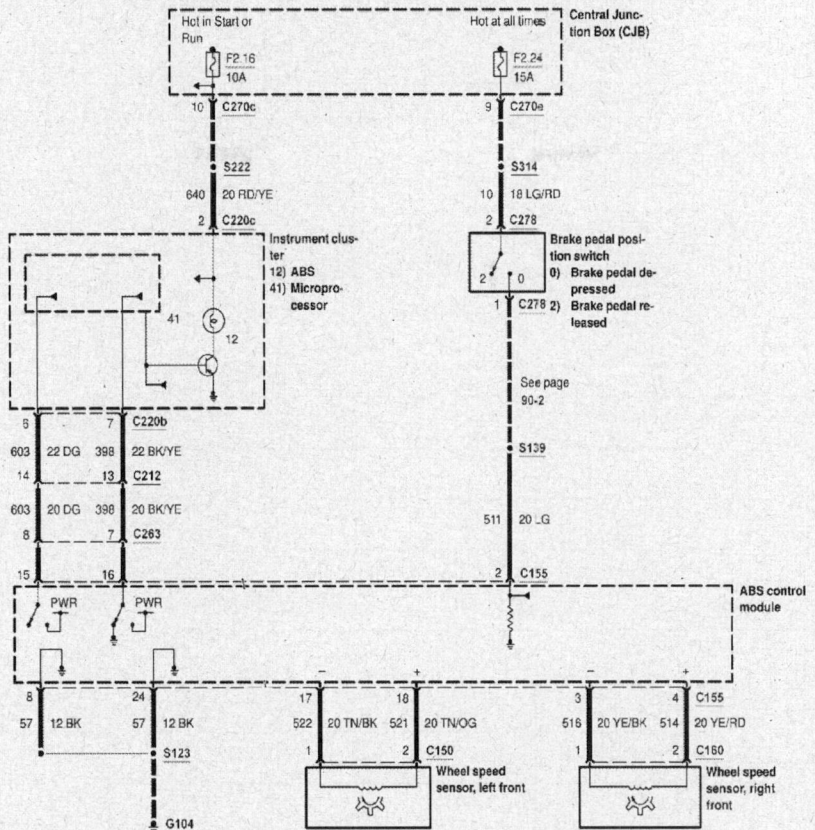

Fig. 6 Wiring diagram (Part 1 of 2). 2002–04

LTV0500000004116

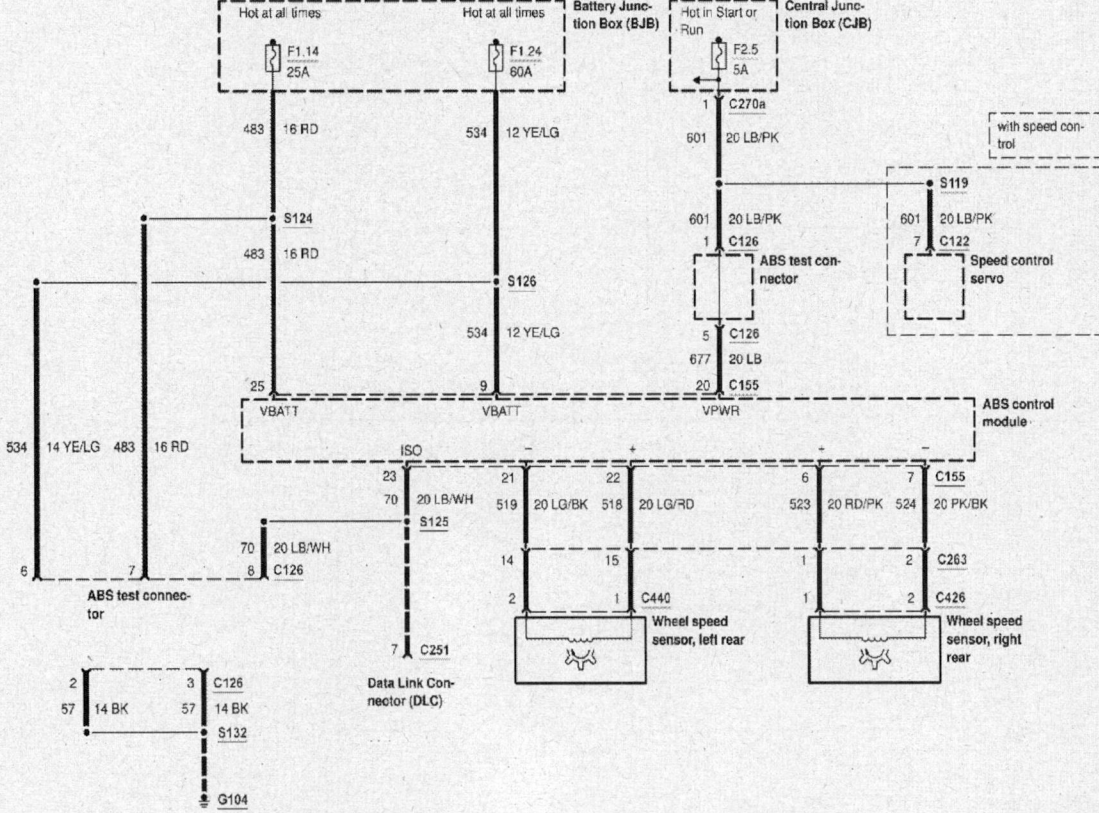

Fig. 6 Wiring diagram (Part 2 of 2). 2002–04

LTV0500000004117

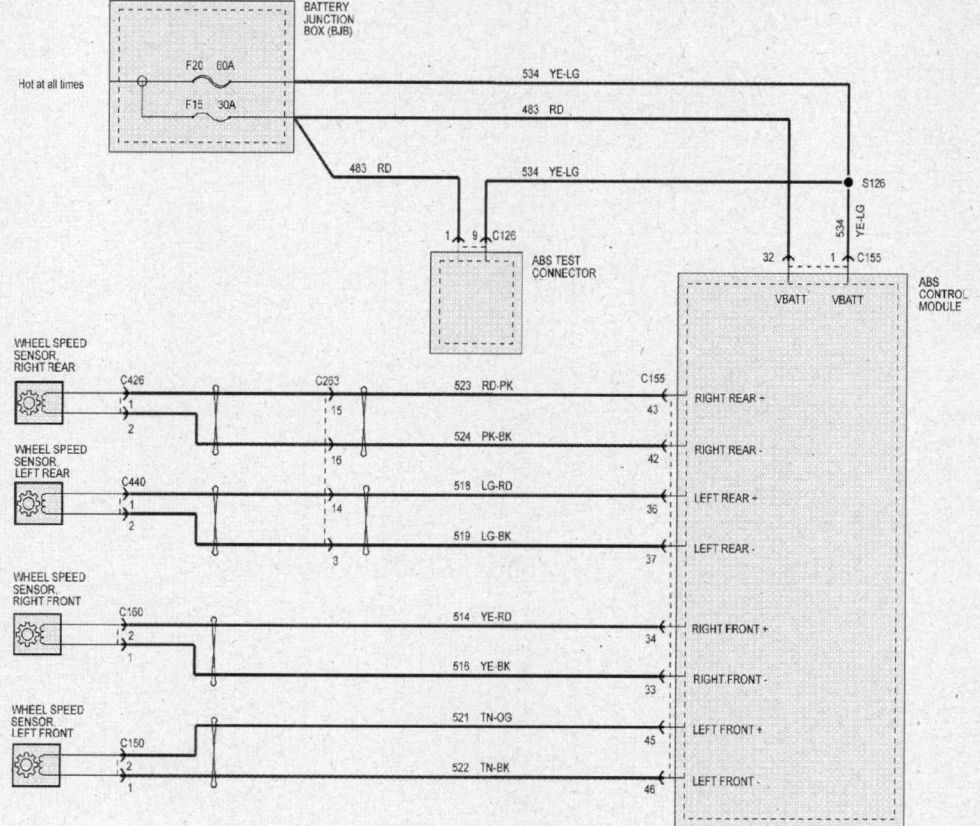

Fig. 7   Wiring diagram (Part 1 of 2). 2005

LTV0500000004118

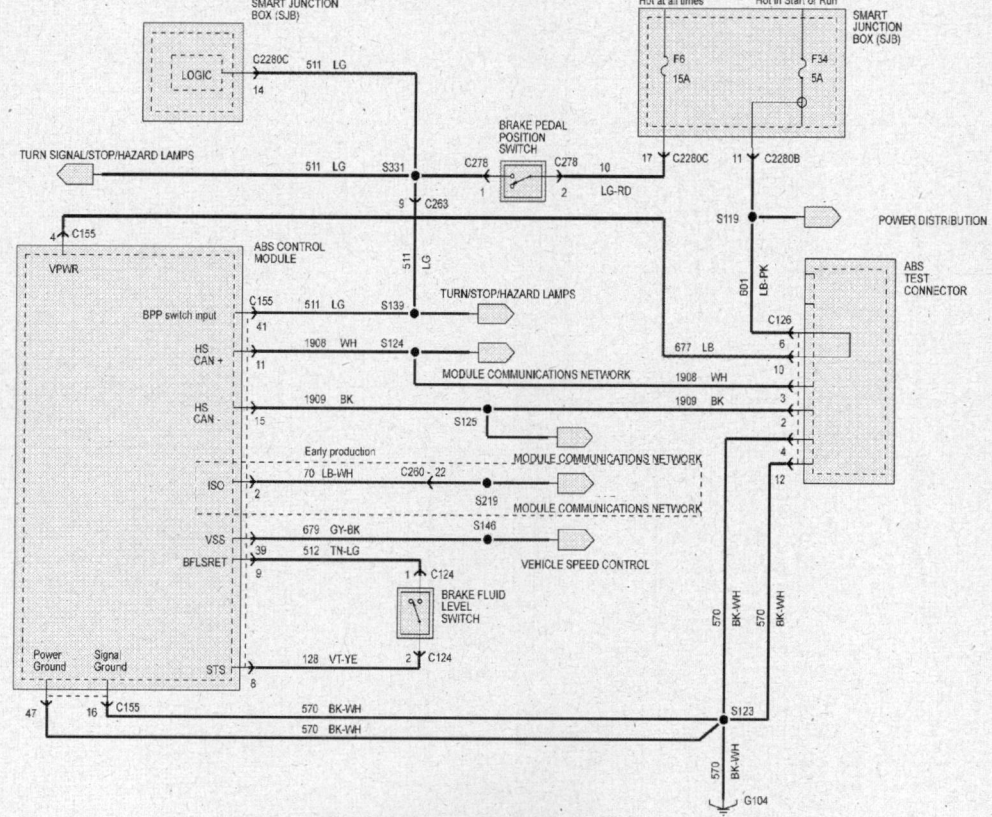

Fig. 7   Wiring diagram (Part 2 of 2). 2005

LTV0500000004119

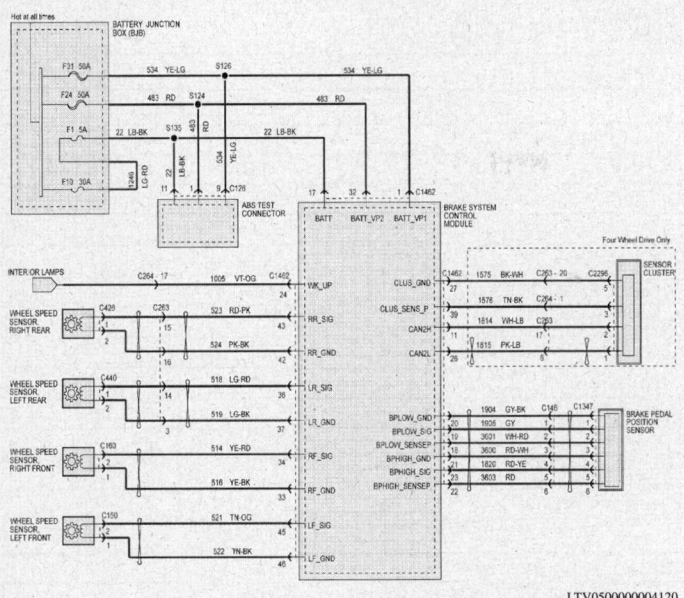

Fig. 8   Wiring diagram (Part 1 of 2). Hybrid

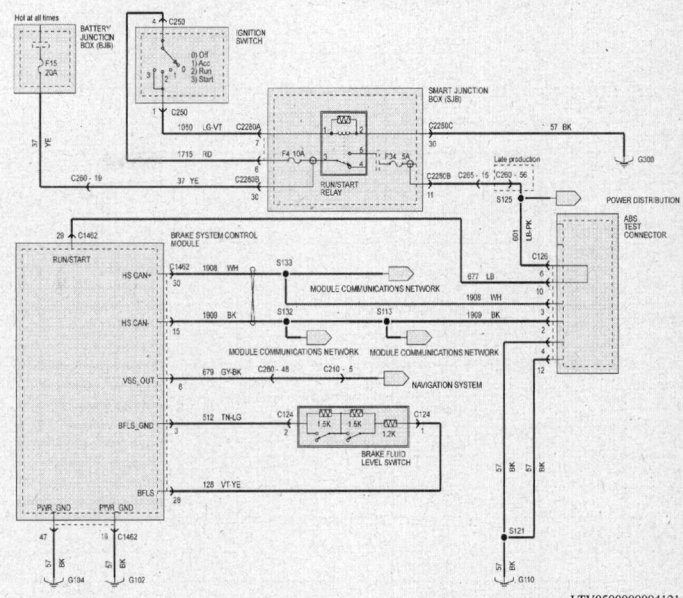

Fig. 8   Wiring diagram (Part 2 of 2). Hybrid

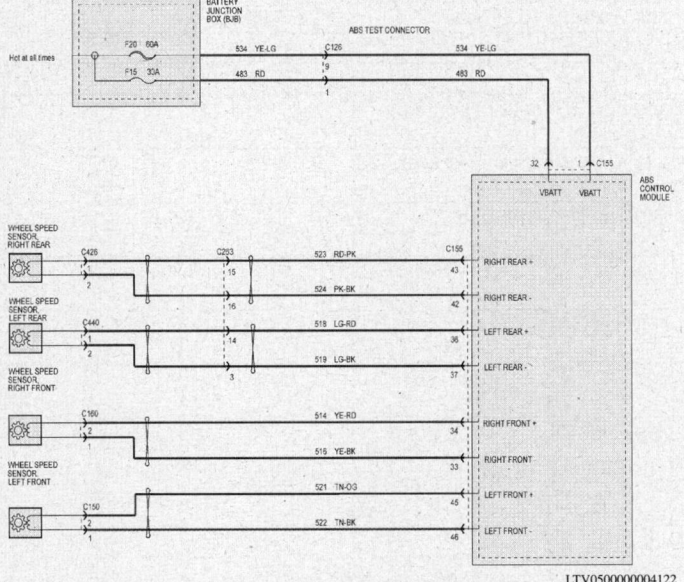

Fig. 9   Wiring diagram (Part 1 of 2). 2006

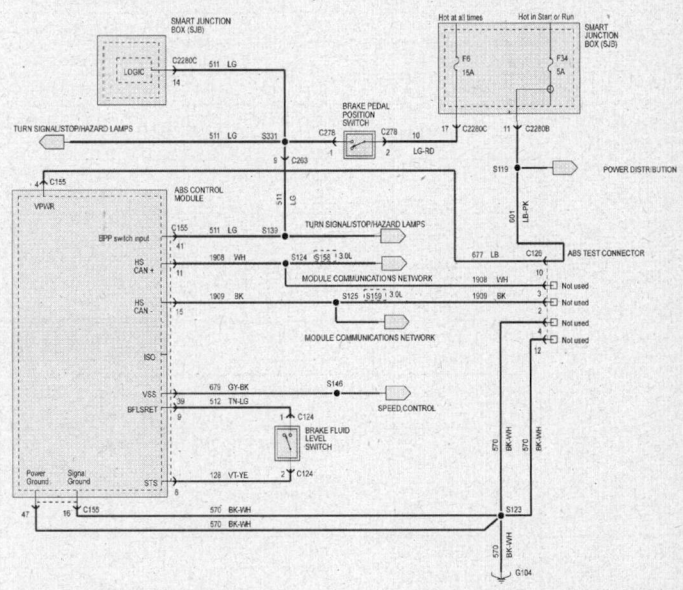

Fig. 9   Wiring diagram (Part 2 of 2). 2006

DIAGNOSTIC CHART INDEX

Test	Code	Description	Page No.	Fig. No.
2002–04				
A	—	No Communication w/ABS Module	5-29	10
B	—	Battery Voltage Out Of Range	5-29	11
C	C1145	Anti–Lock Brake Sensor Input Circuit Failure	5-30	12
	C1155	Anti–Lock Brake Sensor Input Circuit Failure	5-30	12
	C1165	Anti–Lock Brake Sensor Input Circuit Failure	5-30	12
	C1175	Anti–Lock Brake Sensor Input Circuit Failure	5-30	12
D	C1233	Anti–Lock Brake Sensor Output Failure	5-31	13
	C1234	Anti–Lock Brake Sensor Output Failure	5-31	13
	C1235	Anti–Lock Brake Sensor Output Failure	5-31	13
	C1236	Anti–Lock Brake Sensor Output Failure	5-31	13
E	C1095	Hydraulic Pump Motor Circuit Failure	5-32	14
F	—	Yellow ABS Warning Indicator Does Not Self Check	5-33	15
G	—	Yellow ABS Light Always On, No DTCS	5-33	16
2005–06				
F	—	No Communications With Anti-Lock Brake System Module	5-33	17
G	B1317	Battery Voltage High/Low	5-34	18
	B1318	Battery Voltage High/Low	5-34	18
H	C1145	Wheel Speed Sensor Circuit Failure	5-34	19
	C1155	Wheel Speed Sensor Circuit Failure	5-34	19
	C1165	Wheel Speed Sensor Circuit Failure	5-34	19
	C1175	Wheel Speed Sensor Circuit Failure	5-34	19
I	C1141	Wheel Speed Sensor Tone Ring Tooth Missing Fault/Wheel Speed Input Signal Missing	5-35	20
	C1142	Wheel Speed Sensor Tone Ring Tooth Missing Fault/Wheel Speed Input Signal Missing	5-35	20
	C1143	Wheel Speed Sensor Tone Ring Tooth Missing Fault/Wheel Speed Input Signal Missing	5-35	20
	C1144	Wheel Speed Sensor Tone Ring Tooth Missing Fault/Wheel Speed Input Signal Missing	5-35	20
	C1233	Wheel Speed Sensor Tone Ring Tooth Missing Fault/Wheel Speed Input Signal Missing	5-35	20
	C1234	Wheel Speed Sensor Tone Ring Tooth Missing Fault/Wheel Speed Input Signal Missing	5-35	20
	C1235	Wheel Speed Sensor Tone Ring Tooth Missing Fault/Wheel Speed Input Signal Missing	5-35	20
	C1236	Wheel Speed Sensor Tone Ring Tooth Missing Fault/Wheel Speed Input Signal Missing	5-35	20
J	C1305	Sensor Cluster Circuit Failure	5-36	21
	C2768	Sensor Cluster Circuit Failure	5-36	21
	C2769	Sensor Cluster Circuit Failure	5-36	21
	C2778	Sensor Cluster Circuit Failure	5-36	21
	C2783	Sensor Cluster Circuit Failure	5-36	21
	U1901	Sensor Cluster Circuit Failure	5-36	21
	U2527	Sensor Cluster Circuit Failure	5-36	21
K	C1218	Lamp Anti-Lock Brake System Warning Output Failure	5-37	22

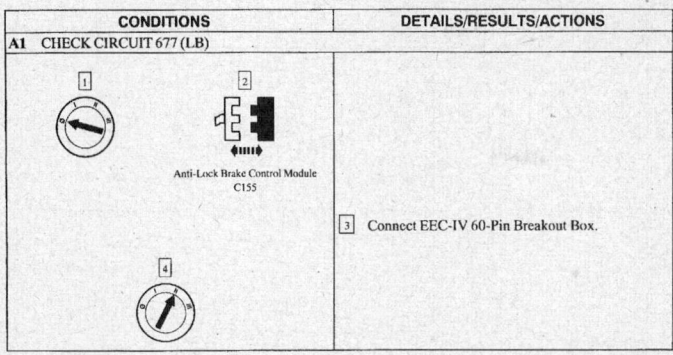

CONDITIONS	DETAILS/RESULTS/ACTIONS
A1 CHECK CIRCUIT 677 (LB)	③ Connect EEC-IV 60-Pin Breakout Box.

FM4020001667010X

Fig. 10   Test A: No Communication w/ABS Module (Part 1 of 2). 2002–04

CONDITIONS	DETAILS/RESULTS/ACTIONS
B1 CHECK RECENT VEHICLE HISTORY	① Check recent vehicle history. • Has the vehicle been jump-started by a tow truck within the past two weeks? → **Yes** The system is OK. CLEAR the DTCs. REPEAT the self-test. → **No** GO to **B2**.
B2 CHECK THE BATTERY VOLTAGE	① Measure the voltage between the positive and negative battery posts. • Is the voltage between 9 and 19 volts? → **Yes** GO to **B3**. → **No** DIAGNOSE charging system.
B3 CHECK THE CHARGING SYSTEM	② With the engine running at 2,000 rpm, measure the voltage between the positive and negative battery posts. • Is the voltage between 9 and 19 volts? → **Yes** GO to **B4**. → **No** REPAIR the charging system.

FM4020001668010X

Fig. 11   Test B: Battery Voltage Out Of Range (Part 1 of 3). 2002–04

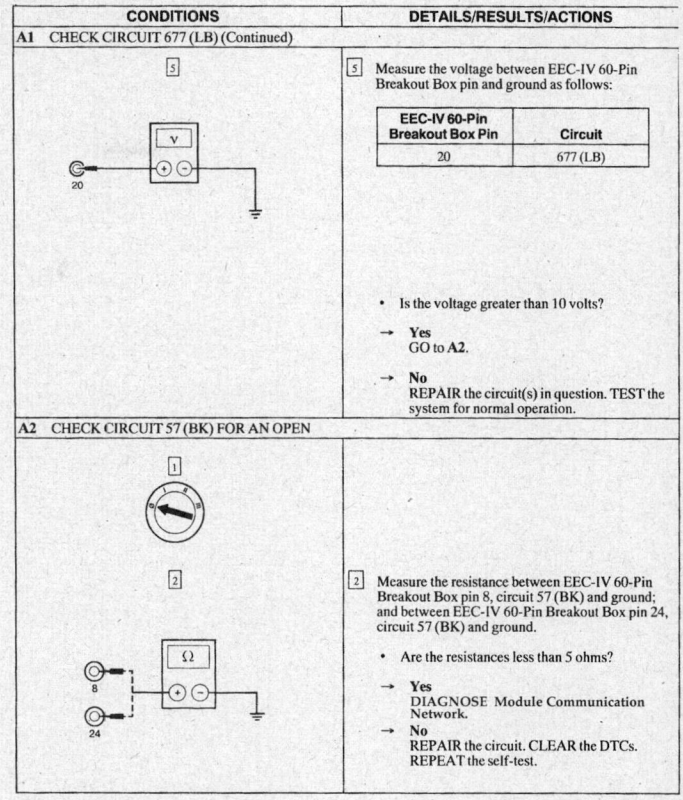

CONDITIONS	DETAILS/RESULTS/ACTIONS
A1 CHECK CIRCUIT 677 (LB) (Continued)	⑤ Measure the voltage between EEC-IV 60-Pin Breakout Box pin and ground as follows: | EEC-IV 60-Pin Breakout Box Pin	Circuit
20	677 (LB) | • Is the voltage greater than 10 volts? → **Yes** GO to **A2**. → **No** REPAIR the circuit(s) in question. TEST the system for normal operation.
A2 CHECK CIRCUIT 57 (BK) FOR AN OPEN	② Measure the resistance between EEC-IV 60-Pin Breakout Box pin 8, circuit 57 (BK) and ground; and between EEC-IV 60-Pin Breakout Box pin 24, circuit 57 (BK) and ground. • Are the resistances less than 5 ohms? → **Yes** DIAGNOSE Module Communication Network. → **No** REPAIR the circuit. CLEAR the DTCs. REPEAT the self-test.

FM4020001667020X

Fig. 10   Test A: No Communication w/ABS Module (Part 2 of 2). 2002–04

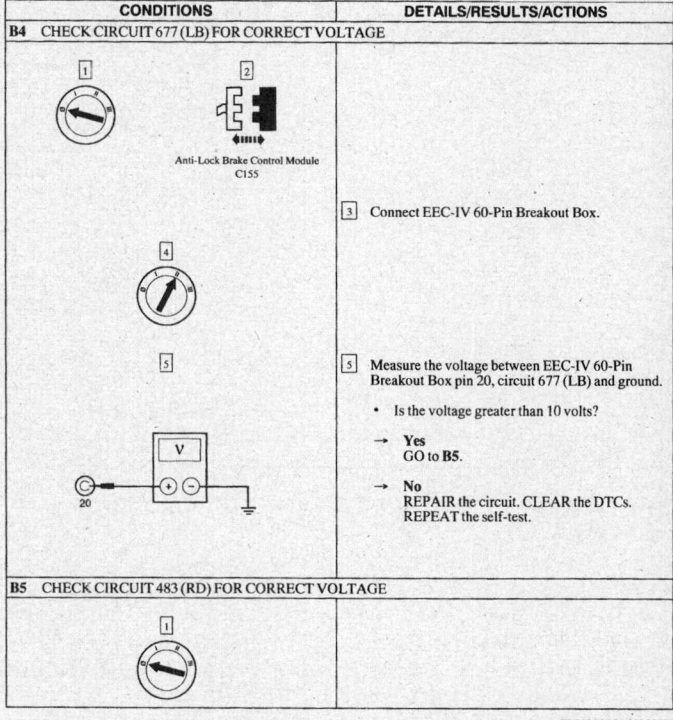

CONDITIONS	DETAILS/RESULTS/ACTIONS
B4 CHECK CIRCUIT 677 (LB) FOR CORRECT VOLTAGE	③ Connect EEC-IV 60-Pin Breakout Box. ⑤ Measure the voltage between EEC-IV 60-Pin Breakout Box pin 20, circuit 677 (LB) and ground. • Is the voltage greater than 10 volts? → **Yes** GO to **B5**. → **No** REPAIR the circuit. CLEAR the DTCs. REPEAT the self-test.
B5 CHECK CIRCUIT 483 (RD) FOR CORRECT VOLTAGE	

FM4020001668020X

Fig. 11   Test B: Battery Voltage Out Of Range (Part 2 of 3). 2002–04

B5 CHECK CIRCUIT 483 (RD) FOR CORRECT VOLTAGE (Continued)

CONDITIONS	DETAILS/RESULTS/ACTIONS
[2]	**2** Measure the voltage between EEC-IV 60-Pin Breakout Box pin 25, circuit 483 (RD) and ground. • Is the voltage greater than 10 volts? → **Yes** GO to **B6**. → **No** REPAIR the circuit. CLEAR the DTCs. REPEAT the self-test.

B6 CHECK CIRCUIT 534 (YE/LG) FOR CORRECT VOLTAGE

CONDITIONS	DETAILS/RESULTS/ACTIONS
[1]	**1** Measure the voltage between EEC-IV 60-Pin Breakout Box pin 9, circuit 534 (YE/LG) and ground. • Is the voltage greater than 10 volts? → **Yes** GO to **B7**. → **No** REPAIR the circuit. CLEAR the DTCs. REPEAT the self-test.

B7 CHECK CIRCUIT 57 (BK) FOR AN OPEN

CONDITIONS	DETAILS/RESULTS/ACTIONS
[1]	**1** Measure the resistance between EEC-IV 60-Pin Breakout Box pin 8, circuit 57 (BK) and ground; and between EEC-IV 60-Pin Breakout Box pin 24, circuit 57 (BK) and ground. • Are the resistances less than 5 ohms? → **Yes** INSTALL a new anti-lock brake control module. REPEAT the self-test. → **No** REPAIR the circuit. CLEAR the DTCs.

FM4020001668030X

Fig. 11 Test B: Battery Voltage Out Of Range (Part 3 of 3). 2002–04

C2 CHECK FOR SHORT TO GROUND (Continued)

CONDITIONS	DETAILS/RESULTS/ACTIONS
[2]	**2** Measure the resistance between EEC-IV 60-Pin Breakout Box pins and ground as follows:

DTC	EEC-IV 60-Pin Breakout Box Pin	EEC-IV 60-Pin Breakout Box Pin
C1145 (RF)	4 (circuit 514 [YE/RD])	3 (circuit 516 [YE/BK])
C1155 (LF)	18 (circuit 521 [TN/OG])	17 (circuit 522 [TN/BK])
C1165 (RR)	6 (circuit 523 [RD/PK])	7 (circuit 524 [PK/BK])
C1175 (LR)	22 (circuit 518 [LG/RD])	21 (circuit 519 [LG/BK])

• Are the resistances greater than 10,000 ohms?

→ **Yes**
 GO to **C3**.

→ **No**
 REPAIR the circuit in question. CLEAR the DTCs. TEST the system for normal operation.

C3 CHECK FOR AN OPEN

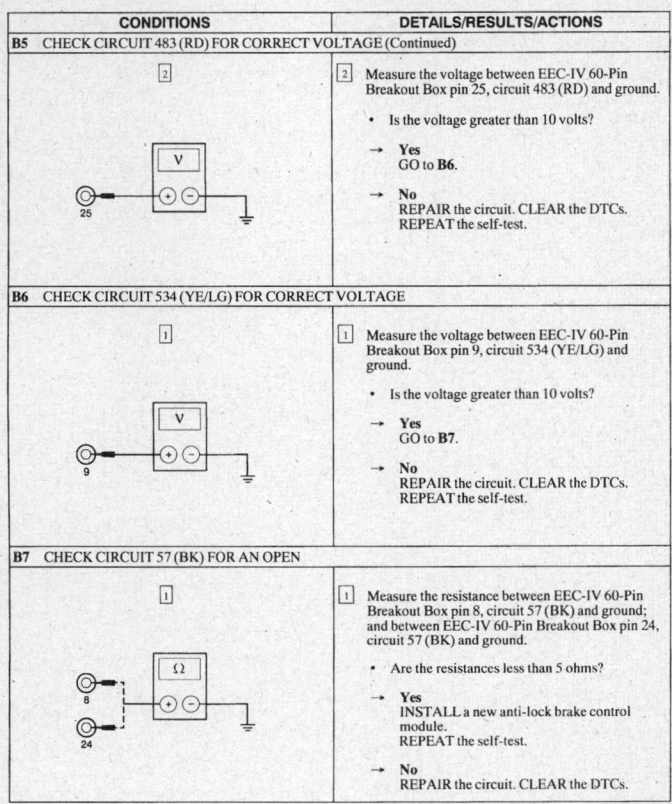

Suspect Anti-Lock Brake Sensor Connector

FM4020001669020X

Fig. 12 Test C: Codes C1145, C1155, C1165 & C1175: Anti-Lock Brake Sensor Input Circuit Failure (Part 2 of 4). 2002–04

C1 CHECK FOR SHORT TO POWER

CONDITIONS	DETAILS/RESULTS/ACTIONS
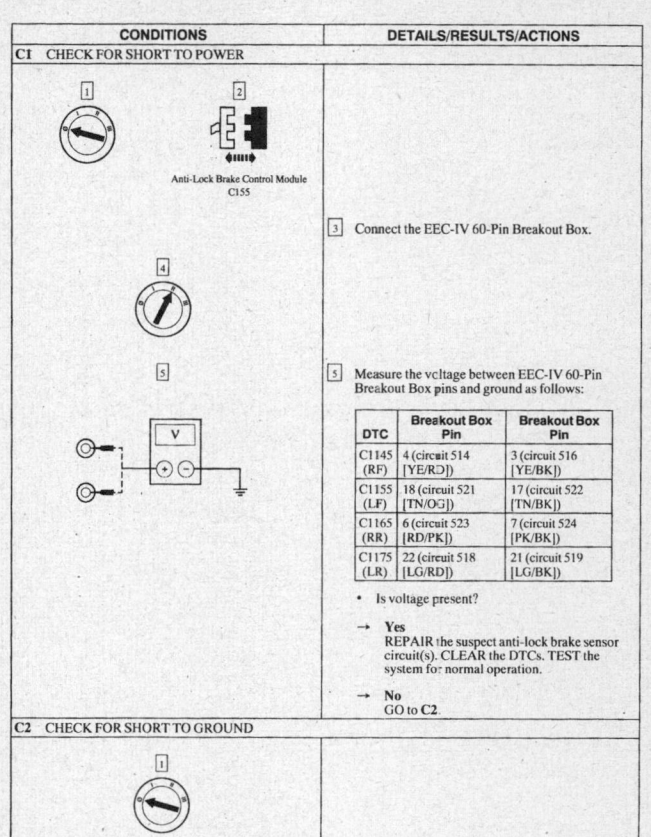 Anti-Lock Brake Control Module C155	**3** Connect the EEC-IV 60-Pin Breakout Box. **5** Measure the voltage between EEC-IV 60-Pin Breakout Box pins and ground as follows:

DTC	Breakout Box Pin	Breakout Box Pin
C1145 (RF)	4 (circuit 514 [YE/RD])	3 (circuit 516 [YE/BK])
C1155 (LF)	18 (circuit 521 [TN/OG])	17 (circuit 522 [TN/BK])
C1165 (RR)	6 (circuit 523 [RD/PK])	7 (circuit 524 [PK/BK])
C1175 (LR)	22 (circuit 518 [LG/RD])	21 (circuit 519 [LG/BK])

• Is voltage present?

→ **Yes**
 REPAIR the suspect anti-lock brake sensor circuit(s). CLEAR the DTCs. TEST the system for normal operation.

→ **No**
 GO to **C2**.

C2 CHECK FOR SHORT TO GROUND

FM4020001669010X

Fig. 12 Test C: Codes C1145, C1155, C1165 & C1175: Anti-Lock Brake Sensor Input Circuit Failure (Part 1 of 4). 2002–04

C3 CHECK FOR AN OPEN (Continued)

CONDITIONS	DETAILS/RESULTS/ACTIONS
[3]	**3** Measure the resistance between EEC-IV 60-Pin Breakout Box pins and anti-lock brake sensor connector as follows:

DTC	EEC-IV 60-Pin Breakout Box Pin	Anti-Lock Brake Sensor Connector
C1145 (RF)	4 (circuit 514 [YE/RD])	C160 (circuit 514 [YE/RD])
C1145 (RF)	3 (circuit 516 [YE/BK])	C160 (circuit 516 [YE/BK])
C1155 (LF)	18 (circuit 521 [TN/OG])	C150 (circuit 521 [TN/OG])
C1155 (LF)	17 (circuit 522 [TN/BK])	C150 (circuit 522 [TN/BK])
C1165 (RR)	6 (circuit 523 [RD/PK])	C426 (circuit 523 [RD/PK])
C1165 (LR)	7 (circuit 524 [PK/BK])	C426 (circuit 524 [PK/BK])
C1175 (LR)	22 (circuit 518 [LG/RD])	C440 (circuit 518 [LG/RD])
C1175 (LR)	21 (circuit 519 [LG/BK])	C440 (circuit 519 [LG/BK])

• Are the resistances less than 5 ohms?

→ **Yes**
 RECONNECT the anti-lock brake control module. GO to **C4**.

→ **No**
 REPAIR the circuit in question. CLEAR the DTCs. TEST the system for normal operation.

C4 CHECK THE ANTI-LOCK BRAKE CONTROL MODULE OUTPUT

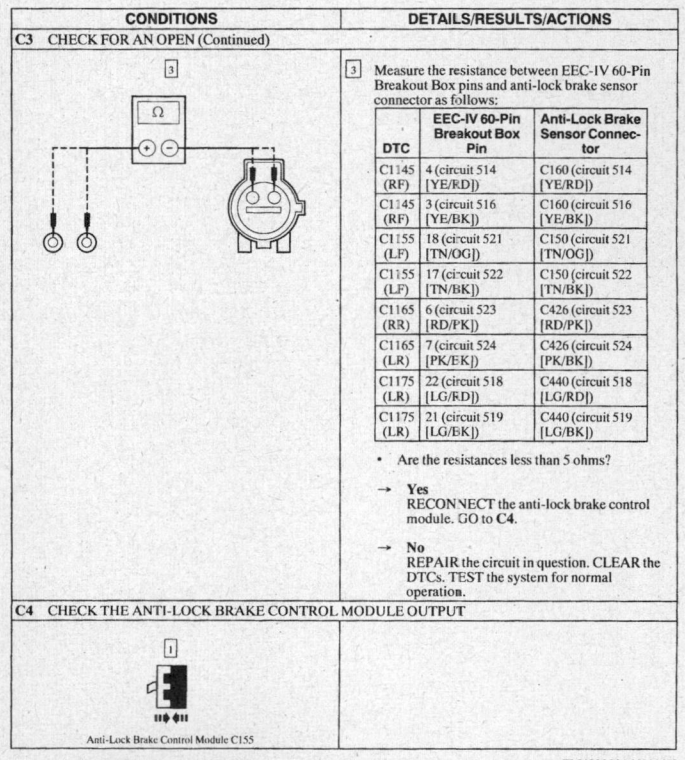

Anti-Lock Brake Control Module C155

FM4020001669030X

Fig. 12 Test C: Codes C1145, C1155, C1165 & C1175: Anti-Lock Brake Sensor Input Circuit Failure (Part 3 of 4). 2002–04

CONDITIONS	DETAILS/RESULTS/ACTIONS
C4 CHECK THE ANTI-LOCK BRAKE CONTROL MODULE OUTPUT (Continued)	

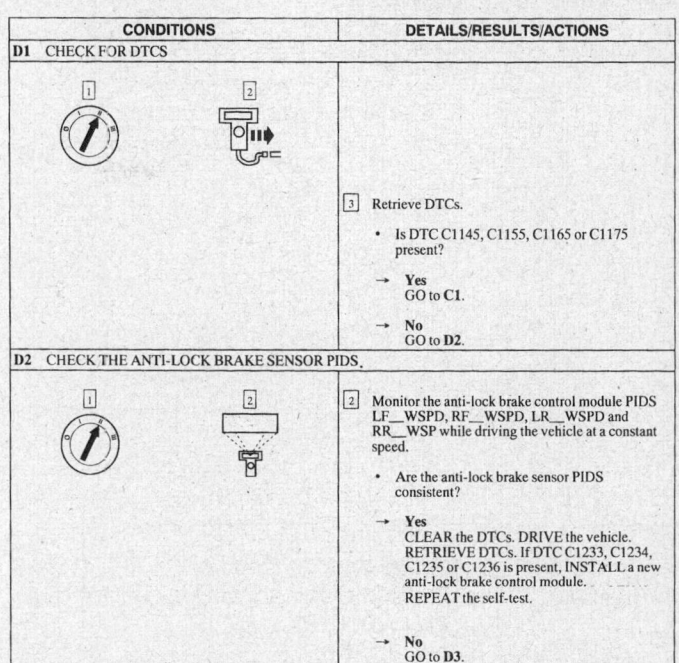

CONDITIONS	DETAILS/RESULTS/ACTIONS
D1 CHECK FOR DTCS	

[2] Measure the voltage between suspect anti-lock brake sensor as follows:

DTC	Suspect Anti-Lock Brake Sensor Circuit	Suspect Anti-Lock Brake Sensor Circuit
C1145 (RF)	514 (YE/RD)	516 (YE/BK)
C1155 (LF)	521 (TN/OG)	522 (TN/BK)
C1165 (RR)	523 (RD/PK)	524 (PK/BK)
C1175 (LR)	518 (LG/RD)	519 (LG/BK)

• Is the voltage greater than 9 volts?

→ **Yes**
INSTALL a new anti-lock brake sensor. CLEAR the DTCs. TEST the system for normal operation.

→ **No**
INSTALL a new anti-lock brake control module. TEST the system for normal operation.

FM4020001669040X

Fig. 12   Test C: Codes C1145, C1155, C1165 & C1175: Anti-Lock Brake Sensor Input Circuit Failure (Part 4 of 4). 2002–04

[3] Retrieve DTCs.

• Is DTC C1145, C1155, C1165 or C1175 present?

→ **Yes**
GO to **C1**.

→ **No**
GO to **D2**.

CONDITIONS	DETAILS/RESULTS/ACTIONS
D2 CHECK THE ANTI-LOCK BRAKE SENSOR PIDS	

[2] Monitor the anti-lock brake control module PIDS LF__WSPD, RF__WSPD, LR__WSPD and RR__WSP while driving the vehicle at a constant speed.

• Are the anti-lock brake sensor PIDS consistent?

→ **Yes**
CLEAR the DTCs. DRIVE the vehicle. RETRIEVE DTCs. If DTC C1233, C1234, C1235 or C1236 is present, INSTALL a new anti-lock brake control module. REPEAT the self-test.

→ **No**
GO to **D3**.

FM4020001670010X

Fig. 13   Test D: Codes C1233, C1234, C1235, C1236: Anti-Lock Brake Sensor Output Failure (Part 1 of 4). 2002–04

CONDITIONS	DETAILS/RESULTS/ACTIONS
D3 CHECK FOR ANTI-LOCK BRAKE SENSOR DAMAGE AND LOOSENESS	
NOTE: Any time an anti-lock brake sensor is removed, thoroughly clean the mounting surfaces. On front anti-lock brake sensors, apply High-Temperature 4x4 Front Axle and Wheel Bearing Grease.	

[2] Raise and support the vehicle.

[3] ⚠ **CAUTION: Examine the anti-lock brake sensor wire carefully with good light. Failure to verify damage in the anti-lock brake sensor wire can lead to unnecessary installation of a new component.**

Inspect the anti-lock brake sensor mounting for looseness. If the anti-lock brake sensor is suspected, inspect the sensor for corrosion on the rear axle housing boss, or on the front anti-lock brake mounting flange. Clean as necessary.

• Is the anti-lock brake sensor OK?

→ **Yes**
GO to **D4**.

→ **No**
If the anti-lock brake sensor mounting is loose or corroded, REMOVE the anti-lock brake sensor, plug the opening, and thoroughly clean the mounting surfaces. On the front anti-lock brake sensors, apply High Temperature 4x4 Front Axle and Wheel Bearing Grease E8TZ-19590-A or equivalent meeting Ford Specification ESA-M1C198-A. REPEAT the self-test.

If the anti-lock brake sensor is damaged, INSTALL a new anti-lock brake sensor. CLEAR the DTCs. REPEAT the self-test.

FM4020001670020X

Fig. 13   Test D: Codes C1233, C1234, C1235, C1236: Anti-Lock Brake Sensor Output Failure (Part 2 of 4). 2002–04

CONDITIONS	DETAILS/RESULTS/ACTIONS
D4 CHECK FOR ANTI-LOCK BRAKE SENSOR INDICATOR DAMAGE	
NOTE: Any time an anti-lock brake sensor is removed, thoroughly clean the mounting surfaces. On front anti-lock brake sensors, apply High Temperature 4x4 Front Axle and Wheel Bearing Grease.	

[1] Remove the anti-lock brake sensor.

[2] ⚠ **CAUTION: Examine the anti-lock brake sensor indicator carefully with good light. Failure to verify damage in the anti-lock brake sensor indicator can lead to unnecessary installation of a new component.**

Inspect the anti-lock brake sensor indicator for damaged or missing teeth. Rotate the wheel to verify that no teeth are missing.

• Is the anti-lock brake sensor indicator OK?

→ **Yes**
GO to **D5**.

→ **No**
INSTALL a new anti-lock brake sensor indicator. CLEAR the DTCs. REPEAT the self-test.

CONDITIONS	DETAILS/RESULTS/ACTIONS
D5 CHECK THE ANTI-LOCK BRAKE CONTROL MODULE OUTPUT	

FM4020001670030X

Fig. 13   Test D: Codes C1233, C1234, C1235, C1236: Anti-Lock Brake Sensor Output Failure (Part 3 of 4). 2002–04

CONDITIONS	DETAILS/RESULTS/ACTIONS
D5 CHECK THE ANTI-LOCK BRAKE CONTROL MODULE OUTPUT (Continued)	

<table>
<tr><td>[2]</td><td>[2] Measure the voltage between the suspect anti-lock brake sensor as follows:</td></tr>
</table>

DTC	Suspect Anti-Lock Brake Sensor Circuit	Suspect Anti-Lock Brake Sensor Circuit
C1234 (RF)	514 (YE/RD)	516 (YE/BK)
C1233 (LF)	521 (TN/OG)	522 (TN/BK)
C1235 (RR)	523 (RD/PK)	524 (PK/BK)
C1236 (LR)	518 (LG/RD)	519 (LG/BK)

- Is the voltage greater than 9 volts?

→ **Yes**
INSTALL a new anti-lock brake sensor.
CLEAR the DTCs.
TEST the system for normal operation.

→ **No**
INSTALL a new anti-lock brake control module.
TEST the system for normal operation.

FM4020001670040X

Fig. 13 Test D: Codes C1233, C1234, C1235, C1236: Anti-Lock Brake Sensor Output Failure (Part 4 of 4). 2002–04

CONDITIONS	DETAILS/RESULTS/ACTIONS
E2 CHECK THE PUMP MOTOR OPERATION	

[1] [2] [3]

Scan Tool

[3] Trigger the anti-lock brake control module active command PMP MOTOR ON.

- Does the pump motor operate?

→ **Yes**
CLEAR the DTC. CHECK the yellow ABS warning indicator while driving the vehicle above 32 km/h (20 mph) and no brakes applied until the vehicle exceeds 32 km/h (20 mph). If the yellow ABS warning indicator illuminates, INSTALL a new anti-lock brake control module. CLEAR the DTCs. REPEAT the self-test. If the yellow ABS warning indicator does not illuminate, CLEAR the DTCs. REPEAT the self-test.

→ **No**
GO to E3.

| E3 CHECK THE PUMP MOTOR | |

[1] [2]

Pump Motor Connector

[3]

50A

[3] Connect a fused 50A jumper wire between the positive battery terminal and red ABS pump motor terminal. Connect a jumper wire between the negative battery terminal and brown ABS pump motor terminal.

- Is the ABS pump motor running?

→ **Yes**
GO to E4.

→ **No**
INSTALL a new HCU.
REPEAT the self-test.

FM4020001671020X

Fig. 14 Test E: Code C1095: Hydraulic Pump Motor Circuit Failure (Part 2 of 4). 2002–04

CONDITIONS	DETAILS/RESULTS/ACTIONS
E1 CHECK THE ABS PUMP MOTOR	

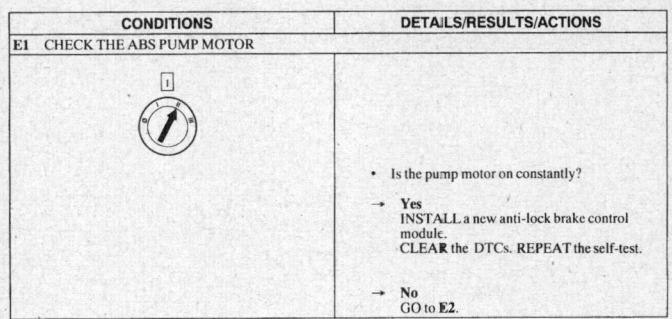

- Is the pump motor on constantly?

→ **Yes**
INSTALL a new anti-lock brake control module.
CLEAR the DTCs. REPEAT the self-test.

→ **No**
GO to E2.

FM4020001671010X

Fig. 14 Test E: Code C1095: Hydraulic Pump Motor Circuit Failure (Part 1 of 4). 2002–04

CONDITIONS	DETAILS/RESULTS/ACTIONS
E4 CHECK CIRCUIT 534 (YE/LG)	

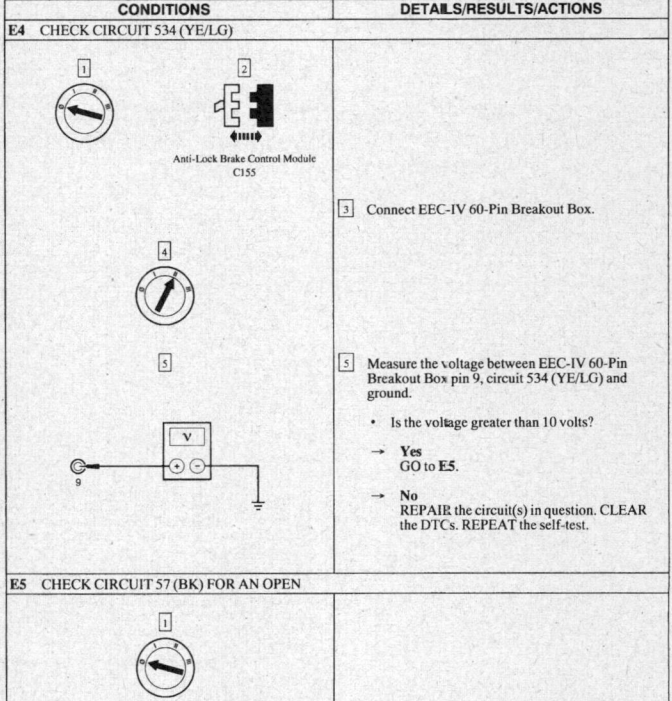

[3] Connect EEC-IV 60-Pin Breakout Box.

[5] Measure the voltage between EEC-IV 60-Pin Breakout Box pin 9, circuit 534 (YE/LG) and ground.

- Is the voltage greater than 10 volts?

→ **Yes**
GO to E5.

→ **No**
REPAIR the circuit(s) in question. CLEAR the DTCs. REPEAT the self-test.

| E5 CHECK CIRCUIT 57 (BK) FOR AN OPEN | |

FM4020001671030X

Fig. 14 Test E: Code C1095: Hydraulic Pump Motor Circuit Failure (Part 3 of 4). 2002–04

CONDITIONS	DETAILS/RESULTS/ACTIONS
E5 CHECK CIRCUIT 57 (BK) FOR AN OPEN (Continued)	

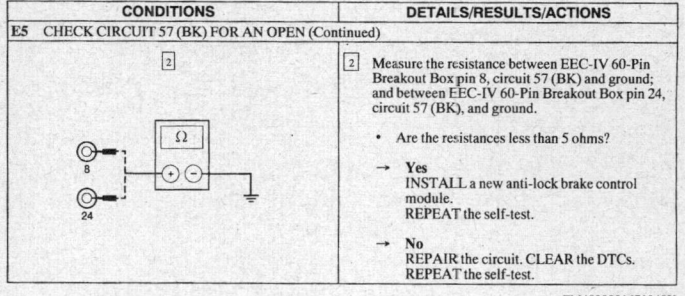

[2] Measure the resistance between EEC-IV 60-Pin Breakout Box pin 8, circuit 57 (BK) and ground; and between EEC-IV 60-Pin Breakout Box pin 24, circuit 57 (BK), and ground.

- Are the resistances less than 5 ohms?

→ **Yes**
INSTALL a new anti-lock brake control module. REPEAT the self-test.

→ **No**
REPAIR the circuit. CLEAR the DTCs. REPEAT the self-test.

FM4020001671040X

Fig. 14 Test E: Code C1095: Hydraulic Pump Motor Circuit Failure (Part 4 of 4). 2002–04

CONDITIONS	DETAILS/RESULTS/ACTIONS
F1 CHECK THE ANTI-LOCK BRAKE CONTROL MODULE	

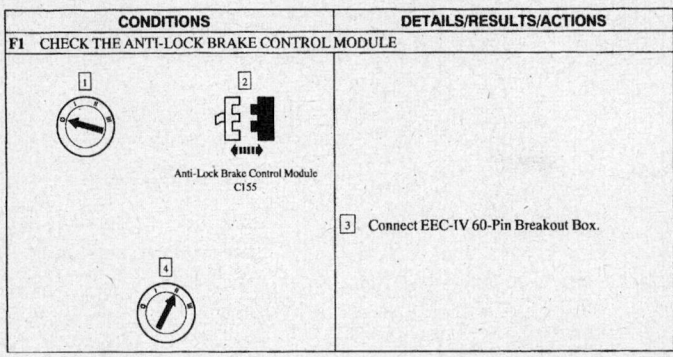

Anti-Lock Brake Control Module
C155

|3| Connect EEC-IV 60-Pin Breakout Box.

FM4020001672010X

Fig. 15 Test F: Yellow ABS Warning Indicator Does Not Self Check (Part 1 of 2). 2002–04

CONDITIONS	DETAILS/RESULTS/ACTIONS
G1 CHECK THE MODULE	

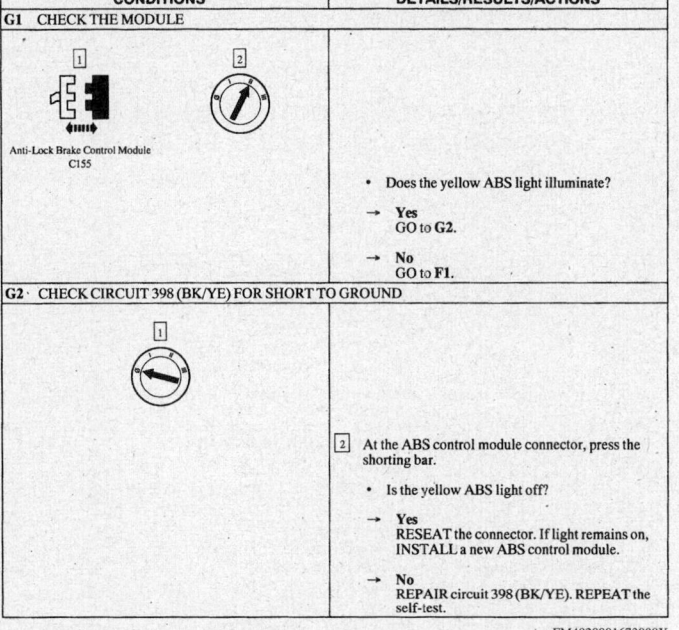

Anti-Lock Brake Control Module
C155

• Does the yellow ABS light illuminate?

→ **Yes**
GO to **G2**.

→ **No**
GO to **F1**.

G2 CHECK CIRCUIT 398 (BK/YE) FOR SHORT TO GROUND

|2| At the ABS control module connector, press the shorting bar.

• Is the yellow ABS light off?

→ **Yes**
RESEAT the connector. If light remains on, INSTALL a new ABS control module.

→ **No**
REPAIR circuit 398 (BK/YE). REPEAT the self-test.

FM4020001673000X

Fig. 16 Test G: Yellow ABS Light Always On, No DTCS. 2002–04

CONDITIONS	DETAILS/RESULTS/ACTIONS
F1 CHECK THE ANTI-LOCK BRAKE CONTROL MODULE (Continued)	

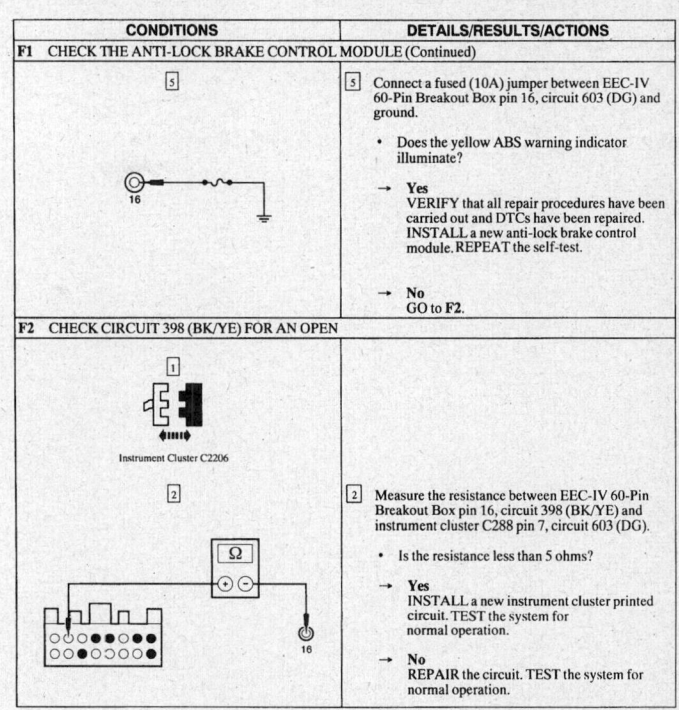

|5| Connect a fused (10A) jumper between EEC-IV 60-Pin Breakout Box pin 16, circuit 603 (DG) and ground.

• Does the yellow ABS warning indicator illuminate?

→ **Yes**
VERIFY that all repair procedures have been carried out and DTCs have been repaired. INSTALL a new anti-lock brake control module. REPEAT the self-test.

→ **No**
GO to **F2**.

F2 CHECK CIRCUIT 398 (BK/YE) FOR AN OPEN

Instrument Cluster C2206

|2| Measure the resistance between EEC-IV 60-Pin Breakout Box pin 16, circuit 398 (BK/YE) and instrument cluster C288 pin 7, circuit 603 (DG).

• Is the resistance less than 5 ohms?

→ **Yes**
INSTALL a new instrument cluster printed circuit. TEST the system for normal operation.

→ **No**
REPAIR the circuit. TEST the system for normal operation.

FM4020001672020X

Fig. 15 Test F: Yellow ABS Warning Indicator Does Not Self Check (Part 2 of 2). 2002–04

Test Step	Result / Action to Take
F1 CHECK THE ABS MODULE POWER SUPPLY	

• Key in OFF position.
• Disconnect: ABS Module C1462.
• Key in ON position.
• Measure the voltage between ABS module C1462, harness side and ground as follows:

ABS Module Connector Pin	Circuit
C1462-1	534 (YE/LG)
C1462-17	22 (LB/BK)
C1462-29	677 (LB)
C1462-32	483 (RD)

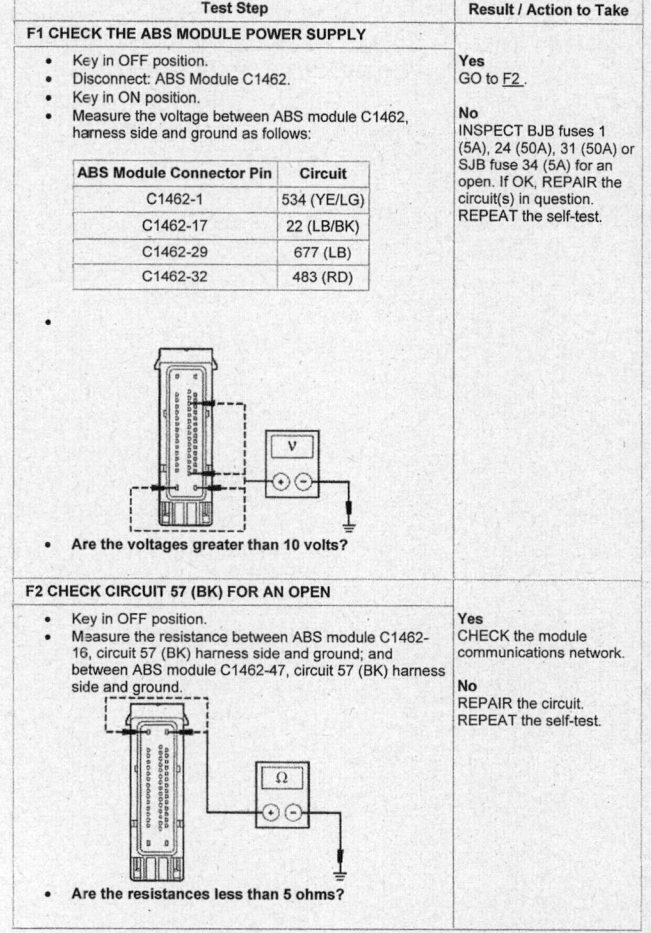

• Are the voltages greater than 10 volts?

Yes
GO to <u>F2</u>.

No
INSPECT BJB fuses 1 (5A), 24 (50A), 31 (50A) or SJB fuse 34 (5A) for an open. If OK, REPAIR the circuit(s) in question. REPEAT the self-test.

F2 CHECK CIRCUIT 57 (BK) FOR AN OPEN

• Key in OFF position.
• Measure the resistance between ABS module C1462-16, circuit 57 (BK) harness side and ground; and between ABS module C1462-47, circuit 57 (BK) harness side and ground.

• Are the resistances less than 5 ohms?

Yes
CHECK the module communications network.

No
REPAIR the circuit. REPEAT the self-test.

LTV0500000004124

Fig. 17 Test F: No Communications With Anti-Lock Brake System Module. 2005-06

Test Step	Result / Action to Take
G1 CHECK THE BATTERY VOLTAGE • Measure the battery voltage between the positive and negative battery posts with the key ON engine OFF (KOEO), and with the engine running. • **Is the battery voltage between 10 and 13 volts with KOEO, and between 11 and 17 volts with the engine running?**	**Yes** GO to G2 . **No** CHECK the charging system. TEST the system for normal operation.
G2 CHECK THE ABS MODULE POWER SUPPLY • Key in OFF position. • Disconnect: ABS Module C1462. • Key in ON position. • Measure the voltage between the ABS module C1462, harness side and ground as follows: | ABS Module Connector Pin	Circuit
C1462-1	534 (YE/LG)
C1462-17	22 (LB/BK)
C1462-29	677 (LB)
C1462-32	483 (RD) | 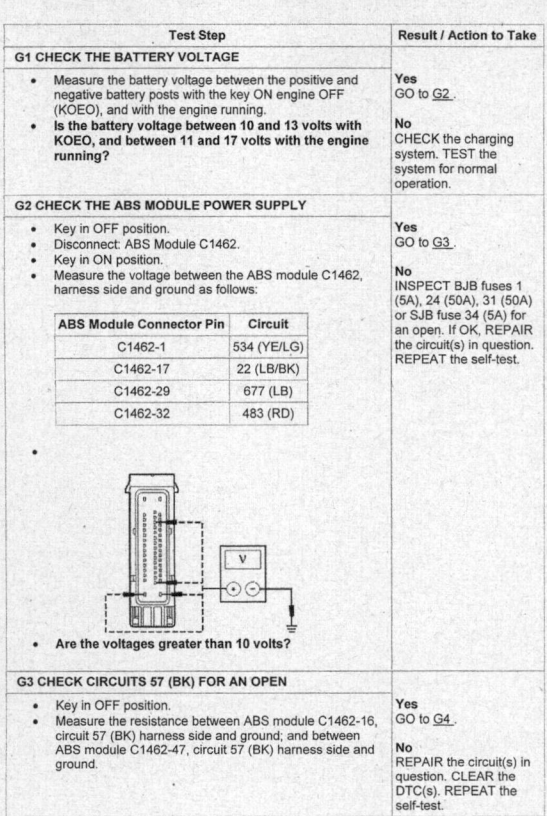 • **Are the voltages greater than 10 volts?**	**Yes** GO to G3 . **No** INSPECT BJB fuses 1 (5A), 24 (50A), 31 (50A) or SJB fuse 34 (5A) for an open. If OK, REPAIR the circuit(s) in question. REPEAT the self-test.
G3 CHECK CIRCUITS 57 (BK) FOR AN OPEN • Key in OFF position. • Measure the resistance between ABS module C1462-16, circuit 57 (BK) harness side and ground; and between ABS module C1462-47, circuit 57 (BK) harness side and ground.	**Yes** GO to G4 . **No** REPAIR the circuit(s) in question. CLEAR the DTC(s). REPEAT the self-test.

LTV0500000004125

Fig. 18 Test G, Codes B1317 & B1318: Battery Voltage High/Low (Part 1 of 2). 2005-06

Test Step	Result / Action to Take
H1 CHECK THE WHEEL SPEED SENSOR CIRCUITS FOR A SHORT TO POWER ⚠ **CAUTION: No measurements should be taken with the wheel speed sensor connected. Damage to the wheel speed sensor will result. NOTE: Both circuits must be checked for each DTC.** • Key in OFF position. • Disconnect: ABS Module C1462. • Disconnect: Suspect Wheel Speed Sensor. • Key in ON position. • Measure the voltage between ABS module C1462, harness side and ground as follows: 	DTC	ABS Module Connector Pin	Circuit
---	---	---
C1145	C1462-33	516 (YE/BK)
C1145	C1462-34	514 (YE/RD)
C1155	C1462-45	521 (TN/OG)
C1155	C1462-46	522 (TN/BK)
C1165	C1462-42	524 (PK/BK)
C1165	C1462-43	523 (RD/PK)
C1175	C1462-36	518 (LG/RD)
C1175	C1462-37	519 (LG/BK)	 • **Is any voltage present?**	**Yes** REPAIR the circuit(s) in question. CLEAR the DTC(s). REPEAT the self-test. **No** GO to H2 .
H2 CHECK THE WHEEL SPEED SENSOR CIRCUITS FOR A SHORT TO GROUND NOTE: Both circuits must be checked for each DTC. • Key in OFF position. • Measure the resistance between ABS module C1462, harness side and ground as follows: 	DTC	ABS Module Connector Pin	Circuit
---	---	---
C1145	C1462-33	516 (YE/BK)
C1145	C1462-34	514 (YE/RD)
C1155	C1462-45	521 (TN/OG)
C1155	C1462-46	522 (TN/BK)
C1165	C1462-42	524 (PK/BK)		**Yes** GO to H3 . **No** REPAIR the circuit(s) in question. CLEAR the DTC(s). REPEAT the self-test.

LTV0500000004127

Fig. 19 Test H, Codes C1145, C1155, C1165 & C1175: Wheel Speed Sensor Circuit Failure (Part 1 of 4). 2005-06

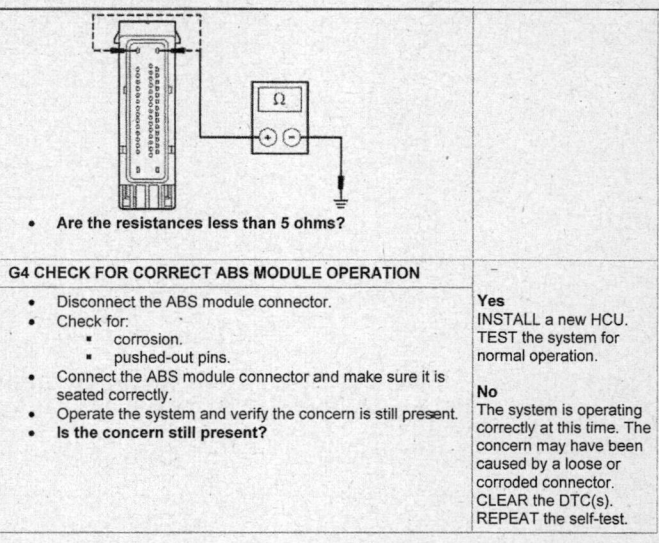

• **Are the resistances less than 5 ohms?**

Test Step	Result / Action to Take

G4 CHECK FOR CORRECT ABS MODULE OPERATION
• Disconnect the ABS module connector.
• Check for:
  ▪ corrosion.
  ▪ pushed-out pins.
• Connect the ABS module connector and make sure it is seated correctly.
• Operate the system and verify the concern is still present.
• **Is the concern still present?**
	Yes
	INSTALL a new HCU. TEST the system for normal operation.
	
	No
	The system is operating correctly at this time. The concern may have been caused by a loose or corroded connector. CLEAR the DTC(s). REPEAT the self-test.

LTV0500000004126

Fig. 18 Test G, Codes B1317 & B1318: Battery Voltage High/Low (Part 2 of 2). 2005-06

C1165	C1462-43	523 (RD/PK)
C1175	C1462-36	518 (LG/RD)
C1175	C1462-37	519 (LG/BK)

• **Are the resistances greater than 10,000 ohms?**

Test Step	Result / Action to Take
H3 CHECK THE WHEEL SPEED SENSOR CIRCUITS FOR AN OPEN NOTE: Both circuits must be checked for each DTC. • Disconnect: Suspect Wheel Speed Sensor. • Measure the resistance between ABS module C1462, harness side and the suspect wheel speed sensor connector, harness side as follows: 	DTC	Circuit	ABS Module Connector Pin	Wheel Speed Sensor Connector Pin
---	---	---	---
C1145	516 (YE/BK)	C1462-33	RH front wheel speed sensor C160-1
C1145	514 (YE/RD)	C1462-34	RH front wheel speed sensor C160-2
C1155	521 (TN/OG)	C1462-45	LH front wheel speed sensor C150-2
C1155	522 (TN/BK)	C1462-46	LH front wheel speed sensor C150-1
C1165	523 (RD/PK)	C1462-43	RH rear wheel speed sensor C426-1
C1165	524 (PK/BK)	C1462-42	RH rear wheel speed sensor C426-2
C1175	518 (LG/RD)	C1462-36	LH rear wheel speed sensor C440-1
C1175	519 (LG/BK)	C1462-37	LH rear wheel speed sensor C440-2 | • **Are the resistances less than 5 ohms?**	**Yes** GO to H4 . **No** REPAIR the circuit(s) in question. CLEAR the DTC(s). REPEAT the self-test.

LTV0500000004128

Fig. 19 Test H, Codes C1145, C1155, C1165 & C1175: Wheel Speed Sensor Circuit Failure (Part 2 of 4). 2005-06

H4 CHECK FOR SHORTED WHEEL SPEED SENSOR CIRCUITS

• Measure the resistance between the suspect wheel speed sensor pins, harness side. 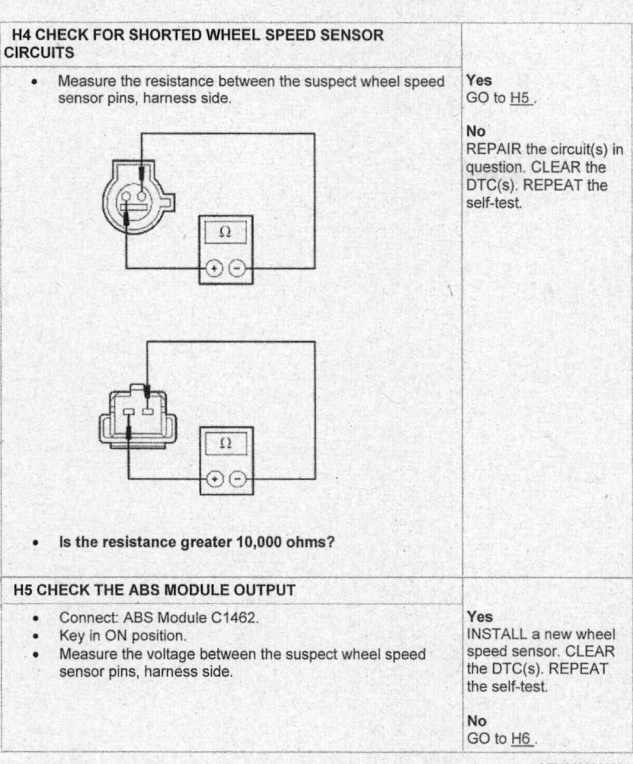 • **Is the resistance greater 10,000 ohms?**	**Yes** GO to H5. **No** REPAIR the circuit(s) in question. CLEAR the DTC(s). REPEAT the self-test.

H5 CHECK THE ABS MODULE OUTPUT

• Connect: ABS Module C1462. • Key in ON position. • Measure the voltage between the suspect wheel speed sensor pins, harness side.	**Yes** INSTALL a new wheel speed sensor. CLEAR the DTC(s). REPEAT the self-test. **No** GO to H6.

LTV0500000004129

Fig. 19 Test H, Codes C1145, C1155, C1165 & C1175: Wheel Speed Sensor Circuit Failure (Part 3 of 4). 2005-06

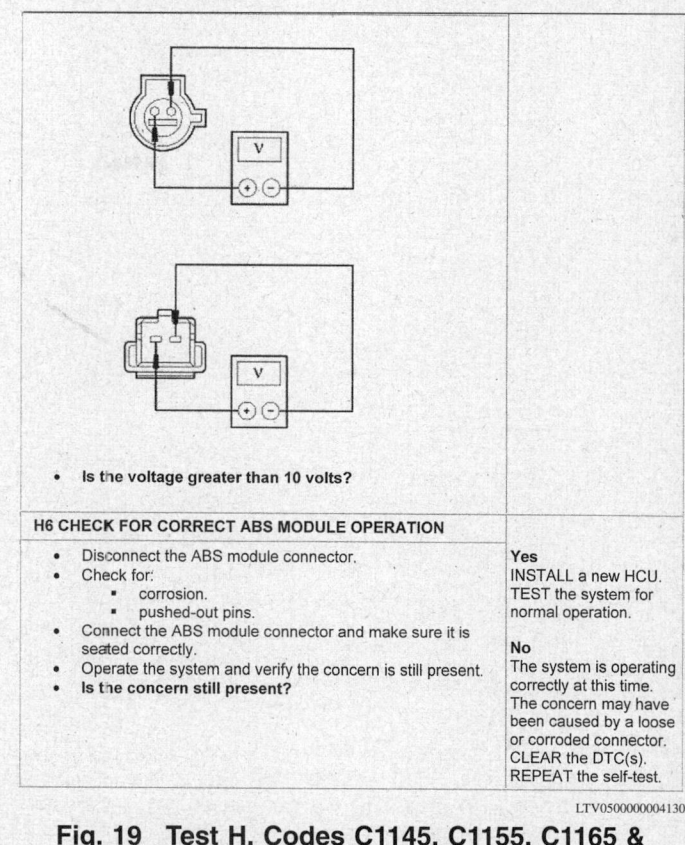

• **Is the voltage greater than 10 volts?**	

H6 CHECK FOR CORRECT ABS MODULE OPERATION

• Disconnect the ABS module connector.
 • Check for:
   ▪ corrosion.
   ▪ pushed-out pins.
 • Connect the ABS module connector and make sure it is seated correctly.
 • Operate the system and verify the concern is still present.
 • **Is the concern still present?**
	Yes
	 INSTALL a new HCU. TEST the system for normal operation.
	
	 No
	 The system is operating correctly at this time. The concern may have been caused by a loose or corroded connector. CLEAR the DTC(s). REPEAT the self-test.

LTV0500000004130

Fig. 19 Test H, Codes C1145, C1155, C1165 & C1175: Wheel Speed Sensor Circuit Failure (Part 4 of 4). 2005-06

Test Step	Result / Action to Take
I1 CHECK THE DTCs FROM THE SELF-TEST • Check the recorded results from the ABS self-test: • **Are DTCs C1141, C1142, C1143 or C1144 present?**	**Yes** GO to I6. **No** If DTC(s) C1222, C1233, C1234, C1235 or C1236 are present, GO to I2. For all other DTC(s) refer to the Anti-Lock Brake System (ABS) Module Diagnostic Trouble Code (DTC) Index.
I2 MONITOR THE WHEEL SPEED PIDS • Connect the diagnostic tool. • Key in ON position. • Enter the following diagnostic mode on the diagnostic tool: ABS Module PIDs. • Monitor the ABS module wheel speed sensor PIDs while driving the vehicle at a constant speed. • **Are all the wheel speed sensor PID values similar?**	**Yes** CLEAR the DTC(s). DRIVE the vehicle. RETRIEVE the DTC(s). If DTC C1233, C1234, C1235 or C1236 is present, GO to I9. **No** GO to I3.
I3 INSPECT THE WHEEL SPEED SENSOR MOUNTING • Key in OFF position. • With the vehicle in NEUTRAL, position it on a hoistInspect the wheel speed sensor for looseness. • **Is the wheel speed sensor loose?**	**Yes** TIGHTEN the wheel speed sensor to specification. CLEAR the DTC(s). GO to I4. **No** GO to I5.
I4 RECHECK THE WHEEL SPEED PIDS • Connect the diagnostic tool. • Key in ON position. • Enter the following diagnostic mode on the diagnostic tool: ABS Module PIDs. • Monitor the ABS module wheel speed sensor PIDs while driving the vehicle at a constant speed. • **Are all the wheel speed sensor PID values similar?**	**Yes** The vehicle is OK. The concern may have been caused by a loose wheel speed sensor. **No** GO to I5.

LTV0500000004131

Fig. 20 Test I, Codes C1141, C1142, C1143, C1144, C1233, C1234, C1235 & C1236: Wheel Speed Sensor Tone Ring Tooth Missing Fault/Wheel Speed Input Signal Missing (Part 1 of 3). 2005-06

I5 CHECK THE WHEEL SPEED SENSOR FOR DAMAGE • Key in OFF position. • With the vehicle in NEUTRAL, position it on a hoist • ⚠ CAUTION: Examine the wheel speed sensor wire carefully with a good light source. Failure to verify damage in the wheel speed sensor wire can lead to unnecessary installation of a new component. • Inspect the wheel speed sensor for general damage. • **Is the wheel speed sensor OK?**	**Yes** GO to I6. **No** INSTALL a new wheel speed sensor. CLEAR the DTC(s). REPEAT the self-test.
I6 CHECK FOR WHEEL SPEED SENSOR RING DAMAGE • Remove the wheel speed sensor ring. • Inspect the wheel speed sensor ring for damaged or missing teeth. Rotate the wheel to verify that no teeth are missing. • **Is the wheel speed sensor ring OK?**	**Yes** GO to I7. **No** INSTALL a new wheel speed sensor ring. CLEAR the DTC(s). REPEAT the self-test.
I7 CHECK FOR BEARING DAMAGE • Inspect the wheel bearings for damage. • **Are the wheel bearings OK?**	**Yes** GO to I8. **No** INSTALL new wheel bearings as necessary. CLEAR the DTC(s). REPEAT the self-test.
I8 CHECK THE ABS MODULE OUTPUT • Key in OFF position. • Disconnect: Suspect Wheel Speed Sensor. • Key in ON position. • Measure the voltage between the suspect wheel speed sensor pins, harness side.	**Yes** INSTALL a new wheel speed sensor ring. section. CLEAR the DTC(s). REPEAT the self-test. **No** GO to I9.

LTV0500000004132

Fig. 20 Test I, Codes C1141, C1142, C1143, C1144, C1233, C1234, C1235 & C1236: Wheel Speed Sensor Tone Ring Tooth Missing Fault/Wheel Speed Input Signal Missing (Part 2 of 3). 2005-06

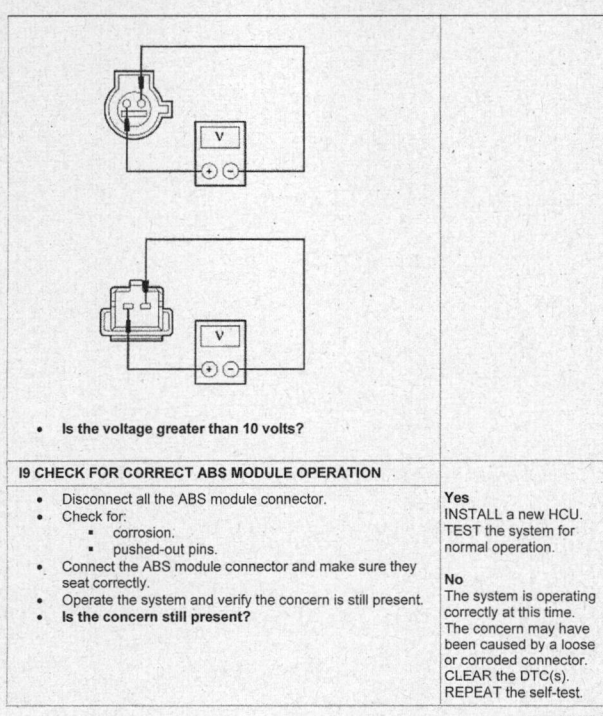

- **Is the voltage greater than 10 volts?**

I9 CHECK FOR CORRECT ABS MODULE OPERATION

Test Step	Result / Action to Take

• Disconnect all the ABS module connector.
• Check for:
  ■ corrosion.
  ■ pushed-out pins.
• Connect the ABS module connector and make sure they seat correctly.
• Operate the system and verify the concern is still present.
• **Is the concern still present?**
	Yes
	INSTALL a new HCU. TEST the system for normal operation.
	
	No
	The system is operating correctly at this time. The concern may have been caused by a loose or corroded connector. CLEAR the DTC(s). REPEAT the self-test.

LTV0500000004133

Fig. 20   Test I, Codes C1141, C1142, C1143, C1144, C1233, C1234, C1235 & C1236: Wheel Speed Sensor Tone Ring Tooth Missing Fault/Wheel Speed Input Signal Missing (Part 3 of 3). 2005-06

- **Are the resistances less than 5 ohms?**

J3 CHECK THE SENSOR CLUSTER CIRCUITRY FOR A SHORT TO POWER

Test Step	Result / Action to Take
• Key in ON position. • Measure the voltage between the sensor cluster, harness side and ground as follows: | Sensor Cluster Connector Pin	Circuit
C2296-1	1815 (PK/LB)
C2296-2	1814 (WH/LB)
C2296-3	1576 (TN/BK)
C2296-5	1575 (BK/WH)		**Yes** REPAIR the circuit(s) in question. CLEAR the DTC(s). CALIBRATE the ABS module. FOLLOW the diagnostic tool directions for the calibration procedure. REPEAT the self-test. **No** GO to J4 .

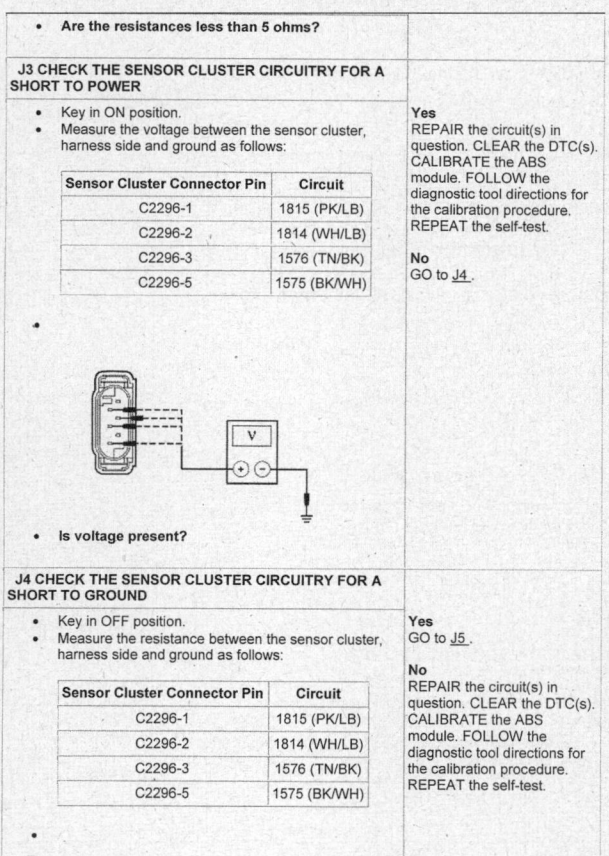

- **Is voltage present?**

J4 CHECK THE SENSOR CLUSTER CIRCUITRY FOR A SHORT TO GROUND

Test Step	Result / Action to Take
• Key in OFF position. • Measure the resistance between the sensor cluster, harness side and ground as follows: | Sensor Cluster Connector Pin	Circuit
C2296-1	1815 (PK/LB)
C2296-2	1814 (WH/LB)
C2296-3	1576 (TN/BK)
C2296-5	1575 (BK/WH)		**Yes** GO to J5 . **No** REPAIR the circuit(s) in question. CLEAR the DTC(s). CALIBRATE the ABS module. FOLLOW the diagnostic tool directions for the calibration procedure. REPEAT the self-test.

LTV0500000004135

Fig. 21   Test J, Codes C1305, C2768, C2769, C2778, C2783, U1901 & U2527: Sensor Cluster Circuit Failure (Part 2 of 3). 2005-06

Test Step	Result / Action to Take
J1 CARRY OUT THE RECALIBRATION PROCEDURE	
NOTE: Make sure the vehicle is not on a hoist and is sitting on level ground before performing stability assist module calibration. • Key in ON position. • Connect the diagnostic tool. • Clear the DTCs. Carry out the sensor cluster recalibration procedure using the diagnostic tool. • Retrieve the DTCs. • **Are any DTCs retrieved or does the recalibration procedure indicate a fault?**	**Yes** GO to J2 . **No** The ABS system is operating correctly. The condition may have been caused by an incomplete or inaccurate calibration.
J2 CHECK THE SENSOR CLUSTER CIRCUITRY FOR AN OPEN	
• Key in OFF position. • Disconnect: ABS Module C1462. • Disconnect: Sensor Cluster C2296. • Measure the resistance between ABS module C1462, harness side and the sensor cluster C2296, harness side as follows: 	ABS Module Connector Pin	Circuit	Sensor Cluster Connector Pin	Circuit
---	---	---	---
C1462-39	1576 (TN/BK)	C2296-3	1576 (TN/BK)
C1462-27	1575 (BK/WH)	C2296-5	1575 (BK/WH)
C1462-26	1815 (PK/LB)	C2296-1	1815 (PK/LB)
C1462-11	1814 (WH/LB)	C2296-2	1814 (WH/LB)		**Yes** GO to J3 . **No** REPAIR the circuit(s) in question. CLEAR the DTC(s). CALIBRATE the ABS module. FOLLOW the diagnostic tool directions for the calibration procedure. REPEAT the self-test.

LTV0500000004134

Fig. 21   Test J, Codes C1305, C2768, C2769, C2778, C2783, U1901 & U2527: Sensor Cluster Circuit Failure (Part 1 of 3). 2005-06

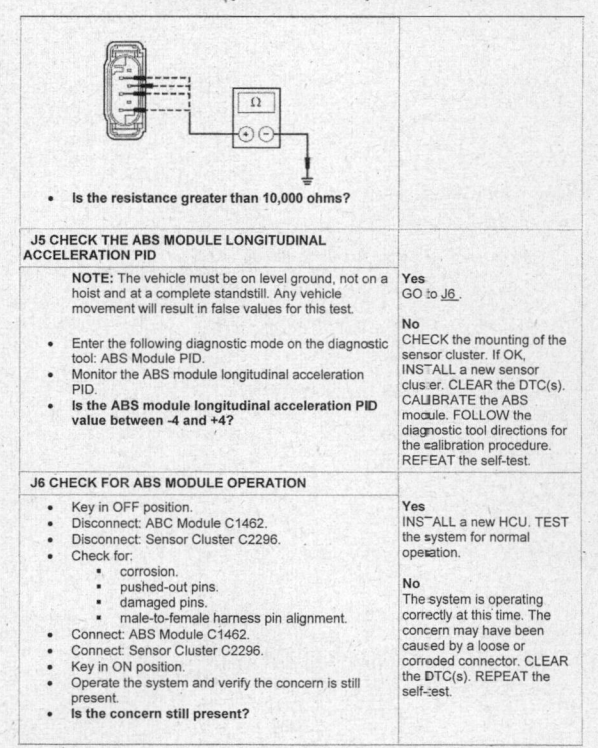

- **Is the resistance greater than 10,000 ohms?**

J5 CHECK THE ABS MODULE LONGITUDINAL ACCELERATION PID

Test Step	Result / Action to Take
NOTE: The vehicle must be on level ground, not on a hoist and at a complete standstill. Any vehicle movement will result in false values for this test. • Enter the following diagnostic mode on the diagnostic tool: ABS Module PID. • Monitor the ABS module longitudinal acceleration PID. • **Is the ABS module longitudinal acceleration PID value between -4 and +4?**	**Yes** GO to J6 . **No** CHECK the mounting of the sensor cluster. If OK, INSTALL a new sensor cluster. CLEAR the DTC(s). CALIBRATE the ABS module. FOLLOW the diagnostic tool directions for the calibration procedure. REPEAT the self-test.
J6 CHECK FOR ABS MODULE OPERATION	

• Key in OFF position.
• Disconnect: ABC Module C1462.
• Disconnect: Sensor Cluster C2296.
• Check for:
  ■ corrosion.
  ■ pushed-out pins.
  ■ damaged pins.
  ■ male-to-female harness pin alignment.
• Connect: ABS Module C1462.
• Connect: Sensor Cluster C2296.
• Key in ON position.
• Operate the system and verify the concern is still present.
• **Is the concern still present?**
	Yes
	INSTALL a new HCU. TEST the system for normal operation.
	
	No
	The system is operating correctly at this time. The concern may have been caused by a loose or corroded connector. CLEAR the DTC(s). REPEAT the self-test.

LTV0500000004136

Fig. 21   Test J, Codes C1305, C2768, C2769, C2778, C2783, U1901 & U2527: Sensor Cluster Circuit Failure (Part 3 of 3). 2005-06

Test Step	Result / Action to Take
K1 RETRIEVE ABS MODULE AND POWERTRAIN CONTROL MODULE (PCM) DTCs	
• Connect the diagnostic tool. • Key in ON position. • Retrieve ABS module and PCM DTCs. • **Are any DTCs retrieved?**	**Yes** For ABS module DTCs, GO to the Anti-Lock Brake System (ABS) Module Diagnostic Trouble Code (DTC) Index. **No** GO to K2 .
K2 RETRIEVE THE TRANSMISSION CONTROL MODULE (TCM) FREEZE FRAME DATA	
• Retrieve the TCM freeze frame data. • Record the ABS status PID and the powertrain control module (PCM) total torque desired PID. • **Does the ABS status PID indicate active and the PCM PID indicate greater than 200 Nm (148 lb-ft)?**	**Yes** GO to K3 . **No** CLEAR the DTCs. REPEAT the self-test. If DTC C1218 returns, GO to K4 . If DTC C1218 does not return, the system is operating correctly at this time.
K3 MONITOR THE TOTAL TORQUE DESIRED PID IN THE TCM	
• Enter the following diagnostic mode on the diagnostic tool: TCM PID. • Road test the vehicle performing an ABS event while monitoring the total torque desired PID. • **Does the total torque desired PID indicate less than 200 Nm (148 lb-ft)?**	**Yes** GO to K4 . **No** GO to K7 .
K4 MONITOR THE ABS STATUS PID IN THE TCM	
• Enter the following diagnostic mode on the diagnostic tool: ABS module PID. • Road test the vehicle performing an ABS event while monitoring the ABS status PID. • **Does the ABS status PID indicate active during the ABS event and inactive during a normal road test?**	**Yes** GO to K6 . **No** GO to K5 .
K5 CHECK FOR ABS MODULE OPERATION	
• Disconnect the ABS module connector. • Check for: ▪ corrosion.	**Yes** INSTALL a new HCU. TEST the system for normal operation.

LTV0500000004137

Fig. 22   Test K, Code C1218: Lamp Anti-Lock Brake System Warning Output Failure (Part 1 of 2). 2005-06

Code	Display	Action
00	NO ERROR	None
01	BFLS (Brake Fluid Level Sensor) LOW	Add brake fluid
02	USER BREAK	Do not press the brake pedal
03	HPA (High Pressure Accumulator) LOADED	Wait for accumulator to discharge
04	STANDSTILL	Block the vehicle from moving
05	VOLTAGE LOW	Start the engine or charge the battery
06	FILL PRESSURE LOW	Maintain brake bleeder pressure at 2 bars
07	FILL PRESSURE NOT REMOVED	Remove the pressure bleeder equipment
08	WRONG BLEEDER	Close the open bleeder and open the correct bleeder as instructed
09	BLEEDER NOT OPEN	Open the correct bleeder screw
0A	BLEEDER OPEN	Close all open bleeder screws
0B	PEDAL FAST	Press brake pedal more slowly
0C	PEDAL WEAK	Press brake pedal more firmly
0D	IGNITION OFF	Turn off the ignition
0E	FATAL ERROR	HCU defect

LTV0500000004142

Fig. 23   Service bleed error code chart. Hybrid

Test Step	Result / Action to Take
▪ pushed-out pins. • Connect the ABS module connector and make sure it seats correctly. • Operate the system and verify the concern is still present. • **Is the concern still present?**	**No** The system is operating correctly at this time. The concern may have been caused by a loose or corroded connector. CLEAR the DTC(s). REPEAT the self-test.
K6 CHECK FOR TCM OPERATION	

• Disconnect the TCM.
• Check for:
  ▪ corrosion.
  ▪ pushed-out pins.
• Connect the TCM and make sure it seats correctly.
• Operate the system and verify the concern is still present.
• **Is the concern still present?**
	Yes
	INSTALL a new TCM.. CLEAR the DTCs. REPEAT the self-test.
	No
	The system is operating correctly at this time. The concern may have been caused by a loose or corroded connector.

K7 CHECK FOR PCM OPERATION	

• Disconnect the PCM.
• Check for:
  ▪ corrosion.
  ▪ pushed-out pins.
• Connect the PCM and make sure it seats correctly.
• Operate the system and verify the concern is still present.
• **Is the concern still present?**
	Yes
	INSTALL a new PCM. CLEAR the DTC(s). REPEAT the self-test.
	No
	The system is operating correctly at this time. The concern may have been caused by a loose or corroded connector. CLEAR the DTC(s). REPEAT the self-test.

LTV0500000004138

Fig. 22   Test K, Code C1218: Lamp Anti-Lock Brake System Warning Output Failure (Part 2 of 2). 2005-06

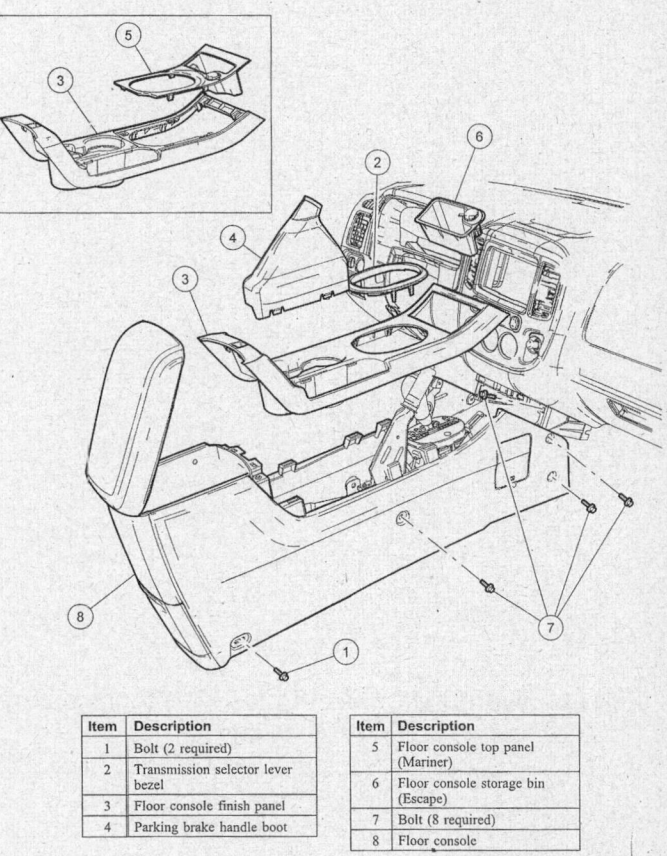

Item	Description		Item	Description
1	Bolt (2 required)		5	Floor console top panel (Mariner)
2	Transmission selector lever bezel		6	Floor console storage bin (Escape)
3	Floor console finish panel		7	Bolt (8 required)
4	Parking brake handle boot		8	Floor console

LTV0500000004143

Fig. 24   Floor console replacement

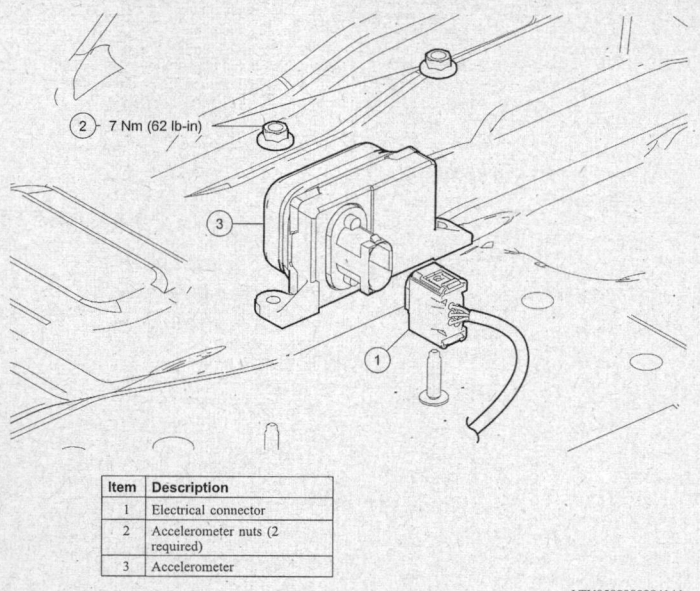

Item	Description
1	Electrical connector
2	Accelerometer nuts (2 required)
3	Accelerometer

LTV0500000004144

Fig. 25 Accelerometer replacement

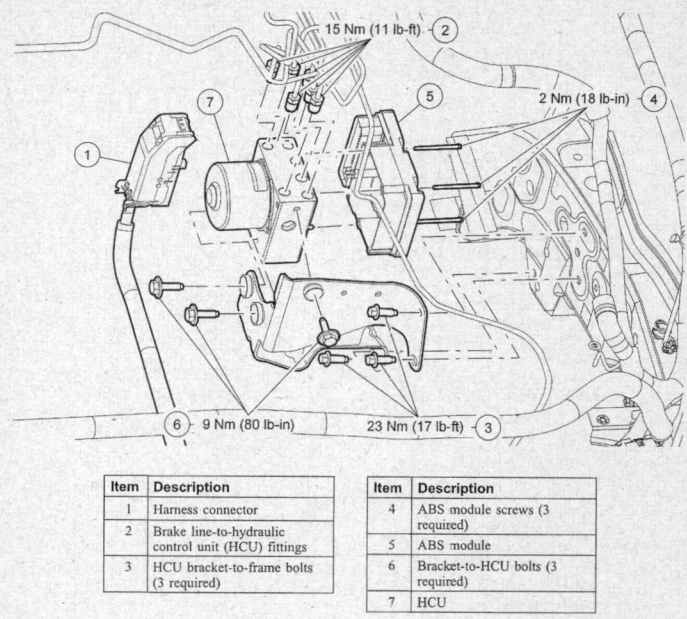

Item	Description	Item	Description
1	Harness connector	4	ABS module screws (3 required)
2	Brake line-to-hydraulic control unit (HCU) fittings	5	ABS module
3	HCU bracket-to-frame bolts (3 required)	6	Bracket-to-HCU bolts (3 required)
		7	HCU

LTV0500000004139

**Fig. 26 Hydraulic Control Unit (HCU) replacement.
Except Hybrid**

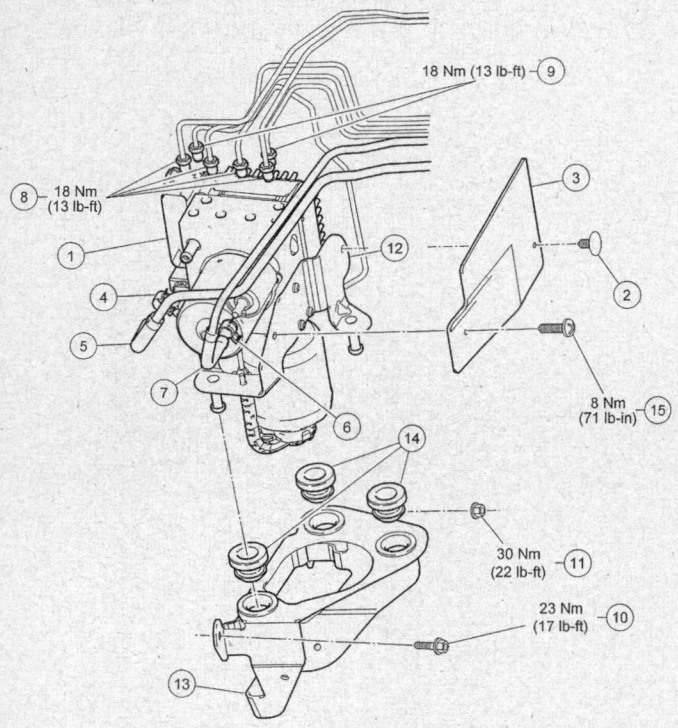

LTV0500000004140

**Fig. 27 Hydraulic Control Unit (HCU) replacement
(Part 1 of 2). Hybrid**

Item	Description
1	Harness connector
2	Heat shield pin-type fasteners (2 required)
3	Heat shield
4	Brake fluid low pressure feed hose clamp
5	Brake fluid low pressure feed hose
6	Brake fluid low pressure return hose clamp
7	Brake fluid low pressure return hose
8	Brake line-to-HCU fittings (10 mm)
9	Brake line-to-HCU fittings (12 mm)
10	HCU bracket-to-frame bolts (3 required) (vehicles built through 9/2005)
11	HCU bracket-to-frame nuts (3 required) (vehicles built after 9/2005)
12	HCU
13	HCU bracket
14	Grommets (3 required)
15	Heat shield screw

LTV0500000004141

**Fig. 27 Hydraulic Control Unit
(HCU) replacement (Part 2 of 2).
Hybrid**

E-Series

NOTE: Electrical Symbol & Wire Color Code Identification Located In The Front Of This Manual May Be Used As An Aid When Using Wiring Circuits Found In This Section.

NOTE: Refer To "Computer Relearn Procedures" Located In The Front Of This Manual When Battery Power To The Computer Has Been Interrupted.

INDEX

	Page No.		Page No.		Page No.
Description	5-39	**Diagnostic Chart Index**	5-45	Hydraulic Control Unit (HCU)	5-40
Diagnosis & Testing	5-39	**Precautions**	5-39	Stability Control Sensor	
Accessing Diagnostic Trouble		Battery Ground Cable	5-39	Cluster	5-40
Codes	5-39	Brake Fluid Handling	5-39	Steering Wheel Rotation	
Clearing Diagnostic Trouble		**System Service**	5-40	Sensor	5-40
Codes	5-39	Brake System Bleed	5-40	Wheel Speed Sensor	5-40
Diagnostic Tests	5-39	Component Replacement	5-40	**Troubleshooting**	5-39
Diagnostic Trouble Code		ABS Control Module	5-40	Symptom Chart	5-39
Interpretation	5-39	Front Wheel Speed Sensor			
Wiring Diagrams	5-39	Ring	5-40		

PRECAUTIONS

BATTERY GROUND CABLE

Prior to service disconnect battery ground cable and isolate as required.

BRAKE FLUID HANDLING

Brake fluid can cause serious injury and vehicle damage if not handled properly. Avoid contact with eyes and do not allow fluid to splash or spill on painted surfaces. Wash hands thoroughly after handling.

DESCRIPTION

The anti-lock brake system (ABS) module, with or without stability assist, simultaneously manages the anti-lock braking, traction control and engine control systems to maintain vehicle control during deceleration and acceleration. The ABS accomplishes this by communicating with the other modules over the high speed controller area network (HS-CAN) bus.

When the ignition switch is in the RUN position, the module carries out a preliminary electrical check and, at approximately 20 km/h (12 mph), the hydraulic pump motor is turned on for approximately one half-second. Any malfunction of the anti-lock brake system disables the traction control and stability assist (if equipped). The ABS module communicates with the instrument cluster over the HS-CAN bus and the cluster illuminates the anti-lock brake warning indicator. However, the power-assist braking system functions normally.

With the ignition switch in the START or RUN positions, the stability assist module functions similarly to a conventional ABS module by monitoring and comparing the rotational speed of each wheel. The wheel

Condition	Possible Source	Action
• No communications with the anti-lock brake control module	• CJB Fuse 1 (20A). • Circuitry. • Anti-lock brake control module.	• GO to Pinpoint Test A.
• Unable to enter self-test	• Anti-lock brake control module.	• GO to Pinpoint Test B.

FM4029901452010X

Fig. 1 Symptom chart (Part 1 of 3). 2002–03

speed sensors electrically sense each tooth of the anti-lock sensor ring as they pass through the sensor magnetic field. When the stability assist module detects an impending wheel lock, wheel spin or vehicle motion that is inconsistent with the driver commands, it modulates brake pressure to the appropriate brake caliper(s). The stability assist module triggers the hydraulic control unit (HCU) to open and close the appropriate solenoid valves. Once the affected wheel(s) return to the desired speed, the stability assist module returns the solenoid valves to their normal position, and normal base brake operation is restored.

TROUBLESHOOTING

Symptom Chart

Refer to **Figs. 1 and 3** for symptom charts.

DIAGNOSIS & TESTING

Accessing Diagnostic Trouble Codes

Connect a suitably programmed scan tool and Vehicle Communication Module (VCM) with appropriate adapters, or equivalents, to the Data Link Connector (DCL) located in the passenger compartment be-

neath the instrument panel. Follow tool manufacturer's instructions for accessing Diagnostic Trouble Codes (DTC).

Diagnostic Trouble Code Interpretation

Refer to **Figs. 4 and 5** for diagnostic trouble code interpretation.

Wiring Diagrams

Refer to **Figs. 6 through 9** for wiring diagram.

Diagnostic Tests

Refer to **Figs. 10 through 47** for pinpoint tests.

Clearing Diagnostic Trouble Codes

Connect a suitably programmed scan tool and Vehicle Communication Module (VCM) with appropriate adapters, or equivalents, to the Data Link Connector (DCL) located in the passenger compartment beneath the instrument panel. Follow tool manufacturer's instructions for clearing Diagnostic Trouble Codes (DTC).

Condition	Possible Source	Action
• ABS misfire, ABS too sensitive, ABS fires on normal stop	• Front anti-lock brake sensor indicator.	• INSPECT for damaged teeth. INSPECT both front anti-lock brake sensor indicators. CHECK anti-lock brake sensor gap.
	• Chafed wire insulation or pinched wire.	• INSPECT the wiring harness from the front anti-lock brake sensor knuckle to the frame and from the rear axle to the frame for worn or chafed wire insulation.
	• Intermittent open or shorted anti-lock brake sensor circuit.	• CARRY OUT the Intermittent Failures for Circuits 514 (YE/RD) and 516 (YE/BK), and 523 (RD/PK) and 519 (LG/BK).
	• Rear anti-lock brake sensor indicator. • Anti-lock brake sensor output.	• INSPECT rear anti-lock brake sensor indicator. • If left front anti-lock brake sensor output is weak, GO to Pinpoint Test G. If right front anti-lock brake sensor output is weak, GO to Pinpoint Test I. If rear anti-lock brake sensor output is weak, GO to Pinpoint Test K.
	• Rear brake adjustment. • Linings.	• ELIMINATE the base brake system as the cause of the problem.
• Wheels lock up	• Hydraulic outlet (dump) valve. • Leaky inlet (isolation) valve during ABS (soft).	• GO to Pinpoint Test L. • INSTALL a new HCU; REFER to Hydraulic Control Unit—(HCU).
	• Rear brake shoe linings, wheel cylinder, rear brakes. • Parking brake. • Rear axle seal.	• ELIMINATE the base brake system as the cause of the problem.
• Soft/excessive pedal travel	• Inlet (isolation) valve or outlet (dump) valve.	• GO to Pinpoint Test L.
	• Brake line or hose, fitting, master cylinder, wheel cylinder or caliper. • Air in brake system. • Little or no vacuum boost. • Wheel cylinder or caliper.	• ELIMINATE the base brake system as the cause of the problem.
• Lack of deceleration during medium/hard brake application	• Inlet (isolation) valve or outlet (dump) valve.	• GO to Pinpoint Test L.
	• Brake line or hose, fitting, master cylinder, wheel cylinder or caliper. • Air in brake system. • Little or no vacuum boost. • Wheel cylinder or caliper. • Brake shoe or pad linings.	• ELIMINATE the base brake system as the cause of the problem.

FM4029901452020X

Fig. 1   Symptom chart (Part 2 of 3). 2002–03

Condition	Possible Source	Action
• Vehicle pulls during braking	• Intermittent sensor failure. • Base brake.	• GO to Sensor Failure. • ELIMINATE the base brake system as the cause of the problem.
• ABS warning indicator illuminated with system pass	• Circuitry. • Anti-lock brake control module.	• DISCONNECT 24-pin connector from anti-lock brake control module. If the lamp is on, REPAIR Circuit 603 (DG). If lamp is off, INSTALL a new anti-lock brake control module;
• The red BRAKE warning indicator does not self-check	• CJB Fuse 2 (15A). • Circuitry. • Red BRAKE warning indicator relay. • Anti-lock brake control module.	• GO to Pinpoint Test D.
• The red BRAKE warning indicator stays on with the ignition switch in RUN	• Circuitry. • Red BRAKE warning indicator relay. • Anti-lock brake control module.	• DIAGNOSE red BRAKE warning indicator that is on continuously.
• The yellow ABS warning indicator does not self-check	• CJB Fuse 2 (15A). • Circuitry. • Anti-lock brake control module.	• GO to Pinpoint Test C.
• The red BRAKE warning indicator and yellow ABS warning indicator are illuminated	• DRP.	• GO to the Anti-Lock Brake Control Module Diagnostic Trouble Code (DTC) Index.

FM4020001693000X

Fig. 1   Symptom chart (Part 3 of 3). 2002–03

SYSTEM SERVICE
Brake System Bleed

Refer to "Hydraulic Brake Systems" chapter for bleeding procedure.

Component Replacement

ABS CONTROL MODULE

1. Remove three bolts, then position degas bottle aside.
2. Remove four ABS module mounting screws, **Fig. 48,** then position module to access electrical connector.
3. Release ABS module connect lock tab, then disconnect electrical connector.
4. Remove ABS control module.
5. Reverse procedure to install. **Torque** ABS control module retaining screws to 44 inch lbs.

FRONT WHEEL SPEED SENSOR RING

1. Raise and support vehicle.
2. Remove front disc brake caliper, then position caliper aside.
3. Remove front disc brake rotor.
4. **On 450–550 models,** remove hub extender and brake disc.
5. **On all models,** remove front wheel speed sensor ring using suitable three jaw puller and step plate adapter tool

No. D80L-630-A, or equivalent.
6. Install front wheel speed sensor ring using an appropriate size cylinder and suitable press.

HYDRAULIC CONTROL UNIT (HCU)

1. Remove three bolts, then position degas bottle aside.
2. Remove four ABS module mounting screws, **Fig. 48,** then position module to access electrical connector.
3. **On models equipped with 6.0L engine,** remove four bolts, then position power steering fluid reservoir and bracket aside.
4. **On all models,** disconnect brake tube fittings from master cylinder.
5. Disconnect two hydraulic brake lines from HCU.
6. Disconnect ABS control module electrical connectors.
7. Remove HCU retaining bolts, then the HCU.
8. Reverse procedure to install, noting the following:
   a. **Torque** HCU retaining bolts to 21 ft. lbs.
   b. **Torque** brake lines to 13 ft. lbs.
   c. **Torque** module screws to 44 inch lbs.
   d. Bleed brake system as outlined under "Brake System Bleed."

STABILITY CONTROL SENSOR CLUSTER

1. Disconnect stability control sensor

cluster electrical connector, **Fig. 49.**
2. Remove two stability control sensor cluster bolts, then the sensor.
3. Reverse procedure to install. Torque sensor bolts to 53 inch lbs.

STEERING WHEEL ROTATION SENSOR

1. Remove lefthand instrument panel under cover.
2. Disconnect steering wheel rotation sensor electrical connector, **Fig. 50.**
3. Remove two rotation sensor retaining screws.
4. Remove steering wheel rotation sensor.
5. Reverse procedure to install.

WHEEL SPEED SENSOR

FRONT

1. Raise and support vehicle.
2. Disconnect speed sensor electrical connector.
3. Separate sensor cable harness from brake hose clips.
4. Remove sensor mounting bolt, then the sensor.
5. Reverse procedure to install. **Torque** sensor mounting bolt to 96 inch lbs.

REAR

1. Raise and support vehicle.
2. Clean area around wheel speed sensor.
3. Disconnect wheel speed sensor electrical connector.
4. Remove sensor retaining bolt, then the sensor.
5. Reverse procedure to install, noting the following:
   a. Install a new O-ring before installing rear axle speed sensor.
   b. Lubricate O-ring with high performance rear axle lubricant F1TZ-19580-B, or equivalent, meeting Ford specification WSL-M2C192-A.
   c. **Torque** speed sensor retaining bolt to 20 ft. lbs.

Condition	Possible Sources	Action
• No communication with the anti-lock brake system (ABS) module	• Circuitry • ABS module	• Go To Pinpoint Test A.
• Soft/excessive brake pedal travel	• Inlet (isolation) valve or hydraulic outlet (dump) valve • Leaky inlet (isolation) valve during ABS applications (soft)	• Go To Pinpoint Test G.
	• Brake line or hose, fitting, master cylinder, wheel cylinder or caliper • Air in brake system • Brake shoe or pad linings • Parking brake • Rear axle seal	• ELIMINATE the base brake system as the cause of the problem.
• ABS false activation, ABS too sensitive, ABS activates on normal stop	• Front anti-lock brake sensor indicators	• INSPECT both front wheel speed sensor rings for damaged teeth. CHECK the wheel speed sensor gap.
	• Chafed wire insulation or	• INSPECT the wiring harness from the

LTV0500000004951

Fig. 2   Symptom chart (Part 1 of 3). 2004-06 less stability assist

Condition	Possible Sources	Action
pinched wire	front wheel speed sensor knuckle to the frame and from the rear axle to the frame.
• Open or shorted wheel speed sensor circuit	• Go To Pinpoint Test B.
• Rear wheel speed sensor indicator	• INSPECT the rear ABS indicator.
• Wheel speed sensor	• Go To Pinpoint Test D.
• Rear brake adjustment • Linings	• ELIMINATE the base brake system as the cause of the problem
• Wheels lock up	• Hydraulic outlet (dump) valve • Leaky inlet (isolation) valve during ABS (soft)	• Go To Pinpoint Test G.
	• Front or rear brakes • Parking brake • Rear axle seal	• ELIMINATE the base brake system as the cause of the problem.
• Vehicle pulls during braking	• Sensor failure	• Go To Pinpoint Test B.
	• Base brake system	• ELIMINATE the base brake system as the cause of the problem.
• Anti-lock brake system (ABS) warning indicator illuminated	• Circuitry • Brake fluid level • ABS module	• REFER to "Dash Gauges & Warning Indicators"

LTV0500000004952

Fig. 2   Symptom chart (Part 2 of 3). 2004-06 less stability assist

Condition	Possible Sources	Action
• The red BRAKE warning indicator stays on when the ignition switch is in RUN	• Circuitry • Brake fluid level • Instrument cluster • Anti-lock brake system (ABS) module	• Check base brake system.
• The yellow anti-lock brake system (ABS) warning indicator does not self-check	• Circuitry • Brake fluid level • Instrument cluster • ABS module	• Continue diagnosis of the warning indicator.
• The red BRAKE warning indicator and yellow anti-lock brake system (ABS) warning indicator are illuminated	• Dynamic rear proportioning (DRP)	• GO to Diagnostic Trouble Code (DTC) Index.

LTV0500000004953

Fig. 2   Symptom chart (Part 3 of 3). 2004-06 less stability assist

Condition	Possible Sources	Action
• No communication with the anti-lock brake system (ABS) module	• Fuse • Circuitry • ABS module	• Go To Pinpoint Test K.
• ABS false activation, ABS too sensitive, ABS activates on normal stop	• Front anti-lock brake sensor indicators	• INSPECT both front wheel speed sensor rings for damaged teeth. CHECK the wheel speed sensor gap.
	• Chafed wire insulation or pinched wire	• INSPECT the wiring harness from the front wheel speed sensor knuckle to the frame and from the rear axle to the frame.
	• Rear wheel speed sensor, excessive variance in air gap between wheel speed sensor and sensor ring	• INSPECT both rear wheel speed sensor rings for damaged teeth. CHECK the wheel speed sensor air gap (0.16-1.65 mm). CHECK the sensor ring run out (0.28 mm max.). If the air gap or run out are not within specification, INSTALL a new hub assembly.
	• Open or shorted wheel speed sensor circuit	• Go To Pinpoint Test N.
	• Rear wheel speed sensor indicator	• INSPECT the rear ABS indicator.
	• Wheel speed sensor	• Go To Pinpoint Test O.
	• Rear brake adjustment	• ELIMINATE the base brake system as the cause of the

LTV0500000004968

Fig. 3   Symptom chart (Part 1 of 2). 2004-06 w/stability assist

	• Linings	problem.
• The red brake warning indicator does not self-check	• Instrument cluster • Brake fluid level • Circuitry • Anti-lock brake system (ABS) module	• Check Communications Area Network (CAN)
• The red brake warning indicator stays on when the ignition is in RUN	• Circuitry • Brake fluid level • Anti-lock brake system (ABS) module • Instrument cluster	• RETRIEVE all DTCs and GO TO the DTC indexes. If no DTCs are present, REFER to "Dash Gauges & Warning Indicators"
• The yellow anti-lock brake system (ABS) warning indicator does not self-check	• Instrument cluster • Brake fluid level • Circuitry • Anti-lock brake system (ABS) module	• REFER to "Dash Gauges & Warning Indicators"
• The Stability/Traction control switch indicator is inoperative.	• Instrument cluster • Circuitry • Traction control switch	• Go To Pinpoint Test V .

LTV0500000004969

Fig. 3   Symptom chart (Part 2 of 2). 2004-06 w/stability assist

DTC	Description
B1317	Battery Voltage High
B1318	Battery Voltage Low
B1342	ECU Is Faulted
B211B	Satellite ECU Is Faulted
B2900	VIN Mismatch
C1095	ABS Hydraulic Pump Motor Circuit Failure
C1096	ABS Hydraulic Pump Motor Circuit Open
C1115	ABS Power Relay Output Short Circuit To Battery
C1145	Speed Wheel Sensor RF Input Circuit Failure
C1155	Speed Wheel Sensor LF Input Circuit Failure
C1165	Speed Wheel Sensor RR Input Circuit Failure
C1175	Speed Wheel Sensor LR Input Circuit Failure
C1185	ABS Power Relay Output Circuit Failure
C1194	ABS Outlet Valve Coil LF Circuit Failure
C1198	ABS Inlet Valve Coil LF Circuit Failure
C1210	ABS Outlet Valve Coil RF Circuit Failure
C1214	ABS Inlet Valve Coil RF Circuit Failure
C1222	Speed Wheel Mismatch
C1233	Speed Wheel LF Input Signal Missing
C1234	Speed Wheel RF Input Signal Missing
C1235	Speed Wheel RR Input Signal Missing
C1236	Speed Wheel LR Input Signal Missing
C1242	ABS Outlet Valve Coil LR Circuit Failure
C1246	ABS Outlet Valve Coil RR Circuit Failure
C1250	ABS Inlet Valve Coil LR Circuit Failure
C1254	ABS Inlet Valve Coil RR Circuit Failure
C1277	Steering Wheel Angle 1 and 2 Circuit Failure
C1278	Steering Wheel Angle 1 and 2 Signal Faulted
C1279	Yaw Rate Sensor Circuit Failure
C1280	Yaw Rate Sensor Signal Fault
C1281	Lateral Accelerometer Circuit Failure
C1282	Lateral Accelerometer Signal Fault
C1288	Brake Pressure Transducer Main/Primary Input Circuit Failure
C1329	ABS Outlet Valve Coil RF Circuit Excessive Temperature
C1330	ABS Outlet Valve Coil LR Circuit Excessive Temperature

LTV0500000004966

Fig. 5   Diagnostic trouble code interpretation (Part 1 of 2). 2004-06

Diagnostic Trouble Code	Description
No Response During DTC Retrieval	Diagnostics
B1342	Anti-Lock Brake Control Module Failure
C1095/C1096	Pump Motor
C1113/C1115	Internal Power Relay
C1145	Right Front Brake Anti-Lock Sensor (Electrical/Static)
C1148/C1234	Right Front Brake Anti-Lock Sensor (Dynamic)
C1155	Left Front Brake Anti-Lock Sensor (Electrical/Static)
C1158/C1233	Left Front Brake Anti-Lock Sensor (Dynamic)
C1169	Excessive Dump Time
C1185	Open Internal Power Relay
C1230	Rear Brake Anti-Lock Sensor (Electrical/Static)
C1229/1237	Rear Brake Anti-Lock Sensor (Dynamic)
C1220	Yellow Anti-Lock Brake System (ABS) Warning Indicator Failure
C1184/C1222	Wheel Speed Error
C1198/C1200	Isolation Valve, Front Left
C1194/C1196	Dump Valve, Front Left
C1214/C1216	Isolation Valve, Front Right
C1210/C1212	Dump Valve, Front Right
C1206/C1208	Isolation Valve, Rear
C1202/C1204	Dump Valve, Rear
C1226	Faulty Red Brake Warning Indicator
C1225	Shorted Red Brake Warning Indicator Lamp Relay
Soft or Excessive Pedal Travel	Anti-Lock Brake Module
C1141(97)	Erratic Left Front Brake Anti-Lock Sensor or Damaged Left Front Sensor Indicator
C1142(97)	Erratic Right Front Wheel Speed Signal or Damaged Right Front Brake Anti-Lock Sensor
C1143(97)	Erratic Rear Wheel Speed Signal or Damaged Rear Sensor Indicator

FM4029901453000X

Fig. 4   Diagnostic trouble code interpretation. 2002–03

C1331	ABS Outlet Valve Coil RR Circuit Excessive Temperature
C1332	ABS Outlet Valve Coil LF Circuit Excessive Temperature
C1333	ABS Inlet Valve Coil LR Circuit Excessive Temperature
C1334	ABS Inlet Valve Coil LF Circuit Excessive Temperature
C1335	ABS Inlet Valve Coil RF Circuit Excessive Temperature
C1336	ABS Inlet Valve Coil RR Circuit Excessive Temperature
C1404	Traction Control Valve Rear Circuit Failure
C1410	Traction Control Valve LF Circuit Failure
C1446	Brake Switch Circuit Failure
C1516	Roll Rate Sensor Signal Fault
C1517	Roll Rate Sensor Circuit Fault
C1527	Traction Control Rear Valve Circuit Excessive Temperature
C1528	Traction Control LF Valve Circuit Excessive Temperature
C1530	Dynamic Stability Control RF Valve Circuit Excessive Temperature
C1531	Dynamic Stability Control LF Valve Circuit Excessive Temperature
C1730	Reference Voltage Out of Range (+5 V)
C1957	Dynamic Stability Control Valve RF Circuit Failure
C1958	Stability Assist Control Valve LF Circuit Failure
C1963	Stability Control Inhibit Warning
C1991	Module Calibration Failure
C2769	Longitudinal Acceleration Sensor Electrical Failure
C2770	Longitudinal Acceleration Sensor Plausibilty Failure
U0073	Control Module Communication Bus Off
U1900	Can Communication Bus Fault - Receive Error
U1901	CAN Network # 2 Comm Bus Fault - Receive Error
C110B	Traction Control Disable Switch Circuit Open

LTV0500000004967

Fig. 5   Diagnostic trouble code interpretation (Part 2 of 2). 2004-06

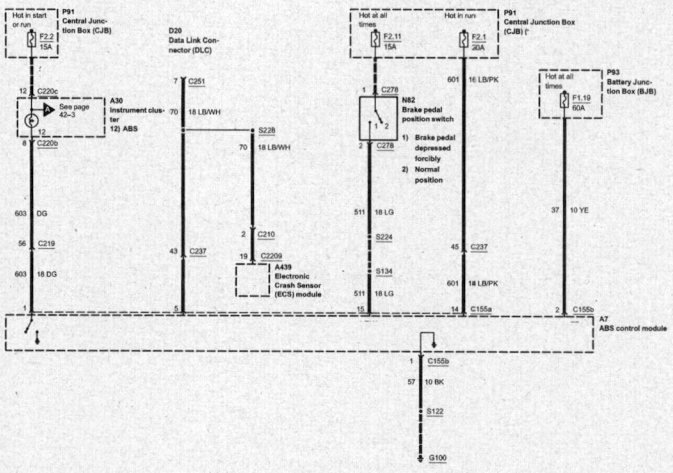

Fig. 6   Wiring diagram (Part 1 of 2). 2002-03 Except striped chassis & E–550

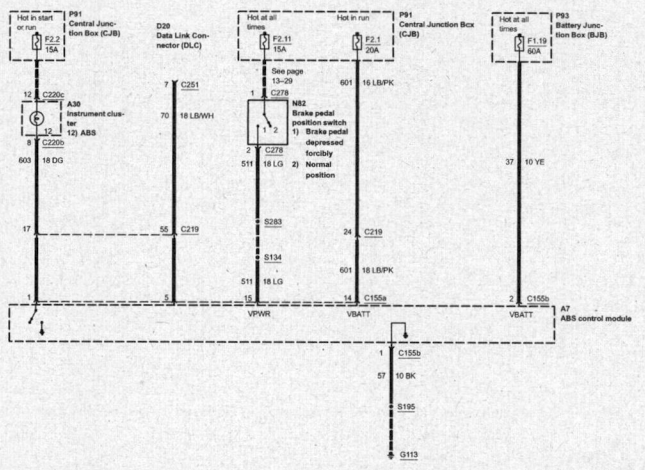

Fig. 7   Wiring diagram (Part 1 of 3). 2002-03 Stripped chassis

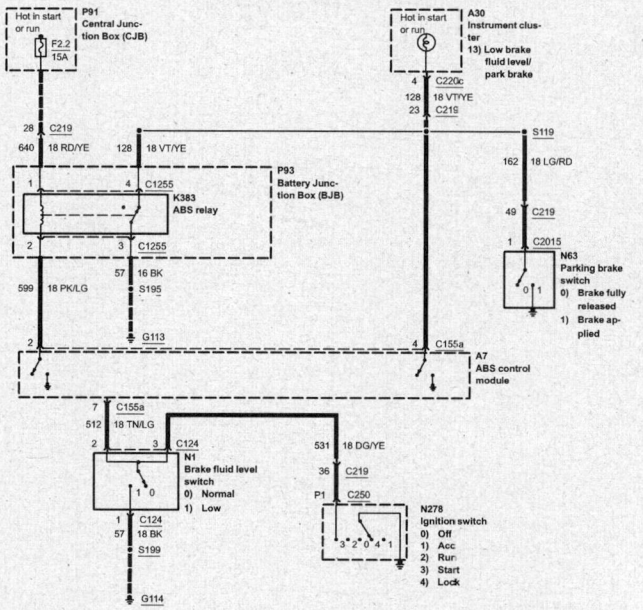

Fig. 7   Wiring diagram (Part 2 of 3). 2002-03 Stripped chassis

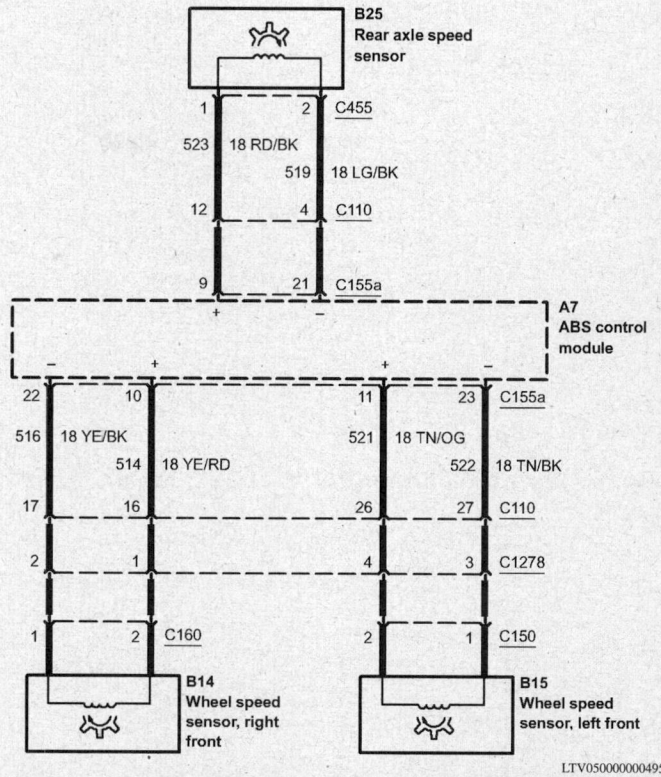

Fig. 6   Wiring diagram (Part 2 of 2). 2002-03 Except striped chassis & E–550

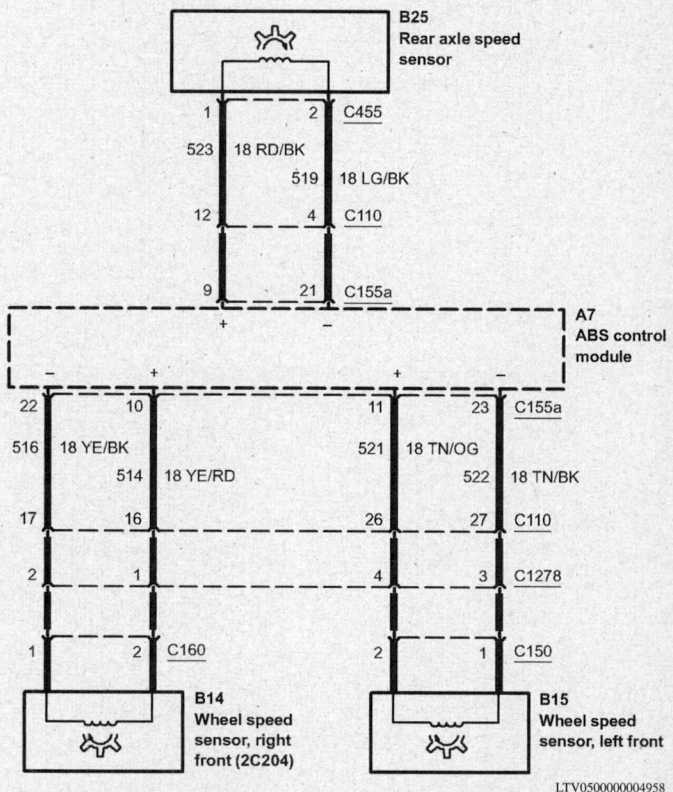

Fig. 7   Wiring diagram (Part 3 of 3). 2002-03 Stripped chassis

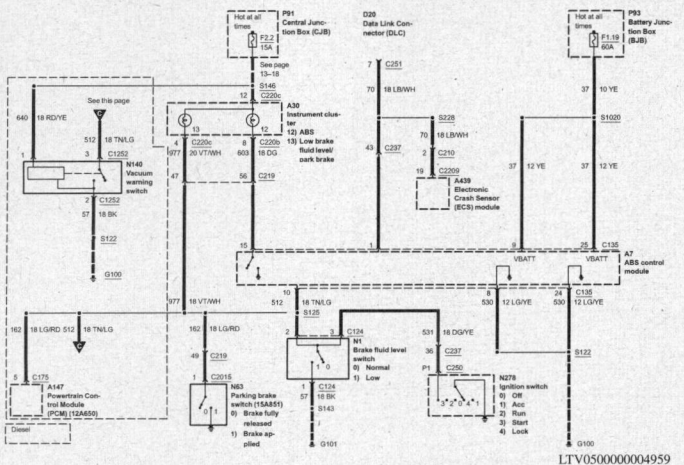

Fig. 8   Wiring diagram (Part 1 of 2). 2002-03 E-550

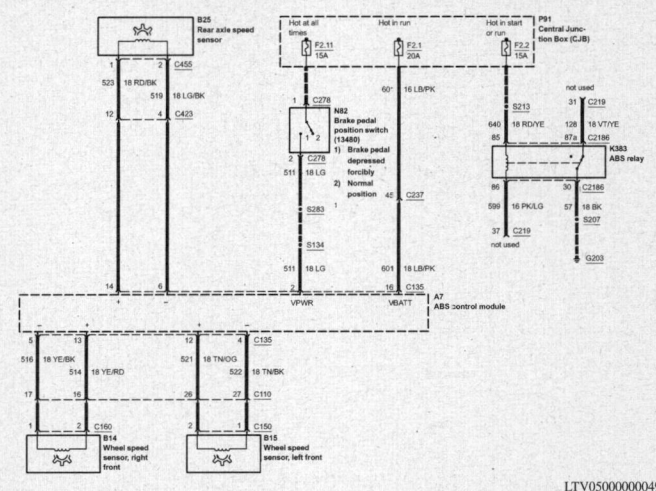

Fig. 8   Wiring diagram (Part 2 of 2). 2002-03 E-550

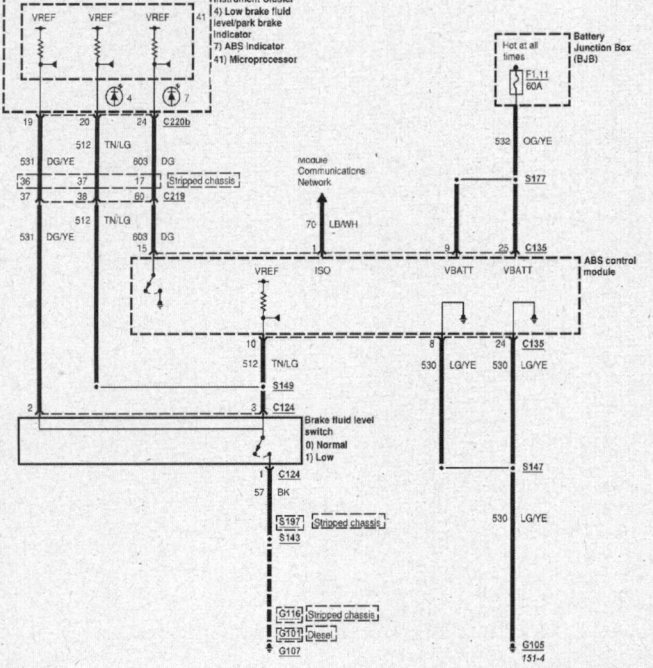

Fig. 9   Wiring diagram (Part 1 of 5). 2004-06

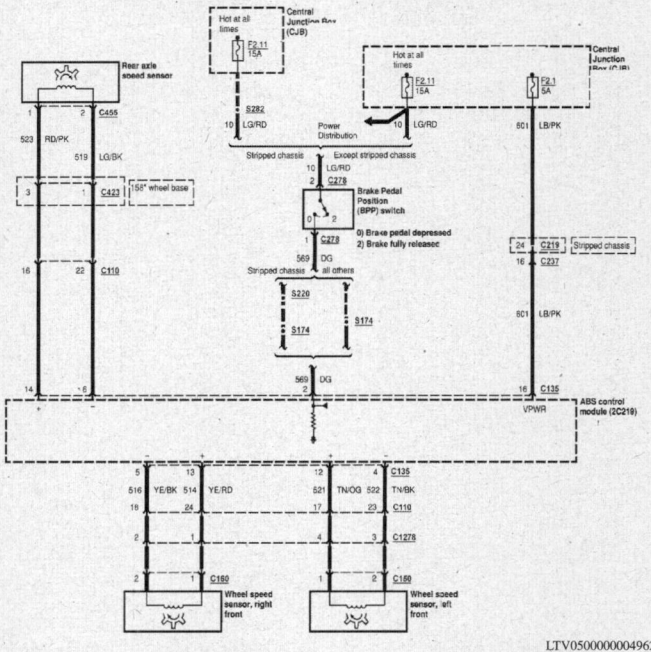

Fig. 9   Wiring diagram (Part 2 of 5). 2004-06

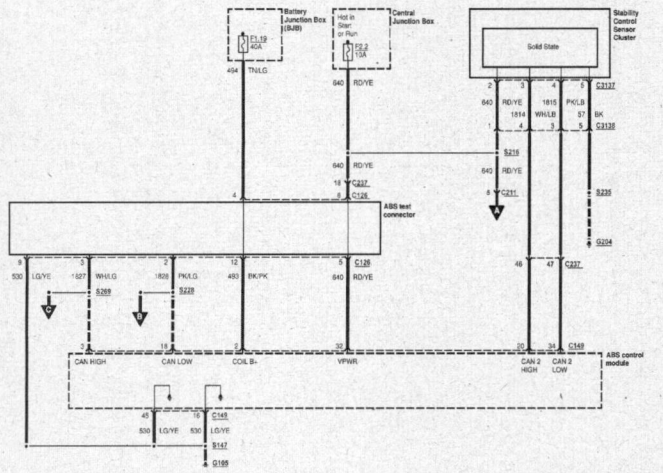

Fig. 9   Wiring diagram (Part 3 of 5). 2004-06

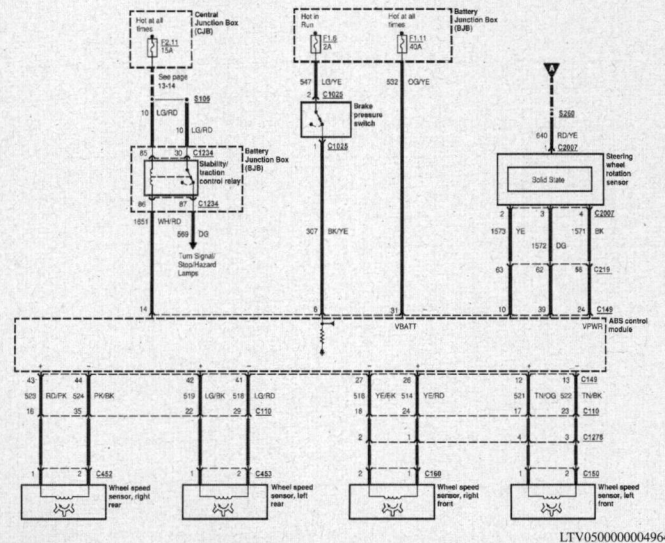

Fig. 9   Wiring diagram (Part 4 of 5). 2004-06

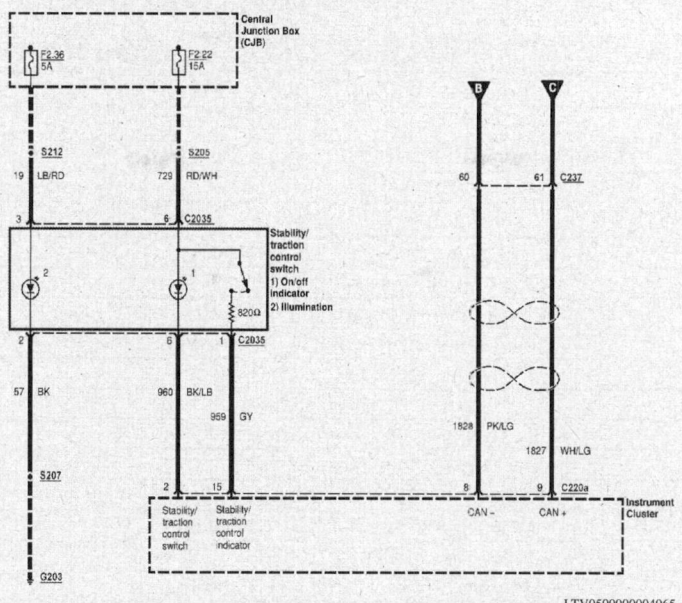

Fig. 9   Wiring diagram (Part 5 of 5). 2004–06

LTV0500000004965

DIAGNOSTIC CHART INDEX

Test	Code	Description	Page No.	Fig. No.
2002–03				
A	—	No Communication w/ABS Control Module	5-47	10
B	—	Unable To Enter Self Test	5-47	11
C	C1220	Yellow ABS Warning Indicator Failure	5-47	12
D	C1225	Faulty Red Brake Warning Indicator/Shorted Red Brake Warning Indicator Relay	5-48	13
	C1226	Faulty Red Brake Warning Indicator/Shorted Red Brake Warning Indicator Relay	5-48	13
E	C1194	Isolation Valve, Dump Valve	5-50	14
	C1196	Isolation Valve, Dump Valve	5-50	14
	C1198	Isolation Valve, Dump Valve	5-50	14
	C1200	Isolation Valve, Dump Valve	5-50	14
	C1202	Isolation Valve, Dump Valve	5-50	14
	C1204	Isolation Valve, Dump Valve	5-50	14
	C1206	Isolation Valve, Dump Valve	5-50	14
	C1208	Isolation Valve, Dump Valve	5-50	14
	C1210	Isolation Valve, Dump Valve	5-50	14
	C1212	Isolation Valve, Dump Valve	5-50	14
	C1214	Isolation Valve, Dump Valve	5-50	14
	C1216	Isolation Valve, Dump Valve	5-50	14
F	C1155	Left Front ABS Sensor, Electrical/Static	5-51	15
G	C1158	Left Front ABS Sensor, Dynamic	5-52	16
	C1233	Left Front ABS Sensor, Dynamic	5-52	16
H	C1145	Right Front ABS Sensor, Electrical/Static	5-53	17
I	C1148	Right Front Anti-Lock Brake Sensor, Dynamic	5-54	18
	C1234	Right Front Anti-Lock Brake Sensor, Dynamic	5-54	18
J	C1230	Rear Anti-Lock Brake Sensor, Electrical/Static	5-55	19
K	C1229	Rear Anti-Lock Brake Sensor, Dynamic	5-56	20
	C1237	Rear Anti-Lock Brake Sensor, Dynamic	5-56	20
L	—	Soft/Excessive Pedal Travel	5-57	21
M	C1095	Pump Motor	5-58	22
	C1096	Pump Motor	5-58	22
N	C1113	Internal Power Relay Failure	5-58	23
	C1115	Internal Power Relay Failure	5-58	23
	C1185	Internal Power Relay Failure	5-58	23

Continued

DIAGNOSTIC CHART INDEX—Continued

Test	Code	Description	Page No.	Fig. No.
2002–03				
O	—	Wheel Speed Error, Dynamic	5-59	24
P	C1169	Excessive Dump Time	5-59	25
2004–06 LESS STABILITY ASSIST				
A	—	No Communication w/ABS Module	5-59	26
B	C1145	Wheel Speed Sensor Input Circuit Failure	5-60	27
	C1155	Wheel Speed Sensor Input Circuit Failure	5-60	27
	C1230	Wheel Speed Sensor Input Circuit Failure	5-60	27
C	C1222	Wheel Speed Mismatch/Missing	5-61	28
	C1233	Wheel Speed Mismatch/Missing	5-61	28
	C1234	Wheel Speed Mismatch/Missing	5-61	28
	C1237	Wheel Speed Mismatch/Missing	5-61	28
D	C1148	Wheel Speed Sensor Coherency Fault	5-62	29
	C1158	Wheel Speed Sensor Coherency Fault	5-62	29
	C1229	Wheel Speed Sensor Coherency Fault	5-62	29
E	C1169	Excessive ABS System Fluid Dump Time	5-63	30
F	C1185	ABS Power Relay Output Circuit Failure	5-63	31
G	—	Soft Or Excessive Brake Pedal Travel	5-63	32
H	C1184	ABS System Time Out	5-64	33
I	C1095	ABS Pump Motor Circuit Failure/Open	5-64	34
	C1096	ABS Pump Motor Circuit Failure/Open	5-64	34
J	C1676	Battery Voltage Out Of Range	5-64	35
2004–06 w/STABILITY ASSIST				
K	—	No Communication w/ABS Module	5-65	36
L	B1317	Battery Voltage High/Low	5-65	37
	B1318	Battery Voltage High/Low	5-65	37
		Battery Voltage High/Low	5-65	37
M	C1095	ABS Hydraulic Pump Motor Circuit Failure/Open	5-66	38
	C1096	ABS Hydraulic Pump Motor Circuit Failure/Open	5-66	38
N	C1145	Wheel Speed Sensor Input Circuit Failure	5-66	39
	C1155	Wheel Speed Sensor Input Circuit Failure	5-66	39
	C1165	Wheel Speed Sensor Input Circuit Failure	5-66	39
	C1175	Wheel Speed Sensor Input Circuit Failure	5-66	39
O	C1222	Wheel Speed Sensor Input Signal Missing/Mismatch	5-67	40
	C1233	Wheel Speed Sensor Input Signal Missing/Mismatch	5-67	40
	C1234	Wheel Speed Sensor Input Signal Missing/Mismatch	5-67	40
	C1235	Wheel Speed Sensor Input Signal Missing/Mismatch	5-67	40
	C1236	Wheel Speed Sensor Input Signal Missing/Mismatch	5-67	40
P	C1277	Steering Wheel Angle 1 & 2 Circuit Failure/Fault	5-68	41
	C1278	Steering Wheel Angle 1 & 2 Circuit Failure/Fault	5-68	41
Q	C1279,	Sensor Cluster Fault	5-69	42
	C1280,	Sensor Cluster Fault	5-69	42
	C1281,	Sensor Cluster Fault	5-69	42
	C1282	Sensor Cluster Fault	5-69	42
	C1516	Sensor Cluster Fault	5-69	42
	C1517	Sensor Cluster Fault	5-69	42
	C2769	Sensor Cluster Fault	5-69	42
	C2770	Sensor Cluster Fault	5-69	42
R	C1288	Pressure Transducer Main/Primary Input Circuit Failure	5-70	43
S	C1446	Brake Pedal Switch Circuit Failure	5-70	44
T	C1991	Module Calibration Failure	5-71	45
U	C1901	Can Network No. 2 Communication Bus Fault-Recieve Error	5-71	46
V	C110B	Traction Control Disable Switch Circuit Open	5-72	47

TEST CONDITIONS	TESTDETAILS/RESULTS/ACTIONS
A1 VERIFY THE CONNECTION BETWEEN THE NGS TESTER AND THE DLC CONNECTOR	

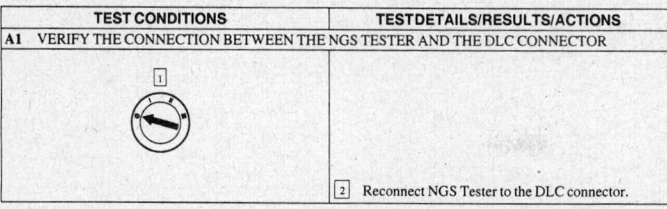

| | 2 Reconnect NGS Tester to the DLC connector. |

FM4029901454010X

Fig. 10   Test A: No Communication w/ABS Control
Module (Part 1 of 3). 2002-03

TEST CONDITIONS	TESTDETAILS/RESULTS/ACTIONS
A3 CHECK VOLTAGE TO THE ANTI-LOCK BRAKE CONTROL MODULE CIRCUIT 37 (YE)	
A4 CHECK THE ANTI-LOCK BRAKE CONTROL MODULE GROUND CIRCUIT 57 (BK)	

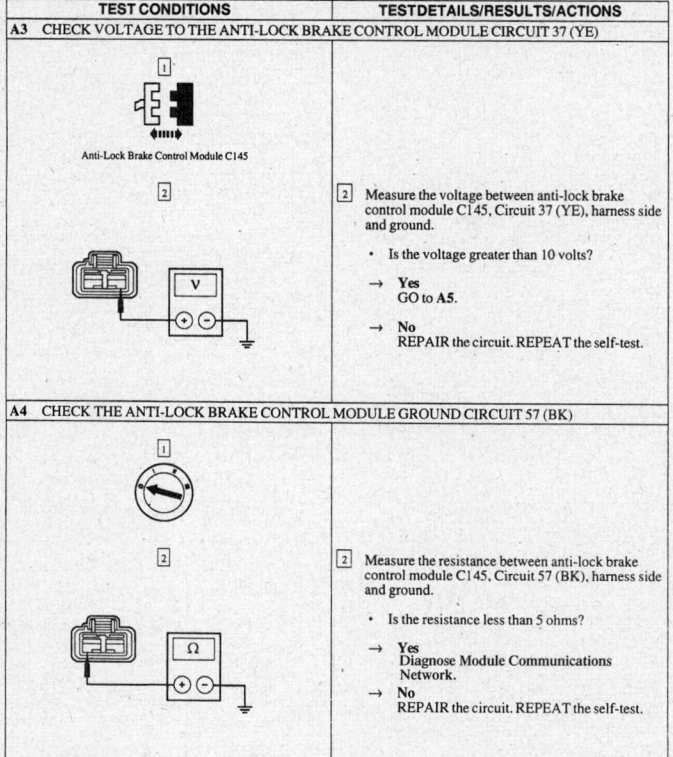

A3 details:

2 Measure the voltage between anti-lock brake control module C145, Circuit 37 (YE), harness side and ground.

• Is the voltage greater than 10 volts?

→ Yes
GO to A5.

→ No
REPAIR the circuit. REPEAT the self-test.

A4 details:

2 Measure the resistance between anti-lock brake control module C145, Circuit 57 (BK), harness side and ground.

• Is the resistance less than 5 ohms?

→ Yes
Diagnose Module Communications Network.

→ No
REPAIR the circuit. REPEAT the self-test.

FM4029901454030X

Fig. 10   Test A: No Communication w/ABS Control
Module (Part 3 of 3). 2002-03

TEST CONDITIONS	TESTDETAILS/RESULTS/ACTIONS
A1 VERIFY THE CONNECTION BETWEEN THE NGS TESTER AND THE DLC CONNECTOR (Continued)	
A2 CHECK VOLTAGE TO THE HCU	

A1 (Continued):

3 Retrieve and document continuous DTCs.

• Are DTCs obtained?

→ Yes
REFER to Diagnostic Chart Index.

→ No
GO to A2.

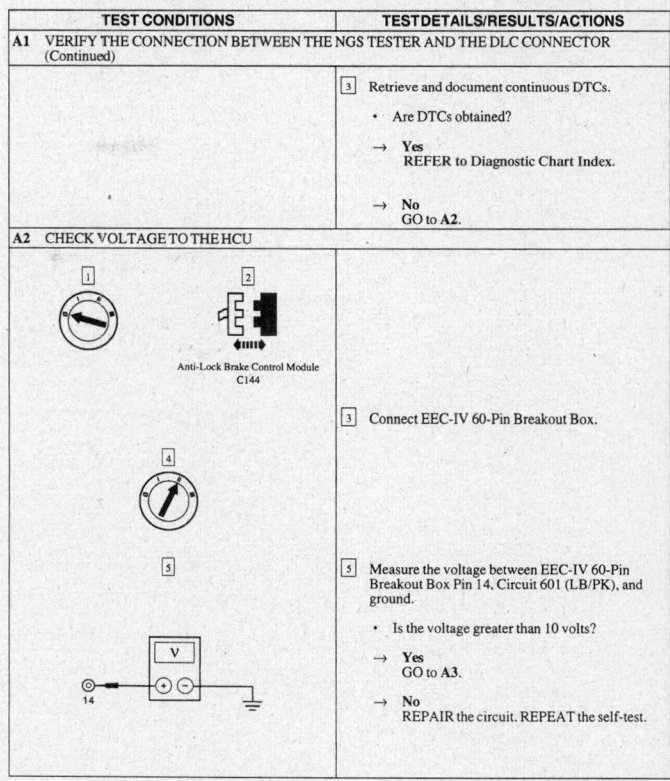

A2:

3 Connect EEC-IV 60-Pin Breakout Box.

5 Measure the voltage between EEC-IV 60-Pin Breakout Box Pin 14, Circuit 601 (LB/PK), and ground.

• Is the voltage greater than 10 volts?

→ Yes
GO to A3.

→ No
REPAIR the circuit. REPEAT the self-test.

FM4029901454020X

Fig. 10   Test A: No Communication w/ABS Control
Module (Part 2 of 3). 2002-03

TEST CONDITIONS	TESTDETAILS/RESULTS/ACTIONS
B1 CHECK THE COMMUNICATIONS TO THE ANTI-LOCK BRAKE CONTROL MODULE	

1 Check the communication to the anti-lock brake control module.

• Does NGS Tester communicate with the anti-lock brake control module?

→ Yes
INSTALL a new anti-lock brake control module. REPEAT the self-test.

→ No
GO to Pinpoint Test A.

FM4029901455000X

Fig. 11   Test B: Unable To Enter Self Test. 2002-03

TEST CONDITIONS	TESTDETAILS/RESULTS/ACTIONS
C1 CHECK YELLOW ABS WARNING INDICATOR FUNCTION	

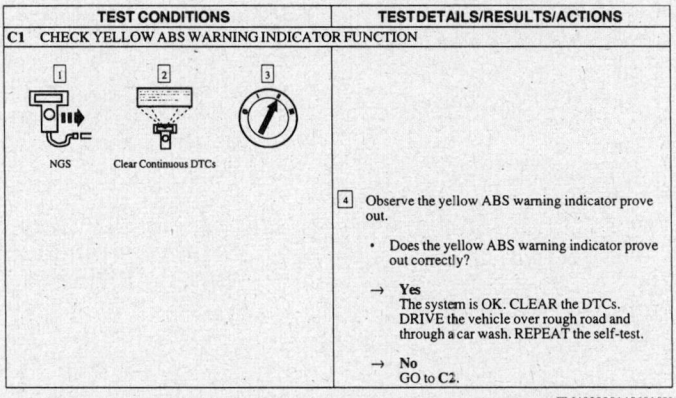

4 Observe the yellow ABS warning indicator prove out.

• Does the yellow ABS warning indicator prove out correctly?

→ Yes
The system is OK. CLEAR the DTCs. DRIVE the vehicle over rough road and through a car wash. REPEAT the self-test.

→ No
GO to C2.

FM4029901456010X

Fig. 12   Test C: Code C1220: Yellow ABS Warning
Indicator Failure (Part 1 of 3). 2002-03

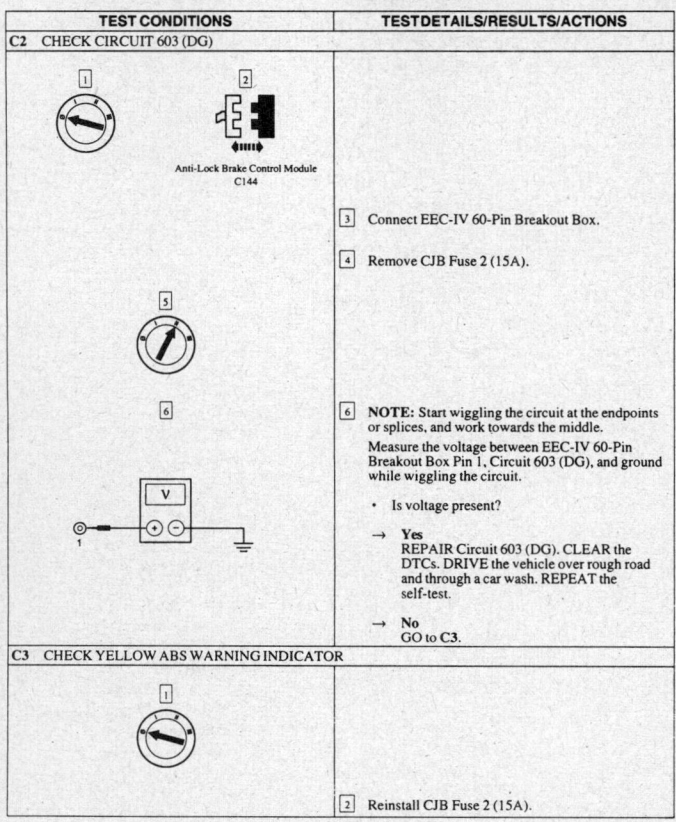

TEST CONDITIONS	TEST DETAILS/RESULTS/ACTIONS
C2 CHECK CIRCUIT 603 (DG)	

Anti-Lock Brake Control Module C144

3. Connect EEC-IV 60-Pin Breakout Box.

4. Remove CJB Fuse 2 (15A).

6. **NOTE:** Start wiggling the circuit at the endpoints or splices, and work towards the middle.
Measure the voltage between EEC-IV 60-Pin Breakout Box Pin 1, Circuit 603 (DG), and ground while wiggling the circuit.

• Is voltage present?

→ **Yes**
REPAIR Circuit 603 (DG). CLEAR the DTCs. DRIVE the vehicle over rough road and through a car wash. REPEAT the self-test.

→ **No**
GO to C3.

| C3 CHECK YELLOW ABS WARNING INDICATOR | |

2. Reinstall CJB Fuse 2 (15A).

FM4029901456020X

Fig. 12 Test C: Code C1220: Yellow ABS Warning Indicator Failure (Part 2 of 3). 2002-03

TEST CONDITIONS	TEST DETAILS/RESULTS/ACTIONS
D1 RED BRAKE WARNING INDICATOR PROVE OUT	

NGS   Clear Continuous DTCs   NGS

4. Make sure the parking brake is disengaged.

6. Observe the red BRAKE warning indicator.

• Does the red BRAKE warning indicator prove out normally?

→ **Yes**
The system is OK. CLEAR the DTCs. DRIVE the vehicle over rough road and through a car wash. REPEAT the self-test.

→ **No**
If the red BRAKE warning indicator is illuminated continuously, GO to D6.

If both the red BRAKE warning indicator and the yellow ABS warning indicator are illuminated continuously, GO to D2.

If the red BRAKE warning indicator never illuminates, GO to D13.

| D2 DETERMINE PROPER FAULT DIAGNOSIS | |

NGS

2. Carry out the Anti-Lock Brake Control On-Demand Self-Test.

FM4029901457010X

Fig. 13 Test D: Codes C1225 & C1226: Faulty Red Brake Warning Indicator/Shorted Red Brake Warning Indicator Relay (Part 1 of 9). 2002-03

TEST CONDITIONS	TEST DETAILS/RESULTS/ACTIONS
C3 CHECK YELLOW ABS WARNING INDICATOR	

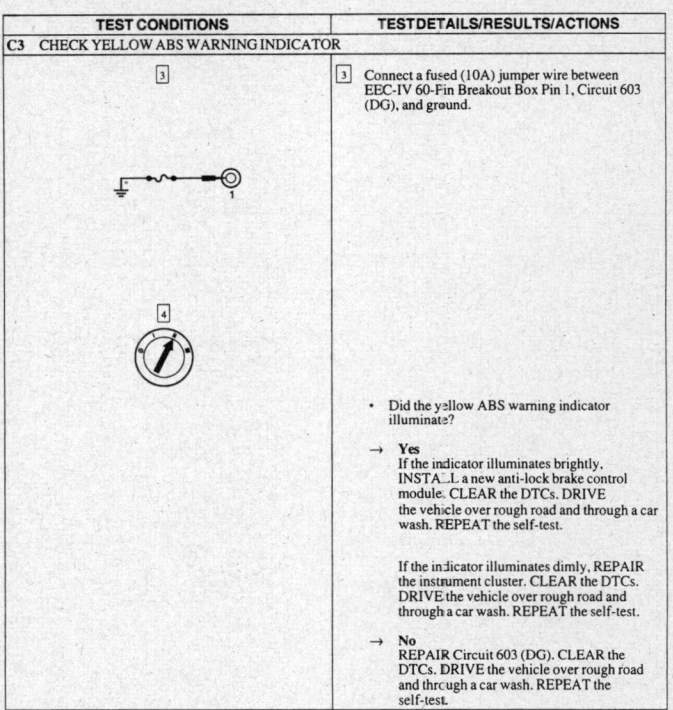

3. Connect a fused (10A) jumper wire between EEC-IV 60-Pin Breakout Box Pin 1, Circuit 603 (DG), and ground.

• Did the yellow ABS warning indicator illuminate?

→ **Yes**
If the indicator illuminates brightly, INSTALL a new anti-lock brake control module. CLEAR the DTCs. DRIVE the vehicle over rough road and through a car wash. REPEAT the self-test.

If the indicator illuminates dimly, REPAIR the instrument cluster. CLEAR the DTCs. DRIVE the vehicle over rough road and through a car wash. REPEAT the self-test.

→ **No**
REPAIR Circuit 603 (DG). CLEAR the DTCs. DRIVE the vehicle over rough road and through a car wash. REPEAT the self-test.

FM4029901456030X

Fig. 12 Test C: Code C1220: Yellow ABS Warning Indicator Failure (Part 3 of 3). 2002-03

TEST CONDITIONS	TEST DETAILS/RESULTS/ACTIONS
D2 DETERMINE PROPER FAULT DIAGNOSIS	

3. Retrieve and document continuous DTCs.

• Was the original DTC C1225 retrieved?

→ **Yes**
GO to D3.

→ **No**
If DTCs C1225 or C1226 are set, diagnose the base brake concern first. GO to D6.

| D3 CHECK CIRCUIT 128 (VT/YE) FOR SHORT TO BATTERY | |

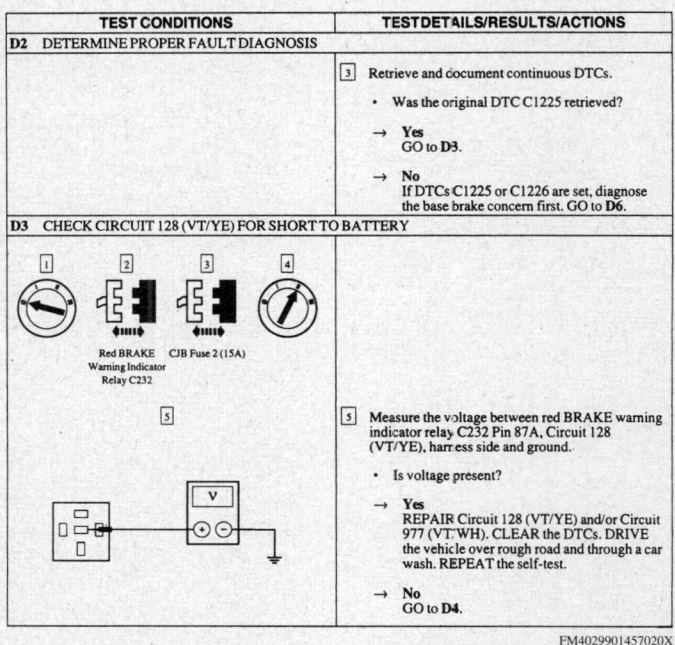

Red BRAKE   CJB Fuse 2 (15A)
Warning Indicator
Relay C232

5. Measure the voltage between red BRAKE warning indicator relay C232 Pin 87A, Circuit 128 (VT/YE), harness side and ground.

• Is voltage present?

→ **Yes**
REPAIR Circuit 128 (VT/YE) and/or Circuit 977 (VT/WH). CLEAR the DTCs. DRIVE the vehicle over rough road and through a car wash. REPEAT the self-test.

→ **No**
GO to D4.

FM4029901457020X

Fig. 13 Test D: Codes C1225 & C1226: Faulty Red Brake Warning Indicator/Shorted Red Brake Warning Indicator Relay (Part 2 of 9). 2002-03

TEST CONDITIONS	TEST DETAILS/RESULTS/ACTIONS
D4 CHECK CIRCUIT 599 (PK/LG) FOR SHORT TO BATTERY	

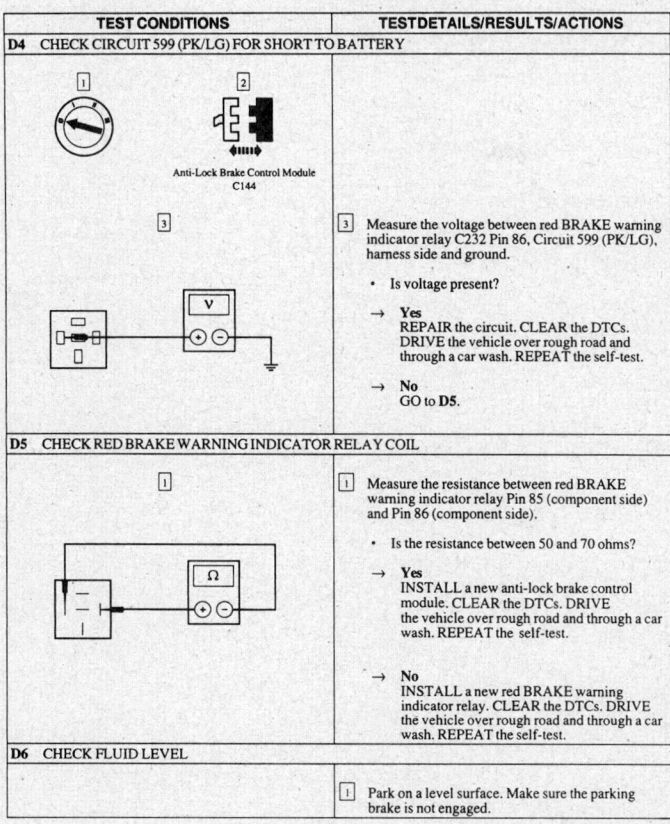

Anti-Lock Brake Control Module C144

③	**3** Measure the voltage between red BRAKE indicator relay C232 Pin 86, Circuit 599 (PK/LG), harness side and ground. • Is voltage present? → **Yes** REPAIR the circuit. CLEAR the DTCs. DRIVE the vehicle over rough road and through a car wash. REPEAT the self-test. → **No** GO to **D5**.
D5 CHECK RED BRAKE WARNING INDICATOR RELAY COIL	
①	**1** Measure the resistance between red BRAKE warning indicator relay Pin 85 (component side) and Pin 86 (component side). • Is the resistance between 50 and 70 ohms? → **Yes** INSTALL a new anti-lock brake control module. CLEAR the DTCs. DRIVE the vehicle over rough road and through a car wash. REPEAT the self-test. → **No** INSTALL a new red BRAKE warning indicator relay. CLEAR the DTCs. DRIVE the vehicle over rough road and through a car wash. REPEAT the self-test.
D6 CHECK FLUID LEVEL	
	1 Park on a level surface. Make sure the parking brake is not engaged.

FM4029901457030X

Fig. 13   Test D: Codes C1226 & C1225: Faulty Red Brake Warning Indicator/Shorted Red Brake Warning Indicator Relay (Part 3 of 9). 2002-03

TEST CONDITIONS	TEST DETAILS/RESULTS/ACTIONS
D8 CHECK THE ANTI-LOCK BRAKE CONTROL MODULE	

Anti-Lock Brake Control Module C144

	• Is the red BRAKE warning indicator illuminated? → **Yes** GO to **D9**. → **No** GO to **D11**.
D9 CHECK THE RED BRAKE WARNING INDICATOR RELAY	

Red BRAKE Warning Indicator Relay C232

	• Is the red BRAKE warning indicator illuminated? → **Yes** REPAIR Circuit 128 (VT/YE), Circuit 977 (VT/WH) and/or Circuit 162 (LG/RD). CLEAR the DTCs. DRIVE the vehicle over rough road and through a car wash. REPEAT the self-test. → **No** GO to **D10**.

FM4029901457050X

Fig. 13   Test D: Codes C1225 & C1226: Faulty Red Brake Warning Indicator/Shorted Red Brake Warning Indicator Relay (Part 5 of 9). 2002-03

TEST CONDITIONS	TEST DETAILS/RESULTS/ACTIONS
D6 CHECK FLUID LEVEL (Continued)	
	2 Check the brake fluid level at the brake master cylinder reservoir (2K478). • Is the fluid within the specified limits? → **Yes** GO to **D7**. → **No** CHECK for leaks in the vehicle brake system. FILL the brake fluid reservoir to the required level. CLEAR the DTCs. DRIVE the vehicle over rough road and through a car wash. REPEAT the self-test.
D7 CHECK BRAKE FLUID LEVEL SWITCH	

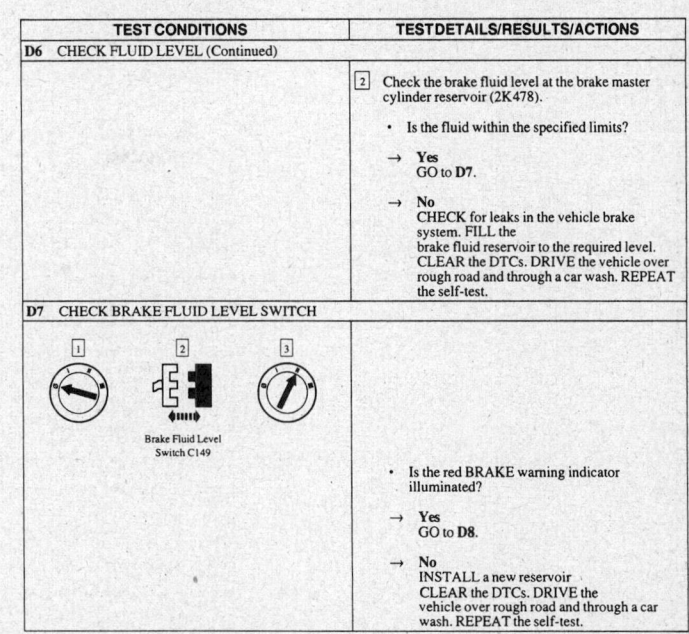

Brake Fluid Level Switch C149

	• Is the red BRAKE warning indicator illuminated? → **Yes** GO to **D8**. → **No** INSTALL a new reservoir. CLEAR the DTCs. DRIVE the vehicle over rough road and through a car wash. REPEAT the self-test.

FM4029901457040X

Fig. 13   Test D: Codes C1225 & C1226: Faulty Red Brake Warning Indicator/Shorted Red Brake Warning Indicator Relay (Part 4 of 9). 2002-03

TEST CONDITIONS	TEST DETAILS/RESULTS/ACTIONS
D10 CHECK CIRCUIT 599 (VT/LG) FOR SHORT TO GROUND	
①	**1** Measure the resistance between red BRAKE warning indicator relay C232 Pin 86, Circuit 599 (VT/LG), harness side and ground. • Is the resistance greater than 10,000 ohms? → **Yes** INSTALL a new red BRAKE warning indicator relay. CLEAR the DTCs. DRIVE the vehicle over rough road and through a car wash. REPEAT the self-test. → **No** REPAIR the circuit. CLEAR the DTCs. DRIVE the vehicle over rough road and through a car wash. REPEAT the self-test.
D11 CHECK CIRCUIT 512 (TN/LG) FOR SHORT TO GROUND	
①	**1** Measure the resistance between brake fluid level switch C149 Pin 2, Circuit 512 (TN/LG), harness side and ground. • Is the resistance greater than 10,000 ohms? → **Yes** GO to **D12**. → **No** REPAIR the circuit. CLEAR the DTCs. DRIVE the vehicle over rough road and through a car wash. REPEAT the self-test.
D12 CHECK CIRCUIT 531 (DG/YE) AND IGNITION SWITCH FOR A SHORT TO GROUND	
①	**1** Measure the resistance between brake fluid level warning switch C149 Pin 3, Circuit 531 (DG/YE), harness side and ground. • Is the resistance greater than 10,000 ohms? → **Yes** INSTALL a new anti-lock brake control module. CLEAR the DTCs. DRIVE the vehicle over rough road and through a car wash. REPEAT the self-test. → **No** GO to **D13**.

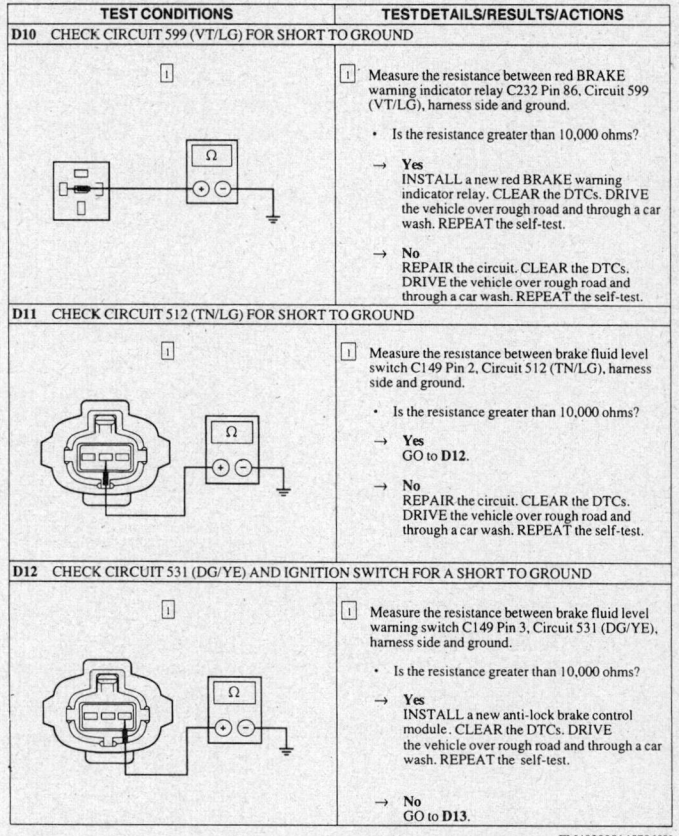

FM4029901457060X

Fig. 13   Test D: Codes C1226 & C1225: Faulty Red Brake Warning Indicator/Shorted Red Brake Warning Indicator Relay (Part 6 of 9). 2002-03

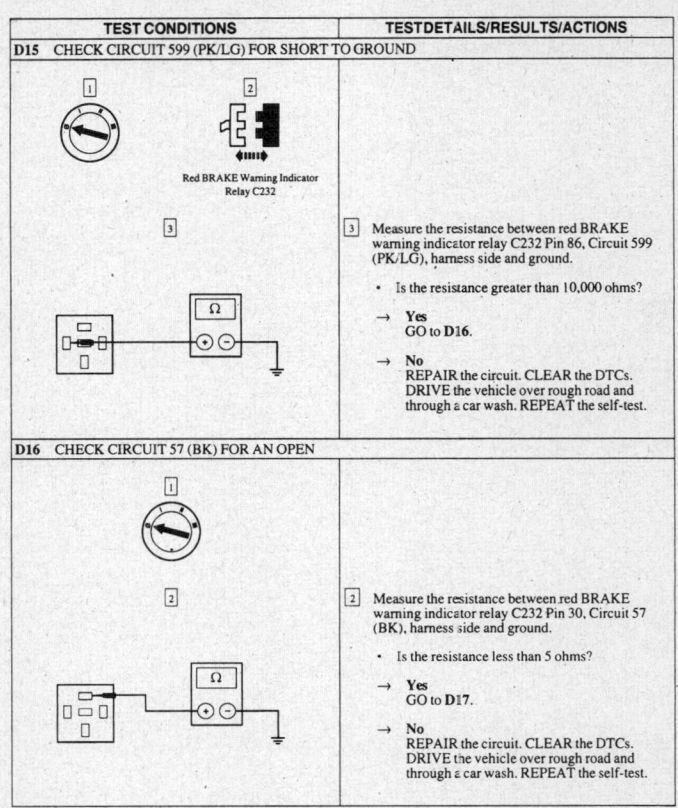

TEST CONDITIONS	TESTDETAILS/RESULTS/ACTIONS
D13 CHECK CIRCUIT 531 (DG/YE) FOR SHORT TO GROUND	
Ignition Switch C240	☐2 Measure the resistance between brake fluid level warning switch C149 Pin 3, Circuit 531 (DG/YE), harness side and ground. • Is the resistance greater than 10,000 ohms? → **Yes** INSTALL a new ignition switch CLEAR the DTCs. DRIVE the vehicle over rough road and through a car wash. REPEAT the self-test. → **No** REPAIR the circuit. CLEAR the DTCs. DRIVE the vehicle over rough road and through a car wash. REPEAT the self-test.
D14 DETERMINE WHETHER THE CONCERN IS IN THE WIRING OR THE ANTI-LOCK BRAKE CONTROL MODULE	
Anti-Lock Brake Control Module C144	• Is the red BRAKE warning indicator illuminated? → **Yes** GO to **D15**. → **No** INSTALL a new anti-lock brake control module. CLEAR the DTCs. DRIVE the vehicle over rough road and through a car wash. REPEAT the self-test.

FM4029901457070X

Fig. 13   Test D: Codes C1225 & C1226: Faulty Red Brake Warning Indicator/Shorted Red Brake Warning Indicator Relay (Part 7 of 9). 2002-03

TEST CONDITIONS	TESTDETAILS/RESULTS/ACTIONS
D15 CHECK CIRCUIT 599 (PK/LG) FOR SHORT TO GROUND	
Red BRAKE Warning Indicator Relay C232	☐3 Measure the resistance between red BRAKE warning indicator relay C232 Pin 86, Circuit 599 (PK/LG), harness side and ground. • Is the resistance greater than 10,000 ohms? → **Yes** GO to **D16**. → **No** REPAIR the circuit. CLEAR the DTCs. DRIVE the vehicle over rough road and through a car wash. REPEAT the self-test.
D16 CHECK CIRCUIT 57 (BK) FOR AN OPEN	
	☐2 Measure the resistance between red BRAKE warning indicator relay C232 Pin 30, Circuit 57 (BK), harness side and ground. • Is the resistance less than 5 ohms? → **Yes** GO to **D17**. → **No** REPAIR the circuit. CLEAR the DTCs. DRIVE the vehicle over rough road and through a car wash. REPEAT the self-test.

FM4029901457080X

Fig. 13   Test D: Codes C1225 & C1226: Faulty Red Brake Warning Indicator/Shorted Red Brake Warning Indicator Relay (Part 8 of 9). 2002-03

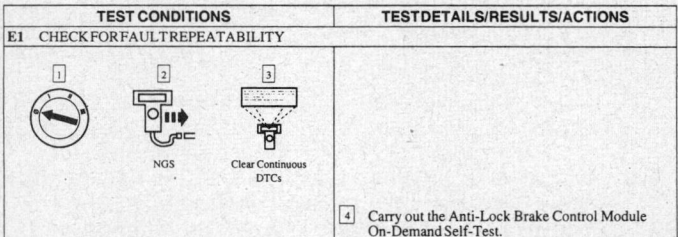

TEST CONDITIONS	TESTDETAILS/RESULTS/ACTIONS
D17 CHECK CIRCUIT 128 (VT/YE) FOR AN OPEN	
	☐2 Measure the voltage between red BRAKE warning indicator relay C232 Pin 87A, Circuit 128 (VT/YE), harness side and ground. • Is the voltage greater than 10 volts? → **Yes** INSTALL a new red BRAKE warning indicator relay. CLEAR the DTCs. DRIVE the vehicle over rough road and through a car wash. REPEAT the self-test. → **No** REPAIR the circuit. DRIVE the vehicle over rough road and through a car wash. REPEAT the self-test. .

FM4029901457090X

Fig. 13   Test D: Codes C1225 & C1226: Faulty Red Brake Warning Indicator/Shorted Red Brake Warning Indicator Relay (Part 9 of 9). 2002-03

TEST CONDITIONS	TESTDETAILS/RESULTS/ACTIONS
E1 CHECK FOR FAULT REPEATABILITY	
NGS Clear Continuous DTCs	☐4 Carry out the Anti-Lock Brake Control Module On-Demand Self-Test.

FM4029901458010X

Fig. 14   Test E: Codes C1194, C1196, C1198, C1200, C1202, C1204, C1206, C1208, C1210, C1212, C1214 & C1216: Isolation Valve, Dump Valve (Part 1 of 2). 2002-03

TEST CONDITIONS	TESTDETAILS/RESULTS/ACTIONS
E1 CHECK FOR FAULT REPEATABILITY	
	☐5 Retrieve and document continuous DTCs. • Is a single valve DTC set? → **Yes** INSTALL a new HCU. CLEAR the DTCs. DRIVE the vehicle over rough road and through a car wash. REPEAT the self-test. → **No** If multiple valve DTCs are set, GO to **E2**. If no DTCs are set, DRIVE the vehicle over rough road and through a car wash. REPEAT the self-test.
E2 CHECK CIRCUIT 37 (YE) FOR AND OPEN	
HCU C145	☐3 Measure the voltage between HCU C145, Circuit 37 (YE), harness side and ground. • Is the voltage greater than 10 volts? → **Yes** INSTALL a new HCU. CLEAR the DTCs. DRIVE the vehicle over rough road and through a car wash. REPEAT the self-test. → **No** REPAIR the circuit. CLEAR the DTCs. DRIVE the vehicle over rough road and through a car wash. REPEAT the self-test.

FM4029901458020X

Fig. 14   Test E: Codes C1194, C1196, C1198, C1200, C1202, C1204, C1206, C1208, C1210, C1212, C1214 & C1216: Isolation Valve, Dump Valve (Part 2 of 2). 2002-03

Part 1 of 4

TEST CONDITIONS	TESTDETAILS/RESULTS/ACTIONS
F1 CHECK FOR FAULT REPEATABILITY 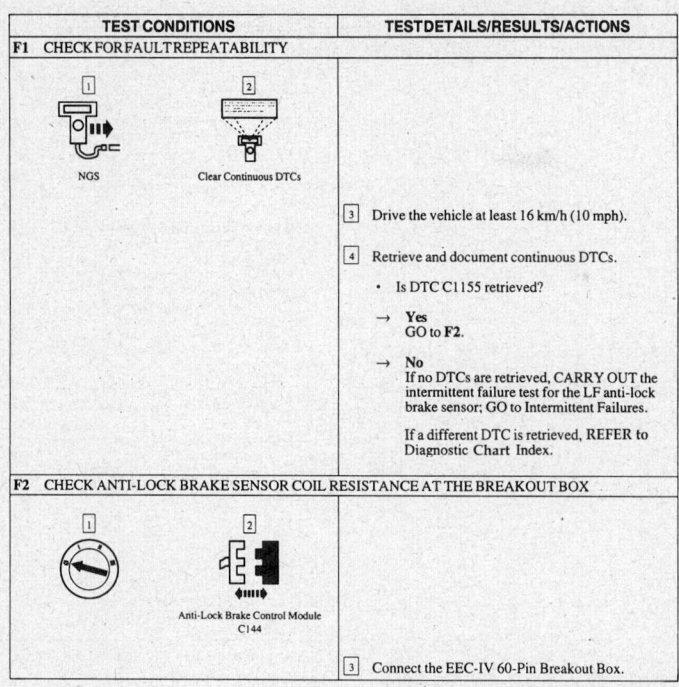 1 NGS 2 Clear Continuous DTCs	3 Drive the vehicle at least 16 km/h (10 mph). 4 Retrieve and document continuous DTCs. • Is DTC C1155 retrieved? → **Yes** GO to **F2**. → **No** If no DTCs are retrieved, CARRY OUT the intermittent failure test for the LF anti-lock brake sensor; GO to Intermittent Failures. If a different DTC is retrieved, REFER to Diagnostic Chart Index.
F2 CHECK ANTI-LOCK BRAKE SENSOR COIL RESISTANCE AT THE BREAKOUT BOX 1 2 Anti-Lock Brake Control Module C144	3 Connect the EEC-IV 60-Pin Breakout Box.

FM4029901459010X

Fig. 15   Test F: Codes C1155: Left Front ABS Sensor, Electrical/Static (Part 1 of 4). 2002-03

Part 2 of 4

TEST CONDITIONS	TESTDETAILS/RESULTS/ACTIONS
F2 CHECK ANTI-LOCK BRAKE SENSOR COIL RESISTANCE AT THE BREAKOUT BOX 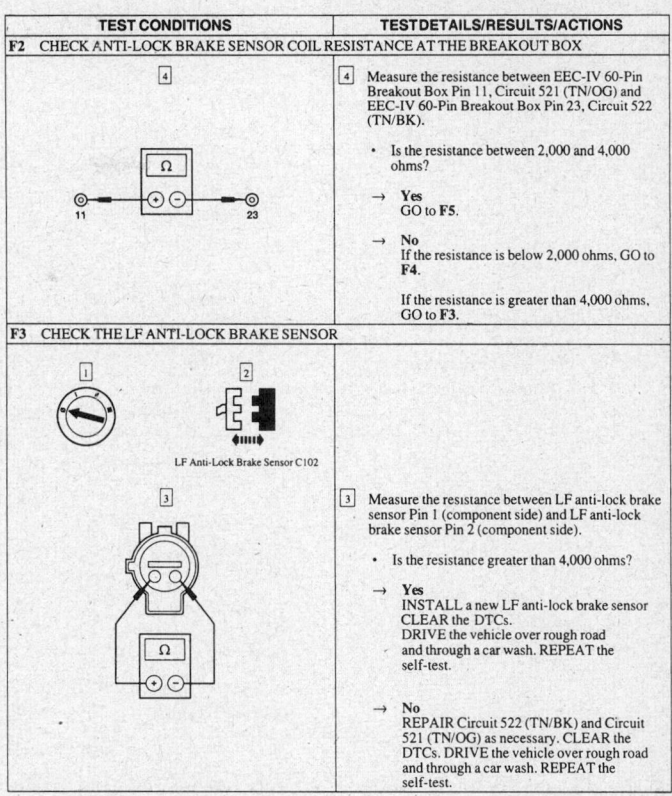 4 11 Ω 23	4 Measure the resistance between EEC-IV 60-Pin Breakout Box Pin 11, Circuit 521 (TN/OG) and EEC-IV 60-Pin Breakout Box Pin 23, Circuit 522 (TN/BK). • Is the resistance between 2,000 and 4,000 ohms? → **Yes** GO to **F5**. → **No** If the resistance is below 2,000 ohms, GO to **F4**. If the resistance is greater than 4,000 ohms, GO to **F3**.
F3 CHECK THE LF ANTI-LOCK BRAKE SENSOR 1 2 LF Anti-Lock Brake Sensor C102 3 Ω	Measure the resistance between LF anti-lock brake sensor Pin 1 (component side) and LF anti-lock brake sensor Pin 2 (component side). • Is the resistance greater than 4,000 ohms? → **Yes** INSTALL a new LF anti-lock brake sensor CLEAR the DTCs. DRIVE the vehicle over rough road and through a car wash. REPEAT the self-test. → **No** REPAIR Circuit 522 (TN/BK) and Circuit 521 (TN/OG) as necessary. CLEAR the DTCs. DRIVE the vehicle over rough road and through a car wash. REPEAT the self-test.

FM4029901459020X

Fig. 15   Test F: Codes C1155: Left Front ABS Sensor, Electrical/Static (Part 2 of 4). 2002-03

Part 3 of 4

TEST CONDITIONS	TESTDETAILS/RESULTS/ACTIONS
F4 CHECK CIRCUIT 521 (TN/OG) AND CIRCUIT 522 (TN/BK) FOR SHORT 1 2 LF Anti-Lock Brake Sensor C102 3 11 Ω 23	3 Measure the resistance between EEC-IV 60-Pin Breakout Box Pin 11, Circuit 521 (TN/OG) and EEC-IV 60-Pin Breakout Box Pin 23, Circuit 522 (TN/BK). • Is the resistance greater than 10,000 ohms? → **Yes** INSTALL a new LF anti-lock brake sensor; CLEAR the DTCs. DRIVE the vehicle over rough road and through a car wash. REPEAT the self-test. → **No** REPAIR Circuit 521 (TN/OG) and Circuit 522 (TN/BK) as necessary. CLEAR the DTCs. DRIVE the vehicle over rough road and through a car wash. REPEAT the self-test.
F5 CHECK FOR SHORT TO GROUND 1 11 Ω 23	1 Measure the resistance between EEC-IV 60-Pin Breakout Box Pin 11, Circuit 521 (TN/OG), and ground; and between EEC-IV 60-Pin Breakout Box Pin 23, Circuit 522 (TN/BK), and ground. • Is the resistance greater than 10,000 ohms? → **Yes** INSTALL a new anti-lock brake control module; CLEAR the DTCs. DRIVE the vehicle over rough road and through a car wash. REPEAT the self-test. → **No** GO to **F6**.

FM4029901459030X

Fig. 15   Test F: Codes C1155: Left Front ABS Sensor, Electrical/Static (Part 3 of 4). 2002-03

Part 4 of 4

TEST CONDITIONS	TESTDETAILS/RESULTS/ACTIONS
F6 CHECK THE LF ANTI-LOCK BRAKE SENSOR 1 LF Anti-Lock Brake Sensor C102 2 Ω	2 Measure the resistance between LF anti-lock brake sensor Pin 1 (component side) and ground; and between LF anti-lock brake sensor Pin 2 (component side) and ground. • Are the resistances greater than 10,000 ohms? → **Yes** REPAIR Circuit 521 (TN/OG) and Circuit 522 (TN/BK) as necessary. CLEAR the DTCs. DRIVE the vehicle over rough road and through a car wash. REPEAT the self-test. → **No** INSTALL a new LF anti-lock brake sensor; CLEAR the DTCs. DRIVE the vehicle over rough road and through a car wash. REPEAT the self-test.

FM4029901459040X

Fig. 15   Test F: Codes C1155: Left Front ABS Sensor, Electrical/Static (Part 4 of 4). 2002-03

TEST CONDITIONS	TEST DETAILS/RESULTS/ACTIONS
G1 RETRIEVE DTCs	
NGS	**4** Retrieve and document continuous DTCs. • Is DTC C1155 retrieved? → **Yes** DIAGNOSE DTC C1155 first. IGNORE all other DTCs retrieved. GO to Pinpoint Test F. → **No** GO to **G2**.
G2 CARRY OUT REPEATABILITY DRIVE TEST (MISMATCHED OUTPUT)	
NOTE: If a hard turn is made, some variation between all three sensors is expected. **NOTE:** Recording the speeds for later plotting will eliminate the necessity of monitoring NGS Tester while driving.	**1** Monitor anti-lock brake control module PIDs LF__WSPD, RF__WSPD and R__WSPD. **2** Drive the vehicle at various speeds. • Does the LF anti-lock brake sensor consistently match the other two? → **Yes** GO to **G7**. → **No** GO to **G3**.
G3 CHECK LF ANTI-LOCK BRAKE SENSOR INDICATOR	
	1 Raise the vehicle on a hoist.

FM4029901460010X

Fig. 16   Test G: Codes C1158 & C1233: Left Front ABS Sensor, Dynamic (Part 1 of 5). 2002-03

TEST CONDITIONS	TEST DETAILS/RESULTS/ACTIONS
G5 CHECK FOR INTERNAL SENSOR SHORT	
LF Anti-Lock Brake Sensor C102	**3** Measure the resistance between LF anti-lock brake sensor Pin 1 (component side) and ground; and between LF anti-lock brake sensor Pin 2 (component side) and ground. • Are the resistances greater than 10,000 ohms? → **Yes** GO to **G6**. → **No** INSTALL a new LF anti-lock brake sensor; CLEAR the DTCs. DRIVE the vehicle over rough road and through a car wash. REPEAT the self-test.
G6 CHECK THE ANTI-LOCK BRAKE SENSOR CIRCUITS	
Anti-Lock Brake Control Module C144	**3** Connect EEC-IV 60-Pin Breakout Box.

FM4029901460030X

Fig. 16   Test G: Codes C1158 & C1233: Left Front ABS Sensor, Dynamic (Part 3 of 5). 2002-03

TEST CONDITIONS	TEST DETAILS/RESULTS/ACTIONS
G3 CHECK LF ANTI-LOCK BRAKE SENSOR INDICATOR	
	2 ⚠ **CAUTION: Examine the anti-lock brake sensor indicator carefully. Failure to correctly diagnose anti-lock brake sensor indicator at this time will lead to unnecessary component replacement and wasted diagnostic time.** Inspect the ant.-lock brake sensor indicator for damaged or missing teeth. Rotate the anti-lock brake sensor indicator to be sure all teeth are checked. • Is the sensor indicator damaged or missing? → **Yes** INSTALL a new anti-lock brake sensor indicator. CLEAR the DTCs. DRIVE the vehicle over rough road and through a car wash. REPEAT the self-test. → **No** GO to **G4**.
G4 CHECK FOR LOOSE LF ANTI-LOCK BRAKE SENSOR MOUNTING	
	1 Wiggle the LF anti-lock brake sensor at the wheel end. • Is the LF anti-lock brake sensor tight and secure? → **Yes** GO to **G5**. → **No** TIGHTEN to specification. CLEAR the DTCs. DRIVE the vehicle over rough road and through a car wash. REPEAT the self-test.

FM4029901460020X

Fig. 16   Test G: Codes C1158 & C1233: Left Front ABS Sensor, Dynamic (Part 2 of 5). 2002-03

TEST CONDITIONS	TEST DETAILS/RESULTS/ACTIONS
G6 CHECK THE ANTI-LOCK BRAKE SENSOR CIRCUITS	
4 11 23	**4** Measure the resistance between EEC-IV 60-Pin Breakout Box Pin 11, Circuit 521 (TN/OG) and EEC-IV 60-Pin Breakout Box Pin 23, Circuit 522 (TN/BK). • Is the resistance greater than 10,000 ohms? → **Yes** GO to **G8**. → **No** REPAIR Circuit 521 (TN/OG) and Circuit 522 (TN/BK) as necessary. CLEAR the DTCs. DRIVE the vehicle over rough road and through a car wash. REPEAT the self-test.
G7 CHECK FOR INTERMITTENT WIRING CONCERN	
	1 CARRY OUT the intermittent failure test for the LF anti-lock brake sensor. Go to Intermittent Failures. • Did the LF anti-lock brake sensor pass the test? → **Yes** GO to **G8**. → **No** REPAIR as necessary. CLEAR the DTCs. DRIVE the vehicle over rough road and through a car wash. REPEAT the self-test.
G8 INSPECT THE LF ANTI-LOCK BRAKE SENSOR FOR DAMAGE	
	2 Remove the LF anti-lock brake sensor. **3** Inspect the housing for stress cracks or breaks.

FM4029901460040X

Fig. 16   Test G: Codes C1158 & C1233: Left Front ABS Sensor, Dynamic (Part 4 of 5). 2002-03

TEST CONDITIONS	TEST DETAILS/RESULTS/ACTIONS
G8 INSPECT THE LF ANTI-LOCK BRAKE SENSOR FOR DAMAGE	
	4 Inspect the sensor connector cavity for evidence of water entry, pin corrosion.
	• Are any of the above conditions evident?
	→ **Yes** REPAIR as necessary. CLEAR the DTCs. DRIVE the vehicle over rough road and through a car wash. REPEAT the self-test.
	→ **No** CLEAR the DTCs. DRIVE the vehicle over rough road and through a car wash. REPEAT the self-test.

FM4029901460050X

Fig. 16 Test G: Codes C1158 & C1233: Left Front ABS Sensor, Dynamic (Part 5 of 5). 2002-03

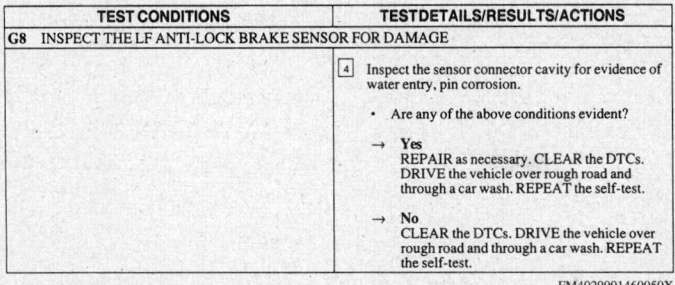

TEST CONDITIONS	TEST DETAILS/RESULTS/ACTIONS
H2 CHECK THE ANTI-LOCK BRAKE SENSOR COIL RESISTANCE	
Anti-Lock Brake Control Module C144	
	3 Connect EEC-IV 60-Pin Breakout Box.
	4 Measure the resistance between EEC-IV 60-Pin Breakout Box Pin 10, Circuit 514 (YE/RD) and EEC-IV 60-Pin Breakout Box Pin 22, Circuit 516 (YE/BK).
	• Is the resistance between 2,000 and 4,000 ohms?
	→ **Yes** GO to **H5**.
	→ **No** If the resistance is below 2,000 ohms, GO to **H4**. If the resistance is greater than 4,000 ohms, GO to **H3**.

FM4029901461020X

Fig. 17 Test H: Code C1145: Right Front ABS Sensor, Electrical/Static (Part 2 of 5). 2002-03

TEST CONDITIONS	TEST DETAILS/RESULTS/ACTIONS
H3 CHECK THE RF ANTI-LOCK BRAKE SENSOR FOR AN OPEN	
RF Anti-Lock Brake Sensor C103	
	3 Measure the resistance between RF anti-lock brake sensor Pin 1 (component side) and RF anti-lock brake sensor Pin 2 (component side).
	• Is the resistance greater than 4,000 ohms?
	→ **Yes** INSTALL a new RF anti-lock brake sensor; CLEAR the DTCs. DRIVE the vehicle over rough road and through a car wash. REPEAT the self-test.
	→ **No** REPAIR Circuit 514 (YE/RD) and/or Circuit 516 (YE/BK). CLEAR the DTCs. DRIVE the vehicle over rough road and through a car wash. REPEAT the self-test.

FM4029901461030X

Fig. 17 Test H: Code C1145: Right Front ABS Sensor, Electrical/Static (Part 3 of 5). 2002-03

TEST CONDITIONS	TEST DETAILS/RESULTS/ACTIONS
H1 CHECK FOR FAULT REPEATABILITY	
NGS	Clear Continuous DTCs
	4 Drive the vehicle at least 16 km/h (10 mph).
	5 Retrieve and document continuous DTCs.
	• Is DTC C1145 retrieved?
	→ **Yes** GO to **H2**.
	→ **No** If no DTC is retrieved, CARRY OUT Intermittent Failure test. GO to Intermittent Failures. If a different DTC is retrieved, REFER to Diagnostic Chart Index.

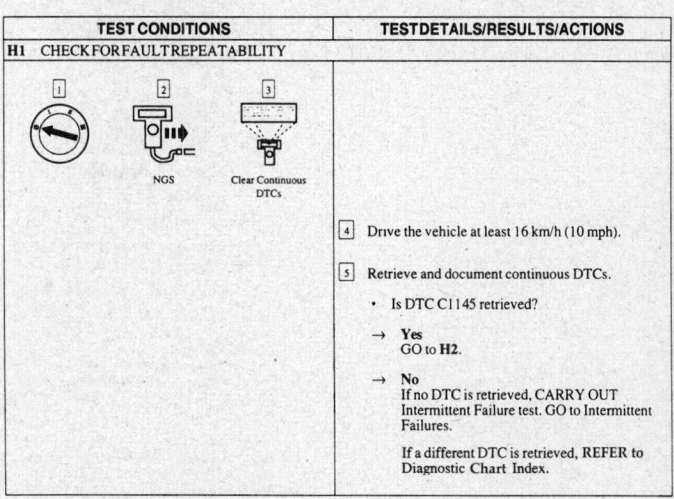

FM4029901461010X

Fig. 17 Test H: Code C1145: Right Front ABS Sensor, Electrical/Static (Part 1 of 5). 2002-03

TEST CONDITIONS	TEST DETAILS/RESULTS/ACTIONS
H4 CHECK THE RF ANTI-LOCK BRAKE SENSOR FOR SHORT	
RF Anti-Lock Brake Sensor C103	
	3 Measure the resistance between EEC-IV 60-Pin Breakout Box Pin 10, Circuit 514 (YE/RD) and EEC-IV 60-Pin Breakout Box Pin 22, Circuit 516 (YE/BK).
	• Is the resistance greater than 10,000 ohms?
	→ **Yes** INSTALL a new RF anti-lock brake sensor; CLEAR the DTCs. DRIVE the vehicle over rough road and through a car wash. REPEAT the self-test.
	→ **No** REPAIR Circuit 514 (YE/RD) and/or Circuit 516 (YE/BK). CLEAR the DTCs. DRIVE the vehicle over rough road and through a car wash. REPEAT the self test.
H5 CHECK THE RF ANTI-LOCK BRAKE SENSOR CIRCUITRY FOR SHORT TO GROUND	
	1 Measure the resistance between EEC-IV 60-Pin Breakout Box Pin 10, Circuit 514 (YE/RD), and ground; and between EEC-IV 60-Pin Breakout Box Pin 22, Circuit 516 (YE/BK), and ground.
	• Are the resistances greater than 10,000 ohms?
	→ **Yes** INSTALL a new anti-lock brake control module. CLEAR the DTCs. DRIVE the vehicle over rough road and through a car wash. REPEAT the self-test.
	→ **No** GO to **H6**.

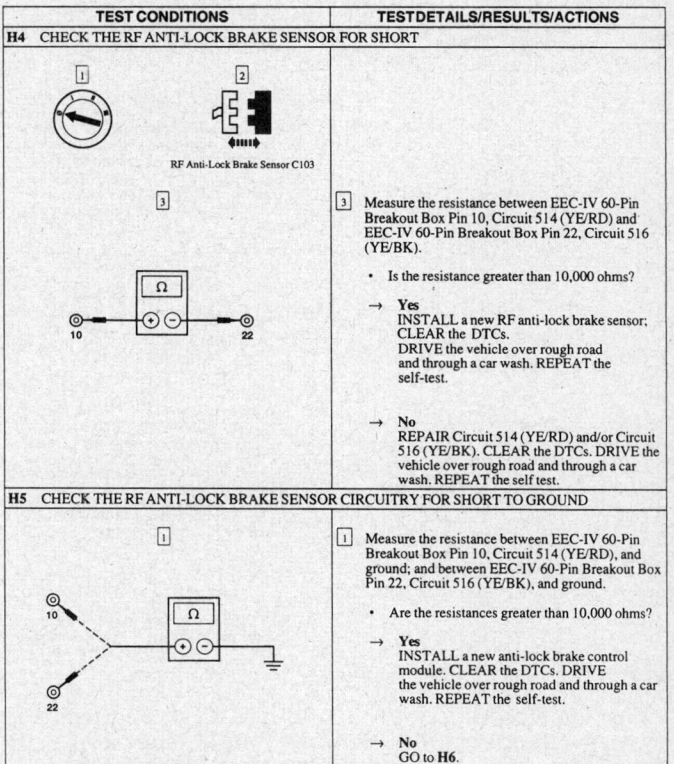

FM4029901461040X

Fig. 17 Test H: Code C1145: Right Front ABS Sensor, Electrical/Static (Part 4 of 5). 2002-03

TEST CONDITIONS	TEST DETAILS/RESULTS/ACTIONS
H6 CHECK RF ANTI-LOCK BRAKE SENSOR FOR SHORT TO GROUND	

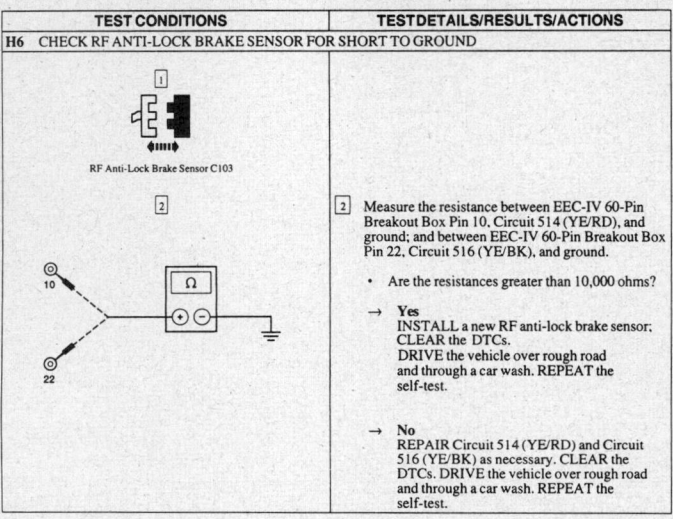

RF Anti-Lock Brake Sensor C103

| | ② Measure the resistance between EEC-IV 60-Pin Breakout Box Pin 10, Circuit 514 (YE/RD), and ground; and between EEC-IV 60-Pin Breakout Box Pin 22, Circuit 516 (YE/BK), and ground.

 • Are the resistances greater than 10,000 ohms?

 → **Yes**
 INSTALL a new RF anti-lock brake sensor; CLEAR the DTCs. DRIVE the vehicle over rough road and through a car wash. REPEAT the self-test.

 → **No**
 REPAIR Circuit 514 (YE/RD) and Circuit 516 (YE/BK) as necessary. CLEAR the DTCs. DRIVE the vehicle over rough road and through a car wash. REPEAT the self-test. |

FM4029901461050X

Fig. 17 Test H: Code C1145: Right Front ABS Sensor, Electrical/Static (Part 5 of 5). 2002-03

TEST CONDITIONS	TEST DETAILS/RESULTS/ACTIONS
I3 CHECK RF ANTI-LOCK BRAKE SENSOR INDICATOR	
	② ⚠ **CAUTION: Examine the anti-lock brake sensor indicator carefully. Failure to correctly diagnose the anti-lock brake sensor indicator at this time will lead to unnecessary component replacement and wasted diagnostic time.** Inspect the anti-lock brake sensor indicator for damaged or missing teeth. Rotate the anti-lock brake sensor indicator to be sure all teeth are checked. • Does the RF anti-lock brake sensor indicator have damaged or missing teeth? → **Yes** INSTALL a new anti-lock brake sensor indicator. CLEAR the DTCs. DRIVE the vehicle over rough road and through a car wash. REPEAT the self-test. → **No** GO to **I4**.
I4 CHECK FOR LOOSE ANTI-LOCK BRAKE SENSOR MOUNTING	
	① Wiggle the RF anti-lock brake sensor at the wheel end. • Is the RF anti-lock brake sensor tight and secure? → **Yes** GO to **I5** → **No** TIGHTEN the sensor to specification. CLEAR the DTCs. DRIVE the vehicle over rough road and through a car wash. REPEAT the self-test.

FM4029901462020X

Fig. 18 Test I: Codes C1148 & C1234: Right Front Anti-Lock Brake Sensor, Dynamic (Part 2 of 5). 2002-03

TEST CONDITIONS	TEST DETAILS/RESULTS/ACTIONS
I1 RETRIEVE DTCs	

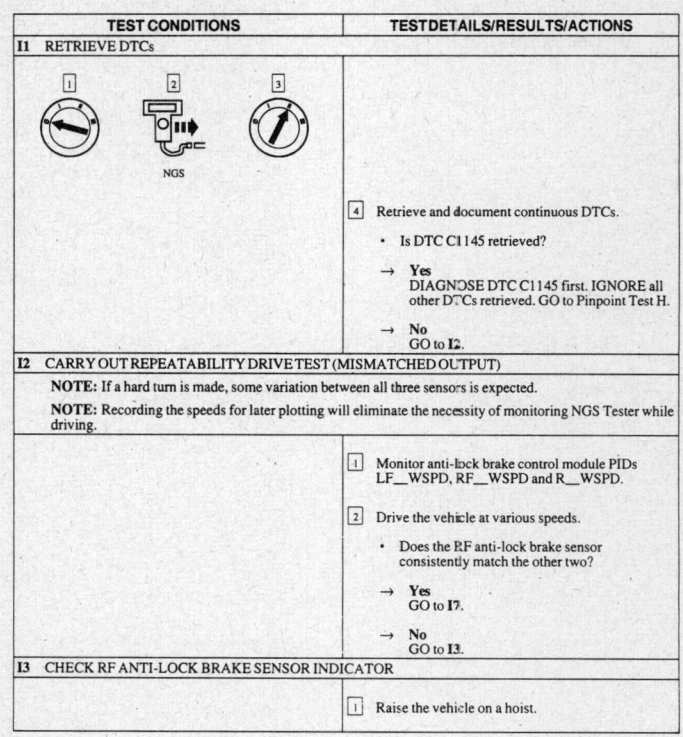

NGS

	④ Retrieve and document continuous DTCs. • Is DTC C1145 retrieved? → **Yes** DIAGNOSE DTC C1145 first. IGNORE all other DTCs retrieved. GO to Pinpoint Test H. → **No** GO to **I2**.
I2 CARRY OUT REPEATABILITY DRIVE TEST (MISMATCHED OUTPUT)	
NOTE: If a hard turn is made, some variation between all three sensors is expected. **NOTE:** Recording the speeds for later plotting will eliminate the necessity of monitoring NGS Tester while driving.	
	① Monitor anti-lock brake control module PIDs LF__WSPD, RF__WSPD and R__WSPD. ② Drive the vehicle at various speeds. • Does the RF anti-lock brake sensor consistently match the other two? → **Yes** GO to **I7**. → **No** GO to **I3**.
I3 CHECK RF ANTI-LOCK BRAKE SENSOR INDICATOR	
	① Raise the vehicle on a hoist.

FM4029901462010X

Fig. 18 Test I: Codes C1148 & C1234: Right Front Anti-Lock Brake Sensor, Dynamic (Part 1 of 5). 2002-03

TEST CONDITIONS	TEST DETAILS/RESULTS/ACTIONS
I5 CHECK FOR INTERNAL SENSOR SHORT	

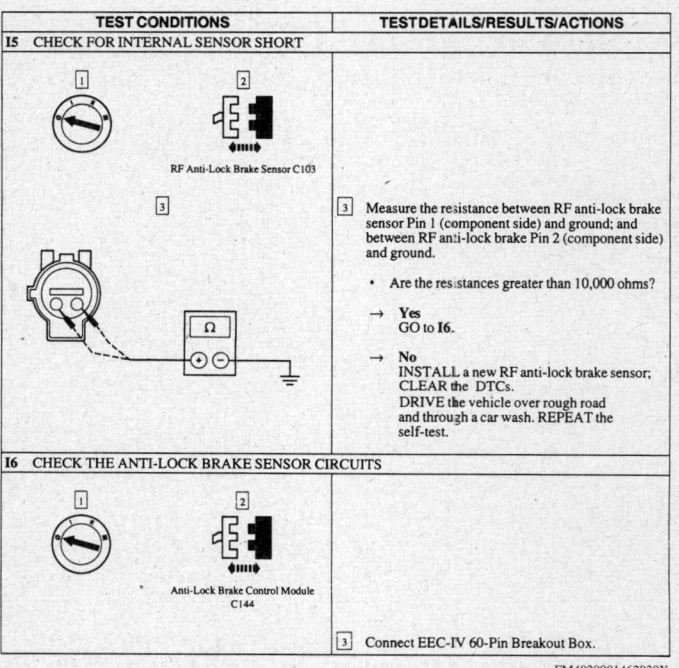

RF Anti-Lock Brake Sensor C103

	③ Measure the resistance between RF anti-lock brake sensor Pin 1 (component side) and ground; and between RF anti-lock brake Pin 2 (component side) and ground. • Are the resistances greater than 10,000 ohms? → **Yes** GO to **I6**. → **No** INSTALL a new RF anti-lock brake sensor; CLEAR the DTCs. DRIVE the vehicle over rough road and through a car wash. REPEAT the self-test.
I6 CHECK THE ANTI-LOCK BRAKE SENSOR CIRCUITS	
	Anti-Lock Brake Control Module C144
	③ Connect EEC-IV 60-Pin Breakout Box.

FM4029901462030X

Fig. 18 Test I: Codes C1148 & C1234: Right Front Anti-Lock Brake Sensor, Dynamic (Part 3 of 5). 2002-03

TEST CONDITIONS	TESTDETAILS/RESULTS/ACTIONS
I6 CHECK THE ANTI-LOCK BRAKE SENSOR CIRCUITS	

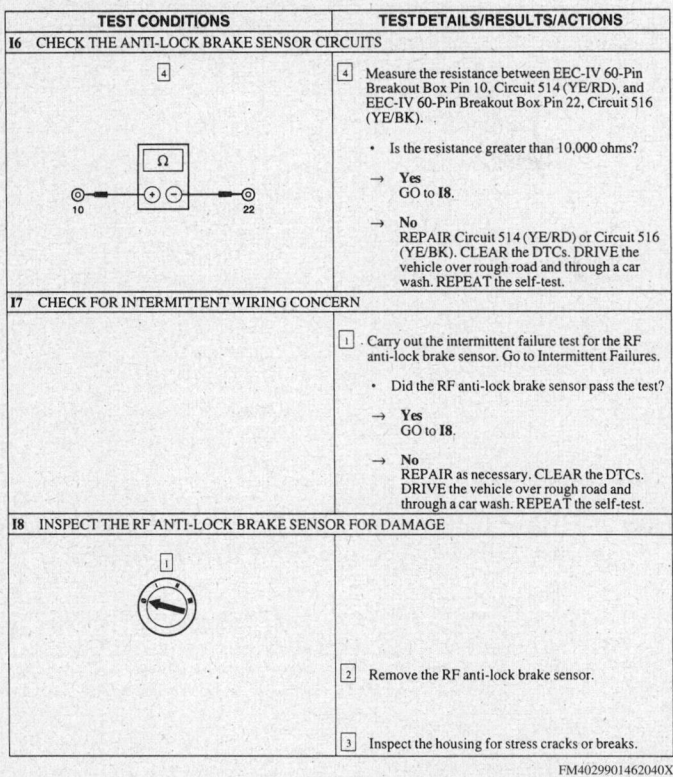	4 Measure the resistance between EEC-IV 60-Pin Breakout Box Pin 10, Circuit 514 (YE/RD), and EEC-IV 60-Pin Breakout Box Pin 22, Circuit 516 (YE/BK).
	
	 • Is the resistance greater than 10,000 ohms?
	
	 → **Yes**
	   GO to **I8**.
	
	 → **No**
	   REPAIR Circuit 514 (YE/RD) or Circuit 516 (YE/BK). CLEAR the DTCs. DRIVE the vehicle over rough road and through a car wash. REPEAT the self-test.

I7 CHECK FOR INTERMITTENT WIRING CONCERN	

	1 Carry out the intermittent failure test for the RF anti-lock brake sensor. Go to Intermittent Failures.
	
	 • Did the RF anti-lock brake sensor pass the test?
	
	 → **Yes**
	   GO to **I8**.
	
	 → **No**
	   REPAIR as necessary. CLEAR the DTCs. DRIVE the vehicle over rough road and through a car wash. REPEAT the self-test.

I8 INSPECT THE RF ANTI-LOCK BRAKE SENSOR FOR DAMAGE	
	2 Remove the RF anti-lock brake sensor. 3 Inspect the housing for stress cracks or breaks.

FM4029901462040X

Fig. 18   Test I: Codes C1148 & C1234: Right Front Anti-Lock Brake Sensor, Dynamic (Part 4 of 5). 2002-03

TEST CONDITIONS	TESTDETAILS/RESULTS/ACTIONS
J1 CHECK FOR FAULT REPEATABILITY	

1   2   3
 	
 NGS   Clear Continuous DTCs
	4 Drive the vehicle at least 16 km/h (10 mph).
	
	 5 Retrieve and document continuous DTCs.
	
	 • Is DTC C1230 retrieved?
	
	 → **Yes**
	   GO to **J2**.
	
	 → **No**
	   If no DTC is retrieved, CARRY OUT intermittent failure test. REFER to Intermittent diagnosis.
	
	   If a different DTC is retrieved, REFER to Diagnostic Chart Index.

FM4029901463010X

Fig. 19   Test J: Code C1230: Rear Anti-Lock Brake Sensor, Electrical/Static (Part 1 of 5). 2002-03

TEST CONDITIONS	TESTDETAILS/RESULTS/ACTIONS
I8 INSPECT THE RF ANTI-LOCK BRAKE SENSOR FOR DAMAGE	

	4 Inspect the sensor connector cavity for evidence of water entry or pin corrosion.
	
	 • Are any of the above conditions present?
	
	 → **Yes**
	   REPAIR as necessary. CLEAR the DTCs. DRIVE the vehicle over rough road and through a car wash. REPEAT the self-test.
	
	 → **No**
	   CLEAR the DTCs. DRIVE the vehicle over rough road and through a car wash. REPEAT the self-test.

FM4029901462050X

Fig. 18   Test I: Codes C1148 & C1234: Right Front Anti-Lock Brake Sensor, Dynamic (Part 5 of 5). 2002-03

TEST CONDITIONS	TESTDETAILS/RESULTS/ACTIONS
J2 CHECK ANTI-LOCK BRAKE SENSOR COIL RESISTANCE	

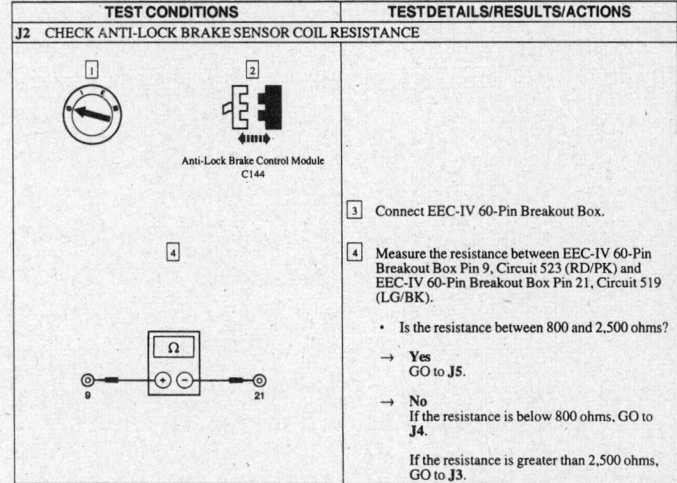
 Anti-Lock Brake Control Module C144
	3 Connect EEC-IV 60-Pin Breakout Box.
	
	 4 Measure the resistance between EEC-IV 60-Pin Breakout Box Pin 9, Circuit 523 (RD/PK) and EEC-IV 60-Pin Breakout Box Pin 21, Circuit 519 (LG/BK).
	
	 • Is the resistance between 800 and 2,500 ohms?
	
	 → **Yes**
	   GO to **J5**.
	
	 → **No**
	   If the resistance is below 800 ohms, GO to **J4**.
	
	   If the resistance is greater than 2,500 ohms, GO to **J3**.

FM4029901463020X

Fig. 19   Test J: Code C1230: Rear Anti-Lock Brake Sensor, Electrical/Static (Part 2 of 5). 2002-03

TEST CONDITIONS	TESTDETAILS/RESULTS/ACTIONS
J3 CHECK THE REAR ANTI-LOCK BRAKE SENSOR FOR AN OPEN	

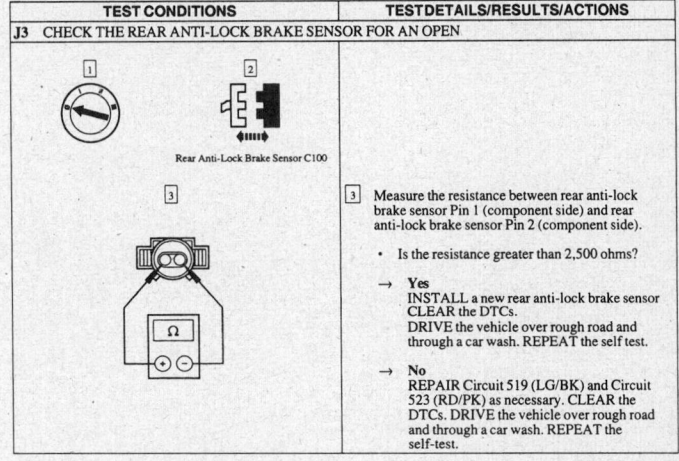
 Rear Anti-Lock Brake Sensor C100
	3 Measure the resistance between rear anti-lock brake sensor Pin 1 (component side) and rear anti-lock brake sensor Pin 2 (component side).
	
	 • Is the resistance greater than 2,500 ohms?
	
	 → **Yes**
	   INSTALL a new rear anti-lock brake sensor. CLEAR the DTCs. DRIVE the vehicle over rough road and through a car wash. REPEAT the self test.
	
	 → **No**
	   REPAIR Circuit 519 (LG/BK) and Circuit 523 (RD/PK) as necessary. CLEAR the DTCs. DRIVE the vehicle over rough road and through a car wash. REPEAT the self-test.

FM4029901463030X

Fig. 19   Test J: Code C1230: Rear Anti-Lock Brake Sensor, Electrical/Static (Part 3 of 5). 2002-03

TEST CONDITIONS	TESTDETAILS/RESULTS/ACTIONS
J4 CHECK THE REAR ANTI-LOCK BRAKE SENSOR FOR SHORT	

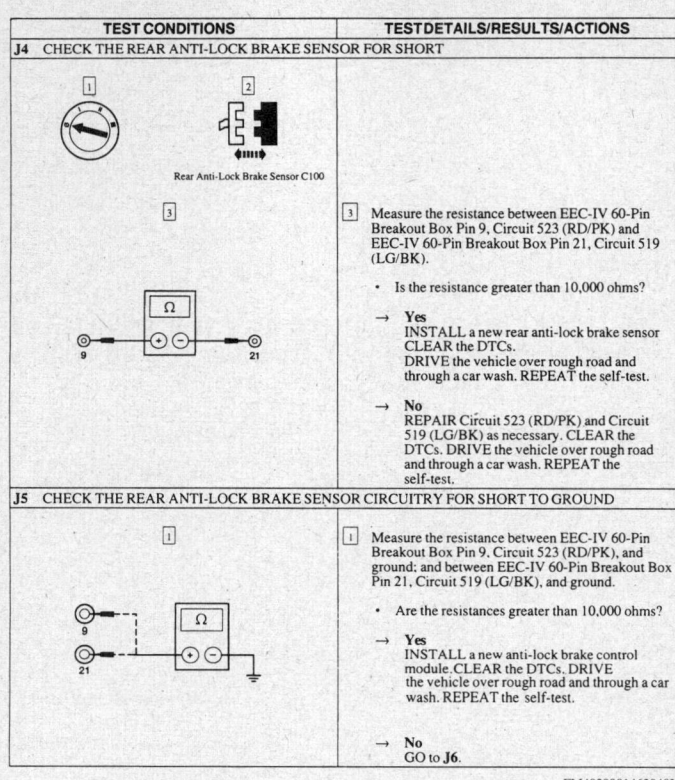

3	Measure the resistance between EEC-IV 60-Pin Breakout Box Pin 9, Circuit 523 (RD/PK) and EEC-IV 60-Pin Breakout Box Pin 21, Circuit 519 (LG/BK). • Is the resistance greater than 10,000 ohms? → **Yes** INSTALL a new rear anti-lock brake sensor CLEAR the DTCs. DRIVE the vehicle over rough road and through a car wash. REPEAT the self-test. → **No** REPAIR Circuit 523 (RD/PK) and Circuit 519 (LG/BK) as necessary. CLEAR the DTCs. DRIVE the vehicle over rough road and through a car wash. REPEAT the self-test.

TEST CONDITIONS	TESTDETAILS/RESULTS/ACTIONS
J5 CHECK THE REAR ANTI-LOCK BRAKE SENSOR CIRCUITRY FOR SHORT TO GROUND	

1	Measure the resistance between EEC-IV 60-Pin Breakout Box Pin 9, Circuit 523 (RD/PK), and ground; and between EEC-IV 60-Pin Breakout Box Pin 21, Circuit 519 (LG/BK), and ground. • Are the resistances greater than 10,000 ohms? → **Yes** INSTALL a new anti-lock brake control module. CLEAR the DTCs. DRIVE the vehicle over rough road and through a car wash. REPEAT the self-test. → **No** GO to **J6**.

FM4029901463040X

Fig. 19   Test J: Code C1230: Rear Anti-Lock Brake Sensor, Electrical/Static (Part 4 of 5). 2002-03

TEST CONDITIONS	TESTDETAILS/RESULTS/ACTIONS
K1 RETRIEVE DTCS	

4	Retrieve and document continuous DTCs. • Is DTC C1230 retrieved? → **Yes** DIAGNOSE DTC C1230 first. IGNORE all other DTCs retrieved. GO to Pinpoint Test J. → **No** GO to **K2**.

FM4029901464010X

Fig. 20   Test K: Codes C1229 & C1237: Rear Anti-Lock Brake Sensor, Dynamic (Part 1 of 5). 2002-03

TEST CONDITIONS	TESTDETAILS/RESULTS/ACTIONS
J6 CHECK REAR ANTI-LOCK BRAKE SENSOR FOR SHORT TO GROUND	

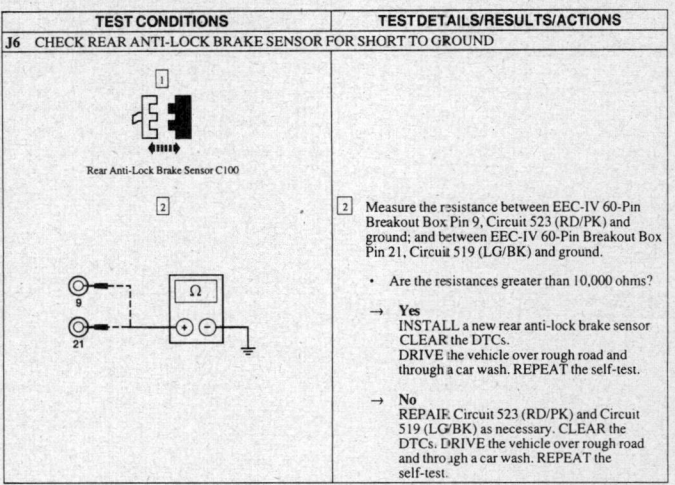

2	Measure the resistance between EEC-IV 60-Pin Breakout Box Pin 9, Circuit 523 (RD/PK) and ground; and between EEC-IV 60-Pin Breakout Box Pin 21, Circuit 519 (LG/BK) and ground. • Are the resistances greater than 10,000 ohms? → **Yes** INSTALL a new rear anti-lock brake sensor CLEAR the DTCs. DRIVE the vehicle over rough road and through a car wash. REPEAT the self-test. → **No** REPAIR Circuit 523 (RD/PK) and Circuit 519 (LG/BK) as necessary. CLEAR the DTCs. DRIVE the vehicle over rough road and through a car wash. REPEAT the self-test.

FM4029901463050X

Fig. 19   Test J: Code C1230: Rear Anti-Lock Brake Sensor, Electrical/Static (Part 5 of 5). 2002-03

TEST CONDITIONS	TESTDETAILS/RESULTS/ACTIONS
K2 CARRY OUT THE REPEATABILITY DRIVE TEST (MISMATCHED OUTPUT)	
	NOTE: If a hard turn is made, some variation between all three sensors is expected.
	NOTE: Recording the speeds for later plotting will eliminate the necessity of monitoring NGS Tester while driving.

1	Monitor anti-lock brake control module PIDs LF__WSPD, RF__WSPD and R__WSPD.
2	Drive the vehicle at various speeds. • Does the rear anti-lock brake sensor consistently match the other two? → **Yes** GO to **K7**. → **No** GO to **K3**.

TEST CONDITIONS	TESTDETAILS/RESULTS/ACTIONS
K3 CHECK REAR ANTI-LOCK BRAKE SENSOR INDICATOR	

1	Raise the vehicle on a hoist
2	⚠ **CAUTION: Examine the anti-lock brake sensor indicator carefully. Failure to correctly diagnose the anti-lock brake sensor indicator at this time will lead to unnecessary component replacement and wasted diagnostic time.** Inspect the anti-lock brake sensor indicator for damaged or missing teeth. Rotate the anti-lock brake sensor indicator to be sure all teeth are checked. • Does the anti-lock brake sensor indicator have damaged or missing teeth? → **Yes** INSTALL a new rear anti-lock brake sensor indicator CLEAR the DTCs. DRIVE the vehicle over rough road and through a car wash. REPEAT the self-test. → **No** GO to **K4**.

FM4029901464020X

Fig. 20   Test K: Codes C1229 & C1237: Rear Anti-Lock Brake Sensor, Dynamic (Part 2 of 5). 2002-03

TEST CONDITIONS	TESTDETAILS/RESULTS/ACTIONS
K4 CHECK FOR LOOSE SENSOR MOUNTING	
	1. Wiggle the rear anti-lock brake sensor at the differential case (4204). • Is the rear anti-lock brake sensor tight and secure? → **Yes** GO to **K5**. → **No** TIGHTEN the sensor to specification. CLEAR the DTCs. DRIVE the vehicle over rough road and through a car wash. REPEAT the self-test.
K5 CHECK FOR INTERNAL SENSOR SHORT	
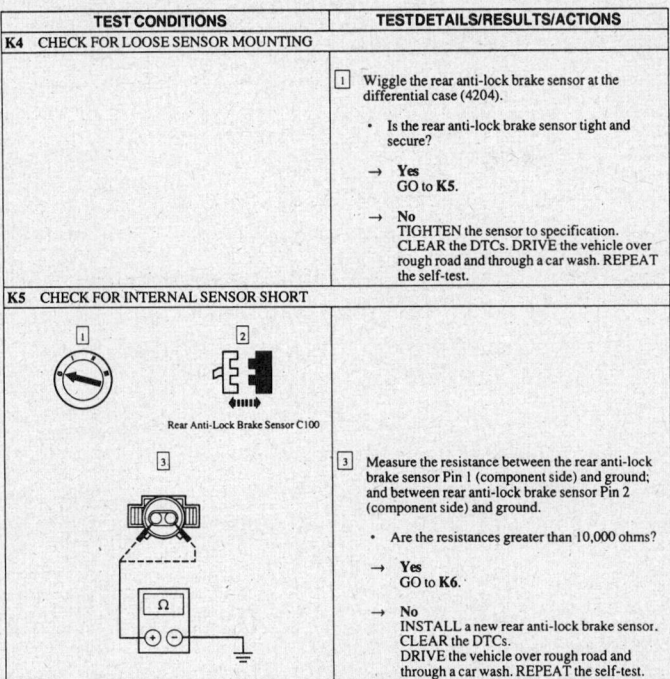	3. Measure the resistance between the rear anti-lock brake sensor Pin 1 (component side) and ground; and between rear anti-lock brake sensor Pin 2 (component side) and ground. • Are the resistances greater than 10,000 ohms? → **Yes** GO to **K6**. → **No** INSTALL a new rear anti-lock brake sensor. CLEAR the DTCs. DRIVE the vehicle over rough road and through a car wash. REPEAT the self-test.

FM4029901464030X

Fig. 20 Test K: Codes C1229 & C1237: Rear Anti-Lock Brake Sensor, Dynamic (Part 3 of 5). 2002-03

TEST CONDITIONS	TESTDETAILS/RESULTS/ACTIONS
K6 CHECK THE ANTI-LOCK BRAKE SENSOR CIRCUIT	
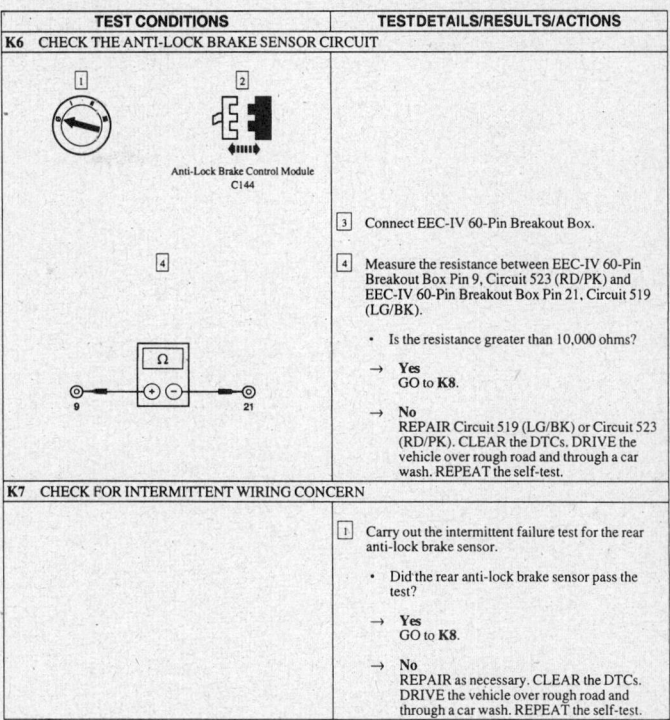	3. Connect EEC-IV 60-Pin Breakout Box. 4. Measure the resistance between EEC-IV 60-Pin Breakout Box Pin 9, Circuit 523 (RD/PK) and EEC-IV 60-Pin Breakout Box Pin 21, Circuit 519 (LG/BK). • Is the resistance greater than 10,000 ohms? → **Yes** GO to **K8**. → **No** REPAIR Circuit 519 (LG/BK) or Circuit 523 (RD/PK). CLEAR the DTCs. DRIVE the vehicle over rough road and through a car wash. REPEAT the self-test.
K7 CHECK FOR INTERMITTENT WIRING CONCERN	
	1. Carry out the intermittent failure test for the rear anti-lock brake sensor. • Did the rear anti-lock brake sensor pass the test? → **Yes** GO to **K8**. → **No** REPAIR as necessary. CLEAR the DTCs. DRIVE the vehicle over rough road and through a car wash. REPEAT the self-test.

FM4029901464040X

Fig. 20 Test K: Codes C1229 & C1237: Rear Anti-Lock Brake Sensor, Dynamic (Part 4 of 5). 2002-03

TEST CONDITIONS	TESTDETAILS/RESULTS/ACTIONS
K8 INSPECT THE REAR ANTI-LOCK BRAKE SENSOR FOR DAMAGE	
	2. Remove the rear anti-lock brake sensor. 3. Inspect the housing for stress cracks or breaks. 4. Inspect the anti-lock brake sensor connector cavity for evidence of water entry or pin corrosion. • Are any of the above conditions evident? → **Yes** REPAIR as necessary. CLEAR the DTCs. DRIVE the vehicle over rough road and through a car wash. REPEAT the self-test. → **No** CLEAR the DTCs. DRIVE the vehicle over rough road and through a car wash. REPEAT the self-test.

FM4029901464050X

Fig. 20 Test K: Codes C1229 & C1237: Rear Anti-Lock Brake Sensor, Dynamic (Part 5 of 5). 2002-03

TEST CONDITIONS	TESTDETAILS/RESULTS/ACTIONS
L1 CHECK BASE BRAKE COMPONENTS	
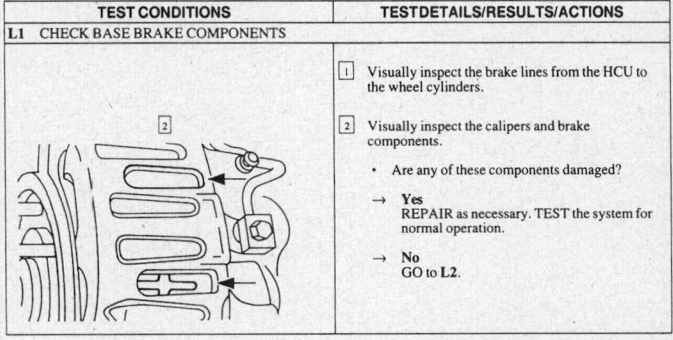	1. Visually inspect the brake lines from the HCU to the wheel cylinders. 2. Visually inspect the calipers and brake components. • Are any of these components damaged? → **Yes** REPAIR as necessary. TEST the system for normal operation. → **No** GO to **L2**.

FM4029901465010X

Fig. 21 Test L: Soft/Excessive Pedal Travel (Part 1 of 3). 2002-03

TEST CONDITIONS	TESTDETAILS/RESULTS/ACTIONS
L2 CHECK FOR LEAKING DUMP VALVE	
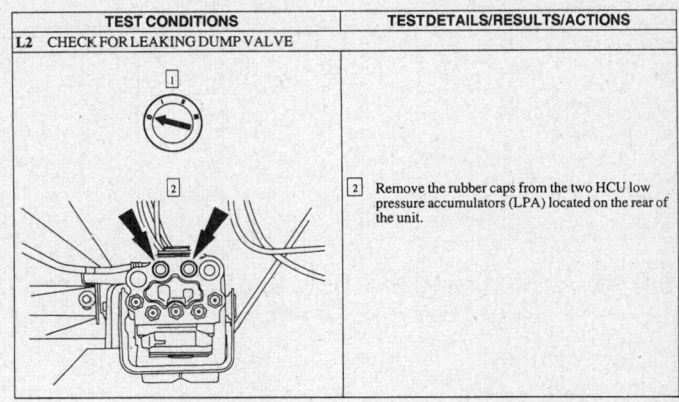	2. Remove the rubber caps from the two HCU low pressure accumulators (LPA) located on the rear of the unit.

FM4029901465020X

Fig. 21 Test L: Soft/Excessive Pedal Travel (Part 2 of 3). 2002-03

TEST CONDITIONS	TESTDETAILS/RESULTS/ACTIONS
L2 CHECK FOR LEAKING DUMP VALVE	
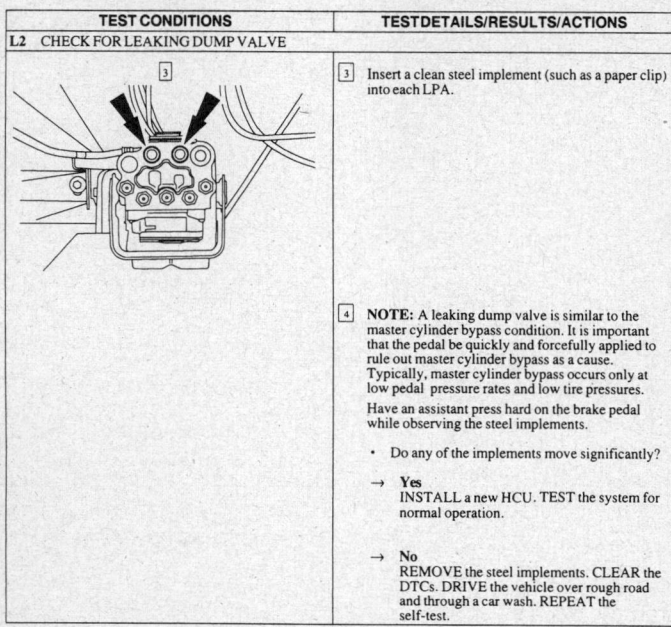	3 Insert a clean steel implement (such as a paper clip) into each LPA.

	4 **NOTE:** A leaking dump valve is similar to the master cylinder bypass condition. It is important that the pedal be quickly and forcefully applied to rule out master cylinder bypass as a cause. Typically, master cylinder bypass occurs only at low pedal pressure rates and low tire pressures. Have an assistant press hard on the brake pedal while observing the steel implements.
	
	• Do any of the implements move significantly?
	
	→ **Yes**
	  INSTALL a new HCU. TEST the system for normal operation.
	
	→ **No**
	  REMOVE the steel implements. CLEAR the DTCs. DRIVE the vehicle over rough road and through a car wash. REPEAT the self-test.

FM4029901465030X

Fig. 21   Test L: Soft/Excessive Pedal Travel (Part 3 of 3). 2002-03

TEST CONDITIONS	TESTDETAILS/RESULTS/ACTIONS
M1 CHECK FOR FAULT REPEATABILITY	

	4 Carry out the Anti-Lock Brake Control Module On-Demand Self-Test.
	
	5 Retrieve and document continuous DTCs.
	
	• Are any DTCs retrieved?
	
	→ **Yes**
	  If DTC C1095 is retrieved, INSTALL a new HCU. CLEAR the DTCs. DRIVE the vehicle over rough road and through a car wash. REPEAT the self-test.
	
	  If DTC C1096 is retrieved, GO to **M2**.
	
	  If a different DTC is retrieved, REFER to Diagnostic Chart Index.
	
	→ **No**
	  CLEAR the DTCs. DRIVE the vehicle over rough road and through a car wash. REPEAT the self-test.

M2 CHECK PUMP MOTOR CIRCUIT 37 (YE) FOR AN OPEN	

HCU C145	3 Measure the voltage between HCU C145, Circuit 37 (YE), harness side and ground.
	
	• Is the voltage greater than 10 volts?
	
	→ **Yes**
	  GO to **M3**.
	
	→ **No**
	  REPAIR Circuit 37 (YE). CLEAR the DTCs. DRIVE the vehicle over rough road and through a car wash. REPEAT the self-test.

FM4029901466020X

Fig. 22   Test M: Codes C1095 & C1096: Pump Motor (Part 2 of 3). 2002-03

TEST CONDITIONS	TESTDETAILS/RESULTS/ACTIONS
M1 CHECK FOR FAULT REPEATABILITY	
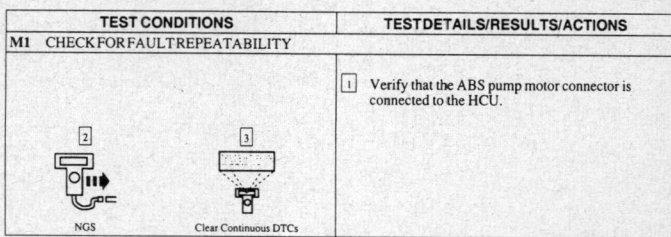	1 Verify that the ABS pump motor connector is connected to the HCU.

FM4029901466010X

Fig. 22   Test M: Codes C1095 & C1096: Pump Motor (Part 1 of 3). 2002-03

TEST CONDITIONS	TESTDETAILS/RESULTS/ACTIONS
M3 CHECK CIRCUIT 57 (BK) FOR AN OPEN	

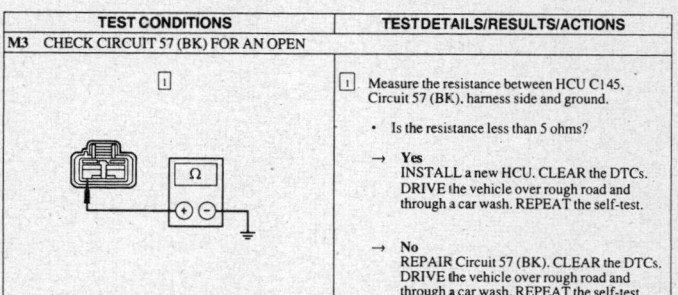	1 Measure the resistance between HCU C145, Circuit 57 (BK), harness side and ground.
	
	• Is the resistance less than 5 ohms?
	
	→ **Yes**
	  INSTALL a new HCU. CLEAR the DTCs. DRIVE the vehicle over rough road and through a car wash. REPEAT the self-test.
	
	→ **No**
	  REPAIR Circuit 57 (BK). CLEAR the DTCs. DRIVE the vehicle over rough road and through a car wash. REPEAT the self-test.

FM4029901466030X

Fig. 22   Test M: Codes C1095 & C1096: Pump Motor (Part 3 of 3). 2002-03

TEST CONDITIONS	TESTDETAILS/RESULTS/ACTIONS
N1 CHECK FOR FAULT REPEATABILITY	

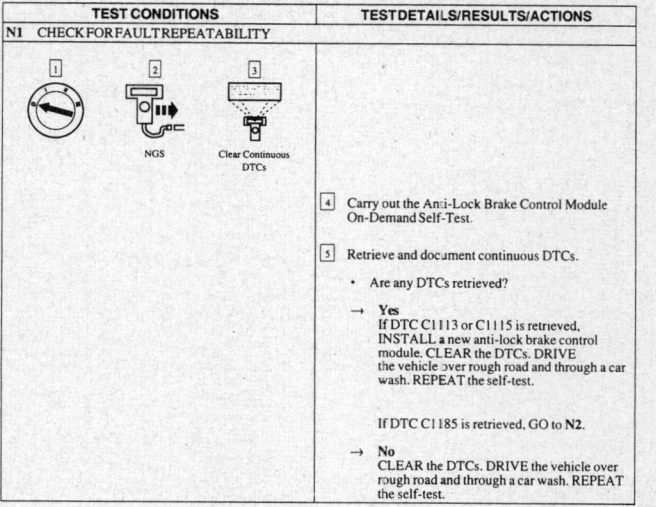	4 Carry out the Anti-Lock Brake Control Module On-Demand Self-Test.
	
	5 Retrieve and document continuous DTCs.
	
	• Are any DTCs retrieved?
	
	→ **Yes**
	  If DTC C1113 or C1115 is retrieved, INSTALL a new anti-lock brake control module. CLEAR the DTCs. DRIVE the vehicle over rough road and through a car wash. REPEAT the self-test.
	
	  If DTC C1185 is retrieved, GO to **N2**.
	
	→ **No**
	  CLEAR the DTCs. DRIVE the vehicle over rough road and through a car wash. REPEAT the self-test.

FM4029901467010X

Fig. 23   Test N: Codes C1113, C1115 & C1185: Internal Power Relay Failure (Part 1 of 2). 2002-03

TEST CONDITIONS	TESTDETAILS/RESULTS/ACTIONS
N2 CHECK VOLTAGE TO THE ANTI-LOCK BRAKE CONTROL MODULE	

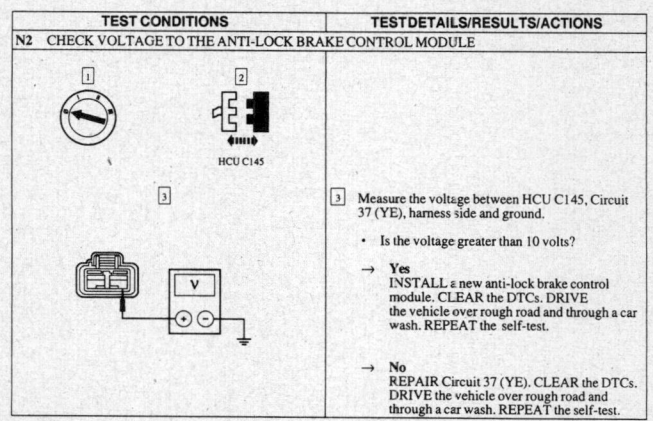	3 Measure the voltage between HCU C145, Circuit 37 (YE), harness side and ground.
	
	• Is the voltage greater than 10 volts?
	
	→ **Yes**
	  INSTALL a new anti-lock brake control module. CLEAR the DTCs. DRIVE the vehicle over rough road and through a car wash. REPEAT the self-test.
	
	→ **No**
	  REPAIR Circuit 37 (YE). CLEAR the DTCs. DRIVE the vehicle over rough road and through a car wash. REPEAT the self-test.

FM4029901467020X

Fig. 23   Test N: Codes C1113, C1115 & C1185: Internal Power Relay Failure (Part 2 of 2). 2002-03

TEST CONDITIONS	TESTDETAILS/RESULTS/ACTIONS
O1 CHECK FOR FAULT REPEATABILITY	

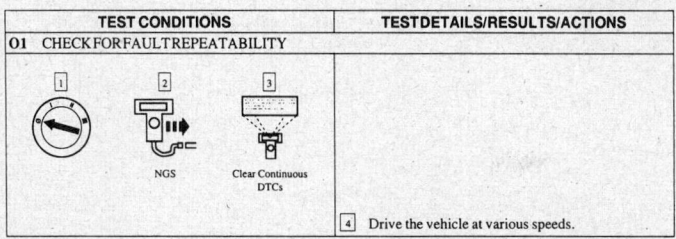

NGS   Clear Continuous DTCs

4   Drive the vehicle at various speeds.

FM4029901468010X

Fig. 24   Test O: Wheel Speed Error, Dynamic (Part 1 of 3). 2002-03

TEST CONDITIONS	TESTDETAILS/RESULTS/ACTIONS
O2 CHECK FOR AN ERRATIC WHEEL SPEED SIGNAL	

Clear Continuous DTCs

2   **NOTE:** When using NGS Tester to monitor the wheel speed signals, monitor one wheel at a time. The information is recorded faster and the likelihood of diagnosing the faulty signal is greater.

Monitor the anti-lock brake control module PIDs LF__WSPD, RF__WSPD and R__WSPD while driving at various speeds.

- Does one wheel speed signal drop out while driving or braking?

→ **Yes**
If LF anti-lock brake sensor, GO to Pinpoint Test G.

If RF anti-lock brake sensor, GO to Pinpoint Test I.

If rear anti-lock brake sensor, GO to Pinpoint Test K.

→ **No**
REPEAT the monitoring of the PIDs. Intermittent signals may not be recorded the first time. INSPECT the sensor indicators and sensor harness for damage. REPAIR as necessary. CLEAR the DTCs. DRIVE the vehicle over rough road and through a car wash. REPEAT the self-test.

FM4029901468030X

Fig. 24   Test O: Wheel Speed Error, Dynamic (Part 3 of 3). 2002-03

TEST CONDITIONS	TESTDETAILS/RESULTS/ACTIONS
P1 CHECK FOR FAULT REPEATABILITY	

NGS   Clear Continuous DTCs

4   Retrieve and document continuous DTCs.

- Is DTC C1169 retrieved?

→ **Yes**
INSTALL a new HCU.

→ **No**
GO to **P2**.

P2 CARRY OUT A LOW SPEED ABS STOP	

1   Drive the vehicle at approximately 16 km/h (10 mph).

2   **NOTE:** Wetting down the area where the stop is to be performed will aid in this test.

NOTE: Momentary lockup is permissible. An assistant should be used to monitor the wheels during ABS stop.

Apply the brakes hard enough to lock all four wheels.

- Does one wheel lock consistently?

→ **Yes**
GO to Symptom Chart.

→ **No**
CLEAR the DTCs. DRIVE the vehicle over rough road and through a car wash. REPEAT the self-test.

FM4029901469000X

Fig. 25   Test P: Code C1169: Excessive Dump Time. 2002-03

TEST CONDITIONS	TESTDETAILS/RESULTS/ACTIONS
O1 CHECK FOR FAULT REPEATABILITY	

5   Retrieve and document continuous DTCs.

- Was a DTC retrieved and did the ABS activate during normal stops?

→ **Yes**
If DTC C1184 is retrieved and the ABS did not activate during normal stops, INSTALL a new anti-lock brake control module

If ABS is activated on normal stops, GO to **O2**.

If DTC C1222 is retrieved, INSPECT the tires for mismatched sizes. INSPECT the sensor indicators for damage. If inspections are normal, INSTALL a new anti-lock brake control module

If a different DTC is retrieved, REFER to Diagnostic Chart Index.

→ **No**
CLEAR the DTCs. DRIVE the vehicle over rough road and through a car wash. REPEAT the self-test.

FM4029901468020X

Fig. 24   Test O: Wheel Speed Error, Dynamic (Part 2 of 3). 2002-03

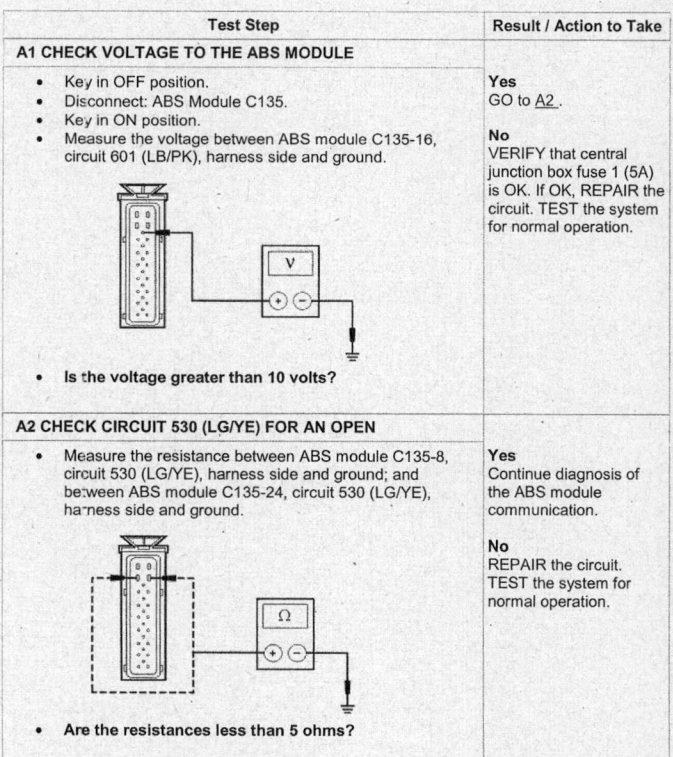

Test Step	Result / Action to Take
A1 CHECK VOLTAGE TO THE ABS MODULE • Key in OFF position. • Disconnect: ABS Module C135. • Key in ON position. • Measure the voltage between ABS module C135-16, circuit 601 (LB/PK), harness side and ground. • Is the voltage greater than 10 volts?	**Yes** GO to A2. **No** VERIFY that central junction box fuse 1 (5A) is OK. If OK, REPAIR the circuit. TEST the system for normal operation.
A2 CHECK CIRCUIT 530 (LG/YE) FOR AN OPEN • Measure the resistance between ABS module C135-8, circuit 530 (LG/YE), harness side and ground; and between ABS module C135-24, circuit 530 (LG/YE), harness side and ground. • Are the resistances less than 5 ohms?	**Yes** Continue diagnosis of the ABS module communication. **No** REPAIR the circuit. TEST the system for normal operation.

LTV0500000004970

Fig. 26   Test A: No Communication w/ABS Module. 2004-06 Less Stability Assist

Test Step	Result / Action to Take
B1 CHECK THE ABS HARNESS AND MODULE FOR WATER INTRUSION • Key in OFF position. • Disconnect: ABS Module C135. • Inspect the ABS module connector and module for water intrusion. • **Is there any evidence of water entry?**	**Yes** CLEAN the connector and dry it out with low pressure compressed air. INSPECT for evidence of water entry and repair as necessary. CLEAR the DTCs. REPEAT the self-test. **No** GO to B2.
B2 CHECK FOR ANTI-LOCK BRAKE SYSTEM (ABS) MODULE DTCs • Enter the following diagnostic mode on the diagnostic tool: Retrieve and record the ABS module DTCs. • **Are any DTCs present?**	**Yes** If DTC C1145, C1155 or C1230 is present, GO to B3 All other DTCs, GO to the Anti-Lock Brake System (ABS) Module Diagnostic Trouble Code (DTC) Index. **No** System is operating correctly at this time.
B3 CHECK THE ANTI-LOCK BRAKE SYSTEM (ABS) CONTROL MODULE OUTPUT • Key in OFF position. • Disconnect: ABS Module C135. • Measure the resistance between ABS module C135 pins harness side as follows:	**Yes** GO to B4. **No** REPAIR the circuit(s) in question. CLEAR the DTCs. REPEAT the self-test.

ABS Module Connector-Pin	Circuit	ABS Module Connector-Pin	Circuit
C135-5	516 (YE/BK)	C135-13	514 (YE/RD)
C135-4	522 (TN/BK)	C135-12	521 (TN/OG)
C135-14	523 (RD/PK)	C135-6	519 (LG/BK)

LTV0500000004971

Fig. 27 Test B, Codes C1145,, C1155 & C1230: Wheel Speed Sensor Input Circuit Failure (Part 1 of 5). 2004-06 Less Stability Assist

---

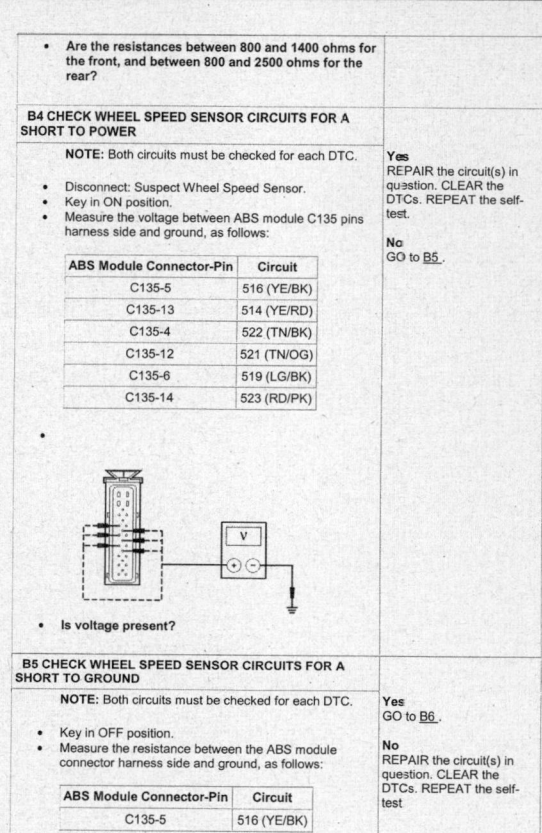

• Are the resistances between 800 and 1400 ohms for the front, and between 800 and 2500 ohms for the rear?	
B4 CHECK WHEEL SPEED SENSOR CIRCUITS FOR A SHORT TO POWER **NOTE:** Both circuits must be checked for each DTC. • Disconnect: Suspect Wheel Speed Sensor. • Key in ON position. • Measure the voltage between ABS module C135 pins harness side and ground, as follows:	**Yes** REPAIR the circuit(s) in question. CLEAR the DTCs. REPEAT the self-test. **No** GO to B5.

ABS Module Connector-Pin	Circuit
C135-5	516 (YE/BK)
C135-13	514 (YE/RD)
C135-4	522 (TN/BK)
C135-12	521 (TN/OG)
C135-6	519 (LG/BK)
C135-14	523 (RD/PK)

• Is voltage present?

| **B5 CHECK WHEEL SPEED SENSOR CIRCUITS FOR A SHORT TO GROUND**

NOTE: Both circuits must be checked for each DTC.

• Key in OFF position.
• Measure the resistance between the ABS module connector harness side and ground, as follows: | **Yes**
GO to B6.

No
REPAIR the circuit(s) in question. CLEAR the DTCs. REPEAT the self-test |

ABS Module Connector-Pin	Circuit
C135-5	516 (YE/BK)

LTV0500000004972

Fig. 27 Test B, Codes C1145,, C1155 & C1230: Wheel Speed Sensor Input Circuit Failure (Part 2 of 5). 2004-06 Less Stability Assist

---

ABS Module Connector-Pin	Circuit
C135-13	514 (YE/RD)
C135-4	522 (TN/BK)
C135-12	521 (TN/OG)
C135-6	519 (LG/BK)
C135-14	523 (RD/PK)

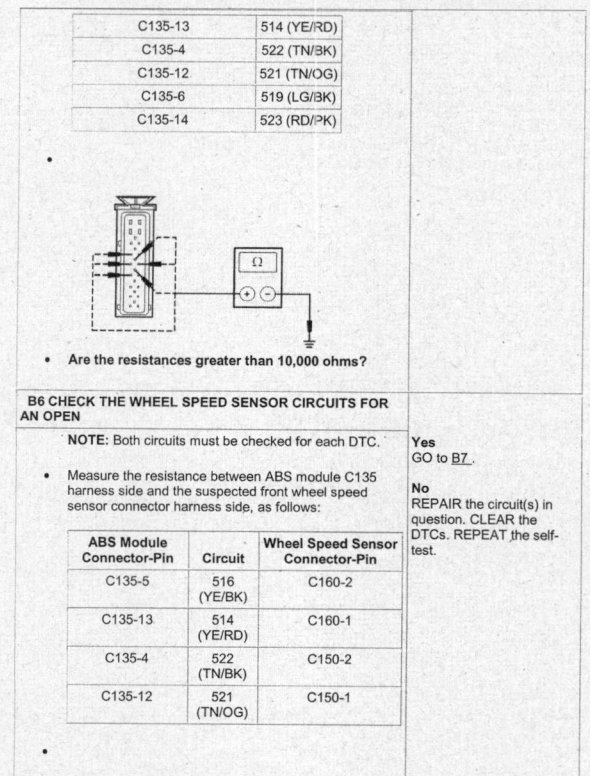

• Are the resistances greater than 10,000 ohms?

| **B6 CHECK THE WHEEL SPEED SENSOR CIRCUITS FOR AN OPEN**

NOTE: Both circuits must be checked for each DTC.

• Measure the resistance between ABS module C135 harness side and the suspected front wheel speed sensor connector harness side, as follows: | **Yes**
GO to B7.

No
REPAIR the circuit(s) in question. CLEAR the DTCs. REPEAT the self-test. |

ABS Module Connector-Pin	Circuit	Wheel Speed Sensor Connector-Pin
C135-5	516 (YE/BK)	C160-2
C135-13	514 (YE/RD)	C160-1
C135-4	522 (TN/BK)	C150-2
C135-12	521 (TN/OG)	C150-1

LTV0500000004973

Fig. 27 Test B, Codes C1145,, C1155 & C1230: Wheel Speed Sensor Input Circuit Failure (Part 3 of 5). 2004-06 Less Stability Assist

---

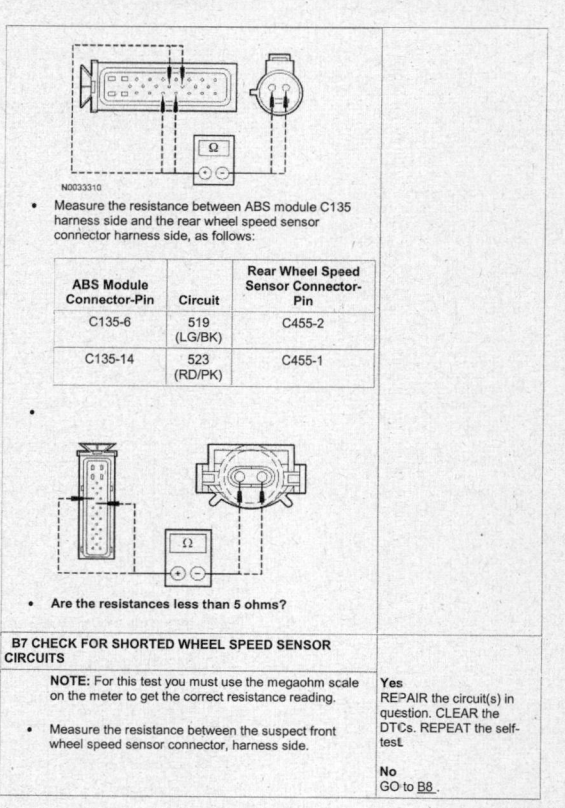

N0033310

• Measure the resistance between ABS module C135 harness side and the rear wheel speed sensor connector harness side, as follows:

ABS Module Connector-Pin	Circuit	Rear Wheel Speed Sensor Connector-Pin
C135-6	519 (LG/BK)	C455-2
C135-14	523 (RD/PK)	C455-1

• Are the resistances less than 5 ohms?

| **B7 CHECK FOR SHORTED WHEEL SPEED SENSOR CIRCUITS**

NOTE: For this test you must use the megaohm scale on the meter to get the correct resistance reading.

• Measure the resistance between the suspect front wheel speed sensor connector, harness side. | **Yes**
REPAIR the circuit(s) in question. CLEAR the DTCs. REPEAT the self-test

No
GO to B8. |

LTV0500000004974

Fig. 27 Test B, Codes C1145,, C1155 & C1230: Wheel Speed Sensor Input Circuit Failure (Part 4 of 5). 2004-06 Less Stability Assist

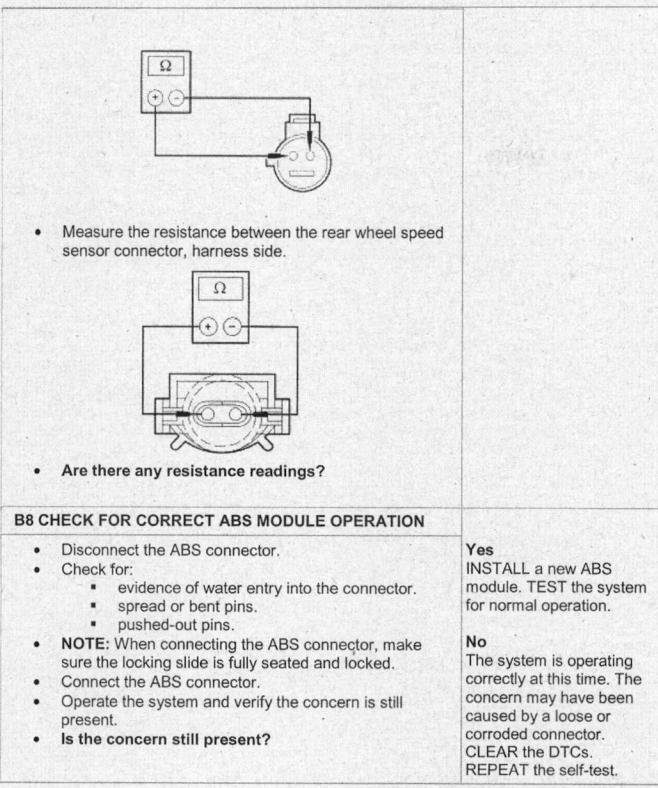

- Measure the resistance between the rear wheel speed sensor connector, harness side.

- **Are there any resistance readings?**

B8 CHECK FOR CORRECT ABS MODULE OPERATION	

- Disconnect the ABS connector.
- Check for:
   - evidence of water entry into the connector.
   - spread or bent pins.
   - pushed-out pins.
- **NOTE:** When connecting the ABS connector, make sure the locking slide is fully seated and locked.
- Connect the ABS connector.
- Operate the system and verify the concern is still present.
- **Is the concern still present?**
	Yes
	INSTALL a new ABS module. TEST the system for normal operation.
	
	No
	The system is operating correctly at this time. The concern may have been caused by a loose or corroded connector. CLEAR the DTCs. REPEAT the self-test.

LTV0500000004975

Fig. 27 Test B, Codes C1145,, C1155 & C1230: Wheel Speed Sensor Input Circuit Failure (Part 5 of 5). 2004-06 Less Stability Assist

Test Step	Result / Action to Take
C1 CHECK THE ABS HARNESS AND MODULE FOR WATER INTRUSION - Key in OFF position. - Disconnect: ABS Module C135. - Inspect the ABS module connector and module for water intrusion. - **Is there any evidence of water entry?**	**Yes** CLEAN the connector and dry it out with low pressure compressed air. INSPECT for evidence of water entry and repair as necessary. CLEAR the DTCs. TEST the system for normal operation. **No** GO to C2 .
C2 CHECK FOR ANTI-LOCK BRAKE SYSTEM (ABS) MODULE DTCs - Enter the following diagnostic mode on the diagnostic tool: Retrieve and record the ABS module DTCs. - **Are any DTCs present?**	**Yes** If DTC C1222 is present, GO to C3 . If DTC C1233, C1234 or C1237 is present, GO to C4 . **No** All other DTCs, GO to the Diagnostic Trouble Code (DTC) Index.
C3 CHECK ALL TIRE SIZES - Make sure that all tire sizes are correct and matching. - **Are the tire sizes correct?**	**Yes** GO to C10 . **No** INSTALL a new tire of the correct size for each tire that is incorrect. CLEAR the DTCs. REPEAT the self-test. TEST the system for normal operation.
C4 MONITOR THE WHEEL SPEED SENSOR PIDs - Use the diagnostic tool to monitor the wheel speed sensor PIDs while driving the vehicle at a constant speed.	**Yes** RETRIEVE the DTCs.

LTV0500000004976

Fig. 28 Test C, Codes C1222, C1233, C1234 & C1237: Wheel Speed Mismatch/Missing (Part 1 of 4). 2004-06 Less Stability Assist

- **Are the wheel speed sensor PID values similar?**	If DTC C1233, C1234 or C1237 is present, GO to C7 . **No** GO to C5 .
C5 CHECK THE WHEEL SPEED SENSOR FOR DAMAGE AND/OR LOOSENESS - Key in OFF position. - Raise and support the vehicle. - ⚠ **CAUTION: Examine the wheel speed sensor wire carefully with a good light. Failure to verify damage in the wheel speed sensor wire can lead to unnecessary installation of a new component.** - Inspect the wheel speed sensor mounting for looseness. If the rear wheel speed sensor is suspected, inspect the sensor for corrosion. If the front wheel speed sensor is suspected, check for corrosion on the front anti-lock brake mounting flange. Clean as necessary. - **Is the wheel speed sensor OK?**	**Yes** GO to C6 . **No** INSTALL a new wheel speed sensor. CLEAR the DTCs. REPEAT the self-test
C6 CHECK FOR WHEEL SPEED SENSOR RING DAMAGE - Remove the wheel speed sensor. - Inspect the wheel speed sensor rings for damaged or missing teeth. - **Is the wheel speed sensor ring OK?**	**Yes** GO to C7 . **No** INSTALL a new wheel speed sensor. CLEAR the DTCs. REPEAT the self-test.
C7 CHECK THE SENSOR OUTPUT TO THE ANTI-LOCK BRAKE SYSTEM (ABS) MODULE - Select NEUTRAL. - Raise and support the vehicle. - **NOTE:** For the rear speed sensor, spinning the wheel will not turn the tone ring. You must spin the driveshaft to get accurate test results. - Measure the A/C voltage between ABS module C135, harness side, while spinning the front tire or the driveshaft by hand as follows:	**Yes** GO to C10 . **No** GO to C8 .

ABS Module Connector-Pin	Circuit	ABS Module Connector-Pin	Circuit
C135-13	514 (YE/RD)	C135-5	516 (YE/BK)
C135-12	521 (TN/OG)	C135-4	522 (TN/BK)
C135-14	523	C135-6	519

LTV0500000004977

Fig. 28 Test C, Codes C1222, C1233, C1234 & C1237: Wheel Speed Mismatch/Missing (Part 2 of 4). 2004-06 Less Stability Assist

(RD/PK)	(LG/BK)

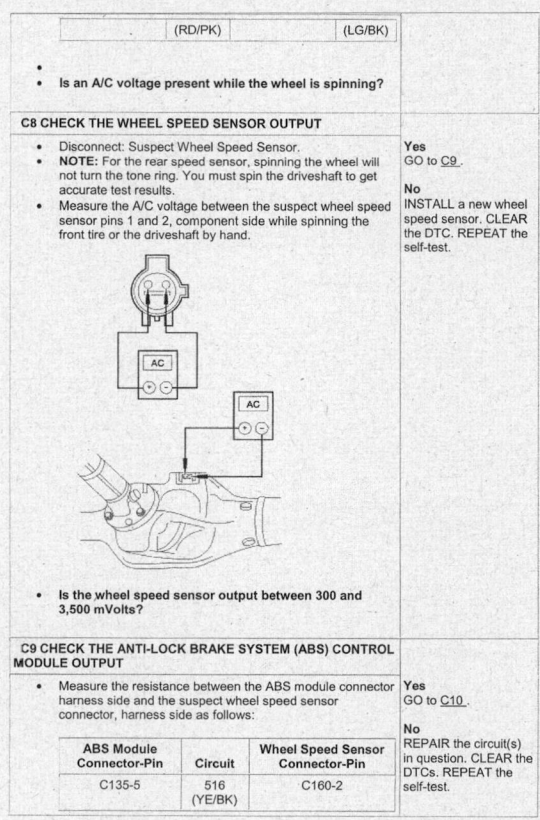

- **Is an A/C voltage present while the wheel is spinning?**	
C8 CHECK THE WHEEL SPEED SENSOR OUTPUT - Disconnect: Suspect Wheel Speed Sensor. - **NOTE:** For the rear speed sensor, spinning the wheel will not turn the tone ring. You must spin the driveshaft to get accurate test results. - Measure the A/C voltage between the suspect wheel speed sensor pins 1 and 2, component side while spinning the front tire or the driveshaft by hand.	**Yes** GO to C9 . **No** INSTALL a new wheel speed sensor. CLEAR the DTC. REPEAT the self-test.
- **Is the wheel speed sensor output between 300 and 3,500 mVolts?**	
C9 CHECK THE ANTI-LOCK BRAKE SYSTEM (ABS) CONTROL MODULE OUTPUT - Measure the resistance between the ABS module connector harness side and the suspect wheel speed sensor connector, harness side as follows:	**Yes** GO to C10 . **No** REPAIR the circuit(s) in question. CLEAR the DTCs. REPEAT the self-test.

ABS Module Connector-Pin	Circuit	Wheel Speed Sensor Connector-Pin
C135-5	516 (YE/BK)	C160-2

LTV0500000004978

Fig. 28 Test C, Codes C1222, C1233, C1234 & C1237: Wheel Speed Mismatch/Missing (Part 3 of 4). 2004-06 Less Stability Assist

C135-13	514 (YE/RD)	C160-1
C135-4	522 (TN/BK)	C150-2
C135-12	521 (TN/OG)	C150-1
C135-14	523 (RD/PK)	C455-1
C135-6	519 (LG/BK)	C455-2

- •
- • Are the resistances less than 5 ohms?

C10 CHECK FOR CORRECT ABS MODULE OPERATION	

• Disconnect the ABS connector.
• Check for:
  ▪ evidence of water entry into the connector.
  ▪ spread or bent pins.
  ▪ pushed-out pins.
• NOTE: When connecting the ABS connector, make sure the locking slide is fully seated and locked.
• Connect the ABS connector.
• Operate the system and verify the concern is still present.
• **Is the concern still present?**
	Yes
	INSTALL a new ABS module. TEST the system for normal operation.
	
	No
	The system is operating correctly at this time. The concern may have been caused by a loose or corroded connector. CLEAR the DTCs. REPEAT the self-test.

LTV0500000004979

Fig. 28 Test C, Codes C1222, C1233, C1234 & C1237: Wheel Speed Mismatch/Missing (Part 4 of 4). 2004-06 Less Stability Assist

D4 CHECK THE ANTI-LOCK BRAKE SYSTEM (ABS) CONTROL MODULE OUTPUT	
• Key in OFF position. • Disconnect: ABS Module C135. • Measure the resistance between ABS module C135 pins as follows:	**Yes** GO to D5. **No** REPAIR the circuit(s) in question. CLEAR the DTCs. REPEAT the self-test.

ABS Module Connector-Pin	Circuit	ABS Module Connector-Pin	Circuit
C135-5	516 (YE/BK)	C135-13	514 (YE/RD)
C135-4	522 (TN/BK)	C135-12	521 (TN/OG)
C135-14	523 (RD/PK)	C135-6	519 (LG/BK)

- •
- • Are the resistances between 800 and 1400 ohms for the front, and between 800 and 2500 ohms for the rear?

D5 CHECK WHEEL SPEED SENSOR RINGS FOR DAMAGE	
• Raise and support the vehicle. • Remove the suspect wheel speed sensor. • Inspect the wheel speed sensor rings for damaged or missing teeth. Rotate the wheel speed sensor rings to verify that all the teeth are checked. • **Is the wheel speed sensor ring OK?**	**Yes** GO to D6. **No** INSTALL a new wheel speed sensor ring. CLEAR the DTCs. REPEAT the self-test.

D6 CHECK THE WHEEL SPEED SENSORS FOR DAMAGE AND LOOSENESS	
• ⚠ CAUTION: Examine the wheel speed sensor wires carefully with a good light. Failure to verify damage in the wheel speed sensor wires at this time will lead to unnecessary component replacement and diagnostic time. • Inspect the wheel speed sensor mounting for looseness. If the wheel speed sensor is suspected, inspect the sensor for corrosion on the rear axle housing boss, or on the front wheel speed sensor mounting flange. Clean as necessary. • **Is the wheel speed sensor OK?**	**Yes** GO to D7. **No** If the wheel speed sensor mounting is loose or corroded, REMOVE the wheel speed sensor, plug the opening and thoroughly clean the mounting surfaces. If the wheel speed sensor is damaged, INSTALL a new wheel speed sensor. CLEAR the DTCs.

LTV0500000004981

Fig. 29 Test D, Codes C1148, C1158 & C1229: Wheel Speed Sensor Coherency Fault: (Part 2 of 4). 2004-06 Less Stability Assist

Test Step	Result / Action to Take
D1 CHECK THE ABS HARNESS AND MODULE FOR WATER INTRUSION • Key in OFF position. • Disconnect: ABS Module C135. • Inspect the ABS module connector and module for water intrusion. • **Is there any evidence of water entry?**	**Yes** CLEAN the connector and dry it out with low pressure compressed air. INSPECT for evidence of water entry and repair as necessary. CLEAR the DTCs. TEST the system for normal operation. **No** GO to D2.
D2 MONITOR THE WHEEL SPEED SENSOR PIDs • Enter the following diagnostic mode on the diagnostic tool: Anti-Lock Brake System (ABS) PIDs. • Use the diagnostic tool to monitor the wheel speed sensor PIDs while driving the vehicle at a constant speed. • **Are the wheel speed sensor PIDs similar?**	**Yes** CLEAR the DTCs. The system is operating correctly at this time. **No** GO to D3.
D3 CHECK ALL TIRE SIZES • Make sure that all tire sizes are correct and matching. • **Are the tire sizes correct?**	**Yes** GO to D4. **No** INSTALL a new tire of the correct size for each tire that is incorrect. CLEAR the DTCs. REPEAT the self-test. TEST the system for normal operation.

LTV0500000004980

Fig. 29 Test D, Codes C1148, C1158 & C1229: Wheel Speed Sensor Coherency Fault: (Part 1 of 4). 2004-06 Less Stability Assist

	REPEAT the self-test.
D7 CHECK WHEEL SPEED SENSOR RESISTANCE • Disconnect: Suspect Wheel Speed Sensor. • Measure the resistance between the suspect wheel speed sensor terminals.	**Yes** GO to D8. **No** INSTALL a new wheel speed sensor. CLEAR the DTCs. REPEAT the self-test.

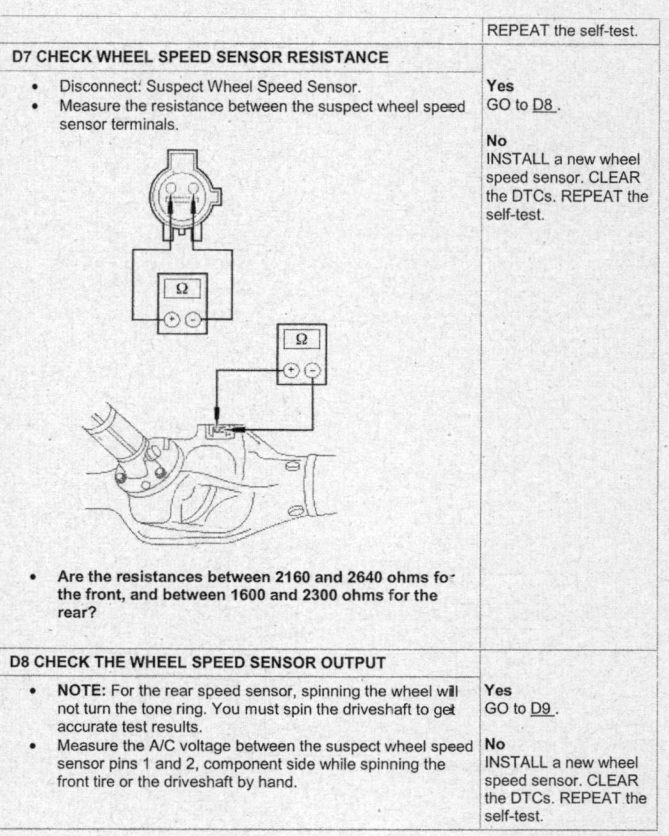

- • Are the resistances between 2160 and 2640 ohms for the front, and between 1600 and 2300 ohms for the rear?

D8 CHECK THE WHEEL SPEED SENSOR OUTPUT	
• NOTE: For the rear speed sensor, spinning the wheel will not turn the tone ring. You must spin the driveshaft to get accurate test results. • Measure the A/C voltage between the suspect wheel speed sensor pins 1 and 2, component side while spinning the front tire or the driveshaft by hand.	**Yes** GO to D9. **No** INSTALL a new wheel speed sensor. CLEAR the DTCs. REPEAT the self-test.

LTV0500000004982

Fig. 29 Test D, Codes C1148, C1158 & C1229: Wheel Speed Sensor Coherency Fault: (Part 3 of 4). 2004-06 Less Stability Assist

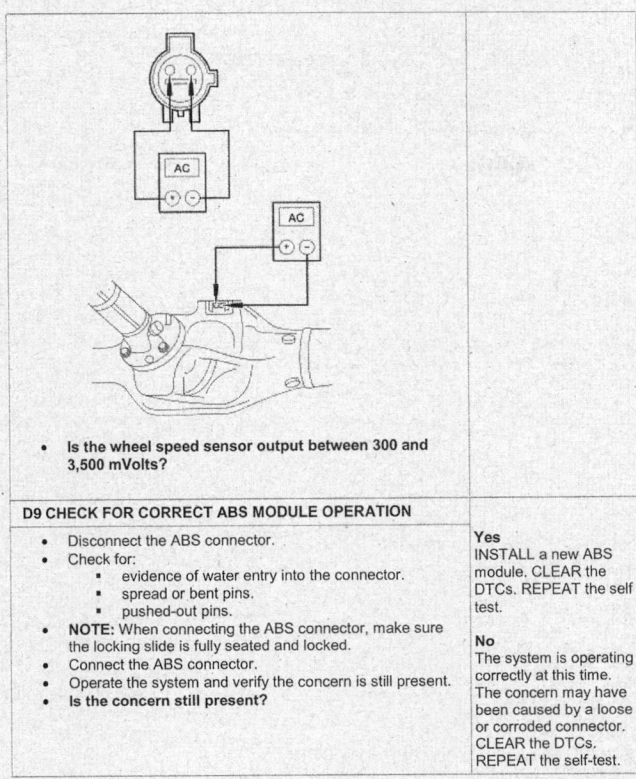

- **Is the wheel speed sensor output between 300 and 3,500 mVolts?**

D9 CHECK FOR CORRECT ABS MODULE OPERATION	
<ul><li>Disconnect the ABS connector.</li><li>Check for:<ul><li>evidence of water entry into the connector.</li><li>spread or bent pins.</li><li>pushed-out pins.</li></ul></li><li>**NOTE:** When connecting the ABS connector, make sure the locking slide is fully seated and locked.</li><li>Connect the ABS connector.</li><li>Operate the system and verify the concern is still present.</li><li>**Is the concern still present?**</li></ul>	**Yes** INSTALL a new ABS module. CLEAR the DTCs. REPEAT the self test. **No** The system is operating correctly at this time. The concern may have been caused by a loose or corroded connector. CLEAR the DTCs. REPEAT the self-test.

LTV0500000004983

Fig. 29   Test D, Codes C1148, C1158 & C1229: Wheel Speed Sensor Coherency Fault: (Part 4 of 4). 2004-06 Less Stability Assist

Test Step	Result / Action to Take
F1 CHECK THE ANTI-LOCK BRAKE SYSTEM (ABS) MODULE FOR DTCs	
<ul><li>Enter the following diagnostic mode on the diagnostic tool: Retrieve and record the ABS module DTCs.</li><li>**Is DTC C1185 retrieved?**</li></ul>	**Yes** GO to F2. **No** CLEAR the DTCs. DRIVE the vehicle over a rough road. REPEAT the self-test. TEST the system for normal operation.
F2 CHECK CIRCUIT 532 (OG/YE) FOR POWER	
<ul><li>Measure the voltage between ABS module C135-9, circuit 532 (OG/YE), harness side and ground; and between ABS module C135-25, circuit 532 (OG/YE), harness side and ground.</li></ul> <ul><li>**Is the voltage greater than 10 volts?**</li></ul>	**Yes** GO to F3. **No** VERIFY battery junction box (BJB) fuse 11 (10A) is OK. If OK, REPAIR the circuit. REPEAT the self-test. TEST the system for normal operation.
F3 CHECK FOR CORRECT ABS MODULE OPERATION	
<ul><li>Disconnect all ABS connectors.</li><li>Check for:<ul><li>corrosion.</li><li>pushed-out pins.</li></ul></li><li>Connect all ABS connectors and make sure they seat correctly.</li><li>Operate the system and verify the concern is still present.</li><li>**Is the concern still present?**</li></ul>	**Yes** INSTALL a new ABS module. CLEAR the DTCs. REPEAT the self-test. **No** The system is operating correctly at this time. The concern may have been caused by a loose or corroded connector. CLEAR the DTCs. REPEAT the self-test.

LTV0500000004985

Fig. 31   Test F, Code C1185: ABS Power Relay Output Circuit Failure. 2004-06 Less Stability Assist

Test Step	Result / Action to Take
E1 CHECK FOR ANTI-LOCK BRAKE SYSTEM (ABS) MODULE DTCs	
<ul><li>Enter the following diagnostic mode on the diagnostic tool: Clear the DTCs and road test the vehicle.</li><li>Retrieve the DTCs.</li><li>**Is DTC C1169 present?**</li></ul>	**Yes** GO to E2. **No** System is operating correctly at this time.
E2 CHECK THE BASE BRAKE SYSTEM	
<ul><li>Check the base brake system.</li><li>**Is the base brake system OK?**</li></ul>	**Yes** INSTALL a new hydraulic control unit (HCU). CLEAR the DTCs. REPEAT the self test. **No** REPAIR the base brake system. CLEAR the DTCs. REPEAT the self test.

LTV0500000004984

Fig. 30   Test E, Code C1169: Excessive ABS System Fluid Dump Time. 2004-06 Less Stability Assist

Test Step	Result / Action to Take
G1 CHECK BASE BRAKE COMPONENTS	
<ul><li>Visually inspect the brake lines from the hydraulic control unit (HCU) to the wheel cylinders.</li><li>Visually inspect the calipers and the brake components.</li><li>**Are any of these components damaged or leaking?**</li></ul>	**Yes** REPAIR as necessary. Continue diagnosis of the base brake system. **No** GO to G2.
G2 CHECK FOR LEAKING DUMP VALVE	
<ul><li>Key in START position.</li><li>Remove the rubber caps from the 2 HCU low pressure accumulators and insert a clean steel implement (such as a paper clip) into each low pressure accumulator.</li></ul> <ul><li>**NOTE:** A leaking dump valve is similar to the master cylinder bypass condition. It is important that the pedal be quickly and forcefully applied to rule out the master cylinder bypass as a cause. Typically a master cylinder bypass occurs only at low pedal pressure rates and low tire pressures.</li><li>Have an assistant press hard on the brake pedal while observing the steel implements.</li><li>**Do any of the steel implements move out 12.7 mm (0.5 in) or more?**</li></ul>	**Yes** INSTALL a new HCU. **No** System is operating correctly at this time. REMOVE the steel implements and INSTALL the rubber caps. CLEAR the DTCs. DRIVE the vehicle over rough roads. REPEAT the self-test. TEST the system for normal operation.

LTV0500000004986

Fig. 32   Test G: Soft Or Excessive Brake Pedal Travel. 2004-06 Less Stability Assist

Test Step	Result / Action to Take
H1 CHECK THE ANTI-LOCK BRAKE SYSTEM (ABS) MODULE FOR DTCs NOTE: Repair all other DTCs before proceeding. • Connect the diagnostic tool. • Retrieve and record the ABS module DTCs. • **Is DTC C1184 retrieved?**	**Yes** GO to <u>H2</u> . **No** CLEAR the DTCs. DRIVE the vehicle over a rough road. REPEAT the self-test. TEST the system for normal operation.
H2 CHECK FOR WHEEL SPEED SENSORS RING DAMAGE • Key in OFF position. • Remove the wheel speed sensors. • ⚠ CAUTION: Examine the wheel speed sensor wire carefully with a good light. Failure to verify damage in the wheel speed sensor wire at this time will lead to unnecessary component replacement and diagnostic time. • Inspect the wheel speed sensor rings for damaged or missing teeth. Rotate the wheel speed sensor rings to verify that all the teeth are checked. • **Are the wheel speed sensor rings damaged or missing teeth?**	**Yes** INSTALL a new wheel speed sensor ring. CLEAR the DTCs. REPEAT the self-test. **No** CLEAR the DTCs. DRIVE the vehicle over rough pavement. REPEAT the self-test.

LTV0500000004987

Fig. 33 Test H, Code C1184: ABS System Time Out. 2004-06 Less Stability Assist

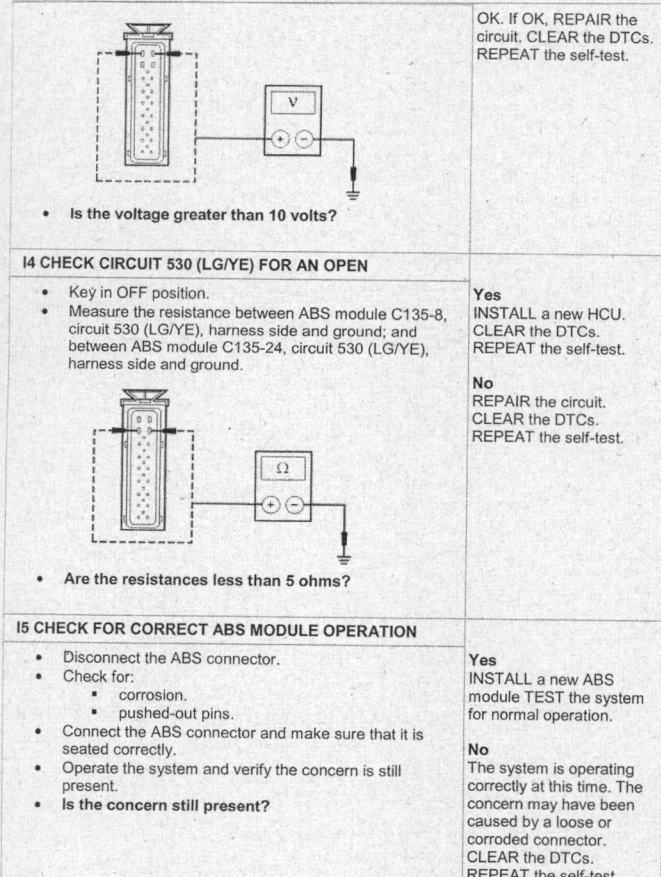

• **Is the voltage greater than 10 volts?**	OK. If OK, REPAIR the circuit. CLEAR the DTCs. REPEAT the self-test.
I4 CHECK CIRCUIT 530 (LG/YE) FOR AN OPEN • Key in OFF position. • Measure the resistance between ABS module C135-8, circuit 530 (LG/YE), harness side and ground; and between ABS module C135-24, circuit 530 (LG/YE), harness side and ground.	**Yes** INSTALL a new HCU. CLEAR the DTCs. REPEAT the self-test. **No** REPAIR the circuit. CLEAR the DTCs. REPEAT the self-test.
• **Are the resistances less than 5 ohms?**	

I5 CHECK FOR CORRECT ABS MODULE OPERATION
 	
• Disconnect the ABS connector.
• Check for:
  • corrosion.
  • pushed-out pins.
• Connect the ABS connector and make sure that it is seated correctly.
• Operate the system and verify the concern is still present.
• **Is the concern still present?**
	Yes
	INSTALL a new ABS module TEST the system for normal operation.
	
	No
	The system is operating correctly at this time. The concern may have been caused by a loose or corroded connector. CLEAR the DTCs. REPEAT the self-test.

LTV0500000004989

Fig. 34 Test I, Codes C1095 & C1096: ABS Pump Motor Circuit Failure/Open (Part 2 of 2). 2004-06 Less Stability Assist

Test Step	Result / Action to Take
I1 CHECK THE ANTI-LOCK BRAKE SYSTEM (ABS) PUMP MOTOR • Key in ON position. • **Is the ABS pump motor running all the time?**	**Yes** INSTALL a new ABS module and hydraulic control unit (HCU) as necessary. CLEAR the DTCs. REPEAT the ABS self-test. **No** GO to <u>I2</u> .
I2 CHECK PUMP MOTOR OPERATION • Enter the following diagnostic mode on the diagnostic tool: ABS Module Active Command. • Trigger the ABS module pump motor ON active command. • **Does the ABS pump motor run for approximately 2 seconds?**	**Yes** CLEAR the DTCs. CHECK the yellow ABS warning indicator while driving the vehicle (brakes must not be applied) above 32 km/h (20 mph). If the yellow ABS warning indicator illuminates, RETRIEVE the DTCs. If DTC C1096 is retrieved, GO to <u>I5</u> . If DTC C1095 is retrieved, INSTALL a new HCU. CLEAR the DTCs. REPEAT the self-test. **No** TRIGGER the ABS module pump motor OFF active command. GO to <u>I3</u> .
I3 CHECK CIRCUIT 532 (OG/YE) FOR AN OPEN • Key in OFF position. • Disconnect: ABS Module C135. • Measure the voltage between ABS module C135-25, circuit 532 (OG/YE), harness side and ground; and between ABS module C135-9, circuit 532 (OG/YE), harness side and ground.	**Yes** GO to <u>I4</u> . **No** VERIFY battery junction box (BJB) fuse 11 (10A) is

LTV0500000004988

Fig. 34 Test I, Codes C1095 & C1096: ABS Pump Motor Circuit Failure/Open (Part 1 of 2). 2004-06 Less Stability Assist

Test Step	Result / Action to Take
J1 CHECK FOR POWER AT THE ANTI-LOCK BRAKE SYSTEM (ABS) MODULE • Key in OFF position. • Disconnect: ABS Module C135. • Key in ON position. • Measure the voltage between ABS module C135 and ground as follows:	**Yes** Continue diagnosis of the charging system. **No** REPAIR the circuit(s) in question. CLEAR the DTCs. REPEAT the self-test.

ABS Module Connector-Pin	Circuit
C135-9	532 (OG/YE)
C135-25	532 (OG/YE)
C135-16	601 (LB/PK)

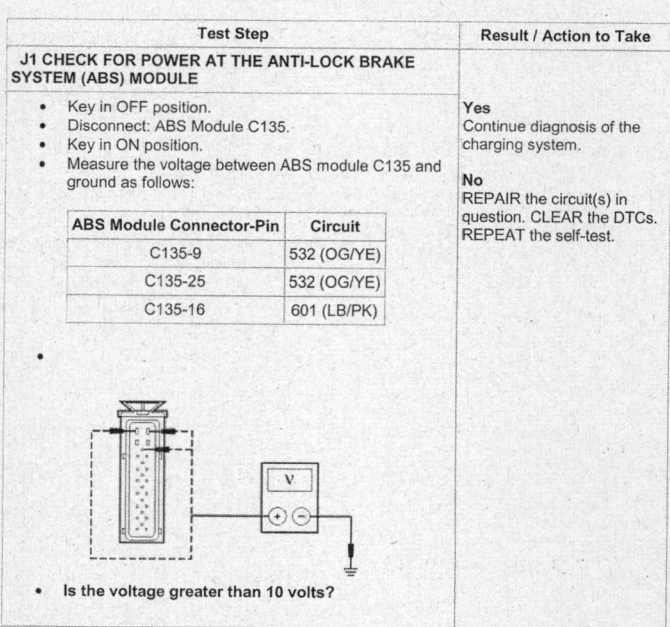

• **Is the voltage greater than 10 volts?**

LTV0500000004990

Fig. 35 Test J, Code C1676: Battery Voltage Out Of Range. 2004-06 Less Stability Assist

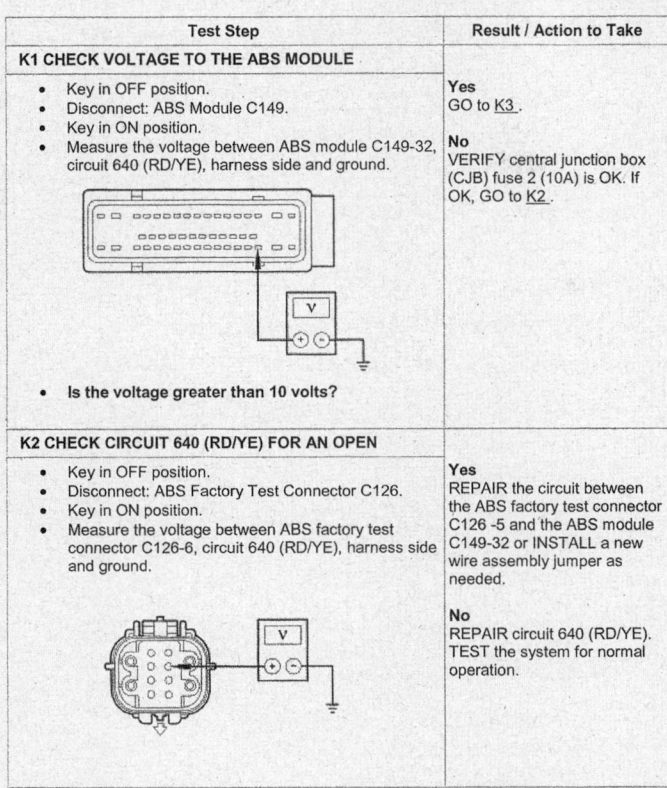

Test Step	Result / Action to Take
K1 CHECK VOLTAGE TO THE ABS MODULE	
• Key in OFF position. • Disconnect: ABS Module C149. • Key in ON position. • Measure the voltage between ABS module C149-32, circuit 640 (RD/YE), harness side and ground. • **Is the voltage greater than 10 volts?**	**Yes** GO to K3. **No** VERIFY central junction box (CJB) fuse 2 (10A) is OK. If OK, GO to K2.
K2 CHECK CIRCUIT 640 (RD/YE) FOR AN OPEN	
• Key in OFF position. • Disconnect: ABS Factory Test Connector C126. • Key in ON position. • Measure the voltage between ABS factory test connector C126-6, circuit 640 (RD/YE), harness side and ground.	**Yes** REPAIR the circuit between the ABS factory test connector C126 -5 and the ABS module C149-32 or INSTALL a new wire assembly jumper as needed. **No** REPAIR circuit 640 (RD/YE). TEST the system for normal operation.

LTV0500000004991

Fig. 36   Test K: No Communication w/ABS Module (Part 1 of 2). 2004-06 w/Stability Assist

Test Step	Result / Action to Take
L1 CHECK THE BATTERY VOLTAGE	
• Measure the voltage between the positive and negative battery terminals with the key ON and the engine OFF (KOEO), and with the engine running. • **Is the battery voltage between 10 and 13 volts with KOEO, and between 13 and 17 volts with the engine running?**	**Yes** GO to L2. **No** Continue diagnosis of the charging system.
L2 CHECK THE VOLTAGE TO THE ANTI-LOCK BRAKE SYSTEM (ABS) MODULE	
• Key in OFF position. • Disconnect: Anti-Lock Brake Module C149. • Key in ON position. • Measure the voltage between ABS module C149-32, circuit 640 (RD/YE), harness side and ground. • **Is the voltage greater 10 volts?**	**Yes** GO to L3. VERIFY central junction box (CJB) fuse 2 (10A) is OK. If OK, REPAIR the circuit. CLEAR the DTCs. CARRY OUT the self-test with the brake pedal not applied.

LTV0500000004993

Fig. 37   Test L, Code B1317 & B1318: Battery Voltage High/Low (Part 1 of 2). 2004-06 w/Stability Assist

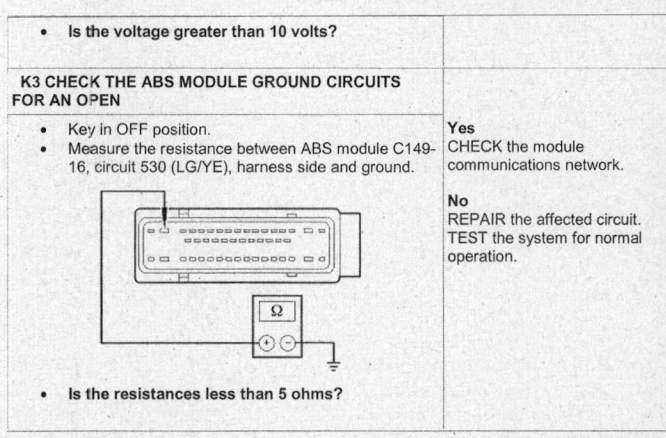

• Is the voltage greater than 10 volts?	
K3 CHECK THE ABS MODULE GROUND CIRCUITS FOR AN OPEN	
• Key in OFF position. • Measure the resistance between ABS module C149-16, circuit 530 (LG/YE), harness side and ground. • **Is the resistances less than 5 ohms?**	**Yes** CHECK the module communications network. **No** REPAIR the affected circuit. TEST the system for normal operation.

LTV0500000004992

Fig. 36   Test K: No Communication w/ABS Module (Part 2 of 2). 2004-06 w/Stability Assist

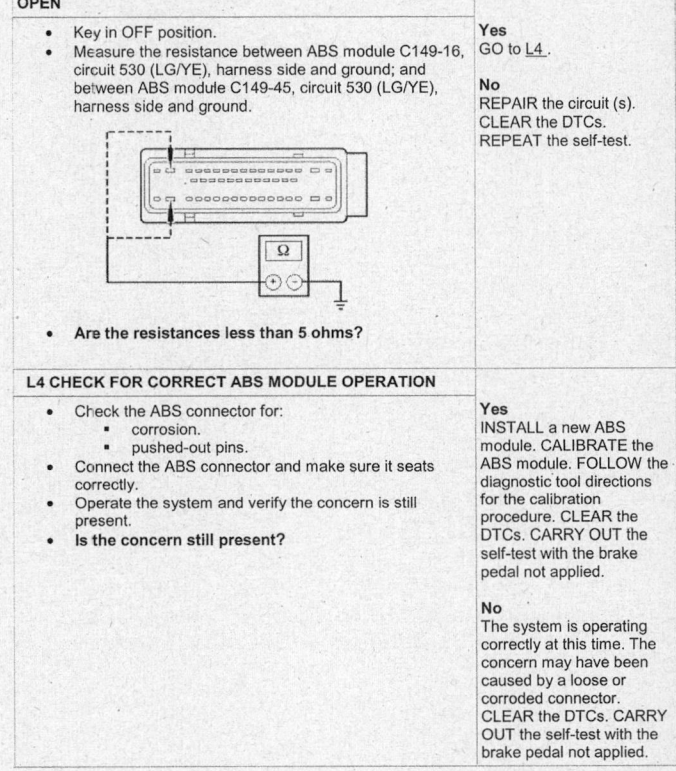

Test Step	Result / Action to Take
L3 CHECK THE ABS MODULE GROUND CIRCUIT FOR AN OPEN	
• Key in OFF position. • Measure the resistance between ABS module C149-16, circuit 530 (LG/YE), harness side and ground; and between ABS module C149-45, circuit 530 (LG/YE), harness side and ground. • **Are the resistances less than 5 ohms?**	**Yes** GO to L4. **No** REPAIR the circuit (s). CLEAR the DTCs. REPEAT the self-test.
L4 CHECK FOR CORRECT ABS MODULE OPERATION	

• Check the ABS connector for:
  ▪ corrosion.
  ▪ pushed-out pins.
• Connect the ABS connector and make sure it seats correctly.
• Operate the system and verify the concern is still present.
• **Is the concern still present?**
	Yes
	INSTALL a new ABS module. CALIBRATE the ABS module. FOLLOW the diagnostic tool directions for the calibration procedure. CLEAR the DTCs. CARRY OUT the self-test with the brake pedal not applied.
	
	No
	The system is operating correctly at this time. The concern may have been caused by a loose or corroded connector. CLEAR the DTCs. CARRY OUT the self-test with the brake pedal not applied.

LTV0500000004994

Fig. 37   Test L, Code B1317 & B1318: Battery Voltage High/Low (Part 2 of 2). 2004-06 w/Stability Assist

Test Step	Result / Action to Take
M1 CHECK THE ANTI-LOCK BRAKE SYSTEM (ABS) PUMP MOTOR • Key in ON position. • **Is the ABS pump motor running all the time?**	**Yes** INSTALL a new ABS module and hydraulic control unit (HCU) as necessary. CALIBRATE the ABS module. FOLLOW the diagnostic tool directions for the calibration procedure. CLEAR the DTCs. CARRY OUT the self-test with the brake pedal not applied. **No** GO to M2.
M2 CHECK PUMP MOTOR OPERATION • Enter the following diagnostic mode on the diagnostic tool: ABS Module Active Command. • Trigger the ABS module pump motor ON active command. • **Does the ABS pump motor run for approximately 2 seconds?**	**Yes** CLEAR the DTCs. CHECK the yellow ABS warning indicator while driving the vehicle (brakes must not be applied) above 32 km/h (20 mph). If the yellow ABS warning indicator illuminates, RETRIEVE the DTCs. If DTC C1096 is retrieved, GO to M5. If DTC C1095 is retrieved, INSTALL a new HCU. CALIBRATE the ABS module. FOLLOW the diagnostic tool directions for the calibration procedure. CLEAR the DTCs. CARRY OUT the self-test with the brake pedal not applied. **No** GO to M3.

LTV0500000004995

Fig. 38   Test M, Codes C1095 & C1096: ABS Hydraulic Pump Motor Circuit Failure/Open (Part 1 of 3). 2004-06 w/Stability Assist

	concern may have been caused by a loose or corroded connector. CLEAR the DTCs. CARRY OUT the self-test with the brake pedal not applied.

LTV0500000004997

Fig. 38   Test M, Codes C1095 & C1096: ABS Hydraulic Pump Motor Circuit Failure/Open (Part 3 of 3). 2004-06 w/Stability Assist

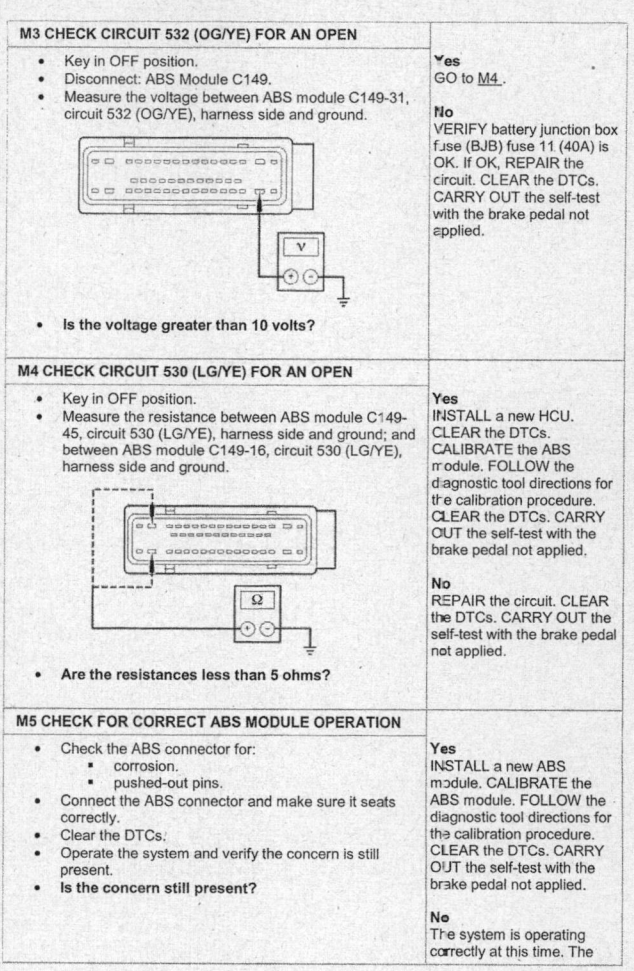

Test Step	Result / Action to Take
M3 CHECK CIRCUIT 532 (OG/YE) FOR AN OPEN • Key in OFF position. • Disconnect: ABS Module C149. • Measure the voltage between ABS module C149-31, circuit 532 (OG/YE), harness side and ground. • **Is the voltage greater than 10 volts?**	**Yes** GO to M4. **No** VERIFY battery junction box fuse (BJB) fuse 11 (40A) is OK. If OK, REPAIR the circuit. CLEAR the DTCs. CARRY OUT the self-test with the brake pedal not applied.
M4 CHECK CIRCUIT 530 (LG/YE) FOR AN OPEN • Key in OFF position. • Measure the resistance between ABS module C149-45, circuit 530 (LG/YE), harness side and ground; and between ABS module C149-16, circuit 530 (LG/YE), harness side and ground. • **Are the resistances less than 5 ohms?**	**Yes** INSTALL a new HCU. CLEAR the DTCs. CALIBRATE the ABS module. FOLLOW the diagnostic tool directions for the calibration procedure. CLEAR the DTCs. CARRY OUT the self-test with the brake pedal not applied. **No** REPAIR the circuit. CLEAR the DTCs. CARRY OUT the self-test with the brake pedal not applied.
M5 CHECK FOR CORRECT ABS MODULE OPERATION • Check the ABS connector for: ▪ corrosion. ▪ pushed-out pins. • Connect the ABS connector and make sure it seats correctly. • Clear the DTCs. • Operate the system and verify the concern is still present. • **Is the concern still present?**	**Yes** INSTALL a new ABS module. CALIBRATE the ABS module. FOLLOW the diagnostic tool directions for the calibration procedure. CLEAR the DTCs. CARRY OUT the self-test with the brake pedal not applied. **No** The system is operating correctly at this time. The

LTV0500000004996

Fig. 38   Test M, Codes C1095 & C1096: ABS Hydraulic Pump Motor Circuit Failure/Open (Part 2 of 3). 2004-06 w/Stability Assist

Test Step	Result / Action to Take
N1 CHECK THE ABS HARNESS AND MODULE FOR WATER INTRUSION • Key in OFF position. • Disconnect: ABS Module C149. • Inspect the ABS module connector and module for water intrusion. • **Is there any evidence of water entry?**	**Yes** CLEAN the connector and dry it out with low pressure compressed air. INSPECT for evidence of water entry and REPAIR as necessary. CALIBRATE the ABS module. FOLLOW the diagnostic tool directions for the calibration procedure. CLEAR the DTCs. CARRY OUT the self-test with the brake pedal not applied. **No** GO to N2.
N2 CHECK FOR A SHORT TO VOLTAGE **NOTE:** Both circuits must be checked for each DTC. • Key in OFF position. • Disconnect: ABS Module C149. • Disconnect: Suspect Wheel Speed Sensor. • Key in ON position. • Measure the voltage between the ABS module connector harness side and ground as follows:	**Yes** REPAIR the circuit(s) in question. CLEAR the DTC(s). CARRY OUT the self test with the brake pedal not applied. **No** GO to N3.

DTC	ABS Module Connector-Pin	Circuit

LTV0500000004998

Fig. 39   Test N, Codes C1145, C1155, C1165 & C1175: Wheel Speed Sensor Input Circuit Failure (Part 1 of 4). 2004-06 w/Stability Assist

C1145	C149-26	514 (YE/RD)
C1145	C149-27	516 (YE/BK)
C1155	C149-13	522 (TN/BK)
C1155	C149-12	521 (TN/OG)
C1165	C149-44	524 (PK/BK)
C1165	C149-43	523 (RD/PK)
C1175	C149-42	519 (LG/BK)
C1175	C149-41	518 (LG/RD)

- Is any voltage present?

N3 CHECK FOR A SHORT TO GROUND

NOTE: Both circuits must be checked for each DTC.

- Key in OFF position.
- Measure the resistance between the ABS module connector harness side and ground as follows:

DTC	ABS Module Connector-Pin	Circuit
C1145	C149-26	514 (YE/RD)
C1145	C149-27	516 (YE/BK)
C1155	C149-13	522 (TN/BK)
C1155	C149-12	521 (TN/OG)
C1165	C149-44	524 (PK/BK)
C1165	C149-43	523 (RD/PK)
C1175	C149-42	519 (LG/BK)
C1175	C149-41	518 (LG/RD)

- Are the resistances greater than 10,000 ohms?

Yes
GO to N4 .

No
REPAIR the circuit(s) in question. CLEAR the DTCs. CARRY OUT the self test with the brake pedal not applied.

N4 CHECK FOR AN OPEN

LTV0500000004999

Fig. 39   Test N, Codes C1145, C1155, C1165 & C1175: Wheel Speed Sensor Input Circuit Failure (Part 2 of 4). 2004-06 w/Stability Assist

---

NOTE: Both circuits must be checked for each DTC.

- Measure the resistance between the ABS module connector harness side and the suspected wheel speed sensor connector harness side as follows:

DTC	Circuit	ABS Module Connector-Pin	Wheel Speed Sensor Connector-Pin
C1145	516 (YE/BK)	C149-27	C160-2
C1145	514 (YE/RD)	C149-26	C160-1
C1155	522 (TN/BK)	C149-13	C150-2
C1155	521 (TN/OG)	C149-12	C150-1
C1165	523 (RD/PK)	C149-43	C452-1
C1165	524 (PK/BK)	C149-44	C452-2
C1175	518 (LG/RD)	C149-41	C453-2
C1175	519 (LG/BK)	C149-42	C453-1

- Are the resistances less than 5 ohms?

Yes
GO to N5 .

No
REPAIR the circuit in question. CLEAR the DTCs. CARRY OUT the self-test with the brake pedal not applied.

N5 CHECK FOR SHORTED WHEEL SPEED SENSOR CIRCUITS

- Measure the resistance between the suspect wheel speed sensor pins, harness side with the meter in the 10 megaohm range.

- Is there any continuity?

Yes
REPAIR the circuit in question. CLEAR the DTCs. CARRY OUT the self-test with the brake pedal not applied.

No
GO to N6 .

LTV0500000005000

Fig. 39   Test N, Codes C1145, C1155, C1165 & C1175: Wheel Speed Sensor Input Circuit Failure (Part 3 of 4). 2004-06 w/Stability Assist

---

N6 CHECK THE ABS MODULE OUTPUT

- Connect: ABS Module C149.
- Key in ON position.
- Measure the voltage between the suspect wheel speed sensor pins, harness side.

- Is the voltage greater than 4.5 volts for the front wheel speed sensor and greater than 10 volts for the rear wheel speed sensors?

Yes
INSTALL a new wheel speed sensor. CLEAR the DTCs. CARRY OUT the self-test with the brake pedal not applied.

No
GO to N7 .

N7 CHECK FOR CORRECT ABS MODULE OPERATION

- Disconnect the ABS connector.
- Check for:
    - evidence of water entry into the connector.
    - spread or bent pins.
    - pushed-out pins.
- **NOTE:** When connecting the ABS connector, make sure the locking slide is fully seated and locked.
- Connect the ABS connector.
- Operate the system and verify the concern is still present.
- **Is the concern still present?**

Yes
INSTALL a new ABS module. CALIBRATE the ABS module. FOLLOW the diagnostic tool directions for the calibration procedure. CLEAR the DTCs. CARRY OUT the self-test with the brake pedal not applied.

No
The system is operating correctly at this time. The concern may have been caused by a loose or corroded connector. CLEAR the DTCs. REPEAT the self-test.

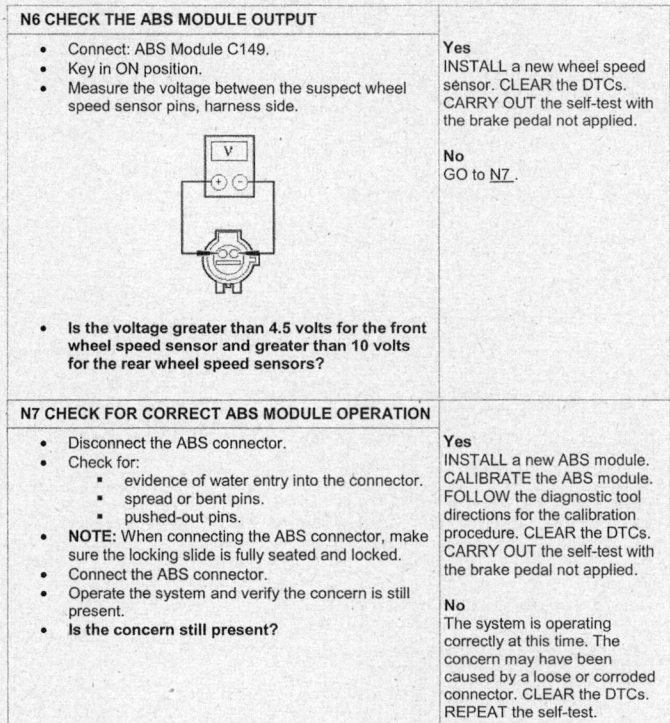

LTV0500000005001

Fig. 39   Test N, Codes C1145, C1155, C1165 & C1175: Wheel Speed Sensor Input Circuit Failure (Part 4 of 4). 2004-06 w/Stability Assist

---

Test Step	Result / Action to Take
O1 CHECK THE ABS HARNESS AND MODULE FOR WATER INTRUSION - Key in OFF position. - Disconnect: ABS Module C149. - Inspect the ABS module connector and module for water intrusion. - **Is there any evidence of water entry?**	**Yes** CLEAN the connector and dry it out with low pressure compressed air. INSPECT for evidence of water entry and repair as necessary. CLEAR the DTCs. CARRY OUT the self-test with the brake pedal not applied. **No** GO to O2 .
O2 RETRIEVE ABS MODULE DTCs - Connect the diagnostic tool. - **Are DTCs C1145, C1155, C1165 or C1175 present?**	**Yes** Go To Pinpoint Test N . **No** If DTC C1222 is present, GO to O5 . For DTC C1233, C1234, GO to O3 . For DTC C1235, C1236, GO to O4 .
O3 CHECK THE FRONT WHEEL SPEED SENSOR OUTPUT - Disconnect: Suspect Wheel Speed Sensor.	**Yes** GO to O5 . **No** INSTALL a new front wheel speed sensor. CLEAR the DTCs. CARRY OUT the self-

LTV0500000005007

Fig. 40   Test O, Codes C1222, C1233, C1234, C1235 & C1236: Wheel Speed Sensor Input Signal Missing/Mismatch (Part 1 of 3). 2004-06 w/Stability Assist

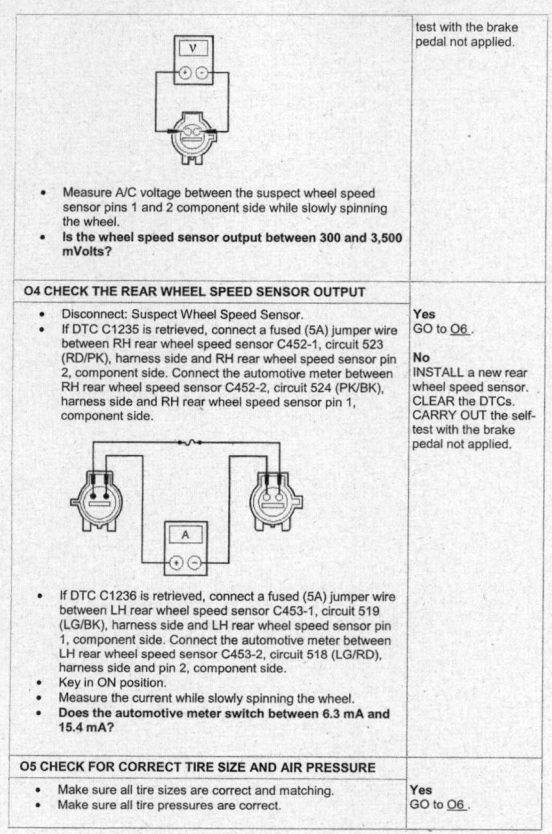

- Measure A/C voltage between the suspect wheel speed sensor pins 1 and 2 component side while slowly spinning the wheel.
- **Is the wheel speed sensor output between 300 and 3,500 mVolts?**

O4 CHECK THE REAR WHEEL SPEED SENSOR OUTPUT

- Disconnect: Suspect Wheel Speed Sensor.
- If DTC C1235 is retrieved, connect a fused (5A) jumper wire between RH rear wheel speed sensor C452-1, circuit 523 (RD/PK), harness side and RH rear wheel speed sensor pin 2, component side. Connect the automotive meter between RH rear wheel speed sensor C452-2, circuit 524 (PK/BK), harness side and RH rear wheel speed sensor pin 1, component side.

Yes
GO to O6.

No
INSTALL a new rear wheel speed sensor. CLEAR the DTCs. CARRY OUT the self-test with the brake pedal not applied.

- If DTC C1236 is retrieved, connect a fused (5A) jumper wire between LH rear wheel speed sensor C453-1, circuit 519 (LG/BK), harness side and LH rear wheel speed sensor pin 1, component side. Connect the automotive meter between LH rear wheel speed sensor C453-2, circuit 518 (LG/RD), harness side and pin 2, component side.
- Key in ON position.
- Measure the current while slowly spinning the wheel.
- **Does the automotive meter switch between 6.3 mA and 15.4 mA?**

O5 CHECK FOR CORRECT TIRE SIZE AND AIR PRESSURE

- Make sure all tire sizes are correct and matching.
- Make sure all tire pressures are correct.

Yes
GO to O6.

LTV0500000005008

Fig. 40 Test O, Codes C1222, C1233, C1234, C1235 & C1236: Wheel Speed Sensor Input Signal Missing/ Mismatch (Part 2 of 3). 2004-06 w/Stability Assist

Test Step	Result / Action to Take
P1 CHECK THE ABS HARNESS AND MODULE FOR WATER INTRUSION • Key in OFF position. • Disconnect: ABS Module C149. • Inspect the ABS module connector and module for water intrusion. • **Is there any evidence of water entry or corrosion?**	**Yes** CLEAN the connector and dry it out with low pressure compressed air. INSPECT for evidence of water entry and repair as necessary. CLEAR the DTCs. CARRY OUT the self-test with the brake pedal not applied. **No** GO to P2.
P2 CARRY OUT THE CALIBRATION PROCEDURE • Key in ON position. • Enter the following diagnostic mode on the diagnostic tool: Clear the DTCs. • Carry out the ABS module calibration procedure following the diagnostic tool directions. • Test drive the vehicle. • Enter the following diagnostic mode on the diagnostic tool: Retrieve DTCs. • **Are any DTCs retrieved or does the calibration procedure indicate a fault?**	**Yes** If DTC C1277 or C1278 is retrieved or the calibration procedure indicates a fault, GO to P3. If any other DTCs are retrieved, GO to the Anti-Lock Brake System (ABS) Module Diagnostic Trouble Code (DTC) Index. If sent here from Pinpoint Test J, GO to P3. **No** The ABS is operating correctly.
P3 MONITOR THE STEERING WHEEL ROTATION SENSOR PIDs • Enter the following diagnostic mode on the diagnostic tool: ABS Module PIDs. • Monitor the ABS module steering wheel rotation sensor PIDs while rotating the steering wheel clockwise and	**Yes** CLEAR the DTCs. DRIVE the vehicle. RETRIEVE the DTCs.

LTV0500000005002

Fig. 41 Test P, Codes C1277 & C1278: Steering Wheel Angle 1 & 2 Circuit Failure/Fault (Part 1 of 5). 2004-06 w/Stability Assist

- Clear the DTCs, drive the vehicle and carry out the self-test.
- **Is DTC C1222 still present?**

No
The system is operating correctly at this time.

O6 CHECK FOR CORRECT ABS MODULE OPERATION

- Disconnect the ABS connector.
- Check for:
  - evidence of water entry into the connector.
  - spread or bent pins.
  - pushed-out pins.
- **NOTE:** When connecting the ABS connector, make sure the locking slide is fully seated and locked.
- Connect the ABS connector.
- Operate the system and verify the concern is still present.
- **Is the concern still present?**

Yes
INSTALL a new ABS module. CALIBRATE the ABS module. FOLLOW the diagnostic tool directions for the calibration procedure. CLEAR the DTCs. CARRY OUT the self-test with the brake pedal not applied.

No
The system is operating correctly at this time. The concern may have been caused by a loose or corroded connector. CLEAR the DTCs. CARRY OUT the self-test with the brake pedal not applied.

LTV0500000005009

Fig. 40 Test O, Codes C1222, C1233, C1234, C1235 & C1236: Wheel Speed Sensor Input Signal Missing/ Mismatch (Part 3 of 3). 2004-06 w/Stability Assist

counterclockwise very slowly. • **Do the PIDs move in intervals of 4.5 degrees?**	If DTC C1277 or C1278 is still present, GO to P11. **No** GO to P4.
P4 CHECK CIRCUIT 640 (RD/YE) FOR VOLTAGE • Key in OFF position. • Disconnect: Steering Wheel Rotation Sensor C2007. • Key in ON position. • Measure the voltage between steering wheel rotation sensor C2007-1, circuit 640 (RD/YE), harness side and ground. • **Is the voltage greater than 10 volts?**	**Yes** GO to P5. **No** REPAIR the circuit. CALIBRATE the ABS module. FOLLOW the diagnostic tool directions for the calibration procedure. CLEAR the DTCs. CARRY OUT the self-test with the brake pedal not applied.
P5 CHECK THE STEERING WHEEL ROTATION SENSOR CIRCUITRY FOR AN OPEN • Key in OFF position. • Disconnect: ABS Module C149. • Measure the resistance between the ABS module connector, harness side and the steering wheel rotation sensor connector, harness side as follows:	**Yes** GO to P6. **No** REPAIR the circuit(s) in question. CALIBRATE the ABS module. FOLLOW the diagnostic tool directions for the calibration procedure. CLEAR the DTCs. CARRY OUT the self-test with the brake pedal not applied.

Steering Wheel Rotation Sensor Connector-Pin	ABS Module Connector-Pin	Circuit
C2007-2	C149-10	1573 (YE)
C2007-3	C149-39	1572 (DG)
C2007-4	C149-24	1571 (BK)

- **Are the resistances less than 5 ohms?**

P6 CHECK THE STEERING WHEEL ROTATION SENSOR CIRCUITS FOR A SHORT TO VOLTAGE • Key in ON position.	**Yes** REPAIR the circuit(s)

LTV0500000005003

Fig. 41 Test P, Codes C1277 & C1278: Steering Wheel Angle 1 & 2 Circuit Failure/Fault (Part 2 of 5). 2004-06 w/Stability Assist

- Measure the voltage between the ABS module connector, harness side and ground as follows:

ABS Module Connector-Pin	Circuit
C149-10	1573 (YE)
C149-39	1572 (DG)
C149-24	1571 (BK)

- **Is voltage present?**

in question. CALIBRATE the ABS module. FOLLOW the diagnostic tool directions for the calibration procedure. CLEAR the DTCs. CARRY OUT the self-test with the brake pedal not applied.

No
GO to P7.

P7 CHECK THE STEERING WHEEL ROTATION SENSOR CIRCUITRY FOR A SHORT TO GROUND

- Key in OFF position.
- Measure the resistance between the ABS module connector, harness side and ground as follows:

ABS Module Connector-Pin	Circuit
C149-10	1573 (YE)
C149-39	1572 (DG)
C149-24	1571 (BK)

- **Are the resistances greater than 10,000 ohms?**

Yes
GO to P8.

No
REPAIR the circuit in question. CALIBRATE the ABS module. FOLLOW the diagnostic tool directions for the calibration procedure. CLEAR the DTCs. CARRY OUT the self-test with the brake pedal not applied.

P8 CHECK THE STEERING WHEEL ROTATION SENSOR OUTPUT SIGNAL A

- Connect: ABS Module C149.
- Connect: Steering Wheel Rotation Sensor C2007.
- Key in ON position.
- With the connector connected, backprobe the connector while measuring the voltage between steering wheel rotation sensor C2007-3, circuit 1572 (DG), harness side and steering wheel rotation sensor C2007-4, circuit 1571 (BK), harness side while rotating the steering wheel slightly.

Yes
GO to P9.

No
GO to P10.

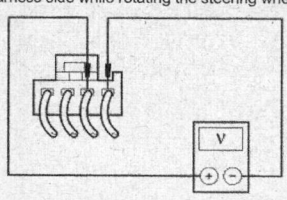

- **Is the voltage between 0.25 volts and 0.75 volts or**

LTV0500000005004

Fig. 41   Test P, Codes C1277 & C1278: Steering Wheel Angle 1 & 2 Circuit Failure/Fault (Part 3 of 5). 2004-06 w/Stability Assist

---

P11 CHECK FOR CORRECT ABS MODULE OPERATION

- Disconnect the ABS connector.
- Check for:
  - evidence of water entry into the connector.
  - spread or bent pins.
  - pushed-out pins.
- NOTE: When connecting the ABS connector, make sure the locking slide is fully seated and locked.
- Connect the ABS connector.
- Operate the system and verify the concern is still present.
- **Is the concern still present?**

Yes
INSTALL a new ABS module. CALIBRATE the ABS module. FOLLOW the diagnostic tool directions for the calibration procedure. CLEAR the DTCs. CARRY OUT the self-test with the brake pedal not applied

No
The system is operating correctly at this time. The concern may have been caused by a loose or corroded connector. CLEAR the DTCs. REPEAT the self-test.

LTV0500000005006

Fig. 41   Test P, Codes C1277 & C1278: Steering Wheel Angle 1 & 2 Circuit Failure/Fault (Part 5 of 5). 2004-06 w/Stability Assist

---

between 4.00 volts and 4.75 volts with the steering wheel stationary and change to the other state when rotating the steering wheel slightly?

P9 CHECK THE STEERING WHEEL ROTATION SENSOR OUTPUT SIGNAL B

- With the connector connected, backprobe the connector while measuring the voltage between the steering wheel rotation sensor C2007-2, circuit 1573 (YE), harness side and the steering wheel rotation sensor C2007-4, circuit 1571 (BK), harness side while rotating the steering wheel slightly.

Yes
CLEAR the DTCs. DRIVE the vehicle. RETRIEVE the DTCs. If DTC C1277 or C1278 is retrieved again, GO to P11.

No
GO to P10.

- **Is the voltage between 0.25 volts and 0.75 volts or between 4.00 volts and 4.75 volts with the steering wheel stationary and change to the other state when rotating the steering wheel slightly?**

P10 CHECK FOR STEERING WHEEL ROTATION SENSOR REFERENCE VOLTAGE

- Key in OFF position.
- Disconnect: Steering Wheel Rotation Sensor C2007.
- Key in ON position.
- Measure the voltage between steering wheel rotation sensor C2007-3, circuit 1572 (DG), harness side and steering wheel rotation sensor C2007-4, circuit 1571 (BK), harness side; and between steering wheel rotation sensor C2007-2, circuit 1573 (YE), harness side and steering wheel rotation sensor C2007-4, circuit 1571 (BK), harness side.

Yes
INSTALL a new steering wheel rotation sensor. CALIBRATE the ABS module. FOLLOW the diagnostic tool directions for the calibration procedure. CLEAR the DTCs. CARRY OUT the self-test with the brake pedal not applied.

No
GO to P11.

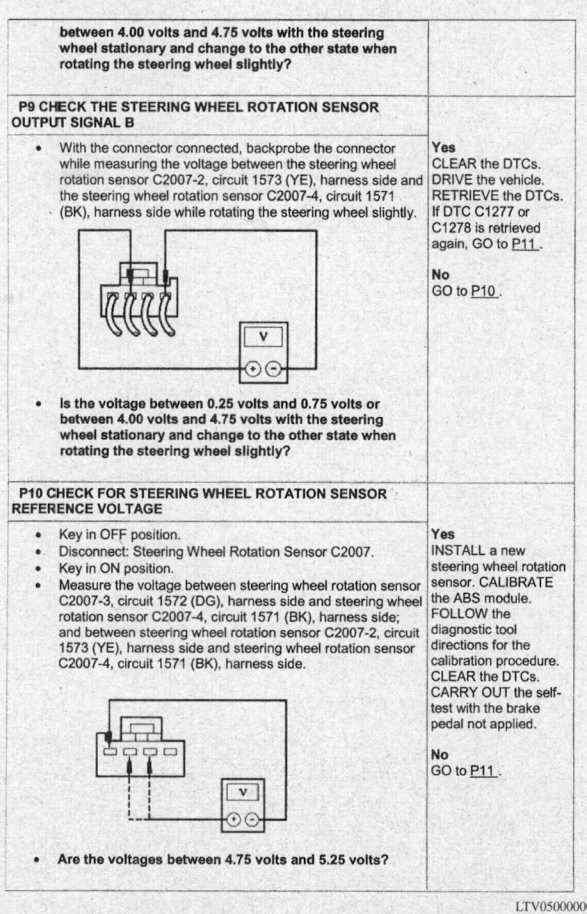

- **Are the voltages between 4.75 volts and 5.25 volts?**

LTV0500000005005

Fig. 41   Test P, Codes C1277 & C1278: Steering Wheel Angle 1 & 2 Circuit Failure/Fault (Part 4 of 5). 2004-06 w/Stability Assist

---

Test Step	Result / Action to Take
Q1 CARRY OUT THE CALIBRATION PROCEDURE • Key in ON position. • Enter the following diagnostic mode on the diagnostic tool: Clear DTCs. • Carry out the sensor cluster module calibration procedure using the diagnostic tool. • Retrieve the DTCs. • **Are any DTCs retrieved or does the recalibration procedure indicate a fault?**	**Yes** GO to Q2. **No** The system is operating correctly. The condition may have been caused by an incomplete or inaccurate sensor cluster module calibration.
Q2 CHECK SENSOR CLUSTER MOUNTING AND MOUNTING SURFACE • Key in OFF position. • Inspect the sensor cluster mounting and make sure that the retaining bolts are fully seated and tightened correctly. Inspect the mounting surface for damage, corrosion or dirt. • **Was the sensor cluster retaining bolts tightened incorrectly or a significant amount of corrosion or dirt found or the mounting surface damaged?**	**Yes** CLEAN and TIGHTEN the bolts to correct specification. REPAIR the mounting surface as necessary. CLEAR the DTCs. RECALIBRATE the ABS module. FOLLOW the diagnostic tool directions for the calibration procedure. REPEAT the self-test. **No** GO to Q3.
Q3 CHECK CIRCUIT 640 (RD/YE) FOR VOLTAGE • Disconnect: Sensor Cluster Module C3137. • Key in ON position. • Measure the voltage between the sensor cluster C3137-2, circuit 640 (RD/YE), harness side and ground.	**Yes** GO to Q4. **No** VERIFY the instrument panel fuse 2 (10A) is OK. If OK, REPAIR the circuit. CLEAR the DTCs. RECALIBRATE the ABS module. FOLLOW the diagnostic tool directions for the calibration procedure. REPEAT the self-test.

LTV0500000005010

Fig. 42   Test Q, Codes C1279, C1280, C1281, C1282, C1516, C1517, C2769 & C2770: Sensor Cluster Fault (Part 1 of 3). 2004-06 w/Stability Assist

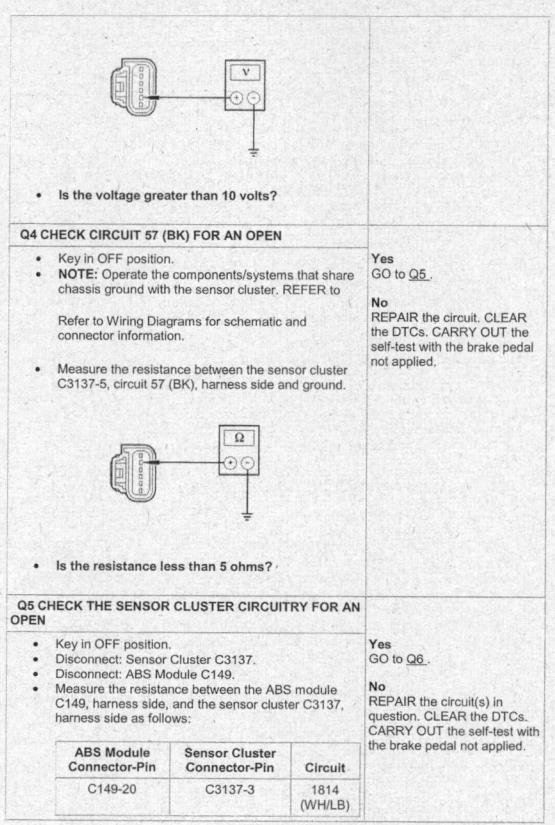

- Is the voltage greater than 10 volts?

Q4 CHECK CIRCUIT 57 (BK) FOR AN OPEN	
<ul><li>Key in OFF position.</li><li>**NOTE:** Operate the components/systems that share chassis ground with the sensor cluster. REFER to</li></ul>Refer to Wiring Diagrams for schematic and connector information.<ul><li>Measure the resistance between the sensor cluster C3137-5, circuit 57 (BK), harness side and ground.</li></ul>	**Yes** GO to Q5 . **No** REPAIR the circuit. CLEAR the DTCs. CARRY OUT the self-test with the brake pedal not applied.

- Is the resistance less than 5 ohms?

Q5 CHECK THE SENSOR CLUSTER CIRCUITRY FOR AN OPEN		
<ul><li>Key in OFF position.</li><li>Disconnect: Sensor Cluster C3137.</li><li>Disconnect: ABS Module C149.</li><li>Measure the resistance between the ABS module C149, harness side, and the sensor cluster C3137, harness side as follows:</li></ul>		**Yes** GO to Q6 . **No** REPAIR the circuit(s) in question. CLEAR the DTCs. CARRY OUT the self-test with the brake pedal not applied.

ABS Module Connector-Pin	Sensor Cluster Connector-Pin	Circuit
C149-20	C3137-3	1814 (WH/LB)

LTV0500000005011

Fig. 42 Test Q, Codes C1279, C1280, C1281, C1282, C1516, C1517, C2769 & C2770: Sensor Cluster Fault (Part 2 of 3). 2004-06 w/Stability Assist

Test Step	Result / Action to Take
R1 CHECK THE SPEED CONTROL<ul><li>Operate the speed control.</li><li>**Does the speed control operate correctly?**</li></ul>	**Yes** GO to R2 . **No** For further diagnosis of the speed control,
R2 CHECK FOR VOLTAGE TO THE ANTI-LOCK BRAKE SYSTEM (ABS) MODULE<ul><li>Key in OFF position.</li><li>Disconnect: ABS Module C149.</li><li>Key in ON position.</li><li>Measure the voltage between ABS module C149-6, circuit 307 (BK/YE), harness side and ground.</li></ul>	**Yes** GO to R3 . **No** REPAIR the circuit. CLEAR the DTCs. TEST DRIVE the vehicle. CARRY OUT the self-test with the brake pedal not applied.

- Is the voltage greater than 10 volts?

R3 MONITOR THE ABS MODULE MASTER CYLINDER PRESSURE PID	
<ul><li>Key in OFF position.</li><li>Connect: ABS Module C149.</li><li>Key in ON position.</li><li>Enter the following diagnostic mode on the diagnostic tool: ABS Module Master Cylinder Pressure PID.</li><li>Press and release the brake pedal while monitoring the master cylinder pressure PID.</li><li>**Does the PID increase with increased brake pedal pressure and decrease with decreased brake pedal pressure?**</li></ul>	**Yes** INSTALL a new ABS module. CALIBRATE the ABS module. FOLLOW the diagnostic tool directions for the calibration procedure. CLEAR the DTCs. CARRY OUT the self-test with the brake pedal not applied. **No** INSTALL a new HCU. in this section. CALIBRATE the ABS module. FOLLOW the diagnostic tool directions for the calibration procedure. CLEAR the DTCs. CARRY OUT the self-test with the brake pedal not applied.

LTV0500000005013

Fig. 43 Test R, Code C1288: Pressure Transducer Main/Primary Input Circuit Failure. 2004-06 w/Stability Assist

C149-34	C3137-4	1815 (PK/LB)

- Are the resistances less than 5 ohms?

Q6 CHECK THE SENSOR CLUSTER CIRCUITRY FOR A SHORT TO VOLTAGE		
<ul><li>Key in ON position.</li><li>Measure the voltage between the sensor cluster C3137, harness side and ground as follows:</li></ul>		**Yes** REPAIR the circuit(s) in question. CLEAR the DTCs. CARRY OUT the self-test the brake pedal not applied. **No** GO to Q7 .

Sensor Cluster Connector-Pin	Circuit
C3137-3	1814 (WH/LB)
C3137-4	1815 (PK/LB)

- Is any voltage present?

Q7 CHECK THE SENSOR CLUSTER CIRCUITRY FOR A SHORT TO GROUND		
<ul><li>Key in OFF position.</li><li>Measure the resistance between the sensor cluster C3137, harness side and ground as follows:</li></ul>		**Yes** INSTALL a new sensor cluster. CLEAR the DTCs. CARRY OUT the self-test with the brake pedal not applied. **No** REPAIR the circuit(s) in question. CLEAR the DTCs. CARRY OUT the self-test with the brake pedal not applied.

Sensor Cluster Connector-Pin	Circuit
C3137-3	1814 (WH/LB)
C3137-4	1815 (PK/LB)

- Are the resistances greater than 10,000 ohms?

LTV0500000005012

Fig. 42 Test Q, Codes C1279, C1280, C1281, C1282, C1516, C1517, C2769 & C2770: Sensor Cluster Fault (Part 3 of 3). 2004-06 w/Stability Assist

Test Step	Result / Action to Take
S1 MONITOR THE POWERTRAIN CONTROL MODULE (PCM) BRAKE PEDAL POSITION PID<ul><li>Enter the following diagnostic mode on the diagnostic tool: PCM Brake ON/OFF PID.</li><li>Press and release the brake pedal while monitoring the PCM brake pedal switch PID.</li><li>**Does the PID agree with the brake pedal position?**</li></ul>	**Yes** GO to S2 . **No** Continue diagnosis of the stoplamps.
S2 MONITOR THE ABS MODULE PID<ul><li>Enter the following diagnostic mode on the diagnostic tool: ABS Module Brake Input Switch Status PID.</li><li>Press and release the brake pedal while monitoring the ABS PID.</li><li>**Did the PID agree with the brake pedal position?**</li></ul>	**Yes** GO to S3 . **No** GO to S4 .
S3 MONITOR THE MODULE MASTER CYLINDER PRESSURE PID<ul><li>Enter the following diagnostic mode on the diagnostic tool: ABS Module Master Cylinder Pressure PID.</li><li>Press and release the brake pedal while monitoring the master cylinder pressure PID.</li><li>**Does the PID value increase with increased brake pedal pressure and decrease with decreased brake pedal pressure?**</li></ul>	**Yes** GO to S4 . **No** INSTALL a new HCU. CALIBRATE the ABS module. FOLLOW the diagnostic tool directions for the calibration procedure. CLEAR the DTCs. CARRY OUT the self-test with the brake pedal not applied.
S4 CHECK FOR CORRECT ABS MODULE OPERATION<ul><li>Disconnect the ABS connector.</li><li>Check for:<ul><li>corrosion.</li><li>pushed-out pins.</li></ul></li><li>Connect the ABS connector and make sure it seats correctly.</li><li>Operate the system and verify the concern is still present.</li><li>**Is the concern still present?**</li></ul>	**Yes** INSTALL a new ABS module. CALIBRATE the ABS module. FOLLOW the diagnostic tool directions for the calibration procedure. CLEAR the DTCs. CARRY OUT the self-test with the brake pedal not applied. **No** The system is operating correctly at this time. The concern may have been caused by a loose or corroded connector. CLEAR the DTCs. CARRY OUT the self-test with the brake pedal not applied.

LTV0500000005015

Fig. 44 Test S, Code C1446: Brake Pedal Switch Circuit Failure. 2004-06 w/Stability Assist

Test Step	Result / Action to Take
T1 CHECK FOR DTCs	
• Connect the diagnostic tool. • Key in ON position. • Retrieve the recorded DTCs. • **Is any other DTC retrieved with C1991?**	**Yes** GO to the Diagnostic Trouble Code (DTC) Index. Some of the pinpoint tests recommend ABS module calibration prior to any further diagnostics. In this case, GO to T2 **No** GO to T2 .
T2 CALIBRATE THE ABS MODULE	
• Key in START position. • **NOTE:** Be sure to rotate the steering wheel lock-to-lock during the calibration of the ABS system. • Carry out the ABS module calibration per the diagnostic tool instructions. • **Does the calibration complete for all of the stability assist sensors, and does the stability assist active/fail lamp stop flashing and turn off?**	**Yes** GO to T3 . **No** GO to T4 . Some concerns cause the calibration not to complete. If sent here from another pinpoint test, return to that pinpoint test for further diagnostics.
T3 CLEAR DTC C1991	
• CLEAR the DTC. • **Does the DTC clear?**	**Yes** TEST DRIVE the vehicle. REPEAT the self-test. If sent here from another pinpoint test, return to that pinpoint test for further diagnostics. **No** GO to T4 .
T4 MONITOR THE STEERING WHEEL ROTATION SENSOR PIDs	
• Key in ON position. • Monitor the ABS module steering wheel rotation sensor PIDs while rotating the steering wheel clockwise and counterclockwise. • **Are the 2 steering wheel rotation sensor PID values switching as the wheel rotates?**	**Yes** Go To Pinpoint Test Q . **No** Go To Pinpoint Test P .

LTV0500000005016

Fig. 45   Test T, Code C1991: Module Calibration Failure. 2004-06 w/Stability Assist

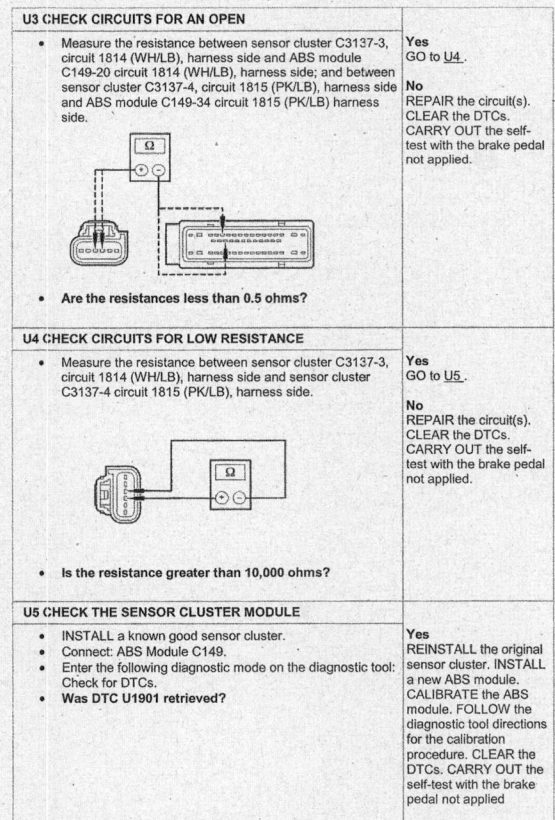

Test Step	Result / Action to Take
U3 CHECK CIRCUITS FOR AN OPEN	
• Measure the resistance between sensor cluster C3137-3, circuit 1814 (WH/LB), harness side and ABS module C149-20 circuit 1814 (WH/LB), harness side; and between sensor cluster C3137-4, circuit 1815 (PK/LB), harness side and ABS module C149-34 circuit 1815 (PK/LB) harness side. • **Are the resistances less than 0.5 ohms?**	**Yes** GO to U4 . **No** REPAIR the circuit(s). CLEAR the DTCs. CARRY OUT the self-test with the brake pedal not applied.
U4 CHECK CIRCUITS FOR LOW RESISTANCE	
• Measure the resistance between sensor cluster C3137-3, circuit 1814 (WH/LB), harness side and sensor cluster C3137-4 circuit 1815 (PK/LB), harness side. • **Is the resistance greater than 10,000 ohms?**	**Yes** GO to U5 . **No** REPAIR the circuit(s). CLEAR the DTCs. CARRY OUT the self-test with the brake pedal not applied.
U5 CHECK THE SENSOR CLUSTER MODULE	
• INSTALL a known good sensor cluster. • Connect: ABS Module C149. • Enter the following diagnostic mode on the diagnostic tool: Check for DTCs. • **Was DTC U1901 retrieved?**	**Yes** REINSTALL the original sensor cluster. INSTALL a new ABS module. CALIBRATE the ABS module. FOLLOW the diagnostic tool directions for the calibration procedure. CLEAR the DTCs. CARRY OUT the self-test with the brake pedal not applied

LTV0500000005018

Fig. 46   Test U, Code C1901: Can Network No. 2 Communication Bus Fault-Recieve Error (Part 2 of 3). 2004-06 w/Stability Assist

Test Step	Result / Action to Take
U1 CHECK CIRCUITS FOR A SHORT TO VOLTAGE	
• Key in OFF position. • Disconnect: ABS Module C149. • Disconnect: Sensor Cluster C3137. • Key in ON position. • Measure the voltage between sensor cluster C3137-3, circuit 1814 (WH/LB), harness side and ground; and between sensor cluster C3137-4, circuit 1815 (PK/LB), harness side and ground. • **Is the voltage less than 0.2 volt?**	**Yes** GO to U2 . **No** REPAIR the circuit. CLEAR the DTCs. CARRY OUT the self-test with the brake pedal not applied.
U2 CHECK CIRCUITS FOR A SHORT TO GROUND	
• Measure the resistance between sensor cluster C3137-3, circuit 1814 (WH/LB), harness side and ground; and between sensor cluster C3137-4, circuit 1815 (PK/LB), harness side and ground. • **Is the resistances greater than 10,000 ohms?**	**Yes** GO to U3 . **No** REPAIR the circuit. CLEAR the DTCs. CARRY OUT the self-test with the brake pedal not applied.

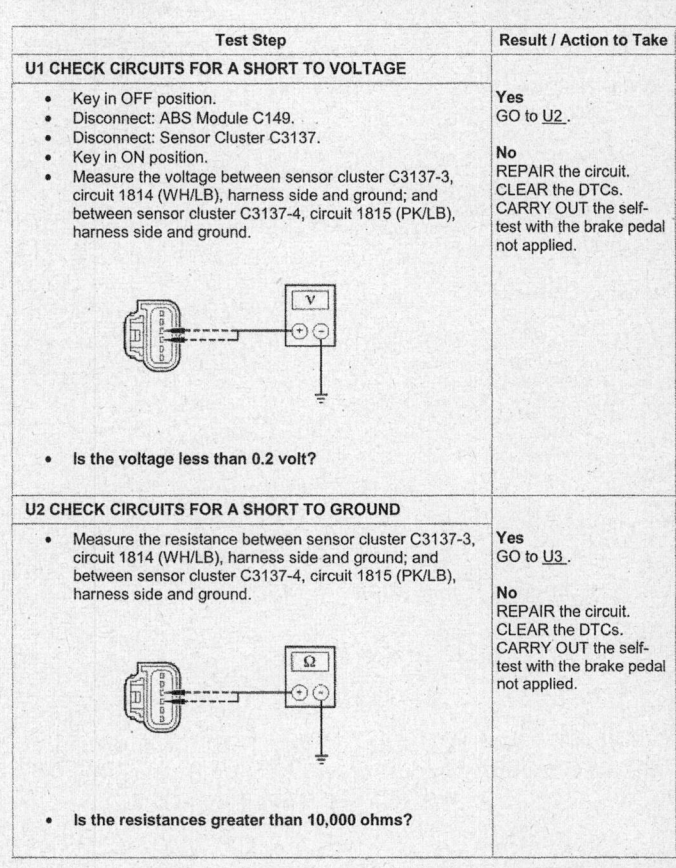

LTV0500000005017

Fig. 46   Test U, Code C1901: Can Network No. 2 Communication Bus Fault-Recieve Error (Part 1 of 3). 2004-06 w/Stability Assist

	Result / Action to Take
	No Fault corrected. CLEAR the DTCs. CARRY OUT the self-test with the brake pedal not applied.

LTV0500000005019

Fig. 46   Test U, Code C1901: Can Network No. 2 Communication Bus Fault-Recieve Error (Part 3 of 3). 2004-06 w/Stability Assist

Test Step	Result / Action to Take
V1 CHECK THE TRACTION CONTROL SWITCH • Key in ON position. • Backprobe the traction control switch between C2035-1, circuit 959 (GY), harness side and ground; and between traction control switch C2035-6, circuit 960 (BK/LB), harness side and ground. • **Is the voltage greater than 4.5 volts at pin 1, when the switch is pressed and 0 volts when released; and 0 volts at pin 6 when the switch is pressed and greater than 10 volts when the switch is released?**	**Yes** GO to <u>V2</u>. **No** GO to <u>V3</u>.
V2 CHECK CIRCUITS FOR AN OPEN • Key in OFF position. • Disconnect: Traction Control Switch C2035. • Disconnect: Instrument Cluster Module C220a. • Measure the resistance between instrument cluster module C220a-2, circuit 960 (BK/LB), harness side and traction control switch C2035-6, circuit 960 (BK/LB), harness side; and between instrument cluster module C220a-15, circuit 959 (GY), harness side and traction control switch C2035-1, circuit 959 (GY), harness side.	**Yes** INSTALL a new instrument cluster module. **No** REPAIR the circuit (s). CLEAR the DTCs. TEST the system for normal operation.

LTV0500000005020

Fig. 47 Test V, Code C110B: Traction Control Disable Switch Circuit Open (Part 1 of 2). 2004-06 w/Stability Assist

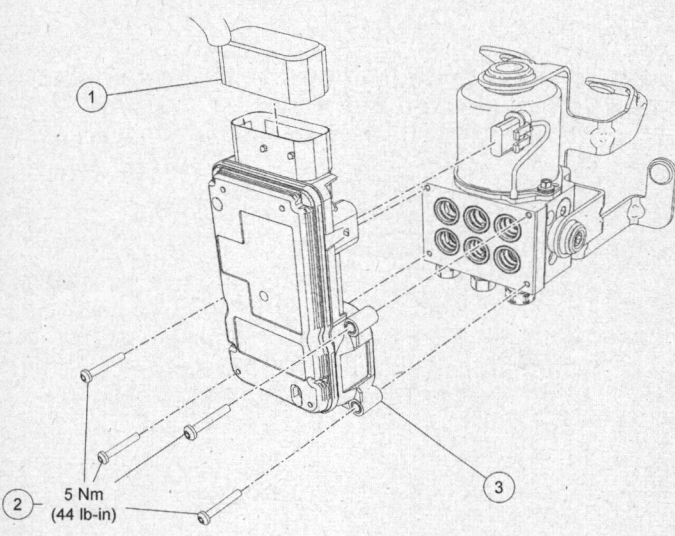

Item	Description
1	Anti-lock brake system (ABS) module electrical connector
2	ABS module screws (4 required)
3	ABS module

LTV0500000005022

Fig. 48 ABS control module replacement

• Is the resistance less than 0.5 ohms?

V3 CHECK FOR VOLTAGE AT THE TRACTION CONTROL SWITCH • Key in OFF position. • Disconnect: Traction Control Switch C2035. • Key in ON position. • Measure the voltage between traction control switch C2035-5, circuit 729 (RD/WH), harness side and ground. • Is the voltage greater than 10 volts?	**Yes** INSTALL a new traction control switch. CLEAR the DTCs. Test the system for normal operation. **No** REPAIR the circuit. CLEAR the DTCs. TEST the system for normal operation.

LTV0500000015000

Fig. 47 Test V, Code C110B: Traction Control Disable Switch Circuit Open (Part 2 of 2). 2004-06 w/Stability Assist

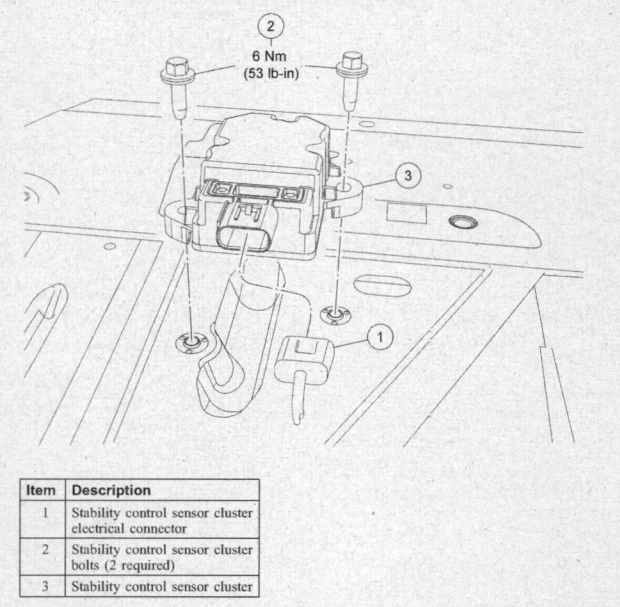

Item	Description
1	Stability control sensor cluster electrical connector
2	Stability control sensor cluster bolts (2 required)
3	Stability control sensor cluster

LTV0500000005024

Fig. 49 Stability control sensor cluster replacement

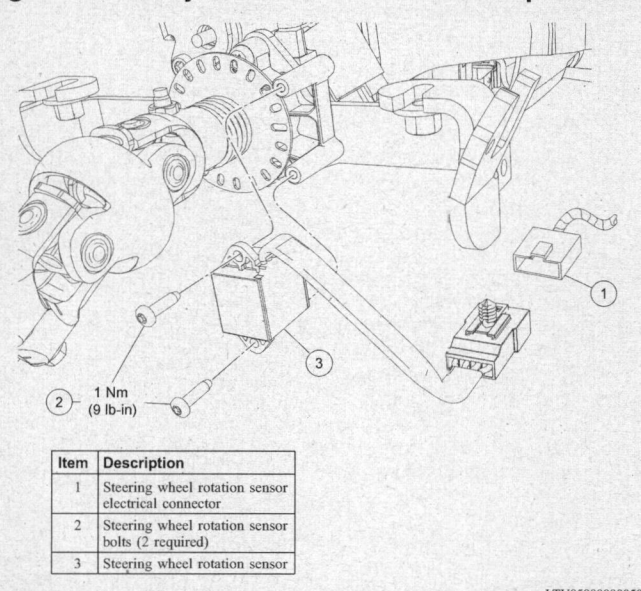

Item	Description
1	Steering wheel rotation sensor electrical connector
2	Steering wheel rotation sensor bolts (2 required)
3	Steering wheel rotation sensor

LTV0500000005023

Fig. 50 Steering wheel rotation sensor replacement

NOTE: Electrical Symbol & Wire Color Code Identification Located In The Front Of This Manual May Be Used As An Aid When Using Wiring Circuits Found In This Section.

NOTE: Refer To "Computer Relearn Procedures" Located In The Front Of This Manual When Battery Power To The Computer Has Been Interrupted.

INDEX

	Page No.		Page No.		Page No.
Description	5-73	Wiring Diagrams	5-73	Front Wheel Speed Sensor	
Diagnosis & Testing	5-73	Diagnostic Chart Index	5-77	Ring	5-74
Accessing Diagnostic Trouble		Precautions	5-73	Hydraulic Control Unit (HCU)	5-74
Codes	5-73	Battery Ground Cable	5-73	Wheel Speed Sensor	5-74
Clearing Diagnostic Trouble		Brake Fluid Handling	5-73	Troubleshooting	5-73
Codes	5-73	System Service	5-73	Symptom Chart	5-73
Diagnostic Tests	5-73	Brake System Bleed	5-73		
Diagnostic Trouble Code		Component Replacement	5-73		
Interpretation	5-73	ABS Control Module	5-73		

PRECAUTIONS

BATTERY GROUND CABLE

Prior to service disconnect battery ground cable and isolate as required.

BRAKE FLUID HANDLING

Brake fluid can cause serious injury and vehicle damage if not handled properly. Avoid contact with eyes and do not allow fluid to splash or spill on painted surfaces. Wash hands thoroughly after handling.

DESCRIPTION

The anti-lock brake system (ABS) module, with or without stability assist, simultaneously manages the anti-lock braking, traction control and engine control systems to maintain vehicle control during deceleration and acceleration. The ABS accomplishes this by communicating with the other modules over the high speed controller area network (HS-CAN) bus.

When the ignition switch is in the RUN position, the module carries out a preliminary electrical check and, at approximately 20 km/h (12 mph), the hydraulic pump motor is turned on for approximately one half-second. Any malfunction of the anti-lock brake system disables the traction control and stability assist (if equipped). The ABS module communicates with the instrument cluster over the HS-CAN bus and the cluster illuminates the anti-lock brake warning indicator. However, the power-assist braking system functions normally.

With the ignition switch in the START or RUN positions, the stability assist module functions similarly to a conventional ABS module by monitoring and comparing the rotational speed of each wheel. The wheel speed sensors electrically sense each tooth of the anti-lock sensor ring as they pass through the sensor magnetic field. When the stability assist module detects an impending wheel lock, wheel spin or vehicle motion that is inconsistent with the driver commands, it modulates brake pressure to the appropriate brake caliper(s). The stability assist module triggers the hydraulic control unit (HCU) to open and close the appropriate solenoid valves. Once the affected wheel(s) return to the desired speed, the stability assist module returns the solenoid valves to their normal position, and normal base brake operation is restored.

TROUBLESHOOTING

Symptom Chart

Refer to **Fig. 1** for symptom charts.

DIAGNOSIS & TESTING

Accessing Diagnostic Trouble Codes

Connect a suitably programmed scan tool and Vehicle Communication Module (VCM) with appropriate adapters, or equivalents, to the Data Link Connector (DCL) located in the passenger compartment beneath the instrument panel. Follow tool manufacturer's instructions for accessing Diagnostic Trouble Codes (DTC).

Diagnostic Trouble Code Interpretation

Refer to **Fig. 2** for diagnostic trouble code interpretation.

Wiring Diagrams

Refer to **Figs. 3 and 4** for wiring diagram.

Diagnostic Tests

Refer to **Figs. 5 through 20** for pinpoint tests.

Clearing Diagnostic Trouble Codes

Connect a suitably programmed scan tool and Vehicle Communication Module (VCM) with appropriate adapters, or equivalents, to the Data Link Connector (DCL) located in the passenger compartment beneath the instrument panel. Follow tool manufacturer's instructions for clearing Diagnostic Trouble Codes (DTC).

SYSTEM SERVICE

Brake System Bleed

Refer to "Hydraulic Brake Systems" chapter for bleeding procedure.

Component Replacement

ABS CONTROL MODULE

1. Remove HCU as outlined under "Hydraulic Control Unit (HCU)."
2. Disconnect pump motor electrical connector from ABS module.
3. Remove ABS control module retaining screws, then the module.
4. Reverse procedure to install. **Torque** ABS control module retaining screws to 36–44 inch lbs.

Condition	Possible Sources	Action
• ABS false activation	• Rear axle speed sensor ring is damaged	• REMOVE the rear axle speed sensor from the differential housing. INSPECT the rear axle speed sensor.
	• Front wheel speed sensor ring is damaged	• INSPECT for damaged teeth. INSPECT both front wheel speed sensor rings.
	• Sensor output is out of sync	• If the left front sensor output is out of sync, Go To Pinpoint Test C . If the right front sensor output is out of sync, Go To Pinpoint Test E . If the rear sensor output is out of sync, Go To Pinpoint Test G .
	• Intermittent open or shorted wheel speed sensor circuit	• Refer to Intermittent Failures to test circuits 514 (YE/RD), 516 (YE/BK), 523 (RD/PK), and 519 (LG/BK).
	• Chafed wire insulation or pinched wire due to incorrect routing causing intermittent short	• INSPECT the wiring harness from the front wheel knuckle to the frame and from the rear axle to the frame for worn or chafed wire insulation.
	• Parking brake adjustment too tight • Brake linings are grabby	• ELIMINATE the base brake system as the cause of the problem.
	• Loose wheel speed sensor(s)	• TIGHTEN the wheel speed sensor bolt to specifications.
• Wheels lock up	• ABS outlet (dump) valve	• Go To Pinpoint Test A .
	• Leaky ABS inlet (isolation) valve during ABS (soft) • Damp or contaminated	• ELIMINATE the base brake system as the cause of the problem.

LTV0500000004847

Fig. 1 Symptom chart (Part 1 of 4)

FRONT WHEEL SPEED SENSOR RING

1. Raise and support vehicle.
2. Remove front disc brake caliper, then position caliper aside.
3. Remove front disc brake rotor.
4. **On F-450–550 models,** remove hub extender and brake disc.
5. **On all models,** remove front wheel speed sensor ring using, suitable three jaw puller and step plate adapter tool No. D80L-630-A, or equivalent.
6. Install front wheel speed sensor ring using an appropriate size cylinder and suitable press.

HYDRAULIC CONTROL UNIT (HCU)

1. Remove air cleaner, then the EVAP canister.

2. Disconnect hydraulic brake lines.
3. Disconnect ABS control module electrical connectors.
4. Remove HCU retaining bolts, then the HCU.
5. Reverse procedure to install, noting the following:
   a. **Torque** HCU retaining bolts to 18 ft. lbs.
   b. **Torque** brake lines to 13–18 ft. lbs.
   c. Bleed brake system as outlined under "Brake System Bleed.".

WHEEL SPEED SENSOR

FRONT

2WD

1. Raise and support vehicle.
2. Remove rotor shield and rotor.
3. Disconnect speed sensor electrical connector.

4. Separate sensor cable from brake hose clips.
5. Remove caliper and anchor plate assembly mounting bolts , then position assembly aside.
6. **On F-450–550 models,** remove hub extender and brake disc.
7. **On all models,** remove sensor retaining bolt, then the sensor.
8. Reverse procedure to install, noting the following:
   a. **Torque** wheel speed sensor retaining bolt to 96 inch lbs.
   b. **Torque** hub extender nut to 130 ft. lbs.
   c. **Torque** caliper and anchor plate assembly mounting bolts to 295 ft. lbs.

4WD

1. Raise and support vehicle.
2. Remove rotor shield and rotor.
3. Disconnect wheel speed sensor wire from vehicle frame.
4. Remove sensor retaining bolt, then the sensor.
5. Reverse procedure to install, noting the following:
   a. **Torque** wheel speed sensor retaining bolt to 71 inch lbs.
   b. Apply high temperature 4X4 front axle and wheel bearing grease E8TZ-19590-A, or equivalent, meeting Ford specification ESA-MIC198-A to sensor mounting surface.

REAR

1. Raise and support vehicle.
2. Clean area around wheel speed sensor.
3. Disconnect wheel speed sensor electrical connector.
4. Remove sensor retaining bolt, then the sensor.
5. Reverse procedure to install, noting the following:
   a. **Torque** wheel speed sensor retaining bolt to 27 ft. lbs.
   b. Clean axle mounting surface.
   c. Lubricate O-ring with high performance rear axle lubricant F1TZ-19580-B, or equivalent, meeting Ford specification WSL-M2C192-A.

Fig. 1 Symptom chart (Part 2 of 4)

	• rear brake linings, or stuck/leaking rear disc brake caliper • Binding parking brake • Leaking rear axle seal	
• Yellow ABS warning indicator does not self check	• Circuitry • Anti-lock brake system (ABS) module	• Go To Pinpoint Test P .
• Hard or soft brake pedal	• Stuck ABS inlet (isolation) valve (hard brake pedal) or leaky ABS outlet (dump) valve (soft brake pedal) • Hydraulic leak in brake line or hose, fitting, master cylinder, or caliper (soft brake pedal) • Air in brake system (soft brake pedal) • Little or no power assist (hard brake pedal) • Stuck or inoperative or caliper (hard brake pedal) • Pinched or crimped brake line or hose (hard brake pedal)	• Go To Pinpoint Test H . • ELIMINATE the base brake system as the cause of the problem.
• Lack of deceleration during medium/hard brake	• Stuck shut ABS inlet (isolation) valve or leaky ABS outlet (dump) valve	• Go To Pinpoint Test H .

LTV0500000004848

Fig. 1 Symptom chart (Part 2 of 4)

Fig. 1 Symptom chart (Part 3 of 4)

application	(rear axle only)	
	• Hydraulic leak in brake line or hose, fitting, master cylinder, or caliper • Air in brake system • Little or no power assist • Stuck or inoperative caliper • Ineffective brake linings	• ELIMINATE the base brake system as the cause of the problem.
• Vehicle pulls during braking	• Frozen or binding caliper (one side of vehicle) • Uneven brake lining wear • Pinched or crimped brake line or hose • Fully or partially blocked front ABS inlet (isolation) valve • Alignment • Front suspension • Rear suspension • Steering components	• ELIMINATE the base brake system as the cause of the problem. • INSTALL a new hydraulic control unit (HCU). • Check wheel alignment.. • Check front suspension • Check rear suspension • Check steering components.
• Yellow ABS warning indicator on with system pass	• Yellow ABS warning indicator circuit • ABS warning lamp circuit open	• DISCONNECT 25-pin connector C135 from the ABS module. Using a jumper wire, GROUND pin 15, circuit 603 (DG). If the lamp is off, INSTALL a new ABS module. If the warning lamp remains

LTV0500000004849

Fig. 1 Symptom chart (Part 3 of 4)

Fig. 1 Symptom chart (Part 4 of 4)

		on, REPAIR circuit 603 (DG).
• Soft or excessive pedal travel	• Hydraulic leak in brake line or hose, fitting, master cylinder, or caliper • Air in brake system • Hydraulic control unit (HCU)	• ELIMINATE the base brake system as the cause of the problem. • Go To Pinpoint Test H .
• No communication with the anti-lock brake control module	• Fuse(s) • Circuitry • Module	• Go To Pinpoint Test L .

LTV0500000004850

Fig. 1 Symptom chart (Part 4 of 4)

Code	Description
B1342	ABS Module Failure
B1485	Brake Pedal Position (BPP) Switch Circuit Failure
B1676	Voltage Out of Range
B2141	NV Memory Configuration Failure
B2477	NV Memory Configuration Failure
C1095	ABS Hydraulic Pump Motor Failure
C1096	ABS Hydraulic Pump Motor Failure
C1113	Shorted Internal Power Relay
C1115	Shorted Internal Power Relay
C1145	RF Wheel Speed Sensor Input Circuit Failure
C1148	RF Wheel Speed Sensor Input Signal Erratic/Missing
C1155	LF Wheel Speed Sensor Input Circuit Failure
C1158	LF Wheel Speed Sensor Input Signal Erratic/Missing
C1169	Excessive Dump Time
C1184	ABS System Timeout
C1185	Open/Shorted Internal Power Relay
C1194	LF ABS Outlet Valve Circuit Failure/Short to Battery
C1196	LF ABS Outlet Valve Circuit Failure/Short to Battery
C1198	LF ABS Inlet Valve Circuit Failure/Short to Battery
C1200	LF ABS Inlet Valve Circuit Failure/Short to Battery
C1202	Rear ABS Outlet Valve Circuit Failure/Short to Battery
C1204	Rear ABS Outlet Valve Circuit Failure/Short to Battery
C1206	Rear ABS Inlet Valve Circuit Failure/Short to Battery
C1208	Rear ABS Inlet Valve Circuit Failure/Short to Battery
C1210	RF ABS Outlet Valve Circuit Failure/Short to Battery
C1212	RF ABS Outlet Valve Circuit Failure/Short to Battery
C1214	RF ABS Inlet Valve Circuit Failure/Short to Battery
C1216	RF ABS Inlet Valve Circuit Failure/Short to Battery
C1222	Wheel Speed Error/Mismatch
C1226	Brake Lamp Warning Output Circuit Short to Ground
C1229	Rear Axle Speed Input Signal Erratic/Missing
C1230	Rear Axle Speed Sensor Input Circuit Failure
C1233	LF Wheel Speed Sensor Input Signal Erratic/Missing
C1234	RF Wheel Speed Sensor Input Signal Erratic/Missing
C1237	Rear Axle Speed Input Signal Erratic/Missing

Fig. 2   Diagnostic trouble code interpretation

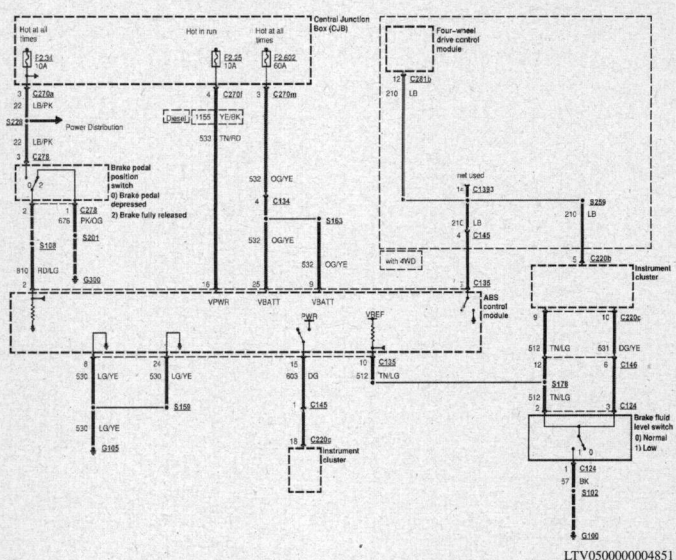

Fig. 3   Wiring diagram (Part 1 of 2). Excursion

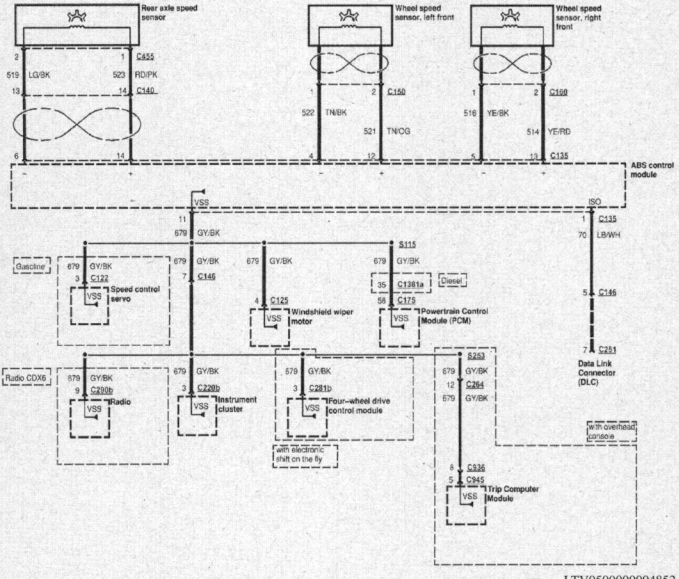

LTV0500000004852

Fig. 3   Wiring diagram (Part 2 of 2). Excursion

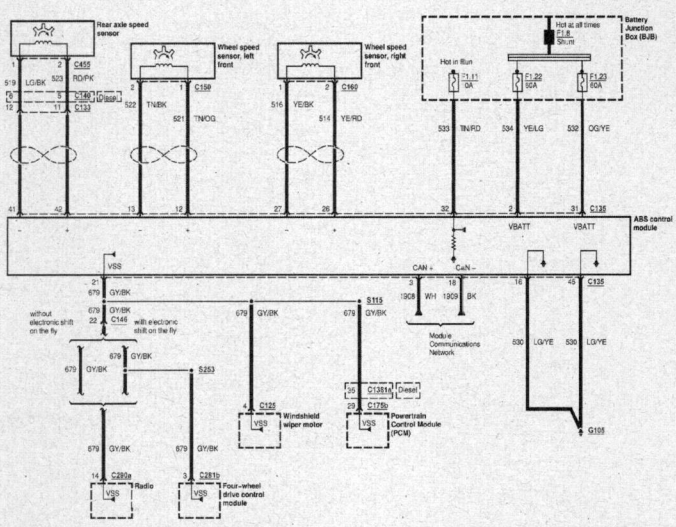

LTV0500000004853

Fig. 4   Wiring diagram. 2004-06 F-Super Duty

DIAGNOSTIC CHART INDEX

Test	Code	Description	Page No.	Fig. No.
A	C1194	ABS Outlet/Inlet Valve Circuit Failure/Short To Battery	5-78	5
	C1196	ABS Outlet/Inlet Valve Circuit Failure/Short To Battery	5-78	5
	C1198	ABS Outlet/Inlet Valve Circuit Failure/Short To Battery	5-78	5
	C1200	ABS Outlet/Inlet Valve Circuit Failure/Short To Battery	5-78	5
	C1202	ABS Outlet/Inlet Valve Circuit Failure/Short To Battery	5-78	5
	C1204	ABS Outlet/Inlet Valve Circuit Failure/Short To Battery	5-78	5
	C1206	ABS Outlet/Inlet Valve Circuit Failure/Short To Battery	5-78	5
	C1208	ABS Outlet/Inlet Valve Circuit Failure/Short To Battery	5-78	5
	C1210	ABS Outlet/Inlet Valve Circuit Failure/Short To Battery	5-78	5
	C1212	ABS Outlet/Inlet Valve Circuit Failure/Short To Battery	5-78	5
	C1214	ABS Outlet/Inlet Valve Circuit Failure/Short To Battery	5-78	5
	C1216	ABS Outlet/Inlet Valve Circuit Failure/Short To Battery	5-78	5
B	C1155	Left Front Wheel Speed Sensor Input Circuit Failure	5-78	6
C	C1158	Left Front Wheel Speed Sensor Input Signal Erratic/Missing	5-78	7
	C1233	Left Front Wheel Speed Sensor Input Signal Erratic/Missing	5-78	7
D	C1145	Right Front Wheel Speed Sensor Input Circuit Failure	5-79	8
E	C1148	Right Front Wheel Speed Sensor Input Signal Erratic/Missing	5-80	9
	C1234	Right Front Wheel Speed Sensor Input Signal Erratic/Missing	5-80	9
F	C1230	Rear Axle Speed Sensor Input Circuit Failure	5-81	10
G	C1229	Rear Axle Speed Sensor Input Signal Erratic/Missing	5-81	11
	C1237	Rear Axle Speed Sensor Input Signal Erratic/Missing	5-81	11
H	—	Soft Or Excessive Pedal Travel	5-82	12
J	C1095	ABS Hydraulic Pump Motor Failure	5-82	13
	C1096	ABS Hydraulic Pump Motor Failure	5-82	13
K	C1113	ABS Power Relay Circuit Failure/Short To Battery	5-82	14
	C1115	ABS Power Relay Circuit Failure/Short To Battery	5-82	14
	C1185	ABS Power Relay Circuit Failure/Short To Battery	5-82	14
L	—	No Communication w/ABS Module	5-83	15
M	C1169	Excessive Dump Time	5-83	16
N	C1184	ABS Time Out/Wheel Speed Error/Mismatch	5-83	17
	C1222	ABS Time Out/Wheel Speed Error/Mismatch	5-83	17
O	B1485	Brake Pedal Position (BPP) Switch Circuit Failure	5-83	18
P	—	Yellow ABS Warning Indicator Does Not Self Check	5-84	19
Q	B1676	Voltage Out Of Range	5-84	20

Test Step	Result / Action to Take
A1 CHECK FOR FAULT REPEATABILITY	
• Connect the diagnostic tool. • Enter the following diagnostic mode on the diagnostic tool: Clear DTCs. • Enter the following diagnostic mode on the diagnostic tool: Carry out the Anti-Lock Brake System (ABS) Module On-Demand Self-Test. • Enter the following diagnostic mode on the diagnostic tool: Retrieve DTCs. • **Is a single inlet or outlet valve DTC set?**	**Yes** INSTALL a new ABS module. **No** If multiple valve DTCs are set, GO to A2. If no DTCs are set, TEST the system for normal operation.
A2 CHECK THE ABS MODULE POWER CIRCUIT 532 (OG/YE)	
⚠ **CAUTION: A blown fuse may be an indication of some other wiring or component concern within the circuit.** • Key in OFF position. • Disconnect: ABS Module C135. • Measure the voltage between ABS module C135 pins 9 and 25, circuit 532 (OG/YE), and ground. • **Is the voltage greater than 10 volts?**	**Yes** INSTALL a new ABS module. TEST the system for normal operation. **No** CONNECT the ABS Module C135. GO to A3.
A3 CHECK THE CENTRAL JUNCTION BOX (CJB) FUSE 4 (60A)	
• Check fuse: CJB Fuse 602 (60A). • **Is the fuse OK?**	**Yes** REPAIR circuit 532 (OG/YE). TEST the system for normal operation. **No** INSTALL a new fuse. TEST the system for normal operation. If the fuse fails again, CHECK for a short to ground. REPAIR as necessary. TEST the system for normal operation.

LTV0500000004854

Fig. 5   Test A, Codes C1194, C1196, C1198, C1200, C1202, C1204, C1206, C1208, C1210, C1212, C1214 & C1216 ABS Outlet/Inlet Valve Circuit Failure/Short To Battery. Excursion & 2004-06 F-Super Duty

Test Step	Result / Action to Take
• Is the resistance between 650 and 800 ohms?	
B4 CHECK THE LEFT FRONT WHEEL SPEED SENSOR CIRCUIT FOR A SHORT TO GROUND	
• Measure the resistance between the EEC-IV 60-Pin Breakout Box pin 12, circuit 521 (TN/OG), and ground; and between the EEC-IV 60-Pin Breakout Box pin 4, circuit 522 (TN/BK), and ground. • Are the resistances greater than 10,000 ohms?	**Yes** GO to B6. **No** GO to B5.
B5 CHECK FOR AN INTERNAL WHEEL SPEED SENSOR SHORT	
• Disconnect: Left Front Wheel Speed Sensor C150. • Measure the resistance between the left front wheel speed sensor C150 terminals and ground. • Are the resistances greater than 10,000 ohms?	**Yes** REPAIR circuit 522 (TN/BK) and/or circuit 521 (TN/OG). TEST the system for normal operation. **No** INSTALL a new left front wheel speed sensor. TEST the system for normal operation.
B6 TEST FOR AN INTERMITTENT SENSOR FAULT	
• Carry out the Sensor Failure test for the left front wheel speed sensor. Refer to Component Test — Intermittent Failures. • **Did the left front wheel speed sensor pass?**	**Yes** System is OK. **No** REPAIR as necessary. TEST the system for normal operation.

LTV0500000004856

Fig. 6   Test B, Code C1155: Left Front Wheel Speed Sensor Input Circuit Failure (Part 2 of 2). Excursion & 2004-06 F-Super Duty

Test Step	Result / Action to Take
B1 CHECK FOR FAULT REPEATABILITY	
• Connect the diagnostic tool. • Enter the following diagnostic mode on the diagnostic tool: Clear Continuous DTCs. • Drive the vehicle at least 6 km/h (10 mph). • Enter the following diagnostic mode on the diagnostic tool: Retrieve and document continuous DTCs. • **Is DTC C1155 retrieved?**	**Yes** GO to B2. **No** If no DTC is retrieved, GO to B6. If a different DTC is retrieved, REFER to Diagnostic Trouble Code (DTC) Chart.
B2 CHECK THE WHEEL SPEED SENSOR INPUT CIRCUIT COIL RESISTANCE AT ABS MODULE CONNECTOR	
• Key in OFF position. • Install the EEC-IV 60-Pin Breakout Box. • Measure the resistance between the EEC-IV 60-Pin Breakout Box pin 12 and the EEC-IV 60-Pin Breakout Box pin 4. • Is the resistance between 650 and 800 ohms?	**Yes** GO to B4. **No** GO to B3.
B3 DETERMINE THE LOCATION OF THE FAULT	
• Disconnect: Left Front Wheel Speed Sensor C150. • Measure the resistance between the left front wheel speed sensor C150 pin 1 and pin 2, component side. 	**Yes** REPAIR circuit 522 (TN/BK) and circuit 521 (TN/OG) as necessary. CLEAR the DTCs. REPEAT the self-test. **No** INSTALL a new left front wheel speed sensor. CLEAR the DTCs. REPEAT the self-test.

LTV0500000004855

Fig. 6   Test B, Code C1155: Left Front Wheel Speed Sensor Input Circuit Failure (Part 1 of 2). Excursion & 2004-06 F-Super Duty

Test Step	Result / Action to Take
C1 RETRIEVE ANY DTCs	
• Connect the diagnostic tool. • Enter the following diagnostic mode on the diagnostic tool: Retrieve and document continuous DTCs. • **Is DTC C1155 retrieved?**	**Yes** DIAGNOSE DTC C1155 first. IGNORE all other DTCs retrieved. **No** GO to C2.
C2 REPEATABILITY DRIVE TEST (MISMATCHED OUTPUT)	
NOTE: If a hard turn is made, some variation between all 3 wheel speeds is expected. **NOTE:** Recording the speeds for later plotting will eliminate the necessity of monitoring the diagnostic tool while driving. • Enter the following diagnostic mode on the diagnostic tool: Monitor ABS module wheel speed PIDs. • Drive the vehicle at various speeds. • **Does the left front wheel speed sensor consistently match the other 2?**	**Yes** GO to C7. **No** GO to C3.
C3 CHECK THE LEFT FRONT WHEEL SPEED SENSOR RING	
• Raise the vehicle on a hoist. • ⚠ **CAUTION: Examine the wheel speed sensor ring carefully. Failure to properly diagnose the sensor ring at this time will lead to unnecessary component replacement and wasted diagnostic time.** • Inspect the wheel speed sensor ring for damaged or missing teeth. Rotate the wheel to be sure all teeth are checked. • **Is the wheel speed sensor ring damaged or missing teeth?**	**Yes** INSTALL a new wheel speed sensor ring. TEST the system for normal operation. **No** GO to C4.

LTV0500000004857

Fig. 7   Test C, Codes C1158 & C1233: Left Front Wheel Speed Sensor Input Signal Erratic/Missing (Part 1 of 3). Excursion & 2004-06 F-Super Duty

Test Step	Result / Action to Take
C4 CHECK FOR LOOSE WHEEL SPEED SENSOR MOUNTING • Wiggle the wheel speed sensor at the wheel end. • **Is any looseness detected?**	**Yes** TIGHTEN the wheel speed sensor bolt to specification. TEST the system for normal operation. **No** GO to C5.
C5 CHECK FOR AN INTERNAL WHEEL SPEED SENSOR SHORT TO GROUND • Key in OFF position. • Disconnect: Left Front Wheel Speed Sensor C150. • Measure the resistance between the left front wheel speed sensor C150 terminals and ground. 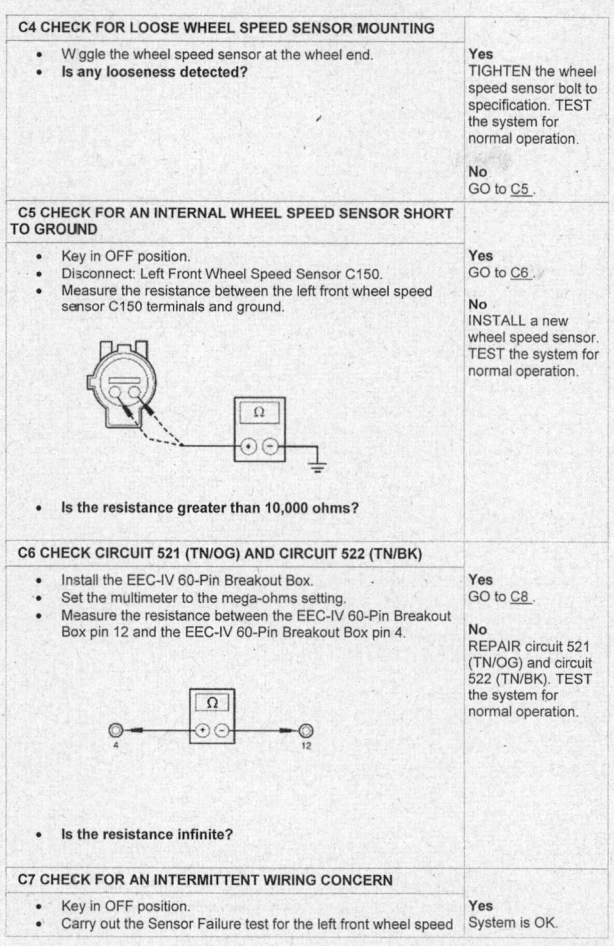 • **Is the resistance greater than 10,000 ohms?**	**Yes** GO to C6. **No** INSTALL a new wheel speed sensor. TEST the system for normal operation.
C6 CHECK CIRCUIT 521 (TN/OG) AND CIRCUIT 522 (TN/BK) • Install the EEC-IV 60-Pin Breakout Box. • Set the multimeter to the mega-ohms setting. • Measure the resistance between the EEC-IV 60-Pin Breakout Box pin 12 and the EEC-IV 60-Pin Breakout Box pin 4. • **Is the resistance infinite?**	**Yes** GO to C8. **No** REPAIR circuit 521 (TN/OG) and circuit 522 (TN/BK). TEST the system for normal operation.
C7 CHECK FOR AN INTERMITTENT WIRING CONCERN • Key in OFF position. • Carry out the Sensor Failure test for the left front wheel speed	**Yes** System is OK.

LTV0500000004858

Fig. 7   Test C, Codes C1158 & C1233: Left Front Wheel Speed Sensor Input Signal Erratic/Missing (Part 2 of 3). Excursion & 2004-06 F-Super Duty

Test Step	Result / Action to Take
D1 CHECK FOR FAULT REPEATABILITY • Connect the diagnostic tool. • Enter the following diagnostic mode on the diagnostic tool: Clear Continuous DTCs. • Drive the vehicle at least 6 km/h (10 mph). • Enter the following diagnostic mode on the diagnostic tool: Retrieve and document continuous DTCs. • **Is DTC C1145 retrieved?**	**Yes** GO to D2. **No** If no DTC is retrieved, GO to D6. If a different DTC is retrieved, refer to Diagnostic Trouble Code (DTC) Index.
D2 CHECK THE WHEEL SPEED SENSOR COIL RESISTANCE AT THE HCU CONNECTOR • Key in OFF position. • Install the EEC-IV 60-Pin Breakout Box. • Measure the resistance between the EEC-IV 60-Pin Breakout Box pin 13, circuit 514 (YE/RD) and the EEC-IV 60-Pin Breakout Box pin 5, circuit 516 (YE/BK). 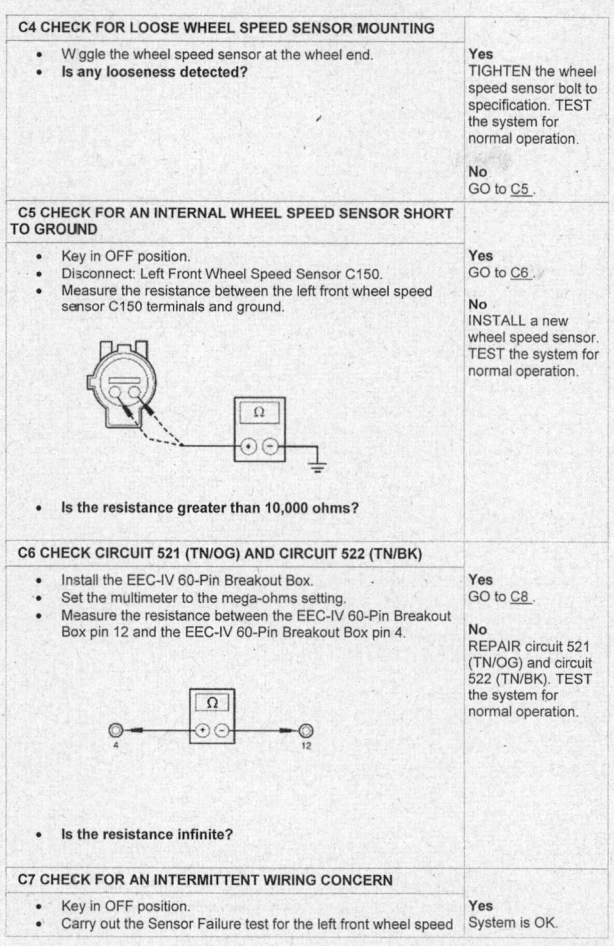 • **Is the resistance between 650 and 800 ohms?**	**Yes** GO to D4. **No** GO to D3.

LTV0500000004860

Fig. 8   Test D, Code C1145: Right Front Wheel Speed Sensor Input Circuit Failure (Part 1 of 3). Excursion & 2004-06 F-Super Duty

Test Step	Result / Action to Take
sensor. Refer to Component Test — Intermittent Failures. • **Did the left front wheel speed sensor pass?**	**No** REPAIR as necessary. TEST the system for normal operation.
C8 INSPECT THE LEFT FRONT WHEEL SPEED SENSOR FOR DAMAGE • Remove the left front wheel speed sensor. • Inspect the housing for stress cracks or breaks. • Inspect the left front wheel speed sensor C150 cavity for evidence of water entry, pin corrosion, or excessive debris. • **Are any of the above conditions evident?**	**Yes** REPAIR as necessary. TEST the system for normal operation. **No** INSTALL a new ABS module.. TEST the system for normal operation.

LTV0500000004859

Fig. 7   Test C, Codes C1158 & C1233: Left Front Wheel Speed Sensor Input Signal Erratic/Missing (Part 3 of 3). Excursion & 2004-06 F-Super Duty

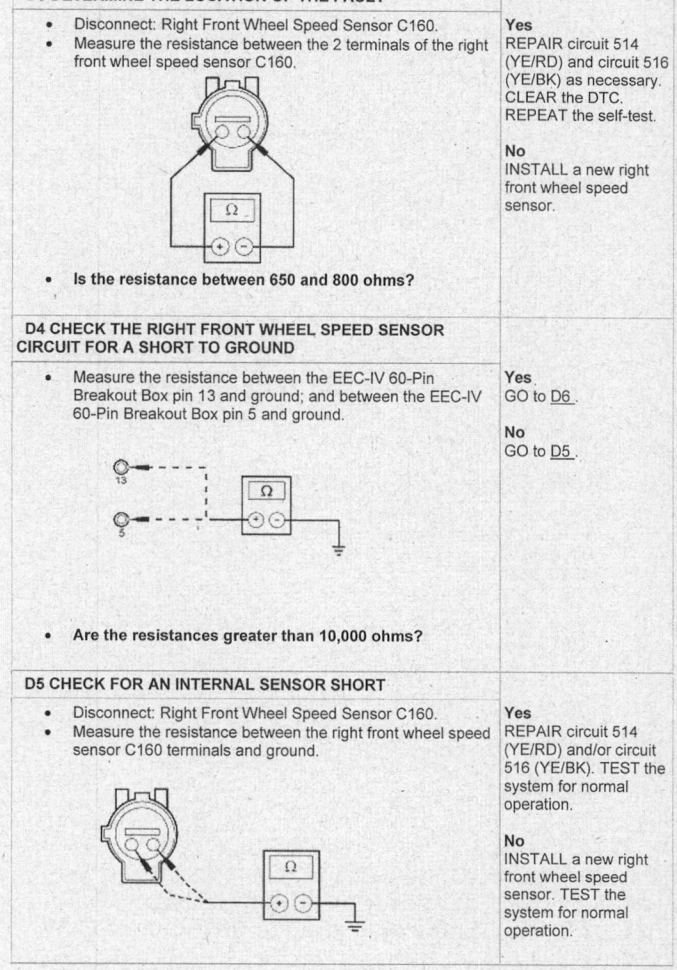

Test Step	Result / Action to Take
D3 DETERMINE THE LOCATION OF THE FAULT • Disconnect: Right Front Wheel Speed Sensor C160. • Measure the resistance between the 2 terminals of the right front wheel speed sensor C160. • **Is the resistance between 650 and 800 ohms?**	**Yes** REPAIR circuit 514 (YE/RD) and circuit 516 (YE/BK) as necessary. CLEAR the DTC. REPEAT the self-test. **No** INSTALL a new right front wheel speed sensor.
D4 CHECK THE RIGHT FRONT WHEEL SPEED SENSOR CIRCUIT FOR A SHORT TO GROUND • Measure the resistance between the EEC-IV 60-Pin Breakout Box pin 13 and ground; and between the EEC-IV 60-Pin Breakout Box pin 5 and ground. • **Are the resistances greater than 10,000 ohms?**	**Yes** GO to D6. **No** GO to D5.
D5 CHECK FOR AN INTERNAL SENSOR SHORT • Disconnect: Right Front Wheel Speed Sensor C160. • Measure the resistance between the right front wheel speed sensor C160 terminals and ground.	**Yes** REPAIR circuit 514 (YE/RD) and/or circuit 516 (YE/BK). TEST the system for normal operation. **No** INSTALL a new right front wheel speed sensor. TEST the system for normal operation.

LTV0500000004861

Fig. 8   Test D, Code C1145: Right Front Wheel Speed Sensor Input Circuit Failure (Part 2 of 3). Excursion & 2004-06 F-Super Duty

• Is the resistance greater than 10,000 ohms?	

D6 TEST FOR AN INTERMITTENT WHEEL SPEED SENSOR FAULT	
• Carry out the Sensor Failure test for the right front wheel speed sensor. Refer to Component Test — Intermittent Failures. • **Did the right front wheel speed sensor pass?**	**Yes** System is OK. **No** REPAIR as necessary. TEST the system for normal operation.

LTV0500000004862

Fig. 8 Test D, Code C1145: Right Front Wheel Speed Sensor Input Circuit Failure (Part 3 of 3). Excursion & 2004-06 F-Super Duty

teeth. Rotate the wheel speed sensor ring to be sure all teeth are checked. • **Is the wheel speed sensor ring damaged or missing teeth?**	**No** GO to E4 .

E4 CHECK FOR LOOSE WHEEL SPEED SENSOR MOUNTING	
• Wiggle the wheel speed sensor at the wheel end. • **Is any looseness detected?**	**Yes** TIGHTEN the wheel speed sensor bolt to specifications. TEST the system for normal operation. **No** GO to E5 .

E5 CHECK FOR AN INTERNAL WHEEL SPEED SENSOR SHORT	
• Key in OFF position. • Disconnect: Right Front Wheel Speed Sensor C160. • Measure the resistance between the right front wheel speed sensor C160 terminals and ground. • Is the resistance greater than 10,000 ohms?	**Yes** GO to E6 . **No** INSTALL a new right front wheel speed sensor. TEST the system for normal operation.

E6 CHECK CIRCUIT 514 (YE/RD) AND CIRCUIT 516 (YE/BK)	
• Install the EEC-IV 60-Pin Breakout Box. • Set the multimeter to the mega-ohms setting. • Measure the resistance between the EEC-IV 60-Pin Breakout Box pin 5 and pin 13. • **Is the resistance infinite?**	**Yes** GO to E8 . **No** REPAIR circuit 514 (YE/RD) and circuit 516 (YE/BK). TEST the system for normal operation.

LTV0500000004864

Fig. 9 Test E, Codes C1148 & C1234: Right Front Wheel Speed Sensor Input Signal Erratic/Missing (Part 2 of 3). Excursion & 2004-06 F-Super Duty

Test Step	Result / Action to Take
E1 RETRIEVE ANY DTCS	
• Connect the diagnostic tool. • Enter the following diagnostic mode on the diagnostic tool: Retrieve and document continuous DTCs. • **Is DTC C1145 retrieved?**	**Yes** DIAGNOSE DTC C1145 first. IGNORE all other DTCs retrieved. **No** GO to E2 .
E2 REPEATABILITY DRIVE TEST (MISMATCHED OUTPUT)	
NOTE: If a hard turn is made, some variation between all 3 wheel speed sensors is expected. **NOTE:** Recording the speeds for later plotting will eliminate the necessity of monitoring the diagnostic tool while driving. • Enter the following diagnostic mode on the diagnostic tool: Monitor the ABS wheel speed PIDs. • Drive the vehicle at various speeds. • **Does the right front wheel speed consistently match the other 2?**	**Yes** GO to E7 . **No** GO to E3 .
E3 CHECK THE RIGHT FRONT WHEEL SPEED SENSOR RING	
• Raise the vehicle on a hoist. • ⚠ **CAUTION: Examine the wheel speed sensor ring carefully. Failure to properly diagnose the sensor ring at this time will lead to unnecessary component replacement and wasted diagnostic time.** • Inspect the wheel speed sensor ring for damaged or missing	**Yes** INSTALL a new wheel speed sensor ring. TEST the system for normal operation.

LTV0500000004863

Fig. 9 Test E, Codes C1148 & C1234: Right Front Wheel Speed Sensor Input Signal Erratic/Missing (Part 1 of 3). Excursion & 2004-06 F-Super Duty

E7 CHECK FOR AN INTERMITTENT WIRING CONCERN	
• Key in OFF position. • Carry out the Sensor Failure test for the right front wheel speed sensor. Refer to Component Test — Intermittent Failures. • **Did the right front wheel speed sensor pass?**	**Yes** System is OK. **No** REPAIR as necessary. TEST the system for normal operation.

E8 INSPECT THE RIGHT FRONT WHEEL SPEED SENSOR FOR DAMAGE	
• Key in OFF position. • Remove the right front wheel speed sensor. • Inspect the housing for stress cracks or breaks. • Inspect the wheel speed sensor C160 for evidence of water entry, pin corrosion, or excessive debris. • **Are any of the above conditions present?**	**Yes** REPAIR as necessary. TEST the system for normal operation. **No** INSTALL a new ABS module. TEST the system for normal operation.

LTV0500000004865

Fig. 9 Test E, Codes C1148 & C1234: Right Front Wheel Speed Sensor Input Signal Erratic/Missing (Part 3 of 3). Excursion & 2004-06 F-Super Duty

Test Step	Result / Action to Take
F1 CHECK FOR FAULT REPEATABILITY	
• Connect the diagnostic tool. • Enter the following diagnostic mode on the diagnostic tool: Clear Continuous DTCs. • Drive the vehicle at least 6 km/h (10 mph). • Enter the following diagnostic mode on the diagnostic tool: Retrieve and document continuous DTCs. • **Is DTC C1230 retrieved?**	**Yes** GO to F2. **No** If no DTC is retrieved, GO to F6. If a different DTC is retrieved, refer to Diagnostic Trouble Code (DTC) Index.
F2 CHECK THE REAR AXLE SPEED SENSOR COIL RESISTANCE AT THE ANTI-LOCK BRAKE SYSTEM (ABS) MODULE	
• Key in OFF position. • Install the EEC-IV 60-Pin Breakout Box. • Measure the resistance between the EEC-IV 60-Pin Breakout Box pin 14 and the EEC-IV 60-Pin Breakout Box pin 6. • **Is the resistance between 800 and 3500 ohms?**	**Yes** GO to F4. **No** GO to F3.
F3 DETERMINE THE LOCATION OF THE FAULT	
• Disconnect: Rear Axle Speed Sensor C455. • Measure the resistance between the 2 terminals of the rear axle speed sensor C455. • **Is the resistance between 800 and 3500 ohms?**	**Yes** REPAIR circuit 519 (LG/BK) and circuit 523 (RD/PK). TEST the system for normal operation. **No** INSTALL a new rear axle speed sensor. TEST the system for normal operation.
F4 CHECK THE REAR AXLE SPEED SENSOR CIRCUIT FOR A SHORT	

LTV0500000004866

Fig. 10   Test F, Code C1230: Rear Axle Speed Sensor Input Circuit Failure (Part 1 of 2). Excursion & 2004-06 F-Super Duty

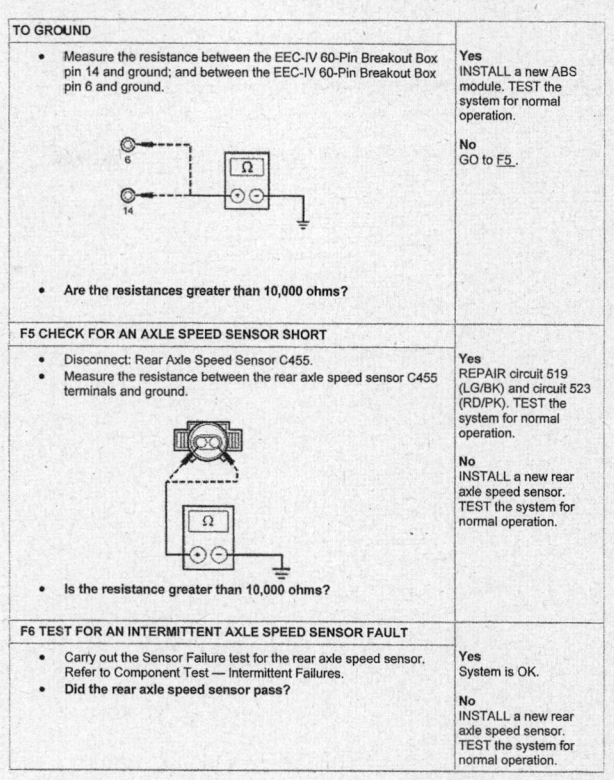

Test Step	Result / Action to Take
TO GROUND	
• Measure the resistance between the EEC-IV 60-Pin Breakout Box pin 14 and ground; and between the EEC-IV 60-Pin Breakout Box pin 6 and ground. • **Are the resistances greater than 10,000 ohms?**	**Yes** INSTALL a new ABS module. TEST the system for normal operation. **No** GO to F5.
F5 CHECK FOR AN AXLE SPEED SENSOR SHORT	
• Disconnect: Rear Axle Speed Sensor C455. • Measure the resistance between the rear axle speed sensor C455 terminals and ground. • **Is the resistance greater than 10,000 ohms?**	**Yes** REPAIR circuit 519 (LG/BK) and circuit 523 (RD/PK). TEST the system for normal operation. **No** INSTALL a new rear axle speed sensor. TEST the system for normal operation.
F6 TEST FOR AN INTERMITTENT AXLE SPEED SENSOR FAULT	
• Carry out the Sensor Failure test for the rear axle speed sensor. Refer to Component Test — Intermittent Failures. • **Did the rear axle speed sensor pass?**	**Yes** System is OK. **No** INSTALL a new rear axle speed sensor. TEST the system for normal operation.

LTV0500000004867

Fig. 10   Test F, Code C1230: Rear Axle Speed Sensor Input Circuit Failure (Part 2 of 2). Excursion & 2004-06 F-Super Duty

Test Step	Result / Action to Take
G1 RETRIEVE ANY DTCs	
• Connect the diagnostic tool. • Enter the following diagnostic mode on the diagnostic tool: Retrieve Continuous DTCs. • **Is DTC C1230 retrieved?**	**Yes** DIAGNOSE DTC C1230 first. IGNORE all other DTCs retrieved. **No** GO to G2.
G2 REPEATABILITY DRIVE TEST (MISMATCHED OUTPUT)	
NOTE: If a hard turn is made, some variation between all 3 wheel speeds is expected. **NOTE:** Recording the speeds for later plotting will eliminate the necessity of monitoring the diagnostic tool while driving. • Enter the following diagnostic mode on the diagnostic tool: Monitor ABS module wheel speed PIDs. • Drive the vehicle at various speeds. • **Does the rear axle speed sensor consistently match the other 2?**	**Yes** GO to G7. **No** GO to G3.
G3 CHECK THE REAR AXLE SPEED SENSOR RING	
• Raise the vehicle on a hoist. • ⚠ **CAUTION: Examine the axle speed sensor ring carefully. Failure to properly diagnose the sensor ring at this time will lead to unnecessary component replacement and wasted diagnostic time.** • Inspect the axle speed sensor ring for damaged or missing teeth. Rotate the wheel to be sure all teeth are checked. • **Is the axle speed sensor ring damaged or missing teeth?**	**Yes** INSTALL a new axle speed sensor ring. TEST the system for normal operation. **No** GO to G4.
G4 CHECK FOR A LOOSE AXLE SPEED SENSOR MOUNTING	
• Wiggle the axle speed sensor at the differential case. • **Is any looseness detected?**	**Yes** TIGHTEN the rear axle speed sensor bolt to specifications. TEST the system for normal operation. **No** GO to G5.
G5 CHECK FOR AN AXLE SPEED SENSOR SHORT	
• Key in OFF position. • Disconnect: Rear Axle Speed Sensor C455. • Measure the resistance between the rear axle speed sensor C455 terminals and ground.	**Yes** GO to G6. **No** INSTALL a new axle speed sensor.. TEST the system for normal operation.

LTV0500000004868

Fig. 11   Test G, Codes C1229 & C1237: Rear Axle Speed Sensor Input Signal Erratic/Missing (Part 1 of 2). Excursion & 2004-06 F-Super Duty

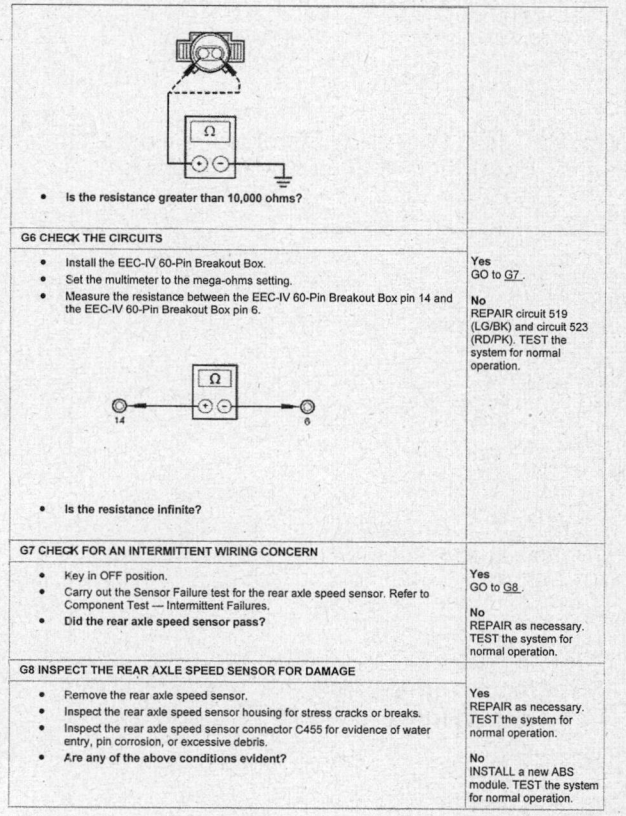

• **Is the resistance greater than 10,000 ohms?**	
G6 CHECK THE CIRCUITS	
• Install the EEC-IV 60-Pin Breakout Box. • Set the multimeter to the mega-ohms setting. • Measure the resistance between the EEC-IV 60-Pin Breakout Box pin 14 and the EEC-IV 60-Pin Breakout Box pin 6. • **Is the resistance infinite?**	**Yes** GO to G7. **No** REPAIR circuit 519 (LG/BK) and circuit 523 (RD/PK). TEST the system for normal operation.
G7 CHECK FOR AN INTERMITTENT WIRING CONCERN	
• Key in OFF position. • Carry out the Sensor Failure test for the rear axle speed sensor. Refer to Component Test — Intermittent Failures. • **Did the rear axle speed sensor pass?**	**Yes** GO to G8. **No** REPAIR as necessary. TEST the system for normal operation.
G8 INSPECT THE REAR AXLE SPEED SENSOR FOR DAMAGE	
• Remove the rear axle speed sensor. • Inspect the rear axle speed sensor housing for stress cracks or breaks. • Inspect the rear axle speed sensor connector C455 for evidence of water entry, pin corrosion, or excessive debris. • **Are any of the above conditions evident?**	**Yes** REPAIR as necessary. TEST the system for normal operation. **No** INSTALL a new ABS module. TEST the system for normal operation.

LTV0500000004869

Fig. 11   Test G, Codes C1229 & C1237: Rear Axle Speed Sensor Input Signal Erratic/Missing (Part 2 of 2). Excursion & 2004-06 F-Super Duty

Test Step	Result / Action to Take
H1 CHECK THE BASE BRAKE COMPONENTS • Visually inspect the brake lines from the HCU to the brake calipers. • Visually inspect the calipers and brake components. • **Are any of these components damaged?**	**Yes** REPAIR or INSTALL new components as necessary. TEST the system for normal operation. **No** GO to <u>H2</u>.
H2 CHECK FOR A LEAKING DUMP VALVE • Key in OFF position. • Remove the rubber boots from the HCU low pressure accumulators (LPA). • Insert a clean steel implement (e.g., paper clip or small screwdriver) into each LPA. • Key in START position. • NOTE: A leaking dump valve is similar to the master cylinder bypass condition. It is important that the pedal be quickly and forcefully applied to rule out master cylinder bypass as a cause. Typically, master cylinder bypass occurs only at low pedal pressure rates and low tire pressure. • Have an assistant press hard on the brake pedal while observing the steel implements. • **Do any of the implements move out 6.35mm (0.25in) or more?**	**Yes** INSTALL a new HCU. **No** REMOVE the steel implements. INSTALL the rubber boots on each LPA. GO to <u>Symptom Chart</u>.

LTV0500000004870

Fig. 12   Test H: Soft Or Excessive Pedal Travel. Excursion & 2004-06 F-Super Duty

Test Step	Result / Action to Take
• **Is the resistance less than 5 ohms?**	
J3 CHECK THE ANTI-LOCK BRAKE SYSTEM (ABS) MODULE FOR DTCS NOTE: Repair all other DTCs before proceeding. • Key in OFF position. • Connect the diagnostic tool. • Clear and retrieve the ABS module DTCs. • **Are DTCs C1095 and C1096 still present?**	**Yes** GO to <u>J4</u>. **No** INSTALL a new ABS module.
J4 CARRY OUT AN ABS EVENT • Clear the DTCs, road test the vehicle and carry out an ABS event. • Retrieve the ABS module DTCs. • **Did DTCs C1095 and C1096 return?**	**Yes** INSTALL a new HCU. **No** The system is operating correctly at this time.

LTV0500000004872

Fig. 13   Test J, Codes C1095, & C1096: ABS Hydraulic Pump Motor Failure (Part 2 of 2). Excursion & 2004-05 F-Super Duty

Test Step	Result / Action to Take
J1 CHECK CIRCUIT 532 (OG/YE) FOR VOLTAGE • Disconnect: ABS Module C135. • Measure the voltage between the ABS module C135 pin 9, circuit 532 (OG/YE), harness side and ground; and between the ABS module C135 pin 25, circuit 532 (OG/YE), harness side and ground. • **Is the voltage greater than 10 volts?**	**Yes** GO to <u>J2</u>. **No** REPAIR the circuit. REPEAT the self-test. DRIVE the vehicle over a rough road. TEST the system for normal operation.
J2 CHECK CIRCUIT 530 (LG/YE) FOR GROUND • Key in OFF position. • Measure the resistance between the ABS module C135 pin 8, circuit 530 (LG/YE), harness side and ground; and between the ABS module C135 pin 24, circuit 530 (LG/YE), harness side and ground.	**Yes** GO to <u>J3</u>. **No** REPAIR the circuit. CLEAR the DTCs. REPEAT the self-test. DRIVE the vehicle over a rough road. TEST the system for normal operation.

LTV0500000004871

Fig. 13   Test J, Codes C1095, & C1096: ABS Hydraulic Pump Motor Failure (Part 1 of 2). Excursion & 2004-05 F-Super Duty

Test Step	Result / Action to Take
K1 CHECK FOR FAULT REPEATABILITY • Connect the diagnostic tool. • Enter the following diagnostic mode on the diagnostic tool: Clear Continuous DTCs. • Enter the following diagnostic mode on the diagnostic tool: Carry out the Anti-Lock Brake System (ABS) Module On-Demand Self-Test. • Enter the following diagnostic mode on the diagnostic tool: Retrieve DTCs. • **Are any DTCs retrieved?**	**Yes** If DTC C1113 or C1115 is retrieved, INSTALL a ABS module. TEST the system for normal operation. If DTC C1185 is retrieved, GO to <u>K2</u>. **No** If no DTCs are retrieved, TEST the system for normal operation.
K2 ELECTRICAL PRECHECKS • Key in OFF position. • Check fuse: CBJ Fuse 602 (60A). • **Is the fuse OK?**	**Yes** GO to <u>K3</u>. **No** INSTALL a new fuse. TEST the system for normal operation. If the fuse fails again, CHECK for a short to ground. REPAIR as necessary. TEST the system for normal operation.
K3 CHECK THE VOLTAGE TO THE ANTI-LOCK BRAKE SYSTEM (ABS) MODULE • Key in OFF position. • Disconnect: ABS Module C135. • Measure the voltage between ABS module C135 pins 9 and 25, circuit 532 (OG/YE) and ground. • **Is voltage greater than 10 volts?**	**Yes** INSTALL a new ABS module. CLEAR the DTCs. DRIVE the vehicle over rough roads and through a car wash. REPEAT the self-test. **No** REPAIR the circuit. CLEAR the DTCs. DRIVE the vehicle over rough roads and through a car wash. REPEAT the self-test.

LTV0500000004873

Fig. 14   Test K, Codes C1113, C1115 & C1185: ABS Power Relay Circuit Failure/Short To Battery. Excursion & 2004-06 F-Super Duty

Test Step	Result / Action to Take
L1 VERIFY THE CONNECTION BETWEEN THE DIAGNOSTIC TOOL AND THE DLC II CONNECTOR • Key in OFF position. • Reconnect the diagnostic tool to the DLC connector. • Enter the following diagnostic mode on the diagnostic tool: Retrieve and document continuous DTCs. • **Are DTCs obtained?**	**Yes** REFER to Diagnostic Trouble Code (DTC) Index. **No** GO to <u>L2</u>.
L2 CHECK THE IGNITION VOLTAGE TO THE HCU • Key in OFF position. • Install the EEC-IV 60-Pin Breakout Box. • Key in ON position. • Measure the voltage between the EEC-IV 60-Pin Breakout Box pin 16 and ground. • Is the voltage greater than 10 volts?	**Yes** GO to <u>L3</u>. **No** CHECK centrarl junction box (CJB) fuse 25 (10A) and/or REPAIR circuit 533 (TN/RD). TEST the system for normal operation.
L3 CHECK THE ABS GROUND • Key in OFF position. • Disconnect: ABS Module C135. • Disconnect the battery. • Measure the resistance between the ABS module C135 pins 8 and 24, circuit 530 (LG/RD), and ground. • Is the resistance less than 5 ohms?	**Yes** Check Communications Area Network (CAN) **No** REPAIR circuit 530 (LG/RD). TEST the system for normal operation.

LTV0500000004874

Fig. 15   Test L: No Communication w/ABS Module. Excursion & 2004-06 F-Super Duty

Test Step	Result / Action to Take
N1 CHECK FOR FAULT REPEATABILITY • Connect the diagnostic tool. • Enter the following diagnostic mode on the diagnostic tool: Clear Continuous DTCs. • Drive the vehicle at various speeds. • Enter the following diagnostic mode on the diagnostic tool: Retrieve and document continuous DTCs. • **Was a DTC retrieved and did the ABS activate during normal stops?**	**Yes** If DTC C1184 is retrieved and the ABS did not activate during normal stops, INSTALL a new ABS module. TEST the system for normal operation. If the ABS activated on normal stops, GO to <u>N2</u>. If DTC C1222 is retrieved, INSPECT the tires for mismatched sizes. INSPECT the sensor rings for damage. If inspections are normal, INSTALL a new ABS module. TEST the system for normal operation. If a different DTC is retrieved, REFER to the Anti-Lock Brake System (ABS) Module Diagnostic Trouble Code (DTC) Index. **No** System is OK. TEST the system for normal operation.
N2 CHECK FOR AN ERRATIC WHEEL SPEED SIGNAL • Enter the following diagnostic mode on the diagnostic tool: Clear Continuous DTCs. • Enter the following diagnostic mode on the diagnostic tool: Monitor the ABS module wheel speed PIDs while driving at various speeds. • **NOTE:** When using the diagnostic tool to monitor the wheel speed signals, monitor one wheel at a time. The information is recorded faster and the likelihood of diagnosing the faulty signal is greater. • **Does one wheel speed signal drop out while driving or braking?**	**Yes** <u>Go To Pinpoint Test C</u> (LF), <u>Go To Pinpoint Test E</u> (RF), <u>Go To Pinpoint Test G</u> (Rear). **No** REPEAT the monitoring of ABS module wheel speed PIDs. Intermittent signals may not be recorded the first time. INSPECT the sensor rings and sensor wiring for damage. If damage is found, REPAIR as necessary. If no damage is found, REFER to Component Test — Intermittent Failures for the suspect wheel sensor. TEST the system for normal operation.

LTV0500000004876

Fig. 17   Test N, Codes C1184 & C1222: ABS Time Out/Wheel Speed Error/Mismatch. Excursion & 2004-06 F-Super Duty

Test Step	Result / Action to Take
M1 CHECK FOR ANTI-LOCK BRAKE SYSTEM (ABS) MODULE DTCS • Connect the diagnostic tool. • Key in ON position. • Clear the DTCs and road test the vehicle. • Retrieve the DTCs. • **If DTC C1169 is present?**	**Yes** GO to <u>M2</u>. **No** System is operating correctly at this time.
M2 CHECK THE BASE BRAKE SYSTEM • Check the base brake system. • **Is the base brake system OK?**	**Yes** INSTALL a new HCU.. TEST the system for normal operation. **No** REPAIR the base brake system. TEST the system for normal operation.

LTV0500000004875

Fig. 16   Test M, Code C1169: Excessive Dump Time. Excursion & 2004-06 F-Super Duty

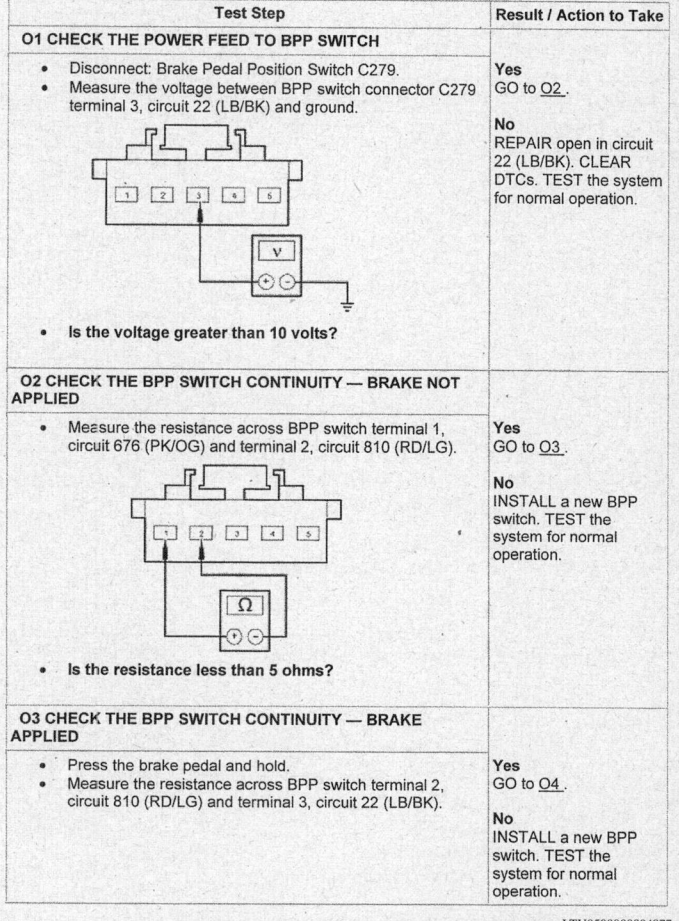

Test Step	Result / Action to Take
O1 CHECK THE POWER FEED TO BPP SWITCH • Disconnect: Brake Pedal Position Switch C279. • Measure the voltage between BPP switch connector C279 terminal 3, circuit 22 (LB/BK) and ground. • Is the voltage greater than 10 volts?	**Yes** GO to <u>O2</u>. **No** REPAIR open in circuit 22 (LB/BK). CLEAR DTCs. TEST the system for normal operation.
O2 CHECK THE BPP SWITCH CONTINUITY — BRAKE NOT APPLIED • Measure the resistance across BPP switch terminal 1, circuit 676 (PK/OG) and terminal 2, circuit 810 (RD/LG). • Is the resistance less than 5 ohms?	**Yes** GO to <u>O3</u>. **No** INSTALL a new BPP switch. TEST the system for normal operation.
O3 CHECK THE BPP SWITCH CONTINUITY — BRAKE APPLIED • Press the brake pedal and hold. • Measure the resistance across BPP switch terminal 2, circuit 810 (RD/LG) and terminal 3, circuit 22 (LB/BK).	**Yes** GO to <u>O4</u>. **No** INSTALL a new BPP switch. TEST the system for normal operation.

LTV0500000004877

Fig. 18   Test O, Code B1485: Brake Pedal Position (BPP) Switch Circuit Failure (Part 1 of 2). Excursion & 2004-05 F-Super Duty

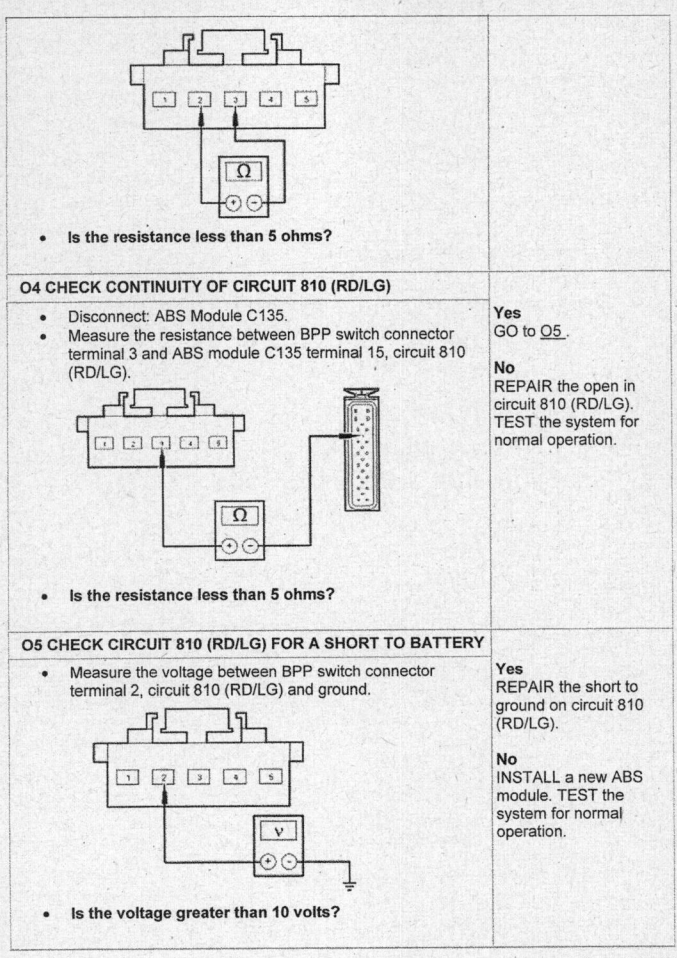

• **Is the resistance less than 5 ohms?**	
O4 CHECK CONTINUITY OF CIRCUIT 810 (RD/LG)	
• Disconnect: ABS Module C135. • Measure the resistance between BPP switch connector terminal 3 and ABS module C135 terminal 15, circuit 810 (RD/LG). • **Is the resistance less than 5 ohms?**	**Yes** GO to O5 . **No** REPAIR the open in circuit 810 (RD/LG). TEST the system for normal operation.
O5 CHECK CIRCUIT 810 (RD/LG) FOR A SHORT TO BATTERY	
• Measure the voltage between BPP switch connector terminal 2, circuit 810 (RD/LG) and ground. • **Is the voltage greater than 10 volts?**	**Yes** REPAIR the short to ground on circuit 810 (RD/LG). **No** INSTALL a new ABS module. TEST the system for normal operation.

LTV0500000004878

Fig. 18   Test O, Code B1485: Brake Pedal Position (BPP) Switch Circuit Failure (Part 2 of 2). Excursion & 2004-05 F-Super Duty

Test Step	Result / Action to Take
P1 CHECK THE YELLOW ABS WARNING INDICATOR OPERATION	
• Key in ON position. • Observe the yellow ABS warning indicator. • **Is the yellow ABS indicator illuminated at all times?**	**Yes** GO to P2 . **No** REFER to "Dash Gauges & Warning Indicators"
P2 CHECK CIRCUIT 533 (TN/RD) FOR AN OPEN	
• Key in OFF position. • Connect the EEC-IV 60-Pin Breakout Box. • Key in ON position. • Measure the voltage between the EEC-IV 60-Pin Breakout Box Pin 16, circuit 533 (TN/RD), and ground. • **Is the voltage greater than 10 volts?**	**Yes** GO to P3 . **No** REPAIR the circuit. REPEAT the self-test.
P3 CHECK CIRCUIT 530 (LG/RD) FOR AN OPEN	
• Key in OFF position. • Disconnect: ABS Module C135. • Measure the resistance between ABS module C135 pins 8 and 24, circuit 530 (LG/RD), and ground. • **Is the resistance less than 5 ohms?**	**Yes** GO to P4 . **No** REPAIR the circuit. REPEAT the self-test.

LTV0500000004879

Fig. 19   Test P: Yellow ABS Warning Indicator Does Not Self Check (Part 1 of 2). Excursion & 2004-06 F-Super Duty

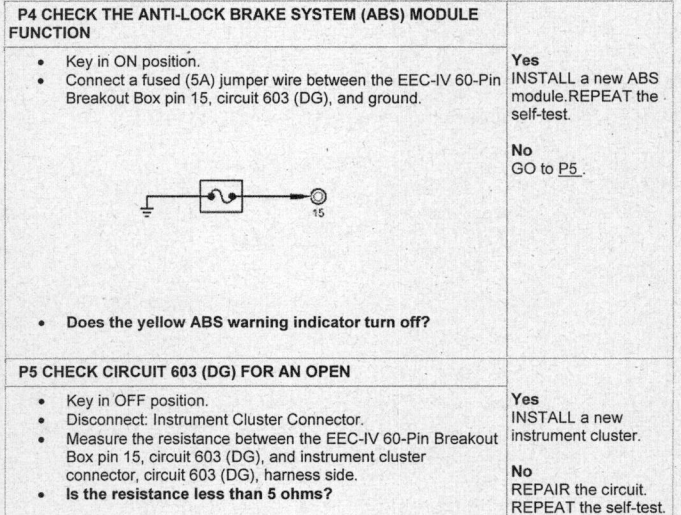

P4 CHECK THE ANTI-LOCK BRAKE SYSTEM (ABS) MODULE FUNCTION	
• Key in ON position. • Connect a fused (5A) jumper wire between the EEC-IV 60-Pin Breakout Box pin 15, circuit 603 (DG), and ground. • **Does the yellow ABS warning indicator turn off?**	**Yes** INSTALL a new ABS module. REPEAT the self-test. **No** GO to P5 .
P5 CHECK CIRCUIT 603 (DG) FOR AN OPEN	
• Key in OFF position. • Disconnect: Instrument Cluster Connector. • Measure the resistance between the EEC-IV 60-Pin Breakout Box pin 15, circuit 603 (DG), and instrument cluster connector, circuit 603 (DG), harness side. • **Is the resistance less than 5 ohms?**	**Yes** INSTALL a new instrument cluster. **No** REPAIR the circuit. REPEAT the self-test.

LTV0500000004880

Fig. 19   Test P: Yellow ABS Warning Indicator Does Not Self Check (Part 2 of 2). Excursion & 2004-06 F-Super Duty

Test Step	Result / Action to Take
Q1 CHECK FOR FAULT REPEATABILITY	
• Connect the diagnostic tool. • Enter the following diagnostic mode on the diagnostic tool: Clear Continuous DTCs. • Drive the vehicle at least 16 km/h (10 mph). • Retrieve and document continuous DTCs. • **Are any DTCs retrieved?**	**Yes** GO to Q2 . **No** If no DTCs are retrieved, RETURN vehicle to owner. If a different DTC is retrieved, GO to the Anti-Lock Brake System (ABS) Diagnostic Trouble Code (DTC) Index.
Q2 CHECK THE IGNITION FEED VOLTAGE	
• Disconnect the wiring at the ABS module. • Start the engine. • Read the voltage across ABS connector pin 16, circuit 533 (TN/RD) and pin 8, circuit 530 (LG/YE). • **Is the voltage greater than 16.6 volts or less than 9.2 volts?**	**Yes** CHECK the charging system. **No** INSTALL a new ABS module. CLEAR DTCs and ROAD TEST.

LTV0500000004881

Fig. 20   Test Q, Code B1676: Voltage Out Of Range. Excursion & F-Super Duty

Expedition & Navigator

NOTE: Electrical Symbol & Wire Color Code Identification Located In The Front Of This Manual May Be Used As An Aid When Using Wiring Circuits Found In This Section.

NOTE: Refer To "Computer Relearn Procedures" Located In The Front Of This Manual When Battery Power To The Computer Has Been Interrupted.

INDEX

	Page No.
Description	5-85
Diagnosis & Testing	5-85
Accessing Diagnostic Trouble Codes	5-85
Clearing Diagnostic Trouble Codes	5-85
Diagnostic Tests	5-85
Pinpoint Tests	5-85
Diagnostic Trouble Code Interpretation	5-85

	Page No.
Wiring Diagrams	5-85
Diagnostic Chart Index	5-88
Precautions	5-85
Battery Ground Cable	5-85
Brake Fluid Handling	5-85
System Service	5-86
Brake System Bleed	5-86
Component Replacement	5-86
ABS Control Module	5-86
Hydraulic Control Unit (HCU)	5-86

	Page No.
Stability Control Sensor Cluster	5-86
Steering Wheel Rotation Sensor	5-86
Wheel Speed Sensor	5-86
Troubleshooting	5-85
Symptom Chart	5-85

PRECAUTIONS

BATTERY GROUND CABLE

Prior to service disconnect battery ground cable and isolate as required.

BRAKE FLUID HANDLING

Brake fluid can cause serious injury and vehicle damage if not handled properly. Avoid contact with eyes and do not allow fluid to splash or spill on painted surfaces. Wash hands thoroughly after handling.

DESCRIPTION

The anti-lock brake system (ABS) module, with or without stability assist, simultaneously manages the anti-lock braking, traction control and engine control systems to maintain vehicle control during deceleration and acceleration. The ABS accomplishes this by communicating with the other modules over the high speed controller area network (HS-CAN) bus.

When the ignition switch is in the RUN position, the module carries out a preliminary electrical check and, at approximately 20 km/h (12 mph), the hydraulic pump motor is turned on for approximately one half-second. Any malfunction of the anti-lock brake system disables the traction control and stability assist (if equipped). The ABS module communicates with the instrument cluster over the HS-CAN bus and the cluster illuminates the anti-lock brake warning indicator. However, the power-assist braking system functions normally.

With the ignition switch in the START or RUN positions, the stability assist module functions similarly to a conventional ABS module by monitoring and comparing the rotational speed of each wheel. The wheel speed sensors electrically sense each tooth of the anti-lock sensor ring as they pass through the sensor magnetic field. When the stability assist module detects an impending wheel lock, wheel spin or vehicle motion that is inconsistent with the driver commands, it modulates brake pressure to the appropriate brake caliper(s). The stability assist module triggers the hydraulic control unit (HCU) to open and close the appropriate solenoid valves. Once the affected wheel(s) returns to the desired speed, the stability assist module returns the solenoid valves to their normal position, and normal base brake operation is restored.

TROUBLESHOOTING

Symptom Chart

Refer to **Figs. 1 and 2** for symptom charts.

DIAGNOSIS & TESTING

Accessing Diagnostic Trouble Codes

Connect a suitably programmed scan tool and Vehicle Communication Module (VCM) with appropriate adapters, or equivalents, to the Data Link Connector (DCL) located in the passenger compartment beneath the instrument panel. Follow tool manufacturer's instructions for accessing Diagnostic Trouble Codes (DTC).

Diagnostic Trouble Code Interpretation

Refer to **Figs. 3** for diagnostic trouble code interpretation.

Wiring Diagrams

Refer to **Fig. 4** for wiring diagrams.

Diagnostic Tests

PINPOINT TESTS

2002–03

Refer to **Figs. 5 through 20** for pinpoint tests.

2004–06

Refer to **Figs. 21 through 36** for pinpoint tests.

Clearing Diagnostic Trouble Codes

Connect a suitably programmed scan tool and Vehicle Communication Module (VCM) with appropriate adapters, or equivalents, to the Data Link Connector (DCL) located in the passenger compartment beneath the instrument panel. Follow tool

Condition	Possible Source	Action
• No communication with the anti-lock brake control module	• CJB Fuse 25 (5A). • Circuitry. • Anti-lock brake control module.	• GO to Pinpoint Test A.
• Unable to enter self-test	• Anti-lock brake control module.	• GO to Pinpoint Test B.
• ABS misfire, ABS too sensitive, ABS fires on normal stop	• Rear anti-lock brake sensor indicator. • Front anti-lock brake sensor indicator(s). • Sensor output. • Sensor circuitry. • Wire insulation. • Rear brake adjustment. • Linings. • Loose anti-lock brake sensor bolt(s).	• REMOVE the rear sensor from the differential housing; INSPECT rear anti-lock brake sensor indicator. • INSPECT for damaged teeth. INSPECT both front anti-lock brake sensor indicator(s). • If left front anti-lock brake sensor output is out of sync, GO to Pinpoint Test F. If right front anti-lock brake sensor output is out of sync, GO to Pinpoint Test H. If rear anti-lock brake sensor output is out of sync, GO to Pinpoint Test J. • INSPECT circuits 514 (YE/RD), 516 (YE/BK), 521 (TN/OG), 522 (TN/BK), 523 (RD/PK) and 519 (LG/BK). • INSPECT the wiring harness from the front anti-lock brake sensor knuckle to the frame and from the rear axle to the frame for worn or chafed wire insulation. • ELIMINATE the base brake system as the cause of the problem. • TIGHTEN the anti-lock brake sensor bolt(s) to specification.
• Wheels lock up	• Hydraulic outlet (dump) valve. • Leaky inlet (isolation) valve during ABS (soft). • Rear brake shoe linings. • Wheel cylinder. • Rear brakes adjustment. • Parking brake. • Rear axle seal.	• GO to Pinpoint Test K. • ELIMINATE the base brake system as cause of the problem.

FM4029901472010X

Fig. 1   Symptom chart (Part 1 of 3). 2002–03

manufacturer's instructions for clearing Diagnostic Trouble Codes (DTC).

SYSTEM SERVICE

Brake System Bleed

Refer to "Hydraulic Brake Systems" chapter for bleeding procedure.

Component Replacement

HYDRAULIC CONTROL UNIT (HCU)

1. Disconnect ABS control module electrical connector.
2. Disconnect hydraulic brake lines.
3. Remove HCU unit retaining bolts, then the HCU.
4. Remove HCU bracket, if required.
5. Reverse procedure to install, noting the following:
   a. **Torque** HCU to bracket bolts to 80 inch lbs.
   b. **Torque** brake lines to 13 ft. lbs.
   c. **Torque** control module retaining screws to 18 inch lbs.

ABS CONTROL MODULE

1. Disconnect pump motor electrical connector from ABS module.
2. Remove ABS control module retaining screws, then the module.
3. Reverse procedure to install. **Torque** ABS control module retaining screws to 18 inch lbs.

STABILITY CONTROL SENSOR CLUSTER

1. Remove driver side front seat.
2. Remove lower B-pillar trim panel.
3. Fold back carpeting flap to gain access to sensor cluster.
4. Disconnect sensor cluster electrical connector.
5. Remove sensor cluster mounting bolts, then the sensor cluster.
6. Reverse procedure to install. **Torque** mounting bolts to 108 inch lbs.

STEERING WHEEL ROTATION SENSOR

1. Remove lefthand instrument panel under cover.
2. Remove two rotation sensor to steering column retaining screws.
3. Remove steering wheel rotation sensor.
4. Reverse procedure to install. **Torque** sensor bolts to 35 inch lbs.

WHEEL SPEED SENSOR

FRONT

1. **On models equipped with 4WD,** remove rotor shield and rotor.

Condition	Possible Source	Action
• Hard or soft brake pedal	• Inlet (isolation) valve (hard brake pedal) or outlet (dump) valve (soft brake pedal). • Brake line or hose, fitting, master cylinder, wheel cylinder or caliper (soft brake pedal). • Air in brake system (soft brake pedal). • Vacuum boost (hard brake pedal). • Wheel cylinder or caliper (hard brake pedal). • Brake line or hose (hard brake pedal).	• GO to Pinpoint Test K. • ELIMINATE the base brake system as cause of the problem.
• Lack of deceleration during medium/hard brake application	• Shut inlet (isolation) valve or outlet (dump) valve (rear axle only). • Brake line or hose, fitting, master cylinder, wheel cylinder or caliper. • Air in brake system. • Vacuum boost. • Wheel cylinder or caliper. • Brake shoe or pad linings.	• GO to Pinpoint Test K. • ELIMINATE the base brake system as cause of the problem.
• Vehicle pulls during braking	• Rear brake adjustment. • Caliper. • Brake pad or shoe. • Brake line or hose. • Front inlet (isolation) valve.	• ELIMINATE the base brake system as cause of the problem. • INSTALL a new hydraulic control unit (HCU)
• Soft/excessive pedal travel	• Electronic hydraulic control unit (EHCU). • Outlet (dump) valve. • Base brake system. • Air in the system.	• GO to Pinpoint Test K. • ELIMINATE the base brake system as cause of the problem.
• The yellow ABS warning indicator does not self-check	• Circuitry. • Yellow ABS warning indicator bulb. • Anti-lock brake control module. • Instrument cluster.	• GO to Pinpoint Test P.
• ABS warning lamp on with system pass	• ABS warning lamp circuit short to ground.	• DISCONNECT the 24-pin connector from the anti-lock brake module. If the lamp is on, REPAIR short to ground in Circuit 603 (DG). If lamp is off, INSTALL a new anti-lock brake control module.

FM4029901472020X

Fig. 1   Symptom chart (Part 2 of 3). 2002–03

Condition	Possible Source	Action
• Spongy brake pedal with no warning indicator	• Outlet (dump) valve. • Brake line or hose, fitting, master cylinder, wheel cylinder or caliper. • Air in the system.	• GO to Pinpoint Test K. • ELIMINATE the base brake system as cause of the problem.

FM4029901472030X

Fig. 1   Symptom chart (Part 3 of 3). 2002–03

2. **On all models,** raise and support vehicle.
3. Disconnect wheel speed sensor wire from vehicle frame.
4. Remove sensor retaining bolt, then the sensor.
5. Reverse procedure to install, noting the following:
   a. **Torque** wheel speed sensor retaining bolt to 96–108 inch lbs.
   b. Apply high temperature 4X4 front axle and wheel bearing grease E8TZ-19590-A, or equivalent, meeting Ford specification ESA-MIC198-A to sensor mounting surface.

REAR

1. Raise and support vehicle.
2. Clean area around wheel speed sensor.
3. Disconnect wheel speed sensor electrical connector.
4. Remove sensor retaining bolt, then the sensor.
5. Reverse procedure to install. **Torque** wheel speed sensor retaining bolt to 13 ft. lbs.

Condition	Possible Sources	Action
• No communication with the anti-lock brake system (ABS) module	• Battery junction box (BJB) fuse(s): ▪ 16 (10A) ▪ 103 (30A) ▪ 112 (30A) • Circuitry. • ABS module.	Go To Pinpoint Test A
• The red brake warning indicator stays on when the ignition switch is in the RUN position	• Circuitry. • Instrument cluster. • Brake fluid level sensor. • Anti-lock brake system (ABS) module.	• REFER to "Dash Gauges & Warning Indicators".
• The yellow anti-lock brake warning indicator does not self-check	• Anti-lock brake system (ABS) module. • Circuitry.	• REFER to "Dash Gauges & Warning Indicators".
• The stability assist system cannot be disabled	• Circuitry. • Stability assist switch. • Anti-lock brake system (ABS) module.	• Go To Pinpoint Test N
• The stability assist switch indicator is never/always on	• Central junction box (CJB) fuse 15 (5A). • Circuitry. • Stability assist switch. • Anti-lock brake system (ABS) module.	• Go To Pinpoint Test P
	• Base brake system.	• Check base brake system.
	• Thermal model.	• Wait for brakes to cool down; the thermal model will reset automatically.

LTV0500000005372

Fig. 2   Symptom chart. 2004-06

DTCs	Description
B1342	Anti-Lock Brake Control Module Failure
C1095/C1096	Pump Motor
C1113/C1115	Internal Power Relay
C1145	Right Front Wheel Speed Sensor (Electrical/Static)
C1148/C1234	Right Front Wheel Speed Sensor (Dynamic)
C1155	Left Front Wheel Speed Sensor (Electrical/Static)
C1158/C1233	Left Front Wheel Speed Sensor (Dynamic)
C1169	Excessive Dump Time
C1184	ABS System Timeout
C1185	Open Internal Power Relay
C1194/C1196	Dump Valve, Front Left
C1198/C1200	Isolation Valve, Front Left
C1202/C1204	Dump Valve, Rear
C1206/C1208	Isolation Valve, Rear
C1210/C1212	Dump Valve, Front Right
C1214/C1216	Isolation Valve, Front Right
C1220	Yellow Anti-Lock Brake System (ABS) Warning Indicator Failure
C1222	Wheel Speed Error (Dynamic)
C1229/C1237	Rear Wheel Speed Sensor (Dynamic)
C1230	Rear Wheel Speed Sensor (Electrical/Static)

FM4029901471000X

Fig. 3   Diagnostic trouble code interpretation. 2002–03

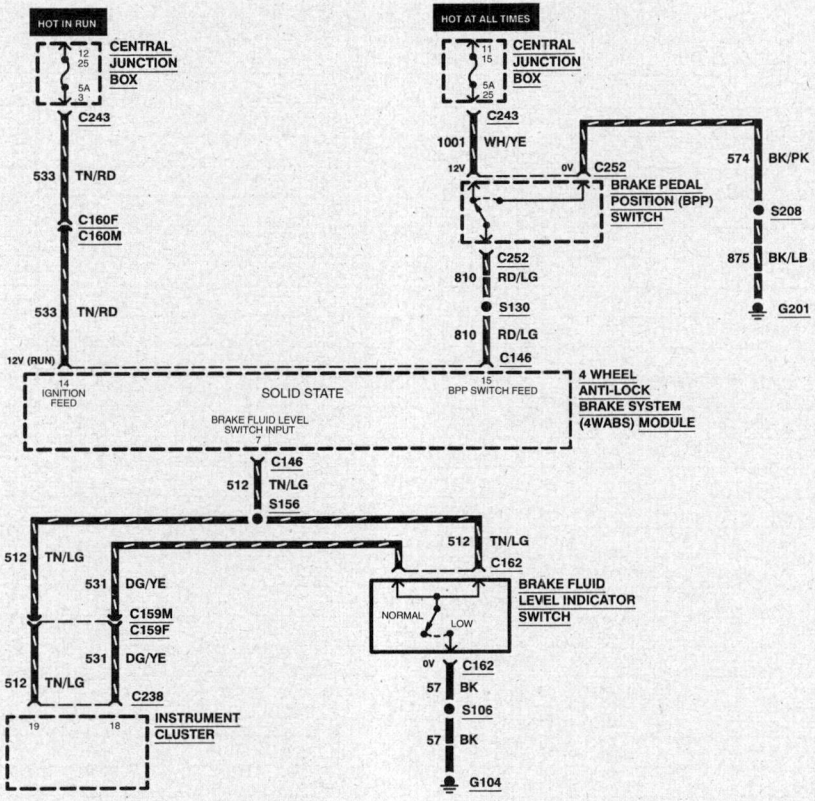

FM4029901489010X

Fig. 4   Wiring diagram (Part 1 of 2). 2002–03

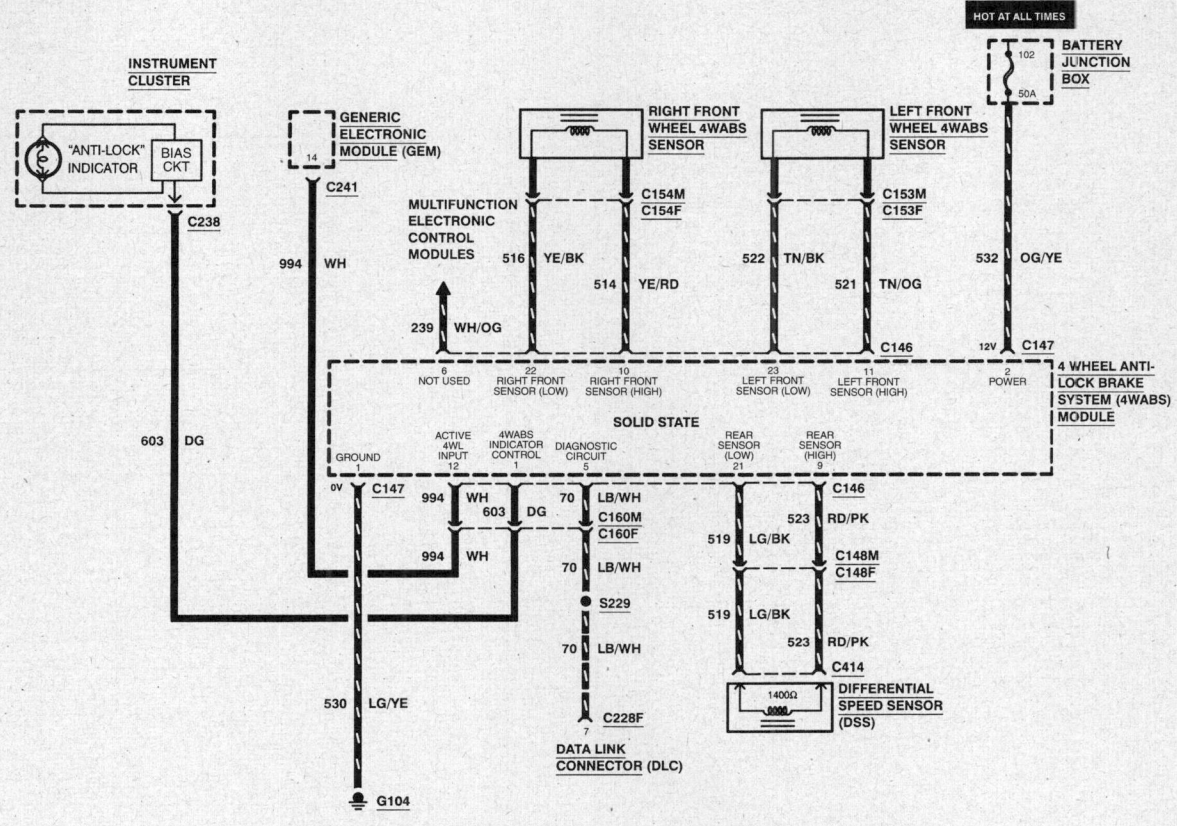

Fig. 4   Wiring diagram (Part 2 of 2). 2002–03

FM4029901489020X

DIAGNOSTIC CHART INDEX

Test		Description	Page No.	Fig. No.
2002–03				
A	—	No Communication w/ABS Control Module	5-90	5
B	—	Unable To Enter Self Test	5-90	6
C	C1220	Yellow ABS Warning Indicator Failure	5-90	7
D	C1194	Isolation Valve, Dump Valve	5-91	8
	C1196	Isolation Valve, Dump Valve	5-91	8
	C1198	Isolation Valve, Dump Valve	5-91	8
	C1200	Isolation Valve, Dump Valve	5-91	8
	C1202	Isolation Valve, Dump Valve	5-91	8
	C1204	Isolation Valve, Dump Valve	5-91	8
	C1206	Isolation Valve, Dump Valve	5-91	8
	C1208	Isolation Valve, Dump Valve	5-91	8
	C1210	Isolation Valve, Dump Valve	5-91	8
	C1212	Isolation Valve, Dump Valve	5-91	8
	C1214	Isolation Valve, Dump Valve	5-91	8
	C1216	Isolation Valve, Dump Valve	5-91	8
E	C1155	Left Front Wheel Speed Sensor, Electrical/Static	5-91	9
F	C1158	Left Front Wheel Speed Sensor, Dynamic	5-92	10
	C1233	Left Front Wheel Speed Sensor, Dynamic	5-92	10
G	C1145	Right Front Wheel Speed Sensor, Electrical/Static	5-93	11
H	C1148	Right Front Wheel Speed Sensor, Dynamic	5-94	12
	C1234	Right Front Wheel Speed Sensor, Dynamic	5-94	12
I	C1230	Rear Wheel Speed Sensor, Electrical/Static	5-95	13
J	C1229	Rear Wheel Speed Sensor, Dynamic	5-96	14
	C1237	Rear Wheel Speed Sensor, Dynamic	5-96	14
K	—	Soft/Excessive Pedal Travel	5-97	15

Continued

DIAGNOSTIC CHART INDEX—Continued

Test		Description	Page No.	Fig. No.
2002–03				
L	C1095	Pump Motor	5-98	16
	C1096	Pump Motor	5-98	16
M	C1113	Internal Power Relay	5-98	17
	C1115	Internal Power Relay	5-98	17
	C1185	Internal Power Relay	5-98	17
N	C1184	ABS System Time-Out/Wheel Speed Error	5-98	18
	C1222	ABS System Time-Out/Wheel Speed Error	5-98	18
O	C1169	Excessive Dump Time	5-99	19
P	—	Yellow ABS Warning Indicator Does Not Self Check	5-99	20
2004–06				
A	—	No Communication w/ABS Module	5-100	21
B	B1483	Brake Pedal Input Circuit Failure	5-100	22
C	B1676	Battery Pack Voltage Out Of Range	5-101	23
D	C1095	ABS Hydraulic Pump Motor Circuit Failure	5-101	24
E	C1145	Wheel Speed Sensor Input Circuit Failure	5-102	25
	C1155	Wheel Speed Sensor Input Circuit Failure	5-102	25
	C1165	Wheel Speed Sensor Input Circuit Failure	5-102	25
	C1175	Wheel Speed Sensor Input Circuit Failure	5-102	25
F	C1233	Wheel Speed Sensor Input Signal Missing	5-102	26
	C1234	Wheel Speed Sensor Input Signal Missing	5-102	26
	C1235	Wheel Speed Sensor Input Signal Missing	5-102	26
	C1236	Wheel Speed Sensor Input Signal Missing	5-102	26
G	C1277	Steering Wheel Angle 1 & 2 Circuit Failure/Signal Fault	5-103	27
	C1278	Steering Wheel Angle 1 & 2 Circuit Failure/Signal Fault	5-103	27
H	C1279	Sensor Cluster Fault	5-104	28
	C1280	Sensor Cluster Fault	5-104	28
	C1281	Sensor Cluster Fault	5-104	28
	C1282	Sensor Cluster Fault	5-104	28
	C1516	Sensor Cluster Fault	5-104	28
	C1517	Sensor Cluster Fault	5-104	28
	C2769	Sensor Cluster Fault	5-104	28
	C2777	Sensor Cluster Fault	5-104	28
	C2778	Sensor Cluster Fault	5-104	28
I	C1285	Booster Solenoid Circuit Failure	5-105	29
J	C1287	Brake Booster Pedal Force Switch Circuit Failure	5-106	30
K	C1288	ABS w/Stability Assist, Brake Pressure Sensor Input Circuit Failure/Signal Fault	5-107	31
	C1440	ABS w/Stability Assist, Brake Pressure Sensor Input Circuit Failure/Signal Fault	5-107	31
L	C1730	Reference Voltage Out Of Range	5-108	32
M	B2734	Pedal Travel Sensor Fault	5-108	33
	B2736	Pedal Travel Sensor Fault	5-108	33
	B2737	Pedal Travel Sensor Fault	5-108	33
	B2738	Pedal Travel Sensor Fault	5-108	33
	B2740	Pedal Travel Sensor Fault	5-108	33
N	—	Stability Assist Cannot Be Disabled	5-109	34
O	C1998	Module Calibration Not Complete	5-110	35
P	—	Stability Assist Switch Indicator Is Never/Always On	5-110	36

TEST CONDITIONS	TESTDETAILS/RESULTS/ACTIONS
A1 VERIFY THE CONNECTION BETWEEN NGS AND THE DLC	
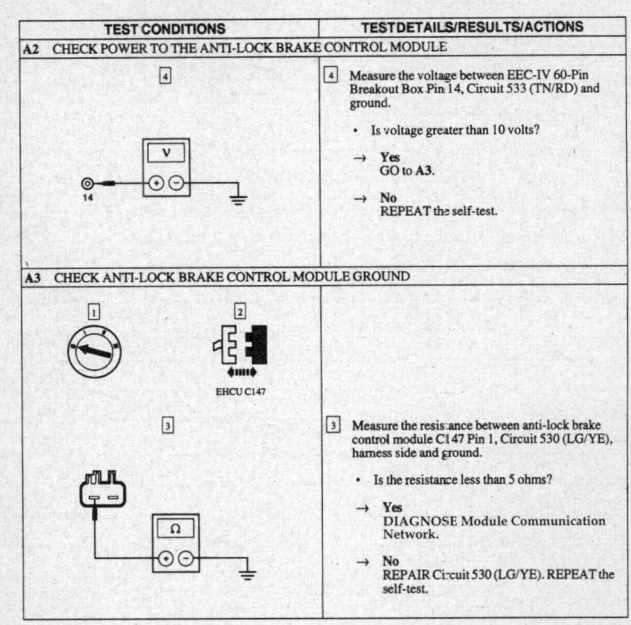	[2] Reconnect NGS Tester to the DLC connector. [3] Retrieve and document continuous DTCs. • Are DTCs obtained? → **Yes** REFER to Diagnostic Chart Index. → **No** GO to A2.
A2 CHECK POWER TO THE ANTI-LOCK BRAKE CONTROL MODULE	
	[2] Connect EEC-IV 60-Pin Breakout Box.

FM4029901473010X

Fig. 5 Test A: No Communication w/ABS Control Module (Part 1 of 2). 2002-03

TEST CONDITIONS	TESTDETAILS/RESULTS/ACTIONS
A2 CHECK POWER TO THE ANTI-LOCK BRAKE CONTROL MODULE	
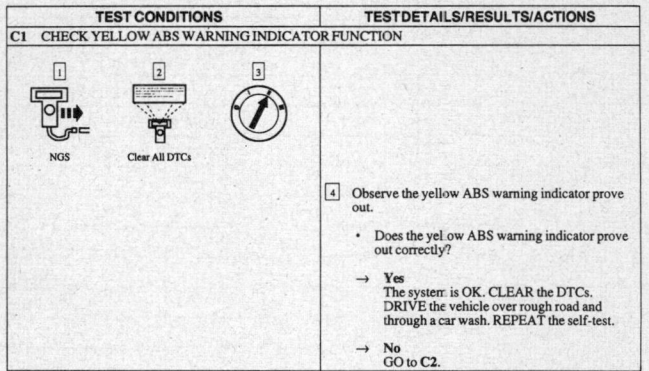	[4] Measure the voltage between EEC-IV 60-Pin Breakout Box Pin 14, Circuit 533 (TN/RD) and ground. • Is voltage greater than 10 volts? → **Yes** GO to A3. → **No** REPEAT the self-test.
A3 CHECK ANTI-LOCK BRAKE CONTROL MODULE GROUND	
	[3] Measure the resistance between anti-lock brake control module C147 Pin 1, Circuit 530 (LG/YE), harness side and ground. • Is the resistance less than 5 ohms? → **Yes** DIAGNOSE Module Communication Network. → **No** REPAIR Circuit 530 (LG/YE). REPEAT the self-test.

FM4029901473020X

Fig. 5 Test A: No Communication w/ABS Control Module (Part 2 of 2). 2002-03

TEST CONDITIONS	TESTDETAILS/RESULTS/ACTIONS
B1 CHECK THE COMMUNICATIONS TO THE ANTI-LOCK BRAKE CONTROL MODULE	
	[1] Check the communication to the anti-lock brake control module. • Does NGS Tester communicate with the anti-lock brake control module? → **Yes** INSTALL a new anti-lock brake control module. REPEAT the self-test. → **No** GO to Pinpoint Test A.

FM4029901474000X

Fig. 6 Test B: Unable To Enter Self Test. 2002-03

TEST CONDITIONS	TESTDETAILS/RESULTS/ACTIONS
C1 CHECK YELLOW ABS WARNING INDICATOR FUNCTION	
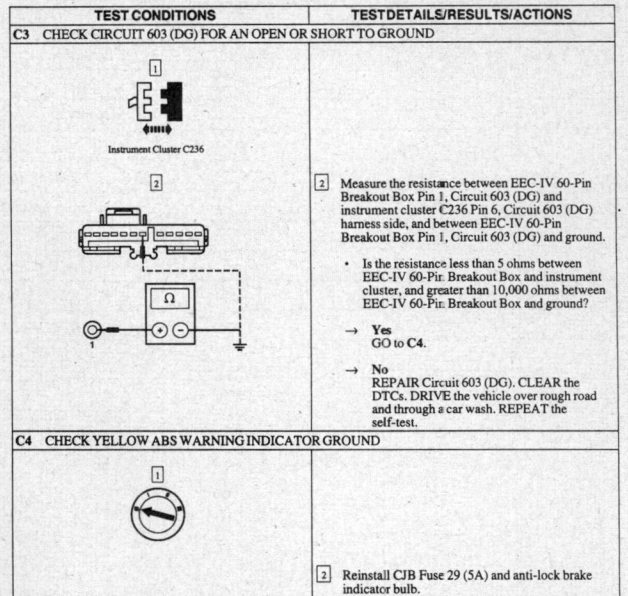	[4] Observe the yellow ABS warning indicator prove out. • Does the yellow ABS warning indicator prove out correctly? → **Yes** The system is OK. CLEAR the DTCs. DRIVE the vehicle over rough road and through a car wash. REPEAT the self-test. → **No** GO to C2.

FM4029901475010X

Fig. 7 Test C: Code C1220: Yellow ABS Warning Indicator Failure (Part 1 of 4). 2002-03

TEST CONDITIONS	TESTDETAILS/RESULTS/ACTIONS
C2 DETERMINE IF THE CAUSE OF THE PROBLEM IS IN THE ANTI-LOCK BRAKE CONTROL MODULE OR THE WIRING	
	[3] Connect EEC-IV 60-Pin Breakout Box. [4] Remove CJB Fuse 29 (5A). [7] **NOTE:** Start wiggling the circuit at the endpoints or splices, and work towards the middle. Measure the voltage between EEC-IV 60-Pin Breakout Box Pin 1, Circuit 603 (DG) and ground while wiggling Circuit 603 (DG). • Is the voltage greater than 0 volts at any time? → **Yes** REPAIR Circuit 603 (DG). CLEAR the DTCs. DRIVE the vehicle over rough road and through a car wash. REPEAT the self-test. → **No** GO to C3.

FM4029901475020X

Fig. 7 Test C: Code C1220: Yellow ABS Warning Indicator Failure (Part 2 of 4). 2002-03

TEST CONDITIONS	TESTDETAILS/RESULTS/ACTIONS
C3 CHECK CIRCUIT 603 (DG) FOR AN OPEN OR SHORT TO GROUND	
	[2] Measure the resistance between EEC-IV 60-Pin Breakout Box Pin 1, Circuit 603 (DG) and instrument cluster C236 Pin 6, Circuit 603 (DG) harness side, and between EEC-IV 60-Pin Breakout Box Pin 1, Circuit 603 (DG) and ground. • Is the resistance less than 5 ohms between EEC-IV 60-Pin Breakout Box and instrument cluster, and greater than 10,000 ohms between EEC-IV 60-Pin Breakout Box and ground? → **Yes** GO to C4. → **No** REPAIR Circuit 603 (DG). CLEAR the DTCs. DRIVE the vehicle over rough road and through a car wash. REPEAT the self-test.
C4 CHECK YELLOW ABS WARNING INDICATOR GROUND	
	[2] Reinstall CJB Fuse 29 (5A) and anti-lock brake indicator bulb.

FM4029901475030X

Fig. 7 Test C: Code C1220: Yellow ABS Warning Indicator Failure (Part 3 of 4). 2002-03

TEST CONDITIONS	TEST DETAILS/RESULTS/ACTIONS
C4 CHECK YELLOW ABS WARNING INDICATOR GROUND	

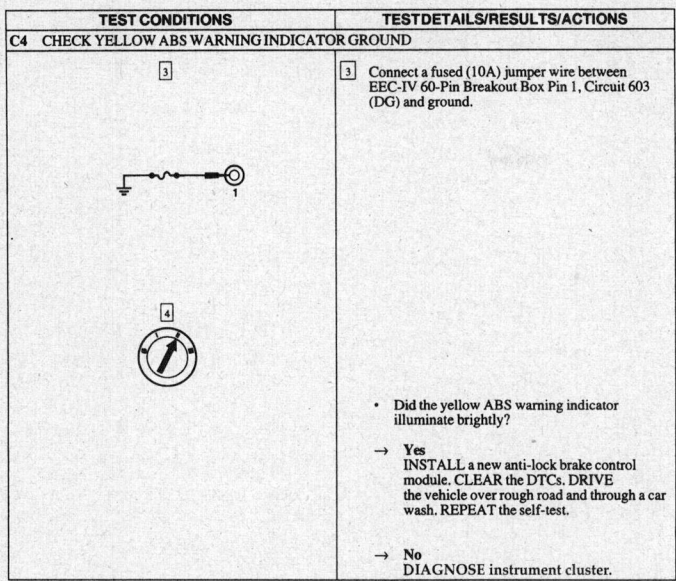

	3 Connect a fused (10A) jumper wire between EEC-IV 60-Pin Breakout Box Pin 1, Circuit 603 (DG) and ground.
	• Did the yellow ABS warning indicator illuminate brightly?
	→ **Yes** INSTALL a new anti-lock brake control module. CLEAR the DTCs. DRIVE the vehicle over rough road and through a car wash. REPEAT the self-test.
	→ **No** DIAGNOSE instrument cluster.

FM4029901475040X

Fig. 7 Test C: Code C1220: Yellow ABS Warning Indicator Failure (Part 4 of 4). 2002-03

TEST CONDITIONS	TEST DETAILS/RESULTS/ACTIONS
E1 CHECK FOR FAULT REPEATABILITY	

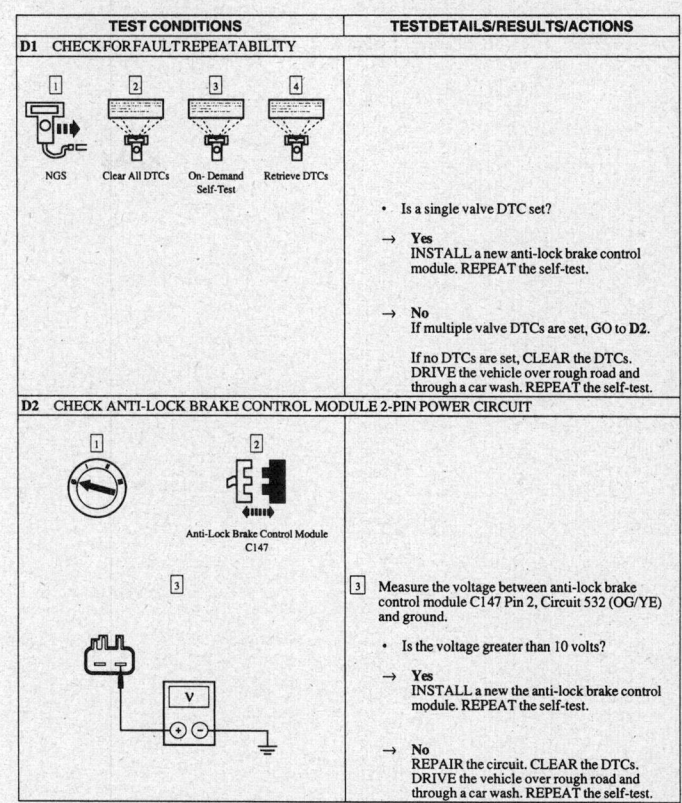

	3 Drive the vehicle over speeds of 16 km/h (10 mph).
	• Is DTC C1155 retrieved?
	→ **Yes** GO to **E2**.
	→ **No** If no DTCs are retrieved, GO to **E6**. If a different DTC is retrieved, REFER to Diagnostic Chart Index.
E2 CHECK SENSOR COIL RESISTANCE AT ANTI-LOCK BRAKE CONTROL MODULE CONNECTOR	
	2 Connect EEC-IV 60-Pin Breakout Box.

FM4029901477010X

Fig. 9 Test E: Code C1155: Left Front Wheel Speed Sensor, Electrical/Static (Part 1 of 4). 2002-03

TEST CONDITIONS	TEST DETAILS/RESULTS/ACTIONS
D1 CHECK FOR FAULT REPEATABILITY	

NGS   Clear All DTCs   On-Demand Self-Test   Retrieve DTCs

	• Is a single valve DTC set?
	→ **Yes** INSTALL a new anti-lock brake control module. REPEAT the self-test.
	→ **No** If multiple valve DTCs are set, GO to **D2**. If no DTCs are set, CLEAR the DTCs. DRIVE the vehicle over rough road and through a car wash. REPEAT the self-test.
D2 CHECK ANTI-LOCK BRAKE CONTROL MODULE 2-PIN POWER CIRCUIT	
Anti-Lock Brake Control Module C147	3 Measure the voltage between anti-lock brake control module C147 Pin 2, Circuit 532 (OG/YE) and ground.
	• Is the voltage greater than 10 volts?
	→ **Yes** INSTALL a new the anti-lock brake control module. REPEAT the self-test.
	→ **No** REPAIR the circuit. CLEAR the DTCs. DRIVE the vehicle over rough road and through a car wash. REPEAT the self-test.

FM4029901476000X

Fig. 8 Test D: Codes C1194, C1196, C1198, C1200, C1202, C1204, C1206, C1208, C1210, C1212, C1214 & C1216: Isolation Valve, Dump Valve. 2002-03

TEST CONDITIONS	TEST DETAILS/RESULTS/ACTIONS
E2 CHECK SENSOR COIL RESISTANCE AT ANTI-LOCK BRAKE CONTROL MODULE CONNECTOR	
	3 Measure the resistance between EEC-IV 60-Pin Breakout Box Pin 11, Circuit 521 (TN/OG), and EEC-IV 60-Pin Breakout Box Pin 23, Circuit 522 (TN/BK).
	• Is the resistance between 2,000 and 4,000 ohms for 4x2 vehicles, and between 300 and 500 ohms for 4x4 vehicles?
	→ **Yes** GO to **E4**.
	→ **No** If the resistance is below 2,000 ohms for 4x2 vehicles or below 300 ohms for 4x4 vehicles, INSTALL a new LF anti-lock brake sensor CLEAR the DTCs. DRIVE the vehicle over rough road and through a car wash. REPEAT the self-test. If the resistance is greater than 4,000 ohms for 4x2 vehicles or greater than 500 ohms for 4x4 vehicles, GO to **E3**.

FM4029901477020X

Fig. 9 Test E: Code C1155: Left Front Wheel Speed Sensor, Electrical/Static (Part 2 of 4). 2002-03

TEST CONDITIONS	TESTDETAILS/RESULTS/ACTIONS
E3 DETERMINE LOCATION OF FAULT	

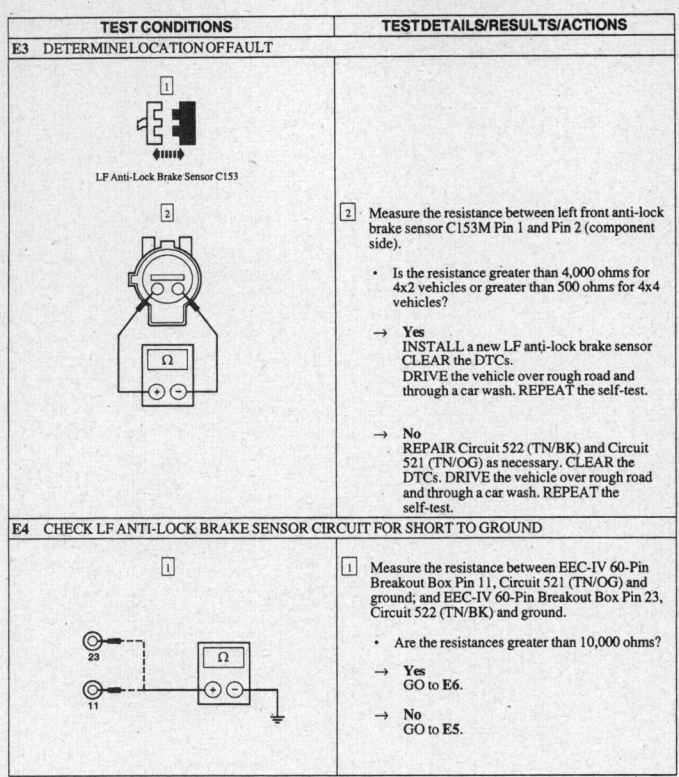

LF Anti-Lock Brake Sensor C153

2   Measure the resistance between left front anti-lock brake sensor C153M Pin 1 and Pin 2 (component side).

- Is the resistance greater than 4,000 ohms for 4x2 vehicles or greater than 500 ohms for 4x4 vehicles?

→ **Yes**
INSTALL a new LF anti-lock brake sensor CLEAR the DTCs.
DRIVE the vehicle over rough road and through a car wash. REPEAT the self-test.

→ **No**
REPAIR Circuit 522 (TN/BK) and Circuit 521 (TN/OG) as necessary. CLEAR the DTCs. DRIVE the vehicle over rough road and through a car wash. REPEAT the self-test.

TEST CONDITIONS	TESTDETAILS/RESULTS/ACTIONS
E4 CHECK LF ANTI-LOCK BRAKE SENSOR CIRCUIT FOR SHORT TO GROUND	

1   Measure the resistance between EEC-IV 60-Pin Breakout Box Pin 11, Circuit 521 (TN/OG) and ground; and EEC-IV 60-Pin Breakout Box Pin 23, Circuit 522 (TN/BK) and ground.

- Are the resistances greater than 10,000 ohms?

→ **Yes**
GO to E6.

→ **No**
GO to E5.

FM4029901477030X

Fig. 9   Test E: Code C1155: Left Front Wheel Speed Sensor, Electrical/Static (Part 3 of 4). 2002-03

TEST CONDITIONS	TESTDETAILS/RESULTS/ACTIONS
E5 CHECK FOR INTERNAL SENSOR SHORT	

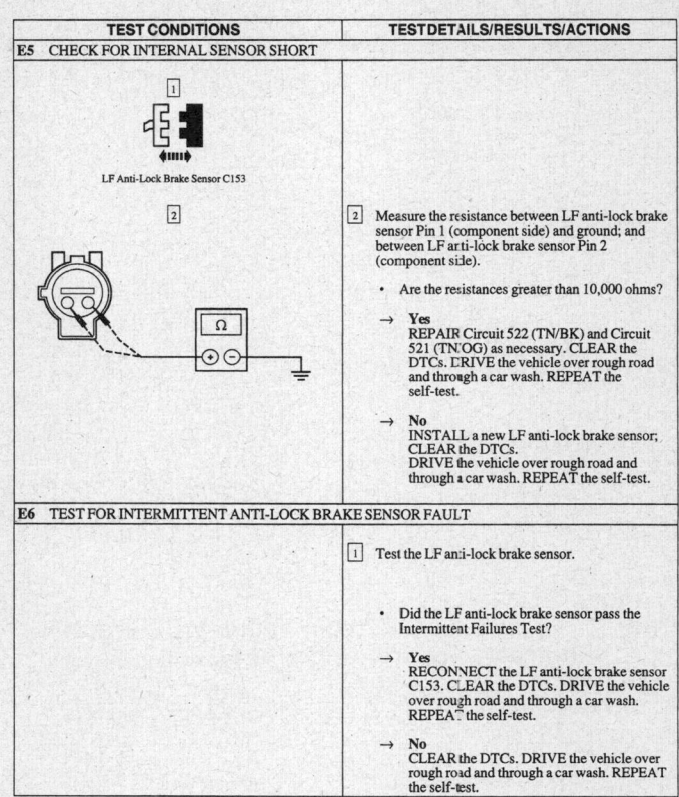

LF Anti-Lock Brake Sensor C153

2   Measure the resistance between LF anti-lock brake sensor Pin 1 (component side) and ground; and between LF anti-lock brake sensor Pin 2 (component side).

- Are the resistances greater than 10,000 ohms?

→ **Yes**
REPAIR Circuit 522 (TN/BK) and Circuit 521 (TN/OG) as necessary. CLEAR the DTCs. DRIVE the vehicle over rough road and through a car wash. REPEAT the self-test.

→ **No**
INSTALL a new LF anti-lock brake sensor; CLEAR the DTCs.
DRIVE the vehicle over rough road and through a car wash. REPEAT the self-test.

TEST CONDITIONS	TESTDETAILS/RESULTS/ACTIONS
E6 TEST FOR INTERMITTENT ANTI-LOCK BRAKE SENSOR FAULT	

1   Test the LF anti-lock brake sensor.

- Did the LF anti-lock brake sensor pass the Intermittent Failures Test?

→ **Yes**
RECONNECT the LF anti-lock brake sensor C153. CLEAR the DTCs. DRIVE the vehicle over rough road and through a car wash. REPEAT the self-test.

→ **No**
CLEAR the DTCs. DRIVE the vehicle over rough road and through a car wash. REPEAT the self-test.

FM4029901477040X

Fig. 9   Test E: Code C1155: Left Front Wheel Speed Sensor, Electrical/Static (Part 4 of 4). 2002-03

TEST CONDITIONS	TESTDETAILS/RESULTS/ACTIONS
F1 RETRIEVE DTCs	

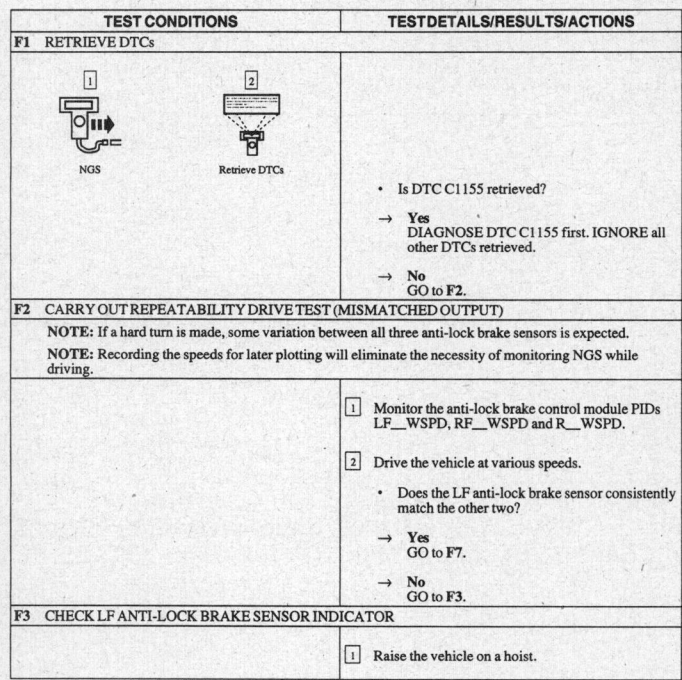

NGS   Retrieve DTCs

- Is DTC C1155 retrieved?

→ **Yes**
DIAGNOSE DTC C1155 first. IGNORE all other DTCs retrieved.

→ **No**
GO to F2.

TEST CONDITIONS	TESTDETAILS/RESULTS/ACTIONS
F2 CARRY OUT REPEATABILITY DRIVE TEST (MISMATCHED OUTPUT)	

NOTE: If a hard turn is made, some variation between all three anti-lock brake sensors is expected.

NOTE: Recording the speeds for later plotting will eliminate the necessity of monitoring NGS while driving.

1   Monitor the anti-lock brake control module PIDs LF__WSPD, RF__WSPD and R__WSPD.

2   Drive the vehicle at various speeds.

- Does the LF anti-lock brake sensor consistently match the other two?

→ **Yes**
GO to F7.

→ **No**
GO to F3.

TEST CONDITIONS	TESTDETAILS/RESULTS/ACTIONS
F3 CHECK LF ANTI-LOCK BRAKE SENSOR INDICATOR	

1   Raise the vehicle on a hoist.

FM4029901478010X

Fig. 10   Test F: Codes C1158 & C1233: Left Front Wheel Speed Sensor, Dynamic (Part 1 of 4). 2002-03

TEST CONDITIONS	TESTDETAILS/RESULTS/ACTIONS
F3 CHECK LF ANTI-LOCK BRAKE SENSOR INDICATOR	

2   **NOTE:** Examine the sensor indicator carefully. Failure to correctly diagnose the sensor indicator at this time will lead to unnecessary component replacement and wasted diagnostic time.

Inspect the sensor indicator for damaged teeth. Rotate the sensor indicator to be sure all teeth are checked.

- Are the anti-lock brake sensor indicator teeth damaged?

→ **Yes**
INSTALL a new anti-lock brake sensor indicator. CLEAR the DTCs.

DRIVE the vehicle over rough road and through a car wash. REPEAT the self-test.

→ **No**
GO to F4.

TEST CONDITIONS	TESTDETAILS/RESULTS/ACTIONS
F4 CHECK FOR LOOSE ANTI-LOCK BRAKE SENSOR MOUNTING	

1   Wiggle the anti-lock brake sensor at wheel end.

- Is any looseness detected?

→ **Yes**
TIGHTEN anti-lock brake sensor to specification. CLEAR the DTCs. DRIVE the vehicle over rough road and through a car wash. REPEAT the self-test.

→ **No**
GO to F5.

FM4029901478020X

Fig. 10   Test F: Codes C1158 & C1233: Left Front Wheel Speed Sensor, Dynamic (Part 2 of 4). 2002-03

TEST CONDITIONS	TESTDETAILS/RESULTS/ACTIONS
F5 CHECK FOR INTERNAL ANTI-LOCK BRAKE SENSOR SHORT	

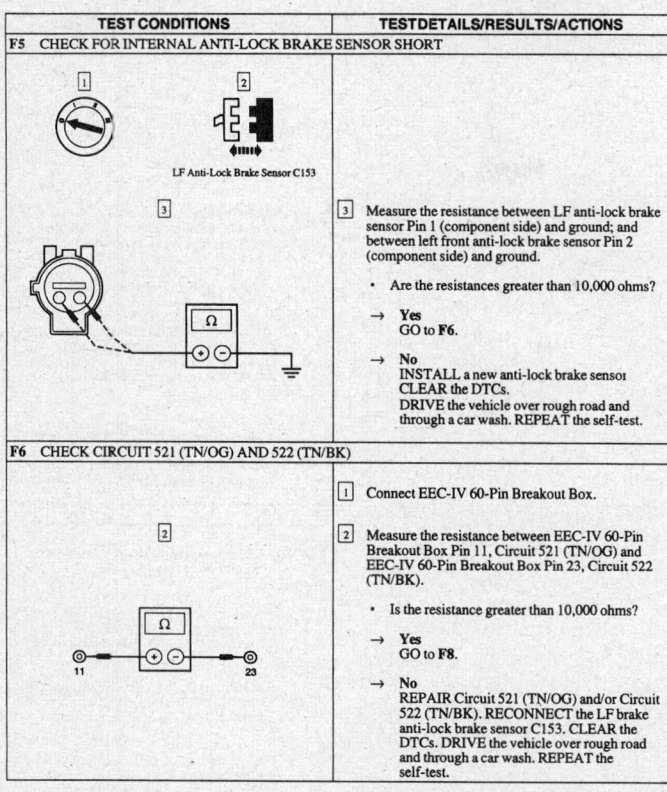

LF Anti-Lock Brake Sensor C153

3 Measure the resistance between LF anti-lock brake sensor Pin 1 (component side) and ground; and between left front anti-lock brake sensor Pin 2 (component side) and ground.

- Are the resistances greater than 10,000 ohms?

→ **Yes**
GO to **F6**.

→ **No**
INSTALL a new anti-lock brake sensor. CLEAR the DTCs.
DRIVE the vehicle over rough road and through a car wash. REPEAT the self-test.

TEST CONDITIONS	TESTDETAILS/RESULTS/ACTIONS
F6 CHECK CIRCUIT 521 (TN/OG) AND 522 (TN/BK)	

1 Connect EEC-IV 60-Pin Breakout Box.

2 Measure the resistance between EEC-IV 60-Pin Breakout Box Pin 11, Circuit 521 (TN/OG) and EEC-IV 60-Pin Breakout Box Pin 23, Circuit 522 (TN/BK).

- Is the resistance greater than 10,000 ohms?

→ **Yes**
GO to **F8**.

→ **No**
REPAIR Circuit 521 (TN/OG) and/or Circuit 522 (TN/BK). RECONNECT the LF brake anti-lock brake sensor C153. CLEAR the DTCs. DRIVE the vehicle over rough road and through a car wash. REPEAT the self-test.

FM4029901478030X

Fig. 10   Test F: Codes C1158 & C1233: Left Front Wheel Speed Sensor, Dynamic (Part 3 of 4). 2002-03

TEST CONDITIONS	TESTDETAILS/RESULTS/ACTIONS
F7 CHECK FOR INTERMITTENT WIRING CONCERN	

2 Test the LF anti-lock brake sensor.

- Did the LF anti-lock brake sensor pass the Intermittent Failures Test?

→ **Yes**
RECONNECT the LF anti-lock brake sensor C153. GO to **F8**.

→ **No**
REPAIR as necessary. CLEAR the DTCs. DRIVE the vehicle over rough road and through a car wash. REPEAT the self-test.

TEST CONDITIONS	TESTDETAILS/RESULTS/ACTIONS
F8 INSPECT THE LF ANTI-LOCK BRAKE SENSOR FOR DAMAGE	

1 Remove the LF anti-lock brake sensor.

2 Inspect the housing for stress cracks or breaks.

3 Inspect the anti-lock brake sensor connector cavity for evidence of water entry and pin corrosion.

- Are any of the above conditions evident?

→ **Yes**
CORRECT the condition(s) as necessary. CLEAR the DTCs. DRIVE the vehicle over rough road and through a car wash. REPEAT the self-test.

→ **No**
RECONNECT the LF anti-lock brake sensor C153. CLEAR the DTCs. DRIVE the vehicle over rough road and through a car wash. REPEAT the self-test.

FM4029901478040X

Fig. 10   Test F: Codes C1158 & C1233: Left Front Wheel Speed Sensor, Dynamic (Part 4 of 4). 2002-03

TEST CONDITIONS	TESTDETAILS/RESULTS/ACTIONS
G1 CHECK FOR FAULT REPEATABILITY	

NGS

Clear All DTCs

Retrieve DTCs

3 Drive the vehicle at least 16 km/h (10 mph).

- Is DTC C1145 retrieved?

→ **Yes**
GO to **G2**.

→ **No**
If no DTCs are retrieved, GO to **G6**.

If a different DTC is retrieved, REFER to Diagnostic Chart Index.

TEST CONDITIONS	TESTDETAILS/RESULTS/ACTIONS
G2 CHECK SENSOR COIL RESISTANCE AT ANTI-LOCK BRAKE CONTROL MODULE CONNECTOR	

1

2 Connect EEC-IV 60-Pin Breakout Box.

FM4029901479010X

Fig. 11   Test G: Code C1145: Right Front Wheel Speed Sensor, Electrical/Static (Part 1 of 4). 2002-03

TEST CONDITIONS	TESTDETAILS/RESULTS/ACTIONS
G2 CHECK SENSOR COIL RESISTANCE AT ANTI-LOCK BRAKE CONTROL MODULE CONNECTOR	

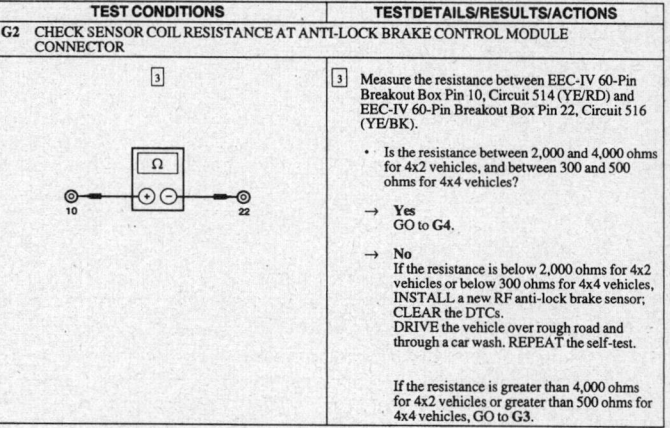

3 Measure the resistance between EEC-IV 60-Pin Breakout Box Pin 10, Circuit 514 (YE/RD) and EEC-IV 60-Pin Breakout Box Pin 22, Circuit 516 (YE/BK).

- Is the resistance between 2,000 and 4,000 ohms for 4x2 vehicles, and between 300 and 500 ohms for 4x4 vehicles?

→ **Yes**
GO to **G4**.

→ **No**
If the resistance is below 2,000 ohms for 4x2 vehicles or below 300 ohms for 4x4 vehicles, INSTALL a new RF anti-lock brake sensor; CLEAR the DTCs.
DRIVE the vehicle over rough road and through a car wash. REPEAT the self-test.

If the resistance is greater than 4,000 ohms for 4x2 vehicles or greater than 500 ohms for 4x4 vehicles, GO to **G3**.

FM4029901479020X

Fig. 11   Test G: Code C1145: Right Front Wheel Speed Sensor, Electrical/Static (Part 2 of 4). 2002-03

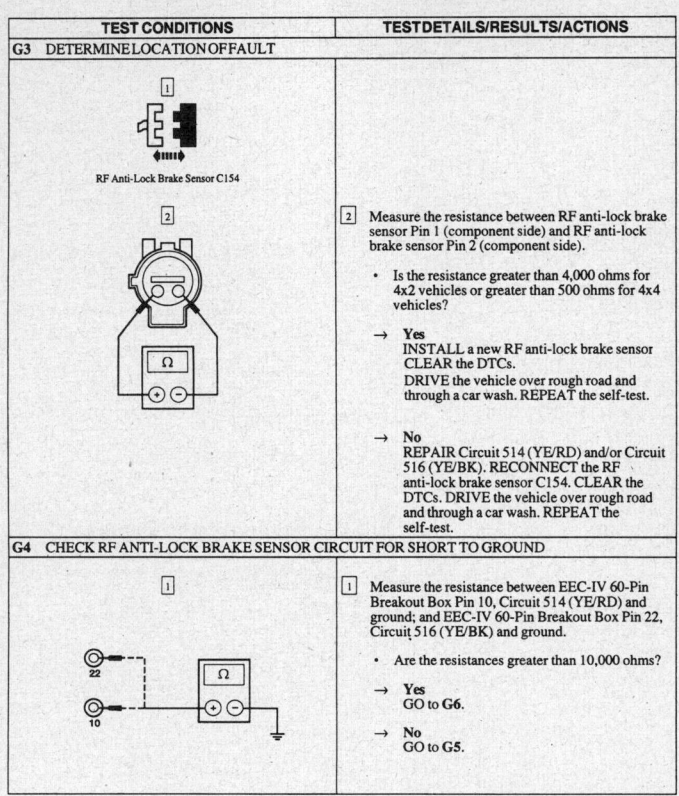

TEST CONDITIONS	TEST DETAILS/RESULTS/ACTIONS
G3 DETERMINE LOCATION OF FAULT	
RF Anti-Lock Brake Sensor C154	2 Measure the resistance between RF anti-lock brake sensor Pin 1 (component side) and RF anti-lock brake sensor Pin 2 (component side). • Is the resistance greater than 4,000 ohms for 4x2 vehicles or greater than 500 ohms for 4x4 vehicles? → **Yes** INSTALL a new RF anti-lock brake sensor CLEAR the DTCs. DRIVE the vehicle over rough road and through a car wash. REPEAT the self-test. → **No** REPAIR Circuit 514 (YE/RD) and/or Circuit 516 (YE/BK). RECONNECT the RF anti-lock brake sensor C154. CLEAR the DTCs. DRIVE the vehicle over rough road and through a car wash. REPEAT the self-test.
G4 CHECK RF ANTI-LOCK BRAKE SENSOR CIRCUIT FOR SHORT TO GROUND	
22 10	1 Measure the resistance between EEC-IV 60-Pin Breakout Box Pin 10, Circuit 514 (YE/RD) and ground; and EEC-IV 60-Pin Breakout Box Pin 22, Circuit 516 (YE/BK) and ground. • Are the resistances greater than 10,000 ohms? → **Yes** GO to G6. → **No** GO to G5.

FM4029901479030X

Fig. 11   Test G: Code C1145: Right Front Wheel Speed Sensor, Electrical/Static (Part 3 of 4). 2002-03

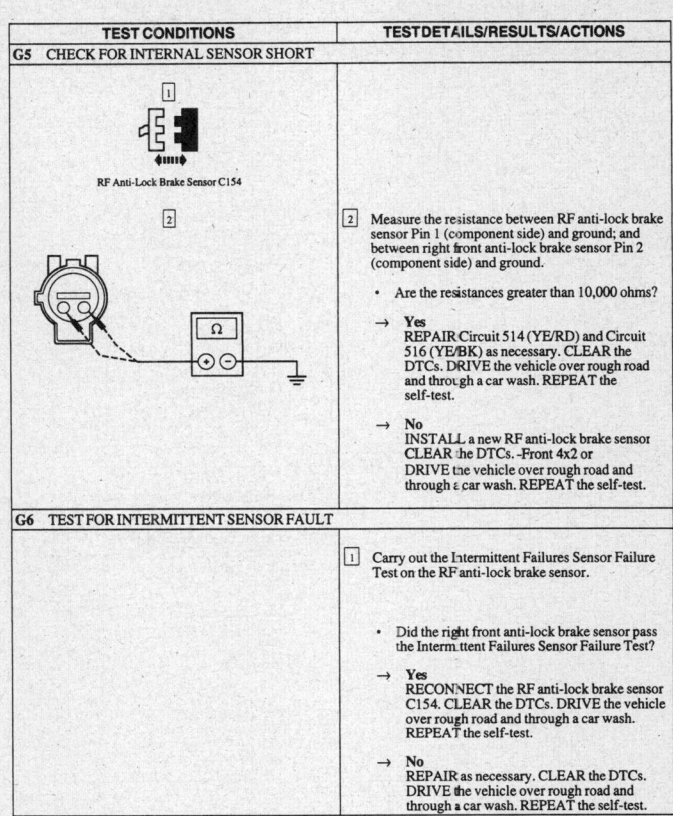

TEST CONDITIONS	TEST DETAILS/RESULTS/ACTIONS
G5 CHECK FOR INTERNAL SENSOR SHORT	
RF Anti-Lock Brake Sensor C154	2 Measure the resistance between RF anti-lock brake sensor Pin 1 (component side) and ground; and between right front anti-lock brake sensor Pin 2 (component side) and ground. • Are the resistances greater than 10,000 ohms? → **Yes** REPAIR Circuit 514 (YE/RD) and Circuit 516 (YE/BK) as necessary. CLEAR the DTCs. DRIVE the vehicle over rough road and through a car wash. REPEAT the self-test. → **No** INSTALL a new RF anti-lock brake sensor CLEAR the DTCs. -Front 4x2 or DRIVE the vehicle over rough road and through a car wash. REPEAT the self-test.
G6 TEST FOR INTERMITTENT SENSOR FAULT	
	1 Carry out the Intermittent Failures Sensor Failure Test on the RF anti-lock brake sensor. • Did the right front anti-lock brake sensor pass the Intermittent Failures Sensor Failure Test? → **Yes** RECONNECT the RF anti-lock brake sensor C154. CLEAR the DTCs. DRIVE the vehicle over rough road and through a car wash. REPEAT the self-test. → **No** REPAIR as necessary. CLEAR the DTCs. DRIVE the vehicle over rough road and through a car wash. REPEAT the self-test.

FM4029901479040X

Fig. 11   Test G: Code C1145: Right Front Wheel Speed Sensor, Electrical/Static (Part 4 of 4). 2002-03

TEST CONDITIONS	TEST DETAILS/RESULTS/ACTIONS
H1 RETRIEVE DTCS	
NGS Retrieve DTCs	• Is DTC C1145 retrieved? → **Yes** DIAGNOSE DTC C1145 first. IGNORE all other DTCs retrieved. → **No** GO to **H2**.
H2 CARRY OUT REPEATABILITY DRIVE TEST (MISMATCHED OUTPUT)	
NOTE: If a hard turn is made, some variation between all three anti-lock brake sensors is expected. **NOTE:** Recording the speeds for later plotting will eliminate the necessity of monitoring NGS Tester while driving. Monitor All Three Wheel Speed Sensors	1 Monitor the anti-lock brake control module PIDs LF__WSPD, RF__WSPD or R__WSPD. 2 Drive the vehicle at various speeds. • Does the RF anti-lock brake sensor consistently match the other two? → **Yes** GO to **H7**. → **No** GO to **H3**.
H3 CHECK RF ANTI-LOCK BRAKE SENSOR INDICATOR	
	1 Raise the vehicle on a hoist.

FM4029901480010X

Fig. 12   Test H: Codes C1148 & C1234: Right Front Wheel Speed Sensor, Dynamic (Part 1 of 5). 2002-03

TEST CONDITIONS	TEST DETAILS/RESULTS/ACTIONS
H3 CHECK RF ANTI-LOCK BRAKE SENSOR INDICATOR	
	2 **NOTE:** Examine the anti-lock brake sensor indicator carefully. Failure to properly diagnose sensor indicator at this time will lead to unnecessary component replacement and wasted diagnostic time. Inspect the anti-lock brake sensor indicator for damaged teeth. Rotate the anti-lock brake sensor indicator to be sure all teeth are checked. • Is the anti-lock brake sensor indicator teeth damaged? → **Yes** INSTALL a new anti-lock brake sensor indicator. CLEAR the DTCs. DRIVE the vehicle over rough road and through a car wash. REPEAT the self-test. → **No** GO to **H4**.
H4 CHECK FOR LOOSE ANTI-LOCK BRAKE SENSOR MOUNTING	
	1 Wiggle the anti-lock brake sensor at wheel end. • Is any looseness detected? → **Yes** TIGHTEN the anti-lock brake sensor to specification. CLEAR the DTCs. DRIVE the vehicle over rough road and through a car wash. REPEAT the self-test. → **No** GO to **H5**.

FM4029901480020X

Fig. 12   Test H: Codes C1148 & C1234: Right Front Wheel Speed Sensor, Dynamic (Part 2 of 5). 2002-03

TEST CONDITIONS	TEST DETAILS/RESULTS/ACTIONS
H5 CHECK FOR INTERNAL ANTI-LOCK BRAKE SENSOR SHORT	

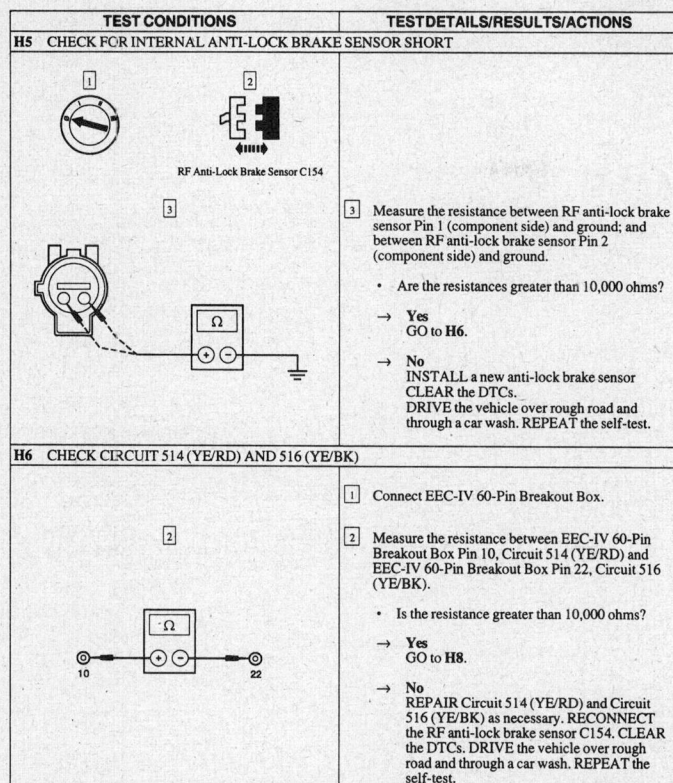

RF Anti-Lock Brake Sensor C154

3 Measure the resistance between RF anti-lock brake sensor Pin 1 (component side) and ground; and between RF anti-lock brake sensor Pin 2 (component side) and ground.

- Are the resistances greater than 10,000 ohms?
- → **Yes**
  GO to **H6**.
- → **No**
  INSTALL a new anti-lock brake sensor CLEAR the DTCs.
  DRIVE the vehicle over rough road and through a car wash. REPEAT the self-test.

TEST CONDITIONS	TEST DETAILS/RESULTS/ACTIONS
H6 CHECK CIRCUIT 514 (YE/RD) AND 516 (YE/BK)	

1 Connect EEC-IV 60-Pin Breakout Box.

2 Measure the resistance between EEC-IV 60-Pin Breakout Box Pin 10, Circuit 514 (YE/RD) and EEC-IV 60-Pin Breakout Box Pin 22, Circuit 516 (YE/BK).

- Is the resistance greater than 10,000 ohms?
- → **Yes**
  GO to **H8**.
- → **No**
  REPAIR Circuit 514 (YE/RD) and Circuit 516 (YE/BK) as necessary. RECONNECT the RF anti-lock brake sensor C154. CLEAR the DTCs. DRIVE the vehicle over rough road and through a car wash. REPEAT the self-test.

FM4029901480030X

Fig. 12   Test H: Codes C1148 & C1234: Right Front Wheel Speed Sensor, Dynamic (Part 3 of 5). 2002-03

TEST CONDITIONS	TEST DETAILS/RESULTS/ACTIONS
H8 INSPECT THE RF ANTI-LOCK BRAKE SENSOR FOR DAMAGE	

4 Inspect the sensor connector cavity for evidence of water entry and pin corrosion.

- Are any of the above conditions present?
- → **Yes**
  CORRECT the condition(s) as necessary. CLEAR the DTCs. DRIVE the vehicle over rough road and through a car wash. REPEAT the self-test.
- → **No**
  RECONNECT the RF anti-lock brake sensor C154. CLEAR the DTCs. DRIVE the vehicle over rough road and through a car wash. REPEAT the self-test.

FM4029901480050X

Fig. 12   Test H: Codes C1148 & C1234: Right Front Wheel Speed Sensor, Dynamic (Part 5 of 5). 2002-03

TEST CONDITIONS	TEST DETAILS/RESULTS/ACTIONS
H7 CHECK FOR INTERMITTENT WIRING CONCERN	

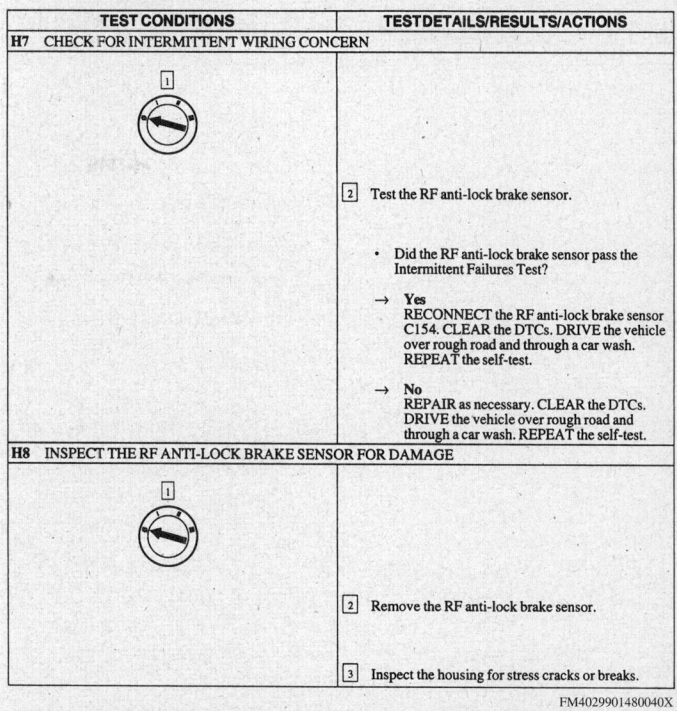

2 Test the RF anti-lock brake sensor.

- Did the RF anti-lock brake sensor pass the Intermittent Failures Test?
- → **Yes**
  RECONNECT the RF anti-lock brake sensor C154. CLEAR the DTCs. DRIVE the vehicle over rough road and through a car wash. REPEAT the self-test.
- → **No**
  REPAIR as necessary. CLEAR the DTCs. DRIVE the vehicle over rough road and through a car wash. REPEAT the self-test.

TEST CONDITIONS	TEST DETAILS/RESULTS/ACTIONS
H8 INSPECT THE RF ANTI-LOCK BRAKE SENSOR FOR DAMAGE	

2 Remove the RF anti-lock brake sensor.

3 Inspect the housing for stress cracks or breaks.

FM4029901480040X

Fig. 12   Test H: Codes C1148 & C1234: Right Front Wheel Speed Sensor, Dynamic (Part 4 of 5). 2002-03

TEST CONDITIONS	TEST DETAILS/RESULTS/ACTIONS
I1 CHECK FOR FAULT REPEATABILITY	

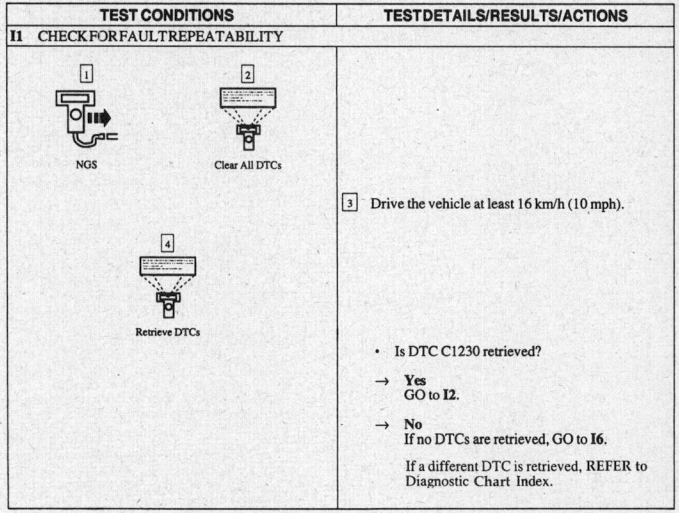

NGS   Clear All DTCs

Retrieve DTCs

3 Drive the vehicle at least 16 km/h (10 mph).

- Is DTC C1230 retrieved?
- → **Yes**
  GO to **I2**.
- → **No**
  If no DTCs are retrieved, GO to **I6**.

  If a different DTC is retrieved, REFER to Diagnostic Chart Index.

FM4029901481010X

Fig. 13   Test I: Code C1230: Rear Wheel Speed Sensor, Electrical/Static (Part 1 of 4). 2002-03

TEST CONDITIONS	TEST DETAILS/RESULTS/ACTIONS
I2 CHECK SENSOR COIL RESISTANCE AT ANTI-LOCK BRAKE CONTROL MODULE CONNECTOR	

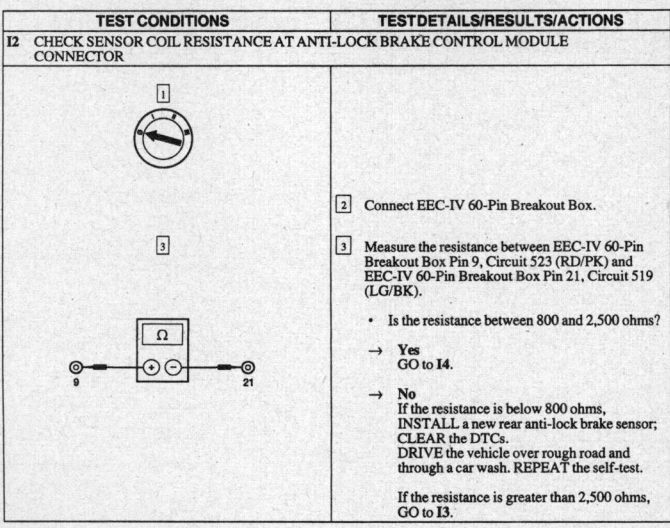

	2 Connect EEC-IV 60-Pin Breakout Box.
	3 Measure the resistance between EEC-IV 60-Pin Breakout Box Pin 9, Circuit 523 (RD/PK) and EEC-IV 60-Pin Breakout Box Pin 21, Circuit 519 (LG/BK).
	• Is the resistance between 800 and 2,500 ohms?
	→ **Yes** GO to **I4**.
	→ **No** If the resistance is below 800 ohms, INSTALL a new rear anti-lock brake sensor; CLEAR the DTCs. DRIVE the vehicle over rough road and through a car wash. REPEAT the self-test.
	If the resistance is greater than 2,500 ohms, GO to **I3**.

FM4029901481020X

Fig. 13   Test I: Code C1230: Rear Wheel Speed Sensor, Electrical/Static (Part 2 of 4). 2002-03

TEST CONDITIONS	TEST DETAILS/RESULTS/ACTIONS
I5 CHECK FOR INTERNAL ANTI-LOCK BRAKE SENSOR SHORT	

Rear Anti-Lock Brake Sensor C414

	2 Measure the resistance between rear anti-lock brake sensor Pin 1 (component side); and between rear anti-lock brake sensor Pin 2 (component side).
	• Are the resistances greater than 10,000 ohms?
	→ **Yes** REPAIR Circuit 519 (LG/BK) and Circuit 523 (RD/PK) as necessary. CLEAR the DTCs. DRIVE the vehicle over rough road and through a car wash. REPEAT the self-test.
	→ **No** INSTALL a new rear anti-lock brake sensor CLEAR the DTCs. DRIVE the vehicle over rough road and through a car wash. REPEAT the self-test.
I6 TEST FOR INTERMITTENT ANTI-LOCK BRAKE SENSOR FAULT	
	1 Test the rear anti-lock brake sensor.
	• Did the rear anti-lock brake sensor pass the Intermittent Failures Test?
	→ **Yes** RECONNECT the rear anti-lock brake sensor C414. CLEAR the DTCs. DRIVE the vehicle over rough road and through a car wash. REPEAT the self-test.
	→ **No** REPAIR as necessary. CLEAR the DTCs. DRIVE the vehicle over rough road and through a car wash. REPEAT the self-test.

FM4029901481040X

Fig. 13   Test I: Code C1230: Rear Wheel Speed Sensor, Electrical/Static (Part 4 of 4). 2002-03

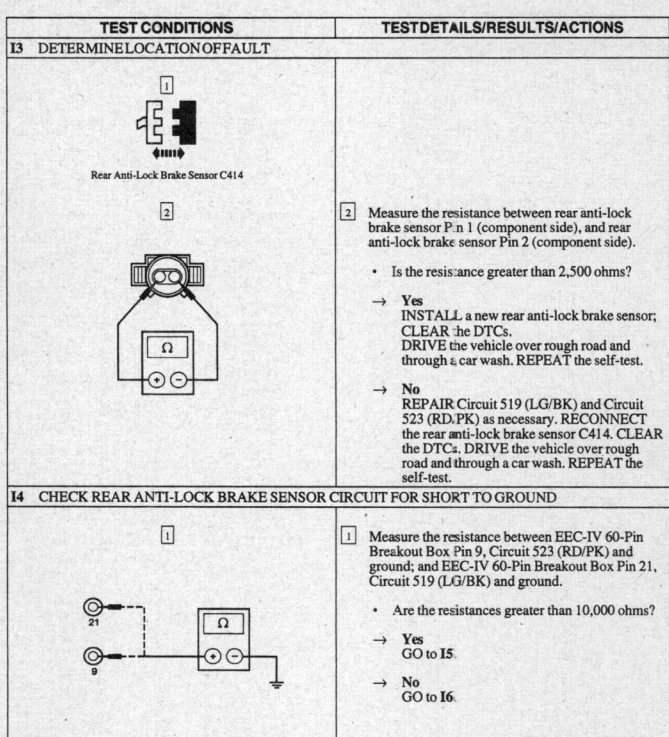

TEST CONDITIONS	TEST DETAILS/RESULTS/ACTIONS
I3 DETERMINE LOCATION OF FAULT	

Rear Anti-Lock Brake Sensor C414

	2 Measure the resistance between rear anti-lock brake sensor Pin 1 (component side), and rear anti-lock brake sensor Pin 2 (component side).
	• Is the resistance greater than 2,500 ohms?
	→ **Yes** INSTALL a new rear anti-lock brake sensor; CLEAR the DTCs. DRIVE the vehicle over rough road and through a car wash. REPEAT the self-test.
	→ **No** REPAIR Circuit 519 (LG/BK) and Circuit 523 (RD/PK) as necessary. RECONNECT the rear anti-lock brake sensor C414. CLEAR the DTCs. DRIVE the vehicle over rough road and through a car wash. REPEAT the self-test.
I4 CHECK REAR ANTI-LOCK BRAKE SENSOR CIRCUIT FOR SHORT TO GROUND	
	1 Measure the resistance between EEC-IV 60-Pin Breakout Box Pin 9, Circuit 523 (RD/PK) and ground; and EEC-IV 60-Pin Breakout Box Pin 21, Circuit 519 (LG/BK) and ground.
	• Are the resistances greater than 10,000 ohms?
	→ **Yes** GO to **I5**.
	→ **No** GO to **I6**.

FM4029901481030X

Fig. 13   Test I: Code C1230: Rear Wheel Speed Sensor, Electrical/Static (Part 3 of 4). 2002-03

TEST CONDITIONS	TEST DETAILS/RESULTS/ACTIONS
J1 RETRIEVE DTCS	

NGS   Retrieve DTCs

	• Is DTC C1230 retrieved?
	→ **Yes** DIAGNOSE DTC C1230 first. IGNORE all other DTCs retrieved.
	→ **No** GO to **J2**.
J2 CARRY OUT REPEATABILITY DRIVE TEST (MISMATCHED OUTPUT)	
NOTE: If a hard turn is made, some variation between all three anti-lock brake sensors is expected.	
NOTE: Recording the speeds for later plotting will eliminate the necessity of monitoring NGS Tester while driving.	
	1 Monitor the anti-lock brake control module PIDs LF__WSPD, RF__WSPD or R__WSPD.
	2 Drive the vehicle at various speeds.
	• Does the rear anti-lock brake sensor consistently match the other two?
	→ **Yes** GO to **J7**.
	→ **No** GO to **J3**.
J3 CHECK REAR ANTI-LOCK BRAKE SENSOR INDICATOR	
	1 Raise the vehicle on a hoist.

FM4029901482010X

Fig. 14   Test J: Codes C1229 & C1237: Rear Wheel Speed Sensor, Dynamic (Part 1 of 4). 2002-03

TEST CONDITIONS	TEST DETAILS/RESULTS/ACTIONS
J3 CHECK REAR ANTI-LOCK BRAKE SENSOR INDICATOR	
	☐2 **NOTE:** Examine the anti-lock brake sensor indicator carefully. Failure to correctly diagnose the sensor indicator at this time will lead to unnecessary component replacement and wasted diagnostic time. Inspect the anti-lock brake sensor indicator for damaged teeth. Rotate the sensor indicator to be sure all teeth are checked. • Are the anti-lock brake sensor indicator teeth damaged? → **Yes** INSTALL a new sensor indicator. CLEAR the DTCs. DRIVE the vehicle over rough road and through a car wash. REPEAT the self-test. → **No** GO to **J4**.
J4 CHECK FOR LOOSE ANTI-LOCK BRAKE SENSOR MOUNTING	
	☐1 Wiggle the anti-lock brake sensor at the differential case. • Is any looseness detected? → **Yes** TIGHTEN the anti-lock brake sensor to specification. CLEAR the DTCs. DRIVE the vehicle over rough road and through a car wash. REPEAT the self-test. → **No** GO to **J5**.

FM4029901482020X

Fig. 14   Test J: Codes C1229 & C1237: Rear Wheel Speed Sensor, Dynamic (Part 2 of 4). 2002-03

TEST CONDITIONS	TEST DETAILS/RESULTS/ACTIONS
J7 CHECK FOR INTERMITTENT WIRING CONCERN	
☐1	☐2 Test the rear anti-lock brake sensor. • Did the rear anti-lock brake sensor pass the Intermittent Failures Test? → **Yes** RECONNECT the rear anti-lock brake sensor C414. CLEAR the DTCs. DRIVE the vehicle over rough road and through a car wash. REPEAT the self-test. → **No** REPAIR as necessary. CLEAR the DTCs. DRIVE the vehicle over rough road and through a car wash. REPEAT the self-test.
J8 INSPECT THE REAR ANTI-LOCK BRAKE SENSOR FOR DAMAGE	
	☐1 Remove the rear anti-lock brake sensor. ☐2 Inspect the anti-lock brake housing for stress cracks or breaks. ☐3 Inspect the anti-lock brake sensor connector cavity for evidence of water entry and pin corrosion. • Are any of the above conditions evident? → **Yes** CORRECT the condition(s) as necessary. CLEAR the DTCs. DRIVE the vehicle over rough road and through a car wash. REPEAT the self-test. → **No** RECONNECT the rear anti-lock brake sensor C414. CLEAR the DTCs. DRIVE the vehicle over rough road and through a car wash. REPEAT the self-test.

FM4029901482040X

Fig. 14   Test J: Codes C1229 & C1237: Rear Wheel Speed Sensor, Dynamic (Part 4 of 4). 2002-03

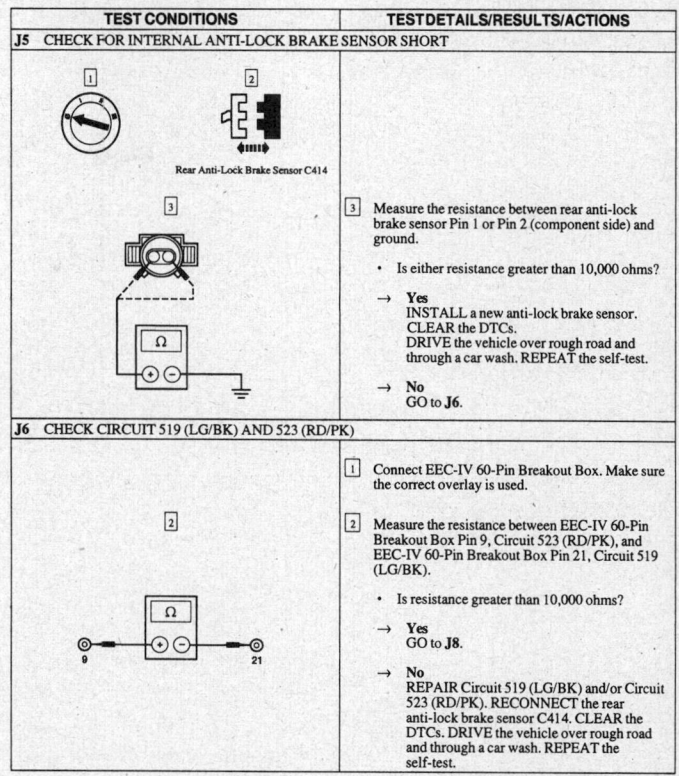

TEST CONDITIONS	TEST DETAILS/RESULTS/ACTIONS
J5 CHECK FOR INTERNAL ANTI-LOCK BRAKE SENSOR SHORT	
☐1 ☐2 Rear Anti-Lock Brake Sensor C414 ☐3	☐3 Measure the resistance between rear anti-lock brake sensor Pin 1 or Pin 2 (component side) and ground. • Is either resistance greater than 10,000 ohms? → **Yes** INSTALL a new anti-lock brake sensor. CLEAR the DTCs. DRIVE the vehicle over rough road and through a car wash. REPEAT the self-test. → **No** GO to **J6**.
J6 CHECK CIRCUIT 519 (LG/BK) AND 523 (RD/PK)	
☐2 9 21	☐1 Connect EEC-IV 60-Pin Breakout Box. Make sure the correct overlay is used. ☐2 Measure the resistance between EEC-IV 60-Pin Breakout Box Pin 9, Circuit 523 (RD/PK), and EEC-IV 60-Pin Breakout Box Pin 21, Circuit 519 (LG/BK). • Is resistance greater than 10,000 ohms? → **Yes** GO to **J8**. → **No** REPAIR Circuit 519 (LG/BK) and/or Circuit 523 (RD/PK). RECONNECT the rear anti-lock brake sensor C414. CLEAR the DTCs. DRIVE the vehicle over rough road and through a car wash. REPEAT the self-test.

FM4029901482030X

Fig. 14   Test J: Codes C1229 & C1237: Rear Wheel Speed Sensor, Dynamic (Part 3 of 4). 2002-03

TEST CONDITIONS	TEST DETAILS/RESULTS/ACTIONS
K1 CHECK BASE BRAKE COMPONENTS	
☐2	☐1 Visually inspect brake lines from the hydraulic control unit (HCU) to wheel cylinders. ☐2 Visually inspect the calipers and brake components. • Are any of these components damaged? → **Yes** REPAIR as necessary. TEST the system for normal operation. → **No** GO to **K2**.
K2 CHECK FOR LEAKING DUMP VALVE	
☐1 ☐3	☐2 Remove the rubber boots from the three HCU low pressure accumulators (LPA). ☐3 Insert a clean steel implement (for example, a paper clip) into each LPA.

FM4029901483010X

Fig. 15   Test K: Soft/Excessive Pedal Travel (Part 1 of 2). 2002-03

TEST CONDITIONS	TESTDETAILS/RESULTS/ACTIONS
K2 CHECK FOR LEAKING DUMP VALVE	
4	4 **NOTE:** A leaking dump valve is similar to the master cylinder bypass condition. It is important that the pedal be quickly and forcefully applied to rule out the master cylinder bypass as a cause. Typically, master cylinder bypass occurs only at low pedal pressure rates. Have an assistant press hard on the brake pedal while observing the steel implements. • Do any of the implements move significantly? → **Yes** INSTALL a new HCU. TEST the system for normal operation. → **No** REMOVE the steel implements. REINSTALL the rubber boots. This is a base brake concern

FM4029901483020X

Fig. 15   Test K: Soft/Excessive Pedal Travel (Part 2 of 2). 2002-03

TEST CONDITIONS	TESTDETAILS/RESULTS/ACTIONS
L1 CHECK FOR FAULT REPEATABILITY	
	• Are any DTCs retrieved? → **Yes** If DTC C1095 is retrieved, INSTALL a new HCU. CLEAR the DTCs. DRIVE the vehicle over rough road and through a car wash. REPEAT the self-test. If DTC C1096 is retrieved, GO to L2. If a different DTC is retrieved, REFER to Diagnostic Chart Index. → **No** CLEAR the DTCs. DRIVE the vehicle over rough road and through a car wash. REPEAT the self-test.
L2 CHECK PUMP MOTOR CIRCUIT	
1 2 Anti-Lock Brake Control Module C147 3	3 Measure the voltage between anti-lock brake control module C147 Pin 2, Circuit 532 (OG/YE), harness side and ground. • Is the voltage greater than 10 volts? → **Yes** GO to L3. → **No** REPAIR Circuit 532 (OG/YE). RECONNECT the anti-lock brake control module C147. CLEAR the DTCs. DRIVE the vehicle over rough road and through a car wash. REPEAT the self-test.

FM4029901484020X

Fig. 16   Test L: Codes C1095 & C1096: Pump Motor (Part 2 of 3). 2002-03

TEST CONDITIONS	TESTDETAILS/RESULTS/ACTIONS
M2 CHECK POWER TO ANTI-LOCK BRAKE CONTROL MODULE	
1 2 Anti-Lock Brake Control Module C147 3	3 Measure the voltage between anti-lock brake control module C147 Pin 2, Circuit 532 (OG/YE), harness side and ground. • Is voltage greater than 10 volts? → **Yes** INSTALL a new anti-lock brake control module. CLEAR the DTCs. DRIVE the vehicle over rough road and through a car wash. REPEAT the self-test. → **No** REPAIR Circuit 532 (OG/YE). RECONNECT the anti-lock brake control module C147. CLEAR the DTCs. DRIVE the vehicle over rough road and through a car wash. REPEAT the self-test.

FM4029901485020X

Fig. 17   Test M: Codes C1113, C1115 & C1185: Internal Power Relay (Part 2 of 2). 2002-03

TEST CONDITIONS	TESTDETAILS/RESULTS/ACTIONS
L1 CHECK FOR FAULT REPEATABILITY	
2 3 4 5 NGS Clear All DTCs On-Demand Self-Test Retrieve DTCs	1 Verify that the ABS pump motor pig tail is connected to the anti-lock brake control module.

FM4029901484010X

Fig. 16   Test L: Codes C1095 & C1096: Pump Motor (Part 1 of 3). 2002-03

TEST CONDITIONS	TESTDETAILS/RESULTS/ACTIONS
L3 CONCLUDE CIRCUIT CHECK	
1 Ω	1 Measure the resistance between anti-lock brake control module C147 Pin 1, Circuit 530 (LG/YE), harness side and ground. • Is the resistance less than 5 ohms? → **Yes** INSTALL a new HCU. CLEAR the DTCs. DRIVE the vehicle over rough road and through a car wash. REPEAT the self-test. → **No** REPAIR Circuit 530 (LG/YE). RECONNECT the anti-lock brake control module C147. CLEAR the DTCs. DRIVE the vehicle over rough road and through a car wash. REPEAT the self-test.

FM4029901484030X

Fig. 16   Test L: Codes C1095 & C1096: Pump Motor (Part 3 of 3). 2002-03

TEST CONDITIONS	TESTDETAILS/RESULTS/ACTIONS
M1 CHECK FOR FAULT REPEATABILITY	
1 2 3 4 NGS Clear All DTCs On-Demand Self-Test Retrieve DTCs	• Are any DTCs retrieved? → **Yes** If DTC C1113 or C1115 is retrieved, INSTALL a new anti-lock brake control module. CLEAR the DTCs. DRIVE the vehicle over rough road and through a car wash. REPEAT the self-test. If DTC C1185 is retrieved, GO to M2. → **No** If no DTCs are retrieved, CLEAR the DTCs. DRIVE the vehicle over rough road and through a car wash. REPEAT the self-test.

FM4029901485010X

Fig. 17   Test M: Codes C1113, C1115 & C1185: Internal Power Relay (Part 1 of 2). 2002-03

TEST CONDITIONS	TESTDETAILS/RESULTS/ACTIONS
N1 CHECK FOR FAULT REPEATABILITY	
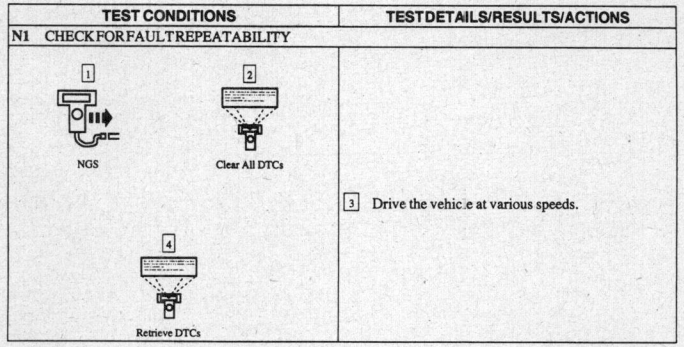	3 Drive the vehicle at various speeds.

FM4029901486010X

Fig. 18   Test N: Codes C1184 & C1222: ABS System Time-Out/Wheel Speed Error (Part 1 of 3). 2002-03

TEST CONDITIONS	TESTDETAILS/RESULTS/ACTIONS
N1 CHECK FOR FAULT REPEATABILITY	
	• Is a DTC retrieved and does the ABS activate during normal stops?
	→ **Yes** If DTC C1184 is retrieved and the ABS does not activate during normal stops, INSTALL a new anti-lock brake control module REPEAT the self-test. If ABS activates on normal stops, GO to **N2**. If DTC C1222 is retrieved, INSPECT tires for mismatched sizes. INSPECT the anti-lock brake sensor indicators for damage. If inspections are normal, INSTALL a new anti-lock brake control module REPEAT the self-test. If a different DTC is retrieved, REFER to Diagnostic Chart Index.
	→ **No** CLEAR the DTCs. DRIVE the vehicle over rough road and through a car wash. REPEAT the self-test.

FM4029901486020X

Fig. 18   Test N: Codes C1184 & C1222: ABS System Time-Out/Wheel Speed Error (Part 2 of 3). 2002-03

TEST CONDITIONS	TESTDETAILS/RESULTS/ACTIONS
N2 CHECK FOR AN ERRATIC WHEEL SPEED SIGNAL	
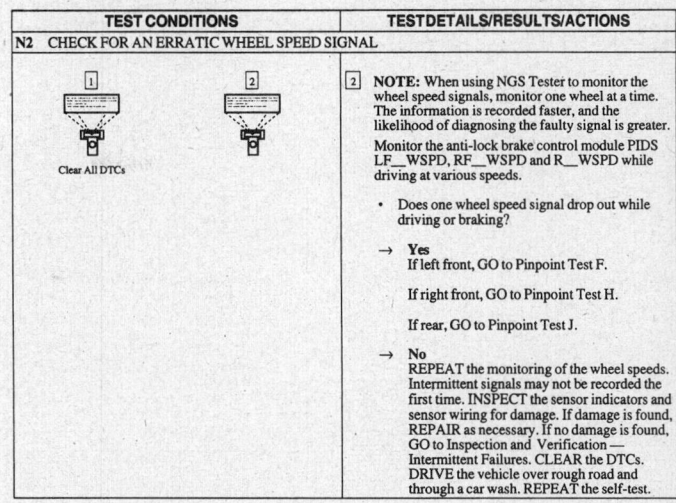	2 **NOTE:** When using NGS Tester to monitor the wheel speed signals, monitor one wheel at a time. The information is recorded faster, and the likelihood of diagnosing the faulty signal is greater. Monitor the anti-lock brake control module PIDS LF__WSPD, RF__WSPD and R__WSPD while driving at various speeds. • Does one wheel speed signal drop out while driving or braking? → **Yes** If left front, GO to Pinpoint Test F. If right front, GO to Pinpoint Test H. If rear, GO to Pinpoint Test J. → **No** REPEAT the monitoring of the wheel speeds. Intermittent signals may not be recorded the first time. INSPECT the sensor indicators and sensor wiring for damage. If damage is found, REPAIR as necessary. If no damage is found, GO to Inspection and Verification — Intermittent Failures. CLEAR the DTCs. DRIVE the vehicle over rough road and through a car wash. REPEAT the self-test.

FM4029901486030X

Fig. 18   Test N: Codes C1184 & C1222: ABS System Time-Out/Wheel Speed Error (Part 3 of 3). 2002-03

TEST CONDITIONS	TESTDETAILS/RESULTS/ACTIONS
O1 CHECK FOR FAULT REPEATABILITY	
1 NGS 2 Clear All DTCs 3 Retrieve DTCs	• Is DTC C1169 retrieved? → **Yes** INSTALL a new EHCU. CLEAR the DTCs. DRIVE the vehicle over rough road and through a car wash. REPEAT the self-test. → **No** GO to **O2**.

FM4029901487010X

Fig. 19   Test O: Code C1169: Excessive Dump Time (Part 1 of 2). 2002-03

TEST CONDITIONS	TESTDETAILS/RESULTS/ACTIONS
O2 LOW SPEED ABS STOP	
	1 Drive the vehicle at approximately 16 km/h (10 mph). 2 **NOTE:** Wetting down the area where the stop is to be performed will aid in performing this test. **NOTE:** An assistant should monitor the wheels during the ABS stop. Momentary lockup is permissible. Apply the brakes hard enough to lock all four wheels. • Does one wheel lock consistently? → **Yes** REFER to Troubleshooting. → **No** CLEAR the DTCs. DRIVE the vehicle over rough road and through a car wash. REPEAT the self-test.

FM4029901487020X

Fig. 19   Test O: Code C1169: Excessive Dump Time (Part 2 of 2). 2002-03

TEST CONDITIONS	TESTDETAILS/RESULTS/ACTIONS
P1 CHECK THE YELLOW ABS WARNING INDICATOR OPERATION	
1	2 Observe the yellow ABS warning indicator. • Is the yellow ABS indicator illuminated at all times? → **Yes** GO to P2. → **No** DIAGNOSE instrument cluster.

FM4029901488010X

Fig. 20   Test P: Yellow ABS Warning Indicator Does Not Self Check (Part 1 of 4). 2002-03

TEST CONDITIONS	TESTDETAILS/RESULTS/ACTIONS
P2 CHECK CIRCUIT 533 (TN/RD) FOR OPEN	
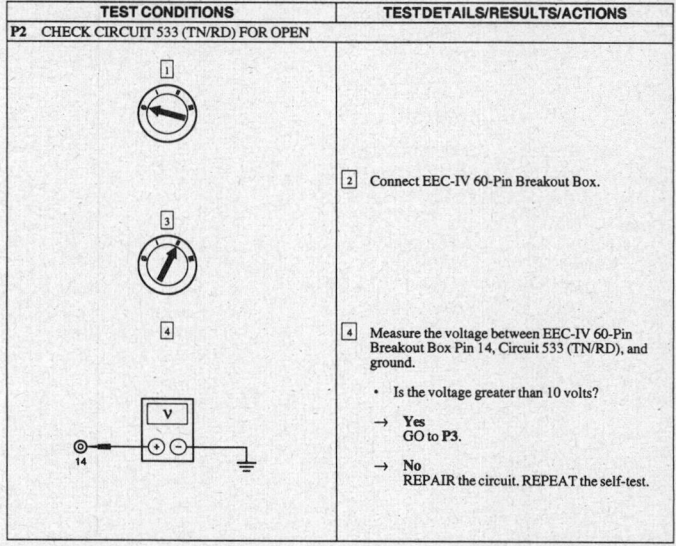	2 Connect EEC-IV 60-Pin Breakout Box. 4 Measure the voltage between EEC-IV 60-Pin Breakout Box Pin 14, Circuit 533 (TN/RD), and ground. • Is the voltage greater than 10 volts? → **Yes** GO to P3. → **No** REPAIR the circuit. REPEAT the self-test.

FM4029901488020X

Fig. 20   Test P: Yellow ABS Warning Indicator Does Not Self Check (Part 2 of 4). 2002-03

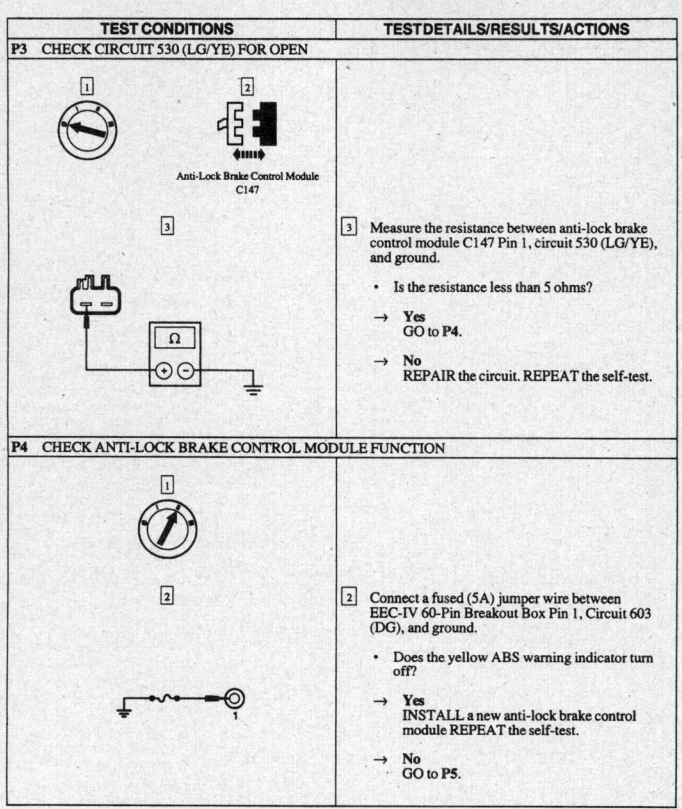

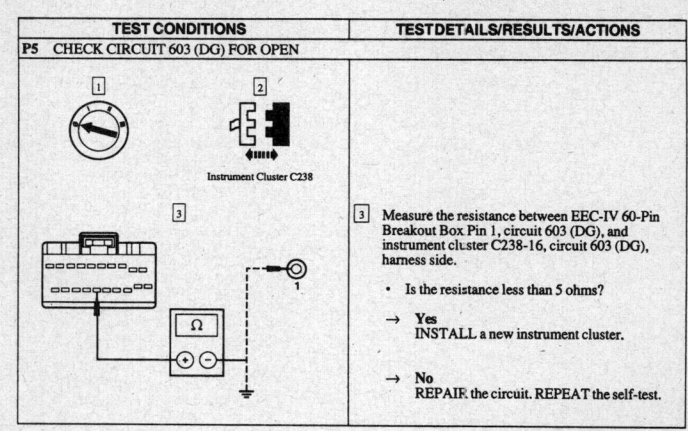

TEST CONDITIONS		TEST DETAILS/RESULTS/ACTIONS
P3 CHECK CIRCUIT 530 (LG/YE) FOR OPEN		

3 Measure the resistance between anti-lock brake control module C147 Pin 1, circuit 530 (LG/YE), and ground.

- Is the resistance less than 5 ohms?
- → **Yes** GO to P4.
- → **No** REPAIR the circuit. REPEAT the self-test.

TEST CONDITIONS		TEST DETAILS/RESULTS/ACTIONS
P5 CHECK CIRCUIT 603 (DG) FOR OPEN		

3 Measure the resistance between EEC-IV 60-Pin Breakout Box Pin 1, circuit 603 (DG), and instrument cluster C238-16, circuit 603 (DG), harness side.

- Is the resistance less than 5 ohms?
- → **Yes** INSTALL a new instrument cluster.
- → **No** REPAIR the circuit. REPEAT the self-test.

FM4029901488040X

Fig. 20 Test P: Yellow ABS Warning Indicator Does Not Self Check (Part 4 of 4). 2002-03

P4 CHECK ANTI-LOCK BRAKE CONTROL MODULE FUNCTION		

2 Connect a fused (5A) jumper wire between EEC-IV 60-Pin Breakout Box Pin 1, Circuit 603 (DG), and ground.

- Does the yellow ABS warning indicator turn off?
- → **Yes** INSTALL a new anti-lock brake control module REPEAT the self-test.
- → **No** GO to P5.

FM4029901488030X

Fig. 20 Test P: Yellow ABS Warning Indicator Does Not Self Check (Part 3 of 4). 2002-03

Test Step	Result / Action to Take
A1 CHECK THE VOLTAGE TO THE ABS MODULE	
• Key in OFF position. • Disconnect: ABS Module C135. • Key in ON position. • Measure the voltage between ABS module C135 pins, harness side and ground as follows:	**Yes** GO to A2 . **No** VERIFY central junction box (CJB) fuse 103 (30A), fuse 112 (30A) and fuse 16 (10A) are OK. If OK, REPAIR the circuit in question. TEST the system for normal operation.

Connector-Pin	Circuit
C135-1	534 (YE/LG)
C135-4	533 (TN/RD)
C135-32	532 (OG/YE)

• Are the voltages greater than 10 volts?	
A2 CHECK THE ABS MODULE GROUNDS	
• Key in OFF position. • Measure the resistance between ABS module C135-16, circuit 530 (LG/YE), harness side and ground; and between ABS module C135-47, circuit 530 (LG/YE), harness side and ground.	**Yes** CHECK the module communication network. **No** REPAIR the circuit. TEST the system for normal operation.
• Are the resistances less than 5 ohms?	

LTV0500000005373

Fig. 21 Test A: No Communication w/ABS Module. 2004-06

Test Step	Result / Action to Take
B1 CHECK THE STOPLAMP OPERATION	
• Press the brake pedal. • **Do the stoplamps operate correctly?**	**Yes** GO to B2 . **No** Check stoplamp operation and circuits..
B2 CHECK CIRCUIT 810 (RD/LG) FOR AN OPEN	
• Key in OFF position. • Disconnect: Anti-Lock Brake System (ABS) Module C135. • Measure the voltage between ABS module C135-41, circuit 810 (RD/LG), harness side and ground, while pressing the brake pedal.	**Yes** GO to B3 . **No** REPAIR the circuit. CLEAR the DTC. REPEAT the self-test.
• **Is the voltage greater than 10 volts?**	
B3 CHECK FOR THE CORRECT ABS MODULE OPERATION	

• Key in OFF position.
• Disconnect all the ABS connectors.
• Check for:
  • corrosion.
  • pushed-out pins.
• Connect all the ABS connectors and make sure they seat correctly.
• Operate the system and verify the concern is still present.
• **Is the concern still present?**
	Yes INSTALL a new ABS module. TEST the system for normal operation.
	
	No The system is operating correctly at this time. The concern may have been caused by a loose or corroded connector. CLEAR the DTCs. REPEAT the self-test.

LTV0500000005374

Fig. 22 Test B, Code B1483: Brake Pedal Input Circuit Failure. 2004-06

Test Step	Result / Action to Take
C1 CHECK THE BATTERY VOLTAGE	
• Key in OFF position. • Measure the battery voltage between the positive and negative battery posts with the key ON engine OFF (KOEO), and with the engine running. • **Is the battery voltage between 10 and 13 volts with KOEO, and between 11 and 17 volts with the engine running?**	**Yes** GO to C2. **No** Check charging system.
C2 CHECK THE VOLTAGE TO THE ANTI-LOCK BRAKE SYSTEM (ABS) MODULE	
• Key in OFF position. • Disconnect: ABS Module C135. • Key in ON position. • Measure the voltage between ABS module C135 pins, harness side and ground as follows: | Pin	Circuit
C135-1	534 (YE/LG)
C135-4	533 (TN/RD)
C135-32	532 (OG/YE) | • **Are the voltages greater than 10 volts?**	**Yes** GO to C3. **No** VERIFY central junction box (CJB) fuse 103 (30A), fuse 112 (30A) and fuse 16 (10A) are OK. If OK, REPAIR the circuit in question. CLEAR the DTC. REPEAT the self-test.
C3 CHECK CIRCUIT 530 (YE/LG) FOR AN OPEN	
• Key in OFF position. • Measure the resistance between ABS module C135-16, circuit 530 (YE/LG), harness side and ground; and between ABS module C135-47, circuit 530 (YE/LG), harness side and ground.	**Yes** GO to C4. **No** REPAIR the circuit in question. CLEAR the DTC. REPEAT the self-test.

LTV0500000005375

Fig. 23   Test C, Code B1676: Battery Pack Voltage Out Of Range (Part 1 of 2). 2004-06

• **Are the resistances less than 5 ohms?**

C4 CHECK FOR THE CORRECT ABS MODULE OPERATION	

• Disconnect all the ABS connectors.
• Check for:
  ▪ corrosion.
  ▪ pushed-out pins.
• Connect all the ABS connectors and make sure they seat correctly.
• Operate the system and verify the concern is still present.
• **Is the concern still present?**
	Yes
	INSTALL a new ABS module. TEST the system for normal operation.
	
	No
	The system is operating correctly at this time. The concern may have been caused by a loose or corroded connector. CLEAR the DTCs. REPEAT the self-test.

LTV0500000005376

Fig. 23   Test C, Code B1676: Battery Pack Voltage Out Of Range (Part 2 of 2). 2004-06

Test Step	Result / Action to Take
D1 CHECK THE ANTI-LOCK BRAKE SYSTEM (ABS) PUMP MOTOR	
• Key in ON position. • **Is the ABS pump motor running all the time?**	**Yes** GO to D5. **No** GO to D2.
D2 CHECK THE PUMP MOTOR OPERATION	
• Enter the following diagnostic mode on the diagnostic tool: ABS Module Active Command. • Trigger the ABS module pump motor ON active command. • **Does the ABS pump motor run for approximately 2 seconds?**	**Yes** CLEAR the DTCs. CHECK the yellow ABS warning indicator while driving the vehicle (the brakes must not be applied) above 20 km/h (12 mph). If the yellow ABS warning indicator illuminates, RETRIEVE the DTCs. If DTC C1095 is retrieved, GO to D5. **No** TRIGGER the ABS module pump motor OFF active command. GO to D3.
D3 CHECK CIRCUIT 534 (YE/LG) FOR AN OPEN	
• Key in OFF position. • Disconnect: ABS Module C135. • Measure the voltage between ABS module C135-1, circuit 534 (YE/LG) harness side, and ground. • **Is the voltage greater than 10 volts?**	**Yes** GO to D4. **No** VERIFY the central junction box (CJB) fuse 103 (30A) is OK. If OK, REPAIR the circuit in question. CLEAR the DTC. REPEAT the self-test.
D4 CHECK CIRCUIT 530 (LG/YE) FOR AN OPEN	
• Measure the resistance between ABS module C135-16, circuit 530 (LG/YE) harness side, and ground; and between ABS module C135-47, circuit 530 (LG/YE) harness side and ground.	**Yes** GO to D5. **No**

LTV0500000005377

Fig. 24   Test D, Code C1095: ABS Hydraulic Pump Motor Circuit Failure (Part 1 of 2). 2004-06

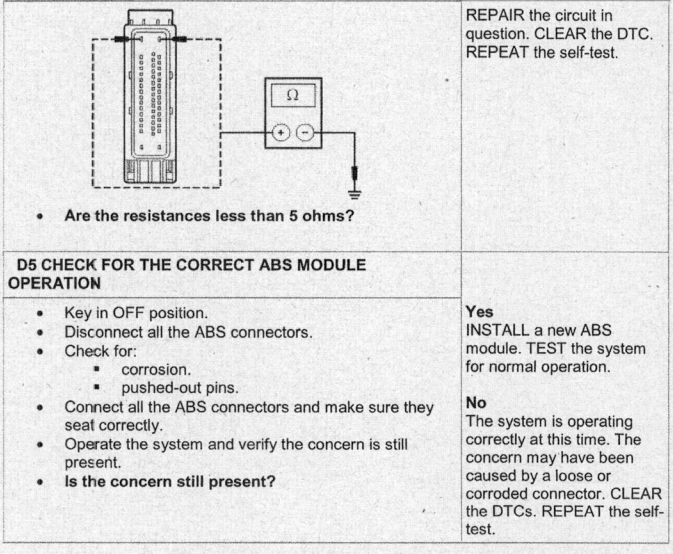

	REPAIR the circuit in question. CLEAR the DTC. REPEAT the self-test.
• **Are the resistances less than 5 ohms?**	
D5 CHECK FOR THE CORRECT ABS MODULE OPERATION	

• Key in OFF position.
• Disconnect all the ABS connectors.
• Check for:
  ▪ corrosion.
  ▪ pushed-out pins.
• Connect all the ABS connectors and make sure they seat correctly.
• Operate the system and verify the concern is still present.
• **Is the concern still present?**
	Yes
	INSTALL a new ABS module. TEST the system for normal operation.
	
	No
	The system is operating correctly at this time. The concern may have been caused by a loose or corroded connector. CLEAR the DTCs. REPEAT the self-test.

LTV0500000005378

Fig. 24   Test D, Code C1095: ABS Hydraulic Pump Motor Circuit Failure (Part 2 of 2). 2004-06

Test Step	Result / Action to Take
E1 CHECK FOR A SHORT TO VOLTAGE ⚠ **CAUTION: No measurements should be taken with the wheel speed sensor connected. Damage to the wheel speed sensor will result. NOTE:** Both circuits must be checked for each DTC. • Key in OFF position. • Disconnect: Anti-Lock Brake System (ABS) Module C135. • Disconnect: Suspect Wheel Speed Sensor. • Key in ON position. • Measure the voltage between ABS module C135, harness side and ground as follows:	**Yes** REPAIR the circuit(s) in question. CLEAR the DTCs. REPEAT the self-test. **No** GO to E2 .

DTC	ABS Module Connector-Pin	Circuit
C1145 (RF)	C135-33	516 (YE/BK)
C1145 (RF)	C135-34	514 (YE/RD)
C1155 (LF)	C135-45	521 (TN/OG)
C1155 (LF)	C135-46	522 (TN/BK)
C1165 (RR)	C135-42	524 (PK/BK)
C1165 (RR)	C135-43	523 (RD/PK)
C1175 (LR)	C135-36	518 (LG/RD)
C1175 (LR)	C135-37	519 (LG/BK)

Test Step	Result / Action to Take
• Is any voltage present?	
E2 CHECK FOR A SHORT TO GROUND **NOTE:** Both circuits must be checked for each diagnostic trouble code (DTC). • Key in OFF position. • Measure the resistance between ABS module C135, harness side and ground as follows:	**Yes** GO to E3 . **No** REPAIR the circuit(s) in question. CLEAR the DTC. REPEAT the self-test.

DTC	ABS Module Connector-Pin	Circuit
C1145 (RF)	C135-33	516 (YE/BK)
C1145 (RF)	C135-34	514 (YE/RD)
C1155 (LF)	C135-45	521 (TN/OG)

LTV0500000005379

Fig. 25 Test E, Codes C1145, C1155, C1165 & C1175: Wheel Speed Sensor Input Circuit Failure (Part 1 of 3). 2004-06

C1155 (LF)	C135-46	522 (TN/BK)
C1165 (RR)	C135-42	524 (PK/BK)
C1165 (RR)	C135-43	523 (RD/PK)
C1175 (LR)	C135-36	518 (LG/RD)
C1175 (LR)	C135-37	519 (LG/BK)

Test Step	Result / Action to Take
• Are the resistances greater than 10,000 ohms?	
E3 CHECK FOR AN OPEN **NOTE:** Both circuits must be checked for each DTC. • Measure the resistance between ABS module C135, harness side and the suspect wheel speed sensor connector, harness side, as follows:	**Yes** GO to E4 . **No** REPAIR the circuit(s) in question. CLEAR the DTCs. REPEAT the self-test.

DTC	Circuit	ABS Module Connector-Pin	Wheel Speed Sensor Connector-Pin
C1145 (RF)	516 (YE/BK)	C135-33	C160-2
C1145 (RF)	514 (YE/RD)	C135-34	C160-1
C1155 (LF)	521 (TN/OG)	C135-45	C150-1
C1155 (LF)	522 (TN/BK)	C135-46	C160-2
C1165 (RR)	523 (RD/PK)	C135-43	C426-2
C1165 (RR)	524 (PK/BK)	C135-42	C426-1
C1175 (LR)	518 (LG/RD)	C135-36	C440-2
C1175 (LR)	519 (LG/BK)	C135-37	C440-1

Test Step	Result / Action to Take
• Are the resistances less than 5 ohms?	
E4 CHECK FOR WHEEL SPEED SENSOR CIRCUITS SHORTED TOGETHER • Measure the resistance across the suspect wheel speed sensor connector, harness side.	**Yes** GO to E5 .

LTV0500000005380

Fig. 25 Test E, Codes C1145, C1155, C1165 & C1175: Wheel Speed Sensor Input Circuit Failure (Part 2 of 3). 2004-06

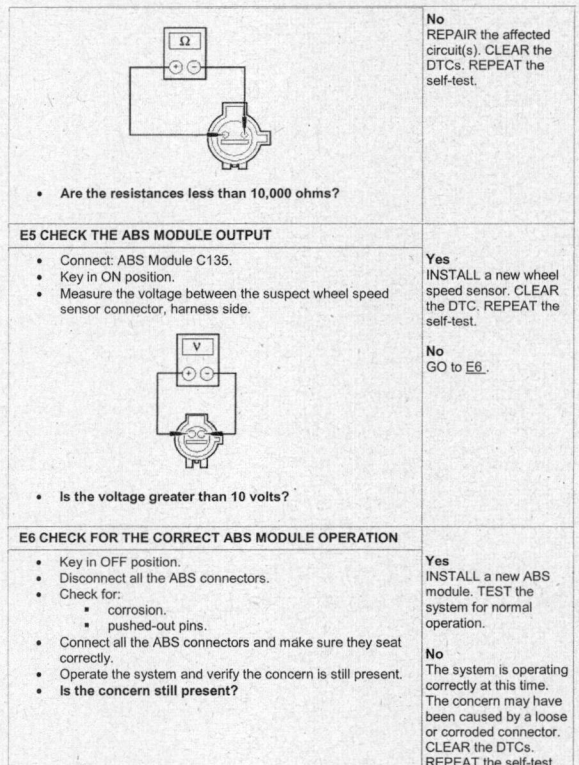

Test Step	Result / Action to Take
	No REPAIR the affected circuit(s). CLEAR the DTCs. REPEAT the self-test.
• Are the resistances less than 10,000 ohms?	
E5 CHECK THE ABS MODULE OUTPUT • Connect: ABS Module C135. • Key in ON position. • Measure the voltage between the suspect wheel speed sensor connector, harness side.	**Yes** INSTALL a new wheel speed sensor. CLEAR the DTC. REPEAT the self-test. **No** GO to E6 .
• Is the voltage greater than 10 volts?	

E6 CHECK FOR THE CORRECT ABS MODULE OPERATION
• Key in OFF position.
• Disconnect all the ABS connectors.
• Check for:
   ▪ corrosion.
   ▪ pushed-out pins.
• Connect all the ABS connectors and make sure they seat correctly.
• Operate the system and verify the concern is still present.
• **Is the concern still present?**
	Yes
	INSTALL a new ABS module. TEST the system for normal operation.
	
	No
	The system is operating correctly at this time. The concern may have been caused by a loose or corroded connector. CLEAR the DTCs. REPEAT the self-test.

LTV0500000005381

Fig. 25 Test E, Codes C1145, C1155, C1165 & C1175: Wheel Speed Sensor Input Circuit Failure (Part 3 of 3). 2004-06

Test Step	Result / Action to Take
F1 CHECK THE ANTI-LOCK BRAKE SYSTEM (ABS) MODULE DTCS • Key in ON position. • Connect the diagnostic tool. • Enter the following diagnostic mode on the diagnostic tool: ABS Module Self-test. • Retrieve the ABS module DTCs. • **Is DTC C1145, C1155, C1165 or C1175 present?**	**Yes** Go To Pinpoint Test E **No** GO to F2 .
F2 MONITOR THE WHEEL SPEED SENSOR PIDS • Enter the following diagnostic mode on the diagnostic tool: ABS Module PIDs. • Monitor the wheel speed PIDs while driving the vehicle at a constant speed. • **Are the wheel speed PIDs consistent?**	**Yes** CLEAR the DTCs. DRIVE the vehicle. RETRIEVE the DTCs. If DTC C1233, C1234, C1235 or C1236 is present, GO to F9 . **No** GO to F3 .
F3 CHECK THE WHEEL SPEED SENSOR AND MOUNTING **NOTE:** Any time a wheel speed sensor is removed, thoroughly clean the mounting surfaces. Apply High-Temperature 4x4 Front Axle and Wheel Bearing Grease before installation. • With the vehicle in NEUTRAL, position it on a hoist. ⚠ **CAUTION: Examine the wheel speed sensor wire carefully, using a good light source. Failure to verify damage in the wheel speed sensor wire can lead to unnecessary installation of a new component.** • Inspect the wheel speed sensor for looseness. • **Is the wheel speed sensor and mounting OK?**	**Yes** TORQUE the wheel speed sensor to specification. CLEAR the DTCs. GO to F4 . **No** GO to F5 .
F4 RECHECK THE WHEEL SPEED PIDS • Enter the following diagnostic mode on the diagnostic tool: ABS Module PIDs. • Use the diagnostic tool to monitor the ABS module wheel speed sensor PIDs while driving the vehicle at a constant speed. • **Are all the wheel speed sensor PID values similar?**	**Yes** The vehicle is OK. The concern may have been caused by a loose wheel speed sensor. **No** GO to F5 .

LTV0500000005382

Fig. 26 Test F, Codes C1233, C1234, C1235 & C1236: Wheel Speed Sensor Input Signal Missing (Part 1 of 3). 2004-06

Test Step	Result / Action to Take
F5 CHECK THE WHEEL SPEED SENSOR FOR DAMAGE	
• Key in OFF position. • With the vehicle in NEUTRAL, position it on a hoist. • ⚠ **CAUTION: Examine the wheel speed sensor wire carefully with a good light source. Failure to verify damage in the wheel speed sensor wire can lead to unnecessary installation of a new component.** • Inspect the wheel speed sensor for general damage. • **Is the wheel speed sensor OK?**	**Yes** GO to F6. **No** INSTALL a new wheel speed sensor. For the front wheel speed sensor, CLEAR the DTC. REPEAT the self-test.
F6 CHECK FOR WHEEL SPEED SENSOR RING DAMAGE	
• Remove the wheel speed sensor. Inspect the wheel speed sensor ring for damaged or missing teeth. Rotate the wheel to verify that no teeth are missing. • **Is the wheel speed sensor ring OK?**	**Yes** GO to F7. **No** INSTALL a new wheel hub and bearing assembly. CLEAR the DTCs. REPEAT the self-test.
F7 CHECK FOR BEARING DAMAGE	
• Inspect the wheel bearings for damage. • **Are the wheel bearings OK?**	**Yes** GO to F8. **No** INSTALL a new wheel hub and bearing assembly. For front 4x2, For front 4x4, CLEAR the DTCs. REPEAT the self-test.
F8 CHECK THE ABS MODULE OUTPUT	
• Disconnect: Suspect Wheel Speed Sensor. • Key in ON position. • Measure the voltage between the suspect wheel speed sensor connector, harness side. • **Is the voltage greater than 10 volts?**	**Yes** INSTALL a new wheel speed sensor. CLEAR the DTCs. REPEAT the self-test. **No** GO to F9.

LTV0500000005383

Fig. 26   Test F, Codes C1233, C1234, C1235 & C1236: Wheel Speed Sensor Input Signal Missing (Part 2 of 3). 2004-06

Test Step	Result / Action to Take
G1 CARRY OUT THE RECALIBRATION PROCEDURE	
• Key in ON position. • Enter the following diagnostic mode on the diagnostic tool: Clear the DTCs. • Carry out the steering wheel angle recalibration procedure using the diagnostic tool. • Test drive the vehicle. • Enter the following diagnostic mode on the diagnostic tool: Retrieve ABS module DTCs. • **Are any DTCs retrieved or does the recalibration procedure indicate a fault?**	**Yes** If DTC C1277 or C1278 is retrieved or the recalibration procedure indicates a fault, GO to G2. If any other DTCs are retrieved, GO to the Anti-Lock Brake System (ABS) Module Diagnostic Trouble Code (DTC) Index. If sent here from Pinpoint Test O, GO to G2. **No** The ABS system is operating correctly.
G2 MONITOR THE STEERING POSITION SENSOR PIDS	
• Make sure the steering wheels are centered straight forward. • Enter the following diagnostic mode on the diagnostic tool: ABS Module PIDs. • Monitor the ABS module steering position sensor PID while rotating the steering wheel clockwise and counterclockwise. • **Are the 2 PID values similar?**	**Yes** CLEAR the DTCs. DRIVE the vehicle. RETRIEVE the DTCs. If DTC C1277 is present, INSTALL a new ABS module. RECALIBRATE the ABS module. FOLLOW the diagnostic tool directions for the calibration procedure. **No** If the value is less than 360, GO to G3. If the value is greater than 360, check alignment, suspension and steering column concerns. CLEAR the DTCs. REPEAT the self-test.
G3 CHECK CIRCUIT 1574 (DB) FOR AN OPEN	
• Key in OFF position. • Disconnect: Steering Position Sensor C226. • Key in ON position. • Measure the voltage between steering position sensor C226-1, circuit 1574 (DB), harness side and ground.	**Yes** GO to G4. **No** REPAIR the circuit. CLEAR the DTCs. RECALIBRATE the ABS module. FOLLOW the diagnostic tool directions for the

LTV0500000005385

Fig. 27   Test G, Codes C1277 & C1278: Steering Wheel Angle 1 & 2 Circuit Failure/Signal Fault (Part 1 of 3). 2004-06

Test Step	Result / Action to Take
F9 CHECK FOR THE CORRECT ABS MODULE OPERATION	

• Key in OFF position.
• Disconnect all the ABS connectors.
• Check for:
  ▪ corrosion.
  ▪ pushed-out pins.
• Connect all the ABS connectors and make sure they seat correctly.
• Operate the system and verify the concern is still present.
• **Is the concern still present?**
	Yes
	INSTALL a new ABS module. TEST the system for normal operation.
	
	No
	The system is operating correctly at this time. The concern may have been caused by a loose or corroded connector. CLEAR the DTCs. REPEAT the self-test.

LTV0500000005384

Fig. 26   Test F, Codes C1233, C1234, C1235 & C1236: Wheel Speed Sensor Input Signal Missing (Part 3 of 3). 2004-06

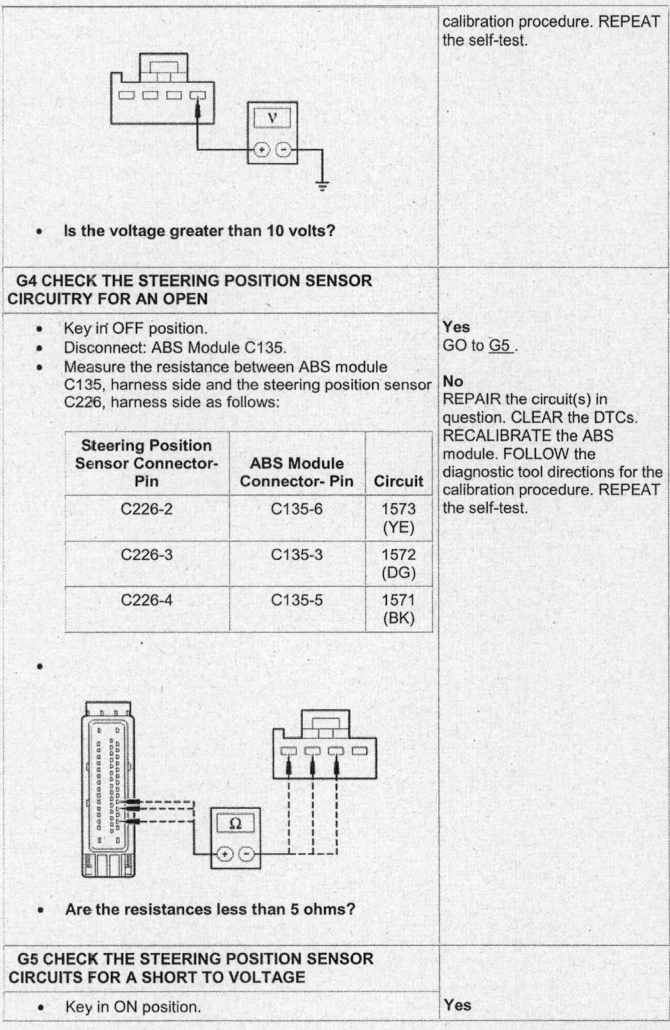

calibration procedure. REPEAT the self-test.

• **Is the voltage greater than 10 volts?**

Test Step	Result / Action to Take
G4 CHECK THE STEERING POSITION SENSOR CIRCUITRY FOR AN OPEN	
• Key in OFF position. • Disconnect: ABS Module C135. • Measure the resistance between ABS module C135, harness side and the steering position sensor C226, harness side as follows:	**Yes** GO to G5. **No** REPAIR the circuit(s) in question. CLEAR the DTCs. RECALIBRATE the ABS module. FOLLOW the diagnostic tool directions for the calibration procedure. REPEAT the self-test.

Steering Position Sensor Connector- Pin	ABS Module Connector- Pin	Circuit
C226-2	C135-6	1573 (YE)
C226-3	C135-3	1572 (DG)
C226-4	C135-5	1571 (BK)

• **Are the resistances less than 5 ohms?**

Test Step	Result / Action to Take
G5 CHECK THE STEERING POSITION SENSOR CIRCUITS FOR A SHORT TO VOLTAGE	
• Key in ON position.	Yes

LTV0500000005386

Fig. 27   Test G, Codes C1277 & C1278: Steering Wheel Angle 1 & 2 Circuit Failure/Signal Fault (Part 2 of 3). 2004-06

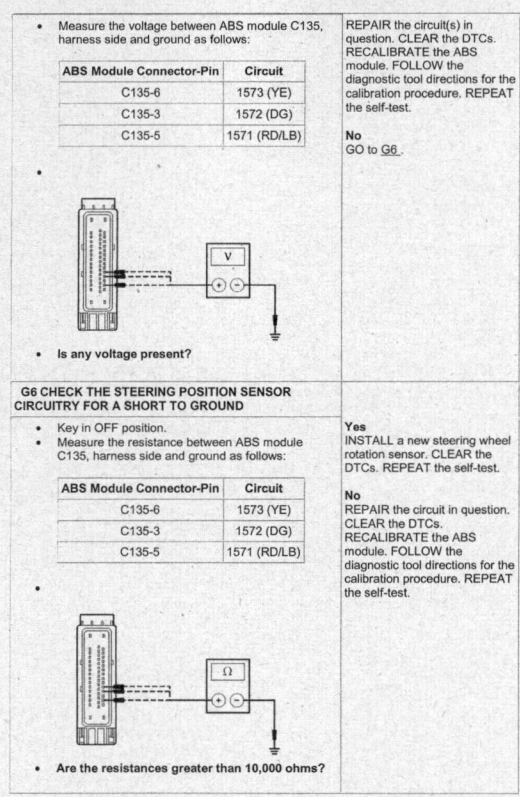

Fig. 27 Test G, Codes C1277 & C1278: Steering Wheel Angle 1 & 2 Circuit Failure/Signal Fault (Part 3 of 3). 2004-06

Test Step	Result / Action to Take
H1 CARRY OUT THE RECALIBRATION PROCEDURE • Key in ON position. • Enter the following diagnostic mode on the diagnostic tool: Clear DTCs. • Carry out the sensor cluster recalibration procedure using the diagnostic tool. • Enter the following diagnostic mode on the diagnostic tool: Retrieve the DTCs. • **Are any DTCs retrieved or does the recalibration procedure indicate a fault?**	**Yes** GO to H2. **No** The anti-lock brake system (ABS) is operating correctly. The condition may have been caused by an incomplete or inaccurate calibration.
H2 CHECK THE ABS MODULE YAW RATE PID • Monitor the ABS module yaw rate PID. • **Is the ABS module yaw rate PID value between -0.05 and 0.05?**	**Yes** GO to H3. **No** INSTALL a new sensor cluster. CLEAR DTCs. RECALIBRATE the ABS module. REPEAT the self-test. FOLLOW the diagnostic tool directions for the calibration procedure. REPEAT the self-test.
H3 CHECK THE ABS MODULE LATERAL ACCELERATION PID • Enter the following diagnostic mode on the diagnostic tool: ABS Module PID. • **NOTE:** The vehicle must be on level ground and at a complete standstill. Any vehicle movement will result in false values for this test. • Monitor the ABS module lateral acceleration PID. • **Is the ABS module lateral acceleration PID value between -7 and 7?**	**Yes** GO to H4. **No** CHECK the mounting of the sensor cluster. If OK, INSTALL a new sensor cluster CLEAR DTCs. RECALIBRATE the ABS module. FOLLOW the diagnostic tool directions for the calibration procedure. REPEAT the self-test.
H4 CHECK THE ABS MODULE LONGITUDINAL ACCELERATION PID • Enter the following diagnostic mode on the diagnostic tool: ABS Module PID. • Monitor the ABS module longitudinal acceleration PID. • **Is the ABS module longitudinal acceleration PID value between -4 and 4?**	**Yes** GO to H5. **No** CHECK the mounting of the sensor cluster. If OK, INSTALL a new sensor cluster. CLEAR

LTV0500000005388

Fig. 28 Test H, Codes C1279, C1280, C1281, C1282, C1516, C1517, C2769, C2777 & C2778: Sensor Cluster Fault (Part 1 of 4). 2004-06

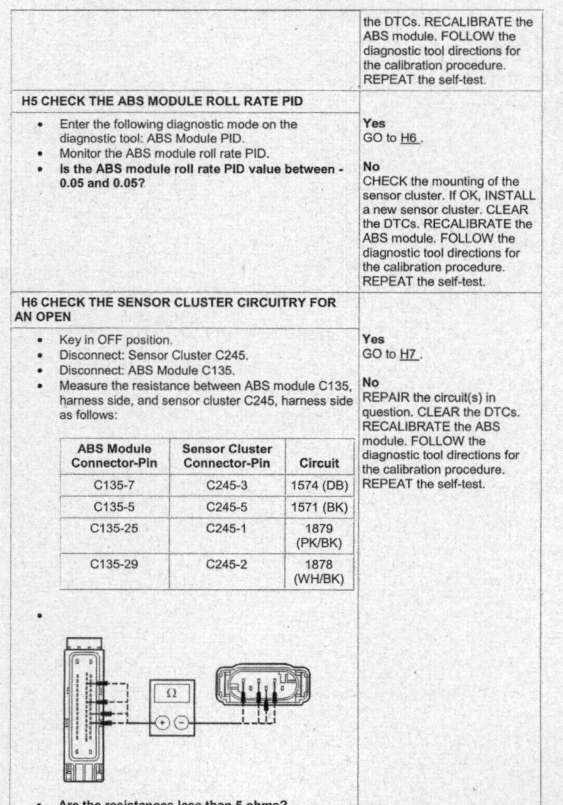

Fig. 28 Test H, Codes C1279, C1280, C1281, C1282, C1516, C1517, C2769, C2777 & C2778: Sensor Cluster Fault (Part 2 of 4). 2004-06

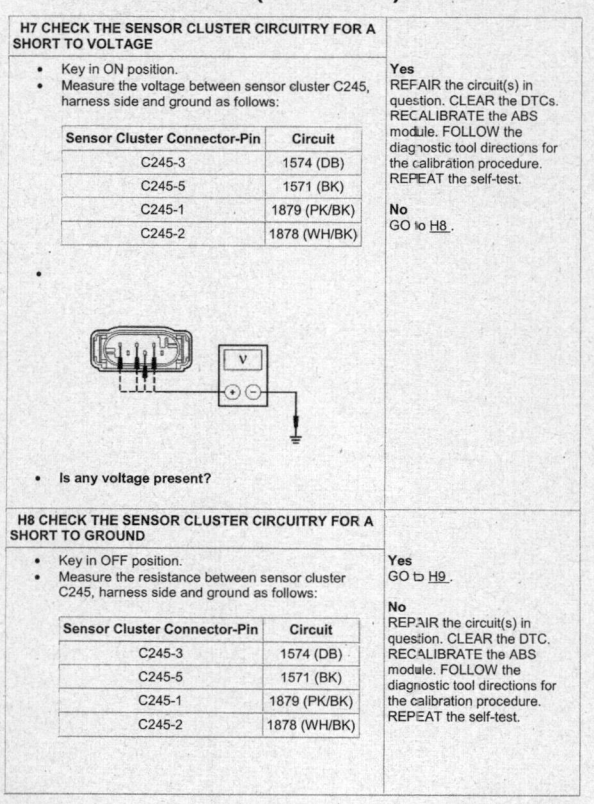

LTV0500000005390

Fig. 28 Test H, Codes C1279, C1280, C1281, C1282, C1516, C1517, C2769, C2777 & C2778: Sensor Cluster Fault (Part 3 of 4). 2004-06

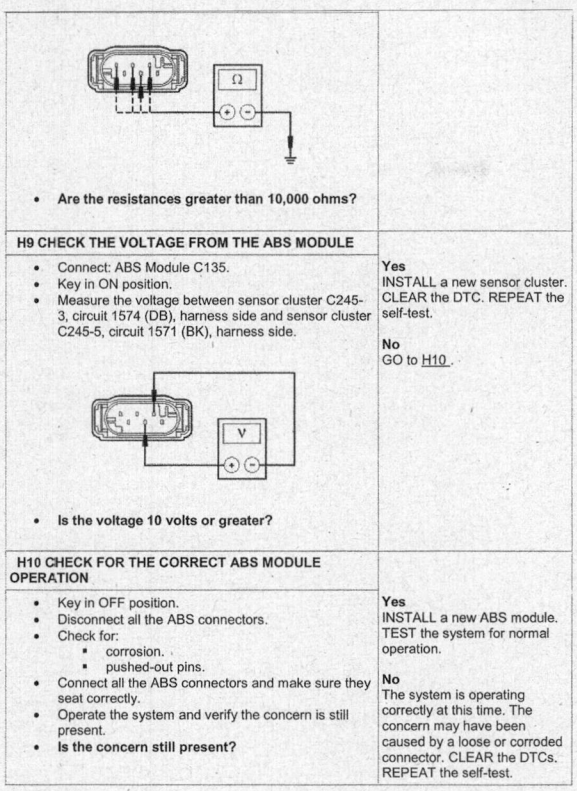

- **Are the resistances greater than 10,000 ohms?**

Test Step	Result / Action to Take
H9 CHECK THE VOLTAGE FROM THE ABS MODULE • Connect: ABS Module C135. • Key in ON position. • Measure the voltage between sensor cluster C245-3, circuit 1574 (DB), harness side and sensor cluster C245-5, circuit 1571 (BK), harness side. • **Is the voltage 10 volts or greater?**	**Yes** INSTALL a new sensor cluster. CLEAR the DTC. REPEAT the self-test. **No** GO to H10.

H10 CHECK FOR THE CORRECT ABS MODULE OPERATION
• Key in OFF position.
• Disconnect all the ABS connectors.
• Check for:
  ▪ corrosion.
  ▪ pushed-out pins.
• Connect all the ABS connectors and make sure they seat correctly.
• Operate the system and verify the concern is still present.
• **Is the concern still present?**
	Yes
	INSTALL a new ABS module. TEST the system for normal operation.
	
	No
	The system is operating correctly at this time. The concern may have been caused by a loose or corroded connector. CLEAR the DTCs. REPEAT the self-test.

LTV0500000005391

Fig. 28   Test H, Codes C1279, C1280, C1281, C1282, C1516, C1517, C2769, C2777 & C2778: Sensor Cluster Fault (Part 4 of 4). 2004-06

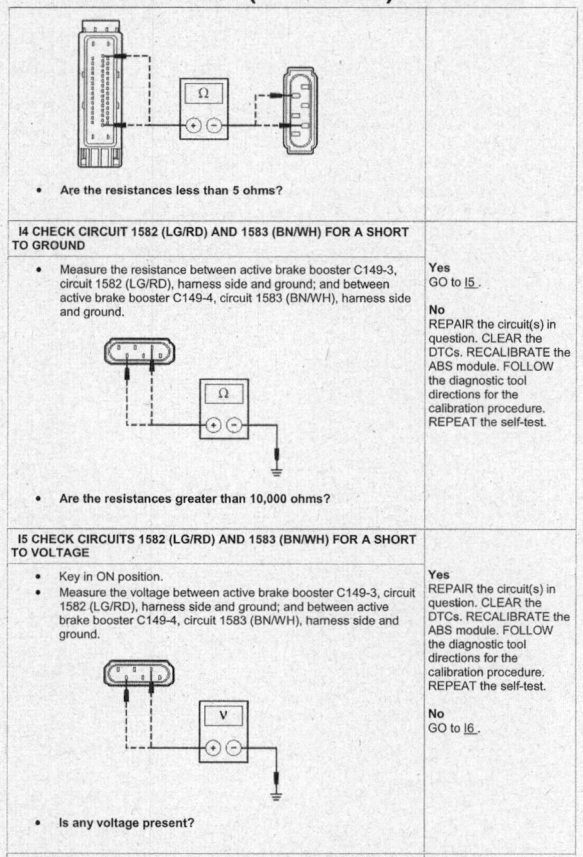

- **Are the resistances less than 5 ohms?**

I4 CHECK CIRCUIT 1582 (LG/RD) AND 1583 (BN/WH) FOR A SHORT TO GROUND • Measure the resistance between active brake booster C149-3, circuit 1582 (LG/RD), harness side and ground; and between active brake booster C149-4, circuit 1583 (BN/WH), harness side and ground. • **Are the resistances greater than 10,000 ohms?**	**Yes** GO to I5. **No** REPAIR the circuit(s) in question. CLEAR the DTCs. RECALIBRATE the ABS module. FOLLOW the diagnostic tool directions for the calibration procedure. REPEAT the self-test.
I5 CHECK CIRCUITS 1582 (LG/RD) AND 1583 (BN/WH) FOR A SHORT TO VOLTAGE • Key in ON position. • Measure the voltage between active brake booster C149-3, circuit 1582 (LG/RD), harness side and ground; and between active brake booster C149-4, circuit 1583 (BN/WH), harness side and ground. • **Is any voltage present?**	**Yes** REPAIR the circuit(s) in question. CLEAR the DTCs. RECALIBRATE the ABS module. FOLLOW the diagnostic tool directions for the calibration procedure. REPEAT the self-test. **No** GO to I6.
I6 CHECK THE ACTIVE BRAKE BOOSTER SOLENOID FOR	

LTV0500000005393

Fig. 29   Test I, Code C1285: Booster Solenoid Circuit Failure (Part 2 of 3). 2004-06

Test Step	Result / Action to Take
I1 CARRY OUT THE RECALIBRATION PROCEDURE • Key in ON position. • Enter the following diagnostic mode on the diagnostic tool: Clear DTCs. • Carry out the active brake booster recalibration procedure using the diagnostic tool. • Enter the following diagnostic mode on the diagnostic tool: Retrieve DTCs. • **Are any DTCs retrieved or does the recalibration procedure indicate a fault?**	**Yes** If DTC C1285 is retrieved, or the brake booster portion of the recalibration procedure indicates a failure, GO to I2. If any other DTC is retrieved, GO to the Anti-Lock Brake System (ABS) Module Diagnostic Trouble Code (DTC) Index. **No** The ABS is operating correctly.
I2 CHECK THE BRAKE BOOSTER SOLENOID • Key in OFF position. • Disconnect: Active Brake Booster C149. • Measure the resistance between active brake booster C149 pin 3, component side and active brake booster C149 pin 4, component side. • **Is the resistance between 1 and 2 ohms?**	**Yes** GO to I3. **No** INSTALL a new active brake booster. CLEAR the DTCs. RECALIBRATE the ABS module. FOLLOW the diagnostic tool directions for the calibration procedure. REPEAT the self-test.
I3 CHECK CIRCUIT 1582 (LG/RD) AND CIRCUIT 1583 (BN/WH) FOR AN OPEN • Disconnect: ABS Module C135. • Measure the resistance between ABS module C135-17, circuit 1582 (LG/RD), harness side and active brake booster C149-3, circuit 1582 (LG/RD), harness side; and between ABS module C135-31, circuit 1583 (BN/WH), harness side and active brake booster C149-4, circuit 1583 (BN/WH).	**Yes** GO to I4. **No** REPAIR the circuit(s) in question. CLEAR the DTCs. RECALIBRATE the ABS module. FOLLOW the diagnostic tool directions for the calibration procedure. REPEAT the self-test.

LTV0500000005392

Fig. 29   Test I, Code C1285: Booster Solenoid Circuit Failure (Part 1 of 3). 2004-06

CORRECT OPERATION • Key in OFF position. • Connect: Active Brake Booster C149. • Connect: ABS Module C135. • Key in ON position. • Start the engine and wait approximately one minute to create vacuum in the brake booster and then place the ignition switch in the OFF position. • Disconnect: ABS Module C135. • Connect a fused (10A) jumper wire between ABS module C135-31, circuit 1583 (BN/WH), harness side and ground. 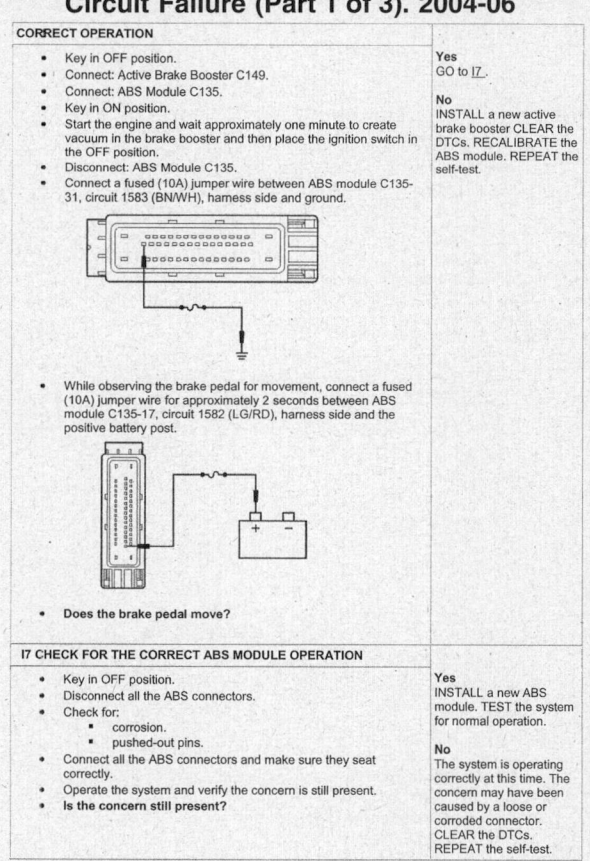 • While observing the brake pedal for movement, connect a fused (10A) jumper wire for approximately 2 seconds between ABS module C135-17, circuit 1582 (LG/RD), harness side and the positive battery post. • **Does the brake pedal move?**	**Yes** GO to I7. **No** INSTALL a new active brake booster CLEAR the DTCs. RECALIBRATE the ABS module. REPEAT the self-test.

I7 CHECK FOR THE CORRECT ABS MODULE OPERATION
• Key in OFF position.
• Disconnect all the ABS connectors.
• Check for:
  ▪ corrosion.
  ▪ pushed-out pins.
• Connect all the ABS connectors and make sure they seat correctly.
• Operate the system and verify the concern is still present.
• **Is the concern still present?**
	Yes
	INSTALL a new ABS module. TEST the system for normal operation.
	
	No
	The system is operating correctly at this time. The concern may have been caused by a loose or corroded connector. CLEAR the DTCs. REPEAT the self-test.

LTV0500000005394

Fig. 29   Test I, Code C1285: Booster Solenoid Circuit Failure (Part 3 of 3). 2004-06

Test Step	Result / Action to Take
J1 CARRY OUT THE RECALIBRATION PROCEDURE • Key in ON position. • Enter the following diagnostic mode on the diagnostic tool: Clear DTCs. • Carry out the active brake booster recalibration procedure using the diagnostic tool. • Enter the following diagnostic mode on the diagnostic tool: Retrieve DTCs. • **Are any DTCs retrieved or does the recalibration procedure indicate a fault?**	**Yes** If DTC C1287 is retrieved or recalibration procedure indicates a fault, GO TO J2. If any other DTC, GO to the Anti-Lock Brake System (ABS) Module Diagnostic Trouble Code (DTC) Index. **No** The system is operating correctly.
J2 CHECK THE NORMALLY CLOSED RELEASE SWITCH • Key in OFF position. • Disconnect: Active Brake Booster C149. • Measure the resistance between active brake booster C149 pin 2, component side and active brake booster C149 pin 5, component side, while pressing and releasing the brake pedal. • **Is the resistance less than 5 ohms with the brake pedal released and greater than 10,000 ohms with the brake pedal applied?**	**Yes** GO to J3. **No** INSTALL a new active brake booster. CLEAR the DTCs. RECALIBRATE the ABS module. FOLLOW the diagnostic tool directions for the calibration procedure. REPEAT the self-test.
J3 CHECK THE NORMALLY OPEN RELEASE SWITCH • Measure the resistance between active brake booster C149 pin 1, component side and active brake booster C149 pin 5, component side, while pressing and releasing the brake pedal.	**Yes** GO to J4. **No** INSTALL a new active brake booster. CLEAR the DTCs. RECALIBRATE the ABS module. FOLLOW the diagnostic tool directions for the calibration procedure.

LTV0500000005395

Fig. 30   Test J, Code C1287: Brake Booster Pedal Force Switch Circuit Failure (Part 1 of 4). 2004-06

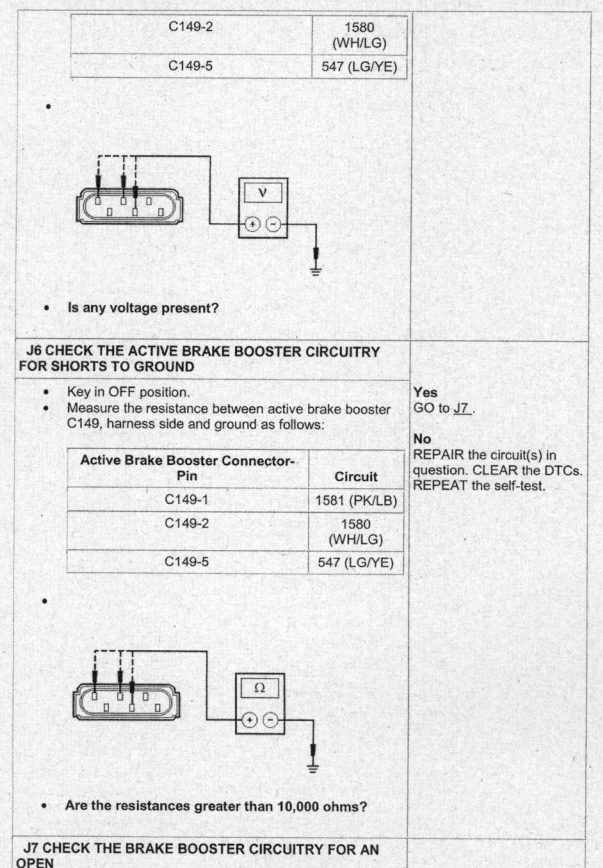

C149-2	1580 (WH/LG)	
C149-5	547 (LG/YE)	

• Is any voltage present?

J6 CHECK THE ACTIVE BRAKE BOOSTER CIRCUITRY FOR SHORTS TO GROUND • Key in OFF position. • Measure the resistance between active brake booster C149, harness side and ground as follows:	**Yes** GO to J7. **No** REPAIR the circuit(s) in question. CLEAR the DTCs. REPEAT the self-test.

Active Brake Booster Connector-Pin	Circuit
C149-1	1581 (PK/LB)
C149-2	1580 (WH/LG)
C149-5	547 (LG/YE)

• Are the resistances greater than 10,000 ohms?

J7 CHECK THE BRAKE BOOSTER CIRCUITRY FOR AN OPEN	

LTV0500000005397

Fig. 30   Test J, Code C1287: Brake Booster Pedal Force Switch Circuit Failure (Part 3 of 4). 2004-06

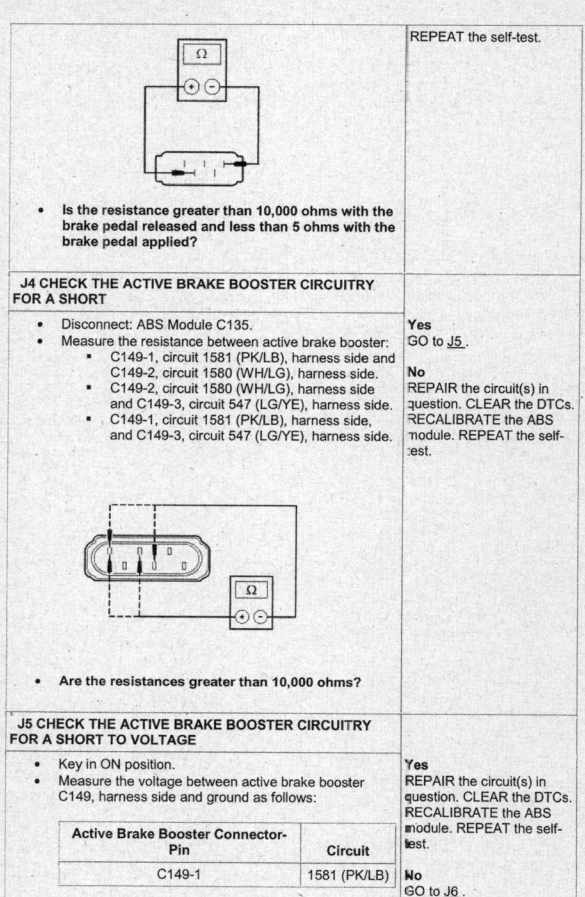

	REPEAT the self-test.
• Is the resistance greater than 10,000 ohms with the brake pedal released and less than 5 ohms with the brake pedal applied?	
J4 CHECK THE ACTIVE BRAKE BOOSTER CIRCUITRY FOR A SHORT • Disconnect: ABS Module C135. • Measure the resistance between active brake booster: ■ C149-1, circuit 1581 (PK/LB), harness side and C149-2, circuit 1580 (WH/LG), harness side. ■ C149-2, circuit 1580 (WH/LG), harness side and C149-3, circuit 547 (LG/YE), harness side. ■ C149-1, circuit 1581 (PK/LB), harness side, and C149-3, circuit 547 (LG/YE), harness side. • Are the resistances greater than 10,000 ohms?	**Yes** GO to J5. **No** REPAIR the circuit(s) in question. CLEAR the DTCs. RECALIBRATE the ABS module. REPEAT the self-test.
J5 CHECK THE ACTIVE BRAKE BOOSTER CIRCUITRY FOR A SHORT TO VOLTAGE • Key in ON position. • Measure the voltage between active brake booster C149, harness side and ground as follows:	**Yes** REPAIR the circuit(s) in question. CLEAR the DTCs. RECALIBRATE the ABS module. REPEAT the self-test. **No** GO to J6.

Active Brake Booster Connector-Pin	Circuit
C149-1	1581 (PK/LB)

LTV0500000005396

Fig. 30   Test J, Code C1287: Brake Booster Pedal Force Switch Circuit Failure (Part 2 of 4). 2004-06

• Measure the resistance between ABS module C135, harness side and active brake booster C149, harness side as follows:	**Yes** GO to J8. **No** REPAIR the circuit(s) in question. CLEAR the DTCs. RECALIBRATE the ABS module. FOLLOW the diagnostic tool directions for the calibration procedure. REPEAT the self-test.

ABS Module Connector-Pin	Active Brake Booster Connector-Pin	Circuit
C135-27	C149-1	1581 (PK/LB)
C135-28	C149-5	547 (LG/YE)
C135-30	C149-2	1580 (WH/LG)

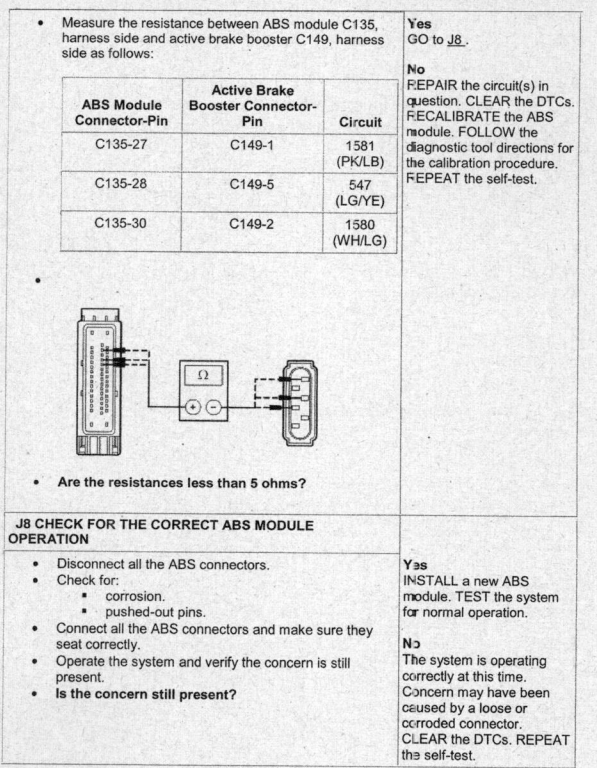

• Are the resistances less than 5 ohms?

J8 CHECK FOR THE CORRECT ABS MODULE OPERATION • Disconnect all the ABS connectors. • Check for: ■ corrosion. ■ pushed-out pins. • Connect all the ABS connectors and make sure they seat correctly. • Operate the system and verify the concern is still present. • **Is the concern still present?**	**Yes** INSTALL a new ABS module. TEST the system for normal operation. **No** The system is operating correctly at this time. Concern may have been caused by a loose or corroded connector. CLEAR the DTCs. REPEAT the self-test.

LTV0500000005398

Fig. 30   Test J, Code C1287: Brake Booster Pedal Force Switch Circuit Failure (Part 4 of 4). 2004-06

Test Step	Result / Action to Take
K1 CHECK FOR DTCS	
• Key in ON position. • Use the recorded results from the ABS module self-test. • **Is DTC C1287, C1483, B2734, B2736, B2737, B2738 or B2740 present?**	**Yes** REPAIR these DTCs first. GO to the Anti-Lock Brake System (ABS) Module Diagnostic Trouble Code (DTC) Index. **No** GO to K2 .
K2 CHECK THE PRIMARY BRAKE PRESSURE SENSOR CIRCUITRY FOR A SHORT TO VOLTAGE	
• Key in OFF position. • Disconnect: ABS Module C135. • Disconnect: Primary Brake Pressure Sensor C147. • Key in ON position. • Measure the voltage between primary brake pressure sensor C147, harness side and ground as follows:	**Yes** REPAIR the circuit(s) in question. CLEAR the DTCs. REPEAT the self-test. **No** GO to K3 .

Primary Brake Pressure Sensor Connector-Pin	Circuit
C147-1	3603 (RD)
C147-2	3600 (RD/WH)
C147-3	3601 (WH/RD)

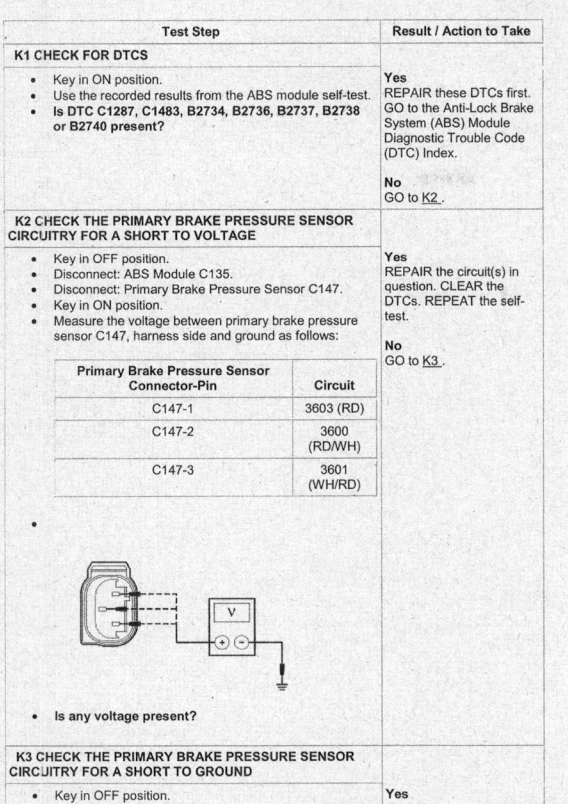

• Is any voltage present?	
K3 CHECK THE PRIMARY BRAKE PRESSURE SENSOR CIRCUITRY FOR A SHORT TO GROUND	
• Key in OFF position.	**Yes**

LTV0500000005399

Fig. 31   Test K, Codes C1288 & C1440: ABS w/Stability Assist, Brake Pressure Sensor Input Circuit Failure/Signal Fault (Part 1 of 4). 2004-06

• Measure the resistance between primary brake pressure sensor C147, harness side and ground as follows:	GO to K4 . **No** REPAIR the circuit(s) in question. CLEAR the DTCs. REPEAT the self-test.

Primary Brake Pressure Sensor Connector-Pin	Circuit
C147-1	3603 (RD)
C147-2	3600 (RD/WH)
C147-3	3601 (WH/RD)

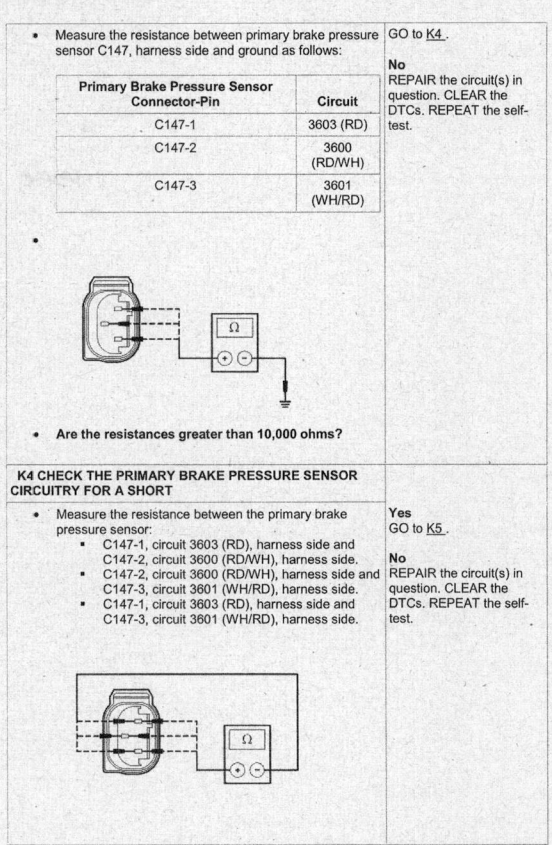

• Are the resistances greater than 10,000 ohms?	
K4 CHECK THE PRIMARY BRAKE PRESSURE SENSOR CIRCUITRY FOR A SHORT	
• Measure the resistance between the primary brake pressure sensor: ▪ C147-1, circuit 3603 (RD), harness side and C147-2, circuit 3600 (RD/WH), harness side. ▪ C147-2, circuit 3600 (RD/WH), harness side and C147-3, circuit 3601 (WH/RD), harness side. ▪ C147-1, circuit 3603 (RD), harness side and C147-3, circuit 3601 (WH/RD), harness side.	**Yes** GO to K5 . **No** REPAIR the circuit(s) in question. CLEAR the DTCs. REPEAT the self-test.

LTV0500000005400

Fig. 31   Test K, Codes C1288 & C1440: ABS w/Stability Assist, Brake Pressure Sensor Input Circuit Failure/Signal Fault (Part 2 of 4). 2004-06

• Are the resistances greater than 10,000 ohms?	
K5 CHECK THE PRIMARY BRAKE PRESSURE SENSOR CIRCUITRY FOR AN OPEN	
• Measure the resistance between ABS module C135, harness side and primary brake pressure sensor C147, harness side as follows:	**Yes** GO to K6 . **No** REPAIR the circuit(s) in question. CLEAR the DTCs. REPEAT the self-test.

ABS Module Connector-Pin	Primary Brake Pressure Sensor Connector-Pin	Circuit
C135-19	C147-1	3603 (RD)
C135-20	C147-2	3600 (RD/WH)
C135-18	C147-3	3601 (WH/RD)

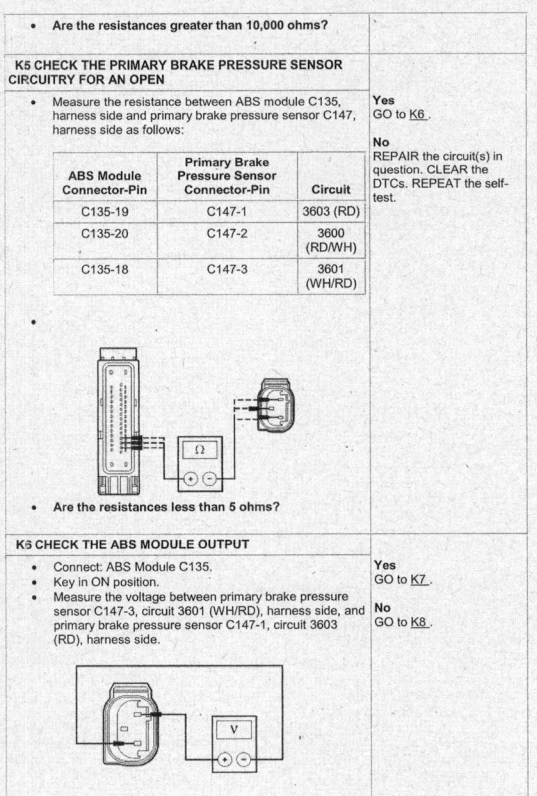

• Are the resistances less than 5 ohms?	
K6 CHECK THE ABS MODULE OUTPUT	
• Connect: ABS Module C135. • Key in ON position. • Measure the voltage between primary brake pressure sensor C147-3, circuit 3601 (WH/RD), harness side, and primary brake pressure sensor C147-1, circuit 3603 (RD), harness side.	**Yes** GO to K7 . **No** GO to K8 .

LTV0500000005401

Fig. 31   Test K, Codes C1288 & C1440: ABS w/Stability Assist, Brake Pressure Sensor Input Circuit Failure/Signal Fault (Part 3 of 4). 2004-06

• Is the voltage approximately 5 volts?	
K7 CHECK THE PRIMARY BRAKE PRESSURE SENSOR OUTPUT	
• Key in OFF position. • Connect: Primary Brake Pressure Sensor C147. • Disconnect: ABS Module C135. • Remove pin 20, circuit 3600 (RD/WH) from the ABS module connector. • Connect: ABS Module C135. • Key in ON position. • Measure the voltage between ABS module C135-20, circuit 3600 (RD/WH), harness side and ground, while pressing and releasing the brake pedal.	**Yes** GO to K8 . **No** INSTALL a new primary brake pressure sensor. CLEAR the DTCs. RECALIBRATE the ABS module. REPEAT the self-test.

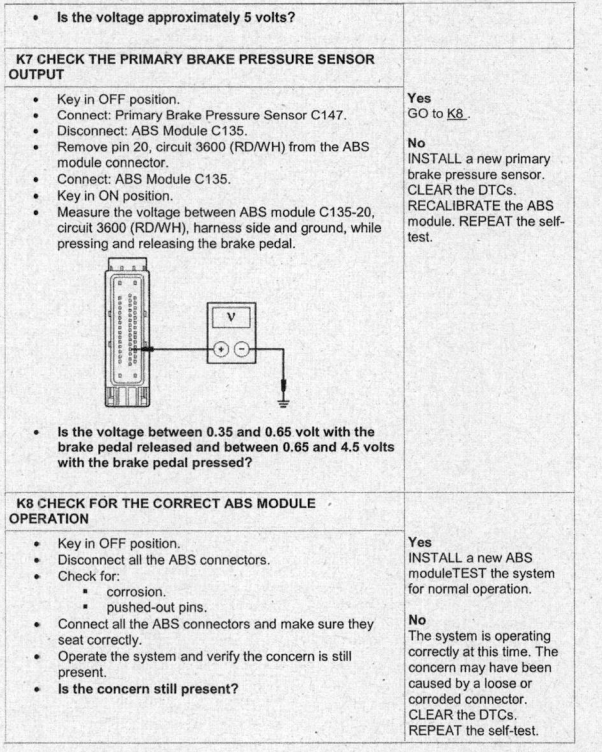

• Is the voltage between 0.35 and 0.65 volt with the brake pedal released and between 0.65 and 4.5 volts with the brake pedal pressed?	
K8 CHECK FOR THE CORRECT ABS MODULE OPERATION	
• Key in OFF position. • Disconnect all the ABS connectors. • Check for: ▪ corrosion. ▪ pushed-out pins. • Connect all the ABS connectors and make sure they seat correctly. • Operate the system and verify the concern is still present. • **Is the concern still present?**	**Yes** INSTALL a new ABS moduleTEST the system for normal operation. **No** The system is operating correctly at this time. The concern may have been caused by a loose or corroded connector. CLEAR the DTCs. REPEAT the self-test.

LTV0500000005402

Fig. 31   Test K, Codes C1288 & C1440: ABS w/Stability Assist, Brake Pressure Sensor Input Circuit Failure/Signal Fault (Part 4 of 4). 2004-06

Test Step	Result / Action to Take
L1 CHECK CIRCUIT 3601 (WH/RD) AND CIRCUIT 1902 (RD) FOR A SHORT TO VOLTAGE • Key in OFF position. • Disconnect: ABS Module C135. • Disconnect: Primary Brake Pressure Sensor C147. • Disconnect: Brake Pedal Travel Sensor C148. • Key in ON position. • Measure the voltage between ABS module C135-18, circuit 3601 (WH/RD), harness side and ground; and between ABS module C135-26, circuit 1902 (RD), harness side and ground. 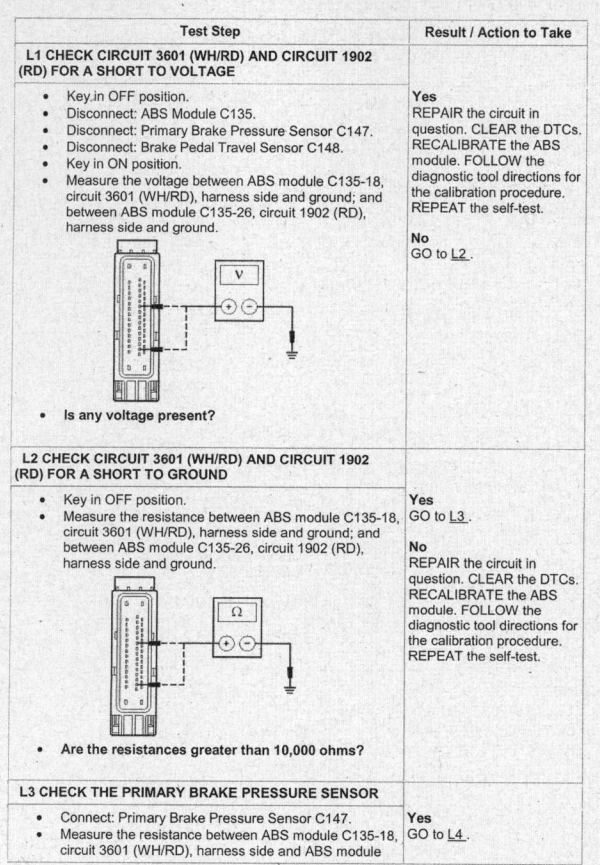 • Is any voltage present?	**Yes** REPAIR the circuit in question. CLEAR the DTCs. RECALIBRATE the ABS module. FOLLOW the diagnostic tool directions for the calibration procedure. REPEAT the self-test. **No** GO to L2.
L2 CHECK CIRCUIT 3601 (WH/RD) AND CIRCUIT 1902 (RD) FOR A SHORT TO GROUND • Key in OFF position. • Measure the resistance between ABS module C135-18, circuit 3601 (WH/RD), harness side and ground; and between ABS module C135-26, circuit 1902 (RD), harness side and ground. • Are the resistances greater than 10,000 ohms?	**Yes** GO to L3. **No** REPAIR the circuit in question. CLEAR the DTCs. RECALIBRATE the ABS module. FOLLOW the diagnostic tool directions for the calibration procedure. REPEAT the self-test.
L3 CHECK THE PRIMARY BRAKE PRESSURE SENSOR • Connect: Primary Brake Pressure Sensor C147. • Measure the resistance between ABS module C135-18, circuit 3601 (WH/RD), harness side and ABS module	**Yes** GO to L4.

LTV0500000005403

Fig. 32 Test L, Code C1730: Reference Voltage Out Of Range (Part 1 of 2). 2004-06

C135-19, circuit 3603 (RD), harness side. 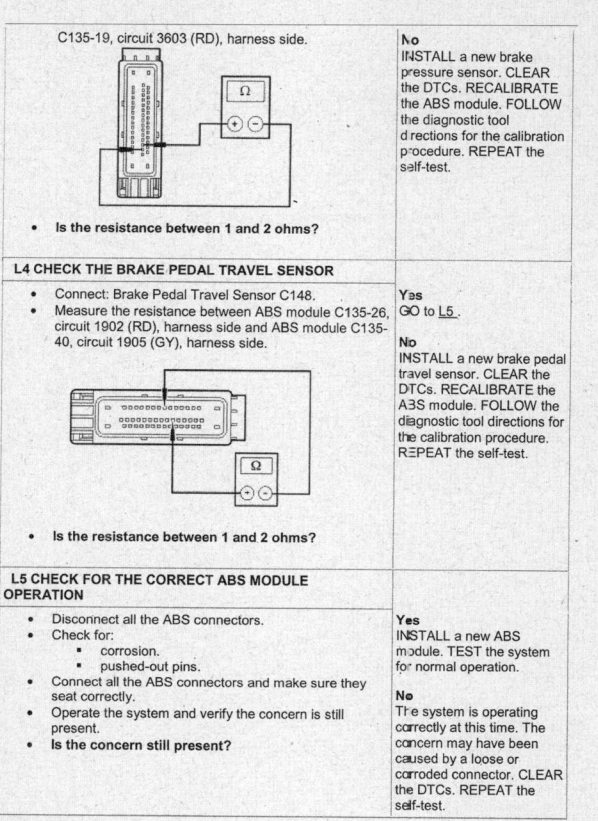 • Is the resistance between 1 and 2 ohms?	**No** INSTALL a new brake pressure sensor. CLEAR the DTCs. RECALIBRATE the ABS module. FOLLOW the diagnostic tool directions for the calibration procedure. REPEAT the self-test.
L4 CHECK THE BRAKE PEDAL TRAVEL SENSOR • Connect: Brake Pedal Travel Sensor C148. • Measure the resistance between ABS module C135-26, circuit 1902 (RD), harness side and ABS module C135-40, circuit 1905 (GY), harness side. • Is the resistance between 1 and 2 ohms?	**Yes** GO to L5. **No** INSTALL a new brake pedal travel sensor. CLEAR the DTCs. RECALIBRATE the ABS module. FOLLOW the diagnostic tool directions for the calibration procedure. REPEAT the self-test.

L5 CHECK FOR THE CORRECT ABS MODULE OPERATION
• Disconnect all the ABS connectors.
• Check for:
     □ corrosion.
     □ pushed-out pins.
• Connect all the ABS connectors and make sure they seat correctly.
• Operate the system and verify the concern is still present.
• Is the concern still present?
	Yes
	INSTALL a new ABS module. TEST the system for normal operation.
	
	No
	The system is operating correctly at this time. The concern may have been caused by a loose or corroded connector. CLEAR the DTCs. REPEAT the self-test.

LTV0500000005404

Fig. 32 Test L, Code C1730: Reference Voltage Out Of Range (Part 2 of 2). 2004-06

Test Step	Result / Action to Take
M1 CHECK THE BRAKE PEDAL TRAVEL SENSOR CIRCUITRY FOR A SHORT TO VOLTAGE • Key in OFF position. • Disconnect: ABS Module C135. • Disconnect: Brake Pedal Travel Sensor C148. • Key in ON position. • Measure the voltage between brake pedal travel sensor C148, harness side and ground as follows:	**Yes** REPAIR the circuit(s) in question. CLEAR the DTCs. REPEAT the self-test. **No** GO to M2.

Brake Pedal Travel Sensor Connector-Pin	Circuit
C148-1	1902 (RD)
C148-2	1904 (GY/BK)
C148-3	1905 (GY)

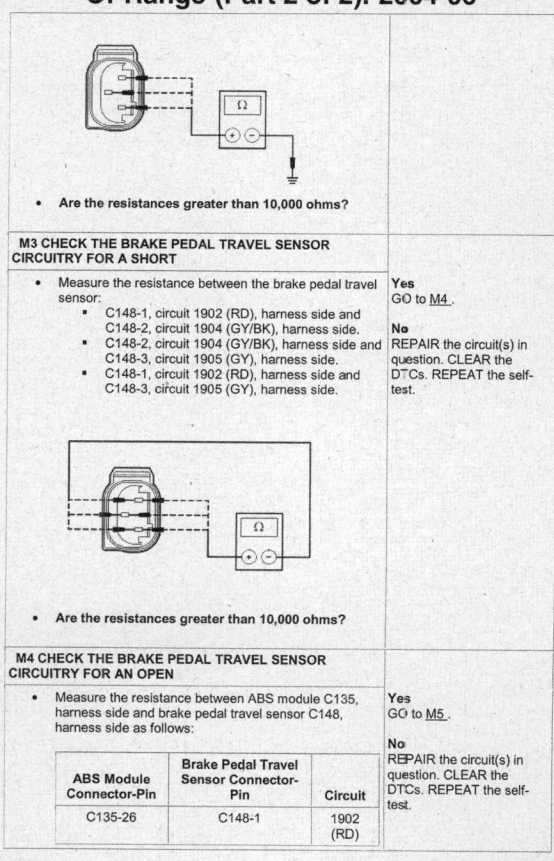

• Is any voltage present?

M2 CHECK THE BRAKE PEDAL TRAVEL SENSOR CIRCUITRY FOR A SHORT TO GROUND • Key in OFF position. • Measure the resistance between brake pedal travel sensor C148, harness side and ground as follows:	**Yes** GO to M3. **No** REPAIR the circuit(s) in question. CLEAR the DTCs. REPEAT the self-test.

Brake Pedal Travel Sensor C148 Pin	Circuit
1	1902 (RD)
2	1904 (GY/BK)
3	1905 (GY)

LTV0500000005405

Fig. 33 Test M Codes B2734, B2736, B2737, B2738 & B2740: Pedal Travel Sensor Fault (Part 1 of 4). 2004-06

• Are the resistances greater than 10,000 ohms?	

M3 CHECK THE BRAKE PEDAL TRAVEL SENSOR CIRCUITRY FOR A SHORT
• Measure the resistance between the brake pedal travel sensor:
     ▪ C148-1, circuit 1902 (RD), harness side and C148-2, circuit 1904 (GY/BK), harness side.
     ▪ C148-2, circuit 1904 (GY/BK), harness side and C148-3, circuit 1905 (GY), harness side.
     ▪ C148-1, circuit 1902 (RD), harness side and C148-3, circuit 1905 (GY), harness side.
• Are the resistances greater than 10,000 ohms?
	Yes
	GO to M4.
	
	No
	REPAIR the circuit(s) in question. CLEAR the DTCs. REPEAT the self-test.

M4 CHECK THE BRAKE PEDAL TRAVEL SENSOR CIRCUITRY FOR AN OPEN • Measure the resistance between ABS module C135, harness side and brake pedal travel sensor C148, harness side as follows:	**Yes** GO to M5. **No** REPAIR the circuit(s) in question. CLEAR the DTCs. REPEAT the self-test.

ABS Module Connector-Pin	Brake Pedal Travel Sensor Connector-Pin	Circuit
C135-26	C148-1	1902 (RD)

LTV0500000005406

Fig. 33 Test M Codes B2734, B2736, B2737, B2738 & B2740: Pedal Travel Sensor Fault (Part 2 of 4). 2004-06

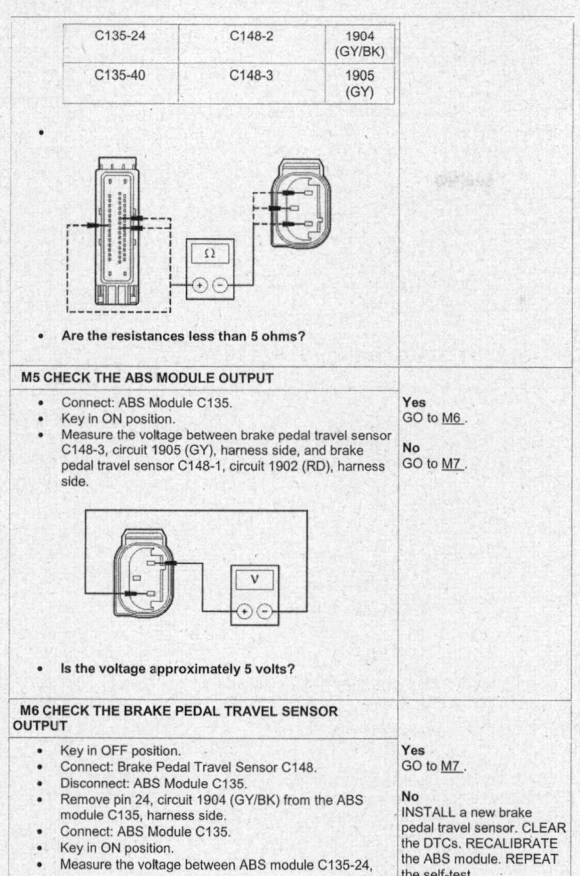

| C135-24 | C148-2 | 1904 (GY/BK) |
| C135-40 | C148-3 | 1905 (GY) |

- Are the resistances less than 5 ohms?

M5 CHECK THE ABS MODULE OUTPUT

- Connect: ABS Module C135.
- Key in ON position.
- Measure the voltage between brake pedal travel sensor C148-3, circuit 1905 (GY), harness side, and brake pedal travel sensor C148-1, circuit 1902 (RD), harness side.

Yes
GO to <u>M6</u>.

No
GO to <u>M7</u>.

- Is the voltage approximately 5 volts?

M6 CHECK THE BRAKE PEDAL TRAVEL SENSOR OUTPUT

- Key in OFF position.
- Connect: Brake Pedal Travel Sensor C148.
- Disconnect: ABS Module C135.
- Remove pin 24, circuit 1904 (GY/BK) from the ABS module C135, harness side.
- Connect: ABS Module C135.
- Key in ON position.
- Measure the voltage between ABS module C135-24,

Yes
GO to <u>M7</u>.

No
INSTALL a new brake pedal travel sensor. CLEAR the DTCs. RECALIBRATE the ABS module. REPEAT the self-test.

LTV0500000005407

Fig. 33   Test M Codes B2734, B2736, B2737, B2738 & B2740: Pedal Travel Sensor Fault (Part 3 of 4). 2004-06

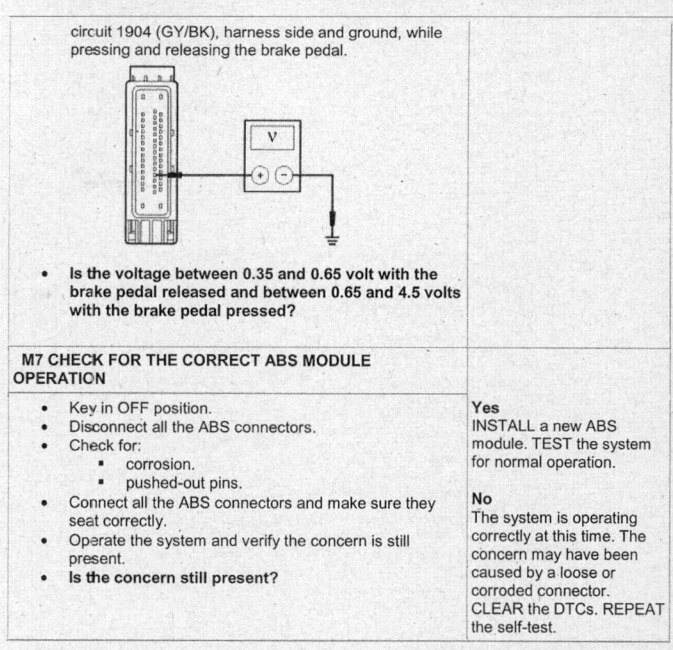

circuit 1904 (GY/BK), harness side and ground, while pressing and releasing the brake pedal.

- Is the voltage between 0.35 and 0.65 volt with the brake pedal released and between 0.65 and 4.5 volts with the brake pedal pressed?

M7 CHECK FOR THE CORRECT ABS MODULE OPERATION

- Key in OFF position.
- Disconnect all the ABS connectors.
- Check for:
  - corrosion.
  - pushed-out pins.
- Connect all the ABS connectors and make sure they seat correctly.
- Operate the system and verify the concern is still present.
- **Is the concern still present?**

Yes
INSTALL a new ABS module. TEST the system for normal operation.

No
The system is operating correctly at this time. The concern may have been caused by a loose or corroded connector. CLEAR the DTCs. REPEAT the self-test.

LTV0500000005408

Fig. 33   Test M Codes B2734, B2736, B2737, B2738 & B2740: Pedal Travel Sensor Fault (Part 4 of 4). 2004-06

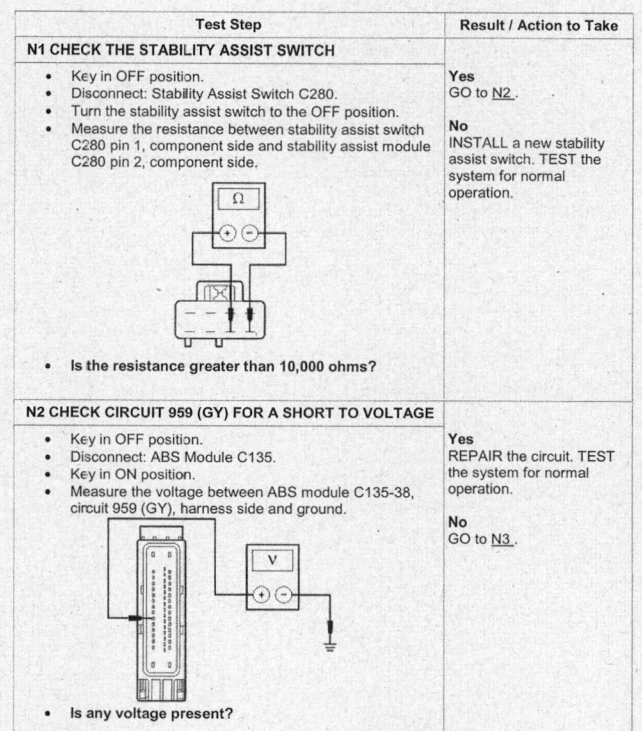

Test Step	Result / Action to Take
N1 CHECK THE STABILITY ASSIST SWITCH • Key in OFF position. • Disconnect: Stability Assist Switch C280. • Turn the stability assist switch to the OFF position. • Measure the resistance between stability assist switch C280 pin 1, component side and stability assist module C280 pin 2, component side. • Is the resistance greater than 10,000 ohms?	**Yes** GO to <u>N2</u>. **No** INSTALL a new stability assist switch. TEST the system for normal operation.
N2 CHECK CIRCUIT 959 (GY) FOR A SHORT TO VOLTAGE • Key in OFF position. • Disconnect: ABS Module C135. • Key in ON position. • Measure the voltage between ABS module C135-38, circuit 959 (GY), harness side and ground. • Is any voltage present?	**Yes** REPAIR the circuit. TEST the system for normal operation. **No** GO to <u>N3</u>.

LTV0500000005409

Fig. 34   Test N: Stability Assist Cannot Be Disabled (Part 1 of 2). 2004-06

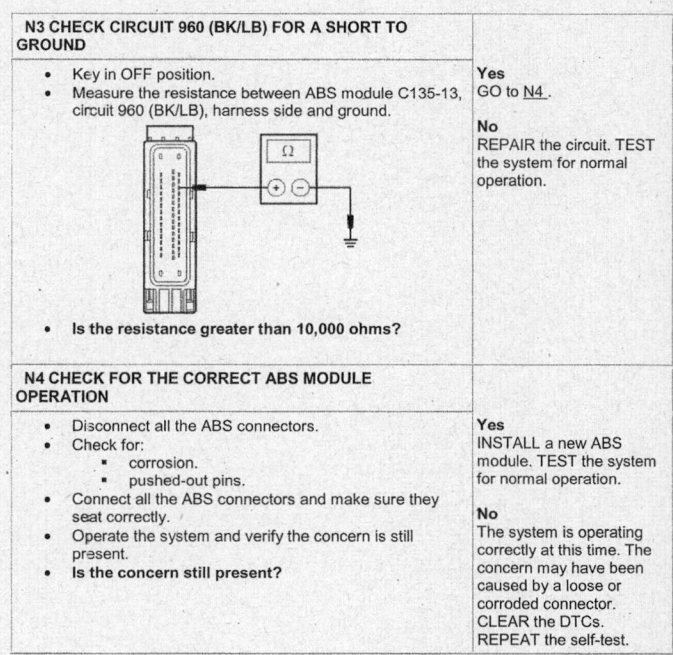

N3 CHECK CIRCUIT 960 (BK/LB) FOR A SHORT TO GROUND • Key in OFF position. • Measure the resistance between ABS module C135-13, circuit 960 (BK/LB), harness side and ground. • Is the resistance greater than 10,000 ohms?	**Yes** GO to <u>N4</u>. **No** REPAIR the circuit. TEST the system for normal operation.

N4 CHECK FOR THE CORRECT ABS MODULE OPERATION
• Disconnect all the ABS connectors.
• Check for:
  • corrosion.
  • pushed-out pins.
• Connect all the ABS connectors and make sure they seat correctly.
• Operate the system and verify the concern is still present.
• **Is the concern still present?**
	Yes
	INSTALL a new ABS module. TEST the system for normal operation.
	
	No
	The system is operating correctly at this time. The concern may have been caused by a loose or corroded connector. CLEAR the DTCs. REPEAT the self-test.

LTV0500000005410

Fig. 34   Test N: Stability Assist Cannot Be Disabled (Part 2 of 2). 2004-06

Test Step	Result / Action to Take
O1 CHECK FOR DTCS • Connect the diagnostic tool. • Key in ON position. • Retrieve the DTCs. • **Are any other DTCs retrieved with C1998?**	**Yes** GO to the Anti-Lock Brake System (ABS) Module Diagnostic Trouble Code (DTC) Index. **NOTE:** Some of the pinpoint tests recommend RSC calibration prior to any further diagnostics, in this case, GO to O2. **No** GO to O2.
O2 ABS CALIBRATION • Start the engine. • **NOTE:** Be sure to rotate the steering wheel lock-to-lock during the calibration of the ABS system. • Carry out the ABS module calibration per the diagnostic tool instructions. • **Did the calibration complete for all of the stability assist sensors; and did the stability assist lamp stop flashing and go off?**	**Yes** GO to O3. **No** GO to O4. Some concerns will cause the calibration not to complete. If sent here from another pinpoint test, return to that pinpoint test for further diagnostics.
O3 CLEAR DTC C1998 • **NOTE:** You must clear DTC C1998 after the completion of the calibration. • Clear the DTC. • **Did the DTC clear?**	**Yes** TEST DRIVE the vehicle. REPEAT the self-test. **NOTE:** If sent here from another pinpoint test, return to that pinpoint test for further diagnostics. **No** GO to O4.
O4 MONITOR THE STEERING WHEEL ROTATION SENSOR PIDS • **NOTE:** You must clear DTC C1998 after the completion of the RSC calibration. Monitor the ABS module steering position sensor PIDS while rotating the steering wheel clockwise and counterclockwise. • **Are the 2 steering position sensor PID values switching as the wheel rotates?**	**Yes** Go To Pinpoint Test H. **No** Go To Pinpoint Test G.

LTV0500000005411

Fig. 35 Test O, Code C1998: Module Calibration Not Complete. 2004-06

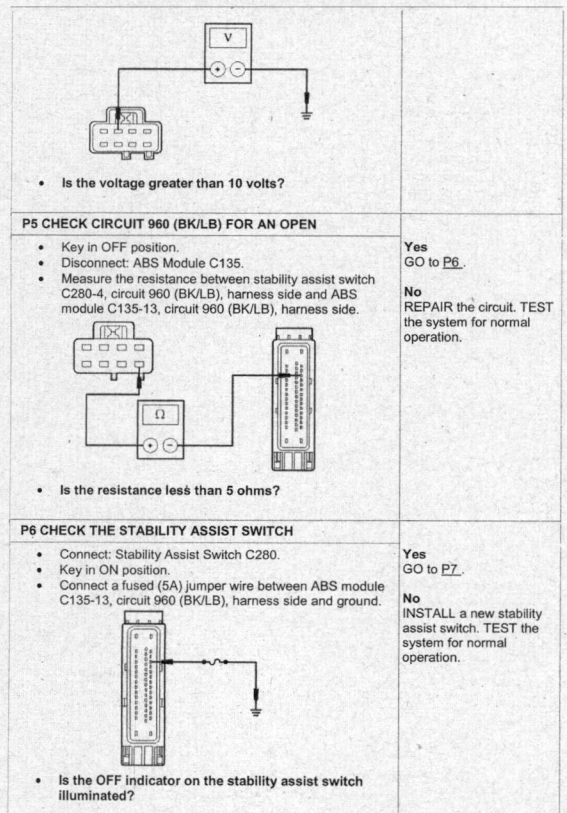

• **Is the voltage greater than 10 volts?**	
P5 CHECK CIRCUIT 960 (BK/LB) FOR AN OPEN • Key in OFF position. • Disconnect: ABS Module C135. • Measure the resistance between stability assist switch C280-4, circuit 960 (BK/LB), harness side and ABS module C135-13, circuit 960 (BK/LB), harness side.	**Yes** GO to P6. **No** REPAIR the circuit. TEST the system for normal operation.
• **Is the resistance less than 5 ohms?**	
P6 CHECK THE STABILITY ASSIST SWITCH • Connect: Stability Assist Switch C280. • Key in ON position. • Connect a fused (5A) jumper wire between ABS module C135-13, circuit 960 (BK/LB), harness side and ground.	**Yes** GO to P7. **No** INSTALL a new stability assist switch. TEST the system for normal operation.
• **Is the OFF indicator on the stability assist switch illuminated?**	

LTV0500000005413

Fig. 36 Test P: Stability Assist Switch Indicator Is Never/Always On (Part 2 of 3). 2004-06

Test Step	Result / Action to Take
P1 DETERMINE THE CONDITION • Key in ON position. • Observe the stability assist switch indicator. • **Is the OFF indicator on the stability assist switch illuminated?**	**Yes** GO to P2. **No** GO to P4.
P2 CHECK THE ABS MODULE • Key in OFF position. • Disconnect: ABS Module C135. • Key in ON position. • **Does the OFF indicator on the stability assist switch continue to illuminate?**	**Yes** GO to P3. **No** GO to P7.
P3 CHECK CIRCUIT 960 (BK/LB) FOR A SHORT TO GROUND • Key in OFF position. • Disconnect: Stability Assist Switch C280. • Measure the resistance between stability assist switch C280-4, circuit 960 (BK/LB), harness side and ground. • **Is the resistance less greater than 10,000 ohms?**	**Yes** INSTALL a new stability assist switch. TEST the system for normal operation. **No** REPAIR the circuit. TEST the system for normal operation.
P4 CHECK CIRCUIT 640 (RD/YE) FOR AN OPEN • Key in OFF position. • Disconnect: Stability Assist Switch C280. • Measure the voltage between stability assist switch C280-6, circuit 640 (RD/YE), harness side and ground.	**Yes** GO to P5. **No** VERIFY central junction box (CJB) fuse 15 (5A) is OK. If OK, REPAIR the circuit. TEST the system for normal operation.

LTV0500000005412

Fig. 36 Test P: Stability Assist Switch Indicator Is Never/Always On (Part 1 of 3). 2004-06

P7 CHECK FOR THE CORRECT ABS MODULE OPERATION
• Key in OFF position.
• Disconnect all the ABS connectors.
• Check for:
   ▪ corrosion.
   ▪ pushed-out pins.
• Connect all the ABS connectors and make sure they seat correctly.
• Operate the system and verify the concern is still present.
• **Is the concern still present?**
	Yes
	INSTALL a new ABS module TEST the system for normal operation.
	No
	The system is operating correctly at this time. The concern may have been caused by a loose or corroded connector. CLEAR the DTCs. REPEAT the self-test.

LTV0500000005414

Fig. 36 Test P: Stability Assist Switch Indicator Is Never/Always On (Part 3 of 3). 2004-06

Explorer & Mountaineer

NOTE: Electrical Symbol & Wire Color Code Identification Located In The Front Of This Manual May Be Used As An Aid When Using Wiring Circuits Found In This Section.

NOTE: Refer To "Computer Relearn Procedures" Located In The Front Of This Manual When Battery Power To The Computer Has Been Interrupted.

INDEX

	Page No.		Page No.		Page No.
Description	5-111	Wiring Diagrams	5-111	Stability Control Sensor	
Diagnosis & Testing	5-111	Diagnostic Chart Index	5-116	Cluster	5-112
Accessing Diagnostic Trouble		Precautions	5-111	Steering Wheel Rotation	
Codes	5-111	Battery Ground Cable	5-111	Sensor	5-112
Clearing Diagnostic Trouble		Brake Fluid Handling	5-111	Wheel Speed Sensor	5-112
Codes	5-111	System Service	5-111	Troubleshooting	5-111
Diagnostic Tests	5-111	Brake System Bleed	5-111	Symptom Chart	5-111
Pinpoint Tests	5-111	Component Replacement	5-111		
Diagnostic Trouble Code		ABS Control Module	5-111		
Interpretation	5-111	Hydraulic Control Unit (HCU)	5-112		

PRECAUTIONS

BATTERY GROUND CABLE

Prior to service disconnect battery ground cable and isolate as required.

BRAKE FLUID HANDLING

Brake fluid can cause serious injury and vehicle damage if not handled properly. Avoid contact with eyes and do not allow fluid to splash or spill on painted surfaces. Wash hands thoroughly after handling.

DESCRIPTION

The anti-lock brake system (ABS) module, with or without stability assist, simultaneously manages the anti-lock braking, traction control and engine control systems to maintain vehicle control during deceleration and acceleration. The ABS accomplishes this by communicating with the other modules over the high speed controller area network (HS-CAN) bus.

When the ignition switch is in the RUN position, the module carries out a preliminary electrical check and, at approximately 20 km/h (12 mph), the hydraulic pump motor is turned on for approximately one half-second. Any malfunction of the anti-lock brake system disables the traction control and stability assist (if equipped). The ABS module communicates with the instrument cluster over the HS-CAN bus and the cluster illuminates the anti-lock brake warning indicator. However, the power-assist braking system functions normally.

With the ignition switch in the START or RUN positions, the stability assist module functions similarly to a conventional ABS module by monitoring and comparing the rotational speed of each wheel. The wheel speed sensors electrically sense each tooth of the anti-lock sensor ring as they pass through the sensor magnetic field. When the stability assist module detects an impending wheel lock, wheel spin or vehicle motion that is inconsistent with the driver commands, it modulates brake pressure to the appropriate brake caliper(s). The stability assist module triggers the hydraulic control unit (HCU) to open and close the appropriate solenoid valves. Once the affected wheel(s) returns to the desired speed, the stability assist module returns the solenoid valves to their normal position, and normal base brake operation is restored.

TROUBLESHOOTING

Symptom Chart

Refer to **Figs. 1 and 2** for symptom charts.

DIAGNOSIS & TESTING

Accessing Diagnostic Trouble Codes

Connect a suitably programmed scan tool and Vehicle Communication Module (VCM) with appropriate adapters, or equivalents, to the Data Link Connector (DCL) located in the passenger compartment beneath the instrument panel. Follow tool manufacturer's instructions for accessing Diagnostic Trouble Codes (DTC).

Diagnostic Trouble Code Interpretation

Refer to **Figs. 3 and 4** for diagnostic trouble code interpretation.

Wiring Diagrams

Refer to **Figs. 5 and 6** for wiring diagrams.

Diagnostic Tests

PINPOINT TESTS

2002–03

Refer to **Figs. 7 through 13** for pinpoint tests.

2004–06

Refer to **Figs. 14 through 24** for pinpoint tests.

Clearing Diagnostic Trouble Codes

Connect a suitably programmed scan tool and Vehicle Communication Module (VCM) with appropriate adapters, or equivalents, to the Data Link Connector (DCL) located in the passenger compartment beneath the instrument panel. Follow tool manufacturer's instructions for clearing Diagnostic Trouble Codes (DTC).

SYSTEM SERVICE

Brake System Bleed

Refer to "Hydraulic Brake Systems" chapter for bleeding procedure.

Component Replacement

ABS CONTROL MODULE

1. Remove HCU as outlined under "Hydraulic Control Unit (HCU)."

Condition	Possible Source	Action
• No communication with the anti-lock brake control module	• BJB Fuse 7 (30A). • CJB Fuse 14 (10A). • Circuitry. • Anti-lock brake control module.	• GO to Pinpoint Test A.
• Loss of sensor signal during vehicle deceleration or sensor signal drops out at low speed	• Anti-lock brake sensor indicator. • Sensor output is weak. • Air gap.	• GO to Pinpoint Test D.
• Unwarranted ABS activity	• Circuitry. • Anti-lock brake sensor.	• GO to Pinpoint Test D.
• Maladjusted rear brakes or "grabby" brake shoe or linings	• Rear brake adjustment. • Linings.	• DIAGNOSE brake system.
• Base brake mechanical concern for wheels lock up	• Rear brakes. • Parking brake. • Rear axle seal.	• DIAGNOSE brake system. • DIAGNOSE parking brake. • DIAGNOSE brake system.
• Base brake hydraulic concern (soft pedal)	• Brake line or hose, fitting, master cylinder, or brake caliper. • Air in brake system.	• DIAGNOSE brake system.

FM4029901435010X

Fig. 1 Symptom chart (Part 1 of 2). 2002–03

2. Remove four control module retaining bolts, then the ABS control module.
3. Reverse procedure to install. **Torque** control module retaining bolts to 18 inch lbs.

HYDRAULIC CONTROL UNIT (HCU)

1. Remove battery and tray.
2. Disconnect control module electrical connector, **Fig. 25**, by lifting up on release tab.
3. Disconnect brake lines from HCU.
4. Remove HCU retaining bolts, then the HCU.
5. Remove ABS module.
6. Reverse procedure to install, noting the following:
   a. **Torque** HCU retaining bolts 17 ft. lbs.
   b. **Torque** brake lines 13 inch lbs.

STABILITY CONTROL SENSOR CLUSTER

When installing a new stability control sensor cluster, the Anti-Lock Brake System (ABS) module must be configured. Follow the diagnostic tool instructions for calibration procedures.

1. Remove pin type retainer, then the driver side floor console finish panel.
2. Remove two bolts, 2 nuts, then the lefthand instrument panel brace.
3. Remove lefthand heater duct.
4. Disconnect stability control sensor cluster electrical connector.
5. Remove sensor cluster electrical harness retainers and position aside harness.
6. Remove two sensor cluster bracket nuts, then the stability control sensor cluster.
7. Reverse procedure to install. **Torque** stability control sensor cluster bolts to 62 inch lbs.

STEERING WHEEL ROTATION SENSOR

1. Remove upper and lower steering column cover bolts, **Fig. 26**, then the lower column covers.
2. Disconnect steering wheel rotation sensor electrical connector.
3. Remove two bolts, then the steering wheel rotation sensor.
4. Reverse procedure to install.

WHEEL SPEED SENSOR

FRONT

1. Raise and support vehicle.
2. Disconnect wheel speed sensor wire from vehicle frame.
3. Remove sensor retaining bolt, then the sensor.
4. Reverse procedure to install, noting the following:

Condition	Possible Source	Action
• Base brake mechanical concern (hard pedal)	• Vacuum boost. • Brake caliper. • Brake line or hose.	• DIAGNOSE brake system.
• Base brake hydraulic concern during medium/hard brake application	• Brake line or hose, fitting, master cylinder, wheel cylinder, or caliper. • Air in brake system.	• DIAGNOSE brake system.
• Base brake mechanical concern during medium/hard brake application	• Vacuum boost. • Wheel cylinder or caliper. • Brake line or hose. • Brake shoe or pad linings.	• DIAGNOSE brake system.
• Base brake mechanical concern for vehicle pulls	• Rear brake. • Caliper. • Brake pad or shoe wear.	• DIAGNOSE brake system.
• Base brake hydraulic concern for vehicle pulls	• Brake line or hose. • Caliper. • Wheel cylinder.	• DIAGNOSE brake system.
• Intermittent loss of voltage to anti-lock brake control module	• Circuitry. • Anti-lock brake control module. • BJB.	• INSPECT Circuit 601 from ignition switch to anti-lock brake control module harness connector for opens or shorts. REPAIR as necessary. • INSPECT anti-lock brake control module grounds for looseness, corrosion or excessive dirt. REPAIR as necessary. • CORRECT condition.
• One wheel locks up; no DTCs recorded	• Base brake. • Dump valve. • ISO valve.	• DIAGNOSE brake system. • INSTALL a new hydraulic control unit.
• The yellow ABS warning indicator does not self-check	• Bulb. • Circuitry. • Instrument cluster. • Anti-lock brake control module.	• GO to Pinpoint Test G.
• Soft or excessive brake pedal	• Brake line or hose, fitting, master cylinder, wheel cylinder, or caliper. • Air in brake system.	• DIAGNOSE brake system.

FM4029901435020X

Fig. 1 Symptom chart (Part 2 of 2). 2002–03

a. **Torque** wheel speed sensor retaining bolt to 13 ft. lbs.
b. Apply high temperature 4X4 front axle and wheel bearing grease E8TZ-19590-A, or equivalent, meeting Ford specification ESA-MIC198-A to sensor mounting surface.

REAR

1. Raise and support vehicle.
2. Clean area around wheel speed sensor.
3. Disconnect wheel speed sensor electrical connector.
4. Remove sensor retaining bolt, then the sensor.
5. Reverse procedure to install, noting the following:
   a. **Torque** wheel speed sensor retaining bolt to 71 inch lbs.
   b. Clean axle mounting surface.
   c. Lubricate O-ring with high performance rear axle lubricant F1TZ-19580-B, or equivalent, meeting Ford specification WSL-M2C192-A.

Condition	Possible Sources	Action
• No communication with the anti-lock brake system (ABS) module	• Circuitry • ABS module	• Go To Pinpoint Test A .
• The red brake warning indicator stays on when the ignition switch is in the RUN position	• Circuitry • Instrument cluster • Brake fluid level sensor • Anti-lock brake system (ABS) module	• REFER to "Dash Gauges & Warning Indicators".
• The yellow anti-lock brake system (ABS) warning indicator does not self-check	• Circuitry • Instrument cluster • ABS module	• REFER to "Dash Gauges & Warning Indicators".
• Spongy brake pedal with no warning indicator	• Air in brake hydraulic system	• REFER to "Brake System Bleed".
• The traction control/roll stability control system cannot be disabled	• Circuitry • Stability traction control switch • Anti-lock brake system (ABS) module	• Go To Pinpoint Test K .

LTV0500000005415

Fig. 2 Symptom chart. 2004-06

DTCs	Description
B1342	Anti-Lock Brake Control Module Failure
B1485	Brake Pedal Position (BPP) Switch Circuit Failure
B1676	Battery Voltage Out Of Range
B2141	Vehicle Speed Calibration Data Not Programmed Into Module
C1095	Hydraulic Pump Motor Circuit Failure
C1102	G-Switch Circuit Failure
C1145	RF Anti-Lock Brake Sensor Circuit Failure
C1155	LF Anti-Lock Brake Sensor Circuit Failure
C1230	Rear Anti-Lock Brake Sensor Circuit Failure
C1233	LF Anti-Lock Brake Sensor Output Failure
C1234	RF Anti-Lock Brake Sensor Output Failure
C1237	Rear Anti-Lock Brake Sensor Output Failure

FM4029901433000X

Fig. 3 Diagnostic trouble code interpretation. 2002–03

DTC	Description
B1342	ECU is Defective
B1483	Brake Pedal Input Circuit Failure
B1676	Battery Pack Voltage Out of Range
B2477	Module Configuration Failure
B2741	Sensor Cluster Is Defective
B2900	VIN Mismatched (normally set when a new ABS module is installed)
C1095	ABS Hydraulic Pump Motor Circuit Failure
C1145	Wheel Speed Sensor RF Input Circuit Failure
C1155	Wheel Speed Sensor LF Input Circuit Failure
C1165	Wheel Speed Sensor RR Input Circuit Failure
C1175	Wheel Speed Sensor LR Input Circuit Failure
C1233	Wheel Speed LF Input Signal Missing
C1234	Wheel Speed RF Input Signal Missing
C1235	Wheel Speed RR Input Signal Missing
C1236	Wheel Speed LR Input Signal Missing
C1277	Steering Wheel Angle 1 and 2 Circuit Failure
C1278	Steering Wheel Angle 1 and 2 Signal Faulted
C1279	Yaw Rate Sensor Circuit Failure
C1280	Yaw Rate Sensor Signal Fault
C1281	Lateral Accelerometer Circuit Failure
C1282	Lateral Accelerometer Signal Fault
C1285	Booster Solenoid Circuit Failure

LTV0500000005416

Fig. 4 Diagnostic trouble code interpretation. 2004-06

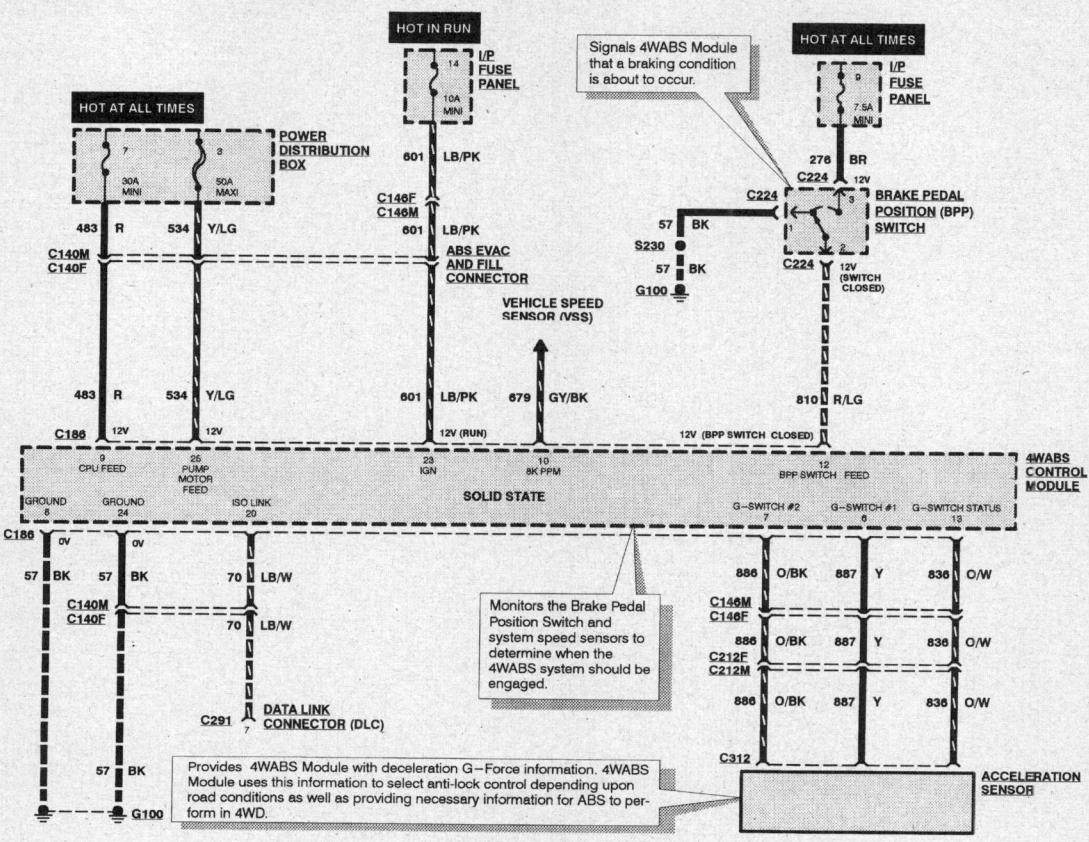

Fig. 5 Wiring diagram (Part 1 of 2). 2002-03

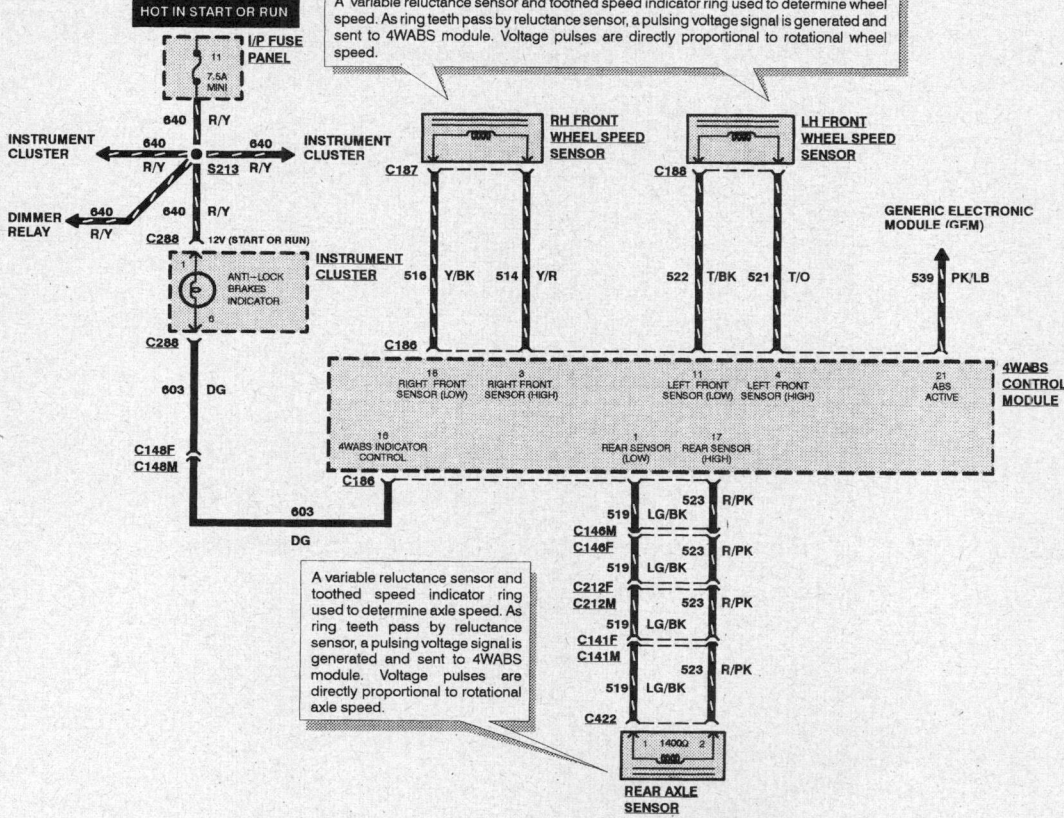

Fig. 5 Wiring diagram (Part 2 of 2). 2002-03

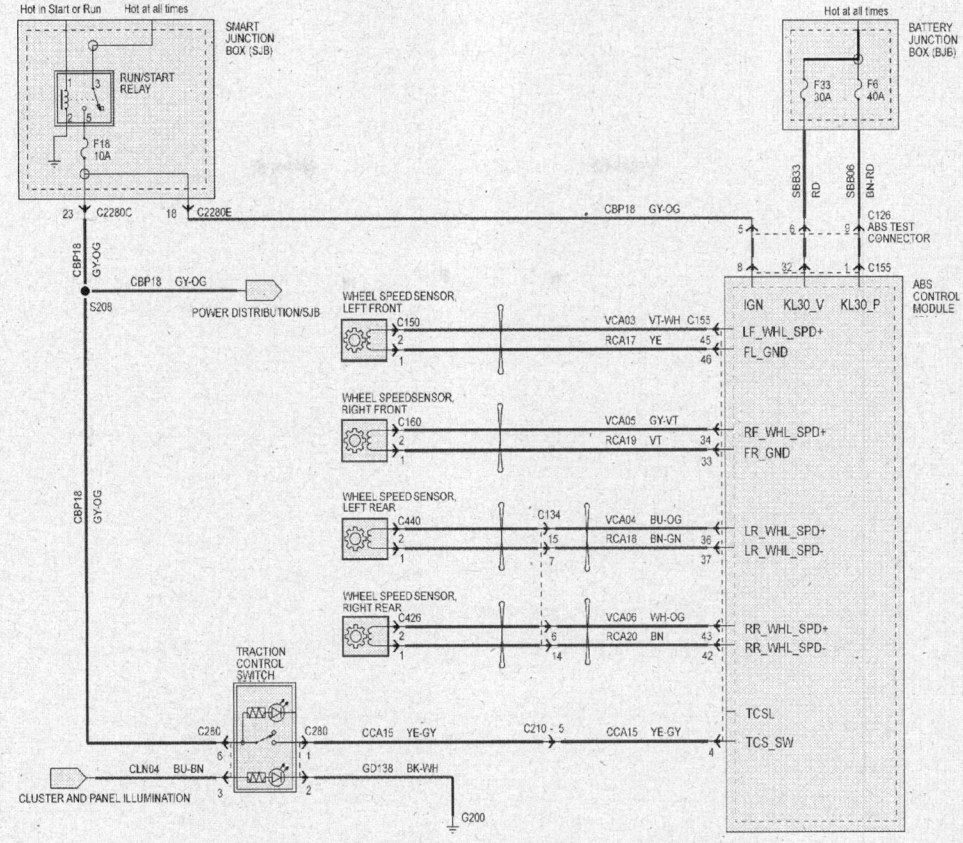

Fig. 6   Wiring diagram (Part 1 of 3). 2004-06

LTV0500000005418

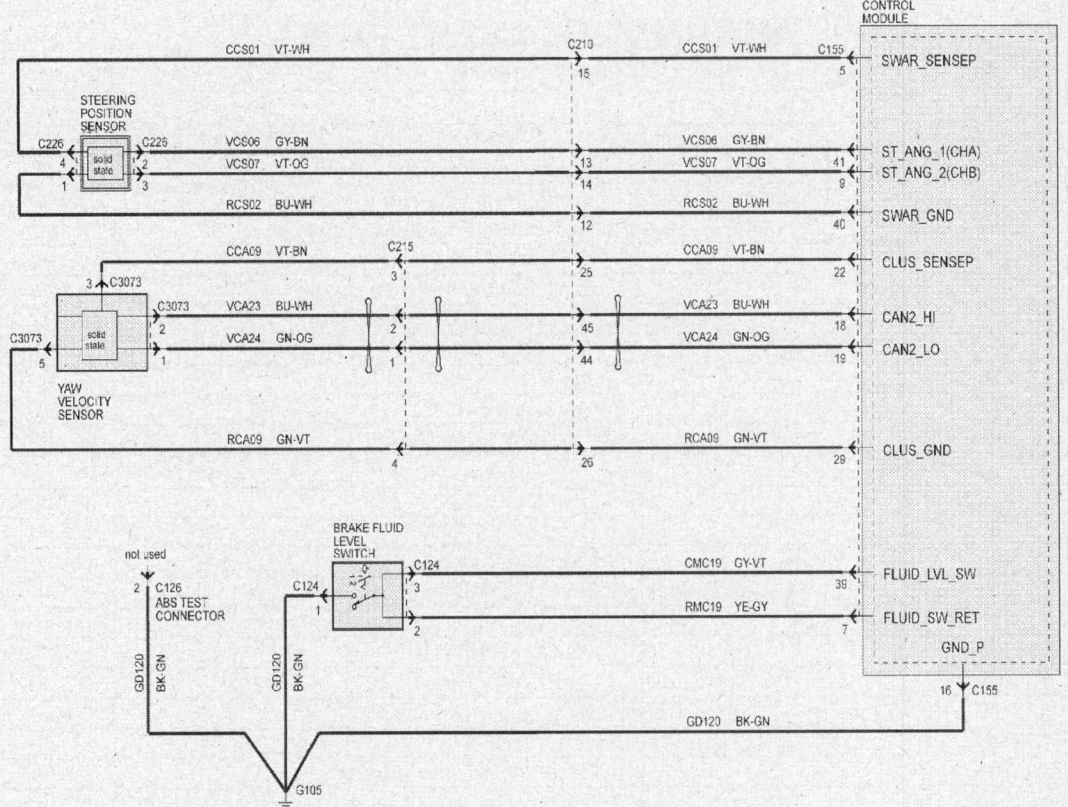

Fig. 6   Wiring diagram (Part 2 of 3). 2004-06

LTV0500000005419

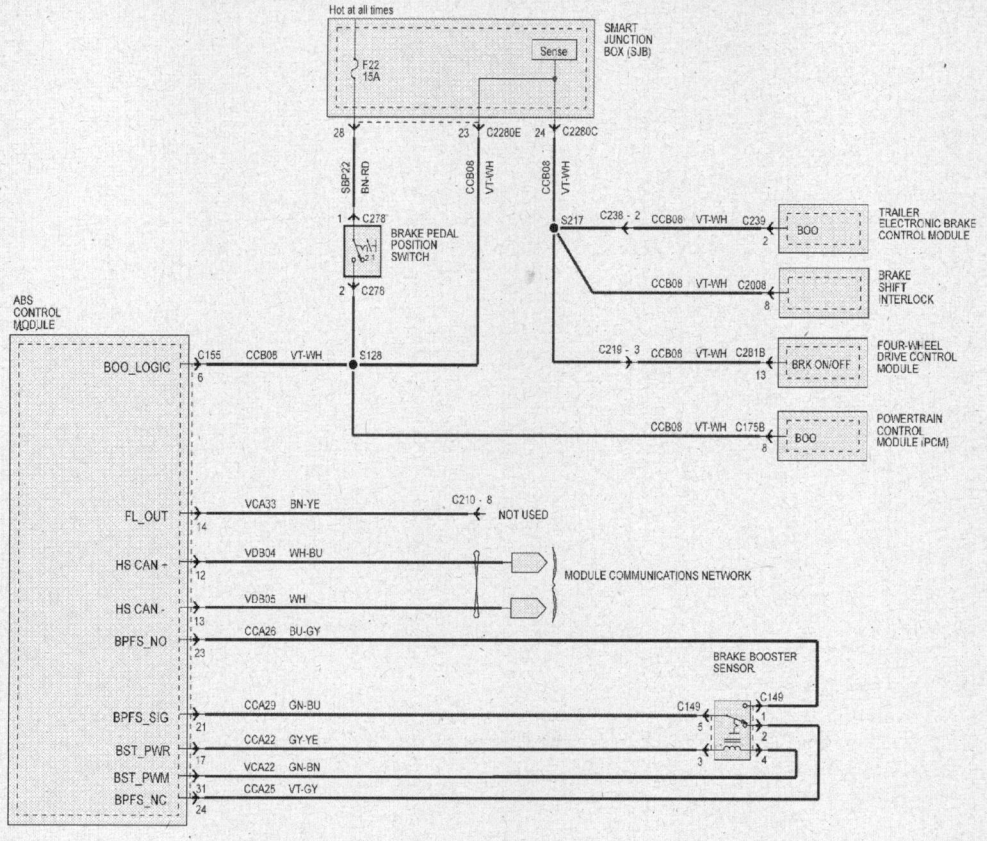

Fig. 6   Wiring diagram (Part 3 of 3). 2004-06

LTV0500000005420

DIAGNOSTIC CHART INDEX

Test	Code	Description	Page No.	Fig. No.
2002–03				
A	—	No Communication w/ABS Control Module	5-117	7
B	B1676	Battery Voltage Out Of Range	5-117	8
C	C1145	Right Front ABS Sensor Circuit Failure (Explorer & Mountaineer)	5-118	9
	C1155	Left Front ABS Sensor Circuit Failure (Explorer & Mountaineer)	5-118	9
	C1230	Rear ABS Sensor Circuit Failure (Explorer & Mountaineer)	5-118	9
D	C1233	Left ABS Sensor Output Failure	5-120	10
	C1234	Right ABS Sensor Output Failure	5-120	10
	C1237	Rear ABS Sensor Output Failure	5-120	10
E	C1095	Hydraulic Pump Motor Circuit Failure	5-121	11
F	C1102	G-Switch Circuit Failure	5-122	12
G	—	Yellow ABS Warning Indicator Does Not Self Check	5-123	13
2004–06				
A	—	No Communication w/ABS Module	5-123	14
B	B1483	Brake Pedal Input Failure	5-124	15
C	B1676	Battery Pack Voltage Out Of Range	5-124	16
D	C1095	ABS Hydraulic Pump Motor Circuit Failure	5-124	17
E	C1145	Wheel Speed Sensor Input Circuit Failure	5-125	18
	C1155	Wheel Speed Sensor Input Circuit Failure	5-125	18
	C1165	Wheel Speed Sensor Input Circuit Failure	5-125	18
	C1175	Wheel Speed Sensor Input Circuit Failure	5-125	18
F	C1233	Wheel Speed Sensor Input Signal Missing	5-126	19
	C1234	Wheel Speed Sensor Input Signal Missing	5-126	19
	C1235	Wheel Speed Sensor Input Signal Missing	5-126	19
	C1236	Wheel Speed Sensor Input Signal Missing	5-126	19

Continued

DIAGNOSTIC CHART INDEX—Continued

Test	Code	Description	Page No.	Fig. No.
2004–06				
G	C1277	Steering Wheel Angle 1 & 2 Circuit Failure/Fault Part	5-126	20
	C1278	Steering Wheel Angle 1 & 2 Circuit Failure/Fault Part	5-126	20
H	B2741	Sensor Cluster Fault	5-127	21
	C1279	Sensor Cluster Fault	5-127	21
	C1280	Sensor Cluster Fault	5-127	21
	C1281	Sensor Cluster Fault	5-127	21
	C1282	Sensor Cluster Fault	5-127	21
	C1516	Sensor Cluster Fault	5-127	21
	C1517	Sensor Cluster Fault	5-127	21
	C2769	Sensor Cluster Fault	5-127	21
	C2770	Sensor Cluster Fault	5-127	21
	C2777	Sensor Cluster Fault	5-127	21
	C2778	Sensor Cluster Fault	5-127	21
	U1900	Sensor Cluster Fault	5-127	21
	U1901	Sensor Cluster Fault	5-127	21
I	C1285	Booster Solenoid Circuit Failure	5-128	22
J	C1287	Brake Booster Pedal Force Switch Failure	5-128	23
K	—	Traction Control/Roll Stability Control System Cannot Be Disabled	5-129	24

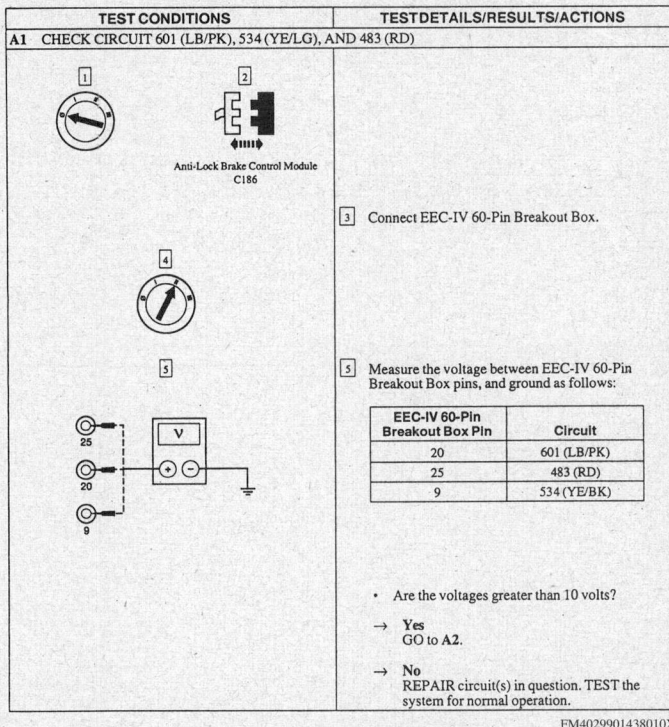

Fig. 7   Test A: No Communication w/ABS Control Module (Part 1 of 2). 2002–03

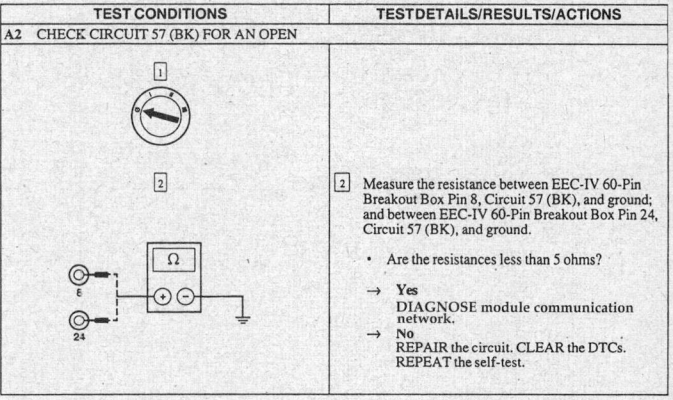

Fig. 7   Test A: No Communication w/ABS Control Module (Part 2 of 2). 2002–03

TEST CONDITIONS	TEST DETAILS/RESULTS/ACTIONS
B1 CHECK RECENT VEHICLE HISTORY	
	1 Check recent vehicle history.
	• Has the vehicle been jump-started by a tow truck within the past two weeks?
	→ **Yes** The system is OK. CLEAR the DTCs. REPEAT the self-test.
	→ **No** GO to B2.

FM4029901439010X

Fig. 8   Test B: Code B1676: Battery Voltage Out Of Range (Part 1 of 4). 2002–03

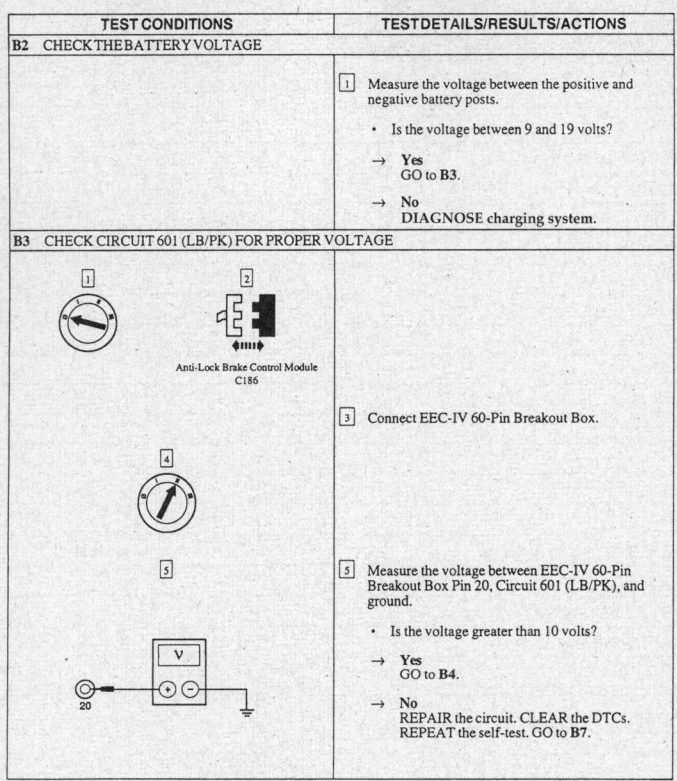

TEST CONDITIONS	TEST DETAILS/RESULTS/ACTIONS
B2 CHECK THE BATTERY VOLTAGE	
	1 Measure the voltage between the positive and negative battery posts.
	• Is the voltage between 9 and 19 volts?
	→ **Yes** GO to **B3**.
	→ **No** DIAGNOSE charging system.
B3 CHECK CIRCUIT 601 (LB/PK) FOR PROPER VOLTAGE	
Anti-Lock Brake Control Module C186	3 Connect EEC-IV 60-Pin Breakout Box.
	5 Measure the voltage between EEC-IV 60-Pin Breakout Box Pin 20, Circuit 601 (LB/PK), and ground.
	• Is the voltage greater than 10 volts?
	→ **Yes** GO to **B4**.
	→ **No** REPAIR the circuit. CLEAR the DTCs. REPEAT the self-test. GO to **B7**.

FM4029901439020X

Fig. 8 Test B: Code B1676: Battery Voltage Out Of Range (Part 2 of 4). 2002–03

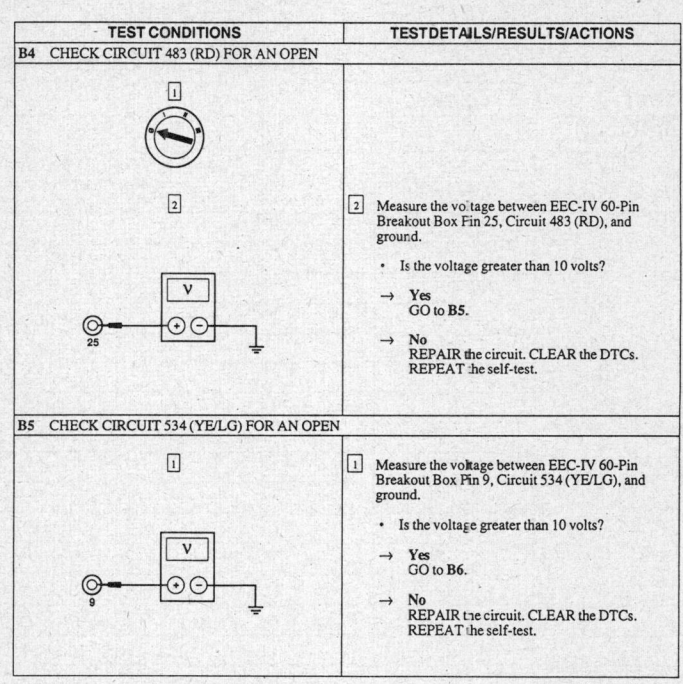

TEST CONDITIONS	TEST DETAILS/RESULTS/ACTIONS
B4 CHECK CIRCUIT 483 (RD) FOR AN OPEN	
	2 Measure the voltage between EEC-IV 60-Pin Breakout Box Pin 25, Circuit 483 (RD), and ground.
	• Is the voltage greater than 10 volts?
	→ **Yes** GO to **B5**.
	→ **No** REPAIR the circuit. CLEAR the DTCs. REPEAT the self-test.
B5 CHECK CIRCUIT 534 (YE/LG) FOR AN OPEN	
	1 Measure the voltage between EEC-IV 60-Pin Breakout Box Pin 9, Circuit 534 (YE/LG), and ground.
	• Is the voltage greater than 10 volts?
	→ **Yes** GO to **B6**.
	→ **No** REPAIR the circuit. CLEAR the DTCs. REPEAT the self-test.

FM4029901439030X

Fig. 8 Test B: Code B1676: Battery Voltage Out Of Range (Part 3 of 4). 2002–03

TEST CONDITIONS	TEST DETAILS/RESULTS/ACTIONS
B6 CHECK CIRCUIT 57 (BK) FOR AN OPEN	
	1 Measure the resistance between EEC-IV 60-Pin Breakout Box Pin 8, Circuit 57 (BK), and ground; and between EEC-IV 60-Pin Breakout Box Pin 24, Circuit 57 (BK), and ground.
	• Are the resistances less than 5 ohms?
	→ **Yes** INSTALL a new anti-lock brake control module. REPEAT the self-test.
	→ **No** REPAIR the circuit. CLEAR the DTCs. REPEAT the self-test.

FM4029901439040X

Fig. 8 Test B: Code B1676: Battery Voltage Out Of Range (Part 4 of 4). 2002–03

TEST CONDITIONS	TEST DETAILS/RESULTS/ACTIONS
C1 CHECK THE ANTI-LOCK BRAKE SENSOR RESISTANCE AT BREAKOUT BOX	
Anti-Lock Brake Control Module C186	3 Connect EEC-IV 60-Pin Breakout Box.
	4 Measure the resistance between EEC-IV 60-Pin Breakout Box pins for the suspect anti-lock brake sensor as follows:

Anti-Lock Brake Sensor	EEC-IV 60-Pin Breakout Box	
	Positive Probe	Negative Probe
LF	17	18
RF	3	4
Rear	22	21

FM4029901440010X

Fig. 9 Test C: Codes C1145, C1155 & C1230: ABS Sensor Circuit Failure (Part 1 of 7). 2002–03

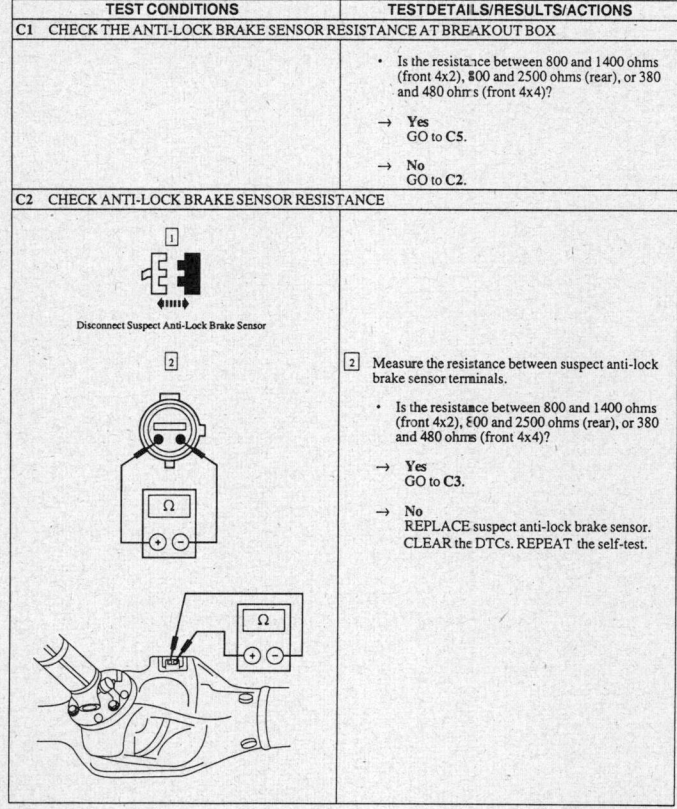

TEST CONDITIONS	TEST DETAILS/RESULTS/ACTIONS
C1 CHECK THE ANTI-LOCK BRAKE SENSOR RESISTANCE AT BREAKOUT BOX	
	• Is the resistance between 800 and 1400 ohms (front 4x2), 800 and 2500 ohms (rear), or 380 and 480 ohms (front 4x4)?
	→ **Yes** GO to **C5**.
	→ **No** GO to **C2**.
C2 CHECK ANTI-LOCK BRAKE SENSOR RESISTANCE	
Disconnect Suspect Anti-Lock Brake Sensor	2 Measure the resistance between suspect anti-lock brake sensor terminals.
	• Is the resistance between 800 and 1400 ohms (front 4x2), 800 and 2500 ohms (rear), or 380 and 480 ohms (front 4x4)?
	→ **Yes** GO to **C3**.
	→ **No** REPLACE suspect anti-lock brake sensor. CLEAR the DTCs. REPEAT the self-test.

FM4029901440020X

Fig. 9 Test C: Codes C1145, C1155 & C1230: ABS Sensor Circuit Failure (Part 2 of 7). 2002–03

TEST CONDITIONS	TEST DETAILS/RESULTS/ACTIONS

C3 CHECK CIRCUIT 521 (TN/OG), 514 (YE/RD), OR 523 (RD/PK)

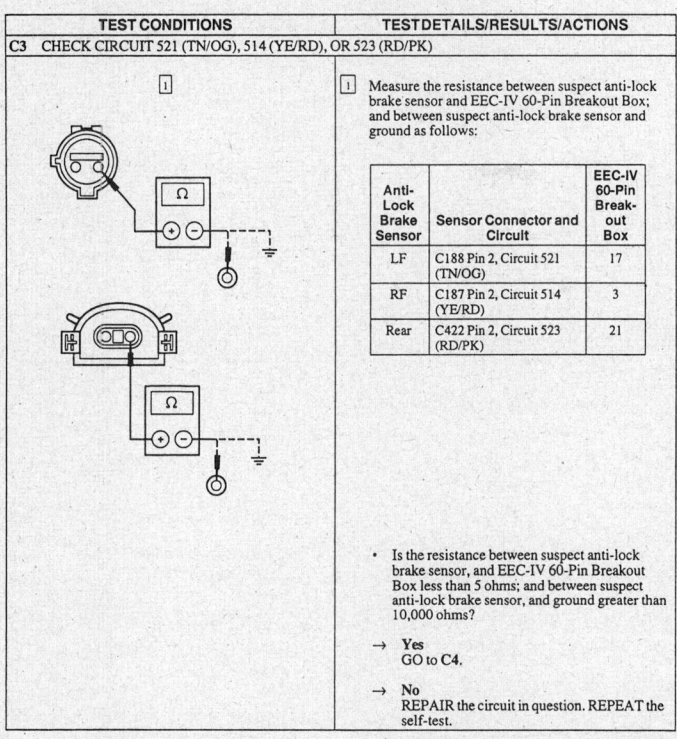

☐ Measure the resistance between suspect anti-lock brake sensor and EEC-IV 60-Pin Breakout Box; and between suspect anti-lock brake sensor and ground as follows:

Anti-Lock Brake Sensor	Sensor Connector and Circuit	EEC-IV 60-Pin Break-out Box
LF	C188 Pin 2, Circuit 521 (TN/OG)	17
RF	C187 Pin 2, Circuit 514 (YE/RD)	3
Rear	C422 Pin 2, Circuit 523 (RD/PK)	21

- Is the resistance between suspect anti-lock brake sensor, and EEC-IV 60-Pin Breakout Box less than 5 ohms; and between suspect anti-lock brake sensor, and ground greater than 10,000 ohms?

→ **Yes**
GO to C4.

→ **No**
REPAIR the circuit in question. REPEAT the self-test.

FM4029901440030X

Fig. 9 Test C: Codes C1145, C1155 & C1230: ABS Sensor Circuit Failure (Part 3 of 7). 2002–03

TEST CONDITIONS	TEST DETAILS/RESULTS/ACTIONS

C4 CHECK CIRCUIT 522 (TN/BK), 516 (YE/BK), OR 519 (LG/BK)

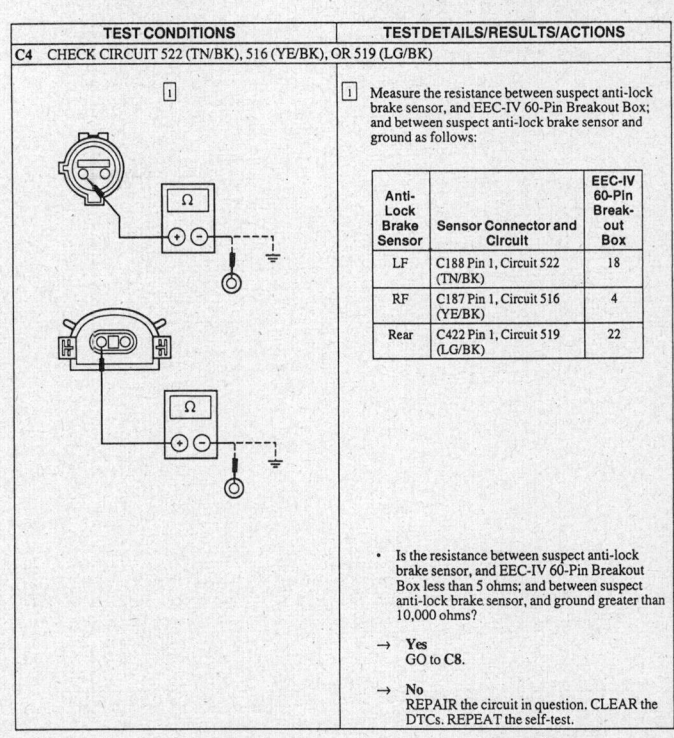

☐ Measure the resistance between suspect anti-lock brake sensor, and EEC-IV 60-Pin Breakout Box; and between suspect anti-lock brake sensor and ground as follows:

Anti-Lock Brake Sensor	Sensor Connector and Circuit	EEC-IV 60-Pin Break-out Box
LF	C188 Pin 1, Circuit 522 (TN/BK)	18
RF	C187 Pin 1, Circuit 516 (YE/BK)	4
Rear	C422 Pin 1, Circuit 519 (LG/BK)	22

- Is the resistance between suspect anti-lock brake sensor, and EEC-IV 60-Pin Breakout Box less than 5 ohms; and between suspect anti-lock brake sensor, and ground greater than 10,000 ohms?

→ **Yes**
GO to C8.

→ **No**
REPAIR the circuit in question. CLEAR the DTCs. REPEAT the self-test.

FM4029901440040X

Fig. 9 Test C: Codes C1145, C1155 & C1230: ABS Sensor Circuit Failure (Part 4 of 7). 2002–03

TEST CONDITIONS	TEST DETAILS/RESULTS/ACTIONS

C5 CHECK THE SUSPECT ANTI-LOCK BRAKE SENSOR CIRCUIT FOR SHORT TO POWER

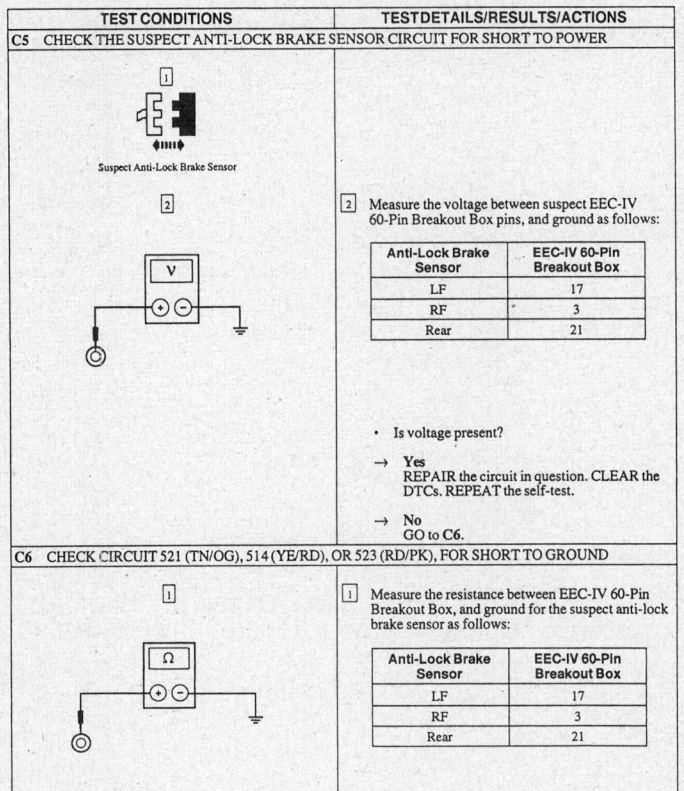

Suspect Anti-Lock Brake Sensor

☐ Measure the voltage between suspect EEC-IV 60-Pin Breakout Box pins, and ground as follows:

Anti-Lock Brake Sensor	EEC-IV 60-Pin Breakout Box
LF	17
RF	3
Rear	21

- Is voltage present?

→ **Yes**
REPAIR the circuit in question. CLEAR the DTCs. REPEAT the self-test.

→ **No**
GO to C6.

C6 CHECK CIRCUIT 521 (TN/OG), 514 (YE/RD), OR 523 (RD/PK), FOR SHORT TO GROUND

☐ Measure the resistance between EEC-IV 60-Pin Breakout Box, and ground for the suspect anti-lock brake sensor as follows:

Anti-Lock Brake Sensor	EEC-IV 60-Pin Breakout Box
LF	17
RF	3
Rear	21

FM4029901440050X

Fig. 9 Test C: Codes C1145, C1155 & C1230: ABS Sensor Circuit Failure (Part 5 of 7). 2002–03

TEST CONDITIONS	TEST DETAILS/RESULTS/ACTIONS

C6 CHECK CIRCUIT 521 (TN/OG), 514 (YE/RD), OR 523 (RD/PK), FOR SHORT TO GROUND

- Is the resistance greater than 10,000 ohms?

→ **Yes**
GO to C7.

→ **No**
REPAIR the circuit in question. CLEAR the DTCs. REPEAT the self-test.

C7 CHECK CIRCUIT 522 (TN/BK), 516 (YE/BK), OR 519 (LG/BK) FOR SHORT TO GROUND

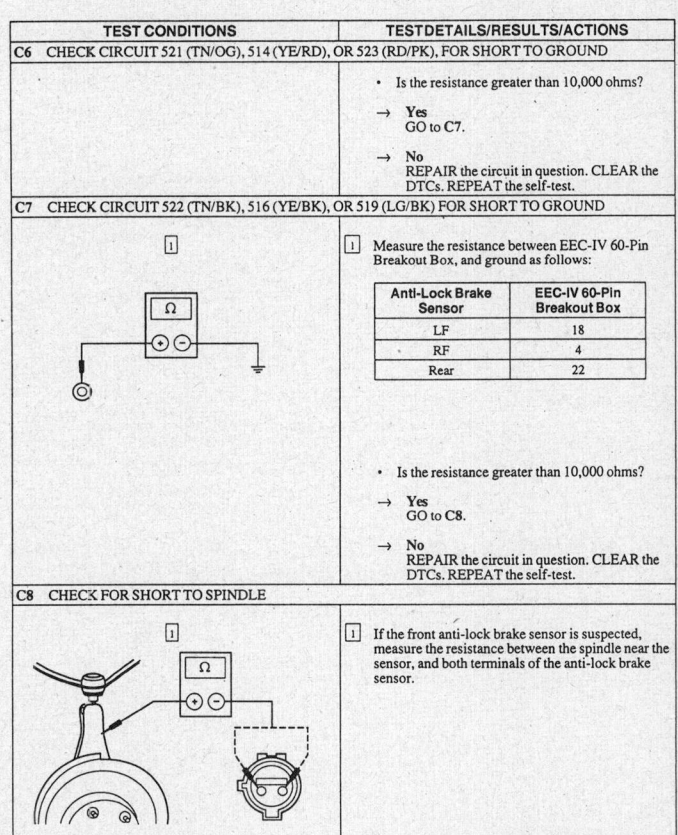

☐ Measure the resistance between EEC-IV 60-Pin Breakout Box, and ground as follows:

Anti-Lock Brake Sensor	EEC-IV 60-Pin Breakout Box
LF	18
RF	4
Rear	22

- Is the resistance greater than 10,000 ohms?

→ **Yes**
GO to C8.

→ **No**
REPAIR the circuit in question. CLEAR the DTCs. REPEAT the self-test.

C8 CHECK FOR SHORT TO SPINDLE

☐ If the front anti-lock brake sensor is suspected, measure the resistance between the spindle near the sensor, and both terminals of the anti-lock brake sensor.

FM4029901440060X

Fig. 9 Test C: Codes C1145, C1155 & C1230: ABS Sensor Circuit Failure (Part 6 of 7). 2002–03

TEST CONDITIONS	TEST DETAILS/RESULTS/ACTIONS
C8 CHECK FOR SHORT TO SPINDLE	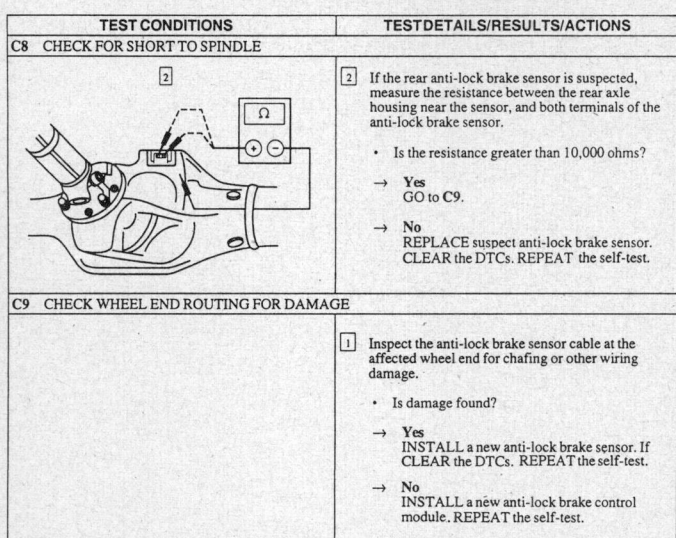
	② If the rear anti-lock brake sensor is suspected, measure the resistance between the rear axle housing near the sensor, and both terminals of the anti-lock brake sensor. • Is the resistance greater than 10,000 ohms? → **Yes** GO to **C9**. → **No** REPLACE suspect anti-lock brake sensor. CLEAR the DTCs. REPEAT the self-test.
C9 CHECK WHEEL END ROUTING FOR DAMAGE	
	① Inspect the anti-lock brake sensor cable at the affected wheel end for chafing or other wiring damage. • Is damage found? → **Yes** INSTALL a new anti-lock brake sensor. If CLEAR the DTCs. REPEAT the self-test. → **No** INSTALL a new anti-lock brake control module. REPEAT the self-test.

FM4029901440070X

Fig. 9 Test C: Codes C1145, C1155 & C1230: ABS Sensor Circuit Failure (Part 7 of 7). 2002–03

TEST CONDITIONS	TEST DETAILS/RESULTS/ACTIONS
D1 CHECK THE ANTI-LOCK BRAKE SENSOR PIDS	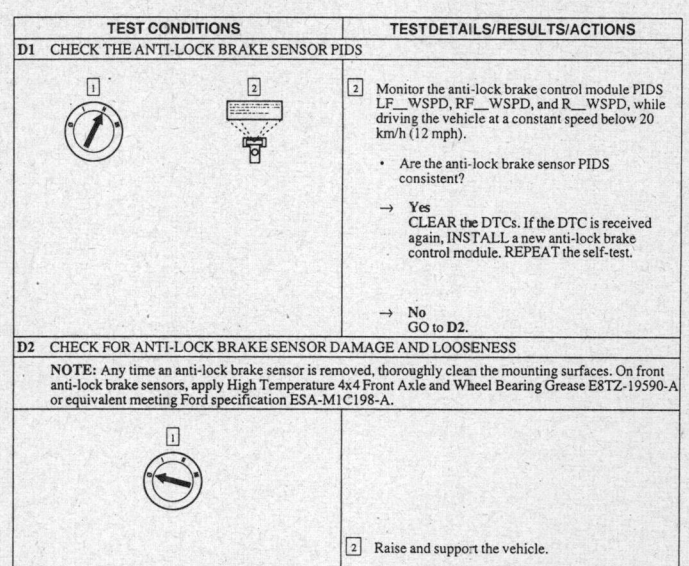
	② Monitor the anti-lock brake control module PIDS LF__WSPD, RF__WSPD, and R__WSPD, while driving the vehicle at a constant speed below 20 km/h (12 mph). • Are the anti-lock brake sensor PIDS consistent? → **Yes** CLEAR the DTCs. If the DTC is received again, INSTALL a new anti-lock brake control module. REPEAT the self-test. → **No** GO to **D2**.
D2 CHECK FOR ANTI-LOCK BRAKE SENSOR DAMAGE AND LOOSENESS	
NOTE: Any time an anti-lock brake sensor is removed, thoroughly clean the mounting surfaces. On front anti-lock brake sensors, apply High Temperature 4x4 Front Axle and Wheel Bearing Grease E8TZ-19590-A or equivalent meeting Ford specification ESA-M1C198-A.	
	② Raise and support the vehicle.

FM4029901441010X

Fig. 10 Test D: Codes C1233, C1234 & C1237: ABS Sensor Output Failure (Part 1 of 5). 2002–03

TEST CONDITIONS	TEST DETAILS/RESULTS/ACTIONS
D2 CHECK FOR ANTI-LOCK BRAKE SENSOR DAMAGE AND LOOSENESS	
	③ ⚠ **CAUTION: Examine the anti-lock brake sensor wire carefully with a good light. Failure to verify damage to the anti-lock brake sensor wire will lead to unnecessary component replacement.** Inspect the anti-lock brake sensor mounting for looseness. If the anti-lock brake sensor is suspected, inspect the sensor for corrosion on the rear axle housing boss, or on the front anti-lock brake mounting flange. Clean as necessary. • Is the anti-lock brake sensor OK? → **Yes** GO to **D3**. → **No** If the anti-lock brake sensor mounting is loose or corroded, REMOVE the anti-lock brake sensor, plug the opening, and thoroughly clean the mounting surfaces. On front anti-lock brake sensors, apply High Temperature 4x4 Front Axle and Wheel Bearing Grease E8TZ-19590-A or equivalent meeting Ford specification ESA-M1C198-A. CLEAR the DTCs. REPEAT the self-test. If the anti-lock brake sensor is damaged, INSTALL a new the anti-lock brake sensor. CLEAR the DTCs. REPEAT the self-test.
D3 CHECK FOR ANTI-LOCK BRAKE SENSOR INDICATOR DAMAGE	
NOTE: Any time an anti-lock brake sensor is removed, thoroughly clean the mounting surfaces. On front anti-lock brake sensors, apply High Temperature 4x4 Front Axle and Wheel Bearing Grease E8TZ-19590-A or equivalent meeting Ford specification ESA-M1C198-A.	
	① Remove the anti-lock brake sensor.

FM4029901441020X

Fig. 10 Test D: Codes C1233, C1234 & C1237: ABS Sensor Output Failure (Part 2 of 5). 2002–03

TEST CONDITIONS	TEST DETAILS/RESULTS/ACTIONS
D3 CHECK FOR ANTI-LOCK BRAKE SENSOR INDICATOR DAMAGE	
	② ⚠ **CAUTION: Examine the anti-lock brake sensor indicator carefully with a good light. Failure to verify damage to the anti-lock brake sensor indicator will lead to unnecessary component replacement.** Inspect the anti-lock brake sensor indicator for damaged or missing teeth. Rotate the wheel to verify that no teeth are missing. • Is the anti-lock brake sensor indicator OK? → **Yes** GO to **D4**. → **No** INSTALL a new anti-lock brake sensor indicator. CLEAR the DTCs. REPEAT the self-test.
D4 CHECK ANTI-LOCK BRAKE SENSOR OUTPUT AT EEC-IV 60-PIN BREAKOUT BOX	
Anti-Lock Brake Control Module C186	① Lower the vehicle so that all wheels are free to spin. ③ Connect EEC-IV 60-Pin Breakout Box.

FM4029901441030X

Fig. 10 Test D: Codes C1233, C1234 & C1237: ABS Sensor Output Failure (Part 3 of 5). 2002–03

TEST CONDITIONS	TEST DETAILS/RESULTS/ACTIONS
D4 CHECK ANTI-LOCK BRAKE SENSOR OUTPUT AT EEC-IV 60-PIN BREAKOUT BOX	

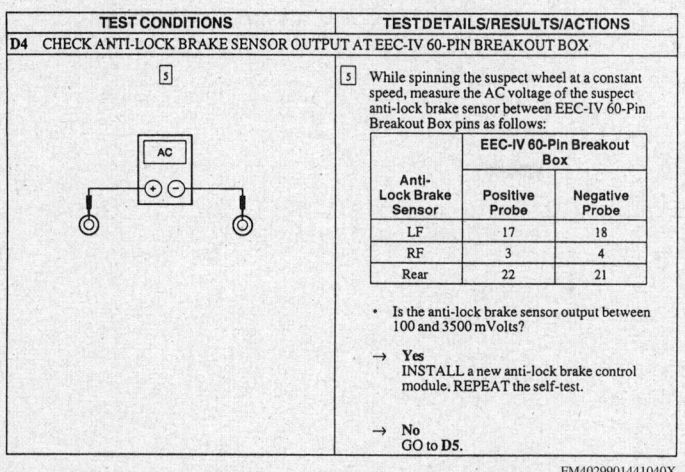

5 | 5 While spinning the suspect wheel at a constant speed, measure the AC voltage of the suspect anti-lock brake sensor between EEC-IV 60-Pin Breakout Box pins as follows:

Anti-Lock Brake Sensor	EEC-IV 60-Pin Breakout Box	
	Positive Probe	Negative Probe
LF	17	18
RF	3	4
Rear	22	21

- Is the anti-lock brake sensor output between 100 and 3500 mVolts?

→ **Yes**
INSTALL a new anti-lock brake control module. REPEAT the self-test.

→ **No**
GO to **D5**.

FM4029901441040X

Fig. 10   Test D: Codes C1233, C1234 & C1237: ABS Sensor Output Failure (Part 4 of 5). 2002–03

TEST CONDITIONS	TEST DETAILS/RESULTS/ACTIONS
E1 CHECK THE ABS PUMP MOTOR	

- Is the pump motor on constantly?

→ **Yes**
INSTALL a new anti-lock brake control module. CLEAR the DTCs. REPEAT the self-test.

→ **No**
GO to **E2**.

TEST CONDITIONS	TEST DETAILS/RESULTS/ACTIONS
E2 CHECK THE PUMP MOTOR OPERATION	

NGS

3 Trigger the anti-lock brake control module active command PMP MOTOR ON.

- Does the pump motor operate?

→ **Yes**
CLEAR the DTC. CHECK the yellow ABS warning indicator while driving the vehicle 32 km/h (20 mph) without brakes applied until the vehicle exceeds 32 km/h (20 mph). If the yellow ABS warning indicator illuminates, INSTALL a new anti-lock brake control module. CLEAR the DTCs. REPEAT the self-test. If the yellow ABS warning indicator does not illuminate, CLEAR the DTCs. REPEAT the self-test.

→ **No**
GO to **E3**.

FM4029901442010X

Fig. 11   Test E: Code C1095: Hydraulic Pump Motor Circuit Failure (Part 1 of 3). 2002–03

TEST CONDITIONS	TEST DETAILS/RESULTS/ACTIONS
D5 CHECK THE ANTI-LOCK BRAKE SENSOR OUTPUT	

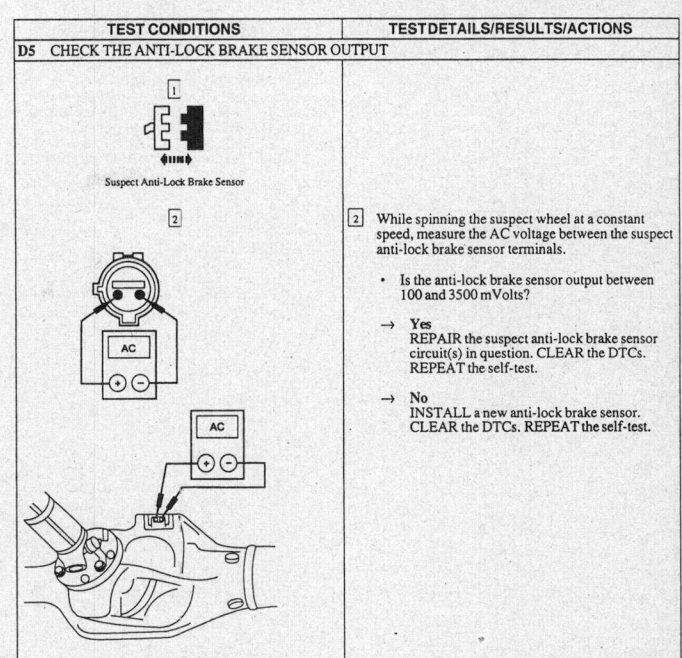

Suspect Anti-Lock Brake Sensor

2 While spinning the suspect wheel at a constant speed, measure the AC voltage between the suspect anti-lock brake sensor terminals.

- Is the anti-lock brake sensor output between 100 and 3500 mVolts?

→ **Yes**
REPAIR the suspect anti-lock brake sensor circuit(s) in question. CLEAR the DTCs. REPEAT the self-test.

→ **No**
INSTALL a new anti-lock brake sensor. CLEAR the DTCs. REPEAT the self-test.

FM4029901441050X

Fig. 10   Test D: Codes C1233, C1234 & C1237: ABS Sensor Output failure (Part 5 of 5). 2002–03

TEST CONDITIONS	TEST DETAILS/RESULTS/ACTIONS
E3 CHECK THE PUMP MOTOR	

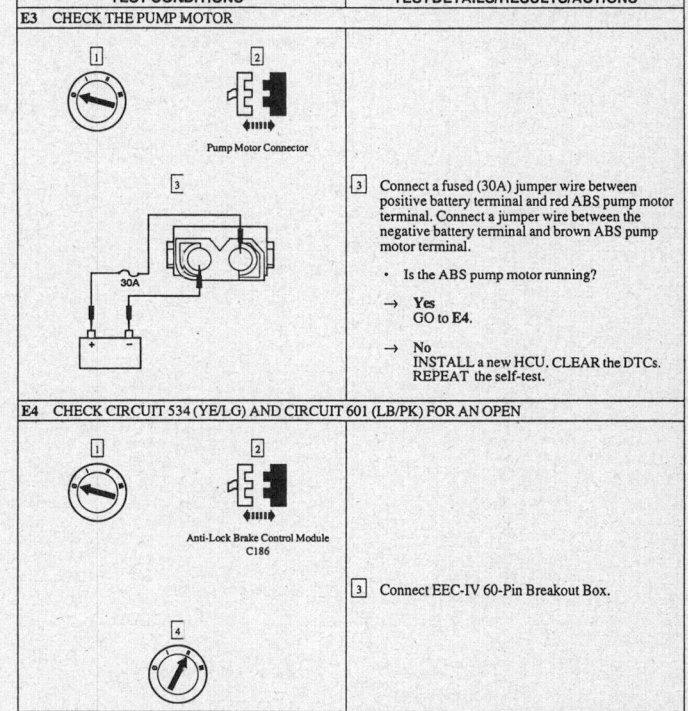

Pump Motor Connector

30A

3 Connect a fused (30A) jumper wire between positive battery terminal and red ABS pump motor terminal. Connect a jumper wire between the negative battery terminal and brown ABS pump motor terminal.

- Is the ABS pump motor running?

→ **Yes**
GO to **E4**.

→ **No**
INSTALL a new HCU. CLEAR the DTCs. REPEAT the self-test.

TEST CONDITIONS	TEST DETAILS/RESULTS/ACTIONS
E4 CHECK CIRCUIT 534 (YE/LG) AND CIRCUIT 601 (LB/PK) FOR AN OPEN	

Anti-Lock Brake Control Module C186

3 Connect EEC-IV 60-Pin Breakout Box.

FM4029901442020X

Fig. 11   Test E: Code C1095: Hydraulic Pump Motor Circuit Failure (Part 2 of 3). 2002–03

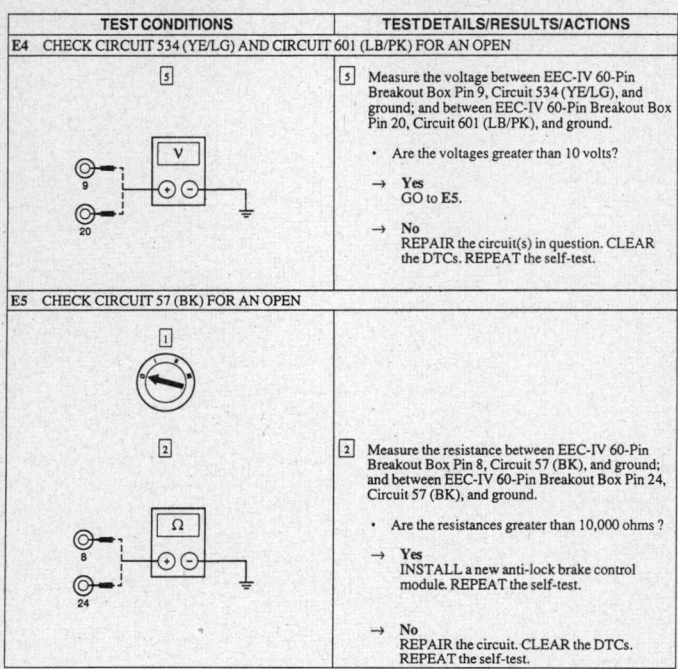

TEST CONDITIONS	TESTDETAILS/RESULTS/ACTIONS
E4 CHECK CIRCUIT 534 (YE/LG) AND CIRCUIT 601 (LB/PK) FOR AN OPEN	
5	5 Measure the voltage between EEC-IV 60-Pin Breakout Box Pins 9, Circuit 534 (YE/LG), and ground; and between EEC-IV 60-Pin Breakout Box Pin 20, Circuit 601 (LB/PK), and ground. • Are the voltages greater than 10 volts? → **Yes** GO to E5. → **No** REPAIR the circuit(s) in question. CLEAR the DTCs. REPEAT the self-test.
E5 CHECK CIRCUIT 57 (BK) FOR AN OPEN	
	2 Measure the resistance between EEC-IV 60-Pin Breakout Box Pin 8, Circuit 57 (BK), and ground; and between EEC-IV 60-Pin Breakout Box Pin 24, Circuit 57 (BK), and ground. • Are the resistances greater than 10,000 ohms? → **Yes** INSTALL a new anti-lock brake control module. REPEAT the self-test. → **No** REPAIR the circuit. CLEAR the DTCs. REPEAT the self-test.

FM4029901442030X

Fig. 11 Test E: Code C1095: Hydraulic Pump Motor Circuit Failure (Part 3 of 3). 2002–03

TEST CONDITIONS	TESTDETAILS/RESULTS/ACTIONS
F1 CHECK THE G-SWITCH	
3	3 Check the table after recording the anti-lock brake control module PIDS ACCLSW1, and ACCLSW2. • Do the G-switch PIDS toggle between ACT and notACT? → **Yes** INSTALL a new anti-lock brake control module. REPEAT the self-test. → **No** GO to F2.
F2 CHECK CIRCUIT 836 (OG/WH) FOR AN OPEN	
Anti-Lock Brake Control Module C186 G-switch C312 4	4 Measure the resistance between EEC-IV 60-Pin Breakout Box Pin 1, Circuit 836 (OG/WH), and G-switch C312 Pin 3, Circuit 836 (OG/WH), harness side. • Is the resistance less than 5 ohms? → **Yes** GO to F3. → **No** REPAIR the circuit . CLEAR the DTCs. REPEAT the self-test.

FM4029901443020X

Fig. 12 Test F: Code C1102: G-Switch Circuit Failure (Part 2 of 5). 2002–03

TEST CONDITIONS	TESTDETAILS/RESULTS/ACTIONS
F1 CHECK THE G-SWITCH	
1 2	2 Monitor and record the anti-lock brake control module PIDS ACCLSW1, and ACCLSW2, while driving the vehicle.

FM4029901443010X

Fig. 12 Test F: Code C1102: G-Switch Circuit Failure (Part 1 of 5). 2002–03

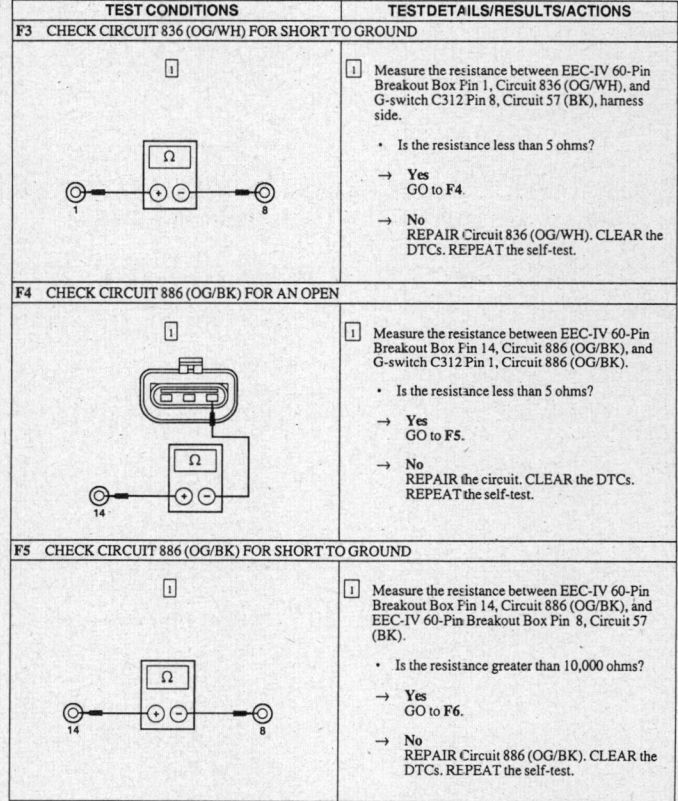

TEST CONDITIONS	TESTDETAILS/RESULTS/ACTIONS
F3 CHECK CIRCUIT 836 (OG/WH) FOR SHORT TO GROUND	
1	1 Measure the resistance between EEC-IV 60-Pin Breakout Box Pin 1, Circuit 836 (OG/WH), and G-switch C312 Pin 8, Circuit 57 (BK), harness side. • Is the resistance less than 5 ohms? → **Yes** GO to F4. → **No** REPAIR Circuit 836 (OG/WH). CLEAR the DTCs. REPEAT the self-test.
F4 CHECK CIRCUIT 886 (OG/BK) FOR AN OPEN	
1	1 Measure the resistance between EEC-IV 60-Pin Breakout Box Pin 14, Circuit 886 (OG/BK), and G-switch C312 Pin 1, Circuit 886 (OG/BK). • Is the resistance less than 5 ohms? → **Yes** GO to F5. → **No** REPAIR the circuit. CLEAR the DTCs. REPEAT the self-test.
F5 CHECK CIRCUIT 886 (OG/BK) FOR SHORT TO GROUND	
1	1 Measure the resistance between EEC-IV 60-Pin Breakout Box Pin 14, Circuit 886 (OG/BK), and EEC-IV 60-Pin Breakout Box Pin 8, Circuit 57 (BK). • Is the resistance greater than 10,000 ohms? → **Yes** GO to F6. → **No** REPAIR Circuit 886 (OG/BK). CLEAR the DTCs. REPEAT the self-test.

FM4029901443030X

Fig. 12 Test F: Code C1102: G-Switch Circuit Failure (Part 3 of 5). 2002–03

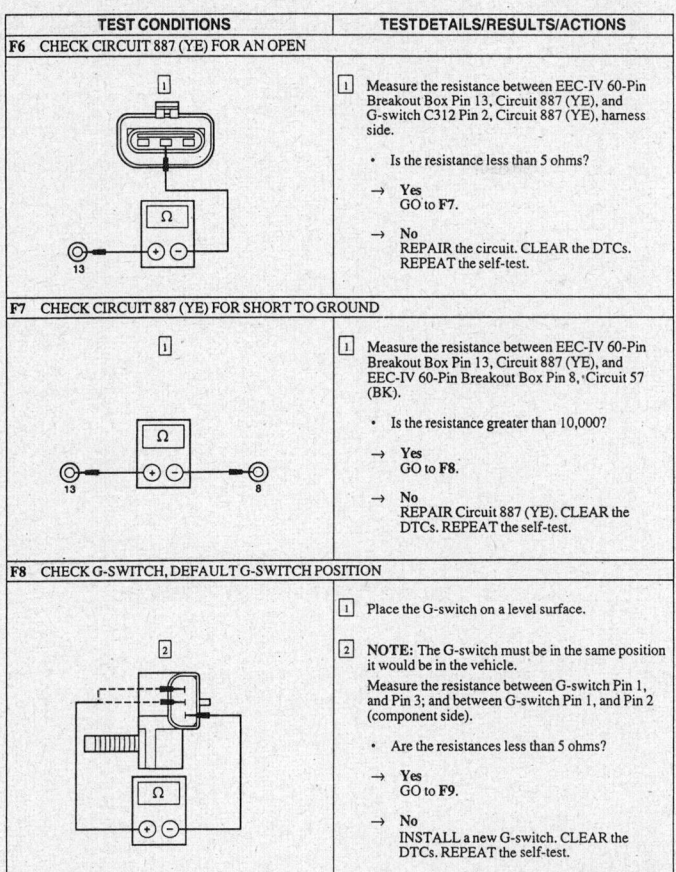

TEST CONDITIONS	TEST DETAILS/RESULTS/ACTIONS
F6 CHECK CIRCUIT 887 (YE) FOR AN OPEN	1. Measure the resistance between EEC-IV 60-Pin Breakout Box Pin 13, Circuit 887 (YE), and G-switch C312 Pin 2, Circuit 887 (YE), harness side. • Is the resistance less than 5 ohms? → **Yes** GO to **F7**. → **No** REPAIR the circuit. CLEAR the DTCs. REPEAT the self-test.
F7 CHECK CIRCUIT 887 (YE) FOR SHORT TO GROUND	1. Measure the resistance between EEC-IV 60-Pin Breakout Box Pin 13, Circuit 887 (YE), and EEC-IV 60-Pin Breakout Box Pin 8, Circuit 57 (BK). • Is the resistance greater than 10,000? → **Yes** GO to **F8**. → **No** REPAIR Circuit 887 (YE). CLEAR the DTCs. REPEAT the self-test.
F8 CHECK G-SWITCH, DEFAULT G-SWITCH POSITION	1. Place the G-switch on a level surface. 2. NOTE: The G-switch must be in the same position it would be in the vehicle. Measure the resistance between G-switch Pin 1, and Pin 3; and between G-switch Pin 1, and Pin 2 (component side). • Are the resistances less than 5 ohms? → **Yes** GO to **F9**. → **No** INSTALL a new G-switch. CLEAR the DTCs. REPEAT the self-test.

FM4029901443040X

Fig. 12 Test F: Code C1102: G-Switch Circuit Failure (Part 4 of 5). 2002–03

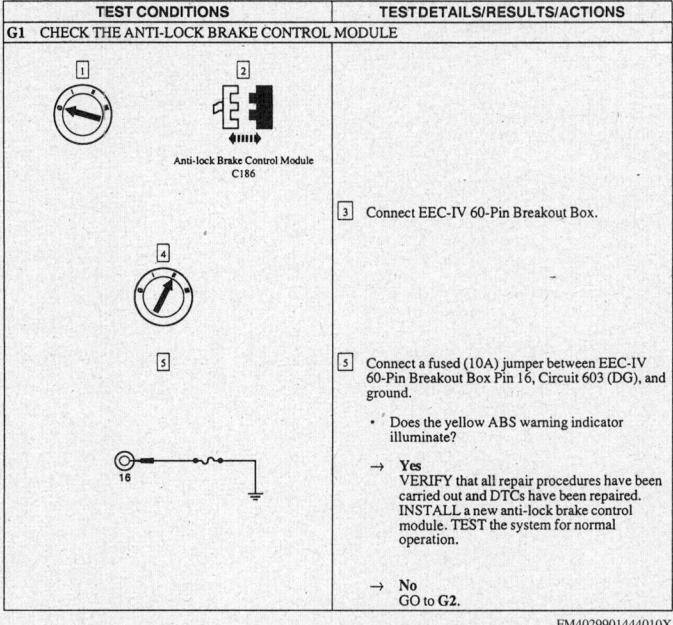

TEST CONDITIONS	TEST DETAILS/RESULTS/ACTIONS
G1 CHECK THE ANTI-LOCK BRAKE CONTROL MODULE	3. Connect EEC-IV 60-Pin Breakout Box. 5. Connect a fused (10A) jumper between EEC-IV 60-Pin Breakout Box Pin 16, Circuit 603 (DG), and ground. • Does the yellow ABS warning indicator illuminate? → **Yes** VERIFY that all repair procedures have been carried out and DTCs have been repaired. INSTALL a new anti-lock brake control module. TEST the system for normal operation. → **No** GO to **G2**.

FM4029901444010X

Fig. 13 Test G: Yellow ABS Warning Indicator Does Not Self Check (Part 1 of 2). 2002–03

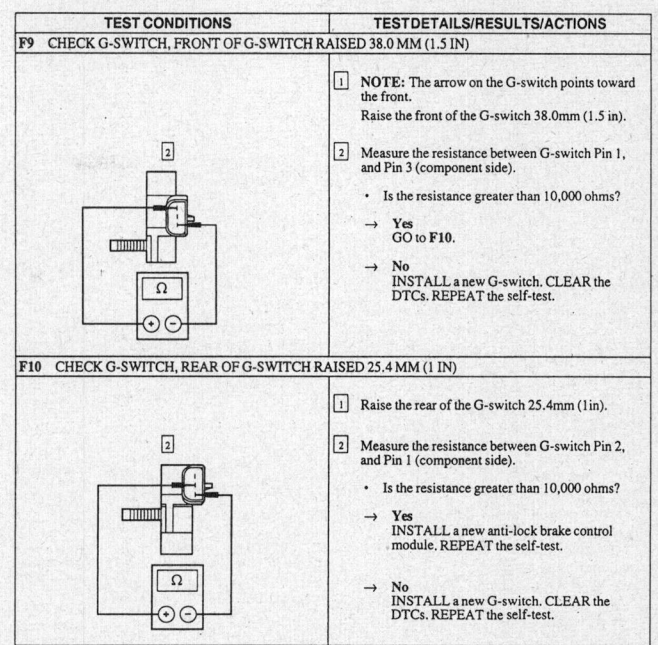

TEST CONDITIONS	TEST DETAILS/RESULTS/ACTIONS
F9 CHECK G-SWITCH, FRONT OF G-SWITCH RAISED 38.0 MM (1.5 IN)	1. NOTE: The arrow on the G-switch points toward the front. Raise the front of the G-switch 38.0mm (1.5 in). 2. Measure the resistance between G-switch Pin 1, and Pin 3 (component side). • Is the resistance greater than 10,000 ohms? → **Yes** GO to **F10**. → **No** INSTALL a new G-switch. CLEAR the DTCs. REPEAT the self-test.
F10 CHECK G-SWITCH, REAR OF G-SWITCH RAISED 25.4 MM (1 IN)	1. Raise the rear of the G-switch 25.4mm (1in). 2. Measure the resistance between G-switch Pin 2, and Pin 1 (component side). • Is the resistance greater than 10,000 ohms? → **Yes** INSTALL a new anti-lock brake control module. REPEAT the self-test. → **No** INSTALL a new G-switch. CLEAR the DTCs. REPEAT the self-test.

FM4029901443050X

Fig. 12 Test F: Code C1102: G-Switch Circuit Failure (Part 5 of 5). 2002–03

TEST CONDITIONS	TEST DETAILS/RESULTS/ACTIONS
G2 CHECK CIRCUIT 603 (DG) FOR AN OPEN	2. Measure the resistance between EEC-IV 60-Pin Breakout Box Pin 16, Circuit 603 (DG), and instrument cluster C288 Pin 6, Circuit 603 (DG), harness side. • Is the resistance less than 5 ohms? → **Yes** INSTALL a new instrument cluster printed circuit. TEST the system for normal operation. → **No** REPAIR the circuit. TEST the system for normal operation.

FM4029901444020X

Fig. 13 Test G: Yellow ABS Warning Indicator Does Not Self Check (Part 2 of 2). 2002–03

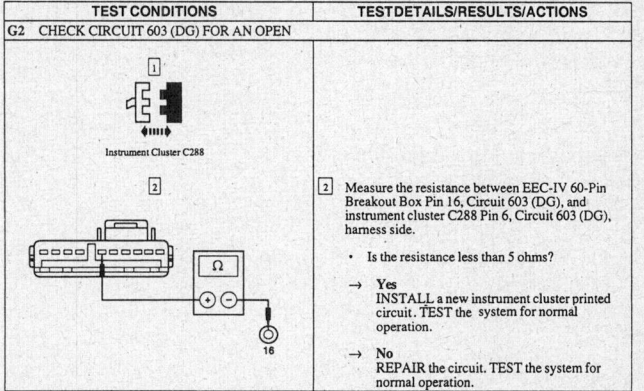

Test Step	Result / Action to Take
A1 CHECK THE ABS MODULE VOLTAGE CIRCUITS FOR AN OPEN • Key in OFF position. • Disconnect: ABS Module C155. • Key in ON position. • Measure the voltage between ground and: ▪ ABS module C155-1, circuit SBB06B (BN/RD), harness side. ▪ ABS module C155-8, circuit CBP18 (GY/OG), harness side. ▪ ABS module C155-32, circuit SBB33B (RD), harness side. • **Are the voltages greater than 10 volts?**	**Yes** GO to A2. **No** VERIFY that BJB fuse 6 (40A) is OK. If OK, REPAIR circuit SBB06B (BN/RD) for an open. VERIFY that BJB fuse 33 (30A) is OK. If OK, REPAIR circuit SBB33B (RD) for an open. VERIFY that SJB fuse 18 (10A) is OK. If OK, REPAIR circuit CBP18 (GY/OG) for an open. REPEAT the self-test.
A2 CHECK THE ABS MODULE GROUND CIRCUIT FOR AN OPEN • Key in OFF position. • Measure the resistance between ABS module C155-16, circuit GD120 (BK/GN), harness side and ground. • **Is the resistance less than 5 ohms?**	**Yes** CHECK the module communications network. **No** REPAIR circuit GD120 (BK/GN) for an open. REPEAT the self-test.

LTV0500000005421

Fig. 14 Test A: No Communication w/ABS Module. 2004-06

Test Step	Result / Action to Take
B1 CHECK THE STOPLAMP OPERATION	
• Key in OFF position. • Observe the stoplamps while pressing and releasing the brake pedal. • **Do the stoplamps operate correctly?**	**Yes** GO to B2. **No** Diagnose the stoplamps. Clear the DTCs. REPEAT the self-test.
B2 CHECK BRAKE ON/OFF (BOO) SWITCH INPUT CIRCUIT FOR AN OPEN	
• Disconnect: ABS Module C155. • Measure the voltage between ABS module C155-6, CCB08 (VT/WH), harness side and ground while pressing the brake pedal. • **Is the voltage greater than 10 volts?**	**Yes** GO to B3. **No** VERIFY SJB fuse 22 (15A) is OK. If OK, REPAIR circuit CCB08 (VT/WH) for an open. CLEAR the DTCs. REPEAT the self-test.
B3 CHECK FOR CORRECT ABS MODULE OPERATION	

• Disconnect the ABS connector.
• Check for:
  ▪ corrosion.
  ▪ pushed-out pins.
  ▪ spread terminals.
• Connect the ABS connector and make sure it seats correctly.
• Operate the system and verify the concern is still present.
• **Is the concern still present?**
	Yes
	INSTALL a new ABS module. TEST the system for normal operation.
	
	No
	The system is operating correctly at this time. The concern may have been caused by a loose or corroded connector. CLEAR the DTCs. REPEAT the self-test.

LTV0500000005422

Fig. 15   Test B, Code B1483: Brake Pedal Input Failure. 2004-06

• Are the voltages greater than 10 volts?	VERIFY that SJB fuse 18 (10A) is OK. If OK, REPAIR circuit CBP18 (GY/OG) for an open. REPEAT the self-test.
C3 CHECK THE ABS MODULE GROUND CIRCUIT FOR AN OPEN	
• Key in OFF position. • Measure the resistance between ABS module C155-16, circuit GD120 (BK/GN), harness side and ground. • **Is the resistance less than 5 ohms?**	**Yes** GO to C4. **No** REPAIR circuit GD120 (BK/GN) for an open. REPEAT the self-test.
C4 CHECK FOR CORRECT ABS MODULE OPERATION	

• Disconnect the ABS connector.
• Check for:
  ▪ corrosion.
  ▪ pushed-out pins.
  ▪ spread terminals.
• Connect the ABS connector and make sure it seats correctly.
• Operate the system and verify the concern is still present.
• **Is the concern still present?**
	Yes
	INSTALL a new ABS module. TEST the system for normal operation.
	
	No
	The system is operating correctly at this time. The concern may have been caused by a loose or corroded connector. CLEAR the DTCs. REPEAT the self-test.

LTV0500000005424

Fig. 16   Test C, Code B1676: Battery Pack Voltage Out Of Range (Part 2 of 2). 2004-06

Test Step	Result / Action to Take
C1 CHECK THE BATTERY VOLTAGE	
• Measure the battery voltage between the positive and negative battery posts with the key ON engine OFF (KOEO) and with the engine running. • **Is the battery voltage greater than 10 volts with KOEO and less than 18 volts with the engine running?**	**Yes** GO to C2. **No** CHECK the charging system. TEST the system for normal operation.
C2 CHECK THE ABS MODULE VOLTAGE CIRCUITS FOR AN OPEN	

• Key in OFF position.
• Disconnect: ABS Module C155.
• Key in ON position.
• Measure the voltage between ground and:
  ▪ ABS module C155-1, circuit SBB06B (BN/RD), harness side.
  ▪ ABS module C155-8, circuit CBP18 (GY/OG), harness side.
  ▪ ABS module C155-32, circuit SBB33B (RD), harness side.
	Yes
	GO to C3.
	
	No
	VERIFY that BJB fuse 6 (40A) is OK. If OK, REPAIR circuit SBB06B (BN/RD) for an open.
	
	VERIFY that BJB fuse 33 (30A) is OK. If OK, REPAIR circuit SBB33B (RD) for an open.

LTV0500000005423

Fig. 16   Test C, Code B1676: Battery Pack Voltage Out Of Range (Part 1 of 2). 2004-06

Test Step	Result / Action to Take
D1 CHECK THE ABS PUMP MOTOR	
• Key in ON position. • **Is the ABS pump motor running all the time?**	**Yes** GO to D5. **No** GO to D2.
D2 CHECK THE PUMP MOTOR OPERATION	
• Key in OFF position. • Connect the diagnostic tool. • Key in ON position. • Using the diagnostic tool, trigger the ABS module pump motor ON active command. • **Does the ABS pump motor run for approximately 2 seconds?**	**Yes** TRIGGER the ABS module pump motor OFF active command. CLEAR the DTCs. CHECK the yellow ABS warning indicator while driving the vehicle (brakes must not be applied) at greater than 20 km/h (12 mph). If the yellow ABS warning indicator illuminates, RETRIEVE the DTCs. If DTC C1095 is retrieved, GO to D5. **No** TRIGGER the ABS module pump motor OFF active command. GO to D3.
D3 CHECK THE PUMP MOTOR VOLTAGE SUPPLY CIRCUIT FOR AN OPEN	
• Disconnect: ABS Module C155. • Measure the voltage between ABS module C155-1, circuit SBB06B (BN/RD), harness side and ground. • **Is the voltage greater than**	**Yes** GO to D4. **No** VERIFY that BJB fuse 6 (40A) is OK. If OK, REPAIR circuit SBB06B (BN/RD) for an open. CLEAR the DTCs. REPEAT the self-test.

LTV0500000005425

Fig. 17   Test D, Code C1095: ABS Hydraulic Pump Motor Circuit Failure (Part 1 of 2). 2004-06

10 volts?	
D4 CHECK THE ABS MODULE GROUND CIRCUIT FOR AN OPEN	
• Key in OFF position. • Measure the resistance between ABS module C155-16, circuit GD120 (BK/GN), harness side and ground. • **Is the resistance less than 5 ohms?**	**Yes** INSTALL a new hydraulic control unit (HCU). CLEAR the DTCs. REPEAT the self-test. **No** REPAIR circuit GD120 (BK/GN) for an open. CLEAR the DTCs. REPEAT the self-test.
D5 CHECK FOR CORRECT ABS MODULE OPERATION	

• Disconnect all the ABS connectors.
• Check for:
  ▪ corrosion.
  ▪ pushed-out pins.
  ▪ spread terminals.
• Connect all the ABS connectors and make sure they seat correctly.
• Operate the system and verify the concern is still present.
• **Is the concern still present?**
	Yes
	INSTALL a new ABS module. TEST the system for normal operation.
	
	No
	The system is operating correctly at this time. The concern may have been caused by a loose or corroded connector. CLEAR the DTCs. REPEAT the self-test.

LTV0500000005426

Fig. 17 Test D, Code C1095: ABS Hydraulic Pump Motor Circuit Failure (Part 2 of 2). 2004-06

• **Are voltages present?**	
E2 CHECK THE WHEEL SPEED CIRCUITS FOR A SHORT TO GROUND	

NOTE: Both circuits must be checked for each DTC.
 	
• Key in OFF position.
• **For DTC C1145**, measure the resistance between ground and:
  ▪ ABS module C155-34, circuit VCA05A (GY/VT), harness side.
  ▪ ABS module C155-33, circuit RCA19A (VT), harness side.
• **For DTC C1155**, measure the resistance between and:
  ▪ ABS module C155-45, circuit VCA03A (VT/WH), harness side.
  ▪ ABS module C155-46, circuit RCA17A (YE), harness side.
• **For DTC C1165**, measure the resistance between ground and:
  ▪ ABS module C155-43, circuit VCA06 (WH/OG), harness side.
  ▪ ABS module C155-42, circuit RCA20 (BN), harness side.
• **For DTC C1175**, measure the resistance between ground and:
  ▪ ABS module C155-36, circuit VCA04A (BU/OG), harness side.
  ▪ ABS module C155-37, circuit RCA18 (BN/GN), harness side.
• **Are the resistances greater than 10,000 ohms?**
	Yes
	GO to E3.
	
	No
	REPAIR the affected circuit(s) for a short to ground. CLEAR the DTCs. REPEAT the self-test.

E3 CHECK THE WHEEL SPEED CIRCUITS FOR AN OPEN	

NOTE: Both circuits must be checked for each DTC.
 	
• **For DTC C1145**, measure the resistance between:
  ▪ ABS module C155-34, circuit VCA05A (GY/VT), harness side and RF wheel speed sensor C160-2, circuit VCA05A (GY/VT), harness side.
  ▪ ABS module C155-33, circuit RCA19A (VT), harness side and RF wheel speed sensor C160-1, circuit RCA19A (VT), harness side.
• **For DTC C1155**, measure the resistance between:
	Yes
	GO to E4.
	
	No
	REPAIR the affected circuit(s) for an open. CLEAR the DTCs. REPEAT the self-test.

LTV0500000005428

Fig. 18 Test E, Codes C1145, C1155, C1165 & C1175: Wheel Speed Sensor Input Circuit Failure (Part 2 of 4). 2004-06

Test Step	Result / Action to Take
E1 CHECK THE WHEEL SPEED CIRCUITS FOR A SHORT TO VOLTAGE	

⚠ **CAUTION: No measurements should be taken with the wheel speed sensor connected. Damage to the wheel speed sensor will result. NOTE:** Both circuits must be checked for each DTC.
 	
• Key in OFF position.
• Disconnect: ABS Module C155.
• Disconnect: Suspect Wheel Speed Sensor.
• Key in ON position.
• For DTC **C1145**, measure the voltage between ground and:
  ▪ ABS module C155-34, circuit VCA05A (GY/VT), harness side.
  ▪ ABS module C155-33, circuit RCA19A (VT), harness side.
• For DTC **C1155**, measure the voltage between ground and:
  ▪ ABS module C155-45, circuit VCA03A (VT/WH), harness side.
  ▪ ABS module C155-46, circuit RCA17A (YE), harness side.
• For DTC **C1165**, measure the voltage between ground and:
  ▪ ABS module C155-43, circuit VCA06 (WH/OG), harness side.
  ▪ ABS module C155-42, circuit RCA20 (BN), harness side.
• For DTC **C1175**, measure the voltage between ground and:
  ▪ ABS module C155-36, circuit VCA04A (BU/OG), harness side.
  ▪ ABS module C155-37, circuit RCA18 (BN/GN), harness side.
	Yes
	REPAIR the affected circuit(s) for a short to voltage. CLEAR the DTCs. REPEAT the self-test.
	
	No
	GO to E2.

LTV0500000005427

Fig. 18 Test E, Codes C1145, C1155, C1165 & C1175: Wheel Speed Sensor Input Circuit Failure (Part 1 of 4). 2004-06

▪ ABS module C155-45, circuit VCA03A (VT/WH), harness side and LF wheel speed sensor C150-2, circuit VCA03A (VT/WH), harness side.
▪ ABS module C155-46, circuit RCA17A (YE), harness side and LF wheel speed sensor C150-1, circuit RCA17A (YE), harness side.
• For DTC **C1165**, measure the resistance between:
  ▪ ABS module C155-43, circuit VCA06 (WH/OG), harness side and RR wheel speed sensor C426-2, circuit VCA06 (WH/OG), harness side.
  ▪ ABS module C155-42, circuit RCA20 (BN), harness side and RR wheel speed sensor C426-1, circuit RCA20 (BN), harness side.
• For DTC **C1175**, measure the resistance between:
  ▪ ABS module C155-36, circuit VCA04A (BU/OG), harness side and LR wheel speed sensor C440-2, circuit VCA04A (BU/OG), harness side.
  ▪ ABS module C155-37, circuit RCA18 (BN/GN), harness side and LR wheel speed sensor C440-1, circuit RCA18 (BN/GN), harness side.
• **Are the resistances less than 5 ohms?**	

E4 CHECK FOR SHORTED WHEEL SPEED SENSOR CIRCUITS	
• **For DTC C1145**, measure the resistance between RF wheel speed sensor C160-1, circuit RCA19A (VT), harness side and RF wheel speed sensor C160-2, circuit VCA05A (GY/VT), harness side. • **For DTC C1155**, measure the resistance between LF wheel speed sensor C150-1, circuit RCA17A (YE), harness side and LF wheel speed sensor C150-2, circuit VCA03A (VT/WH), harness side. • **For DTC C1165**, measure the resistance between RR wheel speed sensor C426-1, circuit RCA20 (BN), harness side and RR wheel speed sensor C426-2, circuit VCA06 (WH/OG), harness side. • **For DTC C1175**, measure the resistance between LR wheel speed sensor C440-1, circuit RCA18 (BN/GN), harness side and LR wheel speed sensor C440-2, circuit VCA04A (BU/OG), harness side. • **Are the resistances greater than 10,000**	**Yes** GO to E5. **No** REPAIR the affected circuit(s) for a short. CLEAR the DTCs. REPEAT the self-test.

LTV0500000005429

Fig. 18 Test E, Codes C1145, C1155, C1165 & C1175: Wheel Speed Sensor Input Circuit Failure (Part 3 of 4). 2004-06

ohms?	

E5 CHECK THE ABS MODULE OUTPUT	
• Connect: ABS Module C155. • Key in ON position. • **For DTC C1145**, measure the voltage between RF wheel speed sensor C160-1, circuit RCA19A (VT), harness side and RF wheel speed sensor C160-2, circuit VCA05A (GY/VT), harness side. • **For DTC C1155**, measure the voltage between LF wheel speed sensor C150-1, circuit RCA17A (YE), harness side and LF wheel speed sensor C150-2, circuit VCA03A (VT/WH), harness side. • **For DTC C1165**, measure the voltage between RR wheel speed sensor C426-1, circuit RCA20 (BN), harness side and RR wheel speed sensor C426-2, circuit VCA06 (WH/OG), harness side. • **For DTC C1175**, measure the voltage between LR wheel speed sensor C440-1, circuit RCA18 (BN/GN), harness side and LR wheel speed sensor C440-2, circuit VCA04A (BU/OG), harness side. • **Are the voltages greater than 10 volts?**	**Yes** INSTALL a new wheel speed sensor. REFER to in this section. CLEAR the DTCs. REPEAT the self-test., **No** GO to E6.

E6 CHECK FOR CORRECT ABS MODULE OPERATION	

• Disconnect all the ABS connectors.
• Check for:
  ▪ corrosion.
  ▪ pushed-out pins.
  ▪ spread terminals.
• Connect all the ABS connectors and make sure they seat correctly.
• Operate the system and verify the concern is still present.
• **Is the concern still present?**
	Yes
	INSTALL a new ABS module. TEST the system for normal operation.
	
	No
	The system is operating correctly at this time. The concern may have been caused by a loose or corroded connector. CLEAR the DTCs. REPEAT the self-test.

LTV0500000005430

Fig. 18   Test E, Codes C1145, C1155, C1165 & C1175: Wheel Speed Sensor Input Circuit Failure (Part 4 of 4). 2004-06

• Key in ON position. • Using the diagnostic tool, monitor the ABS module wheel speed sensor PIDs while driving the vehicle at a constant speed. • **Are all the wheel speed sensor PID values similar?**	CLEAR the DTCs. DRIVE the vehicle, RETRIEVE DTCs. If DTC C1233, C1234, C1235 or C1236 are present, GO to F8. If no DTCs are retrieved, the vehicle is OK. The concern may have been caused by a loose wheel speed sensor. **No** GO to F7.

F7 CHECK THE ABS MODULE OUTPUT	
• Key in OFF position. • Disconnect: Suspect Wheel Speed Sensor. • Key in ON position. • **For DTC C1233**, measure the voltage between LF wheel speed sensor C150-1, circuit RCA17A (YE), harness side and LF wheel speed sensor C150-2, circuit VCA03A (VT/WH), harness side. • **For DTC C1234**, measure the voltage between RF wheel speed sensor C160-1, circuit RCA19A (VT), harness side and RF wheel speed sensor C160-2, circuit VCA05A (GY/VT), harness side. • **For DTC C1235**, measure the voltage between RR wheel speed sensor C426-1, circuit RCA20 (BN), harness side and RR wheel speed sensor C426-2, circuit VCA06 (WH/OG), harness side. • **For DTC C1236**, measure the voltage between LR wheel speed sensor C440-1, circuit RCA18 (BN/GN), harness side and LR wheel speed sensor C440-2, circuit VCA04A (BU/OG), harness side. • **Are the voltages greater than 10 volts?**	**Yes** INSTALL a new wheel speed sensor. CLEAR the DTCs. REPEAT the self-test. **No** GO to F8.

F8 CHECK FOR CORRECT ABS MODULE OPERATION	

• Disconnect all the ABS connectors.
• Check for:
  ▪ corrosion.
  ▪ pushed-out pins.
  ▪ spread terminals.
• Connect all the ABS connectors and make sure they seat correctly.
• Operate the system and verify the concern is still present.
• **Is the concern still present?**
	Yes
	INSTALL a new ABS module TEST the system for normal operation.
	
	No
	The system is operating correctly at this time. The concern may have been caused by a loose or corroded connector. CLEAR the DTCs. REPEAT the self-test.

LTV0500000005432

Fig. 19   Test F, Codes C1233, C1234, C1235 & C1236: Wheel Speed Sensor Input Signal Missing (Part 2 of 2). 2004-06

Test Step	Result / Action to Take
F1 CHECK THE DTCs FROM THE SELF-TEST	
• Check the recorded results from the anti-lock brake system (ABS) self-test. • Are DTCs C1145, C1155, C1165 or C1175 present?	**Yes** Go To Pinpoint Test E. **No** GO to F2.
F2 INSPECT THE WHEEL SPEED SENSOR MOUNTING	
• Key in OFF position. • With the vehicle in NEUTRAL, position it on a hoist. • Inspect the suspect wheel speed sensor for looseness. • Is the wheel speed sensor loose?	**Yes** TIGHTEN the wheel speed sensor to specification. CLEAR the DTCs. GO to F5. **No** GO to F3.
F3 INSPECT THE WHEEL SPEED SENSOR FOR DAMAGE	
• ⚠ **CAUTION: Examine the wheel speed sensor wire carefully with a good light source. Failure to verify damage in the wheel speed sensor wire can lead to unnecessary installation of a new component.** • Inspect the suspect wheel speed sensor for general damage. • Is the wheel speed sensor OK?	**Yes** GO to F5. **No** INSTALL a new wheel speed sensor. CLEAR the DTCs. REPEAT the self-test.
F4 INSPECT THE WHEEL SPEED SENSOR RING FOR DAMAGE	
• Inspect the suspect wheel speed sensor ring for damaged or missing teeth. Rotate the wheel to verify that no teeth are missing. • Is the wheel speed sensor ring OK?	**Yes** GO to F6. **No** INSTALL a new wheel bearing and wheel hub (front sensor ring) or rear halfshaft (rear sensor ring). CLEAR the DTCs. REPEAT the self-test.
F5 INSPECT THE WHEEL BEARING FOR DAMAGE	
• Inspect the wheel bearings for damage. • Are the wheel bearings OK?	**Yes** GO to F7. **No** INSTALL a new wheel bearing and wheel hub as necessary. CLEAR the DTCs. REPEAT the self-test.
F6 RECHECK THE WHEEL SPEED PIDs	
• Connect the diagnostic tool.	**Yes**

LTV0500000005431

Fig. 19   Test F, Codes C1233, C1234, C1235 & C1236: Wheel Speed Sensor Input Signal Missing (Part 1 of 2). 2004-06

Test Step	Result / Action to Take
G1 MONITOR THE STEERING ROTATION SENSOR PIDs	
• Connect the diagnostic tool. • Key in ON position. • Using the diagnostic tool, monitor the ABS module steering rotation sensor PIDs while rotating the steering wheel clockwise and counterclockwise very slowly, from lock to lock. • Do the PIDs move in intervals of 1.5 degrees?	**Yes** CLEAR the DTCs. DRIVE the vehicle. RETRIEVE the DTCs. If DTC C1277 or C1278 is still present, GO to G9. **No** GO to G2.
G2 CHECK CIRCUIT CCS01 (VT/WH) FOR AN OPEN	
• Key in OFF position. • Disconnect: Steering Wheel Rotation Sensor C226. • Key in ON position. • Measure the voltage between steering wheel rotation sensor C226-4, circuit CCS01 (VT/WH), harness side and ground. • Is the voltage greater than 9.5 volts?	**Yes** GO to G3. **No** REPAIR circuit CCS01 (VT/WH) for an open. CLEAR the DTCs. REPEAT the self-test.
G3 CHECK CIRCUIT RSC02 (BU/WH) FOR AN OPEN	
• Measure the voltage between steering wheel rotation sensor C226-4, circuit CCS01 (VT/WH), harness side and steering wheel rotation sensor C226-1, circuit RSC02 (BU/WH) harness side.	**Yes** GO to G4. **No** REPAIR circuit RSC02 (BU/WH) for an open. CLEAR the DTCs. REPEAT the self-test.

LTV0500000005433

Fig. 20   Test G, Codes C1277 & C1278: Steering Wheel Angle 1 & 2 Circuit Failure/Fault Part (Part 1 of 3). 2004-06

Fig. 20 (Part 2 of 3) - Left column

Test Step	Result / Action to Take
• Is the voltage greater than 9.5 volts?	
G4 CHECK CIRCUIT VSC06 (GY/BN) FOR AN OPEN	
• Measure the voltage between steering wheel rotation sensor C226-2, circuit VSC06 (GY/BN), harness side and steering wheel rotation sensor C226-1, circuit RSC02 (BU/WH) harness side. 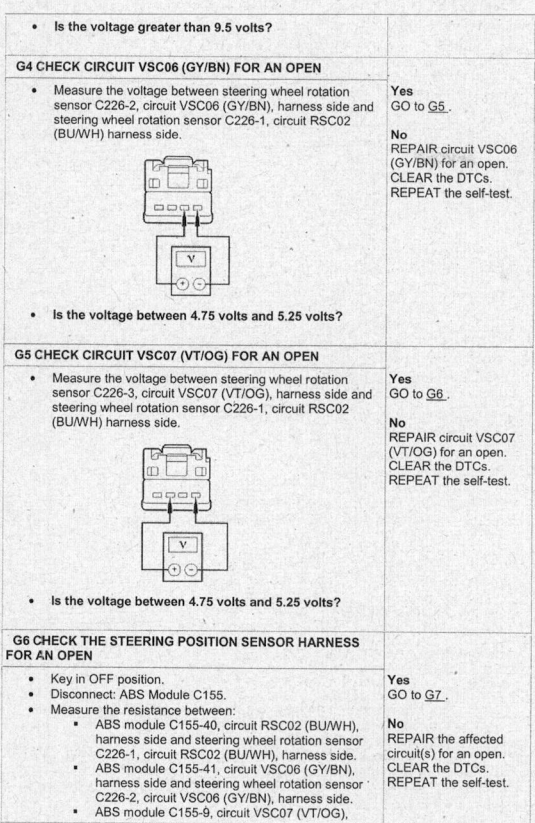 • Is the voltage between 4.75 volts and 5.25 volts?	**Yes** GO to G5. **No** REPAIR circuit VSC06 (GY/BN) for an open. CLEAR the DTCs. REPEAT the self-test.
G5 CHECK CIRCUIT VSC07 (VT/OG) FOR AN OPEN	
• Measure the voltage between steering wheel rotation sensor C226-3, circuit VSC07 (VT/OG), harness side and steering wheel rotation sensor C226-1, circuit RSC02 (BU/WH) harness side. • Is the voltage between 4.75 volts and 5.25 volts?	**Yes** GO to G6. **No** REPAIR circuit VSC07 (VT/OG) for an open. CLEAR the DTCs. REPEAT the self-test.
G6 CHECK THE STEERING POSITION SENSOR HARNESS FOR AN OPEN	
• Key in OFF position. • Disconnect: ABS Module C155. • Measure the resistance between: ▪ ABS module C155-40, circuit RSC02 (BU/WH), harness side and steering wheel rotation sensor C226-1, circuit RSC02 (BU/WH), harness side. ▪ ABS module C155-41, circuit VSC06 (GY/BN), harness side and steering wheel rotation sensor C226-2, circuit VSC06 (GY/BN), harness side. ▪ ABS module C155-9, circuit VSC07 (VT/OG),	**Yes** GO to G7. **No** REPAIR the affected circuit(s) for an open. CLEAR the DTCs. REPEAT the self-test.

LTV0500000005434

Fig. 20   Test G, Codes C1277 & C1278: Steering Wheel Angle 1 & 2 Circuit Failure/Fault (Part 2 of 3). 2004-06

Fig. 20 (Part 3 of 3) - Right column

Test Step	Result / Action to Take
harness side and steering wheel rotation sensor C226-3, circuit VSC07 (VT/OG), harness side. ▪ ABS module C155-5, circuit CCS01 (VT/WH), harness side and steering wheel rotation sensor C226-1, circuit CCS01 (VT/WH), harness side. • Are the resistances less than 5 ohms?	
G7 CHECK THE STEERING POSITION SENSOR CIRCUITS FOR A SHORT TO VOLTAGE	
• Key in ON position. • Measure the voltage between ground and: ▪ ABS module C155-40, circuit RSC02 (BU/WH), harness side. ▪ ABS module C155-41, circuit VSC06 (GY/BN), harness side. ▪ ABS module C155-9, circuit VSC07 (VT/OG), harness side. ▪ ABS module C155-5, circuit CCS01 (VT/WH), harness side. • Is voltage present?	**Yes** REPAIR the affected circuit(s) for a short to voltage. CLEAR the DTCs. REPEAT the self-test. **No** GO to G8.
G8 CHECK THE STEERING POSITION SENSOR CIRCUITRY FOR A SHORT TO GROUND	
• Key in OFF position. • Measure the resistance between ground and: ▪ ABS module C155-40, circuit RSC02 (BU/WH), harness side. ▪ ABS module C155-41, circuit VSC06 (GY/BN), harness side. ▪ ABS module C155-9, circuit VSC07 (VT/OG), harness side. ▪ ABS module C155-5, circuit CCS01 (VT/WH), harness side. • Are the resistances greater than 10,000 ohms?	**Yes** INSTALL a new steering wheel rotation sensor. CLEAR the DTCs. REPEAT the self-test. **No** REPAIR the affected circuit(s) for a short to ground. CLEAR the DTCs. REPEAT the self-test.
G9 CHECK FOR CORRECT ABS MODULE OPERATION	
• Disconnect all the ABS connectors. • Check for: ▪ corrosion. ▪ pushed-out pins. ▪ spread terminals. • Connect all the ABS connectors and make sure they seat correctly. • Operate the system and verify the concern is still present. • Is the concern still present?	**Yes** INSTALL a new ABS module. TEST the system for normal operation. **No** The system is operating correctly at this time. The concern may have been caused by a loose or corroded connector. CLEAR the DTCs. REPEAT the self-test.

LTV0500000005435

Fig. 20   Test G, Codes C1277 & C1278: Steering Wheel Angle 1 & 2 Circuit Failure/Fault (Part 3 of 3). 2004-06

Fig. 21 (Part 1 of 3) - Left column

Test Step	Result / Action to Take
H1 CHECK THE DTCs FROM THE SELF-TEST	
• Connect the diagnostic tool. • Key in ON position. • Using the diagnostic tool, clear the DTCs, carry out the self-test and retrieve any DTCs. • Are any DTCs retrieved?	**Yes** GO to H2. **No** The anti-lock brake system (ABS) system is operating correctly.
H2 CHECK THE VOLTAGE FROM THE ABS MODULE	
• Key in OFF position. • Disconnect: Sensor Cluster C3073. • Key in ON position. • Measure the voltage between sensor cluster C3073-3, circuit CCA09 (VT/BN), harness side and sensor cluster C3073-5, circuit RCA09 (GN/VT), harness side. • Is the voltage greater than 10 volts?	**Yes** GO to H3. **No** GO to H7.
H3 CHECK THE ABS MODULE YAW RATE PID	
• Key in OFF position. • Connect: Sensor Cluster C3073. • Key in ON position. • Using the diagnostic tool, monitor the ABS module yaw rate PID. • Is the ABS module yaw rate PID value between -0.05 and 0.05?	**Yes** GO to H4. **No** CHECK the mounting of the sensor cluster. If OK, INSTALL a new sensor cluster. CLEAR the DTCs. REPEAT the self-test.
H4 CHECK THE ABS MODULE LATERAL ACCELERATION PID	
• NOTE: The vehicle must be on level ground and at a complete standstill. Any vehicle movement results in false values for this test. • Monitor the ABS module lateral acceleration PID. • Is the ABS module lateral acceleration PID value between -7 and 7?	**Yes** GO to H5. **No** CHECK the mounting of the sensor cluster. If OK, INSTALL a new sensor cluster. CLEAR the DTCs. REPEAT the self-test.
H5 CHECK THE ABS MODULE LONGITUDINAL ACCELERATION PID	
• Monitor the ABS module longitudinal acceleration PID. • Is the ABS module longitudinal	**Yes** GO to H6.

LTV0500000005442

Fig. 21   Test H, Codes B2741, C1279, C1280, C1281, C1282, C1516, C1517, C2769, C2770, C2777, C2778, U1900 & U1901: Sensor Cluster Fault (Part 1 of 3). 2004-06

Fig. 21 (Part 2 of 3) - Right column

Test Step	Result / Action to Take
acceleration PID value between -4 and 4?	**No** CHECK the mounting of the sensor cluster. If OK, INSTALL a new sensor cluster. CLEAR the DTCs. REPEAT the self-test.
H6 CHECK THE ABS MODULE ROLL RATE PID	
• Monitor the ABS module roll rate PID. • Is the ABS module roll rate PID value between -0.05 and 0.05?	**Yes** GO to H7. **No** CHECK the mounting of the sensor cluster. If OK, INSTALL a new sensor cluster. REFER to in this section. CLEAR the DTCs.
H7 CHECK THE SENSOR CLUSTER CIRCUITRY FOR AN OPEN	
• Key in OFF position. • Disconnect: Sensor Cluster C3073. • Disconnect: ABS Module C155. • Measure the resistance between: ▪ ABS module C155-18, circuit VCA23 (BU/WH), harness side and sensor cluster C3073-2, circuit VCA23 (BU/WH), harness side. ▪ ABS module C155-19, circuit VCA24 (GN/OG), harness side and sensor cluster C3073-1, circuit VCA24 (GN/OG), harness side. ▪ ABS module C155-22, circuit CCA09 (VT/BN), harness side and sensor cluster C3073-3, circuit CCA09 (VT/BN), harness side. ▪ ABS module C155-29, circuit RCA09 (GN/VT), harness side and sensor cluster C3073-5, circuit RCA09 (GN/VT), harness side. • Are the resistances less than 5 ohms?	**Yes** GO to H8. **No** REPAIR the affected circuit(s) for an open. CLEAR the DTCs. REPEAT the self-test.
H8 CHECK THE SENSOR CLUSTER CIRCUITRY FOR A SHORT TO VOLTAGE	
• Key in ON position. • Measure the voltage between ground and: ▪ Sensor cluster C3073-1, circuit VCA24 (GN/OG), harness side. ▪ Sensor cluster C3073-2, circuit VCA23 (BU/WH), harness side. ▪ Sensor cluster C3073-3, circuit CCA09 (VT/BN), harness side. ▪ Sensor cluster C3073-5, circuit RCA09 (GN/VT),	**Yes** REPAIR the affected circuit(s) for a short to voltage. CLEAR the DTCs. REPEAT the self-test. **No** GO to H9.

LTV0500000005443

Fig. 21   Test H, Codes B2741, C1279, C1280, C1281, C1282, C1516, C1517, C2769, C2770, C2777, C2778, U1900 & U1901: Sensor Cluster Fault (Part 2 of 3). 2004-06

- Are voltages present?

H9 CHECK THE SENSOR CLUSTER CIRCUITRY FOR A SHORT TO GROUND

• Key in OFF position. • Measure the resistance between ground and: ▪ Sensor cluster C3073-1, circuit VCA24 (GN/OG), harness side. ▪ Sensor cluster C3073-2, circuit VCA23 (BU/WH), harness side. ▪ Sensor cluster C3073-3, circuit CCA09 (VT/BN), harness side. ▪ Sensor cluster C3073-5, circuit RCA09 (GN/VT), harness side. • **Are the resistances greater than 10,000 ohms?**	**Yes** GO to H10 . **No** REPAIR the affected circuit(s) for a short to ground. CLEAR the DTCs. REPEAT the self-test.

H10 CHECK FOR CORRECT ABS MODULE OPERATION

• Disconnect all the ABS connectors. • Check for: ▪ corrosion. ▪ pushed-out pins. ▪ spread terminals. • Connect all the ABS connectors and make sure they seat correctly. • Operate the system and verify the concern is still present. • **Is the concern still present?**	**Yes** INSTALL a new ABS module. TEST the system for normal operation. **No** The system is operating correctly at this time. The concern may have been caused by a loose or corroded connector. CLEAR the DTCs. REPEAT the self-test.

LTV0500000005444

Fig. 21 Test H, Codes B2741, C1279, C1280, C1281, C1282, C1516, C1517, C2769, C2770, C2777, C2778, U1900 & U1901: Sensor Cluster Fault (Part 3 of 3). 2004-06

(GY/YE) FOR A SHORT TO VOLTAGE

• Key in ON position. • Measure the voltage between ground and: ▪ Active brake booster C149-4, circuit VCA22 (GN/BN), harness side. ▪ Active brake booster C149-3, circuit CCA22 (GY/YE) harness side. • **Is voltage present?**	**Yes** REPAIR the affected circuit(s) for a short to voltage. CLEAR the DTCs. REPEAT the self-test. **No** GO to I6 .

I6 CHECK THE ACTIVE BRAKE BOOSTER SOLENOID FOR CORRECT OPERATION

• Key in OFF position. • Connect: Active Brake Booster C149. • Connect: ABS Module C155. • Key in ON position. • Start the engine and wait approximately one minute to create vacuum in the brake booster and then turn the ignition switch to the OFF position. • Disconnect: ABS Module C155. • Connect a fused (10A) jumper wire between ABS module C155-31, circuit VCA22 (GN/BN), harness side and ground. • While observing the brake pedal for movement, connect a fused (10A) jumper wire for approximately 2 seconds between ABS module C155-17, circuit CCA22 (GY/YE), harness side and the positive battery post. • **Does the brake pedal move?**	**Yes** GO to I7 . **No** INSTALL a new active brake booster. CLEAR the DTCs. REPEAT the self-test.

I7 CHECK FOR CORRECT ABS MODULE OPERATION

• Disconnect all the ABS connectors. • Check for: ▪ corrosion. ▪ pushed-out pins. ▪ spread terminals. • Connect all the ABS connectors and make sure they seat correctly. • Operate the system and verify the concern is still present. • **Is the concern still present?**	**Yes** INSTALL a new ABS module. TEST the system for normal operation. **No** The system is operating correctly at this time. The concern may have been caused by a loose or corroded connector. CLEAR the DTCs. REPEAT the self-test.

LTV0500000005437

Fig. 22 Test I, Code C1285: Booster Solenoid Circuit Failure (Part 2 of 2). 2004-06

Test Step	Result / Action to Take
I1 CHECK THE DTCs FROM THE SELF-TEST	
• Connect the diagnostic tool. • Key in ON position. • Using the diagnostic tool, clear the DTCs, carry out the self-test and retrieve any DTCs. • **Are any DTCs retrieved?**	**Yes** If DTC C1285 is retrieved GO to I2 . If any other DTC is retrieved, GO to the Anti-Lock Brake System (ABS) Module Diagnostic Trouble Code (DTC) Index. **No** The system is operating correctly at this time.
I2 CHECK THE BRAKE BOOSTER SOLENOID	
• Key in OFF position. • Disconnect: Active Brake Booster C149. • Measure the resistance between active brake booster C149-3, component side and active brake booster C149-4, component side. • **Is the resistance between 1 and 2 ohms?**	**Yes** GO to I3 . **No** INSTALL a new active brake booster. CLEAR the DTCs. REPEAT the self-test.
I3 CHECK CIRCUITS VCA22 (GN/BN) AND CCA22 (GY/YE) FOR AN OPEN	
• Disconnect: ABS Module C155. • Measure the resistance between: ▪ ABS module C155-31, circuit VCA22 (GN/BN), harness side and active brake booster C149-4, circuit VCA22 (GN/BN), harness side. ▪ ABS module C155-17, circuit CCA22 (GY/YE), harness side and active brake booster C149-3, circuit CCA22 (GY/YE) harness side. • **Are the resistances less than 5 ohms?**	**Yes** GO to I4 . **No** REPAIR the affected circuit(s) for an open. CLEAR the DTCs. REPEAT the self-test.
I4 CHECK CIRCUITS VCA22 (GN/BN) AND CCA22 (GY/YE) FOR A SHORT TO GROUND	
• Measure the resistance between ground and: ▪ Active brake booster C149-4, circuit VCA22 (GN/BN), harness side. ▪ Active brake booster C149-3, circuit CCA22 (GY/YE) harness side. • **Are the resistances greater than 10,000 ohms?**	**Yes** GO to I5 . **No** REPAIR the affected circuit(s) for a short to ground. CLEAR the DTCs. REPEAT the self-test.
I5 CHECK CIRCUITS VCA22 (GN/BN) AND CCA22	

LTV0500000005436

Fig. 22 Test I, Code C1285: Booster Solenoid Circuit Failure (Part 1 of 2). 2004-06

Test Step	Result / Action to Take
J1 CHECK THE DTCs FROM THE SELF-TEST	
• Connect the diagnostic tool. • Key in ON position. • Using the diagnostic tool, clear the DTCs, apply and release the brake pedal, carry out the self-test and retrieve any DTCs. • **Are any DTCs retrieved?**	**Yes** If DTC C1287 is retrieved GO to J2 . If any other DTC is retrieved, GO to the Anti-Lock Brake System (ABS) Module Diagnostic Trouble Code (DTC) Index. **No** The system is operating correctly at this time.
J2 CHECK THE BRAKE BOOSTER PEDAL FORCE SWITCH	
• Key in OFF position. • Disconnect: Active Brake Booster C149. • Measure the resistance between active brake booster C149-5, component side and active brake booster C149-2, component side while pressing and releasing the brake pedal. • **Is the resistance less than 5 ohms with the brake pedal released and greater than 10,000 ohms with the brake pedal applied?**	**Yes** GO to J3 . **No** INSTALL a new active brake booster. CLEAR the DTCs. REPEAT the self-test.
J3 CHECK THE BRAKE BOOSTER PEDAL FORCE SWITCH	
• Measure the resistance between active brake booster C149-5, component side and active brake booster C149-1, component side while pressing and releasing the brake pedal. • **Is the resistance greater than 10,000 ohms with the brake pedal released and less than 5 ohms with the brake pedal applied?**	**Yes** GO to J4 . **No** INSTALL a new active brake booster. CLEAR the DTCs. REPEAT the self-test.
J4 CHECK THE ACTIVE BRAKE BOOSTER CIRCUITRY FOR A SHORT	
• Disconnect: ABS Module C155. • Measure the resistance between: ▪ Active brake booster C149-1, circuit CCA26 (BU/GY), harness side and active brake booster C149-2, circuit CCA25 (VT/GY), harness side. ▪ Active brake booster C149-1, circuit CCA26 (BU/GY), harness side and active brake booster C149-5, circuit CCA29 (GN/BU), harness side.	**Yes** GO to J5 . **No** REPAIR the affected circuit(s) for a short. CLEAR the DTCs. REPEAT the self-test

LTV0500000005438

Fig. 23 Test J, Code C1287: Brake Booster Pedal Force Switch Failure (Part 1 of 3). 2004-06

- Active brake booster C149-2, circuit CCA25 (VT/GY), harness side and active brake booster C149-5, circuit CCA29 (GN/BU), harness side.
- **Are the resistances greater than 10,000 ohms?**

Test Step	Result / Action to Take

J5 CHECK THE ACTIVE BRAKE BOOSTER CIRCUITRY FOR A SHORT TO VOLTAGE
• Key in ON position.
• Measure the voltage between ground and:
  ▪ Active brake booster C149-1, circuit CCA26 (BU/GY), harness side.
  ▪ Active brake booster C149-2, circuit CCA25 (VT/GY), harness side.
  ▪ Active brake booster C149-5, circuit CCA29 (GN/BU), harness side.
• **Is voltage present?**
	Yes
	REPAIR the affected circuit(s) for a short to voltage. CLEAR the DTCs. REPEAT the self-test.
	
	No
	GO to J6 .

J6 CHECK THE ACTIVE BRAKE BOOSTER CIRCUITRY FOR A SHORT TO GROUND
• Key in OFF position.
• Measure the resistance between ground and:
  ▪ Active brake booster C149-1, circuit CCA26 (BU/GY), harness side.
  ▪ Active brake booster C149-2, circuit CCA25 (VT/GY), harness side.
  ▪ Active brake booster C149-5, circuit CCA29 (GN/BU), harness side.
• **Are the resistances greater than 10,000 ohms?**
	Yes
	GO to J7 .
	
	No
	REPAIR the affected circuit(s) for a short to ground. CLEAR the DTCs. REPEAT the self-test.

J7 CHECK THE BRAKE BOOSTER CIRCUITRY FOR OPENS
• Key in OFF position.
• Measure the resistance between:
  ▪ ABS module C155-21, circuit CCA29 (GN/BU), harness side and active brake booster C149-5, circuit CCA29 (GN/BU), harness side.
  ▪ ABS module C155-23, circuit CCA26 (BU/GY), harness side and active brake booster C149-1, circuit CCA26 (BU/GY), harness side.
  ▪ ABS module C155-24, circuit CCA25 (VT/GY), harness side and active brake booster C149-2, circuit CCA25 (VT/GY), harness side.
• **Are the resistances less than 5 ohms?**
	Yes
	GO to J8 .
	
	No
	REPAIR the affected circuit(s) for an open. CLEAR the DTCs. REPEAT the self-test.

LTV0500000005439

Fig. 23   Test J, Code C1287: Brake Booster Pedal Force Switch Failure (Part 2 of 3). 2004-06

Test Step	Result / Action to Take
K1 CHECK THE STABILITY TRACTION CONTROL SWITCH • Key in OFF position. • Disconnect: Stability Traction Control Switch C280. • Measure the resistance between the stability traction control switch C280-6, component side and C280-1, component side. • **Is the resistance greater than 10,000 ohms?**	**Yes** GO to K2 . **No** INSTALL a new stability traction control switch. TEST the system for normal operation.
K2 CHECK CIRCUIT CCA15 (YE/GY) FOR A SHORT TO VOLTAGE • Disconnect: ABS Module C155. • Key in ON position. • Measure the voltage between the ABS module C155-4, circuit CCA15 (YE/GY), harness side and ground. • **Is voltage present?**	**Yes** REPAIR circuit CCA15 (YE/GY) for a short to voltage. TEST the system for normal operation. **No** GO to K3 .
K3 CHECK CIRCUIT CCA15 (YE/GY) FOR A SHORT TO GROUND • Key in OFF position. • Measure the resistance between the ABS module C155-4, circuit CCA15 (YE/GY), harness side and ground. • **Is the resistance greater than 10,000 ohms?**	**Yes** GO to K4 . **No** REPAIR circuit CCA15 (YE/GY) for a short to ground. TEST the system for normal operation.

K4 CHECK FOR CORRECT ABS MODULE OPERATION
• Disconnect all the ABS connectors.
• Check for:
  ▪ corrosion.
  ▪ pushed-out pins.
  ▪ spread terminals.
• Connect all the ABS connectors and make sure they seat correctly.
• Operate the system and verify the concern is still present.
• **Is the concern still present?**
	Yes
	INSTALL a new ABS module. TEST the system for normal operation.
	
	No
	The system is operating correctly at this time. The concern may have been caused by a loose or corroded connector. CLEAR the DTCs. REPEAT the self-test

LTV0500000005441

Fig. 24   Test K: Traction Control/Roll Stability Control System Cannot Be Disabled. 2004-06

Test Step	Result / Action to Take

J8 CHECK FOR CORRECT ABS MODULE OPERATION
• Disconnect all the ABS connectors.
• Check for:
  ▪ corrosion.
  ▪ pushed-out pins.
  ▪ spread terminals.
• Connect all the ABS connectors and make sure they seat correctly.
• Operate the system and verify the concern is still present.
• **Is the concern still present?**
	Yes
	INSTALL a new ABS module. TEST the system for normal operation.
	
	No
	The system is operating correctly at this time. The concern may have been caused by a loose or corroded connector. CLEAR the DTCs. REPEAT the self-test.

LTV0500000005440

Fig. 23   Test J, Code C1287: Brake Booster Pedal Force Switch Failure (Part 3 of 3). 2004-06

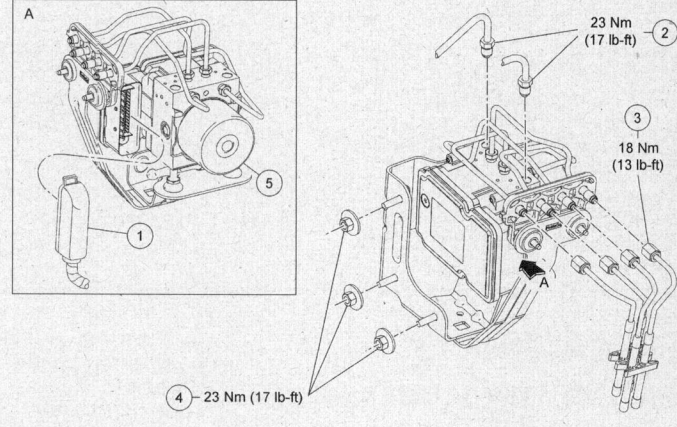

Item	Description	Item	Description
1	Anti-lock brake system (ABS) module electrical connector	4	HCU bracket-to-frame nuts (3 required)
2	Brake tube-to-HCU fittings (M12-1) (2 required)	5	HCU assembly
3	Brake tube-to-HCU extension tube fittings (4 required)		

LTV0500000005445

Fig. 25   Hydraulic Control Unit (HCU) replacement

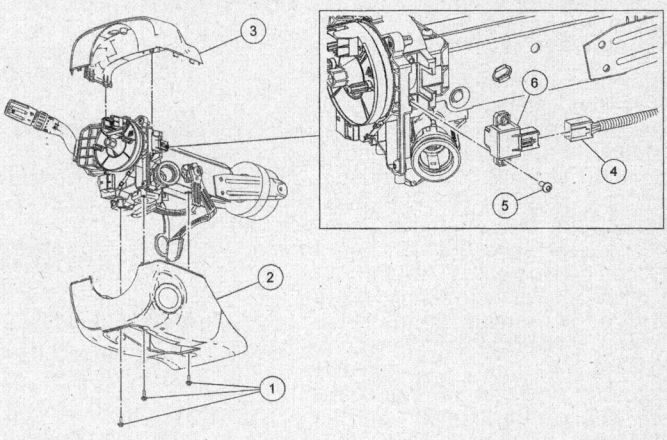

Item	Description
1	Lower steering column cover bolts (3 required)
2	Lower steering column cover
3	Upper steering column cover
4	Steering wheel rotation sensor electrical connector
5	Steering wheel rotation sensor bolt (2 required)
6	Steering wheel rotation sensor

LTV0500000005446

Fig. 26   Steering Wheel Rotation Sensor replacement

Freestar & Monterey

NOTE: Electrical Symbol & Wire Color Code Identification Located In The Front Of This Manual May Be Used As An Aid When Using Wiring Circuits Found In This Section.

NOTE: Refer To "Computer Relearn Procedures" Located In The Front Of This Manual When Battery Power To The Computer Has Been Interrupted.

INDEX

	Page No.		Page No.		Page No.
Description	5-130	Diagnostic Trouble Code		Component Replacement	5-131
Diagnosis & Testing	5-130	Interpretation	5-130	ABS Control Module	5-131
Accessing Diagnostic Trouble		Wiring Diagrams	5-130	Accelerometer	5-131
Codes	5-130	Diagnostic Chart Index	5-134	Hydraulic Control Unit (HCU)	5-131
Clearing Diagnostic Trouble		Precautions	5-130	Steering Wheel Rotation	
Codes	5-130	Battery Ground Cable	5-130	Sensor	5-131
Diagnostic Tests	5-130	Brake Fluid Handling	5-130	Wheel Speed Sensor	5-131
Inspection & Verification	5-130	System Service	5-130	Troubleshooting	5-130
Pinpoint Tests	5-130	Brake System Bleed	5-130	Symptom Chart	5-130

PRECAUTIONS

BATTERY GROUND CABLE

Prior to service disconnect battery ground cable and isolate as required.

BRAKE FLUID HANDLING

Brake fluid can cause serious injury and vehicle damage if not handled properly. Avoid contact with eyes and do not allow fluid to splash or spill on painted surfaces. Wash hands thoroughly after handling.

DESCRIPTION

The anti-lock brake system (ABS) module, with or without stability assist, simultaneously manages the anti-lock braking, traction control and engine control systems to maintain vehicle control during deceleration and acceleration. The ABS accomplishes this by communicating with the other modules over the high speed controller area network (HS-CAN) bus.

When the ignition switch is in the RUN position, the module carries out a preliminary electrical check and, at approximately 20 km/h (12 mph), the hydraulic pump motor is turned on for approximately one half-second. Any malfunction of the anti-lock brake system disables the traction control and stability assist (if equipped). The ABS module communicates with the instrument cluster over the HS-CAN bus and the cluster illuminates the anti-lock brake warning indicator. However, the power-assist braking system functions normally.

With the ignition switch in the START or RUN positions, the stability assist module functions similarly to a conventional ABS module by monitoring and comparing the rotational speed of each wheel. The wheel speed sensors electrically sense each tooth of the anti-lock sensor ring as they pass through the sensor magnetic field. When the stability assist module detects an impending wheel lock, wheel spin or vehicle motion that is inconsistent with the driver commands, it modulates brake pressure to the appropriate brake caliper(s). The stability assist module triggers the hydraulic control unit (HCU) to open and close the appropriate solenoid valves. Once the affected wheel(s) returns to the desired speed, the stability assist module returns the solenoid valves to their normal position, and normal base brake operation is restored.

TROUBLESHOOTING

Symptom Chart

Refer to **Fig. 1** for symptom charts.

DIAGNOSIS & TESTING

Accessing Diagnostic Trouble Codes

Connect a suitably programmed scan tool and Vehicle Communication Module (VCM) with appropriate adapters, or equivalents, to the Data Link Connector (DCL) located in the passenger compartment beneath the instrument panel. Follow tool manufacturer's instructions for accessing Diagnostic Trouble Codes (DTC).

Diagnostic Trouble Code Interpretation

Refer to **Fig. 2** for diagnostic trouble code interpretation.

Wiring Diagrams

Refer to **Fig. 3** for wiring diagram.

Diagnostic Tests

INSPECTION & VERIFICATION

Verify concern by applying brakes under different conditions. Inspect for obvious signs of mechanical and electrical damage such as parking brake cable, tire pressure, tire size or mismatched tires. Check for blown fuse, connectors or connections, harness routing, wire chaffing, circuitry open/shorted and indicator bulb.

PINPOINT TESTS

Refer to **Figs. 4 through 20** for pinpoint tests.

Clearing Diagnostic Trouble Codes

Connect a suitably programmed scan tool and Vehicle Communication Module (VCM) with appropriate adapters, or equivalents, to the Data Link Connector (DCL) located in the passenger compartment beneath the instrument panel. Follow tool manufacturer's instructions for clearing Diagnostic Trouble Codes (DTC).

SYSTEM SERVICE

Brake System Bleed

Refer to "Hydraulic Brake Systems" chapter for bleeding procedure.

Condition	Possible Sources	Action
• No communication with the anti-lock brake system (ABS) module	• Circuitry • ABS module	• Go To Pinpoint Test A .
• No communication with the instrument cluster	• Instrument cluster • Circuitry	• REFER to "Dash Gauges & Warning Indicators"
• The red brake warning indicator does not self-check	• Instrument cluster • Circuitry	• REFER to "Dash Gauges & Warning Indicators"
• The red brake warning indicator stays on when the ignition is in RUN	• Parking brake switch • Base brake system • Circuitry • Instrument cluster • Anti-lock brake system (ABS) module	• RETRIEVE all DTCs and GO TO the DTC indexes. If no DTCs are present, REFER to "Dash Gauges & Warning Indicators"
• The yellow anti-lock brake system (ABS) warning indicator does not self-check	• Instrument cluster • Circuitry • Anti-lock brake system (ABS) module	• REFER to "Dash Gauges & Warning Indicators"
• Spongy/soft/low brake pedal with no warning indicator	• Air in brake hydraulic system • Hydraulic control unit (HCU)	• Go To Pinpoint Test O .

LTV0500000004882

Fig. 1 Symptom Chart (Part 1 of 2)

• The traction control switch indicator is never on	• Circuitry • Traction control switch • Smart junction box (SJB)	• REFER to "Dash Gauges & Warning Indicators"
• The traction control is inoperative	• Circuitry • Traction control switch • Anti-lock brake system (ABS) module	• Go To Pinpoint Test K .
• The traction control system cannot be disabled	• Circuitry • Traction control switch • Anti-lock brake system (ABS) module	• Go To Pinpoint Test C .

LTV0500000004883

Fig. 1 Symptom Chart (Part 2 of 2)

Component Replacement

ABS CONTROL MODULE

1. Raise and support vehicle.
2. Remove three ABS splash shield pin-type retainers, then the shield.
3. Disconnect pump motor electrical connector from ABS module.
4. Remove four ABS control module retaining screws, then the module.
5. Reverse procedure to install. **Torque** ABS control module retaining screws to 27 inch lbs.

ACCELEROMETER

1. Remove driver side front seat.
2. Remove lower B-pillar trim panel.
3. Fold back carpeting flap to gain access to accelerometer.
4. Disconnect accelerometer electrical connector.
5. Remove three accelerometer mounting bolts, then the accelerometer.
6. Reverse procedure to install. **Torque** mounting bolts to 10 ft. lbs.

HYDRAULIC CONTROL UNIT (HCU)

1. Raise and support vehicle.
2. Remove three ABS splash shield pin-type retainers, **Fig. 21,** then the shield.
3. Disconnect brake line to hydraulic control unit (HCU) fittings, then position brake lines aside. Note position of lines for installation.
4. Disconnect ABS control module electrical connectors.
5. Remove three HCU bracket to frame mounting bolts, then the HCU assembly.
6. Remove HCU from bracket.
7. Reverse procedure to install, noting the following:
   a. **Torque** HCU to bracket retaining bolts to 96 inch lbs.
   b. **Torque** HCU retaining bolts to 15 ft. lbs.
   c. **Torque** brake lines to 13 ft. lbs.
   d. Bleed brake system as outlined under "Brake System Bleed.".

STEERING WHEEL ROTATION SENSOR

1. Remove lefthand instrument panel under cover.
2. Disconnect steering wheel rotation sensor electrical connector, **Fig. 22.**
3. Remove two rotation sensor retaining screws.
4. Remove steering wheel rotation sensor.
5. Reverse procedure to install.

WHEEL SPEED SENSOR

FRONT

Front wheel speed sensors and sensor rings are part of the front hub and bearing assembly and must be serviced as an assembly.

REAR

1. Raise and support vehicle.
2. Clean area around wheel speed sensor.
3. Disconnect wheel speed sensor electrical connector.
4. Remove two sensor retaining bolts, then the sensor and harness.
5. Reverse procedure to install.

DTC	Description
B1317	Battery Voltage High
B1318	Battery Voltage Low
B1342	ECU Is Defective
B2477	Module Configuration Failure
C1095	ABS Hydraulic Pump Motor Circuit Failure
C1096	ABS Hydraulic Pump Motor Circuit Open
C1115	ABS Power Relay Output Short Circuit To Battery
C1145	Wheel Speed Sensor RF Input Circuit Failure
C1155	Wheel Speed Sensor LF Input Circuit Failure
C1165	Wheel Speed Sensor RR Input Circuit Failure
C1175	Wheel Speed Sensor LR Input Circuit Failure
C1185	ABS Power Relay Output Circuit Failure
C1194	ABS Outlet Valve Coil LF Circuit Failure
C1198	ABS Inlet Valve Coil LF Circuit Failure
C1210	ABS Outlet Valve Coil RF Circuit Failure
C1214	ABS Inlet Valve Coil RF Circuit Failure
C1222	Speed Wheel Mismatch
C1233	Wheel Speed LF Input Signal Missing
C1234	Wheel Speed RF Input Signal Missing
C1235	Wheel Speed RR Input Signal Missing
C1236	Wheel Speed LR Input Signal Missing
C1242	ABS Outlet Valve Coil LR Circuit Failure
C1246	ABS Outlet Valve Coil RR Circuit Failure
C1250	ABS Inlet Valve Coil LR Circuit Failure
C1254	ABS Inlet Valve Coil RR Circuit Failure
C1277	Steering Wheel Angle 1 and 2 Circuit Failure
C1278	Steering Wheel Angle 1 and 2 Signal Faulted
C1279	Yaw Rate Sensor Circuit Failure
C1280	Yaw Rate Sensor Signal Fault
C1281	Lateral Accelerometer Circuit Failure
C1282	Lateral Accelerometer Signal Fault
C1285	Booster Solenoid Circuit Failure
C1286	Booster Mechanical Failure
C1287	Booster Pedal Force Switch Circuit Failure
C1288	Brake Pressure Transducer Main/Primary Input Circuit Failure

LTV0500000004884

Fig. 2 Diagnostic trouble code interpretation
(Part 1 of 2)

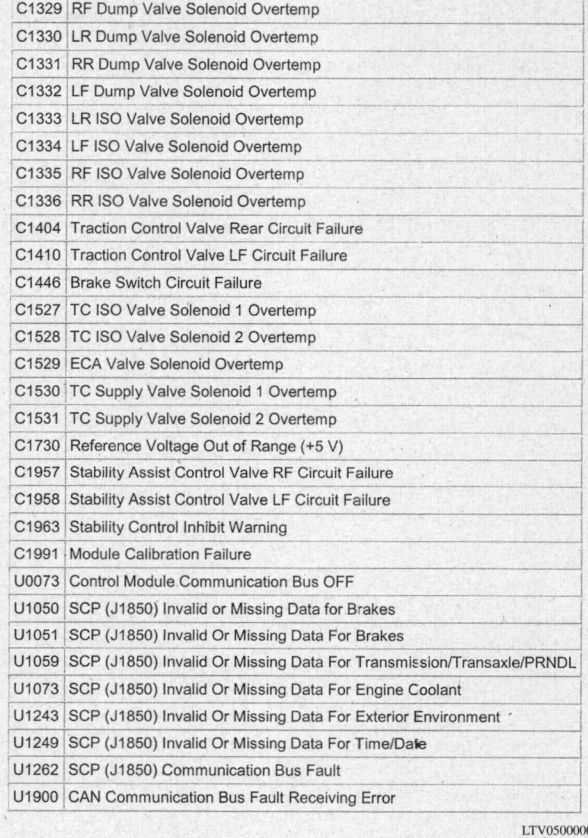

C1329	RF Dump Valve Solenoid Overtemp
C1330	LR Dump Valve Solenoid Overtemp
C1331	RR Dump Valve Solenoid Overtemp
C1332	LF Dump Valve Solenoid Overtemp
C1333	LR ISO Valve Solenoid Overtemp
C1334	LF ISO Valve Solenoid Overtemp
C1335	RF ISO Valve Solenoid Overtemp
C1336	RR ISO Valve Solenoid Overtemp
C1404	Traction Control Valve Rear Circuit Failure
C1410	Traction Control Valve LF Circuit Failure
C1446	Brake Switch Circuit Failure
C1527	TC ISO Valve Solenoid 1 Overtemp
C1528	TC ISO Valve Solenoid 2 Overtemp
C1529	ECA Valve Solenoid Overtemp
C1530	TC Supply Valve Solenoid 1 Overtemp
C1531	TC Supply Valve Solenoid 2 Overtemp
C1730	Reference Voltage Out of Range (+5 V)
C1957	Stability Assist Control Valve RF Circuit Failure
C1958	Stability Assist Control Valve LF Circuit Failure
C1963	Stability Control Inhibit Warning
C1991	Module Calibration Failure
U0073	Control Module Communication Bus OFF
U1050	SCP (J1850) Invalid or Missing Data for Brakes
U1051	SCP (J1850) Invalid Or Missing Data For Brakes
U1059	SCP (J1850) Invalid Or Missing Data For Transmission/Transaxle/PRNDL
U1073	SCP (J1850) Invalid Or Missing Data For Engine Coolant
U1243	SCP (J1850) Invalid Or Missing Data For Exterior Environment
U1249	SCP (J1850) Invalid Or Missing Data For Time/Date
U1262	SCP (J1850) Communication Bus Fault
U1900	CAN Communication Bus Fault Receiving Error

LTV0500000004885

Fig. 2 Diagnostic trouble code interpretation
(Part 2 of 2)

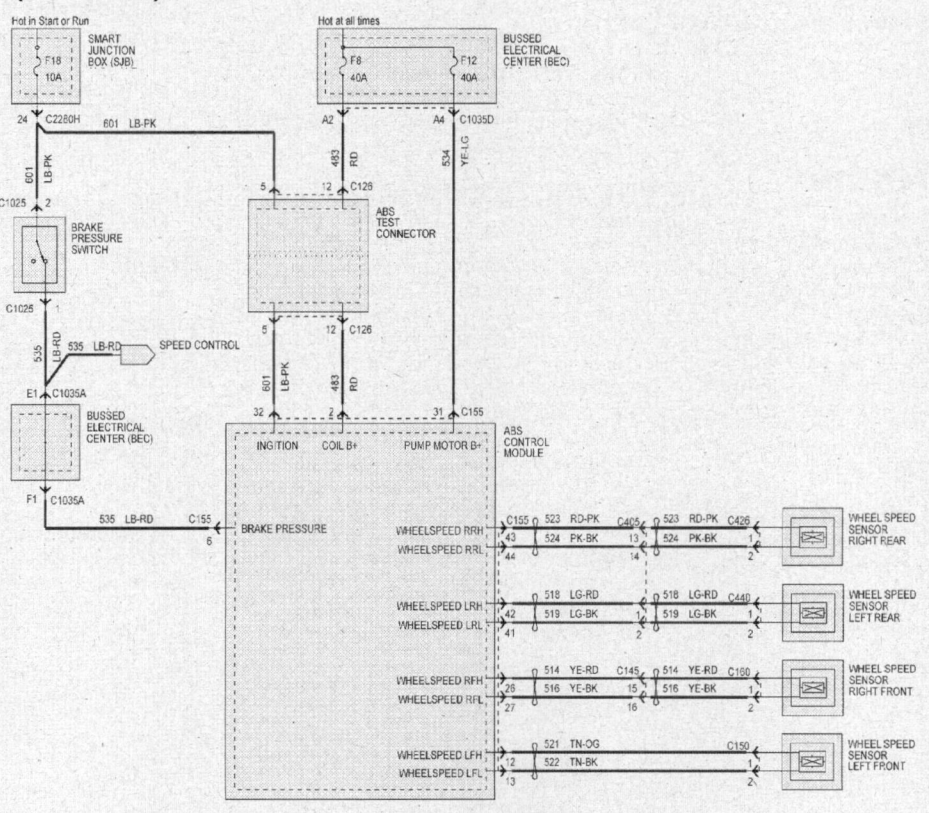

LTV0500000004886

Fig. 3 Wiring diagram (Part 1 of 3)

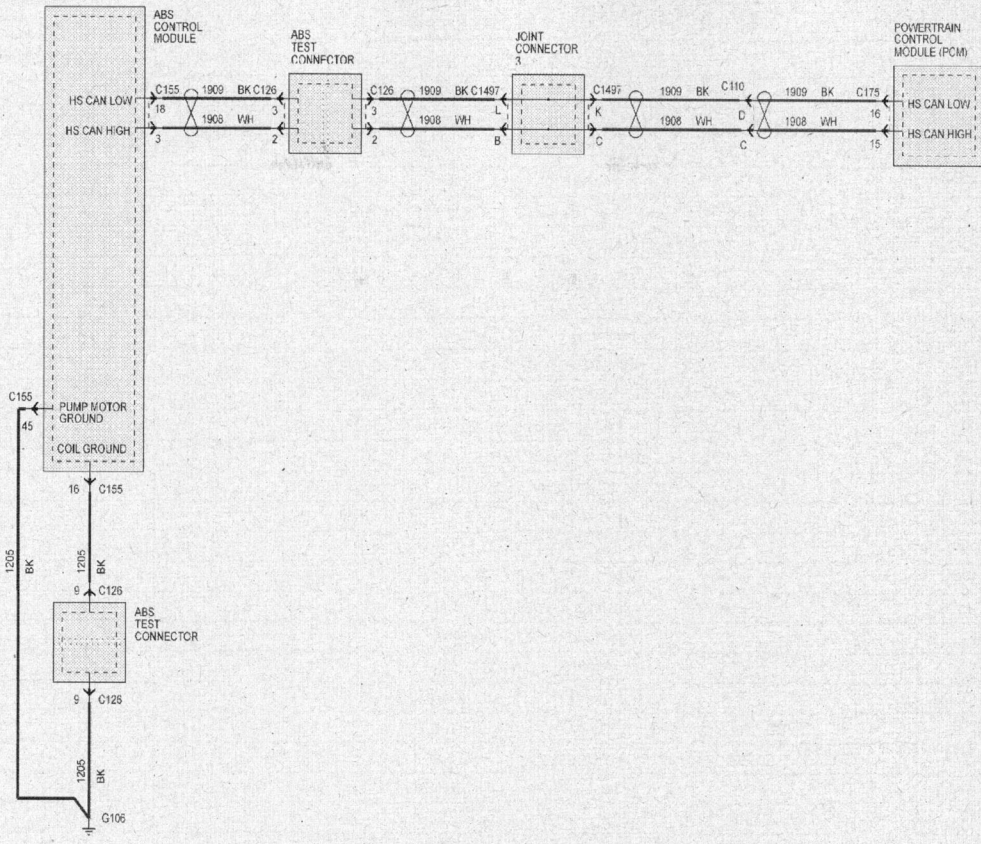

Fig. 3   Wiring diagram (Part 2 of 3)

LTV0500000004887

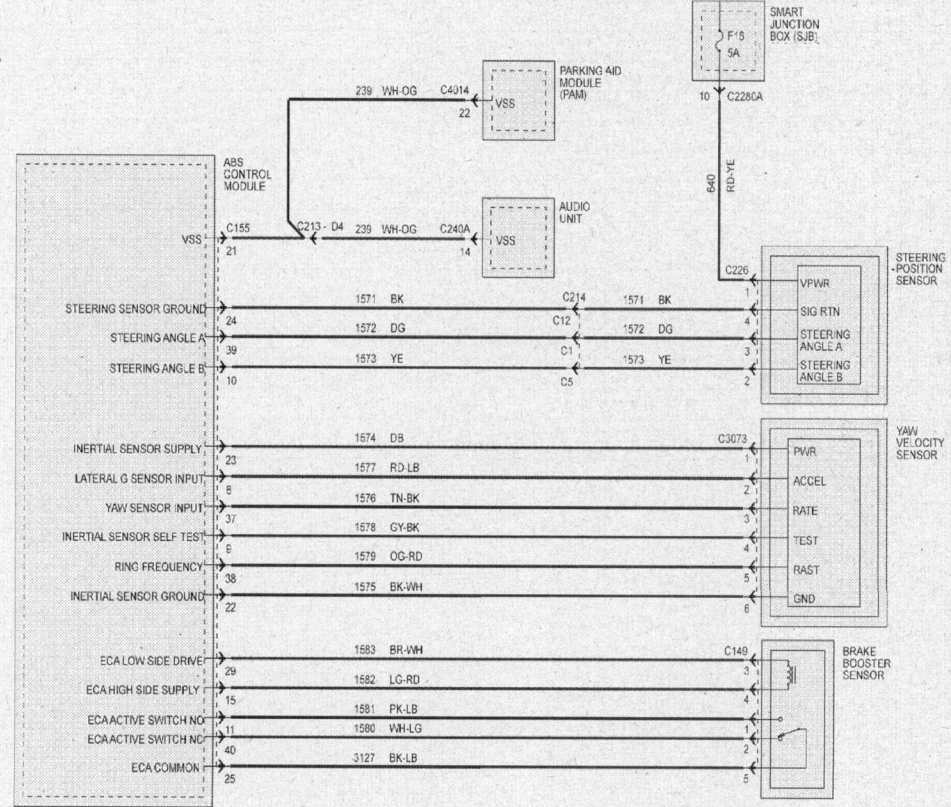

Fig. 3   Wiring diagram (Part 3 of 3)

LTV0500000004888

ANTI-LOCK BRAKES

DIAGNOSTIC CHART INDEX

Test	Code	Description	Page No.	Fig. No.
A	—	No Communication w/Anti-Lock Brake System (ABS) Module	5-135	4
B	C1288	Pressure Transducer Main/Primary Input Circuit Failure	5-135	5
C	—	Traction Control System Cannot Be Disabled	5-135	6
D	C1095	ABS Hydraulic Pump Motor Circuit Failure/Open	5-136	7
	C1096	ABS Hydraulic Pump Motor Circuit Failure/Open	5-136	7
E	C1145	Wheel Speed Sensor Input Circuit Failure	5-136	8
	C1155	Wheel Speed Sensor Input Circuit Failure	5-136	8
	C1165	Wheel Speed Sensor Input Circuit Failure	5-136	8
	C1175	Wheel Speed Sensor Input Circuit Failure	5-136	8
F	C1222	Wheel Speed Sensor Input Signal Missing/Mismatch	5-137	9
	C1233	Wheel Speed Sensor Input Signal Missing/Mismatch	5-137	9
	C1234	Wheel Speed Sensor Input Signal Missing/Mismatch	5-137	9
	C1235	Wheel Speed Sensor Input Signal Missing/Mismatch	5-137	9
	C1236	Wheel Speed Sensor Input Signal Missing/Mismatch	5-137	9
G	C1277	Steering Wheel Angle 1 & 2 Circuit Fault	5-138	10
	C1278	Steering Wheel Angle 1 & 2 Circuit Fault	5-138	10
H	C1279	Sensor Cluster Faults	5-139	11
	C1280	Sensor Cluster Faults	5-139	11
	C1281	Sensor Cluster Faults	5-139	11
	C1282	Sensor Cluster Faults	5-139	11
I	C1285	Booster Solenoid Circuit Failure	5-139	12
	C1286	Booster Mechanical Failure	5-139	12
J	C1287	Brake Booster Pedal Force Switch Circuit Failure	5-140	13
K	—	Traction Control Is Inoperative	5-141	14
L	B1317	Battery Voltage High/Low	5-142	15
	B1318	Battery Voltage High/Low	5-142	15
M	C1991	Module Calibration Failure	5-142	16
N	C1329	Valve Solenoid Overtemp	5-142	17
	C1330	Valve Solenoid Overtemp	5-142	17
	C1331	Valve Solenoid Overtemp	5-142	17
	C1332	Valve Solenoid Overtemp	5-142	17
	C1333	Valve Solenoid Overtemp	5-142	17
	C1334	Valve Solenoid Overtemp	5-142	17
	C1335	Valve Solenoid Overtemp	5-142	17
	C1336	Valve Solenoid Overtemp	5-142	17
	C1527	Valve Solenoid Overtemp	5-142	17
	C1528	Valve Solenoid Overtemp	5-142	17
	C1529	Valve Solenoid Overtemp	5-142	17
	C1530	Valve Solenoid Overtemp	5-142	17
	C1531	Valve Solenoid Overtemp	5-142	17
O	—	Spongy/Soft Brake Pedal w/No Warning Indicator	5-143	18
P	C1446	Brake Pedal Switch Circuit Failure	5-143	19
Q	C1730	Reference Voltage Out Of Range	5-143	20

Test Step	Result / Action to Take
A1 CHECK CIRCUITS 601 (LB/PK) AND 483 (RD) FOR AN OPEN	
• Key in OFF position. • Disconnect: ABS Module C155. • Key in ON position. • Measure the voltage between ABS module C155-32, circuit 601 (LB/PK), harness side and ground; and between ABS module C155-2, circuit 483 (RD), harness side and ground. • **Are the voltages greater than 10 volts?**	**Yes** GO to A2. **No** VERIFY smart junction box (SJB) fuse 18 (10A) and bussed electrical center (BEC) fuse 8 (40A) are OK. If OK, REPAIR the affected circuit(s) for an open. REPEAT the self-test.
A2 CHECK CIRCUIT 1205 (BK) FOR AN OPEN	
• Key in OFF position. • Measure the resistance between ABS module C155-16, circuit 1205 (BK), harness side and ground; and between ABS module C155-45, circuit 1205 (BK), harness side and ground. • **Is the resistance less than 5 ohms?**	**Yes** CHECK the module communications network. **No** REPAIR the affected circuit(s) for an open. REPEAT the self-test.

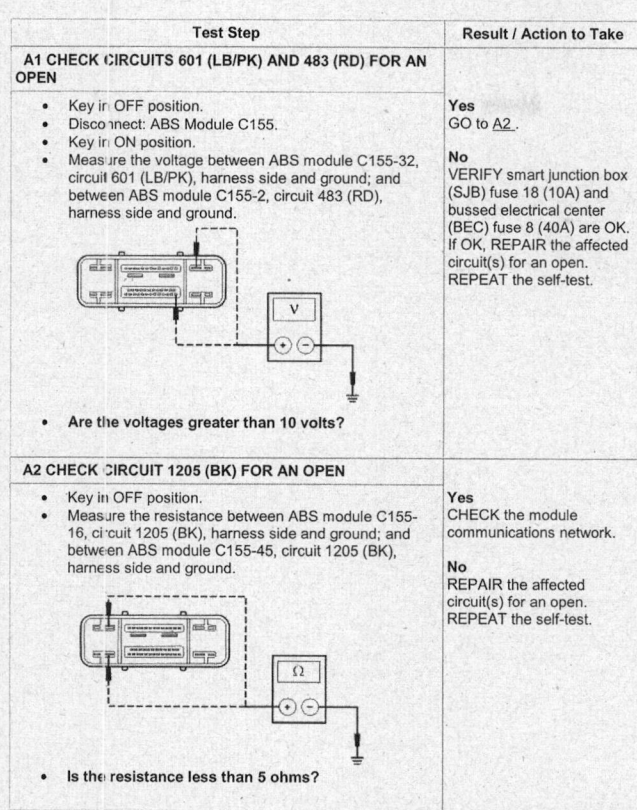

LTV0500000004889

Fig. 4   Test A: No Communication w/Anti-Lock Brake System (ABS) Module

	REPEAT the self-test.
B3 MONITOR THE ABS MODULE BRAKE PRESSURE TRANSDUCER PID	
• Key in OFF position. • Connect: ABS Module C155. • Enter the following diagnostic mode on the diagnostic tool: ABS Module Brake Pressure Transducer PID. • With the key ON and the engine running (KOER), monitor the PID. With no brake pedal application, the PID should toggle back and forth, with light pedal application the PID should display approximately 200 and then increase as pedal pressure increases. • Lightly apply the brake pedal then increase pedal pressure while monitoring the PID. • **Does the PID toggle back and forth with no pedal application and then display approximately 200 with a light application and increase as pedal pressure increases?**	**Yes** GO to B4. **No** INSTALL a new HCU. CLEAR all DTCs. REPEAT the self-test.
B4 CHECK FOR VOLTAGE TO THE ANTI-LOCK BRAKE SYSTEM (ABS) MODULE	
• Key in OFF position. • Disconnect: ABS Module C155. • Key in ON position. • Measure the voltage between ABS module C155-6, circuit 535 (LB/RD), harness side and ground while pressing and releasing the brake pedal. With the brake pedal released, there should be greater than 10 volts and with the pedal pressed, there should be 0 volts. • **Is the voltage greater than 10 volts with the pedal released and 0 volt with the pedal pressed?**	**Yes** INSTALL a new brake pressure switch. **No** VERIFY smart junction box (SJB) fuse 18 (10A) is OK. If OK, REPAIR circuit 535 (LB/RD) for an open. CLEAR the DTCs. TEST DRIVE the vehicle. REPEAT the self-test.

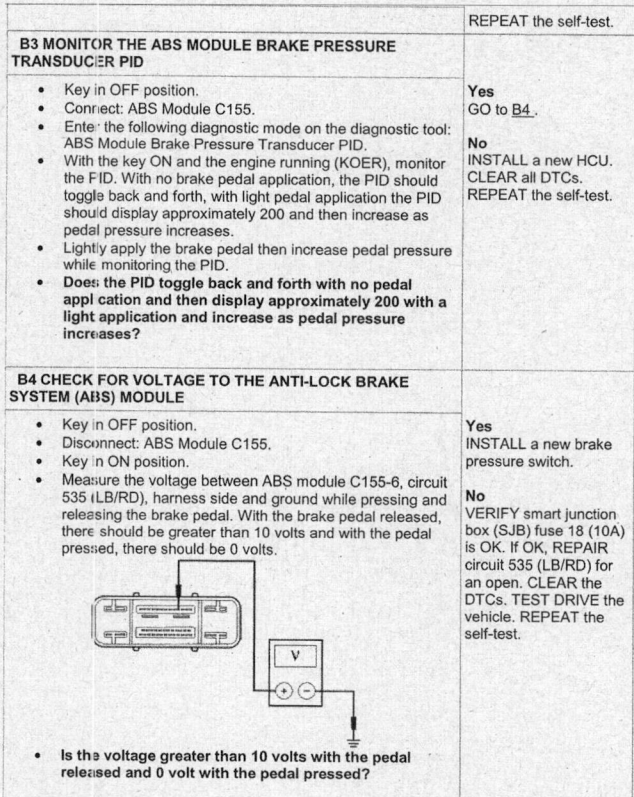

LTV0500000004891

Fig. 5   Test B, Code C1288: Pressure Transducer Main/Primary Input Circuit Failure (Part 2 of 2)

Test Step	Result / Action to Take
B1 CHECK THE SPEED CONTROL	
• Operate the speed control. • **Does the speed control operate correctly?**	**Yes** GO to B2. **No** For further diagnosis of the speed control,
B2 CHECK FOR CORRECT ABS MODULE PART NUMBER	
• Locate the part number of the currently installed ABS module and compare that number to what is currently available. • **Does the vehicle have the latest ABS module installed?**	**Yes** GO to B3. **No** INSTALL a new ABS module. When installing the ABS module check for moisture on the circuit board and/or in the aluminum cavity of the hydraulic control unit (HCU). If moisture is present, INSTALL a new ABS module and a new HCU. CALIBRATE the ABS module.

LTV0500000004890

Fig. 5   Test B, Code C1288: Pressure Transducer Main/Primary Input Circuit Failure (Part 1 of 2)

Test Step	Result / Action to Take
C1 CHECK FOR ANTI-LOCK BRAKE SYSTEM (ABS) DIAGNOSTIC TROUBLE CODES (DTCs)	
• Retrieve the recorded DTCs from the continuous and on demand self-test. • **Are any DTCs retrieved?**	**Yes** GO to Diagnostic Trouble Code (DTC) Index. **No** GO to C2.
C2 CHECK CIRCUIT 1412 (WH/PK) AND 1205 (BK) FOR AN OPEN	
• Key in OFF position. • Disconnect: Traction Control Switch C2114. • Disconnect: Instrument Cluster C220a. • Measure the resistance between traction control switch C2114-10, circuit 1412 (WH/PK), harness side and instrument cluster C220a-5, circuit 1412 (WH/PK), harness side; and between traction control switch C2114-5, circuit 1205 (BK), harness side and ground. • **Is the resistance less than 5 ohms?**	**Yes** GO to C3. **No** REPAIR the affected circuit(s) for an open. TEST the system for normal operation.
C3 CHECK THE TRACTION CONTROL SWITCH	
• Make sure the traction control switch is pressed (traction control disabled). • Measure the resistance between traction control switch C2114-5, component side and C2114-10, component side.	**Yes** GO to C4. **No** INSTALL a new traction control switch. TEST the system for normal operation.

LTV0500000004892

Fig. 6   Test C: Traction Control System Cannot Be Disabled (Part 1 of 2)

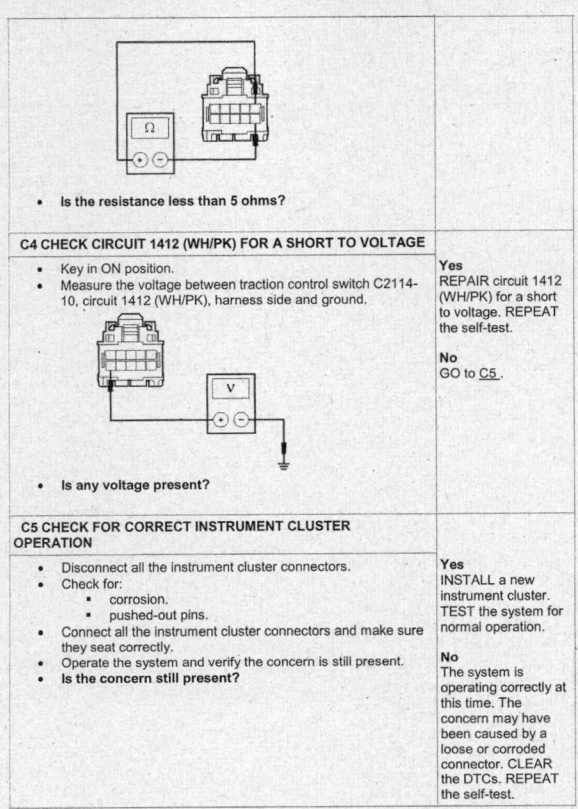

- Is the resistance less than 5 ohms?

C4 CHECK CIRCUIT 1412 (WH/PK) FOR A SHORT TO VOLTAGE	
• Key in ON position. • Measure the voltage between traction control switch C2114-10, circuit 1412 (WH/PK), harness side and ground. • Is any voltage present?	**Yes** REPAIR circuit 1412 (WH/PK) for a short to voltage. REPEAT the self-test. **No** GO to C5 .
C5 CHECK FOR CORRECT INSTRUMENT CLUSTER OPERATION	

• Disconnect all the instrument cluster connectors.
• Check for:
   • corrosion.
   • pushed-out pins.
• Connect all the instrument cluster connectors and make sure they seat correctly.
• Operate the system and verify the concern is still present.
• Is the concern still present?
	Yes
	INSTALL a new instrument cluster. TEST the system for normal operation.
	
	No
	The system is operating correctly at this time. The concern may have been caused by a loose or corroded connector. CLEAR the DTCs. REPEAT the self-test.

LTV0500000004893

Fig. 6   Test C: Traction Control System Cannot Be Disabled (Part 2 of 2)

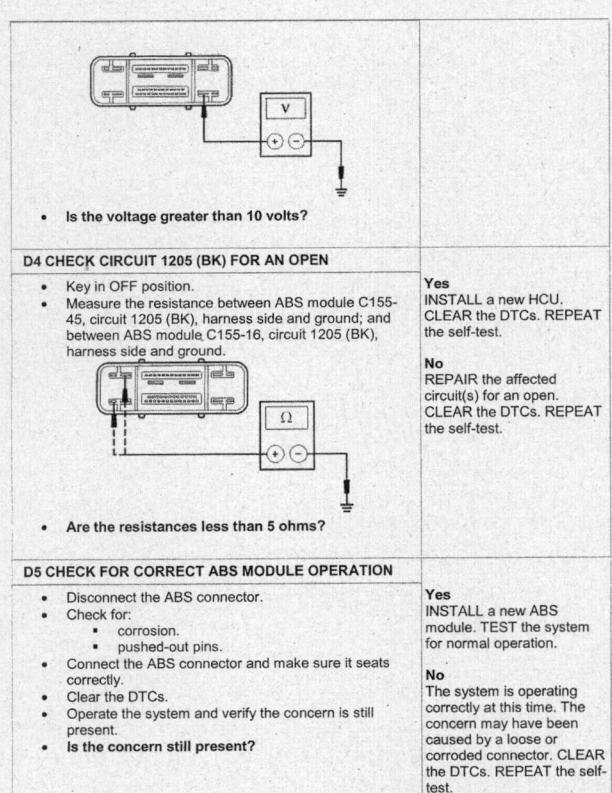

- Is the voltage greater than 10 volts?

D4 CHECK CIRCUIT 1205 (BK) FOR AN OPEN	
• Key in OFF position. • Measure the resistance between ABS module C155-45, circuit 1205 (BK), harness side and ground; and between ABS module C155-16, circuit 1205 (BK), harness side and ground. • Are the resistances less than 5 ohms?	**Yes** INSTALL a new HCU. CLEAR the DTCs. REPEAT the self-test. **No** REPAIR the affected circuit(s) for an open. CLEAR the DTCs. REPEAT the self-test.
D5 CHECK FOR CORRECT ABS MODULE OPERATION	

• Disconnect the ABS connector.
• Check for:
   • corrosion.
   • pushed-out pins.
• Connect the ABS connector and make sure it seats correctly.
• Clear the DTCs.
• Operate the system and verify the concern is still present.
• Is the concern still present?
	Yes
	INSTALL a new ABS module. TEST the system for normal operation.
	
	No
	The system is operating correctly at this time. The concern may have been caused by a loose or corroded connector. CLEAR the DTCs. REPEAT the self-test.

LTV0500000004895

Fig. 7   Test D, Codes C1095 & C1096: ABS Hydraulic Pump Motor Circuit Failure/Open (Part 2 of 2)

Test Step	Result / Action to Take
D1 CHECK THE ANTI-LOCK BRAKE SYSTEM (ABS) PUMP MOTOR	
• Key in ON position. • Is the ABS pump motor running all the time?	**Yes** INSTALL a new ABS module and hydraulic control unit (HCU) as necessary. CLEAR the DTCs. REPEAT the ABS self-test. **No** GO to D2 .
D2 CHECK PUMP MOTOR OPERATION	
• Key in OFF position. • Connect the diagnostic tool. • Key in ON position. • Enter the following diagnostic mode on the diagnostic tool: ABS Module Active Command. • Trigger the ABS module pump motor ON active command. • Does the ABS pump motor run for approximately 2 seconds?	**Yes** CLEAR the DTCs. CHECK the yellow ABS warning indicator while driving the vehicle (brakes must not be applied) above 32 km/h (20 mph). If the yellow ABS warning indicator illuminates, RETRIEVE the DTCs. If DTC C1096 is retrieved, GO to D5 . If DTC C1095 is retrieved, INSTALL a new HCU. CLEAR the DTCs. REPEAT the self-test. **No** TRIGGER the ABS module pump motor OFF active command. GO to D3 .
D3 CHECK CIRCUIT 534 (YE/LG) FOR AN OPEN	
• Disconnect: ABS Module C155. • Measure the voltage between ABS module C155-31, circuit 534 (YE/LG), harness side and ground.	**Yes** GO to D4 . **No** REPAIR circuit 534 (YE/LG) for an open. CLEAR the DTCs. REPEAT the self-test.

LTV0500000004894

Fig. 7   Test D, Codes C1095 & C1096: ABS Hydraulic Pump Motor Circuit Failure/Open (Part 1 of 2)

Test Step	Result / Action to Take
E1 CHECK THE WHEEL SPEED CIRCUITS FOR A SHORT TO VOLTAGE	
NOTE: Both circuits must be checked for each DTC. • Key in OFF position. • Disconnect: Anti-Lock Brake System (ABS) Module C155. • Disconnect: Suspect Wheel Speed Sensor. • Key in ON position. • Measure the voltage between the ABS module connector, harness side and ground as follows:	**Yes** REPAIR the affected circuit(s) for a short to voltage. CLEAR the DTC(s). REPEAT the self-test. **No** GO to E2 .

DTC	ABS Module Connector-Pin	Circuit
C1145	C155-26	514 (YE/RD)
C1145	C155-27	516 (YE/BK)
C1155	C155-13	522 (TN/BK)
C1155	C155-12	521 (TN/OG)
C1165	C155-44	524 (PK/BK)
C1165	C155-43	523 (RD/PK)
C1175	C155-42	518 (LG/RD)
C1175	C155-41	519 (LG/BK)

- Is any voltage present?

E2 CHECK THE WHEEL SPEED CIRCUITS FOR A SHORT TO GROUND	
NOTE: Both circuits must be checked for each DTC. • Key in OFF position. • Measure the resistance between the ABS module connector, harness side and ground as follows:	**Yes** GO to E3 . **No** REPAIR the affected circuit(s) for a short to ground. CLEAR the DTCs. REPEAT the self-test.

DTC	ABS Module Connector-Pin	Circuit
C1145	C155-26	514 (YE/RD)
C1145	C155-27	516 (YE/BK)
C1155	C155-13	522 (TN/BK)
C1155	C155-12	521 (TN/OG)
C1165	C155-44	524 (PK/BK)
C1165	C155-43	523 (RD/PK)
C1175	C155-42	518 (LG/RD)
C1175	C155-41	519 (LG/BK)

LTV0500000004896

Fig. 8   Test E, Codes C1145, C1155, C1165 & C1175: Wheel Speed Sensor Input Circuit Failure (Part 1 of 3)

- Are the resistances greater than 10,000 ohms?

E3 CHECK THE WHEEL SPEED CIRCUITS FOR AN OPEN

NOTE: Both circuits must be checked for each DTC.

- Measure the resistance between the ABS module connector, harness side and the suspect wheel speed sensor connector, harness side as follows:

DTC	Circuit	ABS Module Connector-Pin	Wheel Speed Sensor Connector-Pin
C1145	516 (YE/BK)	C155-27	RH front wheel speed sensor C160-1
C1145	514 (YE/RD)	C155-26	RH front wheel speed sensor C160-2
C1155	522 (TN/BK)	C155-13	LH front wheel speed sensor C150-1
C1155	521 (TN/OG)	C155-12	LH front wheel speed sensor C150-2
C1165 (ABS with stability assist)	523 (RD/PK)	C155-43	RH rear wheel speed sensor C426-2
C1165 (ABS with stability assist)	524 (PK/BK)	C155-44	RH rear wheel speed sensor C426-1
C1175 (ABS with stability assist)	518 (LG/RD)	C155-42	LH rear wheel speed sensor C440-2
C1175 (ABS with stability assist)	519 (LG/BK)	C155-41	LH rear wheel speed sensor C440-1

- Are the resistances less than 5 ohms?

Yes
GO to E4.

No
REPAIR the affected circuit(s) for an open. CLEAR the DTCs. REPEAT the self-test.

E4 CHECK FOR SHORTED WHEEL SPEED SENSOR CIRCUITS

- Measure the resistance between the suspect wheel speed sensor pins, harness side with the meter in the 10 megaohm range.

Yes
REPAIR the affected circuit(s) for a short. CLEAR the DTCs. REPEAT the ABS self-test.

No
GO to E5.

LTV0500000004897

Fig. 8   Test E, Codes C1145, C1155, C1165 & C1175: Wheel Speed Sensor Input Circuit Failure (Part 2 of 3)

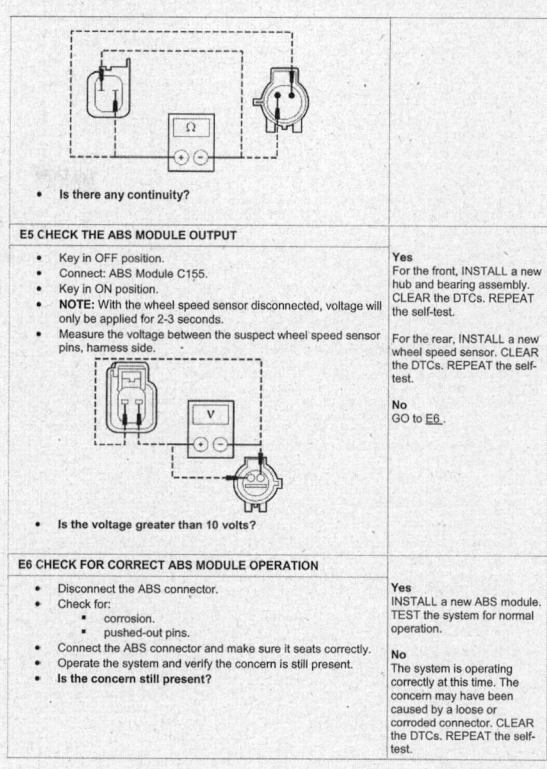

- Is there any continuity?

E5 CHECK THE ABS MODULE OUTPUT

- Key in OFF position.
- Connect: ABS Module C155.
- Key in ON position.
- **NOTE:** With the wheel speed sensor disconnected, voltage will only be applied for 2-3 seconds.
- Measure the voltage between the suspect wheel speed sensor pins, harness side.

- Is the voltage greater than 10 volts?

Yes
For the front, INSTALL a new hub and bearing assembly. CLEAR the DTCs. REPEAT the self-test.

For the rear, INSTALL a new wheel speed sensor. CLEAR the DTCs. REPEAT the self-test.

No
GO to E6.

E6 CHECK FOR CORRECT ABS MODULE OPERATION

- Disconnect the ABS connector.
- Check for:
  - corrosion.
  - pushed-out pins.
- Connect the ABS connector and make sure it seats correctly.
- Operate the system and verify the concern is still present.
- **Is the concern still present?**

Yes
INSTALL a new ABS module. TEST the system for normal operation.

No
The system is operating correctly at this time. The concern may have been caused by a loose or corroded connector. CLEAR the DTCs. REPEAT the self-test.

LTV0500000004898

Fig. 8   Test E, Codes C1145, C1155, C1165 & C1175: Wheel Speed Sensor Input Circuit Failure (Part 3 of 3)

Test Step	Result / Action to Take
F1 CHECK THE DTCs FROM THE SELF-TEST	
- Retrieve the recorded results from the anti-lock brake system (ABS) module continuous and on-demand self-tests. - **Are DTCs C1145, C1155, C1165 or C1175 present?**	**Yes** Go To Pinpoint Test E. **No** If DTC C1222 is present, GO to F3. All others, GO to F2.
F2 CHECK THE WHEEL SPEED SENSOR OUTPUT	

NOTE: The ignition must be in the OFF position until the connections are made or a DTC sets and the ABS light illuminates, cutting voltage to the wheel speed sensors. If this happens, turn the key to the OFF position, and make sure that no jumper connections are shorted to ground or shorted together. Turn the key ON and wait for the ABS light to prove-out.

- Disconnect: Suspect Wheel Speed Sensor.
- If DTC C1233 is retrieved, connect a fused (5A) jumper wire between the LH front wheel speed sensor C150-2, circuit 521 (TN/OG), harness side and the LH front wheel speed sensor, pin 1 component side. Connect the automotive meter between the C150-1, circuit 522 (TN/BK), harness side and the LH front wheel speed sensor pin 2, component side.

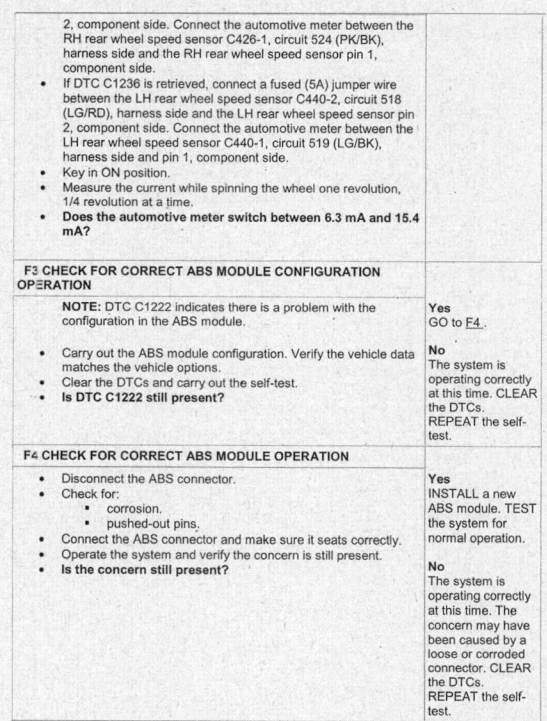

- If DTC C1234 is retrieved, connect a fused (5A) jumper wire between the RH front wheel speed sensor C160-2, circuit 514 (YE/RD), harness side and the RH front wheel speed sensor pin 1, component side. Connect the automotive meter between the RH front wheel speed sensor C160-1, circuit 516 (YE/BK), harness side and the RH front wheel speed sensor pin 2, component side.
- If DTC C1235 is retrieved, connect a fused (5A) jumper wire between the RH rear wheel speed sensor C426-2, circuit 523 (RD/PK), harness side and the RH rear wheel speed sensor pin

Yes
GO to F4.

No
For the front, INSTALL a new hub and bearing assembly. CLEAR the DTCs. REPEAT the self-test.

For the rear, INSTALL a new wheel speed sensor. CLEAR the DTCs. REPEAT the self-test.

LTV0500000004899

Fig. 9   Test F, Codes C1222, C1233, C1234, C1235 & C1236: Wheel Speed Sensor Input Signal Missing/ Mismatch (Part 1 of 2)

2, component side. Connect the automotive meter between the RH rear wheel speed sensor C426-1, circuit 524 (PK/BK), harness side and the RH rear wheel speed sensor pin 1, component side.

- If DTC C1236 is retrieved, connect a fused (5A) jumper wire between the LH rear wheel speed sensor C440-2, circuit 518 (LG/RD), harness side and the LH rear wheel speed sensor pin 2, component side. Connect the automotive meter between the LH rear wheel speed sensor C440-1, circuit 519 (LG/BK), harness side and pin 1, component side.
- Key in ON position.
- Measure the current while spinning the wheel one revolution, 1/4 revolution at a time.
- **Does the automotive meter switch between 6.3 mA and 15.4 mA?**

F3 CHECK FOR CORRECT ABS MODULE CONFIGURATION OPERATION

NOTE: DTC C1222 indicates there is a problem with the configuration in the ABS module.

- Carry out the ABS module configuration. Verify the vehicle data matches the vehicle options.
- Clear the DTCs and carry out the self-test.
- **Is DTC C1222 still present?**

Yes
GO to F4.

No
The system is operating correctly at this time. CLEAR the DTCs. REPEAT the self-test.

F4 CHECK FOR CORRECT ABS MODULE OPERATION

- Disconnect the ABS connector.
- Check for:
  - corrosion.
  - pushed-out pins.
- Connect the ABS connector and make sure it seats correctly.
- Operate the system and verify the concern is still present.
- **Is the concern still present?**

Yes
INSTALL a new ABS module. TEST the system for normal operation.

No
The system is operating correctly at this time. The concern may have been caused by a loose or corroded connector. CLEAR the DTCs. REPEAT the self-test.

LTV0500000004900

Fig. 9   Test F, Codes C1222, C1233, C1234, C1235 & C1236: Wheel Speed Sensor Input Signal Missing/ Mismatch (Part 2 of 2)

Test Step	Result / Action to Take
G1 CARRY OUT THE RECALIBRATION PROCEDURE	
• Key in ON position. • Enter the following diagnostic mode on the diagnostic tool: Clear the DTCs. • Carry out the steering wheel rotation sensor recalibration procedure following the diagnostic tool directions. • Test drive the vehicle. • Enter the following diagnostic mode on the diagnostic tool: Retrieve DTCs. • **Are any DTCs retrieved or does the recalibration procedure indicate a fault?**	**Yes** If DTC C1277 or C1278 is retrieved or the recalibration procedure indicates a fault, GO to G2. If any other DTCs are retrieved, GO to the Anti-Lock Brake System (ABS) Module Diagnostic Trouble Code (DTC) Index. If sent here from Pinpoint Test M, GO to G2. **No** The ABS system is operating correctly.
G2 MONITOR THE STEERING WHEEL ROTATION SENSOR PIDs	
• Enter the following diagnostic mode on the diagnostic tool: ABS Module PIDs. • Monitor the ABS module steering wheel rotation sensor PIDs while rotating the steering wheel clockwise and counterclockwise very slowly. • **Do the PIDs move in intervals of 4.5 degrees?**	**Yes** CLEAR the DTCs. DRIVE the vehicle. RETRIEVE the DTCs. If DTC C1277 or C1278 is still present, GO to G12. **No** GO to G3.
G3 CHECK CIRCUIT 640 (RD/YE) FOR VOLTAGE	
• Key in OFF position. • Disconnect: Steering Wheel Rotation Sensor C226. • Key in ON position. • Measure the voltage between steering wheel rotation sensor C226-1, circuit 640 (RD/YE), harness side and ground. 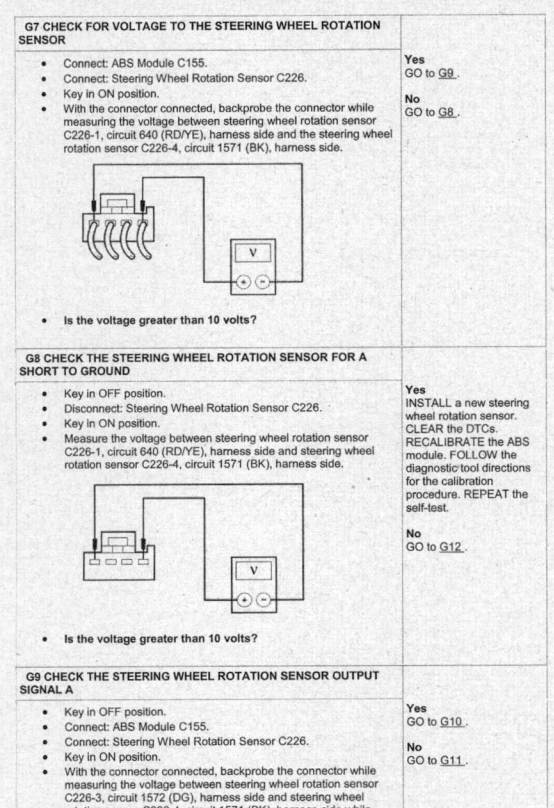 • **Is the voltage greater than 10 volts?**	**Yes** GO to G4. **No** VERIFY SJB fuse 16 (5A) is OK. If OK, REPAIR circuit 640 (RD/YE) for an open. CLEAR the DTCs. RECALIBRATE the ABS module. FOLLOW the diagnostic tool directions for the calibration procedure. REPEAT the self-test.
G4 CHECK THE STEERING WHEEL ROTATION SENSOR CIRCUITRY FOR AN OPEN	

LTV0500000004901

Fig. 10 Test G, Codes C1277 & C1278: Steering Wheel Angle 1 & 2 Circuit Fault (Part 1 of 5)

• Key in OFF position. • Disconnect: ABS Module C155. • Measure the resistance between ABS module connector, harness side and steering wheel rotation sensor connector, harness side as follows:	**Yes** GO to G5. **No** REPAIR the affected circuit(s) for an open. CLEAR the DTCs. RECALIBRATE the ABS module. FOLLOW the diagnostic tool directions for the calibration procedure. REPEAT the self-test.

Steering Wheel Rotation Sensor Connector-Pin	ABS Module Connector-Pin	Circuit
C226-2	C155-10	1573 (YE)
C226-3	C155-39	1572 (DG)
C226-4	C155-24	1571 (BK)

• **Are the resistances less than 5 ohms?**	
G5 CHECK THE STEERING WHEEL ROTATION SENSOR CIRCUITS FOR A SHORT TO VOLTAGE	
• Key in ON position. • Measure the voltage between the ABS module connector, harness side and ground as follows:	**Yes** REPAIR the affected circuit(s) for a short to voltage. CLEAR the DTCs. RECALIBRATE the ABS module. FOLLOW the diagnostic tool directions for the calibration procedure. REPEAT the self-test. **No** GO to G6.

ABS Module Connector-Pin	Circuit
C155-10	1573 (YE)
C155-39	1572 (DG)
C155-24	1571 (BK)

• **Is any voltage present?**	
G6 CHECK THE STEERING WHEEL ROTATION SENSOR CIRCUITRY FOR A SHORT TO GROUND	
• Key in OFF position. • Measure the resistance between the ABS module connector, harness side and ground as follows:	**Yes** GO to G7. **No** REPAIR the affected circuit for a short to ground. CLEAR the DTCs. RECALIBRATE the ABS module. FOLLOW the diagnostic tool directions for the calibration procedure. REPEAT the self-test.

ABS Module Connector-Pin	Circuit
C155-10	1573 (YE)
C155-39	1572 (DG)
C155-24	1571 (BK)

• **Are the resistances greater than 10,000 ohms?**	

LTV0500000004902

Fig. 10 Test G, Codes C1277 & C1278: Steering Wheel Angle 1 & 2 Circuit Fault (Part 2 of 5)

G7 CHECK FOR VOLTAGE TO THE STEERING WHEEL ROTATION SENSOR	
• Connect: ABS Module C155. • Connect: Steering Wheel Rotation Sensor C226. • Key in ON position. • With the connector connected, backprobe the connector while measuring the voltage between steering wheel rotation sensor C226-1, circuit 640 (RD/YE), harness side and the steering wheel rotation sensor C226-4, circuit 1571 (BK), harness side. 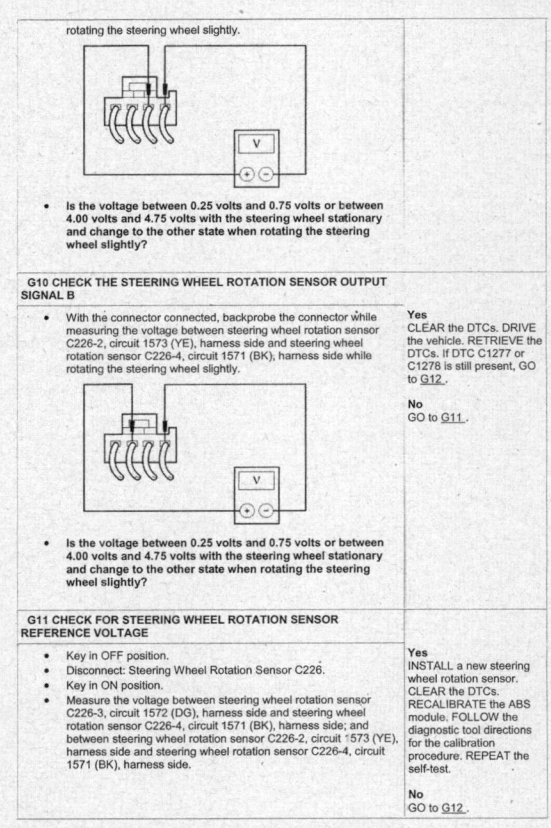 • **Is the voltage greater than 10 volts?**	**Yes** GO to G9. **No** GO to G8.
G8 CHECK THE STEERING WHEEL ROTATION SENSOR FOR A SHORT TO GROUND	
• Key in OFF position. • Disconnect: Steering Wheel Rotation Sensor C226. • Key in ON position. • Measure the voltage between steering wheel rotation sensor C226-1, circuit 640 (RD/YE), harness side and steering wheel rotation sensor C226-4, circuit 1571 (BK), harness side. • **Is the voltage greater than 10 volts?**	**Yes** INSTALL a new steering wheel rotation sensor. CLEAR the DTCs. RECALIBRATE the ABS module. FOLLOW the diagnostic tool directions for the calibration procedure. REPEAT the self-test. **No** GO to G12.
G9 CHECK THE STEERING WHEEL ROTATION SENSOR OUTPUT SIGNAL A	
• Key in OFF position. • Connect: ABS Module C155. • Connect: Steering Wheel Rotation Sensor C226. • Key in ON position. • With the connector connected, backprobe the connector while measuring the voltage between steering wheel rotation sensor C226-3, circuit 1572 (DG), harness side and steering wheel rotation sensor C226-4, circuit 1571 (BK), harness side while	**Yes** GO to G10. **No** GO to G11.

LTV0500000004903

Fig. 10 Test G, Codes C1277 & C1278: Steering Wheel Angle 1 & 2 Circuit Fault (Part 3 of 5)

---

rotating the steering wheel slightly.	
• **Is the voltage between 0.25 volts and 0.75 volts or between 4.00 volts and 4.75 volts with the steering wheel stationary and change to the other state when rotating the steering wheel slightly?**	
G10 CHECK THE STEERING WHEEL ROTATION SENSOR OUTPUT SIGNAL B	
• With the connector connected, backprobe the connector while measuring the voltage between steering wheel rotation sensor C226-2, circuit 1573 (YE), harness side and steering wheel rotation sensor C226-4, circuit 1571 (BK), harness side while rotating the steering wheel slightly. • **Is the voltage between 0.25 volts and 0.75 volts or between 4.00 volts and 4.75 volts with the steering wheel stationary and change to the other state when rotating the steering wheel slightly?**	**Yes** CLEAR the DTCs. DRIVE the vehicle. RETRIEVE the DTCs. If DTC C1277 or C1278 is still present, GO to G12. **No** GO to G11.
G11 CHECK FOR STEERING WHEEL ROTATION SENSOR REFERENCE VOLTAGE	
• Key in OFF position. • Disconnect: Steering Wheel Rotation Sensor C226. • Key in ON position. • Measure the voltage between steering wheel rotation sensor C226-3, circuit 1572 (DG), harness side and steering wheel rotation sensor C226-4, circuit 1571 (BK), harness side; and between steering wheel rotation sensor C226-2, circuit 1573 (YE), harness side and steering wheel rotation sensor C226-4, circuit 1571 (BK), harness side.	**Yes** INSTALL a new steering wheel rotation sensor. CLEAR the DTCs. RECALIBRATE the ABS module. FOLLOW the diagnostic tool directions for the calibration procedure. REPEAT the self-test. **No** GO to G12.

LTV0500000004904

Fig. 10 Test G, Codes C1277 & C1278: Steering Wheel Angle 1 & 2 Circuit Fault (Part 4 of 5)

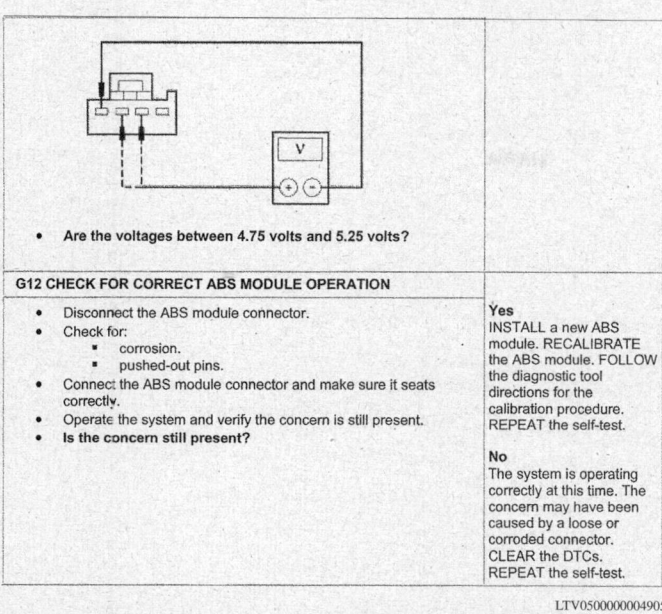

- Are the voltages between 4.75 volts and 5.25 volts?

G12 CHECK FOR CORRECT ABS MODULE OPERATION	

• Disconnect the ABS module connector.
• Check for:
   ▪ corrosion.
   ▪ pushed-out pins.
• Connect the ABS module connector and make sure it seats correctly.
• Operate the system and verify the concern is still present.
• **Is the concern still present?**
	Yes
	INSTALL a new ABS module. RECALIBRATE the ABS module. FOLLOW the diagnostic tool directions for the calibration procedure. REPEAT the self-test.
	
	No
	The system is operating correctly at this time. The concern may have been caused by a loose or corroded connector. CLEAR the DTCs. REPEAT the self-test.

Fig. 10   Test G, Codes C1277 & C1278: Steering Wheel Angle 1 & 2 Circuit Fault (Part 5 of 5)

LTV0500000004905

H3 CHECK THE SENSOR CLUSTER CIRCUITRY FOR A SHORT TO VOLTAGE	
• Key in ON position. • Measure the voltage between the sensor cluster connector, harness side and ground as follows:	**Yes** REPAIR the affected circuit(s) for a short to voltage. CLEAR the DTCs. RECALIBRATE the ABS module. FOLLOW the diagnostic tool directions for the calibration procedure. REPEAT the self-test. **No** GO to H4 .

Sensor Cluster Connector-Pin	Circuit
C3073-1	1574 (DB)
C3073-2	1577 (RD/LB)
C3073-3	1576 (TN/BK)
C3073-4	1578 (GY/BK)
C3073-5	1579 (OG/RD)
C3073-6	1575 (BK/WH)

- Is any voltage present?

H4 CHECK THE SENSOR CLUSTER CIRCUITRY FOR SHORTS TO EACH OTHER	
• Key in OFF position. • Measure the resistance between each of the sensor cluster pins, harness side and the rest of the pins, harness side as follows:	**Yes** GO to H5 . **No** REPAIR the affected circuit(s) for a short. CLEAR the DTCs. RECALIBRATE the ABS module. FOLLOW the diagnostic tool directions for the calibration procedure. REPEAT the self-test.

Sensor Cluster Connector-Pin	Circuit
C3073-1	1574 (DB)
C3073-2	1577 (RD/LB)
C3073-3	1576 (TN/BK)
C3073-4	1578 (GY/BK)
C3073-5	1579 (OG/RD)
C3073-6	1575 (BK/WH)

- Are the resistances greater than 10,000 ohms?

H5 CHECK THE VOLTAGE FROM THE ABS MODULE	
• Key in ON position. • Measure the voltage between sensor cluster C3073-1, circuit 1574 (DB), harness side and sensor cluster C3073-6, circuit 1575 (BK/WH), harness side.	**Yes** INSTALL a new sensor cluster. CARRY OUT the calibration procedure. TEST the system for normal operation. **No**

Fig. 11   Test H, Codes C1279, C1280, C1281 & C1282: Sensor Cluster Faults (Part 2 of 2)

LTV0500000004907

Test Step	Result / Action to Take
H1 CARRY OUT THE RECALIBRATION PROCEDURE	
• Connect the diagnostic tool. • Key in ON position. • Clear the DTCs. • Carry out the anti-lock brake system (ABS) module sensor cluster recalibration procedure using the diagnostic tool. • Retrieve the DTCs. • **Are any DTCs retrieved or does the recalibration procedure indicate a fault?**	**Yes** GO to H2 . **No** The ABS system is operating correctly. The condition may have been caused by an incomplete or inaccurate calibration.
H2 CHECK THE SENSOR CLUSTER CIRCUITRY FOR OPENS AND SHORTS TO GROUND	
• Disconnect: ABS Module C155. • Disconnect: Sensor Cluster C3073. • Measure the resistance between ABS module connector, harness side and sensor cluster connector, harness side; and between ABS module connector, harness side and ground as follows:	**Yes** GO to H3 . **No** REPAIR the affected circuit(s) for an open or a short to ground. CLEAR the DTCs. RECALIBRATE the ABS module. FOLLOW the diagnostic tool directions for the calibration procedure. REPEAT the self-test.

ABS Module Connector-Pin	Sensor Cluster Connector-Pin	Circuit
C155-23	C3073-1	1574 (DB)
C155-8	C3073-2	1577 (RD/LB)
C155-37	C3073-3	1576 (TN/BK)
C155-9	C3073-4	1578 (GY/BK)
C155-38	C3073-5	1579 (OG/RD)
C155-22	C3073-6	1575 (BK/WH)

- Are the resistances less than 5 ohms between the ABS module and the sensor cluster, and greater than 10,000 ohms between the ABS module and ground?

LTV0500000004906

Fig. 11   Test H, Codes C1279, C1280, C1281 & C1282: Sensor Cluster Faults (Part 1 of 2)

Test Step	Result / Action to Take
I1 CARRY OUT THE RECALIBRATION PROCEDURE	
• Key in ON position. • Enter the following diagnostic mode on the diagnostic tool: Clear the Diagnostic Trouble Codes (DTCs). • Carry out the ABS active brake booster recalibration procedure using the diagnostic tool. • Test drive the vehicle. • Enter the following diagnostic mode on the diagnostic tool: Retrieve the DTCs. • **Are any ABS DTCs retrieved or does the recalibration procedure indicate a fault?**	**Yes** If DTC C1285 is retrieved, or the brake booster portion of the recalibration procedure indicates a failure, GO to I2 . If DTC C1286 is retrieved, or the brake booster portion of the recalibration procedure indicates a failure, GO to I6 . If any other DTC is retrieved, GO to the Anti-Lock Brake System (ABS) Module Diagnostic Trouble Code (DTC) Index. **No** The ABS system is operating correctly.
I2 CHECK THE BRAKE BOOSTER SOLENOID	
• Key in OFF position. • Disconnect: Active Brake Booster C149. • Measure the resistance between active brake booster C149-3, circuit 1583 (BN/WH), component side and active brake booster C149-4, circuit 1582 (LG/RD), component side.	**Yes** GO to I3 . **No** INSTALL a new active brake booster. CLEAR the DTCs. RECALIBRATE the ABS module. FOLLOW the diagnostic tool directions for the calibration procedure. REPEAT the self-test.

LTV0500000004908

Fig. 12   Test I, Code C1285: Booster Solenoid Circuit Failure, Code C1286: Booster Mechanical Failure (Part 1 of 4)

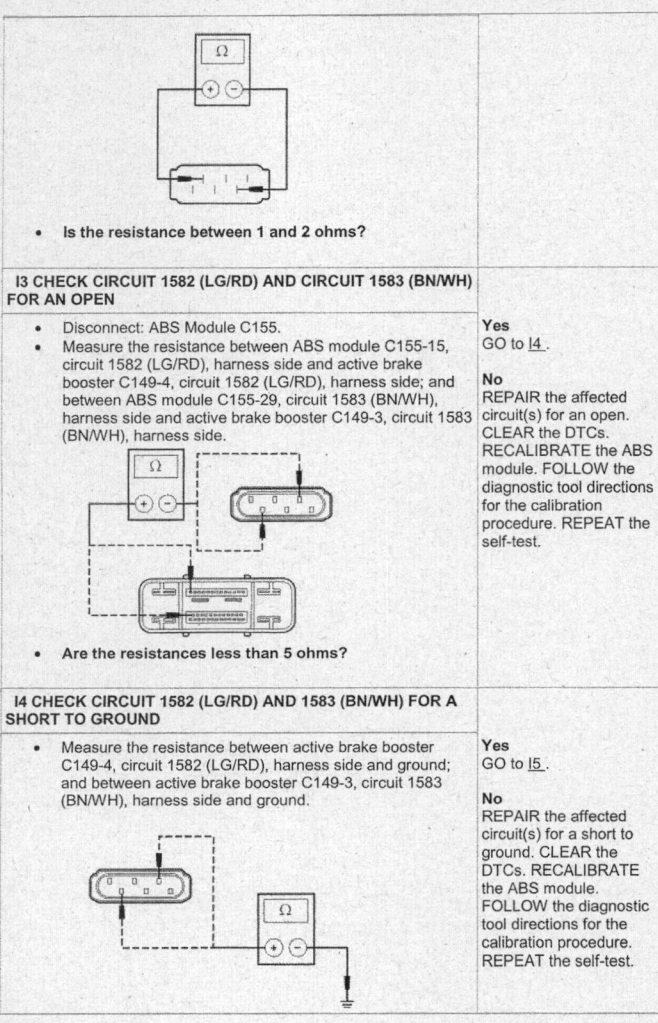

- **Is the resistance between 1 and 2 ohms?**

I3 CHECK CIRCUIT 1582 (LG/RD) AND CIRCUIT 1583 (BN/WH) FOR AN OPEN

- Disconnect: ABS Module C155.
- Measure the resistance between ABS module C155-15, circuit 1582 (LG/RD), harness side and active brake booster C149-4, circuit 1582 (LG/RD), harness side; and between ABS module C155-29, circuit 1583 (BN/WH), harness side and active brake booster C149-3, circuit 1583 (BN/WH), harness side.

Yes
GO to I4 .

No
REPAIR the affected circuit(s) for an open. CLEAR the DTCs. RECALIBRATE the ABS module. FOLLOW the diagnostic tool directions for the calibration procedure. REPEAT the self-test.

- **Are the resistances less than 5 ohms?**

I4 CHECK CIRCUIT 1582 (LG/RD) AND 1583 (BN/WH) FOR A SHORT TO GROUND

- Measure the resistance between active brake booster C149-4, circuit 1582 (LG/RD), harness side and ground; and between active brake booster C149-3, circuit 1583 (BN/WH), harness side and ground.

Yes
GO to I5 .

No
REPAIR the affected circuit(s) for a short to ground. CLEAR the DTCs. RECALIBRATE the ABS module. FOLLOW the diagnostic tool directions for the calibration procedure. REPEAT the self-test.

LTV0500000004909

Fig. 12 Test I, Code C1285: Booster Solenoid Circuit Failure, Code C1286: Booster Mechanical Failure (Part 2 of 4)

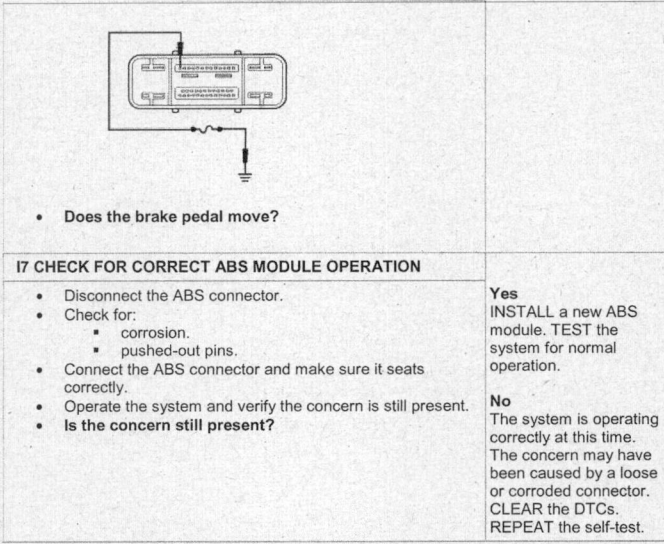

- **Does the brake pedal move?**

I7 CHECK FOR CORRECT ABS MODULE OPERATION

- Disconnect the ABS connector.
- Check for:
  - corrosion.
  - pushed-out pins.
- Connect the ABS connector and make sure it seats correctly.
- Operate the system and verify the concern is still present.
- **Is the concern still present?**

Yes
INSTALL a new ABS module. TEST the system for normal operation.

No
The system is operating correctly at this time. The concern may have been caused by a loose or corroded connector. CLEAR the DTCs. REPEAT the self-test.

LTV0500000004911

Fig. 12 Test I, Code C1285: Booster Solenoid Circuit Failure, Code C1286: Booster Mechanical Failure (Part 4 of 4)

- **Are the resistances greater than 10,000 ohms?**

I5 CHECK CIRCUIT 1583 (BN/WH) FOR A SHORT TO VOLTAGE

- Key in ON position.
- Measure the voltage between active brake booster C149-3, circuit 1583 (BN/WH), harness side and ground.

Yes
REPAIR circuit 1583 (BN/WH) for an open. CLEAR the DTCs. RECALIBRATE the ABS module. FOLLOW the diagnostic tool directions for the calibration procedure. REPEAT the self-test.

No
GO to I6 .

- **Is any voltage present?**

I6 CHECK THE ACTIVE BRAKE BOOSTER SOLENOID FOR CORRECT OPERATION

- Connect: Active Brake Booster C149.
- Connect: ABS Module C155.
- Start the engine and wait a few minutes to create vacuum in the brake booster and then place the ignition switch in the OFF position.
- Disconnect: ABS Module C155.
- Connect a fused (10A) jumper wire between ABS module C155-29, circuit 1583 (BN/WH), harness side and ground.

Yes
GO to I7 .

No
INSTALL a new active brake booster. CLEAR the DTCs. RECALIBRATE the ABS module. REPEAT the self-test.

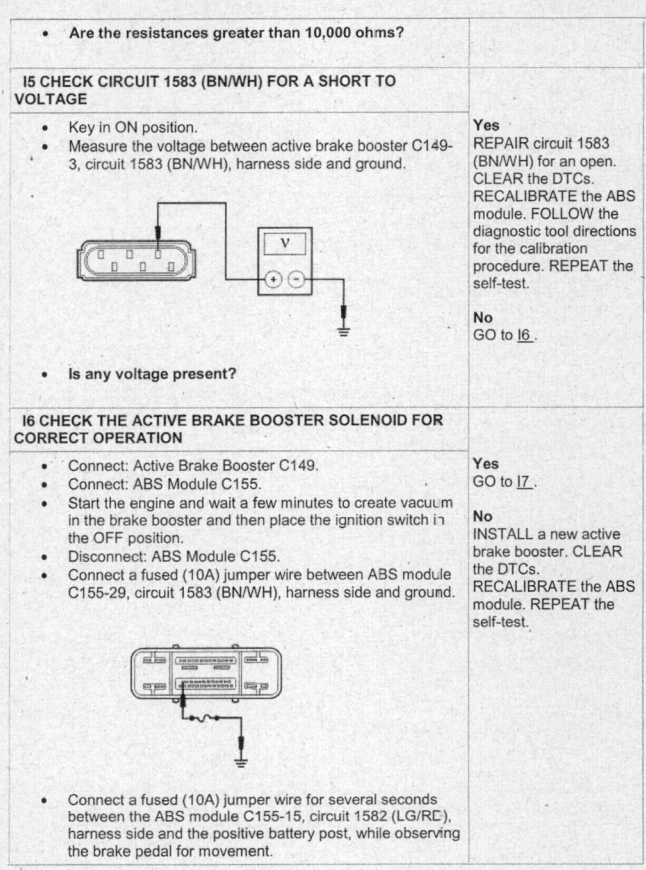

- Connect a fused (10A) jumper wire for several seconds between the ABS module C155-15, circuit 1582 (LG/RD), harness side and the positive battery post, while observing the brake pedal for movement.

LTV0500000004910

Fig. 12 Test I, Code C1285: Booster Solenoid Circuit Failure, Code C1286: Booster Mechanical Failure (Part 3 of 4)

Test Step	Result / Action to Take
J1 CARRY OUT THE RECALIBRATION PROCEDURE • Key in ON position. • Enter the following diagnostic mode on the diagnostic tool: Clear the Diagnostic Trouble Codes (DTCs). • Carry out the active brake booster recalibration procedure using the diagnostic tool. • Enter the following diagnostic mode on the diagnostic tool: Retrieve the DTCs. • **Are any DTCs retrieved or does the recalibration procedure indicate a fault?**	**Yes** If DTC C1287 is retrieved or the recalibration procedure indicates a fault, GO to J2 . If any other DTC is retrieved, GO to the Anti-Lock Brake System (ABS) Module Diagnostic Trouble Code (DTC) Index. **No** The system is operating correctly.
J2 CHECK THE NORMALLY CLOSED RELEASE SWITCH • Key in OFF position. • Disconnect: Active Brake Booster C149. • Measure the resistance between active brake booster C149-2, circuit 1580 (WH/LG), component side and active brake booster C149-5, circuit 3127 (BK/LB), component side, while pressing and releasing the brake pedal. • **Is the resistance less than 5 ohms with the brake pedal released, and greater than 10,000 ohms with the brake pedal applied?**	**Yes** GO to J3 . **No** INSTALL a new active brake booster. CLEAR the DTCs. RECALIBRATE the ABS module. FOLLOW the diagnostic tool directions for the calibration procedure. REPEAT the self-test.
J3 CHECK THE NORMALLY OPEN RELEASE SWITCH • Measure the resistance between active brake booster C149-1, circuit 1581 (PK/LB), component side and active brake booster	**Yes** GO to J4 .

LTV0500000004912

Fig. 13 Test J, Code C1287: Brake Booster Pedal Force Switch Circuit Failure (Part 1 of 3)

C149-5, circuit 3127 (BK/LB), component side while applying and releasing the brake pedal.

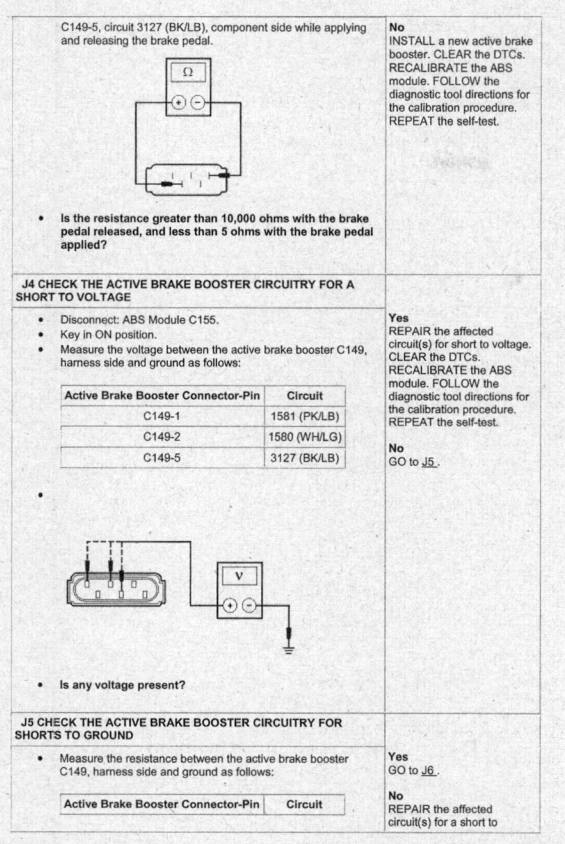

No
INSTALL a new active brake booster. CLEAR the DTCs. RECALIBRATE the ABS module. FOLLOW the diagnostic tool directions for the calibration procedure. REPEAT the self-test.

- Is the resistance greater than 10,000 ohms with the brake pedal released, and less than 5 ohms with the brake pedal applied?

J4 CHECK THE ACTIVE BRAKE BOOSTER CIRCUITRY FOR A SHORT TO VOLTAGE

- Disconnect: ABS Module C155.
- Key in ON position.
- Measure the voltage between the active brake booster C149, harness side and ground as follows:

Active Brake Booster Connector-Pin	Circuit
C149-1	1581 (PK/LB)
C149-2	1580 (WH/LG)
C149-5	3127 (BK/LB)

Yes
REPAIR the affected circuit(s) for short to voltage. CLEAR the DTCs. RECALIBRATE the ABS module. FOLLOW the diagnostic tool directions for the calibration procedure. REPEAT the self-test.

No
GO to J5.

- Is any voltage present?

J5 CHECK THE ACTIVE BRAKE BOOSTER CIRCUITRY FOR SHORTS TO GROUND

- Measure the resistance between the active brake booster C149, harness side and ground as follows:

Active Brake Booster Connector-Pin	Circuit

Yes
GO to J6.

No
REPAIR the affected circuit(s) for a short to

LTV0500000004913

Fig. 13 Test J, Code C1287: Brake Booster Pedal Force Switch Circuit Failure (Part 2 of 3)

C149-1	1581 (PK/LB)
C149-2	1580 (WH/LG)
C149-5	3127 (BK/LB)

ground. CLEAR the DTCs. REPEAT the self-test.

- Are the resistances greater than 10,000 ohms?

J6 CHECK THE BRAKE BOOSTER CIRCUITRY FOR OPENS

- Key in OFF position.
- Measure the resistance between the ABS module connector, harness side and the active brake booster connector, harness side as follows:

ABS Module Connector-Pin	Active Brake Booster Connector-Pin	Circuit
C155-11	C149-1	1581 (PK/LB)
C155-25	C149-5	3127 (BK/LB)
C155-40	C149-2	1580 (WH/LG)

Yes
GO to J7.

No
REPAIR the affected circuit(s) for an open. CLEAR the DTCs. RECALIBRATE the ABS module. FOLLOW the diagnostic tool directions for the calibration procedure. REPEAT the self-test.

- Are the resistances less than 5 ohms?

J7 CHECK FOR CORRECT ABS MODULE OPERATION

- Disconnect the ABS connector.
- Check for:
  - corrosion.
  - pushed-out pins.
- Connect the ABS connector and make sure it seats correctly.
- Operate the system and verify the concern is still present.
- Is the concern still present?

Yes
INSTALL a new ABS module. TEST the system for normal operation.

No
The system is operating correctly at this time. The concern may have been caused by a loose or corroded connector. CLEAR the DTCs. REPEAT the self-test.

LTV0500000004914

Fig. 13 Test J, Code C1287: Brake Booster Pedal Force Switch Circuit Failure (Part 3 of 3)

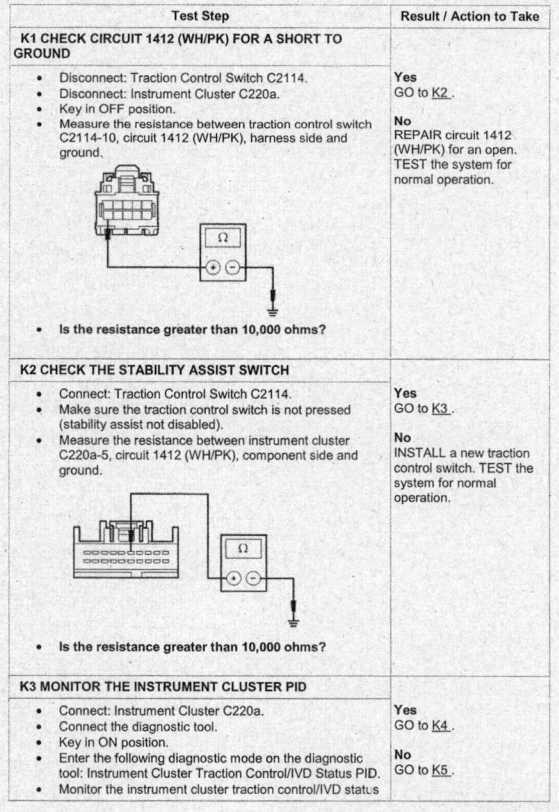

Test Step	Result / Action to Take
K1 CHECK CIRCUIT 1412 (WH/PK) FOR A SHORT TO GROUND • Disconnect: Traction Control Switch C2114. • Disconnect: Instrument Cluster C220a. • Key in OFF position. • Measure the resistance between traction control switch C2114-10, circuit 1412 (WH/PK), harness side and ground. • Is the resistance greater than 10,000 ohms?	**Yes** GO to K2. **No** REPAIR circuit 1412 (WH/PK) for an open. TEST the system for normal operation.
K2 CHECK THE STABILITY ASSIST SWITCH • Connect: Traction Control Switch C2114. • Make sure the traction control switch is not pressed (stability assist not disabled). • Measure the resistance between instrument cluster C220a-5, circuit 1412 (WH/PK), component side and ground. • Is the resistance greater than 10,000 ohms?	**Yes** GO to K3. **No** INSTALL a new traction control switch. TEST the system for normal operation.
K3 MONITOR THE INSTRUMENT CLUSTER PID • Connect: Instrument Cluster C220a. • Connect the diagnostic tool. • Key in ON position. • Enter the following diagnostic mode on the diagnostic tool: Instrument Cluster Traction Control/IVD Status PID. • Monitor the instrument cluster traction control/IVD status	**Yes** GO to K4. **No** GO to K5.

LTV0500000004916

Fig. 14 Test K: Traction Control Is Inoperative (Part 1 of 2)

PID while pressing the traction control/interactive vehicle dynamics (IVD) disable switch repeatedly.
- **Does the PID agree with the switch position?**

Test Step	Result / Action to Take
K4 CHECK FOR CORRECT ABS MODULE OPERATION • Disconnect the ABS connector. • Check for: ▪ corrosion. ▪ pushed-out pins. • Connect the ABS connector and make sure it seats correctly. • Operate the system and verify the concern is still present. • **Is the concern still present?**	**Yes** INSTALL a new ABS module. TEST the system for normal operation. **No** The system is operating correctly at this time. The concern may have been caused by a loose or corroded connector. CLEAR the DTCs. REPEAT the self-test.
K5 CHECK FOR CORRECT INSTRUMENT CLUSTER OPERATION • Disconnect all instrument cluster connectors. • Check for: ▪ corrosion. ▪ pushed-out pins. • Connect all instrument cluster connectors and make sure they seat correctly. • Operate the system and verify the concern is still present. • **Is the concern still present?**	**Yes** INSTALL a new instrument cluster.. TEST the system for normal operation. **No** The system is operating correctly at this time. The concern may have been caused by a loose or corroded connector. CLEAR the DTCs. REPEAT the self-test.

LTV0500000004917

Fig. 14   Test K: Traction Control Is Inoperative (Part 2 of 2)

Test Step	Result / Action to Take
M1 CHECK FOR DTCs • Connect the diagnostic tool. • Key in ON position. • Retrieve the recorded results from the smart junction box (SJB) self-test. • **Is any other DTC retrieved with C1991?**	**Yes** GO to the Anti-Lock Brake System (ABS) Diagnostic Trouble Code (DTC) Index. Some of the pinpoint tests recommend ABS module calibration prior to any further diagnostics. In this case, GO to M2. **No** GO to M2.
M2 CALIBRATE THE ABS MODULE • Key in START position. • **NOTE:** Be sure to rotate the steering wheel lock-to-lock during the calibration of the ABS system. • **NOTE:** To successfully carry out the ABS module calibration, the transmission must be in PARK, the engine must be running and there must be no brake pedal input. • Carry out the ABS module calibration per the diagnostic tool instructions. • **Does the calibration complete for all of the stability assist sensors, and does the stability assist lamp stop flashing and turn off?**	**Yes** GO to M3. **No** GO to M4. Some concerns cause the calibration not to complete. If sent here from another pinpoint test, return to that pinpoint test for further diagnostics.
M3 CLEAR DTC C1991 • **NOTE:** Clear DTC C1991 after completing the calibration. • Connect the diagnostic tool. • Key in ON position. • CLEAR the DTC. • **Does the DTC clear?**	**Yes** TEST DRIVE the vehicle. REPEAT the self-test. If sent here from another pinpoint test, return to that pinpoint test for further diagnostics. **No** GO to M4.
M4 MONITOR THE STEERING WHEEL ROTATION SENSOR PIDs • Key in ON position. • Monitor the ABS module steering wheel rotation sensor PIDs while rotating the steering wheel clockwise and counterclockwise. • **Are the 2 steering wheel rotation sensor PID values switching as the wheel rotates?**	**Yes** Go To Pinpoint Test H. **No** Go To Pinpoint Test G.

LTV0500000004919

Fig. 16   Test M, Code C1991: Module Calibration Failure

Test Step	Result / Action to Take
L1 CHECK RECENT VEHICLE HISTORY • Enter the following diagnostic mode on the diagnostic tool: Clear the Diagnostic Trouble Codes (DTCs). • Drive the vehicle. • Enter the following diagnostic mode on the diagnostic tool: Retrieve the DTCs. • **Is DTC B1317 or B1318 still present?**	**Yes** GO to L2. **No** The system is operating normally.
L2 CHECK THE CHARGING SYSTEM • Key in START position. • With the engine running at 2,000 rpm, measure the voltage between the positive and negative battery posts. • **Is the voltage between 10 and 16 volts?**	**Yes** GO to L3. **No** Continue diagnosis of the charging system.
L3 CHECK CIRCUIT 601 (LB/PK) FOR VOLTAGE • Key in OFF position. • Disconnect: Anti-Lock Brake Module C155. • Key in ON position. • Measure the voltage between ABS module C155-32, circuit 601 (LB/PK), harness side and ground. • **Is the voltage between 10 volts and 16 volts?**	**Yes** GO to L4. **No** VERIFY SJB fuse 18 (10A) is OK. If OK, REPAIR circuit 601 (LB/PK) for an open. CLEAR the DTCs. CARRY OUT the self-test with the brake pedal not applied.
L4 CHECK FOR CORRECT ABS MODULE OPERATION • Disconnect the ABS connector. • Check for: ▪ corrosion. ▪ pushed-out pins. • Connect the ABS connector and make sure it seats correctly. • Operate the system and verify the concern is still present. • **Is the concern still present?**	**Yes** INSTALL a new ABS module. TEST the system for normal operation. **No** The system is operating correctly at this time. The concern may have been caused by a loose or corroded connector. CLEAR the DTCs. CARRY OUT the self-test with the brake pedal not applied.

LTV0500000004918

Fig. 15   Test L, Codes B1317 & B1318: Battery Voltage High/Low

Test Step	Result / Action to Take
N1 RETRIEVE THE DIAGNOSTIC TROUBLE CODES (DTCs) • Connect the diagnostic tool. • Key in ON position. • Retrieve the DTCs. • **Are any other DTCs present?**	**Yes** DIAGNOSE those DTC(s) first. GO to the Anti-Lock Brake System (ABS) Diagnostic Trouble Code (DTC) Index. **No** GO to N2.
N2 CHECK THE WHEELS AND TIRES • Make sure the wheels and tires are correctly inflated and are the correct size. • **Are the wheels and tires OK?**	**Yes** INSTALL a new ABS module CLEAR the DTCs. REPEAT the self-test. **No** CORRECT as necessary. CLEAR the DTCs. REPEAT the self-test.

LTV0500000004920

Fig. 17   Test N, Codes C1329, C1330, C1331, C1332, C1333, C1334, C1335, C1336, C1527, C1528, C1529, C1530 & C1531: Valve Solenoid Overtemp

Test Step	Result / Action to Take
O1 CHECK THE BASE BRAKE COMPONENTS • Visually inspect the brake lines from the hydraulic control unit (HCU) to the wheel cylinders. • Visually inspect the calipers and the brake components. • **Are any of these components damaged or leaking?**	**Yes** REPAIR as necessary. Continue diagnosis of the base brake system. **No** GO to <u>O2</u> .
O2 CHECK FOR A LEAKING DUMP VALVE • Key in OFF position. • Remove the rubber caps from the 2 HCU low pressure accumulators and insert a clean steel implement (such as a paper clip) into each low pressure accumulator. • Key in START position. • **NOTE:** A leaking dump valve is similar to the master cylinder bypass condition. It is important the pedal be quickly and forcefully applied to rule out the master cylinder bypass as a cause. Typically a master cylinder bypass occurs only at low pedal pressure rates and low tire pressures. • Have an assistant press hard on the brake pedal while observing the steel implements. • **Do any of the steel implements move out 6.35 mm (0.25 in) (0.25 in) or more?**	**Yes** INSTALL a new HCU. **No** The system is operating correctly at this time. REMOVE the steel implements and INSTALL the rubber caps. CLEAR the DTCs. DRIVE the vehicle over rough roads. REPEAT the self-test. TEST the system for normal operation.

LTV0500000004921

Fig. 18   Test O: Spongy/Soft Brake Pedal w/No Warning Indicator

	Test Step	Result / Action to Take
		pedal pressure?	
P4 CHECK THE BRAKE FLUID LEVEL SWITCH • Disconnect: Brake Fluid Level Switch C124. • Clear the DTCs. • Test drive the vehicle. • Repeat the self-test. • **Is the DTC retrieved again?**	**Yes** For further diagnosis of the instrument cluster, REFER to "Dash Gauges & Warning Indicators" **No** INSTALL a new brake fluid level switch. CLEAR the DTCs. TEST DRIVE the vehicle. REPEAT the self-test.

P5 CHECK FOR CORRECT ABS MODULE OPERATION
• Disconnect the ABS connector.
• Check for:
  ▪ corrosion.
  ▪ pushed-out pins.
• Connect the ABS connector and make sure it seats correctly.
• Operate the system and verify the concern is still present.
• **Is the concern still present?**
	Yes
	INSTALL a new ABS module. TEST the system for normal operation.
	
	No
	The system is operating correctly at this time. The concern may have been caused by a loose or corroded connector. CLEAR the DTCs. CARRY OUT the self-test with the brake pedal not applied.

LTV0500000004923

Fig. 19   Test P, Code C1446: Brake Pedal Switch Circuit Failure (Part 2 of 2)

Test Step	Result / Action to Take
P1 MONITOR THE SMART JUNCTION BOX (SJB) PIDs • Connect the diagnostic tool. • Key in ON position. • Enter the following diagnostic mode on the diagnostic tool: SJB Stoplamp Switch PID. • Press and release the brake pedal while monitoring the SJB stoplamp switch PID. • **Do the stoplamps illuminate and does the PID agree?**	**Yes** GO to <u>P2</u> . **No** Diagnose the stoplamp circuit.
P2 MONITOR THE ABS MODULE STOPLAMP SWITCH PID • Enter the following diagnostic mode on the diagnostic tool: Anti-lock Brake System (ABS) Module Stoplamp Switch PID. • Press and release the brake pedal while monitoring the stoplamp switch PID and observing the stoplamps. • **Does the PID agree?**	**Yes** GO to <u>P3</u> . **No** GO to <u>P5</u> .
P3 MONITOR THE ABS MODULE BRAKE PRESSURE TRANSDUCER PID • Enter the following diagnostic mode on the diagnostic tool: ABS Module Brake Pressure Transducer PID. • Press and release the brake pedal while monitoring the brake pressure transducer PID. • **Does the PID value increase with increased brake pedal pressure and decrease with decreased brake**	**Yes** GO to <u>P4</u> . **No** INSTALL a new hydraulic control unit (HCU). CLEAR the DTCs. REPEAT the self-test.

LTV0500000004922

Fig. 19   Test P, Code C1446: Brake Pedal Switch Circuit Failure (Part 1 of 2)

Test Step	Result / Action to Take
Q1 CHECK THE VOLTAGE TO THE SENSOR CLUSTER • Key in OFF position. • Disconnect: Sensor Cluster C3073. • Key in ON position. • **NOTE:** Voltage must be tested within 2 seconds of key on, engine off (KOEO). Repeat this step 1 time to verify. • Measure the voltage between sensor cluster C3073-1, circuit 1574 (DB), harness side and ground. 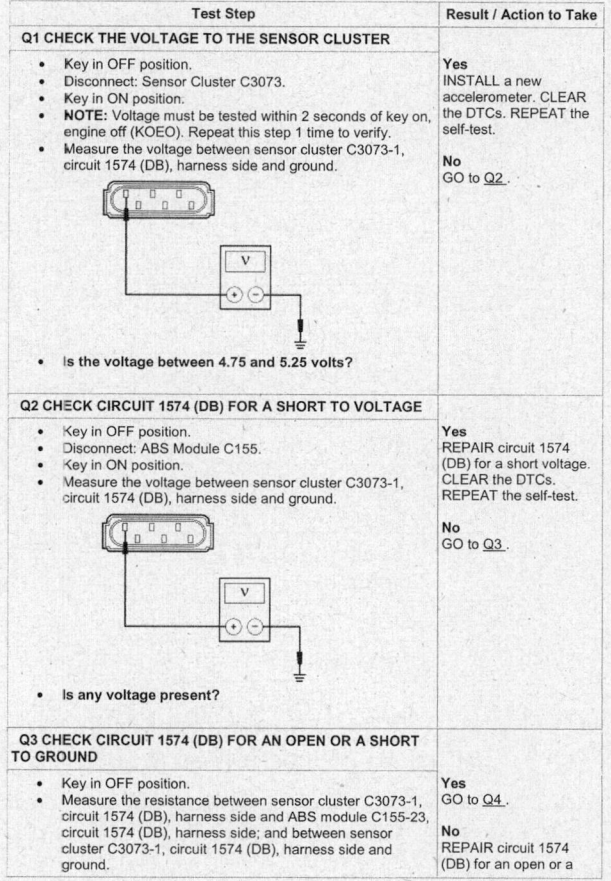 • **Is the voltage between 4.75 and 5.25 volts?**	**Yes** INSTALL a new accelerometer. CLEAR the DTCs. REPEAT the self-test. **No** GO to <u>Q2</u> .
Q2 CHECK CIRCUIT 1574 (DB) FOR A SHORT TO VOLTAGE • Key in OFF position. • Disconnect: ABS Module C155. • Key in ON position. • Measure the voltage between sensor cluster C3073-1, circuit 1574 (DB), harness side and ground. • **Is any voltage present?**	**Yes** REPAIR circuit 1574 (DB) for a short voltage. CLEAR the DTCs. REPEAT the self-test. **No** GO to <u>Q3</u> .
Q3 CHECK CIRCUIT 1574 (DB) FOR AN OPEN OR A SHORT TO GROUND • Key in OFF position. • Measure the resistance between sensor cluster C3073-1, circuit 1574 (DB), harness side and ABS module C155-23, circuit 1574 (DB), harness side; and between sensor cluster C3073-1, circuit 1574 (DB), harness side and ground.	**Yes** GO to <u>Q4</u> . **No** REPAIR circuit 1574 (DB) for an open or a

LTV0500000004924

Fig. 20   Test Q, Code C1730: Reference Voltage Out Of Range (Part 1 of 2)

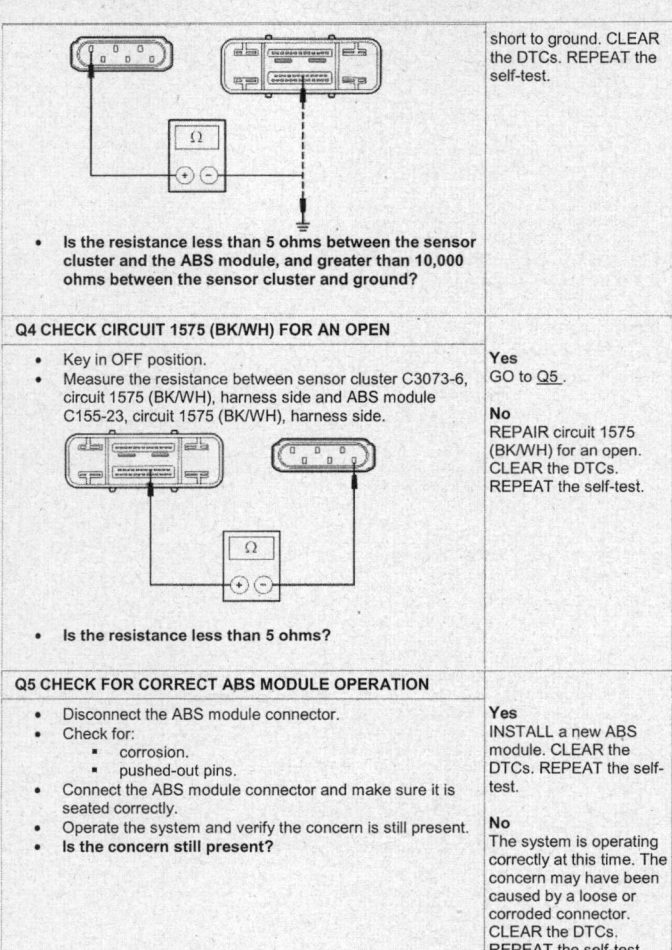

short to ground. CLEAR the DTCs. REPEAT the self-test.

- Is the resistance less than 5 ohms between the sensor cluster and the ABS module, and greater than 10,000 ohms between the sensor cluster and ground?

Q4 CHECK CIRCUIT 1575 (BK/WH) FOR AN OPEN

- Key in OFF position.
- Measure the resistance between sensor cluster C3073-6, circuit 1575 (BK/WH), harness side and ABS module C155-23, circuit 1575 (BK/WH), harness side.

Yes
GO to Q5.

No
REPAIR circuit 1575 (BK/WH) for an open. CLEAR the DTCs. REPEAT the self-test.

- Is the resistance less than 5 ohms?

Q5 CHECK FOR CORRECT ABS MODULE OPERATION

- Disconnect the ABS module connector.
- Check for:
  - corrosion.
  - pushed-out pins.
- Connect the ABS module connector and make sure it is seated correctly.
- Operate the system and verify the concern is still present.
- **Is the concern still present?**

Yes
INSTALL a new ABS module. CLEAR the DTCs. REPEAT the self-test.

No
The system is operating correctly at this time. The concern may have been caused by a loose or corroded connector. CLEAR the DTCs. REPEAT the self-test.

LTV0500000004925

Fig. 20   Test Q, Code C1730: Reference Voltage Out Of Range (Part 2 of 2)

Item	Description
1	Pin-type retainers (3 required)
2	Anti-lock brake system (ABS) splash shield
3	Brake line-to-hydraulic control unit (HCU) fittings
4	HCU electrical connector
5	HCU bracket-to-frame bolts (3 required)
6	Bracket-to-HCU bolts (2 required)
7	HCU
8	HCU bracket

LTV0500000004927

Fig. 21   Hydraulic Control Unit (HCU) replacement (Part 2 of 2)

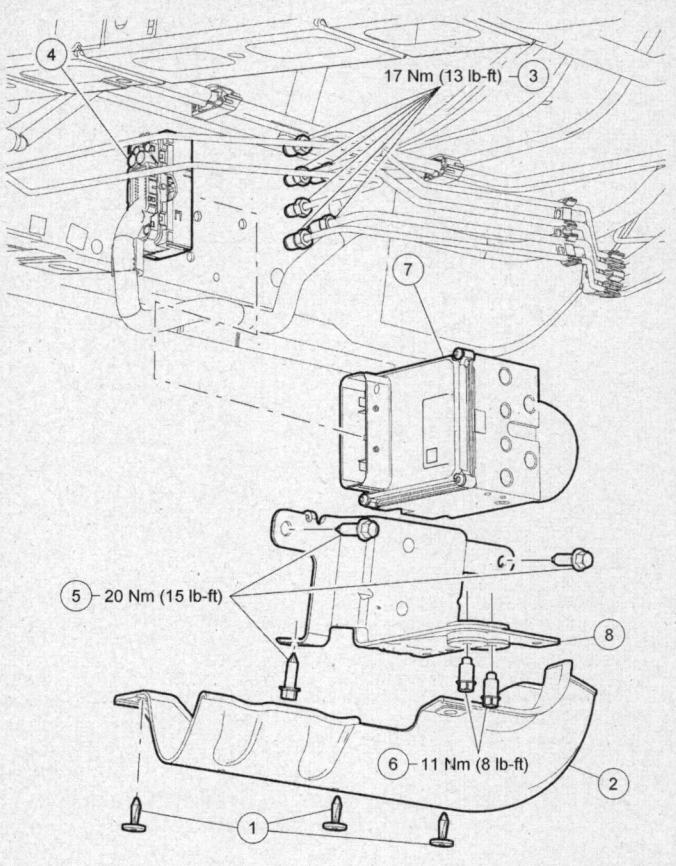

LTV0500000004926

Fig. 21   Hydraulic Control Unit (HCU) replacement (Part 1 of 2)

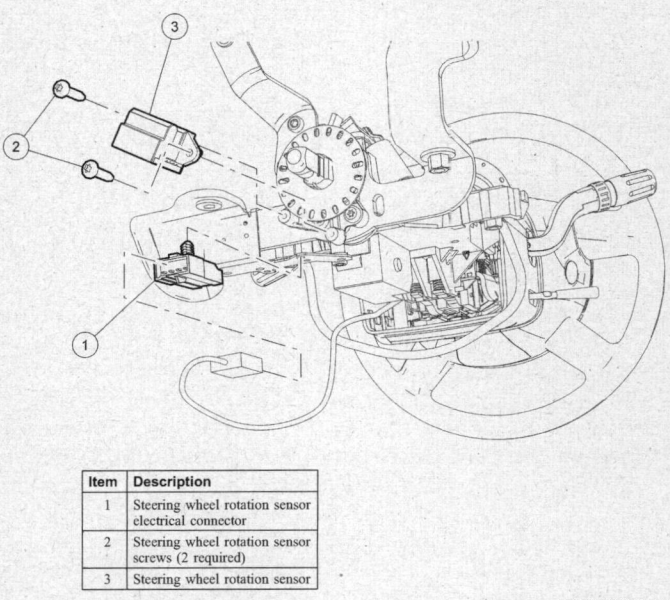

Item	Description
1	Steering wheel rotation sensor electrical connector
2	Steering wheel rotation sensor screws (2 required)
3	Steering wheel rotation sensor

LTV0500000004928

Fig. 22   Steering wheel rotation sensor replacement

F-150 & Mark LT (4WABS)

NOTE: Electrical Symbol & Wire Color Code Identification Located In The Front Of This Manual May Be Used As An Aid When Using Wiring Circuits Found In This Section.

NOTE: Refer To "Computer Relearn Procedures" Located In The Front Of This Manual When Battery Power To The Computer Has Been Interrupted.

INDEX

	Page No.
Description	5-145
Diagnosis & Testing	5-145
Accessing Diagnostic Trouble Codes	5-145
Clearing Diagnostic Trouble Codes	5-145
Diagnostic Tests	5-145
Diagnostic Trouble Code Interpretation	5-145

	Page No.
Wiring Diagrams	5-145
Diagnostic Chart Index	5-148
Precautions	5-145
Battery Ground Cable	5-145
Brake Fluid Handling	5-145
System Service	5-145
Brake System Bleed	5-145
Component Replacement	5-145

	Page No.
ABS Control Module	5-145
Hydraulic Control Unit (HCU)	5-146
Wheel Speed Sensor	5-146
Troubleshooting	5-145
Symptom Chart	5-145

PRECAUTIONS

BATTERY GROUND CABLE

Prior to service disconnect battery ground cable and isolate as required.

BRAKE FLUID HANDLING

Brake fluid can cause serious injury and vehicle damage if not handled properly. Avoid contact with eyes and do not allow fluid to splash or spill on painted surfaces. Wash hands thoroughly after handling.

DESCRIPTION

The anti-lock brake system (ABS) module, with or without stability assist, simultaneously manages the anti-lock braking, traction control and engine control systems to maintain vehicle control during deceleration and acceleration. The ABS accomplishes this by communicating with the other modules over the high speed controller area network (HS-CAN) bus.

When the ignition switch is in the RUN position, the module carries out a preliminary electrical check and, at approximately 20 km/h (12 mph), the hydraulic pump motor is turned on for approximately one half-second. Any malfunction of the anti-lock brake system disables the traction control and stability assist (if equipped). The ABS module communicates with the instrument cluster over the HS-CAN bus and the cluster illuminates the anti-lock brake warning indicator. However, the power-assist braking system functions normally.

With the ignition switch in the START or RUN positions, the stability assist module functions similarly to a conventional ABS module by monitoring and comparing the rotational speed of each wheel. The wheel speed sensors electrically sense each tooth of the anti-lock sensor ring as they pass through the sensor magnetic field. When the stability assist module detects an impending wheel lock, wheel spin or vehicle motion that is inconsistent with the driver commands, it modulates brake pressure to the appropriate brake caliper(s). The stability assist module triggers the hydraulic control unit (HCU) to open and close the appropriate solenoid valves. Once the affected wheel(s) return to the desired speed, the stability assist module returns the solenoid valves to their normal position, and normal base brake operation is restored.

TROUBLESHOOTING

Symptom Chart

Refer to **Fig. 1** for symptom charts.

DIAGNOSIS & TESTING

Accessing Diagnostic Trouble Codes

Connect a suitably programmed scan tool and Vehicle Communication Module (VCM) with appropriate adapters, or equivalents, to the Data Link Connector (DCL) located in the passenger compartment beneath the instrument panel. Follow tool manufacturer's instructions for accessing Diagnostic Trouble Codes (DTC).

Diagnostic Trouble Code Interpretation

Refer to **Fig. 2** for diagnostic trouble code interpretation.

Wiring Diagrams

Refer to **Fig. 3** for wiring diagram.

Diagnostic Tests

Refer to **Figs. 4 through 11** for pinpoint tests.

Clearing Diagnostic Trouble Codes

Connect a suitably programmed scan tool and Vehicle Communication Module (VCM) with appropriate adapters, or equivalents, to the Data Link Connector (DCL) located in the passenger compartment beneath the instrument panel. Follow tool manufacturer's instructions for clearing Diagnostic Trouble Codes (DTC).

SYSTEM SERVICE

Brake System Bleed

Refer to "Hydraulic Brake Systems" chapter for bleeding procedure.

Component Replacement

ABS CONTROL MODULE

1. Remove air cleaner assembly.
2. Disconnect ABS module electrical connector, **Fig. 12**.
3. Remove six screws, then the ABS module.
4. Reverse procedure to install. **Torque** ABS control module retaining screws in sequence, **Fig. 13**, to 27 inch lbs.

Condition	Possible Sources	Action
• No communication with the anti-lock brake system (ABS) module	• Central junction box (CJB) fuse(s): ▪ 14 (10A) ▪ 103 (20A) ▪ 112 (40A) • Circuitry • ABS module	• Go To Pinpoint Test A .
• The yellow anti-lock brake system (ABS) warning indicator is always on	• ABS module • Instrument cluster	• Go To Pinpoint Test H .
• Spongy brake pedal with no warning indicator	• Air in brake hydraulic system	• Check base brake system.
• Unintended anti-lock brake system (ABS) activation	• Wheel speed sensor ring(s)	• INSPECT the sensor ring. INSTALL a new ring if damaged.
	• Wheel speed sensor(s) • ABS module	• Go To Pinpoint Test F .

LTV0500000004931

Fig. 1   Symptom chart

Code	Description
B1342	ABS Module Failure
B1484	Brake Pedal Input Open Circuit Failure
B1676	Battery Pack Voltage Out of Range
B2477	Module Configuration Failure
B2900	VIN Mismatched
C1145	Wheel Speed Sensor RF Input Circuit Failure
C1155	Wheel Speed Sensor LF Input Circuit Failure
C1222	Wheel Speed Mismatch
C1230	Wheel Speed Sensor Rear Center Input Circuit Failure
C1237	Wheel Speed Sensor Rear Center Input Signal Missing
C1266	ABS Valve Power Relay Circuit Failure
C1296	Wheel Speed Sensor LF Input Signal Missing
C1297	Wheel Speed Sensor RF Input Signal Missing
C1300	ABS Hydraulic Pump Motor Circuit Failure
U0073	Control Module Communication Bus Off Fault
U1900	CAN Communication Bus Fault-Receive Error
U2023	Fault-Receive From External Node

Fig. 2   Diagnostic trouble code interpretation

HYDRAULIC CONTROL UNIT (HCU)

1. Remove air cleaner assembly.
2. Disconnect four hydraulic brake lines. Note position of lines for installation.
3. Disconnect ABS control module electrical connectors.
4. Remove two HCU to bracket nuts, then the HCU.
5. Reverse procedure to install, noting the following:
   a. **Torque** HCU retaining nuts to 22 ft. lbs.
   b. **Torque** brake lines to 13 ft. lbs.
   c. Bleed brake system as outlined under "Brake System Bleed.".

WHEEL SPEED SENSOR

FRONT

2WD

1. Disconnect wheel speed sensor electrical connector. Note harness connector is located in engine compartment secured to fender apron.
2. Disconnect three wheel speed sensor harness retainers.
3. Remove speed sensor mounting bolt, then the speed sensor.
4. Reverse procedure to install. **Torque** speed sensor mounting bolt to 71 inch lbs.

4WD

1. Raise and support vehicle.
2. Disconnect wheel speed sensor electrical connector. Note harness connector is located in engine compartment secured to fender apron.
3. Disconnect four wheel speed sensor harness retainers.
4. Remove brake caliper anchor plate bolts, then position brake caliper, pads and anchor plate aside.
5. Index mark brake disc and wheel hub flange, then remove disc.

6. Remove sensor retaining bolt, then the sensor.
7. Reverse procedure to install. **Torque** wheel speed sensor retaining bolt to 71 inch lbs.

REAR

1. Raise and support vehicle.
2. Clean area around wheel speed sensor.
3. Disconnect wheel speed sensor electrical connector, **Fig. 14.**
4. Remove sensor retaining bolt, then the sensor.
5. Reverse procedure to install, noting the following:
   a. Install a new O-ring before installing rear axle speed sensor.
   b. Lubricate O-ring with high performance rear axle lubricant F1TZ-19580-B, or equivalent, meeting Ford specification WSL-M2C192-A.
   c. **Torque** speed sensor retaining bolt to 11 ft. lbs.

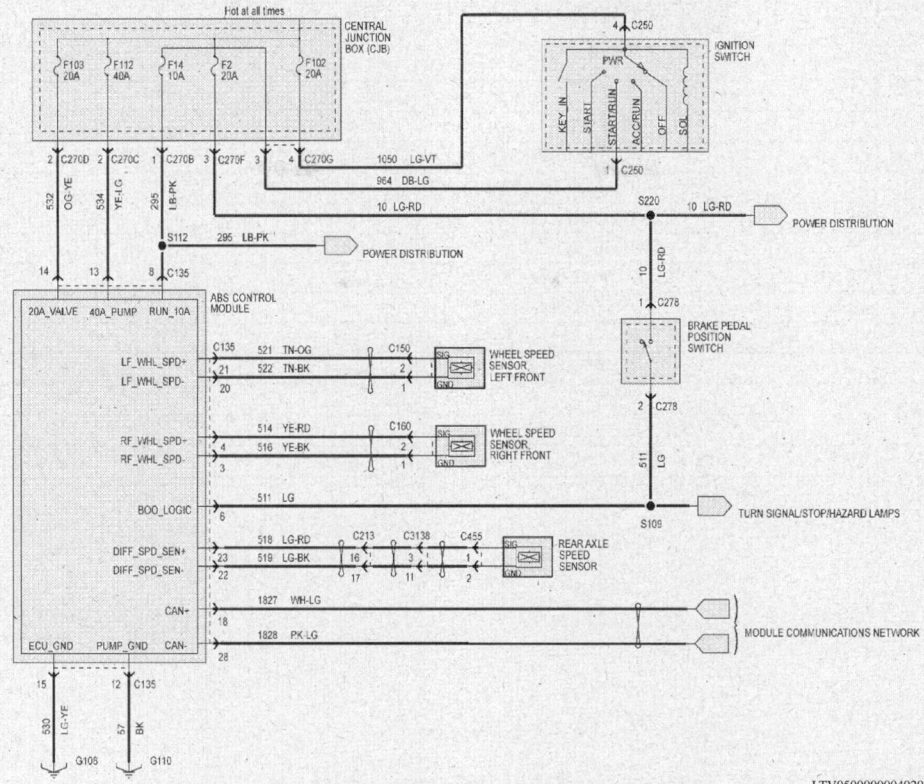

Fig. 3 Wiring diagram (Part 1 of 2)

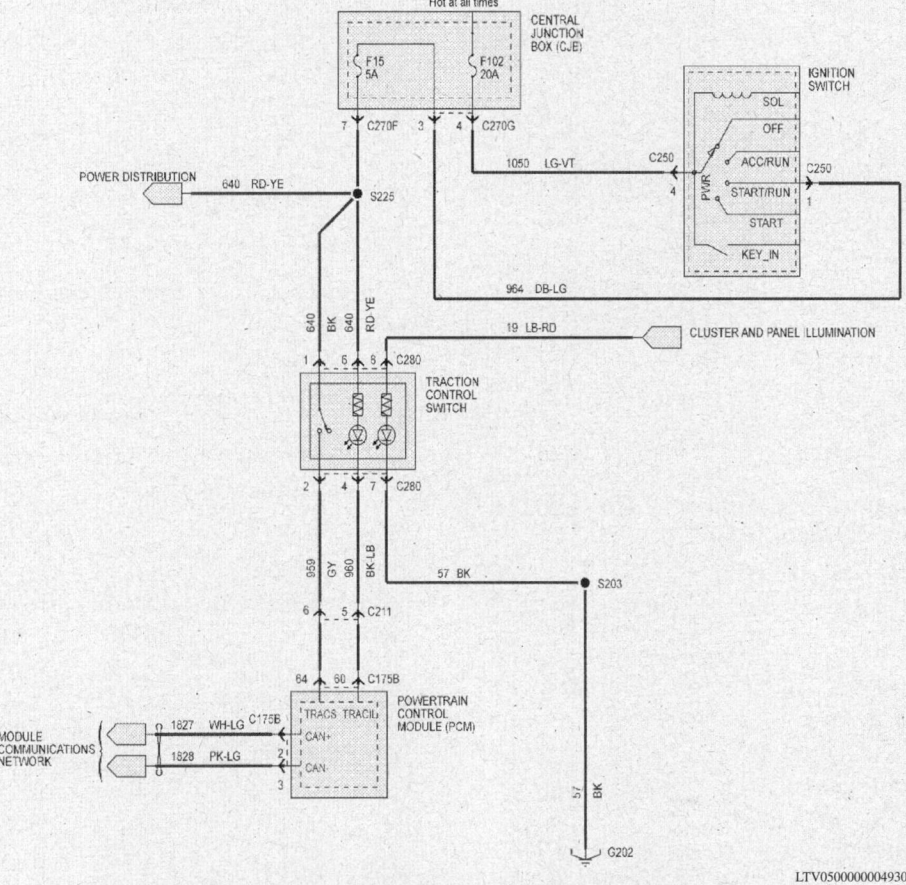

Fig. 3 Wiring diagram (Part 2 of 2)

DIAGNOSTIC CHART INDEX

Test	Code	Description	Page No.	Fig. No.
A	—	No Communication w/Anti-Lock Brake System (ABS)	5-148	4
B	B1484	Brake Pedal Input Open Circuit Failure	5-148	5
C	B1676	Battery Pack Voltage Out Of Range	5-149	6
D	C1300	ABS Hydraulic Pump Motor Circuit Failure/Motor	5-149	7
E	C1145	Wheel Speed Sensor Input Circuit Failure	5-150	8
	C1155	Wheel Speed Sensor Input Circuit Failure	5-150	8
	C1230	Wheel Speed Sensor Input Circuit Failure	5-150	8
F	C1222	Wheel Speed Mismatch	5-151	9
	C1237	Wheel Speed Sensor Signal Fault	5-151	9
	C1296	Wheel Speed Sensor Signal Fault	5-151	9
	C1297	Wheel Speed Sensor Signal Fault	5-151	9
G	C1266	ABS Power Valve Relay Circuit Failure	5-151	10
H	—	Yellow ABS Module Warning Indicator Is Always On	5-152	11

Test Step	Result / Action to Take
A1 CHECK CIRCUIT 295 (LB/PK) FOR AN OPEN • Key in OFF position. • Disconnect: ABS Module C135. • Key in ON position. • Measure the voltage between ABS module C135-8, circuit 295 (LB/PK), harness side and ground. • **Is the voltage greater than 10 volts?**	**Yes** GO to A2 . **No** VERIFY CJB fuse 14 (10A) is OK. If OK, REPAIR circuit 295 (LB/PK) for an open. TEST the system for normal operation.
A2 CHECK CIRCUIT 530 (LG/YE) FOR AN OPEN • Key in OFF position. • Measure the resistance between ABS module C135-15, circuit 530 (LG/YE), harness side, and ground. • **Is the resistance less than 5 ohms?**	**Yes** Continue diagnosis of the communications network. **No** REPAIR circuit 530 (LG/YE) for an open. TEST the system for normal operation.

LTV0500000004932

Fig. 4   Test A: No Communication w/Anti-Lock Brake System (ABS)

Test Step	Result / Action to Take
B1 CHECK FOR CORRECT STOPLAMPS OPERATION • Key in OFF position. • Apply the brake pedal and observe the stoplamps. • **Do the stoplamps operate correctly?**	**Yes** GO to B2 . **No** Continue diagnosis of the stoplamps. CLEAR the DTCs. REPEAT the self-test.
B2 CHECK CIRCUIT 511 (LG) FOR AN OPEN • Disconnect: ABS Module C135. • Measure the voltage between ABS module C135-6, circuit 511 (LG), harness side and ground, while pressing the brake pedal. • **Is the voltage greater than 10 volts?**	**Yes** GO to B3 . **No** REPAIR circuit 511 (LG) for an open. CLEAR the DTCs. REPEAT the self-test.
B3 CHECK FOR CORRECT ABS MODULE OPERATION • Disconnect ABS module C135. • Check for: ▪ corrosion. ▪ pushed-out pins. ▪ spread terminals. • Connect the ABS module connector and make sure it seats correctly. • Operate the system and verify the concern is still present. • **Is the concern still present?**	**Yes** INSTALL a new ABS module. TEST the system for normal operation. **No** The system is operating correctly at this time. The concern may have been caused by a loose or corroded connector. CLEAR the DTCs. REPEAT the self-test.

LTV0500000004933

Fig. 5   Test B, Code B1484: Brake Pedal Input Open Circuit Failure

Test Step	Result / Action to Take
C1 CHECK THE BATTERY VOLTAGE	
• Measure the battery voltage between the positive and negative battery terminals with the key on and the engine off (KOEO) and with the engine running. • **Is the battery voltage between 10 and 13 volts with KOEO, and between 13 and 17 volts with the engine running?**	**Yes** GO to C2. **No** Continue diagnosis of the charging system.
C2 CHECK THE VOLTAGE TO THE ANTI-LOCK BRAKE SYSTEM (ABS) MODULE	

• Key in OFF position.
 • Disconnect: ABS Module C135.
 • Key in ON position.
 • Measure the voltage between ground and:
   ▪ ABS module C135-8, circuit 295 (LB/PK), harness side.
   ▪ ABS module C135-14, circuit 532 (OG/YE), harness side.
   ▪ ABS module C135-13, circuit 534 (YE/LG), harness side.
 	
 • **Are the voltages greater than 10 volts?**
	Yes
	 GO to C3.
	
	 No
	 VERIFY CJB fuses 14 (10A), 103 (20A) and 112 (40A) are OK. If OK, REPAIR the affected circuit(s) for an open. CLEAR the DTCs. REPEAT the self-test.

C3 CHECK THE ANTI-LOCK BRAKE SYSTEM (ABS) MODULE GROUND CIRCUITS FOR AN OPEN	

• Key in OFF position.
 • Measure the resistance between ground and:
   ▪ ABS module C135-15, circuit 530 (LG/YE), harness side.
   ▪ ABS module C135-12, circuit 57 (BK), harness side.
 • **Are the resistances less than 5 ohms?**
	Yes
	 GO to C4.
	
	 No
	 REPAIR the affected circuit(s) for an open. CLEAR the DTCs. REPEAT the self-test

LTV0500000004934

Fig. 6   Test C, Code B1676: Battery Pack Voltage Out Of Range (Part 1 of 2)

Test Step	Result / Action to Take
D1 CHECK THE ANTI-LOCK BRAKE SYSTEM (ABS) PUMP MOTOR	
• Key in ON position. • **Is the ABS pump motor running all the time?**	**Yes** GO to D6. **No** GO to D2.
D2 CHECK THE PUMP MOTOR OPERATION	
• Connect the diagnostic tool. • Key in ON position. • Using the diagnostic tool, trigger the ABS module pump motor ON active command. • **Does the ABS pump motor run for approximately 3 seconds?**	**Yes** TRIGGER the ABS module pump motor OFF active command. CLEAR the DTCs. CHECK the yellow ABS warning indicator while driving the vehicle (the brakes must not be applied) above 32 km/h (20 mph). If the yellow ABS warning indicator illuminates, RETRIEVE the DTCs. If DTC C1300 is retrieved again, GO to D6. If the yellow ABS warning indicator does not illuminate, the system is OK. **No** TRIGGER the ABS module pump motor OFF active command. GO to D3.
D3 CHECK THE PUMP MOTOR CIRCUITS	
• Key in OFF position. • Disconnect: Hydraulic Control Unit (HCU) Connector. • Connect a fused (20A) jumper wire to HCU connector pin 1, component side and momentarily connect the other end of the jumper wire to HCU connector pin 2, component side. • **Does the pump motor run when the jumper wire is**	**Yes** GO to D4. **No** INSTALL a new hydraulic control unit (HCU).

LTV0500000004936

Fig. 7   Test D, Code C1300: ABS Hydraulic Pump Motor Circuit Failure/Motor (Part 1 of 2)

Test Step	Result / Action to Take
C4 CHECK FOR CORRECT ABS MODULE OPERATION	

• Disconnect ABS module C135.
 • Check for:
   ▪ corrosion.
   ▪ pushed-out pins.
   ▪ spread terminals.
 • Connect the ABS module connector and make sure it seats correctly.
 • Operate the system and verify the concern is still present.
 • **Is the concern still present?**
	Yes
	 INSTALL a new ABS module. TEST the system for normal operation.
	
	 No
	 The system is operating correctly at this time. The concern may have been caused by a loose or corroded connector. CLEAR the DTCs. REPEAT the self-test.

LTV0500000004935

Fig. 6   Test C, Code B1676: Battery Pack Voltage Out Of Range (Part 2 of 2)

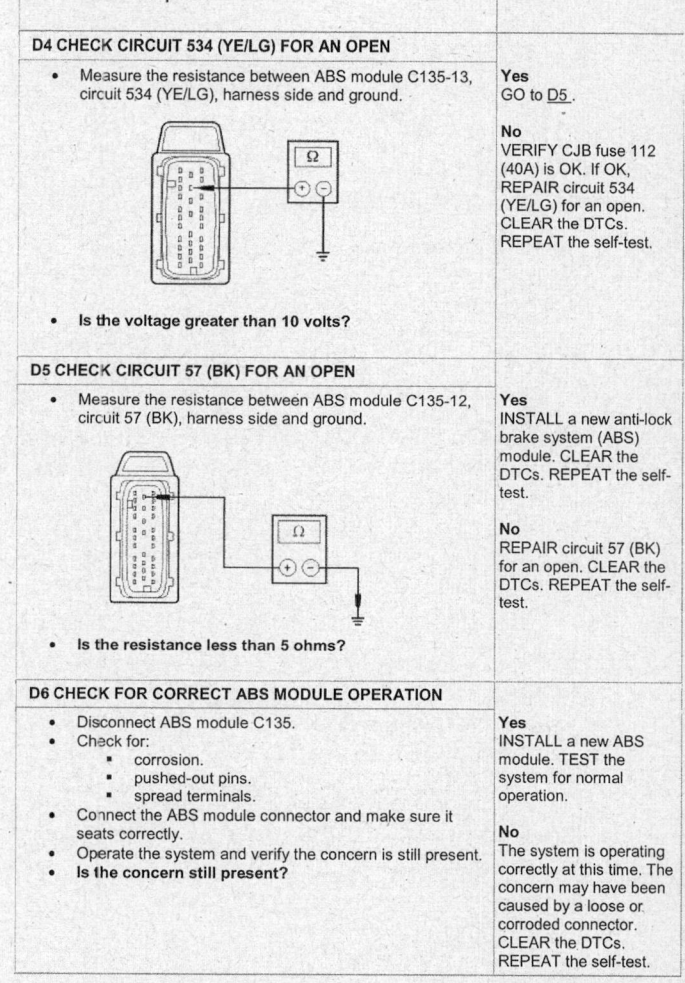

Test Step	Result / Action to Take
connect to pin 2?	
D4 CHECK CIRCUIT 534 (YE/LG) FOR AN OPEN	
• Measure the resistance between ABS module C135-13, circuit 534 (YE/LG), harness side and ground. • **Is the voltage greater than 10 volts?**	**Yes** GO to D5. **No** VERIFY CJB fuse 112 (40A) is OK. If OK, REPAIR circuit 534 (YE/LG) for an open. CLEAR the DTCs. REPEAT the self-test.
D5 CHECK CIRCUIT 57 (BK) FOR AN OPEN	
• Measure the resistance between ABS module C135-12, circuit 57 (BK), harness side and ground. • **Is the resistance less than 5 ohms?**	**Yes** INSTALL a new anti-lock brake system (ABS) module. CLEAR the DTCs. REPEAT the self-test. **No** REPAIR circuit 57 (BK) for an open. CLEAR the DTCs. REPEAT the self-test.
D6 CHECK FOR CORRECT ABS MODULE OPERATION	

• Disconnect ABS module C135.
 • Check for:
   ▪ corrosion.
   ▪ pushed-out pins.
   ▪ spread terminals.
 • Connect the ABS module connector and make sure it seats correctly.
 • Operate the system and verify the concern is still present.
 • **Is the concern still present?**
	Yes
	 INSTALL a new ABS module. TEST the system for normal operation.
	
	 No
	 The system is operating correctly at this time. The concern may have been caused by a loose or corroded connector. CLEAR the DTCs. REPEAT the self-test.

LTV0500000004937

Fig. 7   Test D, Code C1300: ABS Hydraulic Pump Motor Circuit Failure/Motor (Part 2 of 2)

Test Step	Result / Action to Take
E1 CHECK FOR DTCS	
• Connect the diagnostic tool. • Key in ON position. • Using the diagnostic tool, retrieve DTCs from continuous and on-demand self-test. • **Is DTC C1230 present?**	**Yes** If DTC C1230 is present, GO to E3. **No** If DTCs C1145 or C1155 are present, GO to E2. All other DTCs, go to Diagnostic Trouble Code (DTC) Index.
E2 CHECK FOR A SHORTED FRONT WHEEL SPEED SENSOR	

• Disconnect: Wheel Speed Sensor C150 (LF) or C160 (RF).
• Measure the resistance between the suspect front wheel speed sensor pins, component side.
  • **For the LF sensor**, measure between C150-1, component side and C150-2, component side.
  • **For the RF sensor**, measure between C160-1, component side and C160-2, component side.
 	
• **Is the resistance between 3.8 and 5.2 MegOhms?**
	Yes
	INSTALL a new wheel speed sensor. CLEAR the DTCs. TEST the system for normal operation.
	
	No
	GO to E4.

E3 CHECK FOR A SHORTED REAR WHEEL SPEED SENSOR	
• Disconnect: Rear Wheel Speed Sensor C455. • Measure the resistance between rear wheel speed sensor C455-1, component side and rear wheel speed sensor C455-2, component side.	**Yes** GO to E4. **No** INSTALL a new rear wheel speed sensor. CLEAR the DTCs. TEST the system

LTV0500000004938

Fig. 8 Test E, Codes C1145, C1155 & C1230: Wheel Speed Sensor Input Circuit Failure (Part 1 of 4)

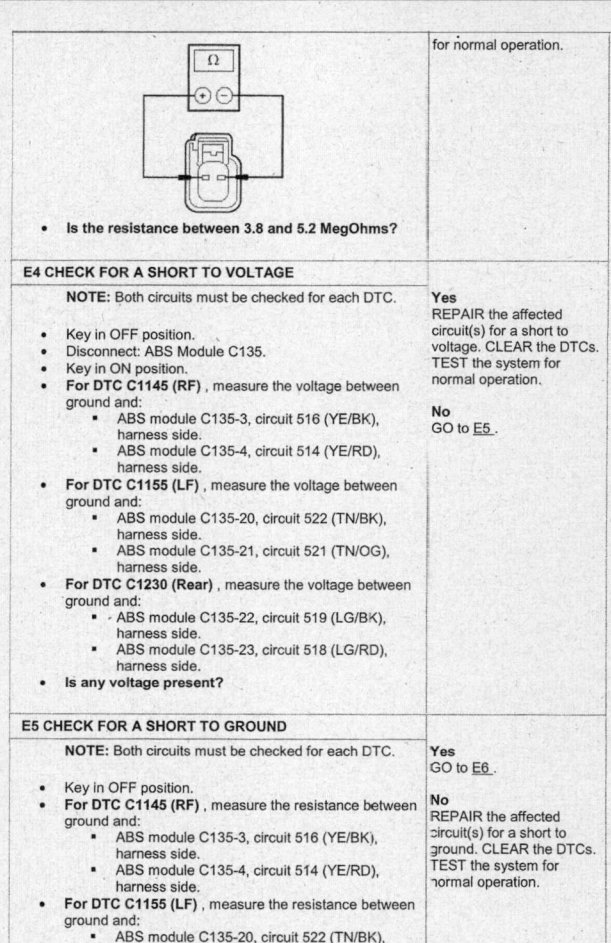

	for normal operation.
• **Is the resistance between 3.8 and 5.2 MegOhms?**	
E4 CHECK FOR A SHORT TO VOLTAGE	

NOTE: Both circuits must be checked for each DTC.
 	
• Key in OFF position.
• Disconnect: ABS Module C135.
• Key in ON position.
• For DTC C1145 (RF), measure the voltage between ground and:
  • ABS module C135-3, circuit 516 (YE/BK), harness side.
  • ABS module C135-4, circuit 514 (YE/RD), harness side.
• For DTC C1155 (LF), measure the voltage between ground and:
  • ABS module C135-20, circuit 522 (TN/BK), harness side.
  • ABS module C135-21, circuit 521 (TN/OG), harness side.
• For DTC C1230 (Rear), measure the voltage between ground and:
  • ABS module C135-22, circuit 519 (LG/BK), harness side.
  • ABS module C135-23, circuit 518 (LG/RD), harness side.
• **Is any voltage present?**
	Yes
	REPAIR the affected circuit(s) for a short to voltage. CLEAR the DTCs. TEST the system for normal operation.
	
	No
	GO to E5.

E5 CHECK FOR A SHORT TO GROUND	

NOTE: Both circuits must be checked for each DTC.
 	
• Key in OFF position.
• For DTC C1145 (RF), measure the resistance between ground and:
  • ABS module C135-3, circuit 516 (YE/BK), harness side.
  • ABS module C135-4, circuit 514 (YE/RD), harness side.
• For DTC C1155 (LF), measure the resistance between ground and:
  • ABS module C135-20, circuit 522 (TN/BK),
	Yes
	GO to E6.
	
	No
	REPAIR the affected circuit(s) for a short to ground. CLEAR the DTCs. TEST the system for normal operation.

LTV0500000004939

Fig. 8 Test E, Codes C1145, C1155 & C1230: Wheel Speed Sensor Input Circuit Failure (Part 2 of 4)

	harness side.
	  • ABS module C135-21, circuit 521 (TN/OG), harness side.
	• For DTC C1230 (Rear), measure the resistance between ground and:
	  • ABS module C135-22, circuit 519 (LG/BK), harness side.
	  • ABS module C135-23, circuit 518 (LG/RD), harness side.
	• **Are the resistances greater than 10,000 ohms?**	

E6 CHECK FOR AN OPEN	

NOTE: Both circuits must be checked for each DTC.
 	
• For DTC C1145 (RF), measure the resistance between:
  • ABS module C135-3, circuit 516 (YE/BK), harness side and RF wheel speed sensor C160-1, circuit 516 (YE/BK), harness side.
  • ABS module C135-4, circuit 514 (YE/RD), harness side and RF wheel speed sensor C160-2, circuit 514 (YE/RD), harness side.
• For DTC C1155 (LF), measure the resistance between:
  • ABS module C135-20, circuit 522 (TN/BK), harness side and LF wheel speed sensor C150-1, circuit 522 (TN/BK), harness side.
  • ABS module C135-21, circuit 521 (TN/OG), harness side and LF wheel speed sensor C150-2, circuit 521 (TN/OG), harness side.
• For DTC C1230 (Rear), measure the resistance between:
  • ABS module C135-23, circuit 518 (LG/RD), harness side and rear wheel speed sensor C455-1, circuit 518 (LG/RD), harness side.
  • ABS module C135-22, circuit 519 (LG/BK), harness side and rear wheel speed sensor C455-2, circuit 519 (LG/BK), harness side.
• **Are the resistances less than 5 ohms?**
	Yes
	GO to E7.
	
	No
	REPAIR the affected circuit(s) for an open. CLEAR the DTCs. TEST the system for normal operation.

E7 CHECK THE ABS MODULE OUTPUT	
• Connect: ABS Module C135. • Key in ON position. • Measure the voltage between the suspect front wheel speed sensor pins, harness side.	**Yes** GO to E8. **No** INSTALL a new wheel speed sensor. CLEAR the DTC. TEST the system for normal operation.

LTV0500000004940

Fig. 8 Test E, Codes C1145, C1155 & C1230: Wheel Speed Sensor Input Circuit Failure (Part 3 of 4)

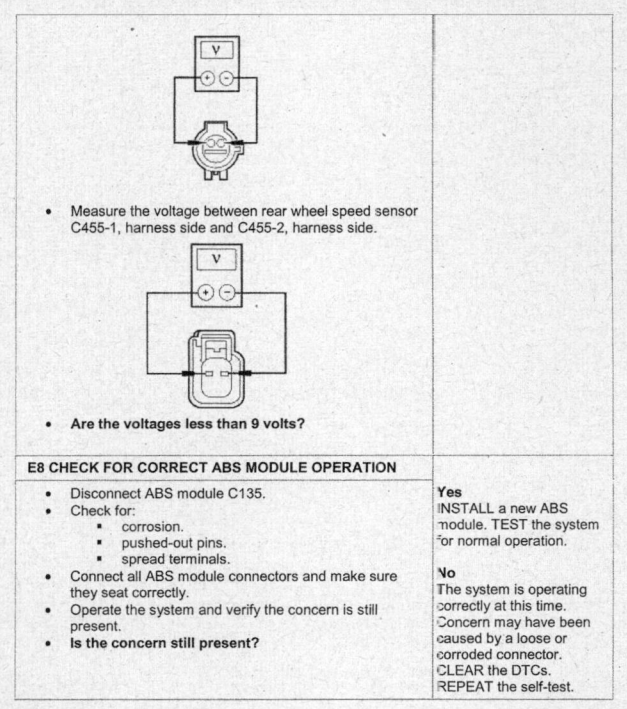

• Measure the voltage between rear wheel speed sensor C455-1, harness side and C455-2, harness side. • **Are the voltages less than 9 volts?**	
E8 CHECK FOR CORRECT ABS MODULE OPERATION	

• Disconnect ABS module C135.
• Check for:
  • corrosion.
  • pushed-out pins.
  • spread terminals.
• Connect all ABS module connectors and make sure they seat correctly.
• Operate the system and verify the concern is still present.
• **Is the concern still present?**
	Yes
	INSTALL a new ABS module. TEST the system for normal operation.
	
	No
	The system is operating correctly at this time. Concern may have been caused by a loose or corroded connector. CLEAR the DTCs. REPEAT the self-test.

LTV0500000004941

Fig. 8 Test E, Codes C1145, C1155 & C1230: Wheel Speed Sensor Input Circuit Failure (Part 4 of 4)

Test Step	Result / Action to Take
F1 CHECK FOR DTCs • Connect the diagnostic tool. • Key in ON position. • Using the diagnostic tool, retrieve the ABS module DTCs. • **Are DTCs C1145, C1155 or C1230 present?**	**Yes** Go To Pinpoint Test E. **No** For DTC C1222, GO to F4. For DTC C1296 or C1297, GO to F2. For DTC C1237, GO to F3. If no DTCs are present, GO to F5.
F2 CHECK THE FRONT WHEEL SPEED SENSOR OUTPUT • Disconnect: Wheel Speed Sensor C150 (LF) or C160 (RF). • If DTC C1296, connect a fused (5A) jumper wire between LF wheel speed sensor, C150 -2, circuit 521 (TN/OG), harness side and component side. Connect the automotive meter between the C150-1, circuit 522 (TN/BK), harness side and component side. 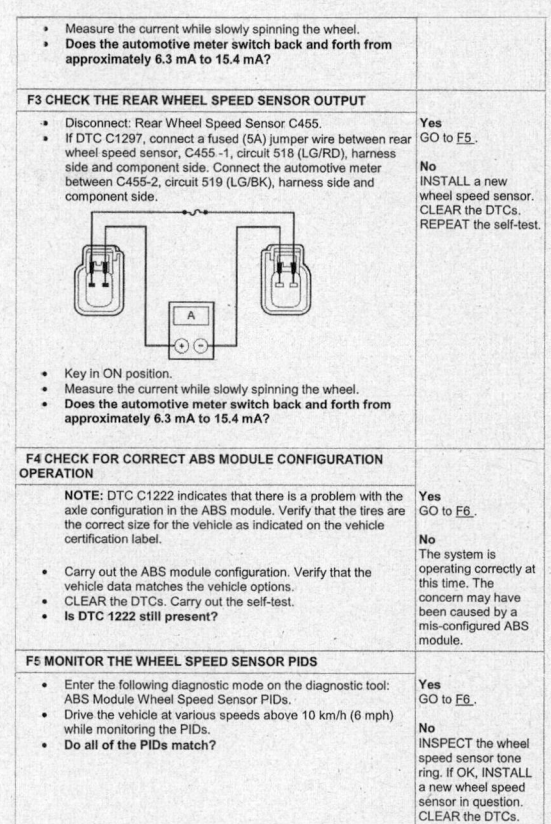 • If DTC C1297, connect a fused (5A) jumper wire between the RF wheel speed sensor, C160 -2, circuit 514 (YE/RD), harness side and component side. Connect the automotive meter between the C160-1, circuit 516 (YE/BK), harness side and component side. • Key in ON position.	**Yes** GO to F5. **No** INSTALL a new wheel speed sensor. CLEAR the DTCs. REPEAT the self-test.

LTV0500000004942

Fig. 9   Test F, Codes C1222 , C1237, C1296 & C1297: Wheel Speed Mismatch/Wheel Speed Sensor Signal Fault (Part 1 of 3)

Test Step	Result / Action to Take
• Measure the current while slowly spinning the wheel. • **Does the automotive meter switch back and forth from approximately 6.3 mA to 15.4 mA?**	
F3 CHECK THE REAR WHEEL SPEED SENSOR OUTPUT • Disconnect: Rear Wheel Speed Sensor C455. • If DTC C1297, connect a fused (5A) jumper wire between rear wheel speed sensor, C455 -1, circuit 518 (LG/RD), harness side and component side. Connect the automotive meter between C455-2, circuit 519 (LG/BK), harness side and component side. 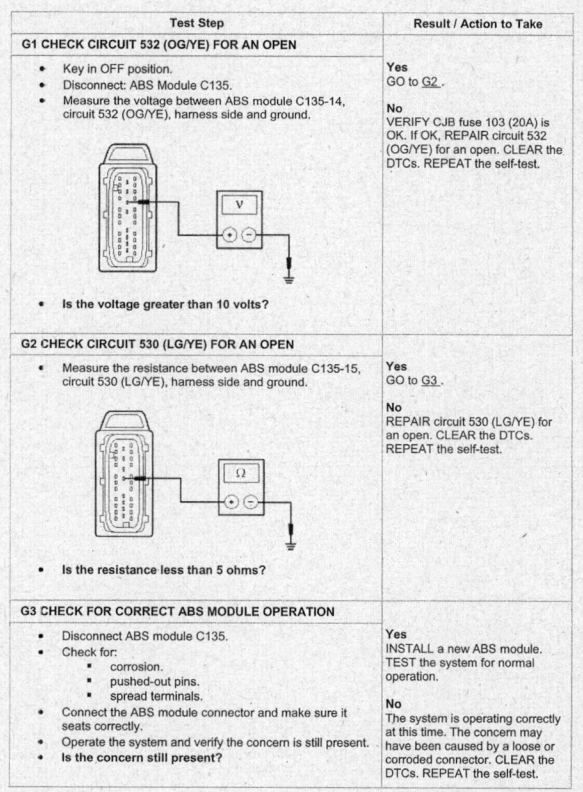 • Key in ON position. • Measure the current while slowly spinning the wheel. • **Does the automotive meter switch back and forth from approximately 6.3 mA to 15.4 mA?**	**Yes** GO to F5. **No** INSTALL a new wheel speed sensor. CLEAR the DTCs. REPEAT the self-test.
F4 CHECK FOR CORRECT ABS MODULE CONFIGURATION OPERATION **NOTE:** DTC C1222 indicates that there is a problem with the axle configuration in the ABS module. Verify that the tires are the correct size for the vehicle as indicated on the vehicle certification label. • Carry out the ABS module configuration. Verify that the vehicle data matches the vehicle options. • CLEAR the DTCs. Carry out the self-test. • **Is DTC 1222 still present?**	**Yes** GO to F6. **No** The system is operating correctly at this time. The concern may have been caused by a mis-configured ABS module.
F5 MONITOR THE WHEEL SPEED SENSOR PIDS • Enter the following diagnostic mode on the diagnostic tool: ABS Module Wheel Speed Sensor PIDs. • Drive the vehicle at various speeds above 10 km/h (6 mph) while monitoring the PIDs. • **Do all of the PIDs match?**	**Yes** GO to F6. **No** INSPECT the wheel speed sensor tone ring. If OK, INSTALL a new wheel speed sensor in question. CLEAR the DTCs.

LTV0500000004943

Fig. 9   Test F, Codes C1222 , C1237, C1296 & C1297: Wheel Speed Mismatch/Wheel Speed Sensor Signal Fault (Part 2 of 3)

REPEAT the self-test.	

F6 CHECK FOR CORRECT ABS MODULE OPERATION
• Disconnect ABS module C135.
• Check for:
  ▪ corrosion.
  ▪ pushed-out pins.
  ▪ spread terminals.
• Connect the ABS module connector and make sure it seats correctly.
• Operate the system and verify the concern is still present.
• **Is the concern still present?**
	Yes
	INSTALL a new ABS module. TEST the system for normal operation.
	
	No
	The system is operating correctly at this time. The concern may have been caused by a loose or corroded connector. CLEAR the DTCs. REPEAT the self-test.

LTV0500000004944

Fig. 9   Test F, Codes C1222 , C1237, C1296 & C1297: Wheel Speed Mismatch/Wheel Speed Sensor Signal Fault (Part 3 of 3)

Test Step	Result / Action to Take
G1 CHECK CIRCUIT 532 (OG/YE) FOR AN OPEN • Key in OFF position. • Disconnect: ABS Module C135. • Measure the voltage between ABS module C135-14, circuit 532 (OG/YE), harness side and ground. • **Is the voltage greater than 10 volts?**	**Yes** GO to G2. **No** VERIFY CJB fuse 103 (20A) is OK. If OK, REPAIR circuit 532 (OG/YE) for an open. CLEAR the DTCs. REPEAT the self-test.
G2 CHECK CIRCUIT 530 (LG/YE) FOR AN OPEN • Measure the resistance between ABS module C135-15, circuit 530 (LG/YE), harness side and ground. • **Is the resistance less than 5 ohms?**	**Yes** GO to G3. **No** REPAIR circuit 530 (LG/YE) for an open. CLEAR the DTCs. REPEAT the self-test.

G3 CHECK FOR CORRECT ABS MODULE OPERATION
• Disconnect ABS module C135.
• Check for:
  ▪ corrosion.
  ▪ pushed-out pins.
  ▪ spread terminals.
• Connect the ABS module connector and make sure it seats correctly.
• Operate the system and verify the concern is still present.
• **Is the concern still present?**
	Yes
	INSTALL a new ABS module. TEST the system for normal operation.
	
	No
	The system is operating correctly at this time. The concern may have been caused by a loose or corroded connector. CLEAR the DTCs. REPEAT the self-test.

LTV0500000004945

Fig. 10   Test G, Code C1266: ABS Power Valve Relay Circuit Failure

Test Step	Result / Action to Take
H1 CHECK FOR DTCs • Connect the diagnostic tool. • Key in ON position. • Using the diagnostic tool, retrieve the ABS module DTCs. • **Are any DTCs present?**	**Yes** REFER to Diagnostic Trouble Code (DTC) Index. **No** GO to <u>H2</u>.
H2 CARRY OUT THE INSTRUMENT CLUSTER ABS WARNING INDICATOR ACTIVE COMMAND • Enter the following diagnostic mode on the diagnostic tool: Instrument Cluster Active Command. • Using the diagnostic tool, select the instrument cluster indicator lamp control active command. Command all warning lamps ON then OFF. • **Does the yellow ABS warning indicator continue to illuminate?**	**Yes** GO to <u>H3</u>. **No** GO to <u>H4</u>.

H3 CHECK FOR CORRECT INSTRUMENT CLUSTER MODULE OPERATION
 	
• Disconnect all the instrument cluster connectors.
• Check for:
  ■ corrosion.
  ■ pushed-out pins.
  ■ spread terminals.
• Connect all the instrument cluster connectors and make sure they seat correctly.
• Operate the system and verify the concern is still present.
• **Is the concern still present?**
	Yes
	INSTALL a new instrument cluster. TEST the system for normal operation.
	
	No
	The system is operating correctly at this time. The concern may have been caused by a loose or corroded connector. TEST the system for normal operation.

H4 CHECK FOR CORRECT ABS MODULE OPERATION
 	
• Disconnect ABS module C135.
• Check for:
  ■ corrosion.
  ■ pushed-out pins.
  ■ spread terminals.
• Connect the ABS module connector and make sure it seats correctly.
• Operate the system and verify the concern is still present.
• **Is the concern still present?**
	Yes
	INSTALL a new ABS module. TEST the system for normal operation.
	
	No
	The system is operating correctly at this time. The concern may have been caused by a loose or corroded connector. TEST the system for normal operation.

LTV0500000004946

Fig. 11   Test H: Yellow ABS Module Warning Indicator Is Always On

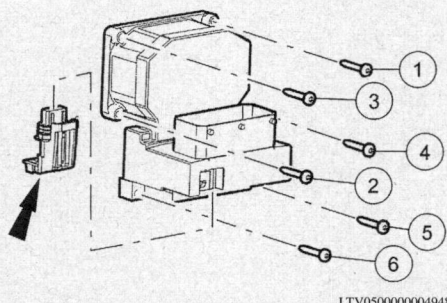

LTV0500000004948

Fig. 13   ABS control module bolt tightening sequence

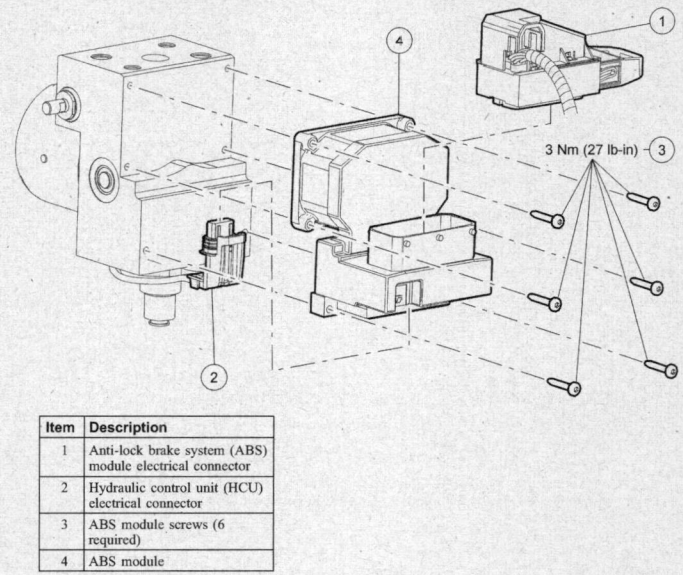

3 Nm (27 lb-in)

Item	Description
1	Anti-lock brake system (ABS) module electrical connector
2	Hydraulic control unit (HCU) electrical connector
3	ABS module screws (6 required)
4	ABS module

LTV0500000004947

Fig. 12   ABS control module replacement

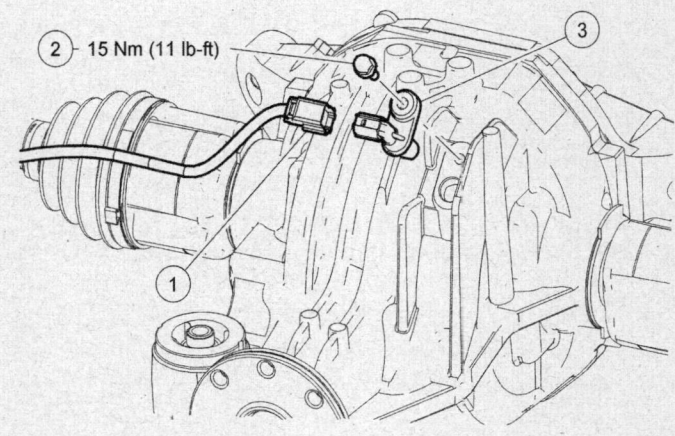

15 Nm (11 lb-ft)

Item	Description
1	Wheel speed sensor electrical connector
2	Wheel speed sensor bolt
3	Wheel speed sensor

LTV0500000004950

Fig. 14   Rear axle/wheel speed sensor replacement

F-150 & 2002-03 F-Super Duty (RABS)

NOTE: Electrical Symbol & Wire Color Code Identification Located In The Front Of This Manual May Be Used As An Aid When Using Wiring Circuits Found In This Section.

NOTE: Refer To "Computer Relearn Procedures" Located In The Front Of This Manual When Battery Power To The Computer Has Been Interrupted.

NOTE: Prior To Performing Any Service Operations Listed In This Section, Consult The "Technical Service Bulletins" Section For Related Information.

INDEX

	Page No.		Page No.		Page No.
Description	5-153	Diagnostic Tests	5-154	Battery Ground Cable	5-153
Diagnosis & Testing	5-153	Intermittent Diagnosis	5-154	Brake Fluid Handling	5-153
Accessing Diagnostic Trouble		Pinpoint Tests	5-154	**System Service**	5-154
Codes	5-153	Quick Check	5-154	Brake System Bleed	5-154
F-150	5-153	System Pre-Check	5-154	Component Replacement	5-154
F-Super Duty	5-154	Diagnostic Trouble Code		RABS Module	5-154
Clearing Diagnostic Trouble		Interpretation	5-154	Rear Wheel Speed Sensor	5-155
Codes	5-154	Wiring Diagrams	5-154	Speed Sensor Ring	5-155
F-150	5-154	**Diagnostic Chart Index**	5-159	**Troubleshooting**	5-153
F-Super Duty	5-154	**Precautions**	5-153	Symptom Charts	5-153

PRECAUTIONS

BATTERY GROUND CABLE

Prior to service disconnect battery ground cable and isolate as required.

BRAKE FLUID HANDLING

Brake fluid can cause serious injury and vehicle damage if not handled properly. Avoid contact with eyes and do not allow fluid to splash or spill on painted surfaces. Wash hands thoroughly after handling.

DESCRIPTION

The anti-lock brake system (ABS) module, with or without stability assist, simultaneously manages the anti-lock braking, traction control and engine control systems to maintain vehicle control during deceleration and acceleration. The ABS accomplishes this by communicating with the other modules over the high speed controller area network (HS-CAN) bus.

When the ignition switch is in the RUN position, the module carries out a preliminary electrical check and, at approximately 20 km/h (12 mph), the hydraulic pump motor is turned on for approximately one half-second. Any malfunction of the anti-lock brake system disables the traction control and stability assist (if equipped). The ABS module communicates with the instrument cluster over the HS-CAN bus and the cluster illuminates the anti-lock brake warning indicator. However, the power-assist braking system functions normally.

With the ignition switch in the START or RUN positions, the stability assist module functions similarly to a conventional ABS module by monitoring and comparing the rotational speed of each wheel. The wheel speed sensors electrically sense each tooth of the anti-lock sensor ring as they pass through the sensor magnetic field. When the stability assist module detects an impending wheel lock, wheel spin or vehicle motion that is inconsistent with the driver commands, it modulates brake pressure to the appropriate brake caliper(s). The stability assist module triggers the hydraulic control unit (HCU) to open and close the appropriate solenoid valves. Once the affected wheel(s) return to the desired speed, the stability assist module returns the solenoid valves to their normal position, and normal base brake operation is restored.

TROUBLESHOOTING

Symptom Charts

Refer to **Figs. 1 and 2** for symptom charts.

DIAGNOSIS & TESTING

Accessing Diagnostic Trouble Codes

F-150

Care must be taken to connect only the black/orange stripe wire to ground. Connecting the mating connector wire to ground will result in a blown fuse.

1. Place ignition switch is in RUN position. Engine does not need to be running.
2. Locate black Rear Anti-Lock Brake System (RABS) diagnostic connector C207. Diagnostic connector C207 has two mating halves, one of which has a black/orange (BK/OG) wire connected to it. Disconnect the two halves.
3. Attach one end of a jumper wire to black/orange (BK/OG) wire side of diagnostic connector C207. Ground opposite end of jumper wire until ABS light begins to flash. If grounding this wire does not start yellow ABS warning indicator flashing, refer to symptom chart.
4. Flash code consists of a number of short flashes and ends with a long flash. Count short flashes and include long flash in the count to obtain code

Condition	Possible Source	Action
• ABS Misfire, ABS Too Sensitive, ABS Fires On Normal Stop	• Rear anti-lock brake sensor indicator is damaged. • Sensor output is out of sync. • Intermittent open or shorted sensor circuit. • Chafed wire insulation or pinched wire due to improper routing causing intermittent short. • Linings are grabby. • Loose sensor(s).	• REMOVE rear sensor from the differential housing; INSPECT rear anti-lock brake sensor indicator for damaged teeth. • GO to Pinpoint Test C. • GO to Component Test — Intermittent Failures to test circuits: 523 (R/PK) and 519 (LG/BK). • INSPECT wiring harness from front sensor knuckle to the frame and from the rear axle to the frame for worn or chafed wire insulation. • ELIMINATE base brake system as cause of problem. • TIGHTEN sensor bolt to specifications.
• Wheels Lock Up	• Hydraulic outlet (dump) valve. • Leaky inlet (isolation) valve during ABS (soft). • Binding parking brake. • Leaking rear axle seal.	• GO to Pinpoint Test F. • ELIMINATE base brake system as cause of problem.
• Hard or Soft Brake Pedal	• Stuck inlet (isolation) valve (hard brake pedal) or leaky outlet (dump) valve (soft brake pedal). • Hydraulic leak in brake line or hose, fitting, master cylinder, wheel cylinder, or caliper (soft brake pedal). • Air in brake system (soft brake pedal). • Little or no vacuum boost (hard brake pedal). • Stuck or inoperative caliper (hard brake pedal). • Pinched or crimped brake line or hose (hard brake pedal).	• GO to Pinpoint Test D. • ELIMINATE base brake system as cause of problem.

FM4029901423010X

Fig. 1   Symptom chart (Part 1 of 2). F-Super Duty

Condition	Possible Source	Action
• Lack of Deceleration During Medium/Hard Brake Application	• Stuck shut inlet (isolation) valve or leaky outlet (dump) valve (rear axle only). • Hydraulic leak in brake line or hose, fitting, master cylinder, wheel cylinder, or caliper. • Air in brake system. • Little or no vacuum boost. • Stuck or inoperative caliper. • Ineffective brake shoe or pad linings.	• GO to Pinpoint Test D. • ELIMINATE base brake system as cause of problem.
• Vehicle Pulls During Braking	• Frozen or binding caliper (one side of vehicle). • Uneven brake pad or shoe wear. • Pinched or crimped brake line or hose. • Fully or partially blocked front inlet (isolation) valve.	• ELIMINATE base brake system as cause of problem. • REPLACE the electronic hydraulic control unit (EHCU).
• ABS Warning Lamp On With System Pass	• ABS warning lamp circuit. • Anti-lock brake control module.	• CHECK circuit 603 (DG) for open or short to B+. REPAIR circuit 603 (DG) if necessary. If OK, REPLACE the anti-lock brake control module. TEST the system for normal operation.
• Soft or Excessive Pedal Travel	• Electronic hydraulic control unit (EHCU).	• GO to Pinpoint Test D.
• No Communication With the Anti-Lock Brake Control Module	• Fuse(s). • Circuitry. • Module.	• GO to Pinpoint Test G.

FM4029901423020X

Fig. 1   Symptom chart (Part 2 of 2). F-Super Duty

number. Example, three short flashes followed by one long flash indicates Diagnostic Trouble Code (DTC) 4.
5. Code will continue to repeat itself until key is turned to Off position.
6. Diagnostic trouble code 16 is obtained when anti-lock brake control module detects normal system operation.

F-SUPER DUTY

1. Connect New Generation STAR (NGS) Tester to Data Link Connector (DLC) located beneath instrument panel.
2. Select vehicle to be tested from NGS menu.
3. If NGS does not communicate with vehicle, proceed as follows:
   a. Ensure program card is properly installed.
   b. Inspect connections to vehicle.
   c. Ensure ignition is in On position.
   d. If NGS still does not communicate with vehicle, refer to NGS Tester manual.
4. Follow NGS Tester instructions to retrieve DTC's.

Diagnostic Trouble Code Interpretation

Refer to **Figs. 3 and 4** for diagnostic trouble code interpretation.

Wiring Diagrams

Refer to **Figs. 5 and 6** for wiring diagrams.

Diagnostic Tests

SYSTEM PRE-CHECK

The system pre-check procedure must be performed first. Failure to do so may result in incorrect system diagnosis and replacement of good components.

The system pre-check is used to diagnose a vehicle for relatively simple diagnostic repairs, such as loose connectors and blown fuses. However, the system pre-check is also used to prepare the vehicle for further diagnostics, including warning lamp diagnostic trouble code diagnosis. Refer to the system pre-check chart, **Fig. 7,** and the related system pre-check test charts, **Figs. 8 through 12** for system pre-check procedures.

INTERMITTENT DIAGNOSIS

Refer to **Fig. 13** for intermittent diagnosis.

QUICK CHECK

Refer **Fig. 14** for quick check procedure.

PINPOINT TESTS

F-SUPER DUTY

Refer to **Figs. 15 through 23** for pinpoint tests.

F-150

Refer to **Figs. 24 through 39** for pinpoint tests.

Clearing Diagnostic Trouble Codes

F-150

To clear the RABS II trouble code memory, turn the ignition switch to the Off position while the diagnostic connector halves are separated as described under "Accessing Diagnostic Trouble Codes."

F-SUPER DUTY

Follow manufacturer's instructions the NGS Tester to clear DTC's.

SYSTEM SERVICE

Brake System Bleed

Refer to "Hydraulic Brake Systems" chapter for bleeding procedure.

Component Replacement

RABS MODULE

F-150

1. Remove radio, instrument panel finish panel, then disconnect cigar lighter connectors.
2. Remove ashtray screws and ash tray.
3. Remove module to instrument panel screw, **Fig. 40.**
4. Slide module to release upper tab from instrument panel brace, then disconnect electrical connectors and remove module.
5. Reverse procedure to install.

F-SUPER DUTY

1. **On models equipped with diesel engine,** remove battery tray.
2. **On models equipped with gasoline engine,** proceed as follows:
   a. Disconnect battery ground cable.
   b. Remove engine air cleaner.
   c. Remove EVAP canister.
3. **On all models,** remove rubber dust cover push pin, then the rubber dust cover.
4. Disconnect ABS control module electrical connector.
5. Remove ABS control module retaining screw, then the module.
6. Reverse procedure to install. **Torque** ABS control module retaining bolt to 35 inch lbs.

Condition	Possible Sources	Action
• The red BRAKE warning indicator is always off	• Circuitry. • Red BRAKE warning indicator bulb. • Instrument cluster.	• DIAGNOSE instrument cluster.
• The red BRAKE warning indicator is always on	• Parking brake switch. • Master cylinder fluid level switch. • Circuitry. • Daytime running lamp (DRL) (if equipped).	• DIAGNOSE brake system.
• The yellow ABS warning indicator is always off	• Circuitry. • Yellow ABS warning indicator bulb. • Instrument cluster.	• DIAGNOSE instrument cluster.
• The yellow ABS warning indicator is always on	• Circuitry. • Anti-lock brake control module.	• GO to Pinpoint Test A.
• The yellow ABS warning indicator self-checks OK but automatically begins flashing	• Circuitry. • Fuse junction panel Fuse 15 (5A). • Anti-lock brake control module.	• GO to Pinpoint Test B.
• The yellow ABS warning indicator self-checks OK but no diagnostic trouble codes are retrieved when diagnostics are started	• Fuse. • Stoplamps. • Circuitry. • Anti-lock brake control module.	• GO to Pinpoint Test C.
• Diagnostic trouble code (DTC) 2 — open RABS isolation solenoid circuit	• Bulkhead connector (between engine compartment and instrument panel). • Anti-lock brake control module or RABS valve connectors not fully seated with component. • Circuitry. • RABS valve. • Anti-lock brake control module.	• GO to Pinpoint Test D.
• Diagnostic trouble code (DTC) 3 — open RABS dump solenoid circuit	• Bulkhead connector (between engine compartment and instrument panel). • Anti-lock brake control module or RABS valve connectors not fully seated with component. • Circuitry. • RABS valve. • Anti-lock brake control module.	• GO to Pinpoint Test E.

FM4020001676010X

Fig. 2 Symptom chart (Part 1 of 5). F-150

REAR WHEEL SPEED SENSOR

REMOVAL

1. Pull wiring harness connector from sensor, mounted in rear axle housing.
2. Remove sensor hold-down bolt, then the sensor from axle housing.

INSTALLATION

1. Clean axle mounting surface. Use care to prevent dirt from entering axle housing.
2. Inspect and clean magnetized sensor pole piece to ensure it is free from loose metal particles which could cause erratic system operation.
3. Inspect sensor O-ring for damage. Replace if necessary.
4. Lightly lubricate the sensor O-ring with clean motor oil. align sensor bolt hole and install sensor. **Do not apply force to plastic sensor connector.**
5. Sensor flange should slide to mounting surface. This will ensure air gap setting is between .005–.045 inch.
6. Install hold-down bolt and **torque** to 25–30 ft. lbs.
7. Push electrical connector onto sensor.

SPEED SENSOR RING

To service the speed sensor ring, the differential case must be removed from the axle housing and the speed sensor ring must be pressed off the case. **Do not reuse speed sensor ring if removed from differential case.**

Condition	Possible Sources	Action
• Diagnostic trouble code (DTC) 4 — open/grounded RABS valve reset circuit	• Bulkhead connector (between engine compartment and instrument panel). • Anti-lock brake control module or RABS valve connectors not fully seated with component. • Circuitry. • RABS valve. • Anti-lock brake control module.	• GO to Pinpoint Test F.
• Diagnostic trouble code (DTC) 5 — excessive dump solenoid activity	• Parking brake. • 4WD indicator switch (4x4 vehicles only). • Rear brake assembly. • Circuitry. • Wire insulation to battery power (4x4 vehicles only).	• GO to Pinpoint Test G.
• Diagnostic trouble code (DTC) 6 — erratic rear anti-lock brake sensor circuit	• Bulkhead connector (between engine compartment and instrument panel). • Anti-lock brake control module or rear anti-lock brake sensor connectors not fully seated with component. • Circuitry. • Rear anti-lock brake sensor. • Rear anti-lock brake sensor indicator. • Anti-lock brake control module.	• GO to Pinpoint Test H.
• Diagnostic trouble code (DTC) 7 — no isolation solenoid during self-check	• Circuitry. • RABS valve. • Anti-lock brake control module.	• GO to Pinpoint Test I.
• Diagnostic trouble code (DTC) 8 — no dump solenoid during self-check	• Circuitry. • Bulkhead connector between engine compartment and instrument panel terminals shorted. • RABS valve. • Anti-lock brake control module.	• GO to Pinpoint Test J.
• Diagnostic trouble code (DTC) 9 — speed sensor high resistance/open circuit	• Anti-lock brake control module or rear anti-lock brake sensor connectors not fully seated with component. • Circuitry. • Rear anti-lock brake sensor. • Anti-lock brake control module.	• GO to Pinpoint Test K.

FM4020001676020X

Fig. 2 Symptom chart (Part 2 of 5). F-150

Condition	Possible Sources	Action
• Diagnostic trouble code (DTC) 10 — speed sensor low resistance/short to ground	• Bulkhead connector between engine compartment and instrument panel sensor terminals shorted together. • Circuitry. • Rear anti-lock brake sensor. • Anti-lock brake control module.	• GO to Pinpoint Test L.
• Diagnostic trouble code (DTC) 11 — brake pedal position (BPP) switch always closed	• Stoplamps. • Circuitry. • BPP switch. • Anti-lock brake control module.	• GO to Pinpoint Test M.
• Diagnostic trouble code (DTC) 12 — loss of hydraulic brake fluid during an anti-lock stop	• Low master cylinder fill level. • Fluid leaks in vehicle brake system. • Brake fluid level warning switch. • Master cylinder float. • Diode/resistor element. • Ignition switch. • Circuitry. • Anti-lock brake control module.	• GO to Pinpoint Test N.
• Diagnostic trouble code (DTC) 13 — RABS module failure	• Anti-lock brake control module.	• INSTALL a new anti-lock brake control module. TEST the system for normal operation. • REPEAT the system pre-check.
• Diagnostic trouble codes (DTC) 16 — RABS system OK	• No system faults detected.	• STOP. Rear anti-lock brake system functioning properly.
• Intermittent problem diagnosis	• Intermittent voltage to anti-lock brake control module. • Less than 11 volts feed to anti-lock brake control module. • Intermittent connections at rear anti-lock brake sensor, RABS valve, anti-lock brake control module.	• GO to Pinpoint Test P.

FM4020001676030X

Fig. 2 Symptom chart (Part 3 of 5). F-150

Condition	Possible Sources	Action
• Unwarranted RABS activity	• Metal chips on sensor pole piece. • Gap between the anti-lock brake sensor and the anti-lock brake sensor indicator is too large. • Anti-lock brake sensor/sensor indicator interference. • Intermittent open rear anti-lock brake sensor circuit at intermediate connections especially bulkhead. • Wire insulation. • Rear brake adjustment. • Brake linings.	• GO to Pinpoint Test H. • GO to Pinpoint Test P. • INSPECT wiring harness from rear axle assembly to frame side rail for chafing or rub marks. • DIAGNOSE brake system. • DIAGNOSE brake system.

• One or both wheels lock up	• Brake related concern:
	    — Rear brake shoe linings.
	    — Rear wheel cylinder.
	    — Rear brake adjustment.
	    — Contaminated brake fluid.
	 • Parking brake.
	 • Rear axle seal.
	
	 • Hubs engaged although shift lever is in 4x2 position.
	 • Faulty 4WD indicator switch or short to 12v in 4x4 circuit 210 (LB).
		• DIAGNOSE brake system.
		
		 • DIAGNOSE brake system.
		 • DIAGNOSE rear axle.
		
		 • DIAGNOSE 4 x 4.
		
		 • GO to Pinpoint Test G.

• Low/soft brake pedal	• Hydraulic leak.
	 • Air in brake system.
	 • Brake related concern:
	    — Vacuum.
	    — Rear wheel cylinder or front disc brake caliper.
	    — Rear brake tube/hose.
	 • Excessive dump solenoid activity
		• DIAGNOSE brake system.
		 • DIAGNOSE brake system.
		 • DIAGNOSE brake system.
		
		 • GO to Pinpoint Test G.

FM4020001676040X

Fig. 2 Symptom chart (Part 4 of 5). F-150

Condition	Possible Sources	Action

• Lack of deceleration during medium/hard brake applications	• RABS valve.
	
	 • Short/open in frame or instrument panel harness (circuits 519 [LG/BK] and/or 523 [RD/BK]).
	    — At anti-lock brake control module connector (pins 3 and 10).
	    — At rear anti-lock brake sensor connector.
	    — At bulkhead or other interconnection.
	    — Wire or insulation due to improper routing.
	    — Test connector (in engine compartment).
	 • Rear anti-lock brake sensor.
	 • Rear anti-lock brake sensor ring radial runout, rear anti-lock brake sensor indicator teeth damaged or missing.
	 • Hydraulic leak.
	 • Air in brake system.
	 • Brake related concern:
	    — Vacuum.
	    — Wheel cylinder or caliper.
	    — Rear brake tube/hose.
	    — Brake shoe and linings.
		• GO to Pinpoint Test F.
		
		 • GO to Pinpoint Test H.
		
		 • GO to Pinpoint Test H.
		 • GO to Pinpoint Test H.
		
		 • DIAGNOSE brake system.
		 • DIAGNOSE brake system.
		 • DIAGNOSE brake system.

FM4020001676050X

Fig. 2 Symptom chart (Part 5 of 5). F-150

Code	Description
2	Open RABS Isolation Solenoid Circuit
3	Open RABS Dump Solenoid Circuit
4	Open/Grounded RABS Valve Reset Circuit
5	Excessive Dump Solenoid Activity
6	Erratic Rear Anti-Lock Brake Sensor Circuit
7	No Isolation Solenoid During Self-Check
8	No Dump Solenoid During Self-Check
9	Speed Sensor High Resistance/Open Circuit
10	Speed Sensor Low Resistance/Short To Ground
11	Brake Pedal Position (BPP) Switch Always
12	Loss Of Brake Fluid During An Anti-Lock Stop
13	RABS Module Failure
16	RABS System OK

Fig. 3 Diagnostic trouble code interpretation. F-150

DTC	Description	Action
B1342	Anti-Lock Brake Control Module Failure	REPLACE anti-lock brake control module.
C1226	Brake Lamp Warning Output Short to Ground	Diagnose Instrument Cluster
C1202/C1204	Dump Valve, Rear	GO to Pinpoint Test A.
C1206/C1208	Isolation Valve, Rear	GO to Pinpoint Test A.
C1230	Rear Brake Anti-Lock Sensor (Electrical/Static)	GO to Pinpoint Test B.
C1229/C1237	Rear Brake Anti-Lock Sensor (Dynamic)	GO to Pinpoint Test C.
C1095/C1096	Pump Motor	GO to Pinpoint Test E.
C1115	Internal Power Relay	GO to Pinpoint Test F.
C1185	Open Internal Power Relay	GO to Pinpoint Test F.
C1169	Excessive Dump Time	GO to Pinpoint Test H.
C1184	ABS System Timeout	GO to Pinpoint Test J.
C1222	Wheel Speed Error (Dynamic)	GO to Pinpoint Test J.
B2141/B2477	Vehicle Speed Calibration Data Not Programmed Into Module	PERFORM the Calibration Procedure using NGS Tester.

FM4029901422000X

Fig. 4 Diagnostic trouble code interpretation. F-Super Duty

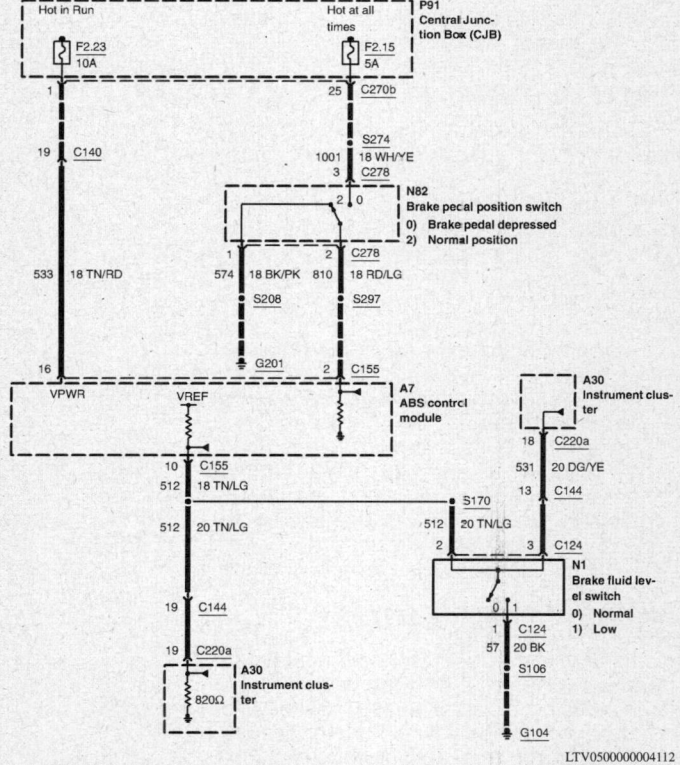

LTV0500000004112

Fig. 5 Wiring diagram. 2002-03 F-150 w/RABS

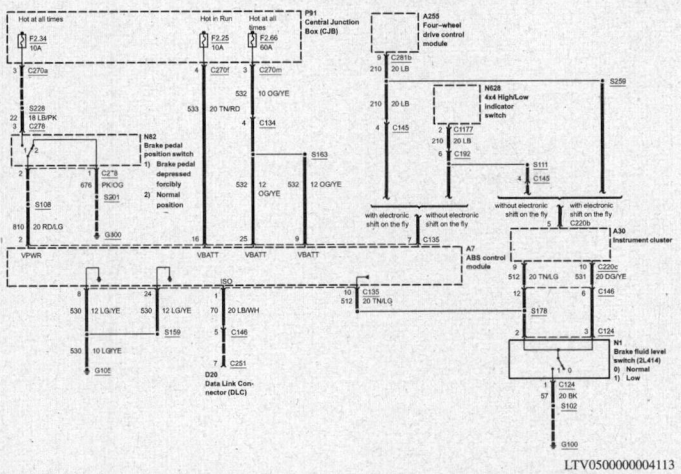

Fig. 6 Wiring diagram (Part 1 of 2). 2002-03 F-Super Duty w/RABS

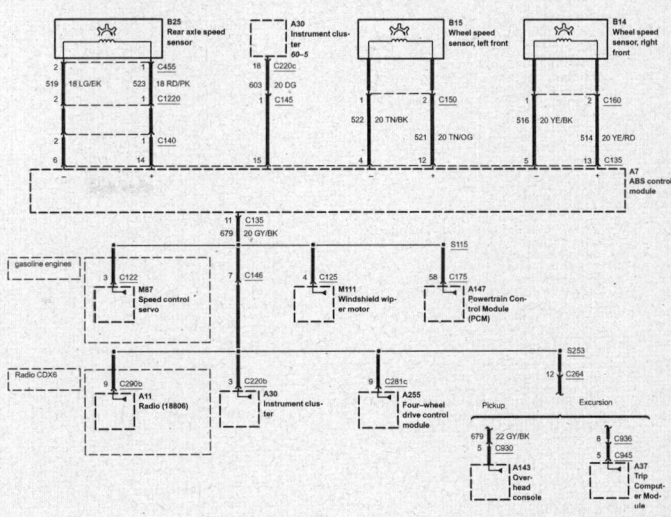

Fig. 6 Wiring diagram (Part 2 of 2). 2002-03 F-Super Duty w/RABS

CONDITION	ACTION TO TAKE
Yellow REAR ABS light OFF and does not self-check.	See System Pre-Check Test A.
Red brake light OFF and does not self-check.	See System Pre-Check Test B.
Yellow REAR ABS light self-check OK, but light automatically begins flashing.	See System Pre-Check Test C.
Yellow REAR ABS light self-check OK, but no diagnostic trouble code when diagnostics started.	See System Pre-Check Test D.
Red brake light ON when key in RUN position.	See System Pre-Check Test E.

FM4029300067000X

Fig. 7 System pre-check reference chart

Test Step	Result	▶	Action to Take
A3 ANTI-LOCK ELECTRONIC CONTROL MODULE GROUND			
NOTE: When checking resistance in the anti-lock system, always disconnect the battery to starter relay cable. Improper resistance may occur with the vehicle battery connected. ● Check for good anti-lock electronic control module ground: — Disconnect battery to starter relay cable. — Remove harness connector from anti-lock electronic control module. — Set multimeter on the 200-ohm scale. — Check for resistance between harness connector Pin 4 and chassis ground. ● Is resistance less than 1.0 ohm?	Yes No	▶ ▶	RECONNECT battery ground cable. GO to A4. CHECK for open in anti-lock electronic control module ground wire. CHECK for loose, dirty or broken connector pins. REPAIR as necessary. REPEAT System Pre-Check.
A4 REAR ABS LIGHT POWER			
● Check for voltage to REAR ABS light: — Remove harness connector from anti-lock electronic control module. — Set multimeter on 20 VDC scale position. — Turn ignition to the ON position. — Check voltage between harness connector Pin 7 and a known good chassis ground. ● Are 9 volts present?	Yes No	▶ ▶	REPLACE anti-lock electronic control module. REPEAT System Pre-Check. GO to A5.
A5 POWER TO REAR ABS LIGHT FUSE			
● Check for voltage to fuse. — Set multimeter to 20 VDC scale. — Turn ignition to the ON position. — Check voltage between panel fuse connector and known good chassis ground. ● Are 9 volts present?	Yes No	▶ ▶	GO to A6. REPAIR fuse panel or vehicle electrical system. REPEAT System Pre-Check.
A6 RABS LIGHT BULB			
● Check REAR ABS light bulb. ● Is the bulb OK?	Yes No	▶ ▶	REPAIR open between RABS light fuse and Pin 7 of the anti-lock electronic control module wiring harness connector. REPEAT System Pre-Check. REPLACE bulb. REPEAT System Pre-Check.

FM4029501202020X

Fig. 8 System Pre-Check Test Chart A (Part 2 of 2)

	TEST STEP	RESULT	▶	ACTION TO TAKE
A1	REAR ABS LIGHT FUSE			
	● Remove and inspect REAR ABS light fuse. ● Is the fuse blown?	Yes No	▶ ▶	CHECK for short to ground between fuse panel and warning lights. REPAIR short and REPLACE fuse. REPEAT System Pre-Check. REINSTALL fuse and GO to A2.
A2	MODULE HARNESS CONNECTOR			
	● Check to make sure module harness is fully plugged into anti-lock electronic control module. ● Are connections secure?	Yes No	▶ ▶	GO to A3. CONNECT harness to anti-lock electronic control module. REPEAT System Pre-Check.

FM4029501202010X

Fig. 8 System Pre-Check Test Chart A (Part 1 of 2)

	TEST STEP	RESULT	▶	ACTION TO TAKE
B1	RED BRAKE WARNING LIGHT/FUSE			
	● Turn ignition to RUN position. ● Apply parking brake. ● Observe red BRAKE warning light. ● Does the BRAKE warning light function?	Yes No	▶ ▶	RELEASE parking brake GO to B2. REPAIR brake warning circuit. CHECK for open fuse. CHECK for burned-out bulb or open Circuits 640 (R/Y), 162 (LG/R). REPEAT System Pre-Check.
B2	CHECK FOR CORRODED FLUID LEVEL CONNECTOR PINS			
	● Remove fluid level switch connector located on brake master cylinder. ● Inspect both halves of fluid level switch connector for corrosion or connector pin back-out. ● Are the connections clean and secure?	Yes No	▶ ▶	GO to B3. REPAIR/REPLACE connector as needed. REPEAT System Pre-Check.

FM4029501203010X

Fig. 9 System Pre-Check Test Chart B (Part 1 of 2)

	TEST STEP	RESULT	▶	ACTION TO TAKE
B3	CHECK FOR UNSEATED CONNECTOR			
	● Key OFF. ● Firmly reconnect fluid level switch connector located on brake master cylinder. ● Turn key to START position. ● Observe red BRAKE light. ● Does the BRAKE light function?	Yes No	▶ ▶	Condition is resolved. REPEAT System Pre-Check. GO to B4.
B4	DIODE RESISTOR ELEMENT/CIRCUIT 531			
	● Disconnect fluid level switch. ● Connect jumper wire from Circuit 531 (DG/Y) to known chassis ground. ● Observe red BRAKE light. ● Does the BRAKE light function?	Yes No	▶ ▶	LEAVE fluid level switch disconnected. GO to B5. REPAIR open Circuits 977 (P/W), 531 (DG/Y) or open diode/resistor element. REPEAT System Pre-Check.
B5	MASTER CYLINDER FLUID LEVEL SWITCH			
	● Connect jumper wire from Circuit 531 (DG/Y) to Circuit 512 (T/LG). ● Turn key to START position. ● Observe red BRAKE light. ● Does the BRAKE light function?	Yes No	▶ ▶	Master cylinder fluid level switch is defective. REPEAT System Pre-Check. Open in Circuit 512 (T/LG) or defective ignition switch. REPAIR/REPLACE and REPEAT System Pre-Check.

FM4029501203020X

Fig. 9 System Pre-Check Test Chart B (Part 2 of 2)

Fig. 10   System Pre-Check Test Chart C

TEST STEP		RESULT	▶	ACTION TO TAKE
C1	OBSERVE REAR ABS LIGHT FOR FLASH SEQUENCE			
	• Observe REAR ABS light and determine if the flashing is a diagnostic trouble code (one or more short pulses followed by one long pulse). • Is the flash sequence a diagnostic trouble code?	Yes	▶	INSPECT Circuits 571 (BK/O) and 483 (R) for short to ground. REPAIR circuit and REPLACE RABS KAM fuse. (See Owner's Manual.) REPEAT System Pre-Check.
		No	▶	GO to C2.
C2	INTERMITTENT POWER TO ANTI-LOCK ELECTRONIC CONTROL MODULE			
	• Remove the anti-lock electronic control module harness connector from the anti-lock electronic control module. • Set multimeter to 20VDC scale. • Turn the ignition to the ON position. • Shake the instrument panel harness while measuring battery voltage between Pin 1, Pin 9 and chassis ground. • Is voltage steady and greater than 9 volts?	Yes	▶	GO to C3.
		No	▶	REPAIR Circuit 601 (LB/PK). REPEAT System Pre-Check.
C3	DAMAGED ANTI-LOCK ELECTRONIC CONTROL MODULE GROUND			
	• Disconnect the battery ground cable. • Set the multimeter on the 200-ohm scale. • Shake the anti-lock electronic control module harness while reading the resistance between Pin 4 and chassis ground. • Is resistance steady and less than 1 ohm?	Yes	▶	REPLACE anti-lock electronic control module. RECONNECT the battery ground cable. REPEAT System Pre-Check.
		No	▶	REPAIR poor ground in Circuit 530 (BK/W). RECONNECT the battery ground cable. REPEAT System Pre-Check.

FM4029501204000X

Fig. 11   System Pre-Check Test Chart D

Test Step		Result	▶	Action to Take
D1	DETERMINE IF SYSTEM IS RABS I OR RABS II			
	• Determine if the ABS system is a RABS I or a RABS II system. • Is module RABS I?	Yes	▶	This shop manual does not cover RABS I anti-lock electronic control module.
		No	▶	GO to D2.
D2	CHECK FOR SHORTED BRAKE SWITCH			
	• Observe rear brake lights. • Are the brake lights on continuously?	Yes	▶	REPAIR shorted stoplight switch. REPEAT System Pre-Check.
		No	▶	GO to D3.
D3	CHECK FOR BURNED-OUT REAR BRAKE LIGHTS			
	• Press on brake pedal while observing rear brake lights. • Do the brake lights function?	Yes	▶	GO to D4.
		No	▶	REPAIR brake light system: Burned-out bulbs or open Circuit 511 (LG). REPEAT System Pre-Check.
D4	CHECK FOR LOSS OF BRAKE INPUT TO ANTI-LOCK ELECTRONIC CONTROL MODULE			
	• Remove the anti-lock electronic control module harness connector from the anti-lock electronic control module. Check for terminal back-out. • Set multimeter to 20 VDC range. • Press on brake pedal hard enough to turn on rear brake lights. • Measure voltage from RABS harness connector Pin 11 to chassis ground while brake pedal is pressed. • Are 9 volts or more present?	Yes	▶	LEAVE anti-lock electronic control module disconnected. GO to D5.
		No	▶	REPAIR open in Circuit 511 (LG). RECONNECT anti-lock electronic control module. REPEAT System Pre-Check.
D5	CHECK POWER TO THE ANTI-LOCK ELECTRONIC CONTROL MODULE			
	• Turn the ignition to the ON position. • Measure the voltage between RABS harness connector Pin 1 (or Pin 9) and chassis ground. • Are 9 volts or more present?	Yes	▶	LEAVE anti-lock electronic control module disconnected. GO to D6.
		No	▶	REPAIR Circuit 601 (LB/PK) or associated fuse. RECONNECT anti-lock electronic control module. REPEAT System Pre-Check.
D6	CHECK FOR SHORTS IN ANTI-LOCK ELECTRONIC CONTROL MODULE HARNESS CONNECTOR			
	• With same set up as in Step D5, observe yellow REAR ABS light. • Is the REAR ABS light on?	Yes	▶	CHECK for short to ground in Circuit 603 (DG). RECONNECT the anti-lock electronic control module. REPEAT System Pre-Check.
		No	▶	LEAVE anti-lock electronic control module disconnected. GO to D7.
D7	CHECK CIRCUIT 571 (BK/O) CONTINUITY			
	• Set the multimeter to the 200-ohm scale. • Disconnect the RABS diagnostic connector from its mating half (Circuits 571 [BK/O] and 483 [R]). • Measure resistance of Circuit 571 (BK/O) from diagnostic connector to module harness connector Pin 12. • Is the resistance less than 20 ohms?	Yes	▶	REPLACE anti-lock electronic control module.
		No	▶	REPAIR Circuit 571 (BK/O). RECONNECT RABS II anti-lock electronic control module. REPEAT System Pre-Check.

FM4029701205000X

Fig. 12   System Pre-Check Test Chart E

TEST STEP		RESULT	▶	ACTION TO TAKE
E1	CHECK IF BOTH WARNING LIGHTS ARE ON			
	• Disengage parking brake. • Key ON. • Do both the red BRAKE warning light and yellow RABS light come on?	Yes	▶	PULL code. DTC 4: GO to Test 4. DTC 12: GO to Test 12.
		No	▶	GO to E2.
E2	CHECK PARKING BRAKE SWITCH			
	• Key OFF. • Disconnect parking brake switch from harness connector. • Key ON. • Does the red BRAKE warning light remain on?	Yes	▶	Aerostar: GO to E3. Ranger: REPAIR ground short in Circuits 977 or 162. REPEAT System Pre-Check Pinpoint Test D.
		No	▶	REPAIR ground short in Circuits 977 or 162. REPEAT System Pre-Check.
E3	CHECK DELTA-P SWITCH (AEROSTAR ONLY)			
	• Key OFF. • Disconnect low vacuum switch from harness connector. • Key ON. • Does the red BRAKE warning light remain on?	Yes	▶	REPAIR ground short in Circuits 977 or 162. REPEAT System Pre-Check.
		No	▶	REPLACE Delta-P switch. REPEAT System Pre-Check.

FM4029501206000X

Fig. 13   Intermittent Wiring Diagnosis Procedure (Part 1 of 2)

TEST STEP		RESULT	▶	ACTION TO TAKE
ID1	CLEAR CODES, RECONNECT COMPONENTS			
	• Remove the pinout box. • Reinstall any components removed and reconnect all connections. • Clear all codes. • Key ON. • Does the REAR ABS warning light prove out?	Yes	▶	GO to ID3.
		No	▶	GO to ID2.

FM4029501207010X

Fig. 13   Intermittent Wiring Diagnosis Procedure (Part 2 of 2)

TEST STEP		RESULT	▶	ACTION TO TAKE
ID2	SERVICE CONNECTOR/TERMINAL FAULT			
	• Most likely problem is at one of the affected component connectors such that terminals unseat or back out upon installation. At each affected connection, look for: — Bent terminals. — Damaged connector terminal locks. — Damaged connector wedge. NOTE: If one of the above conditions is found, check the length of the affected circuit once the connection is remade. If the wire is too tight (short), damage is likely to recur once vehicle is given back to the customer. Service the wire as necessary to correct tight wire conditions. • Are any of the above conditions noted?	Yes	▶	SERVICE connector and terminal as necessary. GO to ID7.
		No	▶	GO to ID6.
ID3	WIGGLE TEST			
	• Leave key on. NOTE: Start at one component and wiggle connector by connector until the whole circuit has been tested. • Wiggle an affected circuit in one location only. • Observe REAR ABS warning light. • Is the REAR ABS warning light on?	Yes	▶	SERVICE the wire terminal or connector as identified in the wiggle test. GO to ID5.
		No	▶	GO to ID4.
ID4	VERIFY ALL CIRCUITS HAVE BEEN TESTED			
	• Have all affected circuits for the code being serviced been tested?	Yes	▶	Key off. GO to ID6.
		No	▶	GO to ID3 and CHECK next circuit.
ID5	RETRIEVE CODE			
	• Retrieve code. • Is this code different than the code being serviced?	Yes	▶	GO to the appropriate pinpoint test.
		No	▶	SERVICE the wire, terminal, or connector as necessary. GO to ID7.
ID6	VERIFY ALL APPROPRIATE DIAGNOSTIC PROCEDURES HAVE BEEN RUN			
	NOTE: All steps of the pinpoint test for the code being serviced must be completed. (If some tests were performed, then go to the pinpoint step last completed and continue.) • Has the System Pre-Check been run and a code been retrieved?	Yes	▶	RETURN to the pinpoint test and PROCEED.
		No	▶	RETURN to procedure(s) not yet performed and PROCEED.
ID7	VERIFY CONDITION RESOLVED			
	• Clear all codes. • Key OFF. • Retrieve code. • Is Code 16 set?	Yes	▶	STOP. Concern has been corrected.
		No	▶	If code being serviced still exists, GO to ID4. If different code is set, GO to appropriate pinpoint test for the code obtained.

FM4029501207020X

Fig. 14   Quick check

Item to Be Tested	Ignition Mode	Measure Between Pin Numbers	Tester Scale/Range	Specification	Pinpoint Test
Battery Power	OFF or ON	3 and Chassis Ground	DC Volts	10 V min	REFER to Symptom Chart
Ignition Feed	OFF	14 and Chassis Ground	DC Volts	0 V	GO to Pinpoint Test F.
	ON	14 and Chassis Ground	DC Volts	10 V min	GO to Pinpoint Test F.
Rear Anti-Lock Brake Sensor Resistance	OFF	9 and 21	kohms	0.8-2.5 kohms	GO to Pinpoint Test B.
Anti-Lock Brake Sensor Continuity to Ground Rear	OFF	9 and Chassis Ground	Continuity	No continuity	GO to Pinpoint Test B.
Anti-Lock Brake Sensor Voltage: Rotate wheel @ one revolution per second Rear	OFF	9 and 21	AC mVolts	100-3500 mV	GO to Pinpoint Test C.

FM4029901421000X

DIAGNOSTIC CHART INDEX

Test	Code	Description	Page No.	Fig. No.
F-SUPER DUTY				
A	C1202	Rear Dump Valve	5-160	15
	C1204	Rear Dump Valve	5-160	15
	C1206	Rear Isolation Dump Valve	5-160	15
	C1208	Rear Isolation Dump Valve	5-160	15
B	C1230	Rear Anti-Lock Brake Sensor, Electrical/Static	5-160	16
C	C1229	Rear Anti-Lock Brake Sensor Diagnosis	5-161	17
C	C1237	Rear Anti-Lock Brake Sensor Diagnosis	5-161	17
D	—	Soft Or Excessive Pedal Travel	5-162	18
E	C1095	Pump Motor Failure	5-163	19
E	C1096	Pump Motor Failure	5-163	19
F	C1113	Internal Power Relay Failure	5-163	20
F	C1115	Internal Power Relay Failure	5-163	20
F	C1185	Internal Power Relay Failure	5-163	20
G	—	No Communication w/ABS Control Module	5-163	21
H	C1169	Excessive Dump Time	5-164	22
J	C1184	Wheel Speed Sensor	5-164	23
J	C1222	ABS System Time-Out	5-164	23
F-150				
A	—	Yellow ABS Warning Indicator Is Always On	5-165	24
B	—	Yellow ABS Warning Indicator Self Check OK But Automatically Begins Flashing	5-165	25
C	—	Yellow ABS Warning Indicator Self-Check OK But No DTCS Are Retrieved When Diagnostics Are Started	5-166	26
D	2	Open RABS Isolation Solenoid Circuit	5-166	27
E	3	Open RABS Dump Solenoid Circuit	5-167	28
F	4	Grounded/Open RABS Valve Reset Switch Circuit	5-168	29
G	5	Excessive Dump Solenoid Activity	5-168	30
H	6	Erratic Rear Anti-Lock Brake Sensor Circuit	5-169	31
I	7	No Isolation Solenoid During Self-Check	5-171	32
J	8	No Dump Solenoid During Self-Check	5-171	33
K	9	Speed Sensor High Resistance/Open Circuit	5-172	34
L	10	Low Speed Sensor Resistance	5-172	35
M	11	Brake Pedal Position Switch Always Closed	5-173	36
N	12	Loss Of Hydraulic Brake Fluid During An Anti-Lock Stop	5-173	37
O	—	Verification Drive Test	5-174	38
P	—	Intermittent Problem Diagnosis	5-174	39

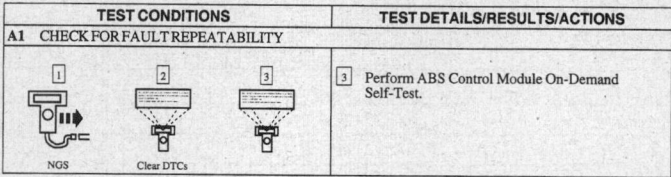

TEST CONDITIONS	TEST DETAILS/RESULTS/ACTIONS
A1 CHECK FOR FAULT REPEATABILITY	
① NGS ② Clear DTCs ③	③ Perform ABS Control Module On-Demand Self-Test.

FM4029901424010X

Fig. 15   Test A: Codes C1202, C1204, C1206, C1208: Isolation Valve, Dump Valve (Part 1 of 3). F-Super Duty

TEST CONDITIONS	TEST DETAILS/RESULTS/ACTIONS
A3 CHECK POWER DISTRIBUTION BOX FUSE 14 (60A)	
① Power Distribution Box Fuse 14 (60A)	• Is the fuse OK? → **Yes** REPAIR circuit 532 (O/Y). TEST the system for normal operation. → **No** REPLACE the fuse. TEST the system for normal operation. If the fuse fails again, CHECK for short to ground. REPAIR as necessary. TEST the system for normal operation.

FM4029901424030X

Fig. 15   Test A: Codes C1202, C1204, C1206, C1208: Isolation Valve, Dump Valve (Part 3 of 3). F-Super Duty

TEST CONDITIONS	TEST DETAILS/RESULTS/ACTIONS
B1 CHECK FOR FAULT REPEATABILITY	
① NGS ② Clear Continuous DTCs ④	③ Drive the vehicle a minimum speed of 6 km/h (10 mph). ④ Retrieve and document continuous DTCs. • Is DTC C1230 retrieved? → **Yes** GO to **B2**. → **No** If no DTC is retrieved, GO to **B6**. If a different DTC is retrieved, REFER to Diagnostic Trouble Code Interpretation

FM4029901425010X

Fig. 16   Test B: Code C1230: Rear Anti-Lock Brake Sensor, Electrical/Static (Part 1 of 4). F-Super Duty

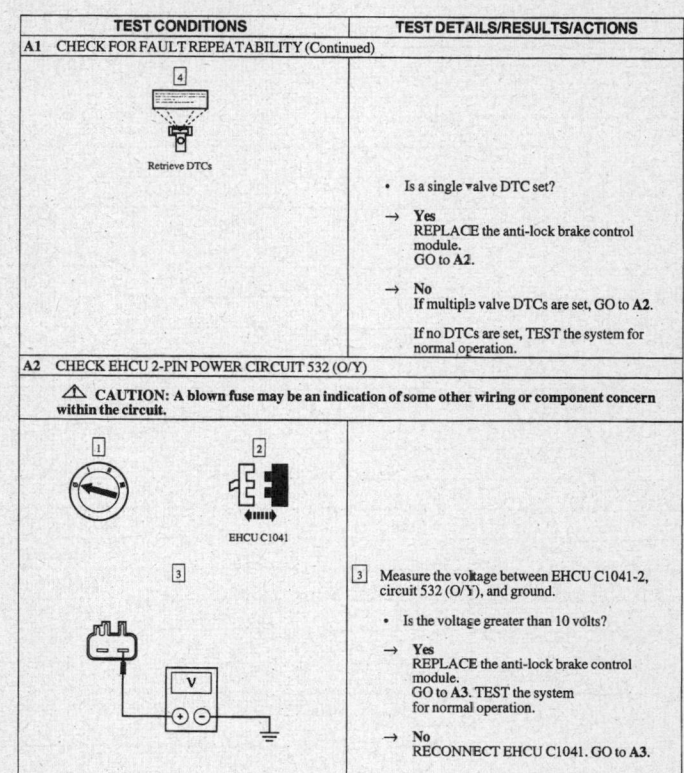

TEST CONDITIONS	TEST DETAILS/RESULTS/ACTIONS
A1 CHECK FOR FAULT REPEATABILITY (Continued)	
④ Retrieve DTCs	• Is a single valve DTC set? → **Yes** REPLACE the anti-lock brake control module. GO to **A2**. → **No** If multiple valve DTCs are set, GO to **A2**. If no DTCs are set, TEST the system for normal operation.
A2 CHECK EHCU 2-PIN POWER CIRCUIT 532 (O/Y)	

⚠ CAUTION: A blown fuse may be an indication of some other wiring or component concern within the circuit.

① ② EHCU C1041 ③ V	③ Measure the voltage between EHCU C1041-2, circuit 532 (O/Y), and ground. • Is the voltage greater than 10 volts? → **Yes** REPLACE the anti-lock brake control module. GO to **A3**. TEST the system for normal operation. → **No** RECONNECT EHCU C1041. GO to **A3**.

FM4029901424020X

Fig. 15   Test A: Codes C1202, C1204, C1206, C1208: Isolation Valve, Dump Valve (Part 2 of 3). F-Super Duty

TEST CONDITIONS	TEST DETAILS/RESULTS/ACTIONS
B2 CHECK ANTI-LOCK BRAKE SENSOR COIL RESISTANCE AT EHCU CONNECTOR	
① ③ Ω 9 21	② Install EEC-IV 60-Pin Breakout Box. ③ Measure the resistance between EEC-IV 60-Pin Breakout Box pin 9, circuit 523 (R/PK), and EEC-IV 60-Pin Breakout Box Pin 21, circuit 519 (LG/BK). • Is the resistance between 800 and 2500 ohms? → **Yes** GO to **B4**. → **No** GO to **B3**.
B3 DETERMINE LOCATION OF FAULT	
① Rear Anti-Lock Brake Sensor C404 ② Ω	② Measure the resistance between the two terminals of the rear anti-lock brake sensor C404. • Is the resistance between 900 and 1500 ohms? → **Yes** REPAIR circuit 519 (LG/BK) and circuit 523 (R/PK). TEST the system for normal operation. → **No** REPLACE the rear anti-lock brake sensor. TEST the system for normal operation.

FM4029901425020X

Fig. 16   Test B: Code C1230: Rear Anti-Lock Brake Sensor, Electrical/Static (Part 2 of 4). F-Super Duty

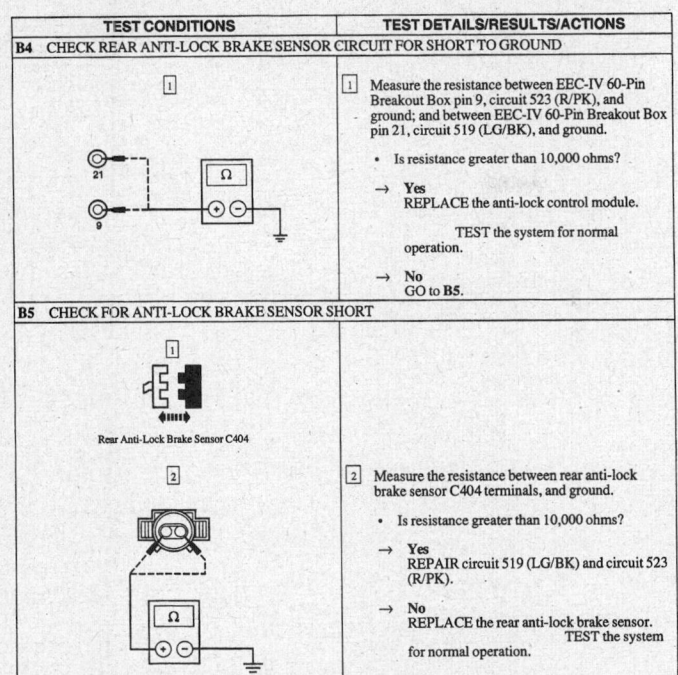

TEST CONDITIONS	TEST DETAILS/RESULTS/ACTIONS
B4 CHECK REAR ANTI-LOCK BRAKE SENSOR CIRCUIT FOR SHORT TO GROUND	
[1]	[1] Measure the resistance between EEC-IV 60-Pin Breakout Box pin 9, circuit 523 (R/PK), and ground; and between EEC-IV 60-Pin Breakout Box pin 21, circuit 519 (LG/BK), and ground. • Is resistance greater than 10,000 ohms? → **Yes** REPLACE the anti-lock control module. TEST the system for normal operation. → **No** GO to **B5**.
B5 CHECK FOR ANTI-LOCK BRAKE SENSOR SHORT	
[1] Rear Anti-Lock Brake Sensor C404 [2]	[2] Measure the resistance between rear anti-lock brake sensor C404 terminals, and ground. • Is resistance greater than 10,000 ohms? → **Yes** REPAIR circuit 519 (LG/BK) and circuit 523 (R/PK). → **No** REPLACE the rear anti-lock brake sensor. TEST the system for normal operation.

FM4029901425030X

Fig. 16 Test B: Code C1230: Rear Anti-Lock Brake Sensor, Electrical/Static (Part 3 of 4). F-Super Duty

TEST CONDITIONS	TEST DETAILS/RESULTS/ACTIONS
B6 TEST FOR INTERMITTENT ANTI-LOCK BRAKE SENSOR FAULT	
	[1] Perform the Sensor Failure test for the rear anti-lock brake sensor. • Did the rear anti-lock brake sensor pass? → **Yes** System is OK. → **No** REPLACE the rear anti-lock brake sensor. TEST the system for normal operation.

FM4029901425040X

Fig. 16 Test B: Code C1230: Rear Anti-Lock Brake Sensor, Electrical/Static (Part 4 of 4). F-Super Duty

TEST CONDITIONS	TEST DETAILS/RESULTS/ACTIONS
C1 RETRIEVE DTCs	
[1] NGS [2] Retrieve Continuous DTCs	• Is DTC C1230 retrieved? → **Yes** DIAGNOSE DTC C1230 first. IGNORE all other DTCs retrieved. → **No** GO to **C2**.

FM4029901426010X

Fig. 17 Test C: Codes C1229, C1237: Rear Anti-Lock Brake Sensor Diagnosis (Part 1 of 6). F-Super Duty

TEST CONDITIONS	TEST DETAILS/RESULTS/ACTIONS
C2 CHECK REAR BRAKE ANTI-LOCK SENSOR SIGNAL	
⚠ **WARNING: The electrical power to the air suspension system must be shut off prior to hoisting, jacking or towing an air suspension vehicle. This can be accomplished by turning off the air suspension switch located in the RH kick panel area. Failure to do so may result in unexpected inflation or deflation of the air springs which may result in shifting of the vehicle during these operations.**	
[1] [2] Anti-Lock Brake Control Module C1040 [4] [5]	[3] Raise and support the vehicle on a hoist so that all wheels are clear of the ground. [5] Turn the rear wheels at a minimum speed of 8 km/h (5 mph).

FM4029901426020X

Fig. 17 Test C: Codes C1229, C1237: Rear Anti-Lock Brake Sensor Diagnosis (Part 2 of 6). F-Super Duty

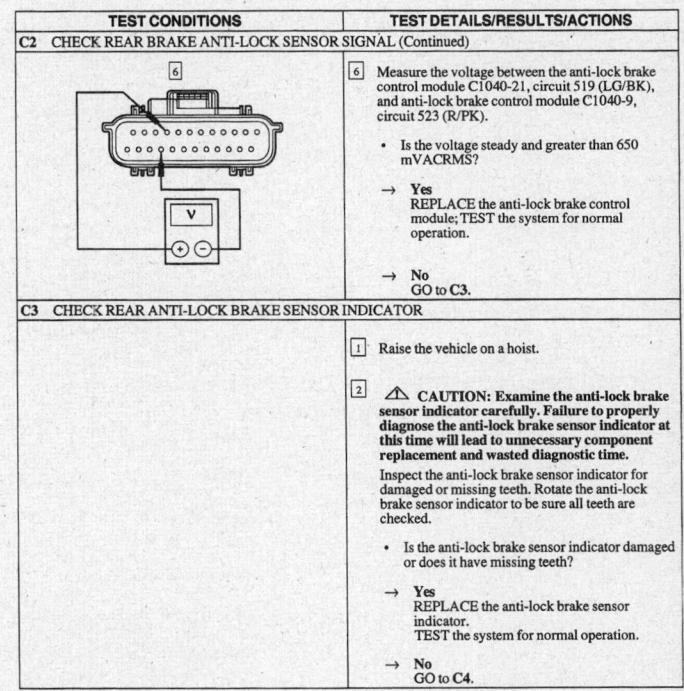

TEST CONDITIONS	TEST DETAILS/RESULTS/ACTIONS
C2 CHECK REAR BRAKE ANTI-LOCK SENSOR SIGNAL (Continued)	
[6]	[6] Measure the voltage between the anti-lock control module C1040-21, circuit 519 (LG/BK), and anti-lock brake control module C1040-9, circuit 523 (R/PK). • Is the voltage steady and greater than 650 mVACRMS? → **Yes** REPLACE the anti-lock brake control module; TEST the system for normal operation. → **No** GO to **C3**.
C3 CHECK REAR ANTI-LOCK BRAKE SENSOR INDICATOR	
	[1] Raise the vehicle on a hoist. [2] ⚠ **CAUTION: Examine the anti-lock brake sensor indicator carefully. Failure to properly diagnose the anti-lock brake sensor indicator at this time will lead to unnecessary component replacement and wasted diagnostic time.** Inspect the anti-lock brake sensor indicator for damaged or missing teeth. Rotate the anti-lock brake sensor indicator to be sure all teeth are checked. • Is the anti-lock brake sensor indicator damaged or does it have missing teeth? → **Yes** REPLACE the anti-lock brake sensor indicator. TEST the system for normal operation. → **No** GO to **C4**.

FM4029901426030X

Fig. 17 Test C: Codes C1229, C1237: Rear Anti-Lock Brake Sensor Diagnosis (Part 3 of 6). F-Super Duty

TEST CONDITIONS	TEST DETAILS/RESULTS/ACTIONS
C4 CHECK FOR LOOSE ANTI-LOCK BRAKE SENSOR MOUNTING	
	1. Wiggle the anti-lock brake sensor at the differential case (4204). • Is any looseness detected? → **Yes** CLEAN the anti-lock brake sensor mounting surface. VERIFY that the anti-lock brake sensor is seated properly. TIGHTEN anti-lock brake sensor bolt to specifications. TEST the system for normal operation. → **No** GO to C5.
C5 CHECK FOR ANTI-LOCK BRAKE SENSOR SHORT	
Rear Anti-Lock Brake Sensor C414	3. Measure the resistance between rear anti-lock brake sensor C414 terminals, and ground. • Is resistance greater than 10,000 ohms? → **Yes** GO to C6. → **No** REPLACE the anti-lock brake sensor. TEST the system for normal operation.
C6 CHECK CIRCUITS	
	1. Install EEC-IV 60-Pin Breakout Box.

FM4029901426040X

Fig. 17   Test C: Codes C1229, C1237: Rear Anti-Lock Brake Sensor Diagnosis (Part 4 of 6). F-Super Duty

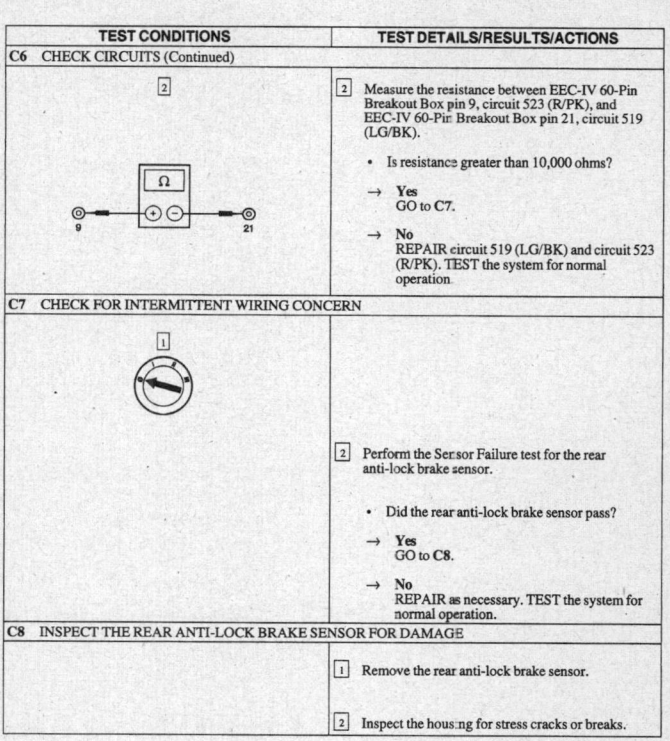

TEST CONDITIONS	TEST DETAILS/RESULTS/ACTIONS
C6 CHECK CIRCUITS (Continued)	
	2. Measure the resistance between EEC-IV 60-Pin Breakout Box pin 9, circuit 523 (R/PK), and EEC-IV 60-Pin Breakout Box pin 21, circuit 519 (LG/BK). • Is resistance greater than 10,000 ohms? → **Yes** GO to C7. → **No** REPAIR circuit 519 (LG/BK) and circuit 523 (R/PK). TEST the system for normal operation.
C7 CHECK FOR INTERMITTENT WIRING CONCERN	
	2. Perform the Sensor Failure test for the rear anti-lock brake sensor. • Did the rear anti-lock brake sensor pass? → **Yes** GO to C8. → **No** REPAIR as necessary. TEST the system for normal operation.
C8 INSPECT THE REAR ANTI-LOCK BRAKE SENSOR FOR DAMAGE	
	1. Remove the rear anti-lock brake sensor. 2. Inspect the housing for stress cracks or breaks.

FM4029901426050X

Fig. 17   Test C: Codes C1229, C1237: Rear Anti-Lock Brake Sensor Diagnosis (Part 5 of 6). F-Super Duty

TEST CONDITIONS	TEST DETAILS/RESULTS/ACTIONS
C8 INSPECT THE REAR ANTI-LOCK BRAKE SENSOR FOR DAMAGE (Continued)	
	3. Inspect the anti-lock brake sensor C404 for evidence of water entry, pin corrosion, or excessive debris. • Are any of the above conditions evident? → **Yes** REPAIR as necessary. TEST the system for normal operation. → **No** REPLACE the anti-lock brake control module; TEST the system for normal operation.

FM4029901426060X

Fig. 17   Test C: Codes C1229, C1237: Rear Anti-Lock Brake Sensor Diagnosis (Part 6 of 6). F-Super Duty

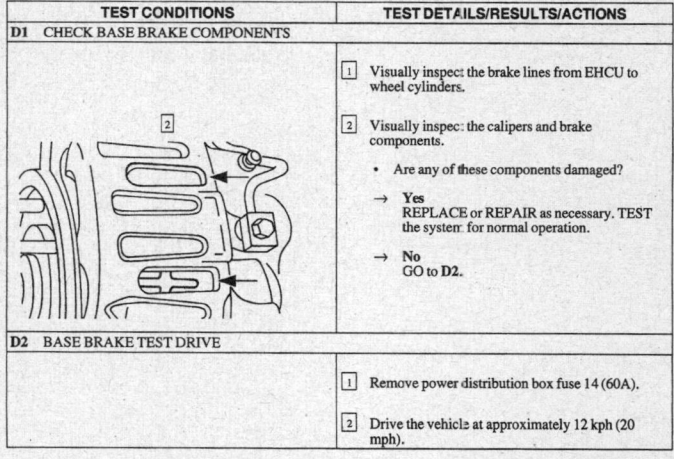

TEST CONDITIONS	TEST DETAILS/RESULTS/ACTIONS
D1 CHECK BASE BRAKE COMPONENTS	
	1. Visually inspect the brake lines from EHCU to wheel cylinders. 2. Visually inspect the calipers and brake components. • Are any of these components damaged? → **Yes** REPLACE or REPAIR as necessary. TEST the system for normal operation. → **No** GO to D2.
D2 BASE BRAKE TEST DRIVE	
	1. Remove power distribution box fuse 14 (60A). 2. Drive the vehicle at approximately 12 kph (20 mph).

FM4029901427010X

Fig. 18   Test D: Soft Or Excessive Pedal Travel (Part 1 of 2). F-Super Duty

TEST CONDITIONS	TEST DETAILS/RESULTS/ACTIONS
D2 BASE BRAKE TEST DRIVE (Continued)	
	3. Perform a light to medium (normal) traffic stop. • Does one wheel lock consistently? → **Yes** GO to Symptom Chart. → **No** GO to Inspection and Verification — System Precheck.

FM4029901427020X

Fig. 18   Test D: Soft Or Excessive Pedal Travel (Part 2 of 2). F-Super Duty

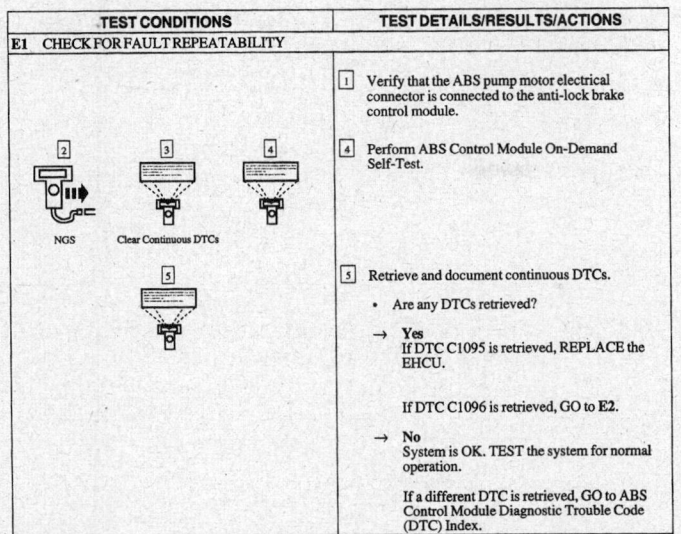

TEST CONDITIONS | **TEST DETAILS/RESULTS/ACTIONS**

E1 CHECK FOR FAULT REPEATABILITY

1. Verify that the ABS pump motor electrical connector is connected to the anti-lock brake control module.

4. Perform ABS Control Module On-Demand Self-Test.

5. Retrieve and document continuous DTCs.

- Are any DTCs retrieved?
  → Yes
    If DTC C1095 is retrieved, REPLACE the EHCU.

    If DTC C1096 is retrieved, GO to E2.
  → No
    System is OK. TEST the system for normal operation.

    If a different DTC is retrieved, GO to ABS Control Module Diagnostic Trouble Code (DTC) Index.

FM4029901428010X

Fig. 19   Test E: Codes C1095, C1096: Pump Motor Failure (Part 1 of 2). F-Super Duty

TEST CONDITIONS | **TEST DETAILS/RESULTS/ACTIONS**

F1 CHECK FOR FAULT REPEATABILITY

3. Perform ABS Control Module On-Demand Self-Test.

FM4029901429010X

Fig. 20   Test F: Codes C1113, C1115, C1185: Internal Power Relay Failure (Part 1 of 3). F-Super Duty

TEST CONDITIONS | **TEST DETAILS/RESULTS/ACTIONS**

F1 CHECK FOR FAULT REPEATABILITY (Continued)

- Are any DTCs retrieved?
  → Yes
    If DTC C1113 or C1115 is retrieved, REPLACE the anti-lock brake control module. TEST the system for normal operation.
  → No
    If DTC C1185 is retrieved, GO to F2.

    If no DTCs are retrieved, TEST the system for normal operation.

F2 ELECTRICAL PRECHECKS

Power Distribution Box Fuse 14 (60A)

- Is the fuse OK?
  → Yes
    GO to F3.
  → No
    REPLACE the fuse. TEST the system for normal operation. If the fuse fails again, CHECK for short to ground. REPAIR as necessary. TEST the system for normal operation.

F3 CHECK POWER TO EHCU

1. Reinstall power distribution box fuse 14 (60A).

FM4029901429020X

Fig. 20   Test F: Codes C1113, C1115, C1185: Internal Power Relay Failure (Part 2 of 3). F-Super Duty

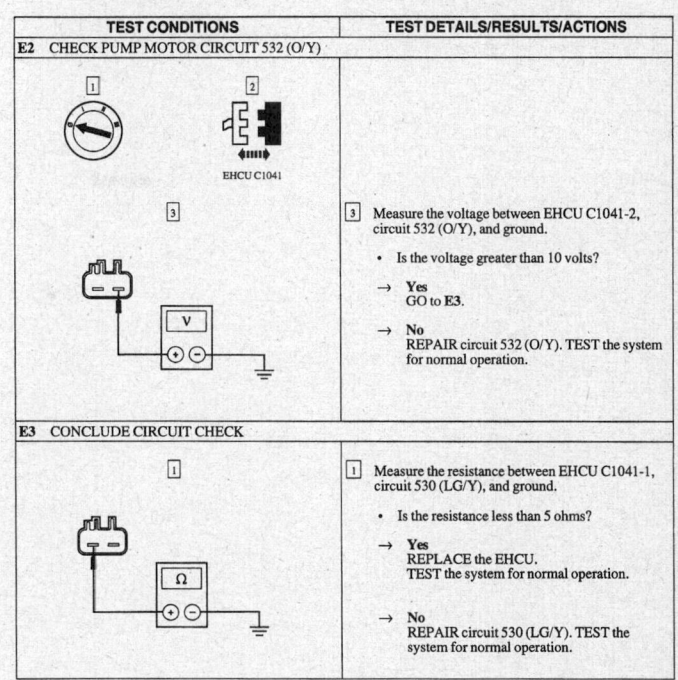

TEST CONDITIONS | **TEST DETAILS/RESULTS/ACTIONS**

E2 CHECK PUMP MOTOR CIRCUIT 532 (O/Y)

EHCU C1041

3. Measure the voltage between EHCU C1041-2, circuit 532 (O/Y), and ground.

- Is the voltage greater than 10 volts?
  → Yes
    GO to E3.
  → No
    REPAIR circuit 532 (O/Y). TEST the system for normal operation.

E3 CONCLUDE CIRCUIT CHECK

1. Measure the resistance between EHCU C1041-1, circuit 530 (LG/Y), and ground.

- Is the resistance less than 5 ohms?
  → Yes
    REPLACE the EHCU. TEST the system for normal operation.
  → No
    REPAIR circuit 530 (LG/Y). TEST the system for normal operation.

FM4029901428020X

Fig. 19   Test E: Codes C1095, C1096: Pump Motor Failure (Part 2 of 2). F-Super Duty

TEST CONDITIONS | **TEST DETAILS/RESULTS/ACTIONS**

F3 CHECK POWER TO EHCU (Continued)

EHCU C1041

3. Measure the voltage between EHCU C1041-2, circuit 532 (O/Y), and ground.

- Is voltage greater than 10 volts?
  → Yes
    REPLACE the anti-lock brake control module. TEST the system for normal operation.
  → No
    REPAIR circuit 532 (O/Y). TEST the system for normal operation.

FM4029901429030X

Fig. 20   Test F: Codes C1113, C1115, C1185: Internal Power Relay Failure (Part 3 of 3). F-Super Duty

TEST CONDITIONS | **TEST DETAILS/RESULTS/ACTIONS**

G1 VERIFY THE CONNECTION BETWEEN NGS TESTER AND THE DLC II CONNECTOR

2. Reconnect NGS Tester to the DLC connector.

3. Retrieve and document continuous DTCs.

- Are DTCs obtained?
  → Yes
    Refer to Diagnostic Trouble Code Interpretation
  → No
    GO to G2.

FM4029901430010X

Fig. 21   Test G: No Communication w/ABS Control Module (Part 1 of 3). F-Super Duty

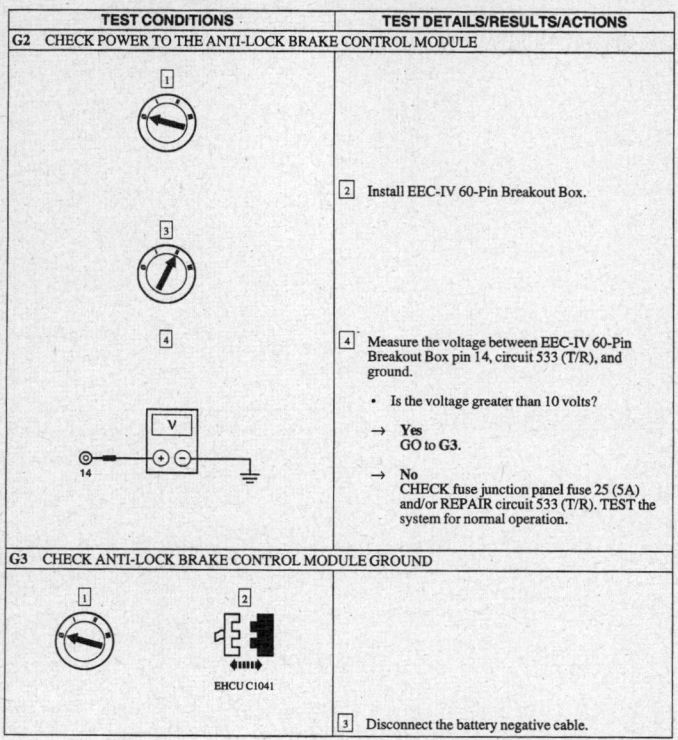

TEST CONDITIONS	TEST DETAILS/RESULTS/ACTIONS
G2 CHECK POWER TO THE ANTI-LOCK BRAKE CONTROL MODULE	
	2 Install EEC-IV 60-Pin Breakout Box.
	4 Measure the voltage between EEC-IV 60-Pin Breakout Box pin 14, circuit 533 (T/R), and ground.
	• Is the voltage greater than 10 volts?
	→ Yes GO to G3.
	→ No CHECK fuse junction panel fuse 25 (5A) and/or REPAIR circuit 533 (T/R). TEST the system for normal operation.
G3 CHECK ANTI-LOCK BRAKE CONTROL MODULE GROUND	
EHCU C1041	3 Disconnect the battery negative cable.

FM4029901430020X

Fig. 21   Test G: No Communication w/ABS Control Module (Part 2 of 3). F-Super Duty

TEST CONDITIONS	TEST DETAILS/RESULTS/ACTIONS
H1 CHECK FOR FAULT REPEATABILITY	
NGS Clear Continuous DTCs	3 Retrieve and document continuous DTCs.
	• Is DTC C1169 retrieved?
	→ Yes REPLACE the EHCU. TEST the system for normal operation.
	→ No GO to H2.
H2 LOW SPEED ABS STOP	
	1 Drive the vehicle at approximately 6 km/h (10 mph).
	2 NOTE: Wetting down the area where the stop is to be performed will aid in this test.
	NOTE: Momentary lock-up is permissible. An assistant should be used to monitor the wheels during ABS stop.
	Apply the brakes hard enough to lock all four wheels.
	• Does one wheel lock consistently?
	→ Yes GO to Symptom Chart.
	→ No System is OK. TEST the system for normal operation.

FM4029901431000X

Fig. 22   Test H: Code C1169: Excessive Dump Time. F-Super Duty

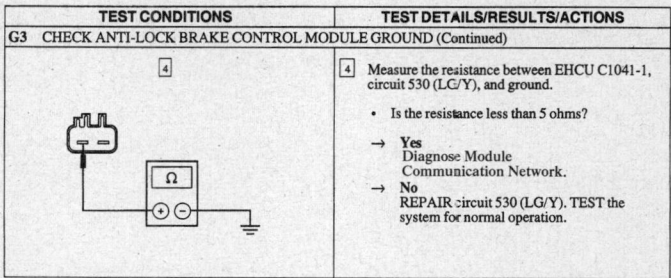

TEST CONDITIONS	TEST DETAILS/RESULTS/ACTIONS
G3 CHECK ANTI-LOCK BRAKE CONTROL MODULE GROUND (Continued)	
	4 Measure the resistance between EHCU C1041-1, circuit 530 (LG/Y), and ground.
	• Is the resistance less than 5 ohms?
	→ Yes Diagnose Module Communication Network.
	→ No REPAIR circuit 530 (LG/Y). TEST the system for normal operation.

FM4029901430030X

Fig. 21   Test G: No Communication w/ABS Control Module (Part 3 of 3). F-Super Duty

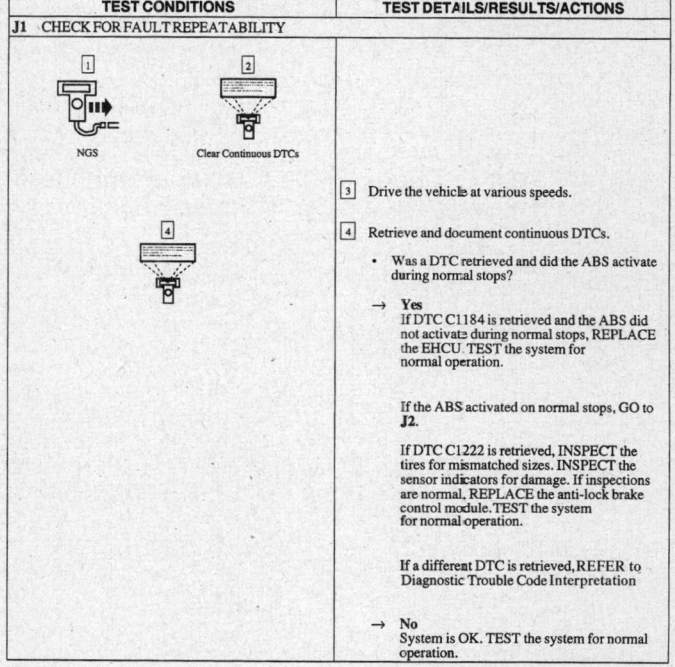

TEST CONDITIONS	TEST DETAILS/RESULTS/ACTIONS
J1 CHECK FOR FAULT REPEATABILITY	
NGS Clear Continuous DTCs	3 Drive the vehicle at various speeds.
	4 Retrieve and document continuous DTCs.
	• Was a DTC retrieved and did the ABS activate during normal stops?
	→ Yes If DTC C1184 is retrieved and the ABS did not activate during normal stops, REPLACE the EHCU. TEST the system for normal operation.
	If the ABS activated on normal stops, GO to J2.
	If DTC C1222 is retrieved, INSPECT the tires for mismatched sizes. INSPECT the sensor indicators for damage. If inspections are normal, REPLACE the anti-lock brake control module. TEST the system for normal operation.
	If a different DTC is retrieved, REFER to Diagnostic Trouble Code Interpretation
	→ No System is OK. TEST the system for normal operation.

FM4029901432010X

Fig. 23   Test J: Code C1184, C1222: ABS System Time-Out/Wheel Speed Sensor (Part 1 of 2). F-Super Duty

TEST CONDITIONS	TEST DETAILS/RESULTS/ACTIONS
J2 CHECK FOR AN ERRATIC WHEEL SPEED SIGNAL	
Clear Continuous DTCs	2 NOTE: When using NGS Tester to monitor the wheel speed signals, monitor one wheel at a time. The information is recorded faster and the likelihood of diagnosing the faulty signal is greater.
	Monitor anti-lock brake control module PID R__WSPD while driving at various speeds.
	• Does the wheel speed signal drop out while driving or braking?
	→ Yes GO to Pinpoint Test C.
	→ No REPEAT the monitoring of anti-lock brake control module PID R__WSPD. (Intermittent signals may not be recorded the first time.) INSPECT the sensor indicator and sensor wiring for damage. If damage is found, REPAIR as necessary. If no damage is found, Inspect system for faulty wiring. TEST the system for normal operation.

FM4029901432020X

Fig. 23   Test J: Code C1184, C1222: ABS System Time-Out/Wheel Speed Sensor (Part 2 of 2). F-Super Duty

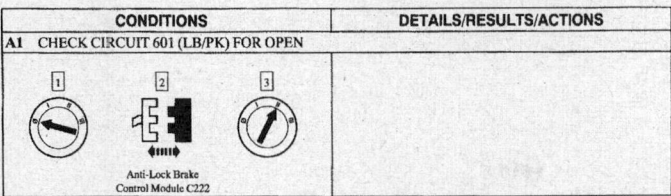

CONDITIONS	DETAILS/RESULTS/ACTIONS
A1 CHECK CIRCUIT 601 (LB/PK) FOR OPEN	

Anti-Lock Brake
Control Module C222

FM4020001677010X

Fig. 24 Test A: Yellow ABS Warning Indicator Is Always On (Part 1 of 3). F-150

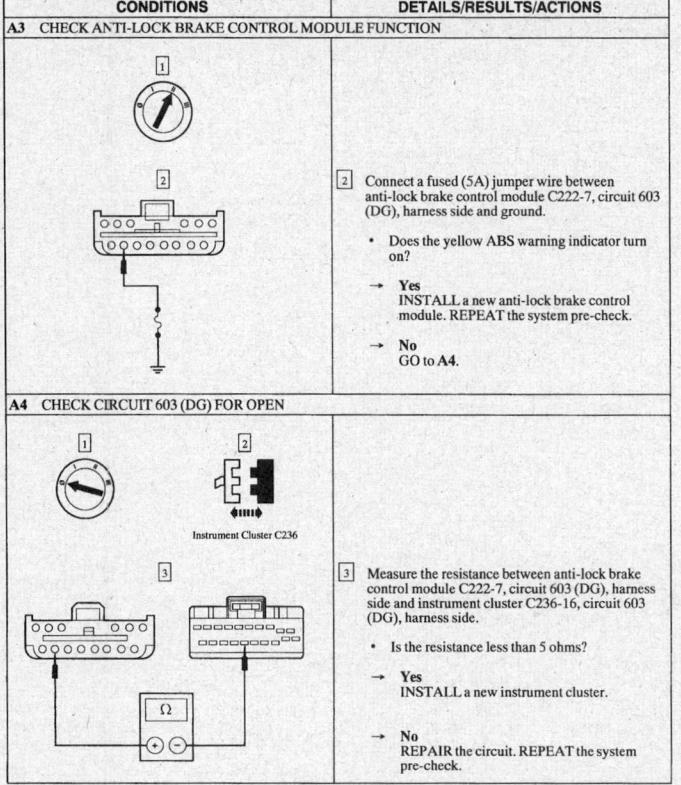

CONDITIONS	DETAILS/RESULTS/ACTIONS
A3 CHECK ANTI-LOCK BRAKE CONTROL MODULE FUNCTION	

2 Connect a fused (5A) jumper wire between anti-lock brake control module C222-7, circuit 603 (DG), harness side and ground.

* Does the yellow ABS warning indicator turn on?

→ **Yes**
INSTALL a new anti-lock brake control module. REPEAT the system pre-check.

→ **No**
GO to A4.

| A4 CHECK CIRCUIT 603 (DG) FOR OPEN | |

Instrument Cluster C236

3 Measure the resistance between anti-lock brake control module C222-7, circuit 603 (DG), harness side and instrument cluster C236-16, circuit 603 (DG), harness side.

* Is the resistance less than 5 ohms?

→ **Yes**
INSTALL a new instrument cluster.

→ **No**
REPAIR the circuit. REPEAT the system pre-check.

FM4020001677030X

Fig. 24 Test A: Yellow ABS Warning Indicator Is Always On (Part 3 of 3). F-150

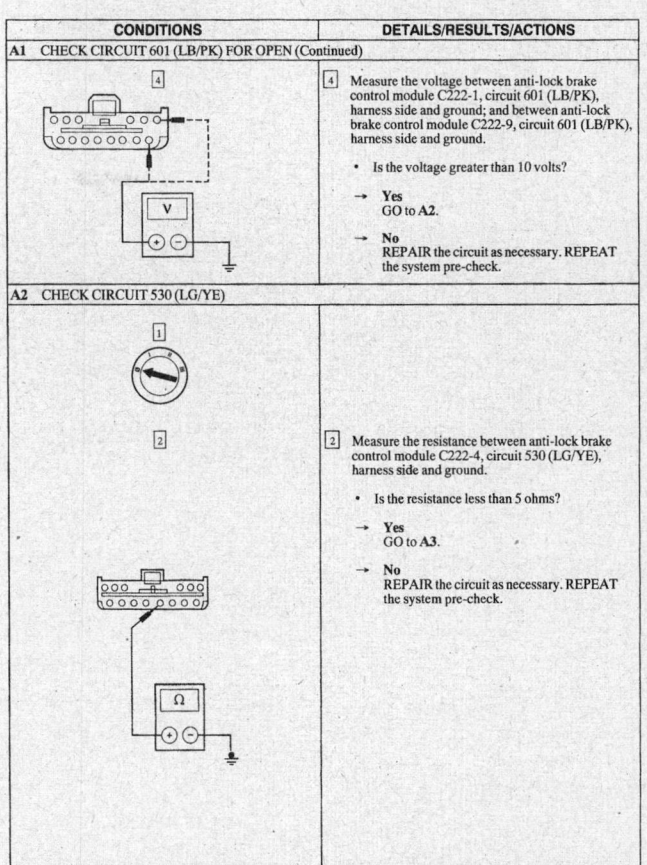

CONDITIONS	DETAILS/RESULTS/ACTIONS
A1 CHECK CIRCUIT 601 (LB/PK) FOR OPEN (Continued)	

4 Measure the voltage between anti-lock brake control module C222-1, circuit 601 (LB/PK), harness side and ground; and between anti-lock brake control module C222-9, circuit 601 (LB/PK), harness side and ground.

* Is the voltage greater than 10 volts?

→ **Yes**
GO to A2.

→ **No**
REPAIR the circuit as necessary. REPEAT the system pre-check.

| A2 CHECK CIRCUIT 530 (LG/YE) | |

2 Measure the resistance between anti-lock brake control module C222-4, circuit 530 (LG/YE), harness side and ground.

* Is the resistance less than 5 ohms?

→ **Yes**
GO to A3.

→ **No**
REPAIR the circuit as necessary. REPEAT the system pre-check.

FM4020001677020X

Fig. 24 Test A: Yellow ABS Warning Indicator Is Always On (Part 2 of 3). F-150

CONDITIONS	DETAILS/RESULTS/ACTIONS
B1 OBSERVE YELLOW ABS WARNING INDICATOR LAMP FOR FLASH SEQUENCE	

NOTE: A diagnostic trouble code (DTC) consists of one or more short pulses and then one long pulse.

2 Observe the yellow ABS warning indicator lamp.

* Is the flash sequence a DTC?

→ **Yes**
RECORD DTC number. GO to B2.

→ **No**
GO to B4.

| B2 CHECK VOLTAGE TO ANTI-LOCK BRAKE CONTROL MODULE | |

Anti-Lock Brake
Control Module C222

4 Measure the voltage between anti-lock brake control module C222-12, circuit 571 (BK/OG), harness side and ground, while shaking the wiring harness.

* Is the voltage greater than 10 volts?

→ **Yes**
GO to B3.

→ **No**
REPAIR circuit 571 (BK/OG) and circuit 483 (RD) as necessary. GO to the Symptom Chart for diagnosis of the DTC recorded in Step B1.

FM4020001678010X

Fig. 25 Test B: Yellow ABS Warning Indicator Self Check OK But Automatically Begins Flashing (Part 1 of 3). F-150

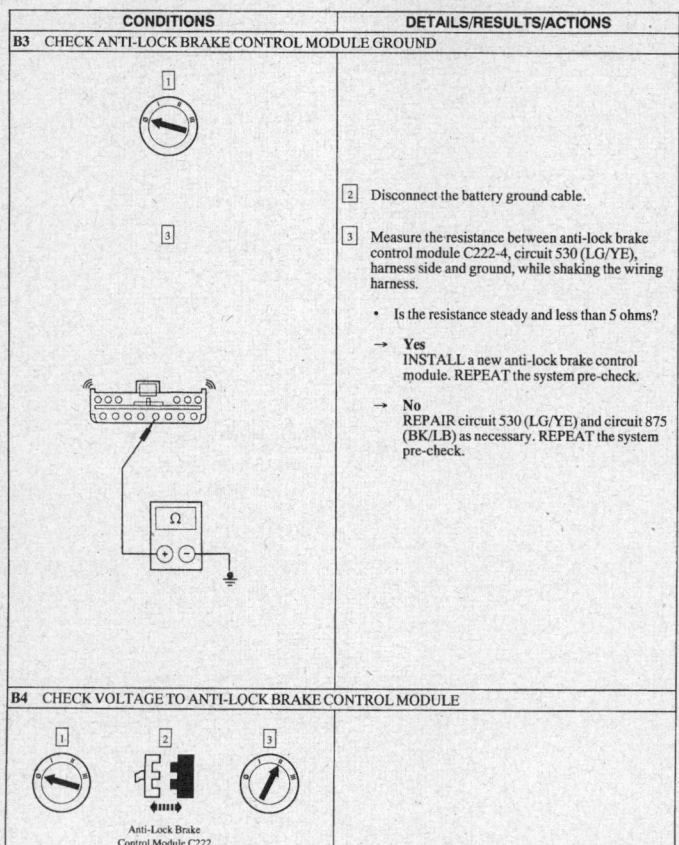

CONDITIONS	DETAILS/RESULTS/ACTIONS
B3 CHECK ANTI-LOCK BRAKE CONTROL MODULE GROUND	
1	2 Disconnect the battery ground cable.
3	3 Measure the resistance between anti-lock brake control module C222-4, circuit 530 (LG/YE), harness side and ground, while shaking the wiring harness.
	• Is the resistance steady and less than 5 ohms?
	→ **Yes** INSTALL a new anti-lock brake control module. REPEAT the system pre-check.
	→ **No** REPAIR circuit 530 (LG/YE) and circuit 875 (BK/LB) as necessary. REPEAT the system pre-check.
B4 CHECK VOLTAGE TO ANTI-LOCK BRAKE CONTROL MODULE	
1 2 3 Anti-Lock Brake Control Module C222	

FM4020001678020X

Fig. 25   Test B: Yellow ABS Warning Indicator Self Check OK But Automatically Begins Flashing (Part 2 of 3). F-150

CONDITIONS	DETAILS/RESULTS/ACTIONS
C1 CHECK POWER FEED TO KEEP ALIVE MEMORY (KAM)	
1 RABS Data Link Connector	2 Measure the voltage between wiring connector C207, circuit 483 (RD) and ground.
	• Is the voltage greater than 10 volts?
	→ **Yes** GO to C2.
	→ **No** REPAIR the open in circuit 483 (RD). REPEAT the system pre-check.
C2 CHECK CIRCUIT 517 (BK/OG) FOR AN OPEN	
1 2 Anti-Lock Brake Control Module C222	

FM4020001679010X

Fig. 26   Test C: Yellow ABS Warning Indicator Self-Check OK But No DTCS Are Retrieved When Diagnostics Are Started (Part 1 of 2). F-150

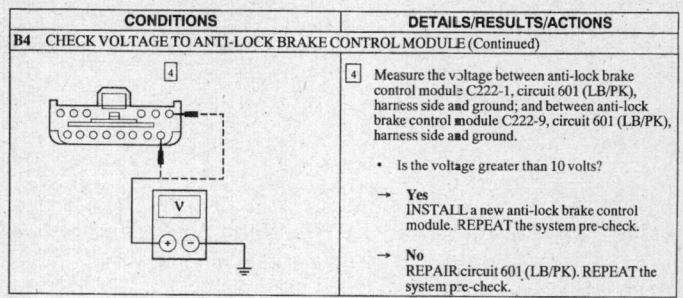

CONDITIONS	DETAILS/RESULTS/ACTIONS
B4 CHECK VOLTAGE TO ANTI-LOCK BRAKE CONTROL MODULE (Continued)	
4	4 Measure the voltage between anti-lock brake control module C222-1, circuit 601 (LB/PK), harness side and ground; and between anti-lock brake control module C222-9, circuit 601 (LB/PK), harness side and ground.
	• Is the voltage greater than 10 volts?
	→ **Yes** INSTALL a new anti-lock brake control module. REPEAT the system pre-check.
	→ **No** REPAIR circuit 601 (LB/PK). REPEAT the system pre-check.

FM4020001678030X

Fig. 25   Test B: Yellow ABS Warning Indicator Self Check OK But Automatically Begins Flashing (Part 3 of 3). F-150

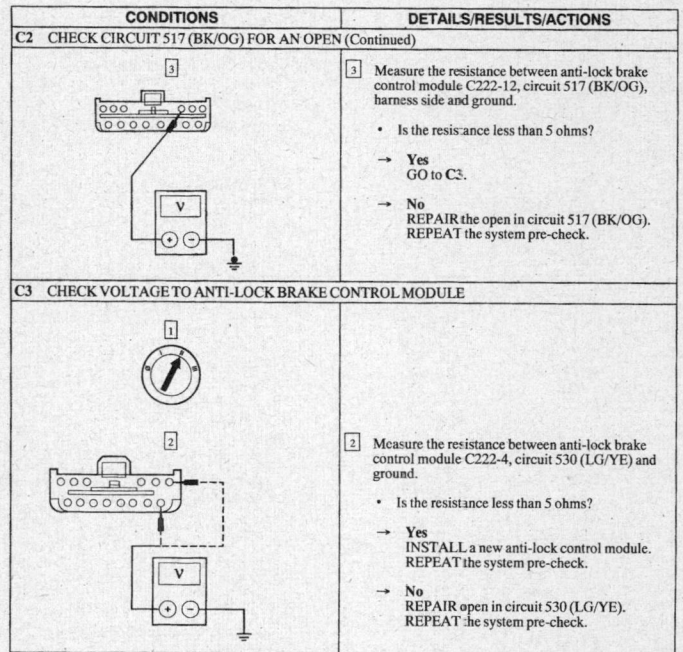

CONDITIONS	DETAILS/RESULTS/ACTIONS
C2 CHECK CIRCUIT 517 (BK/OG) FOR AN OPEN (Continued)	
3	3 Measure the resistance between anti-lock brake control module C222-12, circuit 517 (BK/OG), harness side and ground.
	• Is the resistance less than 5 ohms?
	→ **Yes** GO to C3.
	→ **No** REPAIR the open in circuit 517 (BK/OG). REPEAT the system pre-check.
C3 CHECK VOLTAGE TO ANTI-LOCK BRAKE CONTROL MODULE	
1	
2	2 Measure the resistance between anti-lock brake control module C222-4, circuit 530 (LG/YE) and ground.
	• Is the resistance less than 5 ohms?
	→ **Yes** INSTALL a new anti-lock control module. REPEAT the system pre-check.
	→ **No** REPAIR open in circuit 530 (LG/YE). REPEAT the system pre-check.

FM4020001679020X

Fig. 26   Test C: Yellow ABS Warning Indicator Self-Check OK But No DTCS Are Retrieved When Diagnostics Are Started (Part 2 of 2). F-150

CONDITIONS	DETAILS/RESULTS/ACTIONS
D1 DETERMINE IF FAULT IS HARD OR INTERMITTENT	
1 2 3 4 Diagnostic Test Connector C207 Diagnostic Test Connector C207	• Does the yellow ABS warning indicator illuminate?
	→ **Yes** GO to D2.
	→ **No** Intermittent fault. GO to Pinpoint Test P.
D2 CHECK CIRCUIT 599 (PK/LG) FOR AN OPEN	
1 2 3 RABS Valve C152 Anti-Lock Brake Control Module C222	

FM4020001680010X

Fig. 27   Test D : Code 2: Open RABS Isolation Solenoid Circuit (Part 1 of 3). F-150

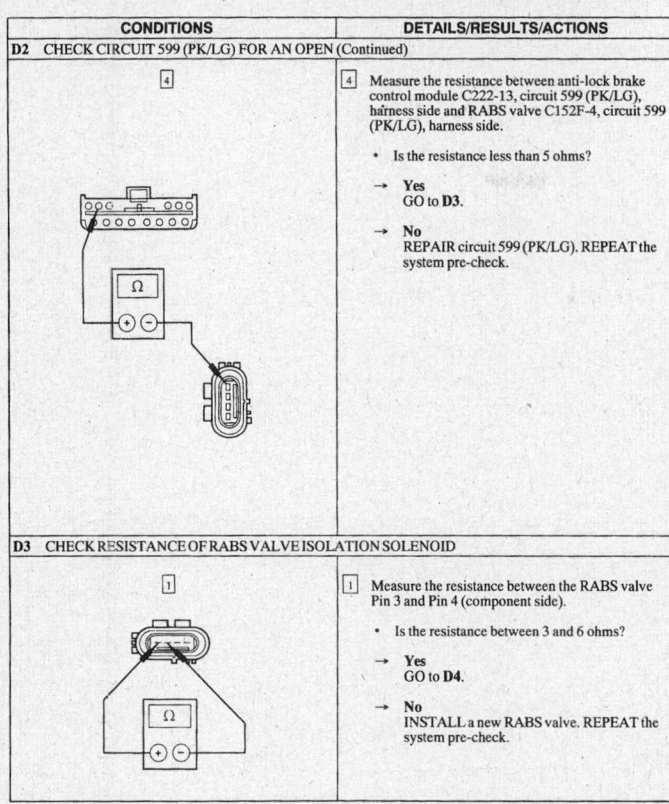

CONDITIONS	DETAILS/RESULTS/ACTIONS
D2 CHECK CIRCUIT 599 (PK/LG) FOR AN OPEN (Continued)	

4   Measure the resistance between anti-lock brake control module C222-13, circuit 599 (PK/LG), harness side and RABS valve C152F-4, circuit 599 (PK/LG), harness side.

- Is the resistance less than 5 ohms?

→ **Yes**
    GO to **D3**.

→ **No**
    REPAIR circuit 599 (PK/LG). REPEAT the system pre-check.

| D3   CHECK RESISTANCE OF RABS VALVE ISOLATION SOLENOID | |

1   Measure the resistance between the RABS valve Pin 3 and Pin 4 (component side).

- Is the resistance between 3 and 6 ohms?

→ **Yes**
    GO to **D4**.

→ **No**
    INSTALL a new RABS valve. REPEAT the system pre-check.

FM4020001680020X

Fig. 27   Test D: Code 2: Open RABS Isolation Solenoid Circuit (Part 2 of 3). F-150

CONDITIONS	DETAILS/RESULTS/ACTIONS
E1 DETERMINE IF FAULT IS HARD OR INTERMITTENT	

Diagnostic Test Connector C207   Diagnostic Test Connector C207

- Does the yellow ABS warning indicator lamp illuminate?

→ **Yes**
    Hard fault. GO to **E2**.

→ **No**
    Intermittent fault. GO to Pinpoint Test P.

| E2   CHECK CIRCUIT 664 (YE/LG) FOR AN OPEN | |

RABS Valve C152   Anti-Lock Brake Control Module C222

FM4020001681010X

Fig. 28   Test E: Code 3: Open RABS Dump Solenoid Circuit (Part 1 of 2). F-150

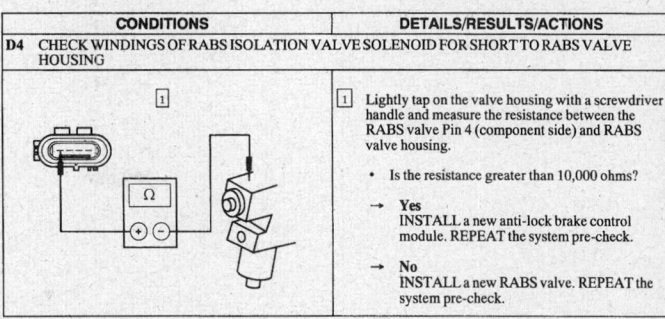

CONDITIONS	DETAILS/RESULTS/ACTIONS
D4 CHECK WINDINGS OF RABS ISOLATION VALVE SOLENOID FOR SHORT TO RABS VALVE HOUSING	

1   Lightly tap on the valve housing with a screwdriver handle and measure the resistance between the RABS valve Pin 4 (component side) and RABS valve housing.

- Is the resistance greater than 10,000 ohms?

→ **Yes**
    INSTALL a new anti-lock brake control module. REPEAT the system pre-check.

→ **No**
    INSTALL a new RABS valve. REPEAT the system pre-check.

FM4020001680030X

Fig. 27   Test D: Code 2: Open RABS Isolation Solenoid Circuit (Part 3 of 3). F-150

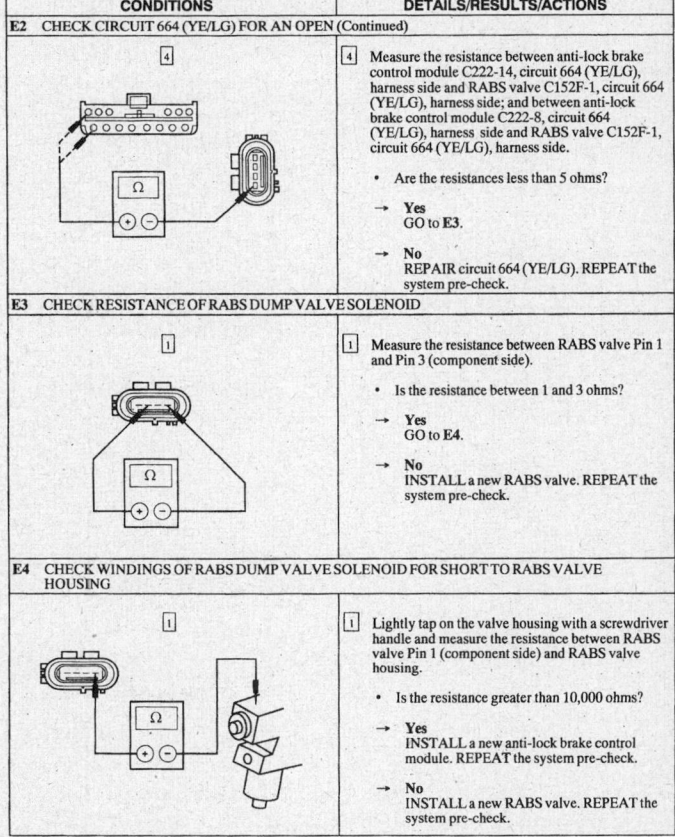

CONDITIONS	DETAILS/RESULTS/ACTIONS
E2 CHECK CIRCUIT 664 (YE/LG) FOR AN OPEN (Continued)	

4   Measure the resistance between anti-lock brake control module C222-14, circuit 664 (YE/LG), harness side and RABS valve C152F-1, circuit 664 (YE/LG), harness side; and between anti-lock brake control module C222-8, circuit 664 (YE/LG), harness side and RABS valve C152F-1, circuit 664 (YE/LG), harness side.

- Are the resistances less than 5 ohms?

→ **Yes**
    GO to **E3**.

→ **No**
    REPAIR circuit 664 (YE/LG). REPEAT the system pre-check.

| E3   CHECK RESISTANCE OF RABS DUMP VALVE SOLENOID | |

1   Measure the resistance between RABS valve Pin 1 and Pin 3 (component side).

- Is the resistance between 1 and 3 ohms?

→ **Yes**
    GO to **E4**.

→ **No**
    INSTALL a new RABS valve. REPEAT the system pre-check.

| E4   CHECK WINDINGS OF RABS DUMP VALVE SOLENOID FOR SHORT TO RABS VALVE HOUSING | |

1   Lightly tap on the valve housing with a screwdriver handle and measure the resistance between RABS valve Pin 1 (component side) and RABS valve housing.

- Is the resistance greater than 10,000 ohms?

→ **Yes**
    INSTALL a new anti-lock brake control module. REPEAT the system pre-check.

→ **No**
    INSTALL a new RABS valve. REPEAT the system pre-check.

FM4020001681020X

Fig. 28   Test E: Code 3: Open RABS Dump Solenoid Circuit (Part 2 of 2). F-150

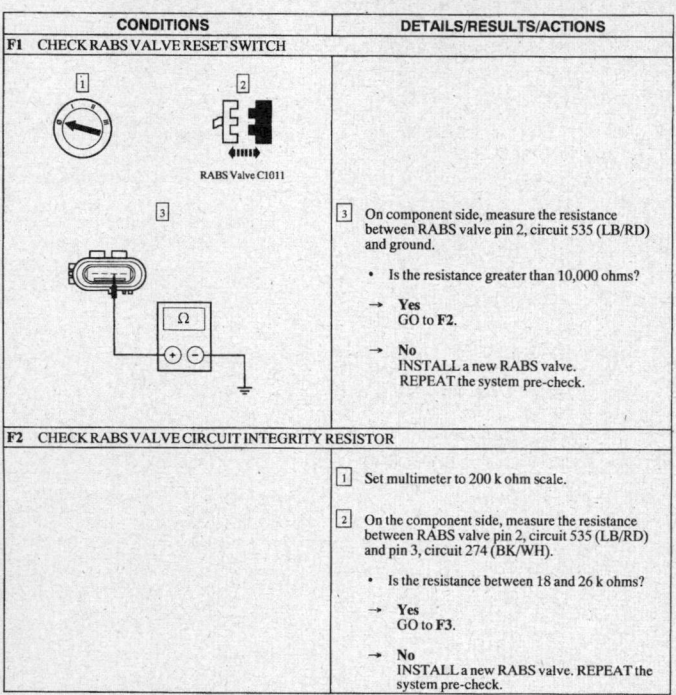

CONDITIONS	DETAILS/RESULTS/ACTIONS
F1 CHECK RABS VALVE RESET SWITCH	
	3 On component side, measure the resistance between RABS valve pin 2, circuit 535 (LB/RD) and ground. • Is the resistance greater than 10,000 ohms? → **Yes** GO to **F2**. → **No** INSTALL a new RABS valve. REPEAT the system pre-check.
F2 CHECK RABS VALVE CIRCUIT INTEGRITY RESISTOR	
	1 Set multimeter to 200 k ohm scale. **2** On the component side, measure the resistance between RABS valve pin 2, circuit 535 (LB/RD) and pin 3, circuit 274 (BK/WH). • Is the resistance between 18 and 26 k ohms? → **Yes** GO to **F3**. → **No** INSTALL a new RABS valve. REPEAT the system pre-check.

FM4020001682010X

Fig. 29 Test F: Code 4: Grounded/Open RABS Valve Reset Switch Circuit (Part 1 of 3). F-150

CONDITIONS	DETAILS/RESULTS/ACTIONS
F5 CHECK CONTINUITY OF CIRCUIT 535 (LG/RD)	
Anti-Lock Brake Control Module C238	**2** On the harness side, measure the resistance between the RABS valve connector pin 2 and module connector pin 6, circuit 535 (LG/RD). • Is the resistance less than 5 ohms? → **Yes** INSTALL a new anti-lock brake control module. REPEAT the system pre-check. → **No** REPAIR the open in circuit 535 (LG/RD).

FM4020001682030X

Fig. 29 Test F: Code 4: Grounded/Open RABS Valve Reset Switch Circuit (Part 3 of 3). F-150

CONDITIONS	DETAILS/RESULTS/ACTIONS
G1 CHECK FOR LEAKING DUMP VALVE	
	2 Remove the rubber caps from the two HCU low pressure accumulators (LPA) located on the rear of the unit.

FM4020001683010X

Fig. 30 Test G: Code 5: Excessive Dump Solenoid Activity (Part 1 of 6). F-150

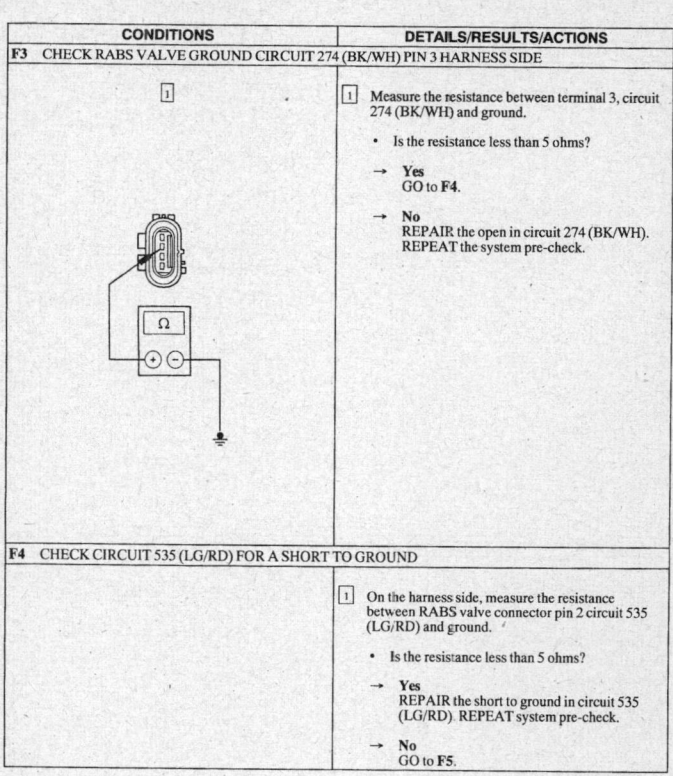

CONDITIONS	DETAILS/RESULTS/ACTIONS
F3 CHECK RABS VALVE GROUND CIRCUIT 274 (BK/WH) PIN 3 HARNESS SIDE	
	1 Measure the resistance between terminal 3, circuit 274 (BK/WH) and ground. • Is the resistance less than 5 ohms? → **Yes** GO to **F4**. → **No** REPAIR the open in circuit 274 (BK/WH). REPEAT the system pre-check.
F4 CHECK CIRCUIT 535 (LG/RD) FOR A SHORT TO GROUND	
	1 On the harness side, measure the resistance between RABS valve connector pin 2 circuit 535 (LG/RD) and ground. • Is the resistance less than 5 ohms? → **Yes** REPAIR the short to ground in circuit 535 (LG/RD). REPEAT system pre-check. → **No** GO to **F5**.

FM4020001682020X

Fig. 29 Test F: Code 4: Grounded/Open RABS Valve Reset Switch Circuit (Part 2 of 3). F-150

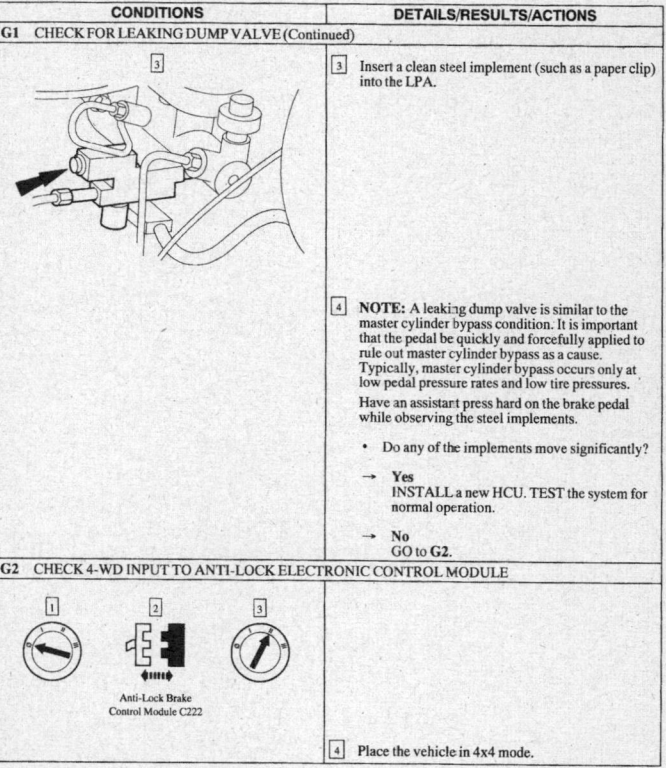

CONDITIONS	DETAILS/RESULTS/ACTIONS
G1 CHECK FOR LEAKING DUMP VALVE (Continued)	
	3 Insert a clean steel implement (such as a paper clip) into the LPA. **4** **NOTE:** A leaking dump valve is similar to the master cylinder bypass condition. It is important that the pedal be quickly and forcefully applied to rule out master cylinder bypass as a cause. Typically, master cylinder bypass occurs only at low pedal pressure rates and low tire pressures. Have an assistant press hard on the brake pedal while observing the steel implements. • Do any of the implements move significantly? → **Yes** INSTALL a new HCU. TEST the system for normal operation. → **No** GO to **G2**.
G2 CHECK 4-WD INPUT TO ANTI-LOCK ELECTRONIC CONTROL MODULE	
Anti-Lock Brake Control Module C222	**4** Place the vehicle in 4x4 mode.

FM4020001683020X

Fig. 30 Test G: Code 5: Excessive Dump Solenoid Activity (Part 2 of 6). F-150

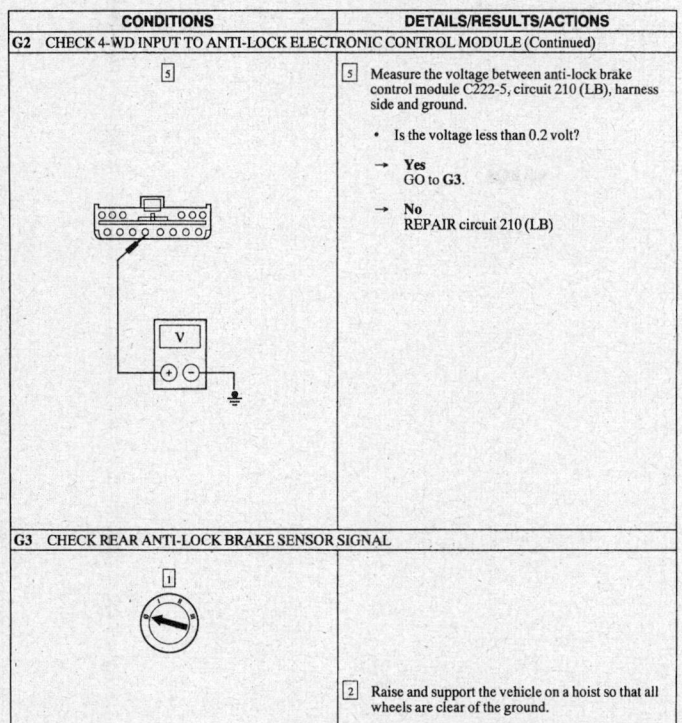

CONDITIONS	DETAILS/RESULTS/ACTIONS
G2 CHECK 4-WD INPUT TO ANTI-LOCK ELECTRONIC CONTROL MODULE (Continued)	
5	5 Measure the voltage between anti-lock brake control module C222-5, circuit 210 (LB), harness side and ground. • Is the voltage less than 0.2 volt? → **Yes** GO to **G3**. → **No** REPAIR circuit 210 (LB)
G3 CHECK REAR ANTI-LOCK BRAKE SENSOR SIGNAL	
1	
	2 Raise and support the vehicle on a hoist so that all wheels are clear of the ground.

FM4020001683030X

Fig. 30 Test G: Code 5: Excessive Dump Solenoid Activity (Part 3 of 6). F-150

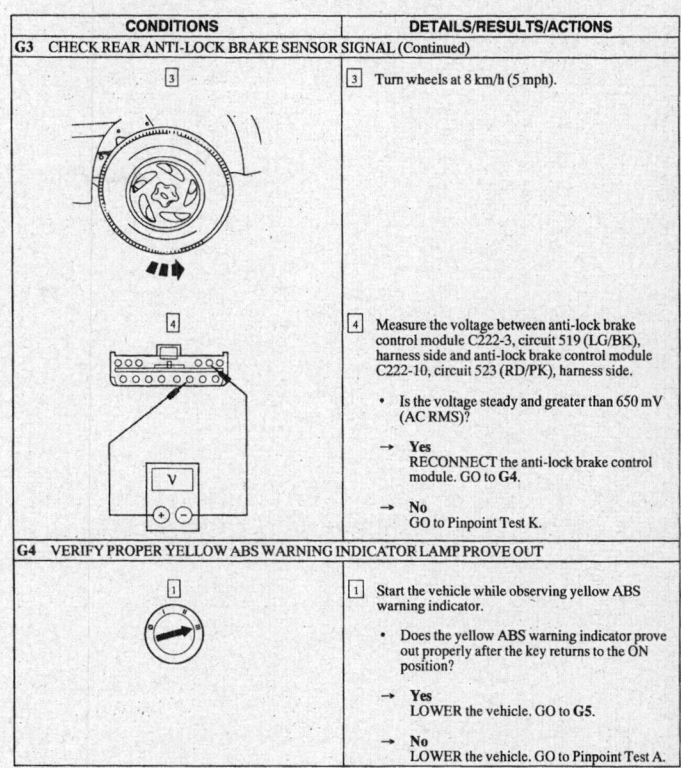

CONDITIONS	DETAILS/RESULTS/ACTIONS
G3 CHECK REAR ANTI-LOCK BRAKE SENSOR SIGNAL (Continued)	
3	3 Turn wheels at 8 km/h (5 mph).
4	4 Measure the voltage between anti-lock brake control module C222-3, circuit 519 (LG/BK), harness side and anti-lock brake control module C222-10, circuit 523 (RD/PK), harness side. • Is the voltage steady and greater than 650 mV (AC RMS)? → **Yes** RECONNECT the anti-lock brake control module. GO to **G4**. → **No** GO to Pinpoint Test K.
G4 VERIFY PROPER YELLOW ABS WARNING INDICATOR LAMP PROVE OUT	
1	1 Start the vehicle while observing yellow ABS warning indicator. • Does the yellow ABS warning indicator prove out properly after the key returns to the ON position? → **Yes** LOWER the vehicle. GO to **G5**. → **No** LOWER the vehicle. GO to Pinpoint Test A.

FM4020001683040X

Fig. 30 Test G: Code 5: Excessive Dump Solenoid Activity (Part 4 of 6). F-150

CONDITIONS	DETAILS/RESULTS/ACTIONS
G5 CHECK BASE BRAKE SYSTEM FUNCTION CHECK	
1 2 Anti-Lock Brake Control Module C222	3 Drive the vehicle at approximately 32 km/h (20 mph). Carry out a normal traffic stop. • Do the rear wheels lock up? → **Yes** DIAGNOSE brake system. → **No** GO to **G6**.
G6 ABS FUNCTION CHECK	
⚠ CAUTION: Do not exceed 16 km/h (10 mph) to prevent flat-spotting of tires.	
1 Anti-Lock Brake Control Module C222	2 Using tape, read is best, mark the wheel and tire with an "X". 3 Have an outside observer watch the "X" marked wheel.

FM4020001683050X

Fig. 30 Test G: Code 5: Excessive Dump Solenoid Activity (Part 5 of 6). F-150

CONDITIONS	DETAILS/RESULTS/ACTIONS
G6 ABS FUNCTION CHECK (Continued)	
	4 On smooth, dry pavement, accelerate the vehicle to 32-40 k m/h (20-25 mph). Press on the brake pedal with enough force to induce wheel lockup. If the "X" turns in a ratcheting motion, the ABS is functioning. If the "X" stops turning and the wheel locks up, the ABS is not functioning. • Do the rear wheels lock up? (Momentary lock up is permissible.) → **Yes** INSTALL a new RABS valve. RECONNECT the module. GO to Pinpoint Test P. → **No** Intermittent fault. GO to Pinpoint Test P.

FM4020001683060X

Fig. 30 Test G: Code 5: Excessive Dump Solenoid Activity (Part 6 of 6). F-150

CONDITIONS	DETAILS/RESULTS/ACTIONS
H1 VERIFY INTEGRITY OF REAR ANTI-LOCK BRAKE SENSOR WIRE ROUTING	
	1 INSPECT wire routing. • Are wires secure, undamaged, and properly routed? → **Yes** GO to **H2**. → **No** REPAIR as necessary. REPEAT the system pre-check.
H2 CHECK REAR ANTI-LOCK BRAKE SENSOR RESISTANCE	
1 2 Anti-Lock Brake Control Module C222	

FM4020001684010X

Fig. 31 Test H: Code 6: Erratic Rear Anti-Lock Brake Sensor Circuit (Part 1 of 6). F-150

CONDITIONS	DETAILS/RESULTS/ACTIONS
H2 CHECK REAR ANTI-LOCK BRAKE SENSOR RESISTANCE (Continued)	
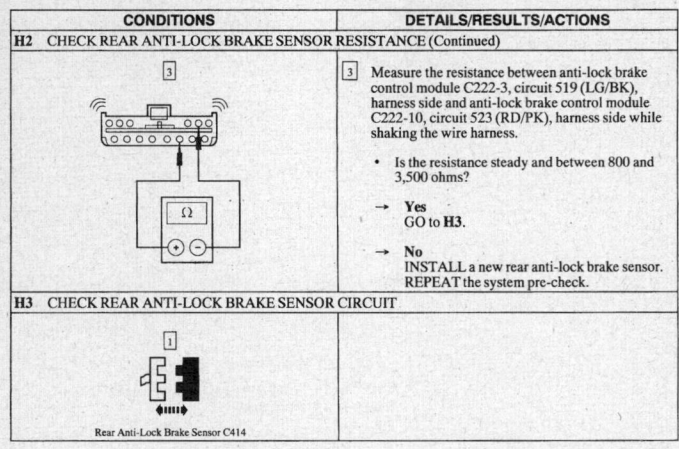	③ Measure the resistance between anti-lock brake control module C222-3, circuit 519 (LG/BK), harness side and anti-lock brake control module C222-10, circuit 523 (RD/PK), harness side while shaking the wire harness. • Is the resistance steady and between 800 and 3,500 ohms? → **Yes** GO to **H3**. → **No** INSTALL a new rear anti-lock brake sensor. REPEAT the system pre-check.
H3 CHECK REAR ANTI-LOCK BRAKE SENSOR CIRCUIT	
Rear Anti-Lock Brake Sensor C414	

FM4020001684020X

Fig. 31   Test H: Code 6: Erratic Rear Anti-Lock Brake Sensor Circuit (Part 2 of 6). F-150

CONDITIONS	DETAILS/RESULTS/ACTIONS
H5 CHECK CIRCUIT 523 (RD/PK) FOR OPEN	
①	① Measure the resistance between anti-lock brake control module C222-10, circuit 523 (RD/PK), harness side and rear anti-lock brake sensor C414, circuit 523 (RD/PK), harness side. • Is the resistance less than 5 ohms? → **Yes** GO to **H6**. → **No** REPAIR circuit 523 (RD/PK) for open. TEST the system for normal operation.
H6 CHECK FOR METAL SHAVINGS ON REAR ANTI-LOCK BRAKE SENSOR MAGNET POLE	
①	① Remove the rear anti-lock brake sensor from the rear differential case (4204) and inspect for metal shavings and chips on the rear brake anti-lock sensor pole piece. • Are metal shavings/chips present? → **Yes** DRAIN and CLEAN the rear differential case. REINSTALL the rear anti-lock brake sensor. GO to **H7**. → **No** REINSTALL the rear anti-lock brake sensor. GO to **H7**.
H7 CHECK REAR ANTI-LOCK BRAKE SENSOR OUTPUT	
	① Raise and support the vehicle on a hoist so that all wheels are clear of the ground.

FM4020001684040X

Fig. 31   Test H: Code 6: Erratic Rear Anti-Lock Brake Sensor Circuit (Part 4 of 6). F-150

CONDITIONS	DETAILS/RESULTS/ACTIONS
H3 CHECK REAR ANTI-LOCK BRAKE SENSOR CIRCUIT (Continued)	
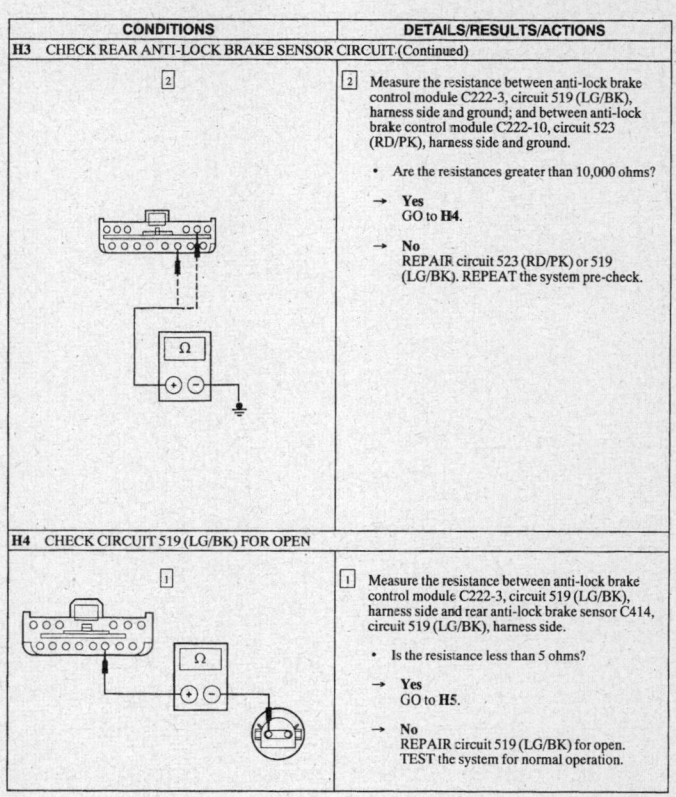	② Measure the resistance between anti-lock brake control module C222-3, circuit 519 (LG/BK), harness side and ground; and between anti-lock brake control module C222-10, circuit 523 (RD/PK), harness side and ground. • Are the resistances greater than 10,000 ohms? → **Yes** GO to **H4**. → **No** REPAIR circuit 523 (RD/PK) or 519 (LG/BK). REPEAT the system pre-check.
H4 CHECK CIRCUIT 519 (LG/BK) FOR OPEN	
①	① Measure the resistance between anti-lock brake control module C222-3, circuit 519 (LG/BK), harness side and rear anti-lock brake sensor C414, circuit 519 (LG/BK), harness side. • Is the resistance less than 5 ohms? → **Yes** GO to **H5**. → **No** REPAIR circuit 519 (LG/BK) for open. TEST the system for normal operation.

FM4020001684030X

Fig. 31   Test H: Code 6: Erratic Rear Anti-Lock Brake Sensor Circuit (Part 3 of 6). F-150

CONDITIONS	DETAILS/RESULTS/ACTIONS
H7 CHECK REAR ANTI-LOCK BRAKE SENSOR OUTPUT (Continued)	
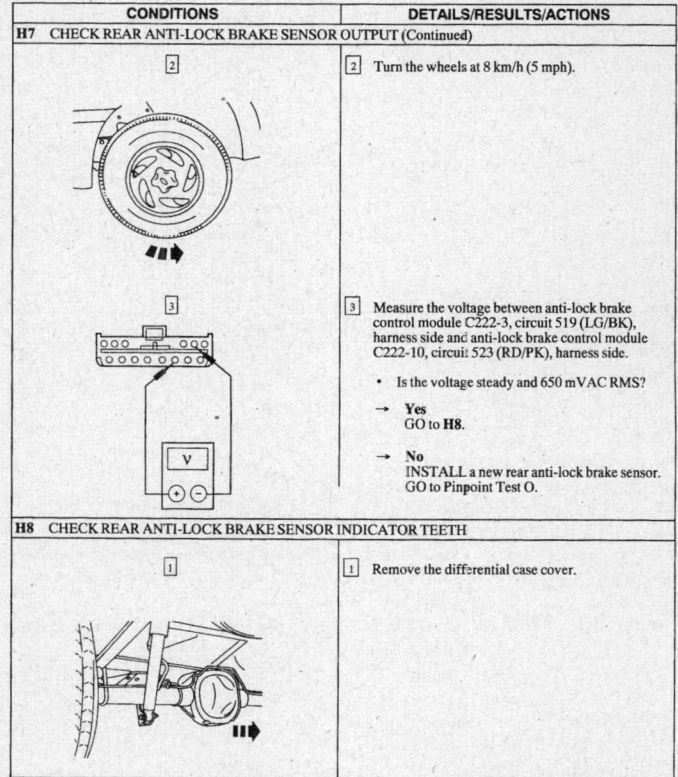	② Turn the wheels at 8 km/h (5 mph).
	③ Measure the voltage between anti-lock brake control module C222-3, circuit 519 (LG/BK), harness side and anti-lock brake control module C222-10, circuit 523 (RD/PK), harness side. • Is the voltage steady and 650 mVAC RMS? → **Yes** GO to **H8**. → **No** INSTALL a new rear anti-lock brake sensor. GO to Pinpoint Test O.
H8 CHECK REAR ANTI-LOCK BRAKE SENSOR INDICATOR TEETH	
	① Remove the differential case cover.

FM4020001684050X

Fig. 31   Test H: Code 6: Erratic Rear Anti-Lock Brake Sensor Circuit (Part 5 of 6). F-150

CONDITIONS	DETAILS/RESULTS/ACTIONS
H8 CHECK REAR ANTI-LOCK BRAKE SENSOR INDICATOR TEETH (Continued)	
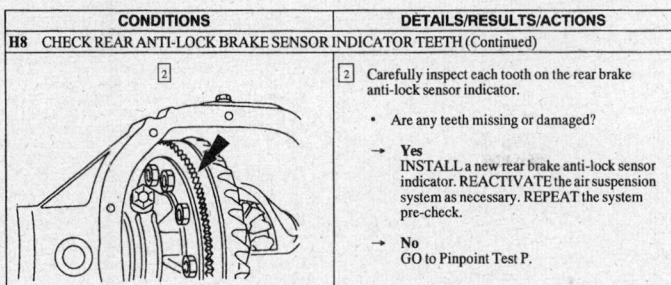	**2** Carefully inspect each tooth on the rear brake anti-lock sensor indicator. • Are any teeth missing or damaged? → **Yes** INSTALL a new rear brake anti-lock sensor indicator. REACTIVATE the air suspension system as necessary. REPEAT the system pre-check. → **No** GO to Pinpoint Test P.

FM4020001684060X

Fig. 31   Test H: Code 6: Erratic Rear Anti-Lock Brake Sensor Circuit (Part 6 of 6). F-150

CONDITIONS	DETAILS/RESULTS/ACTIONS
I1 CHECK CIRCUIT 599 (PK/LG) AND RABS ISOLATION VALVE SOLENOID FOR SHORT TO GROUND (Continued)	
3	**3** Lightly tap on the valve housing with a screwdriver handle and measure the resistance between anti-lock brake control module C222-13, circuit 599 (PK/LG), harness side and ground. • Is the resistance 3-6 ohms? → **Yes** INSTALL a new anti-lock brake control module. REPEAT system pre-check. → **No** GO to **I2**.
I2 CHECK CIRCUIT 599 (PK/LG) FOR OPEN OR SHORT TO GROUND	
1 RABS Valve C152	

FM4020001685020X

Fig. 32   Test I: Code 7: No Isolation Solenoid During Self-Check (Part 2 of 3). F-150

CONDITIONS	DETAILS/RESULTS/ACTIONS
J1 CHECK CIRCUIT 664 (YE/LG) AND RABS DUMP VALVE SOLENOID FOR GROUND (Continued)	
3	**3** Measure the resistance between anti-lock brake control module C222-8, circuit 664 (YE/LG), harness side and ground; and between anti-lock brake control module C222-14, circuit 664 (YE/LG), harness side and ground. • Are the resistances between 1 and 3 ohms? → **Yes** INSTALL a new anti-lock brake control module. REPEAT the system pre-check. → **No** GO to **J2**.
J2 CHECK RABS VALVE DUMP SOLENOID	
1 RABS Valve C152	

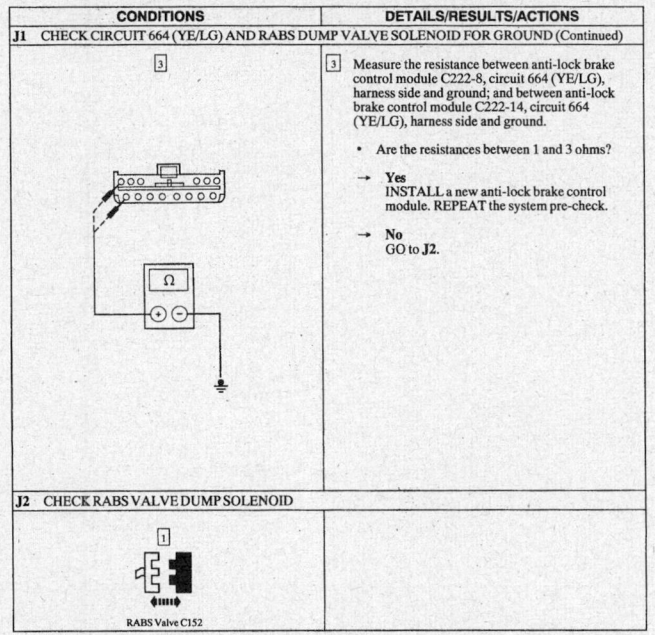

FM4020001686020X

Fig. 33   Test J: Code 8: No Dump Solenoid During Self-Check (Part 2 of 3). F-150

CONDITIONS	DETAILS/RESULTS/ACTIONS
I1 CHECK CIRCUIT 599 (PK/LG) AND RABS ISOLATION VALVE SOLENOID FOR SHORT TO GROUND	
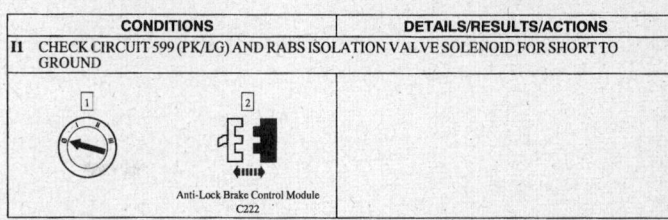 Anti-Lock Brake Control Module C222	

FM4020001685010X

Fig. 32   Test I: Code 7: No Isolation Solenoid During Self-Check (Part 1 of 3). F-150

CONDITIONS	DETAILS/RESULTS/ACTIONS
I2 CHECK CIRCUIT 599 (PK/LG) FOR OPEN OR SHORT TO GROUND (Continued)	
2 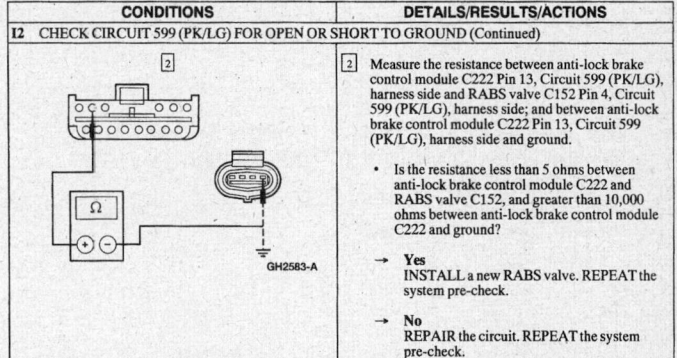 GH2583-A	**2** Measure the resistance between anti-lock brake control module C222 Pin 13, Circuit 599 (PK/LG), harness side and RABS valve C152 Pin 4, Circuit 599 (PK/LG), harness side; and between anti-lock brake control module C222 Pin 13, Circuit 599 (PK/LG), harness side and ground. • Is the resistance less than 5 ohms between anti-lock brake control module C222 and RABS valve C152, and greater than 10,000 ohms between anti-lock brake control module C222 and ground? → **Yes** INSTALL a new RABS valve. REPEAT the system pre-check. → **No** REPAIR the circuit. REPEAT the system pre-check.

FM4020001685030X

Fig. 32   Test I: Code 7: No Isolation Solenoid During Self-Check (Part 3 of 3). F-150

CONDITIONS	DETAILS/RESULTS/ACTIONS
J1 CHECK CIRCUIT 664 (YE/LG) AND RABS DUMP VALVE SOLENOID FOR GROUND	
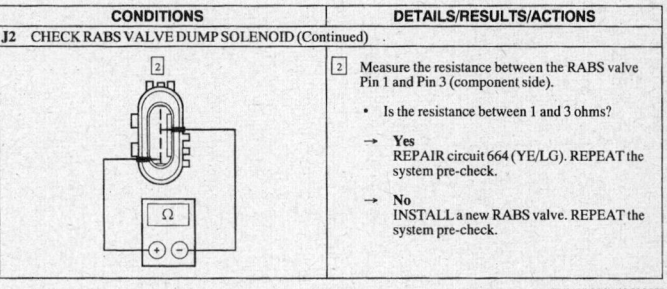 Anti-Lock Brake Control Module C222	

FM4020001686010X

Fig. 33   Test J: Code 8: No Dump Solenoid During Self-Check (Part 1 of 3). F-150

CONDITIONS	DETAILS/RESULTS/ACTIONS
J2 CHECK RABS VALVE DUMP SOLENOID (Continued)	
2	**2** Measure the resistance between the RABS valve Pin 1 and Pin 3 (component side). • Is the resistance between 1 and 3 ohms? → **Yes** REPAIR circuit 664 (YE/LG). REPEAT the system pre-check. → **No** INSTALL a new RABS valve. REPEAT the system pre-check.

FM4020001686030X

Fig. 33   Test J: Code 8: No Dump Solenoid During Self-Check (Part 3 of 3). F-150

CONDITIONS	DETAILS/RESULTS/ACTIONS
K1 VERIFY INTEGRITY OF REAR ANTI-LOCK BRAKE SENSOR WIRE ROUTING	

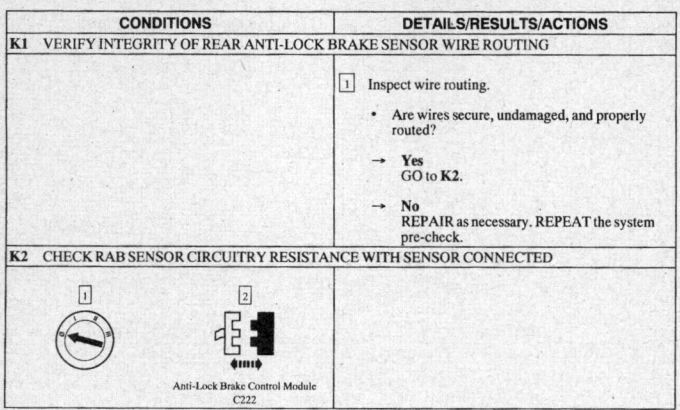

	1 Inspect wire routing.
	• Are wires secure, undamaged, and properly routed?
	→ **Yes** GO to **K2**.
	→ **No** REPAIR as necessary. REPEAT the system pre-check.

CONDITIONS	DETAILS/RESULTS/ACTIONS
K2 CHECK RAB SENSOR CIRCUITRY RESISTANCE WITH SENSOR CONNECTED	

Anti-Lock Brake Control Module C222

FM4020001687010X

Fig. 34 Test K: Code 9: Speed Sensor High Resistance/Open Circuit (Part 1 of 3). F-150

CONDITIONS	DETAILS/RESULTS/ACTIONS
K4 CHECK REAR ANTI-LOCK BRAKE SENSOR	

Rear Anti-Lock Brake Sensor C414

	2 Measure the resistance between the rear anti-lock brake sensor pins (component side).
	• Is the resistance between 800 and 3,500 ohms?
	→ **Yes** REPAIR circuit 519 (LG/BK), and circuit 523 (RD/PK) as necessary. REPEAT the system pre-check.
	→ **No** INSTALL a new rear anti-lock brake sensor. REPEAT the system pre-check.

FM4020001687030X

Fig. 34 Test K: Code 9: Speed Sensor High Resistance/Open Circuit (Part 3 of 3). F-150

CONDITIONS	DETAILS/RESULTS/ACTIONS
L1 CHECK CIRCUITS 519 (LG/BK) AND 523 (RD/PK) FOR SHORT	

Rear Brake Anti-Lock Sensor C414   Anti-Lock Brake Control Module C222

FM4020001688010X

Fig. 35 Test L: Code 10: Low Speed Sensor Resistance (Part 1 of 3). F-150

CONDITIONS	DETAILS/RESULTS/ACTIONS
K2 CHECK RAB SENSOR CIRCUITRY RESISTANCE WITH SENSOR CONNECTED (Continued)	

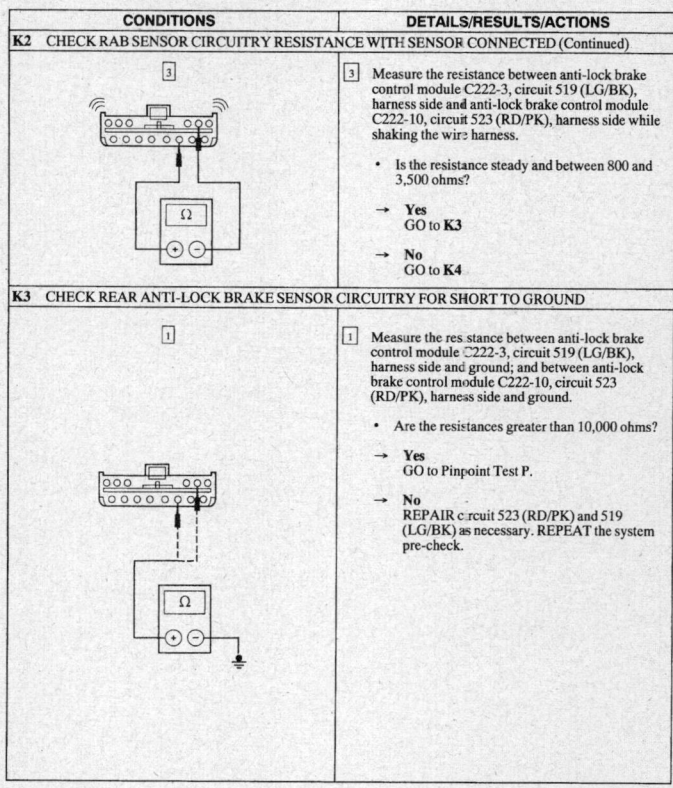

	3 Measure the resistance between anti-lock brake control module C222-3, circuit 519 (LG/BK), harness side and anti-lock brake control module C222-10, circuit 523 (RD/PK), harness side while shaking the wire harness.
	• Is the resistance steady and between 800 and 3,500 ohms?
	→ **Yes** GO to **K3**
	→ **No** GO to **K4**

CONDITIONS	DETAILS/RESULTS/ACTIONS
K3 CHECK REAR ANTI-LOCK BRAKE SENSOR CIRCUITRY FOR SHORT TO GROUND	

	1 Measure the resistance between anti-lock brake control module C222-3, circuit 519 (LG/BK), harness side and ground; and between anti-lock brake control module C222-10, circuit 523 (RD/PK), harness side and ground.
	• Are the resistances greater than 10,000 ohms?
	→ **Yes** GO to Pinpoint Test **P**.
	→ **No** REPAIR circuit 523 (RD/PK) and 519 (LG/BK) as necessary. REPEAT the system pre-check.

FM4020001687020X

Fig. 34 Test K: Code 9: Speed Sensor High Resistance/Open Circuit (Part 2 of 3). F-150

CONDITIONS	DETAILS/RESULTS/ACTIONS
L1 CHECK CIRCUITS 519 (LG/BK) AND 523 (RD/PK) FOR SHORT (Continued)	

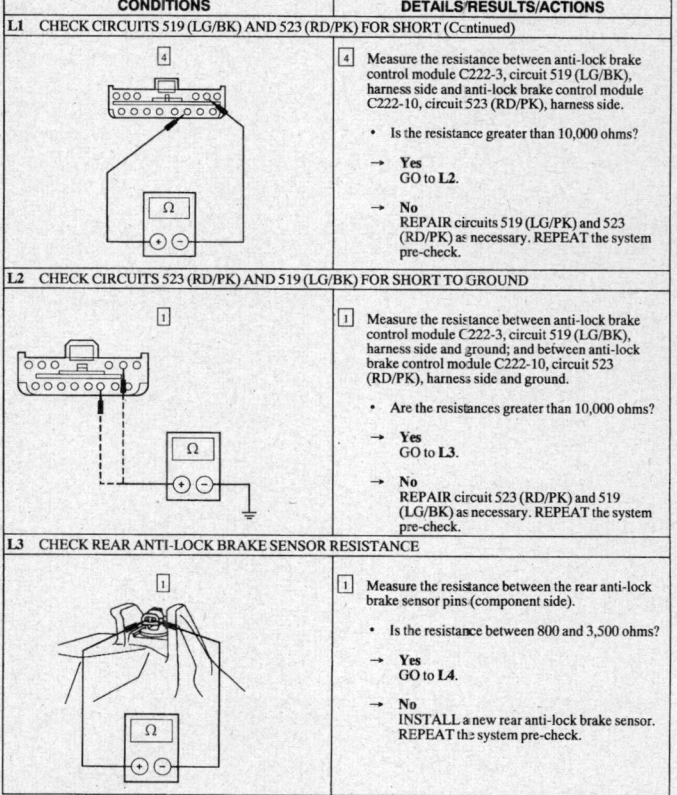

	4 Measure the resistance between anti-lock brake control module C222-3, circuit 519 (LG/BK), harness side and anti-lock brake control module C222-10, circuit 523 (RD/PK), harness side.
	• Is the resistance greater than 10,000 ohms?
	→ **Yes** GO to **L2**.
	→ **No** REPAIR circuits 519 (LG/PK) and 523 (RD/PK) as necessary. REPEAT the system pre-check.

CONDITIONS	DETAILS/RESULTS/ACTIONS
L2 CHECK CIRCUITS 523 (RD/PK) AND 519 (LG/BK) FOR SHORT TO GROUND	

	1 Measure the resistance between anti-lock brake control module C222-3, circuit 519 (LG/BK), harness side and ground; and between anti-lock brake control module C222-10, circuit 523 (RD/PK), harness side and ground.
	• Are the resistances greater than 10,000 ohms?
	→ **Yes** GO to **L3**.
	→ **No** REPAIR circuit 523 (RD/PK) and 519 (LG/BK) as necessary. REPEAT the system pre-check.

CONDITIONS	DETAILS/RESULTS/ACTIONS
L3 CHECK REAR ANTI-LOCK BRAKE SENSOR RESISTANCE	

	1 Measure the resistance between the rear anti-lock brake sensor pins (component side).
	• Is the resistance between 800 and 3,500 ohms?
	→ **Yes** GO to **L4**.
	→ **No** INSTALL a new rear anti-lock brake sensor. REPEAT the system pre-check.

FM4020001688020X

Fig. 35 Test L: Code 10: Low Speed Sensor Resistance (Part 2 of 3). F-150

CONDITIONS	DETAILS/RESULTS/ACTIONS
L4 CHECK REAR ANTI-LOCK BRAKE SENSOR FOR SHORT TO GROUND	

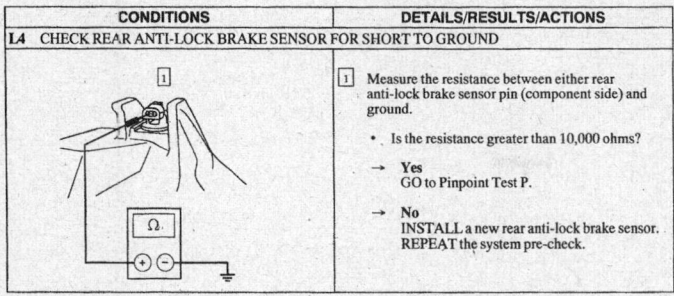

☐1	☐1 Measure the resistance between either rear anti-lock brake sensor pin (component side) and ground. • Is the resistance greater than 10,000 ohms? → **Yes** GO to Pinpoint Test P. → **No** INSTALL a new rear anti-lock brake sensor. REPEAT the system pre-check.

FM4020001688030X

Fig. 35 Test L: Code 10: Low Speed Sensor Resistance (Part 3 of 3). F-150

CONDITIONS	DETAILS/RESULTS/ACTIONS
M2 CHECK FOR OPEN GROUND CIRCUIT	
	☐1 Measure the resistance between BPP switch C252, circuit 574 (BK/PK) and ground. • Is the resistance less than 5 ohms? → **Yes** GO to **M3**. → **No** REPAIR the open in circuit 574 (BK/PK). REPEAT the system pre-check.
M3 CHECK GROUND CIRCUIT FOR SHORT TO BATTERY	
	☐1 Measure the voltage between BPP switch connector C252, circuit 574 (BK/PK) and ground. • Is the voltage greater than 10 volts? → **Yes** REPAIR the short to battery in circuit 574 (BK/PK). REPEAT the system pre-check. → **No** GO to **M4**.
M4 CHECK BPP OUTPUT CIRCUIT FOR SHORT TO BATTERY	
RABS Module C222	☐2 Measure the resistance between module connector C222, circuit 810 (RD/LG) and ground. • Is the voltage greater than 10 volts? → **Yes** REPAIR the short to battery in circuit 810 (RD/LG). REPEAT the system pre-check. → **No** REPLACE the anti-lock brake control module. REPEAT the system pre-check.

FM4020001689020X

Fig. 36 Test M: Code 11: Brake Pedal Position Switch Always Closed (Part 2 of 2). F-150

CONDITIONS	DETAILS/RESULTS/ACTIONS
M1 CHECK FOR SHORTED BPP	
NOTE: Code 11 is caused by the brake pedal position (BPP) switch being closed prior to the vehicle moving. If the BPP switch remains closed when the vehicle begins to move, the REAR ABS warning light will turn on at approximately 26 km/h (16 mph). Code 11 will not be latched in the control module's memory until the speed of the vehicle exceeds 60 km/h (37 mph) for at least 10 seconds. If the vehicle does not exceed 60 km/h (37 mph) for at least 10 seconds, then the REAR ABS warning light will turn on but the module will not latch a code. Code 11 can be caused by a driver who is resting their foot on the brake with just enough pressure to close the BPP switch, while driving at least 60 km/h (37 mph) for a minimum of ten seconds. When this occurs, a Code 11 will be latched by the RABS module.	
Brake Pedal Position (BPP) Switch C252	☐2 Measure the resistance across BPP terminals for circuits 1001 (WH/YE) and 810 (RD/LG). • Is the resistance less than 5 ohms? → **Yes** REPLACE the BPP switch. REPEAT the system pre-check. → **No** GO to **M2**.

FM4020001689010X

Fig. 36 Test M: Code 11: Brake Pedal Position Switch Always Closed (Part 1 of 2). F-150

CONDITIONS	DETAILS/RESULTS/ACTIONS
N1 CHECK BRAKE FLUID LEVEL	
☐1	☐2 Check the brake fluid level in the brake master cylinder reservoir (2K478). • Is the fluid level within specification? → **Yes** GO to **N2**. → **No** CHECK for leaks in the brake system. REPAIR as necessary. FILL the brake master cylinder reservoir to the specified level. REPEAT the system pre-check.
N2 CHECK BRAKE MASTER CYLINDER RESERVOIR FLOAT	
☐1	☐1 Remove the master cylinder filler cap.
	☐2 Push the brake master cylinder reservoir float down to the bottom of the reservoir. • Does the float move to the bottom of the reservoir and then move back to the top of the fluid? → **Yes** GO to **N3**. → **No** INSTALL a new brake master cylinder reservoir. REPEAT the system pre-check.

FM4020001690010X

Fig. 37 Test N: Code 12: Loss Of Hydraulic Brake Fluid During An Anti-Lock Stop (Part 1 of 3). F-150

CONDITIONS	DETAILS/RESULTS/ACTIONS
N3 CHECK CIRCUIT 531 (DG/YE) FOR SHORT TO GROUND	
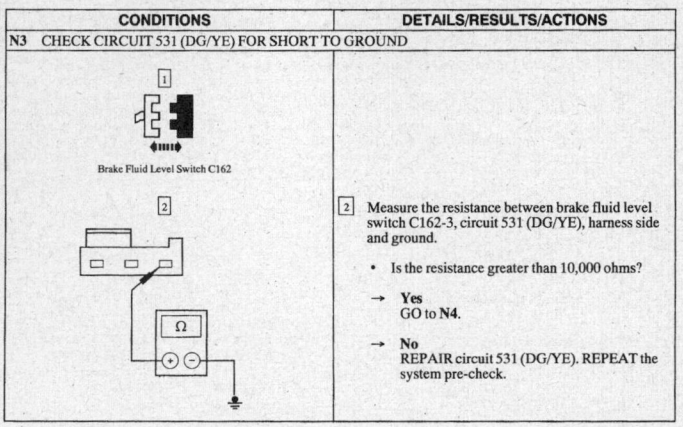 Brake Fluid Level Switch C162	☐2 Measure the resistance between brake fluid level switch C162-3, circuit 531 (DG/YE), harness side and ground. • Is the resistance greater than 10,000 ohms? → **Yes** GO to **N4**. → **No** REPAIR circuit 531 (DG/YE). REPEAT the system pre-check.

Fig. 37 Test N: Code 12: Loss Of Hydraulic Brake Fluid During An Anti-Lock Stop (Part 2 of 3). F-150

FM4020001690020X

CONDITIONS	DETAILS/RESULTS/ACTIONS
N4 CHECK THE BRAKE FLUID LEVEL SWITCH	
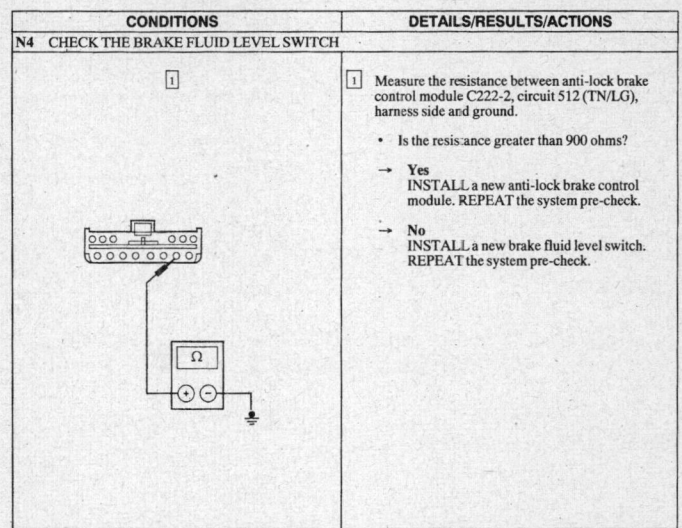	☐1 Measure the resistance between anti-lock brake control module C222-2, circuit 512 (TN/LG), harness side and ground. • Is the resistance greater than 900 ohms? → **Yes** INSTALL a new anti-lock brake control module. REPEAT the system pre-check. → **No** INSTALL a new brake fluid level switch. REPEAT the system pre-check.

FM4020001690030X

Fig. 37 Test N: Code 12: Loss Of Hydraulic Brake Fluid During An Anti-Lock Stop (Part 3 of 3). F-150

CONDITIONS	DETAILS/RESULTS/ACTIONS
O1 CHECK KEEP ALIVE MEMORY (KAM) FUSE	
	☐2 Observe the yellow ABS warning indicator lamp prove out. • Does the yellow ABS warning indicator lamp (10C915) prove out normally? → **Yes** GO to **O2**. → **No** INSTALL a new fuse junction panel fuse 15 (5A). REPEAT the system pre-check.
O2 CHECK LOW SPEED ABS STOP	
NOTE: Wetting down the area where the stop is to be performed will aid in the accomplishment of this test.	
	☐1 Drive at approximately 16 km/h (10 mph). ☐2 Press on the brake pedal hard enough to lock all four wheels and observe the rear wheels in the mirrors or use an observer. • Do one or both of the wheels lock-up consistently? (Momentary lock-up is permissible.) → **Yes** GO to Symptom Chart. → **No** If other symptoms are detected, GO to the Symptom Chart. If yellow ABS warning indicator is not on, GO to **O3**. If yellow ABS warning indicator comes on and stays on, REPEAT the system pre-check.
O3 CHECK FOR UNWARRANTED ABS ACTIVITY	
NOTE: Stopping should be performed on dry pavement.	
NOTE: Windshield wipers should be turned off during this test.	
	☐1 Drive at approximately 32 km/h (20 mph).

FM4020001691010X

Fig. 38 Test O: Verification Drive Test (Part 1 of 2). F-150

CONDITIONS	DETAILS/RESULTS/ACTIONS
O3 CHECK FOR UNWARRANTED ABS ACTIVITY (Continued)	
	☐2 Carry out a normal traffic stop. ☐3 Feel for pulsation in the brake pedal during the stop and within 10 seconds after the vehicle has come to a stop. • Is there any pulsation in the brake pedal at any time during the stop or within 10 seconds after the vehicle has stopped? → **Yes** GO to Symptom Chart for unwarranted RABS activity. → **No** If other symptoms are detected, GO to Symptom Chart. If the yellow ABS warning indicator lamp illuminates and stays illuminated, REPEAT the system pre-check.

FM4020001691020X

Fig. 38 Test O: Verification Drive Test (Part 2 of 2). F-150

CONDITIONS	DETAILS/RESULTS/ACTIONS
P1 CLEAR DTCS; REPEAT SYSTEM PRE-CHECK	
	☐1 Reconnect the system. ☐2 Clear all DTCs. • Does the yellow ABS warning indicator prove out? → **Yes** GO to **P3**. → **No** GO to **P2**.
P2 WIGGLE TEST	
NOTE: Start at one component and wiggle connector by connector until the whole circuit has been tested.	
	☐1 Wiggle an affected circuit in one location only.

FM4020001692010X

Fig. 39 Test P: Intermittent Problem Diagnosis (Part 1 of 2). F-150

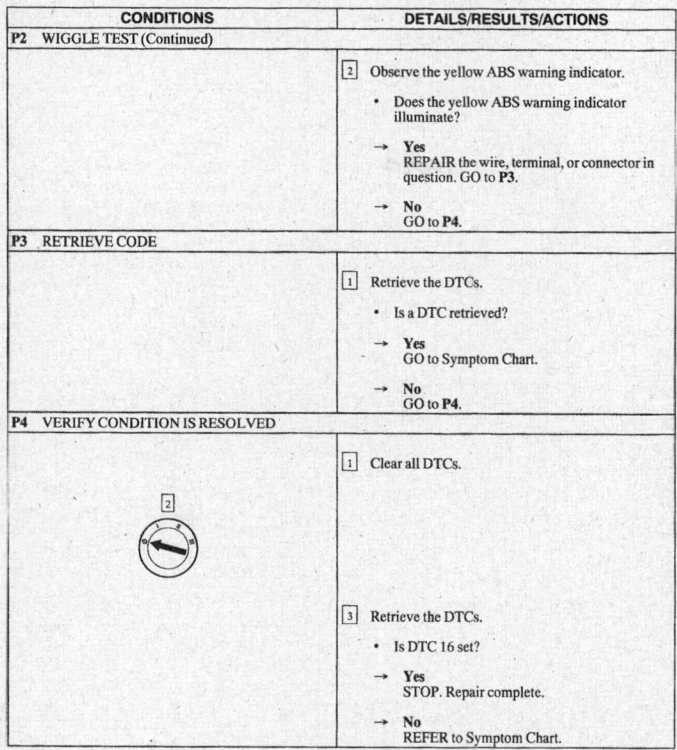

CONDITIONS	DETAILS/RESULTS/ACTIONS
P2 WIGGLE TEST (Continued)	2 Observe the yellow ABS warning indicator. • Does the yellow ABS warning indicator illuminate? → Yes REPAIR the wire, terminal, or connector in question. GO to P3. → No GO to P4.
P3 RETRIEVE CODE	1 Retrieve the DTCs. • Is a DTC retrieved? → Yes GO to Symptom Chart. → No GO to P4.
P4 VERIFY CONDITION IS RESOLVED	1 Clear all DTCs. 3 Retrieve the DTCs. • Is DTC 16 set? → Yes STOP. Repair complete. → No REFER to Symptom Chart.

FM4020001692020X

Fig. 39   Test P: Intermittent Problem Diagnosis (Part 2 of 2). F-150

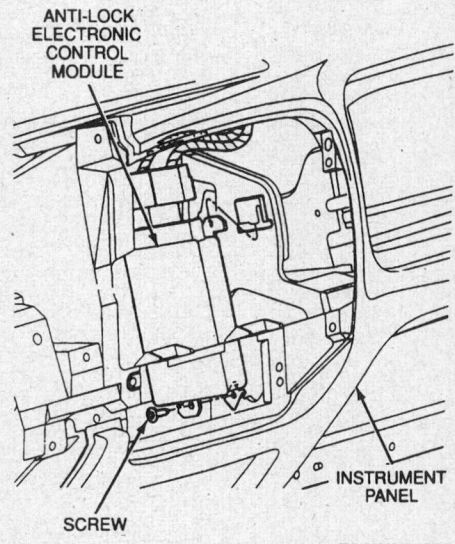

FM4029501045000X

Fig. 40   RABS module removal. F-150

Ranger

NOTE: Electrical Symbol & Wire Color Code Identification Located In The Front Of This Manual May Be Used As An Aid When Using Wiring Circuits Found In This Section.

NOTE: Refer To "Computer Relearn Procedures" Located In The Front Of This Manual When Battery Power To The Computer Has Been Interrupted.

INDEX

	Page No.
Description	5-175
System Operation	5-175
Diagnosis & Testing	5-176
Accessing Diagnostic Trouble Codes	5-176
Clearing Diagnostic Trouble Codes	5-176
Diagnostic Tests	5-176
Pinpoint Tests	5-176

	Page No.
Diagnostic Trouble Code Interpretation	5-176
Wiring Diagrams	5-176
Diagnostic Chart Index	5-179
Precautions	5-175
Battery Ground Cable	5-175
Brake Fluid Handling	5-175
System Service	5-176
Brake System Bleed	5-176

	Page No.
Component Replacement	5-176
ABS Control Module	5-177
G-Switch	5-177
Hydraulic Control Unit (HCU)	5-176
Wheel Speed Sensor	5-177
Troubleshooting	5-176
Symptom Chart	5-176

PRECAUTIONS

BATTERY GROUND CABLE

Prior to service disconnect battery ground cable and isolate as required.

BRAKE FLUID HANDLING

Brake fluid can cause serious injury and vehicle damage if not handled properly. Avoid contact with eyes and do not allow fluid to splash or spill on painted surfaces. Wash hands thoroughly after handling.

DESCRIPTION

SYSTEM OPERATION

The four wheel Anti-Lock Brake System (ABS) prevents wheel lockup by automatically modulating the brake pressure during an emergency stop.

When the brakes are applied, fluid is forced from the master cylinder outlet ports to the Hydraulic Control Unit (HCU) inlet ports. This pressure is transmitted through three normally open solenoid valves contained inside the HCU, then through the outlet ports of the HCU to the wheels.

The ABS Electronic Control Unit (ECU)

Condition	Possible Sources	Action
• No communication with the anti-lock brake system (ABS) module	• Circuitry or connection in the international standards organization (ISO) 9141 network • ABS module	• Go To Pinpoint Test A .
• Incorrectly adjusted rear brakes or brake shoe linings grab.	• Rear brake adjustment • Rear brake shoe linings	• Check base brake system.
• Base brake mechanical concern for wheels lockup	• Rear brake shoe linings • Wheel cylinder • Rear brakes • Parking brake • Rear axle seal	• Check base brake system. • Check base brake system. • Replace axle seal.
• Soft pedal/spongy pedal no warning indicator	• Brake line, hose, fitting, master cylinder, wheel cylinder or caliper • Air in the brake system	• Check base brake system.
• Base brake mechanical concern (hard pedal)	• Vacuum boost • Wheel cylinder or caliper • Brake line or hose	• Check base brake system.
• Base brake hydraulic concern during medium/hard brake application	• Brake line or hose, fitting, master cylinder, wheel cylinder or caliper	• Check base brake system.

LTV0500000005025

Fig. 1   Symptom chart (Part 1 of 3)

Condition	Possible Sources	Action
	• Air in the brake system	
• Base brake mechanical concern during medium/hard brake application	• Vacuum boost • Wheel cylinder or caliper • Brake line or hose • Brake shoe or pad linings	• Check base brake system.
• Base brake mechanical concern for vehicle pulls	• Rear brakes • Caliper • Brake pad or shoe wear	• Check base brake system.
• Base brake hydraulic concern for vehicle pulls	• Brake line or hose	• Check base brake system.
• One wheel locks up; no DTCs recorded	• Caliper • Wheel cylinder • Brake pad/shoe linings	• Check base brake system.
	• Hydraulic control unit (HCU)	• INSTALL a new HCU.
• The red brake warning indicator stays on when the ignition switch is in the RUN position	• Circuitry • Instrument cluster • Anti-lock brake system (ABS) module	• REFER to "Dash Gauges & Warning Indicators"
• The ABS warning indicator stays on when the ignition switch is in the RUN position	• Circuitry • Instrument cluster • Anti-lock brake system (ABS) module	• REFER to "Dash Gauges & Warning Indicators"
• The red brake warning indicator does not self-check	• Circuitry • Instrument cluster • Anti-lock brake	• REFER to REFER to "Dash Gauges & Warning Indicators".

LTV0500000005026

Fig. 1   Symptom chart (Part 2 of 3)

or Electronic Control Module (ECM) monitors the electro-mechanical components of the ABS system. ABS malfunctions will cause the ECU/ECM to shut off or inhibit the system. However, normal power assisted braking operation will continue. System malfunctions will be indicated by the ABS warning lamp.

TROUBLESHOOTING

Symptom Chart

Refer to **Fig. 1** for symptom charts.

DIAGNOSIS & TESTING

Accessing Diagnostic Trouble Codes

Connect a suitably programmed scan tool and Vehicle Communication Module (VCM) with appropriate adapters, or equivalents, to the Data Link Connector (DCL) located in the passenger compartment beneath the instrument panel. Follow tool manufacturer's instructions for accessing Diagnostic Trouble Codes (DTC).

Diagnostic Trouble Code Interpretation

Refer to **Fig. 2** for diagnostic trouble code interpretation.

Wiring Diagrams

Refer to **Fig. 3** for wiring diagrams.

Diagnostic Tests

PINPOINT TESTS

Refer to **Figs. 4 through 12** for pinpoint tests.

Clearing Diagnostic Trouble Codes

Connect a suitably programmed scan tool and Vehicle Communication Module (VCM) with appropriate adapters, or equivalents, to the Data Link Connector (DCL)

located in the passenger compartment beneath the instrument panel. Follow tool manufacturer's instructions for clearing Diagnostic Trouble Codes (DTC).

SYSTEM SERVICE

Brake System Bleed

Refer to "Hydraulic Brake Systems" chapter for bleeding procedure.

Component Replacement

HYDRAULIC CONTROL UNIT (HCU)

1. Disconnect electrical connector by lifting up on release tab.
2. Disconnect brake lines from HCU.
3. Remove HCU retaining bolts, then the HCU.
4. Remove ABS module.

	system (ABS) module	
• The yellow ABS warning indicator does not self-check	• Circuitry • Instrument cluster • Anti-lock brake system (ABS) module	• REFER to "Dash Gauges & Warning Indicators".
• The yellow ABS warning indicator self-checks OK but automatically begins flashing	• Circuitry • Anti-lock brake system (ABS) module • Hydraulic control unit (HCU)	• RETRIEVE the DTCs and REFER to the Diagnostic Trouble Code (DTC) Index.
• Soft/hard/excessive brake pedal travel	• Brake line, hose, fitting, master cylinder, wheel cylinder, wheel cylinder or caliper • Air in the brake system • HCU	• "Bleed Brake System" • Inspect the HCU for visible signs of leaking. If any leaks are present, REPAIR or REPLACE as necessary and bleed the brake system. For additional information.
• The yellow ABS/red brake light always on, no DTCs	• Circuitry • Anti-lock brake system control (ABS) module	• REFER to "Dash Gauges & Warning Indicators".

LTV0500000005027

Fig. 1   Symptom chart (Part 3 of 3)

DTC	Description
B1317	Battery Voltage High
B1318	Battery Voltage Low
B1342	ABS Module Failure
B1485	Brake Pedal Input Circuit Battery Short
C1095	ABS Hydraulic Pump Motor Circuit Failure
C1096	ABS Hydraulic Pump Motor Circuit Open
C1145	RF Wheel Speed Sensor Input Circuit Failure
C1148	RF Wheel Speed Sensor Coherency Fault
C1155	LF Wheel Speed Sensor Input Circuit Failure
C1158	LF Wheel Speed Sensor Coherency Fault
C1186	ABS Power Relay Open
C1187	Brake Fluid Level Sensor Input Open Circuit
C1194	ABS Outlet Valve Coil LF Circuit Failure
C1198	ABS Inlet Valve Coil LF Circuit Failure
C1210	ABS Outlet Valve Coil RF Circuit Failure
C1214	ABS Inlet Valve Coil RF Circuit Failure
C1229	Rear Wheel Speed Sensor Coherency Fault
C1230	Rear Wheel Speed Sensor Input Circuit Failure
C1233	LF Wheel Speed Sensor Signal Incorrect
C1234	RF Wheel Speed Sensor Signal Incorrect
C1237	Rear Wheel Speed Sensor Signal Incorrect
C1246	ABS Outlet Valve Coil Rear Circuit Failure
C1254	ABS Inlet Valve Coil Rear Circuit Failure
C1266	ABS Valve Power Relay Circuit Failure
C1414	Incorrect Module Design Level
C1949 (4x4 only)	G-Sensor Circuit Open
C1950 (4x4 only)	G-Sensor Signal Failure

LTV0500000005028

Fig. 2   Diagnostic trouble code interpretation

5. Reverse procedure to install, noting the following:
   a. **Torque** HCU retaining bolts 91–119 inch lbs.
   b. **Torque** brake lines 11–14 ft. lbs.

ABS CONTROL MODULE

1. Remove HCU retaining bolts.
2. Disconnect ABS control module electrical connector.
3. Remove ABS control module retaining bolts, then the ABS control module.
4. Reverse procedure to install, noting the following:
   a. **Torque** ABS control module retaining bolts to 16–18 inch lbs.
   b. **Torque** HCU retaining bolts to 91–122 inch lbs.
   c. **Torque** brake lines to 79–84 inch lbs.

G-SWITCH

1. Raise and support vehicle.
2. Remove G-switch retaining nuts.
3. Disconnect fuel filter from vehicle frame.
4. Disconnect G-switch electrical connector.
5. Remove G-switch.
6. Reverse procedure to install. **Torque** G-switch retaining nuts to 14–21 ft. lbs.

WHEEL SPEED SENSOR

FRONT

1. **On models equipped with 4WD,** remove rotor shield and rotor.
2. **On all models,** raise and support vehicle.
3. Disconnect wheel speed sensor wire from vehicle frame.

4. Remove sensor retaining bolt, then the sensor.
5. Reverse procedure to install, noting the following:
   a. **Torque** wheel speed sensor retaining bolt to 71–88 inch lbs.
   b. Apply high temperature 4X4 front axle and wheel bearing grease E8TZ-19590-A, or equivalent, meeting Ford specification ESA-MIC198-A to sensor mounting surface.

REAR

1. Raise and support vehicle.
2. Clean area around wheel speed sensor.
3. Disconnect wheel speed sensor electrical connector.
4. Remove sensor retaining bolt, then the sensor.
5. Reverse procedure to install, noting the following:
   a. **Torque** wheel speed sensor retaining bolt to 20 ft. lbs.
   b. Clean axle mounting surface.
   c. Lubricate O-ring with high performance rear axle lubricant F1TZ-19580-B, or equivalent, meeting Ford specification WSL-M2C192-A.

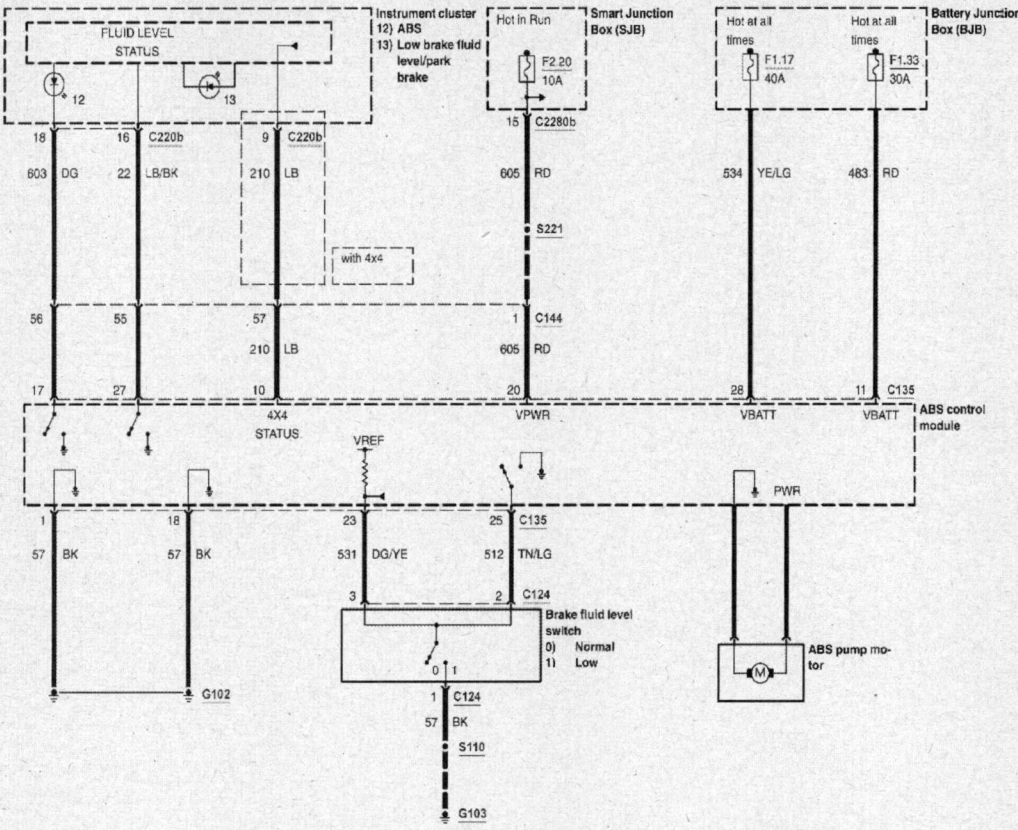

Fig. 3   Wiring diagram (Part 1 of 2)

LTV0500000005029

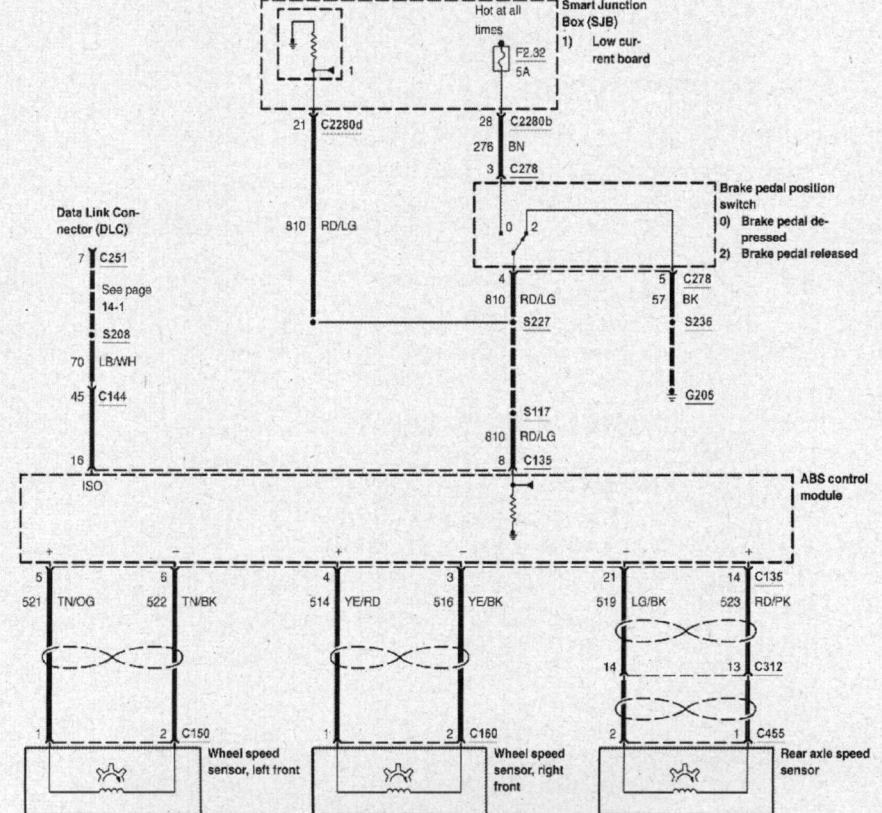

Fig. 3   Wiring diagram (Part 2 of 2)

LTV0500000005030

DIAGNOSTIC CHART INDEX

Test	Code	Description	Page No.	Fig. No.
A	—	No Communication w/ABS Module	5-179	4
B	C1186	ABS Power Relay Output Circuit & Battery Voltage High/Low	5-179	5
	B1317	ABS Power Relay Output Circuit & Battery Voltage High/Low	5-179	5
	B1318	ABS Power Relay Output Circuit & Battery Voltage High/Low	5-179	5
C	C1145	Wheel Speed Sensor Circuit Failure	5-180	6
	C1155	Wheel Speed Sensor Circuit Failure	5-180	6
	C1230	Wheel Speed Sensor Circuit Failure	5-180	6
D	C1148	Wheel Speed Sensor Coherency Fault Signal Incorrect	5-181	7
	C1158	Wheel Speed Sensor Coherency Fault Signal Incorrect	5-181	7
	C1229	Wheel Speed Sensor Coherency Fault Signal Incorrect	5-181	7
	C1233	Wheel Speed Sensor Coherency Fault Signal Incorrect	5-181	7
	C1234	Wheel Speed Sensor Coherency Fault Signal Incorrect	5-181	7
	C1237	Wheel Speed Sensor Coherency Fault Signal Incorrect	5-181	7
E	C1095	ABS Hydraulic Pump Motor Circuit Failure/Open	5-181	8
	C1096	ABS Hydraulic Pump Motor Circuit Failure/Open	5-181	8
F	B1485	Brake Pedal Input Circuit Battery Short	5-182	9
G	C1414	Incorrect Module Design Level	5-182	10
H	C1187	Brake Fluid Level Input Circuit Open	5-183	11
I	—	Check For Correct ABS Module Operation	5-183	12

Test Step	Result / Action to Take
A1 CHECK CIRCUITS 605 (RD), 534 (YE/LG) AND 483 (RD) FOR VOLTAGE • Key in OFF position. • Disconnect: ABS Module C135. • Key in ON position. • Measure the voltage between ground and: ▪ ABS module C135-20, circuit 605 (RD), harness side. ▪ ABS module C135-11, circuit 483 (RD), harness side. ▪ ABS module C135-28, circuit 534 (YE/LG), harness side. • **Are the voltages greater than 10 volts?**	**Yes** GO to A2. **No** VERIFY BJB fuse 17 (40A) is OK. If OK, REPAIR circuit 534 (YE/LG) for an open. VERIFY BJB fuse 33 (30A) is OK. If OK, REPAIR circuit 483 (RD) for an open. VERIFY SJB fuse 20 (10A) is OK. If OK, REPAIR circuit 605 (RD) for an open. CLEAR the DTCs. REPEAT the self-test with the brake pedal not applied.
A2 CHECK CIRCUIT 57 (BK) FOR AN OPEN • Key in OFF position. • Measure the resistance between ground and: ▪ ABS module C135-1, circuit 57 (BK), harness side. ▪ ABS module C135-18, circuit 57 (BK), harness side. • **Are the resistances less than 5 ohms?**	**Yes** CHECK the module communications network. **No** REPAIR circuit 57 (BK) for an open. CLEAR the DTCs. REPEAT the self-test with the brake pedal not applied.

LTV0500000005031

Fig. 4   Test A: No Communication w/ABS module

Test Step	Result / Action to Take
B1 CHECK RECENT VEHICLE HISTORY • Using the diagnostic tool, clear the DTCs. • Drive the vehicle. • Using the diagnostic tool, retrieve the DTCs. • **Is DTC B1317 or B1318 still present?**	**Yes** GO to B2. **No** The system is operating normally at this time.
B2 CHECK THE BATTERY VOLTAGE • Measure the battery voltage between the positive and negative battery posts with the key ON engine OFF (KOEO). • **Is the battery voltage between 10 and 13 volts with KOEO?**	**Yes** GO to B3. **No** REFER to "Dash Gauges & Warning Indicators".
B3 CHECK THE CHARGING SYSTEM • Key in START position. • Measure the battery voltage between the positive and negative battery posts with the engine running. • **Is the battery voltage between 11 and 17 volts with the engine running?**	**Yes** GO to B4. **No** Check charging system.
B4 CHECK CIRCUIT 605 (RD) FOR VOLTAGE • Key in OFF position. • Disconnect: ABS Module C135. • Key in ON position. • Measure the voltage between ABS module C135-20, circuit 605 (RD), harness side and ground. • **Is the voltage greater than 10 volts?**	**Yes** GO to B5. **No** VERIFY SJB fuse 20 (10A) is OK. If OK, REPAIR circuit 605 (RD) for an open. CLEAR the DTCs. CARRY OUT the self-test with the brake pedal not applied.
B5 CHECK CIRCUIT 483 (RD) FOR VOLTAGE • Key in OFF position. • Measure the voltage between ABS module C135-11, circuit 483 (RD), harness side and ground. • **Is the voltage greater than 10**	**Yes** GO to B6. **No** VERIFY BJB fuse 33 (30A) is OK. If OK,

LTV0500000005032

Fig. 5   Test B, Codes C1186, B1317 & B1318: ABS Power Relay Output Circuit & Battery Voltage High/Low (Part 1 of 2)

volts?	REPAIR circuit 483 (RD) for an open. CLEAR the DTCs. CARRY OUT the self-test with the brake pedal not applied.
B6 CHECK CIRCUIT 534 (YE/LG) FOR AN OPEN	
• Measure the voltage between the ABS module C135-28, circuit 534 (YE/LG), harness side and ground. • **Is the voltage greater than 10 volts?**	**Yes** GO to B7 . **No** VERIFY BJB fuse 17 (40A) is OK. If OK, REPAIR circuit 534 (YE/LG) for an open. CLEAR the DTCs. CARRY OUT the self-test with the brake pedal not applied.
B7 CHECK CIRCUIT 57 (BK) FOR AN OPEN	
• Measure the resistance between: ▪ ABS module C135-1, circuit 57 (BK), harness side and ground. ▪ ABS module C135-18, circuit 57 (BK), harness side and ground. • **Are the resistances less than 5 ohms?**	**Yes** GO to B8 . **No** REPAIR circuit 57 (BK) for an open. CLEAR the DTCs. CARRY OUT the self-test with the brake pedal not applied.
B8 CHECK FOR CORRECT ABS MODULE OPERATION	
• Disconnect all ABS connectors. • Check for: ▪ corrosion. ▪ pushed-out pins. ▪ spread terminals. • Connect all ABS connectors and make sure they seat correctly. • Operate the system and verify the concern is still present. • **Is the concern still present?**	**Yes** INSTALL a new ABS module. TEST the system for normal operation. **No** The system is operating correctly at this time. Concern may have been caused by a loose or corroded connector. CLEAR the DTCs. CARRY OUT the self-test with the brake pedal not applied.

LTV0500000005033

Fig. 5 Test B, Codes C1186, B1317 & B1318: ABS Power Relay Output Circuit & Battery Voltage High/Low (Part 2 of 2)

• **Are the resistances greater than 10,000 ohms?**	
C3 CHECK THE WHEEL SPEED SENSOR CIRCUIT(S) FOR AN OPEN	
• **For DTC C1145** , measure the resistance between: ▪ ABS module C135-5, circuit 521 (TN/OG), harness side and LF wheel speed sensor C150-1, circuit 521 (TN/OG), harness side. ▪ ABS module C135-6, circuit 522 (TN/BK), harness side and LF wheel speed sensor C150-2, circuit 522 (TN/BK), harness side. • **For DTC C1155** , measure the resistance between: ▪ ABS module C135-3, circuit 516 (YE/BK), harness side and RF wheel speed sensor C150-1, circuit 516 (YE/BK), harness side. ▪ ABS module C135-4, circuit 514 (YE/RD), harness side and RF wheel speed sensor C150-2, circuit 514 (YE/RD), harness side. • **For DTC C1230** , measure the resistance between: ▪ ABS module C135-21, circuit 519 (LG/BK), harness side and rear wheel speed sensor C455-2, circuit 519 (LG/BK), harness side. ▪ ABS module C135-14, circuit 523 (RD/PK), harness side and rear wheel speed sensor C455-1, circuit 523 (RD/PK), harness side. • **Are the resistances less than 5 ohms?**	**Yes** GO to C4 . **No** REPAIR the affected circuit(s) for an open. CLEAR the DTCs. REPEAT the self-test with the brake pedal not applied.
C4 CHECK WHEEL SPEED SENSOR RESISTANCE	
• **For DTC C1145** , measure the resistance between RF wheel speed sensor C160-1, component side and RF wheel speed sensor C160-2, component side. • **For DTC C1155** , measure the resistance between LF wheel speed sensor C150-1, component side and LF wheel speed sensor C150-2, component side. • **For DTC C1230** , measure the resistance between rear wheel speed sensor C455-1, component side and rear wheel speed sensor C455-2, component side. • **Is the resistance between 800 and 1400**	**Yes** GO to C5 . **No** INSTALL a new wheel speed sensor. For the front wheel speed sensor (4x4), CLEAR the DTCs. REPEAT the self-test with the brake pedal not applied. For the front wheel speed sensor (4x2), CLEAR the DTCs. REPEAT the self-test with the brake pedal not applied.

LTV0500000005035

Fig. 6 Test C, Codes C1145, C1155 & C1230 (Part 2 of 3): Wheel Speed Sensor Circuit Failure

Test Step	Result / Action to Take
C1 CHECK THE WHEEL SPEED SENSOR CIRCUIT(S) FOR A SHORT TO VOLTAGE	
• Key in OFF position. • Disconnect: ABS Module C135. • Disconnect: Suspect Wheel Speed Sensor(s). • Key in ON position. • **For DTC C1145** , measure the voltage between ground and: ▪ ABS module C135-5, circuit 521 (TN/OG), harness side. ▪ ABS module C135-6, circuit 522 (TN/BK), harness side. • **For DTC C1155** , measure the voltage between ground and: ▪ ABS module C135-3, circuit 516 (YE/BK), harness side. ▪ ABS module C135-4, circuit 514 (YE/RD), harness side. • **For DTC C1230** , measure the voltage between ground and: ▪ ABS module C135-21, circuit 519 (LG/BK), harness side. ▪ ABS module C135-14, circuit 523 (RD/PK), harness side. • **Is voltage present?**	**Yes** REPAIR the affected circuit(s) for a short to voltage. CLEAR the DTCs and REPEAT the self-test with the brake pedal not applied. **No** GO to C2 .
C2 CHECK THE WHEEL SPEED SENSOR CIRCUIT(S) FOR A SHORT TO GROUND	
• Key in OFF position. • **For DTC C1145** , measure the resistance between ground and: ▪ ABS module C135-5, circuit 521 (TN/OG), harness side. ▪ ABS module C135-6, circuit 522 (TN/BK), harness side. • **For DTC C1155** , measure the resistance between ground and: ▪ ABS module C135-3, circuit 516 (YE/BK), harness side. ▪ ABS module C135-4, circuit 514 (YE/RD), harness side. • **For DTC C1230** , measure the resistance between ground and: ▪ ABS module C135-21, circuit 519 (LG/BK), harness side. ▪ ABS module C135-14, circuit 523 (RD/PK), harness side.	**Yes** GO to C3 . **No** REPAIR the affected circuit(s) for a short to ground. CLEAR the DTCs. REPEAT the self-test with the brake pedal not applied.

LTV0500000005034

Fig. 6 Test C, Codes C1145, C1155 & C1230: Wheel Speed Sensor Circuit Failure (Part 1 of 3)

ohms (front 4x2), 380 and 480 ohms (front 4x4) or 800 and 2500 ohms (rear all)?	For the rear wheel speed sensor. CLEAR the DTCs. REPEAT the self-test with the brake pedal not applied.
C5 CHECK WHEEL SPEED SENSOR HARNESS FOR DAMAGE	
• Inspect the wheel speed sensor harness at the affected wheel end for chafing or other wiring damage. • **Is damage found?**	**Yes** INSTALL a new wheel speed sensor. For the front wheel speed sensor (4x4), CLEAR the DTCs. REPEAT the self-test with the brake pedal not applied. For the front wheel speed sensor (4x2), CLEAR the DTCs. REPEAT the self-test with the brake pedal not applied. For the rear wheel speed sensor. CLEAR the DTCs. REPEAT the self-test with the brake pedal not applied. **No** GO to C6 .
C6 CHECK FOR CORRECT ABS MODULE OPERATION	
• Disconnect all ABS connectors. • Check for: ▪ corrosion. ▪ pushed-out pins. ▪ spread terminals. • Connect all ABS connectors and make sure they seat correctly. • Operate the system and verify the concern is still present. • **Is the concern still present?**	**Yes** INSTALL a new ABS module. TEST the system for normal operation. **No** The system is operating correctly at this time. Concern may have been caused by a loose or corroded connector. CLEAR the DTCs. REPEAT the self-test with the brake pedal not applied.

LTV0500000005036

Fig. 6 Test C, Codes C1145, C1155 & C1230 (Part 3 of 3): Wheel Speed Sensor Circuit Failure

Test Step	Result / Action to Take
D1 CHECK ALL TIRE SIZES	
NOTE: If DTCs C1145, C1155 or C1230 are present, they must be fixed before C1148, C1158, C1229, C1233, C1234 and C1237. For any other DTCs go to the appropriate pinpoint test. • Make sure that all the tire sizes are correct and matching. • **Are all the tires the correct size?**	**Yes** GO to D2 . **No** INSTALL a new tire of the correct size for each tire that is incorrect. CLEAR the DTCs. Turn the ignition switch to the OFF position. Turn the ignition switch to the ON position, CLEAR the DTCs and DRIVE the vehicle at least 10 km/h (6.25 mph) for at least 3 minutes.
D2 CHECK THE WHEEL SPEED SENSOR PIDs	
• Key in OFF position. • Connect the diagnostic tool. • Key in ON position. • Using the diagnostic tool, monitor the anti-lock brake system (ABS) module PIDs LF, RF and RR while driving the vehicle at a constant speed above 20 km/h (12.43 mph) for at least 10 seconds. • **Are the wheel speed sensor PIDs consistent?**	**Yes** GO to D7 . **No** GO to D3 .
D3 CHECK THE WHEEL SPEED SENSOR OUTPUT(S) AT THE ABS MODULE	
• Key in OFF position. • Disconnect: ABS Module C135. • **For DTC C1148 and C1234**, while spinning the wheel, measure the voltage (A/C) between ABS module C135-5, circuit 521 (TN/OG), harness side and ABS module C135-6, circuit 522 (TN/BK), harness side. • **For DTC C1158 and C1233**, while spinning the wheel measure the voltage (A/C) between ABS module C135-3, circuit 516 (YE/BK), harness side and ABS module C135-4, circuit 514 (YE/RD), harness side. • **For DTC C1229 and C1237**, while spinning the wheel, measure the voltage (A/C) between ABS module C135-21, circuit 519 (LG/BK),	**Yes** GO to D6 . **No** GO to D4 .

LTV0500000005037

Fig. 7   Test D, Codes C1148, C1158, C1229, C1233, C1234 & C1237: Wheel Speed Sensor Coherency Fault Signal Incorrect (Part 1 of 3)

measure the resistance between RF wheel speed sensor C160-1, component side and RF wheel speed sensor C160-2, component side. • **For DTC C1158 and C1233**, measure the resistance between LF wheel speed sensor C150-1, component side and LF wheel speed sensor C150-2, component side. • **For DTC C1229 and C1237**, measure the resistance between rear wheel speed sensor C455-1, component side and rear wheel speed sensor C455-2, component side. • **Is the resistance between 800 and 1400 ohms (front 4x2), 380 and 480 ohms (front 4x4) or 800 and 2500 ohms (rear all)?**	GO to D6 . **No** INSTALL a new wheel speed sensor. For the front wheel speed sensor (4x4), CLEAR the DTCs. Turn the ignition switch to the OFF position. Turn the ignition switch to the ON position, CLEAR the DTCs and DRIVE the vehicle at least 10 km/h (6.25 mph) for at least 3 minutes. For the front wheel speed sensor (4x2), CLEAR the DTCs. Turn the ignition switch to the OFF position. Turn the ignition switch to the ON position, CLEAR the DTCs and DRIVE the vehicle at least 10 km/h (6.25 mph) for at least 3 minutes. For the rear wheel speed sensor, CLEAR the DTCs. Turn the ignition switch to the OFF position. Turn the ignition switch to the ON position, CLEAR the DTCs and DRIVE the vehicle at least 10 km/h (6.25 mph) for at least 3 minutes.
D6 CHECK THE WHEEL SPEED SENSOR OUTPUT	
• **For DTC C1148 and C1234**, while spinning the wheel, measure the voltage (A/C) between RF wheel speed sensor C160-1, component side and RF wheel speed sensor C160-2, component side. • **For DTC C1158 and C1233**, while spinning the wheel, measure the voltage (A/C) between LF wheel speed sensor C150-1, component side and LF wheel speed sensor C150-2, component side. • **For DTC C1229 and C1237**, while spinning the wheel, measure the voltage (A/C) between rear wheel speed sensor C455-1, component side and rear wheel speed sensor C455-2, component side. • **Is the wheel speed sensor output between 150 mvolts and 3500 mvolts?**	**Yes** GO to D7 . **No** INSTALL a new wheel speed sensor ring. For the front wheel speed sensor ring (4x4), INSTALL a new front wheel hub. CLEAR the DTCs. Turn the ignition switch to the OFF position. Turn the ignition switch to the ON position, CLEAR the DTCs and DRIVE the vehicle at least 10 km/h (6.25 mph) for at least 3 minutes. For the front wheel speed sensor ring (4x2), INSTALL a new front brake disc. CLEAR the DTCs. Turn the ignition switch to the OFF position. Turn the ignition switch to the ON position, CLEAR the DTCs and DRIVE the vehicle at least 10 km/h (6.25 mph) for at least 3 minutes. For the rear wheel speed sensor ring, rear drive axle/differential — 7.5-inch ring gear, For the rear drive axle/differential — 8.8-inch ring gear, For the rear drive axle/differential — 8.8-inch ring gear high torque, CLEAR the DTCs. Turn the ignition switch to the OFF

LTV0500000005039

Fig. 7   Test D, Codes C1148, C1158, C1229, C1233, C1234 & C1237: Wheel Speed Sensor Coherency Fault Signal Incorrect (Part 3 of 3)

harness side and ABS module C135-14, circuit 523 (RD/PK), harness side. • **Is the wheel speed sensor output between 150 mvolts and 3500 mvolts?**	
D4 CHECK THE WHEEL SPEED SENSOR CIRCUIT(S) FOR AN OPEN	

• Disconnect: Suspect Wheel Speed Sensor(s).
• **For DTC C1148 and C1234**, measure the resistance between
  ▪ ABS module C135-5, circuit 521 (TN/OG), harness side and LF wheel speed sensor C150-1, circuit 521 (TN/OG), harness side.
  ▪ ABS module C135-6, circuit 522 (TN/BK), harness side and LF wheel speed sensor C150-2, circuit 522 (TN/BK), harness side.
• **For DTC C1158 and C1233**, measure the resistance between:
  ▪ ABS module C135-3, circuit 516 (YE/BK), harness side and RF wheel speed sensor C160-1, circuit 516 (YE/BK), harness side.
  ▪ ABS module C135-4, circuit 514 (YE/RD), harness side and RF wheel speed sensor C160-2, circuit 514 (YE/RD), harness side.
• **For DTC C1229 and C1237**, measure the resistance between:
  ▪ ABS module C135-21, circuit 519 (LG/BK), harness side and rear wheel speed sensor C455-2, circuit 519 (LG/BK), harness side.
  ▪ ABS module C135-14, circuit 523 (RD/PK), harness side and rear wheel speed sensor C455-1, circuit 523 (RD/PK), harness side.
• **Are the resistances less than 5 ohms?**
	Yes
	GO to D5 .
	
	No
	REPAIR the affected circuit(s) for an open, CLEAR the DTCs. Turn the ignition switch to the OFF position. Turn the ignition switch to the ON position, CLEAR the DTCs and DRIVE the vehicle at least 10 km/h (6.25 mph) for at least 3 minutes.

D5 CHECK THE WHEEL SPEED SENSOR(S) RESISTANCE	
• **For DTC C1148 and C1234**,	**Yes**

LTV0500000005038

Fig. 7   Test D, Codes C1148, C1158, C1229, C1233, C1234 & C1237: Wheel Speed Sensor Coherency Fault Signal Incorrect (Part 2 of 3)

Test Step	Result / Action to Take
E1 CHECK THE ABS PUMP MOTOR	
• Key in ON position. • **Is the pump motor on constantly?**	**Yes** GO to E4 . **No** GO to E2 .
E2 CHECK CIRCUIT 534 (YE/LG) FOR AN OPEN	
• Key in OFF position. • Disconnect: ABS Module C135. • Key in ON position. • Measure the voltage between ABS module C135-28, circuit 534 (YE/LG), harness side and ground. • **Is the voltage greater than 10 volts?**	**Yes** GO to E3 . **No** VERIFY BJB fuse 17 (40A) is OK. If OK, REPAIR circuit 534 (YE/LG) for an open. TEST the system for normal operation.
E3 CHECK CIRCUIT 57 (BK) FOR AN OPEN	
• Key in OFF position. • Measure the resistance between ABS module C135-18, circuit 57 (BK), harness side and ground. • **Is the resistance less than 5 ohms?**	**Yes** GO to E4 . **No** REPAIR circuit 57 (BK) for an open. TEST the system for normal

LTV0500000005362

Fig. 8   Test E, Codes C1095 & C1096: ABS Hydraulic Pump Motor Circuit Failure/Open (Part 1 of 2)

	operation.

E4 CHECK FOR CORRECT ABS MODULE OPERATION	

• Disconnect all ABS connectors.
• Check for:
    ▪ corrosion.
    ▪ pushed-out pins.
    ▪ spread terminals.
• Connect all ABS connectors and make sure they seat correctly.
• Operate the system and verify the concern is still present.
• **Is the concern still present?**
	Yes
	GO to <u>E5</u>.
	
	No
	The system is operating correctly at this time. Concern may have been caused by a loose or corroded connector. CLEAR the DTCs. REPEAT the self-test with the brake pedal not applied.

E5 CHECK THE ABS PUMP MOTOR FOR CORRECT OPERATION	
• Key in OFF position. • Remove the ABS module. • Connect a fused (50A) jumper wire between the positive battery terminal and the pump motor positive terminal on the HCU. Momentarily connect a jumper wire between the negative battery terminal and the pump motor negative terminal on the HCU. • **Does the ABS pump motor operate?**	**Yes** INSTALL a new ABS module. After the repairs, CARRY OUT the self-test with the brake pedal not applied. **No** INSTALL a new HCU assembly. CARRY OUT the self-test with the brake pedal not applied.

LTV0500000005363

Fig. 8   Test E, Codes C1095 & C1096: ABS Hydraulic Pump Motor Circuit Failure/Open (Part 2 of 2)

F4 CHECK CIRCUIT 810 (RD/LG) FOR A SHORT TO VOLTAGE	
• Key in OFF position. • Disconnect: Brake Pedal Position (BPP) Switch C278. • Key in ON position. • Using the diagnostic tool, monitor the ABS module BPP switch PID. • **Does the PID read active?**	**Yes** REPAIR circuit 810 (RD/LG) for a short to voltage. CLEAR the DTCs and CARRY OUT the self-test with the brake pedal not applied. **No** INSTALL a new BPP switch. CLEAR the DTCs and CARRY OUT the self-test with the brake pedal not applied.
F5 CHECK FOR CORRECT ABS MODULE OPERATION	

• Disconnect all ABS connectors.
• Check for:
    ▪ corrosion.
    ▪ pushed-out pins.
    ▪ spread terminals.
• Connect all ABS connectors and make sure they seat correctly.
• Operate the system and verify the concern is still present by CARRYING OUT the self-test with the brake pedal not applied.
• **Is the concern still present?**
	Yes
	INSTALL a new ABS module TEST the system for normal operation.
	
	No
	The system is operating correctly at this time. Concern may have been caused by a loose or corroded connector. CLEAR the DTCs. CARRY OUT the self-test with the brake pedal not applied.

LTV0500000005365

Fig. 9   Test F, Code B1485: Brake Pedal Input Circuit Battery Short (Part 2 of 2)

Test Step	Result / Action to Take
F1 CHECK CIRCUIT 810 (RD/LG) FOR VOLTAGE	
• Key in OFF position. • Disconnect: ABS Module C135. • Key in ON position. • Measure the voltage between ABS module C135-8, circuit 810 (RD/LG), harness side and ground while applying and releasing the brake pedal. • **Is the voltage greater than 10 volts with the brake pedal applied and 0 volt with the brake pedal released?**	**Yes** GO to <u>F5</u>. **No** GO to <u>F2</u>.
F2 CHECK ABS MODULE BRAKE PEDAL PID	
• Key in OFF position. • Connect the diagnostic tool. • Key in ON position. • Using the diagnostic tool, monitor the ABS module brake pedal position (BPP) switch PID. • **Does the PID read active with the brake pedal released and read inactive with the brake pedal applied?**	**Yes** GO to <u>F3</u>. **No** GO to <u>F5</u>.
F3 CHECK THE BRAKE SHIFT INTERLOCK SOLENOID	
• Key in OFF position. • Disconnect: Brake Shift Interlock Solenoid. • Key in ON position. • Using the diagnostic tool, monitor the ABS module BPP switch PID. • **Does the PID read active with the brake pedal released?**	**Yes** GO to <u>F4</u>. **No** INSTALL a new brake shift interlock. CLEAR the DTCs and CARRY OUT the self-test with the brake pedal not applied.

LTV0500000005364

Fig. 9   Test F, Code B1485: Brake Pedal Input Circuit Battery Short (Part 1 of 2)

Test Step	Result / Action to Take
G1 CHECK THE 4X4 STATUS CIRCUIT AT THE ABS MODULE	
• Verify the correct operation of the 4x4. If the 4x4 is not operating correctly it must be repaired before proceedingKey in OFF position. • Disconnect: Instrument Cluster C220b. • Measure the voltage between the instrument cluster C220b-9, circuit 210 (LB), harness side and ground. • **Is the voltage greater than 10 volts?**	**Yes** GO to <u>G2</u>. **No** GO to <u>G3</u>.
G2 CHECK FOR CORRECT INSTRUMENT CLUSTER OPERATION	

• Disconnect all instrument cluster connectors.
• Check for:
    ▪ corrosion.
    ▪ pushed-out pins.
    ▪ spread terminals.
• Connect all instrument cluster connectors and make sure they seat correctly.
• Operate the system and verify the concern is still present.
• **Is the concern still present?**
	Yes
	INSTALL a new instrument cluster.
	
	No
	The system is operating correctly at this time. Concern may have been caused by a loose or corroded connector. CLEAR the DTCs. REPEAT the self-test with the brake pedal not applied.

G3 CHECK CIRCUIT 210 (LB) FOR AN OPEN	
• Key in OFF position. • Disconnect: ABS Module C135. • Measure the resistance between ABS module C135-10, circuit 210 (LB), harness side and instrument cluster C220b-9, circuit 210, (LB) harness side. • **Is the resistance less than 5 ohms?**	**Yes** GO to <u>G4</u>. **No** REPAIR circuit 210 (LB) for an open. CLEAR the DTCs. REPEAT the self-test with the brake pedal not applied.
G4 CHECK CIRCUIT 210 (LB) FOR A SHORT TO GROUND	
• Measure the resistance between the ABS module C135-10, circuit 210, (LB) harness side and ground. • **Is the resistance greater than 10,000 ohms?**	**Yes** GO to <u>G5</u>. **No** REPAIR circuit 210 (LB) for a short to ground. CLEAR the DTCs. REPEAT the self-test with the brake pedal not applied.
G5 CHECK CIRCUIT 210 (LB) FOR A SHORT TO POWER	

LTV0500000005366

Fig. 10   Test G, Code C1414: Incorrect Module Design Level (Part 1 of 2)

• Key in ON position. • Measure the voltage between the ABS module C135-10, circuit 210 (LB), harness side and ground. • **Is there any voltage present?**	**Yes** REPAIR circuit 210 (LB) for a short to voltage. CLEAR the DTCs. REPEAT the self-test with the brake pedal not applied. **No** GO to G6 .
G6 CHECK FOR CORRECT ABS MODULE OPERATION	

• Disconnect all ABS connectors.
• Check for:
   ▪ corrosion.
   ▪ pushed-out pins.
   ▪ spread terminals.
• Connect all ABS connectors and make sure they seat correctly.
• Operate the system and verify the concern is still present.
• **Is the concern still present?**
	Yes
	INSTALL a new ABS module. TEST the system for normal operation.
	
	No
	The system is operating correctly at this time. Concern may have been caused by a loose or corroded connector. CLEAR the DTCs. REPEAT the self-test with the brake pedal not applied.

LTV0500000005367

Fig. 10 Test G, Code C1414: Incorrect Module Design Level (Part 2 of 2)

H3 CHECK CIRCUIT 512 (TN/LG) AND 531 (DG/YE) FOR A SHORT TO GROUND	

• Measure the resistance between ground and:
   ▪ ABS module C135-25, circuit 512 (TN/LG), harness side.
   ▪ ABS module C135-23, circuit 531 (DG/YE), harness side.
• **Is the resistance greater than 10,000 ohms?**
	Yes
	GO to H4 .
	
	No
	REPAIR the affected circuit(s) for a short to ground. CLEAR the DTCs. REPEAT the self-test with the brake pedal not applied.

H4 CHECK FOR CORRECT ABS MODULE OPERATION	

• Disconnect all ABS connectors.
• Check for:
   ▪ corrosion.
   ▪ pushed-out pins.
   ▪ spread terminals.
• Connect all ABS connectors and make sure they seat correctly.
• Operate the system and verify the concern is still present.
• **Is the concern still present?**
	Yes
	INSTALL a new ABS module TEST the system for normal operation.
	
	No
	The system is operating correctly at this time. Concern may have been caused by a loose or corroded connector. CLEAR the DTCs. REPEAT the self-test with the brake pedal not applied.

LTV0500000005369

Fig. 11 Test H, Code C1187: Brake Fluid Level Input Circuit Open (Part 2 of 2)

Test Step	Result / Action to Take
H1 CHECK ABS MODULE OPERATION	
• Disconnect: Brake Fluid Level Switch C124. • Connect a fused (10A) jumper wire between the brake fluid level switch C124-2, circuit 512 (TN/LG), harness side and the brake fluid level switch C124-3, circuit 531 (DG/YE), harness side. • Connect the diagnostic tool. • Key in ON position. • Using the diagnostic tool, clear the DTCS and repeat the self-test with the brake pedal not applied. Retrieve the DTCs. • **Is DTC C1187 retrieved again?**	**Yes** GO to H2 . **No** INSTALL a new brake fluid reservoir. CLEAR the DTCs and REPEAT the self-test with the brake pedal not applied.
H2 CHECK CIRCUIT 512 (TN/LG) AND 531 (DG/YE) FOR AN OPEN	

• Key in OFF position.
• Disconnect: ABS Module C135.
• Measure the resistance between:
   ▪ ABS module C135-25, circuit 512 (TN/LG), harness side and brake fluid level switch C124-2, circuit 512 (TN/LG), harness side.
   ▪ ABS module C135-23, circuit 531 (DG/YE), harness side and brake fluid level switch C124-3, circuit 531 (DG/YE), harness side.
• **Are the resistances less than 5 ohms?**
	Yes
	GO to H3 .
	
	No
	REPAIR the affected circuit(s) for an open. CLEAR the DTCs. REPEAT the self-test with the brake pedal not applied.

LTV0500000005368

Fig. 11 Test H, Code C1187: Brake Fluid Level Input Circuit Open (Part 1 of 2)

Test Step	Result / Action to Take
I1 CHECK ALL WHEEL SPEED SENSORS FOR DAMAGE AND LOOSENESS	
NOTE: If DTCs C1148, C1158, C1229, C1233, C1234 and C1237 were originally retrieved and cleared, CARRY OUT the following pinpoint test. **NOTE:** Any time a wheel speed sensor is removed, thoroughly clean the mounting surfaces. On front wheel speed sensors, apply grease. • With the vehicle in NEUTRAL, position it on a hoist. • ⚠ **CAUTION: Examine the wheel speed sensor wire carefully with good light. Failure to verify damage inn the wheel speed sensor wire can lead to unnecessary installation of a new component.** • Inspect the wheel speed sensor mounting for looseness. If the wheel speed sensor is suspected, inspect the sensor for corrosion on the rear axle housing boss or on the front wheel speed sensor mounting flange. Clean as necessary. • **Is the wheel speed sensor OK?**	**Yes** GO to I2 . **No** If the wheel speed sensor mounting is loose or corroded, REMOVE the wheel speed sensor, plug the opening and thoroughly clean the mounting surfaces. CLEAR the DTCS. REPEAT The self-test. If the wheel speed sensor is damaged, INSTALL a new sensor. For the front wheel speed sensor (4x4), CLEAR the DTCs. REPEAT the self-test. For the front wheel speed sensor (4x2), CLEAR the DTCs. REPEAT the self-test. For the rear sensor, CLEAR the DTCs. REPEAT the self-test.
I2 CHECK ALL WHEEL SPEED SENSOR RINGS FOR DAMAGE	
NOTE: Any time a wheel speed sensor is removed, thoroughly clean the mounting surfaces. On front wheel speed sensors, apply grease. • Remove the wheel speed sensor. • ⚠ **CAUTION: Examine the wheel speed sensor wire carefully with good light. Failure to verify damage in the wheel speed sensor wire can lead to unnecessary installation of a new component.**	**Yes** GO to I3 . **No** INSTALL a new wheel speed sensor ring. For the front wheel speed sensor ring (4x4), INSTALL a new front wheel hub. CLEAR the DTCs. REPEAT the self-test with the brake pedal not applied. For the front wheel speed sensor ring

LTV0500000005370

Fig. 12 Test I: Check For Correct ABS Module Operation (Part 1 of 2)

• Inspect the wheel speed sensor ring for damaged or missing teeth. Rotate the wheel to verify that no teeth are missing. • **Is the wheel speed sensor ring OK?**	(4x2), INSTALL a new front brake disc. CLEAR the DTCs. REPEAT the self-test with the brake pedal not applied. For the rear wheel speed sensor ring, rear drive axle/differential — 7.5-inch ring gear, Rear drive axle/differential — 8.8-inch ring gear, Rear drive axle/differential — 8.8-inch ring gear high torque, CLEAR the DTCs. REPEAT the self-test with the brake pedal not applied.
I3 CHECK FOR CORRECT ABS MODULE OPERATION	

• Disconnect all ABS connectors.
• Check for:
   ▪ corrosion.
   ▪ pushed-out pins.
   ▪ spread terminals.
• Connect all ABS connectors and make sure they seat correctly.
• Operate the system and verify the concern is still present.
• **Is the concern still present?**
	Yes
	GO to the Anti-Lock Brake Control Module Diagnostic Trouble Code (DTC) Index to continue diagnosis of the DTCs.
	
	No
	The system is operating correctly at this time. Concern may have been caused by a loose or corroded connector. CLEAR the DTCs. REPEAT the self-test with the brake pedal not applied.

LTV0500000005371

Fig. 12 Test I: Check For Correct ABS Module Operation (Part 2 of 2)

Villager

NOTE: Electrical Symbol & Wire Color Code Identification Located In The Front Of This Manual May Be Used As An Aid When Using Wiring Circuits Found In This Section.

NOTE: Refer To "Computer Relearn Procedures" Located In The Front Of This Manual When Battery Power To The Computer Has Been Interrupted.

INDEX

	Page No.		Page No.		Page No.
Description	5-184	Diagnostic Trouble Code Interpretation	5-185	Wheel Speed Sensor	5-185
Component Locations	5-184	Wiring Diagrams	5-185	**Troubleshooting**	5-185
System Operation	5-184	**Diagnostic Chart Index**	5-188	No Communication w/ABS	
Diagnosis & Testing	5-185	**Precautions**	5-184	Control Module	5-185
Accessing Diagnostic Trouble Codes	5-185	Battery Ground Cable	5-184	Soft/Excessive Pedal Travel	5-185
		Brake Fluid Handling	5-184	Unable To Enter Self Test	5-185
Clearing Diagnostic Trouble Codes	5-185	**System Service**	5-185	Yellow ABS Warning Indicator Does Not Self-Check	5-185
Diagnostic Tests	5-185	Brake System Bleed	5-185		
Pinpoint Tests	5-185	Component Replacement	5-185		
Quick Test	5-185	Electronic Hydraulic Control Unit (EHCU)	5-185		

PRECAUTIONS

BATTERY GROUND CABLE

Prior to service disconnect battery ground cable and isolate as required.

BRAKE FLUID HANDLING

Brake fluid can cause serious injury and vehicle damage if not handled properly. Avoid contact with eyes and do not allow fluid to splash or spill on painted surfaces. Wash hands thoroughly after handling.

DESCRIPTION

SYSTEM OPERATION

The anti-lock brake system (ABS) uses electronic and hydraulic components to prevent wheel lockup during brake application.

The ABS system is controlled by an ABS control module, located behind the control console. The control module receives and compares wheel speed readings from each wheel speed sensor. By monitoring these speed readings, the control module will ac-tivate the ABS system when wheel lockup is about to occur.

The control module also has self-diagnostic capabilities, including diagnostic trouble code memory. If a diagnostic trouble code is stored in memory, the instrument panel "ANTI-LOCK" lamp will illuminate when the engine is running.

COMPONENT LOCATIONS

Refer to **Fig. 1** for component locations.

TROUBLESHOOTING

No Communication w/ABS Control Module

1. Inspect central junction box fuse F35 (10A).
2. Inspect battery junction box fuse F10 (20A), and F18 (40A).
3. Inspect circuit.
4. Inspect ABS control module.

Unable To Enter Self Test

Inspect ABS control module.

Yellow ABS Warning Indicator Does Not Self-Check

Inspect ABS control module.

Soft/Excessive Pedal Travel

1. Inspect for hydraulic leak.
2. Inspect hydraulic control unit.
3. Inspect base brake system.

DIAGNOSIS & TESTING

Accessing Diagnostic Trouble Codes

1. Connect New Generation STAR (NGS) Tester tool No. 007-00500, or equivalent, to Data Link Connector (DLC) located beneath central junction box.
2. Select vehicle.
3. If NGS Tester does not communicate with vehicle, proceed as follows:
   a. Ensure program card is properly installed.
   b. Inspect connections to vehicle.
   c. Ensure ignition switch is in On position.
   d. If NGS Tester still does not communicate with vehicle, refer to NGS Tester manual.
4. Follow NGS Tester instructions to retrieve DTC's.

Diagnostic Trouble Code Interpretation

Refer to **Fig. 2** for diagnostic trouble code interpretation.

Wiring Diagrams

Refer to **Fig. 3** for wiring diagrams.

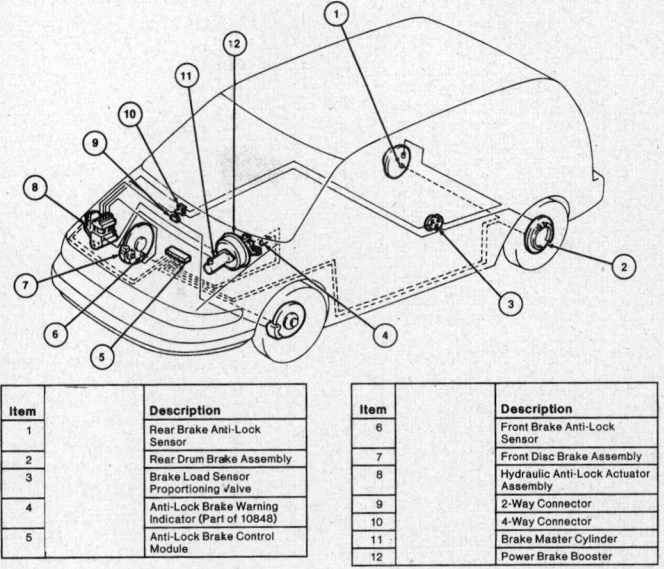

Item	Description
1	Rear Brake Anti-Lock Sensor
2	Rear Drum Brake Assembly
3	Brake Load Sensor Proportioning Valve
4	Anti-Lock Brake Warning Indicator (Part of 10848)
5	Anti-Lock Brake Control Module

Item	Description
6	Front Brake Anti-Lock Sensor
7	Front Disc Brake Assembly
8	Hydraulic Anti-Lock Actuator Assembly
9	2-Way Connector
10	4-Way Connector
11	Brake Master Cylinder
12	Power Brake Booster

FM4029600857000X

Fig. 1   ABS component locations

Diagnostic Tests

QUICK TEST

The Quick Test procedure must be performed first. Failure to do so may result in incorrect system diagnosis and replacement of good components.

The Quick Test is used to diagnose a vehicle for relatively simple repairs, such as loose connectors and blown fuses. However, the Quick Test is also used to prepare the vehicle for further diagnostics, including warning lamp diagnostic trouble code diagnosis. Refer to **Fig. 4** for quick test procedures.

PINPOINT TESTS

Refer to **Figs. 5 through 15** for pinpoint tests.

Clearing Diagnostic Trouble Codes

Follow instructions on the NGS Tester to clear DTC's.

SYSTEM SERVICE

Brake System Bleed

Refer to "Hydraulic Brake Systems" chapter for bleeding procedure.

Component Replacement

ELECTRONIC HYDRAULIC CONTROL UNIT (EHCU)

1. Remove air cleaner outlet tube and air cleaner.
2. Disconnect EHCU connector.
3. Disconnect brake lines from EHCU, then cap brake lines.
4. Disconnect transaxle shift cable from EHCU bracket.
5. Remove EHCU bracket bolts, then loosen bracket nut.
6. Remove EHCU bracket from EHCU.
7. Reverse procedure to install, noting the following:
   a. Bleed brake system.
   b. **Torque** EHCU bracket bolts to 10 ft. lbs.
   c. **Torque** brake lines to 12 ft. lbs.

WHEEL SPEED SENSOR

FRONT

1. **On right anti-lock sensor,** disconnect engine wiring harness bulkhead connector, then the speed control vacuum supply line.
2. **On both anti-lock sensors,** disconnect anti-lock brake sensor electrical connector.
3. Raise and support vehicle.
4. Pull sensor cable and grommet through inner fender well.
5. Remove sensor cable retaining bolts.
6. Remove sensor pin-type retainer and retaining bolt, then the sensor.
7. Reverse procedure to install, noting the following:
   a. **Torque** anti-lock sensor bolt to 15 ft. lbs.
   b. **Torque** anti-lock sensor cable retaining bolts to 44 inch lbs.

REAR

1. Raise and support vehicle.
2. Disconnect anti-lock brake sensor electrical connector.
3. Remove sensor cable upper and lower bracket bolts.
4. Remove sensor cable bushing from axle housing bracket.
5. Remove sensor retaining bolt, then the sensor.
6. Reverse procedure to install. **Torque** sensor retaining bolt to 15 ft. lbs.

DTC	Description
12	No DTCs Retrieved
18	Anti-Lock Brake Sensor Indicator Output Failure
21	RF Anti-Lock Brake Sensor Circuit Open
22	RF Anti-Lock Brake Sensor Circuit Short
25	LF Anti-Lock Brake Sensor Circuit Open
26	LF Anti-Lock Brake Sensor Circuit Short
31	RR Anti-Lock Brake Sensor Circuit Open
32	RR Anti-Lock Brake Sensor Circuit Short
35	LR Anti-Lock Brake Sensor Circuit Open
36	LR Anti-Lock Brake Sensor Circuit Short
41	RF Hydraulic Control Unit Outlet Valve
42	RF Hydraulic Control Unit Inlet Valve
45	LF Hydraulic Control Unit Outlet Valve
46	LF Hydraulic Control Unit Inlet Valve
51	RR Hydraulic Control Unit Outlet Valve
52	RR Hydraulic Control Unit Inlet Valve
55	LR Hydraulic Control Unit Outlet Valve
56	LR Hydraulic Control Unit Inlet Valve
57	Low Battery Voltage
61	Pump Motor or Pump Motor Relay
63	Solenoid Valve Relay
71	ECU Internal Failure

FM4029901355000X

Fig. 2 Diagnostic trouble code interpretation

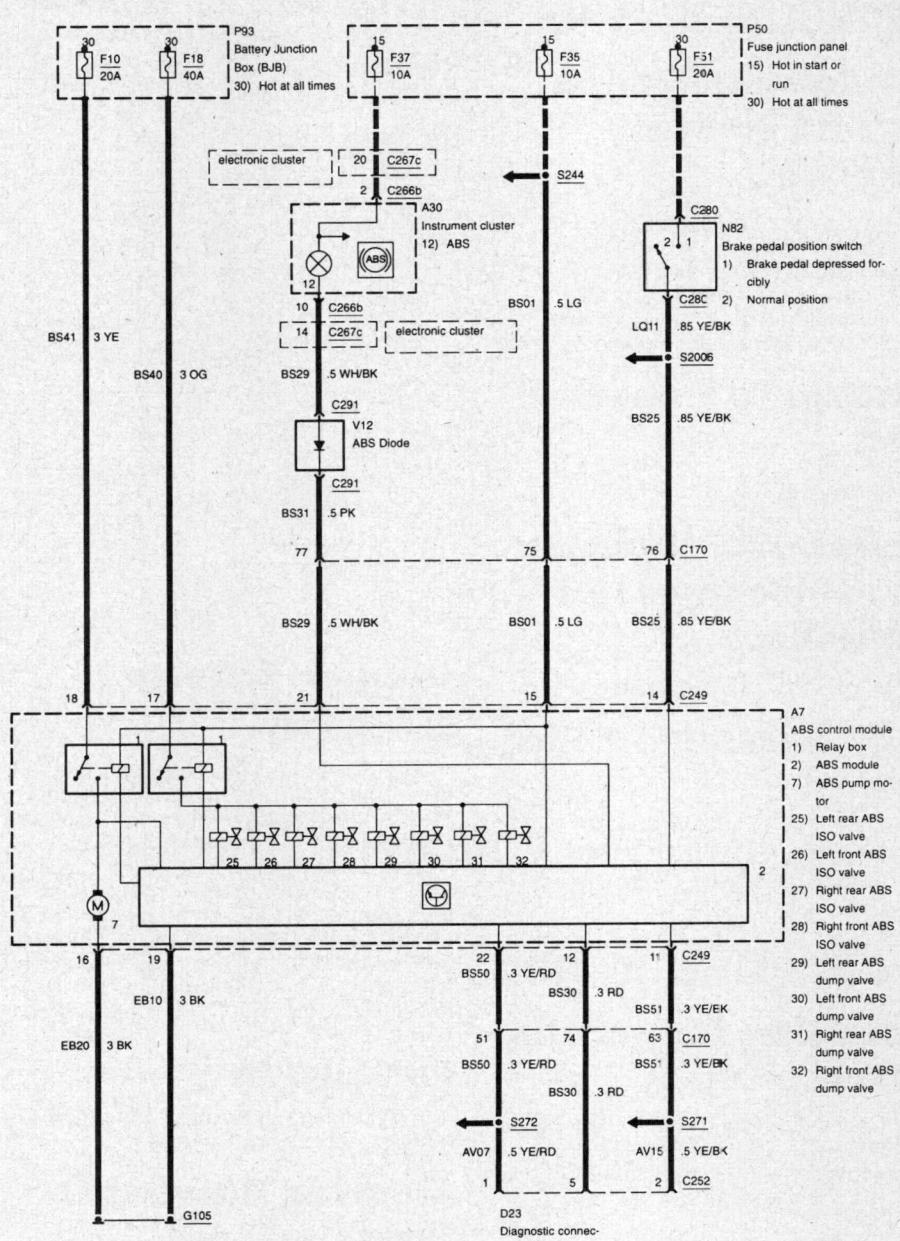

FM4029901357010X

Fig. 3 Wiring diagram (Part 1 of 2)

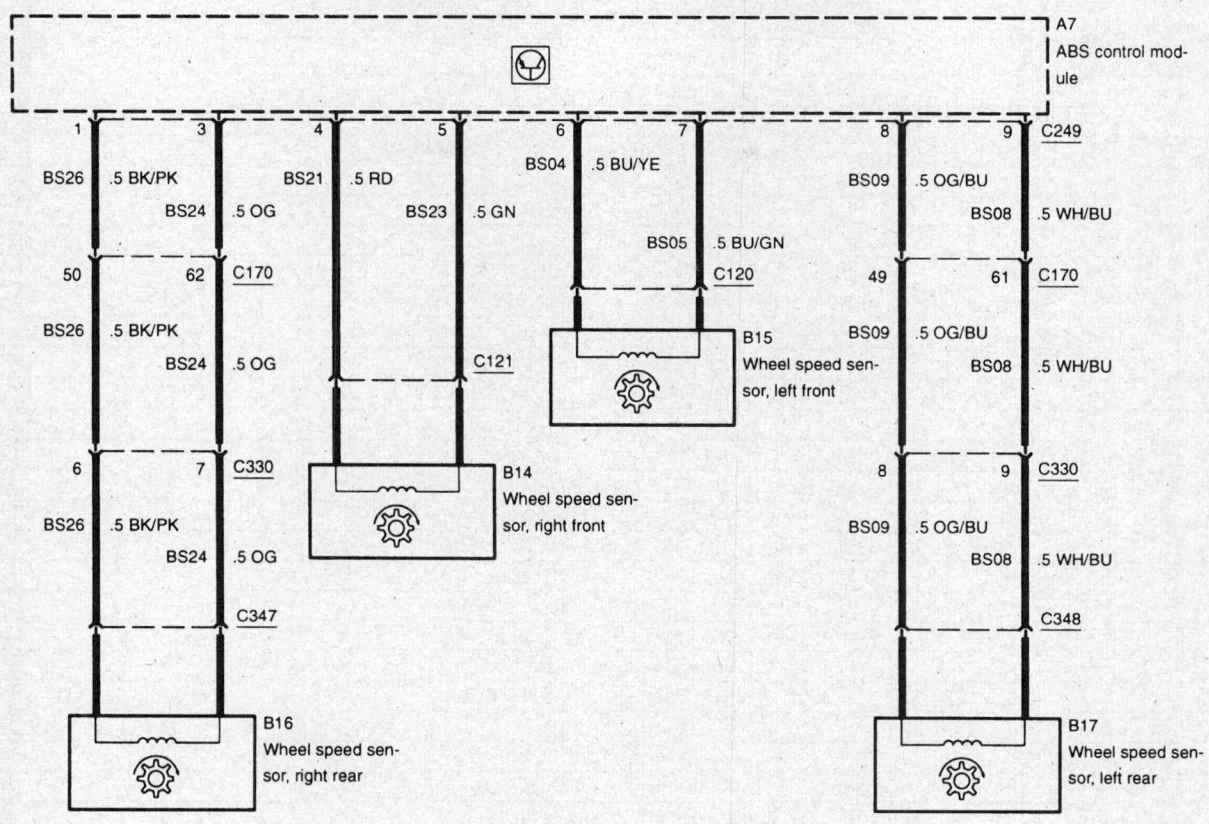

Fig. 3   Wiring diagram (Part 2 of 2)

FM4029901357020X

TEST STEP		RESULT	▶	ACTION TO TAKE
QT1	**PERFORM VISUAL INSPECTION**			
	• Check for insufficient brake fluid, leaks, damaged brake anti-lock sensors or front disc brake rotors, and damaged hydraulic anti-lock actuator assembly. • Check the Anti-lock Brake System (ABS) wiring harness for improper connections, bent or broken pins, corrosion, loose wires, and proper routing. • Check all of the fuses for proper connection or damage. • Check the anti-lock brake control module for physical damage. • **Are all of the components OK?**	Yes No	▶ ▶	GO to **QT2**. SERVICE the fault(s) in question: GO to **QT2**.
QT2	**PERFORM VEHICLE PREPARATION**			
	• Perform all of the following safety steps required to run the Quick Test. — Apply the parking brake. — Place the gearshift lever firmly into the PARK (P) position. — Block the drive wheels. • Turn off all of the electrical loads. — Radios — Lamps — A/C — Heater blower fans, etc. • **Have all of the safety steps been performed and all of the electrical loads been turned off?**	Yes No	▶ ▶	GO to **QT3**. Personal safety and correct diagnostic results are dependent on Test Step **QT2**. DO NOT PROCEED with Quick Test if vehicle preparation cannot be performed.

FM4029500614010X

Fig. 4   Quick test (Part 1 of 2)

TEST STEP		RESULT	▶	ACTION TO TAKE
QT3	**CHECK ANTI-LOCK BRAKE WARNING INDICATOR**			
	• Key ON. • Observe the anti-lock brake warning indicator. • **Does the anti-lock brake warning indicator illuminate for approximately 3 seconds then go out?**	Yes No (Not illuminated) No (Stays illuminated)	▶ ▶ ▶	GO to **QT4**. GO to Pinpoint Test **A1**. GO to **QT4**.
QT4	**CHECK ANTI-LOCK BRAKE WARNING INDICATOR WITH ENGINE RUNNING**			
	• Start the engine. NOTE: Certain ABS faults require that the vehicle be driven in order for the anti-lock brake warning indicator to come on. Other faults will cause the anti-lock brake warning indicator to turn on each time the engine is started. • Drive the vehicle if necessary. (Read note.) • Observe the anti-lock brake warning indicator. • **Does the anti-lock brake warning indicator illuminate?**	Yes No	▶ ▶	Indicates a present failure. GO to **QT5**. Normal operation. If ABS symptoms exists, there may be an intermittent problem. GO to **QT5**. If no ABS symptoms exist, ABS is operating normally.
QT5	**PERFORM ABS TROUBLE CODE RETRIEVAL**			
	• Key OFF. • Jumper Pin 4 of the data link connector to ground. 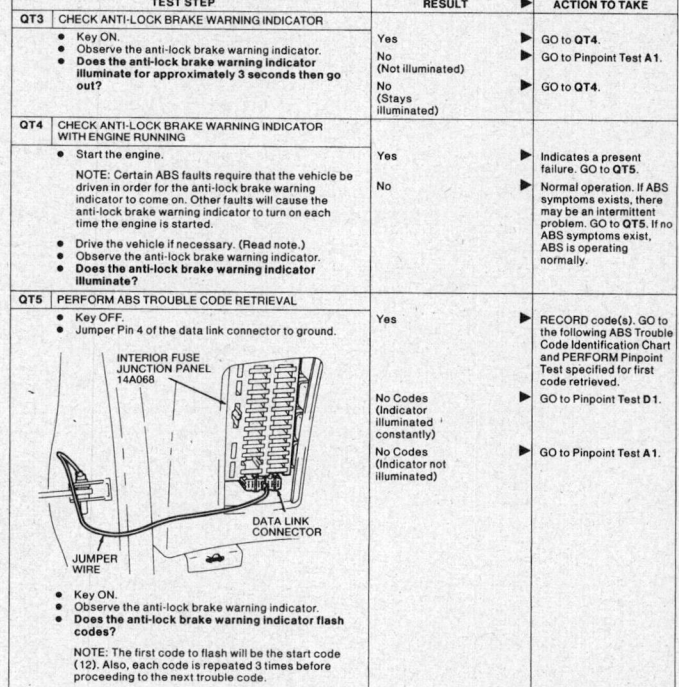 • Key ON. • Observe the anti-lock brake warning indicator. • **Does the anti-lock brake warning indicator flash codes?** NOTE: The first code to flash will be the start code (12). Also, each code is repeated 3 times before proceeding to the next trouble code.	Yes No Codes (Indicator illuminated constantly) No Codes (Indicator not illuminated)	▶ ▶ ▶	RECORD code(s). GO to the following ABS Trouble Code Identification Chart and PERFORM Pinpoint Test specified for first code retrieved. GO to Pinpoint Test **D1**. GO to Pinpoint Test **A1**.

FM4029500614020X

Fig. 4   Quick test (Part 2 of 2)

DIAGNOSTIC CHART INDEX

Test	Code	Description	Page No.	Fig. No.
A	—	No Communications w/ABS Control Module	5-188	5
B	—	Unable To Enter Self Test	5-188	6
C	18	ABS Brake Sensor Indicator Output Failure	5-189	7
D	21	Right Front Anti–Lock Brake Sensor Circuit Open	5-189	8
	22	Right Front Anti–Lock Brake Sensor Circuit Short	5-189	8
	25	Left Front Anti–Lock Brake Sensor Circuit Open	5-189	8
	26	Left Front Anti–Lock Brake Sensor Circuit Short	5-189	8
	31	Right Rear Anti–Lock Brake Sensor Circuit Open	5-189	8
	32	Right Rear Anti–Lock Brake Sensor Circuit Short	5-189	8
	35	Left Rear Anti–Lock Brake Sensor Circuit Open	5-189	8
	36	Left Rear Anti–Lock Brake Sensor Circuit Short	5-189	8
E	41	Right Front Hydraulic Control Unit Output Valve	5-191	9
	42	Right Front Hydraulic Control Unit Inlet Valve	5-191	9
	45	Left Front Hydraulic Control Unit Outlet Valve	5-191	9
	46	Left Front Hydraulic Control Unit Inlet Valve	5-191	9
	51	Right Rear Hydraulic Control Unit Outlet Valve	5-191	9
	52	Right Rear Hydraulic Control Unit Inlet Valve	5-191	9
	55	Left Rear Hydraulic Control Unit Output Valve	5-191	9
	56	Left Rear Hydraulic Control Unit Inlet Valve	5-191	9
F	57	Battery Voltage Low	5-191	10
G	61	Pump Motor Or Pump Motor Relay Failure	5-191	11
H	63	Solenoid Valve Relay	5-191	12
I	71	ECU Internal Failure	5-192	13
J	—	Yellow ABS Warning Indicator Does Not Self Check	5-192	14
K	—	Soft/Excessive Brake Pedal	5-192	15

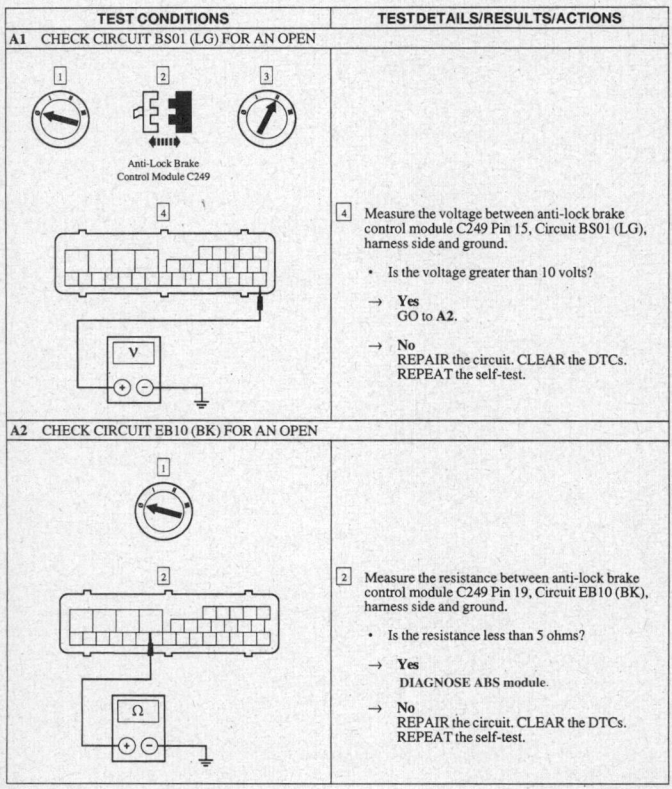

FM4029901358000X

Fig. 5   Test A: No Communications w/ABS Control Module

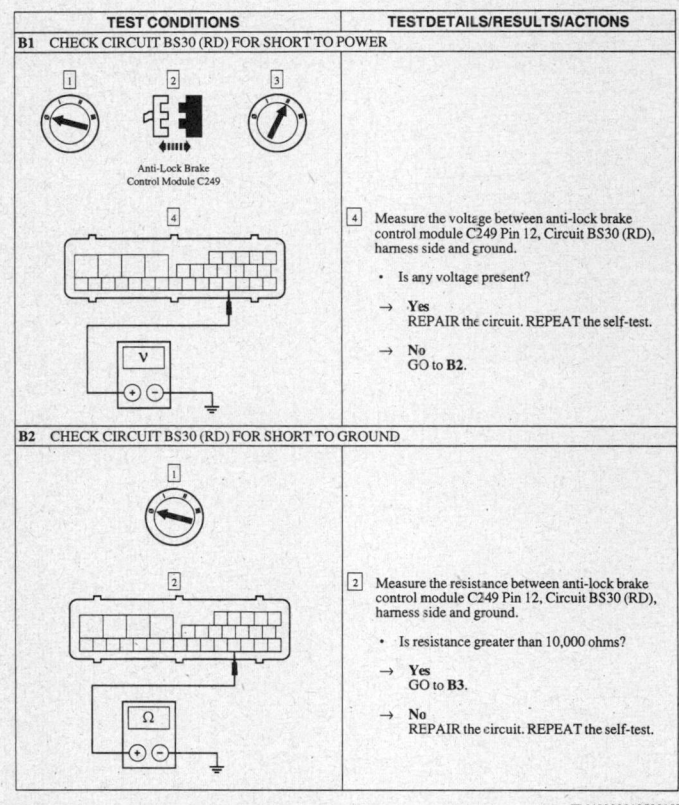

FM4029901359010X

Fig. 6   Test B: Unable To Enter Self Test (Part 1 of 2)

TEST CONDITIONS	TESTDETAILS/RESULTS/ACTIONS
B3 CHECK THE COMMUNICATIONS TO THE ANTI-LOCK BRAKE CONTROL MODULE	

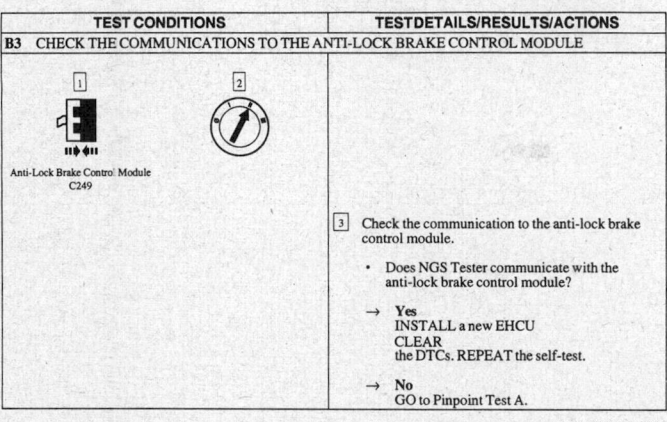

Anti-Lock Brake Control Module
C249

3 Check the communication to the anti-lock brake control module.

- Does NGS Tester communicate with the anti-lock brake control module?

→ **Yes**
INSTALL a new EHCU
CLEAR
the DTCs. REPEAT the self-test.

→ **No**
GO to Pinpoint Test A.

FM4029901359020X

**Fig. 6   Test B: Unable To Enter Self Test
(Part 2 of 2)**

TEST CONDITIONS	TESTDETAILS/RESULTS/ACTIONS
C2 CHECK THE ANTI-LOCK BRAKE SENSOR INDICATOR	

1 Check the anti-lock brake sensor indicator for corrosion, nicks, damaged teeth, correct mounting, alignment, and consistent air gap.

- Are the anti-lock brake sensor indicators OK?

→ **Yes**
GO to C3.

→ **No**
REPAIR or INSTALL a new component as necessary. CLEAR the DTCs. REPEAT the self-test.

TEST CONDITIONS	
C3 CHECK THE ANTI-LOCK BRAKE SENSOR OUTPUT	

Anti-Lock Brake Control Module
C249

3 While spinning the wheel at one revolution per second, measure the AC voltage between anti-lock brake control module C249 (anti-lock brake sensor) pins, harness side as follows:

Anti-Lock Brake Sensor	Anti-lock Brake Control Module C249	Circuit
LF	Pin 6	BS04 (BU/YE)
LF	Pin 7	BS05 (BU/GN)
RF	Pin 4	BS21 (RD)
RF	Pin 5	BS23 (GN)
LR	Pin 8	BS09 (OG/BU)
LR	Pin 9	BS08 (WH/BU)
RR	Pin 1	BS26 (BK/PK)
RR	Pin 3	BS24 (OG)

FM4029901360020X

**Fig. 7   Test C: Code 18: ABS Brake Sensor
Indicator Output Failure (Part 2 of 3)**

TEST CONDITIONS	TESTDETAILS/RESULTS/ACTIONS
C1 CHECK THE ANTI-LOCK BRAKE SENSOR	

1 Check the anti-lock brake sensor mounting. Check the suspect anti-lock brake sensor for excessive dirt build-up, metal obstructions, improper harness routing, and chafing.

- Are the anti-lock brake sensors OK?

→ **Yes**
GO to C2.

→ **No**
REPAIR or INSTALL a new component as necessary. CLEAR the DTCs. REPEAT the self-test.

FM4029901360010X

**Fig. 7   Test C: Code 18: ABS Brake Sensor
Indicator Output Failure (Part 1 of 3)**

TEST CONDITIONS	TESTDETAILS/RESULTS/ACTIONS
C3 CHECK THE ANTI-LOCK BRAKE SENSOR OUTPUT	

- Is the voltage between 100 and 3,500 mVolts AC?

→ **Yes**
INSTALL a new EHCU
CLEAR
the DTCs. REPEAT the self-test.

→ **No**
INSTALL a new anti-lock brake sensor;

CLEAR the DTCs. REPEAT the self-test.

FM4029901360030X

**Fig. 7   Test C: Code 18: ABS Brake Sensor
Indicator Output Failure (Part 3 of 3)**

TEST CONDITIONS	TESTDETAILS/RESULTS/ACTIONS
D1 CHECK FOR SHORT TO POWER	

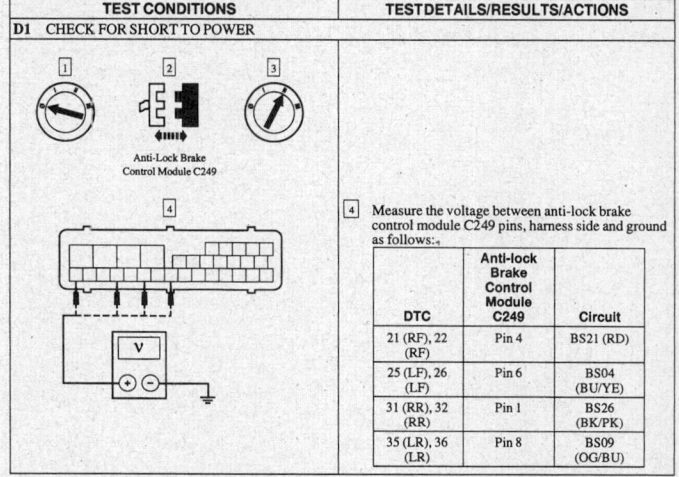

Anti-Lock Brake
Control Module C249

4 Measure the voltage between anti-lock brake control module C249 pins, harness side and ground as follows:

DTC	Anti-lock Brake Control Module C249	Circuit
21 (RF), 22 (RF)	Pin 4	BS21 (RD)
25 (LF), 26 (LF)	Pin 6	BS04 (BU/YE)
31 (RR), 32 (RR)	Pin 1	BS26 (BK/PK)
35 (LR), 36 (LR)	Pin 8	BS09 (OG/BU)

FM4029901361010X

**Fig. 8   Test D: Codes 21, 22, 25, 26, 31, 32, 35, 36:
ABS Sensor Circuit Failure (Part 1 of 5)**

Part 2 (top-left)

TEST CONDITIONS	TEST DETAILS/RESULTS/ACTIONS
D1 CHECK FOR SHORT TO POWER	• Is any voltage present? → **Yes** If DTC 21 or 22, REPAIR Circuit BS21 (RD) or BS23 (GN). CLEAR the DTCs. REPEAT the self-test. If DTC 25 or 26, REPAIR Circuit BS04 (BU/YE) or BS05 (BU/GN). CLEAR the DTCs. REPEAT the self-test. If DTC 31 or 32, REPAIR Circuit BS26 (BK/PK) or BS24 (OG). CLEAR the DTCs. REPEAT the self-test. If DTC 35 or 36, REPAIR Circuit BS09 (OG/BU) or BS08 (WH/BU). CLEAR the DTCs. REPEAT the self-test. → **No** GO to **D2**.
D2 CHECK FOR AN OPEN	

Measure the resistance between anti-lock brake control module C249 pins, harness side as follows:

DTC	Anti-lock Brake Control Module C249	Anti-lock Brake Control Module C249
21 (RF), 22 (RF)	Pin 4, BS21 (RD)	Pin 5, BS23 (GN)
25 (LF), 26 (LF)	Pin 6, BS05 (BU/YE)	Pin 7, BS05 (BU/GN)
31 (RR), 32 (RR)	Pin 1, BS26 (BK/PK)	Pin 3, BS24 (OG)
35 (LR), 36 (LR)	Pin 8, BS09 (OG/BU)	Pin 9, BS08 (WH/BU)

FM4029901361020X

Fig. 8   Test D: Codes 21, 22, 25, 26, 31, 32, 35, 36: ABS Sensor Circuit Failure (Part 2 of 5)

Part 4 (bottom-left)

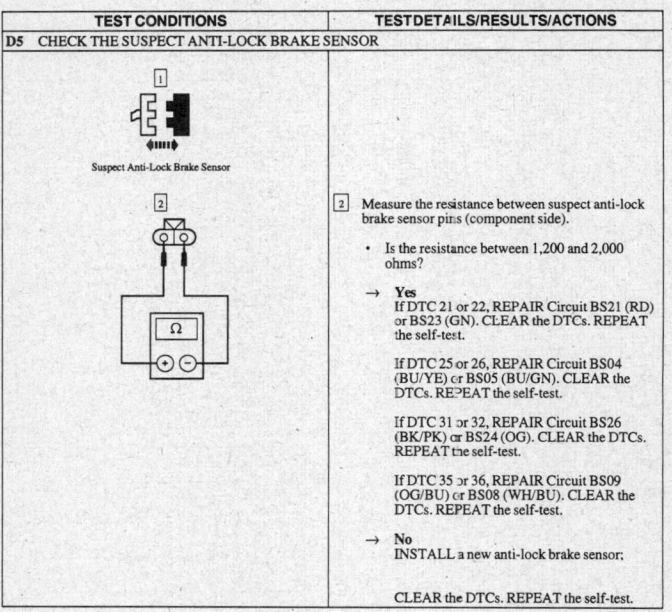

TEST CONDITIONS	TEST DETAILS/RESULTS/ACTIONS
D4 CHECK THE SUSPECT ANTI-LOCK BRAKE SENSOR FOR SHORT TO GROUND	

Suspect Anti-Lock Brake Sensor

2 Measure the resistance between suspect anti-lock brake sensor pin (component side) and ground.

• Is the resistance greater than 10,000 ohms?

→ **Yes**
If DTC 21 or 22, REPAIR Circuit BS21 (RD) or BS23 (GN). CLEAR the DTCs. REPEAT the self-test.

If DTC 25 or 26, REPAIR Circuit BS04 (BU/YE) or BS05 (BU/GN). CLEAR the DTCs. REPEAT the self-test.

If DTC 31 or 32, REPAIR Circuit BS26 (BK/PK) or BS24 (OG). CLEAR the DTCs. REPEAT the self-test.

If DTC 35 or 36, REPAIR Circuit BS09 (OG/BU) or BS08 (WH/BU). CLEAR the DTCs. REPEAT the self-test.

→ **No**
INSTALL a new anti-lock brake sensor;

CLEAR the DTCs. REPEAT the self-test.

FM4029901361040X

Fig. 8   Test D: Codes 21, 22, 25, 26, 31, 32, 35, 36: ABS Sensor Circuit Failure (Part 4 of 5)

Part 3 (top-right)

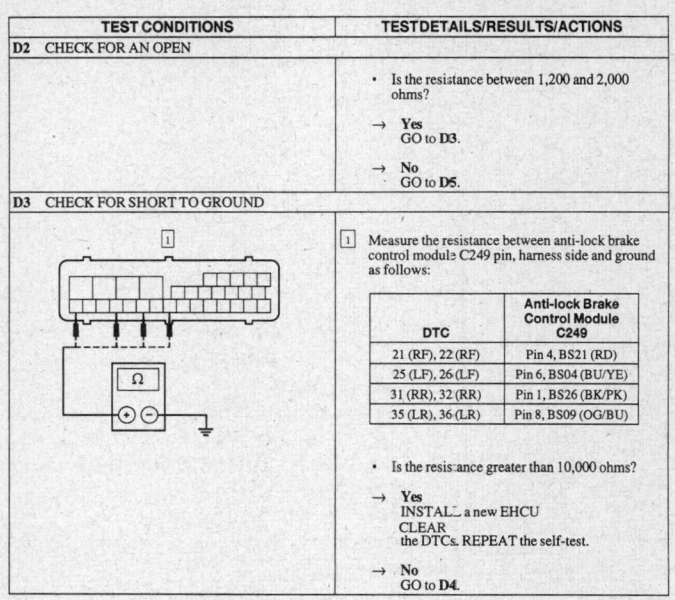

TEST CONDITIONS	TEST DETAILS/RESULTS/ACTIONS
D2 CHECK FOR AN OPEN	• Is the resistance between 1,200 and 2,000 ohms? → **Yes** GO to **D3**. → **No** GO to **D5**.
D3 CHECK FOR SHORT TO GROUND	

1 Measure the resistance between anti-lock brake control module C249 pin, harness side and ground as follows:

DTC	Anti-lock Brake Control Module C249
21 (RF), 22 (RF)	Pin 4, BS21 (RD)
25 (LF), 26 (LF)	Pin 6, BS04 (BU/YE)
31 (RR), 32 (RR)	Pin 1, BS26 (BK/PK)
35 (LR), 36 (LR)	Pin 8, BS09 (OG/BU)

• Is the resistance greater than 10,000 ohms?

→ **Yes**
INSTALL a new EHCU
CLEAR
the DTCs. REPEAT the self-test.

→ **No**
GO to **D4**.

FM4029901361030X

Fig. 8   Test D: Codes 21, 22, 25, 26, 31, 32, 35, 36: ABS Sensor Circuit Failure (Part 3 of 5)

Part 5 (bottom-right)

TEST CONDITIONS	TEST DETAILS/RESULTS/ACTIONS
D5 CHECK THE SUSPECT ANTI-LOCK BRAKE SENSOR	

Suspect Anti-Lock Brake Sensor

2 Measure the resistance between suspect anti-lock brake sensor pins (component side).

• Is the resistance between 1,200 and 2,000 ohms?

→ **Yes**
If DTC 21 or 22, REPAIR Circuit BS21 (RD) or BS23 (GN). CLEAR the DTCs. REPEAT the self-test.

If DTC 25 or 26, REPAIR Circuit BS04 (BU/YE) or BS05 (BU/GN). CLEAR the DTCs. REPEAT the self-test.

If DTC 31 or 32, REPAIR Circuit BS26 (BK/PK) or BS24 (OG). CLEAR the DTCs. REPEAT the self-test.

If DTC 35 or 36, REPAIR Circuit BS09 (OG/BU) or BS08 (WH/BU). CLEAR the DTCs. REPEAT the self-test.

→ **No**
INSTALL a new anti-lock brake sensor;

CLEAR the DTCs. REPEAT the self-test.

FM4029901361050X

Fig. 8   Test D: Codes 21, 22, 25, 26, 31, 32, 35, 36: ABS Sensor Circuit Failure (Part 5 of 5)

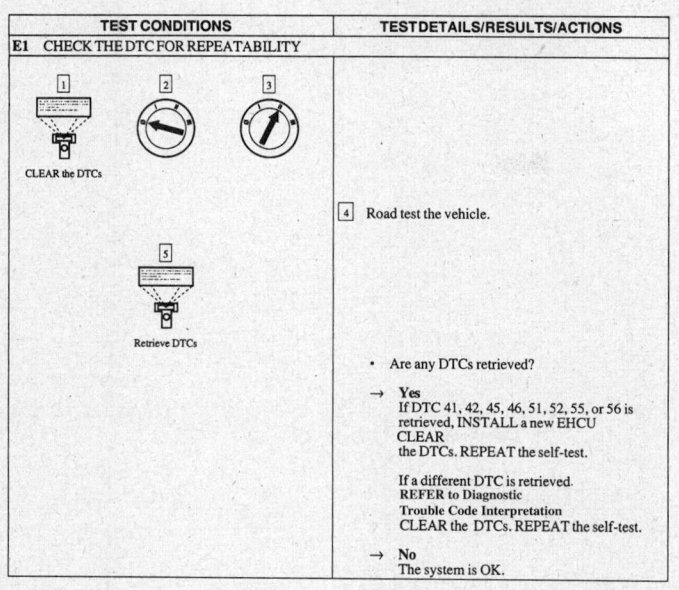

TEST CONDITIONS	TEST DETAILS/RESULTS/ACTIONS
E1 CHECK THE DTC FOR REPEATABILITY	

4 Road test the vehicle.

- Are any DTCs retrieved?
→ **Yes**
  If DTC 41, 42, 45, 46, 51, 52, 55, or 56 is retrieved, INSTALL a new EHCU CLEAR the DTCs. REPEAT the self-test.

  If a different DTC is retrieved, REFER to Diagnostic Trouble Code Interpretation CLEAR the DTCs. REPEAT the self-test.
→ **No**
  The system is OK.

FM4029901362000X

Fig. 9   Test E: Codes 41, 42, 45, 46, 51, 52, 55, 56: Hydraulic Control Unit Valve Failure

TEST CONDITIONS	TEST DETAILS/RESULTS/ACTIONS
G1 CHECK THE PUMP MOTOR	

2 Check the pump motor for continuous operation.

- Does the pump motor run constantly?
→ **Yes**
  INSTALL a new EHCU CLEAR the DTCs. REPEAT the self-test.
→ **No**
  GO to G2.

TEST CONDITIONS	TEST DETAILS/RESULTS/ACTIONS
G2 CHECK CIRCUIT BS40 (OG) FOR AN OPEN	

Anti-Lock Brake Control Module C249

3 Measure the voltage between anti-lock brake control module C249 Pin 17, Circuit BS40 (OG), harness side and ground.

- Is the voltage greater than 10 volts?
→ **Yes**
  GO to G3.
→ **No**
  REPAIR the circuit. CLEAR the DTCs. REPEAT the self-test.

FM4029901364010X

Fig. 11   Test G: Code 61: Pump Motor Or Pump Motor Relay Failure (Part 1 of 2)

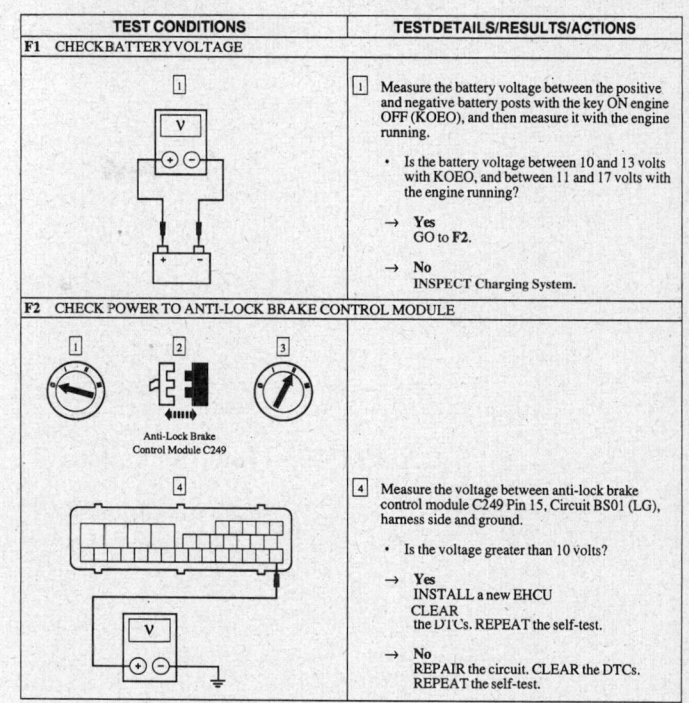

TEST CONDITIONS	TEST DETAILS/RESULTS/ACTIONS
F1 CHECK BATTERY VOLTAGE	

1 Measure the battery voltage between the positive and negative battery posts with the key ON engine OFF (KOEO), and then measure it with the engine running.

- Is the battery voltage between 10 and 13 volts with KOEO, and between 11 and 17 volts with the engine running?
→ **Yes**
  GO to F2.
→ **No**
  INSPECT Charging System.

TEST CONDITIONS	TEST DETAILS/RESULTS/ACTIONS
F2 CHECK POWER TO ANTI-LOCK BRAKE CONTROL MODULE	

Anti-Lock Brake Control Module C249

4 Measure the voltage between anti-lock brake control module C249 Pin 15, Circuit BS01 (LG), harness side and ground.

- Is the voltage greater than 10 volts?
→ **Yes**
  INSTALL a new EHCU CLEAR the DTCs. REPEAT the self-test.
→ **No**
  REPAIR the circuit. CLEAR the DTCs. REPEAT the self-test.

FM4029901363000X

Fig. 10   Test F: Code 57: Battery Voltage Low

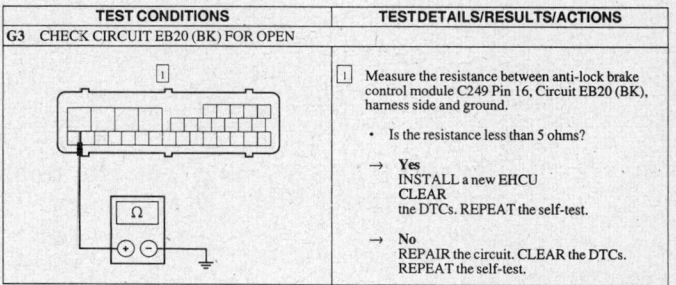

TEST CONDITIONS	TEST DETAILS/RESULTS/ACTIONS
G3 CHECK CIRCUIT EB20 (BK) FOR OPEN	

1 Measure the resistance between anti-lock brake control module C249 Pin 16, Circuit EB20 (BK), harness side and ground.

- Is the resistance less than 5 ohms?
→ **Yes**
  INSTALL a new EHCU CLEAR the DTCs. REPEAT the self-test.
→ **No**
  REPAIR the circuit. CLEAR the DTCs. REPEAT the self-test.

FM4029901364020X

Fig. 11   Test G: Code 61: Pump Motor Or Pump Motor Relay Failure (Part 2 of 2)

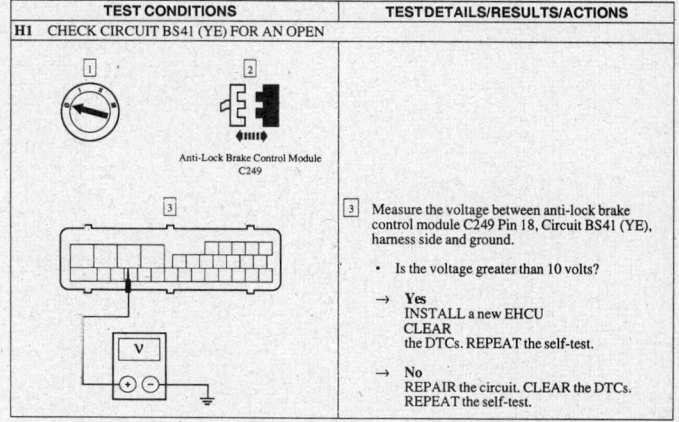

TEST CONDITIONS	TEST DETAILS/RESULTS/ACTIONS
H1 CHECK CIRCUIT BS41 (YE) FOR AN OPEN	

Anti-Lock Brake Control Module C249

3 Measure the voltage between anti-lock brake control module C249 Pin 18, Circuit BS41 (YE), harness side and ground.

- Is the voltage greater than 10 volts?
→ **Yes**
  INSTALL a new EHCU CLEAR the DTCs. REPEAT the self-test.
→ **No**
  REPAIR the circuit. CLEAR the DTCs. REPEAT the self-test.

FM4029901365000X

Fig. 12   Test H: Code 63: Solenoid Valve Relay

TEST CONDITIONS	TEST DETAILS/RESULTS/ACTIONS
I1 CHECK THE DTC FOR REPEATABILITY	

CLEAR the DTCs | Retrieve DTCs

- Are any DTCs retrieved?

→ **Yes**
If DTC 71 is retrieved, INSTALL a new EHCU
CLEAR the DTCs.
REPEAT the self-test.

If a different DTC is retrieved
**REFER to Diagnostic
Trouble Code Interpretation.**
CLEAR the DTCs. REPEAT the self-test.

→ **No**
The system is OK.

FM4029901366000X

Fig. 13   Test I: Code 71: ECU Internal Failure

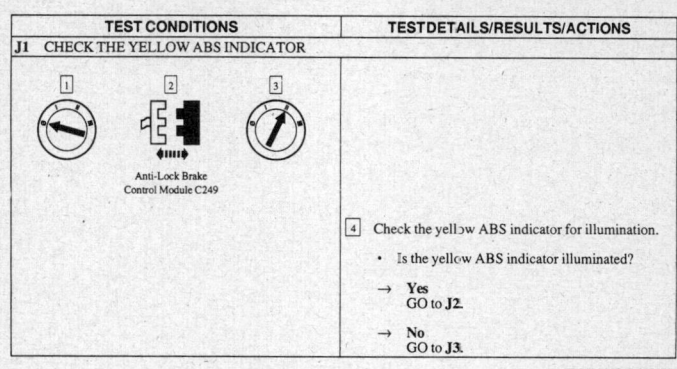

TEST CONDITIONS	TEST DETAILS/RESULTS/ACTIONS
J1 CHECK THE YELLOW ABS INDICATOR	

Anti-Lock Brake
Control Module C249

4 Check the yellow ABS indicator for illumination.

- Is the yellow ABS indicator illuminated?

→ **Yes**
GO to **J2**.

→ **No**
GO to **J3**.

FM4029901367010X

Fig. 14   Test J: Yellow ABS Warning Indicator Does Not Self Check (Part 1 of 3)

TEST CONDITIONS	TEST DETAILS/RESULTS/ACTIONS
J2 CHECK CIRCUIT BS29 (WH/BK) FOR SHORT TO GROUND	

Instrument Cluster C266b
(Conventional Cluster) or C267c
(Electronic Cluster)

3 Measure the resistance between anti-lock brake control module C249 Pin 21, Circuit BS29 (WH/BK), harness side and ground.

- Is the resistance greater than 10,000 ohms?

→ **Yes**
DIAGNOSE
Instrument Cluster

→ **No**
REPAIR the circuit. CLEAR the DTCs.
REPEAT the self-test.

FM4029901367020X

Fig. 14   Test J: Yellow ABS Warning Indicator Does Not Self Check (Part 2 of 3)

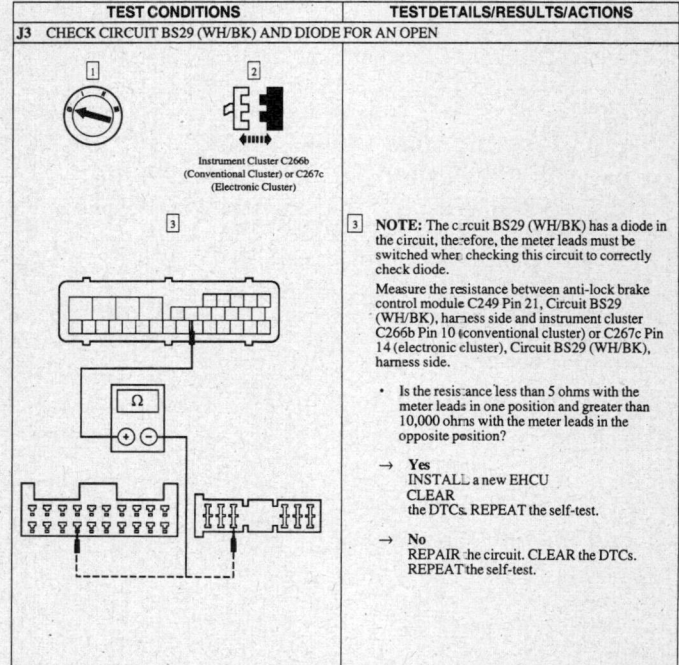

TEST CONDITIONS	TEST DETAILS/RESULTS/ACTIONS
J3 CHECK CIRCUIT BS29 (WH/BK) AND DIODE FOR AN OPEN	

Instrument Cluster C266b
(Conventional Cluster) or C267c
(Electronic Cluster)

3 **NOTE:** The circuit BS29 (WH/BK) has a diode in the circuit, therefore, the meter leads must be switched when checking this circuit to correctly check diode.

Measure the resistance between anti-lock brake control module C249 Pin 21, Circuit BS29 (WH/BK), harness side and instrument cluster C266b Pin 10 (conventional cluster) or C267c Pin 14 (electronic cluster), Circuit BS29 (WH/BK), harness side.

- Is the resistance less than 5 ohms with the meter leads in one position and greater than 10,000 ohms with the meter leads in the opposite position?

→ **Yes**
INSTALL a new EHCU
CLEAR
the DTCs. REPEAT the self-test.

→ **No**
REPAIR the circuit. CLEAR the DTCs.
REPEAT the self-test.

FM4029901367030X

Fig. 14   Test J: Yellow ABS Warning Indicator Does Not Self Check (Part 3 of 3)

TEST CONDITIONS	TEST DETAILS/RESULTS/ACTIONS
K1 BLEED THE BRAKE SYSTEM	

1 Bleed the brake system
2 Check for soft/excessive pedal travel.

- Is the brake pedal travel soft/excessive?

→ **Yes**
GO to **K2**.

→ **No**
The system is OK.

| **K2** CHECK THE BASE BRAKE SYSTEM | |

1 Check the base brake system

- Is the base brake system OK?

→ **Yes**
INSTALL a new EHCU.
CLEAR
the DTCs. REPEAT the self-test.

→ **No**
REPAIR or INSTALL new components as necessary. CLEAR the DTCs. REPEAT the self-test.

FM4029901368000X

Fig. 15   Test K: Soft/Excessive Brake Pedal

Windstar

NOTE: Electrical Symbol & Wire Color Code Identification Located In The Front Of This Manual May Be Used As An Aid When Using Wiring Circuits Found In This Section.

NOTE: Refer To "Computer Relearn Procedures" Located In The Front Of This Manual When Battery Power To The Computer Has Been Interrupted.

INDEX

	Page No.		Page No.		Page No.
Description	5-193	Battery Ground Cable	5-193	Hard Or Soft Brake Pedal	5-193
Diagnosis & Testing	5-194	Brake Fluid Handling	5-193	Lack Of Deceleration During	
Accessing Diagnostic Trouble		**System Service**	5-194	Medium/Hard Brake	
Codes	5-194	Brake System Bleed	5-194	Applications	5-193
Clearing Diagnostic Trouble		Manual	5-194	No Communication w/ABS	
Codes	5-194	Pressure	5-195	Control Module	5-194
Diagnostic Tests	5-194	Component Replacement	5-195	Soft Brake Pedal	5-193
Pinpoint Tests	5-194	ABS Control Module	5-195	Unable To Enter Self-Test	5-194
Diagnostic Trouble Code		Brake Sensors	5-195	Vehicle Pulls During Braking	5-193
Interpretation	5-194	Hydraulic Control Unit (HCU)	5-195	Wheels Lock-Up	5-193
Wiring Diagrams	5-194	**Troubleshooting**	5-193	Yellow ABS Warning Indicator	
Diagnostic Chart Index	5-197	ABS Too Sensitive/Engages On		On w/System Pass	5-194
Precautions	5-193	Normal Stop	5-193		

PRECAUTIONS

BATTERY GROUND CABLE

Prior to service disconnect battery ground cable and isolate as required.

BRAKE FLUID HANDLING

Brake fluid can cause serious injury and vehicle damage if not handled properly. Avoid contact with eyes and do not allow fluid to splash or spill on painted surfaces. Wash hands thoroughly after handling.

DESCRIPTION

The four wheel anti-lock brake system prevents wheel lockup by automatically modulating brake pressure during an emergency stop. The system uses an ABS control module and a hydraulic control unit (HCU) to control both front and rear brakes separately. When the brakes are applied, fluid is forced from the brake master cylinder to the hydraulic control unit (HCU), then to the wheels. One circuit of the master cylinder feeds the left front and right rear brakes. The other circuit feeds the right front and left rear brakes. If the ABS control module senses that a wheel is about to lock, based on speed sensor data, it pulses the normally open solenoid valve for the fluid circuit feeding that wheel.

The anti-lock brake control module is an on-board diagnostic unit responsible for control of the hydraulic valve during ABS operation. It also monitors system operation during normal driving conditions. Most problems that occur in the ABS system will be stored as diagnostic trouble codes in the ABS control module.

The ABS control module and the hydraulic control unit are packaged in one integral unit called the electronic hydraulic control unit (EHCU). The EHCU is located below the battery tray in the left front corner of the engine compartment. Refer to **Fig. 1** for ABS system component locations.

TROUBLESHOOTING

ABS Too Sensitive/Engages On Normal Stop

1. Inspect rear brake anti-lock sensor indicator.
2. Inspect front brake anti-lock sensor indicator.
3. Inspect sensor output.
4. Intermittent open or shorted sensor circuit.
5. Inspect for chaffed wire insulation or pinched wire.
6. Inspect rear brake adjustment too tight.
7. Inspect linings.

Wheels Lock-Up

1. Inspect hydraulic outlet (dump) valve.
2. Damp or contaminated rear brake shoe linings, stuck/leaking wheel cylinder or over adjusted rear brakes.
3. Inspect parking brake.

Hard Or Soft Brake Pedal

1. Inspect for stuck inlet (isolation) valve.

2. Little or no vacuum boost.
3. Inspect for leaking inlet valve during ABS operation.
4. Inspect for stuck or inoperative wheel cylinder or caliper.
5. Inspect for pinched or crimped brake line or hose.

Soft Brake Pedal

1. Inspect for leaking outlet (dump) valve.
2. Inspect for leaking inlet valve during ABS operation.
3. Inspect for hydraulic Leak.
4. Inspect for air in brake system.

Lack Of Deceleration During Medium/Hard Brake Applications

1. Inspect for stuck inlet (isolation) valve.
2. Inspect for leaking outlet (dump) valve, rear axle only.
3. Inspect for hydraulic leak in brake line or hose, fitting, master cylinder, wheel cylinder or caliper.
4. Inspect for air in brake system.
5. Inspect for little or no vacuum boost.
6. Inspect for stuck or inoperative wheel cylinder or caliper.
7. Inspect for ineffective brake shoe or pad linings.

Vehicle Pulls During Braking

1. Inspect for fully or partially blocked right/left inlet (Isolation) valve.
2. Inspect for improperly adjusted rear brake.

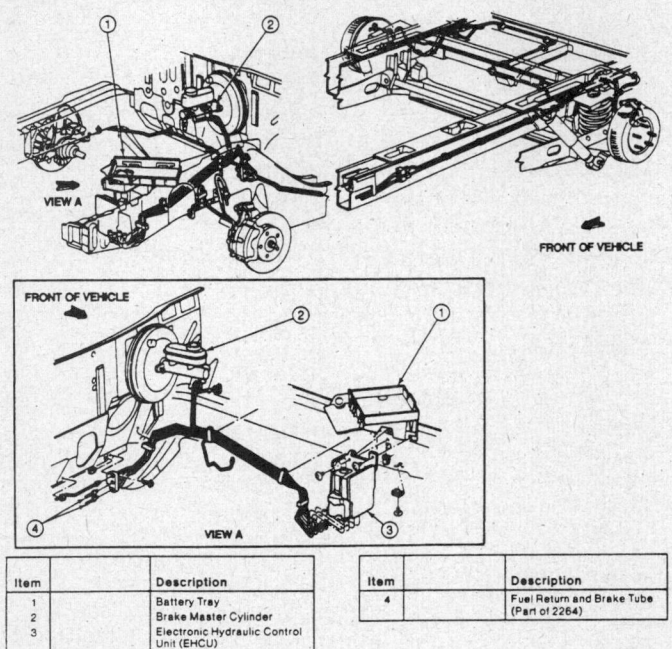

Fig. 1 ABS component locations

Item	Description
1	Battery Tray
2	Brake Master Cylinder
3	Electronic Hydraulic Control Unit (EHCU)

Item	Description
4	Fuel Return and Brake Tube (Part of 2264)

FM4029500593000X

3. Inspect for frozen or binding caliper.
4. Inspect for uneven brake pad or shoe wear.
5. Inspect for pinched or crimped brake line or hose.

Yellow ABS Warning Indicator On w/ System Pass

1. Inspect for ABS brake warning indicator circuit.
2. Inspect ABS control module.

No Communication w/ABS Control Module

1. Inspect for blown fuses 102 (40A), 101 (40A) or fuse junction panel fuse 10 (10A).
2. Inspect for faulty wiring.
3. Inspect ABS control module malfunction.

Unable To Enter Self-Test

Inspect the ABS control module.

DIAGNOSIS & TESTING

Accessing Diagnostic Trouble Codes

1. Connect New Generation Star (NGS) Tester tool No. 007-00500, or equivalent, to Data Link Connector (DLC) lo-cated under instrument panel to right of steering column.
2. Place ignition in RUN position.
3. Follow instructions on NGS Tester screen to retrieve Diagnostic Trouble Codes (DTC). If NGS reports system passed, no DTC's, refer to "Quick Check" in this section. If NGS reports link communication error, module not responding, proceed as follows:
   a. Ensure ignition is in RUN position.
   b. Inspect power distribution box and fuse junction panel for open fuses.
   c. Inspect NGS connection to DLC.
   d. If NGS still reports link communication error, refer to "Quick Check" in this section.

Diagnostic Trouble Code Interpretation

Refer to **Fig. 2** for diagnostic trouble code interpretation.

Wiring Diagrams

Refer to **Fig. 3** for wiring diagrams.

Diagnostic Tests

PINPOINT TESTS

Refer to **Figs. 4 through 14** for pinpoint tests.

Clearing Diagnostic Trouble Codes

To clear the Keep Alive Memory (KAM). Turn ignition switch to the Off position while the diagnostic connector C207 halves are separated as described "Accessing Diagnostic Trouble Codes."

DTC	Description
B1317	Battery Voltage High
B1318	Battery Voltage Low
B1342	ECU is Defective
B2477	Module Configuration Failure
C1095	Hydraulic Pump Motor Circuit Failure
C1096	Hydraulic Pump Motor Circuit Open
C1103	Hydraulic Brake Switch Circuit Failure
C1115	Power Relay Short to Battery
C1145	RF Wheel Speed Input Circuit Failure
C1155	LF Wheel Speed Input Circuit Failure
C1165	RR Wheel Speed Input Circuit Failure
C1175	LR Wheel Speed Input Circuit Failure
C1184	ABS System Timeout
C1185	Power Relay Output Circuit Failure
C1194	LF Dump Valve Circuit Failure
C1198	LF Isolation Valve Circuit Failure
C1210	RF Dump Valve Circuit Failure
C1214	RF Isolation Valve Circuit Failure
C1233	LF Wheel Speed Sensor Signal Missing or Erratic
C1234	RF Wheel Speed Sensor Signal Missing or Erratic
C1235	RR Wheel Speed Sensor Signal Missing or Erratic
C1236	LR Wheel Speed Sensor Signal Missing or Erratic
C1242	LR Dump Valve Circuit Failure

FM4029901336010X

Fig. 2 Diagnostic trouble code interpretation (Part 1 of 2)

SYSTEM SERVICE

Brake System Bleed

MANUAL

Bleed sequence is righthand rear, left-hand rear, righthand front and lefthand front.

1. Clean all dirt from master cylinder filler cap, then remove cap.
2. Fill brake master cylinder reservoir.
3. Attach a rubber drain tube to righthand rear bleeder screw and submerge opposite end in container partially filled with clean brake fluid.
4. With aid of an assistant, pump and hold pressure on brake pedal.
5. Loosen righthand rear bleeder screw until stream of fluid comes out, then tighten bleeder screw.
6. Repeat steps four and five until clear, bubble free fluid comes out.
7. Fill brake master cylinder to proper level.
8. Repeat procedure for remaining brakes.

PRESSURE

Master cylinder pressure bleeder adapter tools are available from various manufactures. Follow instructions of manufacture when installing adapter.

Bleed sequence is righthand rear, lefthand rear, righthand front then lefthand front.

1. Clean all dirt from master cylinder filler cap, then remove cap.
2. Fill brake master cylinder reservoir.
3. Install bleed adapter to brake master cylinder reservoir, then attach bleeder tank hose to fitting on adapter. **Ensure bleeder tank contains enough brake fluid to complete bleed procedure.**
4. Attach a rubber drain tube to righthand rear bleeder screw, then submerge opposite end in a container partially filled with clean brake fluid.
5. Open valve on bleeder tank.
6. Loosen righthand rear bleeder screw.
7. Leave bleeder screw open until clear, bubble free brake fluid flows, then tighten bleeder screw and remove hose.
8. Repeat bleed procedure for remaining brakes.
9. Close bleeder tank valve, then remove tank hose from adapter.
10. Remove adapter.
11. Ensure brake system is operating properly and fluid level is correct.

Component Replacement

HYDRAULIC CONTROL UNIT (HCU)

1. Disconnect harness connector from ABS control module.
2. Disconnect 2-pin power and ground connector from ABS control module.
3. Remove two tubes from inlet ports and four tubes from outlet ports of HCU.
4. Remove three HCU to mounting

DTC	Description	Source	Action
C1246	RR Dump Valve Circuit Failure	ABS	GO to Pinpoint Test I.
C1250	LR Isolation Valve Circuit Failure	ABS	GO to Pinpoint Test I.
C1254	RR Isolation Valve Circuit Failure	ABS	GO to Pinpoint Test I.
C1404	RF Traction Control Valve Circuit Failure	ABS	INSTALL a new anti-lock brake control module.
C1410	LF Traction Control Valve Circuit Failure	ABS	INSTALL a new anti-lock brake control module.
C1446	Pedal Position (BPP)	ABS	DIAGNOSE brake pedal position switch circuit

FM4029901336020X

Fig. 2 Diagnostic trouble code interpretation (Part 2 of 2)

bracket retaining bolts.
5. Lower HCU assembly down and out of engine compartment.
6. Reverse procedure to install, noting the following:
   a. **Torque** HCU to mounting bracket retaining bolts 71–97 inch lbs.
   b. **Torque** tube fittings 11–14 ft. lbs.

ABS CONTROL MODULE

1. Remove battery and battery tray.
2. Disconnect upper radiator hose.
3. Remove fan shroud.
4. Disconnect harness connector, then the 2-pin pump motor harness.
5. Remove four T25H Torx head screws retaining module to HCU assembly.
6. Pull ABS control module straight forward to clear coils away from valve solenoids, then remove module from vehicle.
7. Reverse procedure to install. **Torque** T25H Torx head screws 35–44 inch lbs.

BRAKE SENSORS

FRONT

1. Disconnect sensor assembly 2-pin connector at front frame mounting location.

2. Separate sensor cable from brake hose clips.
3. Remove sensor cable clip retaining bolt from front wheel knuckle.
4. Remove sensor retaining bolt from front wheel knuckle and slide front brake anti-lock sensor out of mating hole.
5. Reverse procedure to install. **Torque** sensor retaining bolt to 72–84 inch lbs.

REAR

1. Disconnect sensor assembly 2-pin connector at rear frame mounting location.
2. Separate sensor cables from brake hose clips and feed through frame.
3. **On models equipped with rear disc brakes,** remove rear brake anti-lock sensor retaining bolt from rear wheel disc brake adapter.
4. **On models equipped with rear drum brakes,** remove rear brake anti-lock sensor retaining bolt from sensor mounting bracket.
5. **On all models,** reverse procedure to install. **Torque** sensor retaining bolt to 71–88 inch lbs.

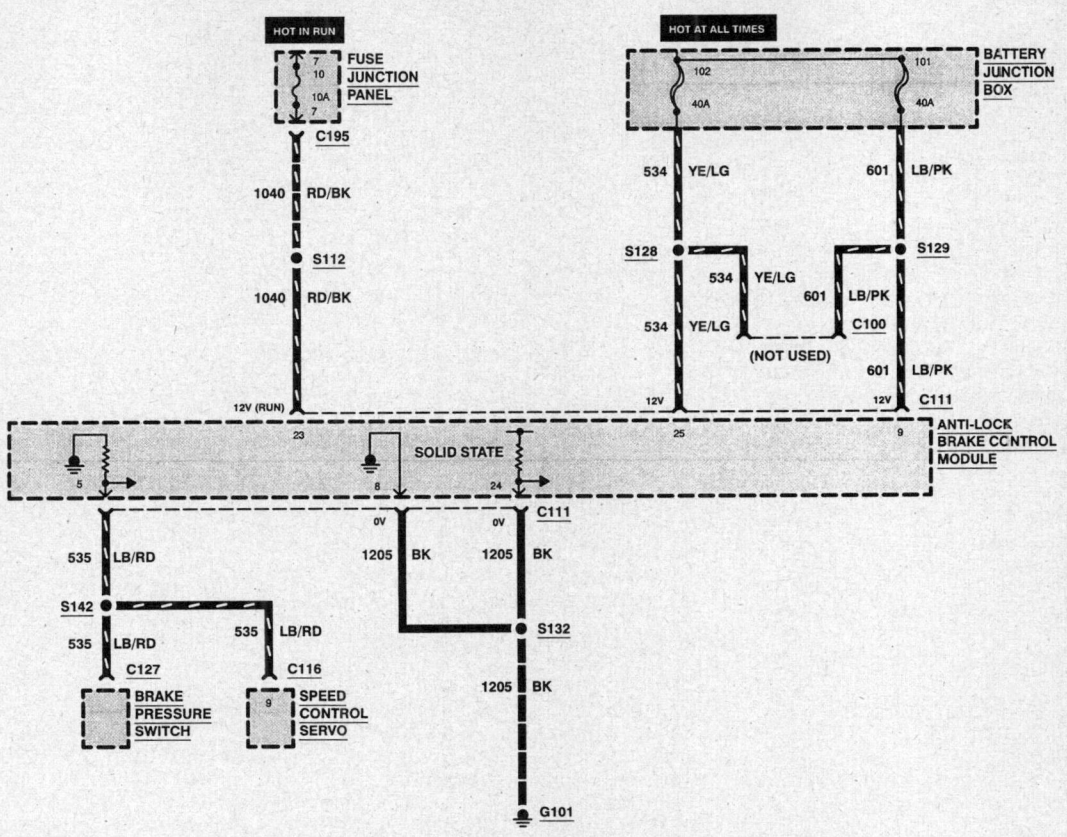

Fig. 3 Wiring diagram (Part 1 of 3)

FM4029901341010X

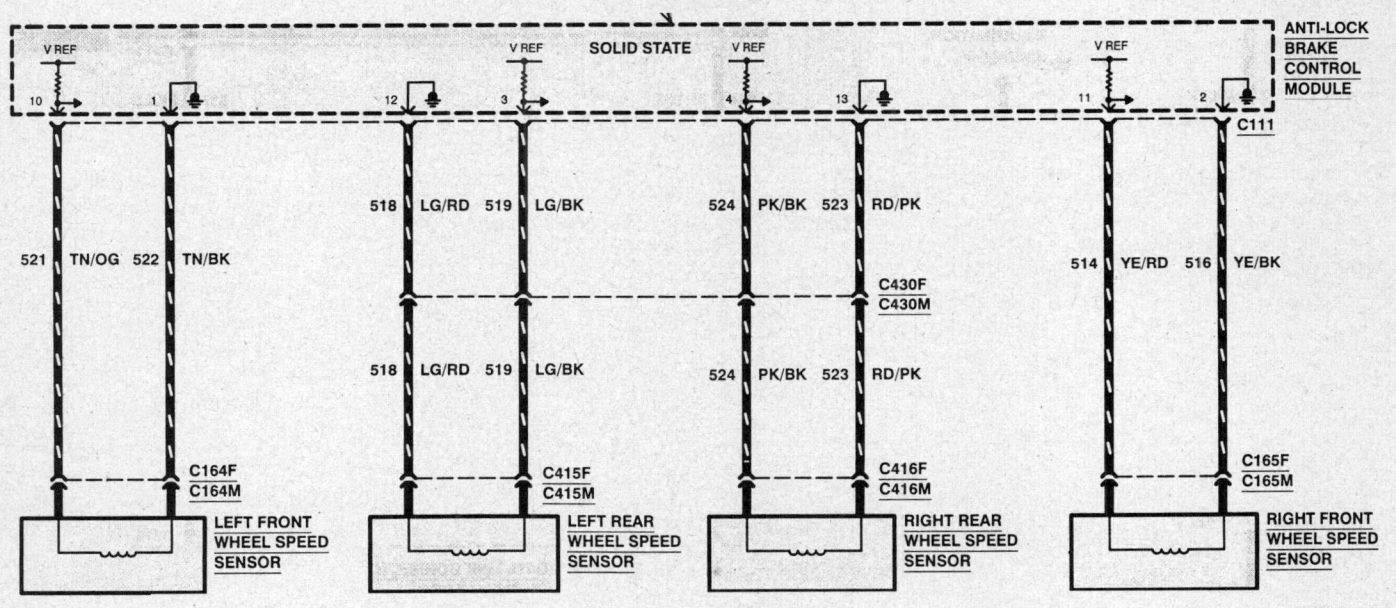

Fig. 3 Wiring diagram (Part 2 of 3)

FM4029901341020X

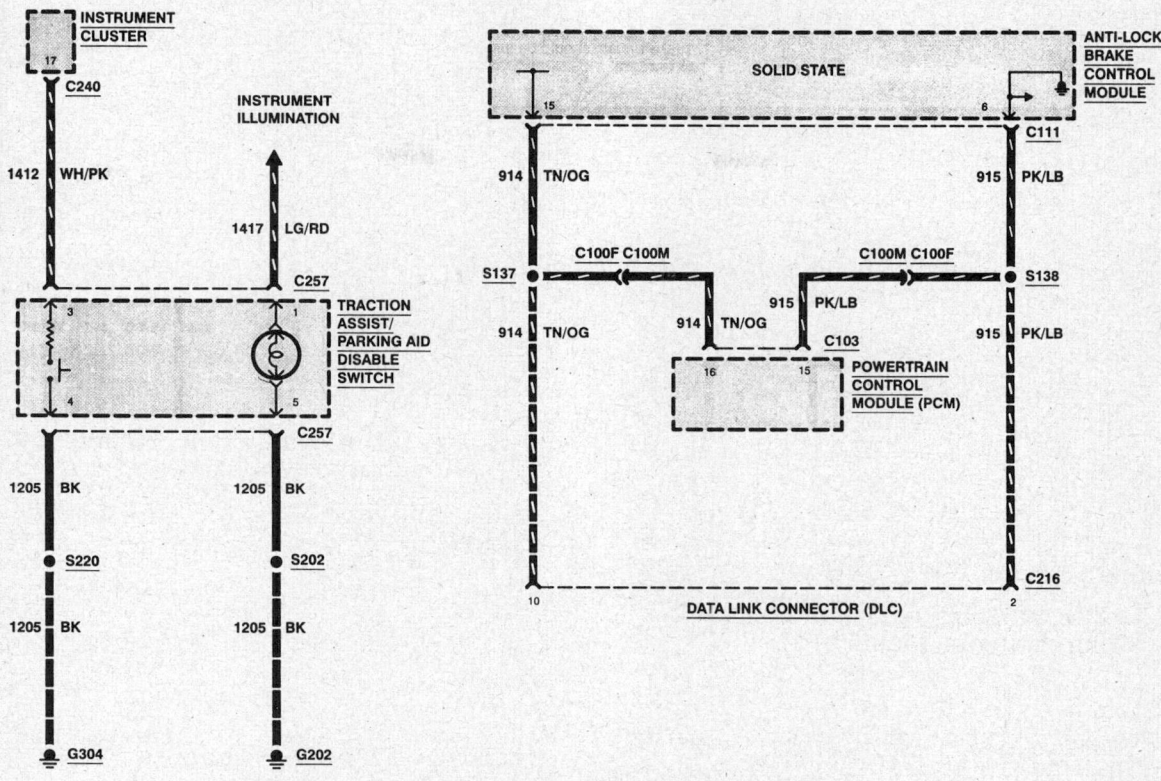

Fig. 3   Wiring diagram (Part 3 of 3)

FM4029901341030X

DIAGNOSTIC CHART INDEX

Test	Code	Description	Page No.	Fig. No.
A	—	No Communication With ABS Control Module	5-198	4
B	—	Unable To Enter Self Test	5-198	5
C	B1317	Battery Voltage High	5-198	6
	B1318	Battery Voltage Low	5-198	6
D	C1095	Hydraulic Pump Motor Circuit Failure	5-198	7
	C1096	Hydraulic Pump Motor Circuit Open	5-198	7
E	C1103	Hydraulic Pressure Switch Circuit Failure	5-199	8
F	C1115	Power Relay Short To Battery	5-199	9
	C1185	Power Relay Output Failure	5-199	9
G	C1145	Right Front Wheel Speed Input Circuit Failure	5-200	10
	C1155	Left Front Wheel Speed Input Circuit Failure	5-200	10
	C1165	Right Rear Wheel Speed Input Circuit Failure	5-200	10
	C1175	Left Front Wheel Speed Input Circuit Failure	5-200	10
H	C1184	ABS System Time-Out	5-201	11
I	C1194	Left Front Dump Valve Circuit Failure	5-201	12
	C1198	Left Front Isolation Valve Circuit Failure	5-201	12
	C1210	Right Front Dump Valve Circuit Failure	5-201	12
	C1214	Right Front Isolation Valve Circuit Failure	5-201	12
	C1242	Left Rear Dump Valve Circuit Failure	5-201	12
	C1246	Right Rear Dump Valve Circuit Failure	5-201	12
	C1250	Left Rear Isolation Valve Circuit Failure	5-201	12
	C1254	Right Rear Isolation Valve Circuit Failure	5-201	12
J	C1233	Left Front Wheel Speed Sensor Signal Missing Or Erratic	5-202	13
	C1234	Right Front Wheel Speed Sensor Signal Missing Or Erratic	5-202	13
	C1235	Right Rear Wheel Speed Sensor Signal Missing Or Erratic	5-202	13
	C1236	Left Rear Wheel Speed Sensor Signal Missing Or Erratic	5-202	13
K	—	Soft Or Excessive Pedal Travel	5-203	14

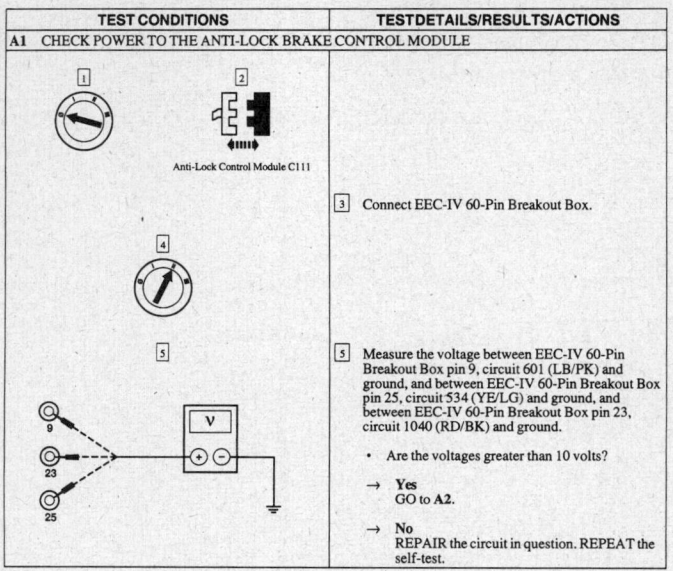

TEST CONDITIONS	TESTDETAILS/RESULTS/ACTIONS
A1 CHECK POWER TO THE ANTI-LOCK BRAKE CONTROL MODULE	
Anti-Lock Control Module C111	
③	Connect EEC-IV 60-Pin Breakout Box.
④	
⑤	Measure the voltage between EEC-IV 60-Pin Breakout Box pin 9, circuit 601 (LB/PK) and ground, and between EEC-IV 60-Pin Breakout Box pin 25, circuit 534 (YE/LG) and ground, and between EEC-IV 60-Pin Breakout Box pin 23, circuit 1040 (RD/BK) and ground. • Are the voltages greater than 10 volts? → **Yes** GO to **A2**. → **No** REPAIR the circuit in question. REPEAT the self-test.

FM4029901343010X

Fig. 4 Test A: No Communication With ABS Control Module (Part 1 of 2)

TEST CONDITIONS	TESTDETAILS/RESULTS/ACTIONS
B1 CHECK THE COMMUNICATIONS TO THE ANTI-LOCK BRAKE CONTROL MODULE	
①	Check the communication to the anti-lock brake control module. • Does NGS Tester communicate with the anti-lock brake control module? → **Yes** INSTALL a new anti-lock brake control module. REPEAT the self-test. → **No** GO to Pinpoint Test A.

FM4029901344000X

Fig. 5 Test B: Unable To Enter Self Test

TEST CONDITIONS	TESTDETAILS/RESULTS/ACTIONS
C3 CHECK CIRCUIT 1205 (BK) FOR AN OPEN	
①	Measure the resistance between EEC-IV 60-Pin Breakout Box pin 8, circuit 1205 (BK) and ground; and between EEC-IV 60-Pin Breakout Box pin 24, circuit 1205 (BK) and ground. • Are the resistances less than 5 ohms? → **Yes** INSTALL a new anti-lock brake control module REPEAT the self-test. → **No** REPAIR circuit 1205 (BK). CLEAR the DTCs. REPEAT the self-test.

FM4029901345020X

Fig. 6 Test C: Codes B1317 & B1318: Battery Voltage High/Low (Part 2 of 2)

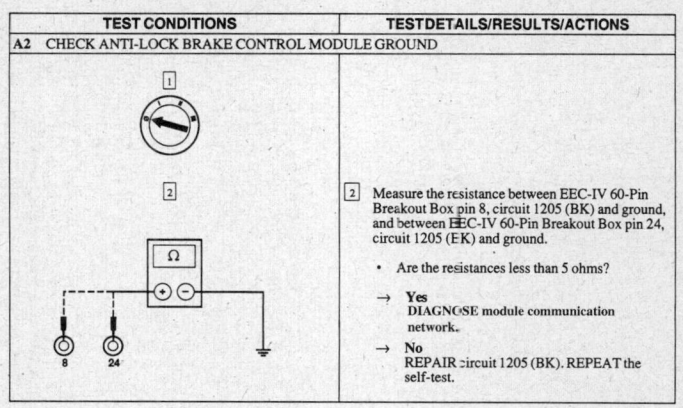

TEST CONDITIONS	TESTDETAILS/RESULTS/ACTIONS
A2 CHECK ANTI-LOCK BRAKE CONTROL MODULE GROUND	
②	Measure the resistance between EEC-IV 60-Pin Breakout Box pin 8, circuit 1205 (BK) and ground, and between EEC-IV 60-Pin Breakout Box pin 24, circuit 1205 (BK) and ground. • Are the resistances less than 5 ohms? → **Yes** DIAGNOSE module communication network. → **No** REPAIR circuit 1205 (BK). REPEAT the self-test.

FM4029901343020X

Fig. 4 Test A: No Communication With ABS Control Module (Part 2 of 2)

TEST CONDITIONS	TESTDETAILS/RESULTS/ACTIONS
C1 CHECK BATTERY VOLTAGE	
Note: A recent jump start may cause these DTCs to set.	
①	Measure the battery voltage between the positive and negative battery posts with the key ON engine OFF (KOEO), and with the engine running. • Is the battery voltage between 10 and 13 volts with KOEO, and between 11 and 17 volts with the engine running? → **Yes** GO to **C2**. → **No** DIAGNOSE charging system.
C2 CHECK POWER TO ANTI-LOCK BRAKE CONTROL MODULE	
Anti-Lock Brake Control Module C111	
③	Connect EEC-IV 60-Pin Breakout Box.
④	
⑤	Measure the voltage between EEC-IV 60-Pin Breakout Box pin 9, circuit 601 (LB/PK) and ground; and between EEC-IV 60-Pin Breakout Box pin 25, circuit 534 (YE/LG) and ground; and between EEC-IV 60-Pin Breakout Box pin 23, circuit 1040 (RD/BK) and ground. • Are the voltages greater than 10 volts? → **Yes** GO to **C3**. → **No** REPAIR the circuit in question. CLEAR the DTCs. REPEAT the self-test.

FM4029901345010X

Fig. 6 Test C: Codes B1317 & B1318: Battery Voltage High/Low (Part 1 of 2)

TEST CONDITIONS	TESTDETAILS/RESULTS/ACTIONS
D1 CHECK FOR FAULT REPEATABILITY	
① NGS ② Clear Continuous DTCs ③	Carry out anti-lock brake control module on-demand self-test.
④	Retrieve and document continuous DTCs. • Are any DTCs retrieved? → **Yes** If DTC C1096 or C1095 is retrieved, GO to **D2**. → **No** System is OK. If a different DTC is retrieved, GO to Anti-Lock Brake Control Module Diagnostic Trouble Code (DTC) Index.

FM4029901346010X

Fig. 7 Test D: Codes C1095 & C1096: Pump Motor Failure (Part 1 of 2)

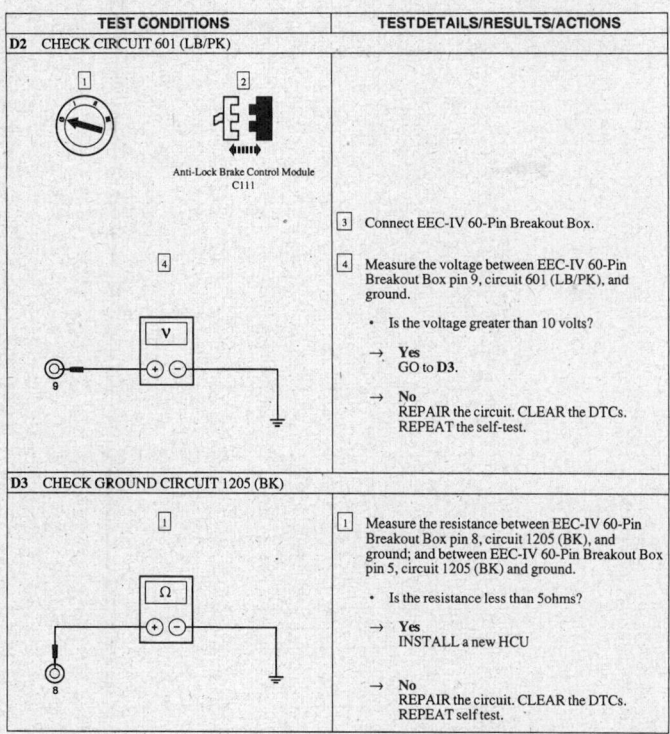

TEST CONDITIONS	TESTDETAILS/RESULTS/ACTIONS
D2 CHECK CIRCUIT 601 (LB/PK)	

3 Connect EEC-IV 60-Pin Breakout Box.

4 Measure the voltage between EEC-IV 60-Pin Breakout Box pin 9, circuit 601 (LB/PK), and ground.

 • Is the voltage greater than 10 volts?

 → **Yes**
   GO to **D3**.

 → **No**
   REPAIR the circuit. CLEAR the DTCs. REPEAT the self-test.

TEST CONDITIONS	TESTDETAILS/RESULTS/ACTIONS
D3 CHECK GROUND CIRCUIT 1205 (BK)	

1 Measure the resistance between EEC-IV 60-Pin Breakout Box pin 8, circuit 1205 (BK), and ground; and between EEC-IV 60-Pin Breakout Box pin 5, circuit 1205 (BK) and ground.

 • Is the resistance less than 5ohms?

 → **Yes**
   INSTALL a new HCU

 → **No**
   REPAIR the circuit. CLEAR the DTCs. REPEAT self test.

FM4029901346020X

Fig. 7 Test D: Codes C1095 & C1096: Pump Motor Failure (Part 2 of 2)

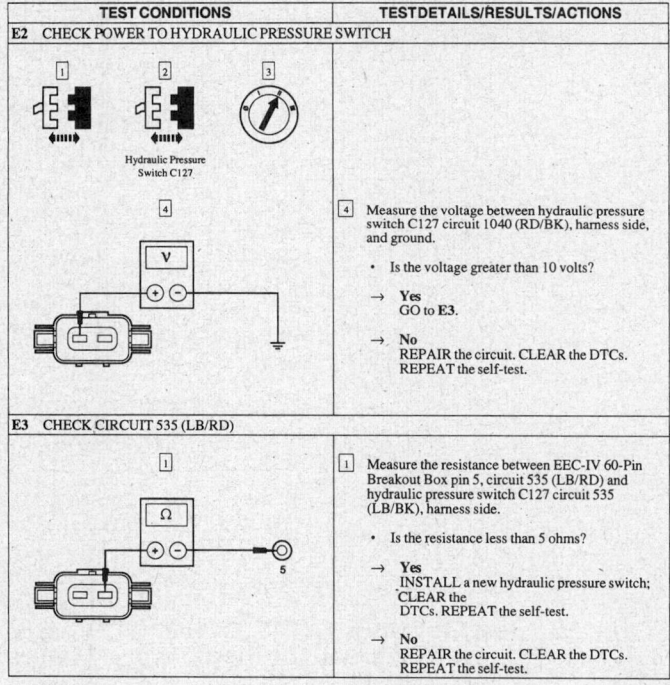

TEST CONDITIONS	TESTDETAILS/RESULTS/ACTIONS
E2 CHECK POWER TO HYDRAULIC PRESSURE SWITCH	

4 Measure the voltage between hydraulic pressure switch C127 circuit 1040 (RD/BK), harness side, and ground.

 • Is the voltage greater than 10 volts?

 → **Yes**
   GO to **E3**.

 → **No**
   REPAIR the circuit. CLEAR the DTCs. REPEAT the self-test.

TEST CONDITIONS	TESTDETAILS/RESULTS/ACTIONS
E3 CHECK CIRCUIT 535 (LB/RD)	

1 Measure the resistance between EEC-IV 60-Pin Breakout Box pin 5, circuit 535 (LB/RD) and hydraulic pressure switch C127 circuit 535 (LB/BK), harness side.

 • Is the resistance less than 5 ohms?

 → **Yes**
   INSTALL a new hydraulic pressure switch; CLEAR the DTCs. REPEAT the self-test.

 → **No**
   REPAIR the circuit. CLEAR the DTCs. REPEAT the self-test.

FM4029901347020X

Fig. 8 Test E: Code C1103: Hydraulic Pressure Switch Failure (Part 2 of 2)

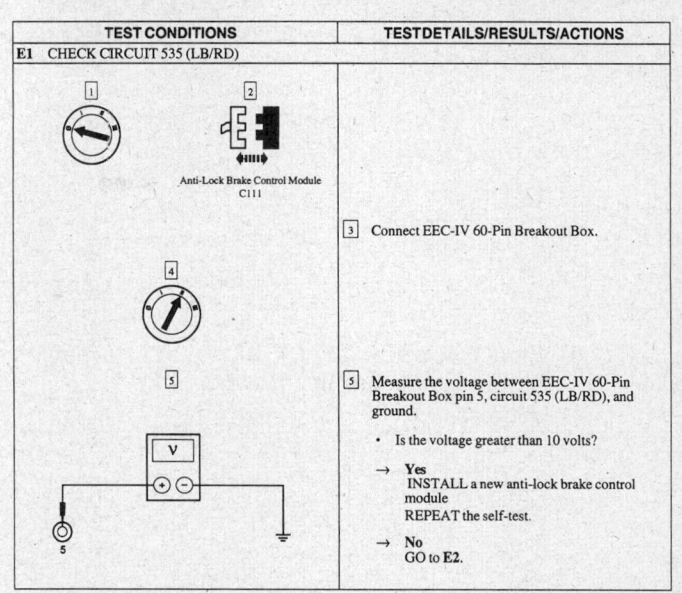

TEST CONDITIONS	TESTDETAILS/RESULTS/ACTIONS
E1 CHECK CIRCUIT 535 (LB/RD)	

3 Connect EEC-IV 60-Pin Breakout Box.

5 Measure the voltage between EEC-IV 60-Pin Breakout Box pin 5, circuit 535 (LB/RD), and ground.

 • Is the voltage greater than 10 volts?

 → **Yes**
   INSTALL a new anti-lock brake control module REPEAT the self-test.

 → **No**
   GO to **E2**.

FM4029901347010X

Fig. 8 Test E: Code C1103: Hydraulic Pressure Switch Failure (Part 1 of 2)

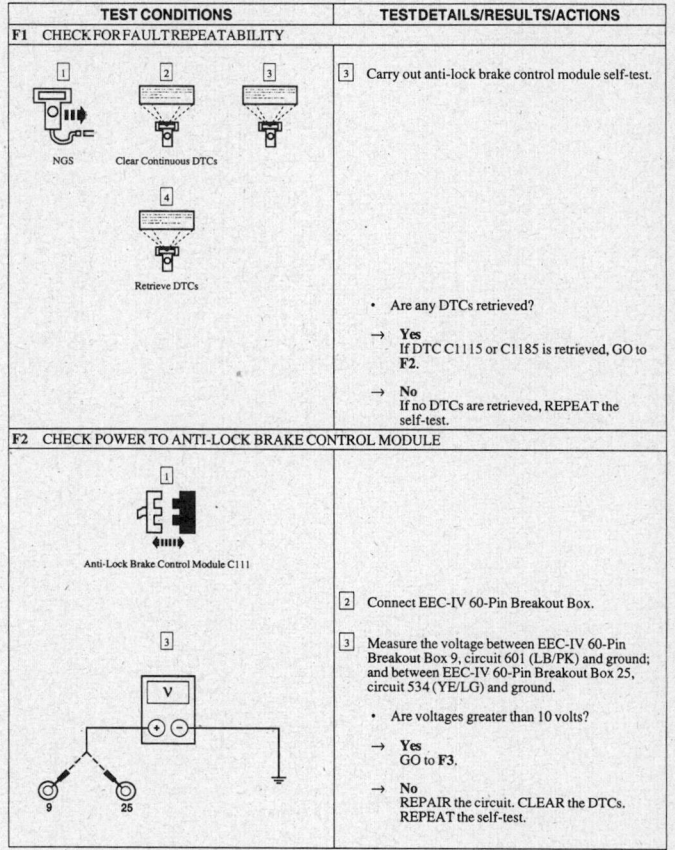

TEST CONDITIONS	TESTDETAILS/RESULTS/ACTIONS
F1 CHECK FOR FAULT REPEATABILITY	

3 Carry out anti-lock brake control module self-test.

 • Are any DTCs retrieved?

 → **Yes**
   If DTC C1115 or C1185 is retrieved, GO to **F2**.

 → **No**
   If no DTCs are retrieved, REPEAT the self-test.

TEST CONDITIONS	TESTDETAILS/RESULTS/ACTIONS
F2 CHECK POWER TO ANTI-LOCK BRAKE CONTROL MODULE	

2 Connect EEC-IV 60-Pin Breakout Box.

3 Measure the voltage between EEC-IV 60-Pin Breakout Box 9, circuit 601 (LB/PK) and ground; and between EEC-IV 60-Pin Breakout Box 25, circuit 534 (YE/LG) and ground.

 • Are voltages greater than 10 volts?

 → **Yes**
   GO to **F3**.

 → **No**
   REPAIR the circuit. CLEAR the DTCs. REPEAT the self-test.

FM4029901348010X

Fig. 9 Test F: Codes C1115 & C1185: Internal Power Relay Failure (Part 1 of 2)

TEST CONDITIONS	TESTDETAILS/RESULTS/ACTIONS
F3 CHECK GROUND CIRCUIT 1205 (BK)	

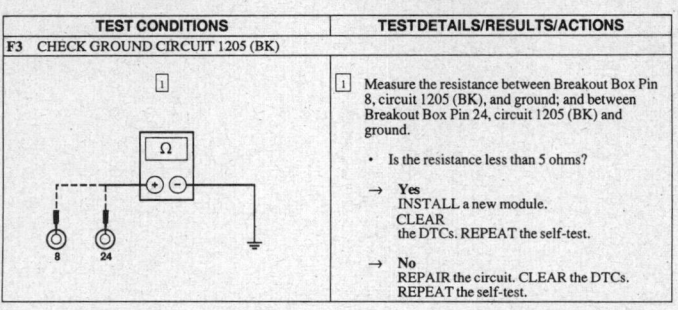

1. Measure the resistance between Breakout Box Pin 8, circuit 1205 (BK), and ground; and between Breakout Box Pin 24, circuit 1205 (BK) and ground.

   • Is the resistance less than 5 ohms?

   → **Yes**
   INSTALL a new module.
   CLEAR
   the DTCs. REPEAT the self-test.

   → **No**
   REPAIR the circuit. CLEAR the DTCs.
   REPEAT the self-test.

FM4029901348020X

Fig. 9   Test F: Codes C1115 & C1185: Internal Power Relay Failure (Part 2 of 2)

TEST CONDITIONS	TESTDETAILS/RESULTS/ACTIONS
G2 CHECK THE ANTI-LOCK BRAKE SENSOR COIL RESISTANCE WITH WIRING HARNESS	

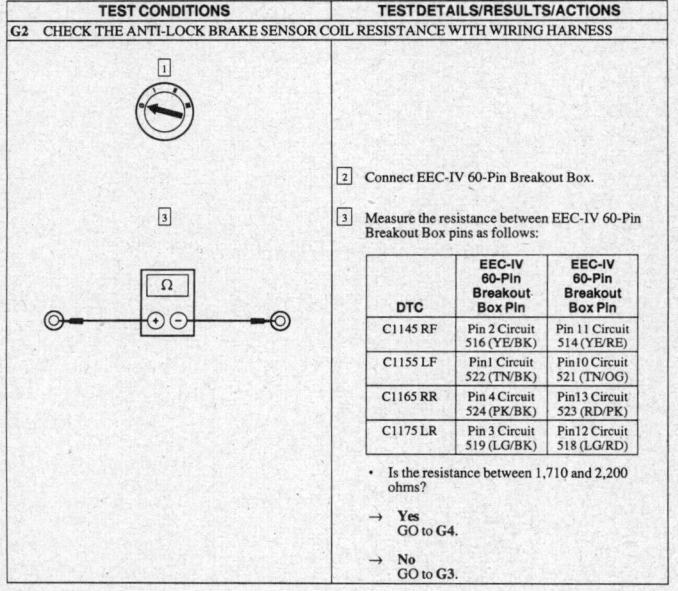

2. Connect EEC-IV 60-Pin Breakout Box.

3. Measure the resistance between EEC-IV 60-Pin Breakout Box pins as follows:

DTC	EEC-IV 60-Pin Breakout Box Pin	EEC-IV 60-Pin Breakout Box Pin
C1145 RF	Pin 2 Circuit 516 (YE/BK)	Pin 11 Circuit 514 (YE/RE)
C1155 LF	Pin1 Circuit 522 (TN/BK)	Pin10 Circuit 521 (TN/OG)
C1165 RR	Pin 4 Circuit 524 (PK/BK)	Pin13 Circuit 523 (RD/PK)
C1175 LR	Pin 3 Circuit 519 (LG/BK)	Pin12 Circuit 518 (LG/RD)

   • Is the resistance between 1,710 and 2,200 ohms?

   → **Yes**
   GO to G4.

   → **No**
   GO to G3.

FM4029901349020X

Fig. 10   Test G: Codes C1145, C1155, C1165 & C1175: Anti-Lock Brake Sensor Input Circuit Failure (Part 2 of 4)

TEST CONDITIONS	TESTDETAILS/RESULTS/ACTIONS
G1 CHECK FOR FAULT REPEATABILITY	

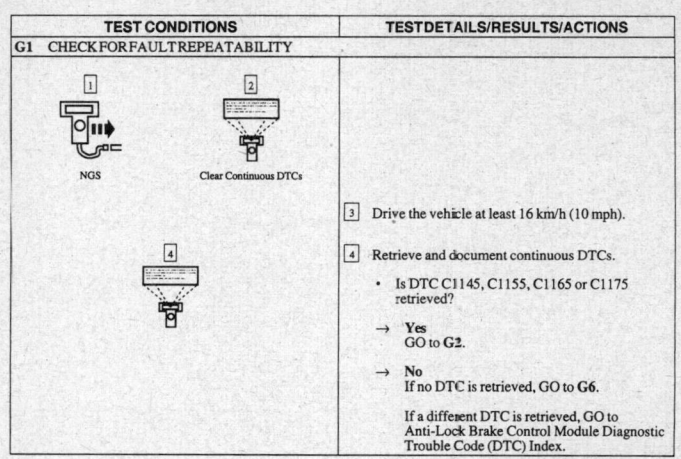

NGS   Clear Continuous DTCs

3. Drive the vehicle at least 16 km/h (10 mph).

4. Retrieve and document continuous DTCs.

   • Is DTC C1145, C1155, C1165 or C1175 retrieved?

   → **Yes**
   GO to G2.

   → **No**
   If no DTC is retrieved, GO to G6.

   If a different DTC is retrieved, GO to Anti-Lock Brake Control Module Diagnostic Trouble Code (DTC) Index.

FM4029901349010X

Fig. 10   Test G: Codes C1145, C1155, C1165 & C1175: Anti-Lock Brake Sensor Input Circuit Failure (Part 1 of 4)

TEST CONDITIONS	TESTDETAILS/RESULTS/ACTIONS
G3 DETERMINE LOCATION OF FAULT	

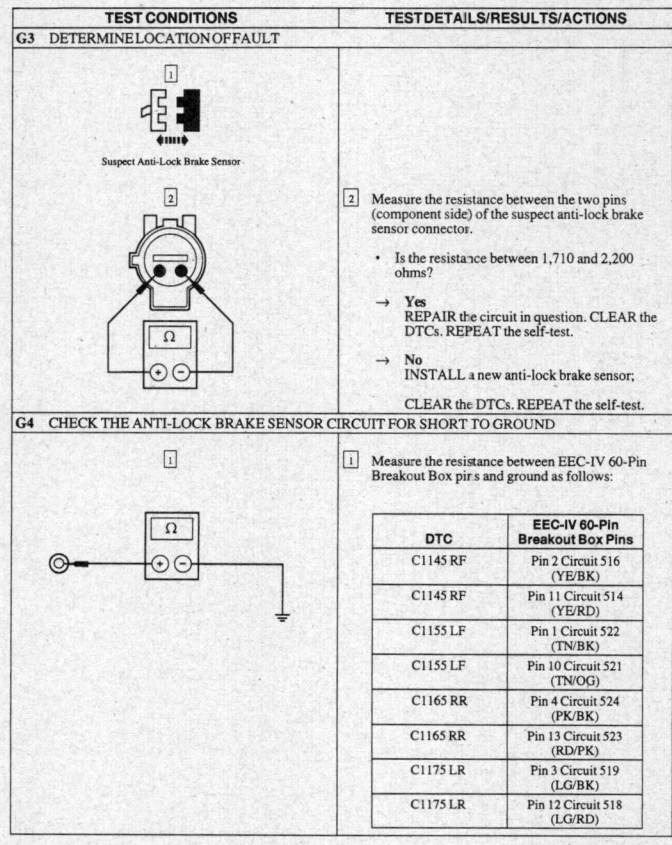

Suspect Anti-Lock Brake Sensor

2. Measure the resistance between the two pins (component side) of the suspect anti-lock brake sensor connector.

   • Is the resistance between 1,710 and 2,200 ohms?

   → **Yes**
   REPAIR the circuit in question. CLEAR the DTCs. REPEAT the self-test.

   → **No**
   INSTALL a new anti-lock brake sensor;

   CLEAR the DTCs. REPEAT the self-test.

G4 CHECK THE ANTI-LOCK BRAKE SENSOR CIRCUIT FOR SHORT TO GROUND	

1. Measure the resistance between EEC-IV 60-Pin Breakout Box pins and ground as follows:

DTC	EEC-IV 60-Pin Breakout Box Pins
C1145 RF	Pin 2 Circuit 516 (YE/BK)
C1145 RF	Pin 11 Circuit 514 (YE/RD)
C1155 LF	Pin 1 Circuit 522 (TN/BK)
C1155 LF	Pin 10 Circuit 521 (TN/OG)
C1165 RR	Pin 4 Circuit 524 (PK/BK)
C1165 RR	Pin 13 Circuit 523 (RD/PK)
C1175 LR	Pin 3 Circuit 519 (LG/BK)
C1175 LR	Pin 12 Circuit 518 (LG/RD)

FM4029901349030X

Fig. 10   Test G: Codes C1145, C1155, C1165 & C1175: Anti-Lock Brake Sensor Input Circuit Failure (Part 3 of 4)

TEST CONDITIONS	TESTDETAILS/RESULTS/ACTIONS
G4 CHECK THE ANTI-LOCK BRAKE SENSOR CIRCUIT FOR SHORT TO GROUND (Continued)	
	• Is the resistance greater than 10,000 ohms? → **Yes** GO to **G6**. → **No** GO to **G5**.
G5 CHECK FOR INTERNAL SENSOR SHORT	

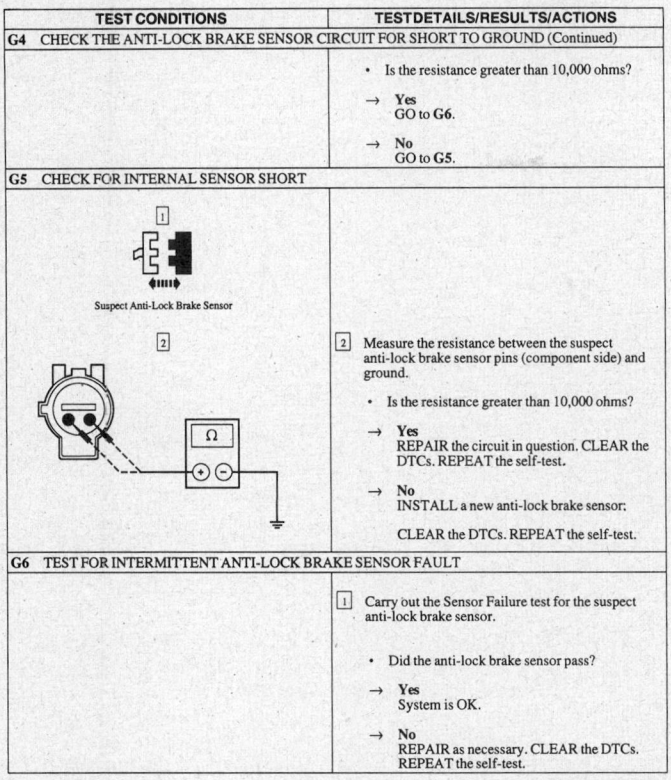

	2 Measure the resistance between the suspect anti-lock brake sensor pins (component side) and ground. • Is the resistance greater than 10,000 ohms? → **Yes** REPAIR the circuit in question. CLEAR the DTCs. REPEAT the self-test. → **No** INSTALL a new anti-lock brake sensor; CLEAR the DTCs. REPEAT the self-test.
G6 TEST FOR INTERMITTENT ANTI-LOCK BRAKE SENSOR FAULT	
	1 Carry out the Sensor Failure test for the suspect anti-lock brake sensor. • Did the anti-lock brake sensor pass? → **Yes** System is OK. → **No** REPAIR as necessary. CLEAR the DTCs. REPEAT the self-test.

FM4029901349040X

Fig. 10   Test G: Codes C1145, C1155, C1165 & C1175: Anti-Lock Brake Sensor Input Circuit Failure (Part 4 of 4)

TEST CONDITIONS	TESTDETAILS/RESULTS/ACTIONS
I1 CHECK FOR FAULT REPEATABILITY	
	3 Carry out anti-lock control module self-test.

FM4029901351010X

Fig. 12   Test I: Codes C1194, C1198, C1210, C1214, C1242, C1246, C1250 & C1254: Isolation Valve, Dump Valve Circuit Failure (Part 1 of 2)

TEST CONDITIONS	TESTDETAILS/RESULTS/ACTIONS
H1 CHECK FOR FAULT REPEATABILITY	

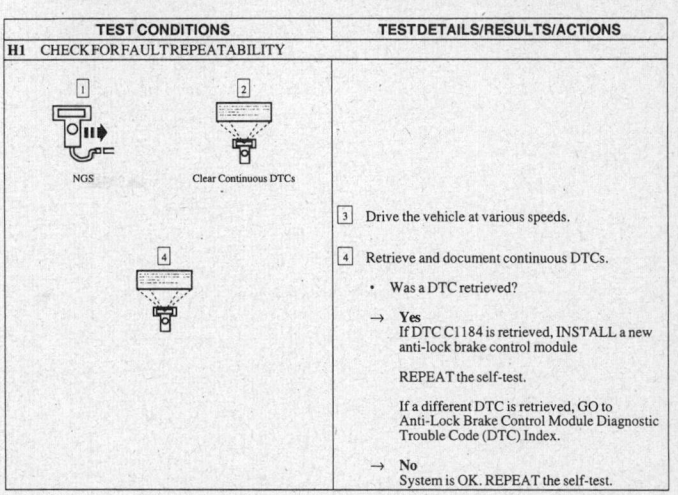

	3 Drive the vehicle at various speeds. 4 Retrieve and document continuous DTCs. • Was a DTC retrieved? → **Yes** If DTC C1184 is retrieved, INSTALL a new anti-lock brake control module REPEAT the self-test. If a different DTC is retrieved, GO to Anti-Lock Brake Control Module Diagnostic Trouble Code (DTC) Index. → **No** System is OK. REPEAT the self-test.

FM4029901350000X

Fig. 11   Test H: Code C1184: ABS System Time-Out

TEST CONDITIONS	TESTDETAILS/RESULTS/ACTIONS
I1 CHECK FOR FAULT REPEATABILITY	
	• Is a single valve DTC set? → **Yes** INSTALL a new anti-lock brake control module. REPEAT the self-test. → **No** If multiple valve DTCs are set, GO to **I2**. If no DTCs are set, the system is OK. REPEAT the self-test.
I2 CHECK CIRCUIT 534 (YE/LG)	

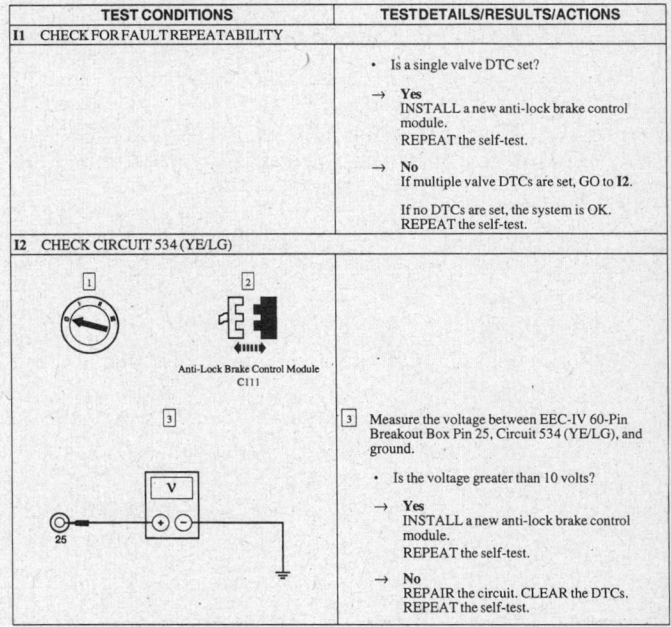

	3 Measure the voltage between EEC-IV 60-Pin Breakout Box Pin 25, Circuit 534 (YE/LG), and ground. • Is the voltage greater than 10 volts? → **Yes** INSTALL a new anti-lock brake control module. REPEAT the self-test. → **No** REPAIR the circuit. CLEAR the DTCs. REPEAT the self-test.

FM4029901351020X

Fig. 12   Test I: Codes C1194, C1198, C1210, C1214, C1242, C1246, C1250 & C1254: Isolation Valve, Dump Valve Circuit Failure (Part 2 of 2)

TEST CONDITIONS	TESTDETAILS/RESULTS/ACTIONS
J1 RETRIEVE DTCS	

| | 2 Retrieve and document continuous DTCs.
• Is DTC C1145, C1155, C1165, or C1175 retrieved?
→ **Yes** DIAGNOSE these DTCs first. REFER to Diagnostic Trouble Code Interpretation.
→ **No** GO to **J2**. |

J2 REPEATABILITY DRIVE TEST (MISMATCHED OUTPUT)

Note: If a hard turn is made, some variation between all four anti-lock brake sensors is expected.

Note: Recording the speeds for later plotting will eliminate the necessity of monitoring NGS Tester while driving.

1 Monitor anti-lock brake control module PIDs LF__WSPD, RF__WSPD, RR__WSPD and LR__WSPD.

2 Drive the vehicle at various speeds.
• Do the anti-lock brake sensors consistently match?
→ **Yes** GO to **J5**.
→ **No** GO to **J3**.

J3 CHECK THE SUSPECT ANTI-LOCK BRAKE SENSOR INDICATOR

1 Raise the vehicle on a hoist.

FM4029901352010X

Fig. 13 Test J: Codes C1233, C1234, C1235 & C1236: Anti-Lock Brake Sensor Signal Missing Or Erratic (Part 1 of 4)

TEST CONDITIONS	TESTDETAILS/RESULTS/ACTIONS
J3 CHECK THE SUSPECT ANTI-LOCK BRAKE SENSOR INDICATOR	
	2 ⚠ **CAUTION: Examine the anti-lock brake sensor indicator carefully. Failure to properly diagnose anti-lock brake sensor indicator at this time will lead to unnecessary component replacement and wasted diagnostic time.** Inspect the anti-lock brake sensor indicator for damaged or missing teeth. Rotate the anti-lock brake sensor indicator to be sure all teeth are checked. • Is the suspect anti-lock brake sensor indicator damaged or missing teeth? → **Yes** INSTALL a new anti-lock brake sensor indicator. CLEAR the DTCs. REPEAT the self-test. → **No** GO to **J4**.
J4 CHECK FOR LOOSE ANTI-LOCK BRAKE SENSOR MOUNTING	
	1 Wiggle the anti-lock brake sensor at wheel end. • Is any looseness detected? → **Yes** TIGHTEN anti-lock brake sensor bolt to specifications. CLEAR the DTCs. TEST DRIVE the vehicle. REPEAT the self-test. → **No** GO to **J6**.

FM4029901352020X

Fig. 13 Test J: Codes C1233, C1234, C1235 & C1236: Anti-Lock Brake Sensor Signal Missing Or Erratic (Part 2 of 4)

TEST CONDITIONS	TESTDETAILS/RESULTS/ACTIONS
J5 CHECK FOR ANTI-LOCK BRAKE SENSOR CIRCUIT SHORT TO GROUND	

Anti-Lock Brake Control Module C111
Suspect Anti-Lock Brake Sensor Connector

4 Measure the resistance between the suspect anti-lock brake sensor connector pins, wiring harness side and ground.
• Are the resistances greater than 10,000 ohms?
→ **Yes** INSTALL a new sensor. CLEAR the DTCs. REPEAT the self-test.
→ **No** REPAIR the circuits. CLEAR the DTCs. REPEAT the self-test.

J6 INSPECT THE SUSPECT ANTI-LOCK BRAKE SENSOR FOR DAMAGE

2 Remove the suspect anti-lock brake sensor.

3 Inspect the housing for stress cracks or breaks.

FM4029901352030X

Fig. 13 Test J: Codes C1233, C1234, C1235 & C1236: Anti-Lock Brake Sensor Signal Missing Or Erratic (Part 3 of 4)

TEST CONDITIONS	TESTDETA LS/RESULTS/ACTIONS
J6 INSPECT THE SUSPECT ANTI-LOCK BRAKE SENSOR FOR DAMAGE	
	4 Inspect the anti-lock brake sensor connector for evidence of water entry, pin corrosion, or excessive debris. • Are any of the above conditions present? → **Yes** INSTALL a new anti-lock brake sensor; CLEAR the DTCs. REPEAT the self-test. → **No** INSTALL a new anti-lock brake control module REPEAT the self-test.

FM4029901352040X

Fig. 13 Test J: Codes C1233, C1234, C1235 & C1236: Anti-Lock Brake Sensor Signal Missing Or Erratic (Part 4 of 4)

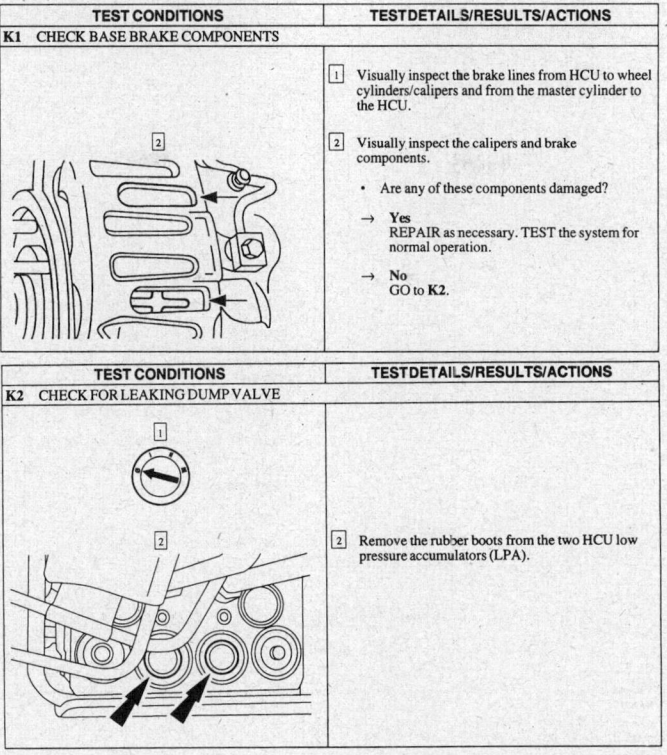

TEST CONDITIONS	TEST DETAILS/RESULTS/ACTIONS
K1 CHECK BASE BRAKE COMPONENTS	

1. Visually inspect the brake lines from HCU to wheel cylinders/calipers and from the master cylinder to the HCU.

2. Visually inspect the calipers and brake components.

   • Are any of these components damaged?

   → **Yes**
   REPAIR as necessary. TEST the system for normal operation.

   → **No**
   GO to **K2**.

TEST CONDITIONS	TEST DETAILS/RESULTS/ACTIONS
K2 CHECK FOR LEAKING DUMP VALVE	

2. Remove the rubber boots from the two HCU low pressure accumulators (LPA).

FM4029901353010X

Fig. 14   Test K: Soft Or Excessive Pedal Travel
(Part 1 of 2)

TEST CONDITIONS	TEST DETAILS/RESULTS/ACTIONS
K2 CHECK FOR LEAKING DUMP VALVE	
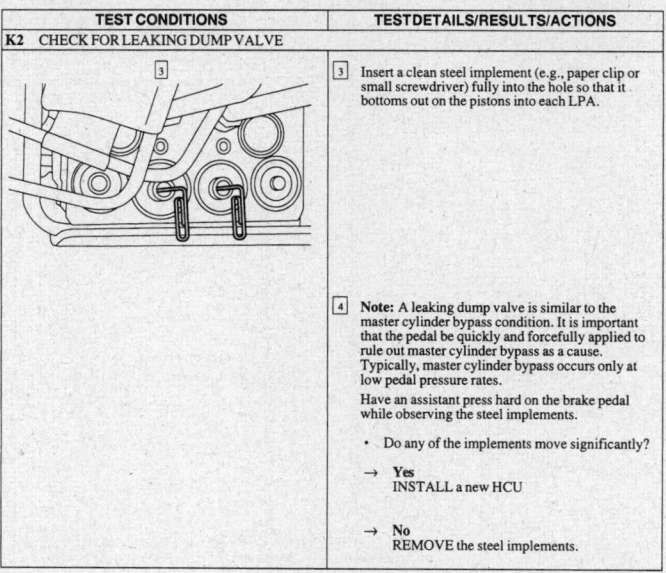	3 Insert a clean steel implement (e.g., paper clip or small screwdriver) fully into the hole so that it bottoms out on the pistons into each LPA.
	4 **Note:** A leaking dump valve is similar to the master cylinder bypass condition. It is important that the pedal be quickly and forcefully applied to rule out master cylinder bypass as a cause. Typically, master cylinder bypass occurs only at low pedal pressure rates.
	Have an assistant press hard on the brake pedal while observing the steel implements.
	• Do any of the implements move significantly?
	→ **Yes** INSTALL a new HCU
	→ **No** REMOVE the steel implements.

FM4029901353020X

Fig. 14   Test K: Soft Or Excessive Pedal Travel
(Part 2 of 2)

ACTIVE SUSPENSION SYSTEMS

TABLE OF CONTENTS

Page No.

APPLICATION CHART 6-1
AUTOMATIC RIDE CONTROL
(ARC) 6-1

Page No.

FOUR WHEEL & REAR LOAD
LEVELING. 6-45
VEHICLE DYNAMIC
SUSPENSION (VDS) 6-98

Application Chart

Model	Year	System
Expedition & Navigator	2002–03	Four Wheel Air Suspension
		Rear Load leveling
	2004–06	Vehicle Dynamic Suspension
Explorer & Mountaineer	2002–03	Automatic Ride Control
		Rear Load Leveling
F–Series	2002–03	Rear Load leveling

Automatic Ride Control (ARC)

NOTE: On Air Bag Equipped Models, Refer To "Air Bag System Precautions" Located In The Front Of This Manual For System Disarming & Arming Procedures.

NOTE: Refer To "Computer Relearn Procedures" Located In The Front Of This Manual When Battery Power To The Computer Has Been Interrupted.

NOTE: "Electrical Symbol & Wire Color Code Identification" Located In The Front Of This Manual May Be Used As An Aid When Using Wiring Circuits Found In This Section.

INDEX

Page No.

Adjustments 6-2
  Ride Height 6-2
Component Replacement 6-43
  Air Compressor & Dryer
    Assembly 6-43
  Air Suspension Switch 6-43
  Automatic Ride Control Module . 6-44
  Front Fill Solenoid 6-44
  Front Height Sensor 6-43
  Front Shock Absorber. 6-43

Page No.

Rear Fill & Gate Solenoid 6-44
Rear Height Sensor. 6-43
Rear Shock Absorber 6-43
Steering Sensor Ring 6-44
Steering Sensor 6-44
Description 6-2
Diagnosis & Testing 6-2
  Accessing Diagnostic Trouble
    Codes 6-2
  Clearing Diagnostic Trouble

Page No.

  Codes 6-2
Diagnostic Tests 6-2
Diagnostic Trouble Code
  Interpretation 6-2
Wiring Diagrams 6-2
Diagnostic Chart Index 6-5
Precautions. 6-1
  Air Bag Systems. 6-1
  Battery Ground Cable. 6-1
  Service 6-1

PRECAUTIONS

Air Bag Systems

Refer to "Air Bag System Precautions" in the front of this manual for system disarming and arming procedures.

Battery Ground Cable

Prior to service, disconnect battery ground cable and isolate as required.

Service

Before servicing an air suspension component, disconnect power to system by turning air suspension switch Off or disconnecting battery ground cable. Do not remove air spring when there is pressure in air spring. Do not remove air spring supporting components without exhausting air or supporting air spring.

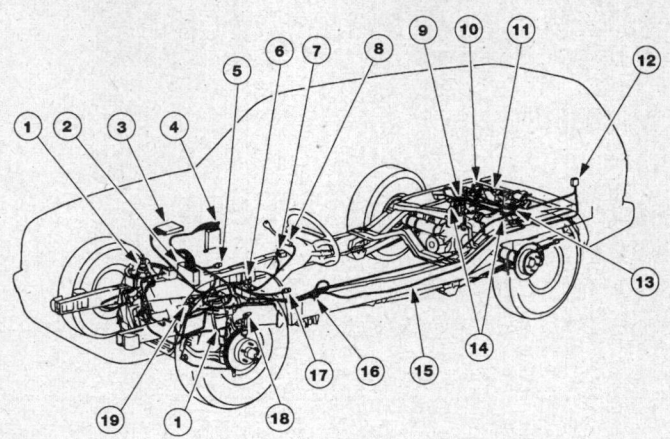

Item	Description
6	Vehicle Speed Sensor (Signal from Transmission)
7	Steering Sensor
8	Ignition Switch
9	Rear Height Sensor
10	Rear Fill Solenoid
11	Air Compressor
12	Automatic Ride Control (ARC) Service Switch

Item	Description
13	Rear Gate Solenoid
14	Rear Shock Absorber
15	Air Line (Part of 3188)
16	Front Fill Solenoid
17	Stoplight Switch
18	Front Height Sensor
19	Compressor Relay

FM2019500302020X

Fig. 1 Automatic ride control component locations (Part 2 of 2)

Item	Description
1	Front Shock Absorber
2	Generic Electronic Module (GEM)
3	Powertrain Control Module

Item	Description
4	Automatic Ride Control (ARC) Module
5	Message Center Indicator

FM2019500302010X

Fig. 1 Automatic ride control component locations (Part 1 of 2)

DTC	Description	Action to Take
P1807	4x4 High Range Input Short to Ground	GO to Pinpoint Test D.
P1808	4x4 Low Range Input Circuit Fault (4.0L) Ride Control Switch Input Circuit Fault (5.0L)	GO to Pinpoint Test E.
C1439	Acceleration Input Signal Circuit Fault	GO to Pinpoint Test F.
C1724	Height Sensor Power Circuit Fault	GO to Pinpoint Test G.
C1725	Front Pneumatic Fault	GO to Pinpoint Test H.
C1726	Rear Pneumatic Fault	GO to Pinpoint Test J.
C1756	Front Height Sensor Circuit Fault	GO to Pinpoint Test K.
C1760	Rear Height Sensor Circuit Fault	GO to Pinpoint Test K.
C1770	Vent Solenoid Circuit Fault	GO to Pinpoint Test L.
C1830	Air Compressor Relay Circuit Fault	GO to Pinpoint Test M.
C1845	Front Fill Solenoid Circuit Fault	GO to Pinpoint Test N.
C1865	Rear Fill Solenoid Circuit Fault	GO to Pinpoint Test N.
C1869	Rear Gate Solenoid Circuit Fault	GO to Pinpoint Test P.
C1901	Right Rear Shock Absorber Circuit Fault	GO to Pinpoint Test Q.
C1905	Left Rear Shock Absorber Circuit Fault	GO to Pinpoint Test R.
C1909	Right Front Shock Absorber Circuit Fault	GO to Pinpoint Test S.
C1913	Left Front Shock Absorber Circuit Fault	GO to Pinpoint Test T.
B1318	Battery Voltage Low	GO to Pinpoint Test U.
B1342	ECU Internal Fault	GO to Pinpoint Test V.
B1485	Brake Lamp Switch Input Short to Battery	GO to Pinpoint Test W.
B1565	Door Ajar Input Short to Power	GO to Pinpoint Test X.

FM2019800476000X

Fig. 2 Diagnostic trouble code chart

DESCRIPTION

The Automatic Ride Control (ARC), **Fig. 1,** is a computer controlled suspension system that uses unique suspension components and two stage (firm and soft) shock absorbers to provide a smooth ride for normal driving conditions without sacrificing handling performance.

The ARC system adjusts vehicle height on front and rear axles separately through use of solenoid valves, air compressor, and air lines. Vehicle height is set based on status of door ajar signal and transfer case mode selected (two-wheel drive, automatic four-wheel drive, or four-wheel drive low). Trim level is maintained even with addition and removal of cargo.

In automatic four-wheel drive with vehicle empty, vehicle is fully supported by front torsion bars and rear leaf springs. This height is referred to as base height. Compressed air is applied to air springs only when a load is added to the vehicle or a transfer case mode or automatic four-wheel drive or four-wheel drive low is selected.

Off-road capability is increased by stiffening the suspension and raising the vehicle about 2 inches above base height. In four-wheel drive low, compressed air is added to both front and rear by approximately 60% over spring rate. Damping is set to firm in four-wheel drive low to minimize relative movement between wheel and body.

ADJUSTMENTS

Ride Height

1. Connect New Generation Star (NGS) Tester, or equivalent to data link connector located below steering column.
2. Select RIDE CONTROL OUTPUT screen and turn on the following sole-

noids to vent the entire system of air and to lower the vehicle to its lowest attainable height as follows:
   a. FRONT-FIL (front fill solenoid).
   b. REAR-FIL (rear fill solenoid).
   c. GATE (gate solenoid).
   d. VENT (vent solenoid).
3. Close all doors including liftgate and liftgate window.
4. Open any door to ensure height will not change until internal electronic calibration is complete.
5. Park vehicle on a flat surface.
6. Raise front of vehicle approximately 5/8 inch, but no more than 3/4 inch with a suitable floor jack. Measure distance from lowest point of lefthand front wheel to fender lip opening. **Failure to perform this step will result in pneumatic fault conditions.**
7. From function menu, quickly select RIDE HEIGHT CALIBRATION, then note warning on NGS tester screen and follow directions.
8. Lower vehicle and clear all stored diagnostic trouble codes.

DIAGNOSIS & TESTING

Accessing Diagnostic Trouble Codes

Connect New Generation Star (NGS)

Tester, or equivalent to Data Link Connector (DLC) located below steering column. Follow scan tool manufacturer's instructions to retrieve Diagnostic Trouble Codes.

Diagnostic Trouble Code Interpretation

Refer to **Fig. 2** for diagnostic trouble code interpretation.

Wiring Diagrams

Refer to **Figs. 3 through 5** for wiring diagrams and connector pin identification.

Diagnostic Tests

Refer to **Figs. 6 through 32** when diagnosing the Automatic Ride Control system.

Clearing Diagnostic Trouble Codes

Connect New Generation Star (NGS) tester, or equivalent, to Data Link Connector (DLC). Select **Retrieve/Clear Continuous Diagnostic Trouble Codes** from menu. Follow tester instructions to clear codes.

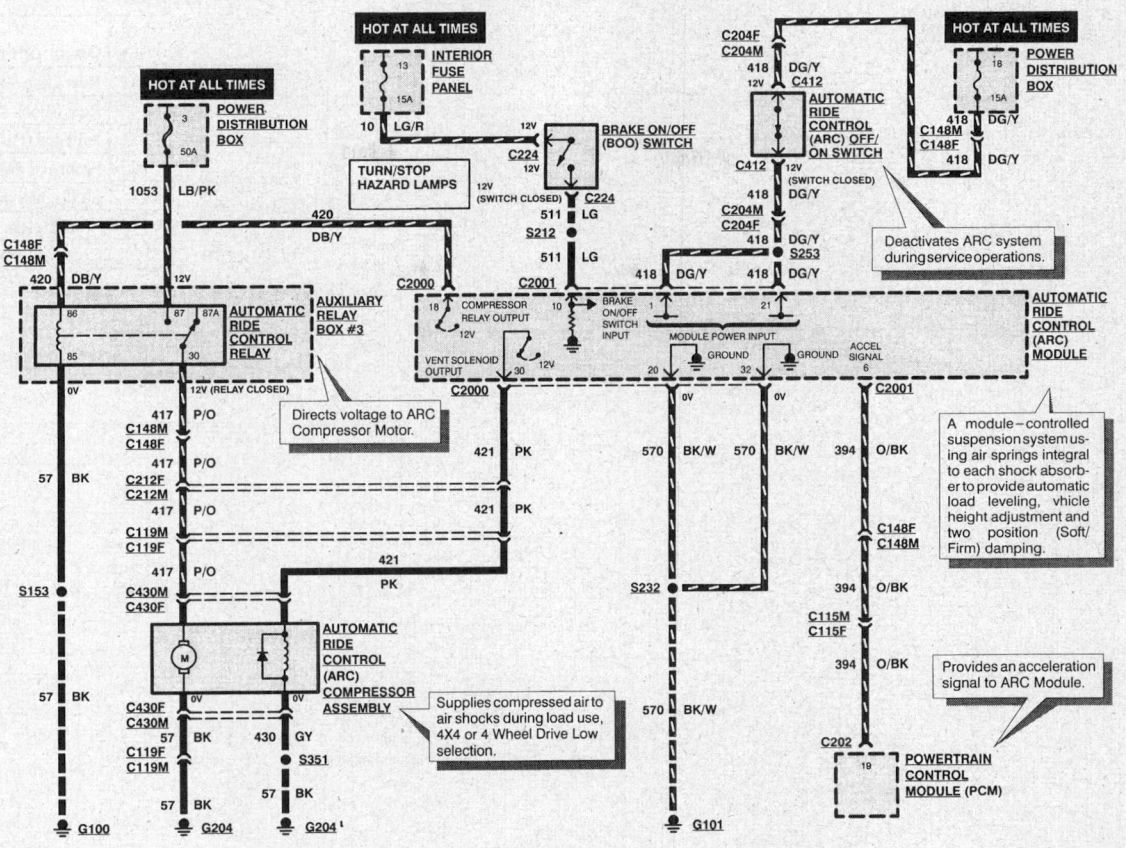

Fig. 3 ARC system wiring circuit (Part 1 of 4)

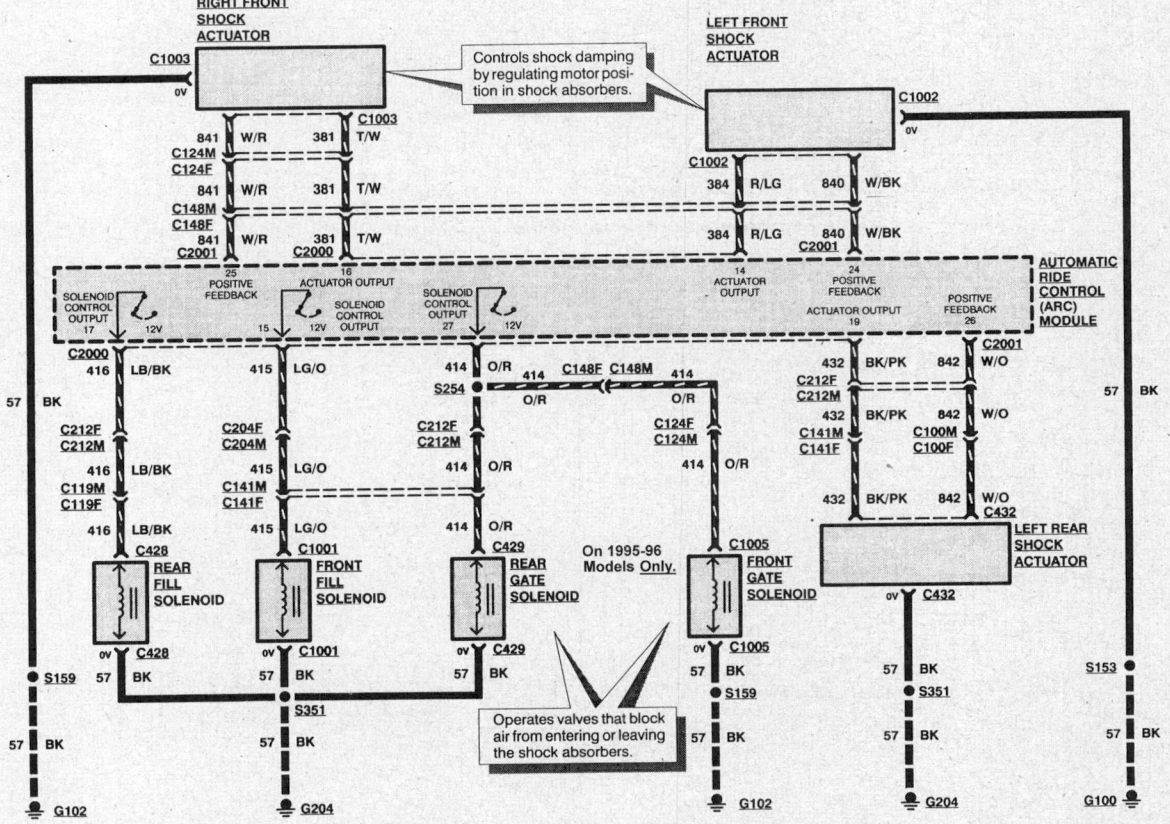

Fig. 3 ARC system wiring circuit (Part 2 of 4)

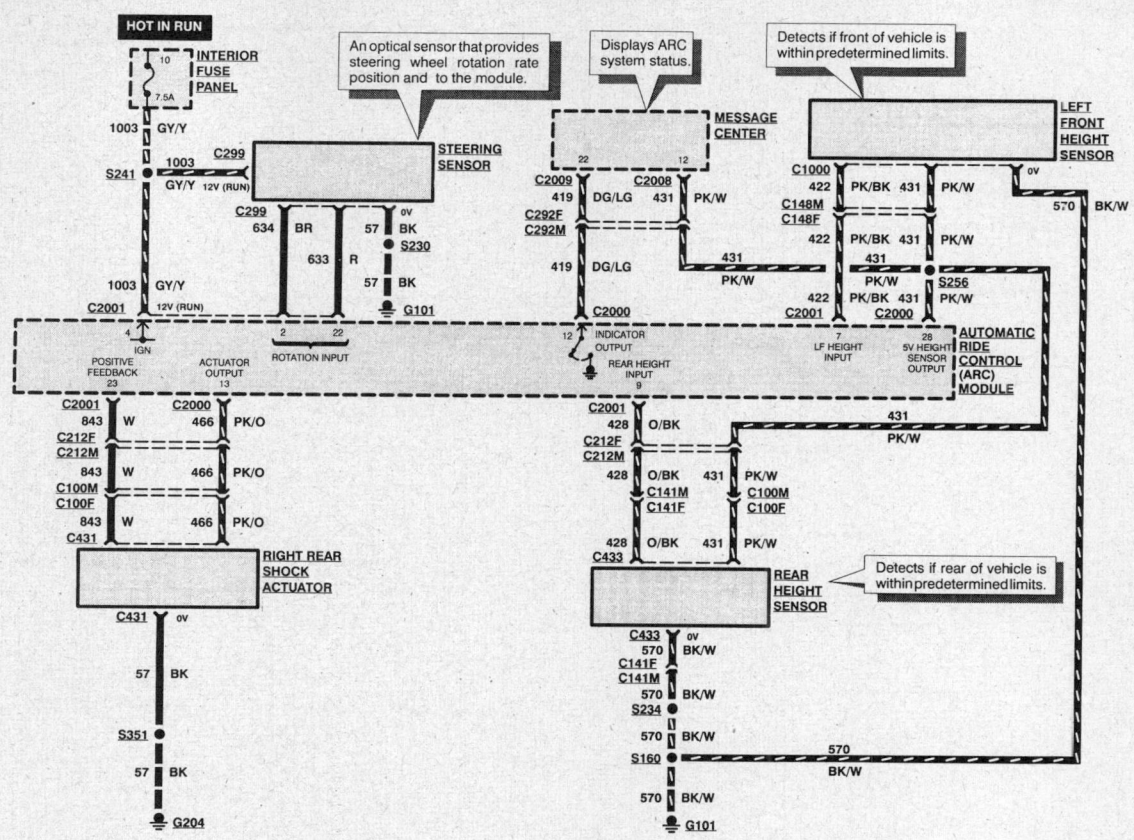

Fig. 3   ARC system wiring circuit (Part 3 of 4)

FM2019500303030X

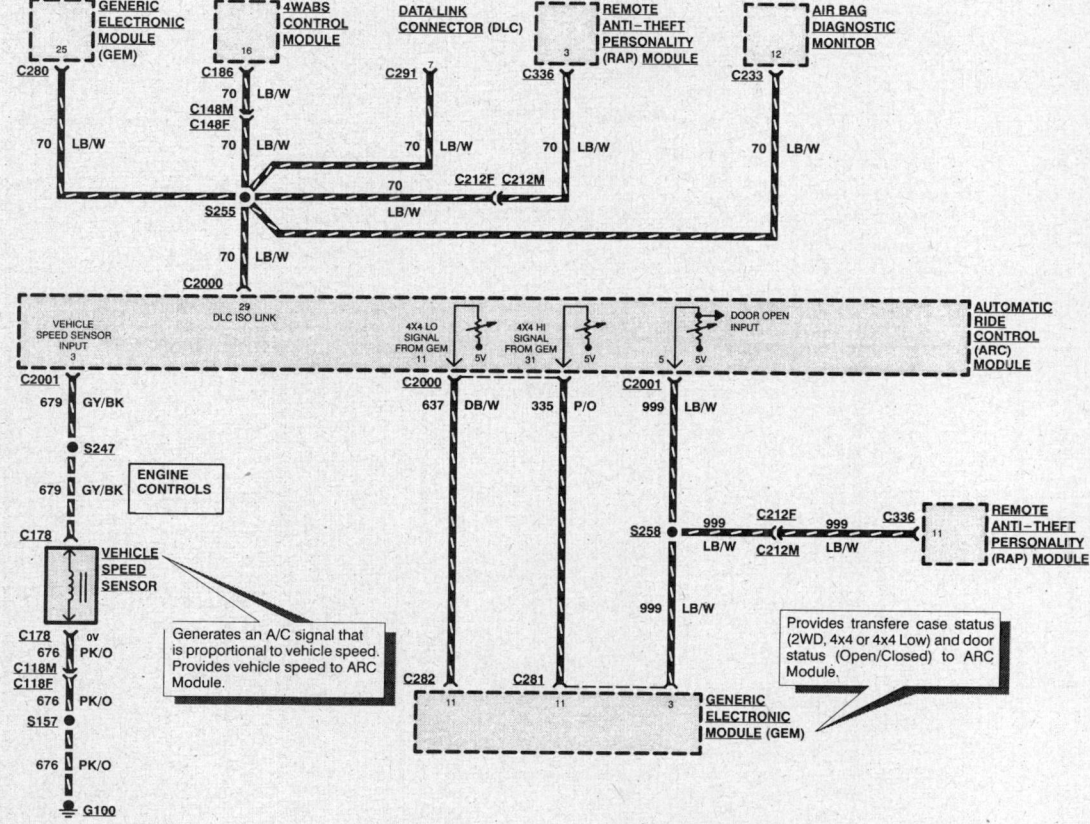

Fig. 3   ARC system wiring circuit (Part 4 of 4)

FM2019500303040X

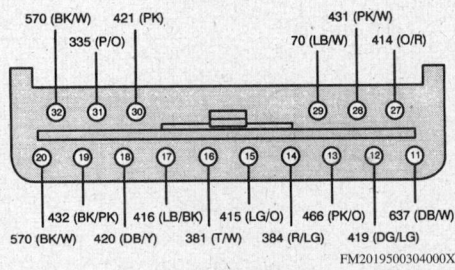

Fig. 4 ARC system gray electrical connector pin identification

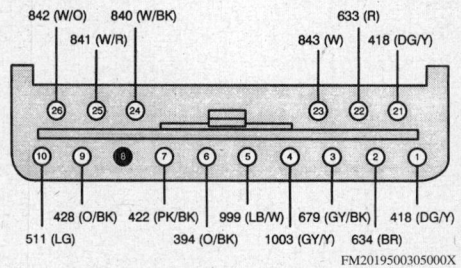

Fig. 5 ARC system black electrical connector pin identification

DIAGNOSTIC CHART INDEX

Test	Code	Description	Page No.	Fig. No.
A	—	Message Center Indicates "Check Air Ride System Within 20 Minutes Of Starting Vehicle"	6-6	6
B	—	Message Center Indicates Air Suspension Switch Is Off	6-6	7
C	—	No Module Communication Or Intermittent	6-7	8
D	P1807	4×4 High Range Input Short To Ground	6-8	9
E	P1808	4×4 Low Range Input Circuit Fault/Ride Control Or Switch Input Circuit Fault	6-8	10
F	C1439	Acceleration Input Signal Circuit Fault	6-9	11
G	C1724	Height Sensor Power Circuit Fault	6-9	12
H	C1725	Front Pneumatic Fault	6-10	13
J	C1726	Rear Pneumatic Fault	6-13	14
K	C1756	Height Sensor Circuit Fault	6-17	15
K	C1760	Height Sensor Circuit Fault	6-17	15
L	C1770	Vent Solenoid Circuit Fault	6-18	16
M	C1830	Air Compressor Relay Circuit Fault	6-21	17
N	C1845	Front–Rear Fill Solenoid Circuit Fault	6-24	18
N	C1865	Front–Rear Fill Solenoid Circuit Fault	6-24	18
P	C1869	Rear Gate Solenoid Circuit Fault	6-28	19
Q	C1901	Righthand Rear Shock Absorber Circuit Fault	6-31	20
R	C1905	Lefthand Rear Shock Absorber Circuit Fault	6-32	21
S	C1909	Righthand Front Shock Absorber Circuit Fault	6-33	22
T	C1913	Lefthand Front Shock Absorber Circuit Fault	6-34	23
U	B1318	Battery Voltage Low	6-35	24
V	B1342	ECU Internal Fault	6-35	25
W	B1485	Brake Lamp Switch Input Short To Power	6-36	26
X	B1565	Door Ajar Input Short To Power	6-36	27
Y	—	ARC System Does Not Seem To Be Working	6-37	28
Z	—	ARC System Functions With Switch Off	6-41	29
AA	—	Compressor Cycles Continuously With Key Off	6-41	30
AB	—	Excessive Compressor Noise	6-41	31
AC	—	Air Compressor Test	6-42	32

TEST CONDITIONS	TEST DETAILS/RESULTS/ACTIONS
A1 CHECK AUTOMATIC RIDE CONTROL (ARC)	

New Generation STAR (NGS) Tester Check ARC Module Communications	• Is the module communicating?
	
	→ **Yes**
	  GO to A2.
	
	→ **No**
	  GO to Pinpoint Test C.

A2 CHECK FOR DTCs	

Retrieve DTCs	Write down all stored DTCs.
	
	• Are there any DTCs retrieved?
	
	→ **Yes**
	  GO to appropriate Pinpoint Test.
	
	→ **No**
	  GO to A3.

FM2019700628010X

Fig. 6   Test A: Message Center Indicates "Check Air Ride System Within 20 Minutes Of Starting Vehicle" (Part 1 of 3)

TEST CONDITIONS	TEST DETAILS/RESULTS/ACTIONS
A3 CHECK BATTERY VOLTAGE	

Monitor VBATARC PID	• Is the displayed voltage greater than 11 volts?
	
	→ **Yes**
	  GO to A4.
	
	→ **No**
	  CHARGE the battery.

A4 CHECK CIRCUIT 419 (DG/LG)	

Cycle Active Command MC NORMAL On and Off	• Does CHECK AIR RIDE SYSTEM message disappear and reappear?
	
	→ **Yes**
	  GO to A5.
	
	→ **No**
	  REPAIR circuit 419 (DG/LG). REPEAT the ARC Module Diagnostics.

FM2019700628020X

Fig. 6   Test A: Message Center Indicates "Check Air Ride System Within 20 Minutes Of Starting Vehicle" (Part 2 of 3)

TEST CONDITIONS	TEST DETAILS/RESULTS/ACTIONS
A5 CHECK INTERMITTENT OPEN CIRCUIT	

Monitor IGN__RUN PID	• Is IGN__RUN set to HIGH?
	
	→ **Yes**
	  CHECK the message center
	  If message center is OK,
	  REPLACE the ARC module. PERFORM ARC module Ride Height procedure. CLEAR all DTCs. REPEAT the ARC Module Diagnostics.
	
	→ **No**
	  REPLACE fuse 10 (15A) and/or REPAIR circuit 1003 (GY/Y).

FM2019700628030X

Fig. 6   Test A: Message Center Indicates "Check Air Ride System Within 20 Minutes Of Starting Vehicle" (Part 3 of 3)

TEST CONDITIONS	TEST DETAILS/RESULTS/ACTIONS
B1 CHECK AIR SUSPENSION SWITCH POSITION	

	Check the position of the air suspension switch.
	
	• Is the air suspension switch in the OFF position?
	
	→ **Yes**
	  TURN the air suspension switch to the ON position. REPEAT the ARC Module Diagnostics.
	
	→ **No**
	  GO to B2.

FM2019700629010X

Fig. 7   Test B: Message Center Indicates Air Suspension Switch Is Off (Part 1 of 5)

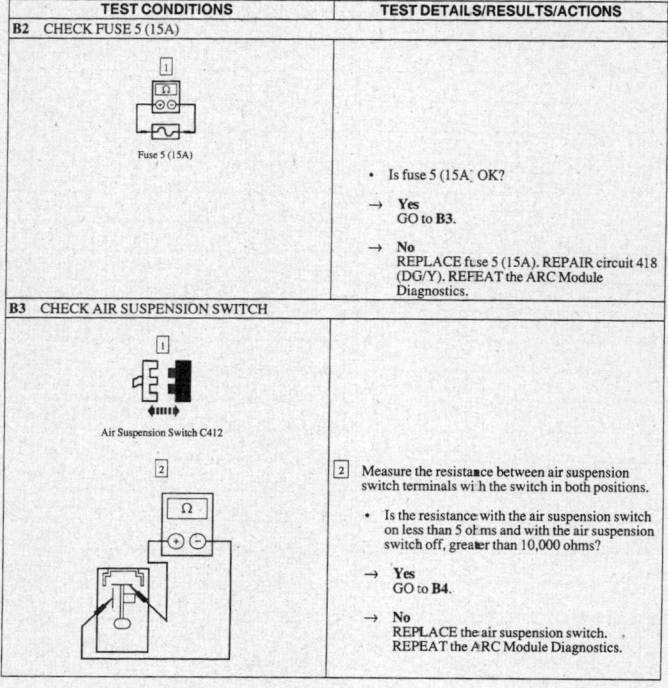

TEST CONDITIONS	TEST DETAILS/RESULTS/ACTIONS
B2 CHECK FUSE 5 (15A)	

Fuse 5 (15A)	• Is fuse 5 (15A) OK?
	
	→ **Yes**
	  GO to B3.
	
	→ **No**
	  REPLACE fuse 5 (15A). REPAIR circuit 418 (DG/Y). REPEAT the ARC Module Diagnostics.

B3 CHECK AIR SUSPENSION SWITCH	

Air Suspension Switch C412	Measure the resistance between air suspension switch terminals with the switch in both positions.
	
	• Is the resistance with the air suspension switch on less than 5 ohms and with the air suspension switch off, greater than 10,000 ohms?
	
	→ **Yes**
	  GO to B4.
	
	→ **No**
	  REPLACE the air suspension switch. REPEAT the ARC Module Diagnostics.

FM2019700629020X

Fig. 7   Test B: Message Center Indicates Air Suspension Switch Is Off (Part 2 of 5)

TEST CONDITIONS	TEST DETAILS/RESULTS/ACTIONS
B4 CHECK CIRCUIT 418 (DG/LG)	
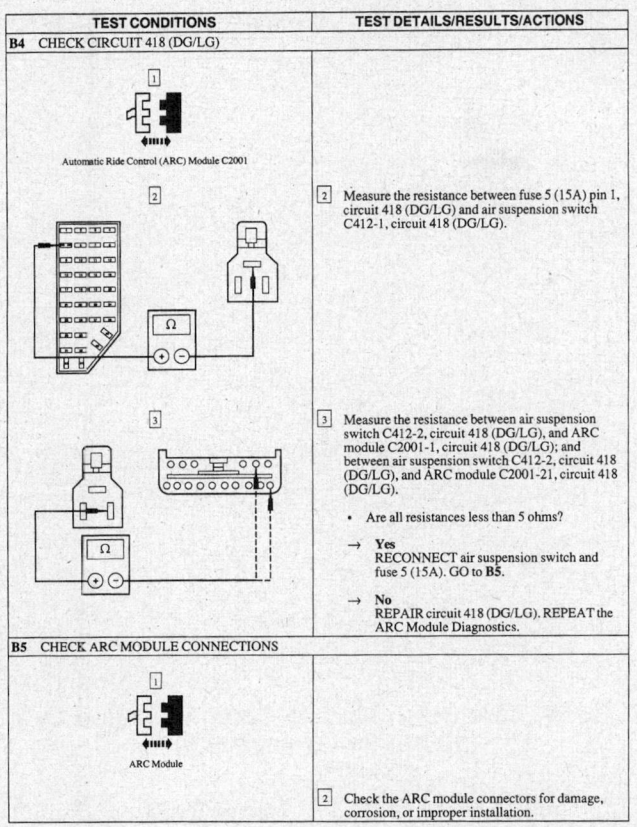	② Measure the resistance between fuse 5 (15A) pin 1, circuit 418 (DG/LG) and air suspension switch C412-1, circuit 418 (DG/LG).
	③ Measure the resistance between air suspension switch C412-2, circuit 418 (DG/LG), and ARC module C2001-1, circuit 418 (DG/LG); and between air suspension switch C412-2, circuit 418 (DG/LG), and ARC module C2001-21, circuit 418 (DG/LG).
	• Are all resistances less than 5 ohms?
	→ **Yes** RECONNECT air suspension switch and fuse 5 (15A). GO to **B5**.
	→ **No** REPAIR circuit 418 (DG/LG). REPEAT the ARC Module Diagnostics.
B5 CHECK ARC MODULE CONNECTIONS	
	② Check the ARC module connectors for damage, corrosion, or improper installation.

FM2019700629030X

Fig. 7   Test B: Message Center Indicates Air Suspension Switch Is Off (Part 3 of 5)

TEST CONDITIONS	TEST DETAILS/RESULTS/ACTIONS
B8 CHECK CIRCUIT 1003 (GY/Y)	
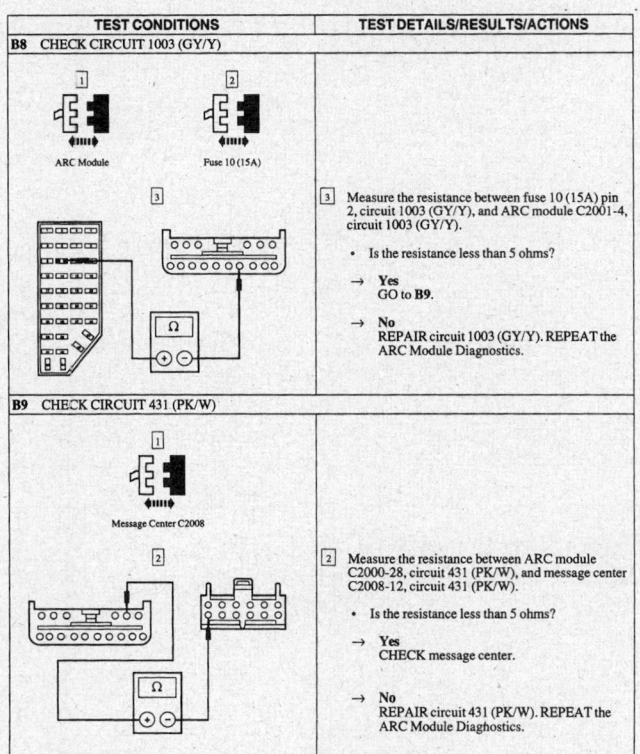	③ Measure the resistance between fuse 10 (15A) pin 2, circuit 1003 (GY/Y), and ARC module C2001-4, circuit 1003 (GY/Y).
	• Is the resistance less than 5 ohms?
	→ **Yes** GO to **B9**.
	→ **No** REPAIR circuit 1003 (GY/Y). REPEAT the ARC Module Diagnostics.
B9 CHECK CIRCUIT 431 (PK/W)	
	② Measure the resistance between ARC module C2000-28, circuit 431 (PK/W), and message center C2008-12, circuit 431 (PK/W).
	• Is the resistance less than 5 ohms?
	→ **Yes** CHECK message center.
	→ **No** REPAIR circuit 431 (PK/W). REPEAT the ARC Module Diagnostics.

FM2019700629050X

Fig. 7   Test B: Message Center Indicates Air Suspension Switch Is Off (Part 5 of 5)

TEST CONDITIONS	TEST DETAILS/RESULTS/ACTIONS
B5 CHECK ARC MODULE CONNECTIONS (Continued)	
	③ Reconnect the ARC module connectors and be sure that connectors are seated properly (a click is heard when connector is properly connected).
	• Are the ARC module connectors OK and connected properly?
	→ **Yes** GO to **B6**.
	→ **No** REPAIR or REPLACE as necessary. REPEAT the ARC Module Diagnostics.
B6 CHECK AUTOMATIC RIDE CONTROL (ARC)	
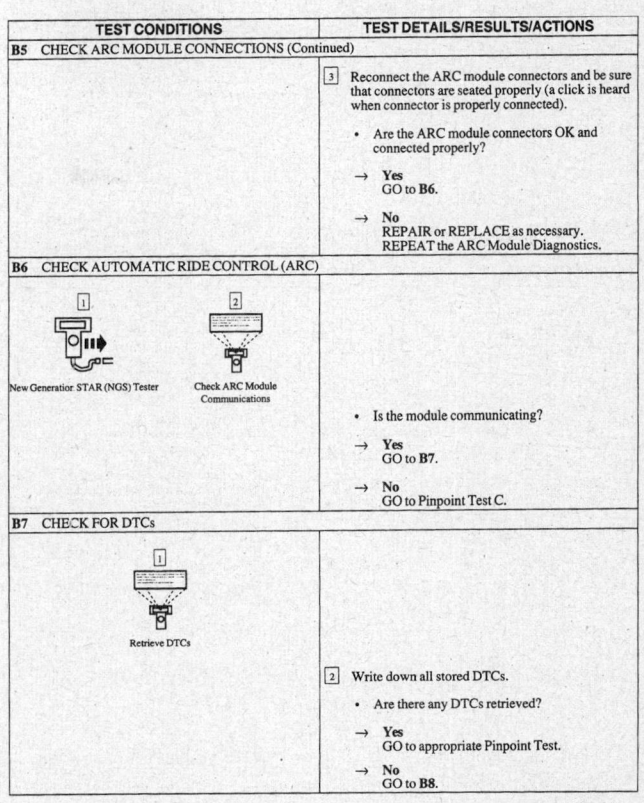	• Is the module communicating?
	→ **Yes** GO to **B7**.
	→ **No** GO to Pinpoint Test C.
B7 CHECK FOR DTCs	
	② Write down all stored DTCs.
	• Are there any DTCs retrieved?
	→ **Yes** GO to appropriate Pinpoint Test.
	→ **No** GO to **B8**.

FM2019700629040X

Fig. 7   Test B: Message Center Indicates Air Suspension Switch Is Off (Part 4 of 5)

TEST CONDITIONS	TEST DETAILS/RESULTS/ACTIONS
C1 CHECK WIRING HARNESS AND CONNECTORS	
New Generation STAR (NGS) Tester	② Check wiring harness and connector on New Generation STAR (NGS) Tester and data link connector (DLC) for damage.
	• Is the connector and wiring okay?
	→ **Yes** GO to **C2**.
	→ **No** REPAIR C291 and or wiring to New Generation STAR (NGS) Tester. REPEAT the ARC Module Diagnostics.
C2 CHECK AIR SUSPENSION SWITCH POSITION	
	① Check position of the air suspension switch.
	• Is the air suspension switch in the ON position?
	→ **Yes** GO to **C3**.
	→ **No** TURN the air suspension switch to the ON position. REPEAT the ARC Module Diagnostics.
C3 CHECK IGNITION SWITCH POSITION	
	NOTE: Automatic Ride Control (ARC) module will provide communication for 40 minutes after ignition switch is turned off.
	① Check the position of the ignition switch.
	• Is the ignition switch in the RUN position?
	→ **Yes** GO to **C4**.
	→ **No** TURN ignition switch to the RUN position. REPEAT the ARC Module Diagnostics.

FM2019700630010X

Fig. 8   Test C: No Module Communication Or Intermittent (Part 1 of 4)

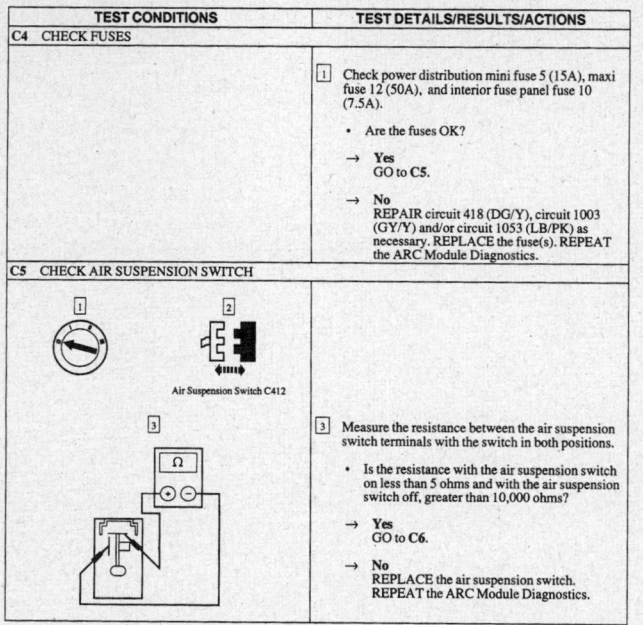

TEST CONDITIONS	TEST DETAILS/RESULTS/ACTIONS
C4 CHECK FUSES	
	☐1 Check power distribution mini fuse 5 (15A), maxi fuse 12 (50A), and interior fuse panel fuse 10 (7.5A).
	• Are the fuses OK?
	→ **Yes** GO to C5.
	→ **No** REPAIR circuit 418 (DG/Y), circuit 1003 (GY/Y) and/or circuit 1053 (LB/PK) as necessary. REPLACE the fuse(s). REPEAT the ARC Module Diagnostics.
C5 CHECK AIR SUSPENSION SWITCH	
Air Suspension Switch C412	☐3 Measure the resistance between the air suspension switch terminals with the switch in both positions.
	• Is the resistance with the air suspension switch on less than 5 ohms and with the air suspension switch off, greater than 10,000 ohms?
	→ **Yes** GO to C6.
	→ **No** REPLACE the air suspension switch. REPEAT the ARC Module Diagnostics.

FM2019700630020X

Fig. 8   Test C: No Module Communication Or Intermittent (Part 2 of 4)

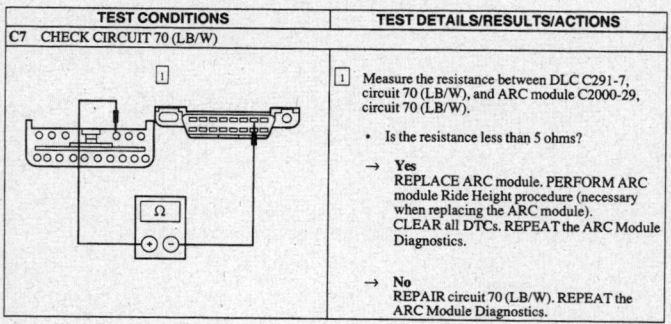

TEST CONDITIONS	TEST DETAILS/RESULTS/ACTIONS
C7 CHECK CIRCUIT 70 (LB/W)	
	☐1 Measure the resistance between DLC C291-7, circuit 70 (LB/W), and ARC module C2000-29, circuit 70 (LB/W).
	• Is the resistance less than 5 ohms?
	→ **Yes** REPLACE ARC module. PERFORM ARC module Ride Height procedure (necessary when replacing the ARC module). CLEAR all DTCs. REPEAT the ARC Module Diagnostics.
	→ **No** REPAIR circuit 70 (LB/W). REPEAT the ARC Module Diagnostics.

FM2019700630040X

Fig. 8   Test C: No Module Communication Or Intermittent (Part 4 of 4)

TEST CONDITIONS	TEST DETAILS/RESULTS/ACTIONS
D1 PERFORM ON-DEMAND SELF-TEST (Continued)	
	• Is DTC P1807 set at the end of self-test?
	→ **Yes** GO to D2.
	→ **No** REPEAT automatic ride control (ARC) module diagnostics and CHECK DTCs.
D2 CHECK CIRCUIT 335 (P/O) FOR SHORT TO GROUND	
ARC Module C2000 Generic Electronic Module (GEM) C281	☐4 Measure the resistance between ARC module C2000-31, circuit 335 (P/O), and ground.
	• Is the resistance less than 5 ohms?
	→ **Yes** REPAIR Circuit 335 (P/O). Clear all DTCs. REPEAT the ARC Module Diagnostics.
	→ **No** Diagnose And Test transfer case indicator signal.

FM2019700631020X

Fig. 9   Test D/DTC 1807: 4×4 High Range Input Short To Ground (Part 2 of 2)

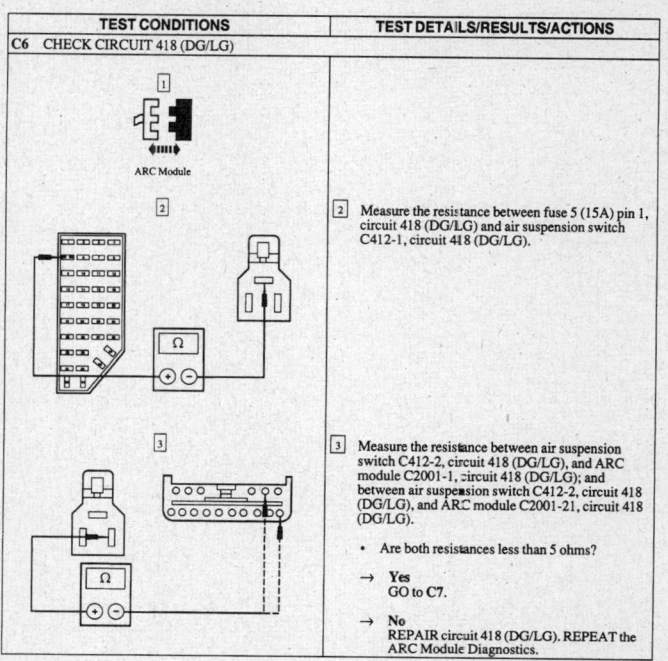

TEST CONDITIONS	TEST DETAILS/RESULTS/ACTIONS
C6 CHECK CIRCUIT 418 (DG/LG)	
ARC Module	
	☐2 Measure the resistance between fuse 5 (15A) pin 1, circuit 418 (DG/LG) and air suspension switch C412-1, circuit 418 (DG/LG).
	☐3 Measure the resistance between air suspension switch C412-2, circuit 418 (DG/LG), and ARC module C2001-1, circuit 418 (DG/LG); and between air suspension switch C412-2, circuit 418 (DG/LG), and ARC module C2001-21, circuit 418 (DG/LG).
	• Are both resistances less than 5 ohms?
	→ **Yes** GO to C7.
	→ **No** REPAIR circuit 418 (DG/LG). REPEAT the ARC Module Diagnostics.

FM2019700630030X

Fig. 8   Test C: No Module Communication Or Intermittent (Part 3 of 4)

TEST CONDITIONS	TEST DETAILS/RESULTS/ACTIONS
D1 PERFORM ON-DEMAND SELF-TEST	
	☐1 Open any door.
	☐2 Set transfer case in 4x4 LOW.
On-Demand Self-Test	

FM2019700631010X

Fig. 9   Test D/DTC 1807: 4×4 High Range Input Short To Ground (Part 1 of 2)

TEST CONDITIONS	TEST DETAILS/RESULTS/ACTIONS
E1 PERFORM ON-DEMAND SELF-TEST	
	☐1 Open any door.

FM2019700632010X

Fig. 10   Test E/DTC P1808: 4×4 Low Range Input Circuit Fault/Ride Control Or Switch Input Circuit Fault (Part 1 of 3)

TEST CONDITIONS	TEST DETAILS/RESULTS/ACTIONS
E1 PERFORM ON-DEMAND SELF-TEST (Continued)	

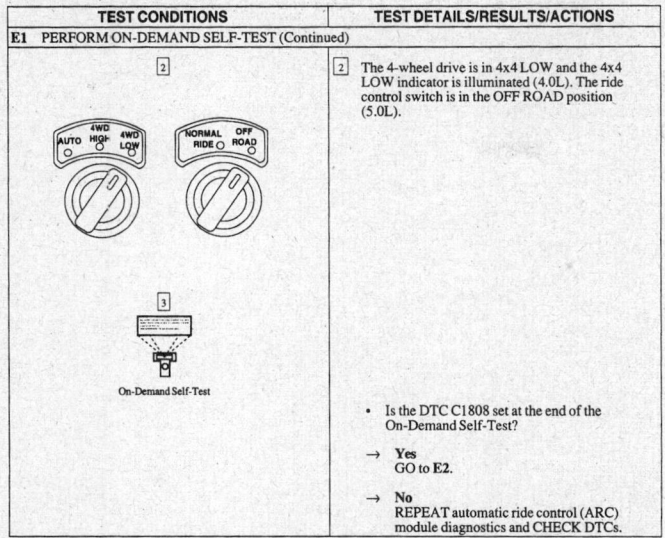

② The 4-wheel drive is in 4x4 LOW and the 4x4 LOW indicator is illuminated (4.0L). The ride control switch is in the OFF ROAD position (5.0L).

- Is the DTC C1808 set at the end of the On-Demand Self-Test?

→ **Yes**
GO to **E2**.

→ **No**
REPEAT automatic ride control (ARC) module diagnostics and CHECK DTCs.

FM2019700632020X

Fig. 10   Test E/DTC P1808: 4×4 Low Range Input Circuit Fault/Ride Control Or Switch Input Circuit Fault (Part 2 of 3)

TEST CONDITIONS	TEST DETAILS/RESULTS/ACTIONS
F1 PERFORM ON-DEMAND SELF TEST	
NOTE: Accelerator pedal should not be touched during self-test.	

① Open any door.

② The 4-wheel drive is in 4x4 LOW and the 4x4 LOW indicator is illuminated (4.0L). The ride control switch is in the OFF ROAD position (5.0L).

FM2019700633010X

Fig. 11   Test F/DTC C1439: Acceleration Input Signal Circuit Fault (Part 1 of 2)

TEST CONDITIONS	TEST DETAILS/RESULTS/ACTIONS
E2 CHECK CIRCUIT 637 (DB/W)	

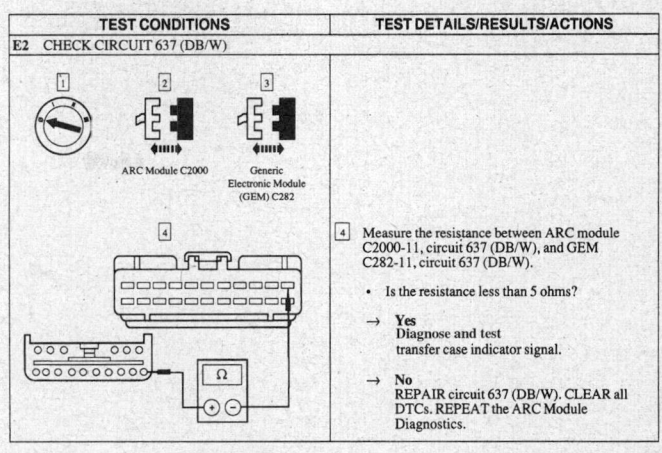

④ Measure the resistance between ARC module C2000-11, circuit 637 (DB/W), and GEM C282-11, circuit 637 (DB/W).

- Is the resistance less than 5 ohms?

→ **Yes**
Diagnose and test transfer case indicator signal.

→ **No**
REPAIR circuit 637 (DB/W). CLEAR all DTCs. REPEAT the ARC Module Diagnostics.

FM2019700632030X

Fig. 10   Test E/DTC P1808: 4×4 Low Range Input Circuit Fault/Ride Control Or Switch Input Circuit Fault (Part 3 of 3)

TEST CONDITIONS	TEST DETAILS/RESULTS/ACTIONS
F1 PERFORM ON-DEMAND SELF TEST (Continued)	

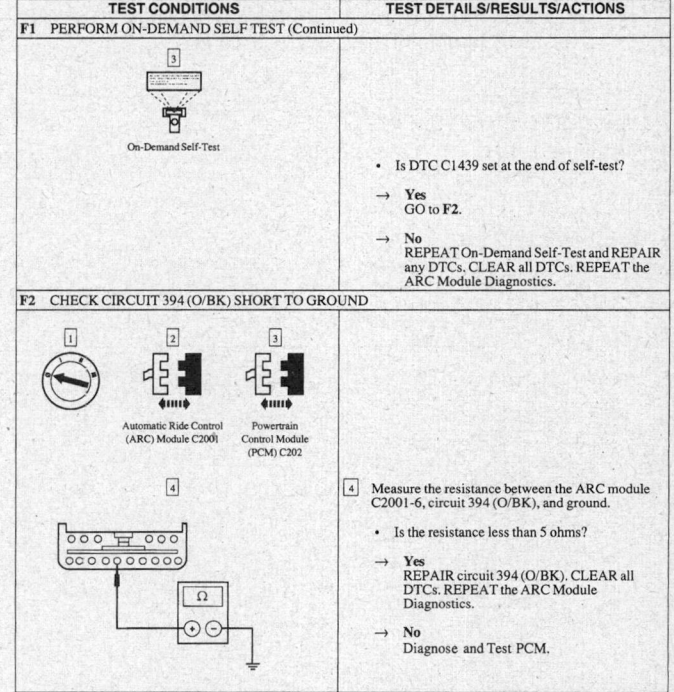

- Is DTC C1439 set at the end of self-test?

→ **Yes**
GO to **F2**.

→ **No**
REPEAT On-Demand Self-Test and REPAIR any DTCs. CLEAR all DTCs. REPEAT the ARC Module Diagnostics.

F2 CHECK CIRCUIT 394 (O/BK) SHORT TO GROUND	

④ Measure the resistance between the ARC module C2001-6, circuit 394 (O/BK), and ground.

- Is the resistance less than 5 ohms?

→ **Yes**
REPAIR circuit 394 (O/BK). CLEAR all DTCs. REPEAT the ARC Module Diagnostics.

→ **No**
Diagnose and Test PCM.

FM2019700633020X

Fig. 11   Test F/DTC C1439: Acceleration Input Signal Circuit Fault (Part 2 of 2)

TEST CONDITIONS	TEST DETAILS/RESULTS/ACTIONS
G1 PERFORM ON-DEMAND SELF-TEST	
	① Open any door.

FM2019700634010X

Fig. 12   Test G/DTC C1724: Height Sensor Power Circuit Fault (Part 1 of 3)

TEST CONDITIONS	TEST DETAILS/RESULTS/ACTIONS
G1 PERFORM ON-DEMAND SELF-TEST (Continued)	

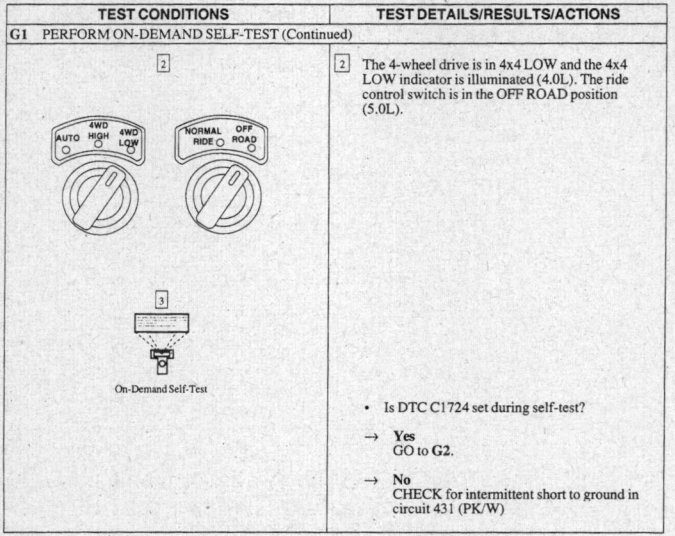

On-Demand Self-Test

②	The 4-wheel drive is in 4x4 LOW and the 4x4 LOW indicator is illuminated (4.0L). The ride control switch is in the OFF ROAD position (5.0L).
	• Is DTC C1724 set during self-test?
	→ **Yes** GO to **G2**.
	→ **No** CHECK for intermittent short to ground in circuit 431 (PK/W)

FM2019700634020X

Fig. 12   Test G/DTC C1724: Height Sensor Power Circuit Fault (Part 2 of 3)

TEST CONDITIONS	TEST DETAILS/RESULTS/ACTIONS
H1 PERFORM FRONT COMPONENT INSPECTION	
	① Inspect the front suspension components for damage, obstructions, or other mechanical failures. • Are any components damaged or obstructed? → **Yes** REPAIR or REPLACE suspension components as necessary. CLEAR all DTCs. REPEAT the ARC Module Diagnostics. → **No** GO to **H2**.
H2 INSPECT FRONT HEIGHT SENSOR	

② Inspect the front height sensor for correct installation at upper and lower ball stud brackets.

FM2019700635010X

Fig. 13   Test H/DTC C1725: Front Pneumatic Fault (Part 1 of 12)

TEST CONDITIONS	TEST DETAILS/RESULTS/ACTIONS
G2 CHECK CIRCUIT 431 (PK/W) FOR SHORT TO GROUND	

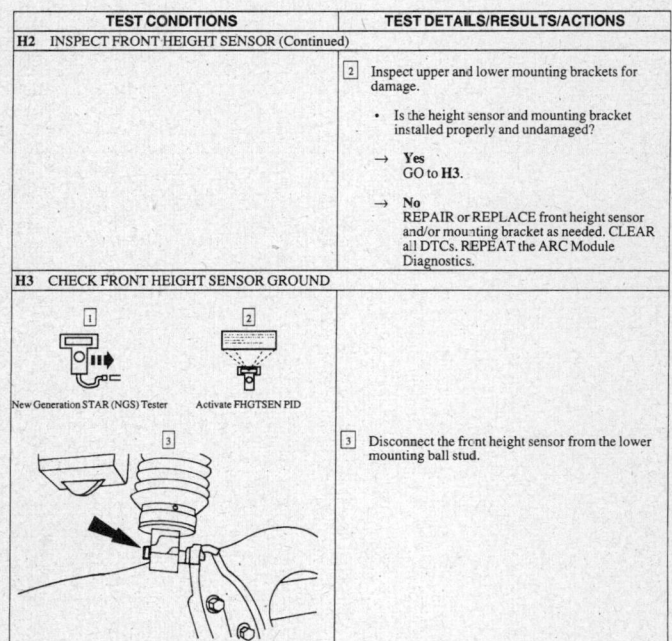

Automatic Ride Control (ARC) Module

②	Turn the air suspension switch to the OFF position.
④	Measure the resistance between ARC module C2000-28, circuit 431 (PK/W), and ground. • Is the resistance less than 5 ohms? → **Yes** REPAIR circuit 431 (PK/W). CLEAR all DTCs. REPEAT the ARC Module Diagnostics. → **No** REPLACE ARC module. PERFORM ARC module Ride Height procedure. CLEAR all DTCs. REPEAT the ARC Module Diagnostics.

FM2019700634030X

Fig. 12   Test G/DTC C1724: Height Sensor Power Circuit Fault (Part 3 of 3)

TEST CONDITIONS	TEST DETAILS/RESULTS/ACTIONS
H2 INSPECT FRONT HEIGHT SENSOR (Continued)	
	② Inspect upper and lower mounting brackets for damage. • Is the height sensor and mounting bracket installed properly and undamaged? → **Yes** GO to **H3**. → **No** REPAIR or REPLACE front height sensor and/or mounting bracket as needed. CLEAR all DTCs. REPEAT the ARC Module Diagnostics.
H3 CHECK FRONT HEIGHT SENSOR GROUND	

New Generation STAR (NGS) Tester   Activate FHGTSEN PID

③ Disconnect the front height sensor from the lower mounting ball stud.

FM2019700635020X

Fig. 13   Test H/DTC C1725: Front Pneumatic Fault (Part 2 of 12)

TEST CONDITIONS	TEST DETAILS/RESULTS/ACTIONS
H3 CHECK FRONT HEIGHT SENSOR GROUND (Continued)	
	④ Slowly move the front height sensor over the full range of travel. • Does the voltage increase as the front height sensor is compressed, and decrease as the front height sensor is expanded? → **Yes** GO to **H4**. → **No** REPAIR circuit 570 (BK/W). CLEAR all DTCs. REPEAT the ARC Module Diagnostics.
H4 VERIFY FRONT PNEUMATIC CIRCUIT CAN RISE	
⚠ **CAUTION: Do not let the air compressor run for more than three minutes at a time.**	
① Turn Active Command FRNT FILL On ② Turn Active Command COMPRESSR On	
	③ Allow front of vehicle to rise for 30 seconds. • Does the front of the vehicle raise and hold the higher position? → **Yes** GO to **H5**. → **No** GO to **H6**.

FM2019700635030X

Fig. 13 Test H/DTC C1725: Front Pneumatic Fault (Part 3 of 12)

TEST CONDITIONS	TEST DETAILS/RESULTS/ACTIONS
H7 PERFORM AIR COMPRESSOR LEAK TEST	
⚠ **CAUTION: Do not allow the air compressor to run for more than three minutes. The air compressor could overheat and stop operating due to an internal temperature sensitive thermal breaker.**	
①	① Disconnect the air line at inlet to the rear fill solenoid.
	② Connect an air pressure gauge (max 1723 kPa [250 psi]) with common fitting to the air line.
③ Turn Active Command COMPRESSR On	
	④ **NOTE:** Within 30 seconds, the pressure should reach 896 kPa (130 psi). Monitor air gauge.
⑤ Turn Active Command COMPRESSR Off	
	⑥ **NOTE:** The pressure should hold steady. Monitor air gauge for 5 minutes.

FM2019700635050X

Fig. 13 Test H/DTC C1725: Front Pneumatic Fault (Part 5 of 12)

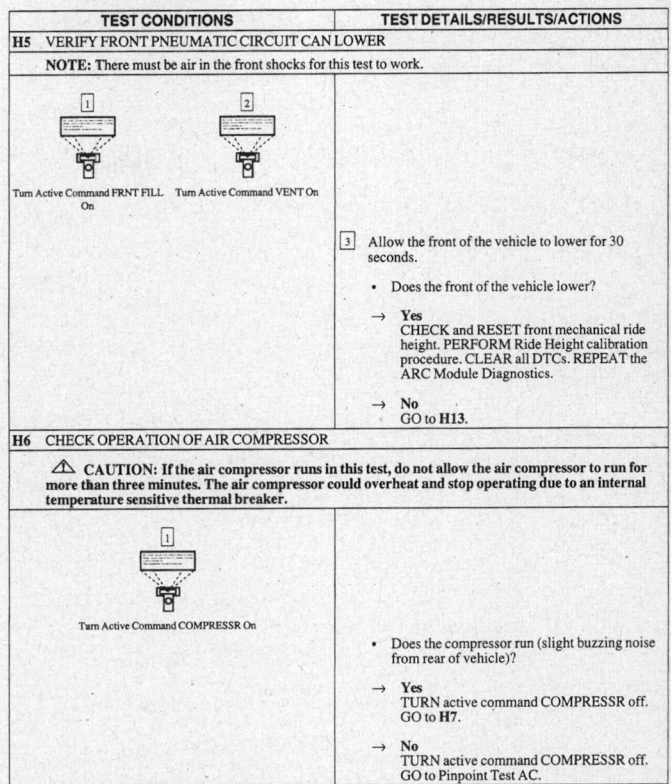

TEST CONDITIONS	TEST DETAILS/RESULTS/ACTIONS
H5 VERIFY FRONT PNEUMATIC CIRCUIT CAN LOWER	
NOTE: There must be air in the front shocks for this test to work.	
① Turn Active Command FRNT FILL On ② Turn Active Command VENT On	
	③ Allow the front of the vehicle to lower for 30 seconds. • Does the front of the vehicle lower? → **Yes** CHECK and RESET front mechanical ride height. PERFORM Ride Height calibration procedure. CLEAR all DTCs. REPEAT the ARC Module Diagnostics. → **No** GO to **H13**.
H6 CHECK OPERATION OF AIR COMPRESSOR	
⚠ **CAUTION: If the air compressor runs in this test, do not allow the air compressor to run for more than three minutes. The air compressor could overheat and stop operating due to an internal temperature sensitive thermal breaker.**	
① Turn Active Command COMPRESSR On	
	• Does the compressor run (slight buzzing noise from rear of vehicle)? → **Yes** TURN active command COMPRESSR off. GO to **H7**. → **No** TURN active command COMPRESSR off. GO to Pinpoint Test AC.

FM2019700635040X

Fig. 13 Test H/DTC C1725: Front Pneumatic Fault (Part 4 of 12)

TEST CONDITIONS	TEST DETAILS/RESULTS/ACTIONS
H7 PERFORM AIR COMPRESSOR LEAK TEST (Continued)	
⑦ Turn Active Command VENT On	
	• Did the air compressor reach and hold a minimum air pressure of 896 kPa (130 psi)? → **Yes** RECONNECT the air line. TURN active command VENT off. GO to **H9**. → **No** RECONNECT the air line. TURN active command VENT off. GO to **H8**.
H8 CHECK AIR LINE TO FILL SOLENOIDS FOR LEAKS	
⚠ **CAUTION: Do not allow the air compressor to run for more than three minutes. The air compressor could overheat and stop operating due to an internal temperature sensitive thermal breaker.**	
① Turn Active Command COMPRESSR On	
	② Check the air line between the air compressor and the two fill solenoids for air leaks.
③ Turn Active Command COMPRESSR Off	
	• Do any of the air lines leak? → **Yes** REPAIR or REPLACE the air lines as necessary. CLEAR all DTCs. REPEAT the ARC Module Diagnostics. → **No** REPLACE the air compressor. CLEAR all DTCs. REPEAT the ARC Module Diagnostics.

FM2019700635060X

Fig. 13 Test H/DTC C1725: Front Pneumatic Fault (Part 6 of 12)

TEST CONDITIONS	TEST DETAILS/RESULTS/ACTIONS
H9 CHECK FRONT FILL SOLENOID OPERATION	

⚠️ CAUTION: Do not let the air compressor run for more than three minutes at a time.

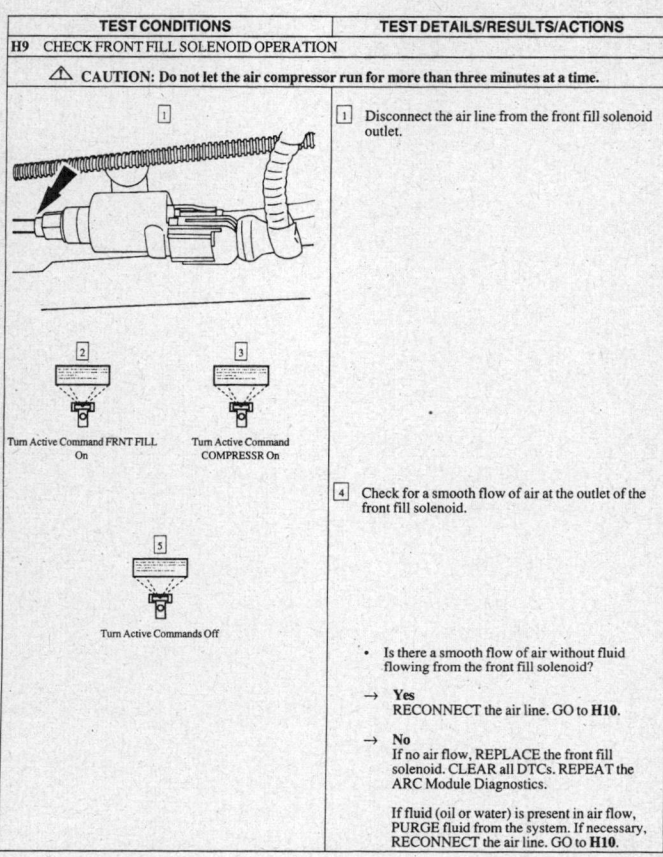

	1 Disconnect the air line from the front fill solenoid outlet.
	4 Check for a smooth flow of air at the outlet of the front fill solenoid.
	• Is there a smooth flow of air without fluid flowing from the front fill solenoid?
	→ Yes RECONNECT the air line. GO to **H10**.
	→ No If no air flow, REPLACE the front fill solenoid. CLEAR all DTCs. REPEAT the ARC Module Diagnostics. If fluid (oil or water) is present in air flow, PURGE fluid from the system. If necessary, RECONNECT the air line. GO to **H10**.

FM2019700635070X

**Fig. 13   Test H/DTC C1725: Front Pneumatic Fault
(Part 7 of 12)**

TEST CONDITIONS	TEST DETAILS/RESULTS/ACTIONS
H11 CHECK FOR RESTRICTED AIR LINE — FRONT FILL SOLENOID TO LEFT FRONT SHOCK ABSORBER	

⚠️ CAUTION: Do not allow the air compressor to run for more than three minutes. The air compressor could overheat and stop operating due to an internal temperature sensitive thermal breaker.

	1 Disconnect the air line from the LF shock absorber.
	4 Check for a smooth flow of air at the LF air shock absorber.

FM2019700635090X

**Fig. 13   Test H/DTC C1725: Front Pneumatic Fault
(Part 9 of 12)**

TEST CONDITIONS	TEST DETAILS/RESULTS/ACTIONS
H10 CHECK FRONT FILL SOLENOID AIR LINES	

⚠️ CAUTION: Do not allow the air compressor to run for more than three minutes. The air compressor could overheat and stop operating due to an internal temperature sensitive thermal breaker.

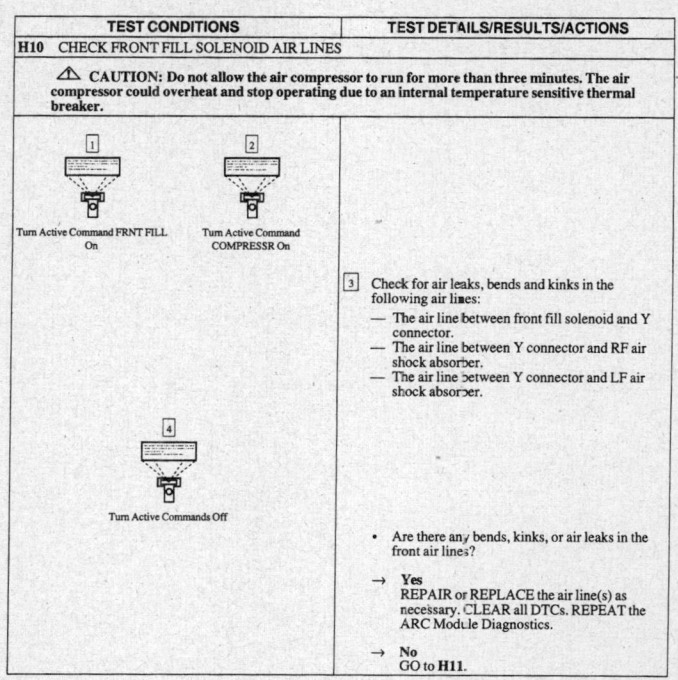

	3 Check for air leaks, bends and kinks in the following air lines: — The air line between front fill solenoid and Y connector. — The air line between Y connector and RF air shock absorber. — The air line between Y connector and LF air shock absorber.
	• Are there any bends, kinks, or air leaks in the front air lines?
	→ Yes REPAIR or REPLACE the air line(s) as necessary. CLEAR all DTCs. REPEAT the ARC Module Diagnostics.
	→ No GO to **H11**.

FM2019700635080X

**Fig. 13   Test H/DTC C1725: Front Pneumatic Fault
(Part 8 of 12)**

TEST CONDITIONS	TEST DETAILS/RESULTS/ACTIONS
H11 CHECK FOR RESTRICTED AIR LINE — FRONT FILL SOLENOID TO LEFT FRONT SHOCK ABSORBER (Continued)	
	• Is there a smooth flow of air without fluid flowing at the LF air shock absorber?
	→ Yes RECONNECT the air line. GO to **H12**.
	→ No If no air flow, REPAIR or REPLACE the air line. CLEAR all DTCs. REPEAT the ARC Module Diagnostics. If fluid (oil or water) is present in air flow, PURGE fluid from the system. If necessary, RECONNECT the air line. GO to **H12**.
H12 CHECK FOR RESTRICTED AIR LINE — FRONT FILL SOLENOID TO RIGHT FRONT SHOCK ABSORBER	

⚠️ CAUTION: Do not allow the air compressor to run for more than three minutes. The air compressor could overheat and stop operating due to an internal temperature sensitive thermal breaker.

	1 Disconnect the air line from the RF shock absorber.
	4 Check for a smooth flow of air at the RF air shock absorber.

FM2019700635100X

**Fig. 13   Test H/DTC C1725: Front Pneumatic Fault
(Part 10 of 12)**

TEST CONDITIONS	TEST DETAILS/RESULTS/ACTIONS
H12 CHECK FOR RESTRICTED AIR LINE — FRONT FILL SOLENOID TO RIGHT FRONT SHOCK ABSORBER (Continued)	
Turn Active Commands Off	• Is there a smooth flow of air without fluid flowing at the RF air shock absorber? → **Yes** If the faulty front shock absorber cannot be identified, REPLACE both front shock absorbers. CLEAR all DTCs. REPEAT the ARC Module Diagnostics. → **No** If no air flow, REPAIR or REPLACE the air line. CLEAR all DTCs. REPEAT the ARC Module Diagnostics. If fluid (oil or water) is present in air flow, PURGE fluid from the system. If necessary, REPLACE faulty front shock absorber.
H13 CHECK FOR RESTRICTED AIR LINE (COMPRESSOR)	
NOTE: If fluid (water or oil) is present when disconnecting the air lines, purge the air line.	
	1 Disconnect the air line between the air compressor air drier and the front fill solenoid. 2 Connect Vacuum Tester to the air line and try to draw a vacuum. • Can a vacuum be drawn and held? → **Yes** REPAIR or REPLACE the air line as necessary. CLEAR all DTCs. REPEAT the ARC Module Diagnostics. → **No** GO to **H14**.
H14 CHECK FOR RESTRICTED AIR LINE (RF AIR SHOCK)	
NOTE: If fluid (water or oil) is present when disconnecting the air lines, purge the air line.	
	1 Disconnect the air line between the front fill solenoid and the RF air shock absorber.

FM2019700635110X

Fig. 13 Test H/DTC C1725: Front Pneumatic Fault (Part 11 of 12)

TEST CONDITIONS	TEST DETAILS/RESULTS/ACTIONS
J1 PERFORM REAR COMPONENT INSPECTION	
	1 Inspect the rear suspension components for damage, obstructions, or other mechanical failures. • Are any components damaged or obstructed? → **Yes** REPAIR or REPLACE suspension components as necessary. CLEAR all DTCs. REPEAT the ARC Module Diagnostics. → **No** GO to **J2**.

FM2019700636010X

Fig. 14 Test J/DTC C1726: Rear Pneumatic Fault (Part 1 of 14)

TEST CONDITIONS	TEST DETAILS/RESULTS/ACTIONS
H14 CHECK FOR RESTRICTED AIR LINE (RF AIR SHOCK) (Continued)	
	2 Connect Vacuum Tester to the air line and try to draw a vacuum. • Can a vacuum be drawn and held? → **Yes** REPAIR or REPLACE the air line as necessary. CLEAR all DTCs. REPEAT the ARC Module Diagnostics. → **No** GO to **H15**.
H15 CHECK FOR RESTRICTED AIR LINE (FRONT)	
NOTE: If fluid (water or oil) is present when disconnecting the air lines, purge the air line.	
	1 Disconnect the air line between the front fill solenoid and the left front air shock absorber. 2 Connect Vacuum Tester to the air line at the left front air shock absorber and try to draw a vacuum. • Can a vacuum be drawn and held? → **Yes** REPAIR or REPLACE the air line as necessary. CLEAR all DTCs. REPEAT the ARC Module Diagnostics. → **No** REPLACE the air compressor. CLEAR all DTCs. REPEAT the ARC Module Diagnostics.

FM2019700635120X

Fig. 13 Test H/DTC C1725: Front Pneumatic Fault (Part 12 of 12)

TEST CONDITIONS	TEST DETAILS/RESULTS/ACTIONS
J2 INSPECT REAR HEIGHT SENSOR	
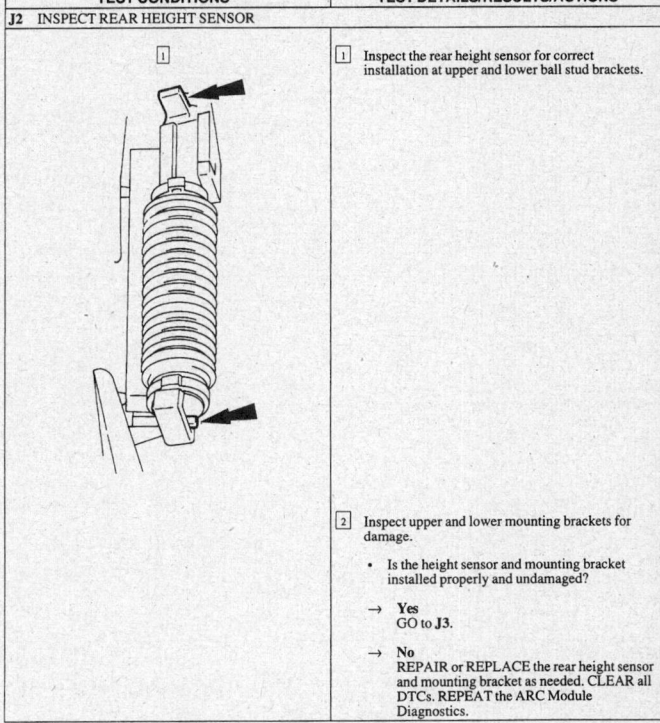	1 Inspect the rear height sensor for correct installation at upper and lower ball stud brackets. 2 Inspect upper and lower mounting brackets for damage. • Is the height sensor and mounting bracket installed properly and undamaged? → **Yes** GO to **J3**. → **No** REPAIR or REPLACE the rear height sensor and mounting bracket as needed. CLEAR all DTCs. REPEAT the ARC Module Diagnostics.

FM2019700636020X

Fig. 14 Test J/DTC C1726: Rear Pneumatic Fault (Part 2 of 14)

TEST CONDITIONS	TEST DETAILS/RESULTS/ACTIONS
J3 CHECK REAR HEIGHT SENSOR GROUND	

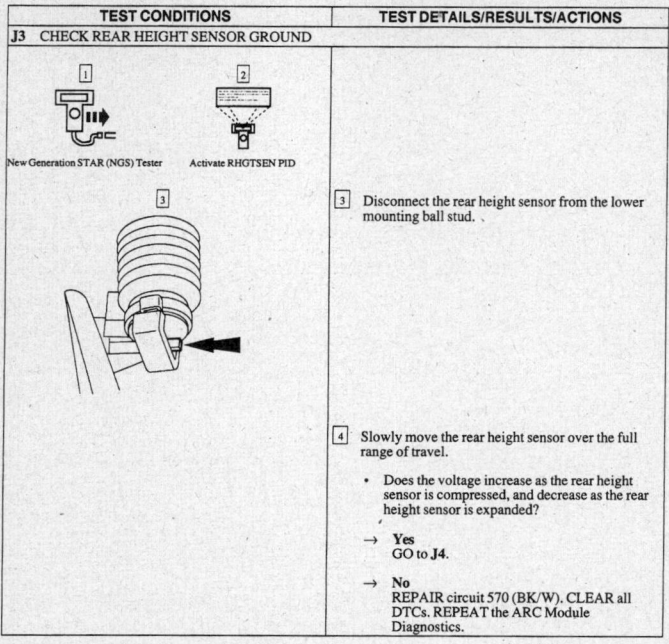

New Generation STAR (NGS) Tester   Activate RHGTSEN PID

3	Disconnect the rear height sensor from the lower mounting ball stud.
4	Slowly move the rear height sensor over the full range of travel. • Does the voltage increase as the rear height sensor is compressed, and decrease as the rear height sensor is expanded? → **Yes** GO to J4. → **No** REPAIR circuit 570 (BK/W), CLEAR all DTCs. REPEAT the ARC Module Diagnostics.

FM2019700636030X

Fig. 14 Test J/DTC C1726: Rear Pneumatic Fault
(Part 3 of 14)

TEST CONDITIONS	TEST DETAILS/RESULTS/ACTIONS
J5 VERIFY REAR PNEUMATIC CIRCUIT CAN RISE (Continued)	
	• Does the rear of the vehicle rise and hold the higher position? → **Yes** GO to J6. → **No** GO to J7.
J6 VERIFY REAR PNEUMATIC CIRCUIT CAN LOWER	

NOTE: There must be air in the rear shocks for this test to work.

1 Turn Active Command REAR FILL On   **2** Turn Active Command GATEVALVE On   **3** Turn Active Command VENT On

4	Allow the rear of the vehicle to lower for 30 seconds. • Does the rear of the vehicle lower? → **Yes** CHECK and RESET rear mechanical ride height. PERFORM Ride Height calibration procedure. CLEAR all DTCs. REPEAT the ARC Module Diagnostics. → **No** GO to J15.

FM2019700636050X

Fig. 14 Test J/DTC C1726: Rear Pneumatic Fault
(Part 5 of 14)

TEST CONDITIONS	TEST DETAILS/RESULTS/ACTIONS
J4 CHECK REAR GATE SOLENOID CONNECTOR	

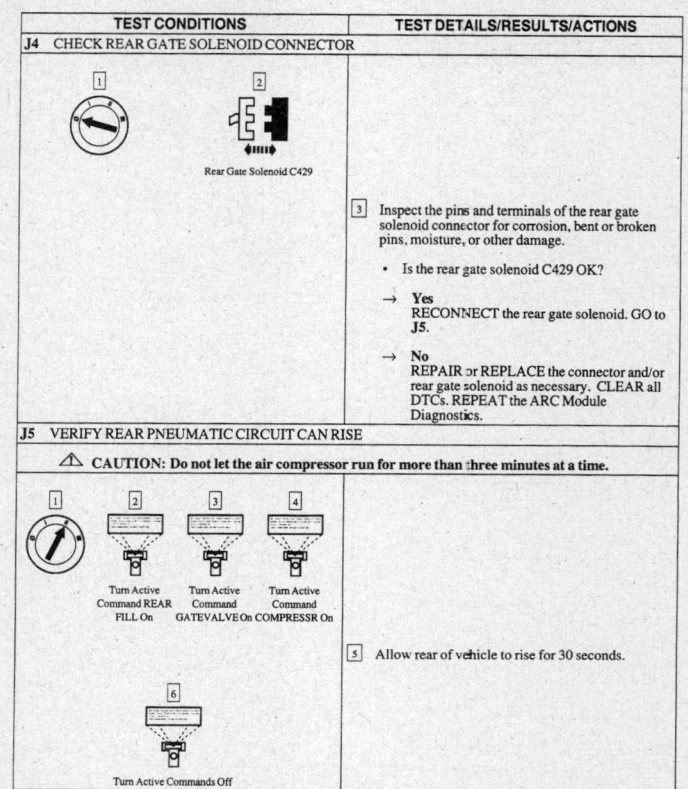

Rear Gate Solenoid C429

3	Inspect the pins and terminals of the rear gate solenoid connector for corrosion, bent or broken pins, moisture, or other damage. • Is the rear gate solenoid C429 OK? → **Yes** RECONNECT the rear gate solenoid. GO to J5. → **No** REPAIR or REPLACE the connector and/or rear gate solenoid as necessary. CLEAR all DTCs. REPEAT the ARC Module Diagnostics.
J5 VERIFY REAR PNEUMATIC CIRCUIT CAN RISE	

⚠ **CAUTION: Do not let the air compressor run for more than three minutes at a time.**

1   **2** Turn Active Command REAR FILL On   **3** Turn Active Command GATEVALVE On   **4** Turn Active Command COMPRESSR On

5	Allow rear of vehicle to rise for 30 seconds.

6 Turn Active Commands Off

FM2019700636040X

Fig. 14 Test J/DTC C1726: Rear Pneumatic Fault
(Part 4 of 14)

TEST CONDITIONS	TEST DETAILS/RESULTS/ACTIONS
J7 CHECK OPERATION OF AIR COMPRESSOR	

⚠ **CAUTION: If the air compressor runs in this test, do not allow the air compressor to run for more than three minutes. The air compressor could overheat and stop operating due to an internal temperature sensitive thermal breaker.**

1 Turn Active Command COMPRESSR On

	• Does the compressor run (slight buzzing noise from rear of vehicle)? → **Yes** TURN active command COMPRESSR Off. GO to J8. → **No** TURN active command COMPRESSR Off. GO to Pinpoint Test AC.
J8 PERFORM AIR COMPRESSOR LEAK TEST	

⚠ **CAUTION: Do not allow the air compressor to run for more than three minutes. The air compressor could overheat and stop operating due to an internal temperature sensitive thermal breaker.**

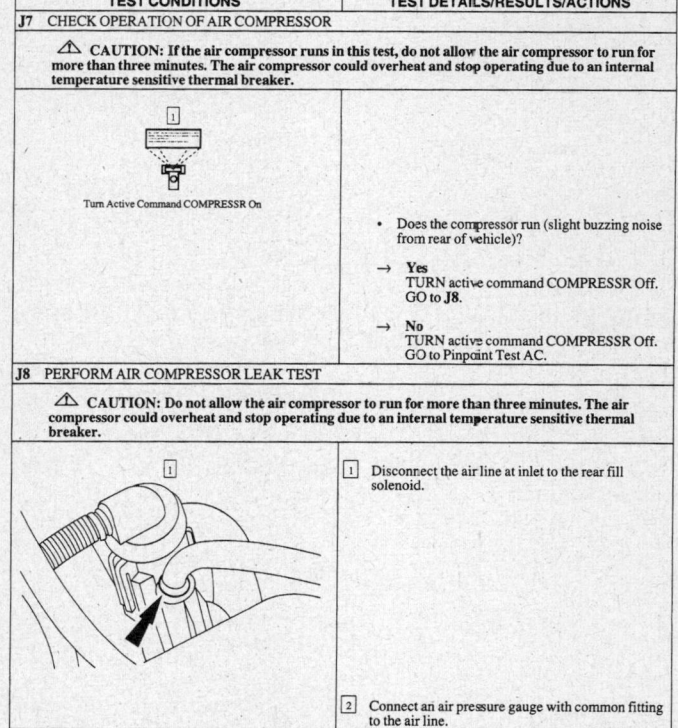

1	Disconnect the air line at inlet to the rear fill solenoid.
2	Connect an air pressure gauge with common fitting to the air line.

FM2019700636060X

Fig. 14 Test J/DTC C1726: Rear Pneumatic Fault
(Part 6 of 14)

TEST CONDITIONS	TEST DETAILS/RESULTS/ACTIONS
J8 PERFORM AIR COMPRESSOR LEAK TEST (Continued)	

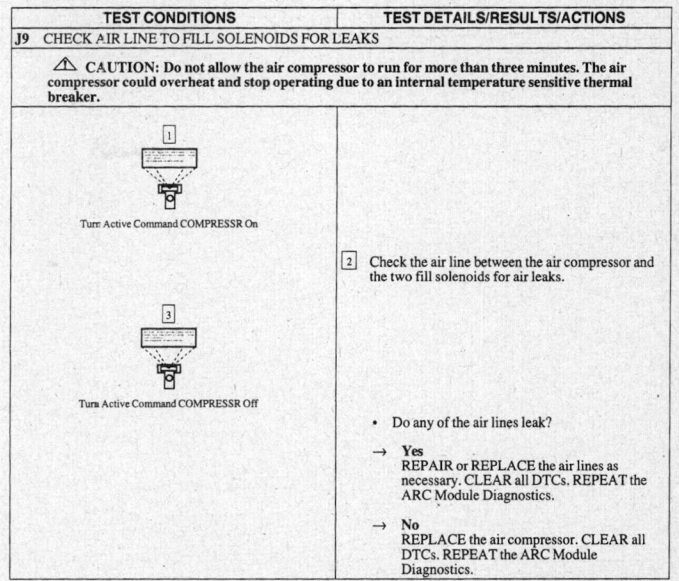

4 **NOTE:** Within 30 seconds, the pressure should reach 896 kPa (130 psi).
Monitor the air pressure gauge.

6 **NOTE:** The pressure should hold steady.
Monitor the air pressure gauge for 5 minutes.

- Did the air compressor reach and hold a minimum air pressure of 896 kPa (130 psi)?

→ **Yes**
RECONNECT the air line. TURN active command VENT off. GO to **J10**.

→ **No**
RECONNECT the air line. TURN active command VENT off. GO to **J9**.

FM2019700636070X

**Fig. 14 Test J/DTC C1726: Rear Pneumatic Fault
(Part 7 of 14)**

TEST CONDITIONS	TEST DETAILS/RESULTS/ACTIONS
J10 CHECK REAR FILL SOLENOID OPERATION	

⚠ **CAUTION: Do not allow the air compressor to run for more than three minutes. The air compressor could overheat and stop operating due to an internal temperature sensitive thermal breaker.**

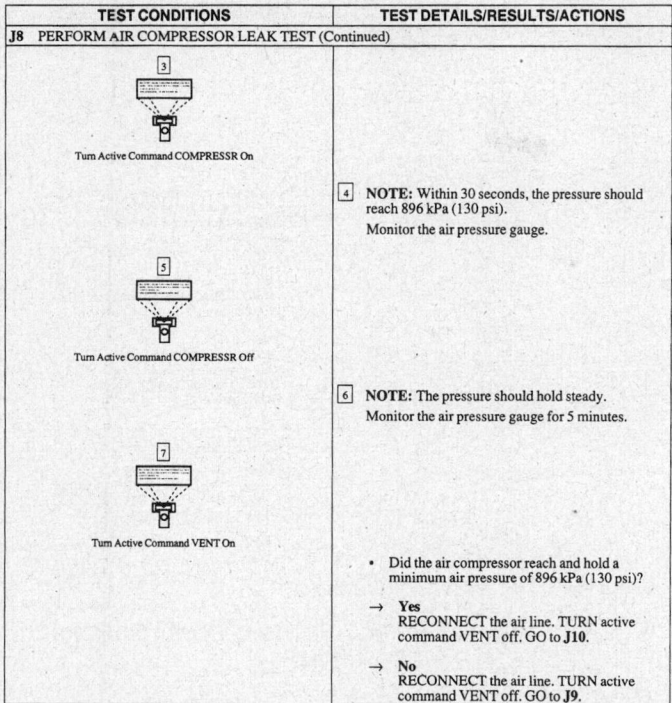

1 Disconnect the air line from the rear fill solenoid outlet.

4 Check for a smooth flow of air at the outlet of the rear fill solenoid.

- Is there a smooth flow of air without fluid flowing from the rear fill solenoid?

→ **Yes**
RECONNECT the air line. GO to **J11**.

→ **No**
If no air flow, REPLACE the rear fill solenoid. CLEAR all DTCs. REPEAT the ARC Module Diagnostics.

If fluid (oil or water) is present in air flow, PURGE fluid from the system. If necessary, RECONNECT the air line. GO to **J11**.

FM2019700636090X

**Fig. 14 Test J/DTC C1726: Rear Pneumatic Fault
(Part 9 of 14)**

TEST CONDITIONS	TEST DETAILS/RESULTS/ACTIONS
J9 CHECK AIR LINE TO FILL SOLENOIDS FOR LEAKS	

⚠ **CAUTION: Do not allow the air compressor to run for more than three minutes. The air compressor could overheat and stop operating due to an internal temperature sensitive thermal breaker.**

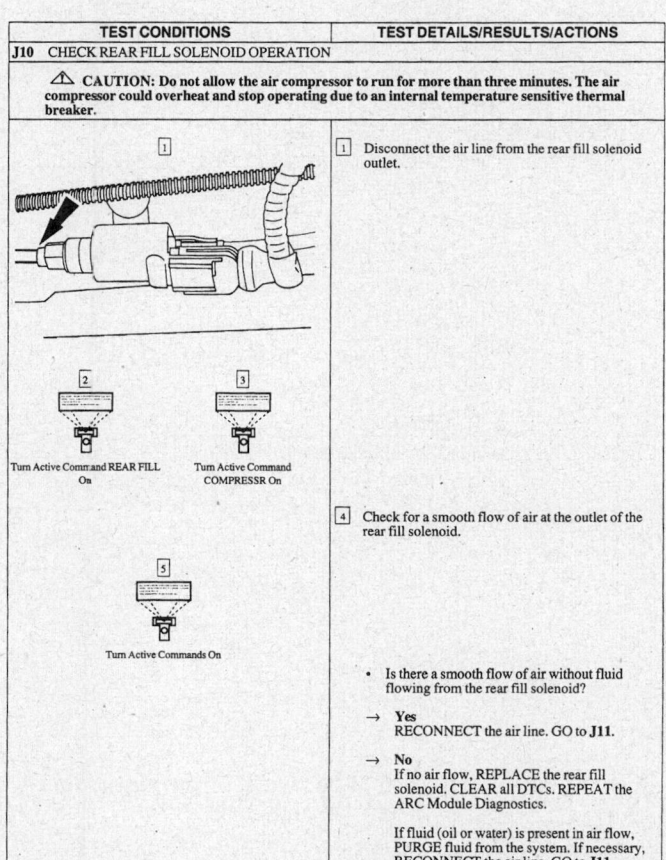

2 Check the air line between the air compressor and the two fill solenoids for air leaks.

- Do any of the air lines leak?

→ **Yes**
REPAIR or REPLACE the air lines as necessary. CLEAR all DTCs. REPEAT the ARC Module Diagnostics.

→ **No**
REPLACE the air compressor. CLEAR all DTCs. REPEAT the ARC Module Diagnostics.

FM2019700636080X

**Fig. 14 Test J/DTC C1726: Rear Pneumatic Fault
(Part 8 of 14)**

TEST CONDITIONS	TEST DETAILS/RESULTS/ACTIONS
J11 CHECK REAR FILL SOLENOID AIR LINES	

⚠ **CAUTION: Do not allow the air compressor to run for more than three minutes. The air compressor could overheat and stop operating due to an internal temperature sensitive thermal breaker.**

3 Check for air leaks, bends and kinks in the following air lines:
— The air line between rear fill solenoid and Y connector.
— The air line between Y connector and RR air shock absorber.
— The air line between Y connector and rear gate solenoid.

- Are there any bends, kinks, or air leaks in the rear air lines?

→ **Yes**
REPAIR or REPLACE the air line(s) as necessary. CLEAR all DTCs. REPEAT the ARC Module Diagnostics.

→ **No**
GO to **J12**.

FM2019700636100X

**Fig. 14 Test J/DTC C1726: Rear Pneumatic Fault
(Part 10 of 14)**

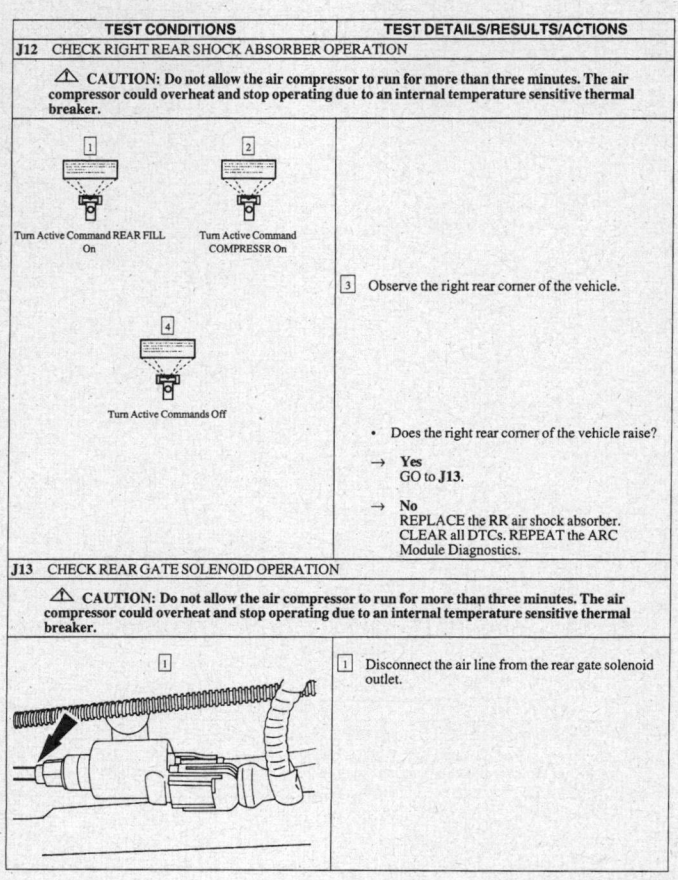

TEST CONDITIONS	TEST DETAILS/RESULTS/ACTIONS
J12 CHECK RIGHT REAR SHOCK ABSORBER OPERATION	
⚠ **CAUTION: Do not allow the air compressor to run for more than three minutes. The air compressor could overheat and stop operating due to an internal temperature sensitive thermal breaker.**	
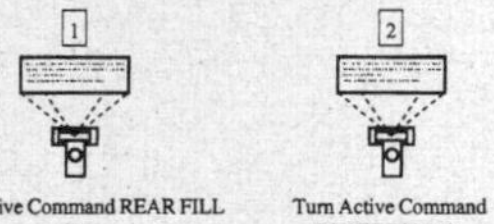 1 Turn Active Command REAR FILL On 2 Turn Active Command COMPRESSR On  4 Turn Active Commands Off	3 Observe the right rear corner of the vehicle. • Does the right rear corner of the vehicle raise? → **Yes** GO to **J13**. → **No** REPLACE the RR air shock absorber. CLEAR all DTCs. REPEAT the ARC Module Diagnostics.
J13 CHECK REAR GATE SOLENOID OPERATION	
⚠ **CAUTION: Do not allow the air compressor to run for more than three minutes. The air compressor could overheat and stop operating due to an internal temperature sensitive thermal breaker.**	
1 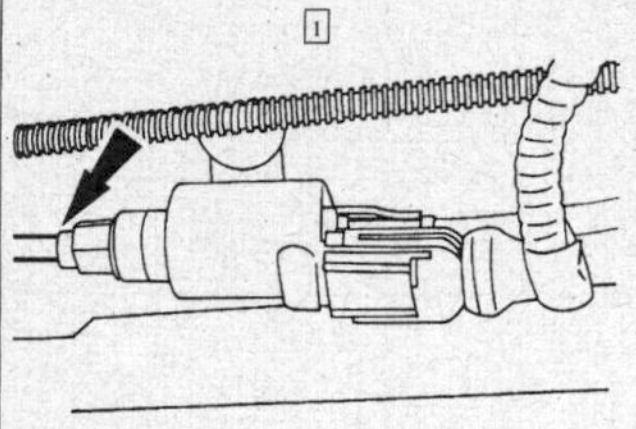	1 Disconnect the air line from the rear gate solenoid outlet.

FM2019700636110X

Fig. 14 Test J/DTC C1726: Rear Pneumatic Fault (Part 11 of 14)

TEST CONDITIONS	TEST DETAILS/RESULTS/ACTIONS
J14 CHECK REAR GATE SOLENOID AIR LINE	
⚠ **CAUTION: Do not allow the air compressor to run for more than three minutes. The air compressor could overheat and stop operating due to an internal temperature sensitive thermal breaker.**	
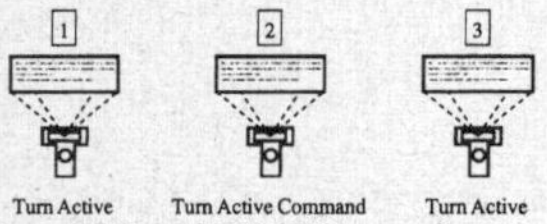 1 Turn Active Command REAR FILL On 2 Turn Active Command GATEVALVE On 3 Turn Active Command COMPRESSR On  5 Turn Active Commands Off	4 Check for air leaks, bends and kinks in the air line between the rear gate solenoid and LR air shock absorber. • Are there any bends, kinks, or air leaks in the rear air line? → **Yes** REPAIR or REPLACE the air line as necessary. CLEAR all DTCs. REPEAT the ARC Module Diagnostics. → **No** REPLACE the LR air shock absorber. CLEAR all DTCs. REPEAT the ARC Module Diagnostics.
J15 CHECK FOR RESTRICTED AIR LINE (COMPRESSOR)	
NOTE: If fluid (water or oil) is present when disconnecting the air lines, purge the air line.	
	1 Disconnect the air line between the air compressor air drier and the rear fill solenoid.

FM2019700636130X

Fig. 14 Test J/DTC C1726: Rear Pneumatic Fault (Part 13 of 14)

TEST CONDITIONS	TEST DETAILS/RESULTS/ACTIONS
J13 CHECK REAR GATE SOLENOID OPERATION (Continued)	
 2 Turn Active Command REAR FILL On 3 Turn Active Command GATEVALVE On 4 Turn Active Command COMPRESSR On  6 Turn Active Commands Off	5 Check for a smooth flow of air at the outlet of the rear gate solenoid. • Is there a smooth flow of air without fluid flowing from the rear gate solenoid? → **Yes** RECONNECT the air line. GO to **J14**. → **No** If no air flow, REPLACE the rear gate solenoid. CLEAR all DTCs. REPEAT the ARC Module Diagnostics. If fluid (oil or water) is present in air flow, PURGE fluid from the system. If necessary, RECONNECT the air line. GO to **J14**.

FM2019700636120X

Fig. 14 Test J/DTC C1726: Rear Pneumatic Fault (Part 12 of 14)

TEST CONDITIONS	TEST DETAILS/RESULTS/ACTIONS
J15 CHECK FOR RESTRICTED AIR LINE (COMPRESSOR) (Continued)	
	2 Connect Vacuum Tester to the air line and try to draw a vacuum. • Can a vacuum be drawn and held? → **Yes** REPAIR or REPLACE the air line as necessary. CLEAR all DTCs. REPEAT the ARC Module Diagnostics. → **No** GO to **J16**.
J16 CHECK FOR RESTRICTED AIR LINE (RR AIR SHOCK)	
NOTE: If fluid (water or oil) is present when disconnecting the air lines, purge the air line.	
	1 Disconnect the air line between the rear gate solenoid and the RR air shock absorber. 2 Connect Vacuum Tester to the air line and try to draw a vacuum. • Can a vacuum be drawn and held? → **Yes** REPAIR or REPLACE the air line as necessary. CLEAR all DTCs. REPEAT the ARC Module Diagnostics. → **No** GO to **J17**.
J17 CHECK FOR RESTRICTED AIR LINE (REAR)	
NOTE: If fluid (water or oil) is present when disconnecting the air lines, purge the air line.	
	1 Disconnect the air line between the rear gate solenoid and the rear fill solenoid. 2 Connect Vacuum Tester to the air line at the rear gate solenoid and try to draw a vacuum. • Can a vacuum be drawn and held? → **Yes** REPAIR or REPLACE the air line as necessary. CLEAR all DTCs. REPEAT the ARC Module Diagnostics. → **No** REPLACE the air compressor. CLEAR all DTCs. REPEAT the ARC Module Diagnostics.

FM2019700636140X

Fig. 14 Test J/DTC C1726: Rear Pneumatic Fault (Part 14 of 14)

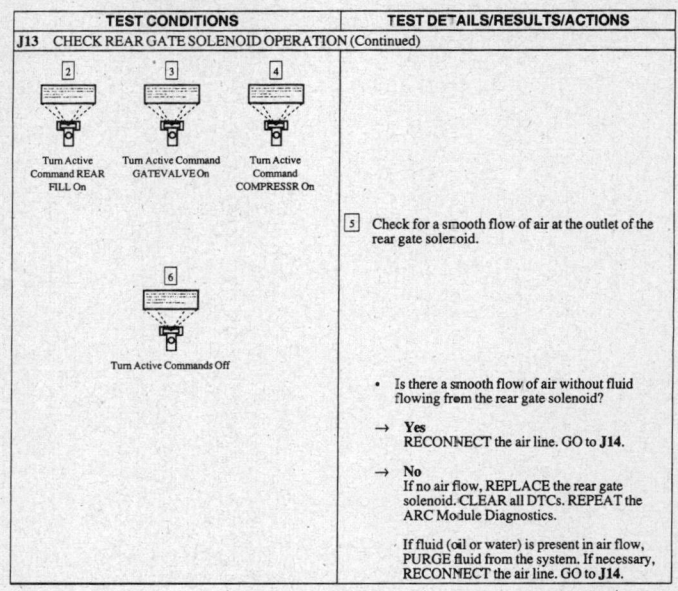

TEST CONDITIONS	TEST DETAILS/RESULTS/ACTIONS
K1 PERFORM ON-DEMAND SELF-TEST	
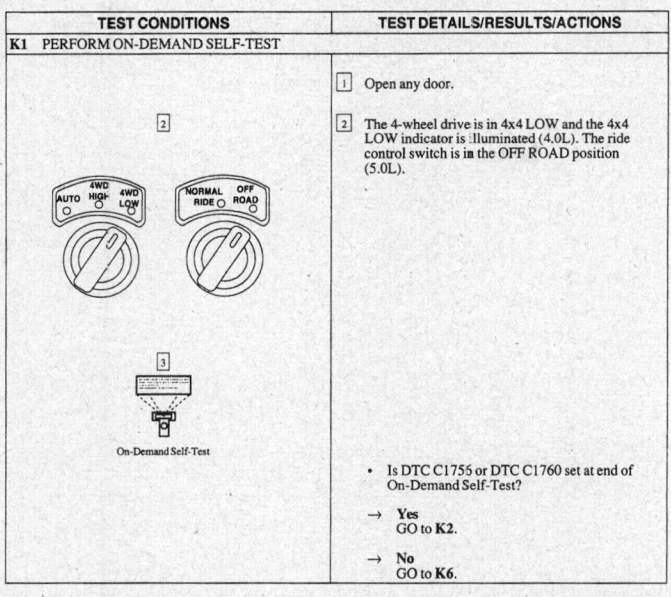	① Open any door.
	② The 4-wheel drive is in 4x4 LOW and the 4x4 LOW indicator is illuminated (4.0L). The ride control switch is in the OFF ROAD position (5.0L).
	• Is DTC C1755 or DTC C1760 set at end of On-Demand Self-Test?
	→ **Yes** GO to **K2**.
	→ **No** GO to **K6**.

FM2019700637010X

Fig. 15   Test K/DTC C1756 & C1760: Height Sensor Circuit Fault (Part 1 of 5)

TEST CONDITIONS	TEST DETAILS/RESULTS/ACTIONS
K2 CHECK SUSPECT HEIGHT SENSOR POWER	
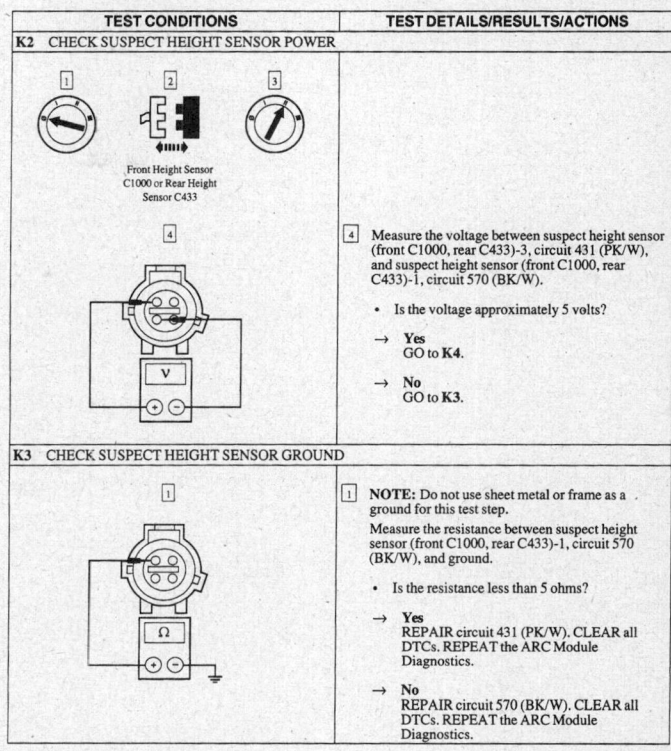	④ Measure the voltage between suspect height sensor (front C1000, rear C433)-3, circuit 431 (PK/W), and suspect height sensor (front C1000, rear C433)-1, circuit 570 (BK/W).
	• Is the voltage approximately 5 volts?
	→ **Yes** GO to **K4**.
	→ **No** GO to **K3**.
K3 CHECK SUSPECT HEIGHT SENSOR GROUND	
①	① **NOTE:** Do not use sheet metal or frame as a ground for this test step.
	Measure the resistance between suspect height sensor (front C1000, rear C433)-1, circuit 570 (BK/W), and ground.
	• Is the resistance less than 5 ohms?
	→ **Yes** REPAIR circuit 431 (PK/W). CLEAR all DTCs. REPEAT the ARC Module Diagnostics.
	→ **No** REPAIR circuit 570 (BK/W). CLEAR all DTCs. REPEAT the ARC Module Diagnostics.

FM2019700637020X

Fig. 15   Test K/DTC C1756 & C1760: Height Sensor Circuit Fault (Part 2 of 5)

TEST CONDITIONS	TEST DETAILS/RESULTS/ACTIONS
K4 CHECK SUSPECT HEIGHT SENSOR OPERATION	
① FHGTSEN or RHGTSEN PID	② Remove the suspect height sensor from the lower ball stud.
	③ While monitoring the FHGTSEN PID, slowly move the front height sensor over the full range of travel.
	• Does the voltage increase as the sensor is compressed, and decrease as the sensor is expanded?
	→ **Yes** GO to **K6**.
	→ **No** GO to **K5**.
K5 CHECK CIRCUIT 422 (PK/BK) OR CIRCUIT 428 (O/BK) FOR OPEN	
① ② Automatic Ride Control (ARC) Module C2001 ③	③ If the suspect height sensor is the front height sensor, measure the resistance between front height sensor C1000-2, circuit 422 (PK/BK), and ARC module C2001-7, circuit 422 (PK/BK).

FM2019700637030X

Fig. 15   Test K/DTC C1756 & C1760: Height Sensor Circuit Fault (Part 3 of 5)

TEST CONDITIONS	TEST DETAILS/RESULTS/ACTIONS
K5 CHECK CIRCUIT 422 (PK/BK) OR CIRCUIT 428 (O/BK) FOR OPEN (Continued)	
④	④ If the suspect height sensor is the rear height sensor, measure the resistance between rear height sensor C433-2, circuit 428 (O/BK), and ARC module C2001-9, circuit 428 (O/BK).
	• Is the resistance less than 5 ohms?
	→ **Yes** REPLACE the suspect height sensor. CLEAR all DTCs. REPEAT the ARC Module Diagnostics.
	→ **No** REPAIR circuit 422 (PK/BK) or circuit 428 (O/BK). CLEAR all DTCs. REPEAT the ARC Module Diagnostics.
K6 CHECK FOR INTERMITTENT OPEN	
① FHGTSEN or RHGTSEN PID	② Monitor the suspect height sensor voltage while wiggling the harnesses between the suspect height sensor and the ARC module.
	• Does the suspect height sensor voltage indicate less than 0.2 volts?
	→ **Yes** REPAIR circuit 422 (PK/BK)(front), circuit 428 (O/BK)(rear) and/or circuit 431 (PK/W). CLEAR all DTCs. REPEAT the ARC Module Diagnostics.
	→ **No** GO to **K7**.

FM2019700637040X

Fig. 15   Test K/DTC C1756 & C1760: Height Sensor Circuit Fault (Part 4 of 5)

TEST CONDITIONS	TEST DETAILS/RESULTS/ACTIONS
K7 CHECK FOR INTERMITTENT SHORT TO POWER	
FHGTSEN or RHGTSEN PID	**2** Monitor the suspect height sensor voltage while wiggling the harnesses between the suspect height sensor and the ARC module. • Does the suspect height sensor voltage indicate more than 4.9 volts? → **Yes** REPAIR circuit 422 (PK/BK)(front) or circuit 428 (O/BK)(rear). CLEAR all DTCs. REPEAT the ARC Module Diagnostics. → **No** REPLACE the front height sensor. CLEAR all DTCs. REPEAT the ARC Module Diagnostics.

FM2019700637050X

Fig. 15 Test K/DTC C1756 & C1760: Height Sensor Circuit Fault (Part 5 of 5)

TEST CONDITIONS	TEST DETAILS/RESULTS/ACTIONS
L1 PERFORM ON-DEMAND SELF-TEST (Continued)	
On-Demand Self-Test	• Is DTC C1770 set at end of self-test? → **Yes** GO to **L2**. → **No** GO to **L10**.
L2 CHECK VENT SOLENOID CONNECTOR	
(switch diagram OFF) Air Compressor C430	**1** Turn the air suspension switch to the OFF position. **3** Check the air compressor connector terminals for damage, corrosion or for pins that may be pushed out. • Are connector and pins OK? → **Yes** RECONNECT air compressor C430. GO to **L3**. → **No** REPAIR or REPLACE the parts as necessary. CLEAR all DTCS. REPEAT the ARC Module Diagnostics.

FM2019700638020X

Fig. 16 Test L/DTC C1770: Vent Solenoid Circuit Fault (Part 2 of 13)

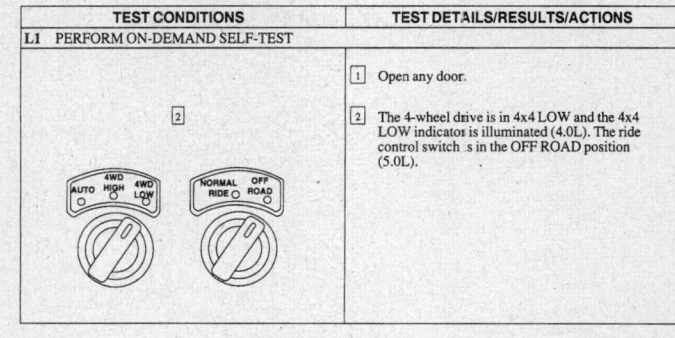

TEST CONDITIONS	TEST DETAILS/RESULTS/ACTIONS
L1 PERFORM ON-DEMAND SELF-TEST	
	1 Open any door. **2** The 4-wheel drive is in 4x4 LOW and the 4x4 LOW indicator is illuminated (4.0L). The ride control switch is in the OFF ROAD position (5.0L).

FM2019700638010X

Fig. 16 Test L/DTC C1770: Vent Solenoid Circuit Fault (Part 1 of 13)

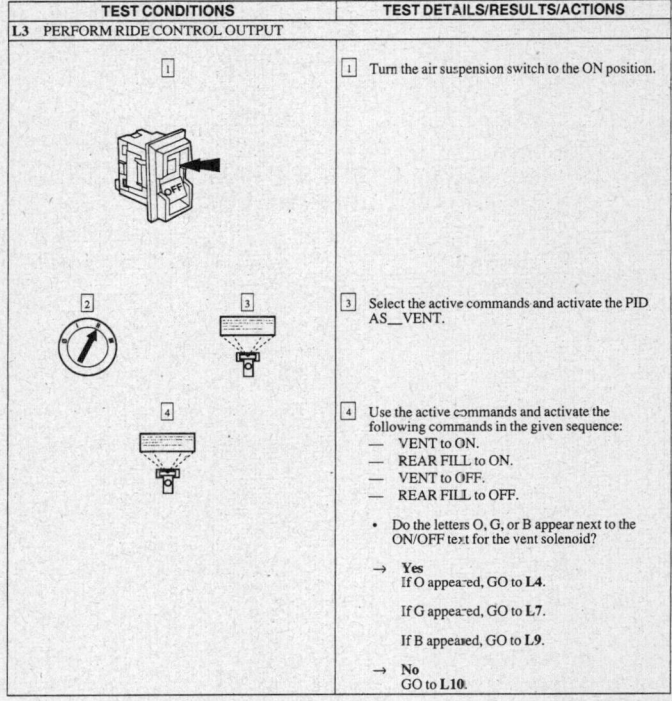

TEST CONDITIONS	TEST DETAILS/RESULTS/ACTIONS
L3 PERFORM RIDE CONTROL OUTPUT	
	1 Turn the air suspension switch to the ON position. **3** Select the active commands and activate the PID AS__VENT. **4** Use the active commands and activate the following commands in the given sequence: — VENT to ON. — REAR FILL to ON. — VENT to OFF. — REAR FILL to OFF. • Do the letters O, G, or B appear next to the ON/OFF text for the vent solenoid? → **Yes** If O appeared, GO to **L4**. If G appeared, GO to **L7**. If B appeared, GO to **L9**. → **No** GO to **L10**.

FM2019700638030X

Fig. 16 Test L/DTC C1770: Vent Solenoid Circuit Fault (Part 3 of 13)

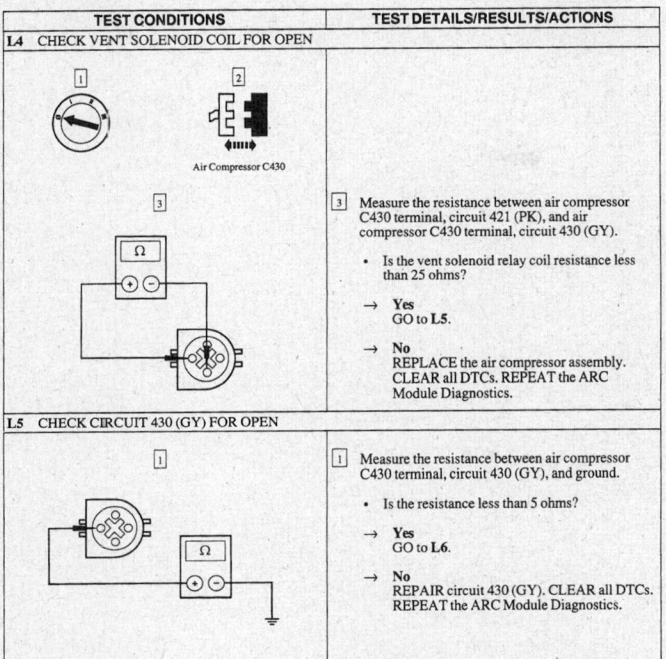

TEST CONDITIONS	TEST DETAILS/RESULTS/ACTIONS
L4 CHECK VENT SOLENOID COIL FOR OPEN	
	3 Measure the resistance between air compressor C430 terminal, circuit 421 (PK), and air compressor C430 terminal, circuit 430 (GY).
	• Is the vent solenoid relay coil resistance less than 25 ohms?
	→ **Yes** GO to **L5**.
	→ **No** REPLACE the air compressor assembly. CLEAR all DTCs. REPEAT the ARC Module Diagnostics.
L5 CHECK CIRCUIT 430 (GY) FOR OPEN	
	1 Measure the resistance between air compressor C430 terminal, circuit 430 (GY), and ground.
	• Is the resistance less than 5 ohms?
	→ **Yes** GO to **L6**.
	→ **No** REPAIR circuit 430 (GY). CLEAR all DTCs. REPEAT the ARC Module Diagnostics.

FM2019700638040X

Fig. 16 Test L/DTC C1770: Vent Solenoid Circuit Fault (Part 4 of 13)

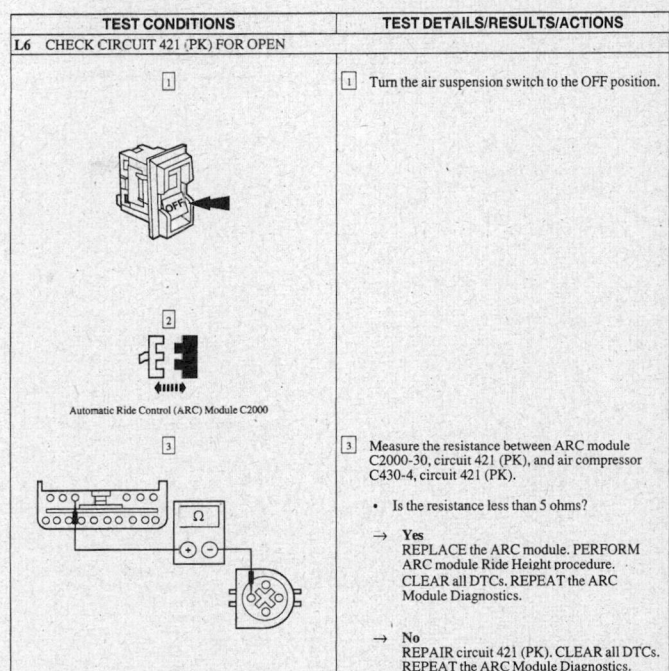

TEST CONDITIONS	TEST DETAILS/RESULTS/ACTIONS
L6 CHECK CIRCUIT 421 (PK) FOR OPEN	
	1 Turn the air suspension switch to the OFF position.
	3 Measure the resistance between ARC module C2000-30, circuit 421 (PK), and air compressor C430-4, circuit 421 (PK).
	• Is the resistance less than 5 ohms?
	→ **Yes** REPLACE the ARC module. PERFORM ARC module Ride Height procedure. CLEAR all DTCs. REPEAT the ARC Module Diagnostics.
	→ **No** REPAIR circuit 421 (PK). CLEAR all DTCs. REPEAT the ARC Module Diagnostics.

FM2019700638050X

Fig. 16 Test L/DTC C1770: Vent Solenoid Circuit Fault (Part 5 of 13)

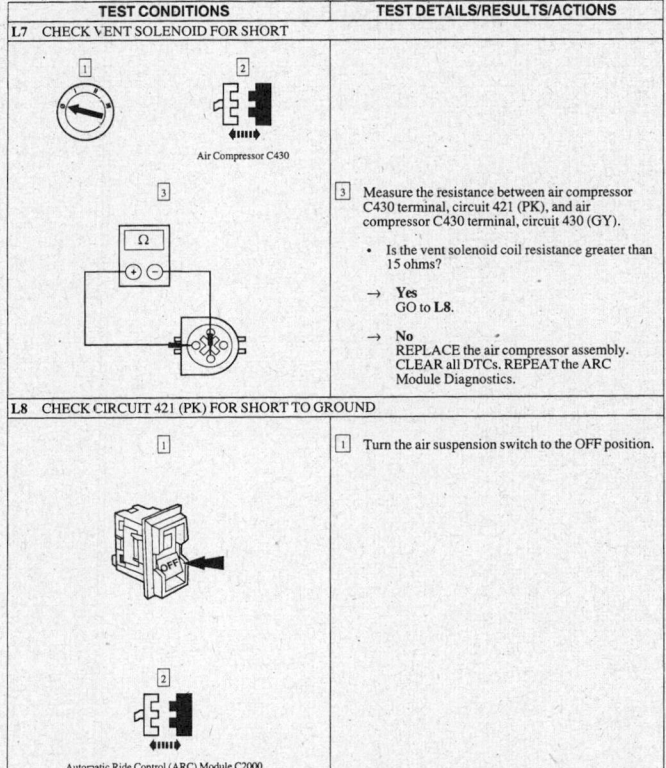

TEST CONDITIONS	TEST DETAILS/RESULTS/ACTIONS
L7 CHECK VENT SOLENOID FOR SHORT	
	3 Measure the resistance between air compressor C430 terminal, circuit 421 (PK), and air compressor C430 terminal, circuit 430 (GY).
	• Is the vent solenoid coil resistance greater than 15 ohms?
	→ **Yes** GO to **L8**.
	→ **No** REPLACE the air compressor assembly. CLEAR all DTCs. REPEAT the ARC Module Diagnostics.
L8 CHECK CIRCUIT 421 (PK) FOR SHORT TO GROUND	
	1 Turn the air suspension switch to the OFF position.

FM2019700638060X

Fig. 16 Test L/DTC C1770: Vent Solenoid Circuit Fault (Part 6 of 13)

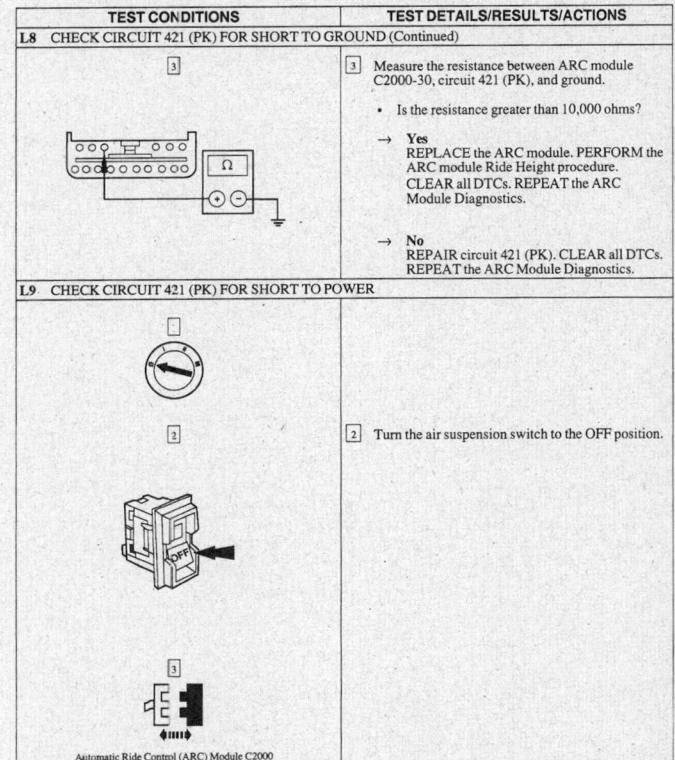

TEST CONDITIONS	TEST DETAILS/RESULTS/ACTIONS
L8 CHECK CIRCUIT 421 (PK) FOR SHORT TO GROUND (Continued)	
	3 Measure the resistance between ARC module C2000-30, circuit 421 (PK), and ground.
	• Is the resistance greater than 10,000 ohms?
	→ **Yes** REPLACE the ARC module. PERFORM the ARC module Ride Height procedure. CLEAR all DTCs. REPEAT the ARC Module Diagnostics.
	→ **No** REPAIR circuit 421 (PK). CLEAR all DTCs. REPEAT the ARC Module Diagnostics.
L9 CHECK CIRCUIT 421 (PK) FOR SHORT TO POWER	
	2 Turn the air suspension switch to the OFF position.

FM2019700638070X

Fig. 16 Test L/DTC C1770: Vent Solenoid Circuit Fault (Part 7 of 13)

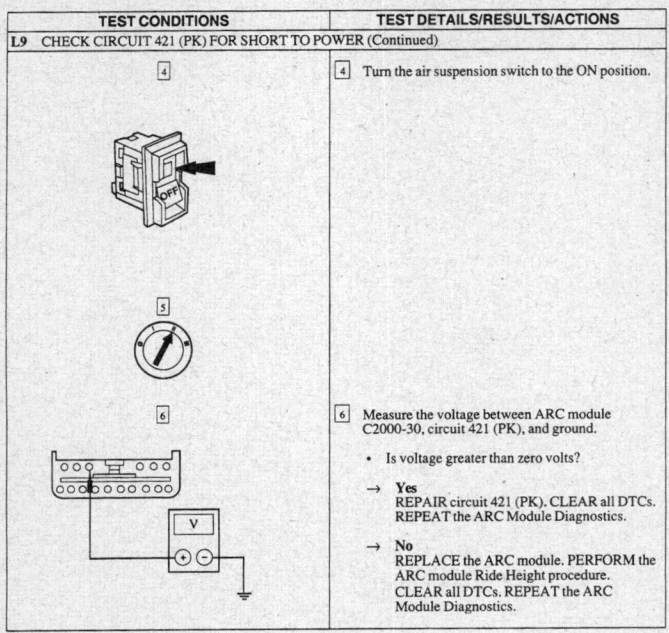

TEST CONDITIONS	TEST DETAILS/RESULTS/ACTIONS
L9 CHECK CIRCUIT 421 (PK) FOR SHORT TO POWER (Continued)	
4	**4** Turn the air suspension switch to the ON position.
5	
6	**6** Measure the voltage between ARC module C2000-30, circuit 421 (PK), and ground.
	• Is voltage greater than zero volts?
	→ **Yes** REPAIR circuit 421 (PK). CLEAR all DTCs. REPEAT the ARC Module Diagnostics.
	→ **No** REPLACE the ARC module. PERFORM the ARC module Ride Height procedure. CLEAR all DTCs. REPEAT the ARC Module Diagnostics.

FM2019700638080X

Fig. 16 Test L/DTC C1770: Vent Solenoid Circuit Fault (Part 8 of 13)

TEST CONDITIONS	TEST DETAILS/RESULTS/ACTIONS
L10 CHECK AIR COMPRESSOR ASSEMBLY CONNECTOR TERMINALS	
1	
2	**2** Turn the air suspension switch to the OFF position.
3 Air Compressor C430	
	4 Inspect the pins and terminals of the air compressor connector for corrosion, bent or broken pins, moisture, or other damage.
	• Are the connectors and pins OK?
	→ **Yes** GO to **L11**.
	→ **No** REPAIR or REPLACE the parts as necessary. CLEAR all DTCs. REPEAT the ARC Module Diagnostics.

FM2019700638090X

Fig. 16 Test L/DTC C1770: Vent Solenoid Circuit Fault (Part 9 of 13)

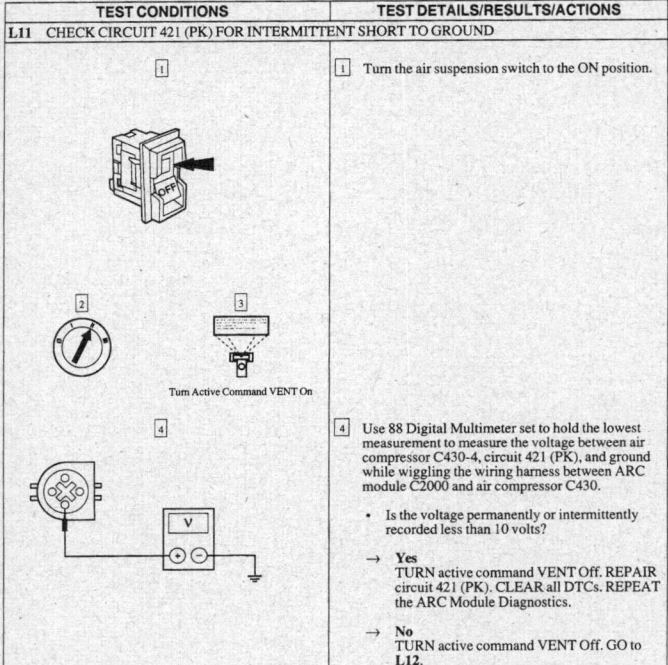

TEST CONDITIONS	TEST DETAILS/RESULTS/ACTIONS
L11 CHECK CIRCUIT 421 (PK) FOR INTERMITTENT SHORT TO GROUND	
1	**1** Turn the air suspension switch to the ON position.
2 **3** Turn Active Command VENT On	
4	**4** Use 88 Digital Multimeter set to hold the lowest measurement to measure the voltage between air compressor C430-4, circuit 421 (PK), and ground while wiggling the wiring harness between ARC module C2000 and air compressor C430.
	• Is the voltage permanently or intermittently recorded less than 10 volts?
	→ **Yes** TURN active command VENT Off. REPAIR circuit 421 (PK). CLEAR all DTCs. REPEAT the ARC Module Diagnostics.
	→ **No** TURN active command VENT Off. GO to **L12**.

FM2019700638100X

Fig. 16 Test L/DTC C1770: Vent Solenoid Circuit Fault (Part 10 of 13)

TEST CONDITIONS	TEST DETAILS/RESULTS/ACTIONS
L12 CHECK CIRCUIT 421 (PK) FOR INTERMITTENT SHORT TO POWER	
1	**1** Use 88 Digital Multimeter set to hold the highest measurement to measure the voltage between air compressor C430-4, circuit 421 (PK), and ground while wiggling the wiring harness between ARC module C2000 and air compressor C430.
	• Is the voltage recorded greater than zero volts?
	→ **Yes** REPAIR circuit 421 (PK). CLEAR all DTCs. REPEAT the ARC Module Diagnostics.
	→ **No** GO to **L13**.
L13 CHECK INTERMITTENT MODULE FUNCTION	
1	
2	**2** Turn the air suspension switch to the OFF position.
	3 Remove circuit 421 (PK) from ARC module C2000-30 (with connector connected to ARC module).

FM2019700638110X

Fig. 16 Test L/DTC C1770: Vent Solenoid Circuit Fault (Part 11 of 13)

TEST CONDITIONS	TEST DETAILS/RESULTS/ACTIONS
L13 CHECK INTERMITTENT MODULE FUNCTION (Continued)	

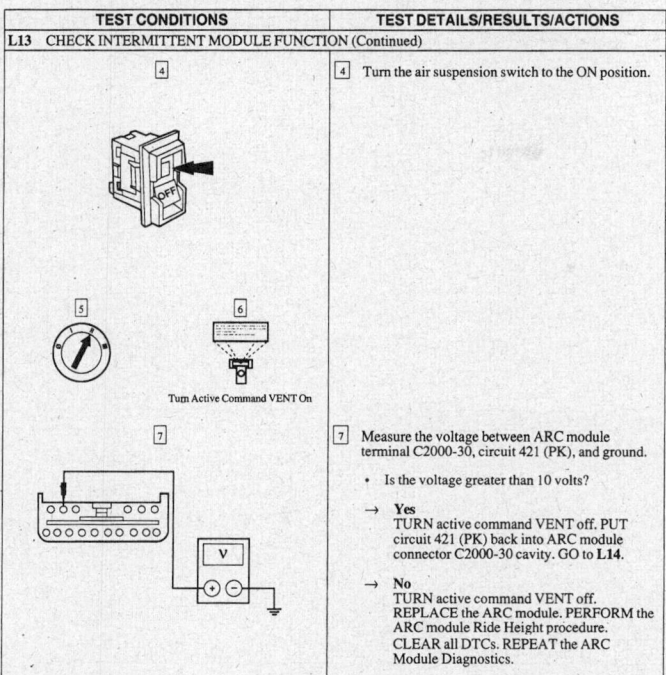

☐4 Turn the air suspension switch to the ON position.

Turn Active Command VENT On

☐7 Measure the voltage between ARC module terminal C2000-30, circuit 421 (PK), and ground.

- Is the voltage greater than 10 volts?

→ **Yes**
TURN active command VENT off. PUT circuit 421 (PK) back into ARC module connector C2000-30 cavity. GO to **L14**.

→ **No**
TURN active command VENT off. REPLACE the ARC module. PERFORM the ARC module Ride Height procedure. CLEAR all DTCs. REPEAT the ARC Module Diagnostics.

FM2019700638120X

Fig. 16   Test L/DTC C1770: Vent Solenoid Circuit Fault (Part 12 of 13)

TEST CONDITIONS	TEST DETAILS/RESULTS/ACTIONS
M1 PERFORM ON-DEMAND SELF-TEST	

☐1 Open any door.

FM2019700639010X

Fig. 17   Test M/DTC C1830: Air Compressor Relay Circuit Fault (Part 1 of 14)

TEST CONDITIONS	TEST DETAILS/RESULTS/ACTIONS
M1 PERFORM ON-DEMAND SELF-TEST (Continued)	

☐3 The 4-wheel drive is in 4x4 LOW and the 4x4 LOW indicator is illuminated (4.0L). The ride control switch is in the OFF ROAD position (5.0L).

On-Demand Self-Test

- Is DTC C1830 set at end of On-Demand Self-Test?

→ **Yes**
GO to **M2**.

→ **No**
GO to **M10**.

FM2019700639020X

Fig. 17   Test M/DTC C1830: Air Compressor Relay Circuit Fault (Part 2 of 14)

TEST CONDITIONS	TEST DETAILS/RESULTS/ACTIONS
L14 PERFORM ROAD TEST	

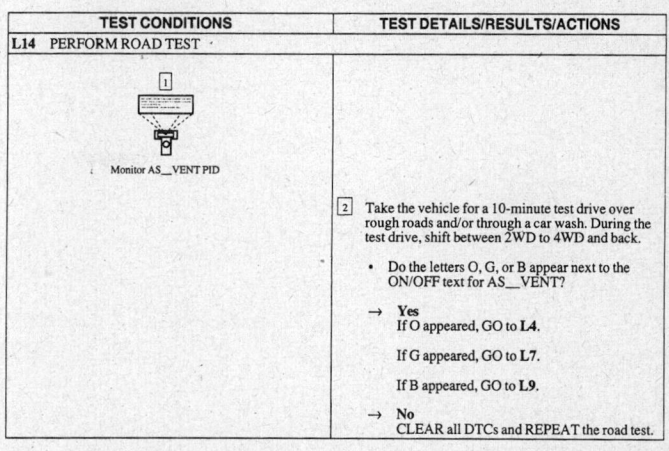

Monitor AS__VENT PID

☐2 Take the vehicle for a 10-minute test drive over rough roads and/or through a car wash. During the test drive, shift between 2WD to 4WD and back.

- Do the letters O, G, or B appear next to the ON/OFF text for AS__VENT?

→ **Yes**
If O appeared, GO to **L4**.

If G appeared, GO to **L7**.

If B appeared, GO to **L9**.

→ **No**
CLEAR all DTCs and REPEAT the road test.

FM2019700638130X

Fig. 16   Test L/DTC C1770: Vent Solenoid Circuit Fault (Part 13 of 13)

TEST CONDITIONS	TEST DETAILS/RESULTS/ACTIONS
M2 CHECK FUSE 12 (50A)	

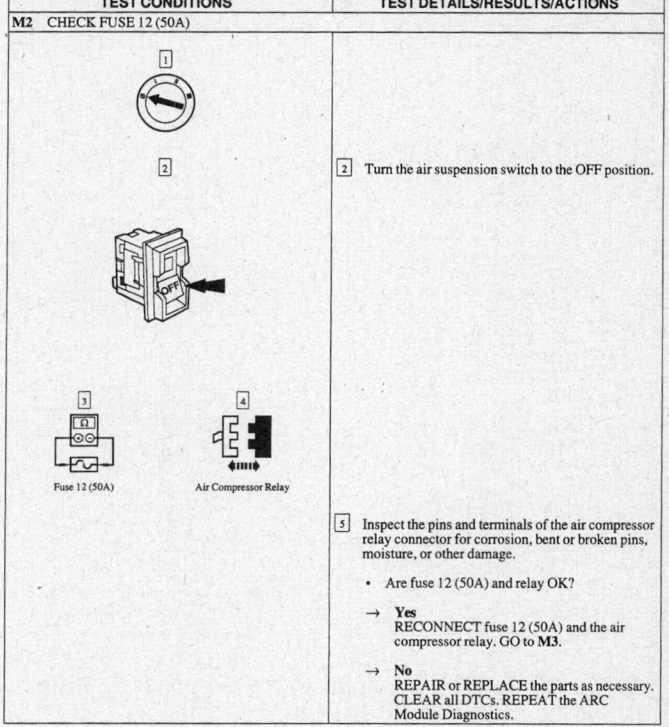

☐2 Turn the air suspension switch to the OFF position.

Fuse 12 (50A)   Air Compressor Relay

☐5 Inspect the pins and terminals of the air compressor relay connector for corrosion, bent or broken pins, moisture, or other damage.

- Are fuse 12 (50A) and relay OK?

→ **Yes**
RECONNECT fuse 12 (50A) and the air compressor relay. GO to **M3**.

→ **No**
REPAIR or REPLACE the parts as necessary. CLEAR all DTCs. REPEAT the ARC Module Diagnostics.

FM2019700639030X

Fig. 17   Test M/DTC C1830: Air Compressor Relay Circuit Fault (Part 3 of 14)

TEST CONDITIONS	TEST DETAILS/RESULTS/ACTIONS
M3 PERFORM RIDE CONTROL OUTPUT	

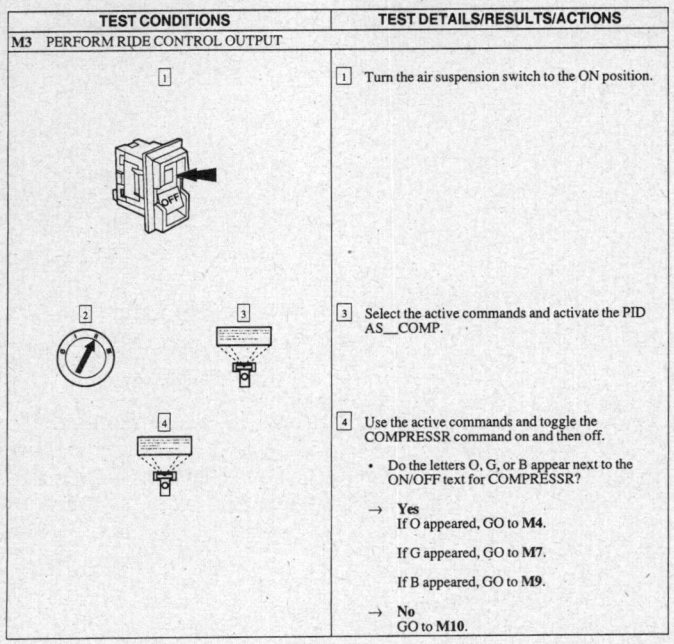

1 Turn the air suspension switch to the ON position.

3 Select the active commands and activate the PID AS__COMP.

4 Use the active commands and toggle the COMPRESSR command on and then off.

- Do the letters O, G, or B appear next to the ON/OFF text for COMPRESSR?

→ **Yes**
If O appeared, GO to **M4**.
If G appeared, GO to **M7**.
If B appeared, GO to **M9**.

→ **No**
GO to **M10**.

FM2019700639040X

Fig. 17 Test M/DTC C1830: Air Compressor Relay Circuit Fault (Part 4 of 14)

TEST CONDITIONS	TEST DETAILS/RESULTS/ACTIONS
M4 CHECK AIR COMPRESSOR RELAY COIL FOR OPEN	

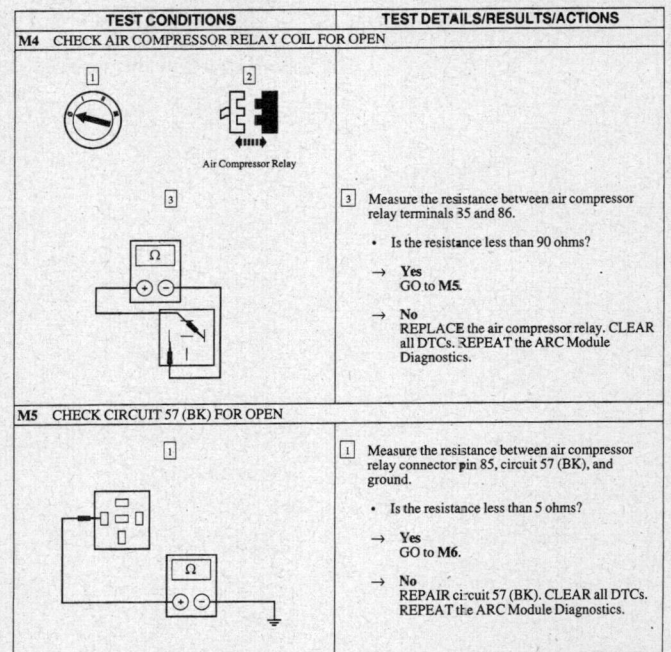

3 Measure the resistance between air compressor relay terminals 35 and 86.

- Is the resistance less than 90 ohms?

→ **Yes**
GO to **M5**.

→ **No**
REPLACE the air compressor relay. CLEAR all DTCs. REPEAT the ARC Module Diagnostics.

M5 CHECK CIRCUIT 57 (BK) FOR OPEN	

1 Measure the resistance between air compressor relay connector pin 85, circuit 57 (BK), and ground.

- Is the resistance less than 5 ohms?

→ **Yes**
GO to **M6**.

→ **No**
REPAIR circuit 57 (BK). CLEAR all DTCs. REPEAT the ARC Module Diagnostics.

FM2019700639050X

Fig. 17 Test M/DTC C1830: Air Compressor Relay Circuit Fault (Part 5 of 14)

TEST CONDITIONS	TEST DETAILS/RESULTS/ACTIONS
M6 CHECK CIRCUIT 420 (DB/Y) FOR OPEN	

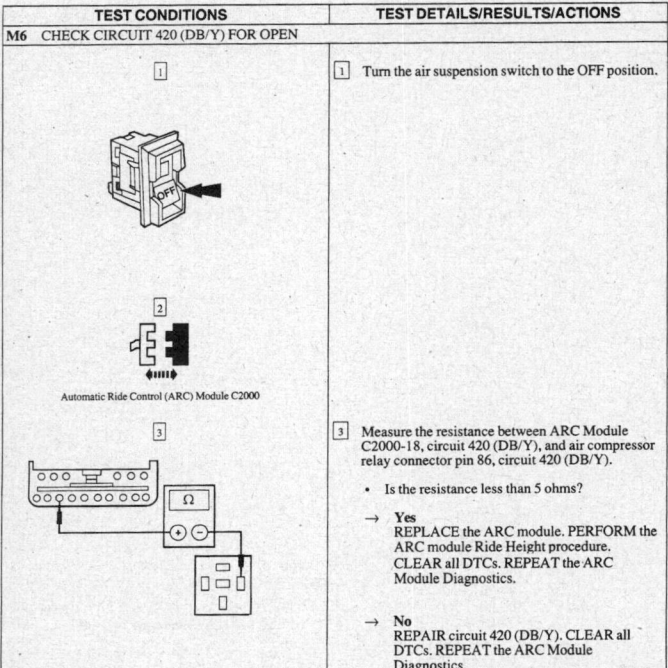

1 Turn the air suspension switch to the OFF position.

3 Measure the resistance between ARC Module C2000-18, circuit 420 (DB/Y), and air compressor relay connector pin 86, circuit 420 (DB/Y).

- Is the resistance less than 5 ohms?

→ **Yes**
REPLACE the ARC module. PERFORM the ARC module Ride Height procedure. CLEAR all DTCs. REPEAT the ARC Module Diagnostics.

→ **No**
REPAIR circuit 420 (DB/Y). CLEAR all DTCs. REPEAT the ARC Module Diagnostics.

FM2019700639060X

Fig. 17 Test M/DTC C1830: Air Compressor Relay Circuit Fault (Part 6 of 14)

TEST CONDITIONS	TEST DETAILS/RESULTS/ACTIONS
M7 CHECK AIR COMPRESSOR RELAY COIL FOR SHORT	

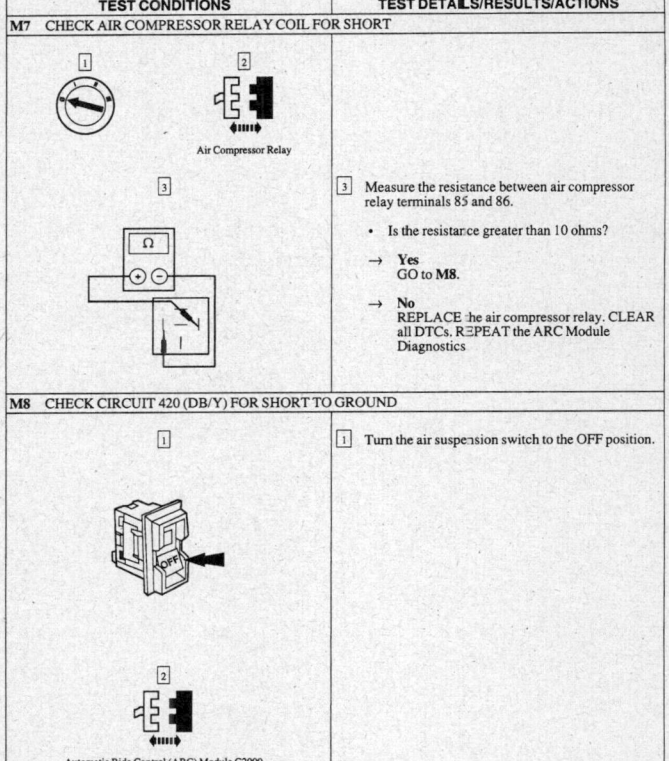

3 Measure the resistance between air compressor relay terminals 85 and 86.

- Is the resistance greater than 10 ohms?

→ **Yes**
GO to **M8**.

→ **No**
REPLACE the air compressor relay. CLEAR all DTCs. REPEAT the ARC Module Diagnostics.

M8 CHECK CIRCUIT 420 (DB/Y) FOR SHORT TO GROUND	

1 Turn the air suspension switch to the OFF position.

FM2019700639070X

Fig. 17 Test M/DTC C1830: Air Compressor Relay Circuit Fault (Part 7 of 14)

TEST CONDITIONS	TEST DETAILS/RESULTS/ACTIONS
M8 CHECK CIRCUIT 420 (DB/Y) FOR SHORT TO GROUND (Continued)	

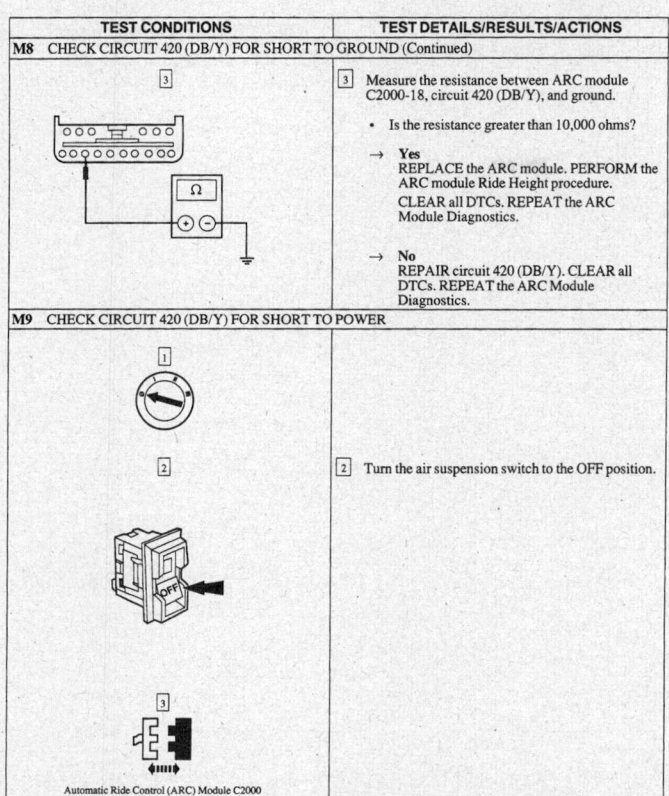

3 Measure the resistance between ARC module C2000-18, circuit 420 (DB/Y), and ground.

- Is the resistance greater than 10,000 ohms?

→ **Yes**
REPLACE the ARC module. PERFORM the ARC module Ride Height procedure. CLEAR all DTCs. REPEAT the ARC Module Diagnostics.

→ **No**
REPAIR circuit 420 (DB/Y). CLEAR all DTCs. REPEAT the ARC Module Diagnostics.

M9 CHECK CIRCUIT 420 (DB/Y) FOR SHORT TO POWER

2 Turn the air suspension switch to the OFF position.

Automatic Ride Control (ARC) Module C2000

FM2019700639080X

Fig. 17 Test M/DTC C1830: Air Compressor Relay Circuit Fault (Part 8 of 14)

TEST CONDITIONS	TEST DETAILS/RESULTS/ACTIONS
M10 CHECK AIR COMPRESSOR RELAY TERMINALS	

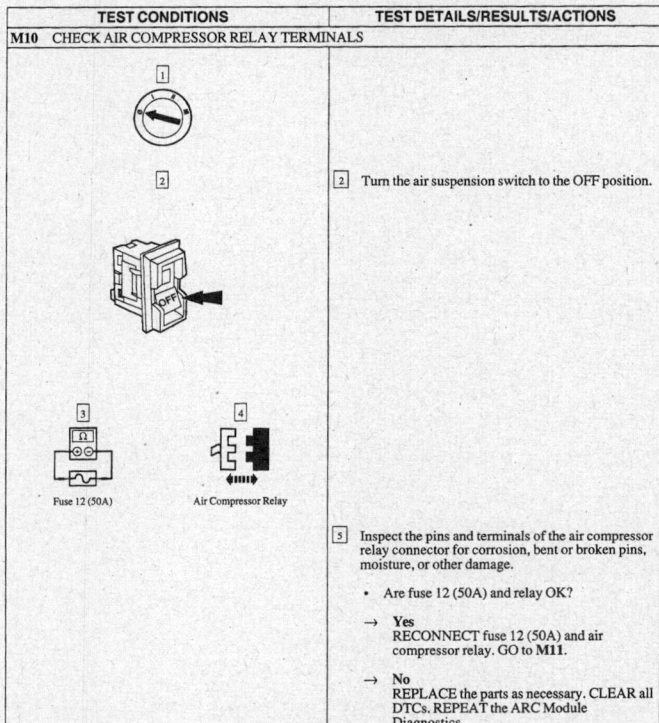

2 Turn the air suspension switch to the OFF position.

Fuse 12 (50A)   Air Compressor Relay

5 Inspect the pins and terminals of the air compressor relay connector for corrosion, bent or broken pins, moisture, or other damage.

- Are fuse 12 (50A) and relay OK?

→ **Yes**
RECONNECT fuse 12 (50A) and air compressor relay. GO to **M11**.

→ **No**
REPLACE the parts as necessary. CLEAR all DTCs. REPEAT the ARC Module Diagnostics.

FM2019700639100X

Fig. 17 Test M/DTC C1830: Air Compressor Relay Circuit Fault (Part 10 of 14)

TEST CONDITIONS	TEST DETAILS/RESULTS/ACTIONS
M9 CHECK CIRCUIT 420 (DB/Y) FOR SHORT TO POWER (Continued)	

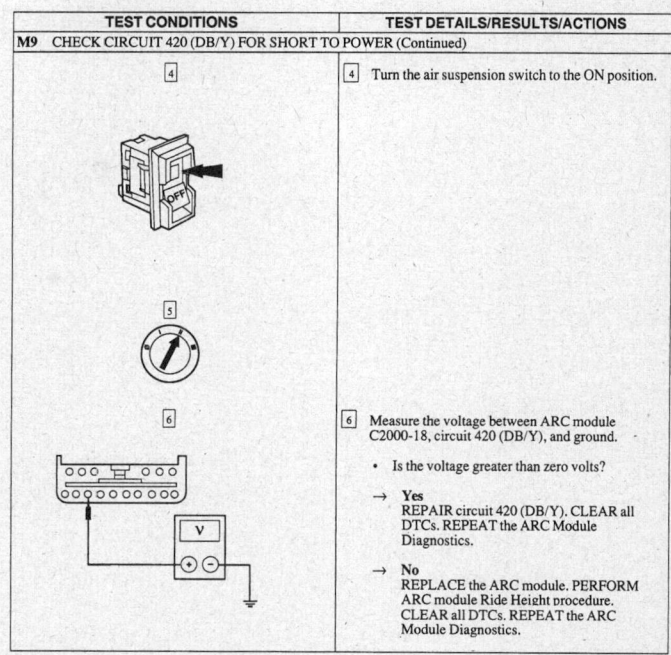

4 Turn the air suspension switch to the ON position.

6 Measure the voltage between ARC module C2000-18, circuit 420 (DB/Y), and ground.

- Is the voltage greater than zero volts?

→ **Yes**
REPAIR circuit 420 (DB/Y). CLEAR all DTCs. REPEAT the ARC Module Diagnostics.

→ **No**
REPLACE the ARC module. PERFORM ARC module Ride Height procedure. CLEAR all DTCs. REPEAT the ARC Module Diagnostics.

FM2019700639090X

Fig. 17 Test M/DTC C1830: Air Compressor Relay Circuit Fault (Part 9 of 14)

TEST CONDITIONS	TEST DETAILS/RESULTS/ACTIONS
M11 CHECK CIRCUIT 420 (DB/Y) FOR INTERMITTENT SHORT TO GROUND	

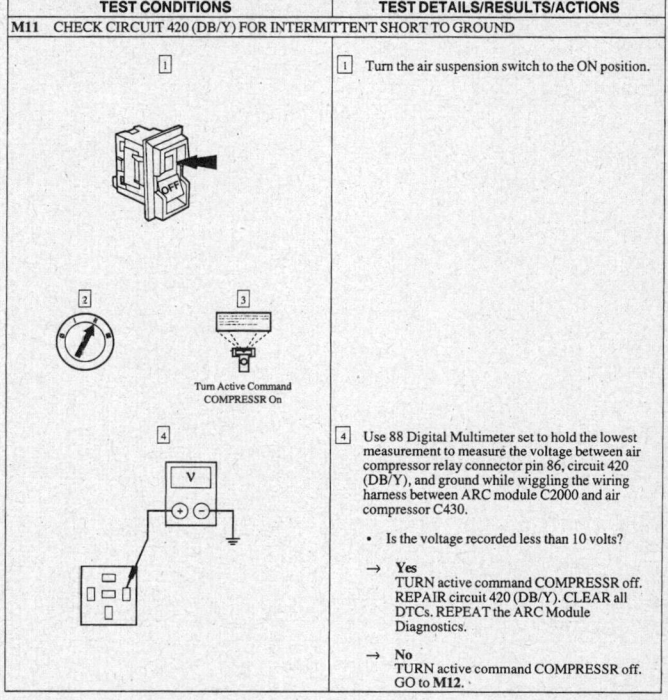

1 Turn the air suspension switch to the ON position.

Turn Active Command COMPRESSR On

4 Use 88 Digital Multimeter set to hold the lowest measurement to measure the voltage between air compressor relay connector pin 86, circuit 420 (DB/Y), and ground while wiggling the wiring harness between ARC module C2000 and air compressor C430.

- Is the voltage recorded less than 10 volts?

→ **Yes**
TURN active command COMPRESSR off. REPAIR circuit 420 (DB/Y). CLEAR all DTCs. REPEAT the ARC Module Diagnostics.

→ **No**
TURN active command COMPRESSR off. GO to **M12**.

FM2019700639110X

Fig. 17 Test M/DTC C1830: Air Compressor Relay Circuit Fault (Part 11 of 14)

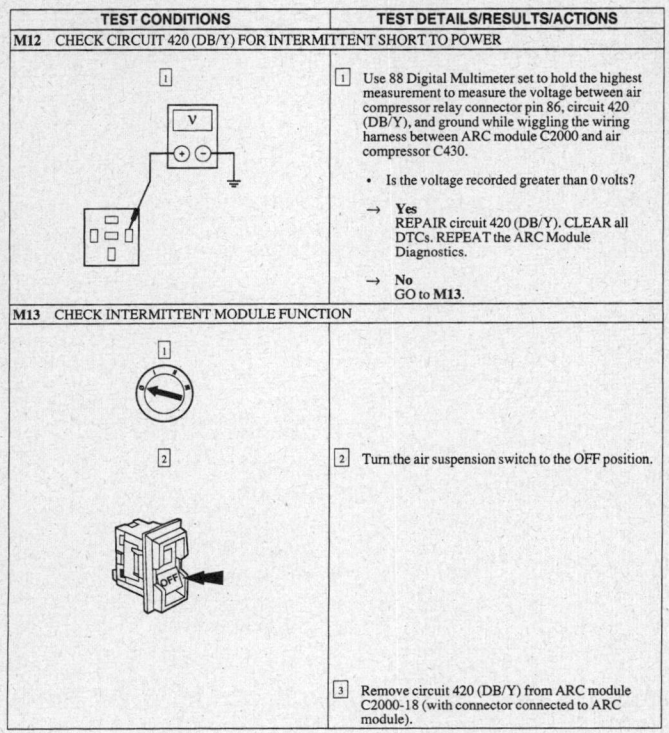

TEST CONDITIONS	TEST DETAILS/RESULTS/ACTIONS
M12 CHECK CIRCUIT 420 (DB/Y) FOR INTERMITTENT SHORT TO POWER	

1. Use 88 Digital Multimeter set to hold the highest measurement to measure the voltage between air compressor relay connector pin 86, circuit 420 (DB/Y), and ground while wiggling the wiring harness between ARC module C2000 and air compressor C430.
   - Is the voltage recorded greater than 0 volts?
   → **Yes**
   REPAIR circuit 420 (DB/Y). CLEAR all DTCs. REPEAT the ARC Module Diagnostics.
   → **No**
   GO to **M13**.

M13 CHECK INTERMITTENT MODULE FUNCTION	

2. Turn the air suspension switch to the OFF position.

3. Remove circuit 420 (DB/Y) from ARC module C2000-18 (with connector connected to ARC module).

FM2019700639120X

Fig. 17 Test M/DTC C1830: Air Compressor Relay Circuit Fault (Part 12 of 14)

TEST CONDITIONS	TEST DETAILS/RESULTS/ACTIONS
M13 CHECK INTERMITTENT MODULE FUNCTION (Continued)	

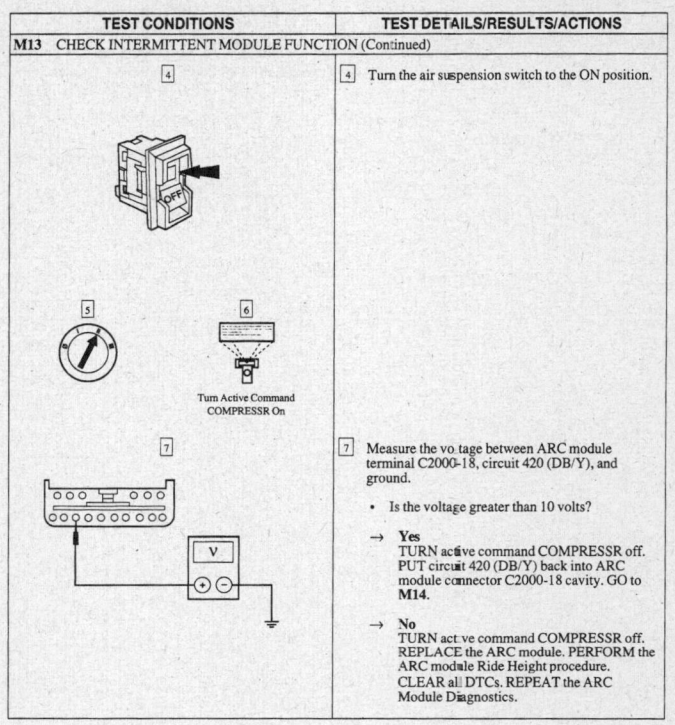

4. Turn the air suspension switch to the ON position.

Turn Active Command COMPRESSR On

7. Measure the voltage between ARC module terminal C2000-18, circuit 420 (DB/Y), and ground.
   - Is the voltage greater than 10 volts?
   → **Yes**
   TURN active command COMPRESSR off. PUT circuit 420 (DB/Y) back into ARC module connector C2000-18 cavity. GO to **M14**.
   → **No**
   TURN active command COMPRESSR off. REPLACE the ARC module. PERFORM the ARC module Ride Height procedure. CLEAR all DTCs. REPEAT the ARC Module Diagnostics.

FM2019700639130X

Fig. 17 Test M/DTC C1830: Air Compressor Relay Circuit Fault (Part 13 of 14)

TEST CONDITIONS	TEST DETAILS/RESULTS/ACTIONS
M14 PERFORM ROAD TEST	

Monitor AS__COMP PID

2. Take the vehicle for a 10-minute test drive over rough roads and/or through a car wash. During the test drive, shift between 2WD to 4WD and back.
   - Do the letters O, G, or B appear next to the ON/OFF text for AS__COMP?
   → **Yes**
   If O appeared, GO to **M4**.
   If G appeared, GO to **M7**.
   If B appeared, GO to **M9**.
   → **No**
   CLEAR all DTCs and REPEAT the road test.

FM2019700639140X

Fig. 17 Test M/DTC C1830: Air Compressor Relay Circuit Fault (Part 14 of 14)

TEST CONDITIONS	TEST DETAILS/RESULTS/ACTIONS
N1 PERFORM ON-DEMAND SELF-TEST	

1. Open any door.

2. The 4-wheel drive is in 4x4 LOW and the 4x4 LOW indicator is illuminated (4.0L). The ride control is in the OFFROAD position (5.0L).

FM2019700640010X

Fig. 18 Test N/DTC C1845 & C1865: Front–Rear Fill Solenoid Circuit Fault (Part 1 of 15)

TEST CONDITIONS	TEST DETAILS/RESULTS/ACTIONS
N1 PERFORM ON-DEMAND SELF-TEST (Continued)	

On-Demand Self-Test

- Is DTC C1845 or C1865 set at the end of On-Demand Self-Test?
→ **Yes**
GO to **N2**.
→ **No**
GO to **N10**.

N2 CHECK SUSPECT FILL SOLENOID CONNECTOR	

2. Turn the air suspension switch to the OFF position.

FM2019700640020X

Fig. 18 Test N/DTC C1845 & C1865: Front-Rear Fill Solenoid Circuit Fault (Part 2 of 15)

TEST CONDITIONS	TEST DETAILS/RESULTS/ACTIONS
N2 CHECK SUSPECT FILL SOLENOID CONNECTOR (Continued)	
[3] Suspect Fill Solenoid (Front C1001, Rear C428)	[3] Inspect the suspect fill solenoid terminals for damage, corrosion or pins that may be pushed out. • Are the suspect fill solenoid connector and pins OK? → **Yes** RECONNECT the suspect fill solenoid. GO to **N3**. → **No** REPAIR or REPLACE parts as necessary. CLEAR all DTCS. REPEAT the ARC Module Diagnostics.
N3 PERFORM RIDE CONTROL OUTPUT	
[1]	[1] Turn the air suspension switch to the ON position.
[2] [3]	[3] Select the active commands and monitor the PID F__FILL or R__FILL as appropriate.

FM2019700640030X

Fig. 18 Test N/DTC C1845 & C1865: Front-Rear Fill Solenoid Circuit Fault (Part 3 of 15)

TEST CONDITIONS	TEST DETAILS/RESULTS/ACTIONS
N5 CHECK CIRCUIT 57 (BK) FOR OPEN IN HARNESS	
[1]	[1] Measure the resistance between the suspect fill solenoid (front C1001, rear C428)-1, circuit 57 (BK), and ground. • Is the resistance less than 5 ohms? → **Yes** GO to **N6**. → **No** REPAIR circuit 57 (BK). CLEAR all DTCs. REPEAT the ARC Module Diagnostics.
N6 CHECK CIRCUIT 415 (LG/O)/CIRCUIT 416 (LB/BK) FOR OPEN	
[1]	[1] Turn the air suspension switch to the OFF position.
[2] Automatic Ride Control (ARC) Module C2000	

FM2019700640050X

Fig. 18 Test N/DTC C1845 & C1865: Front-Rear Fill Solenoid Circuit Fault (Part 5 of 15)

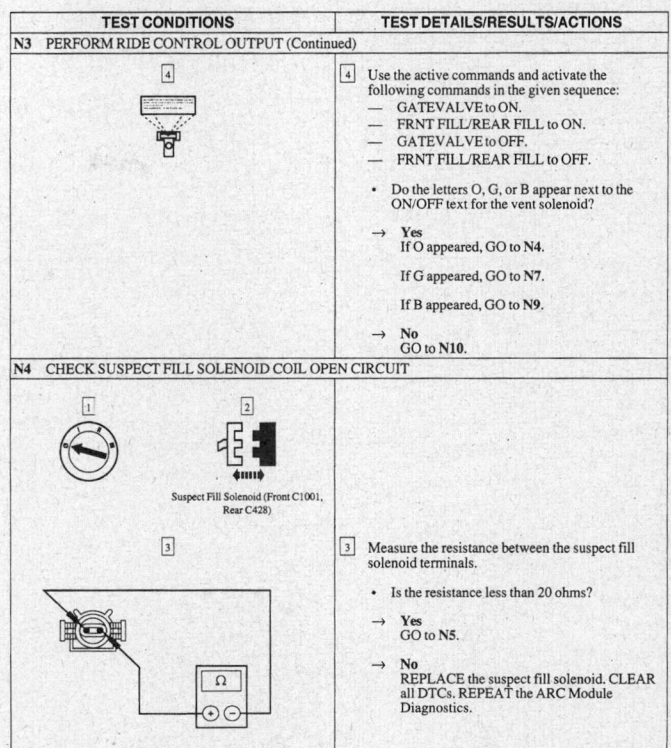

TEST CONDITIONS	TEST DETAILS/RESULTS/ACTIONS
N3 PERFORM RIDE CONTROL OUTPUT (Continued)	
[4]	[4] Use the active commands and activate the following commands in the given sequence: — GATEVALVE to ON. — FRNT FILL/REAR FILL to ON. — GATEVALVE to OFF. — FRNT FILL/REAR FILL to OFF. • Do the letters O, G, or B appear next to the ON/OFF text for the vent solenoid? → **Yes** If O appeared, GO to **N4**. If G appeared, GO to **N7**. If B appeared, GO to **N9**. → **No** GO to **N10**.
N4 CHECK SUSPECT FILL SOLENOID COIL OPEN CIRCUIT	
[1] [2] Suspect Fill Solenoid (Front C1001, Rear C428)	
[3]	[3] Measure the resistance between the suspect fill solenoid terminals. • Is the resistance less than 20 ohms? → **Yes** GO to **N5**. → **No** REPLACE the suspect fill solenoid. CLEAR all DTCs. REPEAT the ARC Module Diagnostics.

FM2019700640040X

Fig. 18 Test N/DTC C1845 & C1865: Front-Rear Fill Solenoid Circuit Fault (Part 4 of 15)

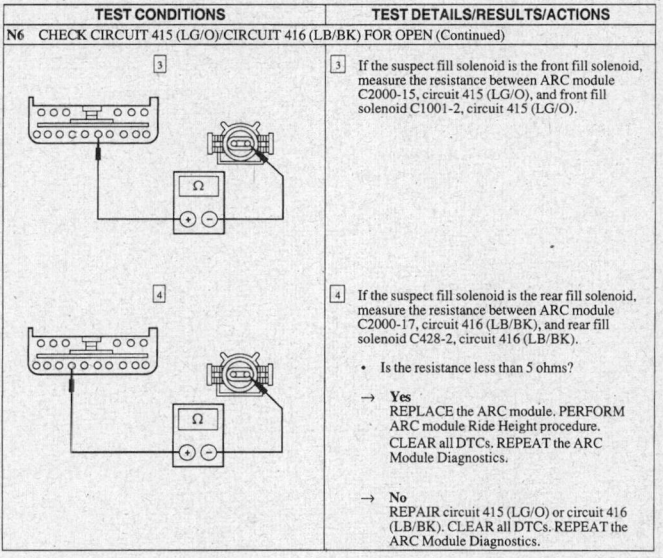

TEST CONDITIONS	TEST DETAILS/RESULTS/ACTIONS
N6 CHECK CIRCUIT 415 (LG/O)/CIRCUIT 416 (LB/BK) FOR OPEN (Continued)	
[3]	[3] If the suspect fill solenoid is the front fill solenoid, measure the resistance between ARC module C2000-15, circuit 415 (LG/O), and front fill solenoid C1001-2, circuit 415 (LG/O).
[4]	[4] If the suspect fill solenoid is the rear fill solenoid, measure the resistance between ARC module C2000-17, circuit 416 (LB/BK), and rear fill solenoid C428-2, circuit 416 (LB/BK). • Is the resistance less than 5 ohms? → **Yes** REPLACE the ARC module. PERFORM ARC module Ride Height procedure. CLEAR all DTCs. REPEAT the ARC Module Diagnostics. → **No** REPAIR circuit 415 (LG/O) or circuit 416 (LB/BK). CLEAR all DTCs. REPEAT the ARC Module Diagnostics.

FM2019700640060X

Fig. 18 Test N/DTC C1845 & C1865: Front-Rear Fill Solenoid Circuit Fault (Part 6 of 15)

TEST CONDITIONS	TEST DETAILS/RESULTS/ACTIONS
N7 CHECK SUSPECT FILL SOLENOID COIL FOR SHORT	

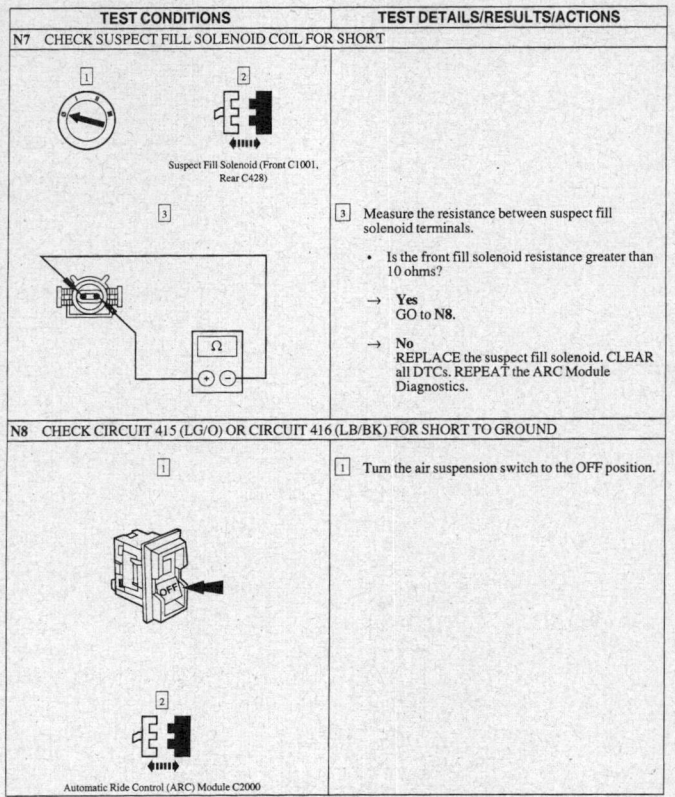

Suspect Fill Solenoid (Front C1001, Rear C428)

3 Measure the resistance between suspect fill solenoid terminals.

- Is the front fill solenoid resistance greater than 10 ohms?

→ **Yes**
GO to **N8**.

→ **No**
REPLACE the suspect fill solenoid. CLEAR all DTCs. REPEAT the ARC Module Diagnostics.

N8 CHECK CIRCUIT 415 (LG/O) OR CIRCUIT 416 (LB/BK) FOR SHORT TO GROUND	

1 Turn the air suspension switch to the OFF position.

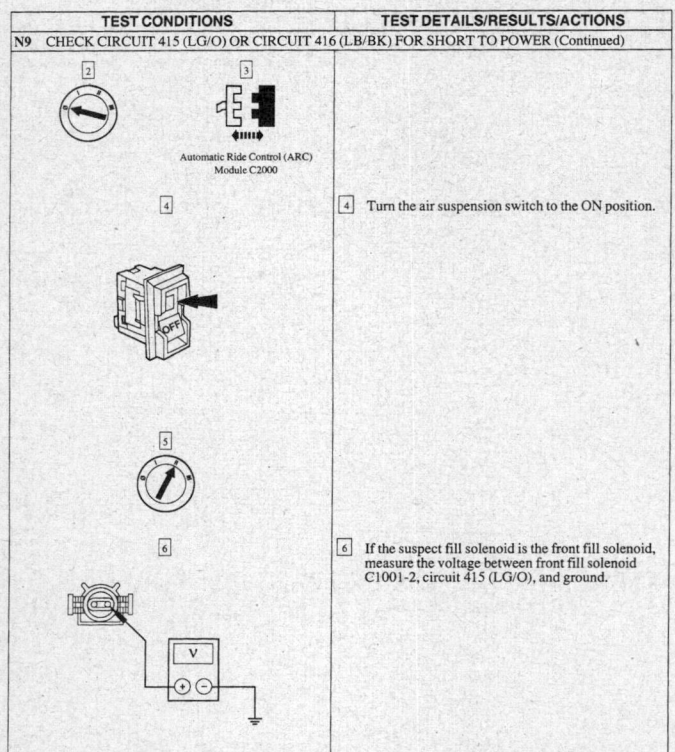

Automatic Ride Control (ARC) Module C2000

FM2019700640070X

Fig. 18 Test N/DTC C1845 & C1865: Front-Rear Fill Solenoid Circuit Fault (Part 7 of 15)

TEST CONDITIONS	TEST DETAILS/RESULTS/ACTIONS
N8 CHECK CIRCUIT 415 (LG/O) OR CIRCUIT 416 (LB/BK) FOR SHORT TO GROUND (Continued)	

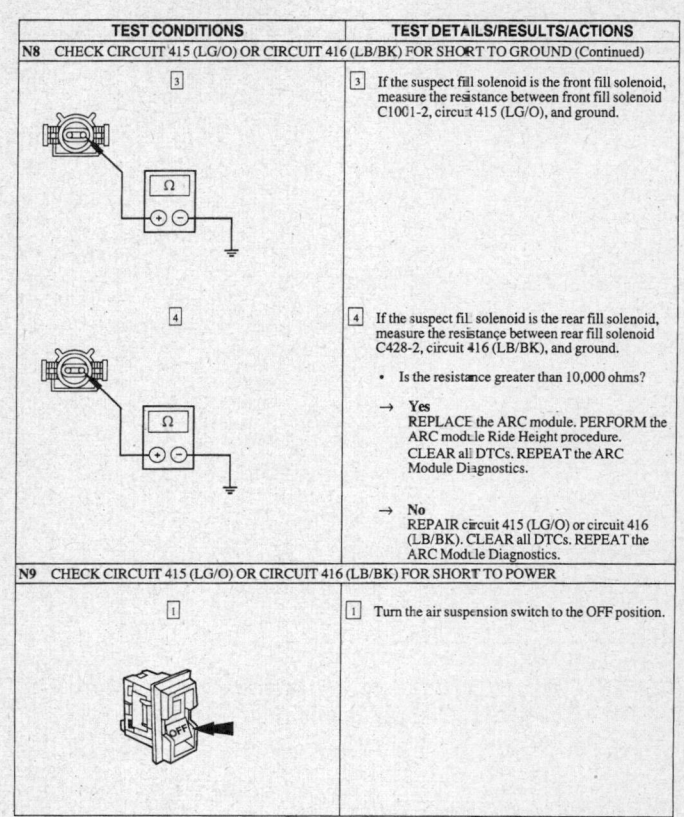

3 If the suspect fill solenoid is the front fill solenoid, measure the resistance between front fill solenoid C1001-2, circuit 415 (LG/O), and ground.

4 If the suspect fill solenoid is the rear fill solenoid, measure the resistance between rear fill solenoid C428-2, circuit 416 (LB/BK), and ground.

- Is the resistance greater than 10,000 ohms?

→ **Yes**
REPLACE the ARC module. PERFORM the ARC module Ride Height procedure. CLEAR all DTCs. REPEAT the ARC Module Diagnostics.

→ **No**
REPAIR circuit 415 (LG/O) or circuit 416 (LB/BK). CLEAR all DTCs. REPEAT the ARC Module Diagnostics.

N9 CHECK CIRCUIT 415 (LG/O) OR CIRCUIT 416 (LB/BK) FOR SHORT TO POWER	

1 Turn the air suspension switch to the OFF position.

FM2019700640080X

Fig. 18 Test N/DTC C1845 & C1865: Front-Rear Fill Solenoid Circuit Fault (Part 8 of 15)

TEST CONDITIONS	TEST DETAILS/RESULTS/ACTIONS
N9 CHECK CIRCUIT 415 (LG/O) OR CIRCUIT 416 (LB/BK) FOR SHORT TO POWER (Continued)	

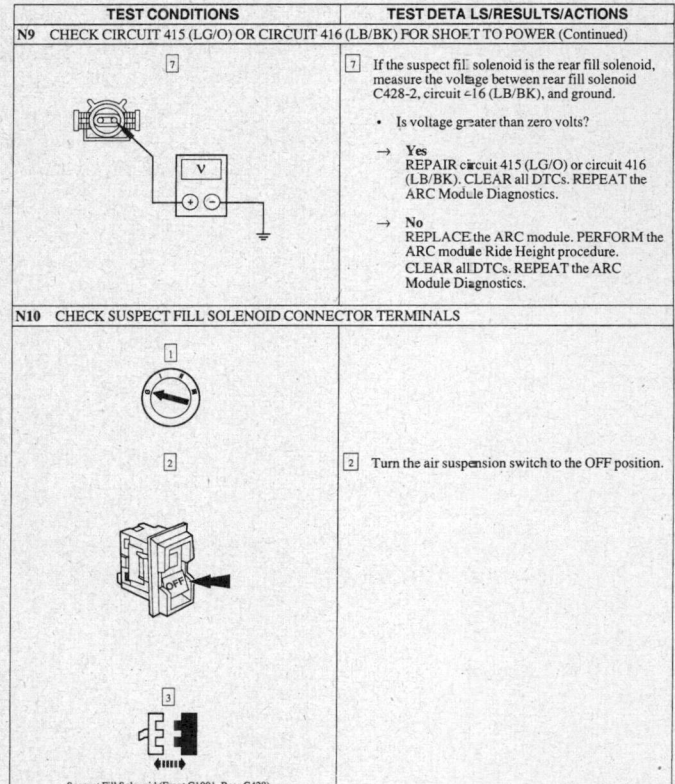

Automatic Ride Control (ARC) Module C2000

4 Turn the air suspension switch to the ON position.

6 If the suspect fill solenoid is the front fill solenoid, measure the voltage between front fill solenoid C1001-2, circuit 415 (LG/O), and ground.

FM2019700640090X

Fig. 18 Test N/DTC C1845 & C1865: Front-Rear Fill Solenoid Circuit Fault (Part 9 of 15)

TEST CONDITIONS	TEST DETAILS/RESULTS/ACTIONS
N9 CHECK CIRCUIT 415 (LG/O) OR CIRCUIT 416 (LB/BK) FOR SHORT TO POWER (Continued)	

7 If the suspect fill solenoid is the rear fill solenoid, measure the voltage between rear fill solenoid C428-2, circuit 416 (LB/BK), and ground.

- Is voltage greater than zero volts?

→ **Yes**
REPAIR circuit 415 (LG/O) or circuit 416 (LB/BK). CLEAR all DTCs. REPEAT the ARC Module Diagnostics.

→ **No**
REPLACE the ARC module. PERFORM the ARC module Ride Height procedure. CLEAR all DTCs. REPEAT the ARC Module Diagnostics.

N10 CHECK SUSPECT FILL SOLENOID CONNECTOR TERMINALS	

2 Turn the air suspension switch to the OFF position.

Suspect Fill Solenoid (Front C1001, Rear C428)

FM2019700640100X

Fig. 18 Test N/DTC C1845 & C1865: Front-Rear Fill Solenoid Circuit Fault (Part 10 of 15)

TEST CONDITIONS	TEST DETAILS/RESULTS/ACTIONS
N10 CHECK SUSPECT FILL SOLENOID CONNECTOR TERMINALS (Continued)	
	4 Inspect the pins and terminals of the suspect fill solenoid connector for corrosion, bent or broken pins, moisture, or other damage. • Are the connectors and pins OK? → **Yes** RECONNECT the suspect fill solenoid. GO to **N11**. → **No** REPLACE the parts as necessary. CLEAR all DTCs. REPEAT the ARC Module Diagnostics.
N11 CHECK CIRCUIT 415 (LG/O) OR CIRCUIT 416 (LB/BK) FOR INTERMITTENT CONDITION	
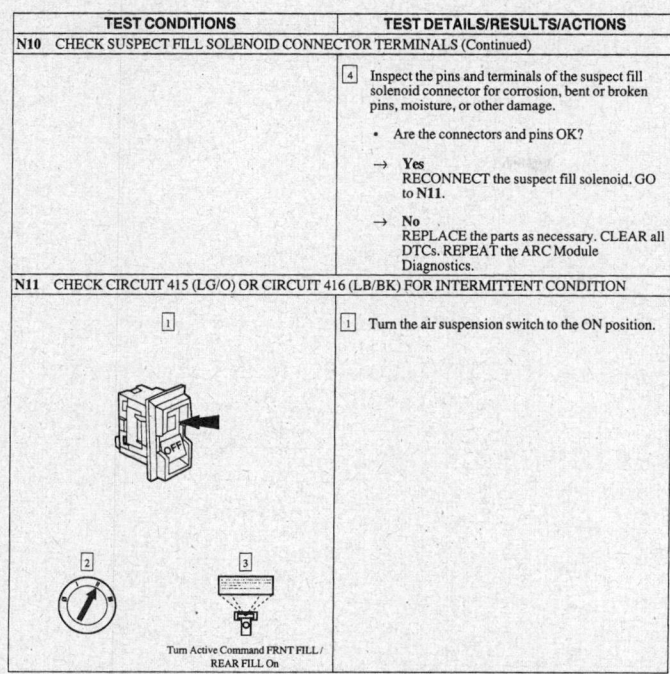	**1** Turn the air suspension switch to the ON position.

FM2019700640110X

Fig. 18   Test N/DTC C1845 & C1865: Front-Rear Fill Solenoid Circuit Fault (Part 11 of 15)

TEST CONDITIONS	TEST DETAILS/RESULTS/ACTIONS
N11 CHECK CIRCUIT 415 (LG/O) OR CIRCUIT 416 (LB/BK) FOR INTERMITTENT CONDITION (Continued)	
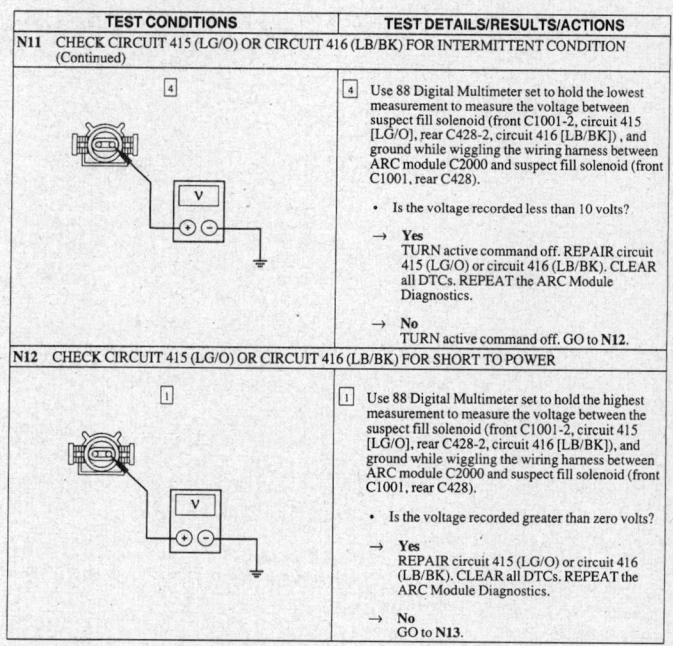	**4** Use 88 Digital Multimeter set to hold the lowest measurement to measure the voltage between suspect fill solenoid (front C1001-2, circuit 415 [LG/O], rear C428-2, circuit 416 [LB/BK]) , and ground while wiggling the wiring harness between ARC module C2000 and suspect fill solenoid (front C1001, rear C428). • Is the voltage recorded less than 10 volts? → **Yes** TURN active command off. REPAIR circuit 415 (LG/O) or circuit 416 (LB/BK). CLEAR all DTCs. REPEAT the ARC Module Diagnostics. → **No** TURN active command off. GO to **N12**.
N12 CHECK CIRCUIT 415 (LG/O) OR CIRCUIT 416 (LB/BK) FOR SHORT TO POWER	
	1 Use 88 Digital Multimeter set to hold the highest measurement to measure the voltage between suspect fill solenoid (front C1001-2, circuit 415 [LG/O], rear C428-2, circuit 416 [LB/BK]), and ground while wiggling the wiring harness between ARC module C2000 and suspect fill solenoid (front C1001, rear C428). • Is the voltage recorded greater than zero volts? → **Yes** REPAIR circuit 415 (LG/O) or circuit 416 (LB/BK). CLEAR all DTCs. REPEAT the ARC Module Diagnostics. → **No** GO to **N13**.

FM2019700640120X

Fig. 18   Test N/DTC C1845 & C1865: Front-Rear Fill Solenoid Circuit Fault (Part 12 of 15)

TEST CONDITIONS	TEST DETAILS/RESULTS/ACTIONS
N13 CHECK INTERMITTENT MODULE FUNCTION	
	2 Turn the air suspension switch to the OFF position.
	3 Remove circuit 415 (LG/O) from ARC module C2000-15 (front) or circuit 416 (LB/BK) from ARC module C2000-17 (rear) (with connector connected to ARC module).

FM2019700640130X

Fig. 18   Test N/DTC C1845 & C1865: Front-Rear Fill Solenoid Circuit Fault (Part 13 of 15)

TEST CONDITIONS	TEST DETAILS/RESULTS/ACTIONS
N13 CHECK INTERMITTENT MODULE FUNCTION (Continued)	
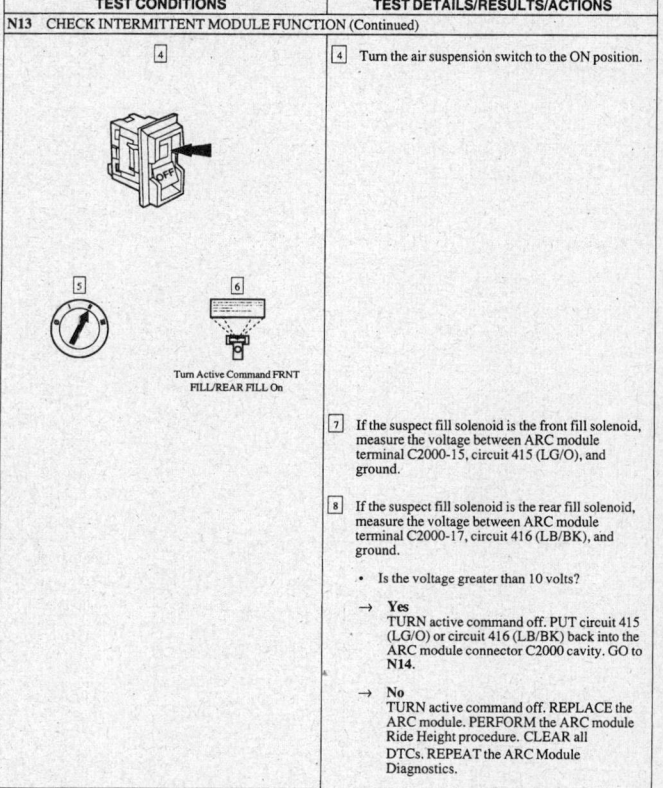	**4** Turn the air suspension switch to the ON position.
	7 If the suspect fill solenoid is the front fill solenoid, measure the voltage between ARC module terminal C2000-15, circuit 415 (LG/O), and ground.
	8 If the suspect fill solenoid is the rear fill solenoid, measure the voltage between ARC module terminal C2000-17, circuit 416 (LB/BK), and ground. • Is the voltage greater than 10 volts? → **Yes** TURN active command off. PUT circuit 415 (LG/O) or circuit 416 (LB/BK) back into the ARC module connector C2000 cavity. GO to **N14**. → **No** TURN active command off. REPLACE the ARC module. PERFORM the ARC module Ride Height procedure. CLEAR all DTCs. REPEAT the ARC Module Diagnostics.

FM2019700640140X

Fig. 18   Test N/DTC C1845 & C1865: Front-Rear Fill Solenoid Circuit Fault (Part 14 of 15)

TEST CONDITIONS	TEST DETAILS/RESULTS/ACTIONS
N14 PERFORM ROAD TEST	

<table>
<tr><td>1
Monitor F__FILL/R__FILL PID</td><td></td></tr>
<tr><td></td><td>2 Take the vehicle for a 10-minute test drive over rough roads and/or through a car wash. During the test drive, shift between 2WD to 4WD and back.

• Do the letters O, G, or B appear next to the ON/OFF text for F__FILL or R__FILL?

→ Yes
If O appeared, GO to N4.

If G appeared, GO to N7.

If B appeared, GO to N9.

→ No
CLEAR all DTCs and REPEAT the road test.</td></tr>
</table>

FM2019700640150X

Fig. 18   Test N/DTC C1845 & C1865: Front-Rear Fill Solenoid Circuit Fault (Part 15 of 15)

TEST CONDITIONS	TEST DETAILS/RESULTS/ACTIONS
P1 PERFORM ON-DEMAND SELF-TEST (Continued)	

<table>
<tr><td>3
On-Demand Self-Test</td><td></td></tr>
<tr><td></td><td>• Is the DTC C1869 set at the end of the On-Demand Self-Test?

→ Yes
GO to P2.

→ No
GO to P10.</td></tr>
<tr><td colspan="2">P2   CHECK REAR GATE SOLENOID CONNECTOR</td></tr>
<tr><td>1</td><td></td></tr>
<tr><td>2</td><td>2 Turn the air suspension switch to the OFF position.</td></tr>
<tr><td>3
Rear Gate Solenoid C429</td><td></td></tr>
</table>

FM2019700641020X

Fig. 19   Test P/DTC C1869: Rear Gate Solenoid Circuit Fault (Part 2 of 14)

TEST CONDITIONS	TEST DETAILS/RESULTS/ACTIONS
P1 PERFORM ON-DEMAND SELF-TEST	

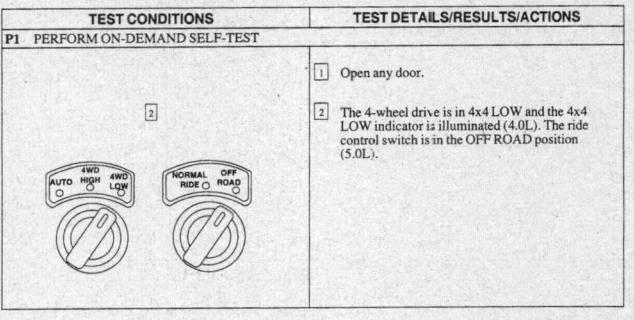

<table>
<tr><td></td><td>1 Open any door.</td></tr>
<tr><td>2</td><td>2 The 4-wheel drive is in 4x4 LOW and the 4x4 LOW indicator is illuminated (4.0L). The ride control switch is in the OFF ROAD position (5.0L).</td></tr>
</table>

FM2019700641010X

Fig. 19   Test P/DTC C1869: Rear Gate Solenoid Circuit Fault (Part 1 of 14)

TEST CONDITIONS	TEST DETAILS/RESULTS/ACTIONS
P2 CHECK REAR GATE SOLENOID CONNECTOR (Continued)	

<table>
<tr><td>4</td><td>4 Inspect the pins and terminals of the rear gate solenoid connector for corrosion, bent or broken pins, moisture, or other damage.

• Is the rear gate solenoid C429 OK?

→ Yes
RECONNECT the rear gate solenoid. GO to P3.

→ No
REPAIR or REPLACE connector as necessary. CLEAR all DTCs. REPEAT the ARC Module Diagnostics.</td></tr>
<tr><td colspan="2">P3   PERFORM RIDE CONTROL OUTPUT</td></tr>
<tr><td>1</td><td>1 Turn the air suspension switch to the ON position.</td></tr>
<tr><td>2   3</td><td>3 Select the active commands and monitor the PID AS__GATE.</td></tr>
</table>

FM2019700641030X

Fig. 19   Test P/DTC C1869: Rear Gate Solenoid Circuit Fault (Part 3 of 14)

TEST CONDITIONS	TEST DETAILS/RESULTS/ACTIONS
P3 PERFORM RIDE CONTROL OUTPUT (Continued)	

<table>
<tr><td>4</td><td>4 Use the active commands and toggle the following commands in the given sequence:
— GATEVALVE to ON.
— REAR FILL to ON.
— GATEVALVE to OFF.
— REAR FILL to OFF.

• Do the letters O, G, or B appear next to the ON/OFF text for the rear gate solenoid?

→ Yes
If O appeared, GO to P4.

If G appeared, GO to P7.

If B appeared, GO to P9.

→ No
GO to P10.</td></tr>
<tr><td colspan="2">P4   CHECK REAR GATE SOLENOID COIL FOR OPEN</td></tr>
<tr><td>1   2
Rear Gate Solenoid C429</td><td></td></tr>
<tr><td>3</td><td>3 Measure the resistance between rear gate solenoid terminals.

• Is the resistance less than 20 ohms?

→ Yes
GO to P5.

→ No
REPLACE the rear gate solenoid. CLEAR all DTCs, REPEAT the ARC Module Diagnostics.</td></tr>
</table>

FM2019700641040X

Fig. 19   Test P/DTC C1869: Rear Gate Solenoid Circuit Fault (Part 4 of 14)

TEST CONDITIONS		TEST DETAILS/RESULTS/ACTIONS
P5 CHECK CIRCUIT 57 (BK)		

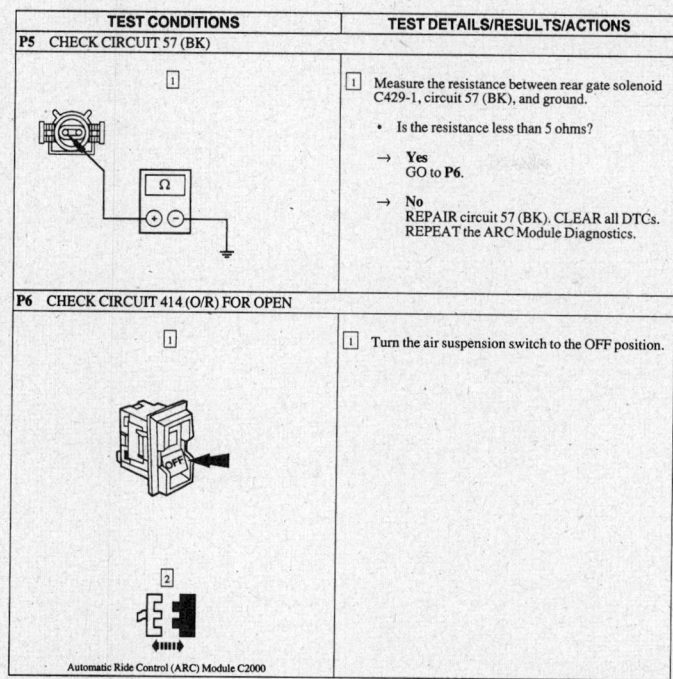

1	Measure the resistance between rear gate solenoid C429-1, circuit 57 (BK), and ground. • Is the resistance less than 5 ohms? → **Yes** GO to **P6**. → **No** REPAIR circuit 57 (BK). CLEAR all DTCs. REPEAT the ARC Module Diagnostics.

TEST CONDITIONS		TEST DETAILS/RESULTS/ACTIONS
P6 CHECK CIRCUIT 414 (O/R) FOR OPEN		

1	Turn the air suspension switch to the OFF position.

Automatic Ride Control (ARC) Module C2000

FM2019700641050X

Fig. 19   Test P/DTC C1869: Rear Gate Solenoid Circuit Fault (Part 5 of 14)

TEST CONDITIONS		TEST DETAILS/RESULTS/ACTIONS
P6 CHECK CIRCUIT 414 (O/R) FOR OPEN (Continued)		

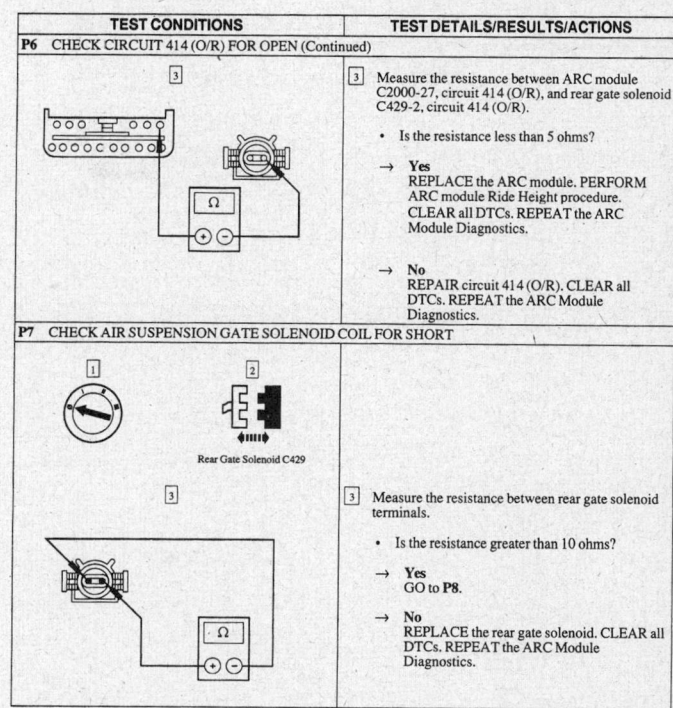

3	Measure the resistance between ARC module C2000-27, circuit 414 (O/R), and rear gate solenoid C429-2, circuit 414 (O/R). • Is the resistance less than 5 ohms? → **Yes** REPLACE the ARC module. PERFORM ARC module Ride Height procedure. CLEAR all DTCs. REPEAT the ARC Module Diagnostics. → **No** REPAIR circuit 414 (O/R). CLEAR all DTCs. REPEAT the ARC Module Diagnostics.

TEST CONDITIONS		TEST DETAILS/RESULTS/ACTIONS
P7 CHECK AIR SUSPENSION GATE SOLENOID COIL FOR SHORT		

Rear Gate Solenoid C429

3	Measure the resistance between rear gate solenoid terminals. • Is the resistance greater than 10 ohms? → **Yes** GO to **P8**. → **No** REPLACE the rear gate solenoid. CLEAR all DTCs. REPEAT the ARC Module Diagnostics.

FM2019700641060X

Fig. 19   Test P/DTC C1869: Rear Gate Solenoid Circuit Fault (Part 6 of 14)

TEST CONDITIONS		TEST DETAILS/RESULTS/ACTIONS
P8 CHECK CIRCUIT 414 (O/R)		

1	Turn the air suspension to the OFF position.

Automatic Ride Control (ARC) Module C2000

3	Measure the resistance between ARC module C2000-27, circuit 414 (O/R), and ground. • Is the resistance greater than 10,000 ohms? → **Yes** REPLACE the ARC module. PERFORM ARC module Ride Height procedure. CLEAR all DTCs. REPEAT the ARC Module Diagnostics. → **No** REPAIR circuit 414 (O/R). CLEAR all DTCs. REPEAT the ARC Module Diagnostics.

FM2019700641070X

Fig. 19   Test P/DTC C1869: Rear Gate Solenoid Circuit Fault (Part 7 of 14)

TEST CONDITIONS		TEST DETAILS/RESULTS/ACTIONS
P9 CHECK CIRCUIT 414 (O/R) FOR SHORT TO POWER		

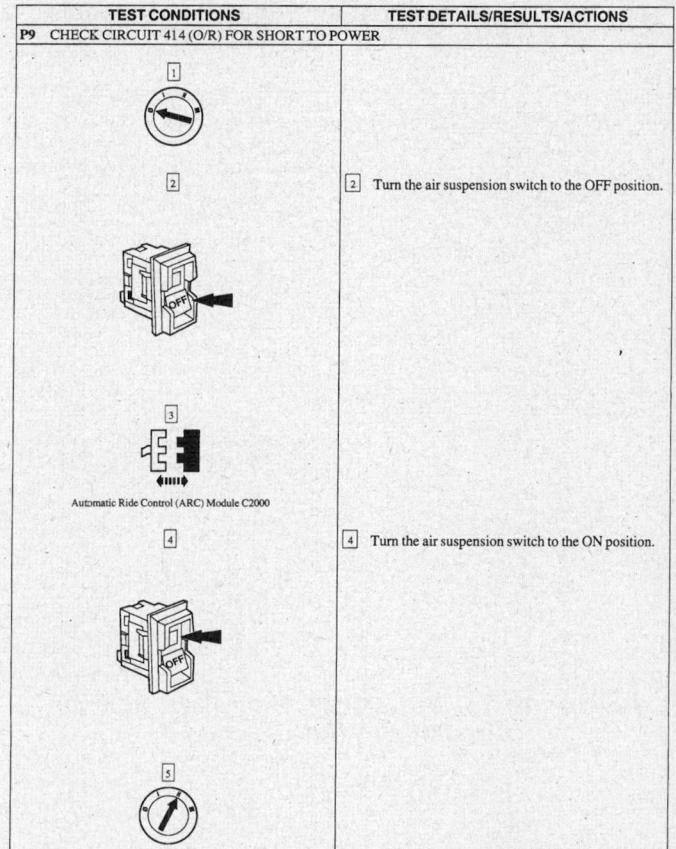

2	Turn the air suspension switch to the OFF position.

Automatic Ride Control (ARC) Module C2000

4	Turn the air suspension switch to the ON position.

FM2019700641080X

Fig. 19   Test P/DTC C1869: Rear Gate Solenoid Circuit Fault (Part 8 of 14)

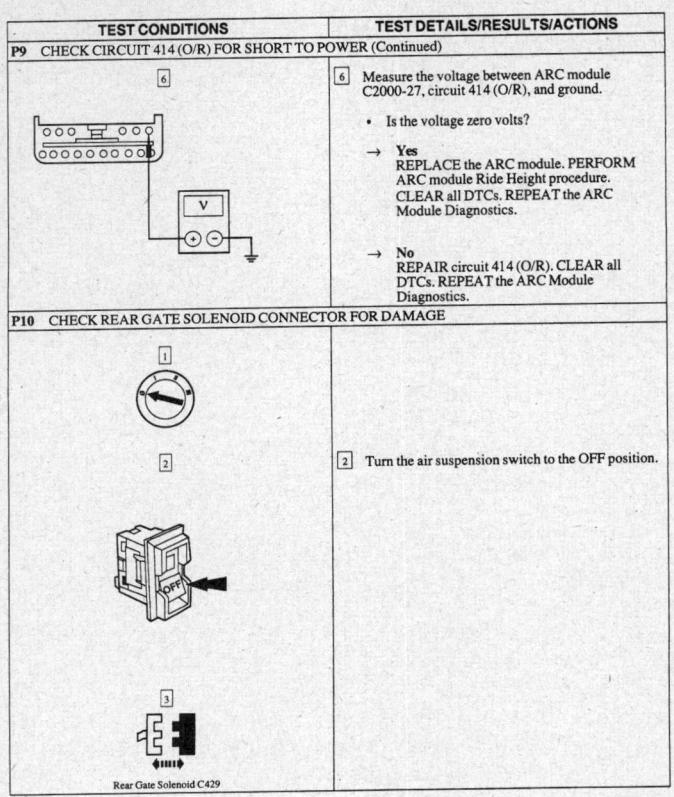

TEST CONDITIONS	TEST DETAILS/RESULTS/ACTIONS
P9 CHECK CIRCUIT 414 (O/R) FOR SHORT TO POWER (Continued)	
[6]	[6] Measure the voltage between ARC module C2000-27, circuit 414 (O/R), and ground. • Is the voltage zero volts? → **Yes** REPLACE the ARC module. PERFORM ARC module Ride Height procedure. CLEAR all DTCs. REPEAT the ARC Module Diagnostics. → **No** REPAIR circuit 414 (O/R). CLEAR all DTCs. REPEAT the ARC Module Diagnostics.
P10 CHECK REAR GATE SOLENOID CONNECTOR FOR DAMAGE	
[1] [2] [3] Rear Gate Solenoid C429	[2] Turn the air suspension switch to the OFF position.

FM2019700641090X

Fig. 19   Test P/DTC C1869: Rear Gate Solenoid Circuit Fault (Part 9 of 14)

TEST CONDITIONS	TEST DETAILS/RESULTS/ACTIONS
P11 CHECK REAR GATE SOLENOID FOR INTERMITTENT FAILURE (Continued)	
[4]	[4] Use 88 Digital Multimeter set to hold the lowest measurement to measure the voltage between rear gate solenoid C429-2, circuit 414 (O/R) , and ground while wiggling the wiring harness between ARC module C2000 and rear gate solenoid C429. • Is the voltage recorded less than 10 volts? → **Yes** TURN active command GATEVALVE off. REPAIR circuit 414 (O/R). CLEAR all DTCs. REPEAT the ARC Module Diagnostics. → **No** TURN active command GATEVALVE off. GO to **P12**.
P12 CHECK CIRCUIT 414 (O/R) FOR SHORT TO POWER	
[1]	[1] Use 88 Digital Multimeter set to hold the highest measurement to measure the voltage between rear gate solenoid C429-2, circuit 414 (O/R), and ground while wiggling the wiring harness between ARC module C2000 and rear gate solenoid C429. • Is the voltage recorded greater than zero volts? → **Yes** REPAIR circuit 414 (O/R). CLEAR all DTCs. REPEAT the ARC Module Diagnostics. → **No** GO to **P13**.

FM2019700641110X

Fig. 19   Test P/DTC C1869: Rear Gate Solenoid Circuit Fault (Part 11 of 14)

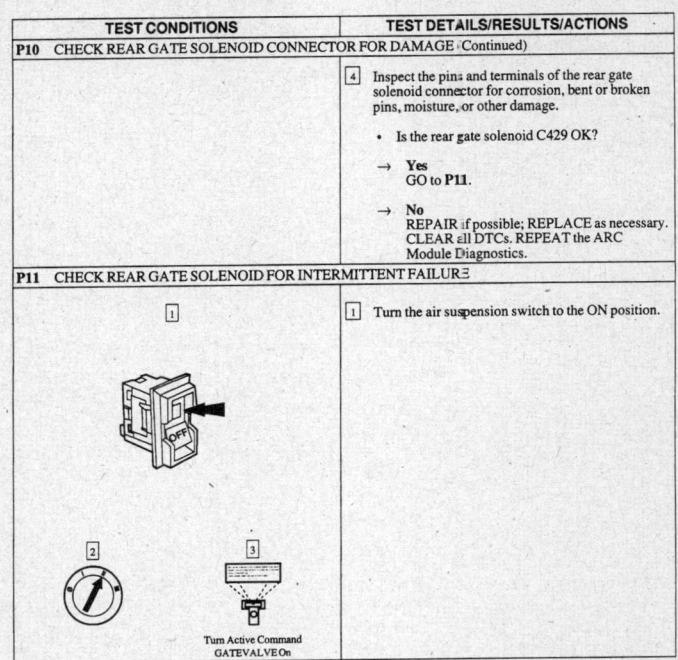

TEST CONDITIONS	TEST DETAILS/RESULTS/ACTIONS
P10 CHECK REAR GATE SOLENOID CONNECTOR FOR DAMAGE (Continued)	
[4]	[4] Inspect the pins and terminals of the rear gate solenoid connector for corrosion, bent or broken pins, moisture, or other damage. • Is the rear gate solenoid C429 OK? → **Yes** GO to **P11**. → **No** REPAIR if possible; REPLACE as necessary. CLEAR all DTCs. REPEAT the ARC Module Diagnostics.
P11 CHECK REAR GATE SOLENOID FOR INTERMITTENT FAILURE	
[1] [2] [3] Turn Active Command GATEVALVE On	[1] Turn the air suspension switch to the ON position.

FM2019700641100X

Fig. 19   Test P/DTC C1869: Rear Gate Solenoid Circuit Fault (Part 10 of 14)

TEST CONDITIONS	TEST DETAILS/RESULTS/ACTIONS
P13 CHECK INTERMITTENT MODULE FUNCTION	
[1] [2] 	[2] Turn the air suspension switch to the OFF position. [3] Remove circuit 414 (O/R) from ARC module C2000-27 (with connector connected to ARC module).

FM2019700641120X

Fig. 19   Test P/DTC C1869: Rear Gate Solenoid Circuit Fault (Part 12 of 14)

TEST CONDITIONS	TEST DETAILS/RESULTS/ACTIONS
P13 CHECK INTERMITTENT MODULE FUNCTION (Continued)	

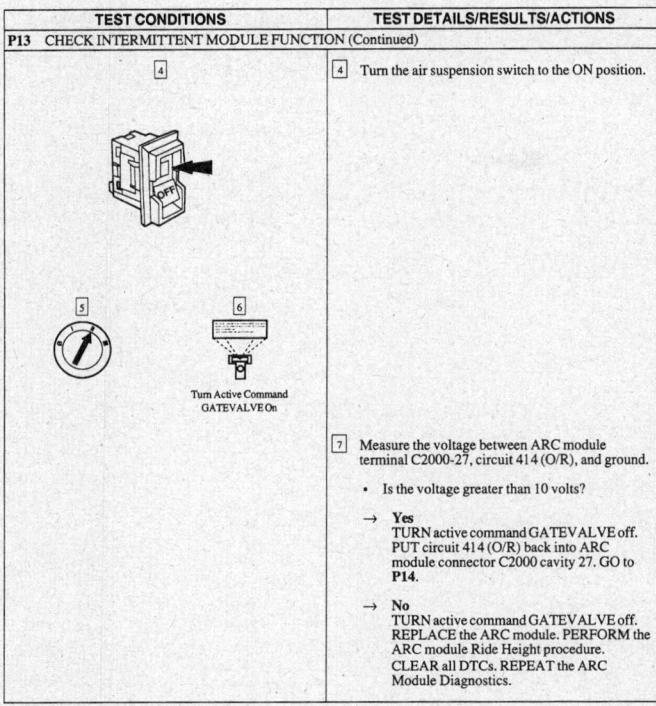

4	4 Turn the air suspension switch to the ON position.
5 6 Turn Active Command GATEVALVE On	7 Measure the voltage between ARC module terminal C2000-27, circuit 414 (O/R), and ground. • Is the voltage greater than 10 volts? → **Yes** TURN active command GATEVALVE off. PUT circuit 414 (O/R) back into ARC module connector C2000 cavity 27. GO to **P14**. → **No** TURN active command GATEVALVE off. REPLACE the ARC module. PERFORM the ARC module Ride Height procedure. CLEAR all DTCs. REPEAT the ARC Module Diagnostics.

FM2019700641130X

Fig. 19 Test P/DTC C1869: Rear Gate Solenoid Circuit Fault (Part 13 of 14)

TEST CONDITIONS	TEST DETAILS/RESULTS/ACTIONS
Q1 CHECK RR SHOCK ABSORBER MOTOR POWER	

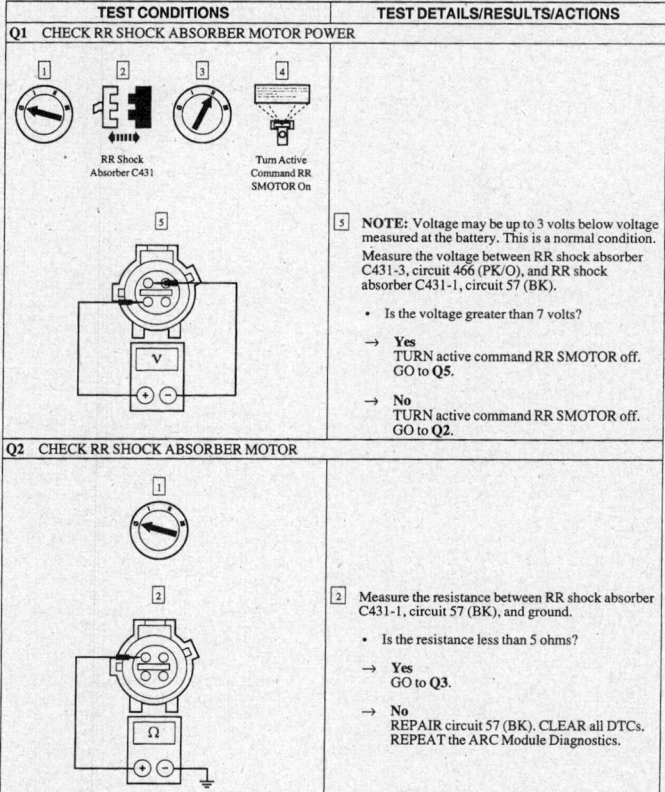

1 2 3 4 RR Shock Absorber C431 Turn Active Command RR SMOTOR On	
5 V	5 **NOTE:** Voltage may be up to 3 volts below voltage measured at the battery. This is a normal condition. Measure the voltage between RR shock absorber C431-3, circuit 466 (PK/O), and RR shock absorber C431-1, circuit 57 (BK). • Is the voltage greater than 7 volts? → **Yes** TURN active command RR SMOTOR off. GO to **Q5**. → **No** TURN active command RR SMOTOR off. GO to **Q2**.
Q2 CHECK RR SHOCK ABSORBER MOTOR	
1 2 Ω	2 Measure the resistance between RR shock absorber C431-1, circuit 57 (BK), and ground. • Is the resistance less than 5 ohms? → **Yes** GO to **Q3**. → **No** REPAIR circuit 57 (BK). CLEAR all DTCs. REPEAT the ARC Module Diagnostics.

FM2019700642010X

Fig. 20 Test Q/DTC C1901: Righthand Rear Shock Absorber Circuit Fault (Part 1 of 4)

TEST CONDITIONS	TEST DETAILS/RESULTS/ACTIONS
P14 PERFORM ROAD TEST	

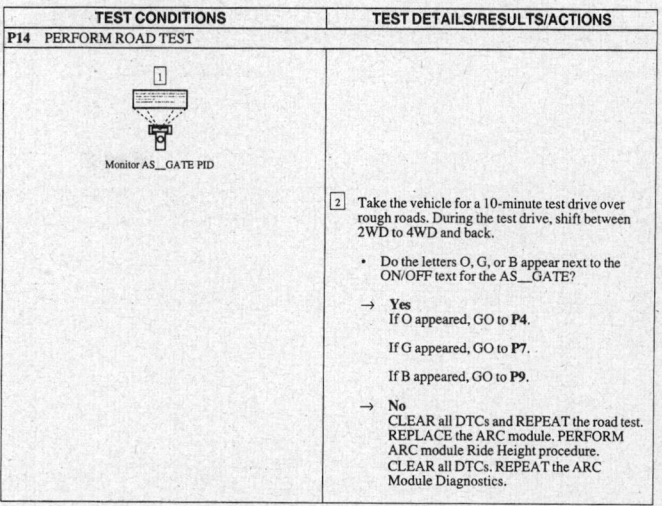

1 Monitor AS__GATE PID	2 Take the vehicle for a 10-minute test drive over rough roads. During the test drive, shift between 2WD to 4WD and back. • Do the letters O, G, or B appear next to the ON/OFF text for the AS__GATE? → **Yes** If O appeared, GO to **P4**. If G appeared, GO to **P7**. If B appeared, GO to **P9**. → **No** CLEAR all DTCs and REPEAT the road test. REPLACE the ARC module. PERFORM ARC module Ride Height procedure. CLEAR all DTCs. REPEAT the ARC Module Diagnostics.

FM2019700641140X

Fig. 19 Test P/DTC C1869: Rear Gate Solenoid Circuit Fault (Part 14 of 14)

TEST CONDITIONS	TEST DETAILS/RESULTS/ACTIONS
Q3 CHECK CIRCUIT 466 (PK/O) FOR OPEN	

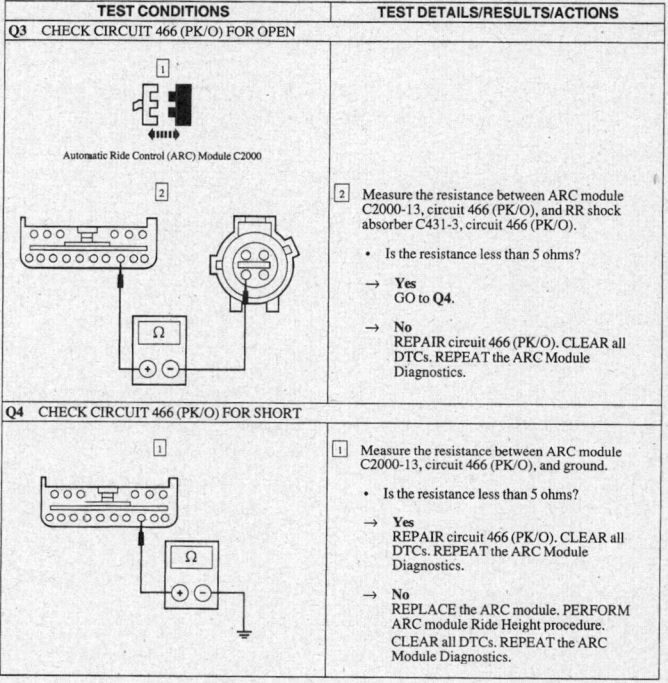

1 Automatic Ride Control (ARC) Module C2000	
2 Ω	2 Measure the resistance between ARC module C2000-13, circuit 466 (PK/O), and RR shock absorber C431-3, circuit 466 (PK/O). • Is the resistance less than 5 ohms? → **Yes** GO to **Q4**. → **No** REPAIR circuit 466 (PK/O). CLEAR all DTCs. REPEAT the ARC Module Diagnostics.
Q4 CHECK CIRCUIT 466 (PK/O) FOR SHORT	
1 Ω	1 Measure the resistance between ARC module C2000-13, circuit 466 (PK/O), and ground. • Is the resistance less than 5 ohms? → **Yes** REPAIR circuit 466 (PK/O). CLEAR all DTCs. REPEAT the ARC Module Diagnostics. → **No** REPLACE the ARC module. PERFORM ARC module Ride Height procedure. CLEAR all DTCs. REPEAT the ARC Module Diagnostics.

FM2019700642020X

Fig. 20 Test Q/DTC C1901: Righthand Rear Shock Absorber Circuit Fault (Part 2 of 4)

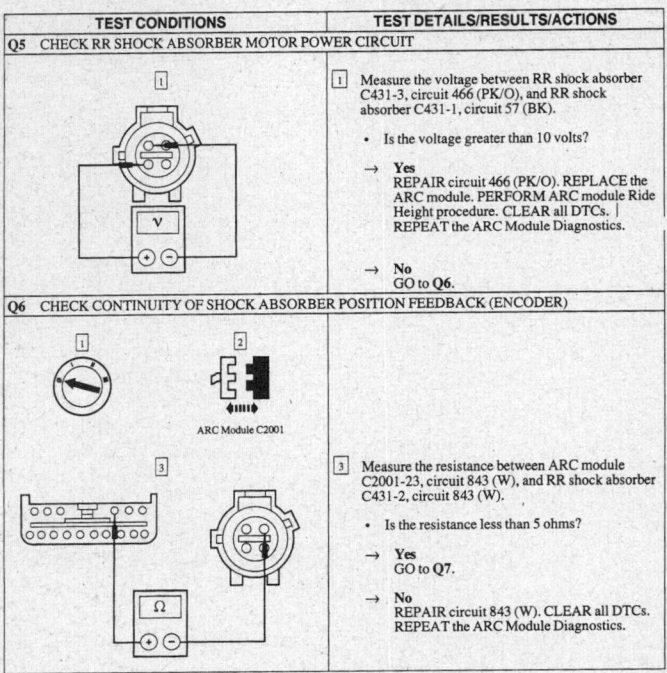

TEST CONDITIONS	TEST DETAILS/RESULTS/ACTIONS

Q5 CHECK RR SHOCK ABSORBER MOTOR POWER CIRCUIT	[1] Measure the voltage between RR shock absorber C431-3, circuit 466 (PK/O), and RR shock absorber C431-1, circuit 57 (BK).
	
	• Is the voltage greater than 10 volts?
	
	→ **Yes**
	  REPAIR circuit 466 (PK/O). REPLACE the ARC module. PERFORM ARC module Ride Height procedure. CLEAR all DTCs. REPEAT the ARC Module Diagnostics.
	
	→ **No**
	  GO to **Q6**.

Q6 CHECK CONTINUITY OF SHOCK ABSORBER POSITION FEEDBACK (ENCODER)	[3] Measure the resistance between ARC module C2001-23, circuit 843 (W), and RR shock absorber C431-2, circuit 843 (W).
	
	• Is the resistance less than 5 ohms?
	
	→ **Yes**
	  GO to **Q7**.
	
	→ **No**
	  REPAIR circuit 843 (W). CLEAR all DTCs. REPEAT the ARC Module Diagnostics.

FM2019700642030X

Fig. 20   Test Q/DTC C1901: Righthand Rear Shock Absorber Circuit Fault (Part 3 of 4)

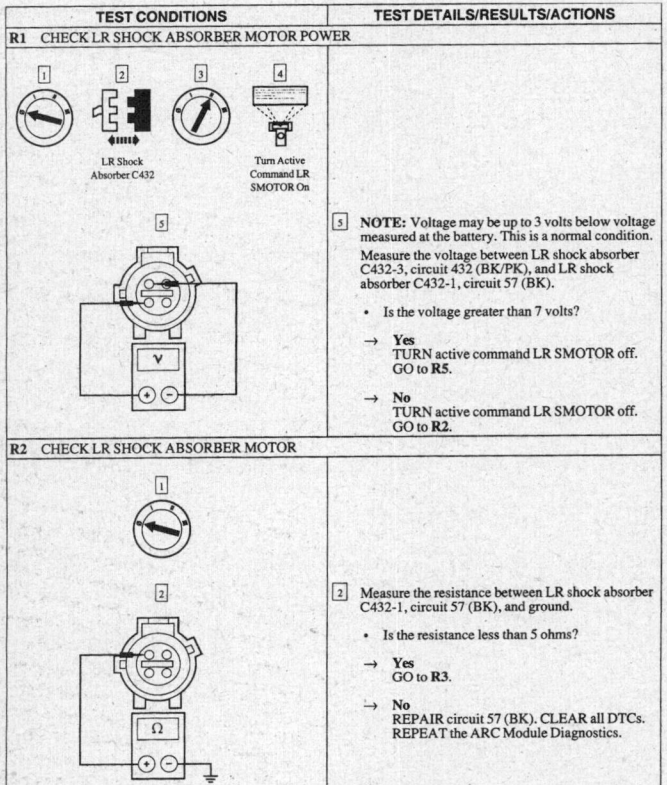

TEST CONDITIONS	TEST DETAILS/RESULTS/ACTIONS

R1 CHECK LR SHOCK ABSORBER MOTOR POWER	[5] **NOTE:** Voltage may be up to 3 volts below voltage measured at the battery. This is a normal condition.
	Measure the voltage between LR shock absorber C432-3, circuit 432 (BK/PK), and LR shock absorber C432-1, circuit 57 (BK).
	
	• Is the voltage greater than 7 volts?
	
	→ **Yes**
	  TURN active command LR SMOTOR off. GO to **R5**.
	
	→ **No**
	  TURN active command LR SMOTOR off. GO to **R2**.

R2 CHECK LR SHOCK ABSORBER MOTOR	[2] Measure the resistance between LR shock absorber C432-1, circuit 57 (BK), and ground.
	
	• Is the resistance less than 5 ohms?
	
	→ **Yes**
	  GO to **R3**.
	
	→ **No**
	  REPAIR circuit 57 (BK). CLEAR all DTCs. REPEAT the ARC Module Diagnostics.

FM2019700643010X

Fig. 21   Test R/DTC C1905: Lefthand Rear Shock Absorber Circuit Fault (Part 1 of 4)

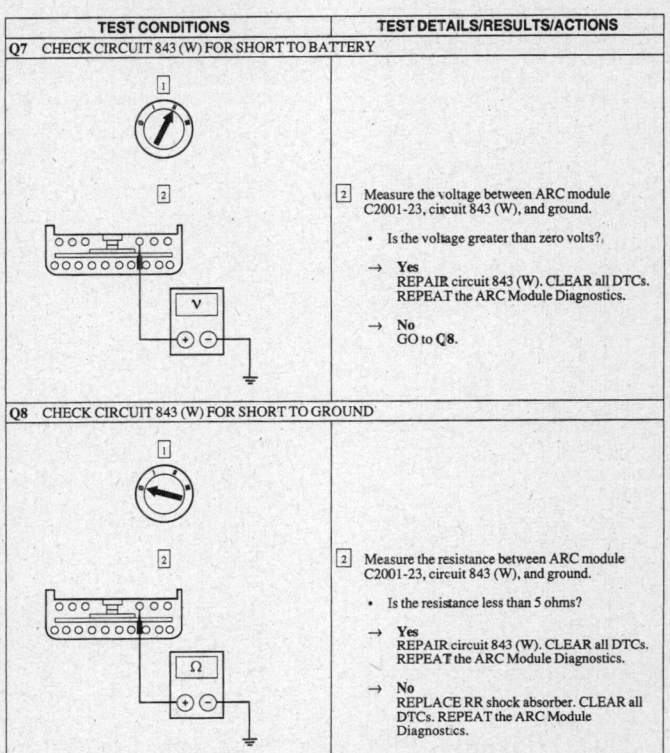

TEST CONDITIONS	TEST DETAILS/RESULTS/ACTIONS

Q7 CHECK CIRCUIT 843 (W) FOR SHORT TO BATTERY	[2] Measure the voltage between ARC module C2001-23, circuit 843 (W), and ground.
	
	• Is the voltage greater than zero volts?
	
	→ **Yes**
	  REPAIR circuit 843 (W). CLEAR all DTCs. REPEAT the ARC Module Diagnostics.
	
	→ **No**
	  GO to **Q8**.

Q8 CHECK CIRCUIT 843 (W) FOR SHORT TO GROUND	[2] Measure the resistance between ARC module C2001-23, circuit 843 (W), and ground.
	
	• Is the resistance less than 5 ohms?
	
	→ **Yes**
	  REPAIR circuit 843 (W). CLEAR all DTCs. REPEAT the ARC Module Diagnostics.
	
	→ **No**
	  REPLACE RR shock absorber. CLEAR all DTCs. REPEAT the ARC Module Diagnostics.

FM2019700642040X

Fig. 20   Test Q/DTC C1901: Righthand Rear Shock Absorber Circuit Fault (Part 4 of 4)

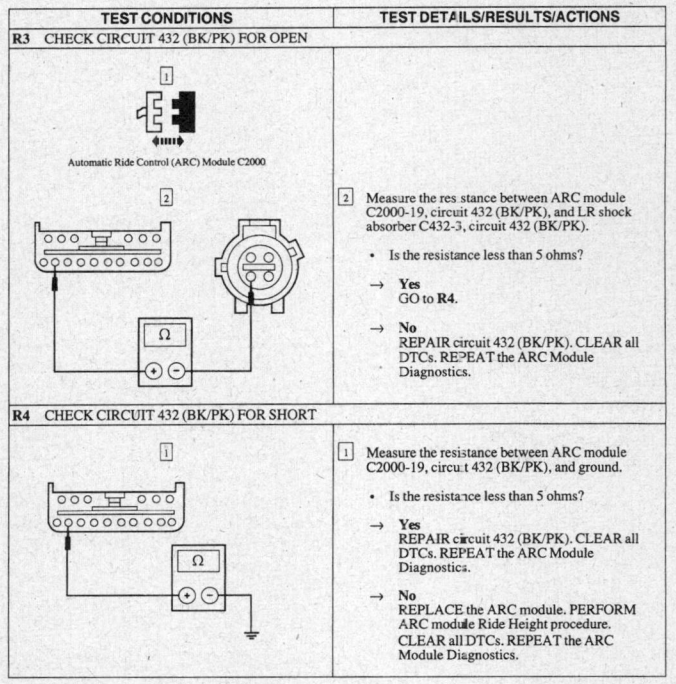

TEST CONDITIONS	TEST DETAILS/RESULTS/ACTIONS

R3 CHECK CIRCUIT 432 (BK/PK) FOR OPEN	[2] Measure the resistance between ARC module C2000-19, circuit 432 (BK/PK), and LR shock absorber C432-3, circuit 432 (BK/PK).
	
	• Is the resistance less than 5 ohms?
	
	→ **Yes**
	  GO to **R4**.
	
	→ **No**
	  REPAIR circuit 432 (BK/PK). CLEAR all DTCs. REPEAT the ARC Module Diagnostics.

R4 CHECK CIRCUIT 432 (BK/PK) FOR SHORT	[1] Measure the resistance between ARC module C2000-19, circuit 432 (BK/PK), and ground.
	
	• Is the resistance less than 5 ohms?
	
	→ **Yes**
	  REPAIR circuit 432 (BK/PK). CLEAR all DTCs. REPEAT the ARC Module Diagnostics.
	
	→ **No**
	  REPLACE the ARC module. PERFORM ARC module Ride Height procedure. CLEAR all DTCs. REPEAT the ARC Module Diagnostics.

FM2019700643020X

Fig. 21   Test R/DTC C1905: Lefthand Rear Shock Absorber Circuit Fault (Part 2 of 4)

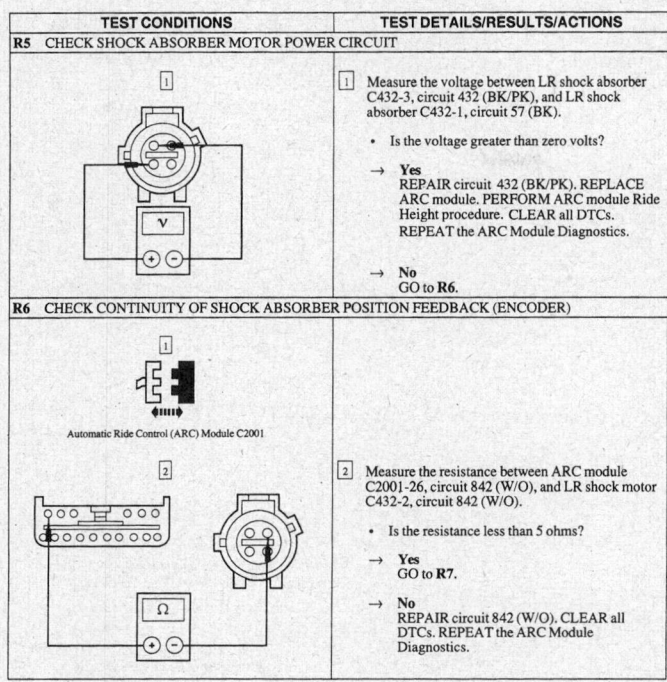

TEST CONDITIONS	TEST DETAILS/RESULTS/ACTIONS
R5 CHECK SHOCK ABSORBER MOTOR POWER CIRCUIT	1 Measure the voltage between LR shock absorber C432-3, circuit 432 (BK/PK), and LR shock absorber C432-1, circuit 57 (BK). • Is the voltage greater than zero volts? → **Yes** REPAIR circuit 432 (BK/PK). REPLACE ARC module. PERFORM ARC module Ride Height procedure. CLEAR all DTCs. REPEAT the ARC Module Diagnostics. → **No** GO to **R6**.
R6 CHECK CONTINUITY OF SHOCK ABSORBER POSITION FEEDBACK (ENCODER) Automatic Ride Control (ARC) Module C2001	2 Measure the resistance between ARC module C2001-26, circuit 842 (W/O), and LR shock motor C432-2, circuit 842 (W/O). • Is the resistance less than 5 ohms? → **Yes** GO to **R7**. → **No** REPAIR circuit 842 (W/O). CLEAR all DTCs. REPEAT the ARC Module Diagnostics.

FM2019700643030X

Fig. 21 Test R/DTC C1905: Lefthand Rear Shock Absorber Circuit Fault (Part 3 of 4)

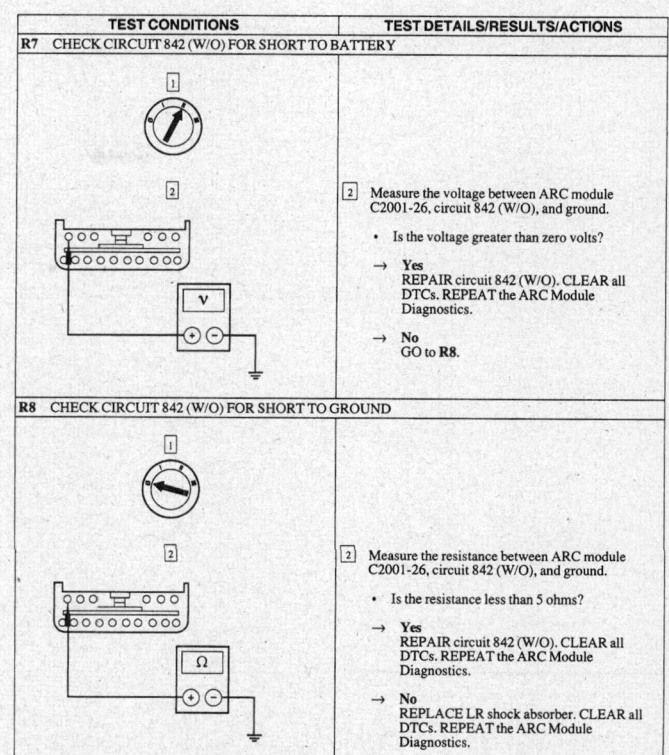

TEST CONDITIONS	TEST DETAILS/RESULTS/ACTIONS
R7 CHECK CIRCUIT 842 (W/O) FOR SHORT TO BATTERY	2 Measure the voltage between ARC module C2001-26, circuit 842 (W/O), and ground. • Is the voltage greater than zero volts? → **Yes** REPAIR circuit 842 (W/O). CLEAR all DTCs. REPEAT the ARC Module Diagnostics. → **No** GO to **R8**.
R8 CHECK CIRCUIT 842 (W/O) FOR SHORT TO GROUND	2 Measure the resistance between ARC module C2001-26, circuit 842 (W/O), and ground. • Is the resistance less than 5 ohms? → **Yes** REPAIR circuit 842 (W/O). CLEAR all DTCs. REPEAT the ARC Module Diagnostics. → **No** REPLACE LR shock absorber. CLEAR all DTCs. REPEAT the ARC Module Diagnostics.

FM2019700643040X

Fig. 21 Test R/DTC C1905: Lefthand Rear Shock Absorber Circuit Fault (Part 4 of 4)

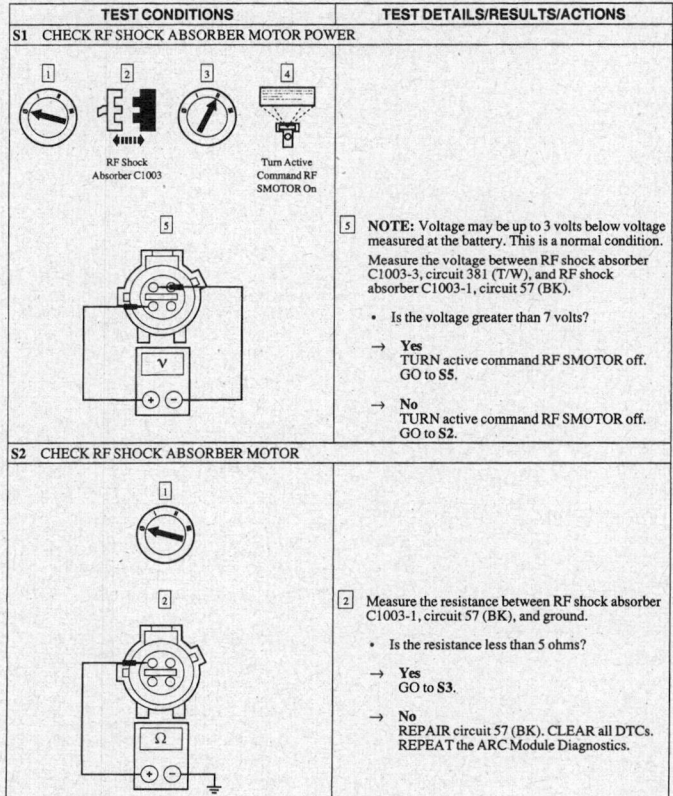

TEST CONDITIONS	TEST DETAILS/RESULTS/ACTIONS
S1 CHECK RF SHOCK ABSORBER MOTOR POWER RF Shock Absorber C1003 Turn Active Command RF SMOTOR On	5 **NOTE:** Voltage may be up to 3 volts below voltage measured at the battery. This is a normal condition. Measure the voltage between RF shock absorber C1003-3, circuit 381 (T/W), and RF shock absorber C1003-1, circuit 57 (BK). • Is the voltage greater than 7 volts? → **Yes** TURN active command RF SMOTOR off. GO to **S5**. → **No** TURN active command RF SMOTOR off. GO to **S2**.
S2 CHECK RF SHOCK ABSORBER MOTOR	2 Measure the resistance between RF shock absorber C1003-1, circuit 57 (BK), and ground. • Is the resistance less than 5 ohms? → **Yes** GO to **S3**. → **No** REPAIR circuit 57 (BK). CLEAR all DTCs. REPEAT the ARC Module Diagnostics.

FM2019700644010X

Fig. 22 Test S/DTC C1909: Righthand Front Shock Absorber Circuit Fault (Part 1 of 4)

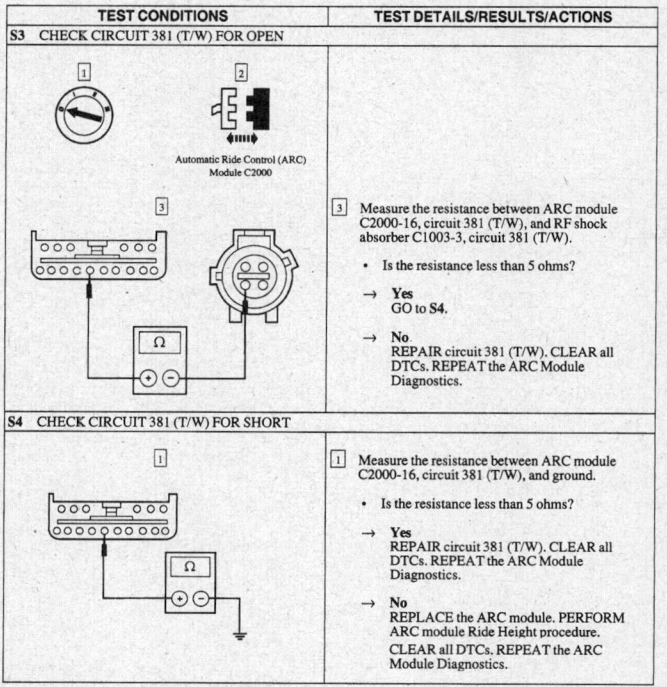

TEST CONDITIONS	TEST DETAILS/RESULTS/ACTIONS
S3 CHECK CIRCUIT 381 (T/W) FOR OPEN Automatic Ride Control (ARC) Module C2000	3 Measure the resistance between ARC module C2000-16, circuit 381 (T/W), and RF shock absorber C1003-3, circuit 381 (T/W). • Is the resistance less than 5 ohms? → **Yes** GO to **S4**. → **No** REPAIR circuit 381 (T/W). CLEAR all DTCs. REPEAT the ARC Module Diagnostics.
S4 CHECK CIRCUIT 381 (T/W) FOR SHORT	1 Measure the resistance between ARC module C2000-16, circuit 381 (T/W), and ground. • Is the resistance less than 5 ohms? → **Yes** REPAIR circuit 381 (T/W). CLEAR all DTCs. REPEAT the ARC Module Diagnostics. → **No** REPLACE the ARC module. PERFORM ARC module Ride Height procedure. CLEAR all DTCs. REPEAT the ARC Module Diagnostics.

FM2019700644020X

Fig. 22 Test S/DTC C1909: Righthand Front Shock Absorber Circuit Fault (Part 2 of 4)

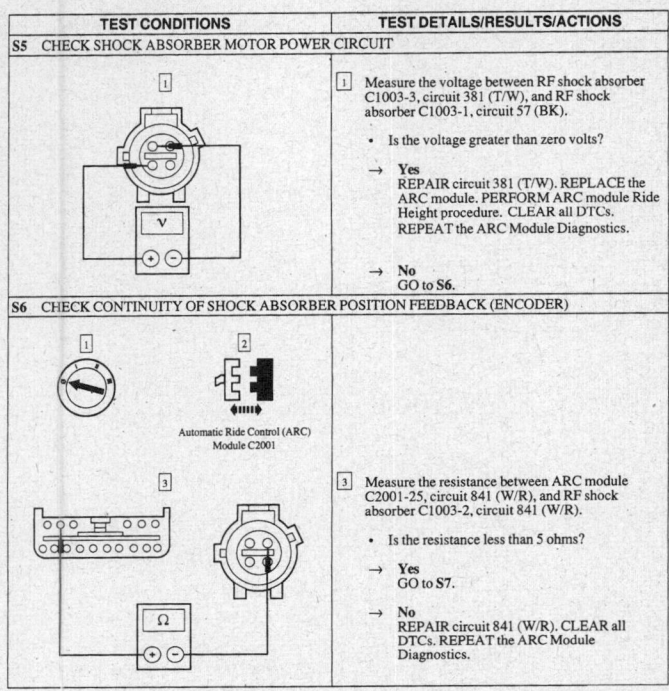

TEST CONDITIONS	TEST DETAILS/RESULTS/ACTIONS
S5 CHECK SHOCK ABSORBER MOTOR POWER CIRCUIT	

1 Measure the voltage between RF shock absorber C1003-3, circuit 381 (T/W), and RF shock absorber C1003-1, circuit 57 (BK).

- Is the voltage greater than zero volts?

→ **Yes**
REPAIR circuit 381 (T/W). REPLACE the ARC module. PERFORM ARC module Ride Height procedure. CLEAR all DTCs. REPEAT the ARC Module Diagnostics.

→ **No**
GO to **S6**.

S6 CHECK CONTINUITY OF SHOCK ABSORBER POSITION FEEDBACK (ENCODER)

3 Measure the resistance between ARC module C2001-25, circuit 841 (W/R), and RF shock absorber C1003-2, circuit 841 (W/R).

- Is the resistance less than 5 ohms?

→ **Yes**
GO to **S7**.

→ **No**
REPAIR circuit 841 (W/R). CLEAR all DTCs. REPEAT the ARC Module Diagnostics.

FM2019700644030X

Fig. 22 Test S/DTC C1909: Righthand Front Shock Absorber Circuit Fault (Part 3 of 4)

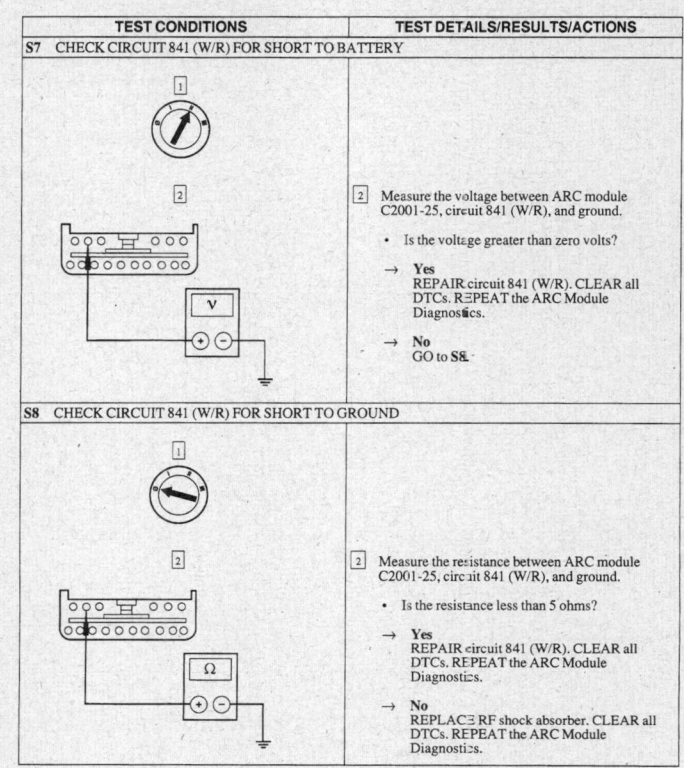

TEST CONDITIONS	TEST DETAILS/RESULTS/ACTIONS
S7 CHECK CIRCUIT 841 (W/R) FOR SHORT TO BATTERY	

2 Measure the voltage between ARC module C2001-25, circuit 841 (W/R), and ground.

- Is the voltage greater than zero volts?

→ **Yes**
REPAIR circuit 841 (W/R). CLEAR all DTCs. REPEAT the ARC Module Diagnostics.

→ **No**
GO to **S8**.

S8 CHECK CIRCUIT 841 (W/R) FOR SHORT TO GROUND

2 Measure the resistance between ARC module C2001-25, circuit 841 (W/R), and ground.

- Is the resistance less than 5 ohms?

→ **Yes**
REPAIR circuit 841 (W/R). CLEAR all DTCs. REPEAT the ARC Module Diagnostics.

→ **No**
REPLACE RF shock absorber. CLEAR all DTCs. REPEAT the ARC Module Diagnostics.

FM2019700644040X

Fig. 22 Test S/DTC C1909: Righthand Front Shock Absorber Circuit Fault (Part 4 of 4)

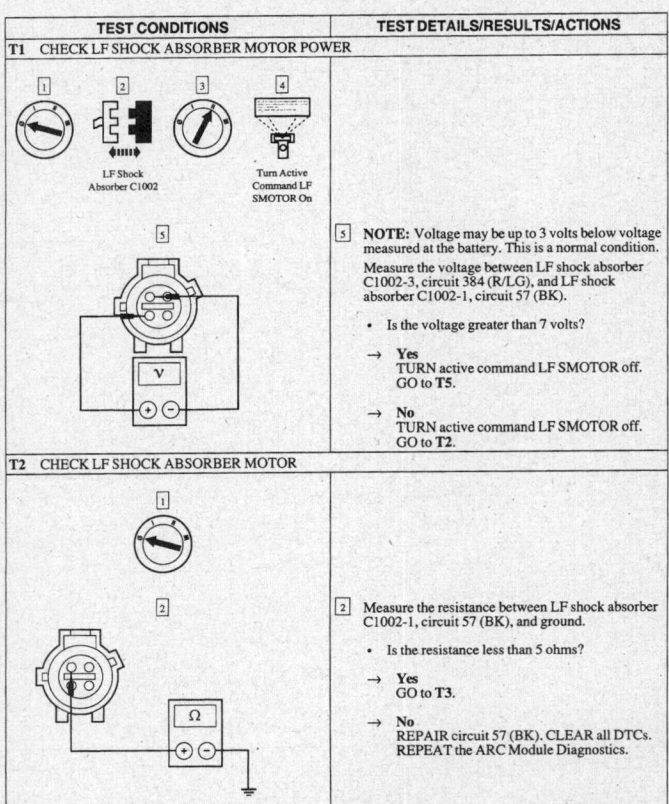

TEST CONDITIONS	TEST DETAILS/RESULTS/ACTIONS
T1 CHECK LF SHOCK ABSORBER MOTOR POWER	

5 **NOTE:** Voltage may be up to 3 volts below voltage measured at the battery. This is a normal condition.
Measure the voltage between LF shock absorber C1002-3, circuit 384 (R/LG), and LF shock absorber C1002-1, circuit 57 (BK).

- Is the voltage greater than 7 volts?

→ **Yes**
TURN active command LF SMOTOR off. GO to **T5**.

→ **No**
TURN active command LF SMOTOR off. GO to **T2**.

T2 CHECK LF SHOCK ABSORBER MOTOR

2 Measure the resistance between LF shock absorber C1002-1, circuit 57 (BK), and ground.

- Is the resistance less than 5 ohms?

→ **Yes**
GO to **T3**.

→ **No**
REPAIR circuit 57 (BK). CLEAR all DTCs. REPEAT the ARC Module Diagnostics.

FM2019700645010X

Fig. 23 Test T/DTC C1913: Lefthand Front Shock Absorber Circuit Fault (Part 1 of 4)

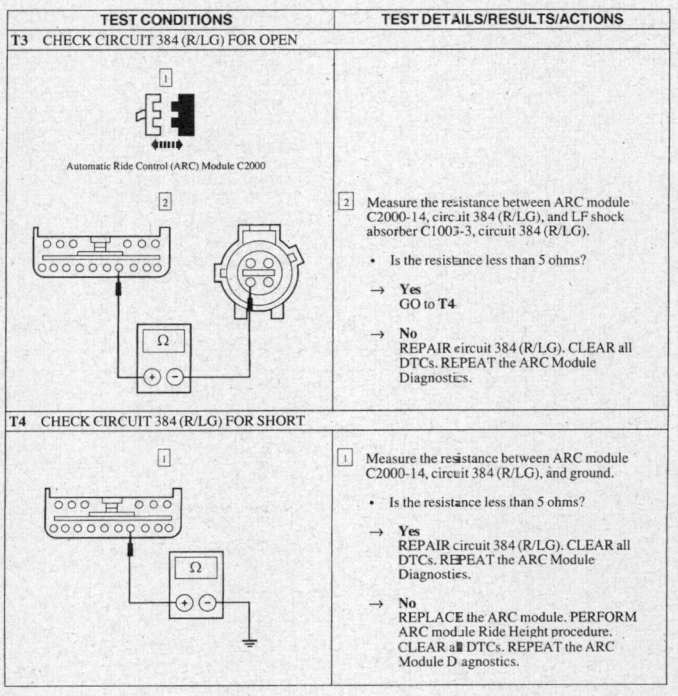

TEST CONDITIONS	TEST DETAILS/RESULTS/ACTIONS
T3 CHECK CIRCUIT 384 (R/LG) FOR OPEN	

2 Measure the resistance between ARC module C2000-14, circuit 384 (R/LG), and LF shock absorber C1003-3, circuit 384 (R/LG).

- Is the resistance less than 5 ohms?

→ **Yes**
GO to **T4**

→ **No**
REPAIR circuit 384 (R/LG). CLEAR all DTCs. REPEAT the ARC Module Diagnostics.

T4 CHECK CIRCUIT 384 (R/LG) FOR SHORT

1 Measure the resistance between ARC module C2000-14, circuit 384 (R/LG), and ground.

- Is the resistance less than 5 ohms?

→ **Yes**
REPAIR circuit 384 (R/LG). CLEAR all DTCs. REPEAT the ARC Module Diagnostics.

→ **No**
REPLACE the ARC module. PERFORM ARC module Ride Height procedure. CLEAR all DTCs. REPEAT the ARC Module Diagnostics.

FM2019700645020X

Fig. 23 Test T/DTC C1913: Lefthand Front Shock Absorber Circuit Fault (Part 2 of 4)

TEST CONDITIONS	TEST DETAILS/RESULTS/ACTIONS
T5 CHECK SHOCK ABSORBER MOTOR POWER CIRCUIT	
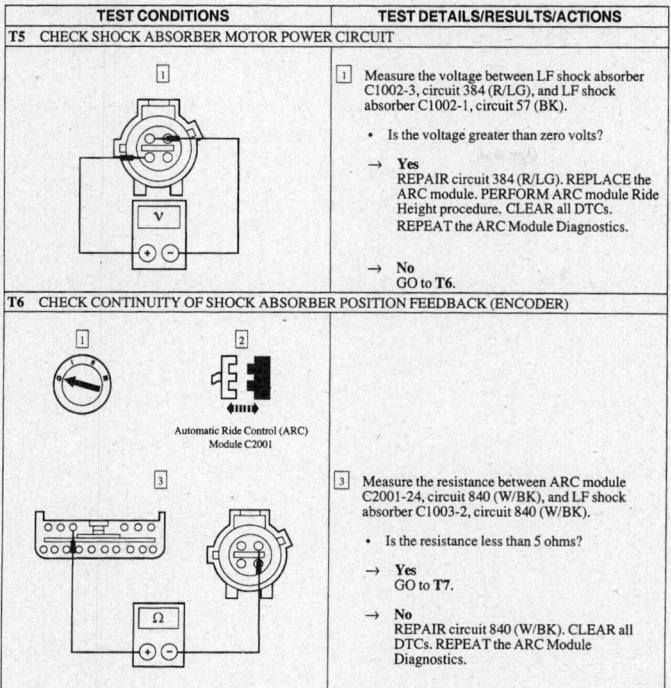	**1** Measure the voltage between LF shock absorber C1002-3, circuit 384 (R/LG), and LF shock absorber C1002-1, circuit 57 (BK). • Is the voltage greater than zero volts? → **Yes** REPAIR circuit 384 (R/LG). REPLACE the ARC module. PERFORM ARC module Ride Height procedure. CLEAR all DTCs. REPEAT the ARC Module Diagnostics. → **No** GO to **T6**.
T6 CHECK CONTINUITY OF SHOCK ABSORBER POSITION FEEDBACK (ENCODER)	
Automatic Ride Control (ARC) Module C2001	**3** Measure the resistance between ARC module C2001-24, circuit 840 (W/BK), and LF shock absorber C1003-2, circuit 840 (W/BK). • Is the resistance less than 5 ohms? → **Yes** GO to **T7**. → **No** REPAIR circuit 840 (W/BK). CLEAR all DTCs. REPEAT the ARC Module Diagnostics.

FM2019700645030X

Fig. 23 Test T/DTC C1913: Lefthand Front Shock Absorber Circuit Fault (Part 3 of 4)

TEST CONDITIONS	TEST DETAILS/RESULTS/ACTIONS
T7 CHECK CIRCUIT 840 (W/BK) FOR SHORT TO BATTERY	
	2 Measure the voltage between ARC module C2001-24, circuit 840 (W/BK), and ground. • Is the voltage greater than zero volts? → **Yes** REPAIR circuit 840 (W/BK). CLEAR all DTCs. REPEAT the ARC Module Diagnostics. → **No** GO to **T8**.
T8 CHECK CIRCUIT 840 (W/BK) FOR SHORT TO GROUND	
	2 Measure the resistance between ARC module C2001-24, circuit 840 (W/BK), and ground. • Is the resistance less than 5 ohms? → **Yes** REPAIR circuit 840 (W/BK). CLEAR all DTCs. REPEAT the ARC Module Diagnostics. → **No** REPLACE LF shock absorber. CLEAR all DTCs. REPEAT the ARC Module Diagnostics.

FM2019700645040X

Fig. 23 Test T/DTC C1913: Lefthand Front Shock Absorber Circuit Fault (Part 4 of 4)

TEST CONDITIONS	TEST DETAILS/RESULTS/ACTIONS
U1 PERFORM ON-DEMAND SELF-TEST	
On-Demand Self-Test	**1** Open any door. **2** The 4-wheel drive is in 4x4 LOW and the 4x4 LOW indicator is illuminated (4.0L). The ride control switch is in the OFF ROAD position (5.0L). • Is DTC C1318 set at the end of On-Demand Self-Test? → **Yes** GO to **U2**. → **No** CHECK the battery and charging system. TEST the system for normal operation.
U2 CHECK FOR INTERMITTENT CONDITION	
Monitor VBATARC PID	**1** Recharge the battery.

FM2019700646010X

Fig. 24 Test U/DTC B1318: Battery Voltage Low (Part 1 of 2)

TEST CONDITIONS	TEST DETAILS/RESULTS/ACTIONS
U2 CHECK FOR INTERMITTENT CONDITION (Continued)	
	• Is the voltage greater than 11 volts? → **Yes** CLEAR all DTCs. REPEAT the ARC Module Diagnostics. → **No** CHECK the battery and charging system. TEST the system for normal operation.

FM2019700646020X

Fig. 24 Test U/DTC B1318: Battery Voltage Low (Part 2 of 2)

TEST CONDITIONS	TEST DETAILS/RESULTS/ACTIONS
V1 PERFORM ON-DEMAND SELF-TEST	
On-Demand Self-Test	**1** Open any door. **2** The 4-wheel drive is in 4x4 LOW and the 4x4 LOW indicator is illuminated (4.0L). The ride control switch is in the OFF ROAD position (5.0L). • Is DTC B1342 set at the end of On-Demand Self-Test? → **Yes** REPLACE the ARC module. PERFORM the ARC module Ride Height procedure. CLEAR all DTCs. REPEAT the ARC Module Diagnostics. → **No** GO to **V2**.

FM2019700647010X

Fig. 25 Test V/DTC B1342: ECU Internal Fault (Part 1 of 3)

TEST CONDITIONS	TEST DETAILS/RESULTS/ACTIONS
V2 CHECK FOR INTERMITTENT FAILURE	
[1] [2] Turn the air suspension switch to the OFF position. [3] Turn the air suspension switch to the ON position. [4] [5] On-Demand Self-Test	[2] Turn the air suspension switch to the OFF position. [3] Turn the air suspension switch to the ON position.

FM2019700647020X

Fig. 25   Test V/DTC B1342: ECU Internal Fault (Part 2 of 3)

TEST CONDITIONS	TEST DETAILS/RESULTS/ACTIONS
V2 CHECK FOR INTERMITTENT FAILURE (Continued)	• Does DTC B1342 set again? → **Yes** REPLACE the ARC module. PERFORM the ARC module Ride Height procedure. CLEAR all DTCs. REPEAT the ARC Module Diagnostics. → **No** CLEAR all DTCs. REPEAT the ARC Module Diagnostics.

FM2019700647030X

Fig. 25   Test V/DTC B1342: ECU Internal Fault (Part 3 of 3)

TEST CONDITIONS	TEST DETAILS/RESULTS/ACTIONS
W1 PERFORM ON-DEMAND SELF-TEST	[1] Open any door. [2] The 4-wheel drive is in 4x4 LOW and the 4x4 LOW indicator is illuminated (4.0L). The ride control switch is in the OFF ROAD position (5.0L).
[2] AUTO 4WD HIGH 4WD LOW NORMAL RIDE OFF ROAD [3] On-Demand Self-Test	• Is DTC B1485 set at the end of On-Demand Self-Test? → **Yes** GO to **W2**. → **No** REPAIR any DTCs that were set. CLEAR all DTCs. REPEAT the ARC Module Diagnostics.

FM2019700648010X

Fig. 26   Test W/DTC B1485: Brake Lamp Switch Input Short To Power (Part 1 of 2)

TEST CONDITIONS	TEST DETAILS/RESULTS/ACTIONS
W2 CHECK CIRCUIT 511 (LG) FOR SHORT TO POWER	[1] Check the stoplamps. • Are any of the stoplamps illuminated? → **Yes** Diagnose Stop lamp System Fault condition. → **No** REPLACE the ARC module. PERFORM the ARC module Ride Height procedure. CLEAR all DTCs. REPEAT the ARC Module Diagnostics.

FM2019700648020X

Fig. 26   Test W/DTC B1485: Brake Lamp Switch Input Short To Power (Part 2 of 2)

TEST CONDITIONS	TEST DETAILS/RESULTS/ACTIONS
X1 PERFORM ON-DEMAND SELF-TEST	[1] Open any door. [2] The 4-wheel drive is in 4x4 LOW and the 4x4 LOW indicator is illuminated (4.0L). The ride control switch is in the OFF ROAD position (5.0L).
[2] AUTO 4WD HIGH 4WD LOW NORMAL RIDE OFF ROAD [3] On-Demand Self-Test	

FM2019700649010X

Fig. 27   Test X/DTC B1565: Door Ajar Input Short To Power (Part 1 of 2)

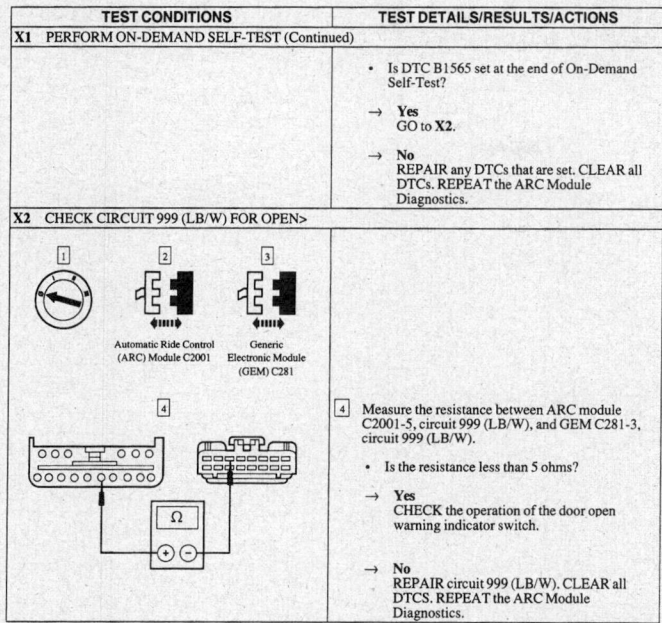

TEST CONDITIONS	TEST DETAILS/RESULTS/ACTIONS
X1 PERFORM ON-DEMAND SELF-TEST (Continued)	
	• Is DTC B1565 set at the end of On-Demand Self-Test? → **Yes** GO to **X2**. → **No** REPAIR any DTCs that are set. CLEAR all DTCs. REPEAT the ARC Module Diagnostics.
X2 CHECK CIRCUIT 999 (LB/W) FOR OPEN>	
	4 Measure the resistance between ARC module C2001-5, circuit 999 (LB/W), and GEM C281-3, circuit 999 (LB/W). • Is the resistance less than 5 ohms? → **Yes** CHECK the operation of the door open warning indicator switch. → **No** REPAIR circuit 999 (LB/W). CLEAR all DTCs. REPEAT the ARC Module Diagnostics.

FM2019700649020X

Fig. 27   Test X/DTC B1565: Door Ajar Input Short To Power (Part 2 of 2)

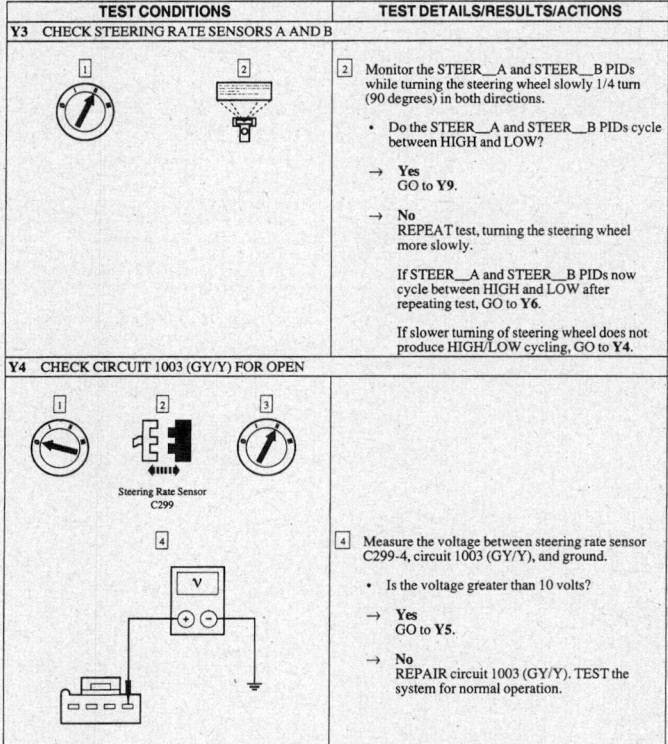

TEST CONDITIONS	TEST DETAILS/RESULTS/ACTIONS
Y3 CHECK STEERING RATE SENSORS A AND B	
	2 Monitor the STEER__A and STEER__B PIDs while turning the steering wheel slowly 1/4 turn (90 degrees) in both directions. • Do the STEER__A and STEER__B PIDs cycle between HIGH and LOW? → **Yes** GO to **Y9**. → **No** REPEAT test, turning the steering wheel more slowly. If STEER__A and STEER__B PIDs now cycle between HIGH and LOW after repeating test, GO to **Y6**. If slower turning of steering wheel does not produce HIGH/LOW cycling, GO to **Y4**.
Y4 CHECK CIRCUIT 1003 (GY/Y) FOR OPEN	
	4 Measure the voltage between steering rate sensor C299-4, circuit 1003 (GY/Y), and ground. • Is the voltage greater than 10 volts? → **Yes** GO to **Y5**. → **No** REPAIR circuit 1003 (GY/Y). TEST the system for normal operation.

FM2019700650020X

Fig. 28   Test Y: ARC System Does Not Seem To Be Working (Part 2 of 17)

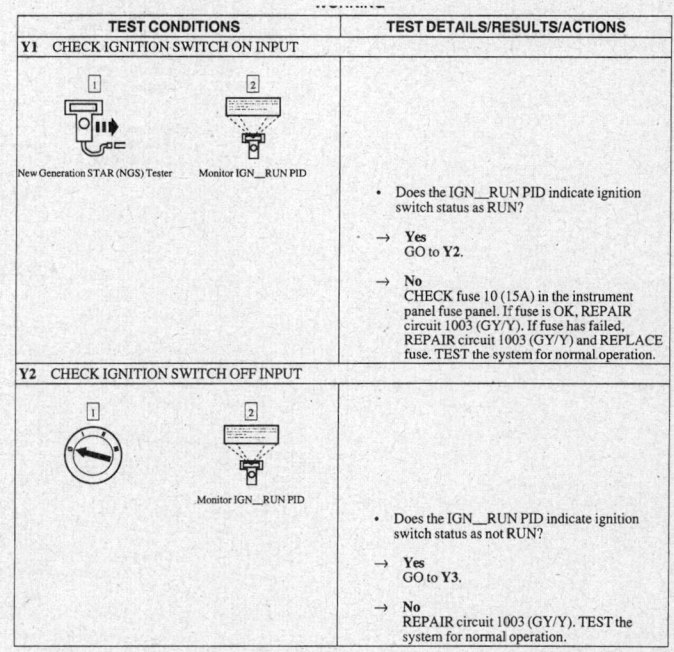

TEST CONDITIONS	TEST DETAILS/RESULTS/ACTIONS
Y1 CHECK IGNITION SWITCH ON INPUT	
	• Does the IGN__RUN PID indicate ignition switch status as RUN? → **Yes** GO to **Y2**. → **No** CHECK fuse 10 (15A) in the instrument panel fuse panel. If fuse is OK, REPAIR circuit 1003 (GY/Y). If fuse has failed, REPAIR circuit 1003 (GY/Y) and REPLACE fuse. TEST the system for normal operation.
Y2 CHECK IGNITION SWITCH OFF INPUT	
	• Does the IGN__RUN PID indicate ignition switch status as not RUN? → **Yes** GO to **Y3**. → **No** REPAIR circuit 1003 (GY/Y). TEST the system for normal operation.

FM2019700650010X

Fig. 28   Test Y: ARC System Does Not Seem To Be Working (Part 1 of 17)

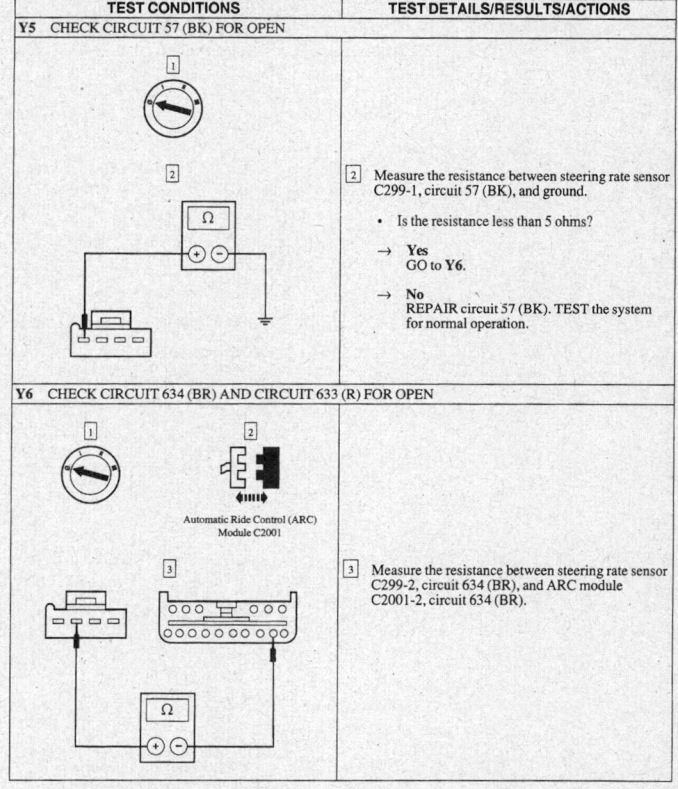

TEST CONDITIONS	TEST DETAILS/RESULTS/ACTIONS
Y5 CHECK CIRCUIT 57 (BK) FOR OPEN	
	2 Measure the resistance between steering rate sensor C299-1, circuit 57 (BK), and ground. • Is the resistance less than 5 ohms? → **Yes** GO to **Y6**. → **No** REPAIR circuit 57 (BK). TEST the system for normal operation.
Y6 CHECK CIRCUIT 634 (BR) AND CIRCUIT 633 (R) FOR OPEN	
	3 Measure the resistance between steering rate sensor C299-2, circuit 634 (BR), and ARC module C2001-2, circuit 634 (BR).

FM2019700650030X

Fig. 28   Test Y: ARC System Does Not Seem To Be Working (Part 3 of 17)

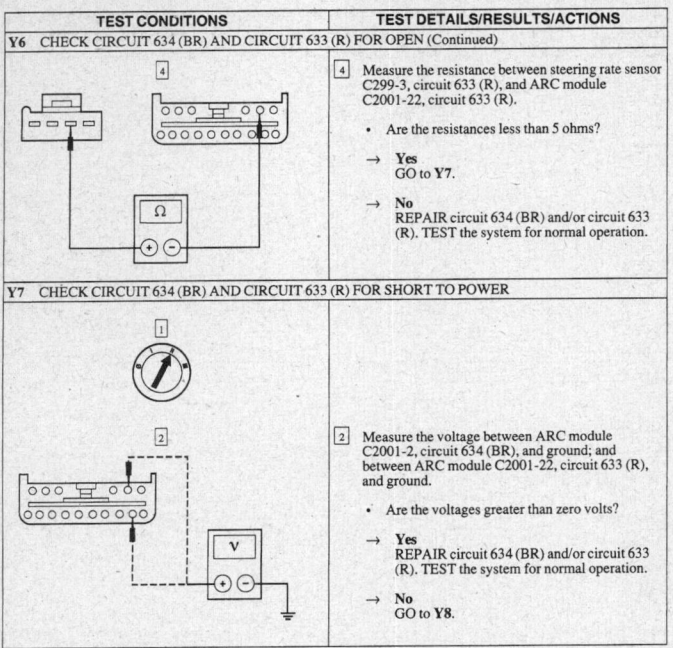

TEST CONDITIONS	TEST DETAILS/RESULTS/ACTIONS
Y6 CHECK CIRCUIT 634 (BR) AND CIRCUIT 633 (R) FOR OPEN (Continued)	**4** Measure the resistance between steering rate sensor C299-3, circuit 633 (R), and ARC module C2001-22, circuit 633 (R). • Are the resistances less than 5 ohms? → **Yes** GO to **Y7**. → **No** REPAIR circuit 634 (BR) and/or circuit 633 (R). TEST the system for normal operation.
Y7 CHECK CIRCUIT 634 (BR) AND CIRCUIT 633 (R) FOR SHORT TO POWER	**2** Measure the voltage between ARC module C2001-2, circuit 634 (BR), and ground; and between ARC module C2001-22, circuit 633 (R), and ground. • Are the voltages greater than zero volts? → **Yes** REPAIR circuit 634 (BR) and/or circuit 633 (R). TEST the system for normal operation. → **No** GO to **Y8**.

FM2019700650040X

Fig. 28   Test Y: ARC System Does Not Seem To Be Working (Part 4 of 17)

TEST CONDITIONS	TEST DETAILS/RESULTS/ACTIONS
Y10 CHECK CIRCUIT 511 (LG) FOR OPEN	**4** Measure the resistance between ARC module C2001-10, circuit 511 (LG), and BOO switch C224, circuit 511 (LG). • Is the resistance less than 5 ohms? → **Yes** REPLACE the ARC module. PERFORM the ARC module Ride Height procedure. TEST the system for normal operation. → **No** REPAIR circuit 511 (LG). TEST the system for normal operation. GO to **Y12**.
Y11 CHECK CIRCUIT 511 (LG) FOR SHORT TO POWER	**3** Check stoplamps to see if they are illuminated. • Are the stoplamps illuminated? → **Yes** Diagnose Stoplamp System Fault Condition → **No** REPLACE the ARC module. PERFORM the ARC module Ride Height procedure. TEST the system for normal operation.

FM2019700650060X

Fig. 28   Test Y: ARC System Does Not Seem To Be Working (Part 6 of 17)

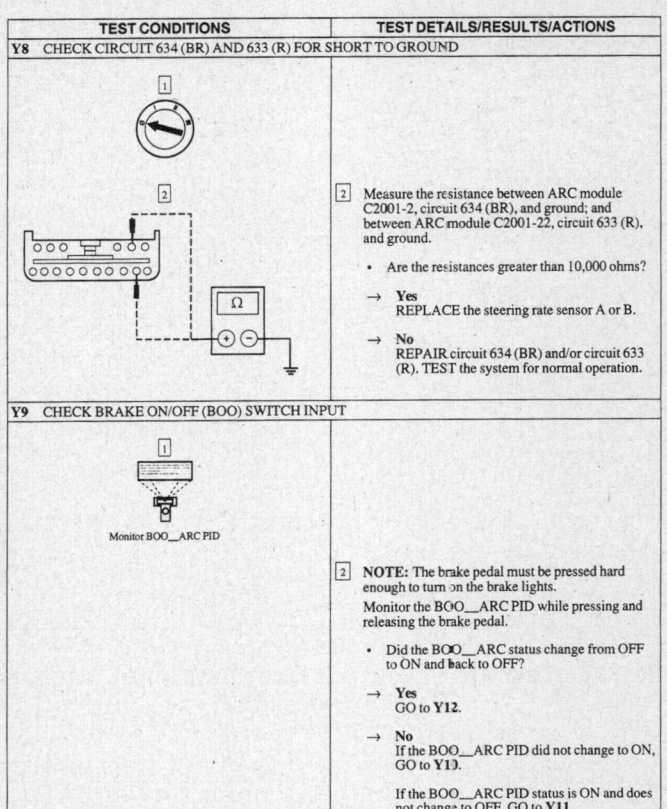

TEST CONDITIONS	TEST DETAILS/RESULTS/ACTIONS
Y8 CHECK CIRCUIT 634 (BR) AND 633 (R) FOR SHORT TO GROUND	**2** Measure the resistance between ARC module C2001-2, circuit 634 (BR), and ground; and between ARC module C2001-22, circuit 633 (R), and ground. • Are the resistances greater than 10,000 ohms? → **Yes** REPLACE the steering rate sensor A or B. → **No** REPAIR circuit 634 (BR) and/or circuit 633 (R). TEST the system for normal operation.
Y9 CHECK BRAKE ON/OFF (BOO) SWITCH INPUT	**2** **NOTE:** The brake pedal must be pressed hard enough to turn on the brake lights. Monitor the BOO__ARC PID while pressing and releasing the brake pedal. • Did the BOO__ARC status change from OFF to ON and back to OFF? → **Yes** GO to **Y12**. → **No** If the BOO__ARC PID did not change to ON, GO to **Y13**. If the BOO__ARC PID status is ON and does not change to OFF, GO to **Y11**.

FM2019700650050X

Fig. 28   Test Y: ARC System Does Not Seem To Be Working (Part 5 of 17)

TEST CONDITIONS	TEST DETAILS/RESULTS/ACTIONS
Y12 CHECK DOOR OPEN WARNING INDICATOR INPUTS	**1** Close all doors, liftgate and liftgate glass (door ajar lamp in instrument cluster is not illuminated). **3** Open any door. • Does the DR__OPEN PID status indicate CLOSED and then AJAR? → **Yes** GO to **Y16**. → **No** GO to **Y13**.
Y13 CHECK DOOR AJAR INPUTS TO GEM	**1** Monitor the following GEM PIDs: — D__DR__SW. — P__DR__SW. — LGATE__SW. — LRDR__SW. — RRDR__SW. **2** Check the GEM door ajar inputs by opening and closing each door individually. • Do all five GEM inputs function correctly? → **Yes** GO to **Y14**. → **No** REFER to diagnostics of the door ajar system.

FM2019700650070X

Fig. 28   Test Y: ARC System Does Not Seem To Be Working (Part 7 of 17)

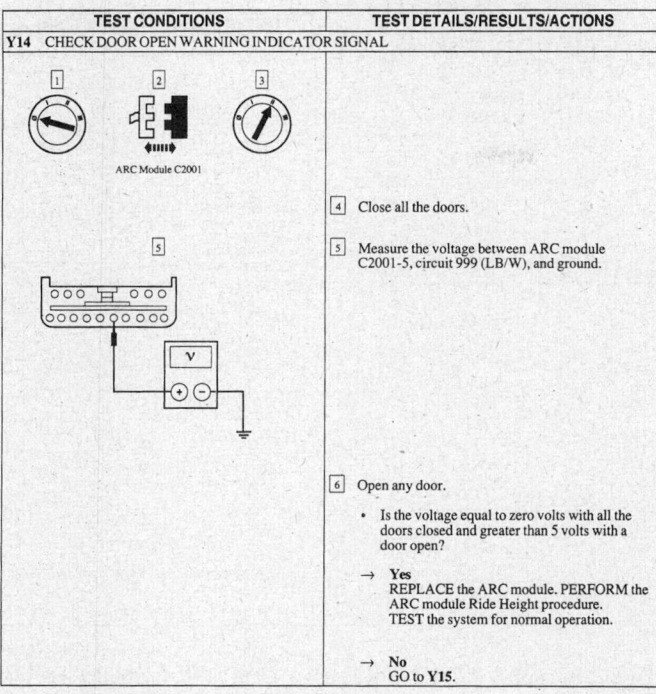

TEST CONDITIONS	TEST DETAILS/RESULTS/ACTIONS
Y14 CHECK DOOR OPEN WARNING INDICATOR SIGNAL	
	4 Close all the doors.
	5 Measure the voltage between ARC module C2001-5, circuit 999 (LB/W), and ground.
	6 Open any door.
	• Is the voltage equal to zero volts with all the doors closed and greater than 5 volts with a door open?
	→ **Yes** REPLACE the ARC module. PERFORM the ARC module Ride Height procedure. TEST the system for normal operation.
	→ **No** GO to **Y15**.

FM2019700650080X

Fig. 28   Test Y: ARC System Does Not Seem To Be Working (Part 8 of 17)

TEST CONDITIONS	TEST DETAILS/RESULTS/ACTIONS
Y16 CHECK 4X4 DISENGAGED INPUT (Continued)	
	• Does the 4X4__LOW (4.0L) or OFF ROAD (5.0L) PID status indicate OUT?
	→ **Yes** GO to **Y19**.
	→ **No** GO to **Y17**.
Y17 CHECK GEM TWO-WHEEL DRIVE OUTPUT	
Monitor GEM 4WDHIGH AND 4WDLOW PIDs	• Are both the GEM PIDs in the OFF state?
	→ **Yes** GO to **Y18**.
	→ **No** CHECK the operation of the transfer case.
Y18 CHECK CIRCUIT 637 (DB/W) FOR SHORT TO GROUND	
GEM C282	**3** Measure the resistance between GEM C282-11, circuit 637 (DB/W), and ground.
	• Is the resistance greater than 10,000 ohms?
	→ **Yes** REPLACE the ARC module. PERFORM the ARC module Ride Height procedure. TEST the system for normal operation.
	→ **No** REPAIR circuit 637 (DB/W). CLEAR all DTCs. TEST the system for normal operation.

FM2019700650100X

Fig. 28   Test Y: ARC System Does Not Seem To Be Working (Part 10 of 17)

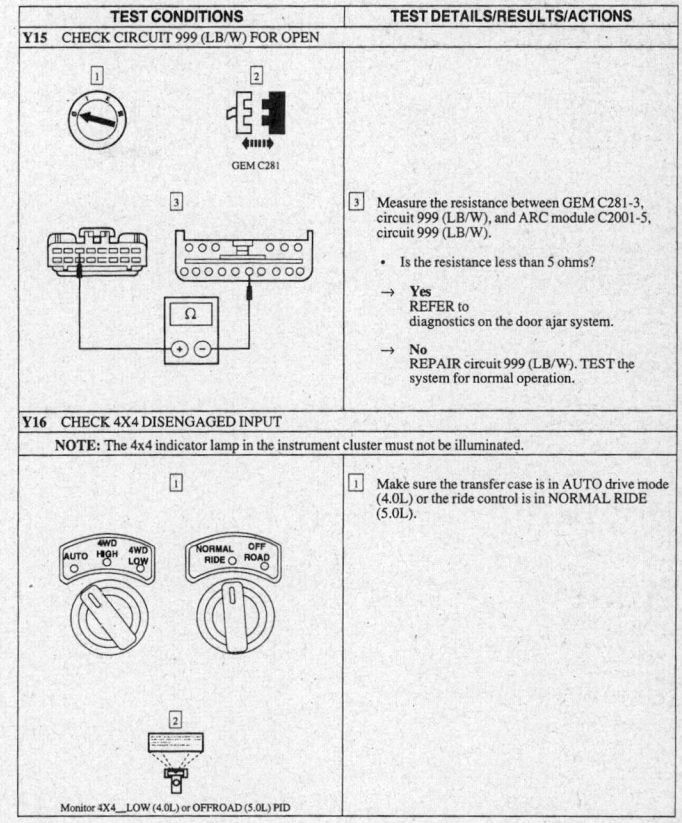

TEST CONDITIONS	TEST DETAILS/RESULTS/ACTIONS
Y15 CHECK CIRCUIT 999 (LB/W) FOR OPEN	
GEM C281	**3** Measure the resistance between GEM C281-3, circuit 999 (LB/W), and ARC module C2001-5, circuit 999 (LB/W).
	• Is the resistance less than 5 ohms?
	→ **Yes** REFER to diagnostics on the door ajar system.
	→ **No** REPAIR circuit 999 (LB/W). TEST the system for normal operation.
Y16 CHECK 4X4 DISENGAGED INPUT	
NOTE: The 4x4 indicator lamp in the instrument cluster must not be illuminated.	
Monitor 4X4__LOW (4.0L) or OFFROAD (5.0L) PID	**1** Make sure the transfer case is in AUTO drive mode (4.0L) or the ride control is in NORMAL RIDE (5.0L).

FM2019700650090X

Fig. 28   Test Y: ARC System Does Not Seem To Be Working (Part 9 of 17)

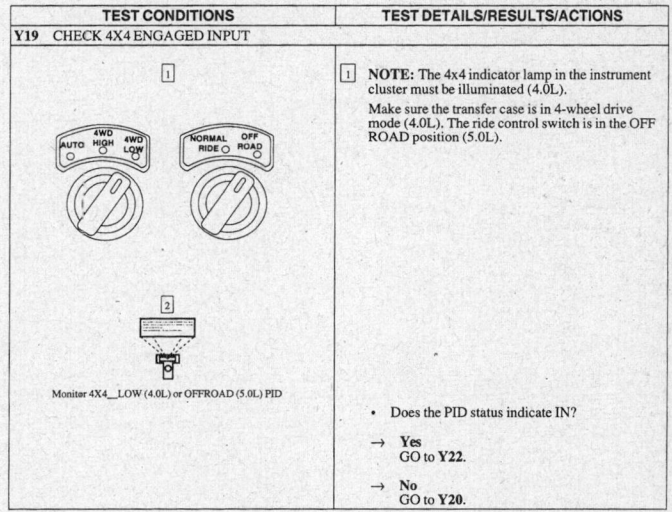

TEST CONDITIONS	TEST DETAILS/RESULTS/ACTIONS
Y19 CHECK 4X4 ENGAGED INPUT	
Monitor 4X4__LOW (4.0L) or OFFROAD (5.0L) PID	**1** **NOTE:** The 4x4 indicator lamp in the instrument cluster must be illuminated (4.0L). Make sure the transfer case is in 4-wheel drive mode (4.0L). The ride control switch is in the OFF ROAD position (5.0L).
	• Does the PID status indicate IN?
	→ **Yes** GO to **Y22**.
	→ **No** GO to **Y20**.

FM2019700650110X

Fig. 28   Test Y: ARC System Does Not Seem To Be Working (Part 11 of 17)

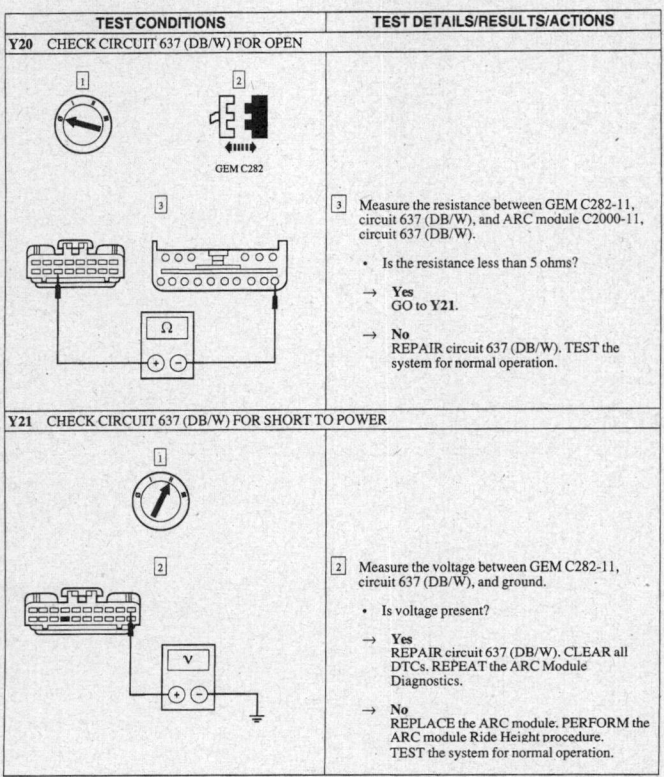

TEST CONDITIONS	TEST DETAILS/RESULTS/ACTIONS
Y20 CHECK CIRCUIT 637 (DB/W) FOR OPEN	
	3 Measure the resistance between GEM C282-11, circuit 637 (DB/W), and ARC module C2000-11, circuit 637 (DB/W). • Is the resistance less than 5 ohms? → **Yes** GO to **Y21**. → **No** REPAIR circuit 637 (DB/W). TEST the system for normal operation.
Y21 CHECK CIRCUIT 637 (DB/W) FOR SHORT TO POWER	
	2 Measure the voltage between GEM C282-11, circuit 637 (DB/W), and ground. • Is voltage present? → **Yes** REPAIR circuit 637 (DB/W). CLEAR all DTCs. REPEAT the ARC Module Diagnostics. → **No** REPLACE the ARC module. PERFORM the ARC module Ride Height procedure. TEST the system for normal operation.

FM2019700650120X

Fig. 28   Test Y: ARC System Does Not Seem To Be Working (Part 12 of 17)

TEST CONDITIONS	TEST DETAILS/RESULTS/ACTIONS
Y24 CHECK CIRCUIT 394 (O/BK) FOR SHORT TO GROUND	
	4 Measure the resistance between ARC module C2001-6, circuit 394 (O/BK), and ground. • Is the resistance greater than 10,000 ohms? → **Yes** REPLACE the ARC module. PERFORM the ARC module Ride Height procedure. TEST the system for normal operation. → **No** REPAIR circuit 394 (O/BK). TEST the system for normal operation.
Y25 CHECK PCM ACCELERATION INPUT — WOT	
	1 **NOTE:** Make sure the accelerator pedal is in the wide-open throttle position. Use NGS Tester to monitor the PCM_ACC PID. • Does the PCM_ACC PID status indicate YES? → **Yes** GO to **Y28**. → **No** GO to **Y26**.

FM2019700650140X

Fig. 28   Test Y: ARC System Does Not Seem To Be Working (Part 14 of 17)

TEST CONDITIONS	TEST DETAILS/RESULTS/ACTIONS
Y22 CHECK PCM ACCELERATION INPUT	
	1 **NOTE:** Make sure the accelerator pedal is fully released. Use NGS Tester to monitor the PCM_ACC PID. • With the accelerator pedal fully released, does the PCM_ACC PID status indicate NO? → **Yes** GO to **Y25**. → **No** GO to **Y23**.
Y23 CHECK PCM ACCELERATION OUTPUT	
Monitor PCM TP V PID	**2** Press and release the accelerator pedal. • Does the PCM acceleration output voltage vary as the acceleration pedal is depressed? → **Yes** GO to **Y24**. → **No** Diagnose and Test the acceleration signal.

FM2019700650130X

Fig. 28   Test Y: ARC System Does Not Seem To Be Working (Part 13 of 17)

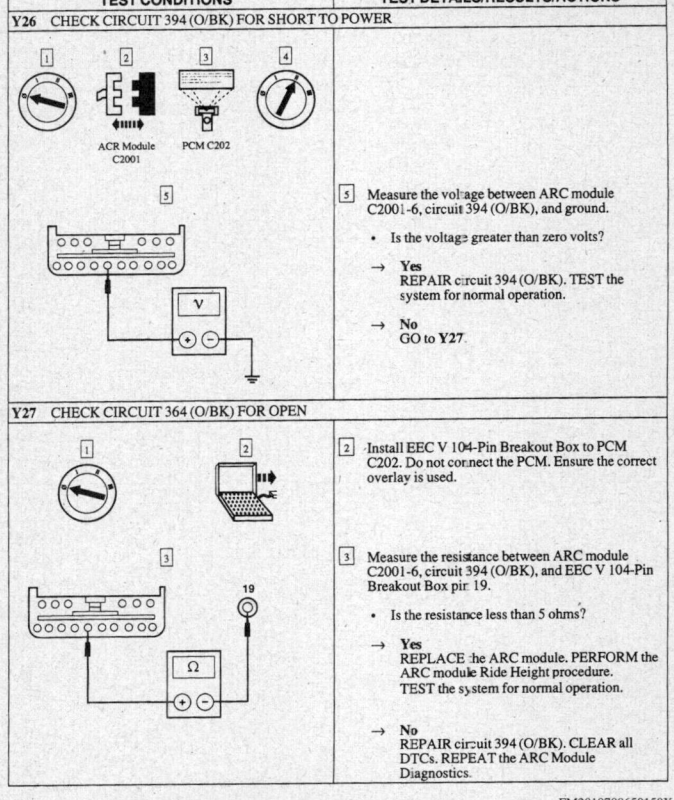

TEST CONDITIONS	TEST DETAILS/RESULTS/ACTIONS
Y26 CHECK CIRCUIT 394 (O/BK) FOR SHORT TO POWER	
	5 Measure the voltage between ARC module C2001-6, circuit 394 (O/BK), and ground. • Is the voltage greater than zero volts? → **Yes** REPAIR circuit 394 (O/BK). TEST the system for normal operation. → **No** GO to **Y27**.
Y27 CHECK CIRCUIT 364 (O/BK) FOR OPEN	
	2 Install EEC V 104-Pin Breakout Box to PCM C202. Do not connect the PCM. Ensure the correct overlay is used. **3** Measure the resistance between ARC module C2001-6, circuit 394 (O/BK), and EEC V 104-Pin Breakout Box pin 19. • Is the resistance less than 5 ohms? → **Yes** REPLACE the ARC module. PERFORM the ARC module Ride Height procedure. TEST the system for normal operation. → **No** REPAIR circuit 394 (O/BK). CLEAR all DTCs. REPEAT the ARC Module Diagnostics.

FM2019700650150X

Fig. 28   Test Y: ARC System Does Not Seem To Be Working (Part 15 of 17)

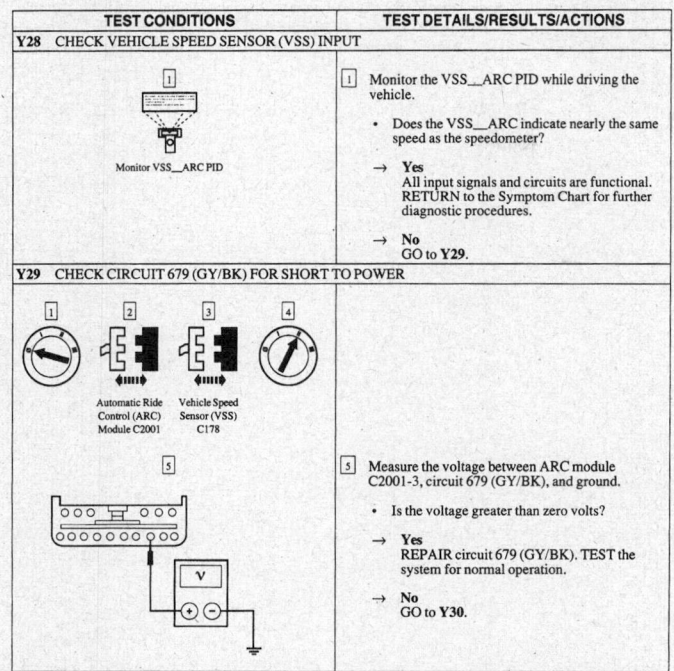

TEST CONDITIONS	TEST DETAILS/RESULTS/ACTIONS
Y28 CHECK VEHICLE SPEED SENSOR (VSS) INPUT	1 Monitor the VSS__ARC PID while driving the vehicle.
	• Does the VSS__ARC indicate nearly the same speed as the speedometer?
	→ **Yes** All input signals and circuits are functional. RETURN to the Symptom Chart for further diagnostic procedures.
	→ **No** GO to **Y29**.
Y29 CHECK CIRCUIT 679 (GY/BK) FOR SHORT TO POWER	5 Measure the voltage between ARC module C2001-3, circuit 679 (GY/BK), and ground.
	• Is the voltage greater than zero volts?
	→ **Yes** REPAIR circuit 679 (GY/BK). TEST the system for normal operation.
	→ **No** GO to **Y30**.

FM2019700650160X

Fig. 28   Test Y: ARC System Does Not Seem To Be Working (Part 16 of 17)

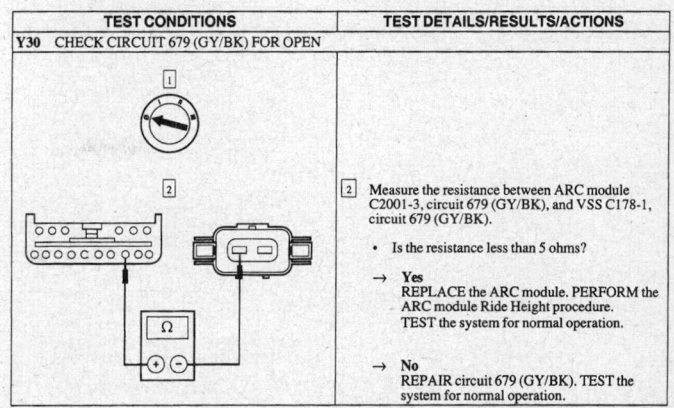

TEST CONDITIONS	TEST DETAILS/RESULTS/ACTIONS
Y30 CHECK CIRCUIT 679 (GY/BK) FOR OPEN	2 Measure the resistance between ARC module C2001-3, circuit 679 (GY/BK), and VSS C178-1, circuit 679 (GY/BK).
	• Is the resistance less than 5 ohms?
	→ **Yes** REPLACE the ARC module. PERFORM the ARC module Ride Height procedure. TEST the system for normal operation.
	→ **No** REPAIR circuit 679 (GY/BK). TEST the system for normal operation.

FM2019700650170X

Fig. 28   Test Y: ARC System Does Not Seem To Be Working (Part 17 of 17)

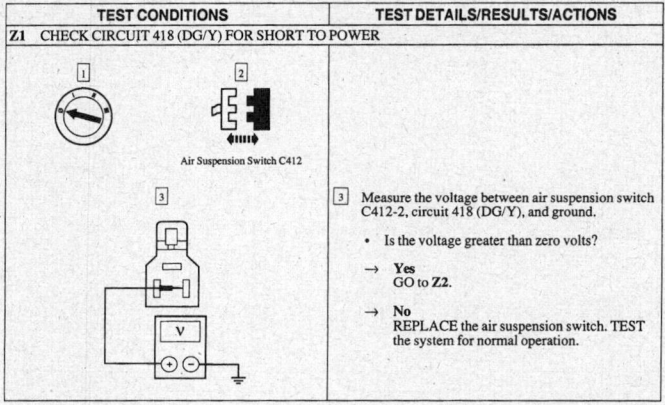

TEST CONDITIONS	TEST DETAILS/RESULTS/ACTIONS
Z1 CHECK CIRCUIT 418 (DG/Y) FOR SHORT TO POWER	3 Measure the voltage between air suspension switch C412-2, circuit 418 (DG/Y), and ground.
	• Is the voltage greater than zero volts?
	→ **Yes** GO to **Z2**.
	→ **No** REPLACE the air suspension switch. TEST the system for normal operation.

FM2019700651010X

Fig. 29   Test Z: ARC System Functions With Switch Off (Part 1 of 2)

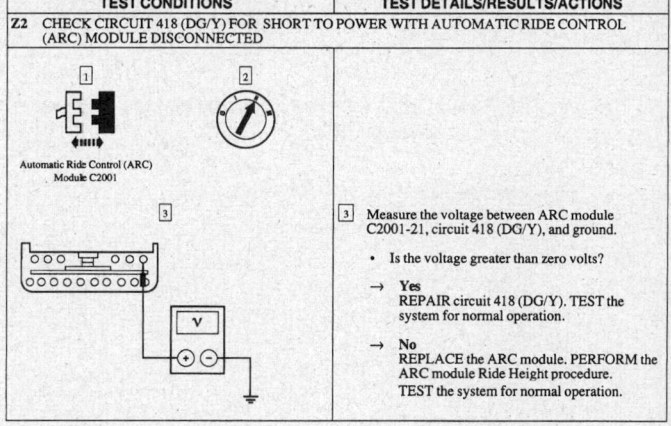

TEST CONDITIONS	TEST DETAILS/RESULTS/ACTIONS
Z2 CHECK CIRCUIT 418 (DG/Y) FOR SHORT TO POWER WITH AUTOMATIC RIDE CONTROL (ARC) MODULE DISCONNECTED	3 Measure the voltage between ARC module C2001-21, circuit 418 (DG/Y), and ground.
	• Is the voltage greater than zero volts?
	→ **Yes** REPAIR circuit 418 (DG/Y). TEST the system for normal operation.
	→ **No** REPLACE the ARC module. PERFORM the ARC module Ride Height procedure. TEST the system for normal operation.

FM2019700651020X

Fig. 29   Test Z: ARC System Functions With Switch Off (Part 2 of 2)

TEST CONDITIONS	TEST DETAILS/RESULTS/ACTIONS
AA1 CHECK CIRCUIT 417 (P/O) FOR SHORT TO POWER	4 Measure the voltage between air compressor connector C430, circuit 417 (P/O), and ground.
	• Is the voltage greater than zero volts?
	→ **Yes** REPAIR circuit 417 (P/O). TEST the system for normal operation.
	→ **No** REPLACE the air compressor relay. TEST the system for normal operation.

FM2019700652000X

Fig. 30   Test AA: Compressor Cycles Continuously With Key Off

TEST CONDITIONS	TEST DETAILS/RESULTS/ACTIONS
AB1 CHECK COMPRESSOR WIRING FOR CONTACT WITH UNDERBODY	1 Check the wiring harness for any contact to the underbody.
	• Is contact being made between the harness and the underbody at any point along the harness?
	→ **Yes** SECURE the air compressor wiring harness away from the vehicle underbody. TEST the system for normal operation.
	→ **No** GO to **AB2**.

FM2019700653010X

Fig. 31   Test AB: Excessive Compressor Noise (Part 1 of 2)

TEST CONDITIONS	TEST DETAILS/RESULTS/ACTIONS
AB2 CHECK FOR BENT AIR COMPRESSOR BRACKET	
	1 Inspect the air compressor bracket for any bends that may contact the underbody of the vehicle at any body height.
	• Is contact being made or the possibility of contact being made at any point in spring compression?
	→ **Yes** REPAIR the bracket or REPLACE the air compressor and bracket assembly. TEST the system for normal operation.
	→ **No** GO to **AB3**.
AB3 CHECK AIR COMPRESSOR MOUNTS FOR DAMAGE	
	1 Inspect the compressor mounts for signs of cracks or the breaking away of insulating material.
	• Are any defects in the mounts present?
	→ **Yes** REPLACE the air compressor and bracket assembly. TEST the system for normal operation.
	→ **No** GO to **AB4**.
AB4 CHECK AIR COMPRESSOR FOR NOISE	
	1 Remove the air compressor from mounting position, but leave it connected to the wiring harness.
	2 Run the air compressor while holding the compressor away from the body and undercarriage.
	• Is the air compressor noisy?
	→ **Yes** REPLACE the air compressor and bracket assembly. TEST the system for normal operation.
	→ **No** RECHECK the mountings and bracket for damage. REPLACE the air compressor and/or bracket assembly if any damage is found. TEST the system for normal operation.

FM2019700653020X

Fig. 31   Test AB: Excessive Compressor Noise (Part 2 of 2)

TEST CONDITIONS	TEST DETAILS/RESULTS/ACTIONS
AC2 CHECK AIR COMPRESSOR RELAY	
Air Compressor Relay	2 Inspect the pins and terminals of the air compressor relay connector for corrosion, bent or broken pins, moisture, or other damage.
	• Is the air compressor relay OK?
	→ **Yes** GO to **AC3**.
	→ **No** REPAIR or REPLACE as necessary. CLEAR all DTCs. REPEAT the ARC Module Diagnostics.
AC3 CHECK CIRCUIT 1053 (LB/PK)	
	1 Measure the voltage between air compressor relay pin 87, circuit 1053 (LB/PK), and ground.
	• Is the voltage greater than 11 volts?
	→ **Yes** GO to **AC4**.
	→ **No** REPAIR circuit 1053 (LB/PK). CLEAR all DTCs. REPEAT the ARC Module Diagnostics.

FM2019700654020X

Fig. 32   Test AC: Air Compressor Test (Part 2 of 5)

TEST CONDITIONS	TEST DETAILS/RESULTS/ACTIONS
AC1 CHECK FUSE 3 (50A)	
	2 Turn the air suspension switch to the OFF position.

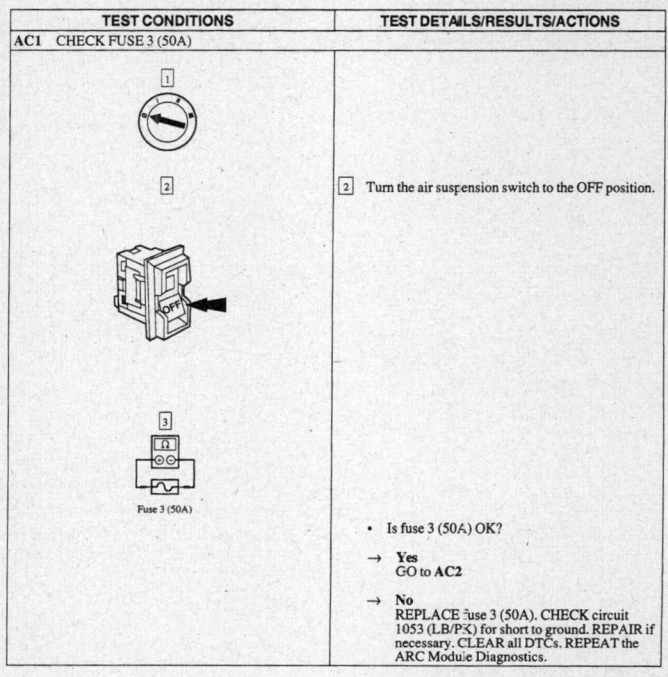

	• Is fuse 3 (50A) OK?
	→ **Yes** GO to **AC2**
	→ **No** REPLACE fuse 3 (50A). CHECK circuit 1053 (LB/PK) for short to ground. REPAIR if necessary. CLEAR all DTCs. REPEAT the ARC Module Diagnostics.

FM2019700654010X

Fig. 32   Test AC: Air Compressor Test (Part 1 of 5)

TEST CONDITIONS	TEST DETAILS/RESULTS/ACTIONS
AC4 CHECK CIRCUIT 417 (P/O)	
Air Compressor Assembly C430	2 Measure the resistance between air compressor relay pin 30, circuit 417 (P/O), and air compressor assembly C430-4, circuit 417 (P/O).
	• Is the resistance less than 5 ohms?
	→ **Yes** GO to **AC5**.
	→ **No** REPAIR circuit 417 (P/O). CLEAR all DTCs. REPEAT the ARC Module Diagnostics.
AC5 CHECK CIRCUIT 57 (BK)	
	1 Measure the resistance between air compressor assembly C430-1, circuit 57 (BK), and ground.
	• Is the resistance less than 5 ohms?
	→ **Yes** RECONNECT air compressor relay and air compressor assembly C430. GO to **AC6**.
	→ **No** REPAIR circuit 57 (BK). CLEAR all DTCs. REPEAT the ARC Module Diagnostics.
AC6 CHECK AIR COMPRESSOR AFTER COOL DOWN PERIOD	
	1 Allow the vehicle to sit for 60 minutes to give the air compressor assembly time to cool off.

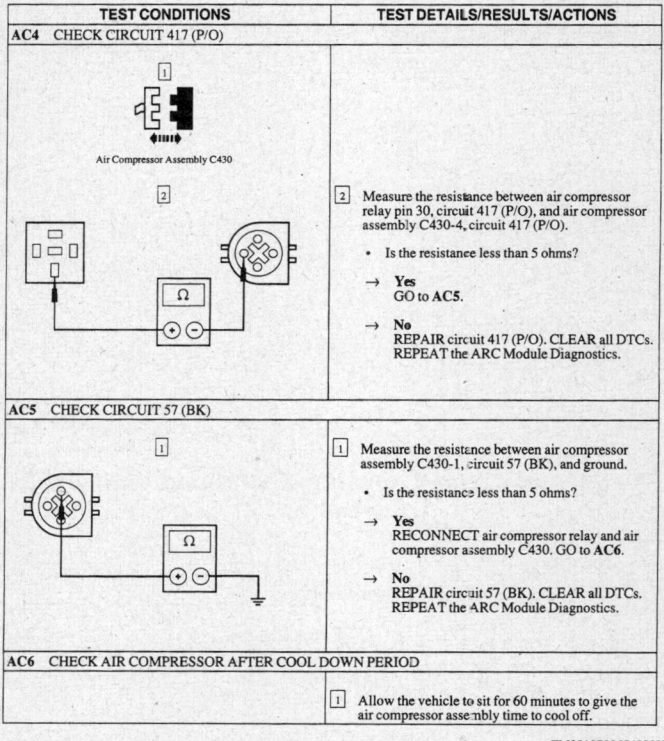

FM2019700654030X

Fig. 32   Test AC: Air Compressor Test (Part 3 of 5)

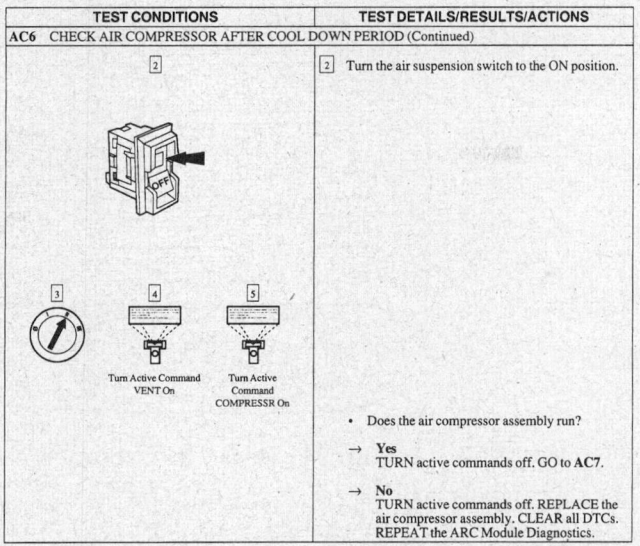

TEST CONDITIONS	TEST DETAILS/RESULTS/ACTIONS
AC6 CHECK AIR COMPRESSOR AFTER COOL DOWN PERIOD (Continued)	

2 — Turn the air suspension switch to the ON position.

3 — Turn Active Command VENT On

5 — Turn Active Command COMPRESSR On

- Does the air compressor assembly run?
- → **Yes**
  TURN active commands off. GO to **AC7.**
- → **No**
  TURN active commands off. REPLACE the air compressor assembly. CLEAR all DTCs. REPEAT the ARC Module Diagnostics.

FM2019700654040X

Fig. 32   Test AC: Air Compressor Test (Part 4 of 5)

TEST CONDITIONS	TEST DETAILS/RESULTS/ACTIONS
AC7 CHECK AIR COMPRESSOR THERMAL BREAKER	

1 — Turn Active Command COMPRESSR On

2 — Run the air compressor assembly for 60 seconds.

- Did the air compressor assembly run for 60 seconds?
- → **Yes**
  The thermal breaker was overheated. CLEAR all DTCs. REPEAT the ARC Module Diagnostics to VERIFY the system is OK.
- → **No**
  REPLACE the air compressor assembly. CLEAR all DTCs. REPEAT the ARC Module Diagnostics.

FM2019700654050X

Fig. 32   Test AC: Air Compressor Test (Part 5 of 5)

COMPONENT REPLACEMENT

Air Compressor & Dryer Assembly

1. **On models equipped with 4.0L engine,** place vehicle in AUTO.
2. **On models equipped with 5.0L engine,** place vehicle in NORMAL.
3. **On all models,** turn air suspension switch Off, then remove spare tire and raise and support vehicle
4. Push in and hold plastic release ring. while holding release ring, disconnect both air lines by pulling firmly.
5. Remove two mounting bracket nuts, then position air compressor bracket to access electrical connector and disconnect.
6. Remove air compressor assembly from vehicle from lefthand side of frame.
7. Remove four bolts and bracket from air compressor.
8. Reverse procedure to install. **Torque** compressor mounting nuts to 13–17 ft. lbs.

Front Height Sensor

1. **On models equipped with 4.0L engine,** place vehicle in AUTO.
2. **On models equipped with 5.0L engine,** place vehicle in NORMAL.
3. **On all models,** turn air suspension switch Off, then raise and support vehicle.
4. Disconnect electrical connector and gently pull electrical connector harness from frame and apron to separate push in fasteners.
5. Release spring clip and pull lower end of height sensor from lower ball stud bracket, **Fig. 33.**
6. Release spring clip and pull upper end of sensor from upper ball stud bracket.

Although the upper and lower height sensor brackets are serviceable, removing them is not required when removing height sensor.

7. Reverse procedure to install.

Rear Height Sensor

1. **On models equipped with 4.0L engine,** place vehicle in AUTO.
2. **On models equipped with 5.0L engine,** place vehicle in NORMAL.
3. **On all models,** turn air suspension switch to the OFF position, then raise and support vehicle.
4. Remove spare tire, then disconnect electrical connector and gently pull electrical connector harness from frame and apron to separate push in fasteners.
5. Release upper and lower spring clip and pull sensor from ball studs.
6. Reverse procedure to install.

Front Shock Absorber

Shock absorbers are charged with nitrogen gas. **Do not apply heat or attempt to open or puncture.** On models equipped with 4.0L engine, place vehicle in AUTO. On models equipped with 5.0L engine, place vehicle in NORMAL.

Prior to replacing air shocks, connect a New Generation Star (NGS) tester to the data link connector. Select the RIDE CONTROL OUTPUT screen and turn on the following solenoids to vent the entire system of air and to lower vehicle to its lowest possible height: FRONT-FIL, REAR-FIL, GATE, and VENT.

1. Turn air suspension switch Off.
2. Raise and support vehicle, then install suitable jack stands under the lower control arm to support axle during removal.
3. Disconnect electrical connector and pry harness retainers from frame.
4. Disconnect air line from shock absorber by pushing in and holding the plastic

ring on the shock. Pull firmly on air line.
5. **On lefthand shock absorber,** disconnect front height sensor from upper bracket.
6. **On right or lefthand shock absorber,** remove upper nut, washer and insulator assembly, then slightly compress front shock absorber by hand and remove from vehicle.
7. Reverse procedure to install. **Torque** upper nut to 25–34 ft. lbs. and lower nut to 18–24 ft. lbs.

Rear Shock Absorber

Shock absorbers are charged with nitrogen gas. **Do not apply heat or attempt to open or puncture.** On models equipped with 4.0L engine, place vehicle in AUTO. On models equipped with 5.0L engine, place vehicle in NORMAL.

Prior to replacing air shocks, connect a New Generation Star (NGS) tester to the data link connector. Select the RIDE CONTROL OUTPUT screen and turn on the following solenoids to vent the entire system of air and to lower vehicle to its lowest possible height: FRONT-FIL, REAR-FIL, GATE, and VENT.

1. Turn air suspension switch Off.
2. Raise and support vehicle, then remove spare tire.
3. Support rear axle with a suitable jack.
4. Disconnect rear shock absorber electrical connector.
5. Push in red ring and remove air line.
6. Remove shock absorber lower retaining nut, then position shock to side.
7. Remove top attaching nuts, then the shock absorber.
8. Reverse procedure to install. **Torque** lower attaching nut to 39–53 ft. lbs. and upper attaching nuts to 15–21 ft. lbs.

Air Suspension Switch

1. Remove door panel at lefthand side of luggage compartment, then turn air suspension switch Off.
2. Remove screw and switch bracket, then disconnect electrical connector.
3. Remove switch and bracket, then press retaining clips on side of switch and pull switch from bracket.
4. Reverse procedure to install.

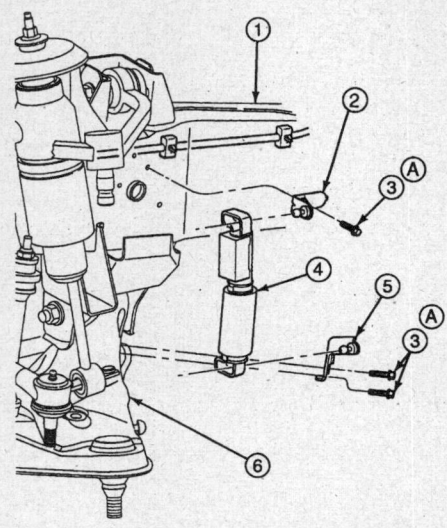

Item	Description
1	Frame
2	Front Height Sensor Upper Bracket
3	Bolt
4	Front Height Sensor
5	Front Height Sensor Lower Bracket
6	Front Suspension Lower Arm (LH)
A	Tighten to 7.5-10.5 N·m (67-93 Lb-In)

FM2019500334000X

Fig. 33 Front height sensor components

Front Fill Solenoid

Prior to replacing fill solenoid, connect a New Generation Star (NGS) tester to the data link connector. Select the RIDE CONTROL OUTPUT screen and turn on the following solenoids to vent the entire system of air and to lower vehicle to its lowest possible height: FRONT-FIL, REAR-FIL, GATE, and VENT.

1. **On models equipped with 4.0L engine,** place vehicle in AUTO.
2. **On models equipped with 5.0L engine,** place vehicle in NORMAL.
3. **On all models,** turn air suspension switch Off, then raise and support vehicle.
4. Pry front fill solenoid valve from left-hand frame rail, then push and hold plastic release ring at front and rear of solenoid valve.
5. While holding release ring, disconnect air line at front and rear of solenoid valve by pulling firmly.
6. Reverse procedure to install.

Rear Fill & Gate Solenoid

Prior to replacing fill solenoid, connect a New Generation Star (NGS) tester to the data link connector. Select the RIDE CONTROL OUTPUT screen and turn on the following solenoids to vent the entire system of air and to lower vehicle to its lowest possible height: FRONT-FIL, REAR-FIL, GATE, and VENT.

1. **On models equipped with 4.0L engine,** place vehicle in AUTO.
2. **On models equipped with 5.0L engine,** place vehicle in NORMAL.
3. **On all models,** turn air suspension switch Off, then raise and support vehicle and remove spare tire.
4. To access air lines pry plastic pushpins from air solenoid and rear frame crossmember and disconnect electrical connector.
5. To release both air lines, push in and hold plastic release ring. While holding release ring, disconnect air lines from both ends of air solenoid by pulling out firmly.
6. Reverse procedure to install.

Automatic Ride Control Module

1. **On models equipped with 4.0L engine,** place vehicle in AUTO.
2. **On models equipped with 5.0L engine,** place vehicle in NORMAL.

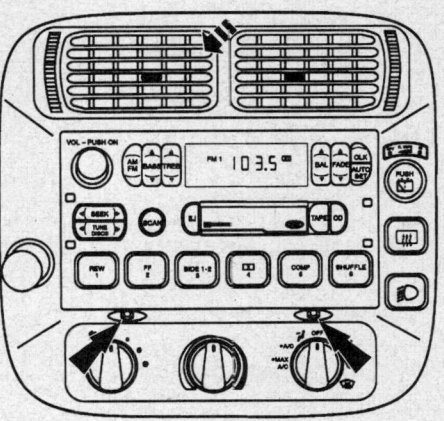

FM2019500336000X

Fig. 34 Radio trim removal

3. **On all models,** remove radio trim center vent assembly, **Fig. 34.**
4. Remove message center, then the control module retaining screw. Slide module down and out from support.
5. Disconnect electrical connectors.
6. Reverse procedure to install. Refer to "Adjustments" to reset ride heights.

Steering Sensor

1. Disconnect electrical connector at lower end of steering column, then pry connector harness retainer from lower steering column bend bracket.
2. Remove two retaining bolts along with steering sensor.
3. Reverse procedure to install.

Steering Sensor Ring

1. Remove steering column as outlined in "Steering Column" section.
2. Remove steering sensor retaining bolts, then using a pair of needle nose pliers, remove steering sensor ring retaining spring.
3. Remove suspension height sensor control ring.
4. Reverse procedure to install.

Four Wheel & Rear Load Leveling

NOTE: On Air Bag Equipped Models, Refer To "Air Bag System Precautions" Located In The Front Of This Manual For System Disarming & Arming Procedures.

NOTE: Refer To "Computer Relearn Procedures" Located In The Front Of This Manual When Battery Power To The Computer Has Been Interrupted.

NOTE: "Electrical Symbol & Wire Color Code Identification" Located In The Front Of This Manual May Be Used As An Aid When Using Wiring Circuits Found In This Section.

INDEX

	Page No.
Adjustments	6-45
Air Line Fluid Purge	6-46
Front	6-46
Rear	6-47
Ride Height	6-45
Expedition, F-Series & Navigator	6-45
Explorer & Mountaineer	6-46
Component Replacement	6-96
Air Compressor	6-96
Expedition, F–Series & Navigator	6-96
Explorer & Mountaineer	6-96
Air Spring Solenoid	6-96
Expedition, F-Series & Navigator	6-96
Air Suspension Switch	6-96
Expedition, F-Series & Navigator	6-96
Explorer & Mountaineer	6-96
Control Module	6-96

	Page No.
Expedition, F-Series & Navigator	6-96
Explorer & Mountaineer	6-96
Dryer	6-97
Explorer & Mountaineer	6-97
Front Shocks	6-96
Expedition, F-Series & Navigator	6-96
Height Sensors	6-96
Expedition, F-Series & Navigator	6-96
Explorer & Mountaineer	6-96
Rear Air Shock Absorber	6-96
Explorer & Mountaineer	6-96
Rear Air Spring	6-96
Expedition, F-Series & Navigator	6-96
Rear Fill Solenoid Valve	6-97
Explorer & Mountaineer	6-97
Rear Gate Solenoid Valve	6-97
Explorer & Mountaineer	6-97

	Page No.
Description	6-45
Expedition, F-Series & Navigator	6-45
Explorer & Mountaineer	6-45
Diagnosis & Testing	6-47
Accessing Diagnostic Trouble Codes	6-47
Clearing Diagnostic Trouble Codes	6-47
Diagnostic Tests	6-47
Four Wheel Air Suspension System	6-47
Rear Load Leveling System	6-47
Diagnostic Trouble Code Interpretation	6-47
Wiring Diagrams	6-47
Diagnostic Chart Index	6-52
Precautions	6-45
Air Bag Systems	6-45
Battery Ground Cable	6-45
Service	6-45

PRECAUTIONS

Air Bag Systems

Refer to "Air Bag System Precautions" in the front of this manual for system disarming and arming procedures.

Battery Ground Cable

Prior to service, disconnect battery ground cable and isolate as required.

Service

Before servicing an air suspension component, disconnect power to system by turning air suspension switch Off or disconnect battery ground cable. Do not remove air spring when there is pressure in air spring. Do not remove air spring supporting components without exhausting air or supporting air spring.

DESCRIPTION

Expedition, F-Series & Navigator

The air suspension system is designed to improve ride, handling and general vehicle performance for on and off-road use. Ride is improved by using an air type spring. Handling is improved by maintaining constant vehicle attitude. Entering and exiting is improved by lowering the vehicle one inch below trim height, then for off-road performance the vehicle is raised one inch above trim height to increase ground clearance.

The system consists of unique rear air springs, front air shocks, the air compressor, air lines, air solenoids, height sensors, and control module, **Figs. 1 and 2.** With these components and signals, the control module commands changes in vehicle height that are required for both load leveling and vertical height adjustment.

Explorer & Mountaineer

Rear load leveling maintains rear vehicle height using a height sensor, steering sensor and other vehicle sensors to measure driver and road inputs. The system maintains vehicle height on the rear axle thorough the use of an air compressor, two air solenoids, air lines and an air spring integrated inside each shock.

ADJUSTMENTS

Ride Height

EXPEDITION, F-SERIES & NAVIGATOR

INFLATING & DEFLATING AIR SUSPENSION

1. Turn ignition to Run, then connect New Generation Star (NGS) tester, or equivalent to Data Link Connector located below steering column.
2. Select 4WAS module, then "Air Suspension Control Mode" under "Active Command Modes" menu.

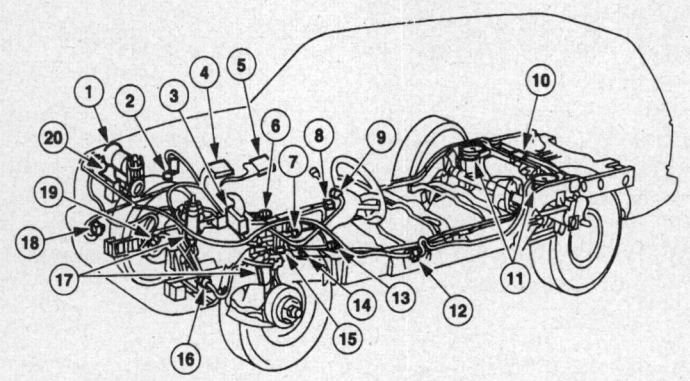

Item	Description
1	Compressor Air Dryer
2	Air Suspension Switch
3	Generic Electronic Module (GEM)
4	Powertrain Control Module
5	Control Module
6	Check Air Suspension Indicator
7	Vehicle Speed Sensor
8	Electronic Steering Sensor
9	Ignition Switch
10	Air Suspension Height Sensor, Rear

Item	Description
11	Rear Air Springs
12	Rear Fill Solenoid
13	Brake On/Off (BOO) Switch
14	Electronic Variable Orifice (EVO) Actuator
15	Air Suspension Height Sensor, Front
16	Front Gate Solenoid
17	Front Air Springs
18	Air Compressor Relay
19	Front Fill Solenoid
20	Air Compressor

FM2019700337000X

Fig. 1   Four wheel air suspension component locations. Expedition, F-Series & Navigator

Item	Description
1	Compressor Air Dryer
2	Air Suspension Switch
3	Generic Electronic Module (GEM)
4	Powertrain Control Module
5	Control Module
6	Check Air Suspension Indicator
7	Vehicle Speed Sensor
8	Electronic Steering Sensor

Item	Description
9	Ignition Switch
10	Air Suspension Height Sensor (Rear)
11	Rear Air Springs
12	Brake On/Off (BOO) Switch
13	Electronic Variable Orifice (EVO) Actuator
14	Air Compressor Relay
15	Air Compressor

FM2019700345000X

Fig. 2   Rear load leveling component locations. Expedition, F-Series & Navigator

3. Select VENT-FRNT to deflate front down, select LIFT-FRNT to inflate front up. Select VENT-REAR to deflate rear down, select LIFT-REAR to inflate rear up.

REAR HEIGHT RESETTING

1. Turn ignition On, then connect New Generation Star (NGS) tester, or equivalent to Data Link Connector (DLC) located below steering column.
2. Select 4WAS module, then measure vehicle rear height on driver's side from bottom of the frame to rear jounce bumper bolt rear side of head base, **Fig. 3.**
3. Select "Active Command Modes" using NGS tester and adjust rear height to 5.78 inches (146.8 mm) by moving rear of vehicle down (VENT-REAR) or up (LIFT-REAR).
4. Monitor on righthand side of NGS screen rear height sensor voltage, then loosen ball stud nut on rear height sensor bracket on track bar and adjust by moving with height sensor up or down until voltage is 2.61 volts.
5. **Torque** ball stud nut to 8–10 ft. lbs.

FRONT HEIGHT SETTING

1. Drive vehicle, then turn ignition Off and back to Run. Exit vehicle, close door and allow system to vent vehicle down to kneel height.
2. Connect New Generation Star (NGS) tester, or equivalent, to data link connector located below steering column.
3. Select 4WAS module, then select "Parameter Reset Command" under "Active Command Modes" menu. Trigger through warning message and reset

"Front" and "Rear" (turn from Off to On).
4. Back out torsion bar adjustment bolt approximately 1½ inches from bolt head to bottom surface of torsion bar adjuster.
5. Deflate front air shocks by using NGS "Vent Front" command in "Air Suspension Control" menu and jounce front of vehicle to fully lower the front.
6. Measure vehicle ride height, which should meet specifications as follows:
   a. **On 2002 models,** ride height should be 3.03–3.27 inches.
   b. **On 2003 models,** ride height should be 3.03–3.23 inches.
7. **On all models, do not under any circumstances save rear ride height. There are pre-calibrated values already stored in control module.**
8. Once mechanically ride heights are set select "Save Calibration Values" under "Active Command Modes" menu to calibrate module. Trigger through warning message and save "Front" (turn from Off to On).

EXPLORER & MOUNTAINEER

1. Connect NGS Tester to DLC.
2. Select RIDE CONTROL OUTPUT screen and turn following solenoids on:
   a. REAR FILL, rear fill solenoid.
   b. GATE VALVE, gate solenoid.
   c. VENT, vent solenoid.
   d. This will vent entire system of air.
3. Close all doors, liftgate and liftgate window.

4. Ensure height will not change by opening any door.
5. Park vehicle on flat surface.
6. Select RIDE HEIGHT CALIBRATION.
7. Follow NGS Tester instructions to adjust ride height.
8. Lower vehicle and clear all DTC's.

Air Line Fluid Purge

FRONT

Perform this procedure if water or oil has found its way into the front or rear air lines.
1. Disconnect air line from compressor air dryer front fill solenoid inlet.
2. Disconnect air line from inlet of front fill solenoid, then connect shop air line and blow out any fluid.
3. Reconnect air line, then disconnect air line from compressor air dryer front fill solenoid inlet.
4. Disconnect air line at righthand front shock, then connect New Generation Star (NGS) tester or equivalent to data link connector located below steering column.
5. Select active command mode for 4WAS and turn on FRNT-FILL solenoid.
6. Connect shop air line to disconnected air line and blow out any fluid.
7. Reconnect air line at righthand front shock, then disconnect lefthand front shock and turn on FRNT-FILL solenoid and then GATEVALVE solenoids.
8. Connect shop air line to disconnected air line and blow out and fluid.
9. **Do not replace shock absorber for presence of water.** If oil is present in air lines, replace both lefthand and righthand shock absorbers.
10. Replace compressor air dryer, then connect air lines to compressor dryer.

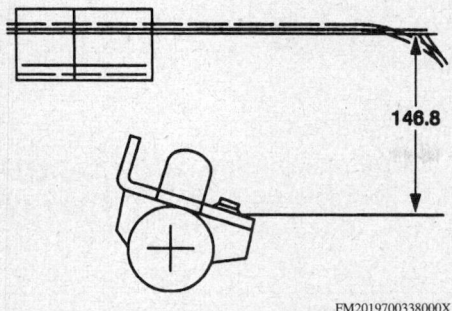

Fig. 3 Frame to rear jounce bumper bolt measurement. Expedition, F-Series & Navigator

DTCs	Description	Source	Action
C1770	Air Suspension Vent Solenoid Output Circuit Failure	Air Suspension Control Module	GO to Pinpoint Test K.
C1790	Air Suspension LR Air Spring Solenoid Output Circuit Failure	Air Suspension Control Module	GO to Pinpoint Test L.
C1795	Air Suspension RR Air Spring Solenoid Output Circuit Failure	Air Suspension Control Module	GO to Pinpoint Test M.
C1830	Air Suspension Compressor Relay Circuit Failure	Air Suspension Control Module	GO to Pinpoint Test N.
C1845	Air Suspension Front Inflator (Fill) Solenoid Output Circuit Failure	Air Suspension Control Module	GO to Pinpoint Test O.
C1865	Air Suspension Rear Inflator (Fill) Solenoid Output Circuit Failure	Air Suspension Control Module	GO to Pinpoint Test P.
C1869	Air Suspension Gate Solenoid Output Circuit Failure	Air Suspension Control Module	GO to Pinpoint Test Q.
C1917	Steering EVO Out-of-Range Fault	Air Suspension Control Module	REPAIR the steering system.
P1807	4x4 High Indicator Circuit Short to Ground	PCM	GO to Pinpoint Test R.
P1808	4x4 Low Indicator Circuit Short to Ground	PCM	GO to Pinpoint Test R.

FM2010100674020X

Fig. 4 Diagnostic trouble code interpretation (Part 2 of 2). four wheel air suspension

REAR

1. Disconnect air line from compressor air dryer rear fill solenoid inlet, then from the inlet of rear fill solenoid.
2. Connect shop air line to disconnected air line and blow out any fluid, then connect air line.
3. Disconnect air line from compressor air dryer rear fill solenoid inlet, then the air lines from rear lefthand and righthand air spring.
4. Connect New Generation Star (NGS) tester, or equivalent to Data Link Connector (DLC) located below steering column.
5. Select active command mode for 4WAS and turn on REAR-FILL, then connect shop air to disconnected air line and blow out any fluid.
6. Connect air line at rear lefthand and righthand air springs.
7. Replace compressor air dryer, then connect air lines to compressor dryer.

DTCs	Description	Source	Action
B1318	Battery Voltage Low	Air Suspension Control Module	GO to Pinpoint Test C.
B1342	ECU Is Defective	Air Suspension Control Module	REPLACE the air suspension control module. RESET front height Clear B2140 DTC. TEST the system for normal operation.
B1485	Brake Pedal Input Circuit Battery Short	Air Suspension Control Module	RERUN On-Demand Self-Test; MAKE SURE that the brake pedal is not pressed. If the DTC is returned again, REPAIR the brake pedal position circuit.
B1566	Door Ajar Circuit Short to Ground	Air Suspension Control Module	GO to Pinpoint Test D.
B1749	Park/Neutral Switch Circuit Failure	Air Suspension Control Module	GO to Pinpoint Test E.
B2140	Initialization Failure (Vehicle Ride Height Not Programmed)	Air Suspension Control Module	REFER to Adjustments Clear B2140 DTC.
C1439	Vehicle Acceleration EEC-IV Circuit Failure	Air Suspension Control Module	GO to Pinpoint Test F.
C1724	Air Suspension Height Sensor Power Circuit Failure	Air Suspension Control Module	GO to Pinpoint Test G.
C1725	Air Suspension Front Pneumatic Failure	Air Suspension Control Module	GO to Pinpoint Test H.
C1726	Air Suspension Rear Pneumatic Failure	Air Suspension Control Module	GO to Pinpoint Test I.
C1756	Air Suspension Front Height Sensor High Signal Circuit Failure	Air Suspension Control Module	GO to Pinpoint Test J.
C1760	Air Suspension Rear Height Sensor High Signal Circuit Failure	Air Suspension Control Module	GO to Pinpoint Test J.

FM2010100674010X

Fig. 4 Diagnostic trouble code interpretation (Part 1 of 2). four wheel air suspension

Condition	Possible Sources	Action
• No communication with the air suspension control module	• CJB Fuse 4 (15A), 6 (5A) and 20 (5A). • Circuitry. • Air suspension control module. • Air suspension switch.	• GO to Pinpoint Test A.
• Unable to enter self-test	• Air suspension control module	• GO to Pinpoint Test B.
• 4x2 vehicle returns front air suspension component DTC	• Circuitry.	• REPAIR Circuit 900 (BK) for possible intermittent short to ground.
• Vehicle changes height with the door open	• Circuitry. • Air suspension control module.	• GO to Pinpoint Test D.
• Vehicle raises and/or lowers too slowly	• Circuitry. • Rear pneumatic fault. • Air compressor assembly. • Air suspension control module.	• GO to Pinpoint Test I.

FM2010100656010X

Fig. 5 Diagnostic trouble code interpretation (Part 1 of 2). Expedition & Navigator w/Rear Load Leveling

DIAGNOSIS & TESTING

Accessing Diagnostic Trouble Codes

Connect New Generation Star (NGS) Tester, or equivalent to Data Link Connector located below steering column.

Diagnostic Trouble Code Interpretation

Refer to **Figs. 4 through 8** for Diagnostic Trouble Code interpretation.

Wiring Diagrams

Refer to **Figs. 9 and 10** for wiring diagrams.

Diagnostic Tests

FOUR WHEEL AIR SUSPENSION SYSTEM

Refer to **Figs. 11 through 34** when diagnosing the Four Wheel Air Suspension system.

REAR LOAD LEVELING SYSTEM

Refer to **Figs. 35 through 51** when diagnosing the Rear Load Leveling system.

Clearing Diagnostic Trouble Codes

Connect New Generation Star (NGS) tester, or equivalent to Data Link Connector (DLC). Select "Retrieve/Clear Continuous Diagnostic Trouble Codes" from menu. Follow tester instructions to clear codes.

ACTIVE SUSPENSION SYSTEMS

Condition	Possible Sources	Action
• Uneven vehicle height	• Circuitry. • Rear pneumatic fault. • Air compressor assembly. • Air suspension control module.	• GO to Pinpoint Test I.
• The air compressor continuously cycles with the ignition switch in the Off position and no DTC is set	• Circuitry. • Air suspension control module. • Air suspension relay.	• GO to Pinpoint Test M.
• The air suspension system is inoperative	• Circuitry.	• GO to Pinpoint Test N.
• Excessive air compressor operation	• Circuitry.	• GO to Pinpoint Test N.
• Harsh or bouncy ride	• Circuitry.	• GO to Pinpoint Test N.
• Ride height changes unexpectedly	• Circuitry.	• GO to Pinpoint Test N.
• The air suspension system operates with the air suspension switch in the OFF position	• Circuitry. • Switch. • Air suspension control module.	• GO to Pinpoint Test O.
• Excessive air compressor noise	• Silencer. • Wire harness. • Mounting bracket.	• GO to Pinpoint Test P.
• The compressor is inoperative	• BJB Fuse 109 (50A). • Air compressor assembly. • Circuitry. • Air suspension relay.	• GO to Pinpoint Test Q.

FM2010100656020X

Fig. 5 Diagnostic trouble code interpretation (Part 2 of 2). Expedition & Navigator w/Rear Load Leveling

DTC	Description	Action
13	Auto Test Failed	—
15	No Drive Cycle Errors Detected	—
35	Drive Cycle Error Codes Erased	—
37	RH Air Spring Solenoid Circuit Shorted to Ground or Open	GO to Pinpoint Test A.
38	RH Air Spring Solenoid Circuit Shorted to Power	GO to Pinpoint Test B.
39	Air Compressor Relay Control Circuit Shorted to Power	GO to Pinpoint Test C.
40	Air Compressor Relay Control Circuit Shorted to Ground	GO to Pinpoint Test C.
42	LH Air Spring Solenoid Circuit Shorted to Ground or Open	GO to Pinpoint Test D.
43	LH Air Spring Solenoid Circuit Shorted to Power	GO to Pinpoint Test E.
44	Vent Solenoid Valve Shorted to Power	GO to Pinpoint Test F.
45	Vent Solenoid Valve Circuit Shorted to Ground or Open	GO to Pinpoint Test G.
46	Air Suspension Height Sensor Supply Circuit Shorted to Power or Ground	GO to Pinpoint Test H.
49	Unable to Detect Lowering of Right Rear	GO to Pinpoint Test J.
51	Unable to Detect Lowering of Left Rear	GO to Pinpoint Test K.
52	Unable to Detect Raising of Right Rear	GO to Pinpoint Test L.
54	Unable to Detect Raising of Left Rear	GO to Pinpoint Test M.
60	Air Suspension Switch Shorted to Power	GO to Pinpoint Test Q.
61	Air Suspension Switch Shorted to Ground or Open	GO to Pinpoint Test R.
66	Short in RH Rear Air Suspension Height Sensor Circuit	GO to Pinpoint Test S.
68	Short in LH Rear Air Suspension Height Sensor Circuit	GO to Pinpoint Test T.
69	RH Rear Air Suspension Height Sensor Circuit Open	GO to Pinpoint Test U.
70	Control Module Failure	REPLACE control module.
71	LH Rear Air Suspension Height Sensor Circuit Open	GO to Pinpoint Test V.
80	Control Module Detects Low Battery Voltage or Over Voltage	GO to Pinpoint Test W.

FM2019800453020X

Fig. 6 Diagnostic trouble code interpretation (Part 2 of 2). F-Series w/Rear Load Leveling

DTC	Description
B1318	Battery Voltage Low
B1342	ECU Is Defective

FM2019900556010X

Fig. 8 Diagnostic trouble code interpretation (Part 1 of 2). Explorer & Mountaineer

DTC	Description	Action
10	Diagnostics Entered, Auto Test in Progress	—
11	Vehicle Passes	If vehicle is still low or high in the rear, check ride height.
12	Auto Test Passed	—

FM2019800453010X

Fig. 6 Diagnostic trouble code interpretation (Part 1 of 2). F-Series w/Rear Load Leveling

Code	Description
23	Rear Right Air Spring Vent
24	Rear Left Air Spring Vent
25	Both Rear Air Springs Vent (4 second stagger)
26	Right Rear Air Spring Compress
27	Left Rear Air Spring Compress
28	Both Rear Air Springs Compress (4 second stagger)

FM2019800451010X

Fig. 7 Functional test code reference chart (Part 1 of 2). F-Series w/Rear Load Leveling

Code	Description
31	Toggle Compressor On and Off Repeatedly
32	Toggle Vent On and Off Repeatedly
33	Toggle Air Spring Solenoid Valves On and Off Repeatedly

FM2019800451020X

Fig. 7 Functional test code reference chart (Part 2 of 2). F-Series w/Rear Load Leveling

DTC	Description
B1485	Brake Pedal Position Switch Input Short to Battery
B1565	Door Ajar Input Short to Power
C1439	Acceleration Input Signal Circuit Failure
C1724	Height Sensor Power Circuit Failure
C1726	Rear Pneumatic Failure
C1760	Rear Height Sensor Circuit Failure
C1770	Vent Solenoid Circuit Failure
C1830	Air Compressor Relay Circuit Failure
C1865	Rear Fill Solenoid Circuit Failure
C1869	Rear Gate Solenoid

FM2019900556020X

Fig. 8 Diagnostic trouble code interpretation (Part 2 of 2). Explorer & Mountaineer

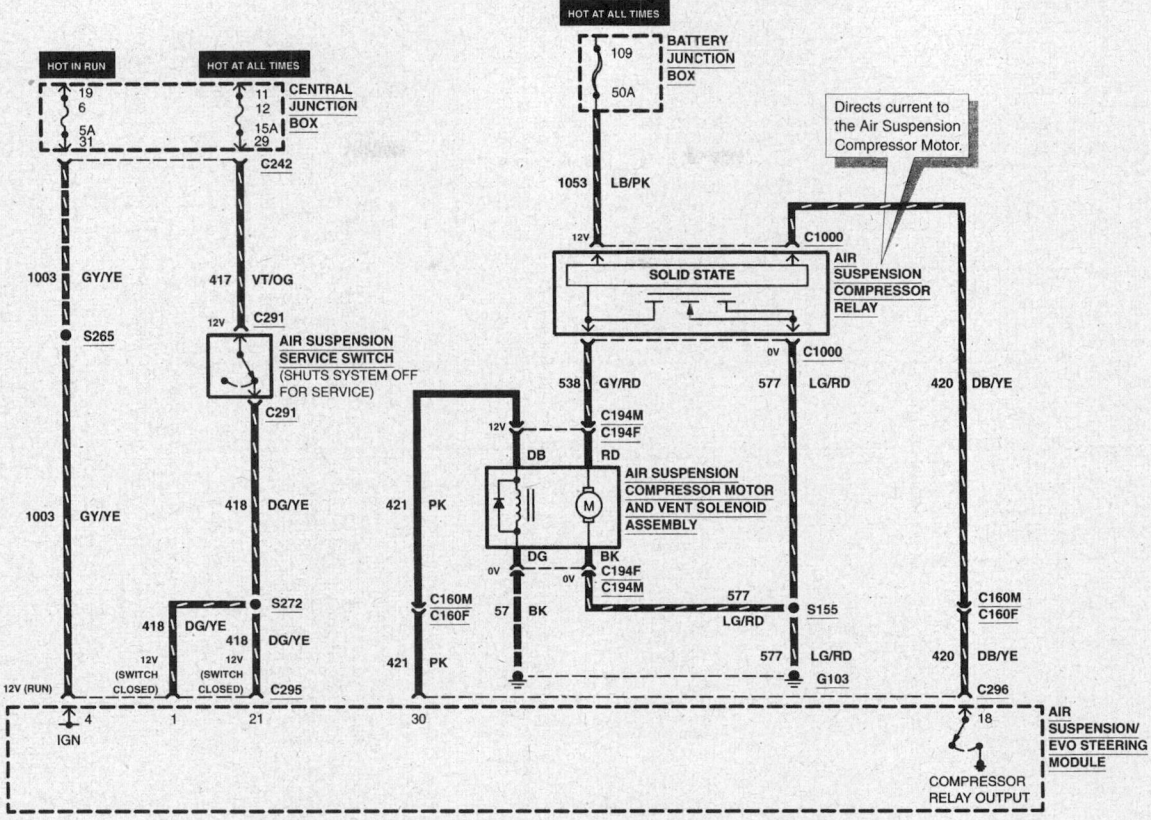

Fig. 9   Air suspension wiring diagram (Part 1 of 4). Expedition & Navigator

FM2010100709010X

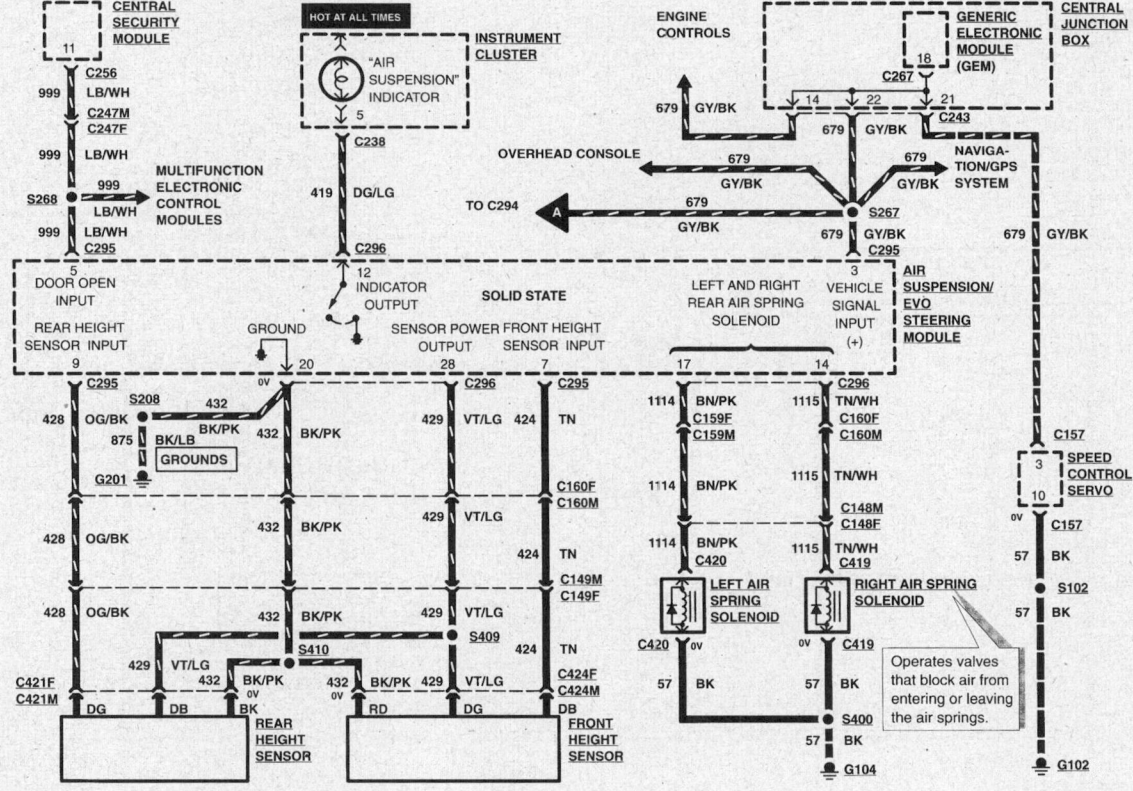

Fig. 9   Air suspension wiring diagram (Part 2 of 4). Expedition & Navigator

FM2010100709020X

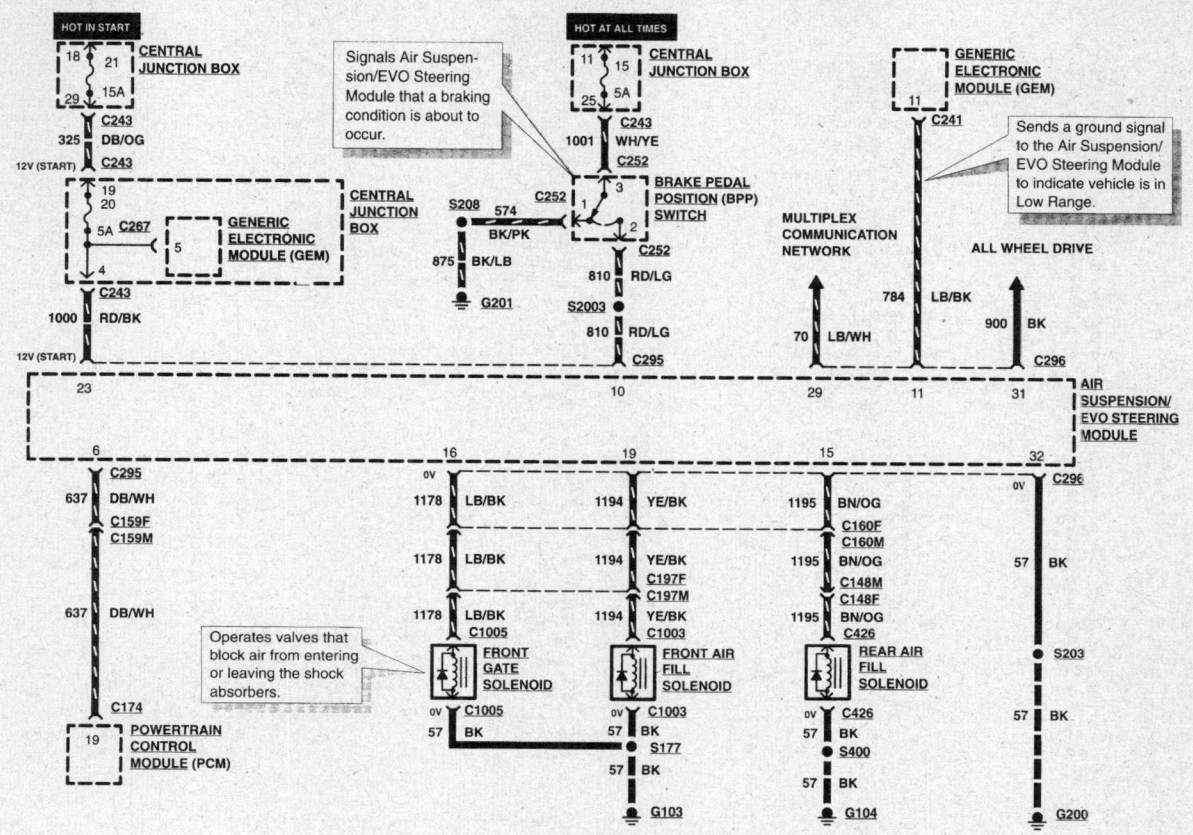

Fig. 9 Air suspension wiring diagram (Part 3 of 4). Expedition & Navigator

FM2010100709030X

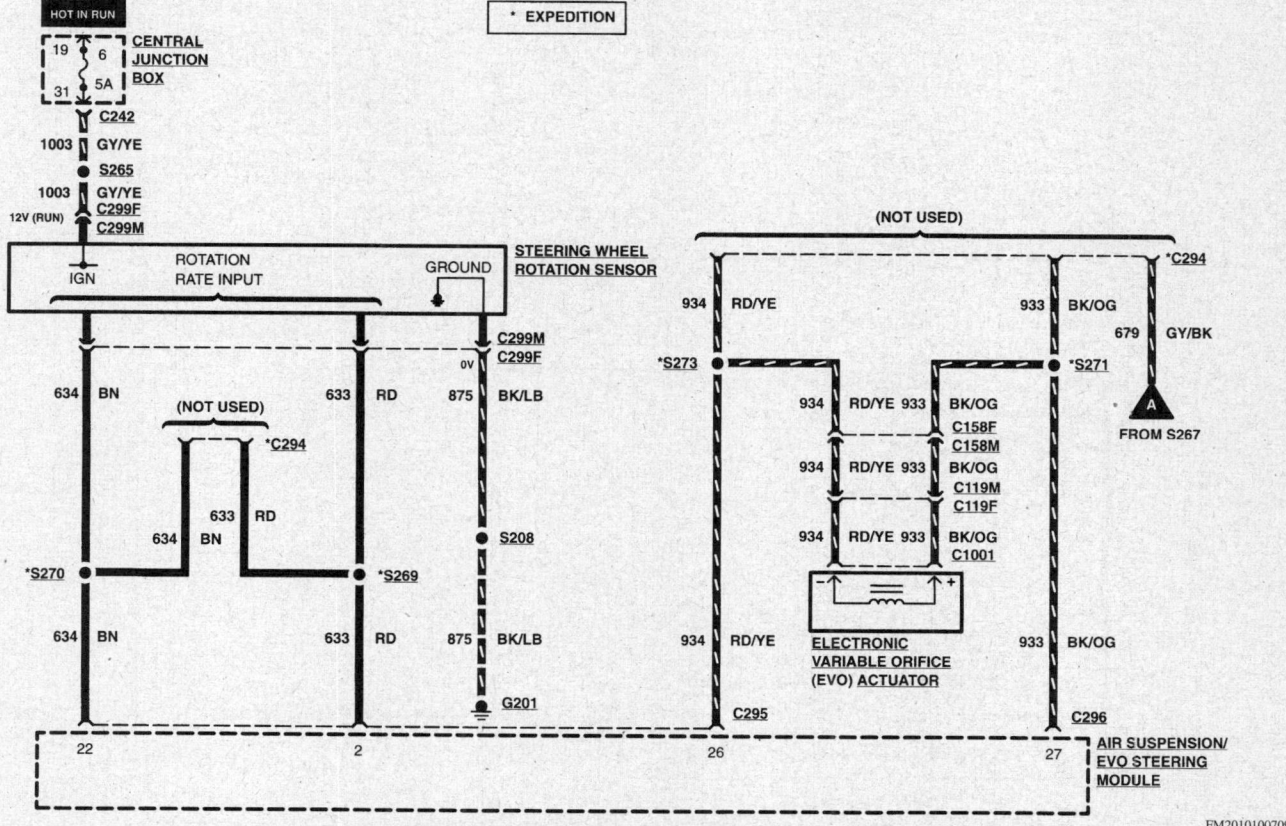

Fig. 9 Air suspension wiring diagram (Part 4 of 4). Expedition & Navigator

FM2010100709040X

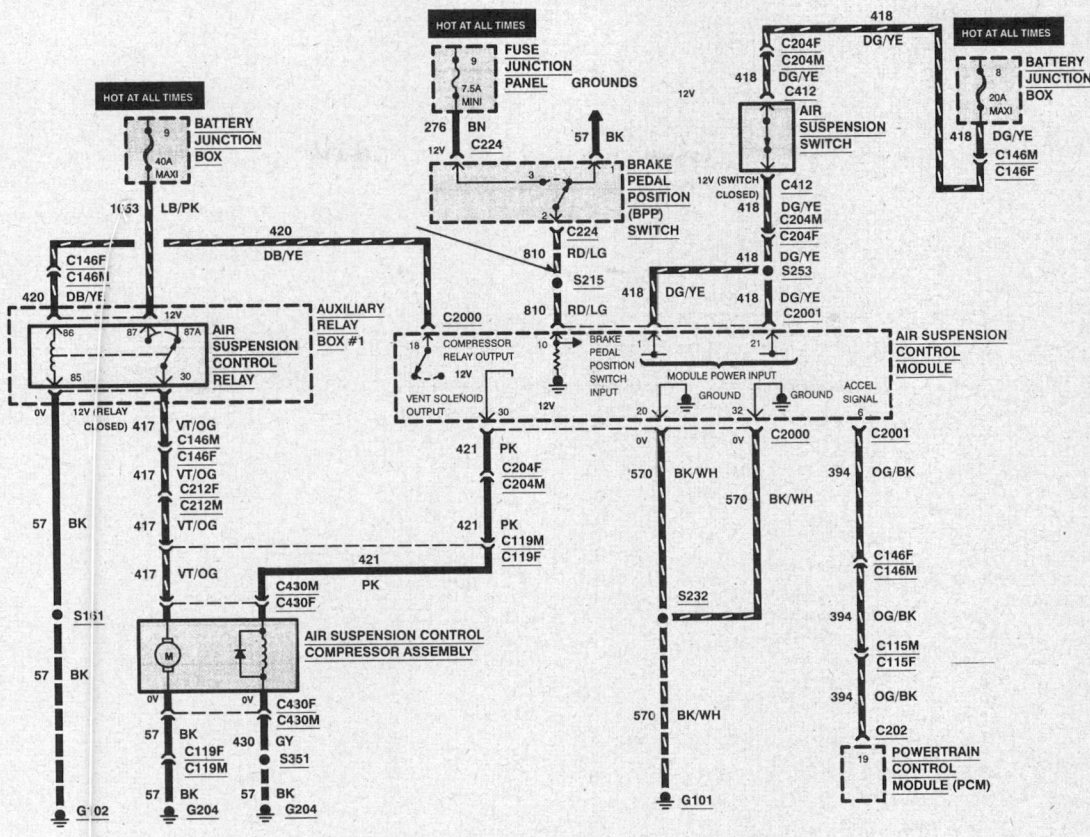

Fig. 10   Wiring diagram (Part 1 of 3). Explorer & Mountaineer

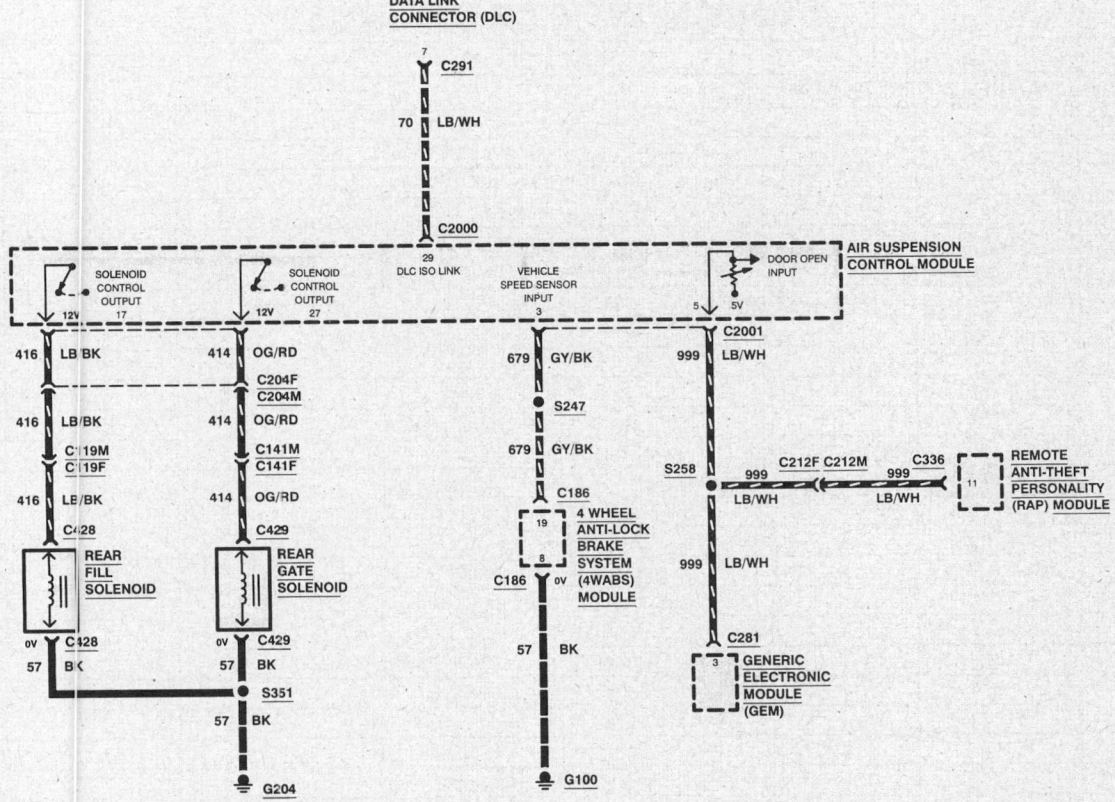

Fig. 10   Wiring diagram (Part 2 of 3). Explorer & Mountaineer

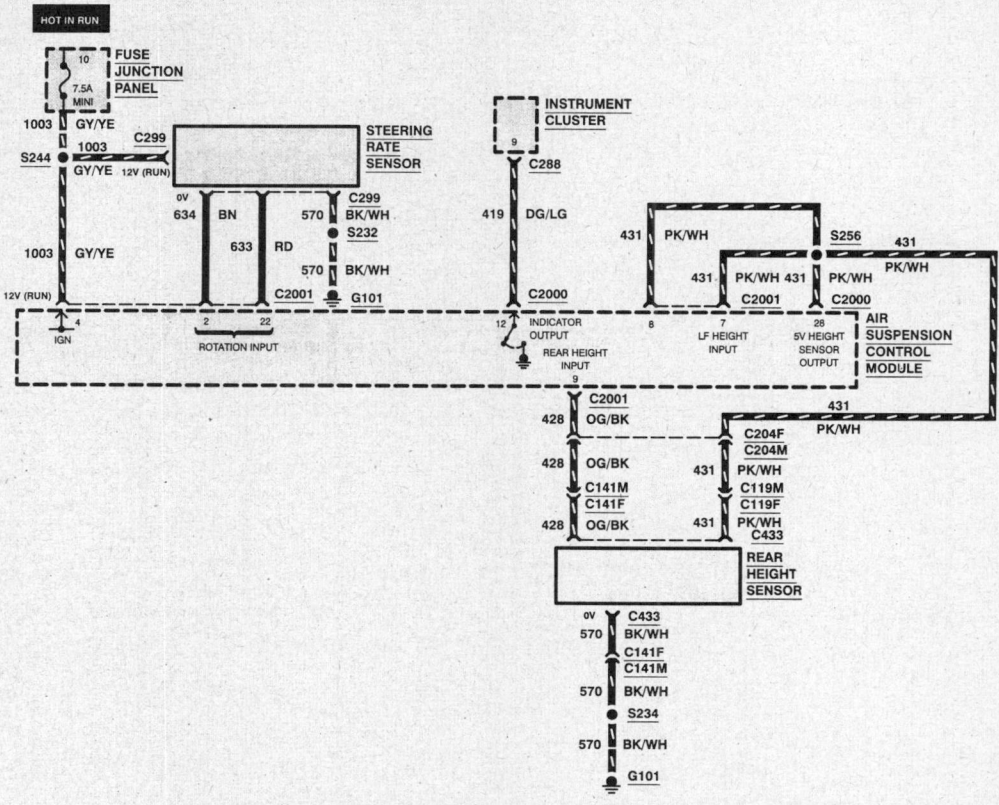

Fig. 10   Wiring diagram (Part 3 of 3). Explorer & Mountaineer

FM2019900557030X

DIAGNOSTIC CHART INDEX

Test	Code	Description	Page No.	Fig. No.
FOUR WHEEL AIR SUSPENSION SYSTEM				
—	—	Symptom Chart	6-53	11
A	—	No Communication w/ASC Module	6-53	12
B	—	Unable To Enter Self-Test	6-54	13
C	B1318	Battery Voltage Low	6-54	14
D	B1566	Door Ajar Circuit Short To Ground	6-55	15
E	B1749	Park-Neutral Switch Circuit Failure	6-55	16
F	C1439	Vehicle Acceleration EEC-IV Circuit Failure	6-55	17
G	C1724	Height Sensor Power Circuit Failure	6-56	18
H	C1725	Front Pneumatic Failure	6-56	19
I	C1726	Rear Pneumatic Failure	6-59	20
J	C1756	Height Sensor High Circuit Failure	6-61	21
	C1760	Height Sensor High Circuit Failure	6-61	21
K	C1770	Vent Solenoid Output Circuit Failure	6-62	22
L	C1790	Lefthand Rear Spring Solenoid Output Circuit Failure	6-64	23
M	C1795	Righthand Rear Spring Solenoid Output Circuit Failure	6-66	24
N	C1830	Compressor Relay Circuit Failure	6-68	25
O	C1845	Front Inflator Fill Solenoid Output Circuit Failure	6-69	26
P	C1865	Rear Inflator Fill Solenoid Output Circuit Failure	6-71	27
Q	C1869	Gate Solenoid Output Circuit Failure	6-73	28
R	P1807	4×4 Indicator Circuit Short To Ground	6-75	29
	P1808	4×4 Indicator Circuit Short To Ground	6-75	29
S	—	Compressor Cycles Continuously w/Ignition Off & No DTC Set	6-75	30
T	—	Air Suspension System Inoperative	6-76	31
U	—	Air Suspension System Operates With Switch Turned Off	6-77	32
V	—	Compressor Noise Excessive	6-77	33
W	—	Compressor Inoperative	6-78	34

Continued

DIAGNOSTIC CHART INDEX—Continued

Test	Code	Description	Page No.	Fig. No.
REAR LOAD LEVELING SYSTEM				
A	—	No Communication w/ASC Module	6-79	35
B	—	Unable To Enter Self-Test	6-79	36
C	B1318	Battery Voltage Low	6-80	37
D	B1566	Door Ajar Circuit Short To Ground	6-80	38
E	C1439	Vehicle Acceleration EEC-V Circuit Failure	6-80	39
F	C1724	Height Sensor Power Circuit	6-81	40
G	C1726	Rear Pneumatic Failure	6-81	41
H	C1760	Rear Height Sensor High Signal Circuit Failure	6-84	42
I	C1770	Air Suspension Vent Solenoid Output Circuit	6-85	43
J	C1790	Lefthand Rear Spring Solenoid Output Circuit Failure	6-87	44
K	C1795	Righthand Rear Spring Solenoid Output Circuit Failure	6-89	45
L	C1830	Compressor Relay Circuit Failure	6-91	46
M	—	Compressor Cycles Continuously w/Ignition Off & No DTC Set	6-92	47
N	—	Air Suspension System Inoperative	6-93	48
O	—	Air Suspension System Operates w/Switch Turned Off	6-94	49
P	—	Compressor Noise Excessive	6-94	50
Q	—	Compressor Inoperative	6-95	51

Condition	Possible Sources	Action
• No communication with the air suspension control module	• CJB fuses 4 (15A), 6 (5A), and 20 (5A). • Circuitry. • Air suspension control module. • Air suspension switch.	• GO to Pinpoint Test A.
• Unable to enter self-test	• Air suspension control module	• GO to Pinpoint Test B.
• 4x4 vehicle only uses rear air suspension components	• Circuitry.	• REPAIR circuit 900 (BK) for open.
• Vehicle changes height with the door ajar	• Circuitry. • Air suspension control module.	• GO to Pinpoint Test D.
• Vehicle raises and/or lowers too slowly	• Front/rear pneumatic fault. • Height sensor brackets. • Air compressor assembly. • Circuitry. • Solenoid. • Air line.	• GO to Pinpoint Test H and Pinpoint Test I.

FM2010100675010X

Fig. 11 Symptom chart (Part 1 of 2). four wheel air suspension system

Condition	Possible Sources	Action
• Uneven vehicle height	• Front/rear pneumatic fault. • Height sensor brackets. • Solenoid. • Air compressor assembly. • Air line. • Circuitry.	• GO to Pinpoint Test H and Pinpoint Test I.
• The air compressor continuously cycles with the ignition switch in the OFF position and no DTC is set	• Circuitry. • Air suspension relay. • Air suspension control module.	• GO to Pinpoint Test S.
• Air suspension system inoperative	• Circuitry.	• GO to Pinpoint Test T.
• Excessive air compressor operation	• Circuitry.	• GO to Pinpoint Test T.
• Harsh or bouncy ride	• Circuitry.	• GO to Pinpoint Test T.
• Ride height changes unexpectedly	• Circuitry.	• GO to Pinpoint Test T.
• Air suspension system operates with air suspension switch in the OFF position	• Circuitry. • Air suspension switch. • Air suspension control module.	• GO to Pinpoint Test U.
• Excessive air compressor noise	• Silencer. • Wire harness. • Mounting bracket. • Air compressor assembly.	• GO to Pinpoint Test V.
• The compressor is inoperative	• BJB Fuse 109 (50A). • Air compressor assembly. • Circuitry. • Suspension relay.	• GO to Pinpoint Test W.

FM2010100675020X

Fig. 11 Symptom chart (Part 2 of 2). four wheel air suspension system

CONDITIONS	DETAILS/RESULTS/ACTIONS
A1 CHECK POSITION OF AIR SUSPENSION SWITCH	
	1 Check to see if the air suspension switch is in the ON position. • Is the air suspension switch ON? → **Yes** GO to A2. → **No** Turn ON the air suspension switch. TEST the system for normal operation.

FM2010100676010X

Fig. 12 Test A: No Communication w/ASC Module (Part 1 of 3). Four wheel air suspension system

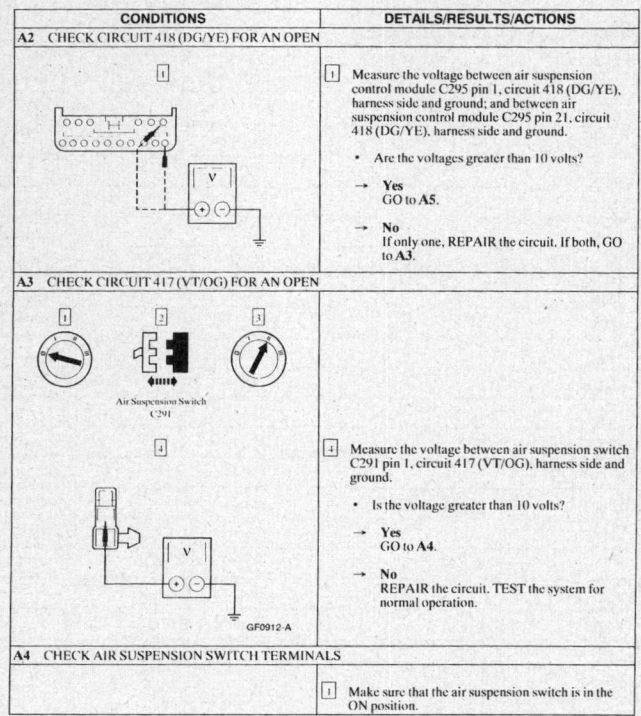

CONDITIONS	DETAILS/RESULTS/ACTIONS
A2 CHECK CIRCUIT 418 (DG/YE) FOR AN OPEN	1. Measure the voltage between air suspension control module C295 pin 1, circuit 418 (DG/YE), harness side and ground; and between air suspension control module C295 pin 21, circuit 418 (DG/YE), harness side and ground. • Are the voltages greater than 10 volts? → **Yes** GO to **A5**. → **No** If only one, REPAIR the circuit. If both, GO to **A3**.
A3 CHECK CIRCUIT 417 (VT/OG) FOR AN OPEN	4. Measure the voltage between air suspension switch C291 pin 1, circuit 417 (VT/OG), harness side and ground. • Is the voltage greater than 10 volts? → **Yes** GO to **A4**. → **No** REPAIR the circuit. TEST the system for normal operation.
A4 CHECK AIR SUSPENSION SWITCH TERMINALS	1. Make sure that the air suspension switch is in the ON position.

FM2010100676020X

Fig. 12   Test A: No Communication w/ASC Module (Part 2 of 3). Four wheel air suspension system

CONDITIONS	DETAILS/RESULTS/ACTIONS
B1 CHECK THE COMMUNICATIONS TO THE AIR SUSPENSION CONTROL MODULE	1. Check the communication to the air suspension control module. • Does scan tool communicate with the air suspension control module? → **Yes** INSTALL a new air suspension control module CLEAR the DTCs. REPEAT the Auto Test. TEST the system for normal operation. → **No** GO to Pinpoint Test A.

FM2010100677000X

Fig. 13   Test B: Unable To Enter Self-Test. Four wheel air suspension system

CONDITIONS	DETAILS/RESULTS/ACTIONS
C1 CHECK BATTERY VOLTAGE	1. Measure the voltage between battery positive post and battery negative post. • Is the voltage greater than 10 volts? → **Yes** GO to **C2**. → **No** REPAIR the charging system for battery does not hold a charge condition.
C2 CHECK CIRCUIT 1003 (GY/YE)	2. Turn the air suspension switch to the OFF position.

FM2010100678010X

Fig. 14   Test C/DTC B1318: Battery Voltage Low (Part 1 of 2). Four wheel air suspension system

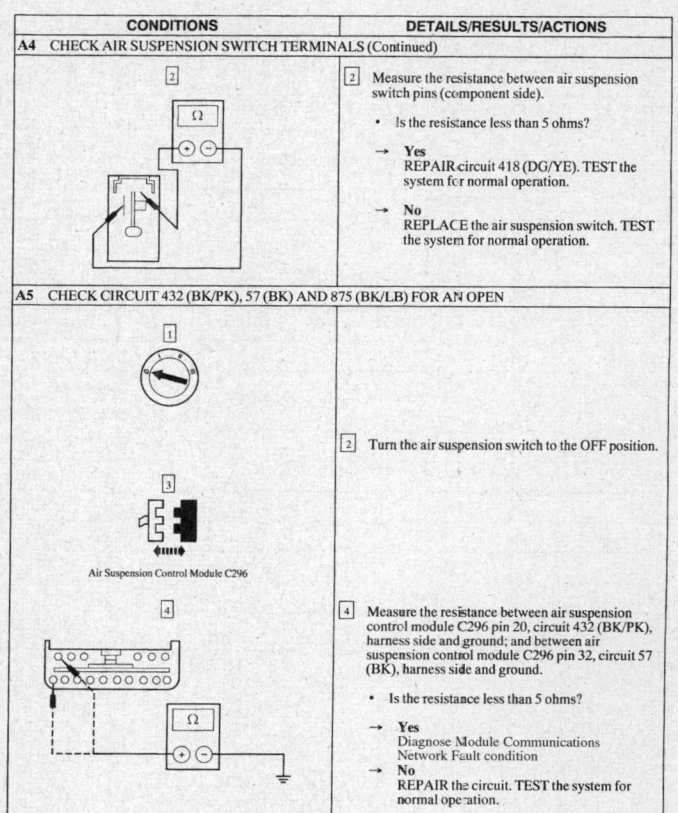

CONDITIONS	DETAILS/RESULTS/ACTIONS
A4 CHECK AIR SUSPENSION SWITCH TERMINALS (Continued)	2. Measure the resistance between air suspension switch pins (component side). • Is the resistance less than 5 ohms? → **Yes** REPAIR circuit 418 (DG/YE). TEST the system for normal operation. → **No** REPLACE the air suspension switch. TEST the system for normal operation.
A5 CHECK CIRCUIT 432 (BK/PK), 57 (BK) AND 875 (BK/LB) FOR AN OPEN	2. Turn the air suspension switch to the OFF position. 4. Measure the resistance between air suspension control module C296 pin 20, circuit 432 (BK/PK), harness side and ground; and between air suspension control module C296 pin 32, circuit 57 (BK), harness side and ground. • Is the resistance less than 5 ohms? → **Yes** Diagnose Module Communications Network Fault condition. → **No** REPAIR the circuit. TEST the system for normal operation.

FM2010100676030X

Fig. 12   Test A: No Communication w/ASC Module (Part 3 of 3). Four wheel air suspension system

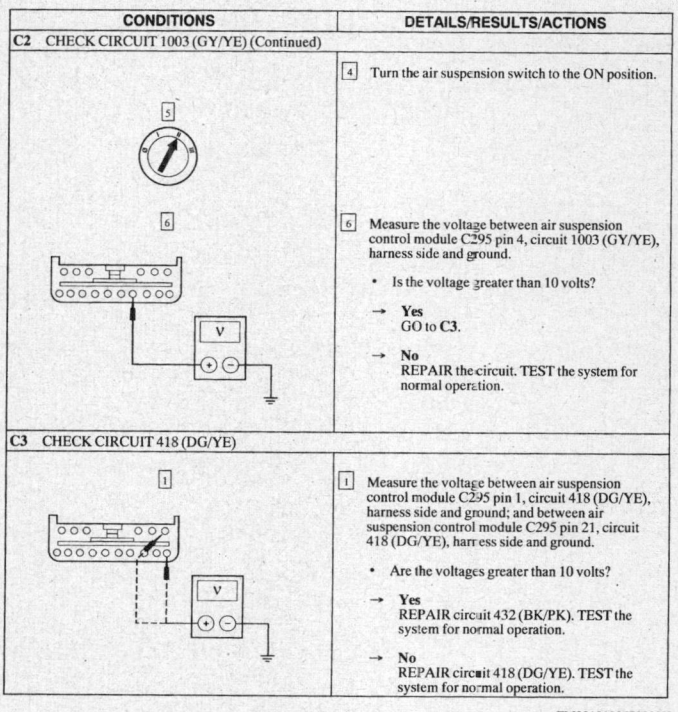

CONDITIONS	DETAILS/RESULTS/ACTIONS
C2 CHECK CIRCUIT 1003 (GY/YE) (Continued)	4. Turn the air suspension switch to the ON position. 6. Measure the voltage between air suspension control module C295 pin 4, circuit 1003 (GY/YE), harness side and ground. • Is the voltage greater than 10 volts? → **Yes** GO to **C3**. → **No** REPAIR the circuit. TEST the system for normal operation.
C3 CHECK CIRCUIT 418 (DG/YE)	1. Measure the voltage between air suspension control module C295 pin 1, circuit 418 (DG/YE), harness side and ground; and between air suspension control module C295 pin 21, circuit 418 (DG/YE), harness side and ground. • Are the voltages greater than 10 volts? → **Yes** REPAIR circuit 432 (BK/PK). TEST the system for normal operation. → **No** REPAIR circuit 418 (DG/YE). TEST the system for normal operation.

FM2010100678020X

Fig. 14   Test C/DTC B1318: Battery Voltage Low (Part 2 of 2). Four wheel air suspension system

CONDITIONS	DETAILS/RESULTS/ACTIONS
D1 CHECK DOOR AJAR INDICATOR	

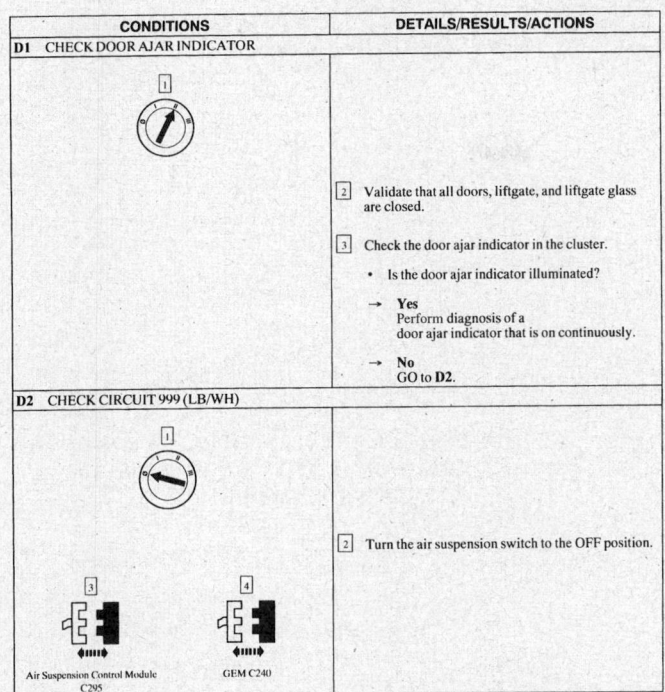

	2 Validate that all doors, liftgate, and liftgate glass are closed.
	3 Check the door ajar indicator in the cluster.
	• Is the door ajar indicator illuminated?
	→ **Yes** Perform diagnosis of a door ajar indicator that is on continuously.
	→ **No** GO to **D2**.

CONDITIONS	DETAILS/RESULTS/ACTIONS
D2 CHECK CIRCUIT 999 (LB/WH)	

	2 Turn the air suspension switch to the OFF position.

Air Suspension Control Module C295   GEM C240

FM2010100679010X

Fig. 15   Test D/DTC B1566: Door Ajar Circuit Short To Ground (Part 1 of 2). Four wheel air suspension system

CONDITIONS	DETAILS/RESULTS/ACTIONS
E1 CHECK CIRCUIT 1000 (RD/BK)	

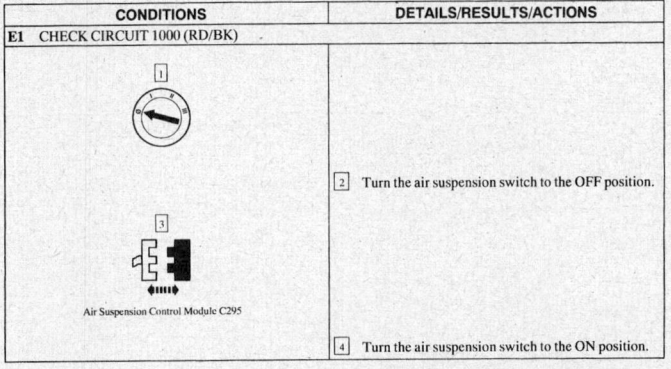

	2 Turn the air suspension switch to the OFF position.

Air Suspension Control Module C295

	4 Turn the air suspension switch to the ON position.

FM2010100680010X

Fig. 16   Test E/DTC B1749: Park-Neutral Switch Circuit Failure (Part 1 of 2). Four wheel air suspension system

CONDITIONS	DETAILS/RESULTS/ACTIONS
D2 CHECK CIRCUIT 999 (LB/WH) (Continued)	

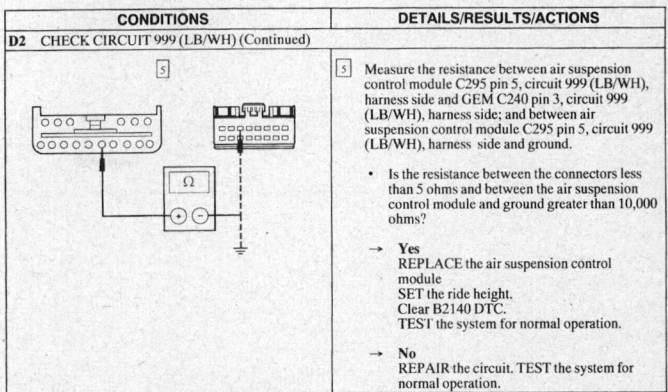

	5 Measure the resistance between air suspension control module C295 pin 5, circuit 999 (LB/WH), harness side and GEM C240 pin 3, circuit 999 (LB/WH), harness side; and between air suspension control module C295 pin 5, circuit 999 (LB/WH), harness side and ground.
	• Is the resistance between the connectors less than 5 ohms and between the air suspension control module and ground greater than 10,000 ohms?
	→ **Yes** REPLACE the air suspension control module SET the ride height. Clear B2140 DTC. TEST the system for normal operation.
	→ **No** REPAIR the circuit. TEST the system for normal operation.

FM2010100679020X

Fig. 15   Test D/DTC B1566: Door Ajar Circuit Short To Ground (Part 2 of 2). Four wheel air suspension system

CONDITIONS	DETAILS/RESULTS/ACTIONS
E1 CHECK CIRCUIT 1000 (RD/BK) (Continued)	

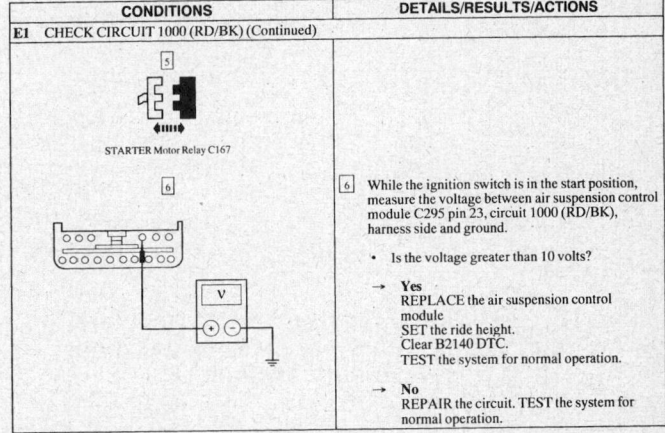

STARTER Motor Relay C167

	6 While the ignition switch is in the start position, measure the voltage between air suspension control module C295 pin 23, circuit 1000 (RD/BK), harness side and ground.
	• Is the voltage greater than 10 volts?
	→ **Yes** REPLACE the air suspension control module SET the ride height. Clear B2140 DTC. TEST the system for normal operation.
	→ **No** REPAIR the circuit. TEST the system for normal operation.

FM2010100680020X

Fig. 16   Test E/DTC B1749: Park-Neutral Switch Circuit Failure (Part 2 of 2). Four wheel air suspension system

CONDITIONS	DETAILS/RESULTS/ACTIONS
F1 CHECK POWERTRAIN CONTROL MODULE (PCM) FOR THROTTLE POSITION INPUT	

	1 Monitor PCM PID TP MODE.
	2 While watching the scan tool display, press and release the accelerator pedal to the floor.
	• Does the PID TP MODE display C/T, P/T, and WOT?
	→ **Yes** GO to **F2**.
	→ **No** Diagnose and Test throttle position input.

FM2010100681010X

Fig. 17   Test F/DTC C1439: Vehicle Acceleration Circuit Failure (Part 1 of 3). Four wheel air suspension system

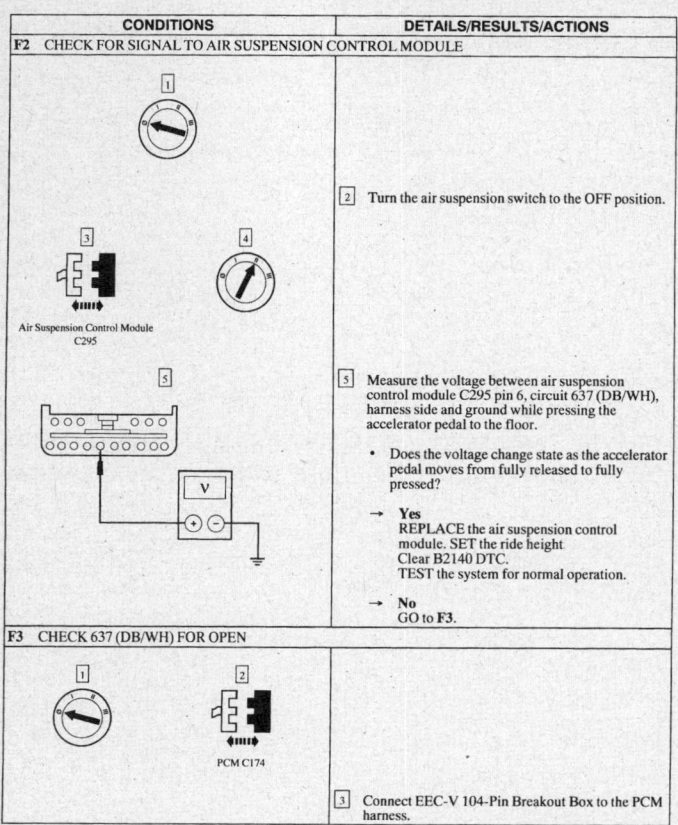

CONDITIONS	DETAILS/RESULTS/ACTIONS
F2 CHECK FOR SIGNAL TO AIR SUSPENSION CONTROL MODULE	
	② Turn the air suspension switch to the OFF position.
Air Suspension Control Module C295	
	⑤ Measure the voltage between air suspension control module C295 pin 6, circuit 637 (DB/WH), harness side and ground while pressing the accelerator pedal to the floor. • Does the voltage change state as the accelerator pedal moves from fully released to fully pressed? → **Yes** REPLACE the air suspension control module. SET the ride height Clear B2140 DTC. TEST the system for normal operation. → **No** GO to **F3**.
F3 CHECK 637 (DB/WH) FOR OPEN	
PCM C174	
	③ Connect EEC-V 104-Pin Breakout Box to the PCM harness.

FM2010100681020X

Fig. 17 Test F/DTC C1439: Vehicle Acceleration Circuit Failure (Part 2 of 3). Four wheel air suspension system

CONDITIONS	DETAILS/RESULTS/ACTIONS
G1 CHECK CIRCUIT 429 (VT/LG) (Continued)	
	④ Measure the resistance between air suspension control module C296 pin 28, circuit 429 (VT/LG), harness side and ground. • Is the resistance greater than 10,000 ohms? → **Yes** CHECK for intermittent short to ground on circuit 429 (VT/LG). REPAIR as necessary. If OK, REPLACE the air suspension control module. SET the ride height Clear B2140 DTC. TEST the system for normal operation. → **No** REPAIR the circuit. TEST the system for normal operation.

FM2010100682020X

Fig. 18 Test G/DTC C1724: Height Sensor Power Circuit Failure (Part 2 of 2). Four wheel air suspension system

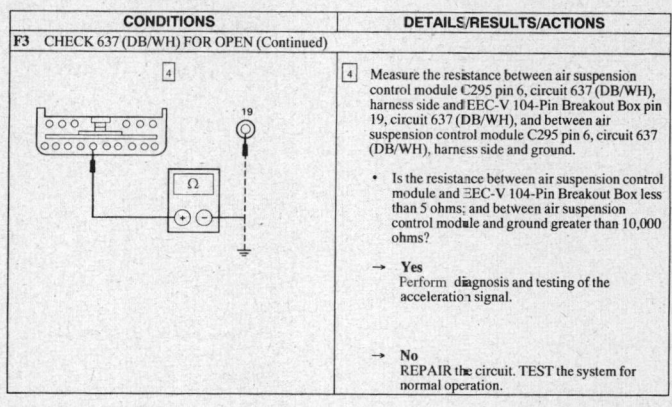

CONDITIONS	DETAILS/RESULTS/ACTIONS
F3 CHECK 637 (DB/WH) FOR OPEN (Continued)	
	④ Measure the resistance between air suspension control module C295 pin 6, circuit 637 (DB/WH), harness side and EEC-V 104-Pin Breakout Box pin 19, circuit 637 (DB/WH), and between air suspension control module C295 pin 6, circuit 637 (DB/WH), harness side and ground. • Is the resistance between air suspension control module and EEC-V 104-Pin Breakout Box less than 5 ohms; and between air suspension control module and ground greater than 10,000 ohms? → **Yes** Perform diagnosis and testing of the acceleration signal. → **No** REPAIR the circuit. TEST the system for normal operation.

FM2010100681030X

Fig. 17 Test F/DTC C1439: Vehicle Acceleration Circuit Failure (Part 3 of 3). Four wheel air suspension system

CONDITIONS	DETAILS/RESULTS/ACTIONS
G1 CHECK CIRCUIT 429 (VT/LG)	
	② Turn the air suspension switch to the OFF position.
	③ Disconnect air suspension control module C296, front air suspension height sensor C308, and rear air suspension height sensor C421.

FM2010100682010X

Fig. 18 Test G/DTC C1724: Height Sensor Power Circuit Failure (Part 1 of 2). Four wheel air suspension system

CONDITIONS	DETAILS/RESULTS/ACTIONS
H1 CHECK FRONT AIR SUSPENSION HEIGHT SENSOR	
	① Inspect the front air suspension height sensor for correct installation at the upper and lower ball stud brackets. **NOTE:** It may become necessary to vent some air out of the front air suspension air shocks during this Pinpoint Test. ② Inspect the air suspension height sensor mounting brackets for damage. ③ Verify that all air lines (front and rear) are fully seated. • Are the air suspension height sensor, mounting brackets, and air lines OK? → **Yes** GO to **H2**. → **No** REPAIR as necessary. TEST the system for normal operation.

FM2010100683010X

Fig. 19 Test H/DTC C1725: Front Pneumatic Failure (Part 1 of 11). Four wheel air suspension system

CONDITIONS	DETAILS/RESULTS/ACTIONS
H2 CHECK FRONT AIR SUSPENSION HEIGHT SENSOR OPERATION	
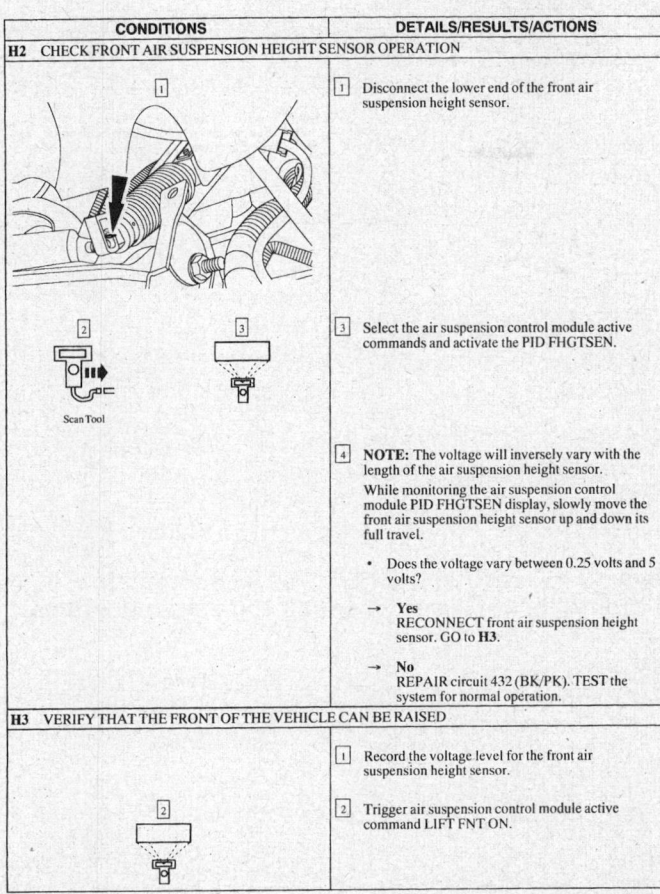	**1** Disconnect the lower end of the front air suspension height sensor.
	3 Select the air suspension control module active commands and activate the PID FHGTSEN.
	4 NOTE: The voltage will inversely vary with the length of the air suspension height sensor. While monitoring the air suspension control module PID FHGTSEN display, slowly move the front air suspension height sensor up and down its full travel. • Does the voltage vary between 0.25 volts and 5 volts? → **Yes** RECONNECT front air suspension height sensor. GO to **H3**. → **No** REPAIR circuit 432 (BK/PK). TEST the system for normal operation.
H3 VERIFY THAT THE FRONT OF THE VEHICLE CAN BE RAISED	
	1 Record the voltage level for the front air suspension height sensor. **2** Trigger air suspension control module active command LIFT FNT ON.

Fig. 19   Test H/DTC C1725: Front Pneumatic Failure (Part 2 of 11). Four wheel air suspension system

FM2010100683020X

CONDITIONS	DETAILS/RESULTS/ACTIONS
H5 CHECK OPERATION OF AIR COMPRESSOR	
⚠ **CAUTION:** If the air compressor runs in this test, do not allow the air compressor to run for more than three minutes. The air compressor could overheat and stop operation due to an internal temperature sensitive thermal breaker.	
	1 Trigger air suspension control module active command COMPRESSR ON. • Does the air compressor run (slight buzzing noise from RF fender)? → **Yes** TRIGGER air suspension control module active command COMPRESSR OFF. GO to **H6**. → **No** TRIGGER air suspension control module active command COMPRESSR OFF. GO to Pinpoint Test W.
H6 CHECK AIR COMPRESSOR PRESSURE OUTPUT	
⚠ **CAUTION:** Do not let the air compressor run for more than three minutes at a time. **NOTE:** If fluid is present when disconnecting and air line, clear the air lines procedure in this section. Check the compressor air drier for water or front air shock for oil.	
	1 Disconnect air line at the rear air line union within the engine compartment. **2** Connect an air pressure gauge (1,723 kPa [250 psi] maximum reading) with common fittings to the air line going to the compressor air drier. **3** Trigger active command COMPRESSR ON. **4** Run the air compressor for only 30 seconds. **5** Wait five minutes.

FM2010100683040X

Fig. 19   Test H/DTC C1725: Front Pneumatic Failure (Part 4 of 11). Four wheel air suspension system

CONDITIONS	DETAILS/RESULTS/ACTIONS
H3 VERIFY THAT THE FRONT OF THE VEHICLE CAN BE RAISED (Continued)	
	Allow the front of the vehicle to raise for only 30 seconds. • Does the front of the vehicle raise and hold the new height? → **Yes** GO to **H4**. → **No** GO to **H5**.
H4 VERIFY THAT THE FRONT OF THE VEHICLE CAN BE LOWERED	
	1 Trigger air suspension control module active command VENT FT ON. **2** Allow the front to lower until the front air suspension height sensor voltage reading matches the one recorded in Step F3 or 30 seconds have passed. • Does the front of the vehicle lower? → **Yes** RESET mechanical ride height. RESET front ride height Clear B2140 DTC. TEST the system for normal operation. → **No** GO to **H8**.

FM2010100683030X

Fig. 19   Test H/DTC C1725: Front Pneumatic Failure (Part 3 of 11). Four wheel air suspension system

CONDITIONS	DETAILS/RESULTS/ACTIONS
H6 CHECK AIR COMPRESSOR PRESSURE OUTPUT (Continued)	
	6 Trigger active command VENT ON. • Does the compressor produce 758 kPa (110 psi) within 30 seconds and hold developed pressure? → **Yes** REMOVE air pressure gauge and RECONNECT the air line. TEST the system for air leaks → **No** GO to **H7**.
H7 CHECK AIR LINES FROM AIR DRIER	
⚠ **CAUTION:** Do not let the air compressor run for more than three minutes at a time.	
	1 Trigger air suspension control module active command COMPRESSR ON. **2** Check for air leaks, bends, or kinks in air lines between the air compressor and front fill solenoid; and between the air compressor and air pressure gauge. • Are there any leaks, bends, or kinks in the air lines? → **Yes** REPLACE the air line. TEST the system for normal operation. → **No** REPLACE the air compressor assembly TEST the system for normal operation.

FM2010100683050X

Fig. 19   Test H/DTC C1725: Front Pneumatic Failure (Part 5 of 11). Four wheel air suspension system

CONDITIONS	DETAILS/RESULTS/ACTIONS
H8 CHECK FOR BLOCKAGE IN AIR LINE TO AIR SUSPENSION FRONT FILL SOLENOID	

⚠ **WARNING: Disconnecting any air line that is connected to an air shock can cause personal injury or damage to components as high pressure air is vented uncontrolled. Before disconnecting air lines connected to air shocks, use scan tool active command VENT FRNT to relieve all pressure.**

NOTE: If fluid is present when disconnecting an air line, clear the air lines Line Fluid Purge. Check the air compressor air drier for water or front air shock for oil.

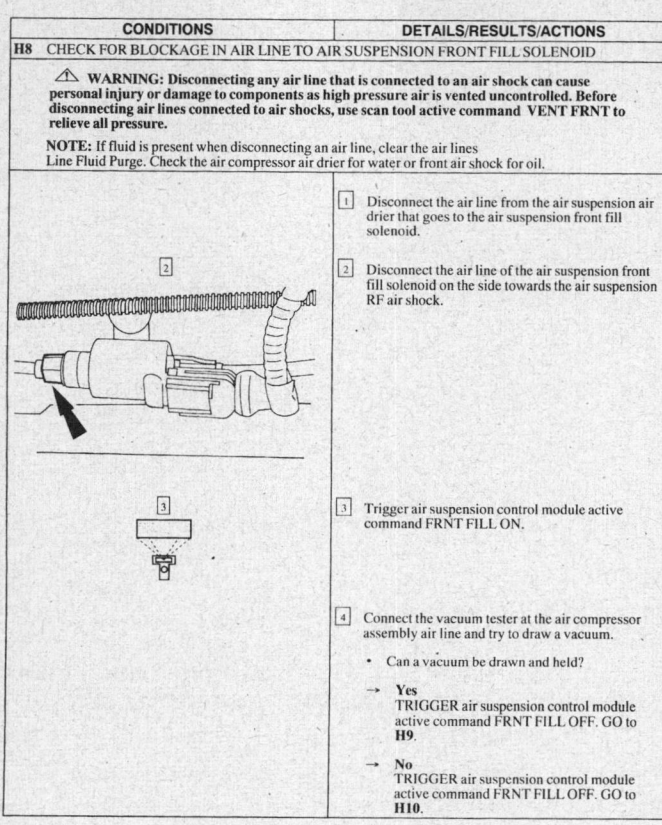

1. Disconnect the air line from the air suspension air drier that goes to the air suspension front fill solenoid.

2. Disconnect the air line of the air suspension front fill solenoid on the side towards the air suspension RF air shock.

3. Trigger air suspension control module active command FRNT FILL ON.

4. Connect the vacuum tester at the air compressor assembly air line and try to draw a vacuum.
   - Can a vacuum be drawn and held?
     → **Yes**
       TRIGGER air suspension control module active command FRNT FILL OFF. GO to **H9**.
     → **No**
       TRIGGER air suspension control module active command FRNT FILL OFF. GO to **H10**.

FM2010100683060X

Fig. 19 Test H/DTC C1725: Front Pneumatic Failure (Part 6 of 11). Four wheel air suspension system

CONDITIONS	DETAILS/RESULTS/ACTIONS
H10 CHECK FOR BLOCKAGE IN AIR LINE TO RF AIR SHOCK	

⚠ **WARNING: Disconnecting any air line that is connected to an air shock can cause personal injury or damage to components as high pressure air is vented uncontrolled. Before disconnecting air lines connected to air shocks, use scan tool active command VENT FRNT to relieve all pressure.**

NOTE: If fluid is present when disconnecting an air line, clear the air lines Check the air compressor air drier for water or front air shock for oil.

1. Disconnect the air line at RF air shock.

2. Connect the vacuum tester at the RF air shock air line and try to draw a vacuum.
   - Can a vacuum be drawn and held?
     → **Yes**
       REPLACE the air line.
     → **No**
       GO to **H11**.

FM2010100683080X

Fig. 19 Test H/DTC C1725: Front Pneumatic Failure (Part 8 of 11). Four wheel air suspension system

CONDITIONS	DETAILS/RESULTS/ACTIONS
H9 CHECK AIR SUSPENSION FRONT FILL SOLENOID	

NOTE: If fluid is present when disconnecting an air line, clear the air lines Check the air compressor air drier for water or front air shock for oil.

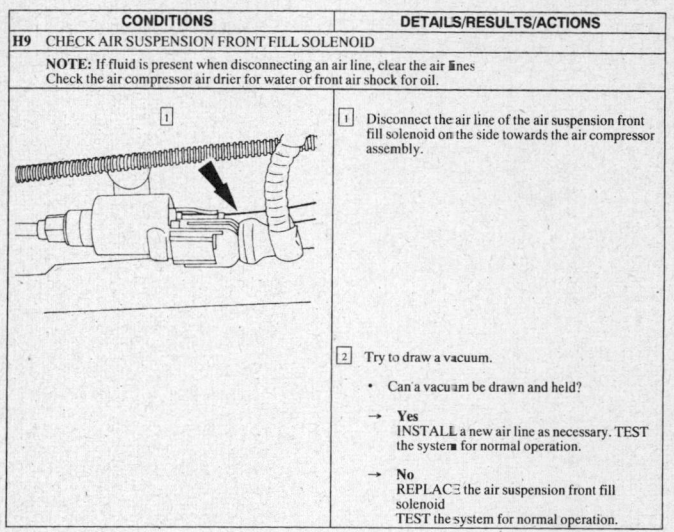

1. Disconnect the air line of the air suspension front fill solenoid on the side towards the air compressor assembly.

2. Try to draw a vacuum.
   - Can a vacuum be drawn and held?
     → **Yes**
       INSTALL a new air line as necessary. TEST the system for normal operation.
     → **No**
       REPLACE the air suspension front fill solenoid TEST the system for normal operation.

FM2010100683070X

Fig. 19 Test H/DTC C1725: Front Pneumatic Failure (Part 7 of 11). Four wheel air suspension system

CONDITIONS	DETAILS/RESULTS/ACTIONS
H11 CHECK FOR BLOCKAGE IN AIR LINE TO LF AIR SHOCK	

⚠ **WARNING: Disconnecting any air line that is connected to an air shock can cause personal injury or damage to components as high pressure air is vented uncontrolled. Before disconnecting air lines connected to air shocks, use scan tool active command VENT FRNT to relieve all pressure.**

NOTE: If fluid is present when disconnecting an air line, clear the air lines; Check the air compressor air drier for water or front air shock for oil.

1. Disconnect the air line at LF air shock.

2. Trigger air suspension control module active command GATE VALVE ON.

3. Connect the vacuum tester at the LF air shock air line and try to draw a vacuum.
   - Can a vacuum be drawn and held?
     → **Yes**
       GO to **H12**.
     → **No**
       REPLACE the air compressor assembly TEST the system for normal operation.

FM2010100683090X

Fig. 19 Test H/DTC C1725: Front Pneumatic Failure (Part 9 of 11). Four wheel air suspension system

CONDITIONS	DETAILS/RESULTS/ACTIONS
H12 CHECK FOR BLOCKAGE IN AIR LINE TO AIR SUSPENSION GATE SOLENOID	

NOTE: If fluid is present when disconnecting an air line, clear the air lines
Check the air compressor air drier for water or front air shock for oil.

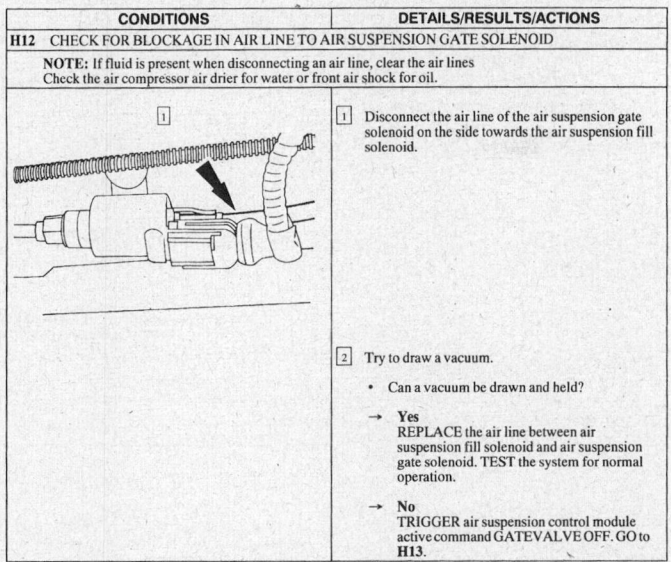

1. Disconnect the air line of the air suspension gate solenoid on the side towards the air suspension fill solenoid.

2. Try to draw a vacuum.

   • Can a vacuum be drawn and held?

   → **Yes**
   REPLACE the air line between air suspension fill solenoid and air suspension gate solenoid. TEST the system for normal operation.

   → **No**
   TRIGGER air suspension control module active command GATEVALVE OFF. GO to **H13**.

FM2010100683100X

Fig. 19   Test H/DTC C1725: Front Pneumatic Failure (Part 10 of 11). Four wheel air suspension system

CONDITIONS	DETAILS/RESULTS/ACTIONS
H13 CHECK FOR BLOCKED AIR SUSPENSION GATE SOLENOID	

NOTE: If fluid is present when disconnecting air line, clear the air lines
Check the air compressor air drier for water or front air shock for oil.

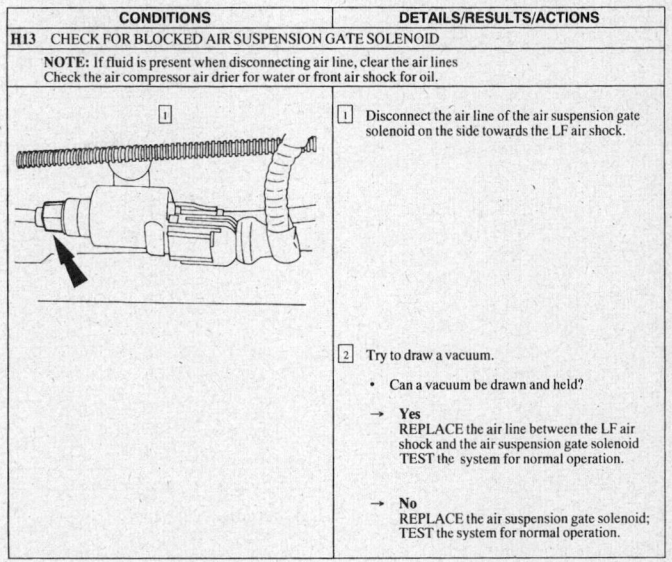

1. Disconnect the air line of the air suspension gate solenoid on the side towards the LF air shock.

2. Try to draw a vacuum.

   • Can a vacuum be drawn and held?

   → **Yes**
   REPLACE the air line between the LF air shock and the air suspension gate solenoid TEST the system for normal operation.

   → **No**
   REPLACE the air suspension gate solenoid; TEST the system for normal operation.

FM2010100683110X

Fig. 19   Test H/DTC C1725: Front Pneumatic Failure (Part 11 of 11). Four wheel air suspension system

CONDITIONS	DETAILS/RESULTS/ACTIONS
I1 CHECK REAR AIR SUSPENSION HEIGHT SENSOR	

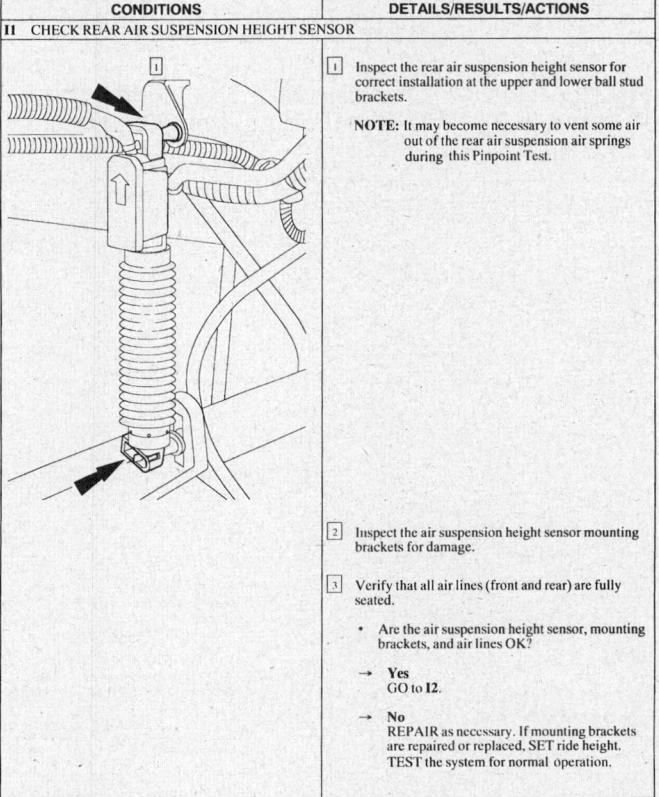

1. Inspect the rear air suspension height sensor for correct installation at the upper and lower ball stud brackets.

   NOTE: It may become necessary to vent some air out of the rear air suspension air springs during this Pinpoint Test.

2. Inspect the air suspension height sensor mounting brackets for damage.

3. Verify that all air lines (front and rear) are fully seated.

   • Are the air suspension height sensor, mounting brackets, and air lines OK?

   → **Yes**
   GO to **I2**.

   → **No**
   REPAIR as necessary. If mounting brackets are repaired or replaced, SET ride height. TEST the system for normal operation.

FM2010100684010X

Fig. 20   Test I/DTC C1726: Rear Pneumatic Failure (Part 1 of 9). Four wheel air suspension system

CONDITIONS	DETAILS/RESULTS/ACTIONS
I2 CHECK REAR AIR SUSPENSION HEIGHT SENSOR OPERATION	

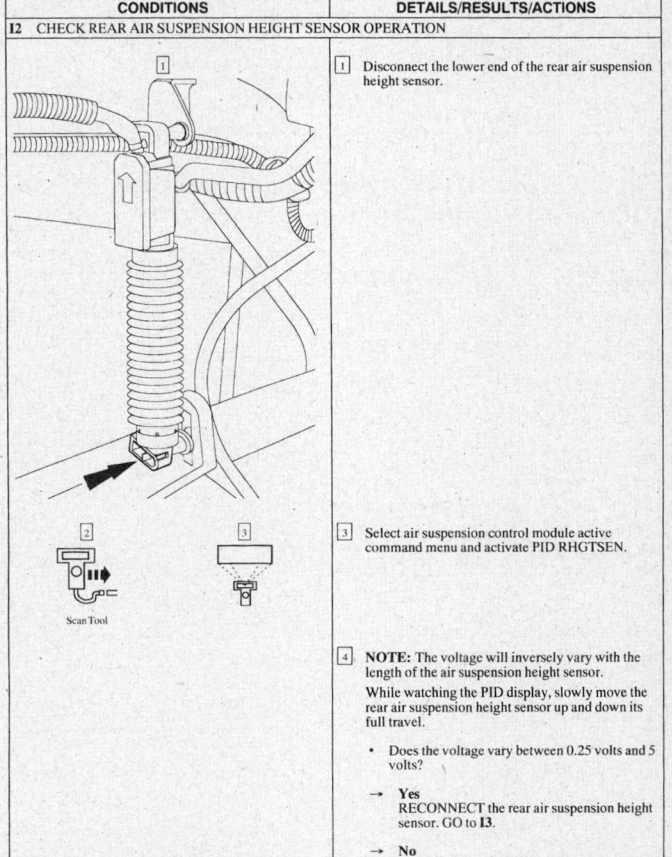

Scan Tool

1. Disconnect the lower end of the rear air suspension height sensor.

3. Select air suspension control module active command menu and activate PID RHGTSEN.

4. NOTE: The voltage will inversely vary with the length of the air suspension height sensor.
   While watching the PID display, slowly move the rear air suspension height sensor up and down its full travel.

   • Does the voltage vary between 0.25 volts and 5 volts?

   → **Yes**
   RECONNECT the rear air suspension height sensor. GO to **I3**.

   → **No**

FM2010100684020X

Fig. 20   Test I/DTC C1726: Rear Pneumatic Failure (Part 2 of 9). Four wheel air suspension system

CONDITIONS	DETAILS/RESULTS/ACTIONS
I2 CHECK REAR AIR SUSPENSION HEIGHT SENSOR OPERATION (Continued)	
	REPAIR circuit 432 (BK/PK). TEST the system for normal operation.
I3 VERIFY THAT THE REAR OF THE VEHICLE CAN BE RAISED	
[2]	[1] Record the voltage level for the rear air suspension height sensor. [2] Trigger air suspension control module active command LIFT REAR ON. [3] Allow the rear of the vehicle to raise for only 30 seconds. • Does the rear of the vehicle raise and hold the new height? → Yes GO to **I4**. → No GO to **I5**.
I4 VERIFY THAT THE REAR OF THE VEHICLE CAN BE LOWERED	
[1]	[1] Trigger air suspension control module active command VENT REAR ON. [2] Allow the rear to lower until the rear air suspension height sensor voltage reading matches the one recorded in Step G3 or 30 seconds have passed. • Does the rear of the vehicle lower? → Yes RESET mechanical ride height. CARRY OUT Rear Ride Height Mechanical Resetting TEST the system for normal operation. → No GO to **I8**.

FM2010100684030X

Fig. 20   Test I/DTC C1726: Rear Pneumatic Failure (Part 3 of 9). Four wheel air suspension system

CONDITIONS	DETAILS/RESULTS/ACTIONS
I6 CHECK AIR COMPRESSOR PRESSURE OUTPUT (Continued)	
[6]	[6] Trigger air suspension control module active command VENT ON. • Does the compressor produce 758 kPa (110 psi) within 30 seconds and hold developed pressure? → Yes REMOVE air pressure gauge and RECONNECT the air line. TEST the system for air leaks → No GO to **I7**.
I7 CHECK AIR LINE FROM AIR DRIER	
⚠ CAUTION: Do not let the air compressor run for more than three minutes at a time.	
[1]	[1] Trigger air suspension control module active command COMPRESSR ON. [2] Check for air leaks, bends, or kinks in air lines between the air compressor and front fill solenoid, and between air compressor and air pressure gauge. • Are there any leaks, bends, or kinks in the air lines? → Yes REPLACE the air line. TEST the system for normal operation. → No REPLACE the air compressor assembly TEST the system for normal operation.
I8 CHECK FOR BLOCKAGE IN AIR LINE TO AIR SUSPENSION REAR FILL SOLENOID	
NOTE: If fluid is present when disconnecting an air line, clear the air lines Check the air compressor air drier for water or front air shock for oil.	
	[1] Disconnect the air line from the air suspension air drier that goes to the air suspension rear fill solenoid.

FM2010100684050X

Fig. 20   Test I/DTC C1726: Rear Pneumatic Failure (Part 5 of 9). Four wheel air suspension system

CONDITIONS	DETAILS/RESULTS/ACTIONS
I5 CHECK OPERATION OF AIR COMPRESSOR	
⚠ CAUTION: If the air compressor runs in this test, do not allow the air compressor to run for more than three minutes. The air compressor could overheat and stop operation due to an internal temperature sensitive thermal breaker.	
[1]	[1] Trigger air suspension control module active command COMPRESSR ON. • Does the air compressor run (slight buzzing noise from RF fender)? → Yes TRIGGER air suspension control module active command COMPRESSR OFF. GO to **I6**. → No TRIGGER air suspension control module active command COMPRESSR OFF. GO to Pinpoint Test W.
I6 CHECK AIR COMPRESSOR PRESSURE OUTPUT	
⚠ CAUTION: Do not let the air compressor run for more than three minutes at a time.	
NOTE: If fluid is present when disconnecting an air line, clear the air lines Check the compressor air drier for water or air compressor for oil.	
[3]	[1] Disconnect the air line at the rear air line union within the engine compartment. [2] Connect an air pressure gauge (1,723 kPa [250 psi] maximum reading) with common fittings to the air line going to the compressor air drier. [3] Trigger air suspension control module active command COMPRESSR ON. [4] Run the air compressor for only 30 seconds. [5] Wait five minutes.

FM2010100684040X

Fig. 20   Test I/DTC C1726: Rear Pneumatic Failure (Part 4 of 9). Four wheel air suspension system

CONDITIONS	DETAILS/RESULTS/ACTIONS
I8 CHECK FOR BLOCKAGE IN AIR LINE TO AIR SUSPENSION REAR FILL SOLENOID (Continued)	
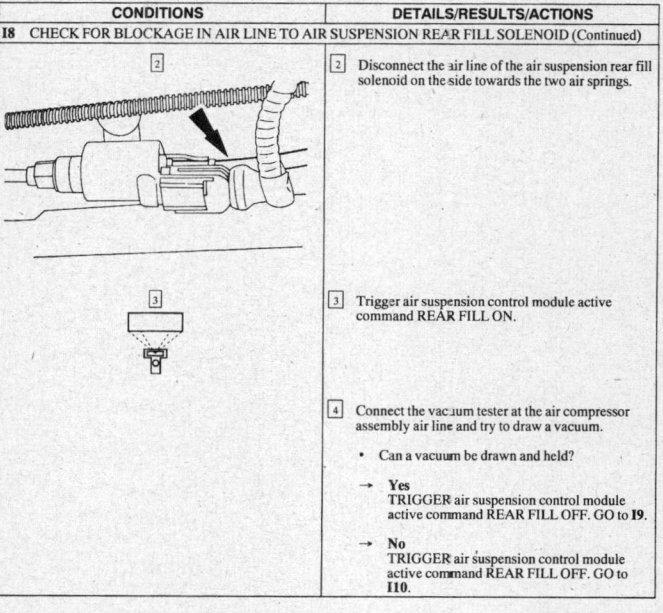	[2] Disconnect the air line of the air suspension rear fill solenoid on the side towards the two air springs. [3] Trigger air suspension control module active command REAR FILL ON. [4] Connect the vacuum tester at the air compressor assembly air line and try to draw a vacuum. • Can a vacuum be drawn and held? → Yes TRIGGER air suspension control module active command REAR FILL OFF. GO to **I9**. → No TRIGGER air suspension control module active command REAR FILL OFF. GO to **I10**.

FM2010100684060X

Fig. 20   Test I/DTC C1726: Rear Pneumatic Failure (Part 6 of 9). Four wheel air suspension system

CONDITIONS	DETAILS/RESULTS/ACTIONS
I9 CHECK AIR SUSPENSION REAR FILL SOLENOID	
NOTE: If fluid is present when disconnecting an air line, clear the air lines; Check the air compressor air drier for water or front air shock for oil.	
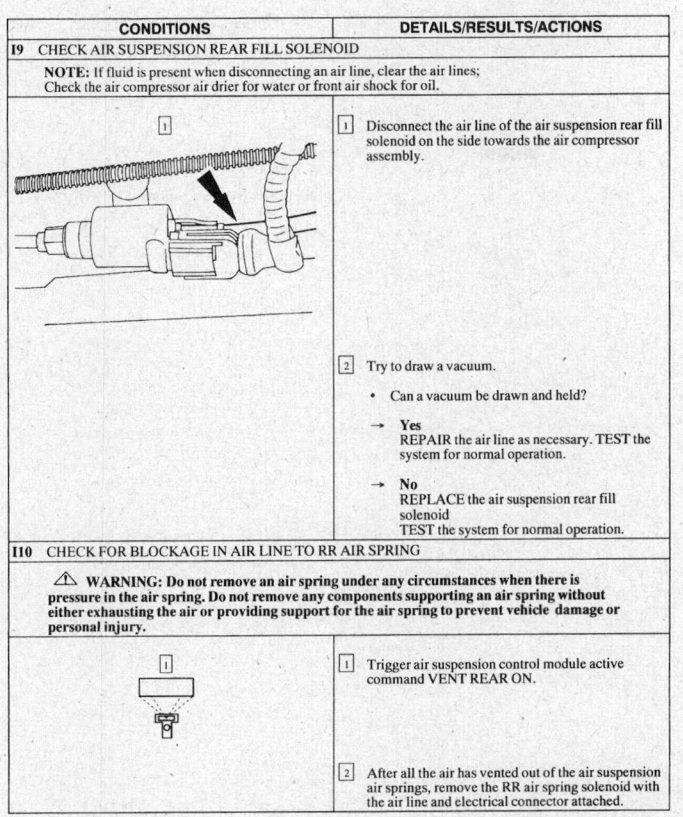	**1** Disconnect the air line of the air suspension rear fill solenoid on the side towards the air compressor assembly.
	2 Try to draw a vacuum.
	• Can a vacuum be drawn and held?
	→ **Yes** REPAIR the air line as necessary. TEST the system for normal operation.
	→ **No** REPLACE the air suspension rear fill solenoid TEST the system for normal operation.
I10 CHECK FOR BLOCKAGE IN AIR LINE TO RR AIR SPRING	
⚠ **WARNING: Do not remove an air spring under any circumstances when there is pressure in the air spring. Do not remove any components supporting an air spring without either exhausting the air or providing support for the air spring to prevent vehicle damage or personal injury.**	
	1 Trigger air suspension control module active command VENT REAR ON.
	2 After all the air has vented out of the air suspension air springs, remove the RR air spring solenoid with the air line and electrical connector attached.

FM2010100684070X

Fig. 20   Test I/DTC C1726: Rear Pneumatic Failure (Part 7 of 9). Four wheel air suspension system

CONDITIONS	DETAILS/RESULTS/ACTIONS
I10 CHECK FOR BLOCKAGE IN AIR LINE TO RR AIR SPRING (Continued)	
	3 Trigger air suspension control module active command RR AIRSP ON.
	4 Connect Vacuum Tester at the air suspension rear fill solenoid air line going to the two air springs and try to draw a vacuum.
	• Can a vacuum be drawn and held?
	→ **Yes** TRIGGER air suspension control module active command RR AIRSP OFF. GO to **I11**.
	→ **No** TRIGGER air suspension control module active command RR AIRSP OFF. GO to **I12**.
I11 CHECK FOR BLOCKED AIR SUSPENSION RR AIR SPRING SOLENOID	
NOTE: If fluid is present when disconnecting an air line, clear the air lines Check the air compressor air drier for water or front air shock for oil.	
	1 Disconnect the air line of the air suspension RR air spring solenoid.
	2 Try to draw a vacuum.
	• Can a vacuum be drawn and held?
	→ **Yes** REPAIR the air line between the RR air spring and the air suspension rear fill solenoid. TEST the system for normal operation.
	→ **No** REPLACE the air suspension RR air spring solenoid. TEST the system for normal operation.
I12 CHECK FOR BLOCKAGE IN AIR LINE TO LR AIR SPRING	
⚠ **WARNING: Do not remove an air spring under any circumstances when there is pressure in the air spring. Do not remove any components supporting an air spring without either exhausting the air or providing support for the air spring to prevent vehicle damage or personal injury.**	
	1 Remove the LR air spring solenoid with the air line and electrical connector attached.

FM2010100684080X

Fig. 20   Test I/DTC C1726: Rear Pneumatic Failure (Part 8 of 9). Four wheel air suspension system

CONDITIONS	DETAILS/RESULTS/ACTIONS
I12 CHECK FOR BLOCKAGE IN AIR LINE TO LR AIR SPRING (Continued)	
	2 Trigger air suspension control module active command LR AIRSP ON.
	3 Connect Vacuum Tester at the air suspension rear fill solenoid air line going to the two air springs and try to draw a vacuum.
	• Can a vacuum be drawn and held?
	→ **Yes** TRIGGER air suspension control module active command LR AIRSP OFF. GO to **I13**.
	→ **No** REPLACE the air compressor assembly. TEST the system for normal operation.
I13 CHECK FOR BLOCKED AIR SUSPENSION LR AIR SPRING SOLENOID	
NOTE: If fluid is present when disconnecting an air line, clear the air lines Check the air compressor air drier for water or front air shock for oil.	
	1 Disconnect the air line of the air suspension LR air spring solenoid.
	2 Try to draw a vacuum.
	• Can a vacuum be drawn and held?
	→ **Yes** REPAIR the air line between the LR air spring and the air suspension rear fill solenoid. TEST the system for normal operation.
	→ **No** REPLACE the air suspension LR air spring solenoid TEST the system for normal operation.

FM2010100684090X

Fig. 20   Test I/DTC C1726: Rear Pneumatic Failure (Part 9 of 9). Four wheel air suspension system

CONDITIONS	DETAILS/RESULTS/ACTIONS
J1 VALIDATEDTCERROR	
	1 Carry out the air suspension control module On-Demand Self-Test.
	• Is the same air suspension height sensor DTC set?
	→ **Yes** GO to **J2**.
	→ **No** If no DTC is retrieved, GO to **J5**. If a different DTC is retrieved, REFER to Air Suspension Control Module Diagnostic Trouble Code (DTC) Index.
J2 CHECK SUSPECT AIR SUSPENSION HEIGHT SENSOR POWER	
	1
	2 Turn the air suspension switch to the OFF position.
Front Air Suspension Height Sensor C424 Rear Air Suspension Height Sensor C421	**3** **4**
	5 Turn the air suspension switch to the ON position.
	6

FM2010100685010X

Fig. 21   Test J/DTC C1756 & C1760: Height Sensor High Circuit Failure (Part 1 of 4). Four wheel air suspension system

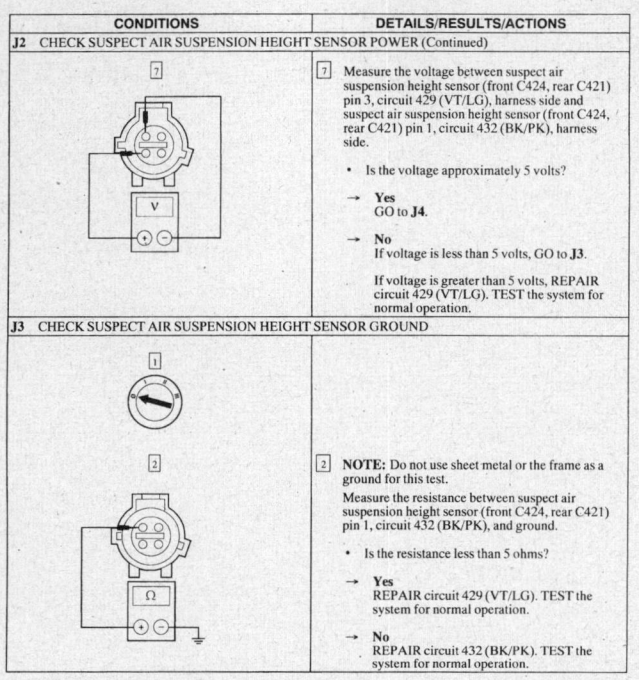

CONDITIONS	DETAILS/RESULTS/ACTIONS
J2 CHECK SUSPECT AIR SUSPENSION HEIGHT SENSOR POWER (Continued)	
7	7 Measure the voltage between suspect air suspension height sensor (front C424, rear C421) pin 3, circuit 429 (VT/LG), harness side and suspect air suspension height sensor (front C424, rear C421) pin 1, circuit 432 (BK/PK), harness side. • Is the voltage approximately 5 volts? → **Yes** GO to **J4**. → **No** If voltage is less than 5 volts, GO to **J3**. If voltage is greater than 5 volts, REPAIR circuit 429 (VT/LG). TEST the system for normal operation.
J3 CHECK SUSPECT AIR SUSPENSION HEIGHT SENSOR GROUND	
1 2	2 **NOTE:** Do not use sheet metal or the frame as a ground for this test. Measure the resistance between suspect air suspension height sensor (front C424, rear C421) pin 1, circuit 432 (BK/PK), and ground. • Is the resistance less than 5 ohms? → **Yes** REPAIR circuit 429 (VT/LG). TEST the system for normal operation. → **No** REPAIR circuit 432 (BK/PK). TEST the system for normal operation.

FM2010100685020X

Fig. 21   Test J/DTC C1756 & C1760: Height Sensor High Circuit Failure (Part 2 of 4). Four wheel air suspension system

CONDITIONS	DETAILS/RESULTS/ACTIONS
J5 CHECK FOR INTERMITTENT (Continued)	
2 3	3 Monitor air suspension control module PIDs FHGTSEN and RHGTSEN while wiggling the wire harness between the suspect air suspension height sensor and the air suspension control module. • Does the suspect air suspension height sensor voltage ever indicate less than 0.2 volts or greater than 5 volts? → **Yes** REPAIR circuits 429 (VT/LG), 432 (BK/PK) or front 424 (TN), rear 428 (OG/BK) for an intermittent fault. TEST the system for normal operation. → **No** REPLACE the suspect air suspension height sensor. TEST the system for normal operation.

FM2010100685040X

Fig. 21   Test J/DTC C1756 & C1760: Height Sensor High Circuit Failure (Part 4 of 4). Four wheel air suspension system

CONDITIONS	DETAILS/RESULTS/ACTIONS
K1 VALIDATE DTC C1770 ERROR	
1	1 Carry out air suspension control module On-Demand Self-Test. • Is the same air suspension DTC set? → **Yes** GO to **K2**. → **No** If no DTC is retrieved, GO to **K10**. If a different DTC is retrieved, REFER to Diagnostic Trouble Code (DTC) Interpretation.
K2 CHECK VENT SOLENOID CONNECTOR	
1	2 Turn the air suspension switch to the OFF position.

FM2010100686010X

Fig. 22   Test K/DTC C1770: Vent Solenoid Output Circuit Failure (Part 1 of 7). Four wheel air suspension system

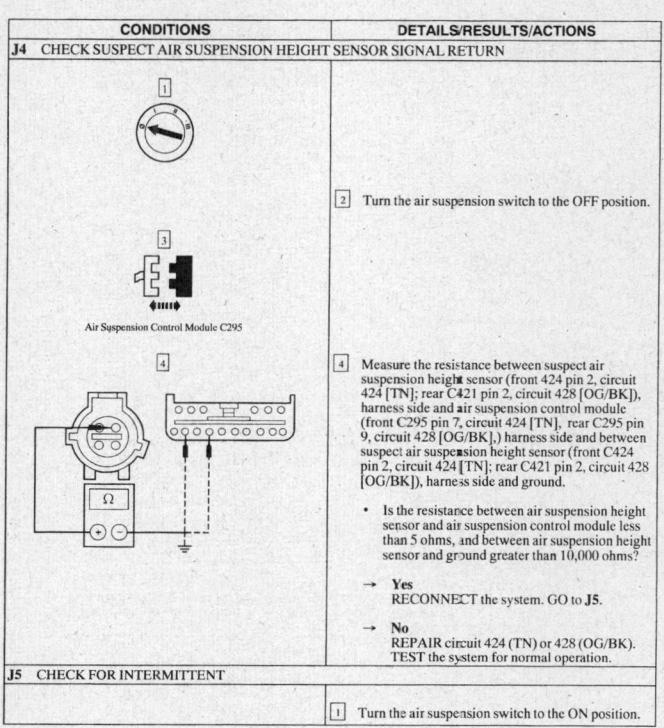

CONDITIONS	DETAILS/RESULTS/ACTIONS
J4 CHECK SUSPECT AIR SUSPENSION HEIGHT SENSOR SIGNAL RETURN	
1	2 Turn the air suspension switch to the OFF position.
3 Air Suspension Control Module C295	
Ω	4 Measure the resistance between suspect air suspension height sensor (front 424 pin 2, circuit 424 [TN]; rear C421 pin 2, circuit 428 [OG/BK]), harness side and air suspension control module (front C295 pin 7, circuit 424 [TN], rear C295 pin 9, circuit 428 [OG/BK],) harness side and between suspect air suspension height sensor (front C424 pin 2, circuit 424 [TN]; rear C421 pin 2, circuit 428 [OG/BK]), harness side and ground. • Is the resistance between air suspension height sensor and air suspension control module less than 5 ohms, and between air suspension height sensor and ground greater than 10,000 ohms? → **Yes** RECONNECT the system. GO to **J5**. → **No** REPAIR circuit 424 (TN) or 428 (OG/BK). TEST the system for normal operation.
J5 CHECK FOR INTERMITTENT	
1	1 Turn the air suspension switch to the ON position.

FM2010100685030X

Fig. 21   Test J/DTC C1756 & C1760: Height Sensor High Circuit Failure (Part 3 of 4). Four wheel air suspension system

CONDITIONS	DETAILS/RESULTS/ACTIONS
K2 CHECK VENT SOLENOID CONNECTOR (Continued)	
3 Air Compressor Assembly C194	4 Inspect the pins and terminals of the air compressor assembly connector for corrosion, bent or broken pins, moisture, or other damage. • Is the air compressor assembly C194 OK? → **Yes** RECONNECT the air compressor assembly C194. GO to **K3**. → **No** REPAIR as necessary. TEST the system for normal operation.
K3 CHECK VENT SOLENOID PID	
	1 Turn the air suspension switch to the ON position.
2 3	3 Select air suspension control module active commands and activate the PID AS__VENT.
4	4 Trigger air suspension control module active command VENT ON and OFF. • Do the letters O, G, or B appear next to the ON/OFF text for the air suspension vent solenoid? → **Yes** If O appeared, GO to **K4**. If G appeared, GO to **K7**. If B appeared, GO to **K9**. → **No** GO to **K10**.

FM2010100686020X

Fig. 22   Test K/DTC C1770: Vent Solenoid Output Circuit Failure (Part 2 of 7). Four wheel air suspension system

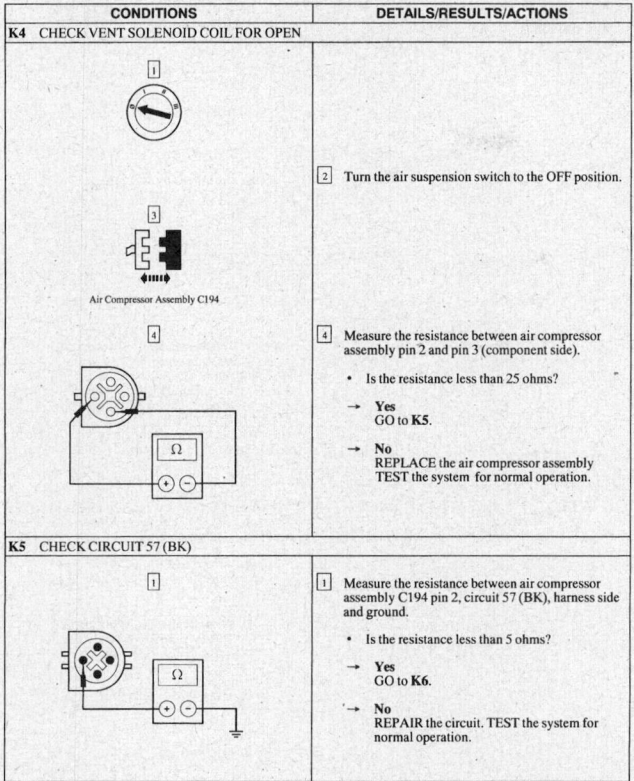

CONDITIONS	DETAILS/RESULTS/ACTIONS
K4 CHECK VENT SOLENOID COIL FOR OPEN	
1	2 Turn the air suspension switch to the OFF position.
3 Air Compressor Assembly C194	
4	4 Measure the resistance between air compressor assembly pin 2 and pin 3 (component side). • Is the resistance less than 25 ohms? → **Yes** GO to **K5**. → **No** REPLACE the air compressor assembly TEST the system for normal operation.
K5 CHECK CIRCUIT 57 (BK)	
1	1 Measure the resistance between air compressor assembly C194 pin 2, circuit 57 (BK), harness side and ground. • Is the resistance less than 5 ohms? → **Yes** GO to **K6**. → **No** REPAIR the circuit. TEST the system for normal operation.

FM2010100686030X

Fig. 22 Test K/DTC C1770: Vent Solenoid Output Circuit Failure (Part 3 of 7). Four wheel air suspension system

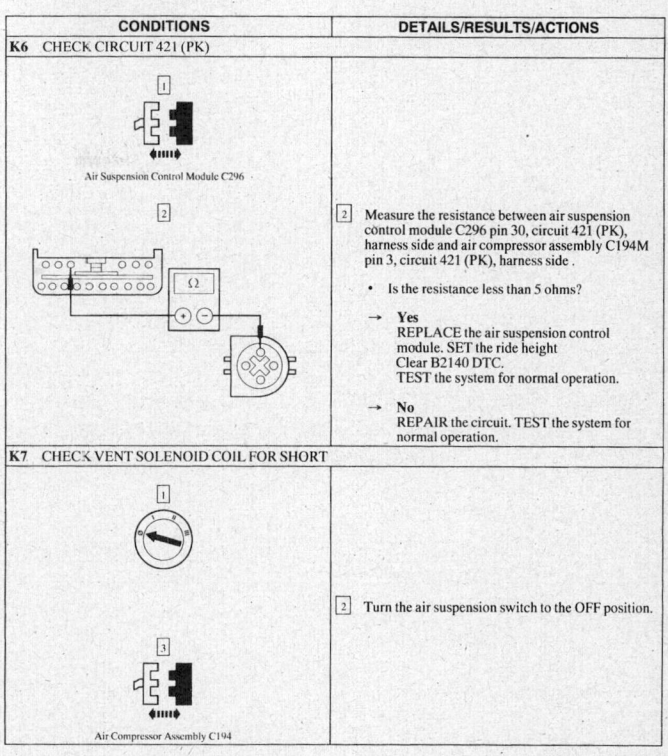

CONDITIONS	DETAILS/RESULTS/ACTIONS
K6 CHECK CIRCUIT 421 (PK)	
1 Air Suspension Control Module C296	
2	2 Measure the resistance between air suspension control module C296 pin 30, circuit 421 (PK), harness side and air compressor assembly C194M pin 3, circuit 421 (PK), harness side . • Is the resistance less than 5 ohms? → **Yes** REPLACE the air suspension control module. SET the ride height Clear B2140 DTC. TEST the system for normal operation. → **No** REPAIR the circuit. TEST the system for normal operation.
K7 CHECK VENT SOLENOID COIL FOR SHORT	
1	2 Turn the air suspension switch to the OFF position.
3 Air Compressor Assembly C194	

FM2010100686040X

Fig. 22 Test K/DTC C1770: Vent Solenoid Output Circuit Failure (Part 4 of 7). Four wheel air suspension system

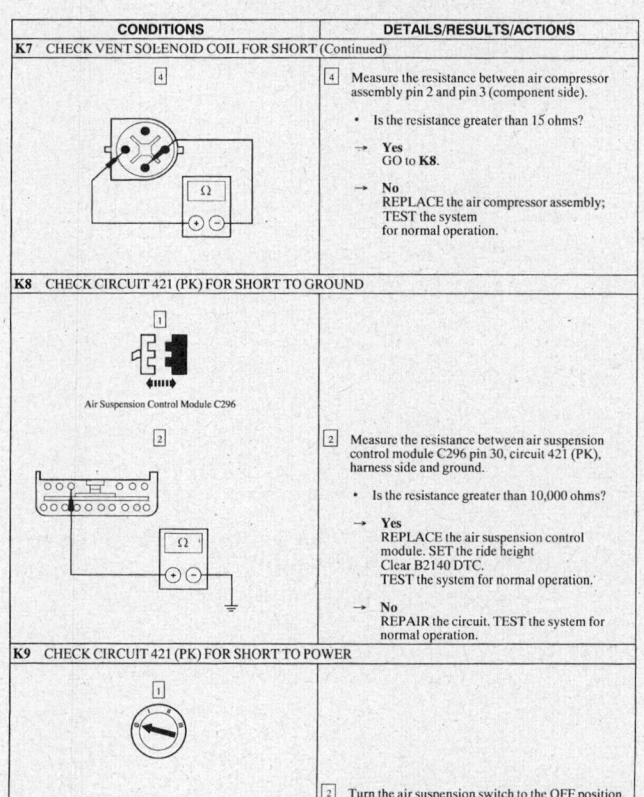

CONDITIONS	DETAILS/RESULTS/ACTIONS
K7 CHECK VENT SOLENOID COIL FOR SHORT (Continued)	
4	4 Measure the resistance between air compressor assembly pin 2 and pin 3 (component side). • Is the resistance greater than 15 ohms? → **Yes** GO to **K8**. → **No** REPLACE the air compressor assembly; TEST the system for normal operation.
K8 CHECK CIRCUIT 421 (PK) FOR SHORT TO GROUND	
1 Air Suspension Control Module C296	
2	2 Measure the resistance between air suspension control module C296 pin 30, circuit 421 (PK), harness side and ground. • Is the resistance greater than 10,000 ohms? → **Yes** REPLACE the air suspension control module. SET the ride height Clear B2140 DTC. TEST the system for normal operation. → **No** REPAIR the circuit. TEST the system for normal operation.
K9 CHECK CIRCUIT 421 (PK) FOR SHORT TO POWER	
1	2 Turn the air suspension switch to the OFF position.

FM2010100686050X

Fig. 22 Test K/DTC C1770: Vent Solenoid Output Circuit Failure (Part 5 of 7). Four wheel air suspension system

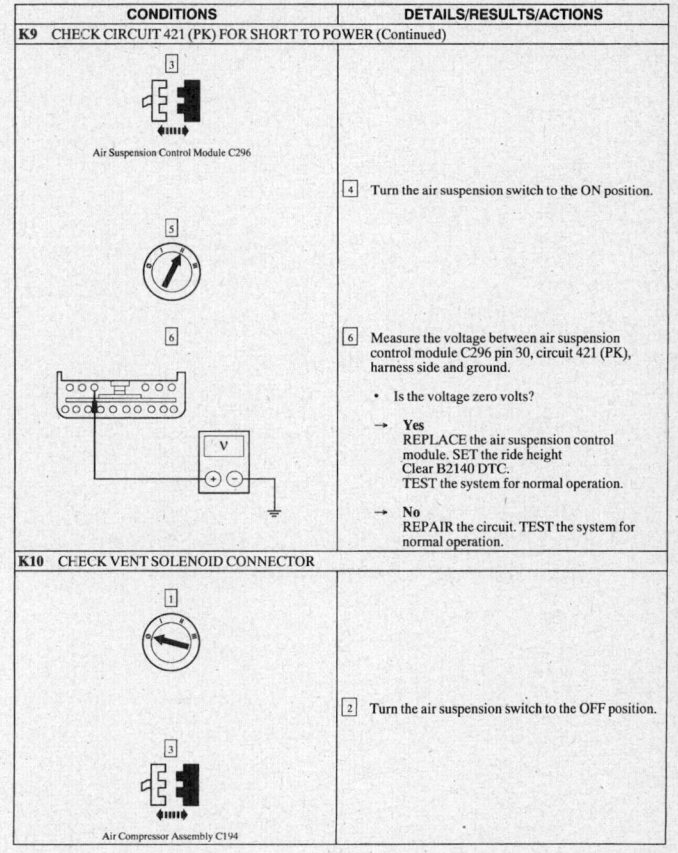

CONDITIONS	DETAILS/RESULTS/ACTIONS
K9 CHECK CIRCUIT 421 (PK) FOR SHORT TO POWER (Continued)	
3 Air Suspension Control Module C296	
4	4 Turn the air suspension switch to the ON position.
5	
6	6 Measure the voltage between air suspension control module C296 pin 30, circuit 421 (PK), harness side and ground. • Is the voltage zero volts? → **Yes** REPLACE the air suspension control module. SET the ride height Clear B2140 DTC. TEST the system for normal operation. → **No** REPAIR the circuit. TEST the system for normal operation.
K10 CHECK VENT SOLENOID CONNECTOR	
1	2 Turn the air suspension switch to the OFF position.
3 Air Compressor Assembly C194	

FM2010100686060X

Fig. 22 Test K/DTC C1770: Vent Solenoid Output Circuit Failure (Part 6 of 7). Four wheel air suspension system

CONDITIONS	DETAILS/RESULTS/ACTIONS
K10 CHECK VENT SOLENOID CONNECTOR (Continued)	

	4 Inspect the pins and terminals of the air compressor assembly connector for corrosion, bent or broken pins, moisture, or other damage; and inspect the wiring near the connector for damage.
	
	• Is the air compressor assembly C194 OK?
	
	→ **Yes**
	  RECONNECT air compressor assembly C194. PLACE the air suspension switch in the ON position. TEST the system for normal operation. If no DTCs are retrieved, the system is OK. If a DTC is retrieved, REFER to Diagnostic Trouble Code (DTC) Interpretation.
	
	→ **No**
	  REPAIR as necessary. TEST the system for normal operation.

FM2010100686070X

Fig. 22   Test K/DTC C1770: Vent Solenoid Output Circuit Failure (Part 7 of 7). Four wheel air suspension system

CONDITIONS	DETAILS/RESULTS/ACTIONS
L2 CHECK AIR SUSPENSION LR AIR SPRING SOLENOID CONNECTOR (Continued)	

Air Suspension LR Air Spring Solenoid C420
	4 Inspect the pins and terminals of the air suspension LR air spring solenoid connector for corrosion, bent or broken pins, moisture, or other damage.
	
	• Is the air suspension LR air spring solenoid C420 OK?
	
	→ **Yes**
	  RECONNECT the air suspension LR air spring solenoid C420. GO to **L3**.
	
	→ **No**
	  REPAIR as necessary. TEST the system for normal operation.

L3 CHECK SOLENOID PID	
	1 Turn the air suspension switch to the ON position. 3 Select air suspension control module active commands and activate the PID ASLRSOL or LR_SOL. 4 **NOTE:** The active command sequence is critical to proper diagnosis. Using the active commands, trigger in the following order: | Active Command	Trigger
RR AIRSP	ON
LR AIRSP	ON
RR AIRSP	OFF
LR AIRSP	OFF	

FM2010100687020X

Fig. 23   Test L/DTC C1790: Lefthand Rear Spring Solenoid Output Circuit Failure (Part 2 of 8). Four wheel air suspension system

CONDITIONS	DETAILS/RESULTS/ACTIONS
L1 VALIDATE DTC C1790 ERROR	

	1 Carry out the air suspension control module On-Demand Self-Test.
	
	• Is the same air suspension DTC set?
	
	→ **Yes**
	  GO to **L10**.
	
	→ **No**
	  If no DTC is retrieved, GO to **L10**. If a different DTC is retrieved, REFER to Diagnostic Trouble Code (DTC) Interpretation.

L2 CHECK AIR SUSPENSION LR AIR SPRING SOLENOID CONNECTOR	
	2 Turn the air suspension switch to the OFF position.

FM2010100687010X

Fig. 23   Test L/DTC C1790: Lefthand Rear Spring Solenoid Output Circuit Failure (Part 1 of 8). Four wheel air suspension system

CONDITIONS	DETAILS/RESULTS/ACTIONS
L3 CHECK SOLENOID PID (Continued)	

	• Do the letters O, G, or B appear next to the ON/OFF text for the air suspension LR air spring solenoid?
	
	→ **Yes**
	  If O appeared, GO to **L4**.
	  If G appeared, GO to **L7**.
	  If B appeared, GO to **L9**.
	
	→ **No**
	  GO to **L10**.

L4 CHECK AIR SUSPENSION LR AIR SPRING SOLENOID COIL FOR OPEN	

Air Suspension LR Air Spring Solenoid C420
 	
	2 Turn the air suspension switch to the OFF position.
	
	4 Measure the resistance between air suspension LR air spring solenoid pin 1 and pin 2 (component side).
	
	• Is the resistance less than 25 ohms?
	
	→ **Yes**
	  GO to **L5**.
	
	→ **No**
	  REPLACE the air suspension LR air spring solenoid; TEST the system for normal operation.

FM2010100687030X

Fig. 23   Test L/DTC C1790: Lefthand Rear Spring Solenoid Output Circuit Failure (Part 3 of 8). Four wheel air suspension system

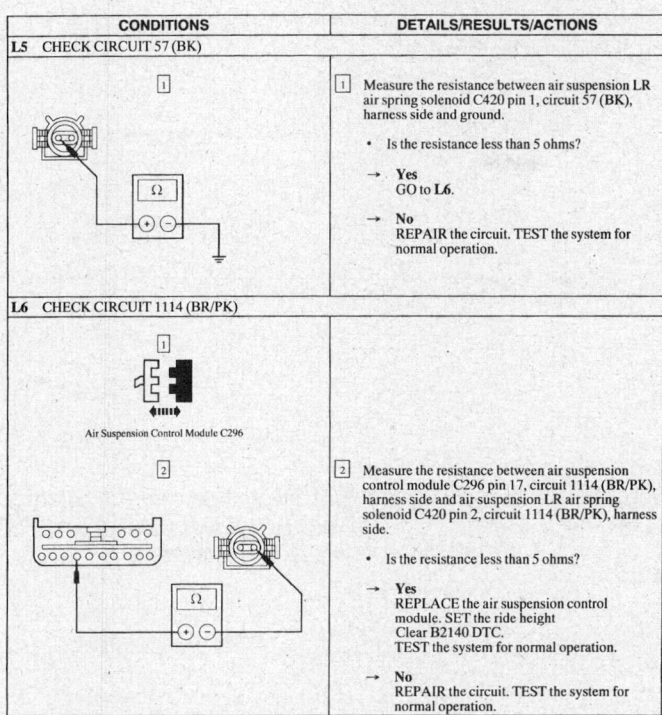

CONDITIONS	DETAILS/RESULTS/ACTIONS
L5 CHECK CIRCUIT 57 (BK)	
1	1 Measure the resistance between air suspension LR air spring solenoid C420 pin 1, circuit 57 (BK), harness side and ground. • Is the resistance less than 5 ohms? → **Yes** GO to **L6**. → **No** REPAIR the circuit. TEST the system for normal operation.
L6 CHECK CIRCUIT 1114 (BR/PK)	
1 Air Suspension Control Module C296 2	2 Measure the resistance between air suspension control module C296 pin 17, circuit 1114 (BR/PK), harness side and air suspension LR air spring solenoid C420 pin 2, circuit 1114 (BR/PK), harness side. • Is the resistance less than 5 ohms? → **Yes** REPLACE the air suspension control module. SET the ride height Clear B2140 DTC. TEST the system for normal operation. → **No** REPAIR the circuit. TEST the system for normal operation.

FM2010100687040X

Fig. 23   Test L/DTC C1790: Lefthand Rear Spring Solenoid Output Circuit Failure (Part 4 of 8). Four wheel air suspension system

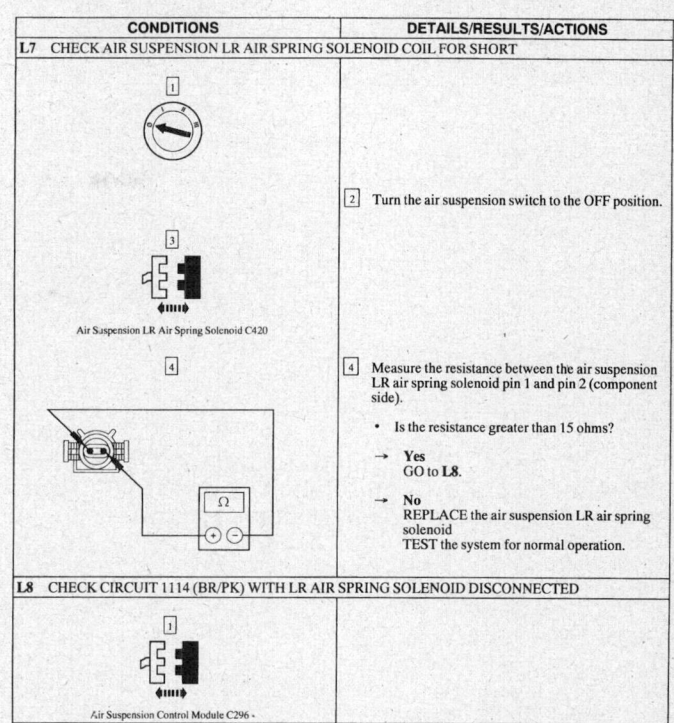

CONDITIONS	DETAILS/RESULTS/ACTIONS
L7 CHECK AIR SUSPENSION LR AIR SPRING SOLENOID COIL FOR SHORT	
1 3 Air Suspension LR Air Spring Solenoid C420	2 Turn the air suspension switch to the OFF position.
4	4 Measure the resistance between the air suspension LR air spring solenoid pin 1 and pin 2 (component side). • Is the resistance greater than 15 ohms? → **Yes** GO to **L8**. → **No** REPLACE the air suspension LR air spring solenoid TEST the system for normal operation.
L8 CHECK CIRCUIT 1114 (BR/PK) WITH LR AIR SPRING SOLENOID DISCONNECTED	
1 Air Suspension Control Module C296	

FM2010100687050X

Fig. 23   Test L/DTC C1790: Lefthand Rear Spring Solenoid Output Circuit Failure (Part 5 of 8). Four wheel air suspension system

CONDITIONS	DETAILS/RESULTS/ACTIONS
L8 CHECK CIRCUIT 1114 (BR/PK) WITH LR AIR SPRING SOLENOID DISCONNECTED (Continued)	
2	2 Measure the resistance between air suspension control module C296 pin 17, circuit 1114 (BR/PK), harness side and ground. • Is the resistance greater than 10,000 ohms? → **Yes** REPLACE the air suspension control module. SET the ride height Clear B2140 DTC. TEST the system for normal operation. → **No** REPAIR the circuit. TEST the system for normal operation.
L9 CHECK CIRCUIT 1114 (BR/PK) FOR SHORT TO POWER	
1	
3 Air Suspension Control Module C296	2 Turn the air suspension switch to the OFF position.
	4 Turn the air suspension switch to the ON position.
5	

FM2010100687060X

Fig. 23   Test L/DTC C1790: Lefthand Rear Spring Solenoid Output Circuit Failure (Part 6 of 8). Four wheel air suspension system

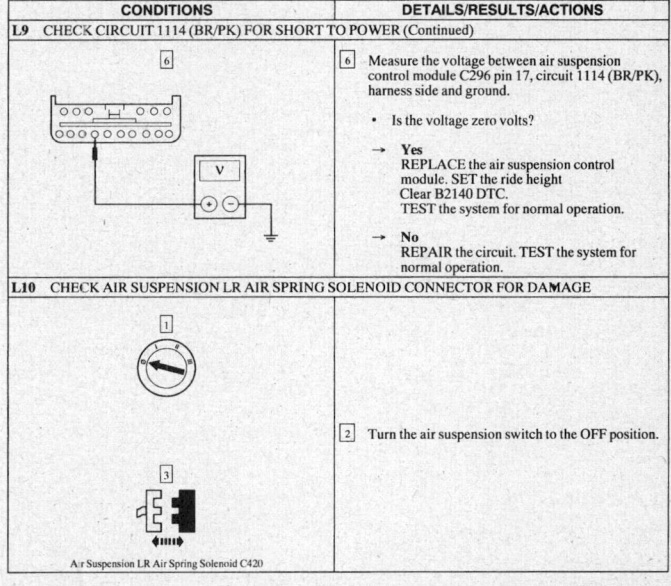

CONDITIONS	DETAILS/RESULTS/ACTIONS
L9 CHECK CIRCUIT 1114 (BR/PK) FOR SHORT TO POWER (Continued)	
6	6 Measure the voltage between air suspension control module C296 pin 17, circuit 1114 (BR/PK), harness side and ground. • Is the voltage zero volts? → **Yes** REPLACE the air suspension control module. SET the ride height Clear B2140 DTC. TEST the system for normal operation. → **No** REPAIR the circuit. TEST the system for normal operation.
L10 CHECK AIR SUSPENSION LR AIR SPRING SOLENOID CONNECTOR FOR DAMAGE	
1 3 Air Suspension LR Air Spring Solenoid C420	2 Turn the air suspension switch to the OFF position.

FM2010100687070X

Fig. 23   Test L/DTC C1790: Lefthand Rear Spring Solenoid Output Circuit Failure (Part 7 of 8). Four wheel air suspension system

CONDITIONS	DETAILS/RESULTS/ACTIONS
L10 CHECK AIR SUSPENSION LR AIR SPRING SOLENOID CONNECTOR FOR DAMAGE (Continued)	
	4 Inspect the pins and terminals of the air suspension LR air spring solenoid C420 for corrosion, bent or broken pins, moisture, or other damage; inspect the wiring near the connector for damage. • Is the air suspension LR air spring solenoid C420 OK? → **Yes** RECONNECT the air suspension LR air spring solenoid C420. PLACE the air suspension switch in the ON position. TEST the system for normal operation. If no DTCs are retrieved, the system is OK. If a DTC is retrieved, REFER to Diagnostic Trouble Code (DTC) Interpretation. → **No** REPAIR as necessary. TEST the system for normal operation.

FM2010100687080X

Fig. 23   Test L/DTC C1790: Lefthand Rear Spring Solenoid Output Circuit Failure (Part 8 of 8). Four wheel air suspension system

CONDITIONS	DETAILS/RESULTS/ACTIONS
M1 VALIDATE DTC C1795 ERROR	
	1 Carry out the air suspension control module On-Demand Self-Test. • Is the same air suspension DTC set? → **Yes** GO to **M2**. → **No** If no DTC is retrieved, GO to **M10**. If a different DTC is retrieved, REFER to Interpretation Diagnostic Trouble Code (DTC).
M2 CHECK AIR SUSPENSION RR AIR SPRING SOLENOID CONNECTOR	
	2 Turn the air suspension switch to the OFF position.

FM2010100688010X

Fig. 24   Test M/DTC C1795: Righthand Rear Spring Solenoid Output Circuit Failure (Part 1 of 8). Four wheel air suspension system

CONDITIONS	DETAILS/RESULTS/ACTIONS
M2 CHECK AIR SUSPENSION RR AIR SPRING SOLENOID CONNECTOR (Continued)	
 Air Suspension RR Air Spring Solenoid C419	4 Inspect the pins and terminals of the air suspension RR air spring solenoid connector for corrosion, bent or broken pins, moisture, or other damage. • Is the air suspension RR air spring solenoid C419 OK? → **Yes** RECONNECT the air suspension RR air spring solenoid C419. GO to **M3**. → **No** REPAIR as necessary. TEST the system for normal operation.
M3 CHECK SOLENOID PID	
	1 Turn the air suspension switch to the ON position. 3 Select air suspension control module active commands and activate PID ASRRSOL. 4 **NOTE:** The active command sequence is critical to proper diagnosis. Using the active commands, trigger in the following order:

Active Command	Trigger
LR AIRSP	ON
RR AIRSP	ON
LR AIRSP	OFF
RR AIRSP	OFF

FM2010100688020X

Fig. 24   Test M/DTC C1795: Righthand Rear Spring Solenoid Output Circuit Failure (Part 2 of 8). Four wheel air suspension system

CONDITIONS	DETAILS/RESULTS/ACTIONS
M3 CHECK SOLENOID PID (Continued)	
	• Do the letters O, G, or B appear next to the ON/OFF text for the air suspension RR air spring solenoid? → **Yes** If O appeared, GO to **M4**. If G appeared, GO to **M7**. If B appeared, GO to **M9**. → **No** GO to **M10**.
M4 CHECK AIR SUSPENSION RR AIR SPRING SOLENOID COIL FOR OPEN	
    Air Suspension RR Air Spring Solenoid C419 	2 Turn the air suspension switch to the OFF position. 4 Measure the resistance between air suspension RR air spring solenoid pin 1 and pin 2 (component side). • Is the resistance less than 25 ohms? → **Yes** GO to **M5**. → **No** REPLACE the air suspension RR air spring solenoid TEST the system for normal operation.

FM2010100688030X

Fig. 24   Test M/DTC C1795: Righthand Rear Spring Solenoid Output Circuit Failure (Part 3 of 8). Four wheel air suspension system

CONDITIONS	DETAILS/RESULTS/ACTIONS
M5 CHECK CIRCUIT 57 (BK)	

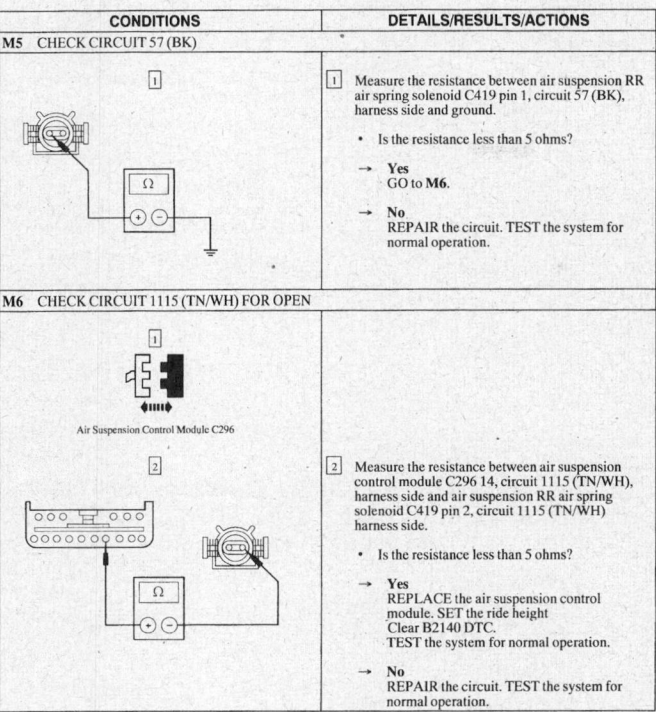

[1]	[1] Measure the resistance between air suspension RR air spring solenoid C419 pin 1, circuit 57 (BK), harness side and ground. • Is the resistance less than 5 ohms? → **Yes** GO to **M6**. → **No** REPAIR the circuit. TEST the system for normal operation.

CONDITIONS	DETAILS/RESULTS/ACTIONS
M6 CHECK CIRCUIT 1115 (TN/WH) FOR OPEN	

[1] Air Suspension Control Module C296	
[2]	[2] Measure the resistance between air suspension control module C296 14, circuit 1115 (TN/WH), harness side and air suspension RR air spring solenoid C419 pin 2, circuit 1115 (TN/WH) harness side. • Is the resistance less than 5 ohms? → **Yes** REPLACE the air suspension control module. SET the ride height Clear B2140 DTC. TEST the system for normal operation. → **No** REPAIR the circuit. TEST the system for normal operation.

FM2010100688040X

Fig. 24   Test M/DTC C1795: Righthand Rear Spring Solenoid Output Circuit Failure (Part 4 of 8). Four wheel air suspension system

CONDITIONS	DETAILS/RESULTS/ACTIONS
M7 CHECK AIR SUSPENSION RR AIR SPRING SOLENOID COIL FOR SHORT	

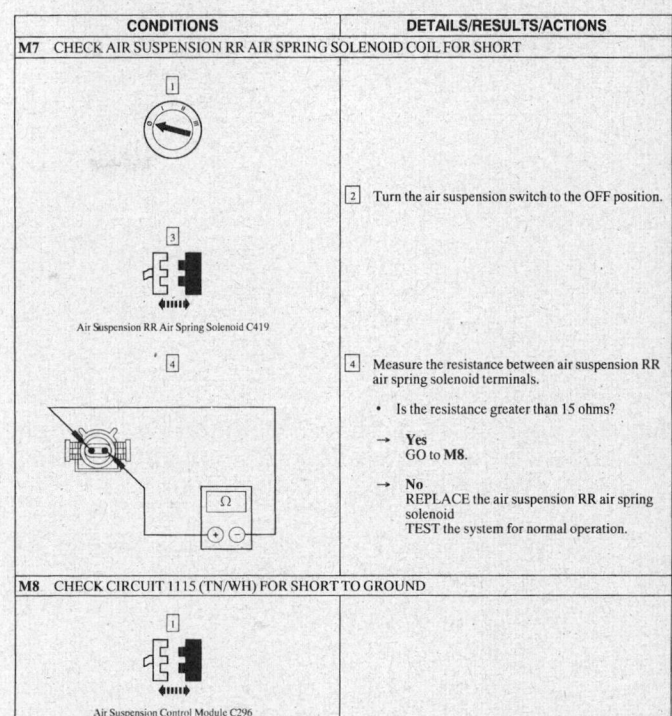

	[2] Turn the air suspension switch to the OFF position.
[3] Air Suspension RR Air Spring Solenoid C419	
[4]	[4] Measure the resistance between air suspension RR air spring solenoid terminals. • Is the resistance greater than 15 ohms? → **Yes** GO to **M8**. → **No** REPLACE the air suspension RR air spring solenoid TEST the system for normal operation.

CONDITIONS	DETAILS/RESULTS/ACTIONS
M8 CHECK CIRCUIT 1115 (TN/WH) FOR SHORT TO GROUND	

[1] Air Suspension Control Module C296	

FM2010100688050X

Fig. 24   Test M/DTC C1795: Righthand Rear Spring Solenoid Output Circuit Failure (Part 5 of 8). Four wheel air suspension system

CONDITIONS	DETAILS/RESULTS/ACTIONS
M8 CHECK CIRCUIT 1115 (TN/WH) FOR SHORT TO GROUND (Continued)	

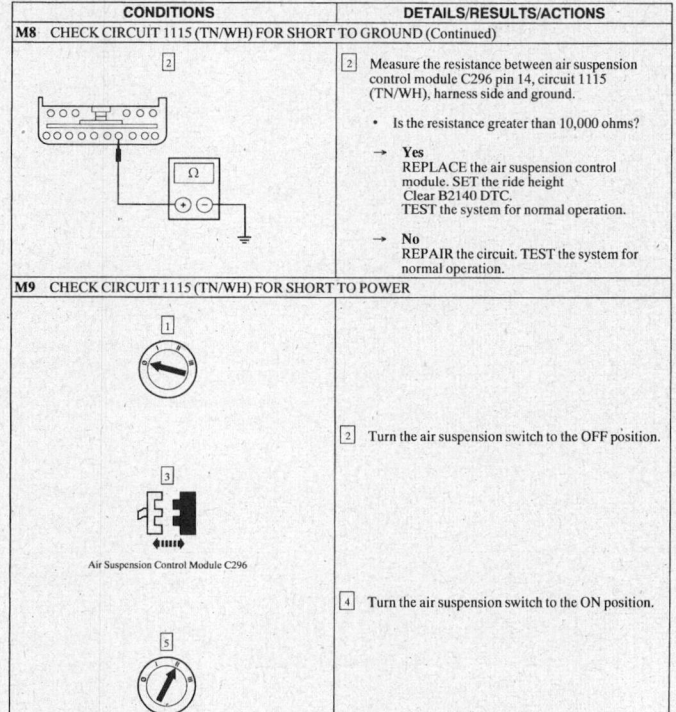

[2]	[2] Measure the resistance between air suspension control module C296 pin 14, circuit 1115 (TN/WH), harness side and ground. • Is the resistance greater than 10,000 ohms? → **Yes** REPLACE the air suspension control module. SET the ride height Clear B2140 DTC. TEST the system for normal operation. → **No** REPAIR the circuit. TEST the system for normal operation.

CONDITIONS	DETAILS/RESULTS/ACTIONS
M9 CHECK CIRCUIT 1115 (TN/WH) FOR SHORT TO POWER	

[1]	
	[2] Turn the air suspension switch to the OFF position.
[3] Air Suspension Control Module C296	
	[4] Turn the air suspension switch to the ON position.
[5]	

FM2010100688060X

Fig. 24   Test M/DTC C1795: Righthand Rear Spring Solenoid Output Circuit Failure (Part 6 of 8). Four wheel air suspension system

CONDITIONS	DETAILS/RESULTS/ACTIONS
M9 CHECK CIRCUIT 1115 (TN/WH) FOR SHORT TO POWER (Continued)	

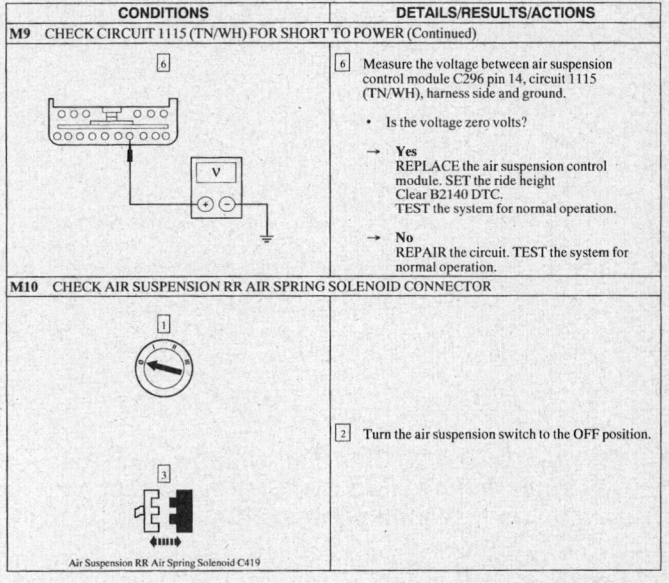

[6]	[6] Measure the voltage between air suspension control module C296 pin 14, circuit 1115 (TN/WH), harness side and ground. • Is the voltage zero volts? → **Yes** REPLACE the air suspension control module. SET the ride height Clear B2140 DTC. TEST the system for normal operation. → **No** REPAIR the circuit. TEST the system for normal operation.

CONDITIONS	DETAILS/RESULTS/ACTIONS
M10 CHECK AIR SUSPENSION RR AIR SPRING SOLENOID CONNECTOR	

[1]	
	[2] Turn the air suspension switch to the OFF position.
[3] Air Suspension RR Air Spring Solenoid C419	

FM2010100688070X

Fig. 24   Test M/DTC C1795: Righthand Rear Spring Solenoid Output Circuit Failure (Part 7 of 8). Four wheel air suspension system

CONDITIONS	DETAILS/RESULTS/ACTIONS
M10 CHECK AIR SUSPENSION RR AIR SPRING SOLENOID CONNECTOR (Continued)	
4	Inspect the pins and terminals of the air suspension RR air spring solenoid C419 for corrosion, bent or broken pins, moisture, or other damage; inspect the wiring near the connector for damage. • Is the air suspension RR air spring solenoid C419 OK? → **Yes** RECONNECT the air suspension RR air spring solenoid C419. PLACE the air suspension switch in the ON position. TEST the system for normal operation. If no DTCs are retrieved, the system is OK. If a DTC is retrieved, REFER to Diagnostic Trouble Code (DTC) Interpretation. → **No** REPAIR as necessary. TEST the system for normal operation.

FM2010100688080X

Fig. 24 Test M/DTC C1795: Righthand Rear Spring Solenoid Output Circuit Failure (Part 8 of 8). Four wheel air suspension system

CONDITIONS	DETAILS/RESULTS/ACTIONS
N2 CHECK AIR COMPRESSOR RELAY CONNECTOR (Continued)	
Air Compressor Relay C1000	4 Inspect the pins and terminals of the air compressor relay for corrosion, bent or broken pins, moisture, or other damage. • Is the connector OK? → **Yes** RECONNECT air compressor relay C1000. GO to **N3**. → **No** REPAIR as necessary. TEST the system for normal operation.
N3 CHECK AIR COMPRESSOR PID	
	1 Turn the air suspension switch to the ON position. 3 Select air suspension control module active commands and activate PID AS__COMP. 4 Trigger active command COMPRESSR ON and OFF. • Do the letters O or B appear next to the ON/OFF text for the air compressor? → **Yes** If O appeared, GO to **N4**. If B appeared, GO to **N7**. → **No** GO to **N8**.

FM2010100689020X

Fig. 25 Test N/DTC C1830: Compressor Relay Circuit Failure (Part 2 of 6). Four wheel air suspension system

CONDITIONS	DETAILS/RESULTS/ACTIONS
N1 VALIDATE DTC C1830 ERROR	
1	1 Carry out the air suspension control module On-Demand Self-Test. • Is the same air suspension DTC set? → **Yes** GO to **N2**. → **No** If no DTC is retrieved, GO to **N8**. If a different DTC is retrieved, REFER to Diagnostic Trouble Code (DTC) Interpretation.
N2 CHECK AIR COMPRESSOR RELAY CONNECTOR	
1	2 Turn the air suspension switch to the OFF position.

FM2010100689010X

Fig. 25 Test N/DTC C1830: Compressor Relay Circuit Failure (Part 1 of 6). Four wheel air suspension system

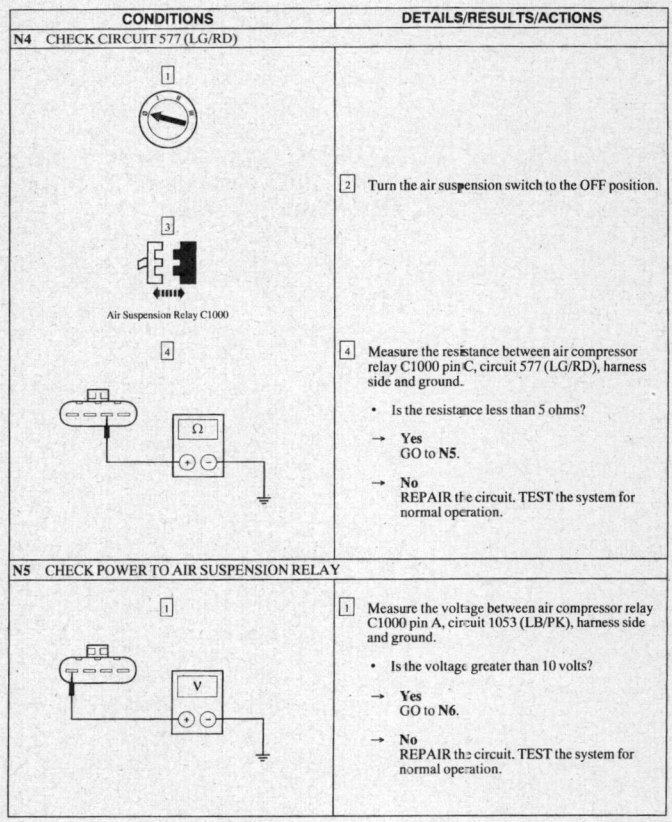

CONDITIONS	DETAILS/RESULTS/ACTIONS
N4 CHECK CIRCUIT 577 (LG/RD)	
Air Suspension Relay C1000	2 Turn the air suspension switch to the OFF position. 4 Measure the resistance between air compressor relay C1000 pin C, circuit 577 (LG/RD), harness side and ground. • Is the resistance less than 5 ohms? → **Yes** GO to **N5**. → **No** REPAIR the circuit. TEST the system for normal operation.
N5 CHECK POWER TO AIR SUSPENSION RELAY	
1	1 Measure the voltage between air compressor relay C1000 pin A, circuit 1053 (LB/PK), harness side and ground. • Is the voltage greater than 10 volts? → **Yes** GO to **N6**. → **No** REPAIR the circuit. TEST the system for normal operation.

FM2010100689030X

Fig. 25 Test N/DTC C1830: Compressor Relay Circuit Failure (Part 3 of 6). Four wheel air suspension system

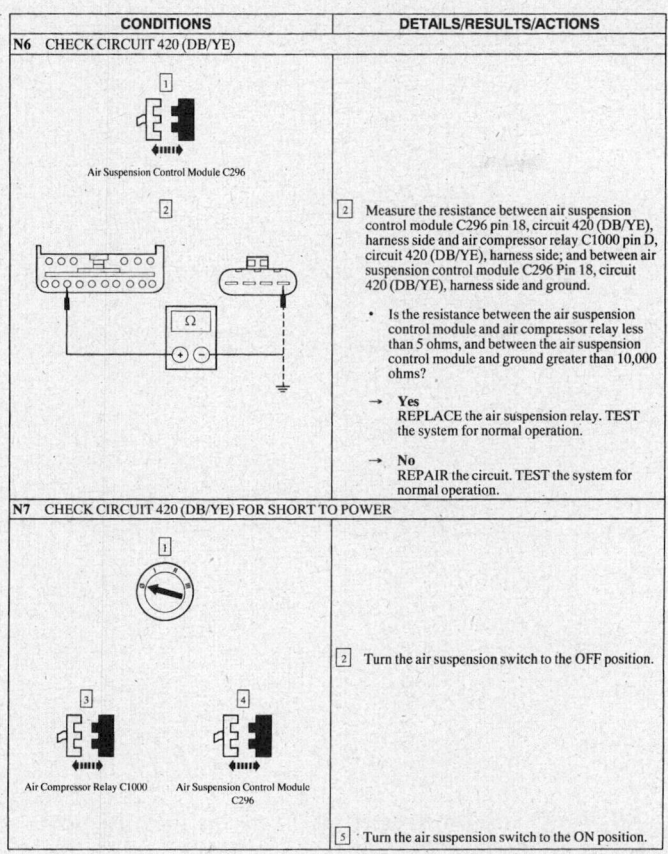

CONDITIONS	DETAILS/RESULTS/ACTIONS
N6 CHECK CIRCUIT 420 (DB/YE)	
	[2] Measure the resistance between air suspension control module C296 pin 18, circuit 420 (DB/YE), harness side and air compressor relay C1000 pin D, circuit 420 (DB/YE), harness side; and between air suspension control module C296 Pin 18, circuit 420 (DB/YE), harness side and ground.
	• Is the resistance between the air suspension control module and air compressor relay less than 5 ohms, and between the air suspension control module and ground greater than 10,000 ohms?
	→ Yes REPLACE the air suspension relay. TEST the system for normal operation.
	→ No REPAIR the circuit. TEST the system for normal operation.
N7 CHECK CIRCUIT 420 (DB/YE) FOR SHORT TO POWER	
	[2] Turn the air suspension switch to the OFF position.
	[5] Turn the air suspension switch to the ON position.

Fig. 25   Test N/DTC C1830: Compressor Relay Circuit Failure (Part 4 of 6). Four wheel air suspension system

FM2010100689040X

CONDITIONS	DETAILS/RESULTS/ACTIONS
N8 CHECK AIR COMPRESSOR RELAY CONNECTOR (Continued)	
	[4] Inspect the pins and terminals of the air compressor relay for corrosion, bent or broken pins, moisture, or other damage; inspect the wiring near the connector for damage.
	• Is the connector OK?
	→ Yes RECONNECT air compressor relay. PLACE the air suspension switch in the ON position. TEST the system for normal operation. If no DTCs are retrieved, the system is OK. If a DTC is retrieved, REFER to Diagnostic Trouble Code (DTC) Interpretation.
	→ No REPAIR as necessary. TEST the system for normal operation.

FM2010100689060X

Fig. 25   Test N/DTC C1830: Compressor Relay Circuit Failure (Part 6 of 6). Four wheel air suspension system

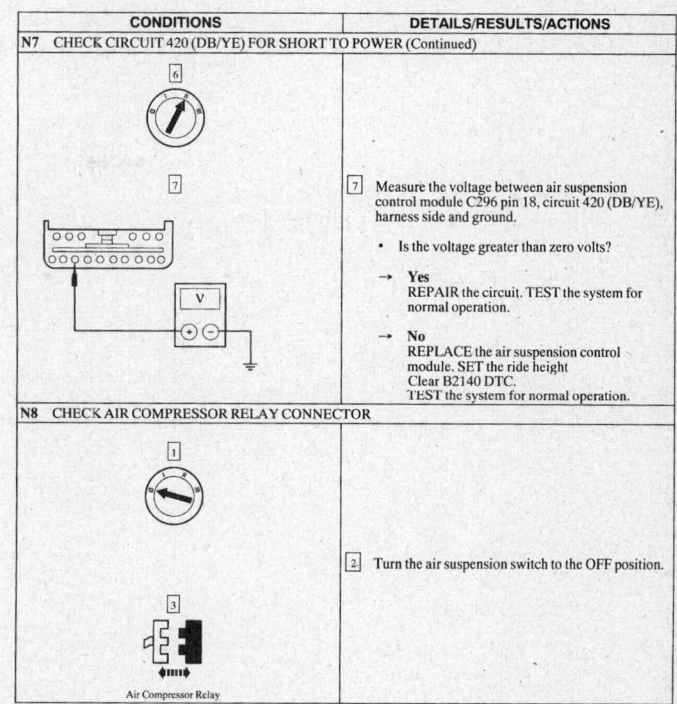

CONDITIONS	DETAILS/RESULTS/ACTIONS
N7 CHECK CIRCUIT 420 (DB/YE) FOR SHORT TO POWER (Continued)	
	[7] Measure the voltage between air suspension control module C296 pin 18, circuit 420 (DB/YE), harness side and ground.
	• Is the voltage greater than zero volts?
	→ Yes REPAIR the circuit. TEST the system for normal operation.
	→ No REPLACE the air suspension control module. SET the ride height Clear B2140 DTC. TEST the system for normal operation.
N8 CHECK AIR COMPRESSOR RELAY CONNECTOR	
	[2] Turn the air suspension switch to the OFF position.

FM2010100689050X

Fig. 25   Test N/DTC C1830: Compressor Relay Circuit Failure (Part 5 of 6). Four wheel air suspension system

CONDITIONS	DETAILS/RESULTS/ACTIONS
O1 VALIDATE DTC C1845 ERROR	
	[1] Carry out the air suspension control module On-Demand Self-Test.
	• Is the same air suspension DTC set?
	→ Yes GO to O2.
	→ No If no DTC is retrieved, GO to O10. If a different DTC is retrieved, REFER to Diagnostic Trouble Code (DTC) Interpretation.
O2 CHECK AIR SUSPENSION FRONT FILL SOLENOID CONNECTOR	
	[2] Turn the air suspension switch to the OFF position.

FM2010100690010X

Fig. 26   Test O/DTC C1845: Front Inflator Fill Solenoid Output Circuit Failure (Part 1 of 7). Four wheel air suspension system

CONDITIONS	DETAILS/RESULTS/ACTIONS
O2 CHECK AIR SUSPENSION FRONT FILL SOLENOID CONNECTOR (Continued)	

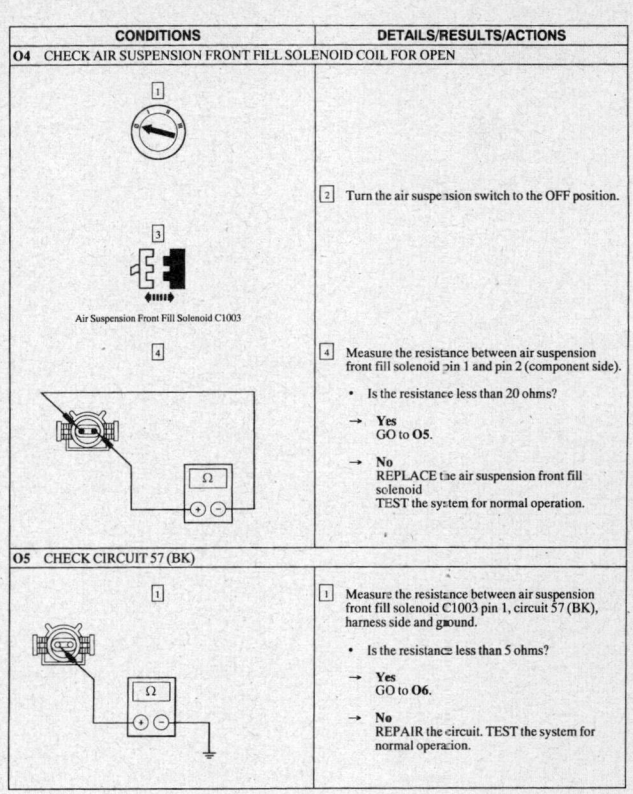

Air Suspension Front Fill Solenoid C1003

4 Inspect the pins and terminals of the air suspension front fill solenoid connector for corrosion, bent or broken pins, moisture, or other damage.

- Is the air suspension front fill solenoid C1003 OK?

→ **Yes**
RECONNECT the air suspension front fill solenoid C1003. GO to **O3**.

→ **No**
REPAIR as necessary. TEST the system for normal operation.

CONDITIONS	DETAILS/RESULTS/ACTIONS
O3 CHECK SOLENOID PID	

1 Turn the air suspension switch to the ON position.

3 Select the air suspension control module active commands and activate PID F__FILL.

4 Trigger active command FRNT FILL ON and OFF.

- Do the letters O, G, or B appear next to the ON/OFF text for the air suspension front fill solenoid?

→ **Yes**
If O appeared, GO to **O4**.

If G appeared, GO to **O7**.

If B appeared, GO to **O10**.

→ **No**
GO to **O10**.

FM2010100690020X

Fig. 26 Test O/DTC C1845: Front Inflator Fill Solenoid Output Circuit Failure (Part 2 of 7). Four wheel air suspension system

CONDITIONS	DETAILS/RESULTS/ACTIONS
O4 CHECK AIR SUSPENSION FRONT FILL SOLENOID COIL FOR OPEN	

2 Turn the air suspension switch to the OFF position.

Air Suspension Front Fill Solenoid C1003

4 Measure the resistance between air suspension front fill solenoid pin 1 and pin 2 (component side).

- Is the resistance less than 20 ohms?

→ **Yes**
GO to **O5**.

→ **No**
REPLACE the air suspension front fill solenoid
TEST the system for normal operation.

CONDITIONS	DETAILS/RESULTS/ACTIONS
O5 CHECK CIRCUIT 57 (BK)	

1 Measure the resistance between air suspension front fill solenoid C1003 pin 1, circuit 57 (BK), harness side and ground.

- Is the resistance less than 5 ohms?

→ **Yes**
GO to **O6**.

→ **No**
REPAIR the circuit. TEST the system for normal operation.

FM2010100690030X

Fig. 26 Test O/DTC C1845: Front Inflator Fill Solenoid Output Circuit Failure (Part 3 of 7). Four wheel air suspension system

CONDITIONS	DETAILS/RESULTS/ACTIONS
O6 CHECK CIRCUIT 1194 (YE/BK)	

Air Suspension Control Module C296

2 Measure the resistance between air suspension control module C296 pin 19, circuit 1194 (YE/BK), harness side and air suspension front fill solenoid C1003 pin 2, circuit 1194 (YE/BK), harness side.

- Is the resistance less than 5 ohms?

→ **Yes**
REPLACE the air suspension control module. SET the ride height
Clear B2140 DTC.
TEST the system for normal operation.

→ **No**
REPAIR the circuit. TEST the system for normal operation.

CONDITIONS	DETAILS/RESULTS/ACTIONS
O7 CHECK AIR SUSPENSION FRONT FILL SOLENOID COIL FOR SHORT	

2 Turn the air suspension switch to the OFF position.

Air Suspension Front Fill Solenoid C1003

FM2010100690040X

Fig. 26 Test O/DTC C1845: Front Inflator Fill Solenoid Output Circuit Failure (Part 4 of 7). Four wheel air suspension system

CONDITIONS	DETAILS/RESULTS/ACTIONS
O7 CHECK AIR SUSPENSION FRONT FILL SOLENOID COIL FOR SHORT (Continued)	

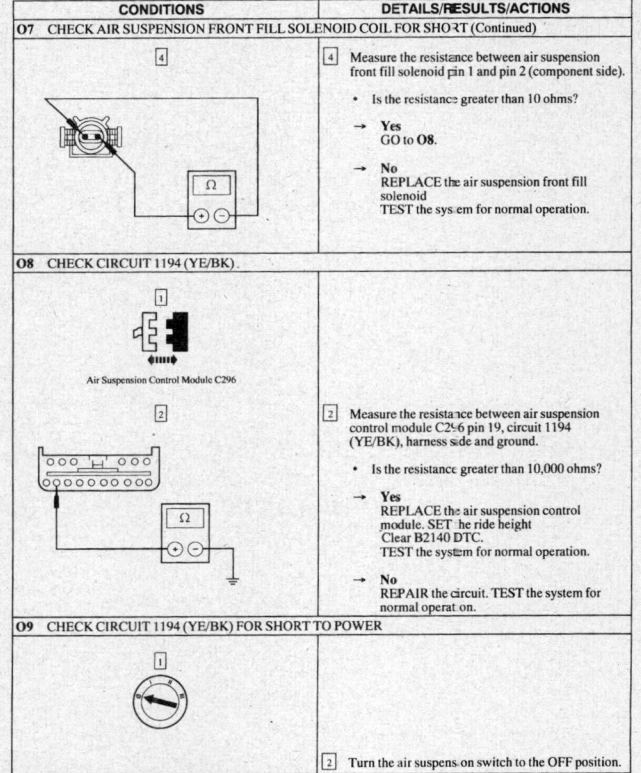

4 Measure the resistance between air suspension front fill solenoid pin 1 and pin 2 (component side).

- Is the resistance greater than 10 ohms?

→ **Yes**
GO to **O8**.

→ **No**
REPLACE the air suspension front fill solenoid
TEST the system for normal operation.

CONDITIONS	DETAILS/RESULTS/ACTIONS
O8 CHECK CIRCUIT 1194 (YE/BK)	

Air Suspension Control Module C296

2 Measure the resistance between air suspension control module C296 pin 19, circuit 1194 (YE/BK), harness side and ground.

- Is the resistance greater than 10,000 ohms?

→ **Yes**
REPLACE the air suspension control module. SET the ride height
Clear B2140 DTC.
TEST the system for normal operation.

→ **No**
REPAIR the circuit. TEST the system for normal operation.

CONDITIONS	DETAILS/RESULTS/ACTIONS
O9 CHECK CIRCUIT 1194 (YE/BK) FOR SHORT TO POWER	

2 Turn the air suspension switch to the OFF position.

FM2010100690050X

Fig. 26 Test O/DTC C1845: Front Inflator Fill Solenoid Output Circuit Failure (Part 5 of 7). Four wheel air suspension system

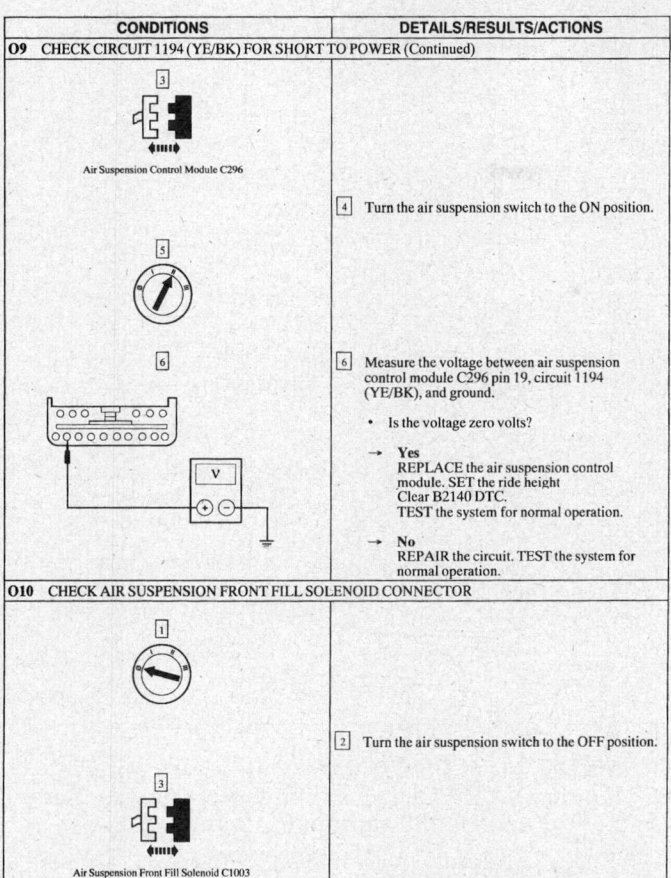

CONDITIONS	DETAILS/RESULTS/ACTIONS
O9 CHECK CIRCUIT 1194 (YE/BK) FOR SHORT TO POWER (Continued)	
Air Suspension Control Module C296	
	4 Turn the air suspension switch to the ON position.
	6 Measure the voltage between air suspension control module C296 pin 19, circuit 1194 (YE/BK), and ground.
	• Is the voltage zero volts?
	→ **Yes** REPLACE the air suspension control module. SET the ride height Clear B2140 DTC. TEST the system for normal operation.
	→ **No** REPAIR the circuit. TEST the system for normal operation.
O10 CHECK AIR SUSPENSION FRONT FILL SOLENOID CONNECTOR	
	2 Turn the air suspension switch to the OFF position.
Air Suspension Front Fill Solenoid C1003	

FM2010100690060X

Fig. 26 Test O/DTC C1845: Front Inflator Fill Solenoid Output Circuit Failure (Part 6 of 7). Four wheel air suspension system

CONDITIONS	DETAILS/RESULTS/ACTIONS
P1 VALIDATE DTC C1865 ERROR	
	1 Carry out the air suspension control module On-Demand Self-Test.
	• Is the same air suspension DTC set?
	→ **Yes** GO to **P2**.
	→ **No** If no DTC is retrieved, GO to **P10**. If a different DTC is retrieved, REFER to Diagnostic Trouble Code (DTC) Interpertation.
P2 CHECK AIR SUSPENSION REAR FILL SOLENOID CONNECTOR	
	2 Turn the air suspension switch to the OFF position.

FM2010100691010X

Fig. 27 Test P/DTC C1865: Rear Inflator Fill Solenoid Output Circuit Failure (Part 1 of 8). Four wheel air suspension system

CONDITIONS	DETAILS/RESULTS/ACTIONS
O10 CHECK AIR SUSPENSION FRONT FILL SOLENOID CONNECTOR (Continued)	
	4 Inspect the pins and terminals of the air suspension front fill solenoid C1003 for corrosion, bent or broken pins, moisture, or other damage; inspect the wiring near the connector for damage.
	• Is the air suspension front fill solenoid C1003 OK?
	→ **Yes** RECONNECT the air suspension front fill solenoid C1003. PLACE the air suspension switch in the ON position. TEST the system for normal operation. If no DTCs are retrieved, the system is OK. If a DTC is retrieved, REFER to Diagnostic Trouble Code (DTC) Interpertation.
	→ **No** REPAIR as necessary. TEST the system for normal operation.

FM2010100690070X

Fig. 26 Test O/DTC C1845: Front Inflator Fill Solenoid Output Circuit Failure (Part 7 of 7). Four wheel air suspension system

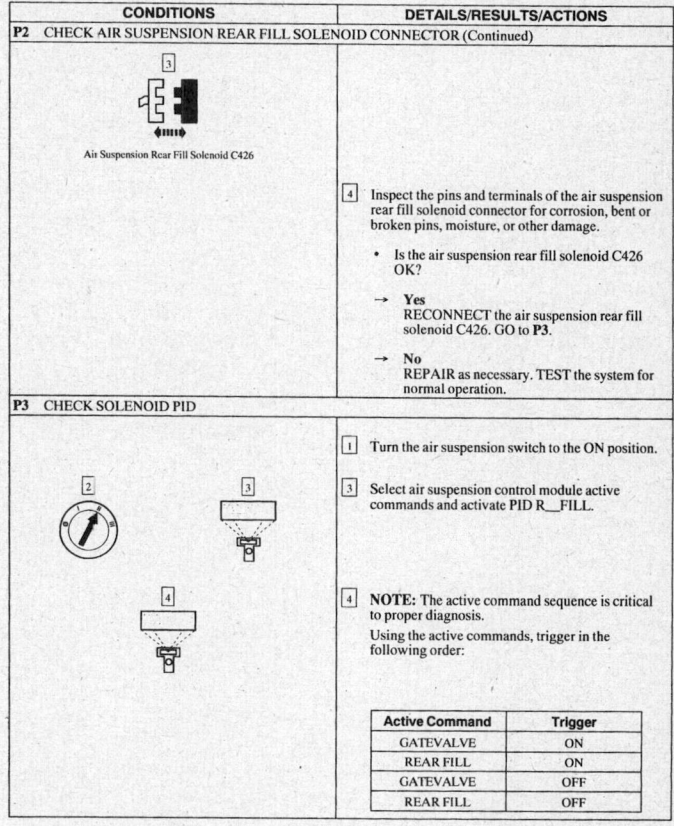

CONDITIONS	DETAILS/RESULTS/ACTIONS
P2 CHECK AIR SUSPENSION REAR FILL SOLENOID CONNECTOR (Continued)	
Air Suspension Rear Fill Solenoid C426	
	4 Inspect the pins and terminals of the air suspension rear fill solenoid connector for corrosion, bent or broken pins, moisture, or other damage.
	• Is the air suspension rear fill solenoid C426 OK?
	→ **Yes** RECONNECT the air suspension rear fill solenoid C426. GO to **P3**.
	→ **No** REPAIR as necessary. TEST the system for normal operation.
P3 CHECK SOLENOID PID	
	1 Turn the air suspension switch to the ON position.
	3 Select air suspension control module active commands and activate PID R__FILL.
	4 **NOTE:** The active command sequence is critical to proper diagnosis. Using the active commands, trigger in the following order:

Active Command	Trigger
GATEVALVE	ON
REAR FILL	ON
GATEVALVE	OFF
REAR FILL	OFF

FM2010100691020X

Fig. 27 Test P/DTC C1865: Rear Inflator Fill Solenoid Output Circuit Failure (Part 2 of 8). Four wheel air suspension system

CONDITIONS	DETAILS/RESULTS/ACTIONS
P3 CHECK SOLENOID PID (Continued)	
	• Do the letters O, G, or B appear next to the ON/OFF text for the air suspension rear fill solenoid? → **Yes** If O appeared, GO to **P4**. If G appeared, GO to **P7**. If B appeared, GO to **P9**. → **No** GO to **P10**.
P4 CHECK AIR SUSPENSION REAR FILL SOLENOID COIL FOR OPEN	
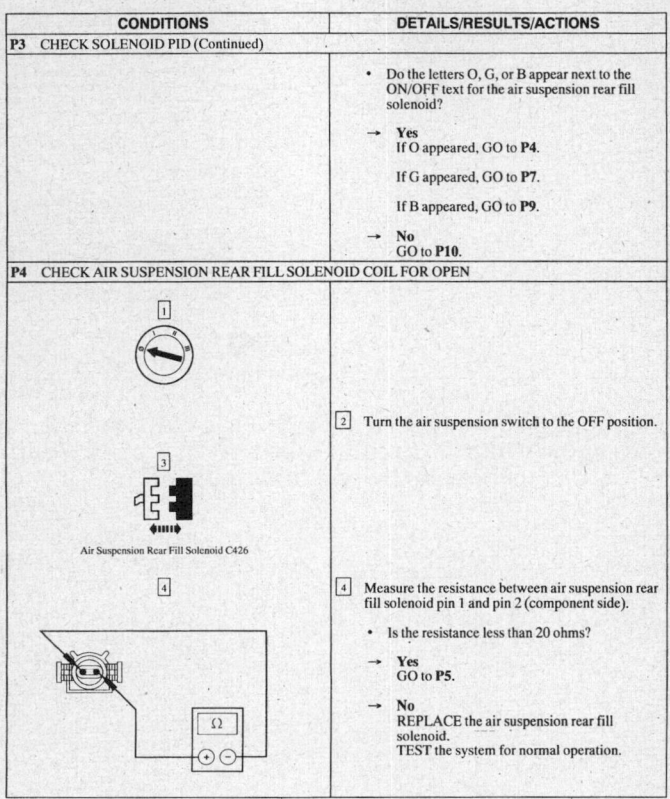	[2] Turn the air suspension switch to the OFF position. [4] Measure the resistance between air suspension rear fill solenoid pin 1 and pin 2 (component side). • Is the resistance less than 20 ohms? → **Yes** GO to **P5**. → **No** REPLACE the air suspension rear fill solenoid. TEST the system for normal operation.

FM2010100691030X

Fig. 27 Test P/DTC C1865: Rear Inflator Fill Solenoid Output Circuit Failure (Part 3 of 8). Four wheel air suspension system

CONDITIONS	DETAILS/RESULTS/ACTIONS
P5 CHECK CIRCUIT 57 (BK)	
[1]	[1] Measure the resistance between air suspension rear fill solenoid C426 pin 1, circuit 57 (BK), harness side and ground. • Is the resistance less than 5 ohms? → **Yes** GO to **P6**. → **No** REPAIR the circuit. TEST the system for normal operation.
P6 CHECK CIRCUIT 1195 (BR/OG)	
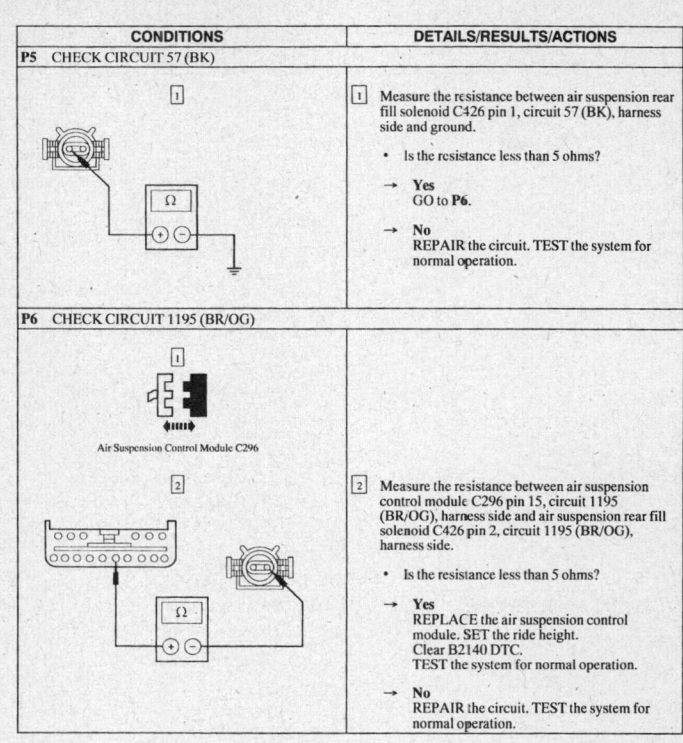	[2] Measure the resistance between air suspension control module C296 pin 15, circuit 1195 (BR/OG), harness side and air suspension rear fill solenoid C426 pin 2, circuit 1195 (BR/OG), harness side. • Is the resistance less than 5 ohms? → **Yes** REPLACE the air suspension control module. SET the ride height. Clear B2140 DTC. TEST the system for normal operation. → **No** REPAIR the circuit. TEST the system for normal operation.

FM2010100691040X

Fig. 27 Test P/DTC C1865: Rear Inflator Fill Solenoid Output Circuit Failure (Part 4 of 8). Four wheel air suspension system

CONDITIONS	DETAILS/RESULTS/ACTIONS
P7 CHECK AIR SUSPENSION REAR FILL SOLENOID COIL FOR SHORT	
[1] [3] Air Suspension Rear Fill Solenoid C426 [4]	[2] Turn the air suspension switch to the OFF position. [4] Measure the resistance between air suspension rear fill solenoid pin 1 and pin 2 (component side). • Is the resistance greater than 10 ohms? → **Yes** GO to **P8**. → **No** REPLACE the air suspension rear fill solenoid. TEST the system for normal operation.
P8 CHECK CIRCUIT 1195 (BR/OG)	
[1] Air Suspension Control Module C296	

FM2010100691050X

Fig. 27 Test P/DTC C1865: Rear Inflator Fill Solenoid Output Circuit Failure (Part 5 of 8). Four wheel air suspension system

CONDITIONS	DETAILS/RESULTS/ACTIONS
P8 CHECK CIRCUIT 1195 (BR/OG) (Continued)	
[2]	[2] Measure the resistance between air suspension control module C296 pin 15, circuit 1195 (BR/OG), harness side and ground. • Is the resistance greater than 10,000 ohms? → **Yes** REPLACE the air suspension control module. SET the ride height. Clear B2140 DTC. TEST the system for normal operation. → **No** REPAIR the circuit. TEST the system for normal operation.
P9 CHECK CIRCUIT 1195 (BR/OG) FOR SHORT TO POWER	
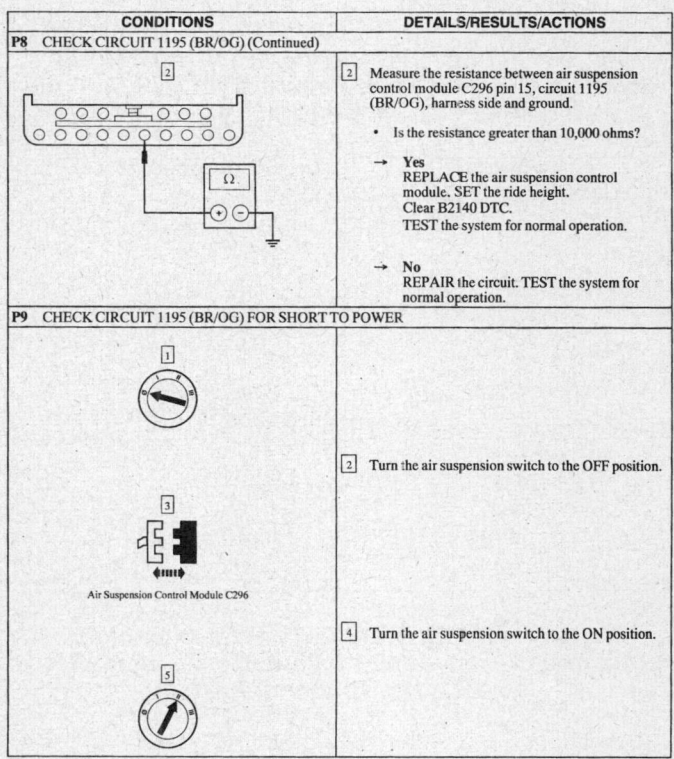	[2] Turn the air suspension switch to the OFF position. [4] Turn the air suspension switch to the ON position.

FM2010100691060X

Fig. 27 Test P/DTC C1865: Rear Inflator Fill Solenoid Output Circuit Failure (Part 6 of 8). Four wheel air suspension system

CONDITIONS	DETAILS/RESULTS/ACTIONS
P9 CHECK CIRCUIT 1195 (BR/OG) FOR SHORT TO POWER (Continued)	
6	6 Measure the voltage between air suspension control module C296 pin 15, circuit 1195 (BR/OG), harness side and ground. • Is the voltage zero volts? → **Yes** REPLACE the air suspension control module. SET the ride height. Clear B2140 DTC. TEST the system for normal operation. → **No** REPAIR the circuit. TEST the system for normal operation.
P10 CHECK AIR SUSPENSION REAR FILL SOLENOID CONNECTOR	
1 2 3 Air Suspension Rear Fill Solenoid C426	2 Turn the air suspension switch to the OFF position.

FM2010100691070X

Fig. 27   Test P/DTC C1865: Rear Inflator Fill Solenoid Output Circuit Failure (Part 7 of 8). Four wheel air suspension system

CONDITIONS	DETAILS/RESULTS/ACTIONS
Q1 VALIDATE DTC C1869 ERROR	
1	1 Carry out the air suspension control module On-Demand Self-Test. • Is the same air suspension DTC set? → **Yes** GO to **Q2**. → **No** If no DTC is retrieved, GO to **Q10**. If a different DTC is retrieved, REFER to Diagnostic Trouble Code (DTC) Interpretation.
Q2 CHECK AIR SUSPENSION GATE SOLENOID CONNECTOR	
1	2 Turn the air suspension switch to the OFF position.

FM2010100692010X

Fig. 28   Test Q/DTC C1869: Gate Solenoid Output Circuit Failure (Part 1 of 7). Four wheel air suspension system

CONDITIONS	DETAILS/RESULTS/ACTIONS
P10 CHECK AIR SUSPENSION REAR FILL SOLENOID CONNECTOR (Continued)	
	4 Inspect the pins of the air suspension rear fill solenoid C426 for corrosion, bent or broken pins, moisture, or other damage; inspect the wiring near the connector for damage. • Is the air suspension rear fill solenoid C426 OK? → **Yes** RECONNECT the air suspension rear fill solenoid C426. PLACE the air suspension switch in the ON position. TEST the system for normal operation. If no DTCs are retrieved, the system is OK. If a DTC is retrieved, REFER to Diagnostic Trouble Code (DTC) Interpretation. → **No** REPAIR as necessary. TEST the system for normal operation.

FM2010100691080X

Fig. 27   Test P/DTC C1865: Rear Inflator Fill Solenoid Output Circuit Failure (Part 8 of 8). Four wheel air suspension system

CONDITIONS	DETAILS/RESULTS/ACTIONS
Q2 CHECK AIR SUSPENSION GATE SOLENOID CONNECTOR (Continued)	
3 Air Suspension Gate Solenoid C1005	4 Inspect the pins and terminals of the air suspension gate solenoid connector for corrosion, bent or broken pins, moisture, or other damage. • Is the air suspension gate solenoid C1005 OK? → **Yes** RECONNECT the air suspension gate solenoid C1005. GO to **Q3**. → **No** REPAIR as necessary. TEST the system for normal operation.
Q3 CHECK SOLENOID PID	
2 3 4	1 Turn the air suspension switch to the ON position. 3 Select air suspension control module active commands and activate PID AS__GATE. 4 **NOTE:** The active command sequence is critical to proper diagnosis. Using the active commands, trigger in the following order:

Active Command	Trigger
REAR FILL	ON
GATE VALVE	ON
REAR FILL	OFF
GATE VALVE	OFF

FM2010100692020X

Fig. 28   Test Q/DTC C1869: Gate Solenoid Output Circuit Failure (Part 2 of 7). Four wheel air suspension system

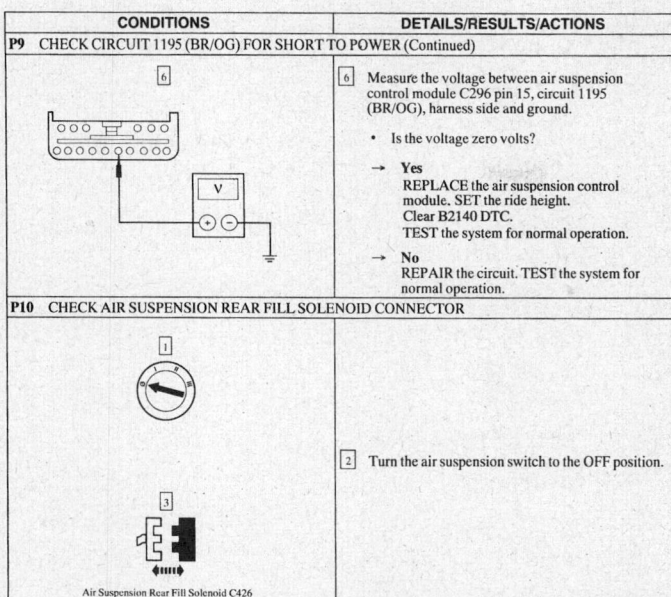

CONDITIONS	DETAILS/RESULTS/ACTIONS
Q3 CHECK SOLENOID PID (Continued)	
	• Do the letters O, G, or B appear next to the ON/OFF text for the air suspension gate solenoid? → **Yes** If O appeared, GO to **Q4**. If G appeared, GO to **Q7**. If B appeared, GO to **Q9**. → **No** GO to **Q10**.
Q4 CHECK AIR SUSPENSION GATE SOLENOID COIL FOR OPEN	
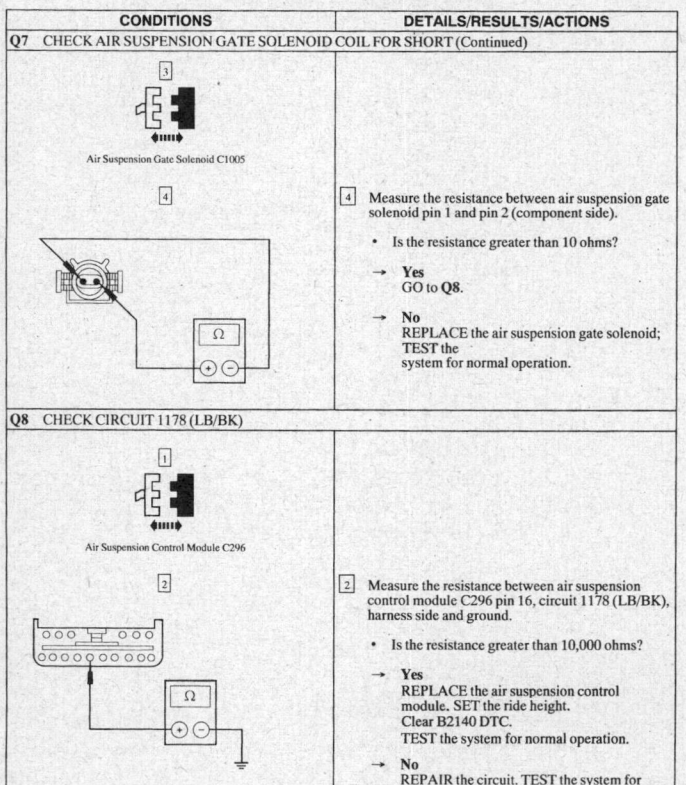	2 Turn the air suspension switch to the OFF position. 4 Measure the resistance between air suspension gate solenoid pin 1 and pin 2 (component side). • Is the resistance less than 20 ohms? → **Yes** GO to **Q5**. → **No** REPLACE the air suspension gate solenoid; TEST the system for normal operation.

FM2010100692030X

Fig. 28   Test Q/DTC C1869: Gate Solenoid Output Circuit Failure (Part 3 of 7). Four wheel air suspension system

CONDITIONS	DETAILS/RESULTS/ACTIONS
Q5 CHECK CIRCUIT 57 (BK)	
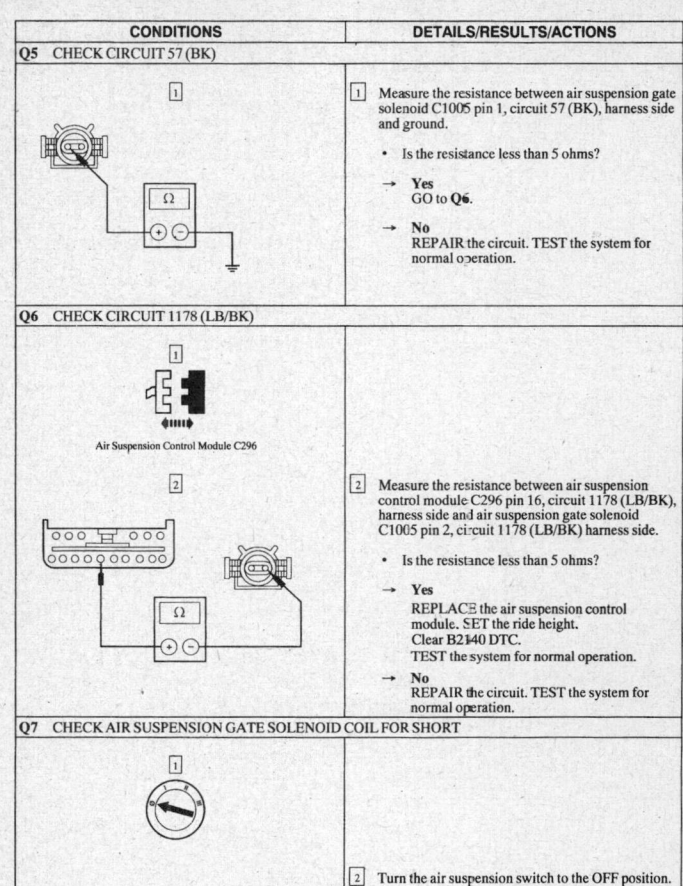	1 Measure the resistance between air suspension gate solenoid C1005 pin 1, circuit 57 (BK), harness side and ground. • Is the resistance less than 5 ohms? → **Yes** GO to **Q6**. → **No** REPAIR the circuit. TEST the system for normal operation.
Q6 CHECK CIRCUIT 1178 (LB/BK)	
Air Suspension Control Module C296	2 Measure the resistance between air suspension control module C296 pin 16, circuit 1178 (LB/BK), harness side and air suspension gate solenoid C1005 pin 2, circuit 1178 (LB/BK) harness side. • Is the resistance less than 5 ohms? → **Yes** REPLACE the air suspension control module. SET the ride height. Clear B2140 DTC. TEST the system for normal operation. → **No** REPAIR the circuit. TEST the system for normal operation.
Q7 CHECK AIR SUSPENSION GATE SOLENOID COIL FOR SHORT	
	2 Turn the air suspension switch to the OFF position.

FM2010100692040X

Fig. 28   Test Q/DTC C1869: Gate Solenoid Output Circuit Failure (Part 4 of 7). Four wheel suspension system

CONDITIONS	DETAILS/RESULTS/ACTIONS
Q7 CHECK AIR SUSPENSION GATE SOLENOID COIL FOR SHORT (Continued)	
Air Suspension Gate Solenoid C1005	4 Measure the resistance between air suspension gate solenoid pin 1 and pin 2 (component side). • Is the resistance greater than 10 ohms? → **Yes** GO to **Q8**. → **No** REPLACE the air suspension gate solenoid; TEST the system for normal operation.
Q8 CHECK CIRCUIT 1178 (LB/BK)	
Air Suspension Control Module C296	2 Measure the resistance between air suspension control module C296 pin 16, circuit 1178 (LB/BK), harness side and ground. • Is the resistance greater than 10,000 ohms? → **Yes** REPLACE the air suspension control module. SET the ride height. Clear B2140 DTC. TEST the system for normal operation. → **No** REPAIR the circuit. TEST the system for normal operation.

FM2010100692050X

Fig. 28   Test Q/DTC C1869: Gate Solenoid Output Circuit Failure (Part 5 of 7). Four wheel air suspension system

CONDITIONS	DETAILS/RESULTS/ACTIONS
Q9 CHECK CIRCUIT 1178 (LB/BK) FOR SHORT TO POWER	
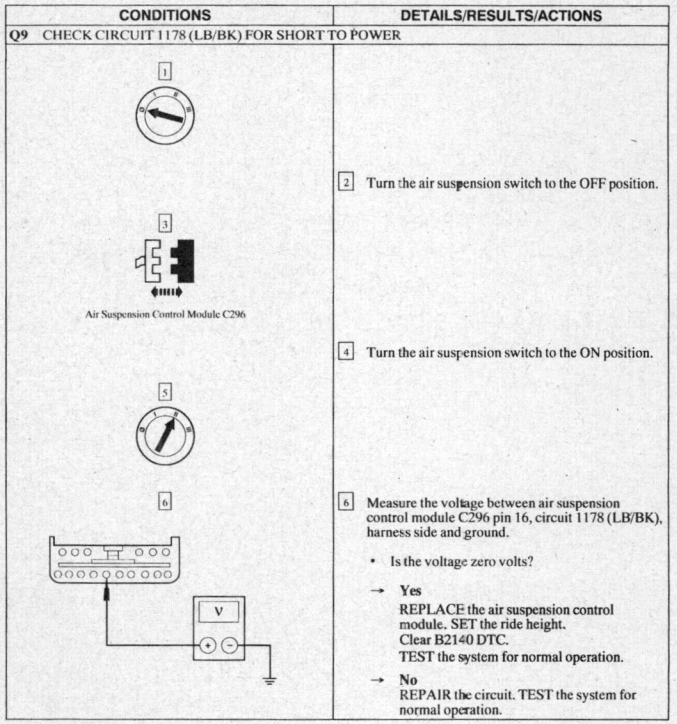 Air Suspension Control Module C296	2 Turn the air suspension switch to the OFF position. 4 Turn the air suspension switch to the ON position. 6 Measure the voltage between air suspension control module C296 pin 16, circuit 1178 (LB/BK), harness side and ground. • Is the voltage zero volts? → **Yes** REPLACE the air suspension control module. SET the ride height. Clear B2140 DTC. TEST the system for normal operation. → **No** REPAIR the circuit. TEST the system for normal operation.

FM2010100692060X

Fig. 28   Test Q/DTC C1869: Gate Solenoid Output Circuit Failure (Part 6 of 7). Four wheel air suspension system

CONDITIONS	DETAILS/RESULTS/ACTIONS
Q10 CHECK AIR SUSPENSION GATE SOLENOID CONNECTOR	
[2]	Turn the air suspension switch to the OFF position.
[3] Air Suspension Gate Solenoid C1005	
[4]	Inspect the pins and terminals of the air suspension gate solenoid C1005 for corrosion, bent or broken pins, moisture, or other damage; inspect the wiring near the connector for damage.
	• Is the air suspension gate solenoid C1005 OK?
	→ **Yes** RECONNECT the air suspension gate solenoid C1005. PLACE the air suspension switch in the ON position. TEST the system for normal operation. If no DTCs are retrieved, the system is OK. If a DTC is retrieved, REFER to Diagnostic Trouble Code (DTC) Interpretation.
	→ **No** REPAIR as necessary. TEST the system for normal operation.

FM2010100692070X

Fig. 28   Test Q/DTC C1869: Gate Solenoid Output Circuit Failure (Part 7 of 7). Four wheel air suspension system

CONDITIONS	DETAILS/RESULTS/ACTIONS
S1 CHECK FOR MODULE ACTIVITY	
NOTE: The air suspension control module is powered for 40 minutes after the ignition is turned OFF. During this time, the air suspension system is still active and may activate system components.	
[1]	
[2]	Check to see if the air compressor still cycles 50 minutes after the ignition is turned OFF.
	• Does the air compressor still cycle after the module goes to sleep?
	→ **Yes** GO to **S2**.
	→ **No** The system is OK. INFORM the owner of system operations.
S2 CHECK THE AIR SUSPENSION CONTROL MODULE	
[1]	Turn the air suspension switch to the OFF position.
[2] Air Suspension Control Module C296	
	• Does the air compressor still cycle?
	→ **Yes** GO to **S3**.
	→ **No** REPLACE the air suspension control module. SET the ride height. Clear B2140 DTC. TEST the system for normal operation.

FM2010100694010X

Fig. 30   Test S: Compressor Cycles Continuously w/Ignition Off & No DTC Set (Part 1 of 2). Four wheel air suspension system

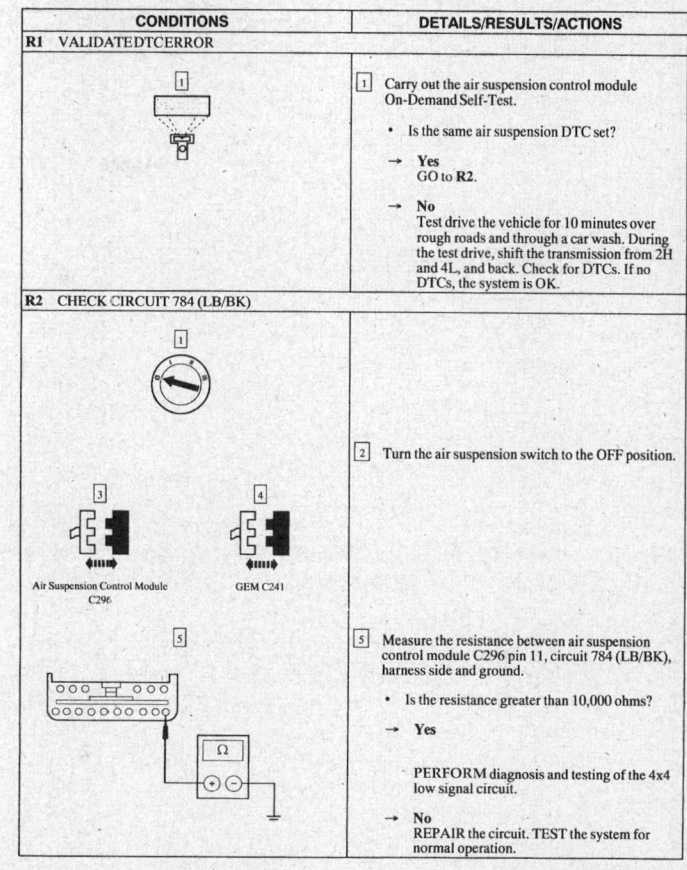

CONDITIONS	DETAILS/RESULTS/ACTIONS
R1 VALIDATE DTC ERROR	
[1]	Carry out the air suspension control module On-Demand Self-Test.
	• Is the same air suspension DTC set?
	→ **Yes** GO to **R2**.
	→ **No** Test drive the vehicle for 10 minutes over rough roads and through a car wash. During the test drive, shift the transmission from 2H and 4L, and back. Check for DTCs. If no DTCs, the system is OK.
R2 CHECK CIRCUIT 784 (LB/BK)	
[1]	
	[2] Turn the air suspension switch to the OFF position.
[3] Air Suspension Control Module C296 [4] GEM C241	
[5]	[5] Measure the resistance between air suspension control module C296 pin 11, circuit 784 (LB/BK), harness side and ground.
	• Is the resistance greater than 10,000 ohms?
	→ **Yes** PERFORM diagnosis and testing of the 4x4 low signal circuit.
	→ **No** REPAIR the circuit. TEST the system for normal operation.

FM2010100693000X

Fig. 29   Test R/DTC P1807 & P1808: 4×4 Indicator Circuit Short To Ground. Four wheel air suspension system

CONDITIONS	DETAILS/RESULTS/ACTIONS
S3 CHECK THE AIR COMPRESSOR RELAY	
[1] Air Compressor Relay C1000	
	• Does the air compressor still cycle?
	→ **Yes** REPAIR circuit 538 (GY/RD). TEST the system for normal operation.
	→ **No** REPLACE the air suspension relay. TEST the system for normal operation.

FM2010100694020X

Fig. 30   Test S: Compressor Cycles Continuously w/Ignition Off & No DTC Set (Part 2 of 2). Four wheel air suspension system

CONDITIONS	DETAILS/RESULTS/ACTIONS
T1 CHECK AIR SUSPENSION CONTROL MODULE FOR IGNITION SWITCH ON INPUT	
[1] [2] (Scan Tool)	[2] Monitor air suspension control module PID IGN__AS. • Does PID IGN__AS show RUN? → **Yes** GO to **T2**. → **No** REPAIR circuit 1003 (GY/YE). TEST the system for normal operation.
T2 CHECK AIR SUSPENSION CONTROL MODULE FOR IGNITION SWITCH OFF INPUT	
[1]	• Does IGN__AS PID show notRUN? → **Yes** GO to **T3**. → **No** REPAIR circuit 1003 (GY/YE). TEST the system for normal operation.

FM2010100695010X

Fig. 31   Test T: Air Suspension System Inoperative (Part 1 of 5). Four wheel air suspension system

CONDITIONS	DETAILS/RESULTS/ACTIONS
T5 CHECK AIR SUSPENSION CONTROL MODULE FOR DOOR AJAR INPUT (Continued)	
	[3] While observing PID DOOR__AS, open and close one door. • Does PID DOOR__AS change between CLOSED and AJAR states? → **Yes** GO to **T6**. → **No** REPAIR circuit 999 (LB/WH). TEST the system for normal operation.
T6 CHECK AIR SUSPENSION CONTROL MODULE FOR 4X4 INPUT	
[1]	[1] Monitor air suspension control module PID 4WDSYS. • Is PID 4WDSYS in the YES state? → **Yes** GO to **T7**. → **No** REPAIR circuit 900 (BK). TEST the system for normal operation.
T7 CHECK AIR SUSPENSION CONTROL MODULE FOR 4X4 STATE INPUT	
[1] [4] P R N D	[1] Monitor air suspension control module PID 4WDLOW. [2] **NOTE:** The 4x4 light on the instrument panel will turn off when the system is in 2H mode. Place the mode switch into 2H mode. [3] Place the mode switch into 4L mode.

FM2010100695030X

Fig. 31   Test T: Air Suspension System Inoperative (Part 3 of 5). Four wheel air suspension system

CONDITIONS	DETAILS/RESULTS/ACTIONS
T3 CHECK AIR SUSPENSION CONTROL MODULE FOR ELECTRONIC STEERING SENSOR INPUT	
[1] [2]	[2] Monitor air suspension control module PIDs STEER__A and STEER__B. [3] Turn steering wheel slowly 1/4 turn in both directions. • Do both PIDs cycle between HIGH and LOW? → **Yes** GO to **T4**. → **No** DIAGNOSE electronic steering sensor.
T4 CHECK AIR SUSPENSION CONTROL MODULE FOR BPP SWITCH INPUT	
[1]	[1] Monitor air suspension control module PID BOO__AS. [2] Press and release the brake pedal while observing PID BOO__AS. • Did the PID change between OFF and ON states? → **Yes** GO to **T5**. → **No** REPAIR circuit 511 (LG). TEST the system for normal operation.
T5 CHECK AIR SUSPENSION CONTROL MODULE FOR DOOR AJAR INPUT	
[1]	[1] Monitor air suspension control module PID DOOR__AS. [2] Close all doors, liftgate, and liftgate glass.

FM2010100695020X

Fig. 31   Test T: Air Suspension System Inoperative (Part 2 of 5). Four wheel air suspension system

CONDITIONS	DETAILS/RESULTS/ACTIONS
T7 CHECK AIR SUSPENSION CONTROL MODULE FOR 4X4 STATE INPUT (Continued)	
	[5] Press the brake pedal. • Did PID 4WDLOW show OFF in 2H and ON in 4L, and did the cluster indicators agree with PID 4WDLOW? → **Yes** GO to **T8**. → **No** REPAIR circuit 784 (LB/BK). TEST the system for normal operation.
T8 CHECK AIR SUSPENSION CONTROL MODULE FOR ACCELERATION INPUT	
[1]	[1] Monitor air suspension control module PID ACC__SIG. [2] While observing PID ACC__SIG, press and release the accelerator pedal. • Did PID ACC__SIG show both notPRE and PRESNT states? → **Yes** GO to **T9**. → **No** REPAIR circuit 637 (DB/WH). TEST the system for normal operation.
T9 CHECK AIR SUSPENSION CONTROL MODULE FOR VSS INPUT	
[1]	[1] Monitor air suspension control module PID VSS__AS or VSS__ARC.

FM2010100695040X

Fig. 31   Test T: Air Suspension System Inoperative (Part 4 of 5). Four wheel air suspension system

FOUR WHEEL & REAR LOAD LEVELING

CONDITIONS	DETAILS/RESULTS/ACTIONS
T9 CHECK AIR SUSPENSION CONTROL MODULE FOR VSS INPUT (Continued)	
	[2] Test drive the vehicle at different speeds. • Does PID VSS__AS or PID VSS__ARC track the speedometer within 8 km/h (5 mph)? → **Yes** GO to **T10**. → **No** REPAIR circuit 679 (GY/BK). TEST the system for normal operation.
T10 CHECK PARK/NEUTRAL INPUT TO AIR SUSPENSION CONTROL MODULE	
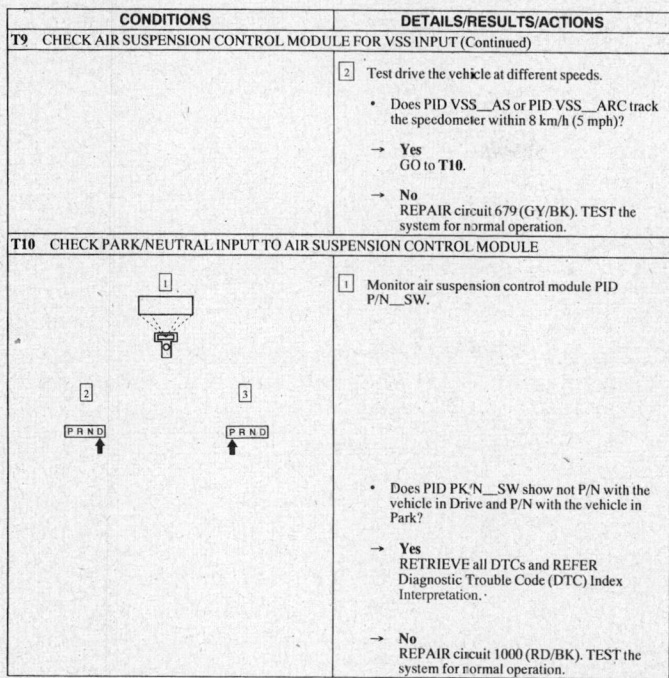	[1] Monitor air suspension control module PID P/N__SW. • Does PID PK/N__SW show not P/N with the vehicle in Drive and P/N with the vehicle in Park? → **Yes** RETRIEVE all DTCs and REFER Diagnostic Trouble Code (DTC) Index Interpretation. → **No** REPAIR circuit 1000 (RD/BK). TEST the system for normal operation.

FM2010100695050X

Fig. 31   Test T: Air Suspension System Inoperative (Part 5 of 5). Four wheel air suspension system

CONDITIONS	DETAILS/RESULTS/ACTIONS
U2 CHECK CIRCUIT 418 (DG/YE) (Continued)	
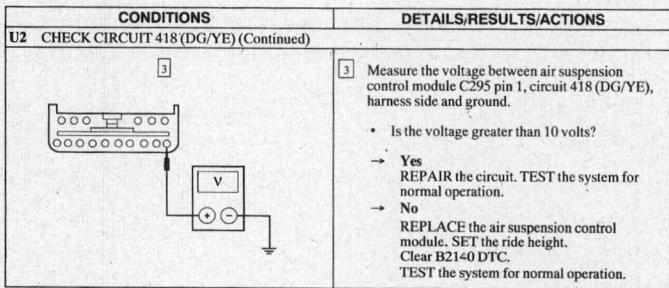	[3] Measure the voltage between air suspension control module C295 pin 1, circuit 418 (DG/YE), harness side and ground. • Is the voltage greater than 10 volts? → **Yes** REPAIR the circuit. TEST the system for normal operation. → **No** REPLACE the air suspension control module. SET the ride height. Clear B2140 DTC. TEST the system for normal operation.

FM2010100696020X

Fig. 32   Test U: Air Suspension System Operates With Switch Turned Off (Part 2 of 2). Four wheel air suspension system

CONDITIONS	DETAILS/RESULTS/ACTIONS
U1 CHECK AIR SUSPENSION SWITCH	
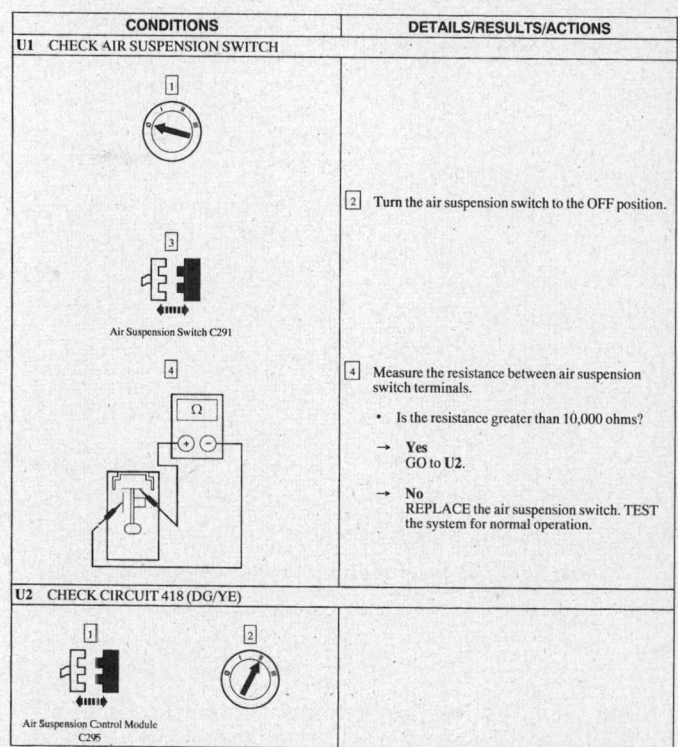	[2] Turn the air suspension switch to the OFF position. [4] Measure the resistance between air suspension switch terminals. • Is the resistance greater than 10,000 ohms? → **Yes** GO to **U2**. → **No** REPLACE the air suspension switch. TEST the system for normal operation.
U2 CHECK CIRCUIT 418 (DG/YE)	

FM2010100696010X

Fig. 32   Test U: Air Suspension System Operates With Switch Turned Off (Part 1 of 2). Four wheel air suspension system

CONDITIONS	DETAILS/RESULTS/ACTIONS
V1 CHECK FOR AIR COMPRESSOR AND/OR AIR COMPRESSOR WIRING CONTACTING OTHER COMPONENTS	
	[1] Check the air compressor wiring to see if it is contacting other components inside the engine compartment at any place other than the mounting points. [2] Check for anything contacting the air compressor (other wire harnesses, loose fasteners, stones or other foreign objects). • Is the air compressor wiring contacting non-mounting components or is anything contacting the compressor assembly besides the mounts? → **Yes** ADJUST air compressor wiring harness so that it does not contact non-mounting components or FASTEN/REMOVE objects so they no longer contact the air compressor assembly. TEST the system for normal operation. → **No** GO to **V2**.

FM2010100697010X

Fig. 33   Test V: Compressor Noise Excessive (Part 1 of 3). Four wheel air suspension system

CONDITIONS	DETAILS/RESULTS/ACTIONS
V2 CHECK FOR BENT AIR COMPRESSOR BRACKET	
	① Check the air compressor bracket for any damage/bends that may contact other components within the engine compartment. • Is the air compressor bracket making contact with other components? → **Yes** REPAIR the air compressor and bracket assembly or other component as necessary. TEST the system for normal operation. → **No** GO to **V3**.
V3 CHECK AIR COMPRESSOR MOUNTS FOR DAMAGE	
	① Check the air compressor mounts for signs of cracks or breaking away of insulation material. • Are any faults in the mounts present? → **Yes** REPAIR the air compressor and bracket assembly or other component as necessary. TEST the system for normal operation. → **No** GO to **V4**.
V4 CHECK AIR COMPRESSOR FOR NOISE	
⚠ **CAUTION: Do not allow the air compressor to run for more than three minutes. The air compressor could overheat and stop operation due to an internal temperature sensitive thermal breaker.**	
	① Remove the air compressor assembly, but leave it connected electrically.

FM2010100697020X

Fig. 33 Test V: Compressor Noise Excessive (Part 2 of 3). Four wheel air suspension system

CONDITIONS	DETAILS/RESULTS/ACTIONS
V4 CHECK AIR COMPRESSOR FOR NOISE (Continued)	
② ③ Scan Tool	③ Trigger air suspension control module active command COMPRESSR ON. • Is the air compressor noisy? → **Yes** REPLACE the air compressor assembly. TEST the system for normal operation. → **No** RECHECK the mountings and bracket for damage. If damaged, REPLACE the air compressor assembly. TEST the system for normal operation.

FM2010100697030X

Fig. 33 Test V: Compressor Noise Excessive (Part 3 of 3). Four wheel air suspension system

CONDITIONS	DETAILS/RESULTS/ACTIONS
W1 CHECK AIR COMPRESSOR RELAY CONNECTOR	
① Air Compressor Relay C1000	② Inspect the pins of the air compressor relay connector for corrosion, bent or broken pins, moisture, or other damage. • Is the air compressor relay C1000 OK? → **Yes** GO to **W2**. → **No** REPAIR as necessary. TEST the system for normal operation.

FM2010100698010X

Fig. 34 Test W: Compressor Inoperative (Part 1 of 4). Four wheel air suspension system

CONDITIONS	DETAILS/RESULTS/ACTIONS
W2 CHECK CIRCUIT 1053 (LB/PK)	
①	① Measure the voltage between air compressor relay C1000 pin A, circuit 1053 (LB/PK), harness side and ground. • Is the voltage greater than 10 volts? → **Yes** GO to **W3**. → **No** REPAIR the circuit. TEST the system for normal operation.
W3 CHECK CIRCUIT 538 (GY/RD)	
① Air Compressor Assembly C194	
②	② Measure the resistance between air compressor relay C1000 pin B, circuit 538 (GY/RD), harness side and air compressor assembly C194M pin 4, circuit 538 (GY/RD), harness side. • Is the resistance less than 5 ohms? → **Yes** GO to **W4**. → **No** REPAIR the circuit. TEST the system for normal operation.

FM2010100698020X

Fig. 34 Test W: Compressor Inoperative (Part 2 of 4). Four wheel air suspension system

CONDITIONS	DETAILS/RESULTS/ACTIONS
W4 CHECK CIRCUIT 577 (LG/RD)	
①	① Measure the resistance between air compressor assembly C194M pin 1, circuit 577 (LG/RD), harness side and ground. • Is the resistance less than 5 ohms? → **Yes** RECONNECT air compressor relay C1000 and air compressor assembly C194. GO to **W5**. → **No** REPAIR the circuit. TEST the system for normal operation.
W5 CHECK AIR COMPRESSOR AFTER COOL DOWN PERIOD	
③ ④ ⑤	① Allow the vehicle to sit for 60 minutes to give the air compressor assembly time to cool off. ② Turn the air suspension switch to the ON position. ④ Trigger air suspension control module active command VENT ON. ⑤ Trigger air suspension control module active command COMPRESSR ON. • Does the air compressor assembly run? → **Yes** GO to **W7**. → **No** GO to **W6**
W6 CHECK AIR COMPRESSOR RELAY	
① ② Air Compressor Relay C1000	

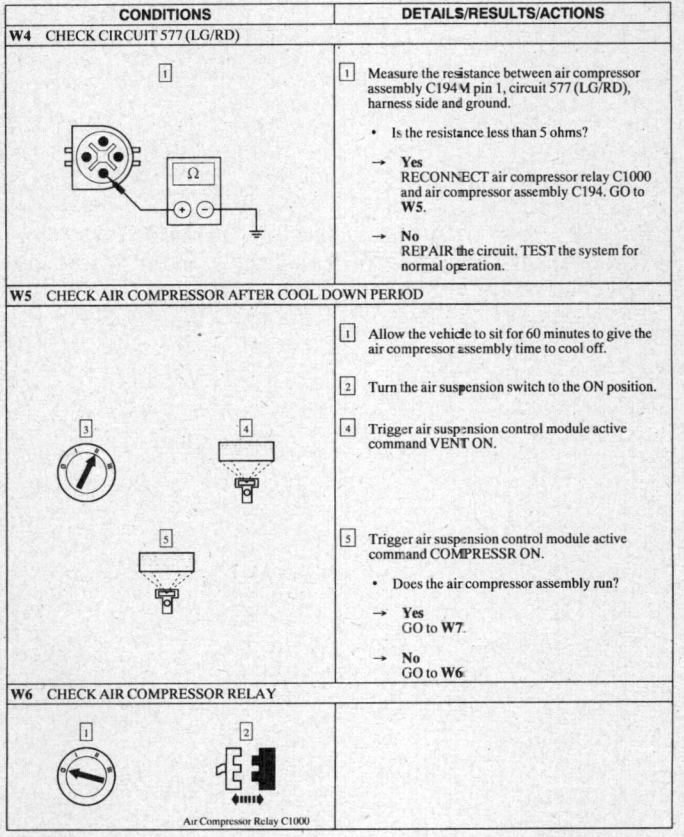

FM2010100698030X

Fig. 34 Test W: Compressor Inoperative (Part 3 of 4). Four wheel air suspension system

CONDITIONS	DETAILS/RESULTS/ACTIONS
W6 CHECK AIR COMPRESSOR RELAY (Continued)	
▢3	▢3 Connect a fused (50A) jumper wire (10 gauge) between air compressor relay C1000 pin A, circuit 1053 (LB/PK), harness side and air compressor relay C1000 pin B, circuit 538 (GY/RD), harness side. • Does the air compressor run? → **Yes** DISCONNECT the jumper wire. REPLACE the air compressor relay. TEST the system for normal operation. → **No** DISCONNECT the jumper wire. REPLACE the air compressor. TEST the system for normal operation.
W7 CHECK AIR COMPRESSOR THERMAL BREAKER	
▢1	▢1 Run the air compressor assembly for 60 seconds. • Did the air compressor assembly run for 60 seconds? → **Yes** The thermal breaker was overheated. RETEST to validate the system is OK. → **No** REPLACE the air compressor assembly. TEST the system for normal operation.

FM2010100698040X

Fig. 34   Test W: Compressor Inoperative (Part 4 of 4). Four wheel air suspension system

CONDITIONS	DETAILS/RESULTS/ACTIONS
A2 CHECK CIRCUIT 418 (DG/YE) FOR AN OPEN	
▢1 Air Suspension Control Module C295 ▢2	▢2 Measure the voltage between air suspension control module C295 Pin 1, Circuit 418 (DG/YE), harness side and ground, and between air suspension control module C295 Pin 21, Circuit 418 (DG/YE), harness side and ground. • Are the voltages greater than 10 volts? → **Yes** GO to **A5**. → **No** If only one, REPAIR the circuit. If both, GO to **A3**.
A3 CHECK CIRCUIT 417 (VT/OG) FOR AN OPEN	
▢1 ▢2 ▢3 Air Suspension Switch C291 ▢4	▢4 Measure the voltage between air suspension switch C291 Pin 1, Circuit 417 (VT/OG), harness side and ground. • Is the voltage greater than 10 volts? → **Yes** GO to **A4**. → **No** REPAIR the circuit. CLEAR the DTCs. REPEAT the self-test.

FM2010100657020X

Fig. 35   Test A: No Communication w/ASC Module (Part 2 of 3). Expedition & Navigator w/Rear Load Leveling

CONDITIONS	DETAILS/RESULTS/ACTIONS
A1 CHECK POSITION OF AIR SUSPENSION SWITCH	
	▢1 Check to see if the air suspension switch is in the ON position. • Is the air suspension switch on? → **Yes** GO to A2. → **No** TURN ON the air suspension switch. CLEAR the DTCs. REPEAT the self-test.

FM2010100657010X

Fig. 35   Test A: No Communication w/ASC Module (Part 1 of 3). Expedition & Navigator w/Rear Load Leveling

CONDITIONS	DETAILS/RESULTS/ACTIONS
A4 CHECK AIR SUSPENSION SWITCH TERMINALS	
▢2	▢1 Make sure that the air suspension switch is in the ON position. ▢2 Measure the resistance between the air suspension switch pins (component side). • Is the resistance less than 5 ohms? → **Yes** REPAIR Circuit 418 (DG/YE). CLEAR the DTCs. REPEAT the self-test. → **No** INSTALL a new air suspension switch. CLEAR the DTCs. REPEAT the self-test.
A5 CHECK CIRCUIT 432 (BK/PK), 57 (BK) AND 875 (BK/LB) FOR AN OPEN	
▢1 ▢3 Air Suspension Control Module C296 ▢4	▢2 Turn the air suspension switch to the OFF position. ▢4 Measure the resistance between air suspension control module C296 Pin 20, Circuit 432 (BK/PK), harness side and ground; and between air suspension control module C296 Pin 32, Circuit 57 (BK), harness side and ground. • Are the resistances less than 5 ohms? → **Yes** Diagnose Module Communications Network. → **No** REPAIR the circuit in question. CLEAR the DTCs. REPEAT the self-test.

FM2010100657030X

Fig. 35   Test A: No Communication w/ASC Module (Part 3 of 3). Expedition & Navigator w/Rear Load Leveling

CONDITIONS	DETAILS/RESULTS/ACTIONS
B1 CHECK THE COMMUNICATIONS TO THE AIR SUSPENSION CONTROL	
▢1	▢1 Check the communication to the air suspension control module. • Does NGS Tester communicate with the air suspension control module? → **Yes** INSTALL a new air suspension control module REPEAT the Auto Test. CLEAR the DTCs. REPEAT the self-test. → **No** GO to Pinpoint Test A.

FM2010100658000X

Fig. 36   Test B: Unable To Enter Self-Test. Expedition & Navigator w/Rear Load Leveling

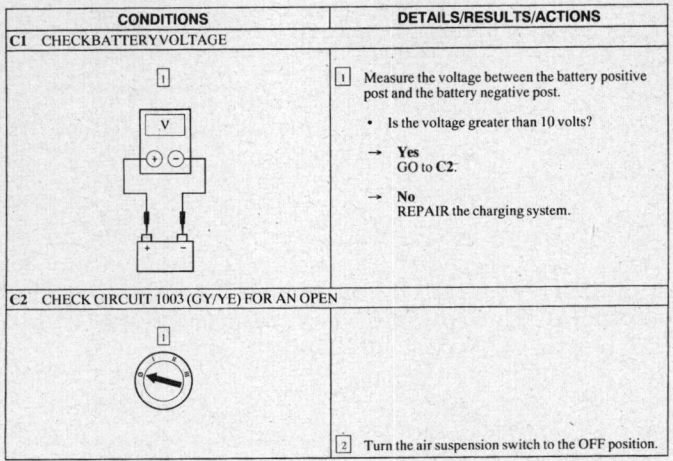

CONDITIONS	DETAILS/RESULTS/ACTIONS
C1 CHECK BATTERY VOLTAGE	
☐1	☐1 Measure the voltage between the battery positive post and the battery negative post. • Is the voltage greater than 10 volts? → **Yes** GO to **C2**. → **No** REPAIR the charging system.
C2 CHECK CIRCUIT 1003 (GY/YE) FOR AN OPEN	
☐1	☐2 Turn the air suspension switch to the OFF position.

FM2010100659010X

Fig. 37 Test C/DTC B1318: Battery Voltage Low (Part 1 of 2). Expedition & Navigator w/Rear Load Leveling

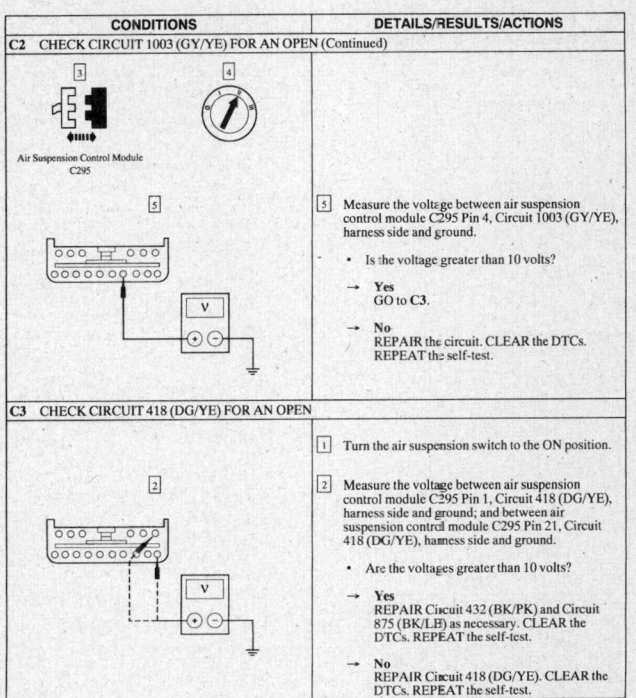

CONDITIONS	DETAILS/RESULTS/ACTIONS
C2 CHECK CIRCUIT 1003 (GY/YE) FOR AN OPEN (Continued)	
☐3 ☐4 Air Suspension Control Module C295 ☐5	☐5 Measure the voltage between air suspension control module C295 Pin 4, Circuit 1003 (GY/YE), harness side and ground. • Is the voltage greater than 10 volts? → **Yes** GO to **C3**. → **No** REPAIR the circuit. CLEAR the DTCs. REPEAT the self-test.
C3 CHECK CIRCUIT 418 (DG/YE) FOR AN OPEN	
☐2	☐1 Turn the air suspension switch to the ON position. ☐2 Measure the voltage between air suspension control module C295 Pin 1, Circuit 418 (DG/YE), harness side and ground; and between air suspension control module C295 Pin 21, Circuit 418 (DG/YE), harness side and ground. • Are the voltages greater than 10 volts? → **Yes** REPAIR Circuit 432 (BK/PK) and Circuit 875 (BK/LB) as necessary. CLEAR the DTCs. REPEAT the self-test. → **No** REPAIR Circuit 418 (DG/YE). CLEAR the DTCs. REPEAT the self-test.

FM2010100659020X

Fig. 37 Test C/DTC B1318: Battery Voltage Low (Part 2 of 2). Expedition & Navigator w/Rear Load Leveling

CONDITIONS	DETAILS/RESULTS/ACTIONS
D1 CHECK DOOR AJAR INDICATOR	
☐1	☐2 Validate that all doors, the liftgate and the liftgate glass are closed. ☐3 Check the door ajar indicator in the cluster. • Is the door ajar indicator illuminated? → **Yes** Diagnose Warning Lamps Fualt condition → **No** GO to **D2**.
D2 CHECK CIRCUIT 999 (LB/WH) FOR AN OPEN AND SHORT TO GROUND	
☐1 ☐3 ☐4 Air Suspension Control Module C295 GEM C240	☐2 Turn the air suspension switch to the OFF position.

FM2010100660010X

Fig. 38 Test D/DTC B1566: Door Ajar Circuit Short To Ground (Part 1 of 2). Expedition & Navigator w/Rear Load Leveling

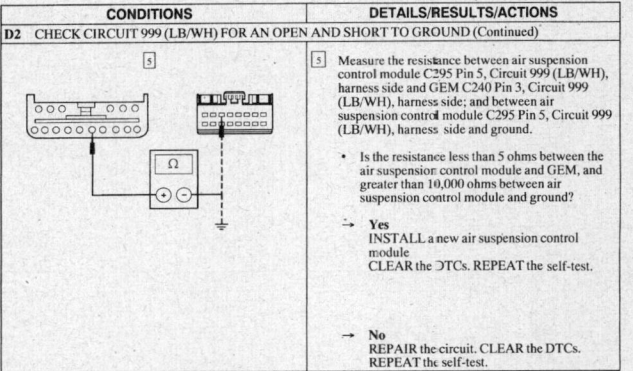

CONDITIONS	DETAILS/RESULTS/ACTIONS
D2 CHECK CIRCUIT 999 (LB/WH) FOR AN OPEN AND SHORT TO GROUND (Continued)	
☐5	☐5 Measure the resistance between air suspension control module C295 Pin 5, Circuit 999 (LB/WH), harness side and GEM C240 Pin 3, Circuit 999 (LB/WH), harness side; and between air suspension control module C295 Pin 5, Circuit 999 (LB/WH), harness side and ground. • Is the resistance less than 5 ohms between the air suspension control module and GEM, and greater than 10,000 ohms between air suspension control module and ground? → **Yes** INSTALL a new air suspension control module CLEAR the DTCs. REPEAT the self-test. → **No** REPAIR the circuit. CLEAR the DTCs. REPEAT the self-test.

FM2010100660020X

Fig. 38 Test D/DTC B1566: Door Ajar Circuit Short To Ground (Part 2 of 2). Expedition & Navigator w/Rear Load Leveling

CONDITIONS	DETAILS/RESULTS/ACTIONS
E1 CHECK POWERTRAIN CONTROL MODULE (PCM) FOR THROTTLE POSITION INPUT	
☐1	☐1 Monitor the PCM PID TP MODE. ☐2 While watching the NGS tester display, press and release the accelerator pedal to the floor. • Does the TP MODE PID display C/T, P/T and WOT? → **Yes** GO to **E2**. → **No** Diagnose throttle position input.

FM2010100661010X

Fig. 39 Test E/DTC C1439: Vehicle Acceleration EEC-V Circuit Failure (Part 1 of 3). Expedition & Navigator w/Rear Load Leveling

CONDITIONS	DETAILS/RESULTS/ACTIONS
E2 CHECK FOR SIGNAL TO AIR SUSPENSION CONTROL MODULE	
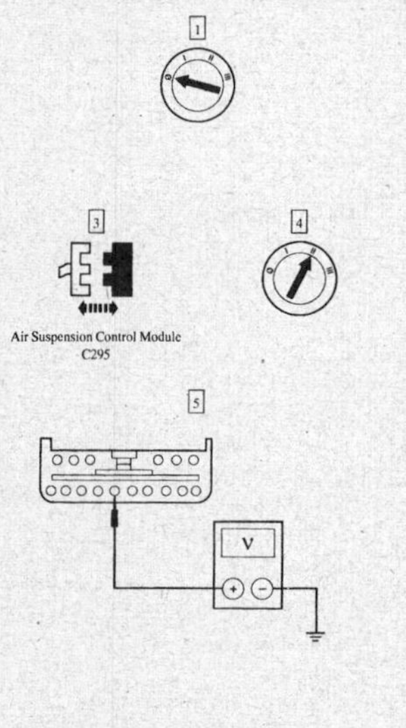 Air Suspension Control Module C295	2 Turn the air suspension switch to the OFF position. 5 Measure the voltage between air suspension control module C295 Pin 6, Circuit 637 (DB/WH), harness side and ground while pressing the accelerator pedal to the floor. • Does the voltage change as the accelerator pedal moves? → **Yes** INSTALL a new air suspension control module. SET the front ride height CLEAR the DTCs. REPEAT the self-test. → **No** GO to **E3**.
E3 CHECK 637 (DB/WH) FOR OPEN AND SHORT TO GROUND	
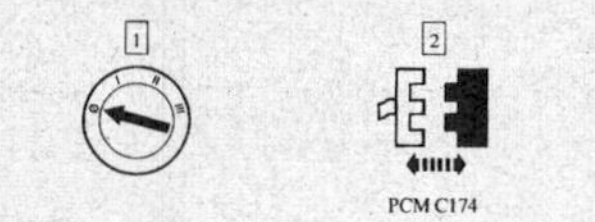 PCM C174	3 Connect EEC-V 104-Pin Breakout Box.

FM2010100661020X

Fig. 39 Test E/DTC C1439: Vehicle Acceleration EEC-V Circuit Failure (Part 2 of 3). Expedition & Navigator w/Rear Load Leveling

CONDITIONS	DETAILS/RESULTS/ACTIONS
E3 CHECK 637 (DB/WH) FOR OPEN AND SHORT TO GROUND (Continued)	
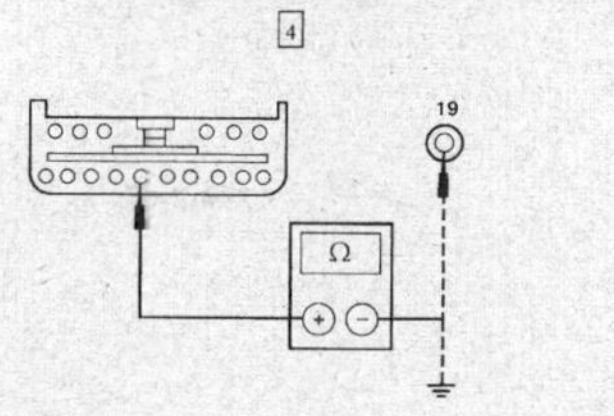	4 Measure the resistance between air suspension control module C295 Pin 6, Circuit 637 (DB/WH), harness side and EEC-V 104-Pin Breakout Box Pin 19, Circuit 637 (DB/WH); and between air suspension control module C295 Pin 6, Circuit 637 (DB/WH), harness side and ground. • Is the resistance less than 5 ohms between the air suspension control module and EEC-V 104-Pin Breakout Box, and greater than 10,000 ohms between air suspension control module and ground? → **Yes** Diagnose and Test acceleration signal. → **No** REPAIR the circuit. CLEAR the DTCs. REPEAT the self-test.

FM2010100661030X

Fig. 39 Test E/DTC C1439: Vehicle Acceleration EEC-V Circuit Failure (Part 3 of 3). Expedition & Navigator w/Rear Load Leveling

CONDITIONS	DETAILS/RESULTS/ACTIONS
F1 CHECK CIRCUIT 429 (VT/LG) FOR AN OPEN	
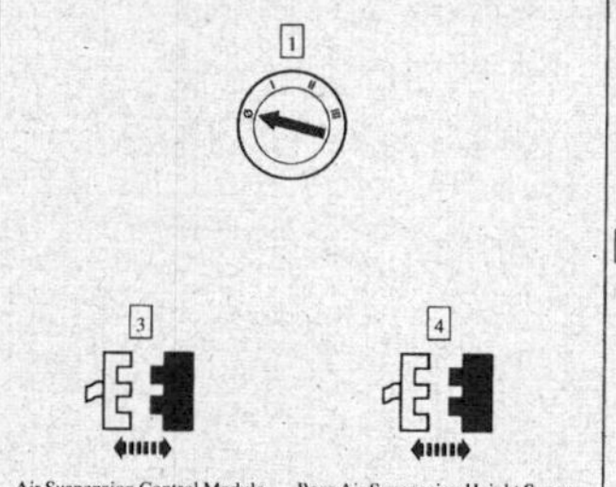 Air Suspension Control Module C296; Rear Air Suspension Height Sensor C421	2 Turn the air suspension switch to the OFF position.

FM2010100662010X

Fig. 40 Test F/DTC C1724: Height Sensor Power Circuit (Part 1 of 2). Expedition & Navigator w/Rear Load Leveling

CONDITIONS	DETAILS/RESULTS/ACTIONS
F1 CHECK CIRCUIT 429 (VT/LG) FOR AN OPEN (Continued)	
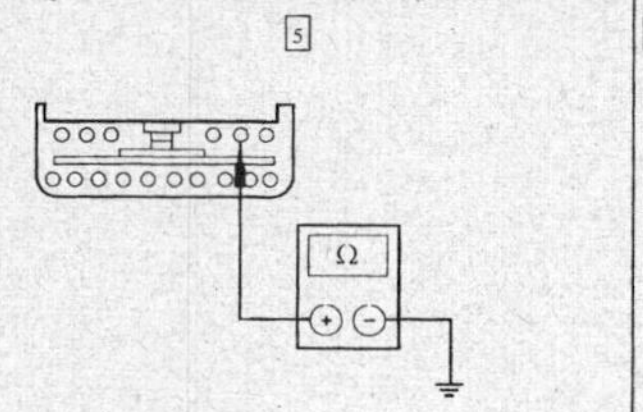	5 Measure the resistance between air suspension control module C296 Pin 28, Circuit 429 (VT/LG), harness side and ground. • Is the resistance greater than 10,000 ohms? → **Yes** CHECK for intermittent short to ground on Circuit 429 (VT/LG). REPAIR as necessary. If OK, INSTALL a new air suspension control module. SET the front ride height (Clear B2140 DTC). REPEAT the self-test. → **No** REPAIR the circuit. CLEAR the DTCs. REPEAT the self-test.

FM2010100662020X

Fig. 40 Test F/DTC C1724: Height Sensor Power Circuit (Part 2 of 2). Expedition & Navigator w/Rear Load Leveling

CONDITIONS	DETAILS/RESULTS/ACTIONS
G1 CHECK REAR AIR SUSPENSION HEIGHT SENSOR	
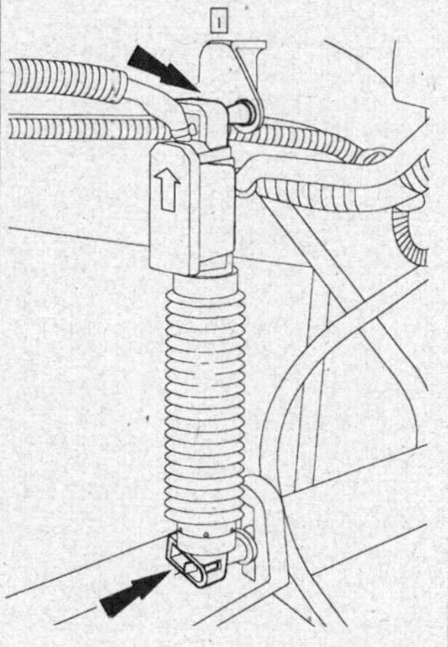	1 Inspect the rear air suspension height sensor for correct installation at the upper and lower ball stud brackets. 2 Inspect the air suspension height sensor mounting brackets for damage. 3 Verify that all air lines are fully seated. • Are the air suspension height sensor, mounting brackets and air lines OK? → **Yes** GO to **G2**. → **No** REPAIR as necessary. If mounting brackets are installed or repaired, SET ride height CLEAR the DTCs. REPEAT the self-test.

FM2010100663010X

Fig. 41 Test G/DTC C1726: Rear Pneumatic Failure (Part 1 of 11). Expedition & Navigator w/Rear Load Leveling

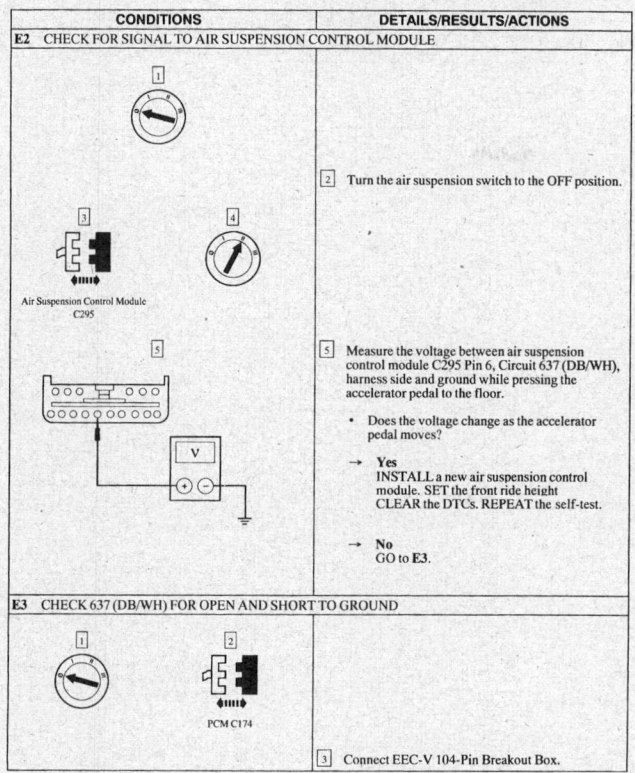

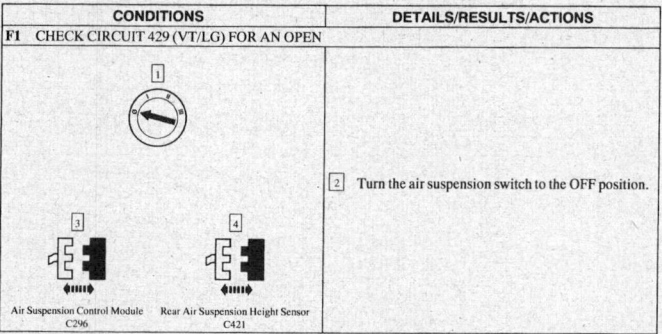

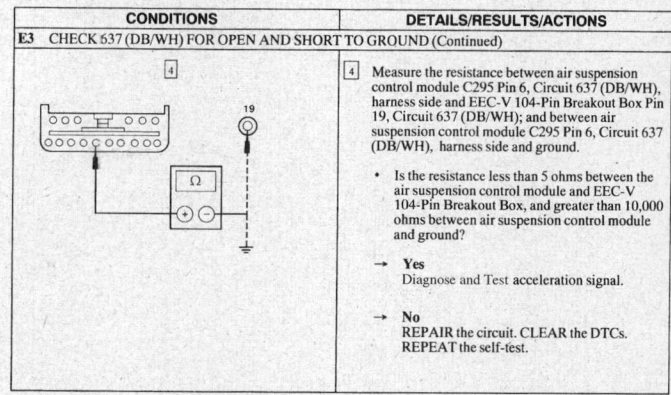

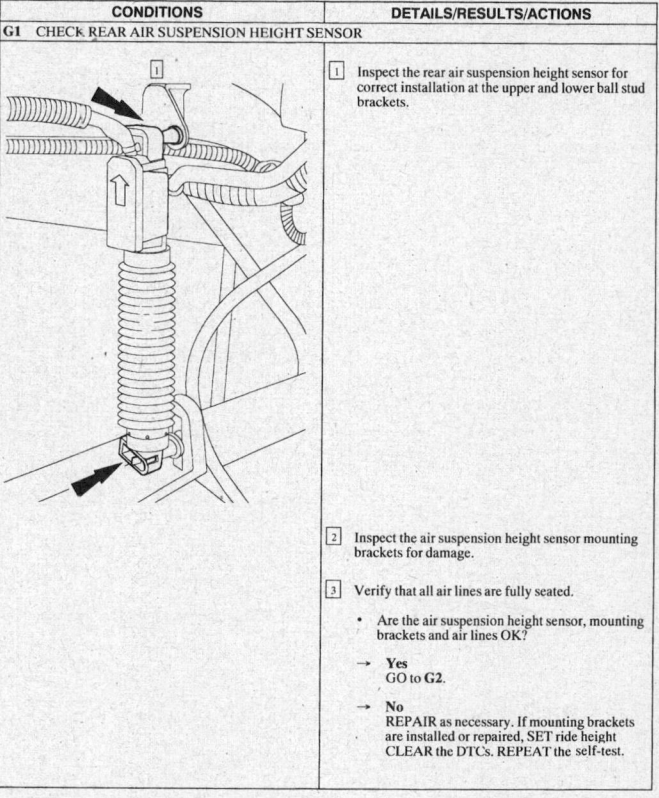

CONDITIONS	DETAILS/RESULTS/ACTIONS
G2 CHECK REAR AIR SUSPENSION HEIGHT SENSOR OPERATION	
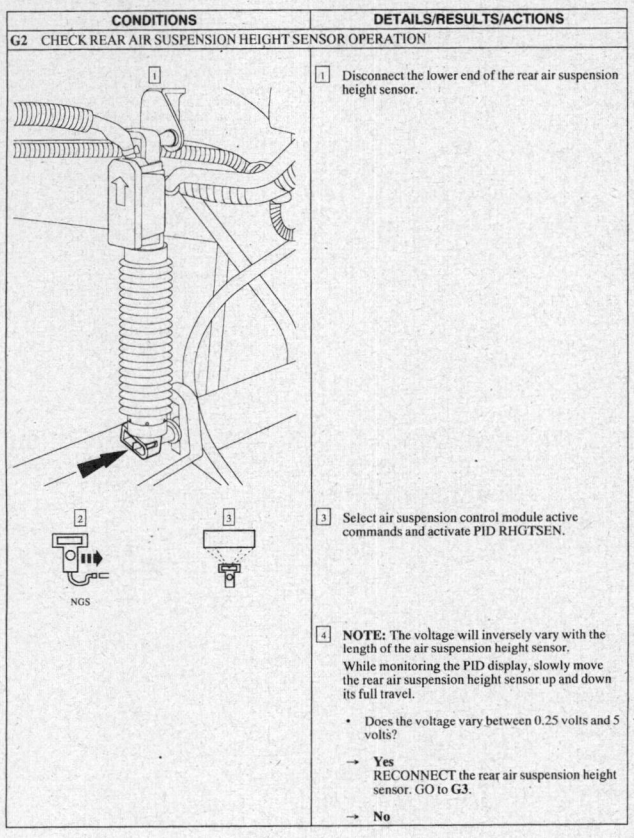	[1] Disconnect the lower end of the rear air suspension height sensor.
	[3] Select air suspension control module active commands and activate PID RHGTSEN.
	[4] **NOTE:** The voltage will inversely vary with the length of the air suspension height sensor. While monitoring the PID display, slowly move the rear air suspension height sensor up and down its full travel. • Does the voltage vary between 0.25 volts and 5 volts? → **Yes** RECONNECT the rear air suspension height sensor. GO to **G3**. → **No**

FM2010100663020X

Fig. 41 Test G/DTC C1726: Rear Pneumatic Failure (Part 2 of 11). Expedition & Navigator w/Rear Load Leveling

CONDITIONS	DETAILS/RESULTS/ACTIONS
G2 CHECK REAR AIR SUSPENSION HEIGHT SENSOR OPERATION (Continued)	
	REPAIR Circuit 432 (BK/PK). CLEAR the DTCs. REPEAT the self-test.
G3 VERIFY THAT THE REAR OF THE VEHICLE CAN BE RAISED	
	[1] Record the voltage level for the rear air suspension height sensor.
	[2] Trigger air suspension control module active command LIFT REAR ON.
	[3] Allow the rear of the vehicle to raise for only 30 seconds. • Does the rear of the vehicle raise and hold the new height? → **Yes** TRIGGER air suspension control module active command OFF. GO to **G4**. → **No** TRIGGER air suspension control module active command OFF. GO to **G5**.
G4 VERIFY THAT THE REAR OF THE VEHICLE CAN BE LOWERED	
	[1] Trigger air suspension control module active command VENT REAR ON.
	[2] Allow the rear to lower until the rear air suspension height sensor voltage reading matches the one recorded in Step G3 or until 30 seconds have passed. • Does the rear of the vehicle lower? → **Yes** RESET mechanical ride height CLEAR the DTCs. REPEAT the self-test. → **No** GO to **G8**.

FM2010100663030X

Fig. 41 Test G/DTC C1726: Rear Pneumatic Failure (Part 3 of 11). Expedition & Navigator w/Rear Load Leveling

CONDITIONS	DETAILS/RESULTS/ACTIONS
G5 CHECK OPERATION OF AIR COMPRESSOR	
⚠ **CAUTION:** If the air compressor runs in this test, do not allow the air compressor to run for more than three minutes. The air compressor could overheat and stop operation due to an internal temperature sensitive thermal breaker.	
	[1] Trigger air suspension control module active command COMPRESSR ON. • Does the air compressor run (slight buzzing noise from RF fender)? → **Yes** TRIGGER air suspension control module active command COMPRESSR OFF. GO to **G6**. → **No** TRIGGER air suspension control module active command COMPRESSR OFF. GO to **G12**.
G6 CHECK AIR COMPRESSOR PRESSURE OUTPUT	
⚠ **CAUTION:** Do not let the air compressor run for more than three minutes at a time. **NOTE:** If fluid is present when disconnecting the air line, clear the air lines Check the compressor air drier (water) or air compressor (oil).	
	[1] Disconnect the air line at the rear air line union within the engine compartment.
	[2] Connect air pressure gauge (1,723 kPa [250 psi] maximum reading) with common fittings to the air line going to the compressor air drier.
	[3] Trigger air suspension control module active command COMPRESSR ON.
	[4] Run the air compressor for only 30 seconds.
	[5] Wait five minutes.

FM2010100663040X

Fig. 41 Test G/DTC C1726: Rear Pneumatic Failure (Part 4 of 11). Expedition & Navigator w/Rear Load Leveling

CONDITIONS	DETAILS/RESULTS/ACTIONS
G6 CHECK AIR COMPRESSOR PRESSURE OUTPUT (Continued)	
	[6] Trigger air suspension control module active command VENT ON. • Does the compressor produce 896 kPa (130 psi) within 30 seconds and hold the developed pressure? → **Yes** TRIGGER air suspension control module active command VENT OFF. GO to **G7**. → **No** REMOVE the air pressure gauge and RECONNECT the air line. TEST the system for air leaks.
G7 CHECK AIR LINE FROM AIR DRIER	
⚠ **CAUTION:** Do not let the air compressor run for more than three minutes at a time.	
	[1] Trigger air suspension control module active command COMPRESSR ON.
	[2] Check for air leaks, bends or kinks in the air line between the air compressor and the air pressure gauge. • Are there any leaks, bends or kinks in the air line? → **Yes** INSTALL a new air line. CLEAR the DTCs. REPEAT the self-test. → **No** INSTALL a new air compressor assembly; CLEAR the DTCs. REPEAT the self-test.

FM2010100663050X

Fig. 41 Test G/DTC C1726: Rear Pneumatic Failure (Part 5 of 11). Expedition & Navigator w/Rear Load Leveling

CONDITIONS	DETAILS/RESULTS/ACTIONS
G8 CHECK FOR BLOCKAGE IN AIR LINE TO RR AIR SPRING	
⚠ **WARNING: Do not remove an air spring under any circumstances when there is pressure in the air spring. Do not remove any components supporting an air spring without either exhausting the air or providing support for the air spring to prevent vehicle damage or personal injury.**	
1	1 Trigger air suspension control module active command VENT REAR ON.
	2 Disconnect the air line from the air suspension air drier.
	3 After all the air has vented out of the air suspension air springs, remove the RR air spring solenoid, with the air line and electrical connector attached.
4	4 Trigger air suspension control module active command RRAIRSP ON.
	5 Connect the vacuum tester at the air suspension air drier and try to draw a vacuum.
	• Can a vacuum be drawn and held?
	→ **Yes** TRIGGER air suspension control module active command RRAIRSP OFF. GO to **G9**.
	→ **No** TRIGGER air suspension control module active command RRAIRSP OFF. GO to **G10**.
G9 CHECK FOR BLOCKED AIR SUSPENSION RR AIR SPRING SOLENOID	
NOTE: If fluid is present when disconnecting the air line, clear the air lines; Check the air compressor air drier (water) or the front air shock (oil).	
	1 Disconnect the air line of the air suspension RR air spring solenoid.

FM2010100663060X

Fig. 41   Test G/DTC C1726: Rear Pneumatic Failure (Part 6 of 11). Expedition & Navigator w/Rear Load Leveling

CONDITIONS	DETAILS/RESULTS/ACTIONS
G9 CHECK FOR BLOCKED AIR SUSPENSION RR AIR SPRING SOLENOID (Continued)	
	2 Try to draw a vacuum.
	• Can a vacuum be drawn and held?
	→ **Yes** REPAIR or INSTALL a new air line(s) between the RR air spring and air suspension air drier. CLEAR the DTCs. REPEAT the self-test.
	→ **No** INSTALL a new air suspension RR air spring solenoid CLEAR the DTCs. REPEAT the self-test.
G10 CHECK FOR BLOCKAGE IN AIR LINE TO LR AIR SPRING	
⚠ **WARNING: Do not remove an air spring under any circumstances when there is pressure in the air spring. Do not remove any components supporting an air spring without either exhausting the air or providing support for the air spring to prevent vehicle damage or personal injury.**	
2	1 Remove the LR air spring solenoid, with the air line and electrical connector attached.
	2 Trigger air suspension control module active command LRAIRSP ON.
	3 Connect the vacuum tester at the air suspension air drier and try to draw a vacuum.
	• Can a vacuum be drawn and held?
	→ **Yes** TURN OFF the active command LRAIRSP. GO to **G11**.
	→ **No** INSTALL a new air compressor assembly CLEAR the DTCs. REPEAT the self-test.
G11 CHECK FOR BLOCKED AIR SUSPENSION LR AIR SPRING SOLENOID	
NOTE: If fluid is present when disconnecting the air line, clear the air lines; Check the air compressor air drier (water) or the front air shock (oil).	
	1 Disconnect the air line of the air suspension LR air spring solenoid.

FM2010100663070X

Fig. 41   Test G/DTC C1726: Rear Pneumatic Failure (Part 7 of 11). Expedition & Navigator w/Rear Load Leveling

CONDITIONS	DETAILS/RESULTS/ACTIONS
G11 CHECK FOR BLOCKED AIR SUSPENSION LR AIR SPRING SOLENOID (Continued)	
	2 Try to draw a vacuum.
	• Can a vacuum be drawn and held?
	→ **Yes** REPAIR or INSTALL a new air line between the LR air spring and the T-fitting. CLEAR the DTCs. REPEAT the self-test.
	→ **No** INSTALL a new air suspension LR air spring solenoid CLEAR the DTCs. REPEAT the self-test.
G12 CHECK AIR COMPRESSOR RELAY CONNECTOR C1000	
1 Air Compressor Relay C1000	
	2 Inspect the pins of the air compressor relay connector C1000 for corrosion, bent or broken pins, moisture or other damage.
	• Is the air compressor relay C1000 OK?
	→ **Yes** GO to **G13**.
	→ **No** REPAIR as necessary. CLEAR the DTCs. REPEAT the self-test.
G13 CHECK CIRCUIT 1053 (LB/PK) FOR AN OPEN	
1	1 Measure the voltage between air compressor relay C1000 Pin A, Circuit 1053 (LB/PK), harness side and ground.
	• Is the voltage greater than 10 volts?
	→ **Yes** GO to **G14**.
	→ **No** REPAIR Circuit 1053 (LB/PK). CLEAR the DTCs. REPEAT the self-test.

FM2010100663080X

Fig. 41   Test G/DTC C1726: Rear Pneumatic Failure (Part 8 of 11). Expedition & Navigator w/Rear Load Leveling

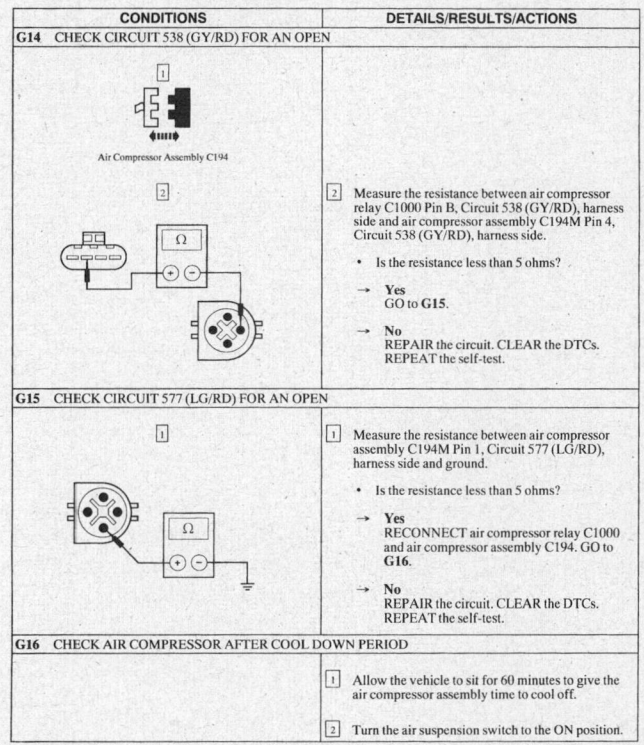

CONDITIONS	DETAILS/RESULTS/ACTIONS
G14 CHECK CIRCUIT 538 (GY/RD) FOR AN OPEN	
1 Air Compressor Assembly C194	
2	2 Measure the resistance between air compressor relay C1000 Pin B, Circuit 538 (GY/RD), harness side and air compressor assembly C194M Pin 4, Circuit 538 (GY/RD), harness side.
	• Is the resistance less than 5 ohms?
	→ **Yes** GO to **G15**.
	→ **No** REPAIR the circuit. CLEAR the DTCs. REPEAT the self-test.
G15 CHECK CIRCUIT 577 (LG/RD) FOR AN OPEN	
1	1 Measure the resistance between air compressor assembly C194M Pin 1, Circuit 577 (LG/RD), harness side and ground.
	• Is the resistance less than 5 ohms?
	→ **Yes** RECONNECT air compressor relay C1000 and air compressor assembly C194. GO to **G16**.
	→ **No** REPAIR the circuit. CLEAR the DTCs. REPEAT the self-test.
G16 CHECK AIR COMPRESSOR AFTER COOL DOWN PERIOD	
	1 Allow the vehicle to sit for 60 minutes to give the air compressor assembly time to cool off.
	2 Turn the air suspension switch to the ON position.

FM2010100663090X

Fig. 41   Test G/DTC C1726: Rear Pneumatic Failure (Part 9 of 11). Expedition & Navigator w/Rear Load Leveling

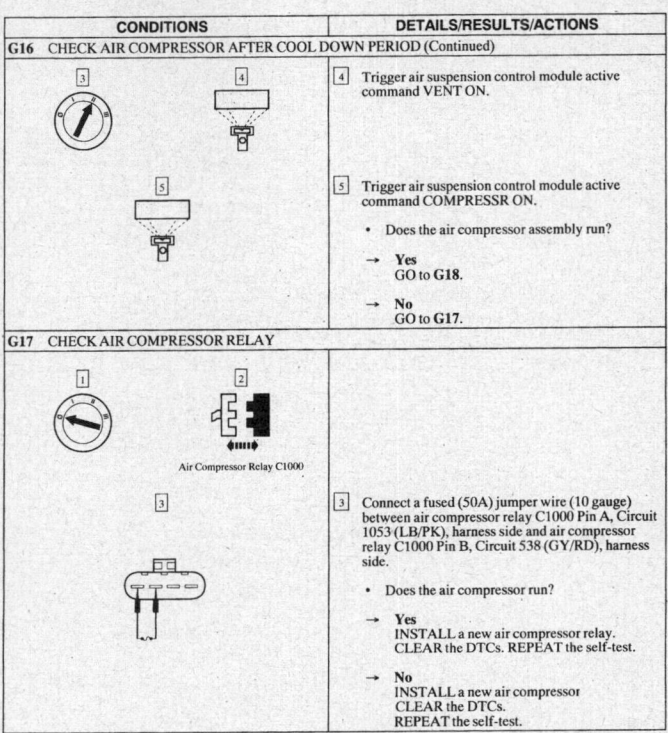

CONDITIONS	DETAILS/RESULTS/ACTIONS
G16 CHECK AIR COMPRESSOR AFTER COOL DOWN PERIOD (Continued)	
3 4 5	4 Trigger air suspension control module active command VENT ON.
	5 Trigger air suspension control module active command COMPRESSR ON.
	• Does the air compressor assembly run?
	→ **Yes** GO to **G18**.
	→ **No** GO to **G17**.
G17 CHECK AIR COMPRESSOR RELAY	
1 2	
Air Compressor Relay C1000	
3	3 Connect a fused (50A) jumper wire (10 gauge) between air compressor relay C1000 Pin A, Circuit 1053 (LB/PK), harness side and air compressor relay C1000 Pin B, Circuit 538 (GY/RD), harness side.
	• Does the air compressor run?
	→ **Yes** INSTALL a new air compressor relay. CLEAR the DTCs. REPEAT the self-test.
	→ **No** INSTALL a new air compressor CLEAR the DTCs. REPEAT the self-test.

FM2010100663100X

Fig. 41   Test G/DTC C1726: Rear Pneumatic Failure (Part 10 of 11). Expedition & Navigator w/Rear Load Leveling

CONDITIONS	DETAILS/RESULTS/ACTIONS
H1 VALIDATE DTC 1760 ERROR	
1	1 Carry out the air suspension control module On-Demand Self-Test.
	• Is the same air suspension DTC set?
	→ **Yes** GO to **H2**.
	→ **No** If no DTC is retrieved, GO to **H5**.
	If a different DTC is retrieved, REFER to Air Suspension Control Module Diagnostic Trouble Code (DTC) Index.
H2 CHECK AIR SUSPENSION REAR HEIGHT SENSOR POWER	
1	
	2 Turn the air suspension switch to the OFF position.
3	
Air Suspension Rear Height Sensor C421	

FM2010100664010X

Fig. 42   Test H/DTC C1760: Rear Height Sensor High Signal Circuit Failure (Part 1 of 4). Expedition & Navigator w/Rear Load Leveling

CONDITIONS	DETAILS/RESULTS/ACTIONS
G18 CHECK AIR COMPRESSOR THERMAL BREAKER	
	1 Run the air compressor assembly for 60 seconds.
	• Did the air compressor assembly run for 60 seconds?
	→ **Yes** The thermal breaker was overheated. CLEAR the DTCs. REPEAT the self-test.
	→ **No** INSTALL a new air compressor assembly; CLEAR the DTCs. REPEAT the self-test.

FM2010100663110X

Fig. 41   Test G/DTC C1726: Rear Pneumatic Failure (Part 11 of 11). Expedition & Navigator w/Rear Load Leveling

CONDITIONS	DETAILS/RESULTS/ACTIONS
H2 CHECK AIR SUSPENSION REAR HEIGHT SENSOR POWER (Continued)	
5 6	4 Turn the air suspension switch to the ON position.
	6 Monitor air suspension control module PID RHGTSEN.
7	7 Measure the voltage between air suspension rear height sensor C421 Pin 3, Circuit 429 (VT/LG), harness side and air suspension rear height sensor C421 Pin 1, Circuit 432 (BK/PK), harness side.
V	• Is the voltage approximately 5 volts?
	→ **Yes** GO to **H4**.
	→ **No** If voltage is less than 5 volts, GO to **H3**.
	If voltage is greater than 5 volts, REPAIR Circuit 429 (VT/LG). TEST the system for normal operation.
H3 CHECK AIR SUSPENSION REAR HEIGHT SENSOR GROUND	
1	
2	2 **NOTE:** Do not use sheet metal or the vehicle frame as a ground for this test.
	Measure the resistance between air suspension rear height sensor C421 Pin 1, Circuit 432 (BK/PK), harness side and ground.
Ω	• Is the resistance less than 5 ohms?
	→ **Yes** REPAIR Circuit 429 (VT/LG). CLEAR the DTCs. REPEAT the self-test.
	→ **No** REPAIR Circuit 432 (BK/PK) and Circuit 875 (BK/LB). CLEAR the DTCs. REPEAT the self-test.

FM2010100664020X

Fig. 42   Test H/DTC C1760: Rear Height Sensor High Signal Circuit Failure (Part 2 of 4). Expedition & Navigator w/Rear Load Leveling

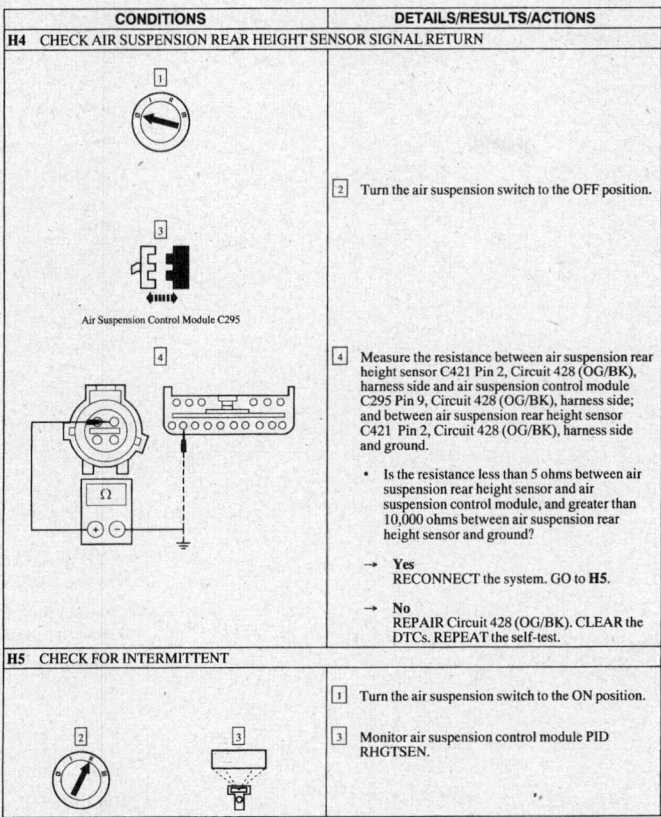

CONDITIONS	DETAILS/RESULTS/ACTIONS
H4 CHECK AIR SUSPENSION REAR HEIGHT SENSOR SIGNAL RETURN	
	2 Turn the air suspension switch to the OFF position.
Air Suspension Control Module C295	
	4 Measure the resistance between air suspension rear height sensor C421 Pin 2, Circuit 428 (OG/BK), harness side and air suspension control module C295 Pin 9, Circuit 428 (OG/BK), harness side; and between air suspension rear height sensor C421 Pin 2, Circuit 428 (OG/BK), harness side and ground.
	• Is the resistance less than 5 ohms between air suspension rear height sensor and air suspension control module, and greater than 10,000 ohms between air suspension rear height sensor and ground?
	→ **Yes** RECONNECT the system. GO to **H5**.
	→ **No** REPAIR Circuit 428 (OG/BK). CLEAR the DTCs. REPEAT the self-test.
H5 CHECK FOR INTERMITTENT	
	1 Turn the air suspension switch to the ON position.
	3 Monitor air suspension control module PID RHGTSEN.

FM2010100664030X

Fig. 42   Test H/DTC C1760: Rear Height Sensor High Signal Circuit Failure (Part 3 of 4). Expedition & Navigator w/Rear Load Leveling

CONDITIONS	DETAILS/RESULTS/ACTIONS
I1 VALIDATE DTC C1770 ERROR	
	1 Carry out the air suspension control module On-Demand Self-Test.
	• Is the same air suspension DTC set?
	→ **Yes** GO to **I2**.
	→ **No** If no DTC is retrieved, GO to **I10**. If a different DTC is retrieved; REFER Diagnostic Trouble Code (DTC) Interpretation.
I2 CHECK AIR COMPRESSOR ASSEMBLY CONNECTOR	
	2 Turn the air suspension switch to the OFF position.

FM2010100665010X

Fig. 43   Test I/DTC C1770: Air Suspension Vent Solenoid Output Circuit (Part 1 of 7). Expedition & Navigator w/Rear Load Leveling

CONDITIONS	DETAILS/RESULTS/ACTIONS
H5 CHECK FOR INTERMITTENT (Continued)	
	4 Monitor the PID display while wiggling the wire harness between the air suspension rear height sensor and the air suspension control module.
	• Does the air suspension rear height sensor voltage ever indicate less than 0.2 volt or greater than 5 volts?
	→ **Yes** REPAIR Circuits 429 (VT/LG), 432 (BK/PK) and 428 (OG/BK) for an intermittent fault as necessary. CLEAR the DTCs. REPEAT the self-test.
	→ **No** INSTALL a new air suspension rear height sensor CLEAR the DTCs. REPEAT the self-test.

FM2010100664040X

Fig. 42   Test H/DTC C1760: Rear Height Sensor High Signal Circuit Failure (Part 4 of 4). Expedition & Navigator w/Rear Load Leveling

CONDITIONS	DETAILS/RESULTS/ACTIONS
I2 CHECK AIR COMPRESSOR ASSEMBLY CONNECTOR (Continued)	
Air Compressor Assembly C194	
	4 Inspect the pins of the air compressor assembly connector for corrosion, bent or broken pins, moisture or other damage.
	• Is air compressor assembly C194 OK?
	→ **Yes** RECONNECT air compressor assembly C194. GO to **I3**.
	→ **No** REPAIR as necessary. CLEAR the DTCs. REPEAT the self-test.
I3 CHECK VENT SOLENOID PID	
	1 Turn the air suspension switch to the ON position.
	3 Select the active commands and activate the PID AS__VENT.
	4 Trigger air suspension control module active command VENT ON and OFF.
	• Do the letters O, G or B appear next to the ON/OFF text for the air suspension vent solenoid?
	→ **Yes** If O appeared, GO to **I4**. If G appeared, GO to **I7**. If B appeared, GO to **I9**.
	→ **No** GO to **I10**.

FM2010100665020X

Fig. 43   Test I/DTC C1770: Air Suspension Vent Solenoid Output Circuit (Part 2 of 7). Expedition & Navigator w/Rear Load Leveling

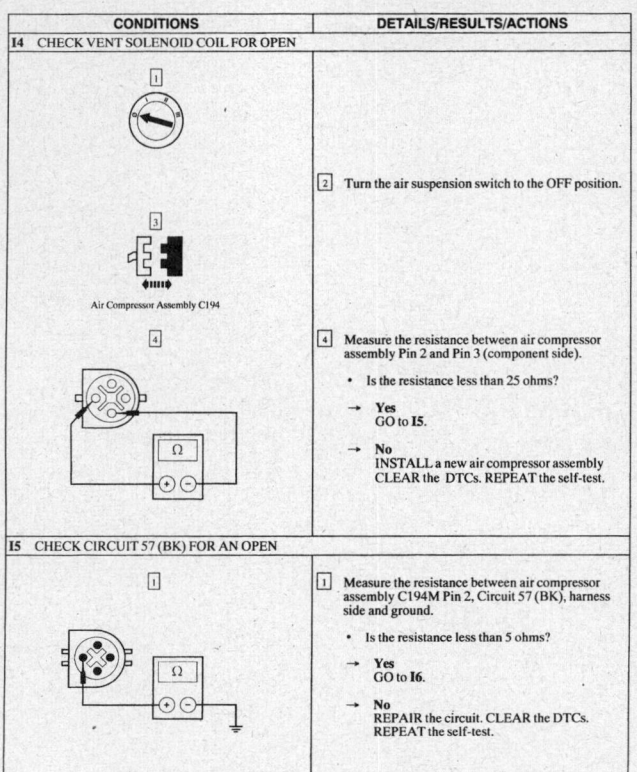

CONDITIONS	DETAILS/RESULTS/ACTIONS
I4 CHECK VENT SOLENOID COIL FOR OPEN	
2	2 Turn the air suspension switch to the OFF position.
3 Air Compressor Assembly C194	
4	4 Measure the resistance between air compressor assembly Pin 2 and Pin 3 (component side). • Is the resistance less than 25 ohms? → **Yes** GO to **I5**. → **No** INSTALL a new air compressor assembly CLEAR the DTCs. REPEAT the self-test.
I5 CHECK CIRCUIT 57 (BK) FOR AN OPEN	
1	1 Measure the resistance between air compressor assembly C194M Pin 2, Circuit 57 (BK), harness side and ground. • Is the resistance less than 5 ohms? → **Yes** GO to **I6**. → **No** REPAIR the circuit. CLEAR the DTCs. REPEAT the self-test.

FM2010100665030X

Fig. 43   Test I/DTC C1770: Air Suspension Vent Solenoid Output Circuit (Part 3 of 7). Expedition & Navigator w/Rear Load Leveling

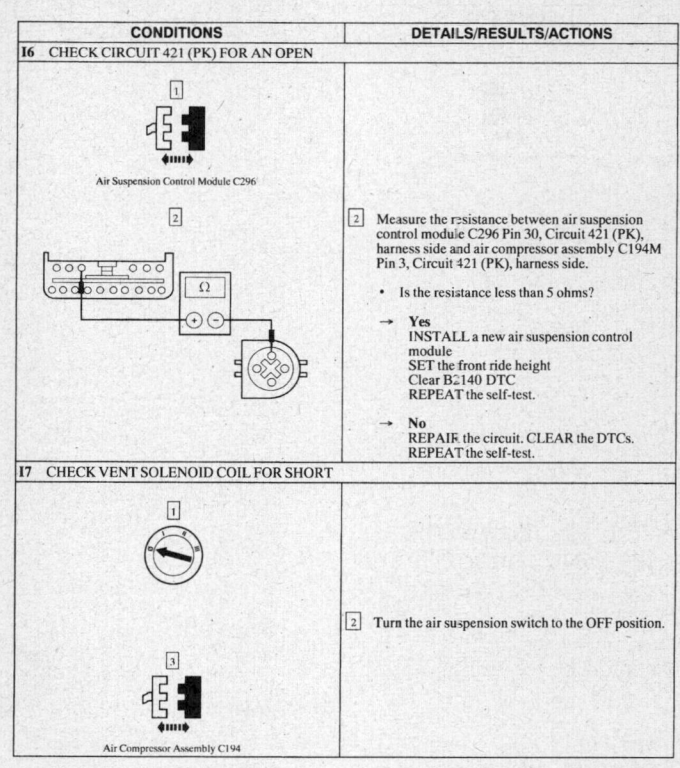

CONDITIONS	DETAILS/RESULTS/ACTIONS
I6 CHECK CIRCUIT 421 (PK) FOR AN OPEN	
1 Air Suspension Control Module C296	
2	2 Measure the resistance between air suspension control module C296 Pin 30, Circuit 421 (PK), harness side and air compressor assembly C194M Pin 3, Circuit 421 (PK), harness side. • Is the resistance less than 5 ohms? → **Yes** INSTALL a new air suspension control module SET the front ride height Clear B2140 DTC REPEAT the self-test. → **No** REPAIR the circuit. CLEAR the DTCs. REPEAT the self-test.
I7 CHECK VENT SOLENOID COIL FOR SHORT	
1	
2	2 Turn the air suspension switch to the OFF position.
3 Air Compressor Assembly C194	

FM2010100665040X

Fig. 43   Test I/DTC C1770: Air Suspension Vent Solenoid Output Circuit (Part 4 of 7). Expedition & Navigator w/Rear Load Leveling

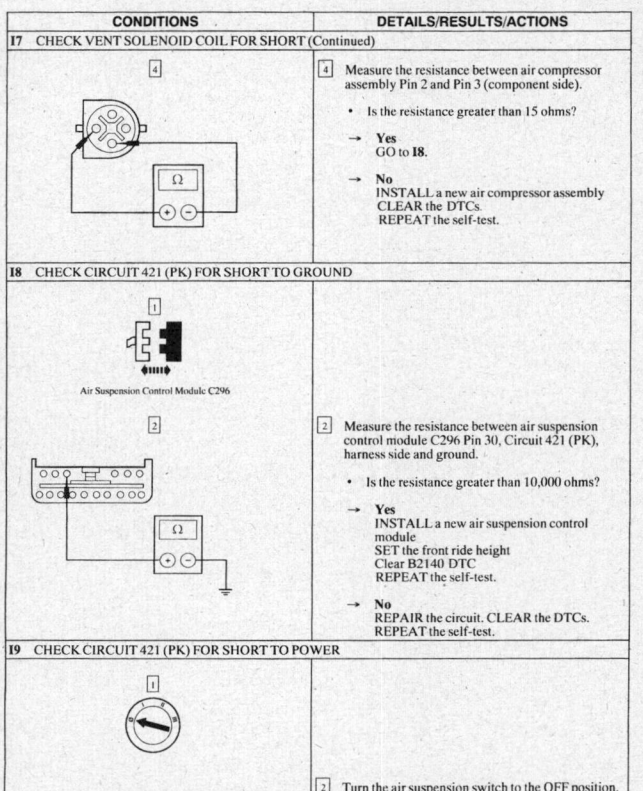

CONDITIONS	DETAILS/RESULTS/ACTIONS
I7 CHECK VENT SOLENOID COIL FOR SHORT (Continued)	
4	4 Measure the resistance between air compressor assembly Pin 2 and Pin 3 (component side). • Is the resistance greater than 15 ohms? → **Yes** GO to **I8**. → **No** INSTALL a new air compressor assembly CLEAR the DTCs. REPEAT the self-test.
I8 CHECK CIRCUIT 421 (PK) FOR SHORT TO GROUND	
1 Air Suspension Control Module C296	
2	2 Measure the resistance between air suspension control module C296 Pin 30, Circuit 421 (PK), harness side and ground. • Is the resistance greater than 10,000 ohms? → **Yes** INSTALL a new air suspension control module SET the front ride height Clear B2140 DTC REPEAT the self-test. → **No** REPAIR the circuit. CLEAR the DTCs. REPEAT the self-test.
I9 CHECK CIRCUIT 421 (PK) FOR SHORT TO POWER	
1	
	2 Turn the air suspension switch to the OFF position.

FM2010100665050X

Fig. 43   Test I/DTC C1770: Air Suspension Vent Solenoid Output Circuit (Part 5 of 7). Expedition & Navigator w/Rear Load Leveling

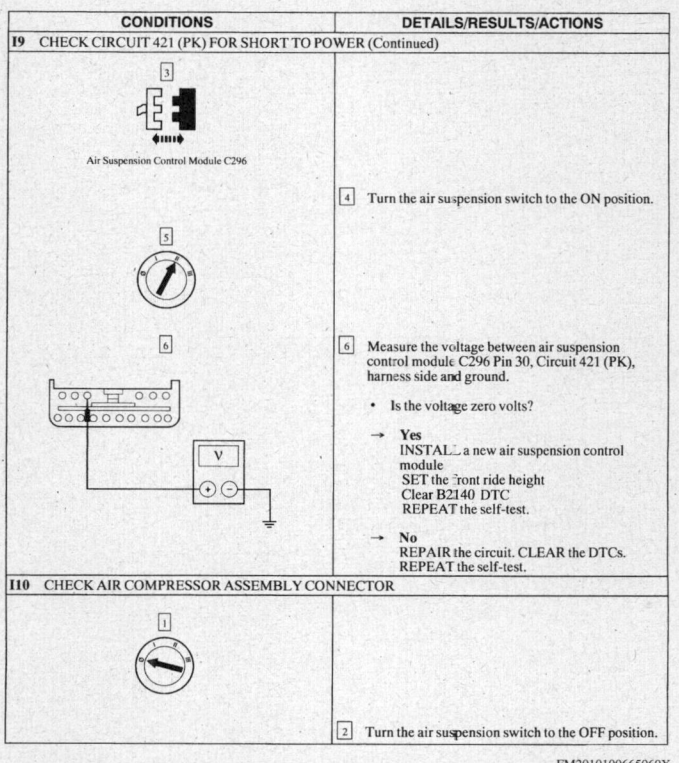

CONDITIONS	DETAILS/RESULTS/ACTIONS
I9 CHECK CIRCUIT 421 (PK) FOR SHORT TO POWER (Continued)	
3 Air Suspension Control Module C296	
	4 Turn the air suspension switch to the ON position.
5	
6	6 Measure the voltage between air suspension control module C296 Pin 30, Circuit 421 (PK), harness side and ground. • Is the voltage zero volts? → **Yes** INSTALL a new air suspension control module SET the front ride height Clear B2140 DTC REPEAT the self-test. → **No** REPAIR the circuit. CLEAR the DTCs. REPEAT the self-test.
I10 CHECK AIR COMPRESSOR ASSEMBLY CONNECTOR	
1	
	2 Turn the air suspension switch to the OFF position.

FM2010100665060X

Fig. 43   Test I/DTC C1770: Air Suspension Vent Solenoid Output Circuit (Part 6 of 7). Expedition & Navigator w/Rear Load Leveling

CONDITIONS	DETAILS/RESULTS/ACTIONS
I10 CHECK AIR COMPRESSOR ASSEMBLY CONNECTOR (Continued)	

Air Compressor Assembly C194

4 | Inspect the pins of the air compressor assembly C194 for corrosion, bent or broken pins, moisture or other damage; inspect the wiring near the connector for damage.

• Is air compressor assembly C194 OK?

→ **Yes**
RECONNECT air compressor assembly C194. PLACE the air suspension switch in the ON position. CLEAR the DTCs. REPEAT the self-test. If no DTCs are retrieved, the system is OK. If a DTC is retrieved, REFER to Diagnostic Trouble Code (DTC) Interpretation.

→ **No**
REPAIR as necessary. CLEAR the DTCs. REPEAT the self-test.

FM2010100665070X

Fig. 43   Test I/DTC C1770: Air Suspension Vent Solenoid Output Circuit (Part 7 of 7). Expedition & Navigator w/Rear Load Leveling

CONDITIONS	DETAILS/RESULTS/ACTIONS
J2 CHECK AIR SUSPENSION LR AIR SPRING SOLENOID CONNECTOR C420	

2 | Turn the air suspension switch to the OFF position.

Air Suspension LR Air Spring Solenoid C420

4 | Inspect the pins of the air suspension LR air spring solenoid connector C420 for corrosion, bent or broken pins, moisture or other damage.

• Is air suspension LR air spring solenoid OK?

→ **Yes**
RECONNECT air suspension LR air spring solenoid C420. GO to **J3**.

→ **No**
REPAIR as necessary. CLEAR the DTCs. REPEAT the self-test.

| J3 CHECK SOLENOID PID | |

1 | Turn the air suspension switch to the ON position.

3 | Select the air suspension control module active commands and activate PID ASLRSOL or LR__SOL.

FM2010100666020X

Fig. 44   Test J/DTC C1790: Lefthand Rear Spring Solenoid Output Circuit Failure (Part 2 of 8). Expedition & Navigator w/Rear Load Leveling

CONDITIONS	DETAILS/RESULTS/ACTIONS
J1 VALIDATE DTC C1790 ERROR	

1 | Carry out the air suspension control module On-Demand Self-Test.

• Is the same air suspension DTC set?

→ **Yes**
GO to **J2**.

→ **No**
If no DTC is retrieved, GO to **J10**. If a different DTC is retrieved, REFER Diagnostic Trouble Code (DTC) Index Interpretation.

FM2010100666010X

Fig. 44   Test J/DTC C1790: Lefthand Rear Spring Solenoid Output Circuit Failure (Part 1 of 8). Expedition & Navigator w/Rear Load Leveling

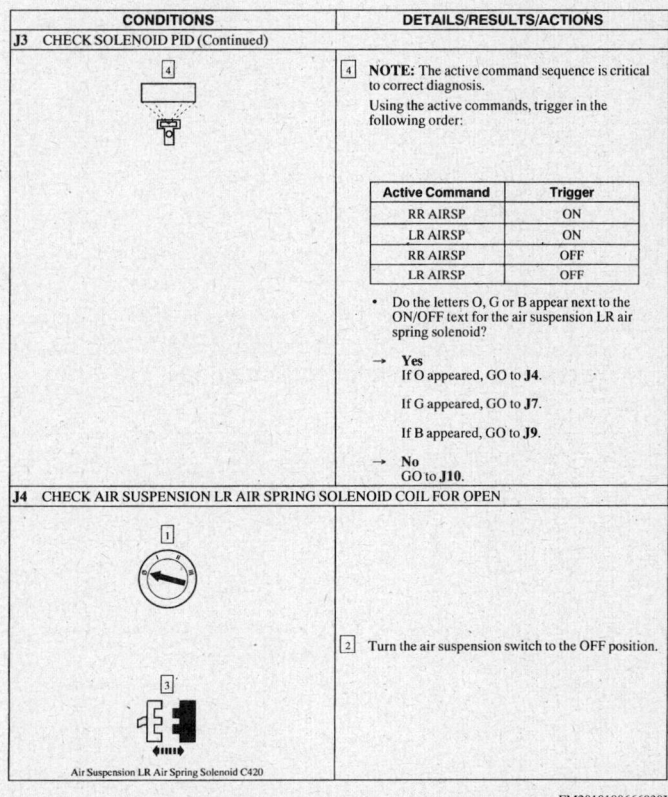

CONDITIONS	DETAILS/RESULTS/ACTIONS
J3 CHECK SOLENOID PID (Continued)	

4 | **NOTE:** The active command sequence is critical to correct diagnosis.

Using the active commands, trigger in the following order:

Active Command	Trigger
RR AIRSP	ON
LR AIRSP	ON
RR AIRSP	OFF
LR AIRSP	OFF

• Do the letters O, G or B appear next to the ON/OFF text for the air suspension LR air spring solenoid?

→ **Yes**
If O appeared, GO to **J4**.

If G appeared, GO to **J7**.

If B appeared, GO to **J9**.

→ **No**
GO to **J10**.

| J4 CHECK AIR SUSPENSION LR AIR SPRING SOLENOID COIL FOR OPEN | |

2 | Turn the air suspension switch to the OFF position.

Air Suspension LR Air Spring Solenoid C420

FM2010100666030X

Fig. 44   Test J/DTC C1790: Lefthand Rear Spring Solenoid Output Circuit Failure (Part 3 of 8). Expedition & Navigator w/Rear Load Leveling

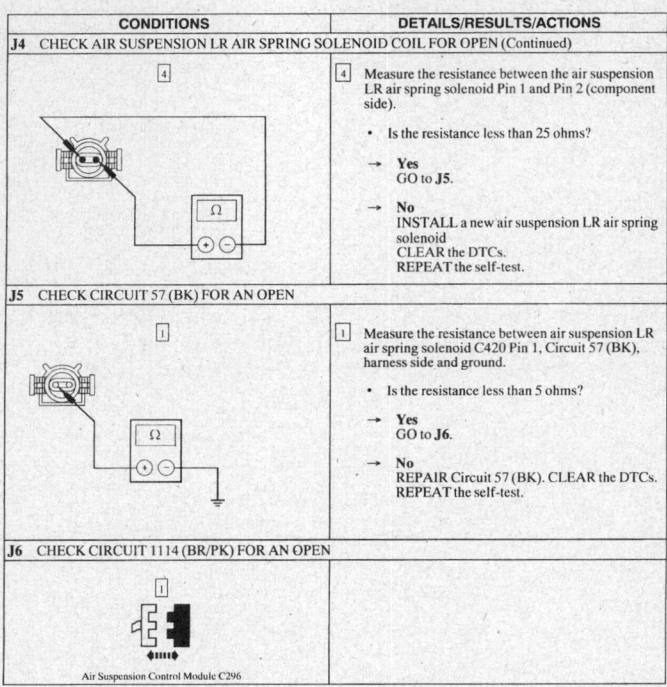

CONDITIONS	DETAILS/RESULTS/ACTIONS
J4 CHECK AIR SUSPENSION LR AIR SPRING SOLENOID COIL FOR OPEN (Continued)	
4	4 Measure the resistance between the air suspension LR air spring solenoid Pin 1 and Pin 2 (component side). • Is the resistance less than 25 ohms? → **Yes** GO to **J5**. → **No** INSTALL a new air suspension LR air spring solenoid CLEAR the DTCs. REPEAT the self-test.
J5 CHECK CIRCUIT 57 (BK) FOR AN OPEN	
1	1 Measure the resistance between air suspension LR air spring solenoid C420 Pin 1, Circuit 57 (BK), harness side and ground. • Is the resistance less than 5 ohms? → **Yes** GO to **J6**. → **No** REPAIR Circuit 57 (BK). CLEAR the DTCs. REPEAT the self-test.
J6 CHECK CIRCUIT 1114 (BR/PK) FOR AN OPEN	
Air Suspension Control Module C296	

FM2010100666040X

Fig. 44   Test J/DTC C1790: Lefthand Rear Spring Solenoid Output Circuit Failure (Part 4 of 8). Expedition & Navigator w/Rear Load Leveling

CONDITIONS	DETAILS/RESULTS/ACTIONS
J8 CHECK CIRCUIT 1114 (BR/PK) FOR SHORT TO GROUND	
1 Air Suspension Control Module C296	
2	2 Measure the resistance between air suspension control module C296 Pin 17, Circuit 1114 (BR/PK), harness side and ground. • Is the resistance greater than 10,000 ohms? → **Yes** INSTALL a new air suspension control module SET the front ride height Clear B2140 DTC REPEAT the self-test. → **No** REPAIR the circuit. CLEAR the DTCs. REPEAT the self-test.
J9 CHECK CIRCUIT 1114 (BR/PK) FOR SHORT TO BATTERY	
1	
2	2 Turn the air suspension switch to the OFF position.
3 Air Suspension Control Module C296	4 Turn the air suspension switch to the ON position.

FM2010100666060X

Fig. 44   Test J/DTC C1790: Lefthand Rear Spring Solenoid Output Circuit Failure (Part 6 of 8). Expedition & Navigator w/Rear Load Leveling

CONDITIONS	DETAILS/RESULTS/ACTIONS
J6 CHECK CIRCUIT 1114 (BR/PK) FOR AN OPEN (Continued)	
2	2 Measure the resistance between air suspension control module C296 Pin 17, Circuit 1114 (BR/PK), harness side and air suspension LR air spring solenoid C420 Pin 2, Circuit 1114 (BR/PK), harness side. • Is the resistance less than 5 ohms? → **Yes** INSTALL a new air suspension control module. SET the front ride height Clear B2140 DTC REPEAT the self-test. → **No** REPAIR the circuit. CLEAR the DTCs. REPEAT the self-test.
J7 CHECK AIR SUSPENSION LR AIR SPRING SOLENOID COIL FOR SHORT	
1	
3 Air Suspension LR Air Spring Solenoid C420	2 Turn the air suspension switch to the OFF position.
4	4 Measure the resistance between air suspension LR air spring solenoid Pin 1 and Pin 2 (component side). • Is the resistance greater than 15 ohms? → **Yes** GO to **J8**. → **No** INSTALL a new air suspension LR air spring solenoid CLEAR the DTCs. REPEAT the self-test.

FM2010100666050X

Fig. 44   Test J/DTC C1790: Lefthand Rear Spring Solenoid Output Circuit Failure (Part 5 of 8). Expedition & Navigator w/Rear Load Leveling

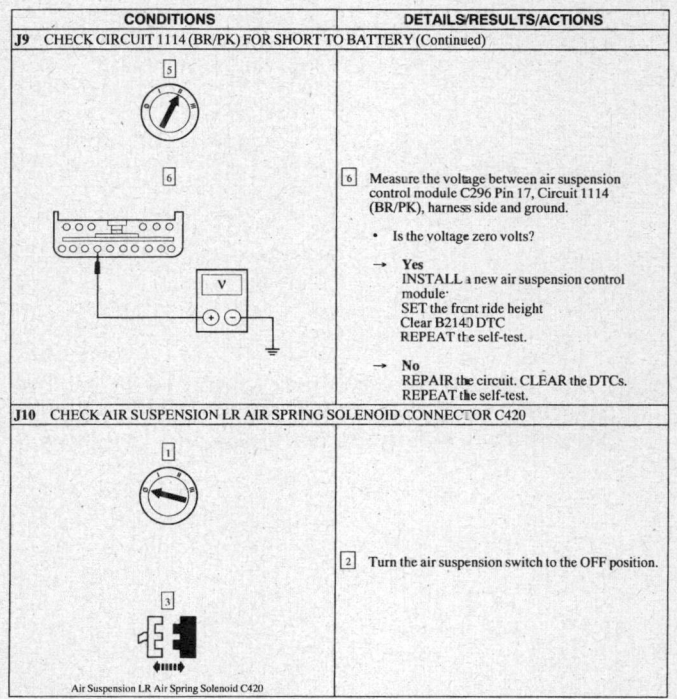

CONDITIONS	DETAILS/RESULTS/ACTIONS
J9 CHECK CIRCUIT 1114 (BR/PK) FOR SHORT TO BATTERY (Continued)	
5	
6	6 Measure the voltage between air suspension control module C296 Pin 17, Circuit 1114 (BR/PK), harness side and ground. • Is the voltage zero volts? → **Yes** INSTALL a new air suspension control module. SET the front ride height Clear B2140 DTC REPEAT the self-test. → **No** REPAIR the circuit. CLEAR the DTCs. REPEAT the self-test.
J10 CHECK AIR SUSPENSION LR AIR SPRING SOLENOID CONNECTOR C420	
1	
3 Air Suspension LR Air Spring Solenoid C420	2 Turn the air suspension switch to the OFF position.

FM2010100666070X

Fig. 44   Test J/DTC C1790: Lefthand Rear Spring Solenoid Output Circuit Failure (Part 7 of 8). Expedition & Navigator w/Rear Load Leveling

CONDITIONS	DETAILS/RESULTS/ACTIONS
J10 CHECK AIR SUSPENSION LR AIR SPRING SOLENOID CONNECTOR C420 (Continued)	
	4 Inspect the pins of the air suspension LR air spring solenoid C420 for corrosion, bent or broken pins, moisture or other damage; inspect the wiring near the connector for damage. • Is air suspension LR air spring solenoid C420 OK? → **Yes** RECONNECT air suspension LR air spring solenoid C420. PLACE the air suspension switch in the ON position. CLEAR the DTCs. REPEAT the self-test. If no DTCs are retrieved, the system is OK. If a DTC is retrieved, REFER to Diagnostic Trouble Code (DTC) Interpretation. → **No** REPAIR as necessary. CLEAR the DTCs. REPEAT the self-test.

FM2010100666080X

Fig. 44   Test J/DTC C1790: Lefthand Rear Spring Solenoid Output Circuit Failure (Part 8 of 8). Expedition & Navigator w/Rear Load Leveling

CONDITIONS	DETAILS/RESULTS/ACTIONS
K2 CHECK AIR SUSPENSION RR AIR SPRING SOLENOID CONNECTOR C419 (Continued)	
  Air Suspension RR Air Spring Solenoid C419	4 Inspect the pins of the air suspension RR air spring solenoid connector C419 for corrosion, bent or broken pins, moisture or other damage. • Is air suspension RR air spring solenoid connector C419 OK? → **Yes** RECONNECT air suspension RR air spring solenoid C419. GO to **K3**. → **No** REPAIR as necessary. CLEAR the DTCs. REPEAT the self-test.
K3 CHECK SOLENOID PID	1 Turn the air suspension switch to the ON position. 3 Select the air suspension control module active commands and activate PID ASRRSOL or RR__SOL. 4 Using the active commands, trigger in the following order:

Active Command	Trigger
LR AIRSP	ON
RR AIRSP	ON
LR AIRSP	OFF
RR AIRSP	OFF

FM2010100667020X

Fig. 45   Test K/DTC C1795: Righthand Rear Spring Solenoid Output Circuit Failure (Part 2 of 8). Expedition & Navigator w/Rear Load Leveling

CONDITIONS	DETAILS/RESULTS/ACTIONS
K1 VALIDATE DTC C1795 ERROR	
	1 Carry out the air suspension control module On-Demand Self-Test. • Is the same air suspension DTC set? → **Yes** GO to **K2**. → **No** If no DTC is retrieved, GO to **K10**. If a different DTC is retrieved, REFER Diagnostic Trouble Code (DTC) Interpretation.
K2 CHECK AIR SUSPENSION RR AIR SPRING SOLENOID CONNECTOR C419	
	2 Turn the air suspension switch to the OFF position.

FM2010100667010X

Fig. 45   Test K/DTC C1795: Righthand Rear Spring Solenoid Output Circuit Failure (Part 1 of 8). Expedition & Navigator w/Rear Load Leveling

CONDITIONS	DETAILS/RESULTS/ACTIONS
K3 CHECK SOLENOID PID (Continued)	• Do the letters O, G or B appear next to the ON/OFF text for the air suspension RR air spring solenoid? → **Yes** If O appeared, GO to **K4**. If G appeared, GO to **K7**. If B appeared, GO to **K9**. → **No** GO to **K10**.
K4 CHECK AIR SUSPENSION RR AIR SPRING SOLENOID COIL FOR OPEN	
  Air Suspension RR Air Spring Solenoid C419	2 Turn the air suspension switch to the OFF position. 4 Measure the resistance between the air suspension RR air spring solenoid Pin 1 and Pin 2 (component side). • Is the resistance less than 25 ohms? → **Yes** GO to **J5**. → **No** INSTALL a new air suspension RR air spring solenoid CLEAR the DTCs. REPEAT the self-test.

FM2010100667030X

Fig. 45   Test K/DTC C1795: Righthand Rear Spring Solenoid Output Circuit Failure (Part 3 of 8). Expedition & Navigator w/Rear Load Leveling

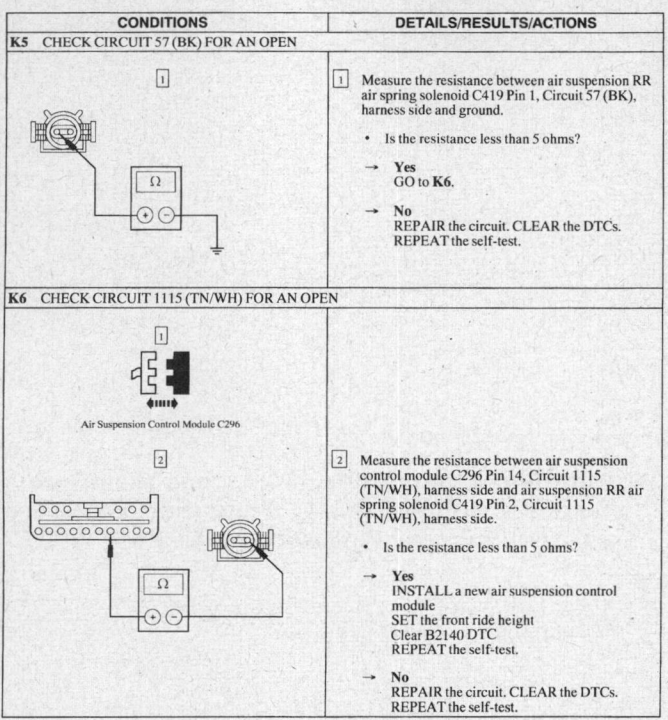

CONDITIONS	DETAILS/RESULTS/ACTIONS
K5 CHECK CIRCUIT 57 (BK) FOR AN OPEN	**1** Measure the resistance between air suspension RR air spring solenoid C419 Pin 1, Circuit 57 (BK), harness side and ground. • Is the resistance less than 5 ohms? → **Yes** GO to **K6**. → **No** REPAIR the circuit. CLEAR the DTCs. REPEAT the self-test.
K6 CHECK CIRCUIT 1115 (TN/WH) FOR AN OPEN *Air Suspension Control Module C296*	**2** Measure the resistance between air suspension control module C296 Pin 14, Circuit 1115 (TN/WH), harness side and air suspension RR air spring solenoid C419 Pin 2, Circuit 1115 (TN/WH), harness side. • Is the resistance less than 5 ohms? → **Yes** INSTALL a new air suspension control module SET the front ride height Clear B2140 DTC REPEAT the self-test. → **No** REPAIR the circuit. CLEAR the DTCs. REPEAT the self-test.

FM2010100667040X

Fig. 45 Test K/DTC C1795: Righthand Rear Spring Solenoid Output Circuit Failure (Part 4 of 8). Expedition & Navigator w/Rear Load Leveling

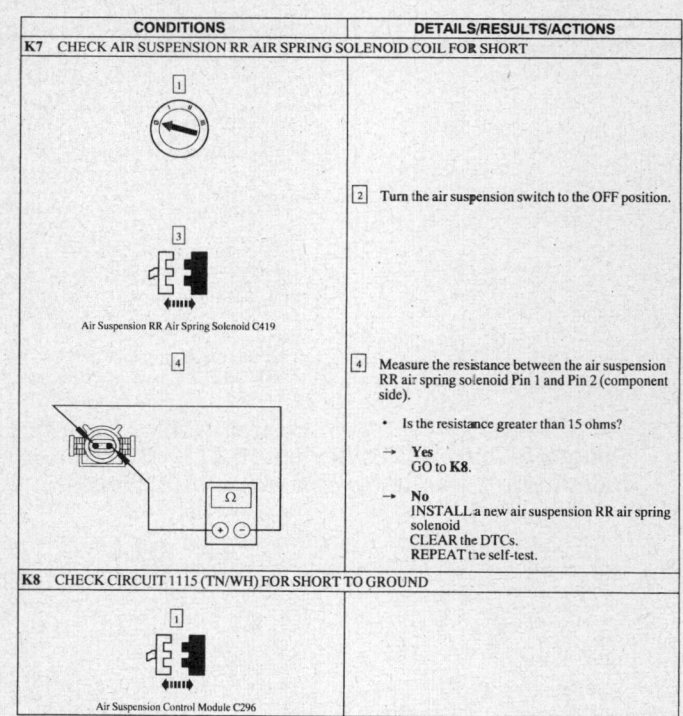

CONDITIONS	DETAILS/RESULTS/ACTIONS
K7 CHECK AIR SUSPENSION RR AIR SPRING SOLENOID COIL FOR SHORT *Air Suspension RR Air Spring Solenoid C419*	**2** Turn the air suspension switch to the OFF position. **4** Measure the resistance between the air suspension RR air spring solenoid Pin 1 and Pin 2 (component side). • Is the resistance greater than 15 ohms? → **Yes** GO to **K8**. → **No** INSTALL a new air suspension RR air spring solenoid CLEAR the DTCs. REPEAT the self-test.
K8 CHECK CIRCUIT 1115 (TN/WH) FOR SHORT TO GROUND *Air Suspension Control Module C296*	

FM2010100667050X

Fig. 45 Test K/DTC C1795: Righthand Rear Spring Solenoid Output Circuit Failure (Part 5 of 8). Expedition & Navigator w/Rear Load Leveling

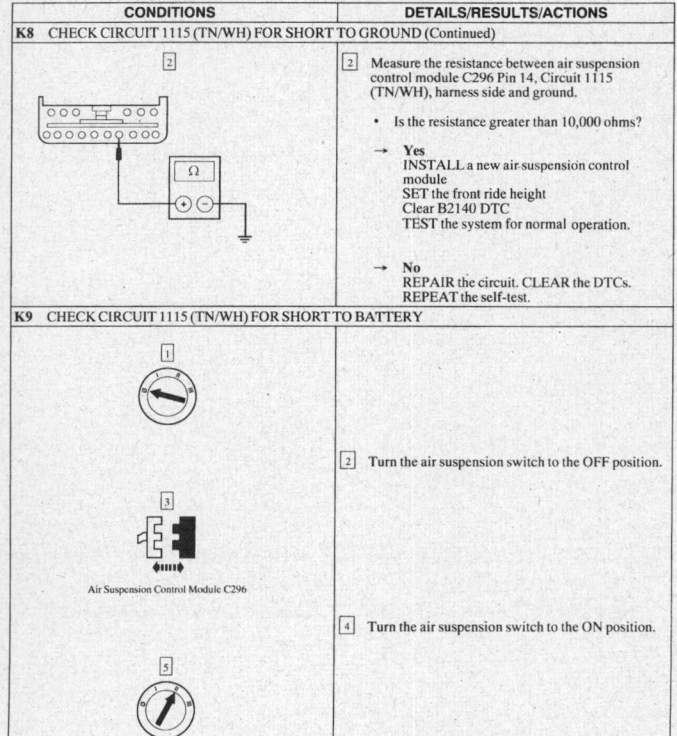

CONDITIONS	DETAILS/RESULTS/ACTIONS
K8 CHECK CIRCUIT 1115 (TN/WH) FOR SHORT TO GROUND (Continued)	**2** Measure the resistance between air suspension control module C296 Pin 14, Circuit 1115 (TN/WH), harness side and ground. • Is the resistance greater than 10,000 ohms? → **Yes** INSTALL a new air suspension control module SET the front ride height Clear B2140 DTC TEST the system for normal operation. → **No** REPAIR the circuit. CLEAR the DTCs. REPEAT the self-test.
K9 CHECK CIRCUIT 1115 (TN/WH) FOR SHORT TO BATTERY *Air Suspension Control Module C296*	**2** Turn the air suspension switch to the OFF position. **4** Turn the air suspension switch to the ON position.

FM2010100667060X

Fig. 45 Test K/DTC C1795: Righthand Rear Spring Solenoid Output Circuit Failure (Part 6 of 8). Expedition & Navigator w/Rear Load Leveling

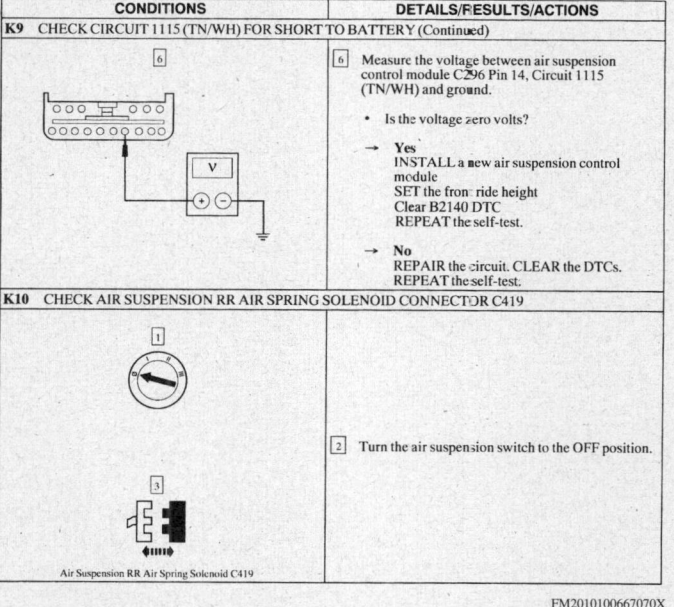

CONDITIONS	DETAILS/RESULTS/ACTIONS
K9 CHECK CIRCUIT 1115 (TN/WH) FOR SHORT TO BATTERY (Continued)	**6** Measure the voltage between air suspension control module C296 Pin 14, Circuit 1115 (TN/WH) and ground. • Is the voltage zero volts? → **Yes** INSTALL a new air suspension control module SET the front ride height Clear B2140 DTC REPEAT the self-test. → **No** REPAIR the circuit. CLEAR the DTCs. REPEAT the self-test.
K10 CHECK AIR SUSPENSION RR AIR SPRING SOLENOID CONNECTOR C419 *Air Suspension RR Air Spring Solenoid C419*	**2** Turn the air suspension switch to the OFF position.

FM2010100667070X

Fig. 45 Test K/DTC C1795: Righthand Rear Spring Solenoid Output Circuit Failure (Part 7 of 8). Expedition & Navigator w/Rear Load Leveling

CONDITIONS	DETAILS/RESULTS/ACTIONS
K10 CHECK AIR SUSPENSION RR AIR SPRING SOLENOID CONNECTOR C419 (Continued)	
	4 Inspect the pins of the air suspension RR air spring solenoid C419 for corrosion, bent or broken pins, moisture or other damage; inspect the wiring near the connector for damage. • Is air suspension RR air spring solenoid C419 OK? → **Yes** RECONNECT air suspension RR air spring solenoid C419. PLACE the air suspension switch in the ON position. CLEAR the DTCs. REPEAT the self-test. If no DTCs are retrieved, the system is OK. If a DTC is retrieved, REFER to Diagnostic Trouble Code (DTC) Interpretation. → **No** REPAIR as necessary. CLEAR the DTCs. REPEAT the self-test.

FM2010100667080X

Fig. 45 Test K/DTC C1795: Righthand Rear Spring Solenoid Output Circuit Failure (Part 8 of 8). Expedition & Navigator w/Rear Load Leveling

CONDITIONS	DETAILS/RESULTS/ACTIONS
L2 CHECK AIR COMPRESSOR RELAY CONNECTOR C1000 (Continued)	
Air Compressor Relay C1000	**4** Inspect the pins of the air compressor relay C1000 for corrosion, bent or broken pins, moisture or other damage. • Is the air compressor relay connector OK? → **Yes** RECONNECT air compressor relay C1000. GO to **L3**. → **No** REPAIR as necessary. CLEAR the DTCs. REPEAT the self-test.
L3 CHECK AIR COMPRESSOR PID	**1** Turn the air suspension switch to the ON position. **3** Select the active commands and activate the PID AS__COMP. **4** Use the active command to toggle the COMPRESSR command ON and OFF. • Do the letters O or B appear next to the ON/OFF text for the air compressor? → **Yes** If O appeared, GO to **L4**. If B appeared, GO to **L7**. → **No** GO to **L8**.

FM2010100668020X

Fig. 46 Test L/DTC C1830: Compressor Relay Circuit Failure (Part 2 of 6). Expedition & Navigator w/Rear Load Leveling

CONDITIONS	DETAILS/RESULTS/ACTIONS
L1 VALIDATE DTC C1830 ERROR	
	1 Carry out the air suspension control module On-Demand Self-Test. • Is the same air suspension DTC set? → **Yes** GO to **L2**. → **No** If no DTC is retrieved, GO to **L8**. If a different DTC is retrieved, REFER to Diagnostic Trouble Code (DTC) Index Interpretation.
L2 CHECK AIR COMPRESSOR RELAY CONNECTOR C1000	
	2 Turn the air suspension switch to the OFF position.

FM2010100668010X

Fig. 46 Test L/DTC C1830: Compressor Relay Circuit Failure (Part 1 of 6). Expedition & Navigator w/Rear Load Leveling

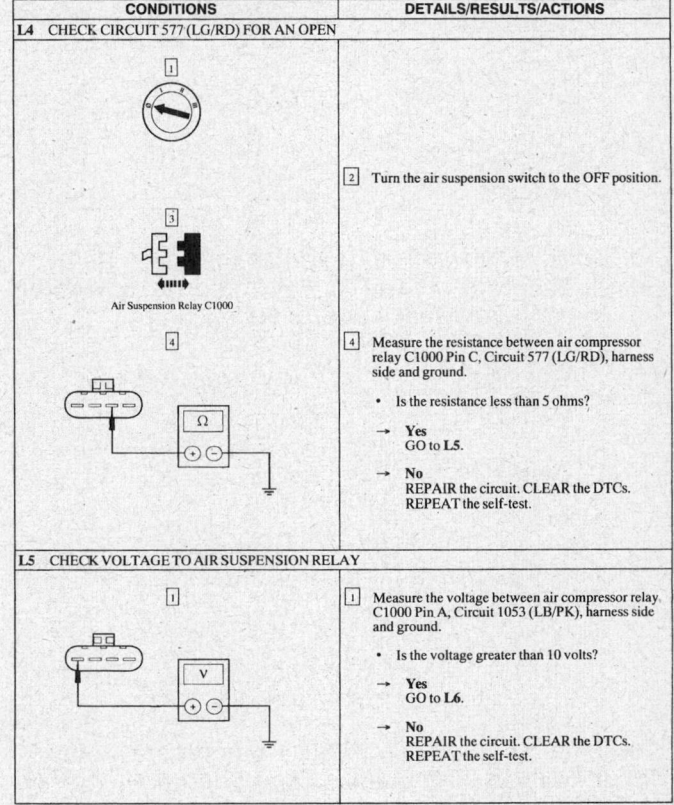

CONDITIONS	DETAILS/RESULTS/ACTIONS
L4 CHECK CIRCUIT 577 (LG/RD) FOR AN OPEN	
Air Suspension Relay C1000	**2** Turn the air suspension switch to the OFF position. **4** Measure the resistance between air compressor relay C1000 Pin C, Circuit 577 (LG/RD), harness side and ground. • Is the resistance less than 5 ohms? → **Yes** GO to **L5**. → **No** REPAIR the circuit. CLEAR the DTCs. REPEAT the self-test.
L5 CHECK VOLTAGE TO AIR SUSPENSION RELAY	
	1 Measure the voltage between air compressor relay C1000 Pin A, Circuit 1053 (LB/PK), harness side and ground. • Is the voltage greater than 10 volts? → **Yes** GO to **L6**. → **No** REPAIR the circuit. CLEAR the DTCs. REPEAT the self-test.

FM2010100668030X

Fig. 46 Test L/DTC C1830: Compressor Relay Circuit Failure (Part 3 of 6). Expedition & Navigator w/Rear Load Leveling

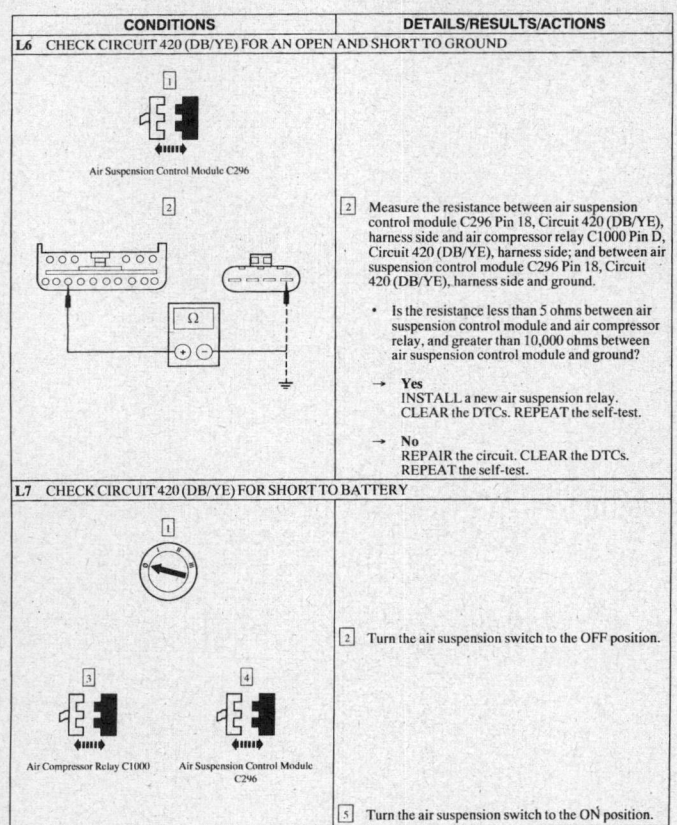

CONDITIONS	DETAILS/RESULTS/ACTIONS
L6 CHECK CIRCUIT 420 (DB/YE) FOR AN OPEN AND SHORT TO GROUND	
	2 Measure the resistance between air suspension control module C296 Pin 18, Circuit 420 (DB/YE), harness side and air compressor relay C1000 Pin D, Circuit 420 (DB/YE), harness side; and between air suspension control module C296 Pin 18, Circuit 420 (DB/YE), harness side and ground. • Is the resistance less than 5 ohms between air suspension control module and air compressor relay, and greater than 10,000 ohms between air suspension control module and ground? → **Yes** INSTALL a new air suspension relay. CLEAR the DTCs. REPEAT the self-test. → **No** REPAIR the circuit. CLEAR the DTCs. REPEAT the self-test.
L7 CHECK CIRCUIT 420 (DB/YE) FOR SHORT TO BATTERY	
	2 Turn the air suspension switch to the OFF position. 5 Turn the air suspension switch to the ON position.

FM2010100668040X

Fig. 46 Test L/DTC C1830: Compressor Relay Circuit Failure (Part 4 of 6). Expedition & Navigator w/Rear Load Leveling

CONDITIONS	DETAILS/RESULTS/ACTIONS
L8 CHECK AIR COMPRESSOR RELAY CONNECTOR C1000 (Continued)	
	4 Inspect the pins of the air compressor relay C1000 for corrosion, bent or broken pins, moisture or other damage; inspect the wiring near the connector for damage. • Is the air compressor relay C1000 OK? → **Yes** RECONNECT air compressor relay C1000. PLACE the air suspension switch in the ON position. CLEAR the DTCs. REPEAT the self-test. If no DTCs are retrieved, the system is OK. If a DTC is retrieved, REFER to Diagnostic Trouble Code (DTC) Interpretation. → **No** REPAIR as necessary. CLEAR the DTCs. REPEAT the self-test.

FM2010100668060X

Fig. 46 Test L/DTC C1830: Compressor Relay Circuit Failure (Part 6 of 6). Expedition & Navigator w/Rear Load Leveling

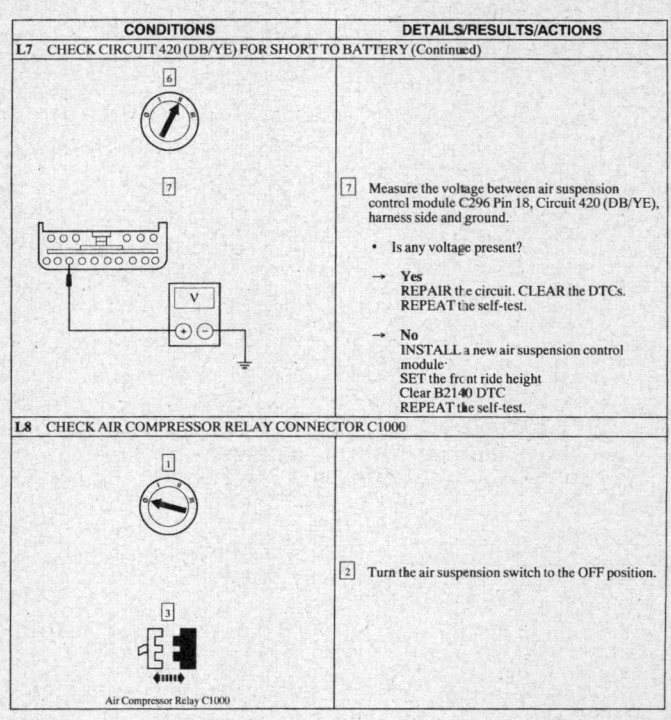

CONDITIONS	DETAILS/RESULTS/ACTIONS
L7 CHECK CIRCUIT 420 (DB/YE) FOR SHORT TO BATTERY (Continued)	
	7 Measure the voltage between air suspension control module C296 Pin 18, Circuit 420 (DB/YE), harness side and ground. • Is any voltage present? → **Yes** REPAIR the circuit. CLEAR the DTCs. REPEAT the self-test. → **No** INSTALL a new air suspension control module. SET the front ride height Clear B2140 DTC REPEAT the self-test.
L8 CHECK AIR COMPRESSOR RELAY CONNECTOR C1000	
	2 Turn the air suspension switch to the OFF position.

FM2010100668050X

Fig. 46 Test L/DTC C1830: Compressor Relay Circuit Failure (Part 5 of 6). Expedition & Navigator w/Rear Load Leveling

CONDITIONS	DETAILS/RESULTS/ACTIONS
M1 CHECK FOR MODULE ACTIVITY	
NOTE: The air suspension control module is powered for 40 minutes after the ignition switch is turned off. During this time, the air suspension system is still active and may activate system components.	
	2 Check to see if the air compressor still cycles 50 minutes after the ignition switch is turned off. • Does the air compressor still cycle after the module times out? → **Yes** GO to M2. → **No** The system is OK. INFORM the owner of system operations.
M2 CHECK THE AIR SUSPENSION CONTROL MODULE	
	1 Turn the air suspension switch to the OFF position.

FM2010100669010X

Fig. 47 Test M: Compressor Cycles Continuously w/Ignition Off & No DTC Set (Part 1 of 2). Expedition & Navigator w/Rear Load Leveling

CONDITIONS	DETAILS/RESULTS/ACTIONS
M2 CHECK THE AIR SUSPENSION CONTROL MODULE (Continued)	

Air Suspension Control Module C296	• Does the air compressor still cycle?
	
	→ **Yes**
	  GO to **M3**.
	
	→ **No**
	  INSTALL a new air suspension control module
	  SET the front ride height
	  Clear B2140 DTC
	  REPEAT the self-test.

M3 CHECK THE AIR COMPRESSOR RELAY	

Air Compressor Relay C1000	• Does the air compressor still cycle?
	
	→ **Yes**
	  REPAIR Circuit 538 (GY/RD). CLEAR the DTCs. REPEAT the self-test.
	
	→ **No**
	  INSTALL a new air compressor relay. CLEAR the DTCs. REPEAT the self-test.

FM2010100669020X

Fig. 47   Test M: Compressor Cycles Continuously w/Ignition Off & No DTC Set (Part 2 of 2). Expedition & Navigator w/Rear Load Leveling

CONDITIONS	DETAILS/RESULTS/ACTIONS
N3 CHECK AIR SUSPENSION CONTROL MODULE FOR ELECTRONIC STEERING SENSOR INPUT	

STEER__A and STEER__B PIDs	[3] Turn steering wheel slowly 1/4 turn in both directions.
	
	• Do both PIDs cycle between HIGH and LOW?
	
	→ **Yes**
	  GO to **N4**.
	
	→ **No**
	  Perform electronic steering sensor diagnostics.

N4 CHECK AIR SUSPENSION CONTROL MODULE FOR BRAKE PEDAL POSITION SWITCH INPUT	

BOO__AS PID	[2] Press and release the break pedal while observing the BOO__AS PID.
	
	• Did the PID change between OFF and ON states?
	
	→ **Yes**
	  GO to **N5**.
	
	→ **No**
	  REPAIR Circuit 810 (RD/LG). CLEAR the DTCs. REPEAT the self-test.

FM2010100670020X

Fig. 48   Test N: Air Suspension System Inoperative (Part 2 of 4). Expedition & Navigator w/Rear Load Leveling

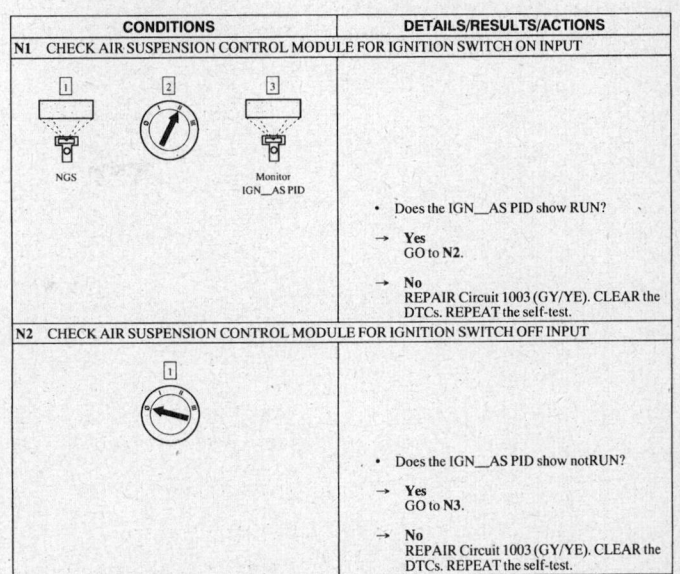

CONDITIONS	DETAILS/RESULTS/ACTIONS
N1 CHECK AIR SUSPENSION CONTROL MODULE FOR IGNITION SWITCH ON INPUT	

NGS Monitor IGN__AS PID	• Does the IGN__AS PID show RUN?
	
	→ **Yes**
	  GO to **N2**.
	
	→ **No**
	  REPAIR Circuit 1003 (GY/YE). CLEAR the DTCs. REPEAT the self-test.

N2 CHECK AIR SUSPENSION CONTROL MODULE FOR IGNITION SWITCH OFF INPUT	

	• Does the IGN__AS PID show notRUN?
	
	→ **Yes**
	  GO to **N3**.
	
	→ **No**
	  REPAIR Circuit 1003 (GY/YE). CLEAR the DTCs. REPEAT the self-test.

FM2010100670010X

Fig. 48   Test N: Air Suspension System Inoperative (Part 1 of 4). Expedition & Navigator w/Rear Load Leveling

CONDITIONS	DETAILS/RESULTS/ACTIONS
N5 CHECK AIR SUSPENSION CONTROL MODULE FOR DOOR AJAR INPUT	

DOOR__AS PID	[2] Close all doors, the liftgate and the liftgate glass.
	
	[3] While observing the DOOR__AS PID, open and close one door.
	
	• Does the DOOR__AS PID change between CLOSED and AJAR states?
	
	→ **Yes**
	  GO to **N6**.
	
	→ **No**
	  REPAIR Circuit 999 (LB/WH). CLEAR the DTCs. REPEAT the self-test.

N6 CHECK AIR SUSPENSION CONTROL MODULE FOR 4X4 INPUT	

4WDSYS PID	• Is the 4WDSYS PID in the NO state?
	
	→ **Yes**
	  GO to **N7**.
	
	→ **No**
	  REPAIR Circuit 900 (BK). CLEAR the DTCs. REPEAT the self-test.

N7 CHECK AIR SUSPENSION CONTROL MODULE FOR ACCELERATION INPUT	
ACC__SIG PID	

FM2010100670030X

Fig. 48   Test N: Air Suspension System Inoperative (Part 3 of 4). Expedition & Navigator w/Rear Load Leveling

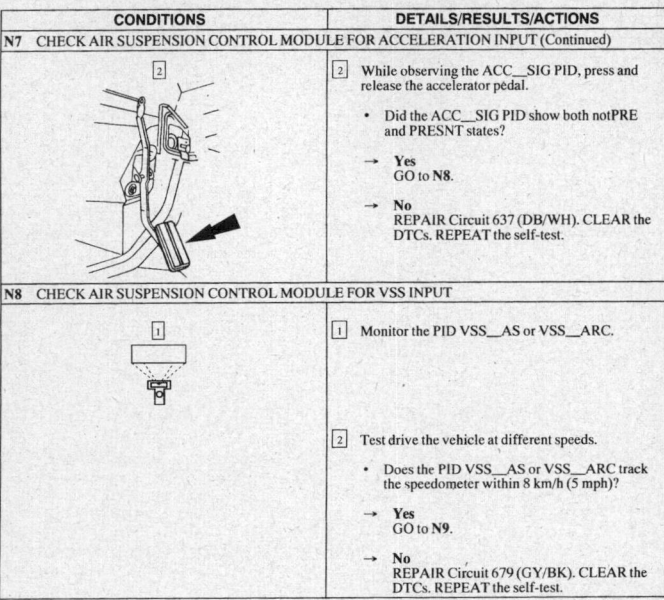

CONDITIONS	DETAILS/RESULTS/ACTIONS
N7 CHECK AIR SUSPENSION CONTROL MODULE FOR ACCELERATION INPUT (Continued)	
[2]	[2] While observing the ACC__SIG PID, press and release the accelerator pedal. • Did the ACC__SIG PID show both notPRE and PRESNT states? → **Yes** GO to N8. → **No** REPAIR Circuit 637 (DB/WH). CLEAR the DTCs. REPEAT the self-test.
N8 CHECK AIR SUSPENSION CONTROL MODULE FOR VSS INPUT	
[1]	[1] Monitor the PID VSS__AS or VSS__ARC. [2] Test drive the vehicle at different speeds. • Does the PID VSS__AS or VSS__ARC track the speedometer within 8 km/h (5 mph)? → **Yes** GO to N9. → **No** REPAIR Circuit 679 (GY/BK). CLEAR the DTCs. REPEAT the self-test.

FM2010100670040X

Fig. 48   Test N: Air Suspension System Inoperative (Part 4 of 4). Expedition & Navigator w/Rear Load Leveling

CONDITIONS	DETAILS/RESULTS/ACTIONS
O1 CHECK AIR SUSPENSION SWITCH (Continued)	
[4]	[4] Measure the resistance between the air suspension switch pins. • Is the resistance greater than 10,000 ohms? → **Yes** GO to O2. → **No** INSTALL a new air suspension switch CLEAR the DTCs. REPEAT the self-test.
O2 CHECK CIRCUIT 418 (DG/YE) FOR SHORT TO BATTERY	
[1] [2] Air Suspension Control Module C295 [3]	[3] Measure the voltage between air suspension control module C295 Pin 1, Circuit 418 (DG/YE) and ground. • Is any voltage present? → **Yes** REPAIR the circuit. CLEAR the DTCs. REPEAT the self-test. → **No** INSTALL a new air suspension control module Control . SET the front ride height Clear B2140 DTC REPEAT the self-test.

FM2010100671020X

Fig. 49   Test O: Air Suspension System Operates w/Switch Turned Off (Part 2 of 2). Expedition & Navigator w/Rear Load Leveling

CONDITIONS	DETAILS/RESULTS/ACTIONS
O1 CHECK AIR SUSPENSION SWITCH	
[1] [3] Air Suspension Switch C291	[2] Turn the air suspension switch to the OFF position.

FM2010100671010X

Fig. 49   Test O: Air Suspension System Operates w/Switch Turned Off (Part 1 of 2). Expedition & Navigator w/Rear Load Leveling

CONDITIONS	DETAILS/RESULTS/ACTIONS
P1 CHECK FOR AIR COMPRESSOR AND AIR COMPRESSOR WIRING CONTACTING OTHER COMPONENTS	
	[1] Check the air compressor wiring to see if it is contacting other components inside the engine compartment at any place other than the mounting points. [2] Check for anything contacting the air compressor. • Is the air compressor wiring contacting non-mounting components or is anything contacting the air compressor assembly beside the mount? → **Yes** ADJUST as necessary. CLEAR the DTCs. REPEAT the self-test. → **No** GO to P2.
P2 CHECK FOR BENT AIR COMPRESSOR BRACKET	
	[1] Check the air compressor bracket for any damage/bends that may contact other components within the engine compartment. • Is the air compressor bracket making contact with other components? → **Yes** REPAIR or INSTALL a new air compressor assembly or other component(s) as necessary; CLEAR the DTCs. REPEAT the self-test. → **No** GO to P3.
P3 CHECK AIR COMPRESSOR MOUNTS FOR DAMAGE	
	[1] Check air compressor mounts for cracks or evidence that insulation material has broken away. • Are any defects in the mounts present? → **Yes** INSTALL a new air compressor and bracket assembly CLEAR the DTCs. REPEAT the self-test. → **No** GO to P4.

FM2010100672010X

Fig. 50   Test P: Compressor Noise Excessive (Part 1 of 2). Expedition & Navigator w/Rear Load Leveling

CONDITIONS	DETAILS/RESULTS/ACTIONS
P4 CHECK AIR COMPRESSOR FOR NOISE	

⚠ **CAUTION: Do not allow the air compressor to run for more than three minutes. The air compressor could overheat and stop operation due to an internal temperature sensitive thermal breaker.**

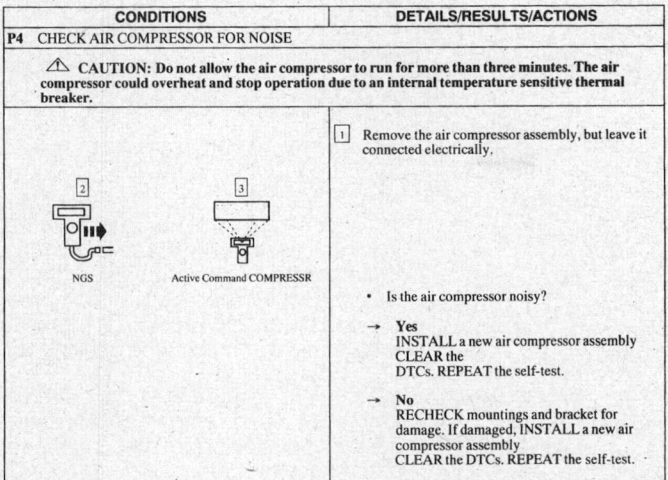

1. Remove the air compressor assembly, but leave it connected electrically.

- Is the air compressor noisy?

  → **Yes**
  INSTALL a new air compressor assembly CLEAR the DTCs. REPEAT the self-test.

  → **No**
  RECHECK mountings and bracket for damage. If damaged, INSTALL a new air compressor assembly CLEAR the DTCs. REPEAT the self-test.

FM2010100672020X

Fig. 50   Test P: Compressor Noise Excessive (Part 2 of 2). Expedition & Navigator w/Rear Load Leveling

CONDITIONS	DETAILS/RESULTS/ACTIONS
Q3 CHECK CIRCUIT 538 (LG/RD) (Continued)	

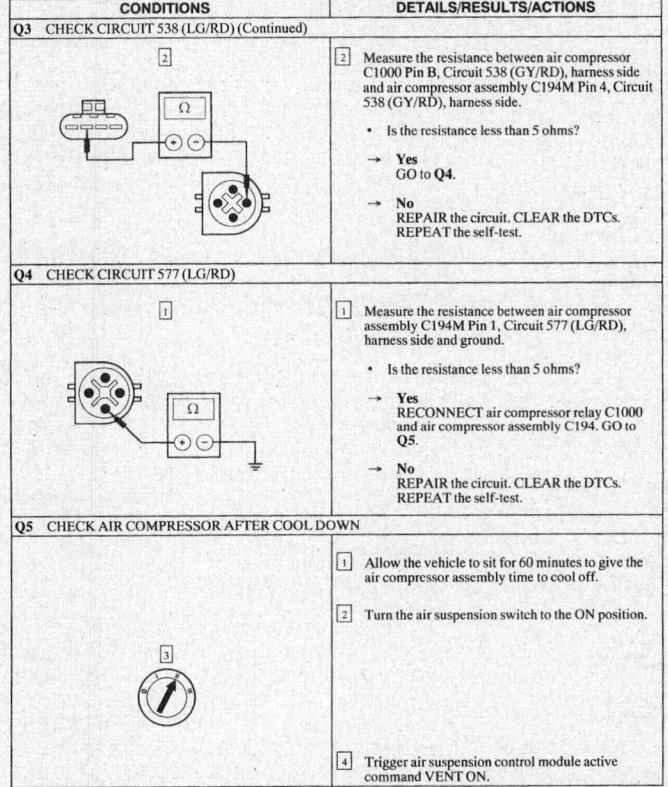

2. Measure the resistance between air compressor C1000 Pin B, Circuit 538 (GY/RD), harness side and air compressor assembly C194M Pin 4, Circuit 538 (GY/RD), harness side.

- Is the resistance less than 5 ohms?

  → **Yes**
  GO to **Q4.**

  → **No**
  REPAIR the circuit. CLEAR the DTCs. REPEAT the self-test.

| Q4   CHECK CIRCUIT 577 (LG/RD) | |

1. Measure the resistance between air compressor assembly C194M Pin 1, Circuit 577 (LG/RD), harness side and ground.

- Is the resistance less than 5 ohms?

  → **Yes**
  RECONNECT air compressor relay C1000 and air compressor assembly C194. GO to **Q5.**

  → **No**
  REPAIR the circuit. CLEAR the DTCs. REPEAT the self-test.

| Q5   CHECK AIR COMPRESSOR AFTER COOL DOWN | |

1. Allow the vehicle to sit for 60 minutes to give the air compressor assembly time to cool off.

2. Turn the air suspension switch to the ON position.

4. Trigger air suspension control module active command VENT ON.

FM2010100673020X

Fig. 51   Test Q: Compressor Inoperative (Part 2 of 3). Expedition & Navigator w/Rear Load Leveling

CONDITIONS	DETAILS/RESULTS/ACTIONS
Q1 CHECK THE AIR COMPRESSOR RELAY CONNECTOR 1000	

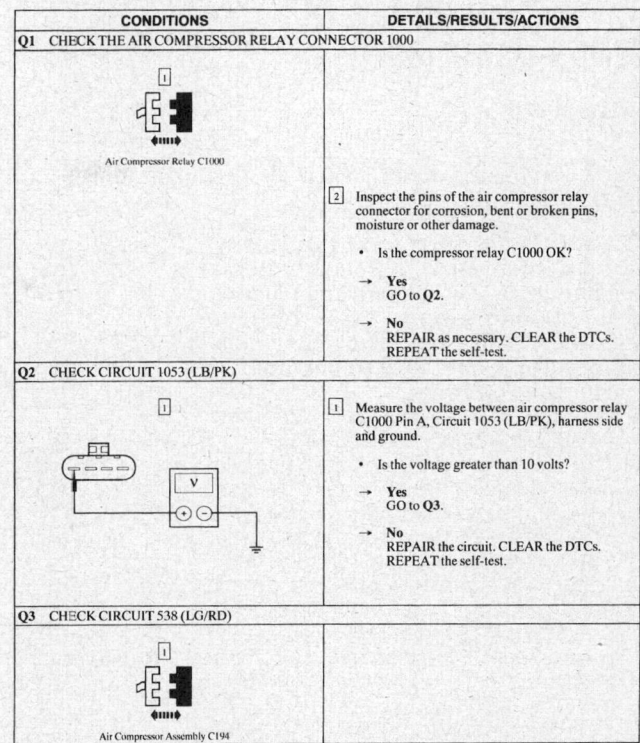

Air Compressor Relay C1000

2. Inspect the pins of the air compressor relay connector for corrosion, bent or broken pins, moisture or other damage.

- Is the compressor relay C1000 OK?

  → **Yes**
  GO to **Q2.**

  → **No**
  REPAIR as necessary. CLEAR the DTCs. REPEAT the self-test.

| Q2   CHECK CIRCUIT 1053 (LB/PK) | |

1. Measure the voltage between air compressor relay C1000 Pin A, Circuit 1053 (LB/PK), harness side and ground.

- Is the voltage greater than 10 volts?

  → **Yes**
  GO to **Q3.**

  → **No**
  REPAIR the circuit. CLEAR the DTCs. REPEAT the self-test.

| Q3   CHECK CIRCUIT 538 (LG/RD) | |

Air Compressor Assembly C194

FM2010100673010X

Fig. 51   Test Q: Compressor Inoperative (Part 1 of 3). Expedition & Navigator w/Rear Load Leveling

CONDITIONS	DETAILS/RESULTS/ACTIONS
Q5 CHECK AIR COMPRESSOR AFTER COOL DOWN (Continued)	

5. Trigger air suspension control module active command COMPRESSOR ON.

- Does the air compressor assembly run?

  → **Yes**
  GO to **Q7.**

  → **No**
  GO to **Q6.**

| Q6   CHECK AIR COMPRESSOR RELAY | |

Air Compressor Relay 1000

3. Connect a fused (50A) jumper wire (10 gauge) between air compressor relay C1000 Pin A, Circuit 1053 (LB/BK), harness side and air compressor relay C1000 Pin B, circuit 538 (GY/RD), harness side.

- Does the air compressor run?

  → **Yes**
  DISCONNECT the jumper wire. INSTALL a new air compressor relay. CLEAR the DTCs. REPEAT the self-test.

  → **No**
  DISCONNECT the jumper wire. INSTALL a new air compressor CLEAR the DTCs. REPEAT the self-test.

| Q7   CHECK THE AIR COMPRESSOR THERMAL BREAKER | |

1. Run the air compressor for 60 seconds.

- Did the air compressor run for 60 seconds?

  → **Yes**
  The thermal breaker was overheated. REPEAT the self-test.

  → **No**
  DISCONNECT the jumper wire. INSTALL a new air compressor assembly CLEAR the DTCs. REPEAT the self-test.

FM2010100673030X

Fig. 51   Test Q: Compressor Inoperative (Part 3 of 3). Expedition & Navigator w/Rear Load Leveling

COMPONENT REPLACEMENT

Front Shocks

EXPEDITION, F–SERIES & NAVIGATOR

Do not remove an air shock under any circumstances when there is pressure in air shock. Do not remove any components supporting an air shock without either exhausting the air or providing support for the air shock to prevent vehicle damage or injury.

1. Bleed air from air suspension system as outlined under "Adjustments."
2. Turn air suspension switch located in righthand kick panel area Off, then raise and support vehicle.
3. Remove air shock lower nut and bolt. For removal of lefthand front air shock absorber disconnect top of front height sensor from upper frame bracket to prevent damage to height sensor.
4. Disconnect air line by pushing red ring in, then remove upper nut and grommet and air shock.
5. Reverse procedure to install. **Torque** upper nut to 37–44 ft. lbs.

Rear Air Spring

EXPEDITION, F–SERIES & NAVIGATOR

1. Bleed air from air suspension system as outlined under "Adjustments."
2. Turn air suspension switch located in righthand kick panel area Off, then raise and support vehicle.
3. Remove rear air spring retainer, **Fig. 52.**
4. Lift bottom of air spring off rear axle, then disconnect air line by pushing green ring in and holding firmly to release air line.
5. Disconnect solenoid electrical connector and remove air spring.
6. Reverse procedure to install.

Air Spring Solenoid

EXPEDITION, F–SERIES & NAVIGATOR

1. Remove air spring as outlined in "Rear Air Spring."
2. Remove any dirt or other debris from air spring assembly prior to removing solenoid from air spring.
3. Remove metal retaining clip from air spring solenoid, then twist solenoid to remove and inspect O-rings and replace if required.
4. Reverse procedure to install.

Height Sensors

EXPEDITION, F–SERIES & NAVIGATOR

1. Turn air suspension switch located in righthand kick panel area Off, then

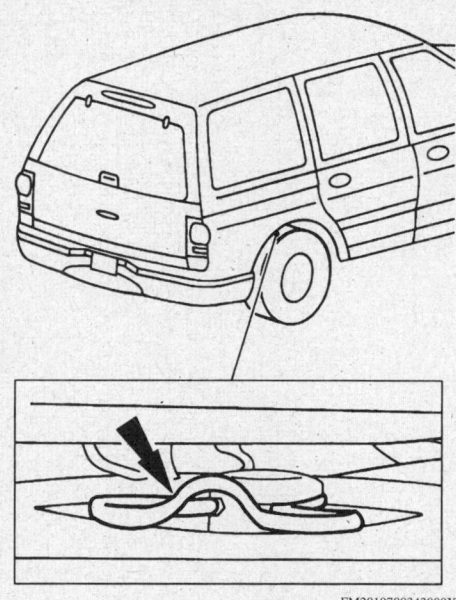

FM2019700343000X

Fig. 52 Rear air spring retainer removal. Expedition, F-Series & Navigator

raise and support vehicle.
2. The air suspension has a plastic harness retainer to suspension that must be disconnected prior to removal.
3. Disconnect electrical connector, then depress metal retaining tabs and remove height sensor from ball stud, **Fig. 53.**
4. Reverse procedure to install.

EXPLORER & MOUNTAINEER

1. Raise and support vehicle.
2. Remove spare tire.
3. Disconnect height sensor electrical connector.
4. Remove electrical connector harness from frame and apron to disconnect push-in fasteners.
5. Remove upper and lower spring clip and pull sensor from ball studs.
6. Reverse procedure to install.

Control Module

EXPEDITION, F–SERIES & NAVIGATOR

Remove EVO/air suspension module as outlined in "Power Steering" section.

EXPLORER & MOUNTAINEER

Electronic modules are sensitive to static electrical charges. Damage may occur if exposed to charges.
1. Remove center instrument panel finish panel.
2. Remove air suspension control module retaining screws, then slide module down and out of support bracket.
3. Disconnect air suspension control module electrical connectors.
4. Remove air suspension control module.

5. Reverse procedure to install. Adjust ride height as described under "Adjustments."

Air Compressor

EXPEDITION, F–SERIES & NAVIGATOR

1. Turn air suspension switch located in righthand kick panel area Off, then remove windshield washer reservoir.
2. Disconnect air lines from air compressor by depressing red plastic retaining rings and hold firmly while pulling out on air lines.
3. Disconnect air compressor electrical connector, then remove air compressor bracket bolts and air compressor and dryer assembly.
4. Reverse procedure to install. **Torque** compressor bracket bolts to 5–7 ft. lbs.

EXPLORER & MOUNTAINEER

1. Raise and support vehicle.
2. Remove spare tire.
3. Disconnect air compressor electrical connector.
4. Disconnect air line from dryer.
5. Remove air compressor retaining bolts, then the compressor.
6. Reverse procedure install. **Torque** compressor retaining bolts 13–17 ft. lbs.

Air Suspension Switch

EXPEDITION, F–SERIES & NAVIGATOR

1. Remove righthand front door scuff plate, then the cowl side trim panel.
2. Disconnect air suspension switch electrical connector, then remove switch bracket mounting bolt.
3. Reverse procedure to install. **Torque** bracket mounting bolt to 8–10 ft. lbs.

EXPLORER & MOUNTAINEER

1. Remove jack storage access cover.
2. Remove air suspension switch bracket retaining screw, then the air switch bracket.
3. Disconnect air switch electrical connector.
4. Press retaining clips, then remove suspension switch from bracket.
5. Reverse procedure to install. **Torque** air suspension switch bracket retaining screw 91–123 inch lbs.

Rear Air Shock Absorber

EXPLORER & MOUNTAINEER

Electrical power to air suspension must be shut off prior to hoisting, jacking or towing. This can be done by turning Off air suspension switch located in rear jack storage area.

Low pressure gas shock absorbers are charged with nitrogen gas 135 psi. Do not open, puncture or apply heat to shock absorbers.

1. Connect NGS Tester to DLC.
2. Select RIDE CONTROL OUTPUT screen and turn on following solenoids:
   a. REAR FILL, rear fill solenoid.
   b. GATEVALVE, gate solenoid.
   c. VENT, vent solenoid.
   d. This will vent entire system of air.
3. Remove spare tire.
4. Support rear axle using high-lift transmission jack tool No. 164-R3508, or equivalent.
5. Remove rear shock absorber electrical connector from rear crossmember, then disconnect electrical connector.
6. Disconnect air line from shock absorber.
7. Remove shock absorber lower retaining bolt, then swing shock absorber out of lower mounting bracket.
8. Remove retaining nuts on top of rear crossmember, then the shock absorber.
9. Reverse procedure to install, noting the following:
   a. **Torque** upper shock absorber retaining nuts 14–19 ft. lbs.
   b. **Torque** lower shock absorber bolt 39–53 ft. lbs.

Dryer
EXPLORER & MOUNTAINEER

1. Remove air compressor as described in this section.
2. Remove air compressor dryer retaining screw.
3. Rotate dryer 90° to unlock.
4. Remove dryer assembly.
5. Reverse procedure to install, noting the following:
   a. Inspect O-ring for damage.
   b. Lubricant solenoid seal area using

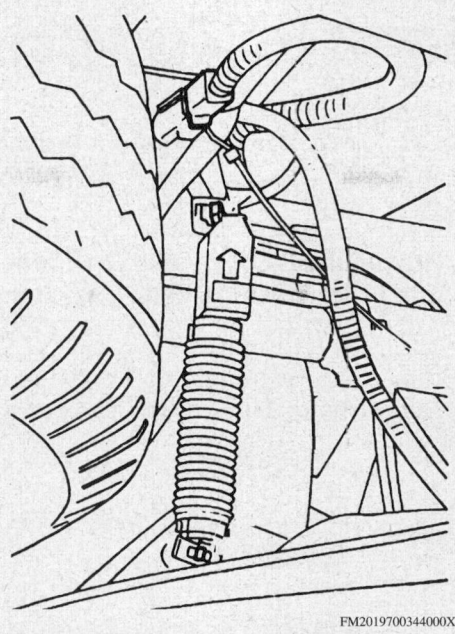

FM2019700344000X

Fig. 53 Height sensor removal. Expedition, F-Series & Navigator

silicone brake caliper grease and dielectric compound part No. D7AZ-19A331-A, or an equivalent meeting Ford specification ESE-M1C171-A.
   c. Ensure white air line is fully inserted into fitting.
   d. Adjust ride height as described under "Adjustments."
   e. **Torque** dryer retaining screw to 18–27 inch lbs.

Rear Fill Solenoid Valve
EXPLORER & MOUNTAINEER

1. Connect NGS Tester to DLC.

2. Select RIDE CONTROL OUTPUT screen and turn on following solenoids:
   a. REAR FILL, rear fill solenoid.
   b. GATEVALVE, gate solenoid.
   c. VENT, vent solenoid.
3. Raise and support vehicle.
4. Remove spare tire.
5. Remove solenoid valve from frame.
6. Compress quick connect locking ring and pull out air line.
7. Disconnect solenoid valve electrical connector.
8. Reverse procedure to install.

Rear Gate Solenoid Valve
EXPLORER & MOUNTAINEER

1. Connect NGS Tester to DLC.
2. Select RIDE CONTROL OUTPUT screen and turn on following solenoids:
   a. REAR FILL, rear fill solenoid.
   b. GATEVALVE, gate solenoid.
   c. VENT, vent solenoid.
3. Raise and support vehicle.
4. Remove spare tire.
5. Remove EVAP canister.
6. Remove solenoid valve from frame.
7. Disconnect solenoid valve electrical connector.
8. Reverse procedure to install.

Vehicle Dynamic Suspension (VDS)

NOTE: On Air Bag Equipped Models, Refer To "Air Bag System Precautions" Located In The Front Of This Manual For System Disarming & Arming Procedures.

NOTE: Refer To "Computer Relearn Procedures" Located In The Front Of This Manual When Battery Power To The Computer Has Been Interrupted.

NOTE: "Electrical Symbol & Wire Color Code Identification" Located In The Front Of This Manual May Be Used As An Aid When Using Wiring Circuits Found In This Section.

INDEX

	Page No.
Adjustments	6-98
Air Line Fluid Purge	6-98
Inflation & Deflation	6-99
Ride Height Calibration & Resetting	6-99
Component Replacement	6-111
Air Compressor	6-112
Air Spring Solenoid Valve	6-111
Control Module	6-112
Dryer	6-112
Front Air Shock	6-111

	Page No.
Height Sensors	6-112
Front	6-112
Rear	6-112
Rear Air Shock	6-111
Description	6-98
Diagnosis & Testing	6-99
Accessing Diagnostic Trouble Codes	6-99
Clearing Diagnostic Trouble Codes	6-99
Diagnostic Trouble Code Interpretation	6-99

	Page No.
Pinpoint Tests	6-99
Wiring Diagrams	6-99
Diagnostic Chart Index	6-102
Precautions	6-98
Air Bag Systems	6-98
Battery Ground Cable	6-98
Service	6-98
Troubleshooting	6-98
Symptom Chart	6-98

PRECAUTIONS

Air Bag Systems

Refer to "Air Bag System Precautions" in the front of this manual for system disarming and arming procedures.

Battery Ground Cable

Prior to service, disconnect battery ground cable and isolate as required.

Service

The service switch for the air suspension system must be shut off prior to hoisting, jacking or towing an air suspension vehicle. This can be accomplished by turning off the air suspension switch located in the rear storage area in the rear of the passenger compartment. Failure to follow these instructions may result in personal injury.

DESCRIPTION

The air suspension Vehicle Dynamics Module (VDM) commands changes in vehicle height that are necessary for both the load leveling and the vertical height adjustment features. The load leveling feature automatically makes adjustments in vehicle height so that the vehicle is always at target height and that constant front-to-rear vehicle attitudes are maintained over the load range of the vehicle. Adjustments in height that are necessary to correct height differences between the vehicle left and right sides for the system are restricted to what can be reliably achieved with three sensors.

The height adjustment feature has three target heights within a 2 inch (51 mm) span: **Kneel height** improves the ease of entering and exiting by lowering the vehicle 25 mm (0.98 in) below the trim height in the front and rear when the vehicle ignition is in the OFF or LOCK positions and the vehicle is stationary and all doors, liftgate and liftgate glass are CLOSED: **Trim height** normal vehicle ride position; vehicle adjusts to trim position when the ignition is ON, when the transmission is initially shifted to DRIVE or REVERSE mode, when all doors and the liftgate are CLOSED or when speed of more than 15 mph is detected: **Off-road height** improves ground clearance by raising the vehicle 0.98 inch (25 mm) above trim height in the front and rear when the vehicle is at 4x4 low modes and the vehicle speed is less than 19 mph.

The 4-Wheel Air Suspension (4WAS) system holds vehicle height when any door or rear liftgate is opened. The system stores front and rear vehicle height the moment any door is detected OPEN. The system then maintains this height regardless of the addition or removal of a load. The system returns to its commanded height when all doors are CLOSED or vehicle speed exceeds 15 mph. The system will remain active for 40 minutes after the ignition is turned OFF to make limited height adjustments as necessary.

TROUBLESHOOTING

Symptom Chart

Refer to **Fig. 1** for symptom chart.

ADJUSTMENTS

Air Line Fluid Purge

If oil is present in the air lines, remove the air spring solenoids and inspect the solenoid filters. If oil is present in a filter, install a new solenoid and shock absorber.
1. Disconnect air line at air compressor drier.
2. Disconnect air line at lefthand and righthand front air spring solenoids.
3. Connect shop air line to disconnected air line (drier end) and blow out any fluid.
4. Reconnect air line at lefthand and righthand front air spring solenoids. When installing air lines, make sure white air line is fully inserted into fitting for correct installation.
5. Disconnect air line at lefthand and righthand rear air spring solenoids.
6. Connect shop air line (drier end) to disconnected air line and blow out any fluid.
7. Reconnect air line at lefthand and righthand rear air spring solenoids.
8. Install a new air compressor drier.
9. Reconnect air line to air compressor drier.

Condition	Possible Sources	Action
• No communication with the VDM	• Fuse(s). • Circuitry. • VDM.	• Go To Pinpoint Test A.
• NOTE: Be sure that the ignition switch is in the ON position and the air suspension service switch is in the ON position before determining that the VDM will not enter the self-test. Unable to enter self-test.	• Air suspension service switch. • VDM.	• Go To Pinpoint Test B.
• Vehicle raises and/or lowers too slowly	• Front/rear pneumatic failure. • Height sensor. • Air compressor assembly. • Circuitry. • Solenoid. • Air line.	• Go To Pinpoint Test E.
• Uneven vehicle height	• Front/rear pneumatic failure. • Height sensor. • Solenoid. • Air compressor assembly. • Air line. • Circuitry.	• Go To Pinpoint Test E.
• The air compressor continuously cycles with the ignition switch in the OFF position and no DTC is set	• Circuitry. • Air suspension relay. • VDM.	• Go To Pinpoint Test K.
• The air suspension system is inoperative without DTCs and vehicle at rest	• CAN network communication fault.	• Go To Pinpoint Test L.
• Air suspension system operates with air suspension service switch in the OFF position	• Circuitry. • Air suspension switch. • VDM.	• Go To Pinpoint Test M.

LTV0500000005448

**Fig. 1 Symptom Chart
(Part 1 of 2)**

Inflation & Deflation

1. Connect suitably programed scan tool to Data Link Connector (DLC).
2. Ensure air suspension switch is in ON position.
3. Turn ignition switch to ON position.
4. Select "Air Suspension Control Module" under "Active Command Mode."
5. Follow diagnostic tool directions to lift or vent, front or rear suspension.

Ride Height Calibration & Resetting

1. Ensure air suspension switch is in ON position.
2. Turn ignition to OFF position, then exit vehicle, close all doors and allow system to vent vehicle down to kneel height, approximately 45 seconds.
3. With ignition in ON position, shift vehicle into DRIVE and then back to PARK, then exit vehicle, close all doors and allow system to pump vehicle up to trim height, approximately 45 seconds.
4. Connect suitably programed scan tool to Data Link Connector (DLC).
5. While outside vehicle, select correct vehicle year, model and engine type.
6. Select "Vehicle Dynamic Module (VDM)." Using active command mode, vent or lift vehicle to achieve correct ride height.
7. Select "Save Calibration Values (Store Ride Height)" diagnostic tool command to calibrate VDM.

DIAGNOSIS & TESTING

Accessing Diagnostic Trouble Codes

Connect a suitably programmed scan tool and Vehicle Communication Module (VCM) with appropriate adapters, or equivalents, to the Data Link Connector (DCL) located in the passenger compartment beneath the instrument panel. Follow tool manufacturer's instructions for accessing Diagnostic Trouble Codes (DTC).

Condition	Possible Sources	Action
• Excessive air compressor noise	• Bracket isolator(s). • Mounting bracket. • Air compressor assembly. • Air compressor assembly in contact with other components.	• Go To Pinpoint Test N.
• The compressor is inoperative	• Fuse(s). • Air compressor assembly. • Circuitry. • Air suspension relay.	• Go To Pinpoint Test O.
• NOTE: Vehicle speed signal is sent through the CAN communication (secondary) network and it is transmitted by hardwire (primary). DTC C1445: Vehicle Speed Signal Circuit Failure	• Circuitry. • PCM. • CAN communication network.	• Check communications area network.

LTV0500000005449

**Fig. 1 Symptom Chart
(Part 2 of 2)**

Diagnostic Trouble Code Interpretation

Refer to **Fig. 2** for diagnostic trouble code interpretation.

Wiring Diagrams

Refer to **Fig. 3** for wiring diagrams.

Pinpoint Tests

Refer to **Figs. 4 through 18** for pinpoint tests

Clearing Diagnostic Trouble Codes

Connect a suitably programmed scan tool and Vehicle Communication Module (VCM) with appropriate adapters, or equivalents, to the Data Link Connector (DCL) located in the passenger compartment beneath the instrument panel. Follow tool manufacturer's instructions for Clearing Diagnostic Trouble Codes (DTC).

Code	Description
B1317	Battery Voltage High
B1318	Battery Voltage Low
B1342	ECU Is Defective
B2477	VAPS II Steering Assist Curve Not Complete
C1445	Vehicle Speed Signal Circuit Failure
C1724	Air Suspension Height Sensor Power Circuit Failure
C1725	Air Suspension Front Pneumatic Failure
C1726	Air Suspension Rear Pneumatic Failure
C1760	Air Suspension Rear Height Sensor Signal Circuit Failure
C1770	Air Suspension Vent Solenoid Output Circuit Failure
C1790	Air Suspension LR Air Spring/Shock Solenoid Output Circuit Failure
C1795	Air Suspension RR Air Spring/Shock Solenoid Output Circuit Failure
C1830	Air Suspension Compressor Relay Circuit Failure
C1840	Air Suspension Disable Switch Circuit Failure
C1873	Air Suspension RF Air Spring Solenoid Output Circuit Failure
C1877	Air Suspension LF Air Spring Solenoid Output Circuit Failure
C1881	Air Suspension RF Height Sensor Circuit Failure
C1889	Air Suspension LF Height Sensor Circuit Failure
C1897	Steering VAPS Circuit Loop Failure
C1964	Air Suspension Compressor Actual Run Time Exceeded Allowed Run Time
C1990	New Control Module Initialization (Requires Ride Height Calibration & Pneumatic Test Pass)
C1991	Plant Ride Height Setting And/Or Tests Incomplete
C2023	Invalid CAN Message(s)
U1900	Missing CAN Message(s)

Fig. 2 Diagnostic trouble code interpretation

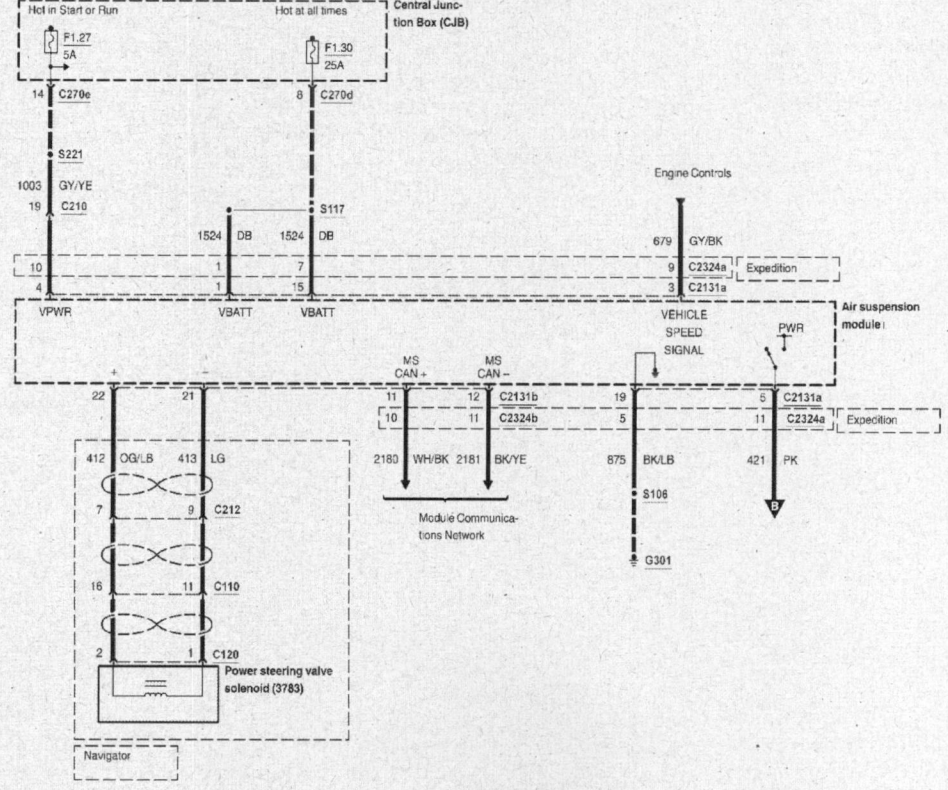

Fig. 3 Wiring diagram (Part 1 of 4)

LTV0500000005450

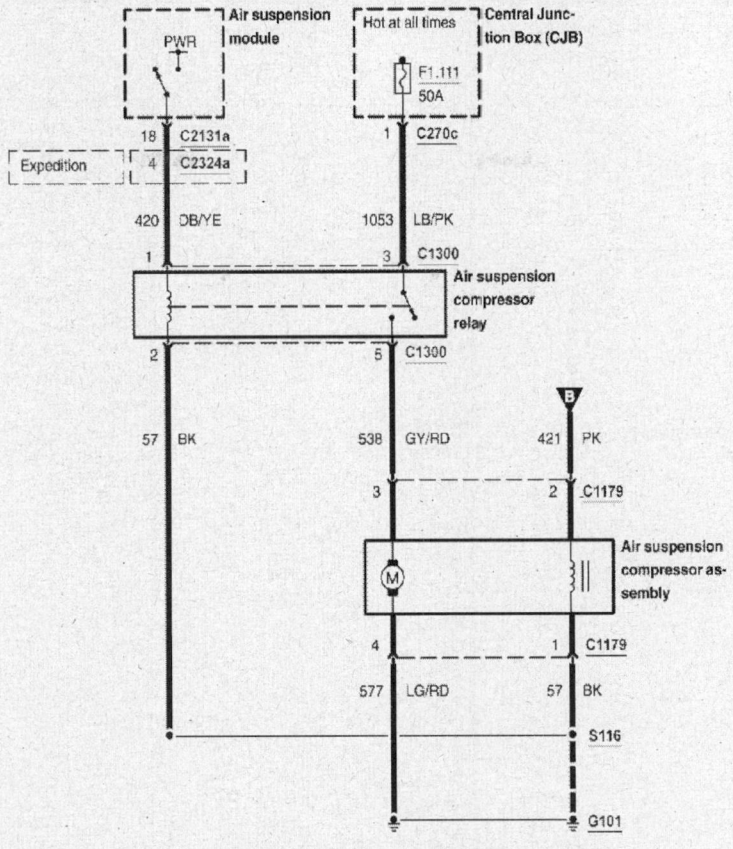

Fig. 3   Wiring diagram (Part 2 of 4)

LTV0500000005451

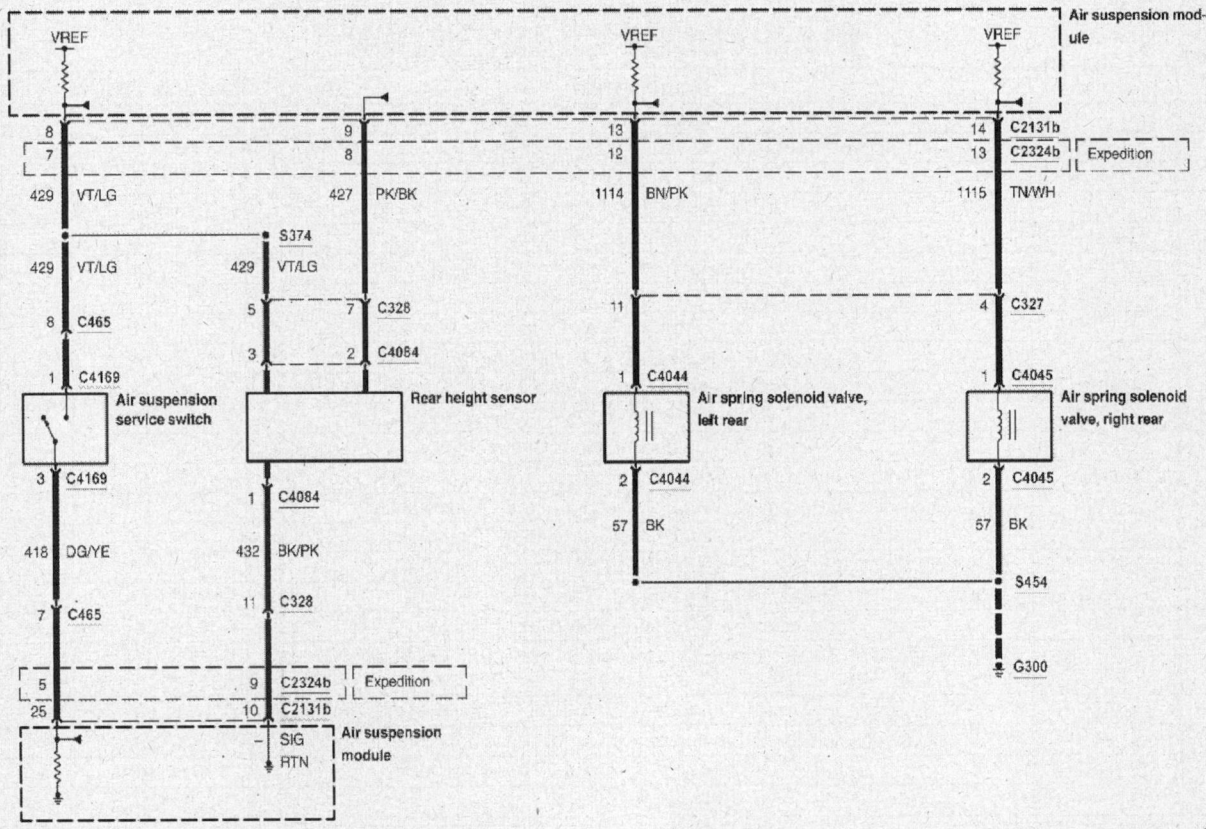

LTV0500000005452

Fig. 3   Wiring diagram (Part 3 of 4)

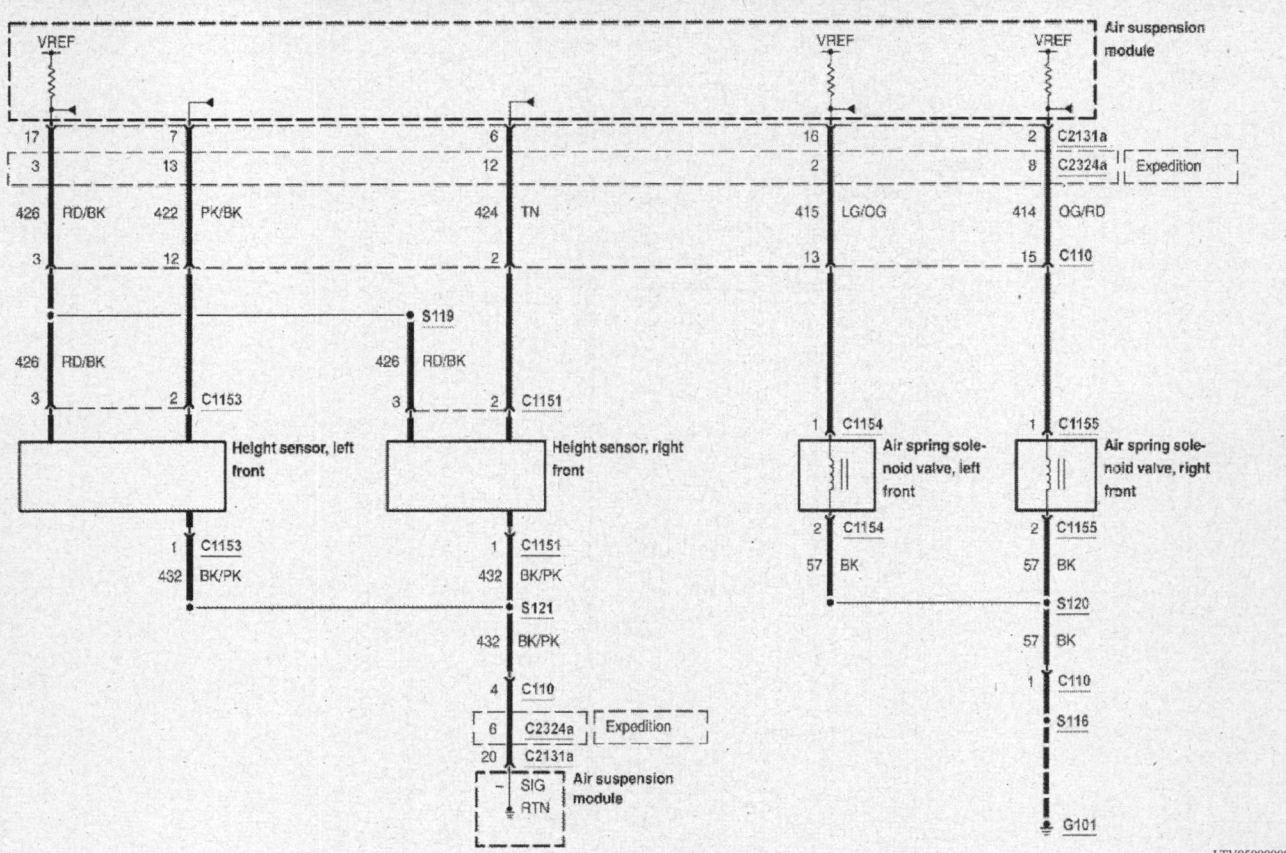

Fig. 3 Wiring diagram (Part 4 of 4)

DIAGNOSTIC CHART INDEX

Test	Code	Description	Page No.	Fig. No.
—	—	Symptom Chart	6-99	1
A	—	No Communication w/Vehicle Dynamics Module (VDM)	6-103	4
B	—	Unable To Enter Self-Test	6-103	5
C	B1317	Battery Voltage High/Low	6-103	6
	B1318	Battery Voltage High/Low	6-103	6
D	C1724	Air Suspension Height Sensor Power Circuit Failure	6-104	7
E	C1725	Air Suspension Front/Rear Pneumatic Failure	6-104	8
	C1726	Air Suspension Front/Rear Pneumatic Failure	6-104	8
F	C1760	Air Suspension Height Sensor Signal Circuit Failure	6-105	9
	C1881	Air Suspension Height Sensor Signal Circuit Failure	6-105	9
	C1889	Air Suspension Height Sensor Signal Circuit Failure	6-105	9
G	C1770	Air Suspension Solenoid Output Circuit Failure	6-106	10
H	C1790	Air Suspension Air Spring Solenoid Output Circuit Failure	6-107	11
	C1795	Air Suspension Air Spring Solenoid Output Circuit Failure	6-107	11
	C1873	Air Suspension Air Spring Solenoid Output Circuit Failure	6-107	11
	C1877	Air Suspension Air Spring Solenoid Output Circuit Failure	6-107	11
I	C1830	Air Suspension Compressor Relay Circuit Failure	6-108	12
J	C1840	Air Suspension Service Switch Circuit Failure	6-108	13
K	—	Air Compressor Continuously Cycles w/Ignition Switch In Off Position & No DTC Is Set	6-109	14
L	—	Air Suspension System Inoperative Without DTC & Vehicle At Rest	6-109	15
M	—	Air Suspension System Operates w/Service Switch In Off Position	6-110	16
N	—	Excessive Air Compressor Noise	6-110	17
O	—	Air Compressor Is Inoperative	6-110	18

Test Step	Result / Action to Take
A1 CHECK CIRCUIT 1524 (DB) FOR VOLTAGE	

• Disconnect: VDM C2131a.
• Measure the voltage between:
  ▪ VDM C2131a-1, circuit 1524 (DB), harness side and ground.
  ▪ VDM C2131a-15, circuit 1524 (DB), harness side and ground.
• **Are the voltages greater than 10 volts?**
	Yes
	GO to <u>A2</u>.
	
	No
	Verify CJB fuse 30 (25A) is OK. If OK, REPAIR circuit 1524 (DB) for an open. TEST the system for normal operation.

A2 CHECK CIRCUIT 1003 (GY/YE) FOR VOLTAGE	
• Key in ON position. • Measure the voltage between VDM C2131a-4, circuit 1003 (GY/YE), harness side and ground. • **Is the voltage greater than 10 volts?**	**Yes** GO to <u>A3</u>. **No** Verify CJB fuse 27 (5A) is OK. If OK, REPAIR circuit 1003 (GY/YE) for an open. TEST the system for normal operation.
A3 CHECK CIRCUIT 875 (BK/LB) FOR AN OPEN	
• Key in OFF position. • Measure the resistance between VDM C2131a-19, circuit 875 (BK/LB), harness side and ground. • **Is the resistance less than 5 ohms?**	**Yes** CHECK the CAN communication network. **No** REPAIR circuit 875 (BK/LB) for an open. TEST the system for normal operation.

LTV0500000005453

Fig. 4 Test A: No Communication w/Vehicle Dynamics Module (VDM)

Test Step	Result / Action to Take
B1 CHECK THE COMMUNICATION TO THE VDM	

• Verify that the following conditions have been met using the diagnostic tool and monitoring PIDs:
  ▪ Ignition switch is in the ON position.
  ▪ Air suspension service switch is in the ON position.
  ▪ Vehicle speed is less than 3 km/h (2 mph).
  ▪ Transmission selector is in PARK.
  ▪ Battery voltage is greater than 10 volts.
  ▪ Verify that the doors, the liftgate and the liftgate glass are CLOSED.
  ▪ Verify that the power running boards (if equipped), are not deployed.
  ▪ Transfer case is **not** in 4L mode.
• **Does diagnostic tool communicate with the VDM?**
	Yes
	INSTALL a new VDM. REPEAT the self-test.
	
	No
	Go To Pinpoint Test A.

LTV0500000005454

Fig. 5 Test B: Unable To Enter Self-Test

Test Step	Result / Action to Take
C1 VERIFY DTC B1317 AND/OR B1318	
• Connect the diagnostic tool. • Key in ON position. • Clear any DTCs and carry out the On-Demand Self Test. • **Is DTC B1317 or B1318 retrieved?**	**Yes** GO to <u>C2</u>. **No** TEST the vehicle for normal operation.
C2 CHECK THE BATTERY VOLTAGE	
• Measure the battery voltage between the positive and negative battery posts with the key ON engine OFF (KOEO), and with the engine running. • **Is the battery voltage between 10 and 13 volts with KOEO, and between 11 and 18 volts with the engine running?**	**Yes** GO to <u>C3</u>. **No** TEST the charging system for normal operation.
C3 CHECK VOLTAGE TO THE VDM	
• Key in OFF position. • Disconnect: VDM C2131a. • Key in ON position. • Measure the voltage between the following VDM C2131a pins, harness side and ground with the key ON engine OFF (KOEO), and with the engine running:	**Yes** GO to <u>C4</u>. **No** Verify CJB fuse 30 (25A) and fuse 27 (5A) are OK. If OK, REPAIR the affected circuit(s) for an open. CLEAR the DTCs. REPEAT the self-test.

LTV0500000005455

Fig. 6 Test C, Codes B1317 & B1318: Battery Voltage High/Low (Part 1 of 2)

VDM Connector C2131a Pin No.	Circuit	
1	1524 (DB)	
4	1003 (GY/YE)	
15	1524 (DB)	

• **Is the voltage between 10 and 13 volts with KOEO, and between 11 and 18 volts with the engine running?**

Test Step	Result / Action to Take
C4 CHECK CIRCUIT 875 (BK/LB) FOR AN OPEN	
• Key in OFF position. • Measure the resistance between VDM C2131a-19, circuit 875 (BK/LB), harness side, and ground. • **Is the resistance less than 5 ohms?**	**Yes** INSTALL a new VDM. REPEAT the self-test. **No** REPAIR circuit 875 (BK/LB) for an open. CLEAR the DTCs. REPEAT the self-test

LTV0500000005456

Fig. 6 Test C, Codes B1317 & B1318: Battery Voltage High/Low (Part 2 of 2)

Test Step	Result / Action to Take

D1 CHECK THE AIR SUSPENSION HEIGHT SENSOR POWER CIRCUITS FOR AN OPEN
• Disconnect: VDM C2131a.
• Disconnect: VDM C2131b.
• Disconnect: LF Height Sensor C1153.
• Disconnect: RF Height Sensor C1151.
• Disconnect: Rear Height Sensor C4084.
• Measure the resistance between:
  ▪ VDM C2131a-17, circuit 426 (RD/BK), harness side and LF height sensor C1153-3, circuit 426 (RD/BK).
  ▪ VDM C2131a-17, circuit 426 (RD/BK), harness side and RF height sensor C1151-3, circuit 426 (RD/BK).
  ▪ VDM C2131b-8, circuit 429 (VT/LG), harness side and rear height sensor C4084-3, circuit 429 (VT/LG).
• **Are the resistances less than 5 ohms?**
	Yes
	GO to <u>D2</u>.
	
	No
	REPAIR the affected circuit(s) for an open. CLEAR the DTCs. REPEAT the self-test.

D2 CHECK THE AIR SUSPENSION HEIGHT SENSOR POWER CIRCUITS FOR A SHORT TO GROUND
• Measure the resistance between ground and:
  ▪ VDM C2131a-17, circuit 426 (RD/BK), harness side.
  ▪ VDM C2131b-8, circuit 429 (VT/LG), harness side.
  ▪ LF height sensor C1153-3, circuit 426 (RD/BK), harness side.
  ▪ RF height sensor C1151-3, circuit 426 (RD/BK), harness side.
  ▪ Rear height sensor C4084-3, circuit 429 (VT/LG), harness side.
• **Are the resistances greater than 10,000 ohms?**
	Yes
	GO to <u>D3</u>.
	
	No
	REPAIR the affected circuit(s) for a short to ground. CLEAR the DTCs. REPEAT the self-test.

D3 CHECK THE AIR SUSPENSION HEIGHT SENSOR SIGNAL RETURN CIRCUITS FOR AN OPEN
• Measure the resistance between:
  ▪ VDM C2131a-20, circuit 432 (BK/PK), harness side and RF height sensor C1153-1, circuit 432 (BK/PK), harness side.
  ▪ VDM C2131a-20, circuit 432 (BK/PK), harness side and LF height sensor C1151-1, circuit 432 (BK/PK), harness side.
  ▪ VDM C2131b-10, circuit 432 (BK/PK), harness side and rear height sensor C4084-1, circuit 432 (BK/PK) harness side.
	Yes
	GO to <u>D4</u>.
	
	No
	REPAIR circuit 432 (BK/PK) for an open. CLEAR the DTCs. REPEAT the self-test.

LTV0500000005457

Fig. 7 Test D, Code C1724: Air Suspension Height Sensor Power Circuit Failure (Part 1 of 2)

Test Step	Result / Action to Take
• **Are the resistances less than 5 ohms?**	
D4 CHECK THE AIR SUSPENSION SWITCH • Place the air suspension switch in the ON position. • Measure the resistance between C2131b-25, circuit 418 (DG/YE), harness side and C2131b-8, circuit 429 (VT/LG), harness side. • **Is the resistance less than 5 ohms?**	**Yes** GO to <u>D5</u>. **No** REPAIR the affected circuit(s) for an open. CLEAR the DTCs. REPEAT the self-test.
D5 CHECK CIRCUITS 426 (RD/BK) AND 429 (VT/LG) FOR A SHORT TO GROUND • Place the air suspension switch in the ON position. • Measure the resistance between VDM C2131a-17, circuit 426 (RD/BK), harness side and ground; and measure the resistance between VDM C2131b-8, circuit 429 (VT/LG), harness side and ground. • **Are the resistances greater than 10,000 ohms?**	**Yes** GO to <u>D6</u>. **No** REPAIR the affected circuit(s) for an open. CLEAR the DTCs. REPEAT the self-test.

D6 CHECK VOLTAGE AT THE LF, RF AND REAR HEIGHT SENSORS
• Connect: VDM C2131a.
• Connect: VDM C2131b.
• Key in ON position.
• Measure the voltage between:
  ▪ LF height sensor C1153-1, circuit 432 (BK/PK), harness side and LF height sensor C1153-3, circuit 432 (BK/PK), harness side.
  ▪ RF height sensor C1151-1, circuit 432 (BK/PK), harness side and RF height sensor C1151-3, circuit 426 (RD/BK) harness side.
• Measure the voltage between rear height sensor C4084-1, circuit 432 (BK/PK), harness side and C4084-3, circuit 429 (VT/LG), harness side.
• **Are the voltages 5 volts?**
	Yes
	INSTALL a new height sensor(s) as necessary. CLEAR the DTCs. REPEAT the self-test.
	
	No
	INSTALL a new VDM. CLEAR the DTCs. REPEAT the self-test.

LTV0500000005458

Fig. 7 Test D, Code C1724: Air Suspension Height Sensor Power Circuit Failure (Part 2 of 2)

Test Step	Result / Action to Take
E1 CHECK THE AIR SUSPENSION HEIGHT SENSORS • Inspect the LF, RF and rear air suspension height sensors for correct installation at the upper and lower ball studs. • Inspect the air suspension height sensor mounting brackets for damage. • Verify that all air lines are fully seated. • **Are the air suspension height sensors, mounting brackets and air lines OK?**	**Yes** GO to <u>E2</u>. **No** REPAIR as necessary. If the height sensor mounting brackets are installed or repaired, RESET front ride height. CLEAR the DTCs. REPEAT the self-test.
E2 CHECK THE AIR SUSPENSION HEIGHT SENSOR OPERATION • Turn the air suspension switch to the OFF position. • Disconnect the sensor arm linkage from the LF, RF and rear air suspension height sensors. • Connect the diagnostic tool. • Key in ON position. • **NOTE:** The voltage will increase as the suspension is compressed. • While monitoring the VDM LF, RF and rear height sensor PID display, slowly move the LF, RF and rear air suspension height sensors through its full travel UP and DOWN. • **Do the voltages vary from approximately 0.50 volt and 4.50 volts?**	**Yes** RECONNECT the sensor arm linkages to the air suspension height sensors. GO to <u>E3</u>. **No** INSTALL a new height sensor(s). CLEAR the DTCs. REPEAT the self-test.
E3 VERIFY THAT THE FRONT CAN BE RAISED • Trigger the VDM LF and RF suspension fill active commands. • Allow the vehicle to raise for 30 seconds. • Monitor all 3 height sensor voltage PIDs. • **Did the LF and RF raise and the rear remain at**	**Yes** TRIGGER the VDM off active command. GO to <u>E4</u>. **No**

LTV0500000005459

Fig. 8 Test E, Codes C1725 & C1726: Air Suspension Front/Rear Pneumatic Failure (Part 1 of 5)

Test Step	Result / Action to Take
the same height?	TRIGGER the VDM off active command. If the front remained at the same height, GO to <u>E6</u>; if the rear raised, GO to <u>E4</u>.
E4 VERIFY THAT THE REAR CAN BE RAISED • Trigger the VDM rear suspension fill active command. • Allow the vehicle to raise for 30 to 45 seconds. • Monitor all 3 height sensor voltage PIDs. • **Did the rear raise and the LF and RF remain at the same height?**	**Yes** TRIGGER the VDM off active command. GO to <u>E6</u>. **No** TRIGGER the VDM off active command. If the rear raised and the LF and RF raised, GO to <u>E5</u>; if the rear did not raise and LF and RF remained at the same height, GO to <u>E7</u>.
E5 VERIFY THAT THE AIR SPRING SOLENOIDS DO NOT LEAK • Disconnect the air line at the right rear air spring solenoid valve. • Use a thumb to block and unblock the end of the disconnected air line as the air escapes. • **Can air pressure be felt when the air line is blocked?**	**Yes** IDENTIFY the leaking air spring solenoid valve by observing which air spring assembly continues to vent with the air line blocked. INSTALL a new air spring solenoid valve. CLEAR the DTCs. REPEAT the self-test. **No** GO to <u>E6</u>.
E6 VERIFY THAT THE VEHICLE CAN BE LOWERED • Trigger the VDM vent front and rear air suspension active commands. • Allow the front and rear to lower for 30 seconds. • **Does the vehicle lower evenly?**	**Yes** INSTALL a new VDM. REPEAT the self-test. **No** GO to <u>E11</u>.
E7 CHECK OPERATION OF THE AIR COMPRESSOR ⚠ **CAUTION:** The VDM limits the air compressor run time. If the air compressor overheats, it will not restart until it cools down. The ignition switch must be in the OFF position to allow the compressor thermal switch to cool. • Trigger the VDM compressor on active command. • **Does the air compressor run (slight buzzing noise from RF fender)?**	**Yes** TRIGGER the VDM compressor off active command. GO to <u>E8</u>. **No** TRIGGER the VDM compressor off active command. Go To Pinpoint Test O.

LTV0500000005460

Fig. 8 Test E, Codes C1725 & C1726: Air Suspension Front/Rear Pneumatic Failure (Part 2 of 5)

E8 CHECK THE AIR COMPRESSOR PRESSURE OUTPUT

⚠ **CAUTION: The VDM limits the air compressor run time. If the air compressor overheats, it will not restart until it cools down. The ignition switch must be in the OFF position to allow the compressor thermal switch to cool. NOTE:** If fluid is present when disconnecting an air line, clear the air lines. Check the compressor air drier for water or the front air spring for oil. **NOTE:** When triggering the compressor ON, the vent solenoid will open as well. To prevent the vent solenoid from opening during this test, first trigger a single spring solenoid ON, then trigger the compressor ON.

- Disconnect air line T-fitting at the right front shock tower.
- Connect an air pressure gauge (1,723 kPa [250 psi] maximum reading) with common fittings to the air line going to the compressor air drier.
- Trigger the VDM compressor on active command.
- Run the air compressor for 30 seconds.
- Wait 5 minutes.
- Trigger the VDM compressor vent on active command.
- **Did the compressor produce 1,034 kPa (150 psi) within 30 seconds and hold developed pressure during the 5 minutes?**

Yes GO to E10.

No GO to E9.

E9 CHECK THE AIR DRIER FOR LEAKS

⚠ **CAUTION: The VDM limits the air compressor run time. If the air compressor overheats, it will not restart until it cools down. The ignition switch must be in the OFF position to allow the compressor thermal switch to cool. NOTE:** Apply a soap and water solution to the air lines and air line connections when checking for air suspension system leakage. **NOTE:** When triggering the compressor ON, the vent solenoid will open as well. To prevent the vent solenoid from opening during this test, first trigger a single spring solenoid ON, then trigger the compressor ON.

- Trigger the VDM compressor on active command.
- Thoroughly inspect the air drier-to-air compressor connection.
- **Is the air drier leaking at the air compressor?**

Yes INSTALL a new air drier. CLEAR the DTCs. REPEAT the self-test.

No GO to E10.

LTV0500000005461

Fig. 8   Test E, Codes C1725 & C1726: Air Suspension Front/Rear Pneumatic Failure (Part 3 of 5)

E10 CHECK THE SPRING SOLENOID OPERATION

NOTE: Start with the vehicle at trim height before carrying out this test step. **NOTE:** Air will vent much faster with the air lines disconnected from each spring solenoid.

- Disconnect the air line at the LF, RF, LR and RR air spring solenoids.
- Trigger the VDM LF, RF, LR and RR air spring solenoid valve vent active commands.
- **Does each air solenoid vent?**

Yes GO to E11.

No INSTALL a new air spring solenoid valve(s). CLEAR the DTCs. REPEAT the self-test. CARRY OUT the Pneumatic Test.

E11 CHECK THE AIR LINE FROM THE AIR DRIER

⚠ **CAUTION: The VDM limits the air compressor run time. If the air compressor overheats, it will not restart until it cools down. The ignition switch must be in the OFF position to allow the compressor thermal switch to cool. NOTE:** Apply a soap and water solution to the air lines and air line connections when checking for air suspension system leakage.

- Trigger the VDM compressor on active command.
- Check for excessive air leaks, kinked or pinched air lines between the air compressor and the LF, RF, LR and RR air spring solenoids and between the air compressor and the air pressure gauge.
- **Are there any excessive leaks, kinks or pinched air lines?**

Yes INSTALL new or REPAIR the air line where necessary. CLEAR the DTCs. REPEAT the self-test.

No GO to E12.

E12 CHECK FOR A PLUGGED AIR LINE

- Disconnect the air line from the air drier.
- Trigger the front and rear suspension vent active commands.
- **Does the vehicle lower at an acceptable rate?**

Yes GO to E13.

No GO to E14.

E13 CHECK FOR A PLUGGED AIR DRIER

- Disconnect the air drier from the air compressor.
- Connect the air line to the air drier
- Trigger the front and rear suspension vent active commands.
- **Does the vehicle lower at an acceptable rate?**

Yes INSTALL a new air drier. CLEAR the DTCs. REPEAT the self-test.

No GO to E14.

E14 CHECK FOR A BLOCKAGE IN THE AIR LINE TO EACH AIR SPRING

NOTE: If fluid is present when disconnecting an air line, clear the air lines. Check the air compressor air drier for water and check the air springs for oil.

Yes REPAIR the blockage in the affected air line(s). CLEAR the

LTV0500000005462

Fig. 8   Test E, Codes C1725 & C1726: Air Suspension Front/Rear Pneumatic Failure (Part 4 of 5)

- Disconnect the air line at the LF, RF, LR and RR air spring.
- Disconnect the air line at the air drier.
- Connect the vacuum tester at the suspect air spring air line and try to draw a vacuum.
- **Can a vacuum be drawn and held?**

DTCs. REPEAT the self-test.

No GO to E15.

E15 CHECK THE AIR SPRINGS FOR LEAKS

NOTE: If fluid is present when disconnecting an air line, clear the air lines. Check the air compressor air drier for water and check the air springs for oil.

- Trigger the VDM to fill the suspect air spring(s).
- Using a soap and water solution, check the air spring for leaks at the upper mount and sleeve areas.
- **Are any leaks detected?**

Yes INSTALL a new air spring(s). CLEAR the DTCs. REPEAT the self-test. CARRY OUT the Pneumatic Test in this section.

No INSTALL a new VDM. REPEAT the self-test.

LTV0500000005463

Fig. 8   Test E, Codes C1725 & C1726: Air Suspension Front/Rear Pneumatic Failure (Part 5 of 5)

Test Step	Result / Action to Take
F1 VALIDATE THE DTC ERROR • Carry out the VDM On-Demand Self Test. • **Is the same air suspension height sensor DTC set?**	**Yes** GO to F2. **No** If no DTC is retrieved, GO to F5. If a different DTC is retrieved, REFER to the VDM Diagnostic Trouble Code (DTC) Index.

F2 CHECK THE AIR SUSPENSION HEIGHT SENSOR SIGNAL RETURN CIRCUIT FOR AN OPEN

- Key in OFF position.
- Turn the air suspension service switch to the OFF position.
- Disconnect: Air Suspension Service Switch C4169.
- Disconnect: VDM C2131a.
- Disconnect: VDM C2131b.
- Disconnect: Suspect Height Sensor.
- Measure the resistance between the suspect height sensor connector pin 1 harness side, circuit 432 (BK/PK) and VDM C2131a-20 (front sensors) or C2131b-10 (rear sensor), harness side.

Yes GO to F3.

No REPAIR circuit 432 (BK/PK) for an open. CLEAR the DTCs. REPEAT the self-test.

Air Suspension Height Sensor	Air Suspension Height Sensor Connector No.
Left Front (LF)	C1153
Right Front (RF)	C1151
Rear	C4084

- **Is the resistance less than 5 ohms?**

F3 CHECK THE VDM POWER AND RETURN CIRCUITS FOR VOLTAGE

- Key in ON position.
- For DTC C1760, measure the voltage between rear height sensor C4084-1, circuit 432 (BK/PK) harness side and rear height sensor C4084-3, circuit 429 (VT/LG) harness side.
- For DTC C1881 (RF), measure the voltage between RF height sensor C1151-1, circuit 432 (BK/PK) harness side

Yes GO to F8.

No GO to F4.

LTV0500000005464

Fig. 9   Test F, Codes C1760, C1881 & C1889: Air Suspension Height Sensor Signal Circuit Failure (Part 1 of 3)

and RF height sensor C1151-3, circuit 426 (RD/BK) harness side.
- For DTC C1889 (LF), measure the voltage between LF height sensor C1153-1, circuit 432 (BK/PK) harness side and LF height sensor C1153-3, circuit 426 (RD/BK) harness side.
- **Is the voltage approximately 5 volts?**

Test Step	Result / Action to Take
F4 CHECK THE AIR SUSPENSION HEIGHT SENSOR POWER CIRCUIT FOR A SHORT TO VOLTAGE • Key in OFF position. • Turn the air suspension service switch to the OFF position. • Measure the voltage between ground and: 　▪ VDM C2131a-17, circuit 426 (RD/BK), harness side. 　▪ VDM C2131b-8, circuit 429 (VT/LG), harness side. • **Is voltage present?**	**Yes** REPAIR the affected circuit(s) for a short to voltage. CLEAR the DTCs. REPEAT the self-test. **No** GO to F5.
F5 CHECK THE AIR SUSPENSION HEIGHT SENSOR SIGNAL RETURN CIRCUITS FOR A SHORT TO VOLTAGE • Key in OFF position. • Disconnect: VDM C2131a. • Disconnect: VDM C2131b. • Turn the air suspension service switch to the OFF position. • Measure the voltage between ground and: 　▪ VDM C2131a-20, circuit 432 (BK/PK), harness side 　▪ VDM C2131b-10, circuit 432 (BK/PK), harness side • **Is voltage present?**	**Yes** REPAIR circuit 432 (BK/PK) for a short to voltage. CLEAR the DTCs. REPEAT the self-test. **No** GO to F6.
F6 CHECK THE AIR SUSPENSION HEIGHT SENSOR SIGNAL RETURN CIRCUITS FOR AN OPEN • **For front** height sensors(s), measure the voltage between VDM C2131a-20, circuit 432 (BK/PK), harness side and the suspect height sensor pin 1, harness side. **For rear** height sensor, measure the voltage between VDM C2131b-10, circuit 432 (BK/PK), harness side rear height sensor pin 1, harness side.	**Yes** GO to F7. **No** REPAIR circuit 432 (BK/PK) for an open. CLEAR the DTCs. REPEAT the self-test.

Air Suspension Height Sensor	Air Suspension Height Sensor Connector No.
Left Front (LF)	C1153
Right Front (RF)	C1151
Rear	C4084

- **Is the resistance less than 5 ohms?**

LTV0500000005465

Fig. 9   Test F, Codes C1760, C1881 & C1889: Air Suspension Height Sensor Signal Circuit Failure (Part 2 of 3)

Test Step	Result / Action to Take
F7 CHECK THE AIR SUSPENSION HEIGHT SENSOR SIGNAL RETURN CIRCUITS FOR A SHORT TO GROUND • **For front** height sensor(s), measure the resistance between VDM C2131a-20, circuit 432 (BK/PK), harness side and ground. **For rear** height sensor, measure the resistance between VDM C2131b-10, circuit 432 (BK/PK), harness side and ground.	**Yes** GO to F8. **No** REPAIR circuit 432 (BK/PK) for a short to ground. CLEAR the DTCs. REPEAT the self-test.

Air Suspension Height Sensor	Air Suspension Height Sensor Connector No.
Left Front (LF)	C1153
Right Front (RF)	C1151
Rear	C4084

- **Is the resistance greater than 10,000 ohms?**

Test Step	Result / Action to Take
F8 CHECK THE HEIGHT SENSOR OUTPUT • Key in OFF position. • Connect: Air Suspension Service Switch C4169. • Connect: VDM C2131a. • Connect: VDM C2131b. • Connect: Height Sensor(s). • Turn the air suspension service switch to the OFF position. • Key in ON position. • Disconnect the suspect height sensor linkage from the height sensor ball stud. • **For LF or RF height sensor:** using a multimeter set to DC voltage, back-probe the VDM C2131a-17 and C2131a-20. **Rear height sensor:** using a multimeter set to DC voltage, back-probe the VDM C2131b-8 and C2131b-10. • Move the suspect height sensor arm through its full range of motion. • **Does the voltage vary from approximately 0.50 volt to 4.5 volts?**	**Yes** INSTALL a new VDM. REPEAT the self-test. **No** INSTALL a new height sensor(s) as necessary. CLEAR the DTCs. REPEAT the self-test.

LTV0500000005466

Fig. 9   Test F, Codes C1760, C1881 & C1889: Air Suspension Height Sensor Signal Circuit Failure (Part 3 of 3)

Test Step	Result / Action to Take
G1 VALIDATE DTC C1770 • Carry out VDM On-Demand Self Test. • **Is the same air suspension DTC set?**	**Yes** GO to G2. **No** CHECK the VDM and air compressor harness connectors for corroded, damaged or backed out pins, moisture or other damage. CARRY OUT the pneumatic test. REPEAT the self-test. If other DTCs are present, REFER to the VDM Diagnostic Trouble Code (DTC) Index.
G2 CHECK THE VENT SOLENOID CONNECTOR • Key in OFF position. • Turn the air suspension service switch to the OFF position. • Disconnect: Air Compressor Assembly C1179. • Inspect the pins and terminals of the air compressor assembly connector for corroded, damaged or backed out pins, moisture or other damage. • **Is the air compressor assembly C1179 OK?**	**Yes** GO to G3. **No** REPAIR the connector as necessary. CLEAR the DTCs. REPEAT the self-test.
G3 CHECK THE VENT SOLENOID PID • Connect: Air Compressor Assembly C1179. • Turn the air suspension service switch to the ON position. • Key in ON position. • Trigger the VDM vent ON and vent OFF active command. • **Do the letters O, G or B appear next to the ON/OFF text for the air suspension vent solenoid?**	**Yes** If O appeared, GO to G4. If G appeared, GO to G5. If B appeared, GO to G7. **No** CLEAR the DTCs. REPEAT the self-test.
G4 CHECK CIRCUIT 57 (BK) FOR AN OPEN • Key in OFF position. • Disconnect: Air Compressor Assembly C1179. • Measure the resistance	**Yes** **No**

LTV0500000005467

Fig. 10   Test G, Code C1770: Air Suspension Solenoid Output Circuit Failure (Part 1 of 2)

Test Step	Result / Action to Take
between air compressor assembly C1179-2, circuit 57 (BK), harness side and ground. • **Is the resistance less than 5 ohms?**	REPAIR circuit 57 (BK) for an open. CLEAR the DTCs. REPEAT the self-test.
G5 CHECK THE VENT SOLENOID FOR AN OPEN OR SHORT • Measure the resistance between air compressor C1179-2 and C1179-1, component side. • **Is the resistance between 17 and 22 ohms?**	**Yes** GO to G6. **No** INSTALL a new air compressor. CLEAR the DTCs. REPEAT the self-test.
G6 CHECK CIRCUIT 421 (PK) FOR AN OPEN • Disconnect: VDM C2131b. • Measure the resistance between VDM C2131b-5, circuit 421 (PK), harness side and air compressor assembly C1179-2, circuit 421 (PK), harness side. • **Is the resistance less than 5 ohms?**	**Yes** GO to G7. **No** REPAIR circuit 421 (PK) for an open. CLEAR the DTCs. REPEAT the self-test.
G7 CHECK CIRCUIT 421 (PK) FOR A SHORT TO GROUND • Measure the resistance between VDM C2131b-5, circuit 421 (PK), harness side and ground. • **Is the resistance greater than 10,000 ohms?**	**Yes** GO to G8. **No** REPAIR circuit 421 (PK) for a short to ground. CLEAR the DTCs. REPEAT the self-test.
G8 CHECK CIRCUIT 421 (PK) FOR A SHORT TO VOLTAGE • Turn the air suspension service switch to the OFF position. • Key in ON position. • Measure the voltage between VDM C2131b-5, circuit 421 (PK), harness side and ground. • **Is the voltage at zero?**	**Yes** INSTALL a new VDM REPEAT the self-test. **No** REPAIR circuit 421 (PK) for a short to voltage. CLEAR the DTCs. REPEAT the self-test.

LTV0500000005468

Fig. 10   Test G, Code C1770: Air Suspension Solenoid Output Circuit Failure (Part 2 of 2)

Test Step	Result / Action to Take
H1 VALIDATE THE DTC	
• Carry out the VDM On-Demand Self Test. • **Is DTC C1790, C1795, C1873 or C1877 set?**	**Yes** GO to H2 . **No** If no DTCs are retrieved, GO to H10 . If different DTCs are retrieved, REFER to VDM Diagnostic Trouble Code (DTC) Index.
H2 CHECK THE AIR SUSPENSION AIR SPRING SOLENOID CONNECTOR(S)	
• Key in OFF position. • Turn the air suspension service switch to the OFF position. • Disconnect: Suspect Air Spring Solenoid Connector. • Inspect the pins and terminals of the air spring solenoid connector(s) for corroded, damaged or backed out pins, moisture or other damage. • **Is the air spring solenoid connector(s) OK?**	**Yes** GO to H3 . **No** REPAIR the connector(s) as necessary. CLEAR the DTCs. REPEAT the self-test.
H3 CHECK THE AIR SPRING SOLENOID PIDs	
• Connect: Air Spring Solenoid Connector. • Turn the air suspension service switch to the ON position. • Key in ON position. • Monitor the air spring solenoid PID. • **Do the letters O, G or B appear next to the ON/OFF text for the air suspension air spring solenoid?**	**Yes** If O appeared, GO to H4 . If G appeared, GO to H7 . If B appeared, GO to H9 . **No** GO to H10 .
H4 CHECK THE AIR SUSPENSION AIR SPRING SOLENOID COIL(S) FOR AN OPEN	
• Key in OFF position. • Turn the air suspension service switch to the OFF position. • Disconnect: Suspect Air Spring Solenoid Connector. • Measure the resistance between the suspect air spring solenoid(s) pin 1 and pin 2, component side.	**Yes** GO to H5 . **No** INSTALL a new air spring solenoid(s). CLEAR the DTCs. REPEAT the self-test.

LTV0500000005469

Fig. 11   Test H, Codes C1790, C1795, C1873 & C1877: Air Suspension Air Spring Solenoid Output Circuit Failure (Part 1 of 4)

	(RF) 2	414 (OG/RD)
	(LF) 16	415 (LG/OG)

• **Is the resistance less than 5 ohms?**

Test Step	Result / Action to Take
H7 CHECK THE AIR SUSPENSION AIR SPRING SOLENOID COIL FOR A SHORT	
• Key in OFF position. • Turn the air suspension service switch to the OFF position. • Disconnect: Suspect Air Spring Solenoid. • Measure the resistance between the suspect air spring solenoid pin 1 and pin 2, component side.	**Yes** GO to H8 . **No** INSTALL a new air spring solenoid(s). CLEAR the DTCs. REPEAT the self-test.

Air Spring Solenoid	Air Spring Solenoid Connector No.
Left Front (LF)	C1154
Right Front (RF)	C1155
Left Rear (LR)	C4044
Right Rear (RR)	C4045

• **Is the resistance between 15 and 18 ohms (if the solenoid is very hot, the resistance may be as high as 22 ohms)?**

Test Step	Result / Action to Take
H8 CHECK THE OUTPUT CIRCUIT FOR A SHORT TO GROUND	
• Disconnect: VDM C2131b. • Measure the resistance between VDM C2131b pin, harness side and ground.	**Yes** INSTALL a new VDM. REPEAT the self-test. **No** REPAIR the affected circuit(s) for a short to ground. CLEAR the DTCs. REPEAT the self-test.

VDM C2131b Pin	Air Spring Solenoid Output Circuit
(LR) 13	1114 (BN/PK)
(RR) 14	1115 (TN/WH)
(RF) 2	414 (OG/RD)
(LF) 16	415 (LG/OG)

LTV0500000005471

Fig. 11   Test H, Codes C1790, C1795, C1873 & C1877: Air Suspension Air Spring Solenoid Output Circuit Failure (Part 3 of 4)

Air Spring Solenoid	Air Spring Solenoid Connector No.
Left Front (LF)	C1154
Right Front (RF)	C1155
Left Rear (LR)	C4044
Right Rear (RR)	C4045

• **Is the resistance between 15 and 18 ohms (if the solenoid is very hot, the resistance may be as high as 22 ohms)?**

Test Step	Result / Action to Take
H5 CHECK GROUND CIRCUIT 57 (BK) FOR AN OPEN	
• Measure the resistance between the suspect air spring solenoid pin 1, circuit 57 (BK), harness side and ground.	**Yes** GO to H6 . **No** REPAIR circuit 57 (BK) for an open. CLEAR the DTCs. REPEAT the self-test.

Air Spring Solenoid	Air Spring Solenoid Connector No.
Left Front (LF)	C1154
Right Front (RF)	C1155
Left Rear (LR)	C4044
Right Rear (RR)	C4045

• **Is the resistance less than 5 ohms?**

Test Step	Result / Action to Take
H6 CHECK THE AIR SPRING SOLENOID OUTPUT CIRCUIT(S) FOR AN OPEN	
• Disconnect: VDM C2131b. • Measure the resistance between the VDM C2131b pin, harness side and the suspect air suspension air spring solenoid pin 2, harness side as follows:	**Yes** INSTALL a new VDM. REPEAT the self-test. **No** REPAIR the affected circuit(s) for an open. CLEAR the DTCs. REPEAT the self-test.

VDM C2131b Pin	Air Spring Solenoid Output Circuit
(LR) 13	1114 (BN/PK)
(RR) 14	1115 (TN/WH)

LTV0500000005470

Fig. 11   Test H, Codes C1790, C1795, C1873 & C1877: Air Suspension Air Spring Solenoid Output Circuit Failure (Part 2 of 4)

• **Is the resistance greater than 10,000 ohms?**

Test Step	Result / Action to Take
H9 CHECK THE OUTPUT CIRCUIT FOR A SHORT TO VOLTAGE	
• Key in OFF position. • Disconnect: VDM C2131b. • Measure the voltage between the following VDM C2131b pin, harness side and ground.	**Yes** REPAIR the affected circuit(s) for a short to voltage. CLEAR the DTCs. REPEAT the self-test. **No** INSTALL a new VDM. REPEAT the self-test.

VDM C2131b Pin	Air Spring Solenoid Output Circuit
(LR) 13	1114 (BN/PK)
(RR) 14	1115 (TN/WH)
(RF) 2	414 (OG/RD)
(LF) 16	415 (LG/OG)

• **Is voltage present?**

Test Step	Result / Action to Take
H10 CHECK THE AIR SUSPENSION AIR SPRING SOLENOID CONNECTOR FOR DAMAGE	
• Key in OFF position. • Turn the air suspension service switch to the OFF position. • Disconnect: Suspect Air Suspension Air Spring Solenoid. • Inspect the pins and terminals of the air suspension air spring solenoid for corroded, damaged or backed out pins, moisture or other damage; inspect the wiring near the connector for damage. • **Is the air suspension air spring solenoid connector OK?**	**Yes** RECONNECT the air suspension air spring solenoid connector. TURN the air suspension service switch to the ON position. REPEAT the self-test. If no DTCs are retrieved, the system is OK. If a DTC is retrieved, REFER to VDM Diagnostic Trouble Code (DTC) Index. **No** REPAIR the connector(s) as necessary. CLEAR the DTCs. REPEAT the self-test.

LTV0500000005472

Fig. 11   Test H, Codes C1790, C1795, C1873 & C1877: Air Suspension Air Spring Solenoid Output Circuit Failure (Part 4 of 4)

Test Step	Result / Action to Take
I1 VALIDATE DTC C1830	
• Carry out the VDM On-Demand Self Test. • **Is the same air suspension DTC set?**	**Yes** GO to I2. **No** CHECK the VDM and air compressor harness connectors for corroded, damaged or backed out pins, moisture or other damage. CARRY OUT the pneumatic test. REPEAT the self-test. If other DTCs are present, REFER to Diagnostic Trouble Code (DTC) Index.
I2 CHECK THE AIR COMPRESSOR RELAY AND CONNECTOR	
• Key in OFF position. • Turn the air suspension service switch to the OFF position. • Disconnect: Air Compressor Relay C1300. • Inspect the pins and terminals of the air compressor relay for corroded, damaged or backed out pins, moisture or other damage. Carry out the Air Compressor Relay Component test. Refer to Wiring. • **Are the relay and connector OK?**	**Yes** GO to I3. **No** REPAIR the connector or INSTALL a new air compressor relay. CLEAR the DTCs. REPEAT the self-test.
I3 CHECK THE AIR COMPRESSOR PID	
• Connect: Air Compressor Relay C1300. • Turn the air suspension service	If O appeared, GO to I4. If G appeared, GO to I7.

LTV0500000005473

Fig. 12   Test I, Code C1830: Air Suspension Compressor Relay Circuit Failure (Part 1 of 3)

10,000 ohms?	
I8 CHECK CIRCUIT 420 (DB/YE) FOR A SHORT TO VOLTAGE	
• Key in OFF position. • Turn the air suspension service switch to the OFF position. • Disconnect: Air Compressor Relay C1300. • Disconnect: VDM C2131a. • Key in ON position. • Measure the resistance between VDM C2131a-18, circuit 420 (DB/YE), harness side and ground. • **Is the voltage greater than 0 volts?**	**Yes** REPAIR circuit 420 (DB/YE) for a short to voltage. CLEAR the DTCs. REPEAT the self-test. **No** INSTALL a new VDM. REPEAT the self-test.

LTV0500000005475

Fig. 12   Test I, Code C1830: Air Suspension Compressor Relay Circuit Failure (Part 3 of 3)

switch to the ON position. • Key in ON position. • Trigger the VDM compressor ON and OFF using active command. • **Do the letters O, G or B appear next to the ON/OFF text for the air compressor?**	If B appeared, GO to I8. **No** CHECK the VDM and air compressor harness connectors for corroded, damaged or backed out pins, moisture, or other damage. CARRY OUT the pneumatic test. REPEAT the self-test. If other DTCs are present, REFER to VDM Diagnostic Trouble Code (DTC) Index.
I4 CHECK THE AIR SUSPENSION RELAY COIL GROUND FOR AN OPEN	
• Key in OFF position. • Turn the air suspension service switch to the OFF position. • Disconnect: Air Compressor Relay C1300. • Measure the resistance between air compressor relay C1300-2, circuit 57 (BK), harness side and ground. • **Is the resistance 5 ohms or less?**	**Yes** GO to I5. **No** REPAIR circuit 57 (BK) for an open. CLEAR the DTCs. REPEAT the self-test.
I5 CHECK THE AIR COMPRESSOR RELAY FOR AN OPEN	
• Measure the resistance between air compressor relay terminals 1 and 2, component side. • **Is the resistance between 49 and 74 ohms?**	**Yes** GO to I6. **No** INSTALL a new relay. CLEAR the DTCs. REPEAT the self-test.
I6 CHECK CIRCUIT 420 (DB/YE) FOR AN OPEN	
• Disconnect: VDM C2131a. • Measure the resistance between VDM C2131a-18, circuit 420 (DB/YE), harness side and air compressor relay C1300-2, circuit 420 (DB/YE), harness side. • **Is the resistance less than 5 ohms?**	**Yes** GO to I7. **No** REPAIR circuit 420 (DB/YE) for an open. CLEAR the DTCs. REPEAT the self-test.
I7 CHECK CIRCUIT 420 (DB/YE) FOR A SHORT TO GROUND	
• Disconnect: VDM C2131a. • Measure the resistance between VDM C2131a-18, circuit 420 (DB/YE), harness side and ground. • **Is the resistance greater than**	**Yes** GO to I8. **No** REPAIR circuit 420 (DB/YE) for an open. CLEAR the DTCs. REPEAT the self-test.

LTV0500000005474

Fig. 12   Test I, Code C1830: Air Suspension Compressor Relay Circuit Failure (Part 2 of 3)

Test Step	Result / Action to Take
J1 CHECK THE POSITION OF THE AIR SUSPENSION SERVICE SWITCH	
• Verify that the air suspension service switch is in the ON position. • **Is the air suspension service switch ON?**	**Yes** GO to J2. **No** TURN the air suspension service switch to the ON position. CLEAR the DTCs. REPEAT the self-test. If DTC C1840 is retrieved, GO to J2.
J2 CHECK THE AIR SUSPENSION SERVICE SWITCH	
• Turn the air suspension service switch to the OFF position. • Disconnect: Air Suspension Service Switch C4169. • Turn the air suspension service switch to the ON position and measure the resistance between air suspension service switch C4169-1 and C4169-3 component side. • **Is the resistance less than 5 ohms?**	**Yes** GO to J3. **No** INSTALL a new air suspension service switch. CLEAR the DTCs. REPEAT the self-test.
J3 CHECK CIRCUIT 418 (DG/YE) FOR AN OPEN	
• Key in OFF position. • Disconnect: VDM C2131b. • Measure the resistance between air suspension service switch C4169-3, circuit 418 (DG/YE), harness side and VDM C2131b-25, circuit 418 (DG/YE) harness side. • **Is the resistance less than 5 ohms?**	**Yes** GO to J4. **No** REPAIR circuit 418 (DG/YE) for an open. CLEAR the DTCs. REPEAT the self-test.

LTV0500000005476

Fig. 13   Test J, Code C1840: Air Suspension Service Switch Circuit Failure (Part 1 of 2)

J4 CHECK CIRCUIT 418 (DG/YE) FOR A SHORT TO GROUND	
• Measure the resistance between air suspension service switch C4169-3, circuit 418 (DG/YE), harness side and ground. • **Is the resistance greater than 10,000 ohms?**	**Yes** GO to J5 . **No** REPAIR circuit 418 (DG/YE) for a short to ground. CLEAR the DTCs. REPEAT the self-test.
J5 CHECK CIRCUIT 429 (VT/LG) FOR VOLTAGE	
• Connect: VDM C2131b. • Key in ON position. • Measure the voltage between air suspension service switch C4169-1, circuit 429 (VT/LG), harness side and ground. • **Is the voltage 5 volts?**	**Yes** INSTALL a new VDM. REPEAT the self-test. **No** REPAIR circuit 429 (VT/LG) for a short to voltage. CLEAR the DTC. REPEAT the self-test.

LTV0500000005477

Fig. 13   Test J, Code C1840: Air Suspension Service Switch Circuit Failure (Part 2 of 2)

Test Step	Result / Action to Take
L1 CHECK FOR DTCs	
• Connect the diagnostic tool. • Key in ON position. • Carry out the VDM On-Demand Self Test. • **Is a DTC retrieved?**	**Yes** If DTCs are retrieved, REFER to the Diagnostic Trouble Code (DTC) Index. **No** GO to L2 .
L2 CHECK THE VDM FOR IGNITION SWITCH ON INPUT	
• Monitor VDM ignition switch position PID. • **Does the PID indicate that the ignition switch is in the ON position?**	**Yes** GO to L3 . **No** VERIFY CJB fuse 27 (5A) is OK. If OK, REPAIR circuit 1003 (GY/YE) for an open. TEST the system for normal operation.
L3 CHECK THE VDM FOR IGNITION SWITCH OFF INPUT	
NOTE: The ignition switch must initially be in the ON position for this test step to be valid. • Key in OFF position. • **Does the PID indicate that the ignition switch is in the ON position?**	**Yes** GO to L4 . **No** VERIFY CJB fuse 27 (5A) is OK. If OK, REPAIR circuit 1003 (GY/YE) for an open. TEST the system for normal operation.
L4 CHECK THE VDM FOR DOOR AJAR INPUT	
• Key in ON position. • Monitor VDM door position status PID. • Close all doors, liftgate, liftgate glass and power running boards. • While observing the diagnostic tool, open and close one door. • **Does the door status PID change between CLOSED and AJAR states?**	**Yes** GO to L5 . **No** CHECK for a CAN network fault.

LTV0500000005479

Fig. 15   Test L: Air Suspension System Inoperative Without DTC & Vehicle At Rest (Part 1 of 2)

Test Step	Result / Action to Take
K1 CHECK FOR MODULE ACTIVITY	
NOTE: The VDM is powered for 40 minutes after the ignition is turned OFF. During this time, the air suspension system is still active and may activate system components. • Key in OFF position. • Check to see if the air compressor still cycles 50 minutes after the ignition is turned OFF. • **Does the air compressor still cycle after the module goes to sleep?**	**Yes** GO to K2 . **No** The system is OK. INFORM the owner of system operations.
K2 CHECK THE VDM	
• Turn the air suspension service switch to the OFF position. • Disconnect: VDM C2131a. • Disconnect: VDM C2131b. • **Does the air compressor still cycle?**	**Yes** GO to K3 . **No** INSTALL a new VDM. REPEAT the self-test.
K3 CHECK THE AIR COMPRESSOR RELAY	
• Disconnect: Air Compressor Relay C1300. • **Does the air compressor still cycle?**	**Yes** REPAIR circuit 538 (GY/RD) for a short to voltage. TEST the system for normal operation. **No** GO to K4 .
K4 CHECK CIRCUIT 420 (DB/YE) FOR A SHORT TO VOLTAGE	
• Measure the voltage between the air compressor relay C1300-4, circuit 420 (DB/YE), harness side and ground. • **Is battery voltage present (approximately)?**	**Yes** REPAIR circuit 420 (DB/YE) for a short to voltage. TEST the system for normal operation. **No** INSTALL a new air suspension relay. TEST the system for normal operation.

LTV0500000005478

Fig. 14   Test K: Air Compressor Continuously Cycles w/Ignition Switch In Off Position & No DTC Is Set

L5 CHECK THE VDM FOR 4x4 STATE INPUT	
• Monitor VDM PID 4WDLOW. • **NOTE:** The 4x4 light on the instrument panel will turn off when the system is in 2H mode. • Place the mode switch into 2H mode. • Place the mode switch into 4L mode. • Select NEUTRAL. • Press the brake pedal. • **Did PID 4WDLOW show OFF in 2H and ON in 4L, and did the cluster indicators agree with PID 4WDLOW?**	**Yes** GO to L6 . **No** CHECK for a CAN network fault.
L6 CHECK THE VDM FOR VSS INPUT	
• Monitor VDM VSS PID. • Test drive the vehicle at different speeds. • **Does VSS PID match the speedometer within 8 km/h (5 mph)?**	**Yes** GO to L7 . **No** REPAIR circuit 679 (GY/BK) for an open. TEST the system for normal operation.
L7 CHECK PARK/NEUTRAL INPUT TO THE VDM	
• Monitor the VDM Park/Neutral switch PID. • Select DRIVE. • Select PARK. • **Does Park/Neutral switch PID correctly indicate that the vehicle is in PARK?**	**Yes** RETRIEVE all DTCs and REFER to the VDM Diagnostic Trouble Code (DTC) Index and Symptom Chart for further diagnostics. **No** CHECK for a CAN network fault.

LTV0500000005480

Fig. 15   Test L: Air Suspension System Inoperative Without DTC & Vehicle At Rest (Part 2 of 2)

Test Step	Result / Action to Take
M1 CHECK THE AIR SUSPENSION SWITCH • Key in OFF position. • Turn the air suspension service switch to the OFF position. • Disconnect: Air Suspension Service Switch C4196. • Measure the resistance between air suspension service switch C4169-1 and C4169-3 component side. • **Is the resistance greater than 10,000 ohms?**	**Yes** GO to <u>M2</u>. **No** INSTALL a new air suspension service switch. TEST the system for normal operation.
M2 CHECK CIRCUIT 418 (DG/YE) FOR VOLTAGE • Disconnect: Air Suspension Service Switch C4196. • Disconnect: VDM C2131b. • Key in ON position. • Measure the voltage between air suspension service switch C4196-2, circuit 418 (DG/YE), harness side and ground. • **Is the voltage approximately 0 volt?**	**Yes** INSTALL a new VDM. REPEAT the self-test. **No** REPAIR circuit 418 (DG/YE) for a short to voltage. TEST the system for normal operation.

LTV0500000005481

Fig. 16   Test M: Air Suspension System Operates w/Service Switch In Off Position

N4 CHECK THE AIR COMPRESSOR FOR NOISE ⚠ **CAUTION: Do not run the air compressor for more than 3 minutes. The air compressor can overheat and stop operating due to an internal temperature sensitive thermal breaker.** **The VDM will limit run time to protect the air compressor. When DTC C1964 is present, the compressor will not operate for approximately 10 minutes.** • Remove the air compressor assembly, but leave it connected electrically. • Connect the diagnostic tool. • Key in ON position. • Trigger the VDM compressor on active command. • **Is the air compressor noisy?**	**Yes** INSTALL a new air compressor bracket. TEST the system for normal operation. **No** RECHECK the mountings and bracket for damage. If damaged, INSTALL a new air compressor assembly. TEST the system for normal operation.

LTV0500000005483

Fig. 17   Test N: Excessive Air Compressor Noise (Part 2 of 2)

Test Step	Result / Action to Take
N1 CHECK FOR AIR COMPRESSOR AND/OR AIR COMPRESSOR WIRING CONTACTING OTHER COMPONENTS • Check the air compressor wiring to see if it is contacting other components inside the engine compartment at any place other than the mounting points. • Check for anything contacting the air compressor (other wire harnesses, air lines, hoses, loose fasteners, stones or other foreign objects). • **Is the air compressor wiring contacting non-mounting components or is anything contacting the compressor assembly other than the mounts?**	**Yes** ADJUST air compressor wiring harness so that it does not contact non-mounting components or FASTEN/REMOVE objects so they no longer contact the air compressor assembly. TEST the system for normal operation. **No** GO to <u>N2</u>.
N2 CHECK FOR A BENT AIR COMPRESSOR BRACKET • Check the air compressor bracket for any damage/bends that may contact other components within the engine compartment. • **Is the air compressor bracket making contact with other components or is the bracket loading the mounts?**	**Yes** REPAIR the air compressor and bracket assembly or other components as necessary. TEST the system for normal operation. **No** GO to <u>N3</u>.
N3 CHECK THE AIR COMPRESSOR MOUNTS FOR DAMAGE • Check the air compressor mounts for signs of cracks or breaking away of insulation material. • **Is there any damage present in the mounts?**	**Yes** INSTALL a new air compressor bracket. TEST the system for normal operation. **No** GO to <u>N4</u>.

LTV0500000005482

Fig. 17   Test N: Excessive Air Compressor Noise (Part 1 of 2)

Test Step	Result / Action to Take
O1 CHECK THE AIR COMPRESSOR RELAY CONNECTOR • Disconnect: Air Compressor Relay C1300. • Inspect the pins of the air compressor relay C1300 for corroded, damaged or backed out pins, moisture or other damage. • **Is the air compressor relay C1300 OK?**	**Yes** GO to <u>O2</u>. **No** REPAIR as necessary. TEST the system for normal operation.
O2 CHECK CIRCUIT 1053 (LB/PK) FOR VOLTAGE • Measure the voltage between air compressor relay C1300-3, circuit 1053 (LB/PK), harness side and ground. • **Is the voltage greater than 10 volts?**	**Yes** GO to <u>O3</u>. **No** Verify CJB fuse 111 (50A) is OK. If OK, REPAIR circuit 1053 (LB/PK) for an open. TEST the system for normal operation.
O3 CHECK CIRCUIT 538 (GY/RD) FOR AN OPEN • Disconnect: Air Compressor Assembly C1179. • Measure the resistance between air compressor relay C1300-5, circuit 538 (GY/RD), harness side and air compressor assembly C1179-3, circuit 538 (GY/RD), harness side. • **Is the resistance less than 5 ohms?**	**Yes** GO to <u>O4</u>. **No** REPAIR circuit 538 (GY/RD) for an open. TEST the system for normal operation.
O4 CHECK CIRCUIT 577 (LG/RD) FOR AN OPEN • Measure the resistance between air compressor assembly C1179-4, circuit 577 (LG/RD), harness side and ground. • **Is the resistance less than 5 ohms?**	**Yes** GO to <u>O5</u>. **No** REPAIR circuit 577 (LG/RD) for an open. TEST the system for normal operation.

LTV0500000005484

Fig. 18   Test O: Air Compressor Is Inoperative (Part 1 of 3)

O5 CHECK THE AIR COMPRESSOR RELAY POWER	
⚠ CAUTION: Do not run the air compressor for more than 3 minutes. The air compressor can overheat and stop operating due to an internal temperature sensitive thermal breaker. The VDM will limit run time to protect the air compressor. • Connect: Air Compressor Assembly C1179. • Connect the diagnostic tool. • Key in ON position. • Trigger the VDM compressor on active command. • Measure the voltage between air compressor relay C1300-1, circuit 420 (DB/YE), harness side and ground. • **Is the voltage greater than 5 volts?**	**Yes** GO to O6. **No** REPAIR circuit 420 (DB/YE) for an open. TEST the system for normal operation.

O6 CHECK THE AIR COMPRESSOR RELAY CIRCUIT 57 (BK) FOR AN OPEN	
• Key in OFF position. • Measure the resistance between air compressor relay C1300-2, circuit 57 (BK), harness side and ground. • **Is the resistance less than 5 ohms?**	**Yes** GO to O7. **No** REPAIR circuit 57 (BK) for an open. TEST the system for normal operation.

O7 CHECK THE AIR COMPRESSOR RELAY	
• Key in OFF position. • Connect a fused (50A) jumper wire (10 gauge) between air compressor relay C1300-3, circuit 1053 (LB/PK), harness side and air compressor relay C1300-5, circuit 538 (GY/RD), harness side. • **Does the air compressor run?**	**Yes** DISCONNECT the jumper wire. INSTALL a new air compressor relay. TEST the system for normal operation. **No** DISCONNECT the jumper wire. GO to O8.

O8 CHECK THE AIR COMPRESSOR STATUS	
• Connect: Air Compressor Relay C1300. • Key in ON position. • Carry out the On-Demand Self Test. • **Is DTC C1964 present?**	**Yes** The air suspension compressor run time has been exceeded. DISCONNECT the VDM harness connectors for 10 minutes. **No** REPEAT the self-test. If DTC C1964 is present, INSTALL a new VDM. If no DTC is present, GO to O9.

LTV0500000005485

Fig. 18   Test O: Air Compressor Is Inoperative (Part 2 of 3)

O9 CHECK THE AIR COMPRESSOR AFTER COOL DOWN PERIOD	
• Key in OFF position. • Turn the air suspension service switch to the OFF position. Allow the vehicle to sit for 60 minutes to give the air compressor assembly time to cool off. • Turn the air suspension service switch to the ON position. • Key in ON position. • Trigger the VDM vent on active command. • Trigger the VDM compressor on active command. • **Does the air compressor assembly run?**	**Yes** GO to O10. **No** INSTALL a new air compressor. TEST the system for normal operation.

O10 CHECK THE AIR COMPRESSOR THERMAL BREAKER	
• Trigger the VDM LR and RR air spring solenoid valve open active commands. • Run the air compressor assembly for 60 seconds. • **Did the air compressor assembly run for 60 seconds?**	**Yes** The thermal breaker was overheated. RETEST to validate the system is OK. **No** INSTALL a new air compressor assembly. TEST the system for normal operation.

LTV0500000005486

Fig. 18   Test O: Air Compressor Is Inoperative (Part 3 of 3)

4. Disconnect air valve electrical connector.
5. Compress orange quick connect lock ring, then pull downward on air supply line to disconnect it from air valve.
6. Remove lower shock mounting nut, then the shock absorber assembly.
7. Remove and discard shock rod nut. Index mark air spring and shock absorber for reference during installation.
8. Depress retainer tabs, **Fig. 20,** then remove air spring assembly.
9. Remove shock rod O-ring seal, washer and jounce bumper.
10. Remove and discard two air spring lower O-ring seals.
11. Remove retaining pins, then the upper mount.
12. Remove and discard two air spring upper O-ring seals.
13. Reverse procedure to install, noting the following:
    a. During installation, use assembly kit No. 5L74-5B302-AA. , or equivalent.
    b. Use a suitable press to install upper mount retaining pins. Do not use a hammer or damage may occur.
    c. Apply a thin coat of grease to new O-ring seals.
    d. **Torque** shock rod nut to 22 ft. lbs.
    e. **Torque** lower shock nut to 350 ft. lbs.
    f. **Torque** upper shock nuts to 30 ft. lbs.

COMPONENT REPLACEMENT

Front Air Shock

Do not remove an air shock under any circumstances when there is pressure in air shock. Do not remove any components supporting an air shock without either exhausting the air or providing support for the air shock to prevent vehicle damage or injury.

1. Using suitably programed scan tool, vent appropriate air spring.
2. Turn air suspension service switch to Off position, then raise and support vehicle.
3. Remove and discard three upper shock mounting nuts, **Fig. 19.**
4. Disconnect air valve electrical connector.
5. Compress orange quick connect lock ring, then pull downward on air supply line to disconnect it from air valve.
6. Remove lower shock mounting nut, then the shock absorber assembly.
7. Remove and discard shock rod nut. Index mark air spring and shock absorber for reference during installation.
8. Depress retainer tabs, **Fig. 20,** then remove air spring assembly.

9. Remove shock rod O-ring seal, washer and jounce bumper.
10. Remove and discard two air spring lower O-ring seals.
11. Remove retaining pins, then the upper mount.
12. Remove and discard two air spring upper O-ring seals.
13. Reverse procedure to install, noting the following:
    a. During installation, use assembly kit No. 5B302, or equivalent.
    b. Use a suitable press to install upper mount retaining pins. Do not use a hammer or damage may occur.
    c. Apply a thin coat of grease to new O-ring seals.
    d. **Torque** shock rod nut to 22 ft. lbs.
    e. **Torque** lower shock nut to 295 ft. lbs.
    f. **Torque** upper shock nuts to 30 ft. lbs.

Rear Air Shock

1. Using suitably programed scan tool, vent appropriate air spring.
2. Turn air suspension service switch to Off position, then raise and support vehicle.
3. Remove and discard three upper shock mounting nuts, **Fig. 21.**

Air Spring Solenoid Valve

1. Using suitably programed scan tool, vent appropriate air spring.
2. Turn air suspension service switch to Off position, then raise and support vehicle.
3. Remove any dirt or other debris from air spring assembly prior to removing solenoid valve from air spring.
4. Disconnect solenoid valve electrical connector.

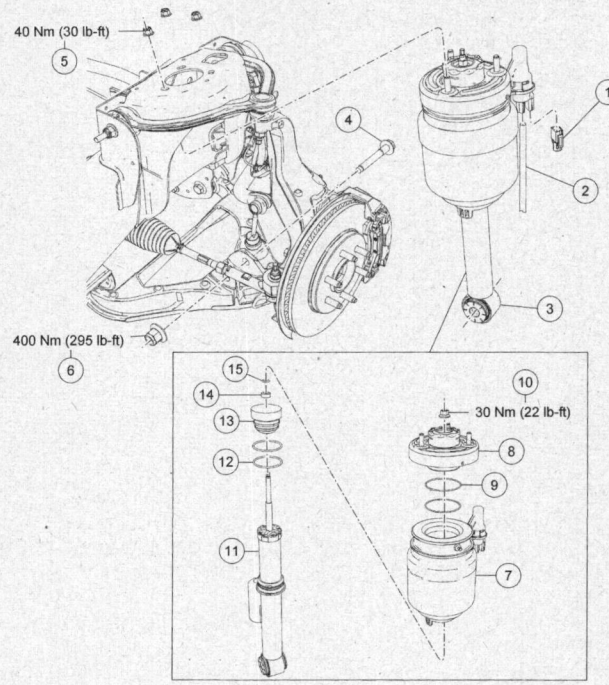

Item	Description
1	Air valve electrical connector
2	Air line
3	Air shock and spring assembly
4	Shock lower bolt
5	Shock upper nut (3 required)
6	Shock lower nut
7	Air spring assembly
8	Upper mount

Item	Description
9	Air spring upper O-ring seal (2 required)
10	Shock rod nut
11	Shock absorber
12	Air spring lower O-ring seal (2 required)
13	Jounce bumper
14	Washer
15	Shock rod O-ring seal

LTV0500000005487

Fig. 19   Front air shock replacement

5. Compress orange quick connect lock ring, then pull downward on air supply line to disconnect it from solenoid valve.
6. Remove solenoid valve metal retaining clip. Air spring solenoid valve has a two stage release, remove solenoid valve as follows:
   a. When removing a non-functional solenoid and air spring is inflated, carefully rotate solenoid counterclockwise until it reaches first stage to release air from air spring.
   b. Turn solenoid to second stage, then remove the solenoid.
7. Reverse procedure to install.
8. Reverse procedure to install.

Height Sensors

FRONT

1. Raise and support vehicle.
2. Disconnect sensor arm from vehicle, **Fig. 22.**
3. Remove two height sensor mounting nuts.
4. Disconnect sensor electrical connector.
5. Remove height sensor.
6. Reverse procedure to install, noting the following:

a. Lefthand and righthand height sensors cannot be used on opposite sides of vehicle.
b. **Torque** mounting nuts to 22 ft. lbs.
c. Calibrate sensor ride height as outlined under "Adjustments."

REAR

1. Raise and support vehicle.
2. Disconnect sensor arm from vehicle, **Fig. 23.**
3. Remove height sensor mounting bolts and nuts.
4. Disconnect sensor electrical connector.
5. Remove height sensor.
6. Reverse procedure to install, noting the following:
   a. Lefthand and righthand height sensors cannot be used on opposite sides of vehicle.
   b. **Torque** mounting nuts to 13 ft. lbs.
   c. Calibrate sensor ride height as outlined under "Adjustments."

Control Module

Electronic modules are sensitive to static electrical charges. Damage may occur if exposed to charges.
1. Control module is mounted to lower lefthand side of dash above parking

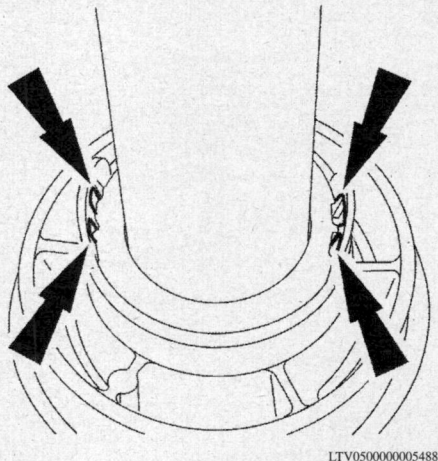

LTV0500000005488

Fig. 20   Air spring retaining tab locations

brake control.
2. Disconnect control module electrical connectors.
3. Pull back dash padding to expose two module bracket nuts.
4. Remove control module mounting nuts, then the control module.
5. Reverse procedure to install. Adjust ride height as described under "Adjustments."

Air Compressor

1. Turn air suspension switch to Off position. then remove windshield washer reservoir.
2. Disconnect air lines from air compressor by depressing orange plastic retaining rings and hold firmly while pulling out on air lines.
3. Disconnect air compressor electrical connector, then remove air compressor bracket bolts and air compressor and dryer assembly.
4. Reverse procedure to install. **Torque** compressor bracket bolts to 80 inch lbs.

Dryer

1. Remove air compressor as described in this section.
2. Remove air compressor dryer retaining screw.
3. Rotate dryer 90° to unlock.
4. Remove dryer assembly.
5. Reverse procedure to install, noting the following:
   a. Inspect O-ring for damage.
   b. Lubricant solenoid seal area using silicone brake caliper grease and suitable dielectric compound.
   c. Ensure white air line is fully inserted into fitting.
   d. Adjust ride height as described under "Adjustments."
   e. **Torque** dryer retaining screw to 27 inch lbs.

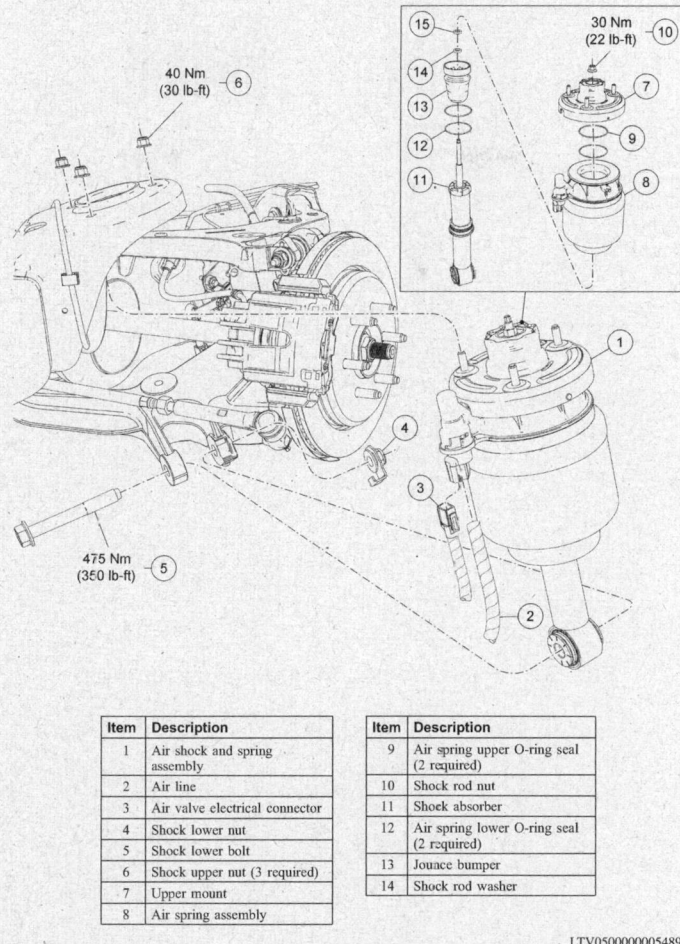

Item	Description
1	Air shock and spring assembly
2	Air line
3	Air valve electrical connector
4	Shock lower nut
5	Shock lower bolt
6	Shock upper nut (3 required)
7	Upper mount
8	Air spring assembly

Item	Description
9	Air spring upper O-ring seal (2 required)
10	Shock rod nut
11	Shock absorber
12	Air spring lower O-ring seal (2 required)
13	Jounce bumper
14	Shock rod washer

LTV0500000005489

Fig. 21   Rear air shock replacement (Part 1 of 2)

Item	Description
1	Air shock and spring assembly
2	Air line
3	Air valve electrical connector
4	Shock lower nut
5	Shock lower bolt
6	Shock upper nut (3 required)
7	Upper mount
8	Air spring assembly
9	Air spring upper O-ring seal (2 required)
10	Shock rod nut
11	Shock absorber
12	Air spring lower O-ring seal (2 required)
13	Jounce bumper
14	Shock rod washer
15	Shock rod O-ring seal

LTV0500000005490

Fig. 21   Rear air shock replacement (Part 2 of 2)

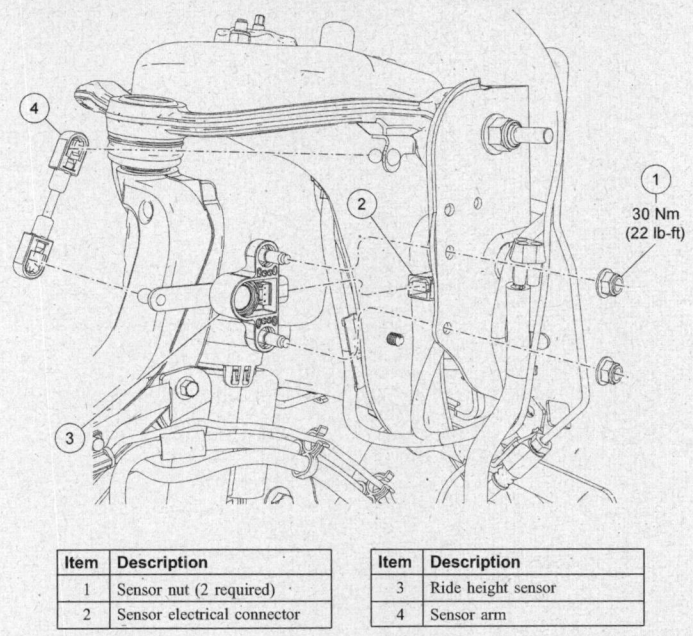

Item	Description	Item	Description
1	Sensor nut (2 required)	3	Ride height sensor
2	Sensor electrical connector	4	Sensor arm

LTV0500000005491

Fig. 22 Front height sensor replacement

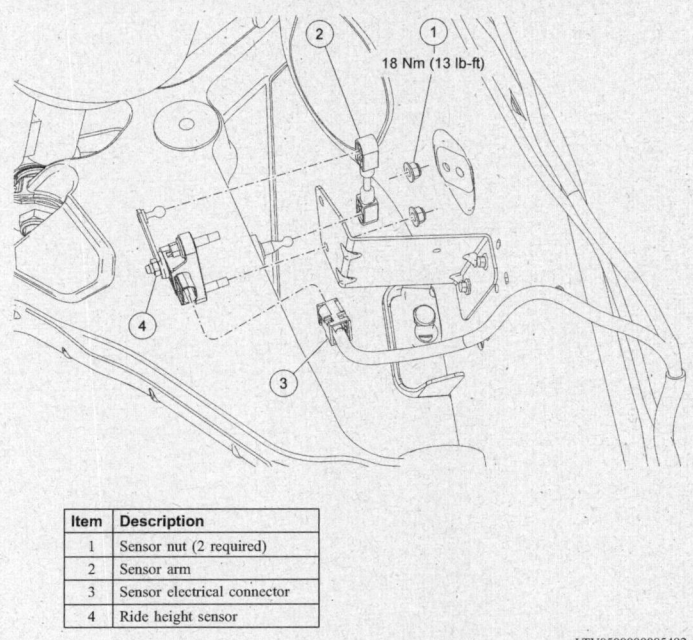

Item	Description
1	Sensor nut (2 required)
2	Sensor arm
3	Sensor electrical connector
4	Ride height sensor

LTV0500000005492

Fig. 23 Rear height sensor replacement

TIRE PRESSURE MONITORING SYSTEM

INDEX

	Page No.
Component Service	7-30
Pressure Monitor Sensor Programming	7-30
Aviator	7-30
Expedition & Navigator	7-30
Explorer, Freestar, Monterey & Mountaineer	7-31
Pressure Monitor Sensor Replacement	7-31
Description	7-1
Diagnosis & Testing	7-1
Accessing Diagnostic Trouble Codes	7-1

	Page No.
Clearing Diagnostic Trouble Codes	7-2
Diagnostic Tests	7-1
Aviator	7-1
Expedition & Navigator	7-1
Explorer, Freestar, Monterey & Mountaineer	7-1
Intermittent & Poor Connections	7-2
Intermittents	7-2
Poor Connections	7-2
Symptom Tests	7-1
Aviator	7-1

	Page No.
Expedition & Navigator	7-2
Explorer & Mountaineer.......	7-2
Freestar & Monterey	7-2
Wiring Diagrams	7-1
Aviator......................	7-1
Expedition & Navigator	7-1
Explorer & Mountaineer	7-1
Freestar & Monterey	7-1
Diagnostic Chart Index	7-10
Precautions...................	7-1
Air Bag Systems	7-1
Battery Ground Cable	7-1
Tightening Specifications	7-32

PRECAUTIONS

Air Bag Systems

Refer to "Air Bag System Precautions" in the front of this manual for system disarming and arming procedures.

Battery Ground Cable

Prior to service, disconnect battery ground cable and isolate as required.

DESCRIPTION

The optional tire pressure monitoring system (TPMS) has the ability to monitor the air pressure of all five tires. The tire-mounted pressure sensors transmit signals to the TPMS module by using the valve stem as an antenna. These transmissions are sent approximately every 30 seconds when the vehicle speed exceeds 32 km/h (20 mph). The TPMS module compares each tire pressure sensor transmission against two pressure limits — low and high. If the TPMS module determines that the tire pressure has exceeded the low or high limit, the TPMS module communicates on the SCP network to the vehicle message center, which then displays a warning message.

DIAGNOSIS & TESTING

Accessing Diagnostic Trouble Codes

Connect a suitably programmed scan tool to Data Link Connector (DLC) and follow manufacturer's instructions.

Wiring Diagrams

AVIATOR

Refer to **Fig. 1** for wiring diagram.

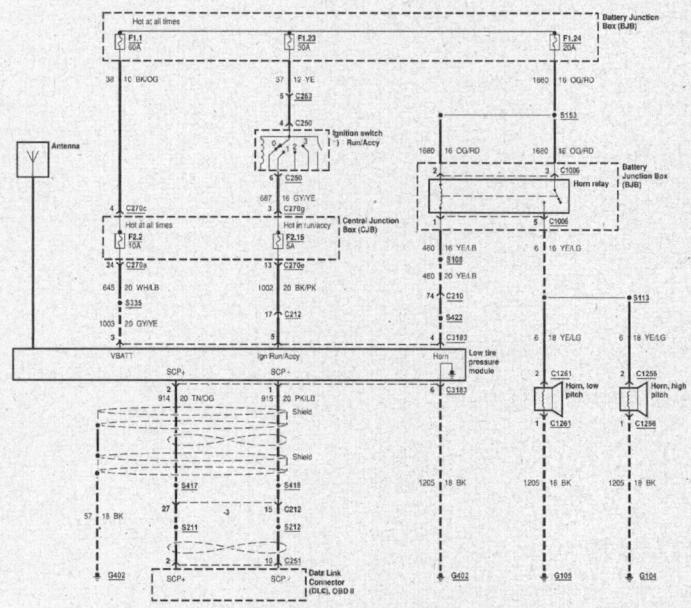

LTV0500000004343

Fig. 1 Wiring diagram. Aviator

EXPEDITION & NAVIGATOR

Refer to **Fig. 2** for wiring diagram.

EXPLORER & MOUNTAINEER

Refer to **Fig. 3** for wiring diagram.

FREESTAR & MONTEREY

Refer to **Fig. 4** for wiring diagram.

Diagnostic Tests

AVIATOR

Refer to **Figs. 5 through 7** for diagnostic test procedures.

EXPEDITION & NAVIGATOR

Refer to **Figs. 8 through 29** for diagnostic test procedures.

EXPLORER, FREESTAR, MONTEREY & MOUNTAINEER

Refer to **Figs. 30 through 34** for diagnostic test procedures.

Symptom Tests

AVIATOR

Refer to **Fig. 35** for symptom test procedures.

EXPEDITION & NAVIGATOR

Refer to **Fig. 36** for symptom test procedures.

EXPLORER & MOUNTAINEER

Refer to **Fig. 37** for symptom test procedures.

FREESTAR & MONTEREY

Refer to **Fig. 38** for symptom test procedures.

Clearing Diagnostic Trouble Codes

Connect a suitably programmed scan tool to Data Link Connector (DLC), and follow manufacturer's instructions.

Intermittent & Poor Connections

INTERMITTENTS

Most intermittents are caused by faulty electrical connections or wiring. Inspect for the following:
1. Wiring broken inside insulation.
2. Poor connection between male and female terminal at connector.
3. Poor terminal to wire connection. Some conditions which fall under this are:
   a. Poor crimps.
   b. Poor solder joints.
   c. Crimping over wire insulation rather than wire.
   d. Corrosion in wire to terminal contact.
4. Wire insulation which is rubbed through. This causes an intermittent short as bare area touches other wiring or components.

POOR CONNECTIONS

1. It is important to test terminal contact at component and any inline connectors before replacing suspect component.
2. Mating terminals must be inspected to ensure good terminal contact.
3. Poor connection between male and female terminal at a connector may be result of contamination or deformation.
4. Contamination may be caused by:
   a. Connector halves being improperly connected.

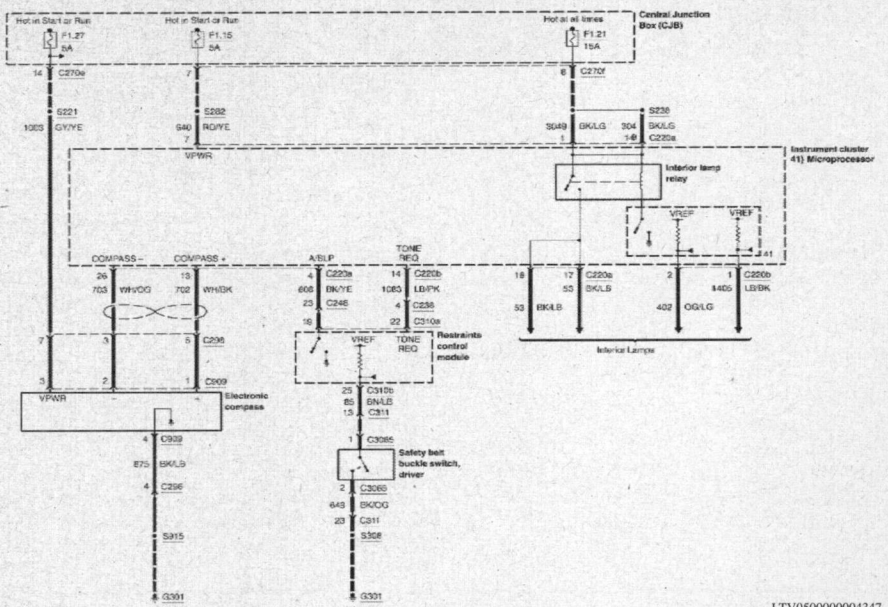

LTV0500000004347

Fig. 2   Wiring diagram (Part 1 of 5). Expedition & Navigator

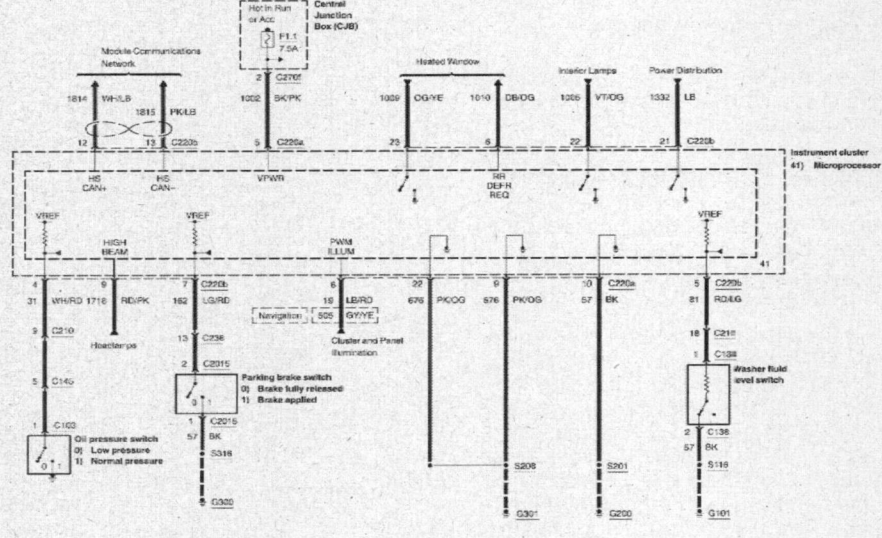

LTV0500000004348

Fig. 2   Wiring diagram (Part 2 of 5). Expedition & Navigator

b. Missing or damaged seal.
c. Damaged connector.
d. Exposing terminals to moisture and dirt.
5. Deformation is caused by:
   a. Probing connector terminal mating

side without proper adapter.
b. Improperly joining connector halves.
c. Repeatedly separating and joining connector halves.

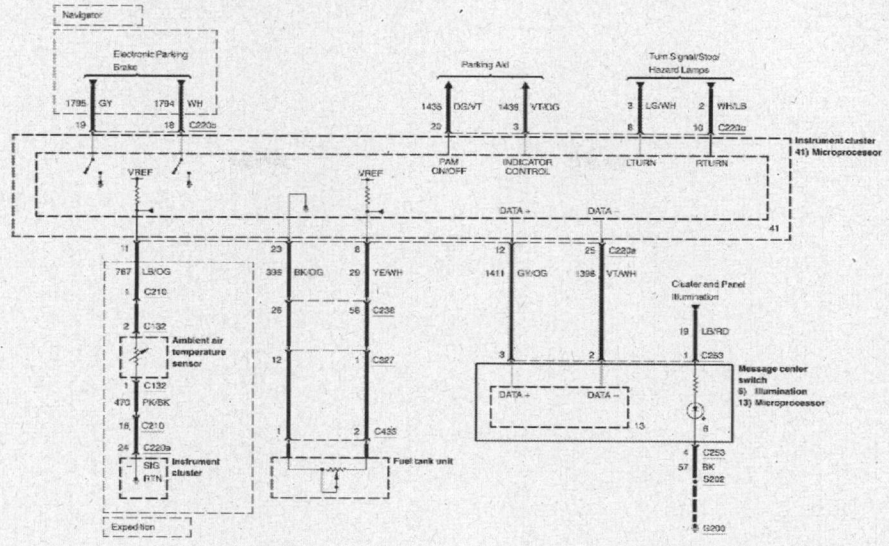

Fig. 2 Wiring diagram (Part 3 of 5). Expedition & Navigator

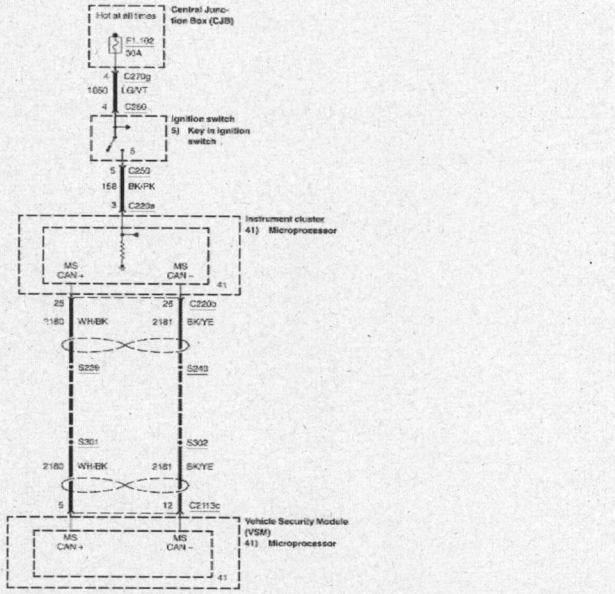

Fig. 2 Wiring diagram (Part 4 of 5). Expedition & Navigator

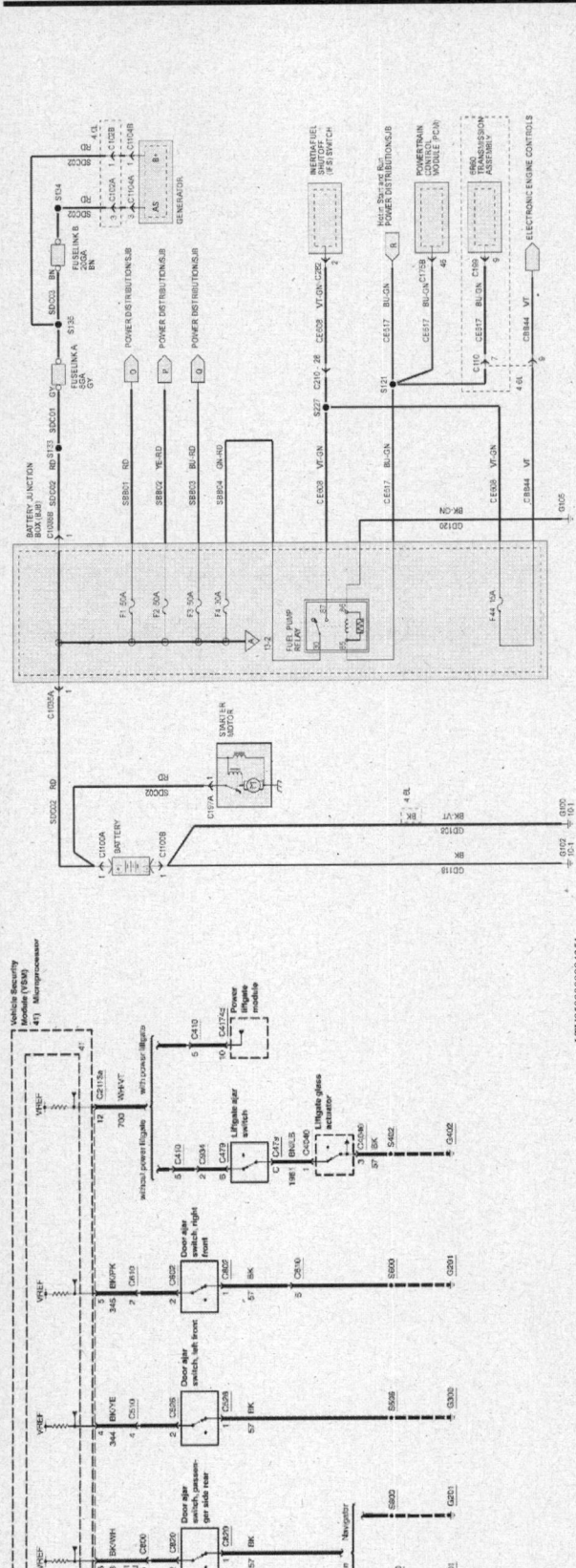

Fig. 2 Wiring diagram (Part 5 of 5). Expedition & Navigator

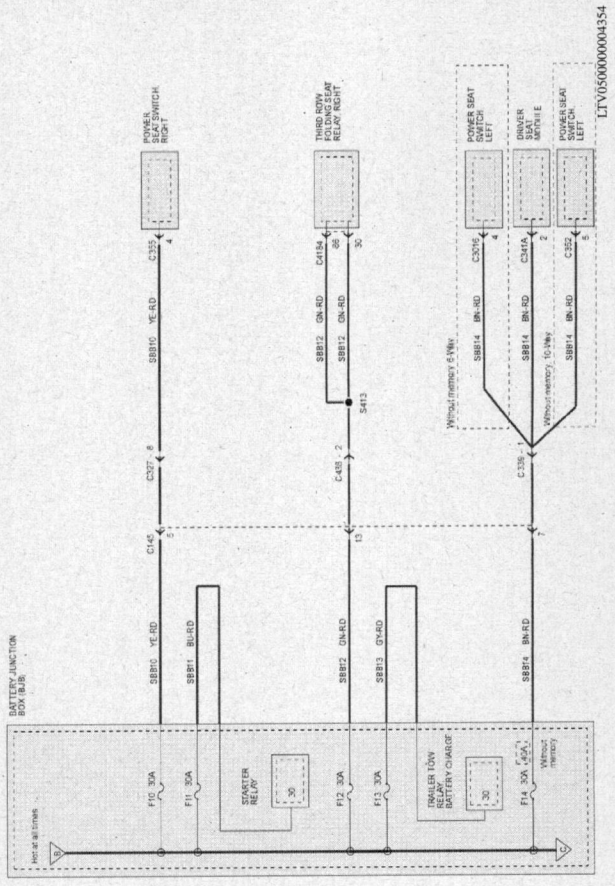

Fig. 3 Wiring diagram (Part 1 of 19). Explorer & Mountaineer

Fig. 3 Wiring diagram (Part 3 of 19). Explorer & Mountaineer

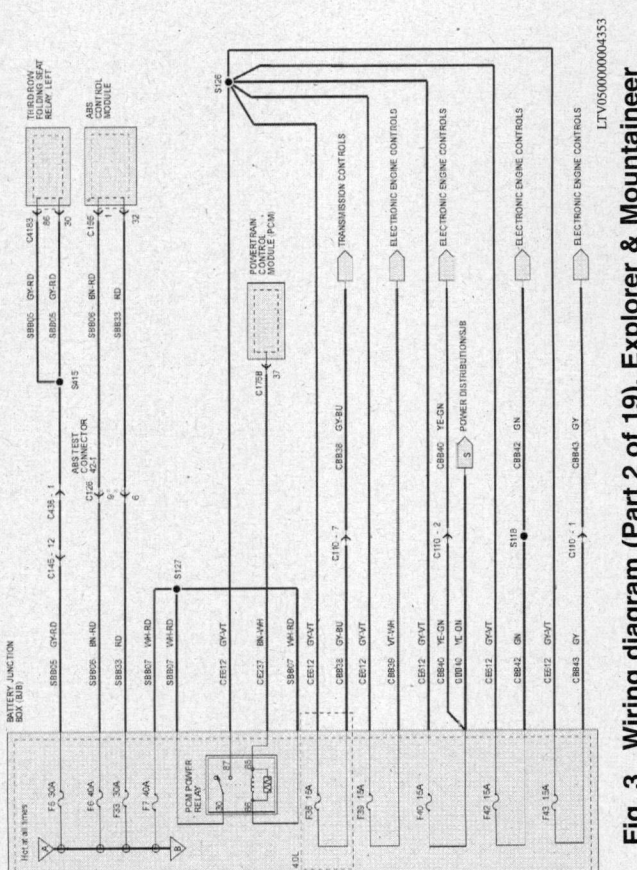

Fig. 3 Wiring diagram (Part 2 of 19). Explorer & Mountaineer

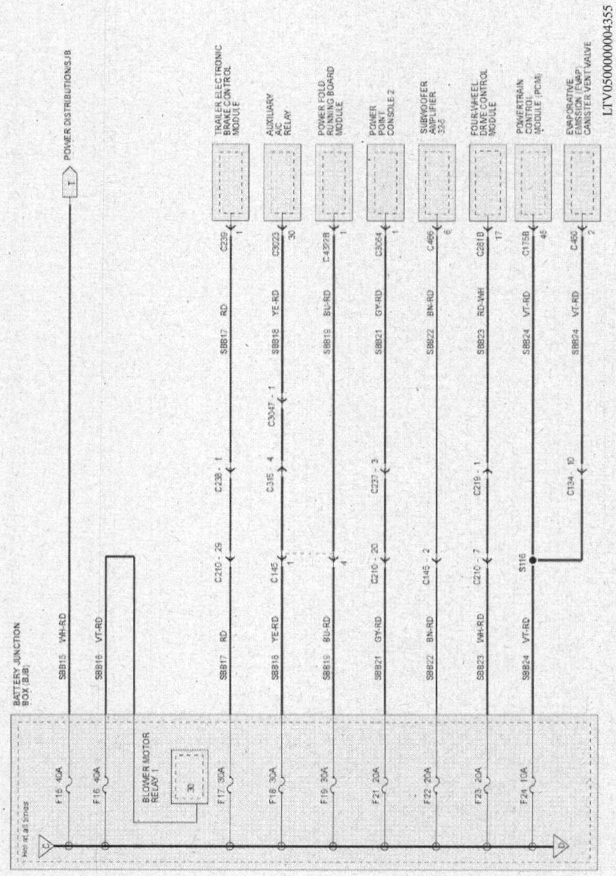

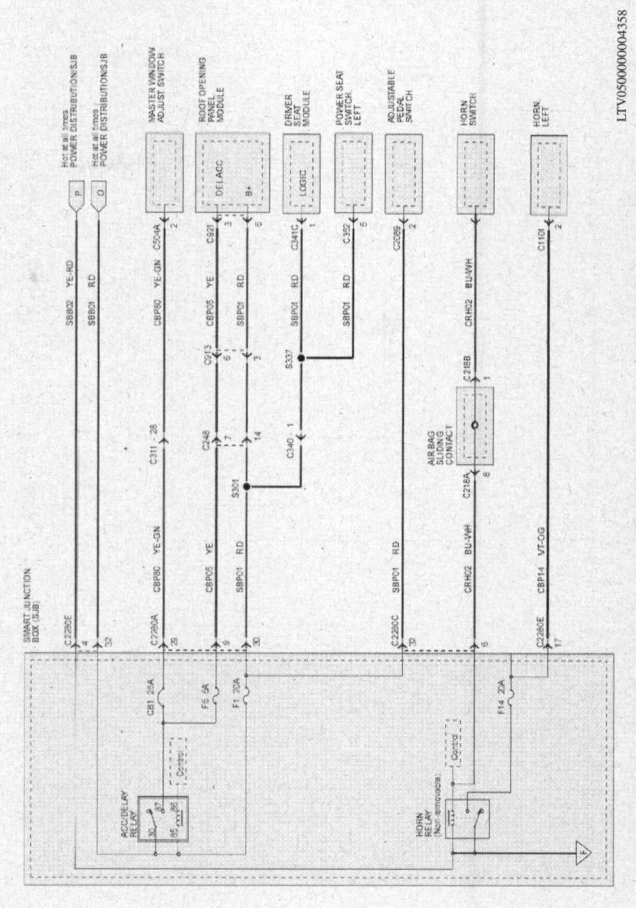

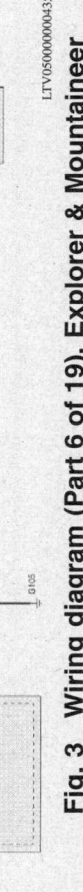

LTV0500000004355

Fig. 3 Wiring diagram (Part 4 of 19). Explorer & Mountaineer

LTV0500000004356

Fig. 3 Wiring diagram (Part 5 of 19). Explorer & Mountaineer

LTV0500000004357

Fig. 3 Wiring diagram (Part 6 of 19). Explorer & Mountaineer

LTV0500000004358

Fig. 3 Wiring diagram (Part 7 of 19). Explorer & Mountaineer

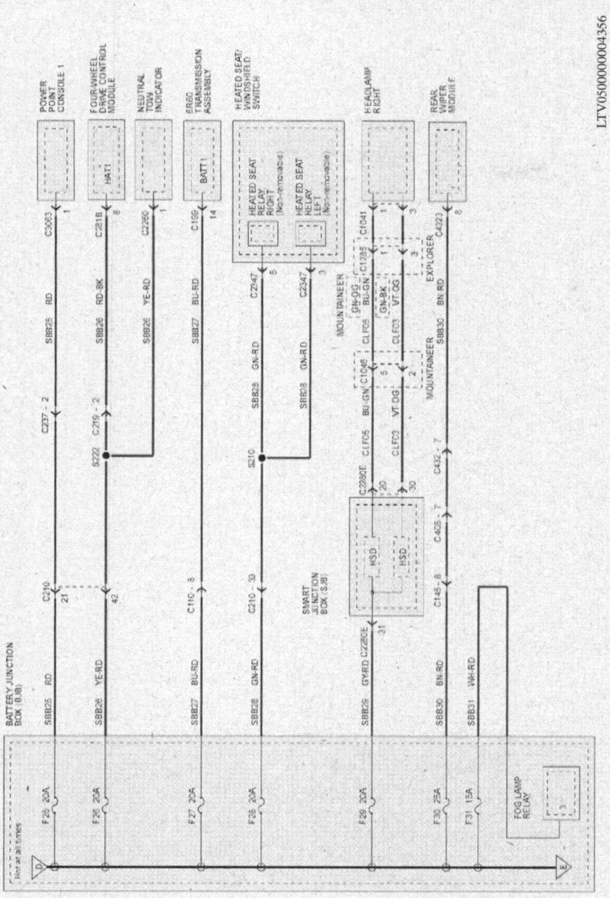

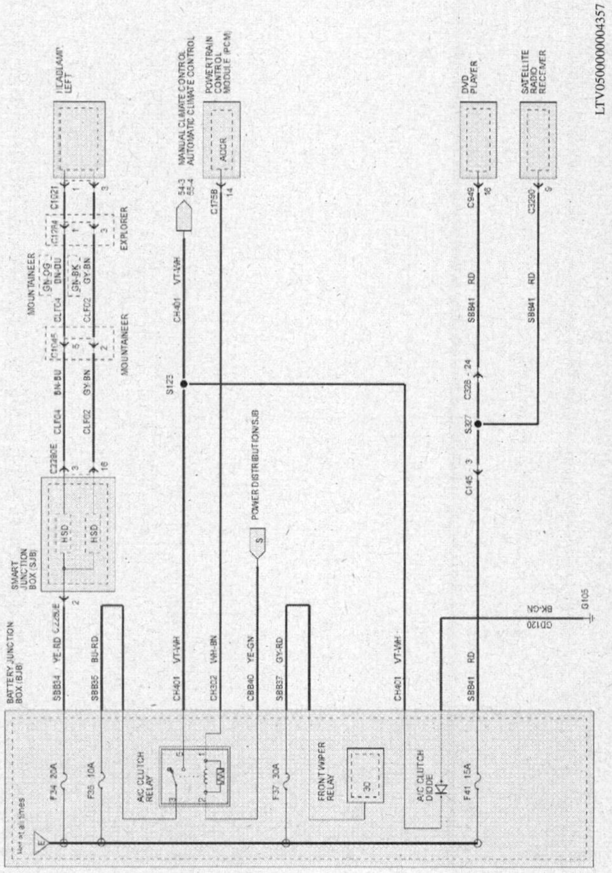

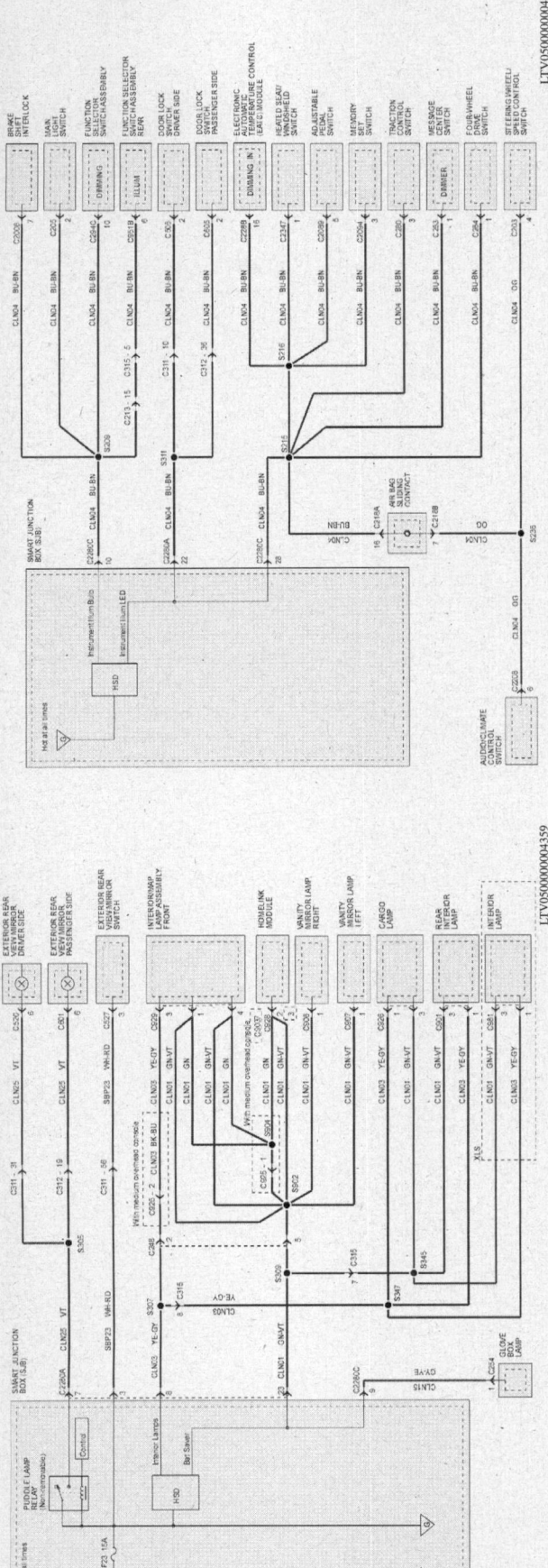

Fig. 3 Wiring diagram (Part 9 of 19). Explorer & Mountaineer

Fig. 3 Wiring diagram (Part 8 of 19). Explorer & Mountaineer

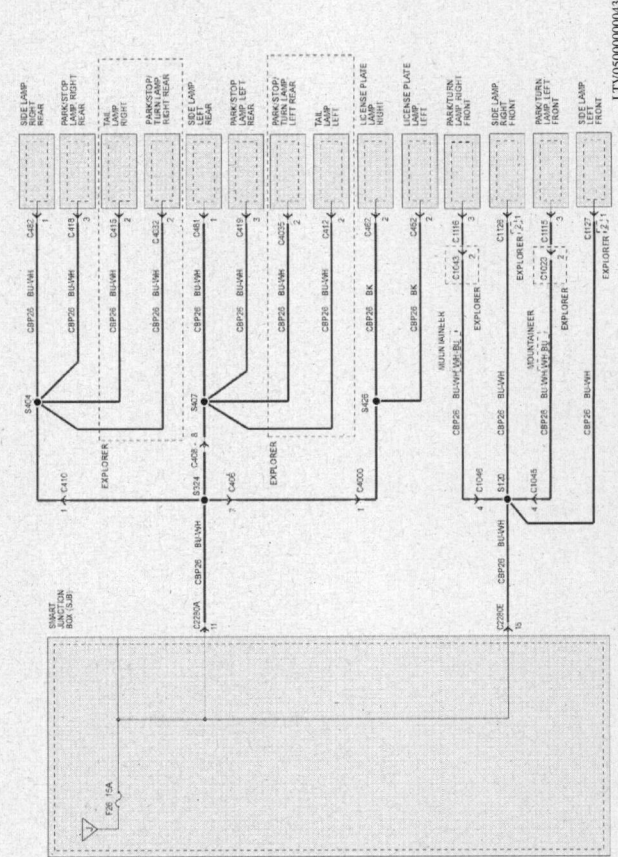

Fig. 3 Wiring diagram (Part 11 of 19). Explorer & Mountaineer

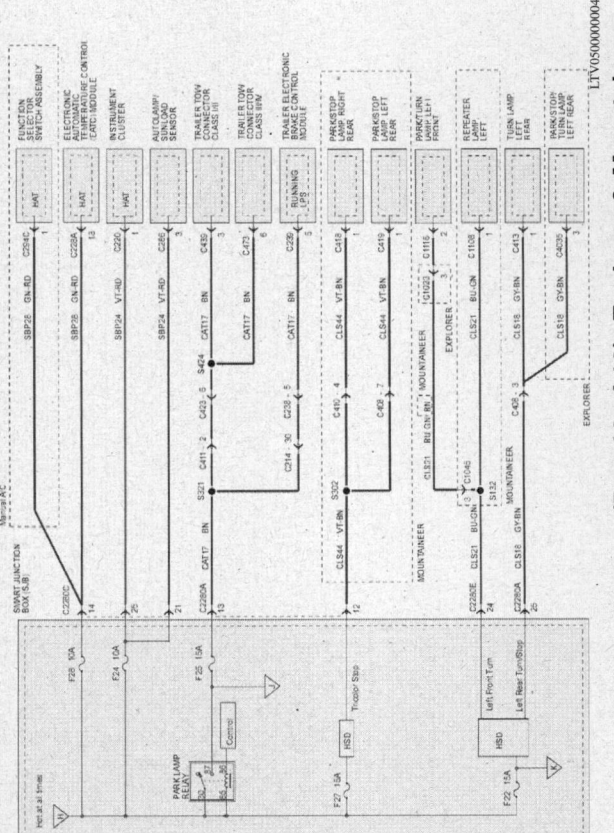

Fig. 3 Wiring diagram (Part 10 of 19). Explorer & Mountaineer

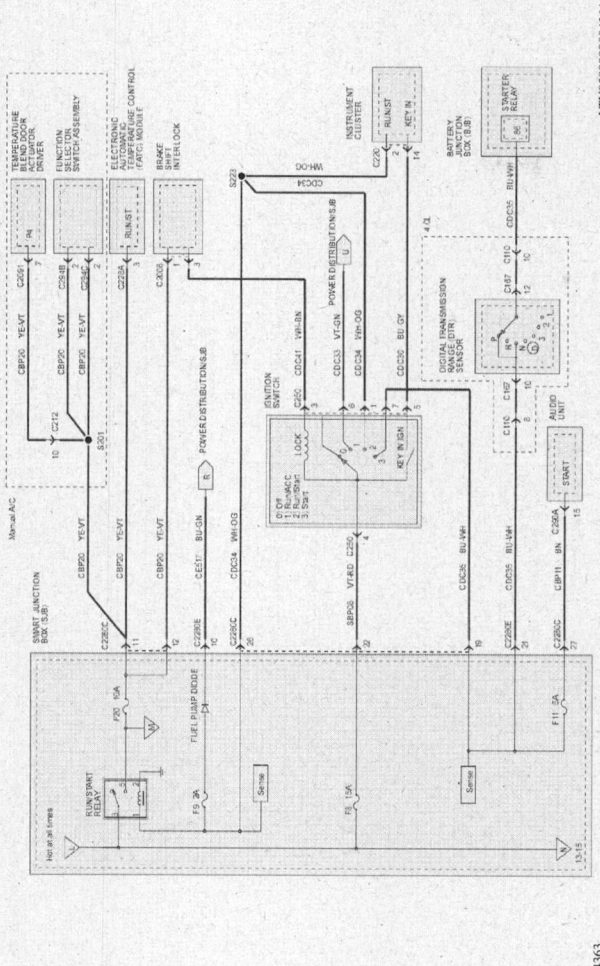

Fig. 3 Wiring diagram (Part 13 of 19). Explorer & Mountaineer

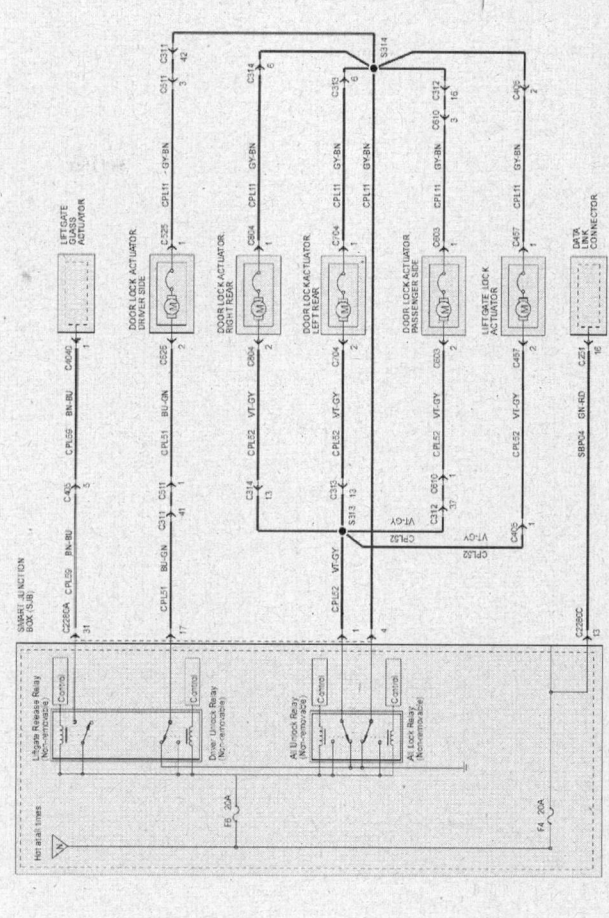

Fig. 3 Wiring diagram (Part 15 of 19). Explorer & Mountaineer

Fig. 3 Wiring diagram (Part 12 of 19). Explorer & Mountaineer

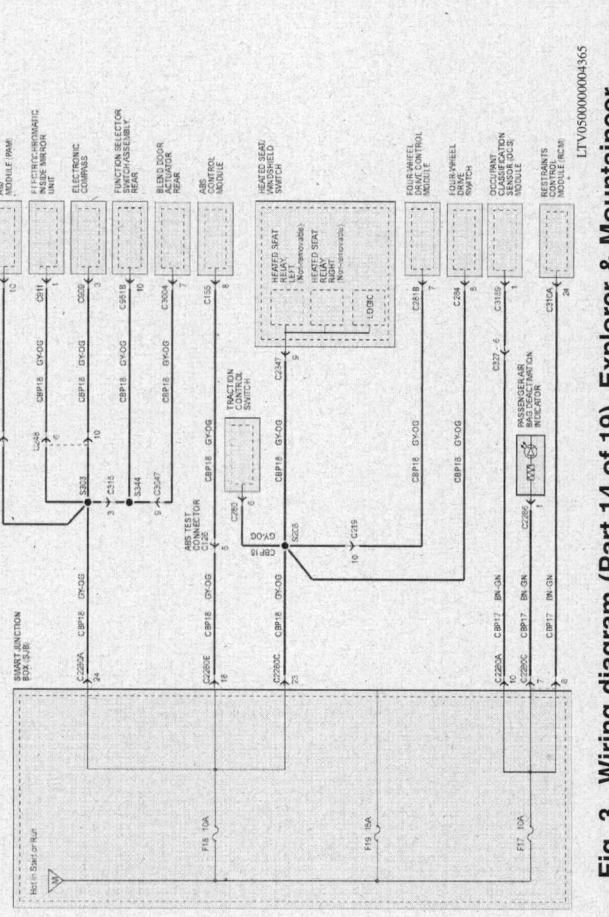

Fig. 3 Wiring diagram (Part 14 of 19). Explorer & Mountaineer

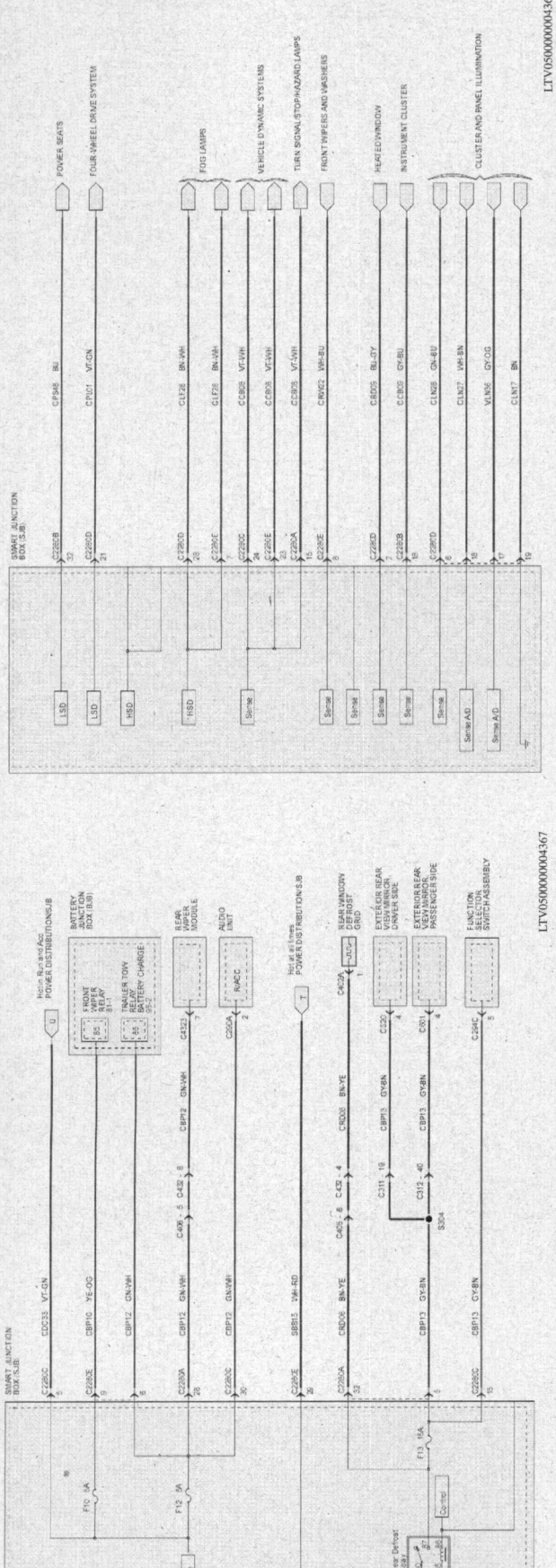

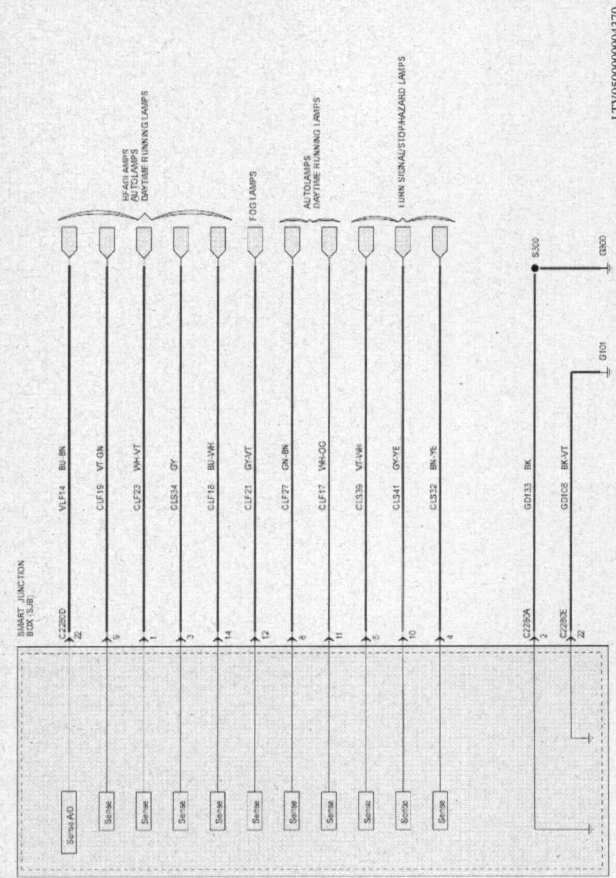

Fig. 3 Wiring diagram (Part 17 of 19). Explorer & Mountaineer

Fig. 3 Wiring diagram (Part 19 of 19). Explorer & Mountaineer

Fig. 3 Wiring diagram (Part 16 of 19). Explorer & Mountaineer

Fig. 3 Wiring diagram (Part 18 of 19). Explorer & Mountaineer

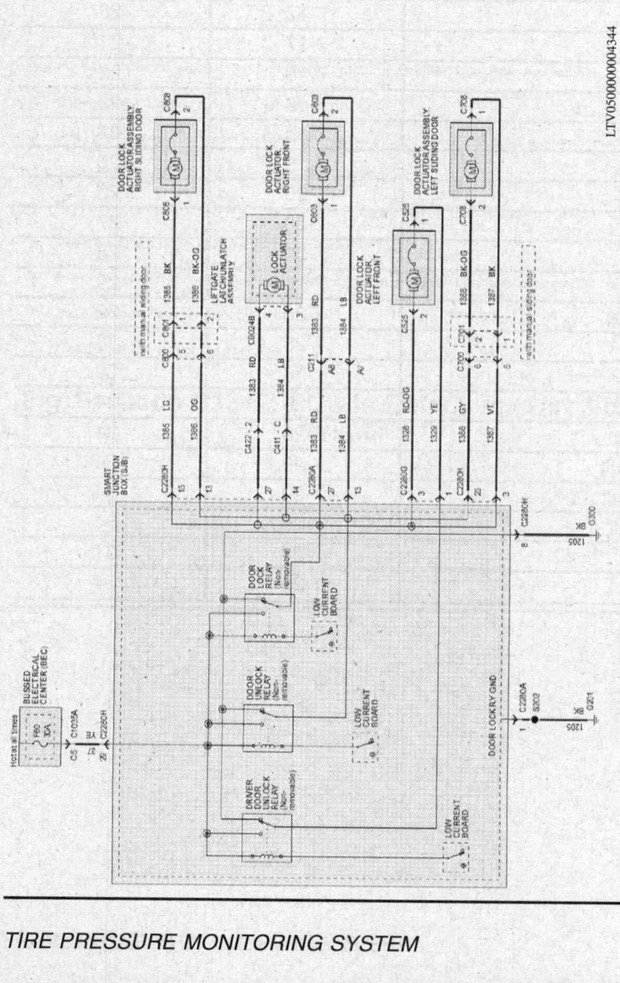

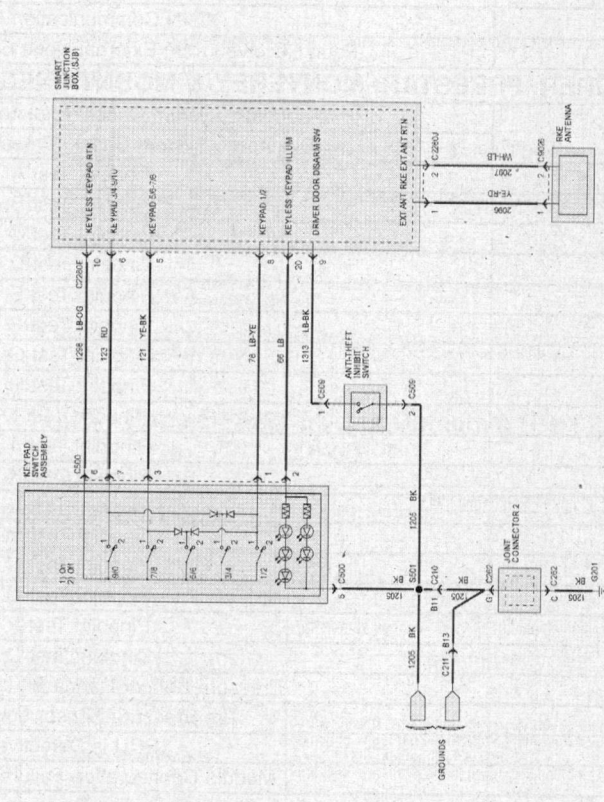

Fig. 4 Wiring diagram (Part 2 of 3). Freestar & Monterey

Fig. 4 Wiring diagram (Part 3 of 3). Freestar & Monterey

Fig. 4 Wiring diagram (Part 1 of 3). Freestar & Monterey

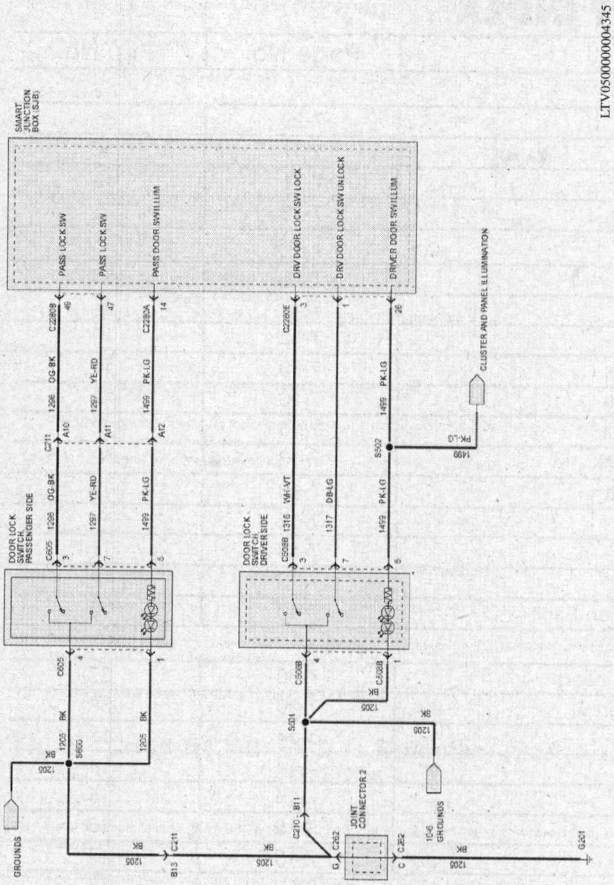

Test Step	Result / Action to Take
E1 CHECK FOR FAULT REPEATABILITY	
• Connect the diagnostic tool. • Carry out the tire pressure sensor training procedure, using the diagnostic tool. • **Does the tire training procedure initiate?**	**Yes** GO to E2 . **No** Go To Pinpoint Test B .
E2 CHECK TIRE PRESSURE SENSOR TRANSMITTING ABILITY	
• Continue to carry out the sensor training procedure. • **Do all of the tire pressure sensors transmit correctly and does the horn sound when each tire pressure sensor transmits to the TPMS module?**	**Yes** GO to E3 . **No** INSTALL a new tire pressure sensor. CLEAR the DTC(s). REPEAT the self-test.
E3 CHECK THE TPMS MODULE	
• Review the continuous and on-demand DTCs. • Review the continuous and on-demand self-test DTCs. • **Were DTCs retrieved?**	**Yes** If DTCs are retrieved, REFER to the DTC index. **No** The system is functioning normally. CLEAR the DTCs.

LTV0500000004380

Fig. 7 Code B2872: Tire Pressure Sensor Fault. Aviator

Test Step	Result / Action to Take
E1 CHECK FOR FAULT REPEATABILITY	
• Carry out the tire pressure sensor training procedure. • **Does the tire training procedure initiate?**	**Yes** GO to E2 . **No** Go To Pinpoint Test B .
E2 CHECK THE TIRE PRESSURE SENSORS TRANSMITTING ABILITY	
• Continue to carry out the sensor training procedure. • **Do all of the tire pressure sensors transmit correctly and does the horn sound when each tire pressure sensor transmits to the TPMS module?**	**Yes** GO to E3 . **No** INSTALL a new tire pressure sensor(s). REFER to Tire Pressure Sensor . CLEAR the DTCs. REPEAT the self-test.
E3 CHECK THE TPMS MODULE	
• Connect the diagnostic tool. • Carry out the on-demand self test. • Review the continuous and on-demand DTCs. • **Are any DTCs present?**	**Yes** If DTCs are retrieved, REFER to the DTC index. **No** The system is functioning normally. CLEAR the DTCs.

LTV0500000004382

Fig. 9 Code B2872: Tire Pressure Sensor Fault. Expedition & Navigator

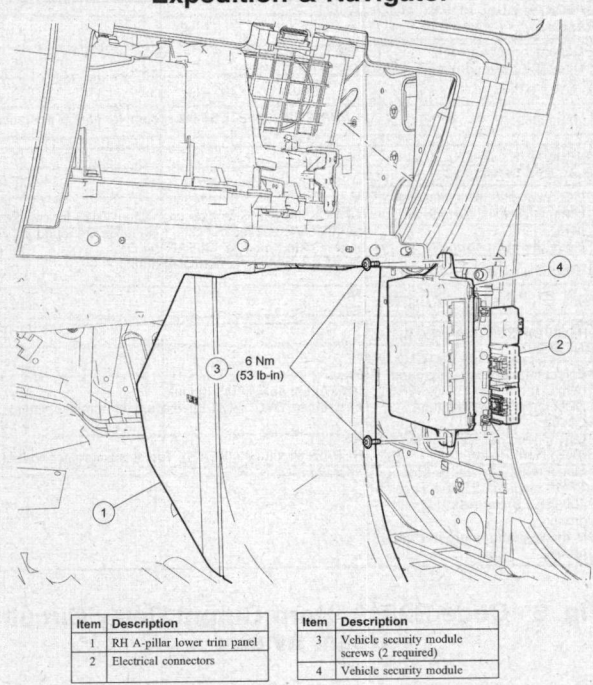

Item	Description
1	RH A-pillar lower trim panel
2	Electrical connectors

Item	Description
3	Vehicle security module screws (2 required)
4	Vehicle security module

LTV0500000004383

Fig. 10 Code B1342: ECU is Defective (Part 1 of 2). Expedition & Navigator

Test Step	Result / Action to Take
D1 CHECK MANUAL HORN OPERATION	
• Confirm horn operation. • **Does the horn sound?**	**Yes** GO to D2 . **No** REPAIR the horn. TEST the system for normal operation.
D2 CHECK HORN OPERATION USING ACTIVE COMMAND	
• Using the diagnostic tool active command menu, actuate the horn. • **Does the horn sound?**	**Yes** CHECK the VSM module connector C2113b for corroded, damaged or backed out pins. If no faults are found, INSTALL a new VSM (TPMS module integral to VSM). TEST the system for normal operation. **No** GO to D3 .
D3 CHECK CIRCUIT 1 (DB) FOR AN OPEN	
• Disconnect the battery ground cable. • Disconnect: VSM C2113b. • Disconnect: Battery Junction Box (BJB) Horn Relay. • Measure the resistance between VSM C2113b-6, circuit 1 (DB) harness side and BJB Horn Relay cavity 2 (ground side). • **Is the resistance less than 5 ohms?**	**Yes** INSTALL a new VSM (TPMS is integral to VSM). TEST the system for normal operation. **No** REPAIR circuit 1 (DB) for an open. TEST the system for normal operation.

LTV0500000004381

Fig. 8 Code B1217: Horn Relay Circuit Failure. Expedition & Navigator

1. **NOTE:** Prior to the removal of the vehicle security module , it is necessary to upload the module configuration information to the diagnostic tool. This information must be downloaded to the new vehicle security module after installation.

   Disconnect the battery.

2. Remove the pin-type retainer and the RH A-pillar lower trim panel.

3. Remove the glove compartment.

4. Disconnect the 3 electrical connectors.

5. Remove the 2 screws and the vehicle security module .

Installation

1. Position the vehicle security module and install the 2 screws.
   • Tighten the screws to 6 Nm (53 lb-in).

2. Connect the 3 electrical connectors.

3. Position the RH A-pillar lower trim panel and install the pin-type retainer.

4. Install the glove compartment.

5. Connect the battery.

6. **NOTE:** When successful, this step provides the calibration necessary for vehicle security module operation and clears DTC B2477. The clearing of the DTC indicates the calibration data has been successfully downloaded to the vehicle security module.

   Download the vehicle security module configuration information from the diagnostic tool to the vehicle security module

7. **NOTE:** When successful, this step clears DTCs B2868, B2869, B2870 and B2871. The clearing of these DTCs indicates the vehicle security module has recognized the tire pressure sensors during the training procedure.

   Train the tire pressure sensors.

8. Clear the DTCs.

9. **NOTE:** DTC C2780 will not clear if any other DTCs are present in the vehicle security module .

   NOTE: This step is required to clear DTC C2780, allow the vehicle security module to exit the manufacturing mode, and to be sure there are no other concerns with the newly programmed vehicle security module

   Carry out the vehicle security module on-demand self-test.

LTV0500000004384

Fig. 10 Code B1342: ECU is Defective (Part 2 of 2). Expedition & Navigator

Using the Vehicle Communication Module (VCM) When the Original Module is Not Available

1. Install the new module.

2. Using the VCM and the latest version of the service function card, SELECT: Programmable Module Installation.

3. Select the module being installed.

4. Follow the on-screen instructions.

5. SELECT: Retrieve Module Configuration — Old ECU and press trigger.

6. Follow the on-screen instructions.

7. The VCM attempts to retrieve the module data.
   - If the module data is available, go to Step A.
   - If the VCM displays: Call the As-Built Data Center, go to Step B.

Step A

1. SELECT: Restore Configuration — New ECU. Press trigger.

2. The VCM completes loading the retrieved data and displays Module Download Successful.

3. Test the module for correct operation.

Step B

1. Press the trigger.

2. If the VCM asks for vehicle data, enter the vehicle data, then press store.

3. The VCM asks for module data line 1. Enter the data and press store.

4. The VCM then asks if there is an additional line of data available for that address. Select YES or NO depending on the information in the As Built Data Sheet.

5. Repeat Steps 3 and 4 until the answer is NO for Step 4.

LTV0500000004385

Fig. 11   Codes B2477 & C2780: Module Configuration Failure & Mismatch / ECU in Manufacturing Mode (Part 1 of 3). Expedition & Navigator

8. Enter the module data (the module address and line are displayed to the left of the 3 entry boxes) and press the check mark.

9. The WDS downloads the data into the new module and displays Operation Successful — Programming Complete.

10. Test the module for correct operation.

Using the Worldwide Diagnostic System (WDS) When the Original Module is Available

1. Connect the WDS and ID the vehicle as normal.

2. From the Toolbox icon, select and highlight Module Programming and press the check mark.

3. Select and highlight Programmable Module Installation.

4. Follow the on-screen instructions, turn the ignition key to the OFF position, and press the check mark.

5. Install the new module and press the check mark.

6. Follow the on-screen instructions, turn the ignition key to the ON position, and press the check mark.

7. The module configuration is complete.

8. Test the module for correct operation.

LTV0500000004387

Fig. 11   Codes B2477 & C2780: Module Configuration Failure & Mismatch / ECU in Manufacturing Mode (Part 3 of 3). Expedition & Navigator

6. The VCM should show a screen stating that the module data was stored. Press the trigger.

7. Follow the on-screen instructions.

8. SELECT: Restore Configuration — New ECU. Press the trigger.

9. The VCM completes loading the retrieved data and displays Module Download Successful.

10. Test the module for correct operation.

Using the Vehicle Communication Module (VCM) When the Original Module is Available

1. With the original module still installed, using the VCM and the latest version of the service function card, SELECT: Programmable Module Installation.

2. Select the module being installed and press the trigger.

3. Follow the on-screen instructions.

4. SELECT: Retrieve Module Configuration — Old ECU. Press the trigger.

5. Follow the on-screen instructions.

6. INSTALL new module, SELECT: Restore Configuration — New ECU. Press the trigger.

7. The VCM completes loading the retrieved data and displays Module Download Successful.

8. Test the module for correct operation.

Using the Worldwide Diagnostic System (WDS) When the Original Module is Not Available

1. Install the new module.

2. Connect the WDS and ID the vehicle as normal.

3. From the Toolbox icon, select and highlight Module Programming. Then highlight the module that was installed and press the check mark.

4. Select and highlight Programmable Module Installation. Then highlight the module that was installed and press the check mark.

5. Follow the on-screen instructions, turn the ignition key to the RUN position and press the check mark.

6. The WDS retrieves the module data, automatically downloads the data into the new module, and displays Module Configuration Complete.

7. If the data is not available in the module, the WDS displays a screen stating to contact the As-Built Data Center. Retrieve the data from WWW.FMCDEALER.COM at this time and press the check mark.

LTV0500000004386

Fig. 11   Codes B2477 & C2780: Module Configuration Failure & Mismatch / ECU in Manufacturing Mode (Part 2 of 3). Expedition & Navigator

Condition	Possible Sources	Action
• The anti-lock brake system (ABS) module does not respond to the diagnostic tool	• Circuit or connection in the high speed controller area network (CAN) • ABS module	• Go To Pinpoint Test A .
• The restraint control module (RCM) does not respond to the diagnostic tool	• Circuit or connection in the international standards organization (ISO) 9141 communications network • RCM	• Go To Pinpoint Test B .
• The vehicle security module does not respond to the diagnostic tool	• Circuit or connection in the medium speed controller area network (CAN) • Vehicle security module	• Go To Pinpoint Test C .
• The tire pressure monitoring system (TPMS) module does not respond to the diagnostic tool	• Circuit or connection in the medium speed controller area network (CAN) • Vehicle security module	• Go To Pinpoint Test C .
• The powertrain control module (PCM) does not respond to the diagnostic tool	• Circuit or connection in the high speed controller area network (CAN) • PCM	• Go To Pinpoint Test D .
• The 4-wheel drive (4WD) control module does not respond to the diagnostic tool	• Circuit or connection in the high speed controller area network (CAN) • PCM	• Go To Pinpoint Test D .
• The electronic automatic temperature control (EATC) module does not respond to the diagnostic tool	• Circuit or connection in the medium speed controller area network (CAN) • EATC module	• Go To Pinpoint Test E .
• The driver seat module (DSM) does not respond to the diagnostic tool	• Circuit or connection in the medium speed controller area network (CAN) • DSM	• Go To Pinpoint Test F .
• The parking aid module does not respond to the diagnostic tool	• Circuit or connection in the international standards organization (ISO) 9141 communications network (Expedition only) • Circuit or connection in the medium speed controller area network (CAN) (Navigator only) • Parking aid module	• Go To Pinpoint Test G .
• The transmission control module (TCM) does not respond to the diagnostic tool	• Circuit or connection in the high speed controller area network (CAN) • TCM	• Go To Pinpoint Test H .

LTV0500000004388

Fig. 12   Codes B2868, B2869, B2870, B2871, U1900 & U2023: Tire Pressure Sensor Fault / CAN Communication Fault (Part 1 of 2). Expedition & Navigator

• The instrument cluster does not respond to the diagnostic tool	• Circuit or connection in the medium speed controller area network (CAN) • Circuit or connection in the high speed CAN • Instrument cluster	• Go To Pinpoint Test I .
• The power liftgate module does not respond to the diagnostic tool	• Circuit or connection in the medium speed controller area network (CAN) • Power liftgate module	• Go To Pinpoint Test J .
• The air suspension control module does not respond to the diagnostic tool	• Circuit or connection in the medium speed controller area network (CAN) • Air suspension control module	• Go To Pinpoint Test K .
• The climate controlled seat module does not respond to the diagnostic tool	• Circuit or connection in the medium speed controller area network (CAN) • Climate controlled seat module	• Go To Pinpoint Test L .
• The navigation system module does not respond to the diagnostic tool	• Circuit or connection in the standard corporate protocol (SCP) communications network • Navigation system module	• Go To Pinpoint Test M .
• No international standards organization (ISO) 9141 communications network communication	• Circuit or connection in the ISO 9141 communications network • ISO 9141 communications network modules	• Go To Pinpoint Test N .
• No high speed controller area network (CAN) communication	• Circuit or connection in the high speed CAN • High speed CAN modules	• Go To Pinpoint Test O .
• No medium speed controller area network (CAN) communication	• Circuit or connection in the medium speed CAN • Medium speed CAN modules	• Go To Pinpoint Test P .
• No module/network communication — no power to the diagnostic tool	• Data link connector (DLC) • Fuse • Circuitry • Diagnostic tool	• Go To Pinpoint Test Q .

LTV0500000004389

Fig. 12 Codes B2868, B2869, B2870, B2871, U1900 & U2023: Tire Pressure Sensor Fault / CAN Communication Fault (Part 2 of 2). Expedition & Navigator

A3 CHECK FOR CORRECT ABS MODULE OPERATION	
• Disconnect all the ABS module connectors. • Check for: 　• corrosion 　• pushed-out pins • Connect all the ABS module connectors and make sure they seat correctly. • Operate the system and verify the concern is still present. • **Is the concern still present?**	**Yes** INSTALL a new ABS module. CLEAR the diagnostic trouble codes (DTCs). REPEAT the self-test. CARRY OUT the data link diagnostics test. **No** The system is operating correctly at this time. The concern may have been caused by a loose or corroded connector. CLEAR the DTCs. REPEAT the self-test. CARRY OUT the data link diagnostics test.

LTV0500000004391

Fig. 13   Pinpoint Test A (Part 2 of 2). Expedition & Navigator

Test Step	Result / Action to Take
A1 CHECK THE ABS MODULE C135	
• Key in OFF position. • Disconnect: ABS Module C135. • Inspect the ABS module C135 for damage. • **Is the ABS module C135 OK?**	**Yes** GO to A2 . **No** REPAIR the ABS module C135. CARRY OUT the data link diagnostics test.
A2 CHECK THE HIGH SPEED CAN CIRCUITS BETWEEN THE ABS MODULE AND THE DLC FOR AN OPEN	
• Measure the resistance between the ABS module C135-11, circuit 1814 (WH/LB) harness side and the DLC C251-6, circuit 1814 (WH/LB), harness side. 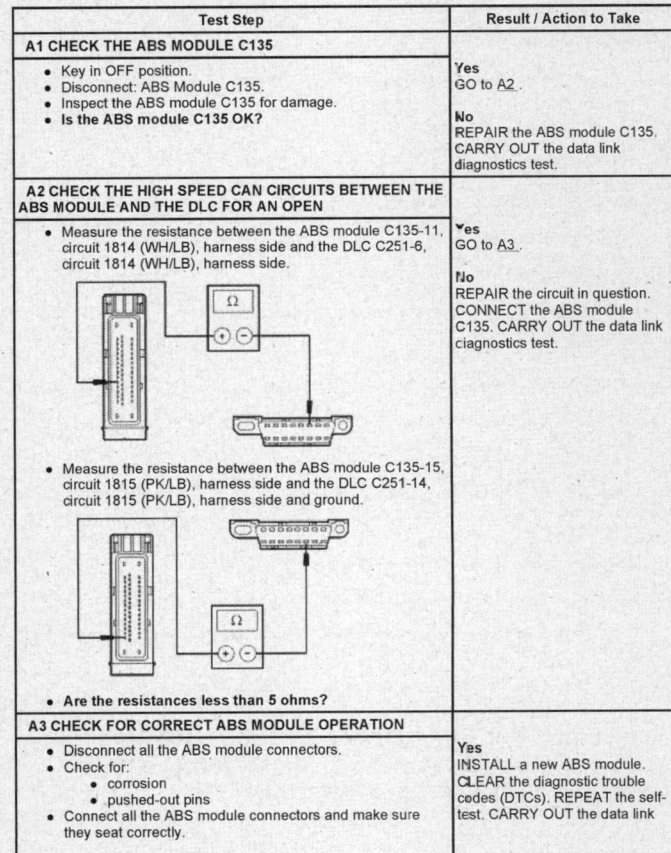 • Measure the resistance between the ABS module C135-15, circuit 1815 (PK/LB), harness side and the DLC C251-14, circuit 1815 (PK/LB), harness side and ground. • **Are the resistances less than 5 ohms?**	**Yes** GO to A3 . **No** REPAIR the circuit in question. CONNECT the ABS module C135. CARRY OUT the data link diagnostics test.
A3 CHECK FOR CORRECT ABS MODULE OPERATION	
• Disconnect all the ABS module connectors. • Check for: 　• corrosion 　• pushed-out pins • Connect all the ABS module connectors and make sure they seat correctly.	**Yes** INSTALL a new ABS module. CLEAR the diagnostic trouble codes (DTCs). REPEAT the self-test. CARRY OUT the data link

LTV0500000004390

Fig. 13   Pinpoint Test A (Part 1 of 2). Expedition & Navigator

Test Step	Result / Action to Take
B1 CHECK THE RCM C310A FOR DAMAGE	
• Key in OFF position. • Depower the supplemental restraint system (SRS). • Disconnect: RCM C310a. • Inspect the RCM C310a for damage. • **Is the RCM C310a OK?**	**Yes** GO to B2 . **No** REPAIR the RCM C310a. CONNECT the RCM C310a. REPOWER the SRS. CARRY OUT the data link diagnostics test.
B2 CHECK THE ISO 9141 CIRCUIT BETWEEN THE DLC AND THE RCM FOR AN OPEN	
• Measure the resistance between the RCM C310a-11, circuit 70 (LB/WH), harness side and the DLC C251-7, circuit 70 (LB/WH), harness side. • **Is the resistance less than 5 ohms?**	**Yes** GO to B3 . **No** REPAIR the circuit. CONNECT the RCM C310a. REPOWER the SRS. CLEAR the diagnostic trouble codes (DTCs). REPEAT the self-test. CARRY OUT the data link diagnostics test.
B3 CHECK FOR CORRECT RCM OPERATION	
• Disconnect all the RCM connectors. • Check for: 　• corrosion 　• pushed-out pins • Connect all the RCM connectors and make sure they seat correctly. • Operate the system and verify the concern is still present. • **Is the concern still present?**	**Yes** INSTALL a new RCM. REPOWER the SRS. CLEAR the DTCs. REPEAT the self-test. CARRY OUT the data link diagnostics test. **No** The system is operating correctly at this time. The concern may have been caused by a loose or corroded connector. CLEAR the DTCs. REPEAT the self-test. CARRY OUT the data link diagnostics test.

LTV0500000004392

Fig. 14   Pinpoint Test B. Expedition & Navigator

Test Step	Result / Action to Take
C1 CHECK THE VEHICLE SECURITY MODULE C2113C FOR DAMAGE • Key in OFF position. • Disconnect: Vehicle Security Module C2113c. • Inspect the vehicle security module C2113c for damage. • **Is the vehicle security module C2113c OK?**	**Yes** GO to C2. **No** REPAIR the vehicle security module C2113c. CARRY OUT the data link diagnostics test.
C2 CHECK THE MEDIUM SPEED CAN CIRCUITS BETWEEN THE DLC AND THE VEHICLE SECURITY MODULE FOR AN OPEN • Measure the resistance between the vehicle security module C2113c-5, circuit 2180 (WH/BK), harness side and the DLC C251-3, circuit 2180 (WH/BK), harness side. 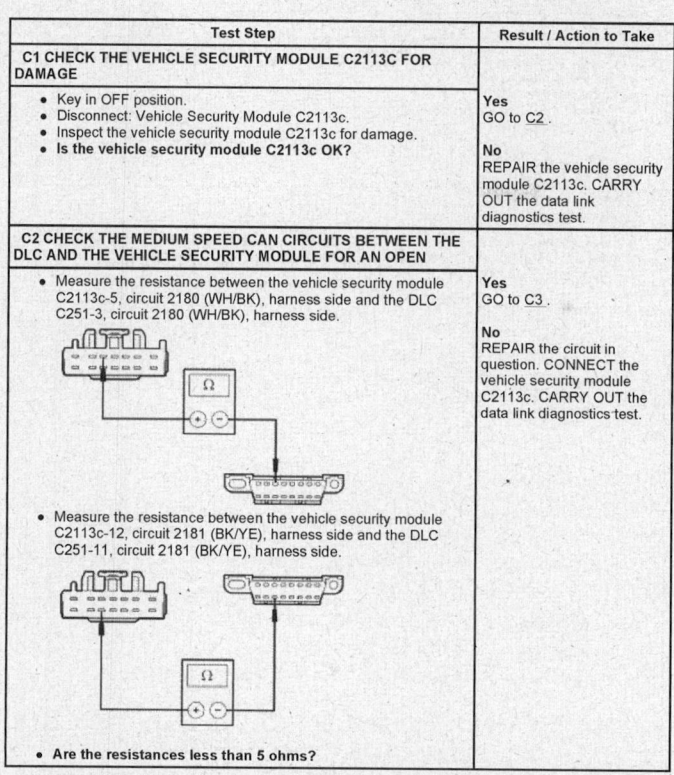 • Measure the resistance between the vehicle security module C2113c-12, circuit 2181 (BK/YE), harness side and the DLC C251-11, circuit 2181 (BK/YE), harness side. • Are the resistances less than 5 ohms?	**Yes** GO to C3. **No** REPAIR the circuit in question. CONNECT the vehicle security module C2113c. CARRY OUT the data link diagnostics test.

LTV0500000004393

Fig. 15 Pinpoint Test C (Part 1 of 2). Expedition & Navigator

Test Step	Result / Action to Take
D1 CHECK THE PCM C175B • Key in OFF position. • Disconnect: PCM C175b. • Inspect the PCM C175b for damage. • **Is the PCM C175b OK?**	**Yes** GO to D2. **No** REPAIR the PCM C175b. CARRY OUT the data link diagnostics test.
D2 CHECK THE HIGH SPEED CAN CIRCUITS BETWEEN THE PCM AND THE DLC FOR AN OPEN • Measure the resistance between the PCM C175b-2, circuit 1814 (WH/LB), harness side and the DLC C251-6, circuit 1814 (WH/LB), harness side. • Measure the resistance between the PCM C175b-3, circuit 1815 (PK/LB), harness side and the DLC C251-14, circuit 1815 (PK/LB), harness side. • Are the resistances less than 5 ohms?	**Yes** GO to D3. **No** REPAIR the circuit in question. CONNECT the PCM C175b. CARRY OUT the data link diagnostics test.

LTV0500000004395

Fig. 16 Pinpoint Test D (Part 1 of 2). Expedition & Navigator

C3 CHECK FOR CORRECT VEHICLE SECURITY MODULE OPERATION	

• Disconnect all the vehicle security module connectors.
• Check for:
  • corrosion
  • pushed-out pins
• Connect all the vehicle security module connectors and make sure they seat correctly.
• Operate the system and verify the concern is still present.
• **Is the concern still present?**
	Yes
	INSTALL a new vehicle security module. CLEAR the diagnostic trouble codes (DTCs). REPEAT the self-test. CARRY OUT the data link diagnostics test.
	
	No
	The system is operating correctly at this time. The concern may have been caused by a loose or corroded connector. CLEAR the DTCs. REPEAT the self-test. CARRY OUT the data link diagnostics test.

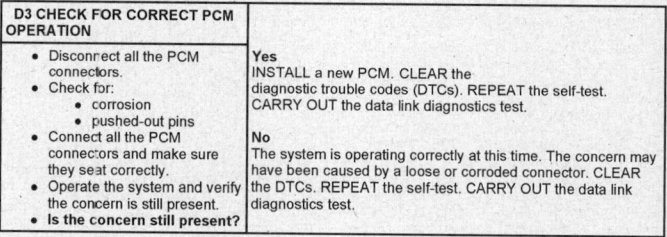

LTV0500000004394

Fig. 15 Pinpoint Test C (Part 2 of 2). Expedition & Navigator

D3 CHECK FOR CORRECT PCM OPERATION	

• Disconnect all the PCM connectors.
• Check for:
  • corrosion
  • pushed-out pins
• Connect all the PCM connectors and make sure they seat correctly.
• Operate the system and verify the concern is still present.
• **Is the concern still present?**
	Yes
	INSTALL a new PCM. CLEAR the diagnostic trouble codes (DTCs). REPEAT the self-test. CARRY OUT the data link diagnostics test.
	
	No
	The system is operating correctly at this time. The concern may have been caused by a loose or corroded connector. CLEAR the DTCs. REPEAT the self-test. CARRY OUT the data link diagnostics test.

LTV0500000004396

Fig. 16 Pinpoint Test D (Part 2 of 2). Expedition & Navigator

Test Step	Result / Action to Take
E1 CHECK THE EATC MODULE C228B FOR DAMAGE • Key in OFF position. • Disconnect: EATC Module C228b. • Inspect the EATC module C228b for damage. • **Is the EATC module C228b OK?**	**Yes** GO to E2. **No** REPAIR the EATC module C228b. CARRY OUT the data link diagnostics test.
E2 CHECK THE MEDIUM SPEED CAN CIRCUITS BETWEEN THE EATC MODULE AND THE DLC FOR AN OPEN • Measure the resistance between the EATC module C228b-2, circuit 2180 (WH/BK), harness side and the DLC C251-3, circuit 2180 (WH/BK), harness side. 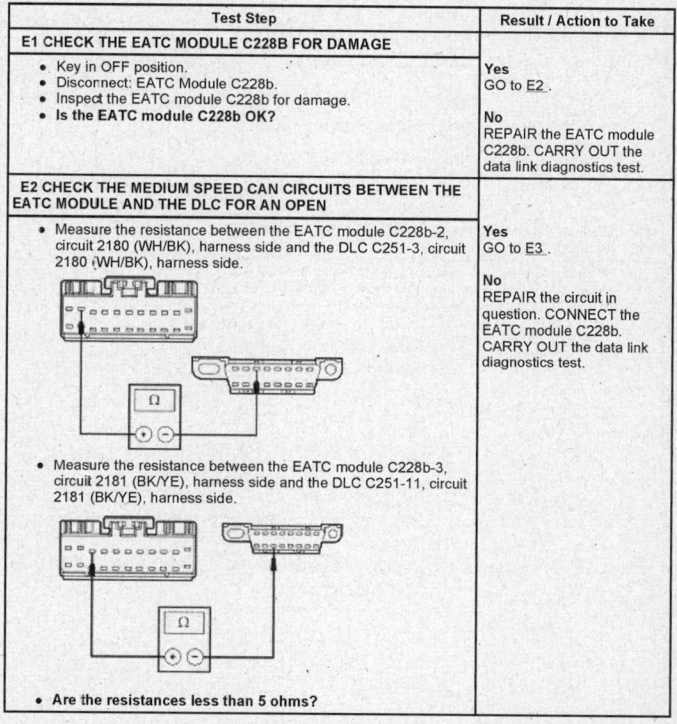 • Measure the resistance between the EATC module C228b-3, circuit 2181 (BK/YE), harness side and the DLC C251-11, circuit 2181 (BK/YE), harness side. • Are the resistances less than 5 ohms?	**Yes** GO to E3. **No** REPAIR the circuit in question. CONNECT the EATC module C228b. CARRY OUT the data link diagnostics test.

LTV0500000004397

Fig. 17 Pinpoint Test E (Part 1 of 2). Expedition & Navigator

E3 CHECK FOR CORRECT EATC OPERATION	
<ul><li>Disconnect all the EATC connectors.</li><li>Check for:<ul><li>corrosion</li><li>pushed-out pins</li></ul></li><li>Connect all the EATC connectors and make sure they seat correctly.</li><li>Operate the system and verify the concern is still present.</li><li>**Is the concern still present?**</li></ul>	**Yes** INSTALL a new EATC module. CLEAR the diagnostic trouble codes (DTCs). REPEAT the self-test. CARRY OUT the data link diagnostics test. **No** The system is operating correctly at this time. The concern may have been caused by a loose or corroded connector. CLEAR the DTCs. REPEAT the self-test. CARRY OUT the data link diagnostics test.

LTV0500000004398

Fig. 17   Pinpoint Test E (Part 2 of 2). Expedition & Navigator

F3 CHECK FOR CORRECT DSM OPERATION	
<ul><li>Disconnect all the DSM connectors.</li><li>Check for:<ul><li>corrosion</li><li>pushed-out pins</li></ul></li><li>Connect all the DSM connectors and make sure they seat correctly.</li><li>Operate the system and verify the concern is still present.</li><li>**Is the concern still present?**</li></ul>	**Yes** INSTALL a new DSM. CLEAR the diagnostic trouble codes (DTCs). REPEAT the self-test. CARRY OUT the data link diagnostics test. **No** The system is operating correctly at this time. The concern may have been caused by a loose or corroded connector. CLEAR the DTCs. REPEAT the self-test. CARRY OUT the data link diagnostics test.

LTV0500000004400

Fig. 18   Pinpoint Test F (Part 2 of 2). Expedition & Navigator

Test Step	Result / Action to Take
G1 CHECK THE PARKING AID MODULE CONNECTOR FOR DAMAGE <ul><li>Key in OFF position.</li><li>Disconnect: Parking Aid Module C4226 (Expedition) or C4014b (Navigator).</li><li>Inspect the parking aid module C4226 (Expedition) or C4014b (Navigator) for damage.</li><li>**Is the parking aid module connector OK?**</li></ul>	**Yes** For Expedition, GO to G2. For Navigator, GO to G3. **No** REPAIR the parking aid module connector in question. CARRY OUT the data link diagnostics test.
G2 CHECK ISO 9141 CIRCUIT BETWEEN THE DLC AND THE PARKING AID MODULE FOR AN OPEN <ul><li>Measure the resistance between the parking aid module C4226-5, circuit 70 (LB/WH), harness side and the DLC C251-7, circuit 70 (LB/WH), harness side.</li></ul> <ul><li>**Is the resistance less than 5 ohms?**</li></ul>	**Yes** GO to G4. **No** REPAIR the circuit in question. CONNECT the parking aid module C4226. CARRY OUT the data link diagnostics test.

LTV0500000004401

Fig. 19   Pinpoint Test G (Part 1 of 2). Expedition & Navigator

Test Step	Result / Action to Take
F1 CHECK THE DSM C341C FOR DAMAGE <ul><li>Key in OFF position.</li><li>Disconnect: DSM C341c.</li><li>Inspect the DSM C341c for damage.</li><li>**Is the DSM C341c OK?**</li></ul>	**Yes** GO to F2. **No** REPAIR the DSM C341c. CARRY OUT the data link diagnostics test.
F2 CHECK THE MEDIUM SPEED CAN CIRCUITS BETWEEN THE DLC AND THE DSM FOR AN OPEN <ul><li>Measure the resistance between the DSM C341c-3, circuit 2180 (WH/BK), harness side and the DLC C251-3, circuit 2180 (WH/BK), harness side.</li></ul> <ul><li>Measure the resistance between the DSM C341c-4, circuit 2181 (BK/YE), harness side and the DLC C251-11, circuit 2181 (BK/YE), harness side.</li></ul> <ul><li>**Are the resistances less than 5 ohms?**</li></ul>	**Yes** GO to F3. **No** REPAIR the circuit in question. CONNECT the DSM C341c. CARRY OUT the data link diagnostics test

LTV0500000004399

Fig. 18   Pinpoint Test F (Part 1 of 2). Expedition & Navigator

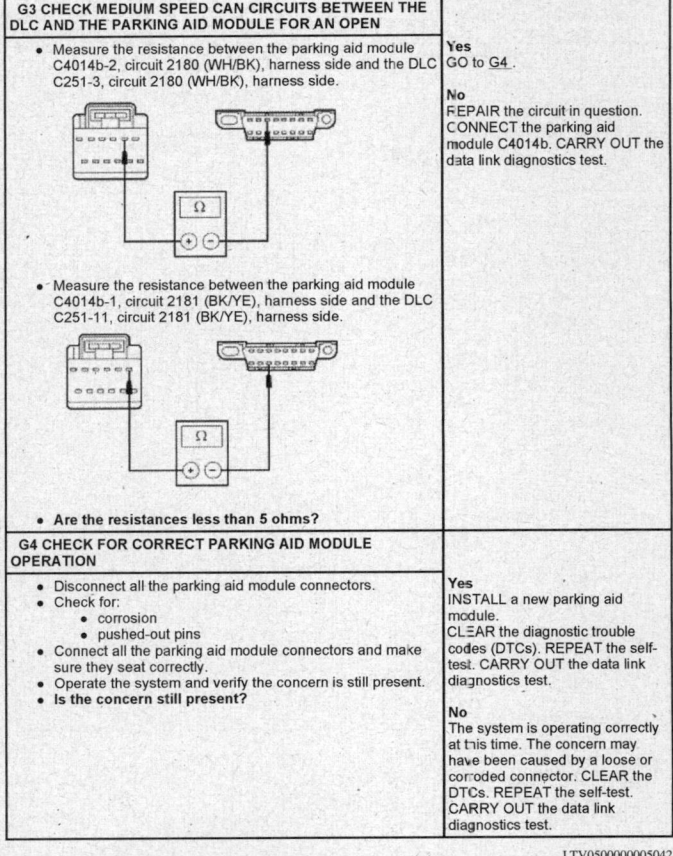

G3 CHECK MEDIUM SPEED CAN CIRCUITS BETWEEN THE DLC AND THE PARKING AID MODULE FOR AN OPEN	
<ul><li>Measure the resistance between the parking aid module C4014b-2, circuit 2180 (WH/BK), harness side and the DLC C251-3, circuit 2180 (WH/BK), harness side.</li></ul> <ul><li>Measure the resistance between the parking aid module C4014b-1, circuit 2181 (BK/YE), harness side and the DLC C251-11, circuit 2181 (BK/YE), harness side.</li></ul> <ul><li>**Are the resistances less than 5 ohms?**</li></ul>	**Yes** GO to G4. **No** REPAIR the circuit in question. CONNECT the parking aid module C4014b. CARRY OUT the data link diagnostics test.
G4 CHECK FOR CORRECT PARKING AID MODULE OPERATION <ul><li>Disconnect all the parking aid module connectors.</li><li>Check for:<ul><li>corrosion</li><li>pushed-out pins</li></ul></li><li>Connect all the parking aid module connectors and make sure they seat correctly.</li><li>Operate the system and verify the concern is still present.</li><li>**Is the concern still present?**</li></ul>	**Yes** INSTALL a new parking aid module. CLEAR the diagnostic trouble codes (DTCs). REPEAT the self-test. CARRY OUT the data link diagnostics test. **No** The system is operating correctly at this time. The concern may have been caused by a loose or corroded connector. CLEAR the DTCs. REPEAT the self-test. CARRY OUT the data link diagnostics test.

LTV0500000005042

Fig. 19   Pinpoint Test G (Part 2 of 2). Expedition & Navigator

Test Step	Result / Action to Take
H1 CHECK THE TCM C1473 FOR DAMAGE	
• Key in OFF position. • Disconnect: TCM C1473. • Inspect the TCM C1473 for damage. • **Is the TCM C1473 OK?**	**Yes** GO to H2 . **No** REPAIR the TCM C1473. CARRY OUT the data link diagnostics test.
H2 CHECK THE HIGH SPEED CAN CIRCUITS BETWEEN THE DLC AND THE TCM FOR AN OPEN	
• Measure the resistance between the TCM C1473-6, circuit 1814 (WH/LB), harness side and the DLC C251-6, circuit 1814 (WH/LB), harness side. 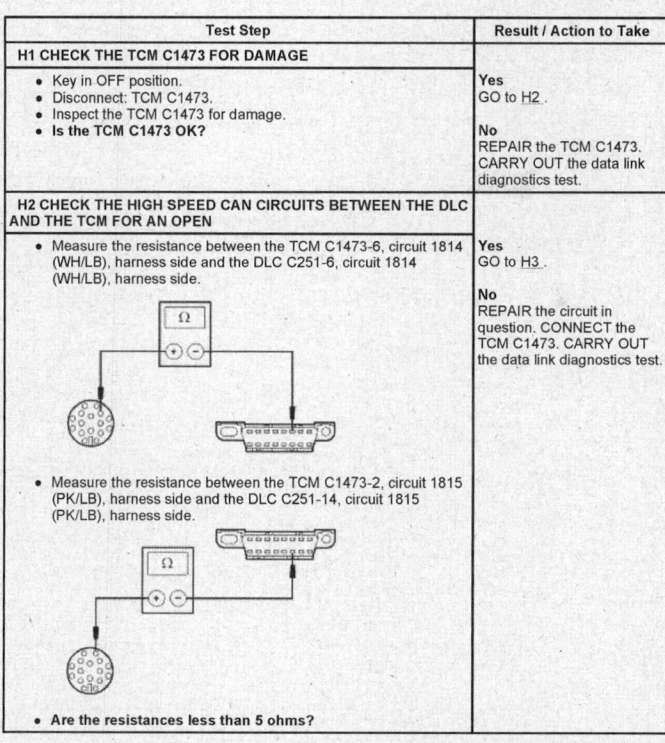 • Measure the resistance between the TCM C1473-2, circuit 1815 (PK/LB), harness side and the DLC C251-14, circuit 1815 (PK/LB), harness side. • **Are the resistances less than 5 ohms?**	**Yes** GO to H3 . **No** REPAIR the circuit in question. CONNECT the TCM C1473. CARRY OUT the data link diagnostics test.

LTV0500000005043

Fig. 20 Pinpoint Test H (Part 1 of 2). Expedition & Navigator

Test Step	Result / Action to Take
I1 CHECK THE INSTRUMENT CLUSTER C220B FOR DAMAGE	
• Key in OFF position. • Depower the supplemental restraint system (SRS). • Disconnect: Instrument Cluster C220b. • Inspect the instrument cluster C220b for damage. • **Is the instrument cluster C220b OK?**	**Yes** GO to I2 . **No** REPAIR the circuit in question. CONNECT the instrument cluster C220b. REPOWER the SRS. CARRY OUT the diagnostic tool data link test.
I2 CHECK THE HIGH SPEED CAN CIRCUITS BETWEEN THE INSTRUMENT CLUSTER AND THE DLC FOR AN OPEN	
• Measure the resistance between the instrument cluster C220b-12, circuit 1814 (WH/LB), harness side and the DLC C251-6, circuit 1814 (WH/LB), harness side. 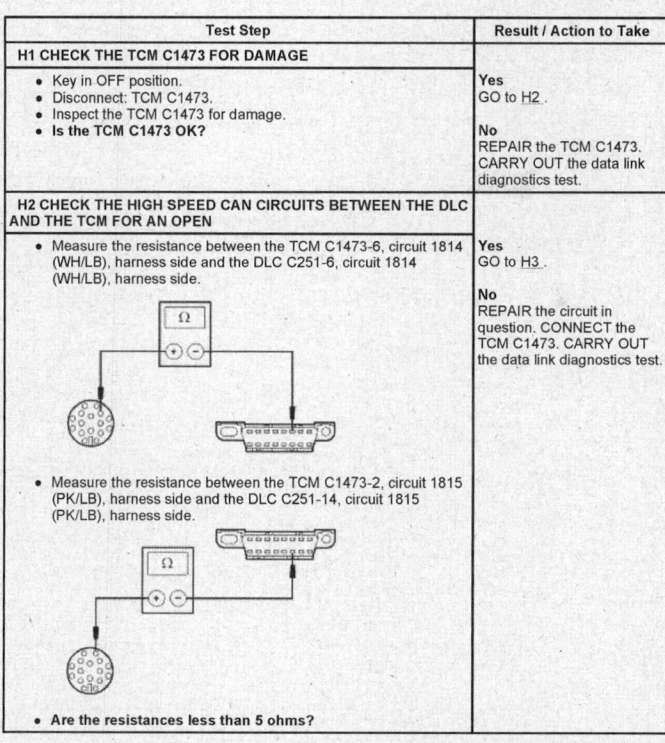 • Measure the resistance between the instrument cluster C220b-13, circuit 1815 (PK/LB), harness side and the DLC C251-14, circuit 1815 (PK/LB), harness side. • **Are the resistances less than 5 ohms?**	**Yes** GO to I3 . **No** REPAIR the circuit in question. CONNECT the instrument cluster C220b. REPOWER the SRS. CARRY OUT the diagnostic tool data link test.

LTV0500000005045

Fig. 21 Pinpoint Test I (Part 1 of 2). Expedition & Navigator

H3 CHECK FOR CORRECT TCM OPERATION	

• Disconnect all the TCM connectors.
• Check for:
  • corrosion
  • pushed-out pins
• Connect all the TCM connectors and make sure they seat correctly.
• Operate the system and verify the concern is still present.
• **Is the concern still present?**
	Yes
	INSTALL a new TCM. CLEAR the
	diagnostic trouble codes (DTCs). REPEAT the self-test.
	CARRY OUT the data link diagnostics test.
	
	No
	The system is operating correctly at this time. The concern may
	have been caused by a loose or corroded connector. CLEAR
	the DTCs. REPEAT the self-test. CARRY OUT the data link
	diagnostics test.

LTV0500000005044

Fig. 20 Pinpoint Test H (Part 2 of 2). Expedition & Navigator

I3 CHECK THE MEDIUM SPEED CAN CIRCUITS BETWEEN THE INSTRUMENT CLUSTER AND THE DLC FOR AN OPEN	
• Measure the resistance between the instrument cluster C220b-25, circuit 2180 (WH/BK), harness side and the DLC C251-3, circuit 2180 (WH/BK), harness side. 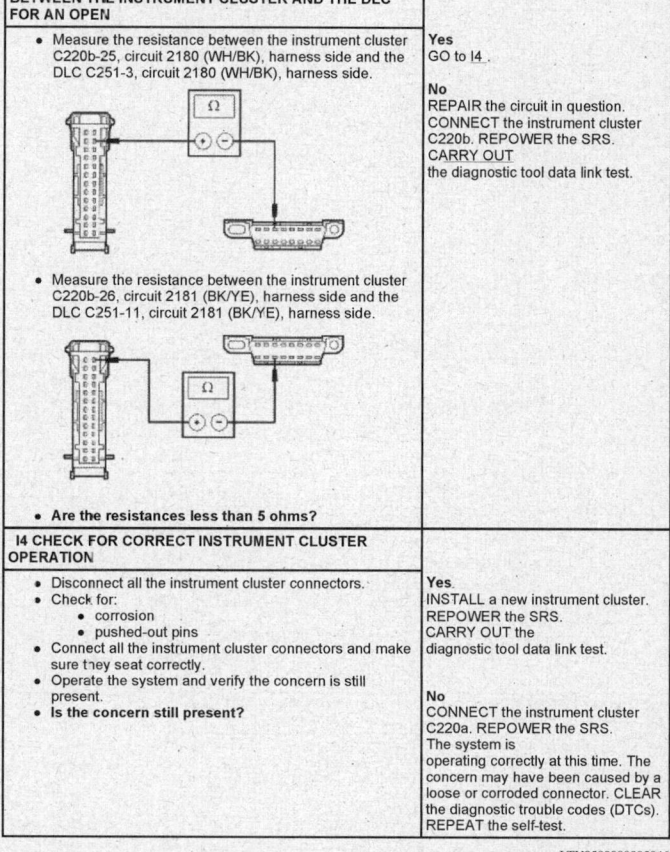 • Measure the resistance between the instrument cluster C220b-26, circuit 2181 (BK/YE), harness side and the DLC C251-11, circuit 2181 (BK/YE), harness side. • **Are the resistances less than 5 ohms?**	**Yes** GO to I4 . **No** REPAIR the circuit in question. CONNECT the instrument cluster C220b. REPOWER the SRS. CARRY OUT the diagnostic tool data link test.
I4 CHECK FOR CORRECT INSTRUMENT CLUSTER OPERATION	

• Disconnect all the instrument cluster connectors.
• Check for:
  • corrosion
  • pushed-out pins
• Connect all the instrument cluster connectors and make sure they seat correctly.
• Operate the system and verify the concern is still present.
• **Is the concern still present?**
	Yes
	INSTALL a new instrument cluster.
	REPOWER the SRS.
	CARRY OUT the
	diagnostic tool data link test.
	
	No
	CONNECT the instrument cluster
	C220a. REPOWER the SRS.
	The system is
	operating correctly at this time. The
	concern may have been caused by a
	loose or corroded connector. CLEAR
	the diagnostic trouble codes (DTCs).
	REPEAT the self-test.

LTV0500000005046

Fig. 21 Pinpoint Test I (Part 2 of 2). Expedition & Navigator

Test Step	Result / Action to Take
J1 CHECK THE POWER LIFTGATE MODULE C4174D FOR DAMAGE • Key in OFF position. • Disconnect: Power Liftgate Module C4174d. • Inspect the power liftgate module C4174d for damage. • **Is the power liftgate module C4174d OK?**	**Yes** GO to J2 . **No** REPAIR the power liftgate module C4174d. CARRY OUT the data link diagnostics test.
J2 CHECK THE MEDIUM SPEED CAN CIRCUITS BETWEEN THE POWER LIFTGATE MODULE AND THE DLC FOR AN OPEN • Measure the resistance between the power liftgate module C4174d-20, circuit 2180 (WH/BK), harness side and the DLC C251-3, circuit 2180 (WH/BK), harness side. 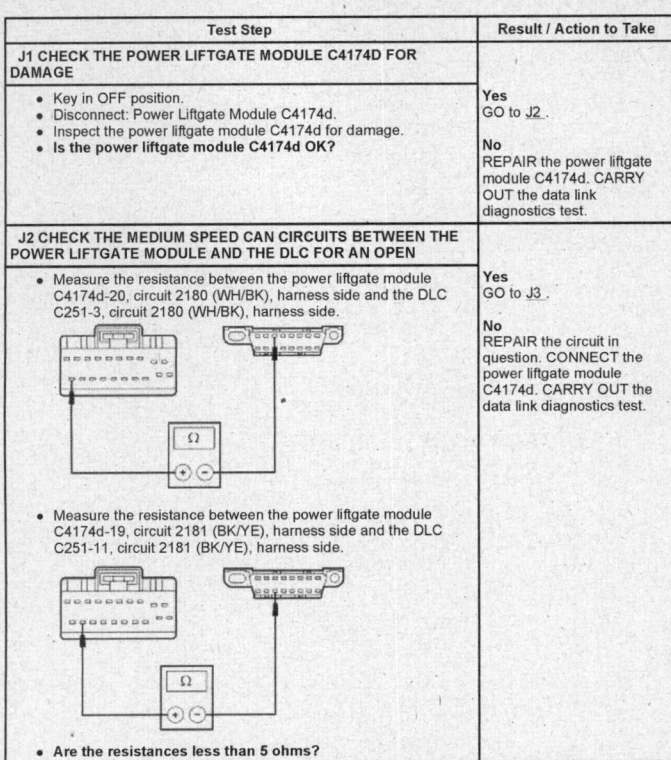 • Measure the resistance between the power liftgate module C4174d-19, circuit 2181 (BK/YE), harness side and the DLC C251-11, circuit 2181 (BK/YE), harness side. • **Are the resistances less than 5 ohms?**	**Yes** GO to J3 . **No** REPAIR the circuit in question. CONNECT the power liftgate module C4174d. CARRY OUT the data link diagnostics test.

LTV0500000005047

Fig. 22   Pinpoint Test J (Part 1 of 2). Expedition & Navigator

Test Step	Result / Action to Take
K1 CHECK THE AIR SUSPENSION CONTROL MODULE C2324B (EXPEDITION) OR C2131B (NAVIGATOR) FOR DAMAGE • Key in OFF position. • Disconnect: Air Suspension Control Module C2324b (Expedition). • Disconnect: Air Suspension Control Module C2131b (Navigator). • Inspect the air suspension control module C2324b (Expedition) or C2131b (Navigator) for damage. • **Is the air suspension control module C2324b (Expedition) or C2131b (Navigator) OK?**	**Yes** GO to K2 . **No** REPAIR the air suspension control module connector. CARRY OUT the data link diagnostics test.
K2 CHECK THE MEDIUM SPEED CAN CIRCUITS BETWEEN THE AIR SUSPENSION CONTROL MODULE AND THE DLC FOR AN OPEN • Measure the resistance between the air suspension control module C2324b-10 (Expedition) or C2131b-11 (Navigator), circuit 2180 (WH/BK), harness side and the DLC C251-3, circuit 2180 (WH/BK), harness side. • Measure the resistance between the air suspension control module C2324b-11 (Expedition) or C2131b-12 (Navigator), circuit 2181 (BK/YE), harness side and the DLC C251-11, circuit 2181 (BK/YE), harness side. • **Are the resistances less than 5 ohms?**	**Yes** GO to K3 . **No** REPAIR the circuit in question. CONNECT the air suspension module connector. CARRY OUT the data link diagnostics test.

LTV0500000005049

Fig. 23   Pinpoint Test K (Part 1 of 2). Expedition & Navigator

J3 CHECK FOR CORRECT POWER LIFTGATE MODULE OPERATION	

• Disconnect all the power liftgate module connectors.
• Check for:
   • corrosion
   • pushed-out pins
• Connect all the power liftgate module connectors and make sure they seat correctly.
• Operate the system and verify the concern is still present.
• **Is the concern still present?**
	Yes
	INSTALL a new power liftgate module. CLEAR the diagnostic trouble codes (DTCs). REPEAT the self-test. CARRY OUT the data link diagnostics test.
	
	No
	The system is operating correctly at this time. The concern may have been caused by a loose or corroded connector. CLEAR the DTCs. REPEAT the self-test. CARRY OUT the data link diagnostics test.

LTV0500000005048

Fig. 22   Pinpoint Test J (Part 2 of 2). Expedition & Navigator

K3 CHECK FOR CORRECT AIR SUSPENSION CONTROL MODULE OPERATION	

• Disconnect all the air suspension control module connectors.
• Check for:
   • corrosion
   • pushed-out pins
• Connect all the air suspension control module connectors and make sure they seat correctly.
• Operate the system and verify the concern is still present.
• **Is the concern still present?**
	Yes
	INSTALL a new air suspension control module. CLEAR the diagnostic trouble codes (DTCs). REPEAT the self-test. CARRY OUT the data link diagnostics test.
	
	No
	The system is operating correctly at this time. The concern may have been caused by a loose or corroded connector. CLEAR the DTCs. REPEAT the self-test. CARRY OUT the data link diagnostics test.

LTV0500000005050

Fig. 23   Pinpoint Test K (Part 2 of 2). Expedition & Navigator

Test Step	Result / Action to Take
L1 CHECK THE CLIMATE CONTROLLED SEAT MODULE CONNECTOR FOR DAMAGE • Key in OFF position. • Disconnect: Climate Controlled Seat Module C3265b. • Inspect the climate controlled seat module C3265b for damage. • **Is the climate controlled seat module C3265b OK?**	**Yes** GO to L2 . **No** REPAIR the climate controlled seat module C3265b. CARRY OUT the data link diagnostics test.
L2 CHECK THE MEDIUM SPEED CAN CIRCUITS BETWEEN THE CLIMATE CONTROLLED SEAT MODULE AND THE DLC FOR AN OPEN • Measure the resistance between the climate controlled seat module C3265b-14, circuit 2180 (WH/BK), harness side and the DLC C251-3, circuit 2180 (WH/BK), harness side. • Measure the resistance between the climate controlled seat module C3265b-15, circuit 2181 (BK/YE), harness side and the DLC C251-11, circuit 2181 (BK/YE), harness side. • **Are the resistances less than 5 ohms?**	**Yes** GO to L3 . **No** REPAIR the circuit in question. CONNECT the climate controlled seat module C3265b. CARRY OUT the data link diagnostic

LTV0500000005051

Fig. 24   Pinpoint Test L (Part 1 of 2). Expedition & Navigator

L3 CHECK FOR CORRECT CLIMATE CONTROLLED SEAT MODULE OPERATION	

• Disconnect all the climate controlled seat module connectors.
• Check for:
   • corrosion
   • pushed-out pins
• Connect all the climate controlled seat module connectors and make sure they seat correctly.
• Operate the system and verify the concern is still present.
• **Is the concern still present?**
	Yes
	INSTALL a new climate controlled seat module. CLEAR the diagnostic trouble codes (DTCs). REPEAT the self-test. CARRY OUT the data link diagnostics test.
	
	No
	The system is operating correctly at this time. The concern may have been caused by a loose or corroded connector. CLEAR the DTCs. REPEAT the self-test. CARRY OUT the data link diagnostics test.

LTV0500000005052

Fig. 24   Pinpoint Test L (Part 2 of 2). Expedition & Navigator

Test Step	Result / Action to Take
M1 CHECK THE DATA LINK CONNECTOR (DLC) C251 FOR DAMAGE • Key in OFF position. • Inspect the DLC C251. • **Is the DLC C251 OK?**	**Yes** GO to M2 . **No** REPAIR the DLC C251. CARRY OUT the data link diagnostics test.
M2 CHECK THE NAVIGATION SYSTEM MODULE C2279A FOR DAMAGE • Key in OFF position. • Disconnect: Navigation System Module C2279a. • Inspect the navigation system module C2279a for damage. • **Is the navigation system module C2279a OK?**	**Yes** GO to M3 . **No** REPAIR the navigation system module C2279a. CARRY OUT the data link diagnostics test.

LTV0500000005053

Fig. 25   Pinpoint Test M (Part 1 of 4). Expedition & Navigator

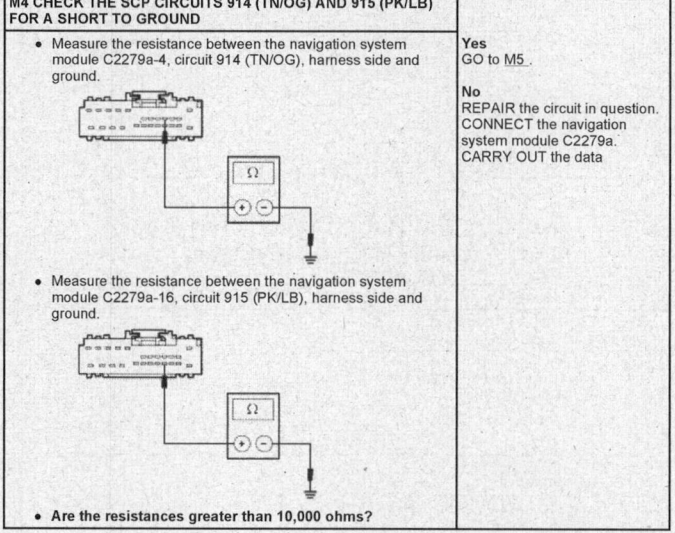

• Are the resistances greater than 10,000 ohms?

M4 CHECK THE SCP CIRCUITS 914 (TN/OG) AND 915 (PK/LB) FOR A SHORT TO GROUND
• Measure the resistance between the navigation system module C2279a-4, circuit 914 (TN/OG), harness side and ground.
• Measure the resistance between the navigation system module C2279a-16, circuit 915 (PK/LB), harness side and ground.

Yes
GO to M5 .

No
REPAIR the circuit in question. CONNECT the navigation system module C2279a. CARRY OUT the data

LTV0500000005055

Fig. 25   Pinpoint Test M (Part 3 of 4). Expedition & Navigator

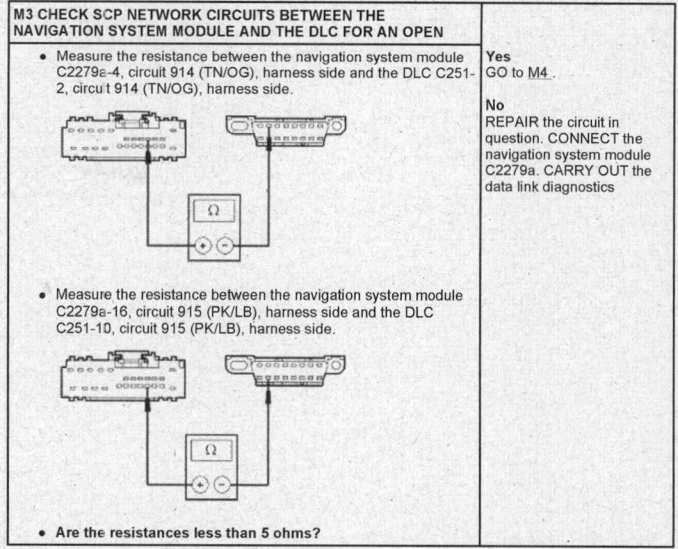

M3 CHECK SCP NETWORK CIRCUITS BETWEEN THE NAVIGATION SYSTEM MODULE AND THE DLC FOR AN OPEN
• Measure the resistance between the navigation system module C2279a-4, circuit 914 (TN/OG), harness side and the DLC C251-2, circuit 914 (TN/OG), harness side.
• Measure the resistance between the navigation system module C2279a-16, circuit 915 (PK/LB), harness side and the DLC C251-10, circuit 915 (PK/LB), harness side.
• Are the resistances less than 5 ohms?

Yes
GO to M4 .

No
REPAIR the circuit in question. CONNECT the navigation system module C2279a. CARRY OUT the data link diagnostics

LTV0500000005054

Fig. 25   Pinpoint Test M (Part 2 of 4). Expedition & Navigator

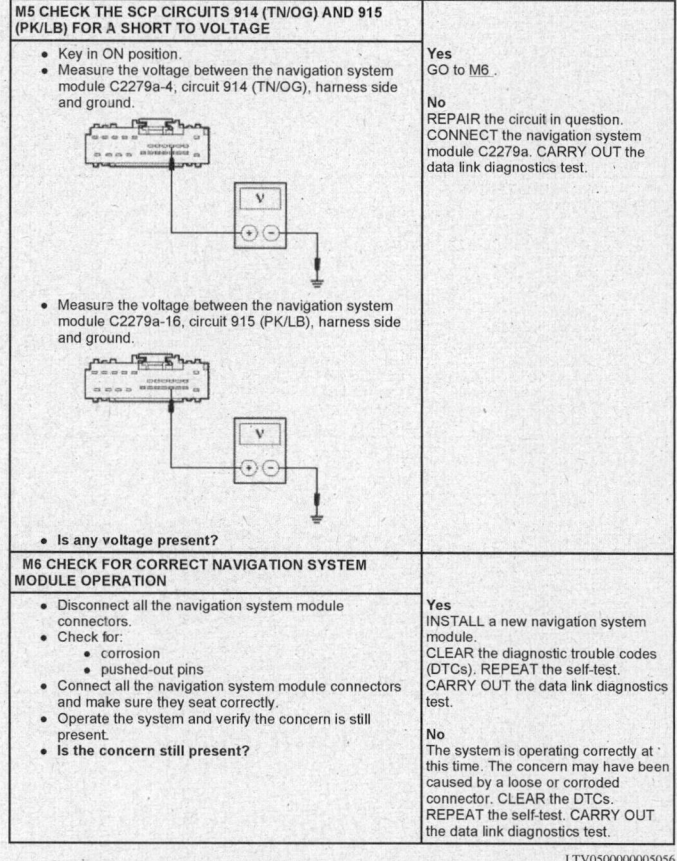

M5 CHECK THE SCP CIRCUITS 914 (TN/OG) AND 915 (PK/LB) FOR A SHORT TO VOLTAGE
• Key in ON position.
• Measure the voltage between the navigation system module C2279a-4, circuit 914 (TN/OG), harness side and ground.
• Measure the voltage between the navigation system module C2279a-16, circuit 915 (PK/LB), harness side and ground.
• Is any voltage present?

Yes
GO to M6 .

No
REPAIR the circuit in question. CONNECT the navigation system module C2279a. CARRY OUT the data link diagnostics test.

M6 CHECK FOR CORRECT NAVIGATION SYSTEM MODULE OPERATION
• Disconnect all the navigation system module connectors.
• Check for:
  • corrosion
  • pushed-out pins
• Connect all the navigation system module connectors and make sure they seat correctly.
• Operate the system and verify the concern is still present.
• Is the concern still present?

Yes
INSTALL a new navigation system module. CLEAR the diagnostic trouble codes (DTCs). REPEAT the self-test. CARRY OUT the data link diagnostics test.

No
The system is operating correctly at this time. The concern may have been caused by a loose or corroded connector. CLEAR the DTCs. REPEAT the self-test. CARRY OUT the data link diagnostics test.

LTV0500000005056

Fig. 25   Pinpoint Test M (Part 4 of 4). Expedition & Navigator

Test Step	Result / Action to Take
N1 CHECK THE DATA LINK CONNECTOR (DLC) C251 FOR DAMAGE • Key in OFF position. • Inspect the DLC C251. • **Is the DLC C251 OK?**	**Yes** GO to N2 . **No** REPAIR the DLC C251. CARRY OUT the data link diagnostics test.
N2 CHECK ISO 9141 CIRCUIT BETWEEN THE DLC AND THE RESTRAINT CONTROL MODULE (RCM) FOR AN OPEN • Depower the supplemental restraint system (SRS). • Disconnect: RCM 310a. • Measure the resistance between the RCM C310a-11, circuit 70 (LB/WH), harness side and the DLC C251-7, circuit 70 (LB/WH), harness side. 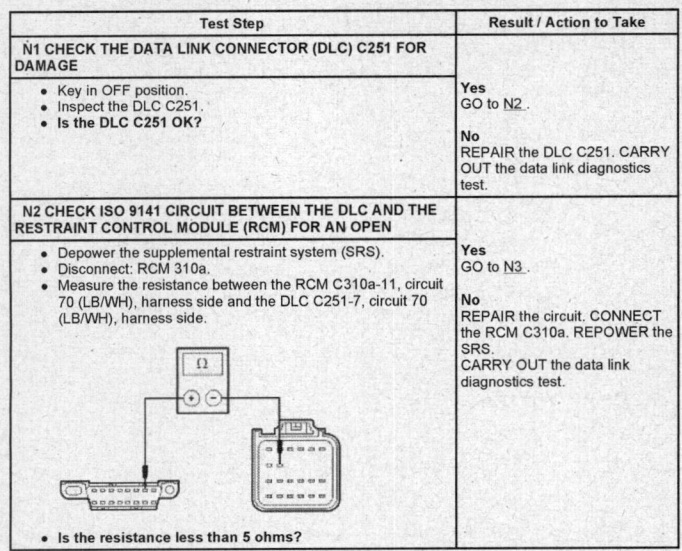 • **Is the resistance less than 5 ohms?**	**Yes** GO to N3 . **No** REPAIR the circuit. CONNECT the RCM C310a. REPOWER the SRS. CARRY OUT the data link diagnostics test.

LTV0500000005057

Fig. 26   Pinpoint Test N (Part 1 of 3).
Expedition & Navigator

N3 CHECK THE ISO 9141 COMMUNICATIONS NETWORK FOR A SHORT TO VOLTAGE • Disconnect: Parking Aid Module C4226 (Expedition equipped with Parking Aid). • Key in ON position. • Measure the voltage between the DLC C251-7, circuit 70 (LB/WH), harness side and ground. 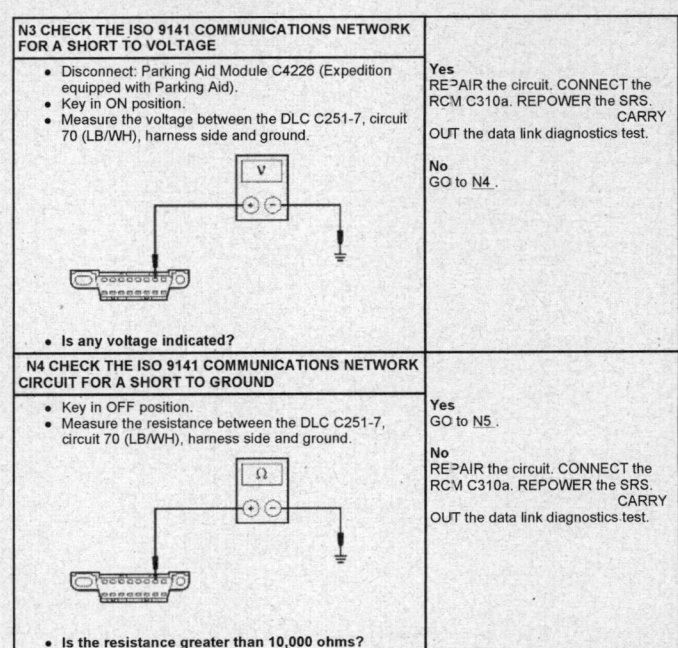 • **Is any voltage indicated?**	**Yes** REPAIR the circuit. CONNECT the RCM C310a. REPOWER the SRS. CARRY OUT the data link diagnostics test. **No** GO to N4 .
N4 CHECK THE ISO 9141 COMMUNICATIONS NETWORK CIRCUIT FOR A SHORT TO GROUND • Key in OFF position. • Measure the resistance between the DLC C251-7, circuit 70 (LB/WH), harness side and ground. • **Is the resistance greater than 10,000 ohms?**	**Yes** GO to N5 . **No** REPAIR the circuit. CONNECT the RCM C310a. REPOWER the SRS. CARRY OUT the data link diagnostics test.

LTV0500000005058

Fig. 26   Pinpoint Test N (Part 2 of 3).
Expedition & Navigator

N5 CHECK THE ISO 9141 COMMUNICATIONS NETWORK • Connect: RCM C310a. • REPOWER the SRS. • Key in ON position. • Carry out the data link diagnostics test. • **Does the diagnostic tool indicate system passed?**	**Yes** For Expedition with parking aid, GO to N7 . For all others, GO to N6 . **No** GO to N6 .

N6 CHECK FOR CORRECT RCM OPERATION
• Depower the SRS.
• Disconnect all the RCM connectors.
• Check for:
  • corrosion
  • pushed-out pins
• Connect all the RCM connectors and make sure they seat correctly.
• Operate the system and verify the concern is still present.
• **Is the concern still present?**
	Yes
	INSTALL a new RCM. REPOWER the SRS. CLEAR the diagnostic trouble codes (DTCs). REPEAT the self-test. CARRY OUT the data link diagnostics test.
	
	No
	The system is operating correctly at this time. The concern may have been caused by a loose or corroded connector. REPOWER the SRS. CLEAR the DTCs. REPEAT the self-test. CARRY OUT the data link diagnostics test.

N7 CHECK FOR CORRECT PARKING AID MODULE OPERATION
• Disconnect all the parking aid module connectors.
• Check for:
  • corrosion
  • pushed-out pins
• Connect all the parking aid module connectors and make sure they seat correctly.
• Operate the system and verify the concern is still present.
• **Is the concern still present?**
	Yes
	INSTALL a new parking aid module. REPOWER the SRS. CLEAR the DTCs. REPEAT the self-test. CARRY OUT the data link diagnostics test.
	
	No
	The system is operating correctly at this time. The concern may have been caused by a loose or corroded connector. REPOWER the SRS. CLEAR the DTCs. REPEAT the self-test. CARRY OUT the data link diagnostics test.

LTV0500000005059

Fig. 26   Pinpoint Test N (Part 3 of 3).
Expedition & Navigator

Test Step	Result / Action to Take
O1 CHECK THE DATA LINK CONNECTOR (DLC) C251 FOR DAMAGE • Key in OFF position. • Inspect the DLC C251 for damage. • **Is the DLC C251 OK?**	**Yes** GO to O2 . **No** REPAIR the DLC C251. CARRY OUT the data link diagnostics test.
O2 CHECK THE HIGH SPEED CAN MODULE CONNECTORS • Disconnect: Anti-Lock Brake System (ABS) Module C135. • Disconnect: Instrument Cluster C220b. • Disconnect: Powertrain Control Module (PCM) C175b. • Disconnect: Transmission Control Module (TCM) C1473 (if equipped). • Inspect the connectors for damage. • **Are the connectors OK?**	**Yes** GO to O3 . **No** REPAIR the module connector in question. CONNECT all network modules. CARRY OUT the data link diagnostics test.

LTV0500000005060

Fig. 27   Pinpoint Test O (Part 1 of 8).
Expedition & Navigator

O3 CHECK THE HIGH SPEED CAN CIRCUITS BETWEEN THE ABS MODULE AND THE DLC FOR AN OPEN • Measure the resistance between the ABS module C135-11, circuit 1814 (WH/LB), harness side and the DLC C251-6, circuit 1814 (WH/LB), harness side. 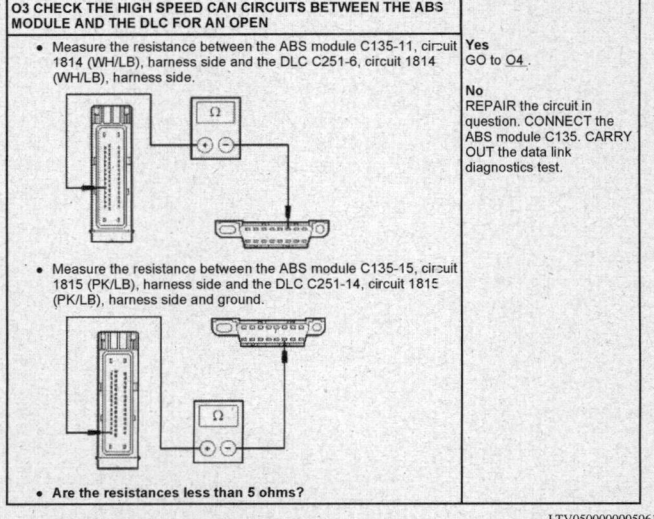 • Measure the resistance between the ABS module C135-15, circuit 1815 (PK/LB), harness side and the DLC C251-14, circuit 1815 (PK/LB), harness side and ground. • **Are the resistances less than 5 ohms?**	**Yes** GO to O4 . **No** REPAIR the circuit in question. CONNECT the ABS module C135. CARRY OUT the data link diagnostics test.

LTV0500000005061

Fig. 27   Pinpoint Test O (Part 2 of 8).
Expedition & Navigator

O4 CHECK THE HIGH SPEED CAN CIRCUITS BETWEEN THE INSTRUMENT CLUSTER AND THE DLC FOR AN OPEN

- Depower the supplemental restraint system (SRS). Refer to Section 501-20B.
- Measure the resistance between the instrument cluster C220b-12, circuit 1814 (WH/LB), harness side and the DLC C251-6, circuit 1814 (WH/LB), harness side.

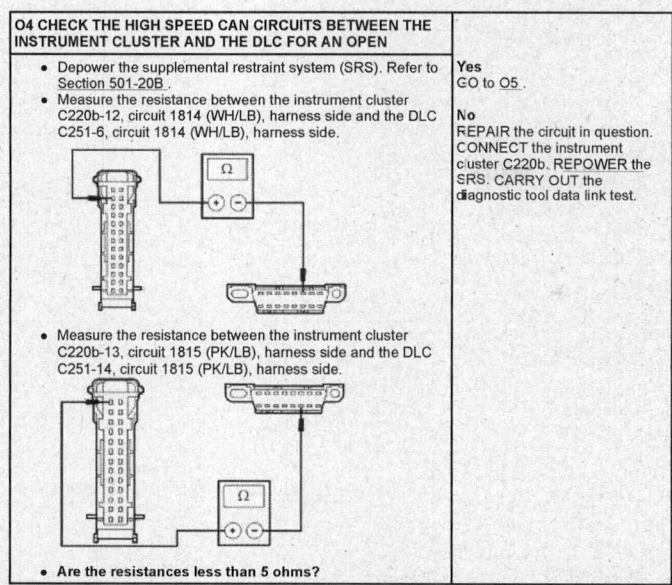

- Measure the resistance between the instrument cluster C220b-13, circuit 1815 (PK/LB), harness side and the DLC C251-14, circuit 1815 (PK/LB), harness side.

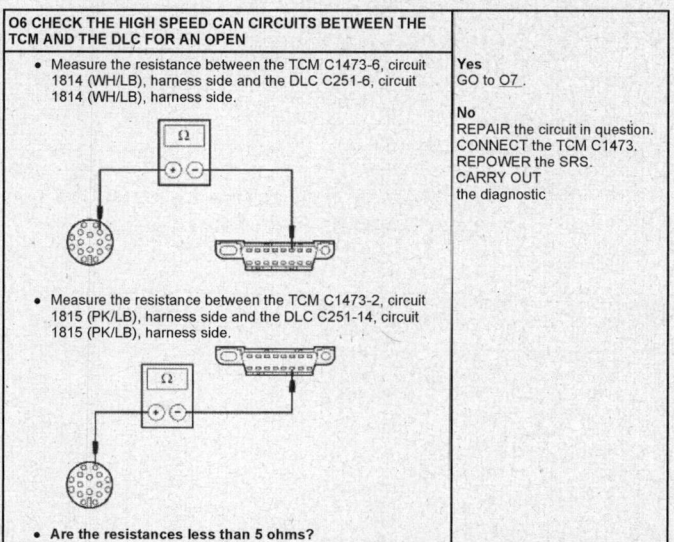

- Are the resistances less than 5 ohms?

Yes
GO to O5.

No
REPAIR the circuit in question. CONNECT the instrument cluster C220b. REPOWER the SRS. CARRY OUT the diagnostic tool data link test.

LTV0500000005062

Fig. 27   Pinpoint Test O (Part 3 of 8).
Expedition & Navigator

O5 CHECK THE HIGH SPEED CAN CIRCUITS BETWEEN THE PCM AND THE DLC FOR AN OPEN

- Measure the resistance between the PCM C175b-2, circuit 1814 (WH/LB), harness side and the DLC C251-6, circuit 1814 (WH/LB), harness side.

- Measure the resistance between the PCM C175b-3, circuit 1815 (PK/LB), harness side and the DLC C251-14, circuit 1815 (PK/LB), harness side.

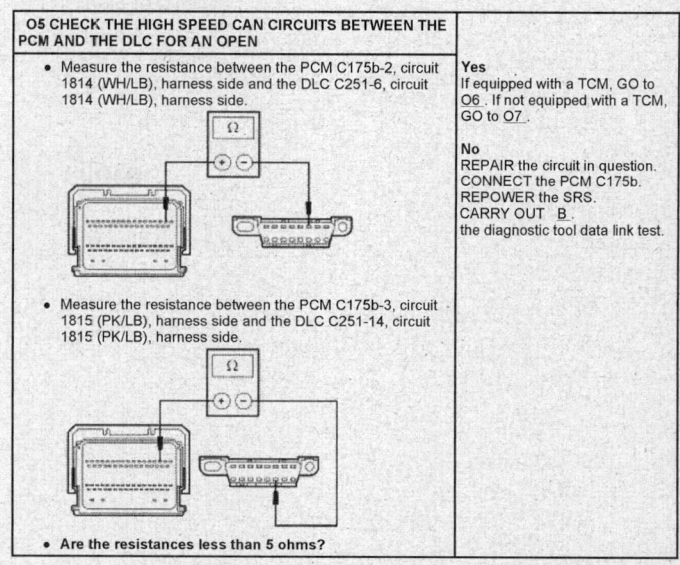

- Are the resistances less than 5 ohms?

Yes
If equipped with a TCM, GO to O6. If not equipped with a TCM, GO to O7.

No
REPAIR the circuit in question. CONNECT the PCM C175b. REPOWER the SRS. CARRY OUT B . the diagnostic tool data link test.

LTV0500000005063

Fig. 27   Pinpoint Test O (Part 4 of 8).
Expedition & Navigator

O6 CHECK THE HIGH SPEED CAN CIRCUITS BETWEEN THE TCM AND THE DLC FOR AN OPEN

- Measure the resistance between the TCM C1473-6, circuit 1814 (WH/LB), harness side and the DLC C251-6, circuit 1814 (WH/LB), harness side.

- Measure the resistance between the TCM C1473-2, circuit 1815 (PK/LB), harness side and the DLC C251-14, circuit 1815 (PK/LB), harness side.

- Are the resistances less than 5 ohms?

Yes
GO to O7.

No
REPAIR the circuit in question. CONNECT the TCM C1473. REPOWER the SRS. CARRY OUT the diagnostic

LTV0500000005064

Fig. 27   Pinpoint Test O (Part 5 of 8).
Expedition & Navigator

O7 CHECK THE HIGH SPEED CAN CIRCUITS FOR A SHORT TO GROUND

- Measure the resistance between the DLC C251-6, circuit 1814 (WH/LB), harness side and ground; and between the DLC C251-14, circuit 1815 (PK/LB), harness side and ground.

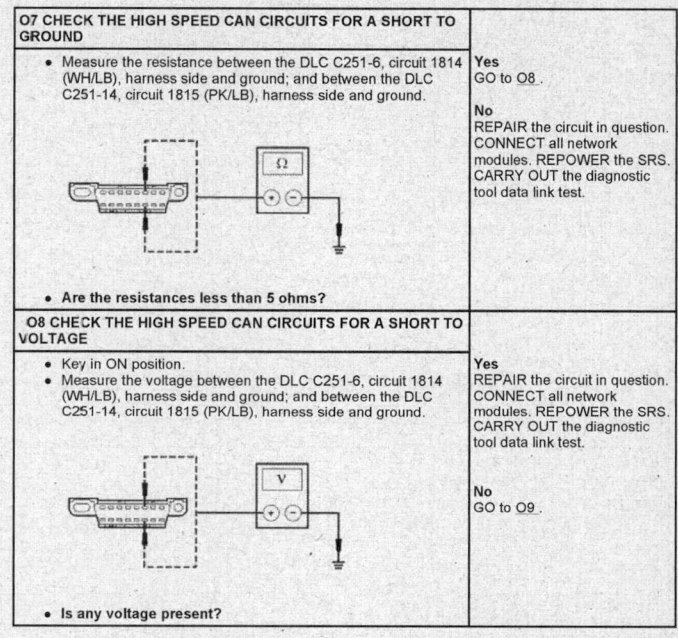

- Are the resistances less than 5 ohms?

Yes
GO to O8.

No
REPAIR the circuit in question. CONNECT all network modules. REPOWER the SRS. CARRY OUT the diagnostic tool data link test.

O8 CHECK THE HIGH SPEED CAN CIRCUITS FOR A SHORT TO VOLTAGE

- Key in ON position.
- Measure the voltage between the DLC C251-6, circuit 1814 (WH/LB), harness side and ground; and between the DLC C251-14, circuit 1815 (PK/LB), harness side and ground.

- Is any voltage present?

Yes
REPAIR the circuit in question. CONNECT all network modules. REPOWER the SRS. CARRY OUT the diagnostic tool data link test.

No
GO to O9.

LTV0500000005065

Fig. 27   Pinpoint Test O (Part 6 of 8).
Expedition & Navigator

O9 CHECK THE HIGH SPEED CAN WITH THE ABS MODULE C135 DISCONNECTED

- Connect: Instrument Cluster C220b.
- Connect: PCM C175b.
- Connect: TCM C1473 (if equipped).
- Key in ON position.
- Enter the following diagnostic mode on the diagnostic tool: Data Link Diagnostics Test.
- **Is system passed obtained?**

Yes
GO to O12.

No
If equipped with a TCM, GO to O10. If not equipped with a TCM, GO to O11.

O10 CHECK THE HIGH SPEED CAN WITH THE TCM C1473 DISCONNECTED

- Connect: ABS Module C135.
- Disconnect: TCM C1473.
- Key in ON position.
- Enter the following diagnostic mode on the diagnostic tool: Data Link Diagnostics Test.
- **Is system passed obtained?**

Yes
GO to O15.

No
GO to O11.

O11 CHECK THE HIGH SPEED CAN WITH A SUBSTITUTED PCM

- Connect: ABS Module C135 (if disconnected).
- Connect: TCM C1473 (if equipped).
- INSTALL a known good PCM.
- Key in ON position.
- Enter the following diagnostic mode on the diagnostic tool: Data Link Diagnostics Test.
- **Is system passed obtained?**

Yes
GO to O14.

No
INSTALL the original PCM. GO to O13.

O12 CHECK FOR CORRECT ABS MODULE OPERATION

- Disconnect all the ABS module connectors.
- Check for:
  - corrosion
  - pushed-out pins
- Connect all the ABS module connectors and make sure they seat correctly.
- Operate the system and verify the concern is still present.
- **Is the concern still present?**

Yes
INSTALL a new ABS module. CONNECT all network modules. REPOWER the SRS. CLEAR the DTCs. REPEAT the self-test. CARRY OUT the data link diagnostics test.

No
The system is operating correctly at this time. The concern may have been caused by a loose or corroded connector. CONNECT all network modules. REPOWER the SRS. CLEAR the DTCs. REPEAT the self-test. CARRY OUT the data link diagnostics test.

LTV0500000005066

**Fig. 27 Pinpoint Test O (Part 7 of 8).
Expedition & Navigator**

O13 CHECK FOR CORRECT INSTRUMENT CLUSTER OPERATION

- Disconnect all the instrument cluster connectors.
- Check for:
  - corrosion
  - pushed-out pins
- Connect all the instrument cluster connectors and make sure they seat correctly.
- Operate the system and verify the concern is still present.
- **Is the concern still present?**

Yes
INSTALL a new instrument cluster. CONNECT all network modules. REPOWER the SRS. CLEAR the DTCs. REPEAT the self-test. CARRY OUT the data link diagnostics test.

No
The system is operating correctly at this time. The concern may have been caused by a loose or corroded connector. CONNECT all network modules. REPOWER the SRS. CLEAR the DTCs. REPEAT the self-test. CARRY OUT the data link diagnostics test.

O14 CHECK FOR CORRECT PCM OPERATION

- Disconnect all the PCM connectors.
- Check for:
  - corrosion
  - pushed-out pins
- Connect all the PCM connectors and make sure they seat correctly.
- Operate the system and verify the concern is still present.
- **Is the concern still present?**

Yes
INSTALL a new PCM. CONNECT all network modules. REPOWER the SRS. CLEAR the DTCs. REPEAT the self-test. CARRY OUT the data link diagnostics test.

No
The system is operating correctly at this time. The concern may have been caused by a loose or corroded connector. CONNECT all network modules. REPOWER the SRS. CLEAR the DTCs. REPEAT the self-test. CARRY OUT the data link diagnostics test.

O15 CHECK FOR CORRECT TCM OPERATION

- Disconnect all the TCM connectors.
- Check for:
  - corrosion
  - pushed-out pins
- Connect all the TCM connectors and make sure they seat correctly.
- Operate the system and verify the concern is still present.
- **Is the concern still present?**

Yes
INSTALL a new TCM. CONNECT all network modules. REPOWER the SRS. CLEAR the DTCs. REPEAT the self-test. CARRY OUT the data link diagnostics test.

No
The system is operating correctly at this time. The concern may have been caused by a loose or corroded connector. CONNECT all network modules. REPOWER the SRS. CLEAR the DTCs. REPEAT the self-test. CARRY OUT the data link diagnostics test.

LTV0500000005067

**Fig. 27 Pinpoint Test O (Part 8 of 8).
Expedition & Navigator**

Test Step	Result / Action to Take
P1 CHECK THE DATA LINK CONNECTOR (DLC) C251 FOR DAMAGE • Key in OFF position. • Inspect the DLC C251 for damage. • **Is the DLC C251 OK?**	**Yes** GO to P2. **No** REPAIR the DLC C251. CARRY OUT the data link diagnostics test.
P2 CHECK THE MEDIUM SPEED CAN MODULE CONNECTORS • Depower the supplemental restraint system (SRS). • Disconnect: Air Suspension Control Module C2131b (Navigator) or C2324n (Expedition) (if equipped). • Disconnect: Climate Controlled Seat Module C3265b (if equipped). • Disconnect: Driver Seat Module (DSM) C341c. • Disconnect: Electronic Automatic Temperature Control (EATC) Module C228b (if equipped). • Disconnect: Instrument Cluster C220b. • Disconnect: Parking Aid Module C4014b (if equipped). • Disconnect: Power Liftgate Module C4174d (if equipped). • Disconnect: Vehicle Security Module C2113c. • Inspect the connectors for damage. • **Are the connectors OK?**	**Yes** GO to P3. **No** REPAIR the module connector in question. REPOWER the SRS. CARRY OUT the diagnostic tool data link test.

LTV0500000005068

**Fig. 28 Pinpoint Test P (Part 1 of 16).
Expedition & Navigator**

P3 CHECK THE MEDIUM SPEED CAN CIRCUITS BETWEEN THE VEHICLE SECURITY MODULE AND THE DLC FOR AN OPEN

- Measure the resistance between the vehicle security module C2113c-5, circuit 2180 (WH/BK), harness side and the DLC C251-3, circuit 2180 (WH/BK), harness side.

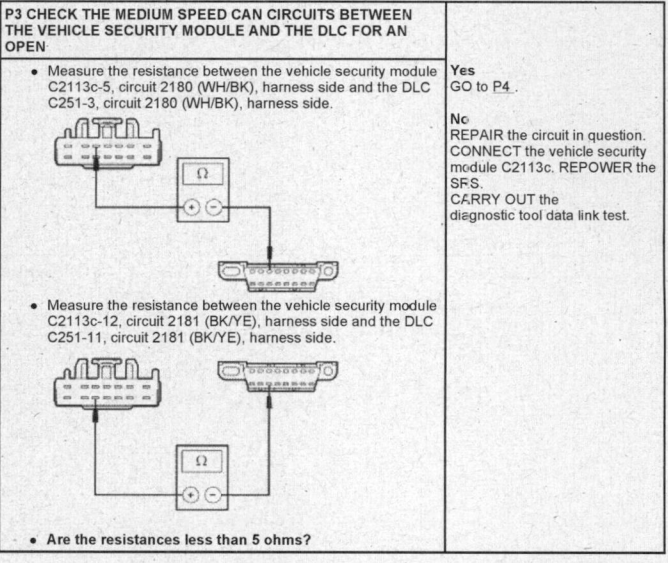

- Measure the resistance between the vehicle security module C2113c-12, circuit 2181 (BK/YE), harness side and the DLC C251-11, circuit 2181 (BK/YE), harness side.

- **Are the resistances less than 5 ohms?**

Yes
GO to P4.

No
REPAIR the circuit in question. CONNECT the vehicle security module C2113c. REPOWER the SRS. CARRY OUT the diagnostic tool data link test.

LTV0500000005069

**Fig. 28 Pinpoint Test P (Part 2 of 16).
Expedition & Navigator**

P4 CHECK THE MEDIUM SPEED CAN CIRCUITS BETWEEN THE INSTRUMENT CLUSTER AND THE DLC FOR AN OPEN

- Measure the resistance between the instrument cluster C220b-25, circuit 2180 (WH/BK), harness side and the DLC C251-3, circuit 2180 (WH/BK), harness side.

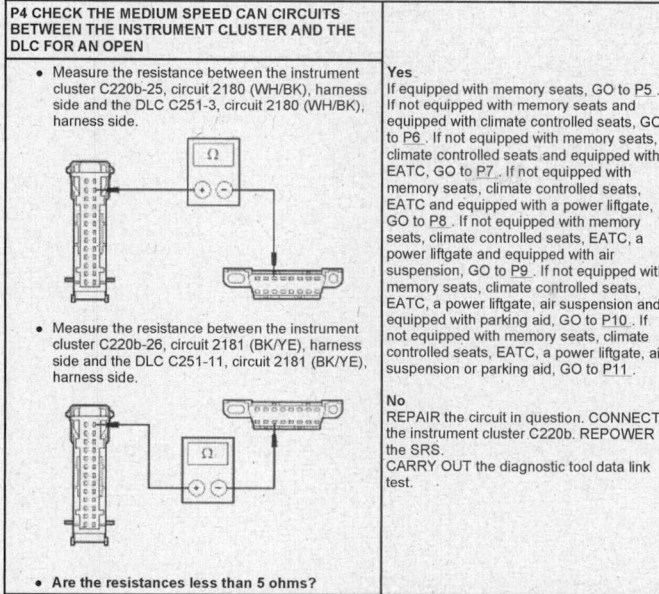

- Measure the resistance between the instrument cluster C220b-26, circuit 2181 (BK/YE), harness side and the DLC C251-11, circuit 2181 (BK/YE), harness side.

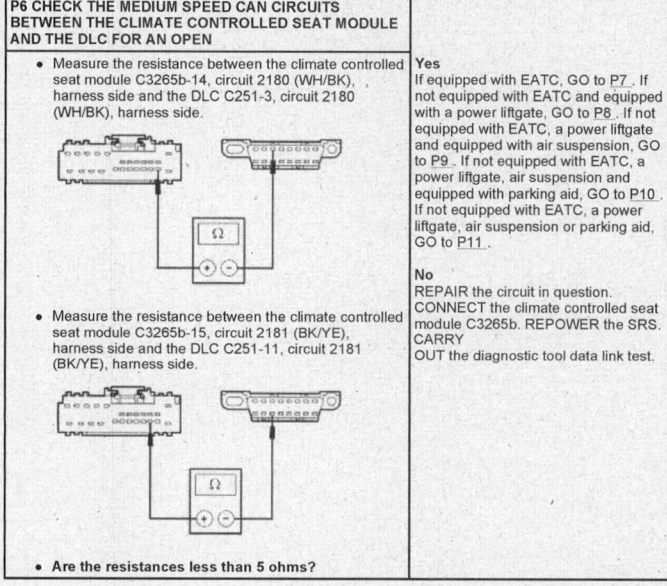

- **Are the resistances less than 5 ohms?**

Yes
If equipped with memory seats, GO to P5. If not equipped with memory seats and equipped with climate controlled seats, GO to P6. If not equipped with memory seats, climate controlled seats and equipped with EATC, GO to P7. If not equipped with memory seats, climate controlled seats, EATC and equipped with a power liftgate, GO to P8. If not equipped with memory seats, climate controlled seats, EATC, a power liftgate and equipped with air suspension, GO to P9. If not equipped with memory seats, climate controlled seats, EATC, a power liftgate, air suspension and equipped with parking aid, GO to P10. If not equipped with memory seats, climate controlled seats, EATC, a power liftgate, air suspension or parking aid, GO to P11.

No
REPAIR the circuit in question. CONNECT the instrument cluster C220b. REPOWER the SRS. CARRY OUT the diagnostic tool data link test.

LTV0500000005070

**Fig. 28 Pinpoint Test P (Part 3 of 16).
Expedition & Navigator**

P5 CHECK THE MEDIUM SPEED CAN CIRCUITS BETWEEN THE DSM AND THE DLC FOR AN OPEN

7-23

- Measure the resistance between the DSM C341c-3, circuit 2180 (WH/BK), harness side and the DLC C251-3, circuit 2180 (WH/BK), harness side.

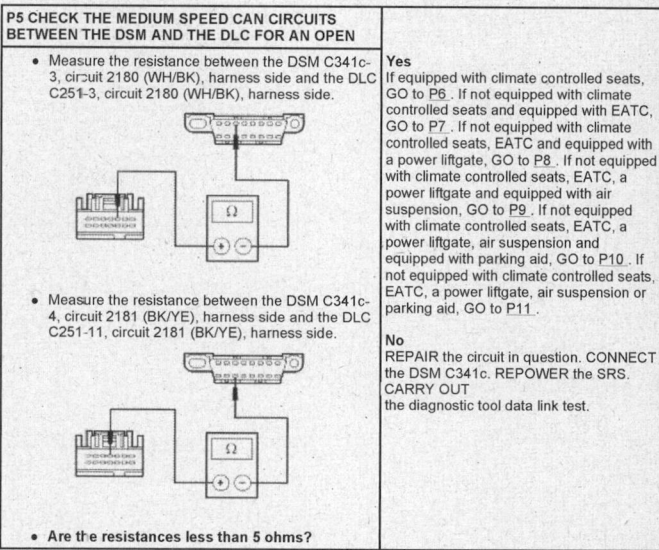

- Measure the resistance between the DSM C341c-4, circuit 2181 (BK/YE), harness side and the DLC C251-11, circuit 2181 (BK/YE), harness side.

- **Are the resistances less than 5 ohms?**

Yes
If equipped with climate controlled seats, GO to P6. If not equipped with climate controlled seats and equipped with EATC, GO to P7. If not equipped with climate controlled seats, EATC and equipped with a power liftgate, GO to P8. If not equipped with climate controlled seats, EATC, a power liftgate and equipped with air suspension, GO to P9. If not equipped with climate controlled seats, EATC, a power liftgate, air suspension and equipped with parking aid, GO to P10. If not equipped with climate controlled seats, EATC, a power liftgate, air suspension or parking aid, GO to P11.

No
REPAIR the circuit in question. CONNECT the DSM C341c. REPOWER the SRS. CARRY OUT the diagnostic tool data link test.

LTV0500000005071

**Fig. 28 Pinpoint Test P (Part 4 of 16).
Expedition & Navigator**

P6 CHECK THE MEDIUM SPEED CAN CIRCUITS BETWEEN THE CLIMATE CONTROLLED SEAT MODULE AND THE DLC FOR AN OPEN

- Measure the resistance between the climate controlled seat module C3265b-14, circuit 2180 (WH/BK), harness side and the DLC C251-3, circuit 2180 (WH/BK), harness side.

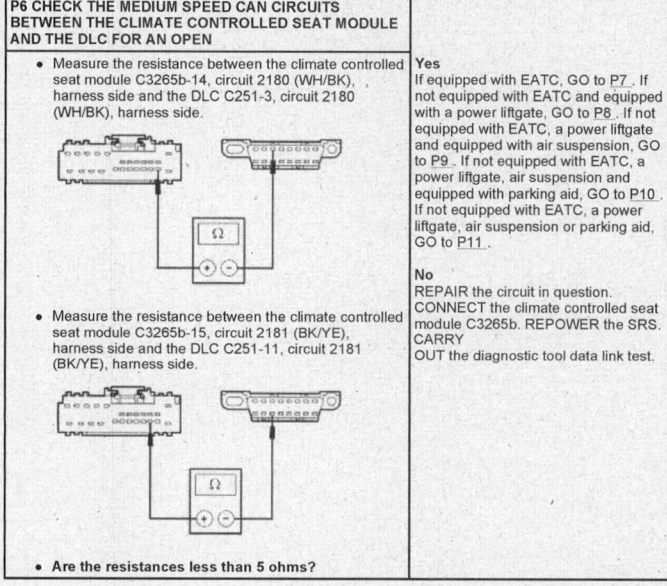

- Measure the resistance between the climate controlled seat module C3265b-15, circuit 2181 (BK/YE), harness side and the DLC C251-11, circuit 2181 (BK/YE), harness side.

- **Are the resistances less than 5 ohms?**

Yes
If equipped with EATC, GO to P7. If not equipped with EATC and equipped with a power liftgate, GO to P8. If not equipped with EATC, a power liftgate and equipped with air suspension, GO to P9. If not equipped with EATC, a power liftgate, air suspension and equipped with parking aid, GO to P10. If not equipped with EATC, a power liftgate, air suspension or parking aid, GO to P11.

No
REPAIR the circuit in question. CONNECT the climate controlled seat module C3265b. REPOWER the SRS. CARRY OUT the diagnostic tool data link test.

LTV0500000005072

**Fig. 28 Pinpoint Test P (Part 5 of 16).
Expedition & Navigator**

P7 CHECK THE MEDIUM SPEED CAN CIRCUITS BETWEEN THE EATC MODULE AND THE DLC FOR AN OPEN

- Measure the resistance between the EATC module C228b-2, circuit 2180 (WH/BK), harness side and the DLC C251-3, circuit 2180 (WH/BK), harness side.

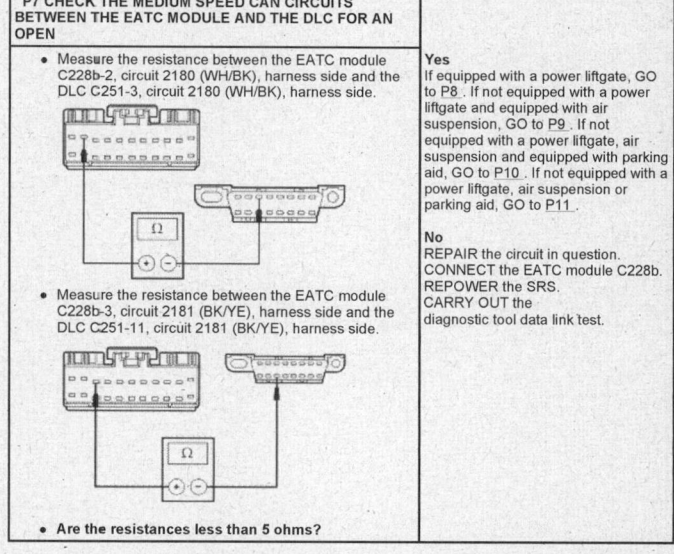

- Measure the resistance between the EATC module C228b-3, circuit 2181 (BK/YE), harness side and the DLC C251-11, circuit 2181 (BK/YE), harness side.

- **Are the resistances less than 5 ohms?**

Yes
If equipped with a power liftgate, GO to P8. If not equipped with a power liftgate and equipped with air suspension, GO to P9. If not equipped with a power liftgate, air suspension and equipped with parking aid, GO to P10. If not equipped with a power liftgate, air suspension or parking aid, GO to P11.

No
REPAIR the circuit in question. CONNECT the EATC module C228b. REPOWER the SRS. CARRY OUT the diagnostic tool data link test.

LTV0500000005073

**Fig. 28 Pinpoint Test P (Part 6 of 16).
Expedition & Navigator**

P8 CHECK THE MEDIUM SPEED CAN CIRCUITS BETWEEN THE POWER LIFTGATE MODULE AND THE DLC FOR AN OPEN

- Measure the resistance between the power liftgate module C4174d-20, circuit 2180 (WH/BK), harness side and the DLC C251-3, circuit 2180 (WH/BK), harness side.

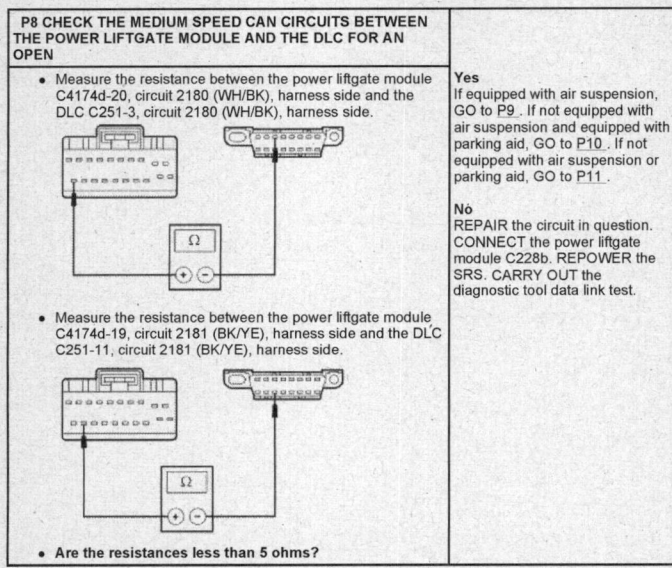

- Measure the resistance between the power liftgate module C4174d-19, circuit 2181 (BK/YE), harness side and the DLC C251-11, circuit 2181 (BK/YE), harness side.

- Are the resistances less than 5 ohms?

Yes
If equipped with air suspension, GO to P9. If not equipped with air suspension and equipped with parking aid, GO to P10. If not equipped with air suspension or parking aid, GO to P11.

No
REPAIR the circuit in question. CONNECT the power liftgate module C228b. REPOWER the SRS. CARRY OUT the diagnostic tool data link test.

LTV0500000005074

Fig. 28 Pinpoint Test P (Part 7 of 16). Expedition & Navigator

P9 CHECK THE MEDIUM SPEED CAN CIRCUITS BETWEEN THE AIR SUSPENSION CONTROL MODULE AND THE DLC FOR AN OPEN

- Measure the resistance between the air suspension control module C2324b-10 (Expedition) or C2131b-11 (Navigator), circuit 2180 (WH/BK), harness side and the DLC C251-3, circuit 2180 (WH/BK), harness side.

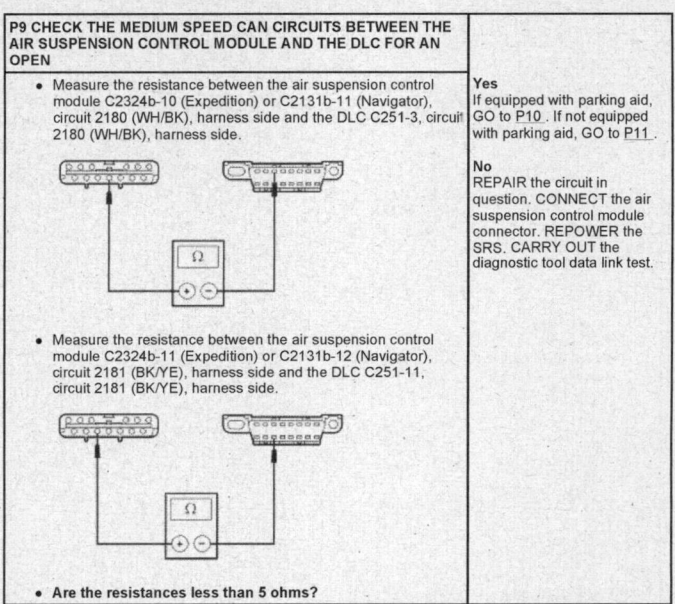

- Measure the resistance between the air suspension control module C2324b-11 (Expedition) or C2131b-12 (Navigator), circuit 2181 (BK/YE), harness side and the DLC C251-11, circuit 2181 (BK/YE), harness side.

- Are the resistances less than 5 ohms?

Yes
If equipped with parking aid, GO to P10. If not equipped with parking aid, GO to P11.

No
REPAIR the circuit in question. CONNECT the air suspension control module connector. REPOWER the SRS. CARRY OUT the diagnostic tool data link test.

LTV0500000005075

Fig. 28 Pinpoint Test P (Part 8 of 16). Expedition & Navigator

P10 CHECK THE MEDIUM SPEED CAN CIRCUITS BETWEEN THE PARKING AID MODULE AND THE DLC FOR AN OPEN

- Measure the resistance between the parking aid module C4014b-2, circuit 2180 (WH/BK), harness side and the DLC C251-3, circuit 2180 (WH/BK), harness side.

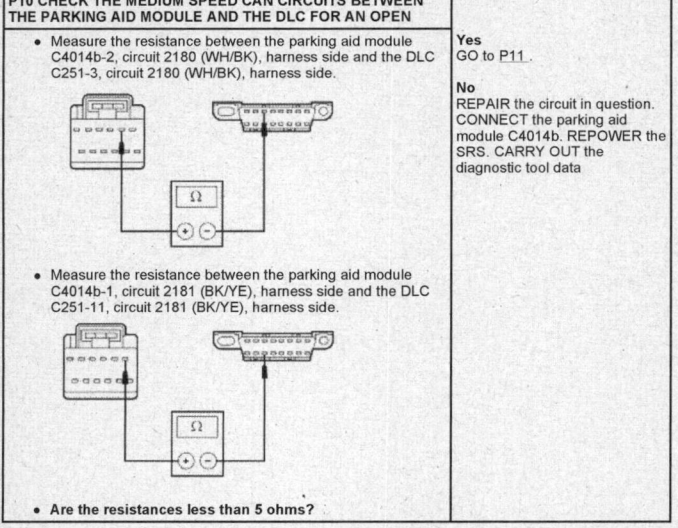

- Measure the resistance between the parking aid module C4014b-1, circuit 2181 (BK/YE), harness side and the DLC C251-11, circuit 2181 (BK/YE), harness side.

- Are the resistances less than 5 ohms?

Yes
GO to P11.

No
REPAIR the circuit in question. CONNECT the parking aid module C4014b. REPOWER the SRS. CARRY OUT the diagnostic tool data

LTV0500000005076

Fig. 28 Pinpoint Test P (Part 9 of 16). Expedition & Navigator

P11 CHECK THE MEDIUM SPEED CAN CIRCUITS FOR A SHORT TO GROUND

- Measure the resistance between the DLC C251-3, circuit 2180 (WH/BK), harness side and ground; and between the DLC C251-11, circuit 2181 (BK/YE), harness side and ground.

- Are the resistances less than 5 ohms?

Yes
GO to P12.

No
REPAIR the circuit in question. REPOWER the SRS. CARRY OUT the diagnostic tool data link test.

P12 CHECK THE MEDIUM SPEED CAN CIRCUITS FOR A SHORT TO VOLTAGE

- Key in ON position.
- Measure the voltage between the DLC C251-3, circuit 2180 (WH/BK), harness side and ground; and between the DLC C251-11, circuit 2181 (BK/YE), harness side and ground.

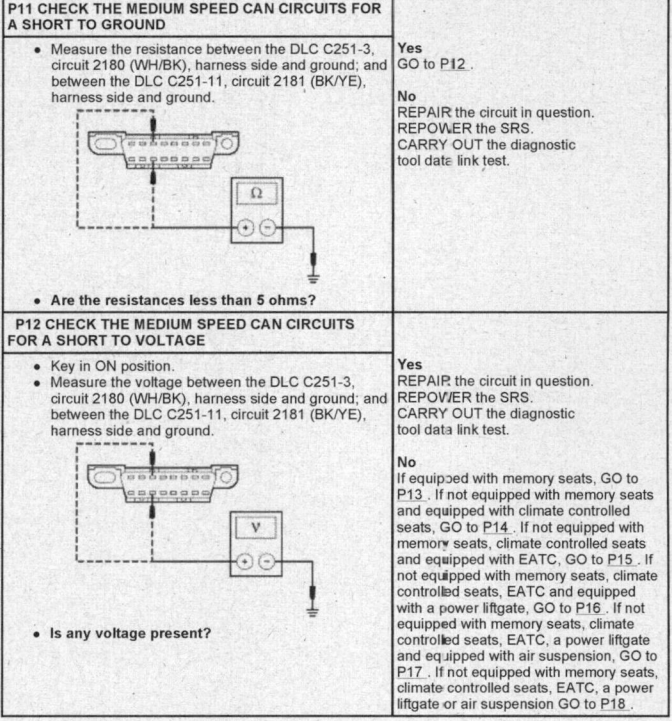

- Is any voltage present?

Yes
REPAIR the circuit in question. REPOWER the SRS. CARRY OUT the diagnostic tool data link test.

No
If equipped with memory seats, GO to P13. If not equipped with memory seats and equipped with climate controlled seats, GO to P14. If not equipped with memory seats, climate controlled seats and equipped with EATC, GO to P15. If not equipped with memory seats, climate controlled seats, EATC and equipped with a power liftgate, GO to P16. If not equipped with memory seats, climate controlled seats, EATC, a power liftgate and equipped with air suspension, GO to P17. If not equipped with memory seats, climate controlled seats, EATC, a power liftgate or air suspension GO to P18.

LTV0500000005077

Fig. 28 Pinpoint Test P (Part 10 of 16). Expedition & Navigator

P13 CHECK THE MEDIUM SPEED CAN WITH THE DSM C341C DISCONNECTED	
• Key in OFF position. • Connect: Air Suspension Control Module C2131b (Navigator) or C2324b (Expedition) (if equipped). • Connect: EATC Module C228b (if equipped). • Connect: Instrument Cluster C220b. • Connect: Parking Aid Module C4014b (if equipped). • Connect: Power Liftgate Module C4174d (if equipped). • Connect: Vehicle Security Module C2113c. • Key in ON position. • Enter the following diagnostic mode on the diagnostic tool: Data Link Diagnostics Test. • **Is system passed obtained?**	**Yes** GO to P20 . **No** If equipped with climate controlled seats, GO to P14 . If not equipped with climate controlled seats and equipped with EATC, GO to P15 . If not equipped with climate controlled seats, EATC and equipped with a power liftgate, GO to P16 . If not equipped with climate controlled seats, EATC, a power liftgate, air suspension and equipped with parking aid, GO to P18 . If not equipped with climate controlled seats, EATC, a power liftgate, air suspension or parking aid, GO to P19

P14 CHECK THE MEDIUM SPEED CAN WITH THE CLIMATE CONTROLLED SEAT MODULE C3265B DISCONNECTED	
• Disconnect: Climate Controlled Seat Module C3265b. • Connect: DSM C341c (if equipped). • Key in ON position. • Enter the following diagnostic mode on the diagnostic tool: Data Link Diagnostics Test. • **Is system passed obtained?**	**Yes** GO to P21 . **No** If equipped with EATC, GO to P15 . If not equipped with EATC and equipped with a power liftgate, GO to P16 . If not equipped with EATC, a power liftgate and equipped with air suspension, GO to P17 . If not equipped with EATC, a power liftgate, air suspension and equipped with parking aid, GO to P18 . If not equipped with EATC, a power liftgate, air suspension or parking aid, GO to P19 .

LTV0500000005078

Fig. 28 Pinpoint Test P (Part 11 of 16).
Expedition & Navigator

P15 CHECK THE MEDIUM SPEED CAN WITH THE EATC MODULE C228B DISCONNECTED	
• Connect: Climate Controlled Seat Module C3265b (if equipped). • Disconnect: EATC Module C228b. • Connect: DSM C341c (if equipped). • Key in ON position. • Enter the following diagnostic mode on the diagnostic tool: Data Link Diagnostics Test. • **Is system passed obtained?**	**Yes** GO to P22 . **No** If equipped with a power liftgate, GO to P16 . If not equipped with a power liftgate and equipped with air suspension, GO to P17 . If not equipped with a power liftgate and equipped with air suspension and equipped with parking aid, GO to P18 . If not equipped with a power liftgate, air suspension or parking aid, GO to P19 .

P16 CHECK THE MEDIUM SPEED CAN WITH THE POWER LIFTGATE MODULE C4174D DISCONNECTED	
• Disconnect: Climate Controlled Seat Module C3265b (if equipped). • Connect: EATC Module C228b (if equipped). • Connect: DSM C341c (if equipped). • Disconnect: Power Liftgate Module C4174d. • Key in ON position. • Enter the following diagnostic mode on the diagnostic tool: Data Link Diagnostics Test. • **Is system passed obtained?**	**Yes** GO to P23 . **No** If equipped with air suspension, GO to P17 . If not equipped with air suspension and equipped with parking aid, GO to P18 . If not equipped with air suspension or parking aid, GO to P19 .

P17 CHECK THE MEDIUM SPEED CAN WITH THE AIR SUSPENSION CONTROL MODULE C2131B DISCONNECTED	
• Disconnect: Air Suspension Control Module C2131b (Navigator) or C2324b (Expedition) (if equipped). • Connect: Climate Controlled Seat Module C3265b (if equipped). • Connect: EATC Module C228b (if equipped). • Connect: DSM C341c (if equipped). • Connect: Power Liftgate Module C4174d (if equipped). • Key in ON position. • Enter the following diagnostic mode on the diagnostic tool: Data Link Diagnostics Test. • **Is system passed obtained?**	**Yes** GO to P24 . **No** If equipped with parking aid, GO to P18 . If not equipped with parking aid, GO to P19 .

LTV0500000005079

Fig. 28 Pinpoint Test P (Part 12 of 16).
Expedition & Navigator

P18 CHECK THE MEDIUM SPEED CAN WITH THE PARKING AID MODULE C4014B DISCONNECTED	
• Connect: Air Suspension Control Module C2131b (Navigator) or C2324b (Expedition) (if equipped). • Connect: Climate Controlled Seat Module C3265b (if equipped). • Connect: EATC Module C228b (if equipped). • Connect: DSM C341c (if equipped). • Disconnect: Parking Aid Module C4014b. • Connect: Power Liftgate Module C4174d (if equipped). • Key in ON position. • Enter the following diagnostic mode on the diagnostic tool: Data Link Diagnostics Test. • **Is system passed obtained?**	**Yes** GO to P25 . **No** GO to P19 .

P19 CHECK THE MEDIUM SPEED CAN WITH A SUBSTITUTED VEHICLE SECURITY MODULE	
• Connect: Air Suspension Control Module C2131b (Navigator) or C2324b (Expedition) (if equipped). • Connect: Climate Controlled Seat Module C3265b (if equipped). • Connect: EATC Module C228b (if equipped). • Connect: DSM C341c (if equipped). • Connect: Parking Aid Module C4014b (if equipped). • Connect: Power Liftgate Module C4174d (if equipped). • INSTALL a known good vehicle security module. • Key in ON position. • Enter the following diagnostic mode on the diagnostic tool: Data Link Diagnostics Test. • **Is system passed obtained?**	**Yes** GO to P26 . **No** INSTALL the original vehicle security module. GO to P27 .

LTV0500000005080

Fig. 28 Pinpoint Test P (Part 13 of 16).
Expedition & Navigator

P20 CHECK FOR CORRECT DSM MODULE OPERATION	

• Disconnect all the DSM connectors.
• Check for:
  • corrosion
  • pushed-out pins
• Connect all the DSM module connectors and make sure they seat correctly.
• Operate the system and verify the concern is still present.
• **Is the concern still present?**
	Yes
	INSTALL a new DSM module. REPOWER the SRS. CLEAR the DTCs. REPEAT the self-test. CARRY OUT the data link diagnostics test.
	
	No
	The system is operating correctly at this time. The concern may have been caused by a loose or corroded connector. REPOWER the SRS. CLEAR the DTCs. REPEAT the self-test. CARRY OUT the data link diagnostics test.

P21 CHECK FOR CORRECT CLIMATE CONTROLLED SEAT MODULE OPERATION	

• Disconnect all the climate controlled seat module connectors.
• Check for:
  • corrosion
  • pushed-out pins
• Connect all the climate controlled seat module connectors and make sure they seat correctly.
• Operate the system and verify the concern is still present.
• **Is the concern still present?**
	Yes
	INSTALL a new climate controlled seat module. REPOWER the SRS. CLEAR the DTCs. REPEAT the self-test. CARRY OUT the data link diagnostics test.
	
	No
	The system is operating correctly at this time. The concern may have been caused by a loose or corroded connector. REPOWER the SRS. CLEAR the DTCs. REPEAT the self-test. CARRY OUT the data link diagnostics test.

P22 CHECK FOR CORRECT EATC MODULE OPERATION	

• Disconnect all the EATC module connectors.
• Check for:
  • corrosion
  • pushed-out pins
• Connect all the EATC module connectors and make sure they seat correctly.
• Operate the system and verify the concern is still present.
• **Is the concern still present?**
	Yes
	INSTALL a new EATC module. REPOWER the SRS. CLEAR the DTCs. REPEAT the self-test. CARRY OUT the data link diagnostics test.
	
	No
	The system is operating correctly at this time. The concern may have been caused by a loose or corroded connector. REPOWER the SRS. CLEAR the DTCs. REPEAT the self-test. CARRY OUT the data link diagnostics test.

LTV0500000005081

Fig. 28 Pinpoint Test P (Part 14 of 16).
Expedition & Navigator

P23 CHECK FOR CORRECT POWER LIFTGATE MODULE OPERATION

- Disconnect all the power liftgate module connectors.
- Check for:
  - corrosion
  - pushed-out pins
- Connect all the power liftgate module connectors and make sure they seat correctly.
- Operate the system and verify the concern is still present.
- **Is the concern still present?**

Yes
INSTALL a new power liftgate module. REPOWER the SRS. CLEAR the DTCs. REPEAT the self-test. CARRY OUT the data link diagnostics test.

No
The system is operating correctly at this time. The concern may have been caused by a loose or corroded connector. REPOWER the SRS. CLEAR the DTCs. REPEAT the self-test. CARRY OUT the data link diagnostics test.

P24 CHECK FOR CORRECT AIR SUSPENSION CONTROL MODULE OPERATION

- Disconnect all the air suspension control module connectors.
- Check for:
  - corrosion
  - pushed-out pins
- Connect all the air suspension control module connectors and make sure they seat correctly.
- Operate the system and verify the concern is still present.
- **Is the concern still present?**

Yes
INSTALL a new air suspension control module. REPOWER the SRS. CLEAR the DTCs. REPEAT the self-test. CARRY OUT the data link diagnostics test.

No
The system is operating correctly at this time. The concern may have been caused by a loose or corroded connector. REPOWER the SRS. CLEAR the DTCs. REPEAT the self-test. CARRY OUT the data link diagnostics test.

P25 CHECK FOR CORRECT PARKING AID MODULE OPERATION

- Disconnect all the parking aid module connectors.
- Check for:
  - corrosion
  - pushed-out pins
- Connect all the parking aid module connectors and make sure they seat correctly.
- Operate the system and verify the concern is still present.
- **Is the concern still present?**

Yes
INSTALL a new parking aid module. REPOWER the SRS. CLEAR the DTCs. REPEAT the self-test. CARRY OUT the data link diagnostics test.

No
The system is operating correctly at this time. The concern may have been caused by a loose or corroded connector. REPOWER the SRS. CLEAR the DTCs. REPEAT the self-test. CARRY OUT the data link diagnostics test.

LTV0500000005082

Fig. 28   Pinpoint Test P (Part 15 of 16). Expedition & Navigator

P26 CHECK FOR CORRECT VEHICLE SECURITY MODULE OPERATION

- Disconnect all the vehicle security module connectors.
- Check for:
  - corrosion
  - pushed-out pins
- Connect all the vehicle security module connectors and make sure they seat correctly.
- Operate the system and verify the concern is still present.
- **Is the concern still present?**

Yes
INSTALL a new vehicle security module. REPOWER the SRS. CLEAR the DTCs. REPEAT the self-test. CARRY OUT the data link diagnostics test.

No
The system is operating correctly at this time. The concern may have been caused by a loose or corroded connector. REPOWER the SRS. CLEAR the DTCs. REPEAT the self-test. CARRY OUT the data link diagnostics test.

P27 CHECK FOR CORRECT INSTRUMENT CLUSTER OPERATION

- Disconnect all the instrument cluster connectors.
- Check for:
  - corrosion
  - pushed-out pins
- Connect all the instrument cluster connectors and make sure they seat correctly.
- Operate the system and verify the concern is still present.
- **Is the concern still present?**

Yes
INSTALL a new instrument cluster. REPOWER the SRS. CLEAR the DTCs. REPEAT the self-test. CARRY OUT the data link diagnostics test.

No
The system is operating correctly at this time. The concern may have been caused by a loose or corroded connector. REPOWER the SRS. CLEAR the DTCs. REPEAT the self-test. CARRY OUT the data link diagnostics test.

LTV0500000005083

Fig. 28   Pinpoint Test P (Part 16 of 16). Expedition & Navigator

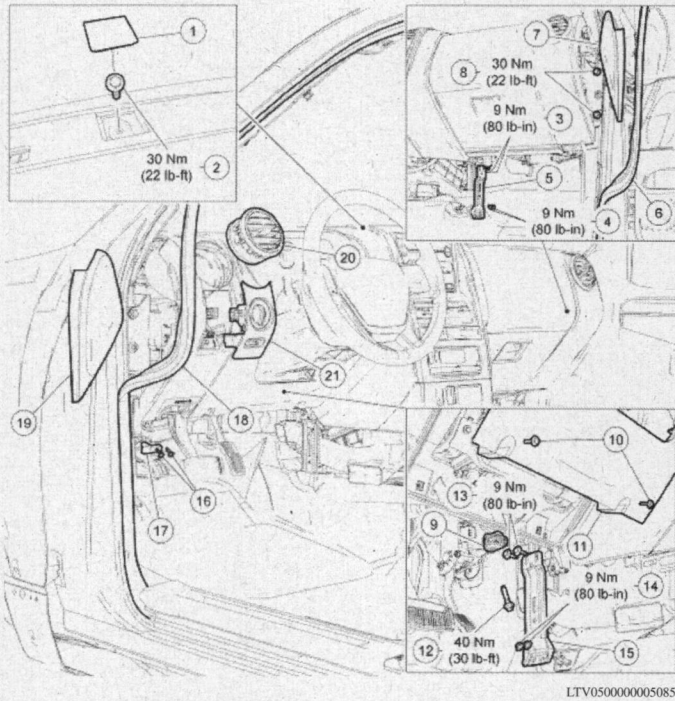

LTV0500000005085

Fig. 30   Code B1342: ECU is Defective (Part 1 of 6). Explorer, Freestar, Monterey & Mountaineer

Test Step	Result / Action to Take
Q1 CHECK THE DIAGNOSTIC TOOL CONNECTOR • Inspect the diagnostic tool pins for damage. • **Are the pins OK?**	**Yes** GO to Q2. **No** REPAIR the diagnostic tool connector. CARRY OUT the data link diagnostics test.
Q2 CHECK THE DATA LINK CONNECTOR (DLC) C251 FOR DAMAGE • Key in OFF position. • Inspect the DLC C251 pins for damage. • **Are the pins OK?**	**Yes** GO to Q3. **No** REPAIR the DLC C251. CARRY OUT the data link diagnostics test.
Q3 CHECK CIRCUIT 40 (LB/WH) FOR VOLTAGE AT THE DLC • Key in ON position. • Measure the voltage between the DLC C251-16, circuit 40 (LB/WH), harness side and ground. • **Is the voltage greater than 10 volts?**	**Yes** GO to Q4. **No** VERIFY central junction box (CJB) fuse 41 (20A) is OK. If OK, REPAIR the circuit. CARRY OUT the diagnostic tool data link test.
Q4 CHECK CIRCUITS 57 (BK) AND 570 (BK/WH) FOR AN OPEN AT THE DLC • Measure the resistance between the DLC C251-4, circuit 57 (BK), harness side and ground; and between the DLC C251-5, circuit 570 (BK/WH), harness side and ground.	**Yes** REPAIR the diagnostic tool. CARRY OUT the data link diagnostics test. **No** REPAIR the circuit in question. CARRY OUT the data link diagnostics test.

LTV0500000005084

Fig. 29   Pinpoint Test Q. Expedition & Navigator

Item	Description
1	Upper instrument panel bolt covers (2 required)
2	Upper instrument panel bolts (2 required)
3	Instrument panel center brace bolts (RH, 2 required)
4	Instrument panel center brace nuts (RH, 2 required)
5	Instrument panel center brace (RH)
6	RH door weather seal
7	RH instrument panel side finish panel
8	RH instrument panel side mount bolts (2 required)
9	Accelerator pedal electrical connector
10	Steering column cover panel screws (2 required)
11	Steering column cover panel
12	Steering column shaft-to-steering column bolt
13	instrument panel center brace bolts (LH, 2 required)
14	Instrument panel center brace nuts (LH, 2 required)
15	Instrument panel center brace (LH)
16	Parking brake release handle bolts (2 required)
17	Parking brake release handle bolts (2 required)
18	LH door weather seal
19	LH instrument panel side finish panel
20	Driver side vent
21	Headlamp switch assembly

LTV0500000005086

Fig. 30   Code B1342: ECU is Defective (Part 2 of 6). Explorer, Freestar, Monterey & Mountaineer

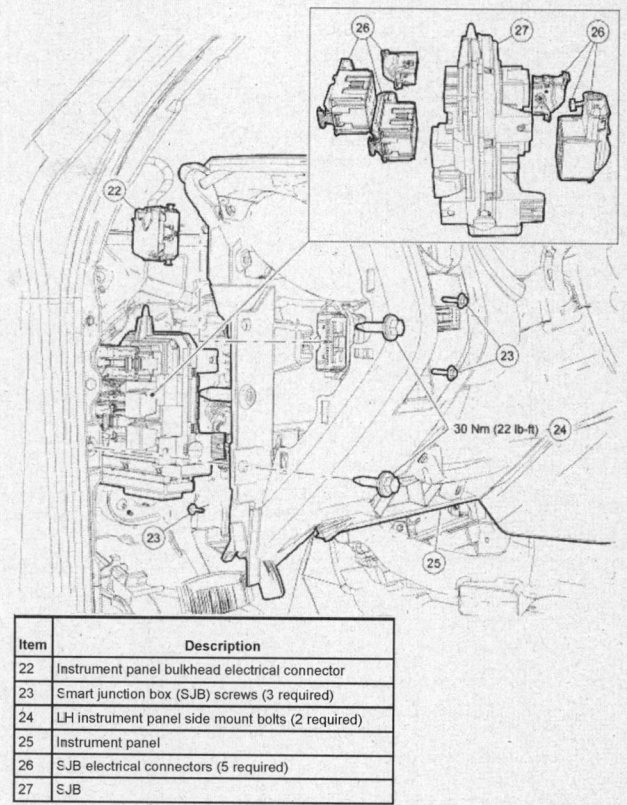

30 Nm (22 lb-ft)

Item	Description
22	Instrument panel bulkhead electrical connector
23	Smart junction box (SJB) screws (3 required)
24	LH instrument panel side mount bolts (2 required)
25	Instrument panel
26	SJB electrical connectors (5 required)
27	SJB

LTV0500000005087

Fig. 30   Code B1342: ECU is Defective (Part 3 of 6). Explorer, Freestar, Monterey & Mountaineer

1. ⚠ CAUTION: The steps included in the SJB removal and installation procedure are critical to restoring the vehicle security and tire pressure monitoring systems to normal operation. A new SJB is delivered in manufacturing mode with 6 pre-set diagnostic trouble codes (DTCs) related to the tire pressure monitoring system. The presence of these DTCs requires the installation procedures be followed in order to clear the DTCs and enable normal SJB operations.

   ⚠ CAUTION: Prior to the removal of the SJB, it is necessary to upload the module configuration information to the diagnostic tool. This information must be downloaded to the new SJB after installation.

   Disconnect the battery.

2. Remove the transmission selector lever.

3. NOTE: Position the front wheels straight forward before removing the ignition key.

   Remove the ignition key from the lock cylinder locking the steering wheel in place.

4. Remove the 2 upper instrument panel bolt covers and bolts.

5. Remove the 4 bolts, 4 nuts and the 2 instrument panel center braces

6. Position the RH door weather seal aside.

7. Remove the RH instrument panel side finish panel.

8. Loosen the RH instrument panel side mount bolts 13 mm (0.51 in).

9. Disconnect the accelerator pedal electrical connector.

10. Disconnect the harness locator at the front of the SJB.

11. Remove the 2 screws and the steering column cover panel.

12. ⚠ CAUTION: Secure the steering wheel to prevent damage to the clock spring assembly.

    Remove the shaft-to-steering column bolt and separate the steering column shaft from the steering column.

13. Remove the 2 bolts and position the parking brake release handle aside.

14. Remove the LH A-pillar trim panel.

15. Remove the LH cowl side trim panel.

16. Position the LH door weather seal aside.

17. Remove the LH instrument panel side finish panel.

LTV0500000005088

Fig. 30   Code B1342: ECU is Defective (Part 4 of 6). Explorer, Freestar, Monterey & Mountaineer

18. ⚠ CAUTION: The bulkhead electrical connector is lever assisted. Do not damage the lever when releasing the electrical connector.

    Disconnect the LH instrument panel bulkhead connector.

19. Remove the driver side vent assembly.

20. Remove the headlamp switch assembly.

21. Remove the 3 SJB mount screws and release the SJB from its locators.

22. Remove the 2 LH instrument panel side mount bolts.

23. ⚠ CAUTION: The SJB electrical connectors are lever assisted. Do not damage the lever when releasing the electrical connectors.

    Disconnect the 5 SJB electrical connectors and remove the SJB.
    • Disconnect the remote keyless entry (RKE) antenna.

Installation

NOTE: When a new SJB is installed, all customer RKE transmitters are required to program the RKE function of the SJB

1. ⚠ CAUTION: The SJB electrical connectors are lever assisted. Do not damage the lever when engaging the electrical connectors.

   Connect the 5 SJB electrical connectors and the RKE antenna connector.

2. Position the SJB in the locators and install the 3 SJB mount screws.

3. Reposition the instrument panel with the cowl and install the 2 LH instrument panel side mount bolts.
   • Tighten to 30 Nm (22 lb-ft).

4. Install the headlamp switch assembly.

5. Install the driver side vent assembly.

6. ⚠ CAUTION: The bulkhead electrical connector is lever assisted. Do not damage the lever when engaging the electrical connector.

   Connect the LH instrument panel bulkhead connector.

7. Install the LH instrument panel side finish panel.

8. Install the LH door weather seal.

9. Install the LH cowl side trim panel.

10. Install the LH A-pillar trim panel.

LTV0500000005089

Fig. 30   Code B1342: ECU is Defective (Part 5 of 6). Explorer, Freestar, Monterey & Mountaineer

11. Position the parking brake release handle and install the 2 parking brake release handle bolts.

12. Position the steering shaft onto the steering column shaft and install the bolt.
    - Tighten to 40 Nm (30 lb-ft).

13. Position the steering column cover panel and install the 2 screws.

14. Connect the harness locator at the front of the SJB.

15. Connect the accelerator pedal electrical connector.

16. Install the RH instrument panel side mount bolts.
    - Tighten to 30 Nm (22 lb-ft).

17. Install the RH instrument panel side finish panel.

18. Install the RH door weather seal.

19. Position the 2 instrument panel center braces and install the 4 bolts, 4 nuts.
    - Tighten to 9 Nm (80 lb-in).

20. Install the 2 upper instrument panel bolts and the 2 bolt covers.
    - Tighten to 30 Nm (22 lb-ft).

21. Install the transmission selector lever.

22. Install the floor console.

23. Connect the battery.

24. NOTE: When successful, this step provides the calibration necessary for SJB operation and clears DTC B2477. The clearing of the DTC indicates the calibration data has been successfully downloaded to the SJB.

    Download the SJB configuration information from the diagnostic tool to the SJB.

25. NOTE: When successful, this step clears DTCs B2868, B2869, B2870 and B2871. The clearing of these DTCs indicates the SJB has recognized the tire pressure sensors during the training procedure.

    Train the tire pressure sensors.

26. Clear the DTCs.

27. NOTE: This step is required to clear DTC C2780, cause the SJB to exit the manufacturing mode, and to be sure there are no other concerns with the newly programmed SJB.

    Carry out the SJB on-demand self-test.

28. ⚠ CAUTION: If the module configuration upload/download is successful, then the RKE transmitters do not need to be reprogrammed to the vehicle. However, if the module configuration upload/download is unsuccessful and as-built data must be used to configure

LTV0500000005090

Fig. 30   Code B1342: ECU is Defective (Part 6 of 6). Explorer, Freestar, Monterey & Mountaineer

C3 CARRY OUT THE SENSOR TRAINING PROCEDURE	
• Train all 4 tire pressure sensors. Refer to Tire Pressure Monitoring System (TPMS) Sensor Training Procedure in this section. • **Did all of the tire pressure sensors transmit correctly and did the horn sound when each tire pressure sensor transmitted to the SJB?**	**Yes** Using the diagnostic tool, locate the updated TPMS sensor IDs trained to the SJB module. COMPARE these values to those recorded prior to the TPMS sensor training procedure. DOCUMENT all TPMS sensor IDs on the applicable warranty claim. VERIFY system operation. **No** **Before installing a new sensor(s)** : If a sensor(s) does not respond to the special tool, ATTEMPT to activate the same sensor(s) with the special tool. If the sensor(s) still does not respond, MOVE the vehicle to rotate the wheels at least 1/4 of a turn and ATTEMPT to activate the same sensor(s) again. If the sensor(s) fail to train a second time, INSTALL a new tire pressure sensor(s). CLEAR the DTCs. REPEAT the self-test. VERIFY system operation.
C4 TPMS SYSTEM STATUS EQUALS "$02 SYSTEM FAULT"	
• Train all 4 tire pressure sensors. Refer to Tire Pressure Monitoring System (TPMS) Sensor Training Procedure in this section. • **Did all of the tire pressure sensors transmit correctly and did the horn sound when each tire pressure sensor transmitted to the SJB?**	**Yes** Using the diagnostic tool, locate the updated TPMS sensor IDs trained to the SJB module. COMPARE these values to those recorded prior to the TPMS sensor training procedure. DOCUMENT all TPMS sensor IDs on the applicable warranty claim. VERIFY system operation. **No** **Before diagnosing the SJB** : If a sensor(s) does not respond to the special tool, ATTEMPT to activate the same sensor(s) with the special tool. If the sensor(s) still does not respond, MOVE the vehicle to rotate the wheels at least 1/4 of a turn and ATTEMPT to activate the same sensor(s) again. If the sensor(s) fail to train a second time,

LTV0500000005092

Fig. 31   Code B2872: Tire Pressure Sensor Fault (Part 2 of 2). Explorer, Freestar, Monterey & Mountaineer

Test Step	Result / Action to Take
C1 CHECK FOR DTCs	
• Connect the diagnostic tool. • Using the diagnostic tool, read the TPMS sensor IDs currently trained to the SJB. • Record the sensor IDs. • Using the diagnostic tool, read the TPMS System Status: TP_STAT. • **Is the TPMS system status (TP_STAT) equal to "$02 SENSOR FAULT"?**	**Yes** GO to C2. **No** If the TPMS system status is equal to "$01 SYSTEM FAULT", GO to C4.
C2 CHECK THE TIRE PRESSURE SENSOR RESPONSE TO THE TRAINING TOOL	
• Position the tire pressure monitor activation tool against the LH tire sidewall 180 degrees from the tire valve stem. • Press the test button on the special tool. • NOTE: The special tool will provide feedback in the form of a flashing green light and a "beep" sound for each successful response from a tire pressure sensor. • Repeat Steps 1 and 2 for the remaining 3 tires. • **Did all tire pressure sensors respond back to the training tool?**	**Yes** GO to C3. **No** The sensor(s) that did not respond to the tool could be the cause. GO to C3.

LTV0500000005091

Fig. 31   Code B2872: Tire Pressure Sensor Fault (Part 1 of 2). Explorer, Freestar, Monterey & Mountaineer

Test Step	Result / Action to Take
D1 DETERMINE IF THE VEHICLE IS EQUIPPED WITH AN INCORRECT SENSOR	
• Train all 4 tire pressure sensors. Refer to Tire Pressure Monitoring System (TPMS) Sensor Training Procedure in this section. • **Did all of the tire pressure sensors transmit correctly and did the horn sound when each tire pressure sensor transmitted to the SJB?**	**Yes** CLEAR the DTCs. REPEAT the self-test. VERIFY system operation. **No** **Before installing a new sensor(s)** : If a sensor(s) does not respond to the special tool, ATTEMPT to activate the same sensor(s) with the special tool. If the sensor(s) still does not respond, MOVE the vehicle to rotate the wheels at least 1/4 of a turn and ATTEMPT to activate the same sensor(s) again. If the sensor(s) fail to train a second time, INSTALL a new tire pressure sensor(s). CLEAR the DTCs. REPEAT the self-test. VERIFY system operation.

LTV0500000005093

Fig. 32   Code B106A: Pressure Sensor Range Bit Incorrect State. Explorer, Freestar, Monterey & Mountaineer

Test Step	Result / Action to Take
E1 DETERMINE WHICH SENSOR HAS A LOW BATTERY	
• Train all 4 tire pressure sensors. Refer to Tire Pressure Monitoring System (TPMS) Sensor Training Procedure in this section. • **Did all of the tire pressure sensors transmit correctly and did the horn sound when each tire pressure sensor transmitted to the SJB?**	**Yes** CLEAR the DTCs. REPEAT the self-test. VERIFY system operation. **No** **Before installing a new sensor(s)** : If a sensor(s) does not respond to the special tool, ATTEMPT to activate the same sensor(s) with the special tool. If the sensor(s) still does not respond, MOVE the vehicle to rotate the wheels at least 1/4 of a turn and ATTEMPT to activate the same sensor(s) again. If the sensor(s) fail to train a second time, INSTALL a new tire pressure sensor(s). CLEAR the DTCs. REPEAT the self-test. VERIFY system operation.

LTV0500000005094

Fig. 33   Code B106B: Tire Pressure Sensor Low Battery. Explorer, Freestar, Monterey & Mountaineer

⚠ CAUTION: Electronic modules are sensitive to static electrical charges. If exposed to these charges, damage can result.

NOTE: The tire pressure monitoring system (TPMS) is integral to the smart junction box (SJB) and is not serviced separately.

NOTE: A new SJB module is delivered in manufacturing mode with pre-set diagnostic trouble codes (DTCs). These DTCs require that a particular set of operations to be carried out in order to clear them and enable the module for normal operations. The pre-set DTCs are as follows:

- B2477 — Module Configuration Failure/Mismatch
- B2868 — Left Front Tire Pressure Sensor Fault
- B2869 — Right Front Tire Pressure Sensor Fault
- B2870 — Left Rear Tire Pressure Sensor Fault
- B2871 — Right Rear Tire Pressure Sensor Fault
- C2780 — ECU in Manufacturing Mode

NOTE: A reconfigured SJB may also set the above codes and will need to go through the same set of procedures as a new module to enable normal operation.

1. NOTE: The steps included in the SJB removal and installation process are critical to tire pressure monitoring system operations and will permit a new or reconfigured module to operate as intended. Each step is designed to carry out a particular operation and clear the manufacturing mode DTCs. Once these DTCs are cleared, the new or reconfigured module will enter into normal operating mode.

Remove the SJB.

LTV0500000005095

Fig. 34 Codes B2477, B2868, B2869, B2870, B2871 & C2780: Module Configuration Failure & Mismatch / Tire Pressure Sensor Fault / ECU in Manufacturing Mode. Explorer, Freestar, Monterey & Mountaineer

Condition	Possible Sources	Action
• Message center (if equipped) displays "CHECK TIRE PRESSURE". TPMS indicator illuminates continuously	• Air pressure not set to placard. • TPMS module. • TPMS sensor.	• Go To Pinpoint Test F .
	• Spare tire currently in use.	• INSTALL a new spare tire with repaired road wheel/tire.
• No communication with the TPMS module	• Fuse(s). • Circuitry. • Module.	• Go To Pinpoint Test A .
• Unable to enter self-test	• TPMS module. • Diagnostic tool.	• Go To Pinpoint Test A .
• TPMS will not enter sensor training mode	• TPMS sensor. • Message center. • TPMS module. • BOO switch. • ABS/TC/IVD module.	• Go To Pinpoint Test B . • Diagnose TPMS

LTV0500000004372

Fig. 35 Diagnostic Test Procedures (Part 2 of 2). Aviator

Condition	Possible Sources	Action
• Message center (if equipped) displays "TIRE PRESSURE SENSOR FAULT". TPMS indicator flashes	• TPMS module.	• Go To Pinpoint Test C .
	• All four TPMS sensor (excluding spare tire) failed, missing or incorrectly trained.	• TRAIN the TPMS sensors.
• Message center (if equipped) displays "TIRE PRESSURE SYSTEM FAULT". TPMS indicator illuminated continuously. No communication with the TPMS module	• Instrument cluster misconfigured.	• RECONFIGURE the instrument cluster.
	• Fuse(s). • Circuitry. • Module.	• Go To Pinpoint Test A .
• Message center (if equipped) displays "TIRE PRESSURE SENSOR FAULT". TPMS indicator flashes	• TPMS sensor.	• Go To Pinpoint Test E .
	• Spare tire currently in use.	• INSTALL a new spare tire with repaired road wheel/tire.
• Message center displays "WARNING — TIRE VERY LOW". TPMS indicator illum nates continuously	• Air pressure not set to placard.	• Go To Pinpoint Test F .
	• Spare tire currently in use.	• INSTALL a new spare tire with repaired road wheel/tire.
	• TPMS module.	• Go To Pinpoint Test F

LTV0500000004371

Fig. 35 Diagnostic Test Procedures (Part 1 of 2). Aviator

Condition	Possible Sources	Action
• Message center (if equipped) displays "TIRE PRESSURE MONITOR FAULT". TPMS indicator flashes	• VSM (TPMS module integral to VSM).	• Go To Pinpoint Test C .
	• CAN Bus fault.	
	• All four TPMS sensors (excluding spare tire) failed, missing or incorrectly trained.	• TRAIN the TPMS sensors.
• Message center (if equipped) displays "TIRE PRESSURE SENSOR FAULT". TPMS indicator flashes	• Up to three TPMS sensors failed, missing or incorrectly trained.	• TRAIN the TPMS sensors.
	• VSM (TPMS module integral to VSM).	• Go To Pinpoint Test C .
• Message center (if equipped) displays "LOW TIRE PRESSURE". TPMS indicator ON continuously	• Air pressure not set to placard. • TPMS module (integral to VSM). • TPMS sensor.	• Go To Pinpoint Test F .
	• Spare tire currently in use.	• INSTALL the repaired road wheel/tire in place of the spare tire.
• No communication with the VSM module	• Fuse(s). • Circuitry. • VSM (TPMS module integral to VSM).	• Go To Pinpoint Test A .
• Unable to enter self-test	• VSM (TPMS module integral to VSM). • Diagnostic tool.	• Go To Pinpoint Test A .
• TPMS will not enter sensor training mode	• Message center. • VSM (TPMS module integral to VSM). • BOO switch. • ABS/TC/IVD module.	• Go To Pinpoint Test B . • Diagnose TPMS.

LTV0500000004373

Fig. 36 Diagnostic System Check. Expedition

Condition	Possible Sources	Action
• Message center (if equipped) displays "CHECK TIRE PRESSURE". TPMS indicator ON continuously	• Air pressure not set to placard.	• Go To Pinpoint Test F .
	• Spare tire currently in use.	• EXCHANGE spare with repaired road wheel/tire.
	• TPMS module. • TPMS sensor.	• Go To Pinpoint Test F .
• Message center (if equipped) displays "CHECK PRESSURE" or "WARNING — TIRE VERY LOW". TPMS indicator ON continuously	• Air pressure not set to placard.	• Go To Pinpoint Test F .
	• Spare tire currently in use.	• EXCHANGE spare with repaired road wheel/tire.
	• TPMS module. • TPMS sensor.	• Go To Pinpoint Test F .
• Message center (if equipped) displays "TIRE PRESSURE MONITOR FAULT". TPMS indicator flashes	• TPMS module. • All four TPMS sensors failed, missing, or incorrectly trained.	• Go To Pinpoint Test C .
• Message center (if equipped) displays "TIRE PRESSURE SENSOR FAULT". TPMS indicator flashes	• TPMS sensor.	• Go To Pinpoint Test E .
	• Spare tire currently in use.	• EXCHANGE spare with repaired road wheel/tire.
• Message center (if equipped) displays "TIRE PRESSURE MONITOR FAULT". TPMS indicator ON continuously. No communication with TPMS module	• Fuse(s). • Circuitry. • Module.	• Go To Pinpoint Test A .
• No communication with the TPMS module	• Fuse(s). • Circuitry. • Module.	• Go To Pinpoint Test A .
• Unable to enter self-test	• TPMS module. • Diagnostic tool.	• Go To Pinpoint Test A .
• TPMS will not enter sensor training mode	• TPMS sensor. • Message center. • TPMS module. • BOO switch. • ABS/TC/IVD module.	• Go To Pinpoint Test B . • Diagnose TPMS.

LTV0500000004374

Fig. 37   Diagnostic System Check. Explorer & Mountaineer

Condition	Possible Sources	Action
• TPMS indicator ON continuously and message center (if equipped) displays "LOW TIRE PRESSURE"	• Air pressure not set to specifications listed on the vehicle certification label	• Go To Pinpoint Test A .
• Message center (if equipped) displays "LOW TIRE PRESSURE"	• Spare tire currently in use	• INSTALL the repaired road wheel/tire in place of the spare tire.
• SJB will not enter sensor training mode when using the TPMS sensor training procedure	• Brake on/off (BOO) switch • Ignition switch • Vehicle communication bus • ABS/TC/IVD module • Smart junction box (SJB)	• Go To Pinpoint Test B .
• TPMS indicator FLASHES when the ignition key is turned to the ON position and DTC B2872 is present	• TPMS sensor(s) • TPMS sensor(s) not trained to the SJB • SJB • SJB antenna damaged or not connected	• Go To Pinpoint Test C . • Diagnose SJB antenna
• TPMS indicator FLASHES when the ignition key is turned to the ON position, the message center (if equipped) displays "TIRE MONITOR FAULT" and DTC B1342 is present	• SJB	• Check Multi-function Modules.
• TPMS indicator FLASHES when the ignition key is turned to the ON position, the message center (if equipped) displays "TIRE MONITOR FAULT" and there are no DTCs present in the SJB	• Vehicle communication bus • SJB • Vehicle communication issue between SJB and instrument cluster	• Check Multi-function Modules. • REFER to "Dash Gauges & Warning Indicators."

LTV0500000004375

Fig. 38   Diagnostic System Check. Freestar & Monterey

COMPONENT SERVICE

Pressure Monitor Sensor Programming

AVIATOR

1. Turn ignition switch to off position.
2. Turn ignition switch to run position three times, ending in run position. Do not wait more than two minutes between each key cycle.
3. Press and release brake pedal.
4. Turn ignition switch to off position.
5. Turn ignition switch to run position three times, ending in run position. Do not wait more than two minutes between each key cycle.
6. Horn will sound once and TPMS indicator will flash if train mode has been entered successfully. If equipped, message center displays "TRAIN LEFT FRONT TIRE". Place magnet on valve stem of LF tire pressure sensor. Horn will sound briefly to indicate that tire pressure sensor has been recognized by TPMS module.
7. Within two minutes after horn sounds, place magnet on valve stem of RF tire pressure sensor.
8. Repeat Step 7 for RR and LR tires. When tire training procedure is complete, horn will sound once and message center (if equipped) will display "TIRE TRAINING MODE COMPLETE". **If TPMS module does not recognize any one of four tire pressure sensors during tire training procedure, horn will sound twice and message center (if equipped) will display "TIRE TRAINING MODE INCOMPLETE". If this occurs, entire procedure must be repeated from Step 1.**

EXPEDITION & NAVIGATOR

Tire pressure monitoring system is not affected by wheel and tire rotation. Tire pressure sensor training procedure must be done on a single vehicle, in an area without radio frequency noise. Radio frequency noise is generated by electrical motor and appliance operation, cellular telephones and remote transmitters, power inverters and portable entertainment equipment.

1. Turn ignition switch to off position.
2. Turn ignition switch from off position to run position 3 times, ending in run position. Do not wait more than 1 minute between each key cycle.
3. Press and release brake pedal.
4. Turn ignition switch to off position.
5. Turn ignition switch from off position to run position 3 times, ending in run position. Do not wait more than 1 minute between each key cycle.
6. Horn will sound once and TPMS indicator will flash if train mode has been entered successfully. If equipped, message center displays "TRAIN LF TIRE", place special tool on valve stem of LF tire pressure sensor. Horn will sound briefly to indicate that tire pressure sensor has been recognized by TPMS module.
7. Within 2 minutes after horn sounds, place special tool on valve stem of RF tire pressure sensor.
8. Repeat Step 7 for RR and LR tires. When tire training procedure is complete, horn will sound once and message center (if equipped) will display "TIRE TRAINING MODE COMPLETE". **If VSM (TPMS module integral to VSM) does not recognize any 1 of 4 tire pressure sensors during tire training procedure, horn will sound twice and message center (if equipped) will display "TIRE NOT TRAINED REPEAT" and procedure must be repeated.**

EXPLORER, FREESTAR, MONTEREY & MOUNTAINEER

Tire pressure monitoring system is not affected by wheel and tire rotation. Tire pressure sensor training procedure must be done on a single vehicle, in an area without radio frequency noise and at least 1 meter (3 feet) away from other vehicles equipped with TPMS. Radio frequency noise is generated by electrical motor and appliance operation, cellular telephones and remote transmitters, power inverters and portable entertainment equipment. If a sensor does not respond to special tool, attempt to activate same sensor with special tool. If sensor still does not respond, move vehicle to rotate wheels at least 1/4 of a turn and attempt to activate same sensor again. A new tire pressure sensor is shipped in an off mode (or battery saver mode) and must be turned on before it can be trained. To turn the sensor on, inflate tire to recommended inflation pressure and wait at least 2 minutes, then continue with sensor training procedure.

1. Turn ignition switch to off position, then press and release brake pedal.
2. Turn ignition switch from off position to run position 3 times, ending in run position. Do not wait more than one minute between each key cycle.
3. Press and release brake pedal.
4. Turn ignition switch to off position.
5. Turn ignition switch from off position to run position 3 times, ending in run position. Do not wait more than one minute between each key cycle.
6. Horn will sound once and TPMS indicator will flash if train mode has been entered successfully. If equipped, message center displays "TRAIN LF TIRE", place special tool on LF tire sidewall opposite (180 degrees) from valve stem. Horn will sound briefly to indicate that tire pressure sensor has

been recognized by the smart junction box (SJB). **It may take up to 6 seconds to activate a tire pressure sensor. During this time, special tool must remain in place 180 degrees from valve stem. If a sensor(s) does not respond to special tool, attempt to activate same sensor(s) with special tool. If sensor(s) still does not respond, move vehicle to rotate wheels at least 1/4 of a turn and attempt to activate same sensor(s) again. If the SJB does not recognize any 1 of 4 tire pressure sensors during tire training procedure, horn will sound twice and message center (if equipped) will display "TIRE NOT TRAINED REPEAT" and procedure must be repeated.**

7. Within 2 minutes of horn sounding, place special tool on RF tire sidewall opposite (180 degrees) from valve stem to train RF tire pressure sensor.
8. Repeat Step 7 for RR and LR tires. Procedure is completed after last tire has been trained. When training procedure is complete, message center (if equipped) will display "TIRE TRAINING MODE COMPLETE". For vehicles not equipped with a message center, successful completion of training procedure will be verified by turning ignition switch to off position without horn sounding. If horn sounds when switch is turned to off position, training procedure was not successful. **Do not wait more than two minutes between training each sensor.**
9. Using diagnostic tool, locate updated TPMS sensor IDs trained to the SJB and document them on applicable warranty claim.

Pressure Monitor Sensor Replacement

Use only tool no. 204-354 anytime tire

pressures are measured to be sure that accurate values are obtained. Place air chuck straight on the valve stem to inflate tire. Do not cock air chuck during inflation cycle. Doing so can damage valve stem and cause air leaks. Ford recommends using a round head air chuck on tire pressure sensors; it is not recommended to use air chucks with long shanks. Doing so can cause tire pressure sensor valve stem damage and loss of tire pressure.

1. Remove wheel and tire assembly.
2. With valve stem at the 6 o'clock position, remove sensor retaining nut and push sensor by hand into tire (with the cap on). **If valve stem core has been removed from valve stem, re-install original valve stem core. If original valve stem core is damaged, a nickel-plated core must be installed. Failure to use a nickel-plated core will result in corrosion and possible loss of tire pressure. Do not remove valve stem core to relieve tire pressure. Release tire pressure by removing sensor retaining nut.**
3. Using a suitable tire machine, separate both beads of tire from wheel. **Make sure that valve stem mounting hole remains in 6 o'clock position while separating beads of tire.**
4. Place wheel and tire on turntable of tire machine so that valve stem hole is positioned 270 degrees from mounting/dismounting fixture. Index-mark valve stem and wheel weight positions. Lubricate bead of tire. Dismount outside bead of tire from rim.
5. Remove tire pressure sensor from tire.
6. Remove and discard grommet from tire pressure sensor.
7. Reverse procedure to install.

TIRE PRESSURE MONITORING SYSTEM

TIGHTENING SPECIFICATIONS

Year	Component	Torque Ft. Lbs.
AVIATOR		
2003–05	Tire Pressure Sensor	44①
	Wheel Lug Nuts	100
EXPLORER, EXPEDITION, MOUNTAINEER & NAVIGATOR		
2002–06	Tire Pressure Sensor	44①
	Wheel Lug Nuts	150
FREESTAR & MONTEREY		
2004–06	Tire Pressure Sensor	44①
	Wheel Lug Nuts	98

① — Inch lbs.

GENERAL MOTORS CORPORATION

Page No.

BUICK
Rainier (Volume 1) 5-1
Rendezvous (Volume 1) 7-1
Terraza (Volume 1) 13-1

CADILLAC
Escalade (Volume 1).......................... 3-1
Escalade ESV (Volume 1)..................... 3-1
Escalade EXT (Volume 1)..................... 1-1
SRX (Volume 1)............................. 11-1

CHEVROLET
Astro (Volume 1)............................. 9-1
Avalanche (Volume 1)......................... 1-1
Blazer (Volume 1) 5-1
Colorado (Volume 1).......................... 4-1
Equinox (Volume 1)........................... 6-1
Express/Van (Volume 1) 2-1
HHR (Volume 1) 8-1
Pickup Trucks (Volume 1) 3-1
S-10 (Volume 1)............................. 4-1
Silverado (Volume 1) 1-1
SSR (Volume 1)............................. 1-1
Suburban (Volume 1) 3-1
Tahoe (Volume 1) 3-1
Tracker (Volume 1) 12-1
TrailBlazer (Volume 1) 5-1
Uplander (Volume 1).......................... 13-1
Venture (Volume 1).......................... 10-1

GMC
Canyon (Volume 1)........................... 4-1
Envoy (Volume 1) 5-1
Jimmy (Volume 1)............................ 5-1
Safari (Volume 1) 9-1
Savana (Volume 1) 2-1
Sierra (Volume 1) 1-1
Sonoma (Volume 1) 4-1
Suburban (Volume 1) 3-1
Yukon (Volume 1) 3-1
Yukon XL (Volume 1) 3-1

HUMMER
H2 (Volume 1) 14-1
H3 (Volume 1) 14-1

OLDSMOBILE
Bravada (Volume 1) 5-1
Silhouette (Volume 1)........................ 10-1

PONTIAC
Aztek (Volume 1)............................ 7-1
Montana (Volume 1).......................... 10-1

Page No.

Montana SV6 (Volume 1) 13-1
Torrent (Volume 1) 6-1

SATURN
Relay (Volume 1)............................ 13-1
VUE (Volume 1)............................. 15-1

GENERAL SERVICE
Active Suspension Systems 6-1
Air Bag Systems............................ 4-1
Air Conditioning (Volume 1)................. 16-1
All-Wheel Drive (Volume 1) 30-1
Alternators (Volume 1)...................... 19-1
Anti-Lock Brake Systems 5-1
Axles, Drive (Volume 1) 31-1
Axles, Front Wheel Drive (Volume 1) 29-1
Brakes
    Anti-Lock Brake Systems 5-1
    Disc Brakes (Volume 1) 23-1
    Drum Brakes (Volume 1) 24-1
    Hydraulic Brake Systems (Volume 1) 25-1
    Power Brake Units (Volume 1)............. 26-1
Cooling Fans (Volume 1)..................... 17-1
Cruise Control Systems...................... 2-1
Dash Gauges 1-1
Dash Panel Service (Volume 1)............... 20-1
Disc Brakes (Volume 1) 23-1
Drive Axles (Volume 1)...................... 31-1
Drum Brakes (Volume 1) 24-1
Electric Cooling Fans (Volume 1) 17-1
Electronic Level Controls 6-1
Engine Cooling Fans (Volume 1).............. 17-1
Engine Rebuilding Specifications (Volume 1) ... 33-1
Fans, Engine Cooling (Volume 1) 17-1
Front Wheel Drive Axle (Volume 1)........... 29-1
Hydraulic Brake Systems (Volume 1).......... 25-1
Machine Shop Specifications (Volume 1) 33-1
Passive Restraint Systems 4-1
Power Brake Units (Volume 1) 26-1
Power Steering (Volume 1) 22-1
Speed Control Systems...................... 2-1
Starter Motors (Volume 1)................... 18-1
Steering
    Power Steering (Volume 1) 22-1
    Steering Columns (Volume 1) 21-1
Steering Columns (Volume 1) 21-1
Tire Pressure Monitoring Systems............ 7-1
Transfer Cases (Volume 1)................... 28-1
Universal Joints (Volume 1).................. 32-1
Vacuum Pumps (Volume 1) 27-1
Variable Speed Fans (Volume 1) 17-1
Warning Indicators......................... 1-1
Wiper Systems 3-1

GENERAL MOTORS CORPORATION

Page No.

BUICK
Rainier (Volume 1) 5-1
Rendezvous (Volume 1) 7-1
Terraza (Volume 1) 13-1

CADILLAC
Escalade (Volume 1)........................... 3-1
Escalade ESV (Volume 1)....................... 3-1
Escalade EXT (Volume 1)....................... 1-1
SRX (Volume 1)................................ 11-1

CHEVROLET
Astro (Volume 1).............................. 9-1
Avalanche (Volume 1).......................... 1-1
Blazer (Volume 1) 5-1
Colorado (Volume 1)........................... 4-1
Equinox (Volume 1)............................ 6-1
Express/Van (Volume 1) 2-1
HHR (Volume 1) 8-1
Pickup Trucks (Volume 1) 3-1
S-10 (Volume 1)............................... 4-1
Silverado (Volume 1) 1-1
SSR (Volume 1)................................ 1-1
Suburban (Volume 1) 3-1
Tahoe (Volume 1) 3-1
Tracker (Volume 1) 12-1
TrailBlazer (Volume 1) 5-1
Uplander (Volume 1)........................... 13-1
Venture (Volume 1)............................ 10-1

GMC
Canyon (Volume 1)............................. 4-1
Envoy (Volume 1) 5-1
Jimmy (Volume 1).............................. 5-1
Safari (Volume 1) 9-1
Savana (Volume 1) 2-1
Sierra (Volume 1) 1-1
Sonoma (Volume 1) 4-1
Suburban (Volume 1) 3-1
Yukon (Volume 1) 3-1
Yukon XL (Volume 1) 3-1

HUMMER
H2 (Volume 1) 14-1
H3 (Volume 1) 14-1

OLDSMOBILE
Bravada (Volume 1) 5-1
Silhouette (Volume 1)......................... 10-1

PONTIAC
Aztek (Volume 1).............................. 7-1
Montana (Volume 1)............................ 10-1

Page No.

Montana SV6 (Volume 1) 13-1
Torrent (Volume 1) 6-1

SATURN
Relay (Volume 1).............................. 13-1
VUE (Volume 1)................................ 15-1

GENERAL SERVICE
Active Suspension Systems 6-1
Air Bag Systems.............................. 4-1
Air Conditioning (Volume 1)................... 16-1
All-Wheel Drive (Volume 1) 30-1
Alternators (Volume 1)........................ 19-1
Anti-Lock Brake Systems 5-1
Axles, Drive (Volume 1) 31-1
Axles, Front Wheel Drive (Volume 1) 29-1
Brakes
    Anti-Lock Brake Systems 5-1
    Disc Brakes (Volume 1) 23-1
    Drum Brakes (Volume 1) 24-1
    Hydraulic Brake Systems (Volume 1) 25-1
    Power Brake Units (Volume 1).............. 26-1
Cooling Fans (Volume 1)....................... 17-1
Cruise Control Systems....................... 2-1
Dash Gauges 1-1
Dash Panel Service (Volume 1) 20-1
Disc Brakes (Volume 1) 23-1
Drive Axles (Volume 1)........................ 31-1
Drum Brakes (Volume 1) 24-1
Electric Cooling Fans (Volume 1) 17-1
Electronic Level Controls 6-1
Engine Cooling Fans (Volume 1)................ 17-1
Engine Rebuilding Specifications (Volume 1) ... 33-1
Fans, Engine Cooling (Volume 1) 17-1
Front Wheel Drive Axle (Volume 1)............. 29-1
Hydraulic Brake Systems (Volume 1)............ 25-1
Machine Shop Specifications (Volume 1) 33-1
Passive Restraint Systems 4-1
Power Brake Units (Volume 1) 26-1
Power Steering (Volume 1) 22-1
Speed Control Systems........................ 2-1
Starter Motors (Volume 1) 18-1
Steering
    Power Steering (Volume 1) 22-1
    Steering Columns (Volume 1) 21-1
Steering Columns (Volume 1) 21-1
Tire Pressure Monitoring Systems............. 7-1
Transfer Cases (Volume 1).................... 28-1
Universal Joints (Volume 1).................. 32-1
Vacuum Pumps (Volume 1) 27-1
Variable Speed Fans (Volume 1)............... 17-1
Warning Indicators.......................... 1-1
Wiper Systems 3-1

DASH GAUGES & WARNING INDICATORS

NOTE: On Air Bag Equipped Models, Refer To "Air Bag System Precautions" Located In The Front Of This Manual For System Disarming & Arming Procedures.

NOTE: Refer To The "Electronic Instrumentation" Section In MOTOR's Domestic Engine Performance & Driveability Manual For Information Related To Electronic Instrumentation.

NOTE: Refer To "Computer Relearn Procedures" Located In The Front Of This Manual When Battery Power To The Computer Has Been Interrupted.

NOTE: "Electrical Symbol & Wire Color Code Identification" Located In The Front Of This Manual May Be Used As An Aid When Using Wiring Circuits Found In This Section.

INDEX

	Page No.		Page No.		Page No.
Diagnosis & Testing	1-3	Bravada	1-3	Check Coolant Temperature	1-2
Symptom Diagnosis	1-3	Canyon & Colorado	1-3	Check Engine Warning Lamp	1-2
Astro & Safari	1-3	Envoy, Rainier & Trailblazer	1-3	Cruise Control Indicator	1-2
Avalanche, Escalade,		Equinox & Torrent	1-3	Fog Lamp	1-2
Suburban, Tahoe & Yukon	1-3	Express & Savana	1-3	Four Wheel Drive (4WD)	
Aztek & Rendezvous	1-3	HHR	1-3	Indicator	1-2
Blazer	1-3	Hummer H2	1-3	High Beam Out	1-2
Bravada	1-3	Hummer H3	1-3	Lights On Indicator	1-2
Canyon & Colorado	1-3	Montana & Venture	1-3	Low Coolant Warning Lamp	1-2
Envoy, Rainier & Trailblazer	1-3	Relay	1-3	Low Fuel Level Warning Lamp	1-2
Equinox & Torrent	1-3	S10 & Sonoma	1-3	Low Oil Level Warning Lamp	1-2
Express & Savana	1-3	SRX	1-3	Low Oil Pressure Warning	
Hummer H2	1-3	SSR	1-3	Lamp	1-2
Hummer H3	1-3	SV6, Terraza & Uplander	1-3	Low Tire Pressure Warning	
Montana & Venture	1-3	Sierra, Silverado, Suburban,		Lamp	1-2
Relay, SV6, Terraza &		Tahoe & Yukon	1-3	Low Washer Fluid Warning	
Uplander	1-3	Silhouette	1-3	Lamp	1-2
S10 & Sonoma	1-3	Tracker	1-3	Reduced Engine Power	1-2
SRX	1-3	Vue	1-3	Safety Belt Warning Lamp	1-2
SSR	1-3	**Precautions**	1-2	Service 4WD	1-2
Sierra & Silverado	1-3	Air Bag Systems	1-2	Service Engine Soon Lamp	1-2
Silhouette	1-3	Battery Ground Cable	1-2	Shift Indicator (Manual	
Tracker	1-3	**Troubleshooting**	1-2	Transmission)	1-2
Vue	1-3	ABS Indicator	1-2	Tow/Haul Indicator (Automatic	
Wiring Diagrams	1-3	Air Bag Warning Lamp	1-2	Transmission)	1-3
Astro & Safari	1-3	Anti-Lock Brake Warning Lamp	1-2	Wait To Start (Diesel)	1-3
Avalanche & Escalade	1-3	Brake Warning Lamp	1-2	Water In Fuel (Diesel)	1-3
Aztek & Rendezvous	1-3	Charging System Warning			
Blazer	1-3	Lamp	1-2		

DASH GAUGES & WARNING INDICATORS

PRECAUTIONS

Air Bag Systems

Refer to "Air Bag System Precautions" in the front of this manual for system disarming and arming procedures.

Battery Ground Cable

Prior to service disconnect battery ground cable and isolate as required.

TROUBLESHOOTING

ABS Indicator

1. EBCM detects fault with ABS system.
2. EBCM displays test at beginning of each ignition cycle.
3. Indicator illuminates at least three seconds.
4. IPC detects loss of communications with EBCM.

Air Bag Warning Lamp

Air bag warning lamp illuminates when there is an air bag system concern.
Refer to **MOTOR's "Air Bag Manual"** or **"Air Bag Diagnostics CD"** for diagnosis and testing.

Anti-Lock Brake Warning Lamp

The Anti-lock brake warning lamp will illuminate if the system controller detects any fault in the anti-lock brake system. Normal brake system operation will remain operational, but wheels could lock during panic stop.

Brake Warning Lamp

1. Brake fluid level switch.
2. Low brake fluid level.
3. Park brake system.
4. Instrument cluster.
5. Daytime Running Lights control module.
6. Wiring circuits and bulb.

Charging System Warning Lamp

1. Wiring circuits and bulb.
2. Instrument cluster and battery.
3. Inspect drive belt.
4. Inspect PCM.
5. Inspect for corroded terminals.
6. Alternator.

Check Coolant Temperature

Check engine or malfunction indicator lamp (MIL) indicator is illuminated by Powertrain Control Module (PCM). Refer to **MOTOR's "Domestic Engine Performance & Driveability Manual"** for lamp diagnosis.

Check Engine Warning Lamp

Check engine or malfunction indicator lamp (MIL) indicator is illuminated by Powertrain Control Module (PCM). Refer to **MOTOR's "Domestic Engine Performance & Driveability Manual"** for lamp diagnosis.

Cruise Control Indicator

1. Cruise control system.
2. Wiring circuits and PCM.
3. Instrument cluster.

Fog Lamp

1. Fog lamp assembly.
2. Wiring circuits and BCM.
3. Instrument cluster.

Four Wheel Drive (4WD) Indicator

The IPC illuminates the 4WD indicator when the PCM detects that the 4WD is requested.

High Beam Out

1. High beam lamp.
2. Wiring circuits and BCM.
3. Instrument cluster.

Lights On Indicator

1. Lamp switch.
2. Wiring circuits and DIM.
3. Instrument cluster.

Low Coolant Warning Lamp

1. Instrument cluster.
2. Wiring circuits and bulb.
3. Low coolant level switch.
4. Inspect BCM.

Low Fuel Level Warning Lamp

1. Fuel gauge and indicator bulb.
2. Instrument cluster circuit.
3. Electrical connections.
4. Low fuel level switch.

Low Oil Pressure Warning Lamp

1. Oil pressure switch.
2. Low engine oil level.
3. Wiring circuits, bulb and fuse.
4. Low engine oil pressure and instrument cluster.

Low Oil Level Warning Lamp

1. Wiring circuits, bulb and fuse.
2. Low engine oil level.
3. Oil pressure switch.
4. Instrument cluster.

Low Tire Pressure Warning Lamp

1. Low tire pressure.
2. Low tire pressure sensor and bulb.
3. Low tire pressure module.
4. Wiring circuits and fuse.

Low Washer Fluid Warning Lamp

1. Wiring circuits and bulb.
2. Windshield washer low fluid switch.
3. Instrument cluster.
4. Low washer fluid level and washer fluid container.
5. Indicator lamp module and sensor.

Reduced Engine Power

1. Wiring circuits and PCM.
2. Instrument cluster.

Safety Belt Warning Lamp

1. Lefthand belt switch and fuse.
2. Wiring circuits and bulb.
3. Instrument cluster

Service Engine Soon Lamp

Service engine soon lamp is illuminated by Powertrain Control Module (PCM). Refer to **MOTOR's "Domestic Engine Performance & Driveability Manual"** for lamp diagnosis.

Service 4WD

1. Transfer case.
2. Wiring circuits and PCM.
3. Instrument cluster.

Shift Indicator (Manual Transmission)

1. Shifter and linkage.
2. Wiring circuits.
3. Instrument cluster.

Tow/Haul Indicator (Automatic Transmission)

1. Tow/haul mode.
2. Wiring circuits and BCS.
3. Instrument cluster.

Wait To Start (Diesel)

1. Engine controls.
2. Wiring circuits and PCM.
3. Instrument cluster.

Water In Fuel (Diesel)

1. Engine controls.
2. Wiring circuits and ECM.
3. Instrument cluster.

DIAGNOSIS & TESTING

Wiring Diagrams

ASTRO & SAFARI

Refer to **Figs. 1 through 4** for wiring diagrams.

AVALANCHE & ESCALADE

Refer to **Figs. 5 and 6** for wiring diagrams.

AZTEK & RENDEZVOUS

Refer to **Figs. 7 through 11** for wiring diagrams.

BLAZER

Refer to **Figs. 12 and 13** for wiring diagrams.

BRAVADA

Refer to **Figs. 14 and 15** for wiring diagrams.

CANYON & COLORADO

Refer to **Figs. 16 through 18** for wiring diagrams.

ENVOY, RAINIER & TRAILBLAZER

Refer to **Figs. 19 through 21** for wiring diagrams.

EQUINOX & TORRENT

Refer to **Figs. 22 and 23** for wiring diagrams.

EXPRESS & SAVANA

Refer to **Figs. 24 through 27** for wiring diagrams.

HUMMER H2

Refer to **Figs. 28 through 31** for wiring diagrams.

HUMMER H3

Refer to **Fig. 32** for wiring diagrams.

HHR

Refer to **Fig. 33** for wiring diagrams.

MONTANA & VENTURE

Refer to **Figs. 34 through 36** for wiring diagrams.

RELAY

Refer to **Figs. 37 and 38** for wiring diagrams.

S10 & SONOMA

Refer to **Fig. 39** for wiring diagrams.

SIERRA, SILVERADO, SUBURBAN, TAHOE & YUKON

Refer to **Figs. 40 and 41** for wiring diagrams.

SILHOUETTE

Refer to **Fig. 42** for wiring diagrams.

SRX

Refer to **Figs. 43 through 45** for wiring diagrams.

SSR

Refer to **Figs. 46 through 49** for wiring diagrams.

SV6, TERRAZA & UPLANDER

Refer to **Figs. 50 and 51** for wiring diagrams.

TRACKER

Refer to **Figs. 52 through 54** for wiring diagrams.

VUE

Refer to **Figs. 55 through 59** for wiring diagrams.

Symptom Diagnosis

ASTRO & SAFARI

Refer to **Figs. 60 through 74** for symptom diagnosis procedures.

AVALANCHE, ESCALADE, SUBURBAN, TAHOE & YUKON

2002

Refer to **Figs. 75 through 96** for symptom diagnosis procedures.

2003–06

Refer to **Figs. 97 through 111** for symptom diagnosis procedures.

AZTEK & RENDEZVOUS

Refer to **Figs. 112 through 132** for symptom diagnosis procedures.

BLAZER

Refer to **Figs. 133 through 149** for symptom diagnosis procedures.

BRAVADA

Refer to **Figs. 150 through 161** for symptom diagnosis procedures.

CANYON & COLORADO

Refer to **Figs. 162 through 171** for symptom diagnosis procedures.

ENVOY, RAINIER & TRAILBLAZER

Refer to **Figs. 172 through 186** for symptom diagnosis procedures.

EQUINOX & TORRENT

Refer to **Figs. 187 through 195** for symptom diagnosis procedures.

EXPRESS & SAVANA

Refer to **Figs. 196 through 208** for symptom diagnosis procedures.

HUMMER H2

Refer to **Figs. 209 through 222** for symptom diagnosis procedures.

HUMMER H3

Refer to **Figs. 223 through 232** for symptom diagnosis procedures.

MONTANA & VENTURE

Refer to **Figs. 233 through 246** for symptom diagnosis procedures.

RELAY, SV6, TERRAZA & UPLANDER

Refer to **Figs. 247 through 258** for symptom diagnosis procedures.

S10 & SONOMA

Refer to **Figs. 259 through 275** for symptom diagnosis procedures.

SIERRA & SILVERADO

Refer to **Figs. 276 through 292** for symptom diagnosis procedures.

SILHOUETTE

Refer to **Figs. 293 through 306** for symptom diagnosis procedures.

SRX

Refer to **Figs. 307 through 318** for symptom diagnosis procedures.

SSR

Refer to **Figs. 319 through 331** for symptom diagnosis procedures.

TRACKER

Refer to **Figs. 332 through 340** for symptom diagnosis procedures.

VUE

Refer to **Figs. 341 through 348** for symptom diagnosis procedures.

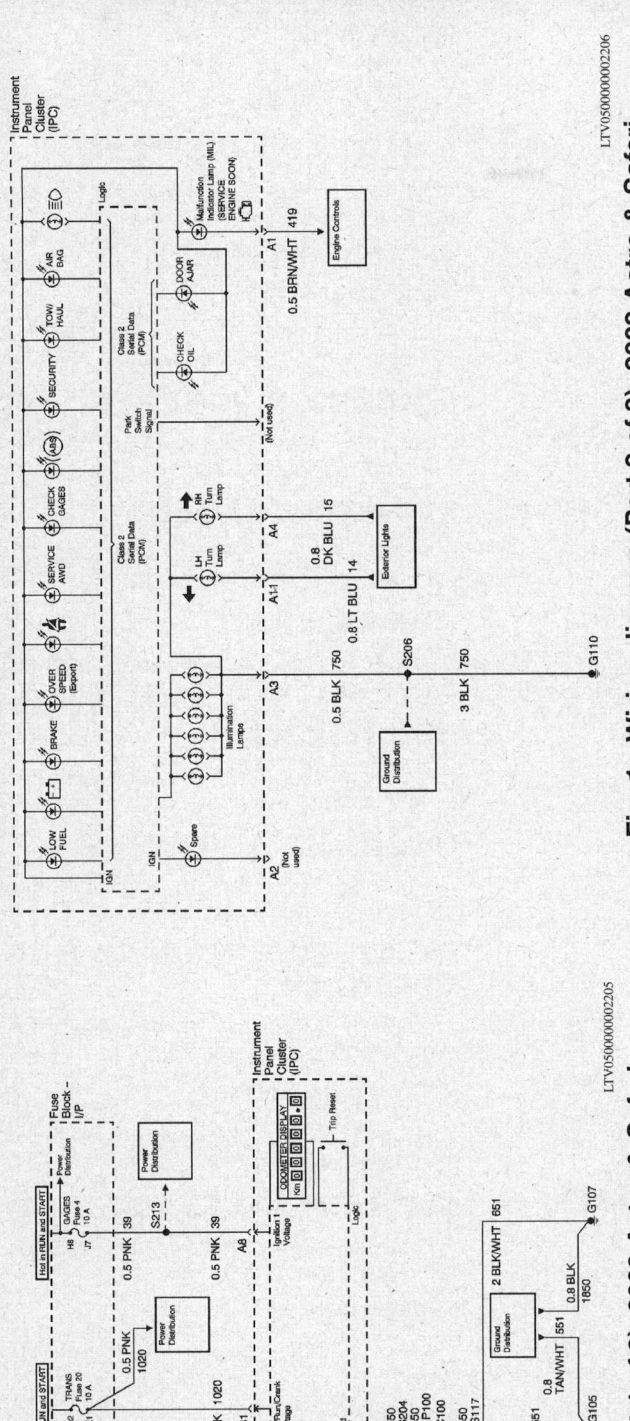

Fig. 1 Wiring diagram (Part 2 of 3). 2002 Astro & Safari

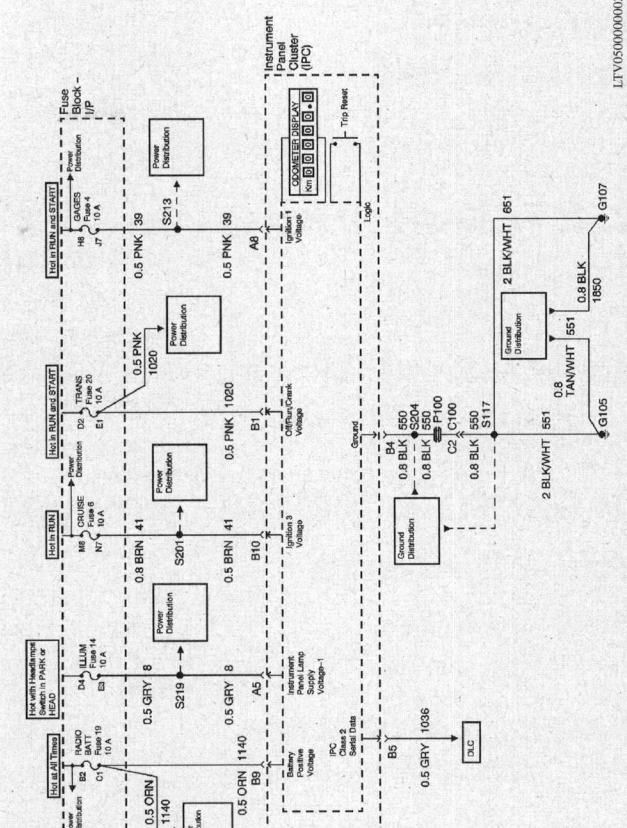

Fig. 2 Wiring diagram (Part 1 of 3). 2003 Astro & Safari

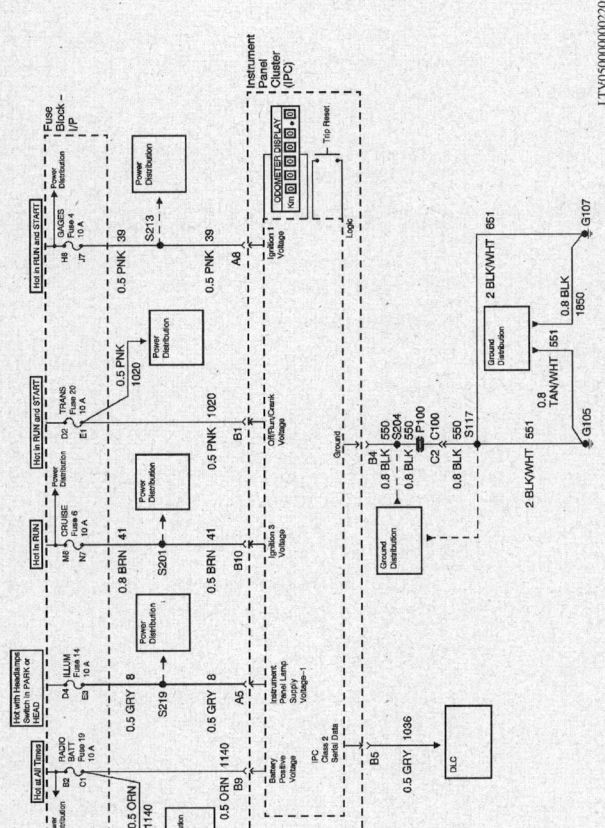

Fig. 1 Wiring diagram (Part 1 of 3). 2002 Astro & Safari

Fig. 1 Wiring diagram (Part 3 of 3). 2002 Astro & Safari

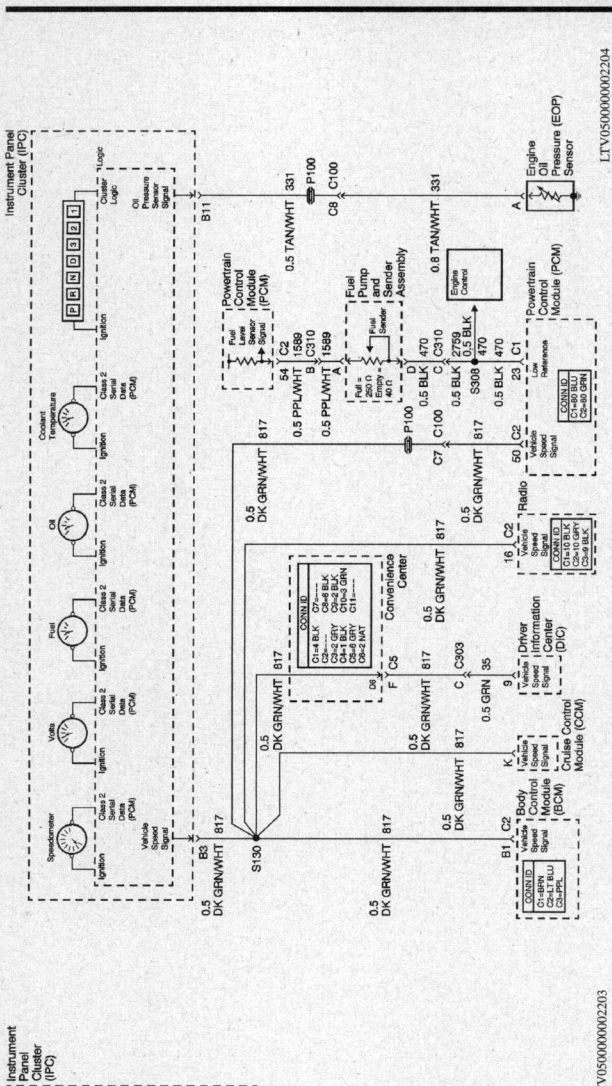

Fig. 2 Wiring diagram (Part 3 of 3). 2003 Astro & Safari

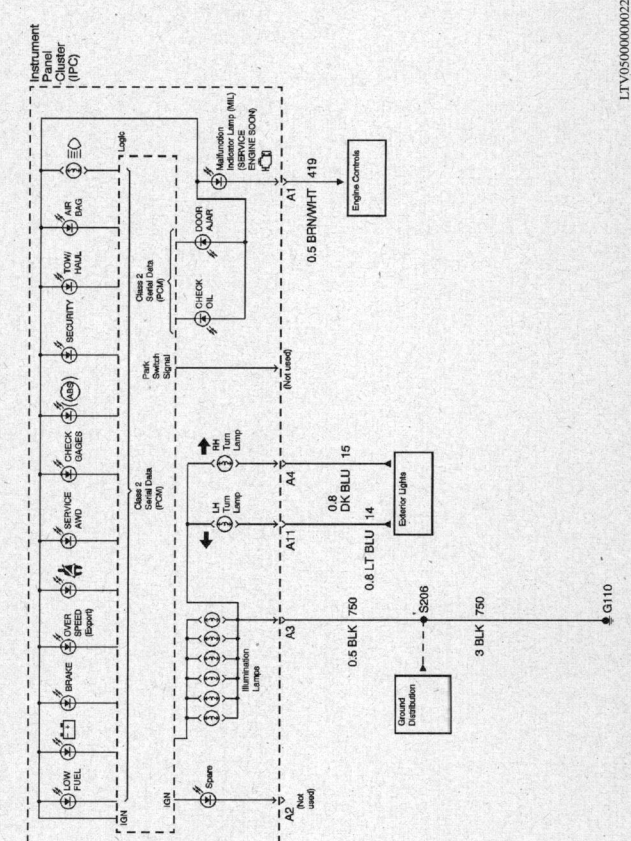

Fig. 3 Wiring diagram (Part 2 of 3). 2004 Astro & Safari

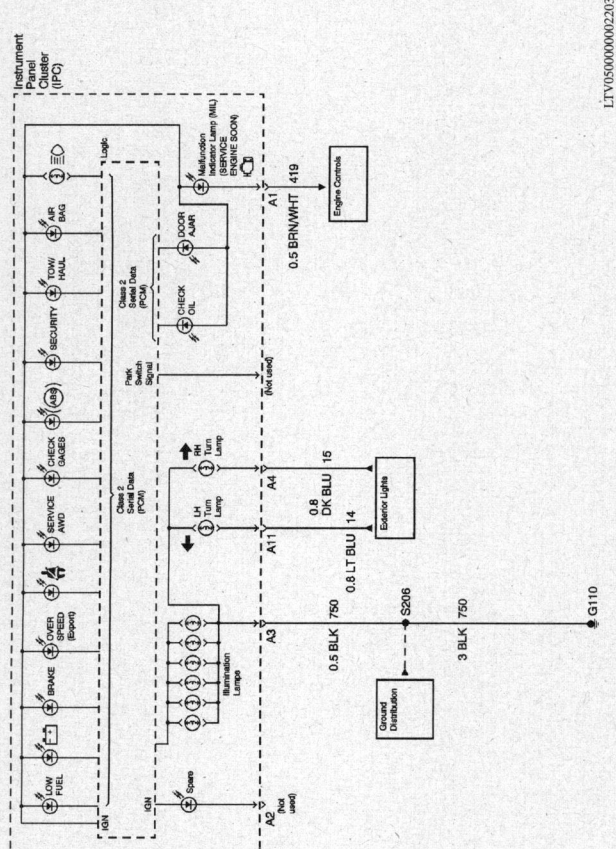

Fig. 2 Wiring diagram (Part 2 of 3). 2003 Astro & Safari

Fig. 3 Wiring diagram (Part 1 of 3). 2004 Astro & Safari

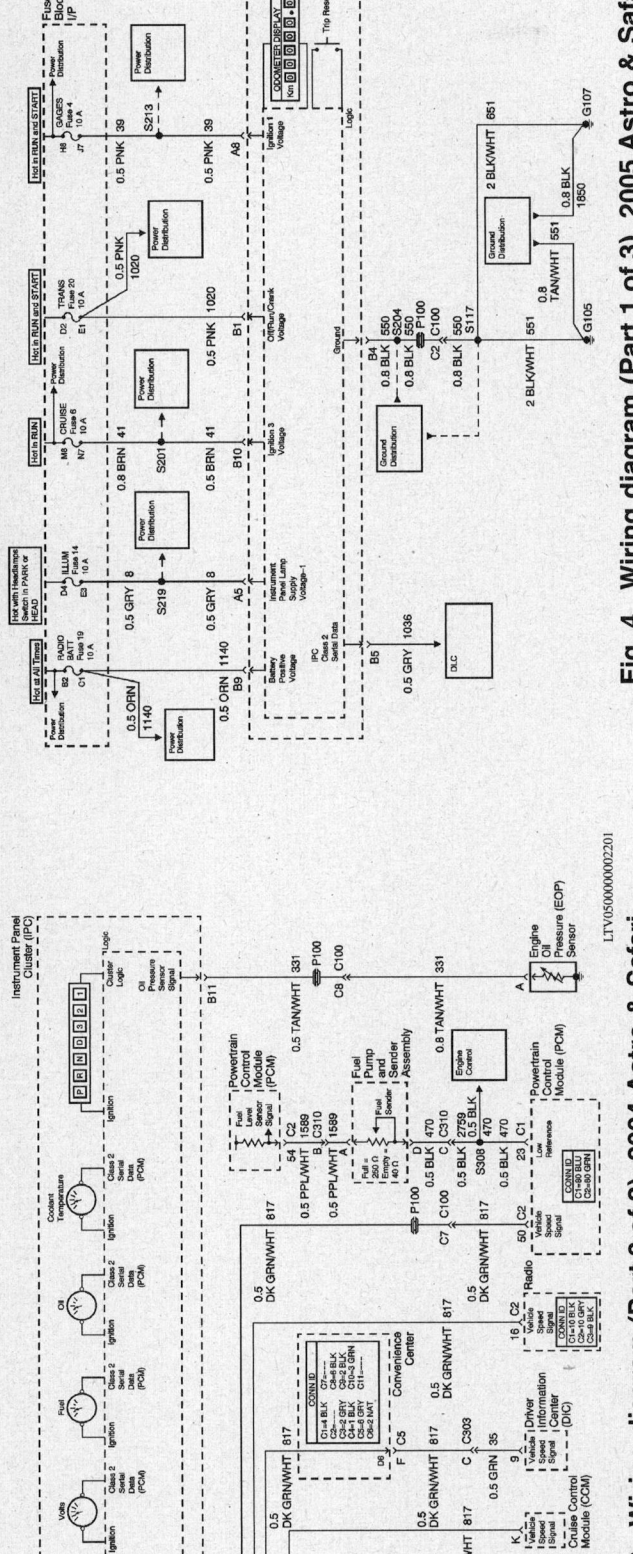

Fig. 4   Wiring diagram (Part 1 of 3). 2005 Astro & Safari

Fig. 3   Wiring diagram (Part 3 of 3). 2004 Astro & Safari

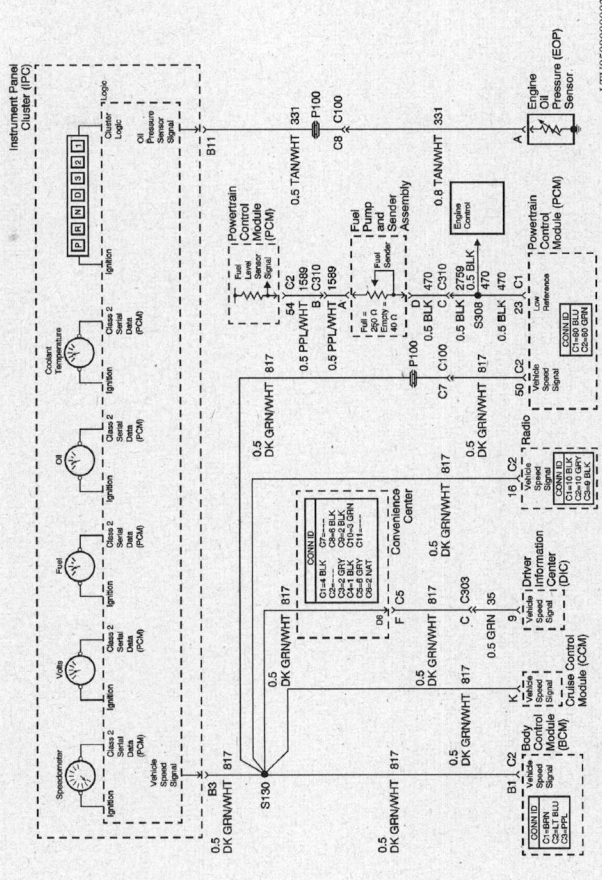

Fig. 4   Wiring diagram (Part 3 of 3). 2005 Astro & Safari

Fig. 4   Wiring diagram (Part 2 of 3). 2005 Astro & Safari

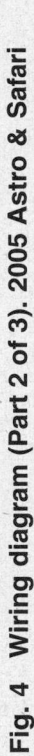

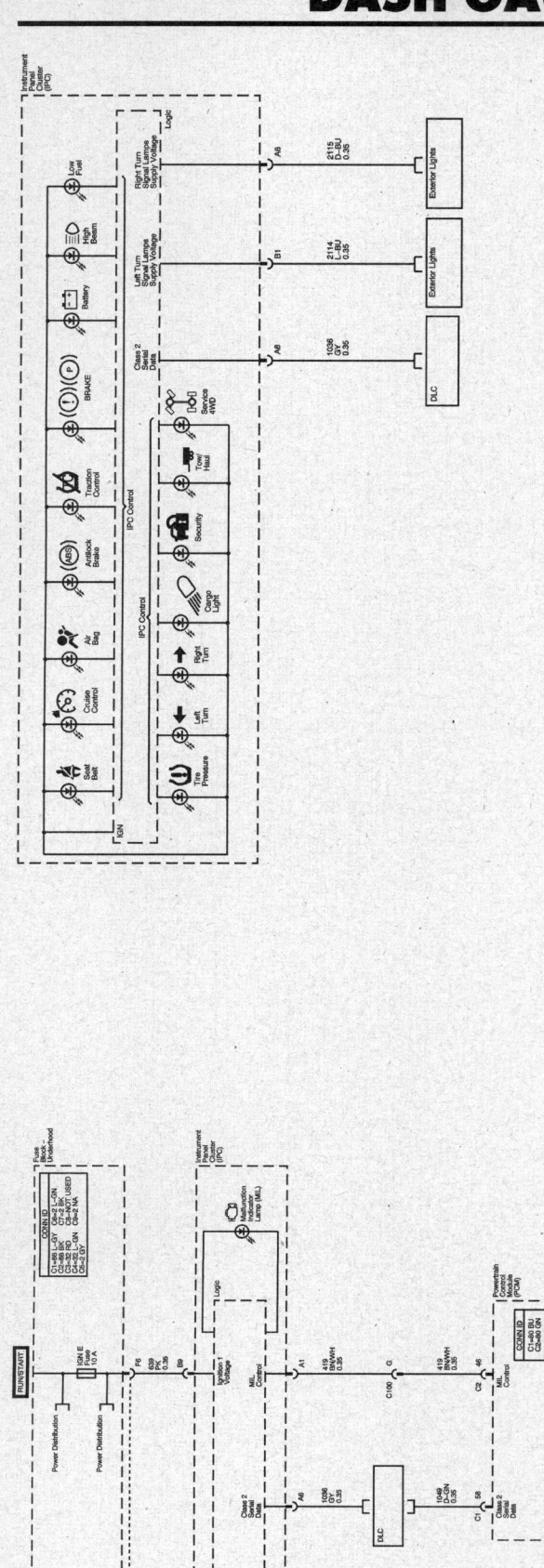

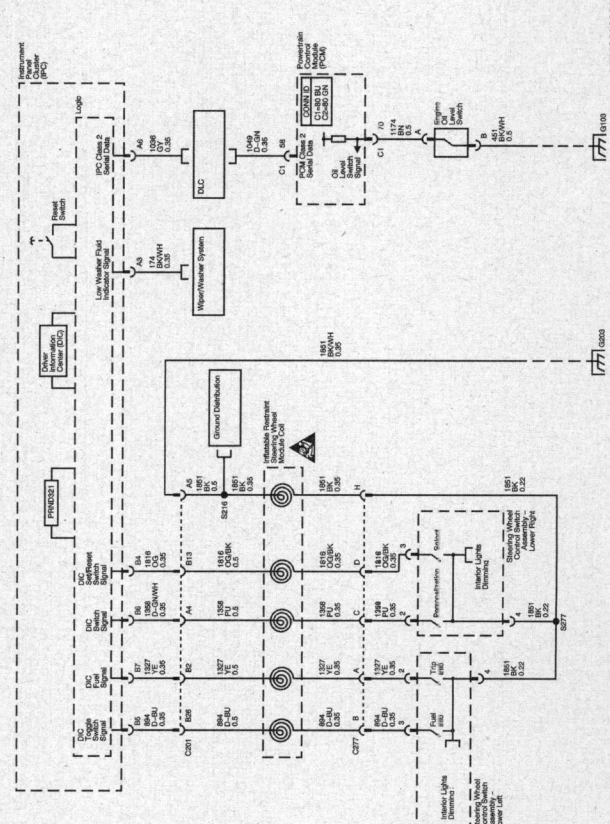

Fig. 5 Wiring diagram (Part 2 of 4). 2002–05 Avalanche & Escalade

Fig. 5 Wiring diagram (Part 4 of 4). 2002–05 Avalanche & Escalade

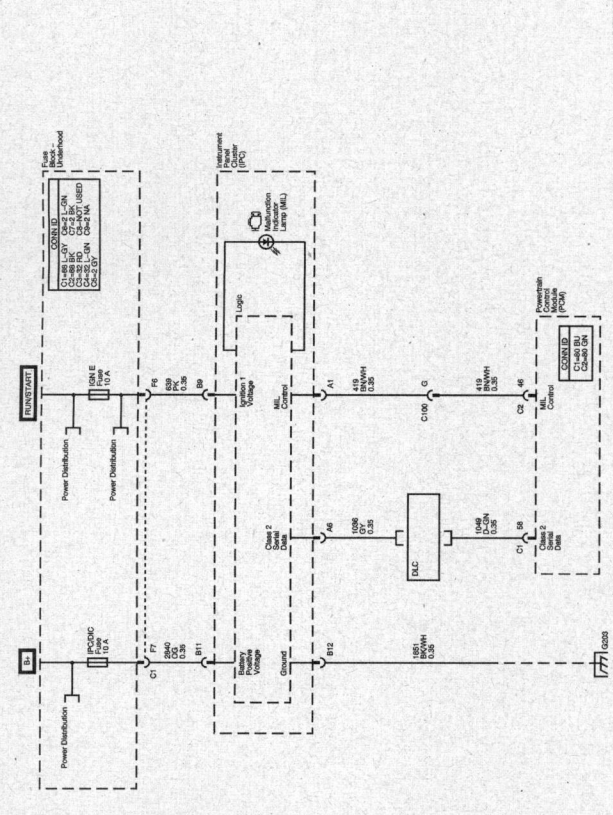

Fig. 5 Wiring diagram (Part 1 of 4). 2002–05 Avalanche & Escalade

Fig. 5 Wiring diagram (Part 3 of 4). 2002–05 Avalanche & Escalade

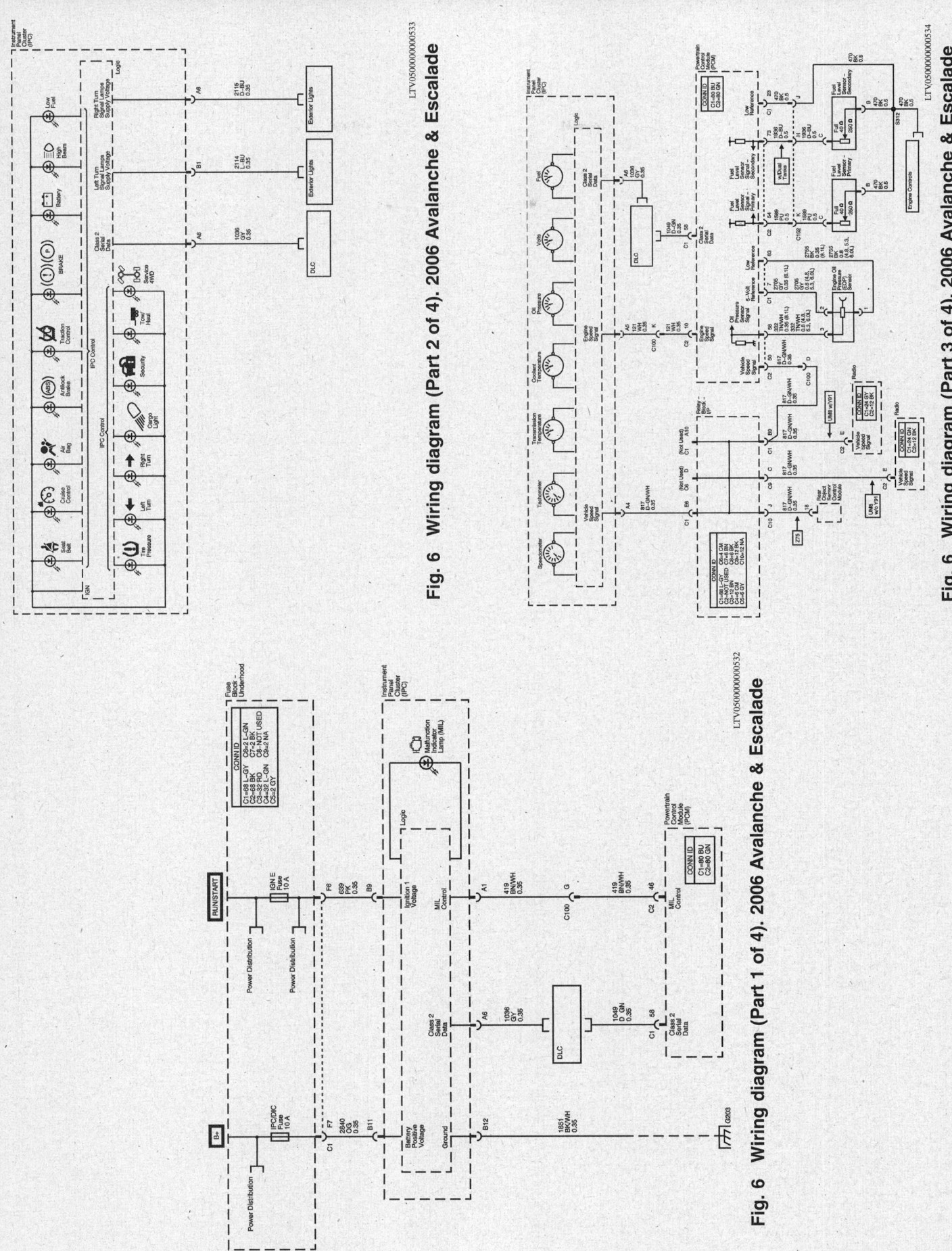

Fig. 6 Wiring diagram (Part 2 of 4). 2006 Avalanche & Escalade

Fig. 6 Wiring diagram (Part 3 of 4). 2006 Avalanche & Escalade

Fig. 6 Wiring diagram (Part 1 of 4). 2006 Avalanche & Escalade

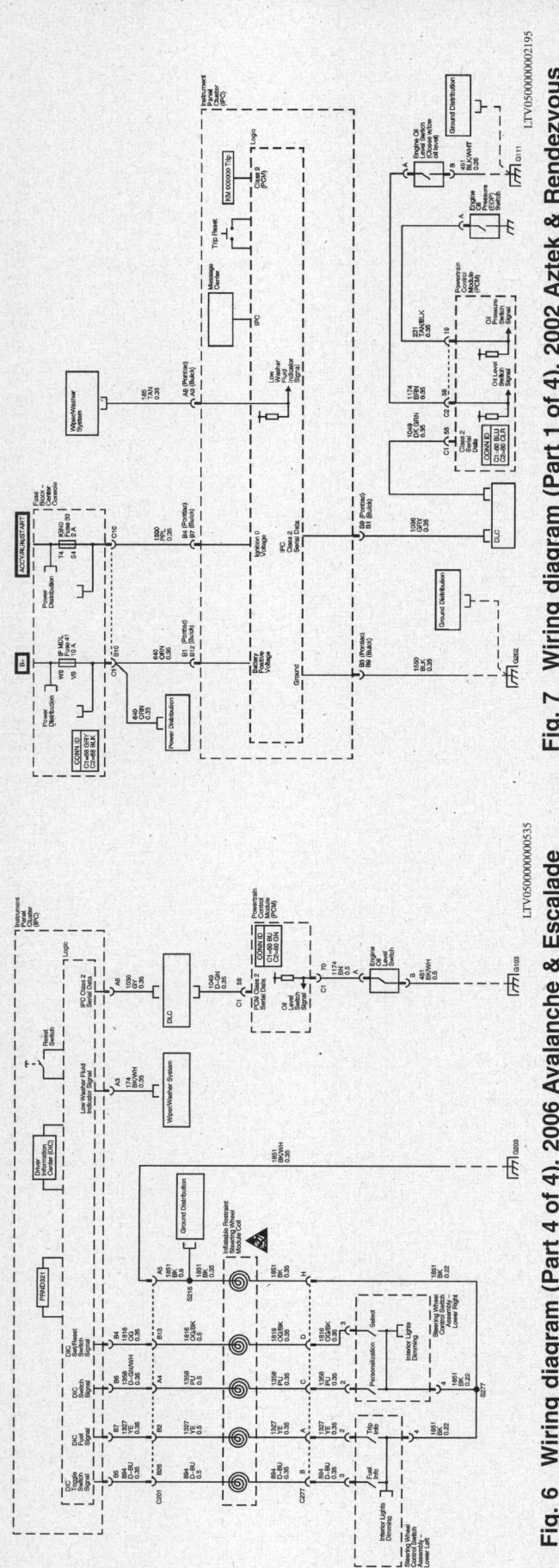

Fig. 7 Wiring diagram (Part 1 of 4). 2002 Aztek & Rendezvous

Fig. 6 Wiring diagram (Part 4 of 4). 2006 Avalanche & Escalade

Fig. 7 Wiring diagram (Part 3 of 4). 2002 Aztek & Rendezvous

Fig. 7 Wiring diagram (Part 2 of 4). 2002 Aztek & Rendezvous

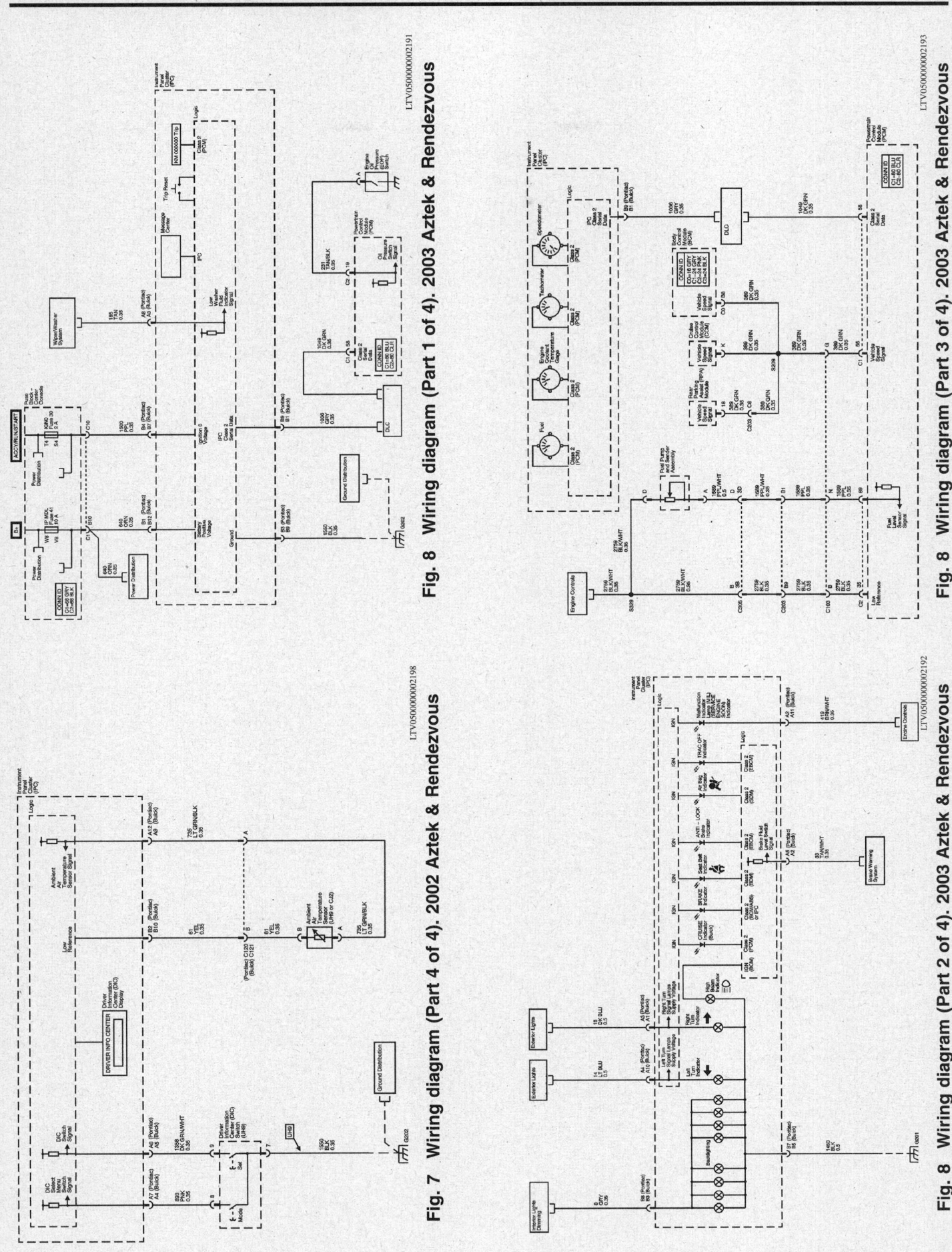

Fig. 8   Wiring diagram (Part 1 of 4). 2003 Aztek & Rendezvous

Fig. 8   Wiring diagram (Part 3 of 4). 2003 Aztek & Rendezvous

Fig. 7   Wiring diagram (Part 4 of 4). 2002 Aztek & Rendezvous

Fig. 8   Wiring diagram (Part 2 of 4). 2003 Aztek & Rendezvous

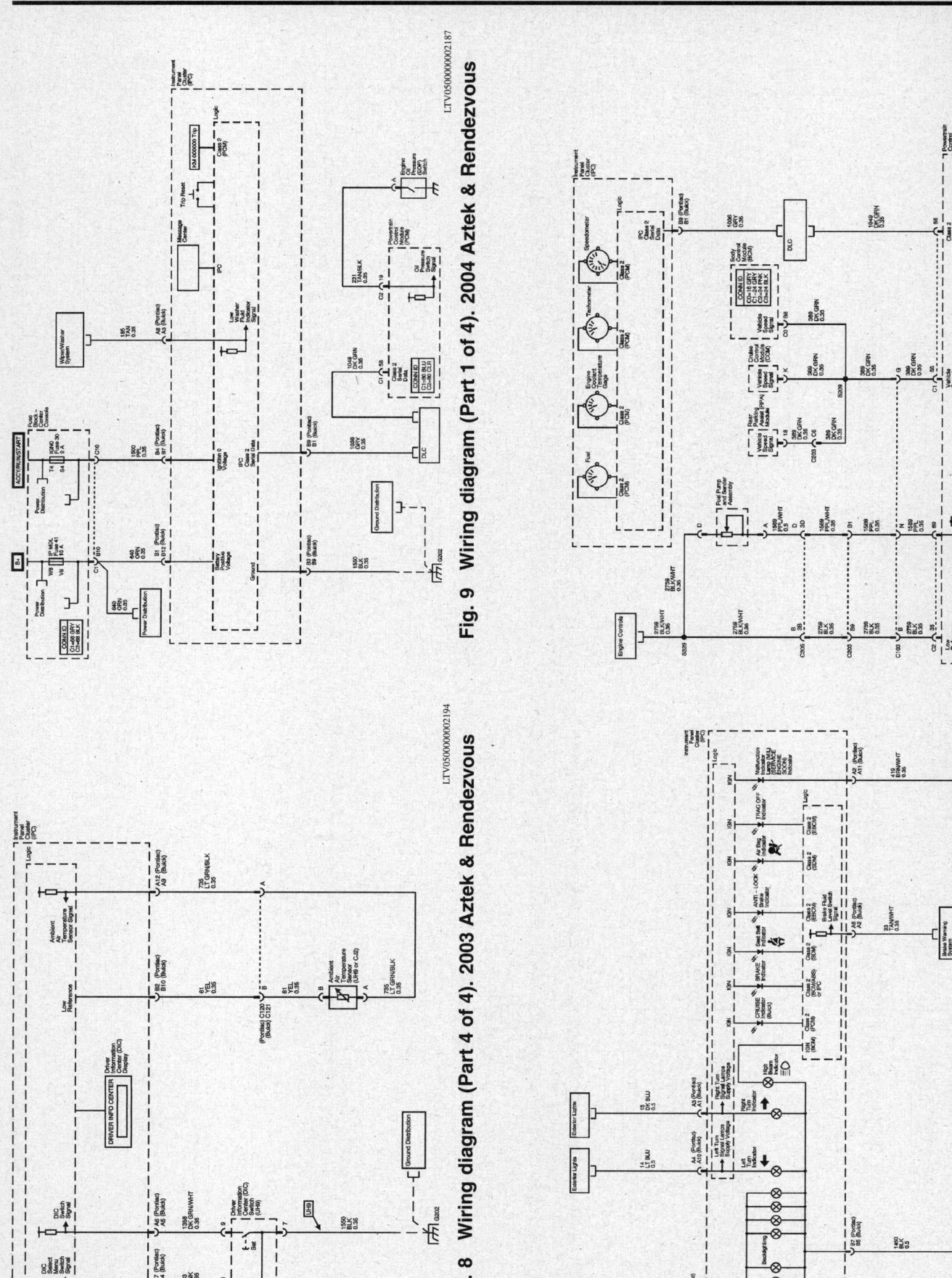

Fig. 9   Wiring diagram (Part 1 of 4). 2004 Aztek & Rendezvous

Fig. 9   Wiring diagram (Part 3 of 4). 2004 Aztek & Rendezvous

Fig. 8   Wiring diagram (Part 4 of 4). 2003 Aztek & Rendezvous

Fig. 9   Wiring diagram (Part 2 of 4). 2004 Aztek & Rendezvous

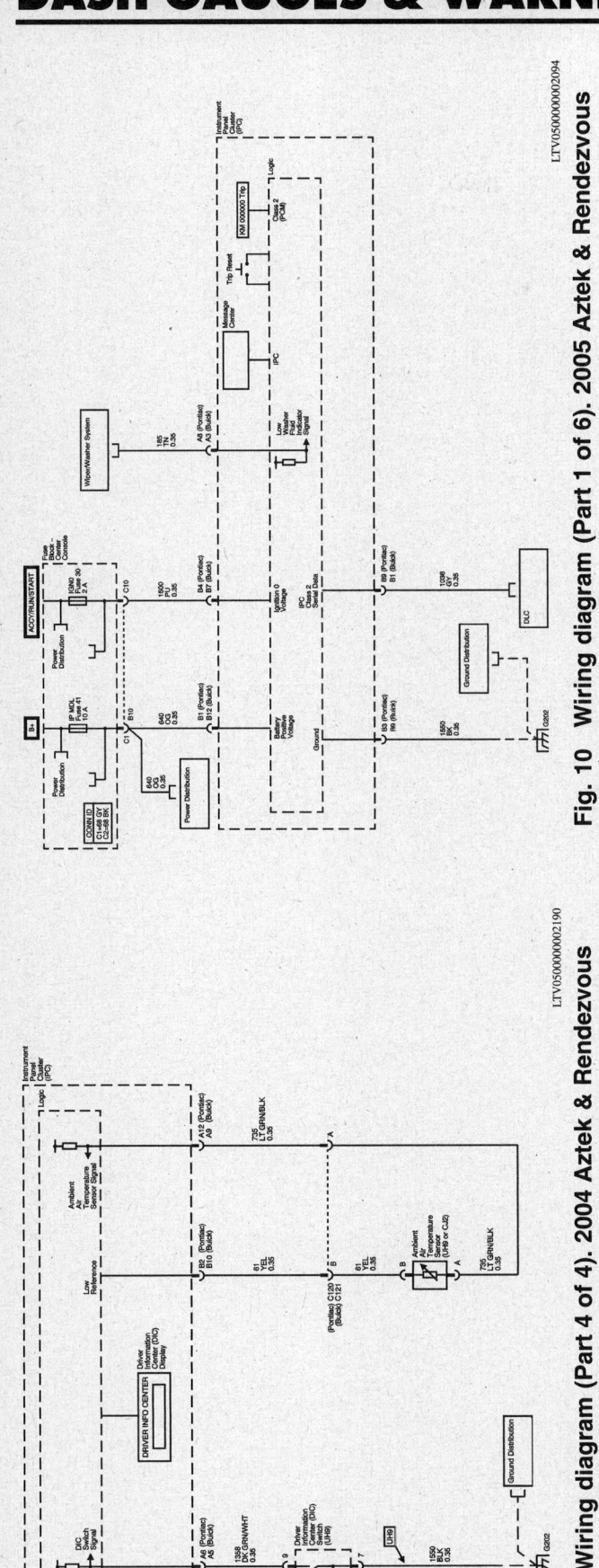

Fig. 10 Wiring diagram (Part 1 of 6). 2005 Aztek & Rendezvous

Fig. 9 Wiring diagram (Part 4 of 4). 2004 Aztek & Rendezvous

Fig. 10 Wiring diagram (Part 3 of 6). 2005 Aztek & Rendezvous

Fig. 10 Wiring diagram (Part 2 of 6). 2005 Aztek & Rendezvous

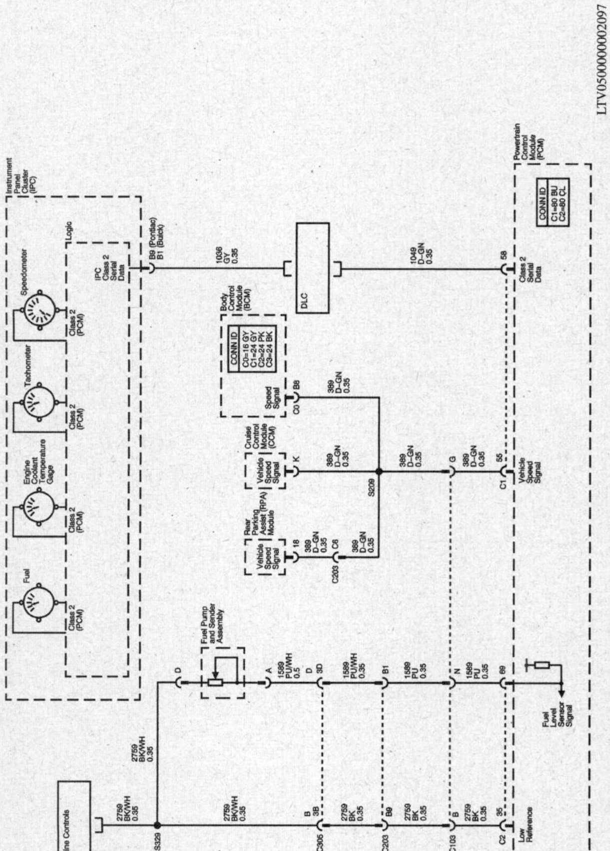

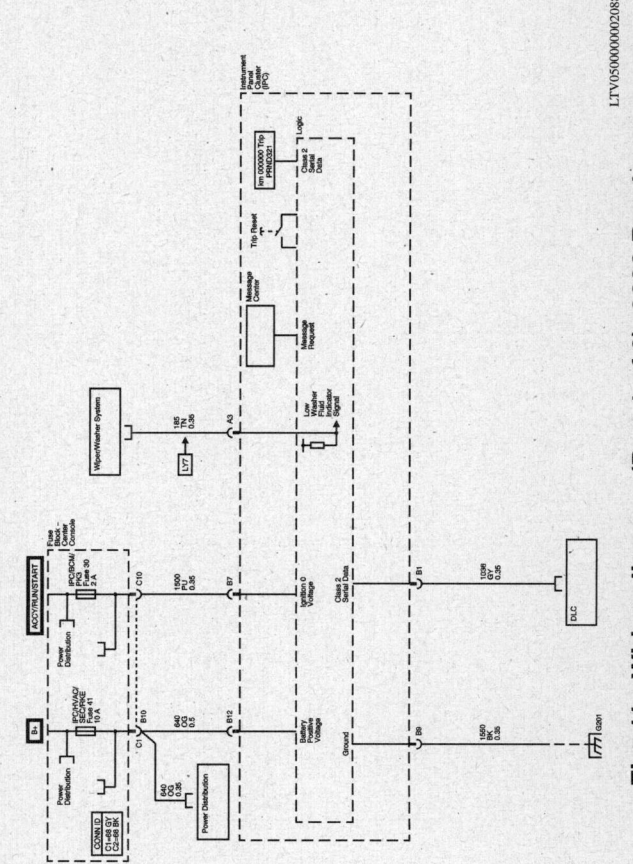

Fig. 10   Wiring diagram (Part 5 of 6). 2005 Aztek & Rendezvous

Fig. 11   Wiring diagram (Part 1 of 6). 2006 Rendezvous

Fig. 10   Wiring diagram (Part 4 of 6). 2005 Aztek & Rendezvous

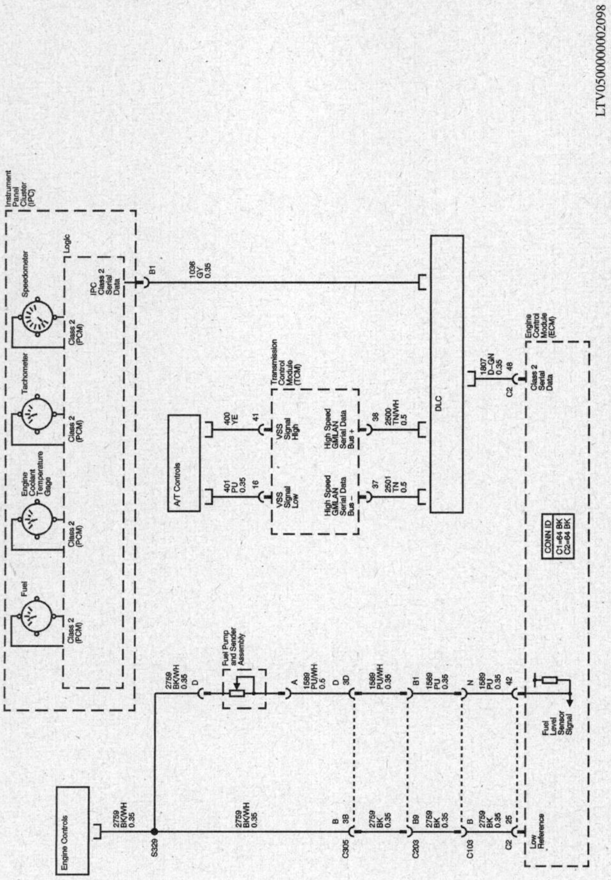

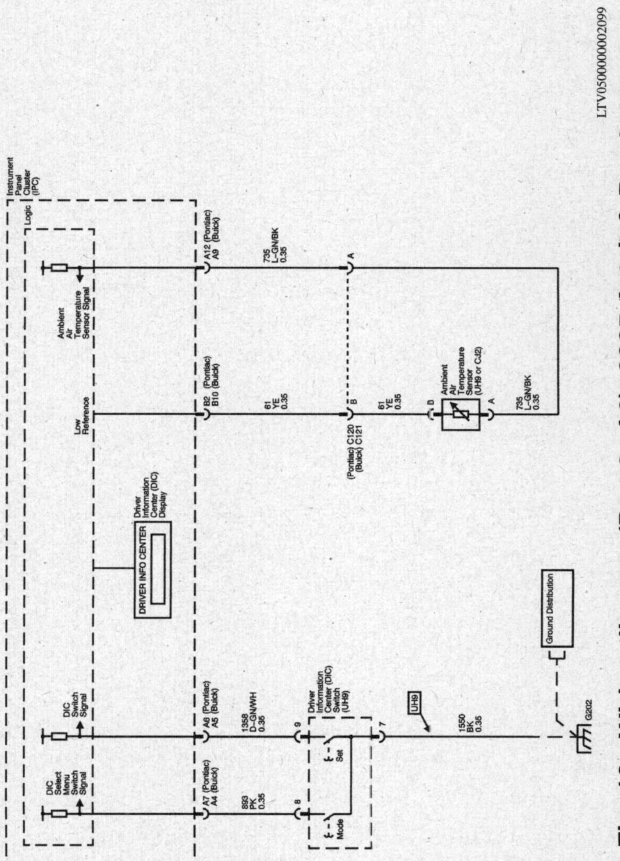

Fig. 10   Wiring diagram (Part 6 of 6). 2005 Aztek & Rendezvous

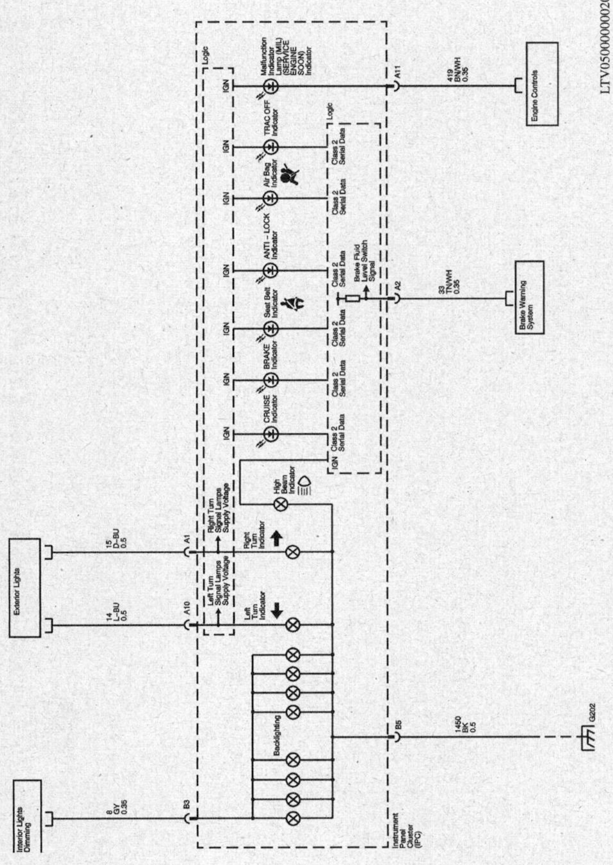

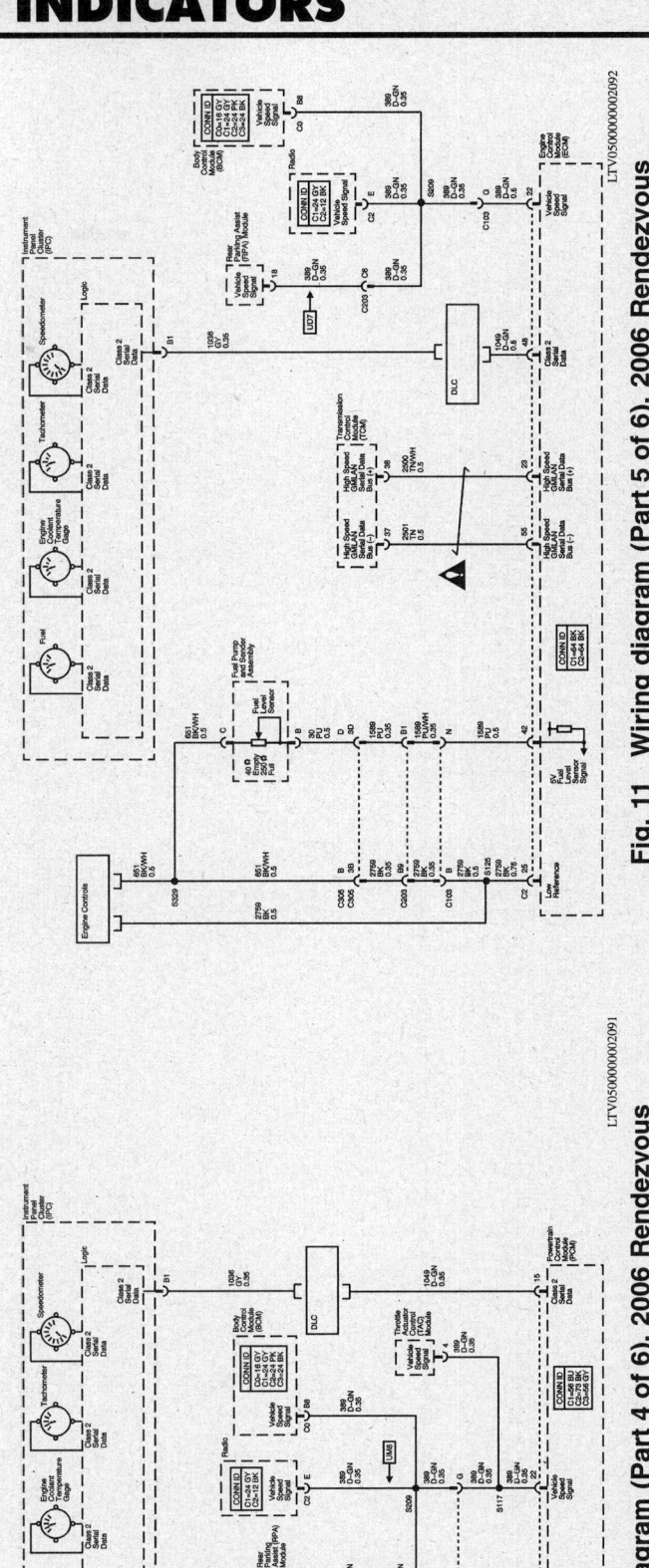

Fig. 11 Wiring diagram (Part 3 of 6). 2006 Rendezvous

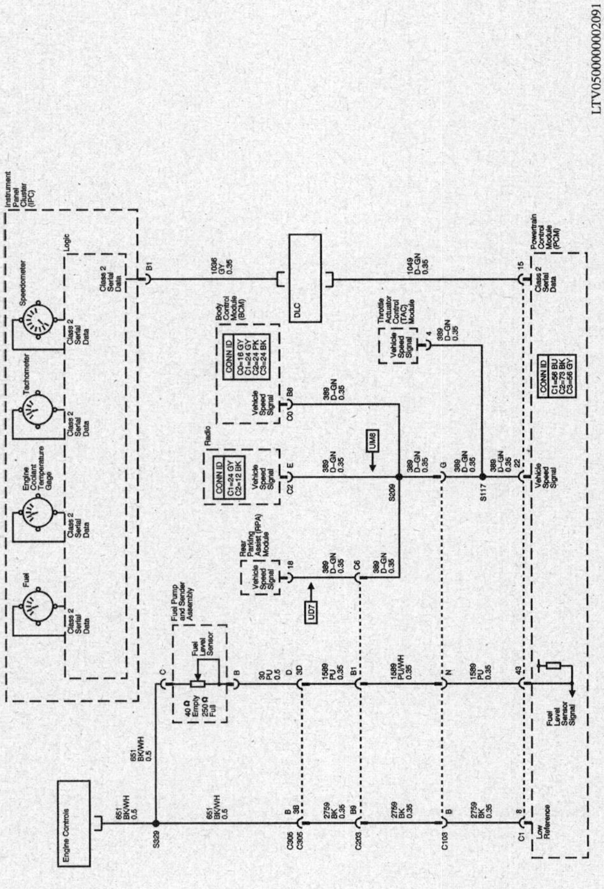

Fig. 11 Wiring diagram (Part 5 of 6). 2006 Rendezvous

Fig. 11 Wiring diagram (Part 2 of 6). 2006 Rendezvous

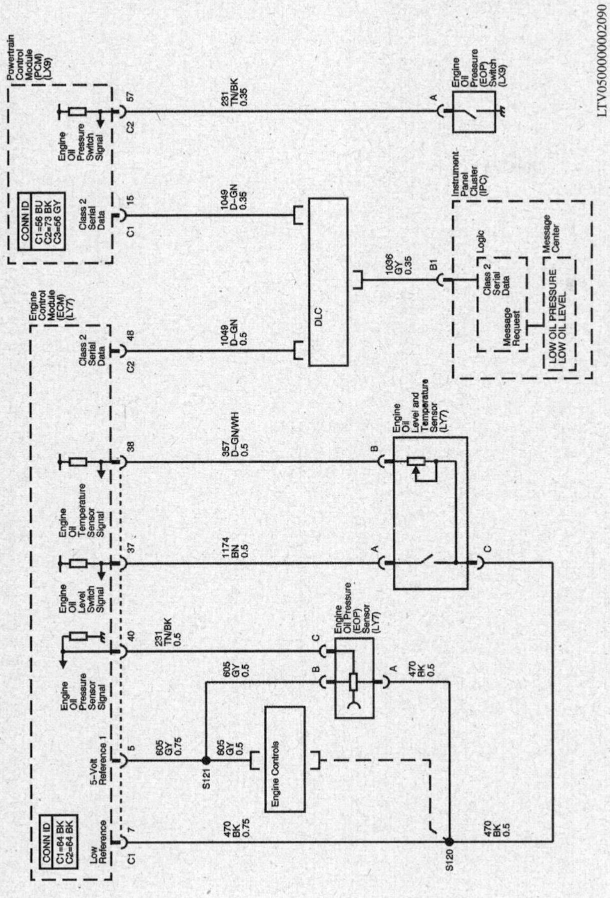

Fig. 11 Wiring diagram (Part 4 of 6). 2006 Rendezvous

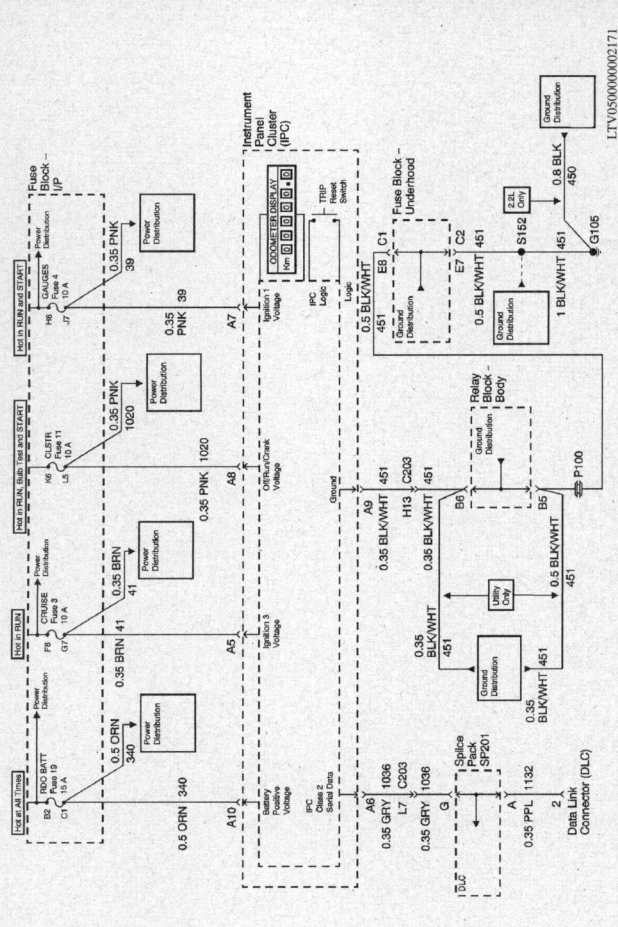

Fig. 12 Wiring diagram (Part 1 of 4). 2002–03 Blazer

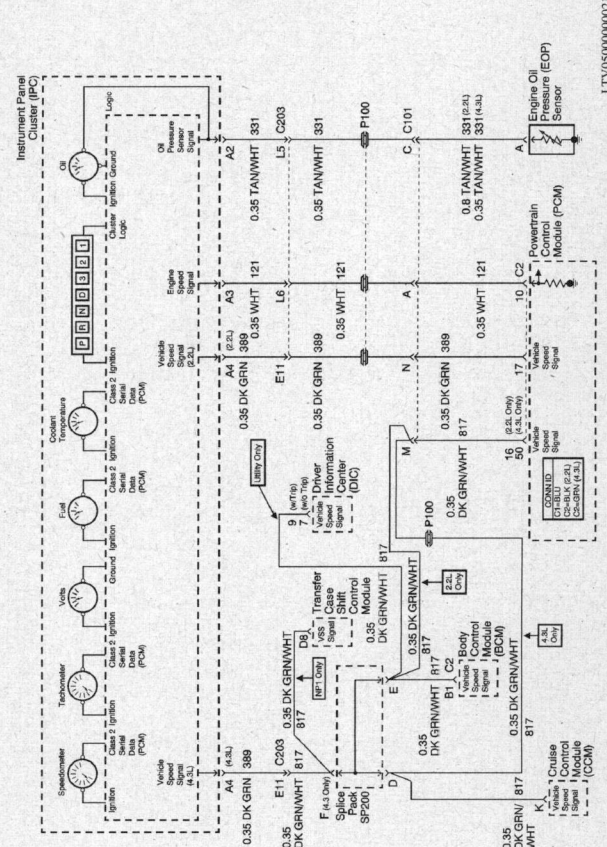

Fig. 12 Wiring diagram (Part 3 of 4). 2002–03 Blazer

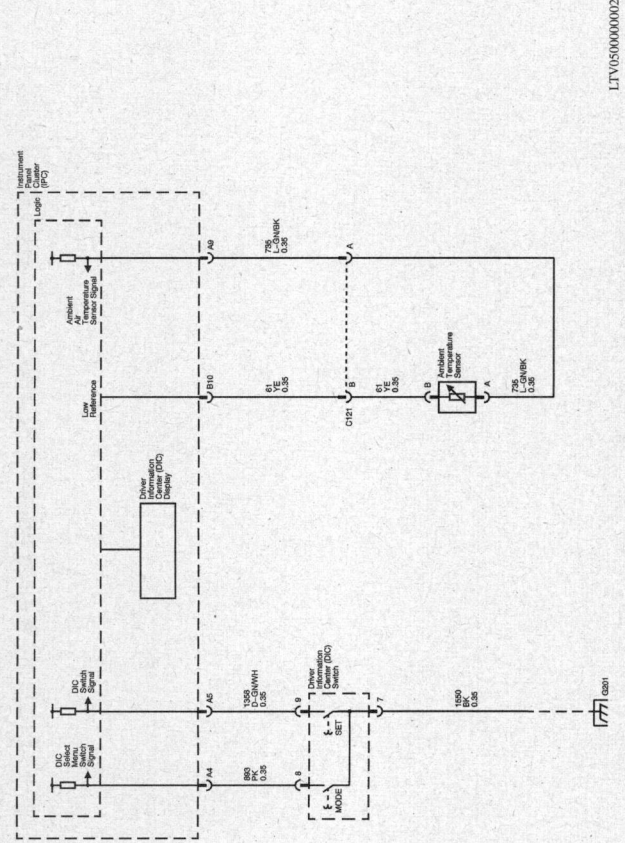

Fig. 11 Wiring diagram (Part 6 of 6). 2006 Rendezvous

Fig. 12 Wiring diagram (Part 2 of 4). 2002–03 Blazer

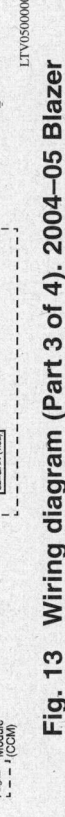

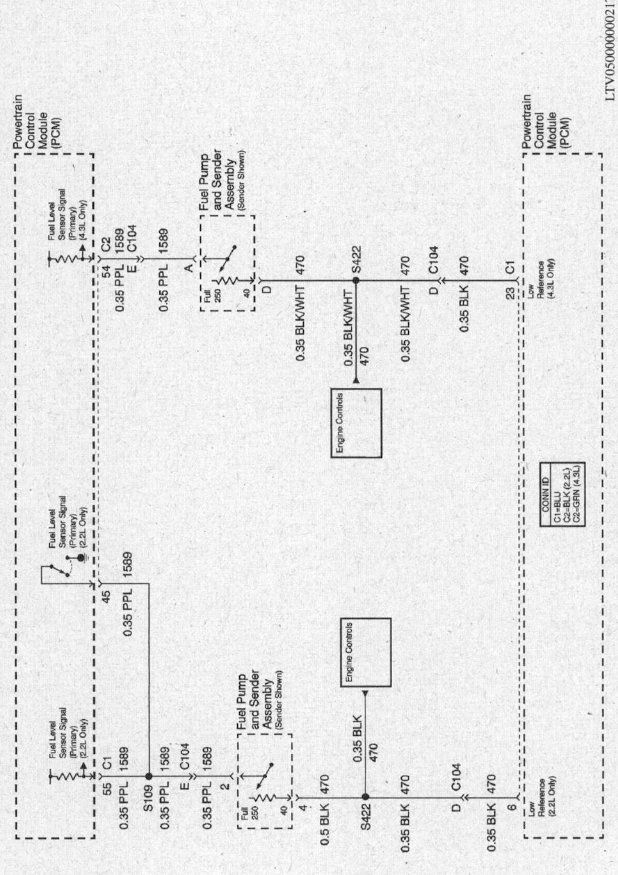

Fig. 13 Wiring diagram (Part 1 of 4). 2004–05 Blazer

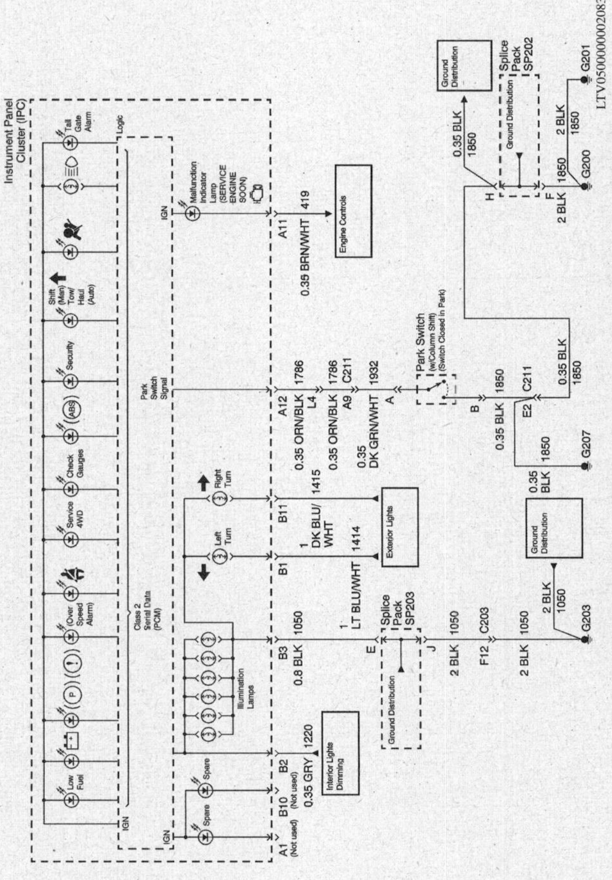

Fig. 13 Wiring diagram (Part 3 of 4). 2004–05 Blazer

Fig. 12 Wiring diagram (Part 4 of 4). 2002–03 Blazer

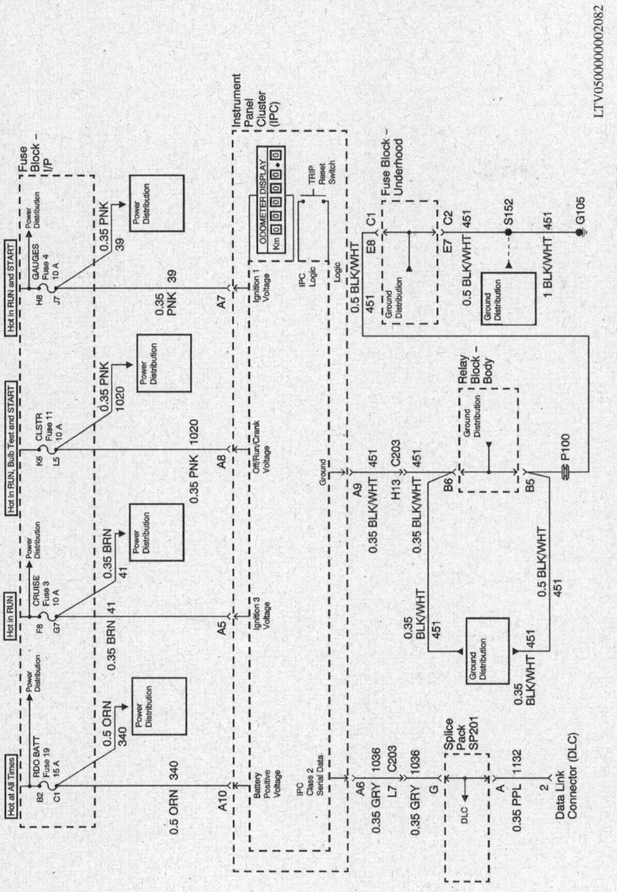

Fig. 13 Wiring diagram (Part 2 of 4). 2004–05 Blazer

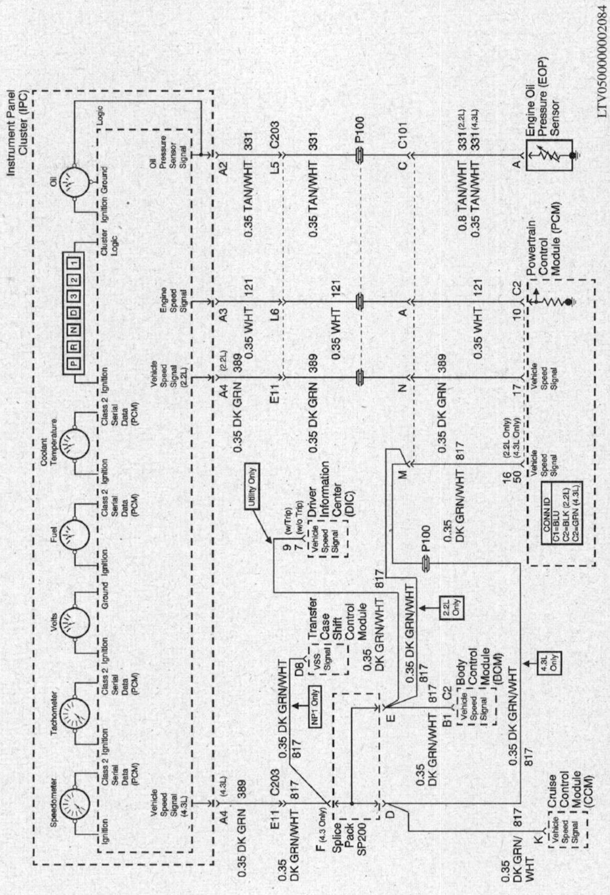

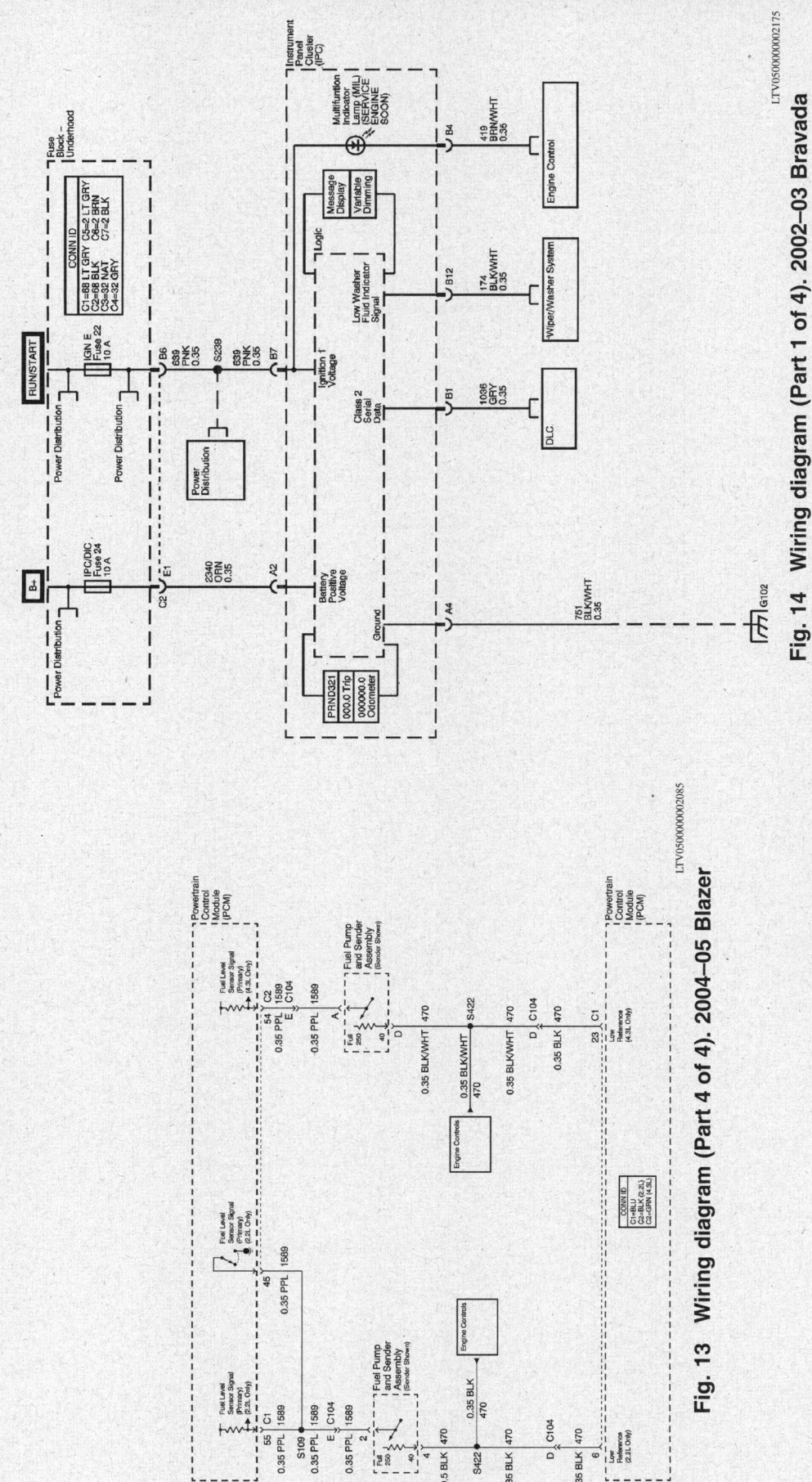

Fig. 14 Wiring diagram (Part 1 of 4). 2002–03 Bravada

Fig. 13 Wiring diagram (Part 4 of 4). 2004–05 Blazer

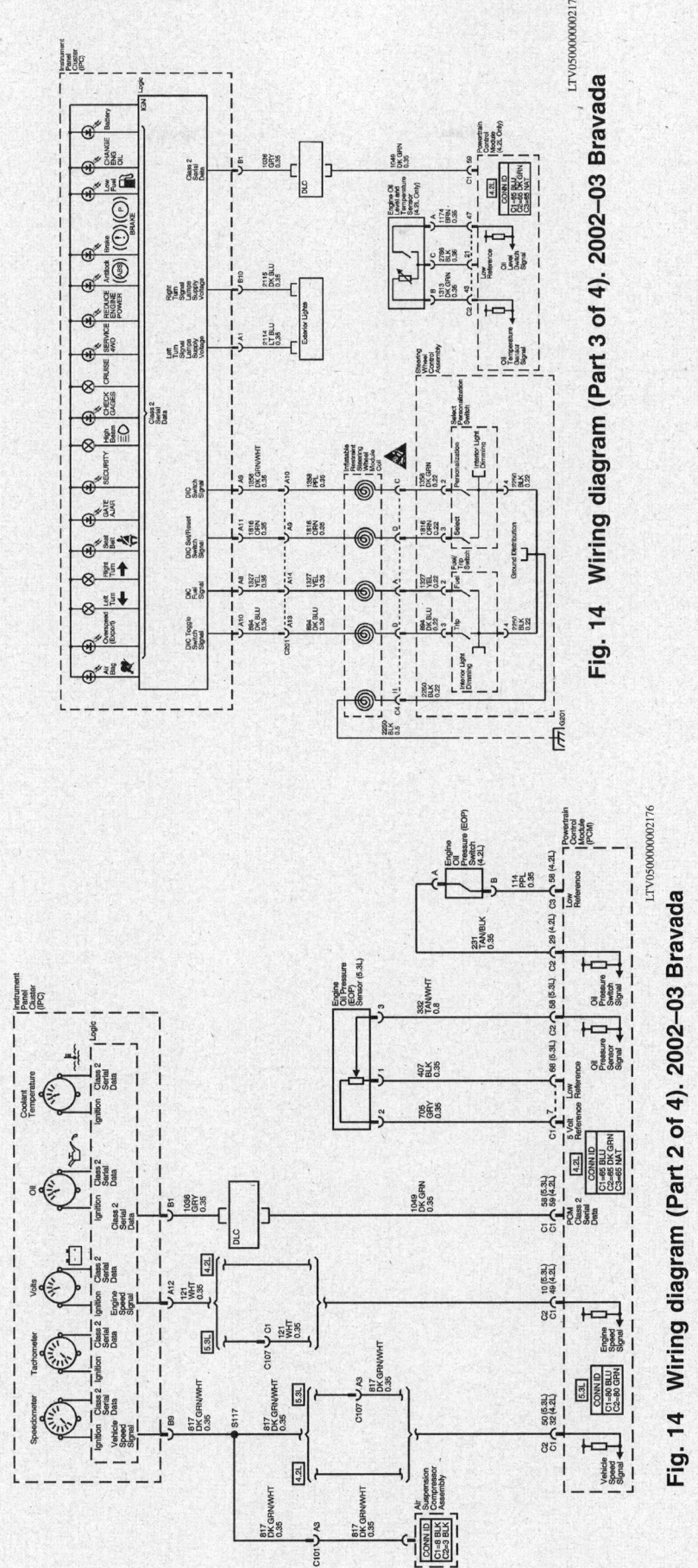

Fig. 14 Wiring diagram (Part 3 of 4). 2002–03 Bravada

Fig. 14 Wiring diagram (Part 2 of 4). 2002–03 Bravada

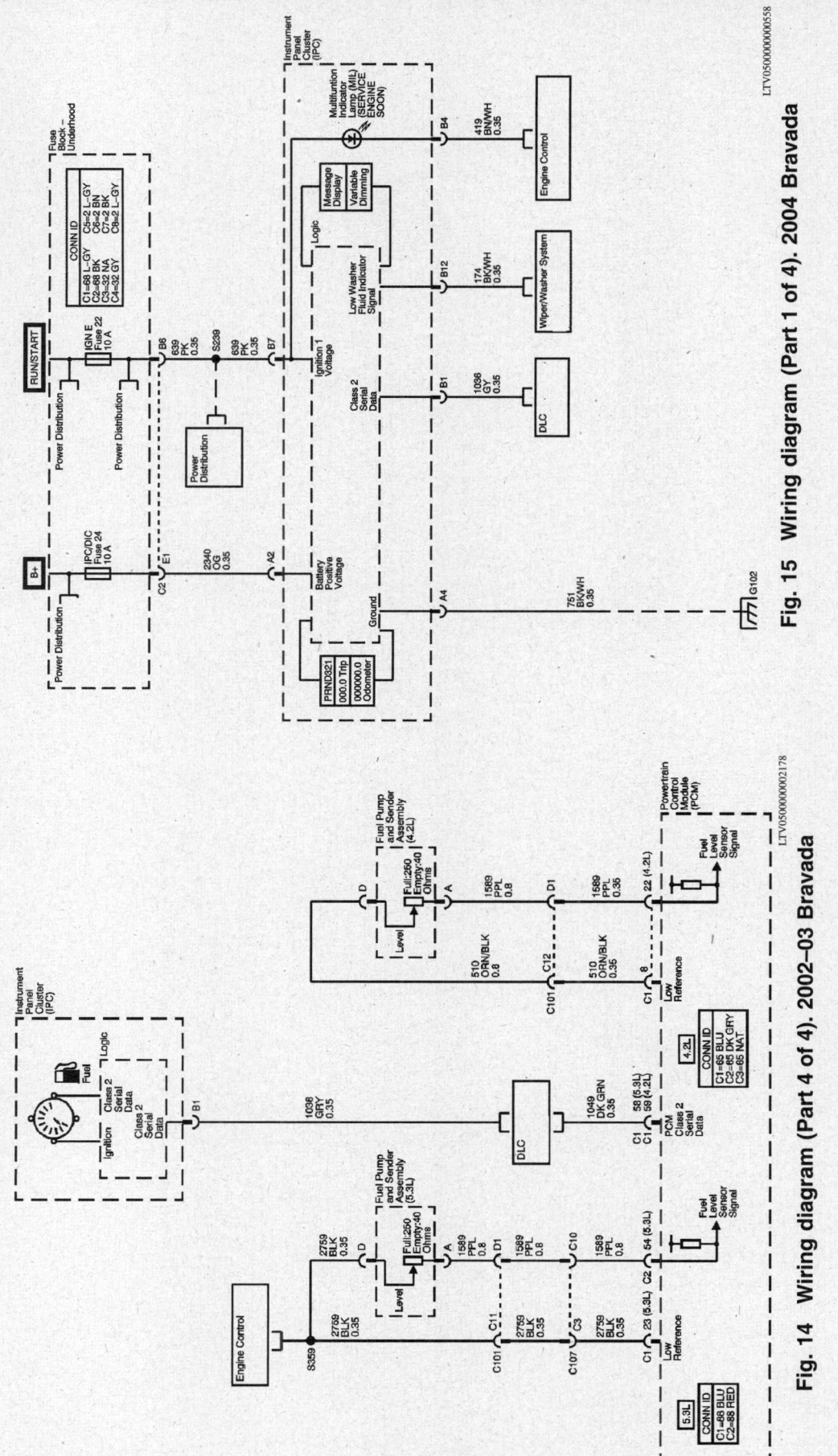

Fig. 15 Wiring diagram (Part 1 of 4). 2004 Bravada

Fig. 14 Wiring diagram (Part 4 of 4). 2002–03 Bravada

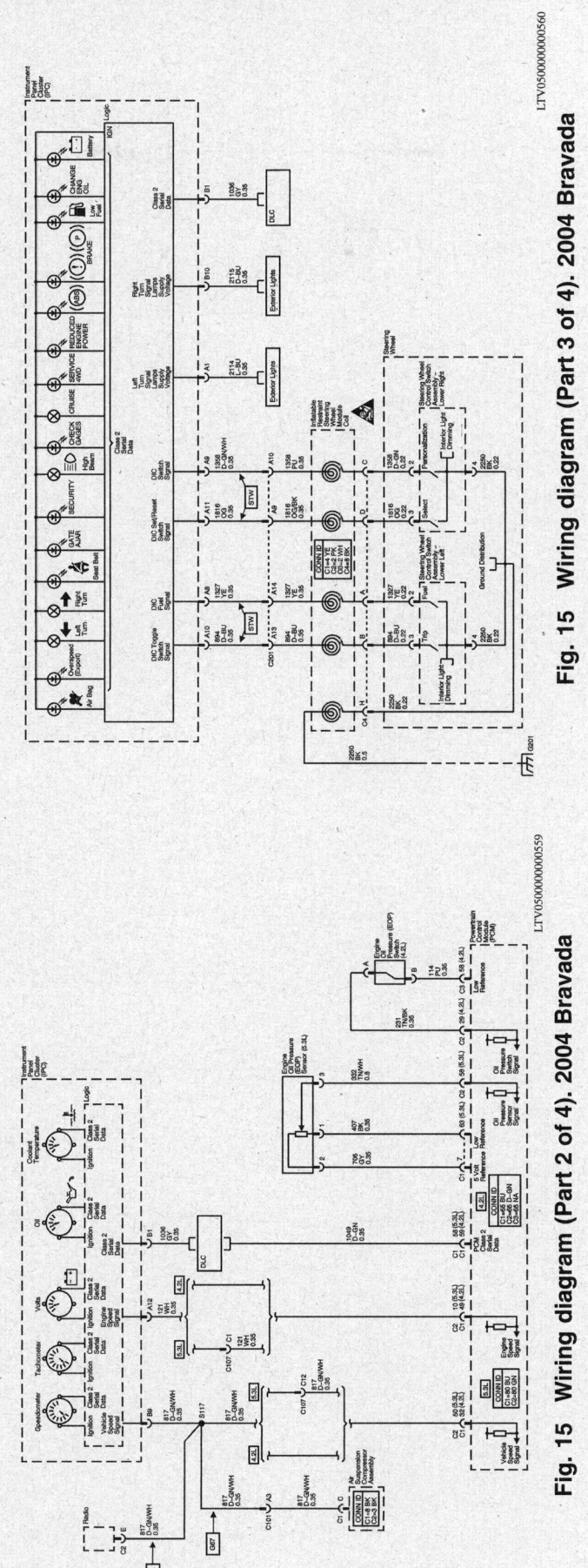

Fig. 15   Wiring diagram (Part 3 of 4). 2004 Bravada

Fig. 15   Wiring diagram (Part 2 of 4). 2004 Bravada

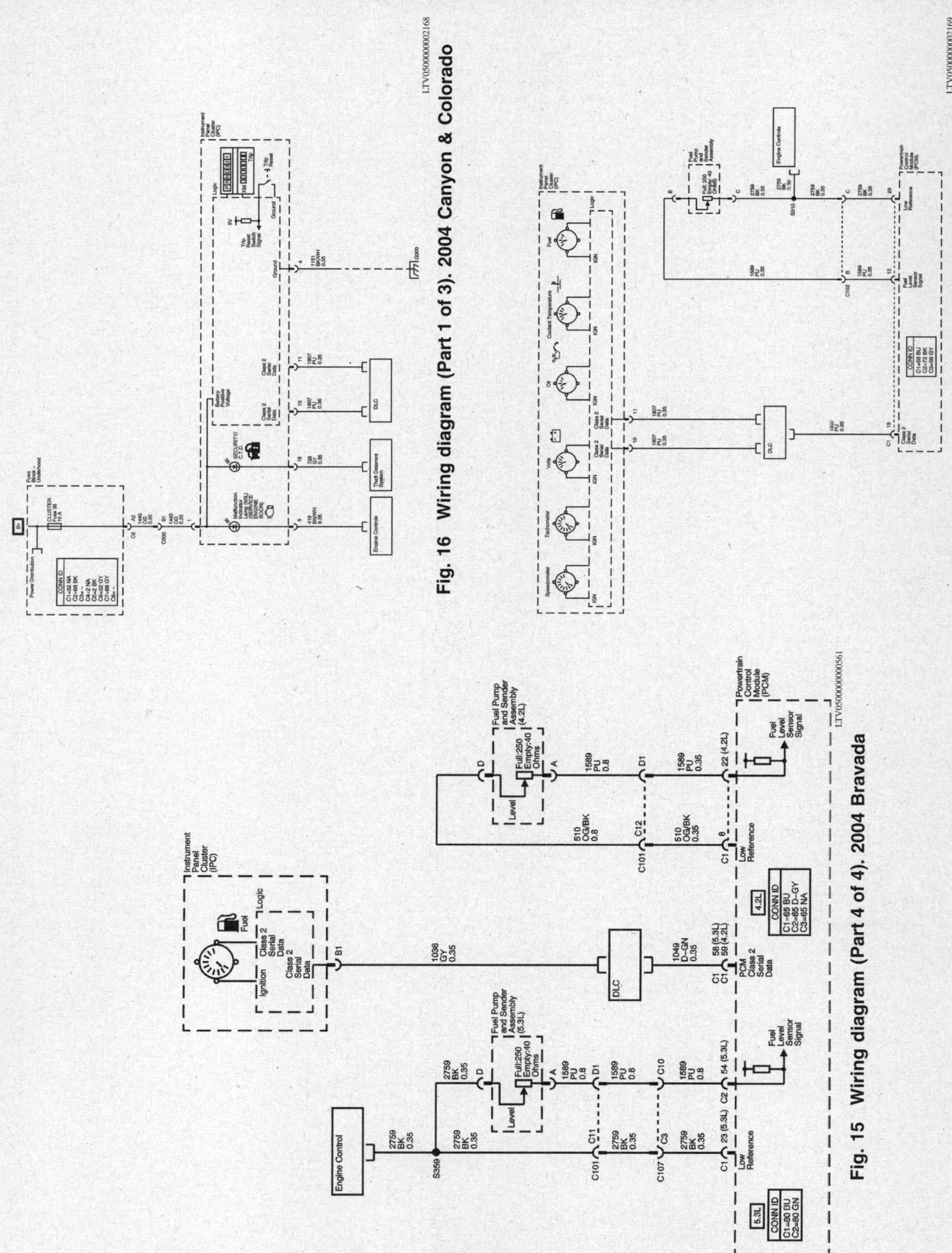

Fig. 16 Wiring diagram (Part 1 of 3). 2004 Canyon & Colorado

Fig. 16 Wiring diagram (Part 2 of 3). 2004 Canyon & Colorado

Fig. 15 Wiring diagram (Part 4 of 4). 2004 Bravada

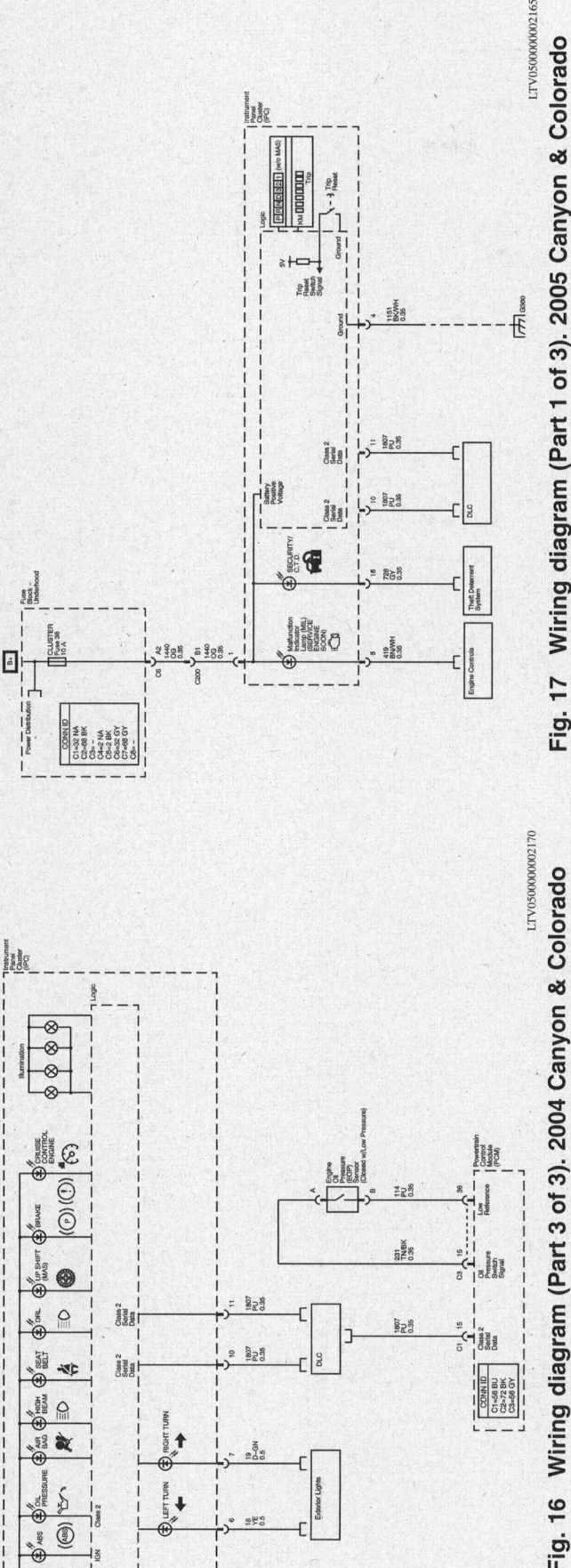

Fig. 17   Wiring diagram (Part 1 of 3). 2005 Canyon & Colorado

Fig. 16   Wiring diagram (Part 3 of 3). 2004 Canyon & Colorado

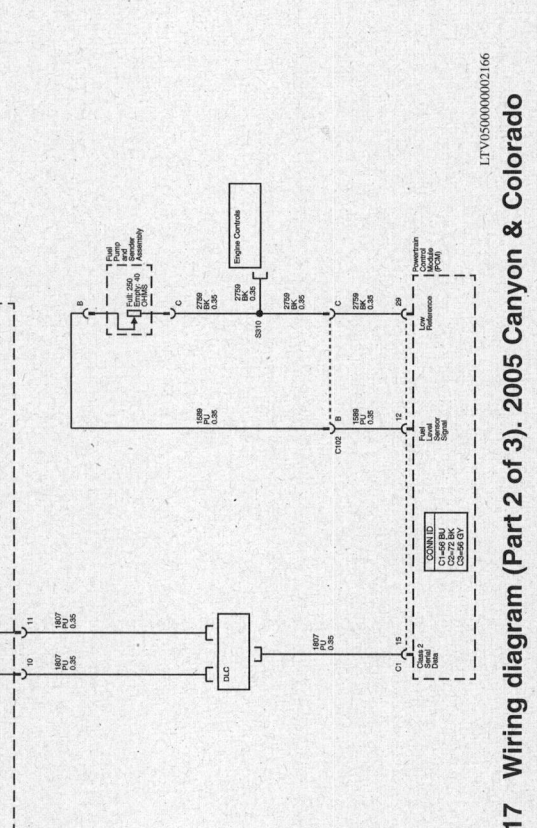

Fig. 17   Wiring diagram (Part 3 of 3). 2005 Canyon & Colorado

Fig. 17   Wiring diagram (Part 2 of 3). 2005 Canyon & Colorado

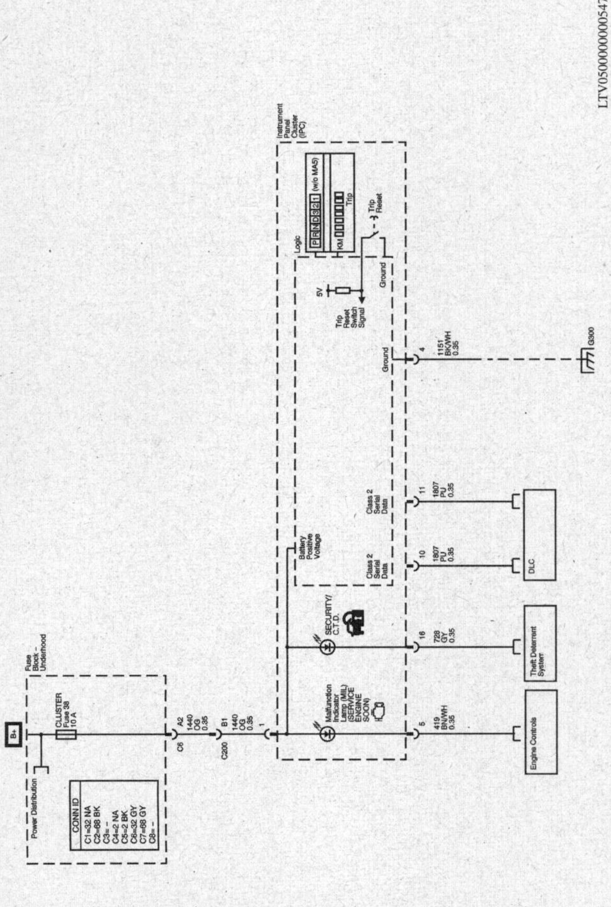

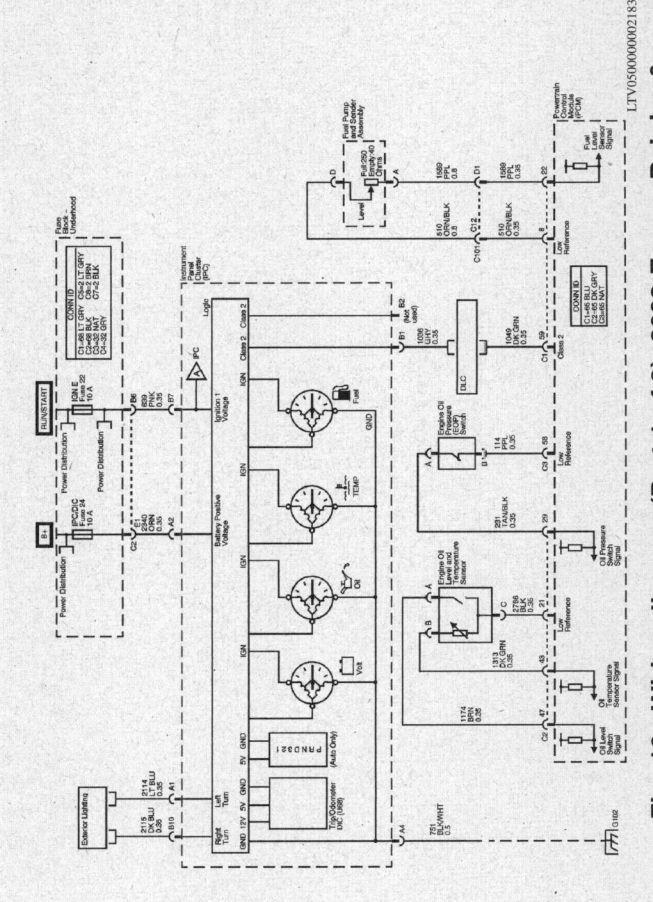

LTV050000000547

Fig. 18 Wiring diagram (Part 1 of 3). 2006 Canyon & Colorado

LTV050000000548

Fig. 18 Wiring diagram (Part 2 of 3). 2006 Canyon & Colorado

LTV050000000549

Fig. 18 Wiring diagram (Part 3 of 3). 2006 Canyon & Colorado

LTV050000002183

Fig. 19 Wiring diagram (Part 1 of 2). 2002 Envoy, Rainier & Trailblazer

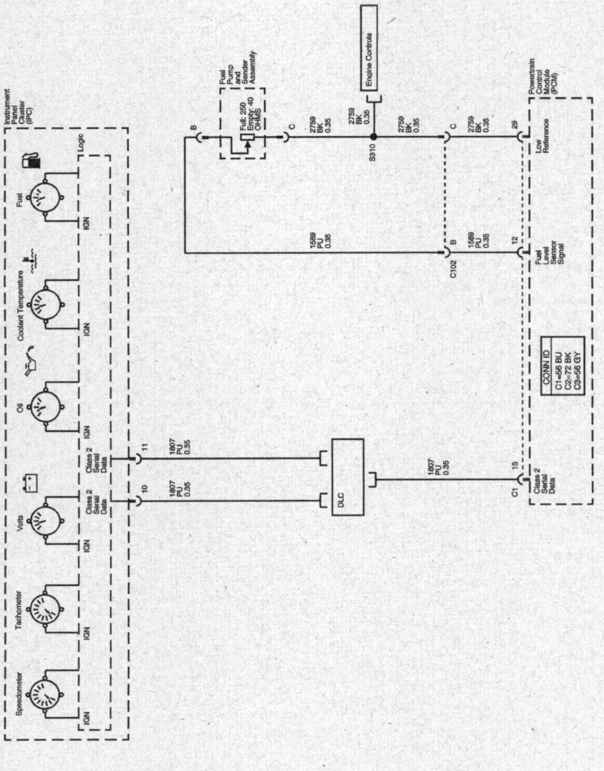

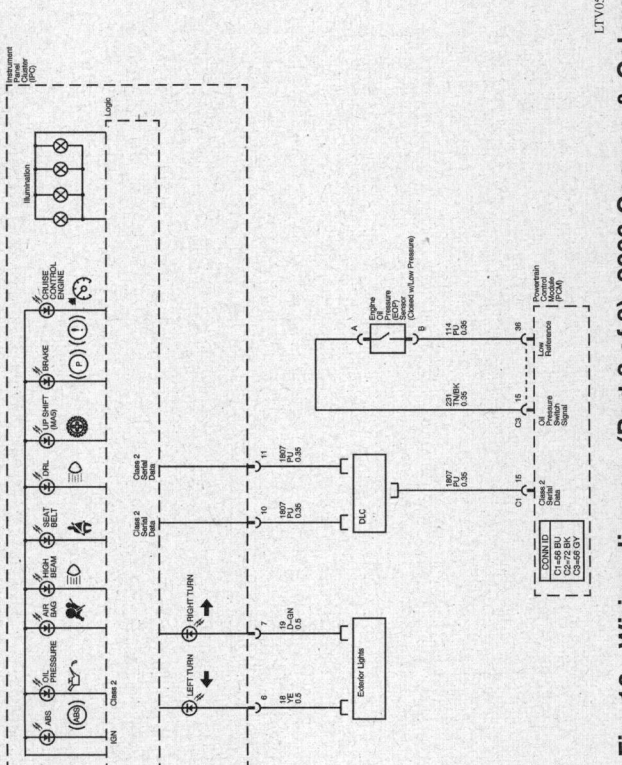

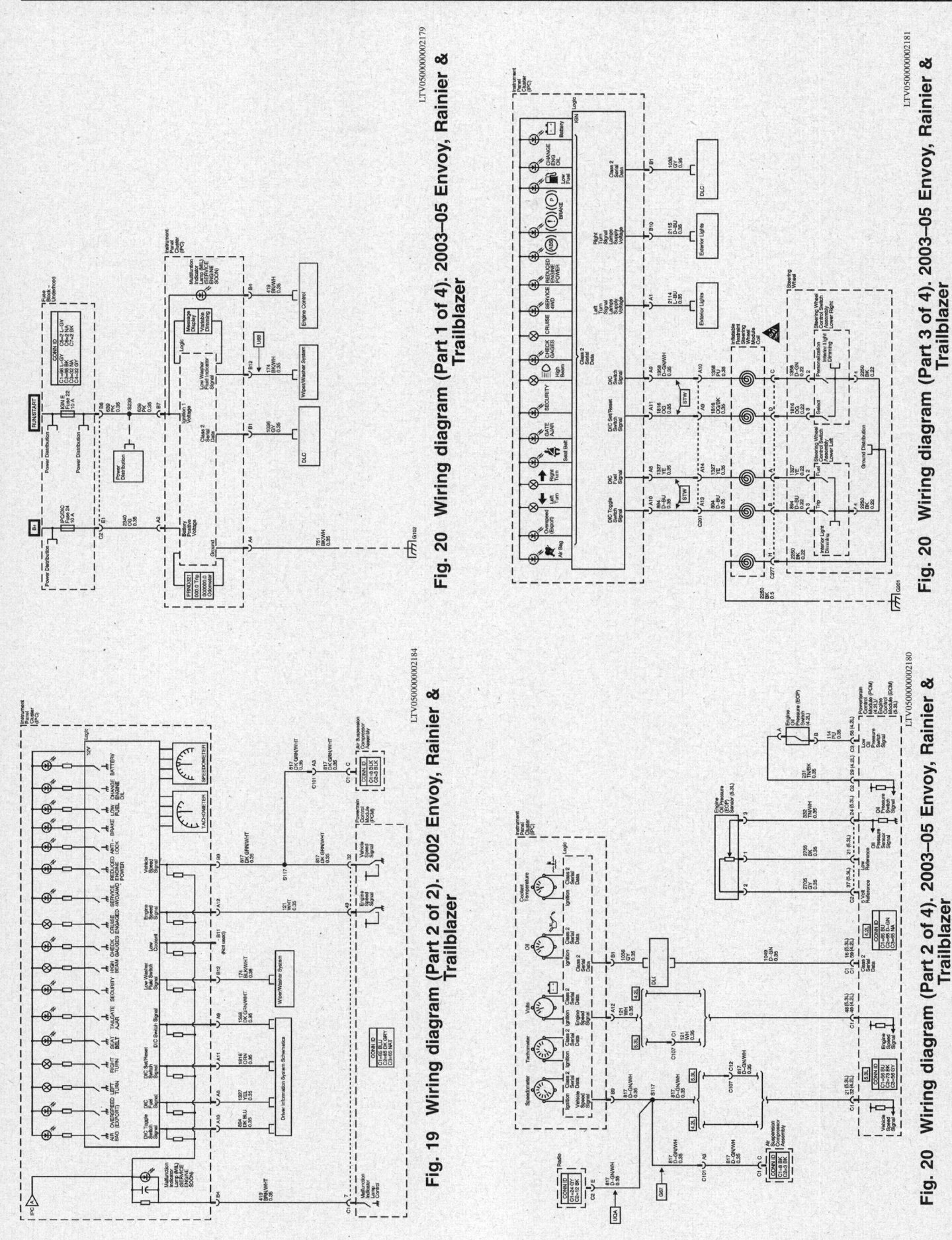

Fig. 20 Wiring diagram (Part 1 of 4). 2003–05 Envoy, Rainier & Trailblazer

Fig. 20 Wiring diagram (Part 3 of 4). 2003–05 Envoy, Rainier & Trailblazer

Fig. 19 Wiring diagram (Part 2 of 2). 2002 Envoy, Rainier & Trailblazer

Fig. 20 Wiring diagram (Part 2 of 4). 2003–05 Envoy, Rainier & Trailblazer

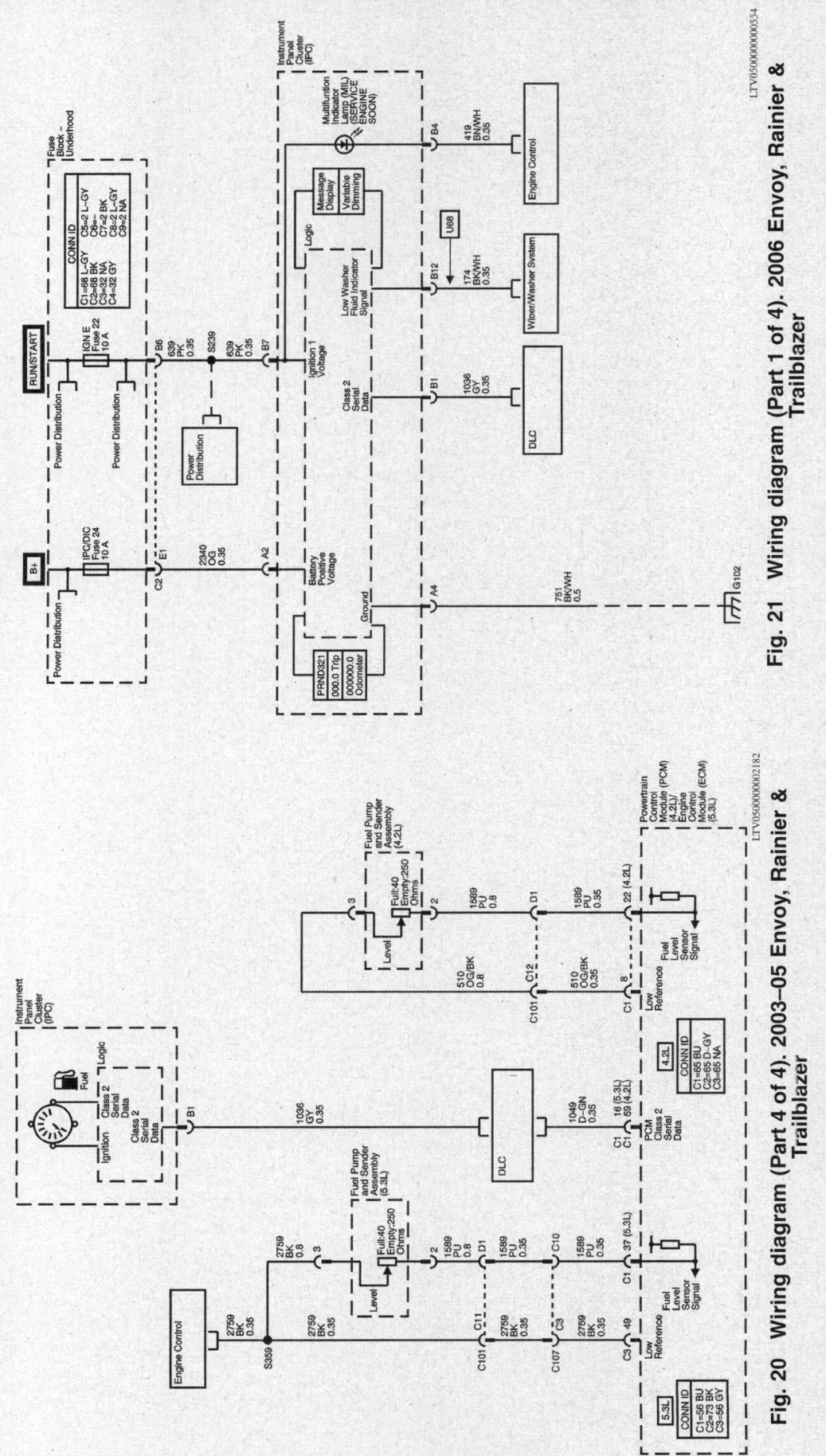

Fig. 21 Wiring diagram (Part 1 of 4). 2006 Envoy, Rainier & Trailblazer

Fig. 20 Wiring diagram (Part 4 of 4). 2003–05 Envoy, Rainier & Trailblazer

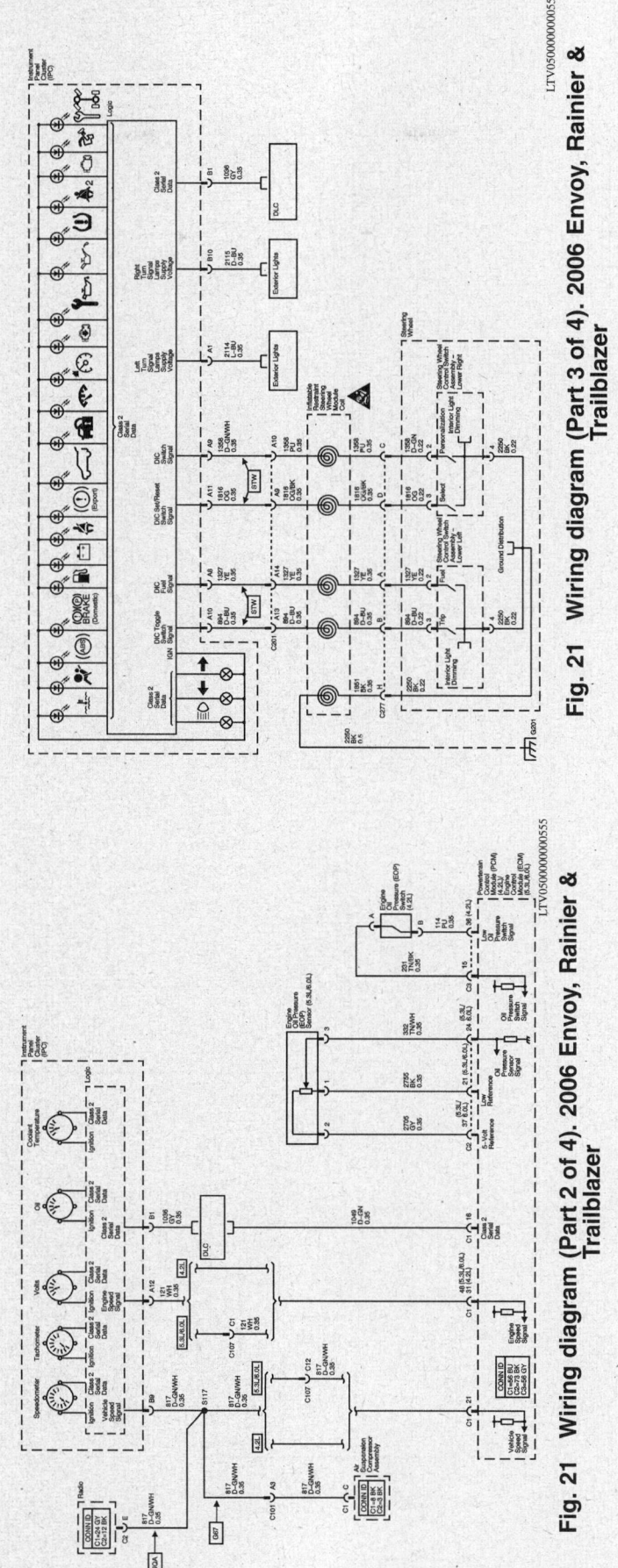

Fig. 21 Wiring diagram (Part 3 of 4). 2006 Envoy, Rainier & Trailblazer

Fig. 21 Wiring diagram (Part 2 of 4). 2006 Envoy, Rainier & Trailblazer

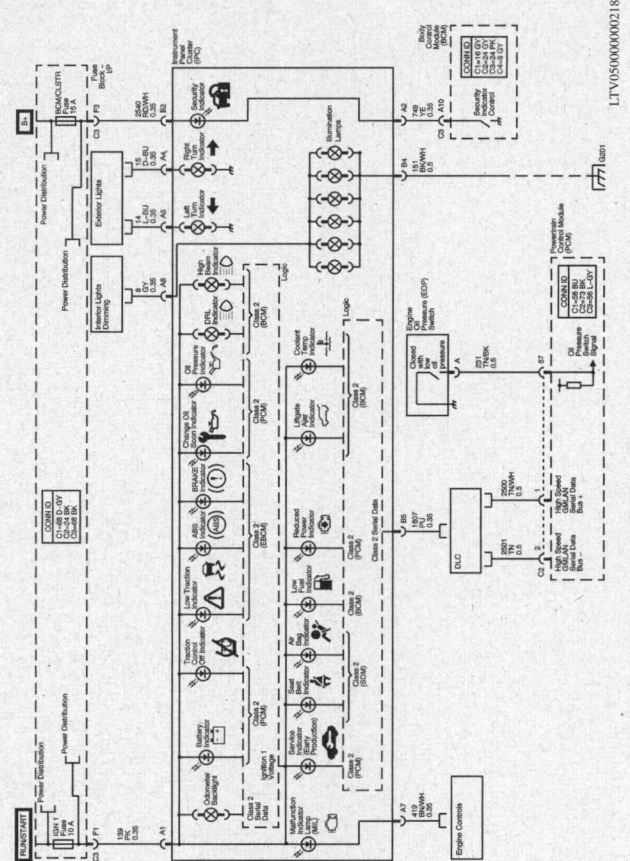

Fig. 22 Wiring diagram (Part 1 of 2). 2005 Equinox

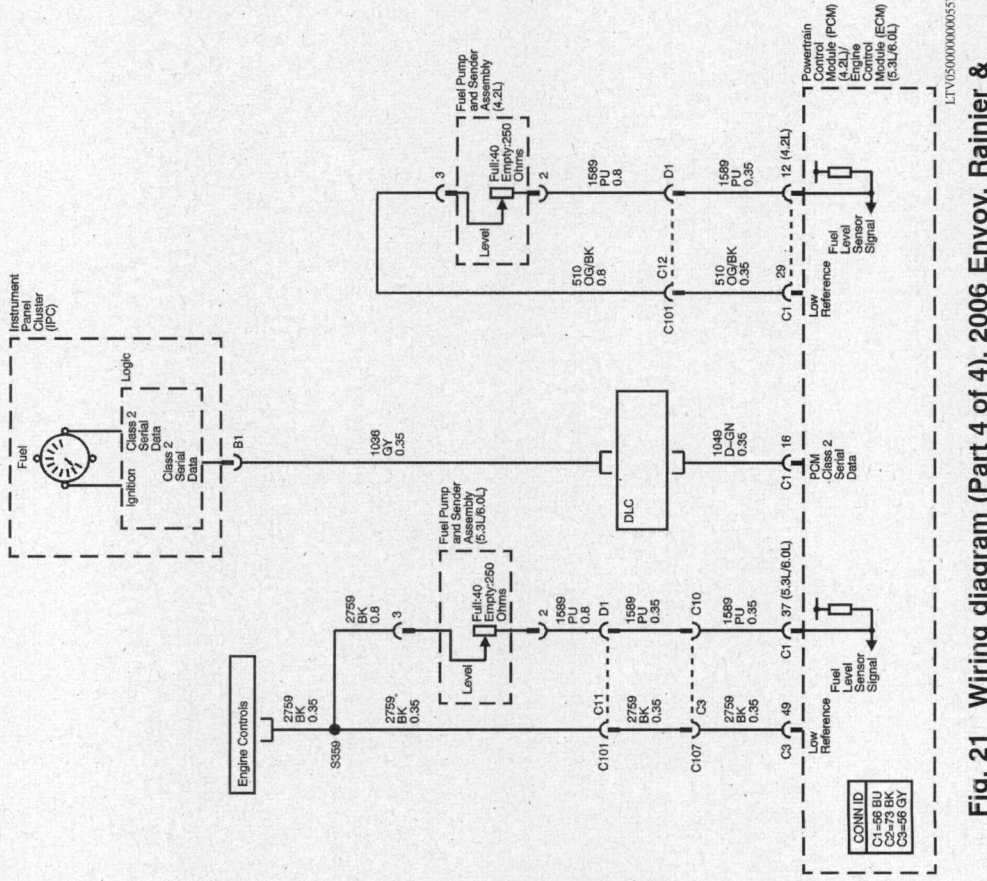

Fig. 21 Wiring diagram (Part 4 of 4). 2006 Envoy, Rainier & Trailblazer

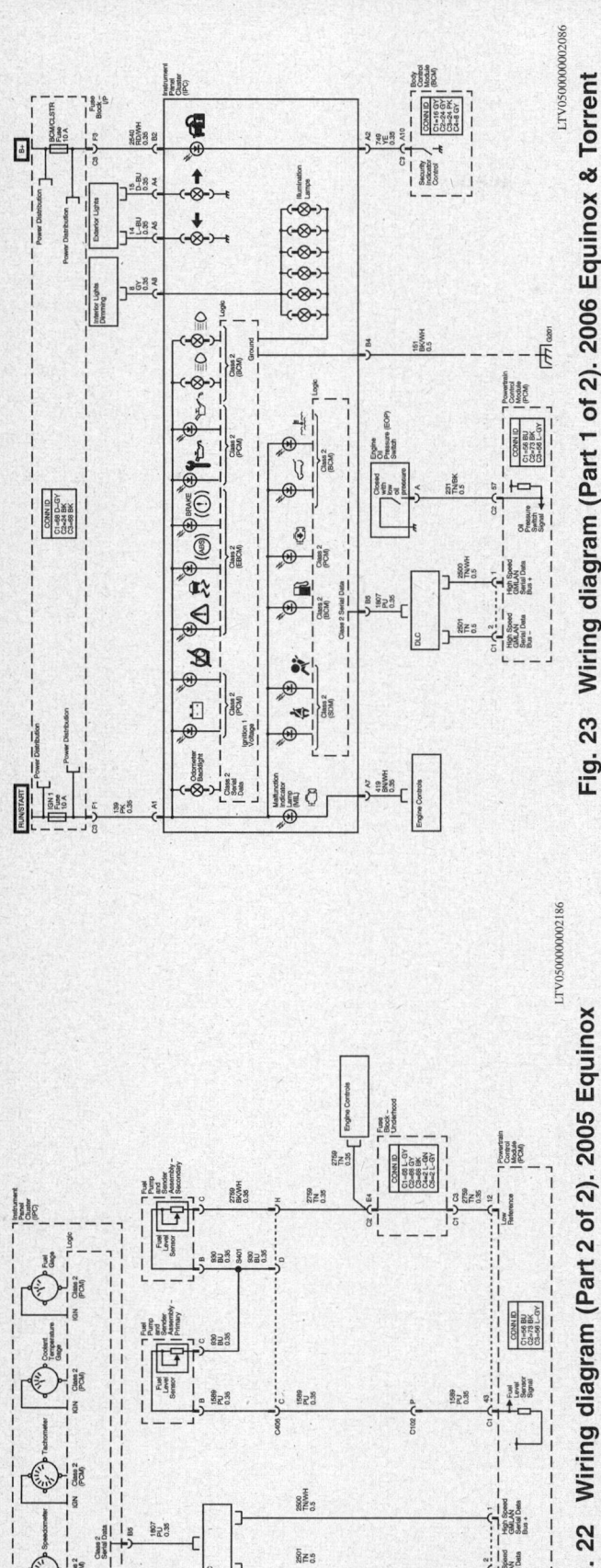

Fig. 22 Wiring diagram (Part 2 of 2). 2005 Equinox

Fig. 23 Wiring diagram (Part 1 of 2). 2006 Equinox & Torrent

Fig. 23 Wiring diagram (Part 2 of 2). 2006 Equinox & Torrent

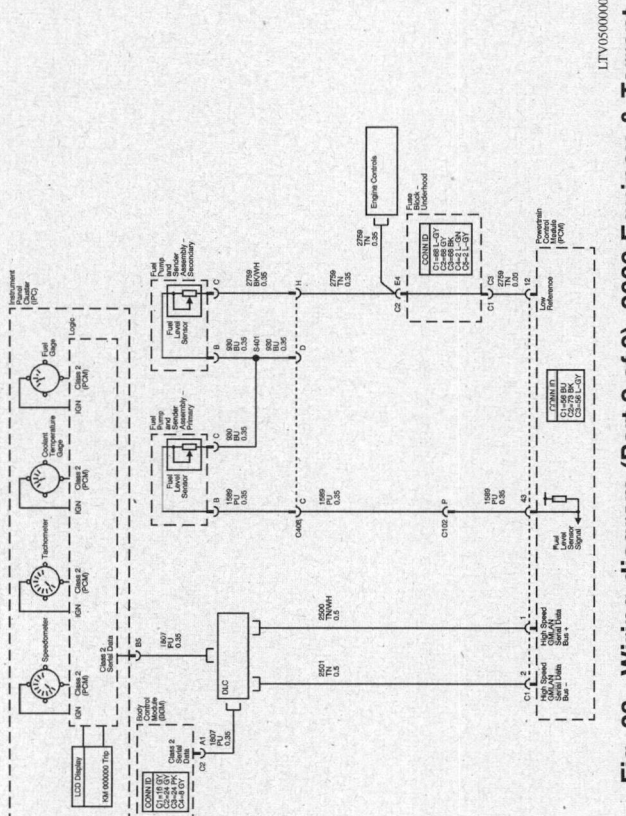

Fig. 24 Wiring diagram (Part 1 of 3). 2003 Express & Savana

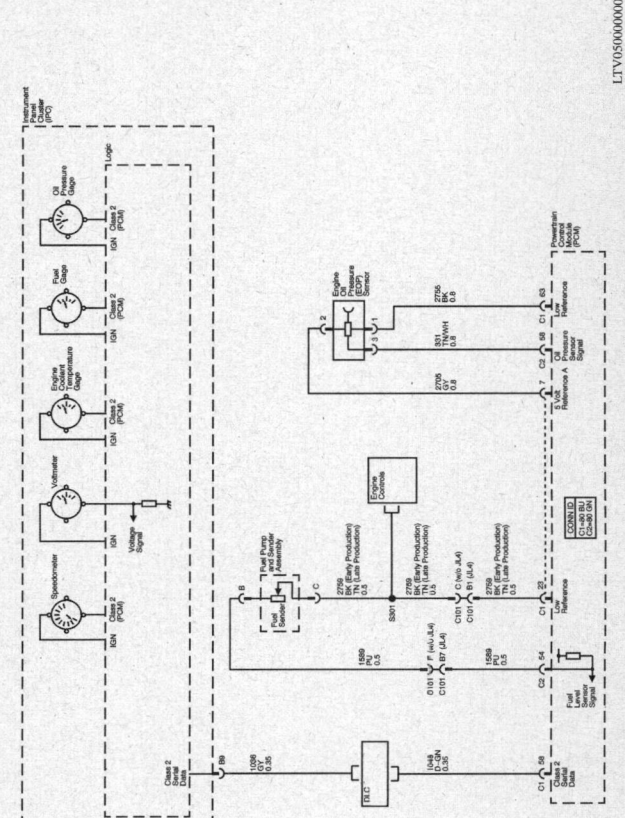

Fig. 25 Wiring diagram (Part 2 of 3). 2004 Express & Savana

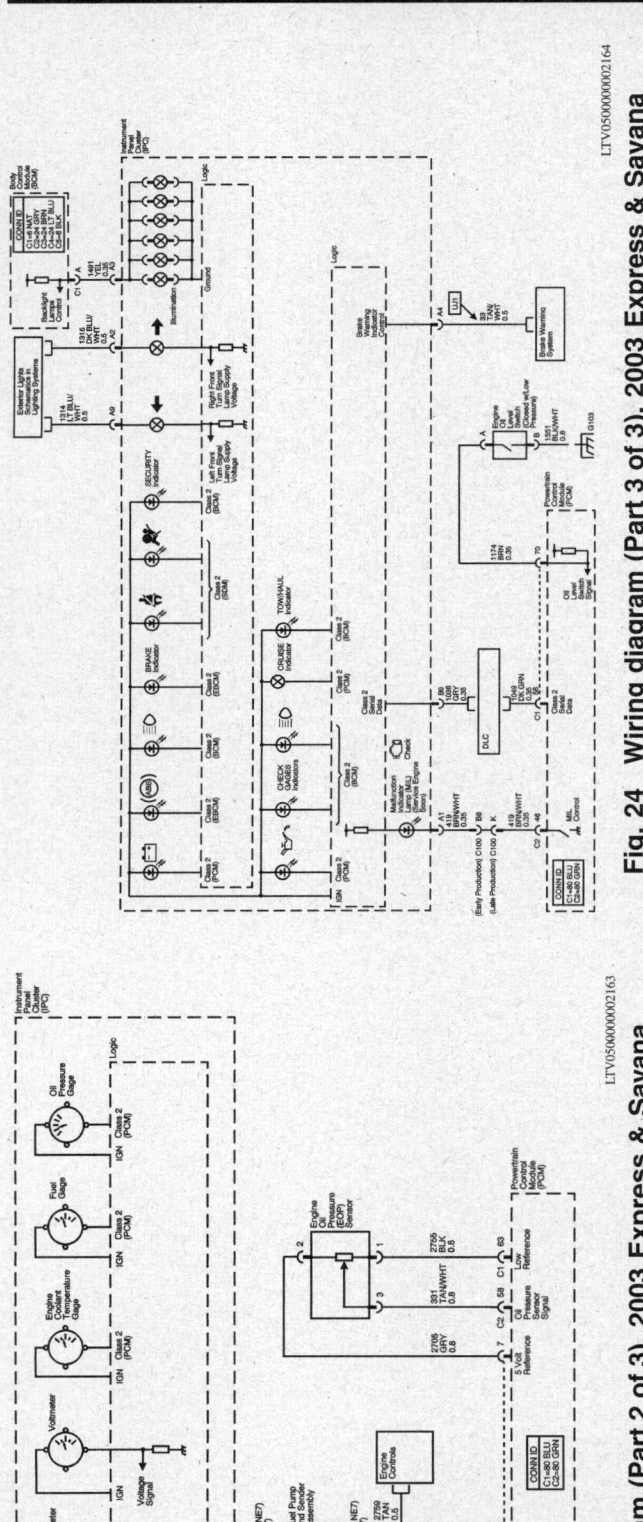

Fig. 24 Wiring diagram (Part 3 of 3). 2003 Express & Savana

Fig. 24 Wiring diagram (Part 2 of 3). 2003 Express & Savana

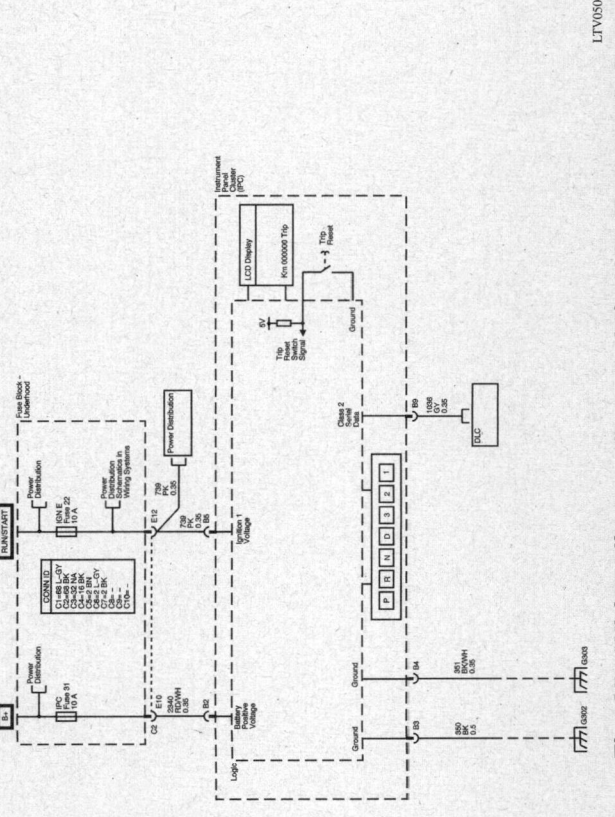

Fig. 25 Wiring diagram (Part 1 of 3). 2004 Express & Savana

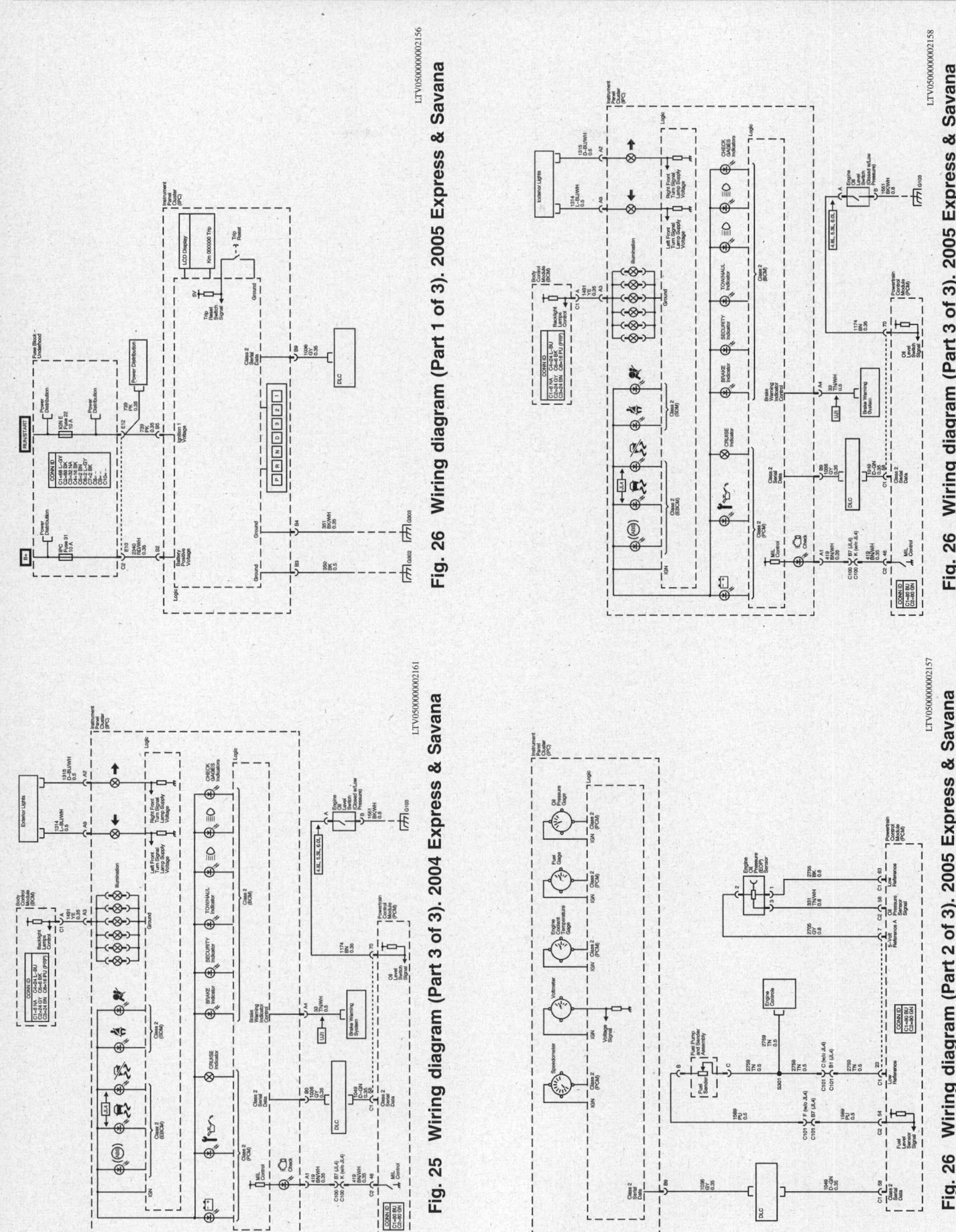

Fig. 26 Wiring diagram (Part 1 of 3). 2005 Express & Savana

Fig. 26 Wiring diagram (Part 3 of 3). 2005 Express & Savana

Fig. 25 Wiring diagram (Part 3 of 3). 2004 Express & Savana

Fig. 26 Wiring diagram (Part 2 of 3). 2005 Express & Savana

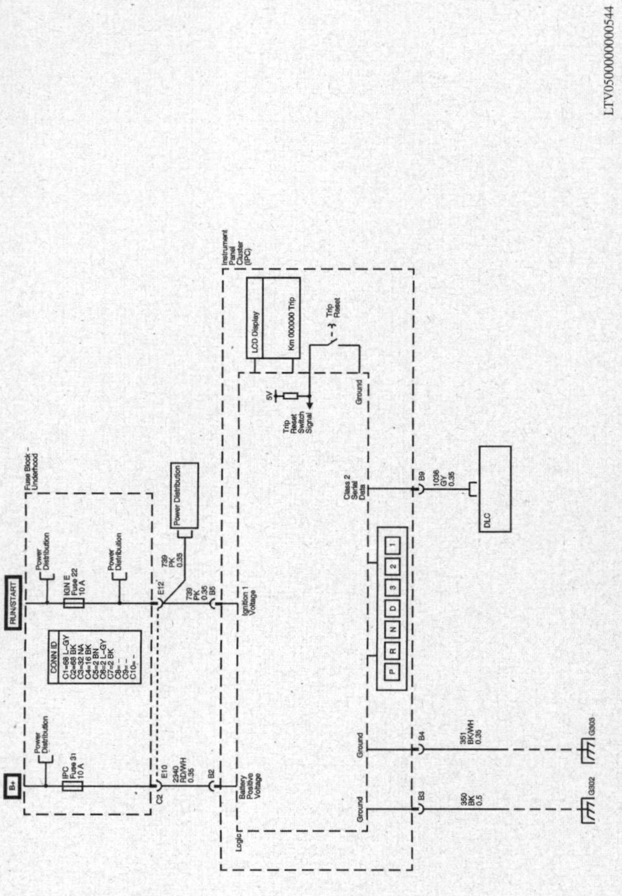

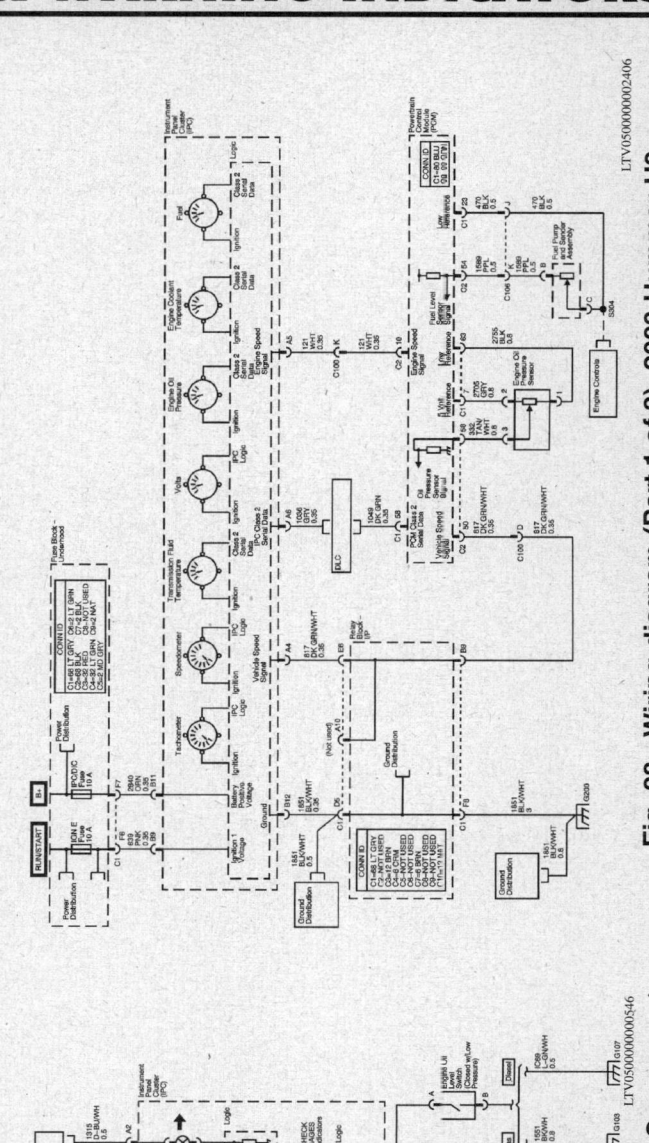

Fig. 27 Wiring diagram (Part 2 of 3). 2006 Express & Savana

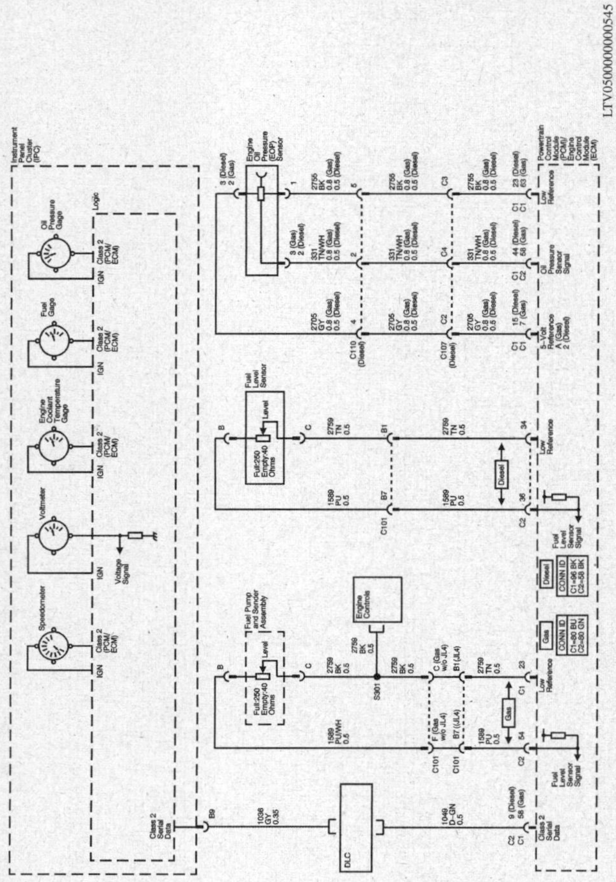

Fig. 28 Wiring diagram (Part 1 of 3). 2003 Hummer H2

Fig. 27 Wiring diagram (Part 1 of 3). 2006 Express & Savana

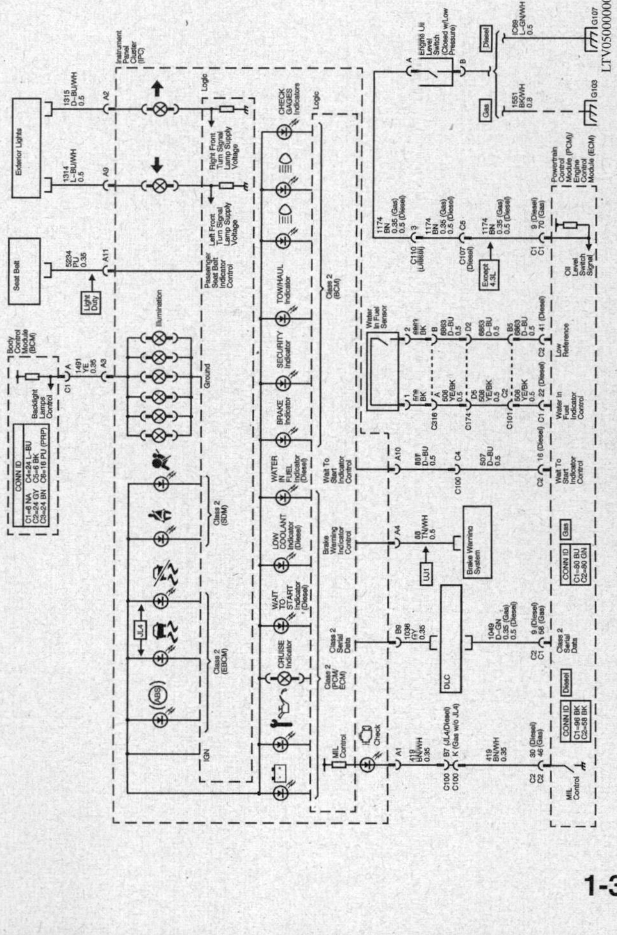

Fig. 27 Wiring diagram (Part 3 of 3). 2006 Express & Savana

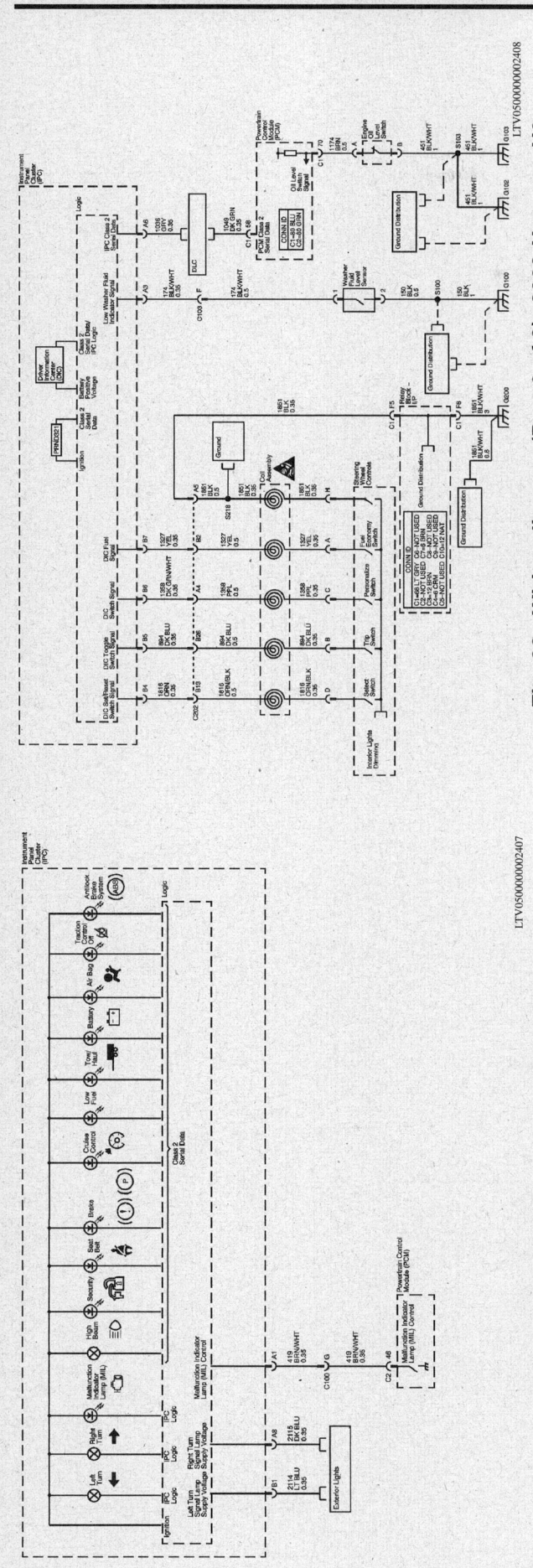

Fig. 28   Wiring diagram (Part 3 of 3). 2003 Hummer H2

Fig. 29   Wiring diagram (Part 2 of 3). 2004 Hummer H2

Fig. 28   Wiring diagram (Part 2 of 3). 2003 Hummer H2

Fig. 29   Wiring diagram (Part 1 of 3). 2004 Hummer H2

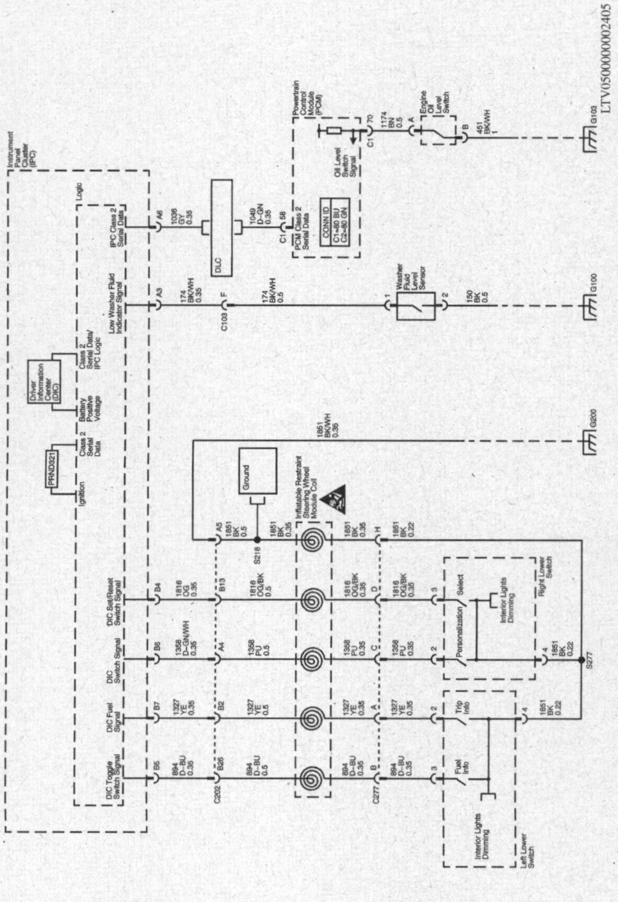

Fig. 30   Wiring diagram (Part 1 of 3). 2005 Hummer H2

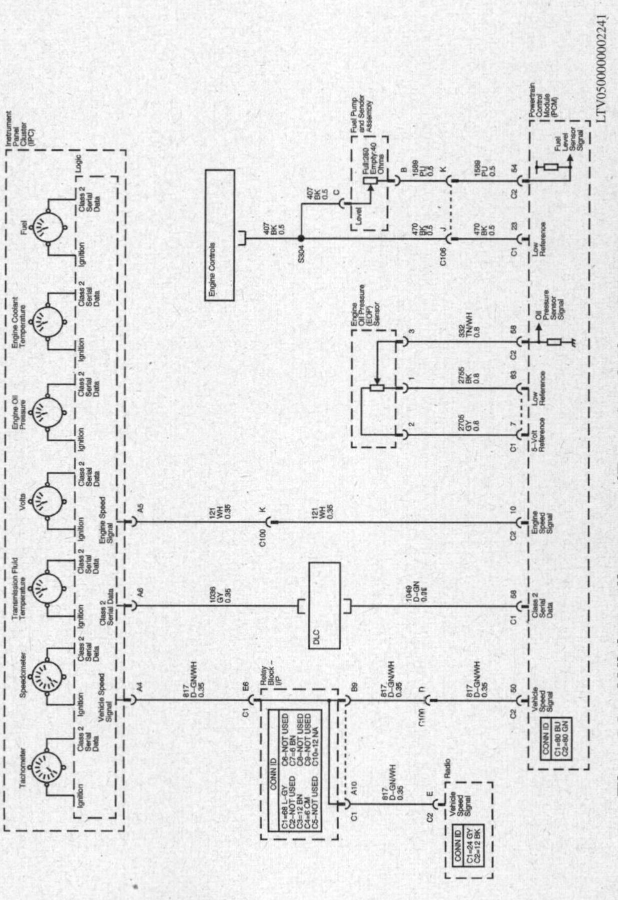

Fig. 30   Wiring diagram (Part 3 of 3). 2005 Hummer H2

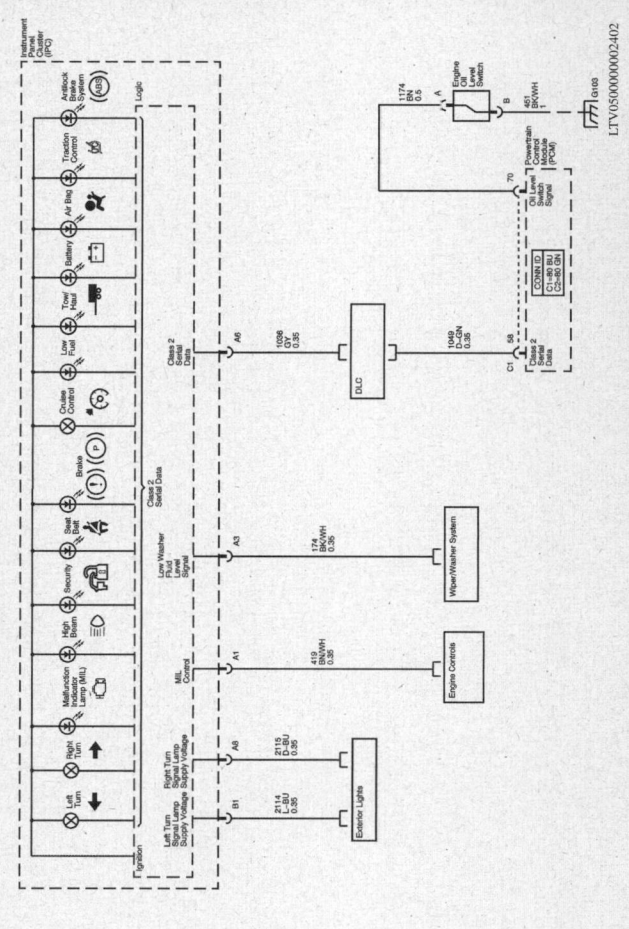

Fig. 29   Wiring diagram (Part 3 of 3). 2004 Hummer H2

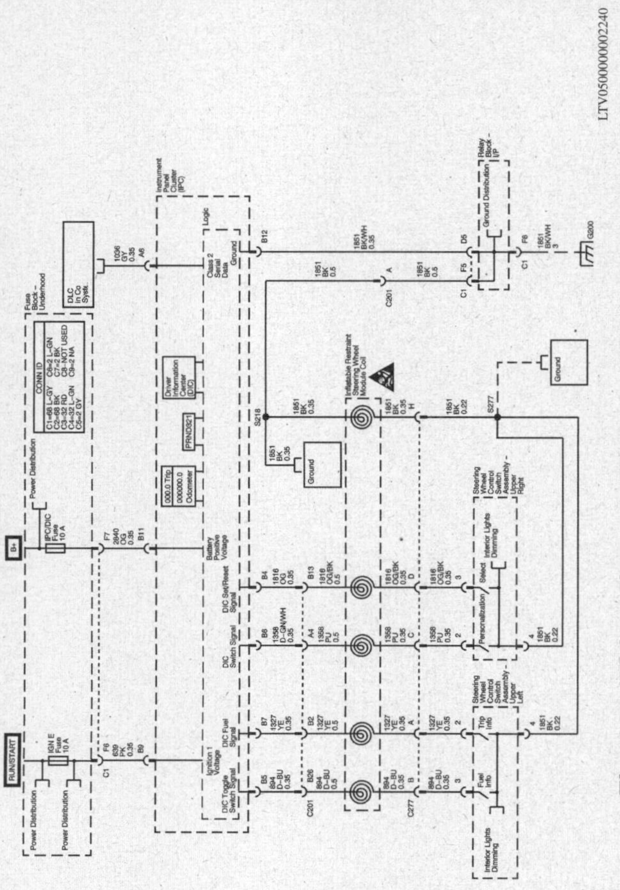

Fig. 30   Wiring diagram (Part 2 of 3). 2005 Hummer H2

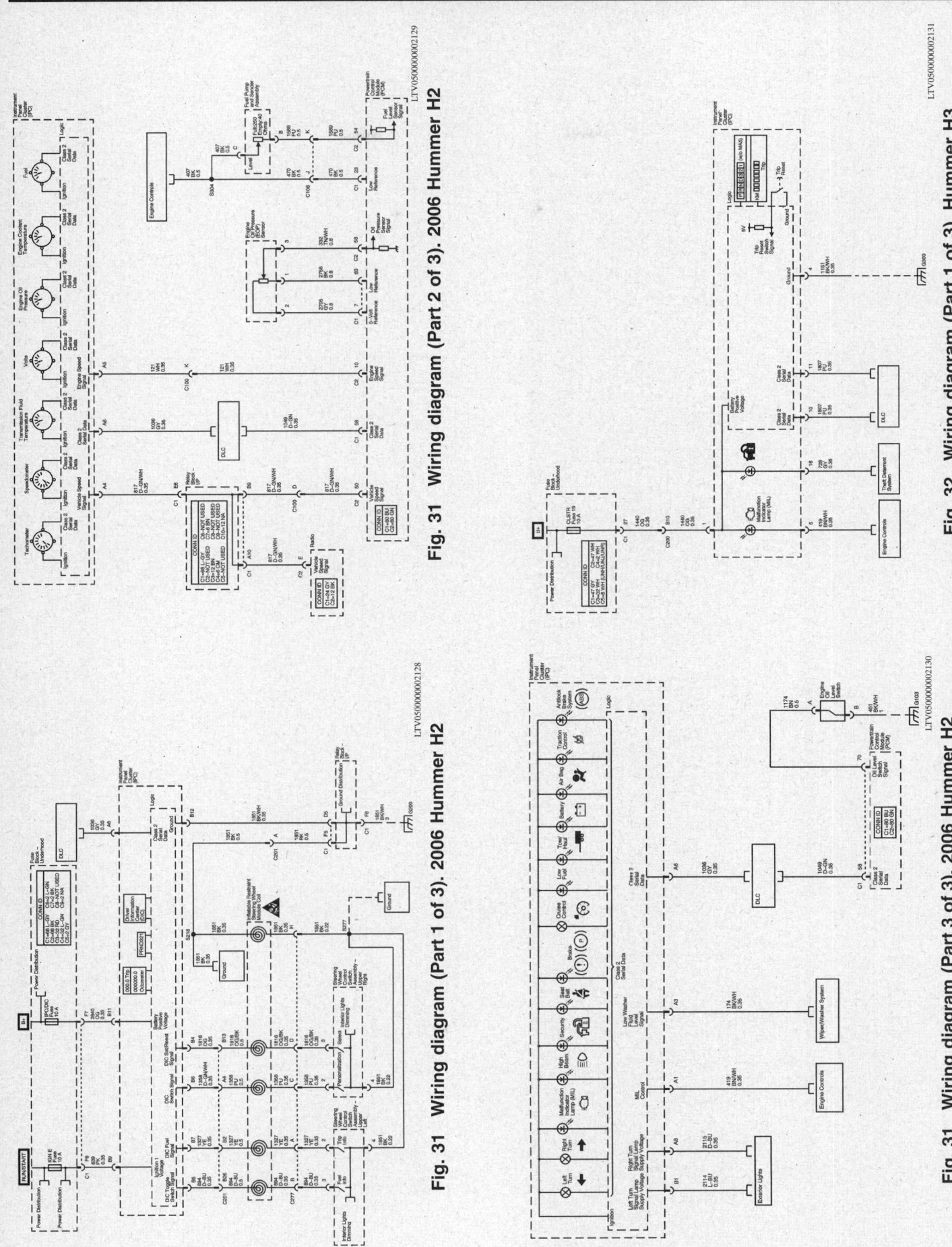

Fig. 31 Wiring diagram (Part 2 of 3). 2006 Hummer H2

Fig. 32 Wiring diagram (Part 1 of 3). Hummer H3

Fig. 31 Wiring diagram (Part 1 of 3). 2006 Hummer H2

Fig. 31 Wiring diagram (Part 3 of 3). 2006 Hummer H2

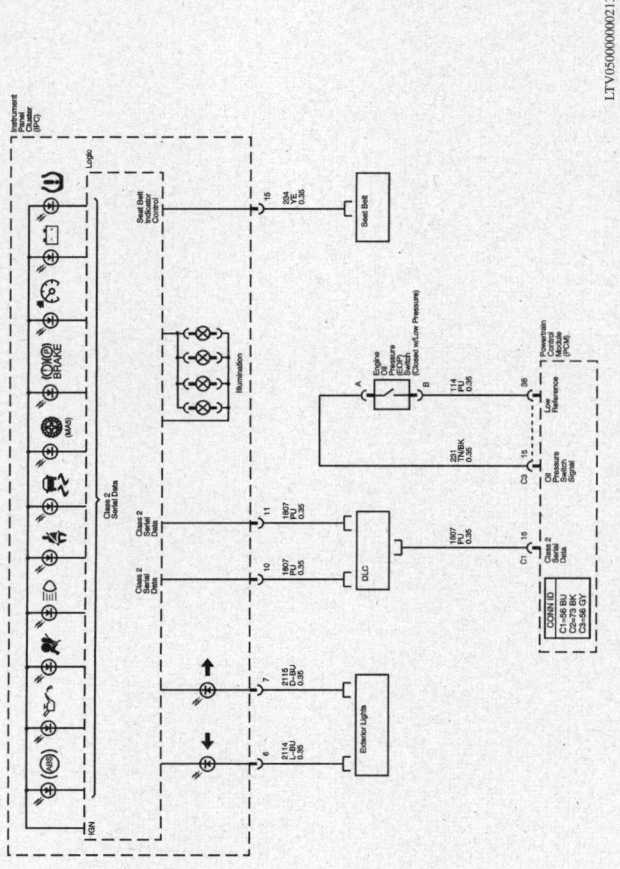

Fig. 32 Wiring diagram (Part 3 of 3). Hummer H3

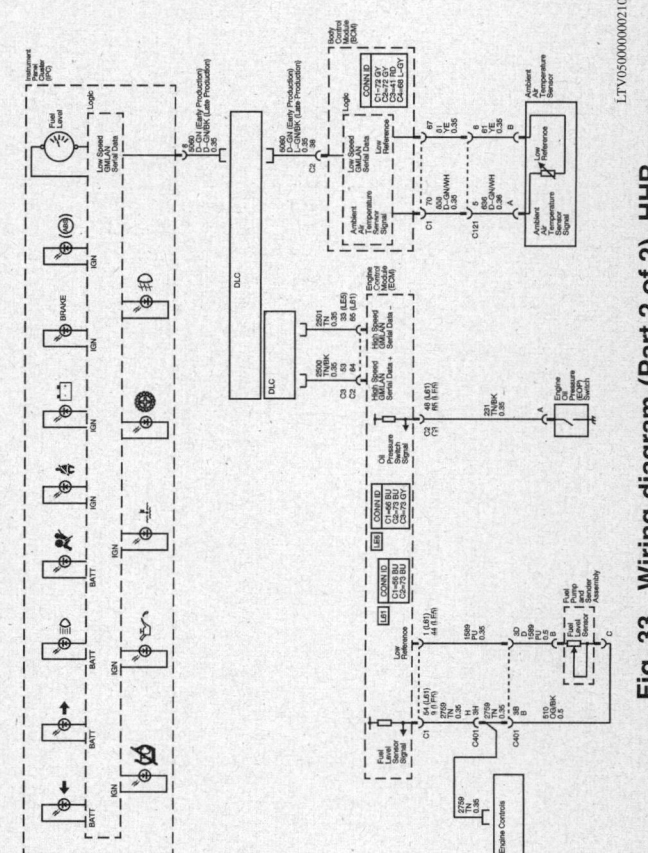

Fig. 33 Wiring diagram (Part 2 of 2). HHR

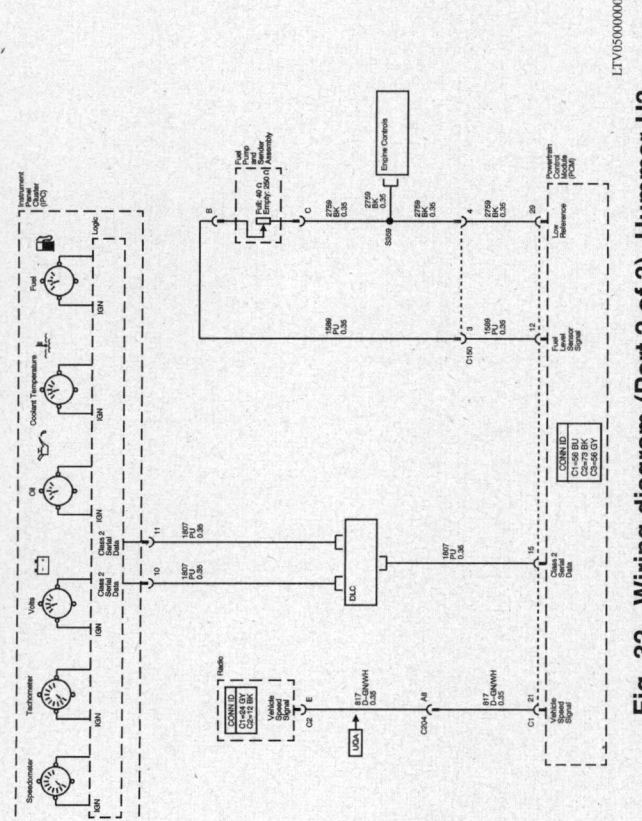

Fig. 32 Wiring diagram (Part 2 of 3). Hummer H3

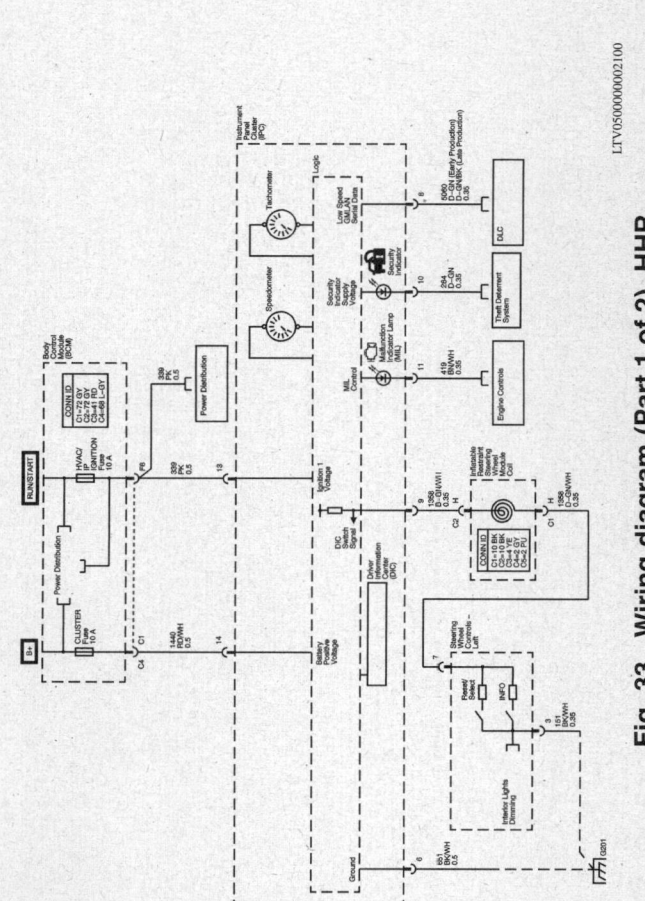

Fig. 33 Wiring diagram (Part 1 of 2). HHR

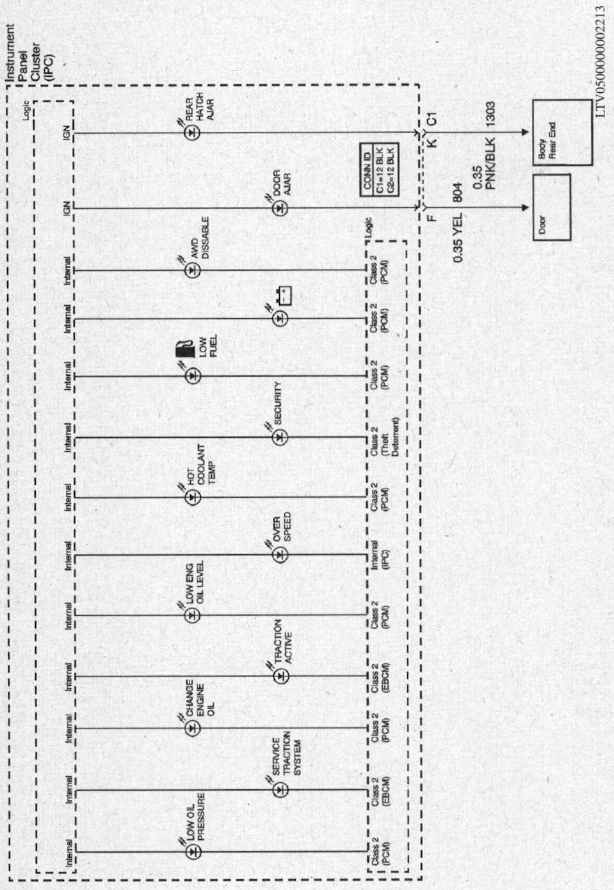

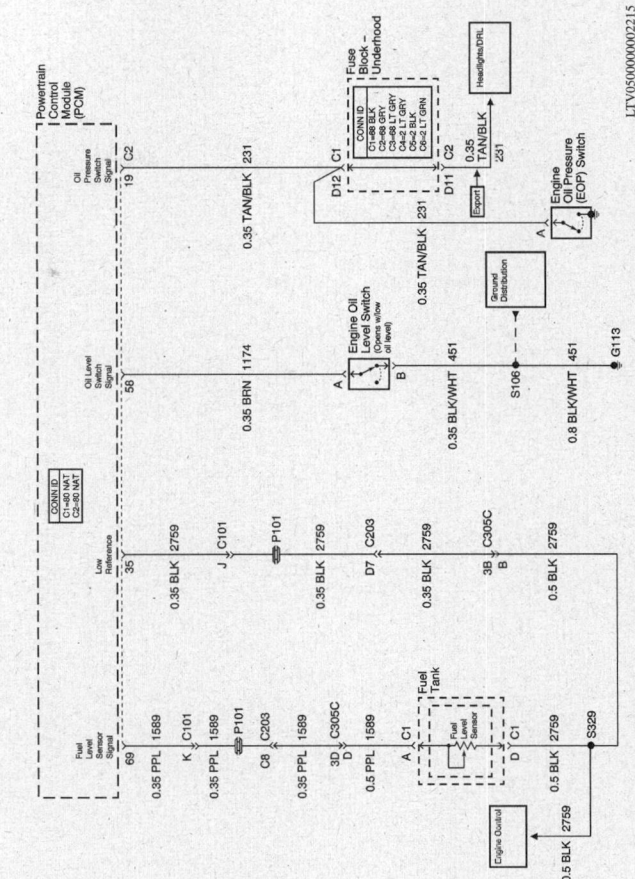

Fig. 34 Wiring diagram (Part 2 of 4). 2002 Montana & Venture

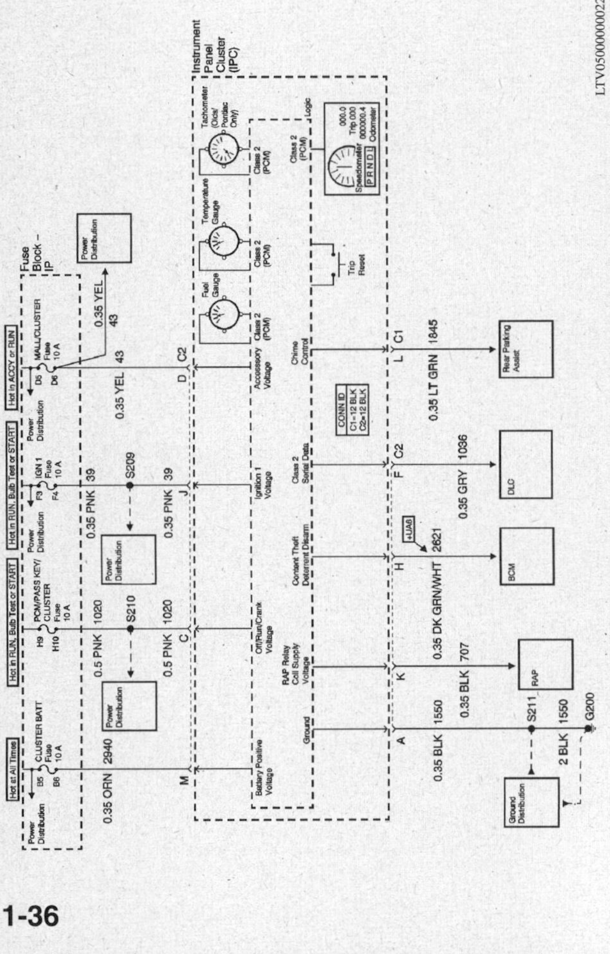

Fig. 34 Wiring diagram (Part 4 of 4). 2002 Montana & Venture

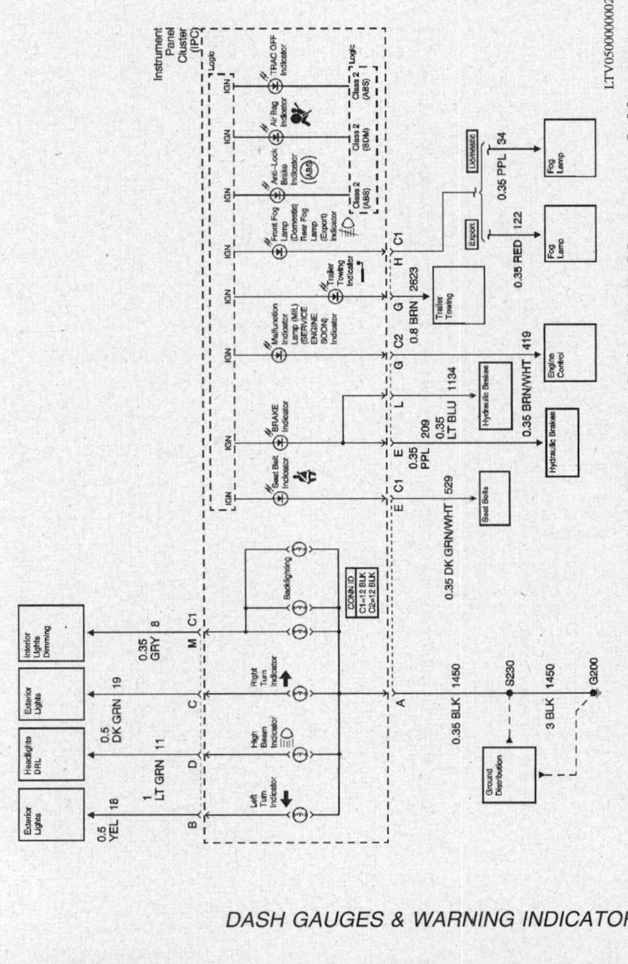

Fig. 34 Wiring diagram (Part 1 of 4). 2002 Montana & Venture

Fig. 34 Wiring diagram (Part 3 of 4). 2002 Montana & Venture

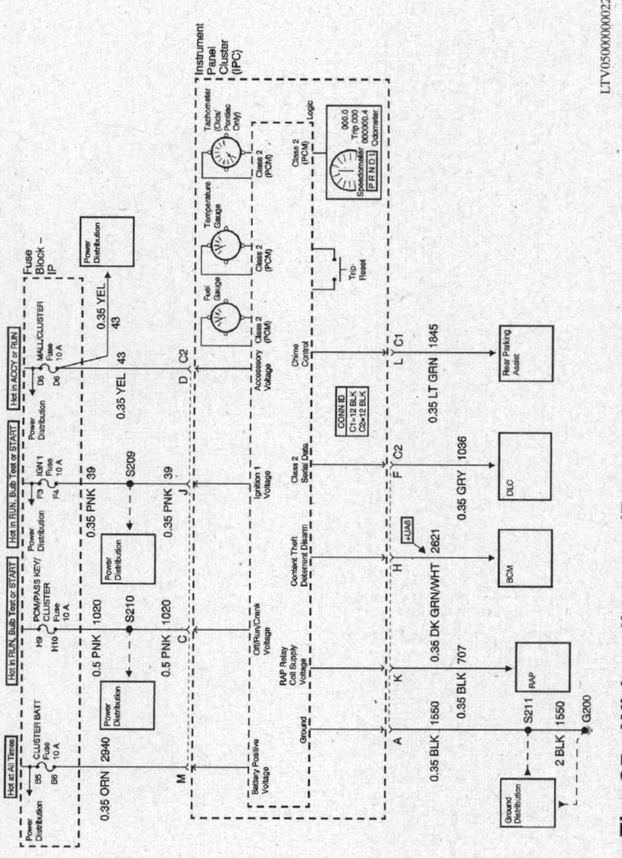

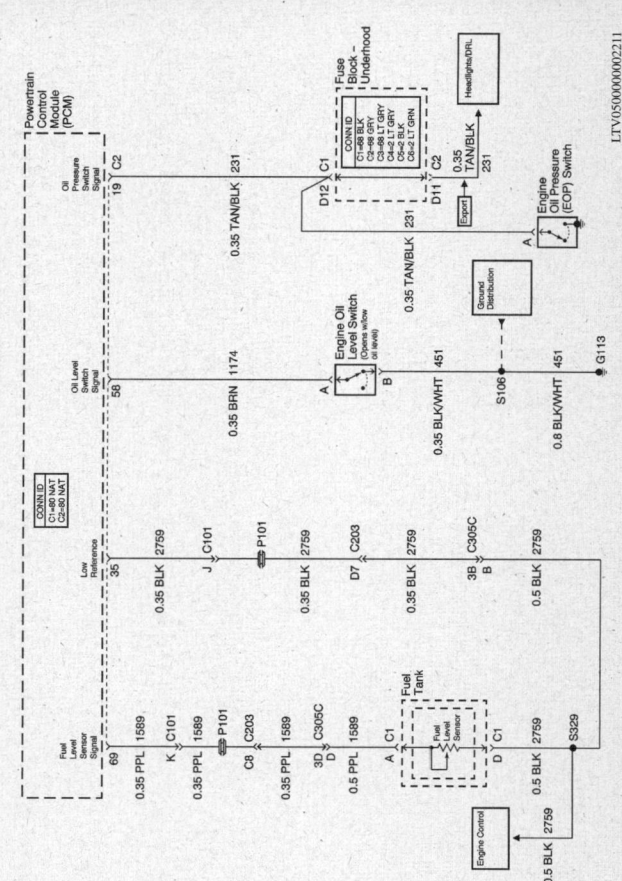

Fig. 35 Wiring diagram (Part 2 of 4). 2003–04 Montana & Venture

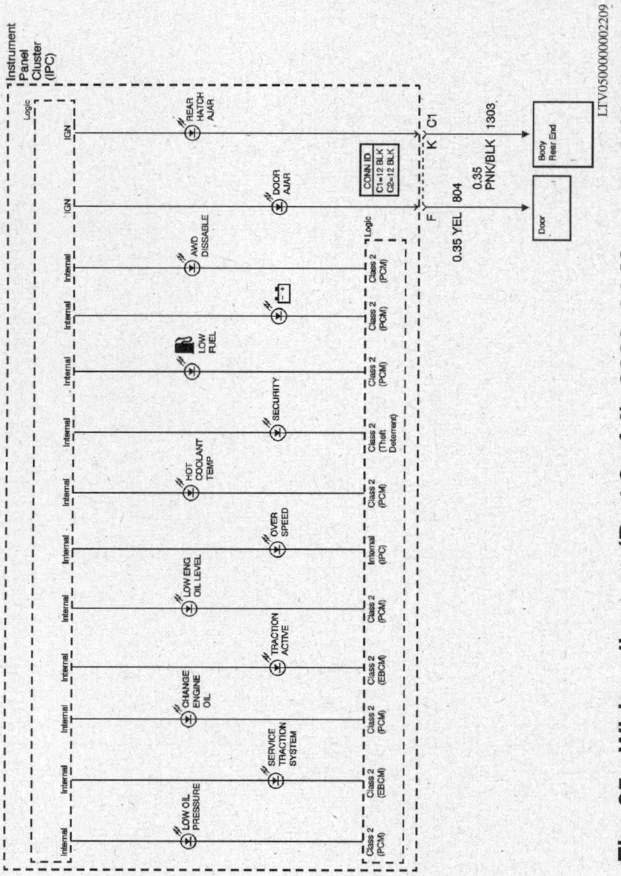

Fig. 35 Wiring diagram (Part 4 of 4). 2003–04 Montana & Venture

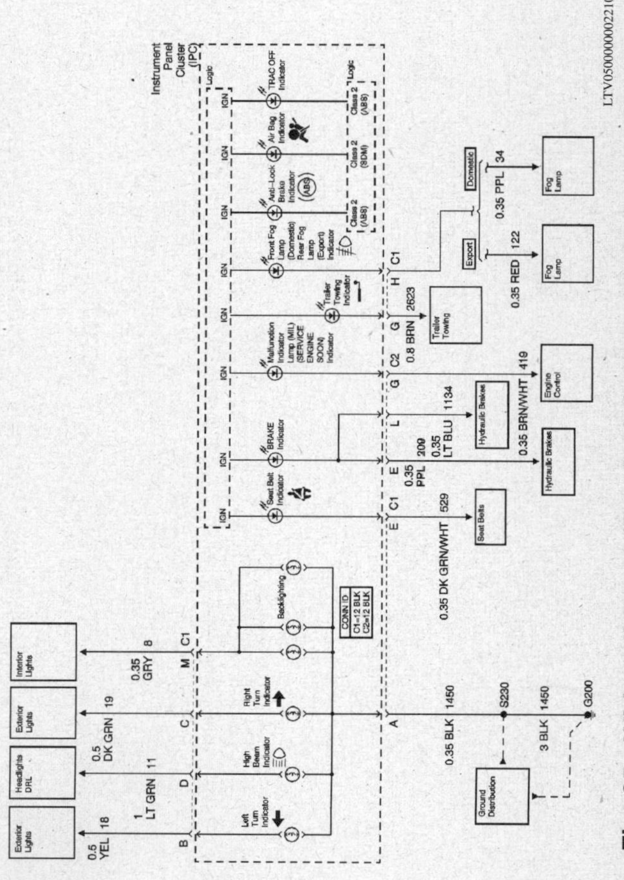

Fig. 35 Wiring diagram (Part 1 of 4). 2003–04 Montana & Venture

Fig. 35 Wiring diagram (Part 3 of 4). 2003–04 Montana & Venture

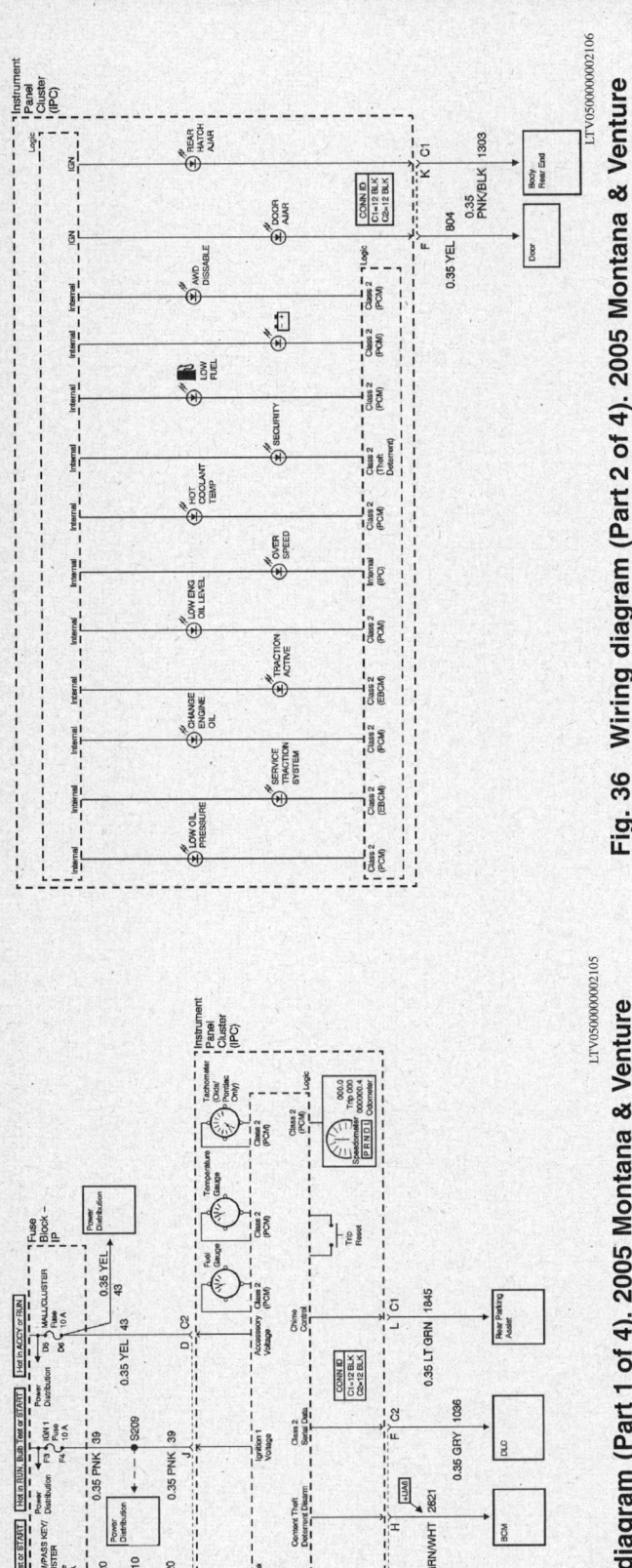

Fig. 36 Wiring diagram (Part 2 of 4). 2005 Montana & Venture

Fig. 36 Wiring diagram (Part 4 of 4). 2005 Montana & Venture

Fig. 36 Wiring diagram (Part 1 of 4). 2005 Montana & Venture

Fig. 36 Wiring diagram (Part 3 of 4). 2005 Montana & Venture

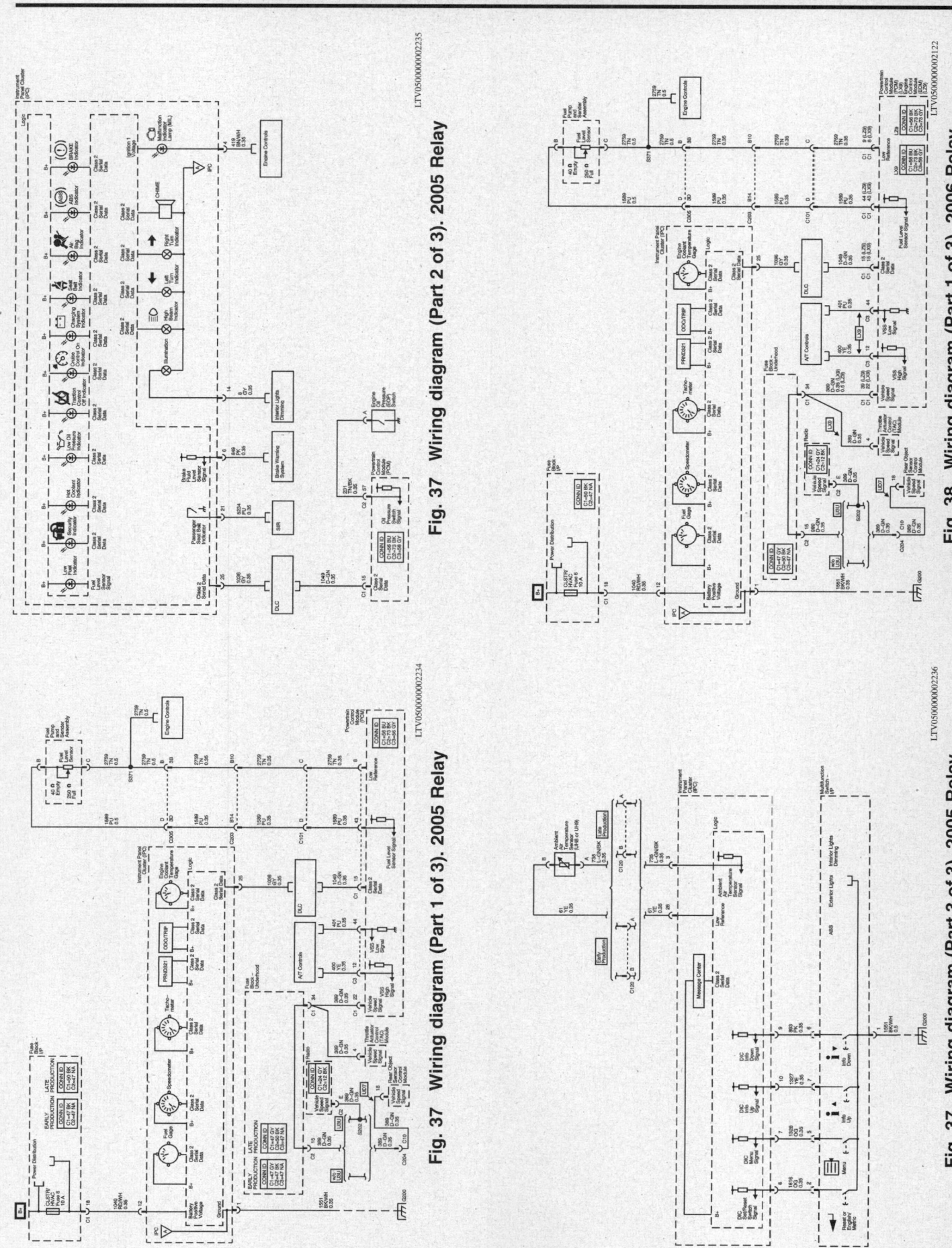

Fig. 37 Wiring diagram (Part 2 of 3). 2005 Relay

Fig. 38 Wiring diagram (Part 1 of 3). 2006 Relay

Fig. 37 Wiring diagram (Part 1 of 3). 2005 Relay

Fig. 37 Wiring diagram (Part 3 of 3). 2005 Relay

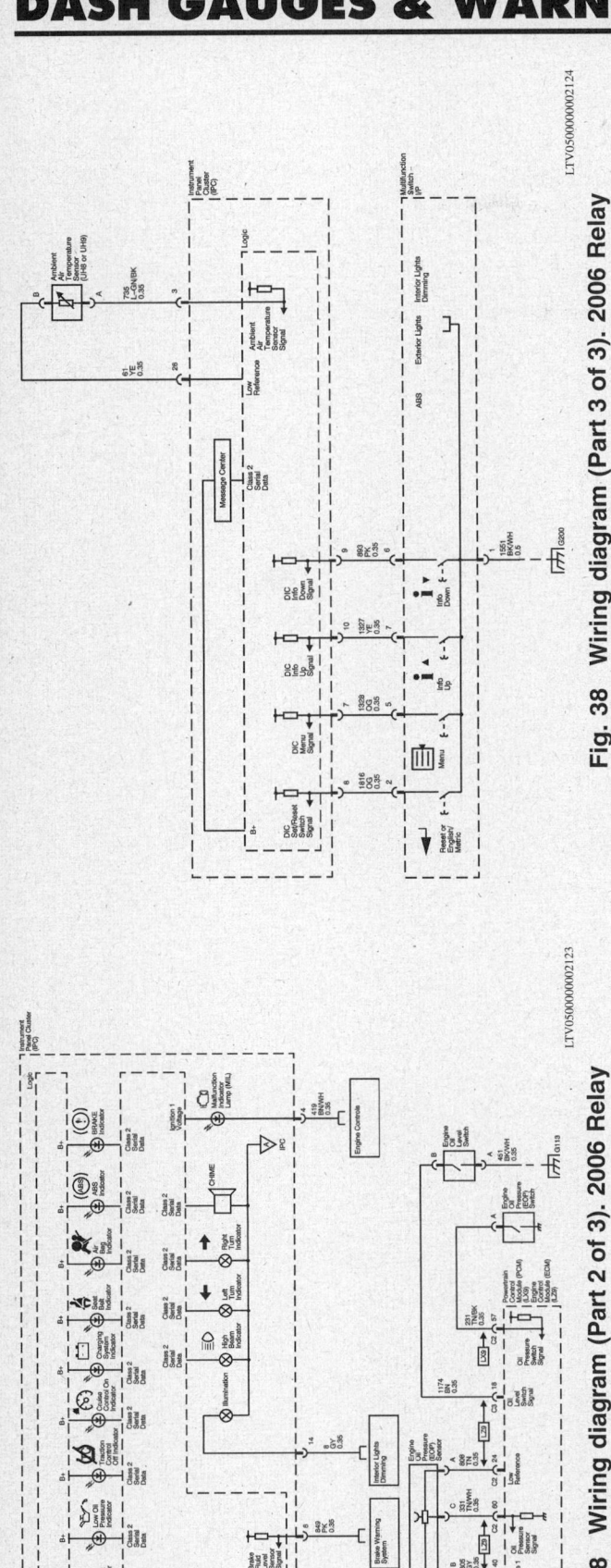

Fig. 38 Wiring diagram (Part 3 of 3). 2006 Relay

Fig. 38 Wiring diagram (Part 2 of 3). 2006 Relay

Fig. 39 Wiring diagram (Part 2 of 4). S10 & Sonoma

Fig. 39 Wiring diagram (Part 1 of 4). S10 & Sonoma

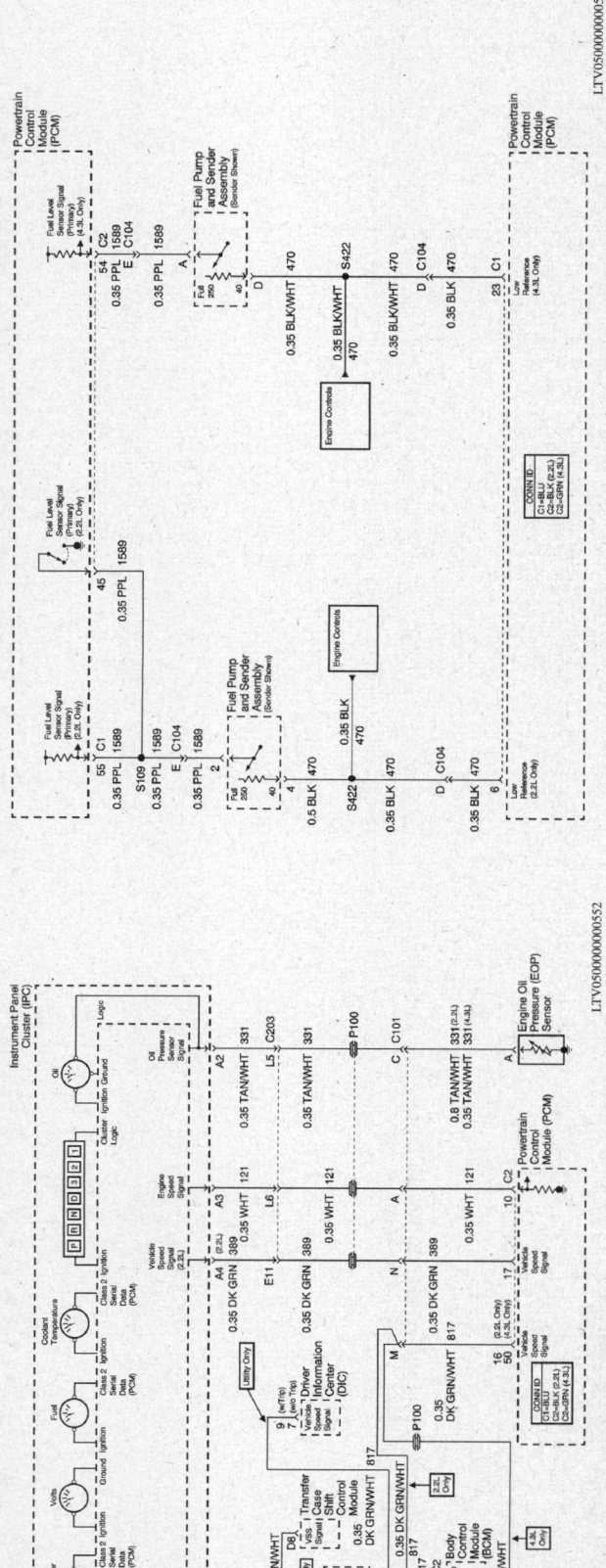

Fig. 39 Wiring diagram (Part 4 of 4). S10 & Sonoma

Fig. 39 Wiring diagram (Part 3 of 4). S10 & Sonoma

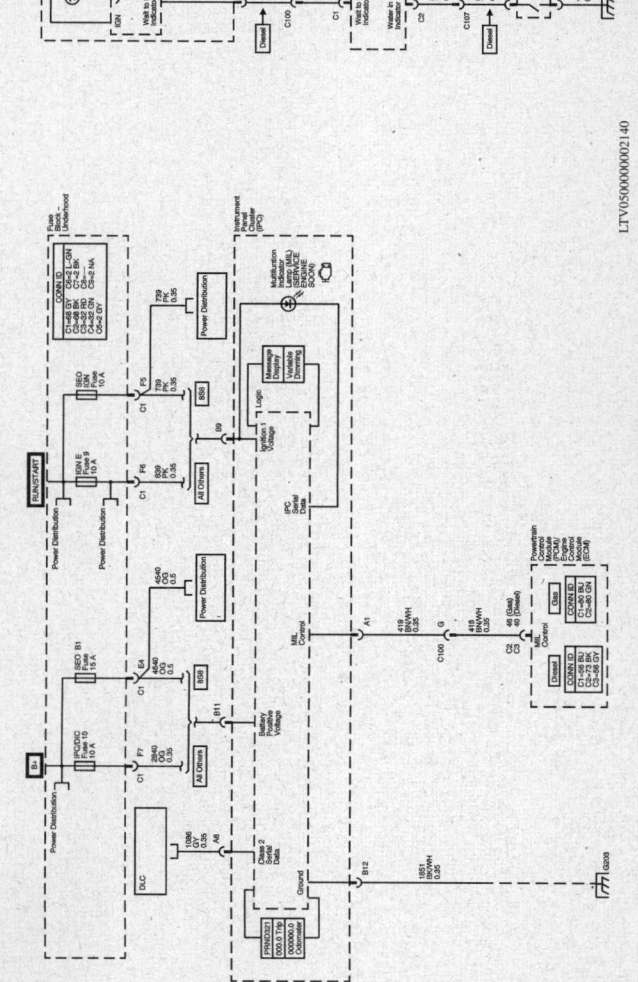

Fig. 40 Wiring diagram (Part 2 of 4). 2002–05 Sierra, Silverado, Suburban, Tahoe & Yukon

Fig. 40 Wiring diagram (Part 1 of 4). 2002–05 Sierra, Silverado, Suburban, Tahoe & Yukon

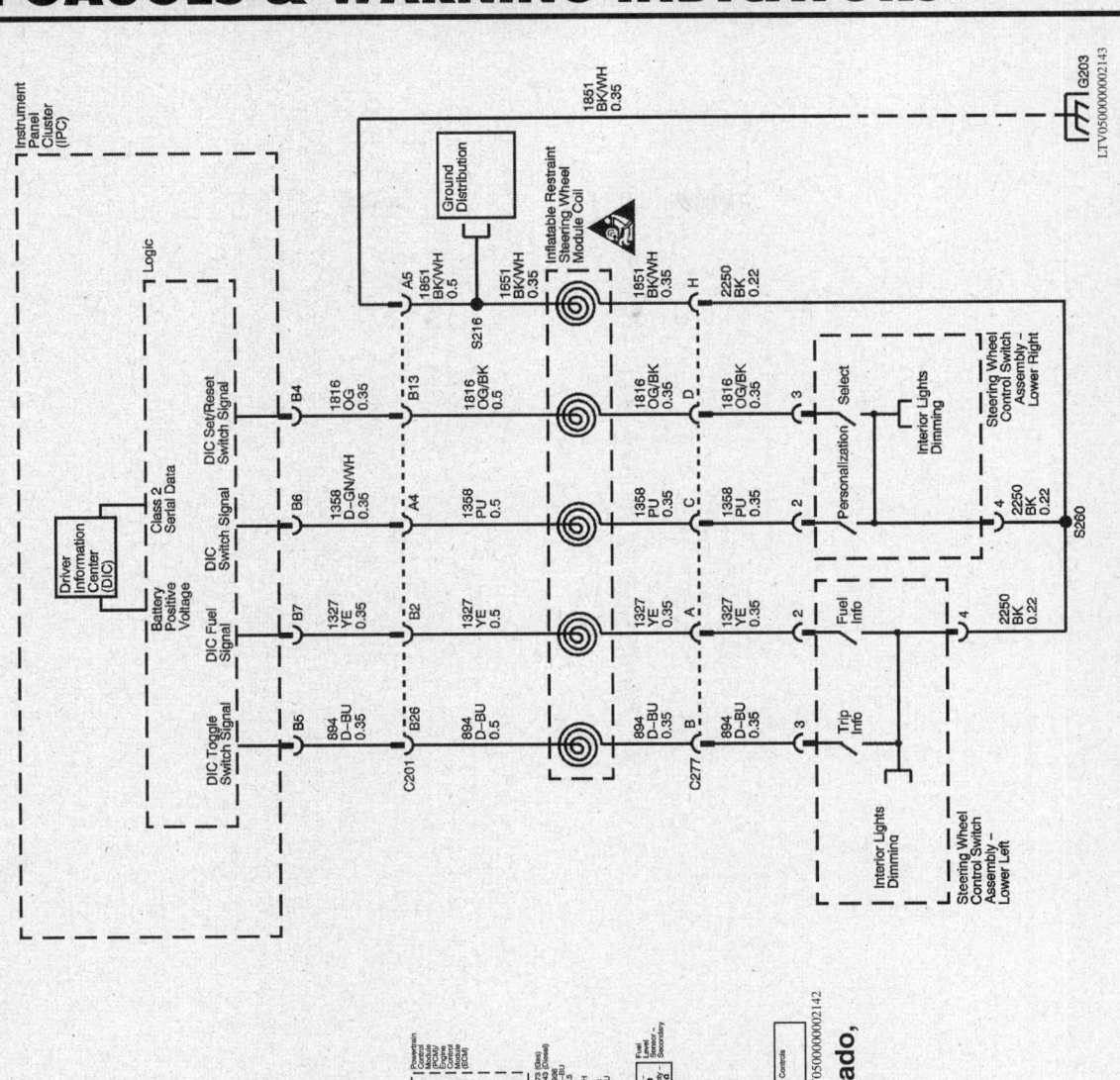

Fig. 40 Wiring diagram (Part 4 of 4). 2002–05 Sierra, Silverado, Suburban, Tahoe & Yukon

Fig. 40 Wiring diagram (Part 3 of 4). 2002–05 Sierra, Silverado, Suburban, Tahoe & Yukon

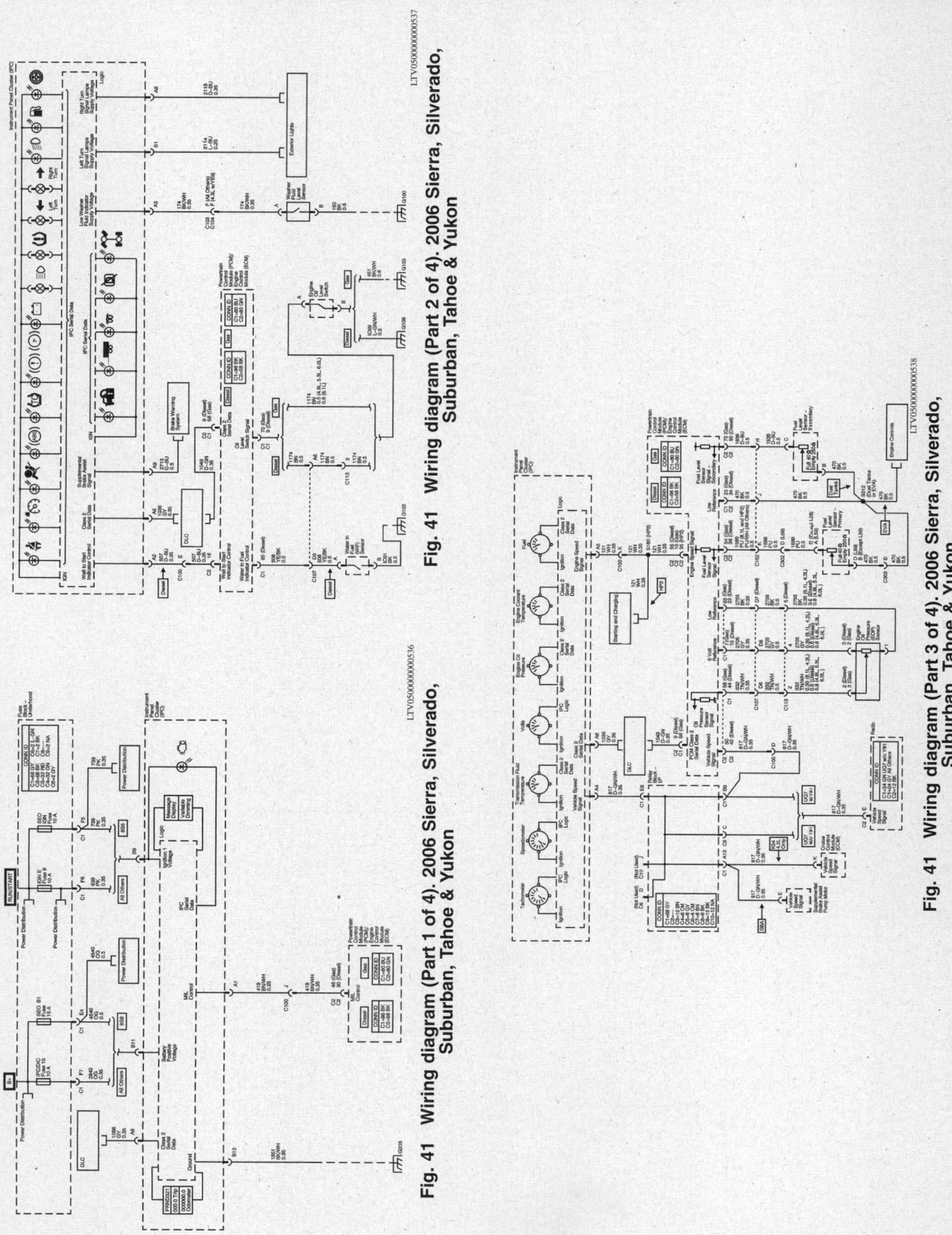

Fig. 41 Wiring diagram (Part 2 of 4). 2006 Sierra, Silverado, Suburban, Tahoe & Yukon

Fig. 41 Wiring diagram (Part 1 of 4). 2006 Sierra, Silverado, Suburban, Tahoe & Yukon

Fig. 41 Wiring diagram (Part 3 of 4). 2006 Sierra, Silverado, Suburban, Tahoe & Yukon

DASH GAUGES & WARNING INDICATORS

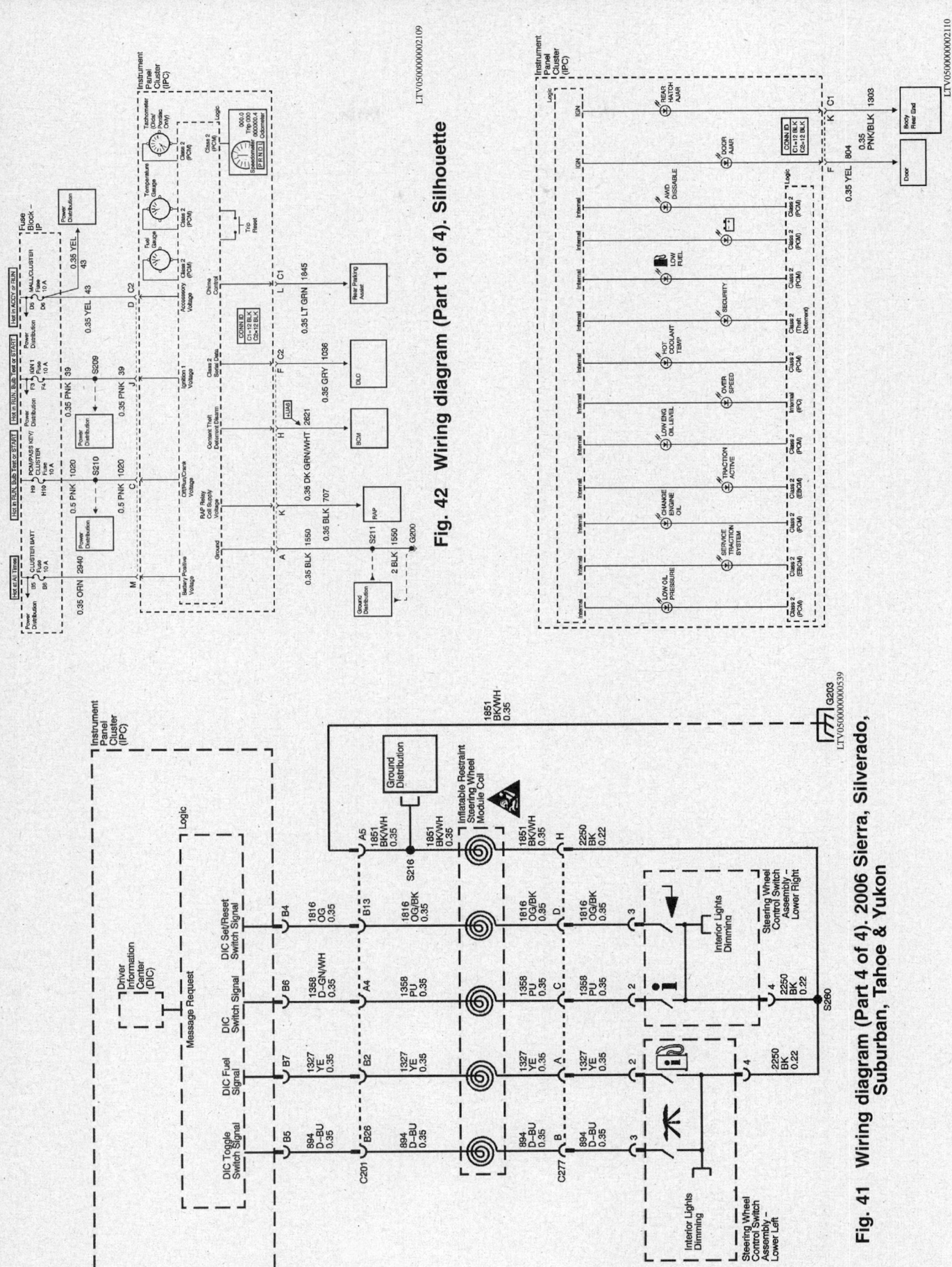

Fig. 42 Wiring diagram (Part 1 of 4). Silhouette

Fig. 42 Wiring diagram (Part 2 of 4). Silhouette

Fig. 41 Wiring diagram (Part 4 of 4). 2006 Sierra, Silverado, Suburban, Tahoe & Yukon

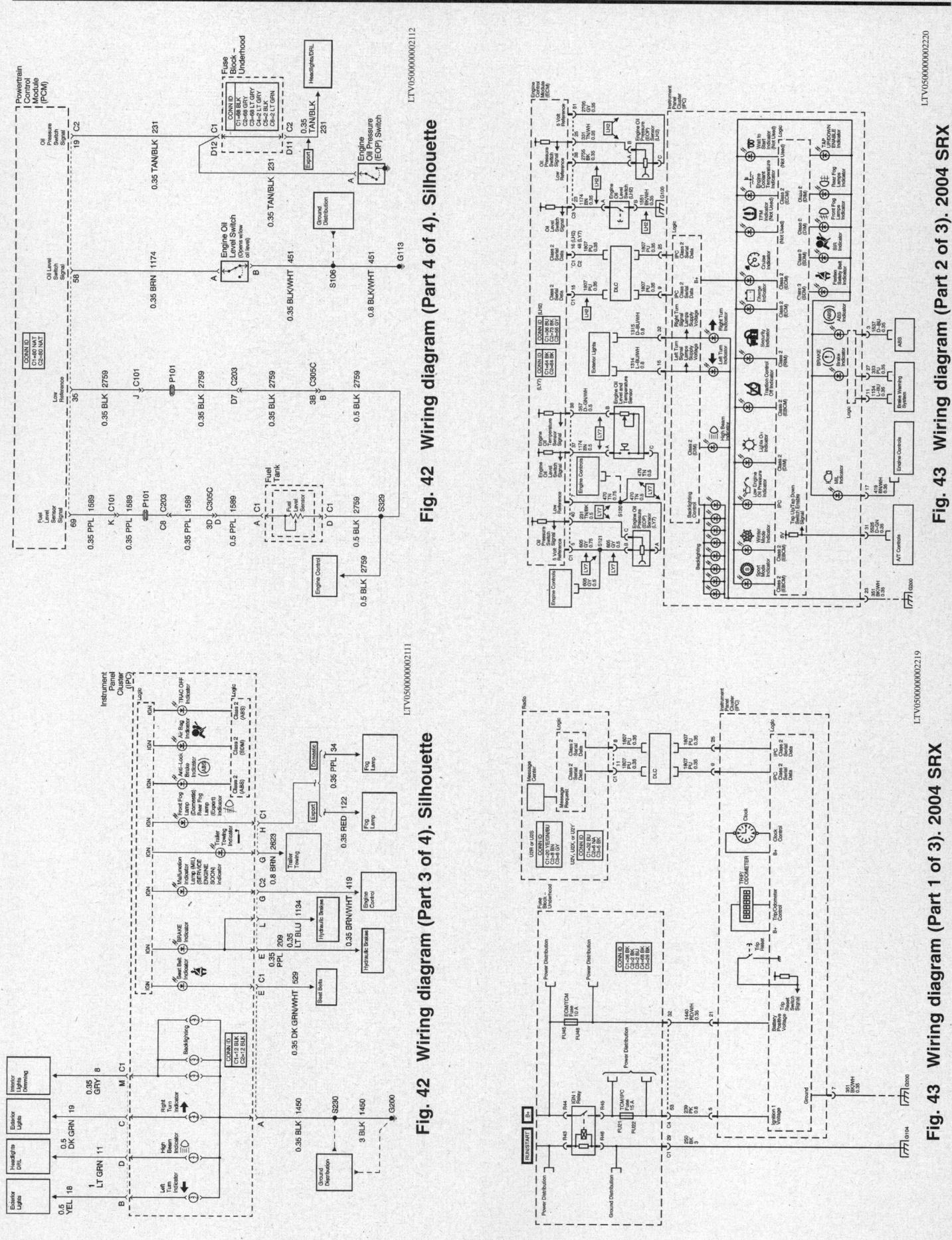

Fig. 42 Wiring diagram (Part 4 of 4). Silhouette

Fig. 42 Wiring diagram (Part 3 of 4). Silhouette

Fig. 43 Wiring diagram (Part 2 of 3). 2004 SRX

Fig. 43 Wiring diagram (Part 1 of 3). 2004 SRX

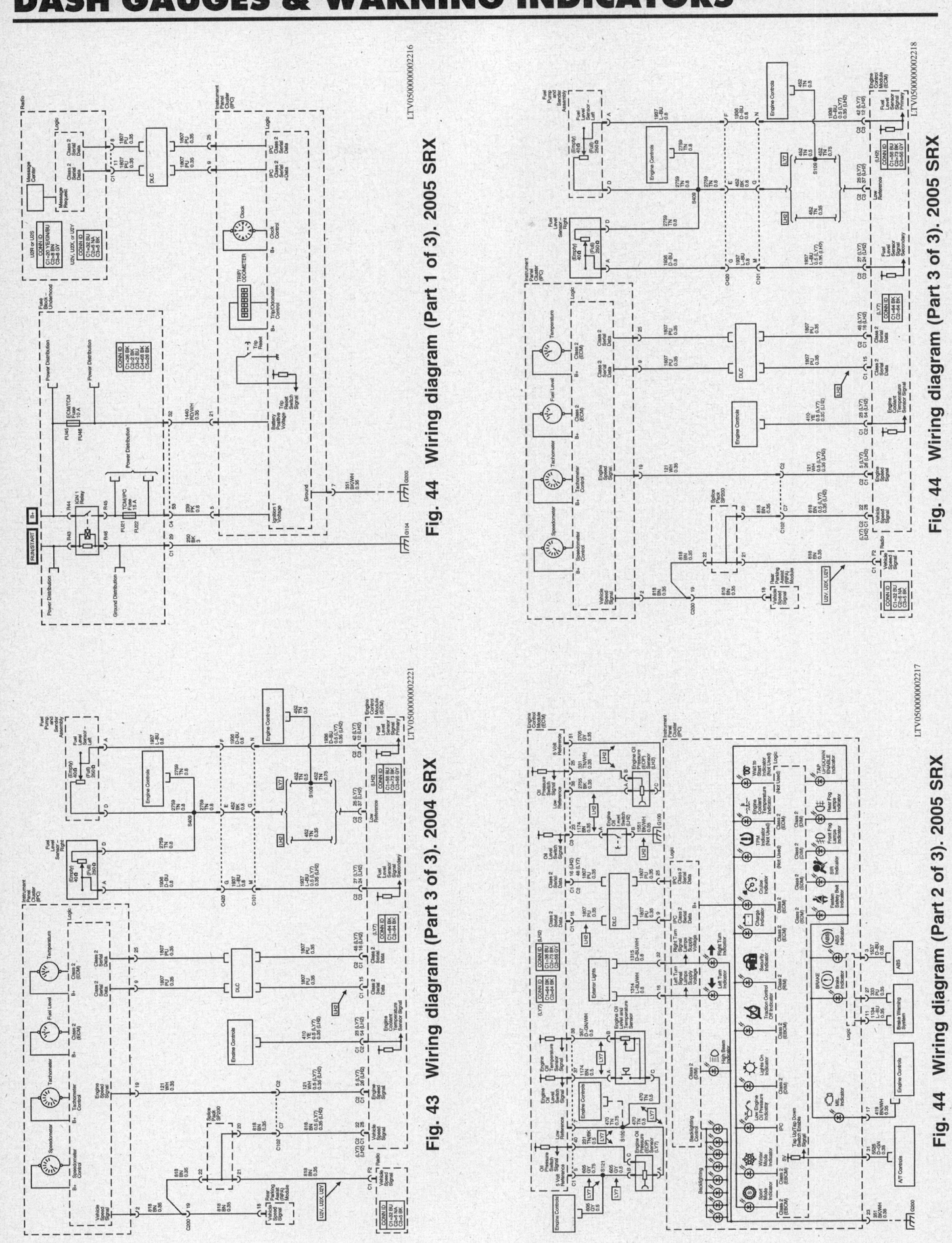

Fig. 44 Wiring diagram (Part 1 of 3). 2005 SRX

Fig. 44 Wiring diagram (Part 3 of 3). 2005 SRX

Fig. 43 Wiring diagram (Part 3 of 3). 2004 SRX

Fig. 44 Wiring diagram (Part 2 of 3). 2005 SRX

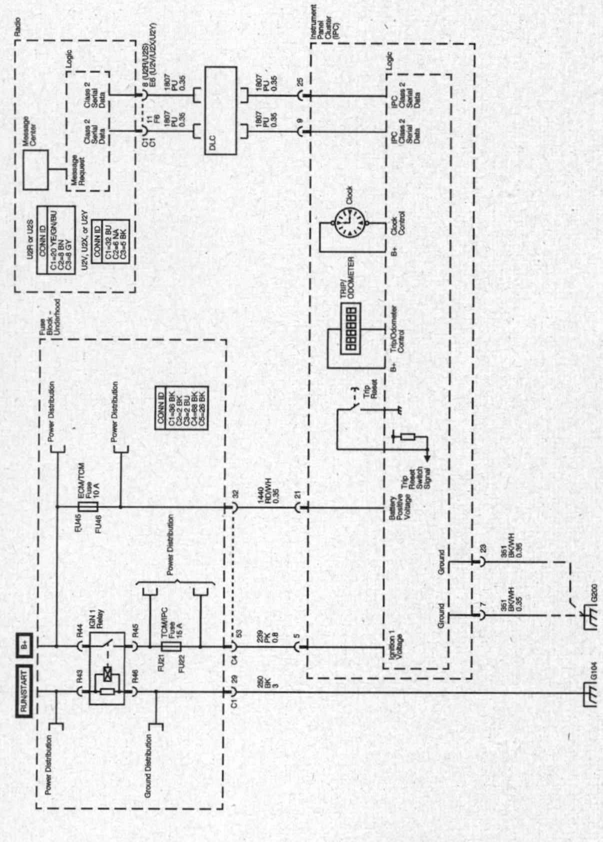

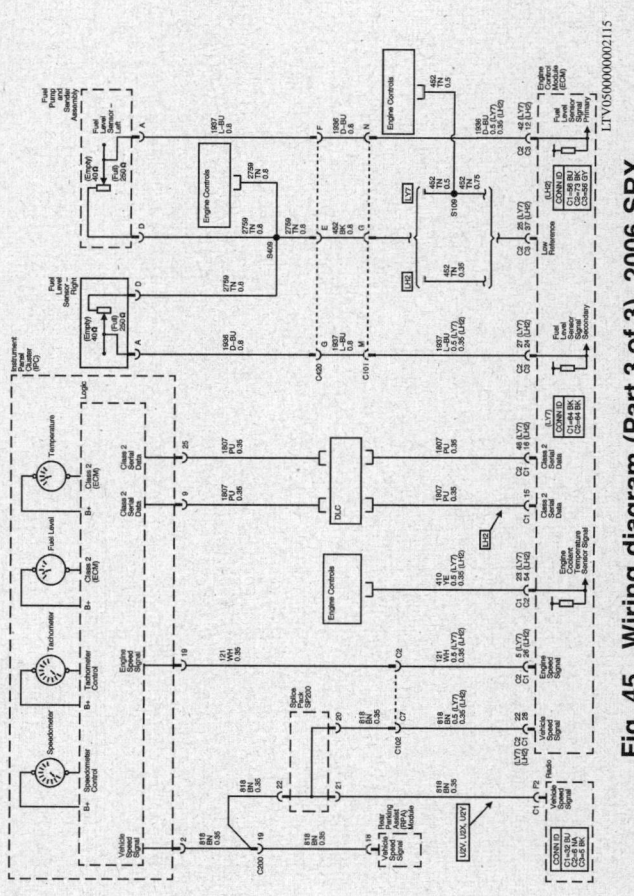

LTV0500000002113

Fig. 45 Wiring diagram (Part 1 of 3). 2006 SRX

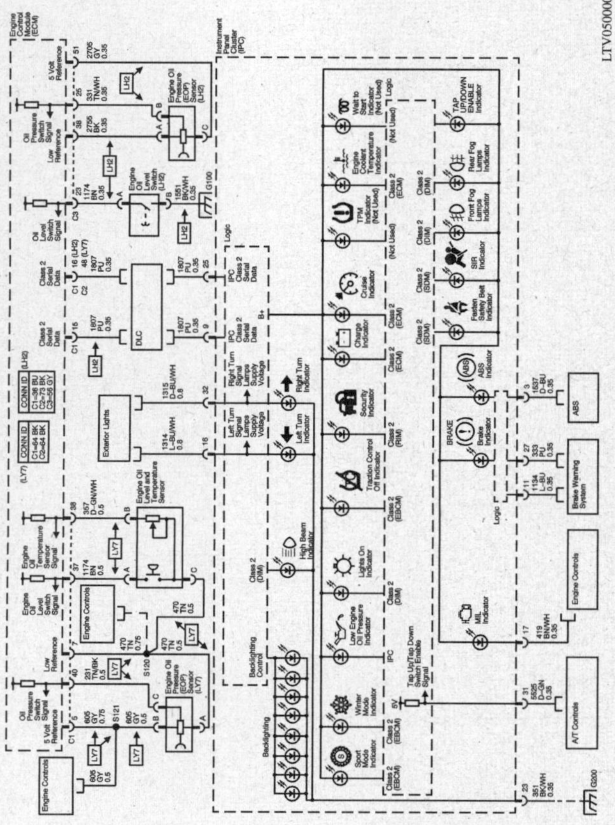

LTV0500000002114

Fig. 45 Wiring diagram (Part 2 of 3). 2006 SRX

LTV0500000002115

Fig. 45 Wiring diagram (Part 3 of 3). 2006 SRX

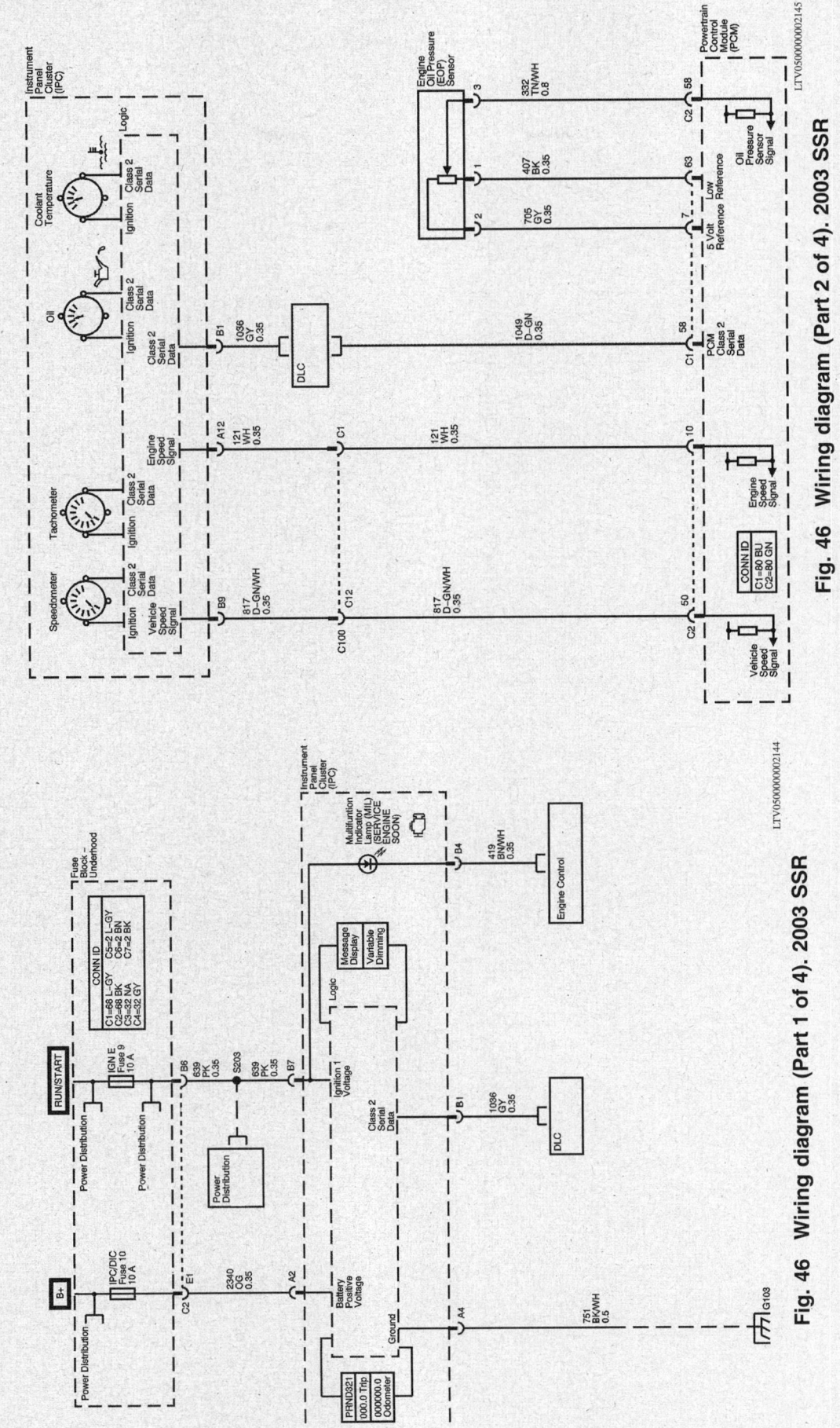

Fig. 46 Wiring diagram (Part 2 of 4). 2003 SSR

Fig. 46 Wiring diagram (Part 1 of 4). 2003 SSR

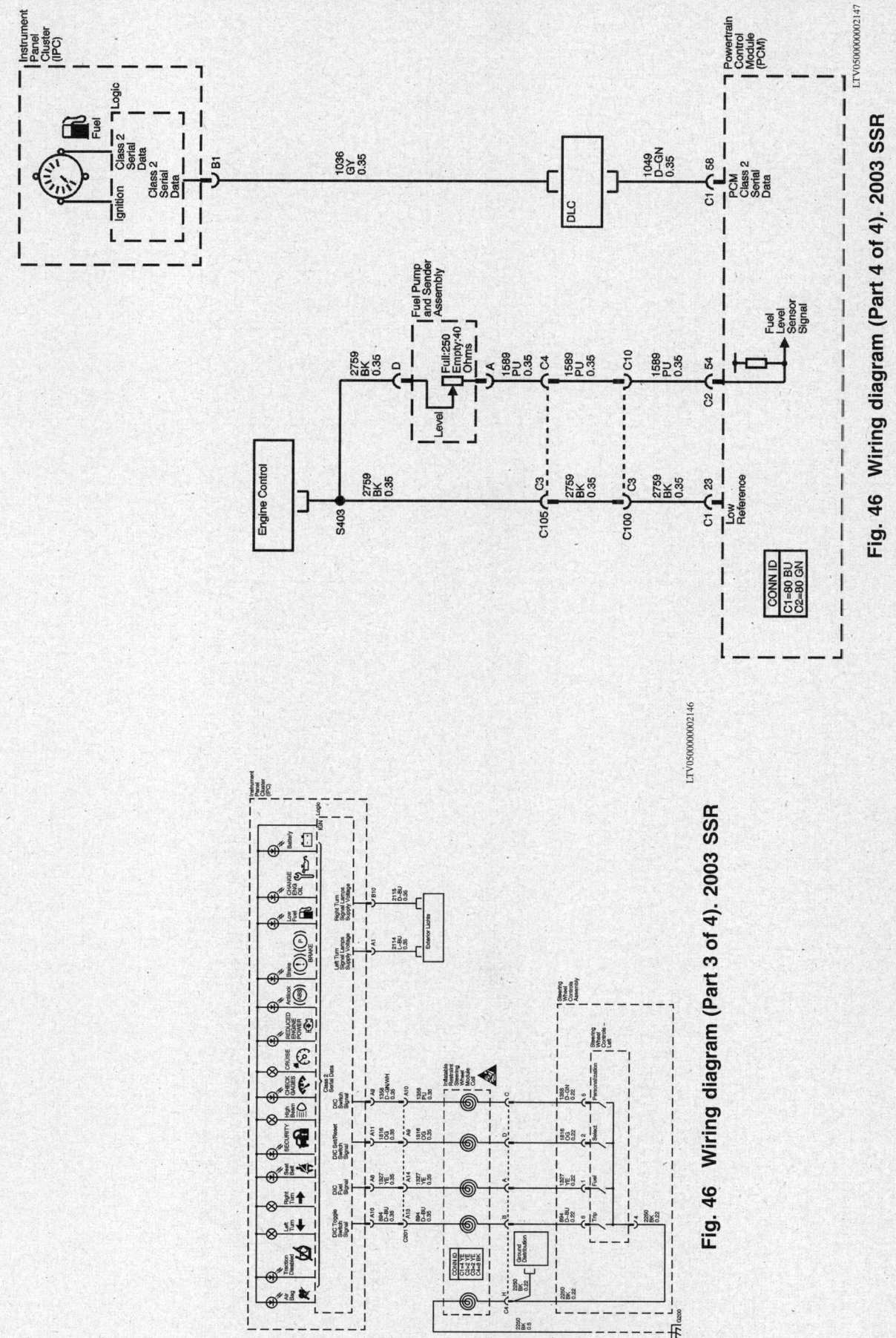

Fig. 46 Wiring diagram (Part 4 of 4). 2003 SSR

Fig. 46 Wiring diagram (Part 3 of 4). 2003 SSR

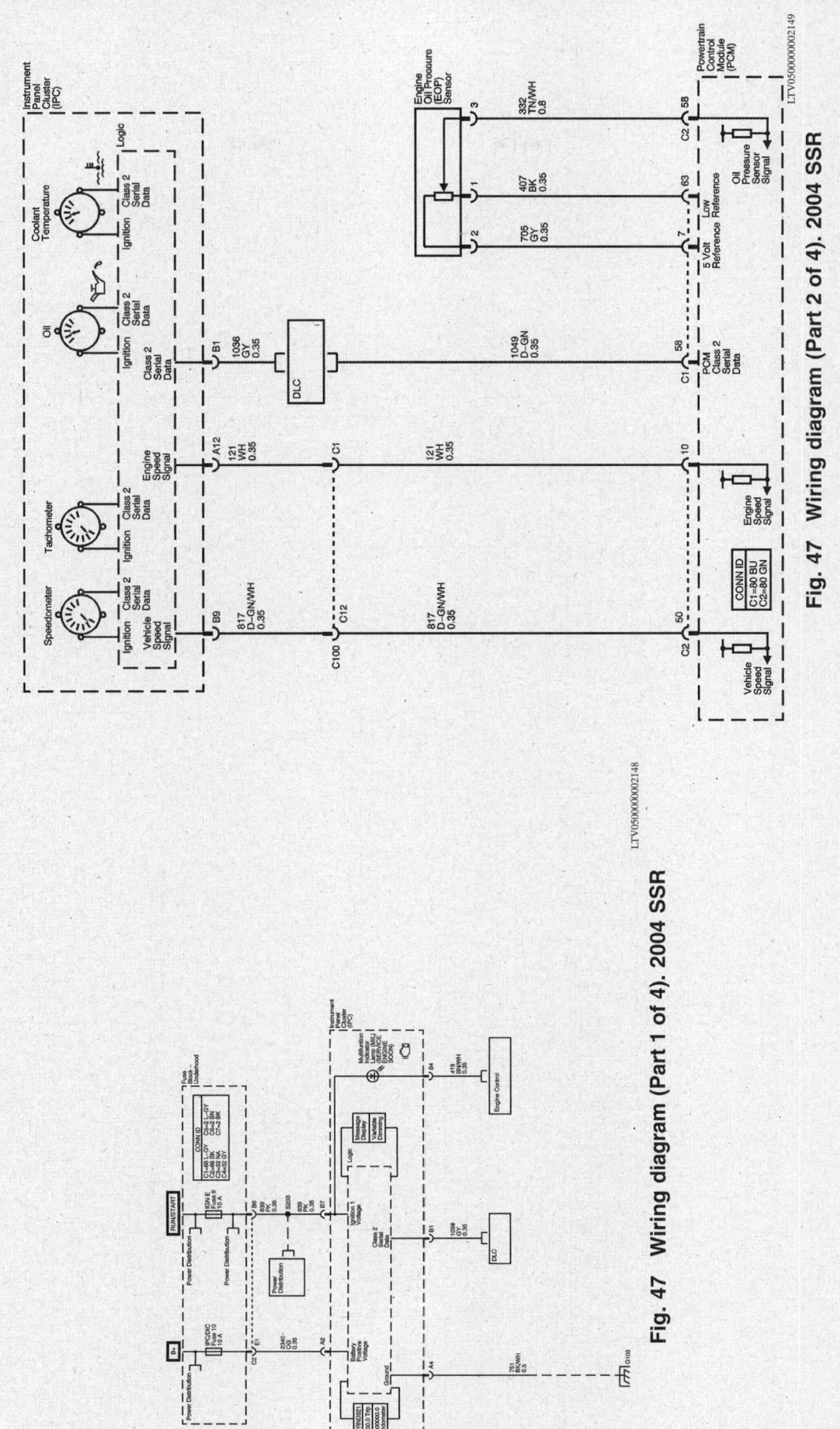

Fig. 47 Wiring diagram (Part 2 of 4). 2004 SSR

Fig. 47 Wiring diagram (Part 1 of 4). 2004 SSR

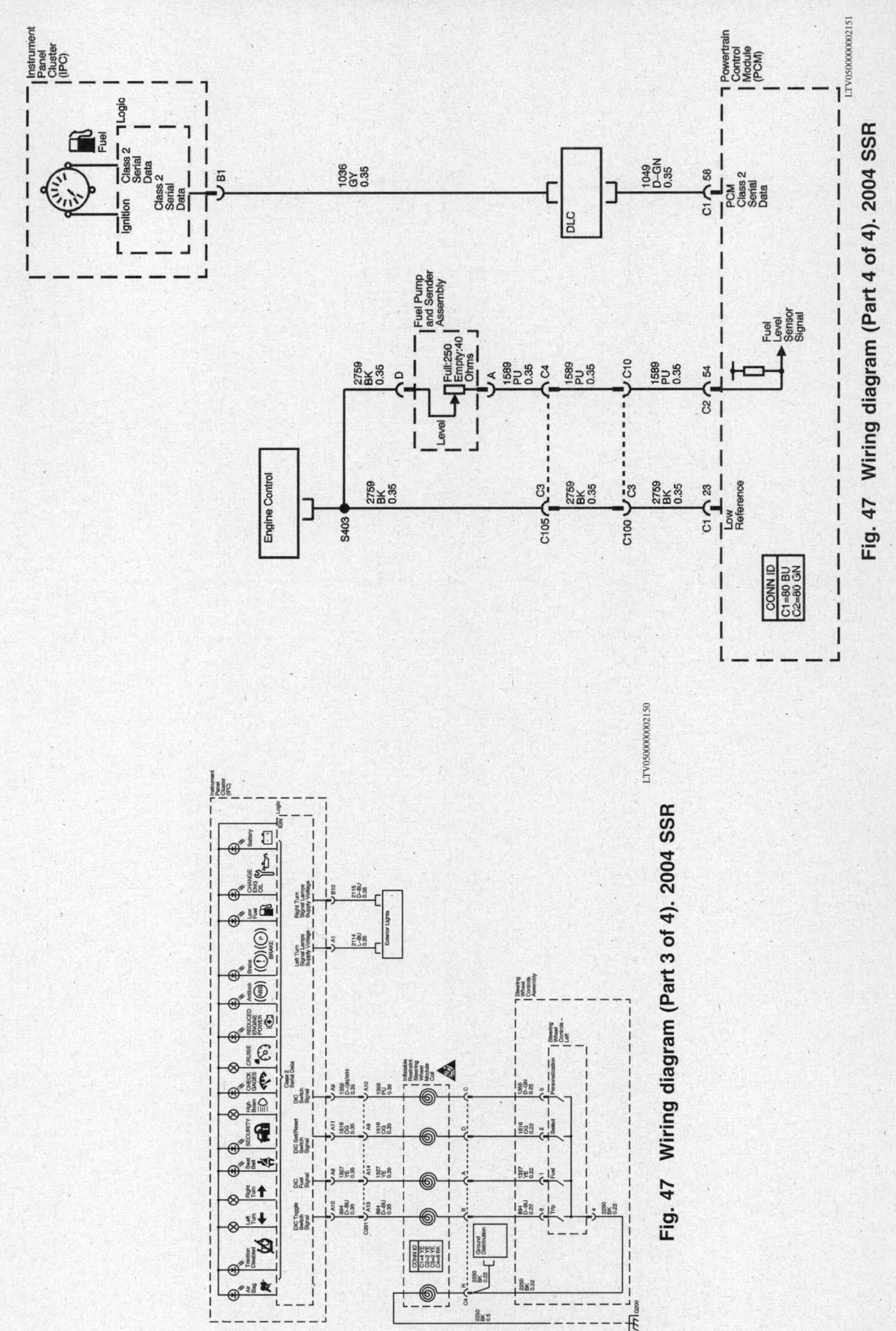

Fig. 47 Wiring diagram (Part 4 of 4). 2004 SSR

Fig. 47 Wiring diagram (Part 3 of 4). 2004 SSR

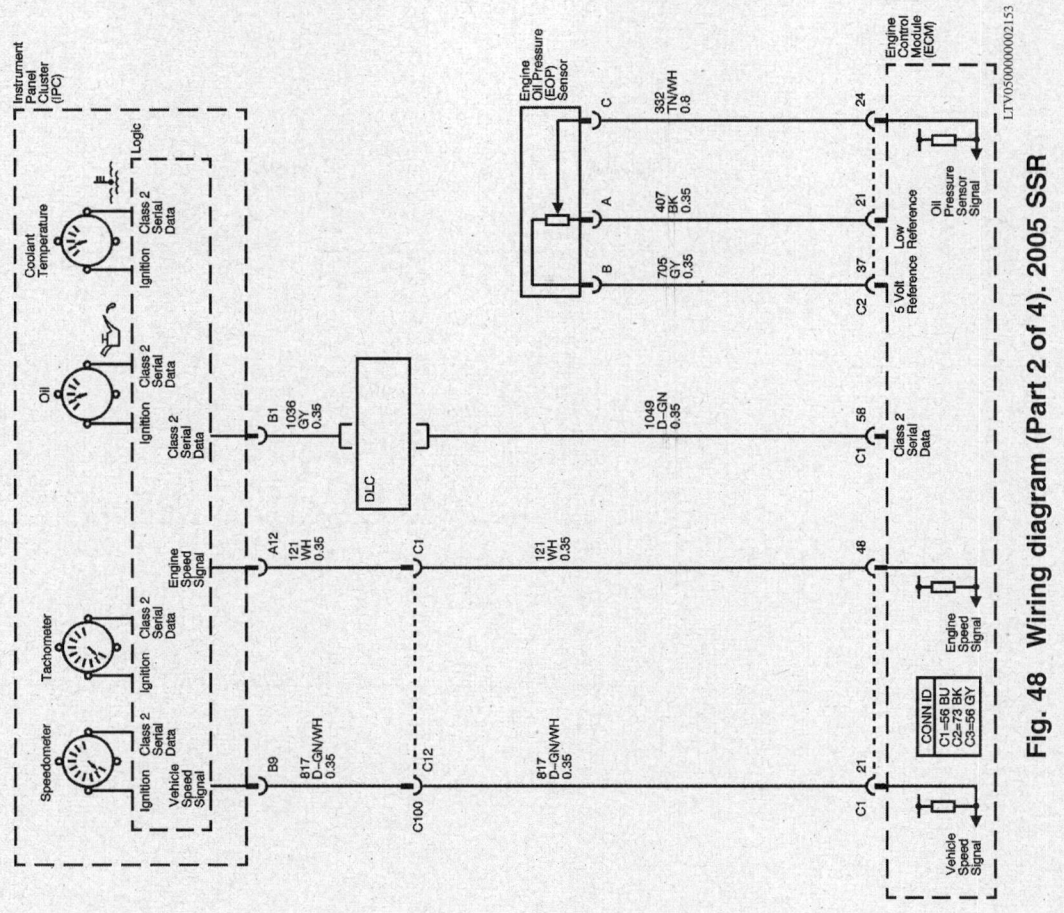

Fig. 48 Wiring diagram (Part 2 of 4). 2005 SSR

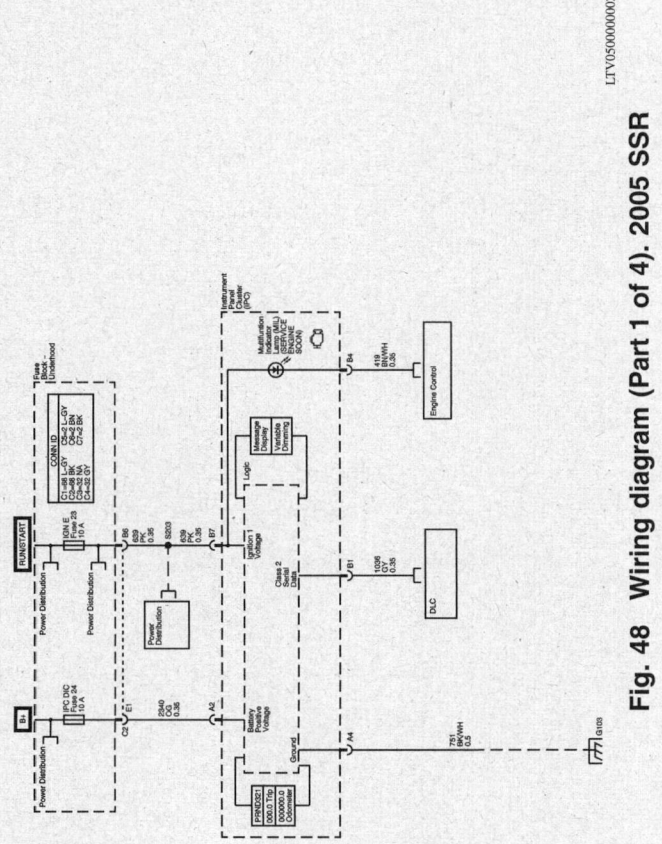

Fig. 48 Wiring diagram (Part 1 of 4). 2005 SSR

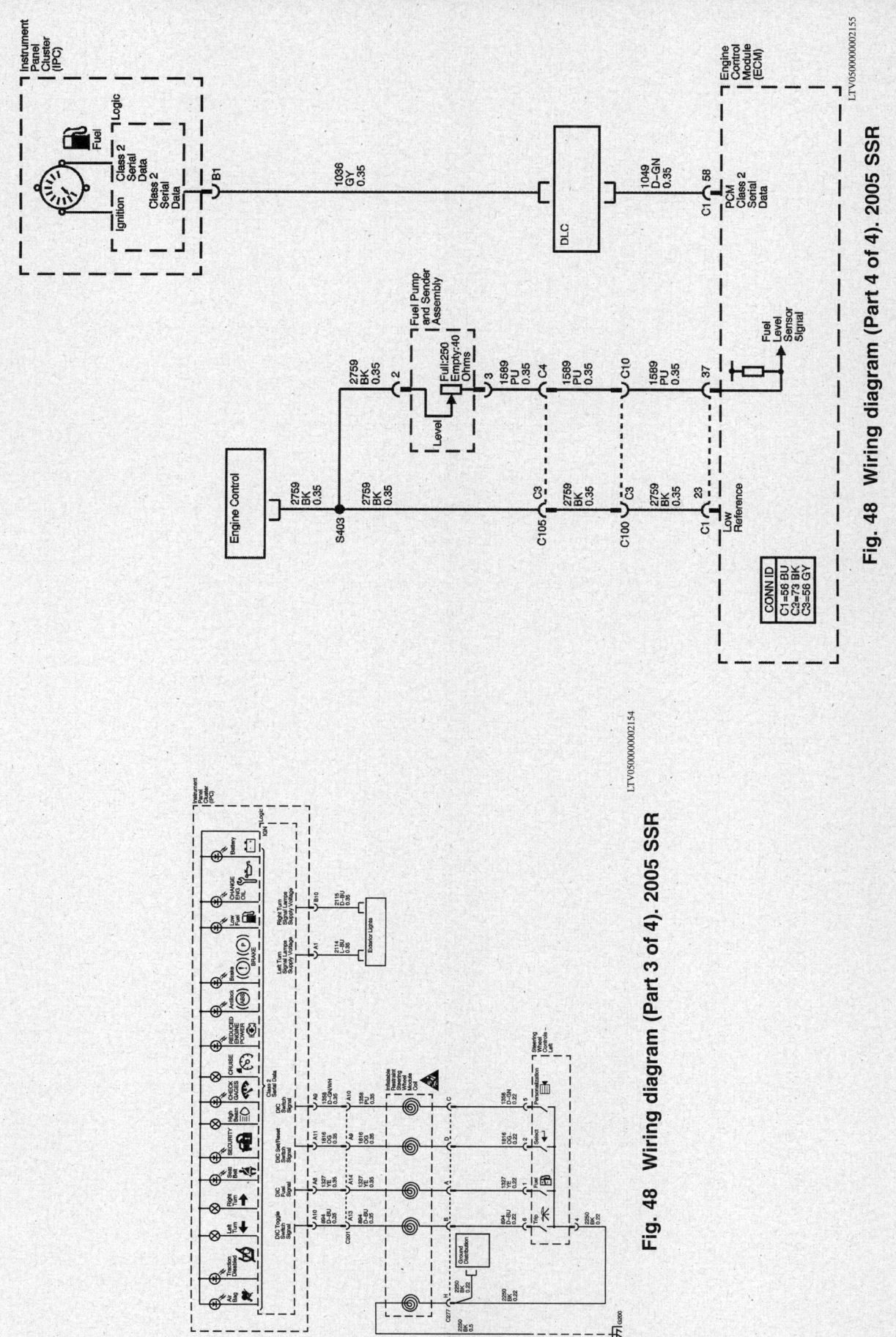

Fig. 48 Wiring diagram (Part 4 of 4). 2005 SSR

Fig. 48 Wiring diagram (Part 3 of 4). 2005 SSR

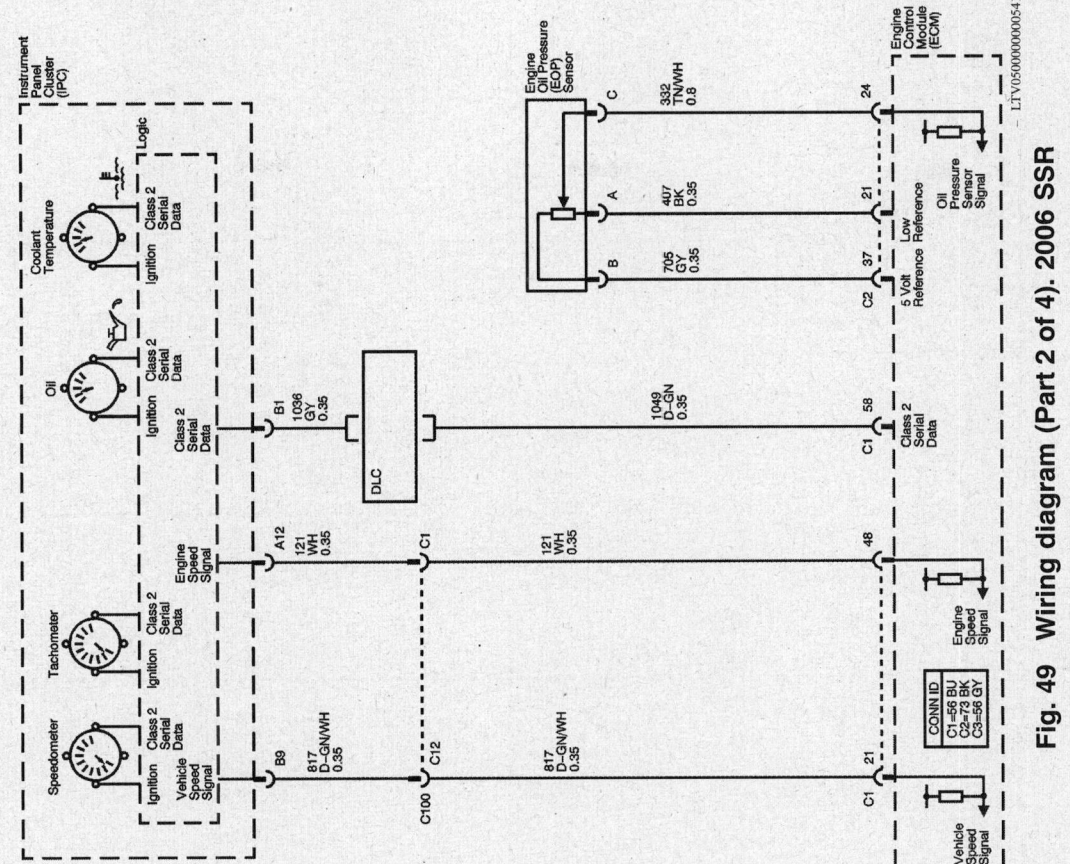

Fig. 49   Wiring diagram (Part 2 of 4). 2006 SSR

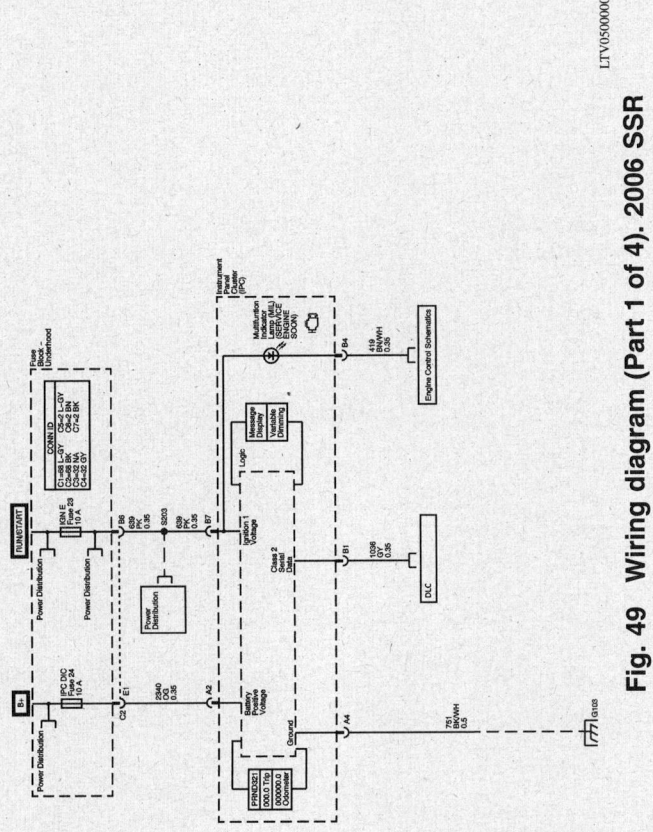

Fig. 49   Wiring diagram (Part 1 of 4). 2006 SSR

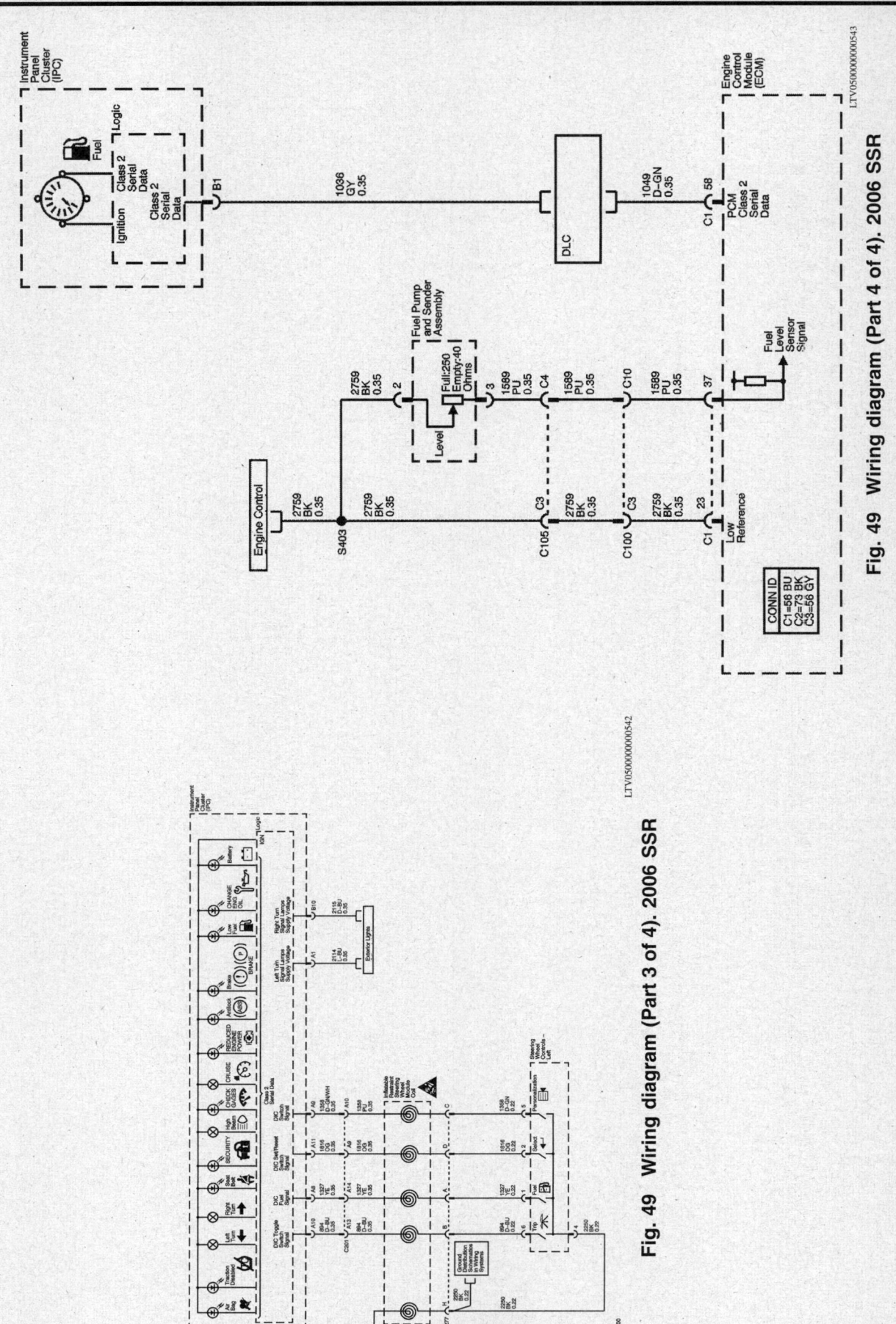

Fig. 49 Wiring diagram (Part 4 of 4). 2006 SSR

Fig. 49 Wiring diagram (Part 3 of 4). 2006 SSR

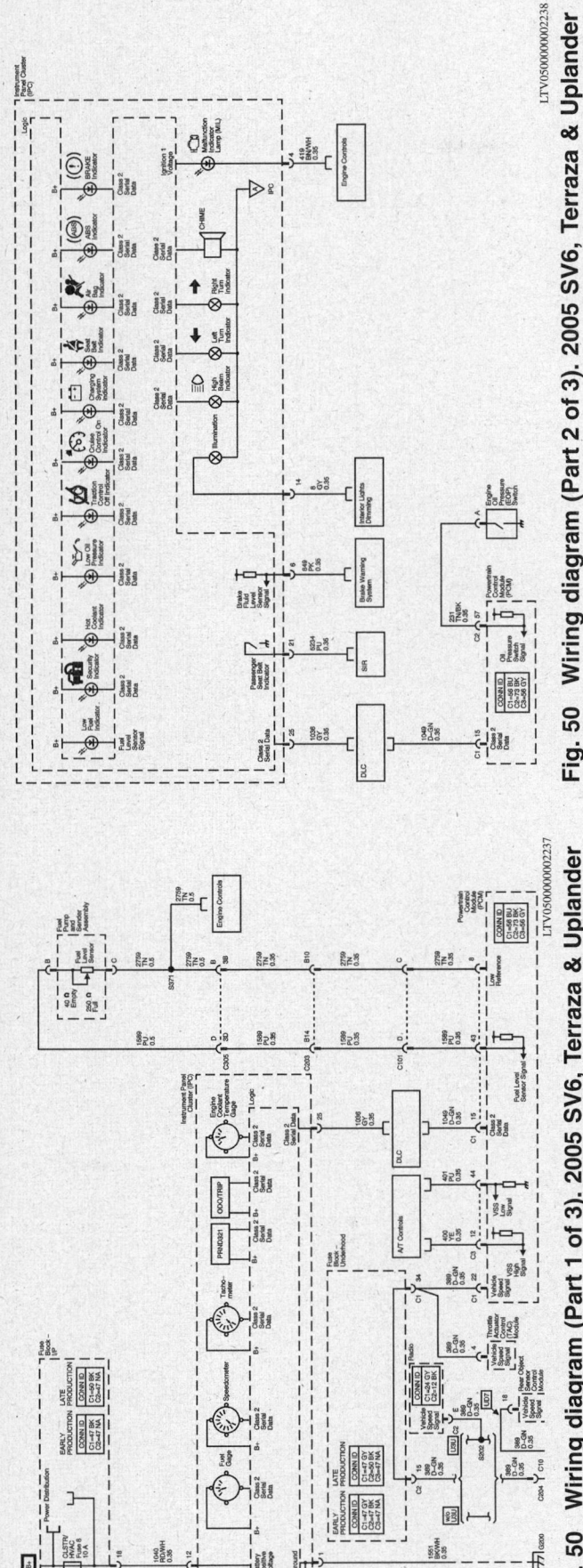

Fig. 50 Wiring diagram (Part 2 of 3). 2005 SV6, Terraza & Uplander

Fig. 51 Wiring diagram (Part 1 of 3). 2006 SV6, Terraza & Uplander

Fig. 50 Wiring diagram (Part 1 of 3). 2005 SV6, Terraza & Uplander

Fig. 50 Wiring diagram (Part 3 of 3). 2005 SV6, Terraza & Uplander

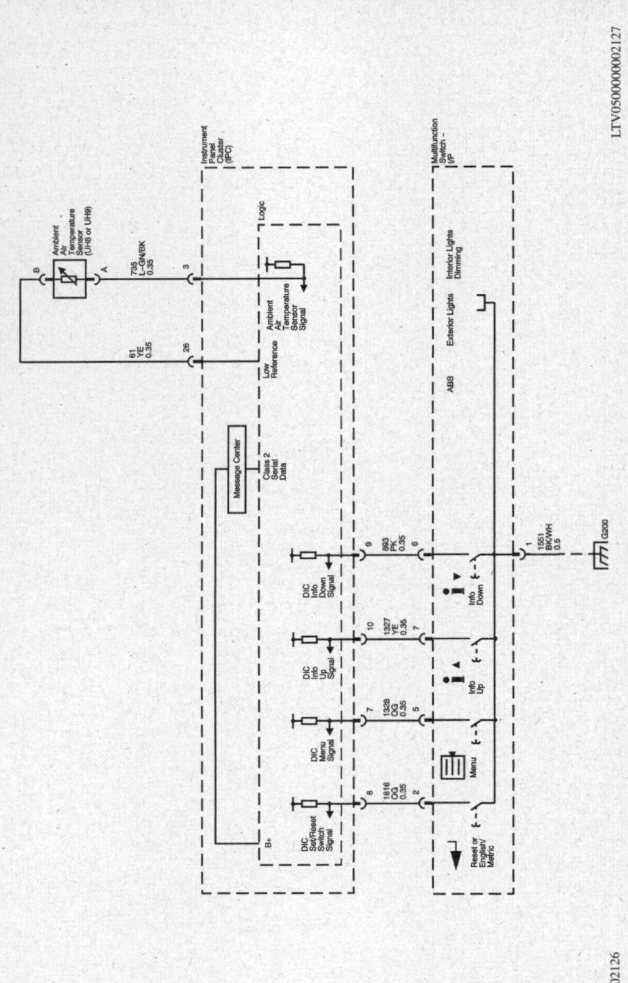

Fig. 51   Wiring diagram (Part 3 of 3). 2006 SV6, Terraza & Uplander

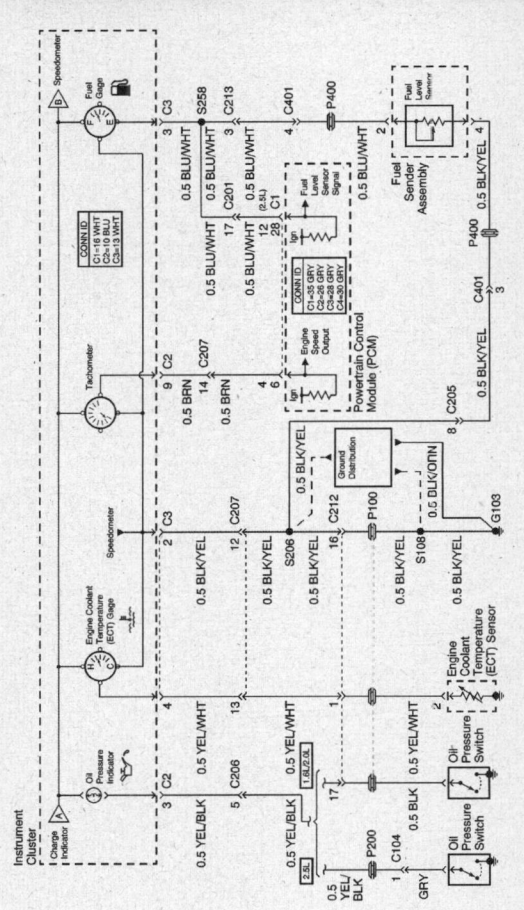

Fig. 52   Wiring diagram (Part 2 of 6). 2002 Tracker

Fig. 51   Wiring diagram (Part 2 of 3). 2006 SV6, Terraza & Uplander

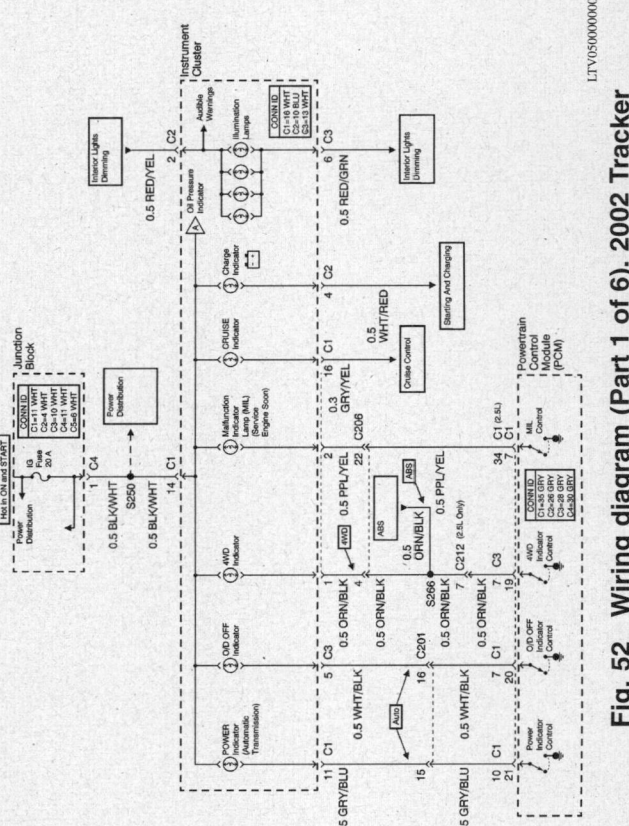

Fig. 52   Wiring diagram (Part 1 of 6). 2002 Tracker

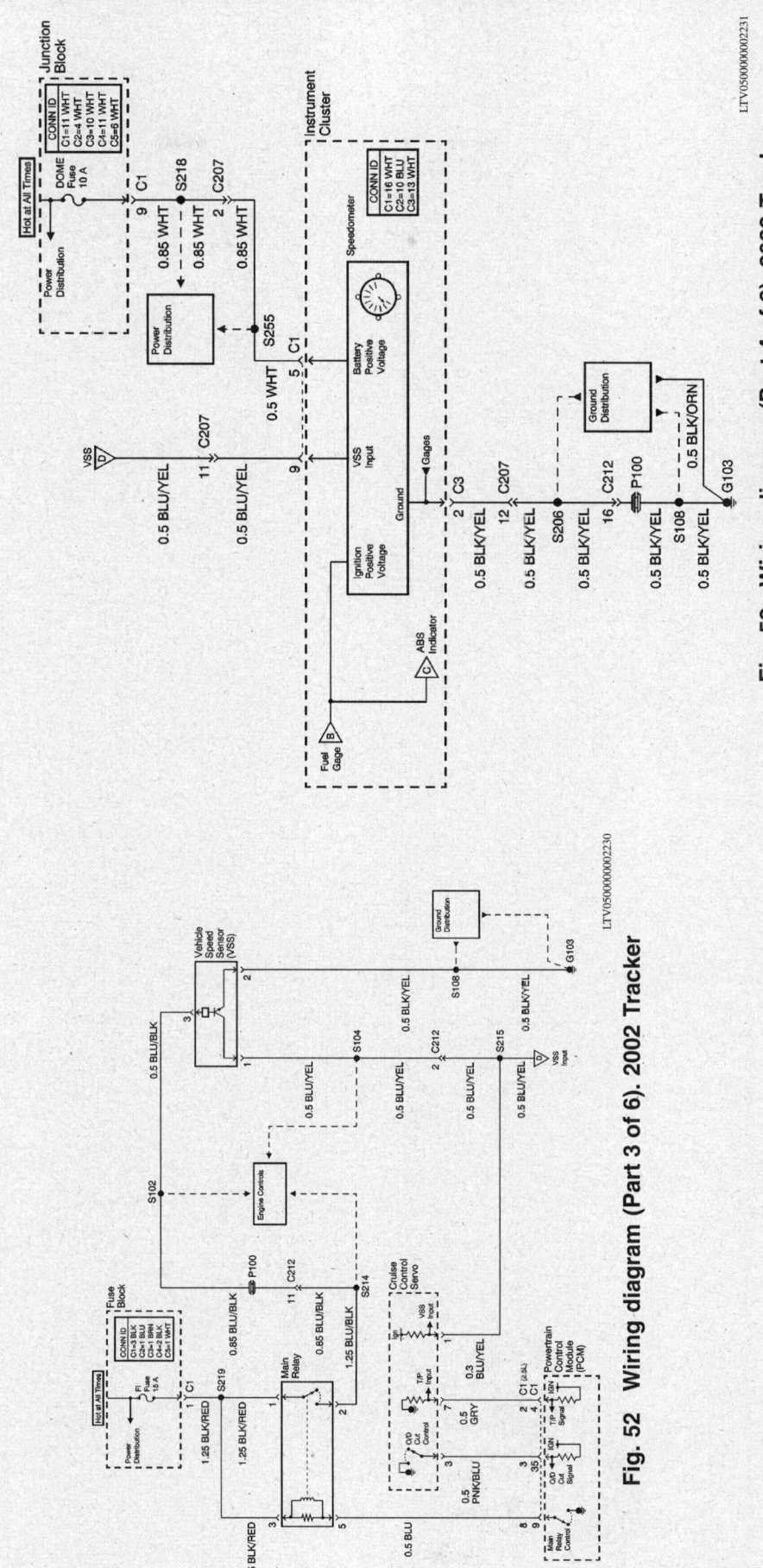

Fig. 52 Wiring diagram (Part 4 of 6). 2002 Tracker

Fig. 52 Wiring diagram (Part 3 of 6). 2002 Tracker

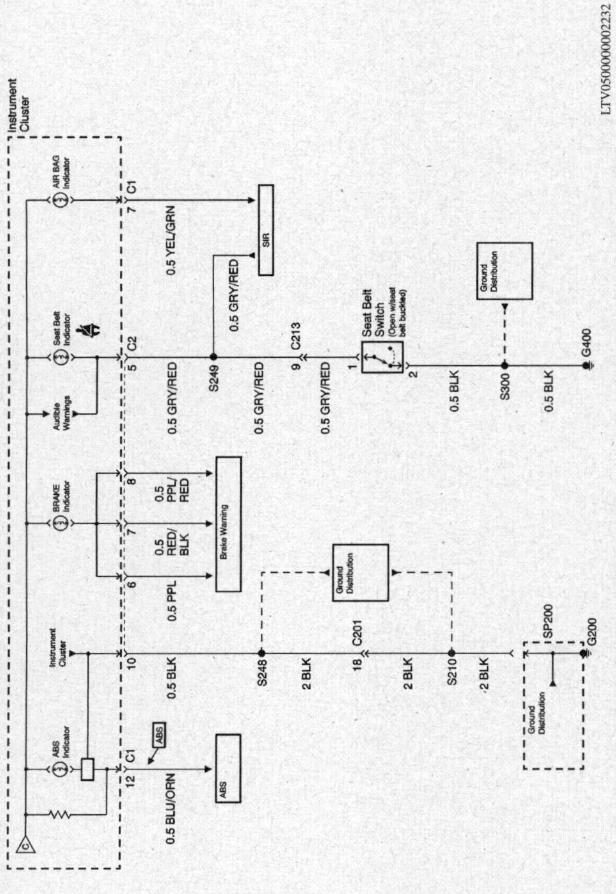

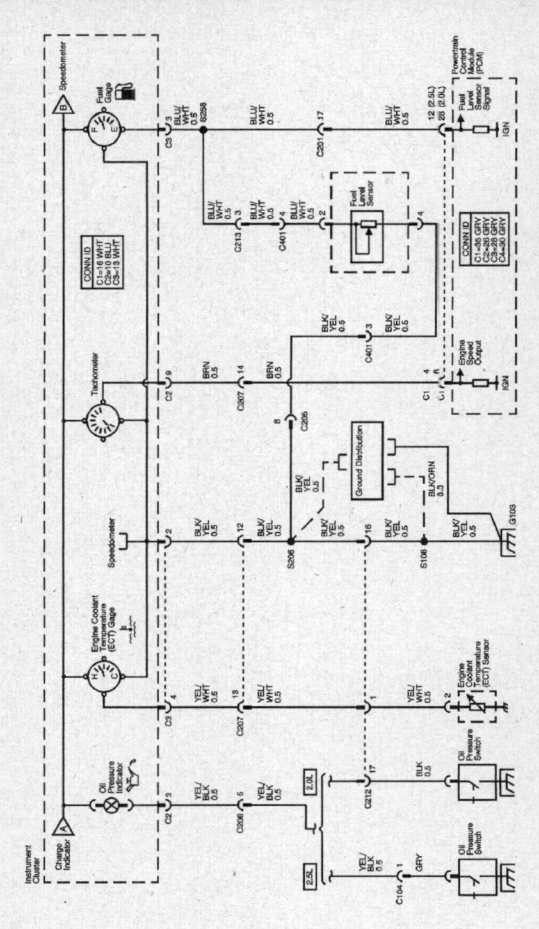

Fig. 52 Wiring diagram (Part 6 of 6). 2002 Tracker

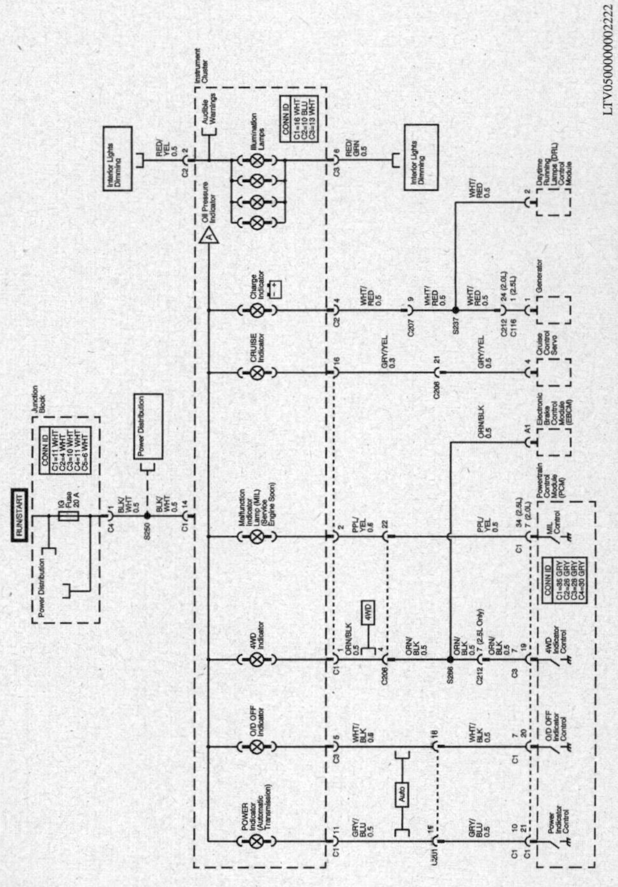

Fig. 53 Wiring diagram (Part 2 of 6). 2003 Tracker

Fig. 52 Wiring diagram (Part 5 of 6). 2002 Tracker

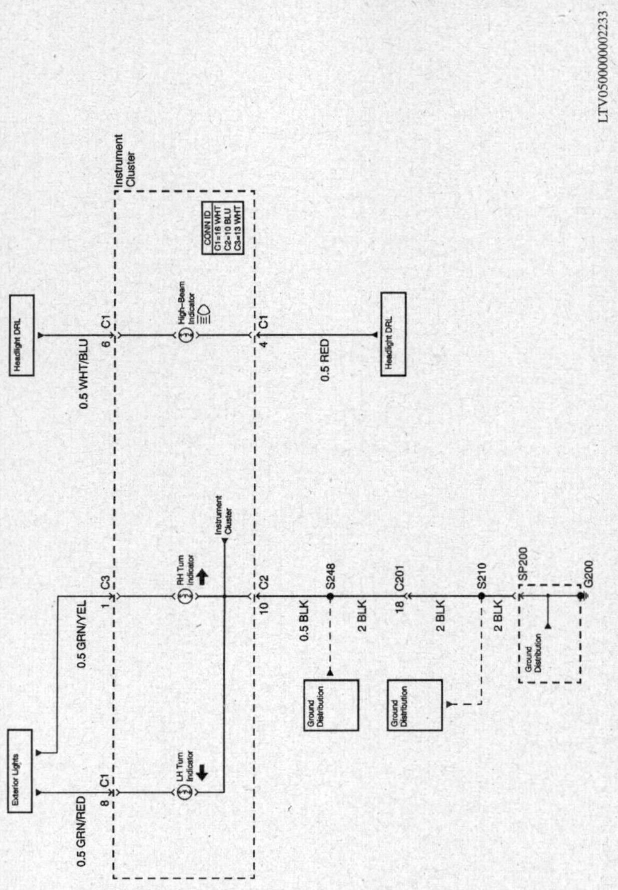

Fig. 53 Wiring diagram (Part 1 of 6). 2003 Tracker

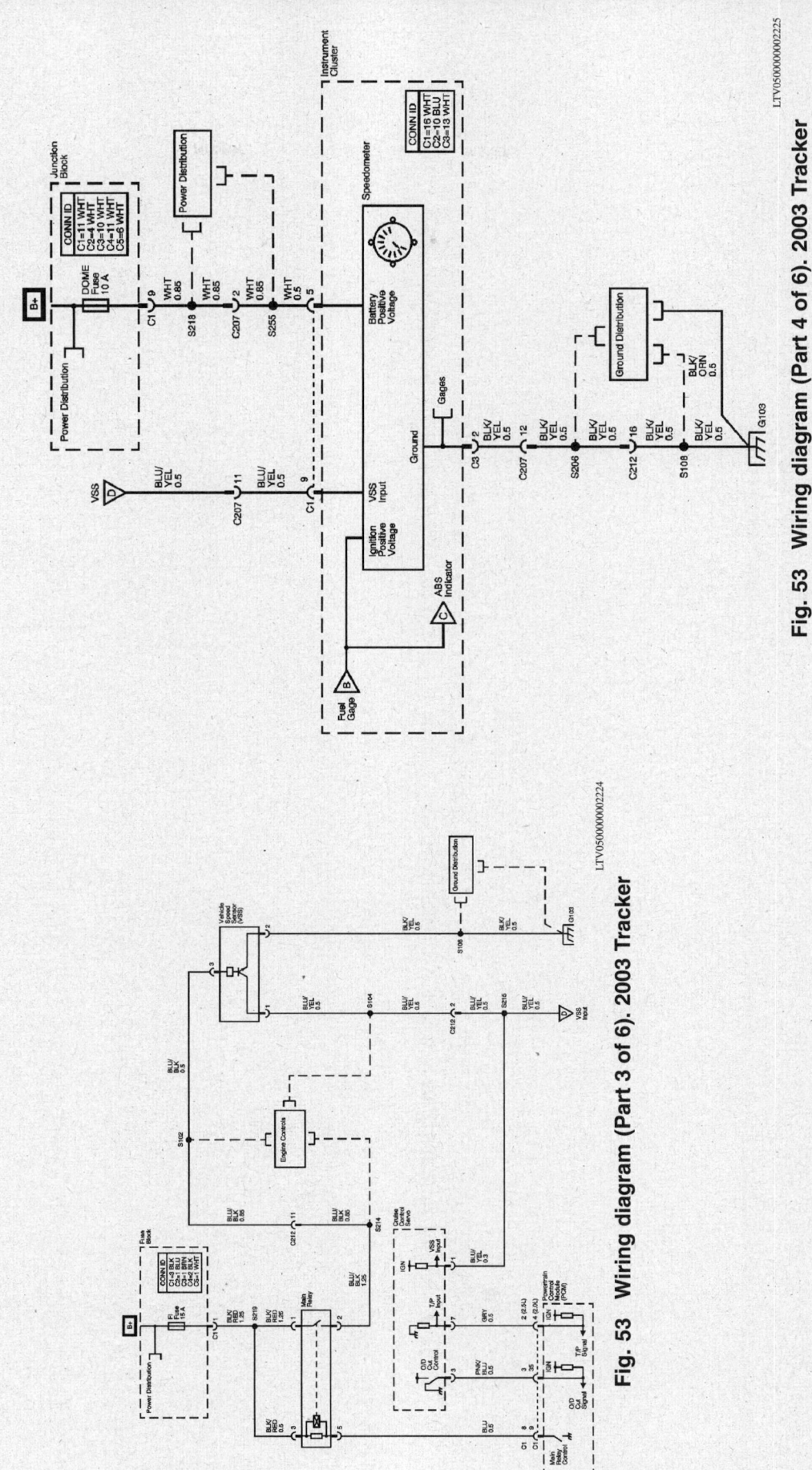

Fig. 53   Wiring diagram (Part 4 of 6). 2003 Tracker

Fig. 53   Wiring diagram (Part 3 of 6). 2003 Tracker

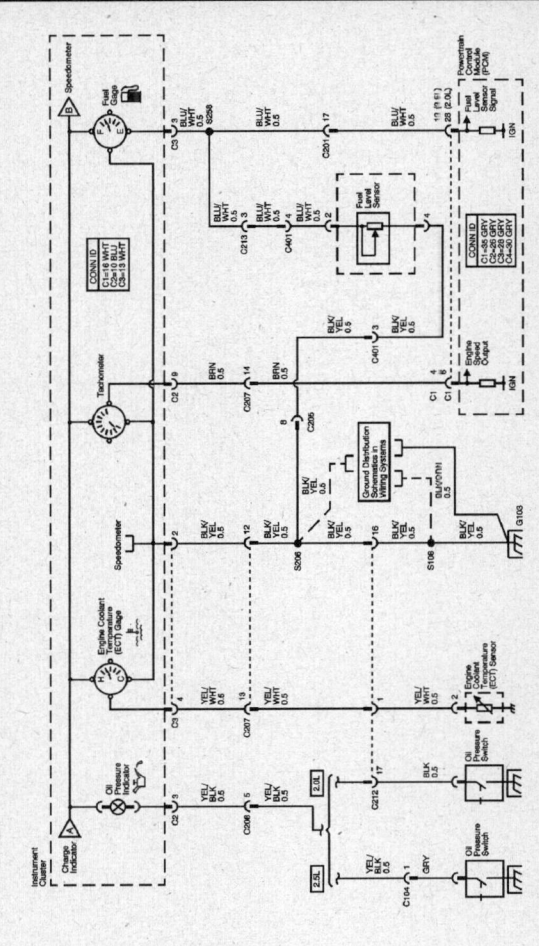

LTV050000002226

Fig. 53 Wiring diagram (Part 5 of 6). 2003 Tracker

LTV050000002227

Fig. 53 Wiring diagram (Part 6 of 6). 2003 Tracker

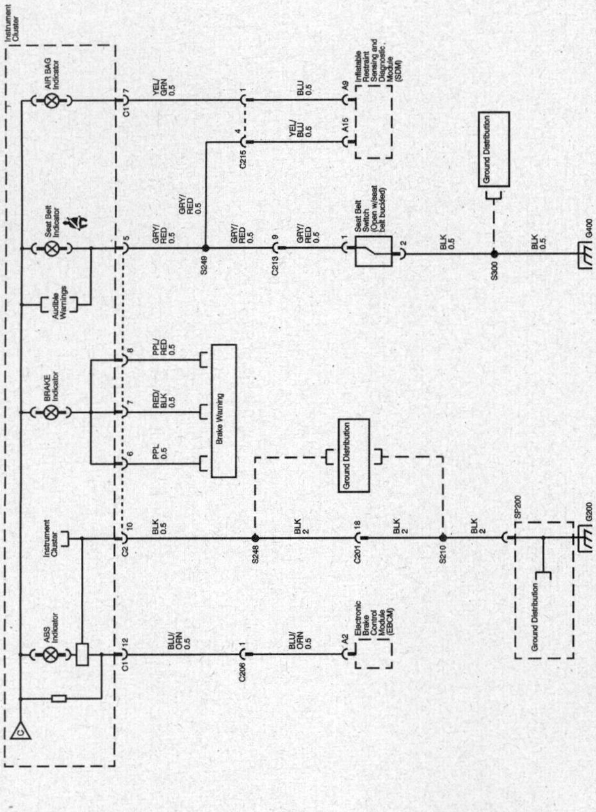

LTV050000002116

Fig. 54 Wiring diagram (Part 1 of 6). 2004 Tracker

LTV050000002117

Fig. 54 Wiring diagram (Part 2 of 6). 2004 Tracker

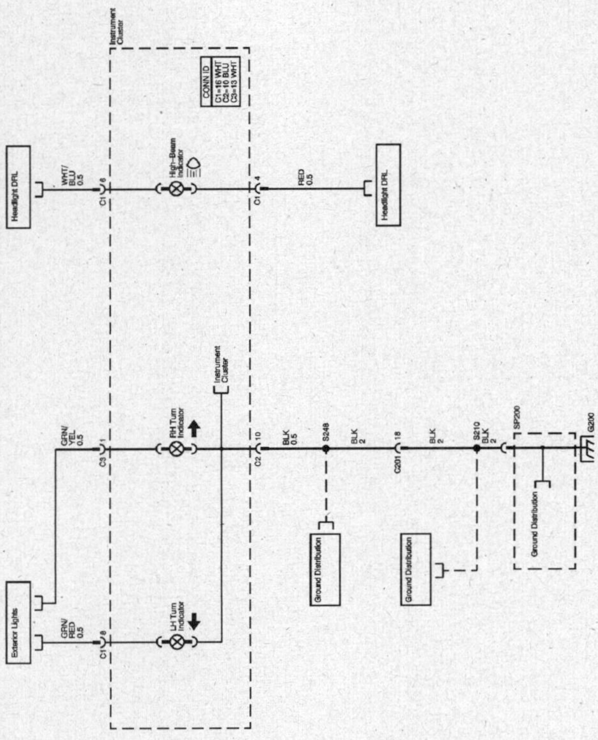

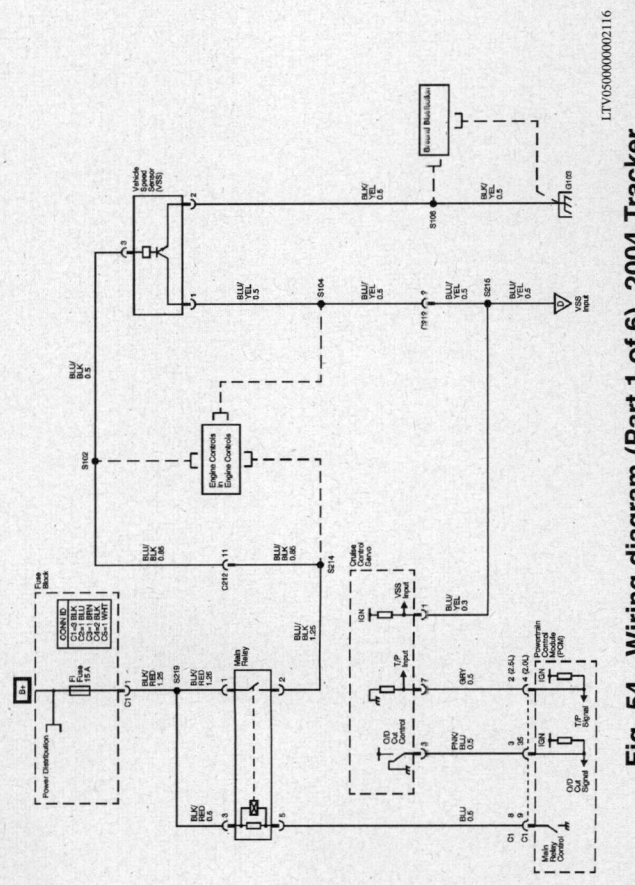

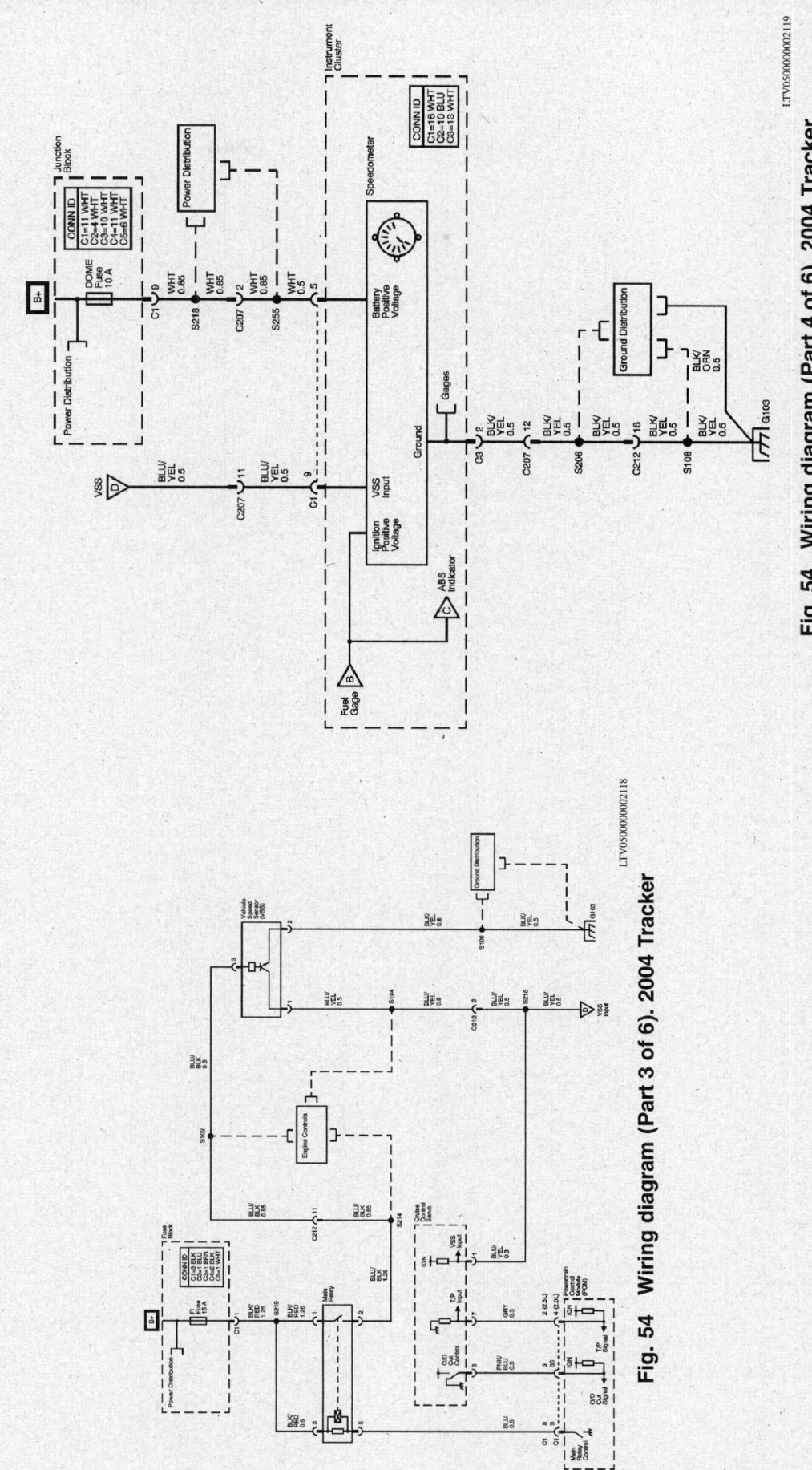

Fig. 54   Wiring diagram (Part 4 of 6). 2004 Tracker

Fig. 54   Wiring diagram (Part 3 of 6). 2004 Tracker

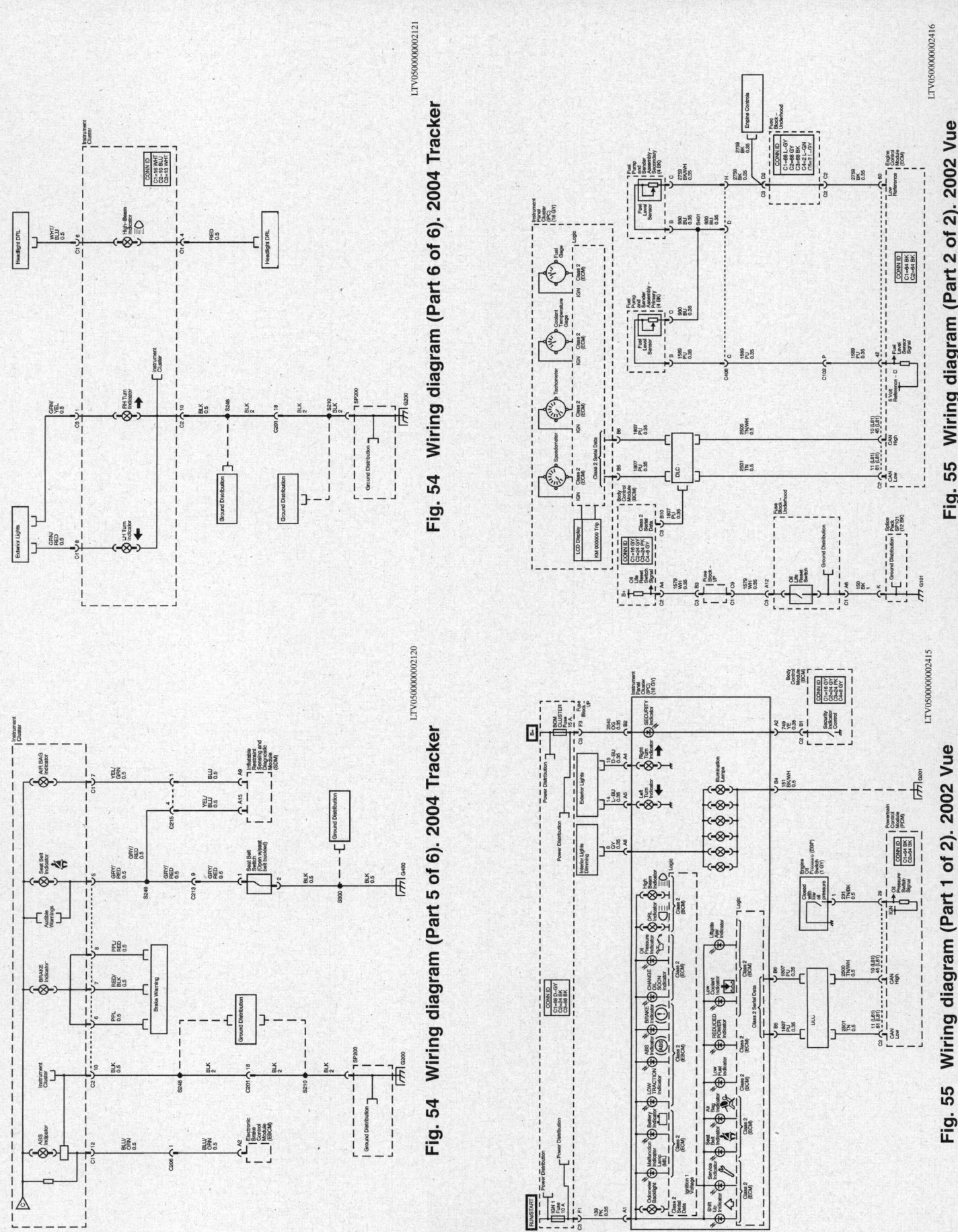

Fig. 54 Wiring diagram (Part 6 of 6). 2004 Tracker

Fig. 55 Wiring diagram (Part 2 of 2). 2002 Vue

Fig. 54 Wiring diagram (Part 5 of 6). 2004 Tracker

Fig. 55 Wiring diagram (Part 1 of 2). 2002 Vue

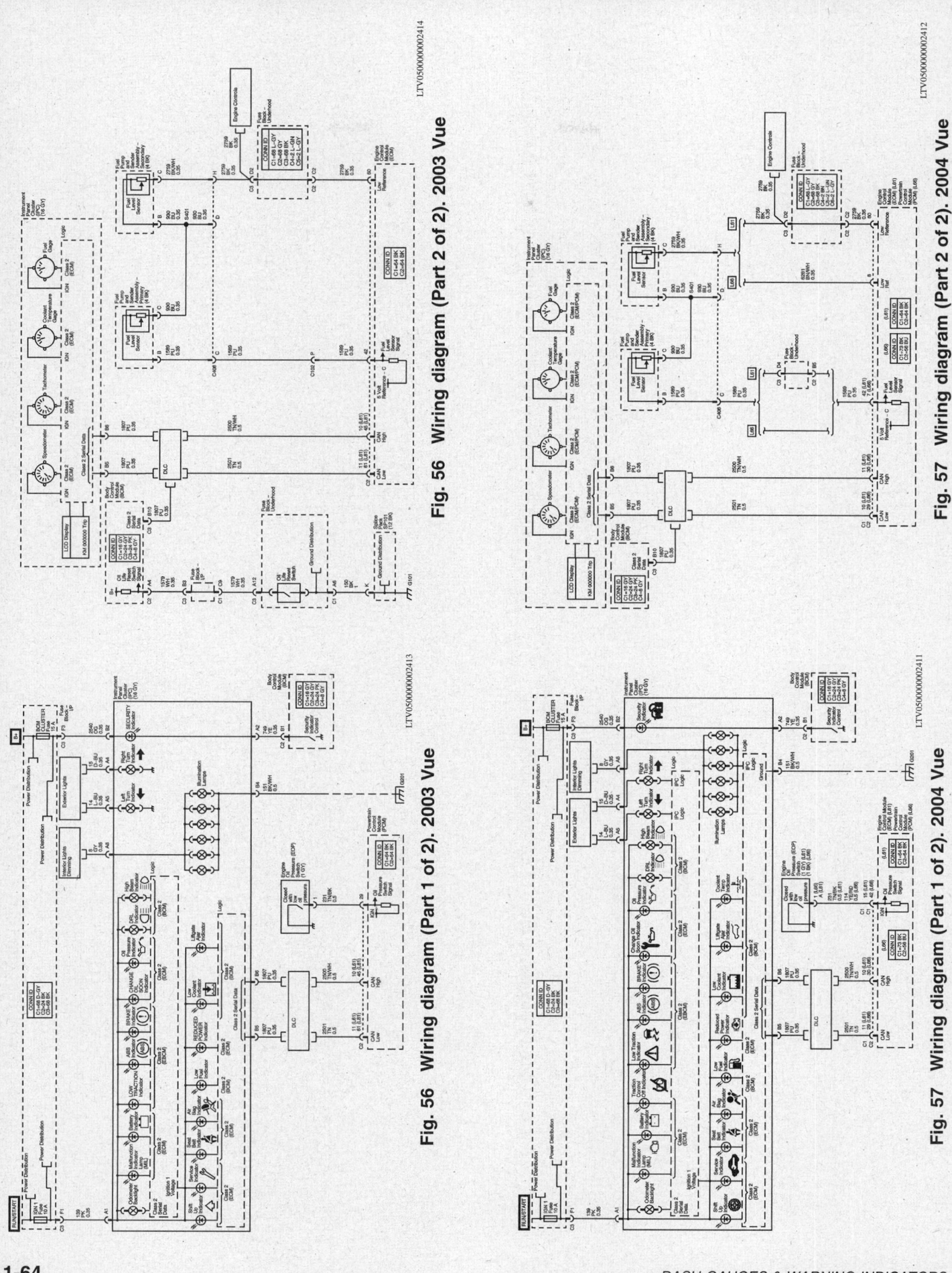

Fig. 56 Wiring diagram (Part 2 of 2). 2003 Vue

Fig. 57 Wiring diagram (Part 2 of 2). 2004 Vue

Fig. 56 Wiring diagram (Part 1 of 2). 2003 Vue

Fig. 57 Wiring diagram (Part 1 of 2). 2004 Vue

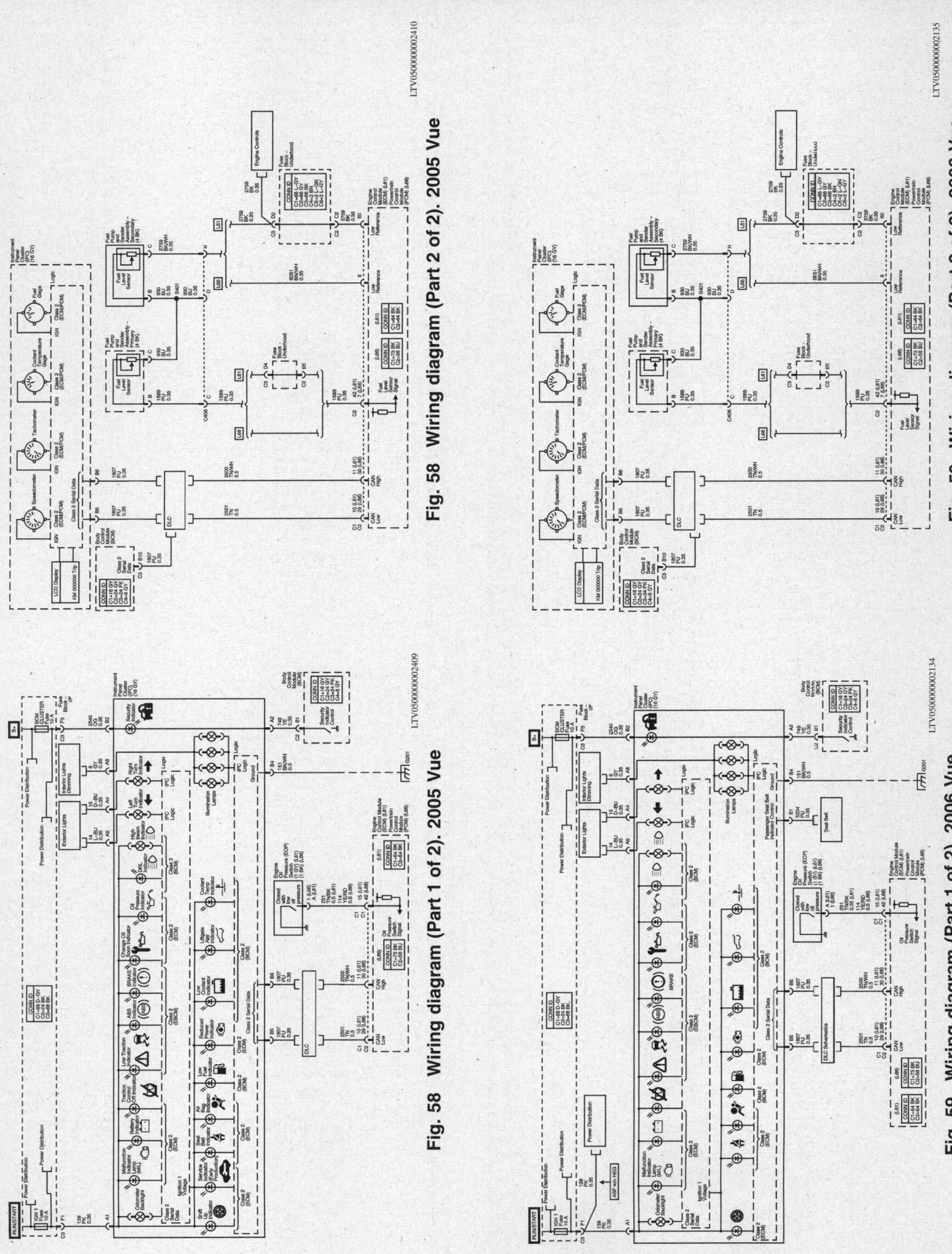

Fig. 58 Wiring diagram (Part 2 of 2). 2005 Vue

Fig. 59 Wiring diagram (Part 2 of 2). 2006 Vue

Fig. 58 Wiring diagram (Part 1 of 2). 2005 Vue

Fig. 59 Wiring diagram (Part 1 of 2). 2006 Vue

Step	Action	Yes	No
1	Did you perform the Diagnostic System Check - Vehicle?	Go to Step 2	Go to Diagnostic System Check
2	1. Install a scan tool. 2. Turn the ignition ON, with the engine OFF. 3. With the scan tool, perform the Coolant Gauge Sweep Test. Does the engine coolant temperature gage move up and down when commanded?	Test for Intermittent and Poor Connections	Go to Step 3
3	Replace the instrument panel cluster (IPC). Did you complete the replacement?	Go to Step 4	--
4	Operate the system in order to verify the repair. Did you correct the condition?	System OK	Go to Step 2

LTV0500000002871

Fig. 60 Engine coolant temperature gage inaccurate or inoperative. Astro & Safari

Step	Action	Value(s)	Yes	No
1	Did you perform the Diagnostic System Check - Vehicle?	--	Go to Step 2	Go to Diagnostic System Check -
2	Start the engine. Does the engine oil pressure gage display that the engine oil pressure is within the specified range?	10-70 psi (69-483 kPa)	Test for Intermittent Conditions and Poor Connections	Go to Step 3
3	1. Turn the ignition OFF. 2. Disconnect the engine oil pressure sensor. 3. Start the engine. Does the engine oil pressure gage display at or above the specified value?	80 psi (550 kPa)	Go to Step 4	Go to Step 6
4	1. Turn the ignition OFF. 2. Connect a 3-amp fused jumper between the signal circuit of the engine oil pressure sensor and a good ground. 3. Start the engine. Does the engine oil pressure gage display at or below the specified value?	0 psi (0 kPa)	Go to Step 7	Go to Step 5
5	Test the signal circuit of the engine oil pressure sensor for an open, for a high resistance, or for a short to voltage. Did you find and correct the condition?	--	Go to Step 12	Go to Step 9
6	Test the signal circuit of the engine oil pressure sensor for a short to ground. Did you find and correct the condition?	--	Go to Step 12	Go to Step 9

LTV0500000002872

Fig. 61 Engine oil pressure gage inaccurate or inoperative (Part 1 of 2). Astro & Safari

Step	Action		Yes	No
7	Inspect for a high resistance or for a poor connection at the case ground of the engine oil pressure sensor. Did you find and correct the condition?		Go to Step 12	Go to Step 8
8	Inspect for poor connections at the harness connector of the engine oil pressure sensor. Did you find and correct the condition?		Go to Step 12	Go to Step 10
9	Inspect for poor connections at the harness connector of the instrument panel cluster (IPC). Did you find and correct the condition?		Go to Step 12	Go to Step 11
10	Replace the engine oil pressure sensor. Did you complete the replacement?		Go to Step 12	--
11	Replace the IPC. Did you complete the replacement?		Go to Step 12	--
12	Operate the system in order to verify the repair. Did you correct the condition?		System OK	Go to Step 2

LTV0500000002873

Fig. 61 Engine oil pressure gage inaccurate or inoperative (Part 2 of 2). Astro & Safari

	Action		Yes	No
1	Did you perform the Instrument Cluster Diagnostic System Check?		Go to Step 2	Go to Diagnostic System Check
2	1. Disconnect C310. 2. Connect the J 33431-C Signal Generator and Instrument Panel Tester between the signal circuit of the fuel level sensor and the low reference circuit of the fuel level sensor on the male terminal side of the connector. 3. Turn ON the ignition, with the engine OFF. **Important:** Verify J 33431-C resistance settings with a DMM. 4. Vary the resistance on the J 33431-C from 40-250 ohms. 5. Check Fuel Level Specifications Does the fuel gage display the correct fuel level?		Go to Step 4	Go to Step 3
3	1. Install a scan tool. 2. Turn ON the ignition, with the engine OFF. **Important:** Verify J 33431-C resistance settings with a DMM. 3. Vary the resistance on the J 33431-C from 40-250 ohms. 4. Check Fuel Level Specifications **Important:** Turn the ignition OFF momentarily between the resistance settings in order to quickly update the scan tool display. 5. With the scan tool, observe the Fuel Level Sensor parameter in the PCM Enhanced EVAP Data list. Does the Fuel Level Sensor parameter display the correct fuel level?		Go to Step 11	Go to Step 5

LTV0500000002874

Fig. 62 Fuel gage inaccurate or inoperative (Part 1 of 3). Astro & Safari

Step	Action	Value(s)	Yes	No
4	Inspect for the following items: • A poor connection at the harness connector of the fuel level sensor • A misaligned fuel level sender • A deformed fuel tank • A high resistance in the signal circuit or low reference circuit of the fuel level sensor between the fuel level sensor and C310 Did you find and correct the condition?	--	Go to Step 13	Go to Step 7
5	Test the signal circuit of the fuel level sensor for a high resistance. Did you find and correct the condition?	--	Go to Step 13	Go to Step 6
6	Test the low reference circuit of the fuel level sensor for a high resistance. Did you find and correct the condition?	--	Go to Step 13	Go to Step 9

7	1. Remove the fuel level sender.
	2. Inspect for the following items:
	  - A stuck fuel level sender such as the fuel strainer interfering with the sender float arm
	  - Foreign material in the fuel tank such as ice
	
	Did you find and correct the condition?
		--	Go to Step 13	Go to Step 8

8	1. With the DMM, measure the resistance of the fuel level sensor while moving the float arm. 2. Observe both the analog and digital displays on the DMM. Does the resistance change smoothly across the specified range?	40-250 ohms	Go to Diagnostic Aids	Go to Step 10

LTV0500000002875

Fig. 62 Fuel gage inaccurate or inoperative (Part 2 of 3). Astro & Safari

Step	Action	Value(s)	Yes	No
9	Inspect for poor connections at the harness connector of the PCM. Did you find and correct the condition?	--	Go to Step 13	Go to Step 12
10	Replace the fuel level sender. Did you complete the replacement?	--	Go to Step 13	--
11	Replace the instrument panel cluster (IPC). Did you complete the replacement?	--	Go to Step 13	--
12	Replace the PCM. Did you complete the replacement?	--	Go to Step 13	--
13	1. Use the scan tool in order to clear the PCM DTCs. 2. Operate the system in order to verify the repair. Did you correct the condition?	--	System OK	Go to Step 2

LTV0500000002876

Fig. 62 Fuel gage inaccurate or inoperative (Part 3 of 3). Astro & Safari

Step	Action	Yes	No
1	Did you perform the Diagnostic System Check - Vehicle?	Go to Step 2	Go to Diagnostic System Check -
2	Activate the trip reset button. Does the odometer display switch between trip and odometer?	Test for Intermittent Conditions and Poor Connections	Go to Step 3
3	Replace the instrument panel cluster (IPC). Did you complete the replacement?	Go to Step 4	--
4	Operate the system in order to verify the repair. Did you correct the condition?	System OK	Go to Step 3

LTV0500000002877

Fig. 63 Odometer trip/reset switch inoperative. Astro & Safari

Step	Action	Value(s)	Yes	No
1	Did you perform the Instrument Cluster Diagnostic System Check?	--	Go to Step 2	Go to Diagnostic System Check
2	1. Install a scan tool. 2. Raise the vehicle drive wheels. 3. Start the engine. 4. Place the transmission into drive for an automatic transmission and third gear for a manual transmission. 5. With the scan tool, observe the Vehicle Speed Sensor parameter in the PCM Engine Data 1 data list. Does the Vehicle Speed Sensor parameter match the speedometer display?	--	Go to Step 3	Go to Step 4
3	Does the odometer operate properly?	--	Test for Intermittent Conditions and Poor Connections	Go to Step 11
4	1. Turn the ignition OFF. 2. Disconnect the driver information center (DIC). 3. Start the engine. 4. Place the transmission into drive. 5. With the scan tool, observe the Vehicle Speed Sensor parameter. Does the Vehicle Speed Sensor parameter match the speedometer display?	--	Go to Step 7	Go to Step 5

LTV0500000002878

Fig. 64 Speedometer and/or odometer inaccurate or inoperative (Part 1 of 2). Astro & Safari

Step	Action		Yes	No
5	1. Turn the ignition OFF. 2. Disconnect the powertrain control module (PCM) connector C2. 3. Turn the ignition ON. 4. Measure the voltage from the vehicle speed signal circuit to a good ground. Does the voltage measure greater than the specified value?	9 V	Go to Step 9	Go to Step 6
6	Test the vehicle speed signal circuit for an open or for a high resistance between the instrument panel cluster (IPC) and the PCM. Did you find and correct the condition?	--	Go to Step 13	Go to Step 8
7	Inspect for poor connections at the harness connector of the DIC. Did you find and correct the condition?	--	Go to Step 13	Go to Step 10
8	Inspect for poor connections at the harness connector of the IPC. Did you find and correct the condition?	--	Go to Step 13	Go to Step 11
9	Inspect for poor connections at the harness connector of the PCM. Did you find and correct the condition?	--	Go to Step 13	Go to Step 12
10	Replace the DIC. Did you complete the replacement?	--	Go to Step 13	--
11	Replace the IPC. Did you complete the replacement?	--	Go to Step 13	--
12	Replace the PCM. Did you complete the replacement?	--	Go to Step 13	--
13	Operate the system in order to verify the repair. Did you correct the condition?	--	System OK	Go to Step 2

LTV0500000002879

Fig. 64   Speedometer and/or odometer inaccurate or inoperative (Part 2 of 2). Astro & Safari

Step	Action	Yes	No
1	Did you perform the Diagnostic System Check - Vehicle?	Go to Step 2	Go to Diagnostic System Check
2	1. Install a scan tool. 2. Turn the ignition ON, with the engine OFF. 3. With the scan tool, perform the Lamp Test in the Instrument Panel Cluster Special Functions. Does the low fuel indicator illuminate when commanded ON?	Test for Intermittent and Poor Connections	Go to Step 3
3	Replace the instrument panel cluster (IPC). Did you complete the replacement?	Go to Step 4	--
4	Operate the system in order to verify the repair. Did you correct the condition?	System OK	Go to Step 2

LTV0500000002881

Fig. 66   Low fuel indicator inoperative. Astro & Safari

Step	Action	Yes	No
1	Did you perform the Diagnostic System Check - Vehicle?	Go to Step 2	Go to Diagnostic System Check -
2	1. Install a scan tool. 2. Turn the ignition ON, with the engine OFF. 3. Compare the scan tool Battery Voltage parameter in the BCM Data data list to the volt gage display. Does the Battery Voltage parameter approximately match the volt gage display?	Go to Diagnostic System Check -	Go to Step 3
3	Replace the instrument panel cluster (IPC). Did you complete the replacement?	Go to Step 4	--
4	Operate the system in order to verify the repair. Did you correct the condition?	System OK	Go to Step 2

LTV0500000002880

Fig. 65   Volt gage inaccurate or inoperative. Astro & Safari

Step	Action	Yes	No
1	Did you review the Driver Information Center (DIC) Description and Operation?	Go to Step 2	Go to Driver Information Center (DIC) Description and Operation
2	Test the instrument panel (I/P) lamp supply voltage circuit of the DIC for an open. Did you find and correct the condition?	Go to Step 7	Go to Step 3
3	Test the RAP fuse supply voltage circuit of the DIC for an open. Did you find and correct the condition?	Go to Step 7	Go to Step 4
4	Test the ground circuit of the DIC for an open or for a high resistance. Did you find and correct the condition?	Go to Step 7	Go to Step 5
5	Inspect for poor connections at the harness connector of the DIC. Did you find and correct the condition?	Go to Step 7	Go to Step 6
6	Replace the DIC. Did you complete the replacement?	Go to Step 7	--
7	Operate the system in order to verify the repair. Did you correct the condition?	System OK	Go to Step 2

LTV0500000003282

Fig. 67   Driver information center (DIC) inoperative. Astro & Safari

Step	Action	Yes	No
1	Did you review the Driver Information Center (DIC) Description and Operation?	Go to Step 2	Go to Driver Information Center (DIC) Description and Operation
2	1. Disconnect the ambient temperature sensor. 2. Connect the J 33431-C Signal Generator and Instrument Panel Tester between the signal circuit of the ambient temperature sensor and the ground circuit of the ambient temperature sensor. 3. Turn ON the ignition, with the engine OFF. **Important** Verify the J 33431-C resistance settings with a DMM. Disconnect one of the J 33431-C leads momentarily between the resistance settings in order to quickly update the DIC display. 4. Vary the resistance on the J 33431-C from 2,500-11,200 ohms. 5. Check Ambient Air Temperature Sensor Resistance in order to convert from resistance to DIC temperature display. Does the DIC display the correct temperature?	Go to Step 4	Go to Step 3
3	Test the signal circuit of the ambient temperature sensor for a short to ground. Did you find and correct the condition?	Go to Step 7	Go to Step 6

LTV0500000003283

Fig. 68 Driver information center (DIC) temperature display always reads SC (Part 1 of 2). Astro & Safari

Step	Action	Yes	No
1	Did you review the Driver Information Center (DIC) Description and Operation?	Go to Step 2	Go to Driver Information Center (DIC) Description and Operation
2	1. Disconnect the ambient temperature sensor. 2. Connect the J 33431-C Signal Generator and Instrument Panel Tester between the signal circuit of the ambient temperature sensor and the ground circuit of the ambient temperature sensor. 3. Turn the ignition ON, with the engine OFF. **Important** Verify the J 33431-C resistance settings with a DMM. Disconnect one of the J 33431-C leads momentarily between the resistance settings in order to quickly update the DIC display. 4. Vary the resistance on the J 33431-C from 2500-11200 ohms. 5. Check Ambient Air Temperature Sensor Resistance in order to convert from resistance to DIC temperature display. Does the DIC display the correct temperature?	Go to Step 5	Go to Step 3
3	Test the signal circuit of the ambient temperature sensor for an open. Did you find and correct the condition?	Go to Step 9	Go to Step 4
4	Test the ground circuit of the ambient temperature sensor for an open. Did you find and correct the condition?	Go to Step 9	Go to Step 6

LTV0500000003285

Fig. 69 Driver information center (DIC) temperature display always reads OC (Part 1 of 2). Astro & Safari

Step	Action	Yes	No
4	Inspect for a poor connection at the harness connector of the ambient temperature sensor. Did you find and correct the condition?	Go to Step 7	Go to Step 5
5	Replace the ambient temperature sensor. Did you complete the replacement?	Go to Step 7	--
6	Replace the DIC. Did you complete the replacement?	Go to Step 7	--
7	Operate the system in order to verify the repair. Did you correct the condition?	System OK	Go to Step 2

LTV0500000003284

Fig. 68 Driver information center (DIC) temperature display always reads SC (Part 2 of 2). Astro & Safari

Step	Action	Yes	No
5	Inspect for poor connections at the harness connector of the ambient temperature sensor. Did you find and correct the condition?	Go to Step 9	Go to Step 7
6	Inspect for poor connections at the harness connector of the DIC. Did you find and correct the condition?	Go to Step 9	Go to Step 8
7	Replace the ambient temperature sensor. Did you complete the replacement?	Go to Step 9	--
8	Replace the DIC. Did you complete the replacement?	Go to Step 9	--
9	Operate the system in order to verify the repair. Did you correct the condition?	System OK	Go to Step 2

LTV0500000003286

Fig. 69 Driver information center (DIC) temperature display always reads OC (Part 2 of 2). Astro & Safari

Step	Action	Yes	No
1	Did you review the Driver Information Center (DIC) Description and Operation?	Go to Step 2	Go to Driver Information Center (DIC) Description and Operation
2	1. Disconnect the ambient temperature sensor connector. 2. Connect the J 33431-C Signal Generator and Instrument Panel Tester between the signal circuit of the ambient temperature sensor and the ground circuit of the ambient temperature sensor. 3. Turn the ignition ON, with the engine OFF. **Important** Verify the J 33431-C resistance settings with a DMM. Disconnect one of the J 33431-C leads momentarily between the resistance settings in order to quickly update the DIC display. 4. Vary the resistance on the J 33431-C from 2500-11200 ohms. 5. Check Ambient Air Temperature Sensor Resistance in order to convert from resistance to DIC temperature display. Does the DIC display the correct temperature?	Go to Step 5	Go to Step 3
3	Test the signal circuit of the ambient temperature sensor for a high resistance. Did you find and correct the condition?	Go to Step 9	Go to Step 4
4	Test the ground circuit of the ambient temperature sensor for a high resistance. Did you find and correct the condition?	Go to Step 9	Go to Step 6

LTV0500000003287

Fig. 70 Driver information center (DIC) temperature inaccurate or inoperative (Part 1 of 2). Astro & Safari

Step	Action	Yes	No
5	Inspect for poor connections at the harness connector of the ambient temperature sensor. Did you find and correct the condition?	Go to Step 9	Go to Step 7
6	Inspect for poor connections at the harness connector of the DIC. Did you find and correct the condition?	Go to Step 9	Go to Step 8
7	Replace the ambient temperature sensor. Did you complete the replacement?	Go to Step 9	--
8	Replace the DIC. Did you complete the replacement?	Go to Step 9	
9	Operate the system in order to verify the repair. Did you correct the condition?	System OK	Go to Step 2

LTV0500000003288

Fig. 70 Driver information center (DIC) temperature inaccurate or inoperative (Part 2 of 2). Astro & Safari

Step	Action	Yes	No
1	Did you review the Driver Information Center (DIC) Description and Operation?	Go to Step 2	Go to Driver Information Center (DIC) Description and Operation
2	Press each of the DIC switches. Do the switches operate normally?	Test for Intermittent and Poor Connections	Go to Step 3
3	Replace the DIC. Did you complete the replacement?	Go to Step 4	--
4	Operate the system in order to verify the repair. Did you correct the condition?	System OK	Go to Step 2

LTV0500000003290

Fig. 72 Driver information center (DIC) switch(es) inoperative. Astro & Safari

Step	Action	Yes	No
1	Did you review the Driver Information Center (DIC) Description and Operation?	Go to Step 2	Go to Driver Information Center (DIC) Description and Operation
2	Verify that the compass is inaccurate or that CAL or C is displayed. Does the system operate normally?	Test for Intermittent and Poor Connections	Go to Step 3
3	Turn the ignition ON, with the engine OFF. Is the compass display blank?	Go to Step 7	Go to Step 4
4	Is CAL or C displayed?	Go to Step 5	Go to Step 6
5	Perform the compass calibration procedure. Does the compass operate properly?	Go to Step 8	Go to Step 6
6	Perform the compass variance procedure. Does the compass operate properly?	Go to Step 8	Go to Step 7
7	Replace the DIC. Did you complete the replacement?	Go to Step 8	--
8	Operate the system in order to verify the repair. Did you correct the condition?	System OK	Go to Step 2

LTV0500000003289

Fig. 71 Driver information center (DIC) compass inaccurate or C displayed. Astro & Safari

Step	Action	Yes	No
1	Did you perform the Diagnostic System Check - Vehicle?	Go to Step 2	Go to Diagnostic System Check
2	1. Turn the headlamps OFF. 2. Turn the ignition OFF. 3. Remove the key from the ignition. 4. Close all doors. Does the chime sound?	Go to Step 3	Test for Intermittent and Poor Connections
3	Do any indicators illuminate when the chime sounds?	Go to Symptoms	Go to Step 4
4	1. Install a scan tool. 2. Turn the ignition ON, with the engine OFF. 3. Observe the Key in Ignition parameter in the BCM Input 1 data List. 4. Turn the ignition OFF. 5. Remove and insert the key from the ignition. Does the Key in Ignition parameter change states?	Go to Step 8	Go to Step 5
5	Test the key in ignition signal circuit for a short to ground. Did you find and correct the condition?	Go to Step 9	Go to Step 6
6	Inspect for poor connections at the harness connector of the ignition key alarm switch. Did you find and correct the condition?	Go to Step 9	Go to Step 7
7	Replace the ignition switch. Did you complete the replacement?	Go to Step 9	--
8	Replace the body control module (BCM). Did you complete the replacement?	Go to Step 9	--
9	Operate the system in order to verify the repair. Did you correct the condition?	System OK	Go to Step 3

LTV0500000003291

Fig. 73 Chime always on. Astro & Safari

Step	Action	Value(s)	Yes	No
1	Did you perform the Diagnostic System Check - Vehicle?	--	Go to Step 2	Go to Diagnostic System Check
2	Replace the body control module (BCM). Did you complete the replacement?	--	Go to Step 3	--
3	Operate the system in order to verify the repair. Did you correct the condition?	--	System OK	Go to Step 1

LTV0500000003292

Fig. 74   Chime inoperative. Astro & Safari

Step	Action	Yes	No
	DEFINITION: This diagnostic applies only to the analog clock (Z75 only) located in the instrument panel upper console.		
1	Did you review the operation and perform the necessary inspections?	Go to Step 2	Go to Symptoms
2	Test the battery positive voltage circuit of the clock for an open, short to ground or a high resistance. Did you find and correct the condition?	Go to Step 6	Go to Step 3
3	Test the ground circuit of the clock for an open or a high resistance. Did you find and correct the condition?	Go to Step 6	Go to Step 4
4	Inspect for poor connections at the harness connector of the clock. Did you find and correct the condition?	Go to Step 6	Go to Step 5
5	Replace the clock. Did you complete the replacement?	Go to Step 6	--
6	Operate the system in order to verify the repair. Did you correct the condition?	System OK	Go to Step 2

LTV0500000002443

Fig. 76   Clock fault. 2002 Avalanche, Escalade, Suburban, Tahoe & Yukon

Step	Action	Value(s)	Yes	No
1	Did you perform the Instrument Cluster Diagnostic System Check?	--	Go to Step 2	Go to Diagnostic System Check
2	1. Install the scan tool. 2. Turn ON the ignition, with the engine OFF. 3. With the scan tool, perform the ECT Gage Sweep Test. Does the ECT gage move up and down when commanded?	--	Test for Intermittent Conditions and Poor Connections	Go to Step 3
3	Replace the IPC. Did you complete the replacement?	--	Go to Step 4	--
4	Operate the system in order to verify the repair.	--	System OK	Go to Step 2

LTV0500000002444

Fig. 77   Engine coolant temperature gage inaccurate or inoperative. 2002 Avalanche, Escalade, Suburban, Tahoe & Yukon

Step	Action	Yes	No
1	Did you perform the Instrument Cluster Diagnostic System Check?	Go to Step 2	Go to Diagnostic System Check
2	1. Turn ON the ignition, with the engine OFF. 2. Observe the instrument cluster. Does the instrument cluster perform the displays test?	Test for Intermittent Conditions and Poor Connections	Go to Step 3
3	1. Turn OFF the ignition. 2. Disconnect the IPC. 3. Turn ON the ignition, with the engine OFF. 4. Connect a test lamp between the ignition 1 voltage circuit and a good ground. Does the test lamp illuminate?	Go to Step 4	Go to Step 7
4	Connect a test lamp between the ignition 1 voltage circuit of the instrument cluster and the ground circuit of the instrument cluster. Does the test lamp illuminate?	Go to Step 5	Go to Step 6
5	Inspect for poor connections at the harness connector of the IPC. Did you find and correct the condition?	Go to Step 9	Go to Step 8
6	Repair the open or a high resistance in the ground circuit. Did you complete the repair?	Go to Step 9	--
7	Repair the open, short to ground or high resistance in the ignition 1 voltage circuit. Did you complete the repair?	Go to Step 9	--
8	Replace the IPC. Did you complete the replacement?	Go to Step 9	--
9	Operate the system in order to verify the repair. Did you find and correct the condition?	System OK	Go to Step 3

LTV0500000002442

Fig. 75   Instrument cluster inoperative. 2002 Avalanche, Escalade, Suburban, Tahoe & Yukon

Step	Action	Value(s)	Yes	No
1	Did you perform the Instrument Cluster Diagnostic System Check?	--	Go to Step 2	Go to Diagnostic System Check -
2	Start the engine. Does the engine oil pressure gage display that the oil pressure is within the specified range?	10-80 psi (69-550 kPa)	Test for Intermittent and Poor Connections Wiring Systems	Go to Step 3
3	1. Turn OFF the ignition. 2. Disconnect the engine oil pressure sensor connector. 3. Start the engine. Does the engine oil pressure gage display at or above the specified value?	80 psi (550 kPa)	Go to Step 4	Go to Step 6
4	1. Turn OFF the ignition. 2. Connect a 3 amp fused jumper wire between the signal circuit of the oil pressure sensor and a good ground. 3. Start the engine. Does the engine oil pressure gage display at or below the specified value?	0 kPa (0 psi)	Go to Step 7	Go to Step 5
5	Test the signal circuit of the oil pressure sensor for an open, a high resistance, or a short to voltage. Did you find and correct the condition?	--	Go to Step 12	Go to Step 9
6	Test the signal circuit of the oil pressure sensor for a short to ground. Did you find and correct the condition?		Go to Step 12	Go to Step 9
7	Inspect for a high resistance or a poor connection at the case ground of the engine oil pressure sensor. Did you find and correct the condition?		Go to Step 12	Go to Step 8

LTV0500000002445

Fig. 78   Engine oil pressure gage in accurate or inoperative (Part 1 of 2). 2002 Avalanche, Escalade, Suburban, Tahoe & Yukon

Step	Action	Value(s)	Yes	No
8	Inspect for poor connections at the harness connector of the engine oil pressure sensor. Did you find and correct the condition?	--	Go to Step 12	Go to Step 10
9	Inspect for poor connections at the harness connector of the IPC. Did you find and correct the condition?	--	Go to Step 12	Go to Step 11
10	Replace the engine oil pressure sensor. Did you complete the replacement?	--	Go to Step 12	--
11	Replace the IPC. Did you complete the replacement?	--	Go to Step 12	--
12	Operate the system in order to verify the repair. Did you correct the condition?	--	System OK	Go to Step 2

LTV0500000002446

Fig. 78 Engine oil pressure gage in accurate or inoperative (Part 2 of 2). 2002 Avalanche, Escalade, Suburban, Tahoe & Yukon

Step	Action	Value(s)	Yes	No
4	Inspect for the following items: • A poor connection at the harness connectors of the fuel level senders • A high resistance in the signal circuits or the low reference circuit between the fuel level senders and C152 • A misaligned primary or secondary fuel level sender • A deformed primary or secondary fuel tank. Did you find and correct the condition?	--	Go to Step 13	Go to Step 7
5	Test the signal circuits of the fuel level senders for a high resistance between C152 and the PCM. Did you find and correct the condition?	--	Go to Step 13	Go to Step 6
6	Test the low reference circuit of the fuel level senders for a high resistance between C152 and the PCM. Did you find and correct the condition?	--	Go to Step 13	Go to Step 9
7	1. Remove the fuel level senders. 2. Inspect for the following items: - A stuck fuel level sender (i.e. the fuel strainer interfering with the sender float arm) - Foreign material in the fuel tanks (ice). Did you find and correct the condition?	--	Go to Step 13	Go to Step 8
8	1. With the J 39200 DMM, measure the resistance of the fuel level senders while moving the float arm. 2. Observe both the analog and digital displays on the DMM. Does the resistance change smoothly across the specified range?	40-250 ohms	Go to Diagnostic Aids	Go to Step 10
9	Inspect for poor connections at the harness connector of the PCM. Did you find and correct the condition?	--	Go to Step 13	Go to Step 12

LTV0500000002448

Fig. 79 Fuel gage inaccurate or inoperative dual tank (Part 2 of 3). 2002 Avalanche, Escalade, Suburban, Tahoe & Yukon

Step	Action	Value(s)	Yes	No
1	Did you perform the Instrument Cluster Diagnostic System Check?	--	Go to Step 2	Go to Diagnostic System Check -
2	1. Disconnect C152. 2. Connect a jumper wire between the signal circuit of the primary fuel level sender and the signal circuit of the secondary fuel level sender (male terminal side). 3. Connect the J 33431-C Signal Generator and Instrument Panel Tester between the signal circuits of the fuel level senders and the low reference circuit of the fuel level senders (male terminal side). 4. Turn ON the ignition, with the engine OFF. 5. Vary the resistance on the J 33431-C from 40-250 ohms. **Important:** Verify the J 33431-C resistance settings with a DMM. 6. Check Fuel Level Specifications. Does the fuel gage display the correct fuel level?	--	Go to Step 4	Go to Step 3
3	1. Install the scan tool. 2. Turn ON the ignition, with the engine OFF. **Important:** Verify the J 33431-C resistance settings with a DMM. 3. Vary the resistance on the J 33431-C from 40-250 ohms. 4. Check Fuel Level Specifications. **Important:** Turn OFF the ignition momentarily between the resistance settings in order to quickly update the scan tool display. 5. With the scan tool, observe the Fuel Tank Level Remaining % parameter in the PCM Enhanced Evap Data list. Does the scan tool display the correct fuel level %?	--	Go to Step 11	Go to Step 5

LTV0500000002447

Fig. 79 Fuel gage inaccurate or inoperative dual tank (Part 1 of 3). 2002 Avalanche, Escalade, Suburban, Tahoe & Yukon

Step	Action	Value(s)	Yes	No
10	Replace the primary or secondary fuel level sender. Did you complete the replacement?		Go to Step 13	--
11	Replace the IPC. Did you complete the replacement?		Go to Step 13	--
12	**Important:** Program the replacement PCM. Replace the PCM. Did you complete the replacement?		Go to Step 13	--
13	1. Use the scan tool in order to clear the PCM DTCs. 2. Operate the system in order to verify the repair. Did you correct the condition?	--	System OK	Go to Step 2

LTV0500000002449

Fig. 79 Fuel gage inaccurate or inoperative dual tank (Part 3 of 3). 2002 Avalanche, Escalade, Suburban, Tahoe & Yukon

Step	Action	Value (s)	Yes	No
1	Did you perform the Instrument Cluster Diagnostic System Check?	--	Go to Step 2	Go to Diagnostic System Check -
2	1. Disconnect C152. 2. Connect the J 33431-C Signal Generator and Instrument Panel Tester between the signal circuit of the fuel level sender and the low reference circuit of the fuel level sender (male terminal side). 3. Turn ON the ignition, with the engine OFF. 4. Vary the resistance on the J 33431-C from 40-250 ohms. **Important:** Verify the J 33431-C resistance settings with a DMM. 5. Check Fuel Level Specifications. Does the fuel gage display the correct fuel level?	--	Go to Step 4	Go to Step 3
3	1. Install the scan tool. 2. Turn ON the ignition, with the engine OFF. 3. Vary the resistance on the J 33431-C from 40-250 ohms. **Important:** Verify the J 33431-C resistance settings with a DMM. 4. Check Fuel Level Specifications. **Important:** Turn OFF the ignition momentarily between the resistance settings in order to quickly update the scan tool display. 5. With the scan tool, observe the Fuel Tank Level Remaining % parameter in the PCM Enhanced Evap Data list. Does the scan tool display the correct fuel level %?	--	Go to Step 11	Go to Step 5

LTV0500000002450

Fig. 80 Fuel gage inaccurate or inoperative single tank (Part 1 of 3). 2002 Avalanche, Escalade, Suburban, Tahoe & Yukon

Step	Action	Value (s)	Yes	No
4	Inspect for the following items: • A poor connection at the harness connector of the fuel level sender • A high resistance in the signal circuit or the low reference circuit between the fuel level sender and C152 • A misaligned fuel level sender • A deformed fuel tank Did you find and correct the condition?	--	Go to Step 13	Go to Step 7
5	Test the signal circuit of the fuel level sender for a high resistance between C152 and the PCM. Did you find and correct the condition?	--	Go to Step 13	Go to Step 6
6	Test the low reference circuit of the fuel level sender for a high resistance between C152 and the PCM. Did you find and correct the condition?	--	Go to Step 13	Go to Step 9
7	1. Remove the fuel level sender. 2. Inspect for the following items: - A stuck fuel level sender (i.e. the fuel strainer interfering with the sender float arm) - Foreign material in the fuel tank (ice) Did you find and correct the condition?	--	Go to Step 13	Go to Step 8
8	1. With the J 39200 DMM, measure the resistance of the fuel level sender while moving the float arm. 2. Observe both the analog and digital displays on the DMM. Does the resistance change smoothly across the specified range?	40-250 ohms	Go to Diagnostic Aids	Go to Step 10

LTV0500000002451

Fig. 80 Fuel gage inaccurate or inoperative single tank (Part 2 of 3). 2002 Avalanche, Escalade, Suburban, Tahoe & Yukon

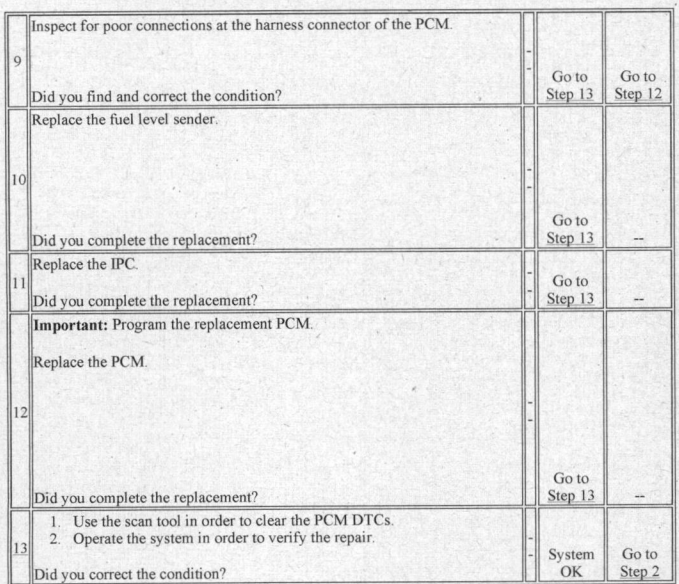

Step	Action	Yes	No
9	Inspect for poor connections at the harness connector of the PCM. Did you find and correct the condition?	Go to Step 13	Go to Step 12
10	Replace the fuel level sender. Did you complete the replacement?	Go to Step 13	--
11	Replace the IPC. Did you complete the replacement?	Go to Step 13	--
12	**Important:** Program the replacement PCM. Replace the PCM. Did you complete the replacement?	Go to Step 13	--
13	1. Use the scan tool in order to clear the PCM DTCs. 2. Operate the system in order to verify the repair. Did you correct the condition?	System OK	Go to Step 2

LTV0500000002452

Fig. 80 Fuel gage inaccurate or inoperative single tank (Part 3 of 3). 2002 Avalanche, Escalade, Suburban, Tahoe & Yukon

Step	Action	Yes	No
1	Did you perform the Instrument Cluster Diagnostic System Check?	Go to Step 2	Go to Diagnostic System Check
2	Verify the hourmeter operation. Does the hourmeter operate normally?	Test for Intermittent Conditions and Poor Connections	Go to Step 3
3	Replace the IPC. Did you complete the replacement?	Go to Step 4	--
4	Operate the system in order to verify the repair. Did you correct the condition?	System OK	Go to Step 2

LTV0500000002453

Fig. 81 Hourmeter inaccurate or inoperative. 2002 Avalanche, Escalade, Suburban, Tahoe & Yukon

Step	Action	Value (s)	Yes	No
1	Did you perform the Instrument Cluster Diagnostic System Check?	--	Go to Step 2	Go to Diagnostic System Check
2	Press in and release the trip odometer reset switch. Does the odometer display toggle between trip and season odometer?	--	Test for Intermittent Conditions and Poor Connections	Go to Step 3
3	Replace the IPC. Did you complete the replacement?	--	Go to Step 4	--
4	Operate the system in order to verify the repair. Did you correct the condition?		System OK	Go to Step 3

LTV0500000002454

Fig. 82 Odometer trip/reset switch inoperative. 2002 Avalanche, Escalade, Suburban, Tahoe & Yukon

Step	Action	Value (s)	Yes	No
1	Did you perform the Instrument Cluster Diagnostic System Check?	--	Go to Step 2	Go to Diagnostic System Check -
2	1. Install a scan tool. 2. Raise the vehicle drive wheels. 3. Start the engine. 4. Place the transmission into drive for an automatic transmission or third gear for a manual transmission. 5. With the scan tool, observe the vehicle speed parameter in the PCM Engine Data 1 data list. Does the vehicle speed parameter match the speedometer display?	--	Go to Step 3	Go to Step 4
3	Does the odometer operate properly?	--	Test for Intermittent and Poor Connections	Go to Step 8
4	1. Turn the ignition OFF. 2. Disconnect the PCM connector C2. 3. Turn the ignition ON. 4. Measure the voltage from the vehicle speed signal circuit to a good ground. Does the voltage measure greater than the specified value?	9.0 V	Go to Step 7	Go to Step 5
5	Test the vehicle speed signal circuit for an open or for a high resistance between the IPC and the PCM. Did you find and correct the condition?	--	Go to Step 10	Go to Step 6
6	Inspect for poor connections at the harness connector of the IPC. Did you find and correct the condition?	--	Go to Step 10	Go to Step 8

LTV0500000002455

Fig. 83 Speedometer and/or odometer inaccurate or inoperative (Part 1 of 2). 2002 Avalanche, Escalade, Suburban, Tahoe & Yukon

Step	Action	Value (s)	Yes	No
7	Inspect for poor connections at the harness connector of the PCM. Did you find and correct the condition?	--	Go to Step 10	Go to Step 9
8	Replace the IPC. Did you complete the replacement?	--	Go to Step 10	--
9	**Important:** Program the replacement PCM. Replace the PCM. Did you complete the replacement?	--	Go to Step 10	--
10	Operate the system in order to verify the repair. Did you correct the condition?	--	System OK	Go to Step 2

LTV0500000002456

Fig. 83 Speedometer and/or odometer inaccurate or inoperative (Part 2 of 2). 2002 Avalanche, Escalade, Suburban, Tahoe & Yukon

Step	Action	Value (s)	Yes	No
7	Replace the IPC. Did you complete the replacement?	--	Go to Step 9	--
8	**Important:** Program the replacement PCM. Replace the PCM. Did you complete the replacement?	--	Go to Step 9	--
9	Operate the system in order to verify the repair. Did you correct the condition?	--	System OK	Go to Step 2

LTV0500000002458

Fig. 84 Tachometer inaccurate or inoperative (Part 2 of 2). 2002 Avalanche, Escalade, Suburban, Tahoe & Yukon

Step	Action	Value (s)	Yes	No
1	Did you perform the Instrument Cluster Diagnostic System Check?	--	Go to Step 2	Go to Diagnostic System Check
2	1. Install the scan tool. 2. Start the engine. 3. With the scan tool, observe the Engine Speed signal parameter in the PCM Engine Data 1 data list. Does the Engine Speed parameter match the tachometer display?	--	Test for Intermittent Conditions and Poor Connections	Go to Step 3
3	1. Turn the ignition OFF. 2. Disconnect the PCM connector C2. 3. Turn the ignition ON, with the engine OFF. 4. Measure the voltage from the engine speed signal circuit to a good ground. Does the voltage measure greater than the specified value?	9.0 V	Go to Step 6	Go to Step 4
4	Test the engine speed signal circuit for an open or for a high resistance. Did you find and correct the condition?	--	Go to Step 9	Go to Step 5
5	Inspect for poor connections at the harness connector of the IPC. Did you find and correct the condition?	--	Go to Step 9	Go to Step 7
6	Inspect for poor connections at the harness connector of the PCM. Did you find and correct the condition?	--	Go to Step 9	Go to Step 8

LTV0500000002457

Fig. 84 Tachometer inaccurate or inoperative (Part 1 of 2). 2002 Avalanche, Escalade, Suburban, Tahoe & Yukon

Step	Action	Value (s)	Yes	No
1	Did you perform the Instrument Cluster Diagnostic System Check?	--	Go to Step 2	Go to Diagnostic System Check -
2	1. Start the engine. 2. Install a scan tool. 3. Idle the engine. 4. With the scan tool observe the Displayed Trans Oil Temp parameter in the IPC data list. Does the Displayed Trans Oil Temp parameter match the transmission fluid temperature gage display?	--	Test for Intermittent and Poor Connections	Go to Step 3
3	1. With the scan tool observe the Monitored Trans Oil Temp parameter in the IPC data list. 2. Compare the Monitored Trans Oil Temp parameter to the Displayed Trans Oil Temp in the IPC data list. Does the scan tool indicate both parameters are approximately the same?	--	Go to Step 4	Go to Step 5
4	With the scan tool observe the Monitored Trans Oil Temp parameter in the IPC data list. Does the scan tool indicate the parameter is within the specified range?	38°C to 130°C (100°F to 265°F)	Go to Step 5	Go to Diagnostic System Check
5	Replace the IPC. Did you complete the replacement?	--	Go to Step 6	--
6	Operate the system in order to verify the repair. Did you correct the condition?	--	System OK	Go to Step 2

LTV0500000002459

Fig. 85 Transmission fluid temperature gage inaccurate or inoperative. 2002 Avalanche, Escalade, Suburban, Tahoe & Yukon

Step	Action	Yes	No
1	Did you perform the Instrument Cluster Diagnostic System Check?	Go to Step 2	Go to Diagnostic System Check -
2	1. Install a scan tool. 2. Turn ON the ignition, with the engine OFF. 3. Compare the scan tool Ignition 1 Signal parameter in the PCM Engine Data 1 data list to the volt gage display. Does the Ignition 1 Signal parameter approximately match the volt gage display?	Go to Diagnostic System Check -	Go to Step 3
3	Replace the IPC. Did you complete the replacement?	Go to Step 4	--
4	Operate the system in order to verify the repair. Did you correct the condition?	System OK	Go to Step 2

LTV0500000002460

Fig. 86 Volt gage inaccurate or inoperative. 2002 Avalanche, Escalade, Suburban, Tahoe & Yukon

Step	Action	Yes	No
1	Did you perform the Instrument Cluster Diagnostic System Check?	Go to Step 2	Go to Diagnostic System Check
2	1. Install a scan tool. 2. Turn ON the ignition, with the engine OFF. 3. With a scan tool, observe the Engine Oil Life Remaining parameter in the PCM Engine Data 2 data list. Does the Engine Oil Life Remaining parameter display 0%?	Go to Step 3	Test for Intermittent Conditions and Poor Connections
3	Replace the IPC. Did you complete the replacement?	Go to Step 4	--
4	Operate the system in order to verify the repair. Did you correct the condition?	System OK	Go to Step 2

LTV0500000002462

Fig. 88 Change engine oil indicator inoperative. 2002 Avalanche, Escalade, Suburban, Tahoe & Yukon

Step	Action	Value (s)	Yes	No
1	Did you perform the Instrument Cluster Diagnostic System Check?	--	Go to Step 2	Go to Diagnostic System Check -
2	Turn ON the ignition with the engine OFF. Does the engine oil pressure indicator display in the message center?	--	Go to Step 3	Test for Intermittent and Poor Connections
3	1. Start the engine. 2. Check the engine oil pressure gage in the IPC. Does the engine oil pressure gage display at or below the specified value?	0 kPa (0 psi)	Go to Engine Oil Pressure Gage Inaccurate or Inoperative	Go to Step 4
4	Replace the IPC. Refer to Instrument Panel Cluster (IPC) Replacement. Did you complete the replacement?	--	Go to Step 5	--
5	Operate the system in order to verify the repair. Did you correct the condition?		System OK	Go to Step 3

LTV0500000002463

Fig. 89 Engine oil pressure indicator always on. 2002 Avalanche, Escalade, Suburban, Tahoe & Yukon

Step	Action	Yes	No
1	Did you perform the Instrument Cluster Diagnostic System Check?	Go to Step 2	Go to Diagnostic System Check
2	Start the engine. Does the CHANGE ENGINE OIL indicator illuminate in the message center?	Go to Step 3	Test for Intermittent and Poor Connections
3	1. Install a scan tool. 2. With a scan tool, observe the Engine Oil Life Remaining parameter in the PCM Engine Data 2 data list. Does the Engine Oil Life Remaining parameter display 0%?	Go to Step 4	Go to Step 5
4	Reset the engine oil life. Does the CHANGE ENGINE OIL indicator turn off?	Go to Step 6	Go to Step 5
5	Replace the IPC. Did you complete the replacement?	Go to Step 6	--
6	Operate the system in order to verify the repair. Did you correct the condition?	System OK	Go to Step 2

LTV0500000002461

Fig. 87 Change engine oil indicator always on. 2002 Avalanche, Escalade, Suburban, Tahoe & Yukon

Step	Action	Value (s)	Yes	No
1	Did you perform the Instrument Cluster Diagnostic System Check?	--	Go to Step 2	Go to Diagnostic System Check
2	Turn the ignition ON, with the engine OFF. Does the CHECK ENGINE OIL LEVEL indicator display in the message center?	--	Go to Step 3	Test for Intermittent Conditions and Poor Connections
3	1. Install a scan tool. 2. With the scan tool observe the Engine Oil Level Switch parameter in the PCM Engine Data 2 data list. Does the Engine Oil Level Switch parameter display OK?		Go to Step 9	Go to Step 4
4	1. Turn the ignition OFF. 2. Disconnect the engine oil level switch. 3. Connect a 3 amp fused jumper wire between the signal circuit of the oil level switch and a good ground. 4. Turn the ignition ON, with the engine OFF. Does the Engine Oil Level Switch parameter display LOW?		Go to Step 5	Go to Step 6
5	Test the signal circuit of the engine oil level switch for an open or for a high resistance. Did you find and correct the condition?		Go to Step 12	Go to Step 8
6	Test the ground circuit of the engine oil level switch for an open or for a high resistance. Did you find and correct the condition?		Go to Step 12	Go to Step 7
7	Inspect for poor connections at the harness connector of the engine oil level switch. Did you find and correct the condition?		Go to Step 12	Go to Step 10

LTV0500000002464

Fig. 90 Low engine oil dipstick always on (Part 1 of 2). 2002 Avalanche, Escalade, Suburban, Tahoe & Yukon

DASH GAUGES & WARNING INDICATORS

Step	Action	Yes	No
8	Inspect for poor connections at the harness connector of the PCM. Did you find and correct the condition?	Go to Step 12	Go to Step 11
9	Replace the IPC. Did you complete the replacement?	Go to Step 12	--
10	Replace the engine oil level switch. Did you complete the replacement?	Go to Step 12	--
11	**Important** Program the replacement PCM. Replace the PCM. Did you complete the replacement?	Go to Step 12	--
12	Operate the system in order to verify the repair. Did you correct the condition?	System OK	Go to Step 3

LTV0500000002465

Fig. 90 Low engine oil dipstick always on (Part 2 of 2). 2002 Avalanche, Escalade, Suburban, Tahoe & Yukon

Step	Action	Yes	No
8	Replace the IPC. Did you complete the replacement?	Go to Step 11	--
9	Replace the engine oil level switch. Did you complete the replacement?	Go to Step 11	--
10	**Important** Program the replacement PCM. Replace the PCM. Did you complete the replacement?	Go to Step 11	--
11	Operate the system in order to verify the repair. Did you correct the condition?	System OK	Go to Step 3

LTV0500000002467

Fig. 91 Low engine oil dipstick inoperative (Part 2 of 2). 2002 Avalanche, Escalade, Suburban, Tahoe & Yukon

Step	Action	Value (s)	Yes	No
1	Did you perform the Instrument Cluster Diagnostic System Check?	--	Go to Step 2	Go to Diagnostic System Check -
2	Turn the ignition ON, with the engine OFF. Does the CHECK ENGINE OIL LEVEL indicator display in the message center?	--	Test for Intermittent and Poor Connections	Go to Step 3
3	1. Install a scan tool. 2. With the scan tool observe the Engine Oil Level Switch parameter in the PCM Engine Data 2 data list. Does the Engine Oil Level Switch parameter display LOW?	--	Go to Step 8	Go to Step 4
4	1. Turn the ignition OFF. 2. Disconnect the engine oil level switch. 3. Turn the ignition ON, with the engine OFF. Does the Engine Oil Level Switch parameter display OK?	--	Go to Step 5	Go to Step 6
5	Test the signal circuit of the engine oil level switch for a short to ground. Did you find and correct the condition?		Go to Step 11	Go to Step 7
6	Inspect for poor connections at the harness connector of the engine oil level switch. Did you find and correct the condition?		Go to Step 11	Go to Step 9
7	Inspect for poor connections at the harness connector of the PCM. Did you find and correct the condition?		Go to Step 11	Go to Step 10

LTV0500000002466

Fig. 91 Low engine oil dipstick inoperative (Part 1 of 2). 2002 Avalanche, Escalade, Suburban, Tahoe & Yukon

Step	Action	Value (s)	Yes	No
1	Did you perform the Instrument Cluster Diagnostic System Check?	--	Go to Step 2	Go to Diagnostic System Check -
2	1. Turn ON the ignition, with the engine OFF. 2. Place the shift lever in the PARK position. Does the PRNDL display identify the PARK position?	--	Test for Intermittent and Poor Connections	Go to Step 3
3	1. Install a scan tool. 2. With the scan tool, observe the Park Switch parameter in the IPC Inputs data list. Does the scan tool display Closed?	--	Go to Diagnostic System Check	Go to Step 4
4	1. Disconnect the park switch. 2. Connect a fused jumper wire between the park switch signal circuit and a good ground. 3. With the scan tool, observe the Park Switch parameter. Does the scan tool display Closed?	--	Go to Step 6	Go to Step 5
5	Test the park switch signal circuit for an open or a high resistance. Did you find and correct the condition?	--	Go to Step 11	Go to Step 8
6	Test the ground circuit of the park switch for an open or a high resistance. Did you find and correct the condition?	--	Go to Step 11	Go to Step 7

LTV0500000002468

Fig. 92 PRNDL display park indicator inoperative (Part 1 of 2). 2002 Avalanche, Escalade, Suburban, Tahoe & Yukon

Step	Action	Yes	No
7	Inspect for poor connections at the harness connector of the park switch. Did you find and correct the condition?	Go to Step 11	Go to Step 9
8	Inspect for poor connections at the harness connector of the IPC. Did you find and correct the condition?	Go to Step 11	Go to Step 10
9	Replace the park switch. Did you complete the replacement?	Go to Step 11	--
10	Replace the IPC. Did you complete the replacement?	Go to Step 11	--
11	Operate the system in order to verify the repair. Did you correct the condition?	System OK	Go to Step 3

LTV0500000002469

Fig. 92 PRNDL display park indicator inoperative (Part 2 of 2). 2002 Avalanche, Escalade, Suburban, Tahoe & Yukon

DASH GAUGES & WARNING INDICATORS

Step	Action	Value (s)	Yes	No
1	Did you perform the Driver Information Center Diagnostic System Check?	--	Go to Step 2	
2	1. Turn ON the ignition, with the engine OFF. 2. Observe the DIC operation. Does the DIC illuminate all segments with the ignition ON?	--		Go to Step 3
3	1. Install the scan tool. 2. With the scan tool, observe the Run/Accy/Rap Voltage parameter in the DIC data list. Does the DIC Run/Accy/Rap Voltage parameter indicate any voltage?	--	Go to Step 4	Go to Step 5
4	Inspect for poor connections at the harness connector of the DIC. Did you find and correct the condition?	--	Go to Step 7	Go to Step 6
5	Repair the open, a short to ground or a high resistance in the RAP fuse supply voltage circuit of the DIC. Did you complete the repair?	--	Go to Step 7	--
6	Replace the DIC. Did you complete the replacement?	--	Go to Step 7	--
7	Operate the system in order to verify the repair. Did you correct the condition?	--	System OK	Go to Step 2

LTV0500000002470

Fig. 93   Driver information center (DIC) inoperative. 2002 Avalanche, Escalade, Suburban, Tahoe & Yukon

Step	Action	Value (s)	Yes	No
1	Did you perform the Audible Warning Diagnostic System Check?	--	Go to Step 2	
2	Are any indicators illuminated?	--	Go to Symptoms	Go to Step 3
3	1. Turn the ignition OFF. 2. Turn the headlamp switch to OFF. 3. Remove the key from the ignition. 4. Open the driver door. Does the chime sound?	--	Go to Step 4	Test for Intermittent and Poor Connections
4	1. Install a scan tool. 2. Turn the ignition ON, with the engine OFF. 3. With the scan tool observe the Head Lamp Relay Feedback parameter in the BCM Input 2 data display. Does the Head Lamp Relay Feedback parameter display ON?	--	Go to Headlamps On in Daylight Conditions	Go to Step 5
5	1. Open and close the driver door. 2. With the scan tool observe the Driver Door Jamb Switch parameter in the BCM Input 1 data list. Does the Driver Door Jamb Switch parameter toggle between ACTIVE and INACTIVE?	--	Go to Step 8	Go to Step 6
6	1. Disconnect the driver door jamb switch. 2. With the scan tool observe the Driver Door Jamb Switch parameter in the BCM Input 1 data list. Does the Driver Door Jamb Switch parameter display ACTIVE?	--	Go to Step 7	Go to Step 11

LTV0500000002472

Fig. 95   Chime always on (Part 1 of 3). 2002 Avalanche, Escalade, Suburban, Tahoe & Yukon

Step	Action	Value (s)	Yes	No
1	Did you perform the Driver Information Center Diagnostic System Check?	--	Go to Step 2	Go to Diagnostic System Check
2	1. Install a scan tool. 2. Turn ON the ignition, with the engine OFF. 3. With a scan tool, observe the suspect DIC switch parameter in the DIC Inputs data list. 4. Depress the suspect DIC switch. Does the switch parameter change state?	--	Test for Intermittent Conditions and Poor Connections	Go to Step 3
3	Replace the DIC. Did you complete the replacement?	--	Go to Step 4	--
4	Operate the system in order to verify the repair. Did you correct the condition?	--	System OK	Go to Step 2

LTV0500000002471

Fig. 94   Driver information center (DIC) switch(es) inoperative. 2002 Avalanche, Escalade, Suburban, Tahoe & Yukon

Step	Action		Yes	No
7	Test the driver door jamb switch signal circuit for a short to ground. Did you find and correct the condition?	-	Go to Step 17	Go to Step 13
8	1. Disconnect the ignition switch connector C201. 2. Install a scan tool. 3. Turn the ignition ON, with the engine OFF. 4. With the scan tool, observe the Key In Ignition parameter in the BCM Input 1 data list. Does the Key In Ignition parameter display YES?	-	Go to Step 9	Go to Step 10
9	Test the key in ignition switch signal circuit for a short to ground between the BCM and C201. Did you find and correct the condition?	-	Go to Step 17	Go to Step 13
10	Test the key in ignition switch signal circuit for a short to ground between the switch and C201. Did you find and correct the condition?	-	Go to Step 17	Go to Step 12
11	Inspect for poor connections at the harness connector of the driver door jamb switch. Did you find and correct the condition?	-	Go to Step 17	Go to Step 14
12	Inspect for poor connections at the harness connector of the ignition key alarm switch. Did you find and correct the condition?	-	Go to Step 17	Go to Step 15
13	Inspect for poor connections at the harness connector of the BCM. Did you find and correct the condition?	-	Go to Step 17	Go to Step 16

LTV0500000002473

Fig. 95   Chime always on (Part 2 of 3). 2002 Avalanche, Escalade, Suburban, Tahoe & Yukon

Step	Action	Value (s)	Yes	No
14	Replace the driver door jamb switch. Did you complete the replacement?	--	Go to Step 17	--
15	Replace the ignition key alarm switch. Did you complete the replacement?	--	Go to Step 17	--
16	**Important** Perform the set up procedure for the replacement BCM. Replace the BCM. Refer to Body Control Module Replacement in Body Control System. Did you complete the replacement?	--	Go to Step 17	--
17	1. Use the scan tool in order to clear the BCM DTCs. 2. Operate the system in order to verify the repair. Did you correct the condition?	--	System OK	Go to Step 3

LTV0500000002474

Fig. 95   Chime always on (Part 3 of 3). 2002 Avalanche, Escalade, Suburban, Tahoe & Yukon

Step	Action	Value (s)	Yes	No
6	Test the driver door jamb switch ground circuit for an open or for a high resistance. Did you find and correct the condition?	--	Go to Step 14	Go to Step 8
7	1. Turn the ignition ON, with the engine OFF. 2. With the scan tool, observe the Key In Ignition parameter in the BCM Input 1 data list. Does the Key In Ignition parameter display YES?	--	Go to Step 10	Go to Step 9
8	Inspect for poor connections at the harness connector of the driver door jamb switch. Did you find and correct the condition?	--	Go to Step 14	Go to Step 11
9	Inspect for poor connections at the harness connector of the ignition key alarm switch. Did you find and correct the condition?	--	Go to Step 14	Go to Step 12
10	Inspect for poor connections at the harness connector of the BCM. Did you find and correct the condition?	--	Go to Step 14	Go to Step 13

LTV0500000002476

Fig. 96   Chime inoperative (Part 2 of 3). 2002 Avalanche, Escalade, Suburban, Tahoe & Yukon

Step	Action	Value (s)	Yes	No
11	Replace the driver door jamb switch. Did you complete the replacement?	--	Go to Step 14	--
12	Replace the ignition key alarm switch. Refer to: Did you complete the replacement?	--	Go to Step 14	--
13	**Important** Perform the set up procedure for the replacement BCM. Replace the BCM. Did you complete the replacement?	--	Go to Step 14	--
14	1. Use the scan tool in order to clear the BCM DTCs. 2. Operate the system in order to verify the repair. Did you correct the condition?	--	System OK	Go to Step 2

LTV0500000002477

Fig. 96   Chime inoperative (Part 3 of 3). 2002 Avalanche, Escalade, Suburban, Tahoe & Yukon

Step	Action	Value (s)	Yes	No
	DEFINITION: One or more chime functions are inoperative.			
1	Did you perform the Audible Warning Diagnostic System Check?	--	Go to Step 2	Go to Diagnostic System Check
2	1. Turn the ignition OFF, with the key in the ignition. 2. Open the driver door. Does the chime sound?	--	Test for Intermittent Conditions and Poor Connections	Go to Step 3
3	1. Install a scan tool. 2. Turn the ignition ON, with the engine OFF. 3. Open the driver door. 4. With the scan tool, observe the Driver Door Jamb Switch parameter in the BCM Input 1 data list. Does the Driver Door Jamb Switch parameter display ACTIVE?	--	Go to Step 7	Go to Step 4
4	1. Turn the ignition OFF. 2. Disconnect the driver door jamb switch connector. 3. Connect a 3 amp fused jumper wire between the signal circuit of the driver door jamb switch and a good ground. 4. Turn the ignition ON, with the engine OFF. 5. With the scan tool, observe the Driver Door Jamb Switch parameter in the BCM Input 1 data list. Does the Driver Door Jamb Switch parameter display ACTIVE?	--	Go to Step 6	Go to Step 5
5	Test the driver door jamb switch signal circuit for an open or for a high resistance. Did you find and correct the condition?		Go to Step 14	Go to Step 10

LTV0500000002475

Fig. 96   Chime inoperative (Part 1 of 3). 2002 Avalanche, Escalade, Suburban, Tahoe & Yukon

Step	Action	Yes	No
1	Did you perform the Diagnostic System Check - Vehicle?	Go to Step 2	Go to Diagnostic System Check
2	1. Turn the ignition ON, with the engine OFF. 2. Observe the instrument cluster. Does the instrument cluster perform the displays test?	Test for Intermittent Conditions and Poor Connections	Go to Step 3
3	1. Turn the ignition OFF. 2. Disconnect the instrument panel cluster (IPC). 3. Turn the ignition ON, with the engine OFF. 4. Connect a test lamp between the ignition 1 voltage circuit and a good ground. Does the test lamp illuminate?	Go to Step 4	Go to Step 7
4	Connect a test lamp between the ignition 1 voltage circuit of the instrument cluster and the ground circuit of the instrument cluster. Does the test lamp illuminate?	Go to Step 5	Go to Step 6
5	Inspect for poor connections at the harness connector of the IPC. Did you find and correct the condition?	Go to Step 9	Go to Step 8
6	Repair the open or a high resistance in the ground circuit. Did you complete the repair?	Go to Step 9	--

LTV0500000002417

Fig. 97   Instrument cluster inoperative (Part 1 of 2). 2003–06 Avalanche, Escalade, Suburban, Tahoe & Yukon

	Action	Yes	No
7	Repair the open, short to ground or high resistance in the ignition 1 voltage circuit. Did you complete the repair?	Go to Step 9	--
8	Replace the IPC. Did you complete the replacement?	Go to Step 9	--
9	Operate the system in order to verify the repair. Did you find and correct the condition?	System OK	Go to Step 3

LTV0500000002418

Fig. 97 Instrument cluster inoperative (Part 2 of 2). 2003–06 Avalanche, Escalade, Suburban, Tahoe & Yukon

	Action	Yes	No
6	Inspect for poor connections at the harness connector of the EOP sensor. Did you find and correct the condition?	Go to Step 11	Go to Step 8
7	Inspect for poor connections at the harness connector of the powertrain control module (PCM). Did you find and correct the condition?	Go to Step 11	Go to Step 9
8	Replace the engine oil pressure sensor. Did you complete the replacement?	Go to Step 11	--
9	Replace the PCM. Did you complete the replacement?	Go to Step 11	--
10	Replace the IPC. Did you complete the replacement?	Go to Step 11	--
11	Operate the system in order to verify the repair. Did you correct the condition?	System OK	Go to Step 2

LTV0500000002420

Fig. 98 Engine oil pressure gage inaccurate or inoperative (Part 2 of 2). 2003–06 Avalanche, Escalade, Suburban, Tahoe & Yukon

Step	Action	Values	Yes	No
1	Did you perform the Diagnostic System Check - Vehicle?	--	Go to Step 2	Go to Diagnostic System Check
2	Start the engine. Does the engine oil pressure (EOP) gage display within the specified range?	34-483 kPa (5-70 psi) - 8.1L only / 207-483 kPa (30-70 psi)	Test for Intermittent Conditions and Poor Connections	Go to Step 3
3	1. Install a scan tool. 2. Turn the ignition ON, with the engine OFF. 3. With a scan tool, perform the Displays Test in the instrument panel cluster (IPC) scan tool Output Controls. Does the EOP gage move up and down when commanded?		Go to Step 4	Go to Step 10
4	1. Turn the ignition OFF. 2. Disconnect the negative battery cable. 3. Disconnect the EOP sensor. 4. Measure the resistance from the low reference circuit of the EOP sensor to a good ground. Does the resistance measure less than the specified value?	5 ohms	Go to Step 6	Go to Step 5
5	Test the low reference circuit of the EOP sensor for high resistance or for an open. Did you find and correct the condition?		Go to Step 11	Go to Step 7

LTV0500000002419

Fig. 98 Engine oil pressure gage inaccurate or inoperative (Part 1 of 2). 2003–06 Avalanche, Escalade, Suburban, Tahoe & Yukon

	Action	Yes	No
1	Did you perform the Diagnostic System Check - Vehicle?	Go to Step 2	Go to Diagnostic System Check
2	1. Disconnect C152. 2. Connect a jumper wire between the signal circuit of the primary fuel level sender and the signal circuit of the secondary fuel level sender, male terminal side. 3. Connect the J 33431-C Signal Generator and Instrument Panel Tester between the signal circuits of the fuel level senders and the low reference circuit of the fuel level senders, male terminal side. 4. Turn ON the ignition, with the engine OFF. **Important:** Verify the J 33431-C resistance settings with a DMM. 5. Vary the resistance on the J 33431-C from 40-250 ohms. Does the fuel gage display the correct fuel level?	Go to Step 4	Go to Step 3
3	1. Install the scan tool. 2. Turn ON the ignition, with the engine OFF. **Important:** Verify the J 33431-C resistance settings with a DMM. 3. Vary the resistance on the J 33431-C from 40-250 ohms. **Important:** Turn OFF the ignition momentarily between the resistance settings in order to quickly update the scan tool display. 4. With the scan tool, observe the Fuel Tank Level Remaining % parameter in the powertrain control module (PCM) Enhanced evaporative emission (EVAP) Data list. Does the scan tool display the correct fuel level percent?	Go to Step 5	Go to Step 5

LTV0500000002421

Fig. 99 Fuel gage inaccurate or inoperative dual tanks (Part 1 of 3). 2003–06 Avalanche, Escalade, Suburban, Tahoe & Yukon

	Action	Yes	No
4	With the scan tool, perform the Displays Test in the instrument panel cluster (IPC) scan tool Output Controls. Does the gage move from 0 to its maximum value and back to 0 when you perform the Displays Test?	Go to Step 5	Go to Step 10
5	Inspect for the following items: • A poor connection at the harness connectors of the fuel level senders-- • A high resistance in the signal circuits or the low reference circuit between the fuel level senders and C152 • A misaligned primary or secondary fuel level sender • A deformed primary or secondary fuel tank Did you find and correct the condition?	Go to Step 15	Go to Step 8
6	Test the signal circuits of the fuel level senders for a high resistance between C152 and the PCM. Did you find and correct the condition?	Go to Step 15	Go to Step 7
7	Test the low reference circuit of the fuel level senders for a high resistance between C152 and the PCM. Did you find and correct the condition?	Go to Step 15	Go to Step 11
8	1. Remove the fuel level senders. 2. Inspect for the following items: - A stuck fuel level sender, i.e. the fuel strainer interfering with the sender float arm - Foreign material in the fuel tanks, ice Did you find and correct the condition?	Go to Step 15	Go to Step 9

LTV0500000002422

Fig. 99 Fuel gage inaccurate or inoperative dual tanks (Part 2 of 3). 2003–06 Avalanche, Escalade, Suburban, Tahoe & Yukon

	Action	Values	Yes	No
10	1. With the DMM, measure the resistance of the fuel level senders while moving the float arm. 2. Observe both the analog and digital displays on the DMM. Does the resistance change smoothly across the specified range?	40-250 ohms	Go to Diagnostic Aids	Go to Step 11
11	Inspect for poor connections at the harness connector of the IPC. Did you find and correct the condition?	--	Go to Step 14	Go to Step 12
12	Inspect for poor connections at the harness connector of the PCM. Did you find and correct the condition?	--	Go to Step 14	13 Go to Step 14
13	Replace the primary or the secondary fuel level sender. Did you complete the replacement?	--	--	Go to Step 15
14	Replace the instrument panel cluster (IPC). Did you complete the replacement?	--	--	Go to Step 14
15	Replace the PCM. Did you complete the replacement?	--	--	Go to Step 14
16	1. Use the scan tool in order to clear the PCM DTCs. 2. Operate the system in order to verify the repair. Did you correct the condition?	--	System OK	Go to Step 2

LTV0500000002423

Fig. 99 Fuel gage inaccurate or inoperative dual tanks (Part 3 of 3). 2003–06 Avalanche, Escalade, Suburban, Tahoe & Yukon

Step	Action	Values	Yes	No
1	Did you perform the Diagnostic System Check - Vehicle?	--	Go to Step 2	Go to Diagnostic System Check -
2	1. Disconnect C152. 2. Connect the J 33431-C Signal Generator and Instrument Panel Tester between the signal circuit of the fuel level sender and the low reference circuit of the fuel level sender (male terminal side). 3. Turn ON the ignition, with the engine OFF. 4. Vary the resistance on the J 33431-C from 40-250 ohms. **Important:** Verify the J 33431-C resistance settings with a DMM. Does the fuel gage display the correct fuel level?	--	Go to Step 5	Go to Step 3
3	1. Install the scan tool. 2. Turn ON the ignition, with the engine OFF. 3. Vary the resistance on the J 33431-C from 40-250 ohms. **Important:** Verify the J 33431-C resistance settings with a DMM. **Important:** Turn OFF the ignition momentarily between the resistance settings in order to quickly update the scan tool display. 4. With the scan tool, observe the Fuel Tank Level Remaining % parameter in the powertrain control module (PCM) Enhanced evaporative emission (EVAP) Data list. Does the scan tool display the correct fuel level percent?	--	Go to Step 3	Go to Step 5

LTV0500000002424

Fig. 100 Fuel gage inaccurate or inoperative single tank (Part 1 of 3). 2003–06 Avalanche, Escalade, Suburban, Tahoe & Yukon

	Action	Values	Yes	No
4	With the scan tool, perform the Displays Test in the instrument panel cluster (IPC) scan tool Output Controls. Does the gage move from 0 to its maximum value and back to 0 when you perform the Displays Test?	--	Go to Step 5	Go to Step 10
5	Inspect for the following items: • A poor connection at the harness connector of the fuel level sender • A high resistance in the signal circuit or the low reference circuit between the fuel level sender and C152 • A misaligned fuel level sender • A deformed fuel tank Did you find and correct the condition?	--	Go to Step 15	Go to Step 8
6	Test the signal circuit of the fuel level sender for a high resistance between C152 and the PCM. Did you find and correct the condition?	--	Go to Step 15	Go to Step 7
7	Test the low reference circuit of the fuel level sender for a high resistance between C152 and the PCM. Did you find and correct the condition?	--	Go to Step 15	Go to Step 11

8	1. Remove the fuel level sender.
	2. Inspect for the following items:
	  - A stuck fuel level sender, i.e. the fuel strainer interfering with the sender float arm
	  - Foreign material in the fuel tank, i.e. ice
	
	Did you find and correct the condition?
		--	Go to Step 15	Go to Step 9

9	1. With the DMM, measure the resistance of the fuel level sender while moving the float arm. 2. Observe both the analog and digital displays on the DMM. Does the resistance change smoothly across the specified range?	40-250 ohms	Go to Diagnostic Aids	Go to Step 12

LTV0500000002425

Fig. 100 Fuel gage inaccurate or inoperative single tank (Part 2 of 3). 2003–06 Avalanche, Escalade, Suburban, Tahoe & Yukon

	Action	Values	Yes	No
10	Inspect for poor connections at the harness connector of the IPC. Did you find and correct the condition?	--	Go to Step 14	Go to Step 12
11	Inspect for poor connections at the harness connector of the PCM. Did you find and correct the condition?	--	Go to Step 14	Go to Step 13
12	Replace the fuel level sender. Did you complete the replacement?	--	Go to Step 14	--
13	Replace the instrument panel cluster (IPC). Did you complete the replacement?	--	Go to Step 14	--
14	Replace the PCM. Did you complete the replacement?	--	Go to Step 15	--
15	1. Use the scan tool in order to clear the PCM DTCs. 2. Operate the system in order to verify the repair. Did you correct the condition?	--	System OK	Go to Step 2

LTV0500000002426

Fig. 100 Fuel gage inaccurate or inoperative single tank (Part 3 of 3). 2003–06 Avalanche, Escalade, Suburban, Tahoe & Yukon

Step	Action	Yes	No
1	Did you perform the Diagnostic System Check - Vehicle?	Go to Step 2	Go to Diagnostic System Check
2	Verify the hourmeter operation. Does the hourmeter operate normally?	Test for Intermittent Conditions and Poor Connections	Go to Step 3
3	Replace the instrument panel cluster (IPC). Did you complete the replacement?	Go to Step 4	--
4	Operate the system in order to verify the repair. Did you correct the condition?	System OK	Go to Step 2

LTV0500000002427

Fig. 101 Hourmeter inaccurate or inoperative. 2003–06 Avalanche, Escalade, Suburban, Tahoe & Yukon

Step	Action	Yes	No
1	Did you perform the Diagnostic System Check - Vehicle?	Go to Step 2	Go to Diagnostic System Check
2	1. Turn the ignition ON, with the engine OFF. 2. Press the trip odometer reset switch. Does the odometer toggle between the season odometer, the trip odometer, and the hourmeter?	Test for Intermittent Conditions and Poor Connections	Go to Step 3
3	Replace the instrument panel cluster (IPC). Did you complete the replacement?	Go to Step 4	--
4	Operate the system in order to verify the repair. Did you correct the condition?	System OK	Go to Step 2

LTV0500000002429

Fig. 103 Odometer trip/reset switch inoperative. 2003–06 Avalanche, Escalade, Suburban, Tahoe & Yukon

Step	Action	Yes	No
	DEFINITION: This diagnostic procedure applies only to the serial data gages located in the instrument cluster which include the engine coolant temperature gage, and the transmission fluid temperature gage.		
1	Did you perform the Diagnostic System Check - Vehicle?	Go to Step 2	Go to Diagnostic System Check
2	1. Turn the ignition ON, with the engine OFF. 2. Install a scan tool. 3. With the scan tool, perform the Displays Test in the IPC scan tool Output Controls. Does the gage move from 0 to its maximum value and back to 0 when you perform the Displays Test?	Go to Step 3	Go to Step 4
3	1. Install a scan tool. 2. Start the engine. 3. Observe the appropriate parameter in the PCM Data list. Does the parameter match the gage display?	Go to Diagnostic System Check	Go to Step 4
4	Replace the instrument panel cluster (IPC). Did you complete the replacement?	Go to Step 5	--
5	1. Use the scan tool in order to clear any induced DTCs. 2. Operate the system in order to verify the repair. Did you correct the condition?	System OK	Go to Step 2

LTV0500000002428

Fig. 102 Instrument panel cluster (IPC) gages inoperative. 2003–06 Avalanche, Escalade, Suburban, Tahoe & Yukon

Step	Action	Yes	No
1	Did you perform the Diagnostic System Check - Vehicle?	Go to Step 2	Go to Diagnostic System Check
2	1. Turn ON the ignition, with the engine OFF. 2. Install a scan tool. 3. With the scan tool, perform the segments test in the instrument panel cluster (IPC) scan tool output controls. Do all of the segments of the driver information center (DIC) illuminate?	Go to Step 3	Go to Step 6
3	1. Install a scan tool. 2. Raise the vehicle drive wheels. 3. Start the engine. 4. Place the transmission into drive for automatic transmission or third gear for manual transmission. 5. With the scan tool, observe the Vehicle Speed Sensor (VSS) parameter in the IPC Data 1 data list. Does the VSS parameter match the speedometer display?	Test for Intermittent Conditions and Poor Connections	Go to Step 4
4	Test the vehicle speed signal circuit for a high resistance between the IPC and the powertrain control module (PCM). Did you find and correct the condition?	Go to Step 7	Go to Step 5
5	Inspect for poor connections at the harness connector of the IPC. Did you find and correct the condition?	Go to Step 7	Go to Step 6
6	Replace the IPC. Did you complete the replacement?	Go to Step 7	--
7	Operate the system in order to verify the repair. Did you correct the condition?	System OK	Go to Step 3

LTV0500000002430

Fig. 104 Speedometer and/or odometer inaccurate or inoperative. 2003–06 Avalanche, Escalade, Suburban, Tahoe & Yukon

Step	Action	Yes	No
1	Did you perform the Diagnostic System Check - Vehicle?	Go to Step 2	Go to Diagnostic System Check
2	1. Install a scan tool. 2. Start the engine. 3. With the scan tool, observe the Engine Speed parameter in the IPC Data 1 data list. Does the Engine Speed parameter match the tachometer display?	Test for Intermittent Conditions and Poor Connections	Go to Step 3
3	Test the engine speed signal circuit for a high resistance between the instrument panel cluster (IPC) and powertrain control module (PCM). Did you find and correct the condition?	Go to Step 6	Go to Step 4
4	Inspect for poor connections at the harness connector of the instrument cluster. Did you find and correct the condition?	Go to Step 6	Go to Step 5
5	Replace the IPC. Did you complete the replacement?	Go to Step 6	--
6	Operate the system in order to verify the repair. Did you correct the condition?	System OK	Go to Step 2

LTV0500000002431

Fig. 105 Tachometer inaccurate or inoperative. 2003–06 Avalanche, Escalade, Suburban, Tahoe & Yukon

Step	Action	Yes	No
1	Did you perform the Diagnostic System Check - Vehicle?	Go to Step 2	Go to Diagnostic System Check
2	1. Turn the ignition ON, with the engine OFF. 2. Install a scan tool. 3. With the scan tool, perform the Displays Test in the IPC scan tool Output Controls. Does the gage move from 0 to its maximum value and back to 0 when you perform the Displays Test?	Go to Step 3	Go to Step 4
3	1. Install a scan tool. 2. Start the engine. 3. With the scan tool, observe the Battery Voltage parameter in the BCM Data list. Does the Battery Voltage parameter match the gage display?	Test for Intermittent Conditions and Poor Connections	Go to Step 4
4	Replace the instrument panel cluster (IPC). Did you complete the replacement?	Go to Step 5	--
5	1. Use the scan tool in order to clear any induced DTCs. 2. Operate the system in order to verify the repair. Did you correct the condition?	System OK	Go to Step 2

LTV0500000002432

Fig. 106 Volt gage inaccurate or inoperative. 2003–06 Avalanche, Escalade, Suburban, Tahoe & Yukon

Step	Action	Yes	No
1	Did you perform the Diagnostic System Check - Vehicle?	Go to Step 2	Go to Diagnostic System Check
2	Start the engine. Does the CHANGE ENGINE OIL indicator illuminate in the Driver Information Center?	Go to Step 3	Test for Intermittent Conditions and Poor Connections
3	1. Install a scan tool. 2. With the scan tool, observe the Engine Oil Life Remaining parameter in the PCM Engine Data 2 data list. Does the Engine Oil Life Remaining parameter display 0%?	Go to Step 4	Go to Step 5
4	Reset the engine oil life. Does the CHANGE ENGINE OIL indicator turn off?	Go to Step 6	Go to Step 5
5	Replace the instrument panel cluster (IPC). Did you complete the replacement?	Go to Step 6	--
6	Operate the system in order to verify the repair. Did you correct the condition?	System OK	Go to Step 2

LTV0500000002433

Fig. 107 Change engine oil indicator always on. 2003–06 Avalanche, Escalade, Suburban, Tahoe & Yukon

Step	Action	Yes	No
1	Did you perform the Diagnostic System Check - Vehicle?	Go to Step 2	Go to Diagnostic System Check
2	1. Install a scan tool. 2. Turn ON the ignition, with the engine OFF. 3. With the scan tool, observe the Engine Oil Level Switch parameter in the powertrain control module (PCM) Engine Data 2 data list. Does the Engine Oil Level Switch parameter display OK?	Go to Step 3	Go to Step 4
3	Does the CHECK ENG OIL LEVEL indicator remain illuminated after the displays test?	Go to Step 11	Test for Intermittent Conditions and Poor Connections
4	1. Turn the ignition OFF. 2. Disconnect the engine oil level switch. 3. Connect a 3-amp fused jumper between the signal circuit of the engine oil level switch and a good ground. 4. Turn ON the ignition, with the engine OFF. 5. With the scan tool, observe the Engine Oil Level Switch parameter. Does the Engine Oil Level Switch parameter display OK?	Go to Step 6	Go to Step 5
5	Test the signal circuit of the engine oil level switch for a short to battery voltage, for an open, or for a high. Did you find and correct the condition?	Go to Step 12	Go to Step 8
6	Test the ground circuit of the engine oil level switch for an open or for a high resistance. Did you find and correct the condition?	Go to Step 12	Go to Step 7

LTV0500000002434

Fig. 108 Low engine oil dipstick always on (Part 1 of 2). 2003–06 Avalanche, Escalade, Suburban, Tahoe & Yukon

Step	Action	Yes	No
7	Inspect for poor connections at the harness connector of the engine oil level switch. Did you find and correct the condition?	Go to Step 12	Go to Step 9
8	Inspect for poor connections at the harness connector of the PCM. Did you find and correct the condition?	Go to Step 12	Go to Step 10
9	Replace the engine oil level switch. Did you complete the replacement?	Go to Step 12	--
10	Replace the PCM. Did you complete the replacement?	Go to Step 12	--
11	Replace the instrument panel cluster (IPC). Did you complete the replacement?	Go to Step 12	--
12	Operate the system in order to verify the repair. Did you correct the condition?	System OK	Go to Step 2

LTV0500000002435

Fig. 108 Low engine oil dipstick always on (Part 2 of 2). 2003–06 Avalanche, Escalade, Suburban, Tahoe & Yukon

Step	Action	Yes	No
7	Test the signal circuit of the suspect DIC switch for a short to ground. Did you find and correct the condition?	Go to Step 14	Go to Step 11
8	Test the signal circuit of the suspect DIC switch for an open or high resistance. Did you find and correct the condition?	Go to Step 14	Go to Step 11
9	Test the ground circuit of the DIC switch for an open or high resistance. Did you find and correct the condition?	Go to Step 14	Go to Step 10
10	Inspect for poor connections at the harness connector of the DIC switch. Did you find and correct the condition?	Go to Step 14	Go to Step 12
11	Inspect for poor connections at the harness connector of the instrument panel cluster (IPC). Did you find and correct the condition?	Go to Step 14	Go to Step 13
12	Replace the DIC switch. Did you complete the replacement?	Go to Step 14	--
13	Replace the IPC. Did you complete the replacement?	Go to Step 14	--
14	Operate the system in order to verify the repair. Did you correct the condition?	System OK	Go to Step 2

LTV0500000002437

Fig. 109 Driver information center (DIC) switch(es) inoperative (Part 2 of 2). 2003–06 Avalanche, Escalade, Suburban, Tahoe & Yukon

Step	Action	Yes	No
1	Did you perform the Diagnostic System Check - Vehicle?	Go to Step 2	Go to Diagnostic System Check
2	1. Install a scan tool. 2. Turn the ignition ON, with the engine OFF. 3. Press and release each of the driver information center (DIC) switches. 4. With a scan tool, observe the DIC switch parameters in the IPC Input/Output data list. Does the scan tool display On when each switch is pressed and Off when each switch is released?	Test for Intermittent Conditions and Poor Connections	Go to Step 3
3	Does the scan tool display Off when each switch is pressed?	Go to Step 5	Go to Step 4
4	Does the scan tool always display On for the suspect switch even when the switch is released?	Go to Step 5	Go to Step 6
5	1. Turn the ignition OFF. 2. Disconnect the DIC switch connector. 3. Turn the ignition ON, with the engine OFF. 4. With a scan tool, observe the suspect DIC switch parameter. Does the scan tool display On for the suspect switch?	Go to Step 7	Go to Step 12
6	1. Turn the ignition OFF. 2. Disconnect the DIC switch connector. 3. Connect a 3-amp fused jumper wire between the signal circuit of the suspect DIC switch and a good ground. 4. Turn the ignition ON, with the engine OFF. 5. With a scan tool, observe the suspect DIC switch parameter. Does the scan tool display On for the suspect switch?	Go to Step 10	Go to Step 8

LTV0500000002436

Fig. 109 Driver information center (DIC) switch(es) inoperative (Part 1 of 2). 2003–06 Avalanche, Escalade, Suburban, Tahoe & Yukon

Step	Action	Yes	No
1	Did you perform the Diagnostic System Check - Vehicle?	Go to Step 2	Go to Diagnostic System Check
2	Do any indicators illuminate when the chime sounds?	Go to Symptoms	Go to Step 3
3	1. Turn the ignition OFF. 2. Remove the key from the ignition. 3. Turn the headlamp switch to OFF. 4. Close all of the vehicle doors. 5. Open one or more of the vehicle doors. Does the chime sound at all times regardless if the doors are open or closed?	Go to Step 16	Go to Step 4
4	1. Close all of the vehicle doors. 2. With a scan tool observe the Driver Door Ajar Switch and the Passenger Door Ajar Switch parameters in the body control module (BCM) inputs data list or the Door Ajar Switch parameters in the DDM/PDM inputs data list. Do all of the Door Ajar Switch parameters display Off or Inactive?	Go to Step 5	Check Courtesy Lamps Always On
5	With a scan tool observe the Left Rear Cargo Door Ajar Switch and the Right Rear Door Ajar Switch parameters in the BCM inputs data list. Do all of the Door Switch parameters display Inactive?	Go to Step 6	Check Courtesy Lamps Always On
6	With a scan tool, observe the Cargo Door Ajar Switch and the Hood Ajar Switch parameters in the BCM inputs data list. Does the Cargo Door Ajar Switch and the Hood Ajar Switch parameters display Inactive?	Go to Step 7	Check Courtesy Lamps Always On
7	1. Turn the ignition OFF. 2. Remove the key from the ignition. 3. Turn the headlamp switch to OFF. 4. Open the driver door. Does the chime sound?	Go to Step 8	Test for Intermittent Conditions and Poor Connections

LTV0500000002438

Fig. 110 Chime always on (Part 1 of 3). 2003–06 Avalanche, Escalade, Suburban, Tahoe & Yukon

8	1. Install a scan tool. 2. Turn the ignition ON, with the engine OFF. 3. With a scan tool, observe the Parklamp Switch parameter in the BCM inputs data list. Does the Parklamp Switch parameter display Inactive?		Go to Step 9	Go to Step 11
9	With a scan tool, observe the Headlamp Switch parameter in the BCM inputs data list. Does the Headlamp Switch parameter display Inactive?		Go to Step 10	Go to Step 11
10	1. Turn the ignition OFF. 2. Remove the key from the ignition. 3. With a scan tool, observe the Key In Ignition parameter in the BCM inputs data list. Does the Key In Ignition parameter display No?		Go to Step 15	Go to Step 12
11	Test the headlamp input signal circuit and the park lamp signal circuit at the BCM for a short to voltage. Did you find and correct the condition?		Go to Step 21	Go to Step 13
12	Test the key in ignition signal circuit for a short to ground. Did you find and correct the condition?		Go to Step 21	Go to Step 14
13	Inspect for poor connections at the harness connector of the headlamp switch. Did you find and correct the condition?		Go to Step 21	Go to Step 17
14	Inspect for poor connections at the harness connector of the ignition key alarm switch. Did you find and correct the condition?		Go to Step 21	Go to Step 18

LTV0500000002439

Fig. 110 Chime always on (Part 2 of 3). 2003–06 Avalanche, Escalade, Suburban, Tahoe & Yukon

15	Inspect for poor connections at the harness connector of the BCM. Did you find and correct the condition?		Go to Step 21	Go to Step 19
16	Inspect for poor connections at the harness connector of the radio or audio amplifier. Did you find and correct the condition?		Go to Step 21	Go to Step 20
17	Replace the headlamp switch. Did you complete the replacement?		Go to Step 21	--
18	Replace the ignition switch. Did you complete the replacement?		Go to Step 21	--
19	Replace the BCM. Did you complete the replacement?		Go to Step 21	--
20	Replace the radio. Did you complete the replacement?		Go to Step 21	--
21	Operate the system in order to verify the repair. Did you correct the condition?		System OK	Go to Step 3

LTV0500000002440

Fig. 110 Chime always on (Part 3 of 3). 2003–06 Avalanche, Escalade, Suburban, Tahoe & Yukon

Step	Action	Yes	No
	DEFINITION: One or more chime functions are inoperative.		
1	Did you perform the Diagnostic System Check - Vehicle?	Go to Step 2	Go to Diagnostic System Check
2	1. Turn the ignition OFF, with the key in the ignition. 2. Open the driver door. Does the chime sound?	Test for Intermittent Conditions and Poor Connections	Go to Step 3
3	Do the courtesy lights turn on when you open the driver door?	Go to Step 4	Go to Courtesy Lamps Inoperative
4	1. Turn the ignition ON, with the engine OFF. 2. Turn the radio ON. 3. Adjust the radio balance and fade to the left front speaker. Does the speaker operate properly?	Go to Step 5	Go to Speakers Inoperative - One or More
5	Replace the radio. Did you complete the replacement?	Go to Step 6	--
6	Operate the system in order to verify the repair. Did you correct the condition?	System OK	Go to Step 1

LTV0500000002441

Fig. 111 Chime inoperative. 2003–06 Avalanche, Escalade, Suburban, Tahoe & Yukon

Step	Action	Values	Yes	No
1	Did you perform the Diagnostic System Check - Vehicle?	--	Go to Step 2	Go to Diagnostic System Check -
2	1. Install a scan tool. 2. Turn ON the ignition, with the engine OFF. 3. With the scan tool, perform the coolant gage sweep test. Does the engine coolant temperature gage move up and down when commanded?	--	Test for Intermittent Conditions and Poor Connections	Go to Step 3
3	Replace the instrument panel cluster (IPC). Did you complete the replacement?	--	Go to Step 4	--
4	Operate the system in order to verify the repair. Did you correct the condition?	--	System OK	Go to Step 2

LTV0500000002839

Fig. 112 Engine coolant temperature gage inaccurate or inoperative. Aztek & Rendezvous

Step	Action	Values	Yes	No
1	Did you perform the Diagnostic System Check - Vehicle?	--	Go to Step 2	Go to Diagnostic System Check -
2	1. Disconnect C305/C305C. 2. Connect the J 33431-C Signal Generator and Instrument Panel Tester between the signal circuit of the fuel level sender and the low reference circuit of the fuel level sender (male terminal side). 3. Turn ON the ignition, with the engine OFF. **Important:** Verify the J 33431-C resistance settings with a DMM. 4. Vary the resistance on the J 33431-C from 40-250 ohms. 5. Check Fuel Level Specifications Does the fuel gage display the correct fuel level?	--	Go to Step 4	Go to Step 3
3	1. Install a scan tool. 2. Turn ON the ignition, with the engine OFF. **Important:** Verify the J 33431-C resistance settings with a DMM. 3. Vary the resistance on the J 33431-C from 40-250 ohms. 4. Check Fuel Level Specifications **Important:** Turn OFF the ignition momentarily between the resistance settings in order to quickly update the scan tool display. 5. With the scan tool, observe the Fuel Level Sensor parameter in the engine control module (ECM)/powertrain control module (PCM) evaporative emission (EVAP) Data, data list. Does the scan tool display the correct fuel level percent or voltage?	--	Go to Step 11	Go to Step 5

LTV0500000002840

Fig. 113   Fuel gage inaccurate or inoperative (Part 1 of 3). Aztek & Rendezvous

Step	Action	Values	Yes	No
4	Inspect for the following items: • A poor connection at the harness connector of the fuel level sender • A high resistance in the signal circuit or the low reference circuit between the fuel level sender and C305/C305C-- • A misaligned fuel level sender • A deformed fuel tank Did you find and correct the condition?	--	Go to Step 13	Go to Step 7
5	Test the signal circuit of the fuel level sender for a high resistance. Did you find and correct the condition?	--	Go to Step 13	Go to Step 6
6	Test the low reference circuit of the fuel level sender for a high resistance. Did you find and correct the condition?	--	Go to Step 13	Go to Step 9
7	1. Remove the fuel level sender. 2. Inspect for the following items: - A stuck fuel level sender, i.e., the fuel strainer interfering with the sender float arm - Foreign material in the fuel tank, i.e. ice Did you find and correct the condition?	--	Go to Step 13	Go to Step 8
8	1. With the DMM, measure the resistance of the fuel level sender while moving the float arm. 2. Observe both the analog and digital displays on the DMM. Does the resistance change smoothly across the specified range?	40-250 ohms	Go to Diagnostic Aids	Go to Step 10

LTV0500000002841

Fig. 113   Fuel gage inaccurate or inoperative (Part 2 of 3). Aztek & Rendezvous

Step	Action		Yes	No
9	Inspect for poor connections at the harness connector of the ECM/PCM. Did you find and correct the condition?	-	Go to Step 13	Go to Step 12
10	Replace the fuel level sender. Did you complete the replacement?	-	Go to Step 13	--
11	Replace the instrument panel cluster (IPC). Did you complete the replacement?	-	Go to Step 13	--
12	Replace the ECM/PCM. Did you complete the replacement?	-	Go to Step 13	--
13	1. Use the scan tool in order to clear the ECM/PCM DTCs. 2. Operate the system in order to verify the repair. Did you correct the condition?		System OK	Go to Step 2

LTV0500000002842

Fig. 113   Fuel gage inaccurate or inoperative (Part 3 of 3). Aztek & Rendezvous

Step	Action	Yes	No
1	Did you perform the Diagnostic System Check - Vehicle?	Go to Step 2	Go to Diagnostic System Check -
2	Replace the instrument panel cluster (IPC). Did you complete the replacement?	Go to Step 3	--
3	Operate the system in order to verify the repair. Did you correct the condition?	System OK	Go to Step 2

LTV0500000002843

Fig. 114   Odometer trip/reset switch inoperative. Aztek & Rendezvous

Step	Action	Yes	No
1	Did you perform the Diagnostic System Check - Vehicle?	Go to Step 2	Go to Diagnostic System Check -
2	1. Install a scan tool. 2. Raise the vehicles drive wheels. 3. Start the engine. 4. Place the transmission into drive. 5. With the scan tool, observe the Vehicle Speed Sensor (VSS) parameter in the engine control module (ECM)/powertrain control module (PCM) Engine Data 1 data list. Does the VSS parameter match the speedometer display?	Go to Step 3	Go to Step 4
3	Does the odometer operate properly?	Test for Intermittent Conditions and Poor Connections	Go to Step 4
4	Replace the instrument panel cluster (IPC). Did you complete the replacement?	Go to Step 5	
5	1. Operate the system in order to verify the repair. 2. Use the scan tool in order to clear the DTCs that may have set in other modules during diagnosis. Did you correct the condition?	System OK	Go to Step 2

LTV0500000002844

Fig. 115   Speedometer and/or odometer inaccurate or inoperative. Aztek & Rendezvous

Step	Action	Yes	No
1	Did you perform the Diagnostic System Check - Vehicle?	Go to Step 2	Go to Diagnostic System Check -
2	1. Turn ON the ignition, with the engine OFF. 2. Install a scan tool. 3. With a scan tool, perform the Tach Gage Sweep Test. Does the tachometer move from 0 RPM to 7000 RPM and back to 0 RPM when you sweep this gage up and down?	Test for Intermittent Conditions and Poor Connections	Go to Step 3
3	Replace the instrument panel cluster (IPC). Did you complete the replacement?	Go to Step 4	--
4	Operate the system in order to verify the repair. Did you correct the condition?	System OK	Go to Step 2

LTV0500000002845

Fig. 116 Tachometer inaccurate or inoperative. Aztek & Rendezvous

Step	Action	Yes	No
1	Did you perform the Diagnostic System Check - Vehicle?	Go to Step 2	Go to Diagnostic System Check -
2	1. Install a scan tool. 2. Turn ON the ignition, with the engine OFF. 3. With a scan tool, observe the Engine Oil Life Remaining parameter in the powertrain control module (PCM) Data 2 data list. Does the scan tool display zero percent with the Change Engine Oil message inoperative?	Go to Step 3	System OK
3	Replace the instrument panel cluster (IPC). Did you complete the replacement?	Go to Step 4	--
4	Operate the system in order to verify the repair. Did you correct the condition?	System OK	Go to Step 2

LTV0500000002847

Fig. 118 Change engine oil indicator inoperative. Aztek & Rendezvous

Step	Action	Yes	No
1	Did you perform the Diagnostic System Check - Vehicle?	Go to Step 2	Go to Diagnostic System Check
2	Start the engine. Does the engine oil pressure indicator illuminate after the displays test?	Go to Step 3	Test for Intermittent Conditions and Poor Connections
3	1. Install a scan tool. 2. Turn ON the ignition. 3. With the scan tool, observe the Engine Oil Pressure Switch parameter in the instrument panel cluster (IPC) powertrain control module (PCM) data list. Does the Engine Oil Pressure Switch parameter display Ok?	Go to Step 10	Go to Step 4
4	1. Turn OFF the ignition. 2. Disconnect the engine oil pressure switch. 3. Start the engine. 4. With the scan tool, observe the Engine Oil Pressure Switch parameter. Does the Engine Oil Pressure Switch parameter display Ok?	Go to Step 6	Go to Step 5
5	Test the signal circuit of the engine oil pressure switch for a short to ground. Did you find and correct the condition?	Go to Step 11	Go to Step 7

LTV0500000002848

Fig. 119 Engine oil pressure indicator always on (Part 1 of 2). Aztek & Rendezvous w/3.5L engine

Step	Action	Yes	No
1	Did you perform the Diagnostic System Check - Vehicle?	Go to Step 2	Go to Diagnostic System Check -
2	1. Install a scan tool. 2. Turn ON the ignition, with the engine OFF. 3. With a scan tool, observe the Engine Oil Life Remaining parameter in the powertrain control module (PCM) Engine Data 2 data list. Does the scan tool display zero percent with the Change Engine Oil message on?	Go to Step 3	Go to Step 4
3	Reset GM engine oil life system. Does the Change Engine Oil message turn off?	Go to Step 5	Go to Step 4
4	Replace the instrument panel cluster (IPC). Did you complete the replacement?	Go to Step 5	--
5	1. Install a scan tool. 2. Turn ON the ignition, with the engine OFF. 3. With a scan tool, observe the Engine Oil Life Remaining parameter in the PCM Engine Data 2 data list. Does the scan tool display 100 percent with the Change Engine Oil message off?	System OK	Go to Diagnostic System Check -

LTV0500000002846

Fig. 117 Change engine oil indicator always on. Aztek & Rendezvous

Step	Action	Yes	No
6	Inspect for poor connections at the harness connector of the engine oil pressure switch. Did you find and correct the condition?	Go to Step 11	Go to Step 8
7	Inspect for poor connections at the harness connector of the PCM. Did you find and correct the condition?	Go to Step 11	Go to Step 9
8	Replace the engine oil pressure switch. Did you complete the replacement?	Go to Step 11	--
9	Replace the PCM. Did you complete the replacement?	Go to Step 11	--
10	Replace the IPC. Did you complete the replacement?	Go to Step 11	--
11	Operate the system in order to verify the repair. Did you correct the condition?	System OK	Go to Step 2

LTV0500000002849

Fig. 119 Engine oil pressure indicator always on (Part 2 of 2). Aztek & Rendezvous w/3.5L engine

Step	Action	Values	Yes	No
1	Did you perform the Diagnostic System Check - Vehicle?	--	Go to Step 2	Go to Diagnostic System Check
2	Does the engine oil pressure (EOP) indicator display in the message center?	--	Go to Step 3	Test for Intermittent Conditions and Poor Connections
3	1. Install a scan tool. 2. Turn ON the ignition, with the engine OFF. 3. With a scan tool, observe the Engine Oil Pressure Sensor parameter in the engine control module (ECM) instrument panel cluster (IPC) Data list. Is the Engine Oil Pressure Sensor parameter within the specified range?	207-483 kPa (30-70 psi)	Go to Step 15	Go to Step 4
4	1. Turn the ignition OFF. 2. Disconnect the EOP sensor. 3. Connect a 3-ampere fused jumper between the EOP sensor signal circuit and the 5-volt reference circuit of the EOP sensor. 4. With the scan tool, observe the Engine Oil Pressure Sensor parameter in the ECM IPC Data list. Does the scan tool indicate that the Engine Oil Pressure Sensor parameter is at or greater than the specified value?	550 kPa (80 psi)	Go to Step 5	Go to Step 6
5	1. Connect a 3-ampere fused jumper between the EOP sensor signal circuit and the low reference circuit of the EOP sensor. 2. With the scan tool, observe the Engine Oil Pressure Sensor parameter in the ECM IPC Data list. Does the scan tool indicate that the Engine Oil Pressure Sensor parameter is at or less than the specified value?	0 kPa (0 psi)	Go to Step 11	Go to Step 7
6	1. Disconnect the fused jumper. 2. Measure the voltage between the 5-volt reference circuit of the EOP sensor and the low reference circuit of the EOP sensor. Does the voltage measure greater than the specified value?	4.6 V	Go to Step 10	Go to Step 8

LTV0500000002850

Fig. 120 Engine oil pressure indicator always on (Part 1 of 3). Aztek & Rendezvous w/3.6L engine

Step	Action	Values	Yes	No
7	1. Disconnect the negative battery cable. 2. Measure the resistance from the low reference circuit of the EOP sensor to a good ground. Does the resistance measure less than the specified value?	5 ohms	Go to Step 12	Go to Step 9
8	Test the EOP 5-volt reference circuit for the following: • An open • A short to ground • A high resistance Did you find and correct the condition?	--	Go to Step 16	Go to Step 9
9	Test the EOP low reference circuit for high resistance or for an open. Did you find and correct the condition?	--	Go to Step 16	Go to Step 10
10	Test the EOP oil pressure sensor signal circuit for the following: • An open • A short to ground • A high resistance Did you find and correct the condition?	--	Go to Step 16	Go to Step 12
11	Inspect for poor connections at the harness connector of the EOP sensor. Did you find and correct the condition?	--	Go to Step 16	Go to Step 13

LTV0500000002851

Fig. 120 Engine oil pressure indicator always on (Part 2 of 3). Aztek & Rendezvous w/3.6L engine

Step	Action	Yes	No
12	Inspect for poor connections at the harness connector of the powertrain control module (PCM). Did you find and correct the condition?	Go to Step 16	Go to Step 14
13	Replace the engine oil pressure sensor. Did you complete the replacement?	Go to Step 16	--
14	Replace the PCM. Did you complete the replacement?	Go to Step 16	--
15	Replace the IPC. Did you complete the replacement?	Go to Step 16	--
16	Operate the system in order to verify the repair. Did you correct the condition?	System OK	Go to Step 2

LTV0500000002852

Fig. 120 Engine oil pressure indicator always on (Part 3 of 3). Aztek & Rendezvous w/3.6L engine

Step	Action	Yes	No
1	Did you perform the Diagnostic System Check - Vehicle?	Go to Step 2	Go to Diagnostic System Check
2	1. Install a scan tool. 2. Turn ON the ignition, with the engine OFF. 3. With a scan tool, observe the Engine Oil Level Switch parameter in the engine control module (ECM) instrument panel cluster (IPC) Data, data list - 3.6L. Does the Engine Oil Level Switch parameter display OK?	Go to Step 3	Go to Step 4
3	Does the low engine oil level indicator remain illuminated after the displays test?	Go to Step 10	Test for Intermittent Conditions and Poor Connections
4	1. Turn OFF the ignition. 2. Disconnect the ECM/powertrain control module (PCM) connector C2. 3. Turn ON the ignition, with the engine OFF. 4. Connect a test lamp between the signal circuit of the engine oil level switch at the ECM/PCM and battery positive voltage. Does the test lamp illuminate?	Go to Step 7	Go to Step 5
5	Test the signal circuit of the engine oil level indicator switch for an open, or for a short to voltage. Did you find and correct the condition?	Go to Step 12	Go to Step 6
6	Test the ground of the engine oil level indicator switch for an open. Did you find and correct the condition?	Go to Step 12	Go to Step 8

LTV0500000002853

Fig. 121 Low engine oil pressure indicator always on (Part 1 of 2). Aztek & Rendezvous

		Yes	No
7	Inspect for poor connections at the ECM/PCM. Did you find and correct the condition?	Go to Step 12	Go to Step 9
8	Inspect for poor connections at the engine oil level switch. Did you find and correct the condition?	Go to Step 12	Go to Step 11
9	Replace the ECM/PCM. Did you complete the replacement?	Go to Step 12	--
10	Replace the IPC. Did you complete the replacement?	Go to Step 12	--
11	Replace the engine oil level switch. Did you complete the replacement?	Go to Step 12	--
12	Operate the system in order to verify the repair. Did you correct the condition?	System OK	Go to Step 2

LTV0500000002854

Fig. 121   Low engine oil pressure indicator always on (Part 2 of 2). Aztek & Rendezvous

1	Did you perform the Diagnostic System Check - Vehicle?	Go to Step 2	Go to Diagnostic System Check
2	1. Turn the ignition OFF. 2. Disconnect the ambient air temperature sensor. 3. Connect a 3-ampere fused jumper wire between the signal circuit and the ground circuit of the ambient air temperature sensor. 4. Turn the ignition ON, with the engine OFF. Does the driver information center (DIC) display SC?	Go to Step 5	Go to Step 3
3	Test the signal circuit of the ambient air temperature sensor for a short to voltage, for a high resistance, or for an open. Did you find and correct the condition?	Go to Step 9	Go to Step 4
4	Test the ground circuit of the ambient air temperature sensor for a high resistance, for a short to voltage, or for an open. Did you find and correct the condition?	Go to Step 9	Go to Step 6
5	Inspect for poor connections at the harness connector of the ambient air temperature sensor. Did you find and correct the condition?	Go to Step 9	Go to Step 7
6	Inspect for poor connections at the harness connector of the instrument panel cluster (IPC). Did you find and correct the condition?	Go to Step 9	Go to Step 8
7	Replace the ambient air temperature sensor. Did you complete the replacement?	Go to Step 9	--
8	Replace the IPC. Did you complete the replacement?	Go to Step 9	--
9	Operate the system in order to verify the repair. Did you correct the condition?	System OK	Go to Step 2

LTV0500000002856

Fig. 123   Driver information center (DIC) temperature display always reads OC. Aztek & Rendezvous

Step	Action	Yes	No
1	Did you perform the Diagnostic System Check - Vehicle?	Go to Step 2	Go to Diagnostic System Check
2	1. Turn the ignition OFF. 2. Disconnect the ambient air temperature sensor. 3. Turn the ignition ON, with the engine OFF. Does the driver information center (DIC) display OC?	Go to Step 4	Go to Step 3
3	Test the signal circuit of the ambient air temperature sensor for a short to ground. Did you find and correct the condition?	Go to Step 7	Go to Step 5
4	Inspect for poor connections at the ambient air temperature sensor. Did you find and correct the condition?	Go to Step 7	Go to Step 6
5	Replace the instrument panel cluster (IPC). Did you complete the replacement?	Go to Step 7	--
6	Replace the ambient air temperature sensor. Did you complete the replacement?	Go to Step 7	--
7	Operate the system in order to verify the repair. Did you correct the condition?	System OK	Go to Step 2

LTV0500000002855

Fig. 122   Driver information center (DIC) temperature display always reads SC. Aztek & Rendezvous

Step	Action	Yes	No
1	Did you perform the Diagnostic System Check - Vehicle?	Go to Step 2	Go to Diagnostic System Check -
2	Verify the compass is inaccurate or C is displayed. Does the system operate normally?	Test for Intermittent Conditions and Poor Connections	Go to Step 3
3	Turn ON the ignition, with the engine OFF. Is the compass display blank?	Go to Step 7	Go to Step 4
4	Is CAL or C displayed?	Go to Step 5	Go to Step 6
5	Perform the compass calibration procedure. Does the compass operate properly?	Go to Step 8	Go to Step 6
6	Perform the compass variance procedure. Does the compass operate properly?	Go to Step 8	Go to Step 7
7	Replace the instrument panel cluster (IPC). Did you complete the replacement?	Go to Step 8	--
8	Operate the system in order to verify the repair. Did you correct the condition?	System OK	Go to Step 2

LTV0500000002857

Fig. 124   Driver information center (DIC) compass inaccurate or C displayed. Aztek & Rendezvous

Step	Action	Yes	No
1	Did you perform the Diagnostic System Check - Vehicle?	Go to Step 2	Go to Diagnostic System Check -
2	1. Turn ON the ignition, with the engine OFF. 2. Install a scan tool. 3. With a scan tool, observe the driver information center (DIC) switch parameters in the instrument panel cluster (IPC) Inputs data list. 4. Press and release each of the DIC switches. Does the scan tool display On when each switch is pressed and Off when each switch is released?	Test for Intermittent Conditions and Poor Connections	Go to Step 3
3	Does the scan tool display Off when each switch is pressed?	Go to Step 9	Go to Step 4
4	Does the scan tool always display On for the suspect switch even when the switch is released?	Go to Step 5	Go to Step 6
5	1. Turn OFF the ignition. 2. Disconnect the DIC switch connector. 3. Turn ON the ignition, with the engine OFF. 4. With a scan tool, observe the suspect DIC switch parameter. Does the scan tool display On for the suspect switch?	Go to Step 7	Go to Step 12
6	1. Turn OFF the ignition. 2. Disconnect the DIC switch connector. 3. Connect a 3-amp fused jumper wire between the signal circuit of the suspect DIC switch and a good ground. 4. Turn ON the ignition, with the engine OFF. 5. With a scan tool, observe the suspect DIC switch parameter. Does the scan tool display On for the suspect switch?	Go to Step 10	Go to Step 8

LTV0500000002858

Fig. 125 Driver information Center (DIC) switch(es) inoperative (Part 1 of 2). Aztek & Rendezvous

Step	Action	Yes	No
7	Test the signal circuit of the suspect DIC switch for a short to ground. Did you find and correct the condition?	Go to Step 14	Go to Step 11
8	Test the signal circuit of the suspect DIC switch for an open or high resistance. Did you find and correct the condition?	Go to Step 14	Go to Step 11
9	Test the ground circuit of the DIC switch for an open or high resistance. Did you find and correct the condition?	Go to Step 14	Go to Step 10
10	Inspect for poor connections at the harness connector of the DIC switch. Did you find and correct the condition?	Go to Step 14	Go to Step 12
11	Inspect for poor connections at the IPC. Did you find and correct the condition?	Go to Step 14	Go to Step 13
12	Replace the DIC switch. Did you complete the replacement?	Go to Step 14	--
13	Replace the IPC. Did you complete the replacement?	Go to Step 14	--
14	Operate the system in order to verify the repair. Did you correct the condition?	System OK	Go to Step 2

LTV0500000002859

Fig. 125 Driver information Center (DIC) switch(es) inoperative (Part 2 of 2). Aztek & Rendezvous

Step	Action	Values	Yes	No
1	Did you perform the Diagnostic System Check - Vehicle?	--	Go to Step 2	Go to Diagnostic System Check -
2	1. Turn ON the ignition, with the engine OFF. 2. Set the driver information center (DIC) to the compass/temperature display. Does the temperature displayed on the DIC match the current room temperature within 2°C (3°F)?	--	Test for Intermittent Conditions and Poor Connections	Go to Step 3
3	**Important:** Verify the J 33431-C Signal Generator and Instrument Panel Tester resistance settings with a DMM. 1. Connect the J 33431-C between the signal circuit of the ambient air temperature sensor and the ground circuit of the ambient air temperature sensor. 2. Turn ON the ignition, with the engine OFF. 3. Vary the resistance on the J 33431-C from 600-97,000 ohms. Does the DIC display the correct value?	--	Go to Step 6	Go to Step 4
4	Test the ambient air temperature sensor signal circuit for a high resistance. Did you find and correct the condition?	--	Go to Step 10	Go to Step 5

LTV0500000002860

Fig. 126 Outside air temperature display inaccurate or inoperative (Part 1 of 2). Aztek & Rendezvous

Step	Action		Yes	No
5	Test the ground circuit of the ambient air temperature sensor for a high resistance. Did you find and correct the condition?		Go to Step 10	Go to Step 7
6	Inspect for poor connections at the harness connector of the ambient air temperature sensor. Did you find and correct the condition?		Go to Step 10	Go to Step 8
7	Inspect for poor connections at the harness connector of the instrument panel cluster (IPC). Did you find and correct the condition?		Go to Step 10	Go to Step 9
8	Replace the ambient air temperature sensor. Did you complete the replacement?		Go to Step 10	--
9	Replace the IPC. Did you complete the replacement?		Go to Step 10	--
10	1. Use the scan tool in order to clear the IPC DTCs. 2. Operate the system in order to verify the repair. Did you correct the condition?		System OK	Go to Step 2

LTV0500000002861

Fig. 126 Outside air temperature display inaccurate or inoperative (Part 2 of 2). Aztek & Rendezvous

Step	Action	Yes	No
1	Did you perform the Diagnostic System Check - Vehicle?	Go to Step 2	Go to Diagnostic System Check -
2	1. Turn the ignition ON, with the engine OFF. 2. Adjust the head up display (HUD) dimmer switch to full intensity. Is the HUD display visible?	Test for Intermittent Conditions and Poor Connections	Go to Step 3
3	1. Turn the ignition OFF. 2. Disconnect the HUD module connector. 3. Turn the ignition ON, with the engine OFF. 4. Test for an open, for a short to ground, and a short to battery in the ignition circuit of the HUD module. Did you find and correct the condition?	Go to Step 11	Go to Step 4
4	1. Connect a test lamp between the dimmer signal circuit of the HUD and battery positive voltage. 2. Turn the HUD dimmer switch to the off position. Does the test lamp illuminate?	Go to Step 5	Go to Step 6
5	Disconnect the HUD dimmer switch. Does the test lamp still illuminate?	Go to Step 8	Go to Step 7

LTV0500000002862

Fig. 127   Head up display (HUD) inoperative (Part 1 of 2). Aztek & Rendezvous

Step	Action	Yes	No
6	Inspect for poor connections at the harness connector of the HUD module. Did you find and correct the condition?	Go to Step 11	Go to Step 9
7	Inspect for poor connections at the harness connector of the HUD dimmer switch. Did you find and correct the condition?	Go to Step 11	Go to Step 10
8	Repair a short to ground in the dimmer signal circuit. Did you complete the repair?	Go to Step 11	--
9	Replace the HUD module. Did you complete the replacement?	Go to Step 11	--
10	Replace the HUD dimmer switch. Did you complete the replacement?	Go to Step 11	--
11	Operate the system in order to verify the repair. Did you correct the condition?	System OK	Go to Step 2

LTV0500000002863

Fig. 127   Head up display (HUD) inoperative (Part 2 of 2). Aztek & Rendezvous

Step	Action	Yes	No
1	Did you perform the Diagnostic System Check - Vehicle?	Go to Step 2	Go to Diagnostic System Check
2	1. Turn ON the ignition, with the engine OFF. 2. Turn ON the inoperative turn signal. 3. Observe the turn signal lamp indicator on the head up display (HUD). Does the turn signal lamp indicator on the HUD operate properly?	Test for Intermittent and Poor Connections	Go to Step 3
3	Does the instrument panel cluster (IPC) turn signal lamp indicator operate properly?	Go to Step 4	Go to Diagnostic System Check
4	Test the suspect turn signal indicator control circuit to the HUD module for high resistance or an open. Did you find and correct the condition?	Go to Step 7	Go to Step 5
5	Inspect for poor connections at the harness connector of the HUD module. Did you find and correct the condition?	Go to Step 7	Go to Step 6
6	Replace the HUD module. Did you complete the replacement?	Go to Step 7	--
7	Operate the system in order to verify the repair. Did you correct the condition?	System OK	Go to Step 2

LTV0500000002864

Fig. 128   Head up display (HUD) turn signal indicator inoperative. Aztek & Rendezvous

Step	Action	Yes	No
1	Did you perform the Diagnostic System Check - Vehicle?	Go to Step 2	Go to Diagnostic System Check -
2	1. Turn the ignition ON, with the engine OFF. 2. Adjust the head up display (HUD) UP, then DOWN. Does the HUD display adjust properly?	Test for Intermittent Conditions and Poor Connections	Go to Step 3
3	Adjust the HUD image to full brightness. Does the image dim?	Go to Step 4	Go to Step 7
4	1. Turn the ignition OFF. 2. Disconnect the HUD module. 3. Connect a test lamp between the UP signal circuit and battery positive voltage. 4. Then connect a test lamp between the DOWN signal circuit and battery positive voltage. Does the test lamp illuminate in either instance?	Go to Step 5	Go to Step 6
5	Disconnect the HUD dimmer switch. Is the test lamp still illuminated?	Go to Step 11	Go to Step 9
6	1. Connect a test lamp between the UP signal circuit and battery positive voltage. 2. Move the HUD up/down switch to the UP position. 3. Connect a test lamp between the DOWN signal circuit and battery positive voltage. 4. Move the HUD up/down switch to the DOWN position. Does the test lamp illuminate in both cases?	Go to Step 10	Go to Step 8

LTV0500000002865

Fig. 129   Head up display (HUD) image adjustment inoperative (Part 1 of 2). Aztek & Rendezvous

Step	Action	Yes	No
7	Test the HUD dimming switch ground circuit for an open. Did you find and correct the condition?	Go to Step 14	Go to Step 9
8	1. Disconnect the HUD dimmer switch. 2. Test the HUD UP and DOWN signal circuits for an open, or for a high resistance. Did you find and correct the condition?	Go to Step 14	Go to Step 9
9	Inspect for poor connections at the harness connector of the HUD dimmer switch. Did you find and correct the condition?	Go to Step 14	Go to Step 13
10	Inspect for poor connections at the harness connector of the HUD module. Did you find and correct the condition?	Go to Step 14	Go to Step 12
11	Repair a short to ground in the HUD UP and DOWN signal circuit. Did you complete the repair?	Go to Step 14	--
12	Replace the HUD module. Did you complete the replacement?	Go to Step 14	--
13	Replace the HUD dimmer switch. Did you complete the replacement?	Go to Step 14	--
14	Operate the system in order to verify the repair. Did you correct the condition?	System OK	Go to Step 2

LTV0500000002866

Fig. 129 Head up display (HUD) image adjustment inoperative (Part 2 of 2). Aztek & Rendezvous

Step	Action	Yes	No
1	Did you perform the Diagnostic System Check - Vehicle?	Go to Step 2	Go to Diagnostic System Check -
2	1. Turn the ignition ON, with the engine OFF. 2. Adjust the head up display (HUD) dimmer switch from the lowest intensity to the highest intensity. Does the HUD dim properly?	Test for Intermittent Conditions and Poor Connections	Go to Step 3
3	Move the HUD image up and down. Does the image move up and down?	Go to Step 4	Go to Step 6
4	1. Turn the ignition OFF. 2. Disconnect the HUD module. 3. Turn the ignition ON, with the engine OFF. 4. Connect a test lamp between the HUD dimmer signal circuit and battery positive voltage. 5. Adjust the HUD from the lowest intensity to the highest intensity. Does the test lamp go from full intensity then to full dim?	Go to Step 7	Go to Step 5
5	Test the HUD dimmer signal circuit for an open. Did you find and correct the condition?	Go to Step 11	Go to Step 8
6	Test the HUD dimming switch ground circuit for an open. Did you find and correct the condition?	Go to Step 12	Go to Step 8

LTV0500000002867

Fig. 130 Head up display (HUD) intensity does not vary (Part 1 of 2). Aztek & Rendezvous

Step	Action	Yes	No
7	Inspect for poor connections at the harness connector of the HUD. Did you find and correct the condition?	Go to Step 11	Go to Step 9
8	Inspect for poor connections at the harness connector of the HUD dimmer switch. Did you find and correct the condition?	Go to Step 11	Go to Step 10
9	Replace the HUD module. Did you complete the replacement?	Go to Step 11	--
10	Replace the HUD dimmer switch. Did you complete the replacement?	Go to Step 11	--
11	Operate the system in order to verify the repair. Did you correct the condition?	System OK	Go to Step 2

LTV0500000002868

Fig. 130 Head up display (HUD) intensity does not vary (Part 2 of 2). Aztek & Rendezvous

Step	Action	Yes	No
1	Did you perform the Diagnostic System Check - Vehicle?	Go to Step 2	Go to Diagnostic System Check -
2	Are any indicators illuminated?	Go to Symptoms	Go to Step 3
3	1. Turn OFF the ignition. 2. Turn the headlamp switch to OFF. 3. Remove the key from the ignition. 4. Open the drivers door. Does the chime sound?	Go to Step 4	Test for Intermittent Conditions and Poor Connections
4	1. Turn OFF the ignition. 2. Disconnect the ignition switch connector. 3. Install a scan tool. 4. Turn ON the ignition, with the engine OFF. 5. With a scan tool, observe the Key In Ignition parameter in the body control module (BCM) data list. Does the Key In Ignition parameter display Inactive?	Go to Step 6	Go to Step 5
5	Test the key in ignition input circuit for a short to ground. Did you find and correct the condition?	Go to Step 8	Go to Step 7
6	Replace the ignition switch. Did you complete the replacement?	Go to Step 8	
7	Replace the BCM. Did you complete the replacement?	Go to Step 8	--
8	Operate the system in order to verify the repair. Did you correct the condition?	System OK	Go to Step 2

LTV0500000002869

Fig. 131 Chime always on. Aztek & Rendezvous

Step	Action	Yes	No
1	Did you perform the Diagnostic System Check - Vehicle?	Go to Step 2	Go to Diagnostic System Check
2	1. Turn OFF the ignition, with the key in the ignition. 2. Open the driver door. Does the chime sound?	Test for Intermittent Conditions and Poor Connections	Go to Step 3
3	Do the courtesy lights turn ON when you open the driver door?	Go to Step 4	Go to Courtesy Lamps Inoperative in Lighting Systems
4	1. Turn ON the ignition, with the engine OFF. 2. Turn ON the radio. 3. Adjust the radio balance and fade to the left front speaker. Does the speaker operate properly?	Go to Step 5	Go to Speakers Inoperative - One or More
5	Replace the radio. Did you complete the replacement?	Go to Step 6	--
6	Operate the system in order to verify the repair. Did you correct the condition?	System OK	Go to Step 2

LTV0500000002870

Fig. 132   Chime inoperative. Aztek & Rendezvous

Step	Action	Yes	No
6	Repair the open or a high resistance in the ground circuit. Did you complete the repair?	Go to Step 9	--
7	Repair the open, short to ground or high resistance in the ignition 1 voltage circuit. Did you complete the repair?	Go to Step 9	--
8	Replace the IPC. Did you complete the replacement?	Go to Step 9	--
9	Operate the system in order to verify the repair. Did you find and correct the condition?	System OK	Go to Step 3

LTV0500000002759

Fig. 133   Instrument cluster inoperative (Part 2 of 2). Blazer

Step	Action	Yes	No
1	Did you perform the Diagnostic System Check - Vehicle?	Go to Step 2	Go to Diagnostic System Check -
2	1. Install a scan tool. 2. Turn the ignition ON, with the engine OFF. 3. With the scan tool, perform the Coolant Gauge Sweep Test. Does the engine coolant temperature gage move up and down when commanded?	Test for Intermittent and Poor Connections	Go to Step 3
3	Replace the instrument panel cluster (IPC). Did you complete the replacement?	Go to Step 4	--
4	Operate the system in order to verify the repair. Did you correct the condition?	System OK	Go to Step 2

LTV0500000002760

Fig. 134   Engine coolant temperature gage inaccurate or inoperative. Blazer

Step	Action	Yes	No
1	Did you perform the Diagnostic System Check - Vehicle?	Go to Step 2	Go to Diagnostic System Check -
2	1. Turn the ignition ON, with the engine OFF. 2. Observe the instrument cluster. Does the instrument cluster perform the displays test?	Test for Intermittent and Poor Connections	Go to Step 3
3	1. Turn the ignition OFF. 2. Disconnect the instrument panel cluster (IPC). 3. Turn the ignition ON, with the engine OFF. 4. Connect a test lamp between the ignition 1 voltage circuit and a good ground. Does the test lamp illuminate?	Go to Step 4	Go to Step 7
4	Connect a test lamp between the ignition 1 voltage circuit of the instrument cluster and the ground circuit of the instrument cluster. Does the test lamp illuminate?	Go to Step 5	Go to Step 6
5	Inspect for poor connections at the harness connector of the IPC. Did you find and correct the condition?	Go to Step 9	Go to Step 8

LTV0500000002758

Fig. 133   Instrument cluster inoperative (Part 1 of 2). Blazer

Step	Action	Value(s)	Yes	No
1	Did you perform the Diagnostic System Check - Vehicle?	--	Go to Step 2	Go to Diagnostic System Check -
2	Start the engine. Does the engine oil pressure gage display that the engine oil pressure is within the specified range?	10-70 psi (69-483 kPa)	Test for Intermittent Conditions and Poor Connections	Go to Step 3
3	1. Turn the ignition OFF. 2. Disconnect the engine oil pressure sensor. 3. Start the engine. Does the engine oil pressure gage display at or above the specified value?	80 psi (550 kPa)	Go to Step 4	Go to Step 6
4	1. Turn the ignition OFF. 2. Connect a 3-amp fused jumper between the signal circuit of the engine oil pressure sensor and a good ground. 3. Start the engine. Does the engine oil pressure gage display at or below the specified value?	0 psi (0 kPa)	Go to Step 7	Go to Step 5
5	Test the signal circuit of the engine oil pressure sensor for an open, for a high resistance, or for a short to voltage. Did you find and correct the condition?	--	Go to Step 12	Go to Step 9

LTV0500000002761

Fig. 135   Engine oil pressure gage inaccurate or inoperative (Part 1 of 2). Blazer

Step	Action		Yes	No
6	Test the signal circuit of the engine oil pressure sensor for a short to ground. Did you find and correct the condition?		Go to Step 12	Go to Step 9
7	Inspect for a high resistance or for a poor connection at the case ground of the engine oil pressure sensor. Did you find and correct the condition?		Go to Step 12	Go to Step 8
8	Inspect for poor connections at the harness connector of the engine oil pressure sensor. Did you find and correct the condition?		Go to Step 12	Go to Step 10
9	Inspect for poor connections at the harness connector of the instrument panel cluster (IPC). Did you find and correct the condition?		Go to Step 12	Go to Step 11
10	Replace the engine oil pressure sensor. Did you complete the replacement?		Go to Step 12	--
11	Replace the IPC. Did you complete the replacement?		Go to Step 12	--
12	Operate the system in order to verify the repair. Did you correct the condition?		System OK	Go to Step 2

LTV0500000002762

Fig. 135   Engine oil pressure gage inaccurate or inoperative (Part 2 of 2). Blazer

Step	Action	Values	Yes	No
1	Did you perform the Diagnostic System Check - Vehicle?	--	Go to Step 2	Go to Diagnostic System Check -
2	1. Disconnect C104. 2. Connect the J 33431-C Signal Generator and Instrument Panel Tester between the signal circuit of the fuel level sensor and the low reference circuit of the fuel level sensor on the male terminal side. 3. Turn the ignition ON, with the engine OFF. **Important:** Verify the J 33431-C resistance settings with a DMM. 4. Vary the resistance on the J 33431-C from 40-250 ohms. 5. Check Fuel Level Specifications. Does the fuel gage display the correct fuel level?	--	Go to Step 4	Go to Step 3
3	1. Install a scan tool. 2. Turn the ignition ON, with the engine OFF. **Important:** Verify the J 33431-C resistance settings with a digital multimeter (DMM). 3. Vary the resistance on the J 33431-C from 40-250 ohms. 4. Check Fuel Level Specifications. **Important:** Turn the ignition OFF momentarily between the resistance settings in order to quickly update the scan tool display. 5. With the scan tool, observe the Fuel Tank Level Remaining parameter in the powertrain control module (PCM) Enhanced evaporative emission (EVAP) Data, data list. Does the scan tool display the correct fuel level percentage?	--	Go to Step 11	Go to Step 5

LTV0500000002763

Fig. 136   Fuel gage inaccurate or inoperative (Part 1 of 3). Blazer

Step	Action		Yes	No
4	Inspect for the following items: • A poor connection at the harness connector of the fuel level sensor • A high resistance in the signal circuit of the fuel level sensor or the low reference circuit of the fuel level sensor between the fuel level sensor and C104 • A misaligned fuel sender • A deformed fuel tank. Did you find and correct the condition?		Go to Step 13	Go to Step 7
5	Test the signal circuit of the fuel level sensor for a high resistance. Did you find and correct the condition?		Go to Step 13	Go to Step 6
6	Test the low reference circuit of the fuel level sensor for a high resistance. Did you find and correct the condition?		Go to Step 13	Go to Step 9
7	1. Remove the fuel level sender. 2. Inspect for the following items: - A stuck fuel level sender, i.e. the fuel strainer interfering with the sender float arm - Foreign material in the fuel tank, i.e. ice. Did you find and correct the condition?		Go to Step 13	Go to Step 8

LTV0500000002764

Fig. 136   Fuel gage inaccurate or inoperative (Part 2 of 3). Blazer

Step	Action	Values	Yes	No
8	1. With the DMM, measure the resistance of the fuel level sensor while moving the float arm. 2. Observe both the analog and digital displays on the DMM. Does the resistance change smoothly across the specified range?	40-250 ohms	Go to Diagnostic Aids	Go to Step 10
9	Inspect for poor connections at the harness connector of the PCM. Did you find and correct the condition?	--	Go to Step 13	Go to Step 12
10	Replace the fuel level sensor. Did you complete the replacement?	--	Go to Step 13	--
11	Replace the instrument panel cluster (IPC). Did you complete the replacement?	--	Go to Step 13	--
12	Replace the PCM. Did you complete the replacement?	--	Go to Step 13	--
13	1. Use the scan tool in order to clear the PCM DTCs. 2. Operate the system in order to verify the repair. Did you correct the condition?	--	System OK	Go to Step 2

LTV0500000002765

Fig. 136   Fuel gage inaccurate or inoperative (Part 3 of 3). Blazer

Step	Action	Yes	No
1	Did you perform the Diagnostic System Check - Vehicle?	Go to Step 2	Go to Diagnostic System Check -
2	Activate the trip reset button. Does the odometer display switch between trip and odometer?	Test for Intermittent and Poor Connections	Go to Step 3
3	Replace the instrument panel cluster (IPC). Did you complete the replacement?	Go to Step 4	--
4	Operate the system in order to verify the repair. Did you correct the condition?	System OK	Go to Step 3

LTV0500000002766

Fig. 137 Odometer trip/reset switch inoperative. Blazer

Step	Action		Yes	No
6	Inspect for poor connections at the harness connector of the IPC. Did you find and correct the condition?		Go to Step 11	Go to Step 9
7	Test the vehicle speed signal circuit for a short to voltage between the IPC and the PCM. Did you find and correct the condition?		Go to Step 11	Go to Step 8
8	Inspect for poor connections at the harness connector of the PCM. Did you find and correct the condition?		Go to Step 11	Go to Step 10
9	Replace the IPC. Did you complete the replacement?		Go to Step 11	--
10	Replace the PCM. Did you complete the replacement?		Go to Step 11	--
11	Operate the system in order to verify the repair. Did you correct the condition?		System OK	Go to Step 2

LTV0500000002768

Fig. 138 Speedometer and/or odometer inaccurate or inoperative (Part 2 of 2). Blazer

Step	Action	Values	Yes	No
1	Did you perform the Diagnostic System Check - Vehicle?	--	Go to Step 2	Go to Diagnostic System Check -
2	1. Install a scan tool. 2. Raise the vehicle drive wheels. 3. Start the engine. 4. Place the transmission into drive for an automatic transmission or third gear for a manual transmission. 5. With the scan tool, observe the Vehicle Speed parameter in the powertrain control module (PCM) Engine Data 1 data list. Does the Vehicle Speed parameter match the speedometer display?	--	Go to Step 3	Go to Step 4
3	Does the odometer operate properly?	--	Test for Intermittent Conditions and Poor Connections	Go to Step 9
4	1. Turn the ignition OFF. 2. Disconnect the PCM connector C2. 3. Turn the ignition ON. 4. Measure the voltage from the vehicle speed signal circuit to a good ground. Does the voltage measure greater than the specified value?	9 V	Go to Step 7	Go to Step 5
5	Test the vehicle speed signal circuit for an open or for a high resistance between the instrument panel cluster (IPC) and the PCM. Did you find and correct the condition?		Go to Step 11	Go to Step 6

LTV0500000002767

Fig. 138 Speedometer and/or odometer inaccurate or inoperative (Part 1 of 2). Blazer

Step	Action	Values	Yes	No
1	Did you perform the Diagnostic System Check - Vehicle?	--	Go to Step 2	Go to Diagnostic System Check -
2	1. Install a scan tool. 2. Start the engine. 3. With the scan tool, observe the Engine Speed parameter in the powertrain control module (PCM) Engine Data 1 data list. Does the Engine Speed parameter match the tachometer display?	--	Test for Intermittent Conditions and Poor Connections	Go to Step 3
3	1. Turn the ignition OFF. 2. Disconnect the PCM connector C2. 3. Turn the ignition ON, with the engine OFF. 4. Measure the voltage from the engine speed signal circuit to a good ground. Does the voltage measure greater than the specified value?	9 V	Go to Step 6	Go to Step 4
4	Test the engine speed signal circuit for an open or for a high resistance. Did you find and correct the condition?	--	Go to Step 10	Go to Step 5

LTV0500000002769

Fig. 139 Tachometer inaccurate or inoperative (Part 1 of 2). Blazer

Step	Action		Yes	No
5	Inspect for poor connections at the harness connector of the instrument panel cluster (IPC). Did you find and correct the condition?		Go to Step 10	Go to Step 8
6	Test the engine speed signal circuit for a short to voltage. Did you find and correct the condition?		Go to Step 10	Go to Step 7
7	Inspect for poor connections at the harness connector of the PCM. Did you find and correct the condition?		Go to Step 10	Go to Step 9
8	Replace the IPC. Did you complete the replacement?		Go to Step 10	--
9	Replace the PCM. Did you complete the replacement?		Go to Step 10	--
10	Operate the system in order to verify the repair. Did you correct the condition?		System OK	Go to Step 2

LTV0500000002770

Fig. 139 Tachometer inaccurate or inoperative (Part 2 of 2). Blazer

Step	Action	Yes	No
1	Did you perform the Diagnostic System Check - Vehicle?	Go to Step 2	Go to Diagnostic System Check
2	1. Install a scan tool. 2. Turn the ignition ON, with the engine OFF. 3. Compare the scan tool Battery Voltage parameter in the BCM Data data list to the volt gage display. Does the Battery Voltage parameter approximately match the volt gage display?	Go to Diagnostic System Check	Go to Step 3
3	Replace the instrument panel cluster (IPC). Did you complete the replacement?	Go to Step 4	--
4	Operate the system in order to verify the repair. Did you correct the condition?	System OK	Go to Step 2

LTV0500000002771

Fig. 140   Volt gage inaccurate or inoperative. Blazer

Step	Action	Yes	No
1	Did you perform the Diagnostic System Check - Vehicle?	Go to Step 2	Go to Diagnostic System Check
2	1. Install a scan tool. 2. Turn the ignition ON, with the engine OFF. 3. With the scan tool, perform the Lamp Test in the Instrument Panel Cluster Special Functions. Does the low fuel indicator illuminate when commanded ON?	Test for Intermittent Conditions and Poor Connections	Go to Step 3
3	Replace the instrument panel cluster (IPC). Did you complete the replacement?	Go to Step 4	--
4	Operate the system in order to verify the repair. Did you correct the condition?	System OK	Go to Step 2

LTV0500000002772

Fig. 141   Low fuel indicator inoperative. Blazer

Step	Action	Yes	No
1	Did you perform the Diagnostic System Check - Vehicle?	Go to Step 2	Go to Diagnostic System Check -
2	Test the instrument panel (I/P) lamp supply voltage circuit of the driver information center (DIC) for an open. Did you find and correct the condition?	Go to Step 8	Go to Step 3
3	Test the battery positive voltage circuit of the DIC for an open. Did you find and correct the condition?	Go to Step 8	Go to Step 4
4	Test the retained accessory power (RAP) fuse supply voltage circuit of the DIC for an open. Did you find and correct the condition?	Go to Step 8	Go to Step 5
5	Test the ground circuit of the DIC for an open. Did you find and correct the condition?	Go to Step 8	Go to Step 6
6	Inspect for poor connections at the harness connector of the DIC. Did you find and correct the condition?	Go to Step 8	Go to Step 7
7	Replace the DIC. Did you complete the replacement?	Go to Step 8	--
8	Operate the system in order to verify the repair. Did you correct the condition?	System OK	Go to Step 2

LTV0500000002773

Fig. 142   Driver information center (DIC) inoperative. Blazer

Step	Action	Yes	No
1	Did you review the Driver Information Center (DIC) Description and Operation?	Go to Step 2	Go to Driver Information Center (DIC) Description and Operation
2	1. Disconnect the ambient temperature sensor. 2. Connect the J 33431-C Signal Generator and Instrument Panel Tester between the signal circuit of the ambient temperature sensor and the ground circuit of the ambient temperature sensor. 3. Turn ON the ignition, with the engine OFF. **Important** Verify the J 33431-C resistance settings with a DMM. Disconnect one of the J 33431-C leads momentarily between the resistance settings in order to quickly update the DIC display. 4. Vary the resistance on the J 33431-C from 2,500-11,200 ohms. 5. Check Ambient Air Temperature Sensor Resistance in order to convert from resistance to DIC temperature display. Does the DIC display the correct temperature?	Go to Step 4	Go to Step 3
3	Test the signal circuit of the ambient temperature sensor for a short to ground. Did you find and correct the condition?	Go to Step 7	Go to Step 6
4	Inspect for a poor connection at the harness connector of the ambient temperature sensor. Did you find and correct the condition?	Go to Step 7	Go to Step 5

LTV0500000002774

Fig. 143   Driver information center (DIC) temperature display always reads SC (Part 1 of 2). Blazer

Step	Action	Yes	No
5	Replace the ambient temperature sensor. Did you complete the replacement?	Go to Step 7	--
6	Replace the DIC. Did you complete the replacement?	Go to Step 7	--
7	Operate the system in order to verify the repair. Did you correct the condition?	System OK	Go to Step 2

LTV0500000002775

Fig. 143   Driver information center (DIC) temperature display always reads SC (Part 2 of 2). Blazer

Step	Action	Yes	No
1	Did you review the Driver Information Center (DIC) Description and Operation?	Go to Step 2	Go to Driver Information Center (DIC) Description and Operation
2	1. Disconnect the ambient temperature sensor. 2. Connect the J 33431-C Signal Generator and Instrument Panel Tester between the signal circuit of the ambient temperature sensor and the ground circuit of the ambient temperature sensor. 3. Turn the ignition ON, with the engine OFF. **Important** Verify the J 33431-C resistance settings with a DMM Disconnect one of the J 33431-C leads momentarily between the resistance settings in order to quickly update the DIC display. 4. Vary the resistance on the J 33431-C from 2500-11200 ohms. 5. Check Ambient Air Temperature Sensor Resistance in order to convert from resistance to DIC temperature display. Does the DIC display the correct temperature?	Go to Step 5	Go to Step 3
3	Test the signal circuit of the ambient temperature sensor for an open. Did you find and correct the condition?	Go to Step 9	Go to Step 4
4	Test the ground circuit of the ambient temperature sensor for an open. Did you find and correct the condition?	Go to Step 9	Go to Step 6
5	Inspect for poor connections at the harness connector of the ambient temperature sensor. Did you find and correct the condition?	Go to Step 9	Go to Step 7

LTV0500000002776

Fig. 144   Driver information center (DIC) temperature display always reads OC (Part 1 of 2). Blazer

Step	Action	Yes	No
6	Inspect for poor connections at the harness connector of the DIC. Did you find and correct the condition?	Go to Step 9	Go to Step 8
7	Replace the ambient temperature sensor. Did you complete the replacement?	Go to Step 9	--
8	Replace the DIC. Did you complete the replacement?	Go to Step 9	--
9	Operate the system in order to verify the repair. Did you correct the condition?	System OK	Go to Step 2

LTV0500000002777

Fig. 144   Driver information center (DIC) temperature display always reads OC (Part 2 of 2). Blazer

Step	Action	Yes	No
4	Test the ground circuit of the ambient temperature sensor for a high resistance. Did you find and correct the condition?	Go to Step 9	Go to Step 6
5	Inspect for poor connections at the harness connector of the ambient temperature sensor. Did you find and correct the condition?	Go to Step 9	Go to Step 7
6	Inspect for poor connections at the harness connector of the DIC. Did you find and correct the condition?	Go to Step 9	Go to Step 8
7	Replace the ambient temperature sensor. Did you complete the replacement?	Go to Step 9	--
8	Replace the DIC. Did you complete the replacement?	Go to Step 9	
9	Operate the system in order to verify the repair. Did you correct the condition?	System OK	Go to Step 2

LTV0500000002779

Fig. 145   Driver information center (DIC) temperature display inaccurate or inoperative (Part 2 of 2). Blazer

Step	Action	Yes	No
1	Did you review the Driver Information Center (DIC) Description and Operation?	Go to Step 2	Go to Driver Information Center (DIC) Description and Operation
2	1. Disconnect the ambient temperature sensor connector. 2. Connect the J 33431-C Signal Generator and Instrument Panel Tester between the signal circuit of the ambient temperature sensor and the ground circuit of the ambient temperature sensor. 3. Turn the ignition ON, with the engine OFF. **Important** Verify the J 33431-C resistance settings with a DMM. Disconnect one of the J 33431-C leads momentarily between the resistance settings in order to quickly update the DIC display. 4. Vary the resistance on the J 33431-C from 2500-11200 ohms. 5. Check Ambient Air Temperature Sensor Resistance in order to convert from resistance to DIC temperature display. Does the DIC display the correct temperature?	Go to Step 5	Go to Step 3
3	Test the signal circuit of the ambient temperature sensor for a high resistance. Did you find and correct the condition?	Go to Step 9	Go to Step 4

LTV0500000002778

Fig. 145   Driver information center (DIC) temperature display inaccurate or inoperative (Part 1 of 2). Blazer

Step	Action	Yes	No
1	Did you review the Driver Information Center (DIC) Description and Operation?	Go to Step 2	Go to Driver Information Center (DIC) Description and Operation
2	Verify that the compass is inaccurate or that CAL or C is displayed. Does the system operate normally?	Test for Intermittent and Poor Connections	Go to Step 3
3	Turn the ignition ON, with the engine OFF. Is the compass display blank?	Go to Step 7	Go to Step 4
4	Is CAL or C displayed?	Go to Step 5	Go to Step 6
5	Perform the compass calibration procedure. Does the compass operate properly?	Go to Step 8	Go to Step 6
6	Perform the compass variance procedure. Does the compass operate properly?	Go to Step 8	Go to Step 7
7	Replace the DIC. Did you complete the replacement?	Go to Step 8	--
8	Operate the system in order to verify the repair. Did you correct the condition?	System OK	Go to Step 2

LTV0500000002780

Fig. 146   Driver information center (DIC) compass inaccurate or C displayed. Blazer

Step	Action	Yes	No
1	Did you review the Driver Information Center (DIC) Description and Operation?	Go to Step 2	Go to Driver Information Center (DIC) Description and Operation
2	Press each of the DIC switches. Do the switches operate normally?	Test for Intermittent and Poor Connections	Go to Step 3
3	Replace the DIC. Did you complete the replacement?	Go to Step 4	--
4	Operate the system in order to verify the repair. Did you correct the condition?	System OK	Go to Step 2

LTV0500000002781

Fig. 147   Driver information center (DIC) switch(es) inoperative. Blazer

Step	Action	Value (s)	Yes	No
	DEFINITION: One or more chime functions are inoperative.			
1	Did you perform the Diagnostic System Check - Vehicle?	--	Go to Step 2	Go to Diagnostic System Check
2	Replace the body control module (BCM). Did you complete the replacement?	--	Go to Step 3	Replace the body control module (BCM).
3	Operate the system in order to verify the repair. Did you correct the condition?	--	System OK	Go to Step 1

LTV0500000002783

Fig. 149   Chime inoperative. Blazer

Step	Action	Yes	No
1	Did you perform the Instrument Panel Cluster (IPC) Diagnostic System Check?	Go to Step 2	Go to Diagnostic System Check -
2	1. Install a scan tool. 2. Turn the ignition ON, with the engine OFF. 3. With the scan tool, perform the instrument panel cluster (IPC) Gages Output Control. Does the engine coolant temperature gage move up and down when commanded?	Test for Intermittent and Poor Connections	Go to Step 3
3	**Important** Program the replacement IPC. Replace the IPC. Did you complete the replacement?	Go to Step 4	--
4	Operate the system in order to verify the repair. Did you correct the condition?	System OK	Go to Step 2

LTV0500000002784

Fig. 150   Engine coolant temperature gage inaccurate or inoperative. Bravada

Step	Action		Yes	No
1	Did you perform the Diagnostic System Check - Vehicle?		Go to Step 2	Go to Diagnostic System Check -
2	1. Turn the headlamps OFF. 2. Turn the ignition OFF. 3. Remove the key from the ignition. 4. Close all doors. Does the chime sound?		Go to Step 3	Test for Intermittent and Poor Connections
3	Do any indicators illuminate when the chime sounds?		Go to Symptoms	Go to Step 4
4	1. Install a scan tool. 2. Turn the ignition ON, with the engine OFF. 3. Observe the Key in Ignition parameter in the BCM Input 1 data List. 4. Turn the ignition OFF. 5. Remove and insert the key from the ignition. Does the Key in Ignition parameter change states?		Go to Step 8	Go to Step 5
5	Test the key in ignition signal circuit for a short to ground. Did you find and correct the condition?		Go to Step 9	Go to Step 6
6	Inspect for poor connections at the harness connector of the ignition key alarm switch. Did you find and correct the condition?		Go to Step 9	Go to Step 7
7	Replace the ignition switch. Did you complete the replacement?		Go to Step 9	--
8	Replace the body control module (BCM). Did you complete the replacement?		Go to Step 9	--
9	Operate the system in order to verify the repair. Did you correct the condition?		System OK	Go to Step 3

LTV0500000002782

Fig. 148   Chime always on. Blazer

Step	Action	Yes	No
1	Did you perform the Instrument Cluster Diagnostic System Check?	Go to Step 2	Go to Diagnostic System Check -
2	Start the engine. Does the engine oil pressure gage display at or below 0 psi (0 kPa)?	Go to Step 3	Test for Intermittent and Poor Connections
3	1. Install a scan tool. 2. Turn the ignition ON. 3. With the scan tool, observe the Engine Oil Pressure Switch parameter in the PCM Engine Data 3 data list. Does the Engine Oil Pressure Switch parameter display Ok?	Go to Step 10	Go to Step 4
4	1. Turn the ignition OFF. 2. Disconnect the engine oil pressure switch. 3. Start the engine. 4. With the scan tool, observe the Engine Oil Pressure Switch parameter. Does the Engine Oil Pressure Switch parameter display Ok?	Go to Step 6	Go to Step 5
5	Test the signal circuit of the engine oil pressure switch for a short to ground. Did you find and correct the condition?	Go to Step 11	Go to Step 7
6	Inspect for poor connections at the harness connector of the engine oil pressure switch. Did you find and correct the condition?	Go to Step 11	Go to Step 8

LTV0500000002785

Fig. 151   Engine oil pressure gage inaccurate or inoperative (Part 1 of 2). Bravada

7	Inspect for poor connections at the harness connector of the PCM. Did you find and correct the condition?	Go to Step 11	Go to Step 9
8	Replace the engine oil pressure switch. Did you complete the replacement?	Go to Step 11	--
9	**Important** Program the replacement PCM. Replace the PCM. Did you complete the replacement?	Go to Step 11	--
10	**Important** Program the replacement IPC. Replace the IPC. Did you complete the replacement?	Go to Step 11	--
11	Operate the system in order to verify the repair. Did you correct the condition?	System OK	Go to Step 2

LTV0500000002786

Fig. 151 Engine oil pressure gage inaccurate or inoperative (Part 2 of 2). Bravada

4	Inspect for the following items: • A poor connection at the harness connector of the fuel level sensor. • A high resistance in the signal circuit of the fuel level sensor or the low reference circuit of the fuel level sensor between the fuel level sensor and C101. • A misaligned fuel level sender • A deformed fuel tank Did you find and correct the condition?	--	Go to Step 13	Go to Step 7
5	Test the signal circuit of the fuel level sensor for a high resistance. Did you find and correct the condition?	--	Go to Step 13	Go to Step 6
6	Test the low reference circuit of the fuel level sensor for a high resistance. Did you find and correct the condition?	--	Go to Step 13	Go to Step 9

7	1. Remove the fuel level sender.
	2. Inspect for the following items:
	  - A stuck fuel level sender (i.e. the fuel strainer interfering with the sender float arm).
	  - Foreign material in the fuel tank (ice).
	
	Did you find and correct the condition?
			Go to Step 13	Go to Step 8

8	1. With the DMM, measure the resistance of the fuel level sensor while moving the float arm. 2. Observe both the analog and digital displays on the DMM. Does the resistance change smoothly across the specified range?	40-250 ohms	Go to Diagnostic Aids	Go to Step 10

LTV0500000002788

Fig. 152 Fuel gage inaccurate or inoperative (Part 2 of 3). Bravada

1	Did you perform the Instrument Cluster Diagnostic System Check?	Go to Step 2	Go to Diagnostic System Check -
2	1. Disconnect C101. 2. Connect the J 33431-C Signal Generator and Instrument Panel Tester between the signal circuit of the fuel level sensor and the low reference circuit of the fuel level sensor on the female terminal side of the connector. 3. Turn the ignition ON, with the engine OFF. **Important:** Verify the J 33431-C resistance settings with a DMM. 4. Vary the resistance on the J 33431-C from 40-250 ohms. 5. Check Fuel Level Specifications Does the fuel gage display the correct fuel level?	Go to Step 4	Go to Step 3

3	1. Install a scan tool.
	2. Turn the ignition ON, with the engine OFF.
	
	Important: Verify the J 33431-C resistance settings with a DMM.
	
	3. Vary the resistance on the J 33431-C from 40-250 ohms.
	4. Check Fuel Level Specifications
	
	Important: Turn the ignition OFF momentarily between the resistance settings in order to quickly update the scan tool display.
	
	5. With the scan tool, observe one of the following Fuel Level parameters:
	  - Fuel Tank Level Remaining parameter in the PCM Enhanced EVAP Data data list.
	  - Fuel Level Sensor parameter in the PCM EVAP Data data list - 4.2L only.
	
	Does the scan tool indicate that the Fuel Tank Level Remaining or the Fuel Level Sensor parameter is less than the specified value?
		Go to Step 11	Go to Step 5

LTV0500000002787

Fig. 152 Fuel gage inaccurate or inoperative (Part 1 of 3). Bravada

9	Inspect for poor connections at the harness connector of the PCM. Did you find and correct the condition?	Go to Step 13	Go to Step 12
10	Replace the fuel level sensor. Did you complete the replacement?	Go to Step 13	--
11	**Important:** Program the replacement instrument panel control (IPC). Replace the IPC. Did you complete the replacement?	Go to Step 13	--
12	**Important:** Program the replacement PCM. Replace the PCM. Did you complete the replacement?	Go to Step 13	--
13	1. Use the scan tool in order to clear the PCM DTCs. 2. Operate the system in order to verify the repair. Did you correct the condition?	System OK	Go to Step 2

LTV0500000002789

Fig. 152 Fuel gage inaccurate or inoperative (Part 3 of 3). Bravada

Step	Action	Yes	No
1	Did you perform the Instrument Cluster Diagnostic System Check?	Go to Step 2	Go to Diagnostic System Check -
2	• Turn the ignition ON. • Activate the trip reset button. Does the odometer display switch between trip and odometer?	Test for Intermittent and Poor Connections	Go to Step 3
3	**Important** Program the replacement instrument panel cluster (IPC). Replace the IPC. Did you complete the replacement?	Go to Step 4	--
4	Operate the system in order to verify the repair. Did you correct the condition?	System OK	Go to Step 2

LTV0500000002790

Fig. 153   Odometer trip/reset switch inoperative. Bravada

Step	Action	Yes	No
1	Did you perform the Instrument Cluster Diagnostic System Check?	Go to Step 2	Go to Diagnostic System Check -
2	1. Install a scan tool. 2. Start the engine. 3. With the scan tool, observe the Engine Speed parameter in the IPC Data 1 data list. Does the Engine Speed parameter match the tachometer display?	Test for Intermittent and Poor Connections	Go to Step 3
3	Test the engine speed signal circuit for a high resistance between the IPC and PCM. Did you find and correct the condition?	Go to Step 6	Go to Step 4
4	Inspect for poor connections at the harness connector of the instrument cluster. Did you find and correct the condition?	Go to Step 6	Go to Step 5
5	**Important** Program the replacement IPC. Replace the IPC. Did you complete the replacement?	Go to Step 6	--
6	Operate the system in order to verify the repair. Did you correct the condition?	System OK	Go to Step 2

LTV0500000002792

Fig. 155   Tachometer inaccurate or inoperative. Bravada

Step	Action	Yes	No
1	Did you perform the Instrument Panel Cluster (IPC) Diagnostic System Check?	Go to Step 2	Go to Diagnostic System Check
2	1. Install a scan tool. 2. Turn the ignition ON, with the engine OFF. 3. With the scan tool, perform the IPC Gages Output Control. Does the volt gauge move up and down when commanded?	Go to Diagnostic System Check	Go to Step 3
3	**Important** Program the replacement IPC. Replace the IPC. Did you complete the replacement?	Go to Step 4	--
4	Operate the system in order to verify the repair. Did you correct the condition?	System OK	Go to Step 2

LTV0500000002793

Fig. 156   Volt gage inaccurate or inoperative. Bravada

Step	Action	Yes	No
1	Did you perform the Instrument Cluster Diagnostic System Check?	Go to Step 2	Go to Diagnostic System Check
2	1. Turn ON the ignition, with the engine OFF. 2. Install a scan tool. 3. With the scan tool, perform the segments test in the instrument panel cluster (IPC) scan tool output controls. Do all of the segments of the driver information center (DIC) illuminate?	Go to Step 3	Go to Step 6
3	1. Install a scan tool. 2. Raise the vehicles drive wheels. 3. Start the engine. 4. Place the transmission into drive for automatic transmission or third gear for manual transmission. 5. With the scan tool, observe the Vehicle Speed Sensor (VSS) parameter in the IPC Data 1 data list. Does the VSS parameter match the speedometer display?	Test for Intermittent Conditions and Poor Connections	Go to Step 4
4	Test the vehicle speed signal circuit for a high resistance between the IPC and the powertrain control module (PCM). Did you find and correct the condition?	Go to Step 7	Go to Step 5
5	Inspect for poor connections at the harness connector of the IPC. Did you find and correct the condition?	Go to Step 7	Go to Step 6
6	**Important** Program the replacement IPC. Replace the IPC. Did you complete the replacement?	Go to Step 7	--
7	Operate the system in order to verify the repair. Did you correct the condition?	System OK	Go to Step 3

LTV0500000002791

Fig. 154   Speedometer and/or odometer inaccurate or inoperative. Bravada

Step	Action	Yes	No
1	Did you perform the Instrument Cluster Diagnostic System Check?	Go to Step 2	Go to Diagnostic System Check
2	Start the engine. Does the CHANGE ENGINE OIL indicator illuminate?	Go to Step 3	Test for Intermittent and Poor Connections
3	1. Install a scan tool. 2. With a scan tool, observe the Engine Oil Life Remaining parameter in the PCM Engine Data 3 data list. Does the Engine Oil Life Remaining parameter display 0%?	Go to Step 4	Go to Step 5
4	Reset the engine oil life. Does the CHANGE ENGINE OIL indicator turn off?	Go to Step 6	Go to Step 5
5	**Important** Program the replacement IPC. Replace the IPC. Did you complete the replacement?	Go to Step 6	--
6	Operate the system in order to verify the repair. Did you correct the condition?	System OK	Go to Step 2

LTV0500000002794

Fig. 157   Change engine oil indicator always on. Bravada

Step	Action	Yes	No
1	Did you perform the Instrument Cluster Diagnostic System Check?	Go to Step 2	Go to Diagnostic System Check -
2	1. Install a scan tool. 2. Turn the ignition ON, with the engine OFF. 3. With the scan tool, perform the Lamp Test in the Instrument Panel Cluster Special Functions. Does the low fuel indicator illuminate when commanded ON?	Test for Intermittent and Poor Connections	Go to Step 3
3	Replace the IPC. Did you complete the replacement?	Go to Step 4	--
4	Operate the system in order to verify the repair. Did you correct the condition?	System OK	Go to Step 2

LTV0500000002795

Fig. 158 Low fuel indicator inoperative. Bravada

Step	Action	Yes	No
7	Test the signal circuit of the suspect DIC switch for a short to ground. Did you find and correct the condition?	Go to Step 14	Go to Step 11
8	Test the signal circuit of the suspect DIC switch for an open or high resistance. Did you find and correct the condition?	Go to Step 14	Go to Step 11
9	Test the ground circuit of the DIC switch for an open or high resistance. Did you find and correct the condition?	Go to Step 14	Go to Step 10
10	Inspect for poor connections at the harness connector of the DIC switch. Did you find and correct the condition?	Go to Step 14	Go to Step 12
11	Inspect for poor connections at the harness connector of the instrument panel cluster (IPC). Did you find and correct the condition?	Go to Step 14	Go to Step 13
12	Replace the DIC switch. Did you complete the replacement?	Go to Step 14	--
13	**Important** Program the replacement IPC. Replace the IPC. Did you complete the replacement?	Go to Step 14	--
14	Operate the system in order to verify the repair. Did you correct the condition?	System OK	Go to Step 2

LTV0500000002797

Fig. 159 Driver information center (DIC) switch(es) inoperative (Part 2 of 2). Bravada

Step	Action	Yes	No
1	Did you perform the Instrument Cluster Diagnostic System Check?	Go to Step 2	Go to Diagnostic System Check -
2	1. Install a scan tool. 2. Turn the ignition ON, with the engine OFF. 3. Press and release each of the DIC switches. 4. With a scan tool, observe the DIC switch parameters in the IPC Inputs/Outputs. Does the scan tool display On when each switch is pressed and Off when each switch is released?	Test for Intermittent Conditions and Poor Connections	Go to Step 3
3	Does the scan tool display Off when each switch is pressed?	Go to Step 9	Go to Step 4
4	Does the scan tool always display On for the suspect switch even when the switch is released?	Go to Step 5	Go to Step 6
5	1. Turn the ignition OFF. 2. Disconnect the DIC switch connector. 3. Turn the ignition ON, with the engine OFF. 4. With a scan tool, observe the suspect DIC switch parameter. Does the scan tool display On for the suspect switch?	Go to Step 7	Go to Step 12
6	1. Turn the ignition OFF. 2. Disconnect the driver information center (DIC) switch connector. 3. Connect a 3 amp fused jumper wire between the signal circuit of the suspect DIC switch and a good ground. 4. Turn the ignition OFF. 5. With a scan tool, observe the suspect DIC switch parameter. Does the scan tool display On for the suspect switch?	Go to Step 10	Go to Step 8

LTV0500000002796

Fig. 159 Driver information center (DIC) switch(es) inoperative (Part 1 of 2). Bravada

Step	Action	Yes	No
1	Did you perform the Audible Warnings Diagnostic System Check?	Go to Step 2	Go to Diagnostic System Check
2	Do any indicators illuminate when the chime sounds?	Go to Symptoms	Go to Step 3
3	1. Turn the ignition OFF. 2. Remove the key from the ignition. 3. Turn the headlamp switch to OFF. 4. Close all of the vehicles doors. 5. Open one or more of the vehicle's doors. Does the chime sound at all times regardless if the doors are open or closed?	Go to Step 16	Go to Step 4
4	1. Close all of the vehicles doors. 2. With a scan tool, observe the Door Ajar Switch parameters in the DDM/PDM Inputs data list. Do all of the Door Ajar Switch parameters display Off?	Go to Step 5	Go to Courtesy Lamps Always On
5	With a scan tool, observe the Left Rear Door Ajar Switch parameter and the Right Rear Door Switch parameter in the BCM Inputs data list. Do all of the Rear Door Switch parameters display Off?	Go to Step 6	Go to Courtesy Lamps Always On
6	With a scan tool, observe the Rear Gate/Door parameter in the IPC Inputs data list. Does the Rear Gate/Door parameter display Closed?	Go to Step 7	Go to Courtesy Lamps Always On
7	1. Turn the ignition OFF. 2. Remove the key from the ignition. 3. Turn the headlamp switch to OFF. 4. Open the driver's door. Does the chime sound?	Go to Step 8	Test for Intermittent Conditions and Poor Connections

LTV0500000002798

Fig. 160 Chime always on (Part 1 of 3). Bravada

Step	Action	Yes	No
8	1. Install a scan tool. 2. Turn the ignition ON, with the engine OFF. 3. With a scan tool, observe the Parklamp Switch parameter in the BCM Inputs data list. Does the Parklamp Switch parameter display inactive?	Go to Step 9	Go to Step 11
9	With a scan tool, observe the Headlamp Switch parameter in the BCM Inputs data list. Does the Headlamp Switch parameter display Inactive?	Go to Step 10	Go to Step 11
10	1. Turn the ignition OFF. 2. Remove the key from the ignition. 3. With a scan tool, observe the Key In Ignition parameter in the BCM Inputs data list. Does the Key In Ignition parameter display No?	Go to Step 15	Go to Step 12
11	Test the headlamp input signal circuit and the parklamp signal circuit at the BCM for a short to voltage. Did you find and correct the condition?	Go to Step 21	Go to Step 13
12	Test the key in ignition signal circuit for a short to ground. Did you find and correct the condition?	Go to Step 21	Go to Step 14
13	Inspect for poor connections at the harness connector of the headlamp switch. Did you find and correct the condition?	Go to Step 21	Go to Step 17
14	Inspect for poor connections at the harness connector of the ignition key alarm switch. Did you find and correct the condition?	Go to Step 21	Go to Step 18
15	Inspect for poor connections at the harness connector of the BCM. Did you find and correct the condition?	Go to Step 21	Go to Step 19

LTV0500000002799

Fig. 160   Chime always on (Part 2 of 3). Bravada

Step	Action	Yes	No
16	Inspect for poor connections at the harness connector of the radio or audio amplifier. Did you find and correct the condition?	Go to Step 21	Go to Step 20
17	Replace the headlamp switch. Did you complete the replacement?	Go to Step 21	--
18	Replace the ignition switch. Did you complete the replacement?	Go to Step 21	--
19	**Important** Program the replacement BCM. Replace the BCM. Did you complete the replacement?	Go to Step 21	--
20	**Important** Program the replacement radio or audio amplifier. Replace the radio. Did you complete the replacement?	Go to Step 21	--
21	Operate the system in order to verify the repair. Did you correct the condition?	System OK	Go to Step 3

LTV0500000002800

Fig. 160   Chime always on (Part 3 of 3). Bravada

Step	Action	Yes	No
	DEFINITION: One or more chime functions are inoperative.		
1	Did you perform the Audible Warning Diagnostic System Check?	Go to Step 2	Go to Diagnostic System Check -
2	1. Turn the ignition OFF, with the key in the ignition. 2. Open the driver's door. Does the chime sound?	Test for Intermittent Conditions and Poor Connections	Go to Step 3
3	Do the courtesy lights turn on when you open the drivers door?	Go to Step 4	Go to Courtesy Lamps Inoperative
4	1. Turn the ignition ON, with the engine OFF. 2. Turn the radio ON. 3. Adjust the radio balance and fade to the left front speaker. Does the speaker operate properly?	Go to Step 5	Go to Speakers Inoperative - One or More
5	**Important** Program the replacement radio or audio amplifier. Replace the radio. Did you complete the replacement?	Go to Step 6	--
6	Operate the system in order to verify the repair. Did you correct the condition?	System OK	Go to Step 1

LTV0500000002801

Fig. 161   Chime inoperative. Bravada

Step	Action	Yes	No
1	Did you perform the Diagnostic System Check - Vehicle?	Go to Step 2	Go to Diagnostic System Check
2	1. Install a scan tool. 2. Turn ON the ignition, with the engine OFF. 3. With the scan tool, perform the instrument panel cluster (IPC) Gages Output Control. Does the engine coolant temperature gage move up and down when commanded?	Test for Intermittent Conditions and Poor Connections	Go to Step 3
3	Replace the IPC. Did you complete the replacement?	Go to Step 4	--
4	Operate the system in order to verify the repair. Did you correct the condition?	System OK	Go to Step 2

LTV0500000002555

Fig. 162   Engine coolant temperature gage inaccurate or inoperative. Canyon & Colorado

Step	Action	Yes	No
1	Did you perform the Diagnostic System Check - Vehicle?	Go to Step 2	Go to Diagnostic System Check
2	Start the engine. Does the engine oil pressure (EOP) gage display at or below 0 psi (0 kPa)?	Go to Step 3	Test for Intermittent Conditions and Poor Connections
3	1. Install a scan tool. 2. Turn the ignition ON. 3. With the scan tool, observe the Engine Oil Pressure Switch parameter in the powertrain control module (PCM) Engine Data 3 data list. Does the Engine Oil Pressure Switch parameter display Ok?	Go to Step 10	Go to Step 4
4	1. Turn the ignition OFF. 2. Disconnect the EOP switch. 3. Start the engine. 4. With the scan tool, observe the Engine Oil Pressure Switch parameter. Does the Engine Oil Pressure Switch parameter display Ok?	Go to Step 6	Go to Step 5
5	Test the signal circuit of the EOP switch for a short to ground. Did you find and correct the condition?	Go to Step 11	Go to Step 7
6	Inspect for poor connections at the harness connector of the EOP switch. Did you find and correct the condition?	Go to Step 11	Go to Step 8

LTV0500000002556

Fig. 163   Engine oil pressure gage inaccurate or inoperative (Part 1 of 2). Canyon & Colorado

Step	Action	Yes	No
7	Inspect for poor connections at the harness connector of the PCM. Did you find and correct the condition?	Go to Step 11	Go to Step 9
8	Replace the EOP switch. Did you complete the replacement?	Go to Step 11	--
9	Replace the PCM. Did you complete the replacement?	Go to Step 11	--
10	Replace the IPC. Did you complete the replacement?	Go to Step 11	--
11	Operate the system in order to verify the repair. Did you correct the condition?	System OK	Go to Step 2

LTV0500000002557

Fig. 163   Engine oil pressure gage inaccurate or inoperative (Part 2 of 2). Canyon & Colorado

Step	Action	Yes	No
1	Did you perform the Diagnostic System Check - Vehicle?	Go to Step 2	Go to Diagnostic System Check
2	1. Disconnect C102. 2. Connect the J 33431-C Signal Generator and Instrument Panel Tester between the signal circuit of the fuel level sensor and the low reference circuit of the fuel level sensor on the female terminal side. 3. Turn ON the ignition, with the engine OFF. **Important:** Verify the J 33431-C resistance settings with a DMM. 4. Vary the resistance on the J 33431-C from 40-250 ohms. 5. Check Fuel Level Specifications. Does the fuel gage display the correct fuel level?	Go to Step 4	Go to Step 3
3	1. Install a scan tool. 2. Turn ON the ignition, with the engine OFF. **Important:** Verify the J 33431-C resistance settings with a DMM. 3. Vary the resistance on the J 33431-C from 40-250 ohms. 4. Check Fuel Level Specifications. **Important:** Turn the ignition OFF momentarily between the resistance settings in order to quickly update the scan tool display. 5. With the scan tool, observe the Fuel Level Sensor parameter in the powertrain control module (PCM) evaporative emission (EVAP) Data, data list. Does the scan tool display the correct fuel level percentage?	Go to Step 11	Go to Step 5

LTV0500000002558

Fig. 164   Fuel gage inaccurate or inoperative (Part 1 of 3). Canyon & Colorado

Step	Action	Yes	No
4	Inspect for the following items: • A poor connection at the harness connector of the fuel level sensor-- • A high resistance in the signal circuit of the fuel level sensor or the low reference circuit of the fuel level sensor between the fuel level sensor and C102 • A misaligned fuel sender • A deformed fuel tank. Did you find and correct the condition?	Go to Step 13	Go to Step 7
5	Test the signal circuit of the fuel level sensor for a high resistance. Did you find and correct the condition?	Go to Step 13	Go to Step 6
6	Test the low reference circuit of the fuel level sensor for a high resistance. Did you find and correct the condition?	Go to Step 13	Go to Step 9
7	1. Remove the fuel level sender. 2. Inspect for the following items: - A stuck fuel level sender, i.e. the fuel strainer interfering with the sender float arm - Foreign material in the fuel tank, i.e. ice. Did you find and correct the condition?	Go to Step 13	Go to Step 8

LTV0500000002559

Fig. 164   Fuel gage inaccurate or inoperative (Part 2 of 3). Canyon & Colorado

Step	Action		Yes	No
8	1. With the J 39200 DMM, measure the resistance of the fuel level sensor while moving the float arm. 2. Observe both the analog and digital displays on the DMM. Does the resistance change smoothly across the specified range?	40-250 ohms	Go to Diagnostic Aids	Go to Step 10
9	Inspect for poor connections at the harness connector of the PCM. Did you find and correct the condition?	--	Go to Step 13	Go to Step 12
10	Replace the fuel level sensor. Did you complete the replacement?	--	Go to Step 13	--
11	Replace the instrument panel cluster (IPC). Did you complete the replacement?	--	Go to Step 13	--
12	Replace the PCM. Did you complete the replacement?	--	Go to Step 13	--
13	1. Use the scan tool in order to clear the PCM DTCs. 2. Operate the system in order to verify the repair. Did you correct the condition?	--	System OK	Go to Step 2

LTV0500000002560

Fig. 164 Fuel gage inaccurate or inoperative (Part 3 of 3). Canyon & Colorado

Step	Action	Yes	No
1	Did you perform the Diagnostic System Check - Vehicle?	Go to Step 2	Go to Diagnostic System Check -
2	1. Install a scan tool. 2. Raise the vehicles drive wheels. 3. Start the engine. 4. Place the transmission into drive. 5. With the scan tool, observe the Vehicle Speed Sensor (VSS) parameter in the powertrain control module (PCM) evaporative emission (EVAP) Data, data list. Does the VSS parameter match the speedometer display?	Go to Step 3	Go to Step 4
3	Does the odometer operate properly?	Test for Intermittent Conditions and Poor Connections	Go to Step 4
4	Replace the instrument panel cluster (IPC). Did you complete the replacement?	Go to Step 5	--
5	1. Operate the system in order to verify the repair. 2. Use the scan tool in order to clear the DTCs that may have set in other modules during diagnosis. Did you correct the condition?	System OK	Go to Step 2

LTV0500000002722

Fig. 166 Speedometer and/or odometer inaccurate or inoperative. Canyon & Colorado

Step	Action	Yes	No
1	Did you perform the Diagnostic System Check - Vehicle?	Go to Step 2	Go to Diagnostic System Check
2	1. Turn ON the ignition. 2. Activate the trip reset button. Does the odometer display switch between trip and odometer?	Test for Intermittent Conditions and Poor Connections	Go to Step 3
3	Replace the instrument panel cluster (IPC). Did you complete the replacement?	Go to Step 4	--
4	Operate the system in order to verify the repair. Did you correct the condition?	System OK	Go to Step 2

LTV0500000002561

Fig. 165 Odometer trip/reset switch inoperative. Canyon & Colorado

Step	Action	Yes	No
1	Did you perform the Diagnostic System Check - Vehicle?	Go to Step 2	Go to Diagnostic System Check
2	1. Turn ON the ignition, with the engine OFF. 2. Install a scan tool. 3. With a scan tool, perform the tach gage sweep test. Does the tachometer gage move up and down when commanded?	Test for Intermittent Conditions and Poor Connections	Go to Step 3
3	Replace the instrument panel cluster (IPC). Did you complete the replacement?	Go to Step 4	--
4	Operate the system in order to verify the repair. Did you correct the condition?	System OK	Go to Step 2

LTV0500000002723

Fig. 167 Tachometer inaccurate or inoperative. Canyon & Colorado

Step	Action	Yes	No
1	Did you perform the Diagnostic System Check - Vehicle?	Go to Step 2	
2	1. Install a scan tool. 2. Turn the ignition ON, with the engine OFF. 3. With the scan tool, perform the instrument panel cluster (IPC) gages output control. Does the volt gauge move up and down when commanded?		Go to Step 3
3	Replace the IPC. Did you complete the replacement?	Go to Step 4	--
4	Operate the system in order to verify the repair. Did you correct the condition?	System OK	Go to Step 2

LTV0500000002724

Fig. 168 Volt gage inaccurate or inoperative. Canyon & Colorado

Step	Action	Yes	No
1	Did you perform the Diagnostic System Check - Vehicle?	Go to Step 2	Go to Diagnostic System Check
2	Start the engine. Does the engine oil pressure indicator illuminate after the display test?	Go to Step 3	Test for Intermittent Conditions and Poor Connections
3	1. Install a scan tool. 2. Turn the ignition ON. 3. With the scan tool, observe the Engine Oil Pressure Switch parameter in the powertrain control module (PCM) Engine Data 3 data list. Does the Engine Oil Pressure Switch parameter display Ok?	Go to Step 10	Go to Step 4
4	1. Turn the ignition OFF. 2. Disconnect the engine oil pressure (EOP) switch. 3. Start the engine. 4. With the scan tool, observe the Engine Oil Pressure Switch parameter. Does the Engine Oil Pressure Switch parameter display Ok?	Go to Step 6	Go to Step 5
5	Test the signal circuit of the EOP switch for a short to ground. Did you find and correct the condition?	Go to Step 11	Go to Step 7
6	Inspect for poor connections at the harness connector of the EOP switch. Did you find and correct the condition?	Go to Step 11	Go to Step 8

LTV0500000002725

Fig. 169 Engine oil pressure indicator always on (Part 1 of 2). Canyon & Colorado

Step	Action	Yes	No
7	Inspect for poor connections at the harness connector of the PCM. Did you find and correct the condition?	Go to Step 11	Go to Step 9
8	Replace the EOP switch. Did you complete the replacement?	Go to Step 11	--
9	Replace the PCM. Did you complete the replacement?	Go to Step 11	--
10	Replace the instrument panel cluster (IPC). Did you complete the replacement?	Go to Step 11	--
11	Operate the system in order to verify the repair. Did you correct the condition?	System OK	Go to Step 2

LTV0500000002726

Fig. 169 Engine oil pressure indicator always on (Part 2 of 2). Canyon & Colorado

Step	Action	Yes	No
1	Did you perform the Diagnostic System Check - Vehicle?	Go to Step 2	Go to Diagnostic System Check
2	Do any indicators illuminate when the chime sounds?	Go to Symptoms	Go to Step 3
3	1. Turn OFF the ignition. 2. Remove the key from the ignition. 3. Turn the headlamp switch to OFF. 4. Close all of the vehicle doors. 5. Open one or more of the vehicle doors Does the chime sound at all times, regardless if the doors are open or closed?	Go to Step 14	Go to Step 4
4	1. Close all of the vehicle doors. 2. With a scan tool, observe the Door Ajar Switch parameters in the body control module (BCM) inputs data list. Do all of the Door Ajar Switch parameters display door closed?	Go to Step 5	Go to Courtesy Lamps Always On
5	1. Turn OFF the ignition. 2. Remove the key from the ignition. 3. Turn the headlamp switch to OFF. 4. Open the driver door. Does the chime sound?	Go to Step 6	Test for Intermittent Conditions and Poor Connections
6	1. Install a scan tool. 2. Turn ON the ignition, with the engine OFF. 3. With a scan tool, observe the Park Lamp Switch parameter in the BCM inputs data list. Does the Park Lamp Switch parameter display OFF?	Go to Step 7	Go to Step 9

LTV0500000002727

Fig. 170 Chime always on (Part 1 of 3). Canyon & Colorado

Step	Action	Yes	No
7	With a scan tool, observe the Headlamp ON Switch parameter in the BCM Inputs data list. Does the Headlamp ON Switch parameter display Inactive?	Go to Step 8	Go to Step 9
8	1. Turn OFF the ignition. 2. Remove the key from the ignition. 3. With a scan tool, observe the Ign. Off/Run/Crank parameter in the BCM inputs data list. Does the Ign. Off/Run/Crank parameter display Inactive?	Go to Step 13	Go to Step 10
9	Test the headlamp input signal circuit and the park lamp signal circuit at the BCM for a short to voltage. Did you find and correct the condition?	Go to Step 19	Go to Step 11
10	Test the key in ignition signal circuit for a short to ground. Did you find and correct the condition?	Go to Step 19	Go to Step 12
11	Inspect for poor connections at the harness connector of the headlamp switch. Did you find and correct the condition?	Go to Step 19	Go to Step 15
12	Inspect for poor connections at the harness connector of the ignition key alarm switch. Did you find and correct the condition?	Go to Step 19	Go to Step 16

LTV0500000002728

Fig. 170 Chime always on (Part 2 of 3). Canyon & Colorado

Step	Action	Yes	No
13	Inspect for poor connections at the harness connector of the BCM. Did you find and correct the condition?	Go to Step 19	Go to Step 17
14	Inspect for poor connections at the harness connector of the radio or audio amplifier. Did you find and correct the condition?	Go to Step 19	Go to Step 18
15	Replace the headlamp switch. Did you complete the replacement?	Go to Step 19	--
16	Replace the ignition switch. Did you complete the replacement?	Go to Step 19	--
17	Replace the BCM. Did you complete the replacement?	Go to Step 19	--
18	Replace the radio. Did you complete the replacement?	Go to Step 19	--
19	Operate the system in order to verify the repair. Did you correct the condition?	System OK	Go to Step 3

LTV0500000002729

Fig. 170 Chime always on (Part 3 of 3). Canyon & Colorado

Step	Action	Yes	No
	DEFINITION: One or more chime functions are inoperative.		
1	Did you perform the Diagnostic System Check - Vehicle?	Go to Step 2	Go to Diagnostic System Check
2	1. Turn OFF the ignition, with the key in the ignition. 2. Open the driver door. Does the chime sound?	Test for Intermittent Conditions and Poor Connections	Go to Step 3
3	Do the courtesy lights turn ON when you open the driver door?	Go to Step 4	Go to Courtesy Lamps Inoperative
4	1. Turn ON the ignition, with the engine OFF. 2. Turn the radio ON. 3. Adjust the radio balance and fade to the left front speaker. Does the speaker operate properly?	Go to Step 5	Go to Speakers Inoperative - One or More
5	Replace the radio. Did you complete the replacement?	Go to Step 6	--
6	Operate the system in order to verify the repair. Did you correct the condition?	System OK	Go to Step 1

LTV0500000002730

Fig. 171   Chime inoperative. Canyon & Colorado

Step	Action	Yes	No
1	Did you perform the Diagnostic System Check - Vehicle?	Go to Step 2	Go to Diagnostic System Check -
2	1. Install a scan tool. 2. Turn ON the ignition, with the engine OFF. 3. With the scan tool, perform the instrument panel cluster (IPC) Gages Output Control. Does the engine coolant temperature gage move up and down when commanded?	Test for Intermittent Conditions and Poor Connections	Go to Step 3
3	Replace the IPC. Did you complete the replacement?	Go to Step 4	--
4	Operate the system in order to verify the repair. Did you correct the condition?	System OK	Go to Step 2

LTV0500000002802

Fig. 172   Engine coolant temperature gage inaccurate or inoperative. Envoy, Rainier & Trailblazer

Step	Action	Yes	No
1	Did you perform the Diagnostic System Check - Vehicle?	Go to Step 2	Go to Diagnostic System Check
2	Start the engine. Does the engine oil pressure gage display at or below 0 psi (0 kPa)?	Go to Step 3	Test for Intermittent Conditions and Poor Connections
3	1. Install a scan tool. 2. Turn ON the ignition. 3. With the scan tool, observe the Engine Oil Pressure Switch parameter in the powertrain control module (PCM) Engine Data 3 data list. Does the Engine Oil Pressure Switch parameter display Ok?	Go to Step 10	Go to Step 4
4	1. Turn OFF the ignition. 2. Disconnect the engine oil pressure (EOP) switch. 3. Start the engine. 4. With the scan tool, observe the Engine Oil Pressure Switch parameter. Does the Engine Oil Pressure Switch parameter display Ok?	Go to Step 6	Go to Step 5
5	Test the signal circuit of the engine oil pressure switch for a short to ground. Did you find and correct the condition?	Go to Step 11	Go to Step 7
6	Inspect for poor connections at the harness connector of the EOP switch. Did you find and correct the condition?	Go to Step 11	Go to Step 8

LTV0500000002803

Fig. 173   Engine oil pressure gage inaccurate or inoperative (Part 1 of 2) . Envoy, Rainier & Trailblazer w/4.2L engine

Step	Action	Yes	No
7	Inspect for poor connections at the harness connector of the PCM. Did you find and correct the condition?	Go to Step 11	Go to Step 9
8	Replace the engine oil pressure switch. Did you complete the replacement?	Go to Step 11	--
9	Replace the PCM. Did you complete the replacement?	Go to Step 11	--
10	Replace the instrument panel cluster (IPC). Did you complete the replacement?	Go to Step 11	--
11	Operate the system in order to verify the repair. Did you correct the condition?	System OK	Go to Step 2

LTV0500000002804

Fig. 173   Engine oil pressure gage inaccurate or inoperative (Part 2 of 2) . Envoy, Rainier & Trailblazer w/4.2L engine

Step	Action	Values	Yes	No
1	Did you perform the Diagnostic System Check - Vehicle?	--	Go to Step 2	Go to Diagnostic System Check -
2	Start the engine. Does the engine oil pressure (EOP) gage display within the specified range?	207-483 kPa (30-70 psi)	Test for Intermittent Conditions and Poor Connections	Go to Step 3
3	1. Install a scan tool. 2. Turn the ignition ON, with the engine OFF. 3. With a scan tool, perform the Displays Test in the instrument panel cluster (IPC) scan tool Output Controls. Does the EOP gage move up and down when commanded?	--	Go to Step 4	Go to Step 10
4	1. Turn the ignition OFF. 2. Disconnect the negative battery cable. 3. Disconnect the EOP sensor. 4. Measure the resistance from the low reference circuit of the EOP sensor to a good ground. Does the resistance measure less than the specified value?	5 ohms	Go to Step 6	Go to Step 5
5	Test the low reference circuit of the EOP sensor for high resistance or for an open. Did you find and correct the condition?	--	Go to Step 11	Go to Step 7
6	Inspect for poor connections at the harness connector of the EOP sensor. Did you find and correct the condition?	--	Go to Step 11	Go to Step 8

LTV0500000002805

Fig. 174   Engine oil pressure gage inaccurate or inoperative (Part 1 of 2). Envoy, Rainier & Trailblazer w/5.3L and 6.0L engines

Step	Action	Values	Yes	No
7	Inspect for poor connections at the harness connector of the powertrain control module (PCM). Did you find and correct the condition?	-	Go to Step 11	Go to Step 9
8	Replace the engine oil pressure sensor. Did you complete the replacement?	-	Go to Step 11	--
9	Replace the PCM. Did you complete the replacement?	-	Go to Step 11	--
10	Replace the IPC. Did you complete the replacement?	-	Go to Step 11	--
11	Operate the system in order to verify the repair. Did you correct the condition?	-	System OK	Go to Step 2

LTV0500000002806

Fig. 174   Engine oil pressure gage inaccurate or inoperative (Part 2 of 2). Envoy, Rainier & Trailblazer w/5.3L and 6.0L engines

Step	Action	Values	Yes	No
4	Inspect for the following items: • A poor connection at the harness connector of the fuel level sensor • A high resistance in the signal circuit of the fuel level sensor or the low reference circuit of the fuel level sensor between the fuel level sensor and C101 • A misaligned fuel level sender • A deformed fuel tank Did you find and correct the condition?	--	Go to Step 13	Go to Step 7
5	Test the signal circuit of the fuel level sensor for a high resistance. Did you find and correct the condition?	--	Go to Step 13	Go to Step 6
6	Test the low reference circuit of the fuel level sensor for a high resistance. Did you find and correct the condition?	--	Go to Step 13	Go to Step 9
7	1. Remove the fuel level sender. 2. Inspect for the following items: - A stuck fuel level sender (i.e. the fuel strainer interfering with the sender float arm) - Foreign material in the fuel tank (ice) Did you find and correct the condition?	--	Go to Step 13	Go to Step 8
8	1. With the DMM, measure the resistance of the fuel level sensor while moving the float arm. 2. Observe both the analog and digital displays on the DMM. Does the resistance change smoothly across the specified range?	40-250 ohms	Go to Diagnostic Aids	Go to Step 10

LTV0500000002808

Fig. 175   Fuel gage inaccurate or inoperative (Part 2 of 3). Envoy, Rainier & Trailblazer

Step	Action		Yes	No
1	Did you perform the Diagnostic System Check - Vehicle?		Go to Step 2	Go to Diagnostic System Check
2	1. Disconnect C101. 2. Connect the J 33431-C Signal Generator and Instrument Panel Tester between the signal circuit of the fuel level sensor and the low reference circuit of the fuel level sensor on the female terminal side of the connector. 3. Turn the ignition ON, with the engine OFF. **Important:** Verify the J 33431-C resistance settings with a DMM. 4. Vary the resistance on the J 33431-C from 40-250 ohms. 5. Check Fuel Level Specifications Does the fuel gage display the correct fuel level?		Go to Step 4	Go to Step 3
3	1. Install a scan tool. 2. Turn the ignition ON, with the engine OFF. **Important:** Verify the J 33431-C resistance settings with a DMM. 3. Vary the resistance on the J 33431-C from 40-250 ohms. 4. Check Fuel Level Specifications **Important:** Turn the ignition OFF momentarily between the resistance settings in order to quickly update the scan tool display. 5. With the scan tool, observe one of the following Fuel Level parameters: - Fuel Tank Level Remaining parameter in the powertrain control module (PCM) Enhanced evaporative emission (EVAP) Data, data list - Fuel Level Sensor parameter in the PCM EVAP Data, data list for the 4.2L only Does the scan tool indicate that the Fuel Tank Level Remaining or the Fuel Level Sensor parameter is less than the specified value?		Go to Step 11	Go to Step 5

LTV0500000002807

Fig. 175   Fuel gage inaccurate or inoperative (Part 1 of 3). Envoy, Rainier & Trailblazer

Step	Action		Yes	No
9	Inspect for poor connections at the harness connector of the PCM. Did you find and correct the condition?		Go to Step 13	Go to Step 12
10	Replace the fuel level sensor. Did you complete the replacement?	-	Go to Step 13	--
11	Replace the instrument panel cluster (IPC). Did you complete the replacement?		Go to Step 13	--
12	Replace the PCM. Did you complete the replacement?		Go to Step 13	--
13	1. Use the scan tool in order to clear the PCM DTCs. 2. Operate the system in order to verify the repair. Did you correct the condition?		System OK	Go to Step 2

LTV0500000002809

Fig. 175   Fuel gage inaccurate or inoperative (Part 3 of 3). Envoy, Rainier & Trailblazer

Step	Action	Yes	No
1	Did you perform the Diagnostic System Check - Vehicle?	Go to Step 2	Go to Diagnostic System Check -
2	1. Turn ON the ignition. 2. Activate the trip reset button. Does the odometer display switch between trip and odometer?	Test for Intermittent Conditions and Poor Connections	Go to Step 3
3	Replace the instrument panel cluster (IPC). Did you complete the replacement?	Go to Step 4	--
4	Operate the system in order to verify the repair. Did you correct the condition?	System OK	Go to Step 2

LTV0500000002810

Fig. 176 Odometer trip/reset switch inoperative. Envoy, Rainier & Trailblazer

Step	Action	Yes	No
5	Test the VSS high signal circuit for a high resistance, a short to ground, or a short to voltage between the PCM and the transmission control module (TCM). Did you find and correct the condition?	Go to Step 8	Go to Step 6
6	Inspect for poor connections at the harness connector of the IPC Did you find and correct the condition?	Go to Step 8	Go to Step 7
7	Replace the IPC. Did you complete the replacement?	Go to Step 8	--
8	Operate the system in order to verify the repair. Did you correct the condition?	System OK	Go to Step 3

LTV0500000002812

Fig. 177 Speedometer and/or odometer inaccurate or inoperative (Part 2 of 2). Envoy, Rainier & Trailblazer w/6.0L engine

Step	Action	Yes	No
1	Did you perform the Diagnostic System Check - Vehicle?	Go to Step 2	Go to Diagnostic System Check
2	1. Turn ON the ignition, with the engine OFF. 2. Install a scan tool. 3. With the scan tool, perform the segments test in the instrument panel cluster (IPC) scan tool output controls. Do all of the segments of the driver information center (DIC) illuminate?	Go to Step 3	Go to Step 6
3	1. Install a scan tool. 2. Raise the vehicle drive wheels. 3. Start the engine. 4. Place the transmission into drive for automatic transmission or third gear for manual transmission. 5. With the scan tool, observe the Vehicle Speed Sensor (VSS) parameter in the IPC Data 1 data list. Does the VSS parameter match the speedometer display?	Test for Intermittent Conditions and Poor Connections	Go to Step 4
4	Test the vehicle speed signal circuit for a high resistance between the IPC and the powertrain control module (PCM). Did you find and correct the condition?	Go to Step 8	Go to Step 5

LTV0500000002811

Fig. 177 Speedometer and/or odometer inaccurate or inoperative (Part 1 of 2). Envoy, Rainier & Trailblazer w/6.0L engine

Step	Action	Yes	No
5	Test the signal high-front circuit for a high resistance, a short to ground, or a short to voltage between the PCM and the transmission control module (TCM). Did you find and correct the condition?	Go to Step 8	Go to Step 6
6	Inspect for poor connections at the harness connector of the IPC. Did you find and correct the condition?	Go to Step 8	Go to Step 7
7	Replace the IPC. Did you complete the replacement?	Go to Step 8	--
8	Operate the system in order to verify the repair. Did you correct the condition?	System OK	Go to Step 3

LTV0500000002814

Fig. 178 Speedometer and/or odometer inaccurate or inoperative (Part 2 of 2). Envoy, Rainier & Trailblazer w/5.3L engine

Step	Action	Yes	No
1	Did you perform the Diagnostic System Check - Vehicle?	Go to Step 2	Go to Diagnostic System Check
2	1. Turn ON the ignition, with the engine OFF. 2. Install a scan tool. 3. With the scan tool, perform the segments test in the instrument panel cluster (IPC) scan tool output controls. Do all of the segments of the driver information center (DIC) illuminate?	Go to Step 3	Go to Step 6
3	1. Install a scan tool. 2. Raise the vehicle drive wheels. 3. Start the engine. 4. Place the transmission into drive for automatic transmission or third gear for manual transmission. 5. With the scan tool, observe the Vehicle Speed Sensor (VSS) parameter in the IPC Data 1 data list. Does the VSS parameter match the speedometer display?	Test for Intermittent Conditions and Poor Connections	Go to Step 4
4	Test the vehicle speed signal circuit for a high resistance between the IPC and the powertrain control module (PCM). Did you find and correct the condition?	Go to Step 8	Go to Step 5

LTV0500000002813

Fig. 178 Speedometer and/or odometer inaccurate or inoperative (Part 1 of 2). Envoy, Rainier & Trailblazer w/5.3L engine

Step	Action	Yes	No
1	Did you perform the Diagnostic System Check - Vehicle?	Go to Step 2	Go to Diagnostic System Check
2	1. Turn ON the ignition, with the engine OFF. 2. Install a scan tool. 3. With the scan tool, perform the segments test in the instrument panel cluster (IPC) scan tool output controls. Do all of the segments of the driver information center (DIC) illuminate?	Go to Step 3	Go to Step 6
3	1. Install a scan tool. 2. Raise the vehicle drive wheels. 3. Start the engine. 4. Place the transmission into drive for automatic transmission or third gear for manual transmission. 5. With the scan tool, observe the Vehicle Speed Sensor (VSS) parameter in the IPC Data 1 data list. Does the VSS parameter match the speedometer display?	Test for Intermittent Conditions and Poor Connections	Go to Step 4
4	Test the vehicle speed signal circuit for a high resistance between the IPC and the powertrain control module (PCM). Did you find and correct the condition?	Go to Step 7	Go to Step 5
5	Inspect for poor connections at the harness connector of the IPC. Did you find and correct the condition?	Go to Step 7	Go to Step 6
6	Replace the IPC. Did you complete the replacement?	Go to Step 7	--
7	Operate the system in order to verify the repair. Did you correct the condition?	System OK	Go to Step 3

LTV0500000002816

Fig. 179 Speedometer and/or odometer inaccurate or inoperative. Envoy, Rainier & Trailblazer w/4.2L engine

Step	Action	Yes	No
1	Did you perform the Diagnostic System Check - Vehicle?	Go to Step 2	Go to Diagnostic System Check -
2	1. Install a scan tool. 2. Turn the ignition ON, with the engine OFF. 3. With the scan tool, perform the instrument panel cluster (IPC) gages output control. Does the volt gauge move up and down when commanded?	Go to Diagnostic System Check -	Go to Step 3
3	Replace the IPC. Did you complete the replacement?	Go to Step 4	--
4	Operate the system in order to verify the repair. Did you correct the condition?	System OK	Go to Step 2

LTV0500000002818

Fig. 181 Volt gage inaccurate or inoperative. Envoy, Rainier & Trailblazer

Step	Action	Yes	No
1	Did you perform the Diagnostic System Check - Vehicle?	Go to Step 2	Go to Diagnostic System Check -
2	1. Install a scan tool. 2. Start the engine. 3. With the scan tool, observe the Engine Speed parameter in the IPC Data 1 data list. Does the Engine Speed parameter match the tachometer display?	Test for Intermittent Conditions and Poor Connections	Go to Step 3
3	Test the engine speed signal circuit for a high resistance between the instrument panel cluster (IPC) and powertrain control module (PCM). Did you find and correct the condition?	Go to Step 6	Go to Step 4
4	Inspect for poor connections at the harness connector of the instrument cluster. Did you find and correct the condition?	Go to Step 6	Go to Step 5
5	Replace the IPC. Did you complete the replacement?	Go to Step 6	--
6	Operate the system in order to verify the repair. Did you correct the condition?	System OK	Go to Step 2

LTV0500000002817

Fig. 180 Tachometer inaccurate or inoperative. Envoy, Rainier & Trailblazer

Step	Action	Yes	No
1	Did you perform the Diagnostic System Check - Vehicle?	Go to Step 2	Go to Diagnostic System Check -
2	Start the engine. Does the CHANGE ENGINE OIL indicator illuminate?	Go to Step 3	Test for Intermittent and Poor Connections
3	1. Install a scan tool. 2. With a scan tool, observe the Engine Oil Life Remaining parameter in the powertrain control module (PCM) Engine Data 2 data list. Does the Engine Oil Life Remaining parameter display 0%?	Go to Step 4	Go to Step 5
4	Reset the engine oil life. Does the CHANGE ENGINE OIL indicator turn off?	Go to Step 6	Go to Step 5
5	Replace the instrument panel cluster (IPC). Did you complete the replacement?	Go to Step 6	--
6	Operate the system in order to verify the repair. Did you correct the condition?	System OK	Go to Step 2

LTV0500000002819

Fig. 182 Change engine oil indicator always on. Envoy, Rainier & Trailblazer

Step	Action	Yes	No
1	Did you perform the Diagnostic System Check - Vehicle?	Go to Step 2	Go to Diagnostic System Check
2	1. Install a scan tool. 2. Turn ON the ignition, with the engine OFF. 3. With the scan tool, perform the Lamp Test in the instrument panel cluster (IPC) Special Functions. Does the low fuel indicator illuminate when commanded ON?	Test for Intermittent Conditions and Poor Connections	Go to Step 3
3	Replace the IPC. Did you complete the replacement?	Go to Step 4	--
4	Operate the system in order to verify the repair. Did you correct the condition?	System OK	Go to Step 2

LTV0500000002820

Fig. 183 Low fuel indicator inoperative. Envoy, Rainier & Trailblazer

Step	Action	Yes	No
1	Did you perform the Diagnostic System Check - Vehicle?	Go to Step 2	Go to Diagnostic System Check -
2	1. Install a scan tool. 2. Turn ON the ignition, with the engine OFF. 3. Press and release each of the driver information center (DIC) switches. 4. With a scan tool, observe the DIC switch parameters in the instrument panel cluster (IPC) Inputs/Outputs. Does the scan tool display On when each switch is pressed and Off when each switch is released?	Test for Intermittent and Poor Connections	Go to Step 3
3	Does the scan tool display Off when each switch is pressed?	Go to Step 9	Go to Step 4
4	Does the scan tool always display On for the suspect switch even when the switch is released?	Go to Step 5	Go to Step 6
5	1. Turn OFF the ignition. 2. Disconnect the DIC switch connector. 3. Turn ON the ignition, with the engine OFF. 4. With a scan tool, observe the suspect DIC switch parameter. Does the scan tool display On for the suspect switch?	Go to Step 7	Go to Step 12
6	1. Turn OFF the ignition. 2. Disconnect the DIC switch connector. 3. Connect a 3-amp fused jumper wire between the signal circuit of the suspect DIC switch and a good ground. 4. Turn ON the ignition, with the engine OFF. 5. With a scan tool, observe the suspect DIC switch parameter. Does the scan tool display On for the suspect switch?	Go to Step 10	Go to Step 8

LTV0500000002821

Fig. 184   Driver information center (DIC) switch(es) inoperative (Part 1 of 2). Envoy, Rainier & Trailblazer

Step	Action	Yes	No
1	Did you perform the Diagnostic System Check - Vehicle?	Go to Step 2	Go to Diagnostic System Check
2	Do any indicators illuminate when the chime sounds?	Go to Symptoms	Go to Step 3
3	1. Turn the ignition OFF. 2. Remove the key from the ignition. 3. Turn the headlamp switch to OFF. 4. Close all of the vehicle doors. 5. Open one or more of the vehicle doors Does the chime sound at all times regardless if the doors are open or closed?	Go to Step 16	Go to Step 4
4	1. Close all of the vehicle doors. 2. With a scan tool, observe the Door Ajar Switch parameters in the driver door module (DDM)/passenger door module (PDM) Inputs data list. Do all of the Door Ajar Switch parameters display Off?	Go to Step 5	Go to Courtesy Lamps Always On
5	With a scan tool, observe the Left Rear Door Ajar Switch parameter and the Right Rear Door Switch parameter in the body control module (BCM) Inputs data list. Do all of the Rear Door Switch parameters display Off?	Go to Step 6	Go to Courtesy Lamps Always On
6	With a scan tool, observe the Rear Gate/Door parameter in the instrument panel cluster (IPC) Inputs data list. Does the Rear Gate/Door parameter display Closed?	Go to Step 7	Go to Courtesy Lamps Always On
7	1. Turn the ignition OFF. 2. Remove the key from the ignition. 3. Turn the headlamp switch to OFF. 4. Open the driver door. Does the chime sound?	Go to Step 8	Test for Intermittent Conditions and Poor Connections

LTV0500000002823

Fig. 185   Chime always on (Part 1 of 3). Envoy, Rainier & Trailblazer

Step	Action	Yes	No
7	Test the signal circuit of the suspect DIC switch for a short to ground. Did you find and correct the condition?	Go to Step 14	Go to Step 11
8	Test the signal circuit of the suspect DIC switch for an open or high resistance. Did you find and correct the condition?	Go to Step 14	Go to Step 11
9	Test the ground circuit of the DIC switch for an open or high resistance. Did you find and correct the condition?	Go to Step 14	Go to Step 10
10	Inspect for poor connections at the harness connector of the DIC switch. Did you find and correct the condition?	Go to Step 14	Go to Step 12
11	Inspect for poor connections at the harness connector of the IPC. Did you find and correct the condition?	Go to Step 14	Go to Step 13
12	Replace the DIC switch. Did you complete the replacement?	Go to Step 14	--
13	Replace the IPC. Did you complete the replacement?	Go to Step 14	--
14	Operate the system in order to verify the repair. Did you correct the condition?	System OK	Go to Step 2

LTV0500000002822

Fig. 184   Driver information center (DIC) switch(es) inoperative (Part 2 of 2). Envoy, Rainier & Trailblazer

Step	Action	Yes	No
8	1. Install a scan tool. 2. Turn the ignition ON, with the engine OFF. 3. With a scan tool, observe the Parklamp Switch parameter in the BCM Inputs data list. Does the Parklamp Switch parameter display inactive?	Go to Step 9	Go to Step 11
9	With a scan tool, observe the Headlamp Switch parameter in the BCM Inputs data list. Does the Headlamp Switch parameter display Inactive?	Go to Step 10	Go to Step 11
10	1. Turn the ignition OFF. 2. Remove the key from the ignition. 3. With a scan tool, observe the Key In Ignition parameter in the BCM Inputs data list. Does the Key In Ignition parameter display No?	Go to Step 15	Go to Step 12
11	Test the headlamp input signal circuit and the parklamp signal circuit at the BCM for a short to voltage. Did you find and correct the condition?	Go to Step 21	Go to Step 13
12	Test the key in ignition signal circuit for a short to ground. Did you find and correct the condition?	Go to Step 21	Go to Step 14
13	Inspect for poor connections at the harness connector of the headlamp switch. Did you find and correct the condition?	Go to Step 21	Go to Step 17
14	Inspect for poor connections at the harness connector of the ignition key alarm switch. Did you find and correct the condition?	Go to Step 21	Go to Step 18
15	Inspect for poor connections at the harness connector of the BCM. Did you find and correct the condition?	Go to Step 21	Go to Step 19

LTV0500000002824

Fig. 185   Chime always on (Part 2 of 3). Envoy, Rainier & Trailblazer

Step	Action	Yes	No
16	Inspect for poor connections at the harness connector of the radio or audio amplifier. Did you find and correct the condition?	Go to Step 21	Go to Step 20
17	Replace the headlamp switch. Did you complete the replacement?	Go to Step 21	--
18	Replace the ignition switch. Did you complete the replacement?	Go to Step 21	--
19	Replace the BCM. Did you complete the replacement?	Go to Step 21	--
20	Replace the radio. Did you complete the replacement?	Go to Step 21	--
21	Operate the system in order to verify the repair. Did you correct the condition?	System OK	Go to Step 3

LTV0500000002825

Fig. 185 Chime always on (Part 3 of 3). Envoy, Rainier & Trailblazer

Step	Action	Yes	No
1	Did you perform the Diagnostic System Check - Vehicle?	Go to Step 2	Go to Diagnostic System Check -
2	1. Install a scan tool. 2. Turn the ignition ON, with the engine OFF. 3. With the scan tool, perform the Lamp and Gauge Check in the IPC Special Functions list. Does the engine coolant temperature gage move up and down when commanded?	Test for Intermittent and Poor Connections	Go to Step 3
3	Replace the instrument panel cluster (IPC). Did you complete the replacement?	Go to Step 4	--
4	Operate the system in order to verify the repair. Did you correct the condition?	System OK	Go to Step 2

LTV0500000002827

Fig. 187 Engine coolant temperature gage inaccurate or inoperative. Equinox & Torrent

Step	Action	Yes	No
1	Did you perform the Diagnostic System Check - Vehicle?	Go to Step 2	Go to Diagnostic System Check
2	1. Disconnect C406. 2. Connect the J 33431-C Signal Generator and Instrument Panel Tester between the signal circuit of the fuel level sensor and the low reference circuit of the fuel level sensor on the male terminal side. 3. Turn ON the ignition, with the engine OFF. **Important:** Verify the J 33431-C resistance settings with a DMM. 4. Vary the resistance on the J 33431-C from 40-250 ohms. 5. Check Fuel Level Specifications Does the fuel gage display the correct fuel level?	Go to Step 4	Go to Step 3
3	1. Install a scan tool. 2. Turn ON the ignition, with the engine OFF. **Important:** Verify the J 33431-C resistance settings with a DMM. 3. Vary the resistance on the J 33431-C from 40-250 ohms. 4. Check Fuel Level Specifications **Important:** Turn OFF the ignition momentarily between the resistance settings in order to quickly update the scan tool display. 5. With the scan tool, observe the Fuel Level Sensor parameter in the Powertrain EVAP Data, data list. Does the Fuel Level Sensor parameter display the correct fuel level amount?	Go to Step 9	Go to Step 5

LTV0500000002828

Fig. 188 Fuel gage inaccurate or inoperative (Part 1 of 3). Equinox & Torrent

Step	Action	Yes	No
	DEFINITION: One or more chime functions are inoperative.		
1	Did you perform the Diagnostic System Check - Vehicle?	Go to Step 2	Go to Diagnostic System Check -
2	1. Turn OFF the ignition, with the key in the ignition. 2. Open the driver door. Does the chime sound?	Test for Intermittent Conditions and Poor Connections	Go to Step 3
3	Do the courtesy lights turn ON when you open the driver door?	Go to Step 4	Go to Courtesy Lamps Inoperative
4	1. Turn ON the ignition, with the engine OFF. 2. Turn the radio ON. 3. Adjust the radio balance and fade to the left front speaker. Does the speaker operate properly?	Go to Step 5	Go to Speakers Inoperative - One or More
5	Replace the radio. Did you complete the replacement?	Go to Step 6	--
6	Operate the system in order to verify the repair. Did you correct the condition?	System OK	Go to Step 1

LTV0500000002826

Fig. 186 Chime inoperative. Envoy, Rainier & Trailblazer

Step	Action	Yes	No
4	Inspect for the following items: • A poor connection at the harness connector of the fuel level sensors • A high resistance in the signal circuit or the low reference circuit between the fuel level sensor and C406 • A misaligned fuel level sender • A deformed fuel tank Did you find and correct the condition?	-- / Go to Step 15	Go to Step 7
5	Test the signal circuit of the fuel level sensor for a high resistance. Did you find and correct the condition?	-- / Go to Step 15	Go to Step 6
6	Test the low reference circuit of the fuel level sensor for a high resistance. Did you find and correct the condition?	-- / Go to Step 15	Go to Step 10

7	1. Remove the fuel level senders.
	2. Inspect for the following items:
	    - A stuck fuel level sensor, i.e. the fuel strainer interfering with the sender float arm.
	    - Foreign material in the fuel tank, i.e. ice.
	
	Did you find and correct the condition?
		Go to Step 15	Go to Step 8

8	1. With the J 39200 DMM, measure the resistance of both fuel level sensors while moving the float arm. 2. Observe both the analog and digital displays on the DMM. Does the resistance change smoothly across the specified range on both fuel level sensors?	20-125 ohms / Go to Diagnostic Aids	Go to Step 11

LTV0500000002829

Fig. 188 Fuel gage inaccurate or inoperative (Part 2 of 3). Equinox & Torrent

9	1. Turn ON the ignition, with the engine OFF. **Important:** Verify the J 33431-C resistance settings with a DMM. 2. Vary the resistance on the J 33431-C from 40-250 ohms. 3. Check Fuel Level Specifications **Important:** Turn the ignition OFF momentarily between the resistance settings in order to quickly update the scan tool display. 4. With the scan tool, observe the Fuel Gage Position parameter in the Body Control Module (BCM) Accessory data list and the Fuel Level Sensor parameter in the Powertrain EVAP Data, data list. Does the Fuel Gage Position parameter match the Fuel Level Sensor parameter?	Go to Step 12	Go to Step 14
10	Inspect for poor connections at the harness connector of the powertrain control module (PCM). Did you find and correct the condition?	Go to Step 15	Go to Step 13
11	Replace the fuel level sensor with the abnormally high resistance. Did you complete the replacement?	Go to Step 15	--
12	Replace the instrument panel cluster (IPC). Did you complete the replacement?	Go to Step 15	--
13	Replace the PCM. Did you complete the replacement?	Go to Step 15	--
14	Replace the BCM. Did you complete the replacement?	Go to Step 15	--
15	1. Use the scan tool in order to clear the PCM DTCs. 2. Operate the system in order to verify the repair. Did you correct the condition?	System OK	Go to Step 2

LTV0500000002830

Fig. 188   Fuel gage inaccurate or inoperative (Part 3 of 3). Equinox & Torrent

Step	Action	Yes	No
1	Did you perform the Diagnostic System Check - Vehicle?	Go to Step 2	Go to Diagnostic System Check -
2	1. Install a scan tool. 2. Start the engine. 3. With the scan tool, observe the Engine Speed parameter in the Powertrain Engine Data 1 data list. Does the Engine Speed parameter match the tachometer display?	Test for Intermittent Conditions and Poor Connections	Go to Step 3
3	Replace the instrument panel cluster (IPC). Did you complete the replacement?	Go to Step 4	--
4	Operate the system in order to verify the repair. Did you correct the condition?	System OK	Go to Step 2

LTV0500000002833

Fig. 191   Tachometer inaccurate or inoperative. Equinox & Torrent

Step	Action	Yes	No
1	Did you perform the Diagnostic System Check - Vehicle?	Go to Step 2	Go to Diagnostic System Check
2	Replace the IPC. Did you complete the replacement?	Go to Step 3	--
3	Operate the system in order to verify the repair. Did you correct the condition?	System OK	Go to Step 2

LTV0500000002831

Fig. 189   Odometer trip/reset switch inoperative. Equinox & Torrent

Step	Action	Yes	No
1	Did you perform the Diagnostic System Check - Vehicle?	Go to Step 2	Go to Diagnostic System Check -
2	1. Install a scan tool. 2. Raise the vehicles drive wheels. 3. Start the engine. 4. Place the transmission into drive for an automatic transmission or third gear for a manual transmission. 5. With the scan tool, observe the Vehicle Speed parameter in the Powertrain Engine Data 1 data list. Does the Vehicle Speed parameter match the speedometer display?	Go to Step 3	Go to Step 4
3	Does the odometer operate properly?	Test for Intermittent Conditions and Poor Connections	Go to Step 4
4	Replace the instrument panel cluster (IPC). Did you complete the replacement?	Go to Step 5	--
5	Operate the system in order to verify the repair. Did you correct the condition?	System OK	Go to Step 2

LTV0500000002832

Fig. 190   Speedometer and/or odometer inaccurate or inoperative. Equinox & Torrent

Step	Action	Yes	No
1	Did you perform the Diagnostic System Check - Vehicle?	Go to Step 2	Go to Diagnostic System Check -
2	Start the engine. Does the engine oil pressure indicator illuminate after the displays test?	Go to Step 3	Test for Intermittent Conditions and Poor Connections
3	1. Install a scan tool. 2. With a scan tool, observe the Engine Oil Pressure Switch parameter in the Powertrain Engine Data 3 data list. Does the Engine Oil Pressure Switch parameter display No?	Go to Step 10	Go to Step 4
4	1. Turn OFF the ignition. 2. Disconnect the engine oil pressure switch. 3. Start the engine. 4. With the scan tool, observe the Engine Oil Pressure Switch parameter. Does the Engine Oil Pressure Switch parameter display Yes?	Go to Step 6	Go to Step 5
5	Test the signal circuit of the oil pressure switch signal for a short to ground. Did you find and correct the condition?	Go to Step 11	Go to Step 7
6	Inspect for poor connections at the harness connector of the engine oil pressure switch. Did you find and correct the condition?	Go to Step 11	Go to Step 8

LTV0500000002834

Fig. 192   Engine oil pressure indicator always on (Part 1 of 2). Equinox & Torrent

Step	Action	Yes	No
7	Inspect for poor connections at the harness connector of the powertrain control module (PCM). Did you find and correct the condition?	Go to Step 11	Go to Step 9
8	Replace the engine oil pressure switch. Did you complete the replacement?	Go to Step 11	--
9	Replace the PCM. Did you complete the replacement?	Go to Step 11	--
10	Replace the IPC. Did you complete the replacement?	Go to Step 11	--
11	Operate the system in order to verify the repair. Did you correct the condition?	System OK	Go to Step 2

LTV0500000002835

Fig. 192 Engine oil pressure indicator always on (Part 2 of 2). Equinox & Torrent

Step	Action	Yes	No
1	Did you perform the Diagnostic System Check - Vehicle?	Go to Step 2	Go to Diagnostic System Check
2	Are any indicators illuminated?	Go to Symptoms	Go to Step 3
3	1. Turn the ignition OFF. 2. Turn the headlamp switch to OFF. 3. Remove the key from the ignition. 4. Open the driver door. Does the chime sound?	Go to Step 4	Test for Intermittent Conditions and Poor Connections
4	1. Turn the ignition OFF. 2. Disconnect the ignition switch. 3. Install a scan tool. 4. Turn the ignition ON, with the engine OFF. 5. With a scan tool, observe the Key in Ignition parameter in the Body Control Module Switch Inputs data list. Does the Key in Ignition parameter display No?	Go to Step 6	Go to Step 5
5	Test the key in ignition signal circuit for a short to ground. Did you find and correct the condition?	Go to Step 8	Go to Step 7
6	Replace the ignition switch. Did you complete the replacement?	Go to Step 8	
7	Replace the body control module (BCM). Did you complete the replacement?	Go to Step 8	
8	Operate the system in order to verify the repair. Did you correct the condition?	System OK	Go to Step 2

LTV0500000002837

Fig. 194 Chime always on. Equinox & Torrent

Step	Action	Yes	No
1	Did you perform the Diagnostic System Check - Vehicle?	Go to Step 2	Go to Diagnostic System Check -
2	1. Place the key in the ignition. 2. Open the driver door. Does the chime sound?	Go to Step 3	Go to Step 4
3	Do the courtesy lamps illuminate when the driver door is opened?	Test for Intermittent Conditions and Poor Connections	Go to Courtesy Lamps Inoperative
4	Replace the body control module (BCM). Did you complete the replacement?	Go to Step 5	--
5	Operate the system in order to verify the repair. Did you correct the condition?	System OK	Go to Step 2

LTV0500000002838

Fig. 195 Chime inoperative. Equinox & Torrent

Step	Action	Yes	No
1	Did you perform the Diagnostic System Check - Vehicle?	Go to Step 2	Go to Diagnostic System Check -
2	Is the shift indicator display inaccurate?	Check Range Selector Displays Incorrect Range	Go to Step 3
3	1. Turn the park lamps ON. 2. Test the park lamp supply voltage circuit of the shift indicator for an open. Did you find and correct the condition?	Go to Step 8	Go to Step 4
4	Test the PRNDL/powertrain fuse supply voltage circuit of the shift indicator for an open. Did you find and correct the condition?	Go to Step 8	Go to Step 5
5	Test the ground circuit of the shift indicator for an open. Did you find and correct the condition?	Go to Step 8	Go to Step 6
6	Inspect for poor connections at the harness connector of the shift indicator. Did you find and correct the condition?	Go to Step 8	Go to Step 7
7	Replace the shift indicator. Did you complete the replacement?	Go to Step 8	--
8	Operate the system in order to verify the repair. Did you correct the condition?	System OK	Go to Step 2

LTV0500000002836

Fig. 193 Shift indicator inaccurate or inoperative. Equinox & Torrent

Step	Action	Yes	No
1	Did you perform the Diagnostic System Check - Vehicle?	Go to Step 2	
2	1. Turn ON the ignition, with the engine OFF. 2. Observe the instrument panel cluster (IPC). Does the IPC perform the displays test?		Go to Step 3
3	1. Turn OFF the ignition. 2. Disconnect the IPC. 3. Turn ON the ignition, with the engine OFF. 4. Connect a test lamp between the ignition 1 voltage circuit of the IPC and a good ground. Does the test lamp illuminate?	Go to Step 4	Go to Step 7
4	Connect a test lamp between the ignition 1 voltage circuit of the IPC and the ground circuit of the IPC. Does the test lamp illuminate?	Go to Step 5	Go to Step 6
5	Inspect for poor connections at the harness connector of the IPC. Did you find and correct the condition?	Go to Step 9	Go to Step 8

LTV0500000002530

Fig. 196 Instrument cluster inoperative (Part 1 of 2). Express & Savana

6	Repair the open or the high resistance in the IPC ground circuit. Did you complete the repair?	Go to Step 9	--
7	Repair the open, the short to ground or the high resistance in the ignition 1 voltage circuit. Did you complete the repair?	Go to Step 9	--
8	Replace the IPC. Did you complete the replacement?	Go to Step 9	--
9	Operate the system in order to verify the repair. Did you find and correct the condition?	System OK	Go to Step 3

LTV0500000002531

Fig. 196 Instrument cluster inoperative (Part 2 of 2). Express & Savana

Step	Action	Yes	No
1	Did you perform the Diagnostic System Check - Vehicle?	Go to Step 2	Go to Diagnostic System Check
2	1. Install a scan tool. 2. Turn ON the ignition, with the engine OFF. 3. With the scan tool, perform the Displays Test. Does the engine oil pressure gage move from 0 to its maximum value and back to 0 when you perform the Displays Test?	Test for Intermittent Conditions and Poor Connections	Go to Step 3
3	Replace the instrument panel cluster (IPC). Did you complete the replacement?	Go to Step 4	--
4	Operate the system in order to verify the repair. Did you correct the condition?	System OK	Go to Step 2

LTV0500000002532

Fig. 197 Engine oil pressure gage inaccurate or inoperative. Express & Savana

1	Did you perform the Diagnostic System Check - Vehicle?	Go to Step 2	Go to Diagnostic System Check
2	1. Disconnect C101. 2. Connect the J 33431-C Signal Generator and Instrument Panel Tester between the signal circuit of the fuel level sensor and the low reference circuit of the fuel level sensor on the female terminal side of the connector. 3. Turn ON the ignition, with the engine OFF. **Important:** Verify the J 33431-C resistance settings with a DMM. 4. Vary the resistance on the J 33431-C from 40-250 ohms. 5. Check Fuel Level Specifications Does the fuel gage display the correct fuel level?	Go to Step 4	Go to Step 3
3	1. Install a scan tool. 2. Turn ON the ignition, with the engine OFF. **Important:** Verify the J 33431-C resistance settings with a DMM. 3. Vary the resistance on the J 33431-C from 40-250 ohms. 4. Check Fuel Level Specifications **Important:** Turn the ignition OFF momentarily between the resistance settings in order to quickly update the scan tool display. 5. With the scan tool, observe one of the following fuel level parameters: - Fuel Tank Level Remaining % parameter in the powertrain control module (PCM) Enhanced EVAP data list - gas only. - Fuel Level Sensor % parameter in the Fuel data list - 6.6L diesel only. Do the Fuel Level % parameters display the correct fuel level percentage?	Go to Step 11	Go to Step 5

LTV0500000002533

Fig. 198 Fuel gage inaccurate or inoperative single tank (Part 1 of 3). Express & Savana

4	Inspect for the following items: - A poor connection at the harness connector of the fuel level sensor - A high resistance in the signal circuit or the low reference circuit between the fuel level sender and C101 - A misaligned fuel level sender - A deformed fuel tank Did you find and correct the condition?	--	Go to Step 13 / Go to Step 7
5	Test the signal circuit of the fuel level sender for a high resistance between C101 and the PCM. Did you find and correct the condition?	--	Go to Step 13 / Go to Step 6
6	Test the low reference circuit of the fuel level sender for a high resistance between C101 and the PCM. Did you find and correct the condition?	--	Go to Step 13 / Go to Step 9
7	1. Remove the fuel level sender. 2. Inspect for the following items: - The fuel level sensor is stuck, perhaps due to an interference with the fuel strainer. - The fuel tank contains foreign material, for instance, ice. Did you find and correct the condition?	--	Go to Step 13 / Go to Step 8
8	1. With the DMM, measure the resistance of the fuel level sender while moving the float arm. 2. Observe both the analog and digital displays on the DMM. Does the resistance change smoothly across the specified range?	40-250 ohms	Go to Diagnostic Aids / Go to Step 10

LTV0500000002534

Fig. 198 Fuel gage inaccurate or inoperative single tank (Part 2 of 3). Express & Savana

9	Inspect for poor connections at the harness connector of the PCM. Did you find and correct the condition?	Go to Step 13	Go to Step 12
10	Replace the fuel level sender. Did you complete the replacement?	Go to Step 13	--
11	Replace the instrument panel cluster (IPC). Did you complete the replacement?	Go to Step 13	--
12	Replace the PCM. Did you complete the replacement?	Go to Step 13	--
13	1. Use the scan tool in order to clear the PCM DTCs. 2. Operate the system in order to verify the repair. Did you correct the condition?	System OK	Go to Step 2

LTV0500000002535

Fig. 198 Fuel gage inaccurate or inoperative single tank (Part 3 of 3). Express & Savana

1	Did you perform the Diagnostic System Check - Vehicle?	Go to Step 2	Go to Diagnostic System Check -
2	1. Disconnect C101. 2. Connect a jumper wire between the signal circuit of the primary fuel level sender and the signal circuit of the secondary fuel level sender, female terminal side. 3. Connect the J 33431-C Signal Generator and Instrument Panel Tester between the signal circuit of the fuel level sensor and the low reference circuit of the fuel level sensor on the female terminal side of the connector. 4. Turn ON the ignition, with the engine OFF. **Important:** Verify the J 33431-C resistance settings with a DMM. 5. Vary the resistance on the J 33431-C from 40-250 ohms. 6. Check Fuel Level Specifications Does the fuel gage display the correct fuel level?	Go to Step 4	Go to Step 3
3	1. Install a scan tool. 2. Turn ON the ignition, with the engine OFF. **Important:** Verify the J 33431-C resistance settings with a DMM. 3. Vary the resistance on the J 33431-C from 40-250 ohms. 4. Check Fuel Level Specifications **Important:** Turn the ignition OFF momentarily between the resistance settings in order to quickly update the scan tool display. 5. With the scan tool, observe one of the following fuel level parameters: - Fuel Tank Level Remaining % parameter in the powertrain control module (PCM) Enhanced EVAP data list - gas only. - Fuel Level Sensor % parameter in the Fuel data list - 6.6L diesel only. Do the Fuel Level % parameters display the correct fuel level percentage?	Go to Step 11	Go to Step 5

LTV0500000002536

Fig. 199   Fuel gage inaccurate or inoperative dual tank (Part 1 of 3). Express & Savana

8	1. With the DMM, measure the resistance of the fuel level senders while moving the float arm. 2. Observe both the analog and digital displays on the DMM. Does the resistance change smoothly across the specified range?	40-250 ohms Go to Diagnostic Aids	Go to Step 10
9	Inspect for poor connections at the harness connector of the PCM. Did you find and correct the condition?	-- Go to Step 13	Go to Step 12
10	Replace the fuel level sender. Did you complete the replacement?	Go to Step 13	--
11	Replace the instrument panel cluster (IPC). Did you complete the replacement?	Go to Step 13	--
12	Replace the PCM. Did you complete the replacement?	Go to Step 13	--
13	1. Use the scan tool in order to clear the PCM DTCs. 2. Operate the system in order to verify the repair. Did you correct the condition?	System OK	Go to Step 2

LTV0500000002538

Fig. 199   Fuel gage inaccurate or inoperative dual tank (Part 3 of 3). Express & Savana

4	Inspect for the following items: - A poor connection at the harness connector of the fuel level senders - A high resistance in the primary and secondary signal circuits or the primary and secondary low reference circuits between the fuel level sender and C101 - A misaligned fuel level sender - A deformed primary or secondary fuel tank Did you find and correct the condition?	Go to Step 13	Go to Step 7
5	Test the signal circuits of the primary and secondary fuel level senders for a high resistance between C101 and the PCM. Did you find and correct the condition?	Go to Step 13	Go to Step 6
6	Test the low reference circuit of the primary and secondary fuel level senders for a high resistance between C101 and the PCM. Did you find and correct the condition?	Go to Step 13	Go to Step 9
7	1. Remove the fuel level senders. 2. Inspect for the following items: - The fuel level sender is stuck, perhaps due to an interference with the fuel strainer. - The fuel tank contains foreign material, for instance, ice. Did you find and correct the condition?	Go to Step 13	Go to Step 8

LTV0500000002537

Fig. 199   Fuel gage inaccurate or inoperative dual tank (Part 2 of 3). Express & Savana

1	Did you perform the Diagnostic System Check - Vehicle?	Go to Step 2	Go to Diagnostic System Check -
2	1. Turn ON the ignition, with the engine OFF. 2. Install a scan tool. 3. With the scan tool, perform the Displays Test. Does the gage move from 0 to its maximum value and back to 0 when you perform the Displays Test?	Go to Step 3	Go to Step 4
3	1. Install a scan tool. **Important:** If the suspect gage is the speedometer, the drive wheels of the vehicle must be raised and the transmission must be placed in drive or first gear. 2. Start the engine. 3. Observe the appropriate parameter in the powertrain control module (PCM) Data list. Does the parameter match the gage display?	Test for Intermittent and Poor Connections	Go to Step 4
4	Replace the instrument panel cluster (IPC). Did you complete the replacement?	Go to Step 5	--
5	1. Use the scan tool in order to clear any induced DTCs. 2. Operate the system in order to verify the repair. Did you correct the condition?	System OK	Go to Step 2

LTV0500000002539

Fig. 200   Instrument panel cluster (IPC) gages inoperative. Express & Savana

Step	Action	Yes	No
1	Did you perform the Diagnostic System Check - Vehicle?	Go to Step 2	Go to Diagnostic System Check
2	Start the engine. Does the change engine oil indicator illuminate in the instrument panel cluster (IPC)?	Go to Step 3	Test for Intermittent Conditions and Poor Connections
3	1. Install a scan tool. 2. With the scan tool, observe one of the following engine oil life remaining parameters: - Engine Oil Life Remaining parameter in the powertrain control module (PCM) Engine Data 2 data list - gas only. - Engine Oil Life Remaining parameter in the PCM Engine Data 1 data list - 6.6L diesel only. Does the Engine Oil Life parameter display 0%?	Go to Step 4	Go to Step 5
4	Reset the engine oil life. Does the change engine oil indicator turn off?	Go to Step 6	Go to Step 5
5	Replace the IPC. Did you complete the replacement?	Go to Step 6	---
6	Operate the system in order to verify the repair. Did you correct the condition?	System OK	Go to Step 2

LTV0500000002540

Fig. 201 Change oil indicator always on. Express & Savana

Step	Action	Yes	No
1	Did you perform the Diagnostic System Check - Vehicle?	Go to Step 2	Go to Diagnostic System Check
2	1. Install a scan tool. 2. Turn ON the ignition, with the engine OFF. 3. With the scan tool, observe one of the engine oil life remaining parameters: - Engine Oil Life Remaining parameter in the powertrain control module (PCM) Engine Data 2 data list - gas only. - Engine Oil Life Remaining parameter in the PCM Engine Data 1 data list - 6.6L diesel only. Does the Engine Oil Life parameter display 0%?	Go to Step 3	Test for Intermittent Conditions and Poor Connections
3	Replace the instrument panel cluster (IPC). Did you complete the replacement?	Go to Step 4	---
4	Operate the system in order to verify the repair. Did you correct the condition?	System OK	Go to Step 2

LTV0500000002541

Fig. 202 Change oil indicator inoperative. Express & Savana

Step	Action	Values	Yes	No
1	Did you perform the Diagnostic System Check - Vehicle?	--	Go to Step 2	Go to Diagnostic System Check
2	1. Install a scan tool. 2. Turn ON the ignition, with the engine OFF. 3. With the scan tool, observe one of the following engine oil level switch parameters: - Engine Oil Level Switch parameter in the powertrain control module (PCM) Engine Data 2 data list - gas only. - Engine Oil Level Switch parameter in the PCM Engine Data 1 data list - 6.6L diesel only Does the Engine Oil Level Switch parameter display Ok?	--	Go to Step 3	Go to Step 4
3	Does the low engine oil level indicator remain illuminated after the displays test?	--	Go to Step 11	Test for Intermittent Conditions and Poor Connections
4	1. Turn OFF the ignition. 2. Disconnect the engine oil level switch. 3. Connect a 3-ampere fused jumper between the signal circuit of the engine oil level switch and a good ground. 4. Turn ON the ignition, with the engine OFF. 5. With the scan tool, observe the Engine Oil Level Switch parameter. Does the Engine Oil Level Switch parameter display Ok?	--	Go to Step 6	Go to Step 5

LTV0500000002542

Fig. 203 Low engine oil dipstick always on (Part 1 of 2). Express & Savana

Step	Action		Yes	No
5	Test the signal circuit of the engine oil level switch for the following: • An open • A high resistance • A short to battery voltage Did you find and correct the condition?		Go to Step 12	Go to Step 8
6	Test the ground circuit of the engine oil level switch for an open or for a high resistance. Did you find and correct the condition?		Go to Step 12	Go to Step 7
7	Inspect for poor connections at the harness connector of the engine oil level switch. Did you find and correct the condition?		Go to Step 12	Go to Step 9
8	Inspect for poor connections at the harness connector of the PCM. Did you find and correct the condition?		Go to Step 12	Go to Step 10
9	Replace the engine oil level switch. Did you complete the replacement?		Go to Step 12	--
10	Replace the PCM. Did you complete the replacement?		Go to Step 12	--
11	Replace the instrument panel cluster (IPC). Did you complete the replacement?		Go to Step 12	--
12	Operate the system in order to verify the repair. Did you correct the condition?		System OK	Go to Step 2

LTV0500000002543

Fig. 203 Low engine oil dipstick always on (Part 2 of 2). Express & Savana

Step	Action	Yes	No
1	Did you perform the Diagnostic System Check - Vehicle?	Go to Step 2	Go to Diagnostic System Check -
2	1. Install a scan tool. 2. Turn ON the ignition, with the engine OFF. 3. With the scan tool, perform the Displays Test in the instrument panel cluster (IPC) Special Functions. Does the low fuel indicator illuminate?	Test for Intermittent Conditions and Poor Connections	Go to Step 3
3	Replace the IPC. Did you complete the replacement?	Go to Step 4	--
4	Operate the system in order to verify the repair. Did you correct the condition?	System OK	Go to Step 2

LTV0500000002544

Fig. 204 Low fuel indicator inoperative. Express & Savana

Step	Action	Yes	No
8	Inspect for poor connections at the harness connector of the IPC. Did you find and correct the condition?	Go to Step 12	Go to Step 11
9	Replace the water in fuel sensor. Did you complete the replacement?	Go to Step 12	--
10	Replace the PCM. Did you complete the replacement?	Go to Step 12	--
11	Replace the IPC. Did you complete the replacement?	Go to Step 12	--
12	Operate the system in order to verify the repair. Did you correct the condition?	System OK	Go to Step 2

LTV0500000002546

Fig. 205 Water-in-fuel lamp always on (Part 2 of 2). Express & Savana

Step	Action	Yes	No
1	Did you perform the Diagnostic System Check - Vehicle?	Go to Step 2	Go to Diagnostic System Check -
2	1. Turn OFF the engine. 2. Disconnect the water in fuel sensor. 3. Connect a 3-ampere fused jumper wire between the signal circuit of the water in fuel sensor and a good ground. 4. Turn ON the ignition, with the engine OFF. Does the water in fuel indicator illuminate in the instrument panel cluster (IPC)?	Go to Step 3	Go to Step 4
3	1. Turn OFF the ignition. 2. Connect a 3-ampere fused jumper wire between the signal circuit of the water in fuel sensor and the ground circuit of the water in fuel sensor. 3. Turn ON the ignition, with the engine OFF. Does the water in fuel indicator illuminate in the IPC?	Go to Step 9	Go to Step 6
4	Test the signal circuit of the water in fuel sensor for an open or for a high resistance. Did you find and correct the condition?	Go to Step 13	Go to Step 5
5	1. Install a scan tool. 2. Turn OFF the engine. 3. Disconnect the water in fuel sensor. 4. Connect a 3-ampere fused jumper wire between the signal circuit of the water in fuel sensor and a good ground. 5. Turn ON the ignition, with the engine OFF. 6. With the scan tool, observe the Water In Fuel Sensor parameter in the PCM Engine Data 1 data list. Does the Water In Fuel Sensor parameter display Water?	Go to Step 7	Go to Step 8

LTV0500000002547

Fig. 206 Water-in-fuel lamp inoperative (Part 1 of 2). Express & Savana

Step	Action	Yes	No
1	Did you perform the Diagnostic System Check - Vehicle?	Go to Step 2	Go to Diagnostic System Check
2	Does the Water In Fuel indicator remain illuminated in the instrument panel cluster (IPC) after the displays test?	Go to Step 3	Test for Intermittent Conditions and Poor Connections
3	1. Turn OFF the ignition. 2. Disconnect the water in fuel sensor. 3. Turn ON the ignition, with the engine OFF. Does the Water In Fuel indicator illuminate in the IPC?	Go to Step 4	Go to Step 6
4	Test the signal circuit of the water in fuel sensor for a short to ground. Did you find and correct the condition?	Go to Step 12	Go to Step 5
5	1. Install a scan tool. 2. Turn OFF the ignition. 3. Disconnect the water in fuel sensor. 4. Turn ON the ignition, with the engine OFF. 5. With the scan tool, observe the Water In Fuel Sensor parameter in the powertrain control module (PCM) Engine Data 1 data list. Does the Water In Fuel Sensor parameter display No Water?	Go to Step 8	Go to Step 7
6	Inspect for poor connections at the harness connector of the water in fuel switch. Did you find and correct the condition?	Go to Step 12	Go to Step 9
7	Inspect for poor connections at the harness connector of the PCM. Did you find and correct the condition?	Go to Step 12	Go to Step 10

LTV0500000002545

Fig. 205 Water-in-fuel lamp always on (Part 1 of 2). Express & Savana

Step	Action	Yes	No
6	Test the low reference circuit of the water in fuel sensor for an open or for a high resistance. Did you find and correct the condition?	Go to Step 13	Go to Step 9
7	Inspect for poor connections at the harness connector of the IPC. Did you find and correct the condition?	Go to Step 13	Go to Step 10
8	Inspect for poor connections at the harness connector of the powertrain control module (PCM). Did you find and correct the condition?	Go to Step 13	Go to Step 11
9	Inspect for poor connections at the harness connector of the water in fuel sensor. Did you find and correct the condition?	Go to Step 13	Go to Step 12
10	Replace the IPC. Did you complete the replacement?	Go to Step 13	--
11	Replace the PCM. Did you complete the replacement?	Go to Step 13	--
12	Replace the water in fuel sensor. Did you complete the replacement?	Go to Step 13	--
13	Operate the system in order to verify the repair. Did you correct the condition?	System OK	Go to Step 2

LTV0500000002548

Fig. 206 Water-in-fuel lamp inoperative (Part 2 of 2). Express & Savana

Step	Action	Value (s)	Yes	No
	DEFINITION: The chime sounds with the driver's door open.			
1	Did you perform the Diagnostic System Check - Vehicle?	--	Go to Step 2	Go to Diagnostic System Check
2	Do any indicators illuminate when the chime sounds?	--	Go to Symptoms	Go to Step 3
3	1. Turn OFF the ignition. 2. Turn the headlamp switch to OFF. 3. Remove the key from the ignition. 4. Open the driver door. Does the chime sound?	--	Go to Step 4	Test for Intermittent Conditions and Poor Connections
4	Disconnect the body control module (BCM). Does the chime sound?	--	Go to Step 5	Go to Step 6
5	Is the vehicle equipped with a chime module (UL5)?	--	Go to Step 10	Go to Step 11
6	1. Turn OFF the ignition. 2. Reconnect the BCM. 3. Install a scan tool. 4. Turn ON the ignition, with the engine OFF. 5. With a scan tool, observe the Parklamp Switch parameter in the BCM Inputs data list. Does the Parklamp Switch parameter display Inactive?	--	Go to Step 7	Go to Diagnostic Trouble Code (DTC)
7	1. Close the driver door. 2. With a scan tool, observe the Driver Door Ajar Switch parameter in the BCM Inputs data list. Does the Driver Door Ajar parameter display Inactive?	--	Go to Step 8	Go to Courtesy Lamps Always On

LTV0500000002549

Fig. 207   Chime always on (Part 1 of 3). Express & Savana

Step	Action	Value (s)	Yes	No
14	Replace the chime module. Did you complete the replacement?	-	Go to Step 18	--
15	Replace the radio. Did you complete the replacement?	-	Go to Step 18	--
16	Replace the BCM. Did you complete the replacement?	-	Go to Step 18	--
17	Replace the ignition key alarm switch. Did you find and correct the condition?	-	Go to Step 18	--
18	Operate the system in order to verify the repair. Did you correct the condition?	-	System OK	Go to Step 2

LTV0500000002551

Fig. 207   Chime always on (Part 3 of 3). Express & Savana

Step	Action	Value (s)	Yes	No
8	1. Turn OFF the ignition. 2. Remove the key from the ignition. 3. Disconnect the BCM connector C4. 4. Connect a test lamp between the key in ignition signal circuit and battery voltage. Does the test lamp illuminate?		Go to Step 9	Go to Step 12
9	Test the key in ignition switch signal circuit for a short to ground. Did you find and correct the condition?		Go to Step 18	Go to Step 13
10	Inspect for poor connections at the harness connector of the chime module. Did you find and correct the condition?		Go to Step 18	Go to Step 14
11	Inspect for poor connections at the harness connector of the radio. Did you find and correct the condition?		Go to Step 18	Go to Step 15
12	Inspect for poor connections at the harness connector of the BCM. Did you find and correct the condition?		Go to Step 18	Go to Step 16
13	Inspect for poor connections at the harness connector of the ignition key alarm switch. Did you find and correct the condition?		Go to Step 18	Go to Step 17

LTV0500000002550

Fig. 207   Chime always on (Part 2 of 3). Express & Savana

Step	Action	Value (s)	Yes	No
	DEFINITION: One or more chime functions are inoperative.			
1	Did you perform the Diagnostic System Check - Vehicle?	--	Go to Step 2	
2	1. Turn OFF the ignition, with the key in the ignition. 2. Open the driver door. Does the chime sound?	--		Go to Step 3
3	Is the vehicle equipped with a chime module (UL5)?	--	Go to Step 5	Go to Step 4
4	1. Turn the radio ON. 2. Adjust the radio balance and fade to the left front speakers. Does the speaker operate properly?	--	Go to Step 5	Go to Speakers Inoperative - One or More
5	1. Install a scan tool. 2. Turn ON the ignition, with the engine OFF. 3. With a scan tool, observe the Key in Ignition parameter in the body control module (BCM) Inputs data list. Does the Key in Ignition parameter display Yes?	--	Go to Step 7	Go to Step 6
6	1. Turn OFF the ignition, with the key in the ignition. 2. Disconnect the BCM connector C4. 3. Connect a test lamp between the signal circuit of the ignition key alarm switch and battery voltage. Does the test lamp illuminate?	--	Go to Step 12	Go to Step 8

LTV0500000002552

Fig. 208   Chime inoperative (Part 1 of 3). Express & Savana

Step	Action	Yes	No
7	1. Turn OFF the ignition. 2. Disconnect the driver door ajar switch. 3. Place the key in the ignition. 4. Connect a 3-ampere fused jumper between the signal circuit of the driver door ajar switch and the ground circuit of the driver door ajar switch. Does the chime sound?	Go to Step 13	Go to Step 10
8	Test the signal circuit of the ignition key alarm switch for an open, for a high resistance, or for a short to voltage. Did you find and correct the condition?	Go to Step 20	Go to Step 9
9	Test the ground circuit of the ignition key alarm switch for an open or for a high resistance. Did you find and correct the condition?	Go to Step 20	Go to Step 14
10	Test the signal circuit of the driver door ajar switch for an open, for a high resistance, or for a short to voltage. Did you find and correct the condition?	Go to Step 20	Go to Step 11
11	Test the ground circuit of the driver door ajar switch for an open or for a high resistance. Did you find and correct the condition?	Go to Step 20	Go to Step 15
12	Inspect for poor connections at the harness connector of the BCM. Did you find and correct the condition?	Go to Step 20	Go to Step 16
13	Inspect for poor connections at the harness connector of the driver door ajar switch. Did you find and correct the condition?	Go to Step 20	Go to Step 17

LTV0500000002553

Fig. 208 Chime inoperative (Part 2 of 3). Express & Savana

Step	Action	Yes	No
14	Inspect for poor connections at the harness connector of the ignition key alarm switch. Did you find and correct the condition?	Go to Step 20	Go to Step 18
15	Inspect for poor connections at the harness connector of the chime module. Did you find and correct the condition?	Go to Step 20	Go to Step 19
16	Replace the BCM. Did you complete the replacement?	Go to Step 20	--
17	Replace the driver door ajar switch. Did you complete the replacement?	Go to Step 20	--
18	Replace the ignition key alarm switch. Did you complete the replacement?	Go to Step 20	--
19	Replace the chime module. Did you complete the replacement?	Go to Step 20	--
20	Operate the system in order to verify the repair. Did you correct the condition?	System OK	Go to Step 2

LTV0500000002554

Fig. 208 Chime inoperative (Part 3 of 3). Express & Savana

Step	Action	Value(s)	Yes	No
1	Did you perform the Diagnostic System Check - Vehicle?	--	Go to Step 2	Go to Diagnostic System Check -
2	Start the engine. Does the engine oil pressure (EOP) gage display within the specified range?	207-483 kPa (30-70 psi)	Test for Intermittent Conditions and Poor Connections	Go to Step 3
3	1. Install a scan tool. 2. Turn the ignition ON, with the engine OFF. 3. With a scan tool, perform the Displays Test in the IPC scan tool Output Controls. Does the engine oil pressure gage move up and down when commanded?	--	Go to Step 4	Go to Step 10
4	1. Turn the ignition OFF. 2. Disconnect the negative battery cable. 3. Disconnect the EOP sensor. 4. Measure the resistance from the low reference circuit of the EOP sensor to a good ground. Does the resistance measure less than the specified value?	5 ohms	Go to Step 6	Go to Step 5
5	Test the low reference circuit of the EOP sensor for high resistance or for an open. Did you find and correct the condition?	--	Go to Step 11	Go to Step 7

LTV0500000003404

Fig. 210 Engine oil pressure gage inaccurate or inoperative (Part 1 of 2). Hummer H2

Step	Action	Yes	No
1	Did you perform the Diagnostic System Check - Vehicle?	Go to Step 2	Go to Diagnostic System Check -
2	1. Turn the ignition ON, with the engine OFF. 2. Observe the instrument cluster. Does the instrument cluster perform the displays test?	Test for Intermittent Conditions and Poor Connections	Go to Step 3
3	1. Turn the ignition OFF. 2. Disconnect the instrument panel cluster (IPC). 3. Turn the ignition ON, with the engine OFF. 4. Connect a test lamp between the ignition 1 voltage circuit and a good ground. Does the test lamp illuminate?	Go to Step 4	Go to Step 7
4	Connect a test lamp between the ignition 1 voltage circuit of the instrument cluster and the ground circuit of the instrument cluster. Does the test lamp illuminate?	Go to Step 5	Go to Step 6
5	Inspect for poor connections at the harness connector of the IPC. Did you find and correct the condition?	Go to Step 9	Go to Step 8
6	Repair the open or a high resistance in the ground circuit. Did you complete the repair?	Go to Step 9	--
7	Repair the open, short to ground or high resistance in the ignition 1 voltage circuit. Did you complete the repair?	Go to Step 9	--
8	Replace the IPC. Did you complete the replacement?	Go to Step 9	--
9	Operate the system in order to verify the repair. Did you find and correct the condition?	System OK	Go to Step 3

LTV0500000003403

Fig. 209 Instrument cluster inoperative. Hummer H2

Step	Action	Value (s)	Yes	No
6	Inspect for poor connections at the harness connector of the EOP sensor. Did you find and correct the condition?	-	Go to Step 11	Go to Step 8
7	Inspect for poor connections at the harness connector of the powertrain control module (PCM). Did you find and correct the condition?	-	Go to Step 11	Go to Step 9
8	Replace the EOP sensor. Did you complete the replacement?	-	Go to Step 11	--
9	Replace the PCM. Did you complete the replacement?	-	Go to Step 11	--
10	Replace the IPC. Did you complete the replacement?	-	Go to Step 11	--
11	Operate the system in order to verify the repair. Did you correct the condition?	-	System OK	Go to Step 2

LTV0500000003405

Fig. 210 Engine oil pressure gage inaccurate or inoperative (Part 2 of 2). Hummer H2

Step	Action	Value (s)	Yes	No
4	Inspect for the following items: • A poor connection at the harness connector of the fuel level sensor • A high resistance in the signal circuit of the fuel level sensor or the low reference circuit of the fuel level sensor between the fuel level sensor and C106. • A misaligned fuel level sender. • A deformed fuel tank. Did you find and correct the condition?	--	Go to Step 13	Go to Step 7
5	Test the signal circuit of the fuel level sensor for a high resistance. Did you find and correct the condition?	--	Go to Step 13	Go to Step 6
6	Test the low reference circuit of the fuel level sensor for a high resistance. Did you find and correct the condition?	--	Go to Step 13	Go to Step 9

7	1. Remove the fuel level sender.
	2. Inspect for the following items:
	  - The fuel level sensor is stuck, perhaps due to an interference with the fuel strainer.
	  - The fuel tank contains foreign material, for instance, ice.
	
	Did you find and correct the condition?
		--	Go to Step 13	Go to Step 8

8	1. With the J 39200 DMM, measure the resistance of the fuel level sensor while moving the float arm. 2. Observe both the analog and digital displays on the DMM. Does the resistance change smoothly across the specified range?	40-250 ohms	Go to Diagnostic Aids	Go to Step 10
9	Inspect for poor connections at the harness connector of the powertrain control module (PCM). Did you find and correct the condition?	--	Go to Step 13	Go to Step 12

LTV0500000003407

Fig. 211 Fuel gage inaccurate or inoperative (Part 2 of 3). Hummer H2

Step	Action	Value (s)	Yes	No
1	Did you perform the Diagnostic System Check - Vehicle?	--	Go to Step 2	Go to Diagnostic System Check -
2	1. Disconnect C106. 2. Connect the J 33431-C Signal Generator and Instrument Panel Tester between the signal circuit of the fuel level sensor and the low reference circuit of the fuel level sensor on the female terminal side of the connector. 3. Turn the ignition ON, with the engine OFF. **Important:** Verify the J 33431-C resistance settings with a DMM. 4. Vary the resistance on the J 33431-C from 40-250 ohms. 5. Check Fuel Level Specifications Does the fuel gage display the correct fuel level?	--	Go to Step 4	Go to Step 3
3	1. Install a scan tool. 2. Turn the ignition ON, with the engine OFF. **Important:** Verify the J 33431-C resistance settings with a DMM. 3. Vary the resistance on the J 33431-C from 40-250 ohms. 4. Check Fuel Level Specifications **Important:** Turn OFF the ignition momentarily between the resistance settings in order to quickly update the scan tool display. 5. With the scan tool, observe the Fuel Tank Level Remaining parameter in the PCM Enhanced EVAP Data List. Does the scan tool display the correct fuel level percentage?	--	Go to Step 11	Go to Step 5

LTV0500000003406

Fig. 211 Fuel gage inaccurate or inoperative (Part 1 of 3). Hummer H2

Step	Action	Value (s)	Yes	No
10	Replace the fuel level sensor. Did you complete the replacement?	-	Go to Step 13	
11	Replace the instrument panel cluster (IPC). Did you complete the replacement?	-	Go to Step 13	
12	Replace the PCM. Did you complete the replacement?	-	Go to Step 13	--
13	1. Use the scan tool in order to clear the PCM DTCs. 2. Operate the system in order to verify the repair. Did you correct the condition?	-	System OK	Go to Step 2

LTV0500000003408

Fig. 211 Fuel gage inaccurate or inoperative (Part 3 of 3). Hummer H2

Step	Action	Yes	No
1	Did you perform the Diagnostic System Check - Vehicle?	Go to Step 2	Go to Diagnostic System Check
2	Verify the hourmeter operation. Does the hourmeter operate normally?	Test for Intermittent Conditions and Poor Connections	Go to Step 3
3	Replace the instrument panel cluster (IPC). Did you complete the replacement?	Go to Step 4	--
4	Operate the system in order to verify the repair. Did you correct the condition?	System OK	Go to Step 2

LTV0500000003409

Fig. 212 Hourmeter inaccurate or inoperative. Hummer H2

Step	Action	Yes	No
1	Did you perform the Diagnostic System Check - Vehicle?	Go to Step 2	Go to Diagnostic System Check -
2	1. Turn the ignition ON, with the engine OFF. 2. Press the trip odometer reset switch. Does the odometer toggle between the season odometer, the trip odometer, and the hourmeter?	Test for Intermittent Conditions and Poor Connections	Go to Step 3
3	Replace the instrument panel cluster (IPC). Did you complete the replacement?	Go to Step 4	--
4	Operate the system in order to verify the repair. Did you correct the condition?	System OK	Go to Step 2

LTV0500000003411

Fig. 214 Odometer trip/reset switch inoperative. Hummer H2

Step	Action	Yes	No
	DEFINITION: This diagnostic procedure applies only to the serial data gages located in the instrument cluster which include the engine coolant temperature gage, and the transmission fluid temperature gage.		
1	Did you perform the Diagnostic System Check - Vehicle?	Go to Step 2	Go to Diagnostic System Check
2	1. Turn the ignition ON, with the engine OFF. 2. Install a scan tool. 3. With the scan tool, perform the Displays Test in the Instrument Panel Cluster (IPC) Scan Tool Output Controls. Does the gage move from 0 to its maximum value and back to 0 when you perform the Displays Test?	Go to Step 3	Go to Step 4
3	1. Install a scan tool. 2. Start the engine. 3. Observe the appropriate parameter in the PCM Data List. Does the parameter match the gage display?	Go to Diagnostic System Check	Go to Step 4
4	Replace the IPC. Did you complete the replacement?	Go to Step 5	--
5	1. Use the scan tool in order to clear any induced DTCs. 2. Operate the system in order to verify the repair. Did you correct the condition?	System OK	Go to Step 2

LTV0500000003410

Fig. 213 Instrument panel cluster (IPC) gages inoperative. Hummer H2

Step	Action	Yes	No
1	Did you perform the Diagnostic System Check - Vehicle?	Go to Step 2	Go to Diagnostic System Check
2	1. Turn ON the ignition, with the engine OFF. 2. Install a scan tool. 3. With the scan tool, perform the segments test in the instrument panel cluster (IPC) scan tool output controls. Do all of the segments of the driver information center (DIC) illuminate?	Go to Step 3	Go to Step 6
3	1. Install a scan tool. 2. Raise the vehicle drive wheels. 3. Start the engine. 4. Place the transmission into drive for automatic transmission or third gear for manual transmission. 5. With the scan tool, observe the Vehicle Speed Sensor (VSS) parameter in the IPC Data 1 data list. Does the VSS parameter match the speedometer display?	Test for Intermittent Conditions and Poor Connections	Go to Step 4
4	Test the vehicle speed signal circuit for a high resistance between the IPC and the powertrain control module (PCM). Did you find and correct the condition?	Go to Step 7	Go to Step 5
5	Inspect for poor connections at the harness connector of the IPC. Did you find and correct the condition?	Go to Step 7	Go to Step 6
6	Replace the IPC. Did you complete the replacement?	Go to Step 7	--
7	Operate the system in order to verify the repair. Did you correct the condition?	System OK	Go to Step 3

LTV0500000003412

Fig. 215 Speedometer and/or odometer inaccurate or inoperative. Hummer H2

Step	Action	Yes	No
1	Did you perform the Diagnostic System Check - Vehicle?	Go to Step 2	Go to Diagnostic System Check -
2	1. Install a scan tool. 2. Start the engine. 3. With the scan tool, observe the Engine Speed parameter in the IPC Data 1 data list. Does the Engine Speed parameter match the tachometer display?	Test for Intermittent Conditions and Poor Connections	Go to Step 3
3	Test the engine speed signal circuit for a high resistance between the instrument panel cluster (IPC) and powertrain control module (PCM). Did you find and correct the condition?	Go to Step 6	Go to Step 4
4	Inspect for poor connections at the harness connector of the instrument cluster. Did you find and correct the condition?	Go to Step 6	Go to Step 5
5	Replace the IPC. Did you complete the replacement?	Go to Step 6	--
6	Operate the system in order to verify the repair. Did you correct the condition?	System OK	Go to Step 2

LTV0500000003413

Fig. 216 Tachometer inaccurate or inoperative. Hummer H2

Step	Action	Yes	No
1	Did you perform the Diagnostic System Check - Vehicle?	Go to Step 2	Go to Diagnostic System Check -
2	1. Turn the ignition ON, with the engine OFF. 2. Install a scan tool. 3. With the scan tool, perform the Displays Test in the IPC scan tool Output Controls. Does the gage move from 0 to its maximum value and back to 0 when you perform the Displays Test?	Go to Step 3	Go to Step 4
3	1. Install a scan tool. 2. Start the engine. 3. With the scan tool, observe the Battery Voltage parameter in the BCM Data list. Does the Battery Voltage parameter match the gage display?	Test for Intermittent Conditions and Poor Connections	Go to Step 4
4	Replace the instrument panel cluster (IPC). Did you complete the replacement?	Go to Step 5	--
5	1. Use the scan tool in order to clear any induced DTCs. 2. Operate the system in order to verify the repair. Did you correct the condition?	System OK	Go to Step 2

LTV0500000003414

Fig. 217 Volt gage inaccurate or inoperative. Hummer H2

Step	Action	Yes	No
1	Did you perform the Diagnostic System Check - Vehicle?	Go to Step 2	Go to Diagnostic System Check
2	Start the engine. Does the CHANGE ENGINE OIL indicator illuminate in the Driver Information Center?	Go to Step 3	Test for Intermittent Conditions and Poor Connections
3	1. Install a scan tool. 2. With the scan tool, observe the Engine Oil Life Remaining parameter in the PCM Engine Data 2 data list. Does the Engine Oil Life Remaining parameter display 0%?	Go to Step 4	Go to Step 5
4	Reset the engine oil life. Does the CHANGE ENGINE OIL indicator turn off?	Go to Step 6	Go to Step 5
5	Replace the instrument panel cluster (IPC). Did you complete the replacement?	Go to Step 6	--
6	Operate the system in order to verify the repair. Did you correct the condition?	System OK	Go to Step 2

LTV0500000003415

Fig. 218 Change engine oil indicator always on. Hummer H2

Step	Action	Yes	No
1	Did you perform the Diagnostic System Check - Vehicle?	Go to Step 2	Go to Diagnostic System Check
2	1. Install a scan tool. 2. Turn the ignition ON, with the engine OFF. 3. With the scan tool, observe the Engine Oil Level Switch parameter in the PCM Engine Data 2 data list. Does the Engine Oil Level Switch parameter display OK?	Go to Step 3	Go to Step 4
3	Does the CHECK ENG OIL LEVEL indicator remain illuminated after the displays test?	Go to Step 11	Test for Intermittent Conditions and Poor Connections
4	1. Turn the ignition OFF. 2. Disconnect the engine oil level switch. 3. Connect a 3-amp fused jumper between the signal circuit of the engine oil level switch and a good ground. 4. Turn the ignition ON, with the engine OFF. 5. With the scan tool, observe the Engine Oil Level Switch parameter. Does the Engine Oil Level Switch parameter display OK?	Go to Step 6	Go to Step 5
5	Test the signal circuit of the engine oil level switch for a short to battery voltage, for an open or for a high resistance. Did you find and correct the condition?	Go to Step 12	Go to Step 8
6	Test the ground circuit of the engine oil level switch for an open or for a high resistance. Did you find and correct the condition?	Go to Step 12	Go to Step 7

LTV0500000003416

Fig. 219 Low engine oil dipstick always on (Part 1 of 2). Hummer H2

7	Inspect for poor connections at the harness connector of the engine oil level switch.		
	Did you find and correct the condition?	Go to Step 12	Go to Step 9
8	Inspect for poor connections at the harness connector of the powertrain control module (PCM).		
	Did you find and correct the condition?	Go to Step 12	Go to Step 10
9	Replace the engine oil level switch.		
	Did you complete the replacement?	Go to Step 12	--
10	Replace the PCM.		
	Did you complete the replacement?	Go to Step 12	--
11	Replace the instrument panel cluster (IPC).		
	Did you complete the replacement?	Go to Step 12	--
12	Operate the system in order to verify the repair.		
	Did you correct the condition?	System OK	Go to Step 2

LTV0500000003417

Fig. 219 Low engine oil dipstick always on (Part 2 of 2). Hummer H2

7	Test the signal circuit of the suspect DIC switch for a short to ground.		
	Did you find and correct the condition?	Go to Step 14	Go to Step 11
8	Test the signal circuit of the suspect DIC switch for an open or high resistance.		
	Did you find and correct the condition?	Go to Step 14	Go to Step 11
9	Test the ground circuit of the DIC switch for an open or high resistance.		
	Did you find and correct the condition?	Go to Step 14	Go to Step 10
10	Inspect for poor connections at the harness connector of the DIC switch.		
	Did you find and correct the condition?	Go to Step 14	Go to Step 12
11	Inspect for poor connections at the harness connector of the instrument panel cluster (IPC).		
	Did you find and correct the condition?	Go to Step 14	Go to Step 13
12	Replace the DIC switch.		
	Did you complete the replacement?	Go to Step 14	--
13	Replace the IPC.		
	Did you complete the replacement?	Go to Step 14	--
14	Operate the system in order to verify the repair.		
	Did you correct the condition?	System OK	Go to Step 2

LTV0500000003419

Fig. 220 Driver information center (DIC) switch(es) inoperative (Part 2 of 2). Hummer H2

Step	Action	Yes	No
1	Did you perform the Diagnostic System Check - Vehicle?	Go to Step 2	Go to Diagnostic System Check -
2	1. Install a scan tool. 2. Turn the ignition ON, with the engine OFF. 3. Press and release each of the driver information center (DIC) switches. 4. With a scan tool, observe the DIC switch parameters in the IPC Input/Output data list. Does the scan tool display On when each switch is pressed and Off when each switch is released?	Test for Intermittent Conditions and Poor Connections	Go to Step 3
3	Does the scan tool display Off when each switch is pressed?	Go to Step 9	Go to Step 4
4	Does the scan tool always display On for the suspect switch even when the switch is released?	Go to Step 5	Go to Step 6
5	1. Turn the ignition OFF. 2. Disconnect the DIC switch connector. 3. Turn the ignition ON, with the engine OFF. 4. With a scan tool, observe the suspect DIC switch parameter. Does the scan tool display On for the suspect switch?	Go to Step 7	Go to Step 12
6	1. Turn the ignition OFF. 2. Disconnect the DIC switch connector. 3. Connect a 3-amp fused jumper wire between the signal circuit of the suspect DIC switch and a good ground. 4. Turn the ignition ON, with the engine OFF. 5. With a scan tool, observe the suspect DIC switch parameter. Does the scan tool display On for the suspect switch?	Go to Step 10	Go to Step 8

LTV0500000003418

Fig. 220 Driver information center (DIC) switch(es) inoperative (Part 1 of 2). Hummer H2

Step	Action	Yes	No
1	Did you perform the Diagnostic System Check - Vehicle?	Go to Step 2	Go to Diagnostic System Check
2	Do any indicators illuminate when the chime sounds?	Go to Symptoms	Go to Step 3
3	1. Turn the ignition OFF. 2. Remove the key from the ignition. 3. Turn the headlamp switch to OFF. 4. Close all of the vehicles doors. 5. Open one or more of the vehicles doors. Does the chime sound at all times regardless if the doors are open or closed?	Go to Step 16	Go to Step 4
4	1. Close all of the vehicles doors. 2. With a scan tool observe the Driver Door Ajar Switch and the Passenger Door Ajar Switch parameters in the BCM inputs data list or the Door Ajar Switch parameters in the DDM/PDM inputs data list. Do all of the Door Ajar Switch parameters display Off or Inactive?	Go to Step 5	Go to Courtesy Lamps Always On
5	With a scan tool observe the Left Rear Cargo Door Ajar Switch and the Right Rear Door Ajar Switch parameters in the BCM inputs data list. Do all of the Door Switch parameters display Inactive?	Go to Step 6	Go to Courtesy Lamps Always On
6	With a scan tool, observe the Cargo Door Ajar Switch and the Hood Ajar Switch parameters in the BCM inputs data list. Does the Cargo Door Ajar Switch and the Hood Ajar Switch parameters display Inactive?	Go to Step 7	Go to Courtesy Lamps Always On
7	1. Turn the ignition OFF. 2. Remove the key from the ignition. 3. Turn the headlamp switch to OFF. 4. Open the drivers door. Does the chime sound?	Go to Step 8	Test for Intermittent Conditions and Poor Connections

LTV0500000003420

Fig. 221 Chime always on (Part 1 of 3). Hummer H2

Step	Action	Yes	No
8	1. Install a scan tool. 2. Turn the ignition ON, with the engine OFF. 3. With a scan tool, observe the Parklamp Switch parameter in the BCM inputs data list. Does the Parklamp Switch parameter display inactive?	Go to Step 9	Go to Step 11
9	With a scan tool, observe the Headlamp Switch parameter in the BCM inputs data list. Does the Headlamp Switch parameter display Inactive?	Go to Step 10	Go to Step 11
10	1. Turn the ignition OFF. 2. Remove the key from the ignition. 3. With a scan tool, observe the Key In Ignition parameter in the BCM inputs data list. Does the Key In Ignition parameter display No?	Go to Step 15	Go to Step 12
11	Test the headlamp input signal circuit and the park lamp signal circuit at the body control module (BCM) for a short to voltage. Did you find and correct the condition?	Go to Step 21	Go to Step 13
12	Test the key in ignition signal circuit for a short to ground. Did you find and correct the condition?	Go to Step 21	Go to Step 14
13	Inspect for poor connections at the harness connector of the headlamp switch. Did you find and correct the condition?	Go to Step 21	Go to Step 17
14	Inspect for poor connections at the harness connector of the ignition key alarm switch. Did you find and correct the condition?	Go to Step 21	Go to Step 18
15	Inspect for poor connections at the harness connector of the BCM. Did you find and correct the condition?	Go to Step 21	Go to Step 19

LTV0500000003421

Fig. 221 Chime always on (Part 2 of 3). Hummer H2

Step	Action	Yes	No
	DEFINITION: One or more chime functions are inoperative.		
1	Did you perform the Diagnostic System Check - Vehicle?	Go to Step 2	Go to Diagnostic System Check
2	1. Turn the ignition OFF, with the key in the ignition. 2. Open the driver door. Does the chime sound?	Test for Intermittent Conditions and Poor Connections	Go to Step 3
3	Do the courtesy lights turn on when you open the driver door?	Go to Step 4	Go to Courtesy Lamps Inoperative
4	1. Turn the ignition ON, with the engine OFF. 2. Turn the radio ON. 3. Adjust the radio balance and fade to the left front speaker. Does the speaker operate properly?	Go to Step 5	Go to Speakers Inoperative - One or More
5	Replace the radio. Did you complete the replacement?	Go to Step 6	--
6	Operate the system in order to verify the repair. Did you correct the condition?	System OK	Go to Step 1

LTV0500000003423

Fig. 222 Chime inoperative. Hummer H2

16	Inspect for poor connections at the harness connector of the radio or audio amplifier. Did you find and correct the condition?	Go to Step 21	Go to Step 20
17	Replace the headlamp switch. Did you complete the replacement?	Go to Step 21	--
18	Replace the ignition switch. Did you complete the replacement?	Go to Step 21	--
19	Replace the BCM. Did you complete the replacement?	Go to Step 21	--
20	Replace the radio. Did you complete the replacement?	Go to Step 21	--
21	Operate the system in order to verify the repair. Did you correct the condition?	System OK	Go to Step 3

LTV0500000003422

Fig. 221 Chime always on (Part 3 of 3). Hummer H2

Step	Action	Yes	No
1	Did you perform the Diagnostic System Check - Vehicle?	Go to Step 2	Go to Diagnostic System Check -
2	1. Install a scan tool. 2. Turn ON the ignition, with the engine OFF. 3. With the scan tool, perform the instrument panel cluster (IPC) Gages Output Control. Does the engine coolant temperature gage move up and down when commanded?	Test for Intermittent Conditions and Poor Connections	Go to Step 3
3	Replace the IPC. Did you complete the replacement?	Go to Step 4	--
4	Operate the system in order to verify the repair. Did you correct the condition?	System OK	Go to Step 2

LTV0500000003387

Fig. 223 Engine coolant temperature gage inaccurate or inoperative. Hummer H3

Step	Action	Yes	No
1	Did you perform the Diagnostic System Check - Vehicle?	Go to Step 2	Go to Diagnostic System Check
2	Start the engine. Does the engine oil pressure (EOP) gage display at or below 0 psi (0 kPa)?	Go to Step 3	Test for Intermittent Conditions and Poor Connections
3	1. Install a scan tool. 2. Turn the ignition ON. 3. With the scan tool, observe the Engine Oil Pressure Switch parameter in the powertrain control module (PCM) Engine Data, data list. Does the Engine Oil Pressure Switch parameter display Ok?	Go to Step 10	Go to Step 4
4	1. Turn the ignition OFF. 2. Disconnect the EOP switch. 3. Start the engine. 4. With the scan tool, observe the Engine Oil Pressure Switch parameter. Does the Engine Oil Pressure Switch parameter display Ok?	Go to Step 6	Go to Step 5
5	Test the signal circuit of the EOP switch for a short to ground. Did you find and correct the condition?	Go to Step 11	Go to Step 7

LTV0500000003388

Fig. 224 Engine oil pressure gage inaccurate or inoperative (Part 1 of 2). Hummer H3

	Action	Yes	No
6	Inspect for poor connections at the harness connector of the EOP switch. Did you find and correct the condition?	Go to Step 11	Go to Step 8
7	Inspect for poor connections at the harness connector of the PCM. Did you find and correct the condition?	Go to Step 11	Go to Step 9
8	Replace the EOP switch. Did you complete the replacement?	Go to Step 11	--
9	Replace the PCM. Did you complete the replacement?	Go to Step 11	--
10	Replace the instrument panel cluster (IPC). Did you complete the replacement?	Go to Step 11	--
11	Operate the system in order to verify the repair. Did you correct the condition?	System OK	Go to Step 2

LTV0500000003389

Fig. 224 Engine oil pressure gage inaccurate or inoperative (Part 2 of 2). Hummer H3

	Action	Values	Yes	No
4	Inspect for the following items: • A poor connection at the harness connector of the fuel level sensor • A high resistance in the signal circuit of the fuel level sensor or the low reference circuit of the fuel level sensor between the fuel level sensor and C150 • A misaligned fuel sender • A deformed fuel tank Did you find and correct the condition?	--	Go to Step 13	Go to Step 7
5	Test the signal circuit of the fuel level sensor for a high resistance. Did you find and correct the condition?	--	Go to Step 13	Go to Step 6
6	Test the low reference circuit of the fuel level sensor for a high resistance. Did you find and correct the condition?	--	Go to Step 13	Go to Step 9

7	1. Remove the fuel level sender.
	2. Inspect for the following items:
	  - A stuck fuel level sender, i.e. the fuel strainer interfering with the sender float arm
	  - Foreign material in the fuel tank, i.e. ice
	
	Did you find and correct the condition?
		--	Go to Step 13	Go to Step 8

8	1. With the J 39200 DMM, measure the resistance of the fuel level sensor while moving the float arm. 2. Observe both the analog and digital displays on the DMM. Does the resistance change smoothly across the specified range?	40-250 ohms	Go to Diagnostic Aids	Go to Step 10

LTV0500000003391

Fig. 225 Fuel gage inaccurate or inoperative (Part 2 of 3). Hummer H3

Step	Action	Values	Yes	No
1	Did you perform the Diagnostic System Check - Vehicle?	--	Go to Step 2	Go to Diagnostic System Check
2	1. Disconnect C150. 2. Connect the J 33431-C Signal Generator and Instrument Panel Tester between the signal circuit of the fuel level sensor and the low reference circuit of the fuel level sensor on the female terminal side. 3. Turn ON the ignition, with the engine OFF. **Important:** Verify the J 33431-C resistance settings with a DMM. 4. Vary the resistance on the J 33431-C from 40-250 ohms. 5. Check Fuel Level Specifications Does the fuel gage display the correct fuel level?	--	Go to Step 4	Go to Step 3
3	1. Install a scan tool. 2. Turn ON the ignition, with the engine OFF. **Important:** Verify the J 33431-C resistance settings with a DMM. 3. Vary the resistance on the J 33431-C from 40-250 ohms. 4. Check Fuel Level Specifications **Important:** Turn the ignition OFF momentarily between the resistance settings in order to quickly update the scan tool display. 5. With the scan tool, observe the Fuel Tank Level Remaining parameter in the powertrain control module (PCM) Engine Data, data list. Does the scan tool display the correct fuel level percentage?	--	Go to Step 11	Go to Step 5

LTV0500000003390

Fig. 225 Fuel gage inaccurate or inoperative (Part 1 of 3). Hummer H3

	Action	Yes	No
9	Inspect for poor connections at the harness connector of the PCM. Did you find and correct the condition?	Go to Step 13	Go to Step 12
10	Replace the fuel level sensor. Did you complete the replacement?	Go to Step 13	--
11	Replace the instrument panel cluster (IPC). Did you complete the replacement?	Go to Step 13	--
12	Replace the PCM. Did you complete the replacement?	Go to Step 13	--
13	1. Use the scan tool in order to clear the PCM DTCs. 2. Operate the system in order to verify the repair. Did you correct the condition?	System OK	Go to Step 2

LTV0500000003392

Fig. 225 Fuel gage inaccurate or inoperative (Part 3 of 3). Hummer H3

Step	Action	Yes	No
1	Did you perform the Diagnostic System Check - Vehicle?	Go to Step 2	Go to Diagnostic System Check -
2	1. Turn ON the ignition. 2. Activate the trip reset button. Does the odometer display switch between trip and odometer?	Test for Intermittent Conditions and Poor Connections	Go to Step 3
3	Replace the instrument panel cluster (IPC). Did you complete the replacement?	Go to Step 4	--
4	Operate the system in order to verify the repair. Did you correct the condition?	System OK	Go to Step 2

LTV0500000003393

Fig. 226 Odometer trip/reset switch inoperative. Hummer H3

Step	Action	Yes	No
1	Did you perform the Diagnostic System Check - Vehicle?	Go to Step 2	Go to Diagnostic System Check
2	1. Install a scan tool. 2. Raise the vehicles drive wheels. 3. Start the engine. 4. Place the transmission into drive. 5. With the scan tool, observe the Vehicle Speed Sensor (VSS) parameter in the powertrain control module (PCM) evaporative emission (EVAP) Data, data list. Does the VSS parameter match the speedometer display?	Go to Step 3	Go to Step 4
3	Does the odometer operate properly?	Test for Intermittent Conditions and Poor Connections	Go to Step 4
4	Replace the instrument panel cluster (IPC). Did you complete the replacement?	Go to Step 5	--
5	1. Operate the system in order to verify the repair. 2. Use the scan tool in order to clear the DTCs that may have set in other modules during diagnosis. Did you correct the condition?	System OK	Go to Step 2

LTV0500000003394

Fig. 227   Speedometer and/or odometer inaccurate or inoperative. Hummer H3

Step	Action	Yes	No
1	Did you perform the Diagnostic System Check - Vehicle?	Go to Step 2	Go to Diagnostic System Check
2	1. Install a scan tool. 2. Turn the ignition ON, with the engine OFF. 3. With the scan tool, perform the instrument panel cluster (IPC) gages output control. Does the volt gauge move up and down when commanded?	Go to Diagnostic System Check	Go to Step 3
3	Replace the IPC. Did you complete the replacement?	Go to Step 4	--
4	Operate the system in order to verify the repair. Did you correct the condition?	System OK	Go to Step 2

LTV0500000003396

Fig. 229   Volt gage inaccurate or inoperative. Hummer H3

Step	Action	Yes	No
1	Did you perform the Diagnostic System Check - Vehicle?	Go to Step 2	Go to Diagnostic System Check -
2	1. Turn ON the ignition, with the engine OFF. 2. Install a scan tool. 3. With a scan tool, perform the tach gage sweep test. Does the tachometer gage move up and down when commanded?	Test for Intermittent Conditions and Poor Connections	Go to Step 3
3	Replace the instrument panel cluster (IPC). Did you complete the replacement?	Go to Step 4	--
4	Operate the system in order to verify the repair. Did you correct the condition?	System OK	Go to Step 2

LTV0500000003395

Fig. 228   Tachometer inaccurate or inoperative. Hummer H3

Step	Action	Yes	No
1	Did you perform the Diagnostic System Check - Vehicle?	Go to Step 2	Go to Diagnostic System Check
2	Start the engine. Does the engine oil pressure indicator illuminate after the display test?	Go to Step 3	Test for Intermittent and Poor Connections
3	1. Install a scan tool. 2. Turn the ignition ON. 3. With the scan tool, observe the Engine Oil Pressure Switch parameter in the powertrain control module (PCM) Engine Data, data list. Does the Engine Oil Pressure Switch parameter display OK?	Go to Step 10	Go to Step 4
4	1. Turn the ignition OFF. 2. Disconnect the EOP switch. 3. Start the engine. 4. With the scan tool, observe the Engine Oil Pressure Switch parameter. Does the Engine Oil Pressure Switch parameter display OK?	Go to Step 6	Go to Step 5
5	Test the signal circuit of the EOP switch for a short to ground. Did you find and correct the condition?	Go to Step 11	Go to Step 7

LTV0500000003397

Fig. 230   Engine oil pressure indicator always on (Part 1 of 2). Hummer H3

6	Inspect for poor connections at the harness connector of the EOP switch. Did you find and correct the condition?	Go to Step 11	Go to Step 8
7	Inspect for poor connections at the harness connector of the PCM. Did you find and correct the condition?	Go to Step 11	Go to Step 9
8	Replace the EOP switch. Did you complete the replacement?	Go to Step 11	--
9	Replace the PCM. Did you complete the replacement?	Go to Step 11	--
10	Replace the instrument panel cluster (IPC). Did you complete the replacement?	Go to Step 11	--
11	Operate the system in order to verify the repair. Did you correct the condition?	System OK	Go to Step 2

LTV0500000003398

Fig. 230   Engine oil pressure indicator always on (Part 2 of 2). Hummer H3

Step	Action	Yes	No
1	Did you perform the Diagnostic System Check - Vehicle?	Go to Step 2	Go to Diagnostic System Check
2	Do any indicators illuminate when the chime sounds?	Go to Symptoms	Go to Step 3
3	1. Turn OFF the ignition. 2. Remove the key from the ignition. 3. Turn the headlamp switch to OFF. 4. Close all of the vehicle doors. 5. Open one or more of the vehicle doors. Does the chime sound at all times, regardless if the doors are open or closed?	Go to Step 14	Go to Step 4
4	1. Close all of the vehicle doors. 2. With a scan tool, observe the Door Ajar Switch parameters in the body control module (BCM) inputs data list. Do all of the Door Ajar Switch parameters display door closed?	Go to Step 5	Go to Courtesy Lamps Always On
5	1. Turn OFF the ignition. 2. Remove the key from the ignition. 3. Turn the headlamp switch to OFF. 4. Open the driver door. Does the chime sound?	Go to Step 6	Test for Intermittent Conditions and Poor Connections
6	1. Install a scan tool. 2. Turn ON the ignition, with the engine OFF. 3. With a scan tool, observe the Park Lamp Switch parameter in the BCM inputs data list. Does the Park Lamp Switch parameter display OFF?	Go to Step 7	Go to Step 9

LTV0500000003399

Fig. 231   Chime always on (Part 1 of 3). Hummer H3

Step	Action	Yes	No
7	With a scan tool, observe the Headlamp ON Switch parameter in the BCM Inputs data list. Does the Headlamp ON Switch parameter display Inactive?	Go to Step 8	Go to Step 9
8	1. Turn OFF the ignition. 2. Remove the key from the ignition. 3. With a scan tool, observe the Ign. Off/Run/Crank parameter in the BCM inputs data list. Does the Ign. Off/Run/Crank parameter display Inactive?	Go to Step 13	Go to Step 10
9	Test the headlamp input signal circuit and the park lamp signal circuit at the BCM for a short to voltage. Did you find and correct the condition?	Go to Step 19	Go to Step 11
10	Test the key in ignition signal circuit for a short to ground. Did you find and correct the condition?	Go to Step 19	Go to Step 12
11	Inspect for poor connections at the harness connector of the headlamp switch. Did you find and correct the condition?	Go to Step 19	Go to Step 15
12	Inspect for poor connections at the harness connector of the ignition key alarm switch. Did you find and correct the condition?	Go to Step 19	Go to Step 16
13	Inspect for poor connections at the harness connector of the BCM. Did you find and correct the condition?	Go to Step 19	Go to Step 17
14	Inspect for poor connections at the harness connector of the radio or audio amplifier. Did you find and correct the condition?	Go to Step 19	Go to Step 18

LTV0500000003400

Fig. 231   Chime always on (Part 2 of 3). Hummer H3

Step	Action	Yes	No
15	Replace the headlamp switch. Did you complete the replacement?	Go to Step 19	--
16	Replace the ignition switch. Did you complete the replacement?	Go to Step 19	--
17	Replace the BCM Did you complete the replacement?	Go to Step 19	--
18	Replace the radio. Did you complete the replacement?	Go to Step 19	--
19	Operate the system in order to verify the repair. Did you correct the condition?	System OK	Go to Step 3

LTV0500000003401

Fig. 231   Chime always on (Part 3 of 3). Hummer H3

Step	Action	Yes	No
1	Did you perform the Diagnostic System Check - Vehicle?	Go to Step 2	Go to Diagnostic System Check
2	1. Turn OFF the ignition, with the key in the ignition. 2. Open the driver door. Does the chime sound?	Test for Intermittent Conditions and Poor Connections	Go to Step 3
3	Do the courtesy lights turn ON when you open the driver door?	Go to Step 4	Go to Courtesy Lamps Inoperative
4	1. Turn ON the ignition, with the engine OFF. 2. Turn the radio ON. 3. Adjust the radio balance and fade to the left front speaker. Does the speaker operate properly?	Go to Step 5	Go to Speakers Inoperative - One or More
5	Replace the radio. Did you complete the replacement?	Go to Step 6	--
6	Operate the system in order to verify the repair. Did you correct the condition?	System OK	Go to Step 1

LTV0500000003402

Fig. 232   Chime inoperative. Hummer H3

Step	Action	Yes	No
1	Did you perform the Diagnostic System Check - Vehicle?	Go to Step 2	Go to Diagnostic System Check
2	1. Install a scan tool. 2. Turn ON the ignition, with the engine OFF. 3. With the scan tool, sweep the engine coolant temperature gage. Does the engine coolant temperature gage sweep from C to H and then back to C?	Test for Intermittent Conditions and Poor Connections	Go to Step 3
3	Replace the instrument panel cluster (IPC). Did you complete the replacement?	Go to Step 4	--
4	Operate the system in order to verify the repair. Did you correct the condition?	System OK	Go to Step 2

LTV0500000003293

Fig. 233   Engine coolant gage inaccurate or inoperative. Montana & Venture

Step	Action	Value(s)	Yes	No
1	Did you perform the Diagnostic System Check - Vehicle?	--	Go to Step 2	Go to Diagnostic System Check
2	1. Disconnect C305. 2. Connect the J 33431-C Signal Generator and Instrument Panel Tester between the signal circuit of the fuel level sensor and the sensor ground circuit of the fuel level sensor (male terminal side). 3. Turn ON the ignition, with the engine OFF. **Important:** Verify the J 33431-C resistance settings with a DMM. 4. Vary the resistance on the J 33431-C from 40-250 ohms. Does the fuel gage display the correct fuel level?	-- / --	Go to Step 4	Go to Step 3
3	1. Install a scan tool. 2. Turn ON the ignition, with the engine OFF. **Important:** Verify the J 33431-C resistance settings with a DMM. 3. Vary the resistance on the J 33431-C from 40-250 ohms. **Important:** Turn OFF the ignition momentarily between the resistance settings in order to quickly update the scan tool display. 4. With the scan tool, observe the Fuel Level % parameter in the PCM EVAP data list. Does the scan tool display the correct fuel level %?	--	Go to Step 11	Go to Step 5

LTV0500000003294

Fig. 234   Fuel gage inaccurate or inoperative (Part 1 of 3). Montana & Venture

Step	Action	Value(s)	Yes	No
8	1. With the DMM, measure the resistance of the fuel level sensor while moving the float arm. 2. Observe both the analog and digital displays on the DMM. Does the resistance change smoothly across the specified range?	40-250 ohms	Go to Diagnostic Aids	Go to Step 10
9	Inspect for poor connections at the harness connector of the powertrain control module (PCM). Did you find and correct the condition?	--	Go to Step 13	Go to Step 12
10	Replace the fuel level sensor. Did you complete the replacement?	--	Go to Step 13	--
11	Replace the instrument panel cluster (IPC). Did you complete the replacement?	--	Go to Step 13	--
12	Replace the PCM. Did you complete the replacement?	--	Go to Step 13	--
13	1. Use a scan tool in order to clear the PCM DTCs. 2. Operate the system in order to verify the repair. Did you correct the condition?	--	System OK	Go to Step 2

LTV0500000003296

Fig. 234   Fuel gage inaccurate or inoperative (Part 3 of 3). Montana & Venture

Step	Action	Yes	No
4	Inspect for the following items: • A poor connection at the harness connector of the fuel level sensor • A high resistance in the signal circuit or the sensor ground circuit between the fuel level sensor and C305 • A misaligned fuel level sensor • A deformed fuel tank. Did you find and correct the condition?	Go to Step 13	Go to Step 7
5	Test the signal circuit of the fuel level sensor for a high resistance. Did you find and correct the condition?	Go to Step 13	Go to Step 6
6	Test the sensor ground circuit of the fuel level sensor for a high resistance. Did you find and correct the condition?	Go to Step 13	Go to Step 9
7	1. Remove the fuel level sensor. 2. Inspect for the following items: - A stuck fuel level sensor (i.e. the fuel strainer interfering with the sensor float arm) - Foreign material in the gas tank (ice). Did you find and correct the condition?	Go to Step 13	Go to Step 8

LTV0500000003295

Fig. 234   Fuel gage inaccurate or inoperative (Part 2 of 3). Montana & Venture

Step	Action	Yes	No
1	Did you perform the Diagnostic System Check - Vehicle?	Go to Step 2	Go to Diagnostic System Check
2	Replace the instrument panel cluster (IPC). Did you complete the replacement?	Go to Step 3	--
3	Operate the system in order to verify the repair. Did you correct the condition?	System OK	Go to Step 2

LTV0500000003297

Fig. 235   Odometer trip/reset switch inoperative. Montana & Venture

Step	Action	Yes	No
1	Did you perform the Diagnostic System Check - Vehicle?	Go to Step 2	Go to Diagnostic System Check
2	1. Install a scan tool. 2. Raise vehicle drive wheels. 3. Start the engine. 4. Place the transmission into drive for automatic transmission and third gear for manual transmission. 5. With the scan tool, observe the vehicle speed parameter in the PCM Engine Data 1 data list. Does the vehicle speed parameter match the speedometer display?	Go to Step 3	Go to Step 4
3	Does the odometer operate properly?	Test for Intermittent Conditions and Poor Connections	Go to Step 4
4	Replace the instrument panel cluster (IPC). Did you complete the replacement?	Go to Step 5	--
5	1. Operate the system in order to verify the repair. 2. Use the scan tool in order to clear the DTCs that may have set in other modules during diagnosis. Did you correct the condition?	System OK	Go to Step 2

LTV0500000003298

Fig. 236   Speedometer and/or odometer inaccurate or inoperative. Montana & Venture

Step	Action	Yes	No
1	Did you perform the Diagnostic System Check - Vehicle?	Go to Step 2	Go to Diagnostic System Check
2	Start the engine. Does the tachometer operate normally?	Test for Intermittent Conditions and Poor Connections	Go to Step 3
3	1. Turn ON the ignition, with the engine OFF. 2. Install a scan tool. 3. With a scan tool, sweep the tachometer. Does the tachometer move from 0 RPM to 7000 RPM and back to 0 RPM when you sweep this gage up and down?	Go to Diagnostic System Check	Go to Step 4
4	Replace the instrument panel cluster (IPC). Did you complete the replacement?	Go to Step 5	--
5	Operate the system in order to verify the repair. Did you correct the condition?	System OK	Go to Step 3

LTV0500000003299

Fig. 237 Tachometer inaccurate or inoperative. Montana & Venture

Step	Action	Yes	No
1	Did you perform the Diagnostic System Check - Vehicle?	Go to Step 2	Go to Diagnostic System Check
2	1. Install a scan tool. 2. Turn ON the ignition, with the engine OFF. 3. With a scan tool, observe the engine oil life percent in the PCM IPC data list. Does the scan tool display zero percent with the change engine oil message on?	Go to Step 3	Go to Step 4
3	Reset GM engine oil life system. Has the GM engine oil life system been reset?	Go to Step 5	--
4	Replace the instrument panel cluster (IPC). Did you complete the replacement?	Go to Step 5	--
5	1. Install a scan tool. 2. Turn ON the ignition, with the engine OFF. 3. With a scan tool, observe the Engine Oil Life percent in PCM IPC data list. Does the scan tool display 100 percent with the engine oil message off?	System OK	Go to Diagnostic System Check

LTV0500000003300

Fig. 238 Change engine oil indicator always on. Montana & Venture

Step	Action	Yes	No
1	Did you perform the Diagnostic System Check - Vehicle?	Go to Step 2	Go to Diagnostic System Check
2	1. Install a scan tool. 2. Turn ON the ignition, with the engine OFF. 3. With a scan tool, observe the Engine Oil Life percent in PCM IPC data list. Does the scan tool display zero percent while the Change Engine Oil message is inoperative?	Go to Step 3	System OK
3	Replace the instrument panel cluster (IPC). Did you complete the replacement?	Go to Step 4	--
4	Operate the system in order to verify the repair. Did you correct the condition?	System OK	Go to Step 2

LTV0500000003301

Fig. 239 Change engine oil indicator inoperative. Montana & Venture

Step	Action	Yes	No
1	Did you perform the Diagnostic System Check - Vehicle?	Go to Step 2	Go to Diagnostic System Check
2	Start the engine. Does the engine oil pressure indicator illuminate after the displays test?	Go to Step 3	Test for Intermittent and Poor Connections
3	1. Install a scan tool. 2. Turn the ignition ON. 3. With the scan tool, observe the Engine Oil Pressure parameter in the PCM IPC data list. Does the Engine Oil Pressure parameter display Ok?	Go to Step 10	Go to Step 4
4	1. Turn the ignition OFF. 2. Disconnect the engine oil pressure switch. 3. Start the engine. 4. With the scan tool, observe the Engine Oil Pressure parameter. Does the Engine Oil Pressure parameter display Ok?	Go to Step 6	Go to Step 5
5	Test the signal circuit of the engine oil pressure switch for a short to ground. Did you find and correct the condition?	Go to Step 11	Go to Step 7

LTV0500000003302

Fig. 240 Engine oil pressure indicator always on (Part 1 of 2). Montana & Venture

Step	Action	Yes	No
6	Inspect for poor connections at the harness connector of the engine oil pressure switch. Did you find and correct the condition?	Go to Step 11	Go to Step 8
7	Inspect for poor connections at the harness connector of the powertrain control module (PCM). Did you find and correct the condition?	Go to Step 11	Go to Step 9
8	Replace the engine oil pressure switch. Did you complete the replacement?	Go to Step 11	--
9	Replace the PCM. Did you complete the replacement?	Go to Step 11	--
10	Replace the instrument panel cluster (IPC). Did you complete the replacement?	Go to Step 11	--
11	Operate the system in order to verify the repair. Did you correct the condition?	System OK	Go to Step 2

LTV0500000003303

Fig. 240 Engine oil pressure indicator always on (Part 2 of 2). Montana & Venture

Step	Action	Yes	No
1	Did you perform the Diagnostic System Check - Vehicle?	Go to Step 2	Go to Diagnostic System Check
2	1. Install a scan tool. 2. Turn the ignition ON, with the engine OFF. 3. With the scan tool, observe the Engine Oil Level parameter in the PCM IPC data list. Does the Engine Oil Level parameter display Ok?	Go to Step 3	Go to Step 4
3	Does the low engine oil indicator remain illuminated after the displays test?	Go to Step 11	Test for Intermittent and Poor Connections
4	1. Turn the ignition OFF. 2. Disconnect the engine oil level switch. 3. Connect a 3-ampere fused jumper between the signal circuit of the engine oil level switch and a good ground. 4. Turn the ignition ON, with the engine OFF. 5. With the scan tool, observe the Engine Oil Level parameter. Does the Engine Oil Level parameter display Ok?	Go to Step 6	Go to Step 5
5	Test the signal circuit of the engine oil level switch for a short to battery voltage, for an open or for a high resistance. Did you find and correct the condition?	Go to Step 12	Go to Step 8

LTV0500000003304

Fig. 241   Low engine oil dipstick always on (Part 1 of 2). Montana & Venture

Step	Action	Yes	No
6	Test the ground circuit of the engine oil level switch for an open or for a high resistance. Did you find and correct the condition?	Go to Step 12	Go to Step 7
7	Inspect for poor connections at the harness connector of the engine oil level switch. Did you find and correct the condition?	Go to Step 12	Go to Step 9
8	Inspect for poor connections at the harness connector of the powertrain control module (PCM). Did you find and correct the condition?	Go to Step 12	Go to Step 10
9	Replace the engine oil level switch. Did you complete the replacement?	Go to Step 12	--
10	Replace the PCM. Did you complete the replacement?	Go to Step 12	--
11	Replace the instrument panel cluster (IPC). Did you complete the replacement?	Go to Step 12	--
12	Operate the system in order to verify the repair. Did you correct the condition?	System OK	Go to Step 2

LTV0500000003305

Fig. 241   Low engine oil dipstick always on (Part 2 of 2). Montana & Venture

Step	Action	Yes	No
1	Did you perform the Diagnostic System Check - Vehicle?	Go to Step 2	Go to Diagnostic System Check
2	Verify the compass is inaccurate or C is displayed. Does the system operate normally?	Test for Intermittent and Poor Connections	Go to Step 3
3	Turn ON the ignition, with the engine OFF. Is the compass display blank?	Go to Step 7	Go to Step 4
4	Is CAL or C displayed?	Go to Step 5	Go to Step 6
5	Perform the compass calibration procedure. Does the compass operate properly?	Go to Step 8	Go to Step 6
6	Perform the compass variance procedure. Does the compass operate properly?	Go to Step 8	Go to Step 7
7	Replace the driver information center (DIC). Did you complete the replacement?	Go to Step 8	--
8	Operate the system in order to verify the repair. Did you correct the condition?	System OK	Go to Step 2

LTV0500000003306

Fig. 242   Driver information center (DIC) compass inaccurate or C displayed. Montana & Venture

Step	Action	Yes	No
1	Did you perform the Diagnostic System Check - Vehicle?	Go to Step 2	Go to Diagnostic System Check
2	Replace the driver information center (DIC). Did you complete the replacement?	Go to Step 3	--
3	Operate the system in order to verify the repair. Did you correct the condition?	System OK	Go to Step 2

LTV0500000003307

Fig. 243   Driver information center (DIC) switch(es) inoperative. Montana & Venture

Step	Action	Yes	No
1	Did you review the operation and perform the necessary inspections?	Go to Step 2	Go to Symptoms
2	Are the rear parking assist (RPA) indicators ON?	Go to Rear Parking Assist Malfunction	Go to Step 3
3	Are any other indicators illuminated?	Go to Symptoms	Go to Step 4
4	Test the control circuit of the instrument panel (I/P) body control module (BCM) chime request for a short to ground. Did you find and correct the condition?	Go to Step 15	Go to Step 5
5	1. Turn OFF the ignition. 2. Make sure the headlamp and I/P lamp dimmer switch is in the OFF position. 3. Disconnect the BCM connector C2. 4. Connect a test lamp between the headlamp and I/P lamp dimmer switch circuit at the BCM and ground. Does the test lamp illuminate?	Go to Step 6	Go to Step 7
6	1. Take the ignition key out of the ignition switch. 2. Connect a test lamp between the control circuit of the ignition key alarm switch and B+. Does the test lamp illuminate?	Go to Step 8	Go to Step 13

LTV0500000003308

Fig. 244   Chime always on (Part 1 of 2). Montana & Venture

Step	Action	Yes	No
7	Test the control circuit of the headlamp and I/P lamp dimmer switch for an open. Did you find and correct the condition?	Go to Step 15	Go to Step 12
8	1. Disconnect C201. 2. Leave the test lamp at the same location. Does the test lamp illuminate?	Go to Step 11	Go to Step 14
9	Inspect for poor connections at the harness connector of the headlamp and I/P lamp dimmer switch. Did you find and correct the condition?	Go to Step 15	Go to Step 12
10	Inspect for poor connections at the harness connector of the BCM connector C2. Did you find and correct the condition?	Go to Step 15	Go to Step 13
11	Repair a short to ground in the control circuit of the ignition key alarm switch. Did you complete the repair?	Go to Step 15	--
12	Replace the headlamp and I/P lamp dimmer switch. Did you complete the replacement?	Go to Step 15	--
13	Replace the BCM. Did you complete the replacement?	Go to Step 15	--
14	Replace the ignition key alarm switch. Did you complete the replacement?	Go to Step 15	--
15	Operate the system in order to verify the repair. Did you correct the condition?	System OK	Go to Step 2

LTV0500000003309

Fig. 244 Chime always on (Part 2 of 2). Montana & Venture

Step	Action	Yes	No
9	Test for an open or a short to B+ in the control circuit of the ignition key warning switch. Did you find and correct the condition?	Go to Step 17	Go to Step 12
10	Test for an open or a short to B+ in the control circuit of the LF side door lock. Did you find and correct the condition?	Go to Step 17	Go to Step 13
11	Inspect the control circuit of the headlamp switch for poor connections at the harness connector of the BCM connector C2. Did you find and correct the condition?	Go to Step 17	Go to Step 14
12	Inspect the control circuit of the ignition key warning switch for poor connections at the harness connector of the BCM connector C2 and the ignition key warning switch. Did you find and correct the condition?	Go to Step 17	Go to Step 16
13	Inspect the control circuit of the LF side door lock for poor connections at the harness connector of the BCM connector C2 and the LF side door lock. Did you find and correct the condition?	Go to Step 17	Go to Step 15
14	Replace the BCM. Did you complete the replacement?	Go to Step 17	--
15	Replace the LF door lock. Did you complete the replacement?	Go to Step 17	--
16	Replace the ignition key alarm switch. Did you complete the replacement?	Go to Step 17	--
17	Operate the system in order to verify the repair. Did you correct the condition?	System OK	Go to Step 2

LTV0500000003311

Fig. 245 Chime inoperative (Part 2 of 2). Montana & Venture

Step	Action	Yes	No
1	Did you review the operation and perform the necessary inspections?	Go to Step 2	Go to Symptoms
2	Is the fasten safety belt indicator off with the ignition ON and the seat belt unbuckled?	Go to Seat Belt Indicator Circuit Malfunction	Go to Step 3
3	Do both of the turn signals operate when turned on?	Go to Step 4	Go to Diagnostic System Check - Vehicle
4	Do the headlamps illuminate when turned on?	Go to Step 5	Go to Headlamps Inoperative - Low and High Beams
5	1. Turn the ignition ON, with the engine OFF. 2. Make sure the rear parking assist on/off switch is in the on position. Do the rear parking assist indicators turn on for 2 seconds and then turn off after bulb check?	Go to Step 6	Go to Symptoms
6	Test the control circuit of the headlamp switch for a short to B+ or a short to ground. Did you find and correct the condition?	Go to Step 17	Go to Step 7
7	1. Place the key in the ignition switch. 2. Connect a test lamp between the control circuit of the ignition key warning switch at the body control module (BCM) and B+. Does the test lamp illuminate?	Go to Step 8	Go to Step 9
8	1. Open the LF door. 2. Connect a test lamp between the control circuit of the LF side door lock at the BCM and B+. Does the test lamp illuminate?	Go to Step 11	Go to Step 10

LTV0500000003310

Fig. 245 Chime inoperative (Part 1 of 2). Montana & Venture

Step	Action	Yes	No
1	Did you review the operation and perform the necessary inspections?	Go to Step 2	Go to Symptoms
2	Inspect for poor connections at the harness connector of the instrument panel cluster (IPC) connector C1. Did you find and correct the condition?	Go to Step 6	Go to Step 3
3	Inspect for poor connections at the harness connector of the body control module (BCM) connector C2. Did you find and correct the condition?	Go to Step 6	Go to Step 4
4	Test the chime request signal circuit of the IPC for a high resistance, an open, and a short to B+. Did you find and correct the condition?	Go to Step 6	Go to Step 5
5	Replace the BCM. Did you complete the replacement?	Go to Step 6	--
6	Operate the system in order to verify the repair. Did you correct the condition?	System OK	Go to Step 2

LTV0500000003312

Fig. 246 Low oil pressure, low fuel chime inoperative. Montana & Venture

Step	Action	Yes	No
1	Did you perform the Diagnostic System Check - Vehicle?	Go to Step 2	Go to Diagnostic System Check
2	1. Install a scan tool. 2. Turn ON the ignition, with the engine OFF. 3. With the scan tool, sweep the engine coolant temperature gage. Does the engine coolant temperature gage sweep from C to H and then back to C?	Test for Intermittent Conditions and Poor Connections	Go to Step 3
3	Replace the instrument panel cluster (IPC). Did you complete the replacement?	Go to Step 4	--
4	Operate the system in order to verify the repair. Did you correct the condition?	System OK	Go to Step 2

LTV0500000003367

Fig. 247 Engine coolant temperature gage inaccurate or inoperative. Relay, SV6, Terraza & Uplander

Step	Action		Yes	No
4	Inspect for the following items: • A poor connection at the harness connector of the fuel level sensor • A high resistance in the signal circuit or the sensor ground circuit between the fuel level sensor and C305 • A misaligned fuel level sensor • A deformed fuel tank Did you find and correct the condition?	--	Go to Step 13	Go to Step 7
5	Test the signal circuit of the fuel level sensor for a high resistance. Did you find and correct the condition?	--	Go to Step 13	Go to Step 6
6	Test the sensor ground circuit of the fuel level sensor for a high resistance. Did you find and correct the condition?	--	Go to Step 13	Go to Step 9
7	1. Remove the fuel level sensor. 2. Inspect for the following items: - A stuck fuel level sensor (i.e. the fuel strainer interfering with the sensor float arm) - Foreign material in the gas tank (ice) Did you find and correct the condition?	--	Go to Step 13	Go to Step 8
8	1. With the DMM, measure the resistance of the fuel level sensor while moving the float arm. 2. Observe both the analog and digital displays on the DMM. Does the resistance change smoothly across the specified range?	40-250 ohms	Go to Diagnostic Aids	Go to Step 10

LTV0500000003369

Fig. 248 Fuel gage inaccurate or inoperative (Part 2 of 3). Relay, SV6, Terraza & Uplander

Step	Action		Yes	No
9	Inspect for poor connections at the harness connector of the ECM/PCM. Did you find and correct the condition?	-	Go to Step 13	Go to Step 12
10	Replace the fuel level sensor. Did you complete the replacement?	-	Go to Step 13	-
11	Replace the instrument panel cluster (IPC). Did you complete the replacement?	-	Go to Step 13	-
12	Replace the ECM/PCM. Did you complete the replacement?	-	Go to Step 13	-
13	1. Use a scan tool in order to clear the ECM/PCM DTCs. 2. Operate the system in order to verify the repair. Did you correct the condition?	-	System OK	Go to Step 2

LTV0500000003370

Fig. 248 Fuel gage inaccurate or inoperative (Part 3 of 3). Relay, SV6, Terraza & Uplander

Step	Action	Values	Yes	No
1	Did you perform the Diagnostic System Check - Vehicle?	--	Go to Step 2	Go to Diagnostic System Check
2	1. Disconnect C305. 2. Connect the J 33431-C Signal Generator and Instrument Panel Tester or SA9205Z Decade Box between the signal circuit of the fuel level sensor and the sensor ground circuit of the fuel level sensor, male terminal side. 3. Turn ON the ignition, with the engine OFF. **Important:** Verify the J 33431-C or SA9205Z resistance settings with a DMM. 4. Vary the resistance on the J 33431-C or SA9205Z from 40-250 ohms. Does the fuel gage display the correct fuel level?	--	Go to Step 4	Go to Step 3
3	1. Install a scan tool. 2. Turn ON the ignition, with the engine OFF. **Important:** Verify the J 33431-C or SA9205Z resistance settings with a DMM. 3. Vary the resistance on the J 33431-C or SA9205Z from 40-250 ohms. **Important:** Turn OFF the ignition momentarily between the resistance settings in order to quickly update the scan tool display. 4. With the scan tool, observe the Fuel Tank Level Remaining parameter in the engine control module (ECM)/powertrain control module (PCM) evaporative emission (EVAP) data list. Does the scan tool display the correct fuel level %?	--	Go to Step 11	Go to Step 5

LTV0500000003368

Fig. 248 Fuel gage inaccurate or inoperative (Part 1 of 3). Relay, SV6, Terraza & Uplander

Step	Action	Yes	No
1	Did you perform the Diagnostic System Check - Vehicle?	Go to Step 2	Go to Diagnostic System Check
2	1. Install a scan tool. 2. Raise vehicle drive wheels. 3. Start the engine. 4. Place the transmission into drive for automatic transmission and third gear for manual transmission. 5. With the scan tool, observe the Vehicle Speed Sensor parameter in the powertrain control module (PCM) Engine Data, data list. Does the vehicle speed parameter match the speedometer display?	Go to Step 3	Go to Step 4
3	Does the odometer operate properly?	Test for Intermittent Conditions and Poor Connections	Go to Step 4
4	Replace the instrument panel cluster (IPC). Did you complete the replacement?	Go to Step 5	--
5	Operate the system in order to verify the repair. Use the scan tool in order to clear the DTCs that may have set in other modules during diagnosis. Did you correct the condition?	System OK	Go to Step 2

LTV0500000003371

Fig. 249 Speedometer and/or odometer inaccurate or inoperative. Relay, SV6, Terraza & Uplander

Step	Action	Yes	No
1	Did you perform the Diagnostic System Check - Vehicle?	Go to Step 2	Go to Diagnostic System Check
2	Start the engine. Does the tachometer operate normally?		Go to Step 3
3	1. Turn ON the ignition, with the engine OFF. 2. Install a scan tool. 3. With a scan tool, sweep the tachometer. Does the tachometer move from 0 RPM to 7000 RPM and back to 0 RPM when you sweep this gage up and down?	Go to Diagnostic System Check	Go to Step 4
4	Replace the instrument panel cluster (IPC). Did you complete the replacement?	Go to Step 5	--
5	Operate the system in order to verify the repair. Did you correct the condition?	System OK	Go to Step 3

LTV0500000003372

Fig. 250 Tachometer inaccurate or inoperative. Relay, SV6, Terraza & Uplander

Step	Action	Yes	No
1	Did you perform the Diagnostic System Check - Vehicle?	Go to Step 2	Go to Diagnostic System Check
2	1. Install a scan tool. 2. Turn ON the ignition, with the engine OFF. 3. With a scan tool, observe the Engine Oil Life Remaining in the instrument panel cluster (IPC) powertrain control module (PCM) data list. Does the scan tool display zero percent while the Change Engine Oil message is inoperative?	Go to Step 3	System OK
3	Replace the IPC. Did you complete the replacement?	Go to Step 4	--
4	Operate the system in order to verify the repair. Did you correct the condition?	System OK	Go to Step 2

LTV0500000003374

Fig. 252 Change oil indicator inoperative. Relay, SV6, Terraza & Uplander

Step	Action	Yes	No
1	Did you perform the Diagnostic System Check - Vehicle?	Go to Step 2	Go to Diagnostic System Check
2	Start the engine. Does the engine oil pressure indicator illuminate after the displays test?	Go to Step 3	Test for Intermittent Conditions and Poor Connections
3	1. Install a scan tool. 2. Turn ON the ignition. 3. With the scan tool, observe the Engine Oil Pressure Switch parameter in the instrument panel cluster (IPC) powertrain control module (PCM) data list. Does the Engine Oil Pressure Switch parameter display Ok?	Go to Step 10	Go to Step 4
4	1. Turn OFF the ignition. 2. Disconnect the engine oil pressure switch. 3. Start the engine. 4. With the scan tool, observe the Engine Oil Pressure Switch parameter. Does the Engine Oil Pressure Switch parameter display Ok?	Go to Step 6	Go to Step 5
5	Test the signal circuit of the engine oil pressure switch for a short to ground. Did you find and correct the condition?	Go to Step 11	Go to Step 7
6	Inspect for poor connections at the harness connector of the engine oil pressure switch. Did you find and correct the condition?	Go to Step 11	Go to Step 8

LTV0500000003375

Fig. 253 Engine oil pressure indicator always on (Part 1 of 2). Relay, SV6, Terraza & Uplander w/3.5L engine

Step	Action	Yes	No
1	Did you perform the Diagnostic System Check - Vehicle?	Go to Step 2	Go to Diagnostic System Check
2	1. Install a scan tool. 2. Turn ON the ignition, with the engine OFF. 3. With a scan tool, observe the Engine Oil Life Remaining in the instrument panel cluster (IPC) powertrain control module (PCM) data list. Does the scan tool display zero percent with the change engine oil message ON?	Go to Step 3	Go to Step 4
3	Reset GM engine oil life system. Has the GM engine oil life system been reset?	Go to Step 5	--
4	Replace the IPC. Did you complete the replacement?	Go to Step 5	--
5	1. Install a scan tool. 2. Turn ON the ignition, with the engine OFF. 3. With a scan tool, observe the Engine Oil Life Remaining in the IPC data list. Does the scan tool display 100 percent with the engine oil message off?	System OK	Go to Diagnostic System Check

LTV0500000003373

Fig. 251 Change engine oil indicator always on. Relay, SV6, Terraza & Uplander

Step	Action	Yes	No
7	Inspect for poor connections at the harness connector of the PCM. Did you find and correct the condition?	Go to Step 11	Go to Step 9
8	Replace the engine oil pressure switch. Did you complete the replacement?	Go to Step 11	--
9	Replace the PCM. Did you complete the replacement?	Go to Step 11	--
10	Replace the IPC. Did you complete the replacement?	Go to Step 11	--
11	Operate the system in order to verify the repair. Did you correct the condition?	System OK	Go to Step 2

LTV0500000003376

Fig. 253 Engine oil pressure indicator always on (Part 2 of 2). Relay, SV6, Terraza & Uplander w/3.5L engine

Step	Action	Values	Yes	No
1	Did you perform the Diagnostic System Check - Vehicle?	--	Go to Step 2	Go to Diagnostic System Check
2	Does the engine oil pressure (EOP) indicator display in the message center?	--	Go to Step 3	Test for Intermittent Conditions and Poor Connections
3	1. Install a scan tool. 2. Turn ON the ignition, with the engine OFF. 3. With a scan tool, observe the Engine Oil Pressure Sensor parameter in the engine control module (ECM) instrument panel cluster (IPC) Data list. Is the Engine Oil Pressure Sensor parameter within the specified range?	207-483 kPa (30-70 psi)	Go to Step 15	Go to Step 4
4	1. Turn the ignition OFF. 2. Disconnect the EOP sensor. 3. Connect a 3-ampere fused jumper between the EOP sensor signal circuit and the 5-volt reference circuit of the EOP sensor. 4. With the scan tool, observe the Engine Oil Pressure Sensor parameter in the ECM IPC Data list. Does the scan tool indicate that the Engine Oil Pressure Sensor parameter is at or greater than the specified value?	550 kPa (80 psi)	Go to Step 5	Go to Step 6
5	1. Connect a 3-ampere fused jumper between the EOP sensor signal circuit and the low reference circuit of the EOP sensor. 2. With the scan tool, observe the Engine Oil Pressure Sensor parameter in the ECM IPC Data list. Does the scan tool indicate that the Engine Oil Pressure Sensor parameter is at or less than the specified value?	0 kPa (0 psi)	Go to Step 11	Go to Step 7
6	1. Disconnect the fused jumper. 2. Measure the voltage between the 5-volt reference circuit of the EOP sensor and the low reference circuit of the EOP sensor. Does the voltage measure greater than the specified value?	4.6 V	Go to Step 10	Go to Step 8

LTV0500000003377

Fig. 254 Engine oil pressure indicator always on (Part 1 of 3). Relay, SV6, Terraza & Uplander w/3.9L engine

Step	Action		Yes	No
12	Inspect for poor connections at the harness connector of the engine control module (ECM). Did you find and correct the condition?	-	Go to Step 16	Go to Step 14
13	Replace the engine oil pressure sensor. Did you complete the replacement?	-	Go to Step 16	--
14	Replace the ECM. Did you complete the replacement?	-	Go to Step 16	--
15	Replace the IPC. Did you complete the replacement?	-	Go to Step 16	--
16	Operate the system in order to verify the repair. Did you correct the condition?	-	System OK	Go to Step 2

LTV0500000003379

Fig. 254 Engine oil pressure indicator always on (Part 3 of 3). Relay, SV6, Terraza & Uplander w/3.9L engine

Step	Action	Values	Yes	No
7	1. Disconnect the negative battery cable. 2. Measure the resistance from the low reference circuit of the EOP sensor to a good ground. Does the resistance measure less than the specified value?	5 ohms	Go to Step 12	Go to Step 9
8	Test the EOP 5-volt reference circuit for the following: • An open • A short to ground • A high resistance Did you find and correct the condition?	--	Go to Step 16	Go to Step 9
9	Test the EOP low reference circuit for high resistance or for an open. Did you find and correct the condition?	--	Go to Step 16	Go to Step 10
10	Test the EOP oil pressure sensor signal circuit for the following: • An open • A short to ground • A high resistance Did you find and correct the condition?	--	Go to Step 16	Go to Step 12
11	Inspect for poor connections at the harness connector of the EOP sensor. Did you find and correct the condition?	--	Go to Step 16	Go to Step 13

LTV0500000003378

Fig. 254 Engine oil pressure indicator always on (Part 2 of 3). Relay, SV6, Terraza & Uplander w/3.9L engine

Step	Action	Yes	No
1	Did you perform the Diagnostic System Check - Vehicle?	Go to Step 2	Go to Diagnostic System Check
2	1. Install a scan tool. 2. Turn ON the ignition, with the engine OFF. 3. With the scan tool, perform the Lamp Test in the instrument panel cluster (IPC) Special Functions. Does the low fuel indicator illuminate when commanded ON?	Test for Intermittent Conditions and Poor Connections	Go to Step 3
3	Replace the IPC. Did you complete the replacement?	Go to Step 4	--
4	Operate the system in order to verify the repair. Did you correct the condition?	System OK	Go to Step 2

LTV0500000003380

Fig. 255 Low fuel indicator inoperative. Relay, SV6, Terraza & Uplander

1	Did you perform the Diagnostic System Check - Vehicle?	Go to Step 2	Go to Diagnostic System Check
2	1. Install a scan tool. 2. Turn ON the ignition, with the engine OFF. 3. Press and release each of the driver information center (DIC) switches. 4. With a scan tool, observe the DIC Switch parameters in the instrument panel cluster (IPC) data list. Does the scan tool display Active when each switch is pressed and Inactive when each switch is released?	Test for Intermittent Conditions and Poor Connections	Go to Step 3
3	Does the scan tool display Inactive when each switch is pressed?	Go to Step 9	Go to Step 4
4	Does the scan tool always display Active for the suspect switch even when the switch is released?	Go to Step 5	Go to Step 6
5	1. Turn OFF the ignition. 2. Disconnect the DIC switch connector. 3. Turn ON the ignition, with the engine OFF. 4. With a scan tool, observe the suspect DIC Switch parameter. Does the scan tool display Active for the suspect switch?	Go to Step 7	Go to Step 12
6	1. Turn OFF the ignition. 2. Disconnect the DIC switch assembly connector. 3. Connect a 3-amp fused jumper wire between the signal circuit of the suspect DIC switch and a good ground. 4. Turn ON the ignition, with the engine OFF. 5. With a scan tool, observe the suspect DIC Switch parameter. Does the scan tool display Active for the suspect switch?	Go to Step 10	Go to Step 8
7	Test the signal circuit of the suspect DIC switch for a short to ground. Did you find and correct the condition?	Go to Step 14	Go to Step 11

LTV0500000003381

Fig. 256 Driver information center (DIC) switch(es) inoperative (Part 1 of 2). Relay, SV6, Terraza & Uplander

8	Test the signal circuit of the suspect DIC switch for an open or high resistance. Did you find and correct the condition?	Go to Step 14	Go to Step 11
9	Test the ground circuit of the DIC switch assembly for an open or high resistance. Did you find and correct the condition?	Go to Step 14	Go to Step 10
10	Inspect for poor connections at the harness connector of the DIC switch assembly. Did you find and correct the condition?	Go to Step 14	Go to Step 12
11	Inspect for poor connections at the harness connector of the IPC. Did you find and correct the condition?	Go to Step 14	Go to Step 13
12	Replace the DIC switch assembly. Did you complete the replacement?	Go to Step 14	--
13	Replace the IPC. Did you complete the replacement?	Go to Step 14	--
14	Operate the system in order to verify the repair. Did you correct the condition?	System OK	Go to Step 2

LTV0500000003382

Fig. 256 Driver information center (DIC) switch(es) inoperative (Part 2 of 2). Relay, SV6, Terraza & Uplander

1	Did you perform the Diagnostic System Check - Vehicle?	Go to Step 2	Go to Diagnostic System Check -
2	Do any indicators illuminate when the chime sounds?	Go to Symptoms	Go to Step 3
3	1. Turn the ignition OFF. 2. Remove the key from the ignition. 3. Turn the headlamp switch to OFF. 4. Close all of the vehicle doors. 5. Open one or more of the vehicle doors. Does the chime sound at all times regardless if the doors are open or closed?	Go to Step 15	Go to Step 4
4	1. Close all of the vehicle doors. 2. With a scan tool, observe the LF Door Ajar Switch parameter and the RF Door Ajar Switch parameter in the instrument panel cluster BCM/Inputs data list. Do all of the Door Ajar Switch parameters display Door Closed?	Go to Step 5	Go to Courtesy Lamps Always On
5	With a scan tool, observe the Left Rear Door Ajar Sw. parameter and the Right Rear Door Sw. parameter in the instrument panel cluster BCM/Inputs data list. Do all of the Rear Door Switch parameters display Closed?	Go to Step 6	Go to Courtesy Lamps Always On
6	1. Turn the ignition OFF. 2. Remove the key from the ignition. 3. Turn the headlamp switch to OFF. 4. Open the driver door. Does the chime sound?	Go to Step 7	Test for Intermittent Conditions and Poor Connections
7	1. Install a scan tool. 2. Turn the ignition ON, with the engine OFF. 3. With a scan tool, observe the Park Lamp Switch parameter in the instrument panel cluster BCM/Inputs data list. Does the Park Lamp Switch parameter display Off?	Go to Step 8	Go to Step 10

LTV0500000003383

Fig. 257 Chime always on (Part 1 of 3). Relay, SV6, Terraza & Uplander

8	With a scan tool, observe the Headlamp Off Switch parameter in the instrument panel cluster BCM/Inputs data list. Does the Headlamp Off Switch parameter display Inactive?	Go to Step 9	Go to Step 10
9	1. Turn the ignition OFF. 2. Remove the key from the ignition. 3. With a scan tool, observe the Key In Ignition parameter in the instrument panel cluster BCM/Inputs data list. Does the Key In Ignition parameter display Inactive?	Go to Step 14	Go to Step 11
10	Test the headlamp input signal circuit and the parklamp signal circuit at the BCM for a short to voltage. Did you find and correct the condition?	Go to Step 20	Go to Step 12
11	Test the key in ignition signal circuit for a short to ground. Did you find and correct the condition?	Go to Step 20	Go to Step 13
12	Inspect for poor connections at the harness connector of the headlamp switch. Did you find and correct the condition?	Go to Step 20	Go to Step 16
13	Inspect for poor connections at the harness connector of the ignition key alarm switch. Did you find and correct the condition?	Go to Step 20	Go to Step 17
14	Inspect for poor connections at the harness connector of the BCM. Did you find and correct the condition?	Go to Step 20	Go to Step 18
15	Inspect for poor connections at the harness connector of the radio or audio amplifier. Did you find and correct the condition?	Go to Step 20	Go to Step 19

LTV0500000003384

Fig. 257 Chime always on (Part 2 of 3). Relay, SV6, Terraza & Uplander

Step	Action	Yes	No
16	Replace the headlamp switch. Did you complete the replacement?	Go to Step 20	--
17	Replace the ignition switch. Did you complete the replacement?	Go to Step 20	--
18	Replace the BCM. Did you complete the replacement?	Go to Step 20	--
19	Replace the radio. Did you complete the replacement?	Go to Step 20	--
20	Operate the system in order to verify the repair. Did you correct the condition?	System OK	Go to Step 3

LTV0500000003385

Fig. 257 Chime always on (Part 3 of 3). Relay, SV6, Terraza & Uplander

Step	Action	Yes	No
1	Did you perform the Instrument Cluster Diagnostic System Check?	Go to Step 2	
2	1. Turn the ignition ON, with the engine OFF. 2. Observe the IPC. Does the IPC perform the displays test?		Go to Step 3
3	1. Turn the ignition OFF. 2. Disconnect the IPC. 3. Turn the ignition ON, with the engine OFF. 4. Connect a test lamp between the ignition 1 voltage circuit and a good ground. Does the test lamp illuminate?	Go to Step 4	Go to Step 7
4	Connect a test lamp between the ignition 1 voltage circuit of the instrument cluster and the ground circuit of the instrument cluster. Does the test lamp illuminate?	Go to Step 5	Go to Step 6
5	Inspect for poor connections at the harness connector of the IPC. Did you find and correct the condition?	Go to Step 9	Go to Step 8

LTV0500000002731

Fig. 259 Instrument cluster inoperative (Part 1 of 2). S10 & Sonoma

Step	Action	Yes	No
1	Did you perform the Diagnostic System Check - Vehicle?	Go to Step 2	Go to Diagnostic System Check -
2	1. Turn OFF the ignition, with the key in the ignition. 2. Open the driver door. Does the chime sound?	Test for Intermittent Conditions and Poor Connections	Go to Step 3
3	Do the courtesy lights turn ON when you open the driver door?	Go to Step 4	Go to Courtesy Lamps Inoperative
4	1. Turn ON the ignition, with the engine OFF. 2. Turn the radio ON. 3. Adjust the radio balance and fade to the left front speaker. Does the speaker operate properly?	Go to Step 5	Go to Speakers Inoperative - One or More
5	Replace the radio. Did you complete the replacement?	Go to Step 6	--
6	Operate the system in order to verify the repair. Did you correct the condition?	System OK	Go to Step 1

LTV0500000003386

Fig. 258 Chime inoperative. Relay, SV6, Terraza & Uplander

Step	Action	Yes	No
6	Repair the open or a high resistance in the ground circuit. Did you complete the repair?	Go to Step 9	--
7	Repair the open, short to ground or a high resistance in the ignition 1 voltage circuit. Did you complete the repair?	Go to Step 9	--
8	Replace the IPC. Did you complete the replacement?	Go to Step 9	--
9	Operate the system in order to verify the repair. Did you find and correct the condition?	System OK	Go to Step 3

LTV0500000002732

Fig. 259 Instrument cluster inoperative (Part 2 of 2). S10 & Sonoma

Step	Action	Yes	No
1	Did you perform the Instrument Cluster Diagnostic System Check?	Go to Step 2	Go to Diagnostic System Check
2	1. Install a scan tool. 2. Turn the ignition ON, with the engine OFF. 3. With the scan tool, perform the Coolant Gauge Sweep Test. Does the engine coolant temperature gage move up and down when commanded?	Test for Intermittent Conditions and Poor Connections	Go to Step 3
3	Replace the IPC. Did you complete the replacement?	Go to Step 4	--
4	Operate the system in order to verify the repair. Did you correct the condition?	System OK	Go to Step 2

LTV0500000002733

Fig. 260 Engine coolant temperature gage inaccurate or inoperative. S10 & Sonoma

Step	Action	Value(s)	Yes	No
1	Did you perform the Instrument Cluster Diagnostic System Check?	--	Go to Step 2	Go to Diagnostic System Check -
2	Start the engine. Does the engine oil pressure gage display that the engine oil pressure is within the specified range?	10-70 psi (69-483 kPa)	Test for Intermittent and Poor Connections	Go to Step 3
3	1. Turn the ignition OFF. 2. Disconnect the engine oil pressure sensor. 3. Start the engine. Does the engine oil pressure gage display at or above the specified value?	80 psi (550 kPa)	Go to Step 4	Go to Step 6
4	1. Turn the ignition OFF. 2. Connect a 3 ampere fused jumper between the signal circuit of the engine oil pressure sensor and a good ground. 3. Start the engine. Does the engine oil pressure gage display at or below the specified value?	0 psi (0 kPa)	Go to Step 7	Go to Step 5
5	Test the signal circuit of the engine oil pressure sensor for an open, for a high resistance, or for a short to voltage. Did you find and correct the condition?	--	Go to Step 12	Go to Step 9
6	Test the signal circuit of the engine oil Did you find and correct the condition?	--	Go to Step 12	Go to Step 9

LTV0500000002734

Fig. 261 Engine oil pressure gage inaccurate or inoperative (Part 1 of 2). S10 & Sonoma

	Action		Yes	No
7	Inspect for a high resistance or for a poor connection at the case ground of the engine oil pressure sensor. Did you find and correct the condition?		Go to Step 12	Go to Step 8
8	Inspect for poor connections at the harness connector of the engine oil pressure sensor. Did you find and correct the condition?		Go to Step 12	Go to Step 10
9	Inspect for poor connections at the harness connector of the IPC. Did you find and correct the condition?		Go to Step 12	Go to Step 11
10	Replace the engine oil pressure sensor. Did you complete the replacement?		Go to Step 12	--
11	Replace the IPC. Did you complete the replacement?		Go to Step 12	--
12	Operate the system in order to verify the repair. Did you correct the condition?		System OK	Go to Step 2

LTV0500000002735

Fig. 261   Engine oil pressure gage inaccurate or inoperative (Part 2 of 2). S10 & Sonoma

Step	Action		Yes	No
4	Inspect for the following items: • A poor connection at the harness connector of the fuel level sensor • A high resistance in the signal circuit of the fuel level sensor or the low reference circuit of the fuel level sensor between the fuel level sensor and C104 • A misaligned fuel sender • A deformed fuel tank Did you find and correct the condition?		Go to Step 13	Go to Step 7
5	Test the signal circuit of the fuel level sensor for a high resistance. Did you find and correct the condition?		Go to Step 13	Go to Step 6
6	Test the low reference circuit of the fuel level sensor for a high resistance. Did you find and correct the condition?		Go to Step 13	Go to Step 9
7	1. Remove the fuel level sender. 2. Inspect for the following items: - A stuck fuel level sender, i.e. the fuel strainer interfering with the sender float arm - Foreign material in the fuel tank, i.e. ice Did you find and correct the condition?		Go to Step 13	Go to Step 8

LTV0500000002737

Fig. 262   Fuel gage inaccurate or inoperative (Part 2 of 3). S10 & Sonoma

Step	Action	Value(s)	Yes	No
8	1. With the J 39200 DMM, measure the resistance of the fuel level sensor while moving the float arm. 2. Observe both the analog and digital displays on the DMM. Does the resistance change smoothly across the specified range?	40-250 ohms	Go to Diagnostic Aids	Go to Step 10
9	Inspect for poor connections at the harness connector of the powertrain control module (PCM). Did you find and correct the condition?	--	Go to Step 13	Go to Step 12
10	Replace the fuel level sensor. Did you complete the replacement?	--	Go to Step 13	--
11	Replace the instrument panel cluster (IPC). Did you complete the replacement?	--	Go to Step 13	--
12	**Important:** Program the replacement PCM. Replace the PCM. Did you complete the replacement?	--	Go to Step 13	--
13	1. Use the scan tool in order to clear the PCM DTCs. 2. Operate the system in order to verify the repair. Did you correct the condition?		System OK	Go to Step 2

LTV0500000002738

Fig. 262   Fuel gage inaccurate or inoperative (Part 3 of 3). S10 & Sonoma

Step	Action	Value(s)	Yes	No
1	Did you perform the Instrument Cluster Diagnostic System Check?	--	Go to Step 2	Go to Diagnostic System Check -
2	1. Disconnect C104. 2. Connect the J 33431-C Signal Generator and Instrument Panel Tester between the signal circuit of the fuel level sensor and the low reference circuit of the fuel level sensor on the male terminal side. 3. Turn the ignition ON, with the engine OFF. **Important:** Verify the J 33431-C resistance settings with a DMM. 4. Vary the resistance on the J 33431-C from 40-250 ohms. 5. Check Fuel Level Specifications Does the fuel gage display the correct fuel level?	--	Go to Step 4	Go to Step 3
3	1. Install a scan tool. 2. Turn the ignition ON, with the engine OFF. **Important:** Verify the J 33431-C resistance settings with a digital multimeter (DMM). 3. Vary the resistance on the J 33431-C from 40-250 ohms. 4. Check Fuel Level Specifications **Important:** Turn the ignition OFF momentarily between the resistance settings in order to quickly update the scan tool display. 5. With the scan tool, observe the Fuel Tank Level Remaining parameter in the PCM Enhanced EVAP Data data list. Does the scan tool display the correct fuel level percentage?	--	Go to Step 11	Go to Step 5

LTV0500000002736

Fig. 262   Fuel gage inaccurate or inoperative (Part 1 of 3). S10 & Sonoma

Step	Action	Yes	No
1	Did you perform the Instrument Cluster Diagnostic System Check?	Go to Step 2	Go to Diagnostic System Check
2	Activate the trip reset button. Does the odometer display switch between trip and odometer?	Test for Intermittent Conditions and Poor Connections	Go to Step 3
3	Replace the IPC. Did you complete the replacement?	Go to Step 4	--
4	Operate the system in order to verify the repair. Did you correct the condition?	System OK	Go to Step 3

LTV0500000002739

Fig. 263   Odometer trip/reset switch inoperative. S10 & Sonoma

Step	Action	Value(s)	Yes	No
1	Did you perform the Instrument Cluster Diagnostic System Check?	--	Go to Step 2	Go to Diagnostic System Check -
2	1. Install a scan tool. 2. Raise the vehicle drive wheels. 3. Start the engine. 4. Place the transmission into drive for an automatic transmission or third gear for a manual transmission. 5. With the scan tool, observe the Vehicle Speed parameter in the PCM Engine Data 1 data list. Does the Vehicle Speed parameter match the speedometer display?	--	Go to Step 3	Go to Step 4
3	Does the odometer operate properly?	--		Go to Step 9
4	1. Turn the ignition OFF. 2. Disconnect the powertrain control module (PCM) connector C2. 3. Turn the ignition ON. 4. Measure the voltage from the vehicle speed signal circuit to a good ground. Does the voltage measure greater than the specified value?	9.0 V	Go to Step 7	Go to Step 5
5	Test the vehicle speed signal circuit for an open or for a high resistance between the instrument panel cluster (IPC) and the PCM. Did you find and correct the condition?	--	Go to Step 11	Go to Step 6

LTV0500000002740

Fig. 264 Speedometer and/or odometer inaccurate or inoperative (Part 1 of 2). S10 & Sonoma

Step	Action		Yes	No
6	Inspect for poor connections at the harness connector of the IPC. Did you find and correct the condition?	-	Go to Step 11	Go to Step 9
7	Test the vehicle speed signal circuit for a short to voltage between the IPC and the PCM. Did you find and correct the condition?	-	Go to Step 11	Go to Step 8
8	Inspect for poor connections at the harness connector of the PCM. Did you find and correct the condition?	-	Go to Step 11	Go to Step 10
9	Replace the IPC. Did you complete the replacement?	-	Go to Step 11	--
10	Important: Program the replacement PCM. Replace the PCM. Did you complete the replacement?	-	Go to Step 11	--
11	Operate the system in order to verify the repair. Did you correct the condition?	-	System OK	Go to Step 2

LTV0500000002741

Fig. 264 Speedometer and/or odometer inaccurate or inoperative (Part 2 of 2). S10 & Sonoma

Step	Action		Yes	No
7	Inspect for poor connections at the harness connector of the PCM. Did you find and correct the condition?	-	Go to Step 10	Go to Step 9
8	Replace the IPC. Did you complete the replacement?	-	Go to Step 10	--
9	Important: Program the replacement PCM. Replace the PCM. Did you complete the replacement?	-	Go to Step 10	--
10	Operate the system in order to verify the repair. Did you correct the condition?	-	System OK	Go to Step 2

LTV0500000002743

Fig. 265 Tachometer inaccurate or inoperative (Part 2 of 2). S10 & Sonoma

Step	Action	Value(s)	Yes	No
1	Did you perform the Instrument Cluster Diagnostic System Check?	--	Go to Step 2	Go to Diagnostic System Check -
2	1. Install a scan tool. 2. Start the engine. 3. With the scan tool, observe the Engine Speed parameter in the PCM Engine Data 1 data list. Does the Engine Speed parameter match the tachometer display?	--	Test for Intermittent and Poor Connections	Go to Step 3
3	1. Turn the ignition OFF. 2. Disconnect the powertrain control module (PCM) connector C2. 3. Turn the ignition ON, with the engine OFF. 4. Measure the voltage from the engine speed signal circuit to a good ground. Does the voltage measure greater than the specified value?	9.0 V	Go to Step 6	Go to Step 4
4	Test the engine speed signal circuit for an open or for a high resistance. Did you find and correct the condition?	--	Go to Step 10	Go to Step 5
5	Inspect for poor connections at the harness connector of the instrument panel cluster (IPC). Did you find and correct the condition?	--	Go to Step 10	Go to Step 8
6	Test the engine speed signal circuit for a short to voltage. Did you find and correct the condition?	--	Go to Step 10	Go to Step 7

LTV0500000002742

Fig. 265 Tachometer inaccurate or inoperative (Part 1 of 2). S10 & Sonoma

Step	Action	Yes	No
1	Did you perform the Instrument Cluster Diagnostic System Check?	Go to Step 2	Go to Diagnostic System Check -
2	1. Install a scan tool. 2. Turn the ignition ON, with the engine OFF. 3. Compare the scan tool Battery Voltage parameter in the BCM Data data list to the volt gage display. Does the Battery Voltage parameter approximately match the volt gage display?	Go to Diagnostic System Check -	Go to Step 3
3	Replace the IPC. Did you complete the replacement?	Go to Step 4	--
4	Operate the system in order to verify the repair. Did you correct the condition?	System OK	Go to Step 2

LTV0500000002744

Fig. 266 Volt gage inaccurate or inoperative. S10 & Sonoma

Step	Action	Yes	No
1	Did you perform the Instrument Cluster Diagnostic System Check?	Go to Step 2	Go to Diagnostic System Check -
2	1. Install a scan tool. 2. Turn the ignition ON, with the engine OFF. 3. With the scan tool, perform the Lamp Test in the Instrument Panel Cluster Special Functions. Does the low fuel indicator illuminate when commanded ON?	Test for Intermittent and Poor Connections	Go to Step 3
3	Replace the IPC Did you complete the replacement?	Go to Step 4	--
4	Operate the system in order to verify the repair. Did you correct the condition?	System OK	Go to Step 2

LTV0500000002745

Fig. 267 Low fuel indicator inoperative. S10 & Sonoma

Step	Action	Yes	No
1	Did you perform the Driver Information Systems Diagnostic System Check?	Go to Step 2	Go to Diagnostic System Check
2	1. Disconnect the ambient temperature sensor. 2. Connect the J 33431-C Signal Generator and Instrument Panel Tester between the signal circuit of the ambient temperature sensor and the ground circuit of the ambient temperature sensor. 3. Turn the ignition ON, with the engine OFF. **Important** Verify the J 33431-C resistance settings with a DMM. Disconnect one of the J 33431-C leads momentarily between the resistance settings in order to quickly update the DIC display. 4. Vary the resistance on the J 33431-C from 2500-11200 ohms. 5. Check Ambient Air Temperature Sensor Resistance in order to convert from resistance to DIC temperature display. Does the DIC display the correct temperature?	Go to Step 4	Go to Step 3
3	Test the signal circuit of the ambient temperature sensor for a short to ground. Did you find and correct the condition?	Go to Step 7	Go to Step 6

LTV0500000002747

Fig. 269 Driver information center (DIC) temperature display always reads SC (Part 1 of 2). S10 & Sonoma

Step	Action	Yes	No
4	Inspect for a poor connection at the harness connector of the ambient temperature sensor. Did you find and correct the condition?	Go to Step 7	Go to Step 5
5	Replace the ambient temperature sensor. Did you complete the replacement?	Go to Step 7	--
6	**Important** Perform the compass calibration and variance procedure on the replacement DIC. Replace the DIC. Did you complete the replacement?	Go to Step 7	--
7	Operate the system in order to verify the repair. Did you correct the condition?	System OK	Go to Step 2

LTV0500000002748

Fig. 269 Driver information center (DIC) temperature display always reads SC (Part 2 of 2). S10 & Sonoma

Step	Action	Yes	No
1	Did you perform the Driver Information Systems Diagnostic System Check?	Go to Step 2	Go to Diagnostic System Check
2	Test the IP lamp supply voltage circuit of the DIC for an open. Did you find and correct the condition?	Go to Step 8	Go to Step 3
3	Test the battery positive voltage circuit of the DIC for an open. Did you find and correct the condition?	Go to Step 8	Go to Step 4
4	Test the RAP fuse supply voltage circuit of the DIC for an open. Did you find and correct the condition?	Go to Step 8	Go to Step 5
5	Test the ground circuit of the DIC for an open. Did you find and correct the condition?	Go to Step 8	Go to Step 6
6	Inspect for poor connections at the harness connector of the DIC. Did you find and correct the condition?	Go to Step 8	Go to Step 7
7	**Important** Perform the compass calibration and variance procedure on the replacement DIC. Replace the DIC. Did you complete the replacement?	Go to Step 8	--
8	Operate the system in order to verify the repair. Did you correct the condition?	System OK	Go to Step 2

LTV0500000002746

Fig. 268 Driver information center (DIC) inoperative. S10 & Sonoma

Step	Action	Yes	No
1	Did you perform the Driver Information Systems Diagnostic System Check?	Go to Step 2	Go to Diagnostic System Check
2	1. Disconnect the ambient temperature sensor. 2. Connect the J 33431-C Signal Generator and Instrument Panel Tester between the signal circuit of the ambient temperature sensor and the ground circuit of the ambient temperature sensor. 3. Turn the ignition ON, with the engine OFF. **Important** Verify the J 33431-C resistance settings with a DMM. Disconnect one of the J 33431-C leads momentarily between the resistance settings in order to quickly update the DIC display. 4. Vary the resistance on the J 33431-C from 2500-11200 ohms. 5. Check Ambient Air Temperature Sensor Resistance in order to convert from resistance to DIC temperature display. Does the DIC display the correct temperature?	Go to Step 5	Go to Step 3
3	Test the signal circuit of the ambient temperature sensor for an open. Did you find and correct the condition?	Go to Step 9	Go to Step 4

LTV0500000002749

Fig. 270 Driver information center (DIC) temperature display always reads OC (Part 1 of 2). S10 & Sonoma

Step	Action	Yes	No
4	Test the ground circuit of the ambient temperature sensor for an open. Did you find and correct the condition?	Go to Step 9	Go to Step 6
5	Inspect for poor connections at the harness connector of the ambient temperature sensor. Did you find and correct the condition?	Go to Step 9	Go to Step 7
6	Inspect for poor connections at the harness connector of the DIC. Did you find and correct the condition?	Go to Step 9	Go to Step 8
7	Replace the ambient temperature sensor. Did you complete the replacement?	Go to Step 9	--
8	**Important** Perform the compass calibration and variance procedure on the replacement DIC. Replace the DIC. Did you complete the replacement?	Go to Step 9	--
9	Operate the system in order to verify the repair. Did you correct the condition?	System OK	Go to Step 2

LTV0500000002750

Fig. 270 Driver information center (DIC) temperature display always reads 0C (Part 2 of 2). S10 & Sonoma

Step	Action	Yes	No
1	Did you perform the Driver Information Systems Diagnostic System Check?	Go to Step 2	Go to Diagnostic System Check
2	1. Disconnect the ambient temperature sensor connector. 2. Connect the J 33431-C Signal Generator and Instrument Panel Tester between the signal circuit of the ambient temperature sensor and the ground circuit of the ambient temperature sensor. 3. Turn the ignition ON, with the engine OFF. **Important** Verify the J 33431-C resistance settings with a DMM. Disconnect one of the J 33431-C leads momentarily between the resistance settings in order to quickly update the DIC display. 4. Vary the resistance on the J 33431-C from 2500-11200 ohms. 5. Check Ambient Air Temperature Sensor Resistance in order to convert from resistance to DIC temperature display. Does the DIC display the correct temperature?	Go to Step 5	Go to Step 3
3	Test the signal circuit of the ambient temperature sensor for a high resistance. Did you find and correct the condition?	Go to Step 9	Go to Step 4

LTV0500000002751

Fig. 271 Driver information center (DIC) temperature display inaccurate or inoperative (Part 1 of 2). S10 & Sonoma

Step	Action	Yes	No
4	Test the ground circuit of the ambient temperature sensor for a high resistance. Did you find and correct the condition?	Go to Step 9	Go to Step 6
5	Inspect for poor connections at the harness connector of the ambient temperature sensor. Did you find and correct the condition?	Go to Step 9	Go to Step 7
6	Inspect for poor connections at the harness connector of the DIC. Did you find and correct the condition?	Go to Step 9	Go to Step 8
7	Replace the ambient temperature sensor. Did you complete the replacement?	Go to Step 9	--
8	**Important** Perform the compass calibration and variance procedure on the replacement DIC. Replace the DIC. Did you complete the replacement?	Go to Step 9	--
9	Operate the system in order to verify the repair. Did you correct the condition?	System OK	Go to Step 2

LTV0500000002752

Fig. 271 Driver information center (DIC) temperature display inaccurate or inoperative (Part 2 of 2). S10 & Sonoma

Step	Action	Yes	No
1	Did you perform the Driver Information Systems Diagnostic System Check?	Go to Step 2	Go to Diagnostic System Check
2	Verify that the compass is inaccurate or that CAL or C is displayed. Does the system operate normally?	Test for Intermittent Conditions and Poor Connections	Go to Step 3
3	Turn the ignition ON, with the engine OFF. Is the compass display blank?	Go to Step 7	Go to Step 4
4	Is CAL or C displayed?	Go to Step 5	Go to Step 6
5	Perform the compass calibration procedure. Does the compass operate properly?	Go to Step 8	Go to Step 6
6	Perform the compass variance procedure. Does the compass operate properly?	Go to Step 8	Go to Step 7
7	**Important** Perform the compass calibration and variance procedure on the replacement DIC. Replace the DIC. Did you complete the replacement?	Go to Step 8	--
8	Operate the system in order to verify the repair. Did you correct the condition?	System OK	Go to Step 2

LTV0500000002753

Fig. 272 Driver information center (DIC) compass inaccurate or C displayed. S10 & Sonoma

Step	Action	Yes	No
1	Did you perform the Driver Information Systems Diagnostic System Check?	Go to Step 2	Go to Diagnostic System Check
2	Press each of the DIC switches. Do the switches operate normally?	Test for Intermittent Conditions and Poor Connections	Go to Step 3
3	**Important** Perform the compass calibration and variance procedure on the replacement DIC. Replace the DIC. Did you complete the replacement?	Go to Step 4	--
4	Operate the system in order to verify the repair. Did you correct the condition?	System OK	Go to Step 2

LTV0500000002754

Fig. 273   Driver information center (DIC) switch(es) inoperative. S10 & Sonoma

Step	Action	Yes	No
1	Did you perform the Audible Warnings Diagnostic System Check?	Go to Step 2	Go to Diagnostic System Check
2	1. Turn the headlamps OFF. 2. Turn the ignition OFF. 3. Remove the key from the ignition. 4. Close all doors. Does the chime sound?	Go to Step 3	
3	Do any indicators illuminate when the chime sounds?	Go to Symptoms	Go to Step 4
4	1. Install a scan tool. 2. Observe the Key in Ignition parameter in the BCM Input 1 data List. 3. Insert and remove the key from the ignition. Does the Key in Ignition parameter change states?	Go to Step 8	Go to Step 5
5	Test the key in ignition signal circuit for a short to ground. Did you find and correct the condition?	Go to Step 9	Go to Step 6

LTV0500000002755

Fig. 274   Chime always on (Part 1 of 2). S10 & Sonoma

Step	Action	Yes	No
6	Inspect for poor connections at the harness connector of the ignition key alarm switch. Did you find and correct the condition?	Go to Step 9	Go to Step 7
7	Replace the ignition switch. Did you complete the replacement?	Go to Step 9	--
8	**Important** Program the replacement BCM. Replace the BCM. Did you complete the replacement?	Go to Step 9	--
9	Operate the system in order to verify the repair. Did you correct the condition?	System OK	Go to Step 3

LTV0500000002756

Fig. 274   Chime always on (Part 2 of 2). S10 & Sonoma

Step	Action	Yes	No
	DEFINITION: One or more chime functions are inoperative.		
1	Did you perform the Audible Warning Diagnostic System Check?	Go to Step 2	Go to Diagnostic System Check
2	**Important** Perform the set up procedure for the replacement BCM. Replace the BCM. Did you complete the replacement?	Go to Step 3	--
3	Operate the system in order to verify the repair. Did you correct the condition?	System OK	Go to Step 1

LTV0500000002757

Fig. 275   Chime inoperative. S10 & Sonoma

Step	Action	Yes	No
1	Did you perform the Diagnostic System Check - Vehicle?	Go to Step 2	Go to Diagnostic System Check
2	1. Turn the ignition ON, with the engine OFF. 2. Observe the instrument cluster. Does the instrument cluster perform the displays test?	Test for Intermittent Conditions and Poor Connections	Go to Step 3
3	1. Turn the ignition OFF. 2. Disconnect the instrument panel cluster (IPC). 3. Turn the ignition ON, with the engine OFF. 4. Connect a test lamp between the ignition 1 voltage circuit and a good ground. Does the test lamp illuminate?	Go to Step 4	Go to Step 7
4	Connect a test lamp between the ignition 1 voltage circuit of the instrument cluster and the ground circuit of the instrument cluster. Does the test lamp illuminate?	Go to Step 5	Go to Step 6
5	Inspect for poor connections at the harness connector of the IPC. Did you find and correct the condition?	Go to Step 9	Go to Step 8

LTV0500000002478

Fig. 276   Instrument cluster inoperative (Part 1 of 2). Sierra & Silverado

Step	Action	Yes	No
6	Repair the open or a high resistance in the ground circuit. Did you complete the repair?	Go to Step 9	--
7	Repair the open, short to ground or high resistance in the ignition 1 voltage circuit. Did you complete the repair?	Go to Step 9	--
8	Replace the IPC. Did you complete the replacement?	Go to Step 9	--
9	Operate the system in order to verify the repair. Did you find and correct the condition?	System OK	Go to Step 3

LTV0500000002479

Fig. 276   Instrument cluster inoperative (Part 2 of 2). Sierra & Silverado

Step	Action	Values	Yes	No
1	Did you perform the Diagnostic System Check - Vehicle?	--	Go to Step 2	Go to Diagnostic System Check -
2	Start the engine. Does the engine oil pressure (EOP) gage display within the specified range?	34-483 kPa (5-70 psi) - 8.1L only 207-483 kPa (30-70 psi)	Test for Intermittent and Poor Connections	Go to Step 3
3	1. Install a scan tool. 2. Turn ON the ignition, with the engine OFF. 3. With a scan tool, perform the Displays Test in the instrument panel cluster (IPC) Scan Tool Output Controls. Does the engine oil pressure gage move up and down when commanded?	--	Go to Step 4	Go to Step 15
4	1. Turn the ignition OFF. 2. Disconnect the EOP sensor. 3. Connect a 3-ampere fused jumper between the EOP sensor signal circuit and the 5-volt reference circuit of the EOP sensor. 4. With the scan tool, observe one of the following engine oil pressure parameters: - Monitored Oil Pressure parameter in the IPC Data 1 data list - 6.6L diesel only. - Engine Oil Pressure Sensor parameter in the powertrain control module (PCM) Engine Data 2 data list - All engines except 6.6L diesel. Does the scan tool indicate that the Engine Oil Pressure parameter is at or greater than the specified value?	550 kPa (80 psi) - 6.6L diesel only 4.6 V - All engines except 6.6L diesel	Go to Step 5	Go to Step 6

LTV0500000002480

Fig. 277   Engine oil pressure gage inaccurate single tank (Part 1 of 3). Sierra & Silverado

Step	Action	Values	Yes	No
5	1. Connect a 3-ampere fused jumper between the EOP sensor signal circuit and the low reference circuit of the EOP sensor. 2. With the scan tool, observe one of the following engine oil pressure parameters: - Monitored Oil Pressure parameter in the IPC Data 1 data list - 6.6L diesel only. - Engine Oil Pressure Sensor parameter in the PCM Engine Data 2 data list - All engines except 6.6L diesel. Does the scan tool indicate that the Engine Oil Pressure parameter is at or less than the specified value?	0 kPa (0 psi) - 6.6L diesel only 0.4 V - All engines except 6.6L diesel	Go to Step 11	Go to Step 7
6	1. Disconnect the fused jumper. 2. Measure the voltage between the 5-volt reference circuit of the EOP sensor and the low reference circuit of the EOP sensor. Does the voltage measure greater than the specified value?	4.6 V	Go to Step 10	Go to Step 8
7	1. Disconnect the negative battery cable. 2. Measure the resistance from the low reference circuit of the EOP sensor to a good ground. Does the resistance measure less than the specified value?	5 ohms	Go to Step 12	Go to Step 9
8	Test the EOP 5-volt reference circuit for the following: • An open • A short to ground • A high resistance Did you find and correct the condition?		Go to Step 16	Go to Step 9
9	Test the EOP low reference circuit for high resistance or for an open. Did you find and correct the condition?	--	Go to Step 16	Go to Step 10

LTV0500000002481

Fig. 277   Engine oil pressure gage inaccurate single tank (Part 2 of 3). Sierra & Silverado

Step	Action		Yes	No
10	Test the EOP oil pressure sensor signal circuit for the following: • An open • A short to ground • A high resistance Did you find and correct the condition?		Go to Step 16	Go to Step 12
11	Inspect for poor connections at the harness connector of the EOP sensor. Did you find and correct the condition?		Go to Step 16	Go to Step 13
12	Inspect for poor connections at the harness connector of the PCM. Did you find and correct the condition?		Go to Step 16	Go to Step 14
13	Replace the engine oil pressure sensor. Did you complete the replacement?		Go to Step 16	--
14	Replace the PCM. Did you complete the replacement?		Go to Step 16	--
15	Replace the IPC. Did you complete the replacement?		Go to Step 16	--
16	Operate the system in order to verify the repair. Did you correct the condition?		System OK	Go to Step 2

LTV0500000002482

Fig. 277   Engine oil pressure gage inaccurate single tank (Part 3 of 3). Sierra & Silverado

Step	Action		Yes	No
1	Did you perform the Diagnostic System Check - Vehicle?	-	Go to Step 2	Go to Diagnostic System Check
2	1. Disconnect C152. 2. Connect the J 33431-C Signal Generator and Instrument Panel Tester between the signal circuit of the fuel level sender and the low reference circuit of the fuel level sender (male terminal side). 3. Turn the ignition ON, with the engine OFF. 4. Vary the resistance on the J 33431-C from 40-250 ohms. **Important:** Verify the J 33431-C resistance settings with a DMM. 5. Check Fuel Level Specifications Does the fuel gage display the correct fuel level?		Go to Step 5	Go to Step 3
3	1. Install the scan tool. 2. Turn the ignition ON, with the engine OFF. 3. Vary the resistance on the J 33431-C from 40-250 ohms. **Important:** Verify the J 33431-C resistance settings with a DMM. 4. Check Fuel Level Specifications **Important:** Turn the ignition OFF momentarily between the resistance settings in order to quickly update the scan tool display. 5. With the scan tool, observe one of the following fuel level parameters: - Fuel Tank Level Remaining parameter in the powertrain control module (PCM) Enhanced EVAP Data list - gas only - Fuel Level Sensor parameter in the PCM Fuel System data list - 6.6L diesel only Does the scan tool display the correct fuel level percent?		Go to Step 4	Go to Step 6

LTV0500000002483

Fig. 278   Fuel gage inaccurate or inoperative single tank (Part 1 of 3). Sierra & Silverado

Step	Action	Yes	No
4	With the scan tool, perform the Displays Test in the instrument panel cluster (IPC) scan tool Output Controls. Does the gage move from 0 to its maximum value and back to 0 when you perform the Displays Test?	Go to Step 5	Go to Step 10
5	Inspect for the following items: • A poor connection at the harness connector of the fuel level sender-- • A high resistance in the signal circuit or the low reference circuit between the fuel level sender and C152 • A misaligned fuel level sender • A deformed fuel tank. Did you find and correct the condition?	Go to Step 15	Go to Step 8
6	Test the signal circuit of the fuel level sender for a high resistance between C152 and the PCM. Did you find and correct the condition?	Go to Step 15	Go to Step 7
7	Test the low reference circuit of the fuel level sender for a high resistance between C152 and the PCM. Did you find and correct the condition?	Go to Step 15	Go to Step 11
8	1. Remove the fuel level sender. 2. Inspect for the following items: - A stuck fuel level sender, i.e. the fuel strainer interfering with the sender float arm - Foreign material in the fuel tank, i.e. ice. Did you find and correct the condition?	Go to Step 15	Go to Step 9

LTV0500000002484

Fig. 278   Fuel gage inaccurate or inoperative single tank (Part 2 of 3). Sierra & Silverado

Step	Action		Yes	No
9	1. With the DMM, measure the resistance of the fuel level sender while moving the float arm. 2. Observe both the analog and digital displays on the DMM. Does the resistance change smoothly across the specified range?	40-250 ohms	Go to Diagnostic Aids	Go to Step 12
10	Inspect for poor connections at the harness connector of the IPC. Did you find and correct the condition?	--	Go to Step 15	Go to Step 13
11	Inspect for poor connections at the harness connector of the PCM. Did you find and correct the condition?	--	Go to Step 15	Go to Step 14
12	Replace the fuel level sender. Did you complete the replacement?	--	Go to Step 15	--
13	Replace the IPC. Did you complete the replacement?	--	Go to Step 15	--
14	Replace the PCM. Did you complete the replacement?	--	Go to Step 15	--
15	1. Use the scan tool in order to clear the PCM DTCs. 2. Operate the system in order to verify the repair. Did you correct the condition?		System OK	Go to Step 2

LTV0500000002485

Fig. 278   Fuel gage inaccurate or inoperative single tank (Part 3 of 3). Sierra & Silverado

Step	Action	Yes	No
1	Did you perform the Diagnostic System Check - Vehicle?	Go to Step 2	Go to Diagnostic System Check
2	1. Disconnect C152. 2. Connect a jumper wire between the signal circuit of the primary fuel level sender and the signal circuit of the secondary fuel level sender-male terminal side. 3. Connect the J 33431-C Signal Generator and Instrument Panel Tester between the signal circuits of the fuel level senders and the low reference circuit of the fuel level senders-male terminal side. 4. Turn ON the ignition, with the engine OFF. 5. Vary the resistance on the J 33431-C from 40-250 ohms. **Important:** Verify the J 33431-C resistance settings with a DMM. 6. Check Fuel Level Specifications. Does the fuel gage display the correct fuel level?	Go to Step 5	Go to Step 3
3	1. Install the scan tool. 2. Turn ON the ignition, with the engine OFF. **Important:** Verify the J 33431-C resistance settings with a DMM. 3. Vary the resistance on the J 33431-C from 40-250 ohms. 4. Check Fuel Level Specifications. **Important:** Turn the ignition OFF momentarily between the resistance settings in order to quickly update the scan tool display. 5. With the scan tool, observe one of the following fuel level parameters: - Fuel Tank Level Remaining parameter in the PCM Enhanced EVAP Data list-gas only - Fuel Level Sensor parameter in the PCM Fuel System data list - 6.6L diesel only. Does the scan tool display the correct fuel level percentage?	Go to Step 4	Go to Step 6

LTV0500000002486

Fig. 279   Fuel gage inaccurate or inoperative dual tank (Part 1 of 3). Sierra & Silverado

Step	Action	Yes	No
4	With the scan tool, perform the Displays Test in the instrument panel cluster (IPC) scan tool Output Controls. Does the gage move from 0 to its maximum value and back to 0 when you perform the Displays Test?	Go to Step 5	Go to Step 10
5	Inspect for the following items: • A poor connection at the harness connectors of the fuel level senders-- • A high resistance in the signal circuits or the low reference circuit between the fuel level senders and C152 • A misaligned primary or secondary fuel level sender • A deformed primary or secondary fuel tank. Did you find and correct the condition?	Go to Step 15	Go to Step 8
6	Test the signal circuits of the fuel level senders for a high resistance between C152 and the powertrain control module (PCM). Did you find and correct the condition?	Go to Step 15	Go to Step 7
7	Test the low reference circuit of the fuel level senders for a high resistance between C152 and the PCM. Did you find and correct the condition?	Go to Step 15	Go to Step 11
8	1. Remove the fuel level senders. 2. Inspect for the following items: - A stuck fuel level sender, i.e. the fuel strainer interfering with the sender float arm - Foreign material in the fuel tanks, i.e. ice. Did you find and correct the condition?	Go to Step 15	Go to Step 9

LTV0500000002487

Fig. 279   Fuel gage inaccurate or inoperative dual tank (Part 2 of 3). Sierra & Silverado

Step	Action		Yes	No
9	1. With the DMM, measure the resistance of the fuel level senders while moving the float arm. 2. Observe both the analog and digital displays on the DMM. Does the resistance change smoothly across the specified range?	40-250 ohms	Go to Diagnostic Aids	Go to Step 12
10	Inspect for poor connections at the harness connector of the IPC. Did you find and correct the condition?	--	Go to Step 15	Go to Step 13
11	Inspect for poor connections at the harness connector of the PCM. Did you find and correct the condition?	--	Go to Step 15	Go to Step 14
12	Replace the primary or the secondary fuel level sender. Did you complete the replacement?	--	Go to Step 15	--
13	Replace the instrument panel cluster (IPC). Did you complete the replacement?	--	Go to Step 15	--
14	Replace the PCM. Did you complete the replacement?	--	Go to Step 15	--
15	1. Use the scan tool in order to clear the PCM DTCs. 2. Operate the system in order to verify the repair. Did you correct the condition?	--	System OK	Go to Step 2

LTV0500000002488

Fig. 279 Fuel gage inaccurate or inoperative dual tank (Part 3 of 3). Sierra & Silverado

Step	Action	Yes	No
	DEFINITION: This diagnostic procedure applies only to the serial data gages located in the instrument cluster which include the engine coolant temperature gage, and the transmission fluid temperature gage.		
1	Did you perform the Diagnostic System Check - Vehicle?	Go to Step 2	Go to Diagnostic System Check -
2	1. Turn the ignition ON, with the engine OFF. 2. Install a scan tool. 3. With the scan tool, perform the Displays Test in the IPC scan tool Output Controls. Does the gage move from 0 to its maximum value and back to 0 when you perform the Displays Test?	Go to Step 3	Go to Step 4
3	1. Install a scan tool. 2. Start the engine. 3. Observe the appropriate parameter in the PCM Data list. Does the parameter match the gage display?	Go to Diagnostic System Check -	Go to Step 4
4	Replace the instrument panel cluster (IPC). Did you complete the replacement?	Go to Step 5	--
5	1. Use the scan tool in order to clear any induced DTCs. 2. Operate the system in order to verify the repair. Did you correct the condition?	System OK	Go to Step 2

LTV0500000002490

Fig. 281 Instrument panel cluster (IPC) gages inoperative. Sierra & Silverado

Step	Action	Yes	No
1	Did you perform the Diagnostic System Check - Vehicle?	Go to Step 2	Go to Diagnostic System Check -
2	Verify the hourmeter operation. Does the hourmeter operate normally?	Test for Intermittent and Poor Connections	Go to Step 3
3	Replace the instrument panel cluster (IPC). Did you complete the replacement?	Go to Step 4	--
4	Operate the system in order to verify the repair. Did you correct the condition?	System OK	Go to Step 2

LTV0500000002489

Fig. 280 Hourmeter inaccurate or inoperative. Sierra & Silverado

Diagnostic Aids

Refer to Instrument Panel Cluster (IPC) Description and Operation in order to determine if the condition described by the customer concerning the season and trip odometers is normal operation.

Step	Action	Yes	No
1	Did you perform the Diagnostic System Check - Vehicle?	Go to Step 2	Go to Diagnostic System Check -
2	1. Turn the ignition ON, with the engine OFF. 2. Press the trip odometer reset switch. Does the odometer toggle between the season odometer, the trip odometer, and the hourmeter?	Test for Intermittent and Poor Connections	Go to Step 3
3	Replace the instrument panel cluster (IPC). Did you complete the replacement?	Go to Step 4	--
4	Operate the system in order to verify the repair. Did you correct the condition?	System OK	Go to Step 2

LTV0500000002491

Fig. 282 Odometer trip/reset switch inoperative. Sierra & Silverado

Step	Action	Yes	No
1	Did you perform the Diagnostic System Check - Vehicle?	Go to Step 2	
2	1. Turn ON the ignition, with the engine OFF. 2. Install a scan tool. 3. With the scan tool, perform the segments test in the instrument panel cluster (IPC) scan tool output controls. Do all of the segments of the driver information center (DIC) illuminate?	Go to Step 3	Go to Step 6
3	1. Install a scan tool. 2. Raise the vehicle drive wheels. 3. Start the engine. 4. Place the transmission into drive for automatic transmission or third gear for manual transmission. 5. With the scan tool, observe the Vehicle Speed Sensor (VSS) parameter in the IPC Data 1 data list. Does the VSS parameter match the speedometer display?		Go to Step 4
4	Test the vehicle speed signal circuit for a high resistance between the IPC and the powertrain control module (PCM). Did you find and correct the condition?	Go to Step 7	Go to Step 5
5	Inspect for poor connections at the harness connector of the IPC. Did you find and correct the condition?	Go to Step 7	Go to Step 6
6	Replace the IPC. Did you complete the replacement?	Go to Step 7	--
7	Operate the system in order to verify the repair. Did you correct the condition?	System OK	Go to Step 3

LTV0500000002492

Fig. 283 Speedometer and/or odometer inaccurate or inoperative. Sierra & Silverado

Step	Action	Yes	No
1	Did you perform the Diagnostic System Check - Vehicle?	Go to Step 2	Go to Diagnostic System Check
2	1. Turn the ignition ON, with the engine OFF. 2. Install a scan tool. 3. With the scan tool, perform the Displays Test in the IPC scan tool Output Controls. Does the gage move from 0 to its maximum value and back to 0 when you perform the Displays Test?	Go to Step 3	Go to Step 4
3	1. Install a scan tool. 2. Start the engine. 3. With the scan tool, observe the Battery Voltage parameter in the BCM Data list. Does the Battery Voltage parameter match the gage display?	Test for Intermittent Conditions and Poor Connections	Go to Step 4
4	Replace the instrument panel cluster (IPC). Did you complete the replacement?	Go to Step 5	--
5	1. Use the scan tool in order to clear any induced DTCs. 2. Operate the system in order to verify the repair. Did you correct the condition?	System OK	Go to Step 2

LTV0500000002494

Fig. 285 Volt gage inaccurate or inoperative. Sierra & Silverado

Step	Action	Yes	No
1	Did you perform the Diagnostic System Check - Vehicle?	Go to Step 2	
2	1. Install a scan tool. 2. Start the engine. 3. With the scan tool, observe the Engine Speed parameter in the IPC Data 1 data list. Does the Engine Speed parameter match the tachometer display?		Go to Step 3
3	Test the engine speed signal circuit for a high resistance between the instrument panel cluster (IPC) and powertrain control module (PCM). Did you find and correct the condition?	Go to Step 6	Go to Step 4
4	Inspect for poor connections at the harness connector of the instrument cluster. Did you find and correct the condition?	Go to Step 6	Go to Step 5
5	Replace the IPC. Did you complete the replacement?	Go to Step 6	--
6	Operate the system in order to verify the repair. Did you correct the condition?	System OK	Go to Step 2

LTV0500000002493

Fig. 284 Tachometer inaccurate or inoperative. Sierra & Silverado

Step	Action	Yes	No
1	Did you perform the Diagnostic System Check - Vehicle?	Go to Step 2	Go to Diagnostic System Check -
2	Start the engine. Does the CHANGE ENGINE OIL indicator illuminate in the Driver Information Center?	Go to Step 3	Test for Intermittent and Poor Connections
3	1. Install a scan tool. 2. With the scan tool, observe the Engine Oil Life Remaining parameter in the PCM Engine Data 2 data list. Does the Engine Oil Life Remaining parameter display 0%?	Go to Step 4	Go to Step 5
4	Reset the engine oil life. Does the CHANGE ENGINE OIL indicator turn off?	Go to Step 6	Go to Step 5
5	Replace the instrument panel cluster (IPC). Did you complete the replacement?	Go to Step 6	--
6	Operate the system in order to verify the repair. Did you correct the condition?	System OK	Go to Step 2

LTV0500000002495

Fig. 286 Change engine oil indicator always on. Sierra & Silverado

Step	Action	Yes	No
1	Did you perform the Diagnostic System Check - Vehicle?	Go to Step 2	Go to Diagnostic System Check
2	1. Install a scan tool. 2. Turn the ignition ON, with the engine OFF. 3. With the scan tool, observe the Engine Oil Level Switch parameter in the PCM Engine Data 2 data list or the PCM Engine Data 1 data list 6.6L diesel. Does the Engine Oil Level Switch parameter display OK?	Go to Step 3	Go to Step 4
3	Does the CHECK ENG OIL LEVEL indicator remain illuminated after the displays test?	Go to Step 11	Test for Intermittent Conditions and Poor Connections
4	1. Turn the ignition OFF. 2. Disconnect the engine oil level switch. 3. Connect a 3-ampere fused jumper between the signal circuit of the engine oil level switch and a good ground. 4. Turn the ignition ON, with the engine OFF. 5. With the scan tool, observe the Engine Oil Level Switch parameter. Does the Engine Oil Level Switch parameter display OK?	Go to Step 6	Go to Step 5
5	Test the signal circuit of the engine oil level switch for a short to battery voltage, for an open or for a high resistance. Did you find and correct the condition?	Go to Step 12	Go to Step 8
6	Test the ground circuit of the engine oil level switch for an open or for a high resistance. Did you find and correct the condition?	Go to Step 12	Go to Step 7

LTV0500000002496

Fig. 287   Low engine oil dipstick always on (Part 1 of 2). Sierra & Silverado

Step	Action	Yes	No
1	Did you perform the Diagnostic System Check - Vehicle?	Go to Step 2	Go to Diagnostic System Check -
2	Does the Water In Fuel message remain illuminated in the driver information center after the displays test?	Go to Step 3	Test for Intermittent and Poor Connections
3	1. Turn the ignition OFF. 2. Disconnect the water in fuel switch. 3. Turn the ignition ON, with the engine OFF. Does the Water In Fuel message illuminate in the driver information center?	Go to Step 4	Go to Step 6
4	Test the signal circuit of the water in fuel switch for a short to ground. Did you find and correct the condition?	Go to Step 12	Go to Step 5
5	1. Install a scan tool. 2. Turn the ignition OFF. 3. Disconnect the water in fuel switch. 4. Turn the ignition ON, with the engine OFF. 5. With the scan tool, observe the Water In Fuel parameter in the PCM Engine Data 1 data list. Does the Water In Fuel parameter display Off?	Go to Step 8	Go to Step 7
6	Inspect for poor connections at the harness connector of the water in fuel switch. Did you find and correct the condition?	Go to Step 12	Go to Step 9

LTV0500000002498

Fig. 288   Water-in-fuel lamp always on (Part 1 of 2). Sierra & Silverado

Step	Action	Yes	No
7	Inspect for poor connections at the harness connector of the engine oil level switch. Did you find and correct the condition?	Go to Step 12	Go to Step 9
8	Inspect for poor connections at the harness connector of the powertrain control module (PCM). Did you find and correct the condition?	Go to Step 12	Go to Step 10
9	Replace the engine oil level switch. Did you complete the replacement?	Go to Step 12	--
10	Replace the PCM. Did you complete the replacement?	Go to Step 12	--
11	Replace the instrument panel cluster (IPC). Did you complete the replacement?	Go to Step 12	--
12	Operate the system in order to verify the repair. Did you correct the condition?	System OK	Go to Step 2

LTV0500000002497

Fig. 287   Low engine oil dipstick always on (Part 2 of 2). Sierra & Silverado

Step	Action	Yes	No
7	Inspect for poor connections at the harness connector of the powertrain control module (PCM). Did you find and correct the condition?	Go to Step 12	Go to Step 10
8	Inspect for poor connections at the harness connector of the instrument panel cluster (IPC). Did you find and correct the condition?	Go to Step 12	Go to Step 11
9	Replace the water in fuel switch. Did you complete the replacement?	Go to Step 12	--
10	Replace the PCM. Did you complete the replacement?	Go to Step 12	--
11	Replace the IPC. Did you complete the replacement?	Go to Step 12	--
12	Operate the system in order to verify the repair. Did you correct the condition?	System OK	Go to Step 2

LTV0500000002499

Fig. 288   Water-in-fuel lamp always on (Part 2 of 2). Sierra & Silverado

Step	Action	Yes	No
1	Did you perform the Diagnostic System Check - Vehicle?	Go to Step 2	Go to Diagnostic System Check
2	1. Turn the engine OFF. 2. Disconnect the water in fuel sensor. 3. Connect a 3-ampere fused jumper wire between the signal circuit of the water in fuel sensor and a good ground. 4. Turn the ignition ON, with the engine OFF. Does the water in fuel indicator illuminate in the driver information center (DIC)?	Go to Step 3	Go to Step 4
3	1. Turn the ignition OFF. 2. Connect a 3-ampere fused jumper wire between the signal circuit of the water in fuel sensor and the ground circuit of the water in fuel sensor. 3. Turn the ignition ON, with the engine OFF. Does the water in fuel indicator illuminate in the DIC?	Go to Step 9	Go to Step 6
4	Test the signal circuit of the water in fuel sensor for an open or for a high resistance. Did you find and correct the condition?	Go to Step 13	Go to Step 5
5	1. Install a scan tool. 2. Turn the engine OFF. 3. Disconnect the water in fuel sensor. 4. Connect a 3 ampere fused jumper wire between the signal circuit of the water in fuel sensor and a good ground. 5. Turn the ignition ON, with the engine OFF. 6. With the scan tool, observe the Water In Fuel parameter in the PCM Engine Data 1 data list. Does the Water In Fuel parameter display On?	Go to Step 7	Go to Step 8

LTV0500000002500

Fig. 289 Water-in-fuel lamp inoperative (Part 1 of 2). Sierra & Silverado

Step	Action	Yes	No
6	Test the ground circuit of the water in fuel sensor for an open or for a high resistance. Did you find and correct the condition?	Go to Step 13	Go to Step 9
7	Inspect for poor connections at the harness connector of the instrument panel cluster (IPC). Did you find and correct the condition?	Go to Step 13	Go to Step 10
8	Inspect for poor connections at the harness connector of the powertrain control module (PCM). Did you find and correct the condition?	Go to Step 13	Go to Step 11
9	Inspect for poor connections at the harness connector of the water in fuel sensor. Did you find and correct the condition?	Go to Step 13	Go to Step 12
10	Replace the IPC. Did you complete the replacement?	Go to Step 13	--
11	Replace the PCM. Did you complete the replacement?	Go to Step 13	--
12	Replace the water in fuel sensor. Did you complete the replacement?	Go to Step 13	--
13	Operate the system in order to verify the repair. Did you correct the condition?	System OK	Go to Step 2

LTV0500000002501

Fig. 289 Water-in-fuel lamp inoperative (Part 2 of 2). Sierra & Silverado

Step	Action	Yes	No
1	Did you perform the Diagnostic System Check - Vehicle?	Go to Step 2	Go to Diagnostic System Check -
2	1. Install a scan tool. 2. Turn the ignition ON, with the engine OFF. 3. Press and release each of the driver information center (DIC) switches. 4. With a scan tool, observe the DIC switch parameters in the IPC Input/Output data list. Does the scan tool display On when each switch is pressed and Off when each switch is released?	Test for Intermittent and Poor Connections	Go to Step 3
3	Does the scan tool display Off when each switch is pressed?	Go to Step 9	Go to Step 4
4	Does the scan tool always display On for the suspect switch even when the switch is released?	Go to Step 5	Go to Step 6
5	1. Turn the ignition OFF. 2. Disconnect the DIC switch connector. 3. Turn the ignition ON, with the engine OFF. 4. With a scan tool, observe the suspect DIC switch parameter. Does the scan tool display On for the suspect switch?	Go to Step 7	Go to Step 12
6	1. Turn the ignition OFF. 2. Disconnect the DIC switch connector. 3. Connect a 3-amp fused jumper wire between the signal circuit of the suspect DIC switch and a good ground. 4. Turn the ignition ON, with the engine OFF. 5. With a scan tool, observe the suspect DIC switch parameter. Does the scan tool display On for the suspect switch?	Go to Step 10	Go to Step 8

LTV0500000002502

Fig. 290 Driver information center (DIC) switch(es) inoperative (Part 1 of 2). Sierra & Silverado

Step	Action	Yes	No
7	Test the signal circuit of the suspect DIC switch for a short to ground. Did you find and correct the condition?	Go to Step 14	Go to Step 11
8	Test the signal circuit of the suspect DIC switch for an open or high resistance. Did you find and correct the condition?	Go to Step 14	Go to Step 11
9	Test the ground circuit of the DIC switch for an open or high resistance. Did you find and correct the condition?	Go to Step 14	Go to Step 10
10	Inspect for poor connections at the harness connector of the DIC switch. Did you find and correct the condition?	Go to Step 14	Go to Step 12
11	Inspect for poor connections at the harness connector of the instrument panel cluster (IPC). Did you find and correct the condition?	Go to Step 14	Go to Step 13
12	Replace the DIC switch. Did you complete the replacement?	Go to Step 14	--
13	Replace the IPC. Did you complete the replacement?	Go to Step 14	--
14	Operate the system in order to verify the repair. Did you correct the condition?	System OK	Go to Step 2

LTV0500000002503

Fig. 290 Driver information center (DIC) switch(es) inoperative (Part 2 of 2). Sierra & Silverado

Step	Action	Yes	No
1	Did you perform the Diagnostic System Check - Vehicle?	Go to Step 2	Go to Diagnostic System Check -
2	Do any indicators illuminate when the chime sounds?	Go to Symptoms	Go to Step 3
3	1. Turn the ignition OFF. 2. Remove the key from the ignition. 3. Turn the headlamp switch to OFF. 4. Close all of the vehicle doors. 5. Open one or more of the vehicle doors. Does the chime sound at all times regardless if the doors are open or closed?	Go to Step 16	Go to Step 4
4	1. Close all of the vehicle doors. 2. With a scan tool observe the Driver Door Ajar Switch and the Passenger Door Ajar Switch parameters in the body control module (BCM) inputs data list or the Door Ajar Switch parameters in the DDM/PDM inputs data list. Do all of the Door Ajar Switch parameters display Off or Inactive?	Go to Step 5	Go to Courtesy Lamps Always On
5	With a scan tool observe the Left Rear Cargo Door Ajar Switch and the Right Rear Door Ajar Switch parameters in the BCM inputs data list. Do all of the Door Switch parameters display Inactive?	Go to Step 6	Go to Courtesy Lamps Always On
6	With a scan tool, observe the Cargo Door Ajar Switch and the Hood Ajar Switch parameters in the BCM inputs data list. Does the Cargo Door Ajar Switch and the Hood Ajar Switch parameters display Inactive?	Go to Step 7	Go to Courtesy Lamps Always On
7	1. Turn the ignition OFF. 2. Remove the key from the ignition. 3. Turn the headlamp switch to OFF. 4. Open the driver door. Does the chime sound?	Go to Step 8	Test for Intermittent and Poor Connections

LTV0500000002504

Fig. 291   Chime always on (Part 1 of 3). Sierra & Silverado

Step	Action	Yes	No
8	1. Install a scan tool. 2. Turn the ignition ON, with the engine OFF. 3. With a scan tool, observe the Parklamp Switch parameter in the BCM inputs data list. Does the Parklamp Switch parameter display Inactive?	Go to Step 9	Go to Step 11
9	With a scan tool, observe the Headlamp Switch parameter in the BCM inputs data list. Does the Headlamp Switch parameter display Inactive?	Go to Step 10	Go to Step 11
10	1. Turn the ignition OFF. 2. Remove the key from the ignition. 3. With a scan tool, observe the Key In Ignition parameter in the BCM inputs data list. Does the Key In Ignition parameter display No?	Go to Step 15	Go to Step 12
11	Test the headlamp input signal circuit and the park lamp signal circuit at the BCM for a short to voltage. Did you find and correct the condition?	Go to Step 21	Go to Step 13
12	Test the key in ignition signal circuit for a short to ground. Did you find and correct the condition?	Go to Step 21	Go to Step 14
13	Inspect for poor connections at the harness connector of the headlamp switch. Did you find and correct the condition?	Go to Step 21	Go to Step 17
14	Inspect for poor connections at the harness connector of the ignition key alarm switch. Did you find and correct the condition?	Go to Step 21	Go to Step 18

LTV0500000002505

Fig. 291   Chime always on (Part 2 of 3). Sierra & Silverado

Step	Action	Yes	No
15	Inspect for poor connections at the harness connector of the BCM. Did you find and correct the condition?	Go to Step 21	Go to Step 19
16	Inspect for poor connections at the harness connector of the radio or audio amplifier. Did you find and correct the condition?	Go to Step 21	Go to Step 20
17	Replace the headlamp switch Did you complete the replacement?	Go to Step 21	--
18	Replace the ignition switch. Did you complete the replacement?	Go to Step 21	--
19	Replace the BCM. Did you complete the replacement?	Go to Step 21	--
20	Replace the radio. Did you complete the replacement?	Go to Step 21	--
21	Operate the system in order to verify the repair. Did you correct the condition?	System OK	Go to Step 3

LTV0500000002506

Fig. 291   Chime always on (Part 3 of 3). Sierra & Silverado

Step	Action	Yes	No
1	Did you perform the Diagnostic System Check - Vehicle?	Go to Step 2	
2	1. Turn the ignition OFF, with the key in the ignition. 2. Open the driver door. Does the chime sound?		Go to Step 3
3	Do the courtesy lights turn on when you open the driver door?	Go to Step 4	Go to Courtesy Lamps Inoperative
4	1. Turn the ignition ON, with the engine OFF. 2. Turn the radio ON. 3. Adjust the radio balance and fade to the left front speaker. Does the speaker operate properly?	Go to Step 5	Go to Speakers Inoperative - One or More
5	Replace the radio. Did you complete the replacement?	Go to Step 6	--
6	Operate the system in order to verify the repair. Did you correct the condition?	System OK	Go to Step 1

LTV0500000002507

Fig. 292   Chime inoperative. Sierra & Silverado

Step	Action	Yes	No
1	Did you perform the IPC Diagnostic System Check?	Go to Step 2	Go to Diagnostic System Check -
2	1. Install a scan tool. 2. Turn ON the ignition, with the engine OFF. 3. With the scan tool, sweep the engine coolant temperature gage. Does the engine coolant temperature gage sweep from C to H and then back to C?	Test for Intermittent and Poor Connections	Go to Step 3
3	**Important** Perform the setup procedure for the replacement IPC. Replace the IPC. Did you complete the replacement?	Go to Step 4	--
4	Operate the system in order to verify the repair. Did you correct the condition?	System OK	Go to Step 2

LTV0500000003313

Fig. 293 Engine coolant temperature gage inaccurate or inoperative. Silhouette

Step	Action	Value(s)	Yes	No
1	Did you perform the IPC Diagnostic System Check?	--	Go to Step 2	Go to Diagnostic System Check -
2	1. Disconnect C305. 2. Connect the J 33431-C Signal Generator and Instrument Panel Tester between the signal circuit of the fuel level sensor and the sensor ground circuit of the fuel level sensor (male terminal side). 3. Turn ON the ignition, with the engine OFF. **Important:** Verify the J 33431-C resistance settings with a DMM. 4. Vary the resistance on the J 33431-C from 40-250 ohms. Does the fuel gage display the correct fuel level?	--	Go to Step 4	Go to Step 3
3	1. Install a scan tool. 2. Turn ON the ignition, with the engine OFF. **Important:** Verify the J 33431-C resistance settings with a DMM. 3. Vary the resistance on the J 33431-C from 40-250 ohms. **Important:** Turn OFF the ignition momentarily between the resistance settings in order to quickly update the scan tool display. 4. With the scan tool, observe the Fuel Level % parameter in the PCM EVAP data list. Does the scan tool display the correct fuel level %?	--	Go to Step 11	Go to Step 5

LTV0500000003314

Fig. 294 Fuel gage inaccurate or inoperative (Part 1 of 3). Silhouette

Step	Action	Value(s)	Yes	No
4	Inspect for the following items: • A poor connection at the harness connector of the fuel level sensor. • A high resistance in the signal circuit or the sensor ground circuit between the fuel level sensor and C305. • A misaligned fuel level sensor • A deformed fuel tank Did you find and correct the condition?	--	Go to Step 13	Go to Step 7
5	Test the signal circuit of the fuel level sensor for a high resistance. Did you find and correct the condition?	--	Go to Step 13	Go to Step 6
6	Test the sensor ground circuit of the fuel level sensor for a high resistance. Did you find and correct the condition?	--	Go to Step 13	Go to Step 9
7	1. Remove the fuel level sensor. 2. Inspect for the following items: - A stuck fuel level sensor (i.e. the fuel strainer interfering with the sensor float arm) - Foreign material in the gas tank (ice) Did you find and correct the condition?	--	Go to Step 13	Go to Step 8
8	1. With the J 39200 DMM, measure the resistance of the fuel level sensor while moving the float arm. 2. Observe both the analog and digital displays on the DMM. Does the resistance change smoothly across the specified range?	40-250 ohms	Go to Diagnostic Aids	Go to Step 10

LTV0500000003315

Fig. 294 Fuel gage inaccurate or inoperative (Part 2 of 3). Silhouette

Step	Action	Value(s)	Yes	No
9	Inspect for poor connections at the harness connector of the PCM. Did you find and correct the condition?	--	Go to Step 13	Go to Step 12
10	Replace the fuel level sensor. Did you complete the replacement?	--	Go to Step 13	--
11	**Important:** Perform the setup procedure for the replacement IPC. Replace the IPC. Did you complete the replacement?	--	Go to Step 13	--
12	**Important:** Perform the programming procedure for the replacement PCM. Replace the PCM. Did you complete the replacement?	--	Go to Step 13	--
13	1. Use a scan tool in order to clear the PCM DTCs. 2. Operate the system in order to verify the repair. Did you correct the condition?	--	System OK	Go to Step 2

LTV0500000003316

Fig. 294 Fuel gage inaccurate or inoperative (Part 3 of 3). Silhouette

Step	Action	Yes	No
1	Did you perform the IPC Diagnostic System Check?	Go to Step 2	Go to Diagnostic System Check
2	**Important** Perform the setup procedure for the replacement IPC. Replace the IPC. Did you complete the replacement?	Go to Step 3	--
3	Operate the system in order to verify the repair. Did you correct the condition?	System OK	Go to Step 2

LTV0500000003317

Fig. 295 Odometer trip/reset switch inoperative. Silhouette

Step	Action	Yes	No
1	Did you perform the IPC Diagnostic System Check?	Go to Step 2	Go to Diagnostic System Check -
2	1. Install a scan tool. 2. Raise vehicle's drive wheels. 3. Start the engine. 4. Place the transmission into drive for automatic transmission and third gear for manual transmission. 5. With the scan tool, observe the vehicle speed parameter in the PCM Engine Data 1 data list. Does the vehicle speed parameter match the speedometer display?	Go to Step 3	Go to Step 4
3	Does the odometer operate properly?	Test for Intermittent and Poor Connections	Go to Step 4
4	**Important** Perform the setup procedure for the replacement IPC. Replace the IPC. Did you complete the replacement?	Go to Step 5	--
5	Operate the system in order to verify the repair. Use the scan tool in order to clear the DTC's that may have set in other modules during diagnosis. Did you correct the condition?	System OK	Go to Step 2

LTV0500000003318

Fig. 296 Speedometer and/or odometer inaccurate or inoperative. Silhouette

Step	Action	Yes	No
1	Did you perform the IPC Diagnostic System Check?	Go to Step 2	Go to Diagnostic System Check
2	1. Install a scan tool. 2. Turn ON the ignition, with the engine OFF. 3. With a scan tool, observe the engine oil life percent in the PCM IPC data list. Does the scan tool display zero percent with the change engine oil message on?	Go to Step 3	Go to Step 4
3	Reset GM engine oil life system. Has the GM engine oil life system been reset?	Go to Step 5	--
4	**Important** Perform the set up procedure for the replacement IPC. Replace the IPC. Did you complete the replacement?	Go to Step 5	--
5	1. Install a scan tool. 2. Turn ON the ignition, with the engine OFF. 3. With a scan tool, observe the Engine Oil Life percent in PCM IPC data list. Does the scan tool display 100 percent with the engine oil message off?	System OK	Go to Diagnostic System Check

LTV0500000003320

Fig. 298 Change engine oil indicator always on. Silhouette

Step	Action	Yes	No
1	Did you perform the IPC Diagnostic System Check?	Go to Step 2	Go to Diagnostic System Check
2	Start the engine. Does the tachometer operate normally?	Test for Intermittent and Poor Connections	Go to Step 3
3	1. Turn ON the ignition, with the engine OFF. 2. Install a scan tool. 3. With a scan tool, sweep the tachometer. Does the tachometer move from 0 RPM to 7000 RPM and back to 0 RPM when you sweep this gage up and down?	Go to Diagnostic System Check	Go to Step 4
4	**Important** Perform the set up procedure for the replacement IPC. Replace the IPC. Did you complete the replacement?	Go to Step 5	--
5	Operate the system in order to verify the repair. Did you correct the condition?	System OK	Go to Step 3

LTV0500000003319

Fig. 297 Tachometer inaccurate or inoperative. Silhouette

Step	Action	Yes	No
1	Did you perform the IPC Diagnostic System Check?	Go to Step 2	Go to Diagnostic System Check
2	1. Install a scan tool. 2. Turn ON the ignition, with the engine OFF. 3. With a scan tool, observe the Engine Oil Life percent in PCM IPC data list. Does the scan tool display zero percent while the Change Engine Oil message is inoperative?	Go to Step 3	System OK
3	**Important** Perform the set up procedure for the replacement IPC. Replace the IPC. Did you complete the replacement?	Go to Step 4	--
4	Operate the system in order to verify the repair. Did you correct the condition?	System OK	Go to Step 2

LTV0500000003321

Fig. 299 Change engine oil indicator inoperative. Silhouette

Step	Action	Yes	No
1	Did you perform the Instrument Cluster Diagnostic System Check?	Go to Step 2	Go to Diagnostic System Check
2	Start the engine. Does the engine oil pressure indicator illuminate after the displays test?	Go to Step 3	Test for Intermittent and Poor Connections
3	1. Install a scan tool. 2. Turn the ignition ON. 3. With the scan tool, observe the Engine Oil Pressure parameter in the PCM IPC data list. Does the Engine Oil Pressure parameter display Ok?	Go to Step 10	Go to Step 4
4	1. Turn the ignition OFF. 2. Disconnect the engine oil pressure switch. 3. Start the engine. 4. With the scan tool, observe the Engine Oil Pressure parameter. Does the Engine Oil Pressure parameter display Ok?	Go to Step 6	Go to Step 5
5	Test the signal circuit of the engine oil pressure switch for a short to ground. Did you find and correct the condition?	Go to Step 11	Go to Step 7

LTV0500000003322

Fig. 300 Engine oil pressure indicator always on (Part 1 of 2). Silhouette

6	Inspect for poor connections at the harness connector of the engine oil pressure switch. Did you find and correct the condition?	Go to Step 11	Go to Step 8
7	Inspect for poor connections at the harness connector of the PCM. Did you find and correct the condition?	Go to Step 11	Go to Step 9
8	Replace the engine oil pressure switch. Did you complete the replacement?	Go to Step 11	--
9	**Important** Program the replacement PCM. Replace the PCM. Did you complete the replacement?	Go to Step 11	--
10	**Important** Program the replacement IPC. Replace the IPC. Did you complete the replacement?	Go to Step 11	--
11	Operate the system in order to verify the repair. Did you correct the condition?	System OK	Go to Step 2

LTV0500000003323

Fig. 300   Engine oil pressure indicator always on (Part 2 of 2). Silhouette

Step	Action	Yes	No
1	Did you perform the Instrument Cluster Diagnostic System Check?	Go to Step 2	Go to Diagnostic System Check
2	1. Install a scan tool. 2. Turn the ignition ON, with the engine OFF. 3. With the scan tool, observe the Engine Oil Level parameter in the PCM IPC data list. Does the Engine Oil Level parameter display Ok?	Go to Step 3	Go to Step 4
3	Does the low engine oil indicator remain illuminated after the displays test?	Go to Step 11	Test for Intermittent and Poor Connections
4	1. Turn the ignition OFF. 2. Disconnect the engine oil level switch. 3. Connect a 3-ampere fused jumper between the signal circuit of the engine oil level switch and a good ground. 4. Turn the ignition ON, with the engine OFF. 5. With the scan tool, observe the Engine Oil Level parameter. Does the Engine Oil Level parameter display Ok?	Go to Step 6	Go to Step 5
5	Test the signal circuit of the engine oil level switch for a short to battery voltage, for an open or for a high resistance. Did you find and correct the condition?	Go to Step 12	Go to Step 8
6	Test the ground circuit of the engine oil level switch for an open or for a high resistance. Did you find and correct the condition?	Go to Step 12	Go to Step 7

LTV0500000003324

Fig. 301   Low engine oil dipstick always on (Part 1 of 2). Silhouette

7	Inspect for poor connections at the harness connector of the engine oil level switch. Did you find and correct the condition?	Go to Step 12	Go to Step 9
8	Inspect for poor connections at the harness connector of the PCM. Did you find and correct the condition?	Go to Step 12	Go to Step 10
9	Replace the engine oil level switch. Did you complete the replacement?	Go to Step 12	--
10	**Important** Program the replacement PCM. Replace the PCM. Did you complete the replacement?	Go to Step 12	--
11	**Important** Program the replacement IPC. Replace the IPC. Did you complete the replacement?	Go to Step 12	--
12	Operate the system in order to verify the repair. Did you correct the condition?	System OK	Go to Step 2

LTV0500000003325

Fig. 301   Low engine oil dipstick always on (Part 2 of 2). Silhouette

Step	Action	Yes	No
1	Did you perform the DIC Diagnostic System Check?	Go to Step 2	Go to Diagnostic System Check
2	Verify the compass is inaccurate or C is displayed. Does the system operate normally?	Test for Intermittent and Poor Connections	Go to Step 3
3	Turn ON the ignition, with the engine OFF. Is the compass display blank?	Go to Step 7	Go to Step 4
4	Is CAL or C displayed?	Go to Step 5	Go to Step 6
5	Perform the compass calibration procedure. Does the compass operate properly?	Go to Step 8	Go to Step 6
6	Perform the compass variance procedure. Does the compass operate properly?	Go to Step 8	Go to Step 7
7	**Important** Perform the set up procedure for the replacement DIC. Replace the DIC. Did you complete the replacement?	Go to Step 8	--
8	Operate the system in order to verify the repair. Did you correct the condition?	System OK	Go to Step 2

LTV0500000003326

Fig. 302   Driver information center (DIC) compass inaccurate or C displayed. Silhouette

Step	Action	Yes	No
1	Did you perform the DIC Diagnostic System Check?	Go to Step 2	Go to Diagnostic System Check
2	**Important** Perform the set up procedure for the replacement DIC. Replace the DIC. Did you complete the replacement?	Go to Step 3	--
3	Operate the system in order to verify the repair. Did you correct the condition?	System OK	Go to Step 2

LTV0500000003327

Fig. 303   Driver information center (DIC) switch(es) inoperative. Silhouette

Step	Action	Yes	No
8	1. Disconnect C201. 2. Leave the test lamp at the same location. Does the test lamp illuminate?	Go to Step 11	Go to Step 14
9	Inspect for poor connections at the harness connector of the headlamp and I/P lamp dimmer switch. Did you find and correct the condition?	Go to Step 15	Go to Step 12
10	Inspect for poor connections at the harness connector of the BCM connector C2. Did you find and correct the condition?	Go to Step 15	Go to Step 13
11	Repair a short to ground in the control circuit of the ignition key alarm switch. Did you complete the repair?	Go to Step 15	--
12	Replace the headlamp and I/P lamp dimmer switch. Did you complete the replacement?	Go to Step 15	--
13	Replace the BCM. Did you complete the replacement?	Go to Step 15	--
14	Replace the ignition key alarm switch. Did you complete the replacement?	Go to Step 15	--
15	Operate the system in order to verify the repair. Did you correct the condition?	System OK	Go to Step 2

LTV0500000003329

Fig. 304   Chime always on (Part 2 of 2). Silhouette

Step	Action	Yes	No
1	Did you review the operation and perform the necessary inspections?	Go to Step 2	Go to Symptoms
2	Are the Rear Parking Assist (RPA) indicators ON?	Go to Rear Parking Assist Malfunction	Go to Step 3
3	Are any other indicators illuminated?	Go to Symptoms	Go to Step 4
4	Test the control circuit of the IP BCM chime request for a short to ground. Did you find and correct the condition?	Go to Step 15	Go to Step 5
5	1. Turn OFF the ignition. 2. Make sure the headlamp and I/P lamp dimmer switch is in the off position. 3. Disconnect the BCM connector C2. 4. Connect a test lamp between the headlamp and I/P lamp dimmer switch circuit at the BCM and ground. Does the test lamp illuminate?	Go to Step 6	Go to Step 7
6	1. Take the ignition key out of the ignition switch. 2. Connect a test lamp between the control circuit of the ignition key alarm switch and B+. Does the test lamp illuminate?	Go to Step 8	Go to Step 13
7	Test the control circuit of the headlamp and I/P lamp dimmer switch for an open. Did you find and correct the condition?	Go to Step 15	Go to Step 12

LTV0500000003328

Fig. 304   Chime always on (Part 1 of 2). Silhouette

Step	Action	Yes	No
1	Did you review the operation and perform the necessary inspections?	Go to Step 2	Go to Symptoms
2	Is the fasten safety belt indicator off with the ignition ON and the seat belt unbuckled?	Go to Seat Belt Indicator Circuit Malfunction	Go to Step 3
3	Do both of the turn signals operate when turned on?	Go to Step 4	Go to Diagnostic System Check
4	Do the headlamps illuminate when turned on?	Go to Step 5	Go to Headlamps Inoperative - Low and High Beams
5	1. Turn the ignition ON, with the engine OFF. 2. Make sure the rear parking assist on/off switch is in the on position. Do the rear parking assist indicators turn on for 2 seconds and then turn off after bulb check?	Go to Step 6	Go to Symptoms
6	Test the control circuit of the headlamp switch for a short to B+ or a short to ground. Did you find and correct the condition?	Go to Step 17	Go to Step 7
7	1. Place the key in the ignition switch. 2. Connect a test lamp between the control circuit of the ignition key warning switch at the BCM and B+. Does the test lamp illuminate?	Go to Step 8	Go to Step 9
8	1. Open the LF door. 2. Connect a test lamp between the control circuit of the LF side door lock at the BCM and B+. Does the test lamp illuminate?	Go to Step 11	Go to Step 10

LTV0500000003330

Fig. 305   Chime inoperative (Part 1 of 2). Silhouette

Step	Action	Yes	No
9	Test for an open or a short to B+ in the control circuit of the ignition key warning switch. Did you find and correct the condition?	Go to Step 17	Go to Step 12
10	Test for an open or a short to B+ in the control circuit of the LF side door lock. Did you find and correct the condition?	Go to Step 17	Go to Step 13
11	Inspect the control circuit of the headlamp switch for poor connections at the harness connector of the BCM connector C2. Did you find and correct the condition?	Go to Step 17	Go to Step 14
12	Inspect the control circuit of the ignition key warning switch for poor connections at the harness connector of the BCM connector C2 and the ignition key warning switch. Did you find and correct the condition?	Go to Step 17	Go to Step 16
13	Inspect the control circuit of the LF side door lock for poor connections at the harness connector of the BCM connector C2 and the LF side door lock. Did you find and correct the condition?	Go to Step 17	Go to Step 15
14	Replace the BCM. Did you complete the replacement?	Go to Step 17	--
15	Replace the LF door lock. Did you complete the replacement?	Go to Step 17	--
16	Replace the ignition key alarm switch. Did you complete the replacement?	Go to Step 17	--
17	Operate the system in order to verify the repair. Did you correct the condition?	System OK	Go to Step 2

LTV0500000003331

Fig. 305 Chime inoperative (Part 2 of 2). Silhouette

Step	Action	Yes	No
1	Did you review the operation and perform the necessary inspections?	Go to Step 2	Go to Symptoms
2	Inspect for poor connections at the harness connector of the IPC connector C1. Did you find and correct the condition?	Go to Step 6	Go to Step 3
3	Inspect for poor connections at the harness connector of the BCM connector C2. Did you find and correct the condition?	Go to Step 6	Go to Step 4
4	Test the chime request signal circuit of the IPC for a high resistance, an open, and a short to B+. Did you find and correct the condition?	Go to Step 6	Go to Step 5
5	Replace the BCM. Did you complete the replacement?	Go to Step 6	--
6	Operate the system in order to verify the repair. Did you correct the condition?	System OK	Go to Step 2

LTV0500000003332

Fig. 306 Low oil pressure, low fuel chime inoperative. Silhouette

Step	Action	Values	Yes	No
1	Did you perform the Diagnostic System Check - Vehicle?	--	Go to Step 2	Go to Diagnostic System Check -
2	1. Turn ON the ignition, with the engine OFF. 2. Install a scan tool. 3. With the scan tool, perform the Displays Test in the instrument panel cluster (IPC) Special Functions Output Controls list. Does the gage move from 0 to its maximum value and back to 0 when you perform the Displays Test?	--	Go to Step 3	Go to Step 16
3	1. Disconnect C420, the fuel level sensor. 2. Connect the J 33431-C Signal Generator and Instrument Panel Tester between the signal circuit of the Fuel Level Sensor Signal Primary and the low reference circuit of the fuel level sensors on the female terminal side. 3. Turn ON the ignition, with the engine OFF. **Important:** Verify the J 33431-C resistance settings with a DMM. 4. Vary the resistance on the J 33431-C from 40-250 ohms. 5. With the scan tool, observe the Fuel Level Sensor Right Volts parameter in engine control module (ECM) evaporative emission (EVAP) Data list. 6. Check Fuel Level Specifications. Does the Fuel Level Sensor Right Volts parameter change smoothly across the specified range?	0.7-2.5 V	Go to Step 4	Go to Step 10

LTV0500000003333

Fig. 307 Fuel gage inaccurate or inoperative (Part 1 of 4). SRX

Step	Action	Values	Yes	No
4	1. Connect the J 33431-C between the signal circuit of the Fuel Level Sensor Signal Secondary and the low reference circuit of the fuel level sensors on the female terminal side. 2. Turn the ignition ON, with the engine OFF. **Important:** Verify the J 33431-C resistance settings with a DMM. 3. Vary the resistance on the J 33431-C from 40-250 ohms. 4. With the scan tool, observe the Fuel Level Sensor Left Volts parameter in ECM EVAP Data list. 5. Check Fuel Level Specifications. Does the Fuel Level Sensor Left Volts parameter change smoothly across the specified range?	0.7-2.5 V	Go to Step 5	Go to Step 11
5	Inspect for the following items: • A poor connection at the harness connector of the suspect fuel level sensor • A high resistance in the Fuel Level Sensor Signal Primary signal circuit or the low reference circuit between the fuel level sensors and C420 • A high resistance in the Fuel Level Sensor Signal Secondary signal circuit or the low reference circuit between the fuel level sensors and C420 • A misaligned fuel level sender • A deformed fuel tank. Did you find and correct the condition?	--	Go to Step 18	Go to Step 6
6	1. Remove the primary fuel level sender. 2. Inspect for the following items: - A stuck fuel level sensor For example: The fuel strainer interfering with the sender float arm - Foreign material in the fuel tank, i.e., ice. Did you find and correct the condition?	--	Go to Step 18	Go to Step 7
7	1. With the DMM, measure the resistance of the primary fuel level sensor while moving the float arm. 2. Observe both the analog and digital displays on the DMM. Does the resistance change smoothly across the specified range?	40-250 ohms	Go to Step 8	Go to Step 14

LTV0500000003334

Fig. 307 Fuel gage inaccurate or inoperative (Part 2 of 4). SRX

Fig. 307 (Part 3 of 4)

Step	Action	Values	Yes	No
8	1. Remove the secondary fuel level sender. 2. Inspect for the following items: - A stuck fuel level sensor For example: The fuel strainer interfering with the sender float arm - Foreign material in the fuel tank, i.e., ice Did you find and correct the condition?	--	Go to Step 18	Go to Step 9
9	1. With the DMM, measure the resistance of the secondary fuel level sensor while moving the float arm. 2. Observe both the analog and digital displays on the DMM. Does the resistance change smoothly across the specified range?	40-250 ohms	Go to Diagnostic Aids	Go to Step 15
10	Test the Fuel Level Sensor Signal Primary signal circuit for a high resistance. Did you find and correct the condition?	--	Go to Step 18	Go to Step 12
11	Test the Fuel Level Sensor Signal Secondary signal circuit for a high resistance. Did you find and correct the condition?	--	Go to Step 18	Go to Step 13
12	Test the low reference circuit of the fuel level sensors for a high resistance. Did you find and correct the condition?	--	Go to Step 18	Go to Step 13
13	Inspect for poor connections at the harness connector of the ECM. Did you find and correct the condition?	--	Go to Step 18	Go to Step 17

LTV0500000003335

Fig. 307   Fuel gage inaccurate or inoperative (Part 3 of 4). SRX

Fig. 307 (Part 4 of 4)

Step	Action	Yes	No
14	Replace the primary fuel level sensor. Did you complete the replacement?	Go to Step 18	--
15	Replace the secondary fuel level sensor. Did you complete the replacement?	Go to Step 18	--
16	Replace the IPC. Did you complete the replacement?	Go to Step 18	--
17	Replace the ECM. Did you complete the replacement?	Go to Step 18	--
18	1. Use the scan tool in order to clear the ECM DTCs. 2. Operate the system in order to verify the repair. Did you correct the condition?	System OK	Go to Step 2

LTV0500000003336

Fig. 307   Fuel gage inaccurate or inoperative (Part 4 of 4). SRX

Fig. 308

Step	Action	Values	Yes	No
1	Did you perform the Diagnostic System Check - Vehicle?	--	Go to Step 2	Go to Diagnostic System Check -
2	1. Turn ON the ignition, with the engine OFF. 2. Install a scan tool. 3. With the scan tool, perform the Displays Test. Does the gage move from 0 to its maximum value and back to 0 when you perform the Displays Test?	--	Go to Step 3	Go to Step 4
3	1. Install a scan tool. **Important:** If the suspect gage is the speedometer, the drive wheels of the vehicle must be raised and the transmission must be placed in drive or first gear. Refer to Lifting and Jacking the Vehicle in General Information. 2. Start the engine. 3. Observe the suspect gage parameter in the engine control module (ECM) Data list. Does the parameter match the gage display?	--	Test for Intermittent Conditions and Poor Connections	Go to Step 4
4	Replace the instrument panel cluster (IPC). Did you complete the replacement?	--	Go to Step 5	--
5	1. Use the scan tool in order to clear any induced DTCs. 2. Operate the system in order to verify the repair. Did you correct the condition?	--	System OK	Go to Step 2

LTV0500000003337

Fig. 308   Instrument panel cluster (IPC) gages inoperative. SRX

Fig. 309 (Part 1 of 3)

Step	Action	Value (s)	Yes	No
1	Did you perform the Diagnostic System Check - Vehicle?	--	Go to Step 2	Go to Diagnostic System Check
2	1. Install a scan tool. 2. Raise the vehicles drive wheels. Refer to Lifting and Jacking the Vehicle. 3. Start the engine. 4. Place the transmission into drive. 5. With the scan tool, observe the Vehicle Speed Sensor parameter in the ECM Engine Data 1 data list. Does the Vehicle Speed Sensor parameter match the speedometer display?	--	Go to Step 3	Go to Step 4
3	Does the odometer operate properly?	--	Test for Intermittent Conditions and Poor Connections	Go to Step 15
4	1. Turn the ignition OFF. 2. Disconnect the radio. 3. Start the engine. 4. Place the transmission into drive. 5. With the scan tool, observe the Vehicle Speed Sensor parameter in the ECM Engine Data 1 data list. Does the Vehicle Speed Sensor parameter match the speedometer display?	--	Go to Step 9	Go to Step 5
5	1. Turn the ignition OFF. 2. Disconnect the rear object alarm detection module. 3. Start the engine. 4. Place the transmission into drive. 5. With the scan tool, observe the Vehicle Speed Sensor parameter in the Engine Data 1 data list. Does the Vehicle Speed Sensor parameter match the speedometer display?	--	Go to Step 10	Go to Step 6

LTV0500000003338

Fig. 309   Speedometer and/or odometer inaccurate or inoperative (Part 1 of 3). SRX

Step	Action	Value(s)	Yes	No
6	1. Turn the ignition OFF. 2. Disconnect the engine control module (ECM) connector C1. 3. Turn the ignition ON. 4. Measure the voltage between the vehicle speed signal circuit and a good ground. Does the voltage measure greater than the specified value?	9 V	Go to Step 8	Go to Step 7
7	Test the vehicle speed signal circuit for the following between the instrument panel cluster (IPC) and the ECM. • An open • A high resistance • A short to ground Did you find and correct the condition?	--	Go to Step 17	Go to Step 11
8	Test the vehicle speed signal circuit for a short to voltage between the IPC and the ECM. Did you find and correct the condition?	--	Go to Step 17	Go to Step 12
9	Inspect for poor connections at the harness connector of the radio. Did you find and correct the condition?	--	Go to Step 17	Go to Step 13
10	Inspect for poor connections at the harness connector of the rear object alarm detection module. Did you find and correct the condition?	--	Go to Step 17	Go to Step 14
11	Inspect for poor connections at the harness connector of the IPC. Did you find and correct the condition?	--	Go to Step 17	Go to Step 15

LTV0500000003339

Fig. 309   Speedometer and/or odometer inaccurate or inoperative (Part 2 of 3). SRX

Step	Action	Value(s)	Yes	No
12	Inspect for poor connections at the harness connector of the ECM. Did you find and correct the condition?	--	Go to Step 17	Go to Step 16
13	Replace the radio. Did you complete the replacement?	--	Go to Step 17	--
14	Replace the rear object alarm detection module. Did you complete the replacement?	--	Go to Step 17	--
15	Replace the IPC. Did you complete the replacement?	--	Go to Step 17	--
16	Replace the ECM. Did you complete the replacement?	--	Go to Step 17	--
17	Operate the system in order to verify the repair. Did you correct the condition?		System OK	Go to Step 2

LTV0500000003340

Fig. 309   Speedometer and/or odometer inaccurate or inoperative (Part 3 of 3). SRX

Step	Action	Value(s)	Yes	No
6	Inspect for poor connections at the harness connector of the instrument panel cluster (IPC). Did you find and correct the condition?	--	Go to Step 10	Go to Step 8
7	Inspect for poor connections at the harness connector of the ECM. Did you find and correct the condition?	--	Go to Step 10	Go to Step 9
8	Replace the IPC. Did you complete the replacement?	--	Go to Step 10	--
9	Replace the ECM. Did you complete the replacement?	--	Go to Step 10	--
10	Operate the system in order to verify the repair. Did you correct the condition?		System OK	Go to Step 2

LTV0500000003342

Fig. 310   Tachometer inaccurate or inoperative (Part 2 of 2). SRX

Step	Action	Value(s)	Yes	No
1	Did you perform the Diagnostic System Check - Vehicle?	--	Go to Step 2	Go to Diagnostic System Check -
2	1. Install a scan tool. 2. Start the engine. 3. With the scan tool, observe the Engine Speed parameter in the engine control module (ECM) Engine Data 1 data list. Does the Engine Speed parameter match the tachometer display?	--	Test for Intermittent Conditions and Poor Connections	Go to Step 3
3	1. Turn OFF the ignition. 2. Disconnect the ECM connector C1. 3. Turn ON the ignition, with the engine OFF. 4. Measure the voltage from the engine speed signal circuit to a good ground. Does the voltage measure greater than the specified value?	9 V	Go to Step 5	Go to Step 4
4	Test the engine speed signal circuit for an open, a high resistance, or a short to ground. Did you find and correct the condition?	--	Go to Step 10	Go to Step 6
5	Test the engine speed signal circuit for a short to voltage. Did you find and correct the condition?	--	Go to Step 10	Go to Step 7

LTV0500000003341

Fig. 310   Tachometer inaccurate or inoperative (Part 1 of 2). SRX

Step	Action	Yes	No
1	Did you perform the Diagnostic System Check - Vehicle?	Go to Step 2	Go to Diagnostic System Check
2	Start the engine. Does the engine oil pressure indicator illuminate after the displays test?	Go to Step 3	Test for Intermittent and Poor Connections
3	1. Install a scan tool. 2. With a scan tool, observe the Engine Oil Pressure Sensor parameter in the engine control module (ECM) instrument panel cluster (IPC) Data, data list. Does the Engine Oil Pressure Sensor parameter display OK?	Go to Step 10	Go to Step 4
4	1. Turn OFF the ignition. 2. Disconnect the engine oil pressure (EOP) switch. 3. Start the engine. 4. With the scan tool, observe the Engine Oil Pressure Sensor parameter. Does the Engine Oil Pressure Sensor parameter display OK?	Go to Step 6	Go to Step 5
5	Test the EOP switch signal circuit for a short to ground. Did you find and correct the condition?	Go to Step 11	Go to Step 7

LTV0500000003343

Fig. 311   Engine oil pressure indicator always on (Part 1 of 2). SRX

	Action		
6	Inspect for poor connections at the harness connector of the EOP switch.		
	Did you find and correct the condition?	Go to Step 11	Go to Step 8
7	Inspect for poor connections at the harness connector of the ECM.		
	Did you find and correct the condition?	Go to Step 11	Go to Step 9
8	Replace the EOP switch.		
	Did you complete the replacement?	Go to Step 11	--
9	Replace the ECM.		
	Did you complete the replacement?	Go to Step 11	--
10	Replace the IPC.		
	Did you complete the replacement?	Go to Step 11	--
11	Operate the system in order to verify the repair.		
	Did you correct the condition?	System OK	Go to Step 2

LTV0500000003344

Fig. 311 Engine oil pressure indicator always on (Part 2 of 2). SRX

	Action		
6	Inspect for poor connections at the harness connector of the engine oil temperature switch.		
	Did you find and correct the condition?	Go to Step 11	Go to Step 8
7	Inspect for poor connections at the harness connector of the engine control module (ECM).		
	Did you find and correct the condition?	Go to Step 11	Go to Step 9
8	Replace the engine oil temperature switch.		
	Did you complete the replacement?	Go to Step 11	--
9	Replace the ECM.		
	Did you complete the replacement?	Go to Step 11	--
10	Replace the instrument panel cluster (IPC).		
	Did you complete the replacement?	Go to Step 11	--
11	Operate the system in order to verify the repair.		
	Did you correct the condition?	System OK	Go to Step 2

LTV0500000003346

Fig. 312 Engine oil temperature indicator always on (Part 2 of 2). SRX

Step	Action	Value(s)	Yes	No
1	Did you perform the Diagnostic System Check - Vehicle?	--	Go to Step 2	Go to Diagnostic System Check
2	Start the engine. Does the OIL TEMP HIGH message display in the driver information center (DIC)?	--	Go to Step 3	Test for Intermittent Conditions and Poor Connections
3	1. Install a scan tool. 2. With the scan tool, observe the Engine Oil Temperature Calculated parameter in the IPC ECM data list. Does the Engine Oil Temperature Calculated parameter display a value within the specified range?	30-140°C (8-284°F)	Go to Step 10	Go to Step 4
4	1. Turn the ignition OFF. 2. Disconnect the engine oil temperature switch. 3. Start the engine. 4. With the scan tool, observe the Engine Oil Temperature Switch parameter in the IPC ECM data list. Does the Engine Oil Level parameter display at or below the specified value?	30°C (86°F)	Go to Step 6	Go to Step 5
5	Test the signal circuit of the engine oil temperature switch for a short to ground. Did you find and correct the condition?	--	Go to Step 11	Go to Step 7

LTV0500000003345

Fig. 312 Engine oil temperature indicator always on (Part 1 of 2). SRX

Step	Action	Value(s)	Yes	No
1	Did you perform the Diagnostic System Check - Vehicle?	--	Go to Step 2	Go to Diagnostic System Check
2	Start the engine. Does the LOW OIL LEVEL message display in the driver information center (DIC)?	--	Go to Step 3	Test for Intermittent Conditions and Poor Connections
3	1. Install a scan tool. 2. With the scan tool, observe the Engine Oil Level Switch parameter in the ECM data lists. Does the Engine Oil Level Switch parameter display OK?	--	Go to Step 11	Go to Step 4
4	1. Turn the ignition OFF. 2. Disconnect the engine oil level switch. 3. Connect a 3-amp fused jumper wire between the engine oil level switch signal circuit and a good ground. 4. Start the engine. 5. With the scan tool, observe the Engine Oil Level Switch parameter. Does the Engine Oil Level parameter display OK?	--	Go to Step 6	Go to Step 5
5	Test the signal circuit of the engine oil level switch for an open, for a high resistance, or for a short to ground. Did you find and correct the condition?	--	Go to Step 12	Go to Step 7
6	Test the low reference circuit or the ground circuit of the engine oil level switch for an open or for a high resistance. Did you find and correct the condition?	--	Go to Step 12	Go to Step 8

LTV0500000003347

Fig. 313 Low engine oil dipstick always on (Part 1 of 2). SRX

Step	Action		Yes	No
7	Inspect for poor connections at the harness connector of the engine control module (ECM). Did you find and correct the condition?		Go to Step 12	Go to Step 9
8	Inspect for poor connections at the harness connector of the engine oil level switch. Did you find and correct the condition?		Go to Step 12	Go to Step 10
9	Replace the ECM. Did you complete the replacement?		Go to Step 12	--
10	Replace the engine oil level switch. Did you complete the replacement?		Go to Step 12	--
11	Replace the instrument panel cluster (IPC). Did you complete the replacement?		Go to Step 12	--
12	Operate the system in order to verify the repair. Did you correct the condition?		System OK	Go to Step 2

LTV0500000003348

Fig. 313   Low engine oil dipstick always on (Part 2 of 2). SRX

Step	Action	Yes	No
1	Did you perform the Diagnostic System Check - Vehicle?	Go to Step 2	Go to Diagnostic System Check
2	1. Turn ON the ignition. 2. With the scan tool, observe the Engine Oil Level Switch parameter in the ECM data list. Does the Engine Oil Level Switch parameter display OK?	Test for Intermittent Conditions and Poor Connections	Go to Step 3
3	Replace the instrument panel cluster (IPC). Did you complete the replacement?	Go to Step 4	--
4	Operate the system in order to verify the repair. Did you correct the condition?	System OK	Go to Step 2

LTV0500000003349

Fig. 314   Low engine oil dipstick inoperative. SRX

Step	Action	Value (s)	Yes	No
1	Did you review the operation and perform the necessary inspections?	--	Go to Step 2	Go to Symptoms
2	Inspect for poor connections at the radio. Did you find and correct the condition?	--	Go to Step 4	Go to Step 3
3	Replace the radio. Did you complete the replacement?	--	Go to Step 4	--
4	Operate the system in order to verify the repair. Did you correct the condition?	--	System OK	Go to Step 2

LTV0500000003351

Fig. 316   Driver information center (DIC) switch(es) inoperative. SRX

Step	Action	Value	Yes	No
1	Did you perform the Diagnostic System Check - Vehicle?	--	Go to Step 2	Go to Diagnostic System Check -
2	1. Turn ON the ignition, with the engine OFF. 2. Press and release the Eng/Met button. Does the MPH indicator and then the km/h indicator illuminate after each button activation?	--	Test for Intermittent Conditions and Poor Connections	Go to Step 3
3	1. Install a scan tool. 2. With a scan tool, observe the English/Metric Status parameter in the Radio System Configuration data list. 3. Press the Eng/Met button. Does the English/Metric Status parameter display Active?	--	Go to Step 4	Go to Step 5
4	Replace the instrument panel cluster (IPC). Did you find and correct the condition?	--	Go to Step 6	--
5	Replace the radio. Did you find and correct the condition?	--	Go to Step 6	--
6	Operate the system in order to verify the repair. Did you correct the condition?	--	System OK	Go to Step 2

LTV0500000003350

Fig. 315   Miles per hour (mph) indicator inoperative. SRX

Step	Action	Yes	No
1	Did you perform the Diagnostic System Check - Vehicle?	Go to Step 2	Go to Diagnostic System Check
2	Are any indicators illuminated?	Go to Symptoms	Go to Step 3
3	1. Turn OFF the ignition. 2. Turn the headlamp switch to OFF. 3. Remove the key from the ignition. 4. Open the driver door. Does the chime sound?	Go to Step 4	Test for Intermittent and Poor Connections
4	1. Turn OFF the ignition. 2. Disconnect the ignition switch. 3. Install a scan tool. 4. Turn ON the ignition, with the engine OFF. 5. With a scan tool, observe the Key in Ignition parameter in the Dash Integration Module Data list. Does the Key in Ignition parameter display No?	Go to Step 6	Go to Step 5
5	Test the ignition key alarm switch signal circuit for a short to ground. Did you find and correct the condition?	Go to Step 10	Go to Step 7

LTV0500000003352

Fig. 317   Chime always on (Part 1 of 2). SRX

Step	Action	Yes	No
6	Inspect for poor connections at the harness connector of the key switch. Did you find and correct the condition?	Go to Step 10	Go to Step 8
7	Inspect for poor connections at the harness connector of the dash integration module (DIM). Did you find and correct the condition?	Go to Step 10	Go to Step 9
8	Replace the ignition switch. Did you complete the replacement?	Go to Step 10	--
9	Replace the DIM. Did you complete the replacement?	Go to Step 10	--
10	Operate the system in order to verify the repair. Did you correct the condition?	System OK	Go to Step 2

LTV0500000003353

Fig. 317 Chime always on (Part 2 of 2). SRX

Step	Action	Yes	No
1	Did you perform the Diagnostic System Check - Vehicle?	Go to Step 2	Go to Diagnostic System Check -
2	1. Turn OFF the ignition, with the key in the ignition. 2. Open the driver door. Does the chime sound?	Test for Intermittent Conditions and Poor Connections	Go to Step 3
3	Do the courtesy lights turn ON when you open the drivers door?	Go to Step 4	Go to Courtesy Lamps Inoperative
4	1. Turn ON the ignition, with the engine OFF. 2. Turn the radio ON. 3. Adjust the radio balance and fade to the driver front speaker. Does the speaker operate properly?	Go to Step 5	Go to Speakers Inoperative - One or More
5	Replace the radio. Did you complete the replacement?	Go to Step 6	--
6	Operate the system in order to verify the repair. Did you correct the condition?	System OK	Go to Step 2

LTV0500000003354

Fig. 318 Chime inoperative. SRX

Step	Action	Yes	No
1	Did you perform the Diagnostic System Check - Vehicle?	Go to Step 2	Go to Diagnostic System Check
2	1. Install a scan tool. 2. Turn ON the ignition, with the engine OFF. 3. With the scan tool, perform the instrument panel cluster (IPC) Gages Output Control. Does the engine coolant temperature gage move up and down when commanded?	Test for Intermittent Conditions and Poor Connections	Go to Step 3
3	Replace the IPC. Did you complete the replacement?	Go to Step 4	--
4	Operate the system in order to verify the repair. Did you correct the condition?	System OK	Go to Step 2

LTV0500000002508

Fig. 319 Engine coolant temperature gage inaccurate or inoperative. SSR

Step	Action	Yes	No
7	Inspect for poor connections at the harness connector of the powertrain control module (PCM). Did you find and correct the condition?	Go to Step 11	Go to Step 9
8	Replace the engine oil pressure sensor. Did you complete the replacement?	Go to Step 11	--
9	Replace the PCM. Did you complete the replacement?	Go to Step 11	--
10	Replace the IPC. Did you complete the replacement?	Go to Step 11	--
11	Operate the system in order to verify the repair. Did you correct the condition?	System OK	Go to Step 2

LTV0500000002510

Fig. 320 Engine oil pressure gage inaccurate or inoperative (Part 2 of 2). SSR

Step	Action	Value(s)	Yes	No
1	Did you perform the Diagnostic System Check - Vehicle?	--	Go to Step 2	
2	Start the engine. Does the engine oil pressure (EOP) gage display within the specified range?	207-483 kPa (30-70 psi)		Go to Step 3
3	1. Install a scan tool. 2. Turn ON the ignition, with the engine OFF. 3. With a scan tool, perform the Displays Test in the instrument panel cluster (IPC) scan tool Output Controls. Does the engine oil pressure gage move up and down when commanded?	--	Go to Step 4	Go to Step 10
4	1. Turn OFF the ignition. 2. Disconnect the negative battery cable. 3. Disconnect the EOP sensor. 4. Measure the resistance from the low reference circuit of the EOP sensor to a good ground. Does the resistance measure less than the specified value?	5 ohms	Go to Step 6	Go to Step 5
5	Test the low reference circuit of the EOP sensor for high resistance or for an open. Did you find and correct the condition?	--	Go to Step 11	Go to Step 7
6	Inspect for poor connections at the harness connector of the EOP sensor. Did you find and correct the condition?		Go to Step 11	Go to Step 8

LTV0500000002509

Fig. 320 Engine oil pressure gage inaccurate or inoperative (Part 1 of 2). SSR

Step	Action	Value(s)	Yes	No
1	Did you perform the Diagnostic System Check - Vehicle?	--	Go to Step 2	
2	1. Disconnect C105. 2. Connect the J 33431-C Signal Generator and Instrument Panel Tester between the signal circuit of the fuel level sensor and the low reference circuit of the fuel level sensor on the female terminal side of the connector. 3. Turn ON the ignition, with the engine OFF. **Important:** Verify the J 33431-C resistance settings with a DMM. 4. Vary the resistance on the J 33431-C from 40-250 ohms. 5. Check Fuel Level Specifications Does the fuel gage display the correct fuel level?	--	Go to Step 4	Go to Step 3
3	1. Install a scan tool. 2. Turn ON the ignition, with the engine OFF. **Important:** Verify the J 33431-C resistance settings with a DMM. 3. Vary the resistance on the J 33431-C from 40-250 ohms. 4. Check Fuel Level Specifications **Important:** Turn the ignition OFF momentarily between the resistance settings in order to quickly update the scan tool display. 5. With the scan tool, observe the Fuel Tank Level Remaining parameter in the powertrain control module (PCM) Enhanced Evaporative Emission (EVAP) Data List. Does the Fuel Tank Level Remaining parameter display the correct fuel level percent?	--	Go to Step 11	Go to Step 5

LTV0500000002511

Fig. 321 Fuel gage inaccurate or inoperative (Part 1 of 3). SSR

Step	Action	Value(s)	Yes	No
4	Inspect for the following items: • A poor connection at the harness connector of the fuel level sensor • A high resistance in the signal circuit of the fuel level sensor or the low reference circuit of the fuel level sensor between the fuel level sensor and C105 • A misaligned fuel level sender • A deformed fuel tank Did you find and correct the condition?	--	Go to Step 13	Go to Step 7
5	Test the signal circuit of the fuel level sensor for a high resistance. Did you find and correct the condition?	--	Go to Step 13	Go to Step 6
6	Test the low reference circuit of the fuel level sensor for a high resistance. Did you find and correct the condition?	--	Go to Step 13	Go to Step 9
7	1. Remove the fuel level sender. 2. Inspect for the following items: - A stuck fuel level sender (i.e. the fuel strainer interfering with the sender float arm) - Foreign material in the fuel tank (ice) Did you find and correct the condition?	--	Go to Step 13	Go to Step 8
8	1. With the DMM, measure the resistance of the fuel level sensor while moving the float arm. 2. Observe both the analog and digital displays on the DMM. Does the resistance change smoothly across the specified range?	40-250 ohms	Go to Diagnostic Aids	Go to Step 10
9	Inspect for poor connections at the harness connector of the PCM. Did you find and correct the condition?	--	Go to Step 13	Go to Step 12

LTV0500000002512

Fig. 321 Fuel gage inaccurate or inoperative (Part 2 of 3). SSR

Step	Action	Value(s)	Yes	No
10	Replace the fuel level sensor. Did you complete the replacement?	-	Go to Step 13	--
11	Replace the instrument panel cluster (IPC). Did you complete the replacement?	-	Go to Step 13	--
12	Replace the PCM. Did you complete the replacement?	-	Go to Step 13	--
13	1. Use the scan tool in order to clear the PCM DTCs. 2. Operate the system in order to verify the repair. Did you correct the condition?	-	System OK	Go to Step 2

LTV0500000002513

Fig. 321 Fuel gage inaccurate or inoperative (Part 3 of 3). SSR

Step	Action	Yes	No
1	Did you perform the Diagnostic System Check - Vehicle?	Go to Step 2	Go to Diagnostic System Check
2	1. Turn ON the ignition, with the engine OFF. 2. Observe the auxiliary gages. Do the auxiliary gages perform the displays test?	Test for Intermittent Conditions and Poor Connections	Go to Step 3
3	1. Turn OFF the ignition. 2. Disconnect the auxiliary gage package. 3. Turn ON the ignition, with the engine OFF. 4. Connect a test lamp between the ignition 1 voltage circuit and a good ground. Does the test lamp illuminate?	Go to Step 4	Go to Step 7
4	Connect a test lamp between the ignition 1 voltage circuit of the auxiliary gage package and the ground circuit of the auxiliary gage package. Does the test lamp illuminate?	Go to Step 5	Go to Step 6
5	Inspect for poor connections at the harness connector of the auxiliary gage package. Did you find and correct the condition?	Go to Step 9	Go to Step 8

LTV0500000002514

Fig. 322 Gages inoperative all auxiliary gage package (Part 1 of 2). SSR

	Action	Yes	No
6	Repair the open or a high resistance in the ground circuit. Did you complete the repair?	Go to Step 9	--
7	Repair to the following in the ignition 1 voltage circuit: • An open • A short to ground • A high resistance Did you complete the repair?	Go to Step 9	--
8	Replace the auxiliary gage package. Did you complete the replacement?	Go to Step 9	--
9	Operate the system in order to verify the repair. Did you find and correct the condition?	System OK	Go to Step 3

LTV0500000002515

Fig. 322   Gages inoperative all auxiliary gage package (Part 2 of 2). SSR

Step	Action	Yes	No
1	Did you perform the Diagnostic System Check - Vehicle?	Go to Step 2	Go to Diagnostic System Check
2	1. Turn ON the ignition, with the engine OFF. 2. Install a scan tool. 3. With the scan tool, perform the segments test in the instrument panel cluster (IPC) scan tool output controls. Do all of the segments of the driver information center (DIC) illuminate?	Go to Step 3	Go to Step 6
3	1. Install a scan tool. 2. Raise the vehicle drive wheels. 3. Start the engine. 4. Place the transmission into drive for automatic transmission or third gear for manual transmission. 5. With the scan tool, observe the Vehicle Speed Sensor (VSS) parameter in the IPC Data 1 data list. Does the VSS parameter match the speedometer display?		Go to Step 4
4	Test the vehicle speed signal circuit for a high resistance between the IPC and the powertrain control module (PCM). Did you find and correct the condition?	Go to Step 8	Go to Step 5

LTV0500000002517

Fig. 324   Speedometer and/or odometer inaccurate or inoperative (Part 1 of 2). SSR w/6.0L engine

Step	Action	Yes	No
1	Did you perform the Diagnostic System Check - Vehicle?	Go to Step 2	Go to Diagnostic System Check
2	1. Turn ON the ignition. 2. Activate the trip reset button. Does the odometer display switch between trip and odometer?	Test for Intermittent Conditions and Poor Connections	Go to Step 3
3	Replace the instrument panel cluster (IPC). Did you complete the replacement?	Go to Step 4	--
4	Operate the system in order to verify the repair. Did you correct the condition?	System OK	Go to Step 2

LTV0500000002516

Fig. 323   Odometer trip/reset switch inoperative. SSR

	Action	Yes	No
5	Test the VSS high signal circuit for a high resistance, a short to ground, or a short to voltage between the PCM and the transmission control module (TCM). Did you find and correct the condition?	Go to Step 8	Go to Step 6
6	Inspect for poor connections at the harness connector of the IPC. Did you find and correct the condition?	Go to Step 8	Go to Step 7
7	Replace the IPC. Did you complete the replacement?	Go to Step 8	--
8	Operate the system in order to verify the repair. Did you correct the condition?	System OK	Go to Step 3

LTV0500000002518

Fig. 324   Speedometer and/or odometer inaccurate or inoperative (Part 2 of 2). SSR w/6.0L engine

Step	Action	Yes	No
1	Did you perform the Diagnostic System Check - Vehicle?	Go to Step 2	Go to Diagnostic System Check
2	1. Install a scan tool. 2. Start the engine. 3. With the scan tool, observe the Engine Speed parameter in the IPC Data 1 data list. Does the Engine Speed parameter match the tachometer display?	Test for Intermittent Conditions and Poor Connections	Go to Step 3
3	Test the engine speed signal circuit for a high resistance between the instrument panel cluster (IPC) and powertrain control module (PCM). Did you find and correct the condition?	Go to Step 6	Go to Step 4
4	Inspect for poor connections at the harness connector of the instrument cluster. Did you find and correct the condition?	Go to Step 6	Go to Step 5
5	Replace the IPC. Did you complete the replacement?	Go to Step 6	--
6	Operate the system in order to verify the repair. Did you correct the condition?	System OK	Go to Step 2

LTV0500000002519

Fig. 325   Tachometer inaccurate or inoperative. SSR

Step	Action	Yes	No
1	Did you perform the Diagnostic System Check - Vehicle?	Go to Step 2	Go to Diagnostic System Check
2	Start the engine. Does the CHANGE ENGINE OIL indicator illuminate?	Go to Step 3	Test for Intermittent Conditions and Poor Connections
3	1. Install a scan tool. 2. With a scan tool, observe the Engine Oil Life Remaining parameter in the powertrain control module (PCM) Engine Data 2 data list. Does the Engine Oil Life Remaining parameter display 0%?	Go to Step 4	Go to Step 5
4	Reset the engine oil life. Does the CHANGE ENGINE OIL indicator turn off?	Go to Step 6	Go to Step 5
5	Replace the instrument panel cluster (IPC). Did you complete the replacement?	Go to Step 6	--
6	Operate the system in order to verify the repair. Did you correct the condition?	System OK	Go to Step 2

LTV0500000002520

Fig. 326   Change engine oil indicator always on. SSR

Step	Action	Yes	No
1	Did you perform the Diagnostic System Check - Vehicle?	Go to Step 2	Go to Diagnostic System Check
2	1. Install a scan tool. 2. Turn ON the ignition, with the engine OFF. 3. With the scan tool, perform the Lamp Test in the instrument panel cluster (IPC) Special Functions. Does the low fuel indicator illuminate when commanded ON?	Test for Intermittent Conditions and Poor Connections	Go to Step 3
3	Replace the IPC. Did you complete the replacement?	Go to Step 4	--
4	Operate the system in order to verify the repair. Did you correct the condition?	System OK	Go to Step 2

LTV0500000002521

Fig. 327   Low fuel indicator inoperative. SSR

Step	Action	Yes	No
1	Did you perform the Diagnostic System Check - Vehicle?	Go to Step 2	Go to Diagnostic System Check
2	1. Install a scan tool. 2. Turn ON the ignition, with the engine OFF. 3. Press and release each of the driver information center (DIC) switches. 4. With a scan tool, observe the DIC switch parameters in the instrument panel cluster (IPC) Inputs/Outputs. Does the scan tool display On when each switch is pressed and Off when each switch is released?	Test for Intermittent Conditions and Poor Connections	Go to Step 3
3	Does the scan tool display Off when each switch is pressed?	Go to Step 9	Go to Step 4
4	Does the scan tool always display On for the suspect switch even when the switch is released?	Go to Step 5	Go to Step 6
5	1. Turn OFF the ignition. 2. Disconnect the DIC switch connector. 3. Turn ON the ignition, with the engine OFF. 4. With a scan tool, observe the suspect DIC switch parameter. Does the scan tool display On for the suspect switch?	Go to Step 7	Go to Step 12
6	1. Turn OFF the ignition. 2. Disconnect the DIC switch connector. 3. Connect a 3-amp fused jumper wire between the signal circuit of the suspect DIC switch and a good ground. 4. Turn ON the ignition, with the engine OFF. 5. With a scan tool, observe the suspect DIC switch parameter. Does the scan tool display On for the suspect switch?	Go to Step 10	Go to Step 8

LTV0500000002522

Fig. 328   Driver information center (DIC) switch(es) inoperative (Part 1 of 2). SSR

Step	Action	Yes	No
7	Test the signal circuit of the suspect DIC switch for a short to ground. Did you find and correct the condition?	Go to Step 14	Go to Step 11
8	Test the signal circuit of the suspect DIC switch for an open or high resistance. Did you find and correct the condition?	Go to Step 14	Go to Step 11
9	Test the ground circuit of the DIC switch for an open or high resistance. Did you find and correct the condition?	Go to Step 14	Go to Step 10
10	Inspect for poor connections at the harness connector of the DIC switch. Did you find and correct the condition?	Go to Step 14	Go to Step 12
11	Inspect for poor connections at the harness connector of the IPC. Did you find and correct the condition?	Go to Step 14	Go to Step 13
12	Replace the DIC switch. Did you complete the replacement?	Go to Step 14	--
13	Replace the IPC. Did you complete the replacement?	Go to Step 14	--
14	Operate the system in order to verify the repair. Did you correct the condition?	System OK	Go to Step 2

LTV0500000002523

Fig. 328   Driver information center (DIC) switch(es) inoperative (Part 2 of 2). SSR

Step	Action	Yes	No
1	Did you perform the Diagnostic System Check - Vehicle?	Go to Step 2	
2	1. Turn ON the ignition, with the engine OFF. 2. Watch the outside temperature gage on the auxiliary gage package Does the temperature displayed on the temperature gage match the current room temperature?		Go to Step 3
3	1. Disconnect the ambient air temperature sensor. 2. Install a scan tool. **Important:** Verify the J 33431-C Signal Generator and Instrument Panel Tester resistance settings with a DMM. 3. Connect the J 33431-C between the signal circuit of the ambient air temperature sensor and the ground circuit of the ambient air temperature sensor. 4. Turn ON the ignition, with the engine OFF. 5. Vary the resistance on the J 33431-C from 1000-80,000 ohms. 6. Observe the Ambient Air Temp. Sensor parameter in the roof and door module Data 1 data list. Does the Ambient Air Temp. Sensor parameter change value with change in resistance?	Go to Step 4	Go to Step 5
4	Does the value of the temperature gage match the value of the Ambient Temp. Sensor parameter with change in resistance?	Go to Step 8	Go to Step 9
5	Test the ambient air temperature sensor signal circuit for a high resistance, a short to voltage, or a short to ground. Did you find and correct the condition?	Go to Step 13	Go to Step 6

LTV0500000002524

Fig. 329 Outside air temperature center inaccurate or inoperative (Part 1 of 2). SSR

Step	Action	Yes	No
6	Test the ground circuit of the ambient air temperature sensor for a high resistance or a short to voltage. Did you find and correct the condition?	Go to Step 13	Go to Step 7
7	Inspect for poor connections at the harness connector of roof and door module. Did you find and correct the condition?	Go to Step 13	Go to Step 10
8	Inspect for poor connections at the harness connector of the ambient air temperature sensor. Did you find and correct the condition?	Go to Step 13	Go to Step 11
9	Inspect for poor connections at the harness connector of the auxiliary gage package. Did you find and correct the condition?	Go to Step 13	Go to Step 12
10	Replace the roof and door module. Did you complete the replacement?	Go to Step 13	--
11	Replace the ambient air temperature sensor. Did you complete the replacement?	Go to Step 13	--
12	Replace the auxiliary gage package. Did you complete the replacement?	Go to Step 13	--
13	1. Use the scan tool in order to clear the IPC DTCs. 2. Operate the system in order to verify the repair. Did you correct the condition?	System OK	Go to Step 2

LTV0500000002525

Fig. 329 Outside air temperature center inaccurate or inoperative (Part 2 of 2). SSR

Step	Action	Yes	No
1	Did you perform the Diagnostic System Check - Vehicle?	Go to Step 2	
2	Do any indicators illuminate when the chime sounds?	Go to Symptoms	Go to Step 3
3	1. Turn OFF the ignition. 2. Remove the key from the ignition. 3. Turn the headlamp switch to OFF. 4. Close all of the vehicles doors. 5. Open one or more of the vehicles doors. Does the chime sound at all times regardless if the doors are open or closed?	Go to Step 16	Go to Step 4
4	1. Close all of the vehicles doors. 2. With a scan tool, observe the Driver Door Ajar Switch parameter and the Passenger Door Ajar Switch parameter in the body control module (BCM) Inputs data list. Do all of the Door Ajar Switch parameters display Off?	Go to Step 5	Go to Courtesy Lamps Always On
5	With a scan tool, observe the Hood Ajar Switch parameter in the BCM Inputs data list. Does the Hood Ajar Switch parameter display Off?	Go to Step 6	Go to Courtesy Lamps Always On
6	With a scan tool, observe the Rear Compartment Lid Ajar parameter in the RDM Inputs data list. Does the Rear Compartment Lid Ajar parameter display Closed?	Go to Step 7	Go to Courtesy Lamps Always On

LTV0500000002526

Fig. 330 Chime always on (Part 1 of 3). SSR

Step	Action	Yes	No
7	1. Turn OFF the ignition. 2. Remove the key from the ignition. 3. Turn the headlamp switch to OFF. 4. Open the drivers door. Does the chime sound?	Go to Step 8	Test for Intermittent and Poor Connections
8	1. Install a scan tool. 2. Turn ON the ignition, with the engine OFF. 3. With a scan tool, observe the Parklamp Switch parameter in the BCM Inputs data list. Does the Parklamp Switch parameter display inactive?	Go to Step 9	Go to Step 11
9	With a scan tool, observe the Headlamp Switch parameter in the BCM Inputs data list. Does the Headlamp Switch parameter display Inactive?	Go to Step 10	Go to Step 11
10	1. Turn OFF the ignition. 2. Remove the key from the ignition. 3. With a scan tool, observe the Key In Ignition parameter in the BCM Inputs data list. Does the Key In Ignition parameter display No?	Go to Step 15	Go to Step 12
11	Test the headlamp input signal circuit and the park lamp signal circuit at the BCM for a short to voltage. Did you find and correct the condition?	Go to Step 21	Go to Step 13
12	Test the key in ignition signal circuit for a short to ground. Did you find and correct the condition?	Go to Step 21	Go to Step 14
13	Inspect for poor connections at the harness connector of the headlamp switch. Did you find and correct the condition?	Go to Step 21	Go to Step 17
14	Inspect for poor connections at the harness connector of the ignition key alarm switch. Did you find and correct the condition?	Go to Step 21	Go to Step 18

LTV0500000002527

Fig. 330 Chime always on (Part 2 of 3). SSR

Step	Action	Yes	No
15	Inspect for poor connections at the harness connector of the BCM. Did you find and correct the condition?	Go to Step 21	Go to Step 19
16	Inspect for poor connections at the harness connector of the radio or audio amplifier. Did you find and correct the condition?	Go to Step 21	Go to Step 20
17	Replace the headlamp switch. Did you complete the replacement?	Go to Step 21	--
18	Replace the ignition switch. Did you complete the replacement?	Go to Step 21	--
19	Replace the BCM. Did you complete the replacement?	Go to Step 21	--
20	Replace the radio. Did you complete the replacement?	Go to Step 21	--
21	Operate the system in order to verify the repair. Did you correct the condition?	System OK	Go to Step 3

LTV0500000002528

Fig. 330 Chime always on (Part 3 of 3). SSR

Step	Action	Yes	No
	DEFINITION: One or more chime functions are inoperative.		
1	Did you perform the Diagnostic System Check - Vehicle?	Go to Step 2	Go to Diagnostic System Check
2	1. Turn OFF the ignition, with the key in the ignition. 2. Open the driver door. Does the chime sound?	Test for Intermittent Conditions and Poor Connections	Go to Step 3
3	Do the courtesy lights turn ON when you open the driver door?	Go to Step 4	Go to Courtesy Lamps Inoperative
4	1. Turn ON the ignition, with the engine OFF. 2. Turn the radio ON. 3. Adjust the radio balance and fade to the left front speaker. Does the speaker operate properly?	Go to Step 5	Go to Speakers Inoperative - One or More
5	Replace the radio. Did you complete the replacement?	Go to Step 6	--
6	Operate the system in order to verify the repair. Did you correct the condition?	System OK	Go to Step 1

LTV0500000002529

Fig. 331 Chime inoperative. SSR

Step	Action	Yes	No
1	Did you review the Instrument Panel Cluster (IPC) Description and Operation and perform the necessary inspections?	Go to Step 2	Go to Symptoms
2	Verify that the engine coolant temperature (ECT) gage is inoperative. Does the ECT gage operate normally?	Test for Intermittent Conditions and Poor Connections	Go to Step 3
3	1. Turn the ignition switch to LOCK. 2. Disconnect the ECT sending unit connector. 3. Connect the red lead from the J 33431-C. Does the ECT gage indicate the appropriate readings within the specified values?	Go to Step 4	Go to Step 5
4	Replace the ECT sending unit. Did you complete the repair?	Go to Step 10	--
5	Test for a short to ground condition from the instrument cluster connector C3, cavity 4 and the ECT sending unit cavity 2. Does a short to ground condition exist?	Go to Step 6	Go to Step 7
6	Repair the open in the YEL/WHT wire between the instrument panel cluster assembly and the ECT sending unit. Did you complete the repair?	Go to Step 10	--
7	Inspect for damage or loose connections in the instrument panel cluster printed circuit. Does damage or loose connections exist?	Go to Step 8	Go to Step 9
8	Replace the instrument panel cluster printed circuit. Did you complete the repair?	Go to Step 10	--
9	Replace the ECT gage. Did you complete the repair?	Go to Step 10	--
10	Operate the system in order to verify the repair. Did you correct the condition?	System OK	Go to Step 3

LTV0500000003355

Fig. 332 Engine coolant temperature gage inaccurate or inoperative. Tracker

Step	Action	Yes	No
1	Did you review the Instrument Panel Cluster (IPC) Description and Operation and perform the necessary inspections?	Go to Step 2	Go to Symptoms
2	Verify that the oil gage indicator is inoperative. Does the oil gage indicator operate normally?	Test for Intermittent and Poor Connections	Go to Step 3
3	1. Disconnect the oil pressure switch connector. 2. Connect a J 36169-A fused jumper from the oil pressure switch connector to chassis ground. Does the oil pressure indicator light?	Go to Step 4	Go to Step 5
4	Replace the oil pressure switch. Did you complete the repair?	Go to Step 8	--
5	1. Disconnect the instrument panel cluster assembly connector C2. 2. Test for a short to ground or open condition. 3. Test the YEL/BLK wire from cavity 3 to the oil pressure switch. Is a short to ground or open condition present?	Go to Step 6	Go to Step 7
6	Repair the open in the YEL/BLK wire between the instrument panel cluster assembly and the oil pressure switch. Did you complete the repair?	Go to Step 8	--
7	Repair or replace the instrument panel cluster printed circuit. Is the repair complete?	Go to Step 8	--
8	Operate the system in order to verify the repair. Did you correct the condition?	System OK	Go to Step 3

LTV0500000003356

Fig. 333 Engine oil pressure gage inaccurate or inoperative. Tracker

Step	Action	Values	Yes	No
1	Did you review the Instrument Panel Cluster (IPC) Description and Operation and perform the necessary inspections?	--	Go to Step 2	Go to Symptoms
2	Verify that the fuel gage is inoperative. Does the fuel gage operate normally?	--	Test for Intermittent and Poor Connections	Go to Step 3
3	1. Turn the ignition switch to ON. 2. Disconnect the fuel level sensor at C401 3. Connect a red lead of the J 33431-C to the BLU/WHT wire on C401. 4. Connect the other red to a known good ground. Does the fuel gage indicate the appropriate reading at the specified resistance values?	Full- 0ohms 3/4- 15ohms 1/2- 35ohms 1/4- 60ohms Empty- 100ohms	Go to Step 4	Go to Step 6
4	Test for an open or high resistance in the BLK/YEL wire between the fuel level sensor and G203. Does an open or high resistance condition exist?	--	Go to Step 5	Go to Step 7
5	Repair the open or high resistance in the BLK/YEL wire between the fuel level sensor and G400. Did you complete the repair?		Go to Step 10	

LTV0500000003357

Fig. 334　Fuel gage inaccurate or inoperative (Part 1 of 2). Tracker

Step	Action		Yes	No
6	Replace the fuel gage. Refer to Instrument Panel Cluster (IPC) Replacement . Did you complete the repair?	-	Go to Step 10	--
7	Test for an open or high resistance condition in the BLU/WHT wire between instrument panel cluster connector C3 and the fuel level sensor. Does an open or high resistance condition exist?	-	Go to Step 8	Go to Step 9
8	Repair the BLU/WHT wire between the instrument panel cluster assembly and the fuel level sensor. Did you complete the repair?	-	Go to Step 10	--
9	Replace the Fuel level sending unit. Did you complete the replacement?	-	Go to Step 10	--
10	Operate the system in order to verify the repair. Did you correct the condition?	-	System OK	Go to Step 3

LTV0500000003358

Fig. 334　Fuel gage inaccurate or inoperative (Part 2 of 2). Tracker

Step	Action	Yes	No
1	Did you review the Instrument Panel Cluster (IPC) Description and Operation and perform the necessary inspections?	Go to Step 2	Go to Symptoms
2	Verify that the instrument cluster gages are inoperative. Do the gages operate normally?	Test for Intermittent and Poor Connections	Go to Step 3
3	1. Disconnect the instrument cluster connector C1. 2. Test for an open condition between cavity 14 and a good ground. Does an open condition exist?	Go to Step 4	Go to Step 5
4	Repair the open in the BLK/WHT wire between the instrument cluster and the junction block C4 cavity 1. Did you complete the repair?	Go to Step 9	--
5	1. Disconnect the instrument cluster connector C3. 2. Test for a open condition between cavity 2 and G103. Does an open condition exist?	Go to Step 6	Go to Step 7
6	Repair the short in the BLK/YEL wire between the instrument cluster and G103. Did you complete the repair?	Go to Step 9	--
7	Inspect the instrument cluster for any damage to the cluster or printed circuit. Is there any damage to the instrument cluster or printed circuit?	Go to Step 8	Test for Intermittent and Poor Connections
8	Repair or replace the instrument cluster or printed circuit. Did you complete the repair?	Go to Step 9	--
9	Operate the system in order to verify the repair. Did you correct the condition?	System OK	Go to Step 3

LTV0500000003359

Fig. 335　Gages inoperative. Tracker

Step	Action	Yes	No
1	Did you review the Instrument Panel Cluster (IPC) Description and Operation and perform the necessary inspections?	Go to Step 2	Go to Symptoms
2	Verify that the speedometer Indicator is inoperative. Does the speedometer operate normally?	Test for Intermittent and Poor Connections	Go to Step 3
3	Test for an open condition from the instrument cluster connector C1, cavity 5 and battery voltage. Does an open condition exist?	Go to Step 4	Go to Step 5
4	Repair the WHT wire from the instrument cluster C1, cavity 5 and the junction block C1, cavity 9. Did you complete the repair?	Go to Step 12	--
5	Test for a short to ground condition from the instrument cluster connector C3, cavity 2. Does a short to ground condition exist?	Go to Step 5	Go to Step 7

LTV0500000003360

Fig. 336　Speedometer and/or odometer inaccurate or inoperative (Part 1 of 2). Tracker

Step	Action	Yes	No
6	Repair the WHT/YEL wire from the instrument cluster C3, cavity 2 and G103. Did you complete the repair?	Go to Step 12	--
7	Inspect the instrument cluster printed circuit for any damage or loose connections. Does any damage or loose connections exist?	Go to Step 8	Go to Step 9
8	Replace the instrument cluster printed circuit. Did you complete the repair?	Go to Step 12	--
9	Test for an open condition from the instrument cluster connector C1, cavity 9 and the vehicle speed sensor cavity 1. Does an open condition exist?	Go to Step 10	Go to Step 11
10	Repair the open condition from the instrument cluster and the VSS. Did you complete the repair?	Go to Step 12	--
11	Replace the speedometer. Did you complete the repair?	Go to Step 12	--
12	Operate the system in order to verify the repair. Did you complete the repair?	System OK	Go to Step 3

LTV0500000003361

Fig. 336　Speedometer and/or odometer inaccurate or inoperative (Part 2 of 2). Tracker

Step	Action	Yes	No
1	Did you review the Instrument Panel Cluster (IPC) Description and Operation and perform the necessary inspections?	Go to Step 2	Go to Symptoms
2	Verify that the engine oil indicator is inoperative. Does the engine oil indicator operate normally?	Test for Intermittent Conditions and Poor Connections	Go to Step 3
3	Disconnect the oil pressure switch connector. Does the oil pressure indicator remain lit?	Go to Step 4	Go to Step 5
4	Repair the short to ground in the YEL/BLK wire or the instrument panel cluster printed circuit. Did you complete the repair?	Go to Step 7	--
5	Test the oil pressure with a mechanical gage. Is the oil pressure normal?	Go to Step 6	Perform Oil Pressure Diagnosis and Testing
6	Replace the oil pressure switch. Did you complete the repair?	Go to Step 7	--
7	Operate the system in order to verify the repair. Did you correct the condition?	System OK	Go to Step 3

LTV0500000003362

Fig. 337   Engine oil pressure indicator always on. Tracker

Step	Action	Yes	No
1	Did you review the Instrument Cluster Description and Operation and perform the necessary inspections?	Go to Step 2	Go to Symptoms
2	Verify that the oil gage indicator is inoperative. Does the oil gage indicator operate normally?	Test for Intermittent and Poor Connections	Go to Step 3
3	1. Disconnect the oil pressure switch connector. 2. Connect fused jumper from the oil pressure switch connector to chassis ground. Does the oil pressure indicator illuminate?	Go to Step 4	Go to Step 5
4	Replace the oil pressure switch. Did you complete the repair?	Go to Step 8	--
5	1. Disconnect the instrument panel cluster assembly connector C2. 2. Test for a short to ground or open condition. 3. Test the YEL/BLK wire from cavity 3 to the oil pressure switch. Is a short to ground or open condition present?	Go to Step 6	Go to Step 7
6	Repair the open in the YEL/BLK wire between the instrument panel cluster assembly and the oil pressure switch. Did you complete the repair?	Go to Step 8	--
7	Repair or replace the instrument panel cluster printed circuit. Is the repair complete?	Go to Step 8	--
8	Operate the system in order to verify the repair. Did you correct the condition?	System OK	Go to Step 3

LTV0500000003363

Fig. 338   Engine oil pressure indicator inoperative. Tracker

Step	Action	Yes	No
1	Did you review the Audible Warning Description and Operation and perform the necessary inspections?	Go to Step 2	Go to Symptoms
2	Verify that the chime is always on. Does the system operate normally?	Test for Intermittent and Poor Connections	Go to Step 3
3	Remove the door jamb switch connector. Does the audible warning remain ON?	Go to Step 5	Go to Step 4
4	Replace the LH front door jamb switch. Did you complete the repair?	Go to Step 8	--
5	1. Reconnect the LH front door jamb switch connector. 2. Disconnect the ignition key alarm switch. Does the alarm stop sounding?	Go to Step 6	Go to Step 7
6	Replace the ignition switch. Is the repair complete?	Go to Step 8	--
7	Replace the multifunction alarm module. Is the repair complete?	Go to Step 8	--
8	Operate the system in order to verify the repair. Did you correct the condition?	System OK	Go to Step 3

LTV0500000003364

Fig. 339   Chime always on. Tracker

Step	Action	Yes	No
1	Did you review the Audible Warning Description and Operation and perform the necessary inspections?	Go to Step 2	Go to Symptoms
2	Verify that the chime is inoperative. Does the system operate normally?	Test for Intermittent and Poor Connections	Go to Step 3
3	1. Disconnect the audio alarm module connector. 2. Turn the ignition switch to ON. 3. Connect a test lamp from the audio alarm module connector cavity 7 to B+. Does the test lamp illuminate?	Go to Step 5	Go to Step 4
4	Use a test lamp in order to backprobe the junction block connector C4 from cavity 16 to B+. Does the test lamp illuminate?	Go to Step 7	Go to Step 6
5	With the audio alarm module still disconnected and the ignition switch turned to ON, connect a test lamp from cavity 5 of the audio alarm module to ground. Does the test lamp illuminate?	Go to Step 9	Go to Step 8

LTV0500000003365

Fig. 340   Chime inoperative (Part 1 of 2). Tracker

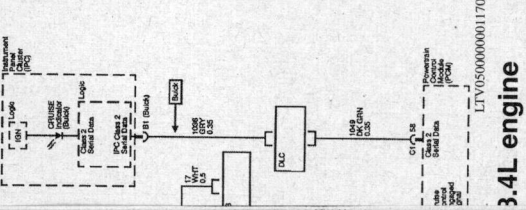

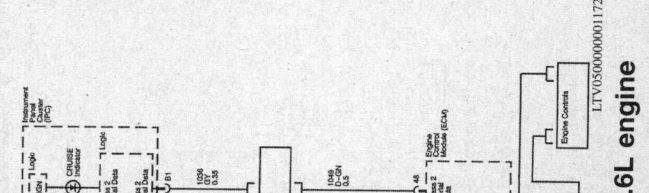

DASH GAUGES & WARNING INDICATORS

DASH GAUGES & WARNING INDICATORS

6	1. Inspect for a poor ground connection at the junction block. 2. If the connection is OK, replace the junction block. Is the repair complete?	Go to Step 10	--
7	Repair the open in the BLK wire between the junction block and the audio alarm module. Is the repair complete?	Go to Step 10	--
8	Repair the open BLK/WHT wire between cavity 5 of the audio alarm module connector and junction block Connector C4 cavity 3. Is the repair complete?	Go to Step 10	--
9	Replace the audio alarm module. Is the repair complete?	Go to Step 10	--
10	Operate the system in order to verify the repair. Did you correct the condition?	System OK	Go to Step 3

LTV0500000003366

Fig. 340 Chime inoperative (Part 2 of 2). Tracker

Step	Action	Value (s)	Yes	No
1	Did you perform the Diagnostic System Check - Vehicle?	--	Go to Step 2	Go to Diagnostic System Check
2	1. Disconnect C406. 2. Connect the J 33431-C Signal Generator and Instrument Panel Tester between the signal circuit of the fuel level sensor and the low reference circuit of the fuel level sensor on the male terminal side. 3. Turn ON the ignition, with the engine OFF. **Important:** Verify the J 33431-C resistance settings with a DMM. 4. Vary the resistance on the J 33431-C from 40-250 ohms. 5. Check Fuel Level Specifications Does the fuel gage display the correct fuel level?	--	Go to Step 4	Go to Step 3
3	1. Install a scan tool. 2. Turn ON the ignition, with the engine OFF. **Important:** Verify the J 33431-C resistance settings with a DMM. 3. Vary the resistance on the J 33431-C from 40-250 ohms. 4. Check Fuel Level Specifications **Important:** Turn OFF the ignition momentarily between the resistance settings in order to quickly update the scan tool display. 5. With the scan tool, observe the Fuel Level parameter Does the Fuel Level parameter display the correct fuel level amount?	--	Go to Step 9	Go to Step 5

LTV0500000003425

Fig. 342 Fuel gage inaccurate or inoperative (Part 1 of 4). Vue

Step	Action	Yes	No
1	Did you perform the Diagnostic System Check - Vehicle?	Go to Step 2	Go to Diagnostic System Check -
2	1. Install a scan tool. 2. Turn the ignition ON, with the engine OFF. 3. With the scan tool, perform the Lamp and Gauge Check in the instrument panel cluster (IPC) Special Functions list. Does the engine coolant temperature gage move up and down when commanded?	Test for Intermittent Conditions and Poor Connections	Go to Step 3
3	Replace the IPC. Did you complete the replacement?	Go to Step 4	--
4	Operate the system in order to verify the repair. Did you correct the condition?	System OK	Go to Step 2

LTV0500000003424

Fig. 341 Engine coolant temperature gage inaccurate or inoperative. Vue

4	Inspect for the following items: • A poor connection at the harness connector of the fuel level sensors • A high resistance in the signal circuit or the low reference circuit between the fuel level sensor and C406 • A misaligned fuel level sender • A deformed fuel tank Did you find and correct the condition?	--	Go to Step 15	Go to Step 7
5	Test the signal circuit of the fuel level sensor for a high resistance. Did you find and correct the condition?	--	Go to Step 15	Go to Step 6
6	Test the low reference circuit of the fuel level sensor for a high resistance. Did you find and correct the condition?	--	Go to Step 15	Go to Step 10
7	1. Remove the fuel level senders. 2. Inspect for the following items: - A stuck fuel level sensor, i.e. the fuel strainer interfering with the sender float arm - Foreign material in the fuel tank, i.e. ice Did you find and correct the condition?	--	Go to Step 15	Go to Step 8
8	1. With the J 39200 DMM, measure the resistance of both fuel level sensors while moving the float arm. 2. Observe both the analog and digital displays on the DMM. Does the resistance change smoothly across the specified range on both fuel level sensors?	20-125 ohms	Go to Diagnostic Aids	Go to Step 11

LTV0500000003426

Fig. 342 Fuel gage inaccurate or inoperative (Part 2 of 4). Vue

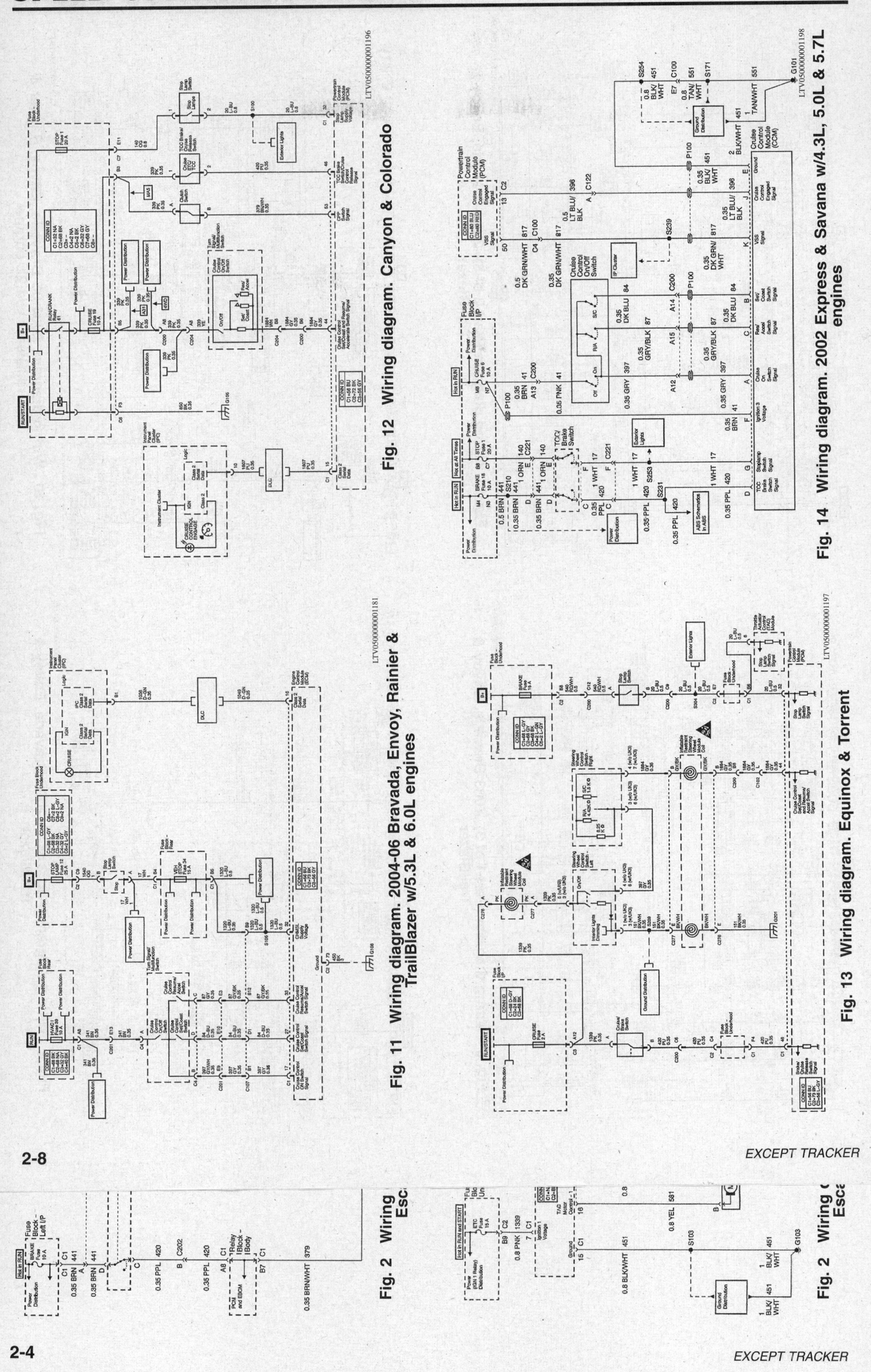

Fig. 12 Wiring diagram. Canyon & Colorado

Fig. 14 Wiring diagram. 2002 Express & Savana w/4.3L, 5.0L & 5.7L engines

Fig. 11 Wiring diagram. 2004-06 Bravada, Envoy, Rainier & TrailBlazer w/5.3L & 6.0L engines

Fig. 13 Wiring diagram. Equinox & Torrent

2-8

EXCEPT TRACKER

Fig. 2 Wiring (Esc

Fig. 2 Wiring (Esc

2-4

EXCEPT TRACKER

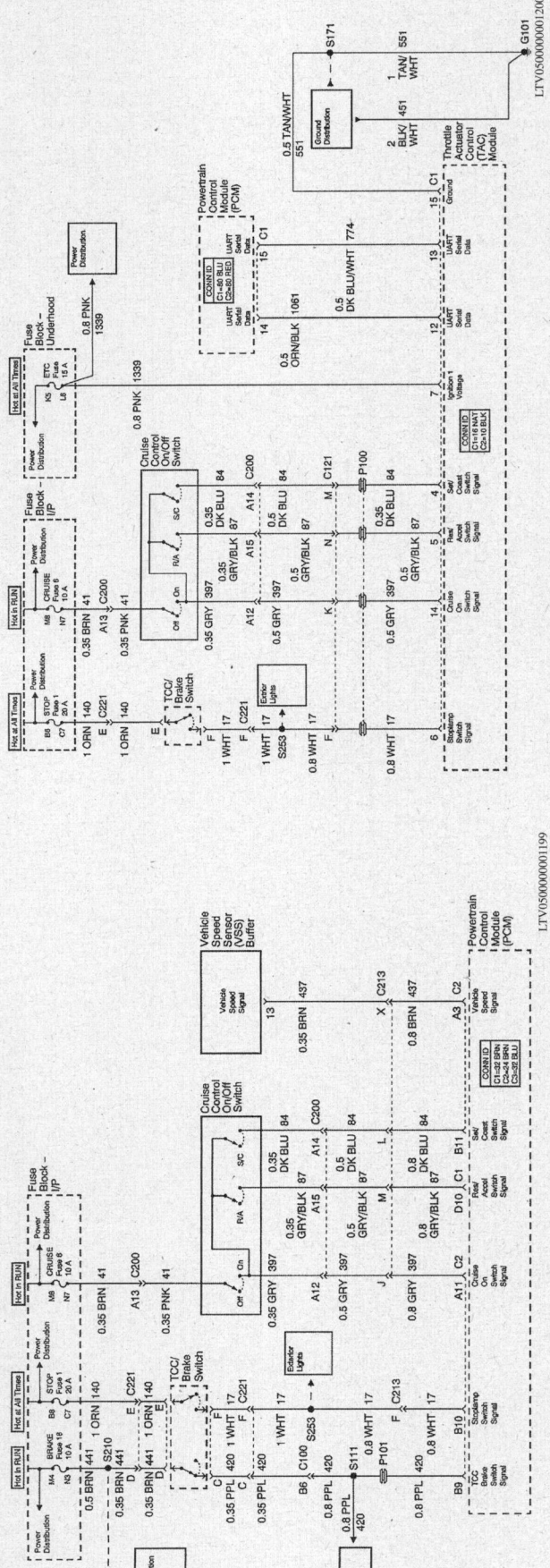

Fig. 16 Wiring diagram. 2002 Express & Savana w/8.1L engine

Fig. 15 Wiring diagram. 2002 Express & Savana w/6.5L diesel engine

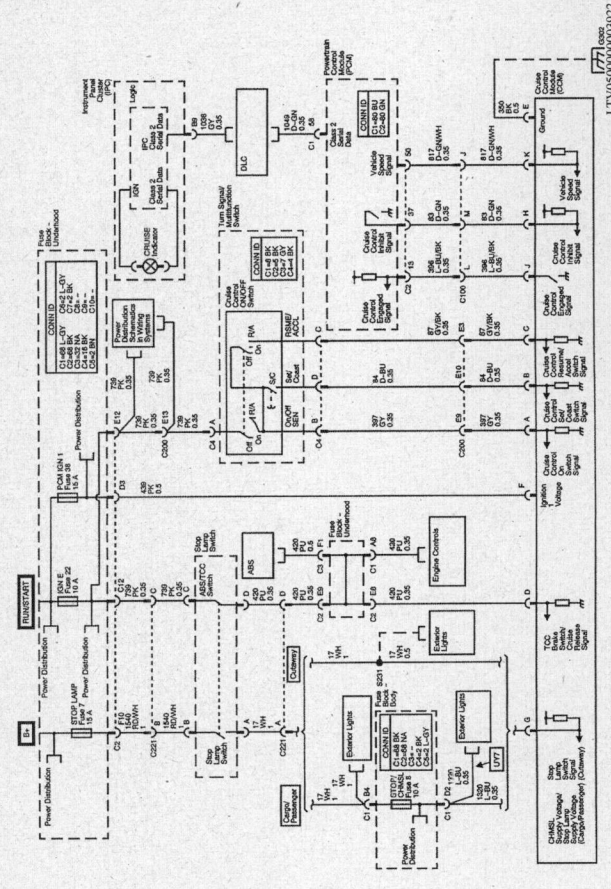

Fig. 18 Wiring diagram. 2003-06 Express & Savana w/gasoline engine less JL4

Fig. 17 Wiring diagram. 2003-06 Express & Savana w/gasoline engine & JL4

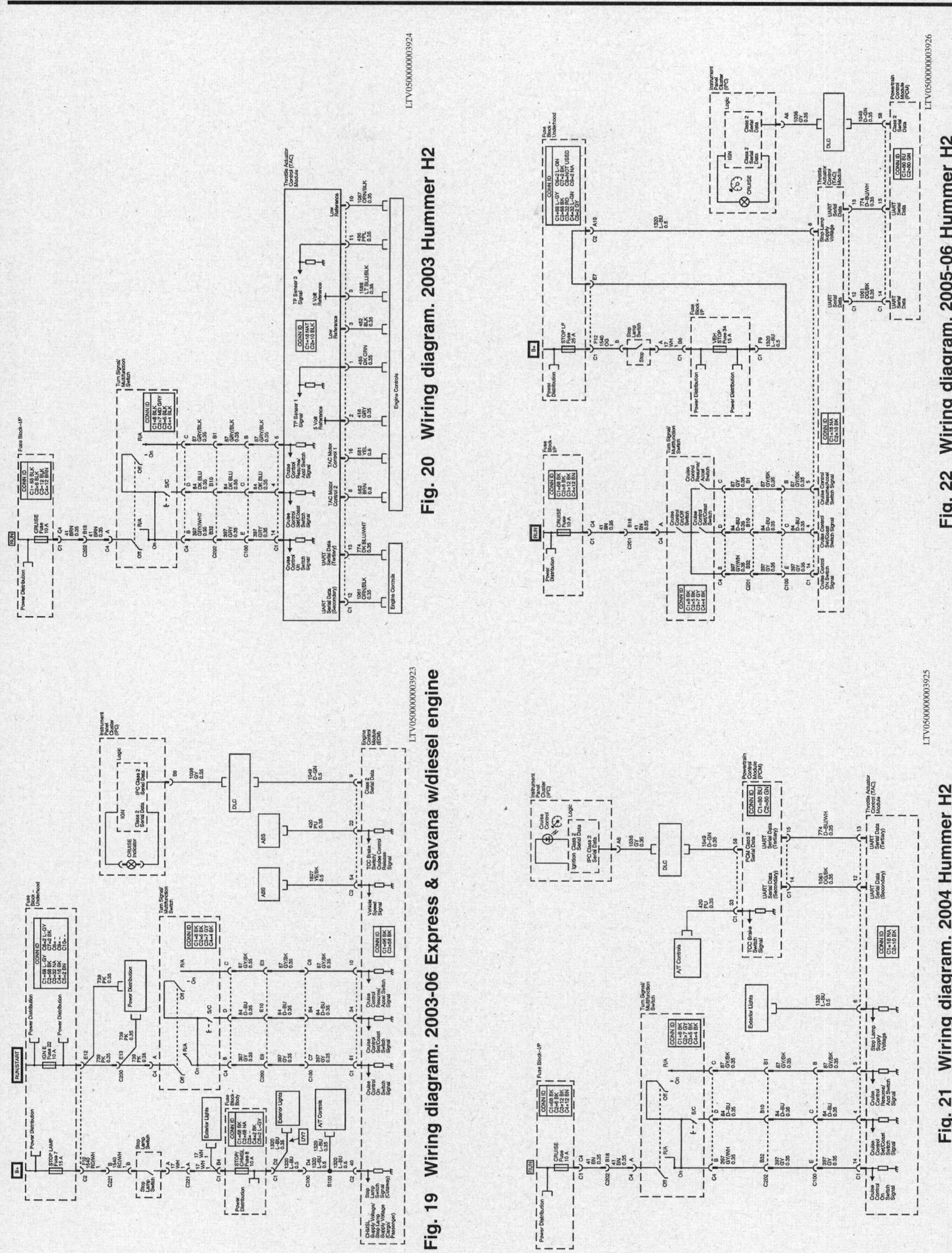

Fig. 19 Wiring diagram. 2003-06 Express & Savana w/diesel engine

Fig. 20 Wiring diagram. 2003 Hummer H2

Fig. 21 Wiring diagram. 2004 Hummer H2

Fig. 22 Wiring diagram. 2005-06 Hummer H2

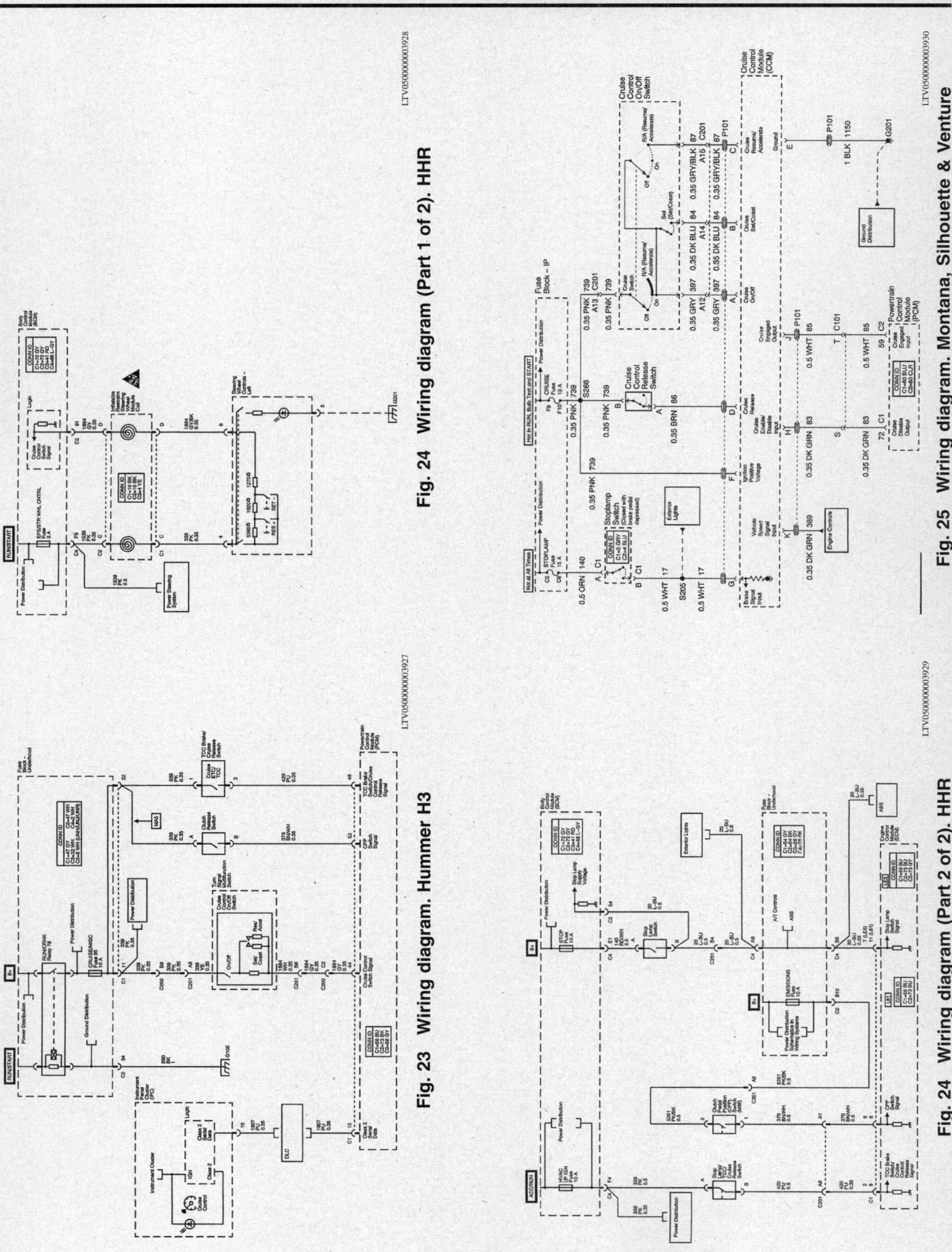

Fig. 24 Wiring diagram (Part 1 of 2). HHR

Fig. 25 Wiring diagram. Montana, Silhouette & Venture

Fig. 23 Wiring diagram. Hummer H3

Fig. 24 Wiring diagram (Part 2 of 2). HHR

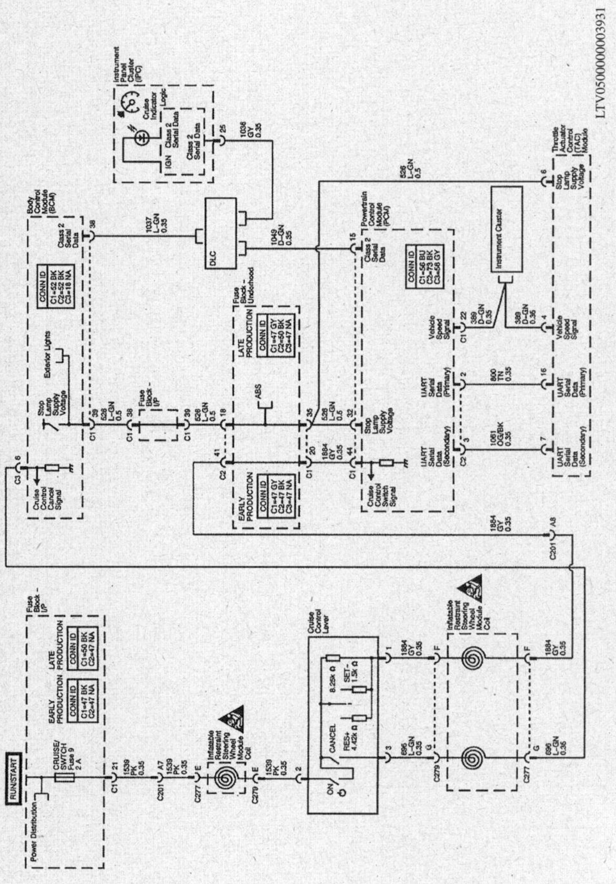

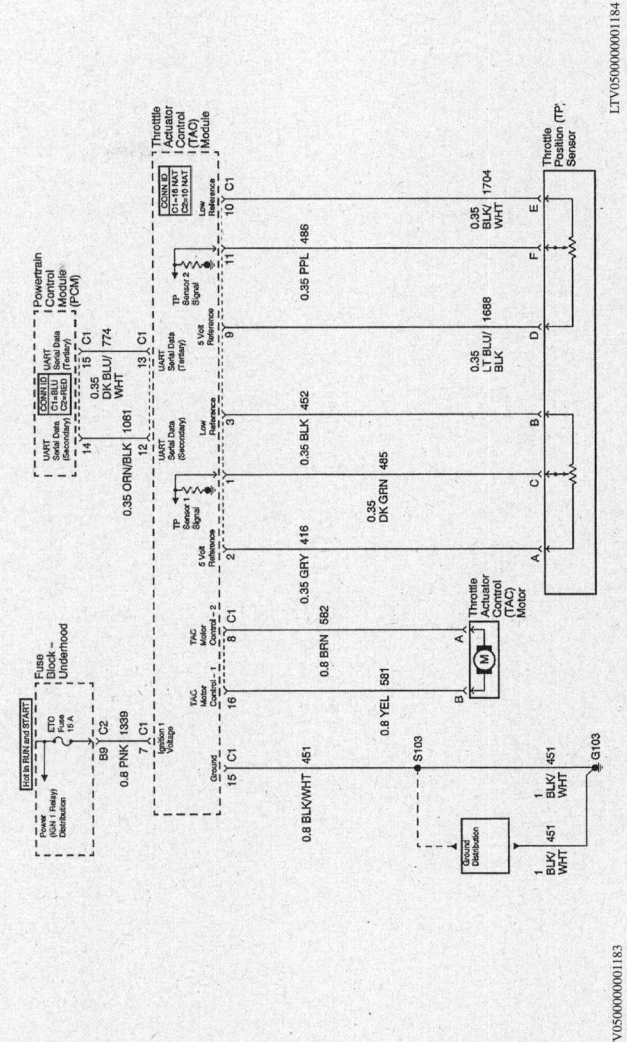

Fig. 27 Wiring diagram (Part 1 of 2). 2002 Sierra & Silverado w/gasoline engine less ETC

Fig. 28 Wiring diagram (Part 1 of 2). 2002 Sierra & Silverado w/gasoline engine & ETC

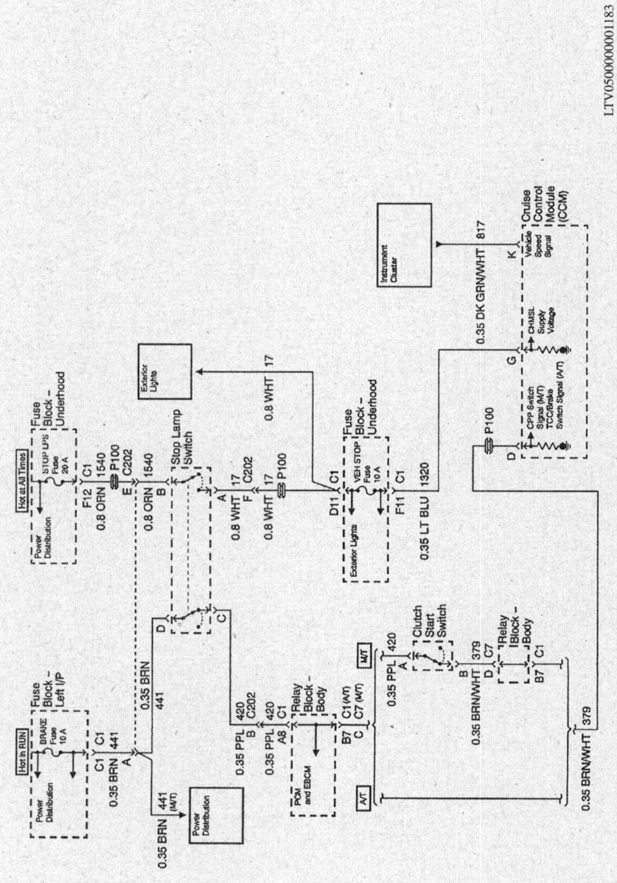

Fig. 26 Wiring diagram. Relay, SV6, Terraza & Uplander

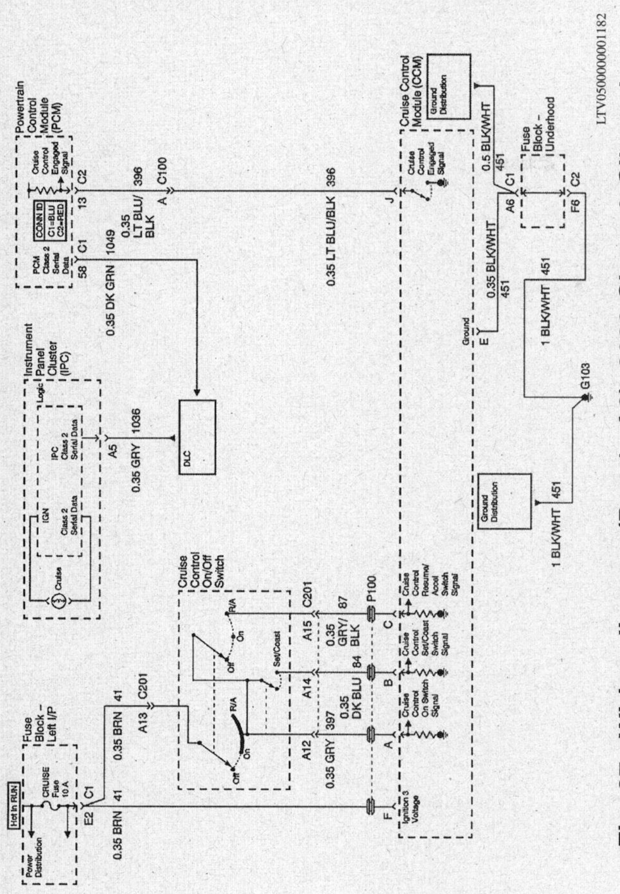

Fig. 27 Wiring diagram (Part 2 of 2). 2002 Sierra & Silverado w/gasoline engine less ETC

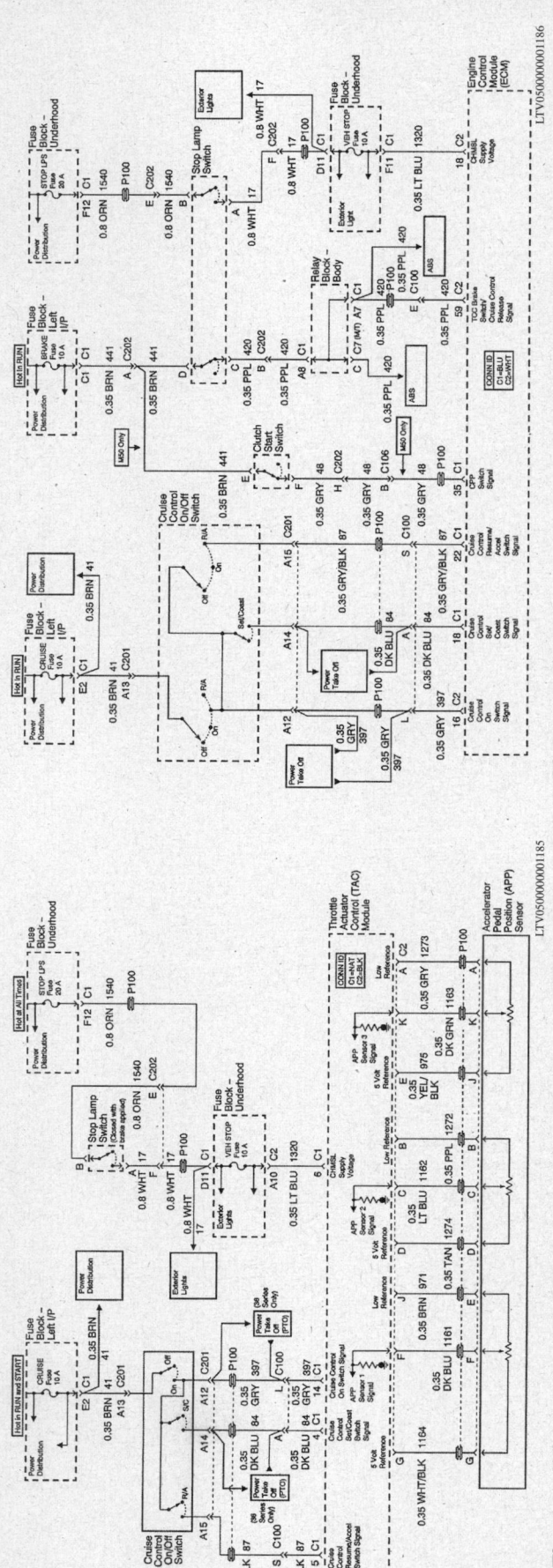

Fig. 29 Wiring diagram. 2002 Sierra & Silverado w/diesel engine

Fig. 30 Wiring diagram (Part 2 of 2). 2003-04 Sierra & Silverado w/4.3L engine

Fig. 28 Wiring diagram (Part 2 of 2). 2002 Sierra & Silverado w/gasoline engine & ETC

Fig. 30 Wiring diagram (Part 1 of 2). 2003-04 Sierra & Silverado w/4.3L engine

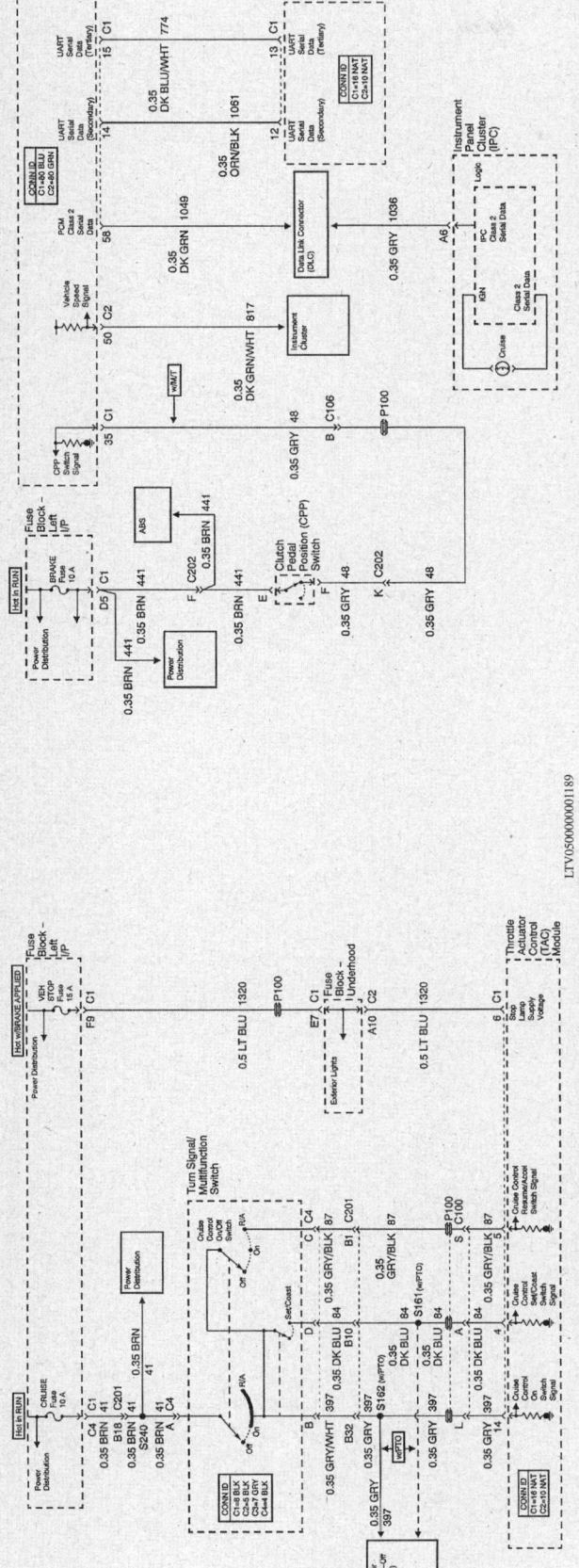

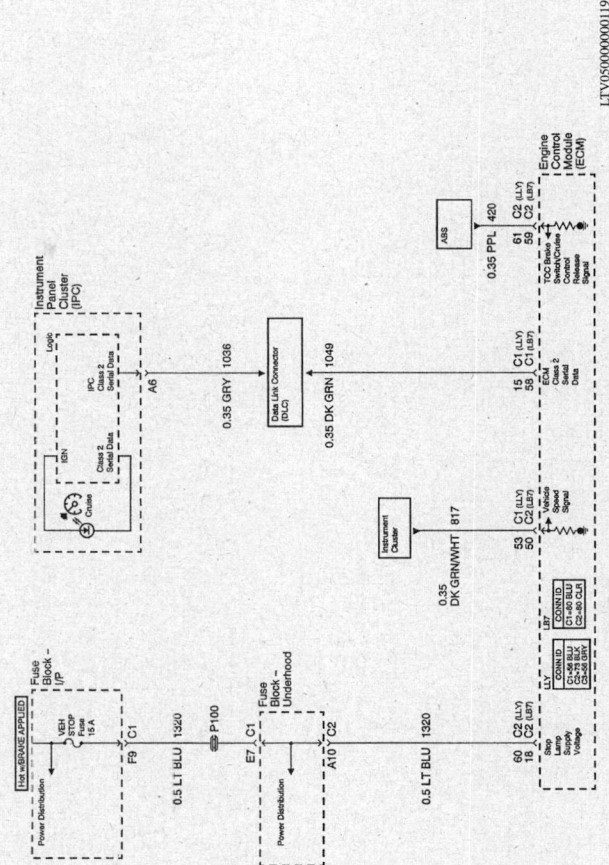

Fig. 31   Wiring diagram (Part 2 of 2). 2003-04 Sierra & Silverado w/4.8L, 5.3L, 6.0L & 8.1L engines

Fig. 32   Wiring diagram (Part 2 of 2). 2003-04 Sierra & Silverado w/diesel engine

Fig. 31   Wiring diagram (Part 1 of 2). 2003-04 Sierra & Silverado w/4.8L, 5.3L, 6.0L & 8.1L engines

Fig. 32   Wiring diagram (Part 1 of 2). 2003-04 Sierra & Silverado w/diesel engine

LTV050000001193

Fig. 33 Wiring diagram. 2005-06 Sierra & Silverado w/4.3L engine

LTV050000001194

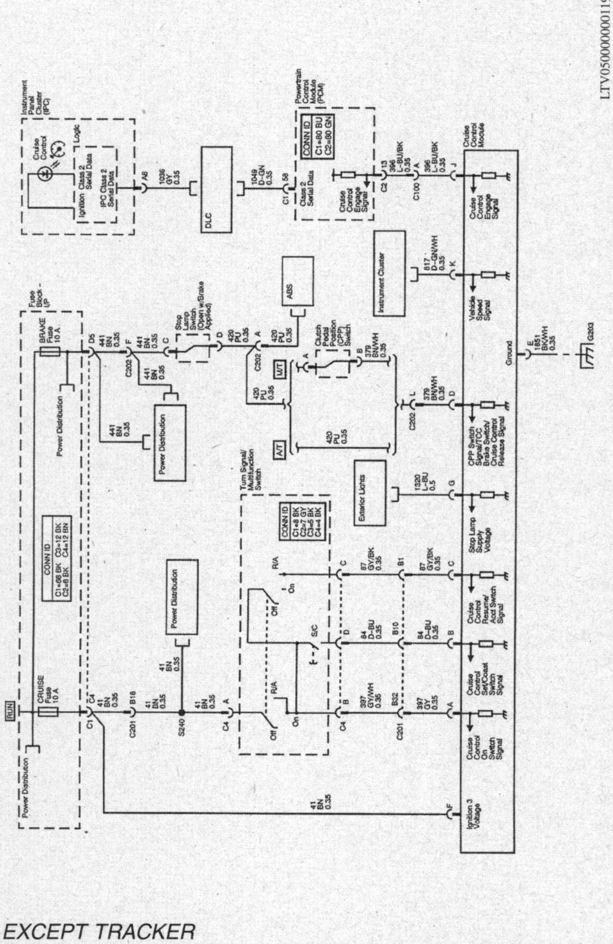

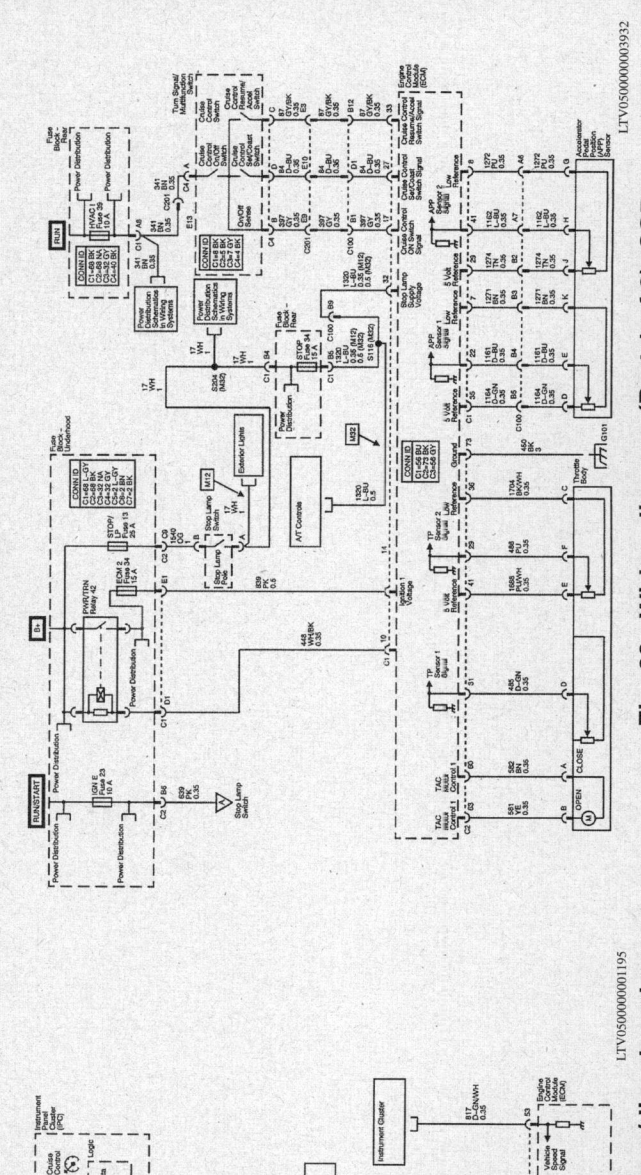

Fig. 34 Wiring diagram. 2005-06 Sierra & Silverado w/4.8L, 5.3L, 6.0L & 8.1L engines

LTV050000001195

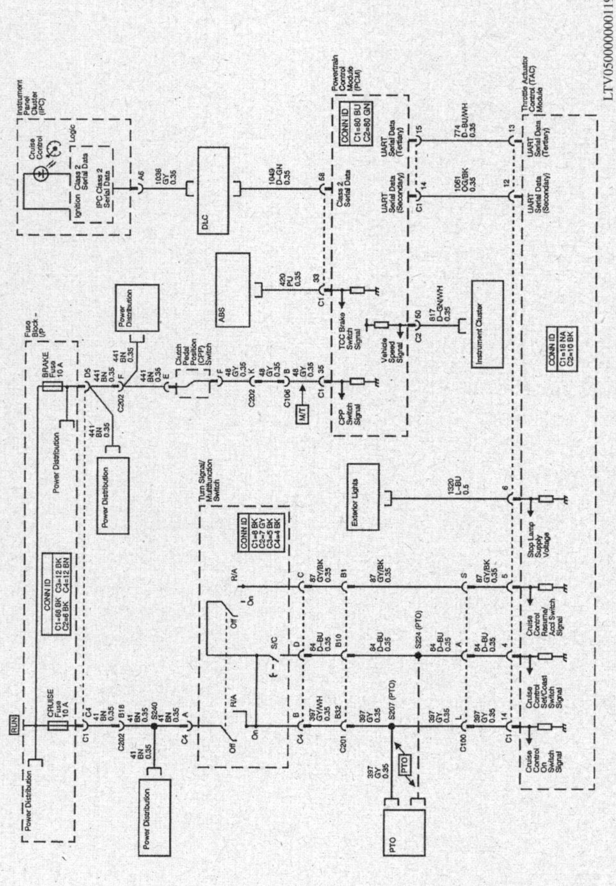

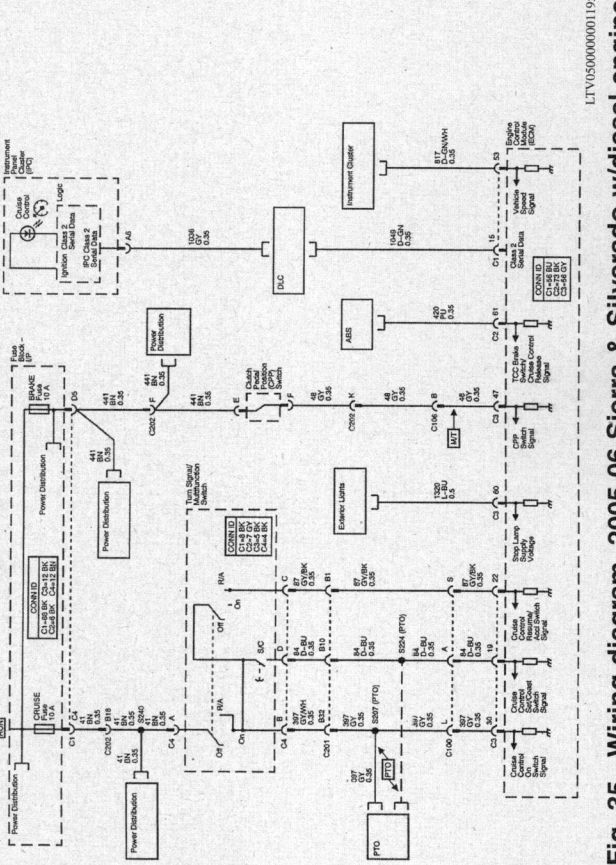

Fig. 35 Wiring diagram. 2005-06 Sierra & Silverado w/diesel engine

LTV050000003932

Fig. 36 Wiring diagram (Part 1 of 2). SSR

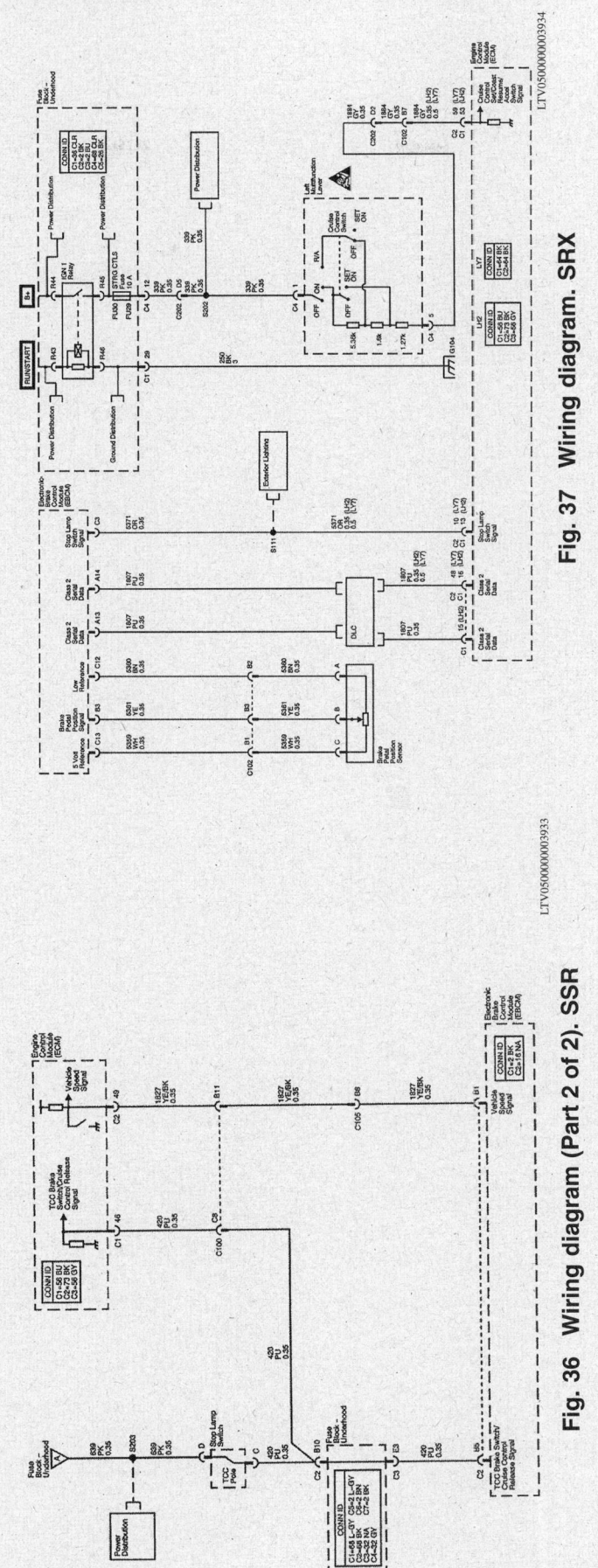

Fig. 37 Wiring diagram. SRX

Fig. 36 Wiring diagram (Part 2 of 2). SSR

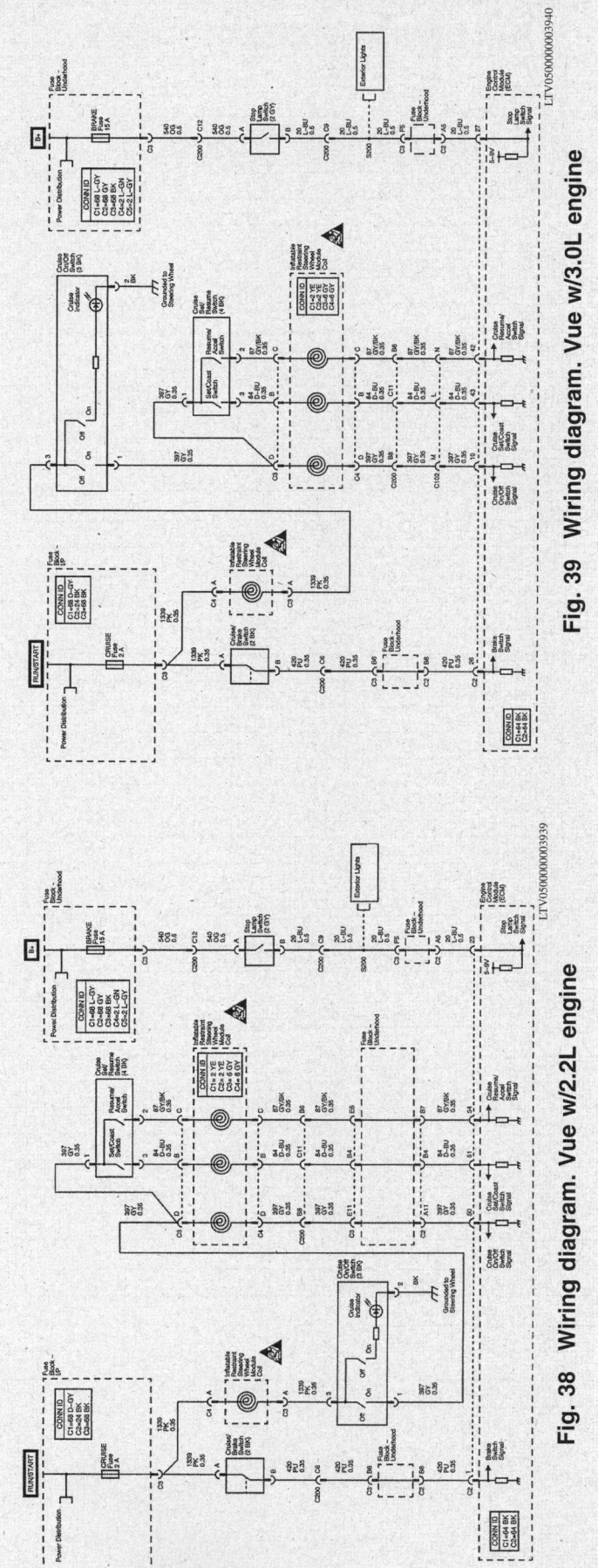

Fig. 39 Wiring diagram. Vue w/3.0L engine

Fig. 38 Wiring diagram. Vue w/2.2L engine

DIAGNOSTIC CHART INDEX

Year	Description	Page No.	Fig. No.
ASTRO & SAFARI			
2002–05	Cruise Control Inoperative/Malfunctioning	2-19	40
AVALANCHE, ESCALADE, ESCALADE EXT, SUBURBAN, TAHOE & YUKON			
2002–06	Cruise Control Indicator Always On	2-21	41
	Cruise Control Indicator Inoperative	2-21	42
2002	Cruise Control Inoperative/Malfunctioning Less ETC	2-21	43
	Cruise Control Inoperative/Malfunctioning w/ETC	2-22	44
2003-06	Cruise Control Inoperative/Malfunctioning	2-23	45
AZTEK & RENDEZVOUS			
2002–06	Cruise Control Indicator Always On w/3.4L & 3.5L Engines	2-25	46
	Cruise Control Indicator Inoperative w/3.4L & 3.5L Engines	2-25	47
	Cruise Control Inoperative/Malfunctioning w/3.4L & 3.5L Engines	2-26	48
	Cruise Control Indicator Always On w/3.6L Engine	2-27	49
	Cruise Control Indicator Inoperative w/3.6L Engine	2-27	50
	Cruise Control Inoperative/Malfunctioning w/3.6L Engine	2-28	51
BLAZER, JIMMY, SONOMA & S10			
2002–05	Cruise Control Inoperative/Malfunctioning	2-29	52
BRAVADA, ENVOY, RAINIER & TRAILBLAZER			
2002	Cruise Control Indicator Always On	2-30	53
	Cruise Control Indicator Inoperative	2-30	54
	Cruise Control Inoperative/Malfunctioning	2-30	55
2003-04	Cruise Control Indicator Always On	2-31	56
	Cruise Control Indicator Inoperative	2-32	57
	Cruise Control Inoperative/Malfunctioning w/4.2L Engine	2-32	58
	Cruise Control Inoperative/Malfunctioning w/5.3L Engine	2-33	59
2005–06	Cruise Control Indicator Always On Less 4.2L Engine	2-34	60
	Cruise Control Indicator Always On w/4.2L Engine	2-34	61
	Cruise Control Indicator Inoperative Less 4.2L Engine	2-35	62
	Cruise Control Inoperative w/4.2L Engine	2-35	63
	Cruise Control Inoperative/Malfunctioning Less 4.2L Engine	2-35	64
	Cruise Control Inoperative/Malfunctioning w/4.2L Engine	2-36	65
CANYON & COLORADO			
2004–06	Cruise Control Inoperative/Malfunctioning	2-37	66
EQUINOX & TORRENT			
2005–06	Cruise Control Inoperative/Malfunction	2-38	67
EXPRESS & SAVANA			
2002	Cruise Control Inoperative/Malfunctioning w/4.3L, 5.0L & 5.7L Engines	2-40	68
	Cruise Control Inoperative/Malfunctioning w/6.5L Diesel Engine	2-41	69
	Cruise Control Inoperative/Malfunctioning w/8.1L Engine	2-42	70
2003	Cruise Control Inoperative/Malfunctioning	2-43	71
2004-06	Cruise Control Inoperative/Malfunctioning Gas Engines w/TAC	2-45	72
	Cruise Control Inoperative/Malfunctioning Gas Engines Less TAC	2-46	73
	Cruise Control Inoperative/Malfunctioning w/Diesel Engine	2-47	74
HHR			
2006	Cruise Control Inoperative/Malfunctioning	2-51	77
HUMMER H2			
2003–06	Cruise Control Inoperative/Malfunctioning	2-48	75
HUMMER H3			
2006	Cruise Control Inoperative/Malfunctioning	2-50	76

Continued

DIAGNOSTIC CHART INDEX—Continued

Year	Description	Page No.	Fig. No.
MONTANA, SILHOUETTE & VENTURE			
2002–03	Cruise Control Inoperative/Malfunctioning	2-52	78
RELAY, SV6, TERRAZA & UPLANDER			
2005–06	Cruise Control Inoperative/Malfunctioning	2-54	79
SIERRA & SILVERADO			
2002–06	Cruise Control Indicator Always On Less TAC	2-56	80
	Cruise Control Indicator Always On w/TAC	2-56	81
	Cruise Control Indicator Inoperative Less TAC	2-56	82
	Cruise Control Indicator Inoperative w/TAC	2-57	83
2002	Cruise Control Inoperative/Malfunction Gas Engines Less ETC	2-57	84
	Cruise Control Inoperative/Malfunctioning Gas Engines w/ETC	2-58	85
	Cruise Control Inoperative/Malfunctioning w/Diesel Engine	2-60	86
2003-06	Cruise Control Inoperative/Malfunctioning w/4.8L, 5.3L, 6.0L & 8.1L Engines	2-61	87
	Cruise Control Inoperative/Malfunctioning w/6.6L Engine	2-62	88
	Cruise Control Inoperative/Malfunctioning w/4.3L Engine	2-64	89
SRX			
2004–06	Cruise Control Inoperative/Malfunctioning w/3.6L Engine	2-66	91
	Cruise Control Inoperative/Malfunctioning w/4.6L Engine	2-67	92
2002–06	Cruise Control Inoperative/Malfunctioning	2-68	93
SSR			
2003–06	Cruise Control Inoperative/Malfunctioning	2-65	90
VUE			
2002–06	Cruise Control Inoperative/Malfunctioning	2-68	93

Diagnostic Aids

To avoid misdiagnosis, inspect for the following:

- Proper operation of brake lamps

- The throttle linkage is not binding.

- The vehicle speed is greater than 40 km/h (25 mph).

- The system voltage is within 9-16 volts.

Electromagnetic interference on the vehicle speed sensor signal circuit may cause erratic cruise control operation.

Step	Action	Values	Yes	No
1	Did you perform the Diagnostic System Check - Vehicle?	--	Go to Step 2	Go to Diagnostic System Check
2	1. Turn OFF the ignition. 2. Disconnect the cruise control module. 3. Turn ON the ignition, with the engine OFF. 4. Connect a test lamp between the ignition 3 voltage circuit and a good ground. Does the test lamp illuminate?	--	Go to Step 3	Go to Step 5
3	Connect a test lamp between the ignition 3 voltage circuit and the ground circuit of the cruise control module. Does the test lamp illuminate?	--	Go to Step 4	Go to Step 26

LTV0500000003941

**Fig. 40 Cruise Control Inoperative/Malfunctioning
(Part 1 of 5). Astro & Safari**

Step	Action	Value	Yes	No
4	1. Turn the cruise control On/Off switch OFF. 2. Connect a test lamp between a good ground and each of the following circuits: - The cruise control ON switch signal circuit - The cruise control set/coast switch signal circuit - The cruise control resume/accel switch signal circuit Does the test lamp illuminate for any of the signal circuits listed above?	-	Go to Step 14	Go to Step 6
5	1. Turn the cruise control On/Off switch OFF. 2. Connect a test lamp between battery voltage and each of the following circuits: - The cruise control ON switch signal circuit - The cruise control set/coast switch signal circuit - The cruise control resume/accel switch signal circuit Does the test lamp illuminate for any of the signal circuits listed above?	-	Go to Step 15	Go to Step 24
6	1. Turn the cruise control On/Off switch ON. 2. Connect a test lamp between the cruise control ON switch signal circuit and a good ground. Does the test lamp illuminate?	-	Go to Step 7	Go to Step 16
7	1. Connect a test lamp between the cruise control set/coast switch signal circuit and a good ground. 2. With the cruise control On/Off switch ON, press and hold the set/coast switch. Does the test lamp illuminate?	-	Go to Step 8	Go to Step 18
8	1. Connect a test lamp between the cruise control resume/accelerate switch signal circuit and a good ground. 2. With the cruise control On/Off switch ON, press and hold the resume/accel switch. Does the test lamp illuminate?	-	Go to Step 9	Go to Step 19
9	1. Connect a test lamp between the stop lamp switch signal circuit and a good ground. 2. Depress the brake pedal. Does the test lamp illuminate?	-	Go to Step 10	Go to Step 27

LTV0500000003942

Fig. 40   Cruise Control Inoperative/Malfunctioning (Part 2 of 5). Astro & Safari

Step	Action	Value	Yes	No
10	Connect a test lamp between the torque converter clutch (TCC) brake switch/cruise control release signal circuit and a good ground. Does the test lamp illuminate?	--	Go to Step 11	Go to Step 25
11	Connect a DMM between the cruise control engaged signal circuit and a good ground. Does the DMM display near the specified voltage?	B+	Go to Step 12	Go to Step 20
12	Connect a DMM between the vehicle speed signal circuit and a good ground. Does the DMM display near the specified voltage?	B+	Go to Diagnostic Aids	Go to Step 13
13	Test the vehicle speed signal circuit for an open or for a high resistance. Did you find and correct the condition?	--	Go to Step 31	Go to Step 23
14	Test the signal circuit that illuminated the test lamp for a short to voltage. Did you find and correct the condition?	--	Go to Step 31	Go to Step 22
15	Test the signal circuit that illuminated the test lamp for a short to ground. Did you find and correct the condition?	--	Go to Step 31	Go to Step 22
16	Test the cruise control On/Off switch signal circuit for an open or for a high resistance. Did you find and correct the condition?	--	Go to Step 31	Go to Step 17
17	Test the ignition 3 voltage circuit for an open or for a high resistance between SP 201 and the multifunction switch. Did you find and correct the condition?	--	Go to Step 31	Go to Step 22
18	Test the cruise control set/coast switch signal circuit for an open or for a high resistance. Did you find and correct the condition?	--	Go to Step 31	Go to Step 22

LTV0500000003943

Fig. 40   Cruise Control Inoperative/Malfunctioning (Part 3 of 5). Astro & Safari

Step	Action	Value	Yes	No
19	Test the cruise control resume/accel switch signal circuit for an open or for a high resistance. Did you find and correct the condition?	-	Go to Step 31	Go to Step 22
20	Test the cruise control engaged signal circuit for an open, for a high resistance, or for a short to ground. Did you find and correct the condition?	-	Go to Step 31	Go to Step 21
21	Inspect for poor connections at the harness connector of the powertrain control module (PCM). Did you find and correct the condition?	-	Go to Step 31	Go to Step 28
22	Inspect for poor connections at the harness connector of the multifunction switch. Did you find and correct the condition?	-	Go to Step 31	Go to Step 29
23	Inspect for poor connections at the harness connector of the cruise control module. Did you find and correct the condition?	-	Go to Step 31	Go to Step 30
24	Repair the open, the high resistance, or the short to ground in the ignition 3 voltage circuit. Did you complete the repair?	-	Go to Step 31	--
25	Repair the open or the high resistance in the TCC brake switch/cruise control release signal circuit. Did you complete the repair?	-	Go to Step 31	--
26	Repair the open or the high resistance in the ground circuit of the cruise control module. Did you complete the repair?	-	Go to Step 31	--

LTV0500000003944

Fig. 40   Cruise Control Inoperative/Malfunctioning (Part 4 of 5). Astro & Safari

Step	Action	Value	Yes	No
27	Repair the open or the high resistance in the stop lamp switch signal circuit. Did you complete the repair?	-	Go to Step 31	--
28	Replace the PCM. Did you complete the replacement?	-	Go to Step 31	--
29	Replace the multifunction switch. Did you complete the replacement?	-	Go to Step 31	--
30	Replace the cruise control module. Did you complete the replacement?	-	Go to Step 31	--
31	Operate the vehicle within the conditions for cruise control operation. Does the cruise control system operate correctly?	-	System OK	Go to Step 2

LTV0500000003945

Fig. 40   Cruise Control Inoperative/Malfunctioning (Part 5 of 5). Astro & Safari

Step	Action	Yes	No
1	Did you perform the Cruise Control Diagnostic System Check?	Go to Step 2	Go to Diagnostic System Check
2	Turn the ignition ON, with the engine OFF. Does the Cruise indicator illuminate after the IPC displays test?	Go to Step 3	Test for Intermittent and Poor Connections
3	1. Turn the ignition OFF. 2. Install a scan tool. 3. Turn the ignition ON, with the engine OFF. 4. With the scan tool, observe the Cruise Control parameter in the IPC data list. Does the Cruise Lamp parameter display On?	Go to Step 4	Go to Step 5
4	**Important** Program the replacement PCM. Replace the PCM. Did you complete the replacement?	Go to Step 6	--
5	Replace the Instrument Panel Cluster (IPC). Did you complete the replacement?	Go to Step 6	--
6	Operate the system in order to verify the repair. Does the system operate properly?	System OK	Go to Step 2

LTV0500000003946

Fig. 41 Cruise Control Indicator Always On. Avalanche, Escalade, Escalade EXT, Suburban, Tahoe & Yukon

Diagnostic Aids

Important: Perform the following in order to avoid misdiagnosis.

- Inspect for proper operation of brake lamps and clutch switch, if equipped.
- Inspect for proper operation of the transmission range switch.
- Inspect throttle linkage for mechanical binding which could cause the system to malfunction.
- Inspect cruise control cable adjustment, should have minimum slack.
- EMI on the speed sensor signal circuit may cause erratic cruise control operation.

Conditions for Enabling Cruise Control

The vehicle speed is greater than 40 km/h (25 mph).

Step	Action	Value(s)	Yes	No
1	Did you perform the Cruise Control Diagnostic System Check?	--	Go to Step 2	Go to Diagnostic System Check
2	1. Turn OFF the ignition. 2. Disconnect the cruise control module. 3. Turn ON the ignition, with the engine OFF. 4. Probe the ignition positive voltage circuit of the cruise control module with a test lamp that is connected to a good ground. Does the test lamp illuminate?	--	Go to Step 3	Go to Step 30
3	Probe the ignition positive voltage circuit of the cruise control module with a test lamp that is connected to the ground circuit of the cruise control module. Does the test lamp illuminate?	--	Go to Step 4	Go to Step 31
4	1. Turn ON the ignition, with the engine OFF. 2. Turn OFF the cruise control. 3. Probe the on/off, the set/coast, and the resume/accelerate signal circuits with a test lamp that is connected to a good ground. Does the test lamp illuminate on any of the circuits?	--	Go to Step 14	Go to Step 5

LTV0500000003948

Fig. 43 Cruise Control Inoperative/Malfunctioning Less ETC (Part 1 of 5). 2002 Avalanche, Escalade, Escalade EXT, Suburban, Tahoe & Yukon

Step	Action	Yes	No
1	Did you perform the Cruise Control Diagnostic System Check?	Go to Step 2	Go to Diagnostic System Check
2	1. Turn the ignition OFF. 2. Install a scan tool. 3. Turn the ignition ON, with the engine OFF. 4. With the scan tool, Command the Cruise Control Lamp Test parameter ON, in the IPC Output Controls. Does the Cruise indicator illuminate in the IPC?	Go to Step 4	Go to Step 3
3	Replace the instrument panel cluster (IPC). Did you complete the replacement?	Go to Step 5	--
4	**Important** Program the replacement PCM. Replace the PCM. Did you complete the replacement?	Go to Step 5	--
5	Operate the system in order to verify the repair. Does the system operate properly?	System OK	Go to Step 2

LTV0500000003947

Fig. 42 Cruise Control Indicator Inoperative. Avalanche, Escalade, Escalade EXT, Suburban, Tahoe & Yukon

Step	Action	Value(s)	Yes	No
5	1. Turn ON the ignition, with the engine OFF. 2. Turn ON the cruise control. 3. Probe the cruise control on/off signal circuit with a test lamp that is connected to a good ground. Does the test lamp illuminate?		Go to Step 6	Go to Step 15
6	1. Probe the cruise control set/coast signal circuit with a test lamp that is connected to a good ground. 2. Press and hold the SET/COAST switch. Does the test lamp illuminate?		Go to Step 7	Go to Step 17
7	1. Probe the cruise control resume/accelerate signal circuit with a test lamp that is connected to a good ground. 2. Press and hold the RESUME/ACCEL switch. Does the test lamp illuminate?		Go to Step 8	Go to Step 18
8	Probe the TCC/brake, cruise release signal circuit with a test lamp that is connected to a good ground. Does the test lamp illuminate?	--	Go to Step 11	Go to Step 9
9	Press the brake pedal while monitoring the test lamp. Does the test lamp illuminate?	--	Go to Step 21	Go to Step 10
10	Probe the stoplamp switch signal circuit with a test lamp that is connected to a good ground. Does the test lamp illuminate?	--	Go to Step 22	Go to Step 11
11	Press the brake pedal while monitoring the test lamp. Does the test lamp illuminate?	--	Go to Step 12	Go to Step 23
12	Probe the cruise engaged signal circuit with a DMM that is connected to a good ground. Does the voltage measure near the specified value?	B+	Go to Step 13	Go to Step 24
13	Check the speedometer for proper operation. Does the speedometer operate properly?	--	Go to Step 25	Go to Symptoms

LTV0500000003949

Fig. 43 Cruise Control Inoperative/Malfunctioning Less ETC (Part 2 of 5). 2002 Avalanche, Escalade, Escalade EXT, Suburban, Tahoe & Yukon

			Yes	No
14	Test the circuit that illuminated the test lamp for a short to voltage. Did you find and correct the condition?	-	Go to Step 36	Go to Step 28
15	Test the cruise control on/off signal circuit for an open, high resistance or short to ground and the set/coast, resume/accel signal circuits for a short to ground. Did you find and correct the condition?	-	Go to Step 36	Go to Step 16
16	Test the ignition positive voltage circuit of the cruise control switch for an open or high resistance. Did you find and correct the condition?	-	Go to Step 36	Go to Step 28
17	Test the set/coast switch signal circuit for an open or a high resistance. Did you find and correct the condition?	-	Go to Step 36	Go to Step 28
18	Test the resume/accelerate switch signal circuit for an open or a high resistance. Did you find and correct the condition?	-	Go to Step 36	Go to Step 28
19	Test the TCC/ brake, cruise release signal circuit for an open or a high resistance . Did you find and correct the condition?	-	Go to Step 36	Go to Step 26
20	Test the TCC/ brake, cruise release signal circuit for an open or a high resistance between the CPP switch and the cruise control module. Did you find and correct the condition?	-	Go to Step 36	Go to Step 32
21	Test the TCC/ brake, cruise release switch signal circuit for a short to voltage. Did you find and correct the condition?	-	Go to Step 36	Go to Step 26
22	Test the stoplamp switch signal circuit for a short to voltage. Did you find and correct the condition?	-	Go to Step 36	Go to Step 26

LTV0500000003950

Fig. 43 Cruise Control Inoperative/Malfunctioning Less ETC (Part 3 of 5). 2002 Avalanche, Escalade, Escalade EXT, Suburban, Tahoe & Yukon

			Yes	No
23	Test the stoplamp switch signal circuit for an open or a high resistance. Did you find and correct the condition?	-	Go to Step 36	Go to Step 26
24	Test the cruise engaged signal circuit for an open, a high resistance, or a short to ground. Did you find and correct the condition?	-	Go to Step 36	Go to Step 27
25	Test the speed sensor circuit for an open or a high resistance between the PCM and cruise control module. Did you find and correct the condition?	-	Go to Step 36	Go to Step 29
26	Inspect for poor connections at the harness connector of the stop lamp switch. Did you find and correct the condition?	-	Go to Step 36	Go to Step 33
27	Inspect for poor connections at the harness connector of the PCM. Did you find and correct the condition?	-	Go to Step 36	Go to Step 34
28	Inspect for poor connections at the harness connector of the cruise control switch. Did you find and correct the condition?	-	Go to Step 36	Go to Step 35
29	Inspect for poor connections at the harness connector of the cruise control module. Did you find and correct the condition?	-	Go to Step 36	Go to Step 36
30	Repair the ignition positive voltage circuit of the cruise control module. Did you complete the repair?	-	Go to Step 36	--

LTV0500000003951

Fig. 43 Cruise Control Inoperative/Malfunctioning Less ETC (Part 4 of 5). 2002 Avalanche, Escalade, Escalade EXT, Suburban, Tahoe & Yukon

			Yes	No
31	Repair the ground circuit of the cruise control module. Did you complete the repair?	-	Go to Step 36	--
32	Replace the stop lamp switch. Did you complete the replacement?	-	Go to Step 36	--
33	**Important:** The PCM must be reprogrammed after replacement. Replace the PCM. Did you complete the replacement?	-	Go to Step 36	--
34	Replace the cruise control switch. Did you complete the replacement?	-	Go to Step 36	--
35	Replace the cruise control module. Did you complete the replacement?	-	Go to Step 36	--
36	Operate the vehicle within the conditions for cruise control operation. Does the cruise control system operate correctly?	-	System OK	Go to Step 2

LTV0500000003952

Fig. 43 Cruise Control Inoperative/Malfunctioning Less ETC (Part 5 of 5). 2002 Avalanche, Escalade, Escalade EXT, Suburban, Tahoe & Yukon

Diagnostic Aids

Important: Perform the following in order to avoid misdiagnosis.

- Inspect for proper operation of brake lamps and clutch switch, if equipped.
- Inspect for proper operation of the transmission range switch.
- EMI on the speed sensor signal circuit may cause erratic cruise control operation.

Conditions for Enabling Cruise Control

The vehicle speed is greater than 40 km/h (25 mph).

Step	Action	Yes	No
1	Did you perform A Diagnostic System Check - Cruise Control?	Go to Step 2	Go to Diagnostic System Check
2	1. Turn OFF the ignition. 2. Disconnect the Throttle Actuator Control (TAC) module. 3. Turn ON the ignition, with the engine OFF. 4. Turn OFF the cruise control switch. 5. Probe the on/off, the set/coast, and the resume/accelerate circuits with a test lamp that is connected to a good ground. Does the test lamp illuminate on any of the circuits?	Go to Step 12	Go to Step 3
3	1. Turn ON the ignition, with the engine OFF. 2. Turn ON the cruise control. 3. Probe the on/off circuit with a test lamp that is connected to a good ground. Does the test lamp illuminate?	Go to Step 4	Go to Step 13
4	1. Probe the set/coast circuit with a test lamp that is connected to a good ground. 2. Press and hold the SET/COAST switch. Does the test lamp illuminate?	Go to Step 5	Go to Step 15

LTV0500000003953

Fig. 44 Cruise Control Inoperative/Malfunctioning w/ETC (Part 1 of 4). 2002 Avalanche, Escalade, Escalade EXT, Suburban, Tahoe & Yukon

5	1. Probe the resume/accelerate circuit with a test lamp that is connected to a good ground. 2. Press and hold the RESUME/ACCEL switch. Does the test lamp illuminate?	Go to Step 6	Go to Step 16
6	Probe the stop lamp switch signal circuit with a test lamp that is connected to a good ground. Does the test lamp illuminate?	Go to Step 19	Go to Step 7
7	Press the brake pedal while monitoring the test lamp. Does the test lamp illuminate?	Go to Step 8	Go to Step 21
8	Probe the brake switch signal circuit of the ECM harness connector with a test lamp connected to a good ground. Does the test lamp illuminate?	Go to Step 9	Go to Step 11
9	Press the brake pedal while monitoring the test lamp. Does the test lamp illuminate?	Go to Step 20	Go to Step 10
10	Check the speedometer for proper operation. Does the speedometer operate properly?	Go to Step 25	Go to Symptoms
11	1. Turn OFF the ignition. 2. Disconnect the brake switch. 3. Probe the brake switch ignition positive voltage circuit with a test lamp connected to a good ground. Does the test lamp illuminate?	Go to Step 21	Go to Step 22
12	Test the circuit that illuminated the test lamp for a short to voltage. Did you find and correct the condition?	Go to Step 29	Go to Step 24
13	Test the on/off signal circuit for a open, high resistance or short to ground and the S/C and R/A signal circuits for a short to ground. Did you find and correct the condition?	Go to Step 29	Go to Step 14

LTV0500000003954

Fig. 44 Cruise Control Inoperative/Malfunctioning w/ETC (Part 2 of 4). 2002 Avalanche, Escalade, Escalade EXT, Suburban, Tahoe & Yukon

22	Repair the open in the ignition positive voltage circuit of the stop lamp switch. Did you complete the repair?	Go to Step 29	--
23	Inspect for poor connections at the harness connector of the stop lamp switch. Did you find and correct the condition?	Go to Step 29	Go to Step 27
24	Inspect for poor connections at the harness connector of the cruise control switch. Did you find and correct the condition?	Go to Step 29	Go to Step 28
25	Inspect for poor connections at the harness connector of the Throttle Actuator Control (TAC) Module. Did you find and correct the condition?	Go to Step 29	Go to Step 29
26	Replace the Stop lamp switch. Did you complete the replacement?	Go to Step 29	--
27	Replace the cruise control switch. Did you complete the replacement?	Go to Step 29	--
28	Replace the Throttle Actuator Control (TAC) Module. Did you complete the replacement?	Go to Step 29	--
29	Operate the vehicle within the conditions for cruise control operation. Does the cruise control system operate correctly?	System OK	Go to Step 2

LTV0500000003956

Fig. 44 Cruise Control Inoperative/Malfunctioning w/ETC (Part 4 of 4). 2002 Avalanche, Escalade, Escalade EXT, Suburban, Tahoe & Yukon

14	Test the ignition positive voltage circuit of the cruise control switch for a open, high resistance or short to ground. Did you find and correct the condition?	Go to Step 29	Go to Step 24
15	Test the set/coast circuit for a open, high resistance or short to ground. Did you find and correct the condition?	Go to Step 29	Go to Step 24
16	Test the resume/accelerate circuit for a open, high resistance or short to ground. Did you find and correct the condition?	Go to Step 29	Go to Step 24
17	Test the stop lamp signal circuit for a open, high resistance or short to ground. Did you find and correct the condition?	Go to Step 29	Go to Step 18
18	Test the stop lamp ignition positive voltage circuit for a open, high resistance or short to ground. Did you find and correct the condition?	Go to Step 29	Go to Step 23
19	Test the stop lamp switch signal circuit for a short to voltage. Did you find and correct the condition?	Go to Step 29	Go to Step 23
20	Test the brake switch circuit for a short to voltage. Did you find and correct the condition?	Go to Step 29	Go to Step 23
21	Test the brake switch signal circuit of the PCM harness for an open or a high resistance. Did you find and correct the condition?	Go to Step 29	Go to Step 23

LTV0500000003955

Fig. 44 Cruise Control Inoperative/Malfunctioning w/ETC (Part 3 of 4). 2002 Avalanche, Escalade, Escalade EXT, Suburban, Tahoe & Yukon

Diagnostic Aids

Perform the following in order to avoid a misdiagnosis:

- Inspect for proper operation of the brake lamps.

- Electromagnetic interference (EMI) on the vehicle speed sensor signal circuit may cause erratic cruise control operation.

Conditions for Enabling Cruise Control

- The vehicle speed is greater than 40 km/h (25 mph).
- The vehicle is not in PARK, REVERSE, NEUTRAL, or 1st gear.
- The system voltage is within 12-16 volts.

Test description

The numbers below refer to the step numbers on the diagnostic table.

8. This step tests the center high mounted stop lamp (CHMSL) supply voltage/stop lamp supply voltage circuit for an open or for a high resistance between the stop lamp switch and the throttle actuator control (TAC) module.

9. This step tests the cruise control set/coast switch signal circuit for an open or for a high resistance.

10. This step tests the cruise control resume/accel switch signal circuit for an open or for a high resistance.

11. This step tests the ignition 3 voltage circuit for an open, for a short to ground, or for a high resistance.

29. DTCs will set in the powertrain control module (PCM) when you perform this table.

LTV0500000003957

Fig. 45 Cruise Control Inoperative/Malfunctioning (Part 1 of 6). 2003-06 Avalanche, Escalade, Escalade EXT, Suburban, Tahoe & Yukon

Step	Action	Yes	No
1	Did you perform the Diagnostic System Check - Vehicle?	Go to Step 2	Go to Diagnostic System Check
2	1. Install a scan tool. 2. Turn ON the ignition, with the engine OFF. 3. Turn the cruise control On/Off switch OFF. 4. With the scan tool, observe the Cruise On/Off Switch parameter in the powertrain control module (PCM) Cruise Control Data, data list. Does the Cruise On/Off Switch parameter display Off?	Go to Step 4	Go to Step 3
3	1. Turn OFF the ignition. 2. Disconnect C4 of the multifunction switch. 3. Turn ON the ignition, with the engine OFF. 4. With the scan tool, observe the Cruise On/Off Switch parameter. Does the Cruise On/Off Switch parameter display Off?	Go to Step 22	Go to Step 13
4	1. Turn the cruise control On/Off switch ON. 2. With the scan tool, observe the Cruise On/Off Switch parameter. Does the Cruise On/Off Switch parameter display On?	Go to Step 5	Go to Step 11
5	1. With the scan tool, observe the Cruise Set/Coast Switch parameter in the PCM Cruise Control Data, data list. 2. Turn the cruise control On/Off switch ON. 3. Press and hold the cruise control Set/Coast button. Does the Cruise Set/Coast Switch parameter display On?	Go to Step 6	Go to Step 9

LTV0500000003958

Fig. 45 Cruise Control Inoperative/Malfunctioning (Part 2 of 6). 2003-06 Avalanche, Escalade, Escalade EXT, Suburban, Tahoe & Yukon

Step	Action	Yes	No
6	1. With the scan tool, observe the Cruise Resume/Accel. Switch parameter in the PCM Cruise Control Data, data list. 2. Press and hold the Resume/Accel switch. Does the Cruise Resume/Accel. Switch parameter display On?	Go to Step 7	Go to Step 10
7	Do the stop lamps operate properly?	Go to Step 8	Diagnose Stop Lamps Inoperative
8	1. With the scan tool, observe the Stoplamp Pedal Switch parameter in the PCM Cruise Control Data, data list. 2. Depress and hold the brake pedal. Does the Stoplamp Pedal Switch parameter display Applied?	Go to Diagnostic Aids	Go to Step 21
9	1. Turn OFF the ignition. 2. Disconnect C4 of the multifunction switch. 3. Turn ON the ignition, with the engine OFF. 4. Connect a 3-amp fused jumper between the cruise control set/coast switch signal circuit and the ignition 3 voltage circuit. 5. With the scan tool, observe the Cruise Set/Coast Switch parameter. Does the Cruise Set/Coast Switch parameter display On?	Go to Step 22	Go to Step 19
10	1. Turn OFF the ignition. 2. Disconnect C4 of the multifunction switch. 3. Turn ON the ignition, with the engine OFF. 4. Connect a 3-amp fused jumper between the cruise control resume/accel switch signal circuit and the ignition 3 voltage circuit. 5. With the scan tool, observe the Cruise Resume/Accel. Switch parameter. Does the Cruise Resume/Accel. Switch parameter display On?	Go to Step 22	Go to Step 20
11	1. Turn OFF the ignition. 2. Disconnect C4 of the multifunction switch. 3. Turn ON the ignition, with the engine OFF. 4. Connect a test lamp between the ignition 3 voltage circuit and a good ground. Does the test lamp illuminate?	Go to Step 12	Go to Step 1

LTV0500000003959

Fig. 45 Cruise Control Inoperative/Malfunctioning (Part 3 of 6). 2003-06 Avalanche, Escalade, Escalade EXT, Suburban, Tahoe & Yukon

Step	Action	Yes	No
12	1. Connect a 3-amp fused jumper between the ignition 3 voltage circuit and the cruise control on switch signal circuit. 2. With the scan tool, observe the Cruise On/Off Switch parameter. Does the Cruise On/Off Switch parameter display On?	Go to Step 22	Go to Step 18
13	Test the cruise control on switch signal circuit for a short to voltage. Did you find and correct the condition?	Go to Step 29	Go to Step 14
14	1. Turn OFF the ignition. 2. Disconnect C1 of the throttle actuator control (TAC) module. 3. Turn ON the ignition, with the engine OFF. 4. With the scan tool, observe the Cruise On/Off Switch parameter. Does the Cruise On/Off Switch parameter display On?	Go to Step 24	Go to Step 23
15	Test the cruise control set/coast switch signal circuit for a short to ground. Did you find and correct the condition?	Go to Step 29	Go to Step 16
16	Test the cruise control resume/accel switch signal circuit for a short to ground. Did you find and correct the condition?	Go to Step 29	Go to Step 17
17	Test the cruise control on switch signal circuit for a short to ground. Did you find and correct the condition?	Go to Step 29	Go to Step 25
18	Test the cruise control on switch signal circuit for the following: • An open • A short to ground • A high resistance Did you find and correct the condition?	Go to Step 29	Go to Step 23

LTV0500000003960

Fig. 45 Cruise Control Inoperative/Malfunctioning (Part 4 of 6). 2003-06 Avalanche, Escalade, Escalade EXT, Suburban, Tahoe & Yukon

Step	Action	Yes	No
19	Test the cruise control set/coast switch signal circuit for the following: • An open • A short to ground • A high resistance Did you find and correct the condition?	Go to Step 29	Go to Step 23
20	Test the cruise control resume/accel switch signal circuit for the following: • An open • A short to ground • A high resistance Did you find and correct the condition?	Go to Step 29	Go to Step 23
21	Test the center high mounted stop lamp (CHMSL) supply voltage/stop lamp supply voltage circuit for an open or for a high resistance between the stop lamp switch and the TAC module. Did you find and correct the condition?	Go to Step 29	Go to Step 23
22	Inspect for poor connections at the harness connector of the cruise control switch. Did you find and correct the condition?	Go to Step 29	Go to Step 26

LTV0500000003961

Fig. 45 Cruise Control Inoperative/Malfunctioning (Part 5 of 6). 2003-06 Avalanche, Escalade, Escalade EXT, Suburban, Tahoe & Yukon

	Action		Yes	No
23	Inspect for poor connections at the harness connector of the TAC module.			
	Did you find and correct the condition?		Go to Step 29	Go to Step 27
24	Inspect for poor connections at the harness connector of the PCM.			
	Did you find and correct the condition?		Go to Step 29	Go to Step 28
25	Repair the open, the high resistance, or the short to ground in the ignition 3 voltage circuit.			
	Did you complete the repair?		Go to Step 29	--
26	Replace the multifunction switch.			
	Did you complete the replacement?		Go to Step 29	--
27	Replace the TAC module.			
	Did you complete the replacement?		Go to Step 29	--
28	Replace the PCM.			
	Did you complete the replacement?		Go to Step 29	--
29	1. Use the scan tool in order to clear the PCM DTCs. 2. Operate the vehicle within the conditions for cruise control operation.			
	Does the cruise control system operate properly?		System OK	Go to Step 2

LTV0500000003962

Fig. 45 Cruise Control Inoperative/Malfunctioning (Part 6 of 6). 2003-06 Avalanche, Escalade, Escalade EXT, Suburban, Tahoe & Yukon

5	Inspect for poor connections at the harness connector of the instrument cluster.			
	Did you find and correct the condition?		Go to Step 8	Go to Step 7
6	**Important** The replacement PCM must be programmed. Replace the PCM.		--	
	Did you complete the replacement?		Go to Step 8	
7	Replace the instrument panel cluster.			
	Did you complete the replacement?		Go to Step 8	
8	Operate the system in order to verify the repair. Did you correct the condition?		System OK	Go to Step 2

LTV0500000003964

Fig. 46 Cruise Control Indicator Always On (Part 2 of 2). Aztek & Rendezvous w/3.4L & 3.5L Engines

Step	Action	Yes	No
1	Did you perform A Diagnostic System Check - Cruise Control?	Go to Step 2	Go to Diagnostic System Check
2	1. Install a scan tool. 2. Turn ON the ignition, with the engine OFF. 3. With a scan tool, observe the cruise lamp parameter in the IPC inputs. Does the scan tool indicate that the cruise lamp is commanded On?	Go to Step 3	Go to Step 5
3	With a scan tool, observe the cruise parameter in the PCM data list. Does the scan tool indicate that the cruise control is engaged?	Go to Step 4	Go to Step 5
4	Inspect for poor connections at the harness connector of the PCM. Did you find and correct the condition?	Go to Step 8	Go to Step 6

LTV0500000003963

Fig. 46 Cruise Control Indicator Always On (Part 1 of 2). Aztek & Rendezvous w/3.4L & 3.5L Engines

Step	Action	Yes	No
1	Did you perform A Diagnostic System Check - Cruise Control?	Go to Step 2	Go to Diagnostic System Check
2	1. Install a scan tool. 2. With a scan tool, command the cruise control indicator ON. Does the cruise control indicator illuminate?	Go to Step 3	Go to Step 4
3	Inspect for poor connections at the harness connector of the PCM. Did you find and correct the condition?	Go to Step 7	Go to Step 5
4	Inspect for poor connections at the harness connector of the IPC. Did you find and correct the condition?	Go to Step 7	Go to Step 6
5	**Important** Replacement PCM must be programmed. Replace the PCM. Did you find and correct the condition?	Go to Step 7	--
6	Replace the Instrument Panel Cluster. Did you complete the repair?	Go to Step 7	--
7	Operate the system in order to verify the repair. Did you correct the condition?	System OK	Go to Step 2

LTV0500000003965

Fig. 47 Cruise Control Indicator Inoperative. Aztek & Rendezvous w/3.4L & 3.5L Engines

Diagnostic Aids

Important

Perform the following in order to avoid misdiagnosis.

- Inspect for proper operation of the brake lamps.
- Inspect for proper operation of the transmission range switch.
- Inspect throttle linkage for mechanical binding which could cause the system to malfunction.

Step	Action	Value (s)	Yes	No
1	Did you perform the Cruise Control Diagnostic System Check?	--	Go to Step 2	Go to Diagnostic System Check -
2	1. Turn OFF the ignition. 2. Disconnect the cruise control module. 3. Turn ON the ignition, with the engine OFF. 4. Probe the ignition 1 voltage circuit of the cruise control module with a test lamp that is connected to a good ground. Does the test lamp illuminate?	--	Go to Step 3	Go to Step 36
3	Probe the ignition 1 voltage circuit of the cruise control module with a test lamp that is connected to the ground circuit of the cruise control module. Does the test lamp illuminate?	--	Go to Step 4	Go to Step 37
4	1. Turn ON the ignition, with the engine OFF. 2. Turn OFF the cruise control. 3. Probe the cruise control on switch signal, the set/coast switch, and the resume/accelerate switch signal circuits with a test lamp that is connected to a good ground. Does the test lamp illuminate on any of the signal circuits?	--	Go to Step 16	Go to Step 5

LTV0500000003966

Fig. 48 Cruise Control Inoperative/Malfunctioning (Part 1 of 7). Aztek & Rendezvous w/3.4L & 3.5L Engines

Step	Action	Yes	No
5	1. Turn ON the ignition, with the engine OFF. 2. Turn ON the cruise control switch. 3. Probe the cruise control on switch signal circuit with a test lamp that is connected to a good ground. Does the test lamp illuminate?	Go to Step 6	Go to Step 17
6	1. Probe the cruise control set/coast switch signal circuit with a test lamp that is connected to a good ground. 2. Press and hold the SET/COAST button. Does the test lamp illuminate?	Go to Step 7	Go to Step 19
7	1. Probe the cruise control resume/accelerate switch signal circuit with a test lamp that is connected to a good ground. 2. Press and hold the RESUME/ACCEL switch. Does the test lamp illuminate?	Go to Step 8	Go to Step 20
8	Probe the cruise control release signal circuit with a test lamp that is connected to a good ground. Does the test lamp illuminate?	Go to Step 9	Go to Step 21
9	Press the brake pedal while monitoring the test lamp. Does the test lamp illuminate?	Go to Step 22	Go to Step 10
10	Probe the stop lamp signal circuit with a test lamp that is connected to a good ground. Does the test lamp illuminate?	Go to Step 23	Go to Step 11
11	Press the brake pedal while monitoring the test lamp. Does the test lamp illuminate?	Go to Step 12	Go to Step 24
12	Probe the cruise control inhibit signal circuit with a test lamp that is connected to B+. Does the test lamp illuminate?	Go to Step 25	Go to Step 13
13	Use a scan tool in order to command the cruise inhibit/enable OFF. Does the test lamp illuminate?	Go to Step 14	Go to Step 26

LTV0500000003967

Fig. 48 Cruise Control Inoperative/Malfunctioning (Part 2 of 7). Aztek & Rendezvous w/3.4L & 3.5L Engines

Step	Action	Value (s)	Yes	No
14	Probe the cruise control engaged signal circuit with a DMM that is connected to a good ground. Does the voltage measure near the specified value?	B+	Go to Step 15	Go to Step 27
15	Check the speedometer for proper operation. Does the speedometer operate properly?	--	Go to Step 28	Go to Symptoms
16	Test the signal circuit that illuminated the test lamp for a short to voltage. Did you find and correct the condition?	--	Go to Step 43	Go to Step 34
17	Test the cruise control on switch signal circuit for an open or a high resistance. Did you find and correct the condition?	--	Go to Step 43	Go to Step 18
18	Test the ignition 1 voltage circuit for an open or high resistance between the cruise control module and the cruise control switch. Did you find and correct the condition?	--	Go to Step 43	Go to Step 34
19	Test the cruise control set/coast signal circuit for an open or a high resistance. Did you find and correct the condition?	--	Go to Step 43	Go to Step 34
20	Test the cruise control resume/accelerate signal circuit for an open or a high resistance. Did you find and correct the condition?	--	Go to Step 43	Go to Step 34
21	Test the cruise control release switch signal circuit for an open or a high resistance. Did you find and correct the condition?	--	Go to Step 43	Go to Step 29

LTV0500000003968

Fig. 48 Cruise Control Inoperative/Malfunctioning (Part 3 of 7). Aztek & Rendezvous w/3.4L & 3.5L Engines

Step	Action	Yes	No
22	Test the cruise control release switch signal circuit for a short to voltage. Did you find and correct the condition?	Go to Step 43	Go to Step 29
23	Test the stoplamp switch signal circuit for a short to voltage. Did you find and correct the condition?	Go to Step 43	Go to Step 30
24	Test the stoplamp switch signal circuit for an open or a high resistance. Did you find and correct the condition?	Go to Step 43	Go to Step 30
25	Test the cruise inhibit signal circuit for a short to ground. Did you find and correct the condition?	Go to Step 43	Go to Step 33
26	Test the cruise inhibit signal circuit for an open, a high resistance, or a short to voltage. Did you find and correct the condition?	Go to Step 43	Go to Step 33
27	Test the cruise engaged signal circuit for an open, a high resistance, or a short to voltage. Did you find and correct the condition?	Go to Step 43	Go to Step 33
28	Test the speed sensor circuit for an open or a high resistance between the PCM and cruise control module. Did you find and correct the condition?	Go to Step 43	Go to Step 35

LTV0500000003969

Fig. 48 Cruise Control Inoperative/Malfunctioning (Part 4 of 7). Aztek & Rendezvous w/3.4L & 3.5L Engines

29	Inspect the cruise control release switch for proper adjustment.	-	
	Did you find and correct the condition?	Go to Step 43	Go to Step 31
30	Inspect the stoplamp switch for proper adjustment.	-	
	Did you find and correct the condition?	Go to Step 43	Go to Step 32
31	Inspect for poor connections at the harness connector of the cruise control release switch.	-	
	Did you find and correct the condition?	Go to Step 43	Go to Step 38
32	Inspect for poor connections at the harness connector of the stoplamp switch.	-	
	Did you find and correct the condition?	Go to Step 43	Go to Step 39
33	Inspect for poor connections at the harness connector of the PCM.	-	
	Did you find and correct the condition?	Go to Step 43	Go to Step 40
34	Inspect for poor connections at the harness connector of the cruise control switch.	-	
	Did you find and correct the condition?	Go to Step 43	Go to Step 41

LTV0500000003970

Fig. 48 Cruise Control Inoperative/Malfunctioning (Part 5 of 7). Aztek & Rendezvous w/3.4L & 3.5L Engines

35	Inspect for poor connections at the harness connector of the cruise control module.	-	
	Did you find and correct the condition?	Go to Step 43	Go to Step 42
36	Repair the ignition positive voltage circuit of the cruise control module.	-	
	Did you complete the repair?	Go to Step 43	--
37	Repair the ground circuit of the cruise control module.	-	
	Did you complete the repair?	Go to Step 43	
38	Replace the cruise control release switch.	-	
	Did you complete the replacement?	Go to Step 43	
39	Replace the stop lamp switch.	-	
	Did you complete the replacement?	Go to Step 43	--
40	**Important** The PCM must be programed after replacement. Replace the PCM.	-	--
	Did you complete the replacement?	Go to Step 43	

LTV0500000003971

Fig. 48 Cruise Control Inoperative/Malfunctioning (Part 6 of 7). Aztek & Rendezvous w/3.4L & 3.5L Engines

41	Replace the multifunction turn signal lever.	-	--
	Did you complete the replacement?	Go to Step 43	
42	Replace the cruise control module.	-	--
	Did you complete the replacement?	Go to Step 43	
43	Operate the vehicle within the conditions for cruise control operation.		
	Does the cruise control system operate correctly?	System OK	Go to Step 2

LTV0500000003972

Fig. 48 Cruise Control Inoperative/Malfunctioning (Part 7 of 7). Aztek & Rendezvous w/3.4L & 3.5L Engines

Step	Action	Yes	No
1	Did you perform the Diagnostic System Check - Vehicle?	Go to Step 2	Go to Diagnostic System Check
2	Turn the ignition ON, with the engine OFF. Does the cruise indicator illuminate after the instrument panel cluster (IPC) displays test?	Go to Step 3	Test for Intermittent and Poor Connections
3	1. Turn the ignition OFF. 2. Install a scan tool. 3. Turn the ignition ON, with the engine OFF. 4. With the scan tool, observe the Cruise Control parameter in the IPC data list. Does the Cruise Lamp parameter display On?	Go to Step 4	Go to Step 5
4	Replace the powertrain control module (PCM). Did you complete the replacement?	Go to Step 6	--
5	Replace the IPC. Did you complete the replacement?	Go to Step 6	--
6	Operate the system in order to verify the repair. Does the system operate properly?	System OK	Go to Step 2

LTV0500000003973

Fig. 49 Cruise Control Indicator Always On. Aztek & Rendezvous w/3.6L Engine

Step	Action	Yes	No
1	Did you perform the Diagnostic System Check - Vehicle?	Go to Step 2	Go to Diagnostic System Check
2	1. Turn the ignition OFF. 2. Install a scan tool. 3. Turn the ignition ON, with the engine OFF. 4. With the scan tool, command the Cruise Control Lamp Test parameter On, in the instrument panel cluster (IPC) Special Functions. Does the Cruise indicator illuminate in the IPC?	Go to Step 4	Go to Step 3
3	Replace the IPC. Did you complete the replacement?	Go to Step 5	--
4	Replace the powertrain control module (PCM). Did you complete the replacement?	Go to Step 5	--
5	Operate the system in order to verify the repair. Does the system operate properly?	System OK	Go to Step 2

LTV0500000003974

Fig. 50 Cruise Control Indicator Inoperative. Aztek & Rendezvous w/3.6L Engine

SPEED CONTROL SYSTEMS

Diagnostic Aids

Perform the following in order to avoid misdiagnosis:

- Inspect for proper operation of the stop lamps.

- Electromagnetic interference (EMI) on the speed sensor signal circuit may cause erratic cruise control operation.

Conditions for Enabling Cruise Control

- The vehicle speed is greater than 40 km/h (25 mph).
- The vehicle is not in PARK, REVERSE, NEUTRAL, or 1st gear.
- The system voltage is between 12 volts and 16 volts.

Step	Action	Yes	No
1	Did you perform the Diagnostic System Check - Vehicle?	Go to Step 2	Go to Diagnostic System Check
2	1. Install a scan tool. 2. Turn ON the ignition, with the engine OFF. 3. Turn the cruise On/Off switch OFF. 4. With the scan tool, observe the Cruise On/Off Switch parameter in the Powertrain-3.6L Cruise/Traction Data, data list. Does the Cruise On/Off Switch parameter display Off?	Go to Step 3	Go to Step 6
3	1. Turn the cruise On/Off switch ON. 2. With the scan tool, observe the Cruise On/Off Switch parameter. Does the Cruise On/Off Switch parameter display On?	Go to Step 4	Go to Step 7

LTV0500000003975

Fig. 51 Cruise Control Inoperative/Malfunctioning (Part 1 of 4). Aztek & Rendezvous w/3.6L Engine

	Action	Yes	No
10	1. Connect a 3-ampere fused jumper between the ignition 3 voltage circuit and the cruise control on switch signal circuit. 2. With the scan tool, observe the Cruise On/Off Switch parameter. Does the Cruise On/Off Switch parameter display On?	Go to Step 20	Go to Step 16
11	Test the stop lamp signal circuit for an open or for a high resistance between the stop lamp switch and the engine control module (ECM). Did you find and correct the condition?	Go to Step 24	Go to Step 21
12	Test the cruise control on switch signal circuit for a short to voltage. Did you find and correct the condition?	Go to Step 24	Go to Step 21
13	Test the cruise control on switch signal circuit for a short to ground. Did you find and correct the condition?	Go to Step 24	Go to Step 14
14	Test the cruise control set/coast switch signal circuit for a short to ground. Did you find and correct the condition?	Go to Step 24	Go to Step 15
15	Test the cruise control resume/accelerate switch signal circuit for a short to ground. Did you find and correct the condition?	Go to Step 24	Go to Step 19
16	Test the cruise control on switch signal circuit for an open, for a short to ground, or for a high resistance. Did you find and correct the condition?	Go to Step 24	Go to Step 21
17	Test the cruise control set/coast signal circuit for an open, for a short to ground, or for a high resistance. Did you find and correct the condition?	Go to Step 24	Go to Step 20

LTV0500000003977

Fig. 51 Cruise Control Inoperative/Malfunctioning (Part 3 of 4). Aztek & Rendezvous w/3.6L Engine

	Action	Yes	No
4	1. With the scan tool, observe the Cruise Set/Coast Switch parameter in the Powertrain-3.6L Cruise/Traction Data, data list. 2. Turn the cruise On/Off switch ON. 3. Press and hold the cruise control Set/Coast button. Does the Cruise Set/Coast Switch parameter Display On?	Go to Step 5	Go to Step 17
5	1. With the scan tool, observe the Cruise Resume/Accel. Switch parameter in the Powertrain-3.6L Cruise/Traction Data, data list. 2. Press and hold the Resume/Accel switch. Does the Cruise Resume/Accel. Switch parameter Display On?	Go to Step 8	Go to Step 18
6	1. Turn OFF the ignition. 2. Disconnect C4 of the multifunction switch. 3. Turn ON the ignition, with the engine OFF. 4. With the scan tool, observe the Cruise On/Off Switch parameter. Does the Cruise On/Off Switch parameter display On?	Go to Step 12	Go to Step 20
7	1. Turn OFF the ignition. 2. Disconnect C4 of the multifunction switch. 3. Turn ON the ignition, with the engine OFF. 4. Connect a test lamp between the ignition 3 voltage circuit and a good ground. Does the test lamp illuminate?	Go to Step 10	Go to Step 13
8	Do the stop lamps operate properly?	Go to Step 9	Diagnose Stop Lamps Inoperative or to Stop Lamps Always On
9	1. With the scan tool, observe the Stoplamp Pedal Switch parameter in the Powertrain-3.6L Cruise/Traction Data, data list. 2. Depress and hold the brake pedal. Does the Stoplamp Pedal Switch parameter Display Applied?	Go to Diagnostic Aids	Go to Step 11

LTV0500000003976

Fig. 51 Cruise Control Inoperative/Malfunctioning (Part 2 of 4). Aztek & Rendezvous w/3.6L Engine

	Action	Yes	No
18	Test the cruise control resume/accelerate signal circuit for an open, for a short to ground, or for a high resistance. Did you find and correct the condition?	Go to Step 24	Go to Step 20
19	Repair the open, the high resistance, or the short to ground in the ignition 3 voltage circuit. Did you complete the repair?	Go to Step 24	--
20	Inspect for poor connections at the harness connector of the multifunction turn signal lever. Did you find and correct the condition?	Go to Step 24	Go to Step 22
21	Inspect for poor connections at the harness connector of the ECM. Did you find and correct the condition?	Go to Step 24	Go to Step 23
22	Replace the multifunction turn signal lever. Did you complete the replacement?	Go to Step 24	--
23	Replace the ECM. Did you complete the replacement?	Go to Step 24	--
24	Operate the vehicle within the conditions for cruise control operation. Does the cruise control system operate properly?	System OK	Go to Step 2

LTV0500000003978

Fig. 51 Cruise Control Inoperative/Malfunctioning (Part 4 of 4). Aztek & Rendezvous w/3.6L Engine

Diagnostic Aids

To avoid misdiagnosis, inspect for the following:

- Proper operation of brake lamps.
- Proper operation of the clutch system, if equipped with a manual transmission.
- The throttle linkage is not binding.
- The vehicle speed is greater than 40 km/h (25 mph).
- The system voltage is within 9-16 volts.

Electromagnetic interference on the vehicle speed sensor signal circuit may cause erratic cruise control operation.

Step	Action	Values	Yes	No
1	Did you perform the Cruise Control Diagnostic System Check?	--	Go to Step 2	Go to Diagnostic System Check
2	1. Turn OFF the ignition. 2. Disconnect the cruise control module. 3. Turn ON the ignition, with the engine OFF. 4. Connect a test lamp between the ignition 3 voltage circuit and a good ground. Does the test lamp illuminate?	--	Go to Step 3	Go to Step 5
3	Connect a test lamp between the ignition 3 voltage circuit and the ground circuit of the cruise control module. Does the test lamp illuminate?	--	Go to Step 4	Go to Step 31
4	1. Turn the cruise control On/Off switch OFF. 2. Connect a test lamp between a good ground and each of the following circuits: - The cruise control ON switch signal circuit - The cruise control set/coast switch signal circuit - The cruise control resume/accel switch signal circuit Does the test lamp illuminate for any of the signal circuits listed above?	--	Go to Step 16	Go to Step 6

Fig. 52 Cruise Control Inoperative/Malfunctioning (Part 1 of 5). Blazer, Jimmy, Sonoma & S10

Step	Action	Yes	No
5	1. Turn the cruise control On/Off switch OFF. 2. Connect a test lamp between battery voltage and each of the following circuits: - The cruise control ON switch signal circuit - The cruise control set/coast switch signal circuit - The cruise control resume/accel switch signal circuit Does the test lamp illuminate for any of the signal circuits listed above?	Go to Step 17	Go to Step 29
6	1. Turn the cruise control On/Off switch ON. 2. Connect a test lamp between the cruise control ON switch signal circuit and a good ground. Does the test lamp illuminate?	Go to Step 7	Go to Step 18
7	1. Connect a test lamp between the cruise control set/coast switch signal circuit and a good ground. 2. With the cruise control On/Off switch ON, press and hold the Set/Coast switch. Does the test lamp illuminate?	Go to Step 8	Go to Step 20
8	1. Connect a test lamp between the cruise control resume/accelerate switch signal circuit and a good ground. 2. With the cruise control On/Off switch ON, press and hold the Resume/Accel switch. Does the test lamp illuminate?	Go to Step 9	Go to Step 21
9	1. Connect a test lamp between the CHMSL supply voltage/stop lamp supply voltage circuit and a good ground. 2. Depress the brake pedal. Does the test lamp illuminate?	Go to Step 10	Go to Step 32
10	Is the vehicle equipped with a manual transmission?	Go to Step 12	Go to Step 11
11	Connect a test lamp between the TCC brake switch/Cruise control release signal circuit and a good ground. Does the test lamp illuminate?	Go to Step 13	Go to Step 30
12	Connect a test lamp between the clutch start switch signal circuit and a good ground. Does the test lamp illuminate?	Go to Step 13	Go to Step 23

Fig. 52 Cruise Control Inoperative/Malfunctioning (Part 2 of 5). Blazer, Jimmy, Sonoma & S10

Step	Action	Values	Yes	No
13	Connect a DMM between the cruise control engaged signal circuit and a good ground. Does the DMM display near the specified voltage?	B+	Go to Step 14	Go to Step 22
14	Connect a DMM between the vehicle speed signal circuit and a good ground. Does the DMM display near the specified voltage?	B+	Go to Diagnostic Aids	Go to Step 15
15	Test the vehicle speed signal circuit for an open or for a high resistance. Did you find and correct the condition?	--	Go to Step 37	Go to Step 28
16	Test the signal circuit that illuminated the test lamp for a short to voltage. Did you find and correct the condition?	--	Go to Step 37	Go to Step 27
17	Test the signal circuit that illuminated the test lamp for a short to ground. Did you find and correct the condition?	--	Go to Step 37	Go to Step 27
18	Test the cruise control on/off switch signal circuit for an open or for a high resistance. Did you find and correct the condition?	--	Go to Step 37	Go to Step 19
19	Test the ignition 3 voltage circuit for an open or for a high resistance between SP 200 and the multifunction switch. Did you find and correct the condition?	--	Go to Step 37	Go to Step 27
20	Test the cruise control set/coast switch signal circuit for an open or for a high resistance. Did you find and correct the condition?	--	Go to Step 37	Go to Step 27
21	Test the cruise control resume/accel switch signal circuit for an open or for a high resistance. Did you find and correct the condition?	--	Go to Step 37	Go to Step 27

Fig. 52 Cruise Control Inoperative/Malfunctioning (Part 3 of 5). Blazer, Jimmy, Sonoma & S10

Step	Action	Yes	No
22	Test the cruise control engaged signal circuit for an open, for a high resistance, or for a short to ground. Did you find and correct the condition?	Go to Step 37	Go to Step 26
23	Test the clutch start switch signal circuit for an open or for a high resistance between the clutch start switch and the cruise control module. Did you find and correct the condition?	Go to Step 37	Go to Step 24
24	Test the TCC brake switch/Cruise control release signal circuit for an open or for a high resistance between the stop lamp switch and the clutch start switch. Did you find and correct the condition?	Go to Step 37	Go to Step 25
25	Inspect for poor connections at the harness connector of the clutch start switch. Did you find and correct the condition?	Go to Step 37	Go to Step 34
26	Inspect for poor connections at the harness connector of the PCM. Did you find and correct the condition?	Go to Step 37	Go to Step 33
27	Inspect for poor connections at the harness connector of the multifunction switch. Did you find and correct the condition?	Go to Step 37	Go to Step 35
28	Inspect for poor connections at the harness connector of the cruise control module. Did you find and correct the condition?	Go to Step 37	Go to Step 36

Fig. 52 Cruise Control Inoperative/Malfunctioning (Part 4 of 5). Blazer, Jimmy, Sonoma & S10

Step	Action	Yes	No
29	Repair the open, the high resistance, or the short to ground in the ignition 3 voltage circuit. Did you complete the repair?	Go to Step 37	--
30	Repair the open or the high resistance in the TCC brake switch/Cruise control release signal circuit between S 138 and the cruise control module. Did you complete the repair?	Go to Step 37	--
31	Repair the open or the high resistance in the ground circuit of the cruise control module. Did you complete the repair?	Go to Step 37	--
32	Repair the open or the high resistance in the CHMSL supply voltage/stop lamp supply voltage circuit Did you complete the repair?	Go to Step 37	--
33	**Important:** Program the replacement PCM. Replace the PCM. Did you complete the replacement?	Go to Step 37	--
34	Replace the clutch start switch. Did you complete the replacement?	Go to Step 37	--
35	Replace the multifunction switch. Did you complete the replacement?	Go to Step 37	--
36	Replace the cruise control module. Did you complete the replacement?	Go to Step 37	--
37	Operate the vehicle within the conditions for cruise control operation. Does the cruise control system operate correctly?	System OK	Go to Step 2

LTV0500000003983

Fig. 52 Cruise Control Inoperative/Malfunctioning (Part 5 of 5). Blazer, Jimmy, Sonoma & S10

Step	Action	Yes	No
1	Did you perform the Cruise Control Diagnostic System Check?	Go to Step 2	Go to Diagnostic System Check -
2	1. Turn OFF the ignition. 2. Install a scan tool. 3. Turn ON the ignition, with the engine OFF. 4. With the scan tool, Command the Cruise Control Lamp Test parameter ON, in the instrument panel cluster (IPC) Output Controls. Does the Cruise indicator illuminate in the IPC?	Go to Step 3	Go to Step 4
3	Inspect for poor connections at the harness connector of the powertrain control module (PCM). Did you find and correct the condition?	Go to Step 7	Go to Step 6
4	Inspect for poor connections at the harness connector of the IPC. Did you find and correct the condition?	Go to Step 7	Go to Step 5
5	**Important:** Program the replacement IPC. Replace the IPC. Did you complete the replacement?	Go to Step 7	--
6	**Important:** Program the replacement PCM. Replace the PCM. Did you complete the replacement?	Go to Step 7	--
7	Operate the system in order to verify the repair. Does the system operate properly?	System OK	Go to Step 2

LTV0500000003985

Fig. 54 Cruise Control Indicator Inoperative. 2002 Bravada, Envoy & TrailBlazer

Step	Action	Yes	No
1	Did you perform A Diagnostic System Check- Cruise Control?	Go to Step 2	Go to Diagnostic System Check -
2	1. Install a scan tool. 2. Turn On the ignition, with the engine OFF. 3. With a scan tool, observer the Cruise Lamp parameter in the IPC data List. Does the scan tool indicate that the cruise lamp is commanded On?	Go to Step 3	Go to Step 4
3	With a scan tool, observe the Cruise parameter in the PCM data list. Does the scan tool indicate that the cruise control is engaged?	Go to Diagnostic System Check	Go to Step 4
4	Inspect for poor connections at the harness connector of the instrument cluster. Did you find and correct the condition?	Go to Step 6	Go to Step 5
5	**Important** The IPC must be reprogrammed Replace the instrument panel cluster. Did you complete the replacement?	Go to Step 6	--
6	Operate the system in order to verify the repair. Did you correct the condition?	System OK	Go to Step 2

LTV0500000003984

Fig. 53 Cruise Control Indicator Always On. 2002 Bravada, Envoy & TrailBlazer

Diagnostic Aids

Important

Perform the following in order to avoid misdiagnosis.

- Inspect for proper operation of brake lamps and clutch switch, if equipped.
- EMI on the speed sensor signal circuit may cause erratic cruise control operation.

Conditions for Enabling Cruise Control

The vehicle speed is greater than 40 km/h (25 mph).

Step	Action	Yes	No
1	Did you perform A Diagnostic System Check - Cruise Control?	Go to Step 2	Go to Diagnostic System Check
2	1. Connect a scan tool. 2. Turn ON the ignition, with the engine OFF. 3. Monitor the Cruise On switch parameter in the powertrain control module (PCM) data list. 4. Turn ON the cruise control switch. Did the scan tool parameter change state?	Go to Step 3	Go to Step 7
3	1. Observe the cruise control set/coast parameter in the PCM data list. 2. Press the cruise control set button. Did the cruise control set/coast parameter change state?	Go to Step 4	Go to Step 11
4	1. Observe the cruise control resume/accelerate parameter in the PCM data list. 2. Press the Resume/Accelerate switch. Did the cruise control resume/accelerate parameter change state?	Go to Step 5	Go to Step 12
5	1. Observe the stop lamp switch parameter in the PCM data list. 2. Press the brake pedal. Did the stop lamp switch parameter change state?	Go to Step 6	Go to Step 8

LTV0500000003986

Fig. 55 Cruise Control Inoperative/Malfunctioning (Part 1 of 4). 2002 Bravada, Envoy & TrailBlazer

Step	Action	Yes	No
6	1. Observe the TCC/Brake switch parameter in the PCM data list. 2. Press the brake pedal. Did the cruise release switch parameter change state?	Go to Step 7	Go to Step 9
7	1. Turn OFF the ignition. 2. Disconnect the multifunction turn signal lever. 3. Turn ON the ignition, with the engine OFF. 4. Probe the multifunction turn signal lever harness connector ignition positive voltage circuit with a test lamp connected to a good ground. Did the test lamp illuminate?	Go to Step 10	Go to Step 17
8	1. Turn OFF the ignition. 2. Disconnect the stop lamp switch harness connector. 3. Turn ON the ignition, with the engine OFF. 4. Probe the stop lamp switch harness connector battery positive voltage feed circuit with a test lamp connected to a good ground. Did the test lamp illuminate?	Go to Step 13	Go to Step 18
9	1. Turn OFF the ignition. 2. Disconnect the TCC/Brake switch harness connector. 3. Turn ON the ignition, with the engine OFF. 4. Probe the TCC/Brake switch harness connector ignition positive voltage circuit with a test lamp connected to a good ground. Did the test lamp illuminate?	Go to Step 15	Go to Step 19
10	Test the cruise control ON switch signal circuit for a open, high resistance, short to ground or short to voltage. Did you find and correct the condition?	Go to Step 28	Go to Step 22
11	Test the cruise control Set/Coast signal circuit for a open, high resistance, short to ground or short to voltage Did you find and correct the condition?	Go to Step 28	Go to Step 22
12	Test the cruise control Resume/Accelerate signal circuit for a open, high resistance, short to ground or short to voltage. Did you find and correct the condition?	Go to Step 28	Go to Step 2

LTV0500000003987

Fig. 55 Cruise Control Inoperative/Malfunctioning (Part 2 of 4). 2002 Bravada, Envoy & TrailBlazer

Step	Action	Yes	No
13	Test the stop lamp switch signal circuit for a open, high resistance, short to ground or short to voltage. Did you find and correct the condition?	Go to Step 28	Go to Step 14
14	Check the stop lamp switch for proper adjustment. Did you find and correct the condition?	Go to Step 28	Go to Step 20
15	Test the TCC/Brake switch signal circuit for a open, high resistance, short to ground or short to voltage. Did you find and correct the condition?	Go to Step 28	Go to Step 16
16	Check the TCC/Brake switch for proper adjustment. Did you find and correct the condition?	Go to Step 28	Go to Step 21
17	Repair the open, high resistance or short to ground in the multifunction turn signal lever ignition positive voltage circuit. Did you complete the repair?	Go to Step 28	--
18	Repair the open, high resistance or short to ground in the stop lamp switch battery positive voltage circuit. Did you complete the repair?	Go to Step 28	--
19	Repair the open, high resistance or short to ground in the TCC/Brake switch battery positive voltage circuit. Did you complete the repair?	Go to Step 28	--

LTV0500000003988

Fig. 55 Cruise Control Inoperative/Malfunctioning (Part 3 of 4). 2002 Bravada, Envoy & TrailBlazer

Step	Action	Yes	No
20	Inspect for poor connections at the harness connector of the stop lamp switch. Did you find and correct the condition?	Go to Step 28	Go to Step 24
21	Inspect for poor connections at the harness connector of the TCC/Brake switch. Did you find and correct the condition?	Go to Step 28	Go to Step 25
22	Inspect for poor connections at the harness connector of the multifunction turn signal lever. Did you find and correct the condition?	Go to Step 28	Go to Step 26
23	Inspect for poor connections at the harness connector of the PCM. Did you find and correct the condition?	Go to Step 28	Go to Step 27
24	Replace the stoplamp switch. Did you complete the repair?	Go to Step 28	--
25	Replace the TCC/Brake switch. Did you complete the repair?	Go to Step 28	--
26	Replace the multifunction turn signal lever Did you complete the repair?	Go to Step 28	--
27	**Important** The PCM must be reprogrammed after replacement. Replace the PCM. Did you complete the replacement?	Go to Step 28	--
28	Operate the vehicle with in the conditions for cruise control operation. Does the cruise control system operate properly?	System OK	Go to Step 2

LTV0500000003989

Fig. 55 Cruise Control Inoperative/Malfunctioning (Part 4 of 4). 2002 Bravada, Envoy & TrailBlazer

Step	Action	Yes	No
1	Did you perform the Cruise Control Diagnostic System Check?	Go to Step 2	Go to Diagnostic System Check
2	Turn ON the ignition, with the engine OFF. Does the Cruise indicator illuminate after the IPC displays test?	Go to Step 3	Test for Intermittent and Poor Connections
3	1. Turn OFF the ignition. 2. Install a scan tool. 3. Turn ON the ignition, with the engine OFF. 4. With the scan tool, observe the Cruise Control parameter in the IPC data list. Does the Cruise Lamp parameter display On?	Go to Step 6	Go to Step 7
4	Inspect for poor connections at the harness connector of the powertrain control module (PCM). Did you find and correct the condition?	Go to Step 8	Go to Step 6
5	Inspect for poor connections at the harness connector of the instrument panel cluster (IPC). Did you find and correct the condition?	Go to Step 8	Go to Step 7

LTV0500000003990

Fig. 56 Cruise Control Indicator Always On (Part 1 of 2). 2003-04 Bravada, Envoy, Rainier & TrailBlazer

Step	Action	Yes	No
6	**Important** Program the replacement PCM. Replace the PCM. Did you complete the replacement?	Go to Step 8	--
7	**Important** Program the replacement IPC. Replace the IPC. Did you complete the replacement?	Go to Step 8	--
8	Operate the system in order to verify the repair. Does the system operate properly?	System OK	Go to Step 2

LTV0500000003991

Fig. 56 Cruise Control Indicator Always On (Part 2 of 2). 2003-04 Bravada, Envoy, Rainier & TrailBlazer

Step	Action	Yes	No
1	Did you perform the Cruise Control Diagnostic System Check?	Go to Step 2	Go to Diagnostic System Check -
2	1. Turn OFF the ignition. 2. Install a scan tool. 3. Turn ON the ignition, with the engine OFF. 4. With the scan tool, Command the Cruise Control Lamp Test parameter ON, in the IPC Output Controls. Does the Cruise indicator illuminate in the instrument panel cluster (IPC)?	Go to Step 3	Go to Step 4
3	Inspect for poor connections at the harness connector of the powertrain control module (PCM). Did you find and correct the condition?	Go to Step 7	Go to Step 6
4	Inspect for poor connections at the harness connector of the IPC. Did you find and correct the condition?	Go to Step 7	Go to Step 5

LTV0500000003992

Fig. 57 Cruise Control Indicator Inoperative (Part 1 of 2). 2003-04 Bravada, Envoy, Rainier & TrailBlazer

Diagnostic Aids

Perform the following in order to avoid misdiagnosis:

- Inspect for proper operation of the stop lamps.

- EMI on the speed sensor signal circuit may cause erratic cruise control operation.

Conditions for Enabling Cruise Control

- The vehicle speed is greater than 40 km/h (25 mph).
- The vehicle is not in PARK, REVERSE, NEUTRAL, or 1st gear.
- The system voltage is between 12 volts and 16 volts.

Step	Action	Yes	No
1	Did you perform the Cruise Control Diagnostic System Check?	Go to Step 2	Go to Diagnostic System Check
2	1. Install a scan tool. 2. Turn ON the ignition, with the engine OFF. 3. Press the cruise On/Off switch Off. 4. With the scan tool, observe the Cruise On/Off Switch parameter in the powertrain control module (PCM) Cruise Control Data data list. Does the Cruise On/Off Switch parameter display Off?	Go to Step 3	Go to Step 6
3	1. Press the cruise On/Off switch On. 2. With the scan tool, observe the Cruise On/Off Switch parameter. Does the Cruise On/Off Switch parameter display On?	Go to Step 4	Go to Step 7

LTV0500000003994

Fig. 58 Cruise Control Inoperative/Malfunctioning (Part 1 of 3). 2003-04 Bravada, Envoy, Rainier & TrailBlazer w/4.2L Engine

Step	Action	Yes	No
5	**Important** Program the replacement IPC. Replace the IPC. Did you complete the replacement?	--	Go to Step 7
6	**Important** Program the replacement PCM. Replace the PCM. Did you complete the replacement?	--	Go to Step 7
7	Operate the system in order to verify the repair. Does the system operate properly?	System OK	Go to Step 2

LTV0500000003993

Fig. 57 Cruise Control Indicator Inoperative (Part 2 of 2). 2003-04 Bravada, Envoy, Rainier & TrailBlazer

Step	Action	Yes	No
4	1. With the scan tool, observe the Cruise Set/Coast Switch parameter in the PCM Cruise Control Data data list. 2. Press the cruise control Set/Coast button. Does the Cruise Set/Coast Switch parameter Display On?	Go to Step 5	Go to Step 13
5	1. With the scan tool, observe the Cruise Resume/Accel. Switch parameter in the PCM Cruise Control Data data list. 2. Press the Resume/Accel switch. Does the Cruise Resume/Accel. Switch parameter Display On?	Go to Diagnostic Aids	Go to Step 14
6	1. Turn OFF the ignition. 2. Disconnect the steering wheel column connector. 3. Turn ON the ignition, with the engine OFF. 4. With the scan tool, observe the Cruise On/Off Switch parameter. Does the Cruise On/Off Switch parameter display On?	Go to Step 8	Go to Step 16
7	1. Turn OFF the ignition. 2. Disconnect the steering wheel column connector. 3. Turn ON the ignition, with the engine OFF. 4. Connect a test lamp between the ignition 3 voltage circuit and a good ground. Does the test lamp illuminate?	Go to Step 12	Go to Step 9
8	Test the cruise control on switch signal circuit for a short to voltage. Did you find and correct the condition?	Go to Step 20	Go to Step 17
9	Test the cruise control on switch signal circuit for a short to ground. Did you find and correct the condition?	Go to Step 20	Go to Step 10
10	Test the cruise control set/coast switch signal circuit for a short to ground. Did you find and correct the condition?	Go to Step 20	Go to Step 11

LTV0500000003995

Fig. 58 Cruise Control Inoperative/Malfunctioning (Part 2 of 3). 2003-04 Bravada, Envoy, Rainier & TrailBlazer w/4.2L Engine

11	Test the cruise control resume/accelerate switch signal circuit for a short to ground. Did you find and correct the condition?	Go to Step 20	Go to Step 15
12	Test the cruise control on switch signal circuit for an open or for a high resistance. Did you find and correct the condition?	Go to Step 20	Go to Step 16
13	Test the cruise control Set/Coast signal circuit for an open or for a high resistance. Did you find and correct the condition?	Go to Step 20	Go to Step 16
14	Test the cruise control Resume/Accelerate signal circuit for an open or for a high resistance. Did you find and correct the condition?	Go to Step 20	Go to Step 16
15	Repair the open, the high resistance, or the short to ground in the ignition 3 voltage circuit. Did you complete the repair?	Go to Step 20	--
16	Inspect for poor connections at the harness connector of the multifunction turn signal lever. Did you find and correct the condition?	Go to Step 20	Go to Step 18
17	Inspect for poor connections at the harness connector of the PCM. Did you find and correct the condition?	Go to Step 20	Go to Step 19
18	Replace the multifunction turn signal lever. Did you complete the replacement?	Go to Step 20	--
19	**Important:** Program the replacement PCM. Replace the PCM. Did you complete the replacement?	Go to Step 20	--
20	Operate the vehicle within the conditions for cruise control operation. Does the cruise control system operate properly?	System OK	Go to Step 2

LTV0500000003996

Fig. 58 Cruise Control Inoperative/Malfunctioning (Part 3 of 3). 2003-04 Bravada, Envoy, Rainier & TrailBlazer w/4.2L Engine

2	1. Install a scan tool. 2. Turn the ignition ON, with the engine OFF. 3. Turn the cruise control On/Off switch OFF. 4. With the scan tool, observe the Cruise On/Off Switch parameter in the powertrain control module (PCM) Cruise Control Data data list. Does the Cruise On/Off Switch parameter display Off?	Go to Step 4	Go to Step 3
3	1. Turn the ignition OFF. 2. Disconnect C4 of the multifunction switch. 3. Turn the ignition ON, with the engine OFF. 4. With the scan tool, observe the Cruise On/Off Switch parameter. Does the Cruise On/Off Switch parameter display Off?	Go to Step 22	Go to Step 13
4	1. Turn the cruise control On/Off switch ON. 2. With the scan tool, observe the Cruise On/Off Switch parameter. Does the Cruise On/Off Switch parameter display On?	Go to Step 5	Go to Step 11
5	1. With the scan tool, observe the Cruise Set/Coast Switch parameter in the PCM Cruise Control Data data list. 2. Turn the cruise control On/Off switch ON. 3. Press and hold the cruise control Set/Coast button. Does the Cruise Set/Coast Switch parameter Display On?	Go to Step 6	Go to Step 9
6	1. With the scan tool, observe the Cruise Resume/Accel. Switch parameter in the PCM Cruise Control Data data list. 2. Press and hold the Resume/Accel switch. Does the Cruise Resume/Accel. Switch parameter Display On?	Go to Step 7	Go to Step 10
7	Do the stop lamps operate properly?	Go to Step 8	Diagnose Stop Lamps Inoperative
8	1. With the scan tool, observe the Stoplamp Pedal Switch parameter in the PCM Cruise Control Data data list. 2. Depress and hold the brake pedal. Does the Stoplamp Pedal Switch parameter Display Applied?	Go to Diagnostic Aids	Go to Step 21

LTV0500000003998

Fig. 59 Cruise Control Inoperative/Malfunctioning (Part 2 of 5). 2003-04 Bravada, Envoy, Rainier & TrailBlazer w/5.3L Engine

Diagnostic Aids

Perform the following in order to avoid a misdiagnosis:

- Inspect for proper operation of the brake lamps.

- EMI on the vehicle speed sensor signal circuit may cause erratic cruise control operation.

Conditions for Enabling Cruise Control

- The vehicle speed is greater than 40 km/h (25 mph).
- The vehicle is not in PARK, REVERSE, NEUTRAL or 1st gear.
- The system voltage is within 12 volts and 16 volts.

Test Description

The numbers below refer to the step numbers on the diagnostic table.

8. This step tests the center high mounted stop lamp (CHMSL) supply voltage/stop lamp supply voltage circuit for an open or for a high resistance between the stop lamp switch and the throttle actuator control (TAC) module.

9. This step tests the cruise control set/coast switch signal circuit for an open or for a high resistance.

10. This step tests the cruise control resume/accel switch signal circuit for an open or for a high resistance.

11. This step tests the ignition 3 voltage circuit for an open, for a short to ground, or for a high resistance.

29. DTCs will set in the powertrain control module (PCM) when you perform this table.

Step	Action	Yes	No
1	Did you perform the Diagnostic System Check - Cruise Control?	Go to Step 2	Go to Diagnostic System Check

LTV0500000003997

Fig. 59 Cruise Control Inoperative/Malfunctioning (Part 1 of 5). 2003-04 Bravada, Envoy, Rainier & TrailBlazer w/5.3L Engine

9	1. Turn the ignition OFF. 2. Disconnect C4 of the multifunction switch. 3. Turn the ignition ON, with the engine OFF. 4. Connect a 3-ampere fused jumper between the cruise control set/coast switch signal circuit and the ignition 3 voltage circuit. 5. With the scan tool, observe the Cruise Set/Coast Switch parameter. Does the Cruise Set/Coast Switch parameter Display On?	Go to Step 22	Go to Step 19
10	1. Turn the ignition OFF. 2. Disconnect C4 of the multifunction switch. 3. Turn the ignition ON, with the engine OFF. 4. Connect a 3-ampere fused jumper between the cruise control resume/accel switch signal circuit and the ignition 3 voltage circuit. 5. With the scan tool, observe the Cruise Resume/Accel. Switch parameter. Does the Cruise Resume/Accel. Switch parameter Display On?	Go to Step 22	Go to Step 20
11	1. Turn the ignition OFF. 2. Disconnect C4 of the multifunction switch. 3. Turn the ignition ON, with the engine OFF. 4. Connect a test lamp between the ignition 3 voltage circuit and a good ground. Does the test lamp illuminate?	Go to Step 12	Go to Step 15
12	1. Connect a 3-ampere fused jumper between the ignition 3 voltage circuit and the cruise control on switch signal circuit. 2. With the scan tool, observe the Cruise On/Off Switch parameter. Does the Cruise On/Off Switch parameter display On?	Go to Step 22	Go to Step 18
13	Test the cruise control on switch signal circuit for a short to voltage. Did you find and correct the condition?	Go to Step 29	Go to Step 14
14	1. Turn the ignition OFF. 2. Disconnect C1 of the TAC module. 3. Turn the ignition ON, with the engine OFF. 4. With the scan tool, observe the Cruise On/Off Switch parameter. Does the Cruise On/Off Switch parameter display On?	Go to Step 24	Go to Step 23

LTV0500000003999

Fig. 59 Cruise Control Inoperative/Malfunctioning (Part 3 of 5). 2003-04 Bravada, Envoy, Rainier & TrailBlazer w/5.3L Engine

15	Test the cruise control set/coast switch signal circuit for a short to ground. Did you find and correct the condition?	Go to Step 29	Go to Step 16
16	Test the cruise control resume/accel switch signal circuit for a short to ground. Did you find and correct the condition?	Go to Step 29	Go to Step 17
17	Test the cruise control on switch signal circuit for a short to ground. Did you find and correct the condition?	Go to Step 29	Go to Step 25
18	Test the cruise control on switch signal circuit for an open or for a high resistance. Did you find and correct the condition?	Go to Step 29	Go to Step 23
19	Test the cruise control set/coast switch signal circuit for an open or for a high resistance. Did you find and correct the condition?	Go to Step 29	Go to Step 23
20	Test the cruise control resume/accel switch signal circuit for an open or for a high resistance. Did you find and correct the condition?	Go to Step 29	Go to Step 23

LTV0500000004000

Fig. 59 Cruise Control Inoperative/Malfunctioning (Part 4 of 5). 2003-04 Bravada, Envoy, Rainier & TrailBlazer w/5.3L Engine

Step	Action	Yes	No
1	Did you perform the Diagnostic System Check - Vehicle?	Go to Step 2	Go to Diagnostic System Check
2	Turn ON the ignition, with the engine OFF. Does the Cruise indicator illuminate after the instrument panel cluster (IPC) displays test?	Go to Step 3	Test for Intermittent and Poor Connections
3	1. Turn OFF the ignition. 2. Install a scan tool. 3. Turn ON the ignition, with the engine OFF. 4. With the scan tool, observe the Cruise Control parameter in the IPC data list. Does the Cruise Lamp parameter display On?	Go to Step 6	Go to Step 7
4	Inspect for poor connections at the harness connector of the engine control module (ECM). Did you find and correct the condition?	Go to Step 8	Go to Step 6

LTV0500000004002

Fig. 60 Cruise Control Indicator Always On (Part 1 of 2). 2005-06 Envoy, Rainier & TrailBlazer Less 4.2L Engine

Step	Action	Yes	No
1	Did you perform the Diagnostic System Check - Vehicle?	Go to Step 2	Go to Diagnostic System Check
2	Turn ON the ignition, with the engine OFF. Does the Cruise indicator illuminate after the instrument panel cluster (IPC) displays test?	Go to Step 3	Test for Intermittent and Poor Connections
3	1. Turn OFF the ignition. 2. Install a scan tool. 3. Turn ON the ignition, with the engine OFF. 4. With the scan tool, observe the Cruise Control parameter in the instrument panel cluster (IPC) data list. Does the Cruise Lamp parameter display On?	Go to Step 6	Go to Step 7
4	Inspect for poor connections at the harness connector of the powertrain control module (PCM). Did you find and correct the condition?	Go to Step 8	Go to Step 6

LTV0500000004004

Fig. 61 Cruise Control Indicator Always On. (Part 1 of 2). 2005-06 Envoy, Rainier & TrailBlazer w/4.2L Engine

21	Test the center high mounted stop lamp (CHMSL) supply voltage/stop lamp supply voltage circuit for an open or for a high resistance between the stop lamp switch and the throttle actuator control (TAC) module. Did you find and correct the condition?	Go to Step 29	Go to Step 23
22	Inspect for poor connections at the harness connector of the cruise control switch. Did you find and correct the condition?	Go to Step 29	Go to Step 26
23	Inspect for poor connections at the harness connector of the TAC module. Did you find and correct the condition?	Go to Step 29	Go to Step 27
24	Inspect for poor connections at the harness connector of the PCM. Did you find and correct the condition?	Go to Step 29	Go to Step 28
25	Repair the open, the high resistance, or the short to ground in the ignition 3 voltage circuit. Did you complete the repair?	Go to Step 29	--
26	Replace the cruise control switch. Did you complete the replacement?	Go to Step 29	--
27	Replace the TAC module. Did you complete the replacement?	Go to Step 29	--
28	**Important:** Program the replacement PCM. Replace the PCM. Did you complete the replacement?	Go to Step 29	--
29	1. Use the scan tool in order to clear the PCM DTCs. 2. Operate the vehicle within the conditions for cruise control operation. Does the cruise control system operate properly?	System OK	Go to Step 2

LTV0500000004001

Fig. 59 Cruise Control Inoperative/Malfunctioning (Part 5 of 5). 2003-04 Bravada, Envoy, Rainier & TrailBlazer w/5.3L Engine

5	Inspect for poor connections at the harness connector of the IPC. Did you find and correct the condition?	Go to Step 8	Go to Step 7
6	Replace the ECM. Did you complete the replacement?	Go to Step 8	--
7	Replace the IPC. Did you complete the replacement?	Go to Step 8	--
8	Operate the system in order to verify the repair. Does the system operate properly?	System OK	Go to Step 2

LTV0500000004003

Fig. 60 Cruise Control Indicator Always On (Part 2 of 2). 2005-06 Envoy, Rainier & TrailBlazer Less 4.2L Engine

5	Inspect for poor connections at the harness connector of the IPC. Did you find and correct the condition?	Go to Step 8	Go to Step 7
6	Replace the PCM. Did you complete the replacement?	Go to Step 8	--
7	Replace the IPC. Did you complete the replacement?	Go to Step 8	--
8	Operate the system in order to verify the repair. Does the system operate properly?	System OK	Go to Step 2

LTV0500000004005

Fig. 61 Cruise Control Indicator Always On. (Part 2 of 2). 2005-06 Envoy, Rainier & TrailBlazer w/4.2L Engine

Step	Action	Yes	No
1	Did you perform the Diagnostic System Check - Vehicle?	Go to Step 2	Go to Diagnostic System Check
2	1. Turn OFF the ignition. 2. Install a scan tool. 3. Turn ON the ignition, with the engine OFF. 4. With the scan tool, Command the Cruise Control Lamp Test parameter ON, in the instrument panel cluster (IPC) output controls. Does the Cruise indicator illuminate in the IPC?	Go to Step 3	Go to Step 4
3	Inspect for poor connections at the harness connector of the engine control module (ECM). Did you find and correct the condition?	Go to Step 7	Go to Step 6
4	Inspect for poor connections at the harness connector of the IPC. Did you find and correct the condition?	Go to Step 7	Go to Step 5

LTV0500000004006

Fig. 62   Cruise Control Indicator Inoperative (Part 1 of 2). 2005-06 Envoy, Rainier & TrailBlazer Less 4.2L Engine

Step	Action	Yes	No
5	Replace the IPC. Did you complete the replacement?	Go to Step 7	--
6	Replace the ECM. Did you complete the replacement?	Go to Step 7	--
7	Operate the system in order to verify the repair. Does the system operate properly?	System OK	Go to Step 2

LTV0500000004007

Fig. 62   Cruise Control Indicator Inoperative (Part 2 of 2). 2005-06 Envoy, Rainier & TrailBlazer Less 4.2L Engine

Step	Action	Yes	No
1	Did you perform the Diagnostic System Check - Vehicle?	Go to Step 2	Go to Diagnostic System Check
2	1. Turn OFF the ignition. 2. Install a scan tool. 3. Turn ON the ignition, with the engine OFF. 4. With the scan tool, Command the Cruise Control Lamp Test parameter ON, in the instrument panel cluster (IPC) Output Controls. Does the Cruise indicator illuminate in the IPC?	Go to Step 3	Go to Step 4
3	Inspect for poor connections at the harness connector of the powertrain control module (PCM). Did you find and correct the condition?	Go to Step 7	Go to Step 6

LTV0500000004008

Fig. 63   Cruise Control Inoperative (Part 1 of 2). 2005-06 Envoy, Rainier & TrailBlazer w/4.2L Engine

Step	Action	Yes	No
4	Inspect for poor connections at the harness connector of the IPC. Did you find and correct the condition?	Go to Step 7	Go to Step 5
5	Replace the IPC. Did you complete the replacement?	Go to Step 7	--
6	Replace the PCM. Did you complete the replacement?	Go to Step 7	--
7	Operate the system in order to verify the repair. Does the system operate properly?	System OK	Go to Step 2

LTV0500000004009

Fig. 63   Cruise Control Inoperative (Part 2 of 2). 2005-06 Envoy, Rainier & TrailBlazer w/4.2L Engine

Diagnostic Aids

- Inspect for proper operation of the stop lamps.

- Ensure that the following cruise control switches are not stuck or sticking in the engaged position:
  - Set/Coast
  - Resume/Accel

Conditions for Enabling Cruise Control

- The vehicle speed is greater than 40 km/h (25 mph).
- The vehicle is not in PARK, REVERSE, NEUTRAL, or 1st gear.
- The system voltage is between 12-16 volts.

Step	Action	Yes	No
1	Did you perform the Diagnostic System Check - Vehicle?	Go to Step 2	Go to Diagnostic System Check
2	1. Install a scan tool. 2. Turn ON the ignition, with the engine OFF. 3. Turn the cruise control ON/OFF switch OFF. 4. With the scan tool, observe the Cruise ON/OFF switch parameter in the engine control module (ECM) Cruise Control Data list. Does the Cruise ON/OFF switch parameter display OFF?	Go to Step 3	Go to Step 8

LTV0500000004010

Fig. 64   Cruise Control Inoperative/Malfunctioning (Part 1 of 5). 2005-06 Envoy, Rainier & TrailBlazer Less 4.2L Engine

Step	Action	Yes	No
3	With the scan tool, observe the following cruise control switch parameters in the engine control module (ECM) Cruise Control Data list: • Cruise Resume/Accel. Switch • Cruise Set/Coast Switch — Do any of the cruise control switch parameters listed above display Applied?	Go to Step 9	Go to Step 4
4	1. Turn the cruise control ON/OFF switch ON. 2. With the scan tool, observe the Cruise ON/OFF switch parameter. Does the Cruise ON/OFF switch parameter display ON?	Go to Step 5	Go to Step 10
5	1. With the scan tool, observe the Cruise Set/Coast Switch parameter. 2. Press and hold the cruise control Set/Coast button. Does the Cruise Set/Coast Switch parameter Display Applied?	Go to Step 6	Go to Step 13
6	1. With the scan tool, observe the Cruise Resume/Accel. Switch parameter. 2. Press and hold the cruise control Resume/Accel switch. Does the Cruise Resume/Accel. Switch parameter Display Applied?	Go to Step 7	Go to Step 12
7	Do the stop lamps work properly?	Go to Step 22	Diagnose Stop Lamps Always On or Stop Lamps Inoperative
8	1. Turn OFF the ignition. 2. Disconnect C4 of the multifunction, turn signal switch. 3. Turn ON the ignition, with the engine OFF. 4. With the scan tool, observe the Cruise ON/OFF switch parameter. Does the Cruise ON/OFF switch parameter display ON?	Go to Step 14	Go to Step 19

LTV0500000004011

Fig. 64   Cruise Control Inoperative/Malfunctioning (Part 2 of 5). 2005-06 Envoy, Rainier & TrailBlazer Less 4.2L Engine

Step	Action	Yes	No

9	1. Turn OFF the ignition.
	2. Disconnect C4 of the multifunction turn signal switch.
	3. Turn ON the ignition, with the engine OFF.
	4. With the scan tool, observe the following cruise control switch parameters in the engine control module (ECM) Cruise Control Data list:
	   - Cruise Resume/Accel. Switch
	   - Cruise Set/Coast Switch
	
	Do any of the cruise control switch parameters listed above display Applied?
		Go to Step 15	Go to Step 19

10	1. Turn OFF the ignition. 2. Disconnect C4 of the multifunction, turn signal switch. 3. Turn ON the ignition, with the engine OFF. 4. Connect a test lamp between the ignition 3 voltage circuit and a good ground. Does the test lamp illuminate?	Go to Step 11	Go to Step 21
11	1. Turn the ignition OFF. 2. Connect a 3-amp fused jumper between the ignition 3 voltage circuit and the cruise control on switch signal circuit. 3. Turn ON the ignition, with the engine OFF. 4. With the scan tool, observe the Cruise ON/OFF switch parameter. Does the Cruise ON/OFF switch parameter display ON?	Go to Step 19	Go to Step 16
12	1. Turn OFF the ignition. 2. Disconnect C4 of the multifunction, turn signal switch. 3. Connect a 3-amp fused jumper between the ignition 3 voltage circuit and the cruise control resume/accel switch signal circuit. 4. Turn ON the ignition, with the engine OFF. 5. With the scan tool, observe the Cruise Resume/Accel. Switch parameter. Does the Cruise Resume/Accel. Switch parameter display Applied?	Go to Step 19	Go to Step 18
13	1. Turn OFF the ignition. 2. Disconnect C4 of the multifunction, turn signal switch. 3. Connect a 3-amp fused jumper between the ignition 3 voltage circuit and the cruise control set/coast switch signal circuit. 4. Turn ON the ignition, with the engine OFF. 5. With the scan tool, observe the Cruise Set/Coast Switch parameter. Does the Cruise Set/Coast Switch parameter display Applied?	Go to Step 19	Go to Step 17
14	Test the cruise control on switch signal circuit for a short to voltage. Did you find and correct the condition?	Go to Step 25	Go to Step 20

LTV0500000004012

Fig. 64 Cruise Control Inoperative/Malfunctioning (Part 3 of 5). 2005-06 Envoy, Rainier & TrailBlazer Less 4.2L Engine

Step	Action	Yes	No
15	Test the cruise control switch signal circuit that displayed Applied on the scan tool for a short to voltage. Did you find and correct the condition?	Go to Step 25	Go to Step 20

16	Test the cruise control on switch signal circuit for the following:
	
	   • An open
	   • A short to ground
	   • A high resistance
	
	Did you find and correct the condition?
		Go to Step 25	Go to Step 20

17	Test the cruise control set/coast switch signal circuit for the following:
	
	   • An open
	   • A short to ground
	   • A high resistance
	
	Did you find and correct the condition?
		Go to Step 25	Go to Step 20

18	Test the cruise control resume/accelerate switch signal circuit for the following:
	
	   • An open
	   • A short to ground
	   • A high resistance
	
	Did you find and correct the condition?
		Go to Step 25	Go to Step 20

19	Inspect for poor connections at C4 of the multifunction, turn signal switch. Did you find and correct the condition?	Go to Step 25	Go to Step 23

LTV0500000004013

Fig. 64 Cruise Control Inoperative/Malfunctioning (Part 4 of 5). 2005-06 Envoy, Rainier & TrailBlazer Less 4.2L Engine

Step	Action	Yes	No
20	Inspect for poor connections at the harness connector of the ECM. Did you find and correct the condition?	Go to Step 25	Go to Step 24

21	Repair the following in the ignition 3 voltage circuit:
	
	   • An open
	   • A short to ground
	   • A high resistance
	
	Did you complete the repair?
		Go to Step 25	--

22	Repair the open or the high resistance in the center high mounted stop lamp (CHMSL) supply voltage circuit. Did you complete the repair?	Go to Step 25	--
23	Replace the cruise control switch. Did you complete the replacement?	Go to Step 25	--
24	Replace the ECM. Did you complete the replacement?	Go to Step 25	--
25	Operate the vehicle within the conditions for cruise control operation. Does the cruise control system operate properly?	System OK	Go to Step 2

LTV0500000004014

Fig. 64 Cruise Control Inoperative/Malfunctioning (Part 5 of 5). 2005-06 Envoy, Rainier & TrailBlazer Less 4.2L Engine

Diagnostic Aids

Perform the following in order to avoid misdiagnosis:

   • Inspect for proper operation of the stop lamps.

   • Electromagnetic interference (EMI) on the speed sensor signal circuit may cause erratic cruise control operation.

Conditions for Enabling Cruise Control

   • The vehicle speed is greater than 40 km/h (25 mph).

   • The vehicle is not in PARK, REVERSE, NEUTRAL, or 1st gear.

   • The system voltage is between 12-16 volts.

Step	Action	Yes	No
1	Did you perform the Diagnostic System Check - Vehicle?	Go to Step 2	Go to Diagnostic System Check
2	1. Install a scan tool. 2. Turn ON the ignition, with the engine OFF. 3. Press the cruise ON/OFF switch OFF. 4. With the scan tool, observe the Cruise ON/OFF switch parameter in the powertrain control module (PCM) Cruise Control Data list. Does the Cruise ON/OFF switch parameter display OFF?	Go to Step 3	Go to Step 6
3	1. Press the cruise ON/OFF switch ON. 2. With the scan tool, observe the Cruise ON/OFF switch parameter. Does the Cruise ON/OFF switch parameter display ON?	Go to Step 4	Go to Step 7

LTV0500000004015

Fig. 65 Cruise Control Inoperative/Malfunctioning (Part 1 of 4). Envoy, Rainier & TrailBlazer w/4.2L Engine

	Action	Yes	No
4	1. With the scan tool, observe the Cruise Set/Coast Switch parameter in the PCM Cruise Control Data list. 2. Press the cruise control Set/Coast button. Does the Cruise Set/Coast Switch parameter Display ON?	Go to Step 5	Go to Step 13
5	1. With the scan tool, observe the Cruise Resume/Accel. Switch parameter in the PCM Cruise Control Data list. 2. Press the Resume/Accel. switch. Does the Cruise Resume/Accel. Switch parameter Display ON?	Go to Diagnostic Aids	Go to Step 14
6	1. Turn OFF the ignition. 2. Disconnect the steering wheel column connector. 3. Turn ON the ignition, with the engine OFF. 4. With the scan tool, observe the Cruise ON/OFF switch parameter. Does the Cruise ON/OFF switch parameter display ON?	Go to Step 8	Go to Step 16
7	1. Turn OFF the ignition. 2. Disconnect the steering wheel column connector. 3. Turn ON the ignition, with the engine OFF. 4. Connect a test lamp between the ignition 3 voltage circuit and a good ground. Does the test lamp illuminate?	Go to Step 12	Go to Step 9
8	Test the cruise control on switch signal circuit for a short to voltage. Did you find and correct the condition?	Go to Step 20	Go to Step 17
9	Test the cruise control on switch signal circuit for a short to ground. Did you find and correct the condition?	Go to Step 20	Go to Step 10
10	Test the cruise control set/coast switch signal circuit for a short to ground. Did you find and correct the condition?	Go to Step 20	Go to Step 11

LTV0500000004016

Fig. 65 Cruise Control Inoperative/Malfunctioning (Part 2 of 4). Envoy, Rainier & TrailBlazer w/4.2L Engine

	Action	Yes	No
11	Test the cruise control resume/accelerate switch signal circuit for a short to ground. Did you find and correct the condition?	Go to Step 20	Go to Step 15
12	Test the cruise control on switch signal circuit for an open or for a high resistance. Did you find and correct the condition?	Go to Step 20	Go to Step 16
13	Test the cruise control Set/Coast signal circuit for an open or for a high resistance. Did you find and correct the condition?	Go to Step 20	Go to Step 16
14	Test the cruise control Resume/Accelerate signal circuit for an open or for a high resistance. Did you find and correct the condition?	Go to Step 20	Go to Step 16
15	Repair the open, the high resistance, or the short to ground in the ignition 3 voltage circuit. Did you complete the repair?	Go to Step 20	--
16	Inspect for poor connections at the harness connector of the multifunction turn signal lever. Did you find and correct the condition?	Go to Step 20	Go to Step 18

LTV0500000004017

Fig. 65 Cruise Control Inoperative/Malfunctioning (Part 3 of 4). Envoy, Rainier & TrailBlazer w/4.2L Engine

	Action	Yes	No
17	Inspect for poor connections at the harness connector of the PCM. Did you find and correct the condition?	Go to Step 20	Go to Step 19
18	Replace the multifunction turn signal lever. Did you complete the replacement?	Go to Step 20	--
19	Replace the PCM. Did you complete the replacement?	Go to Step 20	--
20	Operate the vehicle within the conditions for cruise control operation. Does the cruise control system operate properly?	System OK	Go to Step 2

LTV0500000004018

Fig. 65 Cruise Control Inoperative/Malfunctioning (Part 4 of 4). Envoy, Rainier & TrailBlazer w/4.2L Engine

Diagnostic Aids

Perform the following in order to avoid a misdiagnosis:

- Ensure that the following cruise control switches are not stuck in the engaged position:
  - On/off switch
  - Set/coast switch
  - Resume/accel switch
- Inspect for proper operation of the stop lamps.
- Inspect for proper adjustment of the TCC brake/cruise release switch.
- Inspect for proper adjustment of the clutch release switch.
- Inspect for proper operation of the clutch pedal.

Step	Action	Values	Yes	No
1	Did you perform the Diagnostic System Check - Vehicle?	--	Go to Step 2	Go to Diagnostic System Check

2	1. Install a scan tool.
	2. Turn ON the ignition, with the engine OFF.
	3. Turn the cruise control On/Off switch Off.
	4. With the scan tool, observe the following cruise control parameters in the Cruise Control Data list:
	   - Cruise On/Off Switch
	   - Cruise Resume/Accel Switch
	   - Cruise Set/Coast Switch
	
	Do all of the parameters listed above display Off?
		--	Go to Step 3	Go to Step 13

LTV0500000004019

Fig. 66 Cruise Control Inoperative/Malfunctioning (Part 1 of 5). Canyon & Colorado

	Action	Yes	No
3	1. With the scan tool, observe the Cruise On/Off Switch parameter. 2. Turn the cruise On/Off switch ON. Does the Cruise On/Off Switch parameter display On?	Go to Step 4	Go to Step 11
4	1. With the scan tool, observe the Cruise Set/Coast Switch parameter. 2. Press and hold the set/coast switch. Does the Cruise Set/Coast Switch parameter display On?	Go to Step 5	Go to Step 12
5	1. With the scan tool, observe the Cruise Resume/Accel Switch parameter. 2. Press and hold the resume/accel switch. Does the Cruise Resume/Accel Switch parameter display On?	Go to Step 6	Go to Step 12
6	Do the stop lamps operate properly?	Go to Step 7	Diagnose Stop Lamps Inoperative or to Stop Lamps Always On
7	Test the stop lamp supply voltage circuit for an open or for a high resistance. Did you find and correct the condition?	Go to Step 25	Go to Step 8
8	Is the vehicle equipped with a manual transmission?	Go to Step 9	Go to Step 20

LTV0500000004020

Fig. 66 Cruise Control Inoperative/Malfunctioning (Part 2 of 5). Canyon & Colorado

9	1. Turn OFF the ignition. 2. Disconnect the clutch release switch. 3. With a DMM, measure the resistance of the clutch pedal position (CPP) switch between the ignition 1 voltage circuit and the CPP switch signal circuit. Does the resistance measure between the specified values?	10–15 ohms	Go to Step 10	Go to Step 18
10	1. Depress and hold down the clutch pedal. 2. With a DMM, measure the resistance of the CPP switch between the ignition 1 voltage circuit and the CPP switch signal circuit. Does the resistance measure at the specified value?	O.L.	Go to Step 14	Go to Step 18
11	Connect a DMM between the ignition 1 voltage circuit at the back of C204 and a good ground. Does the voltage measure at the specified value?	B+	Go to Step 12	Go to Step 21
12	Important: The cruise control On/Off switch must be turned ON in order to correctly view the set/coast resistance value with the DMM. 1. Turn OFF the ignition. 2. Disconnect C204. 3. With a DMM, measure the resistance of the cruise control switch between the ignition 1 voltage circuit and the cruise control set/coast and resume/accelerate switch signal circuit. 4. Individually activate and hold the cruise control function switches while measuring the resistance of the cruise control function switches. Do the cruise control function switch resistance values measure between the specified values?	Off = O.L. On = 7.8 K ohms – 8.6 K ohms Resume = 2.7 K ohms – 3.0 K ohms Set = 1.2 K ohms – 1.3 K ohms	Go to Step 17	Go to Step 19

LTV0500000004021

Fig. 66   Cruise Control Inoperative/Malfunctioning (Part 3 of 5). Canyon & Colorado

18	Inspect for poor connections at the harness connector of the clutch switch. Did you find and correct the condition?	–	Go to Step 25	Go to Step 22
19	Inspect for poor connections at the harness connector of the cruise control switch. Did you find and correct the condition?	–	Go to Step 25	Go to Step 23
20	Inspect for poor connections at the harness connector of the powertrain control module (PCM). Did you find and correct the condition?	–	Go to Step 25	Go to Step 24
21	Repair the following in the ignition 1 voltage circuit: • An open • A high resistance • A short to ground Did you complete the repair?	–	Go to Step 25	--
22	Replace the clutch release switch. Did you complete the replacement?	–	Go to Step 25	--
23	Replace the cruise control switch. Did you complete the replacement?	–	Go to Step 25	--
24	Replace the PCM. Did you complete the replacement?	–	Go to Step 25	--
25	Operate the vehicle within the conditions for cruise control operation. Does the cruise control system operate properly?	–	System OK	Go to Step 2

LTV0500000004023

Fig. 66   Cruise Control Inoperative/Malfunctioning (Part 5 of 5). Canyon & Colorado

13	Important: The cruise control On/Off switch must be turned ON in order to correctly view the set coast resistance value with the DMM. 1. Turn OFF the ignition. 2. Disconnect C204. 3. With a DMM, measure the resistance of the cruise control switch between the ignition 1 voltage circuit and the cruise control set/coast and resume/accelerate switch signal circuit. 4. Individually activate and hold the cruise control function switches while measuring the resistance of the cruise control function switches. Do the resistance values measure at the specified values?	Off = O.L. On = 7.8 K ohms – 8.6 K ohms Resume = 2.7 K ohms – 3.0 K ohms Set = 1.2 K ohms – 1.3 K ohms	Go to Step 16	Go to Step 19
14	1. Turn ON the ignition, with the engine OFF. 2. Connect a test lamp between the ignition 1 voltage circuit and a good ground. Does the test lamp illuminate?	--	Go to Step 15	Go to Step 21
15	Test the clutch switch signal circuit for the following: • An open • A short to voltage • A short to ground • A high resistance Did you find and correct the condition?		Go to Step 25	Go to Step 20
16	Test the cruise control set/coast and resume/accelerate switch signal circuit for a short to voltage. Did you find and correct the condition?	--	Go to Step 25	Go to Step 20
17	Test the cruise control set/coast and resume/accelerate switch signal circuit for the following: • An open • A high resistance • A short to ground Did you find and correct the condition?		Go to Step 25	Go to Step 20

LTV0500000004022

Fig. 66   Cruise Control Inoperative/Malfunctioning (Part 4 of 5). Canyon & Colorado

Diagnostic Aids

Disable the inflatable restraint steering wheel module when performing this diagnostic table.

Perform the following in order to avoid misdiagnosis:

• Ensure that the following cruise control switches are not stuck in the engaged position:
  - On/off switch
  - Set/coast switch
  - Resume/accel switch
• Inspect for proper operation of the stop lamps.
• With a scan tool, observe the cruise control function switch parameters, in the powertrain control module (PCM) Cruise Control Data list, while rotating the steering wheel to both steering stops and individually activating each cruise control function switch separately. This will help eliminate the possibility of an internally shorted inflatable restraint steering wheel module coil.

Test Description

The number below refers to the step number on the diagnostic path.

6. This step tests the vehicle speed signal circuit for a short to ground, for a short to voltage, for an open, or for a high resistance between the PCM and the TAC module.

8. This step tests the ignition 1 voltage circuit for a short to ground, for an open, or for a high resistance.

9. This step tests the cruise control set/coast and resume/accelerate switch signal circuit for a short to voltage.

10. This step tests the cruise control set/coast and resume/accelerate switch signal circuit for a short to ground, for a short to voltage, for an open, or for a high resistance.

26. DTCs will set in the powertrain control module (PCM) when you perform this diagnostic table.

LTV0500000004024

Fig. 67   Cruise Control Inoperative/Malfunction (Part 1 of 7). Equinox & Torrent

Step	Action	Values	Yes	No
1	Did you perform the Diagnostic System Check - Vehicle?	--	Go to Step 2	Go to Diagnostic System Check
2	1. Install a scan tool. 2. Turn ON the ignition, with the engine OFF. 3. Turn the cruise control On/Off switch OFF. 4. With the scan tool, observe the following Cruise Control parameters in the Cruise Control data list: - Cruise On/Off Switch - Cruise Resume/Accel. Switch - Cruise Set/Coast Switch Do any of the parameters listed above display On?	--	Go to Step 9	Go to Step 3
3	1. With the scan tool, observe the Cruise On/Off Switch parameter. 2. Turn the cruise control On/Off switch ON. Does the Cruise On/Off Switch parameter display On?	--	Go to Step 4	Go to Step 8
4	1. With the scan tool, observe the Cruise Set/Coast Switch parameter. 2. Press and hold the set/coast switch. Does the Cruise Set/Coast Switch parameter display On?	--	Go to Step 5	Go to Step 10
5	1. With the scan tool, observe the Cruise Resume/Accel. Switch parameter. 2. Press and hold the resume/accel switch. Does the Cruise Resume/Accel. Switch parameter display On?	--	Go to Step 6	Go to Step 10

LTV0500000004025

Fig. 67 Cruise Control Inoperative/Malfunction (Part 2 of 7). Equinox & Torrent

Step	Action	Values	Yes	No
6	1. Turn OFF the ignition. 2. Disconnect the throttle actuator control (TAC) module. 3. Turn ON the ignition, with the engine OFF. 4. With a DMM, measure the voltage of the vehicle speed signal circuit. Does the voltage measure greater than the specified value?	8.5 V	Go to Step 7	Go to Step 11
7	Test the vehicle speed signal circuit for a short to voltage. Did you find and correct the condition?	--	Go to Step 26	Go to Step 21
8	1. Turn OFF the ignition. 2. Remove the inflatable restraint steering wheel module. 3. Disconnect C277. 4. Turn ON the ignition, with the engine OFF. 5. Connect a test lamp between the ignition 1 voltage circuit and a good ground. Does the test lamp illuminate?	--	Go to Step 10	Go to Step 22
9	**Important:** The cruise control On/Off switch must be turned ON in order to correctly view the set/coast switch and the resume/accel switch resistance values with the DMM. 1. Turn OFF the ignition. 2. Remove the inflatable restraint steering wheel module. 3. Disconnect C277. 4. With a DMM, measure the resistance of the cruise control switch between the ignition 1 voltage circuit and the cruise control set/coast and resume/accelerate switch signal circuit. 5. Individually activate and hold the cruise control function switches while measuring the resistance of the cruise control function switches. Do the cruise control function switch resistance values measure between the specified values?	Off = O.L. On = 7.8 K-8.6 K ohms Resume = 2.7 K-3.0 K ohms Set = 1.2 K-1.3 K ohms	Go to Step 12	Go to Step 17

LTV0500000004026

Fig. 67 Cruise Control Inoperative/Malfunction (Part 3 of 7). Equinox & Torrent

Step	Action	Values	Yes	No
10	**Important:** The cruise control On/Off switch must be turned ON in order to correctly view the set/coast switch and the resume/accel switch resistance values with the DMM. 1. Turn OFF the ignition. 2. Remove the inflatable restraint steering wheel module. 3. Disconnect C277. 4. With a DMM, measure the resistance of the cruise control switch between the ignition 1 voltage circuit and the cruise control set/coast and resume/accelerate switch signal circuit. 5. Individually activate and hold the cruise control function switches while measuring the resistance of the cruise control function switches. Do the cruise control function switch resistance values measure between the specified values?	Off = O.L. On = 7.8 K-8.6 K ohms Resume = 2.7 K-3.0 K ohms Set = 1.2 K-1.3 K ohms	Go to Step 13	Go to Step 14
11	Test the vehicle speed signal circuit for an open or for a high resistance. Did you find and correct the condition?	--	Go to Step 26	Go to Step 20
12	Test the cruise control set/coast and resume/accel switch signal circuit for a short to voltage between C277 and the powertrain control module (PCM). Did you find and correct the condition?	--	Go to Step 26	Go to Step 20
13	Test the cruise control set/coast and resume/accel switch signal circuit for the following: • Open • Short to ground • Short to voltage • High resistance Did you find and correct the condition?	--	Go to Step 26	Go to Step 20

LTV0500000004027

Fig. 67 Cruise Control Inoperative/Malfunction (Part 4 of 7). Equinox & Torrent

Step	Action	Values	Yes	No
14	Test the ignition 1 voltage circuit between C277 and the cruise control switch for the following: • Open • Short to ground • High resistance Did you find and correct the condition?	--	Go to Step 26	Go to Step 15
15	Test the cruise control on switch signal circuit for the following: • Open • Short to ground • Short to voltage • High resistance Did you find and correct the condition?	--	Go to Step 26	Go to Step 16
16	Test the cruise control set/coast and resume/accelerate switch signal circuit between C277 and the cruise control switch for the following: • Open • Short to ground • Short to voltage • High resistance Did you find and correct the condition?	--	Go to Step 26	Go to Step 19
17	Test the cruise control on switch signal circuit for a short to voltage. Did you find and correct the condition?	--	Go to Step 26	Go to Step 18

LTV0500000004028

Fig. 67 Cruise Control Inoperative/Malfunction (Part 5 of 7). Equinox & Torrent

Step	Action	Value(s)	Yes	No
18	Test the cruise control set/coast and resume/accelerate switch signal circuit between C277 and the cruise control switch for a short to voltage. Did you find and correct the condition?	-	Go to Step 26	Go to Step 19
19	Inspect for poor connections at the harness connector of the cruise control switch. Did you find and correct the condition?	-	Go to Step 26	Go to Step 23
20	Inspect for poor connections at the harness connector of the PCM. Did you find and correct the condition?	-	Go to Step 26	Go to Step 25
21	Inspect for poor connections at the harness connector of the TAC module. Did you find and correct the condition?	-	Go to Step 26	Go to Step 24
22	Repair the following in the ignition 1 voltage circuit: • Open • Short to ground • High resistance Did you complete the repair?	-	Go to Step 26	--

LTV0500000004029

Fig. 67 Cruise Control Inoperative/Malfunction (Part 6 of 7). Equinox & Torrent

Step	Action	Value(s)	Yes	No
23	Replace the cruise control switch. Did you complete the replacement?	-	Go to Step 26	--
24	Replace the TAC module. Did you complete the replacement?	-	Go to Step 26	--
25	Replace the PCM. Did you complete the replacement?	-	Go to Step 26	--
26	1. Install the inflatable restraint steering wheel module. 2. Enable the inflatable restraint steering wheel module. 3. Use the scan tool in order to clear the PCM DTCs. 4. Operate the Cruise Control System in order to verify the repair. Does the Cruise Control System operate properly?	-	System OK	Go to Step 2

LTV0500000004030

Fig. 67 Cruise Control Inoperative/Malfunction (Part 7 of 7). Equinox & Torrent

Diagnostic Aids

Important: Perform the following in order to avoid misdiagnosis.

- Inspect for proper operation of brake lamps.
- Inspect throttle linkage for mechanical binding which could cause the system to malfunction.
- Inspect cruise control cable adjustment, should have minimum slack.
- EMI on the speed sensor signal circuit may cause erratic cruise control operation.

Conditions for Enabling Cruise Control

The vehicle speed is greater than 40 km/h (25 mph).

Step	Action	Value(s)	Yes	No
1	Did you perform the Cruise Control Diagnostic System Check?	--	Go to Step 2	Go to Diagnostic System Check
2	1. Turn OFF the ignition. 2. Disconnect the cruise control module. 3. Turn ON the ignition, with the engine OFF. 4. Probe the ignition positive voltage circuit of the cruise control module with a test lamp that is connected to a good ground. Does the test lamp illuminate?	--	Go to Step 3	Go to Step 29
3	Probe the ignition positive voltage circuit of the cruise control module with a test lamp that is connected to the ground circuit of the cruise control module. Does the test lamp illuminate?	--	Go to Step 4	Go to Step 30

LTV0500000004031

Fig. 68 Cruise Control Inoperative/Malfunctioning (Part 1 of 5). 2002 Express & Savana w/4.3L, 5.0L & 5.7L Engines

Step	Action	Value(s)	Yes	No
4	1. Turn OFF the cruise control switch. 2. Probe the on/off, the set/coast, and the resume/accelerate signal circuits with a test lamp that is connected to a good ground. Does the test lamp illuminate on any of the circuits?	-	Go to Step 14	Go to Step 5
5	1. Turn ON the cruise control. 2. Probe the cruise control On signal circuit with a test lamp that is connected to a good ground. Does the test lamp illuminate?	-	Go to Step 6	Go to Step 15
6	1. Probe the cruise control set/coast signal circuit with a test lamp that is connected to a good ground. 2. Press and hold the SET/COAST switch. Does the test lamp illuminate?	-	Go to Step 7	Go to Step 17
7	1. Probe the cruise control resume/accelerate signal circuit with a test lamp that is connected to a good ground. 2. Press and hold the RESUME/ACCEL switch. Does the test lamp illuminate?	-	Go to Step 8	Go to Step 18
8	Probe the TCC/Brake signal circuit with a test lamp that is connected to a good ground. Does the test lamp illuminate?	-	Go to Step 9	Go to Step 19
9	Press the brake pedal while monitoring the test lamp. Does the test lamp illuminate?	-	Go to Step 20	Go to Step 10
10	Probe the stop lamp switch signal circuit with a test lamp that is connected to a good ground. Does the test lamp illuminate?	-	Go to Step 21	Go to Step 11
11	Press the brake pedal while monitoring the test lamp. Does the test lamp illuminate?	-	Go to Step 12	Go to Step 22

LTV0500000004032

Fig. 68 Cruise Control Inoperative/Malfunctioning (Part 2 of 5). 2002 Express & Savana w/4.3L, 5.0L & 5.7L Engines

Step	Action		Yes	No
12	Probe the cruise engaged signal circuit with a DMM that is connected to a good ground.	B+	Go to Step 13	Go to Step 23
	Does the voltage measure near the specified value?			
13	Check the speedometer for proper operation.	--	Go to Step 24	Go to Symptoms
	Does the speedometer operate properly?			
14	Test the circuit that illuminated the test lamp for a short to voltage.	--	Go to Step 35	Go to Step 27
	Did you find and correct the condition?			
15	Test the cruise control On signal circuit for an open, high resistance or short to ground, and the cruise control set/coast, resume/accelerate signal circuits for a short to ground.	--	Go to Step 35	Go to Step 16
	Did you find and correct the condition?			
16	Test the ignition positive voltage circuit of the cruise control switch for an open, high resistance or short to ground.	--	Go to Step 35	Go to Step 27
	Did you find and correct the condition?			
17	Test the cruise control set/coast signal circuit for an open or a high resistance.	--	Go to Step 35	Go to Step 27
	Did you find and correct the condition?			
18	Test the cruise control resume/accelerate signal circuit for an open or a high resistance.	--	Go to Step 35	Go to Step 27
	Did you find and correct the condition?			
19	Test the TCC/Brake switch signal circuit for an open or a high resistance.	--	Go to Step 35	Go to Step 25
	Did you find and correct the condition?			

LTV0500000004033

Fig. 68 Cruise Control Inoperative/Malfunctioning (Part 3 of 5). 2002 Express & Savana w/4.3L, 5.0L & 5.7L Engines

Step	Action	Yes	No
20	Test the TCC/Brake switch signal circuit for a short to voltage.	Go to Step 35	Go to Step 25
	Did you find and correct the condition?		
21	Test the stop lamp switch signal circuit for a short to voltage.	Go to Step 35	Go to Step 25
	Did you find and correct the condition?		
22	Test the stop lamp switch signal circuit for an open or a high resistance.	Go to Step 35	Go to Step 25
	Did you find and correct the condition?		
23	Test the cruise engaged signal circuit for an open, a high resistance, or a short to ground.	Go to Step 35	Go to Step 26
	Did you find and correct the condition?		
24	Test the speed sensor circuit for an open or a high resistance between the PCM and cruise control module.	Go to Step 35	Go to Step 28
	Did you find and correct the condition?		
25	Inspect for poor connections at the harness connector of the stop lamp switch.	Go to Step 35	Go to Step 31
	Did you find and correct the condition?		
26	Inspect for poor connections at the harness connector of the PCM.	Go to Step 35	Go to Step 32
	Did you find and correct the condition?		
27	Inspect for poor connections at the harness connector of the cruise control switch.	Go to Step 35	Go to Step 33
	Did you find and correct the condition?		
28	Inspect for poor connections at the harness connector of the cruise control module.	Go to Step 35	Go to Step 34
	Did you find and correct the condition?		

LTV0500000004034

Fig. 68 Cruise Control Inoperative/Malfunctioning (Part 4 of 5). 2002 Express & Savana w/4.3L, 5.0L & 5.7L Engines

Step	Action	Yes	No
29	Repair the ignition positive voltage circuit of the cruise control module.	Go to Step 35	--
	Did you complete the repair?		
30	Repair the ground circuit of the cruise control module.	Go to Step 35	--
	Did you complete the repair?		
31	Replace the stop lamp switch.	Go to Step 35	--
	Did you complete the replacement?		
32	**Important:** The PCM must be reprogrammed after replacement. Replace the PCM.	Go to Step 35	--
	Did you complete the replacement?		
33	Replace the cruise control switch.	Go to Step 35	--
	Did you complete the replacement?		
34	Replace the cruise control module.	Go to Step 35	--
	Did you complete the replacement?		
35	Operate the vehicle within the conditions for cruise control operation.	System OK	Go to Step 2
	Does the cruise control system operate correctly?		

LTV0500000004035

Fig. 68 Cruise Control Inoperative/Malfunctioning (Part 5 of 5). 2002 Express & Savana w/4.3L, 5.0L & 5.7L Engines

Diagnostic Aids

Important: To avoid misdiagnosis, inspect for the following:

- Proper operation of stop lamps.
- The throttle linkage is not binding.

EMI on the speed sensor signal circuit may cause erratic cruise control operation.

Conditions for Enabling Cruise Control

- The vehicle speed is greater than 40 km/h (25 mph).
- The vehicle is not in PARK, REVERSE, NEUTRAL, or 1st gear.
- The system voltage is within 9 volts and 16 volts.

Step	Action	Yes	No
1	Did you perform the Cruise Control Diagnostic System Check?	Go to Step 2	Go to Diagnostic System Check
2	1. Install a scan tool. 2. With the scan tool, observe the Cruise On/Off Switch parameter in the powertrain control module (PCM) data list. 3. Turn the cruise control On/Off switch On and then Off. Does the Cruise On/Off Switch parameter display On and the Off?	Go to Step 3	Go to Step 7
3	1. With the scan tool, observe the Cruise Set/Coast Switch parameter in the PCM data list. 2. Press and then release the cruise control set/coast button. Does the Cruise Set/Coast Switch parameter display On and then Off?	Go to Step 4	Go to Step 11

LTV0500000004036

Fig. 69 Cruise Control Inoperative/Malfunctioning (Part 1 of 4). 2002 Express & Savana w/6.5L Diesel Engine

	Action	Yes	No
4	1. With the scan tool, observe the Cruise Resume/Accel. Switch parameter in the PCM data list. 2. Press and then release the Resume/Accelerate switch. Does the Cruise Resume/Accel. Switch parameter display On and then Off?	Go to Step 5	Go to Step 12
5	1. With the scan tool, observe the Stoplamp Pedal Switch parameter in the PCM data list. 2. Press the brake pedal. Does the Stoplamp Pedal Switch parameter display closed?	Go to Step 6	Go to Step 8
6	1. With the scan tool, observe the TCC Cruise Brake Pedal parameter in the PCM data list. 2. Press the brake pedal. Does the TCC Cruise Brake Pedal parameter display Open?	Go to Step 20	Go to Step 9
7	1. Turn the ignition OFF. 2. Disconnect the cruise control switch. 3. Turn the ignition ON, with the engine OFF. 4. Connect a test lamp between the ignition 3 voltage circuit of the cruise control switch and a good ground. Does the test lamp illuminate?	Go to Step 10	Go to Step 15
8	1. Turn the ignition OFF. 2. Disconnect the stop lamp switch. 3. Turn the ignition ON, with the engine OFF. 4. Connect a test lamp between the battery positive voltage circuit of the stop lamp switch and a good ground. Does the test lamp illuminate?	Go to Step 13	Go to Step 17
9	1. Turn the ignition OFF. 2. Disconnect the stop lamp switch. 3. Turn the ignition ON, with the engine OFF. 4. Connect a test lamp between the ignition 3 voltage circuit of the TCC/Brake switch and a good ground. Does the test lamp illuminate?	Go to Step 14	Go to Step 16
10	Test the cruise control on switch signal circuit for an open, for a high resistance, for a short to ground, or for a short to voltage. Did you find and correct the condition?	Go to Step 24	Go to Step 19

LTV0500000004037

Fig. 69 Cruise Control Inoperative/Malfunctioning (Part 2 of 4). 2002 Express & Savana w/6.5L Diesel Engine

	Action	Yes	No
11	Test the cruise control set/coast switch signal circuit for an open, for a high resistance, for a short to ground, or for a short to voltage. Did you find and correct the condition?	Go to Step 24	Go to Step 19
12	Test the cruise control resume/accelerate switch signal circuit for an open, for a high resistance, for a short to ground, or for a short to voltage. Did you find and correct the condition?	Go to Step 24	Go to Step 19
13	Test the stop lamp switch signal circuit for an open, for a high resistance, for a short to ground, or for a short to voltage. Did you find and correct the condition?	Go to Step 24	Go to Step 18
14	Test the TCC/Brake switch signal circuit for an open, for a high resistance, for a short to ground, or for a short to voltage. Did you find and correct the condition?	Go to Step 24	Go to Step 18
15	Repair the open, the high resistance, or the short to ground in the ignition 3 voltage circuit of the cruise control switch. Did you complete the repair?	Go to Step 24	--
16	Repair the open, the high resistance, or the short to ground in the ignition 3 voltage circuit of the TCC/Brake switch. Did you complete the repair?	Go to Step 24	--
17	Repair the open, the high resistance, or the short to ground in the battery positive voltage circuit. Did you complete the repair?	Go to Step 24	--

LTV0500000004038

Fig. 69 Cruise Control Inoperative/Malfunctioning (Part 3 of 4). 2002 Express & Savana w/6.5L Diesel Engine

	Action	Yes	No
18	Inspect for poor connections at the harness connector of the stop lamp switch. Did you find and correct the condition?	Go to Step 24	Go to Step 21
19	Inspect for poor connections at the harness connector of the cruise control switch. Did you find and correct the condition?	Go to Step 24	Go to Step 22
20	Inspect for poor connections at the harness connector of the PCM. Did you find and correct the condition?	Go to Step 24	Go to Step 23
21	Replace the stop lamp switch. Did you complete the repair?	Go to Step 24	--
22	Replace the multifunction turn signal lever. Did you complete the repair?	Go to Step 24	--
23	**Important:** Program the replacement PCM. Replace the PCM. Did you complete the replacement?	Go to Step 24	--
24	Operate the vehicle within the conditions for cruise control operation. Does the cruise control system operate properly?	System OK	Go to Step 2

LTV0500000004039

Fig. 69 Cruise Control Inoperative/Malfunctioning (Part 4 of 4). 2002 Express & Savana w/6.5L Diesel Engine

Diagnostic Aids

Important: To avoid misdiagnosis, inspect for the following:

- Proper operation of stop lamps.
- The throttle linkage is not binding.

EMI on the speed sensor signal circuit may cause erratic cruise control operation.

Conditions for Enabling Cruise Control

- The vehicle speed is greater than 40 km/h (25 mph).
- The vehicle is not in PARK, REVERSE, NEUTRAL, or 1st gear.
- The system voltage is within 9 volts and 16 volts.

Step	Action	Yes	No
1	Did you perform the Cruise Control Diagnostic System Check?	Go to Step 2	Go to Diagnostic System Check - Cruise Control
2	1. Install a scan tool. 2. With the scan tool, observe the Cruise On/Off Switch parameter in the powertrain control module (PCM) data list. 3. Turn the cruise control On/Off switch On and then Off. Does the Cruise On/Off Switch parameter display On and then Off?	Go to Step 3	Go to Step 6
3	1. With the scan tool, observe the Cruise Set/Coast Switch parameter in the PCM data list. 2. Press and then release the cruise control set/coast button. Does the Cruise Set/Coast Switch parameter display On and then Off?	Go to Step 4	Go to Step 9
4	1. With the scan tool, observe the Cruise Resume/Accel. Switch parameter in the PCM data list. 2. Press and then release the Resume/Accelerate switch. Does the Cruise Resume/Accel. Switch parameter display On and then Off?	Go to Step 5	Go to Step 10

LTV0500000004040

Fig. 70 Cruise Control Inoperative/Malfunctioning (Part 1 of 3). 2002 Express & Savana w/8.1L Engine

Step	Action	Yes	No
5	1. With the scan tool, observe the Stoplamp Pedal Switch parameter in the PCM data list. 2. Press the brake pedal. Does the Stoplamp Pedal Switch parameter display Applied?	Go to Step 16	Go to Step 7
6	1. Turn the ignition OFF. 2. Disconnect the cruise control switch. 3. Turn the ignition ON, with the engine OFF. 4. Connect a test lamp between the ignition 3 voltage circuit and a good ground. Does the test lamp illuminate?	Go to Step 8	Go to Step 12
7	1. Turn the ignition OFF. 2. Disconnect the stop lamp switch. 3. Turn the ignition ON, with the engine OFF. 4. Connect a test lamp between the battery positive voltage circuit and a good ground. Does the test lamp illuminate?	Go to Step 11	Go to Step 13
8	Test the cruise control on switch signal circuit for an open, for a high resistance, for a short to ground, or for a short to voltage. Did you find and correct the condition?	Go to Step 20	Go to Step 15
9	Test the cruise control set/coast switch signal circuit for an open, for a high resistance, for a short to ground, or for a short to voltage. Did you find and correct the condition?	Go to Step 20	Go to Step 15
10	Test the cruise control resume/accelerate switch signal circuit for an open, for a high resistance, for a short to ground, or for a short to voltage. Did you find and correct the condition?	Go to Step 20	Go to Step 15
11	Test the stop lamp switch signal circuit for an open, for a high resistance, for a short to ground, or for a short to voltage. Did you find and correct the condition?	Go to Step 20	Go to Step 14

LTV0500000004041

Fig. 70 Cruise Control Inoperative/Malfunctioning (Part 2 of 3). 2002 Express & Savana w/8.1L Engine

Step	Action	Yes	No
12	Repair the open, the high resistance, or the short to ground in the ignition 3 voltage circuit. Did you complete the repair?	Go to Step 20	--
13	Repair the open, the high resistance, or the short to ground in the battery positive voltage circuit. Did you complete the repair?	Go to Step 20	--
14	Inspect for poor connections at the harness connector of the stop lamp switch. Did you find and correct the condition?	Go to Step 20	Go to Step 17
15	Inspect for poor connections at the harness connector of the cruise control switch. Did you find and correct the condition?	Go to Step 20	Go to Step 18
16	Inspect for poor connections at the harness connector of the TAC module. Did you find and correct the condition?	Go to Step 20	Go to Step 19
17	Replace the stop lamp switch. Did you complete the repair?	Go to Step 20	--
18	Replace the multifunction turn signal lever. Did you complete the repair?	Go to Step 20	--
19	Replace the TAC module. Did you complete the replacement?	Go to Step 20	--
20	Operate the vehicle within the conditions for cruise control operation. Does the cruise control system operate properly?	System OK	Go to Step 2

LTV0500000004042

Fig. 70 Cruise Control Inoperative/Malfunctioning (Part 3 of 3). 2002 Express & Savana w/8.1L Engine

Diagnostic Aids

To avoid a misdiagnosis, inspect for the following:

- Proper operation of the stop lamps.

- Proper adjustment of the cruise control cable.

- The throttle linkage is not binding.

Electromagnetic interference on the speed sensor signal circuit may cause erratic cruise control operation.

Conditions for Enabling Cruise Control

- The vehicle speed is greater than 40 km/h (25 mph).
- The vehicle is not in PARK, REVERSE, NEUTRAL, or 1st gear.
- The system voltage is within 9 volts and 16 volts.

Step	Action	Value(s)	Yes	No
1	Did you perform the Cruise Control Diagnostic System Check?	--	Go to Step 2	Go to Diagnostic System Check
2	1. Turn the ignition OFF. 2. Disconnect the cruise control module. 3. Turn the ignition ON, with the engine OFF. 4. Connect a test lamp between the ignition 1 voltage circuit and a good ground. Does the test lamp illuminate?	--	Go to Step 3	Go to Step 24

LTV0500000004043

Fig. 71 Cruise Control Inoperative/Malfunctioning (Part 1 of 6). 2003 Express & Savana

Step	Action		Yes	No
3	Connect a test lamp between the ignition 1 voltage circuit and the ground circuit of the cruise control module. Does the test lamp illuminate?	-	Go to Step 4	Go to Step 25

4	1. Turn the cruise control On/Off switch OFF.
	2. Connect a test lamp between a good ground and each of the following circuits:
	  - The cruise control on switch signal circuit
	  - The cruise control set/coast switch signal circuit
	  - The cruise control resume/accel switch signal circuit
	
	Does the test lamp illuminate for any of the signal circuits listed above?
		-	Go to Step 15	Go to Step 5

5	1. Turn the cruise control On/Off switch ON. 2. Connect a test lamp between the cruise control on switch signal circuit and a good ground. Does the test lamp illuminate?	-	Go to Step 6	Go to Step 16
6	1. Connect a test lamp between the cruise control set/coast switch signal circuit and a good ground. 2. With the cruise control On/Off switch ON, press and hold the Set/Coast switch. Does the test lamp illuminate?	-	Go to Step 7	Go to Step 20
7	1. Connect a test lamp between the cruise control resume/accelerate switch signal circuit and a good ground. 2. With the cruise control On/Off switch ON, press and hold the Resume/Accel switch. Does the test lamp illuminate?	-	Go to Step 8	Go to Step 21

LTV0500000004044

Fig. 71 Cruise Control Inoperative/Malfunctioning (Part 2 of 6). 2003 Express & Savana

#	Action	Value	Yes	No
8	Connect a test lamp between the TCC brake switch/cruise control release switch signal circuit and a good ground. Does the test lamp illuminate?	--	Go to Step 9	Go to Step 23
9	1. Connect a test lamp between the CHMSL supply voltage/stop lamp supply voltage circuit and a good ground. 2. Depress the brake pedal. Does the test lamp illuminate?	--	Go to Step 10	Go to Step 26
10	With a DMM, measure the voltage of the cruise control engaged signal circuit. Does the voltage measure near the specified value?	9 Volts	Go to Step 11	Go to Step 22
11	With a DMM, measure the voltage at the vehicle speed signal circuit. Does the voltage measure near the specified value?	9 Volts	Go to Step 12	Go to Step 13
12	1. Connect the cruise control module. 2. Disconnect C2 at the PCM. 3. With a DMM, measure the voltage at the cruise inhibit signal circuit. Does the voltage measure near the specified value?	9 Volts	Go to Diagnostic Aids	Go to Step 27
13	Test the vehicle speed signal circuit for an open or for a high resistance. Did you find and correct the condition?	--	Go to Step 33	Go to Step 28
14	Test the cruise control inhibit signal circuit for a short to ground, for an open, or for a high resistance. Did you find and correct the condition?	--	Go to Step 33	Go to Step 29

LTV0500000004045

Fig. 71   Cruise Control Inoperative/Malfunctioning (Part 3 of 6). 2003 Express & Savana

#	Action	Value	Yes	No
15	Test the signal circuit that illuminated the test lamp for a short to voltage. Did you find and correct the condition?	-	Go to Step 33	Go to Step 28
16	Test the cruise control On switch signal circuit for an open, for a high resistance, or for a short to ground. Did you find and correct the condition?	-	Go to Step 33	Go to Step 17
17	Test the cruise control set/coast switch signal circuit for a short to ground. Did you find and correct the condition?	-	Go to Step 33	Go to Step 18
18	Test the cruise control resume/accel switch signal circuit for a short to ground. Did you find and correct the condition?	-	Go to Step 33	Go to Step 19
19	Test the ignition 1 voltage circuit of the cruise control switch for an open, for a high resistance, or for short to ground. Did you find and correct the condition?	-	Go to Step 33	Go to Step 28
20	Test the cruise control set/coast switch signal circuit for an open or for a high resistance. Did you find and correct the condition?	-	Go to Step 33	Go to Step 28
21	Test the cruise control resume/accel switch signal circuit for an open or for a high resistance. Did you find and correct the condition?	-	Go to Step 33	Go to Step 28

LTV0500000004046

Fig. 71   Cruise Control Inoperative/Malfunctioning (Part 4 of 6). 2003 Express & Savana

#	Action	Value	Yes	No
22	Test the cruise control engaged signal circuit for an open, for a high resistance, or for a short to ground. Did you find and correct the condition?	-	Go to Step 33	Go to Step 27
23	Repair the open or the high resistance in the TCC brake switch/cruise control release signal circuit between the fuse block - underhood and the cruise control module. Did you complete the repair?	-	Go to Step 33	--
24	Repair the open, the high resistance, or the short to ground in the ignition 1 voltage circuit of the cruise control module. Did you complete the repair?	-	Go to Step 33	--
25	Repair the open or the high resistance in the ground circuit of the cruise control module. Did you complete the repair?	-	Go to Step 33	--
26	Repair the open or the high resistance in the CHMSL supply voltage/stop lamp supply voltage circuit between the fuse block - underhood and the cruise control module. Did you complete the repair?	-	Go to Step 33	--
27	Inspect for poor connections at the harness connector of the PCM. Did you find and correct the condition?	-	Go to Step 33	Go to Step 30

LTV0500000004047

Fig. 71   Cruise Control Inoperative/Malfunctioning (Part 5 of 6). 2003 Express & Savana

#	Action	Value	Yes	No
28	Inspect for poor connections at the harness connector of the cruise control switch. Did you find and correct the condition?	-	Go to Step 33	Go to Step 31
29	Inspect for poor connections at the harness connector of the cruise control module. Did you find and correct the condition?	-	Go to Step 33	Go to Step 32
30	**Important:** Program the replacement PCM. Replace the PCM. Did you complete the replacement?	-	Go to Step 33	--
31	Replace the cruise control switch. Did you complete the replacement?	-	Go to Step 33	--
32	Replace the cruise control module. Did you complete the replacement?	-	Go to Step 33	--
33	Operate the vehicle within the conditions for cruise control operation. Does the cruise control system operate correctly?	-	System OK	Go to Step 2

LTV0500000004048

Fig. 71   Cruise Control Inoperative/Malfunctioning (Part 6 of 6). 2003 Express & Savana

Diagnostic Aids

Perform the following in order to avoid a misdiagnosis:

- Inspect for proper operation of the brake lamps.
- Electromagnetic interference (EMI) on the vehicle speed sensor signal circuit may cause erratic cruise control operation.

Conditions for Enabling Cruise Control

- The vehicle speed is greater than 40 km/h (25 mph).
- The vehicle is not in PARK, REVERSE, NEUTRAL, or 1st gear.
- The system voltage is within 9-16 volts.

Test description

The numbers below refer to the step numbers on the diagnostic table.

8. This step tests the center high mounted stop lamp (CHMSL) supply voltage/stop lamp supply voltage circuit for an open or for a high resistance between the stop lamp switch and the throttle actuator control (TAC) module.

9. This step tests the cruise control set/coast switch signal circuit for an open or for a high resistance.

10. This step tests the cruise control resume/accel switch signal circuit for an open or for a high resistance.

11. This step tests the ignition 3 voltage circuit for an open, for a short to ground, or for a high resistance.

29. DTCs will set in the powertrain control module (PCM) when you perform this table.

Step	Action	Yes	No
1	Did you perform the Cruise Control Diagnostic System Check?	Go to Step 2	Go to Diagnostic System Check

LTV0500000004049

Fig. 72 Cruise Control Inoperative/Malfunctioning (Part 1 of 6). 2004-06 Express & Savana Gas Engines w/TAC

Step	Action	Yes	No
2	1. Install a scan tool. 2. Turn the ignition ON, with the engine OFF. 3. Turn the cruise control On/Off switch OFF. 4. With the scan tool, observe the Cruise On/Off Switch parameter in the powertrain control module (PCM) Cruise Control Data data list. Does the Cruise On/Off Switch parameter display Off?	Go to Step 4	Go to Step 3
3	1. Turn the ignition OFF. 2. Disconnect C4 of the multifunction switch. 3. Turn the ignition ON, with the engine OFF. 4. With the scan tool, observe the Cruise On/Off Switch parameter. Does the Cruise On/Off Switch parameter display Off?	Go to Step 22	Go to Step 13
4	1. Turn the cruise control On/Off switch ON. 2. With the scan tool, observe the Cruise On/Off Switch parameter. Does the Cruise On/Off Switch parameter display On?	Go to Step 5	Go to Step 11
5	1. With the scan tool, observe the Cruise Set/Coast Switch parameter in the PCM Cruise Control Data data list. 2. Turn the cruise control On/Off switch ON. 3. Press and hold the cruise control Set/Coast button. Does the Cruise Set/Coast Switch parameter Display On?	Go to Step 6	Go to Step 9
6	1. With the scan tool, observe the Cruise Resume/Accel. Switch parameter in the PCM Cruise Control Data data list. 2. Press and hold the Resume/Accel switch. Does the Cruise Resume/Accel. Switch parameter Display On?	Go to Step 7	Go to Step 10
7	Do the stop lamps operate properly?	Go to Step 8	Diagnose Stop Lamps Inoperative

LTV0500000004050

Fig. 72 Cruise Control Inoperative/Malfunctioning (Part 2 of 6). 2004-06 Express & Savana Gas Engines w/TAC

Step	Action	Yes	No
8	1. With the scan tool, observe the Stoplamp Pedal Switch parameter in the PCM Cruise Control Data data list. 2. Depress and hold the brake pedal. Does the Stoplamp Pedal Switch parameter Display Applied?	Go to Diagnostic Aids	Go to Step 21
9	1. Turn the ignition OFF. 2. Disconnect C4 of the multifunction switch. 3. Turn the ignition ON, with the engine OFF. 4. Connect a 3-ampere fused jumper between the cruise control set/coast switch signal circuit and the ignition 3 voltage circuit. 5. With the scan tool, observe the Cruise Set/Coast Switch parameter. Does the Cruise Set/Coast Switch parameter Display On?	Go to Step 22	Go to Step 19
10	1. Turn the ignition OFF. 2. Disconnect C4 of the multifunction switch. 3. Turn the ignition ON, with the engine OFF. 4. Connect a 3-ampere fused jumper between the cruise control resume/accel switch signal circuit and the ignition 3 voltage circuit. 5. With the scan tool, observe the Cruise Resume/Accel. Switch parameter. Does the Cruise Resume/Accel. Switch parameter Display On?	Go to Step 22	Go to Step 20
11	1. Turn the ignition OFF. 2. Disconnect C4 of the multifunction switch. 3. Turn the ignition ON, with the engine OFF. 4. Connect a test lamp between the ignition 3 voltage circuit and a good ground. Does the test lamp illuminate?	Go to Step 12	Go to Step 15
12	1. Connect a 3-ampere fused jumper between the ignition 3 voltage circuit and the cruise control on switch signal circuit. 2. With the scan tool, observe the Cruise On/Off Switch parameter. Does the Cruise On/Off Switch parameter display On?	Go to Step 22	Go to Step 18
13	Test the cruise control on switch signal circuit for a short to voltage. Did you find and correct the condition?	Go to Step 29	Go to Step 14

LTV0500000004051

Fig. 72 Cruise Control Inoperative/Malfunctioning (Part 3 of 6). 2004-06 Express & Savana Gas Engines w/TAC

Step	Action	Yes	No
14	1. Turn the ignition OFF. 2. Disconnect C1 of the throttle actuator contol (TAC) module. 3. Turn the ignition ON, with the engine OFF. 4. With the scan tool, observe the Cruise On/Off Switch parameter. Does the Cruise On/Off Switch parameter display On?	Go to Step 24	Go to Step 23
15	Test the cruise control set/coast switch signal circuit for a short to ground. Did you find and correct the condition?	Go to Step 29	Go to Step 16
16	Test the cruise control resume/accel switch signal circuit for a short to ground. Did you find and correct the condition?	Go to Step 29	Go to Step 17
17	Test the cruise control on switch signal circuit for a short to ground. Did you find and correct the condition?	Go to Step 29	Go to Step 25
18	Test the cruise control on switch signal circuit for an open or for a high resistance. Did you find and correct the condition?	Go to Step 29	Go to Step 23
19	Test the cruise control set/coast switch signal circuit for an open or for a high resistance. Did you find and correct the condition?	Go to Step 29	Go to Step 23
20	Test the cruise control resume/accel switch signal circuit for an open or for a high resistance. Did you find and correct the condition?	Go to Step 29	Go to Step 23

LTV0500000004052

Fig. 72 Cruise Control Inoperative/Malfunctioning (Part 4 of 6). 2004-06 Express & Savana Gas Engines w/TAC

		Yes	No
21	Test the center high mounted stop lamp (CHMSL) supply voltage/stop lamp supply voltage circuit for an open or for a high resistance between the stop lamp switch and the TAC module. Did you find and correct the condition?	Go to Step 29	Go to Step 23
22	Inspect for poor connections at the harness connector of the cruise control switch. Did you find and correct the condition?	Go to Step 29	Go to Step 26
23	Inspect for poor connections at the harness connector of the TAC module. Did you find and correct the condition?	Go to Step 29	Go to Step 27
24	Inspect for poor connections at the harness connector of the PCM. Did you find and correct the condition?	Go to Step 29	Go to Step 28
25	Repair the open, the high resistance, or the short to ground in the Ignition 3 voltage circuit. Did you complete the repair?	Go to Step 29	--
26	Replace the cruise control switch. Did you complete the replacement?	Go to Step 29	--

LTV0500000004053

Fig. 72 Cruise Control Inoperative/Malfunctioning (Part 5 of 6). 2004-06 Express & Savana Gas Engines w/TAC

Diagnostic Aids

To avoid a misdiagnosis, inspect for the following:

- Proper operation of the stop lamps

- Proper adjustment of the cruise control cable

- The throttle linkage is not binding.

Electromagnetic interference on the speed sensor signal circuit may cause erratic cruise control operation.

Conditions for Enabling Cruise Control

- The vehicle speed is greater than 40 km/h (25 mph).
- The vehicle is not in PARK, REVERSE, NEUTRAL, or 1st gear.
- The system voltage is within 9-16 volts.

Step	Action	Value (s)	Yes	No
1	Did you perform the Cruise Control Diagnostic System Check?	--	Go to Step 2	Go to Diagnostic System Check

LTV0500000004055

Fig. 73 Cruise Control Inoperative/Malfunctioning (Part 1 of 6). 2004-06 Express & Savana Gas Engines Less TAC

		Yes	No
27	Replace the TAC module. Did you complete the replacement?	Go to Step 29	--
28	**Important:** Program the replacement PCM. Replace the PCM. Did you complete the replacement?	Go to Step 29	--
29	1. Use the scan tool in order to clear the PCM DTCs. 2. Operate the vehicle within the conditions for cruise control operation. Does the cruise control system operate properly?	System OK	Go to Step 2

LTV0500000004054

Fig. 72 Cruise Control Inoperative/Malfunctioning (Part 6 of 6). 2004-06 Express & Savana Gas Engines w/TAC

		Yes	No
2	1. Turn the ignition OFF. 2. Disconnect the cruise control module. 3. Turn the ignition ON, with the engine OFF. 4. Connect a test lamp between the ignition 1 voltage circuit and a good ground. Does the test lamp illuminate?	Go to Step 3	Go to Step 24
3	Connect a test lamp between the ignition 1 voltage circuit and the ground circuit of the cruise control module. Does the test lamp illuminate?	Go to Step 4	Go to Step 25

4	1. Turn the cruise control On/Off switch OFF.
	2. Connect a test lamp between a good ground and each of the following circuits:
	  - The cruise control on switch signal circuit
	  - The cruise control set/coast switch signal circuit
	  - The cruise control resume/accel switch signal circuit
	
	Does the test lamp illuminate for any of the signal circuits listed above?
		Go to Step 15	Go to Step 5

5	1. Turn the cruise control On/Off switch ON. 2. Connect a test lamp between the cruise control on switch signal circuit and a good ground. Does the test lamp illuminate?	Go to Step 6	Go to Step 16
6	1. Connect a test lamp between the cruise control set/coast switch signal circuit and a good ground. 2. With the cruise control On/Off switch ON, press and hold the Set/Coast switch. Does the test lamp illuminate?	Go to Step 7	Go to Step 20
7	1. Connect a test lamp between the cruise control resume/accelerate switch signal circuit and a good ground. 2. With the cruise control On/Off switch ON, press and hold the Resume/Accel switch. Does the test lamp illuminate?	Go to Step 8	Go to Step 21

LTV0500000004056

Fig. 73 Cruise Control Inoperative/Malfunctioning (Part 2 of 6). 2004-06 Express & Savana Gas Engines Less TAC

		Yes	No
8	Connect a test lamp between the TCC brake switch/cruise control release switch signal circuit and a good ground. Does the test lamp illuminate?	Go to Step 9	Go to Step 23
9	1. Connect a test lamp between the center high mounted stop lamp (CHMSL) supply voltage/stop lamp supply voltage circuit and a good ground. 2. Depress the brake pedal. Does the test lamp illuminate?	Go to Step 10	Go to Step 26
10	With a DMM, measure the voltage of the cruise control engaged signal circuit. Does the voltage measure near the specified value?	9	Go to Step 11	Go to Step 22
11	With a DMM, measure the voltage at the vehicle speed signal circuit. Does the voltage measure near the specified value?	9	Go to Step 12	Go to Step 13
12	1. Connect the cruise control module. 2. Disconnect C2 at the powertrain control module (PCM). 3. With a DMM, measure the voltage at the cruise inhibit signal circuit. Does the voltage measure near the specified value?	9	Go to Diagnostic Aids	Go to Step 27
13	Test the vehicle speed signal circuit for an open or for a high resistance. Did you find and correct the condition?	Go to Step 33	Go to Step 28

LTV0500000004057

Fig. 73 Cruise Control Inoperative/Malfunctioning (Part 3 of 6). 2004-06 Express & Savana Gas Engines Less TAC

14	Test the cruise control inhibit signal circuit for a short to ground, for an open, or for a high resistance. Did you find and correct the condition?	- Go to Step 33	Go to Step 29
15	Test the signal circuit that illuminated the test lamp for a short to voltage. Did you find and correct the condition?	- Go to Step 33	Go to Step 28
16	Test the cruise control On switch signal circuit for an open, for a high resistance, or for a short to ground. Did you find and correct the condition?	- Go to Step 33	Go to Step 17
17	Test the cruise control set/coast switch signal circuit for a short to ground. Did you find and correct the condition?	- Go to Step 33	Go to Step 18
18	Test the cruise control resume/accel switch signal circuit for a short to ground. Did you find and correct the condition?	- Go to Step 33	Go to Step 19
19	Test the ignition 1 voltage circuit of the cruise control switch for an open, for a high resistance, or for short to ground. Did you find and correct the condition?	- Go to Step 33	Go to Step 28
20	Test the cruise control set/coast switch signal circuit for an open or for a high resistance. Did you find and correct the condition?	- Go to Step 33	Go to Step 28

LTV0500000004058

Fig. 73 Cruise Control Inoperative/Malfunctioning (Part 4 of 6). 2004-06 Express & Savana Gas Engines Less TAC

28	Inspect for poor connections at the harness connector of the cruise control switch. Did you find and correct the condition?	- Go to Step 33	Go to Step 31
29	Inspect for poor connections at the harness connector of the cruise control module. Did you find and correct the condition?	- Go to Step 33	Go to Step 32
30	**Important:** Program the replacement PCM. Replace the PCM. Did you complete the replacement?	- Go to Step 33	--
31	Replace the cruise control switch. Did you complete the replacement?	- Go to Step 33	
32	Replace the cruise control module. Did you complete the replacement?	- Go to Step 33	--
33	Operate the vehicle within the conditions for cruise control operation. Does the cruise control system operate correctly?	- System OK	Go to Step 2

LTV0500000004060

Fig. 73 Cruise Control Inoperative/Malfunctioning (Part 6 of 6). 2004-06 Express & Savana Gas Engines Less TAC

21	Test the cruise control resume/accel switch signal circuit for an open or for a high resistance. Did you find and correct the condition?	- Go to Step 33	Go to Step 28
22	Test the cruise control engaged signal circuit for an open, for a high resistance, or for a short to ground. Did you find and correct the condition?	- Go to Step 33	Go to Step 27
23	Repair the open or the high resistance in the torque converter clutch (TCC) brake switch/cruise control release signal circuit between the fuse block - underhood and the cruise control module. Did you complete the repair?	- Go to Step 33	--
24	Repair the open, the high resistance, or the short to ground in the ignition 1 voltage circuit of the cruise control module. Did you complete the repair?	- Go to Step 33	--
25	Repair the open or the high resistance in the ground circuit of the cruise control module. Did you complete the repair?	- Go to Step 33	
26	Repair the open or the high resistance in the CHMSL supply voltage/stop lamp supply voltage circuit between the fuse block - underhood and the cruise control module. Did you complete the repair?	- Go to Step 33	
27	Inspect for poor connections at the harness connector of the PCM. Did you find and correct the condition?	- Go to Step 33	Go to Step 30

LTV0500000004059

Fig. 73 Cruise Control Inoperative/Malfunctioning (Part 5 of 6). 2004-06 Express & Savana Gas Engines Less TAC

Diagnostic Aids

To avoid a misdiagnosis, inspect for the following:

- Proper operation of the stop lamps.
- The throttle linkage is not binding.

EMI on the speed sensor signal circuit may cause erratic cruise control operation.

Conditions for Enabling Cruise Control

- The vehicle speed is greater than 40 km/h (25 mph).
- The vehicle is not in PARK, REVERSE, NEUTRAL, or 1st gear.
- The system voltage is between 12 volts and 16 volts.

Step	Action	Yes	No
1	Did you perform the Diagnostic System Check - Vehicle?	Go to Step 2	Go to Diagnostic System Check
2	1. Install a scan tool. 2. Turn ON the ignition, with the engine OFF. 3. Turn the cruise control On/Off switch OFF. 4. With the scan tool, observe the Cruise On/Off Switch parameter in the Powertrain Engine Data 1 data list. Does the Cruise On/Off Switch parameter display Off?	Go to Step 3	Go to Step 6

LTV0500000004061

Fig. 74 Cruise Control Inoperative/Malfunctioning (Part 1 of 4). 2004-06 Express & Savana w/Diesel Engine

3	1. Turn the cruise control On/Off switch ON. 2. With the scan tool, observe the Cruise On/Off Switch parameter. Does the Cruise On/Off Switch parameter display On?	Go to Step 4	Go to Step 10
4	1. With the scan tool, observe the Cruise Set/Coast Switch parameter in the Powertrain Engine Data 1 data list. 2. Turn the cruise control On/Off switch ON. 3. Press and hold the cruise control Set/Coast switch. Does the Cruise Set/Coast Switch parameter display On?	Go to Step 5	Go to Step 7
5	1. With the scan tool, observe the Cruise Resume/Accel. Switch parameter in the Powertrain Engine Data 1 data list. 2. Press and hold the Resume/Accel switch. Does the Cruise Resume/Accel. Switch parameter display On?	Go to Step 9	Go to Step 8
6	1. Turn OFF the ignition. 2. Disconnect the cruise control switch. 3. Turn ON the ignition, with the engine OFF. 4. Connect a test lamp between the cruise control on switch signal circuit and a good ground. Does the test lamp illuminate?	Go to Step 11	Go to Step 20
7	1. Turn OFF the ignition. 2. Disconnect the cruise control switch. 3. Turn ON the ignition, with the engine OFF. 4. Connect a 3-ampere fused jumper between the cruise control set/coast switch signal circuit and the ignition 3 voltage circuit. 5. With the scan tool, observe the Cruise Set/Coast Switch parameter. Does the Cruise Set/Coast Switch parameter display On?	Go to Step 20	Go to Step 15

LTV0500000004062

Fig. 74   Cruise Control Inoperative/Malfunctioning (Part 2 of 4). 2004-06 Express & Savana w/Diesel Engine

15	Test the cruise control set/coast switch signal circuit for an open or for a high resistance. Did you find and correct the condition?	Go to Step 25	Go to Step 21
16	Test the cruise control resume/accel switch signal circuit for an open or for a high resistance. Did you find and correct the condition?	Go to Step 25	Go to Step 21
17	Test the TCC/Brake switch signal circuit for an open, for a high resistance, or for a short to ground. Did you find and correct the condition?	Go to Step 25	Go to Step 19
18	Repair the open, the high resistance, or the short to ground in the ignition 3 voltage circuit. Did you complete the repair?	Go to Step 25	--
19	Inspect for poor connections at the harness connector of the stop lamp switch. Did you find and correct the condition?	Go to Step 25	Go to Step 22
20	Inspect for poor connections at the harness connector of the cruise control switch. Did you find and correct the condition?	Go to Step 25	Go to Step 23
21	Inspect for poor connections at the harness connector of the engine control module (ECM). Did you find and correct the condition?	Go to Step 25	Go to Step 24
22	Replace the stop lamp switch. Did you complete the replacement?	Go to Step 25	--
23	Replace the multifunction turn signal lever. Did you complete the replacement?	Go to Step 25	--
24	Replace the ECM. Did you complete the replacement?	Go to Step 25	--
25	Operate the vehicle within the conditions for cruise control operation. Does the cruise control system operate properly?	System OK	Go to Step 2

LTV0500000004064

Fig. 74   Cruise Control Inoperative/Malfunctioning (Part 4 of 4). 2004-06 Express & Savana w/Diesel Engine

8	1. Turn OFF the ignition. 2. Disconnect the cruise control switch. 3. Turn ON the ignition, with the engine OFF. 4. Connect a 3-ampere fused jumper between the cruise control resume/accel switch signal circuit and the ignition 3 voltage circuit. 5. With the scan tool, observe the Cruise Resume/Accel. Switch parameter. Does the Cruise Resume/Accel. Switch parameter display On?	Go to Step 20	Go to Step 16
9	1. With the scan tool, observe the TCC/Cruise Brake Pedal Switch parameter in the Powertrain Engine Data 1 data list. 2. Depress the brake pedal. Does the TCC/Cruise Brake Pedal Switch parameter display Applied?	Go to Diagnostic Aids	Go to Step 17
10	1. Turn OFF the ignition. 2. Disconnect the cruise control switch. 3. Turn ON the ignition, with the engine OFF. 4. Connect a test lamp between the ignition 3 voltage circuit and a good ground. Does the test lamp illuminate?	Go to Step 12	Go to Step 18
11	Test the cruise control on switch signal circuit for a short to voltage. Did you find and correct the condition?	Go to Step 25	Go to Step 21
12	Test the cruise control on switch signal circuit for an open, for a high resistance or for a short to ground. Did you find and correct the condition?	Go to Step 25	Go to Step 13
13	Test the cruise control resume/accel switch signal circuit for a short to ground. Did you find and correct the condition?	Go to Step 25	Go to Step 14
14	Test the cruise control set/coast switch signal circuit for a for a short to ground. Did you find and correct the condition?	Go to Step 25	Go to Step 20

LTV0500000004063

Fig. 74   Cruise Control Inoperative/Malfunctioning (Part 3 of 4). 2004-06 Express & Savana w/Diesel Engine

Diagnostic Aids

Perform the following in order to avoid a misdiagnosis:

- Inspect for proper operation of the brake lamps.
- EMI on the vehicle speed sensor signal circuit may cause erratic cruise control operation.

Conditions for Enabling Cruise Control

- The vehicle speed is greater than 40 km/h (25 mph).
- The vehicle is not in PARK, REVERSE, NEUTRAL, or 1st gear.
- The system voltage is within 9 volts and 16 volts.

Test description

The numbers below refer to the step numbers on the diagnostic table.

8. This step tests the CHMSL supply voltage/stop lamp supply voltage circuit for an open or for a high resistance between the stop lamp switch and the TAC module.

9. This step tests the cruise control set/coast switch signal circuit for an open or for a high resistance.

10. This step tests the cruise control resume/accel switch signal circuit for an open or for a high resistance.

11. This step tests the ignition 3 voltage circuit for an open, for a short to ground, or for a high resistance.

29. DTCs will set in the PCM when you perform this table.

LTV0500000004065

Fig. 75   Cruise Control Inoperative/Malfunctioning (Part 1 of 6). Hummer H2

Step	Action	Yes	No
1	Did you perform the Diagnostic System Check - Cruise Control?	Go to Step 2	Go to Diagnostic System Check
2	1. Install a scan tool. 2. Turn ON the ignition, with the engine OFF. 3. Turn the cruise control On/Off switch OFF. 4. With the scan tool, observe the Cruise On/Off Switch parameter in the powertrain control module (PCM) Cruise Control Data data list. Does the Cruise On/Off Switch parameter display Off?	Go to Step 4	Go to Step 3
3	1. Turn OFF the ignition. 2. Disconnect C4 of the multifunction switch. 3. Turn ON the ignition, with the engine OFF. 4. With the scan tool, observe the Cruise On/Off Switch parameter. Does the Cruise On/Off Switch parameter display Off?	Go to Step 22	Go to Step 13
4	1. Turn the cruise control On/Off switch ON. 2. With the scan tool, observe the Cruise On/Off Switch parameter. Does the Cruise On/Off Switch parameter display On?	Go to Step 5	Go to Step 11
5	1. With the scan tool, observe the Cruise Set/Coast Switch parameter in the PCM Cruise Control Data data list. 2. Turn the cruise control On/Off switch ON. 3. Press and hold the cruise control Set/Coast button. Does the Cruise Set/Coast Switch parameter Display On?	Go to Step 6	Go to Step 9

LTV0500000004066

Fig. 75 Cruise Control Inoperative/Malfunctioning (Part 2 of 6). Hummer H2

Step	Action	Yes	No
12	1. Connect a 3 ampere fused jumper between the ignition 3 voltage circuit and the cruise control on switch signal circuit. 2. With the scan tool, observe the Cruise On/Off Switch parameter. Does the Cruise On/Off Switch parameter display On?	Go to Step 22	Go to Step 18
13	Test the cruise control on switch signal circuit for a short to voltage. Did you find and correct the condition?	Go to Step 29	Go to Step 14
14	1. Turn OFF the ignition. 2. Disconnect C1 of the TAC module. 3. Turn ON the ignition, with the engine OFF. 4. With the scan tool, observe the Cruise On/Off Switch parameter. Does the Cruise On/Off Switch parameter display On?	Go to Step 24	Go to Step 23
15	Test the cruise control set/coast switch signal circuit for a short to ground. Did you find and correct the condition?	Go to Step 29	Go to Step 16
16	Test the cruise control resume/accel switch signal circuit for a short to ground. Did you find and correct the condition?	Go to Step 29	Go to Step 17
17	Test the cruise control on switch signal circuit for a short to ground. Did you find and correct the condition?	Go to Step 29	Go to Step 25
18	Test the cruise control on switch signal circuit for the following: • An open • A high resistance • A short to ground Did you find and correct the condition?	Go to Step 29	Go to Step 23

LTV0500000004068

Fig. 75 Cruise Control Inoperative/Malfunctioning (Part 4 of 6). Hummer H2

Step	Action	Yes	No
6	1. With the scan tool, observe the Cruise Resume/Accel. Switch parameter in the PCM Cruise Control Data data list. 2. Press and hold the Resume/Accel switch. Does the Cruise Resume/Accel. Switch parameter Display On?	Go to Step 7	Go to Step 10
7	Do the stop lamps operate properly?	Go to Step 8	Diagnose Stop Lamps Inoperative
8	1. With the scan tool, observe the Stoplamp Pedal Switch parameter in the PCM Cruise Control Data data list. 2. Depress and hold the brake pedal. Does the Stoplamp Pedal Switch parameter Display Applied?	Go to Diagnostic Aids	Go to Step 21
9	1. Turn OFF the ignition. 2. Disconnect C4 of the multifunction switch. 3. Turn ON the ignition, with the engine OFF. 4. Connect a 3 ampere fused jumper between the cruise control set/coast switch signal circuit and the ignition 3 voltage circuit. 5. With the scan tool, observe the Cruise Set/Coast Switch parameter. Does the Cruise Set/Coast Switch parameter Display On?	Go to Step 22	Go to Step 19
10	1. Turn OFF the ignition. 2. Disconnect C4 of the multifunction switch. 3. Turn ON the ignition, with the engine OFF. 4. Connect a 3 ampere fused jumper between the cruise control resume/accel switch signal circuit and the ignition 3 voltage circuit. 5. With the scan tool, observe the Cruise Resume/Accel. Switch parameter. Does the Cruise Resume/Accel. Switch parameter Display On?	Go to Step 22	Go to Step 20
11	1. Turn OFF the ignition. 2. Disconnect C4 of the multifunction switch. 3. Turn ON the ignition, with the engine OFF. 4. Connect a test lamp between the ignition 3 voltage circuit and a good ground. Does the test lamp illuminate?	Go to Step 12	Go to Step 15

LTV0500000004067

Fig. 75 Cruise Control Inoperative/Malfunctioning (Part 3 of 6). Hummer H2

Step	Action	Yes	No
19	Test the cruise control set/coast switch signal circuit for the following: • An open • A high resistance • A short to ground Did you find and correct the condition?	Go to Step 29	Go to Step 23
20	Test the cruise control resume/accel switch signal circuit for the following: • An open • A high resistance • A short to ground Did you find and correct the condition?	Go to Step 29	Go to Step 23
21	Test the CHMSL supply voltage/stop lamp supply voltage circuit for an open or for a high resistance between the stop lamp switch and the TAC module. Did you find and correct the condition?	Go to Step 29	Go to Step 23
22	Inspect for poor connections at the harness connector of the cruise control switch. Did you find and correct the condition?	Go to Step 29	Go to Step 26
23	Inspect for poor connections at the harness connector of the TAC module. Did you find and correct the condition?	Go to Step 29	Go to Step 27
24	Inspect for poor connections at the harness connector of the PCM. Did you find and correct the condition?	Go to Step 29	Go to Step 28

LTV0500000004069

Fig. 75 Cruise Control Inoperative/Malfunctioning (Part 5 of 6). Hummer H2

	Action		Yes	No
25	Repair the open, the high resistance, or the short to ground in the Ignition 3 voltage circuit. Did you complete the repair?		Go to Step 29	--
26	Replace the multifunction switch. Did you complete the replacement?		Go to Step 29	--
27	Replace the TAC module. Did you complete the replacement?		Go to Step 29	--
28	**Important:** Program the replacement PCM. Replace the PCM. Did you complete the replacement?		Go to Step 29	--
29	1. Use the scan tool in order to clear the PCM DTCs. 2. Operate the vehicle within the conditions for cruise control operation. Does the cruise control system operate properly?		System OK	Go to Step 2

LTV0500000004070

Fig. 75   Cruise Control Inoperative/Malfunctioning (Part 6 of 6). Hummer H2

	Action	Values	Yes	No
2	1. Install a scan tool. 2. Turn ON the ignition, with the engine OFF. 3. Turn the cruise control On/Off switch Off. 4. With the scan tool, observe the following cruise control parameters in the Cruise Control Data list: - Cruise On/Off Switch - Cruise Resume/Accel Switch - Cruise Set/Coast Switch Do all of the parameters listed above display Off?		Go to Step 3	Go to Step 13
3	1. With the scan tool, observe the Cruise On/Off Switch parameter. 2. Turn the cruise On/Off switch ON. Does the Cruise On/Off Switch parameter display On?		Go to Step 4	Go to Step 11
4	1. With the scan tool, observe the Cruise Set/Coast Switch parameter. 2. Press and hold the set/coast switch. Does the Cruise Set/Coast Switch parameter display On?		Go to Step 5	Go to Step 12
5	1. With the scan tool, observe the Cruise Resume/Accel Switch parameter. 2. Press and hold the resume/accel switch. Does the Cruise Resume/Accel Switch parameter display On?		Go to Step 6	Go to Step 12
6	Do the stop lamps operate properly?		Go to Step 7	Diagnose Stop Lamps Inoperative or to Stop Lamps Always On

LTV0500000004072

Fig. 76   Cruise Control Inoperative/Malfunctioning (Part 2 of 6). Hummer H3

Diagnostic Aids

Perform the following in order to avoid a misdiagnosis:

- Ensure that the following cruise control switches are not stuck in the engaged position:
  - On/off switch
  - Set/coast switch
  - Resume/accel switch
- Inspect for proper operation of the stop lamps.
- Inspect for proper adjustment of the TCC brake/cruise release switch.
- Inspect for proper adjustment of the clutch release switch.
- Inspect for proper operation of the clutch pedal.

Step	Action	Values	Yes	No
1	Did you perform the Diagnostic System Check - Vehicle?	--	Go to Step 2	Go to Diagnostic System Check

LTV0500000004071

Fig. 76   Cruise Control Inoperative/Malfunctioning (Part 1 of 6). Hummer H3

	Action	Values	Yes	No
7	Test the stop lamp supply voltage circuit for an open or for a high resistance. Did you find and correct the condition?	--	Go to Step 25	Go to Step 8
8	Is the vehicle equipped with a manual transmission?	--	Go to Step 9	Go to Step 20
9	1. Turn OFF the ignition. 2. Disconnect the clutch release switch. 3. With a DMM, measure the resistance of the clutch pedal position (CPP) switch between the ignition 1 voltage circuit and the CPP switch signal circuit. Does the resistance measure between the specified values?	10-15 ohms	Go to Step 10	Go to Step 18
10	1. Depress and hold down the clutch pedal. 2. With a DMM, measure the resistance of the CPP switch between the ignition 1 voltage circuit and the CPP switch signal circuit. Does the resistance measure at the specified value?	O.L.	Go to Step 14	Go to Step 18
11	Connect a DMM between the ignition 1 voltage circuit at the back of C204 and a good ground. Does the voltage measure at the specified value?	B+	Go to Step 12	Go to Step 21
12	**Important:** The cruise control On/Off switch must be turned ON in order to correctly view the set/coast resistance value with the DMM. 1. Turn OFF the ignition. 2. Disconnect C204. 3. With a DMM, measure the resistance of the cruise control switch between the ignition 1 voltage circuit and the cruise control set/coast and resume/accelerate switch signal circuit. 4. Individually activate and hold the cruise control function switches while measuring the resistance of the cruise control function switches. Do the cruise control function switch resistance values measure between the specified values?	Off = O.L. On = 7.8 K ohms - 8.6 K ohms Resume = 2.7 K ohms - 3.0 K ohms Set = 1.2 K ohms - 1.3 K ohms	Go to Step 17	Go to Step 19

LTV0500000004073

Fig. 76   Cruise Control Inoperative/Malfunctioning (Part 3 of 6). Hummer H3

Step	Action	Values	Yes	No
13	**Important:** The cruise control On/Off switch must be turned ON in order to correctly view the set coast resistance value with the DMM. 1. Turn OFF the ignition. 2. Disconnect C204. 3. With a DMM, measure the resistance of the cruise control switch between the ignition 1 voltage circuit and the cruise control set/coast and resume/accelerate switch signal circuit. 4. Individually activate and hold the cruise control function switches while measuring the resistance of the cruise control function switches. Do the resistance values measure at the specified values?	Off = O.L. On = 7.8 K ohms - 8.6 K ohms Resume = 2.7 K ohms - 3.0 K ohms Set = 1.2 K ohms - 1.3 K ohms	Go to Step 16	Go to Step 19
14	1. Turn ON the ignition, with the engine OFF. 2. Connect a test lamp between the ignition 1 voltage circuit and a good ground. Does the test lamp illuminate?	--	Go to Step 15	Go to Step 21
15	Test the clutch switch signal circuit for the following: • An open • A short to voltage • A short to ground • A high resistance Did you find and correct the condition?	--	Go to Step 25	Go to Step 20
16	Test the cruise control set/coast and resume/accelerate switch signal circuit for a short to voltage. Did you find and correct the condition?	--	Go to Step 25	Go to Step 20

LTV0500000004074

Fig. 76   Cruise Control Inoperative/Malfunctioning (Part 4 of 6). Hummer H3

Step	Action	Values	Yes	No
17	Test the cruise control set/coast and resume/accelerate switch signal circuit for the following: • An open • A high resistance • A short to ground Did you find and correct the condition?		Go to Step 25	Go to Step 20
18	Inspect for poor connections at the harness connector of the clutch switch. Did you find and correct the condition?		Go to Step 25	Go to Step 22
19	Inspect for poor connections at the harness connector of the cruise control switch. Did you find and correct the condition?		Go to Step 25	Go to Step 23
20	Inspect for poor connections at the harness connector of the powertrain control module (PCM). Did you find and correct the condition?		Go to Step 25	Go to Step 24
21	Repair the following in the ignition 1 voltage circuit: • An open • A high resistance • A short to ground Did you complete the repair?		Go to Step 25	--

LTV0500000004075

Fig. 76   Cruise Control Inoperative/Malfunctioning (Part 5 of 6). Hummer H3

Step	Action	Values	Yes	No
22	Replace the clutch release switch. Did you complete the replacement?	-	Go to Step 25	--
23	Replace the cruise control switch. Did you complete the replacement?	-	Go to Step 25	--
24	Replace the PCM. Did you complete the replacement?	-	Go to Step 25	--
25	Operate the vehicle within the conditions for cruise control operation. Does the cruise control system operate properly?		System OK	Go to Step 2

LTV0500000004076

Fig. 76   Cruise Control Inoperative/Malfunctioning (Part 6 of 6). Hummer H3

Diagnostic Aids

Caution: Refer to SIR Caution in Cautions and Notices.

Disable the inflatable restraint steering wheel module when performing this diagnostic table.

• Ensure that the following cruise control switches are not stuck in the engaged position:
  - On/off switch
  - - SET switch
  - + RES switch

• With a scan tool, observe the associated cruise control switch parameter in the Body and Accessories, Cruise Control, BCM data list, while rotating the steering wheel to both steering stops and separately activating each cruise control switch. This will help eliminate the possibility of an internally shorted inflatable restraint steering wheel module coil.

Step	Action	Values	Yes	No
1	Did you perform the Diagnostic System Check - Vehicle?	--	Go to Step 2	Go to Diagnostic System Check
2	1. Install a scan tool. 2. Turn ON the ignition, with the engine OFF. 3. Turn the cruise control On/Off switch OFF. 4. With the scan tool, observe the Cruise Control Switch parameter in the Body and Accessories, Cruise Control, BCM data list. Does the Cruise Control Switch parameter display Off?	--	Go to Step 3	Go to Step 6

LTV0500000004077

Fig. 77   Cruise Control Inoperative/Malfunctioning (Part 1 of 5). HHR

Step	Action	Values	Yes	No
3	1. With the scan tool, observe the Cruise Control Switch parameter. 2. Turn the cruise control on/off switch ON. Does the Cruise Control Switch parameter display On?	-	Go to Step 4	Go to Step 7
4	1. With the scan tool, observe the Cruise Control Switch parameter. 2. Press and hold the - SET switch. Does the Cruise Control Switch parameter display Set?	-	Go to Step 5	Go to Step 9
5	1. With the scan tool, observe the Cruise Control Switch parameter. 2. Press and hold the + RES switch. Does the Cruise Control Switch parameter display Resume?	-	Go to Diagnostic Aids	Go to Step 9
6	1. Turn OFF the ignition. 2. Remove the inflatable steering wheel module. 3. Disconnect C1. 4. Turn ON the ignition, with the engine OFF. 5. Observe the Cruise Control Switch parameter in the Cruise Control Data list. Does the Cruise Control Switch parameter display Off?	-	Go to Step 10	Go to Step 15
7	1. Turn OFF the ignition. 2. Remove the inflatable steering wheel module. 3. Disconnect C1. 4. Turn ON the ignition, with the engine OFF. 5. Connect a test lamp between the ignition 1 voltage circuit and a good ground. Does the test lamp illuminate?	-	Go to Step 8	Go to Step 19

LTV0500000004078

Fig. 77   Cruise Control Inoperative/Malfunctioning (Part 2 of 5). HHR

Step	Action	Value (s)	Yes	No
8	**Important:** The cruise control on/off switch must be turned ON in order to correctly view the set/coast switch and the resume/accel switch resistance values with the DMM. 1. Turn OFF the ignition. 2. With a DMM, measure the resistance of the cruise control switch between the ignition 1 voltage circuit and the cruise control set/coast and resume/accelerate switch signal circuit. 3. Individually activate and hold the cruise control function switches while measuring the resistance of the cruise control function switches. Do the cruise control function switch resistance values measure between the specified values?	Off = O.L. On = 7.8-8.6 K ohms Resume = 2.7-3.0 K ohms Set = 1.2-1.3 K ohms	Go to Step 16	Go to Step 12
9	**Important:** The cruise control on/off switch must be turned ON in order to correctly view the set/coast switch and the resume/accel switch resistance values with the DMM. 1. Turn OFF the ignition. 2. Remove the inflatable steering wheel module. 3. Disconnect C1. 4. With a DMM, measure the resistance of the cruise control switch between the ignition 1 voltage circuit and the cruise control set/coast and resume/accelerate switch signal circuit. 5. Individually activate and hold the cruise control function switches while measuring the resistance of the cruise control function switches. Do the cruise control function switch resistance values measure between the specified values?	Off = O.L. On = 7.8-8.6 K ohms Resume = 2.7-3.0 K ohms Set = 1.2-1.3 K ohms	Go to Step 18	Go to Step 17
10	Test the cruise control on switch signal circuit for a short to voltage. Did you find and correct the condition?	--	Go to Step 22	Go to Step 11
11	Test the cruise control set/coast and resume/accelerate switch signal circuit for a short to voltage between C1 and the cruise control switch. Did you find and correct the condition?	--	Go to Step 22	Go to Step 17

LTV0500000004079

Fig. 77   Cruise Control Inoperative/Malfunctioning (Part 3 of 5). HHR

Step	Action	Value (s)	Yes	No
12	Test the ignition 1 voltage circuit for an open or for a high resistance between C1 and the cruise control switch. Did you find and correct the condition?	-	Go to Step 22	Go to Step 13
13	Test the cruise control set/coast and resume/accelerate switch signal circuit between C1 and the cruise control switch for the following: • Open • Short to ground • High resistance Did you find and correct the condition?	-	Go to Step 22	Go to Step 14
14	Test the cruise control on switch signal circuit for the following: • Open • Short to ground • High resistance Did you find and correct the condition?	-	Go to Step 22	Go to Step 17
15	Test the cruise control set/coast and resume/accelerate switch signal circuit for a short to voltage between C1 and the engine control module (ECM). Did you find and correct the condition?	-	Go to Step 22	Go to Step 18
16	Test the cruise control set/coast and resume/accelerate switch signal circuit for the following: • Open • Short to ground • High resistance Did you find and correct the condition?	-	Go to Step 22	Go to Step 18
17	Inspect for poor connections at the harness connector of the cruise control switch. Did you find and correct the condition?	-	Go to Step 22	Go to Step 20

LTV0500000004080

Fig. 77   Cruise Control Inoperative/Malfunctioning (Part 4 of 5). HHR

Step	Action	Value (s)	Yes	No
18	Inspect for poor connections at the harness connector of the ECM. Did you find and correct the condition?	-	Go to Step 22	Go to Step 21
19	Repair the following in the ignition 1 voltage circuit: • Open • Short to ground • High resistance Did you complete the repair?	-	Go to Step 22	--
20	Replace the cruise control switch. Did you complete the replacement?	-	Go to Step 22	--
21	Replace the ECM. Did you complete the replacement?	-	Go to Step 22	--
22	1. Install the inflatable steering wheel module. 2. Enable the inflatable restraint steering wheel module. 3. Operate the vehicle with in the conditions for cruise control operation. Does the cruise control system operate properly?	-	System OK	Go to Step 2

LTV0500000004081

Fig. 77   Cruise Control Inoperative/Malfunctioning (Part 5 of 5). HHR

Diagnostic Aids

Important

Perform the following in order to avoid misdiagnosis:

- Inspect for proper operation of brake lamps.
- Inspect throttle linkage for mechanical binding which could cause the system to malfunction.
- Inspect for stored diagnostic trouble codes (DTCs) in the PCM.
- EMI on the speed sensor signal circuit may cause erratic cruise control operation.

Conditions for Enabling Cruise Control

- When vehicle speed is more than 40 km/h (25 mph).
- When PARK, REVERSE, NEUTRAL, or 1 st gear is not indicated by the park neutral position switch.
- When an over/undercharged battery condition does not exist.
- With normal engine rpm.
- Without high engine rpm e.g. fuel cut off.

Step	Action	Value (s)	Yes	No
1	Did you perform the Cruise Control Diagnostic System Check?	--	Go to Step 2	Go to Diagnostic System Check

LTV0500000004162

Fig. 78   Cruise Control Inoperative/Malfunctioning (Part 1 of 7). Montana, Silhouette & Venture

Step		Yes	No
2	1. Turn OFF the ignition. 2. Disconnect the cruise control module. 3. Turn ON the ignition, with the engine OFF. 4. Probe the ignition positive voltage circuit of the cruise control module with a test lamp that is connected to a good ground. Does the test lamp illuminate?	Go to Step 3	Go to Step 36
3	Probe the ignition positive voltage circuit of the cruise control module with a test lamp that is connected to the ground circuit of the cruise control module. Does the test lamp illuminate?	Go to Step 4	Go to Step 37
4	1. Turn OFF the cruise control switch. 2. Probe the on/off, the set/coast, and the resume/accelerate circuits with a test lamp that is connected to a good ground. Does the test lamp illuminate on any of the circuits?	Go to Step 16	Go to Step 5
5	1. Turn ON the cruise control. 2. Probe the on/off circuit with a test lamp that is connected to a good ground. Does the test lamp illuminate?	Go to Step 6	Go to Step 17
6	1. Probe the set/coast circuit with a test lamp that is connected to a good ground. 2. Press and hold the set/coast switch. Does the test lamp illuminate?	Go to Step 7	Go to Step 19
7	1. Probe the resume/accelerate circuit with a test lamp that is connected to a good ground. 2. Press and hold the resume/accel switch. Does the test lamp illuminate?	Go to Step 8	Go to Step 20

LTV0500000004163

Fig. 78 Cruise Control Inoperative/Malfunctioning (Part 2 of 7). Montana, Silhouette & Venture

Step			Yes	No
8	Probe the cruise release switch circuit with a test lamp that is connected to a good ground. Does the test lamp illuminate?	--	Go to Step 9	Go to Step 21
9	Press the brake pedal while monitoring the test lamp. Does the test lamp go out?	--	Go to Step 10	Go to Step 22
10	Probe the stop lamp switch circuit with a test lamp that is connected to a good ground. Does the test lamp illuminate?	--	Go to Step 23	Go to Step 11
11	Press the brake pedal while monitoring the test lamp. Does the test lamp illuminate?	--	Go to Step 12	Go to Step 24
12	Probe the cruise inhibit circuit with a test lamp that is connected to B+. Does the test lamp illuminate?	--	Go to Step 25	Go to Step 13
13	Use a scan tool in order to command the cruise inhibit OFF. Does the test lamp illuminate?	--	Go to Step 14	Go to Step 26
14	Probe the cruise engaged signal circuit with a DMM that is connected to a good ground. Does the voltage measure near the specified value?	B+	Go to Step 15	Go to Step 27
15	Check the speedometer for proper operation. Does the speedometer operate properly?	--	Go to Step 28	Go to Symptoms

LTV0500000004164

Fig. 78 Cruise Control Inoperative/Malfunctioning (Part 3 of 7). Montana, Silhouette & Venture

Step		Yes	No
16	Test the circuit that illuminated the test lamp for a short to voltage. Did you find and correct the condition?	Go to Step 43	Go to Step 34
17	Test the on/off circuit for an open or a high resistance. Did you find and correct the condition?	Go to Step 43	Go to Step 18
18	Test the ignition positive voltage circuit for an open or high resistance between the cruise control module and the cruise control switch. Did you find and correct the condition?	Go to Step 43	Go to Step 34
19	Test the set/coast circuit for an open or a high resistance. Did you find and correct the condition?	Go to Step 43	Go to Step 34
20	Test the resume/accelerate circuit for an open or a high resistance. Did you find and correct the condition?	Go to Step 43	Go to Step 34
21	Test the cruise release switch circuit for an open or a high resistance. Did you find and correct the condition?	Go to Step 43	Go to Step 29
22	Test the cruise release switch circuit for a short to voltage. Did you find and correct the condition?	Go to Step 43	Go to Step 29
23	Test the stop lamp switch signal circuit for a short to voltage. Did you find and correct the condition?	Go to Step 43	Go to Step 30

LTV0500000004165

Fig. 78 Cruise Control Inoperative/Malfunctioning (Part 4 of 7). Montana, Silhouette & Venture

Step		Yes	No
24	Test the stop lamp switch signal circuit for an open or a high resistance. Did you find and correct the condition?	Go to Step 43	Go to Step 30
25	Test the cruise inhibit circuit for a short to ground. Did you find and correct the condition?	Go to Step 43	Go to Step 33
26	Test the cruise inhibit circuit for an open, a high resistance, or a short to voltage. Did you find and correct the condition?	Go to Step 43	Go to Step 33
27	Test the cruise engaged output circuit for an open, a high resistance, or a short to voltage. Did you find and correct the condition?	Go to Step 43	Go to Step 33
28	Test the speed sensor circuit for an open or a high resistance between the PCM and the cruise control module. Did you find and correct the condition?	Go to Step 43	Go to Step 35
29	Inspect the cruise release switch for proper adjustment. Did you find and correct the condition?	Go to Step 43	Go to Step 31
30	Inspect the stop lamp switch for proper adjustment. Did you find and correct the condition?	Go to Step 43	Go to Step 32

LTV0500000004166

Fig. 78 Cruise Control Inoperative/Malfunctioning (Part 5 of 7). Montana, Silhouette & Venture

Step	Action		Yes	No
31	Inspect for poor connections at the harness connector of cruise release switch. Did you find and correct the condition?	-	Go to Step 43	Go to Step 38
32	Inspect for poor connections at the harness connector of the stop lamp switch. Did you find and correct the condition?	-	Go to Step 43	Go to Step 39
33	Inspect for poor connections at the harness connector of the PCM Did you find and correct the condition?	-	Go to Step 43	Go to Step 40
34	Inspect for poor connections at the harness connector of the cruise control switch. Did you find and correct the condition?	-	Go to Step 43	Go to Step 41
35	Inspect for poor connections at the harness connector of the cruise control module. Did you find and correct the condition?	-	Go to Step 43	Go to Step 42
36	Repair the ignition positive voltage circuit of the cruise control module. Did you complete the repair?	-	Go to Step 43	--
37	Repair the ground circuit of the cruise control module. Did you complete the repair?	-	Go to Step 43	--

LTV0500000004167

Fig. 78   Cruise Control Inoperative/Malfunctioning (Part 6 of 7). Montana, Silhouette & Venture

Diagnostic Aids

Caution: Refer to SIR Caution in Cautions and Notices.

Disable the inflatable restraint steering wheel module when performing this diagnostic table.

Perform the following in order to avoid misdiagnosis:

- Ensure that the following cruise control switches are not stuck in the engaged position:
  - On/Off switch
  - Set/Coast switch
  - Resume/Accel switch
  - Cancel switch
- Inspect for proper operation of the stop lamps.
- Rotate the steering wheel to both steering stops and activate each cruise control switch separately. With a scan tool, observe the associated cruise control switch parameter in the Body and Accessories Cruise Control data list. This will help eliminate the possibility of a internally open or shorted inflatable restraint steering wheel module coil.

Test Description

The number below refers to the step number on the diagnostic path.

26. DTCs will set in the PCM when you perform this diagnostic table.

LTV0500000004169

Fig. 79   Cruise Control Inoperative/Malfunctioning (Part 1 of 6). Relay, Terraza, SV6 & Uplander

Step	Action		Yes	No
38	Replace the cruise release switch. Did you complete the replacement?	-	Go to Step 43	--
39	Replace the stop lamp switch. Did you complete the replacement?	-	Go to Step 43	--
40	**Important** The PCM must be programmed after replacement. Replace the PCM. Did you complete the replacement?	-	Go to Step 43	--
41	Replace the multifunction turn signal lever . Did you complete the replacement?	-	Go to Step 43	--
42	Replace the cruise control module. Did you complete the replacement?	-	Go to Step 43	--
43	Operate the vehicle within the conditions for cruise control operation. Does the cruise control system operate correctly?		System OK	Go to Step 2

LTV0500000004168

Fig. 78   Cruise Control Inoperative/Malfunctioning (Part 7 of 7). Montana, Silhouette & Venture

Step	Action	Values	Yes	No
1	Did you perform the Diagnostic System Check - Vehicle?	--	Go to Step 2	Go to Diagnostic System Check
2	Is DTC P0573 current in the powertrain control module (PCM)?	--	Go to DTC P0573	Go to Step 3

3	1. Install a scan tool.
	 2. Turn ON the ignition, with the engine OFF.
	 3. Turn the cruise control On/Off switch OFF.
	 4. With the scan tool, observe the following cruise control parameters in the Body and Accessories Cruise Control data list:
	   - Cruise On/Off Switch
	   - Cruise Resume/Accel Switch
	   - Cruise Set/Coast Switch
	
	 Do any of the parameters listed above display On?
		--	Go to Step 13	Go to Step 4

4	1. With the scan tool, observe the Cruise On/Off Switch parameter. 2. Turn the cruise On/Off switch ON. Does the Cruise On/Off Switch parameter display On?	--	Go to Step 5	Go to Step 9
5	1. With the scan tool, observe the Cruise Set/Coast Switch parameter. 2. Press and hold the Set/Coast switch. Does the Cruise Set/Coast Switch parameter display On?	--	Go to Step 6	Go to Step 11

LTV0500000004170

Fig. 79   Cruise Control Inoperative/Malfunctioning (Part 2 of 6). Relay, Terraza, SV6 & Uplander

Step	Action	Value	Yes	No
6	1. With the scan tool, observe the Cruise Resume/Accel Switch parameter. 2. Press and hold the Resume/Accel switch. Does the Cruise Resume/Accel Switch parameter display On?	--	Go to Step 7	Go to Step 11
7	1. Turn OFF the ignition. 2. Disconnect C3 at the body control module (BCM). 3. Turn ON the ignition, with the engine OFF. 4. With a DMM, measure the voltage of the cruise control cancel signal circuit. Does the voltage measure at or greater than the specified voltage?	0.5 V	Go to Step 19	Go to Step 8
8	1. Activate and hold the cruise control cancel switch. 2. With a DMM, measure the voltage of the cruise control cancel signal circuit. Does the voltage measure at the specified voltage?	B+	Go to Step 12	Go to Step 20
9	1. Turn OFF the ignition. 2. Remove the inflatable restraint steering wheel module. 3. Disconnect C6. 4. Turn ON the ignition, with the engine OFF. 5. Connect a test lamp between the ignition 1 voltage circuit and a good ground. Does the test lamp illuminate?	--	Go to Step 10	Go to Step 22
10	**Important:** The cruise control on/off switch must be turned ON in order to correctly view the Cancel switch, set/coast switch, and the resume/accel switch resistance values with the DMM. 1. With a DMM, measure the resistance of the cruise control switch between the ignition 1 voltage circuit and the cruise control set/coast and resume/accelerate switch signal circuit at the cruise control switch. 2. Individually activate and hold the cruise control function switches while measuring the resistance of the cruise control function switches. Do the cruise control function switch resistance values measure between the specified values?	Off = O.L. On = 7.8 K-8.6 K ohms Resume = 2.7 K-3.0 K ohms Set = 1.2 K-1.3 K ohms Cancel = 0-1 K ohms	Go to Step 15	Go to Step 16

LTV0500000004171

Fig. 79 Cruise Control Inoperative/Malfunctioning (Part 3 of 6). Relay, Terraza, SV6 & Uplander

Step	Action	Value	Yes	No
11	**Important:** The cruise control on/off switch must be turned ON in order to correctly view the Cancel switch, set/coast switch, and the resume/accel switch resistance values with the DMM. 1. Turn OFF the ignition. 2. Remove the inflatable restraint steering wheel module. 3. Disconnect C6. 4. With a DMM, measure the resistance of the cruise control switch between the ignition 1 voltage circuit and the cruise control set/coast and resume/accelerate switch signal circuit at the cruise control switch. 5. Individually activate and hold the cruise control function switches while measuring the resistance of the cruise control function switches. Do the cruise control function switch resistance values measure between the specified values?	Off = O.L. On = 7.8 K-8.6 K ohms Resume = 2.7 K-3.0 K ohms Set = 1.2 K-1.3 K ohms Cancel = 0-1 K ohms	Go to Step 15	Go to Step 16
12	1. Turn OFF the ignition. 2. Connect C3 at the BCM. 3. Disconnect the throttle actuator control (TAC) module. 4. Turn ON the ignition, with the engine OFF. 5. With a DMM, measure the voltage of the stop lamp switch signal circuit. Does the voltage measure greater than the specified value?	8.5 V	Go to Step 18	Go to Step 21
13	1. Turn OFF the ignition. 2. Remove the inflatable restraint steering wheel module. 3. Disconnect C6. 4. Turn ON the ignition, with the engine OFF. 5. With the scan tool, observe the following cruise control parameters: - Cruise On/Off Switch - Cruise Resume/Accel Switch - Cruise Set/Coast Switch Do any of the parameters listed above display On?	--	Go to Step 14	Go to Step 16
14	Test the cruise control set/coast and resume/accel switch signal circuit for a short to voltage. Did you find and correct the condition?		Go to Step 26	Go to Step 17

LTV0500000004172

Fig. 79 Cruise Control Inoperative/Malfunctioning (Part 4 of 6). Relay, Terraza, SV6 & Uplander

Step	Action	Value	Yes	No
15	Test the cruise control Set/Coast and Resume/Accel switch signal circuit for the following: • Short to ground • Open • High Resistance Did you find and correct the condition?		Go to Step 26	Go to Step 17
16	Inspect for poor connections at the harness connector of the cruise control switch. Did you find and correct the condition?		Go to Step 26	Go to Step 23
17	Inspect for poor connections at the harness connector of the PCM. Did you find and correct the condition?		Go to Step 26	Go to Step 25
18	Inspect for poor connections at the harness connector of the TAC module. Did you find and correct the condition?		Go to Step 26	Go to Step 24
19	Repair the short to voltage in the cruise control cancel signal circuit. Did you complete the repair?		Go to Step 26	--
20	Repair the following in the cruise control cancel signal circuit: • Short to ground • Open • High Resistance Did you complete the repair?		Go to Step 26	--
21	Repair the open or the high resistance in the stop lamp switch signal circuit between the underhood fuse block and the TAC module. Did you complete the repair?		Go to Step 26	--

LTV0500000004173

Fig. 79 Cruise Control Inoperative/Malfunctioning (Part 5 of 6). Relay, Terraza, SV6 & Uplander

Step	Action	Value	Yes	No
22	Repair the open, the short to ground, or the high resistance in the ignition 1 voltage circuit. Did you complete the repair?		Go to Step 26	--
23	Replace the cruise control switch. Did you complete the replacement?		Go to Step 26	--
24	Replace the TAC module. Did you complete the replacement?		Go to Step 26	--
25	Replace the PCM. Did you complete the replacement?		Go to Step 26	--
26	1. Install the inflatable restraint steering wheel module. 2. Enable the inflatable restraint steering wheel module. 3. Use the scan tool in order to clear the PCM DTCs. 4. Operate the cruise control system in order to verify the repair. Does the cruise control system operate properly?		System OK	Go to Step 2

LTV0500000004174

Fig. 79 Cruise Control Inoperative/Malfunctioning (Part 6 of 6). Relay, Terraza, SV6 & Uplander

Step	Action	Values	Yes	No
1	Did you perform the Cruise Control Diagnostic System Check?	--	Go to Step 2	Go to Diagnostic System Check
2	Turn the ignition ON, with the engine OFF. Does the Cruise indicator illuminate after the instrument panel cluster (IPC) displays test?	--	Go to Step 3	Test for Intermittent and Poor Connections
3	1. Turn the ignition OFF. 2. Install a scan tool. 3. Turn the ignition ON, with the engine OFF. 4. With the scan tool, observe the Cruise Control parameter in the IPC data list. Does the Cruise Lamp parameter display On?	--	Go to Step 4	Go to Step 9
4	1. Turn the ignition OFF. 2. Disconnect the cruise control module. 3. Turn the ignition ON, with the engine OFF. 4. With a DMM, measure the voltage of the cruise control engaged signal circuit. Does the voltage measure at approximately the specified voltage?	B+	Go to Step 7	Go to Step 5

LTV0500000004175

Fig. 80 Cruise Control Indicator Always On. (Part 1 of 2). Sierra & Silverado Less TAC

Step	Action	Yes	No
5	Test the Cruise control engaged signal circuit for a short to ground. Did you find and correct the condition?	Go to Step 10	Go to Step 6
6	Inspect for a poor connection at the harness connector of the PCM. Did you find and correct the condition?	Go to Step 10	Go to Step 8
7	Replace the cruise control module. Did you complete the replacement?	Go to Step 10	--
8	**Important:** Program the replacement PCM. Replace the PCM. Did you complete the replacement?	Go to Step 10	--
9	Replace the Instrument Panel Cluster (IPC). Did you complete the replacement?	Go to Step 10	--
10	Operate the system in order to verify the repair. Does the system operate properly?	System OK	Go to Step 2

LTV0500000004176

Fig. 80 Cruise Control Indicator Always On. (Part 2 of 2). Sierra & Silverado Less TAC

Step	Action	Yes	No
1	Did you perform the Cruise Control Diagnostic System Check?	Go to Step 2	Go to Diagnostic System Check
2	Turn the ignition ON, with the engine OFF. Does the Cruise indicator illuminate after the instrument panel cluster (IPC) displays test?	Go to Step 3	Test for Intermittent and Poor Connections
3	1. Turn the ignition OFF. 2. Install a scan tool. 3. Turn the ignition ON, with the engine OFF. 4. With the scan tool, observe the Cruise Control parameter in the IPC data list. Does the Cruise Lamp parameter display On?	Go to Step 4	Go to Step 5

LTV0500000004177

Fig. 81 Cruise Control Indicator Always On (Part 1 of 2). Sierra & Silverado w/TAC

Step	Action	Yes	No
4	**Important:** Program the replacement PCM. Replace the PCM. Did you complete the replacement?	Go to Step 6	--
5	Replace the IPC. Did you complete the replacement?	Go to Step 6	--
6	Operate the system in order to verify the repair. Does the system operate properly?	System OK	Go to Step 2

LTV0500000004178

Fig. 81 Cruise Control Indicator Always On (Part 2 of 2). Sierra & Silverado w/TAC

Step	Action	Values	Yes	No
1	Did you perform the Cruise Control Diagnostic System Check?	--	Go to Step 2	Go to Diagnostic System Check
2	1. Turn the ignition OFF. 2. Install a scan tool. 3. Turn the ignition ON, with the engine OFF. 4. With the scan tool, Command the Cruise Control Lamp Test parameter ON, in the instrument panel cluster (IPC) Special Functions. Does the Cruise indicator illuminate in the IPC?	--	Go to Step 3	Go to Step 8
3	1. Turn the ignition OFF. 2. Disconnect the cruise control module. 3. Turn the ignition ON, with the engine OFF. 4. With a DMM, measure the voltage of the cruise control engaged signal circuit. Does the voltage measure at approximately the specified voltage?	B+	Go to Step 4	Go to Step 5
4	Test the cruise control engaged signal circuit for a short to voltage. Did you find and correct the condition?	--	Go to Step 10	Go to Step 7

LTV0500000004179

Fig. 82 Cruise Control Indicator Inoperative (Part 1 of 2). Sierra & Silvarado Less TAC

Step	Action	Yes	No
5	Test the cruise control engaged signal circuit for an open or for a high resistance. Did you find and correct the condition?	Go to Step 10	Go to Step 6
6	Inspect for poor connections at the harness connector of the PCM. Did you find and correct the condition?	Go to Step 10	Go to Step 9
7	Replace the cruise control module. Did you complete the replacement?	Go to Step 10	--
8	Replace the instrument panel cluster (IPC). Did you complete the replacement?	Go to Step 10	--
9	**Important:** Program the replacement PCM. Replace the PCM. Did you complete the replacement?	Go to Step 10	--
10	Operate the system in order to verify the repair. Does the system operate properly?	System OK	Go to Step 2

LTV0500000004180

Fig. 82 Cruise Control Indicator Inoperative (Part 2 of 2). Sierra & Silvarado Less TAC

Step	Action	Yes	No
1	Did you perform the Cruise Control Diagnostic System Check?	Go to Step 2	Go to Diagnostic System Check
2	1. Turn the ignition OFF. 2. Install a scan tool. 3. Turn the ignition ON, with the engine OFF. 4. With the scan tool, command the Cruise Control Lamp Test parameter On, in the instrument panel cluster (IPC) Special Functions. Does the Cruise indicator illuminate in the IPC?	Go to Step 4	Go to Step 3
3	Replace the IPC. Did you complete the replacement?	Go to Step 5	--
4	**Important:** Program the replacement PCM. Replace the PCM. Did you complete the replacement?	Go to Step 5	--
5	Operate the system in order to verify the repair. Does the system operate properly?	System OK	Go to Step 2

LTV0500000004181

Fig. 83 Cruise Control Indicator Inoperative. Sierra & Silverado w/TAC

Step	Action	Yes	No
4	1. Turn ON the ignition, with the engine OFF. 2. Turn OFF the cruise control. 3. Probe the on/off, the set/coast, and the resume/accelerate signal circuits with a test lamp that is connected to a good ground. Does the test lamp illuminate on any of the circuits?	Go to Step 16	Go to Step 5
5	1. Turn ON the ignition, with the engine OFF. 2. Turn ON the cruise control. 3. Probe the cruise control on/off signal circuit with a test lamp that is connected to a good ground. Does the test lamp illuminate?	Go to Step 6	Go to Step 17
6	1. Probe the cruise control set/coast signal circuit with a test lamp that is connected to a good ground. 2. Press and hold the SET/COAST switch. Does the test lamp illuminate?	Go to Step 7	Go to Step 19
7	1. Probe the cruise control resume/accelerate signal circuit with a test lamp that is connected to a good ground. 2. Press and hold the RESUME/ACCEL switch. Does the test lamp illuminate?	Go to Step 8	Go to Step 20
8	Probe the TCC/brake, cruise release signal circuit with a test lamp that is connected to a good ground. Does the test lamp illuminate?	Go to Step 11	Go to Step 9
9	Is the vehicle equipped with a manual transmission?	Go to Step 10	Go to Step 21
10	1. Turn OFF the ignition. 2. Disconnect the clutch pedal position (CPP) switch. 3. Turn ON the ignition, with the engine OFF. 4. Probe the CPP switch harness connector ignition positive voltage circuit with a test lamp connected to a good ground. Does the test lamp illuminate?	Go to Step 22	Go to Step 21

LTV0500000004183

Fig. 84 Cruise Control Inoperative/Malfunction (Part 2 of 6). 2002 Sierra & Silverado Gas Engines Less ETC

Diagnostic Aids

Important: Perform the following in order to avoid misdiagnosis.

- Inspect for proper operation of brake lamps and clutch switch, if equipped.
- Inspect for proper operation of the transmission range switch.
- Inspect throttle linkage for mechanical binding which could cause the system to malfunction.
- Inspect cruise control cable adjustment, should have minimum slack.
- EMI on the speed sensor signal circuit may cause erratic cruise control operation.

Conditions for Enabling Cruise Control

The vehicle speed is greater than 40 km/h (25 mph).

Step	Action	Value (s)	Yes	No
1	Did you perform the Cruise Control Diagnostic System Check?	--	Go to Step 2	Go to Diagnostic System Check
2	1. Turn OFF the ignition. 2. Disconnect the cruise control module. 3. Turn ON the ignition, with the engine OFF. 4. Probe the ignition positive voltage circuit of the cruise control module with a test lamp that is connected to a good ground. Does the test lamp illuminate?	--	Go to Step 3	Go to Step 33
3	Probe the ignition positive voltage circuit of the cruise control module with a test lamp that is connected to the ground circuit of the cruise control module. Does the test lamp illuminate?	--	Go to Step 4	Go to Step 34

LTV0500000004182

Fig. 84 Cruise Control Inoperative/Malfunction (Part 1 of 6). 2002 Sierra & Silverado Gas Engines Less ETC

Step	Action	Value (s)	Yes	No
11	Press the brake pedal while monitoring the test lamp. Does the test lamp illuminate?	--	Go to Step 23	Go to Step 12
12	Probe the stoplamp switch signal circuit with a test lamp that is connected to a good ground. Does the test lamp illuminate?	--	Go to Step 24	Go to Step 13
13	Press the brake pedal while monitoring the test lamp. Does the test lamp illuminate?	--	Go to Step 14	Go to Step 25
14	Probe the cruise engaged signal circuit with a DMM that is connected to a good ground. Does the voltage measure near the specified value?	B+	Go to Step 15	Go to Step 26
15	Check the speedometer for proper operation. Does the speedometer operate properly?	--	Go to Step 27	Go to Symptoms
16	Test the circuit that illuminated the test lamp for a short to voltage. Did you find and correct the condition?	--	Go to Step 40	Go to Step 30
17	Test the cruise control on/off signal circuit for an open, high resistance or short to ground and the set/coast, resume/accel signal circuits for a short to ground. Did you find and correct the condition?	--	Go to Step 40	Go to Step 18

LTV0500000004184

Fig. 84 Cruise Control Inoperative/Malfunction (Part 3 of 6). 2002 Sierra & Silverado Gas Engines Less ETC

18	Test the ignition positive voltage circuit of the cruise control switch for an open or high resistance. Did you find and correct the condition?	Go to Step 40	Go to Step 30
19	Test the set/coast switch signal circuit for an open or a high resistance. Did you find and correct the condition?	Go to Step 40	Go to Step 30
20	Test the resume/accelerate switch signal circuit for an open or a high resistance. Did you find and correct the condition?	Go to Step 40	Go to Step 30
21	Test the TCC/ brake, cruise release signal circuit for an open or a high resistance . Did you find and correct the condition?	Go to Step 40	Go to Step 28
22	Test the TCC/ brake, cruise release signal circuit for an open or a high resistance between the CPP switch and the cruise control module. Did you find and correct the condition?	Go to Step 40	Go to Step 35
23	Test the TCC/ brake, cruise release switch signal circuit for a short to voltage. Did you find and correct the condition?	Go to Step 40	Go to Step 28
24	Test the stoplamp switch signal circuit for a short to voltage. Did you find and correct the condition?	Go to Step 40	Go to Step 28

LTV0500000004185

Fig. 84 Cruise Control Inoperative/Malfunction (Part 4 of 6). 2002 Sierra & Silverado Gas Engines Less ETC

25	Test the stoplamp switch signal circuit for an open or a high resistance. Did you find and correct the condition?	Go to Step 40	Go to Step 28
26	Test the cruise engaged signal circuit for an open, a high resistance, or a short to ground. Did you find and correct the condition?	Go to Step 40	Go to Step 29
27	Test the speed sensor circuit for an open or a high resistance between the PCM and cruise control module. Did you find and correct the condition?	Go to Step 40	Go to Step 31
28	Inspect for poor connections at the harness connector of the stop lamp switch. Did you find and correct the condition?	Go to Step 40	Go to Step 36
29	Inspect for poor connections at the harness connector of the PCM. Did you find and correct the condition?	Go to Step 40	Go to Step 37
30	Inspect for poor connections at the harness connector of the cruise control switch. Did you complete the replacement?	Go to Step 40	Go to Step 38
31	Inspect for poor connections at the harness connector of the cruise control module. Did you complete the replacement?	Go to Step 40	Go to Step 39

LTV0500000004186

Fig. 84 Cruise Control Inoperative/Malfunction (Part 5 of 6). 2002 Sierra & Silverado Gas Engines Less ETC

32	Inspect for poor connections at the harness connector of the CPP switch. Did you complete the replacement?	Go to Step 40	Go to Step 35
33	Repair the ignition positive voltage circuit of the cruise control module. Did you complete the replacement?	Go to Step 40	--
34	Repair the ground circuit of the cruise control module. Did you complete the replacement?	Go to Step 40	--
35	Replace the CPP switch. Did you complete the replacement?	Go to Step 40	--
36	Replace the stop lamp switch. Did you complete the replacement?	Go to Step 40	--
37	**Important:** The PCM must be reprogrammed after replacement. Replace the PCM. Did you complete the replacement?	Go to Step 40	--
38	Replace the cruise control switch. Did you complete the replacement?	Go to Step 40	--
39	Replace the cruise control module. Did you complete the replacement?	Go to Step 40	--
40	Operate the vehicle within the conditions for cruise control operation. Does the cruise control system operate correctly?	System OK	Go to Step 2

LTV0500000004187

Fig. 84 Cruise Control Inoperative/Malfunction (Part 6 of 6). 2002 Sierra & Silverado Gas Engines Less ETC

Diagnostic Aids

Important: Perform the following in order to avoid misdiagnosis.

- Inspect for proper operation of brake lamps and clutch switch, if equipped.
- Inspect for proper operation of the transmission range switch.
- EMI on the speed sensor signal circuit may cause erratic cruise control operation.

Conditions for Enabling Cruise Control

The vehicle speed is greater than 40 km/h (25 mph).

Step	Action	Yes	No
1	Did you perform A Diagnostic System Check - Cruise Control?	Go to Step 2	Go to Diagnostic System Check
2	1. Turn OFF the ignition. 2. Disconnect the Throttle Actuator Control (TAC) module. 3. Turn ON the ignition, with the engine OFF. 4. Turn OFF the cruise control switch. 5. Probe the on/off, the set/coast, and the resume/accelerate circuits with a test lamp that is connected to a good ground. Does the test lamp illuminate on any of the circuits?	Go to Step 16	Go to Step 3
3	1. Turn ON the ignition, with the engine OFF. 2. Turn ON the cruise control. 3. Probe the on/off circuit with a test lamp that is connected to a good ground. Does the test lamp illuminate?	Go to Step 4	Go to Step 17

LTV0500000004188

Fig. 85 Cruise Control Inoperative/Malfunctioning (Part 1 of 6). 2002 Sierra & Silverado Gas Engines w/ETC

Step	Action	Yes	No
4	1. Probe the set/coast circuit with a test lamp that is connected to a good ground. 2. Press and hold the SET/COAST switch. Does the test lamp illuminate?	Go to Step 5	Go to Step 19
5	1. Probe the resume/accelerate circuit with a test lamp that is connected to a good ground. 2. Press and hold the RESUME/ACCEL switch. Does the test lamp illuminate?	Go to Step 6	Go to Step 20
6	Probe the stop lamp switch signal circuit with a test lamp that is connected to a good ground. Does the test lamp illuminate?	Go to Step 23	Go to Step 7
7	Press the brake pedal while monitoring the test lamp. Does the test lamp illuminate?	Go to Step 8	Go to Step 21
8	Is the vehicle equipped with a manual transmission?	Go to Step 9	Go to Step 11
9	1. Turn OFF the ignition. 2. Disconnect the Powertrain Control Module (PCM). 3. Turn ON the ignition, with the engine OFF. 4. Probe the clutch pedal position (CPP) switch signal circuit of the PCM harness connector with a test lamp connected to a good ground. Does the test lamp illuminate?	Go to Step 10	Go to Step 14
10	Press the clutch pedal while monitoring the test lamp. Does the test lamp illuminate?	Go to Step 27	Go to Step 11
11	Probe the brake switch signal circuit of the ECM harness connector with a test lamp connected to a good ground. Does the test lamp illuminate?	Go to Step 12	Go to Step 15

LTV0500000004189

Fig. 85 Cruise Control Inoperative/Malfunctioning (Part 2 of 6). 2002 Sierra & Silverado Gas Engines w/ETC

Step	Action	Yes	No
12	Press the brake pedal while monitoring the test lamp. Does the test lamp illuminate?	Go to Step 24	Go to Step 13
13	Check the speedometer for proper operation. Does the speedometer operate properly?	Go to Step 33	Go to Symptoms
14	1. Turn OFF the ignition. 2. Disconnect the CPP switch. 3. Turn ON the ignition, with the engine OFF. 4. Probe the CPP switch ignition positive voltage circuit with a test lamp connected to a good ground. Does the test lamp illuminate?	Go to Step 26	Go to Step 28
15	1. Turn OFF the ignition. 2. Disconnect the brake switch. 3. Probe the brake switch ignition positive voltage circuit with a test lamp connected to a good ground. Does the test lamp illuminate?	Go to Step 25	Go to Step 29
16	Test the circuit that illuminated the test lamp for a short to voltage. Did you find and correct the condition?	Go to Step 38	Go to Step 32
17	Test the on/off signal circuit for a open, high resistance or short to ground and the S/C and R/A signal circuits for a short to ground. Did you find and correct the condition?	Go to Step 38	Go to Step 18
18	Test the ignition positive voltage circuit of the cruise control switch for a open, high resistance or short to ground. Did you find and correct the condition?	Go to Step 38	Go to Step 32

LTV0500000004190

Fig. 85 Cruise Control Inoperative/Malfunctioning (Part 3 of 6). 2002 Sierra & Silverado Gas Engines w/ETC

Step	Action	Yes	No
19	Test the set/coast circuit for a open, high resistance or short to ground. Did you find and correct the condition?	Go to Step 38	Go to Step 32
20	Test the resume/accelerate circuit for a open, high resistance or short to ground. Did you find and correct the condition?	Go to Step 38	Go to Step 32
21	Test the stop lamp signal circuit for a open, high resistance or short to ground. Did you find and correct the condition?	Go to Step 38	Go to Step 22
22	Test the stop lamp ignition positive voltage circuit for a open, high resistance or short to ground. Did you find and correct the condition?	Go to Step 38	Go to Step 31
23	Test the stop lamp switch signal circuit for a short to voltage. Did you find and correct the condition?	Go to Step 38	Go to Step 31
24	Test the brake switch circuit for a short to voltage. Did you find and correct the condition?	Go to Step 38	Go to Step 31
25	Test the brake switch signal circuit of the PCM harness for an open or a high resistance. Did you find and correct the condition?	Go to Step 38	Go to Step 31
26	Test the CPP signal circuit for a open, high resistance or short to ground. Did you find and correct the condition?	Go to Step 38	Go to Step 30
27	Test the CPP signal circuit of the PCM harness for a short to voltage. Did you find and correct the condition?	Go to Step 38	Go to Step 30

LTV0500000004191

Fig. 85 Cruise Control Inoperative/Malfunctioning (Part 4 of 6). 2002 Sierra & Silverado Gas Engines w/ETC

Step	Action	Yes	No
28	Repair the open in the ignition positive voltage circuit of the CPF switch. Did you complete the repair?	Go to Step 38	--
29	Repair the open in the ignition positive voltage circuit of the stop lamp switch. Did you complete the repair?	Go to Step 38	--
30	Inspect for poor connections at the harness connector of the CPP switch. Did you find and correct the condition?	Go to Step 38	Go to Step 34
31	Inspect for poor connections at the harness connector of the stop lamp switch. Did you find and correct the condition?	Go to Step 38	Go to Step 35
32	Inspect for poor connections at the harness connector of the cruise control switch. Did you find and correct the condition?	Go to Step 38	Go to Step 36
33	Inspect for poor connections at the harness connector of the Throttle Actuator Control (TAC) Module. Did you find and correct the condition?	Go to Step 38	Go to Step 37
34	Replace the CPP switch. Did you complete the replacement?	Go to Step 38	--

LTV0500000004192

Fig. 85 Cruise Control Inoperative/Malfunctioning (Part 5 of 6). 2002 Sierra & Silverado Gas Engines w/ETC

35	Replace the Stop lamp switch. Did you complete the replacement?	Go to Step 38	--
36	Replace the cruise control switch. Did you complete the replacement?	Go to Step 38	--
37	Replace the Throttle Actuator Control (TAC) Module. Did you complete the replacement?	Go to Step 38	--
38	Operate the vehicle within the conditions for cruise control operation. Does the cruise control system operate correctly?	System OK	Go to Step 2

LTV0500000004193

Fig. 85 Cruise Control Inoperative/Malfunctioning (Part 6 of 6). 2002 Sierra & Silverado Gas Engines w/ETC

4	1. Observe the cruise control Resume/Accelerate parameter in the PCM data list. 2. Press the Resume/Accelerate switch. Did the cruise control Resume Accelerate parameter change state?	Go to Step 5	Go to Step 15
5	1. Observe the stop lamp switch parameter in the PCM data list. 2. Press the brake pedal. Did the stop lamp switch parameter change state?	Go to Step 6	Go to Step 10
6	1. Observe the TCC/Brake switch parameter in the PCM data list. 2. Press the brake pedal. Did the cruise release switch parameter change state?	Go to Step 7	Go to Step 11
7	Is the vehicle equipped with a manual transmission?	Go to Step 8	Go to Step 29
8	1. Observe the clutch pedal position (CPP) switch parameter in the PCM data list. 2. Press the clutch pedal. Did the CPP switch parameter change state?	Go to Step 29	Go to Step 12
9	1. Turn OFF the ignition. 2. Disconnect the multifunction turn signal lever. 3. Turn ON the ignition, with the engine OFF. 4. Probe the multifunction turn signal lever ignition positive voltage circuit with a test lamp connected to a good ground. Did the test lamp illuminate?	Go to Step 13	Go to Step 21
10	1. Turn OFF the ignition. 2. Disconnect the stop lamp switch harness connector. 3. Turn ON the ignition, with the engine OFF. 4. Probe the stop lamp battery positive voltage feed circuit with a test lamp connected to a good ground. Did the test lamp illuminate?	Go to Step 16	Go to Step 22

LTV0500000004195

Fig. 86 Cruise Control Inoperative/Malfunctioning (Part 2 of 5). 2002 Sierra & Silverado w/Diesel Engine

Diagnostic Aids

Important: Perform the following in order to avoid misdiagnosis.

- Inspect for proper operation of brake lamps and clutch switch, if equipped.
- Inspect for proper operation of the transmission range switch.
- EMI on the speed sensor signal circuit may cause erratic cruise control operation.
- Wiring on upfitted equipment must also be tested.

Conditions for Enabling Cruise Control

The vehicle speed is greater than 40 km/h (25 mph).

Step	Action	Yes	No
1	Did you perform A Diagnostic System Check - Cruise Control?	Go to Step 2	Go to Diagnostic System Check
2	1. Connect a scan tool. 2. Monitor the Cruise On switch parameter in the powertrain control module (PCM) data list. 3. Turn ON the cruise control switch. Did the scan tool parameter change state?	Go to Step 3	Go to Step 9
3	1. Observe the cruise control Set/Coast parameter in the PCM data list. 2. Press the cruise control Set button. Did the cruise control Set/Coast parameter change state?	Go to Step 4	Go to Step 14

LTV0500000004194

Fig. 86 Cruise Control Inoperative/Malfunctioning (Part 1 of 5). 2002 Sierra & Silverado w/Diesel Engine

11	1. Turn OFF the ignition. 2. Disconnect the TCC/Brake switch harness connector. 3. Turn ON the ignition, with the engine OFF. 4. Probe the TCC/Brake switch ignition positive voltage circuit with a test lamp connected to a good ground. Did the test lamp illuminate?	Go to Step 18	Go to Step 23
12	1. Turn OFF the ignition. 2. Disconnect the clutch pedal position (CPP) switch. 3. Turn ON the ignition, with the engine OFF. 4. Probe the CPP switch ignition positive voltage circuit with a test lamp connected to a good ground. Did the test lamp illuminate?	Go to Step 20	Go to Step 24
13	Test the cruise control ON switch signal circuit for a open, high resistance, short to ground or short to voltage. Did you find and correct the condition?	Go to Step 35	Go to Step 28
14	Test the cruise control Set/Coast signal circuit for a open, high resistance, short to ground or short to voltage. Did you find and correct the condition?	Go to Step 35	Go to Step 28
15	Test the cruise control Resume/Accelerate signal circuit for a open, high resistance, short to ground or short to voltage. Did you find and correct the condition?	Go to Step 35	Go to Step 28
16	Test the stop lamp switch signal circuit for a open, high resistance, short to ground or short to voltage. Did you find and correct the condition?	Go to Step 35	Go to Step 17
17	Check the stop lamp switch for proper adjustment. Did you find and correct the condition?	Go to Step 35	Go to Step 25

LTV0500000004196

Fig. 86 Cruise Control Inoperative/Malfunctioning (Part 3 of 5). 2002 Sierra & Silverado w/Diesel Engine

		Yes	No
18	Test the TCC/Brake switch signal circuit for a open, high resistance, short to ground or short to voltage. Did you find and correct the condition?	Go to Step 35	Go to Step 19
19	Check the TCC/Brake switch for proper adjustment. Did you find and correct the condition?	Go to Step 35	Go to Step 26
20	Test the CPP switch signal circuit for a open, high resistance, short to ground or short to voltage. Did you find and correct the condition?	Go to Step 35	Go to Step 27
21	Repair the open, high resistance or short to ground in the multifunction turn signal lever ignition positive voltage feed circuit. Did you complete the repair?	Go to Step 35	--
22	Repair the open, high resistance or short to ground in the stop lamp switch battery positive voltage circuit. Did you complete the repair?	Go to Step 35	--
23	Repair the open, high resistance or short to ground in the TCC/Brake switch battery positive voltage circuit. Did you complete the repair?	Go to Step 35	--
24	Repair the open, high resistance or short to ground in the CPP switch battery positive voltage circuit. Did you complete the repair?	Go to Step 35	--
25	Inspect for poor connections at the harness connector of the stop lamp switch. Did you find and correct the condition?	Go to Step 35	Go to Step 30

LTV0500000004197

Fig. 86 Cruise Control Inoperative/Malfunctioning (Part 4 of 5). 2002 Sierra & Silverado w/Diesel Engine

Diagnostic Aids

Perform the following in order to avoid a misdiagnosis:

- Inspect for proper operation of the brake lamps.
- Electromagnetic interference (EMI) on the vehicle speed sensor signal circuit may cause erratic cruise control operation.

Conditions for Enabling Cruise Control

- The vehicle speed is greater than 40 km/h (25 mph).
- The vehicle is not in PARK, REVERSE, NEUTRAL, or 1st gear.
- The system voltage is within 12-16 volts.

Test Description

The numbers below refer to the step numbers on the diagnostic table.

8. This step tests the center high mounted stop lamp (CHMSL) supply voltage/stop lamp supply voltage circuit for an open or for a high resistance between the stop lamp switch and the throttle actuator control (TAC) module.

9. This step tests the cruise control set/coast switch signal circuit for an open or for a high resistance.

10. This step tests the cruise control resume/accel switch signal circuit for an open or for a high resistance.

11. This step tests the ignition 3 voltage circuit for an open, for a short to ground, or for a high resistance.

29. DTCs will set in the powertrain control module (PCM) when you perform this table.

LTV0500000004199

Fig. 87 Cruise Control Inoperative/Malfunctioning (Part 1 of 6). 2003-06 Sierra & Silverado w/4.8L, 5.3L, 6.0L & 8.1L Engines

		Yes	No
26	Inspect for poor connections at the harness connector of the TCC/Brake switch. Did you find and correct the condition?	Go to Step 35	Go to Step 31
27	Inspect for poor connections at the harness connector of the CPP switch. Did you find and correct the condition?	Go to Step 35	Go to Step 32
28	Inspect for poor connections at the harness connector of the multifunction turn signal lever. Did you find and correct the condition?	Go to Step 35	Go to Step 33
29	Inspect for poor connections at the harness connector of the PCM. Did you find and correct the condition?	Go to Step 35	Go to Step 34
30	Replace the stop lamp switch. Did you complete the repair?	Go to Step 35	--
31	Replace the TCC/Brake switch. Did you complete the repair?	Go to Step 35	--
32	Replace the CPP switch. Did you complete the repair?	Go to Step 35	--
33	Replace the multifunction turn signal lever. Did you complete the repair?	Go to Step 35	--
34	Important: The PCM must be reprogrammed after replacement. Replace the PCM.	Go to Step 35	--
35	Operate the vehicle with in the conditions for cruise control operation. Does the cruise control system operate properly?	System OK	Go to Step 2

LTV0500000004198

Fig. 86 Cruise Control Inoperative/Malfunctioning (Part 5 of 5). 2002 Sierra & Silverado w/Diesel Engine

Step	Action	Yes	No
1	Did you perform the Diagnostic System Check - Cruise Control?	Go to Step 2	Go to Diagnostic System Check
2	1. Install a scan tool. 2. Turn the ignition ON, with the engine OFF. 3. Turn the cruise control On/Off switch OFF. 4. With the scan tool, observe the Cruise On/Off Switch parameter in the powertrain control module (PCM) Cruise Control Data data list. Does the Cruise On/Off Switch parameter display Off?	Go to Step 4	Go to Step 3
3	1. Turn the ignition OFF. 2. Disconnect C4 of the multifunction switch. 3. Turn the ignition ON, with the engine OFF. 4. With the scan tool, observe the Cruise On/Off Switch parameter. Does the Cruise On/Off Switch parameter display Off?	Go to Step 22	Go to Step 13
4	1. Turn the cruise control On/Off switch ON. 2. With the scan tool, observe the Cruise On/Off Switch parameter. Does the Cruise On/Off Switch parameter display On?	Go to Step 5	Go to Step 11
5	1. With the scan tool, observe the Cruise Set/Coast Switch parameter in the PCM Cruise Control Data data list. 2. Turn the cruise control On/Off switch ON. 3. Press and hold the cruise control Set/Coast button. Does the Cruise Set/Coast Switch parameter Display On?	Go to Step 6	Go to Step 9
6	1. With the scan tool, observe the Cruise Resume/Accel. Switch parameter in the PCM Cruise Control Data data list. 2. Press and hold the Resume/Accel switch. Does the Cruise Resume/Accel. Switch parameter Display On?	Go to Step 7	Go to Step 10

LTV0500000004200

Fig. 87 Cruise Control Inoperative/Malfunctioning (Part 2 of 6). 2003-06 Sierra & Silverado w/4.8L, 5.3L, 6.0L & 8.1L Engines

Step	Action	Yes	No
7	Do the stop lamps operate properly?	Go to Step 8	Diagnose Stop Lamps Inoperative
8	1. With the scan tool, observe the Stoplamp Pedal Switch parameter in the PCM Cruise Control Data data list. 2. Depress and hold the brake pedal. Does the Stoplamp Pedal Switch parameter Display Applied?	Go to Diagnostic Aids	Go to Step 21
9	1. Turn the ignition OFF. 2. Disconnect the cruise control switch. 3. Turn the ignition ON, with the engine OFF. 4. Connect a 3-ampere fused jumper between the cruise control set/coast switch signal circuit and the ignition 3 voltage circuit. 5. With the scan tool, observe the Cruise Set/Coast Switch parameter. Does the Cruise Set/Coast Switch parameter Display On?	Go to Step 22	Go to Step 19
10	1. Turn the ignition OFF. 2. Disconnect the cruise control switch. 3. Turn the ignition ON, with the engine OFF. 4. Connect a 3-ampere fused jumper between the cruise control resume/accel switch signal circuit and the ignition 3 voltage circuit. 5. With the scan tool, observe the Cruise Resume/Accel. Switch parameter. Does the Cruise Resume/Accel. Switch parameter Display On?	Go to Step 22	Go to Step 20
11	1. Turn the ignition OFF. 2. Disconnect the cruise control switch. 3. Turn the ignition ON, with the engine OFF. 4. Connect a test lamp between the ignition 3 voltage circuit and a good ground. Does the test lamp illuminate?	Go to Step 12	Go to Step 15
12	1. Connect a 3-ampere fused jumper between the ignition 3 voltage circuit and the cruise control on switch signal circuit. 2. With the scan tool, observe the Cruise On/Off Switch parameter. Does the Cruise On/Off Switch parameter display On?	Go to Step 22	Go to Step 18

LTV0500000004201

Fig. 87   Cruise Control Inoperative/Malfunctioning (Part 3 of 6). 2003-06 Sierra & Silverado w/4.8L, 5.3L, 6.0L & 8.1L Engines

Step	Action	Yes	No
20	Test the cruise control resume/accel switch signal circuit for an open or for a high resistance. Did you find and correct the condition?	Go to Step 29	Go to Step 23
21	Test the center high mounted stop lamp (CHMSL) supply voltage/stop lamp supply voltage circuit for an open or for a high resistance between the stop lamp switch and the TAC module. Did you find and correct the condition?	Go to Step 29	Go to Step 23
22	Inspect for poor connections at the harness connector of the cruise control switch. Did you find and correct the condition?	Go to Step 29	Go to Step 26
23	Inspect for poor connections at the harness connector of the TAC module. Did you find and correct the condition?	Go to Step 29	Go to Step 27
24	Inspect for poor connections at the harness connector of the PCM. Did you find and correct the condition?	Go to Step 29	Go to Step 28
25	Repair the open, the high resistance, or the short to ground in the ignition 3 voltage circuit. Did you complete the repair?	Go to Step 29	--
26	Replace the cruise control switch. Did you complete the replacement?	Go to Step 29	--

LTV0500000004203

Fig. 87   Cruise Control Inoperative/Malfunctioning (Part 5 of 6). 2003-06 Sierra & Silverado w/4.8L, 5.3L, 6.0L & 8.1L Engines

Step	Action	Yes	No
13	Test the cruise control on switch signal circuit for a short to voltage. Did you find and correct the condition?	Go to Step 29	Go to Step 14
14	1. Turn the ignition OFF. 2. Disconnect C1 of the throttle actuator control (TAC) module. 3. Turn the ignition ON, with the engine OFF. 4. With the scan tool, observe the Cruise On/Off Switch parameter. Does the Cruise On/Off Switch parameter display On?	Go to Step 24	Go to Step 23
15	Test the cruise control set/coast switch signal circuit for a short to ground. Did you find and correct the condition?	Go to Step 29	Go to Step 16
16	Test the cruise control resume/accel switch signal circuit for a short to ground. Did you find and correct the condition?	Go to Step 29	Go to Step 17
17	Test the cruise control on switch signal circuit for a short to ground. Did you find and correct the condition?	Go to Step 29	Go to Step 25
18	Test the cruise control on switch signal circuit for an open or for a high resistance. Did you find and correct the condition?	Go to Step 29	Go to Step 23
19	Test the cruise control set/coast switch signal circuit for an open or for a high resistance. Did you find and correct the condition?	Go to Step 29	Go to Step 23

LTV0500000004202

Fig. 87   Cruise Control Inoperative/Malfunctioning (Part 4 of 6). 2003-06 Sierra & Silverado w/4.8L, 5.3L, 6.0L & 8.1L Engines

Step	Action	Yes	No
27	Replace the TAC module. Did you complete the replacement?	Go to Step 29	--
28	**Important:** Program the replacement PCM. Replace the PCM. Did you complete the replacement?	Go to Step 29	--
29	1. Use the scan tool in order to clear the PCM DTCs. 2. Operate the vehicle within the conditions for cruise control operation. Does the cruise control system operate properly?	System OK	Go to Step 2

LTV0500000004204

Fig. 87   Cruise Control Inoperative/Malfunctioning (Part 6 of 6). 2003-06 Sierra & Silverado w/4.8L, 5.3L, 6.0L & 8.1L Engines

Diagnostic Aids

To avoid a misdiagnosis, inspect for the following:

- Proper operation of the stop lamps.
- Proper operation of the clutch system, if equipped with a manual transmission.
- The throttle linkage is not binding.

EMI on the speed sensor signal circuit may cause erratic cruise control operation.

Conditions for Enabling Cruise Control

- The vehicle speed is greater than 40 km/h (25 mph).
- The vehicle is not in PARK, REVERSE, NEUTRAL, or 1st gear.
- The system voltage is between 12 volts and 16 volts.

Step	Action	Yes	No
1	Did you perform the Cruise Control Diagnostic System Check?	Go to Step 2	Go to Diagnostic System Check

LTV0500000004205

Fig. 88   Cruise Control Inoperative/Malfunctioning (Part 1 of 5). 2003-06 Sierra & Silverado w/6.6L Engine

Step			
2	1. Install a scan tool. 2. Turn the ignition ON, with the engine OFF. 3. Turn the cruise control On/Off switch OFF. 4. With the scan tool, observe the Cruise On/Off Switch parameter in the PCM Engine Data 1 data list. Does the Cruise On/Off Switch parameter display Off?	Go to Step 3	Go to Step 6
3	1. Turn the cruise control On/Off switch ON. 2. With the scan tool, observe the Cruise On/Off Switch parameter. Does the Cruise On/Off Switch parameter display On?	Go to Step 4	Go to Step 10
4	1. With the scan tool, observe the Cruise Set/Coast Switch parameter in the PCM Engine Data 1 data list. 2. Turn the cruise control On/Off switch ON. 3. Press and hold the cruise control Set/Coast switch. Does the Cruise Set/Coast Switch parameter display On?	Go to Step 5	Go to Step 7
5	1. With the scan tool, observe the Cruise Resume/Accel. Switch parameter in the PCM data list. 2. Press and hold the Resume/Accel switch. Does the Cruise Resume/Accel. Switch parameter display On?	Go to Step 9	Go to Step 8
6	1. Turn the ignition OFF. 2. Disconnect the cruise control switch. 3. Turn the ignition ON, with the engine OFF. 4. Connect a test lamp between the cruise control on switch signal circuit and a good ground. Does the test lamp illuminate?	Go to Step 11	Go to Step 20

LTV0500000004206

Fig. 88 Cruise Control Inoperative/Malfunctioning (Part 2 of 5). 2003-06 Sierra & Silverado w/6.6L Engine

Step			
7	1. Turn the ignition OFF. 2. Disconnect the cruise control switch. 3. Turn the ignition ON, with the engine OFF. 4. Connect a 3 ampere fused jumper between the cruise control set/coast switch signal circuit and the ignition 3 voltage circuit. 5. With the scan tool, observe the Cruise Set/Coast Switch parameter. Does the Cruise Set/Coast Switch parameter display On?	Go to Step 20	Go to Step 15
8	1. Turn the ignition OFF. 2. Disconnect the cruise control switch. 3. Turn the ignition ON, with the engine OFF. 4. Connect a 3 ampere fused jumper between the cruise control resume/accel switch signal circuit and the ignition 3 voltage circuit. 5. With the scan tool, observe the Cruise Resume/Accel. Switch parameter. Does the Cruise Resume/Accel. Switch parameter display On?	Go to Step 20	Go to Step 16
9	1. With the scan tool, observe the TCC Cruise Brake Pedal parameter in the PCM Engine Data 1 data list. 2. Depress the brake pedal. Does the TCC Cruise Brake Pedal parameter display Applied?	Go to Diagnostic Aids	Go to Step 17
10	1. Turn the ignition OFF. 2. Disconnect the cruise control switch. 3. Turn the ignition ON, with the engine OFF. 4. Connect a test lamp between the ignition 3 voltage circuit and a good ground. Does the test lamp illuminate?	Go to Step 12	Go to Step 18
11	Test the cruise control on switch signal circuit for a short to voltage. Did you find and correct the condition?	Go to Step 25	Go to Step 21
12	Test the cruise control on switch signal circuit for an open, for a high resistance or for a short to ground. Did you find and correct the condition?	Go to Step 25	Go to Step 13

LTV0500000004207

Fig. 88 Cruise Control Inoperative/Malfunctioning (Part 3 of 5). 2003-06 Sierra & Silverado w/6.6L Engine

Step			
13	Test the cruise control resume/accel switch signal circuit for a short to ground. Did you find and correct the condition?	Go to Step 25	Go to Step 14
14	Test the cruise control set/coast switch signal circuit for a for a short to ground. Did you find and correct the condition?	Go to Step 25	Go to Step 20
15	Test the cruise control set/coast switch signal circuit for an open or for a high resistance. Did you find and correct the condition?	Go to Step 25	Go to Step 21
16	Test the cruise control resume/accel switch signal circuit for an open or for a high resistance. Did you find and correct the condition?	Go to Step 25	Go to Step 21
17	Test the TCC/Brake switch signal circuit for an open, for a high resistance, or for a short to ground. Did you find and correct the condition?	Go to Step 25	Go to Step 19
18	Repair the open, the high resistance, or the short to ground in the ignition 3 voltage circuit. Did you complete the repair?	Go to Step 25	--
19	Inspect for poor connections at the harness connector of the stop lamp switch. Did you find and correct the condition?	Go to Step 25	Go to Step 22
20	Inspect for poor connections at the harness connector of the cruise control switch. Did you find and correct the condition?	Go to Step 25	Go to Step 23

LTV0500000004208

Fig. 88 Cruise Control Inoperative/Malfunctioning (Part 4 of 5). 2003-06 Sierra & Silverado w/6.6L Engine

Step			
21	Inspect for poor connections at the harness connector of the ECM. Did you find and correct the condition?	Go to Step 25	Go to Step 24
22	Replace the stop lamp switch. Did you complete the replacement?	Go to Step 25	--
23	Replace the multifunction turn signal lever. Did you complete the replacement?	Go to Step 25	--
24	**Important:** Program the replacement ECM. Replace the ECM. Did you complete the replacement?	Go to Step 25	--
25	Operate the vehicle within the conditions for cruise control operation. Does the cruise control system operate properly?	System OK	Go to Step 2

LTV0500000004209

Fig. 88 Cruise Control Inoperative/Malfunctioning (Part 5 of 5). 2003-06 Sierra & Silverado w/6.6L Engine

Diagnostic Aids

To avoid a misdiagnosis, inspect for the following:

- Proper operation of brake lamps.

- Proper operation of the clutch system, if equipped with a manual transmission.

- The throttle linkage is not binding.

EMI on the vehicle speed sensor signal circuit may cause erratic cruise control operation.

Conditions for Enabling Cruise Control

- The vehicle speed is greater than 40 km/h (25 mph).
- The vehicle is not in PARK, REVERSE, NEUTRAL, or 1st gear.
- The system voltage is between 12 volts and 16 volts.

Step	Action	Value	Yes	No
1	Did you perform the Cruise Control Diagnostic System Check?	--	Go to Step 2	Go to Diagnostic System Check
2	1. Turn the ignition OFF. 2. Disconnect the cruise control module. 3. Turn the ignition ON, with the engine OFF. 4. Connect a test lamp between the ignition 3 voltage circuit and a good ground. Does the test lamp illuminate?	--	Go to Step 3	Go to Step 5

LTV0500000004210

Fig. 89   Cruise Control Inoperative/Malfunctioning (Part 1 of 5). 2003-06 Sierra & Silverado w/4.3L Engine

	1. Connect a test lamp between the cruise control resume/accelerate switch signal circuit and a good ground. 2. With the cruise control On/Off switch ON, press and hold the Resume/Accel switch. Does the test lamp illuminate?			
8		--	Go to Step 9	Go to Step 17
9	Connect a test lamp between the stop lamp supply voltage circuit and a good ground. Does the test lamp illuminate?	--	Go to Step 10	Go to Step 19
10	With a DMM, measure the voltage from the vehicle speed signal circuit to a good ground. Does the voltage measure at the specified value?	B+	Go to Step 11	Go to Step 20
11	With a DMM, measure the voltage from the cruise control engaged signal to a good ground. Does the voltage measure at the specified value?	B+	Go to Step 25	Go to Step 18
12	Test the signal circuit that illuminated the test lamp for a short to voltage. Did you find and correct the condition?	--	Go to Step 29	Go to Step 24
13	Test the signal circuit that illuminated the test lamp for a short to ground. Did you find and correct the condition?	--	Go to Step 29	Go to Step 24

LTV0500000004212

Fig. 89   Cruise Control Inoperative/Malfunctioning (Part 3 of 5). 2003-06 Sierra & Silverado w/4.3L Engine

3	Connect a test lamp between the ignition 3 voltage circuit and the ground circuit of the cruise control module. Does the test lamp illuminate?	-	Go to Step 4	Go to Step 22
4	1. Turn the cruise control On/Off switch OFF. 2. Connect a test lamp between a good ground and each of the following circuits: - The cruise control on switch signal circuit - The cruise control set/coast switch signal circuit - The cruise control resume/accel switch signal circuit Does the test lamp illuminate for any of the signal circuits listed above?	-	Go to Step 12	Go to Step 6
5	1. Turn the cruise control On/Off switch OFF. 2. Connect a test lamp between battery voltage and each of the following circuits: - The cruise control on switch signal circuit - The cruise control set/coast switch signal circuit - The cruise control resume/accel switch signal circuit Does the test lamp illuminate for any of the signal circuits listed above?	-	Go to Step 13	Go to Step 21
6	1. Turn the cruise control On/Off switch ON. 2. Connect a test lamp between the cruise control on switch signal circuit and a good ground. Does the test lamp illuminate?	-	Go to Step 7	Go to Step 14
7	1. Connect a test lamp between the cruise control set/coast switch signal circuit and a good ground. 2. With the cruise control On/Off switch ON, press and hold the Set/Coast switch. Does the test lamp illuminate?	-	Go to Step 8	Go to Step 16

LTV0500000004211

Fig. 89   Cruise Control Inoperative/Malfunctioning (Part 2 of 5). 2003-06 Sierra & Silverado w/4.3L Engine

14	Test the cruise control on/off switch signal circuit for an open or for a high resistance. Did you find and correct the condition?	-	Go to Step 29	Go to Step 15
15	Test the ignition 3 voltage circuit for an open or for a high resistance between S204 and the multifunction switch. Did you find and correct the condition?	-	Go to Step 29	Go to Step 24
16	Test the cruise control set/coast switch signal circuit for an open or for a high resistance. Did you find and correct the condition?	-	Go to Step 29	Go to Step 24
17	Test the cruise control resume/accel switch signal circuit for an open or for a high resistance. Did you find and correct the condition?	-	Go to Step 29	Go to Step 24
18	Test the cruise control engaged signal circuit for an open, for a high resistance, or for a short to ground. Did you find and correct the condition?	-	Go to Step 29	Go to Step 23
19	Repair the open, the high resistance, or the short to ground in the stop lamp supply voltage circuit. Did you complete the repair?	-	Go to Step 29	--
20	Repair the open or the high resistance in the vehicle speed signal circuit. Did you complete the repair?	-	Go to Step 29	--

LTV0500000004213

Fig. 89   Cruise Control Inoperative/Malfunctioning (Part 4 of 5). 2003-06 Sierra & Silverado w/4.3L Engine

Step	Action	Yes	No
21	Repair the open, the high resistance, or the short to ground in the ignition 3 voltage circuit. Did you complete the repair?	Go to Step 29	--
22	Repair the open or the high resistance in the ground circuit of the cruise control module. Did you complete the repair?	Go to Step 29	--
23	Inspect for poor connections at the harness connector of the PCM. Did you find and correct the condition?	Go to Step 29	Go to Step 26
24	Inspect for poor connections at the harness connector of the multifunction switch. Did you find and correct the condition?	Go to Step 29	Go to Step 27
25	Inspect for poor connections at the harness connector of the cruise control module. Did you find and correct the condition?	Go to Step 29	Go to Step 28
26	**Important:** Program the replacement PCM. Replace the PCM. Did you complete the replacement?	Go to Step 29	--
27	Replace the multifunction switch. Did you complete the replacement?	Go to Step 29	--
28	Replace the cruise control module. Did you complete the replacement?	Go to Step 29	--
29	Operate the vehicle within the conditions for cruise control operation. Does the cruise control system operate correctly?	System OK	Go to Step 2

LTV0500000004214

Fig. 89 Cruise Control Inoperative/Malfunctioning (Part 5 of 5). 2003-06 Sierra & Silverado w/4.3L Engine

Step	Action	Yes	No
3	With the scan tool, observe the following cruise control switch parameters in the engine control module (ECM) Cruise Control Data list: • Cruise Resume/Accel. Switch • Cruise Set/Coast Switch. Do any of the cruise control switch parameters listed above display Applied?	Go to Step 9	Go to Step 4
4	1. Turn the cruise control On/Off switch ON. 2. With the scan tool, observe the Cruise On/Off Switch parameter. Does the Cruise On/Off Switch parameter display On?	Go to Step 5	Go to Step 10
5	1. With the scan tool, observe the Cruise Set/Coast Switch parameter. 2. Press and hold the cruise control Set/Coast button. Does the Cruise Set/Coast Switch parameter Display Applied?	Go to Step 6	Go to Step 13
6	1. With the scan tool, observe the Cruise Resume/Accel. Switch parameter. 2. Press and hold the cruise control Resume/Accel. switch. Does the Cruise Resume/Accel. Switch parameter Display Applied?	Go to Step 7	Go to Step 12
7	Do the stop lamps work properly?	Go to Step 22	Diagnose Stop Lamps Always On or Stop Lamps Inoperative
8	1. Turn OFF the ignition. 2. Disconnect C4 of the multifunction, turn switch. 3. Turn ON the ignition, with the engine OFF. 4. With the scan tool, observe the Cruise On/Off Switch parameter. Does the Cruise On/Off Switch parameter display On?	Go to Step 14	Go to Step 19

LTV0500000004216

Fig. 90 Cruise Control Inoperative/Malfunctioning (Part 2 of 5). SSR

Diagnostic Aids

- Inspect for proper operation of the stop lamps.

- Ensure that the following cruise control switches are not stuck or sticking in the engaged position:
  - Set/Coast
  - Resume/Accel

Conditions for Enabling Cruise Control

- The vehicle speed is greater than 40 km/h (25 mph).
- The vehicle is not in PARK, REVERSE, NEUTRAL, or 1st gear.
- The system voltage is between 12-16 volts.

Step	Action	Yes	No
1	Did you perform the Diagnostic System Check - Vehicle?	Go to Step 2	Go to Diagnostic System Check
2	1. Install a scan tool. 2. Turn ON the ignition, with the engine OFF. 3. Turn the cruise control On/Off switch OFF. 4. With the scan tool, observe the Cruise On/Off Switch parameter in the engine control module (ECM) Cruise Control Data list. Does the Cruise On/Off Switch parameter display Off?	Go to Step 3	Go to Step 8

LTV0500000004215

Fig. 90 Cruise Control Inoperative/Malfunctioning (Part 1 of 5). SSR

Step	Action	Yes	No
9	1. Turn OFF the ignition. 2. Disconnect C4 of the multifunction turn signal switch. 3. Turn ON the ignition, with the engine OFF. 4. With the scan tool, observe the following cruise control switch parameters in the engine control module (ECM) Cruise Control Data list: - Cruise Resume/Accel. Switch - Cruise Set/Coast Switch. Do any of the cruise control switch parameters listed above display Applied?	Go to Step 15	Go to Step 19
10	1. Turn OFF the ignition. 2. Disconnect C4 of the multifunction, turn signal switch. 3. Turn ON the ignition, with the engine OFF. 4. Connect a test lamp between the ignition 3 voltage circuit and a good ground. Does the test lamp illuminate?	Go to Step 11	Go to Step 21
11	1. Turn the ignition OFF. 2. Connect a 3-amp fused jumper between the ignition 3 voltage circuit and the cruise control on switch signal circuit. 3. Turn ON the ignition, with the engine OFF. 4. With the scan tool, observe the Cruise On/Off Switch parameter. Does the Cruise On/Off Switch parameter display On?	Go to Step 19	Go to Step 16
12	1. Turn OFF the ignition. 2. Disconnect C4 of the multifunction, turn signal switch. 3. Connect a 3-amp fused jumper between the ignition 3 voltage circuit and the cruise control resume/accel switch signal circuit. 4. Turn ON the ignition, with the engine OFF. 5. With the scan tool, observe the Cruise Resume/Accel. Switch parameter. Does the Cruise Resume/Accel. Switch parameter display Applied?	Go to Step 19	Go to Step 18
13	1. Turn OFF the ignition. 2. Disconnect C4 of the multifunction, turn switch. 3. Connect a 3-amp fused jumper between the ignition 3 voltage circuit and the cruise control set/coast switch signal circuit. 4. Turn ON the ignition, with the engine OFF. 5. With the scan tool, observe the Cruise Set/Coast Switch parameter. Does the Cruise Set/Coast Switch parameter display Applied?	Go to Step 19	Go to Step 17
14	Test the cruise control on switch signal circuit for a short to voltage. Did you find and correct the condition?	Go to Step 25	Go to Step 20

LTV0500000004217

Fig. 90 Cruise Control Inoperative/Malfunctioning (Part 3 of 5). SSR

Step	Action	Yes	No
15	Test the cruise control switch signal circuit that displayed Applied on the scan tool for a short to voltage. Did you find and correct the condition?	Go to Step 25	Go to Step 20
16	Test the cruise control on switch signal circuit for the following: • Open • Short to ground • High resistance Did you find and correct the condition?	Go to Step 25	Go to Step 20
17	Test the cruise control set/coast switch signal circuit for the following: • Open • Short to ground • High resistance Did you find and correct the condition?	Go to Step 25	Go to Step 20
18	Test the cruise control resume/accelerate switch signal circuit for the following: • Open • Short to ground • High resistance Did you find and correct the condition?	Go to Step 25	Go to Step 20
19	Inspect for poor connections at C4 of the multifunction, turn signal switch. Did you find and correct the condition?	Go to Step 25	Go to Step 23
20	Inspect for poor connections at the harness connector of the ECM. Did you find and correct the condition?	Go to Step 25	Go to Step 24

LTV0500000004218

Fig. 90 Cruise Control Inoperative/Malfunctioning (Part 4 of 5). SSR

Diagnostic Aids

Perform the following in order to avoid misdiagnosis:

- Ensure that the following cruise control switches are not stuck in the engaged position:
  - On/Off switch
  - Set/Coast switch
  - Resume/Accel switch
- Inspect for proper operation of the stop lamps.

- EMI on the speed sensor signal circuit may cause erratic cruise control operation.

Step	Action	Yes	No
1	Did you perform the Diagnostic System Check - Vehicle?	Go to Step 2	Go to Diagnostic System Check
2	1. Install a scan tool. 2. Turn ON the ignition, with the engine OFF. 3. Turn the cruise control On/Off switch OFF. 4. With the scan tool, observe the following cruise control parameters in the Cruise/Traction Data list: - Cruise Resume/Accel Switch - Cruise Set/Coast Switch Do any of the parameters listed above display ON?	Go to Step 5	Go to Step 3
3	1. Turn the cruise control switch ON. 2. With the scan tool, observe the Cruise Set/Coast Switch parameter. 3. Press and hold the set/coast switch. Does the Cruise Set/Coast Switch parameter display On?	Go to Step 4	Go to Step 6

LTV0500000004220

Fig. 91 Cruise Control Inoperative/Malfunctioning (Part 1 of 3). SRX w/3.6L Engine

Step	Action	Yes	No
21	Repair the following in the ignition 3 voltage circuit. • Open • Short to ground • High resistance Refer to Circuit Testing and Wiring Repairs in Wiring Systems. Did you complete the repair?	Go to Step 25	--
22	Repair the open or the high resistance in the center high mounted stop lamp (CHMSL) supply voltage circuit. Did you complete the repair?	Go to Step 25	--
23	Replace the cruise control switch. Did you complete the replacement?	Go to Step 25	--
24	Replace the ECM. Did you complete the replacement?	Go to Step 25	--
25	Operate the vehicle within the conditions for cruise control operation. Does the cruise control system operate properly?	System OK	Go to Step 2

LTV0500000004219

Fig. 90 Cruise Control Inoperative/Malfunctioning (Part 5 of 5). SSR

Step	Action	Yes	No
4	1. With the scan tool, observe the Cruise Resume/Accel Switch parameter. 2. Press and hold the resume/accel switch. Does the Cruise Resume/Accel Switch parameter display On?	Go to Diagnostic Aids	Go to Step 9
5	1. Turn OFF the ignition. 2. Disconnect the cruise switch. 3. Turn ON the ignition, with the engine OFF. 4. With the scan tool, observe the following cruise control parameters: - Cruise Resume/Accel Switch - Cruise Set/Coast Switch Do any of the parameters listed above display On?	Go to Step 7	Go to Step 9
6	1. Turn OFF the ignition. 2. Disconnect the cruise switch. 3. Turn ON the ignition, with the engine OFF. 4. Connect a test lamp between the ignition 1 voltage circuit and a good ground. Does the test lamp illuminate?	Go to Step 8	Go to Step 11
7	Test the cruise control set/coast and resume/accel switch signal circuit for a short to voltage. Did you find and correct the condition?	Go to Step 14	Go to Step 10
8	Test the cruise control set/coast and resume/accel switch signal circuit for an open, for a short to ground, for a short to voltage, or for a high resistance. Did you find and correct the condition?	Go to Step 14	Go to Step 9
9	Inspect for poor connections at the harness connector of the cruise control switch. Did you find and correct the condition?	Go to Step 14	Go to Step 12

LTV0500000004221

Fig. 91 Cruise Control Inoperative/Malfunctioning (Part 2 of 3). SRX w/3.6L Engine

Step	Action	Yes	No
10	Inspect for poor connections at the harness connector of the engine control module (ECM). Did you find and correct the condition?	Go to Step 14	Go to Step 13
11	Repair the open, the short to ground, or the high resistance in the ignition 1 voltage circuit. Did you complete the repair?	Go to Step 14	--
12	Replace the cruise control switch. Did you complete the replacement?	Go to Step 14	--
13	Replace the ECM. Did you complete the replacement?	Go to Step 14	--
14	Operate the cruise control system in order to verify the repair. Does the cruise control system operate properly?	System OK	Go to Step 2

LTV0500000004222

Fig. 91 Cruise Control Inoperative/Malfunctioning (Part 3 of 3). SRX w/3.6L Engine

Diagnostic Aids

Perform the following in order to avoid a misdiagnosis:

- Ensure that the following cruise control switches are not stuck in the engaged position:
  - On/off switch
  - Set/coast switch
  - Resume/accel switch
- Inspect for proper operation of the stop lamps.

- EMI on the speed sensor signal circuit may cause erratic cruise control operation.

Step	Action	Values	Yes	No
1	Did you perform the Diagnostic System Check - Vehicle?	--	Go to Step 2	Go to Diagnostic System Check - Vehicle in Vehicle DTC Information

LTV0500000004223

Fig. 92 Cruise Control Inoperative/Malfunctioning (Part 1 of 5). SRX w/4.6L Engine

Step	Action	Values	Yes	No
8	1. Turn OFF the ignition. 2. Disconnect the cruise control switch. 3. Turn ON the ignition, with the engine OFF. 4. Observe the Cruise Control Switch parameter in the Cruise/Traction Data list. Does the Cruise Control Switch parameter display Off?	--	Go to Step 15	Go to Step 13
9	1. Turn OFF the ignition. 2. Disconnect the cruise control switch. 3. Connect a test lamp between the ignition 1 voltage circuit and a good ground. Does the test lamp illuminate?	--	Go to Step 11	Go to Step 17
10	**Important:** The cruise control on/off switch must be turned ON in order to correctly view the set/coast resistance value with the DMM. 1. Turn OFF the ignition. 2. Disconnect the cruise control switch. 3. With a DMM, measure the resistance of the cruise control switch between the ignition 1 voltage circuit and the cruise control set/coast and resume/accelerate switch signal circuit. 4. Individually activate and hold the cruise control function switches while measuring the resistance of the cruise control function switches. Do the cruise control function switch resistance values measure between the specified values?	Off = O.L. On = 7.8 K ohms to 8.6 K ohms Resume = 2.7 K ohms to 3.0 K ohms Set = 1.2 K ohms to 1.3 K ohms	Go to Step 14	Go to Step 15

LTV0500000004225

Fig. 92 Cruise Control Inoperative/Malfunctioning (Part 3 of 5). SRX w/4.6L Engine

Step	Action	Values	Yes	No
11	**Important:** The cruise control on/off switch must be turned ON in order to correctly view the set/coast resistance value with the DMM. 1. With a DMM, measure the resistance of the cruise control switch between the ignition 1 voltage circuit and the cruise control set/coast and resume/accelerate switch signal circuit. 2. Individually activate and hold the cruise control function switches while measuring the resistance of the cruise control function switches. Do the cruise control function switch resistance values measure between the specified values?	Off = O.L. On = 7.8 K ohms to 8.6 K ohms Resume = 2.7 K ohms to 3.0 K ohms Set = 1.2 K ohms to 1.3 K ohms	Go to Step 16	Go to Step 15
12	Test the stop lamp switch signal circuit for an open or for a high resistance. Did you find and correct the condition?	--	Go to Step 20	Go to Step 16
13	Test the cruise control set/coast and resume/accelerate switch signal circuit for a short to voltage. Did you find and correct the condition?	--	Go to Step 20	Go to Step 16
14	Test the cruise control set/coast and resume/accelerate switch signal circuit for an open, for a short to voltage, for a short to ground, or for a high resistance. Did you find and correct the condition?	--	Go to Step 20	Go to Step 16

LTV0500000004226

Fig. 92 Cruise Control Inoperative/Malfunctioning (Part 4 of 5). SRX w/4.6L Engine

Step	Action	Values	Yes	No
2	1. Install a scan tool. 2. Turn ON the ignition, with the engine OFF. 3. Turn the cruise control On/Off switch Off. 4. With the scan tool, observe the Cruise Control Switch parameter in the Cruise/Traction Data list. Does the Cruise Control Switch parameter display Off?	-	Go to Step 3	Go to Step 8
3	1. With the scan tool, observe the Cruise Control Switch parameter. 2. Turn the cruise On/Off switch ON. Does the Cruise Control Switch parameter display On?	-	Go to Step 4	Go to Step 9
4	1. With the scan tool, observe the Cruise Control Switch parameter. 2. Press the set/coast switch. Does the Cruise Control Switch parameter display Set?	-	Go to Step 5	Go to Step 10
5	1. With the scan tool, observe the Cruise Control Switch parameter. 2. Press the resume/accel switch. Does the Cruise Control Switch parameter display Resume?	-	Go to Step 6	Go to Step 10
6	Do the stop lamps operate properly?	-	Go to Step 7	Diagnose Stop Lamps Always On or to Stop Lamps Inoperative
7	1. With the scan tool, observe the Stoplamp Pedal Switch parameter. 2. Press and hold the brake pedal. Does the Stoplamp Pedal Switch parameter display Applied?	-	Go to Diagnostic Aids	Go to Step 12

LTV0500000004224

Fig. 92 Cruise Control Inoperative/Malfunctioning (Part 2 of 5). SRX w/4.6L Engine

Step	Action	Values	Yes	No
15	Inspect for poor connections at the harness connector of the cruise control switch. Did you find and correct the condition?	-	Go to Step 20	Go to Step 18
16	Inspect for poor connections at the harness connector of the engine control module (ECM). Did you find and correct the condition?	-	Go to Step 20	Go to Step 19
17	Repair the open, the short to ground, or the high resistance in the ignition 1 voltage circuit. Did you complete the repair?	-	Go to Step 20	--
18	Replace the cruise control switch. Did you complete the replacement?	-	Go to Step 20	--
19	Replace the ECM. Did you complete the replacement?	-	Go to Step 20	--
20	Operate the vehicle with in the conditions for cruise control operation. Does the cruise control system operate properly?	-	System OK	Go to Step 2

LTV0500000004227

Fig. 92 Cruise Control Inoperative/Malfunctioning (Part 5 of 5). SRX w/4.6L Engine

Caution

Diagnostic Aids

Disable the inflatable restraint steering wheel module when performing this diagnostic table.

Perform the following in order to avoid misdiagnosis:

1. Inspect for proper operation of the stop lamps.

2. Inspect for proper operation of the clutch system, if equipped with manual transmission.

3. Observe the cruise set/coast and cruise resume/accel parameters in the scan tool PCM General Info Inputs data list while rotating the steering wheel to both stops and pressing and holding the steering wheel control switches. This will eliminate the possibility of a internally open or shorted inflatable restraint steering wheel module coil.

4. Rotate the steering wheel to both steering stops while separately activating each cruise control switch. With a scan tool, observe the associated cruise control switch parameter in the PCM General Info Inputs data list. This will help eliminate the possibility of a internally open or shorted inflatable restraint steering wheel module coil.

EMI on the vehicle speed sensor signal circuit may cause erratic cruise control operation.

Conditions for Enabling Cruise Control

- The vehicle speed is greater than 40 km/h (25 mph).
- The vehicle is not in PARK, REVERSE, NEUTRAL, or 1st gear.
- The system voltage is between 12-16 volts.

LTV0500000004228

Fig. 93   Cruise Control Inoperative/Malfunctioning (Part 1 of 5). Vue

Step	Action	Yes	No
1	Did you perform the Diagnostic System Check - Vehicle?	Go to Step 2	Go to Diagnostic System Check
2	1. Install a scan tool. 2. Turn ON the ignition, with the engine OFF. 3. Turn the cruise control on/off switch OFF. 4. With the scan tool, observe the Cruise Switch parameter in the powertrain control module (PCM) General Info Inputs data list. Does the Cruise Switch parameter display Off?	Go to Step 3	Go to Step 11
3	1. With the scan tool, observe the Cruise Switch parameter. 2. Turn the cruise on/off switch ON. Does the Cruise Switch parameter display On?	Go to Step 4	Go to Step 12
4	1. With the scan tool, observe the Cruise Set/Coast parameter. 2. Press and hold the set/coast switch. Does the Cruise Set/Coast parameter display On?	Go to Step 5	Go to Step 14
5	1. With the scan tool, observe the Cruise Resume/Accel parameter. 2. Press and hold the resume/accel switch. Does the Cruise Resume/Accel parameter display On?	Go to Step 6	Go to Step 15
6	With a scan tool, observe the Cruise Brake Switch parameter. Does the Cruise Brake Switch parameter display Released?	Go to Step 7	Go to Step 9

LTV0500000004229

Fig. 93   Cruise Control Inoperative/Malfunctioning (Part 2 of 5). Vue

Step	Action	Yes	No
7	1. With a scan tool, observe the Cruise Brake Switch parameter. 2. Press and hold the brake pedal. Does the Cruise Brake Switch parameter display Applied?	Go to Diagnostic Aids	Go to Step 8
8	1. Turn OFF the Ignition. 2. Disconnect the cruise brake switch. 3. Turn ON the ignition, with the engine OFF. 4. With a scan tool, observe the Cruise Brake Switch parameter. Does the Cruise Brake Switch parameter display Applied?	Go to Step 23	Go to Step 18
9	1. Turn OFF the Ignition. 2. Disconnect the cruise brake switch. 3. Turn ON the ignition, with the engine OFF. 4. Connect a test lamp between the ignition 1 voltage circuit and a good ground. Does the test lamp illuminate?	Go to Step 10	Go to Step 22
10	1. Connect a 3-ampere fused jumper between the ignition 1 voltage circuit and the brake switch signal circuit. 2. With the scan tool, observe the Cruise Brake Switch parameter. Does the Cruise Brake Switch parameter display Released?	Go to Step 23	Go to Step 19
11	1. Turn OFF the ignition. 2. Disconnect the cruise switch. 3. Turn ON the ignition, with the engine OFF. 4. Observe the Cruise Switch parameter. Does the Cruise Switch parameter display Off?	Go to Step 20	Go to Step 16
12	1. Turn OFF the ignition. 2. Disconnect the cruise switch. 3. Turn ON the ignition, with the engine OFF. 4. Connect a test lamp between the ignition 1 voltage circuit and a good ground. Does the test lamp illuminate?	Go to Step 13	Go to Step 22

LTV0500000004230

Fig. 93   Cruise Control Inoperative/Malfunctioning (Part 3 of 5). Vue

Step	Action	Yes	No
13	1. Connect a 3-ampere fused jumper between the ignition 1 voltage circuit and the cruise control on switch signal circuit. 2. With the scan tool, observe the Cruise Switch parameter. Does the Cruise Switch parameter display On?	Go to Step 20	Go to Step 17
14	Test the cruise control set/coast switch signal circuit for a short to ground, for an open, or for a high resistance. Did you find and correct the condition?	Go to Step 26	Go to Step 20
15	Test the cruise control resume/accel switch signal circuit for a short to ground, for an open, or for a high resistance. Did you find and correct the condition?	Go to Step 26	Go to Step 20
16	Test the cruise control on switch signal circuit for a short to voltage. Did you find and correct the condition?	Go to Step 26	Go to Step 21
17	Test the cruise control on switch signal circuit for an open, for a short to ground, or for a high resistance. Did you find and correct the condition?	Go to Step 26	Go to Step 21
18	Test the cruise brake switch signal circuit for a short to voltage. Did you find and correct the condition?	Go to Step 26	Go to Step 21

LTV0500000004231

Fig. 93   Cruise Control Inoperative/Malfunctioning (Part 4 of 5). Vue

19	Test the cruise brake switch signal circuit for an open, for a short to ground, or for a high resistance. Did you find and correct the condition?	Go to Step 26	Go to Step 21
20	Inspect for poor connections at the harness connector of the cruise control switch. Did you find and correct the condition?	Go to Step 26	Go to Step 24
21	Inspect for poor connections at the harness connector of the engine control module (ECM)/PCM. Did you find and correct the condition?	Go to Step 26	Go to Step 25
22	Repair the short to ground, the open, or the high resistance in the ignition 1 voltage circuit. Did you complete the repair?	Go to Step 26	--
23	Replace the cruise brake switch. Did you complete the replacement?	Go to Step 26	--
24	Replace the cruise control switch. Did you complete the replacement?	Go to Step 26	--
25	Replace the ECM/PCM. Did you complete the replacement?	Go to Step 26	--
26	1. Enable the inflatable restraint steering wheel module. 2. Operate the vehicle with in the conditions for cruise control operation. Does the cruise control system operate properly?	System OK	Go to Step 2

LTV0500000004232

Fig. 93 Cruise Control Inoperative/Malfunctioning (Part 5 of 5). Vue

COMPONENT REPLACEMENT

Mode Control Switch

Refer to "Multi-Function Switch, Replace" in the "Electrical" section of the appropriate vehicle chapter.

Cruise Control Module

1. Disconnect cruise control cable from module.

2. Remove mounting screws, then disconnect electrical connector and remove module. **Module cannot be serviced.**

3. Reverse procedure to install.

Cruise Control Cable

REMOVAL

1. Disconnect cruise control cable from accelerator lever assembly.
2. Remove cable conduit from engine bracket and module housing.
3. Remove cable bead from cruise module ribbon fitting end, then the cable from vehicle.

INSTALLATION

1. Connect cable bead to cruise module ribbon fitting.
2. Position cable conduit over ribbon fitting and insert tangs into module housing. **Pull engine end fitting until cable is snug, then rotate cable to position ribbon fitting flat and vertical. Ribbon must not be twisted.**
3. Install cable conduit into engine bracket.
4. Unlock cable conduit, then connect engine end fitting of cable to accelerator lever assembly.

SPEED CONTROL SYSTEMS

Tracker

NOTE: On Air Bag Equipped Models, Refer To "Air Bag System Precautions" Located In The Front Of This Manual For System Disarming and Arming Procedures.

NOTE: Refer To "Computer Relearn Procedures" Located In The Front Of This Manual When Battery Power To The Computer Has Been Interrupted.

NOTE: "Electrical Symbol & Wire Color Code Identification" Located In The Front Of This Manual May Be Used As An Aid When Using Wiring Circuits Found In This Section.

INDEX

	Page No.		Page No.		Page No.
Adjustments	2-70	Cruise Control Cable	2-74	Battery Ground Cable	2-70
Actuator Cable	2-70	Cruise Control Switch	2-74	**System Diagnosis & Testing**	2-70
Brake Light Switch	2-70	**Description**	2-70	Intermittents & Poor	
Shift Selector Switch	2-70	**Diagnostic Chart Index**	2-72	Connections	2-70
Component Replacement	2-74	**Precautions**	2-70	Symptom Related Diagnosis	2-70
Cruise Control Actuator	2-74	Air Bag Systems	2-70	Wiring Diagram	2-70

DESCRIPTION

This cruise control system maintains a preset vehicle speed during high speed vehicle operation. The system will maintain any desired constant speed 25 mph or higher, without depressing the accelerator pedal. Other cruise control system functions include the following functions:
1. SET COAST and ACCEL RESUME switches, to change vehicle speed without using accelerator pedal.
2. CANCEL switch, to end cruise control operation.
3. ACCEL RESUME switch, to resume speed stored in memory automatically after cruise control is canceled.

PRECAUTIONS

Air Bag Systems

Refer to "Air Bag System Precautions" in the front of this manual for system disarming and arming procedures.

Battery Ground Cable

Prior to service, disconnect battery ground cable and isolate as required.

ADJUSTMENTS

Actuator Cable

1. Remove actuator cover, then loosen locknuts.
2. Adjust cable to obtain .04–.08 inch play with actuator lever fully closed as shown in **Fig. 1**.
3. **Torque** locknuts to 44 inch lbs.

Brake Light Switch

1. Start engine.
2. Depress brake pedal few times.
3. Apply approximately 66 lbs. of pressure to brake pedal and hold, then measure pedal height. Pedal height should be more than 5.12 inches.
4. Adjust brake light switch as required.

Shift Selector Switch

1. Shift select lever to N position.
2. Ensure engine starts in N and P positions, but does not start in D, 2, L or R positions.
3. Check back-up lamps light in R position.

SYSTEM DIAGNOSIS & TESTING

Wiring Diagram

Refer to **Fig. 2** for wiring diagrams.

Symptom Related Diagnosis

Refer to **Figs. 3 through 7** for system diagnosis and testing procedures.

Intermittents & Poor Connections

Most intermittents are caused by faulty electrical connections or wiring, although occasionally a sticking relay or solenoid can be a problem. Some items to check are:
1. Poor mating of connector halves, or terminals not fully seated in connector body.
2. Dirt or corrosion on terminals. terminals must be clean and free of any foreign material which could impede proper terminal contact.
3. Damage connector body, exposing terminals to moisture and dirt, as well as not maintaining proper terminal orientation with component or mating connector.
4. Improperly formed or damaged terminals. All connector terminals in problem circuits should be checked carefully to ensure good contact tension. Use corresponding mating terminal to check for proper tension.
5. Adapter tool No. J-35616-A or equivalent, must be used whenever diagnostic procedure requests checking or probing terminal. Using adapter will ensure no damage to terminal will occur, as well as giving an idea of whether contact tension is sufficient.
6. Poor terminal to wire connection. Some conditions which fall under this description are poor crimps, but if only one or two strands of multi-strand type wire are intact, resistance could be far too high.

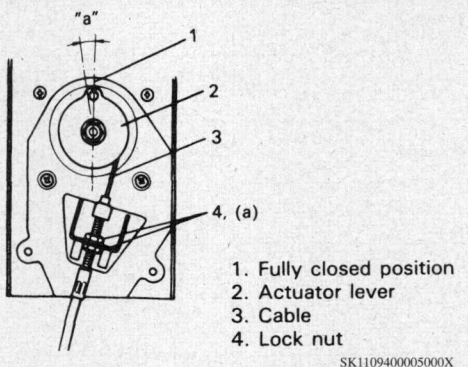

1. Fully closed position
2. Actuator lever
3. Cable
4. Lock nut

SK1109400005000X

Fig. 1   Actuator cable adjustment

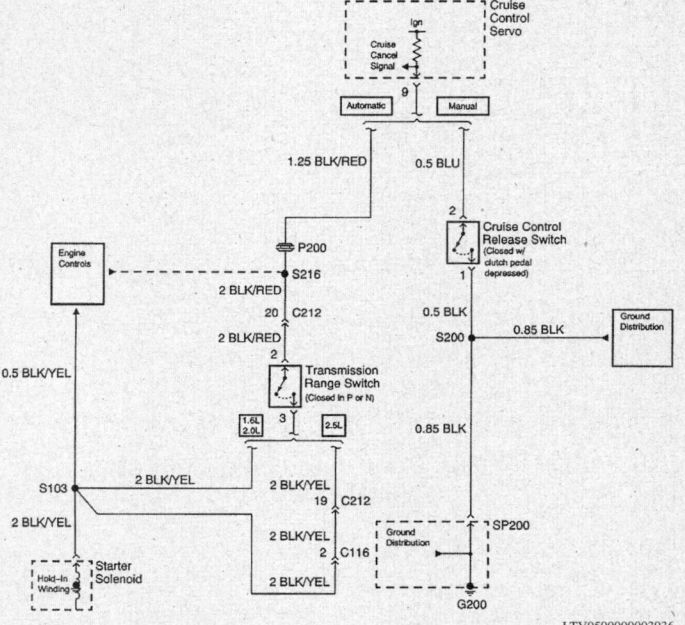

LTV0500000003936

Fig. 2   Wiring diagram (Part 2 of 4). Tracker

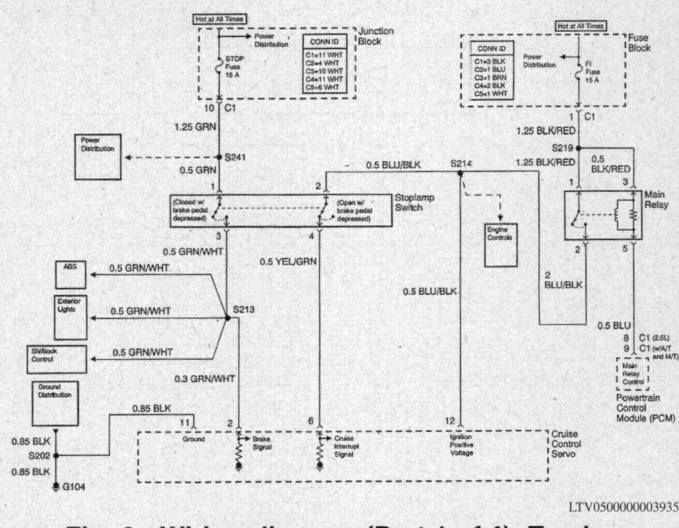

LTV0500000003935

Fig. 2   Wiring diagram (Part 1 of 4). Tracker

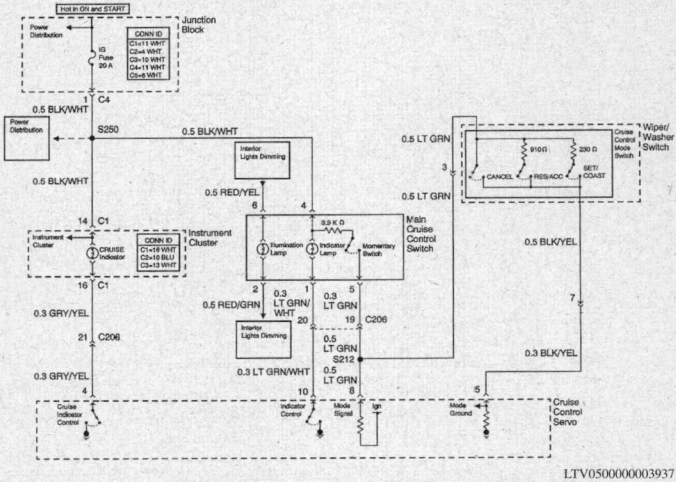

LTV0500000003937

Fig. 2   Wiring diagram (Part 3 of 4). Tracker

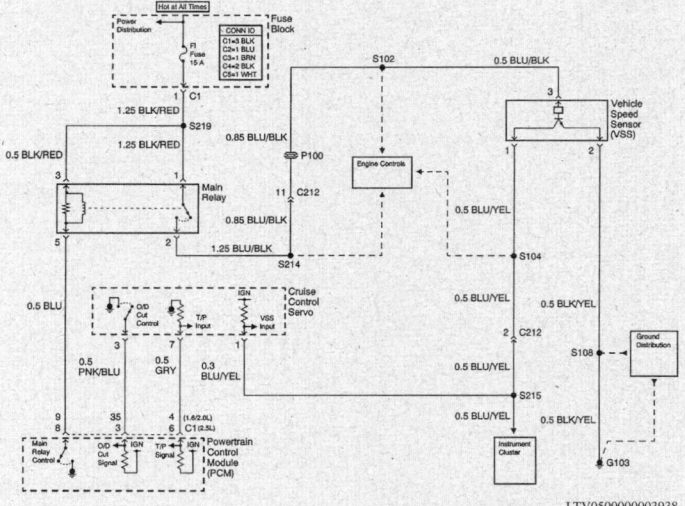

LTV0500000003938

Fig. 2   Wiring diagram (Part 4 of 4). Tracker

DIAGNOSTIC CHART INDEX

Year	Description	Page No.	Fig. No.
2002–04	Cruise Control Always On	2-72	3
	Cruise Control Indicator Inoperative	2-72	4
	Cruise Control Switch Always On	2-72	5
	Cruise Control Switch Indicator Inoperative	2-73	6
	Cruise Control Inoperative/Malfunctioning	2-73	7

Step	Action	Yes	No
1	Did you review the Cruise Control Description and Operation and perform the necessary inspections?	Go to Step 2	Go to Symptoms
2	1. Turn ON the ignition, with the engine OFF. 2. Observe the CRUISE indicator located in the instrument cluster. Is the CRUISE indicator illuminated?	Go to Step 3	Test for Intermittent and Poor Connections
3	1. Turn OFF the ignition. 2. Disconnect the cruise control servo. 3. Turn ON the ignition with the engine OFF. Is the CRUISE indicator illuminated?	Go to Step 5	Go to Step 4
4	Inspect for poor connections at the harness connector of the cruise control servo. Did you find and correct the condition?	Go to Step 7	Go to Step 6
5	Repair the short to ground condition in the CRUISE indicator control circuit between the CRUISE indicator and the cruise control servo. Did you complete the repair?	Go to Step 7	--
6	Replace the cruise control servo. Did you complete the replacement?	Go to Step 7	--
7	Operate the system in order to verify the repair. Did you correct the condition?	System OK	Go to Step 3

LTV0500000004233

Fig. 3 Cruise Control Always On

Step	Action	Yes	No
5	1. Replace the CRUISE lamp in the instrument cluster. 2. Operate the cruise control switch to the ON position. 3. Drive vehicle above 40 km/h (25 mph). 4. Operate the cruise control mode switch to the SET position so that the cruise control system is activated. Does the CRUISE indicator illuminate?	Go to Step 9	Go to Step 6
6	Repair or replace the instrument cluster printed circuit. Did you complete the repair or replacement?	Go to Step 9	--
7	Inspect for poor connections at the harness connector of the cruise control servo. Did you find and correct the condition?	Go to Step 9	Go to Step 8
8	Replace the cruise control servo. Did you complete the replacement?	Go to Step 9	--
9	Operate the system in order to verify the repair. Did you correct the condition?	System OK	Go to Step 3

LTV0500000004235

**Fig. 4 Cruise Control Indicator Inoperative
(Part 2 of 2)**

Step	Action	Yes	No
1	Did you review the Cruise Control Description and Operation and perform the necessary inspections?	Go to Step 2	Go to Symptoms
2	1. Start the vehicle. 2. Operate the cruise control switch to the ON position. 3. Drive vehicle above 40 km/h (25 mph). 4. Operate the cruise control mode switch to the SET position so that the cruise control system is activated. Does the CRUISE indicator illuminate?	Test for Intermittent and Poor Connections	Go to Step 3
3	1. Turn OFF the ignition. 2. Disconnect the cruise control servo connector. 3. Turn ON the ignition, with the engine OFF. 4. Connect a 5 A fused jumper wire between cavity 4 of the cruise control module connector and ground. Does the CRUISE indicator illuminate?	Go to Step 7	Go to Step 4
4	1. Turn OFF the ignition. 2. Test for a high resistance or an open condition between cavity 4 of the cruise control servo and C1 - cavity 16 of the instrument cluster. Refer to Circuit Testing and Wiring Repairs in Wiring Systems. Did you find and repair the condition?	Go to Step 9	Go to Step 5

LTV0500000004234

**Fig. 4 Cruise Control Indicator Inoperative
(Part 1 of 2)**

Step	Action	Yes	No
	DEFINITION: This table diagnoses that the cruise control system operates normally, but the main cruise control switch indicator located in the main cruise control switch is always illuminated.		
1	Did you review the Cruise Control Description and Operation and perform the necessary inspections?	Go to Step 2	Go to Symptoms
2	Verify that the cruise control system is operational and that the main cruise control switch indicator located in the main cruise control switch is always illuminated. Does the main cruise control switch indicator lamp operate normally?	Test for Intermittent and Poor Connections	Go to Step 3
3	1. Turn OFF the ignition. 2. Disconnect the cruise control servo connector. 3. Turn ON the ignition, with the engine OFF. Does the main cruise control switch indicator lamp illuminate?	Go to Step 5	Go to Step 4
4	With the cruise control servo connector still disconnected: 1. Disconnect the main cruise control switch. 2. Test for a short to ground between cavity 10 of the cruise control servo connector and ground. Did you find and correct the condition?	Go to Step 9	Go to Step 6

LTV0500000004236

**Fig. 5 Cruise Control Switch Always On
(Part 1 of 2)**

Step	Action	Yes	No
5	Inspect for poor connections at the harness connector of the cruise control servo. Did you find and correct the condition?	Go to Step 9	Go to Step 7
6	Inspect for poor connections at the harness connector of the main cruise control switch. Did you find and correct the condition?	Go to Step 9	Go to Step 8
7	Replace the cruise control servo. Did you complete the replacement?	Go to Step 9	--
8	Replace the main cruise control switch. Did you complete the replacement?	Go to Step 9	--
9	Operate the system in order to verify the repair. Did you correct the condition?	System OK	Go to Step 3

LTV0500000004237

Fig. 5 Cruise Control Switch Always On (Part 2 of 2)

Step	Action	Yes	No
5	Inspect for poor connections at the harness connector of the cruise control servo. Did you find and correct the condition?	Go to Step 9	Go to Step 7
6	Inspect for poor connections at the harness connector of the main cruise control switch. Did you find and correct the condition?	Go to Step 9	Go to Step 8
7	Replace the cruise control servo. Did you complete the replacement?	Go to Step 9	--
8	Replace the main cruise control switch. Did you complete the replacement?	Go to Step 9	--
9	Operate the system in order to verify the repair. Did you correct the condition?	Go to Step 9	--

LTV0500000004239

Fig. 6 Cruise Control Switch Indicator Inoperative (Part 2 of 2)

Step	Action	Value (s)	Yes	No
	DEFINITION: This table diagnoses the cruise control function is totally inoperative. It does not diagnose the CRUISE indicator or cruise switch indicator only are inoperative or that the overdrive cutoff is inoperative.			
1	Did you review the Cruise Control Description and Operation and perform the necessary inspections?	--	Go to Step 2	Go to Symptoms
2	Verify that the cruise control is inoperative. Does the cruise control system operate normally?	--	Test for Intermittent and Poor Connections	Go to Step 3
3	1. Perform the Powertrain On Board Diagnostic (OBD) System Check. 2. Observe the DTC display using the scan tool. Is DTC P0500 or DTC P0121 stored in memory?	--	Go to Step 4	Go to Step 5
4	For DTC P0121: • Refer to DTC P0121 in Engine Controls - 2.0L. • Refer to DTC P0121 in Engine Controls - 2.5L. For DTC P0500, refer to DTC P0500 in Automatic Transmission - 4 Speed-M41. Did you correct the condition?	--	Go to Step 28	--

LTV0500000004240

Fig. 7 Cruise Control Inoperative/Malfunctioning (Part 1 of 5)

Step	Action	Yes	No
	DEFINITION: This table diagnoses that the cruise control system operates normally, but the main cruise control switch indicator located in the main cruise control switch does not illuminate when the switch is depressed.		
1	Did you review the Cruise Control Description and Operation and perform the necessary inspections?	Go to Step 2	Go to Symptoms
2	Verify that the cruise control system is operational and that the main cruise control switch indicator lamp does not illuminate when the switch is depressed. Does the main cruise control switch indicator lamp operate normally?	Test for Intermittent and Poor Connections	Go to Step 3
3	1. Turn the ignition OFF. 2. Disconnect the cruise control servo connector. 3. Connect a 5 A fused jumper wire between cavity 10 of the cruise control servo connector and a good ground. 4. Turn ON the ignition with the engine OFF. Does the cruise control indicator lamp in the main cruise control switch illuminate?	Go to Step 5	Go to Step 4
4	With the cruise control servo connector still disconnected: 1. Disconnect the main cruise control switch connector. 2. Test for an open condition in the indicator control circuit between the cruise control servo connector and the main cruise control switch connector. Did you find and correct the condition?	Go to Step 9	Go to Step 6

LTV0500000004238

Fig. 6 Cruise Control Switch Indicator Inoperative (Part 1 of 2)

Step	Action	Yes	No
5	1. Disconnect the cruise control servo connector. 2. Remove the cap from cruise control servo. 3. Disconnect the cruise control cable from the cruise control servo. 4. Rotate the cruise control servo lever counterclockwise and release. Did the servo lever turn approximately 1/3 revolution counterclockwise and return to its normal position when released?	Go to Step 6	Go to Step 27
6	With the cruise control servo lever in its normal position, attempt to rotate the lever in a clockwise direction. Did the lever rotate in a clockwise direction?	Go to Step 27	Go to Step 7
7	1. Reconnect the cruise control cable to the cruise control servo. 2. Inspect the amount of play in the cruise control cable. Is the amount of play in the cruise control servo cable within tolerance?	Go to Step 8	Go to Step 26
8	With the cruise control servo connector still disconnected: 1. Turn ON the ignition, with the engine OFF. 2. Connect a test lamp between cavity 12 of the cruise control servo connector and a good ground. Did the test lamp illuminate?	Go to Step 9	Go to Step 20
9	With the cruise control servo connector still disconnected and the ignition ON: 1. Connect the test lamp between cavity 6 of the cruise control servo connector and a good ground. 2. Depress and release the brake pedal. Does the test lamp turn OFF when the brake pedal is depressed and turn ON when the brake pedal is released?	Go to Step 10	Go to Step 18
10	With the cruise control servo connector still disconnected: 1. Connect the test lamp between cavity 2 of the cruise control servo connector and a good ground. 2. Depress and release the brake pedal. Does the test lamp turn ON when the brake pedal is depressed and OFF when the brake pedal is released?	Go to Step 11	Go to Step 18

LTV0500000004241

Fig. 7 Cruise Control Inoperative/Malfunctioning (Part 2 of 5)

11	With the cruise control servo connector still disconnected and the ignition ON: Connect the test lamp between cavity 11 and cavity 12 of the cruise control servo connector. Does the test lamp illuminate?	--	Go to Step 12	Go to Step 22
12	With the cruise control servo connector still disconnected and the ignition ON: 1. Depress and hold the main cruise control switch. 2. Measure the voltage between cavity 8 of the cruise control servo connector and a good ground. Does the voltage measure near the specified value?	12 V	Go to Step 13	Go to Step 23
13	With the cruise control servo connector still disconnected, measure the resistance between cavity 5 and cavity 8 of the cruise control servo connector with the cruise control mode switch in the following positions: • CANCEL • RES/ACC • SET/COAST Does the resistance measure near the specified values?	• CANCEL 0 - 0.5 Ohms • RES/ACC 900 - 920 Ohms • SET/COAST 220 - 240 Ohms	Go to Step 14	Go to Step 24
14	Does the vehicle have an automatic transaxle?	--	Go to Step 15	Go to Step 16
15	1. Move the transmission range switch to any position except P or N. 2. Test for an open condition between cavity 9 of the cruise control servo and ground. Did you measure an open condition?	--	Go to Step 17	Go to Step 25
16	1. Test for an open condition between cavity 9 of the cruise control servo and ground. 2. Make sure the clutch pedal is not depressed. Did you measure an open condition?	--	Go to Step 17	Go to Step 25

LTV0500000004242

Fig. 7 Cruise Control Inoperative/Malfunctioning (Part 3 of 5)

COMPONENT REPLACEMENT

Cruise Control Cable

1. Remove cruise control assembly cover.
2. Loosen cruise control cable locknut.
3. Remove cruise control cable.
4. Remove cruise control cable from underhood guide clips.
5. Remove cruise control cable from accelerator.
6. Unclip cruise control cable from instrument panel, then remove cruise control cable from vehicle.
7. Reverse procedures to install, inspecting cruise control cable for any damage.

Cruise Control Actuator

1. Remove cruise control actuator cover.
2. Loosen cruise control cable locknut.
3. Remove cruise control cable from cruise control actuator lever.
4. Disconnect cruise control actuator electrical connector.
5. Remove bolts and screws from cruise control actuator from mounting bracket.
6. Reverse procedures to install.

Cruise Control Switch

1. Remove lower IP cluster panel screws, then panel.

17	Inspect for poor connections at the harness connector of the cruise control servo. Did you find and correct the condition?		Go to Step 27	--
18	Inspect the stop lamp switch adjustment. Is the stop lamp switch in adjustment?		Go to Step 20	Go to Step 21
19	Adjust the stop lamp switch. Did you complete the adjustment?		Go to Step 27	--
20	Repair the open condition in the BLU/BLK wire between cavity 12 of the cruise control servo connector and cavity 2 of the main relay. Did you complete the repair?		Go to Step 28	--
21	Repair the open or short to voltage condition in the stop lamp switch circuit between the cruise control servo and battery positive voltage. Did you complete the repair or replacement?		Go to Step 28	--
22	Repair the open in the BLK wire of the ground circuit between cavity 11 of the cruise control servo connector and ground. Did you complete the repair?		Go to Step 28	--
23	Repair the open in the battery positive voltage circuit between cavity 8 of the cruise control servo connector and battery positive voltage. Did you complete the repair?		Go to Step 28	--

LTV0500000004243

Fig. 7 Cruise Control Inoperative/Malfunctioning (Part 4 of 5)

24	Repair the open or short to ground condition in the cruise control mode switch control circuit between cavity 5 and cavity 8 of the cruise control servo connector. Did you complete the repair?		Go to Step 28	--
25	Repair the short to ground condition between cavity 9 of the cruise control servo connector and ground. Did you complete the repair?		Go to Step 28	--
26	Adjust the amount of play in the cruise control servo cable. Did you adjust the cruise control cable within adjustment?		Go to Step 28	--
27	Replace the cruise control servo. Did you complete the replacement?		Go to Step 28	--
28	Operate the system in order to verify the repair. Did you correct the condition?		System OK	Go to Step 3

LTV0500000004244

Fig. 7 Cruise Control Inoperative/Malfunctioning (Part 5 of 5)

2. Release retaining tabs from behind instrument panel which secure cruise control switch.
3. Slide cruise control switch out from instrument panel.
4. Disconnect cruise control electrical switch connector.
5. Remove cruise control switch from vehicle.
6. Reverse procedures to install.

WIPER SYSTEMS

NOTE: On Air Bag Equipped Models, Refer To "Air Bag System Precautions" Located In The Front Of This Manual For System Disarming & Arming Procedures.

NOTE: Refer To "Computer Relearn Procedures" Located In The Front Of This Manual When Battery Power To The Computer Has Been Interrupted.

NOTE: "Electrical Symbol & Wire Color Code Identification" Located In The Front Of This Manual May Be Used As An Aid When Using Wiring Circuits Found In This Section.

INDEX

	Page No.		Page No.		Page No.
Description	3-1	Express & Savanna	3-2	Aztek & Rendezvous	3-2
Precautions	3-1	H2	3-2	Blazer, Jimmy, Sonoma &	
Air Bag Systems	3-1	H3	3-2	S10	3-2
Battery Ground Cable	3-1	HHR	3-2	Bravada, Envoy, Rainier &	
System Diagnosis & Testing	3-1	Montana, Silhouette &		Trailblazer	3-2
Accessing Diagnostic Trouble		Venture	3-2	Canyon & Colorado	3-2
Codes	3-1	Relay, SV6, Terraza &		Equinox & Torrent	3-2
Clearing Diagnostic Trouble		Uplander	3-2	Express & Savanna	3-2
Codes	3-2	SRX	3-2	H2	3-2
Diagnostic Chart Index	3-28	SSR	3-2	H3	3-2
Diagnostic Tests	3-2	Suburban, Tahoe & Yukon	3-2	HHR	3-2
Astro & Safari	3-2	Tracker	3-2	Montana, Silhouette &	
Avalanche, Escalade, Sierra &		Vue	3-2	Venture	3-2
Silverado	3-2	Diagnostic Trouble Code		Relay, SV6, Terraza &	
Aztek & Rendezvous	3-2	Interpretation	3-1	Uplander	3-2
Blazer, Jimmy, Sonoma &		Intermittents & Poor		SRX	3-2
S10	3-2	Connections	3-2	SSR	3-2
Bravada, Envoy, Rainier &		Wiring Diagrams	3-2	Suburban, Tahoe & Yukon	3-2
Trailblazer	3-2	Astro & Safari	3-2	Tracker	3-2
Canyon & Colorado	3-2	Avalanche, Escalade, Sierra &		Vue	3-2
Equinox & Torrent	3-2	Silverado	3-2		

PRECAUTIONS

AIR BAG SYSTEMS

Refer to "Air Bag System Precautions" in the front of this manual for system disarming and arming procedures.

BATTERY GROUND CABLE

Prior to service disconnect battery ground cable and isolate as required.

DESCRIPTION

The front wiper system, consists of a permanent magnet positive park pulse wiper, a washer pump mounted on the side of the washer bottle and a turn signal type wiper/washer switch. The die cast aluminum housing of the wiper provides cooling of internal parts and the wiper motor is equipped with radio frequency interference suppression. The wiper motor is protected by an automatic reset type circuit breaker located in the brush holder circuit. A 25 amp Wiper fuse protects the circuit wiring.

An electronic circuit board controls all timing and washer commands. When the washer button is pushed for more than 1 second, washer solvent is sprayed on the windshield for as long as the button is held, followed by approximately 6 seconds of wiper activity.

Turning the switch to either the Lo or Hi speed position completes the circuit and wipers will run at that speed. The pulse and demand wash functions are controlled by a plug-in printed circuit board enclosed in the wiper housing cover. Turning the switch to the Delay position operates the motor intermittently and the delay can be varied by rotating the switch. An instantaneous wipe can be obtained by rotating the switch to the Mist position and a continuous wipe will be performed if the button is held.

The rear window wiper/washer system, has a one-speed, permanent magnet, depressed-park wiper motor assembly with a pulse mode. The motor assembly is either mounted to the rear glass with a wiper arm mounted directly onto the wiper motor or is mounted in the tailgate door. The motor assembly drives a gear box which, in turn, drives a wiper pivot that provides an oscillating output to the arm and blade. Operation is controlled by a two position dash mounted switch. The wiper/washer switch has a momentary wash and wipe position and must be turned off manually. The wiper motor is serviced as an assembly.

On tailgate mounted models, a controller assembly is attached to the wiper motor bracket and is the only replaceable wiper motor component. The controller's printed circuit board controls all wiper motor functions as determined by the position of the wiper/washer switch.

SYSTEM DIAGNOSIS & TESTING

Accessing Diagnostic Trouble Codes

Connect a suitably programmed scan tool to Data Link Connector (DLC) and follow manufacturer's instructions.

Diagnostic Trouble Code Interpretation

Refer to "Diagnostic Chart Index" for diagnostic trouble code interpretation.

WIPER SYSTEMS

Wiring Diagrams

ASTRO & SAFARI

Refer to **Fig. 1** for wiring diagrams.

AVALANCHE, ESCALADE, SIERRA & SILVERADO

Refer to **Figs. 2 through 5** for wiring diagrams.

AZTEK & RENDEZVOUS

Refer to **Figs. 6 and 7** for wiring diagrams.

BLAZER, JIMMY, SONOMA & S10

Refer to **Figs. 8 and 9** for wiring diagrams.

BRAVADA, ENVOY, RAINIER & TRAILBLAZER

Refer to **Figs. 10 through 13** for wiring diagrams.

CANYON & COLORADO

Refer to **Figs. 14 and 15** for wiring diagrams.

EQUINOX & TORRENT

Refer to **Figs. 16 and 17** for wiring diagrams.

EXPRESS & SAVANNA

Refer to **Figs. 18 through 21** for wiring diagrams.

HHR

Refer to **Figs. 22 and 23** for wiring diagrams.

H2

Refer to **Figs. 24 through 29** for wiring diagrams.

H3

Refer to **Figs. 30 through 32** for wiring diagrams.

MONTANA, SILHOUETTE & VENTURE

Refer to **Figs. 33 and 34** for wiring diagrams.

RELAY, SV6, TERRAZA & UPLANDER

Refer to **Figs. 35 and 36** for wiring diagrams.

SRX

Refer to **Figs. 37 through 41** for wiring diagrams.

SSR

Refer to **Fig. 42** for wiring diagram.

SUBURBAN, TAHOE & YUKON

Refer to **Figs. 43 through 48** for wiring diagrams.

TRACKER

Refer to **Figs. 49 and 50** for wiring diagrams.

VUE

Refer to **Figs. 51 and 52** for wiring diagrams.

Diagnostic Tests

ASTRO & SAFARI

Refer to **Figs. 53 through 61** for diagnostic tests.

AVALANCHE, ESCALADE, SIERRA & SILVERADO

Refer to **Figs. 62 through 79** for diagnostic tests.

AZTEK & RENDEZVOUS

Refer to **Figs. 80 through 88** for diagnostic tests.

BLAZER, JIMMY, SONOMA & S10

Refer to **Figs. 89 through 97** for diagnostic system tests.

BRAVADA, ENVOY, RAINIER & TRAILBLAZER

Refer to **Figs. 98 through 112** for diagnostic tests.

CANYON & COLORADO

Refer to **Figs. 113 through 118** for diagnostic tests.

EQUINOX & TORRENT

Refer to **Figs. 119 through 130** for diagnostic tests.

EXPRESS & SAVANNA

Refer to **Figs. 131 through 145** for diagnostic tests.

HHR

Refer to **Figs. 146 through 152** for diagnostic tests.

H2

Refer to **Figs. 153 through 170** for diagnostic tests.

H3

Refer to **Figs. 171 through 181** for diagnostic tests.

MONTANA, SILHOUETTE & VENTURE

Refer to **Figs.182 through 189** for diagnostic tests.

RELAY, SV6, TERRAZA & UPLANDER

Refer to **Figs. 190 through 201** for diagnostic tests.

SRX

Refer to **Figs. 202 through 213** for diagnostic tests.

SSR

Refer to **Figs. 214 through 218** for diagnostic tests.

SUBURBAN, TAHOE & YUKON

Refer to **Figs. 219 through 245** for diagnostic tests.

TRACKER

Refer to **Figs. 246 through 254** for diagnostic tests.

VUE

Refer to **Figs. 255 through 266** for diagnostic tests.

Clearing Diagnostic Trouble Codes

Connect a suitably programmed scan tool to Data Link Connector (DLC) and follow manufacturer's instructions.

Intermittents & Poor Connections

Most intermittents are caused by faulty electrical connections or wiring, although a sticking relay or solenoid can also cause an intermittent condition. Check wiring and connectors for the following:
1. Poor mating of connector halves, or terminals not fully seated in connector body.
2. Dirt or corrosion on terminals.
3. Damaged connector body.
4. Improperly formed or damaged terminals.
5. Poor terminal to wire connection.
6. Rubbed through wiring insulation.
7. Wiring broken inside insulation.

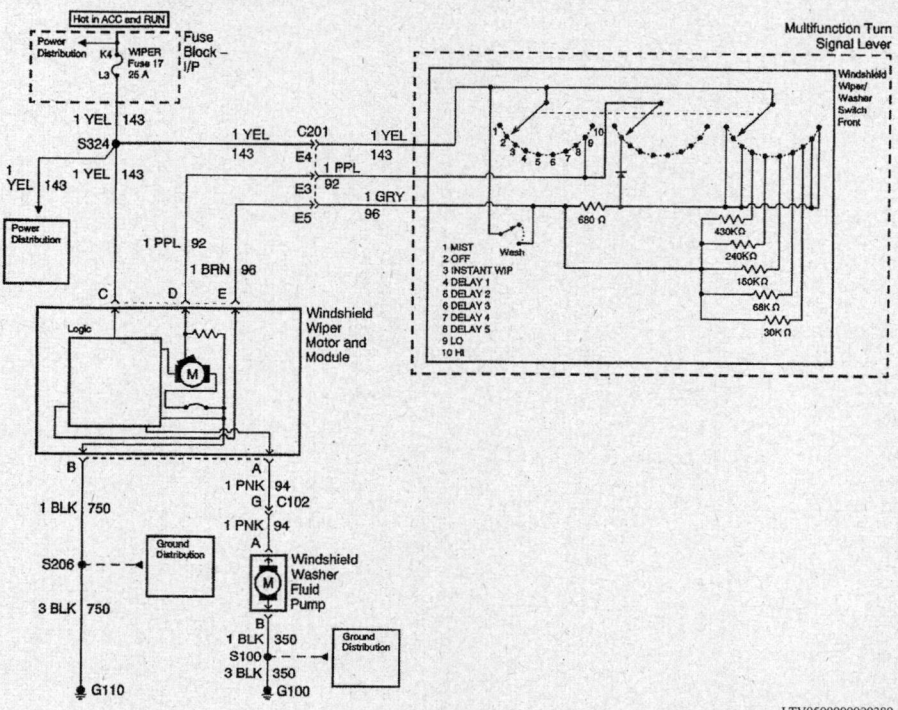

Fig. 1 Wiring diagram (Part 1 of 2). Astro & Safari

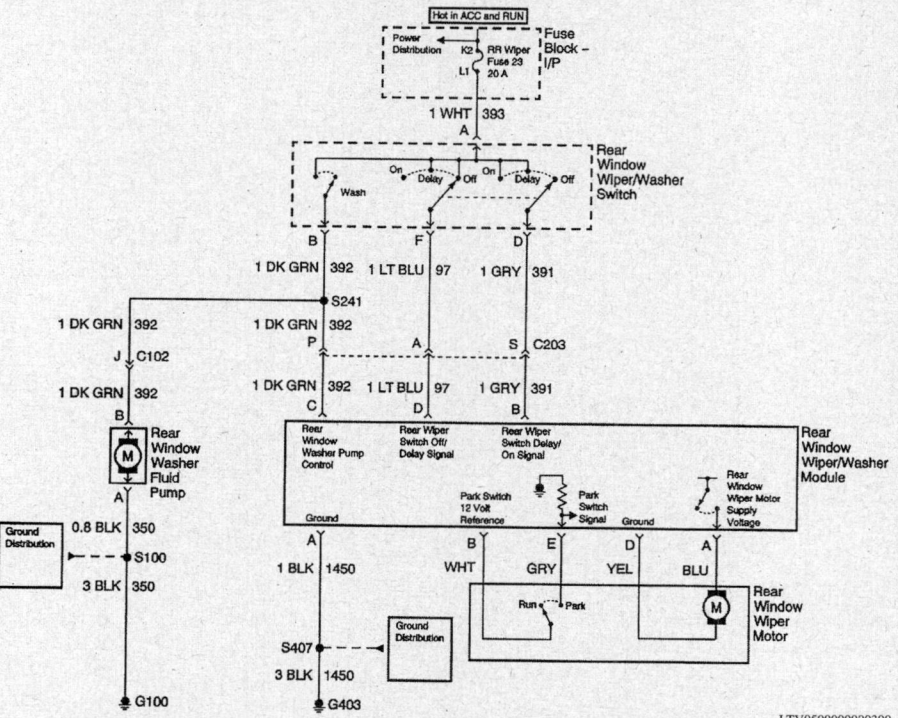

Fig. 1 Wiring diagrams (Part 2 of 2). Astro & Safari

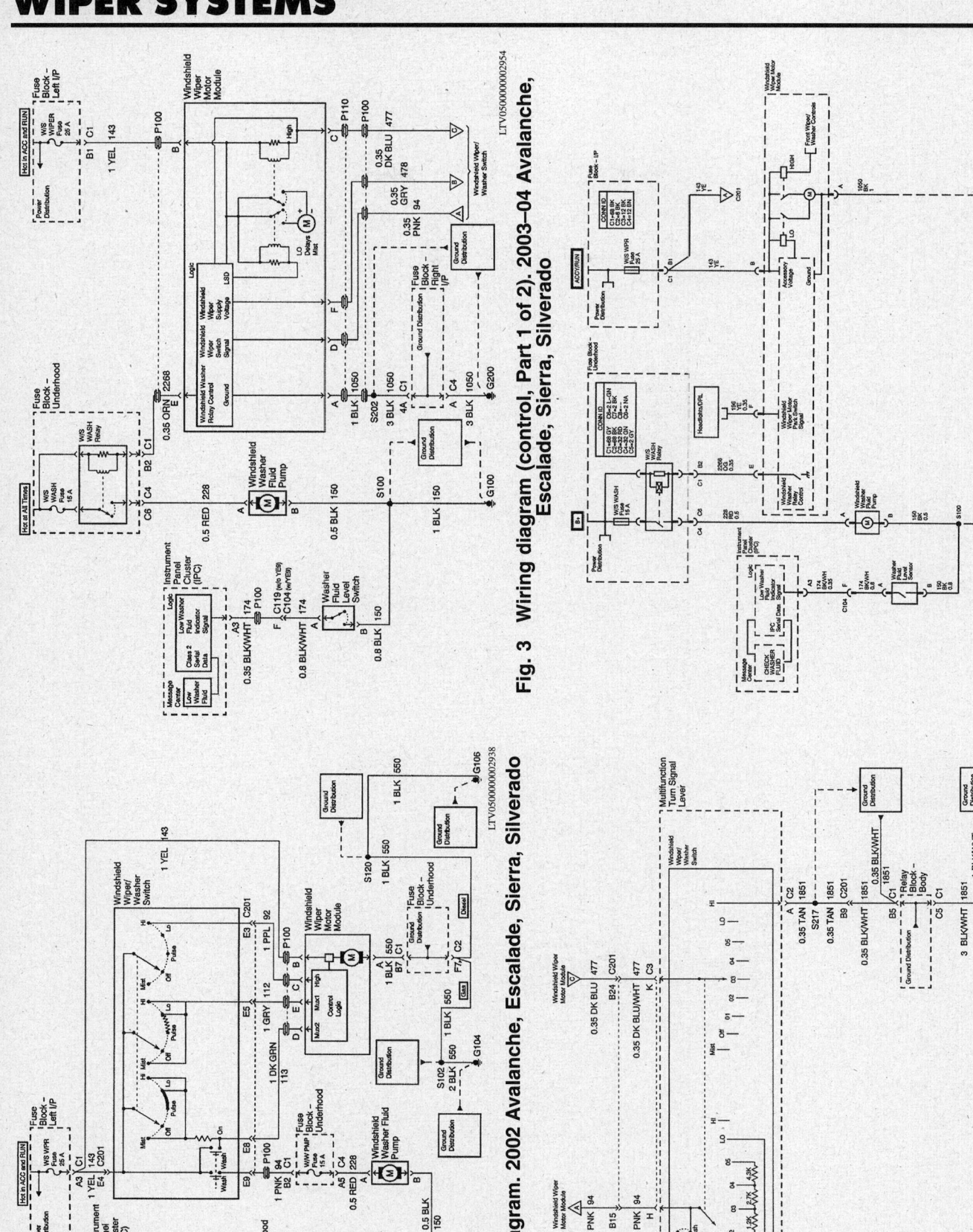

Fig. 3 Wiring diagram (control, Part 1 of 2). 2003–04 Avalanche, Escalade, Sierra, Silverado

Fig. 4 Wiring diagram (power, ground & controls). 2005–06 Avalanche, Escalade, Sierra, Silverado

Fig. 2 Wiring diagram. 2002 Avalanche, Escalade, Sierra, Silverado

Fig. 3 Wiring diagram (control, Part 2 of 2). 2003–04 Avalanche, Escalade, Sierra, Silverado

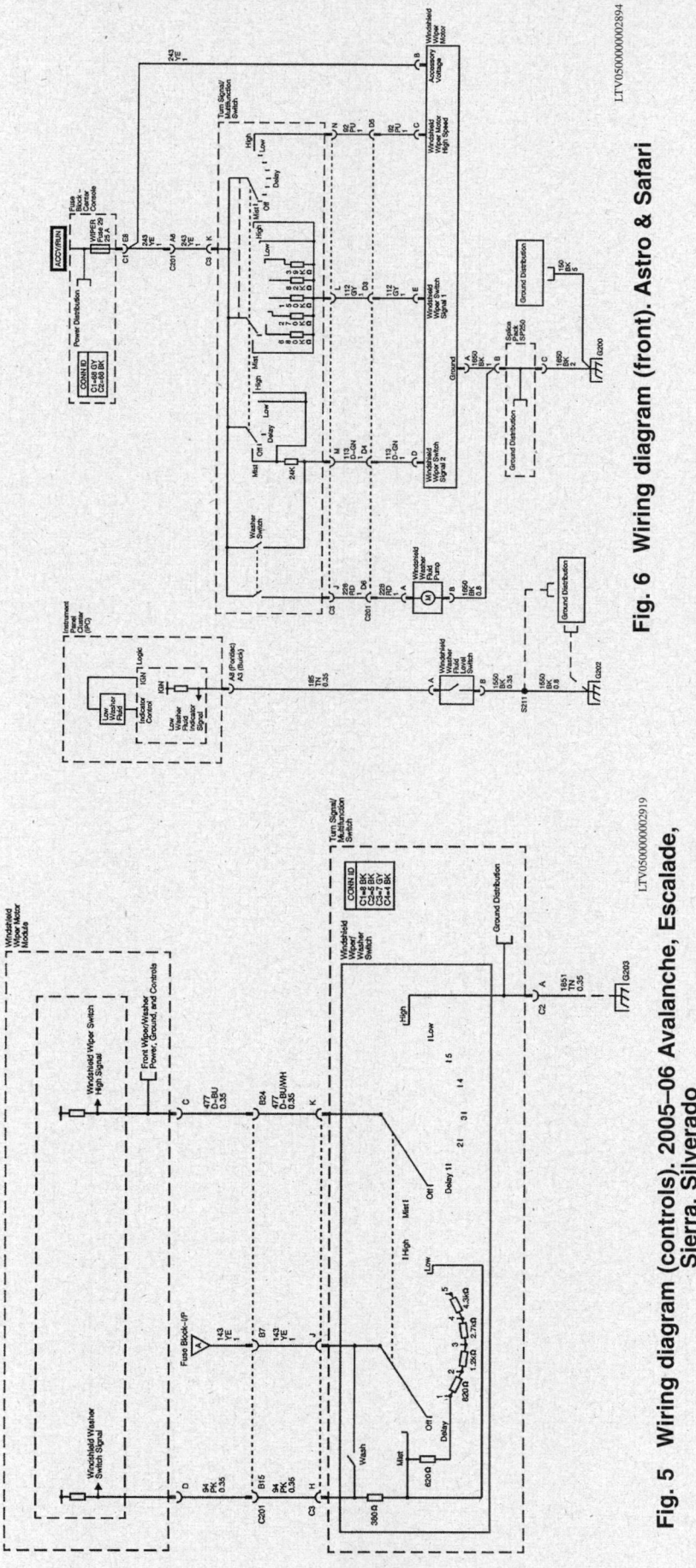

Fig. 6 Wiring diagram (front). Astro & Safari

Fig. 5 Wiring diagram (controls). 2005–06 Avalanche, Escalade, Sierra, Silverado

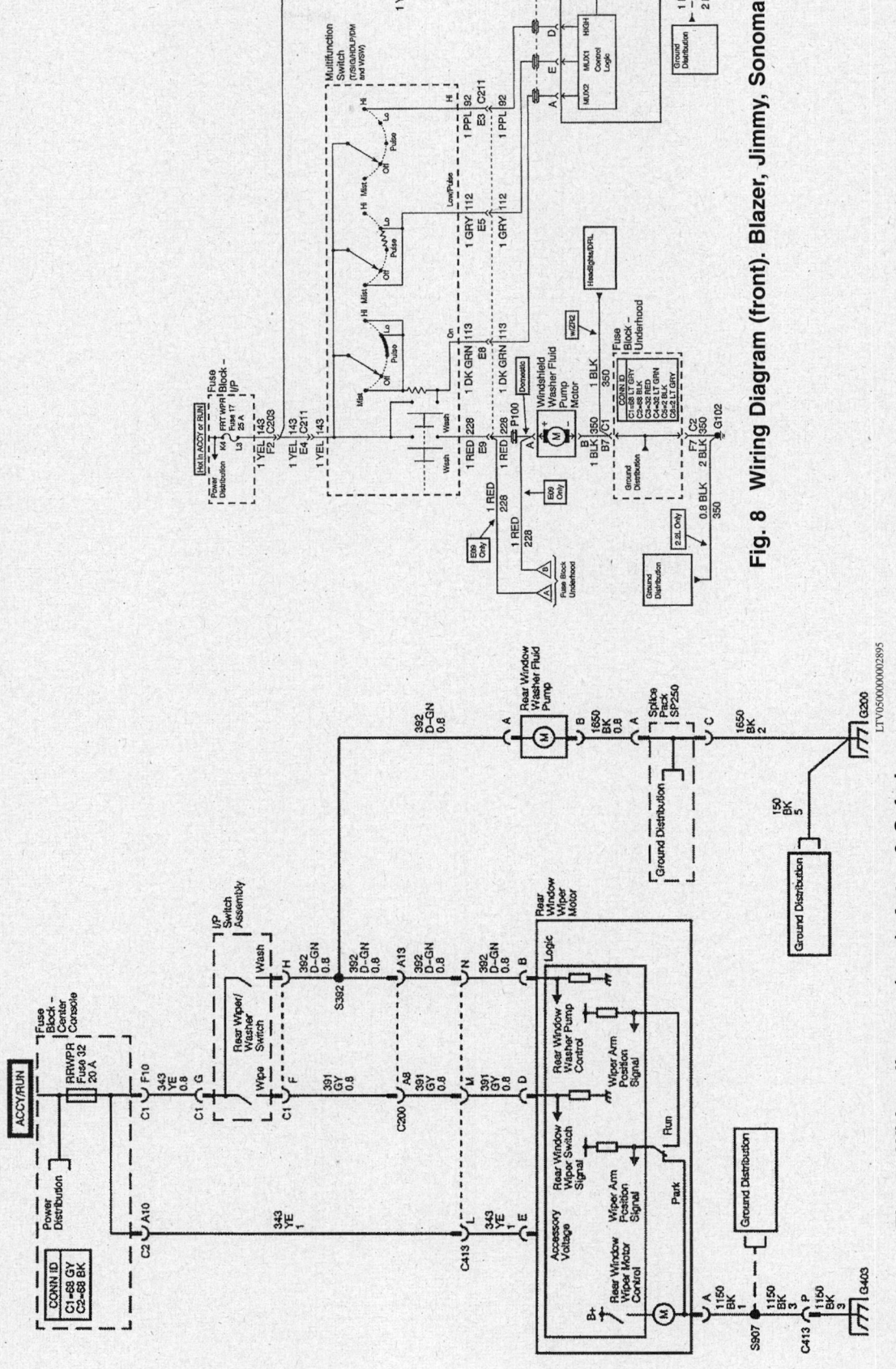

Fig. 8 Wiring Diagram (front). Blazer, Jimmy, Sonoma & S10

Fig. 7 Wiring diagram (rear). Astro & Safari

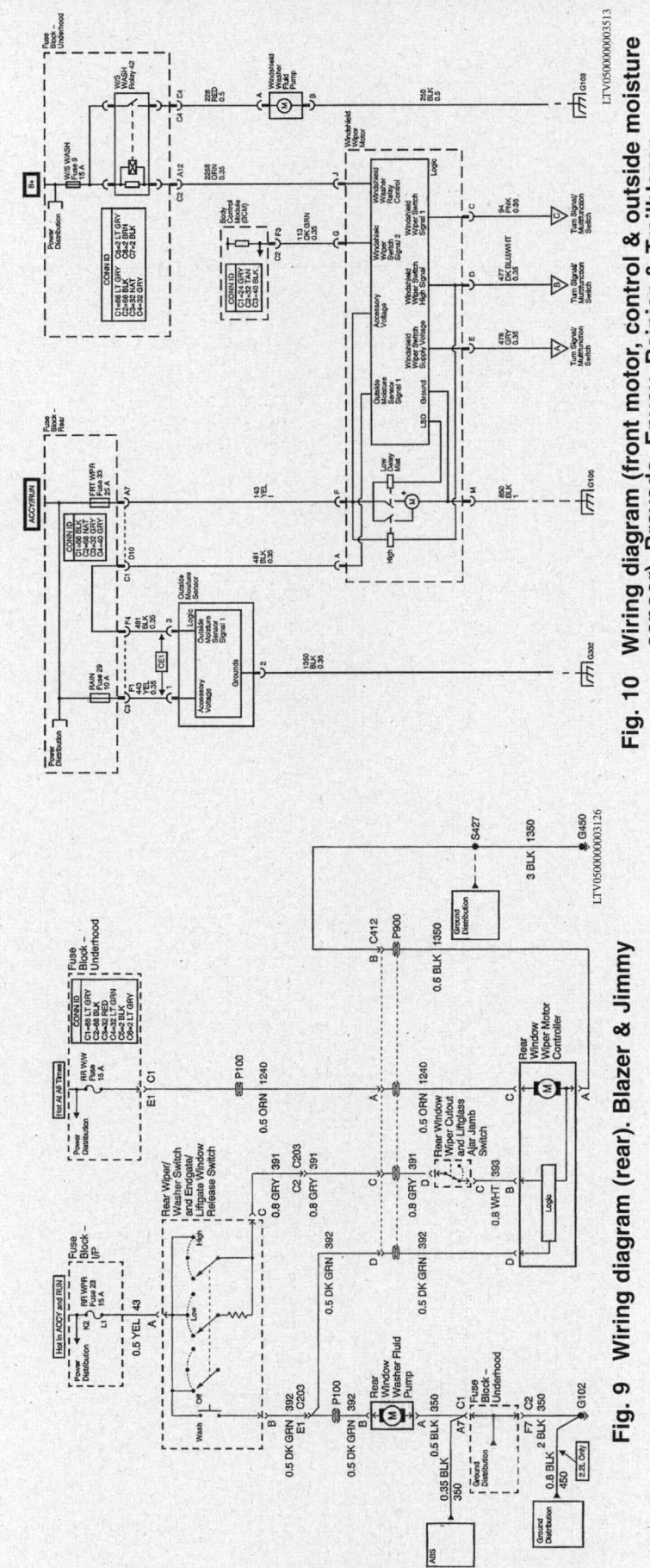

Fig. 10 Wiring diagram (front motor, control & outside moisture sensor). Bravada, Envoy, Rainier & Trailblazer

Fig. 9 Wiring diagram (rear). Blazer & Jimmy

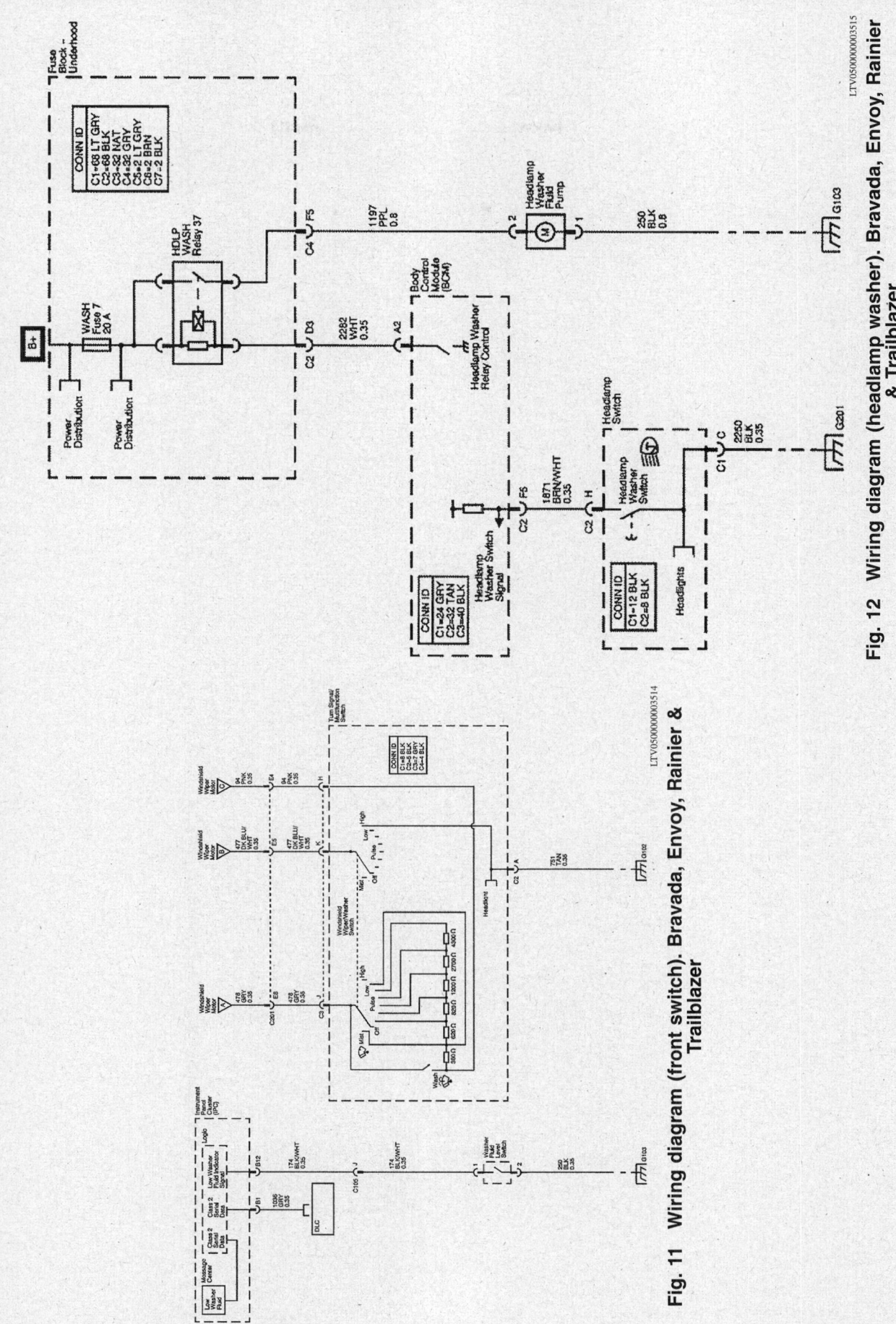

Fig. 12 Wiring diagram (headlamp washer). Bravada, Envoy, Rainier & Trailblazer

Fig. 11 Wiring diagram (front switch). Bravada, Envoy, Rainier & Trailblazer

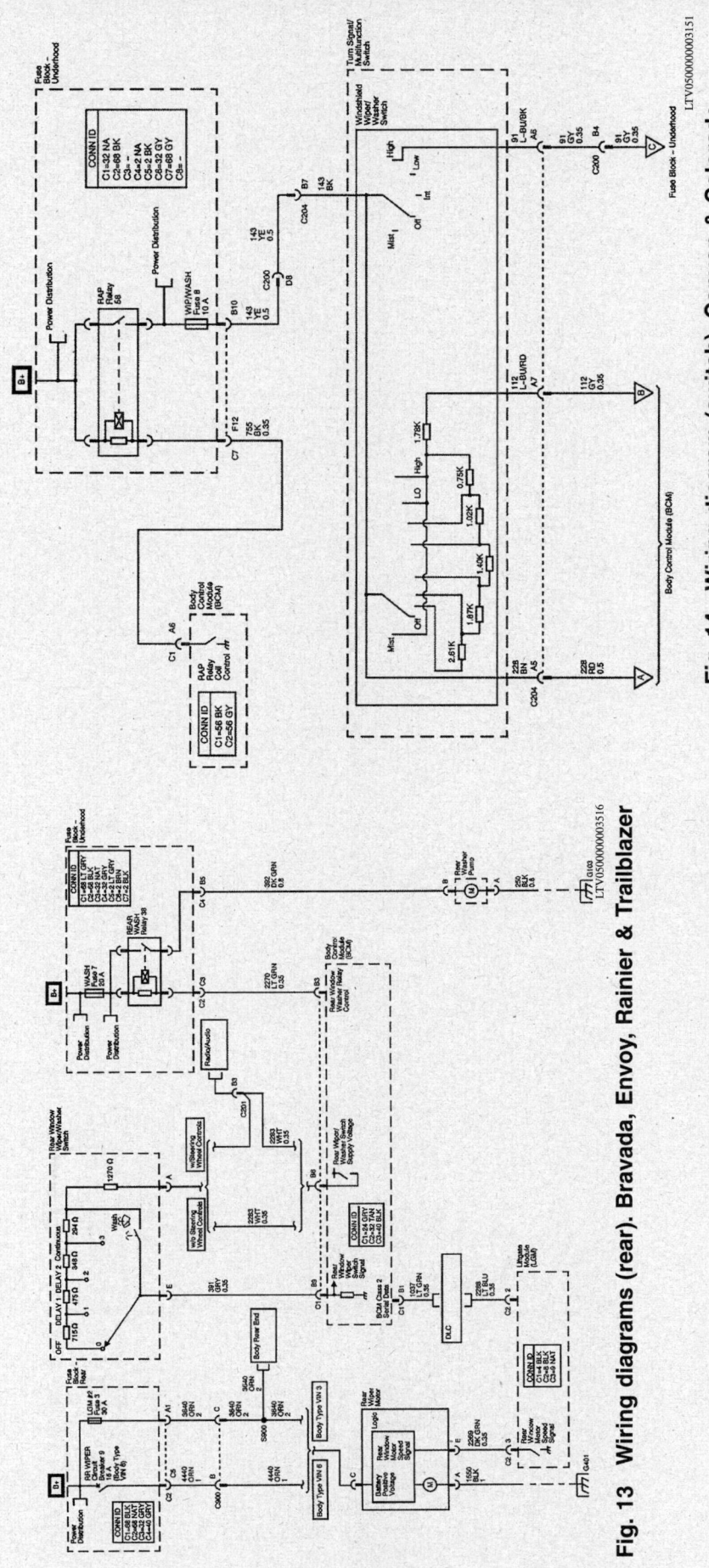

Fig. 14 Wiring diagram (switch). Canyon & Colorado

Fig. 13 Wiring diagrams (rear). Bravada, Envoy, Rainier & Trailblazer

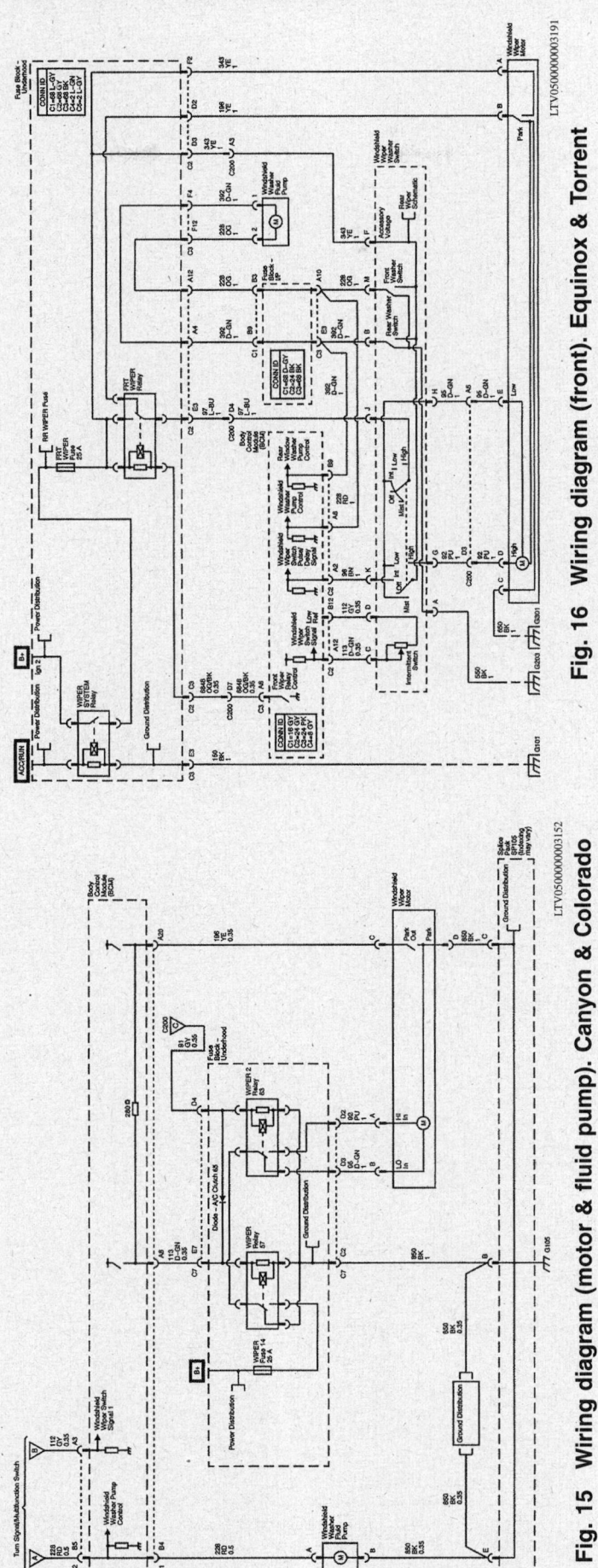

Fig. 16   Wiring diagram (front). Equinox & Torrent

Fig. 15   Wiring diagram (motor & fluid pump). Canyon & Colorado

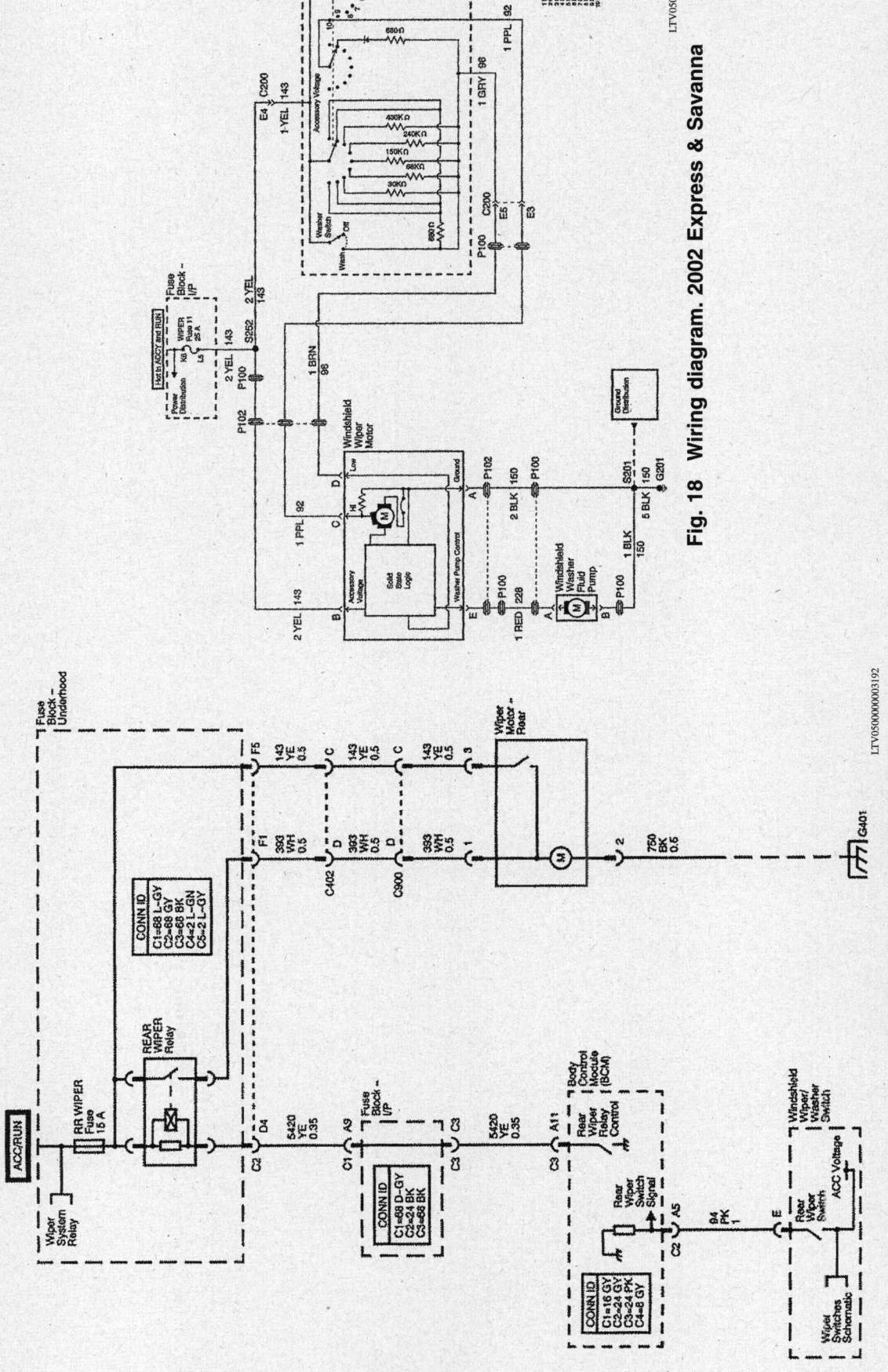

Fig. 18 Wiring diagram. 2002 Express & Savanna

Fig. 17 Wiring diagram (rear). Equinox & Torrent

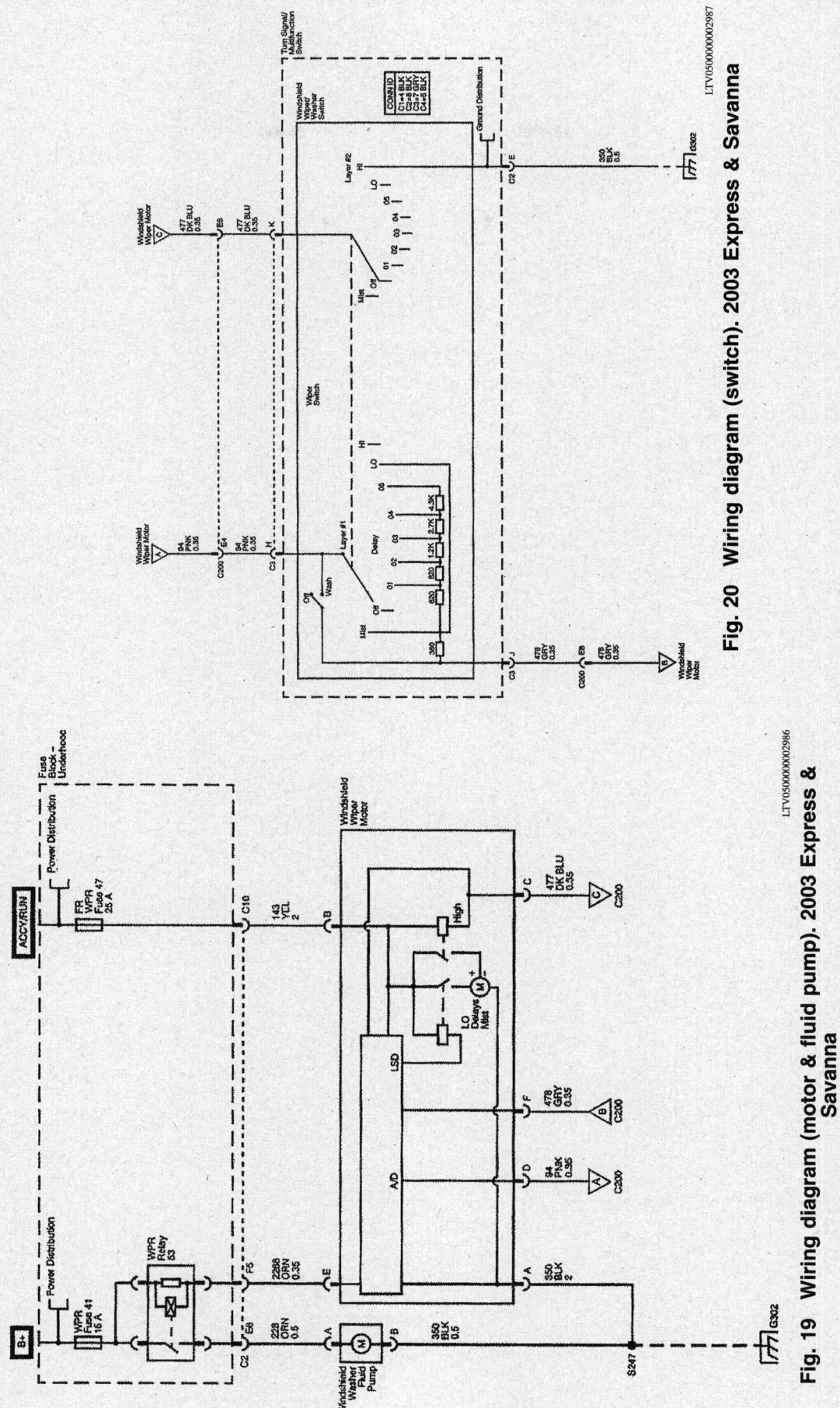

Fig. 20 Wiring diagram (switch). 2003 Express & Savanna

Fig. 19 Wiring diagram (motor & fluid pump). 2003 Express & Savanna

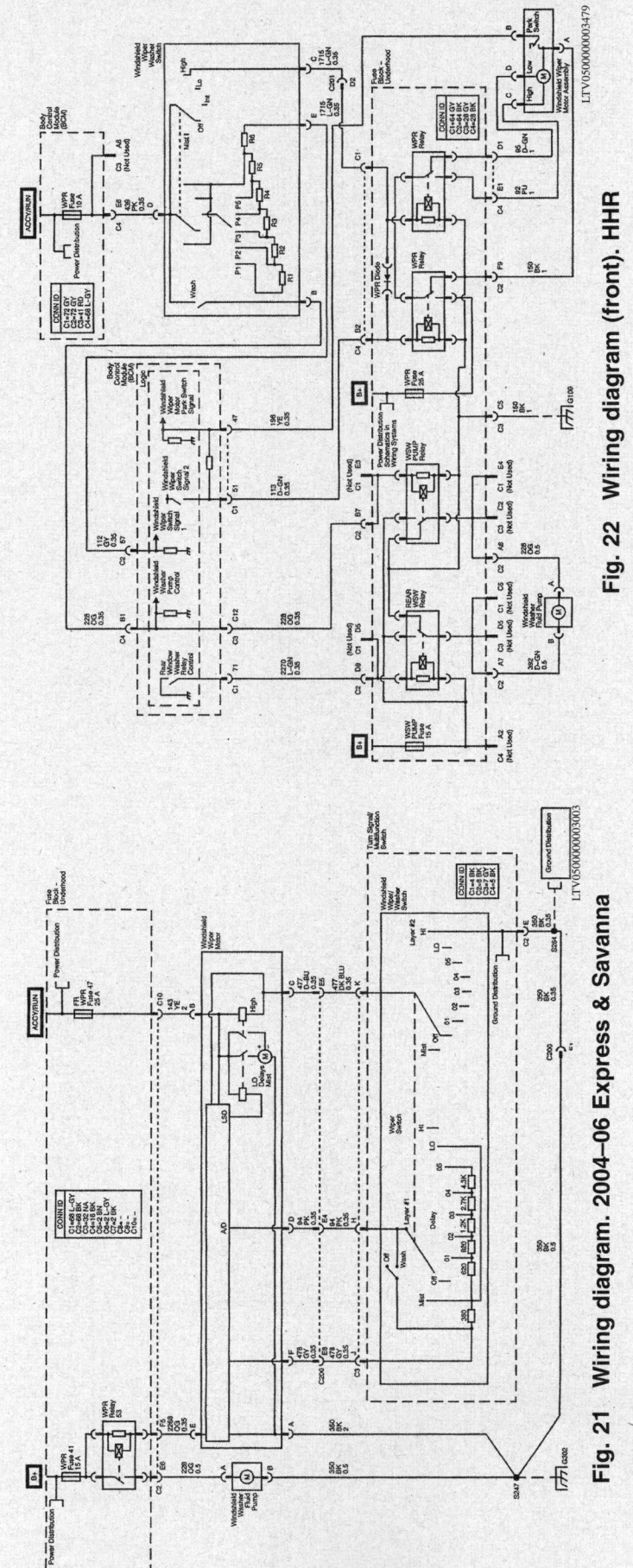

Fig. 22 Wiring diagram (front). HHR

Fig. 21 Wiring diagram. 2004–06 Express & Savanna

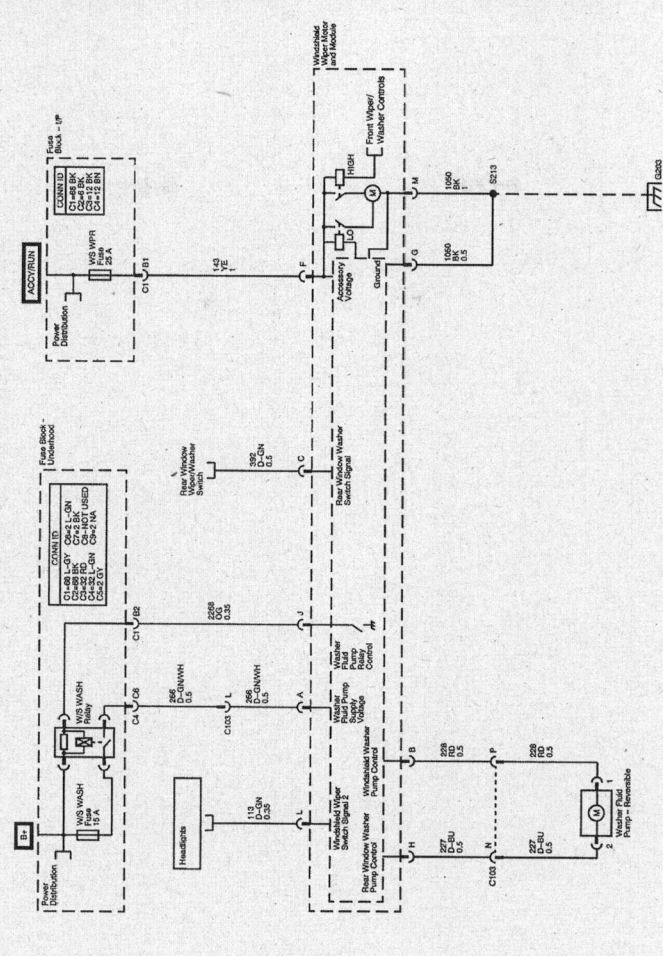

Fig. 24 Wiring diagram (front, power, ground & motors). 2003–04 H2

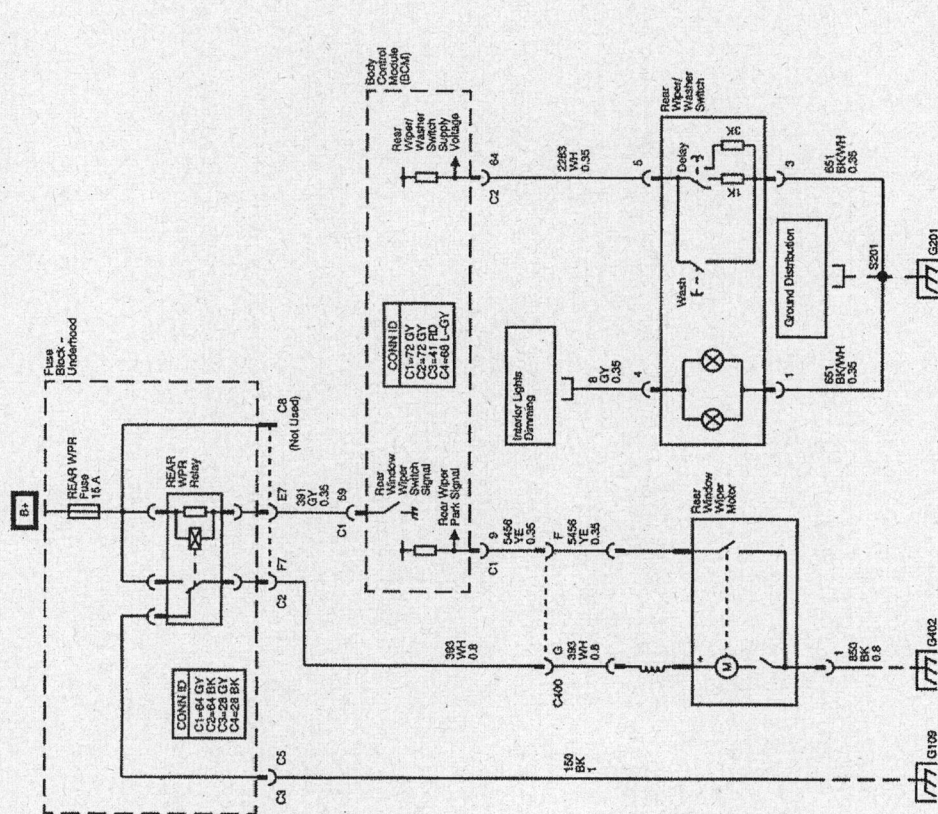

Fig. 23 Wiring diagram (rear). HHR

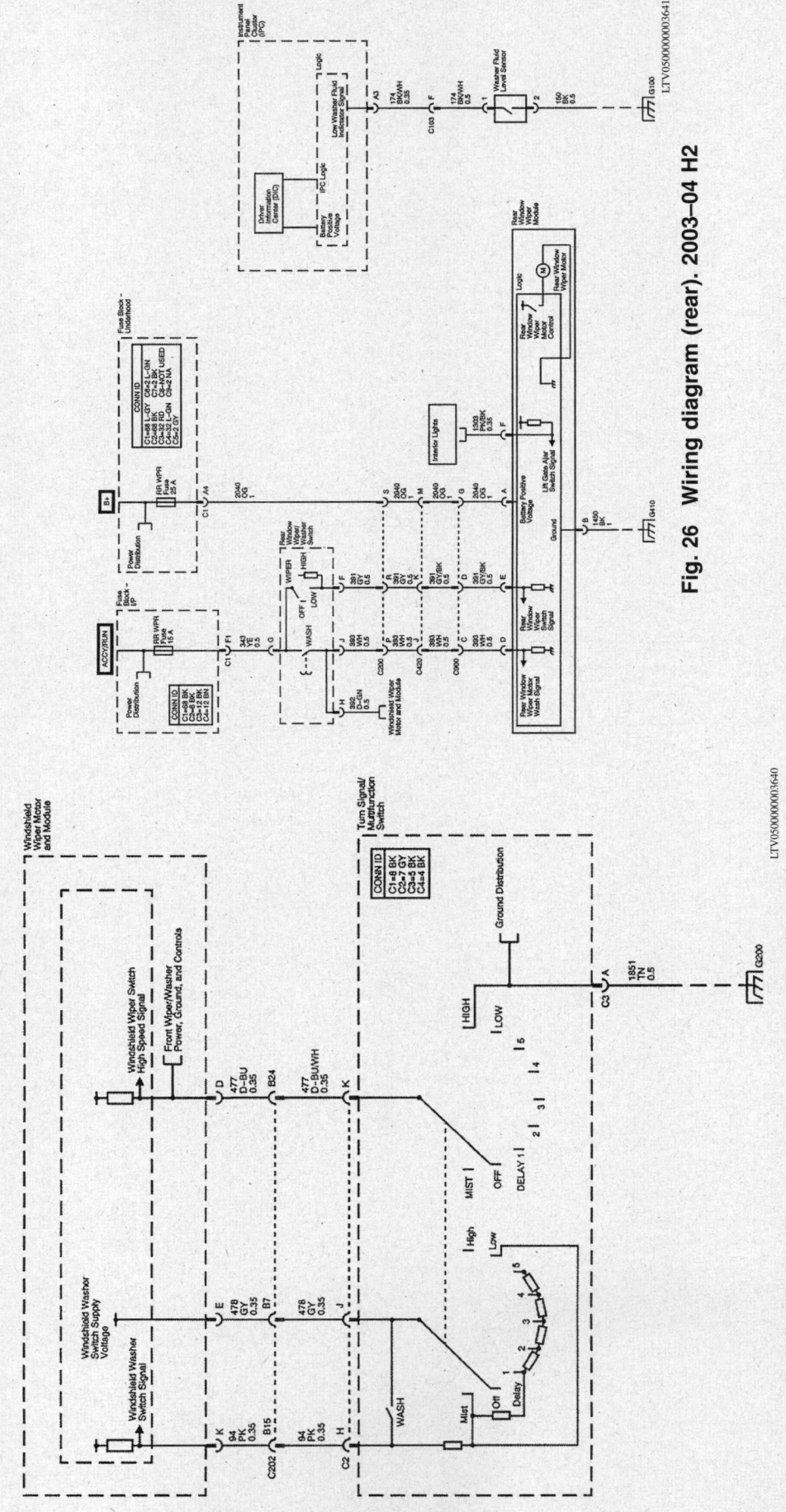

Fig. 26 Wiring diagram (rear). 2003–04 H2

Fig. 25 Wiring diagram (front, controls). 2003–04 H2

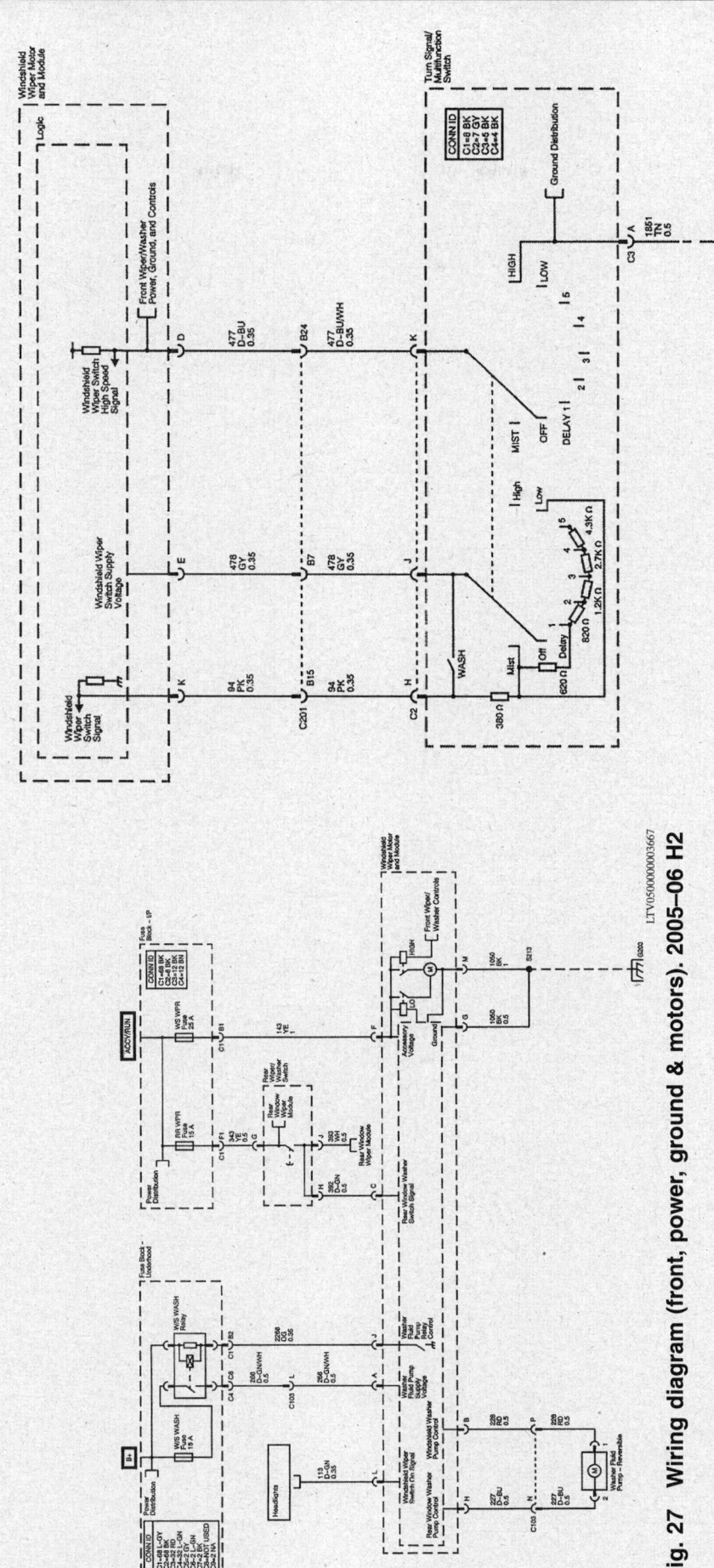

Fig. 28 Wiring diagram (front controls). 2005–06 H2

Fig. 27 Wiring diagram (front, power, ground & motors). 2005–06 H2

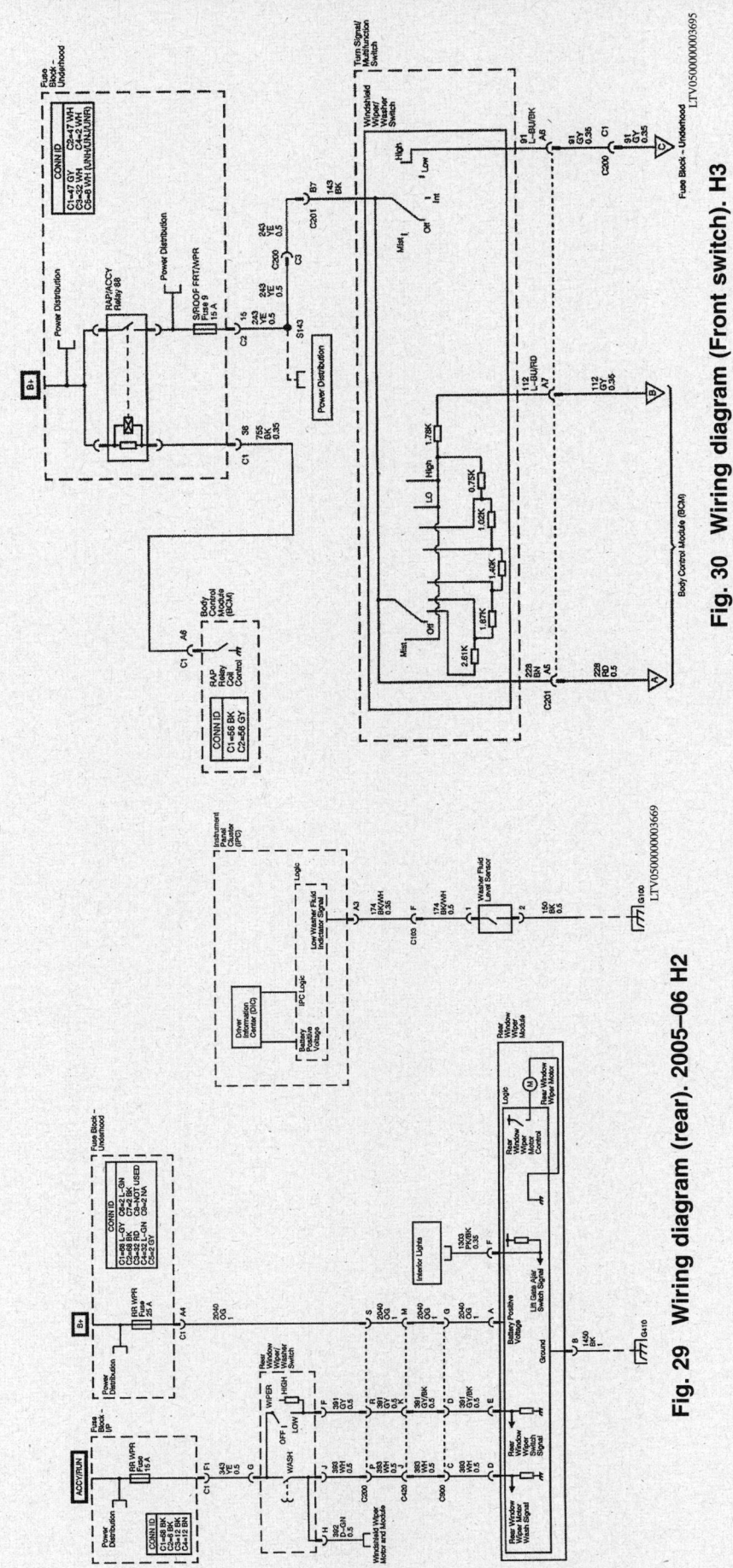

Fig. 30 Wiring diagram (Front switch). H3

Fig. 29 Wiring diagram (rear). 2005–06 H2

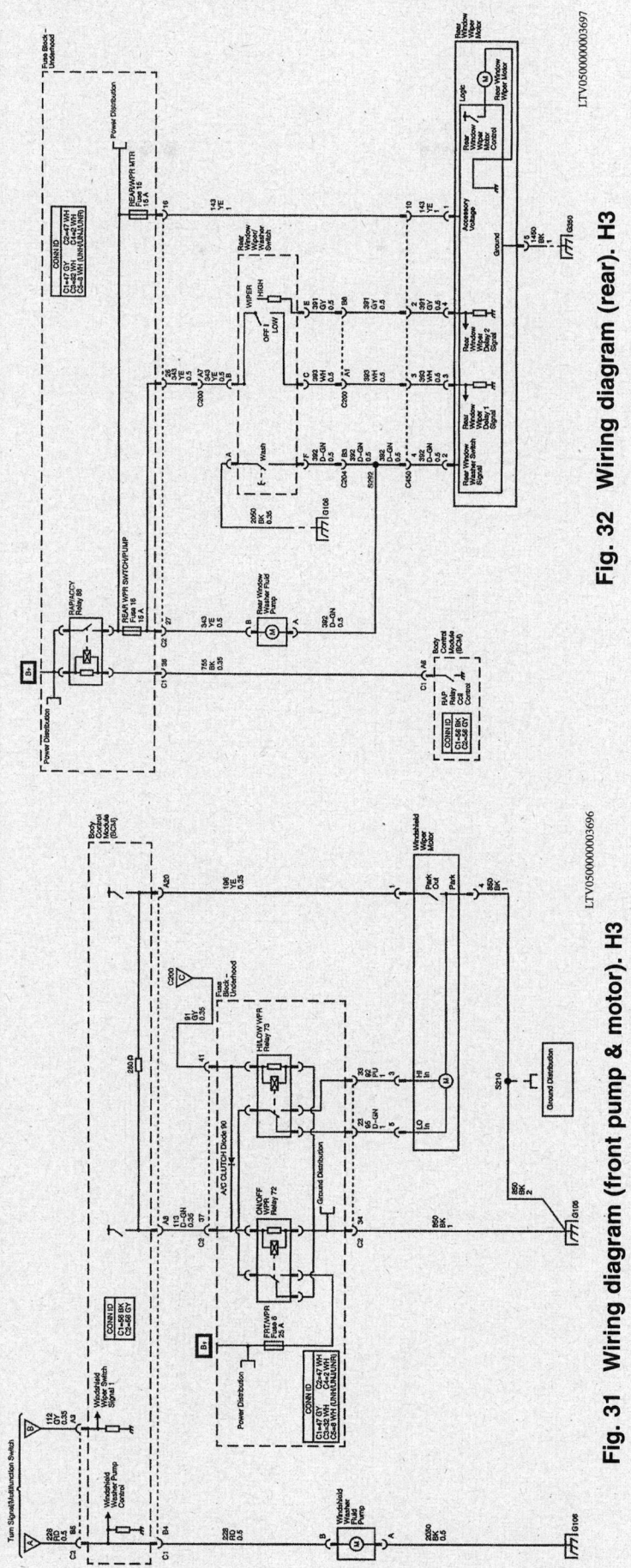

Fig. 32   Wiring diagram (rear). H3

Fig. 31   Wiring diagram (front pump & motor). H3

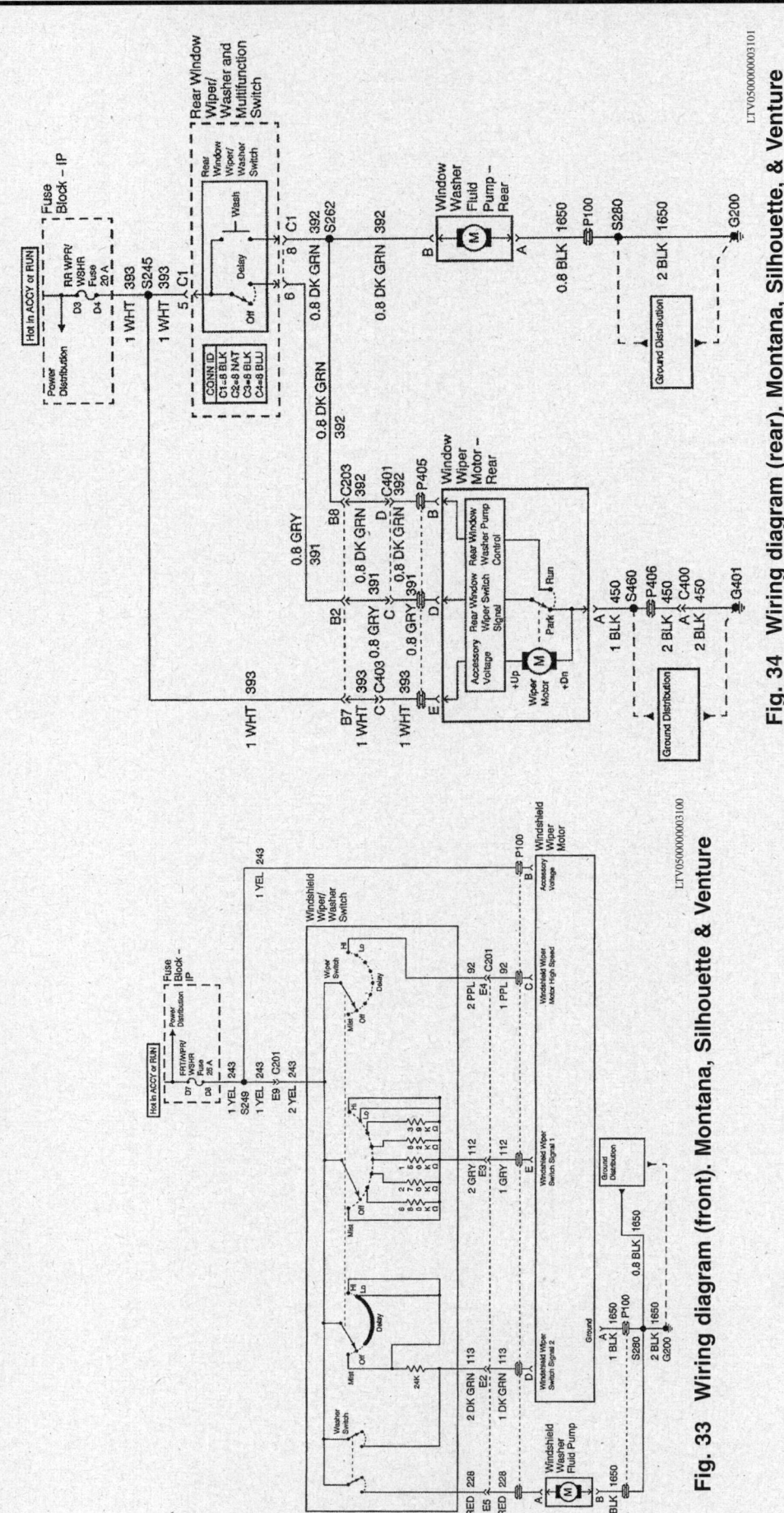

Fig. 34 Wiring diagram (rear). Montana, Silhouette, & Venture

Fig. 33 Wiring diagram (front). Montana, Silhouette & Venture

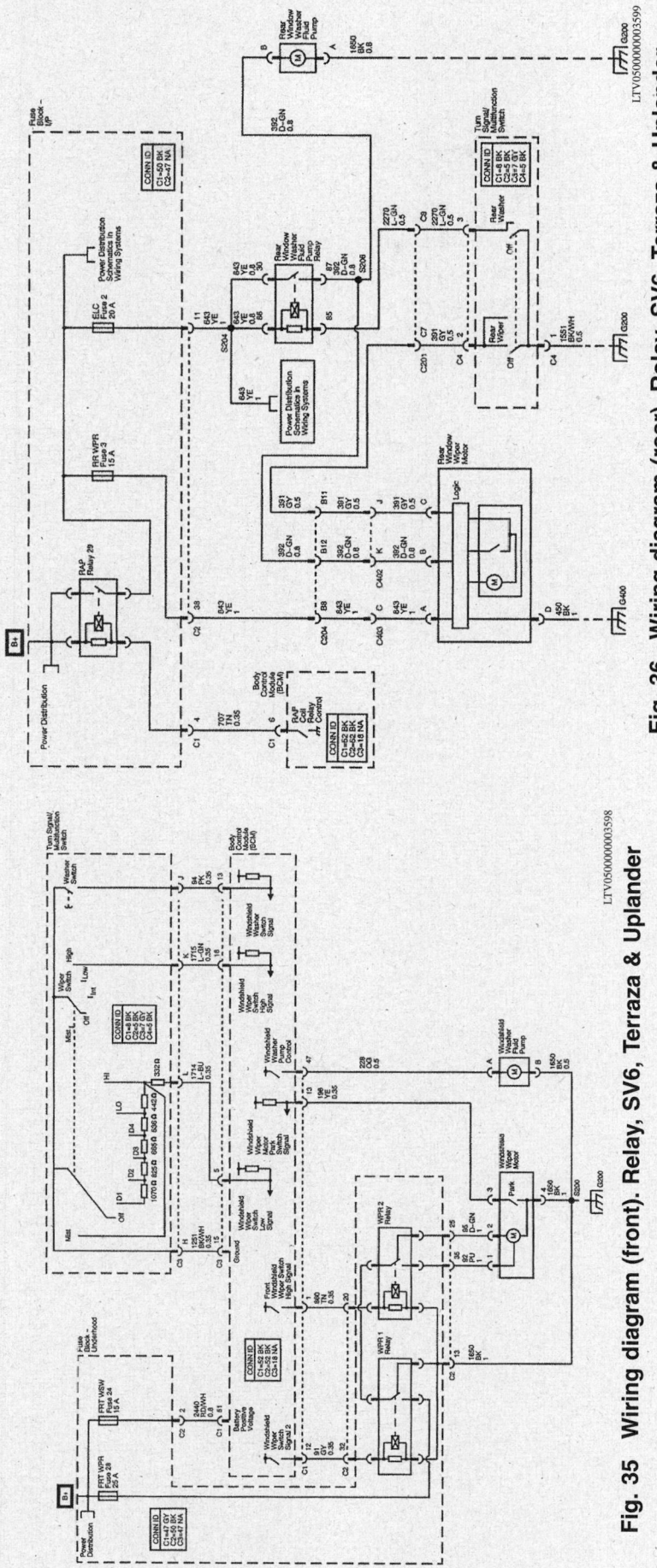

Fig. 36 Wiring diagram (rear). Relay, SV6, Terraza & Uplander

Fig. 35 Wiring diagram (front). Relay, SV6, Terraza & Uplander

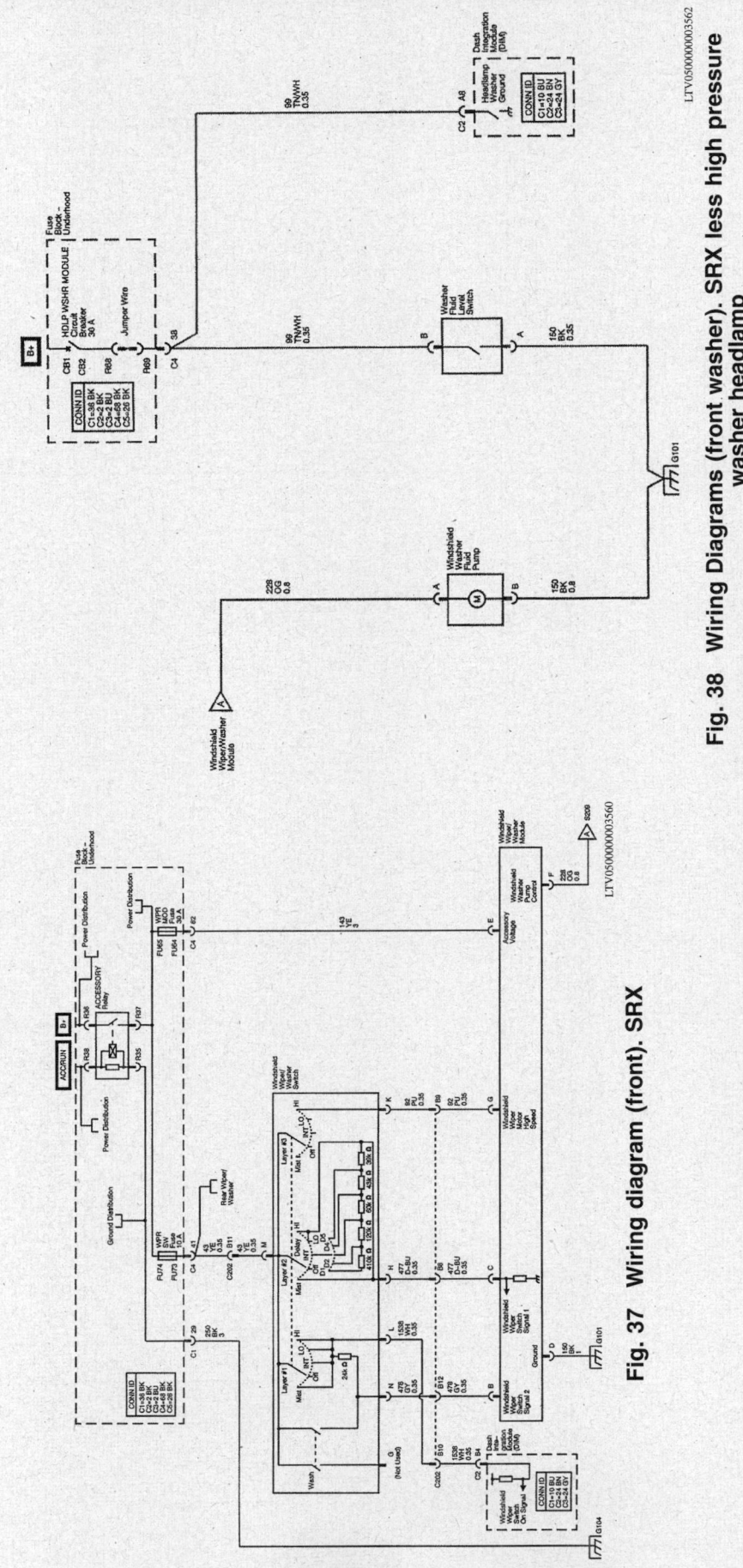

Fig. 38 Wiring Diagrams (front washer). SRX less high pressure washer headlamp

Fig. 37 Wiring diagram (front). SRX

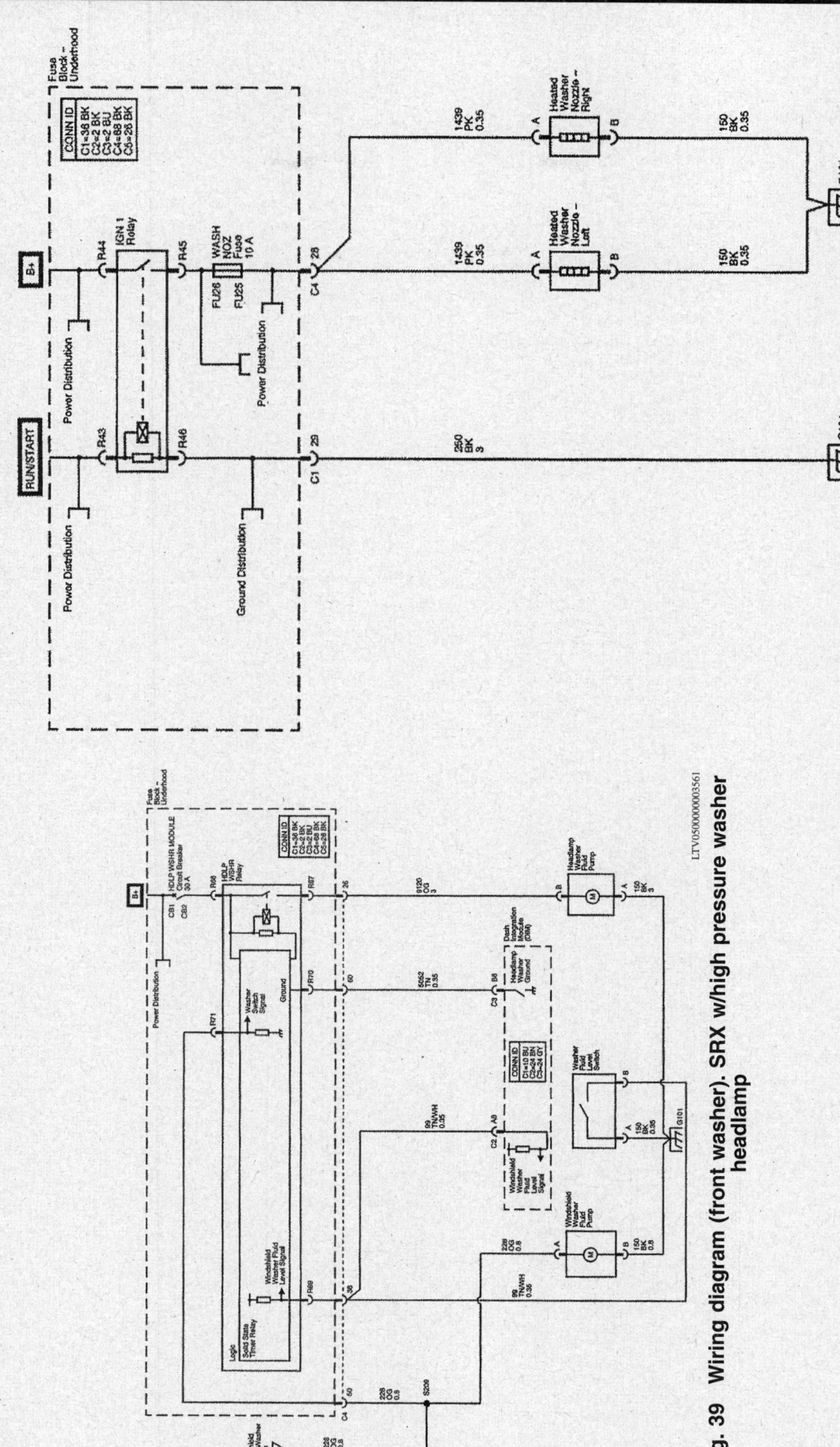

Fig. 40 Wiring diagram (heated washer nozzles). SRX

Fig. 39 Wiring diagram (front washer). SRX w/high pressure washer headlamp

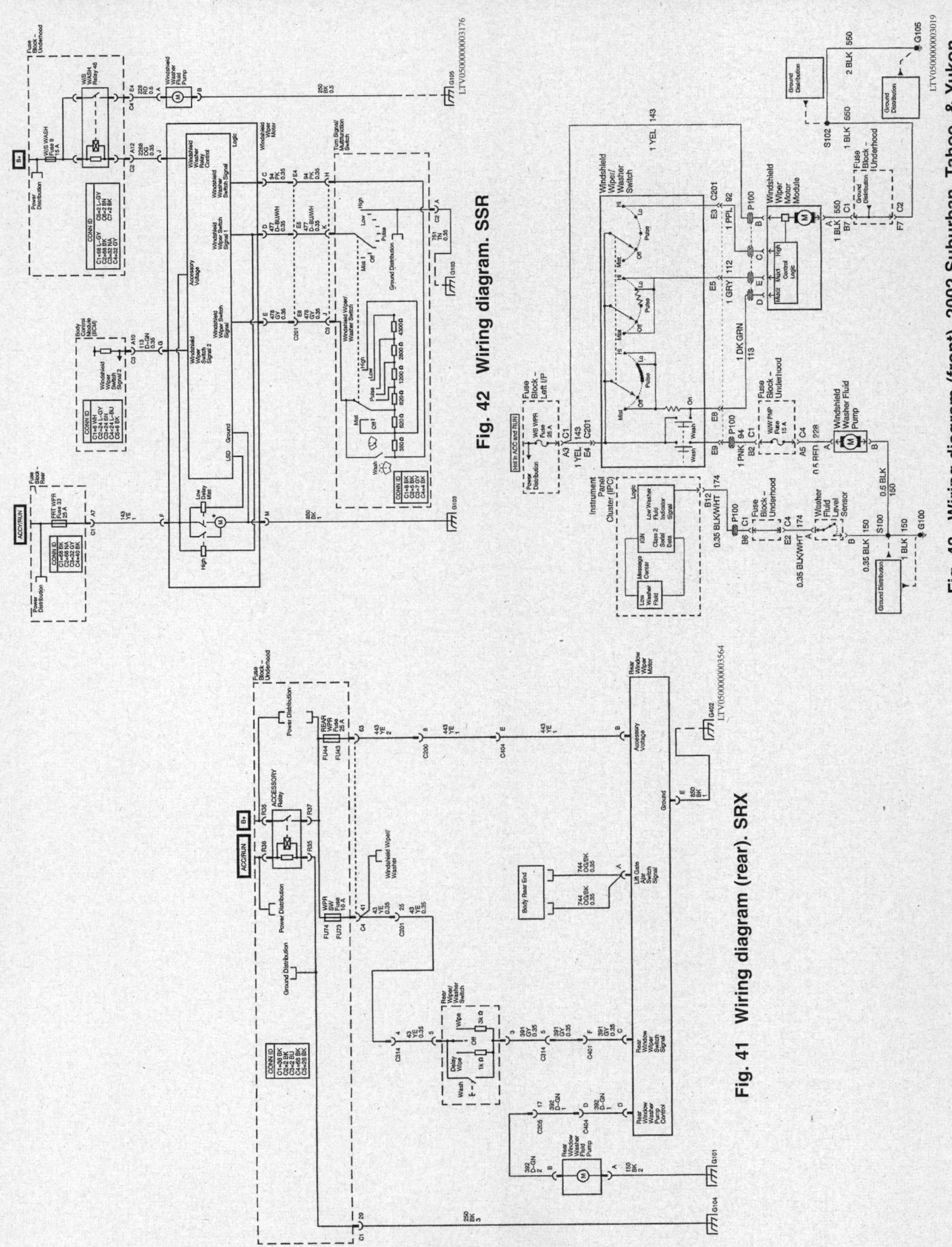

Fig. 42 Wiring diagram. SSR

Fig. 43 Wiring diagram (front). 2002 Suburban, Tahoe, & Yukon

Fig. 41 Wiring diagram (rear). SRX

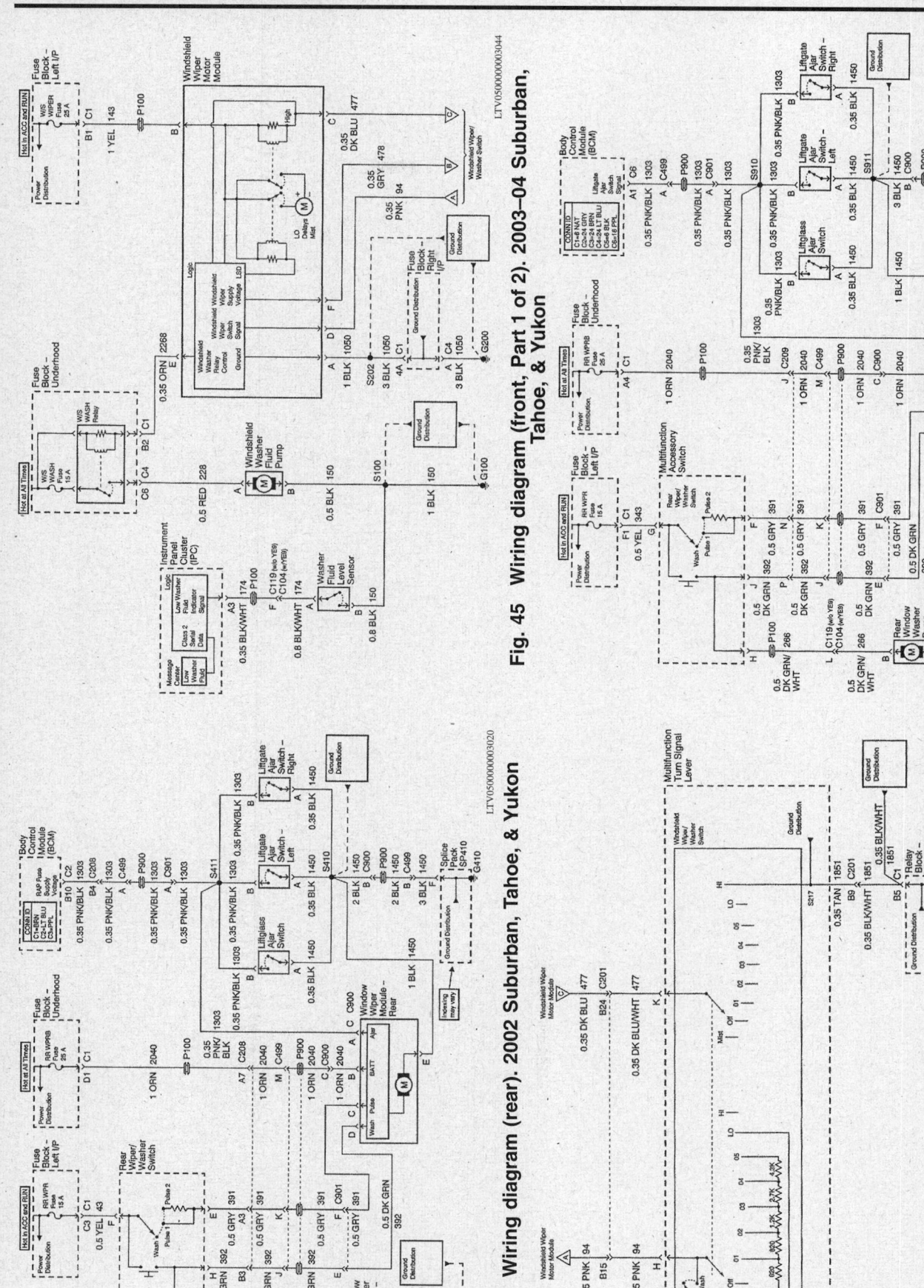

Fig. 45   Wiring diagram (front, Part 1 of 2). 2003–04 Suburban, Tahoe, & Yukon

Fig. 46   Wiring diagram (rear). 2003–04 Suburban, Tahoe, & Yukon

Fig. 44   Wiring diagram (rear). 2002 Suburban, Tahoe, & Yukon

Fig. 45   Wiring diagram (front, Part 2 of 2). 2003–04 Suburban, Tahoe, & Yukon

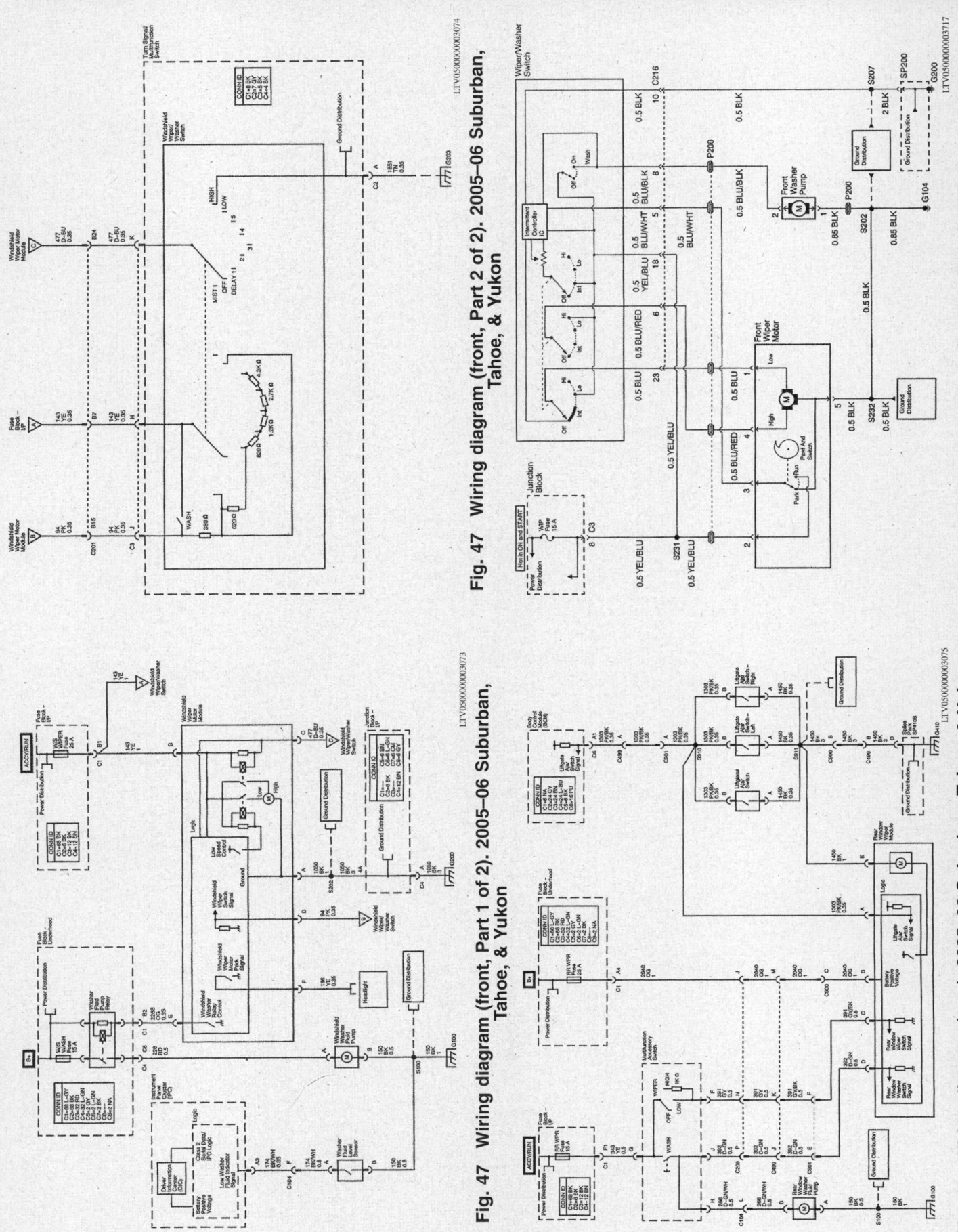

Fig. 47 Wiring diagram (front, Part 2 of 2). 2005–06 Suburban, Tahoe, & Yukon

Fig. 49 Wiring diagram (front). Tracker

Fig. 47 Wiring diagram (front, Part 1 of 2). 2005–06 Suburban, Tahoe, & Yukon

Fig. 48 Wiring diagram (rear). 2005–06 Suburban, Tahoe, & Yukon

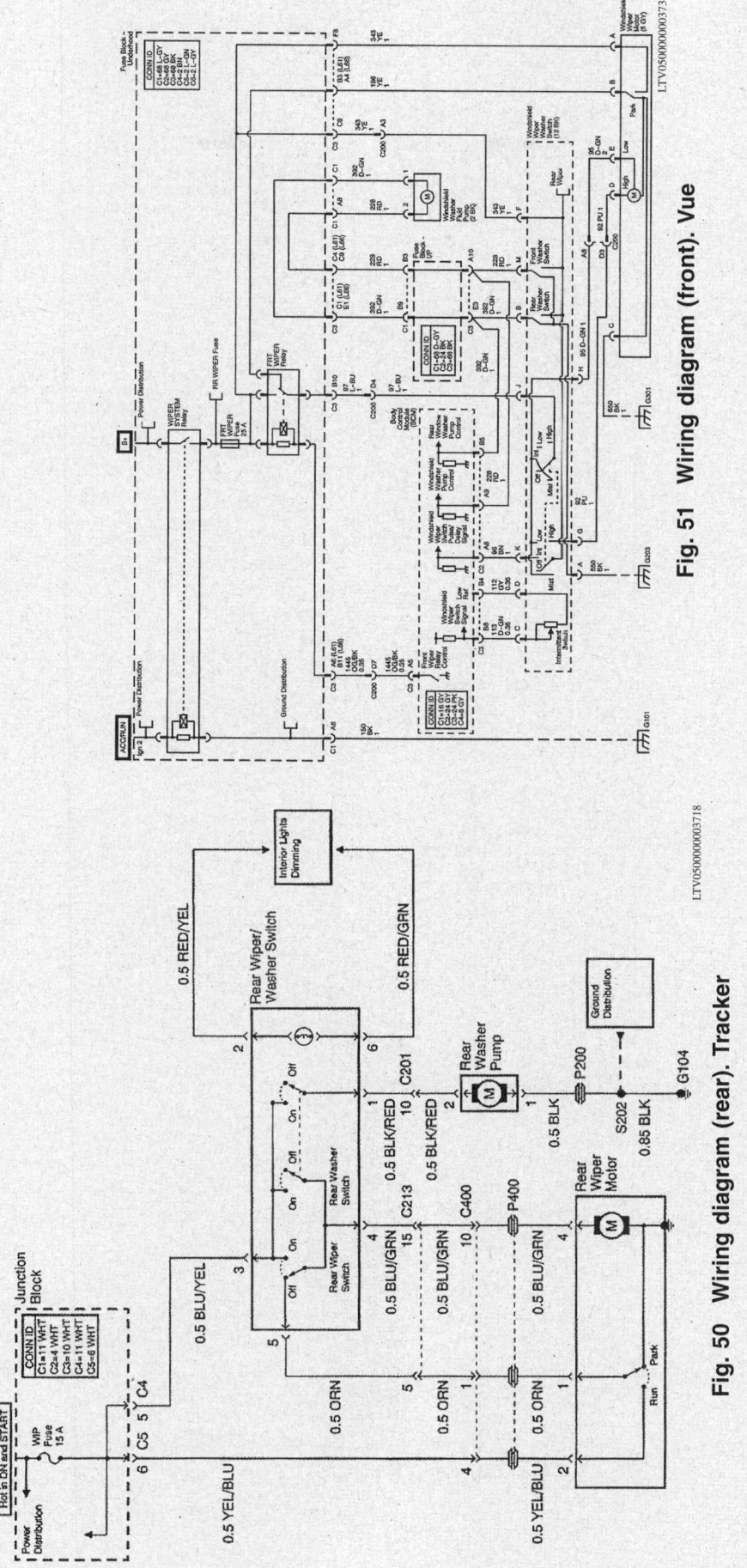

Fig. 51 Wiring diagram (front). Vue

Fig. 50 Wiring diagram (rear). Tracker

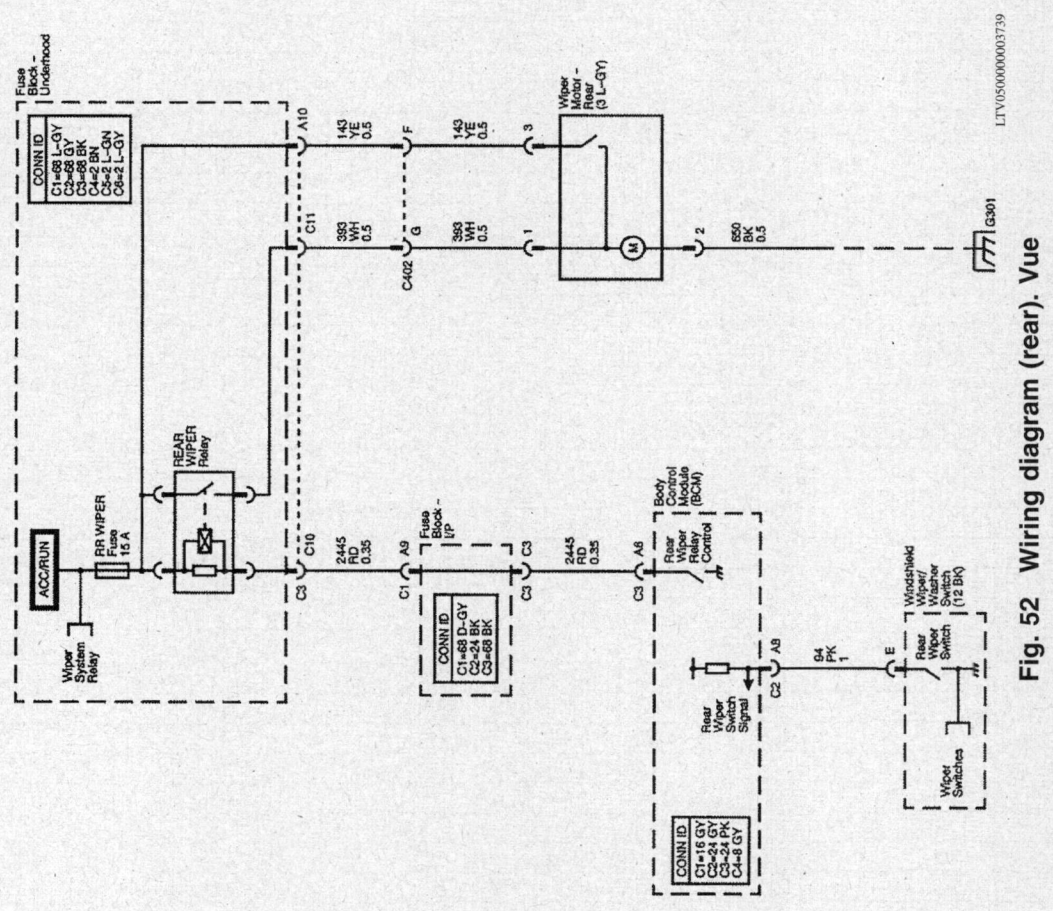

Fig. 52 Wiring diagram (rear). Vue

DIAGNOSTIC CHART INDEX

Code	Description	Page No.	Fig. No.
ASTRO & SAFARI			
—	Washer Always On	3-33	53
—	Washers Inoperative	3-33	54
—	Wipers Always On	3-34	55
—	Wipers Inoperative, All Modes	3-34	56
—	Wipers Inoperative, One Or More Modes	3-35	57
—	Washer Inoperative, Rear	3-35	58
—	Wiper Always On, Rear	3-36	59
—	Wiper Inoperative, Rear	3-37	60
—	Wiper Delay Mode Inoperative, Rear	3-37	61
2002 AVALANCHE, ESCALADE, SIERRA, & SILVERADO			
—	Low Washer Fluid Indicator Fault	3-38	62
—	Washers Always On	3-38	63
—	Washers Inoperative	3-39	64
—	Wipers Always On	3-39	65
—	Wipers Inoperative, All Modes	3-40	66
—	Wipers Inoperative, One Or More Modes	3-40	67
2003–04 AVALANCHE, ESCALADE, SIERRA, & SILVERADO			
—	Low Washer Fluid Indicator Fault	3-41	68
—	Washers Always On	3-42	69
—	Washers Inoperative	3-43	70
—	Wipers Always On	3-43	71
—	Wipers Inoperative, All Modes	3-44	72
—	Wipers Inoperative, One Or More Modes	3-44	73
2005–06 AVALANCHE, ESCALADE, SIERRA, & SILVERADO			
—	Low Washer Fluid Indicator Fault	3-45	74
—	Washers Always On	3-46	75
—	Washers Inoperative	3-46	76
—	Wipers Always On	3-47	77
—	Wipers Inoperative, All Modes	3-48	78
—	Wipers Inoperative, One Or More Modes	3-48	79
AZTEK & RENDEZVOUS			
—	Low Washer Fluid Indicator Fault	3-49	80
—	Washers Always On	3-50	81
—	Washers Inoperative	3-50	82
—	Wipers Always On	3-50	83
—	Wipers Inoperative, All Modes	3-51	84
—	Wipers Inoperative, One Or More Modes	3-51	85
—	Washer Inoperative, Rear	3-52	86
—	Wiper Always On, Rear	3-53	87
—	Wiper Inoperative, Rear	3-53	88
BLAZER & JIMMY			
—	Washers Always On	3-54	89
—	Washers Inoperative	3-54	90
—	Wipers Always On	3-55	91
—	Wipers Inoperative, All Modes	3-55	92
—	Wipers Inoperative, One Or More Modes	3-56	93
—	Washer Inoperative, Rear	3-57	94
—	Washers Inoperative, Headlamp	3-57	95
—	Wiper Always On, Rear	3-58	96
—	Wiper Inoperative, Rear	3-59	97
BRAVADA, ENVOY, RAINIER & TRAILBLAZER			
B1017	Rear Wiper Motor Control Circuit	3-59	98
B2697	Headlamp Washer Switch Signal Circuit	3-60	99
B3970	Rear Wiper Motor Control Circuit	3-59	98
B3799	Rear Wiper/Washer Switch Power Circuit	3-61	100

Continued

DIAGNOSTIC CHART INDEX—Continued

Code	Description	Page No.	Fig. No.
BRAVADA, ENVOY, RAINIER & TRAILBLAZER			
B3810	Washer Relay Control Circuit	3-62	101
B3811	Washer Relay Control Circuit	3-62	101
—	Low Washer Fluid Indicator Fault	3-63	102
—	Moisture Sensing Feature Inoperative	3-66	108
—	Washers Always On, Front	3-63	103
—	Washer Always On, Rear	3-67	109
—	Washers Inoperative, Front	3-64	104
—	Washer Inoperative, Headlamp	3-68	111
—	Washer Inoperative, Rear	3-67	110
—	Wipers Always On	3-65	105
—	Wipers Inoperative, All Modes, Front	3-65	106
—	Wipers Inoperative, One Or More Modes, Front	3-66	107
—	Wiper Inoperative, Rear	3-68	112
CANYON & COLORADO			
B3715	Front Wiper Relay Drive Circuit Low/High	3-69	113
B3716	Front Wiper Relay Drive Circuit Low/High	3-69	113
B3717	Front Wiper Relay Drive Circuit Low/High	3-69	113
B3718	Front Wiper Relay Drive Circuit Low/High	3-69	113
B3719	Front Wiper Relay Drive Circuit Low/High	3-69	113
—	Washers Always On	3-70	114
—	Washers Inoperative	3-71	115
—	Wipers Always On	3-71	116
—	Wipers Inoperative, All Modes	3-72	117
—	Wipers Inoperative, One Or More Modes	3-73	118
EQUINOX & TORRENT			
B3702	Intermittent Wiper Delay Input Circuit Low	3-75	119
B3703	Intermittent Wiper Delay Input Circuit High	3-75	120
B3708	Front Washer Motor Input High	3-76	121
B3713	Rear Washer Motor Input Circuit High	3-77	122
B3715	Front Wiper Relay Drive Circuit High/Low	3-78	123
B3716	Front Wiper Relay Drive Circuit High/Low	3-78	123
B3717	Front Wiper Relay Drive Circuit High/Low	3-78	123
B3718	Front Wiper Relay Drive Circuit High/Low	3-78	123
B3719	Front Wiper Relay Drive Circuit High/Low	3-78	123
B3722	Rear Wiper Relay Drive Circuit Low	3-79	124
B3723	Rear Wiper Relay Drive Circuit High	3-80	125
—	Washers Inoperative	3-81	126
—	Wipers Always On	3-82	127
—	Wipers Inoperative, All Modes	3-82	128
—	Wipers Inoperative, One Or More Modes (Front)	3-83	129
—	Wipers Inoperative, One Or More Modes (Rear)	3-85	130
2002 EXPRESS & SAVANNA			
—	Washers Always On	3-86	131
—	Washers Inoperative	3-86	132
—	Wipers Always On	3-87	133
—	Wipers Inoperative, All Modes	3-87	134
—	Wipers Inoperative, One Or More Modes	3-88	135
2003 EXPRESS & SAVANNA			
—	Washers Always On	3-89	136
—	Wipers Inoperative	3-90	137
—	Wipers Always On	3-91	138
—	Wipers Inoperative, All Modes	3-91	139
—	Wipers Inoperative, One Or More Modes	3-92	140
2004–06 EXPRESS & SAVANNA			
—	Washers Always On	3-92	141

Continued

DIAGNOSTIC CHART INDEX—Continued

Code	Description	Page No.	Fig. No.
2004–06 EXPRESS & SAVANNA			
—	Washers Inoperative	3-93	142
—	Wipers Always On	3-94	143
—	Wipers Inoperative, All Modes	3-94	144
—	Wipers Inoperative, One Or More Modes	3-95	145
HHR			
B3715	Front Wiper Relay Drive Circuit	3-96	146
B3716	Front Wiper Relay Drive Circuit	3-96	146
B3717	Front Wiper Relay Drive Circuit	3-96	146
B3718	Front Wiper Relay Drive Circuit	3-96	146
B3719	Front Wiper Relay Drive Circuit	3-96	146
—	Washers Always On	3-98	147
—	Washers Inoperative	3-98	148
—	Wipers Always On	3-99	149
—	Wipers Inoperative, All Modes	3-100	150
—	Wipers Inoperative, One Or More Modes (Front Wiper)	3-101	151
—	Wipers Inoperative, One Or More Modes (Rear Wiper)	3-102	152
2003–04 H2			
—	Low Washer Fluid Indicator Fault	3-103	153
—	Washers Always On	3-104	154
—	Washers Inoperative, Front	3-104	155
—	Washer Inoperative, Rear	3-107	159
—	Wipers Always On, Front	3-105	156
—	Wiper Always On, Rear	3-108	160
—	Wipers Inoperative, All Modes, Front	3-106	157
—	Wipers Inoperative, One Or More Modes	3-106	158
—	Wiper Inoperative, Rear	3-108	161
2005–06 H2			
—	Low Washer Fluid Indicator Fault	3-109	162
—	Washers Always On	3-110	163
—	Washers Inoperative, Front	3-110	164
—	Washer Inoperative, Rear	3-113	168
—	Wipers Always On, Front	3-111	165
—	Wiper Always On, Rear	3-113	169
—	Wipers Inoperative, All Modes, Front	3-111	166
—	Wipers Inoperative, One Or More Modes, Front	3-112	167
—	Wiper Inoperative, Rear	3-114	170
H3			
B3715	Front Wiper Relay Drive Circuit	3-115	171
B3716	Front Wiper Relay Drive Circuit	3-115	171
B3717	Front Wiper Relay Drive Circuit	3-115	171
B3718	Front Wiper Relay Drive Circuit	3-115	171
B3719	Front Wiper Relay Drive Circuit	3-115	171
—	Front Wipers Inoperative All Modes	3-116	172
—	Front Delay Or Low Speed Wipers Inoperative	3-116	173
—	Front High Speed Wipers Inoperative & Low Speed Wipers Always On	3-116	174
—	Front High Speed Wipers Always On, Washers Inoperative & Washers Always On	3-117	175
—	Front Windshield Wiper Washer Switch High & Wash Circuit	3-117	176
—	Front Windshield Wiper Washer Switch Low Speed Circuit	3-117	177
—	Rear Wiper Motor Inoperative In All Modes & Inoperative In Both Delay Modes	3-117	178
—	Rear Wiper Motor Inoperative In One Delay Mode & Wiper Motor Always On	3-118	179
—	Rear Washer Pump Inoperative, Washer Wiper Inoperative & Washer Wipers/Pump Inoperative	3-118	180
—	Rear Washers Always On	3-118	181
MONTANA, SILHOUETTE & VENTURE			
—	Washers Always On, Front	3-118	182

Continued

DIAGNOSTIC CHART INDEX—Continued

Code	Description	Page No.	Fig. No.
MONTANA, SILHOUETTE & VENTURE			
—	Washers Inoperative, Front	3-119	183
—	Washer Inoperative, Rear	3-121	187
—	Wipers Always On, Front	3-119	184
—	Wiper Always On, Rear	3-122	188
—	Wipers Inoperative, All Modes, Front	3-120	185
—	Wipers Inoperative, One Or More Modes, Front	3-120	186
—	Wiper Inoperative, Rear	3-123	189
RELAY, SV6, TERRAZA & UPLANDER			
B3873	Front Washer Relay Circuit	3-124	190
B3874	Wiper Low Speed Relay Circuit	3-125	191
B3875	WPR2 Relay Circuit	3-126	192
B3922	Front Wiper Select Circuit	3-127	193
—	Washers Always On, Front	3-128	194
—	Washers Inoperative, Front	3-128	195
—	Washer Inoperative, Rear	3-131	199
—	Wipers Always On, Front	3-129	196
—	Wiper Always On, Rear	3-132	200
—	Wipers Inoperative, All Modes, Front	3-129	197
—	Wipers Inoperative, One Or More Modes, Front	3-130	198
—	Wiper Inoperative, Rear	3-132	201
SONOMA & S10			
—	Washers Always On	3-54	89
—	Washers Inoperative	3-54	90
—	Wipers Always On	3-55	91
—	Wipers Inoperative, All Modes	3-55	92
—	Wipers Inoperative, One Or More Modes	3-56	93
—	Washers Inoperative, Headlamp	3-57	95
SRX			
—	Low Washer Fluid Indicator Fault	3-133	202
—	Washers Always On, Front	3-134	203
—	Washer Always On, Rear	3-138	209
—	Washers Inoperative w/Heated Washer Nozzles, Front	3-134	204
—	Washers Inoperative Less Heated Washer Nozzles, Front	3-135	205
—	Washer Inoperative, Rear	3-138	210
—	Wipers Always On, Front	3-135	206
—	Wiper Always On, Rear	3-139	212
—	Wipers Inoperative, All Modes, Front	3-136	207
—	Wipers Inoperative, One Or More Modes, Front	3-137	208
—	Washers Inoperative, Headlamp	3-138	211
—	Wiper Inoperative, Rear	3-140	213
SSR			
—	Washers Always On	3-141	214
—	Washers Inoperative	3-141	215
—	Wipers Always On	3-142	216
—	Wipers Inoperative, All Modes	3-142	217
—	Wipers Inoperative, One Or More Modes	3-143	218
2002 SUBURBAN, TAHOE & YUKON			
—	Low Washer Fluid Indicator Fault	3-144	219
—	Washers Always On, Front	3-144	220
—	Washers Inoperative, Front	3-144	221
—	Washer Inoperative, Rear	3-147	225
—	Wipers Always On, Front	3-145	222
—	Wiper Always On, Rear	3-148	226
—	Wipers Inoperative, All Modes, Front	3-145	223
—	Wipers Inoperative, One Or More Modes, Front	3-146	224

Continued

DIAGNOSTIC CHART INDEX—Continued

Code	Description	Page No.	Fig. No.
MONTANA, SILHOUETTE & VENTURE			
—	Wiper Inoperative, Rear	3-148	227
2003–04 SUBURBAN, TAHOE & YUKON			
—	Low Washer Fluid Indicator Fault	3-149	228
—	Washers Always On, Front	3-149	229
—	Washers Inoperative, Front	3-150	230
—	Washer Inoperative, Rear	3-153	234
—	Wipers Always On, Front	3-151	231
—	Wiper Always On, Rear	3-153	235
—	Wipers Inoperative, All Modes, Front	3-151	232
—	Wipers Inoperative - One Or More Modes, Front	3-152	233
—	Wiper Inoperative, Rear	3-154	236
2005–06 SUBURBAN, TAHOE & YUKON			
—	Low Washer Fluid Indicator Fault	3-155	237
—	Washers Always On, Front	3-155	238
—	Washers Inoperative, Front	3-156	239
—	Washer Inoperative, Rear	3-158	243
—	Wipers Always On, Front	3-156	240
—	Wiper Always On, Rear	3-159	244
—	Wipers Inoperative, All Modes, Front	3-157	241
—	Wipers Inoperative, One Or More Modes, Front	3-157	242
—	Wiper Inoperative, Rear	3-159	245
TRACKER			
—	Washers Inoperative, Front	3-160	246
—	Washer Inoperative, Rear	3-163	251
—	Wipers Always On, Front	3-161	247
—	Wiper Always On, Rear	3-163	252
—	Wipers Blades Do Not Park, Front	3-162	250
—	Wiper Blade Does Not Park, Rear	3-164	254
—	Wipers Inoperative, All Modes, Front	3-161	248
—	Wipers Inoperative, One Mode, Front	3-162	249
—	Wiper Inoperative, Rear	3-164	253
VUE			
B3702	Windshield Wiper Washer Switch	3-165	255
B3703	Windshield Wiper Washer Intermittent Switch	3-165	256
B3708	Body Control Module	3-166	257
B3713	Rear Window Washer Pump Control Circuit	3-167	258
B3715	Front Wiper Relay Control Circuit	3-168	259
B3716	Front Wiper Relay Control Circuit	3-168	259
B3717	Front Wiper Relay Control Circuit	3-168	259
B3718	Front Wiper Relay Control Circuit	3-168	259
B3719	Front Wiper Relay Control Circuit	3-168	259
B3722	Battery Voltage From Rear Wiper Switch	3-169	260
B3723	Rear Wiper Switch Signal Input	3-170	261
—	Washers Inoperative, Front	3-171	262
—	Wipers Always On, Front	3-172	263
—	Wipers Inoperative, All Modes, Front	3-172	264
—	Wipers Inoperative, One Or More Modes, Front	3-173	265
—	Wipers Inoperative, One Or More Modes, Rear	3-174	266

Step	Action	Yes	No
1	Did you review the Wiper/Washer System Description and Operation and perform the necessary inspections?	Go to Step 2	Go to Symptoms
2	Turn the ignition ON. Are the windshield washers always on?	Go to Step 3	Test for Intermittent and Poor Connections
3	Are the windshield washer wipers always on?	Go to Step 4	Go to Step 6
4	1. Turn the ignition OFF. 2. Disconnect the inline harness connector C201. 3. Remove the connector terminal row E from the steering column harness connector half. 4. Connect the inline harness connector C201. 5. Turn the ignition ON. Are the windshield washers always on?	Go to Step 5	Go to Step 7
5	Test the windshield wiper switch pulse delay signal circuit for a short to voltage. Did you find and correct the condition?	Go to Step 9	Go to Step 8
6	Test the windshield washer pump control circuit for a short to voltage. Did you find and correct the condition?	Go to Step 9	Go to Step 8

LTV0500000000392

Fig. 53 Washer Always On (Part 1 of 2). Astro & Safari

Step	Action	Yes	No
7	Replace the windshield wiper/washer switch. Is the repair complete?	Go to Step 9	--
8	Replace the windshield wiper motor module. Is the repair complete?	Go to Step 9	--
9	Operate the system in order to verify the repair. Did you correct the condition?	System OK	Go to Step 3

LTV0500000000393

Fig. 53 Washer Always On (Part 2 of 2). Astro & Safari

Step	Action	Yes	No
6	1. Connect a test lamp from the windshield wiper switch pulse delay signal circuit terminal in the wiper motor harness connector to ground. 2. Turn the ignition ON. 3. Press the windshield washer switch. Does the test lamp illuminate?	Go to Step 12	Go to Step 7
7	Test the windshield wiper switch pulse delay signal circuit for high resistance. Did you find and correct the condition?	Go to Step 14	Go to Step 8
8	Inspect for poor connections at the windshield wiper/washer switch. Did you find and correct the condition?	Go to Step 14	Go to Step 9
9	Replace the windshield wiper/washer switch. Is the repair complete?	Go to Step 14	--
10	Inspect for poor connections at the windshield washer pump. Did you find and correct the condition?	Go to Step 14	Go to Step 11
11	Replace the windshield washer pump. Is the repair complete?	Go to Step 14	--
12	Inspect for poor connections at the windshield wiper motor. Did you find and correct the condition?	Go to Step 14	Go to Step 13
13	Replace the windshield wiper motor module. Is the repair complete?	Go to Step 14	--
14	Operate the system in order to verify the repair. Did you correct the condition?	System OK	Go to Step 3

LTV0500000000395

Fig. 54 Washers Inoperative (Part 2 of 2). Astro & Safari

Step	Action	Yes	No
1	Did you review the Wiper/Washer System Description and Operation and perform the necessary inspections?	Go to Step 2	Go to Symptoms -
2	1. Turn the ignition ON. 2. Press the windshield washer switch. Do the windshield washers operate normal?	Test for Intermittent and Poor Connections	Go to Step 3
3	1. Disconnect the windshield washer pump connector. 2. Connect a test lamp across the washer pump connector terminals. 3. Turn the ignition ON. 4. Press the windshield washer switch. Does the test lamp illuminate?	Go to Step 10	Go to Step 4
4	Test the windshield washer pump ground circuit for an open or high resistance. Did you find and correct the condition?	Go to Step 14	Go to Step 5
5	1. Disconnect the windshield wiper motor connector. 2. Test the windshield washer pump control circuit for an open or short to ground. Did you find and correct the condition?	Go to Step 14	Go to Step 6

LTV0500000000394

Fig. 54 Washers Inoperative (Part 1 of 2). Astro & Safari

Step	Action	Yes	No
1	Did you review the Wiper/Washer System Description and Operation and perform the necessary inspections?	Go to Step 2	Go to Symptoms -
2	1. Turn the ignition ON. 2. Turn the windshield wiper/washer switch to the OFF position. Do the windshield wipers remain in the park position?	Test for Intermittent and Poor Connections	Go to Step 3
3	1. Turn the ignition OFF. 2. Disconnect the inline harness connector C201. 3. Remove the connector terminal row E from the steering column harness connector half. 4. Connect the inline harness connector C201. 5. Turn the ignition ON. Are the windshield wipers always on?	Go to Step 4	Go to Step 6
4	1. Disconnect the windshield wiper motor connector. 2. Test the windshield wiper switch pulse delay signal circuit for a short to voltage. Did you find and correct the condition?	Go to Step 7	Go to Step 5
5	Replace the windshield wiper motor module. Is the repair complete?	Go to Step 7	--
6	Replace the windshield wiper/washer switch. Is the repair complete?	Go to Step 7	--

LTV0500000000396

Fig. 55 Wipers Always On (Part 1 of 2). Astro & Safari

Step	Action	Yes	No
7	Replace the windshield wiper/washer switch. Is the repair complete?	System OK	Go to Step 3

LTV0500000000397

Fig. 55 Wipers Always On (Part 2 of 2). Astro & Safari

Step	Action	Yes	No
6	Test the windshield wiper switch pulse delay signal circuit for an open or short to ground. Did you find and correct the condition?	Go to Step 15	Go to Step 7
7	Test the accessory voltage supply circuit to the windshield wiper/washer switch for an open or short to ground. Did you find and correct the condition?	Go to Step 15	Go to Step 10
8	Repair the accessory voltage supply circuit for an open or high resistance. Is the repair complete?	Go to Step 15	--
9	Repair the windshield wiper motor ground circuit for an open or high resistance. Is the repair complete?	Go to Step 15	--
10	Test the windshield wiper motor high speed circuit for a short to ground. Did you find and correct the condition?	Go to Step 15	Go to Step 11
11	Inspect for poor connections at the windshield wiper/washer switch. Did you find and correct the condition?	Go to Step 15	Go to Step 12
12	Replace the windshield wiper/washer switch. Is the repair complete?	Go to Step 15	--
13	Inspect for poor connections at the windshield wiper motor. Did you find and correct the condition?	Go to Step 15	Go to Step 14

LTV0500000000399

Fig. 56 Wipers Inoperative, All Modes (Part 2 of 3) Astro & Safari

Step	Action	Yes	No
	DEFINITION: The washer pump may operate but all wiper motor functions are inoperative.		
1	Did you review the Wiper/Washer System Description and Operation and perform the necessary inspections?	Go to Step 2	Go to Symptoms -
2	1. Turn the ignition ON. 2. Operate the windshield wiper/washer system in all the switch positions. Does the windshield wiper/washer system operate normally?	Test for Intermittent and Poor Connections	Go to Step 3
3	1. Disconnect the windshield wiper motor connector. 2. Connect a test lamp from the pulse delay signal circuit terminal in the wiper motor harness connector to a good ground. 3. Turn the ignition ON. 4. Press the windshield washer switch. Does the test lamp illuminate?	Go to Step 4	Go to Step 6
4	Connect a test lamp from the accessory voltage supply circuit terminal in the wiper motor harness connector to a good ground. Does the test lamp illuminate?	Go to Step 5	Go to Step 8
5	Connect a test lamp from the accessory voltage supply circuit terminal to the ground circuit terminal in the wiper motor harness connector. Does the test lamp illuminate?	Go to Step 13	Go to Step 9

LTV0500000000398

Fig. 56 Wipers Inoperative, All Modes (Part 1 of 3) Astro & Safari

Step	Action	Yes	No
14	Replace the windshield wiper motor. Is the repair complete?	Go to Step 15	--
15	Operate the system in order to verify the repair. Did you correct the condition?	System OK	Go to Step 3

LTV0500000000400

Fig. 56 Wipers Inoperative, All Modes (Part 3 of 3) Astro & Safari

Test Description

The numbers below refer to the step numbers on the diagnostic table.

6. This step tests for continuity through the 680 ohms resistor in the windshield wiper/washer switch. The connector behind the instrument panel knee bolster is suitable for performing this step.

7. This step tests for continuity through the delay resistors in the windshield wiper/washer switch. The measured resistance will change in sequence from high to low as the delay speed is increased. The connector behind the instrument panel knee bolster is suitable for performing this step.

Step	Action	Value(s)	Yes	No
1	Did you review the Wiper/Washer System Description and Operation and perform the necessary inspections?	--	Go to Step 2	Go to Symptoms -
2	1. Turn the ignition ON. 2. Operate the windshield wiper/washer system in all the switch positions. Does the windshield wiper/washer system operate normally?	--	Test for Intermittent and Poor Connections	Go to Step 3
3	Do the windshield wipers operate in the high speed mode?	--	Go to Step 5	Go to Step 4

LTV0500000000401

Fig. 57   Wipers Inoperative, One Or More Modes (Part 1 of 3). Astro & Safari

Step	Action		Yes	No
8	Test the windshield wiper motor high speed circuit for an open or high resistance. Did you find and correct the condition?	--	Go to Step 15	Go to Step 11
9	Test the windshield wiper switch pulse delay signal circuit for an open or short to ground. Did you find and correct the condition?	--	Go to Step 15	Go to Step 10
10	Test the accessory voltage supply circuit to the windshield wiper switch for an open or high resistance. Did you find and correct the condition?	--	Go to Step 15	Go to Step 11
11	Inspect for poor connections at the windshield wiper/washer switch. Did you find and correct the condition?	--	Go to Step 15	Go to Step 12
12	Replace the windshield wiper/washer switch. Is the repair complete?	--	Go to Step 15	--
13	Inspect for poor connections at the windshield wiper motor. Did you find and correct the condition?	--	Go to Step 15	Go to Step 14
14	Replace the windshield wiper motor module. Is the repair complete?	--	Go to Step 15	--
15	Operate the system in order to verify the repair. Did you correct the condition?	--	System OK	Go to Step 3

LTV0500000002883

Fig. 57   Wipers Inoperative, One Or More Modes (Part 3 of 3). Astro & Safari

4	1. Disconnect the windshield wiper motor connector. 2. Connect a test lamp from the windshield wiper motor high speed circuit terminal in the wiper motor harness connector to ground. 3. Turn the ignition ON. 4. Operate the windshield wiper/washer switch to the high speed position. Does the test lamp illuminate?	--	Go to Step 13	Go to Step 8
5	1. Disconnect the windshield wiper motor connector. 2. Connect a test lamp from the windshield wiper switch pulse delay signal circuit terminal in the wiper motor harness connector to ground. 3. Turn the ignition ON. 4. Press the windshield washer switch. Does the test lamp illuminate?	--	Go to Step 6	Go to Step 9
6	1. Disconnect the windshield wiper/washer switch connector. 2. Measure the resistance through the windshield wiper/washer switch from the pulse delay signal circuit terminal to the accessory voltage supply circuit terminal in the wiper/washer switch connector. 3. Operate the windshield wiper/washer switch to the following positions: - MIST - LO - HI Is the resistance at or near the specified value in all the listed switch positions?	680 ohms	Go to Step 7	Go to Step 11
7	1. Measure the resistance through the windshield wiper/washer switch from the pulse delay signal circuit terminal to the accessory voltage supply circuit terminal in the wiper/washer switch connector. 2. Operate the windshield wiper/washer switch through all of the delay positions. Does the resistance remain within the specified values from high to low as the delay speed is increased?	30K - 450K ohms	Go to Step 13	Go to Step 11

LTV0500000002882

Fig. 57   Wipers Inoperative, One Or More Modes (Part 2 of 3). Astro & Safari

Step	Action	Yes	No
1	Did you review the Rear Wiper/Washer System Description and Operation and perform the necessary inspections?	Go to Step 2	Go to Symptoms -
2	1. Turn the ignition ON. 2. Press the rear window washer switch. Does the rear window washer operate normally?	Test for Intermittent and Poor Connections	Go to Step 3
3	Does the rear window wiper motor operate when the washer switch is pressed?	Go to Step 5	Go to Step 4
4	1. Disconnect the rear window wiper motor module switch input connector. 2. Connect a test lamp from the rear window washer control circuit terminal in the wiper motor module harness connector to a good ground. 3. Turn the ignition ON. 4. Press the rear window washer switch. Does the test lamp illuminate when the rear window washer switch is pressed?	Go to Step 10	Go to Step 5
5	Test the rear window washer control circuit for a short to ground an open or high resistance. Did you find and correct the condition?	Go to Step 15	Go to Step 12

LTV0500000002884

Fig. 58   Washer Inoperative, Rear (Part 1 of 3). Astro & Safari

	Action	Yes	No
6	1. Disconnect the rear window washer fluid pump connector. 2. Connect a test lamp from the rear window washer control circuit terminal in the washer pump harness connector to a good ground. 3. Turn the ignition ON. 4. Press the rear window washer switch. Does the test lamp illuminate when the rear window washer switch is pressed?	Go to Step 7	Go to Step 8
7	1. Connect a test lamp from the rear window washer control circuit terminal to the ground circuit terminal in the washer pump harness connector. 2. Press the rear window washer switch. Does the test lamp illuminate when the rear window washer switch is pressed?	Go to Step 14	Go to Step 9
8	Repair the rear window washer control circuit for an open or high resistance. Is the repair complete?	Go to Step 16	--
9	Repair the rear window washer pump ground circuit for an open or high resistance. Is the repair complete?	Go to Step 16	--
10	Inspect for poor connections at the rear window wiper motor module. Did you find and correct the condition?	Go to Step 16	Go to Step 11
11	Replace the rear window wiper motor module. Is the repair complete?	Go to Step 16	--
12	Inspect for poor connections at the rear window wiper/washer switch. Did you find and correct the condition?	Go to Step 16	Go to Step 13

LTV0500000002885

Fig. 58   Washer Inoperative, Rear (Part 2 of 3). Astro & Safari

	Action	Yes	No
13	Replace the rear window wiper/washer switch. Is the repair complete?	Go to Step 16	--
14	Inspect for poor connections at the rear window washer fluid pump. Did you find and correct the condition?	Go to Step 16	Go to Step 15
15	Replace the rear window washer fluid pump. Is the repair complete?	Go to Step 16	--
16	Operate the system in order to verify the repair. Did you correct the condition?	System OK	Go to Step 3

LTV0500000002886

Fig. 58   Washer Inoperative, Rear (Part 3 of 3). Astro & Safari

Step	Action	Yes	No
1	Did you review the Rear Wiper/Washer System Description and Operation and perform the necessary inspections?	Go to Step 2	Go to Symptoms -
2	1. Turn the ignition ON. 2. Turn the rear window wiper/washer switch to the OFF position. Is the rear wiper always on?	Go to Step 3	Test for Intermittent and Poor Connections
3	1. Disconnect the rear window wiper motor module switch input connector. 2. Turn the rear window wiper/washer switch to the OFF position. 3. Connect a test lamp from the rear window wiper/washer switch delay/on signal circuit terminal in the rear window wiper motor module harness connector to ground. 4. Turn the ignition ON. Does the test lamp illuminate?	Go to Step 5	Go to Step 4
4	1. Connect a test lamp from the rear window washer fluid pump control circuit terminal in the rear window wiper motor module harness connector to ground. 2. Turn the ignition ON. Does the test lamp illuminate?	Go to Step 6	Go to Step 7
5	Test the rear window wiper/washer switch delay/on signal circuit for a short to voltage. Did you find and correct the condition?	Go to Step 11	Go to Step 8
6	Test the rear window washer fluid pump control circuit for a short to voltage. Did you find and correct the condition?	Go to Step 11	Go to Step 8

LTV0500000002887

Fig. 59   Wiper Always On, Rear (Part 1 of 2). Astro & Safari

	Action	Yes	No
7	1. Reconnect the rear window wiper motor module switch input connector. 2. Turn the ignition ON. 3. Turn the rear window wiper/washer switch to the OFF position. 4. Backprobe the rear window wiper motor park switch signal circuit terminal E with a test lamp connected to ground. Is the test lamp off when the wiper arm is in the park position?	Go to Step 10	Go to Step 9
8	Replace the rear window wiper/washer switch. Is the repair complete?	Go to Step 11	--
9	Replace the rear window wiper motor module. Is the repair complete?	Go to Step 11	--
10	Replace the rear window wiper motor. Is the repair complete?	Go to Step 11	--
11	Operate the system in order to verify the repair. Did you correct the condition?	System OK	Go to Step 3

LTV0500000002888

Fig. 59   Wiper Always On, Rear (Part 2 of 2). Astro & Safari

Step	Action	Yes	No
	DEFINITION: The rear wiper motor is inoperative in all modes, the rear washer pump may or may not operate.		
1	Did you review the Rear Wiper/Washer System Description and Operation and perform the necessary inspections?	Go to Step 2	Go to Symptoms -
2	1. Turn the ignition ON. 2. Operate the rear wiper/washer system in all the switch positions. Does the rear wiper/washer system operate normally?	Test for Intermittent and Poor Connections	Go to Step 3
3	Does the rear washer pump operate when the rear washer switch is pressed?	Go to Step 4	Go to Step 6
4	Test the rear wiper motor module ground circuit for an open or high resistance. Did you find and correct the condition?	Go to Step 12	Go to Step 5
5	1. Using a test lamp backprobe across the rear wiper motor control and ground circuit terminals in the rear wiper motor connector at the wiper motor module. 2. Turn the ignition ON. 3. Turn the rear wiper/washer switch to the ON position. Does the test lamp illuminate?	Go to Step 9	Go to Step 7
6	Test the rear wiper/washer switch accessory voltage supply circuit for an open or short to ground. Did you find and correct the condition?	Go to Step 12	Go to Step 10

LTV0500000002889

Fig. 60 Wiper Inoperative, Rear (Part 1 of 2). Astro & Safari

Step	Action	Value(s)	Yes	No
	DEFINITION: The DELAY mode is inoperative or operates at the ON speed, and the wiper does not park.			
1	Did you review the Rear Wiper/Washer System Description and Operation and perform the necessary inspections?	--	Go to Step 2	Go to Symptoms
2	1. Turn the ignition ON. 2. Operate the rear wiper/washer system in all the switch positions. Does the rear wiper/washer system operate normally?	--	Test for Intermittent and Poor Connections	Go to Step 3
3	1. Disconnect the rear wiper motor module switch input connector. 2. Connect a test lamp from the rear wiper washer switch delay/on signal circuit terminal in the harness connector to ground. 3. Turn the ignition ON. 4. Turn the rear wiper/washer switch to the DELAY position. Does the test lamp illuminate?	--	Go to Step 4	Go to Step 10
4	With the test lamp connected as in the previous step, turn the rear wiper/washer switch to the on position. Does the test lamp illuminate?	--	Go to Step 5	Go to Step 14

LTV0500000002891

Fig. 61 Wiper Delay Mode Inoperative, Rear (Part 1 of 3). Astro & Safari

Step	Action	Yes	No
7	Inspect for poor connections at the rear wiper motor module. Did you find and correct the condition?	Go to Step 12	Go to Step 8
8	Replace the rear wiper motor module. Is the repair complete?	Go to Step 12	--
9	Replace the rear wiper motor. Is the repair complete?	Go to Step 12	--
10	Inspect for poor connections at the rear wiper/washer switch. Did you find and correct the condition?	Go to Step 12	Go to Step 11
11	Replace the rear wiper/washer switch. Is the repair complete?	Go to Step 12	--
12	Operate the system in order to verify the repair. Did you correct the condition?	System OK	Go to Step 3

LTV0500000002890

Fig. 60 Wiper Inoperative, Rear (Part 2 of 2). Astro & Safari

Step	Action	Value(s)	Yes	No
5	1. Connect a test lamp from the rear wiper washer switch off/delay signal circuit terminal to ground. 2. Turn the ignition ON. 3. Turn the rear wiper/washer switch to the OFF position. Does the test lamp illuminate?	--	Go to Step 6	Go to Step 11
6	With the test lamp connected as in the previous step, turn the rear wiper/washer switch to the DELAY position. Does the test lamp illuminate?	--	Go to Step 7	Go to Step 14
7	With the test lamp connected as in the previous step, turn the rear wiper/washer switch to the ON position. Does the test lamp illuminate?	--	Go to Step 12	Go to Step 8
8	1. Reconnect the rear wiper motor module switch input connector. 2. Turn the rear wiper/washer switch to the OFF position. Turn the ignition ON. 3. Using a test lamp backprobe from the wiper motor park switch reference voltage circuit terminal B in the wiper motor connector to ground. Does the test lamp illuminate?	--	Go to Step 9	Go to Step 15
9	1. Operate the rear wiper in any mode. 2. Turn the ignition OFF while the wiper arm is in the up position. 3. Disconnect the wiper motor connector. 4. Test the resistance through the wiper motor park switch from the reference voltage circuit terminal B to the signal circuit terminal E. Is the resistance within the specified values?	0-2ohms	Go to Step 15	Go to Step 17
10	Test the delay/on signal circuit for an open or high resistance. Did you find and correct the condition?	--	Go to Step 18	Go to Step 13
11	Test the off/delay signal circuit for an open or high resistance. Did you find and correct the condition?	--	Go to Step 18	Go to Step 13

LTV0500000002892

Fig. 61 Wiper Delay Mode Inoperative, Rear (Part 2 of 3). Astro & Safari

Step	Action	Yes	No
12	Test the off/delay signal circuit for a short to voltage. Did you find and correct the condition?	Go to Step 18	Go to Step 13
13	Inspect for poor connections at the rear wiper/washer switch. Did you find and correct the condition?	Go to Step 18	Go to Step 14
14	Replace the rear wiper/washer switch. Is the repair complete?	Go to Step 18	--
15	Inspect for poor connections at the rear wiper motor module. Did you find and correct the condition?	Go to Step 18	Go to Step 16
16	Replace the rear wiper motor module. Is the repair complete?	Go to Step 18	--
17	Replace the rear wiper motor. Is the repair complete?	Go to Step 18	--
18	Operate the system in order to verify the repair. Did you correct the condition?	System OK	Go to Step 3

LTV0500000002893

Fig. 61 Wiper Delay Mode Inoperative, Rear (Part 3 of 3). Astro & Safari

Step	Action	Yes	No
6	Test the washer fluid level switch signal circuit for a short to ground. Did you find and correct the condition?	Go to Step 13	Go to Step 11
7	Test the washer fluid level switch signal circuit for an open or high resistance. Did you find and correct the condition?	Go to Step 13	Go to Step 11
8	Repair the washer fluid level switch ground circuit for an open or high resistance. Is the repair complete?	Go to Step 13	--
9	Inspect for poor connections at the washer fluid level switch. Did you find and correct the condition?	Go to Step 13	Go to Step 10
10	Replace the washer fluid level switch. Is the repair complete?	Go to Step 13	--
11	Inspect for poor connections at the instrument panel cluster. Did you find and correct the condition?	Go to Step 13	Go to Step 12
12	Replace the instrument panel cluster. Is the repair complete?	Go to Step 13	--
13	Operate the system in order to verify the repair. Did you correct the condition?	System OK	Go to Step 3

LTV0500000002941

Fig. 62 Low Washer Fluid Indicator Fault (Part 2 of 2). 2002 Avalanche, Escalade, Sierra, & Silverado

Step	Action	Yes	No
	DEFINITION: The low washer fluid indicator always indicates low washer fluid or does not turn on with low washer fluid.		
1	Did you review the Wiper/Washer System Description and Operation and perform the necessary inspections?	Go to Step 2	Go to Symptoms -
2	Verify the fault is present. Does the system operate normally?	Test for Intermittent and Poor Connections	Go to Step 3
3	1. Turn the ignition OFF. 2. Disconnect the washer fluid level switch connector. 3. Turn the ignition ON. Does the low washer fluid indicator illuminate for 60 seconds after the ignition is turned ON?	Go to Step 6	Go to Step 4
4	1. Turn the ignition OFF. 2. Connect a fused jumper wire from the washer fluid level switch signal circuit terminal in the washer fluid level switch connector to a good ground. 3. Turn the ignition ON. Does the low washer fluid indicator illuminate for 60 seconds after the ignition is turned ON?	Go to Step 5	Go to Step 7
5	1. Turn the ignition OFF. 2. Connect a fused jumper wire across the washer fluid level switch harness connector terminals. 3. Turn the ignition ON. Does the low washer fluid indicator illuminate for 60 seconds after the ignition is turned ON?	Go to Step 9	Go to Step 8

LTV0500000002940

Fig. 62 Low Washer Fluid Indicator Fault (Part 1 of 2). 2002 Avalanche, Escalade, Sierra, & Silverado

Step	Action	Yes	No
1	Did you review the Wiper/Washer System Description and Operation and perform the necessary inspections?	Go to Step 2	Go to Symptoms
2	Turn the ignition ON. Are the windshield washers always on?	Go to Step 3	Test for Intermittent and Poor Connections
3	1. Turn the ignition OFF. 2. Disconnect the inline harness connector C201. 3. Remove the connector terminal row E from the steering column harness connector half. 4. Connect the inline harness connector C201. 5. Turn the ignition ON. Are the windshield washers always on?	Go to Step 4	Go to Step 5
4	Repair the windshield washer pump control circuit for a short to voltage. Is the repair complete?	Go to Step 6	--
5	Replace the windshield wiper/washer switch. Is the repair complete?	Go to Step 6	--
6	Operate the system in order to verify the repair. Did you correct the condition?	System OK	Go to Step 3

LTV0500000002942

Fig. 63 Washers Always On. 2002 Avalanche, Escalade, Sierra, & Silverado

Step	Action	Yes	No
1	Did you review the Wiper/Washer System Description and Operation and perform the necessary inspections?	Go to Step 2	Go to Symptoms -
2	1. Turn the ignition ON. 2. Press the windshield washer switch. Do the windshield washers operate normally?	Test for Intermittent and Poor Connections	Go to Step 3
3	1. Disconnect the windshield washer pump connector. 2. Connect a test lamp across the washer pump harness connector terminals. 3. Turn the ignition ON. 4. Press the windshield washer switch. Does the test lamp illuminate?	Go to Step 8	Go to Step 4
4	Test the windshield washer pump ground circuit for an open or high resistance. Did you find and correct the condition?	Go to Step 10	Go to Step 5
5	Test the windshield washer pump control circuit for an open or short to ground. Did you find and correct the condition?	Go to Step 10	Go to Step 6
6	Inspect for poor connections at the windshield wiper/washer switch. Did you find and correct the condition?	Go to Step 10	Go to Step 7

LTV0500000002943

Fig. 64 Washers Inoperative (Part 1 of 2). 2002 Avalanche, Escalade, Sierra, & Silverado

Step	Action	Yes	No
7	Replace the windshield wiper/washer switch. Is the repair complete?	Go to Step 10	--
8	Inspect for poor connections at the windshield washer pump. Did you find and correct the condition?	Go to Step 10	Go to Step 9
9	Replace the windshield washer pump. Is the repair complete?	Go to Step 10	--
10	Operate the system in order to verify the repair. Did you correct the condition?	System OK	Go to Step 3

LTV0500000002944

Fig. 64 Washers Inoperative (Part 2 of 2). 2002 Avalanche, Escalade, Sierra, & Silverado

Test Description

The number below refers to the step number on the diagnostic table.

3. Turn the ignition off while the wiper arms are not in the park position. If the wiper arms go to the park position and stop when the ignition is turned on, an internal fault in the windshield wiper/washer switch or short to voltage in the pigtail harness is present.

Step	Action	Yes	No
1	Did you review the Wiper/Washer System Description and Operation and perform the necessary inspections?	Go to Step 2	Go to Symptoms - Step
2	1. Turn the ignition ON. 2. Turn the windshield wiper/washer switch OFF. Are the windshield wipers always on?	Go to Step 3	Test for Intermittent and Poor Connections
3	1. Turn the ignition OFF while the wiper arms are in the upright position. 2. Disconnect the inline harness connector C201. 3. Remove the connector terminal row E from the steering column harness connector half. 4. Connect the inline harness connector C201. 5. Turn the ignition ON. Are the windshield wipers always on?	Go to Step 4	Go to Step 7
4	1. Disconnect the windshield wiper motor connector. 2. Test the windshield wiper switch signal 1 circuit for a short to voltage. Did you find and correct the condition?	Go to Step 11	Go to Step 5

LTV0500000002945

Fig. 65 Wipers Always On (Part 1 of 2). 2002 Avalanche, Escalade, Sierra, & Silverado

Step	Action	Yes	No
5	Test the windshield wiper switch signal 2 circuit for a short to voltage. Did you find and correct the condition?	Go to Step 11	Go to Step 6
6	Test the windshield wiper motor high speed circuit for a short to voltage. Did you find and correct the condition?	Go to Step 11	Go to Step 9
7	Inspect for poor connections at the windshield wiper/washer switch. Did you find and correct the condition?	Go to Step 11	Go to Step 8
8	Replace the windshield wiper/washer switch. Is the repair complete?	Go to Step 11	--
9	Inspect for poor connections at the windshield wiper motor. Did you find and correct the condition?	Go to Step 11	Go to Step 10
10	Replace the windshield wiper motor cover. Is the repair complete?	Go to Step 11	--
11	Operate the system in order to verify the repair. Did you correct the condition?	System OK	Go to Step 3

LTV0500000002946

Fig. 65 Wipers Always On (Part 2 of 2). 2002 Avalanche, Escalade, Sierra, & Silverado

Step	Action	Yes	No
1	Did you review the Wiper/Washer System Description and Operation and perform the necessary inspections?	Go to Step 2	Go to Symptoms -
2	1. Turn the ignition switch ON. 2. Operate the windshield wiper/washer switch through all the switch positions. Does the windshield wiper/washer system operate normally?	Test for Intermittent and Poor Connections	Go to Step 3
3	1. Disconnect the windshield wiper motor connector. 2. Connect a test lamp from the accessory voltage supply circuit terminal in the harness connector to a good ground. 3. Turn the ignition ON. Does the test lamp illuminate?	Go to Step 4	Go to Step 7
4	1. Connect a test lamp from the accessory voltage supply circuit terminal to the ground circuit terminal in the windshield wiper motor harness connector. 2. Turn the ignition ON. Does the test lamp illuminate?	Go to Step 5	Go to Step 8
5	1. Connect a test lamp from the windshield wiper switch signal mux 2 circuit terminal in the windshield wiper motor harness connector to ground. 2. Turn the ignition ON. 3. Press the windshield washer switch. Does the test lamp illuminate?	Go to Step 10	Go to Step 6

LTV0500000002947

Fig. 66   Wipers Inoperative, All Modes (Part 1 of 3). 2002 Avalanche, Escalade, Sierra, & Silverado

Step	Action	Yes	No
11	Replace the windshield wiper motor. Is the repair complete?	Go to Step 14	--
12	Inspect for poor connections at the windshield wiper/washer switch. Did you find and correct the condition?	Go to Step 14	Go to Step 13
13	Replace the windshield wiper/washer switch. Is the repair complete?	Go to Step 14	--
14	Operate the system in order to verify the repair. Did you correct the condition?	System OK	Go to Step 3

LTV0500000002949

Fig. 66   Wipers Inoperative, All Modes (Part 3 of 3). 2002 Avalanche, Escalade, Sierra, & Silverado

Step	Action	Yes	No
6	1. Disconnect the windshield wiper/washer switch connector. 2. Connect a test lamp from the accessory voltage supply circuit terminal in the harness connector to ground. 3. Turn the ignition ON. Does the test lamp illuminate?	Go to Step 12	Go to Step 9
7	Repair the windshield wiper motor accessory voltage supply circuit for an open or short to ground. Is the repair complete?	Go to Step 14	--
8	Repair the windshield wiper motor ground circuit for an open or high resistance. Is the repair complete?	Go to Step 14	--
9	Repair the windshield wiper/washer switch accessory voltage supply circuit for an open or short to ground. Is the repair complete?	Go to Step 14	--
10	Inspect for poor connections at the windshield wiper motor. Did you find and correct the condition?	Go to Step 14	Go to Step 11

LTV0500000002948

Fig. 66   Wipers Inoperative, All Modes (Part 2 of 3). 2002 Avalanche, Escalade, Sierra, & Silverado

Test Description

The number(s) below refer to the step number(s) on the diagnostic table.

8. This step tests for continuity through the 24K ohms resistor in the windshield wiper/washer switch. The connector behind the instrument panel knee bolster is suitable for performing this step.

9. This step tests for continuity through the delay resistors in the windshield wiper/washer switch. The measured resistance will change in sequence from high to low as the delay speed is increased. The connector behind the instrument panel knee bolster is suitable for performing this step.

Step	Action	Value(s)	Yes	No
1	Did you review the Wiper/Washer System Description and Operation and perform the necessary inspections?	--	Go to Step 2	Go to Symptoms -
2	1. Turn the ignition ON. 2. Operate the windshield wiper/washer switch through all the switch positions. Does the windshield wiper/washer system operate normally?	--	Test for Intermittent and Poor Connections	Go to Step 3
3	Do the windshield wipers operate in the high speed mode?	--	Go to Step 5	Go to Step 4

LTV0500000002950

Fig. 67   Wipers Inoperative, One Or More Modes (Part 1 of 4). 2002 Avalanche, Escalade, Sierra, & Silverado

Step	Action	Yes	No
4	1. Disconnect the windshield wiper motor connector. 2. Connect a test lamp from the windshield wiper motor high speed circuit terminal to ground. 3. Turn the ignition ON. 4. Operate the windshield wiper/washer switch to the high speed position. Does the test lamp illuminate?	Go to Step 16	Go to Step 10
5	1. Disconnect the windshield wiper motor connector. 2. Connect a test lamp from the windshield wiper motor accessory voltage supply circuit terminal to ground. 3. Turn the ignition ON. Does the test lamp illuminate?	Go to Step 6	Go to Step 11
6	1. Connect a test lamp from the windshield wiper switch signal mux 2 circuit terminal to ground. 2. Press the windshield washer switch. Does the test lamp illuminate?	Go to Step 7	Go to Step 12
7	1. Connect a test lamp from the windshield wiper switch signal mux 1 circuit terminal to ground. 2. Operate the windshield wiper/washer switch to the following positions: - MIST - LO - HI Does the test lamp illuminate in the listed switch positions?	Go to Step 8	Go to Step 13

LTV0500000002951

Fig. 67   Wipers Inoperative, One Or More Modes (Part 2 of 4). 2002 Avalanche, Escalade, Sierra, & Silverado

Step	Action	Value	Yes	No
8	1. Disconnect the windshield wiper/washer switch connector. 2. Measure the resistance through the windshield wiper/washer switch from the signal mux 2 circuit terminal to the accessory voltage supply circuit terminal in the switch side connector. 3. Operate the windshield wiper/washer switch to the following positions: - MIST - INT - LO - HI Is the resistance at or near the specified value in all the listed switch positions?	24K ohms	Go to Step 9	Go to Step 14
9	1. Measure the resistance through the windshield wiper/washer switch from the signal mux 1 circuit terminal to the accessory voltage supply circuit terminal in the switch side connector. 2. Operate the windshield wiper/washer switch through all of the delay positions. Does the resistance remain within the specified values from high to low as the delay speed is increased?	38K - 690K ohms	Go to Step 16	Go to Step 14
10	Test the windshield wiper motor high speed circuit for an open or high resistance. Did you find and correct the condition?	--	Go to Step 18	Go to Step 14
11	Repair the windshield wiper motor accessory voltage supply circuit for an open or high resistance. Is the repair complete?	--	Go to Step 18	--
12	Test the windshield wiper switch signal mux 2 circuit for an open or short to ground. Did you find and correct the condition?	--	Go to Step 18	Go to Step 14

LTV0500000002952

Fig. 67   Wipers Inoperative, One Or More Modes (Part 3 of 4). 2002 Avalanche, Escalade, Sierra, & Silverado

Step	Action	Yes	No
13	Test the windshield wiper switch signal mux 1 circuit for an open or short to ground. Did you find and correct the condition?	Go to Step 18	Go to Step 14
14	Inspect for poor connections at the windshield wiper/washer switch. Did you find and correct the condition?	Go to Step 18	Go to Step 15
15	Replace the windshield wiper/washer switch. Is the repair complete?	Go to Step 18	--
16	Inspect for poor connections at the windshield wiper motor. Did you find and correct the condition?	Go to Step 18	Go to Step 17
17	Replace the windshield wiper motor cover. Is the repair complete?	Go to Step 18	--
18	Operate the system in order to verify the repair. Did you correct the condition?	System OK	Go to Step 3

LTV0500000002953

Fig. 67   Wipers Inoperative, One Or More Modes (Part 4 of 4). 2002 Avalanche, Escalade, Sierra, & Silverado

Step	Action	Yes	No
	DEFINITION: The low washer fluid indicator always indicates low washer fluid or does not turn on with low washer fluid.		
1	Did you review the Wiper/Washer System Description and Operation and perform the necessary inspections?	Go to Step 2	Go to Symptoms -
2	Verify the fault is present. Does the system operate normally?	Test for Intermittent and Poor Connections	Go to Step 3
3	1. Turn the ignition OFF. 2. Disconnect the washer fluid level switch connector. 3. Turn the ignition ON, with the engine OFF. 4. Wait for about 15 seconds. Does the low washer fluid indicator illuminate?	Go to Step 6	Go to Step 4
4	1. Turn the ignition OFF. 2. Connect a fused jumper wire from the low washer fluid indicator signal circuit terminal in the washer fluid level switch connector to a good ground. 3. Turn the ignition ON, with the engine OFF. 4. Wait for about 15 seconds. Does the low washer fluid indicator illuminate?	Go to Step 5	Go to Step 7

LTV0500000002957

Fig. 68   Low Washer Fluid Indicator Fault (Part 1 of 3). 2003–04 Avalanche, Escalade, Sierra, & Silverado

Step	Action	Yes	No
5	1. Turn the ignition OFF. 2. Connect a fused jumper wire across the washer fluid level switch harness connector terminals. 3. Turn the ignition ON, with the engine OFF. 4. Wait for about 15 seconds. Does the low washer fluid indicator illuminate?	Go to Step 9	Go to Step 8
6	Test the low washer fluid indicator signal circuit for a short to ground. Did you find and correct the condition?	Go to Step 13	Go to Step 11
7	Test the low washer fluid indicator signal circuit for an open or high resistance. Did you find and correct the condition?	Go to Step 13	Go to Step 11
8	Repair the washer fluid level switch ground circuit for an open or high resistance. Did you complete the replacement?	Go to Step 13	--
9	Inspect for poor connections at the washer fluid level switch. Did you find and correct the condition?	Go to Step 13	Go to Step 10
10	Replace the washer fluid level switch. Did you complete the replacement?	Go to Step 13	--

LTV0500000002958

Fig. 68   Low Washer Fluid Indicator Fault (Part 2 of 3). 2003–04 Avalanche, Escalade, Sierra, & Silverado

Step	Action	Yes	No
11	Inspect for poor connections at the instrument panel cluster. Did you find and correct the condition?	Go to Step 13	Go to Step 12
12	Replace the instrument panel cluster. Did you complete the replacement?	Go to Step 13	--
13	Operate the system in order to verify the repair. Did you correct the condition?	System OK	Go to Step 3

LTV0500000002959

Fig. 68   Low Washer Fluid Indicator Fault (Part 3 of 3). 2003–04 Avalanche, Escalade, Sierra, & Silverado

Step	Action	Yes	No
	DEFINITION: The windshield washer pump is always on.		
1	Did you review the Wiper/Washer System Description and Operation and perform the necessary inspections?	Go to Step 2	Go to Symptoms
2	1. Turn the windshield wiper/washer switch to the OFF position. 2. Turn the ignition ON, with the engine OFF. Is the windshield washer pump always ON?	Go to Step 3	Test for Intermittent and Poor Connections
3	Are the windshield wipers always ON, also?	Go to Step 4	Go to Step 6
4	1. Turn the ignition OFF. 2. Disconnect the windshield wiper motor module connector. 3. Turn the ignition ON, with the engine OFF. 4. Connect a test lamp from the windshield wiper switch signal circuit terminal to ground. Does the test lamp illuminate?	Go to Step 5	Go to Step 12
5	Test the windshield wiper switch signal circuit for a short to voltage. Did you find and correct the condition?	Go to Step 16	Go to Step 10
6	1. Turn the ignition OFF. 2. Disconnect the windshield washer relay. 3. Turn the ignition ON, with the engine OFF. Is the windshield washer pump ON?	Go to Step 8	Go to Step 7

LTV0500000002960

Fig. 69   Washers Always On (Part 1 of 3). 2003–04 Avalanche, Escalade, Sierra, & Silverado

Step	Action	Yes	No
7	Connect a test lamp from battery positive voltage to the windshield washer relay control circuit terminal in the underhood fuse block. Does the test lamp illuminate?	Go to Step 9	Go to Step 14
8	Repair the windshield washer pump control circuit for a short to voltage. Is the repair complete?	Go to Step 16	--
9	Test the windshield washer relay control circuit for a short to ground. Did you find and correct the condition?	Go to Step 16	Go to Step 12
10	Inspect for poor connections at the windshield wiper/washer switch. Did you find and correct the condition?	Go to Step 16	Go to Step 11
11	Replace the windshield wiper/washer switch. Did you complete the replacement?	Go to Step 16	--
12	Inspect for poor connections at the windshield wiper motor module. Did you find and correct the condition?	Go to Step 16	Go to Step 13
13	Replace the windshield wiper motor module. Did you complete the replacement?	Go to Step 16	--
14	Inspect for poor connections at the windshield washer relay. Did you find and correct the condition?	Go to Step 16	Go to Step 15
15	Replace the windshield washer relay. Did you complete the replacement?	Go to Step 16	--

LTV0500000002961

Fig. 69   Washers Always On (Part 2 of 3). 2003–04 Avalanche, Escalade, Sierra, & Silverado

Step	Action	Yes	No
16	Operate the system in order to verify the repair. Did you correct the condition?	System OK	Go to Step 3

LTV0500000002962

Fig. 69   Washers Always On (Part 3 of 3). 2003–04 Avalanche, Escalade, Sierra, & Silverado

Step	Action	Values	Yes	No
	DEFINITION: The windshield washer pump is inoperative.			
1	Did you review the Wiper/Washer System Description and Operation and perform the necessary inspections?	--	Go to Step 2	Go to Symptoms
2	1. Turn the ignition ON, with the engine OFF. 2. Press the windshield washer switch. Do the windshield washers operate normally?	--	Test for Intermittent and Poor Connections	Go to Step 3
3	Do the windshield washer wipers operate when the windshield washer switch is pressed?	--	Go to Step 6	Go to Step 4
4	1. Turn the ignition OFF. 2. Disconnect the windshield wiper motor connector. 3. Turn the ignition ON, with the engine OFF. 4. Test the resistance from the windshield wiper switch supply voltage circuit terminal to the windshield wiper switch signal circuit terminal in the windshield wiper motor harness connector. 5. Press the windshield washer switch. Is the resistance near the specified value?	0.5 ohms	Go to Step 15	Go to Step 5

LTV0500000002963

Fig. 70   Washers Inoperative (Part 1 of 3). 2003–04 Avalanche, Escalade, Sierra, & Silverado

Step	Action	Values	Yes	No
5	Test the following circuits for open or high resistance. • Windshield wiper switch supply voltage circuit • Windshield wiper switch signal circuit Did you find and correct the condition?		Go to Step 20	Go to Step 13
6	1. Turn the ignition OFF. 2. Disconnect the windshield washer relay. 3. Turn the ignition ON, with the engine OFF. 4. Connect a test lamp test from each of the windshield washer relay battery positive voltage supply circuit terminals in the underhood fuse block to ground. Does the test lamp illuminate on both terminals?		Go to Step 7	Go to Step 9
7	1. Connect a test lamp from battery positive voltage to the windshield washer relay control circuit terminal in the underhood fuse block. 2. Press the windshield washer switch. Does the test lamp illuminate?		Go to Step 8	Go to Step 10
8	1. Turn the ignition OFF. 2. Connect the windshield washer relay. 3. Disconnect the windshield washer pump connector. 4. Turn the ignition ON, with the engine OFF. 5. Connect a test lamp across the windshield washer pump harness connector terminals. 6. Press the windshield washer switch. Does the test lamp illuminate?		Go to Step 18	Go to Step 11
9	Replace the underhood fuse block. Did you complete the replacement?		Go to Step 20	--
10	Test the windshield washer relay control circuit for an open or high resistance. Did you find and correct the condition?		Go to Step 20	Go to Step 15
11	Test the windshield washer pump control circuit for an open or high resistance. Did you find and correct the condition?		Go to Step 20	Go to Step 12

LTV0500000002964

Fig. 70   Washers Inoperative (Part 2 of 3). 2003–04 Avalanche, Escalade, Sierra, & Silverado

Step	Action	Values	Yes	No
12	Test the windshield washer pump ground circuit for an open or high resistance. Did you find and correct the condition?		Go to Step 20	Go to Step 17
13	Inspect for poor connections at the windshield wiper/washer switch. Did you find and correct the condition?		Go to Step 20	Go to Step 14
14	Replace the windshield wiper/washer switch. Did you complete the replacement?		Go to Step 20	--
15	Inspect for poor connections at the windshield wiper motor module. Did you find and correct the condition?		Go to Step 20	Go to Step 16
16	Replace the windshield wiper motor module. Did you complete the replacement?		Go to Step 20	
17	Replace the windshield washer relay. Did you complete the replacement?		Go to Step 20	--
18	Inspect for poor connections at the windshield washer pump. Did you find and correct the condition?		Go to Step 20	Go to Step 19
19	Replace the windshield washer pump. Did you complete the replacement?		Go to Step 20	--
20	Operate the system in order to verify the repair. Did you correct the condition?		System OK	Go to Step 3

LTV0500000002965

Fig. 70   Washers Inoperative (Part 3 of 3). 2003–04 Avalanche, Escalade, Sierra, & Silverado

Step	Action	Yes	No
	DEFINITION: Windshield wipers are always ON at low or high speed.		
1	Did you review the Wiper/Washer System Description and Operation and perform the necessary inspections?	Go to Step 2	Go to Symptoms -
2	1. Turn the windshield wiper/washer switch OFF. 2. Turn the ignition ON, with the engine OFF. Are the windshield wipers always on?	Go to Step 3	
3	1. Turn the ignition OFF. 2. Disconnect the turn signal multifunction switch connector C3. 3. Turn the ignition ON, with the engine OFF. Are the windshield wipers always on?	Go to Step 4	Go to Step 7
4	Are the windshield wipers always ON at high speed?	Go to Step 5	Go to Step 6
5	Test the windshield wiper switch high signal circuit for a short to ground. Did you find and correct the condition?	Go to Step 11	Go to Step 9
6	Test the windshield wiper switch signal circuit for a short to voltage. Did you find and correct the condition?	Go to Step 11	Go to Step 9
7	Inspect for poor connections at the windshield wiper/washer switch. Did you find and correct the condition?	Go to Step 11	Go to Step 8

LTV0500000002966

Fig. 71   Wipers Always On (Part 1 of 2). 2003–04 Avalanche, Escalade, Sierra, & Silverado

Step	Action	Yes	No
8	Replace the windshield wiper/washer switch. Did you complete the replacement?	Go to Step 11	--
9	Inspect for poor connections at the windshield wiper motor module. Did you find and correct the condition?	Go to Step 11	Go to Step 10
10	Replace the windshield wiper motor module. Did you complete the replacement?	Go to Step 11	--
11	Operate the system in order to verify the repair. Did you correct the condition?	System OK	Go to Step 3

LTV0500000002967

Fig. 71 Wipers Always On (Part 2 of 2). 2003–04 Avalanche, Escalade, Sierra, & Silverado

Step	Action	Yes	No
6	Connect a test lamp from battery positive voltage to the windshield wiper motor ground circuit terminal in the windshield wiper motor harness connector. Does the test lamp illuminate?	Go to Step 11	Go to Step 8
7	Repair the accessory voltage supply circuit to the windshield wiper motor for an open or short to ground. Is the repair complete?	Go to Step 13	--
8	Repair the windshield wiper motor ground circuit for an open or high resistance. Is the repair complete?	Go to Step 13	--
9	Inspect for poor connections at the windshield wiper/washer switch. Did you find and correct the condition?	Go to Step 13	Go to Step 10
10	Replace the windshield wiper/washer switch. Did you complete the replacement?	Go to Step 13	--
11	Inspect for poor connections at the windshield wiper motor. Did you find and correct the condition?	Go to Step 13	Go to Step 12
12	Replace the windshield wiper motor. Did you complete the replacement?	Go to Step 13	--
13	Operate the system in order to verify the repair. Did you correct the condition?	System OK	Go to Step 4

LTV0500000002969

Fig. 72 Wipers Inoperative, All Modes (Part 2 of 2). 2003–04 Avalanche, Escalade, Sierra, & Silverado

Step	Action	Yes	No
	DEFINITION: Wipers are inoperative in all modes.		
1	Did you perform the Wiper/Washer System Description and Operation and perform the necessary inspections?	Go to Step 2	Go to Symptoms -
2	1. Turn the ignition ON, with the engine OFF. 2. Attempt to operate the windshield wipers in all modes. Does the system operate normally?	Test for Intermittent and Poor Connections	Go to Step 3
3	Do the windshield wipers operate in any mode?	Diagnose Wipers Inoperative - One or More Modes	Go to Step 4
4	1. Disconnect the multifunction turn signal harness connector C3. 2. Connect a fused jumper wire from the windshield wiper switch high signal circuit terminal in the multifunction turn signal harness connector to a good ground. 3. Turn the ignition ON. Do the windshield wipers operate at high speed?	Go to Step 9	Go to Step 5
5	1. Disconnect the windshield wiper motor module connector. 2. Connect a test lamp from the accessory voltage supply circuit terminal in the windshield wiper motor harness connector to a good ground. 3. Turn the ignition ON. Does the test lamp illuminate?	Go to Step 6	Go to Step 7

LTV0500000002968

Fig. 72 Wipers Inoperative, All Modes (Part 1 of 2). 2003–04 Avalanche, Escalade, Sierra, & Silverado

Test Description

The numbers below refer to the step numbers on the diagnostic table.

5. This step tests for continuity through the 390 ohms resistor in the windshield wiper/washer switch.

6. This step tests for continuity through the delay resistors in the windshield wiper/washer switch. The measured resistance will change in sequence from low to high as the delay speed is increased.

Step	Action	Values	Yes	No
	DEFINITION: Windshield wipers are inoperative in one or more modes.			
1	Did you perform the Wiper/Washer System Description and Operation and perform the necessary inspections?	--	Go to Step 2	Go to Symptoms -
2	1. Turn the ignition ON, with the engine OFF. 2. Attempt to operate the windshield wipers in all modes. Does the system operate normally?	--	Test for Intermittent and Poor Connections	Go to Step 3
3	Do the windshield wipers operate in the high speed mode?	--	Go to Step 5	Go to Step 4

LTV0500000002970

Fig. 73 Wipers Inoperative, One Or More Modes (Part 1 of 3). 2003–04 Avalanche, Escalade, Sierra, & Silverado

Step	Action		Yes	No
4	1. Turn the ignition OFF. 2. Disconnect the multifunction turn signal harness connector C3. 3. Connect a fused jumper wire from the windshield wiper circuit high signal terminal in the body harness connector half to a good ground. 4. Turn the ignition ON, with the engine OFF. Do the windshield wipers operate at high speed?	--	Go to Step 8	Go to Step 7
5	1. Turn the ignition OFF. 2. Disconnect the windshield wiper motor module connector. 3. Test the resistance from the windshield wiper switch voltage supply circuit terminal to the windshield wiper switch signal circuit terminal in the windshield wiper motor harness connector. 4. Operate the windshield wiper/washer switch in the following positions: - MIST - LO Is the resistance near the specified value in all of the listed switch positions?	390 ohms	Go to Step 6	Go to Step 9
6	1. Test the resistance from the windshield wiper switch voltage supply circuit terminal to the windshield wiper switch signal circuit terminal in the windshield wiper motor harness connector. 2. Operate the windshield wiper/washer switch in all of the delay positions. Does the resistance remain within the specified values from low to high as the delay speed is increased?	1000 ohms-10K ohms	Go to Step 13	Go to Step 11
7	Test the windshield wiper switch high signal circuit for an open or high resistance. Did you find and correct the condition?	--	Go to Step 15	Go to Step 13
8	Repair the wiper switch ground circuit for an open or high resistance. Is the repair complete?	--	Go to Step 15	--

LTV0500000002971

Fig. 73   Wipers Inoperative, One Or More Modes (Part 2 of 3). 2003–04 Avalanche, Escalade, Sierra, & Silverado

Step	Action	Yes	No
	DEFINITION: The low washer fluid indicator always indicates low washer fluid or does not turn on with low washer fluid.		
1	Did you review the Wiper/Washer System Description and Operation and perform the necessary inspections?	Go to Step 2	Go to Symptoms -
2	Verify the fault is present. Does the system operate normally?	Test for Intermittent and Poor Connections	Go to Step 3
3	1. Turn the ignition OFF. 2. Disconnect the washer fluid level switch connector. 3. Turn the ignition ON, with the engine OFF. 4. Wait for about 15 seconds. Does the low washer fluid indicator illuminate?	Go to Step 6	Go to Step 4
4	1. Turn the ignition OFF. 2. Connect a fused jumper wire from the low washer fluid indicator signal circuit terminal in the washer fluid level switch connector to a good ground. 3. Turn the ignition ON, with the engine OFF. 4. Wait for about 15 seconds. Does the low washer fluid indicator illuminate?	Go to Step 5	Go to Step 7

LTV0500000002921

Fig. 74   Low Washer Fluid Indicator Fault (Part 1 of 3). 2005–06 Avalanche, Escalade, Sierra, & Silverado

Step	Action	Yes	No
9	Test the windshield wiper switch voltage supply circuit for an open or short to ground. Did you find and correct the condition?	Go to Step 15	Go to Step 10
10	Test the windshield wiper switch signal circuit for an open or short to ground. Did you find and correct the condition?	Go to Step 15	Go to Step 11
11	Inspect for poor connections at the windshield wiper/washer switch. Did you find and correct the condition?	Go to Step 15	Go to Step 12
12	Replace the windshield wiper/washer switch. Did you complete the replacement?	Go to Step 15	--
13	Inspect for poor connections at the windshield wiper motor module. Did you find and correct the condition?	Go to Step 15	Go to Step 14
14	Replace the windshield wiper motor module. Did you complete the replacement?	Go to Step 15	--
15	Operate the system in order to verify the repair. Did you correct the condition?	System OK	Go to Step 3

LTV0500000002972

Fig. 73   Wipers Inoperative, One Or More Modes (Part 3 of 3). 2003–04 Avalanche, Escalade, Sierra, & Silverado

Step	Action	Yes	No
5	1. Turn the ignition OFF. 2. Connect a fused jumper wire across the washer fluid level switch harness connector terminals. 3. Turn the ignition ON, with the engine OFF. 4. Wait for about 15 seconds. Does the low washer fluid indicator illuminate?	Go to Step 9	Go to Step 8
6	Test the low washer fluid indicator signal circuit for a short to ground. Did you find and correct the condition?	Go to Step 13	Go to Step 11
7	Test the low washer fluid indicator signal circuit for an open or high resistance. Did you find and correct the condition?	Go to Step 13	Go to Step 11
8	Repair the washer fluid level switch ground circuit for an open or high resistance. Did you complete the replacement?	Go to Step 13	--
9	Inspect for poor connections at the washer fluid level switch. Did you find and correct the condition?	Go to Step 13	Go to Step 10
10	Replace the washer fluid level switch. Did you complete the replacement?	Go to Step 13	--

LTV0500000002922

Fig. 74   Low Washer Fluid Indicator Fault (Part 2 of 3). 2005–06 Avalanche, Escalade, Sierra, & Silverado

Step	Action		
11	Inspect for poor connections at the instrument panel cluster (IPC). Did you find and correct the condition?	Go to Step 13	Go to Step 12
12	Replace the IPC. Did you complete the replacement?	Go to Step 13	--
13	Operate the system in order to verify the repair. Did you correct the condition?	System OK	Go to Step 3

LTV0500000002923

Fig. 74 Low Washer Fluid Indicator Fault (Part 3 of 3). 2005–06 Avalanche, Escalade, Sierra, & Silverado

Step	Action		
7	Connect a test lamp from battery positive voltage to the windshield washer relay control circuit terminal in the underhood fuse block. Does the test lamp illuminate?	Go to Step 9	Go to Step 14
8	Repair the windshield washer pump control circuit for a short to voltage. Is the repair complete?	Go to Step 16	--
9	Test the windshield washer relay control circuit for a short to ground. Did you find and correct the condition?	Go to Step 16	Go to Step 12
10	Inspect for poor connections at the windshield wiper/washer switch. Did you find and correct the condition?	Go to Step 16	Go to Step 11
11	Replace the windshield wiper/washer switch. Did you complete the replacement?	Go to Step 16	--
12	Inspect for poor connections at the windshield wiper motor module. Did you find and correct the condition?	Go to Step 16	Go to Step 13
13	Replace the windshield wiper motor module. Did you complete the replacement?	Go to Step 16	--
14	Inspect for poor connections at the windshield washer relay. Did you find and correct the condition?	Go to Step 16	Go to Step 15
15	Replace the windshield washer relay. Did you complete the replacement?	Go to Step 16	--

LTV0500000002925

Fig. 75 Washers Always On (Part 2 of 3). 2005–06 Avalanche, Escalade, Sierra, & Silverado

Step	Action		
16	Operate the system in order to verify the repair. Did you correct the condition?	System OK	Go to Step 3

LTV0500000002926

Fig. 75 Washers Always On (Part 3 of 3). 2005–06 Avalanche, Escalade, Sierra, & Silverado

Step	Action	Yes	No
	DEFINITION: The windshield washer pump is always on.		
1	Did you review the Wiper/Washer System Description and Operation and perform the necessary inspections?	Go to Step 2	Go to Symptoms
2	1. Turn the windshield wiper/washer switch to the OFF position. 2. Turn the ignition ON, with the engine OFF. Is the windshield washer pump always ON?	Go to Step 3	Test for Intermittent and Poor Connections
3	Are the windshield wipers always ON, also?	Go to Step 4	Go to Step 6
4	1. Turn the ignition OFF. 2. Disconnect the windshield wiper motor module connector. 3. Turn the ignition ON, with the engine OFF. 4. Connect a test lamp from the windshield wiper switch signal circuit terminal to ground. Does the test lamp illuminate?	Go to Step 5	Go to Step 12
5	Test the windshield wiper switch signal circuit for a short to voltage. Did you find and correct the condition?	Go to Step 16	Go to Step 10
6	1. Turn the ignition OFF. 2. Disconnect the windshield washer relay. 3. Turn the ignition ON, with the engine OFF. Is the windshield washer pump ON?	Go to Step 8	Go to Step 7

LTV0500000002924

Fig. 75 Washers Always On (Part 1 of 3). 2005–06 Avalanche, Escalade, Sierra, & Silverado

Step	Action	Values	Yes	No
	DEFINITION:The windshield washer pump is inoperative.			
1	Did you review the Wiper/Washer System Description and Operation and perform the necessary inspections?	--	Go to Step 2	Go to Symptoms
2	1. Turn the ignition ON, with the engine OFF. 2. Press the windshield washer switch. Do the windshield washers operate normally?	--	Test for Intermittent and Poor Connections	Go to Step 3
3	Do the windshield washer wipers operate when the windshield washer switch is pressed?	--	Go to Step 6	Go to Step 4
4	1. Turn the ignition OFF. 2. Disconnect the windshield wiper motor connector. 3. Turn the ignition ON, with the engine OFF. 4. Test the resistance from the windshield wiper switch supply voltage circuit terminal to the windshield wiper switch signal circuit terminal in the windshield wiper motor harness connector. 5. Press the windshield washer switch. Is the resistance near the specified value?	0.5 ohms	Go to Step 15	Go to Step 5

LTV0500000002927

Fig. 76 Washers Inoperative (Part 1 of 4). 2005–06 Avalanche, Escalade, Sierra, & Silverado

5	Test the following circuits for open or high resistance. • Windshield wiper switch supply voltage circuit • Windshield wiper switch signal circuit Did you find and correct the condition?	Go to Step 20	Go to Step 13
6	1. Turn the ignition OFF. 2. Disconnect the windshield washer relay. 3. Turn the ignition ON, with the engine OFF. 4. Connect a test lamp test from each of the windshield washer relay battery positive voltage supply circuit terminals in the underhood fuse block to ground. Does the test lamp illuminate on both terminals?	Go to Step 7	Go to Step 9
7	1. Connect a test lamp from battery positive voltage to the windshield washer relay control circuit terminal in the underhood fuse block. 2. Press the windshield washer switch. Does the test lamp illuminate?	Go to Step 8	Go to Step 10
8	1. Turn the ignition OFF. 2. Connect the windshield washer relay. 3. Disconnect the windshield washer pump connector. 4. Turn the ignition ON, with the engine OFF. 5. Connect a test lamp across the windshield washer pump harness connector terminals. 6. Press the windshield washer switch. Does the test lamp illuminate?	Go to Step 18	Go to Step 11
9	Replace the underhood fuse block. Did you complete the replacement?	Go to Step 20	--
10	Test the windshield washer relay control circuit for an open or high resistance. Did you find and correct the condition?	Go to Step 20	Go to Step 15

LTV0500000002928

Fig. 76   Washers Inoperative (Part 2 of 4). 2005–06 Avalanche, Escalade, Sierra, & Silverado

20	Operate the system in order to verify the repair. Did you correct the condition?	--	System OK	Go to Step 3

LTV0500000002930

Fig. 76   Washers Inoperative (Part 4 of 4). 2005–06 Avalanche, Escalade, Sierra, & Silverado

11	Test the windshield washer pump control circuit for an open or high resistance. Did you find and correct the condition?	Go to Step 20	Go to Step 12
12	Test the windshield washer pump ground circuit for an open or high resistance. Did you find and correct the condition?	Go to Step 20	Go to Step 17
13	Inspect for poor connections at the windshield wiper/washer switch. Did you find and correct the condition?	Go to Step 20	Go to Step 14
14	Replace the windshield wiper/washer switch. Did you complete the replacement?	Go to Step 20	--
15	Inspect for poor connections at the windshield wiper motor module. Did you find and correct the condition?	Go to Step 20	Go to Step 16
16	Replace the windshield wiper motor module. Did you complete the replacement?	Go to Step 20	--
17	Replace the windshield washer relay. Did you complete the replacement?	Go to Step 20	--
18	Inspect for poor connections at the windshield washer pump. Did you find and correct the condition?	Go to Step 20	Go to Step 19
19	Replace the windshield washer pump. Did you complete the replacement?	Go to Step 20	--

LTV0500000002929

Fig. 76   Washers Inoperative (Part 3 of 4). 2005–06 Avalanche, Escalade, Sierra, & Silverado

Step	Action	Yes	No
	DEFINITION: Windshield wipers are always ON at low or high speed.		
1	Did you review the Wiper/Washer System Description and Operation and perform the necessary inspections?	Go to Step 2	Go to Symptoms
2	1. Turn the windshield wiper/washer switch OFF. 2. Turn the ignition ON, with the engine OFF. Are the windshield wipers always on?	Go to Step 3	Test for Intermittent and Poor Connections
3	1. Turn the ignition OFF. 2. Disconnect the turn signal multifunction switch connector C3. 3. Turn the ignition ON, with the engine OFF. Are the windshield wipers always on?	Go to Step 4	Go to Step 7
4	Are the windshield wipers always ON at high speed?	Go to Step 5	Go to Step 6
5	Test the windshield wiper switch high signal circuit for a short to ground. Did you find and correct the condition?	Go to Step 11	Go to Step 9
6	Test the windshield wiper switch signal circuit for a short to voltage. Did you find and correct the condition?	Go to Step 11	Go to Step 9
7	Inspect for poor connections at the windshield wiper/washer switch. Did you find and correct the condition?	Go to Step 11	Go to Step 8

LTV0500000002931

Fig. 77   Wipers Always On (Part 1 of 2). 2005–06 Avalanche, Escalade, Sierra, & Silverado

		Yes	No
8	Replace the windshield wiper/washer switch. Did you complete the replacement?	Go to Step 11	--
9	Inspect for poor connections at the windshield wiper motor module. Did you find and correct the condition?	Go to Step 11	Go to Step 10
10	Replace the windshield wiper motor module. Did you complete the replacement?	Go to Step 11	--
11	Operate the system in order to verify the repair. Did you correct the condition?	System OK	Go to Step 3

LTV0500000002932

Fig. 77   Wipers Always On (Part 2 of 2). 2005–06 Avalanche, Escalade, Sierra, & Silverado

		Yes	No
6	Connect a test lamp from battery positive voltage to the windshield wiper motor ground circuit terminal in the windshield wiper motor harness connector. Does the test lamp illuminate?	Go to Step 11	Go to Step 8
7	Repair the accessory voltage supply circuit to the windshield wiper motor for an open or short to ground. Is the repair complete?	Go to Step 13	--
8	Repair the windshield wiper motor ground circuit for an open or high resistance. Is the repair complete?	Go to Step 13	--
9	Inspect for poor connections at the windshield wiper/washer switch. Did you find and correct the condition?	Go to Step 13	Go to Step 10
10	Replace the windshield wiper/washer switch. Did you complete the replacement?	Go to Step 13	--
11	Inspect for poor connections at the windshield wiper motor. Did you find and correct the condition?	Go to Step 13	Go to Step 12
12	Replace the windshield wiper motor. Did you complete the replacement?	Go to Step 13	--
13	Operate the system in order to verify the repair. Did you correct the condition?	System OK	Go to Step 4

LTV0500000002934

Fig. 78   Wipers Inoperative, All Modes (Part 2 of 2). 2005–06 Avalanche, Escalade, Sierra, & Silverado

Step	Action	Yes	No
DEFINITION: Wipers are inoperative in all modes.			
1	Did you perform the Wiper/Washer System Description and Operation and perform the necessary inspections?	Go to Step 2	Go to Symptoms
2	1. Turn the ignition ON, with the engine OFF. 2. Attempt to operate the windshield wipers in all modes. Does the system operate normally?		Go to Step 3
3	Do the windshield wipers operate in any mode?	Diagnose Wipers Inoperative - One or More Modes	Go to Step 4
4	1. Disconnect the multifunction turn signal harness connector C3. 2. Connect a fused jumper wire from the windshield wiper switch high signal circuit terminal in the multifunction turn signal harness connector to a good ground. 3. Turn the ignition ON. Do the windshield wipers operate at high speed?	Go to Step 9	Go to Step 5
5	1. Disconnect the windshield wiper motor module connector. 2. Connect a test lamp from the accessory voltage supply circuit terminal in the windshield wiper motor harness connector to a good ground. 3. Turn the ignition ON. Does the test lamp illuminate?	Go to Step 6	Go to Step 7

LTV0500000002933

Fig. 78   Wipers Inoperative, All Modes (Part 1 of 2). 2005–06 Avalanche, Escalade, Sierra, & Silverado

Test Description

The numbers below refer to the step numbers on the diagnostic table.

5. This step tests for continuity through the 390 ohms resistor in the windshield wiper/washer switch.

6. This step tests for continuity through the delay resistors in the windshield wiper/washer switch. The measured resistance will change in sequence from low to high as the delay speed is increased.

Step	Action	Values	Yes	No
DEFINITION: Windshield wipers are inoperative in one or more modes.				
1	Did you perform the Wiper/Washer System Description and Operation and perform the necessary inspections?	--	Go to Step 2	Go to Symptoms -
2	1. Turn the ignition ON, with the engine OFF. 2. Attempt to operate the windshield wipers in all modes. Does the system operate normally?	--		Go to Step 3
3	Do the windshield wipers operate in the high speed mode?	--	Go to Step 5	Go to Step 4

LTV0500000002935

Fig. 79   Wipers Inoperative, One Or More Modes (Part 1 of 3). 2005–06 Avalanche, Escalade, Sierra, & Silverado

Step	Action	Value	Yes	No
4	1. Turn the ignition OFF. 2. Disconnect the multifunction turn signal harness connector C3. 3. Connect a fused jumper wire from the windshield wiper switch high signal circuit terminal in the body harness connector half to a good ground. 4. Turn the ignition ON, with the engine OFF. Do the windshield wipers operate at high speed?	--	Go to Step 8	Go to Step 7
5	1. Turn the ignition OFF. 2. Disconnect the windshield wiper motor module connector. 3. Test the resistance from the windshield wiper switch voltage supply circuit terminal to the windshield wiper switch signal circuit terminal in the windshield wiper motor harness connector. 4. Operate the windshield wiper/washer switch in the following positions: - MIST - LO Is the resistance near the specified value in all of the listed switch positions?	390 ohms	Go to Step 6	Go to Step 9
6	1. Test the resistance from the windshield wiper switch voltage supply circuit terminal to the windshield wiper switch signal circuit terminal in the windshield wiper motor harness connector. 2. Operate the windshield wiper/washer switch in all of the delay positions. Does the resistance remain within the specified values from low to high as the delay speed is increased?	1000 ohms-10K ohms	Go to Step 13	Go to Step 11
7	Test the windshield wiper switch high signal circuit for an open or high resistance. Did you find and correct the condition?	--	Go to Step 15	Go to Step 13
8	Repair the wiper switch ground circuit for an open or high resistance. Is the repair complete?	--	Go to Step 15	--

LTV0500000002936

Fig. 79 Wipers Inoperative, One Or More Modes (Part 2 of 3). 2005–06 Avalanche, Escalade, Sierra, & Silverado

Step	Action	Yes	No
9	Test the windshield wiper switch voltage supply circuit for an open or short to ground. Did you find and correct the condition?	Go to Step 15	Go to Step 10
10	Test the windshield wiper switch signal circuit for an open or short to ground. Did you find and correct the condition?	Go to Step 15	Go to Step 11
11	Inspect for poor connections at the windshield wiper/washer switch. Did you find and correct the condition?	Go to Step 15	Go to Step 12
12	Replace the windshield wiper/washer switch. Did you complete the replacement?	Go to Step 15	--
13	Inspect for poor connections at the windshield wiper motor module. Did you find and correct the condition?	Go to Step 15	Go to Step 14
14	Replace the windshield wiper motor module. Did you complete the replacement?	Go to Step 15	--
15	Operate the system in order to verify the repair. Did you correct the condition?	System OK	Go to Step 3

LTV0500000002937

Fig. 79 Wipers Inoperative, One Or More Modes (Part 3 of 3). 2005–06 Avalanche, Escalade, Sierra, & Silverado

Step	Action	Yes	No
	DEFINITION: The low washer fluid indicator is always on or does not turn on with low washer fluid.		
1	Did you review the Wiper/Washer System Description and Operation and perform the necessary inspections?	Go to Step 2	Go to Symptoms -
2	Verify the fault is present. Does the system operate normally?	Test for Intermittent and Poor Connections	Go to Step 3
3	1. Turn OFF the ignition. 2. Disconnect the washer fluid level switch connector. 3. Turn ON the ignition. Does the low washer fluid indicator remain illuminated?	Go to Step 6	Go to Step 4
4	1. Turn OFF the ignition. 2. Connect a 3-ampere fused jumper wire from the signal circuit to the ground circuit of the washer fluid level switch. 3. Turn ON the ignition, with the engine OFF. Does the low washer fluid indicator illuminate?	Go to Step 8	Go to Step 5
5	Connect a 3-ampere fused jumper wire from the signal circuit of the washer fluid level switch to a good ground. Does the low washer fluid indicator illuminate?	Go to Step 10	Go to Step 7
6	Test the washer fluid level switch signal circuit for a short to ground. Did you find and correct the condition?	Go to Step 13	Go to Step 9

LTV0500000002897

Fig. 80 Low Washer Fluid Indicator Fault (Part 1 of 2). Aztek & Rendezvous

Step	Action	Yes	No
7	Test the washer fluid level switch signal circuit for an open or high resistance. Did you find and correct the condition?	Go to Step 13	Go to Step 9
8	Inspect for poor connections at the washer fluid level switch. Did you find and correct the condition?	Go to Step 13	Go to Step 11
9	Inspect for poor connections at the instrument panel cluster (IPC). Did you find and correct the condition?	Go to Step 13	Go to Step 12
10	Repair an open or high resistance in the ground circuit of the washer fluid level switch. Did you complete the repair?	Go to Step 13	--
11	Replace the washer fluid level switch. Did you complete the replacement?	Go to Step 13	--
12	Replace the IPC. Did you complete the replacement?	Go to Step 13	--
13	Operate the system in order to verify the repair. Did you correct the condition?	System OK	Go to Step 3

LTV0500000002898

Fig. 80 Low Washer Fluid Indicator Fault (Part 2 of 2). Aztek & Rendezvous

Test Description

The number below refers to the step number on the diagnostic table.

3. Tests for an internal fault in the windshield wiper/washer switch.

Step	Action	Yes	No
1	Did you review the Wiper/Washer System Description and Operation and perform the necessary inspections?	Go to Step 2	Go to Symptoms -
2	Turn the ignition ON. Are the windshield washers always on?	Go to Step 3	Test for Intermittent and Poor Connections
3	Disconnect the windshield wiper/washer switch connector at the multifunction switch assembly. Are the windshield washers always on?	Go to Step 4	Go to Step 5
4	Repair the short to voltage in the windshield washer pump control circuit. Did you complete the repair?	Go to Step 6	--
5	Replace the windshield wiper/washer switch. Is the repair complete?	Go to Step 6	--
6	Operate the system in order to verify the repair. Did you correct the condition?	System OK	Go to Step 3

LTV0500000002899

Fig. 81   Washers Always On. Aztek & Rendezvous

Step	Action	Yes	No
7	Replace the windshield wiper/washer switch. Is the repair complete?	Go to Step 10	--
8	Inspect for poor connections at the windshield washer pump. Did you find and correct the condition?	Go to Step 10	Go to Step 9
9	Replace the windshield washer pump. Is the repair complete?	Go to Step 10	--
10	Operate the system in order to verify the repair. Did you correct the condition?	System OK	Go to Step 3

LTV0500000002901

Fig. 82   Washers Inoperative (Part 2 of 2). Aztek & Rendezvous

Step	Action	Yes	No
1	Did you review the Wiper/Washer System Description and Operation and perform the necessary inspections?	Go to Step 2	Go to Symptoms -
2	1. Turn the ignition ON. 2. Press the windshield washer switch. Do the windshield washers operate normally?	Test for Intermittent and Poor Connections	Go to Step 3
3	1. Disconnect the windshield washer pump connector. 2. Connect a test lamp across the washer pump harness connector terminals. 3. Turn the ignition ON. 4. Press the windshield washer switch. Does the test lamp illuminate?	Go to Step 8	Go to Step 4
4	Test the windshield washer pump ground circuit for an open or high resistance. Did you find and correct the condition?	Go to Step 10	Go to Step 5
5	Test the windshield washer pump control circuit for an open or high resistance. Did you find and correct the condition?	Go to Step 10	Go to Step 6
6	Inspect for poor connections at the windshield wiper/washer switch. Did you find and correct the condition?	Go to Step 10	Go to Step 7

LTV0500000002900

Fig. 82   Washers Inoperative (Part 1 of 2). Aztek & Rendezvous

Test Description

The number below refers to the step number on the diagnostic table.

3. Tests for an internal fault in the windshield wiper/washer switch.

Step	Action	Yes	No
1	Did you review the Wiper/Washer System Description and Operation and perform the necessary inspections?	Go to Step 2	Go to Symptoms -
2	1. Turn the ignition ON. 2. Operate the windshield wiper/washer switch in all of the switch positions. 3. Turn the windshield wiper/washer switch OFF. Are the windshield wipers always on?	Go to Step 3	Test for Intermittent and Poor Connections
3	Disconnect the windshield wiper/washer switch connector at the multifunction switch assembly. Are the windshield wipers always on?	Go to Step 4	Go to Step 7
4	1. Disconnect the windshield wiper motor connector. 2. Test the windshield wiper switch signal 1 circuit for a short to voltage. Did you find and correct the condition?	Go to Step 11	Go to Step 5
5	Test the windshield wiper switch signal 2 circuit for a short to voltage. Did you find and correct the condition?	Go to Step 11	Go to Step 6

LTV0500000002902

Fig. 83   Wipers Always On (Part 1 of 2). Aztek & Rendezvous

Step	Action	Yes	No
6	Test the windshield wiper motor high speed circuit for a short to voltage. Did you find and correct the condition?	Go to Step 11	Go to Step 9
7	Inspect for poor connections at the windshield wiper/washer switch. Did you find and correct the condition?	Go to Step 11	Go to Step 8
8	Replace the windshield wiper/washer switch. Is the repair complete?	Go to Step 11	--
9	Inspect for poor connections at the windshield wiper motor. Did you find and correct the condition?	Go to Step 11	Go to Step 10
10	Replace the windshield wiper motor cover. Is the repair complete?	Go to Step 11	--
11	Operate the system in order to verify the repair. Did you correct the condition?	System OK	Go to Step 3

LTV0500000002903

Fig. 83   Wipers Always On (Part 2 of 2). Aztek & Rendezvous

Step	Action	Yes	No
6	1. Disconnect the windshield wiper/washer switch connector. 2. Connect a test lamp from the accessory voltage supply circuit terminal in the windshield wiper/washer switch harness connector to ground. 3. Turn the ignition ON. Does the test lamp illuminate?	Go to Step 11	Go to Step 9
7	Repair the windshield wiper motor accessory voltage supply circuit for an open or short to ground. Is the repair complete?	Go to Step 12	--
8	Repair the windshield wiper motor ground circuit for an open or high resistance. Is the repair complete?	Go to Step 12	--
9	Repair the windshield wiper/washer switch accessory voltage supply circuit for an open or short to ground. Is the repair complete?	Go to Step 12	--
10	Replace the windshield wiper motor. Is the repair complete?	Go to Step 12	--
11	Replace the windshield wiper/washer switch. Is the repair complete?	Go to Step 12	--
12	Operate the system in order to verify the repair. Did you correct the condition?	System OK	Go to Step 3

LTV0500000002905

Fig. 84   Wipers Inoperative, All Modes (Part 2 of 2). Aztek & Rendezvous

Step	Action	Yes	No
1	Did you review the Wiper/Washer System Description and Operation and perform the necessary inspections?	Go to Step 2	Go to Symptoms -
2	1. Turn the ignition switch ON. 2. Operate the windshield wiper/washer switch through all the switch positions. Does the windshield wiper/washer system operate normally?	Test for Intermittent and Poor Connections	Go to Step 3
3	1. Disconnect the windshield wiper motor connector. 2. Connect a test lamp from the accessory voltage supply circuit terminal in the harness connector to a good ground. 3. Turn the ignition ON. Does the test lamp illuminate?	Go to Step 4	Go to Step 7
4	1. Connect a test lamp from the accessory voltage supply circuit terminal to the ground circuit terminal in the windshield wiper motor harness connector. 2. Turn the ignition ON. Does the test lamp illuminate?	Go to Step 5	Go to Step 8
5	1. Connect a test lamp from the windshield wiper switch signal 2 circuit terminal in the windshield wiper motor harness connector to ground. 2. Turn the ignition ON. 3. Press the windshield washer switch. Does the test lamp illuminate?	Go to Step 10	Go to Step 6

LTV0500000002904

Fig. 84   Wipers Inoperative, All Modes (Part 1 of 2). Aztek & Rendezvous

Test Description

The numbers below refer to the step numbers on the diagnostic table.

8. This step tests for continuity through the 24K ohms resistor in the windshield wiper/washer switch. The connector behind the instrument panel knee bolster is suitable for performing this step.

9. This step tests for continuity through the delay resistors in the windshield wiper/washer switch. The measured resistance will change in sequence from high to low as the delay speed is increased. The connector behind the instrument panel knee bolster is suitable for performing this step.

Step	Action	Value(s)	Yes	No
1	Did you review the Wiper/Washer System Description and Operation and perform the necessary inspections?	--	Go to Step 2	Go to Symptoms -
2	1. Turn the ignition ON. 2. Operate the windshield wiper/washer switch through all the switch positions. Does the windshield wiper/washer system operate normally?	--	Test for Intermittent and Poor Connections	Go to Step 3
3	Do the windshield wipers operate in the high speed mode?	--	Go to Step 5	Go to Step 4

LTV0500000002906

Fig. 85   Wipers Inoperative, One Or More Modes (Part 1 of 4). Aztek & Rendezvous

4	1. Turn OFF the ignition. 2. Disconnect the windshield wiper motor connector. 3. Connect a test lamp from the windshield wiper motor high speed circuit terminal to ground. 4. Turn the ignition ON, with the engine OFF. 5. Place the windshield wiper/washer switch in the high speed position. Does the test lamp illuminate?	Go to Step 16	Go to Step 10
5	1. Turn OFF the ignition. 2. Disconnect the windshield wiper motor connector. 3. Connect a test lamp from the windshield wiper motor accessory voltage supply circuit terminal to ground. 4. Turn the ignition ON, with the engine OFF. Does the test lamp illuminate?	Go to Step 6	Go to Step 11
6	1. Connect a test lamp from the windshield wiper switch signal 2 circuit terminal to ground. 2. Press the windshield washer switch. Does the test lamp illuminate?	Go to Step 7	Go to Step 12

7	1. Connect a test lamp from the windshield wiper switch signal 1 circuit terminal to ground.
	2. Operate the windshield wiper/washer switch to the following positions:
	
	  - MIST
	  - LO
	  - HI
	
	Does the test lamp illuminate in the listed switch positions?
		Go to Step 8	Go to Step 13

LTV0500000002907

Fig. 85 Wipers Inoperative, One Or More Modes (Part 2 of 4). Aztek & Rendezvous

13	Test the windshield wiper switch signal 1 circuit for an open or short to ground. Did you find and correct the condition?	Go to Step 18	Go to Step 14
14	Inspect for poor connections at the windshield wiper/washer switch. Did you find and correct the condition?	Go to Step 18	Go to Step 15
15	Replace the windshield wiper/washer switch. Did you complete the replacement?	Go to Step 18	--
16	Inspect for poor connections at the windshield wiper motor. Did you find and correct the condition?	Go to Step 18	Go to Step 17
17	Replace the windshield wiper motor cover. Did you complete the replacement?	Go to Step 18	--
18	Operate the system in order to verify the repair. Did you correct the condition?	System OK	Go to Step 3

LTV0500000002909

Fig. 85 Wipers Inoperative, One Or More Modes (Part 4 of 4). Aztek & Rendezvous

8	1. Disconnect the windshield wiper/washer switch connector.
	2. Measure the resistance through the windshield wiper/washer switch from the signal 2 circuit terminal to the accessory voltage supply circuit terminal in the switch side connector.
	3. Operate the windshield wiper/washer switch to the following positions:
	
	  - MIST
	  - LO
	  - HI
	
	Is the resistance at or near the specified value in all the listed switch positions?
		24K ohms	Go to Step 9 / Go to Step 14

9	1. Measure the resistance through the windshield wiper/washer switch from the signal 1 circuit terminal to the accessory voltage supply circuit terminal in the switch side connector. 2. Operate the windshield wiper/washer switch through all of the delay positions. Does the resistance remain within the specified values from high to low as the delay speed is increased?	38K - 690K ohms	Go to Step 16 / Go to Step 14
10	Test the windshield wiper motor high speed circuit for an open or high resistance. Did you find and correct the condition?	--	Go to Step 18 / Go to Step 14
11	Repair the open or high resistance in the windshield wiper motor accessory voltage supply circuit. Did you complete the repair?	--	Go to Step 18 / --
12	Test the windshield wiper switch signal 2 circuit for an open or short to ground. Did you find and correct the condition?	--	Go to Step 18 / Go to Step 14

LTV0500000002908

Fig. 85 Wipers Inoperative, One Or More Modes (Part 3 of 4). Aztek & Rendezvous

Step	Action	Yes	No
1	Did you review the Rear Wiper/Washer System Description and Operation and perform the necessary inspections?	Go to Step 2	Go to Symptoms -
2	1. Turn the ignition ON. 2. Press the rear washer switch. Does the rear washer operate normally?	Test for Intermittent and Poor Connections	Go to Step 3
3	Does the rear wiper operate when the washer switch is pressed?	Go to Step 4	Diagnose Wiper Inoperative - Rear
4	1. Turn OFF the ignition. 2. Disconnect the rear washer pump connector. 3. Connect a test lamp from the rear washer control circuit to the ground circuit of the washer pump. 4. Turn the ignition ON, with the engine OFF. 5. Press the rear washer switch. Does the test lamp illuminate when the rear washer switch is pressed?	Go to Step 8	Go to Step 5
5	1. Connect a test lamp from the rear washer control circuit of the washer pump to a good ground. 2. Press the rear washer switch. Does the test lamp illuminate when the rear washer switch is pressed?	Go to Step 7	Go to Step 6

LTV0500000002910

Fig. 86 Washer Inoperative, Rear (Part 1 of 2). Aztek & Rendezvous

Step	Action	Yes	No
6	Repair the rear washer control circuit for an open or high resistance. Did you complete the repair?	Go to Step 10	--
7	Repair the rear washer pump ground circuit for an open or high resistance. Did you complete the repair?	Go to Step 10	--
8	Inspect for poor connections at the rear washer pump. Did you find and correct the condition?	Go to Step 10	Go to Step 9
9	Replace the rear washer pump. Did you complete the replacement?	Go to Step 10	--
10	Operate the system in order to verify the repair. Did you correct the condition?	System OK	Go to Step 3

LTV0500000002911

Fig. 86 Washer Inoperative, Rear (Part 2 of 2). Aztek & Rendezvous

Step	Action	Yes	No
7	Replace the rear wiper/washer switch. Is the repair complete?	Go to Step 9	--
8	Replace the rear wiper motor. Is the repair complete?	Go to Step 9	--
9	Operate the system in order to verify the repair. Did you correct the condition?	System OK	Go to Step 3

LTV0500000002913

Fig. 87 Wiper Always On, Rear (Part 2 of 2). Aztek & Rendezvous

Step	Action	Yes	No
	DEFINITION: The rear wiper motor is inoperative in one or more modes, the rear washer pump may or may not operate.		
1	Did you review the Rear Wiper/Washer System Description and Operation and perform the necessary inspections?	Go to Step 2	Go to Symptoms -
2	1. Turn the ignition ON, with the engine OFF. 2. Operate the rear wiper/washer system in all the switch positions. Does the rear wiper/washer system operate normally?	Test for Intermittent and Poor Connections	Go to Step 3
3	Does the rear wiper motor operate when the rear washer switch is pressed?	Go to Step 9	Go to Step 4
4	1. Turn OFF the ignition. 2. Disconnect the harness connector of the rear wiper/washer switch. 3. Turn the ignition ON, with the engine OFF. 4. Connect a test lamp from the accessory voltage circuit of the rear wiper/washer switch to a good ground. Does the test lamp illuminate?	Go to Step 5	Go to Step 10
5	Connect a 3 ampere fused jumper from the accessory voltage circuit of the rear wiper switch to the signal circuit of the rear wiper motor. Does the rear wiper motor operate?	Go to Step 14	Go to Step 6

LTV0500000002914

Fig. 88 Wiper Inoperative, Rear (Part 1 of 4). Aztek & Rendezvous

Step	Action	Yes	No
1	Did you review the Rear Wiper/Washer System Description and Operation and perform the necessary inspections?	Go to Step 2	Go to Symptoms
2	1. Turn the ignition ON. 2. Turn the rear wiper/washer switch to the OFF position. Is the rear wiper always on?	Go to Step 3	Test for Intermittent and Poor Connections
3	1. Disconnect the rear wiper motor connector. 2. Turn the rear wiper/washer switch to the OFF position. 3. Connect a test lamp from the rear wiper switch signal circuit terminal in the rear wiper motor harness connector to ground. 4. Turn the ignition ON. Does the test lamp illuminate?	Go to Step 5	Go to Step 4
4	1. Connect a test lamp from the rear washer pump control circuit terminal in the rear wiper motor harness connector to ground. 2. Turn the ignition ON. Does the test lamp illuminate?	Go to Step 6	Go to Step 8
5	Test the rear wiper switch signal circuit for a short to voltage. Did you find and correct the condition?	Go to Step 9	Go to Step 7
6	Test the rear washer pump control circuit for a short to voltage. Did you find and correct the condition?	Go to Step 9	Go to Step 7

LTV0500000002912

Fig. 87 Wiper Always On, Rear (Part 1 of 2). Aztek & Rendezvous

Step	Action	Yes	No
6	1. Turn OFF the ignition. 2. Disconnect the harness connector of the rear wiper motor. 3. Turn the ignition ON, with the engine OFF. 4. Connect a test lamp from the signal circuit of the rear wiper/washer switch to a good ground. Does the test lamp illuminate?	Go to Step 7	Go to Step 17
7	Connect a test lamp from the accessory voltage circuit to the ground circuit of the rear wiper motor. Does the test lamp illuminate?	Go to Step 15	Go to Step 8
8	Connect a test lamp from the accessory voltage circuit of the rear wiper motor to a good ground. Does the test lamp illuminate?	Go to Step 19	Go to Step 18
9	1. Turn OFF the ignition. 2. Disconnect the harness connector of the rear wiper motor. 3. Turn the ignition ON, with the engine OFF. 4. Connect a test lamp from the signal circuit of the rear wiper/washer switch to a good ground. 5. Turn ON the rear wiper. Does the test lamp illuminate?	Go to Step 15	Go to Step 13
10	Test the accessory voltage circuit of the rear wiper/washer switch for an open or short to ground. Did you find and correct the condition?	Go to Step 22	Go to Step 11
11	Test the accessory voltage circuit of the rear wiper motor for a short to ground. Did you find and correct the condition?	Go to Step 22	Go to Step 12
12	Test the signal circuit of the rear wiper/washer switch for a short to ground. Did you find and correct the condition?	Go to Step 22	Go to Step 16

LTV0500000002915

Fig. 88 Wiper Inoperative, Rear (Part 2 of 4). Aztek & Rendezvous

Step	Action	Yes	No
13	Test the signal circuit of the rear wiper/washer switch for an open or high resistance. Did you find and correct the condition?	Go to Step 22	Go to Step 14
14	Inspect for poor connections at the rear wiper/washer switch. Did you find and correct the condition?	Go to Step 22	Go to Step 20
15	Inspect for poor connections at the rear wiper motor. Did you find and correct the condition?	Go to Step 22	Go to Step 21
16	Repair a short to ground in the control circuit of the rear washer pump. Did you complete the repair?	Go to Step 22	--
17	Repair an open or high resistance the signal circuit of the rear wiper/washer switch. Did you complete the repair?	Go to Step 22	--
18	Repair an open or high resistance in the accessory voltage circuit of the rear wiper motor. Did you complete the repair?	Go to Step 22	--
19	Repair an open or high resistance in the ground circuit of the rear wiper motor. Did you complete the repair?	Go to Step 22	--
20	Replace the rear wiper/washer switch. Did you complete the replacement?	Go to Step 22	--

LTV0500000002916

Fig. 88   Wiper Inoperative, Rear (Part 3 of 4). Aztek & Rendezvous

Step	Action	Yes	No
1	Did you review the Wiper/Washer System Description and Operation and perform the necessary inspections?	Go to Step 2	Go to Symptoms
2	Turn the ignition ON. Are the windshield washers always on?	Go to Step 3	
3	1. Turn the ignition OFF. 2. Disconnect the inline harness connector C211. 3. Remove the connector terminal row E from the steering column harness connector half. 4. Connect the inline harness connector C211. 5. Turn the ignition ON. Are the windshield washers always on?	Go to Step 4	Go to Step 5
4	Repair the windshield washer pump control circuit for a short to voltage. Is the repair complete?	Go to Step 6	--
5	Replace the windshield wiper/washer switch. Is the repair complete?	Go to Step 6	--
6	Operate the system in order to verify the repair. Did you correct the condition?	System OK	Go to Step 3

LTV0500000003128

Fig. 89   Washers Always On. Blazer, Jimmy, Sonoma & S10

Step	Action	Yes	No
21	Replace the rear wiper motor. Did you complete the replacement?	Go to Step 22	--
22	Operate the system in order to verify the repair. Did you correct the condition?	System OK	Go to Step 3

LTV0500000002917

Fig. 88   Wiper Inoperative, Rear (Part 4 of 4). Aztek & Rendezvous

Step	Action	Yes	No
1	Did you review the Wiper/Washer System Description and Operation and perform the necessary inspections?	Go to Step 2	Go to Symptoms -
2	1. Turn the ignition ON. 2. Press the windshield washer switch. Do the windshield washers operate normally?	Test for Intermittent and Poor Connections	Go to Step 3
3	1. Disconnect the windshield washer pump connector. 2. Connect a test lamp across the washer pump harness connector terminals. 3. Turn the ignition ON. 4. Press the windshield washer switch. Does the test lamp illuminate?	Go to Step 8	Go to Step 4
4	Test the windshield washer pump ground circuit for an open or high resistance. Did you find and correct the condition?	Go to Step 10	Go to Step 5
5	Test the windshield washer pump control circuit for an open or high resistance. Did you find and correct the condition?	Go to Step 10	Go to Step 6
6	Inspect for poor connections at the windshield wiper/washer switch. Did you find and correct the condition?	Go to Step 10	Go to Step 7

LTV0500000003129

Fig. 90   Washers Inoperative (Part 1 of 2). Blazer, Jimmy, Sonoma & S10

Step	Action	Yes	No
7	Replace the windshield wiper/washer switch. Is the repair complete?	Go to Step 10	--
8	Inspect for poor connections at the windshield washer pump. Did you find and correct the condition?	Go to Step 10	Go to Step 9
9	Replace the windshield washer pump. Is the repair complete?	Go to Step 10	--
10	Operate the system in order to verify the repair. Did you correct the condition?	System OK	Go to Step 3

LTV0500000003130

Fig. 90   Washers Inoperative (Part 2 of 2). Blazer, Jimmy, Sonoma & S10

Step	Action	Yes	No
1	Did you review the Wiper/Washer System Description and Operation and perform the necessary inspections?	Go to Step 2	Go to Symptoms -
2	1. Turn the ignition ON. 2. Turn the windshield wiper/washer switch OFF. Do the windshield wipers remain in the park position?	Test for Intermittent and Poor Connections	Go to Step 3
3	1. Turn the ignition OFF. 2. Disconnect the inline harness connector C211. 3. Remove the connector terminal row E from the steering column harness connector half. 4. Connect the inline harness connector C211. 5. Turn the ignition ON. Are the windshield wipers always on?	Go to Step 4	Go to Step 5
4	Test the windshield wiper switch signal 2 circuit for a short to voltage. Did you find and correct the condition?	Go to Step 7	Go to Step 6
5	Replace the windshield wiper/washer switch. Is the repair complete?	Go to Step 7	--
6	Replace the windshield wiper motor module. Is the repair complete?	Go to Step 7	--

LTV0500000003131

Fig. 91 Wipers Always On (Part 1 of 2). Blazer, Jimmy, Sonoma & S10

Step	Action	Yes	No
1	Did you review the Wiper/Washer System Description and Operation and perform the necessary inspections?	Go to Step 2	Go to Symptoms -
2	1. Turn the ignition switch ON. 2. Operate the windshield wiper/washer switch through all the switch positions. Does the windshield wiper/washer system operate normally?	Test for Intermittent and Poor Connections	Go to Step 3
3	1. Disconnect the windshield wiper motor connector. 2. Connect a test lamp from the accessory voltage supply circuit terminal in the harness connector to a good ground. 3. Turn the ignition ON. Does the test lamp illuminate?	Go to Step 4	Go to Step 7
4	1. Connect a test lamp from the accessory voltage supply circuit terminal to the ground circuit terminal in the windshield wiper motor harness connector. 2. Turn the ignition ON. Does the test lamp illuminate?	Go to Step 5	Go to Step 8
5	1. Connect a test lamp from the windshield wiper switch signal 2 circuit terminal in the windshield wiper motor harness connector to ground. 2. Turn the ignition ON. 3. Press the windshield washer switch. Does the test lamp illuminate?	Go to Step 10	Go to Step 6

LTV0500000003133

Fig. 92 Wipers Inoperative, All Modes (Part 1 of 3). Blazer, Jimmy, Sonoma & S10

Step	Action	Yes	No
7	Operate the system in order to verify the repair. Did you correct the condition?	System OK	Go to Step 3

LTV0500000003132

Fig. 91 Wipers Always On (Part 2 of 2). Blazer, Jimmy, Sonoma & S10

Step	Action	Yes	No
6	1. Disconnect the windshield wiper/washer switch connector. 2. Connect a test lamp from the accessory voltage supply circuit terminal in the harness connector to ground. 3. Turn the ignition ON. Does the test lamp illuminate?	Go to Step 12	Go to Step 9
7	Repair the windshield wiper motor accessory voltage supply circuit for an open or short to ground. Is the repair complete?	Go to Step 14	--
8	Repair the windshield wiper motor ground circuit for an open or high resistance. Is the repair complete?	Go to Step 14	--
9	Repair the windshield wiper/washer switch accessory voltage supply circuit for an open or short to ground. Is the repair complete?	Go to Step 14	--
10	Inspect for poor connections at the windshield wiper motor. Did you find and correct the condition?	Go to Step 14	Go to Step 11
11	Replace the windshield wiper motor. Is the repair complete?	Go to Step 14	--
12	Inspect for poor connections at the windshield wiper/washer switch. Did you find and correct the condition?	Go to Step 14	Go to Step 13
13	Replace the windshield wiper/washer switch. Is the repair complete?	Go to Step 14	--

LTV0500000003134

Fig. 92 Wipers Inoperative, All Modes (Part 2 of 3). Blazer, Jimmy, Sonoma & S10

Step	Action	Yes	No
14	Operate the system in order to verify the repair. Did you correct the condition?	System OK	Go to Step 3

LTV0500000003135

Fig. 92 Wipers Inoperative, All Modes (Part 3 of 3). Blazer, Jimmy, Sonoma & S10

Test Description

The numbers below refer to the step numbers on the diagnostic table.

7. This step tests for continuity through the 24K ohms resistor in the windshield wiper/washer switch. The connector behind the instrument panel knee bolster is suitable for performing this step.

8. This step tests for continuity through the delay resistors in the windshield wiper/washer switch. The measured resistance will change in sequence from high to low as the delay speed is increased. The connector behind the instrument panel knee bolster is suitable for performing this step.

Step	Action	Value(s)	Yes	No
1	Did you review the Wiper/Washer System Description and Operation and perform the necessary inspections?	--	Go to Step 2	Go to Symptoms
2	1. Turn the ignition ON. 2. Operate the windshield wiper/washer switch through all the switch positions. Does the windshield wiper/washer system operate normally?	--		Go to Step 3
3	Do the windshield wipers operate in the high speed mode?	--	Go to Step 5	Go to Step 4

LTV0500000003136

Fig. 93   Wipers Inoperative, One Or More Modes (Part 1 of 4). Blazer, Jimmy, Sonoma & S10

Step	Action	Value(s)	Yes	No
4	1. Disconnect the windshield wiper motor connector. 2. Connect a test lamp from the windshield wiper motor high speed circuit terminal to ground. 3. Turn the ignition ON. 4. Operate the windshield wiper/washer switch to the high speed position. Does the test lamp illuminate?		Go to Step 14	Go to Step 9
5	1. Disconnect the windshield wiper motor connector. 2. Connect a test lamp from the windshield wiper switch signal 2 circuit terminal to ground. 3. Turn the ignition ON. 4. Press the windshield washer switch. Does the test lamp illuminate?		Go to Step 6	Go to Step 10
6	1. Connect a test lamp from the windshield wiper switch signal 1 circuit terminal to ground. 2. Operate the windshield wiper/washer switch to the following positions: - MIST - LO - HI Does the test lamp illuminate in the listed switch positions?		Go to Step 7	Go to Step 11

LTV0500000003137

Fig. 93   Wipers Inoperative, One Or More Modes (Part 2 of 4). Blazer, Jimmy, Sonoma & S10

Step	Action	Value(s)	Yes	No
7	1. Disconnect the windshield wiper/washer switch connector. 2. Measure the resistance through the windshield wiper switch from the signal 2 circuit terminal to the accessory voltage supply circuit terminal in the switch side connector. 3. Operate the windshield wiper/washer switch to the following positions: - MIST - INT - LO - HI Is the resistance at or near the specified value in all the listed switch positions?	24K ohms	Go to Step 8	Go to Step 12
8	1. Measure the resistance through the windshield wiper/washer switch from the signal 1 circuit terminal to the accessory voltage supply circuit terminal in the switch side connector. 2. Operate the windshield wiper/washer switch through all of the delay positions. Does the resistance remain within the specified values from high to low as the delay speed is increased?	38K - 690K ohms	Go to Step 14	Go to Step 12
9	Test the windshield wiper motor high speed circuit for an open or high resistance. Did you find and correct the condition?	--	Go to Step 16	Go to Step 12
10	Test the windshield wiper switch signal 2 circuit for an open or short to ground. Did you find and correct the condition?	--	Go to Step 16	Go to Step 12
11	Test the windshield wiper switch signal 1 circuit for an open or short to ground. Did you find and correct the condition?	--	Go to Step 16	Go to Step 12

LTV0500000003138

Fig. 93   Wipers Inoperative, One Or More Modes (Part 3 of 4). Blazer, Jimmy, Sonoma & S10

Step	Action	Value(s)	Yes	No
12	Inspect for poor connections at the windshield wiper/washer switch. Did you find and correct the condition?	--	Go to Step 16	Go to Step 13
13	Replace the windshield wiper/washer switch. Is the repair complete?	--	Go to Step 16	--
14	Inspect for poor connections at the windshield wiper motor. Did you find and correct the condition?	--	Go to Step 16	Go to Step 15
15	Replace the windshield wiper motor module. Is the repair complete?	--	Go to Step 16	--
16	Operate the system in order to verify the repair. Did you correct the condition?	--	System OK	Go to Step 3

LTV0500000003139

Fig. 93   Wipers Inoperative, One Or More Modes (Part 4 of 4). Blazer, Jimmy, Sonoma & S10

Step	Action	Yes	No
1	Did you review the Rear Wiper/Washer System Description and Operation and perform the necessary inspections?	Go to Step 2	Go to Symptoms
2	1. Turn the ignition ON. 2. Press the rear washer switch. Does the rear washer operate normally?	Test for Intermittent and Poor Connections	Go to Step 3
3	Does the rear wiper motor operate when the washer switch is pressed?	Go to Step 6	Go to Step 4
4	1. Disconnect the rear wiper motor connector. 2. Connect a test lamp from the rear washer control circuit terminal in the wiper motor connector to a good ground. 3. Turn the ignition ON. 4. Press the rear washer switch. Does the test lamp illuminate when the rear washer switch is pressed?	Go to Step 10	Go to Step 5
5	Test the rear washer control circuit for an open or high resistance. Did you find and correct the condition?	Go to Step 16	Go to Step 12
6	1. Disconnect the rear washer pump connector. 2. Connect a test lamp from the rear washer control circuit terminal in the washer pump harness connector to a good ground. 3. Turn the ignition ON. 4. Press the rear washer switch. Does the test lamp illuminate when the rear washer switch is pressed?	Go to Step 7	Go to Step 8

LTV0500000003140

Fig. 94   Washer Inoperative, Rear (Part 1 of 3). Blazer & Jimmy

Step	Action	Yes	No
15	Replace the rear washer pump. Is the repair complete?	Go to Step 16	--
16	Operate the system in order to verify the repair. Did you correct the condition?	System OK	Go to Step 3

LTV0500000003142

Fig. 94   Washer Inoperative, Rear (Part 3 of 3). Blazer & Jimmy

Step	Action	Yes	No
7	1. Connect a test lamp from the rear washer control circuit terminal to the ground circuit terminal in the washer pump harness connector. 2. Press the rear washer switch. Does the test lamp illuminate when the rear washer switch is pressed?	Go to Step 14	Go to Step 9
8	Repair the rear washer control circuit for an open or high resistance. Is the repair complete?	Go to Step 16	--
9	Repair the rear washer pump ground circuit for an open or high resistance. Is the repair complete?	Go to Step 16	--
10	Inspect for poor connections at the rear wiper motor. Did you find and correct the condition?	Go to Step 16	Go to Step 11
11	Replace the rear wiper motor. Is the repair complete?	Go to Step 16	--
12	Inspect for poor connections at the rear wiper/washer switch. Did you find and correct the condition?	Go to Step 16	Go to Step 13
13	Replace the rear wiper/washer switch. Is the repair complete?	Go to Step 16	--
14	Inspect for poor connections at the rear washer pump. Did you find and correct the condition?	Go to Step 16	Go to Step 15

LTV0500000003141

Fig. 94   Washer Inoperative, Rear (Part 2 of 3). Blazer & Jimmy

Test Description

The numbers below refer to the step numbers on the diagnostic table.

3. Tests the operation of the headlamp washer pump relay and circuits. If the test lamp illuminates for a few seconds the washer pump is faulty.

4. Tests the battery positive voltage supply circuit to the headlamp washer pump relay.

5. Tests the washer pump control circuit to the headlamp washer pump relay.

6. Tests the front park lamp voltage supply circuit to the headlamp washer pump relay.

Step	Action	Yes	No
	DEFINITION: The headlamp washers are inoperative, the windshield washers, and park lamps operate normal.		
1	Did you review the Headlamp Washer System Description and Operation and perform the necessary inspections?	Go to Step 2	Go to Symptoms
2	1. Turn the ignition ON. 2. Turn the headlamps ON. 3. Press the windshield washer switch. Do the headlamp washers operate normally?		Go to Step 3

LTV0500000003143

Fig. 95   Washers Inoperative, Headlamp (Part 1 of 3). Blazer, Jimmy, Sonoma & S10

Step	Action	Yes	No
3	1. Disconnect the headlamp washer pump connector. 2. Connect a test lamp across the harness connector terminals. 3. Turn the ignition ON. 4. Turn the headlamps ON. 5. Press the windshield washer switch. Does the test lamp illuminate?	Go to Step 14	Go to Step 4
4	1. Disconnect the headlamp washer pump relay. 2. Connect a test lamp from the battery positive voltage supply circuit terminal to a good ground. Does the test lamp illuminate?	Go to Step 5	Go to Step 10
5	1. Connect a test lamp from the windshield washer pump control circuit terminal to a good ground. 2. Turn the ignition ON. 3. Press the windshield washer switch. Does the test lamp illuminate?	Go to Step 6	Go to Step 11
6	1. Connect a test lamp from the front park lamp voltage supply circuit terminal to a good ground. 2. Turn the headlamp switch ON. Does the test lamp illuminate?	Go to Step 7	Go to Step 12
7	Connect a test lamp from battery positive voltage to the headlamp washer pump relay ground circuit terminal. Does the test lamp illuminate?	Go to Step 8	Go to Step 13
8	Test the headlamp washer pump supply circuit for an open or short to ground. Did you find and correct the condition?	Go to Step 18	Go to Step 9
9	Test the headlamp washer pump ground circuit for an open or high resistance. Did you find and correct the condition?	Go to Step 18	Go to Step 16
10	Repair the open or short to ground in the headlamp washer pump relay battery positive voltage supply circuit. Is the repair complete?	Go to Step 18	--

LTV0500000003144

Fig. 95   Washers Inoperative, Headlamp (Part 2 of 3). Blazer, Jimmy, Sonoma & S10

Step	Action	Yes	No
11	Repair the headlamp washer relay control circuit for an open or short to ground. Is the repair complete?	Go to Step 18	--
12	Repair the front park lamp voltage supply circuit for an open or high resistance. Did you find and correct the condition?	Go to Step 18	--
13	Repair the headlamp washer pump relay ground circuit for an open or high resistance. Is the repair complete?	Go to Step 18	--
14	Inspect for poor connections at the headlamp washer pump. Did you find and correct the condition?	Go to Step 18	Go to Step 15
15	Replace the headlamp washer pump. Is the repair complete?	Go to Step 18	--
16	Inspect for poor connections at the headlamp washer pump relay. Did you find and correct the condition?	Go to Step 18	Go to Step 17
17	Replace the headlamp washer pump relay. Is the repair complete?	Go to Step 18	--
18	Operate the system in order to verify the repair. Did you correct the condition?	System OK	Go to Step 3

LTV0500000003145

Fig. 95   Washers Inoperative, Headlamp (Part 3 of 3). Blazer, Jimmy, Sonoma & S10

Step	Action	Yes	No
1	Did you review the Rear Wiper/Washer System Description and Operation and perform the necessary inspections?	Go to Step 2	Go to Symptoms
2	1. Turn the ignition ON. 2. Turn the rear wiper/washer switch to the OFF position. Is the rear wiper always on?	Go to Step 3	Test for Intermittent and Poor Connections
3	1. Disconnect the rear wiper motor connector. 2. Turn the rear wiper/washer switch to the OFF position. 3. Connect a test lamp from the rear wiper switch signal circuit terminal in the rear wiper motor harness connector to ground. 4. Turn the ignition ON. Does the test lamp illuminate?	Go to Step 5	Go to Step 4
4	1. Connect a test lamp from the rear washer pump control circuit terminal in the rear wiper motor harness connector to ground. 2. Turn the ignition ON. Does the test lamp illuminate?	Go to Step 6	Go to Step 8
5	Test the rear wiper switch signal circuit for a short to voltage. Did you find and correct the condition?	Go to Step 9	Go to Step 7
6	Test the rear washer pump control circuit for a short to voltage. Did you find and correct the condition?	Go to Step 9	Go to Step 7
7	Replace the rear wiper/washer switch. Is the repair complete?	Go to Step 9	--

LTV0500000003146

Fig. 96   Wiper Always On, Rear (Part 1 of 2). Blazer & Jimmy

Step	Action	Yes	No
8	Replace the rear wiper motor. Is the repair complete?	Go to Step 9	--
9	Operate the system in order to verify the repair. Did you correct the condition?	System OK	Go to Step 3

LTV0500000003147

Fig. 96   Wiper Always On, Rear (Part 2 of 2). Blazer & Jimmy

Step	Action	Values	Yes	No
	DEFINITION: The rear wiper motor is inoperative in one or more modes, the rear washer pump may or may not operate.			
1	Did you review the Rear Wiper/Washer System Description and Operation and perform the necessary inspections?	--	Go to Step 2	Go to Symptoms
2	1. Turn the ignition ON. 2. Operate the rear wiper/washer system in all the switch positions. Does the rear wiper/washer system operate normally?	--		Go to Step 3
3	Does the rear wiper motor operate when the rear washer switch is pressed?	--	Go to Step 6	Go to Step 4
4	1. Disconnect the rear wiper motor connector. 2. Connect a test lamp from the rear wiper motor accessory voltage supply circuit terminal in the wiper motor harness connector to a good ground. 3. Turn the ignition ON. Does the test lamp illuminate?	--	Go to Step 5	Go to Step 9
5	1. Connect a test lamp from the rear wiper motor accessory voltage supply circuit terminal to the ground circuit terminal in the wiper motor harness connector. 2. Turn the ignition ON. Does the test lamp illuminate?	--	Go to Step 6	Go to Step 10

LTV0500000003148

Fig. 97 Wiper Inoperative, Rear (Part 1 of 3). Blazer & Jimmy

Step	Action	Values	Yes	No
6	1. Disconnect the rear wiper motor connector. 2. Connect a test lamp from the rear wiper switch signal circuit terminal in the wiper motor harness connector to ground. 3. Turn the ignition ON. 4. Operate the rear wiper/washer switch to the LO position. Does the test lamp illuminate?		Go to Step 7	Go to Step 8
7	1. Disconnect the rear wiper/washer switch connector. 2. Operate the rear wiper/washer switch to the HI position. 3. Measure the resistance through the rear wiper/washer switch from the accessory voltage supply circuit terminal to the rear wiper switch signal circuit terminal. Is the resistance at or near the specified value?	1000 ohms	Go to Step 14	Go to Step 13
8	Test the rear wiper switch signal circuit for an open or short to ground. Did you find and correct the condition?	--	Go to Step 16	Go to Step 11
9	Repair the rear wiper motor accessory voltage supply circuit for an open or short to ground. Is the repair complete?	--	Go to Step 16	--
10	Repair the rear wiper motor ground circuit for an open or high resistance. Is the repair complete?	--	Go to Step 16	--
11	Test the rear wiper/washer switch accessory voltage supply circuit for an open or short to ground. Did you find and correct the condition?	--	Go to Step 16	Go to Step 12
12	Inspect for poor connections at the rear wiper/washer switch. Did you find and correct the condition?	--	Go to Step 16	Go to Step 13

LTV0500000003149

Fig. 97 Wiper Inoperative, Rear (Part 2 of 3). Blazer & Jimmy

Step	Action	Values	Yes	No
13	Replace the rear wiper/washer switch. Is the repair complete?	- -	Go to Step 16	--
14	Inspect for poor connections at the rear wiper motor. Did you find and correct the condition?	- -	Go to Step 16	Go to Step 15
15	Replace the rear wiper motor. Is the repair complete?	- -	Go to Step 16	--
16	Operate the system in order to verify the repair. Did you correct the condition?	- -	System OK	Go to Step 3

LTV0500000003150

Fig. 97 Wiper Inoperative, Rear (Part 3 of 3). Blazer & Jimmy

Circuit Description

The rear wiper motor is supplied battery positive voltage and ground. The liftgate control module controls rear wiper motor operation through the rear wiper motor control circuit. The rear wiper motor control circuit is supplied a battery positive reference voltage by the rear wiper motor module and is pulse width modulated to ground by the liftgate control module. The duty cycle of the pulse width modulation determines the rear wiper motor operating mode.

Conditions for Running the DTC

Battery voltage must be between 9-16 volts.

Conditions for Setting the DTC

The rear wiper motor control circuit is shorted to voltage.

Action Taken When the DTC Sets

The rear wiper/washer system will be disabled for as long as the DTC is current.

Conditions for Clearing the DTC

- The DTC will be current for as long as the fault is present and it will be latched for the respective ignition cycle.
- A history DTC will be cleared after 100 error free ignition cycles.

Step	Action	Value(s)	Yes	No
1	Did you perform the Wiper/Washer System Diagnostic System Check?	--	Go to Step 2	Go to Diagnostic System Check

LTV0500000003517

Fig. 98 Codes B1017 & B3970: Rear Wiper Motor Control Circuit (Part 1 of 3). Bravada, Envoy, Rainier & Trailblazer

Step	Action		Yes	No
2	1. Turn ON the ignition, with the engine OFF. 2. Attempt to operate the rear wiper motor through all of the operating modes. Does the rear wiper motor operate normally?	--	Test for Intermittent and Poor Connections	Go to Step 3
3	1. Disconnect the rear wiper motor connector. 2. Connect a test lamp from the battery positive voltage supply circuit terminal in the harness connector to a good ground. Does the test lamp illuminate?	--	Go to Step 4	Go to Step 8
4	Connect a test lamp from the battery positive voltage supply circuit terminal to the ground circuit terminal in the rear wiper motor harness connector. Does the test lamp illuminate?	--	Go to Step 5	Go to Step 9
5	1. Connect the rear wiper motor connector. 2. Disconnect the liftgate control module connector. 3. Using a DMM measure the voltage at the rear wiper motor control circuit terminal in the liftgate control module harness connector. Is the voltage within the specified values?	10-14 V	Go to Step 6	Go to Step 7
6	Test the rear wiper motor control circuit for high resistance. Did you find and correct the condition?	--	Go to Step 14	Go to Step 12
7	Test the rear wiper motor control circuit for an open or short to ground. Did you find and correct the condition?	--	Go to Step 14	Go to Step 10

LTV0500000003518

Fig. 98 Codes B1017 & B3970: Rear Wiper Motor Control Circuit (Part 2 of 3). Bravada, Envoy, Rainier & Trailblazer

Circuit Description

The headlamp washer switch signal circuit is supplied a 12-volt reference through a resistor then monitored within the body control module (BCM). The headlamp washer switch is open when in an inactive state. When the headlamp washer switch is activated the signal circuit is closed to ground. When the headlamp washer switch signal circuit is closed to ground the reference voltage is dropped across the resistor within the BCM. The low voltage on the headlamp washer switch signal circuit indicates to the BCM the switch status is active.

Conditions for Running the DTC

- Battery voltage must be between 9.0-16.0 volts.
- The headlamp washer switch is active.

Conditions for Setting the DTC

The headlamp washer switch signal to the BCM is low longer than 10 seconds.

Action Taken When the DTC Sets

- The DTC will be current for as long as the fault is present.
- The headlamp washers will be disabled for as long as the DTC is current.

Conditions for Clearing the DTC

- The DTC status will change form current to history when the fault is no longer present.
- A history DTC will be cleared after 100 error free ignition cycles.

LTV0500000003520

Fig. 99 Code B2697: Headlamp Washer Switch Signal Circuit (Part 1 of 3). Bravada, Envoy, Rainier & Trailblazer

Step	Action		Yes	No
8	Repair the battery positive voltage circuit to the rear wiper motor. Did you complete the repair?	-	Go to Step 14	--
9	Repair the rear wiper motor ground circuit for an open or high resistance. Did you complete the repair?	-	Go to Step 14	--
10	Inspect for poor connections at the harness connector of the rear wiper motor. Did you find and correct the condition?	-	Go to Step 14	Go to Step 11
11	Replace the rear wiper motor. Did you complete the replacement?	-	Go to Step 14	--
12	Inspect for poor connections at the harness connector of the liftgate control module. Did you find and correct the condition?	-	Go to Step 14	Go to Step 13
13	**Important** Perform the setup procedure for the liftgate control module. Replace the liftgate control module. Did you complete the replacement?	-	Go to Step 14	--
14	1. Use the scan tool in order to clear the DTCs. 2. Operate the system in order to verify the repair. Does the DTC reset?	-	Go to Step 2	System OK

LTV0500000003519

Fig. 98 Codes B1017 & B3970: Rear Wiper Motor Control Circuit (Part 3 of 3). Bravada, Envoy, Rainier & Trailblazer

Test Description

The numbers below refer to the step numbers on the diagnostic table.

2. This step verifies that the fault is current.

3. This step verifies the switch input to the BCM.

4. This step determines if the fault is in the headlamp washer switch. If the switch input to the BCM changes to an inactive state when disconnected the switch contacts are stuck or shorted to ground.

Step	Action	Yes	No
1	Did you perform the Wiper/Washer System Diagnostic System Check?	Go to Step 2	Go to Diagnostic System Check
2	1. Install a scan tool. 2. Turn ON the ignition, with the engine OFF. 3. With a scan tool, observe the headlamp washer switch parameter in the BCM inputs data list. Does the scan tool display OFF?	Go to Step 3	Go to Step 4
3	1. Activate the headlamp washer switch. 2. With the scan tool, observe the headlamp washer switch parameter. Does the headlamp washer switch parameter change state?	Test for Intermittent and Poor Connections	Go to Step 4

LTV0500000003521

Fig. 99 Code B2697: Headlamp Washer Switch Signal Circuit (Part 2 of 3). Bravada, Envoy, Rainier & Trailblazer

4	1. Turn OFF the ignition. 2. Disconnect the headlamp washer switch. 3. Turn ON the ignition, with the engine OFF. 4. With a scan tool, observe the headlamp washer switch parameter. Does the scan tool display OFF?		Go to Step 7	Go to Step 5
5	Test the signal circuit of the headlamp washer switch for a short to ground. Did you find and correct the condition?		Go to Step 10	Go to Step 6
6	Inspect for poor connections at the harness connector of the BCM. Did you find and correct the condition?		Go to Step 10	Go to Step 8
7	Inspect for poor connections at the harness connector of the headlamp washer switch. Did you find and correct the condition?		Go to Step 10	Go to Step 9
8	Important Perform the setup procedure for the BCM. Replace the BCM. Did you complete the replacement?		Go to Step 10	--
9	Replace the headlamp washer switch. Did you complete the replacement?		Go to Step 10	--
10	1. Use the scan tool in order to clear the DTCs. 2. Operate the system in order to verify the repair. Does the DTC reset?		Go to Step 2	System OK

LTV0500000003522

Fig. 99 Code B2697: Headlamp Washer Switch Signal Circuit (Part 3 of 3). Bravada, Envoy, Rainier & Trailblazer

Test Description

The numbers below refer to the step numbers on the diagnostic table.

2. This step verifies that the fault is current.

3. This step tests the resistance through the rear wiper switch. The measured resistance will be highest in the OFF position and reduce as the switch is turned from positions 1 through 3.

Step	Action	Value(s)	Yes	No
1	Did you perform the Wiper/Washer System Diagnostic System Check?	--	Go to Step 2	Go to Diagnostic System Check
2	1. Install a scan tool. 2. Turn ON the ignition, with the engine OFF. 3. Operate the rear wiper/washer switch through all the switch positions. 4. With a scan tool, observe the requested rear wiper parameter. Does the scan too indicate the correct requested rear wiper parameter in relation to the switch position?	--	Test for Intermittent and Poor Connections	Go to Step 3

LTV0500000003524

Fig. 100 Code B3799: Rear Wiper/Washer Switch Power Circuit (Part 2 of 4). Bravada, Envoy, Rainier & Trailblazer

Circuit Description

The switch power circuit to the rear wiper/washer switch is a 12-volt reference supplied by the body control module. The rear wiper/washer switch is a series of resistors and the switch position is determined by the voltage of the rear wiper/washer switch signal circuit to the body control module. The rear wiper/washer switch has continuity at all times and the body control module expects a rear wiper/washer switch signal voltage in all switch positions including OFF.

Conditions for Running the DTC

- Battery voltage must be between 9.0-16.0 volts.
- The rear wiper/washer switch is active or inactive.

Conditions for Setting the DTC

The rear wiper/washer switch signal circuit is higher or lower than normal switch operation allows.

Action Taken When the DTC Sets

- The DTC will be current for as long as the fault is present.
- The rear wiper/washer system will be disabled for as long as the DTC is current.

Conditions for Clearing the DTC

- The DTC status will change from current to history when the fault is no longer present.
- A history DTC will be cleared after 100 error free ignition cycles.

LTV0500000003523

Fig. 100 Code B3799: Rear Wiper/Washer Switch Power Circuit (Part 1 of 4). Bravada, Envoy, Rainier & Trailblazer

3	1. Disconnect the rear wiper/washer switch. 2. Measure the resistance through the rear wiper/washer switch from the switch power circuit terminal to the signal circuit terminal. 3. Operate the rear wiper/washer switch through the following switch positions: - OFF - 1 - 2 - 3 Does the resistance remain within the specified values from high to low as the switch is operated through the listed switch positions?	3100-1500 ohms	Go to Step 4	Go to Step 8
4	While measuring the resistance through the rear wiper/washer switch from the switch power circuit terminal to the signal circuit terminal press the wash switch. Is the resistance near the specified value?	1270 ohms	Go to Step 5	Go to Step 8
5	Test the switch power circuit to the rear wiper/washer switch for an open, short to ground, or short to voltage. Did you find and correct the condition?	--	Go to Step 11	Go to Step 6
6	Test the rear wiper/washer switch signal circuit to the rear wiper switch for an open, short to ground, or short to voltage. Did you find and correct the condition?	--	Go to Step 11	Go to Step 7
7	Inspect for poor connections at the harness connector of the body control module. Did you find and correct the condition?	--	Go to Step 11	Go to Step 9

LTV0500000003525

Fig. 100 Code B3799: Rear Wiper/Washer Switch Power Circuit (Part 3 of 4). Bravada, Envoy, Rainier & Trailblazer

8	Inspect for poor connections at the harness connector of the rear wiper/washer switch. Did you find and correct the condition?	Go to Step 11	Go to Step 10
9	**Important:** Replace the body control module and perform the programing procedure. Did you complete the replacement?	Go to Step 11	--
10	Replace the rear wiper/washer switch. Did you complete the replacement?	Go to Step 11	--
11	1. Use the scan tool in order to clear the DTCs. 2. Operate the system in order to verify the repair. Does the DTC reset?	Go to Step 2	System OK

LTV0500000003526

Fig. 100   Code B3799: Rear Wiper/Washer Switch Power Circuit (Part 4 of 4). Bravada, Envoy, Rainier & Trailblazer

Test Description

The numbers below refer to the step numbers on the diagnostic table.

3. Tests for battery positive voltage to the high side of the relay coil. The WASH fuse supplies power to the headlamp washer and rear washer relays.

4. Tests the ability of the BCM to energize the relay.

5. Tests for a condition which causes the relay to remain energized at all times.

Step	Action	Yes	No
1	Did you perform the Wiper/Washer System Diagnostic System Check?	Go to Step 2	Go to Diagnostic System Check
2	1. Install a scan tool. 2. Turn ON the ignition, with the engine OFF. 3. With a scan tool, command the relay ON and OFF. 4. Refer to Electrical Center Identification Views in Wiring Systems for relay location. Does the relay turn ON and OFF with each command?	Test for Intermittent and Poor Connections	Go to Step 3

LTV0500000003528

Fig. 101   Codes B3810 & B3811: Washer Relay Control Circuit (Part 2 of 4). Bravada, Envoy, Rainier & Trailblazer

Circuit Description

Battery positive voltage is supplied to the coil and switch sides of the rear washer and headlamp washer relays. The BCM energizes a relay by grounding the relay coil through the relay control circuit. When a relay is energized the relay switch is closed and battery positive voltage is supplied to the washer pump control circuit.

Conditions for Running the DTC

Battery voltage must be between 9-16 volts.

Conditions for Setting the DTC

- B3810 - the headlamp washer relay control circuit is shorted to ground or open while the relay is de-energized, or shorted to B+ while the relay is energized.
- B3811 - the rear washer relay control circuit is shorted to ground or open while the relay is de-energized, or shorted to B+ while the relay is energized.

Action Taken When the DTC Sets

- The DTC will be current for as long as the fault is present.
- The headlamp washers will be disabled for as long as the B3810 is current.
- The rear washers will be disabled for as long as the B3811 is current.

Conditions for Clearing the DTC

- A current DTC clears when the malfunction is no longer present.
- A history DTC clears when the module ignition cycle counter reaches the reset threshold, without a repeat of the malfunction.

LTV0500000003527

Fig. 101   Codes B3810 & B3811: Washer Relay Control Circuit (Part 1 of 4). Bravada, Envoy, Rainier & Trailblazer

3	1. Turn OFF the ignition. 2. Disconnect the relay. 3. Turn ON the ignition, with the engine OFF. 4. Probe the battery positive voltage circuit of the relay with a test lamp that is connected to a good ground. Does the test lamp illuminate?	Go to Step 4	Go to Step 10
4	1. Connect a test lamp between the control circuit of the relay and the battery positive voltage circuit of the relay. 2. With a scan tool, command the relay ON and OFF. Does the test lamp turn ON and OFF with each command?	Go to Step 8	Go to Step 5
5	Does the test lamp remain illuminated with each command?	Go to Step 7	Go to Step 6
6	Test the control circuit of the relay for a short to voltage or an open. Did you find and correct the condition?	Go to Step 13	Go to Step 9
7	Test the control circuit of the relay for a short to ground. Did you find and correct the condition?	Go to Step 13	Go to Step 9
8	Inspect for poor connections at the relay. Did you find and correct the condition?	Go to Step 13	Go to Step 11

LTV0500000003529

Fig. 101   Codes B3810 & B3811: Washer Relay Control Circuit (Part 3 of 4). Bravada, Envoy, Rainier & Trailblazer

Step	Action	Yes	No
9	Inspect for poor connections at the harness connector of the BCM. Did you find and correct the condition?	Go to Step 13	Go to Step 12
10	Repair the battery positive voltage circuit of the relay. Did you complete the repair?	Go to Step 13	--
11	Replace the relay. Did you complete the replacement?	Go to Step 13	--
12	**Important** Perform the setup procedure for the BCM. Replace the BCM Did you complete the replacement?	Go to Step 13	--
13	1. Use the scan tool in order to clear the DTCs. 2. Operate the system in order to verify the repair. Does the DTC reset?	Go to Step 2	System OK

LTV0500000003530

Fig. 101 Codes B3810 & B3811: Washer Relay Control Circuit (Part 4 of 4). Bravada, Envoy, Rainier & Trailblazer

Step	Action	Yes	No
6	Test the washer fluid level switch signal circuit for a short to ground. Did you find and correct the condition?	Go to Step 13	Go to Step 11
7	Test the washer fluid level switch signal circuit for an open or high resistance. Did you find and correct the condition?	Go to Step 13	Go to Step 11
8	Test the washer fluid level switch ground circuit for an open or high resistance. Did you find and correct the condition?	Go to Step 13	Go to Step 9
9	Inspect for poor connections at the washer fluid level switch. Did you find and correct the condition?	Go to Step 13	Go to Step 10
10	Replace the washer fluid level switch. Did you complete the replacement?	Go to Step 13	--
11	Inspect for poor connections at the instrument panel cluster. Did you find and correct the condition?	Go to Step 13	Go to Step 12
12	Important. Perform the setup procedure for the instrument panel cluster. Replace the instrument panel cluster. Did you complete the replacement?	Go to Step 13	--
13	Operate the system in order to verify the repair. Did you correct the condition?	System OK	Go to Step 3

LTV0500000003534

Fig. 102 Low Washer Fluid Indicator Fault (Part 2 of 2). Bravada, Envoy, Rainier & Trailblazer

Step	Action	Yes	No
	DEFINITION: The check washer fluid message is always displayed or does not display with low washer fluid.		
1	Did you perform the Wiper/Washer System Diagnostic System Check?	Go to Step 2	Go to Diagnostic System Check
2	Verify the fault is present. Does the system operate normally?		Go to Step 3
3	1. Turn the ignition OFF. 2. Disconnect the washer fluid level switch connector. 3. Turn the ignition ON. Is the check washer fluid message displayed on the driver information center?	Go to Step 6	Go to Step 4
4	1. Turn the ignition OFF. 2. Connect a fused jumper wire from the washer fluid level switch signal circuit terminal in the washer fluid level switch connector to a good ground. 3. Turn the ignition ON. Is the check washer fluid message displayed on the driver information center?	Go to Step 5	Go to Step 7
5	1. Turn the ignition OFF. 2. Connect a fused jumper wire across the washer fluid level switch harness connector terminals. 3. Turn the ignition ON. Is the check washer fluid message displayed on the driver information center?	Go to Step 9	Go to Step 8

LTV0500000003533

Fig. 102 Low Washer Fluid Indicator Fault (Part 1 of 2). Bravada, Envoy, Rainier & Trailblazer

Step	Action	Yes	No
	DEFINITION: The windshield washer pump is always on.		
1	Did you perform the Wiper/Washer System Diagnostic System Check?	Go to Step 2	Go to Diagnostic System Check
2	1. Turn the windshield wiper/washer switch to the OFF position. 2. Turn the ignition ON. Is the windshield washer pump always on?	Go to Step 3	Test for Intermittent and Poor Connections
3	Are the windshield wipers always on?	Go to Step 4	Go to Step 5
4	1. Disconnect the windshield wiper motor connector. 2. Connect a test lamp from the windshield wiper switch signal 1 circuit terminal to ground. 3. Turn the ignition ON. Does the test lamp illuminate?	Go to Step 7	Go to Step 10
5	Disconnect the windshield washer relay. Is the windshield washer pump on?	Go to Step 12	Go to Step 6
6	Connect a test lamp from the control circuit of the windshield washer relay to battery voltage. Does the test lamp illuminate?	Go to Step 8	Go to Step 11
7	Test the windshield wiper switch signal 1 circuit for a short to voltage. Did you find and correct the condition?	Go to Step 16	Go to Step 9
8	Test the windshield washer relay control circuit for a short to ground. Did you find and correct the condition?	Go to Step 16	Go to Step 10

LTV0500000003535

Fig. 103 Washers Always On (Part 1 of 2). Bravada, Envoy, Rainier & Trailblazer

Step	Action	Yes	No
9	Inspect for poor connections at the windshield wiper/washer switch. Did you find and correct the condition?	Go to Step 16	Go to Step 13
10	Inspect for poor connections at the windshield wiper motor. Did you find and correct the condition?	Go to Step 16	Go to Step 14
11	Inspect for poor connections at the windshield washer relay. Did you find and correct the condition?	Go to Step 16	Go to Step 15
12	Repair the windshield washer pump control circuit for a short to voltage. Is the repair complete?	Go to Step 16	--
13	Replace the windshield wiper/washer switch. Did you complete the replacement?	Go to Step 16	--
14	Replace the windshield wiper motor cover. Did you complete the replacement?	Go to Step 16	--
15	Replace the windshield washer relay. Did you complete the replacement?	Go to Step 16	--
16	Operate the system in order to verify the repair. Did you correct the condition?	System OK	Go to Step 3

LTV0500000003536

Fig. 103 Washers Always On (Part 2 of 2). Bravada, Envoy, Rainier & Trailblazer

Step	Action	Yes	No
6	1. Disconnect the windshield washer relay. 2. Connect a test lamp test from each of the windshield washer relay battery positive voltage supply circuit terminals in the underhood fuse block to ground. Does the test lamp illuminate on both terminals?	Go to Step 7	Go to Step 9
7	1. Connect a test lamp from battery positive voltage to the windshield washer relay control circuit terminal in the underhood fuse block. 2. Turn the ignition ON. 3. Press the windshield washer switch. Does the test lamp illuminate?	Go to Step 8	Go to Step 10
8	1. Connect the windshield washer relay. 2. Disconnect the windshield washer pump connector. 3. Connect a test lamp across the windshield washer pump harness connector terminals. 4. Turn the ignition ON. 5. Press the windshield washer switch. Does the test lamp illuminate?	Go to Step 18	Go to Step 11
9	Replace the underhood fuse block. Did you complete the replacement?	Go to Step 20	--
10	Test the windshield washer relay control circuit for an open or high resistance. Did you find and correct the condition?	Go to Step 20	Go to Step 15
11	Test the windshield washer pump control circuit for an open or high resistance. Did you find and correct the condition?	Go to Step 20	Go to Step 12
12	Test the windshield washer pump ground circuit for an open or high resistance. Did you find and correct the condition?	Go to Step 20	Go to Step 17
13	Inspect for poor connections at the windshield wiper/washer switch. Did you find and correct the condition?	Go to Step 20	Go to Step 14

LTV0500000003538

Fig. 104 Washers Inoperative (Part 2 of 3). Bravada, Envoy, Rainier & Trailblazer

Step	Action	Value(s)	Yes	No
1	Did you perform the Wiper/Washer System Diagnostic System Check?	--	Go to Step 2	Go to Diagnostic System Check -
2	1. Turn the ignition ON. 2. Press the windshield washer switch. Do the windshield washers operate normally?	--	Test for Intermittent and Poor Connections	Go to Step 3
3	Do the windshield washer wipers operate when the windshield washer switch is pressed?	--	Go to Step 6	Go to Step 4
4	1. Disconnect the windshield wiper motor connector. 2. Test the resistance from the windshield wiper switch supply voltage circuit terminal to the windshield wiper switch signal 1 circuit terminal in the windshield wiper motor harness connector. 3. Press the windshield washer switch. Is the resistance near the specified value?	0.5 ohms	Go to Step 15	Go to Step 5
5	Test the following circuits for high resistance. • Windshield wiper switch supply voltage circuit • Windshield wiper switch signal 1 circuit. Did you find and correct the condition?		Go to Step 20	Go to Step 13

LTV0500000003537

Fig. 104 Washers Inoperative (Part 1 of 3). Bravada, Envoy, Rainier & Trailblazer

Step	Action	Yes	No
14	Replace the windshield wiper/washer switch. Did you complete the replacement?	Go to Step 20	--
15	Inspect for poor connections at the windshield wiper motor. Did you find and correct the condition?	Go to Step 20	Go to Step 16
16	Replace the windshield wiper motor cover. Did you complete the replacement?	Go to Step 20	--
17	Replace the windshield washer relay. Did you complete the replacement?	Go to Step 20	--
18	Inspect for poor connections at the windshield washer pump. Did you find and correct the condition?	Go to Step 20	Go to Step 19
19	Replace the windshield washer pump. Did you complete the replacement?	Go to Step 20	--
20	Operate the system in order to verify the repair. Did you correct the condition?	System OK	Go to Step 3

LTV0500000003539

Fig. 104 Washers Inoperative (Part 3 of 3). Bravada, Envoy, Rainier & Trailblazer

Step	Action	Yes	No
1	Did you perform the Wiper/Washer System Diagnostic System Check?	Go to Step 2	Go to Diagnostic System Check
2	1. Turn the windshield wiper/washer switch OFF. 2. Turn the ignition ON. Are the windshield wipers always on?	Go to Step 3	Test for Intermittent and Poor Connections
3	1. Disconnect the steering column harness connector. 2. Remove the connector terminal row E from the steering column connector half. 3. Connect the steering column harness connector. 4. Turn the ignition ON. Are the windshield wipers always on?	Go to Step 4	Go to Step 6
4	Test the windshield wiper switch high signal circuit for a short to ground. Did you find and correct the condition?	Go to Step 12	Go to Step 5
5	Test the windshield wiper switch signal 1 circuit for a short to voltage. Did you find and correct the condition?	Go to Step 12	Go to Step 9
6	Test the windshield wiper switch high signal circuit in the steering column harness for a short to ground. Did you find and correct the condition?	Go to Step 12	Go to Step 7
7	Test the windshield wiper switch signal 1 circuit in the steering column harness for a short to voltage. Did you find and correct the condition?	Go to Step 12	Go to Step 8

LTV0500000003540

Fig. 105 Wipers Always On (Part 1 of 2). Bravada, Envoy, Rainier & Trailblazer

Step	Action	Yes	No
8	Inspect for poor connections at the windshield wiper/washer switch. Did you find and correct the condition?	Go to Step 12	Go to Step 10
9	Inspect for poor connections at the windshield wiper motor cover. Did you find and correct the condition?	Go to Step 12	Go to Step 11
10	Replace the windshield wiper/washer switch. Did you complete the replacement?	Go to Step 12	--
11	Replace the windshield wiper motor cover. Did you complete the replacement?	Go to Step 12	--
12	Operate the system in order to verify the repair. Did you correct the condition?	System OK	Go to Step 3

LTV0500000003541

Fig. 105 Wipers Always On (Part 2 of 2). Bravada, Envoy, Rainier & Trailblazer

Step	Action	Yes	No
	DEFINITION: Windshield wipers are inoperative in all modes.		
1	Did you perform the Wiper/Washer Diagnostic System Check?	Go to Step 2	Go to Diagnostic System Check
2	1. Turn ON the ignition. 2. Attempt to operate the windshield wipers in all modes. Are the windshield wipers inoperative in all modes?	Go to Step 3	Test for Intermittent and Poor Connections
3	1. Turn OFF the ignition. 2. Disconnect the windshield wiper motor connector. 3. Turn ON the ignition. 4. Connect a test lamp between the accessory voltage supply circuit terminal and the ground circuit terminal of windshield wiper motor in the windshield wiper motor harness connector. Does the test lamp illuminate?	Go to Step 4	Go to Step 7
4	Connect a test lamp from the accessory voltage supply circuit terminal in the windshield wiper motor harness connector to a good ground. Does the test lamp illuminate?	Go to Step 5	Go to Step 8
5	1. Remove the wiper motor cover from the wiper motor. 2. Connect a test lamp from the wiper motor ground terminal T3 to the low speed supply terminal T1 on the wiper motor cover. 3. With the harness connector connected to the wiper motor cover operate the wiper switch to the low speed position. Does the test lamp illuminate for approximately 15 seconds?	Go to Step 10	Go to Step 6

LTV0500000003542

Fig. 106 Wipers Inoperative, All Modes (Part 1 of 2). Bravada, Envoy, Rainier & Trailblazer

Step	Action	Yes	No
6	Inspect for poor connections at the windshield wiper motor connector. Did you find and correct the condition?	Go to Step 11	Go to Step 9
7	Repair an open or short to ground in the accessory voltage supply circuit to the windshield wiper motor. Is the repair complete?	Go to Step 11	--
8	Repair an open or high resistance in the windshield wiper motor ground circuit. Is the repair complete?	Go to Step 11	--
9	Replace the windshield wiper motor cover. Is the repair complete?	Go to Step 11	--
10	Replace the windshield wiper motor. Is the repair complete?	Go to Step 11	--
11	Operate the system in order to verify the repair. Did you correct the condition?	System OK	Go to Step 3

LTV0500000003543

Fig. 106 Wipers Inoperative, All Modes (Part 2 of 2). Bravada, Envoy, Rainier & Trailblazer

WIPER SYSTEMS

<u>Test Description</u>

The numbers below refer to the step numbers on the diagnostic table.

5. This step tests for continuity through the 390 ohms resistor in the windshield wiper/washer switch.

6. This step tests for continuity through the delay resistors in the windshield wiper/washer switch. The measured resistance will change in sequence from low to high as the delay speed is increased.

Step	Action	Value(s)	Yes	No
1	Did you perform the Wiper/Washer System Diagnostic System Check?	--	Go to Step 2	Go to Diagnostic System Check
2	1. Turn the ignition ON. 2. Attempt to operate the windshield wipers in all modes. Does the system operate normally?	--	Test for Intermittent and Poor Connections	Go to Step 3
3	Do the windshield wipers operate in the high speed mode?	--	Go to Step 5	Go to Step 4
4	1. Disconnect the steering column harness connector. 2. Connect a fused jumper wire from the windshield wiper switch high signal circuit terminal in the body harness connector half to a good ground. 3. Turn the ignition ON. Do the windshield wipers operate at high speed?	--	Go to Step 8	Go to Step 7

LTV0500000003544

Fig. 107 Wipers Inoperative, One Or More Modes (Part 1 of 3). Bravada, Envoy, Rainier & Trailblazer

Step	Action	Value(s)	Yes	No
5	1. Disconnect the windshield wiper motor connector. 2. Test the resistance from the windshield wiper switch voltage supply circuit terminal to the windshield wiper switch signal 1 circuit terminal in the windshield wiper motor harness connector. 3. Operate the windshield wiper/washer switch in the following positions: - MIST - LO Is the resistance near the specified value in the listed switch positions?	380 ohms	Go to Step 6	Go to Step 10
6	1. Test the resistance from the windshield wiper switch voltage supply circuit terminal to the windshield wiper switch signal 1 circuit terminal in the windshield wiper motor harness connector. 2. Operate the windshield wiper/washer switch in all of the delay positions. Does the resistance remain within the specified values from low to high as the delay speed is increased?	1000 ohms-10K ohms	Go to Step 14	Go to Step 12
7	Test the windshield wiper switch high signal circuit for an open or high resistance. Did you find and correct the condition?	--	Go to Step 16	Go to Step 14
8	Test the wiper switch ground circuit for an open or high resistance. Did you find and correct the condition?		Go to Step 16	Go to Step 9
9	Test the windshield wiper switch high signal and ground circuits in the steering column harness for an open or high resistance. Did you find and correct the condition?	--	Go to Step 16	Go to Step 12

LTV0500000003545

Fig. 107 Wipers Inoperative, One Or More Modes (Part 2 of 3). Bravada, Envoy, Rainier & Trailblazer

Step	Action		Yes	No
10	Test the windshield wiper switch voltage supply circuit for an open or short to ground. Did you find and correct the condition?	-	Go to Step 16	Go to Step 11
11	Test the windshield wiper switch signal 1 circuit for an open or high resistance. Did you find and correct the condition?	-	Go to Step 16	Go to Step 12
12	Inspect for poor connections at the windshield wiper/washer switch. Did you find and correct the condition?	-	Go to Step 16	Go to Step 13
13	Replace the windshield wiper/washer switch. Did you complete the replacement?	-	Go to Step 16	--
14	Inspect for poor connections at the windshield wiper motor. Did you find and correct the condition?	-	Go to Step 16	Go to Step 15
15	Replace the windshield wiper motor cover. Did you complete the replacement?	-	Go to Step 16	--
16	Operate the system in order to verify the repair. Did you correct the condition?	-	System OK	Go to Step 3

LTV0500000003546

Fig. 107 Wipers Inoperative, One Or More Modes (Part 3 of 3). Bravada, Envoy, Rainier & Trailblazer

Step	Action	Yes	No
1	Did you perform the Wiper/Washer System Diagnostic System Check?	Go to Step 2	Go to Diagnostic System Check -
2	Verify the fault is present. Does the system operate normally?		Go to Step 3
3	While the windshield wiper/washer system is in the automatic mode does the wiper motor operate at continuous delay intervals?	Go to Step 5	Go to Step 4
4	1. Turn the ignition ON. 2. Operate the windshield wiper/washer switch from the OFF position through all of the delay positions. Does the wiper motor cycle once and stop every time the switch is advanced to the next delay position?	Go to Step 5	Diagnose Wipers Inoperative - One or More Modes
5	1. Disconnect the windshield wipers motor connector. 2. Ensure the outside surface of the windshield in the area of the moisture sensor is clean and dry. 3. Using a DMM, measure the voltage of the moisture sensor signal circuit in the wiper motor harness connector. Does the signal circuit voltage level stabilize at approximately 5 volts?	Go to Step 6	Go to Step 7

LTV0500000003547

Fig. 108 Moisture Sensing Feature Inoperative (Part 1 of 3). Bravada, Envoy, Rainier & Trailblazer

6	While measuring the voltage of the moisture sensor signal circuit, spray water on the outside surface of the windshield in the area of the moisture sensor. Does the signal circuit voltage level fluctuate?	Go to Step 13	Go to Step 9
7	1. Disconnect the moisture sensor connector. 2. Connect a test lamp from the accessory voltage supply circuit terminal in the harness connector to a good ground. Does the test lamp illuminate?	Go to Step 8	Go to Step 10
8	Connect a test lamp from the accessory voltage supply circuit terminal to the ground circuit terminal in the moisture sensor harness connector. Does the test lamp illuminate?	Go to Step 9	Go to Step 11
9	Test the moisture sensor signal 1 circuit for an open, short to ground, or short to voltage. Did you find and correct the condition?	Go to Step 16	Go to Step 12
10	Repair the accessory voltage supply circuit to the moisture sensor for an open or short to ground. Is the repair complete?	Go to Step 16	--
11	Repair the moisture sensor ground circuit for an open or high resistance. Is the repair complete?	Go to Step 16	--
12	Inspect for poor connections at the moisture sensor. Did you find and correct the condition?	Go to Step 16	Go to Step 14
13	Inspect for poor connections at the windshield wiper motor cover. Did you find and correct the condition?	Go to Step 16	Go to Step 15

LTV0500000003548

Fig. 108 Moisture Sensing Feature Inoperative (Part 2 of 3). Bravada, Envoy, Rainier & Trailblazer

Step	Action	Yes	No
	DEFINITION: The rear window washer is always ON and the rear window wiper operates normally.		
1	Did you perform the Wiper/Washer System Diagnostic System Check?	Go to Step 2	Go to Diagnostic System Check
2	Turn the ignition ON. Is the rear washer always on?	Go to Step 3	Test for Intermittent and Poor Connections
3	1. Disconnect the rear washer relay. 2. Turn the ignition ON. Is the rear washer always on?	Go to Step 5	Go to Step 4
4	Inspect for poor connections at the rear washer relay. Did you find and correct the condition?	Go to Step 7	Go to Step 6
5	Repair the rear washer pump control circuit for a short to voltage. Is the repair complete?	Go to Step 7	--
6	Replace the rear washer relay. Did you complete the replacement?	Go to Step 7	--
7	Operate the system in order to verify the repair. Did you correct the condition?	System OK	Go to Step 3

LTV0500000003550

Fig. 109 Washer Always On, Rear. Bravada, Envoy, Rainier & Trailblazer

14	Replace the moisture sensor. Did you complete the replacement?	Go to Step 16	--
15	Replace the windshield wiper motor cover. Did you complete the replacement?	Go to Step 16	--
16	Operate the system in order to verify the repair. Did you correct the condition?	System OK	Go to Step 2

LTV0500000003549

Fig. 108 Moisture Sensing Feature Inoperative (Part 3 of 3). Bravada, Envoy, Rainier & Trailblazer

Step	Action	Yes	No
	DEFINITION: The rear window washer is inoperative and the rear window wiper operates normally.		
1	Did you perform the Wiper/Washer System Diagnostic System Check?	Go to Step 2	Go to Diagnostic System Check
2	1. Turn the ignition ON. 2. Press the rear window washer switch. Does the rear window washer operate normally?		Go to Step 3
3	1. Disconnect the rear washer pump connector. 2. Connect a test lamp across the rear washer pump harness connector terminals. 3. Turn the ignition ON. 4. Press the rear window washer switch. Does the test lamp illuminate?	Go to Step 6	Go to Step 4
4	Test the rear washer pump control circuit for an open or high resistance. Did you find and correct the condition?	Go to Step 9	Go to Step 5
5	Test the rear washer pump ground circuit for an open or high resistance. Did you find and correct the condition?	Go to Step 9	Go to Step 8

LTV0500000003551

Fig. 110 Washer Inoperative, Rear (Part 1 of 2). Bravada, Envoy, Rainier & Trailblazer

6	Inspect for poor connections at the rear washer pump. Did you find and correct the condition?	Go to Step 9	Go to Step 7
7	Replace the rear washer pump. Did you complete the replacement?	Go to Step 9	--
8	Replace the rear washer relay. Did you complete the replacement?	Go to Step 9	--
9	Operate the system in order to verify the repair. Did you correct the condition?	System OK	Go to Step 3

LTV0500000003552

Fig. 110 Washer Inoperative, Rear (Part 2 of 2). Bravada, Envoy, Rainier & Trailblazer

Step	Action	Yes	No
	DEFINITION: The headlamp washers are inoperative.		
1	Did you perform the Wiper/Washer System Diagnostic System Check?	Go to Step 2	Go to Diagnostic System Check -
2	1. Turn the ignition ON. 2. Press the headlamp washer switch. Do the headlamp washers operate normally?	Test for Intermittent and Poor Connections	Go to Step 3
3	1. Install a scan tool. 2. Display the body controller inputs data list. 3. Press the headlamp washer switch. Does the scan tool indicate the headlamp washer switch is ON?	Go to Step 6	Go to Step 4
4	Test the headlamp washer switch signal circuit for an open or high resistance. Did you find and correct the condition?	Go to Step 14	Go to Step 5
5	Test the headlamp washer switch ground circuit for an open or high resistance. Did you find and correct the condition?	Go to Step 14	Go to Step 9

LTV0500000003553

Fig. 111 Washers Inoperative, Headlamp (Part 1 of 2). Bravada, Envoy, Rainier & Trailblazer

Test Description

The numbers below refer to the step numbers on the diagnostic table.

3. If any of the liftgate or liftglass switch fails ajar the rear wiper will not operate.

4. This step determines if the liftgate control module is receiving the correct switch position message from the body control module.

5. This step determines if the liftgate control module is attempting to operate rear wiper motor in the requested operating mode.

6. This step tests the resistance through the rear wiper switch. The measured resistance will be highest in the OFF position and reduce as the switch is turned from positions 1 through 3.

Step	Action	Value(s)	Yes	No
	DEFINITION: One or more of the rear wiper operating modes are inoperative.			
1	Did you perform the Wiper/Washer System Diagnostic System Check?	--	Go to Step 2	Go to Diagnostic System Check -
2	1. Turn the ignition ON. 2. Operate the rear wiper switch through all the switch positions. Does the rear window wiper operate normally?	--	Test for Intermittent and Poor Connections	Go to Step 3

LTV0500000003555

Fig. 112 Wiper Inoperative, Rear (Part 1 of 5). Bravada, Envoy, Rainier & Trailblazer

Step	Action	Yes	No
6	1. Disconnect the headlamp washer pump connector. 2. Connect a test lamp across the headlamp washer pump harness connector terminals. 3. Turn the ignition ON. 4. Press the headlamp washer switch. Does the test lamp illuminate?	Go to Step 11	Go to Step 7
7	Test the headlamp washer pump control circuit for an open or high resistance. Did you find and correct the condition?	Go to Step 14	Go to Step 8
8	Test the headlamp washer pump ground circuit for an open or high resistance. Did you find and correct the condition?	Go to Step 14	Go to Step 13
9	Inspect for poor connections at the headlamp washer switch. Did you find and correct the condition?	Go to Step 14	Go to Step 10
10	Replace the headlamp washer switch. Did you complete the replacement?	Go to Step 14	--
11	Inspect for poor connections at the headlamp washer pump. Did you find and correct the condition?	Go to Step 14	Go to Step 12
12	Replace the headlamp washer pump. Did you complete the replacement?	Go to Step 14	--
13	Replace the headlamp washer relay. Did you complete the replacement?	Go to Step 14	--
14	Operate the system in order to verify the repair. Did you correct the condition?	System OK	Go to Step 3

LTV0500000003554

Fig. 111 Washers Inoperative, Headlamp (Part 2 of 2). Bravada, Envoy, Rainier & Trailblazer

3	1. Install a scan tool. 2. Display the liftgate control module data list. 3. Observe the following parameters while operating the respective switches. Refer to Scan Tool Data List for typical values. - Liftgate Ajar Switch - Liftglass Ajar Switch Did the scan tool indicate the correct switch positions?	Go to Step 4	Diagnose Courtesy Lamps Inoperative
4	1. Observe the requested rear wiper parameter in LGM data list. 2. Operate the rear wiper switch through all the switch positions. Does the scan tool indicate the correct requested rear wiper parameter in relation to the switch position?	Go to Step 5	Go to Step 6
5	1. Close the liftglass and liftgate. 2. Observe the rear wiper mode parameter. 3. Operate the rear wiper switch through all the switch positions. Does the scan tool indicate the correct rear wiper mode parameter in relation to the switch position?	Go to Step 7	Go to Step 18

LTV0500000003556

Fig. 112 Wiper Inoperative, Rear (Part 2 of 5). Bravada, Envoy, Rainier & Trailblazer

6	1. Turn the ignition OFF.
	2. Disconnect the rear wiper switch.
	3. Measure the resistance through the rear wiper switch from the switch power circuit terminal to the signal circuit terminal.
	4. Operate the rear wiper switch through the following switch positions:
	
	  - OFF
	  - 1
	  - 2
	  - 3
	
	Does the resistance remain within the specified values from OFF to 3 as the switch is operated through the listed switch positions?
		3100-1500 ohms	Go to Step 15	Go to Step 11

7	1. Turn the ignition OFF. 2. Disconnect the rear wiper motor connector. 3. Test the rear wiper motor battery voltage supply circuit for an open or short to ground. Did you find and correct the condition?	--	Go to Step 20	Go to Step 8
8	Test the rear wiper motor ground circuit for an open or high resistance. Did you find and correct the condition?	--	Go to Step 20	Go to Step 9
9	1. Connect a test lamp between battery voltage circuit and the control circuit of the rear wiper motor connector. 2. Close the liftglass and liftgate. 3. Turn ON the ignition with the engine OFF. 4. Turn the rear wiper switch from OFF to 3. Did the brightness of the test lamp decrease gradually as the rear wiper switch was turned from OFF to 3?	--	Go to Step 13	Go to Step 10

LTV0500000003557

Fig. 112 Wiper Inoperative, Rear (Part 3 of 5). Bravada, Envoy, Rainier & Trailblazer

18	Inspect for poor connections at the liftgate control module. Did you find and correct the condition?	-	Go to Step 20	Go to Step 19
19	**Important:** Perform the setup procedure for the liftgate control module. Replace the liftgate control module. Is the repair complete?	-	Go to Step 20	--
20	Operate the system in order to verify the repair. Did you correct the condition?	-	System OK	Go to Step 4

LTV0500000003559

Fig. 112 Wiper Inoperative, Rear (Part 5 of 5). Bravada, Envoy, Rainier & Trailblazer

10	Test the rear wiper motor control circuit for an open, a short to ground or a short to voltage. Did you find and correct the condition?	-	Go to Step 20	Go to Step 18
11	Inspect for poor connections at the rear wiper switch. Did you find and correct the condition?	-	Go to Step 20	Go to Step 12
12	Replace the rear wiper switch. Is the repair complete?	-	Go to Step 20	--
13	Inspect for poor connections at the rear wiper motor. Did you find and correct the condition?	-	Go to Step 20	Go to Step 14
14	Replace the rear wiper motor. Is the repair complete?	-	Go to Step 20	--
15	Test the rear window wiper switch signal circuit for an open or short to ground. Did you find and correct the condition?	-	Go to Step 20	Go to Step 16
16	Inspect for poor connections at the BCM. Did you find and correct the condition?	-	Go to Step 20	Go to Step 17
17	Important: Perform the setup procedure for the BCM. Replace the BCM. Is the repair complete?	-	Go to Step 20	--

LTV0500000003558

Fig. 112 Wiper Inoperative, Rear (Part 4 of 5). Bravada, Envoy, Rainier & Trailblazer

Circuit Description

The body control module (BCM) controls and monitors the state of the WIPER relay control circuit. When the windshield wiper switch is placed in to a low speed setting, a signal is applied to the BCM. The BCM then applies battery positive voltage to the coil side of the WIPER relay through the relay control circuit. This energizes the relay, allowing battery positive voltage from the WIPER fuse through the switched side of the WIPER relay through the WIPER 2 relay and to the windshield wiper motor. Ground is applied at all times to the coil sides of the wiper relays and the windshield wiper motor from G105.

DTC Descriptors

This diagnostic procedure supports the following DTCs:

- DTC B3717 Front Wiper Relay Drive Circuit Low
- DTC B3718 Front Wiper Relay Drive Circuit High

Conditions for Running the DTCs

- The ignition is ON.
- The ignition voltage is between 9-18.5 volts.

Conditions for Setting the DTCs

The following conditions will cause these DTCs to set:

- DTC B3717, the BCM detects a low voltage level on the supply circuit of the wiper micro relay for 1 second when the relay is energized.
- DTC B3718, the BCM detects a high voltage level on the supply circuit of the wiper micro relay for 1 second when the relay is de-energized.

Action Taken When the DTC Sets

The BCM de-energizes the wiper micro relay, until the wiper switch is turned OFF and ON.

LTV0500000003153

Fig. 113 Codes B3715, B3716, B3717, B3718 & B3719: Front Wiper Relay Drive Circuit Low/High (Part 1 of 4). Canyon & Colorado

WIPER SYSTEMS

Conditions for Clearing the DTCs

- DTC B3717 will change from current to history when the windshield wiper switch is turned OFF and ON, and the condition is no longer present.
- DTC B3718 will change from current to history when the condition is no longer present.
- A history DTC will clear after 100 ignition cycles, without a repeat of the malfunction.

Step	Action	Yes	No
1	Did you perform the Diagnostic System Check - Vehicle?	Go to Step 2	Go to Diagnostic System Check -
2	1. Turn the ignition to the ON position. 2. Turn the wiper switch to the low position. Do the windshield wipers operate?	Test for Intermittent and Poor Connections	Go to Step 3
3	1. Turn the ignition to the OFF position. 2. Turn the wiper switch OFF. 3. Remove the WIPER relay from the underhood fuse block. 4. Using a test lamp connected to ground, probe the relay control circuit at the underhood fuse block. Does the test lamp illuminate?	Go to Step 8	Go to Step 4
4	1. Leave the test lamp connected. 2. Turn the ignition to the ON position. 3. Turn the wiper switch to the low position. NOTE: Test lamp should illuminate for 3 seconds then turn off. Does the test lamp illuminate?	Go to Step 5	Go to Step 6

LTV0500000003154

Fig. 113 Codes B3715, B3716, B3717, B3718 & B3719: Front Wiper Relay Drive Circuit Low/High (Part 2 of 4). Canyon & Colorado

Step	Action	Yes	No
8	Repair a short to battery positive voltage in the WIPER relay control circuit. Did you complete the repair?	Go to Step 12	--
9	1. Replace the WIPER relay. 2. Operate the vehicle within the Conditions for Running the DTC. Does the DTC reset?	Go to Step 11	Go to Step 12
10	Replace the body control module (BCM). Did you complete the replacement?	Go to Step 12	--
11	Replace the underhood electrical center. Did you complete the replacement?	Go to Step 12	--
12	1. Use the scan tool in order to clear the DTCs. 2. Operate the vehicle within the Conditions For Running the DTC as specified in the supporting text. Does the DTC reset?	Go to Step 2	System OK

LTV0500000003156

Fig. 113 Codes B3715, B3716, B3717, B3718 & B3719: Front Wiper Relay Drive Circuit Low/High (Part 4 of 4). Canyon & Colorado

Step	Action	Yes	No
5	1. Turn the wiper switch to the OFF position. 2. Turn the ignition to the OFF position. 3. Using a test lamp, probe the relay control circuit and the ground circuit of the relay at the underhood fuse block. 4. Turn the ignition to the ON position. 5. Turn the wiper switch to the low position. Does the test lamp illuminate?	Go to Step 9	Go to Step 7
6	Test for the following in the WIPER relay control circuit: • A poor connection • An open • A short to ground Refer to Circuit Testing and Wiring Repairs . Did you find and correct the condition?	Go to Step 12	Go to Step 10
7	Test for a poor connection or an open in the ground circuit of the WIPER relay. Refer to Circuit Testing and Wiring Repairs . Did you find and correct the condition?	Go to Step 12	Go to Step 11

LTV0500000003155

Fig. 113 Codes B3715, B3716, B3717, B3718 & B3719: Front Wiper Relay Drive Circuit Low/High (Part 3 of 4). Canyon & Colorado

Step	Action	Yes	No
1	Did you perform the Diagnostic System Check - Vehicle?	Go to Step 2	Go to Diagnostic System Check
2	1. Turn ON the ignition, with the engine OFF. 2. Ensure that the windshield washer switch is OFF. Is the windshield washer pump ON?	Go to Step 3	Test for Intermittent and Poor Connections
3	Disconnect the windshield wiper/washer switch connector. Do the windshield washers stop?	Go to Step 6	Go to Step 4
4	1. Disconnect the body control module (BCM) J2 connector. 2. Test the windshield washer pump control circuit from the switch for a short to voltage. Did you find and correct the condition?	Go to Step 8	Go to Step 5
5	1. Disconnect the BCM J1 connector. 2. Test the windshield washer pump control circuit to the pump for a short to voltage. Did you find and correct the condition?	Go to Step 8	Go to Step 7
6	Replace the windshield wiper/washer switch. Did you complete the replacement?	Go to Step 8	--

LTV0500000003158

Fig. 114 Washers Always On (Part 1 of 2). Canyon & Colorado

		Yes	No
7	Replace the BCM. Did you complete the replacement?	Go to Step 8	--
8	Operate the system in order to verify the repair. Did you correct the condition?	System OK	Go to Step 3

LTV0500000003159

Fig. 114   Washers Always On (Part 2 of 2). Canyon & Colorado

		Yes	No
5	1. Disconnect the body control module (BCM) J2 connector. 2. Probe the windshield washer switch signal circuit with a test lamp connected to a good ground. 3. Press the windshield washer switch. Does the test lamp illuminate?	Go to Step 12	Go to Step 8
6	Test the windshield washer pump ground circuit for an open or high resistance. Did you find and correct the condition?	Go to Step 16	Go to Step 10
7	1. Disconnect the BCM J1 connector. 2. Test the windshield washer pump control circuit for an open or high resistance. Did you find and correct the condition?	Go to Step 16	Go to Step 12
8	1. Disconnect the windshield washer switch. 2. Test the windshield washer switch voltage supply circuit for an open or high resistance. Did you find and correct the condition?	Go to Step 16	Go to Step 9
9	Test the windshield washer switch signal circuit for an open or high resistance. Did you find and correct the condition?	Go to Step 16	Go to Step 11
10	Inspect for poor connections at the windshield washer pump. Did you find and correct the condition?	Go to Step 16	Go to Step 13
11	Inspect for poor connections at the windshield wiper/washer switch. Did you find and correct the condition?	Go to Step 16	Go to Step 14
12	Inspect for poor connections at the BCM. Did you find and correct the condition?	Go to Step 16	Go to Step 15

LTV0500000003161

Fig. 115   Washers Inoperative (Part 2 of 3). Canyon & Colorado

		Yes	No
13	Replace the windshield washer pump. Did you complete the replacement?	Go to Step 16	--
14	Replace the windshield wiper/washer switch. Did you complete the replacement?	Go to Step 16	--
15	Replace the BCM. Did you complete the replacement?	Go to Step 16	--
16	Operate the system in order to verify the repair. Did you correct the condition?	System OK	Go to Step 3

LTV0500000003162

Fig. 115   Washers Inoperative (Part 3 of 3). Canyon & Colorado

Step	Action	Yes	No
1	Did you perform the Diagnostic System Check - Vehicle?	Go to Step 2	Go to Diagnostic System Check -
2	1. Turn ON the ignition, with the engine OFF. 2. Press the windshield washer switch. Does the windshield washer pump operate?	Test for Intermittent and Poor Connections	Go to Step 3
3	1. Observe the Wash Switch parameter with a scan tool. 2. Press the windshield washer switch. Does the scan tool indicate the Wash Switch is ON?	Go to Step 4	Go to Step 5
4	1. Disconnect the windshield washer pump connector. 2. Probe the windshield washer pump control circuit with a test lamp connected to a good ground. 3. Press the windshield washer switch. Does the test lamp illuminate?	Go to Step 6	Go to Step 7

LTV0500000003160

Fig. 115   Washers Inoperative (Part 1 of 3). Canyon & Colorado

Step	Action	Yes	No
	DEFINITION: The windshield wiper motor operates when the windshield wiper switch is OFF.		
1	Did you perform the Diagnostic System Check - Vehicle?	Go to Step 2	Go to Diagnostic System Check -
2	1. Turn ON the ignition, with the engine OFF. 2. Ensure that the windshield wiper switch is OFF. Does the windshield wiper motor operate?	Go to Step 3	Test for Intermittent and Poor Connections
3	Observe the Wiper Delay Input parameter with a scan tool. Is Wiper Delay Input 0.00 volts?	Go to Step 4	Go to Step 9
4	Observe the Washer Switch parameter with the scan tool. Is Washer Switch OFF?	Go to Step 5	Go to Step 10
5	Remove the wiper diode. Does the windshield wiper motor continue to operate?	Go to Step 6	Go to Step 8
6	Remove the wiper micro relay. Does the windshield wiper motor continue to operate?	Go to Step 7	Go to Step 11
7	Remove the wiper 2 relay. Does the windshield wiper motor continue to operate?	Go to Step 16	Go to Step 20

LTV0500000003163

Fig. 116   Wipers Always On (Part 1 of 3). Canyon & Colorado

Step	Action	Yes	No
8	1. Install the wiper diode. 2. Disconnect the windshield wiper switch. Does the windshield wiper motor continue to operate?	Go to Step 15	Go to Step 19
9	1. Disconnect the windshield wiper switch. 2. Observe the Wiper Delay Input parameter with a scan tool. Is Wiper Delay Input 0.00 volts?	Go to Step 19	Go to Step 13
10	1. Disconnect the windshield wiper switch. 2. Observe the Washer Switch parameter with the scan tool. Is the washer switch OFF?	Go to Step 19	Go to Step 14
11	Probe the windshield wiper switch signal 2 circuit from the body control module (BCM) with a test lamp connected to a good ground. Does the test lamp illuminate?	Go to Step 12	Go to Step 18
12	1. Disconnect the underhood fuse block J7 connector. 2. Probe the windshield wiper switch signal 2 circuit from the BCM with a test lamp connected to a good ground. Does the test lamp illuminate?	Go to Step 17	Go to Step 20
13	1. Disconnect the BCM. 2. Test the windshield wiper switch signal 1 circuit for a short to voltage. Did you find and correct the condition?	Go to Step 22	Go to Step 21
14	1. Disconnect the BCM. 2. Test the windshield washer pump control circuit between the BCM and the wiper switch for a short to voltage. Did you find and correct the condition?	Go to Step 22	Go to Step 21
15	1. Disconnect the underhood fuse block J7 connector. 2. Test the windshield wiper switch signal 2 circuit between the wiper switch and the fuse block for a short to voltage. Did you find and correct the condition?	Go to Step 22	Go to Step 20

LTV0500000003164

Fig. 116   Wipers Always On (Part 2 of 3). Canyon & Colorado

Step	Action	Yes	No
16	1. Disconnect the underhood fuse block J7 connector. 2. Test the windshield wiper motor high speed circuit and the windshield wiper motor low speed circuit for a short to voltage. Did you find and correct the condition?	Go to Step 22	Go to Step 20
17	1. Disconnect the BCM. 2. Test the windshield wiper switch signal 2 circuit between the BCM and the fuse block for a short to voltage. Did you find and correct the condition?	Go to Step 22	Go to Step 21
18	Replace the wiper micro relay. Did you complete the replacement?	Go to Step 22	--
19	Replace the windshield wiper switch. Did you complete the replacement?	Go to Step 22	--
20	Replace the underhood fuse block. Did you complete the replacement?	Go to Step 22	--
21	Replace the BCM. Did you complete the replacement?	Go to Step 22	--
22	1. Reconnect all disconnected components. 2. Clear the DTCs with the scan tool. 3. Operate the system in order to verify the repair. Did you correct the condition?	System OK	Go to Step 2

LTV0500000003165

Fig. 116   Wipers Always On (Part 3 of 3). Canyon & Colorado

Step	Action	Yes	No
	DEFINITION: The windshield wiper motor will not operate in any mode.		
1	Did you perform the Diagnostic System Check - Vehicle? Go to Step 2		Go to Diagnostic System Check
2	1. Turn ON the ignition. 2. Attempt to operate the wipers in each mode. Do the windshield wipers operate in any mode?	Test for Intermittent and Poor Connections	Go to Step 3
3	Are the DTCs B3717 or B3718 stored in the body control module (BCM)?	Go to DTC B3715, B3716, B3717, B3718, or B3719	Go to Step 4
4	1. Turn the wiper switch to the high speed position. 2. Disconnect the windshield wiper motor. 3. Probe the windshield wiper motor high and low speed circuits with a test lamp connected to a good ground. Does the test lamp illuminate for either circuit?	Go to Step 14	Go to Step 5
5	1. Remove the wiper 2 relay from the underhood fuse block. 2. Probe the windshield wiper switch signal 2 circuit from the wiper switch with a test lamp connected to a good ground. Does the test lamp illuminate?	Go to Step 6	Go to Step 10

LTV0500000003166

Fig. 117   Wipers Inoperative, All Modes (Part 1 of 4). Canyon & Colorado

Step	Action	Yes	No
6	Probe the common switched terminal of the wiper 2 relay with a test lamp connected to a good ground. Does the test lamp illuminate?	Go to Step 13	Go to Step 7
7	1. Remove the wiper micro relay from the underhood fuse block. 2. Probe the windshield wiper switch signal 2 circuit from the BCM with a test lamp connected to a good ground. Does the test lamp illuminate?	Go to Step 8	Go to Step 12
8	Connect a test lamp between the windshield wiper switch signal 2 circuit from the BCM and the coil ground circuit. Does the test lamp illuminate?	Go to Step 9	Go to Step 24
9	Probe the wiper micro relay voltage supply circuit with a test lamp connected to a good ground. Does the test lamp illuminate?	Go to Step 16	Go to Step 22
10	1. Disconnect the underhood fuse block J7 connector. 2. Probe the windshield wiper switch signal 2 circuit from the BCM with a test lamp connected to a good ground. Does the test lamp illuminate?	Go to Step 21	Go to Step 11
11	1. Disconnect the wiper/washer switch. 2. Probe the wiper switch voltage supply circuit with a test lamp connected to a good ground. Does the test lamp illuminate?	Go to Step 15	Go to Step 23
12	1. Remove the wiper diode from the underhood fuse block. 2. Connect a 3-amp fused jumper between the diode terminals of the underhood fuse block. 3. Probe the windshield wiper switch signal 2 circuit from the BCM with a test lamp connected to a good ground. Does the test lamp illuminate?	Go to Step 18	Go to Step 30
13	Test the windshield wiper motor high and low speed circuits for an open or a high resistance. Did you find and correct the condition?	Go to Step 31	Go to Step 17

LTV0500000003167

Fig. 117   Wipers Inoperative, All Modes (Part 2 of 4). Canyon & Colorado

	Action	Yes	No
14	Test the windshield wiper motor ground circuit for an open or a high resistance. Did you find and correct the condition?	Go to Step 31	Go to Step 19
15	Test the windshield wiper switch signal 2 circuit from the switch for an open or a high resistance. Did you find and correct the condition?	Go to Step 31	Go to Step 20
16	Inspect for poor connections at the wiper 2 relay. Did you find and correct the condition?	Go to Step 31	Go to Step 25
17	Inspect for poor connections at the wiper 2 relay. Did you find and correct the condition?	Go to Step 31	Go to Step 26
18	Inspect for poor connections at the wiper diode. Did you find and correct the condition?	Go to Step 31	Go to Step 27
19	Inspect for poor connections at the windshield wiper motor. Did you find and correct the condition?	Go to Step 31	Go to Step 28
20	Inspect for poor connections at the windshield wiper/washer switch. Did you find and correct the condition?	Go to Step 31	Go to Step 29
21	Inspect for poor connections at the windshield wiper/washer switch. Did you find and correct the condition?	Go to Step 31	Go to Step 30

LTV0500000003168

Fig. 117 Wipers Inoperative, All Modes (Part 3 of 4). Canyon & Colorado

	Action	Yes	No
22	Repair the open or high resistance in the wiper micro relay voltage supply circuit. Did you complete the repair?	Go to Step 31	--
23	Repair the open or high resistance in the wiper/washer switch voltage supply circuit. Did you complete the repair?	Go to Step 31	--
24	Repair the open or high resistance in the wiper micro relay ground circuit. Did you complete the repair?	Go to Step 31	--
25	Replace the wiper micro relay. Did you complete the replacement?	Go to Step 31	--
26	Replace the wiper 2 relay. Did you complete the replacement?	Go to Step 31	--
27	Replace the wiper diode. Did you complete the replacement?	Go to Step 31	--
28	Replace the windshield wiper motor. Did you complete the replacement?	Go to Step 31	--
29	Replace the windshield wiper/washer switch. Did you complete the replacement?	Go to Step 31	--
30	Replace the underhood fuse block. Did you complete the replacement?	Go to Step 31	--
31	Operate the system in order to verify the repair. Did you correct the condition?	System OK	Go to Step 2

LTV0500000003169

Fig. 117 Wipers Inoperative, All Modes (Part 4 of 4). Canyon & Colorado

Step	Action	Yes	No
1	Did you perform the Diagnostic System Check - Vehicle?	Go to Step 2	Go to Diagnostic System Check
2	Are DTCs B3717 or B3718 stored in the body control module (BCM)?	Go to DTC B3715, B3716, B3717, B3718, or B3719	Go to Step 3
3	1. Turn ON the ignition. 2. Attempt to operate the wipers in each mode. Do the windshield wipers operate correctly in any mode?	Go to Step 4	Diagnose Wipers Inoperative - All Modes
4	Turn the wiper switch to the high speed position. Do the windshield wipers operate at high speed?	Go to Step 5	Go to Step 15
5	1. Turn the wiper switch to the low speed position. 2. Wait 5 seconds. Do the windshield wipers operate at low speed after 5 seconds?	Go to Step 6	Go to Step 9
6	Turn the wiper switch through each delay position. Do the windshield wipers operate correctly in each delay position?	Go to Step 7	Go to Step 33
7	Turn the wiper switch to the mist position. Do the windshield wipers operate at low speed?	Go to Step 8	Go to Step 33

LTV0500000003170

Fig. 118 Wipers Inoperative, One Or More Modes (Part 1 of 6). Canyon & Colorado

	Action	Yes	No
8	Turn the wiper switch to the wash position. Do the windshield wipers operate at low speed?	Test for Intermittent and Poor Connections	Go to Step 11
9	1. Turn the wiper switch to the low speed position. 2. Observe the Wiper Delay Input parameter with a scan tool. Is the Wiper Delay Input equal to 0.00 volts?	Go to Step 21	Go to Step 10
10	Observe the Wiper Relay Cmd. parameter with a scan tool. Is the Wiper Relay Cmd. ON?	Go to Step 13	Go to Step 12
11	1. Turn the wiper switch to the wash position. 2. Observe the Washer Switch parameter with a scan tool. Is the Washer Switch ON?	Go to Step 35	Go to Step 20
12	1. Disconnect the windshield wiper motor. 2. Jumper the windshield wiper motor park switch signal circuit to a good ground with a 3-amp fused jumper. 3. Observe the Wiper Park Switch parameter with a scan tool. Is the Wiper Park Switch Active?	Go to Step 32	Go to Step 28
13	1. Disconnect the windshield wiper motor. 2. Probe the windshield wiper motor low speed circuit with a test lamp connected to a good ground. Does the test lamp illuminate?	Go to Step 32	Go to Step 14
14	1. Remove the wiper 2 relay from the underhood fuse block. 2. Probe the wiper 2 relay voltage supply circuit with a test lamp connected to a good ground. Does the test lamp illuminate?	Go to Step 24	Go to Step 23

LTV0500000003171

Fig. 118 Wipers Inoperative, One Or More Modes (Part 2 of 6). Canyon & Colorado

Step			
15	1. Disconnect the windshield wiper motor. 2. Turn the wiper switch to the high speed position. 3. Probe the windshield wiper motor high speed circuit with a test lamp connected to a good ground. Does the test lamp illuminate?	Go to Step 32	Go to Step 16
16	1. Remove the wiper 2 relay from the underhood fuse block. 2. Probe the windshield wiper switch signal 2 circuit from the wiper switch with a test lamp connected to a good ground. Does the test lamp illuminate?	Go to Step 17	Go to Step 22
17	Connect a test lamp between the windshield wiper switch signal 2 circuit from the wiper switch and the wiper 2 relay coil ground circuit. Does the test lamp illuminate?	Go to Step 18	Go to Step 34
18	Probe the wiper 2 relay voltage supply circuit with a test lamp connected to a good ground. Does the test lamp illuminate?	Go to Step 24	Go to Step 19
19	1. Remove the wiper diode from the underhood fuse block. 2. Probe the windshield wiper switch signal 2 circuit from the wiper switch with a test lamp connected to a good ground. Does the test lamp illuminate?	Go to Step 31	Go to Step 34
20	1. Disconnect the BCM. 2. Probe the windshield washer pump control circuit from the wiper switch with a test lamp connected to a good ground. Does the test lamp illuminate?	Go to Step 35	Go to Step 29

LTV0500000003172

Fig. 118   Wipers Inoperative, One Or More Modes (Part 3 of 6). Canyon & Colorado

Step			
21	1. Disconnect the BCM. 2. Probe the windshield wiper switch signal 1 circuit with a test lamp connected to a good ground. Does the test lamp illuminate?	Go to Step 35	Go to Step 25
22	1. Disconnect the underhood fuse block J7 connector. 2. Probe the windshield wiper switch signal 2 circuit from the wiper switch with a test lamp connected to a good ground. Does the test lamp illuminate?	Go to Step 34	Go to Step 26
23	1. Disconnect the underhood fuse block J7 connector. 2. Probe the windshield wiper switch signal 2 circuit from the BCM with a test lamp connected to a good ground. Does the test lamp illuminate?	Go to Step 34	Go to Step 27
24	Test the windshield wiper motor high and low speed circuits for an open or a high resistance. Did you find and correct the condition?	Go to Step 42	Go to Step 30
25	Test the windshield wiper switch signal 1 circuit for an open or a high resistance. Did you find and correct the condition?	Go to Step 42	Go to Step 33
26	Test the windshield wiper switch signal 2 circuit from the wiper switch for an open or a high resistance. Did you find and correct the condition?	Go to Step 42	Go to Step 33
27	Test the windshield wiper switch signal 2 circuit from the BCM for an open or a high resistance. Did you find and correct the condition?	Go to Step 42	Go to Step 35
28	Test the windshield wiper motor park switch signal circuit for an open or a high resistance. Did you find and correct the condition?	Go to Step 42	Go to Step 35

LTV0500000003173

Fig. 118   Wipers Inoperative, One Or More Modes (Part 4 of 6). Canyon & Colorado

Step			
29	Test the windshield washer pump control circuit from the wiper switch for an open or a high resistance. Did you find and correct the condition?	Go to Step 42	Go to Step 33
30	Inspect for poor connections at the wiper 2 relay. Did you find and correct the condition?	Go to Step 42	Go to Step 36
31	Inspect for poor connections at the wiper diode. Did you find and correct the condition?	Go to Step 42	Go to Step 37
32	Inspect for poor connections at the windshield wiper motor. Did you find and correct the condition?	Go to Step 42	Go to Step 38
33	Inspect for poor connections at the windshield wiper/washer switch. Did you find and correct the condition?	Go to Step 42	Go to Step 39
34	Inspect for poor connections at the underhood fuse block. Did you find and correct the condition?	Go to Step 42	Go to Step 40
35	Inspect for poor connections at the BCM. Did you find and correct the condition?	Go to Step 42	Go to Step 41
36	Replace the wiper 2 relay. Did you complete the replacement?	Go to Step 42	--
37	Replace the wiper diode. Did you complete the replacement?	Go to Step 42	--

LTV0500000003174

Fig. 118   Wipers Inoperative, One Or More Modes (Part 5 of 6). Canyon & Colorado

Step			
38	Replace the windshield wiper motor. Did you complete the replacement?	Go to Step 42	--
39	Replace the windshield wiper/washer switch. Did you complete the replacement?	Go to Step 42	--
40	Replace the underhood fuse block. Did you complete the replacement?	Go to Step 42	--
41	Replace the BCM. Did you complete the replacement?	Go to Step 42	--
42	Operate the system in order to verify the repair. Did you correct the condition?	System OK	Go to Step 2

LTV0500000003175

Fig. 118   Wipers Inoperative, One Or More Modes (Part 6 of 6). Canyon & Colorado

Circuit Description

The intermittent switch in the windshield wiper washer switch is a voltage divider connected across the body control module (BCM) inputs circuits windshield wiper switch signal circuit and windshield wiper switch low reference circuit. The front wiper relay is energized by the BCM switching the front wiper relay control circuit to ground.

The intermittent wiper delay switch has 3 switch positions.

- Delay 1 (500 ohms resistance)
- Delay 2 (1000 ohms resistance)
- Delay 3 (2000 ohms resistance)

DTC Descriptor

This diagnostic procedure supports the following DTC:

DTC B3702 Intermittent Wiper Delay Input Circuit Low

Conditions for Running the DTC

The ignition is in RUN or ACC position.

Conditions for Setting the DTC

The windshield wiper switch signal circuit is shorted to ground or less than 0.20 volts.

Actions Taken When the DTC Sets

- No light will illuminate in the instrument panel (I/P).
- Cannot vary wiper speed
- B3702 is set in the BCM.

LTV0500000003193

Fig. 119   Code B3702: Intermittent Wiper Delay Input Circuit Low (Part 1 of 3). Equinox & Torrent

3	1. Turn OFF the ignition. 2. Disconnect the windshield wiper washer switch. 3. Turn ON the ignition, with the engine OFF. 4. With a scan tool, observe the wiper delay input in the BCM wiper/washer data list. Is the voltage greater than the specified value?	4.5 V	Go to Step 6	Go to Step 4
4	1. Turn OFF the ignition. 2. Disconnect the BCM connector C2. 3. Check continuity between the windshield wiper switch signal circuit and ground, then between the windshield wiper switch signal circuit and the windshield wiper low reference circuit. Is there continuity?	--	Go to Step 5	Go to Step 7
5	Repair a short to ground in the windshield wiper switch signal circuit. Did you complete the repair?	--	Go to Step 8	--
6	Replace the windshield wiper washer switch. Did you complete the replacement?	--	Go to Step 8	--
7	Replace the BCM. Did you complete the replacement?	--	Go to Step 8	--
8	1. Use the scan tool to clear the DTCs. 2. Operate the vehicle within the conditions for running the DTC, as specified in the supporting text. Does the DTC reset?	--	Go to Step 2	System OK

LTV0500000003195

Fig. 119   Code B3702: Intermittent Wiper Delay Input Circuit Low (Part 3 of 3). Equinox & Torrent

Conditions for Clearing the DTC

- A current DTC clears when the fault is no longer present.
- A history DTC clears when the module ignition cycle counter reaches the reset threshold, without a repeat of the fault.

Diagnostic Aids

- Inspect wiring harness for damage. Inspect for broken or chaffed insulation.
- If fault is suspected to be intermittent, wiggling harness wiring may help in locating fault.
- Inspect for poor connection at the BCM. Inspect harness connectors for backed out terminals, improper terminal mating, broken connector locks, improperly formed or damaged terminals and poor terminal-to-wire connection, terminal is crimped over wire insulation and not conductors.

Step	Action	Values	Yes	No
1	Did you perform the Diagnostic System Check - Vehicle?	--	Go to Step 2	Go to Diagnostic System Check
2	1. Turn ON the ignition, with the engine OFF. 2. With a scan tool, observe the wiper delay input in the body control module (BCM) wiper/washer data list. Is the voltage less than the specified value?	0.4 V	Go to Step 3	Go to Diagnostic Aids

LTV0500000003194

Fig. 119   Code B3702: Intermittent Wiper Delay Input Circuit Low (Part 2 of 3). Equinox & Torrent

Circuit Description

The intermittent switch in the windshield wiper washer switch is a voltage divider connected across the body control module (BCM) inputs circuits, windshield wiper switch signal circuit, and windshield wiper switch low reference circuit. The front wiper relay is energized by the BCM switching the front wiper relay control circuit to ground.

The intermittent wiper delay switch has 3 switch positions.

- Delay 1 (500 ohms resistance)
- Delay 2 (1000 ohms resistance)
- Delay 3 (2000 ohms resistance)

DTC Descriptor

This diagnostic procedure supports the following DTC:

DTC B3703 Intermittent Wiper Delay Input Circuit High

Conditions for Running the DTC

The ignition is in RUN or ACC position.

Conditions for Setting the DTC

- The windshield wiper switch signal circuit is greater than 4.71 volts, open or shorted to voltage.
- The windshield wiper switch low reference circuit is open.

Actions Taken When the DTC Sets

- No light will illuminate in the instrument panel (I/P).
- Cannot vary wiper speed

LTV0500000003196

Fig. 120   Code B3703: Intermittent Wiper Delay Input Circuit High (Part 1 of 4). Equinox & Torrent

Conditions for Clearing the DTC

- A current DTC clears when the fault is no longer present.
- A history DTC clears when the module ignition cycle counter reaches the reset threshold, without a repeat of the fault.

Diagnostic Aids

- Inspect wiring harness for damage. Inspect for broken or chaffed insulation.
- If fault is suspected to be intermittent, wiggling harness wiring may help in locating fault.
- Inspect for poor connection at the BCM. Inspect harness connectors for backed out terminals, improper terminal mating, broken connector locks, improperly formed or damaged terminals and poor terminal-to-wire connection, terminal is crimped over wire insulation and not conductors.

Step	Action	Values	Yes	No
1	Did you perform the Diagnostic System Check - Vehicle?	--	Go to Step 2	Go to Diagnostic System Check
2	1. Turn ON the ignition, with the engine OFF. 2. With a scan tool, observe the wiper delay input in the body control module (BCM) wiper/washer data list. Is the voltage greater than the specified value?	4.71 V	Go to Step 3	Go to Diagnostic Aids

LTV0500000003197

Fig. 120 Code B3703: Intermittent Wiper Delay Input Circuit High (Part 2 of 4). Equinox & Torrent

Step	Action	Values	Yes	No
11	Replace the windshield wiper washer switch. Did you complete the replacement?	-	Go to Step 12	--
12	1. Use the scan tool to clear the DTCs. 2. Operate the vehicle within the conditions for running the DTC, as specified in the supporting text. Does the DTC reset?	-	Go to Step 2	System OK

LTV0500000003199

Fig. 120 Code B3703: Intermittent Wiper Delay Input Circuit High (Part 4 of 4). Equinox & Torrent

Step	Action	Values	Yes	No
3	1. Turn OFF the ignition. 2. Disconnect the windshield wiper washer switch. 3. Turn ON the ignition, with the engine OFF. 4. Measure the voltage between the windshield wiper switch signal circuit and the windshield wiper switch low reference circuit at the harness connector. Is the voltage less than the specified value?	4 V	Go to Step 4	Go to Step 5
4	Measure the voltage between the windshield wiper switch signal circuit and a good ground. Is the voltage between the specified values?	4-6 V	Go to Step 7	Go to Step 8
5	Is the voltage between the specified values?	4-6 V	Go to Step 6	Go to Step 9
6	Using a fused jumper, jumper the windshield wiper switch signal circuit to the windshield wiper switch low reference circuit at the harness connector. Is the voltage less than the specified value?	0.4 V	Go to Step 11	Go to Step 10
7	Test the windshield wiper switch low reference circuit for an open Wiring Systems. Did you find and correct the condition?	--	Go to Step 12	Go to Step 10
8	Test the windshield wiper switch signal circuit for an open. Did you find and correct the condition?	--	Go to Step 12	Go to Step 10
9	Test the windshield wiper switch signal circuit for a short to voltage. Did you find and correct the condition?	--	Go to Step 12	Go to Step 10
10	Replace the BCM. Did you complete the replacement?	--	Go to Step 12	--

LTV0500000003198

Fig. 120 Code B3703: Intermittent Wiper Delay Input Circuit High (Part 3 of 4). Equinox & Torrent

Circuit Description

The body control module (BCM) monitors the windshield washer pump control circuit. When a front windshield wash is requested for more than 2 minutes, the BCM will turn OFF the windshield washer pump if the front wiper is NOT requested by the wiper switch.

Battery voltage for the windshield washer pump is supplied through the FRT WIPER 25 A fuse and windshield wiper washer switch. Grounding for the windshield washer pump is through the OFF position of the rear washer switch, when equipped.

DTC Descriptor

This diagnostic procedure supports the following DTC:

DTC B3708 Front Washer Motor Input High

Conditions for Running the DTC

Ignition is in RUN or ACC position.

Conditions for Setting the DTC

Front windshield washer pump control circuit is shorted to battery voltage for 2 minutes.

Actions Taken When the DTC Sets

- No light will illuminate in the instrument panel (I/P).
- Default turns OFF washer motor after failing DTC if wiper input is not active.

Conditions for Clearing the DTC

- A current DTC clears when the fault is no longer present.
- A history DTC clears when the module ignition cycle counter reaches the reset threshold, without a repeat of the fault.

LTV0500000003200

Fig. 121 Code B3708: Front Washer Motor Input High (Part 1 of 3). Equinox & Torrent

Diagnostic Aids

- Inspect for poor connection at the BCM. Inspect harness connectors for backed out terminals, improper terminal mating, broken connector locks, improperly formed or damaged terminals and poor terminal-to-wire connection, terminal crimped over wire insulation and not conductors.
- Inspect wiring harness for damage. Inspect for broken or chaffed insulation.
- If fault is suspected to be intermittent, wiggling harness wiring may help in locating fault.

Step	Action	Yes	No
1	Did you perform the Diagnostic System Check - Vehicle?	Go to Step 2	Go to Diagnostic System Check
2	1. Turn ON the ignition, with the engine OFF. 2. With a scan tool, observe the front washer motor input in the body control module (BCM) wiper/washer data list, while cycling the front washer switch. Does the scan tool indicate the correct washer pump status, ON/OFF?	Go to Diagnostic Aids	Go to Step 3
3	1. Turn OFF the ignition. 2. Disconnect the windshield wiper washer switch. 3. Turn ON the ignition, with the engine OFF. 4. With a scan tool, observe the front washer motor input. Does the scan tool indicate the switch is OFF?	Go to Step 5	Go to Step 4

LTV0500000003201

Fig. 121 Code B3708: Front Washer Motor Input High (Part 2 of 3). Equinox & Torrent

Circuit Description

The body control module (BCM) monitors the rear window washer switch signal circuit. When a rear windshield wash is requested for more than 2 minutes, the BCM will turn OFF the windshield washer fluid pump motor if the rear wiper is NOT requested by the windshield wiper washer switch.

Power for the windshield washer fluid pump is supplied through the FRT WIPER 25 A fuse and windshield wiper washer switch. Grounding for the windshield washer fluid pump is through the OFF position of the windshield washer fluid pump.

DTC Descriptor

This diagnostic procedure supports the following DTC:

DTC B3713 Rear Washer Motor Input Circuit High

Conditions for Running the DTC

Ignition is in RUN or ACC position.

Conditions for Setting the DTC

Rear window washer switch signal circuit at battery voltage for 2 minutes.

Actions Taken When the DTC Sets

No light will illuminate in the instrument panel (I/P).

Conditions for Clearing the DTC

- A current DTC clears when the fault is no longer present.
- A history DTC clears when the module ignition cycle counter reaches the reset threshold, without a repeat of the fault.

LTV0500000003443

Fig. 122 Code B3713: Rear Washer Motor Input Circuit High (Part 1 of 3). Equinox & Torrent

	Action		Yes	No
4	1. Turn OFF the ignition. 2. Disconnect the BCM connector C2. 3. Test the windshield washer pump control circuit for a short to voltage. Did you find and correct the condition?		Go to Step 7	Go to Step 6
5	Replace the windshield wiper washer switch. Did you complete the replacement?		Go to Step 7	--
6	Replace the BCM. Did you complete the replacement?		Go to Step 7	--
7	1. Use the scan tool to clear the DTCs. 2. Operate the vehicle within the conditions for running the DTC, as specified in the supporting text. Does the DTC reset?		Go to Step 2	System OK

LTV0500000003442

Fig. 121 Code B3708: Front Washer Motor Input High (Part 3 of 3). Equinox & Torrent

Diagnostic Aids

- Inspect wiring harness for damage.
- Inspect for broken or chaffed insulation.
- If fault is suspected to be intermittent, wiggling harness wiring may help in locating fault.

Step	Action	Yes	No
1	Did you perform the Diagnostic System Check - Vehicle?	Go to Step 2	Go to Diagnostic System Check
2	1. Turn ON the ignition, with the engine OFF. 2. With a scan tool, observe the rear washer motor input in the body control module (BCM) wiper/washer data list, while cycling the rear washer switch. Does the scan tool indicate the correct washer pump status, ON/OFF?	Go to Diagnostic Aids	Go to Step 3
3	1. Turn OFF the ignition. 2. Disconnect the windshield wiper washer switch. 3. Turn ON the ignition, with the engine OFF. 4. With a scan tool, observe the rear washer motor input. Does the scan tool indicate the switch is OFF?	Go to Step 4	Go to Step 5
4	Using a fused jumper, jumper the windshield wiper washer switch power circuit to the front washer switch circuit and jumper the rear window washer switch circuit to the windshield wiper washer switch ground circuit at the wiper switch harness connector. Does the washer pump motor run?	Go to Step 7	Go to Step 6

LTV0500000003444

Fig. 122 Code B3713: Rear Washer Motor Input Circuit High (Part 2 of 3). Equinox & Torrent

5	1. Turn OFF the ignition. 2. Disconnect the BCM connector C2. 3. Turn ON the ignition, with the engine OFF. 4. Test the front washer switch circuit and the rear washer switch circuit for a short to voltage. Did you find and correct the condition?	Go to Step 9	Go to Step 8
6	Repair an open in the rear window washer switch circuit or the windshield wiper washer switch ground circuit. Did you complete the repair?	Go to Step 9	--
7	Replace the windshield wiper washer switch. Did you complete the replacement?	Go to Step 9	--
8	Replace the BCM. Did you complete the replacement?	Go to Step 9	--
9	1. Use the scan tool to clear the DTCs. 2. Operate the vehicle within the conditions for running the DTC, as specified in the supporting text. Does the DTC reset?	Go to Step 2	System OK

LTV0500000003445

Fig. 122 Code B3713: Rear Washer Motor Input Circuit High (Part 3 of 3). Equinox & Torrent

Action Taken When the DTC Sets

- If the front wiper relay control circuit is open or shorted to battery, the Intermittent wiper mode will not operate.
- If the front wiper relay control circuit is shorted to ground, the wipers will always be on
- If the FRT WIPER relay does not receive battery positive voltage from the WIPER SYSTEM relay, all wiper washer functions will be inoperative.
- If any of the circuits that receive battery positive voltage from the FRT WIPER fuse are shorted to ground, the fuse will be open and all wiper washer functions will be inoperative.

Conditions for Clearing the DTC

- This DTC will change from current to history when the fault is no longer present.
- A history DTC will clear after 100 consecutive ignition cycles if the condition for the malfunction is no longer present.

Diagnostic Aids

DTC B3717 indicates a probable failure of the front wiper relay control circuit. However, the DTC will also set if the WIPER SYSTEM relay fails to supply battery positive voltage to the FRT WIPER relay. This failure may be due to an open FRT WIPER 25 amp fuse, or a malfunction of the WIPER SYSTEM relay or associated circuits. All wiper washer functions will be inoperative for both the front windshield and the rear window. If the fuse is open, a short to ground in any one of the following circuits may be the cause:

- Accessory voltage circuit
- Windshield washer pump control circuit
- Windshield wiper motor high speed circuit
- Windshield wiper motor low speed circuit
- Windshield wiper switch Mist/Off/Low signal circuit
- Windshield wiper switch pulse delay signal circuit
- Windshield wiper motor park switch signal circuit
- Rear wiper switch signal circuit
- Rear window washer pump control circuit

If there is no battery positive voltage supply to the FRT WIPER relay and an open FRT WIPER 25 amp fuse is not the cause, test the WIPER SYSTEM relay and associated circuits.

LTV0500000003447

Fig. 123 Codes B3715, B3716, B3717, B3718 & B3719: Front Wiper Relay Drive Circuit High/Low (Part 2 of 5). Equinox & Torrent

Circuit Description

The body control module (BCM) commands the Intermittent mode of the wipers by switching the front wiper relay control circuit to ground at regular timed intervals. This provides low speed operation of the wiper motor during single swipes of the wipers. Each time the BCM grounds the circuit, the FRT WIPER relay energizes, which closes the switch side contacts of the relay in order to apply battery positive voltage to the windshield wiper motor via the windshield wiper switch MIST/OFF/LOW signal circuit and windshield wiper motor low speed circuit. The BCM monitors the voltage on the front wiper relay control circuit in order to determine when a failure has occurred. When the FRT WIPER relay is energized, the voltage level on the front wiper relay control circuit should be near 0 volts. When the FRT WIPER relay is de-energized, the voltage level should be high, near system voltage.

Control of the wipers during LO or HIGH speed switch settings is direct wired from the windshield wiper washer switch to the wiper motor and is not under the control of the BCM.

DTC Descriptors

This diagnostic procedure supports the following DTCs:

- DTC B3717 Front Wiper Relay Drive Circuit Low
- DTC B3718 Front Wiper Relay Drive Circuit High

Conditions for Running the DTC

The ignition is in the RUN or ACC position.

Conditions for Setting the DTCs

The following conditions will cause these DTCs to set:

- B3717--the BCM detects short to ground or open.
- B3718-- the BCM detects a short to battery voltage.
- For B3718 to set the wiper switch must be in Mist or Intermittent.
- An open FRT WIPER 25 amp fuse
- An open or short to ground in one of the WIPER SYSTEM relay circuits

LTV0500000003446

Fig. 123 Codes B3715, B3716, B3717, B3718 & B3719: Front Wiper Relay Drive Circuit High/Low (Part 1 of 5). Equinox & Torrent

Test Description

The number below refers to the step number on the diagnostic table.

7. Listen for an audible click when the front wiper relay operates. Command both the ON and OFF states. Repeat the commands, as necessary.

Step	Action	Yes	No
1	Did you perform the Diagnostic System Check - Vehicle?	Go to Step 2	Go to Diagnostic System Check
2	1. Turn ON the ignition, with the engine OFF. 2. Operate the windshield wiper washer switch through all the switch positions. Does the windshield wiper/washer system operate normally?	Test for Intermittent and Poor Connections	Go to Step 3
3	Are the wipers always ON?	Go to Step 12	Go to Step 4
4	Inspect the FRT WIPER 25 amp fuse for an open. Is the fuse open?	Go to Step 5	Go to Step 6
5	1. Replace the FRT WIPER 25 amp fuse with a new one. 2. Attempt to operate all functions of the front and rear wipers and washers. Did the new fuse open?	Go to Step 10	Go to Step 15

LTV0500000003448

Fig. 123 Codes B3715, B3716, B3717, B3718 & B3719: Front Wiper Relay Drive Circuit High/Low (Part 3 of 5). Equinox & Torrent

	Action		
6	1. Turn OFF the ignition. 2. Disconnect the FRT WIPER relay in the underhood fuse block (UHFB). 3. Turn ON the ignition, with the engine OFF. 4. With a test lamp connected to a good ground, probe the battery positive voltage supply circuit of the relay at the relay socket terminal. Does the test lamp illuminate?	Go to Step 7	Go to Step 11
7	1. Connect the test lamp between the battery positive voltage circuit and the front wiper relay control circuit at the relay socket terminals. 2. With a scan tool command the front wiper relay ON and OFF under body control module (BCM) special functions. Does the test lamp illuminate when you command the relay ON and go out when you command the relay OFF?	Go to Step 13	Go to Step 8
8	Test the front wiper relay control circuit for an open or a short to voltage. Did you find and correct the condition?	Go to Step 15	Go to Step 9
9	Inspect for poor connections at the harness connector of the BCM. Did you find and correct the condition?	Go to Step 15	Go to Step 14
10	Repair one of the following circuits for a short to ground: • Accessory voltage circuit • Windshield washer pump control circuit • Windshield wiper motor high speed circuit • Windshield wiper motor low speed circuit • Windshield wiper switch Mist/Off/Low signal circuit • Windshield wiper switch pulse delay signal circuit • Windshield wiper motor park switch signal circuit • Rear wiper switch signal circuit • Rear window washer pump control circuit Did you complete the repair?	Go to Step 15	--

LTV0500000003449

Fig. 123 Codes B3715, B3716, B3717, B3718 & B3719: Front Wiper Relay Drive Circuit High/Low (Part 4 of 5). Equinox & Torrent

Circuit Description

When operation of the rear wiper is selected, battery voltage from the rear wiper switch is applied to the rear wiper switch signal input of the body control module (BCM) circuit. The BCM responds by switching the rear wiper relay control circuit to ground. This action energizes the rear wiper relay, providing power to the rear wiper motor.

DTC Descriptor

This diagnostic procedure supports the following DTC:

DTC B3722 Rear Wiper Relay Drive Circuit Low

Conditions for Running the DTC

The ignition is in RUN or ACC position.

Conditions for Setting the DTC

• The rear wiper relay control circuit is shorted to ground or open.
• The accessory voltage circuit to the coil side of the relay is open .
• The accessory voltage circuit is shorted to ground between the fuse and the rear wiper motor.
• The rear window wiper motor control circuit is shorted to ground.
• The RR WIPER 15-amp fuse is open.

Actions Taken When the DTC Sets

Service (wrench) light will illuminate.

Conditions for Clearing the DTC

• A current DTC clears when the fault is no longer present.
• A history DTC clears when the module ignition cycle counter reaches the reset threshold, without a repeat of the fault.

LTV0500000003451

Fig. 124 Code B3722: Rear Wiper Relay Drive Circuit Low (Part 1 of 4). Equinox & Torrent

	Action		
11	Repair an open or a high resistance in the battery positive voltage supply circuit of the FRT WIPER relay. Did you complete the repair?	Go to Step 15	--
12	Repair a short to ground on the front wiper relay control circuit. Did you complete the repair?	Go to Step 15	--
13	Replace the front wiper relay. Did you complete the replacement?	Go to Step 15	--
14	Replace the BCM. Did you complete the replacement?	Go to Step 15	--
15	1. Use the scan tool to clear the DTCs. 2. Operate the vehicle within the Conditions for Running the DTC, as specified in the supporting text. Does the DTC reset?	Go to Step 2	System OK

LTV0500000003450

Fig. 123 Codes B3715, B3716, B3717, B3718 & B3719: Front Wiper Relay Drive Circuit High/Low (Part 5 of 5). Equinox & Torrent

Diagnostic Aids

• Inspect for poor connection at the BCM. Inspect harness connectors for backed out terminals, improper terminal mating, broken connector locks, improperly formed or damaged terminals and poor terminal-to-wire connection, terminal crimped over wire insulation and not conductors.
• If the rear wiper relay control circuit is open, the rear wipers will be inoperative.
• If the rear wiper relay control circuit is shorted to ground, the rear wipers will always be ON.
• If, either the accessory voltage circuit, or the rear window wiper motor control circuit is shorted to ground, the RR WIPER fuse will open and the rear wipers will be inoperative.
• Inspect the wiring harness for damage. Inspect for broken or chaffed insulation.
• If the fault is suspected to be intermittent, wiggling the harness wiring may help in locating fault.

Step	Action	Yes	No
1	Did you perform the Diagnostic System Check - Vehicle?	Go to Step 2	Go to Diagnostic System Check
2	1. Turn OFF the ignition. 2. Remove the rear wiper relay from the underhood fuse block (UHFB). 3. Turn ON the ignition, with the engine OFF. 4. Turn the rear wipers ON. 5. With a test lamp connected to a good ground, probe the coil side accessory voltage supply circuit of the relay. 6. With the test lamp still connected to a good ground, probe the switch side accessory voltage supply circuit of the relay. Does the test lamp illuminate for both accessory voltage circuits?	Go to Step 3	Go to Step 4

LTV0500000003452

Fig. 124 Code B3722: Rear Wiper Relay Drive Circuit Low (Part 2 of 4). Equinox & Torrent

Step	Action	Yes	No
3	1. Connect the test lamp between the accessory voltage supply circuit and the rear wiper relay control circuit of the relay. 2. Using a scan tool, command the rear wipers ON and OFF. Does the test lamp illuminate when you command ON and go out when you command OFF?	Go to Step 8	Go to Step 7
4	Inspect for an open RR WIPER 15-amp fuse. Is the fuse open?	Go to Step 5	Go to Step 11
5	1. Turn OFF the ignition. 2. Install the rear wiper relay. 3. Replace the RR WIPER fuse with a new one. 4. Turn ON the ignition with the engine OFF. 5. Attempt to operate the rear wipers. Does the RR WIPER fuse open again?	Go to Step 6	Go to Step 15
6	Test the following circuits of the rear wiper motor for a short to ground: • Accessory voltage circuit. • Rear window wiper motor control circuit. Did you find and correct the condition?	Go to Step 15	Go to Step 10
7	Test the rear wiper relay control circuit for an open or a short to ground. Did you find and correct the condition?	Go to Step 15	Go to Step 9
8	Inspect for poor connections and terminal damage at the UHFB. Did you find and correct the condition?	Go to Step 15	Go to Step 14
9	Inspect for poor connections at the harness connector of the body control module (BCM). Did you find and correct the condition?	Go to Step 15	Go to Step 13

LTV0500000003453

Fig. 124   Code B3722: Rear Wiper Relay Drive Circuit Low (Part 3 of 4). Equinox & Torrent

Circuit Description

When operation of the rear wiper is selected, battery voltage from the rear wiper switch is applied to the rear wiper switch signal input circuit of the body control module (BCM). The BCM responds by switching the rear wiper relay control circuit to ground. This action energizes the rear wiper relay, providing power to the rear wiper motor.

DTC Descriptor

This diagnostic procedure supports the following DTC:

DTC B3723 Rear Wiper Relay Drive Circuit High

Conditions for Running the DTC

Ignition is in RUN or ACC position.

Conditions for Setting the DTC

• The rear wiper relay control circuit is shorted to battery.
• The rear wiper relay output is ON.

Actions Taken When the DTC Sets

• The service (wrench) light will illuminate.
• The rear wipers are inoperative.

Conditions for Clearing the DTC

• A current DTC clears when the fault is no longer present.
• A history DTC clears when the module ignition cycle counter reaches the reset threshold, without a repeat of the fault.

LTV0500000003455

Fig. 125   Code B3723: Rear Wiper Relay Drive Circuit High (Part 1 of 3). Equinox & Torrent

Step	Action	Yes	No
10	Inspect for poor connections at the harness connector of the rear wiper motor. Did you find and correct the condition?	Go to Step 15	Go to Step 12
11	Repair the open in the accessory voltage supply circuit of the rear wiper relay. Did you complete the repair?	Go to Step 15	--
12	Replace the rear wiper motor. Did you complete the replacement?	Go to Step 15	--
13	Replace the BCM. Did you complete the replacement?	Go to Step 15	--
14	Replace the rear wiper relay. Did you complete the replacement?	Go to Step 15	--
15	1. Use the scan tool to clear the DTCs. 2. Operate the vehicle within the conditions for running the DTC, as specified in the supporting text. Does the DTC reset?	Go to Step 2	System OK

LTV0500000003454

Fig. 124   Code B3722: Rear Wiper Relay Drive Circuit Low (Part 4 of 4). Equinox & Torrent

Diagnostic Aids

• When the BCM has been requested to activate the rear wiper relay, the BCM switches the rear wiper relay control circuit to ground. However, if the circuit is shorted to battery voltage, high current flow will result and the BCM output will go into a protective state. The BCM output will not allow itself to be activated for as much as 3 minutes.
• Inspect the harness connectors at the BCM for improper terminal mating, broken connector locks, and improperly formed or damaged terminals.
• Inspect wiring harness for damage. Inspect for broken or chaffed insulation.
• Review all fail information as this may assist in determining the conditions when the fault occurs.
• If the fault is suspected to be intermittent, wiggling the harness wiring may help in locating the fault.

Test Description

The numbers below refer to the step numbers on the diagnostic table.

2. This step will determine if the rear wiper relay is internally shorted to battery voltage. Once you have disconnected the relay, you should be able to clear DTC B3723 with no recurrence. It is, however, normal for DTC B3722 to set while the relay is disconnected.

3. This step will determine if the rear wiper relay control circuit is shorted to battery voltage, or if the BCM is at fault.

Step	Action	Yes	No
1	Did you perform the Diagnostic System Check - Vehicle?	Go to Step 2	Go to Diagnostic System Check - Vehicle

LTV0500000003456

Fig. 125   Code B3723: Rear Wiper Relay Drive Circuit High (Part 2 of 3). Equinox & Torrent

Step	Action	Yes	No
2	**Important** DTC B3722 may set as a result of disconnecting the REAR WIPER Relay. 1. Turn the front and rear wiper and washer switches OFF. 2. Turn OFF the ignition. 3. Disconnect the REAR WIPER Relay from the underhood fuse block. 4. Turn ON the ignition, with the engine OFF. 5. Use a scan tool to clear DTC B3723. Does DTC B3723 clear?	Go to Step 5	Go to Step 3
3	Test the rear wiper relay control circuit for a short to battery. Did you find and correct the condition?	Go to Step 6	Go to Step 4
4	Replace the body control module (BCM). Did you complete the replacement?	Go to Step 6	--
5	Replace the rear wiper relay. Did you complete the replacement?	Go to Step 6	--
6	1. Use the scan tool to clear the DTCs. 2. Operate the vehicle within the conditions for running the DTC, as specified in the supporting text. Does the DTC reset?	Go to Step 2	System OK

LTV0500000003457

Fig. 125   Code B3723: Rear Wiper Relay Drive Circuit High (Part 3 of 3). Equinox & Torrent

Step	Action	Yes	No
5	1. Connect the test lamp between the windshield washer pump control circuit and the rear window washer pump control circuit at the windshield washer fluid pump. 2. Turn ON the ignition, with the engine OFF. 3. Press the front washer switch. Does the test lamp illuminate?	Go to Step 9	Go to Step 6
6	1. Turn OFF the ignition. 2. Disconnect the harness connector of the windshield wiper washer switch. 3. With a test lamp connected to battery positive voltage, probe the ground circuit of the harness connector. Does the test lamp illuminate?	Go to Step 10	Go to Step 11
7	1. Turn OFF the ignition. 2. Disconnect the harness connector of the windshield wiper washer switch. 3. Test the rear window washer pump control circuit for an open or a short to ground. Did you find and correct the condition?	Go to Step 14	Go to Step 10
8	1. Turn OFF the ignition. 2. Disconnect the harness connector of the windshield wiper washer switch. 3. Test the windshield washer pump control circuit for an open or a short to ground. Did you find and correct the condition?	Go to Step 14	Go to Step 10
9	Inspect for poor connections at the windshield washer fluid pump. Did you find and correct the condition?	Go to Step 14	Go to Step 12
10	Inspect for poor connections at the windshield wiper washer switch. Did you find and correct the condition?	Go to Step 14	Go to Step 13

LTV0500000003460

Fig. 126   Washers Inoperative (Part 2 of 3). Equinox & Torrent

Step	Action	Yes	No
1	Did you perform the Diagnostic System Check - Vehicle?	Go to Step 2	Go to Diagnostic System Check -
2	Verify that the Washers Inoperative complaint is present. Do the washers operate as described in the Description and Operation?	Test for Intermittent and Poor Connections	Go to Step 3
3	1. Turn OFF the ignition. 2. Disconnect the harness connector of the windshield washer fluid pump. 3. Connect a test lamp from the windshield washer pump control circuit to a good ground . 4. Turn ON the ignition, with the engine OFF. 5. Press the front washer switch. Does the test lamp illuminate?	Go to Step 4	Go to Step 8
4	1. Connect the test lamp from the rear window washer pump control circuit to a good ground. 2. Turn ON the ignition, with the engine OFF. 3. Press the rear washer switch. Does the test lamp illuminate?	Go to Step 5	Go to Step 7

LTV0500000003459

Fig. 126   Washers Inoperative (Part 1 of 3). Equinox & Torrent

Step	Action	Yes	No
11	Repair the ground circuit for an open or a high resistance. Did you complete the repair?	Go to Step 14	--
12	Replace the windshield washer fluid pump. Did you complete the replacement?	Go to Step 14	--
13	Replace the windshield wiper washer switch. Did you complete the replacement?	Go to Step 14	--
14	Operate the system in order to verify the repair. Did you correct the condition?	System OK	Go to Step 2

LTV0500000003461

Fig. 126   Washers Inoperative (Part 3 of 3). Equinox & Torrent

Step	Action	Yes	No
1	Did you perform the Diagnostic System Check - Vehicle?	Go to Step 2	Go to Diagnostic System Check -
2	1. Turn ON the ignition, with the engine OFF. 2. Turn both the front windshield and rear window wiper washer switches OFF. Are the wipers OFF?		Go to Step 3
3	Are the rear wipers always ON?	Go to Step 4	Go to Step 7
4	1. The rear wipers are always ON. 2. Turn OFF the ignition. 3. Disconnect the rear wiper relay. 4. Turn ON the ignition, with the engine OFF. Are the rear wipers OFF?	Go to Step 5	Go to Step 6
5	1. Turn OFF the ignition. 2. Connect a test lamp between the rear wiper relay control circuit and the accessory voltage side of the rear wiper relay at the rear wiper relay socket terminals. 3. Turn ON the ignition, with the engine OFF. Does the test lamp illuminate?	Go to Step 8	Go to Step 16
6	Test the rear window wiper motor control circuit for a short to voltage. Did you find and correct the condition?	Go to Step 20	Go to Step 14

LTV0500000003462

Fig. 127   Wipers Always On (Part 1 of 3). Equinox & Torrent

Step	Action	Yes	No
7	1. The front wipers are always ON. 2. Turn OFF the ignition. 3. Disconnect the harness connector of the windshield wiper washer switch. 4. Turn ON the ignition, with the engine OFF. Are the front wipers OFF?	Go to Step 9	Go to Step 15
8	1. Turn OFF the ignition. 2. Disconnect the harness connector C2 of the body control module (BCM). 3. Connect a test lamp between the rear wiper switch signal circuit of the harness connector and a good ground. 4. Turn ON the ignition, with the engine OFF. Does the test lamp illuminate?	Go to Step 10	Go to Step 12
9	Connect a test lamp between the windshield wiper switch pulse delay signal circuit of the harness connector and a good ground. Does the test lamp illuminate?	Go to Step 11	Go to Step 13
10	Test the rear wiper switch signal circuit for a short to voltage. Did you find and correct the condition?	Go to Step 20	Go to Step 13
11	Test the windshield wiper switch pulse delay signal circuit for a short to voltage. Did you find and correct the condition?	Go to Step 20	Go to Step 12
12	Inspect for poor connections at the BCM. Did you find and correct the condition?	Go to Step 20	Go to Step 19
13	Inspect for poor connections at the windshield wiper washer switch. Did you find and correct the condition?	Go to Step 20	Go to Step 18
14	Inspect for poor connections at the rear wiper motor. Did you find and correct the condition?	Go to Step 20	Go to Step 17

LTV0500000003463

Fig. 127   Wipers Always On (Part 2 of 3). Equinox & Torrent

Step	Action	Yes	No
15	Repair the windshield wiper motor high speed circuit or the windshield wiper motor low speed circuit for a short to voltage. Did you complete the repair?	Go to Step 20	--
16	Replace the rear wiper relay. Did you complete the replacement?	Go to Step 20	--
17	Replace the rear wiper motor. Did you complete the replacement?	Go to Step 20	--
18	Replace the windshield wiper washer switch. Did you complete the replacement?	Go to Step 20	--
19	Replace the BCM. Did you complete the replacement?	Go to Step 20	--
20	Operate the system in order to verify the repair. Did you correct the condition?	System OK	Go to Step 2

LTV0500000003464

Fig. 127   Wipers Always On (Part 3 of 3). Equinox & Torrent

Step	Action	Yes	No
	DEFINITION: Both the front and rear wipers are inoperative, however the front and rear washers still operate.		
1	Did you perform the Diagnostic System Check - Vehicle?	Go to Step 2	Go to Diagnostic System Check -
2	1. Turn ON the ignition, with the engine OFF. 2. Operate the front and rear wiper switches through all switch positions. Does the wiper system operate normally?	Test for Intermittent and Poor Connections	Go to Step 3
3	1. Turn OFF the ignition. 2. Disconnect the windshield wiper washer switch connector. 3. Turn ON the ignition, with the engine OFF. 4. With a test lamp connected to a good ground, probe the accessory voltage feed circuit of the harness connector. Does the test lamp illuminate?	Go to Step 4	Go to Step 5
4	Inspect for poor connections at the harness connector of the windshield wiper washer switch. Did you find and correct the condition?	Go to Step 7	Go to Step 6
5	Repair the open or short to ground in the accessory voltage feed circuit. Did you complete the repair?	Go to Step 7	--

LTV0500000003465

Fig. 128   Wipers Inoperative, All Modes (Part 1 of 2). Equinox & Torrent

Step	Action	Yes	No
6	Replace the windshield wiper washer switch. Did you complete the replacement?	Go to Step 7	--
7	Operate the system in order to verify the repair. Did you correct the condition?	System OK	Go to Step 2

LTV0500000003466

Fig. 128   Wipers Inoperative, All Modes (Part 2 of 2). Equinox & Torrent

Step	Action	Yes	No
	DEFINITION: The front windshield wipers are inoperative in one or more modes. The windshield washer still operates.		
1	Did you perform the Diagnostic System Check - Vehicle? Go to Step 2		Go to Diagnostic System Check
2	1. Turn ON the ignition, with the engine OFF. 2. Operate the windshield wiper switch through all switch positions. 3. Turn the windshield wiper switch OFF. 4. With the windshield wiper switch OFF, operate the front windshield washer switch to ON. Do the windshield wipers operate as described in the Description and Operation?		Go to Step 3
3	Are the windshield wipers completely inoperative?	Go to Step 10	Go to Step 4
4	Are the windshield wipers inoperative for every mode except High speed?	Go to Step 11	Go to Step 5
5	Are the wipers inoperative in the Intermittent mode?	Go to Step 6	Go to Step 7
6	In addition to the Intermittent mode, are the windshield wipers inoperative for one or both of the following two modes: • Wash • Park	Go to Step 17	Go to Step 14

LTV0500000003468

Fig. 129   Wipers Inoperative, One Or More Modes (Front Wipers, Part 2 of 7). Equinox & Torrent

Diagnostic Aids

The Wash mode for this diagnostic procedure is defined as the mode when the wiper switch is OFF and only the windshield washer switch has been activated. When the washer switch is activated with the wiper switch OFF, the wipers should wipe the windshield 3-5 times and then park.

Test Description

The numbers below refer to the step numbers on the diagnostic table.

2. This step will pinpoint which specific wiper functions are inoperative. The wipers should operate for all active windshield wiper switch positions. When the wiper switch is OFF and only the windshield washer switch is activated, the wipers should wipe the windshield 3-5 times and then park.

6. This step will help to pinpoint which specific circuit or component may be involved in the malfunction. When the Wash, and Park modes are inoperative as well as the Intermittent mode, the windshield wiper switch mist/off/low signal circuit and associated components are suspect. When the wipers operate for the Park mode but the Intermittent and Wash modes are both inoperative, suspect the accessory voltage feed circuit of the FRT WIPER Relay or an associated component.

12. This step is used when the wipers fail to wipe the windshield while only the washer switch is activated.

13. This step is used when the wipers still operate in all wiping modes, but fail to Park at the full down position. If this condition is present while the wipers are being operated in the Intermittent mode, the wipers typically will not return to the full down position. Instead, they will stop at random positions on the windshield and in between the timed wiper strokes. Or, if the wipers are being operated in either the High or Low mode, the wipers will stop in mid-stroke when the wiper switch is turned OFF.

LTV0500000003467

Fig. 129   Wipers Inoperative, One Or More Modes (Front Wipers, Part 1 of 7). Equinox & Torrent

Step	Action	Yes	No
7	**Important:** When the windshield washer mode is activated with the windshield wiper switch OFF, the windshield wipers should wipe the windshield 3-5 times and then park. Are the wipers inoperative for only the Wash mode.	Go to Step 12	Go to Step 8
8	Are the wipers inoperative for only the Park mode?	Go to Step 13	Go to Step 9
9	The wipers are inoperative for only the High speed mode. 1. Disconnect the windshield wiper motor harness connector. 2. With a test lamp connected to ground, probe the windshield wiper motor high speed circuit of the harness connector. 3. Operate the windshield wiper switch to the high speed position. Does the test lamp illuminate?	Go to Step 24	Go to Step 22
10	The windshield wipers are totally inoperative. 1. Disconnect the windshield wiper motor harness connector. 2. With a test lamp connected to battery positive voltage, probe the windshield wiper motor ground circuit. Does the test lamp illuminate?	Go to Step 16	Go to Step 29
11	The windshield wipers operate only in High speed. 1. Disconnect the windshield wiper motor harness connector. 2. With a test lamp connected to ground, probe the windshield wiper motor low speed circuit of the harness connector. 3. Operate the windshield wiper switch to the low speed position. Does the test lamp illuminate?	Go to Step 24	Go to Step 20

LTV0500000003469

Fig. 129   Wipers Inoperative, One Or More Modes (Front Wipers, Part 3 of 7). Equinox & Torrent

Step	Procedure	Yes	No
12	The windshield wipers are inoperative for only the Wash mode. 1. Disconnect the body control module (BCM) C2 harness connector. 2. With a test lamp connected to ground, probe the windshield washer pump control circuit of the harness connector. 3. Operate the windshield washer switch to ON. Does the test lamp illuminate?	Go to Step 25	Go to Step 21
13	The wipers are inoperative for only the Park mode. 1. Disconnect the windshield wiper motor harness connector. 2. Test for continuity between the windshield wiper motor park switch signal circuit and ground circuit of the wiper motor, at the wiper motor pins. Is there continuity?	Go to Step 15	Go to Step 24
14	The wipers are inoperative for only the Intermittent mode. 1. Disconnect the body control module (BCM) C2 harness connector. 2. With a test lamp connected to ground, probe the windshield wiper switch pulse delay signal circuit of the harness connector. 3. Operate the windshield washer switch through all of the Intermittent positions. Is the test lamp illuminated for all of the Intermittent positions?	Go to Step 25	Go to Step 23
15	1. Connect the windshield wiper motor harness connector. 2. Disconnect the FRT WIPER Relay. 3. With a test lamp connected to battery positive voltage, probe the windshield wiper motor park switch signal circuit of the underhood fuse block. Does the test lamp illuminate?	Go to Step 33	Go to Step 30

LTV0500000003470

Fig. 129 Wipers Inoperative, One Or More Modes (Front Wipers, Part 4 of 7). Equinox & Torrent

Step	Procedure	Yes	No
22	Test the windshield wiper motor high speed circuit for an open. Did you find and correct the condition?	Go to Step 35	Go to Step 26
23	Test the windshield wiper switch pulse delay signal circuit for an open. Did you find and correct the condition?	Go to Step 35	Go to Step 26
24	Inspect for poor connections at the harness connector of the windshield wiper motor. Did you find and correct the condition?	Go to Step 35	Go to Step 32
25	Inspect for poor connections at the harness connector of the body control module (BCM). Did you find and correct the condition?	Go to Step 35	Go to Step 34
26	Inspect for poor connections at the harness connector of the windshield wiper washer switch. Did you find and correct the condition?	Go to Step 35	Go to Step 31
27	Repair the windshield wiper switch mist/off/low signal circuit for an open or a high resistance. Did you complete the repair?	Go to Step 35	--
28	Repair the accessory voltage feed circuit for an open or a high resistance. Did you complete the repair?	Go to Step 35	--
29	Repair the open ground circuit. Did you complete the repair?	Go to Step 35	--

LTV0500000003472

Fig. 129 Wipers Inoperative, One Or More Modes (Front Wipers, Part 6 of 7). Equinox & Torrent

Step	Procedure	Yes	No
16	1. Connect the test lamp between ground and the windshield wiper motor high speed circuit of the harness connector. 2. Operate the windshield wiper switch to the high speed position. 3. Connect the test lamp between ground and the windshield wiper motor low speed circuit of the harness connector. 4. Operate the windshield wiper switch to the low speed position. Does the test lamp illuminate for both the high and the low positions?	Go to Step 24	Go to Step 26
17	1. Turn OFF the ignition. 2. Disconnect the FRT WIPER Relay. 3. Turn ON the ignition, with the engine OFF. 4. With a test lamp connected to ground, probe the accessory voltage feed circuits of the FRT WIPER Relay, at the underhood fuse block. Does the test lamp illuminate?	Go to Step 18	Go to Step 28
18	1. Turn OFF the ignition. 2. Connect a 3 amp fused jumper between the accessory voltage feed circuit and the windshield wiper switch mist/off/low signal circuit, at the underhood fuse block. 3. Turn ON the ignition, with the engine OFF. 4. Turn the windshield wiper switch to the Intermittent position. 5. With a test lamp connected to ground, probe the windshield wiper switch mist/off/low signal circuit, at the windshield wiper switch terminal. Does the test lamp illuminate?	Go to Step 19	Go to Step 27
19	With the test lamp connected to ground, probe the windshield wiper switch low speed circuit, at the windshield wiper switch terminal. Does the test lamp illuminate?	Go to Step 33	Go to Step 26
20	Test the windshield wiper motor low speed circuit for an open. Did you find and correct the condition?	Go to Step 35	Go to Step 26
21	Test the windshield washer pump control circuit for an open. Did you find and correct the condition?	Go to Step 35	Go to Step 26

LTV0500000003471

Fig. 129 Wipers Inoperative, One Or More Modes (Front Wipers, Part 5 of 7). Equinox & Torrent

Step	Procedure	Yes	No
30	Repair the windshield wiper motor park switch signal circuit for an open or a high resistance. Did you complete the repair?	Go to Step 35	--
31	Replace the windshield wiper washer switch. Did you complete the replacement?	Go to Step 35	--
32	Replace the windshield wiper motor. Did you complete the replacement?	Go to Step 35	--
33	Replace the FRT WIPER relay. Did you complete the replacement?	Go to Step 35	--
34	Replace the BCM. Did you complete the replacement?	Go to Step 35	--
35	Operate the system in order to verify the repair. Did you correct the condition?	System OK	Go to Step 2

LTV0500000003473

Fig. 129 Wipers Inoperative, One Or More Modes (Front Wipers, Part 7 of 7). Equinox & Torrent

Diagnostic Aids

Except for when it is in the Wash mode, the rear window wiper wipes the rear window at delay time intervals. With the rear wiper system activated, the length of time between wipes can be adjusted by selecting any one of the three delay speed settings of the windshield wiper switch.

During the Wash mode, if the rear washer switch is momentarily turned to ON, the rear wiper will wipe the rear window 3-5 times and then park. However, if the rear washer switch is held to ON, the rear window wipers will continue to operate until the switch is released.

While the delay speed of both the front and rear wipers is adjusted by the windshield wiper switch selections, the delay time intervals of the rear wiper are not synchronized with the delay time intervals of the front wipers.

The rear wiper should stop at the Park position anytime the rear wiper is not wiping. However, if the ignition switch is turned OFF while the rear wiper is wiping, the wiper will stop at its current location on the glass.

Test Description

The numbers below refer to the step numbers on the diagnostic table.

2. This step will determine if the rear wiper operates properly when only the rear window washer switch is activated. When the rear window washer switch is operated with the rear wiper switch OFF, the rear wiper should wipe the window 3-5 times and then park.

4. This step helps to pinpoint the specific malfunction. The Park mode of the rear window wiper may be the only feature malfunctioning. When the rear wiper switch is ON, the rear wiper should stop at the parked position in between the timed strokes of the wiper. When the rear wiper switch is turned OFF, the rear wiper should park and remain in the parked position until either the wipe or wash mode is operated again.

LTV0500000003474

Fig. 130   Wipers Inoperative, One Or More Modes (Rear Wipers, Part 1 of 5). Equinox & Torrent

Step	Action	Yes	No
	DEFINITION: The rear wiper is inoperative in one or more modes, however the rear washer still operates.		
1	Did you perform the Diagnostic System Check - Vehicle?	Go to Step 2	Go to Diagnostic System Check -
2	1. Turn ON the ignition, with the engine OFF. 2. Turn the rear window wiper switch ON. Does the rear window wiper operate?	Go to Step 3	Go to Step 5
3	1. Turn the rear window wiper switch OFF. 2. With the rear window wiper switch OFF, turn the rear window washer switch ON. Does the rear window wiper operate?	Go to Step 4	Go to Step 7
4	**Important:** Unless the rear window wiper is being operated for the Wash mode, it operates only in the delay modes. When the rear wiper is ON, it should stop at the parked position in between timed strokes of the wiper. When the rear wiper is turned OFF, it should park and remain in the parked position until either the wiper or wash mode is operated again. Does the rear window wiper Park in the full down position as it should?	Test for Intermittent and Poor Connections	Go to Step 9
5	**Turn the rear window washer switch ON.** **Does the rear window wiper operate?**	Go to Step 8	Go to Step 6

LTV0500000003475

Fig. 130   Wipers Inoperative, One Or More Modes (Rear Wipers, Part 2 of 5). Equinox & Torrent

Step	Action	Yes	No
6	1. Turn OFF the ignition. 2. Remove the REAR WIPER Relay from the underhood fuse block. 3. Turn ON the ignition, with the engine OFF. 4. With a test lamp connected to a good ground, probe the accessory voltage feed circuit to the switch side of the relay at the underhood fuse block. Does the test lamp illuminate?	Go to Step 10	Go to Step 20
7	1. Disconnect the body control module (BCM) C2 harness connector. 2. With a test lamp connected to ground, probe the rear window washer pump control circuit. 3. Operate the rear window washer switch to ON while the rear window wiper switch is OFF. Does the test lamp illuminate?	Go to Step 17	Go to Step 13
8	1. Disconnect the body control module (BCM) C2 harness connector. 2. With a test lamp connected to ground, probe the rear wiper switch signal circuit. 3. Operate the rear window wiper switch to ON. Does the test lamp illuminate?	Go to Step 17	Go to Step 14
9	1. Turn OFF the ignition. 2. Disconnect the harness connector of the rear window wiper motor. 3. Turn ON the ignition, with the engine OFF. 4. With a test lamp connected to a good ground, probe the accessory voltage circuit of the rear window wiper motor. Does the test lamp illuminate?	Go to Step 16	Go to Step 19
10	1. Turn OFF the ignition. 2. Connect a 3 amp fused jumper wire between the accessory voltage feed circuit terminal and the rear window wiper motor control circuit terminal at the underhood fuse block. 3. Turn the ignition ON, with the engine OFF. Does the rear wiper operate?	Go to Step 24	Go to Step 11

LTV0500000003476

Fig. 130   Wipers Inoperative, One Or More Modes (Rear Wipers, Part 3 of 5). Equinox & Torrent

Step	Action	Yes	No
11	1. Ensure that the fused jumper wire between the accessory voltage feed circuit terminal and the rear window wiper motor control circuit terminal is still connected. 2. With a test lamp connected to a good ground, probe the rear window wiper motor control circuit at the rear wiper motor. Does the test lamp illuminate?	Go to Step 12	Go to Step 21
12	Connect the test lamp between the rear window wiper motor control circuit and the rear window wiper motor ground circuit. Does the test lamp illuminate?	Go to Step 16	Go to Step 18
13	Test the rear window washer pump control circuit for an open or a high resistance. Did you find and correct the condition?	Go to Step 26	Go to Step 15
14	Test the rear wiper switch signal circuit for an open or a high resistance. Did you find and correct the condition?	Go to Step 26	Go to Step 15
15	Inspect for poor connections at the harness connector of the windshield wiper washer switch. Did you find and correct the condition?	Go to Step 26	Go to Step 22
16	Inspect for poor connections at the harness connector of the rear window wiper motor. Did you find and correct the condition?	Go to Step 26	Go to Step 23
17	Inspect for poor connections at the harness connector of the BCM. Did you find and correct the condition?	Go to Step 26	Go to Step 25
18	Repair the rear window wiper motor ground circuit for an open or a high resistance. Did you complete the repair?	Go to Step 26	--

LTV0500000003477

Fig. 130   Wipers Inoperative, One Or More Modes (Rear Wipers, Part 4 of 5). Equinox & Torrent

19	Repair the accessory voltage circuit, between the REAR WIPER Relay splice and the wiper motor, for an open or a high resistance. Did you complete the repair?	Go to Step 26	--
20	Repair the open or high resistance in the accessory voltage feed circuit. Did you complete the repair?	Go to Step 26	--
21	Repair the open or high resistance in the rear window wiper motor control circuit. Did you complete the repair?	Go to Step 26	--
22	Replace the windshield wiper washer switch. Did you complete the replacement?	Go to Step 26	--
23	Replace the rear window wiper motor. Did you complete the replacement?	Go to Step 26	--
24	Replace the rear wiper relay. Did you complete the replacement?	Go to Step 26	--
25	Replace the BCM. Did you complete the replacement?	Go to Step 26	--
26	Operate the system in order to verify the repair. Did you correct the condition?	System OK	Go to Step 2

LTV0500000003478

Fig. 130   Wipers Inoperative, One Or More Modes (Rear Wipers, Part 5 of 5). Equinox & Torrent

8	Replace the windshield wiper motor module. Is the repair complete?	Go to Step 9	--
9	Operate the system in order to verify the repair. Did you correct the condition?	System OK	Go to Step 3

LTV0500000002975

Fig. 131   Washers Always On (Part 2 of 2). 2002 Express & Savanna

Step	Action	Yes	No
1	Did you review the Wiper/Washer System Description and Operation and perform the necessary inspections?	Go to Step 2	Go to Symptoms
2	Turn the ignition ON. Are the windshield washers always on?	Go to Step 3	
3	Are the windshield washer wipers always on?	Go to Step 4	Go to Step 6
4	1. Turn the ignition OFF. 2. Disconnect the inline harness connector C200. 3. Remove the connector terminal row E from the steering column harness connector half. 4. Connect the inline harness connector C200. 5. Turn the ignition ON. Are the windshield washers always on?	Go to Step 5	Go to Step 7
5	Test the windshield wiper switch pulse delay signal circuit for a short to voltage. Did you find and correct the condition?	Go to Step 9	Go to Step 8
6	Test the windshield washer pump control circuit for a short to voltage. Did you find and correct the condition?	Go to Step 9	Go to Step 8
7	Replace the windshield wiper/washer switch. Is the repair complete?	Go to Step 9	--

LTV0500000002974

Fig. 131   Washers Always On (Part 1 of 2). 2002 Express & Savanna

Step	Action	Yes	No
1	Did you review the Wiper/Washer System Description and Operation and perform the necessary inspections?	Go to Step 2	Go to Symptoms -
2	1. Turn the ignition ON. 2. Press the windshield washer switch. Do the windshield washers operate normally?		Go to Step 3
3	1. Disconnect the windshield washer pump connector. 2. Connect a test lamp across the washer pump connector terminals. 3. Turn the ignition ON. 4. Press the windshield washer switch. Does the test lamp illuminate?	Go to Step 10	Go to Step 4
4	Test the windshield washer pump ground circuit for an open or high resistance. Did you find and correct the condition?	Go to Step 14	Go to Step 5
5	1. Disconnect the windshield wiper motor connector. 2. Test the windshield washer pump control circuit for an open or short to ground. Did you find and correct the condition?	Go to Step 14	Go to Step 6

LTV0500000002976

Fig. 132   Washers Inoperative (Part 1 of 2). 2002 Express & Savanna

	Action	Yes	No
6	1. Connect a test lamp from the low signal circuit terminal in the wiper motor harness connector to ground. 2. Turn the ignition ON. 3. Press the windshield washer switch. Does the test lamp illuminate?	Go to Step 12	Go to Step 7
7	Test the windshield wiper switch pulse delay signal circuit for high resistance. Did you find and correct the condition?	Go to Step 14	Go to Step 8
8	Inspect for poor connections at the windshield wiper/washer switch. Did you find and correct the condition?	Go to Step 14	Go to Step 9
9	Replace the windshield wiper/washer switch. Is the repair complete?	Go to Step 14	--
10	Inspect for poor connections at the windshield washer pump. Did you find and correct the condition?	Go to Step 14	Go to Step 11
11	Replace the windshield washer pump. Is the repair complete?	Go to Step 14	--
12	Inspect for poor connections at the windshield wiper motor. Did you find and correct the condition?	Go to Step 14	Go to Step 13
13	Replace the windshield wiper motor module. Is the repair complete?	Go to Step 14	--
14	Operate the system in order to verify the repair. Did you correct the condition?	System OK	Go to Step 3

LTV0500000002977

Fig. 132   Washers Inoperative (Part 2 of 2). 2002 Express & Savanna

	Action	Yes	No
7	Operate the system in order to verify the repair. Did you correct the condition?	System OK	Go to Step 3

LTV0500000002979

Fig. 133   Wipers Always On (Part 2 of 2). 2002 Express & Savanna

Step	Action	Yes	No
1	Did you review the Wiper/Washer System Description and Operation and perform the necessary inspections?	Go to Step 2	Go to Symptoms -
2	1. Turn the ignition ON. 2. Turn the windshield wiper/washer switch to the OFF position. Do the windshield wipers remain in the park position?	Test for Intermittent and Poor Connections	Go to Step 3
3	1. Turn the ignition OFF. 2. Disconnect the inline harness connector C200. 3. Remove the connector terminal row E from the steering column harness connector half. 4. Connect the inline harness connector C200. 5. Turn the ignition ON. Are the windshield wipers always on?	Go to Step 4	Go to Step 6
4	1. Disconnect the windshield wiper motor connector. 2. Test the windshield wiper switch low circuit for a short to voltage. Did you find and correct the condition?	Go to Step 7	Go to Step 5
5	Replace the windshield wiper motor module. Is the repair complete?	Go to Step 7	--
6	Replace the windshield wiper/washer switch. Is the repair complete?	Go to Step 7	--

LTV0500000002978

Fig. 133   Wipers Always On (Part 1 of 2). 2002 Express & Savanna

Step	Action	Yes	No
	DEFINITION: The washer pump may operate but all of the wiper motor functions are inoperative.		
1	Did you review the Wiper/Washer System Description and Operation and perform the necessary inspections?	Go to Step 2	Go to Symptoms -
2	1. Turn the ignition ON. 2. Operate the windshield wiper/washer system in all the switch positions. Does the windshield wiper/washer system operate normally?		Go to Step 3
3	1. Disconnect the windshield wiper motor connector. 2. Connect a test lamp from the low circuit terminal in the wiper motor harness connector to a good ground. 3. Turn the ignition ON. 4. Press the windshield washer switch. Does the test lamp illuminate?	Go to Step 4	Go to Step 6
4	Connect a test lamp from the accessory voltage supply circuit terminal in the wiper motor harness connector to a good ground. Does the test lamp illuminate?	Go to Step 5	Go to Step 8
5	Connect a test lamp from the accessory voltage supply circuit terminal to the ground circuit terminal in the wiper motor harness connector. Does the test lamp illuminate?	Go to Step 13	Go to Step 9
6	Test the windshield wiper switch low circuit for an open or short to ground. Did you find and correct the condition?	Go to Step 5	Go to Step 7

LTV0500000002980

Fig. 134   Wipers Inoperative, All Modes (Part 1 of 3). 2002 Express & Savanna

Step	Action	Value(s)	Yes	No
7	Test the accessory voltage supply circuit to the windshield wiper/washer switch for an open or short to ground. Did you find and correct the condition?		Go to Step 15	Go to Step 10
8	Repair the accessory voltage supply circuit for an open or high resistance. Is the repair complete?		Go to Step 15	--
9	Repair the windshield wiper motor ground circuit for an open or high resistance. Is the repair complete?		Go to Step 15	--
10	Test the windshield wiper motor high speed circuit for a short to ground. Did you find and correct the condition?		Go to Step 15	Go to Step 11
11	Inspect for poor connections at the windshield wiper/washer switch. Did you find and correct the condition?		Go to Step 15	Go to Step 12
12	Replace the windshield wiper/washer switch Is the repair complete?		Go to Step 15	--

LTV0500000002981

Fig. 134 Wipers Inoperative, All Modes (Part 2 of 3). 2002 Express & Savanna

Test Description

The numbers below refer to the step numbers on the diagnostic table.

6. This step tests for continuity through the 680 ohms resistor in the windshield wiper/washer switch. The connector behind the instrument panel knee bolster is suitable for performing this step.

7. This step tests for continuity through the delay resistors in the windshield wiper/washer switch. The measured resistance will change in sequence from high to low as the delay speed is increased. The connector behind the instrument panel knee bolster is suitable for performing this step.

Step	Action	Value(s)	Yes	No
1	Did you review the Wiper/Washer System Description and Operation and perform the necessary inspections?	--	Go to Step 2	Go to Symptoms -
2	1. Turn the ignition ON. 2. Operate the windshield wiper/washer system in all the switch positions. Does the windshield wiper/washer system operate normally?	--	Test for Intermittent and Poor Connections	Go to Step 3
3	Do the windshield wipers operate in the high speed mode?	--	Go to Step 5	Go to Step 4

LTV0500000002983

Fig. 135 Wipers Inoperative, One Or More Modes (Part 1 of 3). 2002 Express & Savanna

Step	Action	Value(s)	Yes	No
13	Inspect for poor connections at the windshield wiper motor. Did you find and correct the condition?		Go to Step 15	Go to Step 14
14	Replace the windshield wiper motor. Is the repair complete?		Go to Step 15	--
15	Operate the system in order to verify the repair. Did you correct the condition?		System OK	Go to Step 3

LTV0500000002982

Fig. 134 Wipers Inoperative, All Modes (Part 3 of 3). 2002 Express & Savanna

Step	Action	Value(s)	Yes	No
4	1. Disconnect the windshield wiper motor connector. 2. Connect a test lamp from the windshield wiper motor high speed circuit terminal in the wiper motor harness connector to ground. 3. Turn the ignition ON. 4. Operate the windshield wiper/washer switch to the high speed position. Does the test lamp illuminate?	--	Go to Step 13	Go to Step 8
5	1. Disconnect the windshield wiper motor connector. 2. Connect a test lamp from the windshield wiper switch pulse delay signal circuit terminal in the wiper motor harness connector to ground. 3. Turn the ignition ON. 4. Press the windshield washer switch. Does the test lamp illuminate?	--	Go to Step 6	Go to Step 9

6	1. Disconnect the windshield wiper/washer switch connector.
	2. Measure the resistance through the windshield wiper/washer switch from the low circuit terminal to the accessory voltage supply circuit terminal in the wiper/washer switch connector.
	3. Operate the windshield wiper/washer switch to the following positions:
	
	  - MIST
	4.
	  - LO
	5.
	  - HI
	
	Is the resistance at or near the specified value in all the listed switch positions?
		680 ohms	Go to Step 7	Go to Step 11

7	1. Measure the resistance through the windshield wiper/washer switch from the low circuit terminal to the accessory voltage supply circuit terminal in the wiper/washer switch connector. 2. Operate the windshield wiper/washer switch through all of the delay positions. Does the resistance remain within the specified values from high to low as the delay speed is increased?	30K - 450K ohms	Go to Step 13	Go to Step 11

LTV0500000002984

Fig. 135 Wipers Inoperative, One Or More Modes (Part 2 of 3). 2002 Express & Savanna

Step	Action	Yes	No
8	Test the windshield wiper motor high speed circuit for an open or high resistance. Did you find and correct the condition?	Go to Step 15	Go to Step 11
9	Test the windshield wiper switch low circuit for an open or short to ground. Did you find and correct the condition?	Go to Step 15	Go to Step 10
10	Test the accessory voltage supply circuit to the windshield wiper switch for an open or high resistance. Did you find and correct the condition?	Go to Step 15	Go to Step 11
11	Inspect for poor connections at the windshield wiper/washer switch. Did you find and correct the condition?	Go to Step 15	Go to Step 12
12	Replace the windshield wiper/washer switch. Is the repair complete?	Go to Step 15	--
13	Inspect for poor connections at the windshield wiper motor. Did you find and correct the condition?	Go to Step 15	Go to Step 14
14	Replace the windshield wiper motor module. Is the repair complete?	Go to Step 15	--
15	Operate the system in order to verify the repair. Did you correct the condition?	System OK	Go to Step 3

LTV0500000002985

Fig. 135 Wipers Inoperative, One Or More Modes (Part 3 of 3). 2002 Express & Savanna

Step	Action	Yes	No
8	Test the windshield washer relay control circuit for a short to ground. Did you find and correct the condition?	Go to Step 17	Go to Step 12
9	Test the windshield wiper switch signal 1 circuit for a short to voltage. Did you find and correct the condition?	Go to Step 17	Go to Step 11
10	Inspect for poor connections at the windshield washer relay. Did you find and correct the condition?	Go to Step 17	Go to Step 14
11	Inspect for poor connections at the windshield wiper/washer switch. Did you find and correct the condition?	Go to Step 17	Go to Step 15
12	Inspect for poor connections at the windshield wiper motor. Did you find and correct the condition?	Go to Step 17	Go to Step 16
13	Repair the short to voltage in the windshield washer pump control circuit. Did you complete the repair?	Go to Step 17	--
14	Replace the windshield washer relay. Did you complete the replacement?	Go to Step 17	--
15	Replace the windshield wiper/washer switch. Did you complete the replacement?	Go to Step 17	--
16	Replace the windshield wiper motor cover. Did you complete the replacement?	Go to Step 17	--

LTV0500000002990

Fig. 136 Washers Always On (Part 2 of 3). 2003 Express & Savanna

Step	Action	Yes	No
	DEFINITION: The windshield washer pump is always ON.		
1	Did you review the Wiper/Washer System Description and Operation and perform the necessary inspections?	Go to Step 2	Go to Symptoms -
2	1. Turn the windshield wiper/washer switch to the OFF position. 2. Turn the ignition ON. Is the windshield washer pump always ON?	Go to Step 3	
3	Are the windshield wipers always ON?	Go to Step 6	Go to Step 4
4	Remove the windshield washer relay from the underhood fuse block. Is the windshield washer pump ON?	Go to Step 13	Go to Step 5
5	Connect a test lamp from battery positive voltage to the windshield washer relay control circuit terminal in the underhood fuse block. Does the test lamp illuminate?	Go to Step 8	Go to Step 10
6	1. Turn the ignition OFF. 2. Disconnect the windshield wiper motor connector. 3. Turn the ignition ON. 4. Connect a test lamp from the windshield wiper switch signal 1 circuit terminal to ground. Does the test lamp illuminate?	Go to Step 9	Go to Step 7
7	Measure resistance between the windshield wiper switch voltage supply circuit and the signal 1 circuit. Is the resistance less than 380 ohms?	Go to Step 11	Go to Step 12

LTV0500000002989

Fig. 136 Washers Always On (Part 1 of 3). 2003 Express & Savanna

Step	Action	Yes	No
17	Operate the system in order to verify the repair. Did you correct the condition?	System OK	Go to Step 3

LTV0500000002991

Fig. 136 Washers Always On (Part 3 of 3). 2003 Express & Savanna

Step	Action	Values	Yes	No
1	Did you review the Wiper/Washer System Description and Operation and perform the necessary inspections?	--	Go to Step 2	Go to Symptoms
2	1. Turn the ignition ON. 2. Press the windshield washer switch. Do the windshield washers operate normally?	--	Test for Intermittent and Poor Connections	Go to Step 3
3	Do the windshield washer wipers operate when the windshield washer switch is pressed?	--	Go to Step 6	Go to Step 4
4	1. Disconnect the windshield wiper motor connector. 2. Test the resistance from the windshield wiper switch supply voltage circuit terminal to the windshield wiper switch signal 1 circuit terminal in the windshield wiper motor harness connector. 3. Press the windshield washer switch. Is the resistance near the specified value?	0.5 ohms	Go to Step 15	Go to Step 5
5	Test the following circuits for high resistance. • Windshield wiper switch supply voltage circuit • Windshield wiper switch signal 1 circuit Did you find and correct the condition?	--	Go to Step 20	Go to Step 13

LTV0500000002992

Fig. 137 Wipers Inoperative (Part 1 of 4). 2003 Express & Savanna

Step	Action	Values	Yes	No
11	Test the windshield washer pump control circuit for an open or high resistance. Did you find and correct the condition?	-	Go to Step 20	Go to Step 12
12	Test the windshield washer pump ground circuit for an open or high resistance. Did you find and correct the condition?	-	Go to Step 20	Go to Step 17
13	Inspect for poor connections at the windshield wiper/washer switch. Did you find and correct the condition?	-	Go to Step 20	Go to Step 14
14	Replace the windshield wiper/washer switch. Is the repair complete?	-	Go to Step 20	--
15	Inspect for poor connections at the windshield wiper motor. Did you find and correct the condition?	-	Go to Step 20	Go to Step 16
16	Replace the windshield wiper motor cover. Is the repair complete?	-	Go to Step 20	--
17	Replace the windshield washer relay. Is the repair complete?	-	Go to Step 20	--
18	Inspect for poor connections at the windshield washer pump. Did you find and correct the condition?	-	Go to Step 20	Go to Step 19
19	Replace the windshield washer pump. Is the repair complete?	-	Go to Step 20	--

LTV0500000002994

Fig. 137 Wipers Inoperative (Part 3 of 4). 2003 Express & Savanna

Step	Action	Values	Yes	No
6	1. Disconnect the windshield washer relay. 2. Connect a test lamp test from each of the windshield washer relay battery positive voltage supply circuit terminals in the underhood fuse block to ground. Does the test lamp illuminate on both terminals?	--	Go to Step 7	Go to Step 9
7	1. Connect a test lamp from battery positive voltage to the windshield washer relay control circuit terminal in the underhood fuse block. 2. Turn the ignition ON. 3. Press the windshield washer switch. Does the test lamp illuminate?	--	Go to Step 8	Go to Step 10
8	1. Connect the windshield washer relay. 2. Disconnect the windshield washer pump connector. 3. Connect a test lamp across the windshield washer pump harness connector terminals. 4. Turn the ignition ON. 5. Press the windshield washer switch. Does the test lamp illuminate?	--	Go to Step 18	Go to Step 11
9	Replace the underhood fuse block. Is the repair complete?	--	Go to Step 20	--
10	Test the windshield washer relay control circuit for an open or high resistance. Did you find and correct the condition?	--	Go to Step 20	Go to Step 15

LTV0500000002993

Fig. 137 Wipers Inoperative (Part 2 of 4). 2003 Express & Savanna

Step	Action	Values	Yes	No
20	Operate the system in order to verify the repair. Did you correct the condition?	--	System OK	Go to Step 3

LTV0500000002995

Fig. 137 Wipers Inoperative (Part 4 of 4). 2003 Express & Savanna

Step	Action	Yes	No
1	Did you perform the Wiper/Washer System Description and Operation and perform the necessary inspections?	Go to Step 2	Go to Symptoms
2	1. Turn the windshield wiper/washer switch OFF. 2. Turn the ignition ON. Are the windshield wipers always on?	Go to Step 3	
3	1. Disconnect the steering column harness connector. 2. Remove the connector terminal row E from the steering column connector half. 3. Connect the steering column harness connector. 4. Turn the ignition ON. Are the windshield wipers always on?	Go to Step 4	Go to Step 6
4	Test the windshield wiper switch high signal circuit for a short to ground. Did you find and correct the condition?	Go to Step 12	Go to Step 5
5	Test the windshield wiper switch signal 1 circuit for a short to voltage. Did you find and correct the condition?	Go to Step 12	Go to Step 10
6	Test the windshield wiper switch high signal circuit in the steering column harness for a short to ground. Did you find and correct the condition?	Go to Step 12	Go to Step 7

LTV0500000002996

Fig. 138   Wipers Always On (Part 1 of 2). 2003 Express & Savanna

Step	Action	Yes	No
	DEFINITION: The windshield wiper motor will not operate in any mode.		
1	Did you perform the Wiper/Washer System Description and Operation and perform the necessary inspections?	Go to Step 2	Go to Symptoms
2	1. Turn the ignition ON. 2. Attempt to operate the windshield wipers in all modes. Are the windshield wipers inoperative in all modes?	Go to Step 3	Test for Intermittent and Poor Connections
3	1. Disconnect the steering column harness connector. 2. Connect a fused jumper wire from the windshield wiper switch high signal circuit terminal in the body harness connector half to ground. 3. Turn the ignition ON. Do the windshield wipers operate at high speed?	Go to Step 8	Go to Step 4
4	1. Disconnect the windshield wiper motor connector. 2. Connect a test lamp from the accessory voltage supply circuit terminal in the windshield wiper motor harness connector to a good ground. 3. Turn the ignition ON. Does the test lamp illuminate?	Go to Step 5	Go to Step 6
5	Connect a test lamp from battery positive voltage to the windshield wiper motor ground circuit terminal in the windshield wiper motor harness connector. Does the test lamp illuminate?	Go to Step 10	Go to Step 7

LTV0500000002998

Fig. 139   Wipers Inoperative, All Modes (Part 1 of 2). 2003 Express & Savanna

Step	Action	Yes	No
7	Test the windshield wiper switch signal 1 circuit in the steering column harness for a short to voltage. Did you find and correct the condition?	Go to Step 12	Go to Step 8
8	Inspect for poor connections at the windshield wiper/washer switch. Did you find and correct the condition?	Go to Step 12	Go to Step 9
9	Replace the windshield wiper/washer switch. Is the repair complete?	Go to Step 12	--
10	Inspect for poor connections at the windshield wiper motor. Did you find and correct the condition?	Go to Step 12	Go to Step 11
11	Replace the windshield wiper motor cover. Is the repair complete?	Go to Step 12	--
12	Operate the system in order to verify the repair. Did you correct the condition?	System OK	Go to Step 3

LTV0500000002997

Fig. 138   Wipers Always On (Part 2 of 2). 2003 Express & Savanna

Step	Action	Yes	No
6	Repair the accessory voltage supply circuit to the windshield wiper motor for an open or short to ground. Is the repair complete?	Go to Step 12	--
7	Repair the windshield wiper motor ground circuit for an open or high resistance. Is the repair complete?	Go to Step 12	--
8	Inspect for poor connections at the windshield wiper/washer switch. Did you find and correct the condition?	Go to Step 12	Go to Step 9
9	Replace the windshield wiper/washer switch. Is the repair complete?	Go to Step 12	--
10	Inspect for poor connections at the windshield wiper motor. Did you find and correct the condition?	Go to Step 12	Go to Step 11
11	Replace the windshield wiper motor. Is the repair complete?	Go to Step 12	--
12	Operate the system in order to verify the repair. Did you correct the condition?	System OK	Go to Step 3

LTV0500000002999

Fig. 139   Wipers Inoperative, All Modes (Part 2 of 2). 2003 Express & Savanna

Test Description

The numbers below refer to the step numbers on the diagnostic table.

5. This step tests for continuity through the 390 ohms resistor in the windshield wiper/washer switch.

6. This step tests for continuity through the delay resistors in the windshield wiper/washer switch. The measured resistance will change in sequence from low to high as the delay speed is increased.

Step	Action	Values	Yes	No
	DEFINITION: The windshield wiper motor operates in some modes but not all modes.			
1	Did you perform the Wiper/Washer System Description and Operation and perform the necessary inspections?	--	Go to Step 2	Go to Symptoms
2	1. Turn the ignition ON. 2. Attempt to operate the windshield wipers in all modes. Does the system operate normally?	--		Go to Step 3
3	Do the windshield wipers operate in the high speed mode?	--	Go to Step 5	Go to Step 4
4	1. Disconnect the steering column harness connector. 2. Connect a fused jumper wire from the windshield wiper switch high signal circuit terminal in the body harness connector half to a good ground. 3. Turn the ignition ON. Do the windshield wipers operate at high speed?	--	Go to Step 8	Go to Step 7

LTV0500000003000

Fig. 140   Wipers Inoperative, One Or More Modes (Part 1 of 3). 2003 Express & Savanna

Step	Action	Values	Yes	No

5	1. Disconnect the windshield wiper motor connector.
	2. Test the resistance from the windshield wiper switch voltage supply circuit terminal to the windshield wiper switch signal 1 circuit terminal in the windshield wiper motor harness connector.
	3. Operate the windshield wiper/washer switch in the following positions:
	
	  - MIST
	  - LO
	  - HI
	
	Is the resistance near the specified value in all of the listed switch positions?
		390 ohms	Go to Step 6	Go to Step 10

6	1. Test the resistance from the windshield wiper switch voltage supply circuit terminal to the windshield wiper switch signal 1 circuit terminal in the windshield wiper motor harness connector. 2. Operate the windshield wiper/washer switch in all of the delay positions. Does the resistance remain within the specified values from low to high as the delay speed is increased?	1000-10K ohms	Go to Step 14	Go to Step 12
7	Test the windshield wiper switch high signal circuit for an open or high resistance. Did you find and correct the condition?	--	Go to Step 16	Go to Step 14
8	Test the wiper switch ground circuit for an open or high resistance. Did you find and correct the condition?	--	Go to Step 16	Go to Step 9
9	Test the windshield wiper switch high signal circuit in the steering column harness for an open or high resistance. Did you find and correct the condition?	--	Go to Step 16	Go to Step 12
10	Test the windshield wiper switch voltage supply circuit for an open or short to ground. Did you find and correct the condition?	--	Go to Step 16	Go to Step 11

LTV0500000003001

Fig. 140   Wipers Inoperative, One Or More Modes (Part 2 of 3). 2003 Express & Savanna

Step	Action	Values	Yes	No
11	Test the windshield wiper switch signal 1 circuit for an open or short to ground. Did you find and correct the condition?	--	Go to Step 16	Go to Step 12
12	Inspect for poor connections at the windshield wiper/washer switch. Did you find and correct the condition?	--	Go to Step 16	Go to Step 13
13	Replace the windshield wiper/washer switch. Is the repair complete?	--	Go to Step 16	--
14	Inspect for poor connections at the windshield wiper motor. Did you find and correct the condition?	--	Go to Step 16	Go to Step 15
15	Replace the windshield wiper motor cover. Is the repair complete?	--	Go to Step 16	--
16	Operate the system in order to verify the repair. Did you correct the condition?	--	System OK	Go to Step 3

LTV0500000003002

Fig. 140   Wipers Inoperative, One Or More Modes (Part 3 of 3). 2003 Express & Savanna

Step	Action	Yes	No
	DEFINITION: The windshield washer pump is always ON.		
1	Did you review the Wiper/Washer System Description and Operation and perform the necessary inspections?	Go to Step 2	Go to Symptoms
2	1. Turn the windshield wiper/washer switch to the OFF position. 2. Turn the ignition ON. Is the windshield washer pump always ON?	Go to Step 3	Test for Intermittent and Poor Connections
3	Are the windshield wipers always ON?	Go to Step 6	Go to Step 4
4	Remove the windshield washer relay from the underhood fuse block. Is the windshield washer pump ON?	Go to Step 13	Go to Step 5
5	Connect a test lamp from battery positive voltage to the windshield washer relay control circuit terminal in the underhood fuse block. Does the test lamp illuminate?	Go to Step 8	Go to Step 10
6	1. Turn the ignition OFF. 2. Disconnect the windshield wiper motor connector. 3. Turn the ignition ON. 4. Connect a test lamp from the windshield wiper switch signal 1 circuit terminal to ground. Does the test lamp illuminate?	Go to Step 9	Go to Step 7
7	Measure resistance between the windshield wiper switch voltage supply circuit and the signal 1 circuit. Is the resistance less than 380 ohms?	Go to Step 11	Go to Step 12

LTV0500000003005

Fig. 141   Washers Always On (Part 1 of 3). 2004–06 Express & Savanna

Step	Action	Values	Yes	No
8	Test the windshield washer relay control circuit for a short to ground. Did you find and correct the condition?		Go to Step 17	Go to Step 12
9	Test the windshield wiper switch signal 1 circuit for a short to voltage. Did you find and correct the condition?		Go to Step 17	Go to Step 11
10	Inspect for poor connections at the windshield washer relay. Did you find and correct the condition?		Go to Step 17	Go to Step 14
11	Inspect for poor connections at the windshield wiper/washer switch. Did you find and correct the condition?		Go to Step 17	Go to Step 15
12	Inspect for poor connections at the windshield wiper motor. Did you find and correct the condition?		Go to Step 17	Go to Step 16
13	Repair the short to voltage in the windshield washer pump control circuit. Did you complete the repair?		Go to Step 17	--
14	Replace the windshield washer relay. Did you complete the replacement?		Go to Step 17	--
15	Replace the windshield wiper/washer switch. Did you complete the replacement?		Go to Step 17	--
16	Replace the windshield wiper motor cover. Did you complete the replacement?		Go to Step 17	--

LTV0500000003006

Fig. 141 Washers Always On (Part 2 of 3). 2004–06 Express & Savanna

Step	Action	Values	Yes	No
17	Operate the system in order to verify the repair. Did you correct the condition?		System OK	Go to Step 3

LTV0500000003007

Fig. 141 Washers Always On (Part 3 of 3). 2004–06 Express & Savanna

Step	Action	Values	Yes	No
	DEFINITION: The windshield washer pump is inoperative.			
1	Did you review the Wiper/Washer System Description and Operation and perform the necessary inspections?	--	Go to Step 2	Go to Symptoms
2	1. Turn the ignition ON. 2. Press the windshield washer switch. Do the windshield washers operate normally?	--	Test for Intermittent and Poor Connections	Go to Step 3
3	Do the windshield wipers operate when the windshield washer switch is pressed?	--	Go to Step 4	Go to Step 7
4	1. Disconnect the windshield washer relay. Refer to Relay Replacement in Wiring Systems. 2. Probe each of the windshield washer relay battery positive voltage supply circuit terminals in the underhood fuse block with a test lamp connected to a good ground. Does the test lamp illuminate on both terminals?	--	Go to Step 5	Go to Step 19
5	1. Connect a test lamp between the battery positive voltage terminal and the windshield washer relay control circuit terminal in the underhood fuse block. 2. Turn the ignition ON. 3. Press the windshield washer switch. Does the test lamp illuminate?	--	Go to Step 6	Go to Step 9

LTV0500000003008

Fig. 142 Washers Inoperative (Part 1 of 3). 2004–06 Express & Savanna

Step	Action	Values	Yes	No
6	1. Connect the windshield washer relay. 2. Disconnect the windshield washer pump connector. 3. Connect a test lamp across the windshield washer pump harness connector terminals. 4. Turn the ignition ON. 5. Press the windshield washer switch. Does the test lamp illuminate?	--	Go to Step 12	Go to Step 10
7	1. Disconnect the windshield wiper motor connector. 2. Test the resistance from the windshield wiper switch supply voltage circuit terminal to the windshield wiper switch signal 1 circuit terminal in the windshield wiper motor harness connector. 3. Press the windshield washer switch. Is the resistance near the specified value?	0.5 ohms	Go to Step 14	Go to Step 8
8	Test the following circuits for high resistance. • Windshield wiper switch supply voltage circuit • Windshield wiper switch signal 1 circuit. Did you find and correct the condition?	--	Go to Step 20	Go to Step 13
9	Test the windshield washer relay control circuit for an open or high resistance. Did you find and correct the condition?	--	Go to Step 20	Go to Step 14
10	Test the windshield washer pump control circuit for an open or high resistance. Did you find and correct the condition?	--	Go to Step 20	Go to Step 11
11	Test the windshield washer pump ground circuit for an open or high resistance. Did you find and correct the condition?	--	Go to Step 20	Go to Step 15
12	Inspect for poor connections at the windshield washer pump. Did you find and correct the condition?	--	Go to Step 20	Go to Step 16

LTV0500000003009

Fig. 142 Washers Inoperative (Part 2 of 3). 2004–06 Express & Savanna

Step	Action	Values	Yes	No
13	Inspect for poor connections at the windshield wiper/washer switch. Did you find and correct the condition?	--	Go to Step 20	Go to Step 17
14	Inspect for poor connections at the windshield wiper motor. Did you find and correct the condition?	--	Go to Step 20	Go to Step 18
15	Replace the windshield washer relay. Is the repair complete?	--	Go to Step 20	--
16	Replace the windshield washer pump. Is the repair complete?	--	Go to Step 20	--
17	Replace the windshield wiper/washer switch. Is the repair complete?	--	Go to Step 20	--
18	Replace the windshield wiper motor cover. Is the repair complete?	--	Go to Step 20	--
19	Replace the underhood fuse block. Is the repair complete?	--	Go to Step 20	--
20	Operate the system in order to verify the repair. Did you correct the condition?	--	System OK	Go to Step 3

LTV0500000003010

Fig. 142   Washers Inoperative (Part 3 of 3). 2004–06 Express & Savanna

Step	Action	Values	Yes	No
7	Test the windshield wiper switch signal 1 circuit in the steering column harness for a short to voltage. Did you find and correct the condition?	--	Go to Step 12	Go to Step 8
8	Inspect for poor connections at the windshield wiper/washer switch. Did you find and correct the condition?	--	Go to Step 12	Go to Step 10
9	Inspect for poor connections at the windshield wiper motor. Did you find and correct the condition?	--	Go to Step 12	Go to Step 11
10	Replace the windshield wiper/washer switch. Is the repair complete?	--	Go to Step 12	--
11	Replace the windshield wiper motor cover. Is the repair complete?	--	Go to Step 12	--
12	Operate the system in order to verify the repair. Did you correct the condition?	--	System OK	Go to Step 3

LTV0500000003012

Fig. 143   Wipers Always On (Part 2 of 2). 2004–06 Express & Savanna

Step	Action	Yes	No
	DEFINITION: The windshield wiper motor operates when the windshield wiper switch is OFF.		
1	Did you perform the Wiper/Washer System Description and Operation and perform the necessary inspections?	Go to Step 2	Go to Symptoms
2	1. Turn the windshield wiper/washer switch OFF. 2. Turn the ignition ON. Are the windshield wipers always ON?	Go to Step 3	
3	1. Disconnect the steering column harness connector. 2. Remove the connector terminal row E from the steering column connector half. 3. Connect the steering column harness connector. 4. Turn the ignition ON. Are the windshield wipers always ON?	Go to Step 4	Go to Step 6
4	Test the windshield wiper switch high signal circuit for a short to ground. Did you find and correct the condition?	Go to Step 12	Go to Step 5
5	Test the windshield wiper switch signal 1 circuit for a short to voltage. Did you find and correct the condition?	Go to Step 12	Go to Step 9
6	Test the windshield wiper switch high signal circuit in the steering column harness for a short to ground. Did you find and correct the condition?	Go to Step 12	Go to Step 7

LTV0500000003011

Fig. 143   Wipers Always On (Part 1 of 2). 2004–06 Express & Savanna

Step	Action	Yes	No
	DEFINITION: The windshield wiper motor will not operate in any mode.		
1	Did you perform the Wiper/Washer System Description and Operation and perform the necessary inspections?	Go to Step 2	Go to Symptoms
2	1. Turn the ignition ON. 2. Attempt to operate the windshield wipers in all modes. Are the windshield wipers inoperative in all modes?	Go to Step 3	Test for Intermittent and Poor Connections
3	1. Disconnect the steering column harness connector. 2. Connect a fused jumper wire from the windshield wiper switch high signal circuit terminal in the body harness connector half to ground. 3. Turn the ignition ON. Do the windshield wipers operate at high speed?	Go to Step 8	Go to Step 4
4	1. Disconnect the windshield wiper motor connector. 2. Connect a test lamp from the accessory voltage supply circuit terminal in the windshield wiper motor harness connector to a good ground. 3. Turn the ignition ON. Does the test lamp illuminate?	Go to Step 5	Go to Step 6
5	Connect a test lamp from battery positive voltage to the windshield wiper motor ground circuit terminal in the windshield wiper motor harness connector. Does the test lamp illuminate?	Go to Step 10	Go to Step 7

LTV0500000003013

Fig. 144   Wipers Inoperative, All Modes (Part 1 of 2). 2004–06 Express & Savanna

Step	Action	Values	Yes	No
6	Repair the accessory voltage supply circuit to the windshield wiper motor for an open or short to ground. Is the repair complete?		Go to Step 12	--
7	Repair the windshield wiper motor ground circuit for an open or high resistance. Is the repair complete?		Go to Step 12	--
8	Inspect for poor connections at the windshield wiper/washer switch. Did you find and correct the condition?		Go to Step 12	Go to Step 9
9	Replace the windshield wiper/washer switch. Is the repair complete?		Go to Step 12	--
10	Inspect for poor connections at the windshield wiper motor. Did you find and correct the condition?		Go to Step 12	Go to Step 11
11	Replace the windshield wiper motor. Is the repair complete?		Go to Step 12	--
12	Operate the system in order to verify the repair. Did you correct the condition?		System OK	Go to Step 3

LTV0500000003014

Fig. 144 Wipers Inoperative, All Modes (Part 2 of 2). 2004–06 Express & Savanna

Step	Action	Values	Yes	No
5	1. Disconnect the windshield wiper motor connector. 2. Test the resistance from the windshield wiper switch voltage supply circuit terminal to the windshield wiper switch signal 1 circuit terminal in the windshield wiper motor harness connector. 3. Operate the windshield wiper/washer switch in the following positions: - MIST - LO - HI Is the resistance near the specified value in all of the listed switch positions?	390 ohms	Go to Step 6	Go to Step 10
6	1. Test the resistance from the windshield wiper switch voltage supply circuit terminal to the windshield wiper switch signal 1 circuit terminal in the windshield wiper motor harness connector. 2. Operate the windshield wiper/washer switch in all of the delay positions. Does the resistance remain within the specified values from low to high as the delay speed is increased?	1000-10K ohms	Go to Step 14	Go to Step 12
7	Test the windshield wiper switch high signal circuit for an open or high resistance. Did you find and correct the condition?	--	Go to Step 16	Go to Step 14
8	Test the wiper switch ground circuit for an open or high resistance. Did you find and correct the condition?	--	Go to Step 16	Go to Step 9
9	Test the windshield wiper switch high signal circuit in the steering column harness for an open or high resistance. Did you find and correct the condition?	--	Go to Step 16	Go to Step 12
10	Test the windshield wiper switch voltage supply circuit for an open or short to ground. Did you find and correct the condition?	--	Go to Step 16	Go to Step 11

LTV0500000003016

Fig. 145 Wipers Inoperative, One Or More Modes (Part 2 of 3). 2004–06 Express & Savanna

Test Description

The numbers below refer to the step numbers on the diagnostic table.

5. This step tests for continuity through the 390 ohms resistor in the windshield wiper/washer switch.

6. This step tests for continuity through the delay resistors in the windshield wiper/washer switch. The measured resistance will change in sequence from low to high as the delay speed is increased.

Step	Action	Values	Yes	No
	DEFINITION: The windshield wiper motor operates in some modes but not all modes.			
1	Did you perform the Wiper/Washer System Description and Operation and perform the necessary inspections?	--	Go to Step 2	Go to Symptoms
2	1. Turn the ignition ON. 2. Attempt to operate the windshield wipers in all modes. Does the system operate normally?	--	Test for Intermittent and Poor Connections	Go to Step 3
3	Do the windshield wipers operate in the high speed mode?	--	Go to Step 5	Go to Step 4
4	1. Disconnect the steering column harness connector. 2. Connect a fused jumper wire from the windshield wiper switch high signal circuit terminal in the body harness connector half to a good ground. 3. Turn the ignition ON. Do the windshield wipers operate at high speed?		Go to Step 8	Go to Step 7

LTV0500000003015

Fig. 145 Wipers Inoperative, One Or More Modes (Part 1 of 3). 2004–06 Express & Savanna

Step	Action	Values	Yes	No
11	Test the windshield wiper switch signal 1 circuit for an open or short to ground. Did you find and correct the condition?	--	Go to Step 16	Go to Step 12
12	Inspect for poor connections at the windshield wiper/washer switch. Did you find and correct the condition?	--	Go to Step 16	Go to Step 13
13	Replace the windshield wiper/washer switch. Is the repair complete?	--	Go to Step 16	--
14	Inspect for poor connections at the windshield wiper motor. Did you find and correct the condition?	--	Go to Step 16	Go to Step 15
15	Replace the windshield wiper motor cover. Is the repair complete?	--	Go to Step 16	--
16	Operate the system in order to verify the repair. Did you correct the condition?	--	System OK	Go to Step 3

LTV0500000003017

Fig. 145 Wipers Inoperative, One Or More Modes (Part 3 of 3). 2004–06 Express & Savanna

Circuit Description

The body control module (BCM) monitors the supply voltage circuit of the wiper 1 relay. The voltage should be low while the wiper 1 relay is de-energized. The voltage will be near system voltage when the BCM energizes the wiper 1 relay. The supply voltage circuit of the wiper 1 relay is shared with the signal circuit of the windshield wiper motor park switch internally in the BCM. The BCM monitors the signal circuit of the windshield wiper motor park switch to determine if the windshield wiper motor is operating when commanded. The voltage on the signal circuit of the windshield wiper motor park switch should be near system voltage while the wipers are active. This is the result of the windshield wiper motor park switch being open. The voltage is pulled low when wipers are in or return to the Park position. The windshield wiper motor park switch will be closed, pulling the circuit to ground.

DTC Descriptors

This diagnostic procedure supports the following DTCs:

- DTC B3715 Front Wiper Relay Drive Circuit
- DTC B3716 Front Wiper Relay Drive Circuit Range/Performance
- DTC B3717 Front Wiper Relay Drive Circuit Low
- DTC B3718 Front Wiper Relay Drive Circuit High
- DTC B3719 Front Wiper Relay Drive Circuit Open

Conditions for Running the DTC

- The ignition is ON.
- Windshield wiper motor commanded on.

Conditions for Setting the DTCs

The following conditions will cause these DTCs to set:

B3715

The signal circuit of the windshield wiper motor park switch has not transition from a high to low state when the windshield wiper motor was commanded on.

LTV0500000003481

Fig. 146 Codes B3715, B3716, B3717, B3718 & B3719: Front Wiper Relay Drive Circuit (Part 1 of 8). HHR

2	1. Turn ON the ignition, with the engine OFF. 2. Operate the windshield wiper/washer switch through all the switch positions. Does the windshield wiper/washer system operate normally?	--	Test for Intermittent and Poor Connections	Go to Step 3
3	Are the wipers always on?	--	Go to Step 28	Go to Step 4
4	Operate the windshield wiper/washer switch through all the switch positions. Do the windshield wipers park correctly?		Go to Step 5	Go to Step 8
5	Turn the wiper/washer switch to the High position. Do the windshield wipers operate?		Go to Step 8	Go to Step 6
6	1. With a scan tool, observe the Wiper Switch State Data parameter in the body control module (BCM) Wiper/Washer data list. 2. Operate the windshield wiper/washer switch through all the switch positions. Does the scan tool indicate that Off, Delay 1, Delay 2, Delay 3, and Mist/Hi/Lo is correctly displayed each wiper/washer switch position?		Go to Step 10	Go to Step 7

LTV0500000003483

Fig. 146 Codes B3715, B3716, B3717, B3718 & B3719: Front Wiper Relay Drive Circuit (Part 3 of 8). HHR

B3717 or B3719

The BCM detects a low voltage level or open on the supply circuit of the wiper 1 relay when the relay is energized.

B3718

The BCM detects a high voltage level on the supply circuit of the wiper 1 relay when the relay is energized.

Action Taken When the DTC Sets

The windshield wipers will be disabled until the conditions mentioned above are no longer present.

Conditions for Clearing the DTC

- This DTC will change from current to history when the fault is no longer present.
- A history DTC will clear after 100 consecutive ignition cycles if the condition for the malfunction is no longer present.

Test Description

The numbers below refer to the step numbers on the diagnostic table.

10. Listen for an audible click when the Wiper 1 relay operates. Command both the ON and OFF states. Repeat the commands as necessary.

11. Verifies that the BCM is providing voltage to the Wiper 1 relay.

Step	Action	Values	Yes	No
1	Did you perform the Diagnostic System Check - Vehicle?	--	Go to Step 2	Go to Diagnostic System Check -

LTV0500000003482

Fig. 146 Codes B3715, B3716, B3717, B3718 & B3719: Front Wiper Relay Drive Circuit (Part 2 of 8). HHR

7	1. Turn OFF the ignition. 2. Disconnect the harness connector of the wiper/washer switch at the BCM. 3. Operate the windshield wiper/washer switch through all the switch positions. 4. Measure the resistance of the windshield wiper switch from the accessory voltage circuit to the signal circuit of the windshield wiper switch. Is the resistance within the specified range?	1700-9500 ohms	Go to Step 19	Go to Step 24
8	1. With a scan tool, observe the Wiper Park Switch Data parameter from the BCM Wiper/Washer Data list. 2. Disconnect the harness connector of the windshield wiper motor. Does the Wiper Park Switch Data parameter display Off?	--	Go to Step 20	Go to Step 9
9	While observing the Wiper Park Switch Data parameter, connect a 3-ampere fused jumper wire from the signal circuit of the windshield wiper motor park switch to good ground. Does the Wiper Park Switch Data parameter display On?	--	Go to Step 26	Go to Step 21
10	1. Select from miscellaneous test, the wiper from the BCM output controls. 2. Place the wiper/washer switch in the Low speed position. 3. With the scan tool, command the wiper 1 relay ON and OFF. Do you hear a click from the wiper 1 relay in the underhood fuse block, when you command the relay ON and OFF?	--	Go to Step 13	Go to Step 11

LTV0500000003484

Fig. 146 Codes B3715, B3716, B3717, B3718 & B3719: Front Wiper Relay Drive Circuit (Part 4 of 8). HHR

Step	Action		
11	1. Turn OFF the ignition. 2. Disconnect the wiper 1 relay. 3. Turn ON the ignition, with the engine OFF. 4. Connect a test lamp from the supply voltage circuit to the ground circuit of the wiper 1 relay coil. 5. Place the wiper/washer switch in the Low speed position. 6. With the scan tool, command the wiper 1 relay ON. Does the test lamp illuminate?	Go to Step 25	Go to Step 12
12	1. Connect a test lamp from the supply voltage circuit of the wiper 1 relay coil to a good ground. 2. Place the wiper/washer switch in the Low speed position. 3. With the scan tool, command the wiper 1 relay ON. Does the test lamp illuminate?	Go to Step 29	Go to Step 22
13	1. Turn OFF the ignition. 2. Disconnect the wiper 1 relay. 3. Turn ON the ignition, with the engine OFF. 4. Connect a test lamp from the battery voltage circuit of the wiper 1 relay switched input to a good ground. Does the test lamp illuminate?	Go to Step 14	Go to Step 23
14	Connect a 10-ampere fused jumper wire from the wiper 1 relay switched input to the switched output to voltage circuit of the wiper 2 relay switched input. Does the wiper motor operate at low speed?	Go to Step 25	Go to Step 15
15	1. Turn OFF the ignition. 2. Disconnect the wiper 2 relay. 3. Turn ON the ignition, with the engine OFF. 4. Connect a test lamp from the battery voltage circuit supplied from the wiper 1 relay to the wiper 2 relay switched input to a good ground. Does the test lamp illuminate?	Go to Step 16	Go to Step 31
16	Connect a 10-ampere fused jumper wire from the wiper 2 relay switched input to the relay switched output to the low speed circuit of the windshield wiper motor. Does the wiper motor operate?	Go to Step 25	Go to Step 17

LTV0500000003485

Fig. 146   Codes B3715, B3716, B3717, B3718 & B3719: Front Wiper Relay Drive Circuit (Part 5 of 8). HHR

Step	Action		
25	Inspect for poor connections at the inoperative wiper relay. Did you find and correct the condition?	Go to Step 38	Go to Step 35
26	Inspect for poor connections at the harness connector of the windshield wiper motor. Did you find and correct the condition?	Go to Step 38	Go to Step 36
27	Inspect for poor connections at the harness connector of the BCM. Did you find and correct the condition?	Go to Step 38	Go to Step 37
28	Repair a short to voltage in the supply voltage circuits of the wiper 1 and wiper 2 relay coils. Did you complete the repair?	Go to Step 38	--
29	Repair an open or high resistance in the ground circuit of the wiper 1 relay coil. Did you complete the repair?	Go to Step 38	--
30	Repair a short to ground on the low or high speed circuit of the windshield wiper motor. Did you complete the repair?	Go to Step 38	--
31	Repair an open or high resistance in the battery voltage circuit of the wiper 2 relay switched input. Did you complete the repair?	Go to Step 38	--
32	Repair an open or high resistance in the low speed circuit of the windshield wiper motor. Did you complete the repair?	Go to Step 38	--

LTV0500000003487

Fig. 146   Codes B3715, B3716, B3717, B3718 & B3719: Front Wiper Relay Drive Circuit (Part 7 of 8). HHR

Step	Action		
17	1. Turn OFF the ignition. 2. Disconnect the harness connector of the wiper motor. 3. Turn ON the ignition, with the engine OFF. 4. Connect a test lamp from the low speed circuit to the ground circuit of the wiper motor. Does the test lamp illuminate?	Go to Step 26	Go to Step 18
18	Connect a test lamp from the low speed circuit of the wiper motor to a good ground. Does the test lamp illuminate?	Go to Step 33	Go to Step 32
19	Test the signal circuit of the wiper/washer switch for an open or a short to ground. Did you find and correct the condition?	Go to Step 38	Go to Step 27
20	Test the signal circuit of the wiper motor park switch for a short to ground. Did you find and correct the condition?	Go to Step 38	Go to Step 27
21	Test the signal circuit of the wiper motor park switch for an open or a short to voltage. Did you find and correct the condition?	Go to Step 38	Go to Step 27
22	Test the supply voltage circuit of the wiper 1 relay coil for an open or a short to ground. Did you find and correct the condition?	Go to Step 38	Go to Step 27
23	Test the battery voltage circuit of the wiper 1 relay switched input for an open or high resistance. Did you find and correct the condition?	Go to Step 38	Go to Step 30
24	Inspect for poor connections at the harness connector of the windshield wiper/washer switch. Did you find and correct the condition?	Go to Step 38	Go to Step 34

LTV0500000003486

Fig. 146   Codes B3715, B3716, B3717, B3718 & B3719: Front Wiper Relay Drive Circuit (Part 6 of 8). HHR

Step	Action		
33	Repair an open or high resistance in the ground circuit of the windshield wiper motor. Did you complete the repair?	Go to Step 38	--
34	Replace the windshield wiper/washer switch. Did you complete the replacement?	Go to Step 38	--
35	Replace the inoperative wiper relay. Did you complete the replacement?	Go to Step 38	--
36	Replace the windshield wiper motor. Did you complete the replacement?	Go to Step 38	--
37	Replace the BCM. Did you complete the replacement?	Go to Step 38	--
38	1. Use the scan tool to clear the DTCs. 2. Operate the vehicle within the Conditions for Running the DTC as specified in the supporting text. Does the DTC reset?	Go to Step 2	System OK

LTV0500000003488

Fig. 146   Codes B3715, B3716, B3717, B3718 & B3719: Front Wiper Relay Drive Circuit (Part 8 of 8). HHR

Step	Action	Yes	No
1	Did you perform the Diagnostic System Check - Vehicle?	Go to Step 2	Go to Diagnostic System Check -
2	1. Turn the ignition ON. 2. Turn the windshield wiper/washer switch OFF. Do the windshield wipers remain in the Park position?	Test for Intermittent and Poor Connections	Go to Step 3
3	Disconnect the harness connector of the windshield wiper/washer switch. Do the windshield wipers stop?	Go to Step 11	Go to Step 4
4	Connect a test lamp from the signal circuit of the windshield wiper/washer switch at the body control module (BCM) to a good ground. Does the test lamp illuminate?	Go to Step 9	Go to Step 5
5	Connect a test lamp from the supply voltage circuit of the wiper 2 relay coil to a good ground. Does the test lamp illuminate?	Go to Step 14	Go to Step 6
6	Connect a test lamp from the control circuit of the windshield washer pump to a good ground. Does the test lamp illuminate?	Go to Step 15	Go to Step 7
7	Disconnect the wiper 1 relay. Do the windshield wipers stop?	Go to Step 8	Go to Step 16

LTV0500000003490

Fig. 147   Washers Always On (Part 1 of 3). HHR

Step	Action	Yes	No
8	Connect a test lamp from the supply voltage circuit of the wiper 1 relay coil from the BCM to a good ground. Does the test lamp illuminate?	Go to Step 10	Go to Step 12
9	Test the signal circuit of the windshield wiper switch for a short to voltage. Did you find and correct the condition?	Go to Step 20	Go to Step 13
10	Test the supply voltage circuit of the wiper 1 relay for a short to voltage. Did you find and correct the condition?	Go to Step 20	Go to Step 13
11	Inspect for poor connections at the windshield wiper/washer switch. Did you find and correct the condition?	Go to Step 20	Go to Step 17
12	Inspect for poor connections at the wiper 1 relay. Did you find and correct the condition?	Go to Step 20	Go to Step 18
13	Inspect for poor connections at the BCM. Did you find and correct the condition?	Go to Step 20	Go to Step 19
14	Repair a short to voltage on supply voltage circuit of the wiper 2 relay coil. Did you complete the repair?	Go to Step 20	--
15	Repair a short to voltage on control circuit of the windshield washer pump. Did you complete the repair?	Go to Step 20	--

LTV0500000003491

Fig. 147   Washers Always On (Part 2 of 3). HHR

Step	Action	Yes	No
16	Repair a short to voltage on high speed circuit of the windshield wiper motor. Did you complete the repair?	Go to Step 20	--
17	Replace the windshield wiper/washer switch. Did you complete the replacement?	Go to Step 20	--
18	Replace the wiper 1 relay. Did you complete the replacement?	Go to Step 20	--
19	Replace the BCM. Did you complete the replacement?	Go to Step 20	--
20	Operate the system in order to verify the repair. Did you correct the condition?	System OK	Go to Step 3

LTV0500000003492

Fig. 147   Washers Always On (Part 3 of 3). HHR

Step	Action	Yes	No
1	Did you perform the Diagnostic System Check - Vehicle?	Go to Step 2	Go to Diagnostic System Check -
2	1. Turn the ignition ON. 2. Press the windshield washer switch. Do the windshield washers operate normally?	Test for Intermittent and Poor Connections	Go to Step 3
3	1. Turn OFF the ignition. 2. Disconnect the windshield washer pump control circuit harness connector at the windshield washer pump. 3. Turn the ignition ON, with the engine OFF. 4. Connect a test lamp from the control circuit to the ground circuit of the windshield washer pump. 5. Press the windshield washer switch. Does the test lamp illuminate?	Go to Step 10	Go to Step 4
4	1. Connect a test lamp from the control circuit of the windshield washer pump to a good ground. 2. Press the windshield washer switch. Does the test lamp illuminate?	Go to Step 15	Go to Step 5

LTV0500000003493

Fig. 148   Washers Inoperative (Part 1 of 3). HHR

Fig. 148 Washers Inoperative (Part 2 of 3). HHR

Step	Action	Yes	No
5	1. Turn OFF the ignition. 2. Disconnect the accessory voltage circuit harness connector of the windshield wiper/washer switch. 3. Turn the ignition ON, with the engine OFF. 4. Connect a test lamp from the accessory voltage circuit of the windshield wiper/washer switch to a good ground. Does the test lamp illuminate?	Go to Step 6	Go to Step 9
6	1. Turn OFF the ignition. 2. Reconnect the windshield wiper/washer switch. 3. Turn the ignition ON, with the engine OFF. 4. Connect a test lamp from the windshield wiper/washer switch signal circuit of the body control module (BCM) to a good ground. Does the test lamp illuminate?	Go to Step 11	Go to Step 7
7	1. Turn OFF the ignition. 2. Disconnect the harness connector C4 of the BCM. 3. Turn the ignition ON, with the engine OFF. 4. Connect a test lamp from the control circuit of the windshield washer pump to a good ground. Does the test lamp illuminate?	Go to Step 8	Go to Step 14
8	1. Turn OFF the ignition. 2. Reconnect the harness connector C4 of the BCM. 3. Disconnect the harness connector C3 of the BCM. 4. Turn the ignition ON, with the engine OFF. 5. Connect a test lamp from the control circuit of the windshield washer pump in harness connector C3 of the BCM to a good ground. Does the test lamp illuminate?	Go to Step 12	Go to Step 14
9	Test the accessory voltage circuit of the windshield wiper/washer switch for an open or a short to ground. Did you find and correct the condition?	Go to Step 19	Go to Step 13
10	Inspect for poor connections at the windshield washer pump. Did you find and correct the condition?	Go to Step 19	Go to Step 16

LTV0500000003494

Fig. 148 Washers Inoperative (Part 2 of 3). HHR

Fig. 148 Washers Inoperative (Part 3 of 3). HHR

Step	Action	Yes	No
11	Inspect for poor connections at the windshield wiper/washer switch. Did you find and correct the condition?	Go to Step 19	Go to Step 17
12	Inspect for poor connections at the BCM. Did you find and correct the condition?	Go to Step 19	Go to Step 18
13	Repair a short to ground on the control circuit of the windshield washer pump. Did you complete the repair?	Go to Step 19	--
14	Repair an open or high resistance on the control circuit of the windshield washer pump. Did you complete the repair?	Go to Step 19	--
15	Repair an open or high resistance on the ground circuit of the windshield washer pump. Did you complete the repair?	Go to Step 19	--
16	Replace the windshield washer pump. Did you complete the replacement?	Go to Step 19	--
17	Replace the windshield wiper/washer switch. Did you complete the replacement?	Go to Step 19	--
18	Replace the BCM. Did you complete the replacement?	Go to Step 19	--
19	Operate the system in order to verify the repair. Did you correct the condition?	System OK	Go to Step 3

LTV0500000003495

Fig. 148 Washers Inoperative (Part 3 of 3). HHR

Step	Action	Yes	No
1	Did you perform the Diagnostic System Check - Vehicle? Go to Step 2	Go to Step 2	Go to Diagnostic System Check
2	1. Turn the ignition ON. 2. Turn the windshield wiper/washer switch OFF. Do the windshield wipers remain in the Park position?	Test for Intermittent and Poor Connections	Go to Step 3
3	Disconnect the harness connector of the windshield wiper/washer switch. Do the windshield wipers stop?	Go to Step 11	Go to Step 4
4	Connect a test lamp from the signal circuit of the windshield wiper/washer switch at the body control module (BCM) to a good ground. Does the test lamp illuminate?	Go to Step 9	Go to Step 5
5	Connect a test lamp from the supply voltage circuit of the wiper 2 relay coil to a good ground. Does the test lamp illuminate?	Go to Step 14	Go to Step 6
6	Connect a test lamp from the control circuit of the windshield washer pump to a good ground. Does the test lamp illuminate?	Go to Step 15	Go to Step 7
7	Disconnect the wiper 1 relay. Do the windshield wipers stop?	Go to Step 8	Go to Step 16

LTV0500000003496

Fig. 149 Wipers Always On (Part 1 of 3). HHR

Fig. 149 Wipers Always On (Part 2 of 3). HHR

Step	Action	Yes	No
8	Connect a test lamp from the supply voltage circuit of the wiper 1 relay coil to a good ground. Does the test lamp illuminate?	Go to Step 10	Go to Step 12
9	Test the signal circuit of the windshield wiper switch for a short to voltage. Did you find and correct the condition?	Go to Step 20	Go to Step 13
10	Test the supply voltage circuit of the wiper 1 relay for a short to voltage. Did you find and correct the condition?	Go to Step 20	Go to Step 13
11	Inspect for poor connections at the windshield wiper/washer switch. Did you find and correct the condition?	Go to Step 20	Go to Step 17
12	Inspect for poor connections at the wiper 1 relay. Did you find and correct the condition?	Go to Step 20	Go to Step 18
13	Inspect for poor connections at the BCM. Did you find and correct the condition?	Go to Step 20	Go to Step 19
14	Repair a short to voltage on supply voltage circuit of the wiper 2 relay coil. Did you complete the repair?	Go to Step 20	--
15	Repair a short to voltage on control circuit of the windshield washer pump. Did you complete the repair?	Go to Step 20	--

LTV0500000003497

Fig. 149 Wipers Always On (Part 2 of 3). HHR

	Action	Yes	No
16	Repair a short to voltage on high speed circuit of the windshield wiper motor. Did you complete the repair?	Go to Step 20	--
17	Replace the windshield wiper/washer switch. Did you complete the replacement?	Go to Step 20	--
18	Replace the wiper 1 relay. Did you complete the replacement?	Go to Step 20	--
19	Replace the BCM. Did you complete the replacement?	Go to Step 20	--
20	Operate the system in order to verify the repair. Did you correct the condition?	System OK	Go to Step 3

LTV0500000003498

Fig. 149 Wipers Always On (Part 3 of 3). HHR

5	1. Turn OFF the ignition. 2. Disconnect the harness connector of the windshield wiper/washer switch. 3. Turn the ignition ON, with the engine OFF. 4. Connect a test lamp from the accessory voltage circuit of the windshield wiper/washer switch to a good ground. Does the test lamp illuminate?	Go to Step 12	Go to Step 6
6	1. Turn OFF the ignition. 2. Reconnect the harness connector of the windshield wiper/washer switch. 3. Disconnect the harness connector of the windshield wiper/washer switch at the body control module (BCM). 4. Turn the ignition ON, with the engine OFF. 5. Connect a test lamp from the windshield wiper/washer signal circuit to a good ground. 6. Operate the windshield wiper/washer switch. Does the test lamp illuminate?	Go to Step 7	Go to Step 11
7	1. Turn OFF the ignition. 2. Reconnect the harness connector of the windshield wiper/washer switch at the BCM. 3. Disconnect the harness connector C3 of the BCM. 4. Connect a test lamp from the signal circuit of the windshield washer pump at harness connector C3 of the BCM to a good ground. 5. Operate the windshield wiper/washer switch. Does the test lamp illuminate?	Go to Step 8	Go to Step 9
8	Test the following circuits for an open or a short to ground: • The supply voltage circuit for a short to ground. • The control circuit of the windshield washer pump for a short to ground. Did you find and correct the condition?	Go to Step 17	Go to Step 9

LTV0500000003500

Fig. 150 Wipers Inoperative, All Modes (Part 2 of 4). HHR

Step	Action	Yes	No
1	Did you perform the Diagnostic System Check - Vehicle?	Go to Step 2	Go to Diagnostic System Check
2	1. Turn the ignition switch ON. 2. Operate the windshield wiper/washer switch through all the switch positions. Does the windshield wiper/washer system operate normally?	Test for Intermittent and Poor Connections	Go to Step 3
3	1. Turn OFF the ignition. 2. Disconnect the harness connector of the windshield wiper motor. 3. Turn the ignition ON, with the engine OFF. 4. Connect a test lamp from the low speed circuit to the ground circuit of the windshield wiper motor. 5. Press the windshield washer switch. Does the test lamp illuminate?	Go to Step 10	Go to Step 4
4	1. Connect a test lamp from the low speed circuit of the windshield wiper motor to a good ground. 2. Press the windshield washer switch. Does the test lamp illuminate?	Go to Step 13	Go to Step 5

LTV0500000003499

Fig. 150 Wipers Inoperative, All Modes (Part 1 of 4). HHR

9	Inspect for poor connections at the harness connector of the BCM. Did you find and correct the condition?	Go to Step 17	Go to Step 16
10	Inspect for poor connections at the harness connector of the windshield wiper motor. Did you find and correct the condition?	Go to Step 17	Go to Step 14
11	Inspect for poor connections at the harness connector of the windshield wiper/washer switch. Did you find and correct the condition?	Go to Step 17	Go to Step 15
12	Repair the short to ground or an open of the accessory voltage circuit at the wiper/washer switch. Did you complete the repair?	Go to Step 17	--
13	Repair an open or high resistance in the ground circuit of the windshield wiper motor. Did you complete the repair?	Go to Step 17	--
14	Replace the windshield wiper motor. Did you complete the replacement?	Go to Step 17	--
15	Replace the windshield wiper/washer switch. Did you complete the replacement?	Go to Step 17	--
16	Replace the BCM. Did you complete the replacement?	Go to Step 17	--

LTV0500000003501

Fig. 150 Wipers Inoperative, All Modes (Part 3 of 4). HHR

17	Operate the system in order to verify the repair. Did you correct the condition?		System OK	Go to Step 3

LTV0500000003502

Fig. 150 Wipers Inoperative, All Modes (Part 4 of 4). HHR

Step	Action	Values	Yes	No
6	1. Turn OFF the ignition. 2. Disconnect the harness connector of the wiper/washer switch. 3. Turn ON the ignition, with the engine OFF. 4. Operate the windshield wiper/washer switch through all the switch positions. 5. Measure the resistance of the windshield wiper switch from the accessory voltage circuit to the signal circuit of the windshield wiper switch. Is the resistance within the specified range?	1700-9500 ohms	Go to Step 17	Go to Step 24
7	Command the wiper 1 relay ON and OFF by cycling the windshield wiper/washer switch from the High to the Low positions. Do you hear a click when you command the wiper 1 relay ON and OFF?	--	Go to Step 10	Go to Step 8
8	1. Disconnect the wiper 1 relay. 2. Connect a test lamp from the supply voltage circuit to the ground circuit of the wiper 1 relay coil. 3. Place the wiper/washer switch in the Low speed position. Does the test lamp illuminate?	--	Go to Step 23	Go to Step 9
9	Connect a test lamp from the supply voltage circuit of the wiper 1 relay coil to a good ground. Does the test lamp illuminate?	--	Go to Step 27	Go to Step 18
10	1. Disconnect the wiper 1 relay. 2. Connect a test lamp from the battery voltage circuit of the wiper 1 relay switched input to a good ground. Does the test lamp illuminate?	--	Go to Step 23	Go to Step 18
11	Command the wiper 2 relay ON and OFF by cycling the windshield wiper/washer switch from the High to the Low positions. Do you hear a click when you command the wiper 2 relay ON and OFF?	--	Go to Step 14	Go to Step 12

LTV0500000003504

Fig. 151 Wipers Inoperative, One Or More Modes (Front Wiper, Part 2 of 5). HHR

Step	Action	Values	Yes	No
1	Did you perform the Diagnostic System Check - Vehicle?	--	Go to Step 2	Go to Diagnostic System Check -
2	1. Turn the ignition ON, with the engine OFF. 2. Operate the windshield wiper/washer switch through all the switch positions. Does the windshield wiper/washer system operate normally?	--	Test for Intermittent and Poor Connections	Go to Step 3
3	Are the wipers only inoperative when the washer switch is depressed?	--	Go to Step 16	Go to Step 4
4	Are the windshield wipers only inoperative in the high speed mode?	--	Go to Step 11	Go to Step 5
5	1. Turn OFF the ignition. 2. Connect a test lamp from the signal circuit of the windshield wiper switch to a good ground. 3. Turn ON the ignition, with the engine OFF. 4. Operate the windshield wiper switch. Does the test lamp illuminate?	--	Go to Step 7	Go to Step 6

LTV0500000003503

Fig. 151 Wipers Inoperative, One Or More Modes (Front Wiper, Part 1 of 5). HHR

Step	Action	Values	Yes	No
12	1. Disconnect the wiper 2 relay. 2. Connect a test lamp from the voltage supply circuit to the ground circuit of the wiper 2 relay coil. 3. Place the wiper/washer switch in the High speed position. Does the test lamp illuminate?	-	Go to Step 23	Go to Step 13
13	Connect a test lamp from the supply voltage circuit of the wiper 2 relay coil to a good ground. Does the test lamp illuminate?	-	Go to Step 27	Go to Step 20
14	1. Disconnect the wiper 2 relay. 2. Connect a test lamp from the battery voltage circuit supplied from the wiper 1 relay to the wiper 2 relay switched input to a good ground. 3. Place the wiper/washer switch in the Low speed position. Does the test lamp illuminate?	-	Go to Step 15	Go to Step 28
15	1. Reconnect the wiper 2 relay. 2. Connect a test lamp at the wiper 2 relay switched output to a good ground. 3. Place the wiper/washer switch in the Low speed position. Does the test lamp illuminate?	-	Go to Step 21	Go to Step 23
16	1. Turn OFF the ignition. 2. Disconnect the harness connector of the wiper/washer switch. 3. Turn ON the ignition, with the engine OFF. 4. Connect a test lamp from the accessory voltage circuit to the signal circuit of the windshield washer pump control. Does the test lamp illuminate?	-	Go to Step 24	Go to Step 22
17	Test the signal circuit of the wiper/washer switch for an open or a short to ground. Did you find and correct the condition?	-	Go to Step 33	Go to Step 26

LTV0500000003505

Fig. 151 Wipers Inoperative, One Or More Modes (Front Wiper, Part 3 of 5). HHR

18	Test the supply voltage circuit of the wiper 1 relay coil for an open or a short to ground. Did you find and correct the condition?	Go to Step 33	Go to Step 26
19	Test the low speed circuit of the windshield wiper motor for an open or high resistance. Did you find and correct the condition?	Go to Step 33	Go to Step 25
20	Test the supply voltage circuit of the wiper 2 relay coil for an open or a short to ground. Did you find and correct the condition?	Go to Step 33	Go to Step 24
21	Test the high speed circuit of the windshield wiper motor for an open or high resistance. Did you find and correct the condition?	Go to Step 33	Go to Step 25
22	Test the control circuit of the windshield washer pump for an open or high resistance. Did you find and correct the condition?	Go to Step 33	Go to Step 26
23	Inspect for poor connections at the inoperative wiper relay. Did you find and correct the condition?	Go to Step 33	Go to Step 29
24	Inspect for poor connections at the harness connector of the windshield wiper/washer switch. Did you find and correct the condition?	Go to Step 33	Go to Step 30
25	Inspect for poor connections at the harness connector of the windshield wiper motor. Did you find and correct the condition?	Go to Step 33	Go to Step 31

LTV0500000003506

Fig. 151 Wipers Inoperative, One Or More Modes (Front Wiper, Part 4 of 5). HHR

Diagnostic Aids

Except for when it is in the Wash mode, the rear window wiper wipes the rear window at delay time intervals. With the rear wiper system activated, the length of time between wipes can be adjusted by selecting any one of the 3 delay speed settings of the windshield wiper switch.

During the Wash mode, if the rear washer switch is momentarily turned to ON, the rear wiper will wipe the rear window 3-5 times and then park. However, if the rear washer switch is held to ON, the rear window wipers will continue to operate until the switch is released.

While the delay speed of both the front and rear wipers is adjusted by the windshield wiper switch selections, the delay time intervals of the rear wiper are not synchronized with the delay time intervals of the front wipers.

The rear wiper should stop at the Park position anytime the rear wiper is not wiping. However, if the ignition switch is turned OFF while the rear wiper is wiping, the wiper will stop at its current location on the glass.

Test Description

The numbers below refer to the step numbers on the diagnostic table.

2. This step will determine if the rear wiper operates properly when only the rear window washer switch is activated. When the rear window washer switch is operated with the rear wiper switch OFF, the rear wiper should wipe the window 3-5 times and then park.

4. This step helps to pinpoint the specific malfunction. The Park mode of the rear window wiper may be the only feature malfunctioning. When the rear wiper switch is ON, the rear wiper should stop at the parked position in between the timed strokes of the wiper. When the rear wiper switch is turned OFF, the rear wiper should park and remain in the parked position until either the wipe or wash mode is operated again.

LTV0500000003508

Fig. 152 Wipers Inoperative, One Or More Modes (Rear Wiper, Part 1 of 5). HHR

26	Inspect for poor connections at the harness connector of the body control module (BCM). Did you find and correct the condition?	Go to Step 33	Go to Step 32
27	Repair an open or high resistance in the ground circuit of the inoperative wiper relay coil. Did you complete the repair?	Go to Step 33	--
28	Repair an open or high resistance in the battery voltage circuit of the wiper 2 relay switched input. Did you complete the repair?	Go to Step 33	--
29	Replace the inoperative wiper relay. Did you complete the replacement?	Go to Step 33	--
30	Replace the windshield wiper/washer switch. Did you complete the replacement?	Go to Step 33	--
31	Replace the windshield wiper motor. Did you complete the replacement?	Go to Step 33	--
32	Replace the BCM. Did you complete the replacement?	Go to Step 33	--
33	Operate the system in order to verify the repair. Did you correct the condition?	System OK	Go to Step 3

LTV0500000003507

Fig. 151 Wipers Inoperative, One Or More Modes (Front Wiper, Part 5 of 5). HHR

Step	Action	Yes	No
	DEFINITION: The rear wiper is inoperative in one or more modes, however the rear washer still operates.		
1	Did you perform the Diagnostic System Check - Vehicle? Go to Step 2		Go to Diagnostic System Check
2	1. Turn ON the ignition, with the engine OFF. 2. Turn the rear window wiper switch ON. Does the rear window wiper operate?	Go to Step 3	Go to Step 5
3	1. Turn the rear window wiper switch OFF. 2. With the rear window wiper switch OFF, turn the rear window washer switch ON. Does the rear window wiper operate?	Go to Step 4	Go to Step 7
4	**Important:** Unless the rear window wiper is being operated for the Wash mode, it operates only in the delay modes. When the rear wiper is ON, it should stop at the parked position in between timed strokes of the wiper. When the rear wiper is turned OFF, it should park and remain in the parked position until either the wiper or wash mode is operated again. Does the rear window wiper Park in the full down position as it should?	Test for Intermittent and Poor Connections	Go to Step 9
5	**Turn the rear window washer switch ON.** **Does the rear window wiper operate?**	Go to Step 8	Go to Step 6

LTV0500000003509

Fig. 152 Wipers Inoperative, One Or More Modes (Rear Wiper, Part 2 of 5). HHR

Step	Action	Yes	No
6	1. Turn OFF the ignition. 2. Remove the REAR WIPER Relay from the underhood fuse block. 3. Turn ON the ignition, with the engine OFF. 4. With a test lamp connected to a good ground, probe the accessory voltage feed circuit to the switch side of the relay at the underhood fuse block. Does the test lamp illuminate?	Go to Step 10	Go to Step 20
7	1. Disconnect the body control module (BCM) C2 harness connector. 2. With a test lamp connected to ground, probe the rear window washer pump control circuit. 3. Operate the rear window washer switch to ON while the rear window wiper switch is OFF. Does the test lamp illuminate?	Go to Step 17	Go to Step 13
8	1. Disconnect the body control module (BCM) C2 harness connector. 2. With a test lamp connected to ground, probe the rear wiper switch signal circuit. 3. Operate the rear window wiper switch to ON. Does the test lamp illuminate?	Go to Step 17	Go to Step 14
9	1. Turn OFF the ignition. 2. Disconnect the harness connector of the rear window wiper motor. 3. Turn ON the ignition, with the engine OFF. 4. With a test lamp connected to a good ground, probe the accessory voltage circuit of the rear window wiper motor. Does the test lamp illuminate?	Go to Step 16	Go to Step 19
10	1. Turn OFF the ignition 2. Connect a 3 amp fused jumper wire between the accessory voltage feed circuit terminal and the rear window wiper motor control circuit terminal at the underhood fuse block. 3. Turn the ignition ON, with the engine OFF. Does the rear wiper operate?	Go to Step 24	Go to Step 11

LTV0500000003510

Fig. 152   Wipers Inoperative, One Or More Modes (Rear Wiper, Part 3 of 5). HHR

Step	Action	Yes	No
19	Repair the accessory voltage circuit, between the REAR WIPER Relay splice and the wiper motor, for an open or a high resistance. Did you complete the repair?	Go to Step 26	--
20	Repair the open or high resistance in the accessory voltage feed circuit. Did you complete the repair?	Go to Step 26	--
21	Repair the open or high resistance in the rear window wiper motor control circuit. Did you complete the repair?	Go to Step 26	--
22	Replace the windshield wiper washer switch. Did you complete the replacement?	Go to Step 26	--
23	Replace the rear window wiper motor. Did you complete the replacement?	Go to Step 26	--
24	Replace the rear wiper relay. Did you complete the replacement?	Go to Step 26	--
25	Replace the BCM. Did you complete the replacement?	Go to Step 26	--
26	Operate the system in order to verify the repair. Did you correct the condition?	System OK	Go to Step 2

LTV0500000003512

Fig. 152   Wipers Inoperative, One Or More Modes (Rear Wiper, Part 5 of 5). HHR

Step	Action	Yes	No
11	1. Ensure that the fused jumper wire between the accessory voltage feed circuit terminal and the rear window wiper motor control circuit terminal is still connected. 2. With a test lamp connected to a good ground, probe the rear window wiper motor control circuit at the rear wiper motor. Does the test lamp illuminate?	Go to Step 12	Go to Step 21
12	Connect the test lamp between the rear window wiper motor control circuit and the rear window wiper motor ground circuit. Does the test lamp illuminate?	Go to Step 16	Go to Step 18
13	Test the rear window washer pump control circuit for an open or a high resistance. Did you find and correct the condition?	Go to Step 26	Go to Step 15
14	Test the rear wiper switch signal circuit for an open or a high resistance. Did you find and correct the condition?	Go to Step 26	Go to Step 15
15	Inspect for poor connections at the harness connector of the windshield wiper washer switch. Did you find and correct the condition?	Go to Step 26	Go to Step 22
16	Inspect for poor connections at the harness connector of the rear window wiper motor. Did you find and correct the condition?	Go to Step 26	Go to Step 23
17	Inspect for poor connections at the harness connector of the BCM. Did you find and correct the condition?	Go to Step 26	Go to Step 25
18	Repair the rear window wiper motor ground circuit for an open or a high resistance. Did you complete the repair?	Go to Step 26	--

LTV0500000003511

Fig. 152   Wipers Inoperative, One Or More Modes (Rear Wiper, Part 4 of 5). HHR

Step	Action	Yes	No
	DEFINITION: The low washer fluid indicator always indicates low washer fluid or does not turn on with low washer fluid.		
1	Did you review the Wiper/Washer System Description and Operation and perform the necessary inspections?	Go to Step 2	Go to Symptoms
2	Verify the fault is present. Does the system operate normally?		Go to Step 3
3	1. Turn the ignition OFF. 2. Disconnect the washer fluid level switch connector. 3. Turn the ignition ON. Does the low washer fluid indicator illuminate for 60 seconds after the ignition is turned ON?	Go to Step 6	Go to Step 4
4	1. Turn the ignition OFF. 2. Connect a fused jumper wire from the washer fluid level switch signal circuit terminal in the washer fluid level switch connector to a good ground. 3. Turn the ignition ON. Does the low washer fluid indicator illuminate for 60 seconds after the ignition is turned ON?	Go to Step 5	Go to Step 7
5	1. Turn the ignition OFF. 2. Connect a fused jumper wire across the washer fluid level switch harness connector terminals. 3. Turn the ignition ON. Does the low washer fluid indicator illuminate for 60 seconds after the ignition is turned ON?	Go to Step 9	Go to Step 8

LTV0500000003643

Fig. 153   Low Washer Fluid Indicator Fault (Part 1 of 2). 2003–04 H2

Step	Action	Yes	No
6	Test the washer fluid level switch signal circuit for a short to ground. Did you find and correct the condition?	Go to Step 13	Go to Step 11
7	Test the washer fluid level switch signal circuit for an open or high resistance. Did you find and correct the condition?	Go to Step 13	Go to Step 11
8	Repair the washer fluid level switch ground circuit for an open or high resistance. Is the repair complete?	Go to Step 13	--
9	Inspect for poor connections at the washer fluid level switch. Did you find and correct the condition?	Go to Step 13	Go to Step 10
10	Replace the washer fluid level switch. Is the repair complete?	Go to Step 13	--
11	Inspect for poor connections at the instrument panel cluster. Did you find and correct the condition?	Go to Step 13	Go to Step 12
12	Important Perform the module setup procedure if required. Replace the instrument panel cluster. Is the repair complete?	Go to Step 13	--
13	Operate the system in order to verify the repair. Did you correct the condition?	System OK	Go to Step 3

LTV0500000003644

Fig. 153   Low Washer Fluid Indicator Fault (Part 2 of 2). 2003–04 H2

Step	Action	Yes	No
8	Disconnect the windshield wiper motor and module connector. Is the windshield washer pump always ON?	Go to Step 11	Go to Step 9
9	Test the washer fluid pump supply circuit for a short to voltage. Did you find and correct the condition?	Go to Step 17	Go to Step 14
10	1. Disconnect the windshield wiper motor and module connector. 2. Test the washer fluid pump relay control circuit for a short to ground. Did you find and correct the condition?	Go to Step 17	Go to Step 14
11	Repair the windshield washer pump control circuit for a short to voltage. Is the repair complete?	Go to Step 17	--
12	Inspect for poor connections at the turn signal/malfunction switch. Did you find and correct the condition?	Go to Step 17	Go to Step 13
13	Replace the turn signal/malfunction switch. Is the repair complete?	Go to Step 17	--
14	Inspect for poor connections at the windshield wiper motor and module. Did you find and correct the condition?	Go to Step 17	Go to Step 15
15	Replace the windshield wiper motor and module. Is the repair complete?	Go to Step 17	--
16	Replace the windshield washer relay. Is the repair complete?	Go to Step 17	--
17	Operate the system in order to verify the repair. Did you correct the condition?	System OK	Go to Step 3

LTV0500000003646

Fig. 154   Washers Always On (Part 2 of 2). 2003–04 H2

Step	Action	Yes	No
	DEFINITION: The windshield washer pump is always ON.		
1	Did you review the Wiper/Washer System Description and Operation and perform the necessary inspections?	Go to Step 2	Go to Symptoms
2	1. Turn the windshield wiper/washer switch to the OFF position. 2. Turn the ignition ON. Is the windshield washer pump always ON?	Go to Step 3	Test for Intermittent and Poor Connections
3	Are the windshield wipers always ON?	Go to Step 4	Go to Step 6
4	1. Disconnect the windshield wiper motor and module connector. 2. Connect a test lamp from the windshield wiper switch signal circuit terminal in the wiper motor harness connector to battery voltage. 3. Turn the ignition ON. Does the test lamp illuminate?	Go to Step 5	Go to Step 14
5	1. Disconnect the turn signal/malfunction switch connector. 2. Test the windshield wiper switch signal circuit for a short to ground. Did you find and correct the condition?	Go to Step 17	Go to Step 12
6	Disconnect the washer fluid pump relay. Is the windshield washer pump ON?	Go to Step 8	Go to Step 7
7	Connect a test lamp from battery positive voltage to the washer fluid pump relay control circuit terminal in the underhood fuse block. Does the test lamp illuminate?	Go to Step 10	Go to Step 16

LTV0500000003645

Fig. 154   Washers Always On (Part 1 of 2). 2003–04 H2

Step	Action	Values	Yes	No
	DEFINITION: The windshield washer is inoperative.			
1	Did you review the Wiper/Washer System Description and Operation and perform the necessary inspections?	--	Go to Step 2	Go to Symptoms
2	1. Turn the ignition ON. 2. Press the windshield washer switch. Do the windshield washers operate normally?	--		Go to Step 3
3	Do the windshield wipers operate when the windshield washer switch is pressed?	--	Go to Step 6	Go to Step 4
4	1. Disconnect the windshield wiper motor and module connector. 2. Test the resistance from the windshield wiper switch signal circuit terminal to the low reference circuit terminal in the windshield wiper motor harness connector. 3. Press the windshield washer switch. Is the resistance near the specified value?	0.5 ohms	Go to Step 15	Go to Step 5

LTV0500000003647

Fig. 155   Washers Inoperative (Part 1 of 4). 2003–04 H2

Step	Action	Yes	No
5	Test the following circuits for high resistance: • Windshield wiper switch signal circuit • Windshield wiper switch low reference circuit Did you find and correct the condition?	Go to Step 20	Go to Step 13
6	1. Disconnect the washer fluid pump relay. 2. Connect a test lamp from battery positive voltage to the washer fluid pump relay control circuit terminal in the underhood fuse block. 3. Turn the ignition ON. 4. Press the windshield washer switch. Does the test lamp illuminate?	Go to Step 7	Go to Step 8
7	1. Connect the washer fluid pump relay. 2. Disconnect the washer pump connector. 3. Connect a test lamp across the washer pump harness connector terminals. 4. Turn the ignition ON. 5. Press the windshield washer switch. Does the test lamp illuminate?	Go to Step 18	Go to Step 9
8	Test the washer fluid pump relay control circuit for an open or high resistance. Did you find and correct the condition?	Go to Step 20	Go to Step 15
9	1. Disconnect the windshield wiper motor and module connector. 2. Connect a fused jumper wire from the washer fluid pump relay control circuit terminal in the wiper motor harness connector to a good ground. 3. Connect a test lamp from the washer fluid pump supply voltage circuit terminal in the wiper motor harness connector to a good ground. 4. Turn the ignition ON. Does the test lamp illuminate?	Go to Step 11	Go to Step 10

LTV0500000003648

Fig. 155　Washers Inoperative (Part 2 of 4). 2003–04 H2

Step	Action	Yes	No
10	Test the washer fluid pump supply voltage circuit for an open or short to ground. Did you find and correct the condition?	Go to Step 20	Go to Step 17
11	Test the windshield washer pump control circuit for an open or high resistance. Did you find and correct the condition?	Go to Step 20	Go to Step 12
12	Test the rear window washer pump control circuit for an open or high resistance. Did you find and correct the condition?	Go to Step 20	Go to Step 15
13	Inspect for poor connections at the turn signal/multifunction switch switch. Did you find and correct the condition?	Go to Step 20	Go to Step 14
14	Replace the turn signal/multifunction switch. Is the repair complete?	Go to Step 20	--
15	Inspect for poor connections at the windshield wiper motor and module. Did you find and correct the condition?	Go to Step 20	Go to Step 16
16	Replace the windshield wiper motor and module. Is the repair complete?	Go to Step 20	--
17	Replace the washer fluid pump relay. Is the repair complete?	Go to Step 20	--
18	Inspect for poor connections at the washer fluid pump. Did you find and correct the condition?	Go to Step 20	Go to Step 19

LTV0500000003649

Fig. 155　Washers Inoperative (Part 3 of 4). 2003–04 H2

Step	Action	Yes	No
19	Replace the washer fluid pump. Is the repair complete?	Go to Step 20	--
20	Operate the system in order to verify the repair. Did you correct the condition?	System OK	Go to Step 3

LTV0500000003650

Fig. 155　Washers Inoperative (Part 4 of 4). 2003–04 H2

Step	Action	Yes	No
	DEFINITION: Windshield wipers are always ON.		
1	Did you perform the Wiper/Washer System Description and Operation and perform the necessary inspections?	Go to Step 2	Go to Symptoms
2	1. Turn the windshield wiper/washer switch OFF. 2. Turn the ignition ON. Are the windshield wipers always ON?	Go to Step 3	Test for Intermittent and Poor Connections
3	1. Disconnect the turn signal/multifunction switch connectors. 2. Turn the ignition ON. Are the windshield wipers always ON?	Go to Step 4	Go to Step 6
4	1. Turn the ignition OFF. 2. Disconnect the windshield wiper motor and module connector. 3. Test the windshield wiper switch high signal circuit for a short to ground. Did you find and correct the condition?	Go to Step 10	Go to Step 5
5	Test the windshield wiper switch signal circuit for a short to ground. Did you find and correct the condition?	Go to Step 10	Go to Step 8
6	Inspect for poor connections at the windshield wiper/washer switch. Did you find and correct the condition?	Go to Step 10	Go to Step 7

LTV0500000003651

Fig. 156　Wipers Always On (Part 1 of 2). 2003–04 H2

7	Replace the windshield wiper/washer switch.		
	Is the repair complete?	Go to Step 10	--
8	Inspect for poor connections at the windshield wiper motor.		
	Did you find and correct the condition?	Go to Step 10	Go to Step 9
9	Replace the windshield wiper motor.		
	Is the repair complete?	Go to Step 10	--
10	Operate the system in order to verify the repair.		
	Did you correct the condition?	System OK	Go to Step 3

LTV0500000003652

Fig. 156   Wipers Always On (Part 2 of 2). 2003–04 H2

6	1. Connect the wiper motor module connector. 2. Disconnect the wiper motor to module connector. 3. Connect a test lamp across the low speed motor control and ground circuit terminals in the module. 4. Turn the windshield wiper switch to the low position. Does the test lamp illuminate for several seconds?	Go to Step 12	Go to Step 11
7	Repair the accessory voltage supply circuit to the windshield wiper motor and module for an open or short to ground. Is the repair complete?	Go to Step 15	--
8	Repair the windshield wiper motor and module ground circuit for an open or high resistance. Is the repair complete?	Go to Step 15	--
9	Inspect for poor connections at the windshield wiper/washer switch. Did you find and correct the condition?	Go to Step 15	Go to Step 10
10	Replace the windshield wiper/washer switch. Is the repair complete?	Go to Step 15	--
11	Inspect for poor connections at the windshield wiper motor module. Did you find and correct the condition?	Go to Step 15	Go to Step 13
12	Inspect for poor connections at the windshield wiper motor. Did you find and correct the condition?	Go to Step 15	Go to Step 14
13	Replace the windshield wiper motor module. Is the repair complete?	Go to Step 15	--

LTV0500000003654

Fig. 157   Wipers Inoperative, All Modes (Part 2 of 3). 2003–04 H2

14	Replace the windshield wiper motor. Is the repair complete?	Go to Step 15	--
15	Operate the system in order to verify the repair. Did you correct the condition?	System OK	Go to Step 3

LTV0500000003655

Fig. 157   Wipers Inoperative, All Modes (Part 3 of 3). 2003–04 H2

Step	Action	Yes	No
	DEFINITION: Windshield wipers are inoperative in all modes.		
1	Did you perform the Wiper/Washer System Description and Operation and perform the necessary inspections?	Go to Step 2	Go to Symptoms
2	1. Turn the ignition ON. 2. Attempt to operate the windshield wipers in all modes. Are the windshield wipers inoperative in all modes?	Go to Step 3	Test for Intermittent and Poor Connections
3	1. Disconnect the turn signal/multifunction switch connectors. 2. Connect a fused jumper wire from the windshield wiper switch high signal circuit terminal to ground. 3. Turn the ignition ON. Do the windshield wipers operate at high speed?	Go to Step 9	Go to Step 4
4	1. Disconnect the windshield wiper motor module connector. 2. Connect a test lamp from the accessory voltage supply circuit terminal in the windshield wiper motor harness connector to a good ground. 3. Turn the ignition ON. Does the test lamp illuminate?	Go to Step 5	Go to Step 7
5	Connect a test lamp from battery positive voltage to the windshield wiper motor ground circuit terminal in the windshield wiper motor module harness connector. Does the test lamp illuminate?	Go to Step 6	Go to Step 8

LTV0500000003653

Fig. 157   Wipers Inoperative, All Modes (Part 1 of 3). 2003–04 H2

Test Description

The numbers below refer to the step numbers on the diagnostic table.

5. This step tests for continuity through the 390 ohms resistor in the windshield wiper/washer switch.

6. This step tests for continuity through the delay resistors in the windshield wiper/washer switch. The measured resistance will change in sequence from low to high as the delay speed is increased.

Step	Action	Values	Yes	No
	DEFINITION: Windshield wipers are inoperative in one or more modes.			
1	Did you perform the Wiper/Washer System Description and Operation and perform the necessary inspections?	--	Go to Step 2	Go to Symptoms
2	1. Turn ON the ignition. 2. Attempt to operate the windshield wipers in all modes. Does the system operate normally?	--	Test for Intermittent and Poor Connections	Go to Step 3
3	Do the windshield wipers operate in the high speed mode?	--	Go to Step 5	Go to Step 4
4	1. Disconnect the turn signal/multifunction switch connectors. 2. Connect a fused jumper wire from the windshield wiper switch high signal circuit terminal in the body harness connector half to a good ground. 3. Turn ON the ignition. Do the windshield wipers operate at high speed?	--	Go to Step 8	Go to Step 7

LTV0500000003656

Fig. 158   Wipers Inoperative, One Or More Modes (Part 1 of 3). 2003–04 H2

Step	Action		Yes	No
5	1. Disconnect the turn signal/multifunction switch connectors. 2. Test the resistance from the windshield wiper switch signal circuit terminal to the low reference circuit terminal in the turn signal/multifunction switch. 3. Operate the windshield wiper/washer switch in the following positions: - MIST - LO Is the resistance near the specified value in the listed switch positions?	390 ohms	Go to Step 6	Go to Step 11
6	1. Test the resistance from the windshield wiper switch signal circuit terminal to the low reference circuit terminal in the turn signal/multifunction switch. 2. Operate the windshield wiper/washer switch in all of the delay positions. Does the resistance remain within the specified values from low to high as the delay speed is increased?	1K ohms-10K ohms	Go to Step 9	Go to Step 11
7	1. Disconnect the windshield wiper motor and module connector. 2. Test the windshield wiper switch high signal circuit for an open or high resistance. Did you find and correct the condition?	--	Go to Step 16	Go to Step 14
8	Test the windshield wiper switch ground circuit for an open or high resistance. Did you find and correct the condition?	--	Go to Step 16	Go to Step 12
9	Test the windshield wiper switch signal circuit for an open or a high resistance. Did you find and correct the condition?	--	Go to Step 16	Go to Step 10

LTV0500000003657

Fig. 158 Wipers Inoperative, One Or More Modes (Part 2 of 3). 2003–04 H2

Step	Action		Yes	No
10	Test the windshield wiper switch low reference circuit for an open or high resistance. Did you find and correct the condition?	-	Go to Step 16	Go to Step 14
11	Test the windshield wiper switch signal and low reference circuits in the steering column harness for an open or short to ground. Did you find and correct the condition?	-	Go to Step 16	Go to Step 12
12	Inspect for poor connections at the turn signal/malfunction switch. Did you find and correct the condition?	-	Go to Step 16	Go to Step 13
13	Replace the turn signal/malfunction switch. Is the repair complete?	-	Go to Step 16	--
14	Inspect for poor connections at the windshield wiper motor and module. Did you find and correct the condition?	-	Go to Step 16	Go to Step 15
15	Replace the windshield wiper motor and module. Is the repair complete?	-	Go to Step 16	--
16	Operate the system in order to verify the repair. Did you correct the condition?		System OK	Go to Step 3

LTV0500000003658

Fig. 158 Wipers Inoperative, One Or More Modes (Part 3 of 3). 2003–04 H2

Step	Action	Yes	No
	DEFINITION: The rear window washer is inoperative and the windshield washers operate normally.		
1	Did you review the Rear Wiper/Washer System Description and Operation and perform the necessary inspections?	Go to Step 2	Go to Symptoms
2	1. Turn the ignition ON. 2. Press the rear window washer switch. Does the rear window washer operate normally?	Test for Intermittent and Poor Connections	Go to Step 3
3	Does the rear window wiper operate when the washer switch is pressed?	Go to Step 4	Go to Step 8
4	1. Disconnect the washer fluid pump relay. 2. Connect a test lamp from the washer fluid pump relay control circuit terminal to ground. 3. Turn the ignition ON. 4. Press the rear window washer switch. Does the test lamp illuminate when the switch is pressed?	Go to Step 6	Go to Step 5
5	1. Disconnect the windshield wiper motor and module connector. 2. Connect a test lamp from the rear window washer switch signal circuit terminal to ground. 3. Press the rear window washer switch. Does the test lamp illuminate when the switch is pressed?	Go to Step 10	Go to Step 7

LTV0500000003659

Fig. 159 Washer Inoperative, Rear (Part 1 of 2). 2003–04 H2

Step	Action	Yes	No
6	Test the rear window washer pump control circuit for a short to ground. Did you find and correct the condition?	Go to Step 12	Go to Step 10
7	Test the rear window washer switch signal circuit for an open or high resistance. Did you find and correct the condition?	Go to Step 12	Go to Step 8
8	Inspect for poor connections at the rear window wiper/washer switch. Did you find and correct the condition?	Go to Step 12	Go to Step 9
9	Replace the rear window wiper/washer switch. Is the repair complete?	Go to Step 12	--
10	Inspect for poor connections at the windshield wiper motor and module. Did you find and correct the condition?	Go to Step 12	Go to Step 11
11	Replace the windshield wiper motor and module. Is the repair complete?	Go to Step 12	--
12	Operate the system in order to verify the repair. Did you correct the condition?	System OK	Go to Step 3

LTV0500000003660

Fig. 159 Washer Inoperative, Rear (Part 2 of 2). 2003–04 H2

Step	Action	Yes	No
1	Did you review the Rear Wiper/Washer System Description and Operation and perform the necessary inspections?	Go to Step 2	Go to Symptoms
2	1. Turn the ignition ON. 2. Turn the rear window wiper/washer switch to the OFF position. Is the rear window wiper always ON?	Go to Step 3	Test for Intermittent and Poor Connections
3	1. Disconnect the rear window wiper module connector. 2. Connect a test lamp from the rear window wiper switch signal circuit terminal in the harness connector to ground. Does the test lamp illuminate?	Go to Step 5	Go to Step 4
4	Connect a test lamp from the rear window washer switch signal circuit terminal in the rear wiper motor harness connector to ground. Does the test lamp illuminate?	Go to Step 6	Go to Step 9
5	1. Disconnect the rear window wiper/washer switch connector. 2. Test the rear window wiper switch signal circuit for a short to voltage. Did you find and correct the condition?	Go to Step 11	Go to Step 7
6	1. Disconnect the rear window wiper/washer switch connector. 2. Test the rear window washer switch signal circuit for a short to voltage. Did you find and correct the condition?	Go to Step 11	Go to Step 7

LTV0500000003661

Fig. 160   Wiper Always On, Rear (Part 1 of 2). 2003–04 H2

Step	Action	Yes	No
7	Inspect for poor connections at the rear window wiper/washer switch. Did you find and correct the condition?	Go to Step 11	Go to Step 8
8	Replace the rear window wiper/washer switch. Is the repair complete?	Go to Step 11	--
9	Inspect for poor connections at the rear window wiper module. Did you find and correct the condition?	Go to Step 11	Go to Step 10
10	Replace the rear window wiper module. Is the repair complete?	Go to Step 11	--
11	Operate the system in order to verify the repair. Did you correct the condition?	System OK	Go to Step 3

LTV0500000003662

Fig. 160   Wiper Always On, Rear (Part 2 of 2). 2003–04 H2

Step	Action	Yes	No
	DEFINITION: The rear wiper motor is inoperative in one or more modes, the rear washer pump may or may not operate.		
1	Did you review the Rear Wiper/Washer System Description and Operation and perform the necessary inspections?	Go to Step 2	Go to Symptoms
2	1. Turn ON the ignition, with the engine OFF. 2. Operate the rear wiper/washer system in all the switch positions. Does the rear wiper/washer system operate normally?	Test for Intermittent and Poor Connections	Go to Step 3
3	Inspect the courtesy lamps for proper operation. Do the courtesy lamps operate properly?	Go to Step 4	Go to Symptoms
4	Does the rear wiper motor operate when the rear washer switch is pressed?	Go to Step 6	Go to Step 5
5	Is the rear wiper only inoperative when the rear washer switch is pressed?	Go to Step 12	Go to Step 6
6	1. Disconnect the harness connector of the rear wiper switch. 2. Connect a test lamp from the accessory voltage circuit of the rear wiper/washer switch to a good ground. Does the test lamp illuminate?	Go to Step 7	Go to Step 13

LTV0500000003663

Fig. 161   Wiper Inoperative, Rear (Part 1 of 4). 2003–04 H2

Step	Action	Yes	No
7	Connect a 15-amp fused jumper wire from the accessory voltage circuit to the rear window wiper switch signal circuit. Does the rear wiper motor operate?	Go to Step 16	Go to Step 8
8	1. Remove the fused jumper wire and connect the rear wiper switch connector. 2. Disconnect the harness connector of the rear window wiper module. 3. Connect a test lamp from the rear window wiper switch signal circuit to a good ground. 4. Turn the rear wiper switch to the 2 position. Does the test lamp illuminate?	Go to Step 9	Go to Step 18
9	Connect a test lamp from battery voltage to the ground circuit of the rear wiper module. Does the test lamp illuminate?	Go to Step 10	Go to Step 19
10	Connect a test lamp from the battery voltage circuit of the rear wiper module to a good ground. Does the test lamp illuminate?	Go to Step 11	Go to Step 20
11	1. Connect the rear wiper module harness connector. 2. Disconnect the wiper motor to module connector. 3. Connect a test lamp across the motor control circuit terminals in the module. 4. Turn the rear wiper switch to the 2 position. Does the test lamp illuminate?	Go to Step 24	Go to Step 17
12	1. Disconnect the harness connector of the rear wiper/washer module. 2. Connect a test lamp from the rear window washer switch signal circuit to a good ground. 3. Depress the rear washer switch. Does the test lamp illuminate?	Go to Step 17	Go to Step 15
13	Test the accessory voltage circuit of the rear wiper/washer switch for an open or a short to ground. Did you find and correct the condition?	Go to Step 25	Go to Step 14
14	Test the rear window wiper switch signal circuit for a short to ground. Did you find and correct the condition?	Go to Step 25	Go to Step 21

LTV0500000003664

Fig. 161   Wiper Inoperative, Rear (Part 2 of 4). 2003–04 H2

Step	Action	Yes	No
15	Test the rear window washer switch signal circuit for an open or high resistance. Did you find and correct the condition?	Go to Step 25	Go to Step 16
16	Inspect for poor connections at the harness connector of the rear wiper/washer switch. Did you find and correct the condition?	Go to Step 25	Go to Step 22
17	Inspect for poor connections at the harness connector of the rear wiper module. Did you find and correct the condition?	Go to Step 25	Go to Step 23
18	Repair an open or high resistance in the rear window wiper switch signal circuit. Did you complete the repair?	Go to Step 25	--
19	Repair an open or high resistance in the ground circuit of the rear wiper module. Did you complete the repair?	Go to Step 25	--
20	Repair an open or a short to ground in the battery voltage circuit of the rear wiper module. Did you complete the repair?	Go to Step 25	--
21	Repair a short to ground in the rear window washer switch signal circuit. Did you complete the repair?	Go to Step 25	--
22	Replace the rear window wiper/washer switch. Did you complete the replacement?	Go to Step 25	--
23	Replace the rear wiper motor module. Did you complete the replacement?	Go to Step 25	--

LTV0500000003665

Fig. 161   Wiper Inoperative, Rear (Part 3 of 4). 2003–04 H2

Step	Action	Yes	No
24	Replace the rear wiper motor. Did you complete the replacement?	Go to Step 25	--
25	Operate the system in order to verify the repair. Did you correct the condition?	System OK	Go to Step 3

LTV0500000003666

Fig. 161   Wiper Inoperative, Rear (Part 4 of 4). 2003–04 H2

Step	Action	Yes	No
6	Test the washer fluid level switch signal circuit for a short to ground. Did you find and correct the condition?	Go to Step 13	Go to Step 11
7	Test the washer fluid level switch signal circuit for an open or high resistance. Did you find and correct the condition?	Go to Step 13	Go to Step 11
8	Repair the washer fluid level switch ground circuit for an open or high resistance. Is the repair complete?	Go to Step 13	--
9	Inspect for poor connections at the washer fluid level switch. Did you find and correct the condition?	Go to Step 13	Go to Step 10
10	Replace the washer fluid level switch. Is the repair complete?	Go to Step 13	--
11	Inspect for poor connections at the instrument panel cluster (IPC). Did you find and correct the condition?	Go to Step 13	Go to Step 12
12	Replace the IPC. Is the repair complete?	Go to Step 13	--
13	Operate the system in order to verify the repair. Did you correct the condition?	System OK	Go to Step 3

LTV0500000003672

Fig. 162   Low Washer Fluid Indicator Fault (Part 2 of 2). 2005–06 H2

Step	Action	Yes	No
	DEFINITION: The low washer fluid indicator always indicates low washer fluid or does not turn on with low washer fluid.		
1	Did you review the Wiper/Washer System Description and Operation and perform the necessary inspections?	Go to Step 2	Go to Symptoms
2	Verify the fault is present. Does the system operate normally?		Go to Step 3
3	1. Turn OFF the ignition. 2. Disconnect the washer fluid level switch connector. 3. Turn ON the ignition. Does the low washer fluid indicator illuminate for 60 seconds after the ignition is turned ON?	Go to Step 6	Go to Step 4
4	1. Turn OFF the ignition. 2. Connect a fused jumper wire from the washer fluid level switch signal circuit terminal in the washer fluid level switch connector to a good ground. 3. Turn ON the ignition. Does the low washer fluid indicator illuminate for 60 seconds after the ignition is turned ON?	Go to Step 5	Go to Step 7
5	1. Turn OFF the ignition. 2. Connect a fused jumper wire across the washer fluid level switch harness connector terminals. 3. Turn ON the ignition. Does the low washer fluid indicator illuminate for 60 seconds after the ignition is turned ON?	Go to Step 9	Go to Step 8

LTV0500000003671

Fig. 162   Low Washer Fluid Indicator Fault (Part 1 of 2). 2005–06 H2

Step	Action	Yes	No
	DEFINITION: The windshield washer pump is always ON.		
1	Did you review the Wiper/Washer System Description and Operation and perform the necessary inspections?	Go to Step 2	Go to Symptoms
2	1. Turn the windshield wiper/washer switch to the OFF position. 2. Turn the ignition ON. Is the windshield washer pump always ON?	Go to Step 3	Test for Intermittent and Poor Connections
3	Are the windshield wipers always ON?	Go to Step 4	Go to Step 6
4	1. Disconnect the windshield wiper motor and module connector. 2. Connect a test lamp from the windshield wiper switch signal circuit terminal in the wiper motor harness connector to battery voltage. 3. Turn the ignition ON. Does the test lamp illuminate?	Go to Step 5	Go to Step 14
5	1. Disconnect the turn signal/malfunction switch connector. 2. Test the windshield wiper switch signal circuit for a short to ground. Did you find and correct the condition?	Go to Step 17	Go to Step 12
6	Disconnect the washer fluid pump relay. Is the windshield washer pump ON?	Go to Step 8	Go to Step 7
7	Connect a test lamp from battery positive voltage to the washer fluid pump relay control circuit terminal in the underhood fuse block. Does the test lamp illuminate?	Go to Step 10	Go to Step 16

LTV0500000003673

**Fig. 163   Washers Always On (Part 1 of 2).
2005–06 H2**

Step	Action	Yes	No
8	Disconnect the windshield wiper motor and module connector. Is the windshield washer pump always ON?	Go to Step 11	Go to Step 9
9	Test the washer fluid pump supply circuit for a short to voltage. Did you find and correct the condition?	Go to Step 17	Go to Step 14
10	1. Disconnect the windshield wiper motor and module connector. 2. Test the washer fluid pump relay control circuit for a short to ground. Did you find and correct the condition?	Go to Step 17	Go to Step 14
11	Repair the windshield washer pump control circuit for a short to voltage. Is the repair complete?	Go to Step 17	--
12	Inspect for poor connections at the turn signal/malfunction switch. Did you find and correct the condition?	Go to Step 17	Go to Step 13
13	Replace the turn signal/malfunction switch. Is the repair complete?	Go to Step 17	--
14	Inspect for poor connections at the windshield wiper motor and module. Did you find and correct the condition?	Go to Step 17	Go to Step 15
15	Replace the windshield wiper motor and module. Is the repair complete?	Go to Step 17	--
16	Replace the windshield washer relay. Is the repair complete?	Go to Step 17	--
17	Operate the system in order to verify the repair. Did you correct the condition?	System OK	Go to Step 3

LTV0500000003674

**Fig. 163   Washers Always On (Part 2 of 2).
2005–06 H2**

Step	Action	Values	Yes	No
	DEFINITION: The windshield washer is inoperative.			
1	Did you review the Wiper/Washer System Description and Operation and perform the necessary inspections?	--	Go to Step 2	Go to Symptoms
2	1. Turn the ignition ON. 2. Press the windshield washer switch. Do the windshield washers operate normally?	--	Test for Intermittent and Poor Connections	Go to Step 3
3	Do the windshield wipers operate when the windshield washer switch is pressed?	--	Go to Step 6	Go to Step 4
4	1. Disconnect the windshield wiper motor and module connector. 2. Test the resistance from the windshield wiper switch signal circuit terminal to the low reference circuit terminal in the windshield wiper motor harness connector. 3. Press the windshield washer switch. Is the resistance near the specified value?	0.5 ohms	Go to Step 15	Go to Step 5

LTV0500000003675

**Fig. 164   Washers Inoperative (Part 1 of 4).
2005–06 H2**

Step	Action		Yes	No
5	Test the following circuits for high resistance: • Windshield wiper switch signal circuit • Windshield wiper switch low reference circuit Systems. Did you find and correct the condition?		Go to Step 20	Go to Step 13
6	1. Disconnect the washer fluid pump relay. 2. Connect a test lamp from battery positive voltage to the washer fluid pump relay control circuit terminal in the underhood fuse block. 3. Turn the ignition ON. 4. Press the windshield washer switch. Does the test lamp illuminate?		Go to Step 7	Go to Step 8
7	1. Connect the washer fluid pump relay. 2. Disconnect the washer pump connector. 3. Connect a test lamp across the washer pump harness connector terminals. 4. Turn the ignition ON. 5. Press the windshield washer switch. Does the test lamp illuminate?		Go to Step 18	Go to Step 9
8	Test the washer fluid pump relay control circuit for an open or high resistance. Did you find and correct the condition?		Go to Step 20	Go to Step 15
9	1. Disconnect the windshield wiper motor and module connector. 2. Connect a fused jumper wire from the washer fluid pump relay control circuit terminal in the wiper motor harness connector to a good ground. 3. Connect a test lamp from the washer fluid pump supply voltage circuit terminal in the wiper motor harness connector to a good ground. 4. Turn the ignition ON. Does the test lamp illuminate?		Go to Step 11	Go to Step 10

LTV0500000003676

**Fig. 164   Washers Inoperative (Part 2 of 4).
2005–06 H2**

Step	Action	Yes	No
10	Test the washer fluid pump supply voltage circuit for an open or short to ground. Did you find and correct the condition?	Go to Step 20	Go to Step 17
11	Test the windshield washer pump control circuit for an open or high resistance. Did you find and correct the condition?	Go to Step 20	Go to Step 12
12	Test the rear window washer pump control circuit for an open or high resistance. Did you find and correct the condition?	Go to Step 20	Go to Step 15
13	Inspect for poor connections at the turn signal/multifunction switch switch. Did you find and correct the condition?	Go to Step 20	Go to Step 14
14	Replace the turn signal/multifunction switch. Is the repair complete?	Go to Step 20	--
15	Inspect for poor connections at the windshield wiper motor and module. Did you find and correct the condition?	Go to Step 20	Go to Step 16
16	Replace the windshield wiper motor and module. Is the repair complete?	Go to Step 20	--
17	Replace the washer fluid pump relay. Is the repair complete?	Go to Step 20	--

LTV0500000003677

Fig. 164   Washers Inoperative (Part 3 of 4).
2005–06 H2

Step	Action	Yes	No
18	Inspect for poor connections at the washer fluid pump. Did you find and correct the condition?	Go to Step 20	Go to Step 19
19	Replace the washer fluid pump. Is the repair complete?	Go to Step 20	--
20	Operate the system in order to verify the repair. Did you correct the condition?	System OK	Go to Step 3

LTV0500000003678

Fig. 164   Washers Inoperative (Part 4 of 4).
2005–06 H2

Step	Action	Yes	No
7	Replace the windshield wiper/washer switch. Is the repair complete?	Go to Step 10	--
8	Inspect for poor connections at the windshield wiper motor. Did you find and correct the condition?	Go to Step 10	Go to Step 9
9	Replace the windshield wiper motor. Is the repair complete?	Go to Step 10	--
10	Operate the system in order to verify the repair. Did you correct the condition?	System OK	Go to Step 3

LTV0500000003680

Fig. 165   Wipers Always On (Part 2 of 2).
2005–06 H2

Step	Action	Yes	No
	DEFINITION: Windshield wipers are always ON.		
1	Did you perform the Wiper/Washer System Description and Operation and perform the necessary inspections?	Go to Step 2	Go to Symptoms
2	1. Turn the windshield wiper/washer switch OFF. 2. Turn the ignition ON. Are the windshield wipers always ON?	Go to Step 3	Test for Intermittent and Poor Connections
3	1. Disconnect the turn signal/multifunction switch connectors. 2. Turn the ignition ON. Are the windshield wipers always ON?	Go to Step 4	Go to Step 6
4	1. Turn the ignition OFF. 2. Disconnect the windshield wiper motor and module connector. 3. Test the windshield wiper switch high signal circuit for a short to ground. Did you find and correct the condition?	Go to Step 10	Go to Step 5
5	Test the windshield wiper switch signal circuit for a short to ground. Did you find and correct the condition?	Go to Step 10	Go to Step 8
6	Inspect for poor connections at the windshield wiper/washer switch. Did you find and correct the condition?	Go to Step 10	Go to Step 7

LTV0500000003679

Fig. 165   Wipers Always On (Part 1 of 2).
2005–06 H2

Step	Action	Yes	No
	DEFINITION: Windshield wipers are inoperative in all modes.		
1	Did you perform the Wiper/Washer System Description and Operation and perform the necessary inspections?	Go to Step 2	Go to Symptoms
2	1. Turn the ignition ON. 2. Attempt to operate the windshield wipers in all modes. Are the windshield wipers inoperative in all modes?	Go to Step 3	
3	1. Disconnect the turn signal/multifunction switch connectors. 2. Connect a fused jumper wire from the windshield wiper switch high signal circuit terminal to ground. 3. Turn the ignition ON. Do the windshield wipers operate at high speed?	Go to Step 9	Go to Step 4
4	1. Disconnect the windshield wiper motor module connector. 2. Connect a test lamp from the accessory voltage supply circuit terminal in the windshield wiper motor harness connector to a good ground. 3. Turn the ignition ON. Does the test lamp illuminate?	Go to Step 5	Go to Step 7
5	Connect a test lamp from battery positive voltage to the windshield wiper motor ground circuit terminal in the windshield wiper motor module harness connector. Does the test lamp illuminate?	Go to Step 6	Go to Step 8

LTV0500000003681

Fig. 166   Wipers Inoperative, All Modes (Part 1 of 3).
2005–06 H2

Step	Action		Yes	No
6	1. Connect the wiper motor module connector. 2. Disconnect the wiper motor to module connector. 3. Connect a test lamp across the low speed motor control and ground circuit terminals in the module. 4. Turn the windshield wiper switch to the low position. Does the test lamp illuminate for several seconds?		Go to Step 12	Go to Step 11
7	Repair the accessory voltage supply circuit to the windshield wiper motor and module for an open or short to ground. Is the repair complete?		Go to Step 15	--
8	Repair the windshield wiper motor and module ground circuit for an open or high resistance. Is the repair complete?		Go to Step 15	--
9	Inspect for poor connections at the windshield wiper/washer switch. Did you find and correct the condition?		Go to Step 15	Go to Step 10
10	Replace the windshield wiper/washer switch. Is the repair complete?		Go to Step 15	--
11	Inspect for poor connections at the windshield wiper motor module. Did you find and correct the condition?		Go to Step 15	Go to Step 13
12	Inspect for poor connections at the windshield wiper motor. Did you find and correct the condition?		Go to Step 15	Go to Step 14
13	Replace the windshield wiper motor module. Is the repair complete?		Go to Step 15	--

LTV0500000003682

Fig. 166   Wipers Inoperative, All Modes (Part 2 of 3). 2005–06 H2

Test Description

The numbers below refer to the step numbers on the diagnostic table.

5. This step tests for continuity through the 390 ohms resistor in the windshield wiper/washer switch.

6. This step tests for continuity through the delay resistors in the windshield wiper/washer switch. The measured resistance will change in sequence from low to high as the delay speed is increased.

Step	Action	Values	Yes	No
	DEFINITION: Windshield wipers are inoperative in one or more modes.			
1	Did you perform the Wiper/Washer System Description and Operation and perform the necessary inspections?	--	Go to Step 2	Go to Symptoms
2	1. Turn ON the ignition. 2. Attempt to operate the windshield wipers in all modes. Does the system operate normally?	--		Go to Step 3
3	Do the windshield wipers operate in the high speed mode?	--	Go to Step 5	Go to Step 4
4	1. Disconnect the turn signal/multifunction switch connectors. 2. Connect a fused jumper wire from the windshield wiper switch high signal circuit terminal in the body harness connector half to a good ground. 3. Turn ON the ignition. Do the windshield wipers operate at high speed?	--	Go to Step 8	Go to Step 7

LTV0500000003684

Fig. 167   Wipers Inoperative, One Or More Modes (Part 1 of 3). 2005–06 H2

Step	Action		Yes	No
14	Replace the windshield wiper motor. Is the repair complete?		Go to Step 15	--
15	Operate the system in order to verify the repair. Did you correct the condition?		System OK	Go to Step 3

LTV0500000003683

Fig. 166   Wipers Inoperative, All Modes (Part 3 of 3). 2005–06 H2

Step	Action	Values	Yes	No

5	1. Disconnect the turn signal/multifunction switch connectors.
	2. Test the resistance from the windshield wiper switch signal circuit terminal to the low reference circuit terminal in the turn signal/multifunction switch.
	3. Operate the windshield wiper/washer switch in the following positions:
	
	  - MIST
	  - LO
	
	Is the resistance near the specified value in the listed switch positions?
		390 ohms	Go to Step 6	Go to Step 11

6	1. Test the resistance from the windshield wiper switch signal circuit terminal to the low reference circuit terminal in the turn signal/multifunction switch. 2. Operate the windshield wiper/washer switch in all of the delay positions. Does the resistance remain within the specified values from low to high as the delay speed is increased?	1K ohms- 10K ohms	Go to Step 9	Go to Step 11
7	1. Disconnect the windshield wiper motor and module connector. 2. Test the windshield wiper switch high signal circuit for an open or high resistance. Did you find and correct the condition?	--	Go to Step 16	Go to Step 14
8	Test the windshield wiper switch ground circuit for an open or high resistance. Did you find and correct the condition?	--	Go to Step 16	Go to Step 12
9	Test the windshield wiper switch signal circuit for an open or a high resistance. Did you find and correct the condition?	--	Go to Step 16	Go to Step 10

LTV0500000003685

Fig. 167   Wipers Inoperative, One Or More Modes (Part 2 of 3). 2005–06 H2

Step	Action	Yes	No
10	Test the windshield wiper switch low reference circuit for an open or high resistance. Did you find and correct the condition?	Go to Step 16	Go to Step 14
11	Test the windshield wiper switch signal and low reference circuits in the steering column harness for an open or short to ground. Did you find and correct the condition?	Go to Step 16	Go to Step 12
12	Inspect for poor connections at the turn signal/malfunction switch. Did you find and correct the condition?	Go to Step 16	Go to Step 13
13	Replace the turn signal/malfunction switch. Is the repair complete?	Go to Step 16	--
14	Inspect for poor connections at the windshield wiper motor and module. Did you find and correct the condition?	Go to Step 16	Go to Step 15
15	Replace the windshield wiper motor and module. Is the repair complete?	Go to Step 16	--
16	Operate the system in order to verify the repair. Did you correct the condition?	System OK	Go to Step 3

LTV0500000003686

Fig. 167 Wipers Inoperative, One Or More Modes (Part 3 of 3). 2005–06 H2

Step	Action	Yes	No
6	Test the rear window washer pump control circuit for a short to ground. Did you find and correct the condition?	Go to Step 12	Go to Step 10
7	Test the rear window washer switch signal circuit for an open or high resistance. Did you find and correct the condition?	Go to Step 12	Go to Step 8
8	Inspect for poor connections at the rear window wiper/washer switch. Did you find and correct the condition?	Go to Step 12	Go to Step 9
9	Replace the rear window wiper/washer switch. Is the repair complete?	Go to Step 12	--
10	Inspect for poor connections at the windshield wiper motor and module. Did you find and correct the condition?	Go to Step 12	Go to Step 11
11	Replace the windshield wiper motor and module. Is the repair complete?	Go to Step 12	--
12	Operate the system in order to verify the repair. Did you correct the condition?	System OK	Go to Step 3

LTV0500000003688

Fig. 168 Washer Inoperative, Rear (Part 2 of 2). 2005–06 H2

Step	Action	Yes	No
	DEFINITION: The rear window washer is inoperative and the windshield washers operate normally.		
1	Did you review the Rear Wiper/Washer System Description and Operation and perform the necessary inspections?	Go to Step 2	Go to Symptoms
2	1. Turn the ignition ON. 2. Press the rear window washer switch. Does the rear window washer operate normally?	Test for Intermittent and Poor Connections	Go to Step 3
3	Does the rear window wiper operate when the washer switch is pressed?	Go to Step 4	Go to Step 8
4	1. Disconnect the washer fluid pump relay. 2. Connect a test lamp from the washer fluid pump relay control circuit terminal to ground. 3. Turn the ignition ON. 4. Press the rear window washer switch. Does the test lamp illuminate when the switch is pressed?	Go to Step 6	Go to Step 5
5	1. Disconnect the windshield wiper motor and module connector. 2. Connect a test lamp from the rear window washer switch signal circuit terminal to ground. 3. Press the rear window washer switch. Does the test lamp illuminate when the switch is pressed?	Go to Step 10	Go to Step 7

LTV0500000003687

Fig. 168 Washer Inoperative, Rear (Part 1 of 2). 2005–06 H2

Step	Action	Yes	No
1	Did you review the Rear Wiper/Washer System Description and Operation and perform the necessary inspections?	Go to Step 2	Go to Symptoms
2	1. Turn the ignition ON. 2. Turn the rear window wiper/washer switch to the OFF position. Is the rear window wiper always ON?	Go to Step 3	Test for Intermittent and Poor Connections
3	1. Disconnect the rear window wiper module connector. 2. Connect a test lamp from the rear window wiper switch signal circuit terminal in the harness connector to ground. Does the test lamp illuminate?	Go to Step 5	Go to Step 4
4	Connect a test lamp from the rear window washer switch signal circuit terminal in the rear wiper motor harness connector to ground. Does the test lamp illuminate?	Go to Step 6	Go to Step 9
5	1. Disconnect the rear window wiper/washer switch connector. 2. Test the rear window wiper switch signal circuit for a short to voltage. Did you find and correct the condition?	Go to Step 11	Go to Step 7
6	1. Disconnect the rear window wiper/washer switch connector. 2. Test the rear window washer switch signal circuit for a short to voltage. Did you find and correct the condition?	Go to Step 11	Go to Step 7

LTV0500000003689

Fig. 169 Wiper Always On, Rear (Part 1 of 2). 2005–06 H2

Step	Action	Yes	No
7	Inspect for poor connections at the rear window wiper/washer switch. Did you find and correct the condition?	Go to Step 11	Go to Step 8
8	Replace the rear window wiper/washer switch. Is the repair complete?	Go to Step 11	--
9	Inspect for poor connections at the rear window wiper module. Did you find and correct the condition?	Go to Step 11	Go to Step 10
10	Replace the rear window wiper module. Is the repair complete?	Go to Step 11	--
11	Operate the system in order to verify the repair. Did you correct the condition?	System OK	Go to Step 3

LTV0500000003690

Fig. 169   Wiper Always On, Rear (Part 2 of 2).
2005–06 H2

Step	Action	Yes	No
	DEFINITION: The rear wiper motor is inoperative in one or more modes, the rear washer pump may or may not operate.		
1	Did you review the Rear Wiper/Washer System Description and Operation and perform the necessary inspections?	Go to Step 2	Go to Symptoms
2	1. Turn ON the ignition, with the engine OFF. 2. Operate the rear wiper/washer system in all the switch positions. Does the rear wiper/washer system operate normally?	Test for Intermittent and Poor Connections	Go to Step 3
3	Inspect the courtesy lamps for proper operation. Refer to Interior Lighting Systems Description and Operation in Lighting System. Do the courtesy lamps operate properly?	Go to Step 4	Go to Symptoms
4	Does the rear wiper motor operate when the rear washer switch is pressed?	Go to Step 6	Go to Step 5
5	Is the rear wiper only inoperative when the rear washer switch is pressed?	Go to Step 12	Go to Step 6
6	1. Disconnect the harness connector of the rear wiper switch. 2. Connect a test lamp from the accessory voltage circuit of the rear wiper/washer switch to a good ground. Does the test lamp illuminate?	Go to Step 7	Go to Step 13

LTV0500000003691

Fig. 170   Wiper Inoperative, Rear (Part 1 of 4).
2005–06 H2

Step	Action	Yes	No
7	Connect a 15-amp fused jumper wire from the accessory voltage circuit to the rear window wiper switch signal circuit. Does the rear wiper motor operate?	Go to Step 16	Go to Step 8
8	1. Remove the fused jumper wire and connect the rear wiper switch connector. 2. Disconnect the harness connector of the rear window wiper module. 3. Connect a test lamp from the rear window wiper switch signal circuit to a good ground. 4. Turn the rear wiper switch to the 2 position. Does the test lamp illuminate?	Go to Step 9	Go to Step 18
9	Connect a test lamp from battery voltage to the ground circuit of the rear wiper module. Does the test lamp illuminate?	Go to Step 10	Go to Step 19
10	Connect a test lamp from the battery voltage circuit of the rear wiper module to a good ground. Does the test lamp illuminate?	Go to Step 11	Go to Step 20
11	1. Connect the rear wiper module harness connector. 2. Disconnect the wiper motor to module connector. 3. Connect a test lamp across the motor control circuit terminals in the module. 4. Turn the rear wiper switch to the 2 position. Does the test lamp illuminate?	Go to Step 24	Go to Step 17
12	1. Disconnect the harness connector of the rear wiper/washer module. 2. Connect a test lamp from the rear window washer switch signal circuit to a good ground. 3. Depress the rear washer switch. Does the test lamp illuminate?	Go to Step 17	Go to Step 15
13	Test the accessory voltage circuit of the rear wiper/washer switch for an open or a short to ground. Did you find and correct the condition?	Go to Step 25	Go to Step 14
14	Test the rear window wiper switch signal circuit for a short to ground. Did you find and correct the condition?	Go to Step 25	Go to Step 21

LTV0500000003692

Fig. 170   Wiper Inoperative, Rear (Part 2 of 4).
2005–06 H2

Step	Action	Yes	No
15	Test the rear window washer switch signal circuit for an open or high resistance. Did you find and correct the condition?	Go to Step 25	Go to Step 16
16	Inspect for poor connections at the harness connector of the rear wiper/washer switch. Did you find and correct the condition?	Go to Step 25	Go to Step 22
17	Inspect for poor connections at the harness connector of the rear wiper module. Did you find and correct the condition?	Go to Step 25	Go to Step 23
18	Repair an open or high resistance in the rear window wiper switch signal circuit. Did you complete the repair?	Go to Step 25	--
19	Repair an open or high resistance in the ground circuit of the rear wiper module. Did you complete the repair?	Go to Step 25	--
20	Repair an open or a short to ground in the battery voltage circuit of the rear wiper module. Did you complete the repair?	Go to Step 25	--
21	Repair a short to ground in the rear window washer switch signal circuit. Did you complete the repair?	Go to Step 25	--
22	Replace the rear window wiper/washer switch. Did you complete the replacement?	Go to Step 25	--
23	Replace the rear wiper motor module. Did you complete the replacement?	Go to Step 25	--

LTV0500000003693

Fig. 170   Wiper Inoperative, Rear (Part 3 of 4).
2005–06 H2

24	Replace the rear wiper motor. Did you complete the replacement?		Go to Step 25	--
25	Operate the system in order to verify the repair. Did you correct the condition?		System OK	Go to Step 3

LTV0500000003694

Fig. 170 Wiper Inoperative, Rear (Part 4 of 4). 2005–06 H2

Conditions for Clearing the DTCs

- DTC B3717 will change from current to history when the windshield wiper switch is turned OFF and ON, and the condition is no longer present.
- DTC B3718 will change from current to history when the condition is no longer present.
- A history DTC will clear after 100 ignition cycles, without a repeat of the malfunction.

Step	Action	Yes	No
1	Did you perform the Diagnostic System Check - Vehicle? Go to Step 2		Go to Diagnostic System Check -
2	1. Turn the ignition to the ON position. 2. Turn the wiper switch to the low position. Do the windshield wipers operate?	Test for Intermittent and Poor Connections	Go to Step 3
3	1. Turn the ignition to the OFF position. 2. Turn the wiper switch OFF. 3. Remove the ON/OFF WPR relay from the underhood fuse block. 4. Using a test lamp connected to ground, probe the relay control circuit at the underhood fuse block. Does the test lamp illuminate?	Go to Step 8	Go to Step 4

LTV0500000003699

Fig. 171 Codes B3715, B3716, B3717, B3718 & B3719: Front Wiper Relay Drive Circuit (Part 2 of 4). H3

Circuit Description

The body control module (BCM) controls and monitors the state of the ON/OFF wiper relay control circuit. When the windshield wiper switch is placed in to a low speed setting, a signal is applied to the BCM. The BCM then applies battery positive voltage to the coil side of the ON/OFF WPR relay through the relay control circuit. This energizes the relay, allowing battery positive voltage from the FRT/WPR fuse through the switched side of the ON/OFF WPR relay through the HI/LOW WPR relay and to the windshield wiper motor. Ground is applied at all times to the coil sides of the wiper relays and the windshield wiper motor from G105.

DTC Descriptors

This diagnostic procedure supports the following DTCs:

- DTC B3717 Front Wiper Relay Drive Circuit Low
- DTC B3718 Front Wiper Relay Drive Circuit High

Conditions for Running the DTCs

- The ignition is ON.
- The ignition voltage is between 9-18.5 volts.

Conditions for Setting the DTCs

The following conditions will cause these DTCs to set:

- DTC B3717, the BCM detects a low voltage level on the supply circuit of the wiper micro relay for 1 second when the relay is energized.
- DTC B3718, the BCM detects a high voltage level on the supply circuit of the wiper micro relay for 1 second when the relay is de-energized.

Action Taken When the DTC Sets

The BCM de-energizes the wiper micro relay, until the wiper switch is turned OFF and ON.

LTV0500000003698

Fig. 171 Codes B3715, B3716, B3717, B3718 & B3719: Front Wiper Relay Drive Circuit (Part 1 of 4). H3

4	1. Leave the test lamp connected. 2. Turn the ignition to the ON position. 3. Turn the wiper switch to the low position. Does the test lamp illuminate?	Go to Step 5	Go to Step 6
5	1. Turn the wiper switch to the OFF position. 2. Turn the ignition to the OFF position. 3. Using a test lamp, probe the relay control circuit and the ground circuit of the relay at the underhood fuse block. 4. Turn the ignition to the ON position. 5. Turn the wiper switch to the low position. Does the test lamp illuminate?	Go to Step 9	Go to Step 7
6	Test for a poor connection, an open, or short to ground in the ON/OFF wiper relay control circuit. Did you find and correct the condition?	Go to Step 12	Go to Step 10
7	Test for a poor connection or an open in the ground circuit of the ON/OFF WPR relay. Did you find and correct the condition?	Go to Step 12	Go to Step 11
8	Repair a short to battery positive voltage in the ON/OFF wiper relay control circuit. Did you complete the repair?	Go to Step 12	--
9	1. Replace the ON/OFF WPR relay. 2. Operate the vehicle within the Conditions for Running the DTC. Does the DTC reset?	Go to Step 11	Go to Step 12
10	Replace the body control module (BCM). Did you complete the replacement?	Go to Step 12	--
11	Replace the underhood electrical center. Did you complete the replacement?	Go to Step 12	--

LTV0500000003700

Fig. 171 Codes B3715, B3716, B3717, B3718 & B3719: Front Wiper Relay Drive Circuit (Part 3 of 4). H3

12	1. Use the scan tool in order to clear the DTCs. 2. Operate the vehicle within the Conditions For Running the DTC as specified in the supporting text. Does the DTC reset?	Go to Step 2	System OK

LTV0500000003701

Fig. 171 Codes B3715, B3716, B3717, B3718 & B3719: Front Wiper Relay Drive Circuit (Part 4 of 4). H3

Delay or Low Speed Wipers Inoperative

1. Install a scan tool and display the Wiper Delay Input parameter in the BCM data list.
2. Ignition ON, the scan tool should display 0.5 to 3.0 volts in switch positions Mist, Delay 1-5, Low, and High.

    ☐ If the scan tool displays 0.0 volts in any of the listed switch positions test the windshield wiper switch signal 1 circuit for an open or short to ground and perform the windshield wiper washer switch low speed component test. If the circuit and switch test normal replace the body control module.

3. With the wiper switch in the High speed position verify that the Front Wipers Active parameter in the BCM Inputs data list is On.

    ☐ If the scan tool does not display On test the wiper relay control circuit for an open/high resistance. If the circuit tests normal replace the body control module.

4. Disconnect the windshield wiper motor connector.
5. Connect a test lamp between the low speed control circuit and the ground circuit.
6. The test lamp should illuminate with the windshield wiper switch in the Low speed position.

    ☐ If the test lamp does not illuminate test the wiper motor low speed circuit and underhood fuse block for an open/high resistance.

7. If all the circuits test normal replace the windshield wiper motor.

LTV0500000003706

Fig. 173 Front Delay Or Low Speed Wipers Inoperative. H3

Wipers Inoperative All Modes

1. Install a scan tool and display the Wiper Delay Input parameter in the BCM data list.
2. Ignition ON, the scan tool should display 0.5 to 3.0 volts in switch positions Mist, Delay 1-5, Low, and High.

    ☐ If the scan tool displays 0.0 volts in the listed switch positions test the voltage supply circuit to the windshield wiper washer switch for an open or short to ground or the windshield wiper switch signal 2 and the washer pump control circuits for a short to ground.

3. With the windshield wiper switch to the Low speed position the Front Wipers Active parameter in the BCM inputs data list should display On for several seconds.

    ☐ If the scan tool does not display On test the windshield wiper motor high and low speed circuits for a short to ground. If the circuits test normal replace the ON/OFF WPR relay.

4. Disconnect the windshield wiper motor connector.
5. Verify that a test lamp will illuminate when connected from battery voltage to the ground circuit.

    ☐ If the test lamp does not illuminate repair the windshield wiper motor ground circuit for an open/high resistance.

6. If all the circuits test normal replace the windshield wiper motor.

LTV0500000003705

Fig. 172 Front Wipers Inoperative All Modes. H3

High Speed Wipers Inoperative

1. Operate the wiper switch to the High speed position.
2. With the ignition on verify that the Front Wipers Active parameter in the BCM inputs data list is On.

    ☐ If the Front Wipers Active parameter is not On perform the windshield wiper washer switch high speed component test, test the windshield wiper switch signal 2 circuit and underhood fuse block for an open/high resistance. If the circuit and switch test normal replace the wiper diode #90.

3. Disconnect the windshield wiper motor connector.
4. Verify that a test lamp will illuminate when connected between the high speed control circuit and the ground circuit.

    ☐ If the test lamp does not illuminate test the wiper motor high speed circuit for an open/high resistance. If the circuit tests normal replace the HI/LOW WPR relay.

5. If all the circuits test normal replace the windshield wiper motor.

Low Speed Wipers Always On

1. Ignition ON, verify that the Wiper Relay Command parameter on the BCM outputs data list is Off.

    ☐ If the scan tool displays On test the windshield wiper switch signal 1 circuit for a short to voltage and perform the windshield wiper washer switch low speed component test. If the circuit and switch test normal replace the body control module.

2. Verify that the Front Wipers Active parameter on the BCM inputs data list is Off.

    ☐ If the scan tool displays On test the wiper relay control circuit for a short to voltage. If the circuit tests normal replace the BCM.

3. Verify that the wipers stop when the ON/OFF WPR relay is removed.

    ☐ If the wipers remain on test the windshield wiper motor low speed control circuit for a short to voltage.

4. If all the circuits test normal replace the ON/OFF WPR relay.

LTV0500000003707

Fig. 174 Front High Speed Wipers Inoperative & Low Speed Wipers Always On. H3

High Speed Wipers Always On

1. Verify that the Front Wipers Active parameter on the BCM inputs data list is Off.

   ☐ If the scan tool displays On test the windshield wiper washer switch signal 2 circuit for a short to voltage and perform the windshield wiper washer switch high speed component test.

2. Disconnect the windshield wiper motor connector.
3. Wiper switch OFF, verify that a test lamp will not illuminate when connected between the wiper motor high speed control circuit and ground.

   ☐ If the test lamp illuminates repair the wiper motor high speed control circuit for a short to voltage. If the circuit tests normal replace the underhood fuse block.

Washers Inoperative

1. Display the Washer Switch parameter on the BCM Inputs data list.
2. Ignition ON, verify that the Washer Switch parameter is On while the washer switch is pressed.

   ☐ If the scan tool displays Off perform the windshield washer switch component test. If the switch tests normal repair the windshield washer pump control circuit from the switch to the BCM for an open/high resistance.

3. Disconnect the windshield washer pump connector.
4. A test lamp connected between the washer pump control circuits should illuminate while the washer switch is pressed.

   ☐ If the test lamp does not illuminate repair the windshield washer pump control circuit from the BCM to the pump or the ground circuit for an open/high resistance.

5. If all the circuits test normal replace the windshield washer pump.

Washers Always On

1. Disconnect the steering column harness to instrument panel (I/P) harness inline connector C201.
2. Ignition ON, the windshield washers should not be ON.

   ☐ If the windshield washers remain on repair the windshield washer pump control circuit for a short to voltage.

3. If the windshield washers turn off replace the windshield wiper washer switch.

LTV0500000003708

Fig. 175   Front High Speed Wipers Always On, Washers Inoperative & Washers Always On. H3

Windshield Wiper Washer Switch Low Speed Circuit

Important: If the switch tests open in any switch position other than Off test wiper switch signal 1 circuit for a short to ground before replacing the switch.

1. Disconnect the Steering Column harness to I/P harness inline connector C201.
2. Connect a DMM from the accessory voltage supply circuit terminal to the windshield wiper switch signal 2 circuit terminal in the steering column connector half.
3. Operate the windshield wiper switch from Off to Mist, Delay 1 through 5, Low, and High.

   ☐ If the DMM does not display at or near the resistance values provided replace the windshield wiper washer switch.

Switch Position	Resistance
Off	Infinite
Mist	1.78K ohms
Delay 1	9.43K ohms
Delay 2	6.82K ohms
Delay 3	4.95K ohms
Delay 4	3.55K ohms
Delay 5	2.53K ohms
Low	1.78K ohms
High	1.78K ohms

LTV0500000003710

Fig. 177   Front Windshield Wiper Washer Switch Low Speed Circuit Diagnosis. H3

Component Testing

Windshield Wiper Washer Switch High and Wash circuits.

1. Disconnect the steering column harness to I/P harness inline connector C201.
2. Connect a DMM from the accessory voltage supply circuit terminal to the windshield wiper switch signal 2 circuit terminal in the steering column connector half.
3. The DMM should indicate continuity while the wiper switch is in the High speed position.

   ☐ If the DMM does not display 0-2 ohms replace the windshield wiper washer switch.

4. The DMM should indicate no continuity while the wiper switch is in any position other than High.

   ☐ If the DMM does not display infinite resistance replace the windshield wiper washer switch.

5. Connect a DMM from the accessory voltage supply circuit terminal to the windshield washer pump control circuit terminal.
6. The DMM should indicate continuity while the windshield washer switch is pressed.

   ☐ If the DMM does not display 0-2 ohms replace the windshield wiper washer switch.

7. The DMM should indicate no continuity when the windshield washer switch is released.

   ☐ If the DMM does not display infinite resistance replace the windshield wiper washer switch.

LTV0500000003709

Fig. 176   Front Windshield Wiper Washer Switch High & Wash Circuit Diagnosis. H3

Wiper Motor Inoperative in All Modes

1. Disconnect the rear wiper motor connector.
2. Ignition ON, verify that a test lamp will illuminate when connected from the wiper motor supply circuit to ground.

   ☐ If the test lamp does not illuminate repair the wiper motor supply circuit for an open/high resistance or short to ground.

3. Verify that a test lamp will illuminate when connected from the wiper motor ground circuit to battery voltage.

   ☐ If the test lamp does not illuminate repair the wiper motor ground circuit for an open/high resistance.

4. If all the circuits test normal replace the rear wiper motor.

Wiper Motor Inoperative in Both Delay Modes

1. Verify that the wiper fuse is not open.

   ☐ If the wiper fuse is open repair the short to ground in the switch supply, delay 1 signal, delay 2 signal, or washer pump control circuit.

2. Disconnect the wiper switch connector.
3. Ignition ON, verify that a test lamp will illuminate when connected between the wiper switch supply circuit and ground.

   ☐ If the test lamp does not illuminate repair the wiper switch supply circuit for an open/high resistance.

4. Connect the wiper switch connector.
5. Disconnect the wiper motor connector.
6. Connect a test lamp between the delay 1 signal circuit and ground.
7. Turn the rear wiper switch to the delay 1 position, the test lamp should illuminate.

   ☐ If the test lamp does not illuminate replace the rear wiper/washer switch.

8. If all the circuits test normal replace the rear wiper motor.

LTV0500000003713

Fig. 178   Rear Wiper Motor Inoperative In All Modes & Inoperative In Both Delay Modes. H3

WIPER SYSTEMS

Wiper Motor Inoperative in One Delay Mode

1. Disconnect the rear wiper motor connector.
2. Connect a test lamp between the inoperative delay signal circuit and ground.
3. Ignition ON, turn the rear wiper switch to the inoperative delay position, the test lamp should illuminate.

   ☐ If the test lamp does not illuminate test the inoperative delay signal circuit for an open/high resistance. If the circuit tests normal replace the rear wiper switch.

4. If all the circuits test normal replace the rear wiper motor.

Wiper Motor Always On

1. Disconnect the rear wiper motor connector.
2. Connect a test lamp between the delay 1 signal circuit and ground.
3. Ignition ON, wiper switch OFF, the test lamp should not illuminate.

   ☐ If the test lamp illuminates test the delay 1 signal circuit for a short to voltage. If the circuit tests normal replace the rear wiper switch.

4. Connect a test lamp between the delay 2 signal circuit and ground.
5. Ignition ON, wiper switch OFF, the test lamp should not illuminate.

   ☐ If the test lamp illuminates test the delay 2 signal circuit for a short to voltage. If the circuit tests normal replace the rear wiper switch.

6. If all the circuits test normal replace the rear wiper motor.

LTV0500000003714

Fig. 179   Rear Wiper Motor Inoperative In One Delay Mode & Wiper Motor Always On. H3

Washers Always On

1. Disconnect the rear wiper motor connector.
2. Connect a test lamp between battery voltage and the washer pump control circuit.
3. The test lamp should not illuminate while the washer switch is OFF.

   ☐ If the test lamp illuminates repair the washer pump control circuit for a short to ground. If the circuit tests normal replace the rear wiper washer switch.

4. If all the circuits test normal replace the rear wiper motor.

LTV0500000003716

Fig. 181   Rear Washers Always On. H3

Washer Pump Inoperative

1. Disconnect the rear washer pump connector.
2. Connect a test lamp between the washer pump supply circuit and ground.
3. Ignition ON, the test lamp should illuminate.

   ☐ If the test lamp does not illuminate repair the rear washer pump supply circuit for an open/high resistance.

4. Connect a test lamp between the washer pump supply circuit and control circuit.
5. Ignition ON, washer switch pressed, the test lamp should illuminate.

   ☐ If the test lamp does not illuminate test the washer pump control and switch ground circuits for an open/high resistance. If the circuits test normal replace the rear wiper washer switch.

6. If all the circuits test normal replace the rear washer pump.

Washer Wiper Inoperative

1. Disconnect the rear wiper motor connector.
2. Connect a test lamp between battery voltage and the washer pump control circuit.
3. The test lamp should illuminate while the washer switch is pressed.

   ☐ If the test lamp does not illuminate repair the washer pump control circuit for an open/high resistance.

4. If all the circuits test normal replace the rear wiper motor.

Washer Wipers and Pump Inoperative

1. Disconnect the rear washer pump connector.
2. Connect a test lamp between battery voltage and the washer pump control circuit.
3. The test lamp should illuminate while the washer switch is pressed.

   ☐ If the test lamp does not illuminate test the washer pump control and switch ground circuits for an open/high resistance. If the circuits test normal replace the rear wiper washer switch.

LTV0500000003715

Fig. 180   Rear Washer Pump Inoperative, Washer Wiper Inoperative & Washer Wipers/Pump Inoperative. H3

Step	Action	Yes	No
1	Did you review the Wiper/Washer System Description and Operation and perform the necessary inspections?	Go to Step 2	Go to Symptoms
2	Turn the ignition ON. Are the windshield washers always on?	Go to Step 3	
3	1. Turn the ignition OFF. 2. Disconnect the inline harness connector C201. 3. Remove the connector terminal row E from the steering column harness connector half. 4. Connect the inline harness connector C201. 5. Turn the ignition ON. Are the windshield washers always on?	Go to Step 4	Go to Step 5
4	Repair the windshield washer pump control circuit for a short to voltage. Is the repair complete?	Go to Step 6	--
5	Replace the windshield wiper/washer switch. Is the repair complete?	Go to Step 6	--
6	Operate the system in order to verify the repair. Did you correct the condition?	System OK	Go to Step 3

LTV0500000003103

Fig. 182   Washers Always On. Montana, Silhouette & Venture

Step	Action	Yes	No
1	Did you review the Wiper/Washer System Description and Operation and perform the necessary inspections?	Go to Step 2	Go to Symptoms
2	1. Turn the ignition ON. 2. Press the windshield washer switch. Do the windshield washers operate normally?		Go to Step 3
3	1. Disconnect the windshield washer pump connector. 2. Connect a test lamp across the washer pump harness connector terminals. 3. Turn the ignition ON. 4. Press the windshield washer switch. Does the test lamp illuminate?	Go to Step 8	Go to Step 4
4	Test the windshield washer pump ground circuit for an open or high resistance. Did you find and correct the condition?	Go to Step 10	Go to Step 5
5	Test the windshield washer pump control circuit for an open or high resistance. Did you find and correct the condition?	Go to Step 10	Go to Step 6
6	Inspect for poor connections at the windshield wiper/washer switch. Did you find and correct the condition?	Go to Step 10	Go to Step 7

LTV0500000003104

Fig. 183   Washers Inoperative (Part 1 of 2). Montana, Silhouette & Venture

Step	Action	Yes	No
7	Replace the windshield wiper/washer switch. Is the repair complete?	Go to Step 10	--
8	Inspect for poor connections at the windshield washer pump. Did you find and correct the condition?	Go to Step 10	Go to Step 9
9	Replace the windshield washer pump. Is the repair complete?	Go to Step 10	--
10	Operate the system in order to verify the repair. Did you correct the condition?	System OK	Go to Step 3

LTV0500000003105

Fig. 183   Washers Inoperative (Part 2 of 2). Montana, Silhouette & Venture

Step	Action	Yes	No
1	Did you review the Wiper/Washer System Description and Operation and perform the necessary inspections?	Go to Step 2	Go to Symptoms
2	1. Turn the ignition ON. 2. Operate the windshield wiper/washer switch in all of the switch positions. 3. Turn the windshield wiper/washer switch OFF. Are the windshield wipers always on?	Go to Step 3	
3	1. Turn the ignition OFF while the wiper arms are in the up position. 2. Disconnect the inline harness connector C201. 3. Remove the connector terminal row E from the steering column harness connector half. 4. Connect the inline harness connector C201. 5. Turn the ignition ON. Are the windshield wipers always on?	Go to Step 4	Go to Step 7
4	1. Disconnect the windshield wiper motor connector. 2. Test the windshield wiper switch signal 1 circuit for a short to voltage. Did you find and correct the condition?	Go to Step 11	Go to Step 5
5	Test the windshield wiper switch signal 2 circuit for a short to voltage. Did you find and correct the condition?	Go to Step 11	Go to Step 6

LTV0500000003106

Fig. 184   Wipers Always On (Part 1 of 2). Montana, Silhouette & Venture

Step	Action	Yes	No
6	Test the windshield wiper motor high speed circuit for a short to voltage. Did you find and correct the condition?	Go to Step 11	Go to Step 9
7	Inspect for poor connections at the windshield wiper/washer switch. Did you find and correct the condition?	Go to Step 11	Go to Step 8
8	Replace the windshield wiper/washer switch. Is the repair complete?	Go to Step 11	--
9	Inspect for poor connections at the windshield wiper motor. Did you find and correct the condition?	Go to Step 11	Go to Step 10
10	Replace the windshield wiper motor module. Is the repair complete?	Go to Step 11	--
11	Operate the system in order to verify the repair. Did you correct the condition?	System OK	Go to Step 3

LTV0500000003107

Fig. 184   Wipers Always On (Part 2 of 2). Montana, Silhouette, & Venture

Step	Action	Yes	No
1	Did you review the Wiper/Washer System description and operation and perform the necessary inspections?	Go to Step 2	Go to Symptoms -
2	1. Turn ON the ignition ON, with the engine OFF. 2. Operate the windshield wiper/washer switch through all the switch positions. Does the windshield wiper/washer system operate normally?	Test for Intermittent and Poor Connections	Go to Step 3
3	1. Turn OFF the ignition. 2. Disconnect the harness connector of the windshield wiper motor. 3. Turn the ignition ON, with the engine OFF. 4. Connect a test lamp from the accessory voltage circuit of the windshield wiper motor to a good ground. Does the test lamp illuminate?	Go to Step 4	Go to Step 13
4	Connect a test lamp from the accessory voltage circuit to the ground circuit of the windshield wiper motor. Does the test lamp illuminate?	Go to Step 5	Go to Step 14
5	1. Connect a test lamp from the signal 2 circuit of the windshield wiper switch to a good ground. 2. Press the windshield washer switch. Does the test lamp illuminate?	Go to Step 11	Go to Step 6

LTV0500000003108

Fig. 185 Wipers Inoperative, All Modes (Part 1 of 3). Montana, Silhouette & Venture

Step	Action	Yes	No
6	1. Turn OFF the ignition. 2. Disconnect the harness connector of the windshield wiper/washer switch. 3. Turn ON the ignition, with the engine OFF. 4. Connect a test lamp from the accessory voltage circuit of the windshield wiper/washer switch to a good ground. Does the test lamp illuminate?	Go to Step 12	Go to Step 7
7	Test the accessory voltage circuit of the windshield wiper/washer switch for an open or short to ground. Did you find and correct the condition?	Go to Step 18	Go to Step 8
8	Test the signal 1 circuit of the windshield wiper/washer switch for a short to ground. Did you find and correct the condition?	Go to Step 18	Go to Step 9
9	Test the signal 2 circuit of the windshield wiper/washer switch for an open or a short to ground. Did you find and correct the condition?	Go to Step 18	Go to Step 10
10	Test the high speed circuit of the windshield wiper/washer switch for a short to ground. Did you find and correct the condition?	Go to Step 18	Go to Step 15
11	Inspect for poor connections at the windshield wiper motor. Did you find and correct the condition?	Go to Step 18	Go to Step 16
12	Inspect for poor connections at the windshield wiper/washer switch. Did you find and correct the condition?	Go to Step 18	Go to Step 17
13	Repair an open or a short to ground in the accessory voltage circuit of the windshield wiper motor. Did you complete the repair?	Go to Step 18	--

LTV0500000003109

Fig. 185 Wipers Inoperative, All Modes (Part 2 of 3). Montana, Silhouette & Venture

Step	Action	Yes	No
14	Repair an open or high resistance in the ground circuit of the windshield wiper motor. Did you complete the repair?	Go to Step 18	--
15	Repair a short to ground in the control circuit of the windshield washer pump. Did you complete the repair?	Go to Step 18	--
16	Replace the windshield wiper motor module. Did you complete the replacement?	Go to Step 18	--
17	Replace the windshield wiper/washer switch. Did you complete the replacement?	Go to Step 18	--
18	Operate the system in order to verify the repair. Did you correct the condition?	System OK	Go to Step 3

LTV0500000003110

Fig. 185 Wipers Inoperative, All Modes (Part 3 of 3). Montana, Silhouette & Venture

Test Description

The numbers below refer to the step numbers on the diagnostic table.

8. This step tests for continuity through the 24K ohms resistor in the windshield wiper/washer switch.

9. This step tests for continuity through the delay resistors in the windshield wiper/washer switch. The measured resistance will change in sequence from high to low as the delay speed is increased.

Step	Action	Value(s)	Yes	No
1	Did you review the Wiper/Washer System Description and Operation and perform the necessary inspections?	--	Go to Step 2	Go to Symptoms -
2	1. Turn the ignition ON. 2. Operate the windshield wiper/washer switch through all the switch positions. Does the windshield wiper/washer system operate normally?	--	Test for Intermittent and Poor Connections	Go to Step 3
3	Do the windshield wipers operate in the high speed mode?	--	Go to Step 5	Go to Step 4

LTV0500000003111

Fig. 186 Wipers Inoperative, One Or More Modes (Part 1 of 4). Montana, Silhouette & Venture

4	1. Disconnect the windshield wiper motor connector. 2. Connect a test lamp from the windshield wiper motor high speed circuit terminal to ground. 3. Turn the ignition ON. 4. Operate the windshield wiper/washer switch to the high speed position. Does the test lamp illuminate?	- Go to Step 16	Go to Step 10
5	1. Disconnect the windshield wiper motor connector. 2. Connect a test lamp from the windshield wiper motor accessory voltage supply circuit terminal to ground. 3. Turn the ignition ON. Does the test lamp illuminate?	- Go to Step 6	Go to Step 11
6	1. Connect a test lamp from the windshield wiper switch signal 2 circuit terminal to ground. 2. Press the windshield washer switch. Does the test lamp illuminate?	- Go to Step 7	Go to Step 12

7	1. Connect a test lamp from the windshield wiper switch signal 1 circuit terminal to ground.
	2. Operate the windshield wiper/washer switch to the following positions:
	
	  - MIST
	  - LO
	  - HI
	
	Does the test lamp illuminate in the listed switch positions?
		-
		
		Go to Step 8
			Go to Step 13

LTV0500000003112

Fig. 186   Wipers Inoperative, One Or More Modes (Part 2 of 4). Montana, Silhouette & Venture

13	Test the windshield wiper switch signal 1 circuit for an open or short to ground. Did you find and correct the condition?	- Go to Step 18	Go to Step 14
14	Inspect for poor connections at the windshield wiper/washer switch. Did you find and correct the condition?	- Go to Step 18	Go to Step 15
15	Replace the windshield wiper/washer switch. Is the repair complete?	- Go to Step 18	--
16	Inspect for poor connections at the windshield wiper motor. Did you find and correct the condition?	- Go to Step 18	Go to Step 17
17	Replace the windshield wiper motor module. Is the repair complete?	- Go to Step 18	--
18	Operate the system in order to verify the repair. Did you correct the condition?	- System OK	Go to Step 3

LTV0500000003114

Fig. 186   Wipers Inoperative, One Or More Modes (Part 4 of 4). Montana, Silhouette & Venture

8	1. Disconnect the windshield wiper/washer switch connector.
	2. Measure the resistance through the windshield wiper/washer switch from the signal 2 circuit terminal to the accessory voltage supply circuit terminal.
	3. Operate the windshield wiper/washer switch to the following positions:
	
	  - MIST
	  - INT
	  - LO
	  - HI
	
	Is the resistance at or near the specified value in all the listed switch positions?
		24K ohms
		
		Go to Step 9
			Go to Step 14

9	1. Measure the resistance through the windshield wiper/washer switch from the signal 1 circuit terminal to the accessory voltage supply circuit terminal. 2. Operate the windshield wiper/washer switch through all of the delay positions. Does the resistance remain within the specified values from high to low as the delay speed is increased?	38K - 690K ohms Go to Step 16	Go to Step 14
10	Test the windshield wiper motor high speed circuit for an open or high resistance. Did you find and correct the condition?	-- Go to Step 18	Go to Step 14
11	Repair the windshield wiper motor accessory voltage supply circuit for an open or high resistance. Is the repair complete?	Go to Step 18	--
12	Test the windshield wiper switch signal 2 circuit for an open or short to ground. Did you find and correct the condition?	-- Go to Step 18	Go to Step 14

LTV0500000003113

Fig. 186   Wipers Inoperative, One Or More Modes (Part 3 of 4). Montana, Silhouette & Venture

Step	Action	Yes	No
1	Did you review the Rear Wiper/Washer System Description and Operation and perform the necessary inspections?	Go to Step 2	Go to Symptoms -
2	1. Turn the ignition ON. 2. Press the rear washer switch. Does the rear washer operate normally?		Go to Step 3
3	Does the rear wiper motor operate when the washer switch is pressed?	Go to Step 6	Go to Step 4
4	1. Disconnect the rear wiper motor connector. 2. Connect a test lamp from the rear washer control circuit terminal in the wiper motor connector to a good ground. 3. Turn the ignition ON. 4. Press the rear washer switch. Does the test lamp illuminate when the rear washer switch is pressed?	Go to Step 10	Go to Step 5
5	Test the rear washer control circuit for an open or high resistance. Did you find and correct the condition?	Go to Step 16	Go to Step 12

LTV0500000003115

Fig. 187   Washer Inoperative, Rear (Part 1 of 4). Montana, Silhouette & Venture

Step	Action	Yes	No
6	1. Disconnect the rear washer pump connector. 2. Connect a test lamp from the rear washer control circuit terminal in the washer pump harness connector to a good ground. 3. Turn the ignition ON. 4. Press the rear washer switch. Does the test lamp illuminate when the rear washer switch is pressed?	Go to Step 7	Go to Step 8
7	1. Connect a test lamp from the rear washer control circuit terminal to the ground circuit terminal in the washer pump harness connector. 2. Press the rear washer switch. Does the test lamp illuminate when the rear washer switch is pressed?	Go to Step 14	Go to Step 9
8	Repair the rear washer control circuit for an open or high resistance. Is the repair complete?	Go to Step 16	--
9	Repair the rear washer pump ground circuit for an open or high resistance. Is the repair complete?	Go to Step 16	--
10	Inspect for poor connections at the rear wiper motor. Did you find and correct the conditon?	Go to Step 16	Go to Step 11
6	1. Disconnect the rear washer pump connector. 2. Connect a test lamp from the rear washer control circuit terminal in the washer pump harness connector to a good ground. 3. Turn the ignition ON. 4. Press the rear washer switch. Does the test lamp illuminate when the rear washer switch is pressed?	Go to Step 7	Go to Step 8
7	1. Connect a test lamp from the rear washer control circuit terminal to the ground circuit terminal in the washer pump harness connector.	Go to Step 14	Go to Step 9

LTV0500000003116

Fig. 187   Washer Inoperative, Rear (Part 2 of 4). Montana, Silhouette & Venture

Step	Action		
16	Operate the system in order to verify the repair. Did you correct the condition?	System OK	Go to Step 3

LTV0500000003118

Fig. 187   Washer Inoperative, Rear (Part 4 of 4). Montana, Silhouette & Venture

Step	Action	Yes	No
	2. Press the rear washer switch. Does the test lamp illuminate when the rear washer switch is pressed?		
8	Repair the rear washer control circuit for an open or high resistance. Is the repair complete?	Go to Step 16	--
9	Repair the rear washer pump ground circuit for an open or high resistance. Is the repair complete?	Go to Step 16	--
10	Inspect for poor connections at the rear wiper motor. Did you find and correct the conditon?	Go to Step 16	Go to Step 11
11	Replace the rear wiper motor. Is the repair complete?	Go to Step 16	--
12	Inspect for poor connections at the rear wiper/washer switch. Did you find and correct the conditon?	Go to Step 16	Go to Step 13
13	Replace the rear wiper/washer switch. Is the repair complete?	Go to Step 16	--
14	Inspect for poor connections at the rear washer pump. Did you find and correct the conditon?	Go to Step 16	Go to Step 15
15	Replace the rear washer pump Is the repair complete?	Go to Step 16	--

LTV0500000003117

Fig. 187   Washer Inoperative, Rear (Part 3 of 4). Montana, Silhouette & Venture

Step	Action	Yes	No
1	Did you review the Rear Wiper/Washer System Description and Operation and perform the necessary inspections?	Go to Step 2	Go to Symptoms -
2	1. Turn the ignition ON. 2. Turn the rear wiper/washer switch to the OFF position. Is the rear wiper always on?	Go to Step 3	Test for Intermittent and Poor Connections
3	1. Disconnect the rear wiper motor connector. 2. Turn the rear wiper/washer switch to the OFF position. 3. Connect a test lamp from the rear wiper switch signal circuit terminal in the rear wiper motor harness connector to ground. 4. Turn the ignition ON. Does the test lamp illuminate?	Go to Step 5	Go to Step 4
4	1. Connect a test lamp from the rear washer pump control circuit terminal in the rear wiper motor harness connector to ground. 2. Turn the ignition ON. Does the test lamp illuminate?	Go to Step 6	Go to Step 8
5	Test the rear wiper switch signal circuit for a short to voltage. Did you find and correct the condition?	Go to Step 9	Go to Step 7
6	Test the rear washer pump control circuit for a short to voltage. Did you find and correct the condition?	Go to Step 9	Go to Step 7

LTV0500000003119

Fig. 188   Wiper Always On, Rear (Part 1 of 2). Montana, Silhouette & Venture

Step	Action	Yes	No
7	Replace the rear wiper/washer switch. / Is the repair complete?	Go to Step 9	--
8	Replace the rear wiper motor. / Is the repair complete?	Go to Step 9	--
9	Operate the system in order to verify the repair. / Did you correct the condition?	System OK	Go to Step 3

LTV0500000003120

Fig. 188   Wiper Always On, Rear (Part 2 of 2). Montana, Silhouette & Venture

Step	Action	Yes	No
7	1. Turn OFF the ignition. 2. Disconnect the harness connector of the rear wiper motor. 3. Turn the ignition ON, with the engine OFF. 4. Connect a test lamp from the signal circuit of the rear wiper switch to a good ground. / Does the test lamp illuminate?	Go to Step 8	Go to Step 18
8	Connect a test lamp from the accessory voltage circuit of the rear wiper motor to a good ground. / Does the test lamp illuminate?	Go to Step 9	Go to Step 19
9	Connect a test lamp from the accessory voltage circuit to the ground circuit of the rear wiper motor. / Does the test lamp illuminate?	Go to Step 16	Go to Step 20
10	1. Turn OFF the ignition. 2. Disconnect the harness connector of the rear wiper motor. 3. Turn the ignition ON, with the engine OFF. 4. Connect a test lamp from the signal circuit of the rear wiper switch to a good ground. 5. Place the rear wiper switch in the Delay position. / Does the test lamp illuminate?	Go to Step 16	Go to Step 18
11	1. Turn OFF the ignition. 2. Disconnect the harness connector of the rear wiper motor. 3. Turn the ignition ON, with the engine OFF. 4. Connect a test lamp from the control circuit of the rear washer pump to a good ground. 5. Depress the rear washer switch. / Does the test lamp illuminate?	Go to Step 16	Go to Step 21
12	Test the accessory voltage circuit of the rear wiper switch for an open or a short to ground. / Did you find and correct the condition?	Go to Step 24	Go to Step 13
13	Test the accessory voltage circuit of the rear wiper motor for a short to ground. / Did you find and correct the condition?	Go to Step 24	Go to Step 14

LTV0500000003122

Fig. 189   Wiper Inoperative, Rear (Part 2 of 4). Montana, Silhouette & Venture

Step	Action	Yes	No
	DEFINITION: The rear wiper motor is inoperative in one or more modes, the rear washer pump may or may not operate.		
1	Did you review the Rear Wiper/Washer System Description and Operation and perform the necessary inspections?	Go to Step 2	Go to Symptoms
2	1. Turn the ignition ON, with the engine OFF. 2. Operate the rear wiper/washer system in all the switch positions. / Does the rear wiper/washer system operate normally?	Test for Intermittent and Poor Connections	Go to Step 3
3	Does the rear wiper motor operate when the rear washer switch is pressed?	Go to Step 10	Go to Step 4
4	Does the rear washer pump operate when the rear washer switch is pressed?	Go to Step 11	Go to Step 5
5	1. Disconnect the harness connector of the rear wiper switch. 2. Turn the ignition ON, with the engine OFF. 3. Connect a test lamp from the accessory voltage circuit of the rear wiper switch to a good ground. / Does the test lamp illuminate?	Go to Step 6	Go to Step 12
6	Connect a 20-ampere fused jumper wire from the accessory voltage circuit to the signal circuit of the rear wiper switch. / Does the rear wiper motor operate?	Go to Step 15	Go to Step 7

LTV0500000003121

Fig. 189   Wiper Inoperative, Rear (Part 1 of 4). Montana, Silhouette & Venture

Step	Action	Yes	No
14	Test the signal circuit of the rear wiper switch for a short to ground. / Did you find and correct the condition?	Go to Step 24	Go to Step 17
15	Inspect for poor connections at the harness connector of the rear wiper/washer switch. / Did you find and correct the condition?	Go to Step 24	Go to Step 22
16	Inspect for poor connections at the harness connector of the rear wiper motor. / Did you find and correct the condition?	Go to Step 24	Go to Step 23
17	Repair a short to ground in the control circuit of the rear washer pump. / Did you complete the repair?	Go to Step 24	--
18	Repair an open or high resistance in the signal circuit of the rear wiper switch. / Did you complete the repair?	Go to Step 24	--
19	Repair an open or high resistance in the accessory voltage circuit of the rear wiper motor. / Did you complete the repair?	Go to Step 24	--
20	Repair an open or high resistance in the ground circuit of the rear wiper motor. / Did you complete the repair?	Go to Step 24	--
21	Repair an open or high resistance in the control circuit of the rear washer pump. / Did you complete the repair?	Go to Step 24	--

LTV0500000003123

Fig. 189   Wiper Inoperative, Rear (Part 3 of 4). Montana, Silhouette & Venture

Step	Action		Yes	No
22	Replace the rear wiper/washer switch. Did you complete the replacement?		Go to Step 24	--
23	Replace the rear wiper motor. Did you complete the replacement?		Go to Step 24	--
24	Operate the system in order to verify the repair. Did you correct the condition?		System OK	Go to Step 3

LTV0500000003124

Fig. 189 Wiper Inoperative, Rear (Part 4 of 4). Montana, Silhouette & Venture

Step	Action	Yes	No
1	Did you perform the Diagnostic System Check - Vehicle?	Go to Step 2	Go to Diagnostic System Check -
2	1. Turn the ignition to the ON position. 2. Press the windshield washer switch. Does the windshield washer pump operate?	Test for Intermittent and Poor Connections	Go to Step 3
3	1. Turn the ignition to the OFF position. 2. Disconnect the windshield washer fluid pump. 3. Using a test lamp connected to ground, probe the windshield washer pump control circuit at the harness connector of the windshield washer fluid pump. Does the test lamp illuminate?	Go to Step 6	Go to Step 4
4	1. Leave the test lamp connected. 2. Turn the ignition to the ON position. 3. Press the washer switch. Does the test lamp illuminate?	Go to Step 5	Go to Step 7

LTV0500000003601

Fig. 190 Code B3873: Front Washer Relay Circuit (Part 2 of 3). Relay, SV6, Terraza & Uplander

Circuit Description

The body control module (BCM) controls and monitors the windshield washer fluid pump control circuit. The BCM supplies battery positive voltage to the windshield washer fluid pump when commanded ON by the windshield wiper/washer switch. Ground is applied at all times from G200 to the windshield washer fluid pump.

DTC Descriptor

This diagnostic procedure supports the following DTC:

DTC B3873 Front Washer Relay Circuit

Conditions for Running the DTC

- The ignition is ON.
- The ignition voltage is between 9-16 volts.

Conditions for Setting the DTC

The BCM detects a short to ground, an open, or a short to battery positive voltage in the windshield washer pump control circuit.

Action Taken When the DTC Sets

The BCM will not activate the output.

Conditions for Clearing the DTC

- The DTC will clear on current status after the condition for setting the fault is corrected.
- A history DTC will clear after 100 consecutive ignition cycles without a fault present.
- History and current DTCs can be cleared using a scan tool.

LTV0500000003600

Fig. 190 Code B3873: Front Washer Relay Circuit (Part 1 of 3). Relay, SV6, Terraza & Uplander

Step	Action	Yes	No
5	1. Turn the ignition to the OFF position. 2. Using a test lamp, probe between the windshield washer pump control circuit and the windshield washer fluid pump ground circuit at the harness connector of the windshield washer fluid pump. 3. Turn the ignition to the ON position. 4. Press the washer switch. Does the test lamp illuminate?	Go to Step 9	Go to Step 8
6	Test for a short to battery positive voltage in the windshield washer pump control circuit. Did you find and correct the condition?	Go to Step 11	Go to Step 10
7	Test for a short to ground or an open in the windshield washer pump control circuit. Did you find and correct the condition?	Go to Step 11	Go to Step 10
8	Repair a poor connection or an open in the windshield washer fluid pump ground circuit. Did you complete the repair?	Go to Step 11	--
9	Replace the windshield washer fluid pump. Did you complete the replacement?	Go to Step 11	--
10	Replace the body control module (BCM). Did you complete the replacement?	Go to Step 11	--
11	1. Use the scan tool in order to clear the DTCs. 2. Operate the vehicle within the Conditions for Running the DTC as specified in the supporting text. Does the DTC reset?	Go to Step 2	System OK

LTV0500000003602

Fig. 190 Code B3873: Front Washer Relay Circuit (Part 3 of 3). Relay, SV6, Terraza & Uplander

Circuit Description

The body control module (BCM) controls and monitors the state of the wiper control circuit. When the windshield wiper switch is placed in to a low speed setting, a signal is applied to the BCM. The BCM then applies battery positive voltage to the coil side of the WPR1 relay through the WPR1 relay control circuit. This energizes the WPR1 relay, allowing battery positive voltage from the FRT WPR fuse through the switched side of the WPR1 relay to the windshield wiper motor. Ground is applied at all times to the coil side of the WPR1 relay and the windshield wiper motor form G200.

DTC Descriptor

This diagnostic procedure supports the following DTC:

DTC B3874 Wiper Low Speed Relay Circuit

Conditions for Running the DTC

- The ignition is in the ON position.
- The ignition voltage is between 9-16 volts.

Conditions for Setting the DTC

The following conditions will cause the DTC to set:

- The BCM detects an short to battery positive voltage in the WPR1 relay control circuit for over 1 second.
- The BCM detects a short to ground or an open in the WPR1 relay control circuit.

Action Taken When the DTC Sets

The BCM will not activate the output.

LTV0500000003603

Fig. 191   Code B3874: Wiper Low Speed Relay Circuit (Part 1 of 4). Relay, SV6, Terraza & Uplander

3	1. Turn the ignition to the OFF position. 2. Turn the wiper switch OFF. 3. Remove the WPR1 relay from the underhood fuse block. 4. Using a test lamp connected to ground, probe the WPR1 relay control circuit at the underhood fuse block. Does the test lamp illuminate?	Go to Step 8	Go to Step 4
4	1. Leave the test lamp connected. 2. Turn the ignition to the ON position. 3. Turn the wiper switch to a low position. Does the test lamp illuminate?	Go to Step 5	Go to Step 6
5	1. Turn the wiper switch to the OFF position. 2. Turn the ignition to the OFF position. 3. Using a test lamp, probe the WPR1 relay control circuit and the ground circuit of the WPR1 relay at the underhood fuse block. 4. Turn the ignition to the ON position. 5. Turn the wiper switch to a low position. Does the test lamp illuminate?	Go to Step 9	Go to Step 7
6	Test for a poor connection, an open, or short to ground in the WPR1 relay control circuit. Did you find and correct the condition?	Go to Step 12	Go to Step 10
7	Test for a poor connection or an open in the ground circuit of the WPR1 relay. Did you find and correct the condition?	Go to Step 12	Go to Step 11
8	Repair a short to battery positive voltage in the WPR1 relay control circuit. Did you complete the repair?	Go to Step 12	--
9	1. Replace the WPR1 relay. 2. Operate the vehicle within the Conditions for Running the DTC. Does the DTC reset?	Go to Step 11	Go to Step 12

LTV0500000003605

Fig. 191   Code B3874: Wiper Low Speed Relay Circuit (Part 3 of 4). Relay, SV6, Terraza & Uplander

Conditions for Clearing the DTC

- The DTC will clear on current status after the condition for setting the fault is corrected.
- A history DTC will clear after 100 consecutive ignition cycles without a fault present.
- History and current DTCs can be cleared using a scan tool.

Diagnostic Aids

Perform a visual inspection for loose or poor connections at all related components.

Step	Action	Yes	No
1	Did you perform the Diagnostic System Check - Vehicle?	Go to Step 2	Go to Diagnostic System Check
2	1. Turn the ignition to the ON position. 2. On the wiper switch, select a low speed. Do the windshield wipers operate?	Test for Intermittent Conditions and Poor Connections	Go to Step 3

LTV0500000003604

Fig. 191   Code B3874: Wiper Low Speed Relay Circuit (Part 2 of 4). Relay, SV6, Terraza & Uplander

10	Replace the body control module (BCM). Did you complete the replacement?	Go to Step 12	--
11	Replace the underhood electrical center. Did you complete the replacement?	Go to Step 12	--
12	1. Use the scan tool in order to clear the DTCs. 2. Operate the vehicle within the Conditions For Running the DTC as specified in the supporting text. Does the DTC reset?	Go to Step 2	System OK

LTV0500000003606

Fig. 191   Code B3874: Wiper Low Speed Relay Circuit (Part 4 of 4). Relay, SV6, Terraza & Uplander

Circuit Description

The body control module (BCM) controls and monitors the state of the WPR2 relay control circuit. When the windshield wiper switch is placed in to a high speed setting, a signal is applied to the BCM through the windshield wiper switch high signal circuit. The BCM then applies battery positive voltage to the WPR2 relay through the WPR2 relay control circuit. This energizes the WPR2 relay, allowing battery positive voltage to be applies from the FRT WPR fuse, through the switched contacts of the WPR1 relay and through the switched contracts of the WPR2 relay to the windshield wiper motor. Ground is applied at all times to the coil side of the WPR2 relay and to the windshield wiper motor from G200.

DTC Descriptor

This diagnostic procedure supports the following DTC:

DTC B3875 WPR2 Relay Circuit

Conditions for Running the DTC

- The ignition is in the ON position.
- The ignition voltage is between 9-16 volts.

Conditions for Setting the DTC

The following conditions will cause the DTC to set:

- The BCM detects an short to battery positive voltage in the WPR2 relay control circuit for over 1 second.
- The BCM detects an open or a short to ground in the WPR2 relay control circuit for over 1 second.

Action Taken When the DTC Sets

The BCM will not activate the WPR2 relay.

LTV0500000003607

Fig. 192   Code B3875: WPR2 Relay Circuit (Part 1 of 4). Relay, SV6, Terraza & Uplander

3	1. Turn the wiper switch to the OFF position. 2. Turn the ignition to the OFF position. 3. Remove the WPR2 relay from the underhood fuse block. 4. Using a test lamp connected to ground, probe the WPR2 relay control circuit. Does the test lamp illuminate?	Go to Step 6	Go to Step 4
4	1. Leave the test lamp connected. 2. Turn the ignition to the ON position. 3. Turn the wiper switch to HIGH. Does the test lamp illuminate?	Go to Step 5	Go to Step 7
5	Using a test lamp, probe between the WPR2 relay control circuit and the WPR2 relay ground circuit. Does the test lamp illuminate?	Go to Step 9	Go to Step 8
6	Test for a short to battery positive voltage in the WPR2 relay control circuit. Did you find and correct the condition?	Go to Step 12	Go to Step 10
7	Test for a poor connection, an open, or a short to ground in the WPR2 relay control circuit. Did you find and correct the condition?	Go to Step 12	Go to Step 10
8	Test for a poor connection or an open in the ground circuit of the WPR2 relay. Did you find and correct the condition?	Go to Step 12	Go to Step 11
9	Replace the WPR2 relay. Did you complete the replacement?	Go to Step 11	Go to Step 12
10	Replace the body control module (BCM). Did you complete the replacement?	Go to Step 12	--

LTV0500000003609

Fig. 192   Code B3875: WPR2 Relay Circuit (Part 3 of 4). Relay, SV6, Terraza & Uplander

Conditions for Clearing the DTC

- A current DTC B3875 will clear if the short to battery, a short to ground or an open in the WPR2 relay control circuit is no longer detected by the BCM.
- A history DTC B3875 will clear after 100 consecutive ignition cycles if the condition for the malfunction is no longer present.
- The BCM receives a clear code command from the scan tool.

Diagnostic Aids

- If the DTC B3875 is a history DTC, the fault may be intermittent.
- The following conditions may cause an intermittent malfunction or occur:
  - An intermittent short to battery, a short to ground or an open in the WPR2 relay control circuit.
  - The WPR2 relay coil is intermittently shorted to battery.
  - The BCM is intermittently shorted to battery, shorted to ground or an open.

Step	Action	Yes	No
1	Did you perform the Diagnostic System Check - Vehicle?	Go to Step 2	Go to Diagnostic System Check
2	1. Turn the ignition to the ON position. 2. Turn the wiper switch to HIGH. Do the high speed wipers operate?		Go to Step 3

LTV0500000003608

Fig. 192   Code B3875: WPR2 Relay Circuit (Part 2 of 4). Relay, SV6, Terraza & Uplander

11	Replace the underhood electrical center. Did you complete the replacement?	Go to Step 12	--
12	1. Use the scan tool in order to clear the DTCs. 2. Operate the vehicle within the Conditions For Running the DTC as specified in the supporting text. Does the DTC reset?	Go to Step 2	System OK

LTV0500000003610

Fig. 192   Code B3875: WPR2 Relay Circuit (Part 4 of 4). Relay, SV6, Terraza & Uplander

Circuit Description

The body control module (BCM) monitors the windshield wiper switch low signal circuit. When the wiper switch is placed in a low position, a signal is applied to the BCM through the windshield wiper switch low signal circuit. The BCM then applies a battery positive voltage to the WPR1 relay control circuit which energizes the WPR1 relay, allowing the battery positive voltage from FTR WPR fuse through the switched side of the WPR1 relay to the windshield wiper motor.

DTC Descriptor

This diagnostic procedure supports the following DTC:

DTC B3922 Front Wiper Select Circuit

Conditions for Running the DTC

- The ignition switch is in the ON position.
- The ignition voltage is between 9-16 volts.

Conditions for Setting the DTC

The BCM detects an short to battery positive voltage on the windshield wiper switch low signal circuit.

Action Taken When the DTC Sets

The windshield wipers will only function in the high mode.

LTV0500000003611

Fig. 193 Code B3922: Front Wiper Select Circuit (Part 1 of 4). Relay, SV6, Terraza & Uplander

Step	Action	Yes	No
3	1. Turn the ignition to the OFF position. 2. Disconnect the body control module (BCM) connector C3. 3. At the BCM connector C3, install a jumper between ground and ground supply circuit to the windshield wiper/washer switch. 4. Turn the wiper washer switch to the off position. 5. Using a test lamp connected to ground, probe the wiper switch low signal circuit at the BCM connector C3. Does the test lamp illuminate?	Go to Step 7	Go to Step 4
4	1. Remove the ground jumper. 2. Using a test lamp connected to battery positive voltage, probe the wiper switch low signal circuit at the BCM connector C3. Does the test lamp illuminate?	Go to Step 8	Go to Step 5
5	1. Install a jumper between ground and the ground supply circuit to the wiper/washer switch. 2. Using a test lamp connected to battery positive voltage, probe the wiper switch low signal circuit at the BCM connector C3. 3. Turn the wiper switch to all of the low settings. Does the test lamp illuminate at each switch position?	Go to Step 9	Go to Step 6
6	Test for a poor connection or an open in the wiper switch low signal circuit. Did you find and correct the condition?	Go to Step 11	Go to Step 10
7	Repair a short to battery positive voltage in the wiper switch low signal circuit. Did you complete the repair?	Go to Step 11	--
8	Repair a short to ground in the wiper switch low signal circuit. Did you complete the repair?	Go to Step 11	--
9	Replace the BCM. Did you complete the replacement?	Go to Step 11	--

LTV0500000003613

Fig. 193 Code B3922: Front Wiper Select Circuit (Part 3 of 4). Relay, SV6, Terraza & Uplander

Conditions for Clearing the DTC

- The DTC will clear on current status after the condition for setting the fault is corrected.
- A history DTC will clear after 100 consecutive ignition cycles without a fault present.
- History and current DTCs can be cleared using a scan tool.

Diagnostic Aids

Perform a visual inspection for loose or poor connections at all related components.

Step	Action	Yes	No
1	Did you perform the Diagnostic System Check - Vehicle?	Go to Step 2	Go to Diagnostic System Check
2	1. Install a scan tool. 2. Turn the ignition to the ON position. 3. Using a scan tool observe the Wiper Washer Switch parameter in the input list. 4. Rotate the wiper washer switch through all the positions. Does the scan tool display the correct positions?	Test for Intermittent Conditions and Poor Connections	Go to Step 3

LTV0500000003612

Fig. 193 Code B3922: Front Wiper Select Circuit (Part 2 of 4). Relay, SV6, Terraza & Uplander

Step	Action	Yes	No
10	Replace the windshield wiper/washer switch. Refer to 61818. Did you complete the replacement?	Go to Step 11	--
11	1. Use the scan tool in order to clear the DTCs. 2. Operate the vehicle within the Conditions for Running the DTC as specified in the supporting text. Does the DTC reset?	Go to Step 2	System OK

LTV0500000003614

Fig. 193 Code B3922: Front Wiper Select Circuit (Part 4 of 4). Relay, SV6, Terraza & Uplander

Step	Action	Yes	No
1	Did you perform the Diagnostic System Check - Vehicle?	Go to Step 2	Go to Diagnostic System Check
2	Turn the ignition to the ON position. Is the windshield washer pump ON?	Go to Step 3	Test for Intermittent Conditions and Poor Connections
3	Disconnect the windshield wiper/washer switch. Does the washer turn OFF?	Go to Step 7	Go to Step 4
4	Disconnect the body control module (BCM) connector C3. Does the washer turn OFF?	Go to Step 8	Go to Step 5
5	Disconnect the BCM connector C1. Does the washer turn OFF?	Go to Step 9	Go to Step 6
6	Test for a short to battery positive voltage in the windshield washer pump control circuit. Did you find and correct the condition?	Go to Step 11	Go to Step 10
7	Replace the windshield wiper/washer switch. Did you complete the replacement?	Go to Step 11	--
8	Repair a short to ground in the windshield washer switch signal circuit. Did you complete the repair?	Go to Step 11	--

LTV0500000003616

Fig. 194 Washers Always On (Part 1 of 2). Relay, SV6, Terraza & Uplander

Step	Action	Yes	No
9	Replace the BCM. Did you complete the replacement?	Go to Step 11	--
10	Replace the windshield washer fluid pump. Did you complete the replacement?	Go to Step 11	--
11	Operate the system in order to verify the repair. Did you correct the condition?	System OK	Go to Step 3

LTV0500000003617

Fig. 194 Washers Always On (Part 2 of 2). Relay, SV6, Terraza & Uplander

Step	Action	Yes	No
1	Did you perform the Diagnostic System Check - Vehicle?	Go to Step 2	Go to Diagnostic System Check
2	1. Turn the ignition to the ON position. 2. Press the windshield washer switch. Does the windshield washer pump operate?	Test for Intermittent Conditions and Poor Connections	Go to Step 3
3	1. Disconnect the body control module (BCM) connector C1. 2. Install a fused jumper between battery positive voltage and the windshield washer pump control circuit. Does the windshield washer fluid pump operate?	Go to Step 6	Go to Step 4
4	1. Disconnect the windshield washer pump. 2. Connect the BCM connector C1. 3. Using a test lamp probe between windshield washer pump control circuit and ground. 4. Turn the ignition to the ON position. 5. Press the washer switch. Does the test lamp illuminate?	Go to Step 5	Go to Step 8

LTV0500000003618

Fig. 195 Washers Inoperative (Part 1 of 2). Relay, SV6, Terraza & Uplander

Step	Action	Yes	No
5	Test for a poor connection or an open in the ground circuit of the windshield washer fluid pump. Did you find and correct the condition?	Go to Step 12	Go to Step 9
6	1. Disconnect the windshield wiper/washer switch. 2. Install a jumper between windshield washer switch signal circuit and ground. 3. Turn the ignition to the ON position. Does the windshield washer fluid pump operate?	Go to Step 10	Go to Step 7
7	Test for a poor connection, an open, or a short to battery positive voltage in the windshield washer switch signal circuit. Did you find and correct the condition?	Go to Step 12	Go to Step 11
8	Repair a poor connection, an open, or a short to ground in the windshield washer pump control circuit. Did you complete the repair?	Go to Step 12	--
9	Replace the windshield washer fluid pump. Did you complete the replacement?	Go to Step 12	--
10	Replace the windshield washer switch. Did you complete the replacement?	Go to Step 12	--
11	Replace the BCM. Did you complete the replacement?	Go to Step 12	--
12	Operate the system to verify the repair. Did you correct the condition?	System OK	Go to Step 3

LTV0500000003619

Fig. 195 Washers Inoperative (Part 2 of 2). Relay, SV6, Terraza & Uplander

Step	Action	Yes	No
1	Did you perform the Diagnostic System Check - Vehicle?	Go to Step 2	Go to Diagnostic System Check
2	Turn the ignition to the ON position. Are the windshield wipers ON?	Go to Step 3	Test for Intermittent Conditions and Poor Connections
3	Remove the WPR2 relay. Are the windshield wipers ON?	Go to Step 4	Go to Step 7
4	Are the windshield wipers operating at a high speed?	Go to Step 5	Go to Step 6
5	Test for a short to battery positive voltage in the windshield wiper motor high speed circuit. Did you find and correct the condition?	Go to Step 24	Go to Step 20
6	Test for a short to battery positive voltage in the windshield wiper motor low speed circuit. Did you find and correct the condition?	Go to Step 24	Go to Step 20
7	Using a test lamp connected to ground, probe the WPR2 relay control circuit at the underhood fuse block. Does the test lamp illuminate?	Go to Step 13	Go to Step 8
8	1. Install the WPR2 relay. 2. Remove the WPR1 relay. Are the windshield wipers ON?	Go to Step 20	Go to Step 9
9	Using a test lamp connected to ground, probe the WPR1 relay control circuit. Does the test lamp illuminate?	Go to Step 10	Go to Step 21

LTV0500000003620

Fig. 196   Wipers Always On (Part 1 of 3). Relay, SV6, Terraza & Uplander

Step	Action	Yes	No
10	1. Install the WPR1 relay. 2. Disconnect the windshield wiper/washer switch. Are the windshield wipers ON?	Go to Step 11	Go to Step 22
11	1. Disconnect the body control module (BCM) connector C3. 2. Using a test lamp connected to battery positive voltage, probe the windshield wiper switch low signal circuit at the windshield wiper/washer switch. Does the test lamp illuminate?	Go to Step 17	Go to Step 12
12	1. Disconnect the BCM connector C1. 2. Remove the WPR1 relay. 3. Using a test lamp connected to ground, probe the WFR1 relay control circuit at the underhood electrical center. Does the test lamp illuminate?	Go to Step 18	Go to Step 23
13	1. Disconnect the windshield wiper/washer switch. 2. Using a test lamp connected to ground, probe the WPR1 relay control circuit at the underhood electrical center. Does the test lamp illuminate?	Go to Step 14	Go to Step 22
14	1. Disconnect the BCM connector C3. 2. Using a test lamp connected to battery positive voltage, probe the windshield wiper switch high signal circuit. Does the test lamp illuminate?	Go to Step 19	Go to Step 15
15	1. Disconnect the BCM connector C1. 2. Using a test lamp connected to ground, probe the WPR2 relay control circuit at the BCM. Does the test lamp illuminate?	Go to Step 16	Go to Step 23
16	Test for a short to ground in the WPR2 relay control circuit. Did you find and correct the condition?	Go to Step 24	Go to Step 20
17	Repair a short to ground in the windshield wiper switch low signal circuit. Did you complete the repair?	Go to Step 24	--

LTV0500000003621

Fig. 196   Wipers Always On (Part 2 of 3). Relay, SV6, Terraza & Uplander

Step	Action	Yes	No
18	Repair a short to battery positive voltage in the WPR1 relay control circuit. Did you complete the repair?	Go to Step 24	--
19	Repair a short to ground in the windshield wiper switch high signal circuit. Did you complete the repair?	Go to Step 24	--
20	Replace the underhood electrical fuse block. Did you complete the replacement?	Go to Step 24	--
21	Replace the WPR1 relay. Did you complete the replacement?	Go to Step 24	--
22	Replace the windshield wiper/washer switch. Did you complete the repair?	Go to Step 24	--
23	Replace the BCM. Did you complete the replacement?	Go to Step 24	--
24	Operate the system in order to verify the repair. Did you correct the condition?	System OK	Go to Step 3

LTV0500000003622

Fig. 196   Wipers Always On (Part 3 of 3). Relay, SV6, Terraza & Uplander

Step	Action	Yes	No
1	Did you perform the Diagnostic System Check - Vehicle?	Go to Step 2	Go to Diagnostic System Check
2	1. Turn the ignition to the ON position. 2. Attempt to operate the wipers in each mode. Are the wipers inoperative in all modes?	Go to Step 3	Test for Intermittent Conditions and Poor Connections
3	1. Disconnect the windshield wiper motor. 2. Using a test lamp connected to ground, probe the windshield wiper motor low speed circuit. 3. Turn the ignition to the ON position. 4. Turn the windshield wipers to a low speed. Does the test lamp illuminate?	Go to Step 4	Go to Step 5
4	Test for a poor connection or an open in the ground circuit of the windshield wiper motor. Did you find and correct the condition?	Go to Step 16	Go to Step 11
5	1. Connect the windshield wiper motor. 2. Remove the WPR2 relay from the underhood fuse block. 3. Using a test lamp connected to battery positive voltage, probe the WPR2 relay switched input circuit. 4. Turn the wiper switch OFF. 5. Turn the ignition to the OFF position. Does the test lamp illuminate?	Go to Step 9	Go to Step 6

LTV0500000003623

Fig. 197   Wipers Inoperative, All Modes (Part 1 of 3). Relay, SV6, Terraza & Uplander

Step	Action	Yes	No
6	1. Remove the WPR1 relay. 2. Using a test lamp connected to battery positive voltage, probe the ground circuit of the WPR1 relay. Does the test lamp illuminate?	Go to Step 7	Go to Step 12
7	Using a test lamp connected to ground, probe the FRT WPR fuse circuit of the WPR1 relay. Does the test lamp illuminate?	Go to Step 8	Go to Step 13
8	Replace the WPR1 relay. Do the windshield wipers operate normally?	Go to Step 16	Go to Step 13
9	1. Disconnect the windshield wiper/washer switch. 2. Install a jumper between the ground circuit and the windshield wiper switch low signal circuit at the windshield wiper/washer switch connector. 3. Turn the ignition to the ON position. Do the windshield wipers operate normally?	Go to Step 14	Go to Step 10
10	Test for a poor connection or an open in the ground circuit of the windshield wiper/washer switch. Did you find and correct the condition?	Go to Step 16	Go to Step 15
11	Replace the windshield wiper motor. Did you complete the replacement?	Go to Step 16	--
12	Repair a poor connection or an open in the ground circuit of the WPR1 relay. Did you complete the repair?	Go to Step 16	--
13	Replace the underhood fuse block. Did you complete the replacement?	Go to Step 16	--

LTV0500000003624

Fig. 197 Wipers Inoperative, All Modes (Part 2 of 3). Relay, SV6, Terraza & Uplander

Step	Action	Yes	No
14	Replace the windshield wiper/washer switch. Did you complete the replacement?	Go to Step 16	--
15	Replace the body control module (BCM). Did you complete the replacement?	Go to Step 16	--
16	Operate the system in order to verify the repair. Did you correct the condition?	System OK	Go to Step 3

LTV0500000003625

Fig. 197 Wipers Inoperative, All Modes (Part 3 of 3). Relay, SV6, Terraza & Uplander

Step	Action	Yes	No
1	Did you perform the Diagnostic System Check - Vehicle?	Go to Step 2	Go to Diagnostic System Check
2	1. Turn the ignition to the ON position. 2. Attempt to operate the wipers in each mode. Are the wipers inoperative in all modes?	Go to Step 3	Test for Intermittent Conditions and Poor Connections
3	Are the wiper inoperative in high speed mode?	Go to Step 5	Go to Step 4
4	Are all of the low speed mode inoperative?	Go to Step 13	Go to Step 18
5	1. Disconnect the windshield wiper motor. 2. Using a test lamp connected to ground, probe the windshield wiper motor high speed circuit. 3. Turn the ignition to the ON position. 4. Turn the wiper to the high speed setting. Does the test lamp illuminate?	Go to Step 19	Go to Step 6
6	1. Connect the windshield wiper motor. 2. Remove the WPR2 relay. 3. Using a test lamp connected to battery positive voltage, probe the ground circuit of the WPR2 relay. Does the test lamp illuminate?	Go to Step 7	Go to Step 20

LTV0500000003626

Fig. 198 Wipers Inoperative, One Or More Modes (Part 1 of 4). Relay, SV6, Terraza & Uplander

Step	Action	Yes	No
7	1. Using a test lamp connected to ground, probe the WPR2 relay control circuit at the WPR1 relay. 2. Turn the ignition to the ON position. 3. Turn the wipers to the high speed setting. Does the test lamp illuminate?	Go to Step 8	Go to Step 10
8	1. Leave the switch in the high position. 2. Using a test lamp, probe between the WPR2 relay control circuit and the windshield wiper motor high speed circuit. Does the test lamp illuminate?	Go to Step 22	Go to Step 9
9	Test for a poor connection, an open or a short to ground in the windshield wiper motor high speed circuit. Did you find and correct the condition?	Go to Step 23	Go to Step 20
10	1. Disconnect the windshield wiper switch. 2. Install the WPR2 relay. 3. Install a jumper between ground and windshield wiper switch high signal circuit. 4. Turn the ignition to the ON position. Do the high speed wipers operate?	Go to Step 18	Go to Step 11
11	Test for a poor connection, short to battery or an open in the windshield wiper switch high signal circuit. Did you find and correct the condition?	Go to Step 23	Go to Step 12
12	Test for a poor connection, short to ground or an open in the WPR2 relay control circuit. Did you find and correct the condition?	Go to Step 23	Go to Step 21
13	1. Disconnect the windshield wiper motor. 2. Using a test lamp connected to ground, probe the windshield wiper motor low speed circuit. 3. Turn the ignition to the ON position. 4. Turn the wiper switch to a low position. Does the test lamp illuminate?	Go to Step 19	Go to Step 14

LTV0500000003627

Fig. 198 Wipers Inoperative, One Or More Modes (Part 2 of 4). Relay, SV6, Terraza & Uplander

Step	Action	Yes	No
14	1. Connect the windshield wiper motor. 2. Leave the windshield wiper switch in a low position. 3. Disconnect the WPR2 relay. 4. Using a test lamp connected between battery positive voltage and the windshield wiper motor low control circuit. Does the test lamp illuminate?	Go to Step 16	Go to Step 15
15	Test for a poor connection or an open in the windshield wiper motor low control circuit. Did you find and correct the condition?	Go to Step 23	Go to Step 20
16	1. Disconnect the windshield wiper/washer switch. 2. Install the WPR1 relay. 3. Install a jumper between ground and the windshield wiper switch low signal circuit. 4. Turn the ignition to the ON position. Does the windshield wiper turn ON in a low position?	Go to Step 18	Go to Step 17
17	Test for a poor connection or an open in the windshield wiper switch low signal circuit. Did you find and correct the condition?	Go to Step 23	Go to Step 21
18	Replace the windshield wiper/washer switch. Did you complete the replacement?	Go to Step 23	--
19	Replace the windshield wiper motor. Did you complete the replacement?	Go to Step 23	--
20	Replace the underhood fuse block. Did you complete the replacement?	Go to Step 23	--

LTV0500000003628

Fig. 198 Wipers Inoperative, One Or More Modes (Part 3 of 4). Relay, SV6, Terraza & Uplander

Step	Action	Yes	No
21	Replace the body control module (BCM). Did you complete the replacement?	Go to Step 23	--
22	Replace the WPR2 relay. Did you complete the replacement?	Go to Step 23	--
23	Operate the system in order to verify the repair. Did you correct the condition?	System OK	Go to Step 3

LTV0500000003629

Fig. 198 Wipers Inoperative, One Or More Modes (Part 4 of 4). Relay, SV6, Terraza & Uplander

Step	Action	Yes	No
1	Did you review the Rear Wiper/Washer System Description and Operation and perform the necessary inspections?	Go to Step 2	Go to Symptoms
2	1. Turn the ignition ON. 2. Press the rear washer switch. Does the rear washer operate properly?	Test for Intermittent Conditions and Poor Connections	Go to Step 3
3	Does the rear wiper motor operate when the washer switch is pressed?	Go to Step 6	Go to Step 4
4	1. Disconnect the rear wiper motor connector. 2. Connect a test lamp from the rear washer control circuit terminal in the wiper motor connector to a good ground. 3. Turn the ignition ON. 4. Press the rear washer switch. Does the test lamp illuminate when the rear washer switch is pressed?	Go to Step 10	Go to Step 5
5	Test the rear washer control circuit for an open or high resistance. Did you find and correct the condition?	Go to Step 16	Go to Step 12

LTV0500000003630

Fig. 199 Washer Inoperative, Rear (Part 1 of 3). Relay, SV6, Terraza & Uplander

Step	Action	Yes	No
6	1. Disconnect the rear washer pump connector. 2. Connect a test lamp from the rear washer control circuit terminal in the washer pump harness connector to a good ground. 3. Turn the ignition ON. 4. Press the rear washer switch. Does the test lamp illuminate when the rear washer switch is pressed?	Go to Step 7	Go to Step 8
7	1. Connect a test lamp from the rear washer control circuit terminal to the ground circuit terminal in the washer pump harness connector. 2. Press the rear washer switch. Does the test lamp illuminate when the rear washer switch is pressed?	Go to Step 14	Go to Step 9
8	Repair the rear washer control circuit for an open or high resistance. Is the repair complete?	Go to Step 16	--
9	Repair the rear washer pump ground circuit for an open or high resistance. Is the repair complete?	Go to Step 16	--
10	Inspect for poor connections at the rear wiper motor. Did you find and correct the condition?	Go to Step 16	Go to Step 11
11	Replace the rear wiper motor. Is the repair complete?	Go to Step 16	--
12	Inspect for poor connections at the rear wiper/washer switch. Did you find and correct the condition?	Go to Step 16	Go to Step 13

LTV0500000003631

Fig. 199 Washer Inoperative, Rear (Part 2 of 3). Relay, SV6, Terraza & Uplander

Step	Action	Yes	No
13	Replace the rear wiper/washer switch. Is the repair complete?	Go to Step 16	--
14	Inspect for poor connections at the rear washer pump. Did you find and correct the condition?	Go to Step 16	Go to Step 15
15	Replace the rear washer pump. Is the repair complete?	Go to Step 16	--
16	Operate the system in order to verify the repair. Did you correct the condition?	System OK	Go to Step 3

LTV0500000003632

Fig. 199 Washer Inoperative, Rear (Part 3 of 3). Relay, SV6, Terraza & Uplander

Step	Action	Yes	No
7	Replace the rear wiper/washer switch. Is the repair complete?	Go to Step 9	--
8	Replace the rear wiper motor. Is the repair complete?	Go to Step 9	--
9	Operate the system in order to verify the repair. Did you correct the condition?	System OK	Go to Step 3

LTV0500000003634

Fig. 200 Wiper Always On, Rear (Part 2 of 2). Relay, SV6, Terraza & Uplander

Step	Action	Yes	No
1	Did you review the Rear Wiper/Washer System Description and Operation and perform the necessary inspections?	Go to Step 2	Go to Symptoms
2	1. Turn the ignition ON. 2. Turn the rear wiper/washer switch to the OFF position. Is the rear wiper always on?	Go to Step 3	Test for Intermittent Conditions and Poor Connections
3	1. Disconnect the rear wiper motor connector. 2. Turn the rear wiper/washer switch to the OFF position. 3. Connect a test lamp from the rear wiper switch signal circuit terminal in the rear wiper motor harness connector to ground. 4. Turn the ignition ON. Does the test lamp illuminate?	Go to Step 5	Go to Step 4
4	1. Connect a test lamp from the rear washer pump control circuit terminal in the rear wiper motor harness connector to ground. 2. Turn the ignition ON. Does the test lamp illuminate?	Go to Step 6	Go to Step 8
5	Test the rear wiper switch signal circuit for a short to voltage. Did you find and correct the condition?	Go to Step 9	Go to Step 7
6	Test the rear washer pump control circuit for a short to voltage. Did you find and correct the condition?	Go to Step 9	Go to Step 7

LTV0500000003633

Fig. 200 Wiper Always On, Rear (Part 1 of 2). Relay, SV6, Terraza & Uplander

Step	Action	Yes	No
	DEFINITION: The rear wiper motor is inoperative in one or more modes, the rear washer pump may or may not operate.		
1	Did you review the Rear Wiper/Washer System Description and Operation and perform the necessary inspections?	Go to Step 2	Go to Symptoms
2	1. Turn the ignition ON, with the engine OFF. 2. Operate the rear wiper/washer system in all the switch positions. Does the rear wiper/washer system operate normally?	Test for Intermittent Conditions and Poor Connections	Go to Step 3
3	Does the rear wiper motor operate when the rear washer switch is pressed?	Go to Step 10	Go to Step 4
4	Does the rear washer pump operate when the rear washer switch is pressed?	Go to Step 11	Go to Step 5
5	1. Disconnect the harness connector of the rear wiper switch. 2. Turn the ignition ON, with the engine OFF. 3. Connect a test lamp from the accessory voltage circuit of the rear wiper switch to a good ground. Does the test lamp illuminate?	Go to Step 6	Go to Step 12
6	Connect a 20-amp fused jumper wire from the accessory voltage circuit to the signal circuit of the rear wiper switch. Does the rear wiper motor operate?	Go to Step 15	Go to Step 7

LTV0500000003635

Fig. 201 Wiper Inoperative, Rear (Part 1 of 4). Relay, SV6, Terraza & Uplander

Step	Action	Yes	No
7	1. Turn OFF the ignition. 2. Disconnect the harness connector of the rear wiper motor. 3. Turn the ignition ON, with the engine OFF. 4. Connect a test lamp from the signal circuit of the rear wiper switch to a good ground. Does the test lamp illuminate?	Go to Step 8	Go to Step 18
8	Connect a test lamp from the accessory voltage circuit of the rear wiper motor to a good ground. Does the test lamp illuminate?	Go to Step 9	Go to Step 19
9	Connect a test lamp from the accessory voltage circuit to the ground circuit of the rear wiper motor. Does the test lamp illuminate?	Go to Step 16	Go to Step 20
10	1. Turn OFF the ignition. 2. Disconnect the harness connector of the rear wiper motor. 3. Turn the ignition ON, with the engine OFF. 4. Connect a test lamp from the signal circuit of the rear wiper switch to a good ground. 5. Place the rear wiper switch in the Delay position. Does the test lamp illuminate?	Go to Step 16	Go to Step 18
11	1. Turn OFF the ignition. 2. Disconnect the harness connector of the rear wiper motor. 3. Turn the ignition ON, with the engine OFF. 4. Connect a test lamp from the control circuit of the rear washer pump to a good ground. 5. Depress the rear washer switch. Does the test lamp illuminate?	Go to Step 16	Go to Step 21
12	Test the accessory voltage circuit of the rear wiper switch for an open or a short to ground. Did you find and correct the condition?	Go to Step 24	Go to Step 13
13	Test the accessory voltage circuit of the rear wiper motor for a short to ground. Did you find and correct the condition?	Go to Step 24	Go to Step 14

LTV0500000003636

Fig. 201 Wiper Inoperative, Rear (Part 2 of 4). Relay, SV6, Terraza & Uplander

Step	Action	Yes	No
14	Test the signal circuit of the rear wiper switch for a short to ground. Did you find and correct the condition?	Go to Step 24	Go to Step 17
15	Inspect for poor connections at the harness connector of the rear wiper/washer switch. Did you find and correct the condition?	Go to Step 24	Go to Step 22
16	Inspect for poor connections at the harness connector of the rear wiper motor. Did you find and correct the condition?	Go to Step 24	Go to Step 23
17	Repair a short to ground in the control circuit of the rear washer pump. Did you complete the repair?	Go to Step 24	--
18	Repair an open or high resistance in the signal circuit of the rear wiper switch. Did you complete the repair?	Go to Step 24	--
19	Repair an open or high resistance in the accessory voltage circuit of the rear wiper motor. Did you complete the repair?	Go to Step 24	--
20	Repair an open or high resistance in the ground circuit of the rear wiper motor. Did you complete the repair?	Go to Step 24	--
21	Repair an open or high resistance in the control circuit of the rear washer pump. Did you complete the repair?	Go to Step 24	--

LTV0500000003637

Fig. 201   Wiper Inoperative, Rear (Part 3 of 4). Relay, SV6, Terraza & Uplander

Step	Action	Yes	No
22	Replace the rear wiper/washer switch. Did you complete the replacement?	Go to Step 24	--
23	Replace the rear wiper motor. Did you complete the replacement?	Go to Step 24	--
24	Operate the system in order to verify the repair. Did you correct the condition?	System OK	Go to Step 3

LTV0500000003638

Fig. 201   Wiper Inoperative, Rear (Part 4 of 4). Relay, SV6, Terraza & Uplander

Step	Action	Yes	No
	DEFINITION: The check washer fluid message is always displayed or does not display with low washer fluid.		
1	Did you perform the Diagnostic System Check - Vehicle?	Go to Step 2	Go to Diagnostic System Check
2	Verify the fault is present. Does the system operate normally?	Test for Intermittent and Poor Connections	Go to Step 3
3	1. Turn OFF the ignition. 2. Disconnect the washer fluid level switch connector. 3. Turn ON the ignition. Does the radio display the check washer fluid message?	Go to Step 7	Go to Step 4
4	1. Turn OFF the ignition. 2. Connect a fused jumper wire from the washer fluid level switch signal circuit terminal in the washer fluid level switch connector to a good ground. 3. Turn ON the ignition. Does the radio display the check washer fluid message?	Go to Step 6	Go to Step 5
5	1. Install a scan tool. 2. Display the dash integration module inputs data list. Is the washer fluid level switch parameter displayed as low?	Go to Step 15	Go to Step 9

LTV0500000003567

Fig. 202   Low Washer Fluid Indicator Fault (Part 1 of 3). SRX

Step	Action	Yes	No
6	1. Turn OFF the ignition. 2. Connect a fused jumper wire across the washer fluid level switch harness connector terminals. 3. Turn ON the ignition. Does the radio display the check washer fluid message?	Go to Step 11	Go to Step 10
7	1. Install a scan tool. 2. Display the dash integration module inputs data list. Is the washer fluid level switch parameter displayed as low?	Go to Step 8	Go to Step 15
8	Test the washer fluid level switch signal circuit for a short to ground. Did you find and correct the condition?	Go to Step 17	Go to Step 13
9	Test the washer fluid level switch signal circuit for an open or high resistance. Did you find and correct the condition?	Go to Step 17	Go to Step 13
10	Repair the washer fluid level switch ground circuit for an open or high resistance. Is the repair complete?	Go to Step 17	--
11	Inspect for poor connections at the washer fluid level switch. Did you find and correct the condition?	Go to Step 17	Go to Step 12
12	Replace the washer fluid level switch. Is the repair complete?	Go to Step 17	--
13	Inspect for poor connections at the dash integration module (DIM). Did you find and correct the condition?	Go to Step 17	Go to Step 14
14	Replace the DIM. Is the repair complete?	Go to Step 17	--

LTV0500000003568

Fig. 202   Low Washer Fluid Indicator Fault (Part 2 of 3). SRX

Step	Action	Yes	No
15	Inspect for poor connections at the radio. Did you find and correct the condition?	Go to Step 17	Go to Step 16
16	Replace the radio. Is the repair complete?	Go to Step 17	--
17	Operate the system in order to verify the repair. Did you correct the condition?	System OK	Go to Step 3

LTV0500000003569

Fig. 202 Low Washer Fluid Indicator Fault (Part 3 of 3). SRX

Step	Action	Yes	No
10	Replace the windshield wiper motor module. Is the repair complete?	Go to Step 11	--
11	Operate the system in order to verify the repair. Did you correct the condition?	System OK	Go to Step 3

LTV0500000003571

Fig. 203 Washers Always On (Part 2 of 2). SRX

Step	Action	Yes	No
1	Did you perform the Diagnostic System Check - Vehicle?	Go to Step 2	Go to Diagnostic System Check -
2	1. Turn ON the ignition. 2. Press the windshield washer switch. Do the windshield washers operate normally?	Test for Intermittent Conditions and Poor Connections	Go to Step 3
3	While listening for washer pump operation, press the windshield washer switch. Does the washer pump operate when the washer switch is pressed?	Go to Step 10	Go to Step 4
4	Do the windshield wipers operate when the washer switch is pressed?	Go to Step 5	Go to Step 8
5	1. Disconnect the windshield washer pump connector. 2. Connect a test lamp across the washer pump connector terminals. 3. Turn ON the ignition. 4. Press the windshield washer switch. Does the test lamp illuminate?	Go to Step 15	Go to Step 6
6	Test the windshield washer pump ground circuit for an open or high resistance. Did you find and correct the condition?	Go to Step 21	Go to Step 7

LTV0500000003572

Fig. 204 Washers Inoperative (Part 1 of 3). SRX w/Heated Washer Nozzles

Step	Action	Yes	No
1	Did you perform the Diagnostic System Check - Vehicle?	Go to Step 2	Go to Diagnostic System Check
2	Turn ON the ignition. Are the windshield washers always ON?	Go to Step 3	Test for Intermittent Conditions and Poor Connections
3	Are the windshield wipers always ON?	Go to Step 4	Go to Step 6
4	Remove the WPR SW 10A fuse. Are the windshield washers always ON?	Go to Step 5	Go to Step 7
5	Test the windshield wiper switch signal 2 circuit for a short to voltage. Did you find and correct the condition?	Go to Step 11	Go to Step 9
6	Test the windshield washer pump control circuit for a short to voltage. Did you find and correct the condition?	Go to Step 11	Go to Step 9
7	Inspect for poor connections at the windshield wiper/washer switch. Did you find and correct the condition?	Go to Step 11	Go to Step 8
8	Replace the windshield wiper/washer switch. Is the repair complete?	Go to Step 11	--
9	Inspect for poor connections at the windshield wiper motor. Did you find and correct the condition?	Go to Step 11	Go to Step 10

LTV0500000003570

Fig. 203 Washers Always On (Part 1 of 2). SRX

Step	Action	Yes	No
7	1. Disconnect the windshield wiper motor connector. 2. Test the windshield washer pump control circuit for an open or short to ground. Did you find and correct the condition?	Go to Step 21	Go to Step 17
8	1. Disconnect the windshield wiper motor connector. 2. Connect a test lamp from the windshield wiper switch signal 2 circuit terminal in the wiper motor harness connector to ground. 3. Turn ON the ignition. 4. Press the windshield washer switch. Does the test lamp illuminate?	Go to Step 17	Go to Step 9
9	Test the windshield wiper switch signal 2 circuit for high resistance. Did you find and correct the condition?	Go to Step 21	Go to Step 13
10	1. Disconnect an inoperative heated washer nozzle connector. 2. Connect a test lamp from the ignition 1 voltage circuit terminal in the harness connector to a good ground. 3. Turn ON the ignition. Does the test lamp illuminate?	Go to Step 12	Go to Step 11
11	Repair the ignition 1 voltage circuit for an open or short to ground. Is the repair complete?	Go to Step 21	--
12	Test the heated washer nozzle ground circuit for an open or high resistance. Did you find and correct the condition?	Go to Step 21	Go to Step 19
13	Inspect for poor connections at the windshield wiper/washer switch. Did you find and correct the condition?	Go to Step 21	Go to Step 14
14	Replace the windshield wiper/washer switch. Is the repair complete?	Go to Step 21	--

LTV0500000003573

Fig. 204 Washers Inoperative (Part 2 of 3). SRX w/Heated Washer Nozzles

Step	Action		
15	Inspect for poor connections at the windshield washer pump. Did you find and correct the condition?	Go to Step 21	Go to Step 16
16	Replace the windshield washer pump. Is the repair complete?	Go to Step 21	--
17	Inspect for poor connections at the windshield wiper motor. Did you find and correct the condition?	Go to Step 21	Go to Step 18
18	Replace the windshield wiper motor cover. Is the repair complete?	Go to Step 21	--
19	Inspect for poor connections at the heated washer nozzle. Did you find and correct the condition?	Go to Step 21	Go to Step 20
20	Replace the inoperative heated washer nozzle. Is the repair complete?	Go to Step 21	--
21	Operate the system in order to verify the repair. Did you correct the condition?	System OK	Go to Step 3

LTV0500000003574

Fig. 204　Washers Inoperative (Part 3 of 3). SRX w/Heated Washer Nozzles

Step	Action		
6	Test the control circuit of the windshield washer pump for an open or high resistance. Did you find and correct the condition?	Go to Step 12	Go to Step 8
7	Inspect for poor connections at the harness connector of the windshield washer pump. Did you find and correct the condition?	Go to Step 12	Go to Step 10
8	Inspect for poor connections at the harness connector of the windshield wiper motor. Did you find and correct the condition?	Go to Step 12	Go to Step 11
9	Repair an open or high resistance in the ground circuit of the windshield washer pump. Did you complete the repair?	Go to Step 12	--
10	Replace the windshield washer pump. Did you complete the replacement?	Go to Step 12	--
11	Replace the windshield wiper motor cover. Did you complete the replacement?	Go to Step 12	--
12	Operate the system in order to verify the repair. Did you correct the condition?	System OK	Go to Step 3

LTV0500000003576

Fig. 205　Washers Inoperative (Part 2 of 2). SRX Less Heated Washer Nozzles

Step	Action	Yes	No
1	Did you perform the Diagnostic System Check - Vehicle?	Go to Step 2	Go to Diagnostic System Check -
2	1. Turn ON the ignition. 2. Press the windshield washer switch. Do the windshield washers operate normally?	Test for Intermittent and Poor Connections	Go to Step 3
3	Do the wipers operate when the windshield washer switch is pressed?	Go to Step 4	Diagnose Wipers Inoperative - One or More Modes
4	1. Turn OFF the ignition. 2. Disconnect the harness connector of the windshield washer pump. 3. Connect a test lamp between the control circuit and the ground circuit of the windshield washer pump. 4. Turn ON the ignition. 5. Press the windshield washer switch. Does the test lamp illuminate?	Go to Step 7	Go to Step 5
5	1. Connect a test lamp from the control circuit of the windshield washer pump to a good ground. 2. Press the windshield washer switch. Does the test lamp illuminate?	Go to Step 9	Go to Step 6

LTV0500000003575

Fig. 205　Washers Inoperative (Part 1 of 2). SRX Less Heated Washer Nozzles

Step	Action	Yes	No
1	Did you perform the Diagnostic System Check - Vehicle?	Go to Step 2	Go to Diagnostic System Check -
2	1. Turn ON the ignition. 2. Turn the windshield wiper/washer switch OFF. Are the windshield wipers always ON?	Test for Intermittent and Poor Connections	Go to Step 3
3	Remove the WPR SW 10A fuse. Are the windshield wipers always ON?	Go to Step 4	Go to Step 7
4	1. Disconnect the windshield wiper motor connector. 2. Test the windshield wiper switch signal 1 circuit for a short to voltage. Did you find and correct the condition?	Go to Step 11	Go to Step 5
5	Test the windshield wiper switch signal 2 circuit for a short to voltage. Did you find and correct the condition?	Go to Step 11	Go to Step 6
6	Test the windshield wiper motor high speed circuit for a short to voltage. Did you find and correct the condition?	Go to Step 11	Go to Step 9
7	Inspect for poor connections at the windshield wiper/washer switch. Did you find and correct the condition?	Go to Step 11	Go to Step 8

LTV0500000003577

Fig. 206　Wipers Always On (Part 1 of 2). SRX

Step	Action	Yes	No
8	Replace the windshield wiper/washer switch. Is the repair complete?	Go to Step 11	--
9	Inspect for poor connections at the windshield wiper motor. Did you find and correct the condition?	Go to Step 11	Go to Step 10
10	Replace the windshield wiper motor cover. Is the repair complete?	Go to Step 11	--
11	Operate the system in order to verify the repair. Did you correct the condition?	System OK	Go to Step 3

LTV0500000003578

Fig. 206 Wipers Always On (Part 2 of 2). SRX

Step	Action	Yes	No
6	1. Turn OFF the ignition. 2. Disconnect the harness connector of the windshield wiper/washer switch. 3. Turn ON the ignition. 4. Connect a test lamp from the accessory voltage circuit of the windshield wiper/washer switch to a good ground. Does the test lamp illuminate?	Go to Step 14	Go to Step 9
7	Test the windshield wiper motor accessory voltage circuit for an open or short to ground. Did you find and correct the condition?	Go to Step 18	Go to Step 8
8	Test the windshield washer pump control circuit for a short to ground. Did you find and correct the condition?	Go to Step 18	Go to Step 13
9	Test the windshield wiper/washer switch accessory voltage circuit for an open or short to ground. Did you find and correct the condition?	Go to Step 18	Go to Step 10
10	Test the windshield wiper motor high speed circuit for a short to ground. Did you find and correct the condition?	Go to Step 18	Go to Step 11
11	Test the windshield wiper switch signal 1 circuit for a short to ground. Did you find and correct the condition?	Go to Step 18	Go to Step 12
12	Test the windshield wiper switch signal 2 circuit for a short to ground. Did you find and correct the condition?	Go to Step 18	Go to Step 13
13	Inspect for poor connections at the windshield wiper motor. Did you find and correct the condition?	Go to Step 18	Go to Step 16

LTV0500000003580

Fig. 207 Wipers Inoperative, All Modes (Part 2 of 3). SRX

Step	Action	Yes	No
1	Did you perform the Diagnostic System Check - Vehicle?	Go to Step 2	Go to Diagnostic System Check -
2	1. Turn ON the ignition, with the engine OFF. 2. Turn the windshield wiper/washer switch through all the switch positions. Does the windshield wiper/washer system operate normally?	Test for Intermittent Conditions and Poor Connections	Go to Step 3
3	1. Turn OFF the ignition. 2. Disconnect the harness connector of the windshield wiper motor. 3. Turn ON the ignition, with the engine OFF. 4. Connect a test lamp from the accessory voltage circuit to the ground circuit of the windshield wiper motor. Does the test lamp illuminate?	Go to Step 5	Go to Step 4
4	Connect a test lamp from the accessory voltage circuit of the windshield wiper motor to a good ground. Does the test lamp illuminate?	Go to Step 15	Go to Step 7
5	1. Connect the test lamp from the windshield wiper switch signal 2 circuit to a good ground. 2. Press the windshield washer switch. Does the test lamp illuminate?	Go to Step 13	Go to Step 6

LTV0500000003579

Fig. 207 Wipers Inoperative, All Modes (Part 1 of 3). SRX

Step	Action	Yes	No
14	Inspect for poor connections at the windshield wiper/washer switch. Did you find and correct the condition?	Go to Step 18	Go to Step 17
15	Repair the windshield wiper motor ground circuit for an open or high resistance. Did you complete the repair?	Go to Step 18	--
16	Replace the windshield wiper motor. Did you complete the replacement?	Go to Step 18	--
17	Replace the windshield wiper/washer switch. Did you complete the replacement?	Go to Step 18	--
18	Operate the system in order to verify the repair. Did you correct the condition?	System OK	Go to Step 3

LTV0500000003581

Fig. 207 Wipers Inoperative, All Modes (Part 3 of 3). SRX

Test Description

The numbers below refer to the step numbers on the diagnostic table.

7. This step tests for continuity through the 24K ohms resistor in the windshield wiper/washer switch. The connector behind the instrument panel knee bolster is suitable for performing this step.

8. This step tests for continuity through the delay resistors in the windshield wiper/washer switch. The measured resistance will change in sequence from high to low as the delay speed is increased. The connector behind the instrument panel knee bolster is suitable for performing this step.

Step	Action	Values	Yes	No
1	Did you perform the Diagnostic System Check - Vehicle?	--	Go to Step 2	Go to Diagnostic System Check -
2	1. Turn ON the ignition. 2. Operate the windshield wiper/washer switch through all the switch positions. Does the windshield wiper/washer system operate normally?	--	Test for Intermittent Conditions and Poor Connections Go to Step 3	Go to Step 3
3	Do the windshield wipers operate in the high speed mode?	--	Go to Step 5	Go to Step 4

LTV0500000003582

Fig. 208   Wipers Inoperative, One Or More Modes (Part 1 of 4). SRX

	Action		Yes	No
4	1. Disconnect the windshield wiper motor connector. 2. Connect a test lamp from the windshield wiper motor high speed circuit terminal to ground. 3. Turn ON the ignition. 4. Operate the windshield wiper/washer switch to the high speed position. Does the test lamp illuminate?		Go to Step 14	Go to Step 9
5	1. Disconnect the windshield wiper motor connector. 2. Connect a test lamp from the windshield wiper switch signal 2 circuit terminal to ground. 3. Turn ON the ignition. 4. Press the windshield washer switch. Does the test lamp illuminate?		Go to Step 6	Go to Step 10
6	1. Connect a test lamp from the windshield wiper switch signal 1 circuit terminal to ground. 2. Operate the windshield wiper/washer switch to the following positions: - MIST - LO - HI Does the test lamp illuminate in the listed switch positions?		Go to Step 7	Go to Step 11

LTV0500000003583

Fig. 208   Wipers Inoperative, One Or More Modes (Part 2 of 4). SRX

	Action	Values	Yes	No
7	1. Disconnect the windshield wiper/washer switch connector. 2. Measure the resistance through the windshield wiper/washer switch from the signal 2 circuit terminal to the accessory voltage circuit terminal of the wiper/washer switch. 3. Operate the windshield wiper/washer switch to the following positions: - MIST - INT - LO - HI Is the resistance at or near the specified value in all the listed switch positions?	24K ohms	Go to Step 8	Go to Step 12
8	1. Measure the resistance through the windshield wiper/washer switch from the signal 1 circuit terminal to the accessory voltage circuit terminal of the wiper/washer switch. 2. Operate the windshield wiper/washer switch through all of the delay positions. Does the resistance remain within the specified values from high to low as the delay speed is increased?	38K-69K ohms	Go to Step 14	Go to Step 12
9	Test the windshield wiper motor high speed circuit for an open or high resistance. Did you find and correct the condition?	--	Go to Step 16	Go to Step 12
10	Test the windshield wiper switch signal 2 circuit for an open or short to ground. Did you find and correct the condition?	--	Go to Step 16	Go to Step 12
11	Test the windshield wiper switch signal 1 circuit for an open or short to ground. Did you find and correct the condition?	--	Go to Step 16	Go to Step 12

LTV0500000003584

Fig. 208   Wipers Inoperative, One Or More Modes (Part 3 of 4). SRX

	Action		Yes	No
12	Inspect for poor connections at the windshield wiper/washer switch. Did you find and correct the condition?		Go to Step 16	Go to Step 13
13	Replace the windshield wiper/washer switch. Is the repair complete?		Go to Step 16	--
14	Inspect for poor connections at the windshield wiper motor. Did you find and correct the condition?		Go to Step 16	Go to Step 15
15	Replace the windshield wiper motor cover. Is the repair complete?		Go to Step 16	--
16	Operate the system in order to verify the repair. Did you correct the condition?		System OK	Go to Step 3

LTV0500000003585

Fig. 208   Wipers Inoperative, One Or More Modes (Part 4 of 4). SRX

Step	Action	Yes	No
1	Did you review the <u>Wiper/Washer System Description and Operation</u> and perform the necessary inspections?	Go to <u>Step 2</u>	Go to <u>Diagnostic Starting Point -</u>
2	1. Disconnect the wiper/washer switch connector. 2. Turn the ignition switch ON, engine OFF. Is the washer still on?	Go to <u>Step 3</u>	Go to <u>Step 4</u>
3	Test the control circuit between the wiper/washer switch and the rear window wiper module for a short to voltage. Did you find and correct the condition?	Go to <u>Step 7</u>	Go to <u>Step 5</u>
4	Replace the wiper/washer switch. Is the replacement complete?	Go to <u>Step 7</u>	--
5	Test the control circuit between the rear window washer fluid pump and the rear window wiper module for a short to voltage. Did you find and correct the condition?	Go to <u>Step 7</u>	Go to <u>Step 6</u>
6	Replace the rear window wiper module. setup, and programming. Is the replacement complete?	Go to <u>Step 7</u>	--
7	Operate the system in order to verify the repair. Did you correct the condition?	System OK	--

LTV0500000003586

Fig. 209 Washer Always On, Rear. SRX

Step	Action	Yes	No
7	Repair the rear washer pump ground circuit for an open or high resistance. Did you complete the repair?	Go to <u>Step 10</u>	--
8	Inspect for poor connections at the rear washer pump. Did you find and correct the condition?	Go to <u>Step 10</u>	Go to <u>Step 9</u>
9	Replace the rear washer pump. Did you complete the replacement?	Go to <u>Step 10</u>	--
10	Operate the system in order to verify the repair. Did you correct the condition?	System OK	Go to <u>Step 3</u>

LTV0500000003588

Fig. 210 Washer Inoperative, Rear (Part 2 of 2). SRX

Step	Action	Yes	No
1	Did you review the Rear Wiper/Washer System Description and Operation and perform the necessary inspections?	Go to <u>Step 2</u>	Go to <u>Symptoms -</u>
2	1. Turn the ignition ON. 2. Press the rear washer switch. Does the rear washer operate normally?	Test for <u>Intermittent and Poor Connections</u>	Go to <u>Step 3</u>
3	Does the rear wiper operate when the washer switch is pressed?	Go to <u>Step 4</u>	Diagnose <u>Wiper Inoperative - Rear</u>
4	1. Turn OFF the ignition. 2. Disconnect the rear washer pump connector. 3. Connect a test lamp from the rear washer control circuit to the ground circuit of the washer pump. 4. Turn the ignition ON, with the engine OFF. 5. Press the rear washer switch. Does the test lamp illuminate when the rear washer switch is pressed?	Go to <u>Step 8</u>	Go to <u>Step 5</u>
5	1. Connect a test lamp from the rear washer control circuit of the washer pump to a good ground. 2. Press the rear washer switch. Does the test lamp illuminate when the rear washer switch is pressed?	Go to <u>Step 7</u>	Go to <u>Step 6</u>
6	Repair the rear washer control circuit for an open or high resistance. Did you complete the repair?	Go to <u>Step 10</u>	--

LTV0500000003587

Fig. 210 Washer Inoperative, Rear (Part 1 of 2). SRX

Step	Action	Yes	No
	DEFINITION: The headlamp washers are inoperative. The windshield washers and headlamps operate normally. The CHECK WASHER FLUID LEVEL message isn't displayed.		
1	Did you perform the Diagnostic System Check - Vehicle? Go to <u>Step 2</u>		Go to <u>Diagnostic System Check</u>
2	1. Turn ON the ignition, with the engine OFF. 2. Turn the headlamps ON. 3. Press the windshield washer switch. Do the headlamp washers operate normally?	Test for <u>Intermittent and Poor Connections</u>	Go to <u>Step 3</u>
3	1. Turn OFF the ignition. 2. Turn the headlamps OFF. 3. Disconnect the headlamp washer relay. 4. Turn ON the ignition, with the engine OFF. 5. Connect a test lamp from the windshield washer pump control circuit to a good ground. 6. Press the windshield washer switch. Does the test lamp illuminate?	Go to <u>Step 4</u>	Go to <u>Step 14</u>
4	Connect a test lamp from the battery voltage circuit of the headlamp washer relay switched input to a good ground. Does the test lamp illuminate?	Go to <u>Step 5</u>	Go to <u>Step 9</u>

LTV0500000003589

Fig. 211 Washers Inoperative, Headlamp (Part 1 of 3). SRX

Step	Action	Yes	No
5	1. Connect a test lamp from the battery voltage circuit of the headlamp washer relay switched input to the ground circuit of the headlamp washer relay. 2. Turn the headlamps ON. Does the test lamp illuminate?	Go to Step 6	Go to Step 10
6	Connect a 30-ampere fused jumper wire from battery voltage to the headlamp washer relay switched input to relay switched output to the supply voltage circuit of the headlamp washer pump. Does the headlamp washer pump operate?	Go to Step 11	Go to Step 7
7	1. Disconnect the harness connector of the headlamp washer pump. 2. Connect a test lamp from the supply voltage circuit to the ground circuit of headlamp washer pump. Does the test lamp illuminate?	Go to Step 12	Go to Step 8
8	Connect a test lamp from the supply voltage circuit of headlamp washer pump to a good ground. Does the test lamp illuminate?	Go to Step 17	Go to Step 16
9	Test the battery voltage circuit of the headlamp washer relay switched input for an open or short to ground. Did you find and correct the condition?	Go to Step 21	Go to Step 15
10	Test the ground circuit of the headlamp washer relay for an open or short to voltage. Did you find and correct the condition?	Go to Step 21	Go to Step 13
11	Inspect for poor connections at the headlamp washer relay. Did you find and correct the condition?	Go to Step 21	Go to Step 18
12	Inspect for poor connections at the headlamp washer pump. Did you find and correct the condition?	Go to Step 21	Go to Step 19

LTV0500000003590

Fig. 211 Washers Inoperative, Headlamp (Part 2 of 3). SRX

Step	Action	Yes	No
13	Inspect for poor connections at the dash integration module (DIM). Did you find and correct the condition?	Go to Step 21	Go to Step 20
14	Repair the windshield washer pump control circuit for an open or short to ground. Is the repair complete?	Go to Step 21	--
15	Repair a short to ground on the windshield washer pump supply voltage circuit. Is the repair complete?	Go to Step 21	--
16	Repair an open or high resistance on the windshield washer pump supply voltage circuit. Is the repair complete?	Go to Step 21	--
17	Repair an open or high resistance on the windshield washer pump ground circuit. Is the repair complete?	Go to Step 21	--
18	Replace the headlamp washer relay. Is the repair complete?	Go to Step 21	--
19	Replace the headlamp washer pump. Is the repair complete?	Go to Step 21	--
20	Replace the DIM. Is the repair complete?	Go to Step 21	--
21	Operate the system in order to verify the repair. Did you correct the condition?	System OK	Go to Step 3

LTV0500000003591

Fig. 211 Washers Inoperative, Headlamp (Part 3 of 3). SRX

Step	Action	Yes	No
7	Replace the rear wiper/washer switch. Is the repair complete?	Go to Step 9	--
8	Replace the rear wiper motor. Is the repair complete?	Go to Step 9	--
9	Operate the system in order to verify the repair. Did you correct the condition?	System OK	Go to Step 3

LTV0500000003593

Fig. 212 Wiper Always On, Rear (Part 2 of 2). SRX

Step	Action	Yes	No
1	Did you review the Rear Wiper/Washer System Description and Operation and perform the necessary inspections?	Go to Step 2	Go to Symptoms
2	1. Turn the ignition ON. 2. Turn the rear wiper/washer switch to the OFF position. Is the rear wiper always on?	Go to Step 3	Test for Intermittent and Poor Connections
3	1. Disconnect the rear wiper motor connector. 2. Turn the rear wiper/washer switch to the OFF position. 3. Connect a test lamp from the rear wiper switch signal circuit terminal in the rear wiper motor harness connector to ground. 4. Turn the ignition ON. Does the test lamp illuminate?	Go to Step 5	Go to Step 4
4	1. Connect a test lamp from the rear washer pump control circuit terminal in the rear wiper motor harness connector to ground. 2. Turn the ignition ON. Does the test lamp illuminate?	Go to Step 6	Go to Step 8
5	Test the rear wiper switch signal circuit for a short to voltage. Did you find and correct the condition?	Go to Step 9	Go to Step 7
6	Test the rear washer pump control circuit for a short to voltage. Did you find and correct the condition?	Go to Step 9	Go to Step 7

LTV0500000003592

Fig. 212 Wiper Always On, Rear (Part 1 of 2). SRX

WIPER SYSTEMS

Step	Action	Yes	No
	DEFINITION: The rear wiper motor is inoperative in one or more modes, the rear washer pump may or may not operate.		
1	Did you review the Rear Wiper/Washer System Description and Operation and perform the necessary inspections?	Go to Step 2	Go to Symptoms -
2	1. Turn the ignition ON, with the engine OFF. 2. Operate the rear wiper/washer system in all the switch positions. Does the rear wiper/washer system operate normally?	Test for Intermittent and Poor Connections	Go to Step 3
3	Does the rear wiper motor operate when the rear washer switch is pressed?	Go to Step 9	Go to Step 4
4	1. Turn OFF the ignition. 2. Disconnect the harness connector of the rear wiper/washer switch. 3. Turn the ignition ON, with the engine OFF. 4. Connect a test lamp from the accessory voltage circuit of the rear wiper/washer switch to a good ground. Does the test lamp illuminate?	Go to Step 5	Go to Step 10
5	Connect a 3-amp fused jumper from the accessory voltage circuit of the rear wiper switch to the signal circuit of the rear wiper motor. Does the rear wiper motor operate?	Go to Step 14	Go to Step 6

LTV0500000003594

Fig. 213   Wiper Inoperative, Rear (Part 1 of 4). SRX

Step	Action	Yes	No
6	1. Turn OFF the ignition. 2. Disconnect the harness connector of the rear wiper motor. 3. Turn the ignition ON, with the engine OFF. 4. Connect a test lamp from the signal circuit of the rear wiper/washer switch to a good ground. Does the test lamp illuminate?	Go to Step 7	Go to Step 17
7	Connect a test lamp from the accessory voltage circuit to the ground circuit of the rear wiper motor. Does the test lamp illuminate?	Go to Step 15	Go to Step 8
8	Connect a test lamp from the accessory voltage circuit of the rear wiper motor to a good ground. Does the test lamp illuminate?	Go to Step 19	Go to Step 18
9	1. Turn OFF the ignition. 2. Disconnect the harness connector of the rear wiper motor. 3. Turn the ignition ON, with the engine OFF. 4. Connect a test lamp from the signal circuit of the rear wiper/washer switch to a good ground. 5. Turn ON the rear wiper. Does the test lamp illuminate?	Go to Step 15	Go to Step 13
10	Test the accessory voltage circuit of the rear wiper/washer switch for an open or short to ground. Did you find and correct the condition?	Go to Step 22	Go to Step 11
11	Test the accessory voltage circuit of the rear wiper motor for a short to ground. Did you find and correct the condition?	Go to Step 22	Go to Step 12
12	Test the signal circuit of the rear wiper/washer switch for a short to ground. Did you find and correct the condition?	Go to Step 22	Go to Step 16

LTV0500000003595

Fig. 213   Wiper Inoperative, Rear (Part 2 of 4). SRX

Step	Action	Yes	No
22	Operate the system in order to verify the repair. Did you correct the condition?	System OK	Go to Step 3

LTV0500000003597

Fig. 213   Wiper Inoperative, Rear (Part 4 of 4). SRX

Step	Action	Yes	No
13	Test the signal circuit of the rear wiper/washer switch for an open or high resistance. Did you find and correct the condition?	Go to Step 22	Go to Step 14
14	Inspect for poor connections at the rear wiper/washer switch. Did you find and correct the condition?	Go to Step 22	Go to Step 20
15	Inspect for poor connections at the rear wiper motor. Did you find and correct the condition?	Go to Step 22	Go to Step 21
16	Repair a short to ground in the control circuit of the rear washer pump. Did you complete the repair?	Go to Step 22	--
17	Repair an open or high resistance in the signal circuit of the rear wiper/washer switch. Did you complete the repair?	Go to Step 22	--
18	Repair an open or high resistance in the accessory voltage circuit of the rear wiper motor. Did you complete the repair?	Go to Step 22	--
19	Repair an open or high resistance in the ground circuit of the rear wiper motor. Did you complete the repair?	Go to Step 22	--
20	Replace the rear wiper/washer switch. Did you complete the replacement?	Go to Step 22	--
21	Replace the rear wiper motor. Did you complete the replacement?	Go to Step 22	--

LTV0500000003596

Fig. 213   Wiper Inoperative, Rear (Part 3 of 4). SRX

WIPER SYSTEMS

Step	Action	Yes	No
	DEFINITION: The windshield washer pump is always on.		
1	Did you perform the Diagnostic System Check - Vehicle?	Go to Step 2	Go to Diagnostic System Check
2	1. Turn the windshield wiper/washer switch to the OFF position. 2. Turn ON the ignition. Is the windshield washer pump always on?	Go to Step 3	Test for Intermittent and Poor Connections
3	Are the windshield wipers always ON?	Go to Step 6	Go to Step 4
4	Remove the windshield washer relay from the underhood fuse block. Is the windshield washer pump on?	Go to Step 13	Go to Step 5
5	Connect a test lamp from battery positive voltage to the windshield washer relay control circuit terminal in the underhood fuse block. Does the test lamp illuminate?	Go to Step 8	Go to Step 10
6	1. Turn OFF the ignition. 2. Disconnect the windshield wiper motor connector. 3. Turn ON the ignition. 4. Connect a test lamp from the windshield wiper switch signal 1 circuit terminal to ground. Does the test lamp illuminate?	Go to Step 9	Go to Step 7
7	Measure resistance between the windshield wiper switch voltage supply circuit and the signal 1 circuit. Is the resistance less than 380 ohms?	Go to Step 11	Go to Step 12

LTV0500000003178

Fig. 214   Washers Always On (Part 1 of 3). SSR

Step	Action	Yes	No
8	Test the windshield washer relay control circuit for a short to ground. Did you find and correct the condition?	Go to Step 17	Go to Step 12
9	Test the windshield wiper switch signal 1 circuit for a short to voltage. Did you find and correct the condition?	Go to Step 17	Go to Step 11
10	Inspect for poor connections at the windshield washer relay. Did you find and correct the condition?	Go to Step 17	Go to Step 14
11	Inspect for poor connections at the windshield wiper/washer switch. Did you find and correct the condition?	Go to Step 17	Go to Step 15
12	Inspect for poor connections at the windshield wiper motor. Did you find and correct the condition?	Go to Step 17	Go to Step 16
13	Repair the short to voltage in the windshield washer pump control circuit. Did you complete the repair?	Go to Step 17	--
14	Replace the windshield washer relay. Did you complete the replacement?	Go to Step 17	--
15	Replace the windshield wiper/washer switch. Did you complete the replacement?	Go to Step 17	--
16	Replace the windshield wiper motor. Did you complete the replacement?	Go to Step 17	--

LTV0500000003179

Fig. 214   Washers Always On (Part 2 of 3). SSR

Step	Action	Yes	No
17	Operate the system in order to verify the repair. Did you correct the condition?	System OK	Go to Step 3

LTV0500000003180

Fig. 214   Washers Always On (Part 3 of 3). SSR

Step	Action	Values	Yes	No
	DEFINITION: The windshield washer pump is inoperative.			
1	Did you perform the Diagnostic System Check - Vehicle?	--	Go to Step 2	Go to Diagnostic System Check -
2	1. Turn ON the ignition. 2. Press the windshield washer switch. Do the windshield washers operate normally?	--		Go to Step 3
3	Do the windshield wipers operate when the windshield washer switch is pressed?	--	Go to Step 4	Go to Step 7
4	1. Disconnect the windshield washer relay. 2. Probe each of the windshield washer relay battery positive voltage supply circuit terminals in the underhood fuse block with a test lamp connected to a good ground. Does the test lamp illuminate on both terminals?	--	Go to Step 5	Go to Step 19

LTV0500000003181

Fig. 215   Washers Inoperative (Part 1 of 3). SSR

Step	Action	Values	Yes	No
5	1. Connect a test lamp between the battery positive voltage terminal and the windshield washer relay control circuit terminal in the underhood fuse block. 2. Turn ON the ignition. 3. Press the windshield washer switch. Does the test lamp illuminate?	--	Go to Step 6	Go to Step 9
6	1. Connect the windshield washer relay. 2. Disconnect the windshield washer pump connector. 3. Connect a test lamp across the windshield washer pump harness connector terminals. 4. Turn ON the ignition. 5. Press the windshield washer switch. Does the test lamp illuminate?		Go to Step 12	Go to Step 10
7	1. Disconnect the windshield wiper motor connector. 2. Test the resistance from the windshield wiper switch supply voltage circuit terminal to the windshield wiper switch signal 1 circuit terminal in the windshield wiper motor harness connector. 3. Press the windshield washer switch. Is the resistance near the specified value?	0.5 ohms	Go to Step 14	Go to Step 8
8	Test the following circuits for high resistance: • Windshield wiper switch supply voltage circuit • Windshield wiper switch signal 1 circuit Did you find and correct the condition?	--	Go to Step 20	Go to Step 13
9	Test the windshield washer relay control circuit for an open or high resistance. Did you find and correct the condition?	--	Go to Step 20	Go to Step 14
10	Test the windshield washer pump control circuit for an open or high resistance. Did you find and correct the condition?	--	Go to Step 20	Go to Step 11
11	Test the windshield washer pump ground circuit for an open or high resistance. Did you find and correct the condition?	--	Go to Step 20	Go to Step 15

LTV0500000003182

Fig. 215   Washers Inoperative (Part 2 of 3). SSR

12	Inspect for poor connections at the windshield washer pump. Did you find and correct the condition?	-	Go to Step 20	Go to Step 16
13	Inspect for poor connections at the windshield wiper/washer switch. Did you find and correct the condition?	-	Go to Step 20	Go to Step 17
14	Inspect for poor connections at the windshield wiper motor. Did you find and correct the condition?	-	Go to Step 20	Go to Step 18
15	Replace the windshield washer relay. Is the repair complete?	-	Go to Step 20	--
16	Replace the windshield washer pump. Is the repair complete?	-	Go to Step 20	--
17	Replace the windshield wiper/washer switch. Is the repair complete?	-	Go to Step 20	--
18	Replace the windshield wiper motor. Is the repair complete?	-	Go to Step 20	--
19	Replace the underhood fuse block. Is the repair complete?	-	Go to Step 20	--
20	Operate the system in order to verify the repair. Did you correct the condition?	-	System OK	Go to Step 3

LTV0500000003183

Fig. 215   Washers Inoperative (Part 3 of 3). SSR

Step	Action	Yes	No
7	Test the windshield wiper switch signal 1 circuit in the steering column harness for a short to voltage. Did you find and correct the condition?	Go to Step 10	Go to Step 8
8	Replace the windshield wiper/washer switch. Did you complete the replacement?	Go to Step 10	--
9	Replace the windshield wiper motor cover. Did you complete the replacement?	Go to Step 10	--
10	Operate the system in order to verify the repair. Did you correct the condition?	System OK	Go to Step 3

LTV0500000003185

Fig. 216   Wipers Always On (Part 2 of 2). SSR

Step	Action	Yes	No
	DEFINITION: The wiper motor is ON when the wiper switch is OFF.		
1	Did you perform the Diagnostic System Check - Vehicle?	Go to Step 2	Go to Diagnostic System Check -
2	1. Turn the windshield wiper/washer switch OFF. 2. Turn ON the ignition. Are the windshield wipers always on?	Go to Step 3	Test for Intermittent Conditions and Poor Connections
3	1. Disconnect the steering column harness connector. 2. Remove the connector terminal row E from the steering column connector half. 3. Connect the steering column harness connector. 4. Turn ON the ignition. Are the windshield wipers always on?	Go to Step 4	Go to Step 6
4	Test the windshield wiper switch high signal circuit for a short to ground. Did you find and correct the condition?	Go to Step 10	Go to Step 5
5	Test the windshield wiper switch signal 1 circuit for a short to voltage. Did you find and correct the condition?	Go to Step 10	Go to Step 9
6	Test the windshield wiper switch high signal circuit in the steering column harness for a short to ground. Did you find and correct the condition?	Go to Step 10	Go to Step 7

LTV0500000003184

Fig. 216   Wipers Always On (Part 1 of 2). SSR

Step	Action	Yes	No
	DEFINITION: The windshield wiper motor does not operate in any mode.		
1	Did you perform the Diagnostic System Check - Vehicle?	Go to Step 2	Go to Diagnostic System Check
2	1. Turn ON the ignition. 2. Attempt to operate the windshield wipers in all modes. Are the windshield wipers inoperative in all modes?	Go to Step 3	Test for Intermittent and Poor Connections
3	1. Disconnect the steering column harness connector. 2. Connect a fused jumper wire from the windshield wiper switch high signal circuit terminal in the body harness connector half to ground. 3. Turn ON the ignition. Do the windshield wipers operate at high speed?	Go to Step 6	Go to Step 4
4	1. Disconnect the windshield wiper motor connector. 2. Connect a test lamp from the accessory voltage supply circuit terminal in the windshield wiper motor harness connector to a good ground. 3. Turn ON the ignition. Does the test lamp illuminate?	Go to Step 5	Go to Step 8
5	Connect a test lamp from battery positive voltage to the windshield wiper motor ground circuit terminal in the windshield wiper motor harness connector. Does the test lamp illuminate?	Go to Step 7	Go to Step 9

LTV0500000003186

Fig. 217   Wipers Inoperative, All Modes (Part 1 of 2). SSR

Step	Action	Value(s)	Yes	No
6	Inspect for poor connections at the windshield wiper/washer switch. Did you find and correct the condition?		Go to Step 12	Go to Step 10
7	Inspect for poor connections at the windshield wiper motor. Did you find and correct the condition?		Go to Step 12	Go to Step 11
8	Repair the accessory voltage supply circuit to the windshield wiper motor for an open or short to ground. Did you complete the repair?		Go to Step 12	--
9	Repair the windshield wiper motor ground circuit for an open or high resistance. Did you complete the repair?		Go to Step 12	--
10	Replace the windshield wiper/washer switch. Did you complete the replacement?		Go to Step 12	--
11	Replace the windshield wiper motor. Is the repair complete?		Go to Step 12	--
12	Operate the system in order to verify the repair. Did you correct the condition?		System OK	Go to Step 2

LTV0500000003187

Fig. 217 Wipers Inoperative, All Modes (Part 2 of 2). SSR

Step	Action	Value(s)	Yes	No
5	1. Disconnect the windshield wiper motor connector. 2. Test the resistance from the windshield wiper switch voltage supply circuit terminal to the windshield wiper switch signal 1 circuit terminal in the windshield wiper motor harness connector. 3. Operate the windshield wiper/washer switch in the following positions: - MIST - LO - HI Is the resistance near the specified value in the listed switch positions?	390 ohms	Go to Step 6	Go to Step 10
6	1. Test the resistance from the windshield wiper switch voltage supply circuit terminal to the windshield wiper switch signal 1 circuit terminal in the windshield wiper motor harness connector. 2. Operate the windshield wiper/washer switch in all of the delay positions. Does the resistance remain within the specified values from low to high as the delay speed is increased?	1000 ohms-10K ohms	Go to Step 14	Go to Step 12
7	Test the windshield wiper switch high signal circuit for an open or high resistance. Did you find and correct the condition?	--	Go to Step 16	Go to Step 14
8	Test the wiper switch ground circuit for an open or high resistance. Did you find and correct the condition?	--	Go to Step 16	Go to Step 9
9	Test the windshield wiper switch high signal and ground circuits in the steering column harness for an open or high resistance. Did you find and correct the condition?		Go to Step 16	Go to Step 12

LTV0500000003189

Fig. 218 Wipers Inoperative, One Or More Modes (Part 2 of 3). SSR

Test Description

The numbers below refer to the step numbers on the diagnostic table.

5. This step tests for continuity through the 390 ohms resistor in the windshield wiper/washer switch.

6. This step tests for continuity through the delay resistors in the windshield wiper/washer switch. The measured resistance will change in sequence from low to high as the delay speed is increased.

Step	Action	Value(s)	Yes	No
1	Did you perform the Wiper/Washer System Description and Operation and perform the necessary inspections?	--	Go to Step 2	Go to Symptoms
2	1. Turn ON the ignition. 2. Attempt to operate the windshield wipers in all modes. Does the system operate normally in every mode?	--	Test for Intermittent Conditions and Poor Connections	Go to Step 3
3	Do the windshield wipers operate in the high speed mode?	--	Go to Step 5	Go to Step 4
4	1. Disconnect the steering column harness connector. 2. Connect a fused jumper wire from the windshield wiper switch high signal circuit terminal in the body harness connector half to a good ground. 3. Turn ON the ignition. Do the windshield wipers operate at high speed?	--	Go to Step 8	Go to Step 7

LTV0500000003188

Fig. 218 Wipers Inoperative, One Or More Modes (Part 1 of 3). SSR

Step	Action	Value(s)	Yes	No
10	Test the windshield wiper switch voltage supply circuit for an open or short to ground. Did you find and correct the condition?	--	Go to Step 16	Go to Step 11
11	Test the windshield wiper switch signal 1 circuit for an open or high resistance. Wiring Systems. Did you find and correct the condition?		Go to Step 16	Go to Step 12
12	Inspect for poor connections at the windshield wiper/washer switch. Did you find and correct the condition?		Go to Step 16	Go to Step 13
13	Replace the windshield wiper/washer switch. Is the repair complete?		Go to Step 16	--
14	Inspect for poor connections at the windshield wiper motor. Did you find and correct the condition?		Go to Step 16	Go to Step 15
15	Replace the windshield wiper motor. Is the repair complete?		Go to Step 16	--
16	Operate the system in order to verify the repair. Did you correct the condition?		System OK	Go to Step 3

LTV0500000003190

Fig. 218 Wipers Inoperative, One Or More Modes (Part 3 of 3). SSR

Step	Action	Yes	No
	DEFINITION: The low washer fluid indicator always indicates low washer fluid or does not turn on with low washer fluid.		
1	Did you review the Wiper/Washer System Description and Operation and perform the necessary inspections?	Go to Step 2	Go to Symptoms -
2	Verify the fault is present. Does the system operate normally?	Test for Intermittent and Poor Connections	Go to Step 3
3	1. Turn the ignition OFF. 2. Disconnect the washer fluid level switch connector. 3. Turn the ignition ON. Does the low washer fluid indicator illuminate for 60 seconds after the ignition is turned ON?	Go to Step 6	Go to Step 4
4	1. Turn the ignition OFF. 2. Connect a fused jumper wire from the washer fluid level switch signal circuit terminal in the washer fluid level switch connector to a good ground. 3. Turn the ignition ON. Does the low washer fluid indicator illuminate for 60 seconds after the ignition is turned ON?	Go to Step 5	Go to Step 7
5	1. Turn the ignition OFF. 2. Connect a fused jumper wire across the washer fluid level switch harness connector terminals. 3. Turn the ignition ON. Does the low washer fluid indicator illuminate for 60 seconds after the ignition is turned ON?	Go to Step 9	Go to Step 8

LTV0500000003022

Fig. 219 Low Washer Fluid Indicator Fault (Part 1 of 2). 2002 Suburban, Tahoe & Yukon

Step	Action	Yes	No
6	Test the washer fluid level switch signal circuit for a short to ground. Did you find and correct the condition?	Go to Step 13	Go to Step 11
7	Test the washer fluid level switch signal circuit for an open or high resistance. Did you find and correct the condition?	Go to Step 13	Go to Step 11
8	Repair the washer fluid level switch ground circuit for an open or high resistance. Is the repair complete?	Go to Step 13	--
9	Inspect for poor connections at the washer fluid level switch. Did you find and correct the condition?	Go to Step 13	Go to Step 10
10	Replace the washer fluid level switch. Is the repair complete?	Go to Step 13	--
11	Inspect for poor connections at the instrument panel cluster. Did you find and correct the condition?	Go to Step 13	Go to Step 12
12	Replace the instrument panel cluster. Is the repair complete?	Go to Step 13	--
13	Operate the system in order to verify the repair. Did you correct the condition?	System OK	Go to Step 3

LTV0500000003023

Fig. 219 Low Washer Fluid Indicator Fault (Part 2 of 2). 2002 Suburban Tahoe, & Yukon

Step	Action	Yes	No
1	Did you review the Wiper/Washer System Description and Operation and perform the necessary inspections?	Go to Step 2	Go to Symptoms
2	Turn the ignition ON. Are the windshield washers always on?	Go to Step 3	
3	1. Turn the ignition OFF. 2. Disconnect the inline harness connector C201. 3. Remove the connector terminal row E from steering column harness connector half. 4. Connect the inline harness connector C201. 5. Turn the ignition ON. Are the windshield washers always on?	Go to Step 4	Go to Step 5
4	Repair the windshield washer pump control circuit for a short to voltage. Is the repair complete?	Go to Step 6	--
5	Replace the windshield wiper/washer switch. Is the repair complete?	Go to Step 6	--
6	Operate the system in order to verify the repair. Did you correct the condition?	System OK	Go to Step 3

LTV0500000003024

Fig. 220 Washers Always On. 2002 Suburban, Tahoe & Yukon

Step	Action	Yes	No
1	Did you review the Wiper/Washer System Description and Operation and perform the necessary inspections?	Go to Step 2	Go to Symptoms -
2	1. Turn the ignition ON. 2. Press the windshield washer switch. Do the windshield washers operate normally?	Test for Intermittent and Poor Connections	Go to Step 3
3	1. Disconnect the windshield washer pump connector. 2. Connect a test lamp across the washer pump harness connector terminals. 3. Turn the ignition ON. 4. Press the windshield washer switch. Does the test lamp illuminate?	Go to Step 8	Go to Step 4
4	Test the windshield washer pump ground circuit for an open or high resistance. Did you find and correct the condition?	Go to Step 10	Go to Step 5
5	Test the windshield washer pump control circuit for an open or short to ground. Did you find and correct the condition?	Go to Step 10	Go to Step 6
6	Inspect for poor connections at the windshield wiper/washer switch. Did you find and correct the condition?	Go to Step 10	Go to Step 7

LTV0500000003025

Fig. 221 Washers Inoperative (Part 1 of 2). 2002 Suburban, Tahoe, & Yukon

7	Replace the windshield wiper/washer switch. Is the repair complete?	Go to Step 10	--
8	Inspect for poor connections at the windshield washer pump. Did you find and correct the condition?	Go to Step 10	Go to Step 9
9	Replace the windshield washer pump. Is the repair complete?	Go to Step 10	--
10	Operate the system in order to verify the repair. Did you correct the condition?	System OK	Go to Step 3

LTV0500000003026

Fig. 221   Washers Inoperative (Part 2 of 2). 2002 Suburban, Tahoe & Yukon

5	Test the windshield wiper switch signal 2 circuit for a short to voltage. Did you find and correct the condition?	Go to Step 11	Go to Step 6
6	Test the windshield wiper motor high speed circuit for a short to voltage. Did you find and correct the condition?	Go to Step 11	Go to Step 9
7	Inspect for poor connections at the windshield wiper/washer switch. Did you find and correct the condition?	Go to Step 11	Go to Step 8
8	Replace the windshield wiper/washer switch. Is the repair complete?	Go to Step 11	--
9	Inspect for poor connections at the windshield wiper motor. Did you find and correct the condition?	Go to Step 11	Go to Step 10
10	Replace the windshield wiper motor cover. Is the repair complete?	Go to Step 11	--
11	Operate the system in order to verify the repair. Did you correct the condition?	System OK	Go to Step 3

LTV0500000003028

Fig. 222   Wipers Always On (Part 2 of 2). 2002 Suburban, Tahoe & Yukon

Test Description

The number below refers to the step number on the diagnostic table.

3.   Turn the ignition off while the wiper arms are not in the park position. If the wiper arms go to the park position and stop when the ignition is turned on, an internal fault in the windshield wiper/washer switch or short to voltage in the pigtail harness is present.

Step	Action	Yes	No
1	Did you review the Wiper/Washer System Description and Operation and perform the necessary inspections?	Go to Step 2	Go to Symptoms
2	1. Turn the ignition ON. 2. Operate the windshield wiper/washer switch through all of the switch positions. 3. Turn the windshield wiper/washer switch OFF. Are the windshield wipers always on?	Go to Step 3	
3	1. Turn the ignition OFF while the wiper arms are in the upright position. 2. Disconnect the inline harness connector C201. 3. Remove the connector terminal row E from the steering column harness connector half. 4. Connect the inline harness connector C201. 5. Turn the ignition ON. Are the windshield wipers always on?	Go to Step 4	Go to Step 7
4	1. Disconnect the windshield wiper motor connector. 2. Test the windshield wiper switch signal 1 circuit for a short to voltage. Did you find and correct the condition?	Go to Step 11	Go to Step 5

LTV0500000003027

Fig. 222   Wipers Always On (Part 1 of 2). 2002 Suburban, Tahoe & Yukon

Step	Action	Yes	No
1	Did you review the Wiper/Washer System Description and Operation and perform the necessary inspections?	Go to Step 2	Go to Symptoms -
2	1. Turn the ignition switch ON. 2. Operate the windshield wiper/washer switch through all the switch positions. Does the windshield wiper/washer system operate normally?	Test for Intermittent and Poor Connections	Go to Step 3
3	1. Disconnect the windshield wiper motor connector. 2. Connect a test lamp from the accessory voltage supply circuit terminal in the harness connector to a good ground. 3. Turn the ignition ON. Does the test lamp illuminate?	Go to Step 4	Go to Step 7
4	1. Connect a test lamp from the accessory voltage supply circuit terminal to the ground circuit terminal in the windshield wiper motor harness connector. 2. Turn the ignition ON. Does the test lamp illuminate?	Go to Step 5	Go to Step 8
5	1. Connect a test lamp from the windshield wiper switch signal 2 circuit terminal in the windshield wiper motor harness connector to ground. 2. Turn the ignition ON. 3. Press the windshield washer switch. Does the test lamp illuminate?	Go to Step 10	Go to Step 6

LTV0500000003029

Fig. 223   Wipers Inoperative, All Modes (Part 1 of 3). 2002 Suburban, Tahoe, & Yukon

Step	Action		Yes	No
6	1. Disconnect the windshield wiper/washer switch connector. 2. Connect a test lamp from the accessory voltage supply circuit terminal in the harness connector to ground. 3. Turn the ignition ON. Does the test lamp illuminate?		Go to Step 12	Go to Step 9
7	Repair the windshield wiper motor accessory voltage supply circuit for an open or short to ground. Is the repair complete?		Go to Step 14	--
8	Repair the windshield wiper motor ground circuit for an open or high resistance. Is the repair complete?		Go to Step 14	--
9	Repair the windshield wiper/washer switch accessory voltage supply circuit for an open or short to ground. Is the repair complete?		Go to Step 14	--
10	Inspect for poor connections at the windshield wiper motor. Did you find and correct the condition?		Go to Step 14	Go to Step 11
11	Replace the windshield wiper motor. Is the repair complete?		Go to Step 14	--
12	Inspect for poor connections at the windshield wiper/washer switch. Did you find and correct the condition?		Go to Step 14	Go to Step 13
13	Replace the windshield wiper/washer switch. Is the repair complete?		Go to Step 14	--

LTV0500000003030

Fig. 223 Wipers Inoperative, All Modes (Part 2 of 3). 2002 Suburban, Tahoe, & Yukon

Step	Action		Yes	No
14	Operate the system in order to verify the repair. Did you correct the condition?		System OK	Go to Step 3

LTV0500000003031

Fig. 223 Wipers Inoperative, All Modes (Part 3 of 3). 2002 Suburban, Tahoe, & Yukon

Step	Action		Yes	No
4	1. Disconnect the windshield wiper motor connector. 2. Connect a test lamp from the windshield wiper motor high speed circuit terminal to ground. 3. Turn the ignition ON. 4. Operate the windshield wiper/washer switch to the high speed position. Does the test lamp illuminate?		Go to Step 16	Go to Step 10
5	1. Disconnect the windshield wiper motor connector. 2. Connect a test lamp from the windshield wiper motor accessory voltage supply circuit terminal to ground. 3. Turn the ignition ON. Does the test lamp illuminate?		Go to Step 6	Go to Step 11
6	1. Connect a test lamp from the windshield wiper switch signal 2 circuit terminal to ground. 2. Press the windshield washer switch. Does the test lamp illuminate?		Go to Step 7	Go to Step 12
7	1. Connect a test lamp from the windshield wiper switch signal 1 circuit terminal to ground. 2. Operate the windshield wiper/washer switch to the following positions: - MIST - LO - HI Does the test lamp illuminate in the listed switch positions?		Go to Step 8	Go to Step 13

LTV0500000003033

Fig. 224 Wipers Inoperative, One Or More Modes (Part 2 of 4). 2002 Suburban, Tahoe, & Yukon

Test Description

The numbers below refer to the step numbers on the diagnostic table.

8. This step tests for continuity through the 24K ohms resistor in the windshield wiper/washer switch. The connector behind the instrument panel knee bolster is suitable for performing this step.

9. This step tests for continuity through the delay resistors in the windshield wiper/washer switch. The measured resistance will change in sequence from high to low as the delay speed is increased. The connector behind the instrument panel knee bolster is suitable for performing this step.

Step	Action	Value(s)	Yes	No
1	Did you review the Wiper/Washer System Description and Operation and perform the necessary inspections?	--	Go to Step 2	Go to Symptoms
2	1. Turn the ignition ON. 2. Operate the windshield wiper/washer switch through all the switch positions. Does the windshield wiper/washer system operate normally?	--	Test for Intermittent and Poor Connections	Go to Step 3
3	Do the windshield wipers operate in the high speed mode?	--	Go to Step 5	Go to Step 4

LTV0500000003032

Fig. 224 Wipers Inoperative, One Or More Modes (Part 1 of 4). 2002 Suburban, Tahoe & Yukon

Step	Action	Value(s)	Yes	No
8	1. Disconnect the windshield wiper/washer switch connector. 2. Measure the resistance through the windshield wiper switch from the signal 2 circuit terminal to the accessory voltage supply circuit terminal in the switch side connector. 3. Operate the windshield wiper/washer switch to the following positions: - MIST - INT - LO - HI Is the resistance at or near the specified value in all the listed switch positions?	24K ohms	Go to Step 9	Go to Step 14
9	1. Measure the resistance through the windshield wiper/washer switch from the signal 1 circuit terminal to the accessory voltage supply circuit terminal in the switch side connector. 2. Operate the windshield wiper/washer switch through all of the delay positions. Does the resistance remain within the specified values from high to low as the delay speed is increased?	38K - 690K ohms	Go to Step 16	Go to Step 14
10	Test the windshield wiper motor high speed circuit for an open or high resistance. Did you find and correct the condition?	--	Go to Step 18	Go to Step 14
11	Repair the windshield wiper motor accessory voltage supply circuit for an open or high resistance. Is the repair complete?	--	Go to Step 18	--
12	Test the windshield wiper switch signal 2 circuit for an open or short to ground. Did you find and correct the condition?	--	Go to Step 18	Go to Step 14

LTV0500000003034

Fig. 224 Wipers Inoperative, One Or More Modes (Part 3 of 4). 2002 Suburban, Tahoe & Yukon

Step	Action	Yes	No
13	Test the windshield wiper switch signal 1 circuit for an open or short to ground. Did you find and correct the condition?	Go to Step 18	Go to Step 14
14	Inspect for poor connections at the windshield wiper/washer switch. Did you find and correct the condition?	Go to Step 18	Go to Step 15
15	Replace the windshield wiper/washer switch. Is the repair complete?	Go to Step 18	--
16	Inspect for poor connections at the windshield wiper motor. Did you find and correct the condition?	Go to Step 18	Go to Step 17
17	Replace the windshield wiper motor cover. Is the repair complete?	Go to Step 18	--
18	Operate the system in order to verify the repair. Did you correct the condition?	System OK	Go to Step 3

LTV0500000003035

Fig. 224 Wipers Inoperative, One Or More Modes (Part 4 of 4). 2002 Suburban, Tahoe, & Yukon

Step	Action	Yes	No
7	1. Connect a test lamp from the rear washer pump supply circuit terminal to the ground circuit terminal in the washer pump harness connector. 2. Press the rear washer switch. Does the test lamp illuminate when the rear washer switch is pressed?	Go to Step 14	Go to Step 9
8	Test the rear washer pump supply circuit for an open or high resistance. Did you find and correct the condition?	Go to Step 16	Go to Step 12
9	Repair the rear washer pump ground circuit for an open or high resistance. Is the repair complete?	Go to Step 16	--
10	Inspect for poor connections at the rear wiper motor. Did you find and correct the condition?	Go to Step 16	Go to Step 11
11	Replace the rear wiper motor. Is the repair complete?	Go to Step 16	--
12	Inspect for poor connections at the rear wiper/washer switch. Did you find and correct the condition?	Go to Step 16	Go to Step 13
13	Replace the rear wiper/washer switch. Is the repair complete?	Go to Step 16	--
14	Inspect for poor connections at the rear washer pump. Did you find and correct the condition?	Go to Step 16	Go to Step 15

LTV0500000003037

Fig. 225 Washer Inoperative, Rear (Part 2 of 3). 2002 Suburban, Tahoe & Yukon

Step	Action	Yes	No
1	Did you review the Rear Wiper/Washer System Description and Operation and perform the necessary inspections?	Go to Step 2	Go to Symptoms -
2	1. Turn the ignition ON. 2. Press the rear washer switch. Does the rear washer operate normally?	Test for Intermittent and Poor Connections	Go to Step 3
3	Does the rear wiper motor operate when the washer switch is pressed?	Go to Step 6	Go to Step 4
4	1. Disconnect the rear wiper motor connector. 2. Connect a test lamp from the rear washer pump control circuit terminal in the wiper motor connector to a good ground. 3. Turn the ignition ON. 4. Press the rear washer switch. Does the test lamp illuminate when the rear washer switch is pressed?	Go to Step 10	Go to Step 5
5	Test the rear washer pump control circuit for an open or high resistance. Did you find and correct the condition?	Go to Step 16	Go to Step 12
6	1. Disconnect the rear washer pump connector. 2. Connect a test lamp from the rear washer pump supply circuit terminal in the washer pump harness connector to a good ground. 3. Turn the ignition ON. 4. Press the rear washer switch. Does the test lamp illuminate when the rear washer switch is pressed?	Go to Step 7	Go to Step 8

LTV0500000003036

Fig. 225 Washer Inoperative, Rear (Part 1 of 3). 2002 Suburban, Tahoe, & Yukon

Step	Action	Yes	No
15	Replace the rear washer pump. Is the repair complete?	Go to Step 16	--
16	Operate the system in order to verify the repair. Did you correct the condition?	System OK	Go to Step 3

LTV0500000003038

Fig. 225 Washer Inoperative, Rear (Part 3 of 3). 2002 Suburban, Tahoe, & Yukon

Step	Action	Yes	No
1	Did you review the Rear Wiper/Washer System Description and Operation and perform the necessary inspections?	Go to Step 2	Go to Symptoms
2	1. Turn the ignition ON. 2. Turn the rear wiper/washer switch to the OFF position. Is the rear wiper always on?	Go to Step 3	Test for Intermittent and Poor Connections
3	1. Disconnect the rear wiper motor connector. 2. Turn the rear wiper/washer switch to the OFF position. 3. Connect a test lamp from the rear wiper switch signal circuit terminal in the rear wiper motor harness connector to ground. 4. Turn the ignition ON. Does the test lamp illuminate?	Go to Step 5	Go to Step 4
4	1. Connect a test lamp from the rear washer pump control circuit terminal in the rear wiper motor harness connector to ground. 2. Turn the ignition ON. Does the test lamp illuminate?	Go to Step 6	Go to Step 9
5	Test the rear wiper switch signal circuit for a short to voltage. Did you find and correct the condition?	Go to Step 11	Go to Step 7
6	Test the rear washer pump control circuit for a short to voltage. Did you find and correct the condition?	Go to Step 11	Go to Step 7

LTV0500000003039

Fig. 226   Wiper Always On, Rear (Part 1 of 2). 2002 Suburban, Tahoe & Yukon

Step	Action	Yes	No
7	Inspect for poor connections at the rear wiper/washer switch. Did you find and correct the condition?	Go to Step 11	Go to Step 8
8	Replace the rear wiper/washer switch. Is the repair complete?	Go to Step 11	--
9	Inspect for poor connections at the rear wiper motor. Did you find and correct the condition?	Go to Step 11	Go to Step 10
10	Replace the rear wiper motor. Is the repair complete?	Go to Step 11	--
11	Operate the system in order to verify the repair. Did you correct the condition?	System OK	Go to Step 3

LTV0500000003040

Fig. 226   Wiper Always On, Rear (Part 2 of 2). 2002 Suburban, Tahoe & Yukon

Step	Action	Values	Yes	No
	DEFINITION: The rear wiper motor is inoperative in one or more modes, the rear washer pump may or may not operate.			
1	Did you review the Rear Wiper/Washer System Description and Operation and perform the necessary inspections?	--	Go to Step 2	Go to Symptoms
2	1. Turn the ignition ON. 2. Operate the rear wiper/washer system in all the switch positions. Does the rear wiper/washer system operate normally?	--	Test for Intermittent and Poor Connections	Go to Step 3
3	Does the rear wiper motor operate when the rear washer switch is pressed?	--	Go to Step 6	Go to Step 4
4	1. Disconnect the rear wiper motor connector. 2. Connect a test lamp from the rear wiper motor battery voltage supply circuit terminal in the wiper motor harness connector to a good ground. 3. Turn the ignition ON. Does the test lamp illuminate?	--	Go to Step 5	Go to Step 10
5	1. Connect a test lamp from the rear wiper motor battery voltage supply circuit terminal to the ground circuit terminal in the wiper motor harness connector. 2. Turn the ignition ON. Does the test lamp illuminate?	--	Go to Step 6	Go to Step 11

LTV0500000003041

Fig. 227   Wiper Inoperative, Rear (Part 1 of 3). 2002 Suburban, Tahoe & Yukon

Step	Action	Values	Yes	No
6	1. Disconnect the rear wiper motor connector. 2. Connect a test lamp from the rear wiper switch signal circuit terminal in the wiper motor harness connector to ground. 3. Turn the ignition ON. 4. Operate the rear wiper/washer switch to the 1 position. Does the test lamp illuminate?	--	Go to Step 7	Go to Step 9
7	1. Disconnect the rear wiper/washer switch connector. 2. Operate the rear wiper/washer switch to the 2 position. 3. Measure the resistance through the rear wiper/washer switch from the accessory voltage supply circuit terminal to the rear wiper switch signal circuit terminal. Is the resistance at or near the specified value?	1000 ohms	Go to Step 8	Go to Step 13
8	1. Using a DMM measure the voltage from the negitive side rear window defogger grid terminal to a known good ground. 2. Turn the rear window defogger on. Is the voltage measurement less than the specitied value?	0.5 V	Go to Step 15	Go to Step 11
9	Test the rear wiper switch signal circuit for an open or short to ground. Did you find and correct the condition?	--	Go to Step 17	Go to Step 12
10	Repair the rear wiper motor accessory voltage supply circuit for an open or short to ground. Is the repair complete?	--	Go to Step 17	--
11	Repair the rear wiper motor ground circuit for an open or high resistance. Is the repair complete?	--	Go to Step 17	--
12	Test the rear wiper/washer switch accessory voltage supply circuit for an open or short to ground. Did you find and correct the condition?	--	Go to Step 17	Go to Step 13

LTV0500000003042

Fig. 227   Wiper Inoperative, Rear (Part 2 of 3). 2002 Suburban, Tahoe & Yukon

Step	Action		Yes	No
13	Inspect for poor connections at the rear wiper/washer switch. Did you find and correct the condition?	--	Go to Step 17	Go to Step 14
14	Replace the rear wiper/washer switch. Is the repair complete?	--	Go to Step 17	--
15	Inspect for poor connections at the rear wiper motor. Did you find and correct the condition?	--	Go to Step 17	Go to Step 16
16	Replace the rear wiper motor. Is the repair complete?	--	Go to Step 17	--
17	Operate the system in order to verify the repair. Did you correct the condition?	--	System OK	Go to Step 3

LTV0500000003043

Fig. 227 Wiper Inoperative, Rear (Part 3 of 3). 2002 Suburban, Tahoe & Yukon

Step	Action	Yes	No
5	1. Turn the ignition OFF. 2. Connect a fused jumper wire across the washer fluid level switch harness connector terminals. 3. Turn the ignition ON, with the engine OFF. 4. Wait for about 15 seconds. Does the low washer fluid indicator illuminate?	Go to Step 9	Go to Step 8
6	Test the low washer fluid indicator signal circuit for a short to ground. Did you find and correct the condition?	Go to Step 13	Go to Step 11
7	Test the low washer fluid indicator signal circuit for an open or high resistance. Did you find and correct the condition?	Go to Step 13	Go to Step 11
8	Repair the washer fluid level switch ground circuit for an open or high resistance. Did you complete the replacement?	Go to Step 13	--
9	Inspect for poor connections at the washer fluid level switch. Did you find and correct the condition?	Go to Step 13	Go to Step 10
10	Replace the washer fluid level switch. Did you complete the replacement?	Go to Step 13	--
11	Inspect for poor connections at the instrument panel cluster. Did you find and correct the condition?	Go to Step 13	Go to Step 12
12	Replace the instrument panel cluster. Did you complete the replacement?	Go to Step 13	--

LTV0500000003049

Fig. 228 Low Washer Fluid Indicator Fault (Part 2 of 3). 2003–04 Suburban, Tahoe, & Yukon

Step	Action	Yes	No
13	Operate the system in order to verify the repair. Did you correct the condition?	System OK	Go to Step 3

LTV0500000003050

Fig. 228 Low Washer Fluid Indicator Fault (Part 3 of 3). 2003–04 Suburban, Tahoe & Yukon

Step	Action	Yes	No
	DEFINITION: The low washer fluid indicator always indicates low washer fluid or does not turn on with low washer fluid.		
1	Did you review the Wiper/Washer System Description and Operation and perform the necessary inspections?	Go to Step 2	Go to Symptoms -
2	Verify the fault is present. Does the system operate normally?	Test for Intermittent and Poor Connections	Go to Step 3
3	1. Turn the ignition OFF. 2. Disconnect the washer fluid level switch connector. 3. Turn the ignition ON, with the engine OFF. 4. Wait for about 15 seconds. Does the low washer fluid indicator illuminate?	Go to Step 6	Go to Step 4
4	1. Turn the ignition OFF. 2. Connect a fused jumper wire from the low washer fluid indicator signal circuit terminal in the washer fluid level switch connector to a good ground. 3. Turn the ignition ON, with the engine OFF. 4. Wait for about 15 seconds. Does the low washer fluid indicator illuminate?	Go to Step 5	Go to Step 7

LTV0500000003048

Fig. 228 Low Washer Fluid Indicator Fault (Part 1 of 3). 2003–04 Suburban, Tahoe, & Yukon

Step	Action	Yes	No
	DEFINITION: The windshield washer pump is always on.		
1	Did you review the Wiper/Washer System Description and Operation and perform the necessary inspections?	Go to Step 2	Go to Symptoms -
2	1. Turn the windshield wiper/washer switch to the OFF position. 2. Turn the ignition ON, with the engine OFF. Is the windshield washer pump always ON?	Go to Step 3	
3	Are the windshield wipers always ON, also?	Go to Step 4	Go to Step 6
4	1. Turn the ignition OFF. 2. Disconnect the windshield wiper motor module connector. 3. Turn the ignition ON, with the engine OFF. 4. Connect a test lamp from the windshield wiper switch signal circuit terminal to ground. Does the test lamp illuminate?	Go to Step 5	Go to Step 12
5	Test the windshield wiper switch signal circuit for a short to voltage. Did you find and correct the condition?	Go to Step 16	Go to Step 10
6	1. Turn the ignition OFF. 2. Disconnect the windshield washer relay. 3. Turn the ignition ON, with the engine OFF. Is the windshield washer pump ON?	Go to Step 8	Go to Step 7

LTV0500000003051

Fig. 229 Washers Always On (Part 1 of 3). 2003–04 Suburban, Tahoe & Yukon

Step	Action	Yes	No
7	Connect a test lamp from battery positive voltage to the windshield washer relay control circuit terminal in the underhood fuse block. Does the test lamp illuminate?	Go to Step 9	Go to Step 14
8	Repair the windshield washer pump control circuit for a short to voltage. Is the repair complete?	Go to Step 16	--
9	Test the windshield washer relay control circuit for a short to ground. Did you find and correct the condition?	Go to Step 16	Go to Step 12
10	Inspect for poor connections at the windshield wiper/washer switch. Did you find and correct the condition?	Go to Step 16	Go to Step 11
11	Replace the windshield wiper/washer switch. Did you complete the replacement?	Go to Step 16	--
12	Inspect for poor connections at the windshield wiper motor module. Did you find and correct the condition?	Go to Step 16	Go to Step 13
13	Replace the windshield wiper motor module. Did you complete the replacement?	Go to Step 16	--
14	Inspect for poor connections at the windshield washer relay. Did you find and correct the condition?	Go to Step 16	Go to Step 15
15	Replace the windshield washer relay. Did you complete the replacement?	Go to Step 16	--

LTV0500000003052

Fig. 229 Washers Always On (Part 2 of 3). 2003–04 Suburban, Tahoe & Yukon

Step	Action	Yes	No
16	Operate the system in order to verify the repair. Did you correct the condition?	System OK	Go to Step 3

LTV0500000003053

Fig. 229 Washers Always On (Part 3 of 3). 2003–04 Suburban, Tahoe & Yukon

Step	Action	Values	Yes	No
	DEFINITION: The windshield washer pump is inoperative.			
1	Did you review the Wiper/Washer System Description and Operation and perform the necessary inspections?	--	Go to Step 2	Go to Symptoms
2	1. Turn the ignition ON, with the engine OFF. 2. Press the windshield washer switch. Do the windshield washers operate normally?	--	Test for Intermittent and Poor Connections	Go to Step 3
3	Do the windshield washer wipers operate when the windshield washer switch is pressed?	--	Go to Step 6	Go to Step 4
4	1. Turn the ignition OFF. 2. Disconnect the windshield wiper motor connector. 3. Turn the ignition ON, with the engine OFF. 4. Test the resistance from the windshield wiper switch supply voltage circuit terminal to the windshield wiper switch signal circuit terminal in the windshield wiper motor harness connector. 5. Press the windshield washer switch. Is the resistance near the specified value?	0.5 ohms	Go to Step 15	Go to Step 5

LTV0500000003054

Fig. 230 Washers Inoperative (Part 1 of 4). 2003–04 Suburban, Tahoe & Yukon

Step	Action	Values	Yes	No
5	Test the following circuits for open or high resistance. • Windshield wiper switch supply voltage circuit • Windshield wiper switch signal circuit Did you find and correct the condition?	-	Go to Step 20	Go to Step 13
6	1. Turn the ignition OFF. 2. Disconnect the windshield washer relay. 3. Turn the ignition ON, with the engine OFF. 4. Connect a test lamp test from each of the windshield washer relay battery positive voltage supply circuit terminals in the underhood fuse block to ground. Does the test lamp illuminate on both terminals?	-	Go to Step 7	Go to Step 9
7	1. Connect a test lamp from battery positive voltage to the windshield washer relay control circuit terminal in the underhood fuse block. 2. Press the windshield washer switch. Does the test lamp illuminate?	-	Go to Step 8	Go to Step 10
8	1. Turn the ignition OFF. 2. Connect the windshield washer relay. 3. Disconnect the windshield washer pump connector. 4. Turn the ignition ON, with the engine OFF. 5. Connect a test lamp across the windshield washer pump harness connector terminals. 6. Press the windshield washer switch. Does the test lamp illuminate?	-	Go to Step 18	Go to Step 11
9	Replace the underhood fuse block. Did you complete the replacement?	-	Go to Step 20	--
10	Test the windshield washer relay control circuit for an open or high resistance. Did you find and correct the condition?	-	Go to Step 20	Go to Step 15

LTV0500000003055

Fig. 230 Washers Inoperative (Part 2 of 4). 2003–04 Suburban, Tahoe & Yukon

			Go to	Go to
11	Test the windshield washer pump control circuit for an open or high resistance. Did you find and correct the condition?		Go to Step 20	Go to Step 12
12	Test the windshield washer pump ground circuit for an open or high resistance. Did you find and correct the condition?		Go to Step 20	Go to Step 17
13	Inspect for poor connections at the windshield wiper/washer switch. Did you find and correct the condition?		Go to Step 20	Go to Step 14
14	Replace the windshield wiper/washer switch. Did you complete the replacement?		Go to Step 20	--
15	Inspect for poor connections at the windshield wiper motor module. Did you find and correct the condition?		Go to Step 20	Go to Step 16
16	Replace the windshield wiper motor module. Did you complete the replacement?		Go to Step 20	--
17	Replace the windshield washer relay. Did you complete the replacement?		Go to Step 20	--
18	Inspect for poor connections at the windshield washer pump. Did you find and correct the condition?		Go to Step 20	Go to Step 19
19	Replace the windshield washer pump. Did you complete the replacement?		Go to Step 20	--

LTV0500000003056

Fig. 230   Washers Inoperative (Part 3 of 4). 2003–04 Suburban, Tahoe & Yukon

Step	Action	Yes	No
	DEFINITION: Windshield wipers are always ON at low or high speed.		
1	Did you review the Wiper/Washer System Description and Operation and perform the necessary inspections?	Go to Step 2	Go to Symptoms
2	1. Turn the windshield wiper/washer switch OFF. 2. Turn the ignition ON, with the engine OFF. Are the windshield wipers always on?	Go to Step 3	
3	1. Turn the ignition OFF. 2. Disconnect the turn signal multifunction switch connector C3. 3. Turn the ignition ON, with the engine OFF. Are the windshield wipers always on?	Go to Step 4	Go to Step 7
4	Are the windshield wipers always ON at high speed?	Go to Step 5	Go to Step 6
5	Test the windshield wiper switch high signal circuit for a short to ground. Did you find and correct the condition?	Go to Step 11	Go to Step 9
6	Test the windshield wiper switch signal circuit for a short to voltage. Did you find and correct the condition?	Go to Step 11	Go to Step 9
7	Inspect for poor connections at the windshield wiper/washer switch. Did you find and correct the condition?	Go to Step 11	Go to Step 8

LTV0500000003058

Fig. 231   Wipers Always On (Part 1 of 2). 2003–04 Suburban, Tahoe & Yukon

20	Operate the system in order to verify the repair. Did you correct the condition?	--	System OK	Go to Step 3

LTV0500000003057

Fig. 230   Washers Inoperative (Part 4 of 4). 2003–04 Suburban, Tahoe & Yukon

8	Replace the windshield wiper/washer switch. Did you complete the replacement?		Go to Step 11	--
9	Inspect for poor connections at the windshield wiper motor module. Did you find and correct the condition?		Go to Step 11	Go to Step 10
10	Replace the windshield wiper motor module. Did you complete the replacement?		Go to Step 11	--
11	Operate the system in order to verify the repair. Did you correct the condition?		System OK	Go to Step 3

LTV0500000003059

Fig. 231   Wipers Always On (Part 2 of 2). 2003–04 Suburban, Tahoe & Yukon

Step	Action	Yes	No
	DEFINITION: Wipers are inoperative in all modes.		
1	Did you perform the Wiper/Washer System Description and Operation and perform the necessary inspections?	Go to Step 2	Go to Symptoms -
2	1. Turn the ignition ON, with the engine OFF. 2. Attempt to operate the windshield wipers in all modes. Does the system operate normally?	Test for Intermittent and Poor Connections	Go to Step 3
3	Do the windshield wipers operate in any mode?	Diagnose Wipers Inoperative - One or More Modes	Go to Step 4
4	1. Disconnect the multifunction turn signal harness connector C3. 2. Connect a fused jumper wire from the windshield wiper switch high signal circuit terminal in the multifunction turn signal harness connector to a good ground. 3. Turn the ignition ON. Do the windshield wipers operate at high speed?	Go to Step 9	Go to Step 5
5	1. Disconnect the windshield wiper motor module connector. 2. Connect a test lamp from the accessory voltage supply circuit terminal in the windshield wiper motor harness connector to a good ground. 3. Turn the ignition ON. Does the test lamp illuminate?	Go to Step 6	Go to Step 7

LTV0500000003060

Fig. 232   Wipers Inoperative, All Modes (Part 1 of 2). 2003–04 Suburban, Tahoe & Yukon

Step	Action	Yes	No
6	Connect a test lamp from battery positive voltage to the windshield wiper motor ground circuit terminal in the windshield wiper motor harness connector. Does the test lamp illuminate?	Go to Step 11	Go to Step 8
7	Repair the accessory voltage supply circuit to the windshield wiper motor for an open or short to ground. Is the repair complete?	Go to Step 13	--
8	Repair the windshield wiper motor ground circuit for an open or high resistance. Is the repair complete?	Go to Step 13	--
9	Inspect for poor connections at the windshield wiper/washer switch. Did you find and correct the condition?	Go to Step 13	Go to Step 10
10	Replace the windshield wiper/washer switch. Did you complete the replacement?	Go to Step 13	--
11	Inspect for poor connections at the windshield wiper motor. Did you find and correct the condition?	Go to Step 13	Go to Step 12
12	Replace the windshield wiper motor. Did you complete the replacement?	Go to Step 13	--
13	Operate the system in order to verify the repair. Did you correct the condition?	System OK	Go to Step 4

LTV0500000003061

Fig. 232   Wipers Inoperative, All Modes (Part 2 of 2). 2003–04 Suburban, Tahoe & Yukon

Step	Action	Values	Yes	No
4	1. Turn the ignition OFF. 2. Disconnect the multifunction turn signal harness connector C3. 3. Connect a fused jumper wire from the windshield wiper switch high signal circuit terminal in the body harness connector half to a good ground. 4. Turn the ignition ON, with the engine OFF. Do the windshield wipers operate at high speed?	--	Go to Step 8	Go to Step 7
5	1. Turn the ignition OFF. 2. Disconnect the windshield wiper motor module connector. 3. Test the resistance from the windshield wiper switch voltage supply circuit terminal to the windshield wiper switch signal circuit terminal in the windshield wiper motor harness connector. 4. Operate the windshield wiper/washer switch in the following positions: - MIST - LO. Is the resistance near the specified value in all of the listed switch positions?	390 ohms	Go to Step 6	Go to Step 9
6	1. Test the resistance from the windshield wiper switch voltage supply circuit terminal to the windshield wiper switch signal circuit terminal in the windshield wiper motor harness connector. 2. Operate the windshield wiper/washer switch in all of the delay positions. Does the resistance remain within the specified values from low to high as the delay speed is increased?	1000 ohms-10K ohms	Go to Step 13	Go to Step 11
7	Test the windshield wiper switch high signal circuit for an open or high resistance. Did you find and correct the condition?	--	Go to Step 15	Go to Step 13
8	Repair the wiper switch ground circuit for an open or high resistance. Is the repair complete?	--	Go to Step 15	--

LTV0500000003063

Fig. 233   Wipers Inoperative - One Or More Modes (Part 2 of 3). 2003–04 Suburban, Tahoe & Yukon

Test Description

The numbers below refer to the step numbers on the diagnostic table.

5. This step tests for continuity through the 390 ohms resistor in the windshield wiper/washer switch.

6. This step tests for continuity through the delay resistors in the windshield wiper/washer switch. The measured resistance will change in sequence from low to high as the delay speed is increased.

Step	Action	Values	Yes	No
	DEFINITION: Windshield wipers are inoperative in one or more modes.			
1	Did you perform the Wiper/Washer System Description and Operation and perform the necessary inspections?	--	Go to Step 2	Go to Symptoms -
2	1. Turn the ignition ON, with the engine OFF. 2. Attempt to operate the windshield wipers in all modes. Does the system operate normally?	--	Test for Intermittent and Poor Connections	Go to Step 3
3	Do the windshield wipers operate in the high speed mode?	--	Go to Step 5	Go to Step 4

LTV0500000003062

Fig. 233   Wipers Inoperative - One Or More Modes (Part 1 of 3). 2003–04 Suburban, Tahoe & Yukon

Step	Action	Values	Yes	No
9	Test the windshield wiper switch voltage supply circuit for an open or short to ground. Did you find and correct the condition?	-	Go to Step 15	Go to Step 10
10	Test the windshield wiper switch signal circuit for an open or short to ground. Did you find and correct the condition?	-	Go to Step 15	Go to Step 11
11	Inspect for poor connections at the windshield wiper/washer switch. Did you find and correct the condition?	-	Go to Step 15	Go to Step 12
12	Replace the windshield wiper/washer switch. Did you complete the replacement?	-	Go to Step 15	--
13	Inspect for poor connections at the windshield wiper motor module. Did you find and correct the condition?	-	Go to Step 15	Go to Step 14
14	Replace the windshield wiper motor module. Did you complete the replacement?	-	Go to Step 15	--
15	Operate the system in order to verify the repair. Did you correct the condition?	-	System OK	Go to Step 3

LTV0500000003064

Fig. 233   Wipers Inoperative - One Or More Modes (Part 3 of 3). 2003–04 Suburban, Tahoe & Yukon

Step	Action	Yes	No
	DEFINITION: The rear washers are inoperative. The rear wipers operate normally.		
1	Did you review the Rear Wiper/Washer System Description and Operation and perform the necessary inspections?	Go to Step 2	Go to Symptoms -
2	1. Turn the ignition ON. 2. Press the rear washer switch. Does the rear washer operate normally?	Test for Intermittent and Poor Connections	Go to Step 3
3	Press the rear washer switch. Does the rear wiper motor operate when the washer switch is pressed?	Go to Step 4	Go to Step 8
4	1. Disconnect the rear washer pump connector. 2. Connect a test lamp from the rear washer pump supply circuit terminal in the washer pump harness connector to a good ground. 3. Turn the ignition ON. 4. Press the rear washer switch. Does the test lamp illuminate when the rear washer switch is pressed?	Go to Step 5	Go to Step 6
5	1. Connect a test lamp from the rear washer pump supply circuit terminal to the ground circuit terminal in the washer pump harness connector. 2. Press the rear washer switch. Does the test lamp illuminate when the rear washer switch is pressed?	Go to Step 10	Go to Step 7

LTV0500000003065

**Fig. 234   Washer Inoperative, Rear (Part 1 of 2).
2003–04 Suburban, Tahoe & Yukon**

Step	Action	Yes	No
	DEFINITION: Rear wiper is always ON.		
1	Did you review the Rear Wiper/Washer System Description and Operation and perform the necessary inspections?	Go to Step 2	Go to Symptoms
2	1. Turn the ignition ON. 2. Turn the rear wiper/washer switch to the OFF position. Is the rear wiper always on?	Go to Step 3	Test for Intermittent and Poor Connections
3	1. Turn the ignition OFF. 2. Disconnect the rear wiper/washer switch. 3. Turn the ignition ON. Is the rear wiper always on?	Go to Step 4	Go to Step 6
4	1. Turn the ignition OFF. 2. Disconnect the window wiper module-rear. 3. Turn the ignition ON. Test the rear wiper switch signal circuit for a short to voltage. Did you find and correct the condition?	Go to Step 11	Go to Step 5
5	Test the rear window washer switch signal circuit for a short to voltage. Did you find and correct the condition?	Go to Step 11	Go to Step 9
6	Test the rear window washer pump supply voltage circuit for a short to voltage. Did you find and correct the condition?	Go to Step 11	Go to Step 7

LTV0500000003067

**Fig. 235   Wiper Always On, Rear (Part 1 of 2).
2003–04 Suburban, Tahoe & Yukon**

Step	Action	Yes	No
6	Test the rear washer pump supply circuit for an open or high resistance. Did you find and correct the condition?	Go to Step 12	Go to Step 8
7	Repair the rear washer pump ground circuit for an open or high resistance. Is the repair complete?	Go to Step 12	--
8	Inspect for poor connections at the rear wiper/washer switch. Did you find and correct the condition?	Go to Step 12	Go to Step 9
9	Replace the rear wiper/washer switch. Is the repair complete?	Go to Step 12	--
10	Inspect for poor connections at the rear washer pump. Did you find and correct the condition?	Go to Step 12	Go to Step 11
11	Replace the rear washer pump. Is the repair complete?	Go to Step 12	--
12	Operate the system in order to verify the repair. Did you correct the condition?	System OK	Go to Step 1

LTV0500000003066

**Fig. 234   Washer Inoperative, Rear (Part 2 of 2).
2003–04 Suburban, Tahoe & Yukon**

Step	Action	Yes	No
7	Inspect for poor connections at the rear wiper/washer switch. Did you find and correct the condition?	Go to Step 11	Go to Step 8
8	Replace the rear wiper/washer switch. Is the repair complete?	Go to Step 11	--
9	Inspect for poor connections at the window wiper module-rear. Did you find and correct the condition?	Go to Step 11	Go to Step 10
10	Replace the window wiper module-rear. Is the repair complete?	Go to Step 11	--
11	Operate the system in order to verify the repair. Did you correct the condition?	System OK	Go to Step 3

LTV0500000003068

**Fig. 235   Wiper Always On, Rear (Part 2 of 2).
2003–04 Suburban, Tahoe & Yukon**

Step	Action	Yes	No
	DEFINITION: The rear wiper motor is inoperative in one or more modes, the rear washer pump may or may not operate.		
1	Did you review the Rear Wiper/Washer System Description and Operation and perform the necessary inspections?	Go to Step 2	Go to Symptoms
2	1. Turn the ignition ON. 2. Operate the rear wiper/washer system in all the switch positions, including the washer position. Does the rear wiper/washer system operate normally?		Go to Step 3
3	Did the rear wipers operate in any of the rear wiper/washer switch position?	Go to Step 12	Go to Step 4
4	Does the rear washer pump operate when the rear washer switch is pressed?	Go to Step 5	Go to Step 10
5	1. Install a scan tool. 2. Turn the ignition ON, with the engine OFF. 3. Observe the Cargo Door Ajar Switch parameter in body control module (BCM) inputs display screen, with the liftgate closed and opened. Did the parameter displayed Open and the Closed accordingly?	Go to Step 6	Diagnose Courtesy Lamps Always On in Lighting Systems

LTV0500000003069

Fig. 236   Wiper Inoperative, Rear (Part 1 of 4). 2003–04 Suburban, Tahoe & Yukon

Step	Action	Yes	No
6	1. Disconnect the window wiper module-rear connector. 2. Connect a test lamp from the battery voltage circuit terminal in the wiper motor harness connector to a good ground. Does the test lamp illuminate?	Go to Step 7	Go to Step 9
7	Connect a test lamp from the battery voltage circuit terminal to the ground circuit terminal in the wiper motor harness connector. Does the test lamp illuminate?	Go to Step 20	Go to Step 8
8	Repair the rear wiper motor ground circuit for an open or high resistance. Is the repair complete?	Go to Step 22	--
9	Repair the battery voltage supply circuit for an open or short to ground. Is the repair complete?	Go to Step 22	--
10	1. Turn the ignition OFF. 2. Disconnect the rear wiper/washer switch. 3. Connect a test lamp from the accessory voltage circuit terminal in the rear wiper/washer switch harness connector to a good ground. 4. Turn the ignition ON, with the engine OFF. Does the test lamp illuminate?	Go to Step 18	Go to Step 11
11	Repair the accessory voltage circuit for an open or short to ground. Is the repair complete?	Go to Step 22	--
12	Does the rear wipers operate when the rear washer switch is pressed?	Go to Step 13	Go to Step 16

LTV0500000003070

Fig. 236   Wiper Inoperative, Rear (Part 2 of 4). 2003–04 Suburban, Tahoe & Yukon

Step	Action	Yes	No
13	1. Turn the ignition OFF. 2. Disconnect the window wiper module-rear connector. 3. Connect a test lamp from the rear window wiper switch signal circuit terminal in the wiper motor harness connector to a good ground. 4. Turn the ignition ON, with the engine OFF. 5. Turn the rear wiper switch to the 1 and 2 positions. Does the test lamp illuminate for both rear wiper switch positions?	Go to Step 20	Go to Step 14
14	Did the test lamp illuminate in any of the rear wiper switch position?	Go to Step 18	Go to Step 15
15	1. Turn the ignition OFF. 2. Disconnect the rear wiper/washer switch. 3. Test the rear window wiper switch signal circuit for an open or short to ground. Did you find and correct the condition?	Go to Step 22	Go to Step 18
16	1. Turn the ignition OFF. 2. Disconnect the window wiper module-rear connector. 3. Connect a test lamp from the rear window washer switch signal circuit terminal in the wiper motor harness connector to a good ground. 4. Turn the ignition ON, with the engine OFF. 5. Press the rear washer switch. Does the test lamp illuminate?	Go to Step 20	Go to Step 17
17	1. Turn the ignition OFF. 2. Disconnect the rear wiper/washer switch. 3. Test the rear window washer switch signal circuit for an open or short to ground. Did you find and correct the condition?	Go to Step 22	Go to Step 18
18	Inspect for poor connections at the rear wiper/washer switch. Did you find and correct the condition?	Go to Step 22	Go to Step 19
19	Replace the rear wiper/washer switch. Is the repair complete?	Go to Step 22	--

LTV0500000003071

Fig. 236   Wiper Inoperative, Rear (Part 3 of 4). 2003–04 Suburban, Tahoe & Yukon

Step	Action	Yes	No
20	Inspect for poor connections at the rear wiper motor. Did you find and correct the condition?	Go to Step 22	Go to Step 21
21	Replace the rear wiper motor. Is the repair complete?	Go to Step 22	--
22	Operate the system in order to verify the repair. Did you correct the condition?	System OK	Go to Step 1

LTV0500000003072

Fig. 236   Wiper Inoperative, Rear (Part 4 of 4). 2003–04 Suburban, Tahoe & Yukon

Step	Action	Yes	No
	DEFINITION: The low washer fluid indicator always indicates low washer fluid or does not turn on with low washer fluid.		
1	Did you review the Wiper/Washer System Description and Operation and perform the necessary inspections?	Go to Step 2	Go to Symptoms -
2	Verify the fault is present. Does the system operate normally?	Test for Intermittent and Poor Connections	Go to Step 3
3	1. Turn the ignition OFF. 2. Disconnect the washer fluid level switch connector. 3. Turn the ignition ON, with the engine OFF. 4. Wait for about 15 seconds. Does the low washer fluid indicator illuminate?	Go to Step 6	Go to Step 4
4	1. Turn the ignition OFF. 2. Connect a fused jumper wire from the low washer fluid indicator signal circuit terminal in the washer fluid level switch connector to a good ground. 3. Turn the ignition ON, with the engine OFF. 4. Wait for about 15 seconds. Does the low washer fluid indicator illuminate?	Go to Step 5	Go to Step 7

LTV0500000003077

Fig. 237   Low Washer Fluid Indicator Fault (Part 1 of 3). 2005–06 Suburban, Tahoe & Yukon

Step	Action	Yes	No
13	Operate the system in order to verify the repair. Did you correct the condition?	System OK	Go to Step 3

LTV0500000003079

Fig. 237   Low Washer Fluid Indicator Fault (Part 3 of 3). 2005–06 Suburban, Tahoe & Yukon

Step	Action	Yes	No
5	1. Turn the ignition OFF. 2. Connect a fused jumper wire across the washer fluid level switch harness connector terminals. 3. Turn the ignition ON, with the engine OFF. 4. Wait for about 15 seconds. Does the low washer fluid indicator illuminate?	Go to Step 9	Go to Step 8
6	Test the low washer fluid indicator signal circuit for a short to ground. Did you find and correct the condition?	Go to Step 13	Go to Step 11
7	Test the low washer fluid indicator signal circuit for an open or high resistance. Did you find and correct the condition?	Go to Step 13	Go to Step 11
8	Repair the washer fluid level switch ground circuit for an open or high resistance. Did you complete the replacement?	Go to Step 13	--
9	Inspect for poor connections at the washer fluid level switch. Did you find and correct the condition?	Go to Step 13	Go to Step 10
10	Replace the washer fluid level switch. Did you complete the replacement?	Go to Step 13	--
11	Inspect for poor connections at the instrument panel cluster (IPC). Did you find and correct the condition?	Go to Step 13	Go to Step 12
12	Replace the IPC. Did you complete the replacement?	Go to Step 13	--

LTV0500000003078

Fig. 237   Low Washer Fluid Indicator Fault (Part 2 of 3). 2005–06 Suburban, Tahoe & Yukon

Step	Action	Yes	No
	DEFINITION: The windshield washer pump is always on.		
1	Did you review the Wiper/Washer System Description and Operation and perform the necessary inspections?	Go to Step 2	Go to Symptoms
2	1. Turn the windshield wiper/washer switch to the OFF position. 2. Turn the ignition ON, with the engine OFF. Is the windshield washer pump always ON?	Go to Step 3	Test for Intermittent and Poor Connections
3	Are the windshield wipers always ON, also?	Go to Step 4	Go to Step 6
4	1. Turn the ignition OFF. 2. Disconnect the windshield wiper motor module connector. 3. Turn the ignition ON, with the engine OFF. 4. Connect a test lamp from the windshield wiper switch signal circuit terminal to ground. Does the test lamp illuminate?	Go to Step 5	Go to Step 12
5	Test the windshield wiper switch signal circuit for a short to voltage. Did you find and correct the condition?	Go to Step 16	Go to Step 10
6	1. Turn the ignition OFF. 2. Disconnect the windshield washer relay. 3. Turn the ignition ON, with the engine OFF. Is the windshield washer pump ON?	Go to Step 8	Go to Step 7

LTV0500000003080

Fig. 238   Washers Always On (Part 1 of 2). 2005–06 Suburban, Tahoe & Yukon

Step	Action	Yes	No
7	Connect a test lamp from battery positive voltage to the windshield washer relay control circuit terminal in the underhood fuse block. Does the test lamp illuminate?	Go to Step 9	Go to Step 14
8	Repair the windshield washer pump control circuit for a short to voltage. Is the repair complete?	Go to Step 16	--
9	Test the windshield washer relay control circuit for a short to ground. Did you find and correct the condition?	Go to Step 16	Go to Step 12
10	Inspect for poor connections at the windshield wiper/washer switch. Did you find and correct the condition?	Go to Step 16	Go to Step 11
11	Replace the windshield wiper/washer switch. Did you complete the replacement?	Go to Step 16	--
12	Inspect for poor connections at the windshield wiper motor module. Did you find and correct the condition?	Go to Step 16	Go to Step 13
13	Replace the windshield wiper motor module. Did you complete the replacement?	Go to Step 16	--
14	Inspect for poor connections at the windshield washer relay. Did you find and correct the condition?	Go to Step 16	Go to Step 15
15	Replace the windshield washer relay. Did you complete the replacement?	Go to Step 16	--
16	Operate the system in order to verify the repair. Did you correct the condition?	System OK	Go to Step 3

LTV0500000003081

Fig. 238   Washers Always On (Part 2 of 2). 2005–06 Suburban, Tahoe & Yukon

Step	Action	Values	Yes	No
	DEFINITION: The windshield washer pump is inoperative.			
1	Did you review the Wiper/Washer System Description and Operation and perform the necessary inspections?	--	Go to Step 2	Go to Symptoms
2	1. Turn the ignition ON, with the engine OFF. 2. Press the windshield washer switch. Do the windshield washers operate normally?	--	Test for Intermittent and Poor Connections	Go to Step 3
3	Do the windshield washer wipers operate when the windshield washer switch is pressed?	--	Go to Step 6	Go to Step 4
4	1. Turn the ignition OFF. 2. Disconnect the windshield wiper motor connector. 3. Turn the ignition ON, with the engine OFF. 4. Test the resistance from the windshield wiper switch supply voltage circuit terminal to the windshield wiper switch signal circuit terminal in the windshield wiper motor harness connector. 5. Press the windshield washer switch. Is the resistance near the specified value?	0.5 ohms	Go to Step 15	Go to Step 5

LTV0500000003082

Fig. 239   Washers Inoperative (Part 1 of 3). 2005–06 Suburban, Tahoe & Yukon

Step	Action	Yes	No
11	Test the windshield washer pump control circuit for an open or high resistance. Did you find and correct the condition?	Go to Step 20	Go to Step 12
12	Test the windshield washer pump ground circuit for an open or high resistance. Did you find and correct the condition?	Go to Step 20	Go to Step 17
13	Inspect for poor connections at the windshield wiper/washer switch. Did you find and correct the condition?	Go to Step 20	Go to Step 14
14	Replace the windshield wiper/washer switch. Did you complete the replacement?	Go to Step 20	--
15	Inspect for poor connections at the windshield wiper motor module. Did you find and correct the condition?	Go to Step 20	Go to Step 16
16	Replace the windshield wiper motor module. Did you complete the replacement?	Go to Step 20	--
17	Replace the windshield washer relay. Did you complete the replacement?	Go to Step 20	--
18	Inspect for poor connections at the windshield washer pump. Did you find and correct the condition?	Go to Step 20	Go to Step 19
19	Replace the windshield washer pump. Did you complete the replacement?	Go to Step 20	--
20	Operate the system in order to verify the repair. Did you correct the condition?	System OK	Go to Step 3

LTV0500000003084

Fig. 239   Washers Inoperative (Part 3 of 3). 2005–06 Suburban, Tahoe & Yukon

Step	Action	Yes	No
5	Test the following circuits for open or high resistance. • Windshield wiper switch supply voltage circuit • Windshield wiper switch signal circuit Did you find and correct the condition?	Go to Step 20	Go to Step 13
6	1. Turn the ignition OFF. 2. Disconnect the windshield washer relay. 3. Turn the ignition ON, with the engine OFF. 4. Connect a test lamp test from each of the windshield washer relay battery positive voltage supply circuit terminals in the underhood fuse block to ground. Does the test lamp illuminate on both terminals?	Go to Step 7	Go to Step 9
7	1. Connect a test lamp from battery positive voltage to the windshield washer relay control circuit terminal in the underhood fuse block. 2. Press the windshield washer switch. Does the test lamp illuminate?	Go to Step 8	Go to Step 10
8	1. Turn the ignition OFF. 2. Connect the windshield washer relay. 3. Disconnect the windshield washer pump connector. 4. Turn the ignition ON, with the engine OFF. 5. Connect a test lamp across the windshield washer pump harness connector terminals. 6. Press the windshield washer switch. Does the test lamp illuminate?	Go to Step 18	Go to Step 11
9	Replace the underhood fuse block. Did you complete the replacement?	Go to Step 20	--
10	Test the windshield washer relay control circuit for an open or high resistance. Did you find and correct the condition?	Go to Step 20	Go to Step 15

LTV0500000003083

Fig. 239   Washers Inoperative (Part 2 of 3). 2005–06 Suburban, Tahoe & Yukon

Step	Action	Yes	No
	DEFINITION: Windshield wipers are always ON at low or high speed.		
1	Did you review the Wiper/Washer System Description and Operation and perform the necessary inspections?	Go to Step 2	Go to Symptoms
2	1. Turn the windshield wiper/washer switch OFF. 2. Turn the ignition ON, with the engine OFF. Are the windshield wipers always on?	Go to Step 3	
3	1. Turn the ignition OFF. 2. Disconnect the turn signal multifunction switch connector C3. 3. Turn the ignition ON, with the engine OFF. Are the windshield wipers always on?	Go to Step 4	Go to Step 7
4	Are the windshield wipers always ON at high speed?	Go to Step 5	Go to Step 6
5	Test the windshield wiper switch high signal circuit for a short to ground. Did you find and correct the condition?	Go to Step 11	Go to Step 9
6	Test the windshield wiper switch signal circuit for a short to voltage. Did you find and correct the condition?	Go to Step 11	Go to Step 9

LTV0500000003085

Fig. 240   Wipers Always On (Part 1 of 2). 2005–06 Suburban, Tahoe & Yukon

Step	Action	Yes	No
7	Inspect for poor connections at the windshield wiper/washer switch. Did you find and correct the condition?	Go to Step 11	Go to Step 8
8	Replace the windshield wiper/washer switch. Did you complete the replacement?	Go to Step 11	--
9	Inspect for poor connections at the windshield wiper motor module. Did you find and correct the condition?	Go to Step 11	Go to Step 10
10	Replace the windshield wiper motor module. Did you complete the replacement?	Go to Step 11	--
11	Operate the system in order to verify the repair. Did you correct the condition?	System OK	Go to Step 3

LTV0500000003086

Fig. 240 Wipers Always On (Part 2 of 2). 2005–06 Suburban, Tahoe & Yukon

Step	Action	Yes	No
6	Connect a test lamp from battery positive voltage to the windshield wiper motor ground circuit terminal in the windshield wiper motor harness connector. Does the test lamp illuminate?	Go to Step 11	Go to Step 8
7	Repair the accessory voltage supply circuit to the windshield wiper motor for an open or short to ground. Is the repair complete?	Go to Step 13	--
8	Repair the windshield wiper motor ground circuit for an open or high resistance. Is the repair complete?	Go to Step 13	--
9	Inspect for poor connections at the windshield wiper/washer switch. Did you find and correct the condition?	Go to Step 13	Go to Step 10
10	Replace the windshield wiper/washer switch. Did you complete the replacement?	Go to Step 13	--
11	Inspect for poor connections at the windshield wiper motor. Did you find and correct the condition?	Go to Step 13	Go to Step 12
12	Replace the windshield wiper motor. Did you complete the replacement?	Go to Step 13	--
13	Operate the system in order to verify the repair. Did you correct the condition?	System OK	Go to Step 4

LTV0500000003088

Fig. 241 Wipers Inoperative, All Modes (Part 2 of 2). 2005–06 Suburban, Tahoe & Yukon

Step	Action	Yes	No
	DEFINITION: Wipers are inoperative in all modes.		
1	Did you perform the Wiper/Washer System Description and Operation and perform the necessary inspections?	Go to Step 2	Go to Symptoms -
2	1. Turn the ignition ON, with the engine OFF. 2. Attempt to operate the windshield wipers in all modes. Does the system operate normally?	Test for Intermittent and Poor Connections	Go to Step 3
3	Do the windshield wipers operate in any mode?	Diagnose Wipers Inoperative - One or More Modes	Go to Step 4
4	1. Disconnect the multifunction turn signal harness connector C3. 2. Connect a fused jumper wire from the windshield wiper switch high signal circuit terminal in the multifunction turn signal harness connector to a good ground. 3. Turn the ignition ON. Do the windshield wipers operate at high speed?	Go to Step 9	Go to Step 5
5	1. Disconnect the windshield wiper motor module connector. 2. Connect a test lamp from the accessory voltage supply circuit terminal in the windshield wiper motor harness connector to a good ground. 3. Turn the ignition ON. Does the test lamp illuminate?	Go to Step 6	Go to Step 7

LTV0500000003087

Fig. 241 Wipers Inoperative, All Modes (Part 1 of 2). 2005–06 Suburban, Tahoe & Yukon

Test Description

The numbers below refer to the step numbers on the diagnostic table.

5. This step tests for continuity through the 390 ohms resistor in the windshield wiper/washer switch.

6. This step tests for continuity through the delay resistors in the windshield wiper/washer switch. The measured resistance will change in sequence from low to high as the delay speed is increased.

Step	Action	Values	Yes	No
	DEFINITION: Windshield wipers are inoperative in one or more modes.			
1	Did you perform the Wiper/Washer System Description and Operation and perform the necessary inspections?	--	Go to Step 2	Go to Symptoms -
2	1. Turn the ignition ON, with the engine OFF. 2. Attempt to operate the windshield wipers in all modes. Does the system operate normally?	--	Test for Intermittent and Poor Connections	Go to Step 3
3	Do the windshield wipers operate in the high speed mode?	--	Go to Step 5	Go to Step 4

LTV0500000003089

Fig. 242 Wipers Inoperative, One Or More Modes (Part 1 of 3). 2005–06 Suburban, Tahoe & Yukon

Step	Action		Yes	No
4	1. Turn the ignition OFF. 2. Disconnect the multifunction turn signal harness connector C3. 3. Connect a fused jumper wire from the windshield wiper switch high signal circuit terminal in the body harness connector half to a good ground. 4. Turn the ignition ON, with the engine OFF. Do the windshield wipers operate at high speed?	--	Go to Step 8	Go to Step 7

5	1. Turn the ignition OFF.
	2. Disconnect the windshield wiper motor module connector.
	3. Test the resistance from the windshield wiper switch voltage supply circuit terminal to the windshield wiper switch signal circuit terminal in the windshield wiper motor harness connector.
	4. Operate the windshield wiper/washer switch in the following positions:
	
	  - MIST
	
	  - LO
	
	Is the resistance near the specified value in all of the listed switch positions?
		390 ohms	Go to Step 6	Go to Step 9

6	1. Test the resistance from the windshield wiper switch voltage supply circuit terminal to the windshield wiper switch signal circuit terminal in the windshield wiper motor harness connector. 2. Operate the windshield wiper/washer switch in all of the delay positions. Does the resistance remain within the specified values from low to high as the delay speed is increased?	1000 ohms-10K ohms	Go to Step 13	Go to Step 11
7	Test the windshield wiper switch high signal circuit for an open or high resistance. Did you find and correct the condition?	--	Go to Step 15	Go to Step 13
8	Repair the wiper switch ground circuit for an open or high resistance. Is the repair complete?	--	Go to Step 15	--

LTV0500000003090

Fig. 242   Wipers Inoperative, One Or More Modes (Part 2 of 3). 2005–06 Suburban, Tahoe & Yukon

Step	Action	Yes	No
	DEFINITION: The rear washers are inoperative. The rear wipers operate normally.		
1	Did you review the Rear Wiper/Washer System Description and Operation and perform the necessary inspections?	Go to Step 2	Go to Symptoms -
2	1. Turn the ignition ON. 2. Press the rear washer switch. Does the rear washer operate normally?	Test for Intermittent and Poor Connections	Go to Step 3
3	Press the rear washer switch. Does the rear wiper motor operate when the washer switch is pressed?	Go to Step 4	Go to Step 8
4	1. Disconnect the rear washer pump connector. 2. Connect a test lamp from the rear washer pump supply circuit terminal in the washer pump harness connector to a good ground. 3. Turn the ignition ON. 4. Press the rear washer switch. Does the test lamp illuminate when the rear washer switch is pressed?	Go to Step 5	Go to Step 6
5	1. Connect a test lamp from the rear washer pump supply circuit terminal to the ground circuit terminal in the washer pump harness connector. 2. Press the rear washer switch. Does the test lamp illuminate when the rear washer switch is pressed?	Go to Step 10	Go to Step 7

LTV0500000003092

Fig. 243   Washer Inoperative, Rear (Part 1 of 2). 2005–06 Suburban, Tahoe & Yukon

Step	Action		Yes	No
9	Test the windshield wiper switch voltage supply circuit for an open or short to ground. Repairs in Wiring Systems. Did you find and correct the condition?		Go to Step 15	Go to Step 10
10	Test the windshield wiper switch signal circuit for an open or short to ground. Did you find and correct the condition?	-	Go to Step 15	Go to Step 11
11	Inspect for poor connections at the windshield wiper/washer switch. Did you find and correct the condition?	-	Go to Step 15	Go to Step 12
12	Replace the windshield wiper/washer switch. Did you complete the replacement?	-	Go to Step 15	--
13	Inspect for poor connections at the windshield wiper motor module. Did you find and correct the condition?	-	Go to Step 15	Go to Step 14
14	Replace the windshield wiper motor module. Did you complete the replacement?	-	Go to Step 15	--
15	Operate the system in order to verify the repair. Did you correct the condition?		System OK	Go to Step 3

LTV0500000003091

Fig. 242   Wipers Inoperative, One Or More Modes (Part 3 of 3). 2005–06 Suburban, Tahoe & Yukon

Step	Action		Yes	No
6	Test the rear washer pump supply circuit for an open or high resistance. Did you find and correct the condition?		Go to Step 12	Go to Step 8
7	Repair the rear washer pump ground circuit for an open or high resistance. Is the repair complete?		Go to Step 12	--
8	Inspect for poor connections at the rear wiper/washer switch. Did you find and correct the condition?		Go to Step 12	Go to Step 9
9	Replace the rear wiper/washer switch. Is the repair complete?		Go to Step 12	--
10	Inspect for poor connections at the rear washer pump. Did you find and correct the condition?		Go to Step 12	Go to Step 11
11	Replace the rear washer pump. Is the repair complete?		Go to Step 12	--
12	Operate the system in order to verify the repair. Did you correct the condition?		System OK	Go to Step 1

LTV0500000003093

Fig. 243   Washer Inoperative, Rear (Part 2 of 2). 2005–06 Suburban, Tahoe & Yukon

Step	Action	Yes	No
	DEFINITION: Rear wiper is always ON.		
1	Did you review the Rear Wiper/Washer System Description and Operation and perform the necessary inspections?	Go to Step 2	Go to Symptoms
2	1. Turn the ignition ON. 2. Turn the rear wiper/washer switch to the OFF position. Is the rear wiper always on?	Go to Step 3	
3	1. Turn the ignition OFF. 2. Disconnect the rear wiper/washer switch. 3. Turn the ignition ON. Is the rear wiper always on?	Go to Step 4	Go to Step 6
4	1. Turn the ignition OFF. 2. Disconnect the window wiper module-rear. 3. Turn the ignition ON. Test the rear wiper switch signal circuit for a short to voltage. Did you find and correct the condition?	Go to Step 11	Go to Step 5
5	Test the rear window washer switch signal circuit for a short to voltage. Did you find and correct the condition?	Go to Step 11	Go to Step 9
6	Test the rear window washer pump supply voltage circuit for a short to voltage. Did you find and correct the condition?	Go to Step 11	Go to Step 7

LTV0500000003094

**Fig. 244   Wiper Always On, Rear (Part 1 of 2).
2005–06 Suburban, Tahoe & Yukon**

Step	Action	Yes	No
7	Inspect for poor connections at the rear wiper/washer switch. Did you find and correct the condition?	Go to Step 11	Go to Step 8
8	Replace the rear wiper/washer switch. Is the repair complete?	Go to Step 11	--
9	Inspect for poor connections at the window wiper module-rear. Did you find and correct the condition?	Go to Step 11	Go to Step 10
10	Replace the window wiper module-rear. Is the repair complete?	Go to Step 11	--
11	Operate the system in order to verify the repair. Did you correct the condition?	System OK	Go to Step 3

LTV0500000003095

**Fig. 244   Wiper Always On, Rear (Part 2 of 2).
2005–06 Suburban, Tahoe & Yukon**

Step	Action	Yes	No
	DEFINITION: The rear wiper motor is inoperative in one or more modes, the rear washer pump may or may not operate.		
1	Did you review the Rear Wiper/Washer System Description and Operation and perform the necessary inspections?	Go to Step 2	Go to Symptoms -
2	1. Turn the ignition ON. 2. Operate the rear wiper/washer system in all the switch positions, including the washer position. Does the rear wiper/washer system operate normally?		Go to Step 3
3	Did the rear wipers operate in any of the rear wiper/washer switch position?	Go to Step 12	Go to Step 4
4	Does the rear washer pump operate when the rear washer switch is pressed?	Go to Step 5	Go to Step 10
5	1. Install a scan tool. 2. Turn the ignition ON, with the engine OFF. 3. Observe the Cargo Door Ajar Switch parameter in body control module (BCM) inputs display screen, with the liftgate closed and opened. Did the parameter displayed Open and the Closed accordingly?	Go to Step 6	Diagnose Courtesy Lamps Always On

LTV0500000003096

**Fig. 245   Wiper Inoperative, Rear (Part 1 of 4).
2005–06 Suburban, Tahoe & Yukon**

Step	Action	Yes	No
6	1. Disconnect the window wiper module-rear connector. 2. Connect a test lamp from the battery voltage circuit terminal in the wiper motor harness connector to a good ground. Does the test lamp illuminate?	Go to Step 7	Go to Step 9
7	Connect a test lamp from the battery voltage circuit terminal to the ground circuit terminal in the wiper motor harness connector. Does the test lamp illuminate?	Go to Step 20	Go to Step 8
8	Repair the rear wiper motor ground circuit for an open or high resistance. Is the repair complete?	Go to Step 22	--
9	Repair the battery voltage supply circuit for an open or short to ground. Is the repair complete?	Go to Step 22	--
10	1. Turn the ignition OFF. 2. Disconnect the rear wiper/washer switch. 3. Connect a test lamp from the accessory voltage circuit terminal in the rear wiper/washer switch harness connector to a good ground. 4. Turn the ignition ON, with the engine OFF. Does the test lamp illuminate?	Go to Step 18	Go to Step 11
11	Repair the accessory voltage circuit for an open or short to ground. Is the repair complete?	Go to Step 22	--
12	Does the rear wipers operate when the rear washer switch is pressed?	Go to Step 13	Go to Step 16

LTV0500000003097

**Fig. 245   Wiper Inoperative, Rear (Part 2 of 4).
2005–06 Suburban, Tahoe & Yukon**

	Action	Yes	No
13	1. Turn the ignition OFF. 2. Disconnect the window wiper module-rear connector. 3. Connect a test lamp from the rear window wiper switch signal circuit terminal in the wiper motor harness connector to a good ground. 4. Turn the ignition ON, with the engine OFF. 5. Turn the rear wiper switch to the 1 and 2 positions. Does the test lamp illuminate for both rear wiper switch positions?	Go to Step 20	Go to Step 14
14	Did the test lamp illuminate in any of the rear wiper switch position?	Go to Step 18	Go to Step 15
15	1. Turn the ignition OFF. 2. Disconnect the rear wiper/washer switch. 3. Test the rear window wiper switch signal circuit for an open or short to ground. Did you find and correct the condition?	Go to Step 22	Go to Step 18
16	1. Turn the ignition OFF. 2. Disconnect the window wiper module-rear connector. 3. Connect a test lamp from the rear window washer switch signal circuit terminal in the wiper motor harness connector to a good ground. 4. Turn the ignition ON, with the engine OFF. 5. Press the rear washer switch. Does the test lamp illuminate?	Go to Step 20	Go to Step 17
17	1. Turn the ignition OFF. 2. Disconnect the rear wiper/washer switch. 3. Test the rear window washer switch signal circuit for an open or short to ground. Did you find and correct the condition?	Go to Step 22	Go to Step 18
18	Inspect for poor connections at the rear wiper/washer switch. Did you find and correct the condition?	Go to Step 22	Go to Step 19

LTV0500000003098

Fig. 245   Wiper Inoperative, Rear (Part 3 of 4). 2005–06 Suburban, Tahoe & Yukon

	Action	Yes	No
19	Replace the rear wiper/washer switch. Is the repair complete?	Go to Step 22	--
20	Inspect for poor connections at the rear wiper motor. Did you find and correct the condition?	Go to Step 22	Go to Step 21
21	Replace the rear wiper motor. Is the repair complete?	Go to Step 22	--
22	Operate the system in order to verify the repair. Did you correct the condition?	System OK	Go to Step 1

LTV0500000003099

Fig. 245   Wiper Inoperative, Rear (Part 4 of 4). 2005–06 Suburban, Tahoe & Yukon

	Action	Yes	No
5	Test the washer pump ground circuit for a high resistance or an open condition. Did you find and correct the condition?	Go to Step 10	Go to Step 7
6	Inspect for poor connections at the harness connector of the wiper/washer switch. Did you find and correct the condition?	Go to Step 10	Go to Step 8
7	Inspect for poor connections at the harness connector of the washer pump. Did you find and correct the condition?	Go to Step 10	Go to Step 9
8	Replace the wiper/washer switch. Did you complete the replacement?	Go to Step 10	--
9	Replace the washer pump. Did you complete the replacement?	Go to Step 10	--
10	Operate the front washers in order to verify the repair. Did you correct the condition?	System OK	Go to Step 3

LTV0500000003721

Fig. 246   Washers Inoperative (Part 2 of 2). Tracker

Step	Action	Yes	No
	DEFINITION: This table diagnoses the front washer pump inoperative and assumes that the front wipers operate normally.		
1	Did you review the Wiper/Washer System Description and Operation and perform the necessary inspections?	Go to Step 2	Go to Symptoms
2	1. Turn ON the ignition, with the engine OFF. 2. Pull the washer switch to the wash position. Do the washers operate normally?	Test for Intermittent and Poor Connections	Go to Step 3
3	1. Disconnect the front washer pump. Refer to Washer Pump Replacement for access. 2. Turn ON the ignition with the engine OFF. 3. Connect a test light between cavity 2 of the front washer pump connector and a good ground. 4. Pull and hold the wiper/washer switch to the wash position. Does the test light illuminate when the wiper/washer switch is pulled to the wash position?	Go to Step 5	Go to Step 4
4	1. Disconnect the wiper/washer switch connector. 2. Test for a high resistance or an open condition in the washer pump control circuit between the wiper/washer switch connector and the front washer pump connector. Did you find and correct the condition?	Go to Step 10	Go to Step 6

LTV0500000003720

Fig. 246   Washers Inoperative (Part 1 of 2). Tracker

Step	Action	Yes	No
	DEFINITION: This table diagnoses the front wipers are always on when the wiper/washer switch is turned to the off position.		
1	Did you review the Wiper/Washer System Description and Operation and perform the necessary inspections?	Go to Step 2	Go to Symptoms
2	Verify that the front wipers are always on when the wiper/washer switch is turned to the OFF position. Do the front wipers operate normally?	Test for Intermittent and Poor Connections	Go to Step 3
3	1. Turn the front wiper switch to the OFF position. 2. Disconnect the front wiper motor connector. 3. Test the following circuits for a short to voltage condition at the wiper motor connector: - Run/Park - High - Low. Did any of the circuits measure a short to voltage?	Go to Step 4	Go to Step 6
4	1. Disconnect the wiper/washer switch. 2. Retest the circuit that measured shorted to voltage at the wiper motor connector. Does the circuit still have a short to voltage condition?	Go to Step 7	Go to Step 5

LTV0500000003722

Fig. 247 Wipers Always On (Part 1 of 2). Tracker

Step	Action	Yes	No
5	Inspect for poor connections at the harness connector of the wiper/washer switch. Did you find and correct the condition?	Go to Step 10	Go to Step 8
6	Inspect for poor connections at the harness connector of the wiper motor. Did you find and correct the condition?	Go to Step 10	Go to Step 9
7	Repair the short to voltage condition. Did you complete the repair?	Go to Step 10	--
8	Replace the front wiper/washer switch. Did you complete the replacement?	Go to Step 10	--
9	Replace the front wiper motor. Did you complete the replacement?	Go to Step 10	--
10	Operate the system in order to verify the repair. Did you correct the condition?	Go to Step 10	--

LTV0500000003723

Fig. 247 Wipers Always On (Part 2 of 2). Tracker

Step	Action	Yes	No
	DEFINITION: This table diagnoses the front wipers inoperative in the LO, HI, and INT modes.		
1	Did you review the Wiper/Washer System Description and Operation and perform the necessary inspections?	Go to Step 2	Go to Symptoms
2	1. Turn ON the ignition, with the engine OFF. 2. Operate the wiper switch to the LO, HI, and INT positions. 3. Verify that the front wipers are inoperative in all modes. Do the front wipers operate normally?		Go to Step 3
3	1. Disconnect the front wiper motor connector. 2. Turn ON the ignition, with the engine OFF. 3. Turn the front wiper switch to the HI position. 4. Test the High speed voltage supply circuit at the wiper motor connector. Did you measure ignition positive voltage at the wiper motor connector?	Go to Step 5	Go to Step 4
4	1. Disconnect the front wiper/washer switch connector. 2. Turn ON the ignition, with the engine OFF. 3. Test the voltage supply circuit at the front wiper/washer switch connector. Did you find and correct the condition?	Go to Step 10	Go to Step 6

LTV0500000003724

Fig. 248 Wipers Inoperative, All Modes (Part 1 of 2). Tracker

Step	Action	Yes	No
5	Test the ground circuit of the wiper motor for a high resistance or an open condition. Did you find and correct the condition?	Go to Step 10	Go to Step 7
6	Inspect for poor connections at the harness connector of the wiper/washer switch. Did you find and correct the condition?	Go to Step 10	Go to Step 8
7	Inspect for poor connections at the harness connector of the wiper motor. Did you find and correct the condition?	Go to Step 10	Go to Step 9
8	Replace the front wiper/washer switch. Did you complete the replacement?	Go to Step 10	--
9	Replace the front wiper motor. Did you complete the replacement?	Go to Step 10	--
10	Operate the system in order to verify the repair. Did you correct the condition?	System OK	Go to Step 3

LTV0500000003725

Fig. 248 Wipers Inoperative, All Modes (Part 2 of 2). Tracker

Step	Action	Yes	No
1	Did you review the Wiper/Washer System Description and Operation and perform the necessary inspections?	Go to Step 2	Go to Symptoms
2	1. Turn ON the ignition, with the engine OFF. 2. Turn the wiper switch to the LO, HI, and INT positions. Do the front wipers operate in the LO, HI, and INT positions?		Go to Step 3
3	Do the wipers operate in the LO and HI position, but not the INT position?	Go to Step 6	Go to Step 4
4	1. Disconnect the wiper motor. Refer to Wiper Motor Replacement for access. 2. Turn ON the ignition, with the engine OFF. 3. Turn the wiper switch to the affected speed. 4. Test the corresponding voltage supply circuit at the wiper motor connector for ignition positive voltage. Did you measure ignition positive voltage?	Go to Step 7	Go to Step 5
5	1. Disconnect the wiper/washer switch. 2. Turn the wiper switch to the affected speed. 3. Test the wiper/washer switch for a high resistance or an open of the affected speed. Did you measure a high resistance or an open condition in the wiper switch?	Go to Step 6	Go to Step 8

LTV0500000003726

Fig. 249   Wipers Inoperative, One Mode (Part 1 of 2). Tracker

Step	Action	Yes	No
6	Inspect for poor connections at the harness connector of the wiper/washer switch. Did you find and correct the condition?	Go to Step 11	Go to Step 9
7	Inspect for poor connections at the harness connector of the wiper motor. Did you find and correct the condition?	Go to Step 11	Go to Step 10
8	Repair the high resistance or open condition in the voltage supply circuit to the wiper motor. Did you complete the repair?	Go to Step 11	--
9	Replace the front wiper/washer switch. Did you complete the replacement?	Go to Step 11	--
10	Replace the front wiper motor. Did you complete the replacement?	Go to Step 11	--
11	Operate the system in order to verify the repair. Did you correct the condition?	System OK	Go to Step 3

LTV0500000003727

Fig. 249   Wipers Inoperative, One Mode (Part 2 of 2). Tracker

Step	Action	Yes	No
	DEFINITION: This table diagnoses the wipers operates normally but will not return to the park position when the wiper operation is cancelled.		
1	Did you review the Wiper/Washer System Description and Operation and perform the necessary inspections?	Go to Step 2	Go to Symptoms
2	1. Turn ON the ignition, with the engine OFF. 2. Move the wiper switch to the LO position. 3. Move wiper switch to the OFF position. Do the front wipers advance to the park position?		Go to Step 3
3	1. Disconnect the front wiper motor connector. 2. Turn ON the ignition, with the engine OFF. 3. Test the Run circuit for ignition positive voltage at the wiper motor connector. Did you find and correct the condition?	Go to Step 11	Go to Step 4
4	1. Turn OFF the ignition. 2. Make sure the wiper switch is in the OFF position. 3. Test for a high resistance or an open condition in the Run circuit between cavity 1 and cavity 3 of the wiper motor connector. Did you measure a high resistance or an open condition?	Go to Step 5	Go to Step 7

LTV0500000003728

Fig. 250   Wipers Blades Do Not Park (Part 1 of 2). Tracker

Step	Action	Yes	No
5	1. Disconnect the wiper/washer switch connector. 2. Make sure the wiper switch is in the OFF position. 3. Test for a high resistance or an open condition between cavity 23 and cavity 5 of the wiper/washer switch connector. Did you measure a high resistance or an open condition?	Go to Step 6	Go to Step 8
6	Inspect for poor connections at the harness connector of the wiper/washer switch. Did you find and correct the condition?	Go to Step 11	Go to Step 9
7	Inspect for poor connections at the harness connector of the wiper motor. Did you find and correct the condition?	Go to Step 11	Go to Step 10
8	Repair the open in the Run/Park circuit between the wiper motor connector and wiper/washer switch connector. Did you complete the repair?	Go to Step 11	
9	Replace the front wiper/washer switch. Did you complete the replacement?	Go to Step 11	
10	Replace the front wiper motor. Did you complete the replacement?	Go to Step 11	
11	Operate the system in order to verify the repair. Did you correct the condition?	System OK	Go to Step 3

LTV0500000003729

Fig. 250   Wipers Blades Do Not Park (Part 2 of 2). Tracker

Step	Action	Yes	No
	DEFINITION: This table diagnoses the rear washer pump inoperative and assumes that the rear wiper operates normally.		
1	Did you review the Rear Wiper/Washer System Description and Operation and perform the necessary inspections?	Go to Step 2	Go to Symptoms
2	1. Turn ON the ignition, with the engine OFF. 2. Press the washer switch to the wash position. Do the washers operate normally?	Test for Intermittent and Poor Connections	Go to Step 3
3	1. Disconnect the rear washer pump. 2. Turn ON the ignition, with the engine OFF. 3. Connect a test light between the voltage supply side of the rear washer pump connector and a good ground. 4. Depress the rear washer switch to the wash position. Does the test light illuminate when the rear washer switch is pressed to the wash position?	Go to Step 5	Go to Step 4
4	1. Disconnect the rear wiper/washer switch connector. 2. Test for a high resistance or an open condition in the rear washer pump control circuit between the rear wiper/washer switch connector and the rear washer pump connector. Did you find and correct the condition?	Go to Step 10	Go to Step 6

LTV0500000003730

Fig. 251   Washer Inoperative, Rear (Part 1 of 2). Tracker

Step	Action	Yes	No
5	Test the rear washer pump ground circuit for a high resistance or an open condition. Did you find and correct the condition?	Go to Step 10	Go to Step 7
6	Inspect for poor connections at the harness connector of the rear wiper/washer switch. Did you find and correct the condition?	Go to Step 10	Go to Step 8
7	Inspect for poor connections at the harness connector of the rear washer pump. Did you find and correct the condition?	Go to Step 10	Go to Step 9
8	Replace the rear wiper/washer switch. Did you complete the replacement?	Go to Step 10	--
9	Replace the rear washer pump. Did you complete the replacement?	Go to Step 10	--
10	Operate the rear washers in order to verify the repair. Did you correct the condition?	System OK	Go to Step 3

LTV0500000003731

Fig. 251   Washer Inoperative, Rear (Part 2 of 2). Tracker

Step	Action	Yes	No
	DEFINITION: This table diagnoses the rear wipers are always on when the rear wiper/washer switch is in the OFF position.		
1	Did you review the Rear Wiper/Washer System Description and Operation and perform the necessary inspections?	Go to Step 2	Go to Symptoms
2	Verify that the rear wipers are always on when the wiper/washer switch is in the OFF position. Do the rear wipers operate normally?		Go to Step 3
3	1. Turn the front wiper switch to the OFF position. 2. Disconnect the front wiper motor connector. 3. Test the following circuits for a short to voltage condition at the wiper motor connector: - Wiper motor control circuit - Run/Park Did either of the circuits measure a short to voltage?	Go to Step 4	Go to Step 6
4	1. Disconnect the wiper/washer switch. 2. Retest the circuit that measured short to voltage at the wiper motor connector. Does the circuit still have a short to voltage condition?	Go to Step 7	Go to Step 5

LTV0500000003732

Fig. 252   Wiper Always On, Rear (Part 1 of 2). Tracker

Step	Action	Yes	No
5	Inspect for poor connections at the harness connector of the wiper/washer switch. Did you find and correct the condition?	Go to Step 10	Go to Step 8
6	Inspect for poor connections at the harness connector of the wiper motor. Did you find and correct the condition?	Go to Step 10	Go to Step 9
7	Repair the short to voltage condition. Did you complete the repair?	Go to Step 10	--
8	Replace the rear wiper/washer switch. Did you complete the replacement?	Go to Step 10	--
9	Replace the rear wiper motor. Did you complete the replacement?	Go to Step 10	--
10	Operate the system in order to verify the repair. Did you correct the condition?	System OK	Go to Step 3

LTV0500000003733

Fig. 252   Wiper Always On, Rear (Part 2 of 2). Tracker

Step	Action	Yes	No
1	Did you review the Rear Wiper/Washer System Description and Operation and perform the necessary inspections?	Go to Step 2	Go to Symptoms
2	1. Turn ON the ignition, with the engine OFF. 2. Depress the rear wiper switch to operate the rear wiper. Does the rear wiper operate normally?		Go to Step 3
3	1. Disconnect the rear wiper motor connector. 2. Turn ON the ignition, with the engine OFF. 3. Depress the rear wiper switch to the On position. 4. Connect a test light between cavity 4 of the rear wiper motor connector and a good ground. Does the test light illuminate?	Go to Step 7	Go to Step 4
4	1. Disconnect the rear wiper/washer switch connector. 2. Turn ON the ignition, with the engine OFF. 3. Test the voltage supply circuit at the rear wiper/washer switch connector. Did you find and correct the condition?	Go to Step 12	Go to Step 5

LTV0500000003734

Fig. 253 Wiper Inoperative, Rear (Part 1 of 2). Tracker

Step	Action	Yes	No
	DEFINITION: This table diagnoses the rear wiper operates normally but will not return to the park position when the rear wiper operation is cancelled.		
1	Did you review the Rear Wiper/Washer System Description and Operation and perform the necessary inspections?	Go to Step 2	Go to Symptoms
2	Verify that the rear wiper will not park when the wiper operation is cancelled. Does the rear wiper park?	Test for Intermittent and Poor Connections	Go to Step 3
3	1. Disconnect the rear wiper motor connector. 2. Turn ON the ignition, with the engine OFF. 3. Test for ignition positive supply voltage at the rear wiper motor connector. Did you find and correct the condition?	Go to Step 10	Go to Step 4
4	1. Disconnect the rear wiper/washer switch connector. 2. Test for a high resistance or an open condition between cavity 1 of the rear wiper motor connector and cavity 5 of the rear wiper/washer switch connector. Did you find and correct the condition?	Go to Step 10	Go to Step 5

LTV0500000003736

Fig. 254 Wiper Blade Does Not Park, Rear (Part 1 of 2). Tracker

Step	Action	Yes	No
5	With the rear wiper/washer switch still disconnected: 1. Depress the rear wiper switch to the On position. 2. Test the ON circuit of the rear wiper/washer switch for a high resistance or an open condition. Did you measure a high resistance or an open condition in the rear wiper/washer switch?	Go to Step 8	Go to Step 6
6	Repair the open in the BLU/GRN wire between cavity 4 of the rear wiper motor connector and cavity 4 of the rear wiper/washer switch connector. Did you complete the repair?	Go to Step 12	--
7	Test the ground circuit of the wiper motor for a high resistance or an open condition. Did you find and correct the condition?	Go to Step 12	Go to Step 9
8	Inspect for poor connections at the harness connector of the wiper/washer switch. Did you find and correct the condition?	Go to Step 12	Go to Step 10
9	Inspect for poor connections at the harness connector of the wiper motor. Did you find and correct the condition?	Go to Step 12	Go to Step 11
10	Replace the rear wiper/washer switch. Did you complete the replacement?	Go to Step 12	--
11	Replace the rear wiper motor. Did you complete the replacement?	Go to Step 12	--
12	Operate the system in order to verify the repair. Did you correct the condition?	System OK	Go to Step 3

LTV0500000003735

Fig. 253 Wiper Inoperative, Rear (Part 2 of 2). Tracker

Step	Action	Yes	No
5	With the rear wiper/washer switch still disconnected: 1. Make sure the wiper switch is in the Off position. 2. Test for a high resistance or an open condition between cavity 4 and cavity 5 of the rear wiper/washer switch. Did you measure a high resistance or an open condition?	Go to Step 6	Go to Step 7
6	Inspect for poor connections at the harness connector of the wiper/washer switch. Did you find and correct the condition?	Go to Step 10	Go to Step 8
7	Inspect for poor connections at the harness connector of the wiper motor. Did you find and correct the condition?	Go to Step 10	Go to Step 9
8	Replace the rear wiper/washer switch. Did you complete the replacement?	Go to Step 10	--
9	Replace the rear wiper motor. Did you complete the replacement?	Go to Step 10	--
10	Operate the system in order to verify the repair. Did you correct the condition?	System OK	Go to Step 3

LTV0500000003737

Fig. 254 Wiper Blade Does Not Park, Rear (Part 2 of 2). Tracker

Circuit Description

The intermittent switch in the windshield wiper washer switch is a voltage divider connected across the body control module (BCM) inputs circuits windshield wiper switch signal circuit and windshield wiper switch low reference circuit. The front wiper relay is energized by the BCM switching the front wiper relay control circuit to ground.

The intermittent wiper delay switch has 3 switch positions.

- Delay 1 (500 ohms resistance)
- Delay 2 (1000 ohms resistance)
- Delay 3 (2000 ohms resistance)

DTC Descriptor

This diagnostic procedure supports the following DTC:

DTC B3702 Intermittent Wiper Delay Input Circuit Low

Conditions for Running the DTC

The ignition is in RUN or ACC position.

Conditions for Setting the DTC

The windshield wiper switch signal circuit is shorted to ground or less than 0.20 volts.

Actions Taken When the DTC Sets

- No light will illuminate in the instrument panel (I/P).
- Cannot vary wiper speed
- B3702 is set in the BCM.

LTV0500000003740

Fig. 255 Code B3702: Windshield Wiper Washer Switch (Part 1 of 3). Vue

		Action	Values	Yes	No
3	1. Turn OFF the ignition. 2. Disconnect the windshield wiper washer switch. 3. Turn ON the ignition, with the engine OFF. 4. With a scan tool, observe the wiper delay input in the BCM wiper/washer data list. Is the voltage greater than the specified value?	4.5 V	Go to Step 6	Go to Step 4
4	1. Turn OFF the ignition. 2. Disconnect the BCM connector C2. 3. Check continuity between the windshield wiper switch signal circuit and ground, then between the windshield wiper switch signal circuit and the windshield wiper low reference circuit. Is there continuity?	--	Go to Step 5	Go to Step 7
5	Repair a short to ground in the windshield wiper switch signal circuit. Did you complete the repair?	--	Go to Step 8	--
6	Replace the windshield wiper washer switch. Did you complete the replacement?	--	Go to Step 8	--
7	Replace the BCM. Did you complete the replacement?	--	Go to Step 8	--
8	1. Use the scan tool to clear the DTCs. 2. Operate the vehicle within the conditions for running the DTC, as specified in the supporting text. Does the DTC reset?	--	Go to Step 2	System OK

LTV0500000003742

Fig. 255 Code B3702: Windshield Wiper Washer Switch (Part 3 of 3). Vue

Conditions for Clearing the DTC

- A current DTC clears when the fault is no longer present.
- A history DTC clears when the module ignition cycle counter reaches the reset threshold, without a repeat of the fault.

Diagnostic Aids

- Inspect wiring harness for damage. Inspect for broken or chaffed insulation.
- If fault is suspected to be intermittent, wiggling harness wiring may help in locating fault.
- Inspect for poor connection at the BCM. Inspect harness connectors for backed out terminals, improper terminal mating, broken connector locks, improperly formed or damaged terminals and poor terminal-to-wire connection, terminal is crimped over wire insulation and not conductors.

Step	Action	Values	Yes	No
1	Did you perform the Diagnostic System Check - Vehicle?	--	Go to Step 2	Go to Diagnostic System Check
2	1. Turn ON the ignition, with the engine OFF. 2. With a scan tool, observe the wiper delay input in the body control module (BCM) wiper/washer data list. Is the voltage less than the specified value?	0.4 V	Go to Step 3	Go to Diagnostic Aids

LTV0500000003741

Fig. 255 Code B3702: Windshield Wiper Washer Switch (Part 2 of 3). Vue

Circuit Description

The intermittent switch in the windshield wiper washer switch is a voltage divider connected across the body control module (BCM) inputs circuits, windshield wiper switch signal circuit, and windshield wiper switch low reference circuit. The front wiper relay is energized by the BCM switching the front wiper relay control circuit to ground.

The intermittent wiper delay switch has 3 switch positions.

- Delay 1 (500 ohms resistance)
- Delay 2 (1000 ohms resistance)
- Delay 3 (2000 ohms resistance)

DTC Descriptor

This diagnostic procedure supports the following DTC:

DTC B3703 Intermittent Wiper Delay Input Circuit High

Conditions for Running the DTC

The ignition is in RUN or ACC position.

Conditions for Setting the DTC

- The windshield wiper switch signal circuit is greater than 4.71 volts, open or shorted to voltage.
- The windshield wiper switch low reference circuit is open.

Actions Taken When the DTC Sets

- No light will illuminate in the instrument panel (I/P).
- Cannot vary wiper speed

LTV0500000003743

Fig. 256 Code B3703: Windshield Wiper Washer Intermittent Switch (Part 1 of 4). Vue

Conditions for Clearing the DTC

- A current DTC clears when the fault is no longer present.
- A history DTC clears when the module ignition cycle counter reaches the reset threshold, without a repeat of the fault.

Diagnostic Aids

- Inspect wiring harness for damage. Inspect for broken or chaffed insulation.
- If fault is suspected to be intermittent, wiggling harness wiring may help in locating fault.
- Inspect for poor connection at the BCM. Inspect harness connectors for backed out terminals, improper terminal mating, broken connector locks, improperly formed or damaged terminals and poor terminal-to-wire connection, terminal is crimped over wire insulation and not conductors.

Step	Action	Values	Yes	No
1	Did you perform the Diagnostic System Check - Vehicle?	--	Go to Step 2	Go to Diagnostic System Check
2	1. Turn ON the ignition, with the engine OFF. 2. With a scan tool, observe the wiper delay input in the body control module (BCM) wiper/washer data list. Is the voltage greater than the specified value?	4.71 V	Go to Step 3	Go to Diagnostic Aids

LTV0500000003744

Fig. 256 Code B3703: Windshield Wiper Washer Intermittent Switch (Part 2 of 4). Vue

	Replace the windshield wiper washer switch.			
11	Did you complete the replacement?	-	Go to Step 12	--
12	1. Use the scan tool to clear the DTCs. 2. Operate the vehicle within the conditions for running the DTC, as specified in the supporting text. Does the DTC reset?		Go to Step 2	System OK

LTV0500000003746

Fig. 256 Code B3703: Windshield Wiper Washer Intermittent Switch (Part 4 of 4). Vue

Step	Action	Values	Yes	No
3	1. Turn OFF the ignition. 2. Disconnect the windshield wiper washer switch. 3. Turn ON the ignition, with the engine OFF. 4. Measure the voltage between the windshield wiper switch signal circuit and the windshield wiper switch low reference circuit at the harness connector. Is the voltage less than the specified value?	4 V	Go to Step 4	Go to Step 5
4	Measure the voltage between the windshield wiper switch signal circuit and a good ground. Is the voltage between the specified values?	4-6 V	Go to Step 7	Go to Step 8
5	Is the voltage between the specified values?	4-6 V	Go to Step 6	Go to Step 9
6	Using a fused jumper, jumper the windshield wiper switch signal circuit to the windshield wiper switch low reference circuit at the harness connector. Is the voltage less than the specified value?	0.4 V	Go to Step 11	Go to Step 10
7	Test the windshield wiper switch low reference circuit for an open. Did you find and correct the condition?	--	Go to Step 12	Go to Step 10
8	Test the windshield wiper switch signal circuit for an open. Did you find and correct the condition?	--	Go to Step 12	Go to Step 10
9	Test the windshield wiper switch signal circuit for a short to voltage. Did you find and correct the condition?	--	Go to Step 12	Go to Step 10
10	Replace the BCM. Did you complete the replacement?	--	Go to Step 12	--

LTV0500000003745

Fig. 256 Code B3703: Windshield Wiper Washer Intermittent Switch (Part 3 of 4). Vue

Circuit Description

The body control module (BCM) monitors the windshield washer pump control circuit. When a front windshield wash is requested for more than 2 minutes, the BCM will turn OFF the windshield washer pump if the front wiper is NOT requested by the wiper switch.

Battery voltage for the windshield washer pump is supplied through the FRT WIPER 25 A fuse and windshield wiper washer switch. Grounding for the windshield washer pump is through the OFF position of the rear washer switch, when equipped.

DTC Descriptor

This diagnostic procedure supports the following DTC:

DTC B3708 Front Washer Motor Input High

Conditions for Running the DTC

Ignition is in RUN or ACC position.

Conditions for Setting the DTC

Front windshield washer pump control circuit is shorted to battery voltage for 2 minutes.

Actions Taken When the DTC Sets

- No light will illuminate in the instrument panel (I/P).
- Default turns OFF washer motor after failing DTC if wiper input is not active.

Conditions for Clearing the DTC

- A current DTC clears when the fault is no longer present.
- A history DTC clears when the module ignition cycle counter reaches the reset threshold, without a repeat of the fault.

LTV0500000003747

Fig. 257 Code B3708: Body Control Module (Part 1 of 3). Vue

Diagnostic Aids

- Inspect for poor connection at the BCM. Inspect harness connectors for backed out terminals, improper terminal mating, broken connector locks, improperly formed or damaged terminals and poor terminal-to-wire connection, terminal crimped over wire insulation and not conductors.
- Inspect wiring harness for damage. Inspect for broken or chaffed insulation.
- If fault is suspected to be intermittent, wiggling harness wiring may help in locating fault.

Step	Action	Yes	No
1	Did you perform the Diagnostic System Check - Vehicle? Go to Step 2	Go to Step 2	Go to Diagnostic System Check
2	1. Turn ON the ignition, with the engine OFF. 2. With a scan tool, observe the front washer motor input in the body control module (BCM) wiper/washer data list, while cycling the front washer switch. Does the scan tool indicate the correct washer pump status, ON/OFF?	Go to Diagnostic Aids	Go to Step 3
3	1. Turn OFF the ignition. 2. Disconnect the windshield wiper washer switch. 3. Turn ON the ignition, with the engine OFF. 4. With a scan tool, observe the front washer motor input. Does the scan tool indicate the switch is OFF?	Go to Step 5	Go to Step 4

LTV0500000003748

Fig. 257   Code B3708: Body Control Module (Part 2 of 3). Vue

Circuit Description

The body control module (BCM) monitors the rear window washer switch signal circuit. When a rear windshield wash is requested for more than 2 minutes, the BCM will turn OFF the windshield washer fluid pump motor if the rear wiper is NOT requested by the windshield wiper washer switch.

Power for the windshield washer fluid pump is supplied through the FRT WIPER 25 A fuse and windshield wiper washer switch. Grounding for the windshield washer fluid pump is through the OFF position of the windshield washer fluid pump.

DTC Descriptor

This diagnostic procedure supports the following DTC:

DTC B3713 Rear Washer Motor Input Circuit High

Conditions for Running the DTC

Ignition is in RUN or ACC position.

Conditions for Setting the DTC

Rear window washer switch signal circuit at battery voltage for 2 minutes.

Actions Taken When the DTC Sets

No light will illuminate in the instrument panel (I/P).

Conditions for Clearing the DTC

- A current DTC clears when the fault is no longer present.
- A history DTC clears when the module ignition cycle counter reaches the reset threshold, without a repeat of the fault.

LTV0500000003750

Fig. 258   Code B3713: Rear Window Washer Pump Control Circuit (Part 1 of 3). Vue

Step	Action	Yes	No
4	1. Turn OFF the ignition. 2. Disconnect the BCM connector C2. 3. Test the windshield washer pump control circuit for a short to voltage. Did you find and correct the condition?	Go to Step 7	Go to Step 6
5	Replace the windshield wiper washer switch. Did you complete the replacement?	Go to Step 7	--
6	Replace the BCM. Did you complete the replacement?	Go to Step 7	--
7	1. Use the scan tool to clear the DTCs. 2. Operate the vehicle within the conditions for running the DTC, as specified in the supporting text. Does the DTC reset?	Go to Step 2	System OK

LTV0500000003749

Fig. 257   Code B3708: Body Control Module (Part 3 of 3). Vue

Diagnostic Aids

- Inspect wiring harness for damage.
- Inspect for broken or chaffed insulation.
- If fault is suspected to be intermittent, wiggling harness wiring may help in locating fault.

Step	Action	Yes	No
1	Did you perform the Diagnostic System Check - Vehicle? Go to Step 2	Go to Step 2	Go to Diagnostic System Check
2	1. Turn ON the ignition, with the engine OFF. 2. With a scan tool, observe the rear washer motor input in the body control module (BCM) wiper/washer data list, while cycling the rear washer switch. Does the scan tool indicate the correct washer pump status, ON/OFF?	Go to Diagnostic Aids	Go to Step 3
3	1. Turn OFF the ignition. 2. Disconnect the windshield wiper washer switch. 3. Turn ON the ignition, with the engine OFF. 4. With a scan tool, observe the rear washer motor input. Does the scan tool indicate the switch is OFF?	Go to Step 4	Go to Step 5
4	Using a fused jumper, jumper the windshield wiper washer switch power circuit to the front washer switch circuit and jumper the rear window washer switch circuit to the windshield wiper washer switch ground circuit at the wiper switch harness connector. Does the washer pump motor run?	Go to Step 7	Go to Step 6

LTV0500000003751

Fig. 258   Code B3713: Rear Window Washer Pump Control Circuit (Part 2 of 3). Vue

5	1. Turn OFF the ignition. 2. Disconnect the BCM connector C2. 3. Turn ON the ignition, with the engine OFF. 4. Test the front washer switch circuit and the rear washer switch circuit for a short to voltage. Did you find and correct the condition?	Go to Step 9	Go to Step 8
6	Repair an open in the rear window washer switch circuit or the windshield wiper washer switch ground circuit. Did you complete the repair?	Go to Step 9	--
7	Replace the windshield wiper washer switch. Did you complete the replacement?	Go to Step 9	--
8	Replace the BCM. Did you complete the replacement?	Go to Step 9	--
9	1. Use the scan tool to clear the DTCs. 2. Operate the vehicle within the conditions for running the DTC, as specified in the supporting text. Does the DTC reset?	Go to Step 2	System OK

LTV0500000003752

Fig. 258 Code B3713: Rear Window Washer Pump Control Circuit (Part 3 of 3). Vue

Action Taken When the DTC Sets

- If the front wiper relay control circuit is open or shorted to battery , the Intermittent wiper mode will not operate.
- If the front wiper relay control circuit is shorted to ground, the wipers will always be on
- If the FRT WIPER relay does not receive battery positive voltage from the WIPER SYSTEM relay, all wiper washer functions will be inoperative.
- If any of the circuits that receive battery positive voltage from the FRT WIPER fuse are shorted to ground, the fuse will be open and all wiper washer functions will be inoperative.

Conditions for Clearing the DTC

- This DTC will change from current to history when the fault is no longer present.
- A history DTC will clear after 100 consecutive ignition cycles if the condition for the malfunction is no longer present.

Diagnostic Aids

DTC B3717 indicates a probable failure of the front wiper relay control circuit. However, the DTC will also set if the WIPER SYSTEM relay fails to supply battery positive voltage to the FRT WIPER relay. This failure may be due to an open FRT WIPER 25 amp fuse, or a malfunction of the WIPER SYSTEM relay or associated circuits. All wiper washer functions will be inoperative for both the front windshield and the rear window. If the fuse is open, a short to ground in any one of the following circuits may be the cause:

- Accessory voltage circuit
- Windshield washer pump control circuit
- Windshield wiper motor high speed circuit
- Windshield wiper motor low speed circuit
- Windshield wiper switch Mist/Off/Low signal circuit
- Windshield wiper switch pulse delay signal circuit
- Windshield wiper motor park switch signal circuit
- Rear wiper switch signal circuit
- Rear window washer pump control circuit

If there is no battery positive voltage supply to the FRT WIPER relay and an open FRT WIPER 25 amp fuse is not the cause, test the WIPER SYSTEM relay and associated circuits.

LTV0500000003754

Fig. 259 Codes B3715, B3716, B3717, B3718 & B3719: Front Wiper Relay Control Circuit (Part 2 of 5). Vue

Circuit Description

The body control module (BCM) commands the Intermittent mode of the wipers by switching the front wiper relay control circuit to ground at regular timed intervals. This provides low speed operation of the wiper motor during single swipes of the wipers. Each time the BCM grounds the circuit, the FRT WIPER relay energizes, which closes the switch side contacts of the relay in order to apply battery positive voltage to the windshield wiper motor via the windshield wiper switch MIST/OFF/LOW signal circuit and windshield wiper motor low speed circuit. The BCM monitors the voltage on the front wiper relay control circuit in order to determine when a failure has occurred. When the FRT WIPER relay is energized, the voltage level on the front wiper relay control circuit should be near 0 volts. When the FRT WIPER relay is de-energized, the voltage level should be high, near system voltage.

Control of the wipers during LO or HIGH speed switch settings is direct wired from the windshield wiper washer switch to the wiper motor and is not under the control of the BCM.

DTC Descriptors

This diagnostic procedure supports the following DTCs:

- DTC B3717 Front Wiper Relay Drive Circuit Low
- DTC B3718 Front Wiper Relay Drive Circuit High

Conditions for Running the DTC

The ignition is in the RUN or ACC position.

Conditions for Setting the DTCs

The following conditions will cause these DTCs to set:

- B3717--the BCM detects short to ground or open.
- B3718-- the BCM detects a short to battery voltage.
- For B3718 to set the wiper switch must be in Mist or Intermittent.
- An open FRT WIPER 25 amp fuse
- An open or short to ground in one of the WIPER SYSTEM relay circuits

LTV0500000003753

Fig. 259 Codes B3715, B3716, B3717, B3718 & B3719: Front Wiper Relay Control Circuit (Part 1 of 5). Vue

Test Description

The number below refers to the step number on the diagnostic table.

7. Listen for an audible click when the front wiper relay operates. Command both the ON and OFF states. Repeat the commands, as necessary.

Step	Action	Yes	No
1	Did you perform the Diagnostic System Check - Vehicle?	Go to Step 2	Go to Diagnostic System Check
2	1. Turn ON the ignition, with the engine OFF. 2. Operate the windshield wiper washer switch through all the switch positions. Does the windshield wiper/washer system operate normally?	Test for Intermittent and Poor Connections	Go to Step 3
3	Are the wipers always ON?	Go to Step 12	Go to Step 4
4	Inspect the FRT WIPER 25 amp fuse for an open. Is the fuse open?	Go to Step 5	Go to Step 6
5	1. Replace the FRT WIPER 25 amp fuse with a new one. 2. Attempt to operate all functions of the front and rear wipers and washers. Did the new fuse open?	Go to Step 10	Go to Step 15

LTV0500000003755

Fig. 259 Codes B3715, B3716, B3717, B3718 & B3719: Front Wiper Relay Control Circuit (Part 3 of 5). Vue

6	1. Turn OFF the ignition. 2. Disconnect the FRT WIPER relay in the underhood fuse block (UHFB). 3. Turn ON the ignition, with the engine OFF. 4. With a test lamp connected to a good ground, probe the battery positive voltage supply circuit of the relay at the relay socket terminal. Does the test lamp illuminate?	Go to Step 7	Go to Step 11
7	1. Connect the test lamp between the battery positive voltage circuit and the front wiper relay control circuit at the relay socket terminals. 2. With a scan tool command the front wiper relay ON and OFF under body control module (BCM) special functions. Does the test lamp illuminate when you command the relay ON and go out when you command the relay OFF?	Go to Step 13	Go to Step 8
8	Test the front wiper relay control circuit for an open or a short to voltage. Did you find and correct the condition?	Go to Step 15	Go to Step 9
9	Inspect for poor connections at the harness connector of the BCM. Did you find and correct the condition?	Go to Step 15	Go to Step 14
10	Repair one of the following circuits for a short to ground: • Accessory voltage circuit • Windshield washer pump control circuit • Windshield wiper motor high speed circuit • Windshield wiper motor low speed circuit • Windshield wiper switch Mist/Off/Low signal circuit • Windshield wiper switch pulse delay signal circuit • Windshield wiper motor park switch signal circuit • Rear wiper switch signal circuit • Rear window washer pump control circuit Did you complete the repair?	Go to Step 15	--

LTV0500000003756

Fig. 259 Codes B3715, B3716, B3717, B3718 & B3719: Front Wiper Relay Control Circuit (Part 4 of 5). Vue

Circuit Description

When operation of the rear wiper is selected, battery voltage from the rear wiper switch is applied to the rear wiper switch signal input of the body control module (BCM) circuit. The BCM responds by switching the rear wiper relay control circuit to ground. This action energizes the rear wiper relay, providing power to the rear wiper motor.

DTC Descriptor

This diagnostic procedure supports the following DTC:

DTC B3722 Rear Wiper Relay Drive Circuit Low

Conditions for Running the DTC

The ignition is in RUN or ACC position.

Conditions for Setting the DTC

• The rear wiper relay control circuit is shorted to ground or open.
• The accessory voltage circuit to the coil side of the relay is open .
• The accessory voltage circuit is shorted to ground between the fuse and the rear wiper motor.
• The rear window wiper motor control circuit is shorted to ground.
• The RR WIPER 15-amp fuse is open.

Actions Taken When the DTC Sets

Service (wrench) light will illuminate.

Conditions for Clearing the DTC

• A current DTC clears when the fault is no longer present.
• A history DTC clears when the module ignition cycle counter reaches the reset threshold, without a repeat of the fault.

LTV0500000003758

Fig. 260 Code B3722: Battery Voltage From Rear Wiper Switch (Part 1 of 4). Vue

11	Repair an open or a high resistance in the battery positive voltage supply circuit of the FRT WIPER relay. Did you complete the repair?	Go to Step 15	--
12	Repair a short to ground on the front wiper relay control circuit. Did you complete the repair?	Go to Step 15	--
13	Replace the front wiper relay. Did you complete the replacement?	Go to Step 15	--
14	Replace the BCM. Did you complete the replacement?	Go to Step 15	--
15	1. Use the scan tool to clear the DTCs. 2. Operate the vehicle within the Conditions for Running the DTC, as specified in the supporting text. Does the DTC reset?	Go to Step 2	System OK

LTV0500000003757

Fig. 259 Codes B3715, B3716, B3717, B3718 & B3719: Front Wiper Relay Control Circuit (Part 5 of 5). Vue

Diagnostic Aids

• Inspect for poor connection at the BCM. Inspect harness connectors for backed out terminals, improper terminal mating, broken connector locks, improperly formed or damaged terminals and poor terminal-to-wire connection, terminal crimped over wire insulation and not conductors.
• If the rear wiper relay control circuit is open, the rear wipers will be inoperative.
• If the rear wiper relay control circuit is shorted to ground, the rear wipers will always be ON.
• If, either the accessory voltage circuit, or the rear window wiper motor control circuit is shorted to ground, the RR WIPER fuse will open and the rear wipers will be inoperative.
• Inspect the wiring harness for damage. Inspect for broken or chaffed insulation.
• If the fault is suspected to be intermittent, wiggling the harness wiring may help in locating fault.

Step	Action	Yes	No
1	Did you perform the Diagnostic System Check - Vehicle?	Go to Step 2	Go to Diagnostic System Check
2	1. Turn OFF the ignition. 2. Remove the rear wiper relay from the underhood fuse block (UHFB). 3. Turn ON the ignition, with the engine OFF. 4. Turn the rear wipers ON. 5. With a test lamp connected to a good ground, probe the coil side accessory voltage supply circuit of the relay. 6. With the test lamp still connected to a good ground, probe the switch side accessory voltage supply circuit of the relay. Does the test lamp illuminate for both accessory voltage circuits?	Go to Step 3	Go to Step 4

LTV0500000003759

Fig. 260 Code B3722: Battery Voltage From Rear Wiper Switch (Part 2 of 4). Vue

Step	Action	Yes	No
3	1. Connect the test lamp between the accessory voltage supply circuit and the rear wiper relay control circuit of the relay. 2. Using a scan tool, command the rear wipers ON and OFF. Does the test lamp illuminate when you command ON and go out when you command OFF?	Go to Step 8	Go to Step 7
4	Inspect for an open RR WIPER 15-amp fuse. Is the fuse open?	Go to Step 5	Go to Step 11
5	1. Turn OFF the ignition. 2. Install the rear wiper relay. 3. Replace the RR WIPER fuse with a new one. 4. Turn ON the ignition with the engine OFF. 5. Attempt to operate the rear wipers. Does the RR WIPER fuse open again?	Go to Step 6	Go to Step 15
6	Test the following circuits of the rear wiper motor for a short to ground: • Accessory voltage circuit. • Rear window wiper motor control circuit. Did you find and correct the condition?	Go to Step 15	Go to Step 10
7	Test the rear wiper relay control circuit for an open or a short to ground. Did you find and correct the condition?	Go to Step 15	Go to Step 9
8	Inspect for poor connections and terminal damage at the UHFB. Did you find and correct the condition?	Go to Step 15	Go to Step 14
9	Inspect for poor connections at the harness connector of the body control module (BCM). Did you find and correct the condition?	Go to Step 15	Go to Step 13

LTV0500000003760

Fig. 260   Code B3722: Battery Voltage From Rear Wiper Switch (Part 3 of 4). Vue

Circuit Description

When operation of the rear wiper is selected, battery voltage from the rear wiper switch is applied to the rear wiper switch signal input circuit of the body control module (BCM). The BCM responds by switching the rear wiper relay control circuit to ground. This action energizes the rear wiper relay, providing power to the rear wiper motor.

DTC Descriptor

This diagnostic procedure supports the following DTC:

DTC B3723 Rear Wiper Relay Drive Circuit High

Conditions for Running the DTC

Ignition is in RUN or ACC position.

Conditions for Setting the DTC

• The rear wiper relay control circuit is shorted to battery.
• The rear wiper relay output is ON.

Actions Taken When the DTC Sets

• The service (wrench) light will illuminate.
• The rear wipers are inoperative.

Conditions for Clearing the DTC

• A current DTC clears when the fault is no longer present.
• A history DTC clears when the module ignition cycle counter reaches the reset threshold, without a repeat of the fault.

LTV0500000003762

Fig. 261   Code B3723: Rear Wiper Switch Signal Input (Part 1 of 3). Vue

Step	Action	Yes	No
10	Inspect for poor connections at the harness connector of the rear wiper motor. Did you find and correct the condition?	Go to Step 15	Go to Step 12
11	Repair the open in the accessory voltage supply circuit of the rear wiper relay. Did you complete the repair?	Go to Step 15	--
12	Replace the rear wiper motor. Did you complete the replacement?	Go to Step 15	--
13	Replace the BCM. Did you complete the replacement?	Go to Step 15	--
14	Replace the rear wiper relay. Did you complete the replacement?	Go to Step 15	--
15	1. Use the scan tool to clear the DTCs. 2. Operate the vehicle within the conditions for running the DTC, as specified in the supporting text. Does the DTC reset?	Go to Step 2	System OK

LTV0500000003761

Fig. 260   Code B3722: Battery Voltage From Rear Wiper Switch (Part 4 of 4). Vue

Diagnostic Aids

• When the BCM has been requested to activate the rear wiper relay, the BCM switches the rear wiper relay control circuit to ground. However, if the circuit is shorted to battery voltage, high current flow will result and the BCM output will go into a protective state. The BCM output will not allow itself to be activated for as much as 3 minutes.
• Inspect the harness connectors at the BCM for improper terminal mating, broken connector locks, and improperly formed or damaged terminals.
• Inspect wiring harness for damage. Inspect for broken or chaffed insulation.
• Review all fail information as this may assist in determining the conditions when the fault occurs.
• If the fault is suspected to be intermittent, wiggling the harness wiring may help in locating the fault.

Test Description

The numbers below refer to the step numbers on the diagnostic table.

2. This step will determine if the rear wiper relay is internally shorted to battery voltage. Once you have disconnected the relay, you should be able to clear DTC B3723 with no recurrence. It is, however, normal for DTC B3722 to set while the relay is disconnected.

3. This step will determine if the rear wiper relay control circuit is shorted to battery voltage, or if the BCM is at fault.

Step	Action	Yes	No
1	Did you perform the Diagnostic System Check - Vehicle?	Go to Step 2	Go to Diagnostic System Check

LTV0500000003763

Fig. 261   Code B3723: Rear Wiper Switch Signal Input (Part 2 of 3). Vue

Important

DTC B3722 may set as a result of disconnecting the REAR WIPER Relay.

	Action	Go to Step 5	Go to Step 3
2	1. Turn the front and rear wiper and washer switches OFF. 2. Turn OFF the ignition. 3. Disconnect the REAR WIPER Relay from the underhood fuse block. 4. Turn ON the ignition, with the engine OFF. 5. Use a scan tool to clear DTC B3723. Does DTC B3723 clear?	Go to Step 5	Go to Step 3
3	Test the rear wiper relay control circuit for a short to battery. Did you find and correct the condition?	Go to Step 6	Go to Step 4
4	Replace the body control module (BCM). Did you complete the replacement?	Go to Step 6	--
5	Replace the rear wiper relay. Did you complete the replacement?	Go to Step 6	--
6	1. Use the scan tool to clear the DTCs. 2. Operate the vehicle within the conditions for running the DTC, as specified in the supporting text. Does the DTC reset?	Go to Step 2	System OK

LTV0500000003764

Fig. 261 Code B3723: Rear Wiper Switch Signal Input (Part 3 of 3). Vue

	Action	Yes	No
5	1. Connect the test lamp between the windshield washer pump control circuit and the rear window washer pump control circuit at the windshield washer fluid pump. 2. Turn ON the ignition, with the engine OFF. 3. Press the front washer switch. Does the test lamp illuminate?	Go to Step 9	Go to Step 6
6	1. Turn OFF the ignition. 2. Disconnect the harness connector of the windshield wiper washer switch. 3. With a test lamp connected to battery positive voltage, probe the ground circuit of the harness connector. Does the test lamp illuminate?	Go to Step 10	Go to Step 11
7	1. Turn OFF the ignition. 2. Disconnect the harness connector of the windshield wiper washer switch. 3. Test the rear window washer pump control circuit for an open or a short to ground. Did you find and correct the condition?	Go to Step 14	Go to Step 10
8	1. Turn OFF the ignition. 2. Disconnect the harness connector of the windshield wiper washer switch. 3. Test the windshield washer pump control circuit for an open or a short to ground. Did you find and correct the condition?	Go to Step 14	Go to Step 10
9	Inspect for poor connections at the windshield washer fluid pump. Did you find and correct the condition?	Go to Step 14	Go to Step 12
10	Inspect for poor connections at the windshield wiper washer switch. Did you find and correct the condition?	Go to Step 14	Go to Step 13

LTV0500000003767

Fig. 262 Washers Inoperative (Part 2 of 3). Vue

Step	Action	Yes	No
1	Did you perform the Diagnostic System Check - Vehicle?	Go to Step 2	Go to Diagnostic System Check
2	Verify that the Washers Inoperative complaint is present. Do the washers operate as described in the Description and Operation?	Test for Intermittent Conditions and Poor Connections	Go to Step 3
3	1. Turn OFF the ignition. 2. Disconnect the harness connector of the windshield washer fluid pump. 3. Connect a test lamp from the windshield washer pump control circuit to a good ground . 4. Turn ON the ignition, with the engine OFF. 5. Press the front washer switch. Does the test lamp illuminate?	Go to Step 4	Go to Step 8
4	1. Connect the test lamp from the rear window washer pump control circuit to a good ground. 2. Turn ON the ignition, with the engine OFF. 3. Press the rear washer switch. Does the test lamp illuminate?	Go to Step 5	Go to Step 7

LTV0500000003766

Fig. 262 Washers Inoperative (Part 1 of 3). Vue

	Action	Yes	No
11	Repair the ground circuit for an open or a high resistance. Did you complete the repair?	Go to Step 14	--
12	Replace the windshield washer fluid pump. Did you complete the replacement?	Go to Step 14	--
13	Replace the windshield wiper washer switch. Did you complete the replacement?	Go to Step 14	--
14	Operate the system in order to verify the repair. Did you correct the condition?	System OK	Go to Step 2

LTV0500000003768

Fig. 262 Washers Inoperative (Part 3 of 3). Vue

Step	Action	Yes	No
1	Did you perform the Diagnostic System Check - Vehicle?	Go to Step 2	Go to Diagnostic System Check
2	1. Turn ON the ignition, with the engine OFF. 2. Turn both the front windshield and rear window wiper washer switches OFF. Are the wipers OFF?	Test for Intermittent and Poor Connections	Go to Step 3
3	Are the rear wipers always ON?	Go to Step 4	Go to Step 7
4	1. The rear wipers are always ON. 2. Turn OFF the ignition. 3. Disconnect the rear wiper relay. 4. Turn ON the ignition, with the engine OFF. Are the rear wipers OFF?	Go to Step 5	Go to Step 6
5	1. Turn OFF the ignition. 2. Connect a test lamp between the rear wiper relay control circuit and the accessory voltage side of the rear wiper relay at the rear wiper relay socket terminals. 3. Turn ON the ignition, with the engine OFF. Does the test lamp illuminate?	Go to Step 8	Go to Step 16
6	Test the rear window wiper motor control circuit for a short to voltage. Did you find and correct the condition?	Go to Step 20	Go to Step 14

LTV0500000003769

Fig. 263 Wipers Always On (Part 1 of 3). Vue

Step	Action	Yes	No
7	1. The front wipers are always ON. 2. Turn OFF the ignition. 3. Disconnect the harness connector of the windshield wiper washer switch. 4. Turn ON the ignition, with the engine OFF. Are the front wipers OFF?	Go to Step 9	Go to Step 15
8	1. Turn OFF the ignition. 2. Disconnect the harness connector C2 of the body control module (BCM). 3. Connect a test lamp between the rear wiper switch signal circuit of the harness connector and a good ground. 4. Turn ON the ignition, with the engine OFF. Does the test lamp illuminate?	Go to Step 10	Go to Step 12
9	Connect a test lamp between the windshield wiper switch pulse delay signal circuit of the harness connector and a good ground. Does the test lamp illuminate?	Go to Step 11	Go to Step 13
10	Test the rear wiper switch signal circuit for a short to voltage. Did you find and correct the condition?	Go to Step 20	Go to Step 13
11	Test the windshield wiper switch pulse delay signal circuit for a short to voltage. Did you find and correct the condition?	Go to Step 20	Go to Step 12
12	Inspect for poor connections at the BCM. Did you find and correct the condition?	Go to Step 20	Go to Step 19
13	Inspect for poor connections at the windshield wiper washer switch. Did you find and correct the condition?	Go to Step 20	Go to Step 18
14	Inspect for poor connections at the rear wiper motor. Did you find and correct the condition?	Go to Step 20	Go to Step 17

LTV0500000003770

Fig. 263 Wipers Always On (Part 2 of 3). Vue

Step	Action	Yes	No
15	Repair the windshield wiper motor high speed circuit or the windshield wiper motor low speed circuit for a short to voltage. Did you complete the repair?	Go to Step 20	--
16	Replace the rear wiper relay. Did you complete the replacement?	Go to Step 20	--
17	Replace the rear wiper motor. Did you complete the replacement?	Go to Step 20	--
18	Replace the windshield wiper washer switch. Did you complete the replacement?	Go to Step 20	--
19	Replace the BCM. Did you complete the replacement?	Go to Step 20	--
20	Operate the system in order to verify the repair. Did you correct the condition?	System OK	Go to Step 2

LTV0500000003771

Fig. 263 Wipers Always On (Part 3 of 3). Vue

Step	Action	Yes	No
	DEFINITION: Both the front and rear wipers are inoperative, however the front and rear washers still operate.		
1	Did you perform the Diagnostic System Check - Vehicle?	Go to Step 2	Go to Diagnostic System Check
2	1. Turn ON the ignition, with the engine OFF. 2. Operate the front and rear wiper switches through all switch positions. Does the wiper system operate normally?	Test for Intermittent and Poor Connections	Go to Step 3
3	1. Turn OFF the ignition. 2. Disconnect the windshield wiper washer switch connector. 3. Turn ON the ignition, with the engine OFF. 4. With a test lamp connected to a good ground, probe the accessory voltage feed circuit of the harness connector. Does the test lamp illuminate?	Go to Step 4	Go to Step 5
4	Inspect for poor connections at the harness connector of the windshield wiper washer switch. Did you find and correct the condition?	Go to Step 7	Go to Step 6
5	Repair the open or short to ground in the accessory voltage feed circuit. Did you complete the repair?	Go to Step 7	--

LTV0500000003772

Fig. 264 Wipers Inoperative, All Modes (Part 1 of 2). Vue

Step	Action	Yes	No
6	Replace the windshield wiper washer switch. Did you complete the replacement?	Go to Step 7	--
7	Operate the system in order to verify the repair. Did you correct the condition?	System OK	Go to Step 2

LTV0500000003773

Fig. 264   Wipers Inoperative, All Modes (Part 2 of 2). Vue

Step	Action	Yes	No
7	Important: When the windshield washer mode is activated with the windshield wiper switch OFF, the windshield wipers should wipe the windshield 3-5 times and then park. Are the wipers inoperative for only the Wash mode.	Go to Step 12	Go to Step 8
8	Are the wipers inoperative for only the Park mode?	Go to Step 13	Go to Step 9
9	The wipers are inoperative for only the High speed mode. 1. Disconnect the windshield wiper motor harness connector. 2. With a test lamp connected to ground, probe the windshield wiper motor high speed circuit of the harness connector. 3. Operate the windshield wiper switch to the high speed position. Does the test lamp illuminate?	Go to Step 24	Go to Step 22
10	The windshield wipers are totally inoperative. 1. Disconnect the windshield wiper motor harness connector. 2. With a test lamp connected to battery positive voltage, probe the windshield wiper motor ground circuit. Does the test lamp illuminate?	Go to Step 16	Go to Step 29

LTV0500000003776

Fig. 265   Wipers Inoperative, One Or More Modes, Front (Part 2 of 6). Vue

Step	Action	Yes	No
	DEFINITION: The front windshield wipers are inoperative in one or more modes. The windshield washer still operates.		
1	Did you perform the Diagnostic System Check - Vehicle?	Go to Step 2	Go to Diagnostic System Check
2	1. Turn ON the ignition, with the engine OFF. 2. Operate the windshield wiper switch through all switch positions. 3. Turn the windshield wiper switch OFF. 4. With the windshield wiper switch OFF, operate the front windshield washer switch to ON. Do the windshield wipers operate as described in the Description and Operation?	Test for Intermittent and Poor Connections	Go to Step 3
3	Are the windshield wipers completely inoperative?	Go to Step 10	Go to Step 4
4	Are the windshield wipers inoperative for every mode except High speed?	Go to Step 11	Go to Step 5
5	Are the wipers inoperative in the Intermittent mode?	Go to Step 6	Go to Step 7
6	In addition to the Intermittent mode, are the windshield wipers inoperative for one or both of the following two modes: • Wash • Park	Go to Step 17	Go to Step 14

LTV0500000003775

Fig. 265   Wipers Inoperative, One Or More Modes, Front (Part 1 of 6). Vue

Step	Action	Yes	No
11	The windshield wipers operate only in High speed. 1. Disconnect the windshield wiper motor harness connector. 2. With a test lamp connected to ground, probe the windshield wiper motor low speed circuit of the harness connector. 3. Operate the windshield wiper switch to the low speed position. Does the test lamp illuminate?	Go to Step 24	Go to Step 20
12	The windshield wipers are inoperative for only the Wash mode. 1. Disconnect the body control module (BCM) C2 harness connector. 2. With a test lamp connected to ground, probe the windshield washer pump control circuit of the harness connector. 3. Operate the windshield washer switch to ON. Does the test lamp illuminate?	Go to Step 25	Go to Step 21
13	The wipers are inoperative for only the Park mode. 1. Disconnect the windshield wiper motor harness connector. 2. Test for continuity between the windshield wiper motor park switch signal circuit and ground circuit of the wiper motor, at the wiper motor pins. Is there continuity?	Go to Step 15	Go to Step 24
14	The wipers are inoperative for only the Intermittent mode. 1. Disconnect the body control module (BCM) C2 harness connector. 2. With a test lamp connected to ground, probe the windshield wiper switch pulse delay signal circuit of the harness connector. 3. Operate the windshield washer switch through all of the Intermittent positions. Is the test lamp illuminated for all of the Intermittent positions?	Go to Step 25	Go to Step 23

LTV0500000003777

Fig. 265   Wipers Inoperative, One Or More Modes, Front (Part 3 of 6). Vue

Step	Action	Yes	No
15	1. Connect the windshield wiper motor harness connector. 2. Disconnect the FRT WIPER Relay. 3. With a test lamp connected to battery positive voltage, probe the windshield wiper motor park switch signal circuit of the underhood fuse block. Does the test lamp illuminate?	Go to Step 33	Go to Step 30
16	1. Connect the test lamp between ground and the windshield wiper motor high speed circuit of the harness connector. 2. Operate the windshield wiper switch to the high speed position. 3. Connect the test lamp between ground and the windshield wiper motor low speed circuit of the harness connector. 4. Operate the windshield wiper switch to the low speed position. Does the test lamp illuminate for both the high and the low positions?	Go to Step 24	Go to Step 26
17	1. Turn OFF the ignition. 2. Disconnect the FRT WIPER Relay. 3. Turn ON the ignition, with the engine OFF. 4. With a test lamp connected to ground, probe the accessory voltage feed circuits of the FRT WIPER Relay, at the underhood fuse block. Does the test lamp illuminate?	Go to Step 18	Go to Step 28
18	1. Turn OFF the ignition. 2. Connect a 3 amp fused jumper between the accessory voltage feed circuit and the windshield wiper switch mist/off/low signal circuit, at the underhood fuse block. 3. Turn ON the ignition, with the engine OFF. 4. Turn the windshield wiper switch to the Intermittent position. 5. With a test lamp connected to ground, probe the windshield wiper switch mist/off/low signal circuit, at the windshield wiper switch terminal. Does the test lamp illuminate?	Go to Step 19	Go to Step 27
19	With the test lamp connected to ground, probe the windshield wiper switch low speed circuit, at the windshield wiper switch terminal. Does the test lamp illuminate?	Go to Step 33	Go to Step 26

LTV0500000003778

Fig. 265 Wipers Inoperative, One Or More Modes, Front (Part 4 of 6). Vue

Step	Action	Yes	No
20	Test the windshield wiper motor low speed circuit for an open. Did you find and correct the condition?	Go to Step 35	Go to Step 26
21	Test the windshield washer pump control circuit for an open. Did you find and correct the condition?	Go to Step 35	Go to Step 26
22	Test the windshield wiper motor high speed circuit for an open. Did you find and correct the condition?	Go to Step 35	Go to Step 26
23	Test the windshield wiper switch pulse delay signal circuit for an open. Did you find and correct the condition?	Go to Step 35	Go to Step 26
24	Inspect for poor connections at the harness connector of the windshield wiper motor. Did you find and correct the condition?	Go to Step 35	Go to Step 32
25	Inspect for poor connections at the harness connector of the body control module (BCM). Did you find and correct the condition?	Go to Step 35	Go to Step 34
26	Inspect for poor connections at the harness connector of the windshield wiper washer switch. Did you find and correct the condition?	Go to Step 35	Go to Step 31
27	Repair the windshield wiper switch mist/off/low signal circuit for an open or a high resistance. Did you complete the repair?	Go to Step 35	--

LTV0500000003779

Fig. 265 Wipers Inoperative, One Or More Modes, Front (Part 5 of 6). Vue

Step	Action	Yes	No
28	Repair the accessory voltage feed circuit for an open or a high resistance. Did you complete the repair?	Go to Step 35	--
29	Repair the open ground circuit. Did you complete the repair?	Go to Step 35	--
30	Repair the windshield wiper motor park switch signal circuit for an open or a high resistance. Did you complete the repair?	Go to Step 35	--
31	Replace the windshield wiper washer switch. Did you complete the replacement?	Go to Step 35	--
32	Replace the windshield wiper motor. Did you complete the replacement?	Go to Step 35	--
33	Replace the FRT WIPER relay. Did you complete the replacement?	Go to Step 35	--
34	Replace the BCM. Did you complete the replacement?	Go to Step 35	--
35	Operate the system in order to verify the repair. Did you correct the condition?	System OK	Go to Step 2

LTV0500000003780

Fig. 265 Wipers Inoperative, One Or More Modes, Front (Part 6 of 6). Vue

Step	Action	Yes	No
	DEFINITION: The rear wiper is inoperative in one or more modes, however the rear washer still operates.		
1	Did you perform the Diagnostic System Check - Vehicle?	Go to Step 2	Go to Diagnostic System Check
2	1. Turn ON the ignition, with the engine OFF. 2. Turn the rear window wiper switch ON. Does the rear window wiper operate?	Go to Step 3	Go to Step 5
3	1. Turn the rear window wiper switch OFF. 2. With the rear window wiper switch OFF, turn the rear window washer switch ON. Does the rear window wiper operate?	Go to Step 4	Go to Step 7
4	**Important:** Unless the rear window wiper is being operated for the Wash mode, it operates only in the delay modes. When the rear wiper is ON, it should stop at the parked position in between timed strokes of the wiper. When the rear wiper is turned OFF, it should park and remain in the parked position until either the wiper or wash mode is operated again. Does the rear window wiper Park in the full down position as it should?	Test for Intermittent and Poor Connections	Go to Step 9
5	**Turn the rear window washer switch ON.** **Does the rear window wiper operate?**	Go to Step 8	Go to Step 6

LTV0500000003782

Fig. 266 Wipers Inoperative, One Or More Modes, Rear (Part 1 of 4). Vue

Step	Action		
6	1. Turn OFF the ignition. 2. Remove the REAR WIPER Relay from the underhood fuse block. 3. Turn ON the ignition, with the engine OFF. 4. With a test lamp connected to a good ground, probe the accessory voltage feed circuit to the switch side of the relay at the underhood fuse block. Does the test lamp illuminate?	Go to Step 10	Go to Step 20
7	1. Disconnect the body control module (BCM) C2 harness connector. 2. With a test lamp connected to ground, probe the rear window washer pump control circuit. 3. Operate the rear window washer switch to ON while the rear window wiper switch is OFF. Does the test lamp illuminate?	Go to Step 17	Go to Step 13
8	1. Disconnect the body control module (BCM) C2 harness connector. 2. With a test lamp connected to ground, probe the rear wiper switch signal circuit. 3. Operate the rear window wiper switch to ON. Does the test lamp illuminate?	Go to Step 17	Go to Step 14
9	1. Turn OFF the ignition. 2. Disconnect the harness connector of the rear window wiper motor. 3. Turn ON the ignition, with the engine OFF. 4. With a test lamp connected to a good ground, probe the accessory voltage circuit of the rear window wiper motor. Does the test lamp illuminate?	Go to Step 16	Go to Step 19
10	1. Turn OFF the ignition 2. Connect a 3 amp fused jumper wire between the accessory voltage feed circuit terminal and the rear window wiper motor control circuit terminal at the underhood fuse block. 3. Turn the ignition ON, with the engine OFF. Does the rear wiper operate?	Go to Step 24	Go to Step 11

LTV0500000003783

Fig. 266   Wipers Inoperative, One Or More Modes, Rear (Part 2 of 4). Vue

Step	Action		
11	1. Ensure that the fused jumper wire between the accessory voltage feed circuit terminal and the rear window wiper motor control circuit terminal is still connected. 2. With a test lamp connected to a good ground, probe the rear window wiper motor control circuit at the rear wiper motor. Does the test lamp illuminate?	Go to Step 12	Go to Step 21
12	Connect the test lamp between the rear window wiper motor control circuit and the rear window wiper motor ground circuit. Does the test lamp illuminate?	Go to Step 16	Go to Step 18
13	Test the rear window washer pump control circuit for an open or a high resistance. Did you find and correct the condition?	Go to Step 26	Go to Step 15
14	Test the rear wiper switch signal circuit for an open or a high resistance. Systems. Did you find and correct the condition?	Go to Step 26	Go to Step 15
15	Inspect for poor connections at the harness connector of the windshield wiper washer switch. Did you find and correct the condition?	Go to Step 26	Go to Step 22
16	Inspect for poor connections at the harness connector of the rear window wiper motor. Did you find and correct the condition?	Go to Step 26	Go to Step 23
17	Inspect for poor connections at the harness connector of the BCM. Did you find and correct the condition?	Go to Step 26	Go to Step 25
18	Repair the rear window wiper motor ground circuit for an open or a high resistance. Did you complete the repair?	Go to Step 26	--

LTV0500000003784

Fig. 266   Wipers Inoperative, One Or More Modes, Rear (Part 3 of 4). Vue

19	Repair the accessory voltage circuit, between the REAR WIPER Relay splice and the wiper motor, for an open or a high resistance. Did you complete the repair?	Go to Step 26	--
20	Repair the open or high resistance in the accessory voltage feed circuit. Did you complete the repair?	Go to Step 26	--
21	Repair the open or high resistance in the rear window wiper motor control circuit.] Did you complete the repair?	Go to Step 26	--
22	Replace the windshield wiper washer switch. Did you complete the replacement?	Go to Step 26	--
23	Replace the rear window wiper motor. Did you complete the replacement?	Go to Step 26	--
24	Replace the rear wiper relay. Did you complete the replacement?	Go to Step 26	--
25	Replace the BCM. Did you complete the replacement?	Go to Step 26	--
26	Operate the system in order to verify the repair. Did you correct the condition?	System OK	Go to Step 2

LTV0500000003785

Fig. 266 Wipers Inoperative, One Or More Modes, Rear (Part 4 of 4). Vue

AIR BAG SYSTEM

NOTE: Refer To "Computer Relearn Procedures" Located In The Front Of This Manual When Battery Power To The Computer Has Been Interrupted.

INDEX

	Page No.
Air Bag System Disarming &	
Arming	4-2
Arming	4-2
Disarming	4-2
Collision Inspection	4-2
Accident With Deployment	4-2
Accident With Or Without	
Deployment	4-2
General	4-2
Sensor Replacement	
Guidelines	4-3
Component Locations	4-2
Component Service	4-3
Driver Air Bag Module, Replace	4-3
Astro & Safari	4-3
Avalanche, Escalade EXT,	
Sierra, Silverado & SSR	4-3
Aztez & Rendezvous	4-3
Blazer, Bravada, Envoy,	
Rainier & Trailblazer	4-3
Canyon, Colorado, Sonoma &	
S10	4-4
Equinox & Torrent	4-4
Escalade, Escalade ESV,	
Suburban, Tahoe & Yukon	4-4
Express & Savana	4-4
HHR	4-4
Hummer H2 & H3	4-4
Montana, Silhouette &	
Venture	4-4
Relay, SV6, Terraza &	
Uplander	4-4
SRX	4-4
Tracker	4-5
VUE	4-5
Forward Discriminating Sensors,	
Replace	4-7
Astro & Safari	4-7
Avalanche, Escalade EXT,	
Sierra, Silverado & SSR	4-8
Aztez & Rendezvous	4-8
Blazer, Bravada, Envoy,	
Rainier & Trailblazer	4-8
Canyon, Colorado, Sonoma &	
S10	4-8
Equinox & Torrent	4-9
Escalade, Escalade ESV,	
Suburban, Tahoe & Yukon	4-9
Express & Savana	4-9
HHR	4-9
Hummer H2 & H3	4-9
Montana, Silhouette &	
Venture	4-9
Relay, SV6, Terraza &	
Uplander	4-10
SRX	4-10
Passenger Air Bag Module,	
Replace	4-5
Astro & Safari	4-5

	Page No.
Avalanche, Escalade,	
Escalade ESV, Escalade	
EXT, Sierra, Silverado, SSR,	
Suburban, Tahoe, Yukon	4-5
Aztek & Rendezvous	4-5
Blazer, Bravada, Envoy,	
Rainier & Trailblazer	4-5
Canyon, Colorado, Sonoma &	
S10	4-5
Equinox & Torrent	4-5
Express & Savana	4-6
HHR	4-6
Hummer H2 & H3	4-6
Montana, Silhouette, Trans	
Sport & Venture	4-6
Relay, SV6, Terraza &	
Uplander	4-6
SRX	4-6
Tracker	4-6
VUE	4-6
SIR Coil Assembly, Replace	4-14
Astro & Safari	4-14
Avalanche, Escalade EXT,	
Sierra, Silverado & SSR	4-15
Aztez & Rendezvous	4-15
Blazer, Bravada, Envoy,	
Rainier & Trailblazer	4-16
Canyon, Colorado, Sonoma &	
S10	4-16
Equinox & Torrent	4-16
Escalade, Escalade ESV,	
Suburban, Tahoe & Yukon	4-17
Express & Savana	4-17
HHR	4-18
Hummer H2 & H3	4-18
Montana, Silhouette &	
Venture	4-18
Relay, SV6, Terraza &	
Uplander	4-19
SRX	4-19
Tracker	4-19
VUE	4-19
Seat Belt Pretensioner,	
Replace	
Aztez & Rendezvous	4-10
Canyon, Colorado, Sonoma &	
S10	4-10
Equinox & Torrent	4-10
Express & Savana	4-10
HHR	4-10
Montana, Silhouette &	
Venture	4-10
Relay, SV6, Terraza &	
Uplander	4-10
SRX	4-11
VUE	4-11
Sensing & Diagnostic Module	
(SDM), Replace	4-11
Astro & Safari	4-11

	Page No.
Avalanche, Escalade EXT,	
Sierra, Silverado & SSR	4-11
Aztez & Rendezvous	4-11
Blazer, Bravada, Envoy,	
Rainier & Trailblazer	4-11
Canyon, Colorado, Sonoma &	
S10	4-11
Equinox & Torrent	4-12
Escalade, Escalade ESV,	
Suburban, Tahoe & Yukon	4-12
Express & Savana	4-12
HHR	4-12
Hummer H2 & H3	4-12
Montana, Silhouette &	
Venture	4-12
Relay, SV6, Terraza &	
Uplander	4-12
SRX	4-13
Tracker	4-13
VUE	4-13
Side Impact Air Bag Module,	
Replace	4-7
Avalanche, Escalade EXT,	
Sierra, Silverado & SSR	4-7
Aztez & Rendezvous	4-7
Montana, Silhouette &	
Venture	4-7
Relay, SV6, Terraza &	
Uplander	4-7
SRX	4-7
Side Impact Sensor, Replace	4-13
Avalanche, Escalade EXT,	
Sierra, Silverado & SSR	4-13
Aztez & Rendezvous	4-13
Blazer, Bravada, Envoy,	
Rainier & Trailblazer	4-13
Canyon, Colorado, Sonoma &	
S10	4-13
Equinox & Torrent	4-13
Escalade, Escalade ESV,	
Suburban, Tahoe & Yukon	4-14
HHR	4-14
Hummer H2 & H3	4-14
Montana, Silhouette &	
Venture	4-14
Relay, SV6, Terraza &	
Uplander	4-14
SRX	4-14
VUE	4-14
Description & Operation	4-2
Diagnosis & Testing	4-2
Precautions	4-2
Battery Ground Cable	4-2
Deployed Air Bags	4-2
Live Air Bags	4-2
Sensors	4-2
Seat Belt Pretensioner Arming	
& Disarming	4-2
Tightening Specifications	4-21

AIR BAG SYSTEM DISARMING & ARMING

Disarming

Refer to "Air Bag System Procedures" in the front of this manual for air bag system disarming procedures.

Arming

Refer to "Air Bag System Procedures" in the front of this manual for air bag system arming procedures.

SEAT BELT PRETENSIONER ARMING & DISARMING

On models with seat belt pretensioners, refer to "Air Bag System Disarming & Arming" for arming and disarming procedures.

DESCRIPTION & OPERATION

The SIR system helps supplement the protection offered by the seat belt by deploying an driver air bag module from the center of the steering wheel, passenger air bag module, side impact air bag module, roof panel air bag module, door panel air bag module, rear side impact air bag module and or a knee blocker air bag module.

PRECAUTIONS

Battery Ground Cable

Prior to service, disconnect battery ground cable and isolate as required.

Live Air Bags

When carrying a live air bag module, ensure air bag opening is pointed away from body. This will reduce the chance of injury in the event of accidental deployment. Never carry module by the wires or connector on underside of module. When placing a live module on a bench or other surface, always face the bag and trim cover upward.

Do not expose modules to temperatures above 150°F. Verify correct replacement part number. Do not substitute a component from different vehicle. Use only OEM replacement components. Do not use salvaged components for repairs to the SIR system. Discard any component if it has been dropped from a height more than 3 ft.

Deployed Air Bags

Always wear gloves and safety glasses when handling a deployed air bag and module. After deployment, the metal sur-

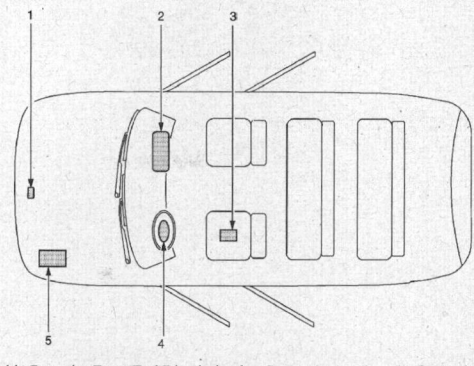

(1) Inflatable Restraint Front End Discriminating Sensor-Located on the front of the vehicle in the engine compartment
(2) Inflatable Restraint I/P Module-Located at the top right under the instrument panel
(3) Inflatable Restraint Sensing and Diagnostic Module (SDM)-Located underneath the LF/driver seat
(4) Inflatable Restraint Steering Wheel Module-Located on the steering wheel
(5) Battery-Located under Hood on the left side

LTV0500000003437

Fig. 1 SIR component location. Astro & Safari

faces of the module will be very hot and the surface of the deployed air bag may be covered with sodium hydroxide which can irritate skin.

Sensors

Caution should be used to ensure proper location of sensor to the mounting brackets. The keying of the sensors through the wiring harness connectors must not be modified for any reason.

COMPONENT LOCATIONS

Refer to **Figs. 1 through 22** for air bag system component locations.

DIAGNOSIS & TESTING

Refer to **MOTOR's "Air Bag Manual" or "Air Bag Diagnostics CD"** for air bag system diagnosis and testing procedures.

COLLISION INSPECTION

General

Proper operation of sensors and the Supplemental Inflatable Restraint (SIR) system requires any repairs to the vehicle structure return it to the original production configuration. Deployment requires, at a minimum, replacement of sensors in the area of accident damage, module and dimensional inspection of the steering column. Any visible damage to the DERM mounting brackets requires replacement. Any visible damage to the sensors in the area of accident damage must be replaced and the steering column must be dimensionally inspected whether deployment occurred or not.

1. If any SIR system components are damaged, they must be replaced. If

SIR component mounting points are damaged, they must be repaired or replaced.
2. Never use SIR components from another vehicle. This does not include remanufactured components purchased from an authorized GM dealer; they may be used for SIR repairs.
3. Do not attempt to service discriminating sensors, arming sensor, DERM, SIR coil assembly or module. Service of these items is by replacement only.
4. Verify part number of replacement module. Some GM modules look identical but contain different internal components.
5. After deployment has occurred, SIR diagnostic trouble codes (DTCs) must be cleared using scan tool "Clear Codes" command. This must be done to cause air bag warning lamp to go off.

Accident With Deployment

The following SIR components must be replaced or inspected for damage after a frontal crash involving air bag deployment:
1. Air bag module(s).
2. Sensors, if in area of accident damage. Refer to "Sensor Replacement Guidelines" for important information on sensor replacement in crashes.
3. SIR coil assembly. Inspect wiring and connector for any signs of scorching, melting or damage due to excessive heat. Replace if damaged as outlined under "Component Service."

Accident With Or Without Deployment

The following SIR and restraint system components must be inspected after any crash, whether the air bag deployed or not:
1. Steering column. Inspect dimensions.
2. Sensors, if in area of accident damage. Refer to "Sensor Replacement Guidelines" for important information on sensor replacement in both deployment

and non-deployment crashes.

3. Knee bolster and mounting points. Inspect for any distortion, bending, cracking or other damage.
4. Instrument panel braces. Inspect for any distortion, bending, cracking or other damage.
5. Seat belts and mounting points.

Sensor Replacement Guidelines

SIR sensor replacement policy requires replacement of the sensors in the area of accident damage only.

The area of accident damage is defined as that area of the vehicle which is crushed, bent or damaged in other ways. An example might be a significant front-end collision in which forward portions of vehicle have contacted another vehicle, tree, guardrail, etc. In this example, a sensor on the front of the vehicle, such as the radiator tie bar, would require replacement, since that portion of the vehicle was damaged in the accident.

Sensors in the area of accident damage should be replaced even if those sensors do not appear to be damaged. Do not attempt to determine whether a sensor is satisfactory. Always replace the sensor if it is in the area of accident damage.

Also, if a sensor is in an area of accident damage but the SIR system has not been deployed, replace the sensor. The sensor bracket may be slightly bent, wiring may be damaged, etc., and the sensor might not work properly in another collision. Again, do not attempt to determine whether a sensor is satisfactory. Always replace the sensor if it is in the area of accident damage.

COMPONENT SERVICE

Prior to service, disconnect battery ground cable and isolate as required.

Refer to "Tightening Specifications" chart when installing components. **All sensors and mounting bracket bolts must be carefully torqued to ensure proper operation. never power up the air bag system when any sensor is not rigidly attached to the vehicle, since the sensor could be activated when not attached, causing air bag deployment.**

Driver Air Bag Module, Replace

ASTRO & SAFARI

1. Disarm system as outlined under "Air Bag System Disarming & Arming."
2. Turn steering wheel 90° to access rear shroud holes, insert screwdriver and push leaf spring to release pin.
3. Turn steering wheel 180° to access rear shroud holes, insert screwdriver and push leaf spring to release pin.
4. Tilt module rearward from top, remove SIR lead wire from module and steering wheel.

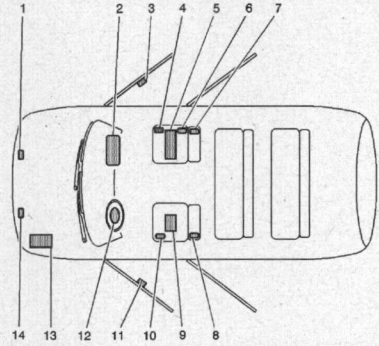

(1) Inflatable Restraint Front End Sensor-Right-Located on the front frame crossmember
(2) Inflatable Restraint I/P Module-Located at the right front of the instrument panel cluster (IPC)
(3) Inflatable Restraint Side Impact Sensor (SIS)-Right-Located under the right front door trim near the lower rear of the door frame
(4) Inflatable Restraint Seat Position Sensor (SPS)-Right-Located on the right front outboard seat track
(5) Inflatable Restraint Passenger Presence System (PPS)-Located under the right front seat mounted to the seat frame
(6) Inflatable Restraint Seat Belt Tension Retractor Sensor-Located on the outboard lower seat belt anchor
(7) Inflatable Restraint Side Impact Module-Right-Located on the side of the right front seat back
(8) Inflatable Restraint Side Impact Module-Left-Located on the side of the left front seat back
(9) Inflatable Restraint Sensing and Diagnostic Module (SDM)-Located under the left front seat under the carpet
(10) Inflatable Restraint Seat Position Sensor (SPS)-Left-Located on the left front outboard seat track
(11) Inflatable Restraint Side Impact Sensor (SIS)-Left-Located under the left front door trim near the lower rear of the door frame
(12) Inflatable Restraint Steering Wheel Module-Located on the steering wheel
(13) Battery-Located under the hood on the left side
(14) Inflatable Restraint Front End Sensor-Left-Located on the front frame crossmember

LTV0500000003438

Fig. 2 SIR component location. Avalanche, Escalade, Escalade ESV, Escalade EXT, Suburban, Tahoe & Yukon

5. Remove CPA and retainer, then the module.
6. Reverse procedure to install, then arm system as outlined under "Air Bag System Disarming & Arming."

AVALANCHE, ESCALADE EXT, SIERRA, SILVERADO & SSR

1. Disarm system as outlined under "Air Bag System Disarming & Arming."
2. Turn steering wheel 90° to access rear shroud holes, insert screwdriver and push leaf spring to release pin.
3. Turn steering wheel 180° to access rear shroud holes, insert screwdriver and push leaf spring to release pin.
4. Tilt module rearward from top, remove SIR lead wire from module and steering wheel.
5. Remove CPA and retainer, then the module.
6. Reverse procedure to install, then arm system as outlined under "Air Bag System Disarming & Arming."

AZTEZ & RENDEZVOUS

1. Disarm system as outlined under "Air Bag System Disarming & Arming."
2. Install and adjust tool No. J 44298, or equivalent into back two holes of steering wheel.
3. Push handle back toward IP releasing two spring loaded fasteners.
4. Turn steering wheel to open air bag tool.

5. Remove cruise control lever cover, then insert air bag tool around cruise control lever to release cruise control.
6. Remove driver air bag module.
7. Remove connector position assurance (CPA).
8. Remove driver air bag module electrical connector.
9. Remove horn ground lead.
10. Rotate horn contact lead ¼ turn counterclockwise, then remove.
11. Remove inflatable restraint steering module.
12. Reverse procedure to install, then arm system as outlined under "Air Bag System Disarming & Arming."

BLAZER, BRAVADA, ENVOY, RAINIER & TRAILBLAZER

1. Disarm system as outlined under "Air Bag System Disarming & Arming."
2. Turn steering wheel 90° to access rear shroud holes, insert screwdriver and push leaf spring to release pin.
3. Turn steering wheel 180° to access rear shroud holes, insert screwdriver and push leaf spring to release pin.
4. Tilt module rearward from top, remove SIR lead wire from module and steering wheel.
5. Remove CPA and retainer, then the module.
6. Reverse procedure to install, then arm system as outlined under "Air Bag System Disarming & Arming."

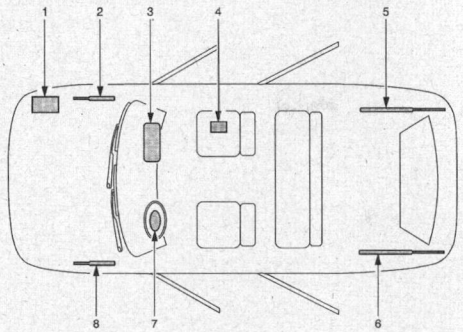

(1) Vehicle Battery - Located under the hood on the right side

(2) Front Hood Assist Rod - A gas shock located under the front hood on the passenger side

(3) I/P Air Bag - Located at the top right under the instrument panel

(4) Sensing and Diagnostic Module (SDM) - Located underneath the passenger front seat

(5) Rear Compartment Lid Assist Rod - A gas shock is located under the rear trunk lid on the passenger side

(6) Rear Compartment Lid Assist Rod - A gas shock is located under the rear trunk lid on the driver side

(7) Steering Wheel Air Bag - Located on the steering wheel

(8) Front Hood Assist Rod - A gas shock located under the front hood on the driver side

LTV0500000003439

Fig. 3 SIR component location. Aztek

CANYON, COLORADO, SONOMA & S10

1. Disarm system as outlined under "Air Bag System Disarming & Arming."
2. Turn steering wheel 90° to access rear shroud holes, insert screwdriver and push leaf spring to release pin.
3. Turn steering wheel 180° to access rear shroud holes, insert screwdriver and push leaf spring to release pin.
4. Tilt module rearward from top, remove SIR lead wire from module and steering wheel.
5. Remove CPA and retainer, then the module.
6. Reverse procedure to install, then arm system as outlined under "Air Bag System Disarming & Arming."

EQUINOX & TORRENT

1. Disarm system as outlined under "Air Bag System Disarming & Arming."
2. Rotate steering wheel until one of triangular openings is accessible with a small flat-bladed tool.
3. Insert small flat-bladed tool into triangular opening to release steering wheel inflatable restraint module from steering wheel.
4. Rotate steering wheel 180° and insert small flat-bladed tool into triangular opening to release steering wheel inflatable restraint module from steering wheel.
5. Disconnect horn switch and inflatable restraint electrical connectors.
6. Remove inflatable restraint steering wheel module.
7. Reverse procedure to install, then arm system as outlined under "Air Bag System Disarming & Arming."

ESCALADE, ESCALADE ESV, SUBURBAN, TAHOE & YUKON

1. Disarm system as outlined under "Air Bag System Disarming & Arming."
2. Turn steering wheel 90° to access rear

shroud holes, insert screwdriver and push leaf spring to release pin.
3. Turn steering wheel 180° to access rear shroud holes, insert screwdriver and push leaf spring to release pin.
4. Tilt module rearward from top, remove SIR lead wire from module and steering wheel.
5. Remove CPA and retainer, then the module.
6. Reverse procedure to install, then arm system as outlined under "Air Bag System Disarming & Arming."

EXPRESS & SAVANA

1. Disarm system as outlined under "Air Bag System Disarming & Arming."
2. Turn steering wheel 90° to access rear shroud holes, insert screwdriver and push leaf spring to release pin.
3. Turn steering wheel 180° to access rear shroud holes, insert screwdriver and push leaf spring to release pin.
4. Tilt module rearward from top, remove SIR lead wire from module and steering wheel.
5. Remove CPA and retainer, then the module.
6. Reverse procedure to install, then arm system as outlined under "Air Bag System Disarming & Arming."

HHR

1. Disarm system as outlined under "Air Bag System Disarming & Arming."
2. On back side of steering wheel are two openings, place wheel so that one opening is on top.
3. Using a blunt-ended tool, push spring fastener inward through access hole. Repeat step for other opening.
4. Remove connector position assurance (CPA) retainer.
5. Disconnect electrical connectors.
6. Remove module.
7. Reverse procedure to install, then arm system as outlined under "Air Bag System Disarming & Arming."

HUMMER H2 & H3

1. Disarm system as outlined under "Air Bag System Disarming & Arming."
2. Using a blunt-ended tool, push leaf spring fasteners inward through access holes. Access holes are located on both sides of steering wheel shroud.
3. Lift and partially remove inflatable restraint steering wheel module from steering wheel in order to expose electrical connectors.
4. Disconnect connector-position assurance (CPA) retainers from electrical connectors.
5. Disconnect electrical connectors from inflatable restraint steering wheel module.
6. Remove inflatable restraint module from steering wheel. **Do not attempt to repair inflatable restraint steering wheel module. Inflatable restraint steering wheel module is replaced only as an assembly.**
7. Fully deploy module before disposal. If module was replaced under warranty, fully deploy and dispose of module after required retention period.
8. Reverse procedure to install, then arm system as outlined under "Air Bag System Disarming & Arming."

MONTANA, SILHOUETTE & VENTURE

1. Disarm system as outlined under "Air Bag System Disarming & Arming."
2. Insert suitable screwdriver into back of steering wheel, turn screwdriver counterclockwise to disengage spring from slot in module.
3. Remove driver air bag module from steering wheel.
4. Perform previous steps for remaining holes.
5. Remove CPA connector.
6. Remove electrical connectors from module.
7. Remove horn ground connector.
8. Remove horn contact lead from steering column cam tower.
9. Reverse procedure to install, then arm system as outlined under "Air Bag System Disarming & Arming."

RELAY, SV6, TERRAZA & UPLANDER

1. Disarm system as outlined under "Air Bag System Disarming & Arming."
2. On back side of steering wheel are 4 openings; place wheel so that two openings are on top.
3. Install tool no. J 44298 and pull handle back toward steering wheel, away from steering column, releasing spring loaded fasteners at same time. Repeat steps for other two openings.
4. Remove module.
5. Reverse procedure to install, then arm system as outlined under "Air Bag System Disarming & Arming."

SRX

1. Disarm system as outlined under "Air Bag System Disarming & Arming."

2. On back side of steering wheel are three openings for removing steering wheel module.
3. Adjust and install tool no. J 44298 into one of holes.
4. Pull handle of air bag tool away from instrument panel releasing one of spring loaded fasteners. **Seat air bag removal tool all way in to perform properly.**
5. Repeat this step for other two fasteners.
6. Pull inflatable restraint module gently away from steering wheel.
7. Remove connector position assurance and electrical connector from steering wheel module.
8. Remove horn contact lead from steering column cam tower.
9. Remove steering wheel module.
10. Reverse procedure to install, then Arm system as outlined under "Air Bag System Disarming & Arming."

TRACKER

1. Disarm system as outlined under "Air Bag System Disarming & Arming."
2. Remove module bolts and screws from steering wheel back.
3. Remove inflatable restraint steering wheel module.
4. Remove electrical connectors from module.
5. Reverse procedure to install, then Arm system as outlined under "Air Bag System Disarming & Arming."

VUE

1. Disarm system as outlined under "Air Bag System Disarming & Arming."
2. On back side of steering wheel are two circular openings, place wheel so that one opening is on top.
3. Using a blunt-ended tool, push spring fastener inward through access hole. Repeat step for other opening.
4. Release connector position assurance retainer.
5. Disconnect electrical connectors.
6. Remove module.
7. Fully deploy module before disposal. If module was replaced under warranty, fully deploy and dispose of module after required retention period.
8. Reverse procedure to install, then Arm system as outlined under "Air Bag System Disarming & Arming."

Passenger Air Bag Module, Replace

ASTRO & SAFARI

1. Disarm system as outlined under "Air Bag System Disarming & Arming."
2. Remove passenger knee bolster panel.
3. Disconnect CPA connector, electrical connectors and pigtail connector mounting clip.
4. Remove passenger air bag module mounting bolts, then the air bag module.
5. Reverse procedure to install, tighten to specifications, then Arm system as

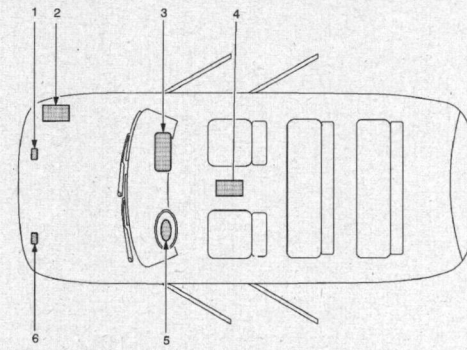

(1) Inflatable Restraint Front End Sensor - Right-Located on the front of the vehicle in the engine compartment
(2) Battery-Located under Hood on the right side
(3) Inflatable Restraint I/P Module-Located at the top right under the instrument panel
(4) Inflatable Restraint Sensing and Diagnostic Module (SDM)-Located under center floor console
(5) Inflatable Restraint Steering Wheel Module-Located on the steering wheel
(6) Inflatable Restraint Front End Sensor - Left-Located on the front of the vehicle in the engine compartment

LTVC500000003441

Fig. 4   SIR component location. Blazer

outlined under "Air Bag System Disarming & Arming."

AZTEK & RENDEZVOUS

1. Disarm system as outlined under "Air Bag System Disarming & Arming."
2. Remove glove compartment and lamp electrical connector.
3. Remove passenger air bag module pigtail harness clips from bracket.
4. Remove passenger air bag module attaching fasteners to IP.
5. Remove passenger air bag module attaching bolts to cross-car beam.
6. Remove passenger air bag module.
7. Reverse procedure to install, tighten to specifications, then Arm system as outlined under "Air Bag System Disarming & Arming."

BLAZER, BRAVADA, ENVOY, RAINIER & TRAILBLAZER

1. Disarm system as outlined under "Air Bag System Disarming & Arming."
2. Remove instrument panel as outlined in "Dash Panel Service" chapter.
3. Disconnect air bag module pigtail connector.
4. Remove air bag module to instrument panel carrier attaching bolts.
5. Remove module from instrument panel.
6. Reverse procedure to install, tighten to specifications, then Arm system as outlined under "Air Bag System Disarming & Arming."

CANYON, COLORADO, SONOMA & S10

1. Disarm system as outlined under "Air Bag System Disarming & Arming."
2. Remove instrument panel as outlined in "Dash Panel Service" chapter.
3. Disconnect air bag module pigtail connector.
4. Remove air bag module to instrument panel carrier attaching bolts.
5. Remove module from instrument panel.

6. Reverse procedure to install, tighten to specifications, then Arm system as outlined under "Air Bag System Disarming & Arming."

EQUINOX & TORRENT

1. Disarm system as outlined under "Air Bag System Disarming & Arming."
2. Remove instrument panel top cover.
3. Remove radio.
4. Remove fastener from passenger side air outlet duct.
5. Remove air outlet duct.
6. Reach through radio and air outlet duct areas to access fasteners. Remove fasteners securing SIR to instrument panel beam.
7. Unsnap module from instrument panel carrier retainers.
8. Remove module from vehicle.
9. Reverse procedure to install, tighten to specifications, then Arm system as outlined under "Air Bag System Disarming & Arming."

AVALANCHE, ESCALADE, ESCALADE ESV, ESCALADE EXT, SIERRA, SILVERADO, SSR, SUBURBAN, TAHOE, YUKON

EXCEPT SIERRA, SILVERADO, SUBURBAN, TAHOE & YUKON

1. Disarm system as outlined under "Air Bag System Disarming & Arming."
2. Roll instrument panel forward to access air bag module mounting. Refer to "Dash Panel Service" chapter.
3. Remove nuts attaching inflatable restraint IP module, then the module.
4. Remove connector position assurance from yellow 2-way connector.
5. Disconnect yellow 2-way connector.
6. Remove inflatable restraint IP module from IP.
7. Reverse procedure to install, tighten to specifications, then Arm system as outlined under "Air Bag System Disarming & Arming."

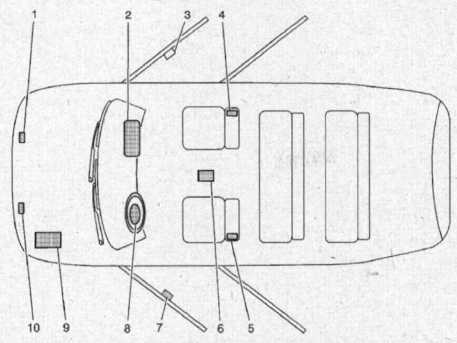

(1) Inflatable Restraint Front End Sensor-right- Right-Located on the front of the vehicle in the engine compartment

(2) Inflatable Restraint IP Module-Located at the top right under the instrument panel

(3) Inflatable Restraint Side Impact Sensor (SIS)-right-Located under right front door trim near the lower rear of door frame

(4) Inflatable Restraint Side Impact Module-right-Located on the side of the right front seat

(5) Inflatable Restraint Side Impact Module-left-Located on the side of the left front seat

(6) Inflatable Restraint Sensing and Diagnostic Module (SDM)-Located under center floor console

(7) Inflatable Restraint Side Impact Sensor (SIS)-left-Located under left front door trim near the lower rear of door frame

(8) Inflatable Restraint Steering Wheel Module-Located on the steering wheel

(9) Battery-Located under hood on the left side

(10) Inflatable Restraint Front End Sensor-left-Located on the front of the vehicle in the engine compartment

LTV0500000004322

Fig. 5   SIR component location. Bravada

SIERRA, SILVERADO, SUBURBAN, TAHOE, YUKON

1. Disarm system as outlined under "Air Bag System Disarming & Arming."
2. Remove upper IP trim panel to access 2 of 4 bolts.
3. Open glove compartment door, remove lift stop to allow door to fall fully open.
4. Disconnect yellow two-way connector at lefthand side of mounting bracket.
5. Disconnect CPA from yellow two-way connector.
6. Disconnect air bag module yellow pigtail connector from yellow two-way connector.
7. Remove air bag mounting bolts, then the air bag module assembly.
8. Reverse procedure to install, tighten to specifications, then Arm system as outlined under "Air Bag System Disarming & Arming."

EXPRESS & SAVANA

1. Disarm system as outlined under "Air Bag System Disarming & Arming."
2. Remove passenger side knee bolster.
3. Remove CPA, then disconnect module electrical connector.
4. Remove module attaching bolts, then the module from instrument panel.
5. Reverse procedure to install, tighten to specifications, then Arm system as outlined under "Air Bag System Disarming & Arming."

HHR

1. Disarm system as outlined under "Air Bag System Disarming & Arming."
2. Remove the right windshield pillar garnish molding.
3. Loosen the front passenger side of the instrument panel upper trim panel.
4. Remove the right hinge pillar trim.
5. Remove insulator panel retainer.
6. Remove insulator panel assembly.

7. Remove instrument panel compartment assembly.
8. Remove instrument panel accessory trim plate.
9. Remove instrument panel inflatable restraint module.
10. To release instrument panel inflatable restraint door from the upper trim panel, push in on tabs to separate module door from trim panel.
11. Remove connector position assurance (CPA) retainer.
12. Disconnect electrical connector.
13. Fully deploy module before disposal. If module was replaced under warranty, fully deploy and dispose of module after required period.
14. Reverse procedure to install, tighten to specifications, then Arm system as outlined under "Air Bag System Disarming & Arming."

HUMMER H2 & H3

1. Disarm system as outlined under "Air Bag System Disarming & Arming."
2. Remove instrument panel right accessory trim replacement from the instrument panel substraight.
3. Remove connector from instrument panel.
4. Remove inflatable restraint instrument panel module retaining bolts.
5. Ensure that you keep a firm hold on instrument panel module.
6. Reverse procedure to install, tighten to specifications, then Arm system as outlined under "Air Bag System Disarming & Arming."

MONTANA, SILHOUETTE, TRANS SPORT & VENTURE

1. Disarm system as outlined under "Air Bag System Disarming & Arming."
2. Remove glove compartment and disconnect light electrical connector.
3. Disconnect air bag pigtail harness

clips from bracket.
4. Remove air bag to cross beam and instrument panel attaching bolts, then the air bag module.
5. Reverse procedure to install, tighten to specifications, then Arm system as outlined under "Air Bag System Disarming & Arming."

RELAY, SV6, TERRAZA & UPLANDER

1. Disarm system as outlined under "Air Bag System Disarming & Arming."
2. Remove instrument panel insulator retainers.
3. Remove instrument panel insulator panel.
4. Remove instrument panel compartment screws.
5. Remove instrument panel compartment assembly.
6. Remove instrument panel inflatable restraint module bolts.
7. Remove instrument panel inflatable restraint module.
8. Release tabs while pushing up module.
9. Fully deploy module before disposal. If module was replaced under warranty, fully deploy and dispose of module, after required retention period.
10. Reverse procedure to install, tighten to specifications, then Arm system as outlined under "Air Bag System Disarming & Arming."

SRX

1. Disarm system as outlined under "Air Bag System Disarming & Arming."
2. Remove instrument panel retainer.
3. Note wire harness routing position on instrument panel module, to help in assembly.
4. Remove instrument panel module mounting fasteners.
5. Remove the instrument panel module from the instrument panel.
6. Reverse procedure to install, tighten to specifications, then Arm system as outlined under "Air Bag System Disarming & Arming."

TRACKER

1. Disarm system as outlined under "Air Bag System Disarming & Arming."
2. Remove glove compartment assembly as outlined under "Dash Panel Service" chapter.
3. Remove passenger air bag module fasteners, then the air bag module.
4. Disconnect electrical connectors.
5. Remove passenger air bag module.
6. Reverse procedure to install, tighten to specifications, then Arm system as outlined under "Air Bag System Disarming & Arming."

VUE

1. Disarm system as outlined under "Air Bag System Disarming & Arming."
2. Remove instrument panel top cover.
3. Remove radio.
4. Remove fastener from passenger side air outlet duct.
5. Remove air outlet duct.

6. Reach through radio and air outlet duct areas to access fasteners. Remove fasteners securing SIR to instrument panel beam.
7. Unsnap module from instrument panel carrier retainers.
8. Remove module from vehicle.
9. Reverse procedure to install, tighten to specifications, then Arm system as outlined under "Air Bag System Disarming & Arming."

Side Impact Air Bag Module, Replace

AVALANCHE, ESCALADE EXT, SIERRA, SILVERADO & SSR

1. Disarm system as outlined under "Air Bag System Disarming & Arming."
2. Remove front seat assembly from vehicle.
3. Remove seat back cover.
4. Remove side impact air bag module retaining bolts, then the side impact air bag module from seat frame.
5. Remove side impact air bag module retainer.
6. Remove side impact air bag module wiring harness retaining clips from seat frame. **NOTE: Routing of the inflatable restraint side impact module wiring harness and retaining clips within seat frame. It is crucial that the wiring harness be routed the exact same way as from the factory to eliminate the possibility of any cutting or chafing of the wiring harness.**
7. Remove side impact air bag module wiring harness from seat frame.
8. Remove side impact air bag module from seat frame.
9. Reverse procedure to install, tighten to specifications, then Arm system as outlined under "Air Bag System Disarming & Arming."

AZTEZ & RENDEZVOUS

1. Disarm system as outlined under "Air Bag System Disarming & Arming."
2. Remove passenger seat.
3. Remove J-clip from lower rear seat back.
4. Remove seat back cover.
5. Remove air bag fasteners.
6. Note routing of air bag wiring harness and retaining clip attachments within passenger seat.
7. Remove retaining clips on air bag wiring harness from passenger seat frame.
8. Gently pull air bag wiring harness up into seat back while guiding harness through wire triangle of seat frame.
9. Remove air bag from seat back frame.
10. Fully deploy module before disposal. If module was replaced under warranty, fully deploy and dispose of module after required retention period.
11. Reverse procedure to install, tighten to specifications, then Arm system as outlined under "Air Bag System Disarming & Arming."

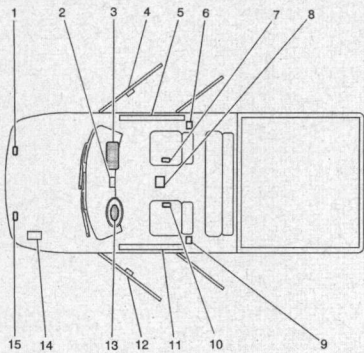

(1) Inflatable Restraint Front End Sensor-Right-Located on the front of the vehicle in the engine compartment
(2) Inflatable Restraint I/P Module Disable Switch-Located in the Center of the I/P
(3) Inflatable Restraint I/P Module-Located at the top right under the instrument panel
(4) Inflatable Restraint Side Impact Sensor (SIS)-Right-Located under right front door trim near the lower rear of door frame
(5) Inflatable Restraint Roof Rail Module-Right-Located in the headliner along roof rail
(6) Seat Belt Retractor Pretensioner-Right-Located on the floor next to the right front seat
(7) Inflatable Restraint Seat Position Switch-Right-Located on the side of the right front seat
(8) Inflatable Restraint Sensing and Diagnostic Module (SDM)-Located under center floor console
(9) Seat Belt Retractor Pretensioner-Left-Located on the floor next to the left front seat
(10) Inflatable Restraint Seat Position Switch-Left-Located on the side of the left front seat
(11) Inflatable Restraint Side Roof Rail Module-Left-Located in the headliner along roof rail
(12) Inflatable Restraint Side Impact Sensor (SIS)-Left-Located under left front door trim near the lower rear of door frame
(13) Inflatable Restraint Steering Wheel Module-Located on the steering wheel
(14) Battery and Underhood Fuse Block-SIR Fuse-Located in engine compartment on left side
(15) Inflatable Restraint Front End Sensor-Left-Located on the front of the vehicle in the engine compartment

LTV0500000004323

Fig. 6 SIR component location. Canyon & Colorado

MONTANA, SILHOUETTE & VENTURE

1. Disarm system as outlined under "Air Bag System Disarming & Arming."
2. Remove front seat.
3. Remove seat back cover.
4. Remove plastic molding that holds air bag inflator module to seat back frame.
5. Note routing of wiring harness to air bag inflator module and retaining clip attachments within seat.
6. Remove wiring harness retaining clips from seat frame.
7. Remove wiring harness from seat frame.
8. Remove inflator module from seat back frame.
9. Fully deploy module before disposal. If module was replaced under warranty, fully deploy and dispose of module after required retention period.
10. Reverse procedure to install, tighten to specifications, then Arm system as outlined under "Air Bag System Disarming & Arming."

RELAY, SV6, TERRAZA & UPLANDER

1. Disarm system as outlined under "Air Bag System Disarming & Arming."
2. Remove front bucket seat.
3. Remove front seat back panel.
4. Remove armrest assembly.
5. Remove head restraint assembly.
6. Remove seat back cushion cover.
7. Disconnect electrical connector.
8. Remove inflatable restraint module.
9. Fully deploy module before disposal. If module was replaced under warranty,

fully deploy and dispose of module, after required retention period.
10. Reverse procedure to install, tighten to specifications, then Arm system as outlined under "Air Bag System Disarming & Arming."

SRX

1. Disarm system as outlined under "Air Bag System Disarming & Arming."
2. Move seat to full forward position.
3. Remove seat back panel cover from seat by pulling out top of panel and lifting bottom away from seat to release hook retainers.
4. Remove two bolts from inflatable restraint side impact module bracket.
5. Remove module from seat.
6. Remove Connector Position Assurance from module electrical connector.
7. Disconnect electrical connector from module.
8. Reverse procedure to install, tighten to specifications, then Arm system as outlined under "Air Bag System Disarming & Arming."

Forward Discriminating Sensors, Replace

ASTRO & SAFARI

1. Disarm system as outlined under "Air Bag System Disarming & Arming."
2. Disconnect MAF and IAT electrical connectors.
3. Loosen clamp, then remove air tube from throttle body air intake cover.

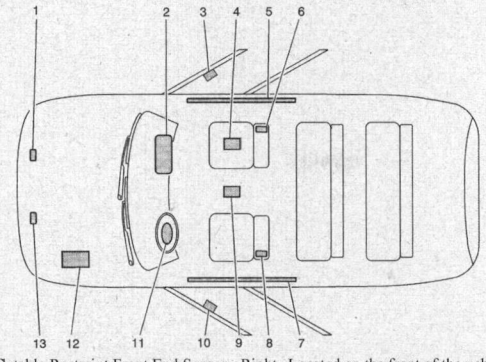

(1) Inflatable Restraint Front End Sensor - Right--Located on the front of the vehicle in the engine compartment

(2) Inflatable Restraint I/P Module--Located at the top right under the instrument panel

(3) Inflatable Restraint Side Impact Sensor (SIS) - Right--Located under right front door trim near the lower rear of door frame

(4) Inflatable Restraint Passenger Presence System (PPS)--Located under the right front seat

(5) Inflatable Restraint Roof Rail Module - Right--Located on the roof rail along the right front seat

(6) Inflatable Restraint Seat Belt Pretensioner - Right--Located inside the right front seat

(7) Inflatable Restraint Roof Rail Module - Left--Located on the roof rail along the left front seat

(8) Inflatable Restraint Seat Belt Pretensioner - Left--Located inside the left front seat

(9) Inflatable Restraint Sensing and Diagnostic Module (SDM)--Located under center floor console

(10) Inflatable Restraint Side Impact Sensor (SIS) - Left--Located under left front door trim near the lower rear of door frame

(11) Inflatable Restraint Steering Wheel Module--Located on the steering wheel

(12) Battery--Located under hood on the left side

(13) Inflatable Restraint Front End Sensor - Left--Located on the front of the vehicle in the engine compartment

LTV0500000004324

Fig. 7 SIR component location. Envoy, Rainier & Trailblazer

4. Remove upper radiator shroud bolts, then the upper radiator shroud.
5. Remove fan and clutch assembly.
6. Remove lower radiator shroud.
7. Remove front end discriminating sensor electrical connector at top of cradle.
8. Remove front end discriminating sensor bolts, then the front end discriminating sensor.
9. The following procedures should be utilized in the event that sensor mounting holes or fasteners are damaged to the extent that the sensor may no longer be properly mounted:
   a. **First fastener repair,** remove and discard improperly installed rivet. Install sensor with new rivet No. GM P/N 15715058, or equivalent.
   b. **Second fastener repair,** remove improperly installed rivet.
   c. Enlarge mounting holes in lower radiator support to .35 inch.
   d. Install new seat rivet No. GM P/N 15699834, or equivalent.
   e. Install sensor with screw No. GM P/N 11515664, or equivalent.
10. Reverse procedure to install, tighten to specifications, then Arm system as outlined under "Air Bag System Disarming & Arming."

AVALANCHE, ESCALADE EXT, SIERRA, SILVERADO & SSR

1. Disarm system as outlined under "Air Bag System Disarming & Arming."
2. Remove connector position assurance (CPA).
3. Disconnect electrical connector.

4. Remove front end discriminating sensor fasteners, then the front end discriminating sensor.
5. The following procedures should be utilized in the event that sensor mounting holes or fasteners are damaged to the extent that the sensor may no longer be properly mounted:
   a. Remove and discard fastener.
   b. Chisel off damaged weld nut.
   c. Condition front end lower tie surface where the new weld nut is to be installed.
   d. Install new weld nut No. GM P/N 11514034, or equivalent.
   e. Migweld new nut into position.
   f. Use new fastener No. GM P/N 11515926, or equivalent.
6. Reverse procedure to install, tighten to specifications, then Arm system as outlined under "Air Bag System Disarming & Arming."

AZTEZ & RENDEZVOUS

1. Disarm system as outlined under "Air Bag System Disarming & Arming."
2. Remove grille.
3. Remove retainers that hold upper front bumper fascia to radiator support.
4. Pull fascia from radiator support to gain access to sensor bolts.
5. Remove orange connector position assurance from yellow sensor harness connector.
6. Disconnect harness connector from sensor.
7. Remove sensor bolts.
8. Remove sensor from upper radiator core support.
9. Reverse procedure to install.

BLAZER, BRAVADA, ENVOY, RAINIER & TRAILBLAZER

1. Disarm system as outlined under "Air Bag System Disarming & Arming."
2. Remove off road skid plate, if equipped.
3. Remove connector position assurance from inflatable restraint front end discriminating sensor harness connector.
4. Disconnect inflatable restraint front end discriminating sensor harness connector from sensor.
5. Drill out mounting rivets.
6. Remove inflatable restraint front end discriminating sensor from vehicle. **Following procedures should be utilized in event that sensor mounting holes or fasteners are damaged to extent that sensor can no longer be properly mounted.**
7. Perform following steps in order to complete first fastener repair:
   a. Remove and discard improperly installed rivet.
   b. Reattach sensor with new rivet.
8. Perform following steps in order to complete second fastener repair:
   a. Remove improperly installed rivet.
   b. Enlarge mounting holes in lower radiator support to 0.35 in.
   c. Insert and properly seat rivet. **Use correct fastener in correct location. Replacement fasteners must be correct part number for that application. Fasteners requiring replacement or fasteners requiring use of thread locking compound or sealant are identified in service procedure. Do not use paints, lubricants, or corrosion inhibitors on fasteners or fastener joint surfaces unless specified. These coatings affect fastener torque and joint clamping force and may damage fastener. Use correct tightening sequence and specifications when installing fasteners in order to avoid damage to parts and systems.**
   d. Install sensor with screw and **torque** to 71 inch lbs.
9. Reverse procedure to install.

CANYON, COLORADO, SONOMA & S10

1. Disarm system as outlined under "Air Bag System Disarming & Arming."
2. Remove off road skid plate, if equipped.
3. Disconnect connector position assurance (CPA) lock.
4. Drill out mounting rivets from sensor.
5. Remove sensor from vehicle.
6. The following procedures should be utilized in the event that sensor mounting holes or fasteners are damaged to the extent that the sensor may no longer be properly mounted:

a. **First fastener repair,** remove improperly installed rivet. Install sensor with new rivet GM P/N 15955523, or equivalent.

b. **Second fastener repair,** remove improperly installed rivet.

c. Enlarge mounting holes in lower radiator support to .35 inch.

d. Install seat rivet GM P/N 15699834, or equivalent.

e. Install sensor with screw GM P/N 11515664, or equivalent.

7. Reverse procedure to install, tighten to specifications, then Arm system as outlined under "Air Bag System Disarming & Arming."

EQUINOX & TORRENT

1. Disarm system as outlined under "Air Bag System Disarming & Arming."
2. Loosen torx head bolt on supplemental inflatable restraint front end discriminating sensor in order to remove sensor.
3. Slide sensor towards front of vehicle to guide sensor bolt out of release slot.
4. Disconnect electrical connector.
5. Remove module.
6. Reverse procedure to install.

ESCALADE, ESCALADE ESV, SUBURBAN, TAHOE & YUKON

1. Disarm system as outlined under "Air Bag System Disarming & Arming."
2. Remove connector position assurance (CPA).
3. Disconnect electrical connector.
4. Remove front end discriminating sensor fasteners, then the front end discriminating sensor.
5. The following procedures should be utilized in the event that sensor mounting holes or fasteners are damaged to the extent that the sensor may no longer be properly mounted:
   a. Remove and discard fastener.
   b. Chisel off damaged weld nut.
   c. Condition front end lower tie surface where the new weld nut is to be installed.
   d. Install new weld nut No. GM P/N 11514034, or equivalent.
   e. Migweld new nut into position.
   f. Use new fastener No. GM P/N 11515926, or equivalent.
6. Reverse procedure to install, tighten to specifications, then Arm system as outlined under "Air Bag System Disarming & Arming."

EXPRESS & SAVANA

1. Disarm system as outlined under "Air Bag System Disarming & Arming."
2. Raise and support vehicle.
3. Remove connector position assurance from inflatable restraint front end discriminating sensor electrical connector.
4. Disconnect inflatable restraint front end sensor electrical connector.
5. Loosen inflatable restraint front end sensor mounting nut.
6. Slide inflatable restraint front end sensor towards front of vehicle.
7. Remove sensor from keyhole slot in lower radiator support.
8. Reverse procedure to install.

HHR

1. Disarm system as outlined under "Air Bag System Disarming & Arming."
2. Loosen forward discriminating sensor bolt in order to remove sensor.
3. Remove connector position assurance retainer.
4. Disconnect electrical connector.
5. Remove module.
6. Reverse procedure to install.

HUMMER H2 & H3

1. Disarm system as outlined under "Air Bag System Disarming & Arming."
2. Remove engine protection shield, if equipped.
3. Remove connector position assurance from inflatable restraint front end discriminator sensor harness connector.
4. Disconnect inflatable restraint front end discriminating sensor harness connector from sensor.
5. Remove mounting fasteners.
6. Remove inflatable restraint front end discriminating sensor from vehicle.
7. Perform following steps in order to complete fastener repair: **Following procedure should be utilized in event that sensor mounting holes or fasteners are damaged to extent that sensor may no longer be properly mounted:**
   a. Remove and discard improperly installed fastener.
   b. Chisel off damaged weld nut.
   c. Condition front end lower tie surface where new weld nut is to be installed.
   d. Install new weld nut tool no. 11514034 or equivalent into position.
   e. Migweld new weld nut to front end lower tie surface in the correct
   f. Use the new fastener tool no. 11514034 or equivalent.
8. Reverse procedure to install.

MONTANA, SILHOUETTE & VENTURE

1. Disarm system as outlined under "Air Bag System Disarming & Arming."
2. Remove connector position assurance (CPA).
3. Disconnect electrical connector.
4. Remove front end discriminating sensor fasteners, then the front end discriminating sensor.
5. The following procedures should be utilized in the event that sensor mounting holes or fasteners are damaged to the extent that the sensor may no longer be properly mounted:
   a. Remove and discard fastener.
   b. Chisel off damaged weld nut.
   c. Condition front end lower tie surface where the new weld nut is to be installed.
   d. Install new weld nut No. GM P/N 11514034, or equivalent.
   e. Migweld new nut into position.
   f. Use new fastener No. GM P/N 11515926, or equivalent.
6. Reverse procedure to install, tighten to specifications, then Arm system as outlined under "Air Bag System Disarming & Arming."

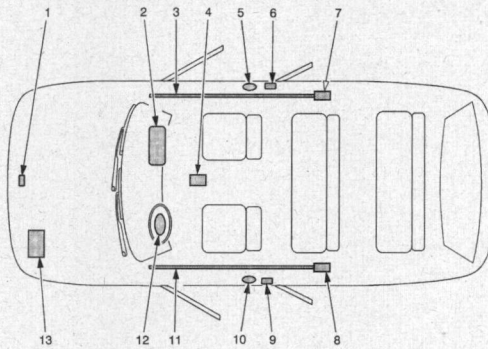

(1) Electrical Frontal Sensor (EFS)--Located under the front hood in the engine compartment

(2) I/P Air Bag--Located at the top right under the instrument panel

(3) Roof Rail Air Bag - Right--Located under the headliner, extending from the passenger front windshield pillar to the passenger rear windshield pillar

(4) Sensing and Diagnostic Module (SDM)--Located underneath the vehicle carpet under the center console

(5) Side Impact Sensor (SIS) and Seat Belt Pretensioner - RF--Located under the trim near the bottom of the center pillar

(6) Seat Belt Pretensioner - RF--Located under the trim near the bottom of the center pillar

(7) Roof Rail Module - Right--Located behind the garnish molding on the upper rear pillar

(8) Roof Rail Module - Left--Located behind garnish molding on the upper rear pillar

(9) Seat Belt Pretensioner - LF--Located under the trim near the bottom of the center pillar

(10) Side Impact Sensor (SIS) - LF--Located under the trim near the bottom of the center pillar

(11) Roof Rail Air Bag - Left--Located under the headliner, extending from the driver front windshield pillar to the driver rear windshield pillar

(12) Steering Wheel Air Bag--Located on the steering wheel

(13) Vehicle Battery--Located at the front left of the engine compartment.

LTV0500000004325

Fig. 8 SIR component location. Equinox & Torrent

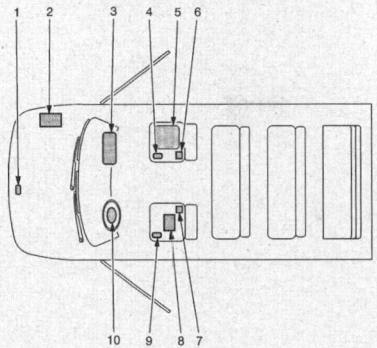

(1) Inflatable Restraint Front End Sensor--Located on the front frame crossmember at center

(2) Battery--Located under the hood on the right side

(3) Inflatable Restraint I/P Module--Located at the right front of the instrument panel cluster

(4) Inflatable Restraint Seat Position Sensor (SPS) - Right--Located on the right front inboard seat track

(5) Passenger Presence System (PPS)--Located in passenger seat

(6) Seat Belt Buckle Pretensioner--Located in RF seat belt buckle

(7) Seat Belt Buckle Pretensioner--Located in LF seat belt buckle

(8) Inflatable Restraint Sensing and Diagnostic Module (SDM)-Located under the left front seat under the carpet

(9) Inflatable Restraint Seat Position Sensor (SPS)--Left--Located on the left front outboard seat track

(10) Inflatable Restraint Steering Wheel Module--Located on the steering wheel

LTV0500000004326

Fig. 9 SIR component location. Express & Savana

RELAY, SV6, TERRAZA & UPLANDER

1. Disarm system as outlined under "Air Bag System Disarming & Arming."
2. Remove front fascia.
3. Remove front end inflatable restraint discriminating sensor bolts.
4. Disconnect electrical connector.
5. Remove orange connector position assurance from yellow sensor harness connector.
6. Remove front end inflatable restraint discriminating sensor.
7. Reverse procedure to install.

SRX

1. Disarm system as outlined under "Air Bag System Disarming & Arming."
2. Remove connector position assurance from wiring harness connector to inflatable restraint front end sensor.
3. Disconnect wiring harness connector from front end sensor.
4. Loosen front end sensor mounting fastener, which is located in upper tie bar. **Front end sensor mounting fastener has left handed threads.**
5. Remove front end sensor from upper tie bar.
6. Reverse procedure to install.

Seat Belt Pretensioner, Replace

AZTEZ & RENDEZVOUS

1. Disarm system as outlined under "Air Bag System Disarming & Arming."
2. Remove front bucket seat.
3. Remove front seat belt anchor from rear outboard stud.
4. Open seat belt guide loop cover.

5. Remove nut from seat belt guide loop.
6. Remove seat belt guide loop from guide adjuster bracket.
7. Remove center pillar lower trim.
8. Remove bolt from seat belt retractor.
9. Remove seat belt retractor from center pillar.
10. Remove front seat belt from vehicle.
11. Reverse procedure to install, tighten to specifications, then Arm system as outlined under "Air Bag System Disarming & Arming."

CANYON, COLORADO, SONOMA & S10

1. Disarm system as outlined under "Air Bag System Disarming & Arming."
2. Open front seat belt upper guide shoulder bolt trim cover.
3. Remove front seat belt upper guide shoulder bolt.
4. Remove body rear corner trim panel.
5. Remove front seat belt anchor bolt.
6. Disconnect electrical connector from retractor/pretensioner.
7. Remove bolt that retains seat belt retractor/pretensioner assembly to body.
8. Remove front seat belt assembly from vehicle.
9. Reverse procedure to install, tighten to specifications, then Arm system as outlined under "Air Bag System Disarming & Arming."

EQUINOX & TORRENT

1. Disarm system as outlined under "Air Bag System Disarming & Arming."
2. Remove front bucket seat.
3. Remove front seat belt anchor from rear outboard stud.
4. Open seat belt guide loop cover
5. Remove nut from seat belt guide loop.
6. Remove seat belt guide loop from guide adjuster bracket.
7. Remove center pillar lower trim.

8. Remove bolt from seat belt retractor.
9. Remove seat belt retractor from center pillar.
10. Remove front seat belt from vehicle.
11. Reverse procedure to install, tighten to specifications, then Arm system as outlined under "Air Bag System Disarming & Arming."

EXPRESS & SAVANA

1. Disarm system as outlined under "Air Bag System Disarming & Arming."
2. Lift buckle cover.
3. Remove seat belt buckle pretensioner retaining bolt from seat.
4. Disconnect electrical connector from seat belt buckle pretensioner, if equipped.
5. Remove seat belt buckle pretensioner from seat.
6. Reverse procedure to install, tighten to specifications, then Arm system as outlined under "Air Bag System Disarming & Arming."

HHR

1. Disarm system as outlined under "Air Bag System Disarming & Arming."
2. Move seat to full forward position to gain access to seat belt anchor bolt.
3. Remove seat belt anchor bolt.
4. Remove seat belt adjuster cover.
5. Remove seat belt adjuster bolt.
6. Remove center pillar lower trim panel to gain access to seat belt retractor bolt.
7. Disconnect belt tension sensor electrical connector.
8. Remove seat belt retractor assembly.
9. Reverse procedure to install, tighten to specifications, then Arm system as outlined under "Air Bag System Disarming & Arming."

MONTANA, SILHOUETTE & VENTURE

1. Disarm system as outlined under "Air Bag System Disarming & Arming."
2. Remove seat.
3. Remove seat adjuster track cover.
4. Remove nut from seat belt pretensioner.
5. Remove seat belt pretensioner wiring harness through the seat bottom frame.
6. Remove seat belt pretensioner from seat bottom frame.
7. Fully deploy module before disposal. If module was replaced under warranty, fully deploy and dispose of module after required retention period.
8. Reverse procedure to install, tighten to specifications, then Arm system as outlined under "Air Bag System Disarming & Arming."

RELAY, SV6, TERRAZA & UPLANDER

1. Disarm system as outlined under "Air Bag System Disarming & Arming."
2. Remove front bucket seat.
3. Remove front seat belt anchor from rear outboard stud.
4. Open seat belt guide loop cover.
5. Remove nut from seat belt guide loop.

6. Remove seat belt guide loop from guide adjuster bracket.
7. Remove center pillar lower trim.
8. Remove bolt from seat belt retractor.
9. Remove seat belt retractor from center pillar.
10. Remove front seat belt from vehicle.
11. Reverse procedure to install, tighten to specifications, then Arm system as outlined under "Air Bag System Disarming & Arming."

SRX

1. Disarm system as outlined under "Air Bag System Disarming & Arming."
2. Disconnect pretensioner electrical connector from side air bag connector.
3. Disconnect electrical connector from seat belt switch.
4. Remove seat from vehicle.
5. Remove pretensioner trim cover by pulling out on cover.
6. Remove pretensioner fastener and remove pretensioner from seat.
7. Fully deploy module before disposal. If module was replaced under warranty, fully deploy and dispose of module after required retention period.
8. Reverse procedure to install, tighten to specifications, then Arm system as outlined under "Air Bag System Disarming & Arming."

VUE

1. Disarm system as outlined under "Air Bag System Disarming & Arming."
2. Remove recliner handle trim by pulling firmly on trim.
3. Remove side trim cover from front seat.
4. Remove seat belt anchor from front seat.
5. Remove lower garnish molding from center pillar.
6. Disconnect electrical connector from pretensioner retractor.
7. Remove height adjuster cover
8. Remove retractor fasteners and remove retractor.
9. Remove shoulder belt from vehicle.
10. Reverse procedure to install, tighten to specifications, then Arm system as outlined under "Air Bag System Disarming & Arming."

Sensing & Diagnostic Module (SDM), Replace

ASTRO & SAFARI

1. Disarm system as outlined under "Air Bag System Disarming & Arming."
2. Remove driver's seat, then the seat belt from floor.
3. Remove carpet retaining sill trim molding.
4. Remove center floor console, if equipped.
5. Fold back carpet to access SDM.
6. Disconnect connector position assurance (CPA), then the electrical connector from SDM.
7. Remove SDM attaching nuts, then the SDM module.
8. Reverse procedure to install, tighten to specifications, then Arm system as outlined under "Air Bag System Disarming & Arming."

AVALANCHE, ESCALADE EXT, SIERRA, SILVERADO & SSR

1. Disarm system as outlined under "Air Bag System Disarming & Arming."
2. Remove driver's seat, then the seat belt from floor.
3. Remove carpet retaining sill trim molding.
4. Remove center floor console, if equipped.
5. Fold back carpet to access SDM.
6. Disconnect connector position assurance (CPA), then the electrical connector from SDM.
7. Remove SDM attaching nuts, then the SDM module.
8. Reverse procedure to install, tighten to specifications, then Arm system as outlined under "Air Bag System Disarming & Arming."

AZTEZ & RENDEZVOUS

1. Disarm system as outlined under "Air Bag System Disarming & Arming."
2. Remove front passenger seat.
3. Fold back carpet to access SDM.
4. Disconnect connector position assurance (CPA), then the electrical connector from SDM.
5. Remove SDM attaching nuts, then the SDM module.
6. Reverse procedure to install, tighten to specifications, then Arm system as outlined under "Air Bag System Disarming & Arming."

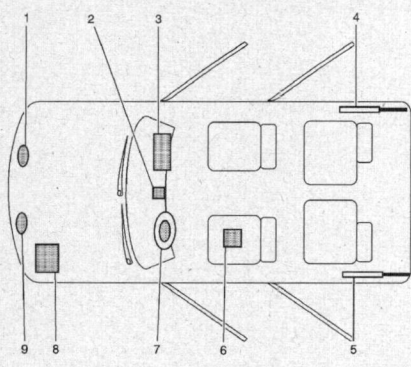

(1) Inflatable Restraint Electronic Frontal Sensor (EFS)-Located on the front of the vehicle in the engine compartment
(2) Inflatable Restraint I/P Module Disable Switch-Located at the top right under the instrument panel
(3) Inflatable Restraint I/P Module-Located at the top right under the instrument panel
(4) Rear Lift Gate Strut-A gas shock is located between rear lift gate and body on the passenger side
(5) Rear Lift Gate Strut-A gas shock is located between rear lift gate and body on the driver side
(6) Inflatable Restraint Sensing and Diagnostic Module (SDM)-Located underneath the LF/driver seat
(7) Inflatable Restraint Steering Wheel Module-Located on the steering wheel
(8) Battery-Located under Hood on the left side
(9) Inflatable Restraint Electronic Frontal Sensor (EFS)-Located on the front of the vehicle in the engine compartment

LTV0500000004327

Fig. 10   SIR component location. Hummer H2

BLAZER, BRAVADA, ENVOY, RAINIER & TRAILBLAZER

1. Disarm system as outlined under "Air Bag System Disarming & Arming."
2. Remove driver's seat, then the seat belt from floor.
3. Remove carpet retaining sill trim molding.
4. Remove center floor console, if equipped.
5. Fold back carpet to access SDM.
6. Disconnect connector position assurance (CPA), then the electrical connector from SDM.
7. Remove SDM attaching nuts, then the SDM module.
8. Reverse procedure to install, tighten to specifications, then Arm system as outlined under "Air Bag System Disarming & Arming."

CANYON, COLORADO, SONOMA & S10

1. Disarm system as outlined under "Air Bag System Disarming & Arming."
2. Remove driver's seat, then the seat belt from floor.
3. Remove carpet retaining sill trim molding.
4. Remove center floor console, if equipped.
5. Fold back carpet to access SDM.
6. Disconnect connector position assurance (CPA), then the electrical connector from SDM.
7. Remove SDM attaching nuts, then the SDM module.
8. Reverse procedure to install, tighten to specifications, then Arm system as outlined under "Air Bag System Disarming & Arming."

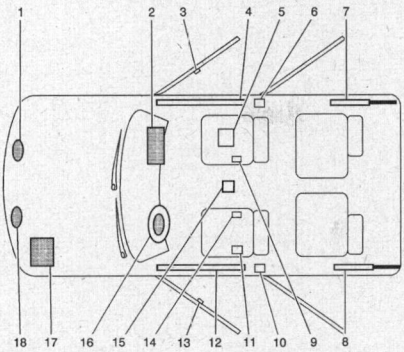

(1) Inflatable Restraint Front End Sensor - Right--Located on the front of the vehicle in the engine compartment

(2) Inflatable Restraint I/P Module--Located at the top right under the instrument panel

(3) Inflatable Restraint Side Impact Sensor (SIS) - Right--Located under right front door trim near the lower rear of door frame

(4) Inflatable Restraint Roof Rail Module - Right--Located in the headliner along roof rail

(5) Passenger Presence System--Located under passenger seat

(6) Seat Belt Retractor Pretensioner - Right--Located on the floor next to the right front seat

(7) Rear Liftgate Start-A Gas Shock--Located at rear of vehicle

(8) Rear Liftgate Start-A Gas Shock--Located at rear of vehicle

(9) Inflatable Restraint Seat Position Switch - Right--Located on the side of the right front seat

(10) Seat Belt Retractor Pretensioner - Left--Located on the floor next to the left front seat

(11) Inflatable Restraint Vehicle Rollover Sensor--Located under driver seat

(12) Inflatable Restraint Side Roof Rail Module - Left--Located in the headliner along the roof rail

(13) Inflatable Restraint Side Impact Sensor (SIS) - Left--Located under left front door trim near the lower rear of door frame

(14) Inflatable Restraint Seat Position Switch - Left--Located on the side of the left front seat

(15) Inflatable Restraint Sensing and Diagnostic Module (SDM)--Located under center floor console

(16) Inflatable Restraint Steering Wheel Module--Located on the steering wheel

(17) Battery and Underhood Fuse Block - SIR Fuse--Located in engine compartment on left side

(18) Inflatable Restraint Front End Sensor - Left--Located on the front of the vehicle in the engine compartment

LTV0500000004328

Fig. 11 SIR component location. Hummer H3

EQUINOX & TORRENT

1. Disarm system as outlined under "Air Bag System Disarming & Arming."
2. Remove console assembly.
3. Remove retainers from connector position assurance and disconnect electrical connectors.
4. Remove nuts and remove sensing and diagnostic module.
5. Reverse procedure to install, tighten to specifications, then Arm system as outlined under "Air Bag System Disarming & Arming."

ESCALADE, ESCALADE ESV, SUBURBAN, TAHOE & YUKON

1. Disarm system as outlined under "Air Bag System Disarming & Arming."
2. Remove driver's seat, then the seat belt from floor.
3. Remove carpet retaining sill trim molding.
4. Remove center floor console, if equipped.
5. Fold back carpet to access SDM.
6. Disconnect connector position assurance (CPA), then the electrical connector from SDM.
7. Remove SDM attaching nuts, then the SDM module.
8. Reverse procedure to install, tighten to specifications, then Arm system as outlined under "Air Bag System Disarming & Arming."

EXPRESS & SAVANA

1. Disarm system as outlined under "Air Bag System Disarming & Arming."
2. Remove driver's seat, then the seat belt from floor.
3. Remove carpet retaining sill trim molding.
4. Remove center floor console, if equipped.
5. Fold back carpet to access SDM.
6. Disconnect connector position assurance (CPA), then the electrical connector from SDM.
7. Remove SDM attaching nuts, then the SDM module.
8. Reverse procedure to install, tighten to specifications, then Arm system as outlined under "Air Bag System Disarming & Arming."

HHR

1. Disarm system as outlined under "Air Bag System Disarming & Arming."
2. Remove center console.
3. Remove inflatable restraint sensing and diagnostic module nuts.
4. Disconnect wire harness.
5. Remove inflatable restraint sensing and diagnostic module.
6. Reverse procedure to install, tighten to specifications, then Arm system as outlined under "Air Bag System Disarming & Arming."

HUMMER H2 & H3

1. Disarm system as outlined under "Air

Bag System Disarming & Arming."
2. Remove drivers seat.
3. Remove driver side door sill plate.
4. Fold back carpet to access inflatable restraint sensing and diagnostic module.
5. Remove connector position assurance from inflatable restraint sensing and diagnostic module wiring harness connector.
6. Push down flex lock button and slide connector locking cover to open position.
7. Disconnect SDM wiring harness connector from SDM.
8. Remove SDM mounting fasteners.
9. Remove SDM from vehicle.
10. Repair fasteners using following procedure: **Following repair procedures should only be used in event that the inflatable restraint sensing and diagnostic module (SDM) mounting studs and/or fasteners are damaged to extent that SDM may no longer be properly mounted.**
    a. Remove stripped nut and discard nut.
    b. Drill out weld spots to weld stud from floor pan side, then remove and discard stud.
    c. Condition floor panel attaching surface where new stud is to be installed.
    d. Install new weld stud tool no. 115115602 and clamp weld stud.
    e. Migweld stud at drilled holes from above or below floor pan, as required.
    f. Apply body sealer tool no. 9984248 around any exposed openings.
    g. Install a new fastener tool no. 11515933.
11. Reverse procedure to install, tighten to specifications, then Arm system as outlined under "Air Bag System Disarming & Arming."

MONTANA, SILHOUETTE & VENTURE

1. Disarm system as outlined under "Air Bag System Disarming & Arming."
2. Remove front passenger seat.
3. Fold back carpet to access SDM.
4. Disconnect connector position assurance (CPA), then the electrical connector from SDM.
5. Remove SDM attaching nuts, then the SDM module.
6. Reverse procedure to install, tighten to specifications, then Arm system as outlined under "Air Bag System Disarming & Arming."

RELAY, SV6, TERRAZA & UPLANDER

1. Disarm system as outlined under "Air Bag System Disarming & Arming."
2. Remove passenger front seat.
3. Remove passenger front carpet retainer. Roll back carpet.
4. Remove right side cowl trim panel.
5. Remove right side insulator panel.
6. Remove the connector position assurance.

7. Remove inflatable restraint sensing and diagnostic module.
8. Reverse procedure to install, tighten to specifications, then Arm system as outlined under "Air Bag System Disarming & Arming."

SRX

1. Disarm system as outlined under "Air Bag System Disarming & Arming."
2. Remove center console.
3. Remove connector position assurance from wiring harness connector to inflatable restraint sensing and diagnostic module.
4. Push flex lock button down and move sliding connector locking cover to open position.
5. Disconnect wiring harness connector from SDM.
6. Remove SDM mounting fasteners.
7. Remove SDM from console floor.
8. Reverse procedure to install, tighten to specifications, then Arm system as outlined under "Air Bag System Disarming & Arming."

TRACKER

1. Disarm system as outlined under "Air Bag System Disarming & Arming."
2. Remove rear console, then the front console to access SDM.
3. Remove connector position assurance (CPA), then disconnect electrical connector.
4. Remove SDM attaching screws, then the SDM.
5. Reverse procedure to install, tighten to specifications, then Arm system as outlined under "Air Bag System Disarming & Arming."

VUE

1. Disarm system as outlined under "Air Bag System Disarming & Arming."
2. Remove console assembly.
3. Remove retainers from connector position assurance and disconnect electrical connectors.
4. Remove nuts and remove sensing and diagnostic module.
5. Reverse procedure to install, tighten to specifications, then Arm system as outlined under "Air Bag System Disarming & Arming."

Side Impact Sensor, Replace

AVALANCHE, ESCALADE EXT, SIERRA, SILVERADO & SSR

1. Disarm system as outlined under "Air Bag System Disarming & Arming."
2. Remove front door trim panel.
3. Loosen two inflatable restraint side impact sensor fasteners.
4. Remove inflatable restraint side impact sensor from door.
5. Remove connector position assurance and disconnect inflatable restraint side impact sensor yellow 2-way harness connector.

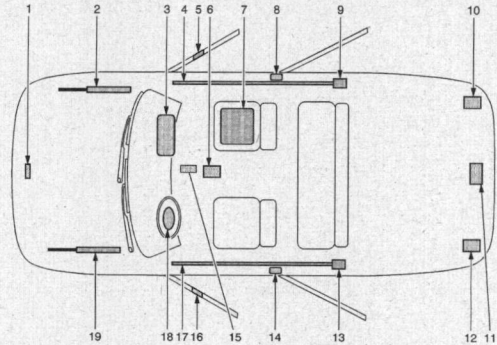

(1) Front End Sensor--Located under the hood at the front of the vehicle
(2) Front Hood Assist Rod--A gas shock located under the front hood on the passenger side
(3) I/P Air Bag--Located at the top right under the instrument panel
(4) Roof Rail Air Bag--Located under the headliner, extending from the passenger front windshield pillar to the passenger rear windshield pillar
(5) Side Impact Sensor (SIS)--Located behind door panel on the passenger front door
(6) Sensing and Diagnostic Module (SDM)--Located underneath the vehicle carpet under the center console
(7) Passenger Presence System--Located on the front passenger seat under the seat bottom trim
(8) Seat Belt Retractor Pretensioner--Located under the trim near the bottom of the center pillar on the passenger side of vehicle
(9) Inflator Module for Roof Rail Air Bag--Located behind the garnish molding on the upper rear pillar
(10) Rear Hood Assist Rod--A gas shock located under the rear truck lid on the passenger side
(11) Vehicle Battery--Located in the trunk under the carpet
(12) Rear Hood Assist Rod--A gas shock located under the rear truck lid on the driver side
(13) Inflator Module for Roof Rail Air Bag--Located behind garnish molding on the upper rear pillar
(14) Seat Belt Retractor Pretensioner--Located under the trim near the bottom of the center pillar on the driver side of vehicle
(15) Body Control Module/Fuse Block-Air Bag and SDM Fuse--Located on RH side of the center console
(16) Side Impact Sensor (SIS)--Located behind door panel on the driver front door
Roof Rail Air Bag--Located under the headliner, extending from the driver front windshield pillar

LTV0500000004329

Fig. 12 SIR component location. HHR

6. Reverse procedure to install, tighten to specifications, then Arm system as outlined under "Air Bag System Disarming & Arming."

AZTEZ & RENDEZVOUS

1. Disarm system as outlined under "Air Bag System Disarming & Arming."
2. Remove center pillar lower trim.
3. Remove connector position assurance from yellow 2-way harness connector on inflatable restraint side impact sensor.
4. Disconnect wiring harness connector from side impact sensor.
5. Loosen two fasteners on side impact sensor.
6. Remove side impact sensor from center pillar.
7. Reverse procedure to install, tighten to specifications, then Arm system as outlined under "Air Bag System Disarming & Arming."

BLAZER, BRAVADA, ENVOY, RAINIER & TRAILBLAZER

1. Disarm system as outlined under "Air Bag System Disarming & Arming."
2. Remove front door trim panel.
3. Peel rear half of water deflector away from door in order to access side impact sensor.
4. Remove screws that retain side impact sensor to door.
5. Disconnect impact sensor electrical connector from side impact sensor.
6. Remove side impact sensor from door.

7. Reverse procedure to install, tighten to specifications, then Arm system as outlined under "Air Bag System Disarming & Arming."

CANYON, COLORADO, SONOMA & S10

1. Disarm system as outlined under "Air Bag System Disarming & Arming."
2. Remove front door trim panel.
3. Peel rear half of water deflector away from door in order to access side impact sensor.
4. Remove screws that retain side impact sensor to door.
5. Disconnect impact sensor electrical connector from side impact sensor.
6. Remove side impact sensor from door.
7. Reverse procedure to install, tighten to specifications, then Arm system as outlined under "Air Bag System Disarming & Arming."

EQUINOX & TORRENT

1. Disarm system as outlined under "Air Bag System Disarming & Arming."
2. Remove center pillar lower molding.
3. Loosen fasteners on the side impact sensor.
4. Remove SIS by sliding module up and out of key slots in sheet metal.
5. Disconnect SIS electrical connector.
6. Reverse procedure to install, tighten to specifications, then Arm system as outlined under "Air Bag System Disarming & Arming."

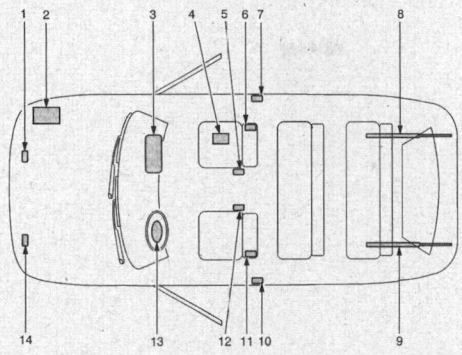

(1) Inflatable Restraint Front End Sensor - Right--Located on the lower right section of the core support

(2) Battery-Located under the hood on the right side

(3) Inflatable Restraint I/P Module--Located at the right front of the instrument panel cluster (IPC)

(4) Inflatable Restraint Sensing and Diagnostic Module (SDM)-Located under the right front seat under the carpet

(5) Inflatable Restraint Seat Belt Pretensioner - Right--Located on the right front inboard seat belt anchor

(6) Inflatable Restraint Side Impact Module - Right--Located on the side of the right front seat back

(7) Inflatable Restraint Side Impact Sensor (SIS) - Right--Located under the right side B-pillar trim near the bottom

(8) Rear Liftgate Strut--Located under the rear liftgate on the right

(9) Rear Liftgate Strut--Located under the rear liftgate on the left

(10) Inflatable Restraint Side Impact Sensor (SIS) - Left--Located under the left side B-pillar trim near the bottom

(11) Inflatable Restraint Seat Belt Pretensioner - Left--Located on the left front inboard seat belt anchor

(12) Inflatable Restraint Side Impact Module - Left--Located on the side of the left front seat back

(13) Inflatable Restraint Steering Wheel Module--Located on the steering wheel

(14) Inflatable Restraint Front End Sensor - Left--Located on the lower left section of the core support

LTV0500000004330

Fig. 13 SIR component location. Montana, Silhouette & Venture

ESCALADE, ESCALADE ESV, SUBURBAN, TAHOE & YUKON

1. Disarm system as outlined under "Air Bag System Disarming & Arming."
2. Remove front door trim panel.
3. Loosen two inflatable restraint side impact sensor fasteners.
4. Remove inflatable restraint side impact sensor from door.
5. Remove connector position assurance and disconnect inflatable restraint side impact sensor yellow 2-way harness connector.
6. Reverse procedure to install, tighten to specifications, then Arm system as outlined under "Air Bag System Disarming & Arming."

HHR

1. Disarm system as outlined under "Air Bag System Disarming & Arming."
2. Remove door trim panel.
3. Loosen the bolts and slide inflatable restraint side impact sensor out of key hole slots
4. Disconnect electrical connectors.
5. Reverse procedure to install, tighten to specifications, then Arm system as outlined under "Air Bag System Disarming & Arming."

HUMMER H2 & H3

1. Disarm system as outlined under "Air Bag System Disarming & Arming."
2. Remove door trim panel.
3. Loosen the bolts and slide inflatable restraint side impact sensor out of key hole slots
4. Disconnect electrical connectors.
5. Reverse procedure to install, tighten to specifications, then Arm system as outlined under "Air Bag System Disarming & Arming."

MONTANA, SILHOUETTE & VENTURE

1. Disarm system as outlined under "Air Bag System Disarming & Arming."
2. Remove seat belt retractor trim cover.
3. Loosen inflatable restraint side impact sensor fasteners.
4. Remove inflatable restraint side impact sensor from center pillar.
5. Remove connector position assurance from inflatable restraint side impact sensor yellow 2-way wiring harness connector.
6. Disconnect inflatable restraint side impact sensor wiring harness connector.
7. Reverse procedure to install, tighten to specifications, then Arm system as outlined under "Air Bag System Disarming & Arming."

RELAY, SV6, TERRAZA & UPLANDER

1. Disarm system as outlined under "Air Bag System Disarming & Arming."
2. Remove center pillar lower trim.
3. Remove connector position assurance from yellow harness connector.
4. Loosen the inflatable restraint side impact sensor bolts only.

5. Remove inflatable restraint side impact sensor.
6. Reverse procedure to install, tighten to specifications, then Arm system as outlined under "Air Bag System Disarming & Arming."

SRX

1. Disarm system as outlined under "Air Bag System Disarming & Arming."
2. Move seat to full forward position.
3. Remove center pillar trim panel.
4. Remove connector position assurance from harness connector to inflatable restraint side impact sensor.
5. Disconnect harness connector from the SIS.
6. Remove SIS mounting fasteners.
7. Remove SIS from center pillar.
8. Reverse procedure to install, tighten to specifications, then Arm system as outlined under "Air Bag System Disarming & Arming."

VUE

1. Disarm system as outlined under "Air Bag System Disarming & Arming."
2. Remove center pillar lower molding.
3. Loosen fasteners on side impact sensor.
4. Remove SIS by sliding module up and out of key slots in sheet metal.
5. Disconnect SIS electrical connector.
6. Reverse procedure to install, tighten to specifications, then Arm system as outlined under "Air Bag System Disarming & Arming."

SIR Coil Assembly, Replace

SIR coil assembly will become uncentered if steering column is separated from steering gear and is allowed to rotate or centering spring is pushed down, letting hub rotate while coil assembly is removed from steering column.

ASTRO & SAFARI

1. Disarm system as outlined under "Air Bag System Disarming & Arming."
2. Remove driver air bag module as outlined under "Driver Air Bag Module, Replace."
3. Remove steering wheel nut, then disconnect horn lead assembly.
4. Mark relationship of steering wheel to steering shaft, then remove steering wheel using steering wheel puller tool No. J-1859-03, or equivalent.
5. Remove coil assembly retaining ring, then the wave washer.
6. **On models equipped with tilt steering,** proceed as follows:
   a. Place ignition switch in Run position, then rotate steering shaft assembly until block tooth is at 7 o'clock position and bolt guard screws are accessible through wide slots in shaft lock.
   b. Loosen screws on lock bolt guard until guard can be removed. Screws will be attached to lock bolt guard.

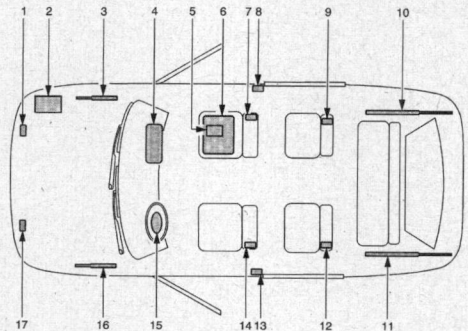

(1) Right Front End Sensor--Located on the front of the vehicle in the engine compartment

(2) Vehicle Battery--Located under the hood on the right side

(3) Front Hood Assist Rod--A gas shock located under the front hood on the passenger side

(4) I/P Air Bag--Located at the top right under the instrument panel

(5) Sensing and Diagnostic Module (SDM)--Located underneath the passenger front seat

(6) Passenger Presence System (PPS)--Located on the passenger front seat underneath the seat bottom trim

(7) RF Side Impact Air Bag--Located on the seat back of the passenger front seat

(8) Right Seat Belt Retractor Pretensioner and Right Side Impact Sensor (SIS)--The right SIS is located above the right seat belt retractor pretensioner under the center pillar trim near the bottom on passenger side of vehicle

(9) RR Side Impact Air Bag--Located on the seat back of the right rear bucket seat

(10) Rear Compartment Lid Assist Rod--A gas shock is located under the rear trunk lid on the passenger side

(11) Rear Compartment Lid Assist Rod--A gas shock is located under the rear trunk lid on the driver side

(12) LR Side Impact Air Bag--Located on the seat back of the left rear bucket seat

(13) Left Seat Belt Retractor Pretensioner and Left Side Impact Sensor (SIS)--The left SIS is located above the left seat belt retractor pretensioner under the center pillar trim near the bottom on driver side of vehicle

(14) LF Side Impact Air Bag--Located on the seat back of the driver front seat

(15) Steering Wheel Air Bag--Located on the steering wheel

(16) Front Hood Assist Rod--A gas shock located under the front hood on the driver side

LTV0500000004331

Fig. 14 SIR component location. Relay

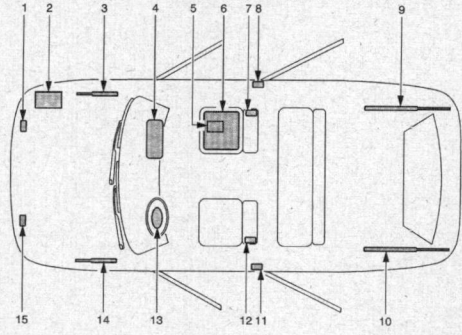

(1) Right Front End Sensor - Located on the front of the vehicle in the engine compartment

(2) Vehicle Battery - Located under the hood on the right side

(3) Front Hood Assist Rod - A gas shock located under the front hood on the passenger side

(4) I/P Air Bag - Located at the top right under the instrument panel

(5) Sensing and Diagnostic Module (SDM) - Located underneath the passenger front seat

(6) Passenger Presence System (PPS) - Located on the passenger front seat underneath the seat bottom trim

(7) RF Side Impact Air Bag - Located on the seat back of the passenger front seat

(8) Side Impact Sensor (SIS) and Right Seat Belt Retractor Pretensioner - The right SIS is located under the center pillar trim near the bottom and the seat belt retractor pretensioner is located above the SIS on passenger side of vehicle

(9) Rear Compartment Lid Assist Rod - A gas shock is located under the rear trunk lid on the passenger side

(10) Rear Compartment Lid Assist Rod - A gas shock is located under the rear trunk lid on the driver side

(11) Side Impact Sensor (SIS) and Left Seat Belt Retractor Pretensioner - The left SIS is located under the center pillar trim near the bottom and the seat belt retractor pretensioner is located above the SIS on driver side of vehicle

(12) LF Side Impact Air Bag - Located on the seat back of the driver front seat

(13) Steering Wheel Air Bag - Located on the steering wheel

(14) Front Hood Assist Rod - A gas shock located under the front hood on the driver side

(15) Left Front End Sensor - Located on the front of the vehicle in the engine compartment

LTV0500000003440

Fig. 15 SIR component location. Rendezvous

c. Place ignition switch in Lock position.

7. **On all models,** remove shaft lock retaining ring using lock plate compressor tool No. J-23653-SIR, or equivalent, to push down shaft lock. Discard ring.

8. Remove shaft lock, then the turn signal cancel cam.

9. Remove upper bearing spring, inner race seat and inner race.

10. Position turn signal lever in righthand turn (up) position, then remove multifunction switch as outlined under appropriate chassis chapter.

11. Remove round washer head screw and signal switch arm, then the oval head cross recess screw.

12. Remove hazard warning button with hazard warning spring and hazard warning switch knob.

13. Remove binding head cross recess screws, then the turn signal switch assembly, noting the following:
   a. Let switch hang freely if removal is not required.
   b. Disconnect turn signal switch connector from connector body bracket and vehicle wire harness.
   c. Disconnect socket and bracket assembly connector terminal from slot "D" of turn signal switch connector.
   d. Remove connector body bracket, then the wiring protector.
   e. Gently pull wire harness through column.

14. Remove SIR coil assembly with wire harness from column assembly.

15. Reverse procedure to install, tighten to specifications, then Arm system as outlined under "Air Bag System Disarming & Arming," noting the following:

AVALANCHE, ESCALADE EXT, SIERRA, SILVERADO & SSR

1. Disarm system as outlined under "Air Bag System Disarming & Arming."

2. Lower or remove steering column from vehicle as outlined in "Steering Columns" chapter.

3. Remove tilt lever.

4. Remove two lower steering column shroud pan head tapping screws from lower steering column shroud, then tilt shroud down and slide back to disengage locking tabs and remove from vehicle.

5. Remove two upper steering column shroud Torx head screws, then lift upper shroud to gain access to lock cylinder hole.

6. Hold ignition key in Start position, then, using 1/16 inch Allen wrench, push on lock cylinder pin.

7. Release key to Run position and pull steering column lock cylinder set from lock module assembly.

8. Remove upper steering column shroud.

9. Remove shift lever clevis, then the shift lever from vehicle.

10. Remove driver air bag module as outlined under "Driver Air Bag Module, Replace."

11. Remove steering wheel as outlined in appropriate chassis chapter.

12. Remove retaining ring, then the SIR coil assembly.

13. Remove wave washer, then disconnect wire harness strap from steering column wire harness.

14. Disconnect two wire harness straps from steering column wire harness.

15. Reverse procedure to install, tighten to specifications, then Arm system as outlined under "Air Bag System Disarming & Arming," noting the following:
   a. Ensure wheels are positioned straight ahead with block tooth and centering mark on steering shaft assembly at 12 o'clock position.
   b. Ensure SIR coil assembly is centered. If installing new SIR coil assembly, coil assembly will be pre-centered. Install coil, then remove and dispose of centering tab.

AZTEZ & RENDEZVOUS

1. Disarm system as outlined under "Air Bag System Disarming & Arming."

2. Remove inflatable restraint steering wheel module.

3. Remove steering wheel.

4. Remove upper and lower shrouds.

5. Remove wire harness straps from steering wheel column wire harness.

6. Remove inflatable restraint steering wheel module coil from steering shaft.

7. Reverse procedure to install, tighten to specifications, then Arm system as outlined under "Air Bag System Disarming & Arming."

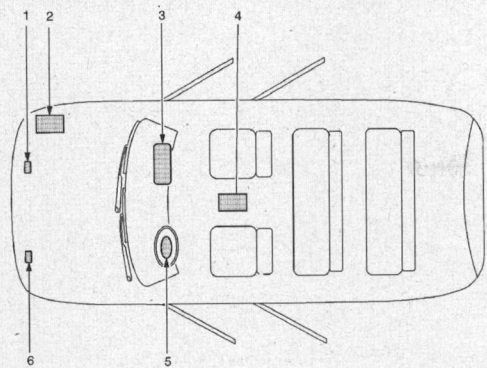

(1) Inflatable Restraint Front End Sensor - Right-Located on the front of the vehicle in the engine compartment

(2) Battery-Located under Hood on the right side

(3) Inflatable Restraint I/P Module-Located at the top right under the instrument panel

(4) Inflatable Restraint Sensing and Diagnostic Module (SDM)-Located under center floor console

(5) Inflatable Restraint Steering Wheel Module-Located on the steering wheel

(6) Inflatable Restraint Front End Sensor - Left-Located on the front of the vehicle in the engine compartment

LTV0500000004332

Fig. 16 SIR component location. S10 & Sonoma

BLAZER, BRAVADA, ENVOY, RAINIER & TRAILBLAZER

1. Disarm system as outlined under "Air Bag System Disarming & Arming."
2. Lower or remove steering column from vehicle as outlined in "Steering Columns" chapter.
3. Remove tilt lever.
4. Remove two lower steering column shroud pan head tapping screws from lower steering column shroud, then tilt shroud down and slide back to disengage locking tabs and remove from vehicle.
5. Remove two upper steering column shroud Torx head screws, then lift upper shroud to gain access to lock cylinder hole.
6. Hold ignition key in Start position, then, using 1/16 inch Allen wrench, push on lock cylinder pin.
7. Release key to Run position and pull steering column lock cylinder set from lock module assembly.
8. Remove upper steering column shroud.
9. Remove shift lever clevis, then the shift lever from vehicle.
10. Remove driver air bag module as outlined under "Driver Air Bag Module, Replace."
11. Remove steering wheel as outlined in appropriate chassis chapter.
12. Remove retaining ring, then the SIR coil assembly.
13. Remove wave washer, then disconnect wire harness strap from steering column wire harness.
14. Disconnect two wire harness straps from steering column wire harness.
15. Reverse procedure to install, tighten to specifications, then Arm system as outlined under "Air Bag System Disarming & Arming," noting the following:
    a. Ensure wheels are positioned straight ahead with block tooth and centering mark on steering shaft assembly at 12 o'clock position.
    b. Ensure SIR coil assembly is centered. If installing new SIR coil assembly, coil assembly will be precentered. Install coil, then remove and dispose of centering tab.

CANYON, COLORADO, SONOMA & S10

1. Disarm system as outlined under "Air Bag System Disarming & Arming."
2. Lower or remove steering column from vehicle as outlined in "Steering Columns" chapter.
3. Remove tilt lever.
4. Remove two lower steering column shroud pan head tapping screws from lower steering column shroud, then tilt shroud down and slide back to disengage locking tabs and remove from vehicle.
5. Remove two upper steering column shroud Torx head screws, then lift upper shroud to gain access to lock cylinder hole.
6. Hold ignition key in Start position, then, using 1/16 inch Allen wrench, push on lock cylinder pin.
7. Release key to Run position and pull steering column lock cylinder set from lock module assembly.
8. Remove upper steering column shroud.
9. Remove shift lever clevis, then the shift lever from vehicle.
10. Remove driver air bag module as outlined under "Driver Air Bag Module, Replace."
11. Remove steering wheel as outlined in appropriate chassis chapter.

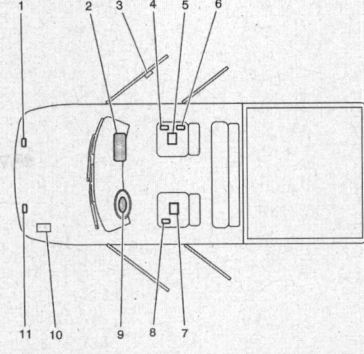

(1) Inflatable Restraint Front End Sensor-Right-Located on the front frame crossmember

(2) Inflatable Restraint I/P Module-Located at the right front of the instrument panel cluster (IPC)

(3) Inflatable Restraint Side Impact Sensor (SIS)-Right-Located under the right front door trim near the lower rear of the door frame-with RPO HP2

(4) Inflatable Restraint Seat Position Sensor (SPS)-Right-Located on the right front outboard seat track

(5) Inflatable Restraint Passenger Presence System (PPS)-Located under the right front seat mounted to the seat frame

(6) Inflatable Restraint Seat Belt Tension Retractor Sensor-Located on the outboard lower seat belt anchor

(7) Inflatable Restraint Sensing and Diagnostic Module (SDM)-Located under the left front seat under the carpet

(8) Inflatable Restraint Seat Position Sensor (SPS)-Left-Located on the left front outboard seat track

(9) Inflatable Restraint Steering Wheel Module-Located on the steering wheel

(10) Battery-Located under the hood on the left side

(11) Inflatable Restraint Front End Sensor-Left-Located on the front frame crossmember

LTV0500000004333

Fig. 17 SIR component location. Sierra & Silverado

12. Remove retaining ring, then the SIR coil assembly.
13. Remove wave washer, then disconnect wire harness strap from steering column wire harness.
14. Disconnect two wire harness straps from steering column wire harness.
15. Reverse procedure to install, tighten to specifications, then Arm system as outlined under "Air Bag System Disarming & Arming," noting the following:
    a. Ensure wheels are positioned straight ahead with block tooth and centering mark on steering shaft assembly at 12 o'clock position.
    b. Ensure SIR coil assembly is centered. If installing new SIR coil assembly, coil assembly will be precentered. Install coil, then remove and dispose of centering tab.

EQUINOX & TORRENT

1. Place front wheels in straight forward position with steering wheel centered.
2. Disarm system as outlined under "Air Bag System Disarming & Arming."
3. Remove inflatable restraint steering wheel module.
4. Remove steering wheel.
5. Remove steering column covers.
6. Release SIR coil harness clips from bracket below column.
7. Disconnect both SIR coil and horn/cruise connectors.
8. Using a small flat-bladed tool, carefully pry retaining tabs away from SIR coil assembly and slide SIR coil assembly off steering column.
9. Reverse procedure to install, tighten to specifications, then Arm system as outlined under "Air Bag System Disarming & Arming."

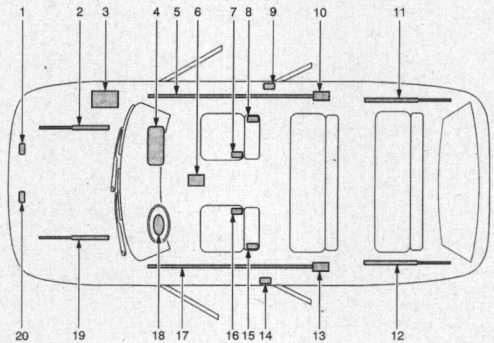

(1) Right Front End Sensor-Located on the front of the vehicle in the engine compartment

(2) Front Hood Assist Rod-A gas shock located under the front hood on the passenger side

(3) Vehicle Battery-Located under the hood on the right side

(4) I/P Air Bag-Located at the top right under the instrument panel

(5) Right Roof Rail Air Bag-Located under the headliner, extending from the passenger front windshield pillar all the way to rear of passenger rear door

(6) Sensing and Diagnostic Module (SDM)-Located underneath the vehicle carpet under the center console

(7) Seat Belt Pretensioner-Located on the inboard side of the passenger seat

(8) RF Side Impact Air Bag-Located on the seat back of passenger seat

(9) Side Impact Sensor (SIS)-Located under the center pillar trim near the bottom on passenger side of vehicle

(10) Inflator Module for Right Roof Rail Air Bag-Located behind passenger rear door opening under trim attach to C pillar

(11) Rear Hatch Assist Rod-A gas shock is located under the rear hatch on the passenger side

(12) Rear Hatch Assist Rod-A gas shock is located under the rear hatch on the driver side

(13) Inflator Module for Left Roof Rail Air Bag-Located behind driver rear door opening under trim attach to C pillar

(14) Side Impact Sensor (SIS)-Located near the center pillar trim near the bottom on driver side of vehicle

(15) LF Side Impact Air Bag-Located on the seat back of driver seat

(16) Seat Belt Pretensioner-Located on the inboard side of the driver seat

Left Roof Rail Air Bag-Located under the headliner, extending from the driver front windshield

LTV0500000004334

Fig. 18   SIR component location. SRX

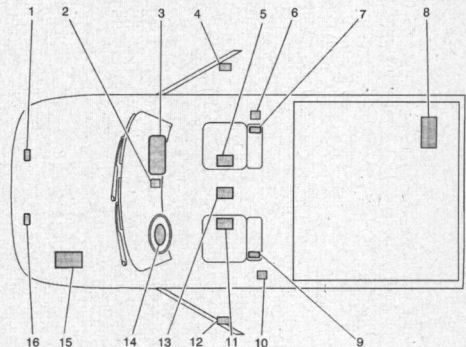

(1) Inflatable Restraint Front End Sensor - Right - Right--Located on the front of the vehicle in the engine compartment

(2) Inflatable Restraint I/P Module Disable Switch--Located in glove box

(3) Inflatable Restraint I/P Module--Located at the top right under the instrument panel

(4) Inflatable Restraint Side Impact Sensor (SIS) - Right--Located under right front door trim near the lower rear of door frame

(5) Inflatable Restraint Seat Position Switch - Right--Located on the side of the right front seat

(6) Seat Belt Retractor Pretensioner - Right--Located on the floor next to the right front seat

(7) Inflatable Restraint Side Impact Module - Right--Located on the side of the right front seat

(8) Battery--Located underneath the rear of the vehicle on the right side

(9) Inflatable Restraint Side Impact Module - Left--Located on the side of the left front seat

(10) Seat Belt Retractor Pretensioner - Left--Located on the floor next to the left front seat

(11) Inflatable Restraint Seat Position Switch - Left--Located on the side of the left front seat

(12) Inflatable Restraint Side Impact Sensor (SIS) - Left--Located under left front door trim near the lower rear of door frame

(13) Inflatable Restraint Sensing and Diagnostic Module (SDM)-Located under center floor console

(14) Inflatable Restraint Steering Wheel Module--Located on the steering wheel

(15) Underhood Fuse Block - SIR Fuse--Located under hood on the left side

(16) Inflatable Restraint Front End Sensor - Left--Located on the front of the vehicle in the engine compartment

LTV0500000003436

Fig. 19   SIR component location. SSR

ESCALADE, ESCALADE ESV, SUBURBAN, TAHOE & YUKON

1. Disarm system as outlined under "Air Bag System Disarming & Arming."
2. Lower or remove steering column from vehicle as outlined in "Steering Columns" chapter.
3. Remove tilt lever.
4. Remove two lower steering column shroud pan head tapping screws from lower steering column shroud, then tilt shroud down and slide back to disengage locking tabs and remove from vehicle.
5. Remove two upper steering column shroud Torx head screws, then lift upper shroud to gain access to lock cylinder hole.
6. Hold ignition key in Start position, then, using 1/16 inch Allen wrench, push on lock cylinder pin.
7. Release key to Run position and pull steering column lock cylinder set from lock module assembly.
8. Remove upper steering column shroud.
9. Remove shift lever clevis, then the shift lever from vehicle.
10. Remove driver air bag module as outlined under "Driver Air Bag Module, Replace."
11. Remove steering wheel as outlined in appropriate chassis chapter.
12. Remove retaining ring, then the SIR coil assembly.
13. Remove wave washer, then disconnect wire harness strap from steering column wire harness.
14. Disconnect two wire harness straps from steering column wire harness.
15. Reverse procedure to install, tighten to specifications, then Arm system as outlined under "Air Bag System Disarming & Arming," noting the following:
    a. Ensure wheels are positioned straight ahead with block tooth and centering mark on steering shaft assembly at 12 o'clock position.
    b. Ensure SIR coil assembly is centered. If installing new SIR coil assembly, coil assembly will be pre-centered. Install coil, then remove and dispose of centering tab.

EXPRESS & SAVANA

1. Disarm system as outlined under "Air Bag System Disarming & Arming."
2. Remove driver air bag module as outlined under "Driver Air Bag Module, Replace."
3. Remove steering wheel nut, then disconnect horn lead assembly.
4. Mark relationship of steering wheel to steering shaft, then remove steering wheel using steering wheel puller tool No. J-1859-03, or equivalent.
5. Remove coil assembly retaining ring, then the wave washer.
6. **On models equipped with tilt steering,** proceed as follows:
    a. Place ignition switch in Run position, then rotate steering shaft as-sembly until block tooth is at 7 o'clock position and bolt guard screws are accessible through wide slots in shaft lock.
    b. Loosen screws on lock bolt guard until guard can be removed. Screws will be attached to lock bolt guard.
    c. Place ignition switch in Lock position.
7. **On all models,** remove shaft lock retaining ring using lock plate compressor tool No. J-23653-SIR, or equivalent, to push down shaft lock. Discard ring.
8. Remove shaft lock, then the turn signal cancel cam.
9. Remove upper bearing spring, inner race seat and inner race.
10. Position turn signal lever in righthand turn (up) position, then remove multi-function switch as outlined under appropriate chassis chapter.
11. Remove round washer head screw and signal switch arm, then the oval head cross recess screw.
12. Remove hazard warning button with hazard warning spring and hazard warning switch knob.
13. Remove binding head cross recess screws, then the turn signal switch assembly, noting the following:
    a. Let switch hang freely if removal is not required.
    b. Disconnect turn signal switch connector from connector body bracket and vehicle wire harness.
    c. Disconnect socket and bracket assembly connector terminal from

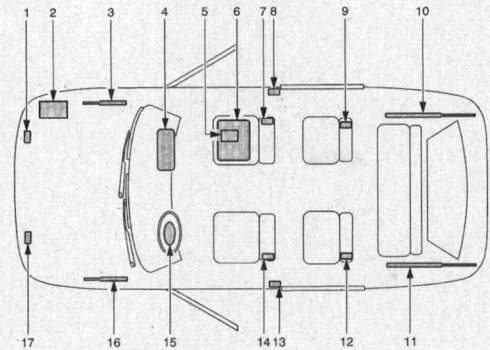

(1) Right Front End Sensor--Located on the front of the vehicle in the engine compartment

(2) Vehicle Battery--Located under the hood on the right side

(3) Front Hood Assist Rod--A gas shock located under the front hood on the passenger side

(4) I/P Air Bag--Located at the top right under the instrument panel

(5) Sensing and Diagnostic Module (SDM)--Located underneath the passenger front seat

(6) Passenger Presence System (PPS)--Located on the passenger front seat underneath the seat bottom trim

(7) RF Side Impact Air Bag--Located on the seat back of the passenger front seat

(8) Right Seat Belt Retractor Pretensioner and Right Side Impact Sensor (SIS)--The right SIS is located above the right seat belt retractor pretensioner under the center pillar trim near the bottom on passenger side of vehicle

(9) RR Side Impact Air Bag--Located on the seat back of the right rear bucket seat

(10) Rear Compartment Lid Assist Rod--A gas shock is located under the rear trunk lid on the passenger side

(11) Rear Compartment Lid Assist Rod--A gas shock is located under the rear trunk lid on the driver side

(12) LR Side Impact Air Bag--Located on the seat back of the left rear bucket seat

(13) Left Seat Belt Retractor Pretensioner and Left Side Impact Sensor (SIS)--The left SIS is located above the left seat belt retractor pretensioner under the center pillar trim near the bottom on driver side of vehicle

(14) LF Side Impact Air Bag--Located on the seat back of the driver front seat

(15) Steering Wheel Air Bag--Located on the steering wheel

(16) Front Hood Assist Rod--A gas shock located under the front hood on the driver side

LTV0500000004335

Fig. 20   SIR component location. SV6, Terraza & Uplander

slot "D" of turn signal switch connector.

d. Remove connector body bracket, then the wiring protector.

e. Gently pull wire harness through column.

14. Remove SIR coil assembly with wire harness from column assembly.

15. Reverse procedure to install, tighten to specifications, then Arm system as outlined under "Air Bag System Disarming & Arming," noting the following:

HHR

1. Place front wheels in straight forward position with steering wheel centered.
2. Disarm system as outlined under "Air Bag System Disarming & Arming."
3. Remove inflatable restraint steering wheel module.
4. Remove steering wheel.
5. Remove steering column covers.
6. Disconnect SIR coil harness connector from SIR coil module assembly.
7. Disconnect headlamp/turn signal harness connector from SIR coil module assembly.
8. Disconnect wiper/washer harness connector for SIR coil module assembly.
9. Using a small flat-bladed tool, carefully pry two retaining tabs away at base of the SIR coil assembly and slide SIR coil assembly off of steering column.
10. Remove headlamp/turn signal switch from SIR coil module assembly.
11. Remove wiper washer switch from SIR coil module assembly.
12. Reverse procedure to install, tighten to specifications, then Arm system as outlined under "Air Bag System Disarming & Arming."

HUMMER H2 & H3

1. Disarm system as outlined under "Air Bag System Disarming & Arming."
2. Make sure wheels on vehicle are straight ahead.
3. Make sure that tool no. J 42640 is installed or ignition switch is in lock position.

4. Remove steering wheel from steering shaft.
5. On vehicles with a tilt column, pull tilt lever straight out from steering column.
6. Remove two torx head screws from lower trim cover.
7. Remove lower trim cover.
8. Remove two torx head screws from upper trim cover.
9. Remove upper trim cover.
10. Remove wire harness straps from steering wheel column wire harness.
11. Remove retaining ring.
12. Remove SIR coil from steering shaft.
13. If replacing, discard SIR coil.
14. Reverse procedure to install, tighten to specifications, then Arm system as outlined under "Air Bag System Disarming & Arming."

MONTANA, SILHOUETTE & VENTURE

1. Disarm system as outlined under "Air Bag System Disarming & Arming."
2. Lower or remove steering column from vehicle as outlined in "Steering Columns" chapter.
3. Remove tilt lever.
4. Remove two lower steering column shroud pan head tapping screws from lower steering column shroud, then tilt shroud down and slide back to disengage locking tabs and remove from vehicle.
5. Remove two upper steering column shroud Torx head screws, then lift upper shroud to gain access to lock cylinder hole.
6. Hold ignition key in Start position, then, using 1/16 inch Allen wrench, push on lock cylinder pin.
7. Release key to Run position and pull steering column lock cylinder set from lock module assembly.
8. Remove upper steering column shroud.
9. Remove shift lever clevis, then the shift lever from vehicle.
10. Remove driver air bag module as outlined under "Driver Air Bag Module, Replace."
11. Remove steering wheel as outlined in appropriate chassis chapter.
12. Remove retaining ring, then the SIR coil assembly.
13. Remove wave washer, then disconnect wire harness strap from steering column wire harness.
14. Disconnect two wire harness straps from steering column wire harness.
15. Reverse procedure to install, tighten to specifications, then Arm system as outlined under "Air Bag System Disarming & Arming," noting the following:
    a. Ensure wheels are positioned

straight ahead with block tooth and centering mark on steering shaft assembly at 12 o'clock position.

b. Ensure SIR coil assembly is centered. If installing new SIR coil assembly, coil assembly will be pre-centered. Install coil, then remove and dispose of centering tab.

RELAY, SV6, TERRAZA & UPLANDER

1. Disarm system as outlined under "Air Bag System Disarming & Arming."
2. Remove steering wheel inflatable restraint module.
3. Remove steering wheel.
4. Remove steering column lower shroud.
5. Remove steering column upper shroud.
6. Remove upper steering column.
7. Remove inflatable restraint steering wheel module coil.
8. Reverse procedure to install, tighten to specifications, then Arm system as outlined under "Air Bag System Disarming & Arming."

SRX

1. Disarm system as outlined under "Air Bag System Disarming & Arming."
2. Remove steering column trim covers.
3. Remove wire harness assembly from wire harness strap.
4. Remove wire harness straps from wire harness assembly.
5. Remove wire harness strap from upper tilt head assembly.
6. Remove SIR steering wheel module coil retaining clip.
7. Remove SIR steering wheel module coil.
8. Remove wave washer from steering column upper shaft.
9. Reverse procedure to install, tighten to specifications, then Arm system as outlined under "Air Bag System Disarming & Arming."

TRACKER

1. Disarm system as outlined under "Air Bag System Disarming & Arming."
2. Remove driver air bag module as outlined under "Driver Air Bag Module, Replace."
3. Remove steering wheel nut, then disconnect horn lead assembly.
4. Mark relationship of steering wheel to steering shaft, then remove steering wheel using steering wheel puller tool

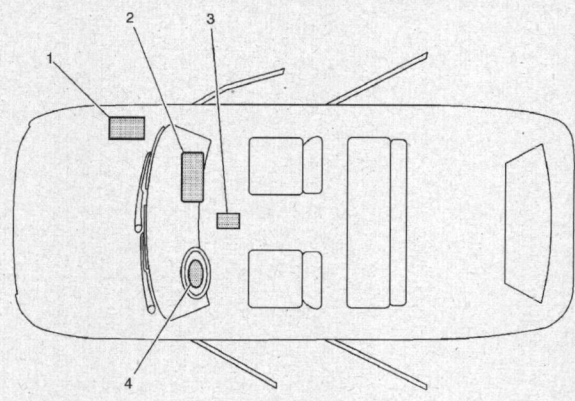

(1) Vehicle Battery-Located under the hood on the right side
(2) IP Air Bag-Located at the top right under the instrument panel
(3) Sensing and Diagnostic Module (SDM)-Located underneath the center console
(4) Steering Wheel Air Bag-Located on the steering wheel

LTV0500000004336

Fig. 21   SIR component location. Tracker

No. J-1859-03, or equivalent.
5. Remove coil assembly retaining ring, then the wave washer.
6. Remove shaft lock retaining ring using lock plate compressor tool No. J-23653-SIR, or equivalent, to push down shaft lock. Discard ring.
7. Remove shaft lock, then the turn signal cancel cam.
8. Remove upper bearing spring, inner race seat and inner race.
9. Position turn signal lever in righthand turn (up) position, then remove multifunction switch as outlined under appropriate chassis chapter.
10. Remove round washer head screw and signal switch arm, then the oval head cross recess screw.
11. Remove hazard warning button with hazard warning spring and hazard warning switch knob.
12. Remove binding head cross recess screws, then the turn signal switch assembly, noting the following:
    a. Let switch hang freely if removal is not required.
    b. Disconnect turn signal switch connector from connector body bracket and vehicle wire harness.
    c. Disconnect socket and bracket assembly connector terminal from slot "D" of turn signal switch connector.

d. Remove connector body bracket, then the wiring protector.
e. Gently pull wire harness through column.
13. Remove SIR coil assembly with wire harness from column assembly.
14. Reverse procedure to install, tighten to specifications, then Arm system as outlined under "Air Bag System Disarming & Arming," noting the following:

VUE

1. Place front wheels in straight forward position with steering wheel centered.
2. Disarm system as outlined under "Air Bag System Disarming & Arming."
3. Remove inflatable restraint steering wheel module.
4. Remove steering wheel.
5. Remove steering column covers.
6. Release SIR coil harness clips from bracket below column.
7. Disconnect both SIR coil and horn/cruise connectors.
8. Using a small flat-bladed tool, carefully pry retaining tabs away from SIR coil assembly and slice SIR coil assembly off steering column.
9. Reverse procedure to install, tighten to specifications, then Arm system as outlined under "Air Bag System Disarming & Arming."

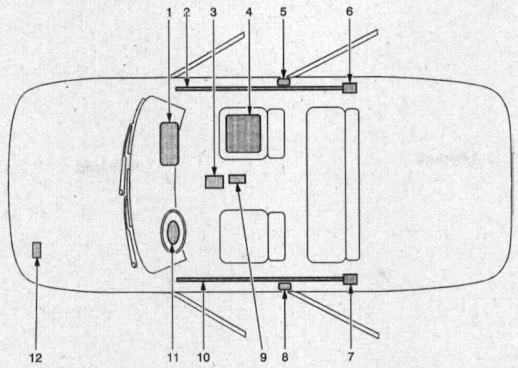

(1) I/P Air Bag--Located at the top right under the instrument panel

(2) Right Roof Rail Air Bag--Located under the headliner, extending from the passenger front windshield pillar to the passenger rear windshield pillar

(3) Sensing and Diagnostic Module (SDM)--Located underneath the vehicle carpet under the center console

(4) Passenger Presence System (PPS)--Located in passenger seat

(5) Passenger/Right Side Impact Sensor (SIS) and Seat Belt Pretensioner--Located under the trim near the bottom of the center pillar

(6) Inflator Module for Right Roof Rail Module--Located behind the garnish molding on the upper rear pillar

(7) Inflator Module for Left Roof Rail Module--Located behind garnish molding on the upper rear pillar

(8) Driver/Left Side Impact Sensor (SIS) and Seat Belt Pretensioner-Located under the trim near the bottom of the center pillar

(9) Vehicle Rollover Sensor--Located under center console

(10) Left Roof Rail Air Bag--Located under the headliner, extending from the driver front windshield pillar to the driver rear windshield pillar

(11) Steering Wheel Air Bag--Located on the steering wheel

(12) Vehicle Battery--Located at the front left of the engine compartment.

LTV0500000004337

Fig. 22   SIR component location. VUE

TIGHTENING SPECIFICATIONS

Year	Component	Torque Inch Lbs.
ASTRO & SAFARI		
2002–05	Inflatable Restraint Front End Discriminating Sensor Fastener	58
	Inflatable Restraint Instrument Panel Module Fastener	80
	Inflatable Restraint Sensing And Diagnostic Module Fastener	106
AVALANCHE, ESCALADE EXT, SIERRA, SILVERADO & SSR		
2002–06	Inflatable Restraint Front End Discriminating Sensor Bolt	80
	Inflatable Restraint Instrument Panel Module Bolt	80
	Inflatable Restraint Sensing And Diagnostic Module Retaining Nuts	89
	Inflatable Restraint Side Impact Module Bolts	89
	Inflatable Restraint Side Impact Sensor Bolts	89
	Passenger Presence System Electronic Control Unit Bolts	18
AZTEK & RENDEZVOUS		
2002–05	Inflatable Front End Discriminating Sensor Bolts	71
	Inflatable Restraint Instrument Panel Module Nuts - Buick	89
	Inflatable Restraint Instrument Panel Module Nuts - Pontiac	89
	Inflatable Restraint Sensing And Diagnostic Module Fasteners	89
	Inflatable Restraint Side Impact Sensor Fasteners	89
	Inflatable Restraint Side Impact Module Fasteners	45
BLAZER, BRAVADA, ENVOY, RAINIER & TRAILBLAZER		
2002–06	Inflatable Restraint Front End Discriminating Sensor Fasteners	71
	Inflatable Restraint Instrument Panel Module Fasteners	71
	Inflatable Restraint Sensing And Diagnostic Module Fasteners	106
CANYON, COLORADO, SONOMA & S10		
2002–06	Front Seat Belt Retractor / Pretensioner Assembly Bolts	39①
	Passenger Supplemental Inflatable Restraint Bracket Fasteners	79
	Passenger Supplemental Inflatable Restraint Fasteners	②
	SIR Roof Rail Air Bag Bolts	79
	SIR Seat Position Sensor Nuts	18①
	SIR Sensing And Diagnostic Module Nuts	79
	SIR Side Impact Sensor Screws	79
	Supplemental Inflatable Restraint Front End Discriminating Sensor Bolts	79

TIGHTENING SPECIFICATIONS—Continued

Year	Component	Torque Inch Lbs.
EQUINOX & TORRENT		
2005–06	Instrument Panel Inflator Module-To-Instrument Panel Screws	89
	Roof Rail Inflator Module-To-Roof Screws	44
	Sensing And Diagnostic Module-To-Floor Nuts	44
	Side Impact Sensor-To-Lock Pillar Screws	89
ESCALADE, ESCALADE ESV, SUBURBAN, TAHOE & YUKON		
2002–06	Inflatable Restraint Front End Discriminating Sensor Bolt	80
	Inflatable Restraint Instrument Panel Module Bolt	80
	Inflatable Restraint Sensing And Diagnostic Module Retaining Nuts	89
	Inflatable Restraint Side Impact Module Bolts	89
	Inflatable Restraint Side Impact Sensor Bolts	89
	Passenger Presence System Electronic Control Unit Bolts	18
EXPRESS & SAVANA		
2002–06	Inflatable Restraint Front End Discriminating Sensor Nut	89
	Inflatable Restraint Instrument Panel Module Bolts	89
	Inflatable Restraint Sensing And Diagnostic Module Nut	89
	Pretensioner Bolt	30①
	Pretensioner Trim Cover Screws	18
HHR		
2006	Forward Discriminating Sensor Bolt	71
	Inflatable Restraint Roof Side Rail Module Bolt	80
	Inflatable Restraint Sensing And Diagnostic Module Nut	89
	Inflatable Restraint Side Impact Sensor Bolt	80
	Instrument Panel Compartment Dampener Screw	25
	Instrument Panel Inflatable Restraint Module Nut	89
	Seat Belt Adjuster Bolt	33①
	Seat Belt Anchor Bolt	33①
	Seat Belt Retractor Bolt	33①
H2		
2003–06	Inflatable Restraint Front End Sensor	89
	Inflatable Restraint Instrument Panel Module	89
	Inflatable Restraint Sensing And Diagnostic Module	89

Continued

TIGHTENING SPECIFICATIONS—Continued

Year	Component	Torque Inch Lbs.
H3		
2006	Inflatable Restraint Front End Sensor	80
	Inflatable Restraint Instrument Panel Module	80
	Inflatable Restraint Passenger Presence System	71
	Inflatable Restraint Roof Rail Module Bolts	71
	Inflatable Restraint Roof Rail Module Screws	18
	Inflatable Restraint Seat Position Sensor	80
	Inflatable Restraint Sensing And Diagnostic Module	89
	Inflatable Restraint Side Impact Sensor	80
	Inflatable Restraint Vehicle Rollover Sensor	89
	Seat Belt Retractor / Pretensioner	38①
MONTANA, SILHOUETTE & VENTURE		
2002–05	Driver Seat Belt Pretensioner Fastener	26①
	Inflatable Restraint Instrument Module Fasteners	89
	Inflatable Restraint Sensing And Diagnostic Module Fasteners	89
	Inflatable Restraint Side Impact Sensor Fasteners	89
	Passenger Seat Belt Pretensioner Fastener	26①
RELAY, SV6, TERRAZA & UPLANDER		
2005–06	Driver Information Center Display Switch Screw	18
	Electronic Control Unit Screw	18
	Front End Inflatable Restraint Discriminating Sensor Bolt	80
	Inflatable Restraint Sensing And Diagnostic Module Bolt	89
	Inflatable Restraint Side Impact Module Nut	44
	Inflatable Restraint Side Impact Sensor Bolt	89
	Inflatable Restraint Steering Wheel Module Coil	22
	Instrument Panel Compartment Screw	18
	Instrument Panel Inflatable Restraint Module	89
	Seat Belt Guide Loop Nut	31①
	Seat Belt Retractor Bolt	31①
	Steering Column Lower Shroud Bolt	13
	Steering Column Upper Shroud Bolt	31
	Steering Wheel Nut	30①

TIGHTENING SPECIFICATIONS—Continued

Year	Component	Torque Inch Lbs.
SRX		
2006	Inflatable Restraint Front End Sensor	80
	Inflatable Restraint Instrument Panel Module Fasteners	16①
	Inflatable Restraint Roof Rail Module Fasteners	80
	Inflatable Restraint Sensing And Diagnostic Module Fasteners	80
	Inflatable Restraint Side Impact Module Bracket Bolts	80
	Inflatable Restraint Side Impact Module Bracket To Seat Frame Bolts	80
	Inflatable Side Impact Sensor Bolts	80
	Seat Belt Buckle Pretensioner Bolt	31①
	Steering Column Shrouds	18
	Steering Wheel Nut	30①
TRACKER		
2002–04	Inflatable Restraint Instrument Panel Module Fasteners Four Bottom Center Bolts	16.5①
	Inflatable Restraint Instrument Panel Module Fasteners Two Upper Side Screws	4①
	Inflatable Restraint Sensing And Diagnostic Module Fasteners	4.5①
	Inflatable Restraint Steering Wheel Module Fasteners Two Upper Side Bolts	6.5①
VUE		
2002–06	Instrument Panel Inflator Module-To-Instrument Panel Screws	89
	Roof Rail Inflator Module-To-Roof Screws	44
	Sensing And Diagnostic Module-To-Floor Nuts	89
	Side Impact Sensor-To-Lock Pillar Screw	89

① — Ft. lbs.

② — Fully Driven, seated and not stripped.

ANTI-LOCK BRAKES

TABLE OF CONTENTS

	Page No.		Page No.
ADVICS	5-2	**DELPHI 7.0**	5-88
APPLICATION CHART	5-1	**DELPHI 7.2**	5-110
BOSCH 5.3 & 8.0	5-38	**DELPHI 7.4**	5-144
CONTINENTAL TEVES MK-70	5-76	**KELSEY-HAYES**	5-169

Application Chart

Make/Model	Year	Type
BUICK		
Rainier	2004–06	Kelsey-Hayes 325
Rendezvous	2002–06	Bosch 5.3
Terraza	2005–06	Delphi 7.4
CADILLAC		
Escalade	2002–05	Kelsey-Hayes 325
	2003–06	Kelsey-Hayes 430
Escalade ESV	2003–05	Kelsey-Hayes 325
	2003–06	Kelsey-Hayes 430
Escalade EXT	2002–05	Kelsey-Hayes 325
	2003–06	Kelsey-Hayes 430
SRX	2004–06	Delphi 7.2
CHEVROLET		
Astro	2002–05	Kelsey-Hayes 325
Avalanche	2002–05	Kelsey-Hayes 325
	2003–06	Kelsey-Hayes 430
Colorado	2004–06	Advics
Equinox	2005–06	Bosch 5.3
Express	2002	Kelsey-Hayes 310
	2003–06	Kelsey-Hayes 325
	2004–06	Kelsey-Hayes 430
HHR	2006	Continental Teves MK-70
Uplander	2006	Delphi 7.4
Venture	2002–05	Delphi 7.0
Blazer (S-Series)	2002–05	Kelsey-Hayes 325
S10 Pickup	2002–04	Kelsey-Hayes 325
Silverado	2002–06	Kelsey-Hayes 325
SSR	2203–06	Kelsey-Hayes 325
Suburban	2002–05	Kelsey-Hayes 325
	2003–06	Kelsey-Hayes 430
Tahoe	2002–05	Kelsey-Hayes 325
	2003–06	Kelsey-Hayes 430
Tracker	2002–04	—
Trailblazer	2002–05	Kelsey-Hayes 325
	2006	Kelsey-Hayes 445
GMC		
Canyon	2004–06	Advics
Envoy	2002–05	Kelsey-Hayes 325
	2006	Kelsey-Hayes 445
Safari	2002–05	Kelsey-Hayes 325
Sierra	2002–06	Kelsey-Hayes 325
Sonoma	2002–04	Kelsey-Hayes 325

Continued

ANTI-LOCK BRAKES

Make/Model	Year	Type
GMC		
Yukon	2002–05	Kelsey-Hayes 325
	2003–06	Kelsey-Hayes 430
Yukon XL	2002–05	Kelsey-Hayes 325
	2003–06	Kelsey-Hayes 430
HUMMER		
H2	2003–06	Bosch 5.3
H3	2006	Advics
OLDSMOBILE		
Bravada	2002–04	Kelsey-Hayes 325
Silhouette	2002–03	Delphi 7.0
PONTIAC		
Aztek	2002–05	Bosch 5.3
Montana	2002–05	Delphi 7.0
SV6	2005–06	Delphi 7.4
Torrent	2006	Bosch 5.3
SATURN		
Vue	2002–04	—
	2005–06	Bosch 8.0
Relay	2006	Delphi 7.4

ADVICS

NOTE: On Air Bag Equipped Models, Refer To "Air Bag System Precautions" Located In The Front Of This Manual For System Disarming & Arming Procedures.

NOTE: Electrical Symbol & Wire Color Code Identification Located In The Front Of This Manual May Be Used As An Aid When Using Wiring Circuits Found In This Section.

NOTE: Refer To "Computer Relearn Procedures" Located In The Front Of This Manual For Computer Relearn Procedures.

INDEX

	Page No.
Description	5-2
Diagnosis & Testing	5-3
Accessing Diagnostic Trouble Codes	5-3
Clearing Diagnostic Trouble Codes	5-3
Connector Pin Identification	5-3
Canyon & Colorado	5-3
Hummer H3	5-3
Diagnostic Tests	5-3
Canyon & Colorado	5-3
Hummer H3	5-3

	Page No.
Diagnostic Trouble Code Interpretation	5-3
Intermittents & Poor Connections	5-3
Symptom Tests	5-3
Canyon & Colorado	5-3
Hummer H3	5-3
Temperature Vs. Resistance	5-3
Wiring Diagrams	5-3
Diagnostic Chart Index	5-13
Precautions	5-2
Air Bag Systems	5-2

	Page No.
Battery Ground Cable	5-2
System Service	5-3
Brake System Bleed	5-3
ABS Automated Bleed Procedure	5-3
Hydraulic Brake System Bleeding – Manual	5-4
Hydraulic Brake System Bleeding – Pressure	5-6
Component Replacement	5-7
Canyon & Colorado	5-7
Hummer H3	5-9

PRECAUTIONS

Air Bag Systems

Refer to "Air Bag System Precautions" in the front of this manual for system disarming and arming procedures.

Battery Ground Cable

Prior to service disconnect battery ground cable and isolate as required.

DESCRIPTION

When wheel slip is detected during a brake application, the ABS enters anti-lock mode. During anti-lock braking, hydraulic pressure in the individual wheel circuits is controlled to prevent any wheel from slipping. A separate hydraulic line and specific solenoid valves are provided for each wheel. The ABS can decrease, hold, or increase hydraulic pressure to each wheel

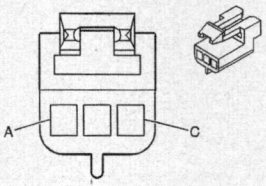

Connector Part Information	• 12064758 • 3-Way F Metri-Pack 150 Series (BK)		
Pin	Wire Color	Circuit No.	Function
A	TN/BK	371	I/P Module Disable Switch - Signal
B	TN/BK	723	I/P Module Disable Switch - Signal
C	YE	1139	Ignition 1 Voltage

LTV050000000615

Fig. 1   Connector pin identification (Accessory switch C1). Canyon & Colorado

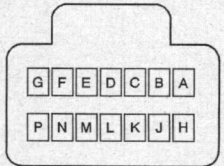

Connector Part Information	• 15332169 • 14-Way F GT 150 (BK)		
Pin	Wire Color	Circuit No.	Function
A	PK	339	Ignition 1 Voltage
B	PU/WH	1572	TCS Requested Indicator Control
C	BN	9	Park Lamp Supply Voltage
D	TN/BK	723	I/P Module Disable Switch - Signal (C99)
E	PK	353	I/P Module Supression Indicator Control (C99)
F	--	--	Not Used
G	GY	8	Instrument Panel Lamp Dimmer Switch Signal
H	BK	2050	Ground
J	BN/WH	1571	Traction Control Switch Signal
K-P	--	--	Not Used

LTV050000000616

Fig. 2   Connector pin identification (Accessory switch C2). Canyon & Colorado

brake. The ABS cannot, however, increase hydraulic pressure above the amount which is transmitted by the master cylinder during braking.

During anti-lock braking, a series of rapid pulsations is felt in the brake pedal. These pulsations are caused by the rapid changes in position of the individual solenoid valves as the EBCM responds to wheel speed sensor inputs and attempts to prevent wheel slip. These pedal pulsations are present only during anti-lock braking and stop when normal braking is resumed or when the vehicle comes to a stop. A ticking or popping noise may also be heard as the solenoid valves cycle rapidly. During anti-lock braking on dry pavement, intermittent chirping noises may be heard as the tires approach slipping. These noises and pedal pulsations are considered normal during anti-lock operation.

Vehicles equipped with ABS may be stopped by applying normal force to the brake pedal. Brake pedal operation during normal braking is no different than that of previous non-ABS systems. Maintaining a constant force on the brake pedal provides the shortest stopping distance while maintaining vehicle stability.

DIAGNOSIS & TESTING

Accessing Diagnostic Trouble Codes

Connect a suitably programmed scan tool to Data Link Connector (DLC) and follow manufacturers instructions.

Diagnostic Trouble Code Interpretation

Refer to "Diagnostic Chart Index" for diagnostic trouble code interpretation.

Connector Pin Identification

CANYON & COLORADO

Refer to **Figs. 1 through 6** for connector pin identification.

HUMMER H3

Refer to **Figs. 7 through 16** for connector pin identification.

Wiring Diagrams

Refer to **Figs. 17 and 18** for wiring diagrams.

Diagnostic Tests

CANYON & COLORADO

Refer to **Figs. 19 through 37** for diagnostic test procedures.

HUMMER H3

Refer to **Figs. 38 through 58** for diagnostic test procedures.

Symptom Tests

CANYON & COLORADO

Refer to **Figs. 59 through 61** for symptom test procedures.

HUMMER H3

Refer to **Figs. 62 through 68** for symptom test procedures.

Temperature Vs. Resistance

Refer to **Fig. 69** for temperature vs. resistance values.

Intermittents & Poor Connections

Most Intermittents are caused by faulty electrical connections or wiring, although a sticking relay or solenoid can also cause an intermittent condition. Inspect wiring and connectors for the following:

1. Poor mating of connector halves, or terminals not fully seated in connector body.
2. Dirt or corrosion on terminals.
3. Damaged connector body.
4. Improperly formed or damaged terminals.
5. Poor terminal to wire connection.
6. Rubbed through wiring insulation.
7. Wiring broken inside insulation.

Clearing Diagnostic Trouble Codes

Connect a suitably programmed scan tool to Data Link Connector (DLC) and follow manufacturers instructions.

SYSTEM SERVICE

Brake System Bleed

ABS AUTOMATED BLEED PROCEDURE

Do not remove the reservoir cap while depressing and releasing the brake pedal. If the cap is removed while depressing and releasing the brake pedal, pressurized brake fluid being returned to the reservoir may leave the reservoir. Personal injury or vehicle damage could result.

Do not allow the HBCi pump and motor to run more than one minute continuously. Allow two minutes cool down time between pump run times. Extended pump and motor run time could create excessive heat and damage the pump and motor assembly.

Perform steps 1–4 below to bleed the HBCi accumulator circuit prior to performing a base brake bleed.

1. Turn ignition On. Allow pump and motor to run as required. Pump and motor will stop automatically and may run up to 10 seconds.
2. Depress brake pedal 4 times.
3. Confirm that brake fluid returns to reservoir.
4. Repeat steps 1–3 until all air is purged

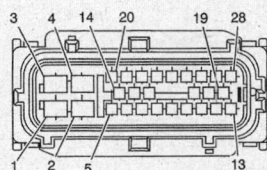

Connector Part Information	• 15409795		
	• 28-Way F Sealed (GY)		
Pin	Wire Color	Circuit No.	Function
1	OG	540	Battery Positive Voltage
2	BK	2050	Ground
3	BK	850	Ground
4	RD	542	Battery Positive Voltage
5	L-BU	20	Stop Lamp Supply Voltage
6	--	--	Not Used
7	PU	1807	Class 2 Serial Data
8-9	--	--	Not Used
10	BN	718	Low Reference (4WD)
11	TN	833	Right Front Wheel Speed Sensor Signal
12	D-GN	872	Right Front Wheel Speed Supply Voltage
13-15	--	--	Not Used
16	PU	1807	Class 2 Serial Data
17	D-BU	716	LNG Rate Signal (4WD)
18	L-BU	830	Left Front Wheel Speed Supply Voltage
19-20	--	--	Not Used
21	PK	1439	Ignition 1 Voltage
22	TN/BK	464	Delivered Torque Signal (2WD)
23	OG/BK	463	Requested Torque Signal (2WD)
24-25	--	--	Not Used
26	YE	873	Left Front Wheel Speed Sensor Signal
27	--	--	Not Used
28	YE/BK	1827	Vehicle Speed Signal

LTV0500000000617

Fig. 3 Connector pin identification (EBCM). Canyon & Colorado

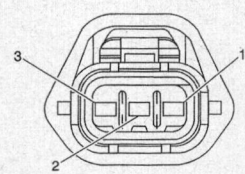

Connector Part Information	• 15383379		
	• 3-Way F 050 SSD Sealed (BK)		
Pin	Wire Color	Circuit No.	Function
1	PK	1439	Ignition 1 Voltage
2	D-BU	716	LNG Rate Signal
3	BN	718	Low Reference

LTV0500000000618

Fig. 4 Connector pin identification (G-sensor). Canyon & Colorado

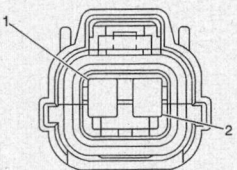

Connector Part Information	• 15409340		
	• 2-Way F Sealed (D-GY)		
Pin	Wire Color	Circuit No.	Function
1	L-BU	830	Left Front Wheel Speed Supply Voltage
2	YE	873	Left Front Wheel Speed Sensor Signal

LTV0500000000619

Fig. 5 Connector pin identification (LF WSS). Canyon & Colorado

from accumulator circuit (return fluid is clear and free from air).

5. **Base hydraulic brake system must be bled before proceeding. If you have not yet performed base hydraulic brake system bleeding procedure, refer to "Hydraulic Brake System Bleeding" for hydraulic brakes before proceeding.**

6. With ignition Off, depress and release brake pedal 20 times to deplete accumulator pressure. If brake fluid clouds and has air mixed with fluid, wait until fluid clears to proceed.

7. Turn ignition On and depress pedal 20 times quickly. Pump and motor will be activated.

8. Turn ignition Off and repeat step procedure 5 again. If brake fluid clouds and has air mixed with fluid, wait until fluid clears to proceed.

9. Turn ignition On to activate pump and motor. Allow pump and motor to stop automatically. Pump and motor will run approximately 10 seconds.

10. Install a suitably programmed scan tool to vehicle.

11. Start engine and allow to idle.

12. Depress brake pedal firmly and maintain steady pressure on pedal.

13. Begin automated bleed procedure using scan tool.

14. Follow instructions on scan tool to complete automated bleed procedure. Release brake pedal between each test sequence.

15. Turn ignition Off.

16. Remove scan tool from vehicle.

17. Fill brake master cylinder reservoir to maximum-fill level with Delco Supreme 11® GM part No. 12377967 or equivalent DOT-3 brake fluid from a clean, sealed brake fluid container.

18. Bleed hydraulic brake system as outlined in "Hydraulic Brake System Bleeding" for hydraulic brakes.

19. With ignition Off, apply brakes 2– times or until brake pedal becomes firm, in order to deplete brake booster power reserve.

20. Slowly depress and release brake pedal. Observe feel of brake pedal.

21. If pedal feels spongy, repeat automated bleeding procedure. If brake pedal still feels spongy after repeating automated bleeding procedure inspect brake system for external leaks.

22. Turn ignition key On, with engine Off, inspect to see if brake system warning lamp remains illuminated.

23. If brake system warning lamp remains illuminated, Do Not allow vehicle to be driven until it is diagnosed and repaired.

24. Drive vehicle to exceed 8 mph to allow ABS initialization to occur while observing pedal feel.

25. If brake pedal feels spongy, repeat automated bleeding procedure until firm brake pedal is obtained.

HYDRAULIC BRAKE SYSTEM BLEEDING – MANUAL

Do not remove the reservoir cap while depressing and releasing the brake pedal. If the cap is removed while depressing and releasing the brake pedal, pressurized brake fluid being returned to the reservoir may leave the reservoir. Personal injury or vehicle damage could result.

Do not allow the HBCi pump and motor to run more than one minute continuously. Allow two minutes cool down time between pump run times. Extended pump and motor run time could create excessive heat and damage the pump and motor assembly.

1. Place a clean shop cloth beneath brake master cylinder to prevent brake fluid spills.

2. If you disconnected brake pipes from master cylinder, you must perform following steps:

a. Ensure that brake master cylinder reservoir is full to maximum-fill level. If required, add Delco Supreme 11 GM part No. 12377967 or equivalent DOT-3 brake fluid from a clean, sealed brake fluid container. If removal of reservoir cap and diaphragm is required, clean outside of reservoir on and around cap prior to removal.

b. With all brake pipes installed securely to master cylinder, loosen and separate lefthand side front brake pipe from lefthand side front port of brake master cylinder.

c. Allow a small amount of brake fluid

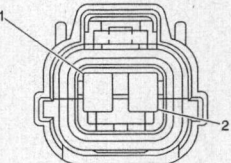

Connector Part Information	• 15409340		
	• 2-Way F Sealed (D-GY)		
Pin	Wire Color	Circuit No.	Function
1	D-GN	872	Right Front Wheel Speed Supply Voltage
2	TN	833	Right Front Wheel Speed Sensor Signal

LTV0500000000620

Fig. 6 Connector pin identification (RF WSS). Canyon & Colorado

to gravity bleed from open port of master cylinder.

d. Reconnect brake pipe to master cylinder port and tighten.

e. Have an assistant slowly depress brake pedal fully and maintain steady pressure on pedal.

f. Loosen same brake pipe to purge air from open port of master cylinder.

g. Tighten brake pipe, then have assistant slowly release brake pedal.

h. Wait 15 seconds, then repeat steps e through g until all air is purged from same port of master cylinder.

i. With lefthand front brake pipe installed securely to master cylinder, after all air has been purged from lefthand front port master cylinder, loosen and separate righthand front brake pipe from master cylinder, then repeat steps e through i.

j. Turn ignition key to On position.

k. With righthand front brake pipe installed to master cylinder, after all air has been purged from righthand front port of master cylinder, loosen and separate lefthand rear brake pipe from master cylinder, then repeat steps e through h.

l. With lefthand rear brake pipe installed securely to master cylinder, after all air has been purged from lefthand rear port of master cylinder, loosen and separate righthand rear brake pipe from master cylinder, then repeat steps e through h.

m. After completing final master cylinder port bleeding procedure, ensure that all brake pipe-to-master cylinder fittings are properly tightened.

n. Turn ignition key to Off position. Depress brake pedal 20 times.

3. Fill brake master cylinder reservoir with Delco Supreme 11® GM part No. 12377967 or equivalent DOT-3 brake fluid from a clean, sealed brake fluid container. Ensure that brake master cylinder reservoir remains at least half-full during this bleeding procedure. Add fluid as required to maintain proper level. Clean outside of reservoir on and around reservoir cap prior to removing cap and diaphragm.

4. Install proper box-end wrench onto righthand rear wheel hydraulic circuit bleeder valve.

5. Install a transparent hose over end of bleeder valve.

6. Submerge open end of transparent hose into a transparent container partially filled with Delco Supreme 11® GM part No. 12377967 or equivalent DOT-3 brake fluid from a clean, sealed brake fluid container.

7. Have an assistant turn ignition On, then partially apply and hold brake pedal. Do Not pump brake pedal. Fluid will flow when bleed valves are opened.

8. Loosen bleeder valve to purge air from wheel hydraulic circuit.

9. Tighten bleeder valve, then have assistant slowly release brake pedal.

10. Wait 15 seconds, then repeat steps 7–9 until all air is purged from same wheel hydraulic circuit.

11. With righthand rear wheel hydraulic circuit bleeder valve tightened securely, after all air has been purged from righthand rear hydraulic circuit, install a proper box-end wrench onto lefthand rear wheel hydraulic circuit bleeder valve.

12. Install a transparent hose over end of bleeder valve, then repeat steps 6–10.

13. Turn ignition Off, assistant will now have to pump brake pedal for fluid to flow from open bleed valves.

14. With lefthand rear wheel hydraulic circuit bleeder valve tightened securely, after all air has been purged from lefthand rear hydraulic circuit, install a proper box-end wrench onto righthand

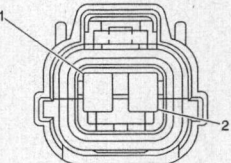

Connector Part Information

• OEM: 15394150
• Service: See Catalog
• Description: 16-Way F Micro 64 Series (BK)

Terminal Part Information

• Terminal/Tray: 15359541 / 4
• Core/Insulation Crimp: M / M
• Release Tool/Test Probe: 15381651-2 / J-35616-64A (L-BU)

Pin	Wire Color	Circuit No.	Function
1	PU/WH	1565	4 LO LOCK Indicator Control
2	YE	234	Seat Belt Indicator Control
3	D-BU	2307	Passenger Air Bag On Indicator Control
4	--	--	Not Used
5	YE	1139	Ignition 1 Voltage
6	D-GN	2308	Passenger Air Bag Off Indicator Control
7	BN	241	Ignition 3 Voltage
8	PK	1561	Differential Lock Indicator Control
9	TN/BK	1566	4 HI LOCK Indicator Control
10	BN	1560	Neutral Indicator Control
11	L-GN/BK	1563	4 HI Indicator Control
12	GY	8	Instrument Panel Lamps Dimmer Switch Signal
13	BK	2050	Ground
14	BN/WH	1571	Traction Control Switch Signal
15	L-BU	1693	Switch Signal
16	GY	596	5-Volt Reference

LTV0500000000621

Fig. 7 Connector pin identification (Accessory switch). Hummer H3

front wheel hydraulic circuit bleeder valve.

15. Install a transparent hose over end of bleeder valve, then repeat steps 7–11.

16. With righthand front wheel hydraulic circuit bleeder valve tightened securely, after all air has been purged from righthand front hydraulic circuit, install a proper box-end wrench onto lefthand front wheel hydraulic circuit bleeder valve.

17. Install a transparent hose over end of bleeder valve, then repeat steps 7–11.

18. After completing final wheel hydraulic circuit bleeding procedure, ensure that each 4 wheel hydraulic circuit bleeder valves are properly tightened.

19. Fill brake master cylinder reservoir to maximum-fill level with Delco Supreme 11® GM part No. 12377967 or equivalent DOT-3 brake fluid from a clean, sealed brake fluid container.

20. Slowly depress and release brake pedal. Observe feel of brake pedal.

21. If brake pedal feels spongy, repeat bleeding procedure. If brake pedal still feels spongy after repeating bleed procedure, perform following steps:

a. Inspect brake system for external leaks.

b. Pressure bleed hydraulic brake system in order to purge any air that may still be trapped in system.

22. Turn ignition key On, with engine Off. Inspect to see if brake system warning lamp remains illuminated. **If brake**

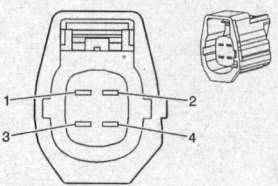

Connector Part Information

- OEM: 6189-1048
- Service: See Catalog
- Description: 4-Way F 025/187 Sealed (BK)

Terminal Part Information

- Pins: 1
- Terminal/Tray: 8100-3455 / 22
- Core/Insulation Crimp: 7 / 7
- Release Tool/Test Probe: 15315247 / J-35616-64A (L-BU)

- Pins: 3, 4
- Terminal/Tray: 8100-0468 / 6
- Core/Insulation Crimp: F / 5
- Release Tool/Test Probe: 12094430 / J-35616-40 (BU)

Pin	Wire Color	Circuit No.	Function
1	PK	1439	Ignition 1 Voltage
2	OG	540	Battery Positive Voltage
3	--	--	Not Used
4	BK	850	Ground

LTV0500000000622

Fig. 8   Connector pin identification (EBCM C1). Hummer H3

system warning lamp remains illuminated, **DO NOT** allow vehicle to be driven until it is diagnosed and repaired.

23. If brake system warning lamp remains illuminated, diagnose and troubleshoot as required.

HYDRAULIC BRAKE SYSTEM BLEEDING – PRESSURE

Do not remove the reservoir cap while depressing and releasing the brake pedal. If the cap is removed while depressing and releasing the brake pedal, pressurized brake fluid being returned to the reservoir may leave the reservoir. Personal injury or vehicle damage could result.

Do not allow the HBCi pump and motor to run more than one minute continuously. Allow two minutes cool down time between pump run times. Extended pump and motor run time could create excessive heat and damage the pump and motor assembly.

1. Place a clean shop cloth beneath brake master cylinder to prevent brake fluid spills.
2. If you disconnected brake pipes from master cylinder, you must perform following steps:
   a. Ensure that brake master cylinder reservoir is full to maximum-fill level. If required, add Delco Supreme 11® GM part No. 12377967 or equivalent DOT-3 brake fluid from a clean, sealed brake fluid container. If removal of reservoir cap and diaphragm is required, clean outside of cap and around cap prior to removal.
   b. With all brake pipes installed securely to master cylinder, loosen and separate lefthand side front brake pipe from lefthand side front port of brake master cylinder.
   c. Allow a small amount of brake fluid to gravity bleed from open port of master cylinder.
   d. Reconnect brake pipe to master cylinder port and tighten.
   e. Have an assistant slowly depress brake pedal fully and maintain steady pressure on pedal.
   f. Loosen same brake pipe to purge air from open port of master cylinder.
   g. Tighten brake pipe, then have assistant slowly release brake pedal.
   h. Wait 15 seconds, then repeat steps e through g until all air is purged from same port of master cylinder.
   i. With lefthand front brake pipe installed securely to master cylinder, after all air has been purged from lefthand front port master cylinder, loosen and separate righthand front brake pipe from master cylinder, then repeat steps e through i.
   j. Turn ignition key to On position.
   k. With righthand front brake pipe installed to master cylinder, after all air has been purged from righthand front port of master cylinder, loosen and separate lefthand rear brake pipe from master cylinder, then repeat steps e through h.
   l. With lefthand rear brake pipe installed securely to master cylinder, after all air has been purged from lefthand rear port of master cylinder, loosen and separate righthand rear brake pipe from master cyl-

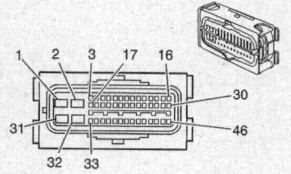

Connector Part Information

- OEM: 6189-1136
- Service: See Catalog
- Description: 46-Way F 025/187 Sealed (BK)

Terminal Part Information

- Pins: 1, 2, 31, 32
- Terminal/Tray: 8100-0468 / 6
- Core/Insulation Crimp: F / 5
- Release Tool/Test Probe: 12094430 / J-35616-40 (BU)

- Pins: 3-27, 38-46
- Terminal/Tray: 8100-3455 / 22
- Core/Insulation Crimp: Pins 3-6, 9-10, 17-20, 42, 45: 8 / 8
- Core/Insulation Crimp: Pins 8, 11, 22-27, 38-41, 43-44, 46: 7 / 7
- Release Tool/Test Probe: 15315247 / J-35616-64A (L-BU)

Pin	Wire Color	Circuit No.	Function
1	BK	850	Ground
2	OG	540	Battery Positive Voltage
3	D-GN	872	Right Front Wheel Speed Sensor Signal
4	YE	873	Left Front Wheel Speed Sensor Low Reference
5	BN	882	Right Rear Wheel Speed Sensor Signal
6	RD	885	Left Rear Wheel Speed Sensor Low Reference
7	--	--	Not Used
8	WH	1765	Steering Wheel Position Marker Pulse Signal (JL4)
9	OG/BK	463	Requested Torque Signal
10	TN/BK	464	Delivered Torque Signal

LTV0500000000623

Fig. 9   Connector pin identification (EBCM C2⟩ (Part 1 of 2). Hummer H3

der, then repeat steps e through h.
   m. After completing final master cylinder port bleeding procedure, ensure that all brake pipe-to-master cylinder fittings are properly tightened.
   n. Turn ignition key to Off position. Depress brake pedal 20 times.
3. Fill brake master cylinder reservoir with Delco Supreme 11® GM part No. 12377967 or equivalent DOT-3 brake fluid from a clean, sealed brake fluid container. Ensure that brake master cylinder reservoir remains at least half-full during this bleeding procedure. Add fluid as required to maintain proper level. Clean outside of reservoir on and around reservoir cap prior to removing cap and diaphragm.
4. Install tool No. J 44894-A or equivalent, to brake master cylinder reservoir.
5. Inspect brake fluid level in tool No. J 29532 or equivalent. Add Delco Supreme 11® GM part No. 12377967 or equivalent DOT-3 brake fluid from a clean, sealed brake fluid container as required to bring level to approximately half-full point.
6. Connect tool No. J 29532 or equivalent, to tool No. J 44894-A or equivalent.
7. Charge tool No. J 29532 or equivalent, air tank to 25–30 psi.
8. Open tool No. J 29532 or equivalent, fluid tank valve to allow pressurized brake fluid to enter brake system.
9. Wait approximately 30 seconds, then inspect entire hydraulic brake system

11	D-BU	716	CAN HI (JL4)
12-16	--	--	Not Used
17	TN	833	Right Front Wheel Speed Sensor Low Reference
18	L-BU	830	Left Front Wheel Speed Sensor Signal
19	WH	883	Right Rear Wheel Speed Sensor Low Reference
20	BK	884	Left Rear Wheel Speed Sensor Signal
21	--	--	Not Used
22	L-BU	1764	Steering Wheel Position Signal B (JL4)
23	L-GN	1763	Steering Wheel Position Signal A (JL4)
24	--	--	Not Used
25	L-BU	2088	CAN LO (JL4)
26	--	--	Not Used
27	PK	849	Brake Fluid Level Sensor Signal
28-30	--	--	Not Used
31	OG	2340	Battery Positive Voltage
32	BK	850	Ground
33-37	--	--	Not Used
38	BK	1835	Low Reference (JL4)
	L-BU	2088	Low Reference (w/o JL4)
39	L-BU	1059	Steering Wheel Position Sensor Signal (JL4)
40	GY	1056	Steering Wheel Position Sensor 5-Volt Reference (JL4)
	D-GN	2087	5-Volt Reference (w/o JL4)
41	YE	5353	Longitudinal Accelerometer Sensor Signal (w/o JL4)
42	L-GN	24	Backup Lamp Supply Voltage
43	--	--	Not Used
44	PU	1807	Class 2 Serial Data
45	L-BU	20	Stop Lamp Supply Voltage
46	BN	441	Ignition 3 Voltage

LTV0500000000624

Fig. 9 Connector pin identification (EBCM C2) (Part 2 of 2). Hummer H3

in order to ensure that there are no existing external brake fluid leaks. Any brake fluid leaks identified require repair prior to completing this procedure.

10. Install a suitable box-end wrench onto righthand rear wheel hydraulic circuit bleeder valve.
11. Install a transparent hose over end of bleeder valve.
12. Submerge open end of transparent hose into a transparent container partially filled with Delco Supreme 11® GM part No. 12377967 or equivalent DOT-3 brake fluid from a clean, sealed brake fluid container.
13. Loosen bleeder valve to purge air from wheel hydraulic circuit. Allow fluid to flow until air bubbles stop flowing from bleeder, then tighten bleeder valve.
14. With righthand rear wheel hydraulic circuit bleeder valve tightened securely, after all air has been purged from righthand rear hydraulic circuit, install a suitable box-end wrench onto lefthand rear wheel hydraulic circuit bleeder valve.
15. Install a transparent hose over end of bleeder valve, then repeat steps 13 and 14.
16. With lefthand rear wheel hydraulic circuit bleeder valve tightened securely, after all air has been purged from lefthand rear hydraulic circuit, install a suitable box-end wrench onto righthand front wheel hydraulic circuit bleeder valve.
17. Install a transparent hose over end of bleeder valve, then repeat steps 13 and 14.

18. With righthand front wheel hydraulic circuit bleeder valve tightened securely, after all air has been purged from righthand front hydraulic circuit, install a suitable box-end wrench onto lefthand front wheel hydraulic circuit bleeder valve.
19. Install a transparent hose over end of bleeder valve, then repeat steps 13 and 14.
20. After completing final wheel hydraulic circuit bleeding procedure, ensure that each (4) wheel hydraulic circuit bleeder valves are properly tightened.
21. Close tool No. J 29532 or equivalent, fluid tank valve, then disconnect tool No. J 29532 or equivalent, from tool No. J 44894-A or equivalent.
22. Remove tool No. J 44894-A or equivalent, from brake master cylinder reservoir.
23. Fill brake master cylinder reservoir.
24. Slowly depress and release brake pedal. Observe feel of brake pedal.
25. If brake pedal feels spongy, perform following steps:
   a. Inspect brake system for external leaks.
   b. Perform "ABS Automated Bleed Procedure" to remove any air that may have been trapped in HBCi.
26. Turn ignition key On, with engine Off. Inspect to indicate if brake system warning lamp remains illuminated. **If brake system warning lamp remains illuminated, DO NOT allow vehicle to be driven until it is diagnosed and repaired.**
27. If brake system warning lamp remains

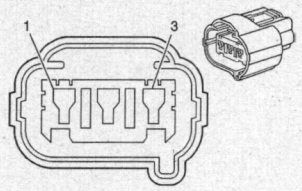

Connector Part Information

- OEM: 6189-0099
- Service: See Catalog
- Description: 3-Way F HX 090 Series (BK)

Terminal Part Information

- Terminal/Tray: 8100-0460 / 6
- Core/Insulation Crimp: E / 1
- Release Tool/Test,Probe: 15315247 / J-35616-2A (GY)

Pin	Wire Color	Circuit No.	Function
1	YE	5353	Longitudinal Accelerometer Sensor Signal
2	L-BU	2088	Low Reference
3	D-GN	2087	5-Volt Reference

LTV0500000000625

Fig. 10 Connector pin identification (Longitudinal accelerometer sensor). Hummer H3 less vehicle stability system

illuminated, diagnose and troubleshoot as required.

Component Replacement

CANYON & COLORADO

BRAKE PRESSURE MODULATOR VALVE (BPMV)

To reduce the possibility of contaminating the brake system or the ABS module, ensure that the work area is clean. Do not wear gloves or use shop towels when working with the ABS module.

1. Clean master cylinder and EBCM assembly with denatured alcohol.
2. Remove EBCM assembly from vehicle as outlined in "Electronic Brake Control Module, Replace."
3. Loosen mounting bolts for BPMV.
4. Remove BPMV from mounting bracket.
5. Reverse procedure to install, noting the following:
   a. **Torque** mounting nuts to 71 inch lbs.
   b. Bleed system as outlined in "Brake System Bleed" section.

ELECTRONIC BRAKE CONTROL MODULE (EBCM)

1. Install clean paper and or shop towels between EBCM assembly and inner fender.
2. Remove electrical connector from EBCM.
3. Relocate electrical connector behind brake booster.
4. **Before removing brake pipes from EBCM module, clean module and master cylinder with denatured alcohol.** Remove brakes pipes from master cylinder to EBCM assembly.

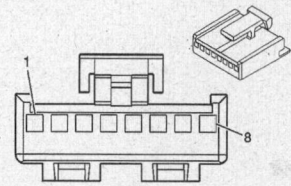

Connector Part Information

- OEM: 12052444
- Service: 12101874
- Description: 8-Way F Micro-Pack 100 Series (BK)

Terminal Part Information

- Terminal/Tray: 12089660 / 3
- Core/Insulation Crimp: See Terminal Kit
- Release Tool/Test Probe: See Terminal Kit

Pin	Wire Color	Circuit No.	Function
1	GY	1056	Steering Wheel Position Sensor 5-Volt Reference
2	BK	1835	Low Reference
3	L-GN	1763	Steering Wheel Position Signal A
4	L-BU	1764	Steering Wheel Position Signal B
5	WH	1765	Steering Wheel Position Marker Pulse Signal
6	L-BU	1059	Steering Wheel Position Sensor Signal
7	BN	441	Ignition 3 Voltage
8	BK/WH	1151	Ground

LTV0500000000626

Fig. 11 Connector pin identification (Steering wheel position sensor). Hummer H3 w/vehicle stability system

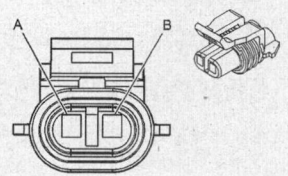

Connector Part Information

- OEM: 12052641
- Service: 12102747
- Description: 2-Way F Metri-Pack 150 Series Sealed (BK)

Terminal Part Information

- Terminal/Tray: 12048074 / 2
- Core/Insulation Crimp: E / 1
- Release Tool/Test Probe: 12094429 / J-35616-2A (GY)

Pin	Wire Color	Circuit No.	Function
A	RD	885	Left Rear Wheel Speed Sensor Low Reference
B	BK	884	Left Rear Wheel Speed Sensor Signal

LTV0500000000628

Fig. 13 Connector pin identification (LR WSS). Hummer H3

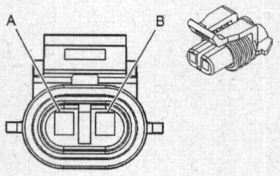

Connector Part Information

- OEM: 12052641
- Service: 12102747
- Description: 2-Way F Metri-Pack 150 Series Sealed (BK)

Terminal Part Information

- Terminal/Tray: 12048074 / 2
- Core/Insulation Crimp: E / 1
- Release Tool/Test Probe: 12094429 / J-35616-2A (GY)

Pin	Wire Color	Circuit No.	Function
A	YE	873	Left Front Wheel Speed Sensor Low Reference
B	L-BU	830	Left Front Wheel Speed Sensor Signal

LTV0500000000627

Fig. 12 Connector pin identification (LF WSS). Hummer H3

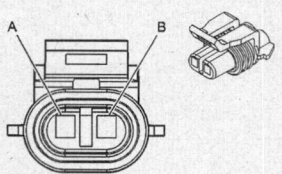

Connector Part Information

- OEM: 12052641
- Service: 12102747
- Description: 2-Way F Metri-Pack 150 Series Sealed (BK)

Terminal Part Information

- Terminal/Tray: 12048074 / 2
- Core/Insulation Crimp: E / 1
- Release Tool/Test Probe: 12094429 / J-35616-2A (GY)

Pin	Wire Color	Circuit No.	Function
A	TN	833	Right Front Wheel Speed Sensor Low Reference
B	D-GN	872	Right Front Wheel Speed Sensor Signal

LTV0500000000629

Fig. 14 Connector pin identification (RF WSS). Hummer H3

5. Remove rear brake pipe from retainers at cowl.
6. Remove brake pipes from EBCM assembly.
7. Install rubber plugs into BPMV. **Install rubber plugs into brake pipes to limit loss of brake fluid and prevent contamination.**
8. Install rubber plugs into master cylinder. **Install rubber plugs into brake pipes to limit loss of brake fluid and prevent contamination.**
9. Remove mounting nuts from EBCM.
10. Remove EBCM from vehicle.
11. Position EBCM module on its side.
12. Remove four mounting screws from ABS module. **Discard screws, use NEW only.**
13. Remove four collars between EBCM and BPMV. **Discard collars, use NEW only.**

14. Rotate ABS module so that BPMV is facing up.
15. Separate EBCM from BPMV. **When handling EBCM or BPMV, use care so as not to cause any misalignment of either of two electrical connectors for EBCM or solenoids on BPMV. When separating EBCM from BPMV, DO NOT use a pry bar. If EBCM and BPMV cannot be separated, without use of force, replace ABS module as an assembly.**
16. Remove solenoid plate from EBCM. **Discard solenoid plate, use new only. DO NOT reuse solenoid plate or O-rings once EBCM and BPMV have been separated. Discard and use NEW only.**
17. Remove foreign material from BPMV assembly using a suitable paper towel.
18. Apply a small amount of DOT-3 brake

fluid and clean surface area of BPMV using a clean paper towel.
19. Inspect solenoids for any contamination or corrosion.
20. Inspect surface of BPMV for any contamination or corrosion.
21. Remove old O-rings from EBCM.
22. Reverse procedure to install, noting the following:
    a. **Torque** EBCM mounting screws to 44 inch lbs.
    b. **Torque** ABS mounting nuts to 80 inch lbs.
    c. **Torque** brake pipe fittings to EBCM to 14 ft. lbs.
    d. **Torque** brake pipe fittings from EBCM to master cylinder to 14 ft. lbs.
    e. Bleed system as outlined in "Brake System Bleed" section.

LONGITUDINAL ACCELEROMETER

1. Remove lefthand side split bench or bucket seat as follows:
    a. Ensure that seat is rearward.
    b. Remove front bolts.
    c. Ensure that seat is forward.
    d. Remove rear bolts.

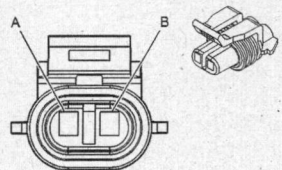

Connector Part Information

- OEM: 12052641
- Service: 12102747
- Description: 2-Way F Metri-Pack 150 Series Sealed (BK)

Terminal Part Information

- Terminal/Tray: 12048074 / 2
- Core/Insulation Crimp: E / 1
- Release Tool/Test Probe: 12094429 / J-35616-2A (GY)

Pin	Wire Color	Circuit No.	Function
A	WH	883	Right Rear Wheel Speed Sensor Low Reference
B	BN	882	Right Rear Wheel Speed Sensor Signal

LTV0500000000630

Fig. 15 Connector pin identification (RR WSS). Hummer H3

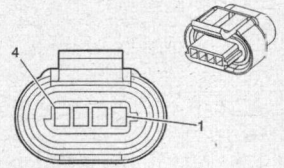

Connector Part Information

- OEM: 6189-0551
- Service: 15165777
- Description: 4-Way F DL 040 Sealed (WH)

Terminal Part Information

- Terminal/Tray: 8100-1466 / 6
- Core/Insulation Crimp: 7 / 7
- Release Tool/Test Probe: 15315247 / J-35616-64A (L-BU)

Pin	Wire Color	Circuit No.	Function
1	BN	441	Ignition 3 Voltage
2	D-BU	716	CAN HI
3	L-BU	2088	CAN LO
4	BK/WH	1151	Ground

LTV0500000000631

Fig. 16 Connector pin identification (Yaw rate & longitudinal accelerometer sensor). Hummer H3 w/vehicle stability system

e. Disconnect seat electrical connectors to body harness.
f. Remove seat from vehicle.
2. Access sensor through service slit provided in carpet.
3. Remove electrical connector from sensor.
4. Remove two nuts retaining sensor to floor panel.
5. Remove sensor from vehicle.
6. Reverse procedure to install, noting the following:
   a. **Torque** two sensor retaining nuts to 80 inch lbs.
   b. **Torque** seat mounting bolts to 39 ft. lbs.

HUMMER H3

BRAKE MASTER CYLINDER w/POWER BRAKE BOOSTER & CHASSIS CONTROL MODULE

Plug the brake pipes to avoid dirt or any type of contaminates to enter the brake system. Depress the brake pedal 20 times to release accumulator pressure.
1. Remove rear and lefthand front brake pipes from brake master cylinder.
2. Remove righthand front brake pipe from brake master cylinder.
3. Remove electrical connectors at BPMV.
4. Remove electrical connector for fluid level sensor.
5. Remove driver side knee bolster panel and bracket.
6. Remove clevis pin retainer from clevis pin.
7. Remove clevis pin from master cylinder push rod.
8. Remove mounting nuts for brake master cylinder.
9. Remove brake master cylinder assembly.
10. Reverse procedure to install, noting the following:
    a. **Torque** brake master cylinder nuts to 22 ft. lbs.
    b. **Torque** brake master cylinder fittings to 14 ft. lbs.
    c. Bleed system as outlined in "Brake System Bleed" section.

BRAKE PRESSURE MODULATOR VALVE (BPMV)

1. Remove brake master cylinder assembly as outlined in "Brake Master Cylinder w/Power Brake Booster & Chassis Control Module, Replace."
2. Install brake master cylinder assembly in a suitable vise using holding fixture tool No. CH-47830 or equivalent.
3. Remove brake master cylinder reservoir as follows:
   a. Drain brake fluid from reservoir.
   b. Install brake master cylinder in a suitable vise.
   c. Disconnect electrical connector for fluid level sensor.
   d. Remove retaining bolt for brake master cylinder.
   e. Remove roll pin for brake master cylinder reservoir. **Grommets for brake master cylinder should remain in brake master cylinder body.**
   f. There are two different size grommets. Two outer grommets are larger than center grommet. Remove grommets as required.
   g. Remove brake master cylinder reservoir assembly.
4. Remove hydraulic brake booster motor.
5. Remove mounting bolts for BPMV.
6. Remove mounting bolt for fluid level sensor.
7. Remove bracket for fluid level sensor wiring harness.
8. Remove BPMV module from brake master cylinder. **When removing BPMV from brake master cylinder, ensure that locating pin remains in brake master cylinder body.**
9. Remove gasket from brake master cylinder. **Do not reuse BPMV gasket, use only New gasket.**
10. Reverse procedure to install, noting the following:
    a. Install new BPMV module gasket on master cylinder.
    b. **Torque** BPMV module mounting bolts to 24 inch lbs.
    c. **Torque** fluid level sensor bracket mounting bolts to 71 inch lbs.
    d. Bleed system as outlined in "Brake System Bleed" section.

FRONT WHEEL SPEED SENSOR

1. Raise and support vehicle using a suitable lift.
2. Remove front tire and wheel assembly.
3. Remove front brake caliper assembly as outlined in "Disc Brakes" chapter.
4. Remove brake rotor as outlined in "Disc Brakes" chapter.
5. Remove front wheel speed sensor electrical connector.
6. Remove front wheel speed sensor wiring harness retaining clips.
7. Remove front wheel speed sensor retaining bolt.
8. Remove front wheel speed sensor.
9. Reverse procedure to install. **Torque** front wheel speed sensor to 13 ft. lbs.

REAR WHEEL SPEED SENSOR

1. Raise and support vehicle using a suitable lift.
2. Remove rear tire and wheel assembly.
3. Remove rear ABS electrical connector.
4. Remove rear ABS wiring harness frame retaining clip.
5. Remove rear ABS wiring harness axle housing retaining clip.
6. Remove rear wheel speed sensor bolts, then the sensor.
7. Reverse procedure to install. **Torque** speed sensor bolts to 13 ft. lbs.

REAR WHEEL SPEED SENSOR RING

1. Raise and support vehicle using a suitable lift.
2. Remove rear tire and wheel assembly.
3. Remove rear wheel speed sensor as outlined in "Rear Wheel Speed Sensor."
4. Remove bolt for rear brake pipe retainer.
5. Remove bolt for mounting bracket.

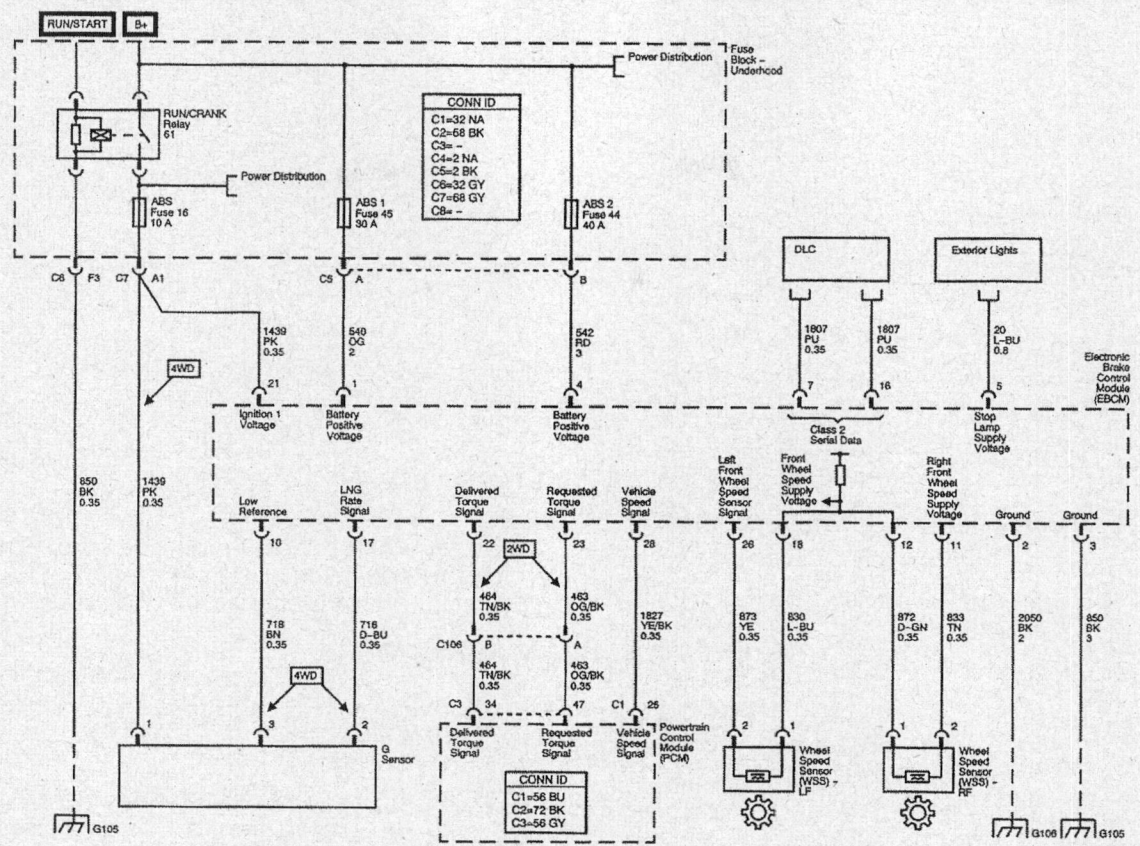

Fig. 17 Wiring diagram (Part 1 of 2). Canyon & Colorado

6. Remove mounting brackets from rear axle cover.
7. Position a suitable drain pan under axle.
8. Remove rear cover mounting bolts.
9. Remove rear cover and gasket from differential housing.
10. Drain rear axle.
11. Remove rear axle shaft as outlined in "Rear Axle & Suspension" section in chassis chapter.
12. Remove axle shaft seal, bearing and wheel speed sensor ring from axle housing using tool Nos. J 45857 and J 2619-01 or equivalents.

13. Reverse procedure to install, noting the following:
    a. **Torque** axle housing cover bolts to 20 ft. lbs.
    b. **Torque** retaining bolt to brake pipe retainer bolts to 14 ft. lbs.
    c. **Torque** pinion shaft locking bolt to 187 ft. lbs.

YAW RATE SENSOR/LATERAL & LONGITUDINAL ACCELEROMETER

1. Disable SIR system as outlined in "Air Bag System Precautions" in front of this manual.

2. Remove driver rear seat assembly.
3. Remove driver rear door sill plates.
4. Remove carpet enough to access yaw rate sensor.
5. Remove longitudinal accelerometer nuts, then the sensor.
6. Reverse procedure to install, noting the following:
    a. **Torque** rear seat center belt nuts to 38 ft. lbs.
    b. **Torque** rear seat and seat back cushion nut to 41 ft. lbs.
    c. **Torque** longitudinal accelerometer nut to 80 inch lbs.

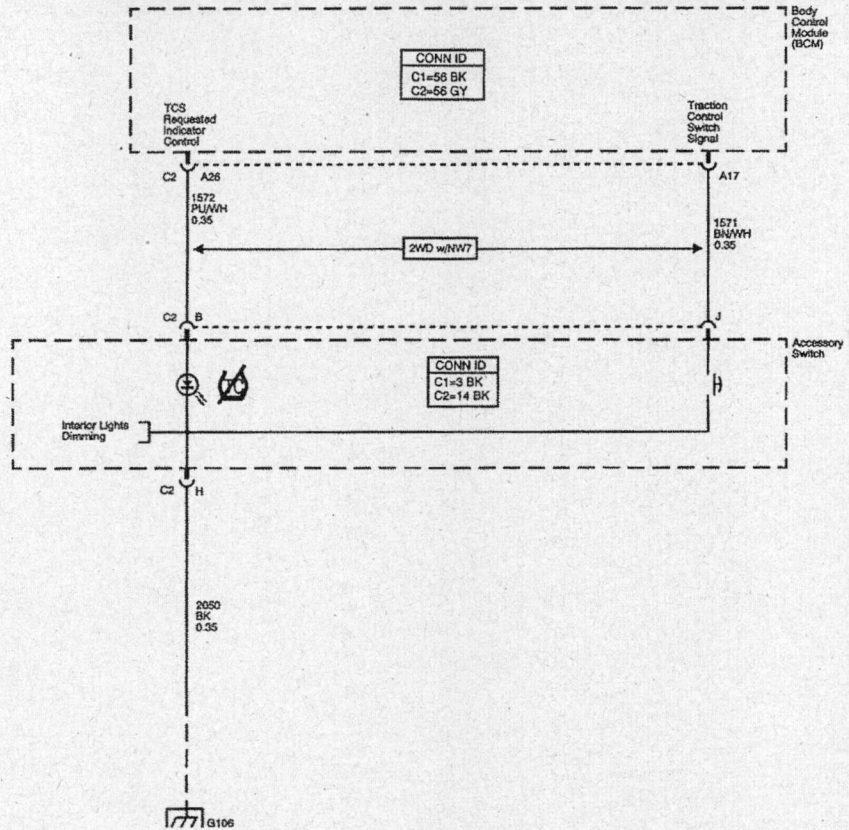

Fig. 17   Wiring diagram (Part 2 of 2). Canyon & Colorado

LTV0500000000610

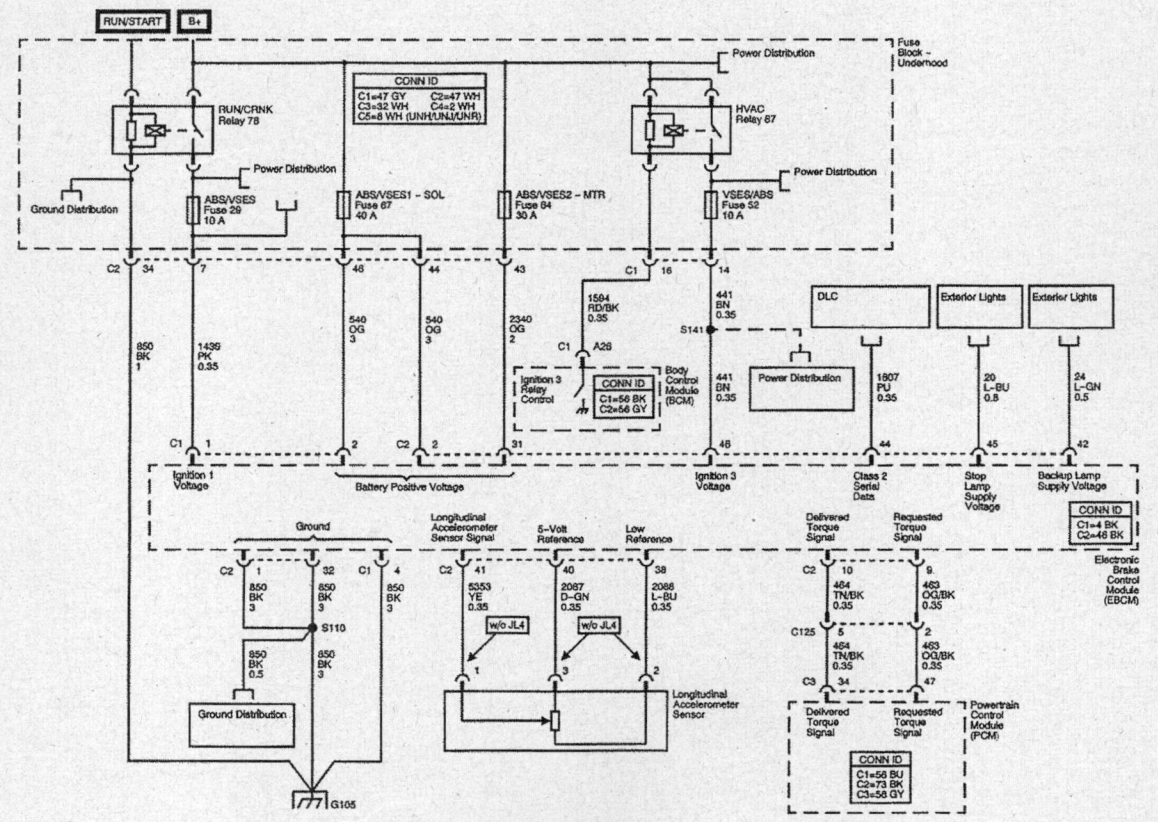

Fig. 18   Wiring diagram (Part 1 of 4). Hummer H3

LTV0500000000611

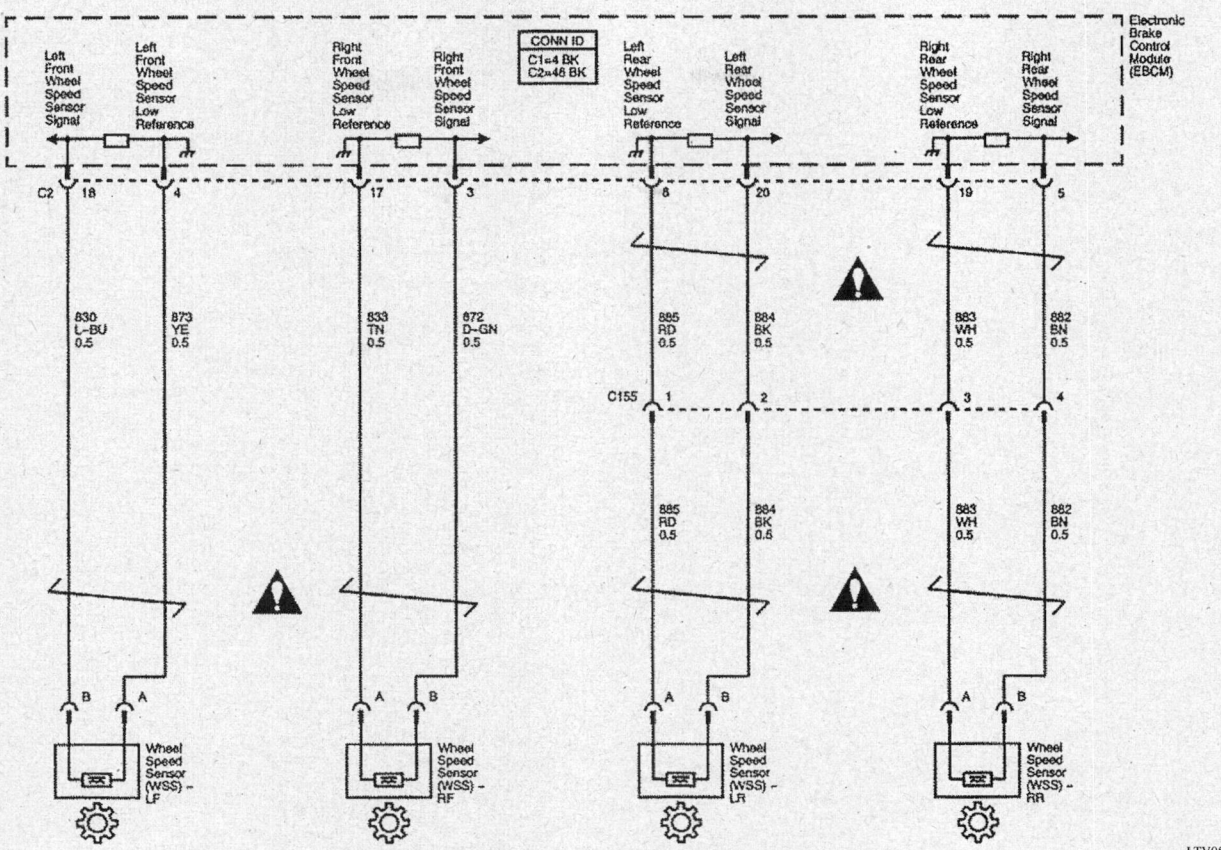

Fig. 18   Wiring diagram (Part 2 of 4). Hummer H3

LTV0500000000612

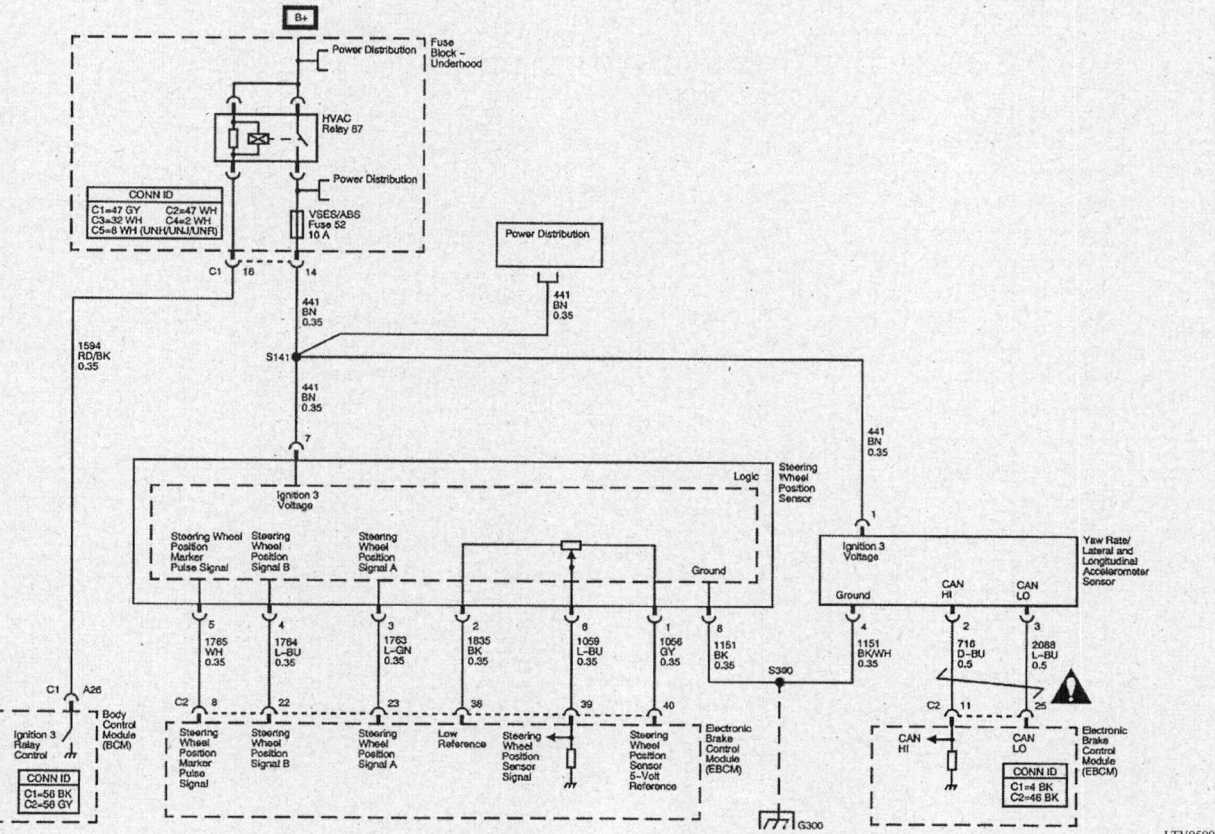

Fig. 18   Wiring diagram (Part 3 of 4). Hummer H3

LTV0500000000613

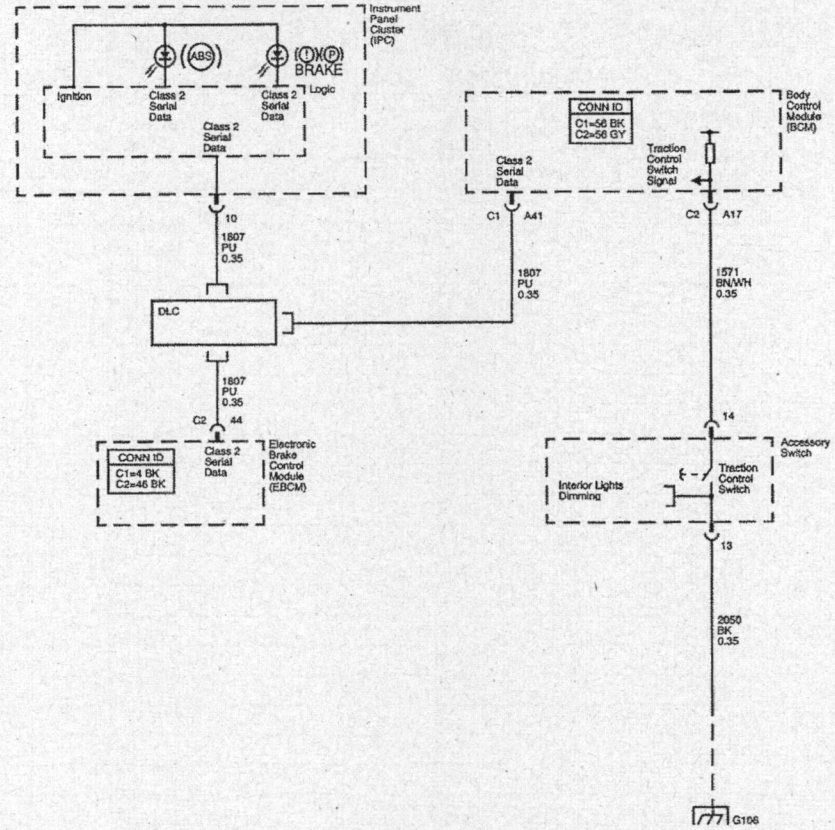

Fig. 18 Wiring diagram (Part 4 of 4). Hummer H3

LTV0500000000614

DIAGNOSTIC CHART INDEX

Code	Description	Page No.	Fig. No.
CANYON & COLORADO			
—	Diagnostic System Check	5-15	19
—	ABS Indicator Always On	5-35	59
—	ABS Indicator Inoperative	5-35	60
—	Traction Control Indicator Inoperative	5-36	61
B0827	Traction Control System Off Indicator Circuit Low	5-15	20
B0828	Traction Control System Off Indicator Circuit High	5-15	21
B2745	Traction Control Switch Circuit	5-16	22
C0035	Lefthand Front Wheel Speed Sensor Circuit	5-16	23
C0040	Righthand Front Wheel Speed Sensor Circuit	5-17	24
C0055	Rear Wheel Speed Sensor Circuit	5-18	25
C0110	Pump Motor Circuit	5-19	26
C0191	All Wheel Drive/Four Wheel Drive Reference Accelerometer Circuit	5-20	27
C0201	Anti-Lock Brake System Enable Relay Contact Circuit	5-20	28
C0220	Anti-Lock Brake System Channel In Release Too Long	5-21	29
C0221	Anti-Lock Brake System Channel In Release Too Long	5-21	29
C0222	Anti-Lock Brake System Channel In Release Too Long	5-21	29
C0240	EBCM Receives Invalid Message	5-21	30
C0244	Pulse Width Modulated Delivered Torque	5-22	31
C0245	Wheel Speed Sensor Frequency Error	5-23	32
C0267	Class 2 Data Error Reported	5-23	33
C0268	Class 2 Data Error Reported	5-23	33
C0550	Electronic Control Unit Performance	5-23	34
C0569	EBCM Detects Longitudinal Accelerometer Signal Voltage	5-24	35
C0899	Device Voltage Low	5-24	36
C0900	Device Voltage High	5-25	37

Continued

DIAGNOSTIC CHART INDEX—Continued

Code	Description	Page No.	Fig. No.
CANYON & COLORADO			
P0856	PCM Receives Invalid Message	5-21	30
P1689	Traction Control Delivered Torque Output Circuit	5-22	31
HUMMER H3			
—	Diagnostic System Check	5-25	38
—	ABS Indicator Always On	5-36	62
—	ABS Indicator Inoperative	5-36	63
—	Stability System Caution Indicator Always On	5-36	64
—	Stability System Caution Indicator Inoperative	5-36	65
—	Traction Off Indicator Always On	5-37	66
—	Traction Off Indicator Inoperative	5-37	67
—	Vehicle Stability Enhancement System Poor Performance	5-37	68
B0010	Reverse Gear Signal Circuit	5-26	39
B2745	Traction Control Switch Circuit	5-26	40
C0035	Lefthand Front Wheel Speed Sensor Circuit	5-27	41
C0040	Righthand Front Wheel Speed Sensor Circuit	5-27	41
C0045	Lefthand Rear Wheel Speed Sensor Circuit	5-27	41
C0050	Righthand Rear Wheel Speed Sensor Circuit	5-27	41
C0110	Pump Motor Circuit	5-27	42
C0131	Anti-Lock Brake System Pressure Circuit	5-28	43
C0136	Base Brake System Pressure Circuit	5-28	44
C0161	ABS Brake Switch Circuit	5-29	45
C0179	System Thermal High	5-29	46
C0186	Lateral Accelerometer Circuit	5-30	47
C0191	Four Wheel Drive Reference Accelerometer Circuit	5-30	48
C0196	Yaw Rate Circuit	5-30	47
C0201	Anti-Lock Brake System Enable Relay Contact Circuit	5-31	49
C0240	PCM Traction Control Not Allowed	5-31	50
C0244	Pulse Width Modulated Delivered Torque	5-32	51
C0245	Wheel Speed Sensor Frequency Error	5-33	52
C0268	Class 2 Data Error Reported	5-33	53
C0276	Transmission Control Module Traction Control Not Allowed	5-33	54
C0550	Electronic Control Unit Performance	5-33	55
C0710	Steering Position Signal	5-34	56
C0899	Device 1 Voltage Low	5-34	57
C0901	Device 2 Voltage Low	5-35	58
P0856	Traction Control Torque Request Circuit	5-31	50
P1689	Traction Control Delivered Torque Output Circuit	5-32	51

Step	Action	Yes	No
1	Install a scan tool. Does the scan tool power up?	Go to Step 2	Diagnose Scan Tool Does Not Power Up
2	1. Turn the ignition ON. 2. Use the scan tool in order to establish communication with the following modules. - ABS - Powertrain - Instrument Panel Cluster - Body Control Module Does the scan tool communicate with all of the control modules listed above?	Go to Step 3	Diagnose Scan Tool Does Not Communicate with Class 2 Device
3	Use the scan tool in order to display DTCs for the following control modules. • ABS • Powertrain • Instrument Panel Cluster • Body Control Module Does the scan tool display any DTCs for the control modules listed above?	Go to Step 4	Go to Symptoms
4	Does the scan tool display any DTCs that begin with a "U"?	Diagnose Scan Tool Does Not Communicate with Class 2 Device	Go to Step 5
5	Does the scan tool display DTC P0500, P0502, P0503, P0562, P0563, P0601-P0607, P1381, P1621, P1627 or P1683?	Go to Diagnostic Trouble Code (DTC)	Go to Diagnostic Trouble Code (DTC) List

LTV0500000000632

Fig. 19 Diagnostic System Check. Canyon & Colorado

Step	Action	Yes	No
1	Did you perform the Diagnostic System Check - Vehicle?	Go to Step 2	Go to Diagnostic System Check -
2	1. Turn OFF the ignition for 5 seconds. 2. Turn ON the ignition. 3. Press and release the traction control switch once. Does the DTC set?	Go to Step 3	Go to Diagnostic Aids
3	1. Turn OFF the ignition. 2. Remove the instrument panel center trim bezel to access the traction control switch harness connector. 3. Disconnect the traction control switch harness connector. 4. Turn ON the ignition. Does DTC B0828 set?	Go to Step 6	Go to Step 4
4	Test the traction control switch (TCS) requested indicator control circuit for a short to ground. Did you find and correct the condition?	Go to Step 7	Go to Step 5
5	Replace the body control module (BCM). Did you complete the replacement?	Go to Step 7	--
6	Replace the traction control switch. Did you complete the replacement?	Go to Step 7	--
7	1. Use the scan tool in order to clear the DTCs. 2. Operate the vehicle within the Conditions for Running the DTC as specified in the supporting text. Does the DTC reset?	Go to Step 3	System OK

LTV0500000000634

Fig. 20 Code B0827: Traction Control System Off Indicator Circuit Low (Part 2 of 2). Canyon & Colorado

Circuit Description

After the traction control switch (TCS) is pressed and released, the LED on the switch illuminates. The body control module (BCM) illuminates the LED by supplying adequate current to the high side of the LED.

DTC Descriptor

This diagnostic procedure supports the following DTC:

DTC B0827 Traction Control System Off Indicator Circuit Low

Conditions for Running the DTC

- The ignition is ON.
- The body control module (BCM) is commanding the traction control switch LED ON.

Conditions for Setting the DTC

The BCM detects low voltage on the TCS requested indicator control circuit when the LED is switched ON.

Action Taken When the DTC Sets

The BCM sets DTC B0827 as a current DTC for as long as the condition is present.

Conditions for Clearing the DTC

The DTC clears automatically from Current status when the fault is corrected or when the Conditions for Running the DTC are not being met. Use a scan tool to clear the DTC from History status.

Diagnostic Aids

An intermittent short to ground on the TCS requested indicator control circuit is the most likely cause of a history DTC when no problem is found. When the Conditions for Setting this DTC are present, the traction control switch LED cannot illuminate.

Test Description

The numbers below refer to the step numbers on the diagnostic table.

3. This step tests for a short in the traction control switch. Normally, DTC B0823 sets when the TCS requested indicator control circuit is opened.

LTV0500000000633

Fig. 20 Code B0827: Traction Control System Off Indicator Circuit Low (Part 1 of 2). Canyon & Colorado

Circuit Description

After the traction control switch (TCS) is pressed and released, the LED on the switch illuminates. The body control module (BCM) illuminates the LED by supplying adequate current to the high side of the LED. The BCM supplies a low current, 12-volt signal to the TCS requested indicator control circuit, when the LED is commanded OFF. The BCM monitors the feedback from this signal to detect opens or shorts to voltage in the LED control circuitry.

DTC Descriptor

This diagnostic procedure supports the following DTC:

DTC B0828 Traction Control System Off Indicator Circuit High

Conditions for Running the DTC

- The ignition is ON.
- The BCM is commanding the traction control switch LED OFF.

Conditions for Setting the DTC

The BCM detects high voltage on the LED control circuit when the TCS requested indicator is switched OFF.

Action Taken When the DTC Sets

The BCM sets DTC B0828 as a current DTC for as long as the condition is present.

Conditions for Clearing the DTC

The DTC clears automatically from Current status when the fault is corrected or when the Conditions for Running the DTC are not being met. Use a scan tool to clear the DTC from History status.

Diagnostic Aids

An intermittent open or short to voltage on the TCS requested indicator control circuit is the most likely cause of a history DTC, when no problem is found. When the Conditions for Setting this DTC are present, the traction control switch LED may not illuminate when the traction control switch is pressed, or may remain illuminated whenever the ignition is ON.

LTV0500000000635

Fig. 21 Code B0828: Traction Control System Off Indicator Circuit High (Part 1 of 2). Canyon & Colorado

Step	Action	Yes	No
1	Did you perform the Diagnostic System Check - Vehicle?	Go to Step 2	Go to Diagnostic System Check
2	1. Turn OFF the ignition for 5 seconds. 2. Turn ON the ignition. Does DTC B0828 set as a Current DTC?	Go to Step 3	Go to Diagnostic Aids
3	Observe the traction control switch LED. Is the traction control switch LED illuminated?	Go to Step 4	Go to Step 5
4	Test the traction control switch (TCS) requested indicator control circuit for a short to voltage. Did you find and correct the condition?	Go to Step 11	Go to Step 8
5	1. Turn OFF the ignition. 2. Remove the instrument panel center trim bezel to access the traction control switch harness connector. 3. Disconnect the traction control switch harness connector. 4. Use a fused jumper wire to connect the TCS requested indicator control circuit to the traction control switch ground circuit. 5. Turn ON the ignition. Does the DTC set?	Go to Step 6	Go to Step 9
6	Test the TCS requested indicator control circuit and the TCS ground circuit for opens. Did you find and correct the condition?	Go to Step 11	Go to Step 7
7	Test for poor connections at the harness connector of the body control module (BCM). Did you find and correct the condition?	Go to Step 11	Go to Step 8
8	Replace the BCM. Did you complete the replacement?	Go to Step 11	--
9	Test for poor connections at the harness connector of the TCS. Did you find and correct the condition?	Go to Step 11	Go to Step 10
10	Replace the TCS. Did you complete the replacement?	Go to Step 11	--
11	1. Use the scan tool in order to clear the DTCs. 2. Operate the vehicle within the Conditions for Running the DTC, as specified in the supporting text. Does the DTC reset?	Go to Step 3	System OK

LTV0500000000636

Fig. 21   Code B0828: Traction Control System Off Indicator Circuit High (Part 2 of 2). Canyon & Colorado

Step	Action	Value	Yes	No
1	Did you perform the Diagnostic System Check - Vehicle?	--	Go to Step 2	Go to Diagnostic System Check
2	1. Turn OFF the ignition for 5 seconds. 2. Turn ON the ignition and wait at least 60 seconds for the DTC to reset. Does DTC B2745 set as a Current DTC?	--	Go to Step 3	Go to Diagnostic Aids
3	1. Turn OFF the ignition. 2. Remove the instrument panel center trim bezel to access the traction control switch harness connector. 3. Disconnect the traction control switch harness connector. 4. Turn ON the ignition. Does the DTC set?	--	Go to Step 4	Go to Step 7
4	Use a DMM to measure the voltage between the traction control signal circuit and a good ground. Does the voltage measure greater than the specified value?	11 V	Go to Step 6	Go to Step 5
5	Test the traction control signal circuit for a short to ground. Did you find and correct the condition?	--	Go to Step 8	Go to Step 6
6	Replace the body control module (BCM). Did you complete the replacement?	--	Go to Step 8	--
7	Replace the traction control switch. Did you complete the replacement?	--	Go to Step 8	--
8	1. Use the scan tool to clear the DTCs. 2. Operate the vehicle within the Conditions for Running the DTC, as specified in the supporting text. Does the DTC reset?	--	Go to Step 3	System OK

LTV0500000000638

Fig. 22   Code B2745: Traction Control Switch Circuit (Part 2 of 2). Canyon & Colorado

Circuit Description

The driver may disable the traction control system (TCS) by pressing the traction control switch. The body control module (BCM) supplies a 12-volt signal on the traction control signal circuit. When the traction control switch is pressed, this voltage signal is grounded.

DTC Descriptor

This diagnostic procedure supports the following DTC:

DTC B2745 Traction Control Switch Circuit

Conditions for Running the DTC

The ignition is ON.

Conditions for Setting the DTC

The BCM detects low voltage on the traction control signal circuit for 60 seconds.

Action Taken When the DTC Sets

- The BCM sends a serial data message to the electronic brake control module (EBCM) informing the EBCM that the desired TCS state cannot be determined.
- The EBCM defaults the TCS status to enabled.

Conditions for Clearing the DTC

The DTC clears automatically from Current status when the fault is corrected. Use a scan tool to clear the DTC from History status.

Diagnostic Aids

An intermittent short to ground on the traction control signal circuit is the most likely cause of a history DTC when no problem is found. When the Conditions for Setting this DTC are present, the driver is not able to disable traction control.

Test Description

The number below refers to the step number on the diagnostic table.

3. This step tests for a short to ground within the traction control switch. DTC B0828 may set during this step.

LTV0500000000637

Fig. 22   Code B2745: Traction Control Switch Circuit (Part 1 of 2). Canyon & Colorado

Circuit Description

The electronic brake control module (EBCM) provides a common supply voltage to each digital front wheel speed sensor. As the front wheels spin, each wheel speed sensor produces a digital square wave signal. The EBCM uses the frequency of the wheel speed sensor signal to determine wheel speed.

DTC Descriptor

This diagnostic procedure supports the following DTC:

DTC C0035 LF Wheel Speed Sensor Circuit

Conditions for Running the DTC

Both of the conditions listed below may be required to set the DTC.

- The ignition is ON.
- The vehicle achieves a speed greater than 40 km/h (25 mph).

Conditions for Setting the DTC

Any of the following conditions may cause this DTC to set.

- The EBCM detects an open or shorted wheel speed sensor for 200 milliseconds.
- The EBCM detects a missing wheel speed sensor signal for one second. If more than one absent wheel speed sensor signal is detected, the condition must be present for 20 seconds to set DTCs.
- The EBCM detects an erratic wheel speed sensor signal for 40 continuous or cumulative milliseconds.
- The supply voltage to the front wheel speed sensors is detected as being at least 5 volts less than the monitored ignition voltage.

Action taken when the DTC sets

If equipped, the following actions occur.

- The EBCM disables the Antilock Brake System (ABS).
- The EBCM disables the TCS.
- The EBCM disables dynamic rear proportion (DRP), if all wheel speed inputs have failed.
- The ABS indicator turns ON.
- The ABS fault message is displayed.
- The traction fault message is displayed.
- The brake warning indicator turns ON, if DRP is disabled.
- The brakes message is displayed.
- An ECE 13 response occurs.

LTV0500000000639

Fig. 23   Code C0035: Lefthand Front Wheel Speed Sensor Circuit (Part 1 of 5). Canyon & Colorado

Conditions for Clearing the DTC

The Conditions for Setting the DTC are no longer present and you use the scan tool Clear DTCs function.

Diagnostic Aids

Thoroughly inspect connections or circuitry that may cause an intermittent malfunction.

If the customer's concern is that the ABS indicator is on only during humid conditions, such as rain, snow, or vehicle wash, thoroughly inspect the wheel speed sensor circuits for signs of water intrusion. Use the following procedure in order to help isolate the problem area:

1. Spray the suspected area with a 5 percent salt water solution.
2. Drive the vehicle at a speed greater than 19 km/h (12 mph) for at least 30 seconds.

Repair or replace the suspect harness, if the DTC sets.

Test Description

The numbers below refer to the step numbers on the diagnostic table.

3. If the DTC sets when the vehicle is not moving, the EBCM is detecting an open or shorted wheel speed sensor or wheel speed sensor circuit.

5. A short to ground in the right front wheel speed sensor supply voltage circuit appears electrically the same to the EBCM as a short to ground in the left front wheel speed sensor supply voltage circuit. Therefore, a short to ground in either circuit sets DTC C0035 and each circuit must be tested.

12. The front wheel speed sensors produce a high resolution signal. Therefore, the slightest rotation of the wheel causes the signal to toggle from high to low.

LTV0500000000640

Fig. 23 Code C0035: Lefthand Front Wheel Speed Sensor Circuit (Part 2 of 5). Canyon & Colorado

	Action	Values	Yes	No
9	1. Disconnect the left front wheel speed sensor harness connector. 2. Test the left front wheel speed sensor signal circuit for an open or a short to ground. Did you find and correct the condition?	--	Go to Step 17	Go to Step 11
10	Test the left front wheel speed sensor supply voltage circuit for an open. Did you find and correct the condition?	--	Go to Step 17	Go to Step 11
11	1. Reconnect the wheel speed sensor harness connector. 2. At the EBCM harness connector, use a fused jumper wire to connect the left front wheel speed sensor supply voltage circuit to battery positive voltage. 3. Set-up the DMM to measure current flow (mA/A). 4. Connect the positive lead of the DMM to the left front wheel speed sensor signal circuit at the EBCM harness connector. 5. Connect the negative lead of the DMM to ground. Does the amperage measure within the specified range?	4-16 mA	Go to Step 15	Go to Step 13
12	1. Turn OFF the ignition. 2. Disconnect the EBCM harness connector. 3. Raise the vehicle so that the left front wheel is 2 cm (1 in) off of the floor. 4. At the EBCM harness connector, use a fused jumper wire to connect the left front wheel speed sensor supply voltage circuit to battery positive voltage. 5. Set-up the DMM to measure current flow (mA/A). 6. Connect the positive lead of the DMM to the left front wheel speed sensor signal circuit at the EBCM harness connector. 7. Connect the negative lead of the DMM to ground. 8. Slowly rotate the left front wheel by hand while observing the DMM. Does the amperage toggle from lower measurement to higher measurement within the specified ranges?	Low signal: 4-8 mA High signal: 12-16 mA	Go to Step 15	Go to Step 13
13	Inspect for poor connections at the harness connector of the left front wheel speed sensor. Did you find and correct the condition?	--	Go to Step 17	Go to Step 14

LTV0500000004562

Fig. 23 Code C0035: Lefthand Front Wheel Speed Sensor Circuit (Part 4 of 5). Canyon & Colorado

	Action			
14	Replace the wheel speed sensor. Did you complete the replacement?	-	Go to Step 17	--
15	Inspect for poor connections at the harness connector of the EBCM. Did you find and correct the condition?	-	Go to Step 17	Go to Step 16
16	Replace the EBCM. Did you complete the replacement?	-	Go to Step 17	--
17	1. Reconnect all electrical components. 2. Operate the vehicle within the Conditions for Running the DTC, as specified in the supporting text. Does the DTC reset?	-	Go to Step 3	System OK

LTV0500000004563

Fig. 23 Code C0035: Lefthand Front Wheel Speed Sensor Circuit (Part 5 of 5). Canyon & Colorado

Step	Action	Values	Yes	No
1	Did you perform the Diagnostic System Check - Vehicle?	--	Go to Step 2	Go to Diagnostic System Check
2	1. Use a scan tool in order to clear the DTCs. 2. Operate the vehicle within the Conditions for Setting the DT, as specified in the supporting text. Does the DTC set?	--	Go to Step 3	Go to Diagnostic Aids
3	1. Turn OFF the ignition for at least 5 seconds. 2. Turn ON the ignition. 3. Use the scan tool to display Current DTCs. Is DTC C0035 set as a current DTC?	--	Go to Step 4	Go to Step 12
4	1. Turn OFF the ignition. 2. Disconnect the electronic brake control module (EBCM) harness connector. 3. Use a DMM to measure the resistance between the left front wheel speed sensor voltage supply circuit and a good ground. Does the resistance measure less than the specified value?	45 ohms	Go to Step 6	Go to Step 5
5	Use a DMM to measure the resistance between the right front wheel speed sensor voltage supply circuit and a good ground. Does the resistance measure less than the specified value?	45 ohms	Go to Step 6	Go to Step 9
6	1. Disconnect the wheel speed sensor corresponding with the supply voltage circuit that showed a resistance level below specification. 2. Use a DMM to again measure the resistance between the supply voltage circuit that measured low resistance and a good ground. Does the resistance measure less than the specified value?	0 L	Go to Step 8	Go to Step 7
7	Replace the wheel speed sensor corresponding with the supply voltage circuit that showed a resistance level below specification before the sensor was disconnected. Did you complete the replacement?	--	Go to Step 17	--
8	Repair the short to ground in the corresponding wheel speed sensor supply voltage circuit. Did you complete the repair?	--	Go to Step 17	--

LTV0500000000641

Fig. 23 Code C0035: Lefthand Front Wheel Speed Sensor Circuit (Part 3 of 5). Canyon & Colorado

Circuit Description

As the front wheels spin, each wheel speed sensor produces a digital square wave signal. The electronic brake control module (EBCM) uses the frequency of the wheel speed sensor signal to determine wheel speed.

DTC Descriptor

This diagnostic procedure supports the following DTC:

DTC C0040 RF Wheel Speed Sensor Circuit

Conditions for Running the DTC

Both of the conditions listed below may be required to set the DTC.

- The ignition is ON.
- The vehicle achieves a speed greater than 40 km/h (25 mph).

Conditions for Setting the DTC

Any of the following conditions may cause this DTC to set.

- The EBCM detects an open or shorted wheel speed sensor for 200 milliseconds.
- The EBCM detects a missing wheel speed sensor signal for one second. If more than one absent wheel speed sensor signal is detected, the condition must be present for 20 seconds to set DTCs.
- The EBCM detects an erratic wheel speed sensor signal for 40 continuous or cumulative milliseconds.

Action taken when the DTC sets

If equipped, the following actions occur.

- The EBCM disables the Antilock Brake System (ABS).
- The EBCM disables the TCS.
- The EBCM disables dynamic rear proportion (DRP) if all wheel speed inputs have failed.
- The ABS indicator turns ON.
- The ABS fault message is displayed.
- The traction fault message is displayed.
- The brake warning indicator turns ON, if DRP is disabled.
- The brakes message is displayed, if DRP is disabled.
- An ECE 13 response occurs.

LTV0500000004564

Fig. 24 Code C0040: Righthand Front Wheel Speed Sensor Circuit (Part 1 of 3). Canyon & Colorado

Conditions for Clearing the DTC

The Conditions for Setting the DTC are no longer present and you use the scan tool Clear DTCs function.

Diagnostic Aids

Thoroughly inspect connections or circuitry that may cause an intermittent malfunction.

If the customer's concern is that the ABS indicator is on only during humid conditions, such as rain, snow, or vehicle wash, thoroughly inspect the wheel speed sensor circuits for signs of water intrusion. Use the following procedure in order to help isolate the problem area:

1. Spray the suspected area with a 5 percent salt water solution.
2. Drive the vehicle at a speed greater than 19 km/h (12 mph) for at least 30 seconds.

Repair or replace the suspect harness, if the DTC sets.

Test Description

The numbers below refer to the step numbers on the diagnostic table.

3. If the DTC sets when the vehicle is not moving, the EBCM is detecting an open or shorted wheel speed sensor or wheel speed sensor circuit.

7. The front wheel speed sensors produce a high resolution signal. Therefore, the slightest rotation of the wheel causes the signal to toggle from high to low.

Step	Action	Values	Yes	No
1	Did you perform the Diagnostic System Check - Vehicle?	--	Go to Step 2	Go to Diagnostic System Check -
2	1. Use a scan tool in order to clear the DTCs. 2. Operate the vehicle within the Conditions for Setting the DTC, as specified in the supporting text. Does the DTC set?	--	Go to Step 3	Go to Diagnostic Aids
3	1. Turn OFF the ignition for at least 5 seconds. 2. Turn ON the ignition. 3. Use the scan tool to display Current DTCs. Is DTC C0040 set as a current DTC?	--	Go to Step 4	Go to Step 7
4	Test the right front wheel speed sensor signal circuit for an open or a short to ground. Refer to Did you find and correct the condition?	--	Go to Step 12	Go to Step 5
5	Test the right front wheel speed sensor supply voltage circuit for an open. Did you find and correct the condition?	--	Go to Step 12	Go to Step 6

LTV0500000004565

Fig. 24 Code C0040: Righthand Front Wheel Speed Sensor Circuit (Part 2 of 3). Canyon & Colorado

Circuit Description

The powertrain control module (PCM) converts the signal from the vehicle speed sensor (VSS) to a 128k pulses/mile signal. The electronic brake control module (EBCM) uses the vehicle speed signal from the PCM to calculate the rear wheel speed.

DTC Descriptor

This diagnostic procedure supports the following DTC:

DTC C0055 Rear Wheel Speed Sensor Circuit

Conditions for Running the DTC

- The ignition is ON.
- The vehicle speed is greater than 30 km/h (19 mph).

Conditions for Setting the DTC

- The EBCM detects an open or shorted vehicle speed signal circuit for 200 milliseconds.
- The EBCM detects the absence of the vehicle speed signal for one second. If more than one absent wheel speed sensor signal is detected, the condition must be present for 20 seconds to set DTCs.
- The EBCM detects an erratic vehicle speed signal for 40 continuous or cumulative milliseconds.

Action Taken When the DTC Sets

If equipped, the following actions occur:

- The EBCM disables the Antilock Brake System (ABS).
- The ABS indicator turns ON.
- The EBCM disables the traction control switch (TCS).
- The traction fault message is displayed.
- The EBCM disables the dynamic rear proportion (DRP), if all wheel speed inputs have failed.
- The brake warning indicator turns ON, if DRP is disabled.
- The brakes message is displayed, if DRP is disabled.
- An ECE 13 response occurs.

Conditions for Clearing the DTC

The Conditions for Setting the DTC are no longer present and you use the scan tool Clear DTCs function.

Diagnostic Aids

Thoroughly inspect connections or circuitry that may cause an intermittent malfunction

LTV0500000004567

Fig. 25 Code C0055: Rear Wheel Speed Sensor Circuit (Part 1 of 4). Canyon & Colorado

Step	Action	Values	Yes	No
6	1. Reconnect the wheel speed sensor harness connector. 2. Disconnect the electronic brake control module (EBCM) harness connector and use a fused jumper wire to connect the right front wheel speed sensor supply voltage circuit to battery positive voltage. 3. Setup the DMM to measure current flow (mA/A). 4. Connect the positive lead of the DMM to the right front wheel speed sensor signal circuit at the EBCM harness connector. 5. Connect the negative lead of the DMM to ground. Does the amperage measure within the specified range?	4-16 mA	Go to Step 10	Go to Step 8
7	1. Turn OFF the ignition. 2. Disconnect the EBCM harness connector. 3. Raise the vehicle so that the right front wheel is 2 cm (1 in) off of the floor. Refer to Lifting and Jacking the Vehicle in General Information. 4. At the EBCM harness connector, use a fused jumper wire to connect the right front wheel speed sensor supply voltage circuit to battery positive voltage. 5. Setup the DMM to measure current flow (mA/A). 6. Connect the positive lead of the DMM to the right front wheel speed sensor signal circuit at the EBCM harness connector. 7. Connect the negative lead of the DMM to ground. 8. Slowly rotate the right front wheel by hand while observing the DMM. Does the amperage toggle from lower measurement to higher measurement within the specified ranges?	Low signal: 4-8 mA High signal: 12-16 mA	Go to Step 10	Go to Step 8
8	Inspect for poor connections at the harness connector of the right front wheel speed sensor. Did you find and correct the condition?	--	Go to Step 12	Go to Step 9
9	Replace the right front wheel speed sensor. Did you complete the replacement?	--	Go to Step 12	--
10	Inspect for poor connections at the harness connector of the EBCM. Did you find and correct the condition?	--	Go to Step 12	Go to Step 11
11	Replace the EBCM. Did you complete the replacement?	--	Go to Step 12	--
12	1. Reconnect all electrical components. 2. Operate the vehicle within the Conditions for Running the DTC, as specified in the supporting text. Does the DTC reset?	--	Go to Step 3	System OK

LTV0500000004566

Fig. 24 Code C0040: Righthand Front Wheel Speed Sensor Circuit (Part 3 of 3). Canyon & Colorado

Test Description

The numbers below refer to the step numbers on the diagnostic table.

3. This step tests for a voltage signal from the PCM.

4. This step tests for a missing or erratic vehicle speed signal from the PCM. An assistant may be required to perform this test.

LTV0500000004568

Fig. 25 Code C0055: Rear Wheel Speed Sensor Circuit (Part 2 of 4). Canyon & Colorado

Step	Action	Values	Yes	No
1	Did you perform the Diagnostic System Check - Vehicle?	--	Go to Step 2	Go to Diagnostic System
2	1. Use a scan tool in order to clear the DTCs. 2. Operate the vehicle at a speed greater than the specified value. Does the DTC set?	30 km/h (19 mph)	Go to Step 3	Go to Diagnostic Aids
3	1. Turn OFF the ignition. 2. Disconnect from the electronic brake control module (EBCM), the harness connector containing the vehicle speed signal circuit. 3. Turn ON the ignition. 4. Use a DMM in order to measure the DC voltage between the vehicle speed signal circuit and a good ground. Does the voltage measure greater than the specified value?	10 V	Go to Step 4	Go to Step 7
4	1. Raise and support the vehicle. 2. Place the transmission in neutral (N). 3. Setup the DMM in order to measure the DC voltage between the vehicle speed signal circuit and a good ground. 4. Slowly spin the rear wheels by hand for at least 30 seconds and while ensuring the driveshaft is rotating, observe the DMM. Does the voltage measure within the specified range for the entire time that the driveshaft is rotating?	5-7 V	Go to Step 5	Go to Step 7
5	Inspect for poor connections at the harness connector of the EBCM. Did you find and correct the condition?	--	Go to Step 10	Go to Step 6
6	Replace the EBCM. Did you complete the replacement?	--	Go to Step 10	--
7	Test the vehicle speed signal circuit for an open, a short to ground, or a short to voltage. Did you find and correct the condition?	--	Go to Step 10	Go to Step 8

LTV0500000004569

Fig. 25   Code C0055: Rear Wheel Speed Sensor Circuit (Part 3 of 4). Canyon & Colorado

Step	Action	Yes	No
1	Did you perform the Diagnostic System Check - Vehicle?	Go to Step 2	Go to Diagnostic System Check
2	1. Use a scan tool in order to clear the DTCs. 2. Select the Antilock Brake System (ABS) Special Functions menu on the scan tool. 3. Select ABS Motor. 4. Use the scan tool to command the ABS Motor On and then Off. 5. Press the Exit key on the scan tool. Does the DTC reset?	Go to Step 3	Go to Diagnostic Aids
3	1. Turn OFF the ignition. 2. Disconnect the electronic brake control module (EBCM) harness connector. 3. Connect a test lamp between the battery positive voltage circuit at terminal 4 of the EBCM harness connector and a good ground. Does the test lamp illuminate?	Go to Step 5	Go to Step 4
4	Repair the open in the battery positive voltage circuit. Did you complete the repair?	Go to Step 12	--
5	Connect a test lamp between the battery positive voltage circuit at terminal 4 of the EBCM harness connector and the ground circuit at terminal 3 of the EBCM harness connector. Does the test lamp illuminate?	Go to Step 7	Go to Step 6
6	Repair the open in the motor ground circuit. Did you complete the repair?	Go to Step 12	--
7	1. Separate the EBCM from the brake pressure modulator valve (BPMV). 2. Inspect for poor connections at the pump motor connectors. Did you find and correct the condition?	Go to Step 12	Go to Step 8

LTV0500000004572

Fig. 26   Code C0110: Pump Motor Circuit (Part 2 of 3). Canyon & Colorado

	Action		Yes	No
8	Inspect for poor connections at the harness connector of the powertrain control module (PCM). Did you find and correct the condition?		Go to Step 10	Go to Step 9
9	Replace the PCM. Did you complete the replacement?		Go to Step 10	--
10	1. Use the scan tool in order to clear the DTCs. 2. Operate the vehicle within the Conditions for Running the DTC, as specified in the supporting text. Does the DTC reset?		Go to Step 3	System OK

LTV0500000004570

Fig. 25   Code C0055: Rear Wheel Speed Sensor Circuit (Part 4 of 4). Canyon & Colorado

Circuit Description

Ground is continuously supplied to the low side of the Antilock Brake System (ABS) pump motor. The electronic brake control module (EBCM) activates the ABS pump by supplying adequate current to the high side of the motor.

DTC Descriptor

This diagnostic procedure supports the following DTC:

DTC C0110 Pump Motor Circuit

Conditions for Running the DTC

- The ignition is ON.
- The EBCM has commanded the pump motor ON at least once during the current ignition cycle.

Conditions for Setting the DTC

The EBCM detects an open pump motor circuit, a shorted pump motor, or a seized pump motor or ABS pump.

Action Taken When the DTC Sets

- The EBCM disables the ABS.
- The ABS indicator turns ON.
- The ABS fault message is displayed.
- An ECE 13 response occurs.

Conditions for Clearing the DTC

The Conditions for Setting the DTC are no longer present and you use the scan tool Clear DTCs function.

Diagnostic Aids

Separate the EBCM from the brake pressure modulator valve (BPMV) in order to inspect for corrosion or any other condition that may cause a poor connection at the pump motor connectors. If severe corrosion or other damage exists, the BPMV or the EBCM may need to be replaced.

Inspect for poor connections that may affect the battery positive voltage circuit to terminal 4 or the ground circuit to terminal 3 of the EBCM harness connector, if this DTC continues to set intermittently. Replace the EBCM, if no wiring concerns are found.

LTV0500000004571

Fig. 26   Code C0110: Pump Motor Circuit (Part 1 of 3). Canyon & Colorado

	Action		Yes	No
8	**Important:** The test lamp must remain properly connected to the pump motor terminals whenever the ignition is ON, or incorrect test results may be obtained. 1. Connect a test lamp between the 2 pump motor connectors on the EBCM. 2. Turn ON the ignition. 3. Select the ABS Special Functions menu on the scan tool. 4. Select ABS Motor. 5. Use the scan tool to command the ABS Motor On and then Off. Does the test lamp illuminate and then turn Off with each command?		Go to Step 9	Go to Step 11
9	Press the Exit key on the scan tool. Does the DTC reset?		Go to Step 11	Go to Step 10
10	Replace the BPMV. Did you complete the replacement?		Go to Step 12	--
11	Replace the EBCM and the BPMV. Did you complete the replacements?		Go to Step 12	--
12	1. Use a scan tool in order to clear the DTCs. 2. Operate the vehicle within the Conditions for Running the DTC, as specified in the supporting text. Does the DTC reset?		Go to Step 3	System OK

LTV0500000004573

Fig. 26   Code C0110: Pump Motor Circuit (Part 3 of 3). Canyon & Colorado

Circuit Description

The ignition 1 circuit supplies 12 volts to the longitudinal accelerometer. When the vehicle is not moving, or is being driven at a constant, steady speed, longitudinal acceleration is 0 m/sec/sec (0 ft/sec/sec), and the longitudinal accelerometer signal voltage is very near 2.5 volts. This is referred to as longitudinal accelerometer bias voltage. Vehicle acceleration or deceleration causes the longitudinal accelerometer signal voltage to increase or decrease. The harder the acceleration or deceleration, the greater the change in signal voltage.

DTC Descriptor

This diagnostic procedure supports the following DTC:

DTC C0191 All Wheel Drive (AWD)/Four Wheel Drive (4WD) Reference Accelerometer Circuit

Conditions for Running the DTC

Both of the conditions listed below may be required to set the DTC.

- The ignition is ON.
- The vehicle is accelerated rapidly to a speed greater than 11 km/h (7 mph) before decelerating rapidly to a stop.

Conditions for Setting the DTC

Any of the following conditions may cause the DTC to set.

- Open longitudinal accelerometer circuitry is detected.
- Shorted longitudinal accelerometer circuitry is detected.
- An erratic longitudinal accelerometer signal is detected.
- The electronic brake control module (EBCM) detects that the longitudinal accelerometer sensor signal does not correspond with signals from other sensors.

Action Taken When the DTC Sets

- The EBCM disables the Antilock Brake System (ABS).
- The ABS indicator turns ON.
- The ABS fault message is displayed.

Conditions for Clearing the DTC

The conditions for setting the DTC are no longer present and you use the scan tool Clear DTCs function.

LTV0500000004574

Fig. 27   Code C0191: All Wheel Drive/Four Wheel Drive Reference Accelerometer Circuit (Part 1 of 3). Canyon & Colorado

Step	Action	Values	Yes	No
7	Use a DMM to measure the voltage between the ignition 1 voltage circuit and the longitudinal accelerometer ground circuit. Does the voltage measure greater than the specified value?	11 V	Go to Step 10	Go to Step 8
8	Test the longitudinal accelerometer ground circuit for an open or high resistance. Did you find and correct the condition?	--	Go to Step 15	Go to Step 11
9	Repair the open in the ignition 1 circuit. Did you complete the repair?	--	Go to Step 15	--
10	1. Inspect for poor connections at the harness connector of the longitudinal accelerometer. 2. Ensure the longitudinal accelerometer is mounted properly. Did you find and correct the condition?	--	Go to Step 15	Go to Step 12
11	Inspect for poor connections at the harness connector of the electronic brake control module (EBCM). Did you find and correct the condition?	--	Go to Step 15	Go to Step 14
12	Replace the longitudinal accelerometer. Did you complete the replacement?	--	Go to Step 15	--
13	Test the LNG rate signal circuit for a short to voltage. Did you find and correct the condition?	--	Go to Step 15	Go to Step 14
14	Replace the EBCM. Did you complete the replacement?	--	Go to Step 15	--
15	1. Use the scan tool to Clear the DTCs. 2. Operate the vehicle within the Conditions for Running the DTC, as specified in the supporting text. Does the DTC reset?	--	Go to Step 3	System OK

LTV0500000004576

Fig. 27   Code C0191: All Wheel Drive/Four Wheel Drive Reference Accelerometer Circuit (Part 3 of 3). Canyon & Colorado

Diagnostic Aids

Thoroughly inspect connections or circuitry that may cause an intermittent malfunction. Refer to Testing for Electrical Intermittents , Testing for Intermittent Conditions and Poor Connections , Wiring Repairs , and Connector Repairs in Wiring Systems.

Diagnostic Aids

Thoroughly inspect connections or circuitry that may cause an intermittent malfunction.

Step	Action	Values	Yes	No
1	Did you perform the Diagnostic System Check - Vehicle?	--	Go to Step 2	Go to Diagnostic System Check
2	1. Use the scan tool to clear the DTCs. 2. Operate the vehicle within the Conditions for Running the DTC, as specified in the supporting text. Does the DTC reset?	--	Go to Step 3	Go to Diagnostic Aids
3	1. Turn OFF the ignition. 2. Disconnect the longitudinal accelerometer harness connector. 3. Turn ON the ignition. 4. Connect a test lamp between the ignition 1 circuit and a good ground. Does the test lamp illuminate?	--	Go to Step 4	Go to Step 9
4	1. Select the Antilock Brake System (ABS) Data Display function on the scan tool. 2. Observe the Longitudinal Accelerometer Sensor Input on the scan tool. Is the Longitudinal Accelerometer Sensor Input voltage less than the specified value?	0.6 V	Go to Step 5	Go to Step 13
5	1. Connect a 3-amp fused jumper wire between the ignition 1 circuit and the LNG rate signal circuit. 2. Observe the Longitudinal Accelerometer Sensor Input on the scan tool. Is the Longitudinal Accelerometer Sensor Input voltage greater than the specified value?	4.75 V	Go to Step 7	Go to Step 6
6	Test the LNG rate signal circuit for the following conditions. - An open - A high resistance - A short to ground Did you find and correct the condition?	--	Go to Step 15	Go to Step 11

LTV0500000004575

Fig. 27   Code C0191: All Wheel Drive/Four Wheel Drive Reference Accelerometer Circuit (Part 2 of 3). Canyon & Colorado

Circuit Description

The solenoid relay, located within the electronic brake control module (EBCM), supplies battery voltage to all of the valve solenoids.

DTC Descriptor

This diagnostic procedure supports the following DTC:

DTC C0201 Antilock Brake System (ABS) Enable Relay Contact Circuit

Conditions for Running the DTC

The ignition is ON.

Conditions for Setting the DTC

The EBCM detects that the solenoid relay is open for 200 milliseconds, when the relay is supposed to be closed.

Action Taken When the DTC Sets

- The EBCM disables the ABS/dynamic rear proportion (DRP).
- The ABS indicator turns ON.
- The ABS fault message turns ON.
- The brake warning indicator turns ON.
- The brakes message is displayed.

Conditions for Clearing the DTC

The Conditions for Setting the DTC are no longer present and you use the scan tool Clear DTCs function.

Diagnostic Aids

Inspect for poor connections that may affect the battery positive voltage circuit to terminal 1 of the EBCM, if this DTC continues to set intermittently. Replace the EBCM, if no wiring concerns are found.

LTV0500000004577

Fig. 28   Code C0201: Anti-Lock Brake System Enable Relay Contact Circuit (Part 1 of 2). Canyon & Colorado

Step	Action	Yes	No
1	Did you perform the Diagnostic System Check - Vehicle?	Go to Step 2	Go to Diagnostic System Check -
2	Use a scan tool to clear the DTCs. Does the DTC set?	Go to Step 3	Go to Diagnostic Aids
3	1. Turn OFF the ignition. 2. Disconnect the electronic brake control module (EBCM) harness connector. 3. Connect a test lamp between the battery positive voltage circuit at terminal 1 of the EBCM harness connector and a good ground. Does the test lamp illuminate?	Go to Step 5	Go to Step 4
4	Repair the open in the battery positive voltage circuit. Did you complete the repair?	Go to Step 7	--
5	Test for poor connections at the harness connector of the EBCM. Did you find and correct the condition?	Go to Step 7	Go to Step 6
6	Replace the EBCM. Did you complete the replacement?	Go to Step 7	--
7	1. Use a scan tool in order to clear the DTCs. 2. Operate the vehicle within the Conditions for Running the DTC, as specified in the supporting text. Does the DTC reset?	Go to Step 3	System OK

LTV0500000004578

Fig. 28 Code C0201: Anti-Lock Brake System Enable Relay Contact Circuit (Part 2 of 2). Canyon & Colorado

Test Description

The number below refers to the step number on the diagnostic table:

2. Performing solenoid tests determines if there is a mechanical malfunction inside the brake pressure modulator valve (BPMV).

Step	Action	Yes	No
1	Did you perform the Diagnostic System Check - Vehicle?	Go to Step 2	Go to Diagnostic System Check
2	1. Use a scan tool in order to clear the DTCs. 2. Use the scan tool in order to perform the necessary Solenoid Tests. Refer to Scan Tool Output Controls . Do the Solenoid Tests show the system to be functioning normally?	Go to Diagnostic Aids	Go to Step 3
3	Replace the brake pressure modulator valve (BPMV). Did you complete the replacement?	Go to Step 4	--
4	Use the scan tool in order to perform the necessary Solenoid Tests. Do the Solenoid Tests show the system to be functioning normally?	System OK	Go to Step 3

LTV0500000004580

Fig. 29 Codes C0220–C0222: Anti-Lock Brake System Channel In Release Too Long (Part 2 of 2). Canyon & Colorado

Circuit Description

The electronic brake control module (EBCM) energizes the appropriate isolation and dump valve solenoids to control hydraulic pressure applied to a brake circuit during an Antilock Brake System (ABS) event.

DTC Descriptors

This diagnostic procedure supports the following DTCs:

- DTC C0220 Left Front ABS Channel in Release Too Long
- DTC C0221 Right Front ABS Channel in Release Too Long
- DTC C0222 Rear Antilock Brake System (ABS) Channel in Release Too Long

Conditions for Running the DTC

- The ignition is ON.
- The vehicle is experiencing an ABS event.

Conditions for Setting the DTC

An ABS event lasting 36 seconds or longer occurs on any brake circuit.

Action Taken When the DTC Sets

- The EBCM disables the ABS/TCS/dynamic rear proportion (DRP).
- The ABS indicator turns ON.
- The brake warning indicator turns ON.
- The ABS fault message is displayed.
- The traction fault message is displayed.
- The brakes message is displayed.

Conditions for Clearing the DTC

The conditions for setting the DTC are no longer present and you use the scan tool Clear DTCs function.

Diagnostic Aids

Always diagnose and repair any wheel speed sensor failures prior to diagnosing DTC C0220, C0221 or C0222.

These DTCs may set, theoretically, when the ABS is activated on surfaces that are nearly impossible to get traction on. If the DTC sets within these conditions, diagnosis of the ABS system is not necessary.

LTV0500000004579

Fig. 29 Codes C0220–C0222: Anti-Lock Brake System Channel In Release Too Long (Part 1 of 2). Canyon & Colorado

Circuit Description

C0240

The powertrain control module (PCM) and the electronic brake control module (EBCM) communicate on the serial data link whenever the ignition is ON.

P0856

The PCM supplies 5 volts through an internal resistor, to the EBCM on the requested torque signal circuit. The EBCM toggles this voltage to ground to create a valid requested torque signal at the PCM.

Conditions for Running the DTC

C0240

The ignition is ON.

P0856
- The ignition is ON.
- The engine is running at a speed greater than 450 RPM for 5-20 seconds.

Conditions for Setting the DTC

C0240

The EBCM receives a serial data message stating that the PCM has lost the ability to reduce engine torque.

P0856

The PCM receives an invalid requested torque signal for 3 seconds.

Action Taken When the DTC Sets

C0240
- The EBCM disables the TCS.
- The traction fault message is displayed.

P0856
- The PCM sends a serial data message to the EBCM stating that the PCM has lost the ability to reduce engine torque.
- The EBCM sets DTC C0240 as a current DTC for as long as the malfunction is present.

Conditions for Clearing the DTC

C0240

The conditions for setting the DTC are no longer present and you use the scan tool Clear DTCs function.

P0856
- The conditions for setting the DTC are no longer present and you use the scan tool Clear DTCs function.
- A history DTC clears automatically after 40 consecutive warm-up cycles without a PCM detected failure.

LTV0500000004581

Fig. 30 Codes C0240 or P0856: EBCM/PCM Receives Invalid Message (Part 1 of 4). Canyon & Colorado

Diagnostic Aids

C0240

A requested torque signal malfunction is only one possible cause for the PCM to lose the ability to perform traction control. DTC C0240 may set due to engine overheating, throttle actuator control failure, loss of ignition timing control by the PCM, etc. If DTC P1571 has not set, refer to Diagnostic System Check - Engine Controls in Engine Controls - 2.8L (LK5) or Diagnostic System Check - Engine Controls in Engine Controls - 3.5L (L52) to identify other possible causes of DTC C0240.

P0856

Thoroughly inspect connections or circuitry that may cause an intermittent malfunction.

Test Description

The numbers below refer to the step numbers on the diagnostic table.

4. This step tests for voltage supplied to the EBCM from the PCM.

5. This step tests for a shorted resistor in the PCM or a short to voltage within the requested torque signal circuit by verifying that a large voltage drop occurs when a test lamp is connected in parallel with the DMM.

LTV0500000004582

Fig. 30 Codes C0240 or P0856: EBCM/PCM Receives Invalid Message (Part 2 of 4). Canyon & Colorado

	Action	Values	Yes	No
9	Inspect for poor connections at the harness connector of the EBCM. Did you find and correct the condition?	-	Go to Step 12	Go to Step 11
10	**Important** Perform the setup procedure for the PCM. Replace the PCM. Did you complete the replacement?		Go to Step 12	--
11	Replace the EBCM. Did you complete the replacement?	-	Go to Step 12	--
12	1. Use the scan tool in order to clear the DTCs. 2. Operate the vehicle within the Conditions for Running the DTC as specified in the supporting text. Does DTC P0856 reset?	-	Go to Step 4	System OK

LTV0500000004584

Fig. 30 Codes C0240 or P0856: EBCM/PCM Receives Invalid Message (Part 4 of 4). Canyon & Colorado

Circuit Description

The electronic brake control module (EBCM) supplies approximately 12 volts through an internal resistor to the powertrain control module (PCM) on the delivered torque signal circuit. The PCM toggles this voltage to ground in order to create a valid delivered torque signal at the EBCM.

DTC Descriptors

This diagnostic procedure supports the following DTCs:

- DTC C0244 Pulse Width Modulated (PWM) Delivered Torque
- DTC P1689 Traction Control Delivered Torque Output Circuit

Conditions for Running the DTC

The ignition is ON.

Conditions for Setting the DTC

The EBCM receives an invalid delivered torque signal for 1 second.

Action Taken When the DTC Sets

- The EBCM disables the traction control switch (TCS).
- The traction fault message is displayed.

Conditions for Clearing the DTC

The conditions for setting the DTC are no longer present and you use the scan tool Clear DTCs function.

Diagnostic Aids

Thoroughly inspect connections or circuitry that may cause an intermittent malfunction.

Test Description

The numbers below refer to the step numbers on the diagnostic table.

3. This step tests for voltage supplied to the PCM from the EBCM.

4. This step tests for a shorted resistor in the EBCM or a short to voltage within the circuit, by verifying that a large voltage drop occurs in the circuit, when the test lamp is placed in parallel with the DMM. The PCM may be damaged, if either of these conditions are present.

LTV0500000004585

Fig. 31 Codes C0244 or P1689: Pulse Width Modulated Delivered Torque/Traction Control Delivered Torque Output Circuit (Part 1 of 3). Canyon & Colorado

Step	Action	Values	Yes	No
1	Did you perform the Antilock Brake System (ABS) Diagnostic System Check?	--	Go to Step 2	Go to Diagnostic System Check -
2	Is DTC P0856 set?	--	Go to Step 3	Go to Diagnostic Aids
3	1. Use a scan tool in order to clear the DTCs. 2. Start the engine. 3. Does DTC P0856 set?	--	Go to Step 4	Go to Diagnostic Aids
4	1. Turn OFF the ignition. 2. Disconnect from the electronic brake control module (EBCM), the harness connector containing the requested torque signal circuit. 3. Turn ON the ignition. 4. Use a DMM to measure the voltage between the requested torque signal circuit and a good ground. Does the voltage measure greater than the specified value?	4.75 V	Go to Step 5	Go to Step 6
5	1. With the DMM still connected to monitor the requested torque circuit, connect one end of a test lamp to a good ground. 2. Connect the other end of the test lamp to the positive lead of the DMM. Does the voltage measure less than the specified value?	0.15 V	Go to Step 9	Go to Step 7
6	Test the requested torque signal circuit for an open or a short to ground. Did you find and correct the condition?	--	Go to Step 12	Go to Step 8
7	Test the requested torque signal circuit for a short to voltage. Did you find and correct the condition?	--	Go to Step 12	Go to Step 10
8	Inspect for poor connections at the harness connector of the powertrain control module (PCM). Did you find and correct the condition?	--	Go to Step 12	Go to Step 10

LTV0500000004583

Fig. 30 Codes C0240 or P0856: EBCM/PCM Receives Invalid Message (Part 3 of 4). Canyon & Colorado

Step	Action	Values	Yes	No
1	Did you perform the Diagnostic System Check - Vehicle?	--	Go to Step 2	Go to Diagnostic System Check
2	1. Use a scan tool in order to clear the DTCs. 2. Turn OFF the ignition for 5 seconds. 3. Start the engine. Does the DTC set?	--	Go to Step 3	Go to Diagnostic Aids
3	1. Turn OFF the ignition. 2. Disconnect from the powertrain control module (PCM), the harness connector containing the delivered torque signal circuit. 3. Turn ON the ignition. 4. Use a DMM in order to measure the voltage between the delivered torque signal circuit and a good ground. Does the voltage measure greater than the specified value?	10 V	Go to Step 4	Go to Step 5
4	1. With the DMM still connected to monitor the delivered torque signal circuit, connect one end of a test lamp to a good ground. 2. Connect the other end of the test lamp to the positive lead of the DMM, while observing the DMM display. Does the voltage measure less than the specified value?	0.15 V	Go to Step 6	Go to Step 8
5	Test the delivered torque signal circuit for an open or a short to ground. Did you find and correct the condition?	--	Go to Step 11	Go to Step 9
6	Inspect for poor connections at the harness connector of the electronic brake control module (EBCM). Did you find and correct the condition?	--	Go to Step 11	Go to Step 7
7	Replace the EBCM. Did you complete the replacement?	--	Go to Step 11	
8	Test the delivered torque signal circuit for a short to voltage. Did you find and correct the condition?	--	Go to Step 11	Go to Step 10
9	Inspect for poor connections at the harness connector of the PCM. Did you find and correct the condition?	--	Go to Step 11	Go to Step 10

LTV0500000004586

Fig. 31 Codes C0244 or P1689: Pulse Width Modulated Delivered Torque/Traction Control Delivered Torque Output Circuit (Part 2 of 3). Canyon & Colorado

10	Replace the PCM. Did you complete the replacement?	--	Go to Step 11	--
11	1. Use the scan tool to clear the DTCs. 2. Operate the vehicle within the Conditions for Running the DTC, as specified in the supporting text. Does the DTC reset?	--	Go to Step 3	System OK

LTV0500000004587

Fig. 31   Codes C0244 or P1689: Pulse Width Modulated Delivered Torque/Traction Control Delivered Torque Output Circuit (Part 3 of 3). Canyon & Colorado

Step	Action	Yes	No
1	Did you perform the Diagnostic System Check - Vehicle?	Go to Step 2	Go to Diagnostic System Check
2	Inspect all of the tires on the vehicle to ensure that all of the tires are of equal size. Did you find and correct the condition?	Go to Step 4	Go to Step 3
3	Inspect the wheel speed sensors and tone rings for damage, incorrect application, or incorrect installation. Did you find and correct the condition?	Go to Step 4	Go to Diagnostic Aids
4	1. Use a scan tool to clear the DTCs. 2. Operate the vehicle within the Conditions for Running the DTC, as specified in the supporting text. Does the DTC reset?	Go to Step 2	System OK

LTV0500000004589

Fig. 32   Code C0245: Wheel Speed Sensor Frequency Error (Part 2 of 2). Canyon & Colorado

Circuit Description

The electronic brake control module (EBCM) receives various serial data messages from other modules, during normal system operation. In vehicles that are equipped with traction control, the EBCM is much more dependant on serial data messages, than the EBCM in vehicles not equipped with traction control.

DTC Descriptor

This diagnostic procedure supports the following DTC:

DTC C0268 Class 2 Data Error Reported

Conditions for Running the DTC

The ignition is ON.

Conditions for Setting the DTC

The EBCM does not receive any one of a number of required serial data messages after the message is requested.

Action Taken When the DTC Sets

- The EBCM sets DTC C0268 for as long as the Condition for Setting the DTC is present.
- The EBCM disables the traction control switch (TCS), if the vehicle is equipped with traction control.
- The traction fault message is displayed, if the vehicle is equipped with traction control.

Conditions for Clearing the DTC

The conditions for setting the DTC are no longer present and you use the scan tool Clear DTCs function.

Step	Action	Yes	No
1	Did you perform the Diagnostic System Check - Vehicle?	Diagnose Scan Tool Does Not Communicate with Class 2 Device	Go to Diagnostic System Check

LTV0500000004590

Fig. 33   Codes C0267 or C0268: Class 2 Data Error Reported. Canyon & Colorado

Circuit Description

As the wheels spin, each wheel speed sensor produces a digital square wave signal. The electronic brake control module (EBCM) uses the frequency of these signals to calculate each wheel speed.

DTC Descriptor

This diagnostic procedure supports the following DTC:

DTC C0245 Wheel Speed Sensor Frequency Error

Conditions for Running the DTC

- The ignition is ON.
- The vehicle speed is between 22 km/h (14 mph) and 110 km/h (69 mph).
- No brake application or deceleration is detected.
- No wheel slip is detected.
- No turning maneuvers are detected.

Conditions for Setting the DTC

The average front wheel speed differs from the rear wheel speed by at least 20 percent for 4 seconds.

Action Taken When the DTC Sets

- The EBCM disables the Antilock Brake System (ABS)/traction control switch (TCS)/dynamic rear proportion (DRP).
- The ABS Fault message is displayed.
- The traction fault message is displayed.
- The brake warning indicator turns ON.

Conditions for Clearing the DTC

The Conditions for Setting the DTC are no longer present and you use the scan tool Clear DTCs function.

Diagnostic Aids

Operating the vehicle with a tire that has very low air pressure may set this DTC.

LTV0500000004588

Fig. 32   Code C0245: Wheel Speed Sensor Frequency Error (Part 1 of 2). Canyon & Colorado

Circuit Description

The electronic brake control module (EBCM) performs several self-tests, for any internal problems, which may affect proper operation.

DTC Descriptor

This diagnostic procedure supports the following DTC:

DTC C0550 Electronic Control Unit (ECU) Performance

Conditions for Running the DTC

- The ignition is ON.
- The vehicle has achieved a speed greater than 10 km/h (7 mph).

Conditions for Setting the DTC

The EBCM detects an internal malfunction.

Action Taken When the DTC Sets

The following actions may occur.

- The EBCM disables the Antilock Brake System (ABS)/dynamic rear proportion (DRP).
- The ABS indicator turns ON.
- The brake warning indicator turns ON.
- The traction fault message is displayed.
- The brake message is displayed.

Conditions for Clearing the DTC

Certain failures that may cause this DTC to set cannot be cleared. Other failures that may cause this DTC to set may be cleared, at least temporarily, by using the scan tool Clear DTCs function.

Diagnostic Aids

Replace the EBCM, if this DTC continues to set intermittently.

LTV0500000004591

Fig. 34   Code C0550: Electronic Control Unit Performance (Part 1 of 2). Canyon & Colorado

Step	Action	Yes	No
1	Did you perform the Diagnostic System Check - Vehicle?	Go to Step 2	Go to Diagnostic System Check
2	Use a scan tool in order to clear the DTCs. Can the DTC be cleared?	Go to Step 3	Go to Step 4
3	Operate the vehicle within the Conditions for Running the DTC, as specified in the supporting text. Does the DTC reset?	Go to Step 4	Go to Diagnostic Aids
4	Replace the electronic brake control module (EBCM). Did you complete the replacement?	Go to Step 5	--
5	1. Use the scan tool to clear the DTCs. 2. Operate the vehicle within the Conditions for Running the DTC, as specified in the supporting text. Does the DTC reset?	Go to Step 3	System OK

LTV0500000004592

Fig. 34   Code C0550: Electronic Control Unit Performance (Part 2 of 2). Canyon & Colorado

Circuit Description

The electronic brake control module (EBCM) is wired to the ignition 1 voltage circuit to indicate the ignition ON/OFF state. The EBCM monitors this voltage and the voltage on the front wheel speed sensor voltage supply circuits to ensure that the voltages remain within an acceptable operating range. The EBCM cannot operate properly when the system voltage is too low.

DTC Descriptor

This diagnostic procedure supports the following DTC:

DTC C0899 Device Voltage Low

Conditions for Running the DTC

- The ignition is ON.
- The power mode is not detected as being CRANK.

Conditions for Setting the DTC

Either of the following conditions may cause the DTC to set.

- The EBCM detects voltage below 9.5 volts at the ignition 1 circuit for 2 seconds.
- The EBCM detects voltage below 7.3 volts at either of the front wheel speed sensor voltage supply circuits for 20 seconds.

Action Taken When the DTC Sets

The following actions may occur when this DTC sets.

- The EBCM disables the ABS/TCS.
- The EBCM disables the dynamic rear proportion (DRP).
- The Antilock Brake System (ABS) indicator turns ON.
- The brake warning indicator turns ON.
- The ABS fault message is displayed.
- The traction fault message is displayed.
- The brakes message is displayed.

Conditions for Clearing the DTC

The Conditions for Setting the DTC are no longer present and you use the scan tool Clear DTCs function.

LTV0500000004594

Fig. 36   Code C0899: Device Voltage Low (Part 1 of 2). Canyon & Colorado

Circuit Description

Two-wheel drive vehicles are not equipped with a longitudinal accelerometer. The electronic brake control module (EBCM) for two-wheel drive vehicles sets a DTC if a longitudinal accelerometer signal voltage is detected at any time.

Conditions for Running the DTC

The ignition is ON.

Conditions for Setting the DTC

The EBCM detects a longitudinal accelerometer signal voltage for 400 milliseconds.

Action Taken When the DTC Sets

If equipped, the following actions may occur.

- The EBCM disables the ABS.
- The EBCM disables the TCS.
- The ABS fault message is displayed.
- The traction fault message is displayed.

Conditions for Clearing the DTC

The Conditions for Setting the DTC are no longer present and you use the scan tool Clear DTCs function.

Diagnostic Aids

This DTC sets when an EBCM that is programmed for a two-wheel drive vehicle is inadvertently installed in a four wheel drive vehicle.

LTV0500000004593

Fig. 35   Code C0569: EBCM Detects Longitudinal Accelerometer Signal Voltage. Canyon & Colorado

Diagnostic Aids

Although 2-20 seconds of low voltage detection are required to set this DTC, ABS related systems may be disabled by the EBCM during the fault detection process, and prior to setting this DTC. This means that the instrument panel cluster (IPC) may turn ON indicators, and fault messages, intermittently, without the EBCM setting any DTCs if low voltage faults are intermittent.

Step	Action	Values	Yes	No
1	Did you perform the Diagnostic System Check - Vehicle?	--	Go to Step 2	Go to Diagnostic System Check
2	Is DTC C0035 set as either a Current or History DTC?	--	Go to DTC C0035	Go to Step 3
3	1. Use a scan tool to clear the DTCs. 2. Operate the vehicle within the Conditions for Setting the DTC, as specified in the supporting text. Does the DTC set?	--	Go to Step 4	Go to Diagnostic Aids
4	Perform the Diagnostic System Check - Vehicle in Vehicle DTC Information. Did you find and correct the condition?	--	Go to Step 9	Go to Step 5
5	1. Turn OFF the ignition. 2. Disconnect the electronic brake control module (EBCM) harness connector. 3. Remove the 10-amp ABS fuse from the underhood fuse panel. 4. Use a DMM to measure the resistance between the unpowered side of the ABS fuse cavity and the ignition 1 voltage circuit at the EBCM harness connector. Does the resistance measure within the specified range?	0-0.2 ohms	Go to Step 7	Go to Step 6
6	Repair the high resistance in the ignition 3 voltage circuit. Did you complete the repair?	--	Go to Step 9	
7	Inspect for poor connections at the harness connector of the EBCM. Did you find and correct the condition?	--	Go to Step 9	Go to Step 8
8	Replace the EBCM. Did you complete the replacement?	--	Go to Step 9	
9	1. Use the scan tool to clear the DTCs. 2. Operate the vehicle within the Conditions for Running the DTC, as specified in the supporting text. Does the DTC reset?	--	Go to Step 3	System OK

LTV0500000004595

Fig. 36   Code C0899: Device Voltage Low (Part 2 of 2). Canyon & Colorado

Circuit Description

The electronic brake control module (EBCM) cannot operate normally, when system voltage is too high.

DTC Descriptor

This diagnostic procedure supports the following DTC:

DTC C0900 Device Voltage High

Conditions for Running the DTC

The ignition is ON.

Conditions for Setting the DTC

- The EBCM detects ignition voltage is greater than 17.5 volts.
- The vehicle achieves a speed greater than 7 km/h (4 mph).

Action Taken When the DTC Sets

If equipped, the following actions occur:

- The EBCM disables the ABS/dynamic rear proportion (DRP).
- The EBCM disables the TCS.
- The Antilock Brake System (ABS) indicator turns ON.
- The brakes message is displayed.
- The traction fault message is displayed.

Conditions for Clearing the DTC

The conditions for setting the DTC are no longer present and you use the scan tool Clear DTCs function.

LTV0500000004596

Fig. 37   Code C0900: Device Voltage High (Part 1 of 2). Canyon & Colorado

Step	Action	Yes	No
1	Did you perform the Diagnostic System Check - Vehicle?	Go to Step 2	Go to Diagnostic System Check
2	Perform the Diagnostic System Check - Vehicle in Vehicle DTC Information. Did you find and correct the condition?	Go to Step 4	Go to Step 3
3	Replace the electronic brake control module (EBCM). Did you complete the replacement?	Go to Step 4	--
4	1. Use the scan tool to clear the DTCs. 2. Operate the vehicle within the Conditions for Running the DTC, as specified in the supporting text. Does the DTC reset?	Go to Step 2	System OK

LTV0500000004597

Fig. 37   Code C0900: Device Voltage High (Part 2 of 2). Canyon & Colorado

Step	Action	Yes	No
1	Perform the following preliminary inspections: • Ensure that the battery is fully charged. • Ensure that the battery cables are clean and tight. • Inspect for any open fuses. • Inspect the easily accessible systems or the visible system components for obvious damage or conditions that could cause the symptom. • Ensure that the grounds are clean, tight, and in the correct location. • Inspect for aftermarket devices that could affect the operation of the system. • Search for applicable service bulletins. Did you find and correct the condition?	System OK	Go to Step 2
2	Install a scan tool. Does the scan tool power up?	Go to Step 3	Diagnose Scan Tool Does Not Power Up
3	1. Turn ON the ignition, with the engine OFF. 2. Attempt to establish communication with all of the control modules on the vehicle. Does the scan tool communicate with all of the expected vehicle control modules?	Go to Step 4	Diagnose Scan Tool Does Not Communicate with Class 2 Device
4	**Important:** 1. To ensure that RAP mode is inactive, if equipped, open the drivers door during the following step. 2. The engine may start during the following step. Turn OFF the engine as soon as you have observed the crank power mode. 1. Access the Power Mode parameter on the scan tool. 2. Rotate the ignition switch, operate the ignition mode switch, through all positions while observing the Power Mode parameter. Does the Power Mode parameter reading on the scan tool match the ignition switch position for all switch positions?	Go to Step 5	Diagnose Power Mode Mismatch
5	Attempt to start the engine. Does the engine crank?	Go to Step 6	Go to Symptoms

LTV0500000004602

Fig. 38   Diagnostic System Check (Part 1 of 2). Hummer H3

Step	Action	Yes	No
6	Attempt to start the engine. Does the engine start and idle?	Go to Step 7	Go to Engine Cranks but Does Not Run
7	**Important:** Do not clear any DTCs unless instructed by a diagnostic procedure. Use the appropriate scan tool selections to obtain DTCs for each of the control modules. Does the scan tool display any DTCs?	Go to Step 8	Go to Step 12
8	Does the scan tool display any DTCs that begin with a "U"?	Go to Diagnostic Trouble Code (DTC)	Go to Step 9
9	**Important:** If any of these DTCs are displayed, diagnose them before diagnosing any other DTCs or symptoms. Does the scan tool display DTC B1000, B1001, B1004, B1007, B1009, C0550, P0601, P0602, P0603, P0604, P0606, P0607, P1621, or P2610?	Go to Diagnostic Trouble Code (DTC)	Go to Step 10
10	**Important:** If any of these DTCs are displayed, diagnose them before diagnosing any other DTCs or symptoms. Does the scan tool display DTC B1372, B1373, B1420, B1442, B1443, C0899, P0562, P0563, or P1682?	Go to Diagnostic Trouble Code (DTC)	Go to Step 11
11	**Important:** If any of the remaining DTCs are powertrain DTCs, select Capture Info in order to store the powertrain DTC information with a scan tool. If multiple DTCs are stored, diagnose the DTCs in the following order: 1. Component level DTCs, such as sensor DTCs, solenoid DTCs, and relay DTCs. 2. System level DTCs, such as misfire DTCs, EVAP system DTCs, and fuel trim DTCs. Diagnose the remaining DTCs.	Go to Diagnostic Trouble Code (DTC)	--
12	Is the customers concern with inspection/maintenance (I/M) testing?	Diagnose (I/M) System Check	Go to Symptoms

LTV0500000004603

Fig. 38   Diagnostic System Check (Part 2 of 2). Hummer H3

DTC Descriptor

DTC B0010: Reverse Gear Signal Circuit

Diagnostic Fault Information

Important: Always perform the Diagnostic System Check - Vehicle prior to using this diagnostic procedure.

Circuit	Short to Ground	Open/High Resistance	Short to Voltage	Signal Performance
Backup Lamp Supply Voltage	--	B0010	1	--
1. Reverse lamp always illuminated				

Circuit/System Description

The electronic brake module (EBCM) receives a 12-volt signal from the backup lamp supply voltage circuit when the vehicle transmission is in reverse. The EBCM uses the backup lamp supply voltage circuit to perform traction control and vehicle stability in reverse.

Conditions for Running the DTC

- The ignition is ON.
- The vehicle speed is greater than 15 km/h (9 mph) for 2 seconds continuously.
- The vehicle is equipped with a manual transmission.

Conditions for Setting the DTC

The EBCM detects an open in the backup lamp supply voltage circuit.

Action Taken When the DTC Sets

- The EBCM disables the Traction Control System (TCS)/Vehicle Stability Enhancement System (VSES) for the duration of the ignition cycle.
- Driver information center (DIC) displays the TRACTION FAILED message.
- DIC displays the SERVICE STAB SYS message.
- Stability Caution indicator turns on.

Conditions for Clearing the DTC

The DTC clears automatically from current status when the fault is corrected and the ignition is cycled. Use a scan tool to clear the DTC from history status.

LTV0500000004604

Fig. 39 Code B0010: Reverse Gear Signal Circuit (Part 1 of 2). Hummer H3

DTC Descriptor

DTC B2745: Traction Control Switch Circuit

Diagnostic Fault Information

Important: Always perform the Diagnostic System Check - Vehicle prior to using this diagnostic procedure.

Circuit	Short to Ground	Open/High Resistance	Short to Voltage	Signal Performance
TCS switch signal circuit	B2745	12	--	--
1. Traction control cannot be manually disabled.				

Circuit/System Description

The driver may disable the Traction Control System (TCS) by pressing the traction control switch. The body control module (BCM) supplies a 12-volt signal on the traction control signal circuit. When the traction control switch is pressed, this voltage signal is grounded.

Conditions for Running the DTC

The ignition is ON.

Conditions for Setting the DTC

The BCM detects low voltage on the traction control signal circuit for 60 seconds.

Action Taken When the DTC Sets

- The BCM sends a serial data message to the electronic brake control module (EBCM) informing the EBCM that the desired TCS state cannot be determined.
- The EBCM defaults the TCS status to enabled.

Conditions for Clearing the DTC

The DTC clears automatically from Current status when the fault is corrected. Use a scan tool to clear the DTC from history status.

Diagnostic Aids

An intermittent short to ground on the traction control signal circuit is the most likely cause of a history DTC when no problem is found. When the Conditions for Setting this DTC are present, the driver is not able to disable traction control.

LTV0500000004606

Fig. 40 Code B2745: Traction Control Switch Circuit (Part 1 of 2). Hummer H3

Diagnostic Aids

B0010 sets if all of the reverse lamp bulbs are open.

Reference Information

Schematic Reference

- ABS Schematics
- Exterior Lights Schematics

Connector End View Reference

- ABS Connector End Views
- Computer/Integrating Systems Connector End Views

Electrical Information Reference

- Circuit Testing
- Connector Repairs
- Testing for Intermittent Conditions and Poor Connections
- Wiring Repairs

Scan Tool Reference

Scan Tool Data List

Circuit/System Testing

1. Turn ON the ignition with the engine OFF. Place the gear selector of the transmission in reverse. The reverse lamps should illuminate.
   ⇒ If the reverse lamps do not illuminate, go to Diagnostic Aids or Symptoms - Lighting Systems.
2. Turn the ignition OFF. Disconnect the EBCM harness connector. Connect a test lamp between the backup lamp supply voltage circuit of the harness connector and ground. Turn the ignition ON and place the gear selector of the transmission in reverse.
   ⇒ If the test lamp does not illuminate, repair open in the backup lamp supply voltage circuit between the splice and the EBCM connector.
   ⇒ If the test lamp illuminates, replace the EBCM/brake pressure modulator valve (BPMV) assembly.

Repair Instructions

Important: Always perform the Diagnostic Repair Verification after completing the diagnostic procedure.

- Control Module References for EBCM and BPMV replacement, setup, and programming.
- Symptoms - Lighting Systems

LTV0500000004605

Fig. 39 Code B0010: Reverse Gear Signal Circuit (Part 2 of 2). Hummer H3

Schematic Reference

ABS Schematics

Connector End View Reference

- SIR Connector End Views
- Computer/Integrating Systems Connector End Views

Electrical Information Reference

- Circuit Testing
- Connector Repairs
- Testing for Intermittent Conditions and Poor Connections
- Wiring Repairs

Scan Tool Reference

Scan Tool Data List

Circuit/System Verification

Traction control can be disabled/enabled when the traction control switch is pressed and released.

Circuit/System Testing

1. Turn OFF the ignition for 5 seconds, then turn ON the ignition and wait at least 60 seconds.
   ⇒ If DTC B2745 does not reset, go to Diagnostic Aids
2. Turn the ignition OFF. Disconnect the traction control switch harness connector. Turn the ignition ON and wait at least 60 seconds.
   ⇒ If DTC B2745 does not reset, replace the traction control switch.
   ⇒ If the DTC B2745 resets, check the TCS switch signal circuit for a short to ground or replace the BCM.

Repair Instructions

Important: Always perform the Diagnostic Repair Verification after completing the diagnostic procedure.

- Accessory Switch Replacement
- Control Module References for BCM replacement, setup, and programming.

LTV0500000004607

Fig. 40 Code B2745: Traction Control Switch Circuit (Part 2 of 2). Hummer H3

DTC Descriptor

DTC C0035: Left Front Wheel Speed Sensor Circuit

DTC C0040: Right Front Wheel Speed Sensor Circuit

DTC C0045: Left Rear Wheel Speed Sensor Circuit

DTC C0050: Right Rear Wheel Speed Sensor Circuit

Diagnostic Fault Information

Important: Always perform the Diagnostic System Check - Vehicle prior to using this diagnostic procedure.

Circuit	Short to Ground	Open or High Resistance	Short to Voltage	Signal Performance
Left Front Sensor Signal	C0035	C0035	C0035	C0035
Left Front Sensor Low Reference	C0035	C0035	C0035	C0035
Right Front Sensor Signal	C0040	C0040	C0040	C0040
Right Front Sensor Low Reference	C0040	C0040	C0040	C0040
Left Rear Sensor Signal	C0045	C0045	C0045	C0045
Left Rear Sensor Low Reference	C0045	C0045	C0045	C0045
Right Rear Sensor Signal	C0050	C0050	C0050	C0050
Right Rear Sensor Low Reference	C0050	C0050	C0050	C0050

Circuit/System Description

The wheel speed sensor receives a 12-volt power supply voltage from the electronic brake control module (EBCM) and provides an output signal to the EBCM. As the wheel spins, the wheel speed sensor sends the EBCM a DC square wave signal. The EBCM uses the frequency of the square wave signal to calculate the wheel speed.

Conditions for Running the DTC

C0035-C0050

- The ignition is ON.
- Ignition voltage is greater than 9 volts.
- Vehicle speed is greater than 10 km/h (6 mph) is required to detect rolling wheel speed failures.

LTV0500000004608

Fig. 41   Codes C0035, C0040, C0045 & C0050: Wheel Speed Sensor Circuit (Part 1 of 4). Hummer H3

Circuit/System Verification

With scan tool installed drive the vehicle in a straight line at a speed greater than 10 km/h (6 mph), all wheel speed sensors should read the same speed.

Circuit/System Testing

Note: It is recommend that Component Testing is performed before Circuit Testing when diagnosing wheel speed sensors.

Note: Performing Circuit Testing with EBCM connector disconnected and key on will cause U codes to set. Clear DTCs after performing the test.

1. With the ignition OFF, Disconnect the wheel speed sensor connector. Ignition ON, Measure for voltage above 7.5 V on the wheel speed sensor signal circuit.
   ⇒ If voltage is below 7.5 check for a short to ground, open or replace EBCM.
2. Ignition OFF, disconnect the EBCM connector. With the EBCM connector disconnected and the ignition ON, measure for 0 volts between the wheel speed sensor signal circuit or the wheel speed sensor low reference circuit and ground at the EBCM connector.
   ⇒ If over 0 volts, repair short to voltage in the wheel speed sensor signal circuit or the wheel speed sensor supply voltage circuit.
3. With the ignition OFF and the wheel speed sensor harness disconnected, Measure for infinite ohms of resistance between ground and the wheel speed sensor signal and the wheel speed sensor low reference circuit from the EBCM connector.
   ⇒ If less than infinite ohms, repair short to ground in the sensor signal or the low reference circuit.
4. Measure for infinite ohms of resistance between the wheel speed sensor signal circuit and the wheel speed low reference circuit at the EBCM connector.
   ⇒ If less than infinite ohms, repair short between the wheel speed sensor signal circuit and the wheel speed sensor low reference circuit.
   ⇒ If all circuits test normal replace the suspect wheel speed sensor.

Component Testing

1. ignition OFF, disconnect the wheel speed sensor connector. Measure for 12 volts on the wheel speed sensor signal circuit.
   ⇒ If the If voltage is below 7.5 check for a short to ground, open or replace EBCM.
2. At the wheel speed sensor, connect a 3 Amp fused jumper wire between wheel speed sensor low reference terminal and the low reference terminal of the wheel speed harness connector. Set-up a DMM to measure current flow (mA/A). Connect the positive terminal of the DMM to the wheel speed sensor signal terminal at the wheel speed sensor

LTV0500000004610

Fig. 41   Codes C0035, C0040, C0045 & C0050: Wheel Speed Sensor Circuit (Part 3 of 4). Hummer H3

harness connector and the negative lead to the wheel speed sensor signal terminal of the wheel speed sensor. Spin the wheel very slowly. Measure for 4-8 mA on the low reading and 12-16 mA on the high reading.
   ⇒ If the low amperage output of the wheel speed sensor signal circuit is below 4 mA or above 8 mA replace the wheel speed sensor.
   ⇒ If the high amperage output of the wheel speed sensor signal circuit is below 12 mA or above 16 mA replace the wheel speed sensor.

Repair Instructions

Important: Always perform the Diagnostic Repair Verification after completing the diagnostic procedure.

- Wheel Hub, Bearing, and Seal Replacement
- Control Module References for EBCM and BPMV replacement, setup, and programming

LTV0500000004611

Fig. 41   Codes C0035, C0040, C0045 & C0050: Wheel Speed Sensor Circuit (Part 4 of 4). Hummer H3

Conditions for Setting the DTC

C0035-C0050

- An erratic signal output of the wheel speed sensor is detected.
- A short to voltage, open or ground is detected on the wheel speed sensor signal circuit.
- A open or short to ground in the wheel speed sensor circuit supply voltage.
- Wheel speed sensor power supply is less than 7.6 volts.
- A missing wheel speed sensor signal

Action Taken When the DTC Sets

- The EBCM disables the Antilock Brake System (ABS)/Traction Control System (TCS)/Vehicle Stability Enhancement System (VSES) for the duration of the ignition cycle.
- ABS indicator turns ON.
- Driver information center (DIC) displays the ABS FAULT message.
- Stability Caution indicator turns on.
- DIC displays the SERVICE STAB SYS message.
- DIC displays the TRACTION FAILED message.
- If both rear wheel speed DTCs are set, the dynamic rear proportioning (DRP) is disabled and the Brake Warning indicator turns ON.

Conditions for Clearing the MIL/DTC

- The condition for setting the DTC is no longer present and the DTC is cleared with a scan tool.
- The EBCM automatically clears the history DTC when a current DTC is not detected in 100 consecutive drive cycles.
- An ECE 13 response may occur. If an ECE 13 response is present the vehicle must be operated at a speed greater than 15 km/h (9 mph) to turn off the ABS warning lamp.

Diagnostic Aids

If 2 or more wheel speed sensors are inoperative diagnose each wheel speed sensor individually.

If the customer comments that the ABS indicator is ON only during moist environmental conditions: rain, snow, vehicle wash, etc., inspect the wheel speed sensor wiring for signs of water intrusion. If the DTC is not current, clear all DTCs and simulate the effects of water intrusion by using the following procedure:

1. Spray the suspected area with a 5 percent saltwater solution. To create a 5 percent saltwater solution, add 2 teaspoons of salt to 8 fl oz of water (10 g of salt to 200 ml of water).
2. Test drive the vehicle over various road surfaces, bumps, turns, etc., above 40 km/h (25 mph) for at least 30 seconds.
3. If the DTC returns, replace the suspected wheel speed sensor or repair the wheel speed sensor wiring.
4. Rinse the area thoroughly when completed.

LTV0500000004609

Fig. 41   Codes C0035, C0040, C0045 & C0050: Wheel Speed Sensor Circuit (Part 2 of 4). Hummer H3

DTC Descriptor

DTC C0110 : Pump Motor Circuit

Diagnostic Fault Information

Important: Always perform the Diagnostic System Check - Vehicle prior to using this diagnostic procedure.

Circuit/System Description

The ABS pump motor recharges the brake fluid accumulator during antilock braking and normal power brake assist. The ABS pump motor is part of the hydraulic brake booster assembly.

Conditions for Running the DTC

Ignition voltage is greater than 9.5 volts.

Conditions for Setting the DTC

- The ABS pump runs continuously for 178 seconds.
- The EBCM detects an open in the pump motor circuit when the pump motor is activated.

Action Taken When the DTC Sets

- EBCM disables the Antilock Brake System (ABS)/Traction Control System (TCS)/Vehicle Stability Enhancement System (VSES) for the duration of the ignition cycle.
- ABS indicator turns ON.
- Brake warning indicator turns ON.
- Driver information center (DIC) displays the SERVICE ABS/TRACTION System message.
- DIC displays the SERVICE STAB SYS message.
- An ECE 13 response may occur.
- ABS pump motor runs intermittently, 2 seconds on and 8 seconds off.

Conditions for Clearing the DTC

- The condition for setting the DTC is no longer present and the DTC is cleared with a scan tool.
- The EBCM automatically clears the history DTC when a current DTC is not detected in 100 consecutive drive cycles.

LTV0500000004612

Fig. 42   Code C0110: Pump Motor Circuit (Part 1 of 2). Hummer H3

Circuit/System Verification

With the scan tool, access the ABS special functions menu and perform the ABS Motor test. The pump motor should function and no DTCs should be set.

Circuit/System Testing

1. With the ignition OFF, disconnect the main EBCM harness connector (C2) an the small 4-way EBCM harness connector (C1). At both EBCM harness connectors, test for 12 volts on the battery positive voltage circuits.
   ⇒ If the voltage is below 10 volts, repair open or short to ground on the battery positive voltage circuit.
2. Connect one end of a test lamp to battery positive voltage. At the EBCM connector, touch the other end of the test lamp to each of the three ground circuits. The test lamp should illuminate.
   ⇒ If the test lamp does not illuminate when touched to each ground circuit, repair open in the suspected ground circuit.
3. Remove the two small rubber caps that cover the ABS pump motor connections to the EBCM. Connect a test lamp between the two terminals located under the rubber plugs. Turn the ignition ON. Use the scan tool to command the ABS pump motor ON.
   ⇒ If the test lamp illuminates, replace the hydraulic brake booster.
   ⇒ If the test lamp does not illuminate, replace the EBCM / BPMV assembly.

Repair Instructions

Important: Always perform the Diagnostic Repair Verification after completing the diagnostic procedure.

- Control Module References for EBCM replacement, setup, and programming
- Hydraulic Brake Booster Replacement

LTV0500000004613

Fig. 42   Code C0110: Pump Motor Circuit (Part 2 of 2). Hummer H3

Diagnostic Aids

The accumulator pressure sensor is located internally in the BPMV and is not serviceable.

Reference Information

Schematic Reference

ABS Schematics

Connector End View Reference

ABS Connector End Views

Electrical Information Reference

- Circuit Testing
- Connector Repairs
- Testing for Intermittent Conditions and Poor Connections
- Wiring Repairs

Scan Tool Reference

Scan Tool Data List

Circuit/System Testing

Important: If present, diagnose DTC C0110 or C0201 before DTC C0131. An inoperative ABS motor or control can cause DTC C0131 to set.

1. Cycle the ignition from OFF to ON. Observe the accumulator pressure data parameter on the scan tool. Fully apply and release the brake pedal once, the accumulator pressure should hold steady above 16.7 MPa.
   ⇒ If the accumulator pressure data parameter does not hold steady above 16.7 MPa, replace the accumulator.
2. Wait 60 seconds without depressing the pedal. The pump motor should not turn on.
   ⇒ If the ABS pump motor turns ON and OFF several times, replace the EBCM/brake pressure modulator valve (BPMV) assembly.
3. Cycle the ignition from OFF to ON. Apply and release the brake pedal continuously. The accumulator pressure should not be below 14.9 for 100 seconds consecutively.
   ⇒ If the accumulator pressure stays below 14.9 MPa for 100 seconds, replace the EBCM/BPMV assembly.
4. Test drive the vehicle and observe the accumulator pressure data parameter while driving. The accumulator should not fluctuate rapidly.
   ⇒ If the accumulator pressure fluctuates rapidly replace the EBCM/BPMV assembly.

Repair Instructions

Important: Always perform the Diagnostic Repair Verification after completing the diagnostic procedure.

- Control Module References for EBCM and BPMV replacement, setup, and programming
- Hydraulic Brake Booster Accumulator Replacement

LTV0500000004615

Fig. 43   Code C0131: Anti-Lock Brake System Pressure Circuit (Part 2 of 2). Hummer H3

DTC Descriptor

DTC C0131 : Antilock Brake System (ABS) Pressure Circuit

Diagnostic Fault Information

Important: Always perform the Diagnostic System Check - Vehicle prior to using this diagnostic procedure.

Circuit/System Description

The ABS pump motor and accumulator operates the ABS and base brake power assist systems. Pressurized brake fluid is stored in the accumulator and used for ABS and base brake power assist functions. An accumulator pressure sensor located internally in the electronic brake control module (EBCM) monitors the accumulator pressure. If accumulator pressure becomes too low, the ABS pump motor is commanded ON.

Conditions for Running the DTC

The ignition is ON

Conditions for Setting the DTC

- The accumulator internal power supply is out of range.
- The accumulator pressure sensor value changes more than 15 MPa in 0.08 seconds.
- The accumulator pressure signal fails to change at least 0.12 MPa during the accumulator pressure test.
- The EBCM detects that the accumulator pressure signal is too low when the vehicle is driven.

Action Taken When the DTC Sets

- The EBCM disables the Antilock Brake System (ABS)/Traction Control System (TCS)/Vehicle Stability Enhancement System (VSES) for the duration of the ignition cycle.
- The ABS indicator turns ON.
- The driver information center (DIC) displays the ABS FAULT message.
- The Stability Caution indicator turns on.
- The DIC displays the SERVICE STAB SYS message.
- The DIC displays the TRACTION FAILED message.

Conditions for Clearing the DTC

- The condition for the DTC is no longer present and the DTC is cleared with a scan tool.
- The EBCM automatically clears the history DTC when a current DTC is not detected in 100 consecutive drive cycles.

LTV0500000004614

Fig. 43   Code C0131: Anti-Lock Brake System Pressure Circuit (Part 1 of 2). Hummer H3

DTC Descriptor

DTC C0136: Base Brake System Pressure Circuit

Diagnostic Fault Information

Important: Always perform the Diagnostic System Check - Vehicle prior to using this diagnostic procedure.

Circuit/System Description

The electronic brake control module (EBCM) monitors an internal input from the master cylinder pressure sensor to enhance Antilock Brake System (ABS) braking and vehicle stability if equipped.

Conditions for Running the DTC

The ignition is ON.

Conditions for Setting the DTC

- When vehicle speed is more than 7 km/h (4 mph), the master cylinder pressure does not change for 30 seconds with the brake applied.
- When vehicle speed is more than 10 km/h (6 mph), the master cylinder pressure signal is erratic.
- Master cylinder pressure signal is out of range.
- Master cylinder pressure is high for 5 seconds with the stop lamp switch signal OFF.

Action Taken When the DTC Sets

- The EBCM disables traction control system (TCS) and vehicle stability enhancement system (VSES) for the duration of the ignition cycle.
- The Stability Caution indicator turns on.
- The driver information center (DIC) displays the TRACTION FAILED message.
- DIC displays the SERVICE STAB SYS message.
- An ECE 13 response may occur.

Conditions for Clearing the DTC

- The condition for the DTC is no longer present and the DTC is cleared with a scan tool.
- The EBCM automatically clears the history DTC when a current DTC is not detected in 100 consecutive drive cycles.

Diagnostic Aids

The master cylinder pressure sensor is located internally in the BPMV and is not serviceable.

LTV0500000004616

Fig. 44   Code C0136: Base Brake System Pressure Circuit (Part 1 of 2). Hummer H3

Circuit/System Testing

Note: Inspect for brake lamp related DTCs and symptoms before diagnosing DTC C0136.

Note: A binding brake pedal or misadjusted brake switch can cause DTC C0136 to set. Correct any hydraulic brake symptoms before diagnosing this DTC.

Disconnect the EBCM harness connector. Connect a test lamp between the stop lamp switch signal circuit and ground. Apply the brake.

⇒ If the test lamp does not illuminate but the center high mounted stop lamp (CHMSL) does illuminate, repair open in the stop lamp switch signal circuit.

⇒ If the test lamp and CHMSL does not illuminate, go to Symptoms - Lighting Systems .

⇒ If the test lamp and CHMSL illuminates, replace the EBCM/brake pressure modulator valve (BPMV).

Repair Instructions

Important: Always perform the Diagnostic Repair Verification after completing the diagnostic procedure.

- Control Module References for EBCM and BPMV replacement, setup, and programming
- Symptoms - Lighting Systems

LTV0500000004617

Fig. 44 Code C0136: Base Brake System Pressure Circuit (Part 2 of 2). Hummer H3

ABS Connector End Views

Electrical Information Reference

- Circuit Testing
- Connector Repairs
- Testing for Intermittent Conditions and Poor Connections
- Wiring Repairs

Scan Tool Reference

Scan Tool Data List

Circuit/System Verification

With the scan tool, observe the Brake Switch Status data parameter. Apply and release the brake pedal. The brake pedal switch status should change from OFF to ON.

Circuit/System Testing

1. Release the brake pedal. With the scan tool observe the Brake Switch Status data parameter.
   ⇒ If the fault is current, the scan tool brake switch status displays ON.

   ⇒ If the scan tool displays OFF, go to Testing for Intermittent Conditions and Poor Connections.

2. With the ignition OFF, disconnect the EBCM connector. With the Ignition ON release the brake pedal and connect a test lamp between the stop lamp switch signal circuit and ground.
   ⇒ If the test lamp illuminates go to Symptoms - Lighting Systems.

   ⇒ If the test lamp does not illuminate, replace the EBCM/ brake pressure modulator valve (BPMV) assembly.

Repair Instructions

Important: Always perform the Diagnostic Repair Verification after completing the diagnostic procedure.

- Symptoms - Lighting Systems
- Control Module References for EBCM or BPMV replacement, setup, and programming

LTV0500000004619

Fig. 45 Code C0161: ABS Brake Switch Circuit (Part 2 of 2). Hummer H3

DTC Descriptor

DTC C0161: ABS Brake Switch Circuit

Diagnostic Fault Information

Important: Always perform the Diagnostic System Check - Vehicle prior to using this diagnostic procedure.

Circuit/System Description

The brake switch supplies battery positive voltage to the electronic brake control module (EBCM) when the brake pedal is applied.

Conditions for Running the DTC

Ignition voltage is greater than 9.5 volts.

Conditions for Setting the DTC

Stop switch is on and vehicle speed is greater than 15 km/h (9 mph) for 15 minutes continuously.

Action Taken When the DTC Sets

- EBCM disables traction control system (TCS) and vehicle stability enhancement system (VSES) for the duration of the ignition cycle.
- Stability Caution indicator turns on.
- Driver information center (DIC) displays the TRACTION FAILED message.
- A ECE 13 responce occurs.

Conditions for Clearing the DTC

- The condition for setting the DTC is no longer present and the DTC is cleared with a scan tool.
- The EBCM automatically clears the history DTC when a current DTC is not detected in 100 consecutive drive cycles.

LTV0500000004618

Fig. 45 Code C0161: ABS Brake Switch Circuit (Part 1 of 2). Hummer H3

DTC Descriptor

DTC C0179: System Thermal High

Diagnostic Fault Information

Important: Always perform the Diagnostic System Check - Vehicle prior to using this diagnostic procedure.

Circuit/System Description

The electronic brake control module (EBCM) monitors Traction Control System (TCS) activation in order to calculate an estimate of the EBCM solenoid valve temperatures. In most cases high solenoid valve temperatures are caused by extended TCS activation. If the EBCM calculates that the solenoid valve temperatures are too high, the EBCM will temporarily suspend the TCS function until the solenoid valves cool.

Conditions for Running the DTC

The ignition is ON.

Conditions for Setting the DTC

The estimated solenoid coil temperature reaches the temperature limit.

Action Taken When the DTC Sets

- The EBCM disables the Antilock Brake System (ABS)/TCS/Vehicle Stability Enhancement System (VSES) for the duration of the ignition cycle.
- The ABS indicator turns ON.
- The driver information center (DIC) displays the ABS system message.
- The DIC displays the TRACTION FAILED system message.

Conditions for Clearing the DTC

- After the solenoid valves have cooled the EBCM automatically re-enables TCS function.
- The EBCM automatically clears the history DTC when a current DTC is not detected in 100 consecutive drive cycles.

LTV0500000004620

Fig. 46 Code C0179: System Thermal High (Part 1 of 2). Hummer H3

Circuit/System Verification

With the scan tool, observe the Brake Switch Status data parameter. Apply and release the brake pedal. The brake pedal switch status should change from OFF to ON.

Circuit/System Testing

1. Most occurrences of this DTC are caused by excessive TCS activation or braking. Review with the customer to verify the conditions under which the DTC set.
   ⇒ If vehicle operation caused this DTC to set, clear the DTC.
2. Test drive the vehicle under normal conditions
   ⇒ If the DTC resets under normal driving conditions, replace the EBCM/brake pressure modulator valve (BPMV).

Repair Instructions

Important: Always perform the Diagnostic Repair Verification after completing the diagnostic procedure.

Control Module References for EBCM and BPMV replacement, setup, and programming

LTV0500000004621

Fig. 46   Code C0179: System Thermal High (Part 2 of 2). Hummer H3

- Communication is lost between the EBCM and the combination sensor.

Action Taken When the DTC Sets

C0186

- The EBCM disables the Antilock Brake System (ABS)/Traction Control System (TCS)/Vehicle Stability Enhancement System (VSES) for the duration of the ignition cycle.
- The ABS indicator turns ON.
- The driver information center (DIC) displays the ABS FAULT message.
- The Stability Caution indicator turns on.
- The DIC displays the SERVICE STAB SYS message.
- The DIC displays the TRACTION FAILED message.

C0196

- The EBCM disables the VSES for the duration of the ignition cycle.
- The DIC displays the SERVICE STAB SYS message.
- The Stability Caution indicator turns on.

Conditions for Clearing the DTC

- The condition for the DTC is no longer present and the DTC is cleared with a scan tool.
- The EBCM automatically clears the history DTC when a current DTC is not detected in 100 consecutive drive cycles.

Diagnostic Aids

The yaw rate and lateral accelerometer sensors are located in one unit and cannot be serviced separately. The master cylinder pressure sensor is located internally in the EBCM and is not serviceable.

Reference Information

Schematic Reference

ABS Schematics

Connector End View Reference

ABS Connector End Views

Electrical Information Reference

- Circuit Testing
- Connector Repairs
- Testing for Intermittent Conditions and Poor Connections

LTV0500000004623

Fig. 47   Codes C0186 or C0196: Lateral Accelerometer Circuit/Yaw Rate Circuit (Part 2 of 3). Hummer H3

Circuit/System Testing

Note: If set, diagnose DTC U1561 before any other DTC.

1. With the scan tool, clear the DTCs. Cycle the ignition from OFF to ON.
   ⇒ Test drive the vehicle to re-set the DTC. If the DTC re-sets only after the vehicle is in motion, replace the combination sensor.
2. Disconnect the yaw / lateral combination sensor harness connector. Connect a test lamp between the ignition voltage circuit at the harness connector, and a good ground.
   ⇒ If the test lamp does not illuminate, repair open in the ignition voltage circuit.
3. With the harness connector disconnected, connect a test lamp between the ground circuit at the harness connector, and battery positive voltage.
   ⇒ If the test lamp does not illuminate, repair open in the ground circuit.
   ⇒ If no wiring faults or loose harness connections can be found, replace the EBCM / brake pressure modulator valve (BPMV) assembly.

Repair Instructions

Important: Always perform the Diagnostic Repair Verification after completing the diagnostic procedure.

- Yaw Rate Sensor/Lateral and Longitudinal Accelerometer Replacement
- Control Module References for EBCM and BPMV replacement, setup, and programming

LTV0500000004624

Fig. 47   Codes C0186 or C0196: Lateral Accelerometer Circuit/Yaw Rate Circuit (Part 3 of 3). Hummer H3

DTC Descriptor

DTC C0186: Lateral Accelerometer Circuit

DTC C0196 : Yaw Rate Circuit

Diagnostic Fault Information

Important: Always perform the Diagnostic System Check - Vehicle prior to using this diagnostic procedure.

Circuit/System Description

The yaw rate, lateral and longitudinal accelerometers are combined into one combination sensor external to the electronic brake control module (EBCM). The combination sensor receives ignition power and a ground that is separate from the EBCM. The combination sensor sends dedicated serial data messages to the EBCM regarding vehicle yaw rate, lateral and longitudinal acceleration.

Conditions for Running the DTC

The ignition is ON.

Conditions for Setting the DTC

C0186

- Lateral acceleration does not change when reducing speed from 30 km/h to 0 km/h and the condition occurs 16 times in a row
- Yaw rate, lateral and longitudinal acceleration do not correlate with the vehicle stationary
- Yaw rate, lateral and longitudinal acceleration do not correlate based on estimated wheel speed.
- Combination sensor fails an internal self test.
- Ignition voltage to the yaw / lateral combination sensor is less than 9.5 volts.
- Communication is lost between the EBCM and the combination sensor.

C0196

- Vehicle speed has reached at least 15 km/h (9 mph) from a stop more three times during the same ignition cycle. During the time the vehicle is stationary, the yaw rate signal value is more than 7 deg/sec for 2 seconds.
- When vehicle speed is more than 25 km/h (16 mph) in a turn the difference between the yaw rate, steering angle, lateral acceleration, and wheel speed sensor values are not correlated three consecutive times.
- Yaw rate changes greater than 20 deg/sec in 6 ms four times in one second.
- Combination sensor fails an internal self test.
- Ignition voltage to the combination sensor is less than 9.5 volts.

LTV0500000004622

Fig. 47   Codes C0186 or C0196: Lateral Accelerometer Circuit/Yaw Rate Circuit (Part 1 of 3). Hummer H3

DTC Descriptor

DTC C0191: Four Wheel Drive (4WD) Reference Accelerometer Circuit

Diagnostic Fault Information

Important: Always perform the Diagnostic System Check - Vehicle prior to using this diagnostic procedure.

Circuit/System Description

The electronic brake control module (EBCM) supplies a 5-volt reference to the longitudinal accelerometer. When the vehicle is not moving, or is being driven at a constant steady speed, longitudinal acceleration is 0 m/sec/sec, and the longitudinal accelerometer signal voltage is very near 2.5 volts. This is referred to as longitudinal accelerometer bias voltage. Vehicle acceleration or deceleration causes the longitudinal accelerometer signal voltage to increase or decrease.

Conditions for Running the DTC

- The ignition is ON.
- Ignition voltage is greater than 8 volts.

Conditions for Setting the DTC

- The 5-volt reference to the longitudinal accelerometer is less than 4.4 volts or greater than 5.6 volts.
- The longitudinal accelerometer output is greater than 1.5 g or less than -1.5 g for 1.2 seconds.
- The longitudinal accelerometer output is greater than 1.5 g or less than -1.5 g for 7 200 ms periods during the same ignition cycle.
- The longitudinal accelerometer output does not change when the vehicle decelerates from 30 km/h (19 mph) to 0 km/h. If the condition occurs 16 consecutive times, the DTC is set.

Action Taken When the DTC Sets

- The EBCM disables the Antilock Brake System (ABS)/Traction Control System (TCS) for the duration of the ignition cycle.
- The ABS indicator turns ON.
- The driver information center (DIC) displays the ABS FAULT message.
- The DIC displays the TRACTION FAILED message.

Conditions for Clearing the DTC

- The condition for setting the DTC is no longer present and the DTC is cleared with a scan tool.
- The EBCM automatically clears the history DTC when a current DTC is not detected in 100 consecutive drive cycles.

LTV0500000004625

Fig. 48   Code C0191: Four Wheel Drive Reference Accelerometer Circuit (Part 1 of 2). Hummer H3

Circuit/System Verification

With scan tool installed drive the vehicle in a straight line at a speed greater than 30 km/h (19 mph) and decelerate the vehicle to a stop several times. The scan tool Longitudinal Accelerometer Sensor Signal parameter should show a change in M/S² output in sequence to the vehicle deceleration.

Circuit/System Testing

1. Turn OFF the ignition. Disconnect the longitudinal accelerometer harness connector. Turn ON the ignition. With a DMM, verify voltage between 4.4 and 5.6 on the LNG rate sensor 5-volt reference circuit.
   ⇒ If the voltage is above 5.6 volts, test for a short to power on the LNG rate sensor circuit. If the circuit tests normal, replace the EBCM.
   ⇒ If voltage is below 4.4, test for an open or a short to ground on the LNG rate sensor circuit. If the circuit tests normal, replace the EBCM assembly.
2. Turn OFF the ignition. At the longitudinal accelerometer harness connector, connect a test lamp between the LNG low reference circuit and battery positive voltage. Verify the test lamp illuminates.
   ⇒ If the test lamp does not illuminate check for an open in the LGN low reference circuit. If the circuit tests normal, replace the EBCM assembly.
3. Connect a 3-amp fused jumper wire between the LNG rate sensor 5-volt reference circuit and the longitudinal accelerometer signal circuit. Turn ON the ignition and observe the longitudinal accelerometer parameter.
   ⇒ If the scan tool displays greater than 1.5g, replace the longitudinal position sensor.
   ⇒ If the scan tool displays less than 1.5g, test for an open or short to ground on the longitudinal accelerometer signal circuit. If the circuit tests normal, replace the EBCM assembly.

Repair Instructions

Important: Always perform the Diagnostic Repair Verification after completing the diagnostic procedure.

- Yaw Rate Sensor/Lateral and Longitudinal Accelerometer Replacement
- Control Module References for EBCM and BPMV replacement, setup, and programming

LTV0500000004626

Fig. 48   Code C0191: Four Wheel Drive Reference Accelerometer Circuit (Part 2 of 2). Hummer H3

Conditions for Clearing the DTC

- The condition for setting the DTC is no longer present and the DTC is cleared with a scan tool.
- The EBCM automatically clears the history DTC when a current DTC is not detected in 100 consecutive drive cycles.

Reference Information

Schematic Reference

ABS Schematics

Connector End View Reference

ABS Connector End Views

Electrical Information Reference

- Circuit Testing
- Connector Repairs
- Testing for Intermittent Conditions and Poor Connections
- Wiring Repairs

Scan Tool Reference

Scan Tool Data List

Circuit/System Verification

With the scan tool, access the ABS special functions menu and perform the Solenoid Test and ABS Motor test. The pump motor and solenoids should function without setting DTCs.

Circuit/System Testing

Disconnect the EBCM harness connector. Connect a test lamp to ground, at the EBCM harness connector touch the test lamp probe to each of the 3 battery positive voltage circuits. The test lamp should illuminate on all 3 circuits.

⇒ If the test lamp does not illuminate on one of the battery positive voltage circuits, repair open or short to ground on the suspected circuit.

Connect a test lamp to battery positive voltage, at the EBCM harness connector touch the test lamp probe to each of the 3 ground circuits. The test lamp should illuminate on all 3 circuits.

⇒ If the test lamp does not illuminate on one of the ground circuits, repair open or short to voltage on the suspected circuit.

⇒ If no wiring faults can be found, replace the EBCM/brake pressure modulator valve (BPMV) assembly.

Repair Instructions

Important: Always perform the Diagnostic Repair Verification after completing the diagnostic procedure.

Control Module References for EBCM and BPMV replacement, setup, and programming

LTV0500000004628

Fig. 49   Code C0201: Anti-Lock Brake System Enable Relay Contact Circuit (Part 2 of 2). Hummer H3

DTC Descriptor

DTC C0201 : Antilock Brake System (ABS) Enable Relay Contact Circuit

Diagnostic Fault Information

Important: Always perform the Diagnostic System Check - Vehicle prior to using this diagnostic procedure.

Circuit/System Description

The solenoid and pump motor relay are located within the electronic brake control module (EBCM). The solenoid relay supplies battery voltage to all of the valve solenoids. Three pump motor relays supply battery positive voltage to the pump motor when the EBCM commands the pump motor on.

Conditions for Running the DTC

- Ignition voltage is greater than 9.5 volts.
- The solenoid relay is commanded ON.

Conditions for Setting the DTC

One or more of the following conditions exists:

- The EBCM detects an open in the battery positive voltage circuit to the solenoid valve relay.
- The EBCM detects a stuck open solenoid valve relay or an open circuit between the solenoid valve relay and solenoid valves.
- The EBCM detects an open in the battery positive voltage circuit to the solenoid valve relay.
- The EBCM detects that one or more of the pump motor relays is off when commanded on.

Action Taken When the DTC Sets

- The EBCM disables the Antilock Brake System (ABS)/Traction Control System (TCS)/Vehicle Stability Enhancement System (VSES) for the duration of the ignition cycle.
- The ABS indicator turns ON.
- The driver information center (DIC) displays the ABS FAULT message.
- The Stability Caution indicator turns ON.
- The DIC displays the SERVICE STAB SYS message.
- The DIC displays the TRACTION FAILED message.
- The Brake Warning indicator turns ON.

LTV0500000004627

Fig. 49   Code C0201: Anti-Lock Brake System Enable Relay Contact Circuit (Part 1 of 2). Hummer H3

DTC Descriptor

DTC C0240 : PCM Traction Control Not Allowed

DTC P0856 : Traction Control Torque Request Circuit

Diagnostic Fault Information

Important: Always perform the Diagnostic System Check - Vehicle prior to using this diagnostic procedure.

Circuit/System Description

C0240

The powertrain control module (PCM) and the electronic brake control module (EBCM) communicate on the serial data link, whenever the ignition is ON.

P0856

The PCM supplies 5 volts through an internal resistor, to the EBCM on the requested torque signal circuit. The EBCM toggles this voltage to ground to create a valid requested torque signal at the PCM.

Conditions for Running the DTC

C0240

The ignition is ON.

P0856

- The ignition is ON.
- The engine is running at a speed greater than 450 RPM for 5-20 seconds.

Conditions for Setting the DTC

C0240

The EBCM receives a serial data message stating that the PCM has lost the ability to reduce engine torque.

P0856

LTV0500000004629

Fig. 50   Codes C0240 or P0856: PCM Traction Control Not Allowed/Traction Control Torque Request Circuit (Part 1 of 3). Hummer H3

The PCM receives an invalid requested torque signal for 3 seconds.

Action Taken When the DTC Sets

C0240

- The EBCM disables the traction control system (TCS) and vehicle stability enhancement system (VSES).
- The TRACTION FAILED message is displayed.
- The Stability Caution indicator turns ON.
- The DIC displays the SERVICE STAB SYS message.

P0856

- The PCM sends a serial data message to the EBCM stating that the PCM has lost the ability to reduce engine torque.
- The EBCM sets DTC C0240 as a current DTC for as long as the malfunction is present.

Conditions for Clearing the DTC

C0240

The conditions for setting the DTC are no longer present and you use the scan tool Clear DTCs function.

P0856

- The conditions for setting the DTC are no longer present and you use the scan tool Clear DTCs function.
- A history DTC clears automatically after 40 consecutive warm-up cycles without a PCM detected failure.

Diagnostic Aids

C0240

A requested torque signal malfunction is only one possible cause for the PCM to lose the ability to perform traction control. DTC C0240 may set due to engine overheating, throttle actuator control failure, loss of ignition timing control by the PCM, etc. If DTC P1571 has not set, refer to Diagnostic System Check - Vehicle to identify other possible causes of DTC C0240.

P0856

Thoroughly inspect connections or circuitry that may cause an intermittent malfunction.

LTV0500000004630

Fig. 50 Codes C0240 or P0856: PCM Traction Control Not Allowed/Traction Control Torque Request Circuit (Part 2 of 3). Hummer H3

DTC Descriptor

DTC C0244 : Pulse Width Modulated (PWM) Delivered Torque

DTC P1689 : Traction Control Delivered Torque Output Circuit

Diagnostic Fault Information

Important: Always perform the Diagnostic System Check - Vehicle prior to using this diagnostic procedure.

Circuit/System Description

The electronic brake control module (EBCM) and the powertrain control module (PCM) simultaneously control the Traction Control System (TCS). The PCM sends a Delivered Torque message via a pulse width modulated (PWM) signal to the EBCM. The duty cycle of the signal is used to determine how much engine torque the PCM is delivering.

Conditions for Running the DTC

The ignition is ON and the engine is running.

Conditions for Setting the DTC

- Pulse signals from the Delivered Torque signal are not detected or are abnormal.
- The Duty Cycle is less than 5 percent or more than 95 percent.

Action Taken When the DTC Sets

- The EBCM disables TCS and vehicle stability enhancement system (VSES) for the duration of the ignition cycle.
- The Stability Caution indicator turns on.
- The driver information center (DIC) displays the TRACTION FAILED message.
- The DIC displays the SERVICE STAB SYS message.

Conditions for Clearing the DTC

- The condition for the DTC is no longer present and the DTC is cleared with a scan tool.
- The EBCM automatically clears the history DTC when a current DTC is not detected in 100 consecutive drive cycles.

Diagnostic Aids

Thoroughly inspect connections or circuitry that may cause an intermittent malfunction.

LTV0500000004632

Fig. 51 Codes C0244 or P1689: Pulse Width Modulated Delivered Torque/Traction Control Delivered Torque Output Circuit (Part 1 of 2). Hummer H3

- ABS Connector End Views
- Powertrain Control Module (PCM) Connector End Views

Electrical Information Reference

- Circuit Testing
- Connector Repairs
- Testing for Intermittent Conditions and Poor Connections
- Wiring Repairs

Scan Tool Reference

Scan Tool Data List

Circuit/System Testing

1. Use a scan tool in order to clear the DTCs. Cycle the ignition to OFF and then start the engine. A current failure will set a DTC.
   ⇒ If the DTC does not reset, go to Diagnostic Aids.
2. Turn OFF the ignition and disconnect the EBCM harness connector. At the EBCM harness connector, use a DMM to measure for 5 volts on the requested torque circuit. Turn ON the ignition.
   ⇒ If the voltage is below 4.5 volts, test for an open or short to ground on the requested torque circuit or replace the PCM.
   ⇒ If the voltage is above 6 volts, test for a short to power or replace the PCM.
3. Connect one end of a test lamp to ground. With the DMM still connected to the EBCM harness connector, touch the other end of the test lamp to the DMM lead connected to the EBCM harness connector. The DMM voltage reading should drop below 0.5 volts.
   ⇒ If the voltage does not drop to below 0.5 volts, check for a short to voltage on the requested torque circuit or replace the PCM.

Repair Instructions

Important: Always perform the Diagnostic Repair Verification after completing the diagnostic procedure.

Control Module References for EBCM or PCM replacement, setup, and programming

LTV0500000004631

Fig. 50 Codes C0240 or P0856: PCM Traction Control Not Allowed/Traction Control Torque Request Circuit (Part 3 of 3). Hummer H3

Circuit/System Testing

1. Use a scan tool in order to clear the DTCs. Cycle the ignition to OFF and then start the engine. A current failure will set a DTC.
   ⇒ If the DTC does not reset, go to Diagnostic Aids.
2. Turn OFF the ignition and disconnect the PCM harness connector. At the PCM harness connector, use a DMM to measure for 12 volts on the delivered torque circuit. Turn ON the ignition.
   ⇒ If the voltage is below 10 volts, test for an open or short to ground on the requested torque circuit or replace the EBCM/brake pressure modulator valve (BPMV) assembly.
3. Connect one end of a test lamp to ground. With the DMM still connected to the PCM harness connector, touch the other end of the test lamp to the DMM lead connected to the PCM harness connector. The DMM voltage reading should drop below 0.5 volts.
   ⇒ If the voltage does not drop to below 0.5 volts, check for a short to voltage on the requested torque circuit. If a short to voltage cannot be found, replace the EBCM/brake pressure modulator valve (BPMV) assembly.

Repair Instructions

Important: Always perform the Diagnostic Repair Verification after completing the diagnostic procedure.

Control Module References for EBCM/BPMV or PCM replacement, setup, and programming

LTV0500000004633

Fig. 51 Codes C0244 or P1689: Pulse Width Modulated Delivered Torque/Traction Control Delivered Torque Output Circuit (Part 2 of 2). Hummer H3

DTC Descriptor

DTC C0245 : Wheel Speed Sensor Frequency Error

Diagnostic Fault Information

Important: Always perform the Diagnostic System Check - Vehicle prior to using this diagnostic procedure.

Circuit/System Description

The wheel speed sensor receives a 12-volt reference voltage from the electronic brake control module (EBCM). As the wheel spins, the wheel speed sensor sends the EBCM a DC square wave signal via the wheel speed sensor output circuit . The EBCM uses the frequency of the square wave signal to calculate the wheel speed.

Conditions for Running the DTC

- Ignition voltage is greater than 8 volts.
- Vehicle must be moving at a speed greater than 30 km/h.

Conditions for Setting the DTC

- The difference between 2 wheel speeds exceeds 20 percent.
- The fault must be present for greater than 60 seconds.

Action Taken When the DTC Sets

- The EBCM disables the Antilock Brake System (ABS)/Traction Control System (TCS)/Vehicle Stability Enhancement System (VSES) for the duration of the ignition cycle.
- The ABS indicator turns ON.
- The driver information center (DIC) displays the ABS FAULT message.
- The Stability Caution indicator turns on.
- The DIC displays the SERVICE STAB SYS message.
- The DIC displays the TRACTION FAILED message.

Conditions for Clearing the DTC

- The condition for the DTC is no longer present and the DTC is cleared with a scan tool.
- The EBCM automatically clears the history DTC when a current DTC is not detected in 100 consecutive drive cycles.

Diagnostic Aids

Inspect tires for improper air pressure or improper size.

LTV0500000004634

Fig. 52   Code C0245: Wheel Speed Sensor Frequency Error. Hummer H3

Repair Instructions

Important: Always perform the Diagnostic Repair Verification after completing the diagnostic procedure.

Control Module References - Electronic Brake Control Module

LTV0500000004636

Fig. 53   Code C0268: Class 2 Data Error Reported (Part 2 of 2). Hummer H3

DTC Descriptor

DTC C0276: Transmission Control Module (TCM) Traction Control Not Allowed

Diagnostic Fault Information

Important: Always perform the Diagnostic System Check - Vehicle prior to using this diagnostic procedure.

Circuit/System Description

The electronic brake control module (EBCM) may inhibit the Traction Control System (TCS) if a failure occurs with the locking differential or the transfer case.

Conditions for Running the DTC

The ignition is ON.

Conditions for Setting the DTC

- The transfer case selected range has been reported as invalid by the transmission control module (TCM).
- The rear differential status has been reported as locked by the TCM when the vehicle speed is greater than 50 km/h (31 mph) for 10 seconds.

Action Taken When the DTC Sets

- The EBCM disables the TCS and Vehicle Stability Enhancement System (VSES) for the duration of the ignition cycle.
- The driver information center (DIC) displays the SERVICE TRACTION message.
- The DIC displays the SERVICE STAB SYS message.

Conditions for Clearing the DTC

- The condition for the DTC is no longer present.
- Using a scan tool, clear the DTC function.

Diagnostic Aids

Check the transmission control module (TCM) for DTCs.

LTV0500000004637

Fig. 54   Code C0276: Transmission Control Module Traction Control Not Allowed. Hummer H3

DTC Descriptor

DTC C0268: Class 2 Data Error Reported

Diagnostic Fault Information

Important: Always perform the Diagnostic System Check - Vehicle prior to using this diagnostic procedure.

Circuit/System Description

The electronic brake control module (EBCM) disables the traction control when other electronic control modules set DTCs for components that effect the operation of the traction control system.

Conditions for Running the DTC

The ignition switch is in the ON position.

Conditions for Setting the DTC

The PCM or BCM diagnoses a condition preventing the engine control portion of the traction control function and sends a serial data message to the EBCM indicating that torque reduction is not allowed. The PCM or BCM will typically set a DTC and the EBCM will set this DTC.

Action Taken When the DTC Sets

One or more of the following actions may occur:

- The EBCM disables the Antilock Brake System (ABS)/Traction Control System (TCS)/Vehicle Stability Enhancement System (VSES) for the duration of the ignition cycle.
- DRP may be disabled and the Brake Warning indicator may turn ON.
- Stability Caution indicator turns ON.
- DIC displays the SERVICE STAB SYS message.
- DIC displays the TRACTION FAILED message.

Conditions for Clearing the MIL/DTC

- The condition for the DTC is no longer present and the DTC is cleared with a scan tool.
- The EBCM automatically clears the history DTC when a current DTC is not detected in 100 consecutive drive cycles.

Circuit/System Verification

This DTC is for information only. As an aid to the technician, this DTC indicates that there are no problems in the ABS/TCS system.

LTV0500000004635

Fig. 53   Code C0268: Class 2 Data Error Reported (Part 1 of 2). Hummer H3

DTC Descriptor

DTC C0550: Electronic Control Unit (ECU) Performance

Diagnostic Fault Information

Important: Always perform the Diagnostic System Check - Vehicle prior to using this diagnostic procedure.

Circuit/System Description

The electronic brake control module (EBCM) detects an internal malfunction.

Conditions for Running the DTC

The ignition switch is in the ON position.

Conditions for Setting the DTC

An internal EBCM malfunction exists.

Action Taken When the DTC Sets

One or more of the following actions may occur:

- The EBCM disables the Antilock Brake System (ABS)/Traction Control System (TCS)/Vehicle Stability Enhancement System (VSES) for the duration of the ignition cycle.
- The dynamic rear proportioning (DRP) may be disabled and the Brake Warning indicator may turn ON.
- The Stability Caution indicator turns ON.
- The DIC displays the SERVICE STAB SYS message.
- The DIC displays the TRACTION FAILED message.

Conditions for Clearing the MIL/DTC

- The condition for the DTC is no longer present and the DTC is cleared with a scan tool.
- The EBCM automatically clears the history DTC when a current DTC is not detected in 100 consecutive drive cycles.

LTV0500000004638

Fig. 55   Code C0550: Electronic Control Unit Performance (Part 1 of 2). Hummer H3

Circuit/System Verification

DTC C0550 will set as result of internal EBCM circuit failure.

⇒ Replace the EBCM.

Repair Instructions

Important: Always perform the Diagnostic Repair Verification after completing the diagnostic procedure.

Control Module References - for EBCM replacement, setup, and programming

LTV0500000004639

Fig. 55   Code C0550: Electronic Control Unit Performance (Part 2 of 2). Hummer H3

Circuit/System Verification

Test drive the vehicle at a speed greater than 15 km/h (9 mph) and make several turns. The DTC should not reset.

Circuit/System Testing

1. Disconnect the SWPS harness connector. At the SWPS harness connector, connect a test lamp between the ignition 3 voltage circuit and ground. Turn ON the ignition, the test lamp should illuminate.
   ⇒ If the test lamp does not illuminate repair open or short to ground on the ignition 3 circuit
2. Connect a test lamp between battery positive voltage and the ground circuit of the SWPS harness connector. The test lamp should illuminate.
   ⇒ If the test lamp does not illuminate, repair open ground circuit.
3. Ignition ON, at the SWPS harness connector measure for 5 volts between the steering wheel position sensor 5 volt reference circuit and low reference circuit.
   ⇒ If voltage is below 4.5, test for an open or short to ground in the steering wheel position sensor 5 volt reference circuit or replace the EBCM/brake pressure modulator valve (BPMV) assembly.
   ⇒ If voltage is above 5.5, test for a short to voltage in the steering wheel position sensor 5 volt reference circuit or replace the EBCM/BPMV assembly.
4. Ignition OFF, Reconnect the SWPS harness connector and disconnect the EBCM connector. Connect a test lamp between battery positive voltage and the low reference circuit at the EBCM harness connector. The test lamp should illuminate.
   ⇒ If the test lamp does not illuminate, repair open low reference circuit.
5. Ignition ON, at the EBCM harness connector, test for a 12 volt pulse on the steering wheel position A and B circuits while slowly turning the steering wheel.
   ⇒ If the A and B steering wheel position circuits do not pulse, repair short to voltage, short to ground or open in the A or B steering wheel position circuits or replace the SWPS.
6. Center the front wheels and steering wheel. Ignition ON, At the EBCM harness connector test for 12 volts at the steering wheel position marker pulse signal circuit.

   Important: The steering wheel must be within 10° of center.

   ⇒ If the voltage is below 10 volts, repair open or short to ground in steering wheel position marker pulse signal circuit or replace the SWPS.
   ⇒ If the voltage is near 12 volts, repair open or short to ground in steering wheel position sensor signal circuit or replace the SWPS.

LTV0500000004641

Fig. 56   Code C0710: Steering Position Signal (Part 2 of 3). Hummer H3

DTC Descriptor

DTC C0899: Device 1 Voltage Low

Diagnostic Fault Information

Important: Always perform the Diagnostic System Check - Vehicle prior to using this diagnostic procedure.

Circuit/System Description

The electronic brake control module (EBCM) monitors the ignition 3 voltage (IGN3) level available for system operation. A low voltage condition prevents the system from operating properly.

Conditions for Running the DTC

The ignition is ON.

Conditions for Setting the DTC

This fault will be set if the ignition voltage to EBCM is less than 9.5 volts for 10 seconds and the vehicle speed is greater than 3 km/h (2 mph).

Action Taken When the DTC Sets

- The EBCM disables the Antilock Brake System (ABS)/Traction Control System (TCS)/Vehicle Stability Enhancement System (VSES) for the duration of the ignition cycle.
- The ABS indicator turns ON.
- The driver information center (DIC) displays the ABS FAULT message.
- The Stability Caution indicator turns on.
- The DIC displays the SERVICE STAB SYS message.
- The DIC displays the TRACTION FAILED message.
- The Brake Warning indicator turns ON if system voltage drops below 8.5 volts.

Conditions for Clearing the DTC

- The condition for the DTC is no longer present and the DTC is cleared with a scan tool.
- The EBCM automatically clears the history DTC when a current DTC is not detected in 100 consecutive drive cycles.

LTV0500000004643

Fig. 57   Code C0899: Device 1 Voltage Low (Part 1 of 2). Hummer H3

DTC Descriptor

DTC C0710 : Steering Position Signal

Diagnostic Fault Information

Important: Always perform the Diagnostic System Check - Vehicle prior to using this diagnostic procedure.

Circuit/System Description

The electronic brake control module (EBCM) receives a digital and an analog steering wheel position signal from one sensor. The EBCM uses the steering wheel position sensor (SWPS) signals to perform Vehicle Stability Enhancement System (VSES). The analog and digital data parameters on the scan tool normally range from 220° to -220°. With the steering and steering wheel centered, the analog data parameter on the scan tool should display near 0°. The digital data parameter will calibrate to 0° after each key cycle regardless of actual steering wheel position. The EBCM verifies the accuracy of the steering wheel position signal by correlating the digital and analog signals together

Conditions for Running the DTC

The ignition is ON.

Conditions for Setting the DTC

- Vehicle speed is greater than 15 km/h (9 mph), the steering angle does not change more than 10 degrees in 20 seconds and the yaw rate is 8.6°/sec or more.
- The digital and analog steering wheel position signals do not correlate.

Action Taken When the DTC Sets

- The EBCM disables the VSES for the duration of the ignition cycle.
- Stability Caution indicator turns on.
- The driver information center (DIC) displays the SERVICE STAB SYS message.

Conditions for Clearing the DTC

- The condition for the DTC is no longer present and the DTC is cleared with a scan tool.
- The EBCM automatically clears the history DTC when a current DTC is not detected in 100 consecutive drive cycles.

LTV0500000004640

Fig. 56   Code C0710: Steering Position Signal (Part 1 of 3). Hummer H3

7. With the Ignition ON, Install a scan tool and Center the front wheels and steering wheel. Observe the Analog Steering Position Sensor data parameter for less than 180° or greater than -180°.
   ⇒ If Analog Steering Position Sensor data parameter is greater than 180° or less than -180°, replace the SWPS.

Repair Instructions

Important: Always perform the Diagnostic Repair Verification after completing the diagnostic procedure.

- Yaw Rate Sensor/Lateral and Longitudinal Accelerometer Replacement
- Control Module References

LTV0500000004642

Fig. 56   Code C0710: Steering Position Signal (Part 3 of 3). Hummer H3

Circuit/System Testing

1. Measure and record the voltage at the battery terminals.
   ⇒ If the battery voltage is low, diagnose the starting and charging system.
2. Disconnect the EBCM connector and turn the ignition ON. At the EBCM harness connector, measure voltage on the IGN3 circuit.
   ⇒ If the voltage is more than one volt less than battery positive voltage, repair open or high resistance in IGN3 circuit.
   ⇒ If the battery positive voltage and IGN3 voltage is within 1-volt, repair open or high resistance in the EBCM ground circuits.
   ⇒ If no electrical faults are present, replace the EBCM/brake pressure modulator valve (BPMV) assembly.

Repair Instructions

Important: Always perform the Diagnostic Repair Verification after completing the diagnostic procedure.

Control Module References for EBCM and BPMV replacement, setup, and programming

LTV0500000004644

Fig. 57   Code C0899: Device 1 Voltage Low (Part 2 of 2). Hummer H3

DTC Descriptor

DTC C0901: Device 2 Voltage Low

Diagnostic Fault Information

Important: Always perform the Diagnostic System Check - Vehicle prior to using this diagnostic procedure.

Circuit/System Description

The electronic brake control module (EBCM) monitors the ignition 1 voltage (IGN1) level available for system operation. A low voltage condition prevents the system from operating properly.

Conditions for Running the DTC

The ignition is ON.

Conditions for Setting the DTC

- Ignition 1 (IGN1) voltage to EBCM is less than 6.5 volts for 7 seconds.
- Vehicle speed is greater than 3 km/h (2 mph).

Action Taken When the DTC Sets

Brake Warning indicator turns ON.

Conditions for Clearing the DTC

- The condition for the DTC is no longer present and the DTC is cleared with a scan tool.
- The EBCM automatically clears the history DTC when a current DTC is not detected in 100 consecutive drive cycles.

LTV0500000004645

Fig. 58   Code C0901: Device 2 Voltage Low (Part 1 of 2). Hummer H3

Circuit Description

The instrument panel cluster (IPC) illuminates the ABS indicator by supplying ground to the lamp. The electronic brake control module (EBCM) sends class 2 serial data messages to the IPC, in order to command the indicator ON or OFF.

Diagnostic Aids

The malfunction must be present during diagnosis in order to prevent unnecessary parts replacement. Always begin diagnosis with Diagnostic System Check - Vehicle in Vehicle DTC Information.

Test Description

The number below refers to the step number on the diagnostic table.

3. This step tests if the IPC is able to turn OFF the ABS indicator.

Step	Action	Yes	No
	Important: After a DTC is cleared and the ignition is ON, the ABS indicator may remain ON until the EBCM completes a power-up self test. This test concludes when the vehicle reaches a speed greater than 10 km/h (7 mph) and the wheel speeds are verified by the EBCM.		
1	Did you perform the Diagnostic System Check - Vehicle?	Go to Step 2	Go to Diagnostic System Check
2	1. Turn OFF the ignition for 5 seconds. 2. Turn ON the ignition while observing the Antilock Brake System (ABS) indicator. Does the ABS indicator illuminate for 2 seconds, then turn OFF?	Go to Diagnostic Aids	Go to Step 3
3	1. Install a scan tool. 2. Select the instrument panel cluster (IPC) Special Functions menu on the scan tool. 3. Select Lamp Tests. 4. Command all of the IPC indicator lamps OFF. Does the ABS indicator turn OFF?	Go to Step 5	Go to Step 4
4	Replace the IPC. Did you complete the replacement?	Go to Step 6	--
5	Replace the electronic brake control module (EBCM). Did you complete the replacement?	Go to Step 6	
6	1. Turn OFF the ignition for 5 seconds. 2. Turn ON the ignition while observing the ABS indicator. Does the ABS indicator illuminate for 2 seconds, then turn OFF?	System OK	Go to Step 3

LTV0500000004598

Fig. 59   ABS Indicator Always On. Canyon & Colorado

Circuit/System Testing

1. Measure and record the voltage at the battery terminals.
   ⇒ If the battery voltage is low, diagnose the starting and charging system.
2. Disconnect the EBCM connector and turn the ignition ON. At the EBCM harness connector, measure voltage on the IGN1 circuit.
   ⇒ If the voltage is more than one volt less than battery positive voltage, repair open or high resistance in IGN1 circuit.
   ⇒ If the battery positive voltage and IGN1 voltage is within 1-volt, repair open or high resistance in the EBCM ground circuits.
   ⇒ If no electrical faults are present, replace the EBCM/brake pressure modulator valve (BPMV) replacement.

Repair Instructions

Important: Always perform the Diagnostic Repair Verification after completing the diagnostic procedure.

Control Module References for EBCM and BPMV replacement, setup, and programming

LTV0500000004646

Fig. 58   Code C0901: Device 2 Voltage Low (Part 2 of 2). Hummer H3

Circuit Description

The instrument panel cluster (IPC) illuminates the ABS indicator by supplying ground to the lamp. The electronic brake control module (EBCM) sends class 2 serial data messages to the IPC in order to command the indicator ON or OFF.

Diagnostic Aids

Replace the IPC if the ABS indicator intermittently fails to operate during the bulb check.

Test Description

The number below refers to the step number on the diagnostic table.

2. This step tests if the IPC is able to illuminate the ABS indicator during the bulb check.

Step	Action	Yes	No
1	Did you perform the Diagnostic System Check - Vehicle?	Go to Step 2	Go to Diagnostic System Check
2	1. Turn OFF the ignition for 5 seconds. 2. Turn ON the ignition while observing the Antilock Brake System (ABS) indicator. Does the ABS indicator illuminate?	Go to Diagnostic Aids	Go to Step 3
3	Replace the instrument panel cluster (IPC). Did you complete the replacement?	Go to Step 4	--
4	1. Turn OFF the ignition for 5 seconds. 2. Turn ON the ignition while observing the ABS indicator. Does the ABS indicator illuminate?	System OK	Go to Step 3

LTV0500000004599

Fig. 60   ABS Indicator Inoperative. Canyon & Colorado

Circuit Description

The body control module (BCM) illuminates the LED on the traction control switch (TCS), by supplying adequate current to the high side of the LED. This LED is referred to as the traction off indicator.

Diagnostic Aids

Thoroughly inspect connections or circuitry that may cause an intermittent malfunction.

Test Description

The number below refers to the step number on the diagnostic table.

6. The traction control switch may be damaged if the traction control switch signal circuit is shorted to voltage.

Step	Action	Yes	No
1	Did you perform the Diagnostic System Check - Vehicle?	Go to Step 2	Go to Diagnostic System Check
2	1. Turn ON the ignition. 2. Press and release the traction control switch. Does the traction off indicator illuminate?	Go to Diagnostic Aids	Go to Step 3
3	**Important:** Do not press the traction control switch continuously for more than 60 seconds to avoid setting DTC B2745. 1. Select body control module (BCM)/Data Display/Inputs on the scan tool. 2. Observe the traction control system (TCS) Switch State parameter while pressing the traction control switch. Does the scan tool display the switch state as Pressed?	Go to Step 8	Go to Step 4
4	**Important:** DTC B0828 sets when this test is performed. 1. Turn OFF the ignition. 2. Disconnect the traction control switch harness connector. 3. Turn ON the ignition. 4. Use a test lamp connected to a good ground to carefully probe the traction control switch signal circuit terminal within the traction control switch harness connector. Does the test lamp illuminate?	Go to Step 6	Go to Step 5

LTV0500000004600

Fig. 61 Traction Control Indicator Inoperative (Part 1 of 2). Canyon & Colorado

Diagnostic Fault Information

Important: Always perform the Diagnostic System Check - Vehicle prior to using this diagnostic procedure.

Circuit/System Description

The instrument panel cluster (IPC) illuminates the Antilock Brake System (ABS) indicator by supplying ground to the lamp. The electronic brake control module (EBCM) sends a serial data messages to the IPC, in order to command the indicator ON or OFF.

Circuit/System Testing

Note: Diagnose all vehicle DTCs before using this diagnostic.

With the scan tool, select instrument panel special functions Lamp Test. Command the instrument panel warning lamps OFF.

⇒ If the ABS warning lamp does not turn OFF, replace the IPC.

⇒ If the ABS lamp turns off and there are no DTCs stored in any vehicle systems, replace the EBCM.

Repair Instructions

Important: Always perform the Diagnostic Repair Verification after completing the diagnostic procedure.

Control Module References for EBCM or IPC replacement, setup, and programming

LTV0500000004647

Fig. 62 ABS Indicator Always On. Hummer H3

Diagnostic Fault Information

Important: Always perform the Diagnostic System Check - Vehicle prior to using this diagnostic procedure.

Circuit/System Description

The instrument panel cluster (IPC) illuminates the stability system caution indicator by supplying ground to the lamp. The electronic brake control module (EBCM) sends a serial data messages to the IPC, in order to command the indicator ON or OFF.

Circuit/System Testing

Note: Diagnose all vehicle DTCs before using this diagnostic.

With the scan tool, select instrument panel special functions Lamp Test. Command the instrument panel warning lamps OFF.

⇒ If the stability system caution indicator lamp does not turn off, replace the IPC.

⇒ If the stability system caution indicator lamp turns off and there are no DTCs stored in any vehicle systems, replace the EBCM.

Repair Instructions

Important: Always perform the Diagnostic Repair Verification after completing the diagnostic procedure.

Control Module References for EBCM and IPC replacement, setup and programming

LTV0500000004649

Fig. 64 Stability System Caution Indicator Always On. Hummer H3

		Yes	No
5	Observe the TCS Switch State parameter on the scan tool while the test lamp is connected. Does the scan tool display the switch state as Pressed?	Go to Step 8	Go to Step 7
6	Test the traction control switch signal circuit for a short to voltage. Did you find and correct the condition?	Go to Step 12	Go to Step 11
7	Test the traction control switch signal circuit for an open. Did you find and correct the condition?	Go to Step 12	Go to Step 9
8	Test for poor connections at the harness connector of the traction control switch. Did you find and correct the condition?	Go to Step 12	Go to Step 10
9	Test for poor connections at the harness connector of the BCM. Did you find and correct the condition?	Go to Step 12	Go to Step 11
10	Replace the accessory switch. Did you complete the replacement?	Go to Step 12	--
11	Replace the BCM. Did you complete the replacement?	Go to Step 12	--
12	1. Turn ON the ignition. 2. Press and release the traction control switch. Does the traction off indicator illuminate?	System OK	Go to Step 3

LTV0500000004601

Fig. 61 Traction Control Indicator Inoperative (Part 2 of 2). Canyon & Colorado

Diagnostic Fault Information

Important: Always perform the Diagnostic System Check - Vehicle prior to using this diagnostic procedure.

Circuit/System Description

The instrument panel cluster (IPC) illuminates the Antilock Brake System (ABS) indicator by supplying ground to the lamp. The electronic brake control module (EBCM) sends a serial data messages to the IPC, in order to command the indicator ON or OFF.

Circuit/System Testing

Note: Diagnose all vehicle DTCs before using this diagnostic.

With the scan tool, select instrument panel special functions Lamp Test. Command the instrument panel warning lamps ON.

⇒ If the ABS warning lamp does not turn on, replace the IPC.

Repair Instructions

Important: Always perform the Diagnostic Repair Verification after completing the diagnostic procedure.

Control Module References for EBCM or IPC replacement, setup, and programming

LTV0500000004648

Fig. 63 ABS Indicator Inoperative. Hummer H3

Diagnostic Fault Information

Important: Always perform the Diagnostic System Check - Vehicle prior to using this diagnostic procedure.

Circuit/System Description

The instrument panel cluster (IPC) illuminates the stability system caution indicator by supplying ground to the lamp. The electronic brake control module (EBCM) sends a serial data messages to the IPC, in order to command the indicator ON or OFF.

Circuit/System Testing

Note: Diagnose all vehicle DTCs before using this diagnostic.

With the scan tool, select instrument panel special functions Lamp Test. Command the instrument panel warning lamps ON.

⇒ If the stability system caution indicator does not turn on, replace the IPC.

Repair Instructions

Important: Always perform the Diagnostic Repair Verification after completing the diagnostic procedure.

Control Module References for EBCM and IPC replacement, setup, and programming

LTV0500000004650

Fig. 65 Stability System Caution Indicator Inoperative. Hummer H3

Diagnostic Fault Information

Important: Always perform the Diagnostic System Check - Vehicle prior to using this diagnostic procedure.

Circuit/System Description

The instrument panel cluster (IPC) illuminates the traction off indicator by supplying ground to the lamp. The electronic brake control module (EBCM) sends a serial data messages to the IPC, in order to command the indicator ON or OFF.

Circuit/System Testing

Note: Diagnose all vehicle DTCs before using this diagnostic.

With the scan tool, select instrument panel special functions Lamp Test. Command the instrument panel warning lamps OFF.

⇒ If the traction off indicator does not turn off, replace the IPC.

⇒ If the traction off indicator turns off and there are no DTCs stored in any vehicle systems, replace the EBCM.

Repair Instructions

Important: Always perform the Diagnostic Repair Verification after completing the diagnostic procedure.

Control Module References for EBCM or IPC replacement, setup, and programming

LTV0500000004651

Fig. 66 Traction Off Indicator Always On. Hummer H3

Diagnostic Fault Information

Important: Always perform the Diagnostic System Check - Vehicle prior to using this diagnostic procedure.

Circuit/System Description

Proper operation of the Vehicle Stability Enhancement System (VSES) is highly dependent on the ability to apply brake pressure to a selected wheel, through the brake pressure modulator valve (BPMV), as commanded by the electronic brake control module (EBCM). The EBCM may not be able to detect certain mechanical failures that may cause the VSES to perform poorly. This diagnostic procedure is designed to help diagnose concerns of poor vehicle stability that may occur without the presence of any DTCs, by verifying the following.

- The tires are the correct size, properly inflated and in acceptable condition.
- There are no mechanical problems in the steering system.
- There are no mechanical problems in the suspension system.
- There are no mechanical problems in the base brake system.
- There are no mechanical problems in the locking differential or transfer case.
- All of the VSES related hydraulic controls within the BPMV are functioning correctly.

Repair Instructions

Important: Always perform the Diagnostic Repair Verification after completing the diagnostic procedure.

- Symptoms - Antilock Brake System
- Symptoms - Hydraulic Brakes
- Symptoms - Locking/Limited Slip Rear Axle
- Symptoms - Steering Wheel and Column
- Symptoms - Suspension General Diagnosis

LTV0500000004653

Fig. 68 Vehicle Stability Enhancement System Poor Performance. Hummer H3

Diagnostic Fault Information

Important: Always perform the Diagnostic System Check - Vehicle prior to using this diagnostic procedure.

Circuit/System Description

The instrument panel cluster (IPC) illuminates the traction off indicator by supplying ground to the lamp. The electronic brake control module (EBCM) sends a serial data messages to the IPC, in order to command the indicator ON or OFF.

Circuit/System Testing

Note: Diagnose all vehicle DTCs before using this diagnostic.

1. With the scan tool, select instrument panel special functions Lamp Test. Command the instrument panel warning lamps ON.
   ⇒ If the ABS warning lamp does not turn on, replace the IPC.

2. Turn the ignition OFF. Disconnect the traction control switch harness connector. Turn the ignition ON. Touch and release a 3-amp fused jumper wire between ground and the Traction Control System (TCS) switch signal circuit.
   ⇒ If the traction off indicator illuminates, replace the traction control switch.

3. Disconnect the body control module (BCM) harness connector. Touch and release a 3-amp fused jumper wire between ground and the TCS switch signal circuit at the BCM.
   ⇒ If the traction off indicator illuminates, repair an open in the TCS switch signal circuit.
   ⇒ If the traction off indicator does not illuminate replace the BCM.

Repair Instructions

Important: Always perform the Diagnostic Repair Verification after completing the diagnostic procedure.

Control Module References for EBCM, IPC, or BCM replacement, setup, and programming

LTV0500000004652

Fig. 67 Traction Off Indicator Inoperative. Hummer H3

°C	°F	OHMS
Temperature vs Resistance Values (Approximate)		
150	302	47
140	284	60
130	266	77
120	248	100
110	230	132
100	212	177
90	194	241
80	176	332
70	158	467
60	140	667
50	122	973
45	113	1188
40	104	1459
35	95	1802
30	86	2238
25	77	2796
20	68	3520
15	59	4450
10	50	5670
5	41	7280
0	32	9420
-5	23	12300
-10	14	16180
-15	5	21450
-20	-4	28680
-30	-22	52700
-40	-40	100700

LTV0500000004654

Fig. 69 Temperature vs. resistance values

Bosch 5.3 & 8.0

NOTE: On Air Bag Equipped Models, Refer To "Air Bag System Precautions" Located In The Front Of This Manual For System Disarming & Arming Procedures.

NOTE: Electrical Symbol & Wire Color Code Identification Located In The Front Of This Manual May Be Used As An Aid When Using Wiring Circuits Found In This Section.

NOTE: Refer To "Computer Relearn Procedures" Located In The Front Of This Manual For Computer Relearn Procedures.

INDEX

	Page No.		Page No.		Page No.
Description	5-38	Intermittents & Poor		Brake System Bleed	5-39
Diagnosis & Testing	5-38	Connections	5-39	ABS Automated Bleed	5-39
Accessing Diagnostic Trouble		Symptom Tests	5-38	Hydraulic Brake System	
Codes	5-38	Aztek & Rendezvous	5-38	Bleeding – Manual	5-40
Clearing Diagnostic Trouble		Equinox, Torrent & Vue	5-38	Hydraulic Brake System	
Codes	5-39	Hummer H2	5-39	Bleeding – Pressure	5-40
Connector Pin Identification	5-38	Temperature Vs. Resistance	5-39	Component Replacement	5-40
Diagnostic Tests	5-38	Wiring Diagrams	5-38	Brake Pressure Modulator	
Aztek & Rendezvous	5-38	**Diagnostic Chart Index**	5-49	Valve (BPMV)	5-40
Equinox, Torrent & Vue	5-38	**Precautions**	5-38	Electronic Brake Control	
Hummer H2	5-38	Air Bag Systems	5-38	Module (EBCM)	5-40
Diagnostic Trouble Code		Battery Ground Cable	5-38	Wheel Speed Sensor	5-40
Interpretation	5-38	**System Service**	5-39		

PRECAUTIONS

Air Bag Systems

Refer to "Air Bag System Precautions" in the front of this manual for system disarming and arming procedures.

Battery Ground Cable

Prior to service disconnect battery ground cable and isolate as required.

DESCRIPTION

When wheel slip is detected during a brake application, the ABS enters anti-lock mode. During anti-lock braking, hydraulic pressure in the individual wheel circuits is controlled to prevent any wheel from slipping. A separate hydraulic line and specific solenoid valves are provided for each wheel. The ABS can decrease, hold, or increase hydraulic pressure to each wheel brake. The ABS cannot, however, increase hydraulic pressure above the amount which is transmitted by the master cylinder during braking.

During anti-lock braking, a series of rapid pulsations is felt in the brake pedal. These pulsations are caused by the rapid changes in position of the individual solenoid valves as the EBCM responds to wheel speed sensor inputs and attempts to prevent wheel slip. These pedal pulsations are present only during anti-lock braking and stop when normal braking is resumed or when the vehicle comes to a stop. A ticking or popping noise may also be heard as the solenoid valves cycle rapidly. During anti-lock braking on dry pavement, intermittent chirping noises may be heard as the tires approach slipping. These noises and pedal pulsations are considered normal during anti-lock operation.

Vehicles equipped with ABS may be stopped by applying normal force to the brake pedal. Brake pedal operation during normal braking is no different than that of previous non-ABS systems. Maintaining a constant force on the brake pedal provides the shortest stopping distance while maintaining vehicle stability.

DIAGNOSIS & TESTING

Accessing Diagnostic Trouble Codes

Connect a suitably programmed scan tool to Data Link Connector (DLC) and follow manufacturers instructions.

Diagnostic Trouble Code Interpretation

Refer to "Diagnostic Chart Index" for trouble code interpretation.

Connector Pin Identification

Refer to **Figs. 1 through 4** for connector pin identifications.

Wiring Diagrams

Refer to **Figs. 5 through 9** for wiring diagrams.

Diagnostic Tests

AZTEK & RENDEZVOUS

Refer to **Figs. 10 through 25** for diagnostic test procedures.

EQUINOX, TORRENT & VUE

Refer to **Figs. 26 through 38** for diagnostic test procedures.

HUMMER H2

Refer to **Figs. 39 through 49** for diagnostic test procedures.

Symptom Tests

AZTEK & RENDEZVOUS

Refer to **Figs. 50 through 55** for symptom procedures.

EQUINOX, TORRENT & VUE

Refer to **Figs. 56 through 59** for symptom procedures.

HUMMER H2

Refer to **Figs. 60 through 63** for symptom procedures.

Temperature Vs. Resistance

Refer to **Fig. 64** for temperature vs. resistance values.

Intermittents & Poor Connections

Most Intermittents are caused by faulty electrical connections or wiring, although a sticking relay or solenoid can also cause an intermittent condition. Inspect wiring and connectors for the following:

1. Poor mating of connector halves, or terminals not fully seated in connector body.
2. Dirt or corrosion on terminals.
3. Damaged connector body.
4. Improperly formed or damaged terminals.
5. Poor terminal to wire connection.
6. Rubbed through wiring insulation.
7. Wiring broken inside insulation.

Clearing Diagnostic Trouble Codes

Connect a suitably programmed scan tool to Data Link Connector (DLC) and follow manufacturers instructions.

SYSTEM SERVICE

Brake System Bleed

ABS AUTOMATED BLEED

In most circumstances a base brake bleed is all that is required for most component replacements (such as wheel cylinders, calipers, brake tubes, and master cylinder) except for BPMV replacement.

The following automated ABS bleed procedure is required when one of the following occur: Manual bleeding at the wheel cylinders does not achieve the desired pedal height or feel. Brake Pressure Modulator Valve replacement (BPMV). Extreme loss of brake fluid has occurred. Air ingestion is suspected.

If none of the above conditions apply use standard bleed procedures as outlined in "Hydraulic Brake System Bleeding – Manual" or "Hydraulic Brake System Bleeding – Pressure"

The "Automated Bleed Procedure" may be terminated at any time during the process by pressing the EXIT button. No further scan tool prompts pertaining to the "Automated Bleed Procedure" will be given. After exiting the bleed procedure, relieve bleed pressure and disconnect bleed equipment per manufacturers instructions. Failure to properly relieve pressure may result in spilled brake fluid causing damage to components and painted surfaces.

Connector Part Information		• 15326390 • 30-Way F GT 150 280 SEALED 4.0 5.8 (BLK)	
Pin	**Wire Color**	**Circuit No.**	**Function**
1	—	—	Not Used
2	BRN	882	Right Rear Wheel Speed Sensor Signal
3	WHT	883	Right Rear Wheel Speed Sensor Low Reference
4	GRN DK	872	Right Front Wheel Speed Sensor Signal
5	TAN	833	Right Front Wheel Speed Sensor Low Reference
6	WHT	17	Stop Lamp Switch Signal
7	—	—	Not Used
8	PNK	1039	Ignition 1 Voltage
9	TAN/BLK	464	Delivered Torque Signal
10	—	—	Not Used
11	WHT	121	Engine Speed Signal
12	BLK/WHT	251	Ground
13	RED	1442	Battery Positive Voltage
14	ORN	1740	Battery Positive Voltage
15	BLK/WHT	251	Ground
12-19	—	—	Not Used
20	BLU LT	830	Left Front Wheel Speed Sensor Signal
21	YEL	873	Left Front Wheel Speed Sensor Low Reference
22	BLK	884	Left Rear Wheel Speed Sensor Signal
23	RED	885	Left Rear Wheel Speed Sensor Low Reference
24	—	—	Not Used
25	BLU LT	1122	ABS/TCS Class 2 Serial Data
26	—	—	Not Used
27	ORN/BLK	463	Requested Torque Signal
28-30	—	—	Not Used

GC=020152439000X

Fig. 1   Connector pin identification. Aztek & Rendezvous

1. Preliminary Inspection:
   a. Inspect battery for full charge, repair battery and charging system as required.
   b. Connect a scan tool to Data Link Connector (DLC) and select current and history DTCs. Repair any DTCs prior to performing ABS bleed procedure.
   c. Inspect for visual damage and leaks and repair as required.
2. Preliminary Setup:
   a. Raise and support vehicle on a suitable lift.
   b. Turn ignition switch to Off position.
   c. Remove all four tires.
   d. Connect pressure bleeding tool according to manufacturer's instructions.
   e. Turn ignition switch to RUN position, engine off.
   f. Connect a scan tool and establish communications with ABS system.
   g. Pressurize bleeding tool to 30–35 psi.
3. Automated Bleed Procedure:
   a. With pressure bleeding tool at 30–35 psi, and all bleeder screws in closed position, select "Automated Bleed Procedure" on scan tool and

follow instructions.
   b. First part of automated bleed procedure will cycle pump and front release valves for one minute. After cycling has stopped scan tool will enter a "cool down" mode and display a 3 minute timer. Auto bleed will not continue until this timer expired, and cannot be overridden.
   c. During next step, scan tool will request technician to open one of bleeder screws. Scan tool will then cycle respective release valve and pump motor for 1 minute.
   d. Scan tool will repeat step 3 for remaining bleeder screws.
   e. With bleeder tool still attached to vehicle and maintaining 35 psi, scan tool will instruct technician to independently open each bleeder screw for approximately 20 seconds. This should allow any remaining air to be purged from brake lines.
   f. When automated bleed procedure is completed scan tool will display appropriate message.
   g. Install all four tires.
   h. Remove pressure from pressure bleeding tool and then disconnect

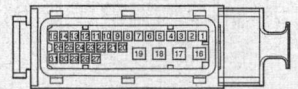

Connector Part Information

- OEM: 1928403008
- Service: See Catalog
- Description: 31-Way F (BK)

Pin	Wire Color	Circuit No.	Function
1	WH	883	RR Wheel Speed Sensor Low Reference
2	--	--	Not Used
3	BN	882	RR Wheel Speed Sensor Signal
4	TN	833	RF Wheel Speed Sensor Low Reference
5	D-GN	872	RF Wheel Speed Sensor Signal
6	YE	873	LF Wheel Speed Sensor Low Reference
7	L-BU	830	LF Wheel Speed Sensor Signal
8	OG	885	LR Wheel Speed Sensor Low Reference
9	TN	884	LR Wheel Speed Sensor Signal
10-14	--	--	Not Used
15	PK	1039	Ignition 1 Voltage
16	BK	350	Ground
17	RD/BK	702	Battery Positive Voltage
18	RD/WH	140	Battery Positive Voltage
19	BK	350	Ground
20-24	--	--	Not Used
25	TN	2501	High Speed GMLAN Serial Data (-)
26	--	--	Not Used
27	TN/BK	2500	High Speed GMLAN Serial Data (+)
28	--	--	Not Used
29	TN	2501	High Speed GMLAN Serial Data (-)
30	TN/BK	2500	High Speed GMLAN Serial Data (+)
31	--	--	Not Used

LTV0500000004245

Fig. 2   Connector pin identification. Equinox & Torrent

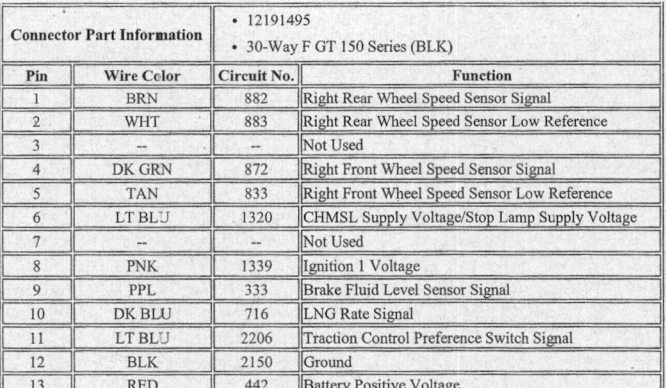

| **Connector Part Information** | • 12191495 | | |
| | • 30-Way F GT 150 Series (BLK) | | |
Pin	Wire Color	Circuit No.	Function
1	BRN	882	Right Rear Wheel Speed Sensor Signal
2	WHT	883	Right Rear Wheel Speed Sensor Low Reference
3	--	--	Not Used
4	DK GRN	872	Right Front Wheel Speed Sensor Signal
5	TAN	833	Right Front Wheel Speed Sensor Low Reference
6	LT BLU	1320	CHMSL Supply Voltage/Stop Lamp Supply Voltage
7	--	--	Not Used
8	PNK	1339	Ignition 1 Voltage
9	PPL	333	Brake Fluid Level Sensor Signal
10	DK BLU	716	LNG Rate Signal
11	LT BLU	2206	Traction Control Preference Switch Signal
12	BLK	2150	Ground
13	RED	442	Battery Positive Voltage
14	ORN	2340	Battery Positive Voltage
15	BLK	2851	Ground
16	ORN	2554	Traction Control Preference Switch Indicator
17	--	--	Not Used
18	LT BLU	2088	LNG Rate Low Reference
19	--	--	Not Used
20	LT BLU	830	Left Front Wheel Speed Sensor Signal
21	YEL	873	Left Front Wheel Speed Sensor Low Reference

LTV0500000004246

Fig. 3   Connector pin identification (Part 1 of 2). Hummer H2

tool from vehicle.
  i. Depress brake pedal to gauge pedal height and feel. Repeat steps 1–8 until pedal is acceptable.
  j. Remove scan tool from DLC connector.
  k. Lower vehicle.
  l. Inspect brake fluid level in master cylinder.
  m. Road test vehicle while making sure brake pedal remains high and firm.
  n. If vehicle is equipped TCS scan tool will cycle both ABS and TCS solenoids valves. This bleed procedure is same as above.

HYDRAULIC BRAKE SYSTEM BLEEDING – MANUAL

Refer to "Continental Teves MK-70" section for bleed procedure.

HYDRAULIC BRAKE SYSTEM BLEEDING – PRESSURE

Refer to "Continental Teves MK-70" section for bleed procedure.

Component Replacement

ELECTRONIC BRAKE CONTROL MODULE (EBCM)

1. Turn ignition switch to Off position.
2. **On Hummer H2 models,** raise and support vehicle.
3. **On all models,** pull out lock tab from EBCM harness connector.
4. Disconnect EBCM harness connector.
5. Disconnect pump motor connector at bottom of EBCM.
6. Remove EBCM to BPMV screws and discard.
7. Separate EBCM from BPMV.
8. Reverse procedure to install, noting the following:
   a. **Torque** mounting screws to 26 inch lbs.
   b. Complete diagnostic system check as outlined in **Fig. 10.**

BRAKE PRESSURE MODULATOR VALVE (BPMV)

The BPMV must not be repaired, the complete unit must be replaced. With the exception of the EBCM/EBTCM, no screws may be loosened. If screws are loosened, it will not be possible to get brake circuits leak-tight and injury may result.
1. Turn ignition switch to Off position.
2. **On Hummer H2 models,** raise and support vehicle.
3. **On all models,** pull out lock tab from EBCM harness connector.
4. Disconnect EBCM harness connector.
5. Disconnect wheel cylinder brake pipes from BPMV.
6. Disconnect master cylinder brake pipes from BPMV.
7. Remove nuts that connect BPMV to BPMV bracket.
8. Remove BPMV and EBCM as an assembly from vehicle.
9. Remove EBCM if replacing BPMV only.
10. Reverse procedure to install, noting the following:
    a. **Torque** BPMV to BPMV bracket to 96 inch lbs.
    b. If a new BPMV is being installed, remove shipping plugs from valve openings.
    c. Ensure brake pipes are correctly installed to brake pressure modulator valve by using a properly programmed scan tool.
    d. **Torque** brake pipe fittings to 18 ft. lbs.

WHEEL SPEED SENSOR

The front and rear speed sensors and rings are integral with hub and bearing assemblies. If a speed sensor or a ring needs replacement, replace entire hub and bearing assembly.
1. Raise and support vehicle.
2. Remove front or rear tire and wheel assembly.
3. Remove front or rear wheel speed sensor jumper harness electrical connector from front or rear wheel speed sensor connector.
4. Remove hub and bearing assembly.
5. Reverse procedure to install.

22	BLK	884	Left Rear Wheel Speed Sensor Signal
23	RED	885	Left Rear Wheel Speed Sensor Low Reference
24	--	--	Not Used
25	LT BLU	1122	ABS/TCS Class 2 Serial Data
26-27	--	--	Not Used
28	DK GRN	2087	LNG Rate Sensor 5 Volt Reference
29-30	--	--	Not Used

LTV0500000004247

Fig. 3 Connector pin identification (Part 2 of 2). Hummer H2

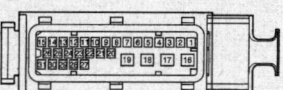

Connector Part Information		• 1928403008 • 31-Way F (BK)	
Pin	**Wire Color**	**Circuit Number**	**Function**
1	BN	882	RR WSS Signal
2	--	--	Not Used
3	WH	883	RR WSS Low Reference
4	D GN	872	RF WSS Signal
5	TN	833	RF WSS Low Reference
6	YE	873	LF WSS Low Reference
7	L-BU	830	LF WSS Signal
8	BK	884	LR WSS Signal
9	RD	885	LR WSS Low Reference
10	--	--	Not Used
11	BN/WH	2960	Keyword Serial Data (w/L81)
11	WH/BK	5043	Keyword Serial Data (w/L61)
12-14	--	--	Not Used
15	PK	1039	Ignition 1 Voltage
16	BK	350	Ground
17	RD	702	Battery Positive Voltage
18	OG	140	Battery Positive Voltage
19	BK	350	Ground
20-24	--	--	Not Used
25	TN	2501	CAN Low
26	--	--	Not Used

LTV0500000004248

Fig. 4 Connector pin identification (Part 1 of 2). Vue

27	TN/WH	2500	CAN High
28	D-BU	1660	Traction Control Indicator Control
29	TN	2501	CAN Low
30	TN/WH	2500	CAN High
31	BN/WH	1571	Traction Control Switch Signal

LTV0500000004249

Fig. 4 Connector pin identification (Part 2 of 2). Vue

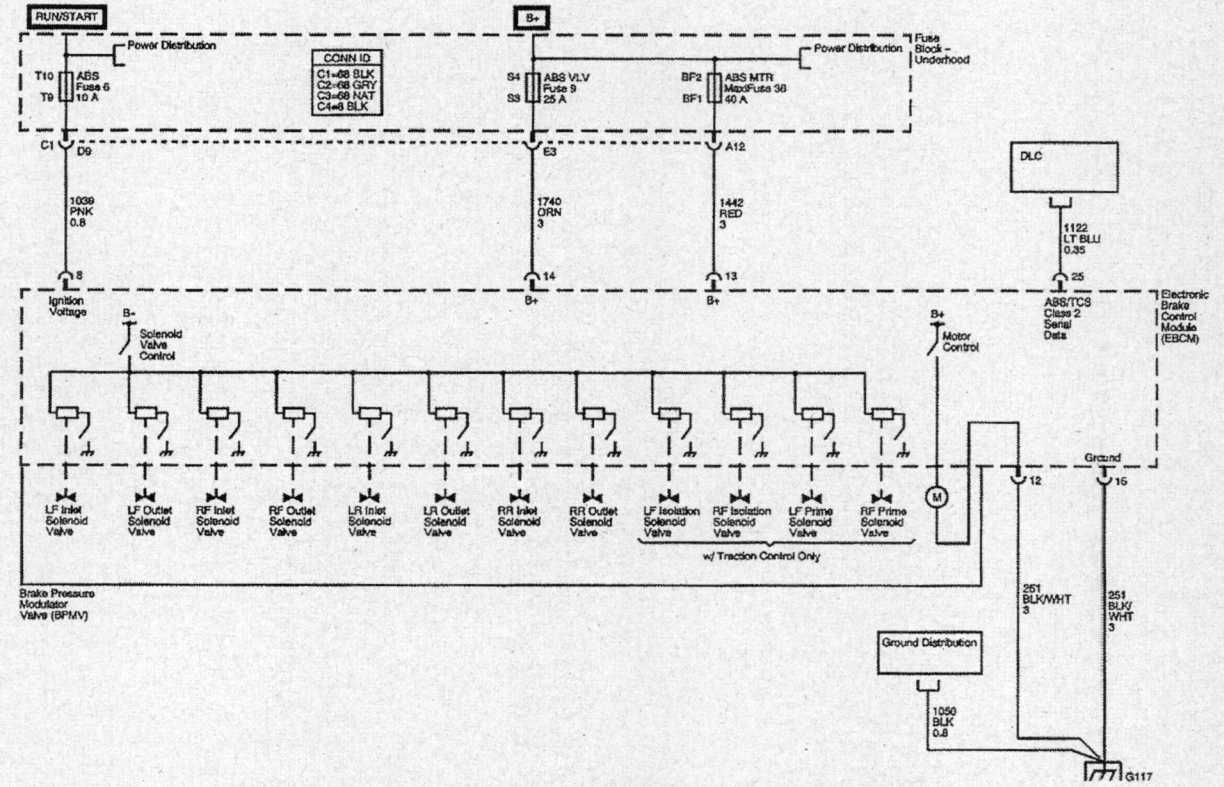

LTV0500000004250

Fig. 5 Wiring diagram (Part 1 of 3). 2002–04 Aztek & Rendezvous

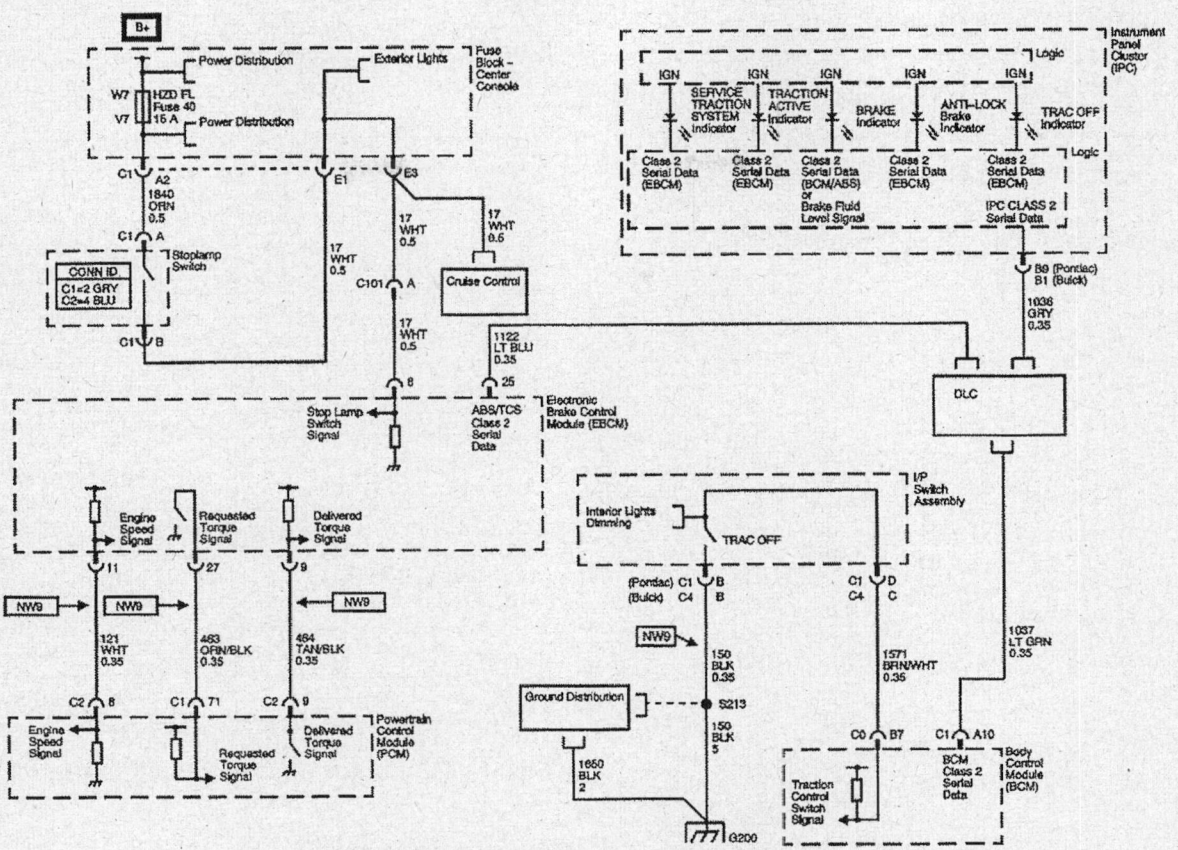

Fig. 5   Wiring diagram (Part 2 of 3). 2002–04 Aztek & Rendezvous

LTV0500000004251

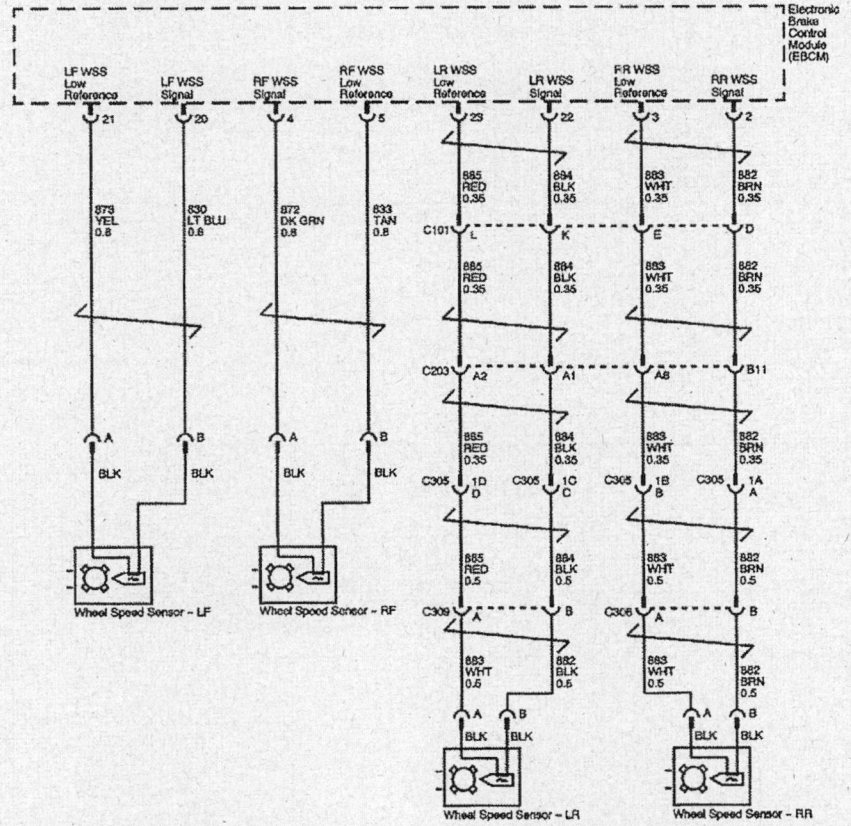

Fig. 5   Wiring diagram (Part 3 of 3). 2002–04 Aztek & Rendezvous

LTV0500000004252

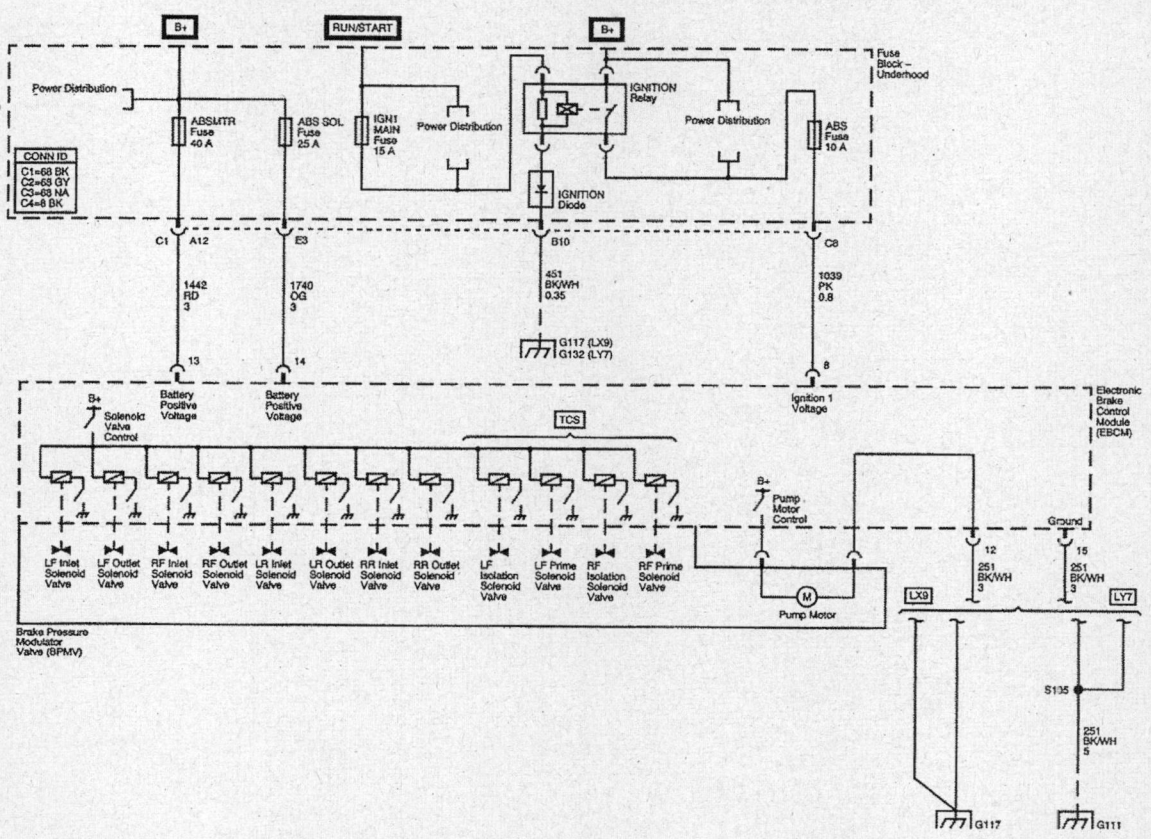

Fig. 6 Wiring diagram (Part 1 of 3). 2005–06 Aztek & Rendezvous

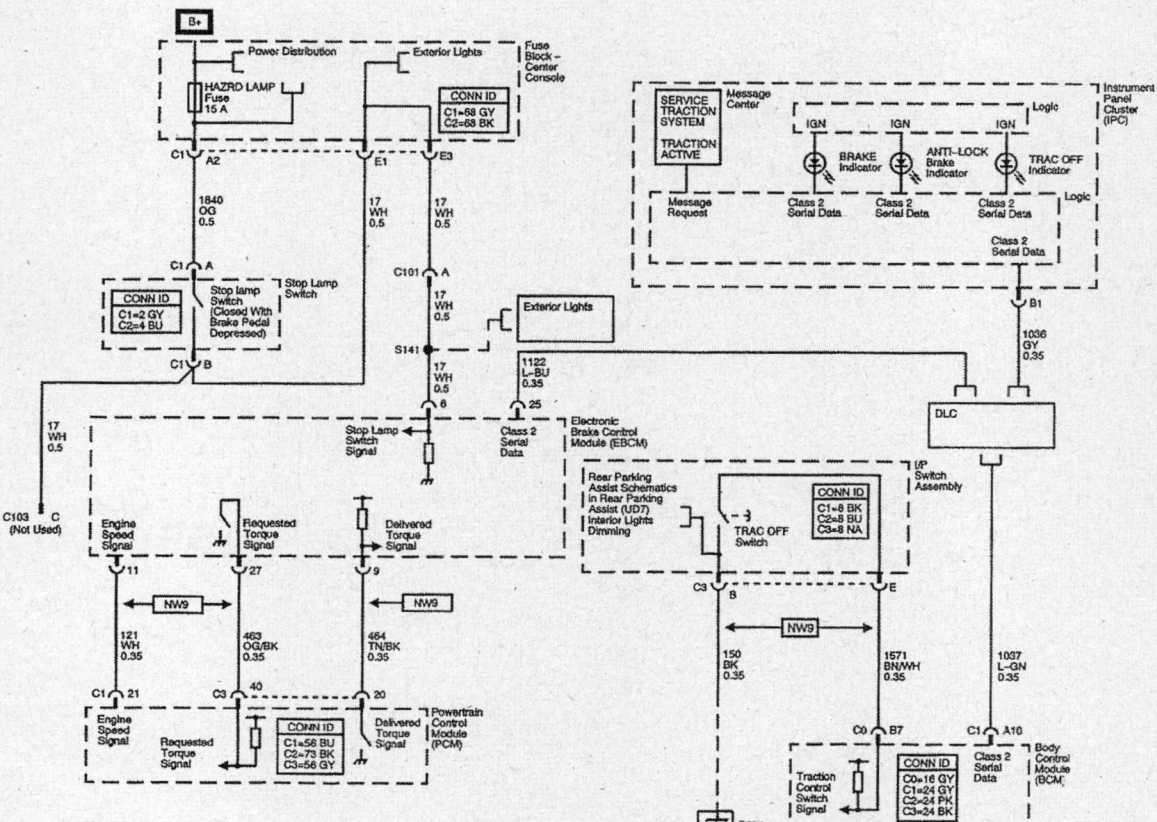

Fig. 6 Wiring diagram (Part 2 of 3). 2005–06 Aztek & Rendezvous w/3.5L engine

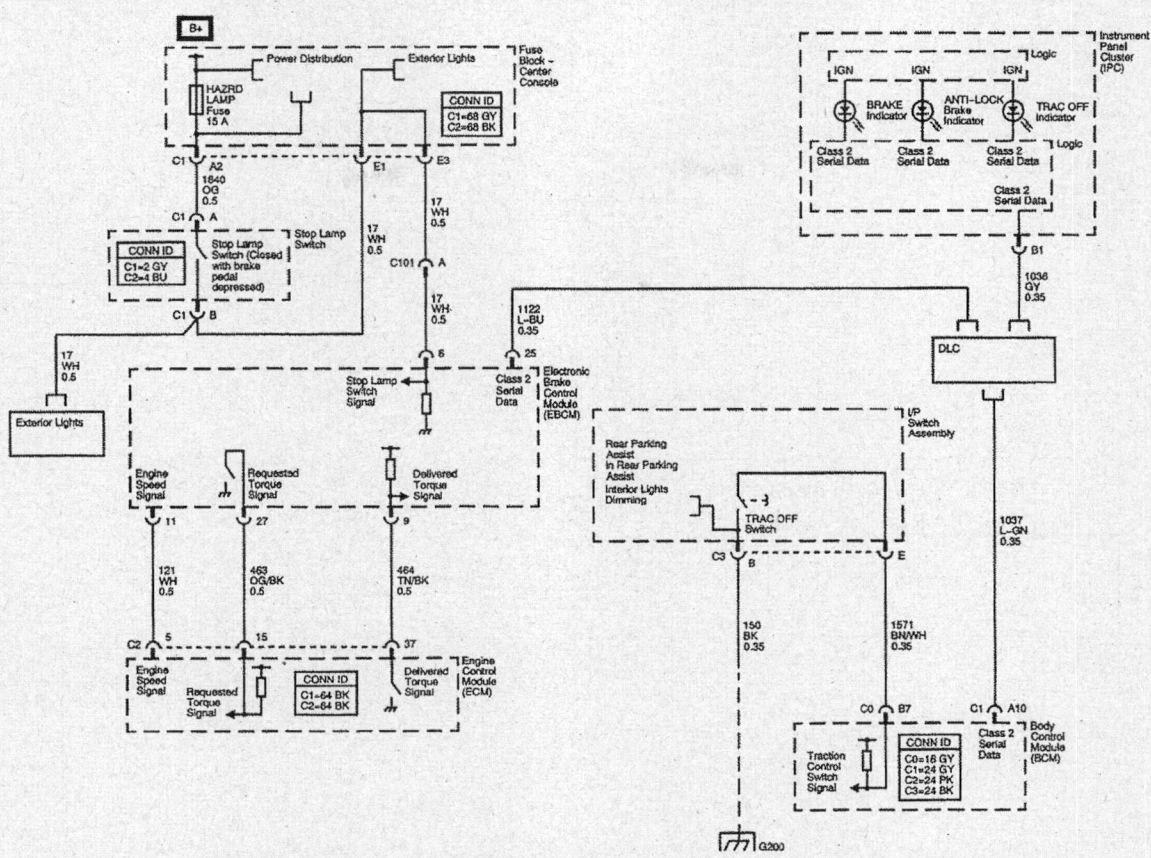

Fig. 6 Wiring diagram (Part 2 of 3). 2005–06 Aztek & Rendezvous w/3.6L engine

LTV0500000004255

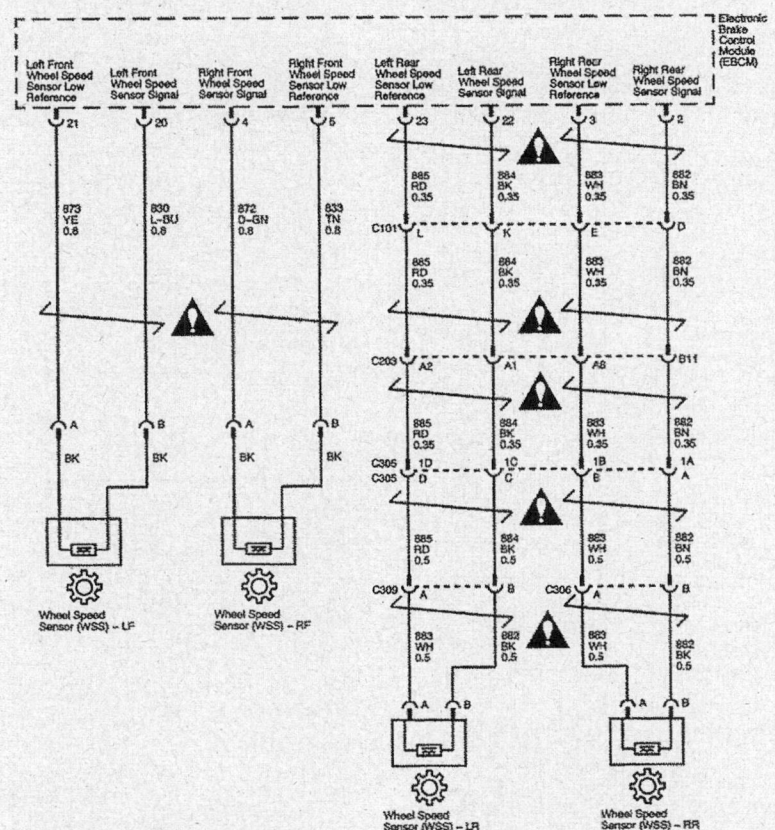

Fig. 6 Wiring diagram (Part 3 of 3). 2005–06 Aztek & Rendezvous

LTV0500000004256

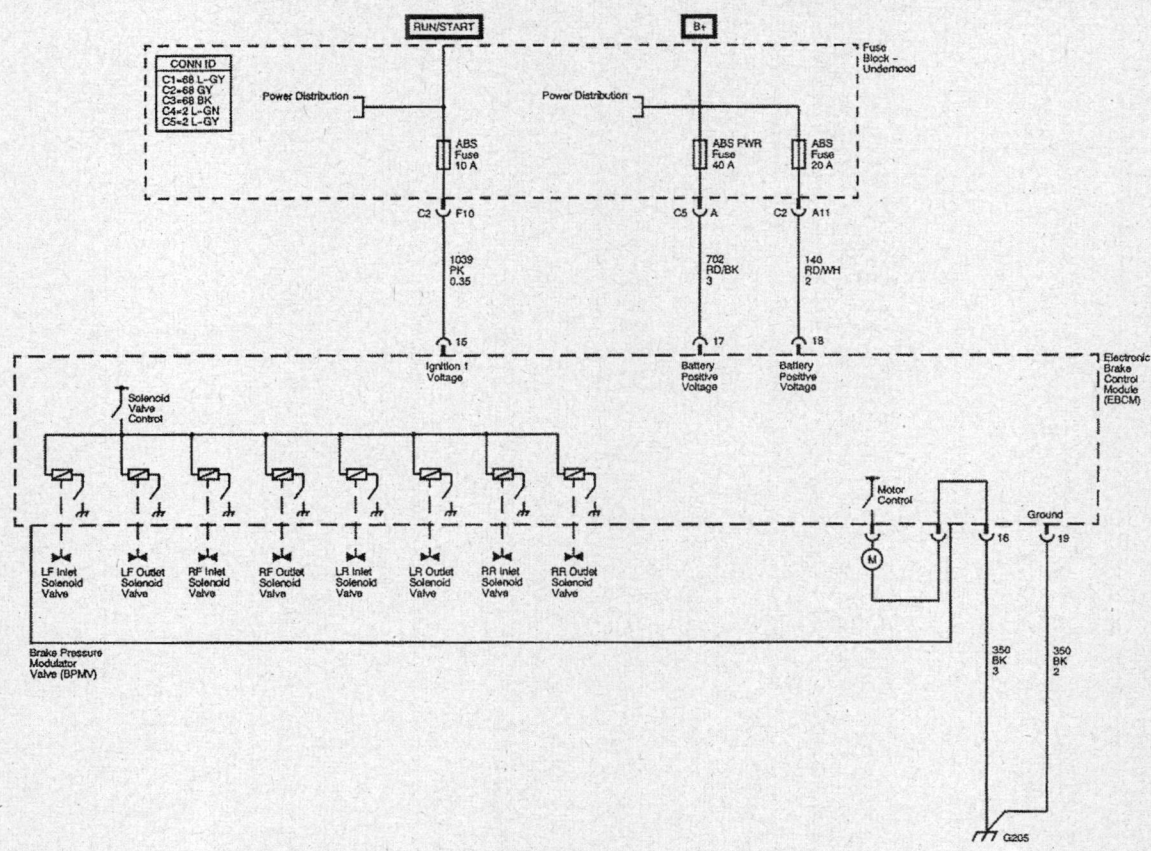

Fig. 7 Wiring diagram (Part 1 of 3). Equinox & Torrent

LTV0500000004257

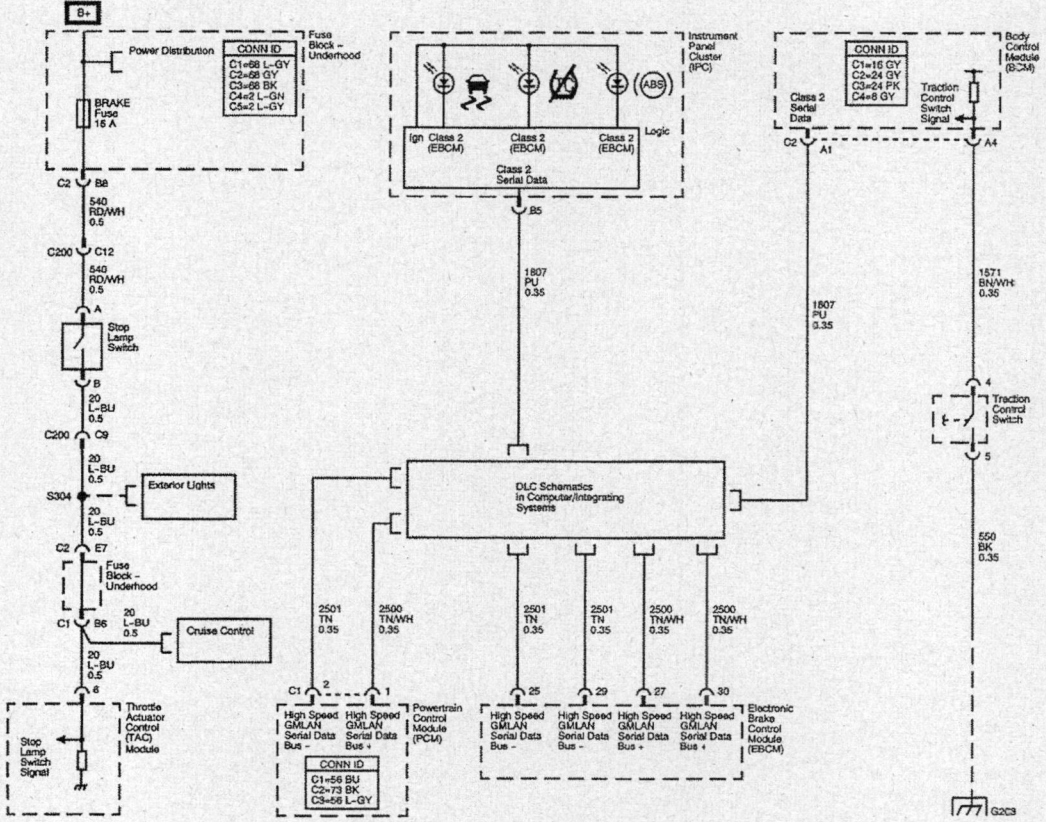

Fig. 7 Wiring diagram (Part 2 of 3). Equinox & Torrent

LTV0500000004258

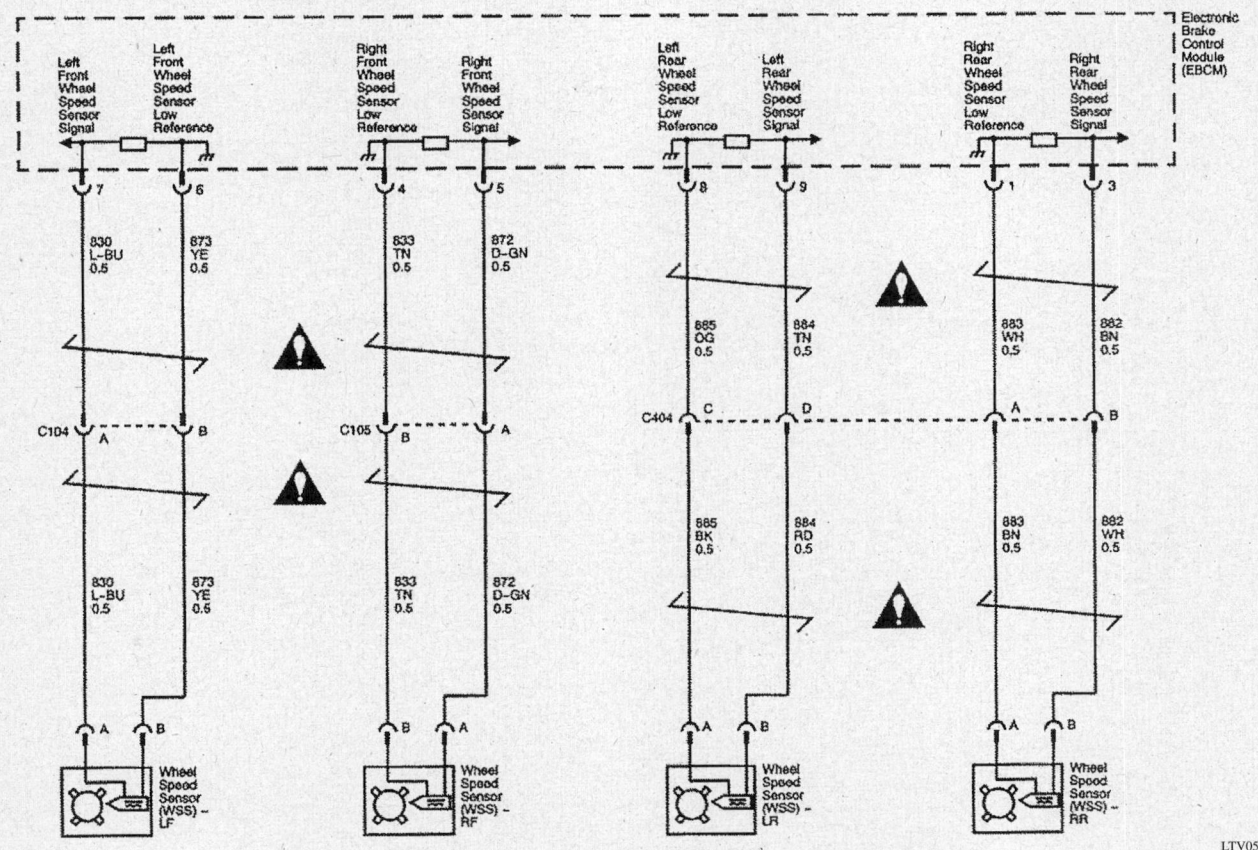

Fig. 7 Wiring diagram (Part 3 of 3). Equinox & Torrent

LTV0500000004259

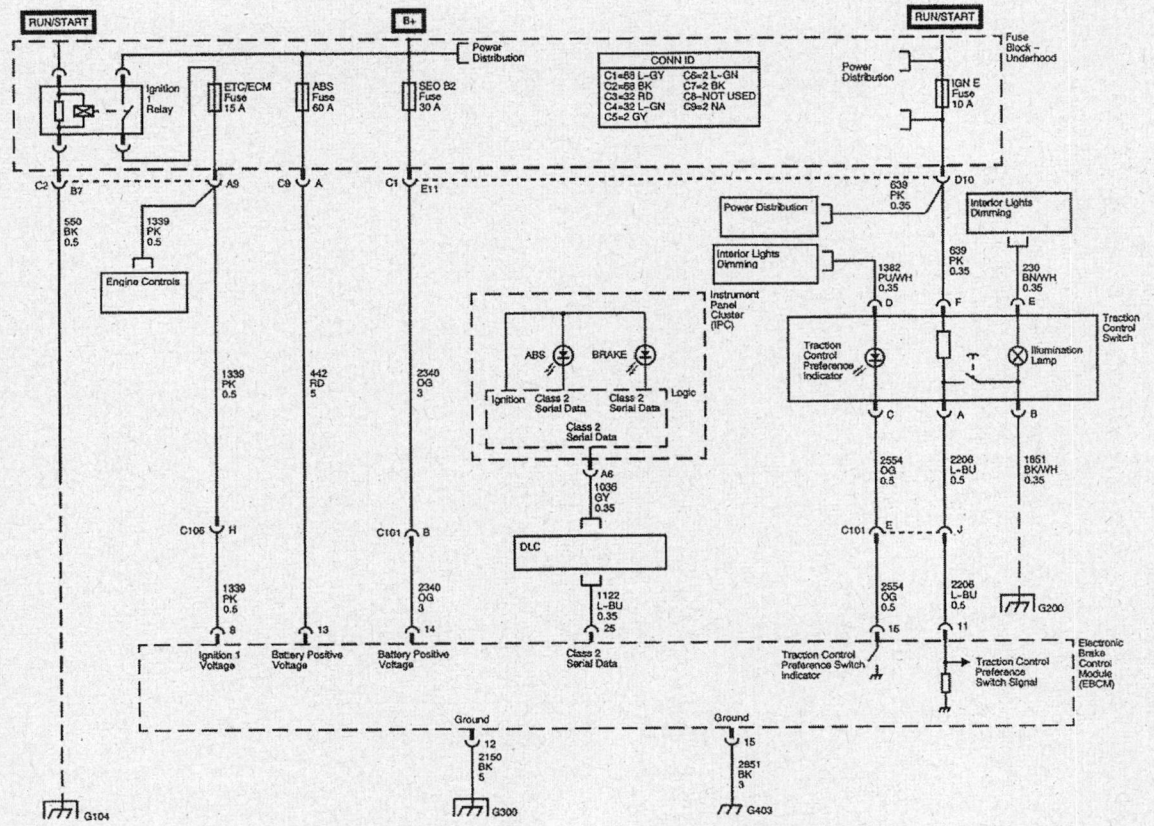

Fig. 8 Wiring diagram (Part 1 of 3). Hummer H2

LTV0500000004260

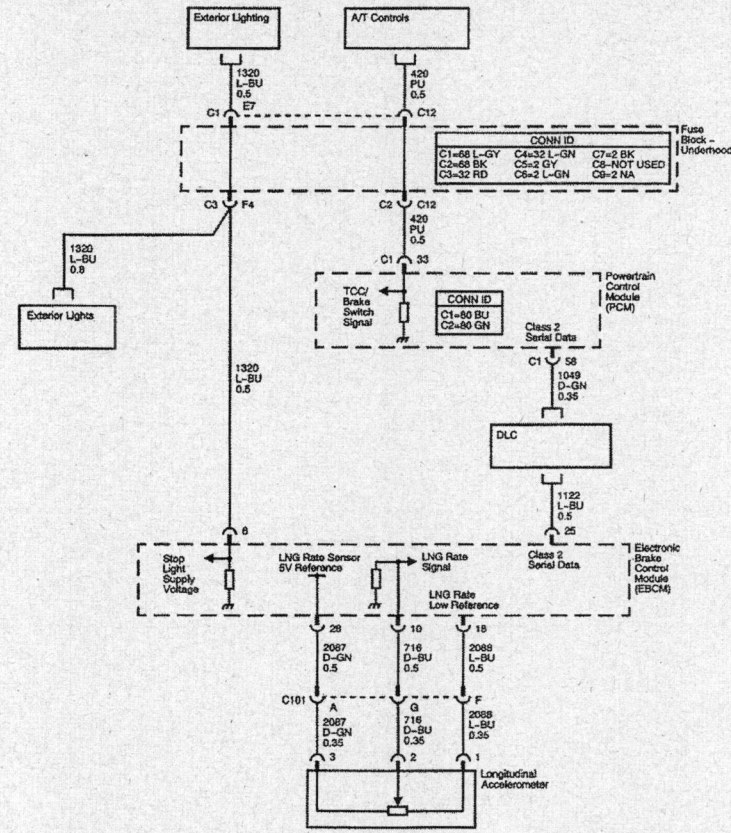

Fig. 8   Wiring diagram (Part 2 of 3). Hummer H2

LTV0500000004261

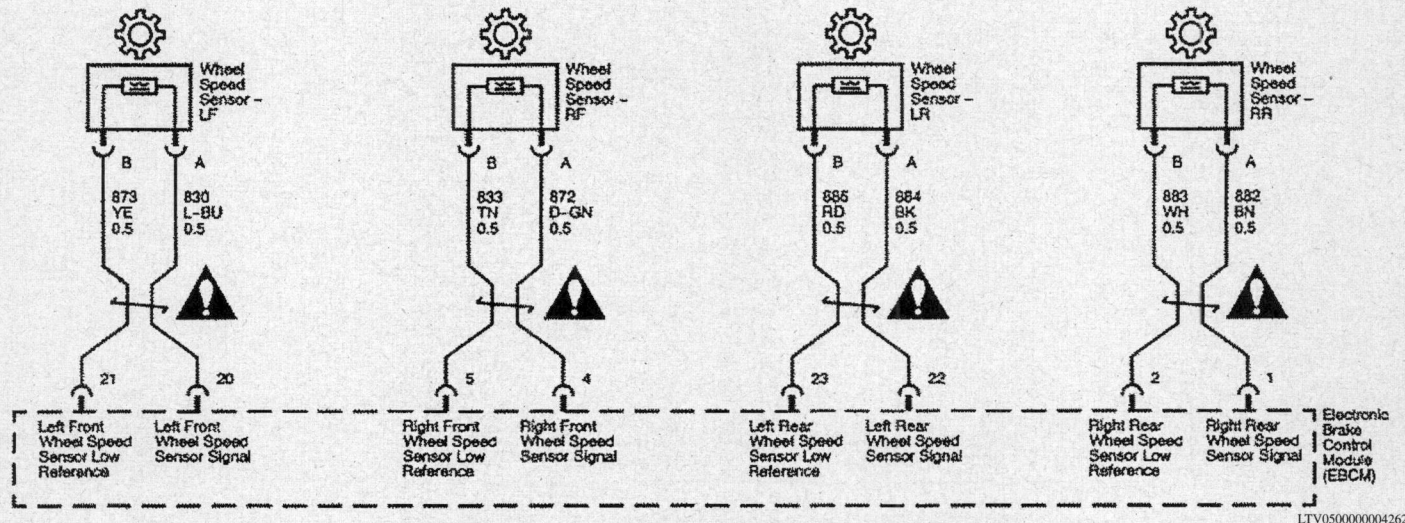

Fig. 8   Wiring diagram (Part 3 of 3). Hummer H2

LTV0500000004262

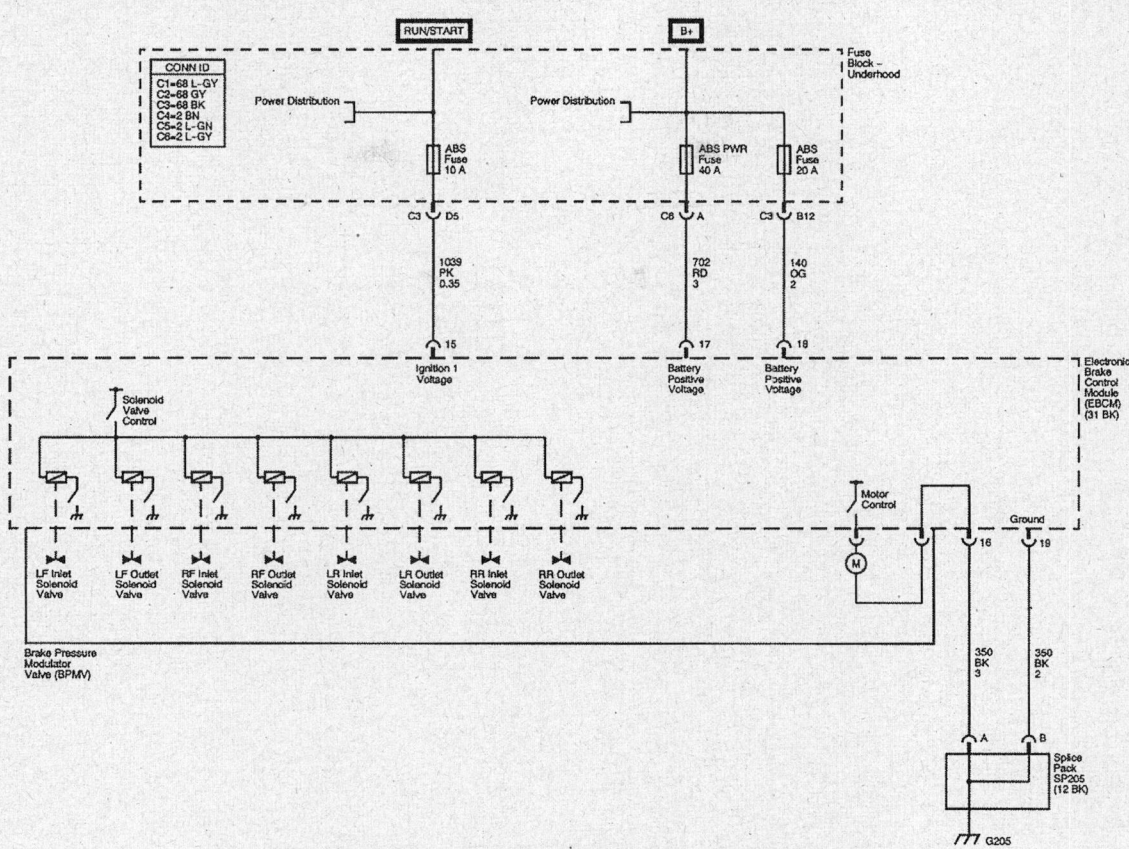

Fig. 9 Wiring diagram (Part 1 of 3). Vue

LTV0500000004263

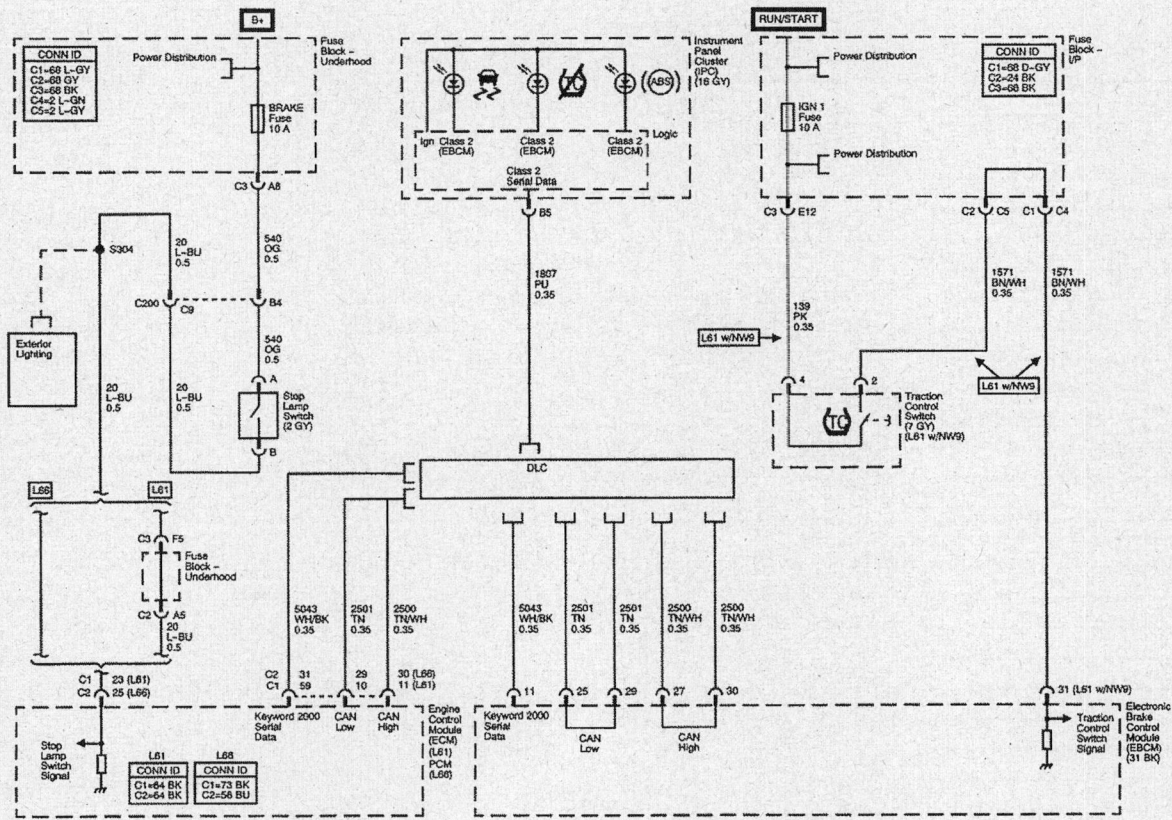

Fig. 9 Wiring diagram (Part 2 of 3). Vue

LTV0500000004264

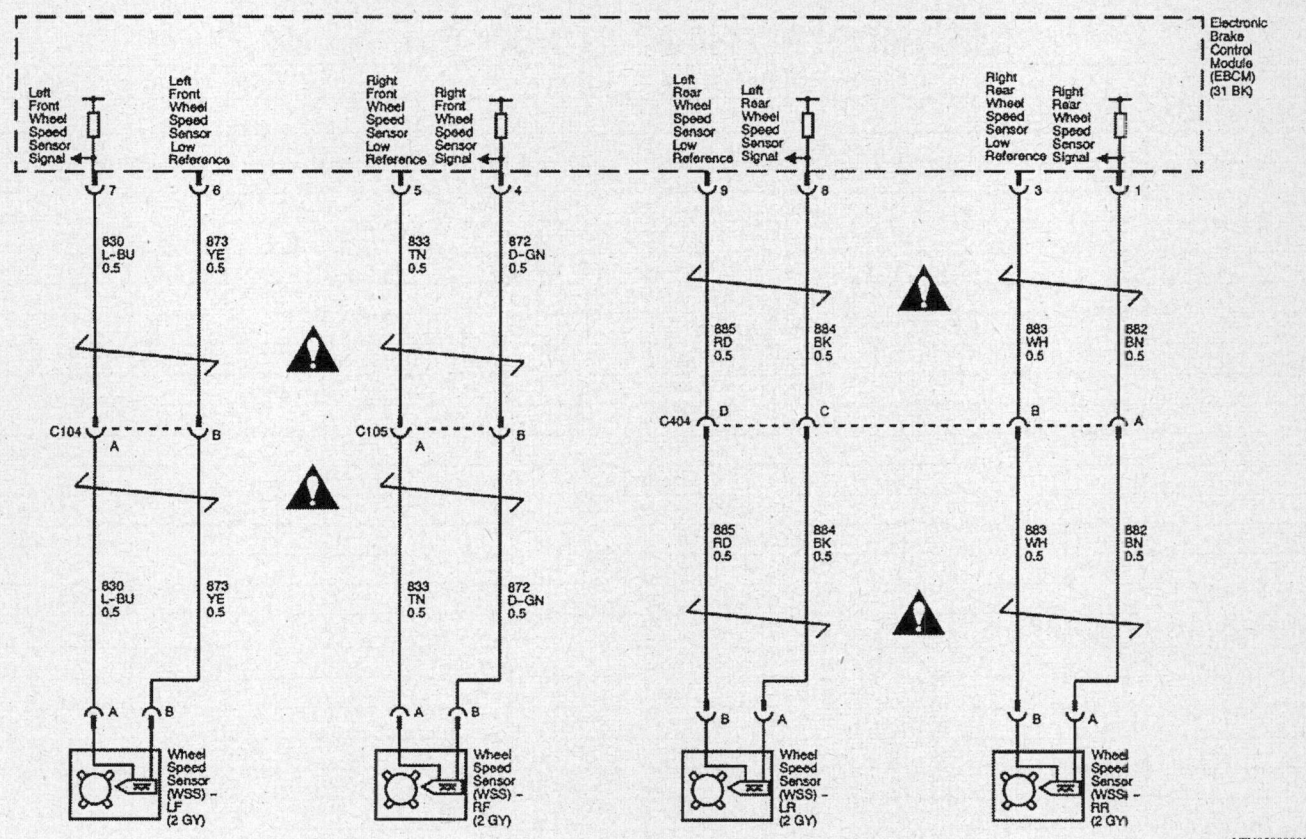

Fig. 9   Wiring diagram (Part 3 of 3). Vue

LTV0500000004265

DIAGNOSTIC CHART INDEX

Code	Description	Page No.	Fig. No.
AZTEK & RENDEZVOUS			
—	Anti-Lock Indicator Always On	5-70	50
—	Anti-Lock Indicator Inoperative	5-70	51
—	Tow Traction Indicator Always On	5-71	52
—	Tow Traction Indicator Inoperative	5-71	53
—	Traction Off Indicator Always On	5-71	54
—	Traction Off Indicator Inoperative	5-71	55
—	Diagnostic System Check	5-51	10
B2747	Traction Control Switch Fault	5-51	11
C0035	Wheel Speed Sensor Fault	5-52	12
C0036	Wheel Speed Sensor Fault	5-52	12
C0040	Wheel Speed Sensor Fault	5-52	12
C0041	Wheel Speed Sensor Fault	5-52	12
C0045	Wheel Speed Sensor Fault	5-52	12
C0046	Wheel Speed Sensor Fault	5-52	12
C0050	Wheel Speed Sensor Fault	5-52	12
C0051	Wheel Speed Sensor Fault	5-52	12
C0060	Short To Ground Or Voltage Solenoid Coil	5-52	13
C0065	Short To Ground Or Voltage Solenoid Coil	5-52	13
C0070	Short To Ground Or Voltage Solenoid Coil	5-52	13
C0075	Short To Ground Or Voltage Solenoid Coil	5-52	13
C0080	Short To Ground Or Voltage Solenoid Coil	5-52	13
C0085	Short To Ground Or Voltage Solenoid Coil	5-52	13
C0090	Short To Ground Or Voltage Solenoid Coil	5-52	13
C0095	Short To Ground Or Voltage Solenoid Coil	5-52	13
C0110	Pump Motor Voltage Fault	5-52	14

Continued

DIAGNOSTIC CHART INDEX—Continued

Code	Description	Page No.	Fig. No.
AZTEK & RENDEZVOUS			
C0121	Solenoid Valve Relay Fault	5-52	15
C0141	Short To Ground Or Voltage Solenoid Fault	5-52	16
C0146	Short To Ground Or Voltage Solenoid Fault	5-52	16
C0151	Short To Ground Or Voltage Solenoid Fault	5-52	16
C0156	Short To Ground Or Voltage Solenoid Fault	5-52	16
C0161	Stoplamp Switch Voltage Fault	5-52	17
C0235	RPM Input Signal	5-53	18
C0236	RPM Input Signal	5-53	18
C0237	RPM Input Signal	5-53	18
C0240	PCM Detects TCS Fault	5-53	19
C0241	PWM Signal Fault To EBCM	5-53	20
C0244	PWM Signal Out Of Range	5-54	21
C0245	Speed Sensor Fault	5-54	22
C0550	EBCM Fault	5-55	23
C0565	EBCM Detects Incorrect VIN	5-55	24
C0896	EBCM Detects High Or Low Voltage	5-55	25
EQUINOX, TORRENT & VUE			
—	ABS Active Indicator Always On	5-72	56
—	ABS Active Indicator Inoperative	5-72	57
—	Traction Control Indicator Always On	5-72	58
—	Traction Control Indicator Inoperative	5-73	59
—	Diagnostic System Check	5-55	26
C0035	Wheel Speed Sensor Fault	5-56	27
C0036	Wheel Speed Sensor Fault	5-56	27
C0040	Wheel Speed Sensor Fault	5-56	27
C0041	Wheel Speed Sensor Fault	5-56	27
C0045	Wheel Speed Sensor Fault	5-56	27
C0046	Wheel Speed Sensor Fault	5-56	27
C0050	Wheel Speed Sensor Fault	5-56	27
C0051	Wheel Speed Sensor Fault	5-56	27
C0060	Short To Ground Or Voltage Solenoid Coil	5-57	28
C0065	Short To Ground Or Voltage Solenoid Coil	5-57	28
C0070	Short To Ground Or Voltage Solenoid Coil	5-57	28
C0075	Short To Ground Or Voltage Solenoid Coil	5-57	28
C0080	Short To Ground Or Voltage Solenoid Coil	5-57	28
C0085	Short To Ground Or Voltage Solenoid Coil	5-57	28
C0090	Short To Ground Or Voltage Solenoid Coil	5-57	28
C0095	Short To Ground Or Voltage Solenoid Coil	5-57	28
C0110	Pump Motor Circuit Fault	5-57	29
C0121	Solenoid Valve Relay Circuit Fault	5-58	30
C0161	ABS/TCS Brake Switch Circuit Fault	5-58	31
C0236	TCS RPM Signal Circuit Fault	5-59	32
C0241	PCM Indicated Requested Torque Fault	5-60	33
C0245	Wheel Speed Sensor Frequency Error	5-60	34
C0275	TCM Traction Control Not Allowed	5-61	35
C0276	TCM Traction Control Not Allowed	5-61	35
C0550	ECU Fault	5-62	36
C0551	Option Configuration Error	5-62	37
C0896	Device Voltage Range Performance	5-62	38
HUMMER H2			
—	ABS Indicator Always On	5-73	60
—	ABS Indicator Inoperative	5-74	61
—	Traction Off Indicator Always On	5-74	62
—	Traction Off Indicator Inoperative	5-75	63
—	Diagnostic System Check	5-63	39
B3632	TC2 Mode Switch Signal Fault	5-64	40

Continued

DIAGNOSTIC CHART INDEX—Continued

Code	Description	Page No.	Fig. No.
HUMMER H2			
C0035	Wheel Speed Sensor Fault	5-64	41
C0036	Wheel Speed Sensor Fault	5-64	41
C0040	Wheel Speed Sensor Fault	5-64	41
C0041	Wheel Speed Sensor Fault	5-64	41
C0045	Wheel Speed Sensor Fault	5-64	41
C0046	Wheel Speed Sensor Fault	5-64	41
C0050	Wheel Speed Sensor Fault	5-64	41
C0051	Wheel Speed Sensor Fault	5-64	41
C0110	Pump Motor Circuit Fault	5-65	42
C0121	Valve Relay Circuit Fault	5-66	43
C0161	Stoplamp Switch Voltage Fault	5-66	44
C0191	Longitudinal Accelerometer Sensor Voltage Fault	5-67	45
C0192	Longitudinal Accelerometer Signal Fault	5-68	46
C0245	Wheel Speed Sensor Frequency Error	5-68	47
C0550	ECU Fault	5-69	48
C0896	Device Voltage Range Performance	5-70	49

GC4020152417000X

Fig. 10   Diagnostic System Check. Aztek & Rendezvous

GC4020152424000X

Fig. 11   Code B2747: Traction Control Switch Fault. Aztek & Rendezvous

Step	Action	Value(s)	Yes	No
1	Did you perform the ABS Diagnostic System Check?	—	Go to Step 2	Go to A Diagnostic System Check
2	1. Install a scan tool. 2. Turn ON the ignition. 3. Set up the scan tool snap shot feature to trigger for this DTC. 4. Drive the vehicle at a speed greater than the specified value. Does the scan tool indicate that this wheel speed DTC set?	8 km/h (5 mph)	Go to Step 3	Go to Diagnostic Aids
3	1. Raise and support the vehicle. 2. Disconnect the wheel speed sensor connector. 3. Measure the resistance across the wheel speed sensor. Does the resistance measure within the specified range?	800–1600 Ω	Go to Step 4	Go to Step 8
4	1. Spin the wheel. 2. Measure the AC voltage across the wheel speed sensor. Does the AC voltage measure greater than the specified value?	100 mV	Go to Step 5	Go to Step 8
5	Inspect for poor connections at the harness connector of the wheel speed sensor. Did you find and correct the condition?	—	Go to Step 10	Go to Step 6
6	1. Disconnect the EBCM harness connector. 2. Install the J 39700 using J 39700-530 to the EBCM harness connector only. 3. Test the wheel speed sensor circuits for the following: • An open • A short to ground • A short to voltage • Shorted together Did you find and correct the condition?	—	Go to Step 10	Go to Step 7
7	Inspect for poor connections at the harness connector for the EBCM. Did you find and correct the condition?	—	Go to Step 10	Go to Step 9
8	Replace the wheel speed sensor. Did you complete the replacement?	—	Go to Step 10	—
9	Replace the EBCM. Did you complete the repair?	—	Go to Step 10	—
10	1. Use the scan tool in order to clear the DTCs. 2. Operate the vehicle within the Conditions for Running the DTC as specified in the supporting text. Does the DTC reset?	—	Go to Step 2	System OK

GC4020152425000X

Fig. 12   Codes C0035–C0051: Wheel Speed Sensor Fault. Aztek & Rendezvous

Step	Action	Value(s)	Yes	No
1	Did you perform the ABS Diagnostic System Check?	—	Go to Step 2	Go to A Diagnostic System Check
2	1. Disconnect the EBCM harness connector 2. Connect the J 39700 universal pinout box using the J 39700-530 cable adapter to the EBCM harness connector only. 3. Test both ground circuits of the EBCM including the EBCM ground for a high resistance or an open. 4. Test the Battery Positive Voltage circuits for an open, high resistance, or a short to ground. Did you find and correct the condition?	—	Go to Step 8	Go to Step 3
3	1. Disconnect the pump motor harness pigtail connector of the BPMV. 2. Measure the resistance between each pump motor control circuit and the housing of the BPMV at the pump motor harness pigtail connector of the BPMV. Does the resistance measure less than the specified value?	5 Ω	Go to Step 4	Go to Step 5
4	Inspect for poor connections at the pump motor harness pigtail connector of the BPMV. Did you find and correct the condition?	—	Go to Step 8	Go to Step 6
5	Inspect for poor connections at the harness connector of the EBCM. Did you find and correct the condition?	—	Go to Step 8	Go to Step 7
6	Replace the BPMV. Did you complete the repair?	—	Go to Step 8	—
7	Replace the EBCM. Did you complete the repair?	—	Go to Step 8	—
8	1. Use the scan tool in order to clear the DTCs. 2. Operate the vehicle within the conditions for Running the DTC as specified in the supporting text Does the DTC reset?	—	Go to Step 2	System OK

GC4020152426000X

Fig. 14   Code C0110: Pump Motor Voltage Fault. Aztek & Rendezvous

Step	Action	Value(s)	Yes	No
1	Did you perform the Diagnostic System Check?	—	Go to Step 2	Go to A Diagnostic System Check
2	1. Using a scan tool clear the DTC. 2. Remove the scan tool from the DLC. 3. Carefully drive the vehicle above 12 km/h (8 mph) for several minutes. 4. Turn the ignition switch to the OFF position. 5. Install a scan tool. 6. Turn the ignition switch to the ON position, engine off. 7. Using the scan tool in Diagnostic Trouble Codes, check for DTCs. Did any one of the DTCs C0060-C0095 reset as a current DTC?	—	Go to Step 3	Go to Intermittent and Poor Connections
3	Replace the EBCM. Is the repair complete?	—	Go to Step 4	
4	1. Use the scan tool in order to clear the DTCs. 2. Operate the vehicle within the Conditions for Running the DTC as specification in the supporting text. Does the DTC reset?	—	Go to Step 2	System OK

GC4020152438000X

Fig. 13   Codes C0060–C0095: Short To Ground Or Voltage Solenoid Coil. Aztek & Rendezvous

Step	Action	Value(s)	Yes	No
1	Did you perform the Diagnostic System Check?	—	Go to Step 2	Go to A Diagnostic System Check
2	1. Install a scan tool. 2. Turn ON the ignition, with the engine OFF. 3. Use the scan tool in order to clear the DTCs. Does the DTC reset?	—	Go to Step 3	Go to Diagnostic Aids
3	1. Connect the J 39700 universal pinout box using the J 39700-530 cable adapter to the EBCM harness connector only. 2. Test the battery positive voltage circuit for an open, high resistance, or a short to ground. Did you find and correct the condition?	—	Go to Step 5	Go to Step 4
4	Replace the Electronic Brake Control Module (EBCM). Did you complete the replacement?	—	Go to Step 5	
5	1. Use the scan tool in order to clear the DTCs. 2. Operate the vehicle within the Conditions for Running the DTC as specified in the supporting text. Does the DTC reset?	—	Go to Step 2	System OK

GC4020152427000X

Fig. 15   Code C0121: Solenoid Valve Relay Fault. Aztek & Rendezvous

Step	Action	Value(s)	Yes	No
1	Did you perform the Diagnostic System Check?	—	Go to Step 2	Go to A Diagnostic System Check
2	1. Using a scan tool clear the DTC. 2. Remove the scan tool from the DLC. 3. Carefully drive the vehicle above 12 km/h (8 mph) for several minutes. 4. Turn the ignition switch to the OFF position. 5. Install a scan tool. 6. Turn the ignition switch to the ON position, engine off. 7. Using the scan tool in Diagnostic Trouble Codes, check for DTCs. Did any one of the DTCs C0141-C0151 reset as a current DTC?	—	Go to Step 3	Go to Diagnostic Aids
3	Replace the EBCM. Is the repair complete?	—	Go to Step 4	
4	1. Use the scan tool in order to clear the DTCs. 2. Operate the vehicle within the Conditions for Running the DTC as specified in the supporting text. Does the DTC reset?	—	Go to Step 2	System OK

GC4020152428000X

Fig. 16   Codes C0141–C0156: Short To Ground Or Voltage Solenoid Fault. Aztek & Rendezvous

Step	Action	Value(s)	Yes	No
1	Did you perform the AES Diagnostic System Check?	—	Go to Step 2	Go to A Diagnostic System Check
2	1. Press the brake pedal. 2. With the scan tool, observe the Brake Switch Status parameter in the ABS data list. Does the Brake Switch Status parameter display Applied?	—	Go to Step 4	Go to Step 3
3	Test the signal circuit of the stoplamp switch for an open. Did you find and correct the condition?	—	Go to Step 15	Go to Step 11
4	Press the brake pedal. Are all of the stoplamps OFF?	—	Go to Step 5	Go to Step 7

GC4020152429010X

Fig. 17   Code C0161: Stoplamp Switch Voltage Fault (Part 1 of 2). Aztek & Rendezvous

Step	Action	Value(s)	Yes	No
5	Test the feed circuit of the stoplamps for an open or high resistance. / Did you find and correct the condition?	—	Go to Step 15	Go to Step 6
6	Test the ground circuit of the stoplamps for an open or high resistance. / Did you find and correct the condition?	—	Go to Step 15	Go to Diagnostic Aids
7	1. Press the brake pedal. 2. With a scan tool, observe the Brake Switch Status parameter. / Does the Brake Switch Status parameter change state?	—	Go to Diagnostic Aids	Go to Step 8
8	1. Turn OFF the ignition. 2. Inspect the stoplamp switch and adjust and/or calibrate if needed. / Did you find and correct the condition?	—	Go to Step 15	Go to Step 9
9	1. Turn OFF the ignition switch. 2. Disconnect the stoplamp switch connector. 3. Turn ON the ignition, with the engine OFF. 4. With a scan tool, observe the Brake Switch Status parameter. / Does the scan tool display Released?	—	Go to Step 11	Go to Step 10
10	Test the stoplamp signal circuit for a short to voltage. / Did you find and correct the condition?	—	Go to Step 15	Go to Step 12
11	Inspect for poor connections at the harness connector of the stoplamp switch. / Did you find and correct the condition?	—	Go to Step 15	Go to Step 13
12	Inspect for poor connections at the harness connector of the EBCM. / Did you find and correct the condition?	—	Go to Step 15	Go to Step 14
13	Replace the stoplamp switch. / Did you complete the repair?	—	Go to Step 15	—
14	Replace the EBCM. / Did you complete the replacement?	—	Go to Step 15	—
15	1. Use the scan tool in order to clear the DTCs. 2. Operate the vehicle within the Conditions for Running the DTC as specified in the supporting text. / Does the DTC reset?	—	Go to Step 2	System OK

GC4020152429020X

Fig. 17 Code C0161: Stoplamp Switch Voltage Fault (Part 2 of 2). Aztek & Rendezvous

Step	Action	Value(s)	Yes	No
6	1. Inspect the PCM connector C2 for the following: • Inspect for damage. • Inspect for poor terminal contact. • Inspect for corrosion. 2. Inspect the EBCM connector for the following: • Inspect for damage. • Inspect for poor terminal contact. • Inspect for corrosion. 3. Ensure both the PCM connector C2 and the EBCM connector are properly retained when connected. Are the following signs present on either connector: • Is poor terminal contact present? • Is corrosion present? • Is damaged terminals present?	—	Go to Step 13	Go to Step 7
7	1. Reconnect all the connectors. 2. Using scan tool clear the DTC. 3. Disconnect the scan tool from the DLC. 4. Start the engine. Did DTC C0236 reset?	—	Go to Step 8	Go to A Diagnostic System Check
8	Replace the EBCM. Is the repair complete?	—	Go to Step 14	—
9	Check the PCM. Is the repair complete?	—	Go to Step 14	—
10	Repair an open between PCM and EBCM tach signal circuit. Is the repair complete?	—	Go to Step 14	—
11	Repair a short to ground in tach signal circuit. Is the repair complete?	—	Go to Step 14	—
12	Repair a short to voltage in TACH signal circuit. Is the repair complete?	—	Go to Step 14	—
13	Replace all the terminals or replace the connectors that exhibit signs of the following: • That exhibit signs of poor terminal contact. • That exhibit signs of corrosion. • That exhibit signs of damaged terminals. Is the repair complete?	—	Go to Step 14	—
14	1. Use the scan tool in order to clear the DTCs. 2. Operate the vehicle within the Conditions for Running the DTC as specified in the supporting text. Dose the DTC reset?	—	Go to Step 2	System OK

GC4020152430020X

Fig. 18 Codes C0235–C0237: RPM Input Signal (Part 2 of 2). Aztek & Rendezvous

Step	Action	Value(s)	Yes	No
1	Did you perform the Diagnostic System Check?	—	Go to Step 2	Go to A Diagnostic System Check
2	1. Start the engine. 2. Vary the engine RPM with the throttle while observing the IP tachometer. Does the IP tachometer work properly as the engine RPM changes?	—	Go to Step 3	Go to Step 9
3	1. Turn the ignition switch to the OFF position. 2. Disconnect the PCM connector C2 from the PCM. 3. Disconnect the EBCM connector from the EBCM. 4. Install the J 39200 with the J 39700-530 cable adapter to the EBTCM harness only. 5. Use a J 39200 to measure the resistance between the PCM harness connector tach signal circuit, and the universal breakout box terminal 11. Is the resistance within the specified range?	0–5 Ω	Go to Step 4	Go to Step 10
4	Use a J 39200 to measure the resistance between the universal breakout box terminal 11 and a good ground. Is the resistance within the specified range?	OL	Go to Step 5	Go to Step 11
5	1. Turn the ignition switch to the ON position. 2. Use a J 39200 to measure the voltage between the universal breakout box terminal 11 and a good ground. Is the voltage within the specified range?	0–2 V	Go to Step 6	Go to Step 12

GC4020152430010X

Fig. 18 Codes C0235–C0237: RPM Input Signal (Part 1 of 2). Aztek & Rendezvous

Step	Action	Value(s)	Yes	No
1	Did you perform the Diagnostic System Check?	—	Go to Step 2	Go to A Diagnostic System Check
2	1. Turn the ignition switch to the RUN position with the engine off. 2. Using a Scan Tool, read the ABS/TCS DTCs. Are any other DTCs set?	—	Go to Diagnostic Trouble Code (DTC) List	Go to Step 3
3	Is DTC C0240 set as a current code?	—	Go to Step 5	Go to Step 4
4	1. Using the scan tool clear the DTC. 2. Remove the scan tool from the DLC. 3. Carefully drive the vehicle above 12 Km/h (8 mph) for several minutes. Did DTC C0240 set as a current DTC?	—	Go to Step 5	Go to A Diagnostic System Check
5	Perform the Powertrain OBD System Check. Did the vehicle pass the OBD System Check?	—	Go to Step 6	Go to Diagnostic Trouble Code (DTC) List
6	1. Use the scan tool in order to clear the DTCs. 2. Operate the vehicle within the Conditions for Running the DTC as specified in the supporting text. Did the DTC reset?	—	Go to Step 2	System OK

GC4020152431000X

Fig. 19 Code C0240: PCM Detects TCS Fault. Aztek & Rendezvous

Step	Action	Value(s)	Yes	No
1	Did you perform the ABS Diagnostic System Check?	—	Go to Step 2	Go to A Diagnostic System Check
2	Inspect the EBCM ground and PCM ground, making sure each ground is clean and torqued to the proper specification. Did you find and correct the condition?	—	Go to Step 13	Go to Step 3
3	1. Install a scan tool. 2. Start the engine. 3. With the scan tool, observe the Torque Request Signal parameter in the Powertrain Control Module data list. Does the scan tool display less than the specified value?	100%	Go to Intermittent and Poor Connections	Go to Step 4
4	1. Turn OFF the ignition. 2. Disconnect the EBCM harness connector. 3. Install the J 39700 universal breakout box using the J 39700-530 cable adapter to the EBCM harness connector and the EBCM connector. 4. Start the engine. 5. Measure the DC duty cycle between the requested torque signal circuit and a good ground. Is the duty cycle within the specified range?	5–95%	Go to Step 5	Go to Step 6

GC4020152432010X

Fig. 20 Code C0241: PWM Signal Fault To EBCM (Part 1 of 2). Aztek & Rendezvous

Step	Action	Value(s)	Yes	No
5	Measure the DC Hz between the requested torque signal circuit and a good ground. Does the frequency measure within the specified range?	121–134 Hz	Go to Step 8	Go to Step 6
6	1. Turn OFF the ignition. 2. Disconnect the cable adapter from the EBCM connector. **Important:** Disconnecting the EBCM connector and turning ON the ignition could cause other modules to set loss of communication DTCs (Uxxxx). Once the EBCM is reconnected, the EBCM may set DTC C0241. 3. Turn ON the ignition, with the engine OFF. 4. Measure the voltage from the requested torque signal circuit to a good ground. Does the voltage measure within the specified range?	4 – 6 V	Go to Step 10	Go to Step 7
7	1. Turn OFF the ignition. 2. Disconnect the powertrain control module (PCM) harness connector. 3. Test the requested torque signal circuit for the following conditions: • A short to voltage • A short to ground Did you find and correct the condition?	—	Go to Step 13	Go to Step 10
8	1. Turn OFF the ignition. 2. Disconnect the powertrain control module (PCM) harness connector. 3. Test the requested torque signal circuit for the following conditions: • An open • A high resistance Did you find and correct the condition?	—	Go to Step 13	Go to Step 9
9	Inspect for poor connections at the harness connector of the PCM. Did you find and correct the condition?	—	Go to Step 13	Go to Step 11
10	Inspect for poor connections at the harness connector of the EBCM. Did you find and correct the condition?	—	Go to Step 13	Go to Step 12
11	**Important:** The replacement PCM must be programmed. Replace the PCM. Did you complete the repair?	—	Go to Step 13	—
12	Replace the EBCM. Did you complete the repair?	—	Go to Step 13	—
13	1. Use the scan tool in order to clear the DTCs. 2. Operate the vehicle within the Conditions for Running the DTC as specified in the supporting text. Does the DTC reset?	—	Go to Step 2	System OK

GC4020152432020X

Fig. 20   Code C0241: PWM Signal Fault To EBCM (Part 2 of 2). Aztek & Rendezvous

Step	Action	Value(s)	Yes	No
4	1. Turn OFF the ignition. 2. Disconnect the EBCM harness connector. 3. Install the J 39700 universal breakout box using the J 39700-530 cable adapter to the EBCM harness connector and the EBCM connector. 4. Disconnect the powertrain control module (PCM) harness connector. 5. Turn ON the ignition, with the engine OFF. 6. Measure the voltage from the delivered torque signal circuit to a good ground. Does the voltage measure near the specified value?	B+	Go to Step 5	Go to Step 6
5	1. Turn OFF the ignition. 2. Disconnect the cable adapter from the EBCM connector. 3. Turn ON the ignition, with the engine OFF. 4. Test the delivered torque signal circuit for a short to voltage. Did you find and correct the condition?	—	Go to Step 11	Go to Step 7
6	1. Turn OFF the ignition. 2. Disconnect the J 39700-530 cable adapter from the EBCM connector. 3. Test the delivered torque signal circuit for the following conditions: • An open • A short to ground • A high resistance Did you find and correct the condition?	—	Go to Step 11	Go to Step 8
7	Inspect for poor connections the harness connector of the PCM. Did you find and correct the condition?	—	Go to Step 11	Go to Step 9
8	Inspect for poor connections the harness connector of the EBCM. Did you find and correct the condition?	—	Go to Step 11	Go to Step 10
9	**Important:** The replacement PCM must be programmed. Replace the PCM. Did you complete the repair?	—	Go to Step 11	—
10	Replace the EBCM. Did you complete the repair?	—	Go to Step 11	—
11	1. Use the scan tool in order to clear the DTCs. 2. Operate the vehicle within the Conditions for Running the DTC as specified in the supporting text. Does the DTC reset?	—	Go to Step 2	System OK

GC4020152433020X

Fig. 21   Code C0244: PWM Signal Out Of Range (Part 2 of 2). Aztek & Rendezvous

Step	Action	Value(s)	Yes	No
1	Did you perform the ABS Diagnostic System Check?	—	Go to Step 2	Go to A Diagnostic System Check
2	Inspect the EBCM ground and PCM ground, making sure each ground is clean and torqued to the proper specification. Did you find and correct the condition?	—	Go to Step 11	Go to Step 3
3	1. Install a scan tool. 2. Start the engine. 3. With a scan tool, observe the PCM to EBTCM Delivered parameter in the Powertrain Control Module data list. Does the scan tool display the specified value?	90%	Go to Step 4	Go to Intermittent and Poor Connections

GC4020152433010X

Fig. 21   Code C0244: PWM Signal Out Of Range (Part 1 of 2). Aztek & Rendezvous

Step	Action	Value(s)	Yes	No
1	Did you perform the diagnostic system check?	—	Go to Step 2	Go to A Diagnostic System Check
2	Is the following DTC(s) set concurrently with a history DTC C0245? • DTC C0036 • DTC C0041 • DTC C0046 • DTC C0051 • DTC C0056	—	Go to DTC Diagnostic Trouble Code (DTC) List	Go to Step 3
3	Inspect the wheel speed sensor for physical damage. Is physical damage of the wheel speed sensor evident?	—	Go to Step 4	Go to Step 5
4	Replace the wheel speed sensor. Is the replacement complete?	—	Go to Step 14	—
5	Inspect the jumper harness for physical damage. Is physical damage of the jumper harness evident?	—	Go to Step 6	Go to Step 7
6	Replace the jumper harness. Is the replacement complete?	—	Go to Step 14	—
7	Check for Proper routing of the wheel speed sensor harness. Check that the wheel speed sensor harness is routed away from the spark plug wires. Is the wheel speed sensor harness properly routed?	—	Go to Step 9	Go to Step 8
8	Reroute the wheel speed sensor harness away from the spark plug wires. Is the reroute complete?	—	Go to Step 14	—
9	1. Install a scan tool. 2. Turn the ignition switch to the RUN position. 3. Set the scan tool to Snap Shot Auto Trigger mode and monitor the wheel speed sensors. 4. Carefully drive the vehicle above 12 Km/h (8 mph) for several minutes. Did the scan tool trigger on any of the wheel speed sensors?	—	Go to Step 10	Go to Step 11
10	Note which wheel speed sensor triggered the scan tool. Follow the appropriate Wheel Speed Sensor Malfunction DTC table for the wheel speed sensor that triggered. Refer to DTC Table. Is the repair complete?	—	Go to Step 14	—
11	1. Reconnect all previously disconnected components. 2. Using a scan tool clear the DTC. 3. Remove the scan tool from the DLC. 4. Carefully drive the vehicle above 12 Km/h (8 mph) for several minutes. Does the DTC reset as a current DTC?	—	Go to Step 13	Go to Step 12
12	Malfunction is intermittent. Inspect all connectors and harnesses for damage that may result in an open or high resistance when connected. Is the repair complete?	—	Go to Step 14	—

GC4020152434010X

Fig. 22   Code C0245: Speed Sensor Fault (Part 1 of 2). Aztek & Rendezvous

Step	Action	Value(s)	Yes	No
13	Replace the EBCM. Is the replacement complete?	—	Go to Step 14	—
14	1. Use the scan tool in order to clear the DTCs. 2. Operate the vehicle within the conditions for running the DTC as specified in the supporting text. Does the DTC reset?	—	Go to Step 2	System OK

GC4020152434020X

Fig. 22   Code C0245: Speed Sensor Fault (Part 2 of 2). Aztek & Rendezvous

Step	Action	Value(s)	Yes	No
	Schematic Reference: *ABS Schematics*			
1	Did you perform the Diagnostic System Check?	—	Go to Step 2	Go to *A Diagnostic System Check*
2	Are any other DTC(s) present besides C0550?	—	Go to *Diagnostic Trouble Code (DTC) List*	Go to Step 3
3	Replace the EBCM. Is the replacement complete?	—	Go to Step 4	—
4	1. Use the scan tool in order to clear the DTCs. 2. Operate the vehicle within the Conditions for Running the DTC as specified in the supporting text. Does the DTC reset?	—	Go to Step 2	System OK

GC4020152435000X

Fig. 23   Code C0550: EBCM Fault. Aztek & Rendezvous

Step	Action	Value(s)	Yes	No
1	Did you perform the Diagnostic System Check?	—	Go to Step 2	Go to *A Diagnostic System Check*
2	1. Turn all the accessories off. 2. Install a scan tool. 3. Start the engine. 4. Use the scan tool to monitor the battery voltage while running the engine at approximately 2000 RPM. Is the monitored battery voltage within the specified range?	0–17.4 V	Go to Step 4	Go to Step 3
3	Use a J 39200 DMM to measure the voltage between the battery positive terminal and ground. Is the voltage within the specified range?	0–17.4 V	Go to Step 5	Go to *Symptoms*
4	Continue to monitor the battery voltage with the scan tool while running the engine at approximately 2000 RPM. Is the monitored battery voltage within the specified range?	0–9.4 V	Go to Step 6	Go to Step 5
5	1. Turn the ignition switch to the OFF position. 2. Disconnect the scan tool if still connected. 3. Test drive the vehicle above 6 km/h (3.5 mph). Did DTC C0896 reset?	—	Go to Step 10	Go to *A Diagnostic System Check - ABS*
6	1. Turn the ignition switch to the OFF position. 2. Disconnect the EBCM connector. 3. Install the J 39700 with the J 39700-530 to the EBCM harness connector only. 4. Use a J 39200 DMM to measure the resistance between the J 39700 terminal 15 and a good ground. Is the resistance within the specified range?	0–5Ω	Go to Step 8	Go to Step 7
7	Repair open or high resistance in the ground circuit. Is the repair complete?	—	Go to Step 11	—
8	1. Turn the ignition switch to the RUN position. 2. Use a J 39200 DMM to measure the voltage between the J 39700 terminal 8 and 15. Is the voltage within the specified range?	Above 9.4 Volts	Go to Step 9	Go to *Symptoms*
9	1. Turn the ignition switch to the OFF position. 2. Reconnect the EBCM connector. 3. Disconnect the scan tool if the scan tool is still connected. 4. Test drive the vehicle above 6 km/h (3.5 mph). Did DTC C0896 reset?	—	Go to Step 10	Go to Step 11
10	Replace the EBCM. Is the repair complete?	—	Go to Step 11	—
11	1. Use the scan tool in order to clear clear the DTCs. 2. Operate the vehicle within the Conditions for Running the DTC as specified in the supporting text. Does the DTC reset?	—	Go to Step 2	System OK

GC4020152437000X

Fig. 25   Code C0896: EBCM Detects High Or Low Voltage. Aztek & Rendezvous

Test Description

The numbers below refer to the step numbers on the diagnostic table.

1. This step insures that the battery, and the vehicle primary power and ground systems are functioning correctly.

3. Lack of communication may be due to a particular malfunction of a serial data circuit. The information in Data Link References will provide a list of modules and the associated data network no communication diagnostic link.

4. A module that is operating in the incorrect power mode based on key position may cause other vehicle symptoms and/or DTCs to set. The information in Power Mode Mismatch will correct the condition before checking for module DTCs or symptoms.

8. This step insures that all data link communication DTCs are diagnosed before system level DTCs.

9. This step insures that all ECU internal DTCs are diagnosed before other system level DTCs.

10. This step insures that all device voltage DTCs are diagnosed before other system level DTCs.

Step	Action	Yes	No
1	Perform the following preliminary inspections: • Ensure that the battery is fully charged. • Ensure that the battery cables are clean and tight. • Inspect for any open fuses. • Inspect the easily accessible systems or the visible system components for obvious damage or conditions that could cause the symptom. • Ensure that the grounds are clean, tight, and in the correct location. • Inspect for aftermarket devices that could affect the operation of the system. • Search for applicable service bulletins. Did you find and correct the condition?	System OK	Go to Step 2

LTV0500000004266

Fig. 26   Diagnostic System Check (Part 1 of 3). Equinox, Torrent & Vue

Step	Action	Value(s)	Yes	No
1	Did you perform the Diagnostic System Check?	—	Go to Step 2	Go to *A Diagnostic System Check*
2	Are any other DTC(s) present besides C0565?	—	Go to *Diagnostic Trouble Code (DTC) List*	Go to Step 3
3	Replace the EBCM with the correct module, and part number. Is the replacement complete?	—	Go to Step 4	—
4	1. Use the scan tool in order to clear the DTCs. 2. Operate the vehicle within the Conditions for Running the DTC as specified in the supporting text. Does the DTC reset?	—	Go to Step 2	System OK

GC4020152436000X

Fig. 24   Code C0565: EBCM Detects Incorrect VIN. Aztek & Rendezvous

Step	Action	Yes	No
2	Install a scan tool. Does the scan tool power up?	Go to Step 3	Check Scan Tool Does Not Power Up
3	1. Turn ON the ignition, with the engine OFF. 2. Attempt to establish communication with all of the control modules on the vehicle. Does the scan tool communicate with all of the expected vehicle control modules?	Go to Step 4	Check Data Link References
4	**Important:** • To ensure that RAP mode is inactive (if equipped), open the drivers door during the following step. • The engine may start during the following step. Turn OFF the engine as soon as you have observed the crank power mode. 1. Access the Power Mode parameter on the scan tool. 2. Rotate the ignition switch (operate the ignition mode switch) through all positions while observing the Power Mode parameter. Does the Power Mode parameter reading on the scan tool match the ignition switch position for all switch positions?	Go to Step 5	Check Power Mode Mismatch
5	Attempt to start the engine. Does the engine crank?	Go to Step 6	Go to *Symptoms*
6	Attempt to start the engine. Does the engine start and idle?	Go to Step 7	Go to Engine Cranks but Does Not Run
7	**Important:** Do not clear the DTCs unless instructed by a diagnostic procedure. Use the appropriate scan tool selections to obtain DTCs for each of the control modules. Does the scan tool display any DTCs?	Go to Step 8	Go to Step 12
8	Does the scan tool display and DTCs that begin with a "U"?	Go to *Diagnostic Trouble Code (DTC) List -*	Go to Step 9
9	**Important:** If any of these DTCs are displayed, diagnose them before diagnosing any other DTCs or symptoms. Does the scan tool display DTC B1000, B1004, B1008, B1009, C0550, C0551, P0601, P0602, P0603, P0604, P0606, or P2610?	Go to *Diagnostic Trouble Code (DTC) List -*	Go to Step 10
10	**Important:** If any of these DTCs are displayed, diagnose them before diagnosing any other DTCs or symptoms. Does the scan tool display DTC B1327, B1328, C0896, C0899, C0900, P0560, P0562, or P0563?	Go to *Diagnostic Trouble Code (DTC) List -*	Go to Step 11

LTV0500000004267

Fig. 26   Diagnostic System Check (Part 2 of 3). Equinox, Torrent & Vue

	Important: If any of the remaining DTCs are powertrain DTCs, select Captured Info in order to store the powertrain DTC information with a scan tool.		
11	If multiple DTCs are stored, diagnose the DTCs in the following order 1. Component level DTCs, such as sensor DTCs, solenoid DTCs, and relay DTCs. 2. System level DTCs, for example, misfire DTCs, EVAP system DTCs, and fuel trim DTCs. Diagnose the remaining DTCs.	Go to *Diagnostic Trouble Code (DTC) List*	—
12	Is the customers concern with inspection/maintenance (I/M) testing?	Go to *Inspection/Maintenance (I/M) System Check*	Go to *Symptoms*

LTV0500000004268

Fig. 26   Diagnostic System Check (Part 3 of 3). Equinox, Torrent & Vue

Circuit Description

The wheel speed sensor produces an alternating current signal whose amplitude and frequency vary, depending on the velocity of the wheel. The electronic brake control module (EBCM) uses the frequency of the AC signal to calculate the wheel speed.

DTC Descriptors

This diagnostic procedure supports the following DTCs:

- DTC C0035 Left Front Wheel Speed Sensor Circuit
- DTC C0036 Left Front Wheel Speed Sensor Circuit Range Performance
- DTC C0040 Right Front Wheel Speed Sensor Circuit
- DTC C0041 Right Front Wheel Speed Sensor Circuit Range Performance
- DTC C0045 Left Rear Wheel Speed Sensor Circuit
- DTC C0046 Left Rear Wheel Speed Sensor Circuit Range Performance
- DTC C0050 Right Rear Wheel Speed Sensor Circuit
- DTC C0051 Right Rear Wheel Speed Sensor Circuit Range Performance

Conditions for Running the DTC

C0035, C0040, C0045, C0050

The ignition is ON.

C0036, C0041, C0046, C0051

- Vehicle speed is over 40 km/h (25 mph).
- The brake pedal is not pressed.
- The antilock brake system (ABS) is not active.

Conditions for Setting the DTC

C0035, C0040, C0045, C0050

One of the following conditions exists for 0.02 seconds:

- The DTC will set if one wheel equals 0 while the other wheel speeds are greater than 40 km/h (25 mph).
- A short to voltage exists in the wheel speed sensor (WSS) in one of the WSS circuits.
- An open exists in the WSS signal circuit.
- A short to ground--The WSS signal circuit is shorted to ground.

LTV0500000004269

Fig. 27   Codes C0035–C0051: Wheel Speed Sensor Fault (Part 1 of 4). Equinox, Torrent & Vue

Diagnostic Aids

C0035, C0040, C0045, C0050

If the customer comments that the ABS indicator is ON only during moist environmental conditions (rain, snow, vehicle wash, etc.), inspect the WSS wiring for signs of water intrusion. If the DTC is not current, clear all DTCs and simulate the effects of water intrusion by using the following procedure:

1. Spray the suspected area with a 5 percent saltwater solution. To create a 5 percent saltwater solution, add 2 teaspoons of salt to 354 ml (12 oz) of water.
2. Test drive the vehicle over various road surfaces (bumps, turns, etc.) above 40 km/h (25 mph) for at least 30 seconds.
3. If the DTC returns, replace the suspected WSS or repair the WSS wiring.
4. Rinse the area thoroughly when completed.

C0036, C0041, C0046, C0051

A possible cause of this DTC is electrical noise on the WSS harness wiring. Electrical noise could result from the WSS wires being routed to close to high energy ignition system components, such as spark plug wires.

Test Description

The numbers below refer to the step numbers on the diagnostic table.

3. This step tests the WSS for the proper resistance value.

4. This step ensures that the WSS generates the proper voltage.

Step	Action	Values	Yes	No
1	Did you perform the Diagnostic System Check - Vehicle?	--	Go to Step 2	Go to Diagnostic System Check
2	1. Install a scan tool. 2. Turn ON the ignition. 3. Set up the scan tool snap shot feature to trigger for this DTC. 4. Drive the vehicle at a speed greater than the specified value. Does the scan tool indicate that this wheel speed DTC set?	64 km/h (40 mph)	Go to Step 3	Go to Diagnostic Aids

LTV0500000004271

Fig. 27   Codes C0035–C0051: Wheel Speed Sensor Fault (Part 3 of 4). Equinox, Torrent & Vue

C0036, C0041, C0046, C0051

All of the following conditions exists for 0.02 seconds:

- The DTC will set if one wheel speed is less than 2.75 km/h (1.7 mph), and the other WSS are greater than 40 km/h (25 mph).
- The brake pedal is not pressed.
- DTC C0035, C0040, C0045, and C0050 is not set.
- The DTC will set if there is interference on the wheel speed circuits for 20 seconds with the brake pedal applied or 5 seconds when the brake pedal is not applied.

Action Taken When the DTC Sets

If equipped, the following actions occur:

- The EBCM disables the ABS and traction control system (TCS) for the duration of the ignition cycle.
- A DTC malfunction will set.
- The ABS telltale turns ON.
- The traction control switch light emitting diode (LED) will turn OFF.

Conditions for Clearing the DTC

- The condition for the DTC is no longer present.
- Using a scan tool, clear the DTC function.
- The EBCM automatically clears the history DTC when a current DTC is not detected in 100 consecutive drive cycles.

LTV0500000004270

Fig. 27   Codes C0035–C0051: Wheel Speed Sensor Fault (Part 2 of 4). Equinox, Torrent & Vue

	Action	Values	Yes	No
3	1. Raise and support the vehicle. 2. Disconnect the wheel speed sensor (WSS) connector. 3. Measure the resistance across the WSS. Does the resistance measure within the specified range?	800-1700 ohms	Go to Step 4	Go to Step 8
4	1. Spin the wheel. 2. Measure the AC voltage across the WSS. Does the AC voltage measure greater than the specified value?	100 mV	Go to Step 5	Go to Step 8
5	Inspect for poor connections at the harness connector of the WSS. Did you find and correct the condition?	--	Go to Step 10	Go to Step 6
6	1. Disconnect the electronic brake control module (EBCM) harness connector. 2. Connect the digital multimeter (DMM) between the sensor signal and the low reference circuit of the EBCM connector. 3. Test the WSS circuits for the following: - An open - A short to ground - A short to voltage - Shorted together Did you find and correct the condition?	--	Go to Step 10	Go to Step 7
7	Inspect for poor connections at the harness connector for the EBCM. Did you find and correct the condition?	--	Go to Step 10	Go to Step 9
8	Replace the wheel speed sensor. Did you complete the replacement?	--	Go to Step 10	--
9	Replace the EBCM. Did you complete the repair?	--	Go to Step 10	--
10	1. Use the scan tool in order to clear the DTCs. 2. Operate the vehicle within the Conditions for Running the DTC as specified in the supporting text. Does the DTC reset?	--	Go to Step 2	System OK

LTV0500000004272

Fig. 27   Codes C0035–C0051: Wheel Speed Sensor Fault (Part 4 of 4). Equinox, Torrent & Vue

Circuit Description

The inlet and outlet valve solenoid circuits are supplied with battery power when the ignition is in the ON position. The electronic brake control module (EBCM) controls the valve functions by grounding the circuit when necessary.

DTC Descriptors

This diagnostic procedure supports the following DTCs:

- DTC C0060 Left Front ABS Solenoid 1 circuit malfunction
- DTC C0065 Left Front ABS Solenoid 2 circuit Malfunction
- DTC C0070 Right Front ABS Solenoid 1 circuit Malfunction
- DTC C0075 Right Front ABS Solenoid 2 circuit Malfunction
- DTC C0080 Left Rear ABS Solenoid 1 circuit Malfunction
- DTC C0085 Left Rear ABS Solenoid 2 circuit Malfunction
- DTC C0090 Right Rear ABS Solenoid 1 circuit Malfunctiont
- DTC C0095 Right Rear ABS Solenoid 2 circuit Malfunction

Conditions for Running the DTC

The DTC can set anytime the ignition switch is in the ON position.

Conditions for Setting the DTC

The DTC will set when the EBCM detects one of the following internal to the EBCM only:

- An open in the solenoid coil or circuit
- A short to ground in the solenoid coil or circuit
- A short to voltage in the solenoid coil or circuit

Action Taken When the DTC Sets

If equipped, the following actions occur:

- The EBCM disables the antilock brake system (ABS), traction control system (TCS), and dynamic rear proportion (DRP) for the duration of the ignition cycle.
- A malfunction DTC will set.
- The ABS telltale turns ON.

LTV0500000004273

Fig. 28   Codes C0060–C0095: Short To Ground Or Voltage Solenoid Coil (Part 1 of 2). Equinox, Torrent & Vue

Circuit Description

The pump motor is an integral part of the brake pressure modulator valve (BPMV), while the pump motor relay is integral to the electronic brake control module (EBCM). The pump motor relay is not engaged during normal system operation. When antilock brake system (ABS) or traction control system (TCS) operation is required, the EBCM activates the pump motor relay and battery power is provided to the pump motor.

DTC Descriptor

This diagnostic procedure supports the following DTC:

DTC C0110 Pump Motor Circuit Malfunction

Conditions for Running the DTC

- The ignition switch is in the ON position.
- Initialization is complete.

Conditions for Setting the DTC

- Pump motor voltage is not present 100 milliseconds after activation of the pump motor relay.
- Pump motor voltage is present for more than 1 second with no activation of the pump motor relay within 5 seconds.

Action Taken When the DTC Sets

If equipped, the following actions occur:

- The EBCM disables the ABS, TCS, and dynamic rear proportion (DRP) for the duration of the ignition cycle.
- A malfunction DTC will set.
- The ABS telltale turns ON.

Conditions for Clearing the DTC

- The condition for the DTC is no longer present.
- Using a scan tool, clear the DTC function.
- The EBCM automatically clears the history DTC when a current DTC is not detected in 100 consecutive drive cycles.

LTV0500000004275

Fig. 29   Code C0110: Pump Motor Circuit Fault (Part 1 of 3). Equinox, Torrent & Vue

Conditions for Clearing the DTC

- The condition for the DTC is no longer present.
- Using a scan tool, clear the DTC function.
- The EBCM automatically clears the history DTC when a current DTC is not detected in 100 consecutive drive cycles.

Diagnostic Aids

The solenoid valve circuit and the solenoid coil are internal to the EBCM. No part of the solenoid circuit is diagnosable external to the EBCM. The DTC sets when there is a malfunction in the solenoid circuit internal to the EBCM only.

Test Description

The number below refer to step number on the diagnostic table.

2. This step determines if the DTC is current.

Step	Action	Yes	No
1	Did you perform the Diagnostic System Check - Vehicle?	Go to Step 2	Go to Diagnostic System Check
2	1. Using a scan tool clear the DTC. 2. Remove the scan tool from the data link connector. 3. Carefully drive the vehicle above 15 km/h (9 mph) for several minutes. 4. Turn the ignition switch to the OFF position. 5. Install a scan tool. 6. Turn the ignition switch to the ON position, engine off. 7. Using the scan tool in Diagnostic Trouble Codes, retrieve current DTCs. Did any one of the DTCs C0060-C0095 reset as a current DTC?	Go to Step 3	Test for Intermittent Conditions and Poor Connections
3	Replace the electronic brake control module (EBCM). Did you complete the repair?	Go to Step 4	--
4	1. Use the scan tool in order to clear the DTCs. 2. Operate the vehicle within the Conditions for Running the DTC as specification in the supporting text. Does the DTC reset?	Go to Step 2	System OK

LTV0500000004274

Fig. 28   Codes C0060–C0095: Short To Ground Or Voltage Solenoid Coil (Part 2 of 2). Equinox, Torrent & Vue

Diagnostic Aids

- It is very important that a thorough inspection of the wiring and connectors be performed. Failure to carefully and fully inspect wiring and connectors may result in misdiagnosis, causing part replacement with reappearance of the malfunction.
- Thoroughly inspect any circuitry that may be causing the complaint for the following conditions:
  - Backed out terminals
  - Improper mating
  - Broken locks
  - Improperly formed or damaged terminals
  - Poor terminal-to-wiring connections
  - Physical damage to the wiring harness
- The following conditions may cause an intermittent malfunction:
  - A poor connection
  - Rubbed-through wire insulation
  - A broken wire inside the insulation

Test Description

The number below refers to the step number on the diagnostic table.

3. This step tests the pump motor circuits of the BPMV for a short to the housing of the BPMV.

Step	Action	Values	Yes	No
1	Did you perform the Diagnostic System Check - Vehicle?	--	Go to Step 2	Go to Diagnostic System Check
2	1. Disconnect the electronic brake control module (EBCM) harness connector. 2. Test both ground circuits of the EBCM including the EBCM ground for a high resistance or an open. 3. Test the battery positive voltage circuits for an open, high resistance, or a short to ground. Did you find and correct the condition?	--	Go to Step 8	Go to Step 3

LTV0500000004276

Fig. 29   Code C0110: Pump Motor Circuit Fault (Part 2 of 3). Equinox, Torrent & Vue

	Action	Spec	Yes	No
3	1. Remove the EBCM from the brake pressure modulator valve (BPMV) to gain access to the pump motor circuits. 2. Measure the resistance between each pump motor control circuit and the housing of the BPMV. Does the resistance measure less than the specified value?	5 ohms	Go to Step 4	Go to Step 5
4	Inspect for poor connections at the pump motor connector of the BPMV. Did you find and correct the condition?	--	Go to Step 8	Go to Step 6
5	Inspect for poor connections at the harness connector of the EBCM. Did you find and correct the condition?	--	Go to Step 8	Go to Step 7
6	Replace the BPMV. Did you complete the repair?	--	Go to Step 8	--
7	Replace the EBCM. Did you complete the repair?	--	Go to Step 8	--
8	1. Use the scan tool in order to clear the DTCs. 2. Operate the vehicle within the conditions for Running the DTC as specified in the supporting text. Does the DTC reset?	--	Go to Step 2	System OK

LTV0500000004277

Fig. 29 Code C0110: Pump Motor Circuit Fault (Part 3 of 3). Equinox, Torrent & Vue

Diagnostic Aids

- It is very important that a thorough inspection of the wiring and connectors be performed. Failure to carefully and fully inspect wiring and connectors may result in misdiagnosis, causing part replacement with reappearance of the malfunction.
- Thoroughly inspect any circuitry that may be causing the complaint for the following conditions:
  - Backed out terminals
  - Improper mating
  - Broken locks
  - Improperly formed or damaged terminals
  - Poor terminal-to-wiring connections
  - Physical damage to the wiring harness
- The following conditions may cause an intermittent malfunction:
  - A poor connection
  - Rubbed-through wire insulation
  - A broken wire inside the insulation
- The solenoid valve relay is an integral part of the EBCM and is not serviced separately.

Test Description

The number below refers to step number on the diagnostic table.

2. This step determines if the DTC is current.

Step	Action	Yes	No
1	Did you perform the Diagnostic System Check - Vehicle?	Go to Step 2	Go to Diagnostic System Check

LTV0500000004279

Fig. 30 Code C0121: Solenoid Valve Relay Circuit Fault (Part 2 of 3). Equinox, Torrent & Vue

	Action	Yes	No
2	1. Install a scan tool. 2. Turn ON the ignition, with the engine OFF. 3. Use the scan tool in order to clear the DTCs. Does the DTC reset?	Go to Step 3	Go to Diagnostic Aids
3	1. Disconnect the electronic brake control module (EBCM) harness connector. 2. Test the battery positive voltage circuit for an open, high resistance, or a short to ground. Did you find and correct the condition?	Go to Step 5	Go to Step 4
4	Replace the EBCM. Did you complete the repair?	Go to Step 5	--
5	1. Use the scan tool in order to clear the DTCs. 2. Operate the vehicle within the Conditions for Running the DTC as specified in the supporting text. Does the DTC reset?	Go to Step 2	System OK

LTV0500000004280

Fig. 30 Code C0121: Solenoid Valve Relay Circuit Fault (Part 3 of 3). Equinox, Torrent & Vue

Circuit Description

The solenoid valve relay supplies power to the solenoid valve coils in the electronic brake control module (EBCM). The solenoid valve relay, located in the EBCM, is activated whenever the ignition switch is in the RUN position and no faults are present. The solenoid valve relay remains engaged until the ignition is turned OFF or a failure is detected.

DTC Descriptor

This diagnostic procedure supports the following DTC:

DTC C0121 Valve Relay Circuit Malfunction

Conditions for Running the DTC

The ignition switch is in the ON position.

Conditions for Setting the DTC

- DTC C0121 will set anytime the solenoid valve relay is commanded on and the EBCM does not see battery voltage at the solenoid valves.
- DTC C0121 will set anytime the EBCM commands the solenoid valve relay off and battery voltage is still present at the solenoid valves.

Action Taken When the DTC Sets

If equipped, the following actions occur:

- The EBCM disables the antilock brake system (ABS), traction control system (TCS), and dynamic rear proportion (DRP) for the duration of the ignition cycle.
- A malfunction DTC is set.
- The ABS telltale turns ON.

Conditions for Clearing the DTC

- The condition for the DTC is no longer present.
- Using a scan tool, clear the DTC function.
- The EBCM automatically clears the history DTC when a current DTC is not detected in 100 consecutive drive cycles.

LTV0500000004278

Fig. 30 Code C0121: Solenoid Valve Relay Circuit Fault (Part 1 of 3). Equinox, Torrent & Vue

Circuit Description

The normally-open stop lamp switch supplies battery voltage to the engine control module (ECM) when the brake pedal is pressed. The ECM sends a brake pedal applied serial data message to the electronic brake and traction control module (EBTCM) and to the transmission control module (TCM).

DTC Descriptor

This diagnostic procedure supports the following DTC:

DTC C0161 ABS/TCS Brake Switch Circuit Malfunction

Conditions for Running the DTC

The ignition switch is ON.

Conditions for Setting the DTC

- The EBCM detects an open in the brake signal circuit.
- Both brake lamps are faulty.

Action Taken When the DTC Sets

If equipped, the following actions occur:

- A malfunction DTC will set.
- The EBCM stores this information-only DTC for as long as the condition is present.
- The antilock brake system (ABS) remains functional.
- The ABS indicator remains OFF.

Conditions for Clearing the DTC

- The condition for the DTC is no longer present.
- Using a scan tool, clear the DTC function.
- The EBCM automatically clears the history DTC when a current DTC is not detected in 100 consecutive drive cycles.

LTV0500000004281

Fig. 31 Code C0161: ABS/TCS Brake Switch Circuit Fault (Part 1 of 3). Equinox, Torrent & Vue

Diagnostic Aids

- It is very important that a thorough inspection of the wiring and connectors be performed. Failure to carefully and fully inspect wiring and connectors may result in misdiagnosis, causing part replacement with reappearance of the malfunction.
- Thoroughly inspect any circuitry that may be causing the complaint for the following conditions:
  - Backed out terminals
  - Improper mating
  - Broken locks
  - Improperly formed or damaged terminals
  - Poor terminal-to-wiring connections
  - Physical damage to the wiring harness
- Possible causes of this DTC are the following conditions:
  - A signal circuit of the stop lamp switch is open.
  - The stop lamp switch is not adjusted properly.
  - Verify proper stop lamp switch operation using the data list of the scan tool. As the brake is applied, the data list displays the stop lamp switch ON within 2.54 cm (1 in) of travel.
  - All brake lamps are open.
  - All brake lamp grounds are open.
  - A circuit has a wiring problem, terminal corrosion, or poor connection.
  - A loose or corroded EBCM ground exists.

Test Description

The numbers below refer to the step numbers on the diagnostic table.

3. This DTC detects an open stop lamp switch signal circuit from the stop lamp side of the splice pack to the EBCM.

4. The EBCM sources 5 volts on the stop lamp switch signal circuit. This small voltage has a ground path through the stop lamp bulbs. This DTC sets if the path to ground is open.

Step	Action	Yes	No
1	Did you perform the Diagnostic System Check - Vehicle?	Go to Step 2	Go to Diagnostic System Check

LTV0500000004282

Fig. 31 Code C0161: ABS/TCS Brake Switch Circuit Fault (Part 2 of 3). Equinox, Torrent & Vue

Circuit Description

The controller area network (CAN) serial data circuit is a high speed serial data bus used to communicate information between the engine control module (ECM) and the electronic brake control module (EBCM). The ECM provides the EBCM with engine RPM data via the serial data message. The EBCM uses this information for traction control system (TCS) operation.

The CAN bus circuit is monitored continuously after the ignition switch is turned to the ON position.

DTC Descriptor

This diagnostic procedure supports the following DTC:

DTC C0236 TCS RPM Signal Circuit Malfunction

Conditions for Running the DTC

The ignition is ON.

Conditions for Setting the DTC

- The EBCM receives an incorrect engine RPM message 3 seconds after start-up from the ECM.
- The EBCM continuously monitors for invalid data.

Action Taken When the DTC Sets

If equipped, the following actions occur:

- The EBCM will disable the TCS.
- The antilock brake system (ABS) telltale is not illuminated.
- The ABS is not disabled.

Conditions for Clearing the DTC

- The condition for the DTC is no longer present.
- Using a scan tool, clear the DTC function.
- The EBCM automatically clears the history DTC when a current DTC is not detected in 100 consecutive drive cycles.

LTV0500000004284

Fig. 32 Code C0236: TCS RPM Signal Circuit Fault (Part 1 of 3). Equinox, Torrent & Vue

Step	Action	Yes	No
2	1. Press the brake pedal. 2. With the scan tool, observe the Brake Switch Status parameter in the ABS data list. Does the Brake Switch Status parameter display Applied?	Go to Step 4	Go to Step 3
3	Test the signal circuit of the stop lamp switch for an open. Did you find and correct the condition?	Go to Step 9	Go to Step 7
4	Press the brake pedal. Are all of the stop lamps OFF?	Go to Step 5	Go to Diagnostic Aids
5	Test the feed circuit of the stop lamps for an open or high resistance. Did you find and correct the condition?	Go to Step 9	Go to Step 6
6	Test the ground circuit of the stop lamps for an open or high resistance. Did you find and correct the condition?	Go to Step 9	Go to Diagnostic Aids
7	Inspect for poor connections at the harness connector of the electronic brake control module (EBCM). Did you find and correct the condition?	Go to Step 9	Go to Step 8
8	Replace the EBCM. Did you complete the repair?	Go to Step 9	--
9	1. Use the scan tool in order to clear the DTCs. 2. Operate the vehicle within the Conditions for Running the DTC as specified in the supporting text. Does the DTC reset?	Go to Step 2	System OK

LTV0500000004283

Fig. 31 Code C0161: ABS/TCS Brake Switch Circuit Fault (Part 3 of 3). Equinox, Torrent & Vue

Diagnostic Aids

Possible causes of this DTC are as follows:

- Check the ECM DTCs.
- Check the EBCM for any communication DTCs, and diagnose any powertrain or communication DTCs first.
- The EBCM is not receiving the message from the ECM.
- The CAN HI and CAN LO circuits are shorted together.
- The CAN HI and CAN LO circuit is shorted to ground.
- The CAN HI and CAN LO circuit is shorted to voltage.

Test Description

The numbers below refer to the step numbers on the diagnostic table.

2. This step tests for a short to ground between the CAN HI and CAN LO circuits.

3. This step tests the CAN HI and CAN LO circuits for a short together.

4. This step checks to see if the DTC will reset as current.

Step	Action	Yes	No
1	Did you perform the Diagnostic System Check - Vehicle?	Go to Step 2	Go to Diagnostic System Check - Vehicle in Vehicle DTC Information

LTV0500000004285

Fig. 32 Code C0236: TCS RPM Signal Circuit Fault (Part 2 of 3). Equinox, Torrent & Vue

Step	Action	Yes	No
2	1. Turn OFF the ignition. 2. Disconnect the electronic brake control module (EBCM). 3. Disconnect the engine control module (ECM) connector. 4. Using the DMM, test the controller area network (CAN) HI and CAN LO circuits for a short to ground between the ECM and the EBCM. Did you find and correct the condition?	Go to Step 6	Go to Step 3
3	Using the DMM, test the CAN HI and CAN LO circuits between the ECM and the EBCM for being shorted together or shorted to voltage. Did you find and correct the condition?	Go to Step 6	Go to Step 4
4	1. Use the scan tool in order to clear the DTCs. 2. Test drive the vehicle. Did DTC C0236 reset?	Go to Step 5	Go to Step 6
5	Replace the EBCM Did you complete the repair?	Go to Step 6	--
6	1. Use the scan tool in order to clear the DTCs. 2. Operate the vehicle within the Conditions for Running the DTC as specified in the supporting text. Does the DTC reset?	Go to Step 2	System OK

LTV0500000004286

Fig. 32 Code C0236: TCS RPM Signal Circuit Fault (Part 3 of 3). Equinox, Torrent & Vue

ANTI-LOCK BRAKES

Circuit Description

The controller area network (CAN) serial data circuit is a high speed serial data bus used to communicate information between the engine control module (ECM) and the electronic brake control module (EBCM). Traction control is simultaneously controlled by the ECM and the EBCM. The ECM sends engine torque data via serial data communications to the EBCM. The EBCM uses this message to determine traction control operation.

The CAN bus circuit is monitored continuously after the ignition switch is turned to the ON position.

DTC Descriptor

This diagnostic procedure supports the following DTC:

DTC C0241 PCM Indicated Requested Torque Malfunction

Conditions for Running the DTC

The ignition is ON.

Conditions for Setting the DTC

- The EBCM receives an incorrect engine torque message 3 seconds after start-up from the ECM.
- The EBCM continuously monitors for invalid data.

Action Taken When the DTC Sets

If equipped, the following actions occur:

- The EBCM will disable the TCS.
- The antilock brake system (ABS) telltale is not illuminated.
- The ABS is not disabled.

Conditions for Clearing the DTC

- The condition for the DTC is no longer present.
- Using a scan tool, clear the DTC function.
- The EBCM automatically clears the history DTC when a current DTC is not detected in 100 consecutive drive cycles.

LTV0500000004287

Fig. 33   Code C0241: PCM Indicated Requested Torque Fault (Part 1 of 3). Equinox, Torrent & Vue

	Action		Yes	No
2	1. Turn OFF the ignition. 2. Disconnect the electronic brake control module (EBCM). 3. Disconnect the engine control module (ECM) connector. 4. Using the DMM, test the controller area network (CAN) HI and CAN LO circuits for a short to ground between the ECM and the EBCM. Did you find and correct the condition?		Go to Step 6	Go to Step 3
3	Using the DMM, test the CAN HI and CAN LO circuits between the ECM and the EBCM for being shorted together or shorted to voltage. Did you find and correct the condition?		Go to Step 6	Go to Step 4
4	1. Use the scan tool in order to clear the DTCs. 2. Test drive the vehicle. Did DTC C0241 reset?		Go to Step 5	Go to Step 6
5	Replace the EBCM. Did you complete the repair?		Go to Step 6	--
6	1. Use the scan tool in order to clear the DTCs. 2. Operate the vehicle within the Conditions for Running the DTC as specified in the supporting text. Does the DTC reset?		Go to Step 2	System OK

LTV0500000004289

Fig. 33   Code C0241: PCM Indicated Requested Torque Fault (Part 3 of 3). Equinox, Torrent & Vue

Diagnostic Aids

Possible causes of this DTC are as follows:

- Check the ECM DTCs.
- Check the EBCM for any communication DTCs, and diagnose any powertrain or communication DTCs first.
- The EBCM is not receiving the message from the ECM.
- The CAN HI and CAN LO circuits are shorted together.
- The CAN HI and CAN LO circuit is shorted to ground.
- The CAN HI and CAN LO circuit is shorted to voltage.

Test Description

The numbers below refer to the step numbers on the diagnostic table.

2. This step tests for a short to ground between the CAN HI and CAN LO circuits.

3. This step tests the CAN HI and CAN LO circuits for a short together.

4. This step checks to see if the DTC will reset as current.

Step	Action	Yes	No
1	Did you perform the Diagnostic System Check - Vehicle?	Go to Step 2	Go to Diagnostic System Check

LTV0500000004288

Fig. 33   Code C0241: PCM Indicated Requested Torque Fault (Part 2 of 3). Equinox, Torrent & Vue

Circuit Description

As the wheel spins, the wheel speed sensor produces an alternating current signal. The electronic brake control module (EBCM) uses the frequency of the AC signal to calculate the wheel speed.

DTC Descriptors

This diagnostic procedure supports the following DTCs:

DTC C0245 Wheel Speed Sensor Frequency Error

Conditions for Running the DTC

- The ignition switch is ON
- The DTC can be set after system initialization.

Conditions for Setting the DTC

- The EBCM detects a deviation between 2 wheel speeds at either side of the vehicle, or at the front or rear axle of greater than 6 km/h (3.75 mph) at a vehicle speed of less than 100 km/h (62 mph).
- The EBCM detects a deviation between 2 wheel speeds at either side of the vehicle, or at the front or rear axle of greater than 6 percent of the vehicle speed at greater than 100 km/h (62 mph).

This DTC will set when the EBCM cannot specifically identify which wheel speed sensor is causing the malfunction. If the EBCM can identify the specific wheel speed sensor causing the malfunction, DTC C0245 will become a history DTC, and the DTC associated with the sensor (DTC C0036, DTC C0041, DTC C0046, DTC C0051) will be set concurrent with DTC C0245.

Diagnose each wheel speed sensor individually.

Action Taken When the DTC Sets

If equipped, the following actions occur:

- A malfunction DTC stores.
- The antilock brake system (ABS) and the traction control system (TCS) disable.
- The amber ABS indicator turns ON.
- The traction control switch light emitting diode (LED) turns OFF.

Conditions for Clearing the DTC

- The condition for the DTC is no longer present.
- Using a scan tool, clear the DTC function.
- The EBCM automatically clears the history DTC when a current DTC is not detected in 100 consecutive drive cycles.

LTV0500000004290

Fig. 34   Code C0245: Wheel Speed Sensor Frequency Error (Part 1 of 4). Equinox, Torrent & Vue

Diagnostic Aids

- It is very important that a thorough inspection of the wiring and connectors be performed. Failure to carefully and fully inspect wiring and connectors may result in misdiagnosis, causing part replacement with reappearance of the malfunction.
- Thoroughly inspect any circuitry that may be causing the complaint for the following conditions:
  - Backed out terminals
  - Improper mating
  - Broken locks
  - Improperly formed or damaged terminals
  - Poor terminal-to-wiring connections
  - Physical damage to the wiring harness
- The following conditions may cause an intermittent malfunction:
  - A poor connection
  - Rubbed-through wire insulation
  - A broken wire inside the insulation
- If the customer's comments reflect that the amber ABS/TCS indicator is on only during moist environmental conditions (rain, snow, vehicle wash), inspect all the wheel speed sensor circuitry for signs of water intrusion. If the DTC is not current, clear all DTCs and simulate the effects of water intrusion by using the following procedure:

1. Spray the suspected area with a 5 percent saltwater solution. Add 2 teaspoons of salt to 12 ounces of water to make a 5 percent saltwater solution.
2. Test drive the vehicle over various road surfaces (bumps, turns, etc.) above 40 km/h (25 mph) for at least 30 seconds.
3. If the DTC returns, replace the suspected harness.

Test Description

The numbers below refer to the step numbers on the diagnostic table.

2. If DTC C0245 is a history code, this step checks if a specific Wheel Speed Circuit Malfunction DTC is set concurrently with DTC C0245.

7. This step checks if the wheel speed sensor harness is routed in close proximity to the spark plug wires.

9. In this step, if the scan tool can record any erroneous wheel speed sensor signals, diagnose that sensors first.

LTV0500000004291

Fig. 34 Code C0245: Wheel Speed Sensor Frequency Error (Part 2 of 4). Equinox, Torrent & Vue

			Go to	Go to
9	1. Install a scan tool. 2. Turn the ignition switch to the RUN position. 3. Set the scan tool to Snap Shot Auto Trigger mode and monitor the wheel speed sensors. 4. Carefully drive the vehicle above 40 km/h (25 mph) for several minutes. Did the scan tool trigger on any of the wheel speed sensors?		Go to Step 10	Go to Step 11
10	Note which wheel speed sensor triggered the scan tool. Follow the appropriate Wheel Speed Sensor Malfunction DTC table for the wheel speed sensor that triggered. Is the repair complete?		Go to Step 14	--
11	1. Reconnect all previously disconnected components. 2. Using a scan tool clear the DTC. 3. Remove the scan tool from the DLC. 4. Carefully drive the vehicle above 40 km/h (25 mph) for several minutes. Does the DTC reset as a current DTC?		Go to Step 13	Go to Step 12
12	The malfunction is intermittent. Inspect all connectors and harnesses for damage that may result in an open or high resistance when connected. Is the repair complete?		Go to Step 14	--
13	Replace the EBCM. Did you complete the repair?		Go to Step 14	--
14	1. Use the scan tool in order to clear the DTCs. 2. Operate the vehicle within the conditions for running the DTC as specified in the supporting text. Does the DTC reset?		Go to Step 2	System OK

LTV0500000004293

Fig. 34 Code C0245: Wheel Speed Sensor Frequency Error (Part 4 of 4). Equinox, Torrent & Vue

Step	Action	Yes	No
1	Did you perform the Diagnostic System Check - Vehicle?	Go to Step 2	Go to Diagnostic System Check
2	Are the following DTCs set concurrently with a history DTC C0245? • DTC C0036 • DTC C0041 • DTC C0046 • DTC C0051	Go to Diagnostic Trouble Code (DTC) List	Go to Step 3
3	Inspect the wheel speed sensor for physical damage. Is physical damage of the wheel speed sensor evident?	Go to Step 4	Go to Step 5
4	Replace the wheel speed sensor. Is the replacement complete?	Go to Step 14	--
5	Inspect the wiring harness for physical damage. Is physical damage of the wiring harness evident?	Go to Step 6	Go to Step 7
6	Repair the wiring harness or connector. Is the replacement complete?	Go to Step 14	--
7	Inspect wiring harness for proper routing of the wheel speed sensor harness. Verify that the wheel speed sensor harness is routed away from the spark plug wires. Is the wheel speed sensor harness properly routed?	Go to Step 9	Go to Step 8
8	Reroute the wheel speed sensor harness away from the spark plug wires. Is the reroute complete?	Go to Step 14	--

LTV0500000004292

Fig. 34 Code C0245: Wheel Speed Sensor Frequency Error (Part 3 of 4). Equinox, Torrent & Vue

Circuit Description

The transmission control module (TCM) monitors various parameters and will not allow traction control operation if any parameter falls outside a specified range.

DTC Descriptor

This diagnostic procedure supports the following DTC:

DTC C0276 TCM Traction Control Not Allowed

Conditions for Running the DTC

- The ignition is ON.
- Ignition voltage is greater than 8 volts.

Conditions for Setting the DTC

The TCM sends a serial data message to the electronic brake control module (EBCM) indicating that torque reduction is temporarily not allowed.

Action Taken When the DTC Sets

- The EBCM disables the engine management portion of the Traction Control System (TCS).
- The Traction Off indicator turns ON.
- The Antilock Brake System (ABS) remains functional.

Conditions for Clearing the DTC

- The condition for the DTC is no longer present and the DTC is cleared with a scan tool.
- The EBCM automatically clears the history DTC when a current DTC is not detected in 100 consecutive drive cycles.

Diagnostic Aids

This DTC is for information only. As an aid to the technician, this DTC indicates that there are no problems in the ABS/TCS System. This DTC C0276 will set in addition to TCM P codes, verify and correct the DTCs in the transmission control module.

Step	Action	Yes	No
1	Did you perform the Diagnostic System Check - Vehicle?	--	Go to Diagnostic System Check

LTV0500000004294

Fig. 35 Codes C0275 Or C0276: TCM Traction Control Not Allowed. Equinox, Torrent & Vue

Circuit Description

The internal fault detection is handled inside the control module. No external circuits are involved.

DTC Descriptor

This diagnostic procedure supports the following DTC:

DTC C0550 ECU Malfunction

Conditions for Running the DTC

The microprocessor runs the program to detect an internal fault when power up is commanded. The only requirements are voltage and ground. This program runs even if the voltage is out of the valid operating range.

Conditions for Setting the DTC

- The control module detects an internal write malfunction.
- The control module detects an internal checksum malfunction.

Action Taken When the DTC Sets

If equipped, the following module specific actions may occur:

- The antilock brake system (ABS) telltale turns ON.
- The BRAKE warning telltale turns ON.
- The traction control system (TCS) telltale light emitting diode (LED) turns OFF.

Conditions for Clearing the DTC

- The condition for the DTC is no longer present.
- Using a scan tool, clear the DTC function.
- The EBCM automatically clears the history DTC when a current DTC is not detected in 100 consecutive drive cycles.

Diagnostic Aids

- This DTC may be stored as a history DTC without affecting the operation of the module. If stored only as a history DTC and not retrieved as a current DTC, do not replace the module.
- If this DTC is retrieved as both a current and history DTC, replace the module.

LTV0500000004295

Fig. 36   Codes C0550: ECU Fault (Part 1 of 2). Equinox, Torrent & Vue

Step	Action	Yes	No
1	Did you perform the Diagnostic System Check - Vehicle?	Go to Step 2	Go to Diagnostic System Check
2	1. Install a scan tool 2. Turn ON the ignition, with the engine OFF. 3. Retrieve DTCs. Is DTC retrieved as a current DTC?	Go to Step 3	Go to Diagnostic Aids
3	Replace the control module setting the DTC as current. Did you complete the replacement?	Go to Step 4	--
4	1. Use the scan tool in order to clear the DTCs. 2. Operate the vehicle within the Conditions for Running the DTC as specified in the supporting text. Does the DTC reset?	Go to Step 2	System OK

LTV0500000004296

Fig. 36   Codes C0550: ECU Fault (Part 2 of 2). Equinox, Torrent & Vue

Step	Action	Yes	No
1	Did you perform the Diagnostic System Check - Vehicle?	Go to Step 2	Go to Diagnostic System Check
2	Are any other DTCs present besides DTC C0551?	Go to Diagnostic Trouble Code (DTC) List	Go to Step 3
3	Replace the electronic brake control module (EBCM). Did you complete the repair?	Go to Step 4	--
4	1. Use the scan tool in order to clear the DTCs. 2. Operate the vehicle within the Conditions for Running the DTC as specified in the supporting text. Does the DTC reset?	Go to Step 2	System OK

LTV0500000004298

Fig. 37   Code C0551: Option Configuration Error (Part 2 of 2). Equinox, Torrent & Vue

Circuit Description

The electronic brake control module (EBCM) learns the model options that it is installed in by using the Vehicle ID information from the body control module (BCM) via the class 2 serial data line. Each time the vehicle is in the RUN position the BCM communicates this information via class 2. The EBCM internally compares the VIN and option information with that information stored in the BCM.

DTC Descriptor

This diagnostic procedure supports the following DTC:

DTC C0551 Option Configuration Error

Condition for Running the DTC

- The EBCM detects digit 2-9 of the VIN, and is not zeros.
- The condition must occur when the ignition switch is first turned on.

Conditions for Setting the DTC

- The EBCM detects information from the BCM that the options are incorrect, FWD or AWD.
- The condition must occur when the ignition switch is first turned on.

Action Taken When the DTC Sets

If equipped, the following actions occur:

- The EBCM disables the ABS/traction control system (TCS) for the duration of the ignition cycle.
- A DTC malfunction will set.
- The ABS indicator turns.
- The traction control indicator turns ON.
- The red brake warning light turns ON.

Conditions for Clearing the DTC

- The EBCM recognizes that information from the BCM is valid information, FWD or AWD.
- A history DTC will clear after 100 consecutive ignition cycles if the condition for the malfunction is no longer present.

Diagnostic Aids

DTC C0551 is set when the EBCM detects a mismatch between itself and the programmed BCM in the vehicle by monitoring the BCM class 2 message.

LTV0500000004297

Fig. 37   Code C0551: Option Configuration Error (Part 1 of 2). Equinox, Torrent & Vue

Circuit Description

The electronic brake control module (EBCM) is required to operate within a specified range of voltage to function properly. During antilock brake system (ABS) and traction control system (TCS) operation, there are current requirements that will cause the voltage to drop. Because of this, voltage is monitored out of ABS/TCS control to indicate a good charging system condition, and also during ABS/TCS control when voltage may drop significantly. The EBCM also monitors for high voltage conditions which could damage the EBCM.

DTC Descriptor

This diagnostic procedure supports the following DTC:

DTC C0896 Device Voltage Range Performance

Conditions for Running the DTC

- The ignition switch is ON.
- The DTC can be set after system initialization.

Conditions for Setting the DTC

- The EBCM operating voltage falls below 9.4 volts.
- The EBCM operating voltage rises above 17.4 volts.
- The low voltage or the high voltage is detected for more than 500 milliseconds with the vehicle speed above 6.5 km/h (4 mph).

Action Taken When the DTC Sets

If equipped, the following actions occur:

- A malfunction DTC is stored.
- The ABS telltale turns ON.
- The ABS, TCS, and dynamic rear proportion (DRP) are disabled.

Conditions for Clearing the DTC

- The condition for the DTC is no longer present.
- Using a scan tool, clear the DTC function.
- The EBCM automatically clears the history DTC when a current DTC is not detected in 100 consecutive drive cycles.

LTV0500000004299

Fig. 38   Code C0896: Device Voltage Range Performance (Part 1 of 3). Equinox, Torrent & Vue

Diagnostic Aids

- It is very important that a thorough inspection of the wiring and connectors be performed. Failure to carefully and fully inspect wiring and connectors may result in misdiagnosis, causing part replacement with reappearance of the malfunction.
- Thoroughly inspect any circuitry that may be causing the complaint for the following conditions:
  - Backed out terminals
  - Improper mating
  - Broken locks
  - Improperly formed or damaged terminals
  - Poor terminal-to-wiring connections
  - Physical damage to the wiring harness
- The following conditions may cause an intermittent malfunction:
  - A poor connection
  - Rubbed-through wire insulation
  - A broken wire inside the insulation

Test Description

The numbers below refer to the step numbers on the diagnostic table.

2. This step checks if the voltage is above the maximum of the range.

4. This step checks if the voltage is below the minimum of the range.

6. This step checks for the integrity of the ground circuit.

Step	Action	Values	Yes	No
1	Did you perform the Diagnostic System Check - Vehicle?	--	Go to Step 2	Go to Diagnostic System Check

LTV0500000004300

Fig. 38 Code C0896: Device Voltage Range Performance (Part 2 of 3). Equinox, Torrent & Vue

Test Description

The numbers below refer to the step numbers on the diagnostic table.

1. This step ensures that the battery and the vehicle primary power and ground systems are functioning correctly.

3. Lack of communication may be due to a particular malfunction of a serial data circuit. The information in Scan Tool does not Communicate with Class 2 Device will provide a list of modules, and the associated data network no communication diagnostic link.

4. A module that is operating in the incorrect power mode, based on key position, may cause other vehicle symptoms, and/or DTCs to set. The information in Power Mode Mismatch will correct the condition before checking for module DTCs or symptoms.

8. This step ensures that all data link communication DTCs are diagnosed before system level DTCs.

9. This step ensures that all electronic control unit (ECU) internal DTCs are diagnosed before other system level DTCs.

10. This step ensures that all device voltage DTCs are diagnosed before other system level DTCs.

Step	Action	Yes	No
1	Perform the following preliminary inspections: • Ensure that the battery is fully charged. • Ensure that the battery cables are clean and tight. • Inspect for any open fuses. • Inspect the easily accessible systems or the visible system components for obvious damage or conditions that could cause the symptom. • Ensure that the grounds are clean, tight, and in the correct location. • Inspect for aftermarket devices that could affect the operation of the system. • Search for applicable service bulletins. Did you find and correct the condition?	System OK	Go to Step 2
2	Install a scan tool. Does the scan tool power up?	Go to Step 3	Check Scan Tool Does Not Power Up
3	1. Turn ON the ignition, with the engine OFF. 2. Attempt to establish communication with all of the control modules on the vehicle. Does the scan tool communicate with all of the expected vehicle control modules?	Go to Step 4	Check Scan Tool Does Not Communicate with Class 2 Device

LTV0500000004312

Fig. 39 Diagnostic System Check (Part 1 of 3). Hummer H2

Step	Action	Values	Yes	No
2	1. Turn all the accessories OFF. 2. Install a scan tool. 3. Start the engine. 4. Use the scan tool to monitor the Ignition Battery Voltage parameter in the electronic brake control module (EBCM) Data List, while running the engine at approximately 2000 RPM. Is the monitored battery voltage within the specified range?	9.4-17.4 V	Go to Step 4	Go to Step 3
3	Use a DMM to measure the voltage between the battery positive terminal and ground. Is the voltage within the specified range?	0-17.4 V	Go to Step 5	Go to Symptoms
4	Continue to monitor the battery voltage with the scan tool while running the engine at approximately 2000 RPM. Is the monitored battery voltage within the specified range?	0-9.4 V	Go to Step 6	Go to Step 5
5	1. Turn the ignition switch to the OFF position. 2. Disconnect the scan tool if still connected. 3. Test drive the vehicle above 6.5 km/h (4 mph). Did DTC C0896 reset?	--	Go to Step 10	Go to Diagnostic System Check
6	1. Turn the ignition switch to the OFF position. 2. Disconnect the EBCM connector. 3. Use a DMM to measure the resistance between the connector terminal 4 and a good ground. Is the resistance within the specified range?	0-5 ohms	Go to Step 8	Go to Step 7
7	Repair open or high resistance in the ground circuit. Is the repair complete?	--	Go to Step 11	--
8	1. Turn the ignition switch to the RUN position. 2. Use a DMM to measure the voltage between terminal 18 and 4. Is the voltage within the specified range?	Above 9.4 V	Go to Step 9	Go to Symptoms
9	1. Turn the ignition switch to the OFF position. 2. Reconnect the EBCM connector. 3. Disconnect the scan tool if the scan tool is still connected. 4. Test drive the vehicle above 6 km/h (3.5 mph). Did DTC C0896 reset?	--	Go to Step 10	Go to Step 11
10	Replace the EBCM. Did you complete the repair?	--	Go to Step 11	--
11	1. Use the scan tool in order to clear the DTCs. 2. Operate the vehicle within the Conditions for Running the DTC as specified in the supporting text. Does the DTC reset?	--	Go to Step 2	System OK

LTV0500000004301

Fig. 38 Code C0896: Device Voltage Range Performance (Part 3 of 3). Equinox, Torrent & Vue

Step	Action	Yes	No
	Important: 1. To ensure that retained accessory power (RAP) mode is inactive, if equipped, open the driver door during the following step. 2. The engine may start during the following step. Turn OFF the engine as soon as you have observed the crank power mode.		
4	1. Access the Power Mode parameter on the scan tool. 2. Rotate the ignition switch (operate the ignition mode switch) through all positions while observing the Power Mode parameter. Refer to Body Control System Description and Operation for a list of the power mode states that correspond with each switch position. Does the Power Mode parameter reading on the scan tool match the ignition switch position for all switch positions?	Go to Step 5	Check Power Mode Mismatch
5	Attempt to start the engine. Does the engine crank?	Go to Step 6	Go to Symptoms
6	Attempt to start the engine. Does the engine start and idle?	Go to Step 7	Go to Engine Cranks but Does Not Run
7	**Important:** Do not clear any DTCs unless instructed by a diagnostic procedure. Use the appropriate scan tool selections to obtain DTCs for each of the control modules. Does the scan tool display any DTCs?	Go to Step 8	Go to Step 12
8	Does the scan tool display any DTCs that begin with a "U"?	Go to Diagnostic Trouble Code (DTC)	Go to Step 9
9	**Important:** If any of these DTCs are displayed, diagnose them before diagnosing any other DTCs or symptoms. Does the scan tool display DTC B1000, B1004, B1007, B1009, C0550, C0563, P0601, P0602, P0604, P0606, or P2610?	Go to Diagnostic Trouble Code (DTC)	Go to Step 10

LTV0500000004313

Fig. 39 Diagnostic System Check (Part 2 of 3). Hummer H2

10	**Important:** If any of these DTCs are displayed, diagnose them before diagnosing any other DTCs or symptoms. Does the scan tool display DTC B1440, C0896, P0562, or P0563?		Go to Diagnostic Trouble Code (DTC) List - Vehicle	Go to Step 11
11	**Important:** If any of the remaining DTCs are powertrain DTCs, select Captured Info in order to store the powertrain DTC information with a scan tool. If multiple DTCs are stored, diagnose the DTCs in the following order: 1. Component level DTCs, such as sensor DTCs, solenoid DTCs, and relay DTCs. 2. System level DTCs, such as misfire DTCs, evaporative emission (EVAP) system DTCs, and fuel trim DTCs. Diagnose the remaining DTCs.		Go to Diagnostic Trouble Code (DTC) List - Vehicle	--
12	Is the customers concern with inspection/maintenance (I/M) testing?		Go to Inspection/Maintenance (I/M) System Check	Go to Symptoms - Vehicle

LTV0500000004314

**Fig. 39   Diagnostic System Check (Part 3 of 3).
Hummer H2**

Step	Action	Values	Yes	No
1	Did you perform the ABS Diagnostic System Check?	--	Go to Step 2	Go to Diagnostic System Check
2	1. Use a scan tool in order to clear the DTCs. 2. Turn OFF the ignition for 5 seconds. 3. Start the engine. 4. Observe the scan tool for up to 60 seconds in order to verify the DTC resets. Does the DTC set?	--	Go to Step 3	Go to Diagnostic Aids
3	1. Turn OFF the ignition. 2. Disconnect the TC2 mode switch harness connector. 3. Turn ON the ignition. 4. Connect a test lamp between the IGN 1 voltage circui, IGN E fuse, and a good ground. Does the test lamp illuminate?	--	Go to Step 4	Go to Step 11
4	1. Turn OFF the ignition. 2. Reconnect the TC2 mode switch harness connector. 3. Turn ON the ignition. 4. Backprobe the TC2 mode switch harness connector in order to connect a DMM between the TC2 mode switch signal circuit and a good ground. 5. Measure the DC voltage on the TC2 mode switch signal circuit. Does the TC2 mode switch signal measure with in the specified range?	12 V	Go to Step 5	Go to Step 6
5	1. Press and hold the TC2 mode switch. 2. Use a DMM in order to measure the DC voltage on the TC2 mode switch signal circuit. Does the TC2 mode switch signal measure within the specified range?	0.5 V	Go to Step 7	Go to Step 13
6	Test the TC2 mode switch signal circuit for a short to ground. Did you find and correct the condition?	--	Go to Step 14	Go to Step 12
7	1. Turn OFF the ignition. 2. Disconnect the wiring harness connector from the EBCM. 3. Connect the J 39700 universal pinout box using the J 39700-530 cable adapter to the EBCM harness connector only. 4. Turn ON the ignition. 5. Use a DMM in order to measure the DC voltage on the TC2 mode switch signal circuit. Does the TC2 mode switch signal measure within the specified range?	12 V	Go to Step 9	Go to Step 8

LTV0500000004316

**Fig. 40   Code B3632: TC2 Mode Switch Signal Fault
(Part 2 of 3). Hummer H2**

8	Repair the open in the TC2 mode switch signal circuit. Did you complete the repair?		Go to Step 14	--
9	Inspect for poor connections at the harness connector of the EBCM. Did you find and correct the condition?		Go to Step 14	Go to Step 10
10	Replace the EBCM. Did you complete the replacement?		Go to Step 14	--
11	Repair the open or short to ground in the IGN 1 voltage circuit, IGN E fuse. Did you complete the repair?		Go to Step 14	--
12	Inspect for open in the TC2 switch ground circuit or poor connections at the harness connector of the TC2 mode switch. Did you find and correct the condition?		Go to Step 14	Go to Step 13
13	Replace the TC2 mode switch. Did you complete the replacement?		Go to Step 14	--
14	1. Use the scan tool in order to clear the DTCs. 2. Operate the vehicle within the Conditions for Running the DTC as specified in the supporting text. Does the DTC reset?		Go to Step 3	System OK

LTV0500000004317

**Fig. 40   Code B3632: TC2 Mode Switch Signal Fault
(Part 3 of 3). Hummer H2**

Circuit Description

The TC2 mode switch is a momentary-contact switch that can be used to limit the traction control function. Each time the TC2 mode switch is pressed, the TC2 switch full traction limited status changes. When the TC2 mode switch is released, voltage on the TC2 mode switch signal circuit is approximately 12 volts. When the TC2 mode switch is pressed, voltage on the TC2 mode switch signal circuit is approximately 0.5 volts.

Conditions for Running the DTC

In order to detect a continuously low or high TC2 mode switch signal:

The ignition is ON.

OR:

In order to detect a continuously pressed TC2 mode switch:

- The ignition is ON.
- The engine speed is greater than 450 RPM.

Conditions for Setting the DTC

Either of the following conditions may cause DTC B3626 to set:

- The TC2 mode switch signal is detected as excessively low or high for 200 milliseconds.
- The TC2 mode switch is detected as pressed for 60 seconds.

Action Taken When the DTC Sets

- The EBCM disables the traction assist.
- The TCS LED switch telltale is disable.

Conditions for Clearing the DTC

The conditions for setting the DTC are no longer present and you use the scan tool Clear DTCs function.

Diagnostic Aids

Press and release the TC2 mode switch several times while observing the traction LED switch telltale in order to verify that the TC2 full traction limited status changes each time the switch is pressed and that DTC B3626 does not set. Using the scan tool in order to observe the Mode Switch Pressed or Released status may also be helpful in diagnosing an intermittent fault within the switch.

Thoroughly inspect connections or circuitry that may cause an intermittent malfunction.

Test Description

The number below refers to the step number on the diagnostic table.

4. This step tests for voltage on the TC2 mode switch signal circuit indicating an unpressed TC2 mode switch.

5. This step tests for voltage on the TC2 mode switch signal circuit indicating a pressed TC2 mode switch.

LTV0500000004315

**Fig. 40   Code B3632: TC2 Mode Switch Signal Fault
(Part 1 of 3). Hummer H2**

Circuit Description

As the wheel spins, the wheel speed sensor produces an AC signal. The electronic brake control module (EBCM) uses the frequency of the AC signal to calculate the wheel speed.

Conditions for Running the DTC

C0035 C0040 C0045 C0050

The ignition is ON.

C0036 C0041 C0046 C0051
- Vehicle speed is over 40 km/h (25 mph).
- The brake pedal is not pressed.
- The ABS is not active.

Conditions for Setting the DTC

C0035 C0040 C0045 C0050

One of the following conditions exists for 0.02 seconds:

- A short to voltage in the wheel speed sensor signal circuit.
- An open in the wheel speed sensor signal circuit.

C0036 C0041 C0046 C0051

All of the following conditions exists for 0.01 seconds:

- The suspect wheel speed equals zero.
- The other wheel speeds are greater than 40 km/h (25 mph) for 0.01 seconds.
- The suspect wheel equals zero during drive off, and the other wheels are greater than 18 km/h (11 mph).
- A short to ground the wheel speed sensor signal circuit is shorted to ground.
- A deviation of two wheel speeds at either side of the vehicle greater than 6 km/h (4 mph), or at the front axle greater than 10 km/h (6 mph) for a time period of 10 to 20 seconds.

Action Taken When the DTC Sets

If equipped, the following actions occur:

- The EBCM disables the ABS/TCS for the duration of the ignition cycle.
- A DTC malfunction will set.
- The ABS indicator turns ON.
- The Red BRAKE Warning indicator could turn on.

Conditions for Clearing the DTC

- The condition for the DTC is no longer present and the DTC is cleared with a scan tool.
- The electronic brake control module (EBCM) automatically clears the history DTC when a current DTC is not detected in 100 consecutive drive cycles.

LTV0500000004318

**Fig. 41   Codes C0035–C0051: Wheel Speed Sensor
Fault (Part 1 of 3). Hummer H2**

Diagnostic Aids

C0035 C0040 C0045 C0050

If the customer comments that the ABS indicator is ON only during moist environmental conditions (rain, snow, vehicle wash, etc.), inspect the wheel speed sensor wiring for signs of water intrusion. If the DTC is not current, clear all DTCs and simulate the effects of water intrusion by using the following procedure:

1. Spray the suspected area with a 5 percent saltwater solution. To create a 5 percent saltwater solution, add 2 teaspoons of salt to 354 ml (12 oz) of water.
2. Test drive the vehicle over various road surfaces (bumps, turns, etc.) above 40 km/h (25 mph) for at least 30 seconds.
3. If the DTC returns, replace the suspected wheel speed sensor or repair the wheel speed sensor wiring.
4. Rinse the are thoroughly when completed.

C0036 C0041 C0046 C0051

Under the following conditions, 2 Wheel Speed Sensor Input is 0 DTCs are set:

- The 2 suspect wheel speeds equal zero for 10-20 seconds.
- The other wheel speeds are greater than 16 km/h (10 mph).
- The other wheel speeds are within 11 km/h (7 mph) of each other.

Diagnose each wheel speed sensor individually.

C0036 C0041 C0046 C0051

A possible cause of this DTC is electrical noise on the wheel speed sensor harness wiring. Electrical noise could result from the wheel speed sensor wires being routed to close to high energy ignition system components, such as spark plug wires.

Test Description

The numbers below refer to the step numbers on the diagnostic table.

3. This step tests the wheel speed sensor for the proper resistance value.

4. This step ensures that the wheel speed sensor generates the proper voltage.

Step	Action	Value(s)	Yes	No
1	Did you perform the ABS Diagnostic System Check?	--	Go to Step 2	Go to Diagnostic System Check
2	1. Install a scan tool. 2. Turn ON the ignition. 3. Set up the scan tool snap shot feature to trigger for this DTC. 4. Drive the vehicle at a speed greater than the specified value. Does the scan tool indicate that this wheel speed DTC set?	40 km/h (25 mph)	Go to Step 3	Go to Diagnostic Aids

LTV0500000004319

Fig. 41 Codes C0035–C0051: Wheel Speed Sensor Fault (Part 2 of 3). Hummer H2

Step	Action	Value(s)	Yes	No
3	1. Raise and support the vehicle. 2. Disconnect the wheel speed sensor connector. 3. Measure the resistance across the wheel speed sensor. Does the resistance measure within the specified range?	Front Wheels 800-1600 ohms Rear Wheels 4500-5400 ohms	Go to Step 4	Go to Step 8
4	1. Spin the wheel. 2. Measure the AC voltage across the wheel speed sensor. Does the AC voltage measure greater than the specified value?	100 mV	Go to Step 5	Go to Step 8
5	Inspect for poor connections at the harness connector of the wheel speed sensor. Did you find and correct the condition?	--	Go to Step 10	Go to Step 6

6	1. Disconnect the EBCM harness connector.
	2. Install the J 39700 using J 39700-530 to the EBCM harness connector only.
	3. Test the wheel speed sensor circuits for the following:
	  - An open
	  - A short to ground
	  - A short to voltage
	  - Shorted together
	
	Did you find and correct the condition?
		--	Go to Step 10	Go to Step 7

7	Inspect for poor connections at the harness connector for the EBCM. Did you find and correct the condition?	--	Go to Step 10	Go to Step 9
8	Replace the wheel speed sensor. Did you complete the replacement?	--	Go to Step 10	--
9	Replace the EBCM. Did you complete the repair?	--	Go to Step 10	--
10	1. Use the scan tool in order to clear the DTCs. 2. Operate the vehicle within the Conditions for Running the DTC as specified in the supporting text. Does the DTC reset?	--	Go to Step 2	System OK

LTV0500000004320

Fig. 41 Codes C0035–C0051: Wheel Speed Sensor Fault (Part 3 of 3). Hummer H2

Circuit Description

The pump motor is an integral part of the BPMV, while the pump motor relay is integral to the EBCM. The pump motor relay is not engaged during normal system operation. When ABS or TCS operation is required the EBCM activates the pump motor relay and battery power is provided to the pump motor.

Conditions for Running the DTC

- The ignition switch is in the ON position.
- Initialization is complete.

Conditions for Setting the DTC

- Pump motor voltage is not present 60 milliseconds after activation of the pump motor relay.
- Pump motor voltage is present for more than 2.5 seconds with no activation of the pump motor relay.
- Pump motor voltage is not present for 40 milliseconds after the pump motor relay is commanded off.

Action Taken When the DTC Sets

If equipped, the following actions occur:

- The EBCM disables the ABS/TCS for the duration of the ignition cycle.
- A malfunction DTC will set.
- The ABS indicator turns ON.
- The Red BRAKE Warning indicator could turn on.

Conditions for Clearing the DTC

- The condition for the DTC is no longer present and the DTC is cleared with a scan tool.
- The electronic brake control module (EBCM) automatically clears the history DTC when a current DTC is not detected in 100 consecutive drive cycles.

LTV0500000004321

Fig. 42 Code C0110: Pump Motor Circuit Fault (Part 1 of 3). Hummer H2

Diagnostic Aids

- It is very important that a thorough inspection of the wiring and connectors be performed. Failure to carefully and fully inspect wiring and connectors may result in misdiagnosis, causing part replacement with reappearance of the malfunction.
- Thoroughly inspect any circuitry that may be causing the complaint for the following conditions:
  - Backed out terminals
  - Improper mating
  - Broken locks
  - Improperly formed or damaged terminals
  - Poor terminal-to-wiring connections
  - Physical damage to the wiring harness
- The following conditions may cause an intermittent malfunction:
  - A poor connection
  - Rubbed-through wire insulation
  - A broken wire inside the insulation

Test Description

The number below refers to the step number on the diagnostic table.

3. Tests the pump motor circuits of the BPMV for a short to the housing of the BPMV. The wiring from the BPMV to the EBCM should not be repaired.

Step	Action	Value(s)	Yes	No
1	Did you perform the ABS Diagnostic System Check?	--	Go to Step 2	Go to Diagnostic System Check
2	1. Disconnect the EBCM harness connector. 2. Connect the J 39700 Universal Pinout Box using the J 39700-530 Cable Adapter to the EBCM harness connector only. 3. Test both ground circuits of the EBCM including the EBCM ground for a high resistance or an open. 4. Test the Battery Positive Voltage circuits for an open, high resistance, or a short to ground. Did you find and correct the condition?	--	Go to Step 8	Go to Step 3

LTV0500000005202

Fig. 42 Code C0110: Pump Motor Circuit Fault (Part 2 of 3). Hummer H2

Step	Action		Yes	No
3	1. Disconnect the pump motor harness pigtail connector of the BPMV. 2. Measure the resistance between each pump motor control circuit and the housing of the BPMV at the pump motor harness pigtail connector of the BPMV. Does the resistance measure less than the specified value?	5 ohms	Go to Step 4	Go to Step 5
4	Inspect for poor connections at the pump motor harness pigtail connector of the BPMV. Did you find and correct the condition?	--	Go to Step 8	Go to Step 6
5	Inspect for poor connections at the harness connector of the EBCM. Did you find and correct the condition?	--	Go to Step 8	Go to Step 7
6	Replace the BPMV. Did you complete the repair?	--	Go to Step 8	--
7	Replace the EBCM. Did you complete the repair?	--	Go to Step 8	--
8	1. Use the scan tool in order to clear the DTCs. 2. Operate the vehicle within the conditions for Running the DTC as specified in the supporting text. Does the DTC reset?	--	Go to Step 2	System OK

LTV0500000005203

Fig. 42   Code C0110: Pump Motor Circuit Fault (Part 3 of 3). Hummer H2

Diagnostic Aids

- It is very important that a thorough inspection of the wiring and connectors be performed. Failure to carefully and fully inspect wiring and connectors may result in misdiagnosis, causing part replacement with reappearance of the malfunction.
- Thoroughly inspect any circuitry that may be causing the complaint for the following conditions:
  - Backed out terminals
  - Improper mating
  - Broken locks
  - Improperly formed or damaged terminals
  - Poor terminal-to-wiring connections
  - Physical damage to the wiring harness
- The following conditions may cause an intermittent malfunction:
  - A poor connection
  - Rubbed-through wire insulation
  - A broken wire inside the insulation
- The solenoid valve relay is an integral part of the EBCM and is not serviced separately.

Test Description

The number below refers to step number on the diagnostic table.

2. This step determines if the DTC is current.

Step	Action	Yes	No
1	Did you perform the Diagnostic System Check?	Go to Step 2	Go to Diagnostic System Check
2	1. Install a scan tool. 2. Turn ON the ignition, with the engine OFF. 3. Use the scan tool in order to clear the DTCs. Does the DTC reset?	Go to Step 3	Go to Diagnostic Aids

LTV0500000005205

Fig. 43   Code C0121: Valve Relay Circuit Fault (Part 2 of 3). Hummer H2

Circuit Description

The stoplamp switch is a normally open switch, when the brake pedal is depressed the EBCM will sense battery voltage. This allows the EBCM to determine the state of the brake lamps. The EBCM sources 5 volts on the stop lamp switch signal circuit when the stop lamp switch is inactive. The voltage is supplied a ground path through the stop lamp bulbs.

Conditions for Running the DTC

The ignition switch is ON.

Conditions for Setting the DTC

- EBCM detects open in the brake signal circuit.
- Both brake lamps are faulty.
- The stoplamp switch input voltage is between 6.6 and 9 volts for 0.5 second.

Action Taken When the DTC Sets

If equiped, the following actions occur:

- A malfunction DTC will set.
- The EBCM stores this information-only DTC for as long as the condition is present.
- The ABS remains functional.
- The ABS indicator remains OFF.

Conditions for Clearing the DTC

- The condition for the DTC is no longer present and the DTC is cleared with a scan tool.
- The electronic brake control module (EBCM) automatically clears the history DTC when a current DTC is not detected in 100 consecutive drive cycles.

LTV0500000005207

Fig. 44   Code C0161: Stoplamp Switch Voltage Fault (Part 1 of 3). Hummer H2

Circuit Description

The solenoid valve relay supplies power to the solenoid valve coils in the EBCM. The solenoid valve relay, located in the EBCM, is activated whenever the ignition switch is in the RUN position and no faults are present. The solenoid valve relay remains engaged until the ignition is turned OFF or a failure is detected.

Conditions for Running the DTC

The ignition switch is in the ON position.

Conditions for Setting the DTC

- DTC C0121 will set anytime the solenoid valve relay is commanded on and the EBCM does not see battery voltage at the solenoid valves.
- DTC C0121 will set anytime the EBCM commands the solenoid valve relay off and battery voltage is still present at the solenoid valves.

Action Taken When the DTC Sets

If equipped, the following actions occur:

- The EBCM disables the ABS/TCS/DRP for the duration of the ignition cycle.
- A malfunction DTC is set.
- The ABS indicator turns ON.
- The TRAC Off indicator turns ON.
- The Red BRAKE Warning indicator could turn on.

Conditions for Clearing the DTC

- The condition for the DTC is no longer present and the DTC is cleared with a scan tool.
- The electronic brake control module (EBCM) automatically clears the history DTC when a current DTC is not detected in 100 consecutive drive cycles.

LTV0500000005204

Fig. 43   Code C0121: Valve Relay Circuit Fault (Part 1 of 3). Hummer H2

Step	Action	Yes	No
3	1. Connect the J 39700 universal pinout box using the J 39700-530 cable adapter to the EBCM harness connector only. 2. Test the battery positive voltage circuit for an open, high resistance, or a short to ground. Did you find and correct the condition?	Go to Step 5	Go to Step 4
4	Replace the Electronic Brake Control Module (EBCM). Did you complete the replacement?	Go to Step 5	--
5	1. Use the scan tool in order to clear the DTCs. 2. Operate the vehicle within the Conditions for Running the DTC as specified in the supporting text. Does the DTC reset?	Go to Step 2	System OK

LTV0500000005206

Fig. 43   Code C0121: Valve Relay Circuit Fault (Part 3 of 3). Hummer H2

Diagnostic Aids

- It is very important that a thorough inspection of the wiring and connectors be performed. Failure to carefully and fully inspect wiring and connectors may result in misdiagnosis, causing part replacement with reappearance of the malfunction.
- Thoroughly inspect any circuitry that may be causing the complaint for the following conditions:
  - Backed out terminals
  - Improper mating
  - Broken locks
  - Improperly formed or damaged terminals
  - Poor terminal-to-wiring connections
  - Physical damage to the wiring harness
- Possible causes of this DTC are the following conditions:
  - A signal circuit of the stop lamp switch is open
  - The stop lamp switch is misadjusted
  - Verify proper stop lamp switch operation using the data list of the scan tool. As the brake is applied, the data list displays the stop lamp switch ON within 2.54 cm (1 in) of travel
  - All brake lamps are open
  - All brake lamp grounds are open
  - Circuit has a wiring problem, terminal corrosion, or poor connections
  - Loose or corroded EBCM ground

Test Description

The numbers below refer to the step numbers on the diagnostic table.

3. This DTC detects an open stop lamp switch signal circuit from the stop lamp side of the splice pack to the EBCM.

4. The EBCM sources 5 volts on the stop lamp switch signal circuit. This small voltage has a ground path through the stop lamp bulbs. This DTC sets if the path to ground is open.

Step	Action	Yes	No
1	Did you perform the ABS Diagnostic System Check?	Go to Step 2	Go to Diagnostic System Check

LTV0500000005208

Fig. 44   Code C0161: Stoplamp Switch Voltage Fault (Part 2 of 3). Hummer H2

	Action		Yes	No
2	1. Press the brake pedal. 2. With the scan tool, observe the Brake Switch Status parameter in the ABS data list. Does the Brake Switch Status parameter display Applied?		Go to Step 4	Go to Step 3
3	Test the signal circuit of the stop lamp switch for an open. Did you find and correct the condition?		Go to Step 9	Go to Step 7
4	Press the brake pedal. Are all of the stoplamps OFF?		Go to Step 5	Go to Diagnostic Aids
5	Test the feed circuit of the stop lamps for an open or high resistance. Did you find and correct the condition?		Go to Step 9	Go to Step 6
6	Test the ground circuit of the stop lamps for an open or high resistance. Did you find and correct the condition?		Go to Step 9	Go to Diagnostic Aids
7	Inspect for poor connections at the harness connector of the EBCM. Did you find and correct the condition?		Go to Step 9	Go to Step 8
8	Replace the EBCM. Did you complete the replacement?		Go to Step 9	--
9	1. Use the scan tool in order to clear the DTCs. 2. Operate the vehicle within the Conditions for Running the DTC as specified in the supporting text. Does the DTC reset?		Go to Step 2	System OK

LTV0500000005209

Fig. 44 Code C0161: Stoplamp Switch Voltage Fault (Part 3 of 3). Hummer H2

Test Description

The number(s) below refer to the step number(s) on the diagnostic table.

2. Tests for specified voltage on the LNG accelerometer signal circuit.

3. Checks to see if voltage was below or above specified voltage.

4. Checks to see if voltage was above specified voltage.

5. Checks to see if voltage was below specified voltage.

6. Checks to see if voltage was above specified voltage.

7. Checks to see if resistance of ground circuit is less than 5 ohms.

8. Tests for a short to voltage on the 5 volt reference circuit.

9. Tests for a short to ground, a high resistance, or an open in the 5 volt reference circuit.

10. Tests for a short to ground, a high resistance, or an open in the lateral accelerometer signal circuit.

11. Tests for a short to voltage in the lateral accelerometer signal circuit.

12. Tests for a high resistance or an open in the ground circuit.

13. Checks the LNG accelerometer sensor connector for poor connections.

Step	Action	Value(s)	Yes	No
1	Did you perform the ABS Diagnostic System Check?	--	Go to Step 2	Go to Diagnostic System Check
2	1. Turn OFF the ignition. 2. Disconnect the EBCM. 3. Install the J 39700 universal pinout box with the J 39700-530 cable adapter between the EBCM and the EBCM harness connector. 4. Turn ON the ignition, with the engine OFF. 5. Using the J 39200 , measure the voltage between pin 10 and pin 15 of the J 39700 universal pinout box. Is the voltage within the specified value?	0.48 V - 4.82 V	Go to Diagnostic Aids	Go to Step 3

LTV0500000005211

Fig. 45 Code C0191: Longitudinal Accelerometer Sensor Voltage Fault (Part 2 of 4). Hummer H2

Circuit Description

The EBCM provides power 5 volts reference to the longitudinal accelerometer. The longitudinal accelerometer converts the change in vehicle motion, or inertia, into a voltage signal. This signal is sent to the EBCM.

The voltage signal ranges, from 2.4 to 2.6 volts at zero speed change, constant motion, or stationary. The longitudinal accelerometer voltage signal drops when the vehicle is under acceleration. The longitudinal accelerometer voltage signal increases when the vehicle is under deceleration. The usable output voltage range for the longitudinal accelerometer is 0.48-4.82 volts. The longitudinal accelerometer sensor bias compensates for sensor mounting alignment errors and electronic signal errors.

Conditions for Running the DTC

- The ignition is ON.
- The DTC can be set after system initialization.

Conditions for Setting the DTC

Voltage at the longitudinal accelerometer signal output to the EBCM falls outside the 0.48 V - 4.82 V range for more than 100 milliseconds.

Action Taken When the DTC Sets

- A malfunction DTC is set.
- TCS is disabled.
- The ABS warning indicator turns ON.

Conditions for Clearing the DTC

- The condition for the DTC is no longer present.
- A history DTC will clear after 100 consecutive ignition cycles if the condition for the malfunction is no longer present.
- Using a scan tool.

Diagnostic Aids

- A thorough inspection of the wiring system and connectors be performed. Failure to carefully and fully inspect the wiring system and connectors may result in misdiagnosis which may result in replacing good parts and the reappearance of the malfunction.
- Inspection for poor connections, broken insulation, or a wire that is broken inside the insulation.

LTV0500000005210

Fig. 45 Code C0191: Longitudinal Accelerometer Sensor Voltage Fault (Part 1 of 4). Hummer H2

	Action	Value(s)	Yes	No
3	1. Reconnect the LNG accelerometer sensor. 2. Using a J 39200 , measure the voltage between pin 10 and pin 15 of the J 39700 universal pinout box. Is the voltage less than the specified value?	4.82 V	Go to Step 4	Go to Step 11
4	Using a DMM, measure the voltage between pin 10 and pin 15 of the J 39700 universal pinout box. Is the voltage greater than the specified value?	0.48 V	Go to Step 5	Go to Step 10
5	Using a DMM, measure the voltage between the 5 volt reference circuit pin 28 and the ground circuit pin 15 on the J 39700 universal pinout box. Does the voltage measure less than the specified value?	2 V	Go to Step 9	Go to Step 6
6	Using a DMM, measure the voltage between the 5 volt reference circuit pin 28 and ground circuit pin 15 on the J 39700 universal pinout box. Does the voltage measure greater than the specified voltage?	3 V	Go to Step 8	Go to Step 7
7	1. Turn OFF the ignition. 2. Disconnect the negative battery cable. 3. Measure the resistance from the ground circuit of the LNG accelerometer to a good ground. Does the resistance measure less than the specified value?	5 ohms	Go to Step 14	Go to Step 12
8	Test the 5 volt reference circuit of the LNG accelerometer sensor for a short to voltage. Did you find and correct the condition?	--	Go to Step 17	Go to Step 13
9	Test the 5 volt reference circuit of the LNG accelerometer sensor for a short to ground, a high resistance, or an open. Did you find and correct the condition?	--	Go to Step 17	Go to Step 10
10	Test the LNG accelerometer signal circuit of the LNG accelerometer sensor for a short to ground, a high resistance, or an open. Did you find and correct the condition?	--	Go to Step 17	Go to Step 13

LTV0500000005212

Fig. 45 Code C0191: Longitudinal Accelerometer Sensor Voltage Fault (Part 3 of 4). Hummer H2

Step	Action		Yes	No
11	Test the LNG accelerometer signal circuit of the yaw/lateral accelerometer sensor for a short to voltage. Did you find and correct the condition?	-	Go to Step 17	Go to Step 13
12	1. Disconnect the EBCM. 2. Test the ground circuit of the LNG accelerometer sensor for a high resistance or an open. Did you find and correct the condition?	-	Go to Step 17	Go to Step 13
13	Inspect for poor connections at the harness connector of the LNG accelerometer sensor. Did you find and correct the condition?	-	Go to Step 17	Go to Step 15
14	Inspect for poor connections at the harness connector of the EBCM. Did you find and correct the condition?	-	Go to Step 17	Go to Step 16
15	Replace the vehicle LNG accelerometer sensor. Did you complete the replacement?	-	Go to Step 17	--
16	Replace the EBCM. Did you complete the replacement?	-	Go to Step 17	--
17	1. Use the scan tool in order to clear the DTCs. 2. Operate the vehicle within the Conditions for Running the DTC as specified in the supporting text. Does the DTC reset?	-	Go to Step 2	System OK

LTV0500000005213

Fig. 45 Code C0191: Longitudinal Accelerometer Sensor Voltage Fault (Part 4 of 4). Hummer H2

Test Description

The numbers below refer to the step numbers on the diagnostic table.

2. Checks for specified voltage on the longitudinal accelerometer signal circuit.

3. Checks for specified 5-volt reference on the longitudinal accelerometer reference circuit.

Step	Action	Value (s)	Yes	No
1	Did you perform the ABS Diagnostic System Check?	--	Go to Step 2	Go to Diagnostic System Check
2	1. Turn OFF the ignition. 2. Disconnect the EBCM connector. 3. Install the J 39700 universal pinout box with the J 39700-530 cable adapter between the EBCM and the EBCM harness connector. 4. Turn the ignition ON, with the engine OFF. 5. Using the DMM, measure the voltage between pin 10 and pin 15 of the J 39700 universal pinout box. Is the voltage within the specified value?	2.3-2.7 V	Go to Step 3	Go to Step 6
3	Using the DMM, measure the voltage between pin 28 and pin 15 of the J 39700 universal pinout box. Is the voltage within the specified value?	4.5-5 V	Go to Step 4	Go to Step 6
4	1. Use the scan tool in order to clear the DTCs. 2. Perform the Diagnostic Test Drive. Does the DTC reset?	--	Go to Step 5	Go to Diagnostic Aids
5	Replace the EBCM Did you complete the replacement?	--	Go to Step 7	--
6	Replace the vehicle longitudinal accelerometer sensor. Did you complete the repair?	--	Go to Step 7	--
7	1. Use the scan tool in order to clear the DTCs. 2. Operate the vehicle within the Conditions for Running the DTC as specified in the supporting text. Does the DTC reset?	--	Go to Step 2	System OK

LTV0500000005215

Fig. 46 Code C0192: Longitudinal Accelerometer Signal Fault (Part 2 of 2). Hummer H2

Circuit Description

The vehicle uses the longitudinal accelerometer input when calculating the desired traction control. The usable output voltage range for the longitudinal accelerometer 0.48-4.84 volts. The scan tool will report zero longitudinal acceleration as 2.5 volts with no sensor bias present.

The longitudinal accelerometer sensor bias compensates for sensor mounting alignment errors and electronic signal errors.

Conditions for Running the DTC

- The ignition is ON.
- The vehicle speed is greater than 40 km/h (25 mph).

Conditions for Setting the DTC

- If during stable driving conditions, the longitudinal accelerometer signal becomes larger than 0.26 g, the EBCM controller will disregard the signal so that a false EBCM intervention is prevented. A malfunction is detected if this condition continues for more than two seconds.
- Under normal driving conditions, the long time filtered driving direction is straight ahead. The long time filtered longitudinal accelerometer value is called the offset. If the offset value is higher than 0.23 g, a malfunction is detected. Malfunction time depends on driving distance, vehicle speed and the amount of malfunctioning longitudinal accelerometer signal.
- The longitudinal accelerometer signal is limited to an electrical stop of 1.8 g. If the longitudinal accelerometer signal is greater than 1.5 g for more than 500 milliseconds, a malfunction is detected.
- At a standstill, the range of the longitudinal accelerometer signal is less than 0.7 g. If the longitudinal accelerometer signal is greater than 0.7 g at standstill, a malfunction is detected.
- longitudinal accelerometer signal cannot change rapidly under normal driving conditions. If the longitudinal accelerometer signal is changing faster than 55 g per second, a malfunction is detected.

Action Taken When the DTC Sets

- A malfunction DTC is set
- TCS is disabled for the duration of the ignition cycle
- ABS remains functional
- ABS lamp indicators turn on

Conditions for Clearing the DTC

- The condition for the DTC is no longer present
- A history DTC will clear after 100 consecutive ignition cycles if the condition for the malfunction is no longer present.
- Using a scan tool.

Diagnostic Aids

Any circuitry that is suspected of causing an intermittent complaint should be thoroughly checked for improper mating, improperly formed or damaged terminals, poor terminal to wiring connections, or physical damage to the wiring harness.

LTV0500000005214

Fig. 46 Code C0192: Longitudinal Accelerometer Signal Fault (Part 1 of 2). Hummer H2

Circuit Description

The speed sensors used on the front of this vehicle are multiple pole and the rear uses a single pole magnetic pickup. This sensor produces an AC signal that the EBCM uses the frequency from to calculate the wheel speed.

Conditions for Running the DTC

- The ignition switch is ON.
- The DTC can be set after system initialization.

Conditions for Setting the DTC

- The EBCM detects a deviation between two wheel speeds at either side of the vehicle greater than 6 km/h (3.75 mph) at a vehicle speed of less than 100 km/h (62 mph).
- The EBCM detects a deviation between the left and right front wheel speeds of greater than 10 km/h (6.25 mph) at a vehicle speed of less than 100 km/h (62 mph).
- The EBCM detects a deviation between the left and right front wheel speeds of greater than 4 km/h (2.5 mph) plus 6 percent of the vehicle speed at greater than 100 km/h (62 mph).

This DTC will set when the EBCM cannot specifically identify which wheel speed sensor is causing the malfunction. If the EBCM can identify the specific wheel speed sensor causing the malfunction, DTC C0245 will become a history DTC, and the DTC associated with the sensor DTC C0036, DTC C0041, DTC C0046, DTC C0051, will be set concurrent with DTC C0245.

Action Taken When the DTC Sets

If equipped, the following actions occur:

- The EBCM disables the ABS if the exact fault can be determined and after ABS control has terminated.
- A malfunction DTC will set.
- The ABS indicator turns on.
- The TCS indicator turns on.
- The Red BRAKE Warning indicator turns on.

Conditions for Clearing the DTC

- The condition for the DTC is no longer present and the DTC is cleared with a scan tool.
- The electronic brake control module (EBCM) automatically clears the history DTC when a current DTC is not detected in 100 consecutive drive cycles.

LTV0500000005216

Fig. 47 Code C0245: Wheel Speed Sensor Frequency Error (Part 1 of 4). Hummer H2

Diagnostic Aids

- It is very important that a thorough inspection of the wiring and connectors be performed. Failure to carefully and fully inspect wiring and connectors may result in misdiagnosis, causing part replacement with reappearance of the malfunction.
- Thoroughly inspect any circuitry that may be causing the complaint for the following conditions:
  - Backed out terminals
  - Improper mating
  - Broken locks
  - Improperly formed or damaged terminals
  - Poor terminal-to-wiring connections
  - Physical damage to the wiring harness
- The following conditions may cause an intermittent malfunction:
  - A poor connection
  - Rubbed-through wire insulation
  - A broken wire inside the insulation
- If the customer's comments reflect that the amber ABS/TCS indicator is on only during moist environmental conditions (rain, snow, vehicle wash), inspect all the wheel speed sensor circuitry for signs of water intrusion. If the DTC is not current, clear all DTCs and simulate the effects of water intrusion by using the following procedure:

1. Spray the suspected area with a five percent saltwater solution. Add two teaspoons of salt to twelve ounces of water to make a five percent saltwater solution.
2. Test drive the vehicle over various road surfaces (bumps, turns, etc.) above 40 km/h (25 mph) for at least 30 seconds.
3. If the DTC returns, replace the suspected harness.

Test Description

The numbers below refer to step numbers on the diagnostic table.

2. If DTC C0245 is a history code, this step checks if a specific Wheel Speed Circuit Malfunction DTC is set concurrently with DTC C0245.

7. This step checks if the wheel speed sensor harness is routed in close proximity to the spark plug wires.

9. In this step, if the scan tool can record any erroneous wheel speed sensor signals, diagnose that sensors first.

Step	Action	Yes	No
1	Did you perform the diagnostic system check?	Go to Step 2	Go to Diagnostic System Check - ABS

LTV0500000005217

Fig. 47   Code C0245: Wheel Speed Sensor Frequency Error (Part 2 of 4). Hummer H2

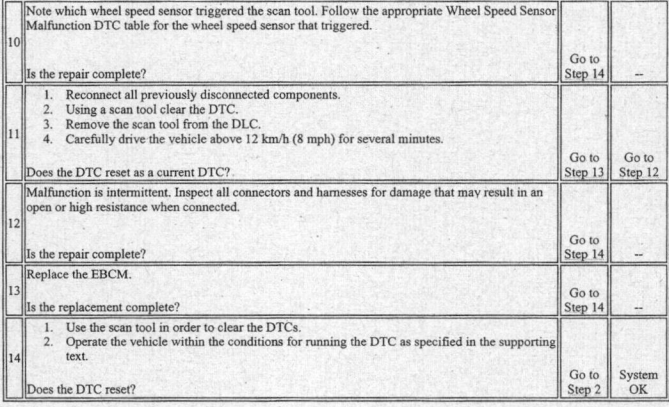

	Action		
10	Note which wheel speed sensor triggered the scan tool. Follow the appropriate Wheel Speed Sensor Malfunction DTC table for the wheel speed sensor that triggered. Is the repair complete?	Go to Step 14	--
11	1. Reconnect all previously disconnected components. 2. Using a scan tool clear the DTC. 3. Remove the scan tool from the DLC. 4. Carefully drive the vehicle above 12 km/h (8 mph) for several minutes. Does the DTC reset as a current DTC?	Go to Step 13	Go to Step 12
12	Malfunction is intermittent. Inspect all connectors and harnesses for damage that may result in an open or high resistance when connected. Is the repair complete?	Go to Step 14	--
13	Replace the EBCM. Is the replacement complete?	Go to Step 14	--
14	1. Use the scan tool in order to clear the DTCs. 2. Operate the vehicle within the conditions for running the DTC as specified in the supporting text. Does the DTC reset?	Go to Step 2	System OK

LTV0500000005219

Fig. 47   Code C0245: Wheel Speed Sensor Frequency Error (Part 4 of 4). Hummer H2

	Action		
2	Is the following DTCs set concurrently with a history DTC C0245? - DTC C0036 - DTC C0041 - DTC C0046 - DTC C0051	Go to DTC Diagnostic Trouble Code (DTC) List	Go to Step 3
3	Inspect the WSS for physical damage. Is physical damage of the WSS evident?	Go to Step 4	Go to Step 5
4	Replace the WSS. Is the replacement complete?	Go to Step 14	--
5	Inspect the wiring harness for physical damage. Is physical damage of the wiring harness evident?	Go to Step 6	Go to Step 7
6	Repair the wiring harness. Is the replacement complete?	Go to Step 14	--
7	Check for proper routing of the wheel speed sensor harness. Check that the wheel speed sensor harness is routed away from the spark plug wires. Is the wheel speed sensor harness properly routed?	Go to Step 9	Go to Step 8
8	Reroute the wheel speed sensor harness away from the spark plug wires. Is the reroute complete?	Go to Step 14	--
9	1. Install a scan tool. 2. Turn the ignition switch to the RUN position. 3. Set the scan tool to Snap Shot Auto Trigger mode and monitor the wheel speed sensors. 4. Carefully drive the vehicle above 12 km/h (8 mph) for several minutes Did the scan tool trigger on any of the wheel speed sensors?	Go to Step 10	Go to Step 11

LTV0500000005218

Fig. 47   Code C0245: Wheel Speed Sensor Frequency Error (Part 3 of 4). Hummer H2

Circuit Description

This DTC identifies a malfunction within the EBCM.

Conditions for Running the DTC

The ignition switch is in the ON position.

Conditions for Setting the DTC

DTC C0550 is set when an internal EBCM or solenoid malfunction exists.

Action Taken When the DTC Sets

If equipped, the following actions occur:

- The EBCM disables the ABS/TCS for the duration of the ignition cycle.
- A malfunction DTC will set.
- The ABS indicator turns on.
- The TCS indicator turns on.

Conditions for Clearing the DTC

- The condition for the DTC is no longer present and you used the scan tool Clear DTC function.
- The EBCM automatically clears the history DTC when a current DTC is not detected in 100 consecutive drive cycles.

Step	Action	Yes	No
1	Did you perform the Diagnostic System Check?	Go to Step 2	Go to Diagnostic System Check
2	Are any other DTC(s) present besides C0550?	Go to Diagnostic Trouble Code (DTC) List	Go to Step 3
3	Replace the EBCM. Is the replacement complete?	Go to Step 4	--
4	1. Use the scan tool in order to clear the DTCs. 2. Operate the vehicle within the Conditions for Running the DTC as specified in the supporting text. Does the DTC reset?	Go to Step 2	System OK

LTV0500000005220

Fig. 48   Code C0550: ECU Fault. Hummer H2

Circuit Description

The EBCM is required to operate within a specified range of voltage to function properly. During ABS and TCS operation, there are current requirements that will cause the voltage to drop. Because of this, voltage is monitored out of ABS/TCS control to indicate a good charging system condition, and also during ABS/TCS control when voltage may drop significantly. The EBCM also monitors for high voltage conditions which could damage the EBCM.

Conditions for Running the DTC

- The ignition switch is ON.
- The DTC can be set after system initialization.

Conditions for Setting the DTC

- The EBCM operating voltage falls below 9.4 volts out of ABS/TCS control, or 8.8 volts during ABS/TCS control.
- The EBCM operating voltage rises above 17.4 volts.
- The low voltage or the high voltage is detected for more than 500 milliseconds with the vehicle speed above 6 km/h (3.6 mph).

Action Taken When the DTC Sets

If equipped, the following actions occur:

- A malfunction DTC is stored.
- The ABS and the Traction Control indicators are turned on.
- The ABS/TCS is disabled.
- The Brake warning indicator turns on.

Conditions for Clearing the DTC

- The condition for the DTC is no longer present and the DTC is cleared with a scan tool.
- The electronic brake control module (EBCM) automatically clears the history DTC when a current DTC is not detected in 100 consecutive drive cycles.

LTV0500000005221

Fig. 49 Code C0896: Device Voltage Range Performance (Part 1 of 3). Hummer H2

Step	Action	Value(s)		
3	Use a J 39200 to measure the voltage between the battery positive terminal and ground. Is the voltage within the specified range?	0-17.4 V	Go to Step 5	Go to Symptoms
4	Continue to monitor the battery voltage with the scan tool while running the engine at approximately 2000 RPM. Is the monitored battery voltage within the specified range?	0-9.4 V	Go to Step 6	Go to Step 5
5	1. Turn the ignition switch to the OFF position. 2. Disconnect the scan tool if still connected. 3. Test drive the vehicle above 6 km/h (3.5 mph). Did DTC C0896 reset?	--	Go to Step 10	Go to Diagnostic System Check
6	1. Turn the ignition switch to the OFF position. 2. Disconnect the EBCM connector. 3. Install the J 39700 with the J 39700-530 to the EBCM harness connector only. 4. Use a J 39200 to measure the resistance between the J 39700 terminal 15 and a good ground. Is the resistance within the specified range?	0-5ohms	Go to Step 8	Go to Step 7
7	Repair open or high resistance in the ground circuit. Is the repair complete?	--	Go to Step 11	--
8	1. Turn the ignition switch to the RUN position. 2. Use a J 39200 to measure the voltage between the J 39700 terminal 8 and 15. Is the voltage within the specified range?	Above 9.4 V	Go to Step 9	Go to Symptoms
9	1. Turn the ignition switch to the OFF position. 2. Reconnect the EBCM connector. 3. Disconnect the scan tool if the scan tool is still connected. 4. Test drive the vehicle above 6 km/h (3.5 mph). Did DTC C0896 reset?	--	Go to Step 10	Go to Step 11
10	Replace the EBCM. Is the repair complete?	--	Go to Step 11	--
11	1. Use the scan tool in order to clear the DTCs. 2. Operate the vehicle within the Conditions for Running the DTC as specified in the supporting text. Does the DTC reset?	--	Go to Step 2	System OK

LTV0500000005223

Fig. 49 Code C0896: Device Voltage Range Performance (Part 3 of 3). Hummer H2

Diagnostic Aids

- It is very important that a thorough inspection of the wiring and connectors be performed. Failure to carefully and fully inspect wiring and connectors may result in misdiagnosis, causing part replacement with reappearance of the malfunction.
- Thoroughly inspect any circuitry that may be causing the complaint for the following conditions:
  - Backed out terminals
  - Improper mating
  - Broken locks
  - Improperly formed or damaged terminals
  - Poor terminal-to-wiring connections
  - Physical damage to the wiring harness
- The following conditions may cause an intermittent malfunction:
  - A poor connection
  - Rubbed-through wire insulation
  - A broken wire inside the insulation

Test Description

The number(s) below refer to the step number(s) on the diagnostic table.

2. This step checks if the voltage is above the maximum of the range.

4. Step 4 checks if the voltage is below the minimum of the range.

6. This step checks for the integrity of the ground circuit.

Step	Action	Value (s)	Yes	No
1	Did you perform the Diagnostic System Check?	--	Go to Step 2	Go to Diagnostic System Check
2	1. Turn all the accessories off. 2. Install a scan tool. 3. Start the engine. 4. Use the scan tool to monitor the battery voltage while running the engine at approximately 2000 RPM. Is the monitored battery voltage within the specified range?	0-17.4 V	Go to Step 4	Go to Step 3

LTV0500000005222

Fig. 49 Code C0896: Device Voltage Range Performance (Part 2 of 3). Hummer H2

Step	Action	Value(s)	Yes	No
1	Was the Diagnostic System Check performed?	—	Go to Step 2	Go to A Diagnostic System Check
2	1. Using a scan tool in the Instrument Panel Cluster Special Functions. 2. Go to Lamps Test in Output Control. 3. In the Lamps Test mode you can turn on or off the instrument panel indicators. All indicators will turn ON when commanded on. Does the ABS indicator turn on then off?	—	Go to Step 3	Go to Step 4
3	Replace the EBCM. Is the replacement complete?	—	Go to A Diagnostic System Check	—
4	1. Disconnect the Instrument Cluster and connect a Test Light across the appropriate power and ground terminals. 2. Test Light OFF, repair open in power or ground circuit to cluster. 3. Test Light ON, check connector for poor connection to cluster. 4. If OK, replace the Instrument Cluster. Is the Instrument Cluster replacement complete?	—	Go to A Diagnostic System Check	—

GC4020152418000X

Fig. 50 Anti-Lock Indicator Always On. Aztek & Rendezvous

Step	Action	Value(s)	Yes	No
1	Was the Diagnostic System Check performed?	—	Go to Step 2	Go to A Diagnostic System Check
2	1. Using a scan tool in the Instrument Panel Cluster Special Functions. 2. Go to Lamps Test in Output Control. 3. In the Lamps Test mode you can turn on or off the instrument panel indicators. All indicators will turn ON when commanded on. Does the ABS Indicator turn on then off?	—	Go to Step 3	Go to Step 4
3	Replace the EBCM. Is the replacement complete?	—	Go to A Diagnostic System Check	—
4	1. Disconnect the Instrument Cluster and connect a Test Light across the appropriate power and ground terminals. 2. Test Light OFF, repair open in power or ground circuit to cluster. 3. Test Light ON, check connector for poor connection to the cluster. 4. If OK, replace the Instrument Cluster. Is the instrument cluster replacement complete?	—	Go to A Diagnostic System Check	—

GC4020152419000X

Fig. 51 Anti-Lock Indicator Inoperative. Aztek & Rendezvous

Step	Action	Value(s)	Yes	No
1	Was the Diagnostic System Check performed?	—	Go to Step 2	Go to A Diagnostic System Check
2	1. Using a scan tool in the Instrument Panel Cluster Special Functions. 2. Go to Lamps Test in Output Control. 3. In the Lamps Test mode you can turn on or off the instrument panel indicators. All indicators will turn ON when commanded on. Does the LOW TRAC Indicator turn on then off?	—	Go to Step 3	Go to Step 4
3	Replace the EBCM. Is the replacement complete?	—	Go to A Diagnostic System Check	
4	1. Disconnect the instrument cluster and connect a Test Light across the appropriate power and ground terminals. 2. Test Light OFF, repair open in power or ground circuit to cluster. 3. Test Light ON, check connector for poor connection to cluster. 4. If OK, replace the instrument cluster Is the instrument cluster replacement complete?	—	Go to A Diagnostic System Check	

GC4020152420000X

Fig. 52 Low Traction Indicator Always On. Aztek & Rendezvous

Step	Action	Value(s)	Yes	No
1	Was the Diagnostic System Check performed?	—	Go to Step 2	Go to A Diagnostic System Check
2	1. Using a scan tool in the Instrument Panel Cluster Special Functions. 2. Go to Lamps Test in Output Control. 3. In the Lamps Test mode you can turn on or off the instrument panel indicators. All indicators will turn ON when commanded on. Does the LOW TRAC Indicator turn on then off?	—	Go to Step 3	Go to Step 4
3	Replace the EBCM. Is the replacement complete?	—	Go to A Diagnostic System Check	
4	1. Disconnect the Instrument Cluster and connect a Test Light across the Appropriate power and ground terminals. 2. Test Light OFF, repair open in power or ground circuit to cluster. 3. Test Light ON, check connector for poor connection to the cluster. 4. If OK, replace the Instrument Cluster Is the instrument cluster replacement complete?	—	Go to A Diagnostic System Check	

GC4020152421000X

Fig. 53 Low Traction Indicator Inoperative. Aztek & Rendezvous

Step	Action	Value(s)	Yes	No
1	Did you perform the ABS Diagnostic System Check?	—	Go to Step 2	Go to A Diagnostic System Check
2	1. Install a scan tool. 2. Turn ON the ignition, with the engine OFF. 3. With a scan tool, observe the Traction Switch parameter in the Body Control Module data list. Does the scan tool display Off?	—	Go to Step 3	Go to Step 4
3	1. Activate the traction control switch. 2. With the scan tool, observe the Traction Switch parameter. Does the Traction Switch parameter change state?	—	Go to Intermittent and Poor Connections	Go to Step 4
4	1. Turn OFF the ignition. 2. Disconnect the traction control switch connector. 3. Turn ON the ignition, with the engine OFF. 4. With a scan tool, observe the Traction Switch parameter. Does the scan tool display Off?	—	Go to Step 7	Go to Step 5
5	Test the signal circuit of the traction control switch for a short to ground. Did you find and correct the condition?	—	Go to Step 10	Go to Step 6
6	Inspect for poor connections at the harness connector of the body control module (BCM). Did you find and correct the condition?	—	Go to Step 10	Go to Step 8
7	Inspect for poor connections at the harness connector of the traction control switch. Did you find and correct the condition?	—	Go to Step 10	Go to Step 9
8	Replace the body control module (BCM). Did you complete the replacement?	—	Go to Step 10	—
9	Replace the traction control switch. Did you complete the replacement?	—	Go to Step 10	—
10	Operate the system in order to verify the repair. Did you correct the condition?	—	System OK	Go to Step 2

GC4020152422000X

Fig. 54 Traction Off Indicator Always On. Aztek & Rendezvous

Step	Action	Value(s)	Yes	No
1	Did you perform the ABS Diagnostic System Check?	—	Go to Step 2	Go to A Diagnostic System Check
2	1. Install a scan tool. 2. Turn ON the ignition, with the engine OFF. 3. With a scan tool, observe the Traction Switch parameter in the Body Control Module data list. 4. Activate the traction control switch. Does the Traction Switch parameter change state?	—	Go to Intermittent and Poor Connections	Go to Step 3
3	1. Turn OFF the ignition. 2. Disconnect the traction control switch connector. 3. Connect a fused jumper from the signal circuit of the traction control switch harness connector to a good ground. 4. Turn ON the ignition, with the engine OFF. 5. With a scan tool, observe the Traction Switch parameter. Does the scan tool display On?	—	Go to Step 5	Go to Step 4
4	Test the signal circuit of the traction control switch for an open or high resistance. Did you find and correct the condition?	—	Go to Step 10	Go to Step 6
5	Test the ground circuit of the traction control switch for an open or high resistance. Did you find and correct the condition?	—	Go to Step 10	Go to Step 7
6	Inspect for poor connections at the harness connector of the body control module (BCM). Did you find and correct the condition?	—	Go to Step 10	Go to Step 8
7	Inspect for poor connections at the harness connector of the traction control switch. Did you find and correct the condition?	—	Go to Step 10	Go to Step 9
8	Replace the body control module (BCM). Did you complete the replacement?	—	Go to Step 10	—
9	Replace the traction control switch. Did you complete the replacement?	—	Go to Step 10	—
10	Operate the system in order to verify the repair. Did you correct the condition?	—	System OK	Go to Step 2

GC4020152423000X

Fig. 55 Traction Off Indicator Inoperative. Aztek & Rendezvous

Circuit Description

The instrument panel cluster (IPC) turns the ABS indicator on during the IPC bulb check for approximately 3 seconds when the ignition switch is turned to the ON position. If the electronic brake control module (EBCM) sets a diagnostic trouble code (DTC) the EBCM sends a class 2 message to the body control module (BCM) and the BCM sends a class 2 message to the IPC to command the antilock brake system (ABS) indicator ON.

Diagnostic Aids

- It is very important that a thorough inspection of the wiring and connectors be performed. Failure to carefully and fully inspect wiring and connectors may result in misdiagnosis, causing part replacement with reappearance of the malfunction.
- Thoroughly inspect any circuitry that may be causing the complaint for the following conditions:
  - Backed out terminals
  - Improper mating
  - Broken locks
  - Improperly formed or damaged terminals
  - Poor terminal-to-wiring connections
  - Physical damage to the wiring harness
- The following conditions may cause an intermittent malfunction:
  - A poor connection
  - Rubbed-through wire insulation
  - A broken wire inside the insulation

Test Description

The numbers below refer to the step numbers on the diagnostic table.

2. Confirm if the scan tool can turn ON and OFF all indicator lamps on the instrument cluster.

4. Verify if the circuits going to the instrument cluster or the cluster is at fault.

LTV0500000004302

Fig. 56 ABS Active Indicator Always On (Part 1 of 2). Equinox, Torrent & Vue

Circuit Description

The instrument panel cluster (IPC) turns the ABS indicator on during the IPC bulb check for approximately 3 seconds when the ignition switch is turned to the ON position. If the electronic brake control module (EBCM) sets a diagnostic trouble code (DTC) the EBCM sends a class 2 message to the body control module (BCM) and the BCM sends a class 2 message to the IPC to command the ABS indicator on.

Diagnostic Aids

- It is very important that a thorough inspection of the wiring and connectors be performed. Failure to carefully and fully inspect wiring and connectors may result in misdiagnosis, causing part replacement with reappearance of the malfunction.
- Thoroughly inspect any circuitry that may be causing the complaint for the following conditions:
  - Backed out terminals
  - Improper mating
  - Broken locks
  - Improperly formed or damaged terminals
  - Poor terminal-to-wiring connections
  - Physical damage to the wiring harness
- The following conditions may cause an intermittent malfunction:
  - A poor connection
  - Rubbed-through wire insulation
  - A broken wire inside the insulation

Test Description

The numbers below refer to the step numbers on the diagnostic table.

2. Confirm if the scan tool can turn on and off all the indicator lamps in the instrument cluster.

4. Verify if the circuits going to the instrument cluster or the cluster is at fault.

LTV0500000004304

Fig. 57 ABS Active Indicator Inoperative (Part 1 of 2). Equinox, Torrent & Vue

Step	Action	Yes	No
1	Did you perform the Diagnostic System Check - Vehicle?	Go to Step 2	Go to Diagnostic System Check
2	1. Using a scan tool, select the brake control module (BCM), Special Functions mode. 2. Select Output Control, Solenoid Test. 3. Select the antilock brake system (ABS) Telltale Indicator. 4. In the ABS Telltale test mode you can turn the instrument panel indicators ON or OFF. All indicators will turn ON when commanded on. Does the ABS indicator turn on then OFF?	Go to Step 3	Go to Step 4
3	Replace the electronic brake control module (EBCM). Is the replacement complete?	Go to Diagnostic System Check	--
4	1. Disconnect the instrument cluster and connect a test light across the appropriate power and ground terminals. 2. With the test light OFF, repair the open in power or ground circuit to cluster. 3. With the test light ON, check the connector for poor connection to cluster. 4. If OK, replace the instrument cluster. Is the instrument cluster replacement complete?	Go to Diagnostic System Check	--

LTV0500000004303

Fig. 56 ABS Active Indicator Always On (Part 2 of 2). Equinox, Torrent & Vue

Step	Action	Yes	No
1	Did you perform the Diagnostic System Check - Vehicle?	Go to Step 2	Go to Diagnostic System Check
2	1. Using a scan tool, select the Brake Control Module, Special Functions mode, Output Control. 2. Select Solenoid Test. 3. Select ABS Telltale Indicator. 4. In the ABS Telltale Test mode you can turn the instrument panel indicators ON or OFF. All indicators will turn ON when commanded on. Does the ABS indicator turn on then off?	Go to Step 3	Go to Step 4
3	Replace the ABS module. Is the replacement complete?	Go to Diagnostic System Check	--
4	1. Disconnect the instrument cluster and connect a test light across the appropriate power and ground terminals. 2. With the test light OFF, repair the open in power or ground circuit to cluster. 3. With the test light ON, check the connector for poor connection to the cluster. 4. If OK, replace the instrument cluster. Is the instrument cluster replacement complete?	Go to Diagnostic System Check	--

LTV0500000004305

Fig. 57 ABS Active Indicator Inoperative (Part 2 of 2). Equinox, Torrent & Vue

Circuit Description

The TRAC OFF indicator is controlled by the instrument cluster via class 2 serial data messages from the electronic brake control module (EBCM). When the body control module (BCM) sees the traction control switch input grounded through the momentary traction control switch, it sends a class 2 message to the EBCM that tells the EBCM that the traction control switch has been pressed. The EBCM then disables traction control and sends a message to the instrument cluster to turn the TRAC OFF indicator ON. Each time the ignition is cycled from OFF to ON, the traction control system (TCS) is enabled.

The following conditions will cause the TRAC OFF indicator to illuminate:

- The EBCM has disabled the TCS due to a DTC.
- The driver manually disabling the TCS via the traction control switch.
- The instrument cluster bulb check. When the ignition switch is turned to ON, the TRAC OFF indicator will turn on for approximately 3 seconds and then turn OFF.

Diagnostic Aids

- It is very important that a thorough inspection of the wiring and connectors be performed. Failure to carefully and fully inspect wiring and connectors may result in misdiagnosis, causing part replacement with reappearance of the malfunction.
- Thoroughly inspect any circuitry that may be causing the complaint for the following conditions:
  - Backed out terminals
  - Improper mating
  - Broken locks
  - Improperly formed or damaged terminals
  - Poor terminal-to-wiring connections
  - Physical damage to the wiring harness
- The following conditions may cause an intermittent malfunction:
  - A poor connection
  - Rubbed-through wire insulation
  - A broken wire inside the insulation

LTV0500000004306

Fig. 58 Traction Control Indicator Always On (Part 1 of 3). Equinox, Torrent & Vue

Step	Action	Yes	No
1	Did you perform the Diagnostic System Check - Vehicle?	Go to Step 2	Go to Diagnostic System Check
2	1. Install a scan tool. 2. Turn ON the ignition, with the engine OFF. 3. With a scan tool, observe the Traction Switch parameter in the EBCM data display. 4. Activate the traction control switch. Does the Traction Switch parameter change state?	Test for Intermittent and Poor Connections	Go to Step 3
3	1. Turn OFF the ignition. 2. Disconnect the traction control switch connector. 3. Connect a fused jumper from the signal circuit of the traction control switch harness connector to a good ground. 4. Turn ON the ignition, with the engine OFF. 5. With a scan tool, observe the Traction Switch parameter. Does the scan tool display Applied?	Go to Step 5	Go to Step 4
4	Test the signal circuit of the traction control switch for an open or high resistance. Did you find and correct the condition?	Go to Step 10	Go to Step 6
5	Test the ground circuit of the traction control switch for an open or high resistance. Did you find and correct the condition?	Go to Step 10	Go to Step 7

LTV0500000004307

Fig. 58   Traction Control Indicator Always On (Part 2 of 3). Equinox, Torrent & Vue

Circuit Description

The TRAC OFF indicator is controlled by the instrument cluster via class 2 serial data messages from the electronic brake control module (EBCM). When the body control module (BCM) sees the traction control switch input grounded through the momentary traction control switch, it sends a class 2 message to the EBCM that tells the EBCM that the traction control switch has been pressed. The EBCM then disables traction control and sends a message to the instrument cluster to turn the TRAC OFF indicator ON. Each time the ignition is cycled from OFF to ON, the traction control system (TCS) is enabled.

The following conditions will cause the TRAC OFF indicator to illuminate:

- The EBCM has disabled the TCS due to a DTC.
- The driver manually disabling the TCS via the traction control switch
- The instrument cluster bulb check--When the ignition switch is turned to ON, the TRAC OFF indicator will turn on for approximately 3 seconds and then turn OFF.

Diagnostic Aids

- It is very important that a thorough inspection of the wiring and connectors be performed. Failure to carefully and fully inspect wiring and connectors may result in misdiagnosis, causing part replacement with reappearance of the malfunction.
- Thoroughly inspect any circuitry that may be causing the complaint for the following conditions:
  - Backed out terminals
  - Improper mating
  - Broken locks
  - Improperly formed or damaged terminals
  - Poor terminal-to-wiring connections
  - Physical damage to the wiring harness
- The following conditions may cause an intermittent malfunction:
  - A poor connection
  - Rubbed-through wire insulation
  - A broken wire inside the insulation

LTV0500000004309

Fig. 59   Traction Control Indicator Inoperative (Part 1 of 3). Equinox, Torrent & Vue

Step	Action	Yes	No
6	Inspect for poor connections at the harness connector of the body control module (BCM). Did you find and correct the condition?	Go to Step 10	Go to Step 8
7	Inspect for poor connections at the harness connector of the traction control switch. Did you find and correct the condition?	Go to Step 10	Go to Step 9
8	Replace the BCM. Did you complete the replacement?	Go to Step 10	--
9	Replace the traction control switch. Did you complete the replacement?	Go to Step 10	--
10	Operate the system in order to verify the repair. Did you correct the condition?	System OK	Go to Step 2

LTV0500000004311

Fig. 59   Traction Control Indicator Inoperative (Part 3 of 3). Equinox, Torrent & Vue

Step	Action	Yes	No
6	Inspect for poor connections at the harness connector of the body control module (BCM). Did you find and correct the condition?	Go to Step 10	Go to Step 8
7	Inspect for poor connections at the harness connector of the traction control switch. Did you find and correct the condition?	Go to Step 10	Go to Step 9
8	Replace the BCM. Did you complete the replacement?	Go to Step 10	--
9	Replace the traction control switch. Did you complete the replacement?	Go to Step 10	--
10	Operate the system in order to verify the repair. Did you correct the condition?	System OK	Go to Step 2

LTV0500000004308

Fig. 58   Traction Control Indicator Always On (Part 3 of 3). Equinox, Torrent & Vue

Step	Action	Yes	No
1	Did you perform the Diagnostic System Check - Vehicle?	Go to Step 2	Go to Diagnostic System Check
2	1. Install a scan tool. 2. Turn ON the ignition, with the engine OFF. 3. With a scan tool, observe the Traction Switch parameter in the EBCM data display. Does the scan tool display Released?	Go to Step 3	Go to Step 4
3	1. Activate the traction control switch. 2. With the scan tool, observe the Traction Switch parameter. Does the Traction Switch parameter change state?		Go to Step 4
4	1. Turn OFF the ignition. 2. Disconnect the traction control switch connector. 3. Turn ON the ignition, with the engine OFF. 4. With a scan tool, observe the Traction Switch parameter. Does the scan tool display Inactive?	Go to Step 7	Go to Step 5
5	Test the signal circuit of the traction control switch for a short to ground. Did you find and correct the condition?	Go to Step 10	Go to Step 6

LTV0500000004310

Fig. 59   Traction Control Indicator Inoperative (Part 2 of 3). Equinox, Torrent & Vue

Circuit Description

The instrument panel cluster (IPC) turns the ABS Indicator on during the IPC bulb check for approximately 3 seconds when the ignition switch is turned to the ON position. If the EBCM sets a diagnostic trouble code (DTC) the EBCM sends the IPC the command to turn the ABS indicator on.

Diagnostic Aids

- It is very important that a thorough inspection of the wiring and connectors be performed. Failure to carefully and fully inspect wiring and connectors may result in misdiagnosis, causing part replacement with reappearance of the malfunction.
- Thoroughly inspect any circuitry that may be causing the complaint for the following conditions:
  - Backed out terminals
  - Improper mating
  - Broken locks
  - Improperly formed or damaged terminals
  - Poor terminal-to-wiring connections
  - Physical damage to the wiring harness
- The following conditions may cause an intermittent malfunction:
  - A poor connection
  - Rubbed-through wire insulation
  - A broken wire inside the insulation

Test Description

The numbers below refer to step numbers on the diagnostic table.

2. Checks if the instrument panel cluster has the ability to turn the ABS indicator off or if the EBCM is sending an incorrect command to turn the ABS indicator on.

LTV0500000005224

Fig. 60   ABS Indicator Always On (Part 1 of 2). Hummer H2

Step	Action	Yes	No
1	Did you perform the ABS Diagnostic System Check?	Go to Step 2	Go to Diagnostic System Check
2	Using a scan tool in the Instrument Panel Cluster Special Functions attempt to turn off the ABS indicator. Did the ABS indicator turn off?	Go to Step 3	Go to Step 4
3	Replace the EBCM. Is the replacement complete?	Go to Step 5	--
4	Replace the instrument panel cluster. Is the replacement complete?	Go to Step 5	--
5	Operate the system in order to verify the repair. Did you correct the condition?	System OK	Go to Step 2

LTV0500000005225

Fig. 60   ABS Indicator Always On (Part 2 of 2). Hummer H2

Test Description

The number(s) below refer to the step number(s) on the diagnostic table.

2. Checks if the scan tool can turn on and off all the indicator lamps in the instrument cluster.

4. Checks if the circuits going to the instrument Cluster or the cluster is at fault.

Step	Action	Yes	No
1	Did you perform the Diagnostic System Check?	Go to Step 2	Go to Diagnostic System Check
2	1. Using a scan tool, select the Instrument Panel Cluster Special Functions mode. 2. Go to Lamp Test. 3. In the Lamp Test mode you can turn on or off the instrument panel indicators. All indicators will turn ON when commanded on. Does the ABS Indicator turn on then off?	Go to Step 3	Go to Step 4
3	Replace the EBCM. Is the replacement complete?	Go to Diagnostic System Check	--
4	1. Disconnect the Instrument Cluster and connect a Test Light across the appropriate power and ground terminals. 2. Test Light OFF, repair open in power or ground circuit to cluster. 3. Test Light ON, check connector for poor connection to the cluster. 4. If OK, replace the Instrument Cluster. Refer to Instrument Panel Cluster (IPC) Replacement in Instrument Panel, Gages, and Console. Is the instrument cluster replacement complete?	Go to Diagnostic System Check	--

LTV0500000005227

Fig. 61   ABS Indicator Inoperative (Part 2 of 2). Hummer H2

Circuit Description

The instrument panel cluster (IPC) turns the ABS Indicator on during the IPC bulb check for approximately 3 seconds when the ignition switch is turned to the ON position. If the EBCM sets a diagnostic trouble code (DTC) the EBCM sends the IPC the command to turn the ABS indicator on.

Diagnostic Aids

- It is very important that a thorough inspection of the wiring and connectors be performed. Failure to carefully and fully inspect wiring and connectors may result in misdiagnosis, causing part replacement with reappearance of the malfunction.
- Thoroughly inspect any circuitry that may be causing the complaint for the following conditions:
  - Backed out terminals
  - Improper mating
  - Broken locks
  - Improperly formed or damaged terminals
  - Poor terminal-to-wiring connections
  - Physical damage to the wiring harness
- The following conditions may cause an intermittent malfunction:
  - A poor connection
  - Rubbed-through wire insulation
  - A broken wire inside the insulation

LTV0500000005226

Fig. 61   ABS Indicator Inoperative (Part 1 of 2). Hummer H2

Circuit Description

The TRAC OFF indicator is controlled by the instrument cluster via class 2 serial data messages from the EBCM. When the EBCM sees the traction control switch fault, the EBCM then disables the traction control and sends a message to the instrument cluster to turn the TRAC OFF indicator ON. Each time the ignition is cycled from OFF to ON, the traction control system is enabled.

The following conditions will cause the TRAC OFF indicator to illuminate:

- The EBCM has disabled the TCS due to a DTC.
- The EBCM has disabled the TCS due to a overheated ABS/TCS hydraulic unit.
- The instrument cluster bulb check. When the ignition switch is turned to ON, the TRAC OFF indicator will turn on for approximately 5 seconds and then turn OFF.

Diagnostic Aids

- It is very important that a thorough inspection of the wiring and connectors be performed. Failure to carefully and fully inspect wiring and connectors may result in misdiagnosis, causing part replacement with reappearance of the malfunction.
- Thoroughly inspect any circuitry that may be causing the complaint for the following conditions:
  - Backed out terminals
  - Improper mating
  - Broken locks
  - Improperly formed or damaged terminals
  - Poor terminal-to-wiring connections
  - Physical damage to the wiring harness
- The following conditions may cause an intermittent malfunction:
  - A poor connection
  - Rubbed-through wire insulation
  - A broken wire inside the insulation

Test Description

The number(s) below refer to the step number(s) on the diagnostic table.

2. Checks if the scan tool can turn on and off all the indicator lamps in the instrument cluster.

4. Checks if the circuits going to the instrument cluster or the cluster is at fault.

LTV0500000005228

Fig. 62   Traction Off Indicator Always On (Part 1 of 2). Hummer H2

Step	Action	Yes	No
1	Did you perform the Diagnostic System Check?	Go to Step 2	Go to Diagnostic System Check
2	1. Using a scan tool, select the Instrument Cluster Special Functions mode. 2. Go to Displays Test in Output Control. 3. In the Displays Test mode you can turn on or off the instrument panel indicators. All indicators will turn ON when commanded on. Does the TRAC OFF indicator turn on then off?	Go to Step 3	Go to Step 4
3	Replace the EBCM. Is the replacement complete?	Go to Diagnostic System Check	--
4	1. Disconnect the Instrument Cluster and connect a Test Light across the appropriate power and ground terminals. 2. Test Light OFF, repair open in power or ground circuit to cluster 3. Test Light ON, check connector for poor connection to cluster. 4. If OK, replace the Instrument Cluster. Is the Instrument Cluster replacement complete?	Go to Diagnostic System Check	--

LTV0500000005229

Fig. 62   Traction Off Indicator Always On (Part 2 of 2). Hummer H2

Circuit Description

The TRAC OFF indicator is controlled by the instrument cluster via class 2 serial data messages from the EBCM. When the EBCM sees the traction control switch fault, the EBCM then disables the traction control, and sends a message to the instrument cluster to turn the TRAC OFF indicator ON. Each time the ignition is cycled from OFF to ON, the traction control system is enabled.

The following conditions will cause the TRAC OFF indicator to illuminate:

- The EBCM has disabled the TCS due to a DTC.
- The EBCM has disabled the TCS due to a overheated ABS/TCS hydraulic unit.
- The instrument cluster bulb check. When the ignition switch is turned to ON, the TRAC OFF indicator will turn on for approximately 5 seconds and then turn OFF.

Diagnostic Aids

- It is very important that a thorough inspection of the wiring and connectors be performed. Failure to carefully and fully inspect wiring and connectors may result in misdiagnosis, causing part replacement with reappearance of the malfunction.
- Thoroughly inspect any circuitry that may be causing the complaint for the following conditions:
  - Backed out terminals
  - Improper mating
  - Broken locks
  - Improperly formed or damaged terminals
  - Poor terminal-to-wiring connections
  - Physical damage to the wiring harness
- The following conditions may cause an intermittent malfunction:
  - A poor connection
  - Rubbed-through wire insulation
  - A broken wire inside the insulation

Test Description

The number(s) below refer to the step number(s) on the diagnostic table.

2. Checks if the scan tool can turn on and off all the indicator lamps in the instrument cluster.

4. Checks if the circuits going to the instrument Cluster or the cluster is at fault.

LTV0500000005230

Fig. 63 Traction Off Indicator Inoperative (Part 1 of 2). Hummer H2

Step	Action	Yes	No
1	Did you perform the Diagnostic System Check?	Go to Step 2	Go to Diagnostic System Check
2	1. Using a scan tool, select the Instrument Panel Cluster Special Functions mode. 2. Go to Displays Test in Output Control. 3. In the Displays Test mode you can turn on or off the instrument panel indicators. All indicators will turn ON when commanded on. Does the TRAC OFF Indicator turn on then off?	Go to Step 3	Go to Step 4
3	Replace the EBCM. Is the replacement complete?	Go to Diagnostic System Check	--
4	1. Disconnect the Instrument Cluster and connect a Test Light across the appropriate power and ground terminals. 2. Test Light OFF, repair open in power or ground circuit to cluster. 3. Test Light ON, check connector for poor connection to the cluster. 4. If OK, replace the Instrument Cluster. Is the instrument cluster replacement complete?	Go to Diagnostic System Check	--

LTV0500000005231

Fig. 63 Traction Off Indicator Inoperative (Part 2 of 2). Hummer H2

°C	°F	OHMS
Temperature vs Resistance Values (Approximate)		
100	212	177
90	194	241
80	176	332
70	158	467
60	140	667
50	122	973
45	113	1188
40	104	1459
35	95	1802
30	86	2238
25	77	2796
20	68	3520
15	59	4450
10	50	5670
5	41	7280
0	32	9420
-5	23	12300
-10	14	16180
-15	5	21450
-20	-4	28680
-30	-22	52700
-40	-40	100700

GC4020152440000X

Fig. 64 Temperature vs. resistance values

Continental Teves MK-70

NOTE: On Air Bag Equipped Models, Refer To "Air Bag System Precautions" Located In The Front Of This Manual For System Disarming & Arming Procedures.

NOTE: Electrical Symbol & Wire Color Code Identification Located In The Front Of This Manual May Be Used As An Aid When Using Wiring Circuits Found In This Section.

NOTE: Refer To "Computer Relearn Procedures" Located In The Front Of This Manual For Computer Relearn Procedures.

INDEX

	Page No.		Page No.		Page No.
Description	5-76	Symptom Tests	5-76	Bleeding – Manual	5-77
Diagnosis & Testing	5-76	Temperature Vs. Resistance	5-76	Hydraulic Brake System	
Accessing Diagnostic Trouble		Wiring Diagrams	5-76	Bleeding – Pressure	5-78
Codes	5-76	**Diagnostic Chart Index**	5-81	Component Replacement	5-79
Clearing Diagnostic Trouble		**Precautions**	5-76	Brake Pressure Modulator	
Codes	5-77	Air Bag Systems	5-76	Valve (BPMV) Bracket	5-80
Connector Pin Identification	5-76	Battery Ground Cable	5-76	Brake Pressure Modulator	
Diagnostic Tests	5-76	**System Service**	5-77	Valve (BPMV)	5-79
Diagnostic Trouble Code		Brake System Bleed	5-77	Electronic Brake Control	
Interpretation	5-76	ABS Automated Bleed		Module (EBCM)	5-80
Intermittents & Poor		Procedure	5-77		
Connections	5-76	Hydraulic Brake System			

PRECAUTIONS

Air Bag Systems

Refer to "Air Bag System Precautions" in the front of this manual for system disarming and arming procedures.

Battery Ground Cable

Prior to service disconnect battery ground cable and isolate as required.

DESCRIPTION

When wheel slip is detected during a brake application, the ABS enters anti-lock mode. During anti-lock braking, hydraulic pressure in the individual wheel circuits is controlled to prevent any wheel from slipping. A separate hydraulic line and specific solenoid valves are provided for each wheel. The ABS can decrease, hold, or increase hydraulic pressure to each wheel brake. The ABS cannot, however, increase hydraulic pressure above the amount which is transmitted by the master cylinder during braking.

During anti-lock braking, a series of rapid pulsations is felt in the brake pedal. These pulsations are caused by the rapid changes in position of the individual solenoid valves as the EBCM responds to wheel speed sensor inputs and attempts to prevent wheel slip. These pedal pulsations are present only during anti-lock braking and

stop when normal braking is resumed or when the vehicle comes to a stop. A ticking or popping noise may also be heard as the solenoid valves cycle rapidly. During anti-lock braking on dry pavement, intermittent chirping noises may be heard as the tires approach slipping. These noises and pedal pulsations are considered normal during anti-lock operation.

Vehicles equipped with ABS may be stopped by applying normal force to the brake pedal. Brake pedal operation during normal braking is no different than that of previous non-ABS systems. Maintaining a constant force on the brake pedal provides the shortest stopping distance while maintaining vehicle stability.

DIAGNOSIS & TESTING

Accessing Diagnostic Trouble Codes

Connect a suitably programmed scan tool to Data Link Connector (DLC) and follow manufacturers instructions.

Diagnostic Trouble Code Interpretation

Refer to "Diagnostic Chart Index" for diagnostic trouble code interpretation.

Connector Pin Identification

Refer to **Figs. 1 through 5** for connector pin identifications.

Wiring Diagrams

Refer to **Fig. 6** for wiring diagrams.

Diagnostic Tests

Refer to **Figs. 7 through 18** for diagnostic test procedures.

Symptom Tests

Refer to **Figs. 19 and 20** for symptom test procedures.

Temperature Vs. Resistance

Refer to **Fig. 21** for temperature vs. resistance.

Intermittents & Poor Connections

Most Intermittents are caused by faulty electrical connections or wiring, although a sticking relay or solenoid can also cause an

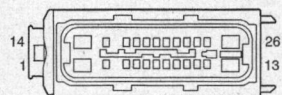

Connector Part Information

- OEM: 1452643-1
- Service: 88988362
- Description: 26-Way F (BK)

Terminal Part Information

- Pins:
- Terminal:
- Core/Insulation Crimp:
- Release Tool/Test Probe:

Pin	Wire Color	Circuit No.	Function
1	RD/WH	740	Battery Positive Voltage
2	OG	885	Left Rear Wheel Speed Sensor Low Reference
3	TN	884	Left Rear Wheel Speed Sensor Signal
4	L-BU	20	Stop Lamp Supply Voltage
5	D-GN	872	Right Front Wheel Speed Sensor Signal
6	TN	833	Right Front Wheel Speed Sensor Low Reference
7	--	--	Not Used
8	YE	873	Left Front Wheel Speed Sensor Low Reference
9	L-BU	830	Left Front Wheel Speed Sensor Signal
10	--	--	Not Used
11	BN	882	Right Rear Wheel Speed Sensor Signal
12	WH	883	Right Rear Wheel Speed Sensor Low Reference
13	--	--	Not Used
14	RD/BK	542	Battery Positive Voltage
15-19	--	--	Not Used

LTV0500000004657

Fig. 1   Connector pin identification
(EBCM – Part 1 of 2)

20	PK	1439	Ignition 1 Voltage
21	TN	2501	High Speed GMLAN Serial Data (-)
22	TN	2501	High Speed GMLAN Serial Data (-)
23	TN/BK	2500	High Speed GMLAN Serial Data (+)
24	TN/BK	2500	High Speed GMLAN Serial Data (+)
25	--	--	Not Used
26	BK	350	Ground

LTV0500000004658

Fig. 1   Connector pin identification
(EBCM – Part 2 of 2)

intermittent condition. Inspect wiring and connectors for the following:

1. Poor mating of connector halves, or terminals not fully seated in connector body.
2. Dirt or corrosion on terminals.
3. Damaged connector body.
4. Improperly formed or damaged terminals.
5. Poor terminal to wire connection.
6. Rubbed through wiring insulation.
7. Wiring broken inside insulation.

Clearing Diagnostic Trouble Codes

Connect a suitably programmed scan tool to Data Link Connector (DLC) and follow manufacturers instructions.

SYSTEM SERVICE

Brake System Bleed

ABS AUTOMATED BLEED PROCEDURE

Before performing the ABS Automated Bleed Procedure, first perform "Manual" or "Pressure" bleed of the base brake system. The automated bleed procedure is recommended when one of the following conditions exist: Base brake system bleeding does not achieve the desired pedal height or feel. Extreme loss of brake fluid has occurred. Air ingestion is suspected in the secondary circuits of the brake modulator assembly.

The ABS automated bleed procedure uses a scan tool to cycle the system sole-noid valves and run the pump in order to purge any air from the secondary circuits. These circuits are normally closed off, and are only opened during system initialization at vehicle start up and during ABS operation. The automated bleed procedure opens these secondary circuits and allows any air trapped in these circuits to flow out toward the brake corners.

The automated bleed procedure may be terminated at any time during the process by pressing the "EXIT" button. No further scan tool prompts pertaining to the automated bleed procedure will be given. After exiting the bleed procedure, relieve bleed pressure and disconnect bleed equipment per manufacturers instructions. Failure to properly relieve pressure may result in spilled brake fluid causing damage to components and painted surfaces.

1. Raise and support vehicle.
2. Remove all four wheel and tire assemblies.
3. Inspect brake system for leaks and visual damage.
4. Lower vehicle.
5. Ensure that battery is at full charge.
6. Install a suitably programmed scan tool to Data Link Connector (DLC).
7. Turn ignition On, with engine Off.
8. Follow scan tool instructions to communicate with ABS system.
9. Raise and support vehicle.
10. Follow directions through scan tool ABS system program. **Pressure bleed base brake system as outlined in "Hydraulic Brake System Bleeding – Pressure."**
11. Follow scan tool directions until desired brake pedal height is achieved.
12. If bleed procedure is aborted, a fault exists. Perform following steps before resuming bleed procedure:
    a. If a DTC is detected, refer to "Diagnostic Trouble Code Interpretation" for information and diagnose as required.
    b. If brake pedal feels spongy, perform conventional brake bleed procedure as outlined in "Hydraulic Brake System Bleeding – Pressure" or "Hydraulic Brake System Bleeding – Manual."
13. When desired pedal height is achieved, press brake pedal to inspect for firmness.
14. Lower vehicle.
15. Remove scan tool.
16. Install tire and wheel assemblies.
17. Inspect brake fluid level.
18. Road test vehicle.

HYDRAULIC BRAKE SYSTEM BLEEDING – MANUAL

1. Place a clean shop cloth beneath brake master cylinder to catch brake fluid spills.
2. With ignition Off and brakes cool, apply brakes 3–5 times, or until brake pedal effort increases significantly, in order to deplete brake booster power reserve.
3. If you have performed a brake master cylinder bench bleeding on this vehicle, or if you disconnected brake pipes from master cylinder, or if you have disconnected brake pipes from proportioning valve assembly or brake modulator assembly, you must perform following steps to bleed air at ports of hydraulic component:
    a. Fill brake master cylinder reservoir to maximum-fill level with GM approved or equivalent DOT-3 brake fluid from a clean, sealed brake fluid container. If removal of reservoir cap and diaphragm is required, clean outside of reservoir on and around cap prior to removal.
    b. With brake pipes installed securely to master cylinder, proportioning valve assembly, or brake modulator assembly, loosen and separate one of brake pipes from port of component. For proportioning valve assembly or brake modulator assembly, perform these steps in sequence of system flow; begin with fluid feed pipes from master cylinder.
    c. Allow a small amount of brake fluid to gravity bleed from open port of component.
    d. Connect brake pipe to component and tighten securely.

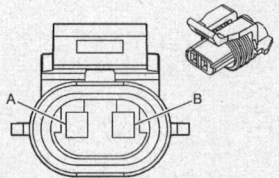

Connector Part Information

- OEM: 12052644
- Service: 22710405
- Description: 2-Way F Metri-Pack 150 Series Sealed (GY)

Terminal Part Information

- Pins:
- Terminal:
- Core/Insulation Crimp:
- Release Tool/Test Probe:

Pin	Wire Color	Circuit No.	Function
A	D-GN	872	Right Front Wheel Speed Sensor Signal
B	TN	833	Right Front Wheel Speed Sensor Low Reference

LTV0500000004659

Fig. 2 Connector pin identification (Lefthand front WSS)

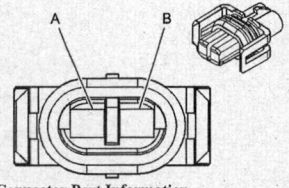

Connector Part Information

- OEM: 15305168
- Service: 12167117
- Description: 2-Way F Metri-Pack 150 Series Sealed (GY)

Terminal Part Information

- Pins:
- Terminal:
- Core/Insulation Crimp:
- Release Tool/Test Probe:

Pin	Wire Color	Circuit No.	Function
A	TN	884	Left Rear Wheel Speed Sensor Signal
B	OG	885	Left Rear Wheel Speed Sensor Low Reference

LTV0500000004660

Fig. 3 Connector pin identification (Lefthand rear WSS)

e. Have an assistant slowly depress brake pedal fully and maintain steady pressure on pedal.

f. Loosen same brake pipe to purge air from open port of component.

g. Tighten brake pipe, then have assistant slowly release brake pedal.

h. Wait 15 seconds, then repeat steps c through g until all air is purged from same port of component.

i. With brake pipe installed securely to master cylinder, proportioning valve assembly, or brake modulator assembly after all air has been purged from first port of component that was bled, loosen and separate next brake pipe from component, then repeat steps c through h until each of ports on component has been bled.

j. After completing final component port bleeding procedure, ensure that each of brake pipe-to-component fittings is properly tightened.

4. Fill brake master cylinder reservoir to maximum-fill level with GM approved or equivalent DOT-3 brake fluid from a clean, sealed brake fluid container. Ensure brake master cylinder reservoir remains at least half-full during this bleeding procedure. Add fluid as required to maintain proper level. Clean outside of reservoir on and around reservoir cap prior to removing cap and diaphragm.

5. Install a suitable box-end wrench onto righthand rear wheel hydraulic circuit bleeder valve.

6. Install a transparent hose over end of bleeder valve.

7. Submerge open end of transparent hose into a transparent container partially filled with GM approved or equivalent DOT-3 brake fluid from a clean, sealed brake fluid container.

8. Have an assistant slowly depress brake pedal fully and maintain steady pressure on pedal.

9. Loosen bleeder valve to purge air from wheel hydraulic circuit.

10. Tighten bleeder valve, then have assistant slowly release brake pedal.

11. Wait 15 seconds, then repeat steps 8–10 until all air is purged from same wheel hydraulic circuit.

12. With righthand rear wheel hydraulic circuit bleeder valve tightened securely and after all air has been purged from righthand rear hydraulic circuit, install a suitable box-end wrench onto lefthand front wheel hydraulic circuit bleeder valve.

13. Install a transparent hose over end of bleeder valve, then repeat steps 7–11.

14. With lefthand front wheel hydraulic circuit bleeder valve tightened securely after all air has been purged from lefthand front hydraulic circuit, install a suitable box-end wrench onto lefthand rear wheel hydraulic circuit bleeder valve.

15. Install a transparent hose over end of bleeder valve, then repeat steps 7–11.

16. With lefthand rear wheel hydraulic circuit bleeder valve tightened securely after all air has been purged from lefthand rear hydraulic circuit, install a suitable box-end wrench onto righthand front wheel hydraulic circuit bleeder valve.

17. Install a transparent hose over end of bleeder valve, then repeat steps 7–11.

18. After completing final wheel hydraulic circuit bleeding procedure, ensure that each of 4 wheel hydraulic circuit bleeder valves is properly tightened.

19. Fill brake master cylinder reservoir to maximum-fill level with GM approved or equivalent DOT-3 brake fluid from a clean, sealed brake fluid container.

20. Slowly depress and release brake pedal. Observe feel of brake pedal.

21. If brake pedal feels spongy, repeat bleeding procedure again. If brake pedal still feels spongy after repeating bleeding procedure, perform the following steps:

a. Inspect brake system for external leaks.

b. Pressure bleed hydraulic brake system in order to purge any air that may still be trapped in system.

22. Turn ignition key On, with engine Off. Inspect to see if brake system warning lamp remains illuminated.

23. If brake system warning lamp remains illuminated, diagnose and troubleshoot as required. **Do not allow vehicle to be driven until it is diagnosed and repaired.**

HYDRAULIC BRAKE SYSTEM BLEEDING – PRESSURE

1. Place a clean shop cloth beneath brake master cylinder to catch brake fluid spills.

2. With ignition Off and brakes cool, apply brakes 3–5 times, or until brake pedal becomes firm, in order to deplete brake booster power reserve.

3. If you have performed a brake master cylinder bench bleeding on this vehicle, or if you disconnected brake pipes from master cylinder, or if you have disconnected brake pipes from proportioning valve assembly or brake modulator assembly, you must perform following steps to bleed air at ports of hydraulic component:

a. Fill brake master cylinder reservoir to maximum-fill level with GM approved or equivalent DOT-3 brake fluid from a clean sealed brake fluid container. If removal of reservoir cap and diaphragm is required, clean outside of reservoir on and around cap prior to removal.

b. With brake pipes installed securely to master cylinder, proportioning valve assembly, or brake modulator assembly, loosen and separate one brake pipe from port of component. For proportioning valve assembly or brake modulator assembly, perform these steps in sequence of system flow; begin with fluid feed pipes from master cylinder.

c. Allow a small amount of brake fluid to gravity bleed from open port of component.

d. Connect brake pipe to component

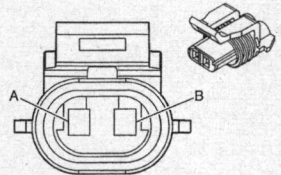

Connector Part Information

- OEM: 12052644
- Service: 22710405
- Description: 2-Way F Metri-Pack 150 Series Sealed (GY)

Terminal Part Information

- Pins:
- Terminal:
- Core/Insulation Crimp:
- Release Tool/Test Probe:

Pin	Wire Color	Circuit No.	Function
A	D-GN	872	Right Front Wheel Speed Sensor Signal
B	TN	833	Right Front Wheel Speed Sensor Low Reference

LTV0500000004661

Fig. 4 Connector pin identification (Righthand front WSS)

Connector Part Information

- OEM: 15305168
- Service: 12167117
- Description: 2-Way F Metri-Pack 150 Series Sealed (GY)

Terminal Part Information

- Pins:
- Terminal:
- Core/Insulation Crimp:
- Release Tool/Test Probe:

Pin	Wire Color	Circuit No.	Function
A	BN	882	Right Rear Wheel Speed Sensor Signal
B	WH	883	Right Rear Wheel Speed Sensor Low Reference

LTV0500000004662

Fig. 5 Connector pin identification (Righthand rear WSS)

and tighten securely.

e. Have an assistant slowly depress brake pedal fully and maintain steady pressure on pedal.

f. Loosen same brake pipe to purge air from open port of component.

g. Tighten brake pipe, then have assistant slowly release brake pedal.

h. Wait 15 seconds, then repeat steps c through g until all air is purged from same port of component.

i. With brake pipe installed securely to master cylinder, proportioning valve assembly, or brake modulator assembly after all air has been purged from first port of component that was bled loosen and separate next brake pipe from component, then repeat steps c through h until each of ports on component has been bled.

j. After completing final component port bleeding procedure, ensure that each of brake pipe-to-component fittings is properly tightened.

4. Fill brake master cylinder reservoir to maximum-fill level with GM approved or equivalent DOT-3 brake fluid from a clean sealed brake fluid container. Clean outside of reservoir on and around reservoir cap prior to removing cap and diaphragm.

5. Install tool No. J 44894-A, or equivalent to brake master cylinder reservoir.

6. Inspect brake fluid level in tool No. J 29532, or equivalent. Add GM approved or equivalent DOT-3 brake fluid from a clean, sealed brake fluid container as required to bring level to approximately half-full point.

7. Connect tool No. J 29532, or equivalent to tool No. J 44894-A, or equivalent.

8. Charge tool No. J 29532, or equivalent air tank to 25–30 psi.

9. Open tool No. J 29532, or equivalent fluid tank valve to allow pressurized brake fluid to enter brake system.

10. Wait approximately 30 seconds, then inspect entire hydraulic brake system in order to ensure that there are no existing external brake fluid leaks. Any brake fluid leaks identified require repair prior to completing this procedure.

11. Install a suitable box-end wrench onto righthand rear wheel hydraulic circuit bleeder valve.

12. Install a transparent hose over end of bleeder valve.

13. Submerge open end of transparent hose into transparent container partially filled with GM approved or equivalent DOT-3 brake fluid from a clean, sealed brake fluid container.

14. Loosen bleeder valve to purge air from wheel hydraulic circuit. Allow fluid to flow until air bubbles stop flowing from bleeder, then tighten bleeder valve.

15. With righthand rear wheel hydraulic circuit bleeder valve tightened securely after all air has been purged from righthand rear hydraulic circuit, install a suitable box-end wrench onto lefthand front wheel hydraulic circuit bleeder valve.

16. Install a transparent hose over end of bleeder valve, then repeat steps 13–14.

17. With lefthand front wheel hydraulic circuit bleeder valve tightened securely after all air has been purged from lefthand front hydraulic circuit, install a suitable box-end wrench onto lefthand rear wheel hydraulic circuit bleeder valve.

18. Install a transparent hose over end of bleeder valve, then repeat steps 13–14.

19. With lefthand rear wheel hydraulic circuit bleeder valve tightened securely after all air has been purged from lefthand rear hydraulic circuit, install a suitable box-end wrench onto righthand front wheel hydraulic circuit bleeder valve.

20. Install a transparent hose over end of bleeder valve, then repeat steps 13–14.

21. After completing final wheel hydraulic circuit bleeding procedure, ensure that each of 4 wheel hydraulic circuit bleeder valves is properly tightened.

22. Close tool No. J 29532, or equivalent fluid tank valve, then disconnect tool No. J 29532, or equivalent from tool No. J 44894-A, or equivalent.

23. Remove tool No. J 44894-A, or equivalent from brake master cylinder reservoir.

24. Fill brake master cylinder reservoir to maximum-fill level with GM approved or equivalent DOT-3 brake fluid from a clean, sealed brake fluid container.

25. Slowly depress and release brake pedal. Observe feel of brake pedal.

26. If brake pedal feels spongy perform the following steps:

a. Inspect brake system for external leaks.

b. Perform "ABS Automated Bleed Procedure" to remove any air that may have been trapped in brake pressure modulator valve (BPMV).

27. Turn ignition key On, with engine Off. Inspect to see if brake system warning lamp remains illuminated.

28. If brake system warning lamp remains illuminated, diagnose and troubleshoot as required. **Do not allow vehicle to be driven until it is diagnosed and repaired.**

Component Replacement

BRAKE PRESSURE MODULATOR VALVE (BPMV)

1. Retrieve percentage of remaining engine oil using suitable scan tool. Record remaining engine oil life.

2. Disconnect battery ground cable as outlined in "Precautions."

3. Remove engine control module (ECM) and transaxle control module (TCM) cover.

4. Disconnect body harness electrical connector from ECM.

5. Disconnect engine harness electrical connector from ECM. **Control module damage may result when metal**

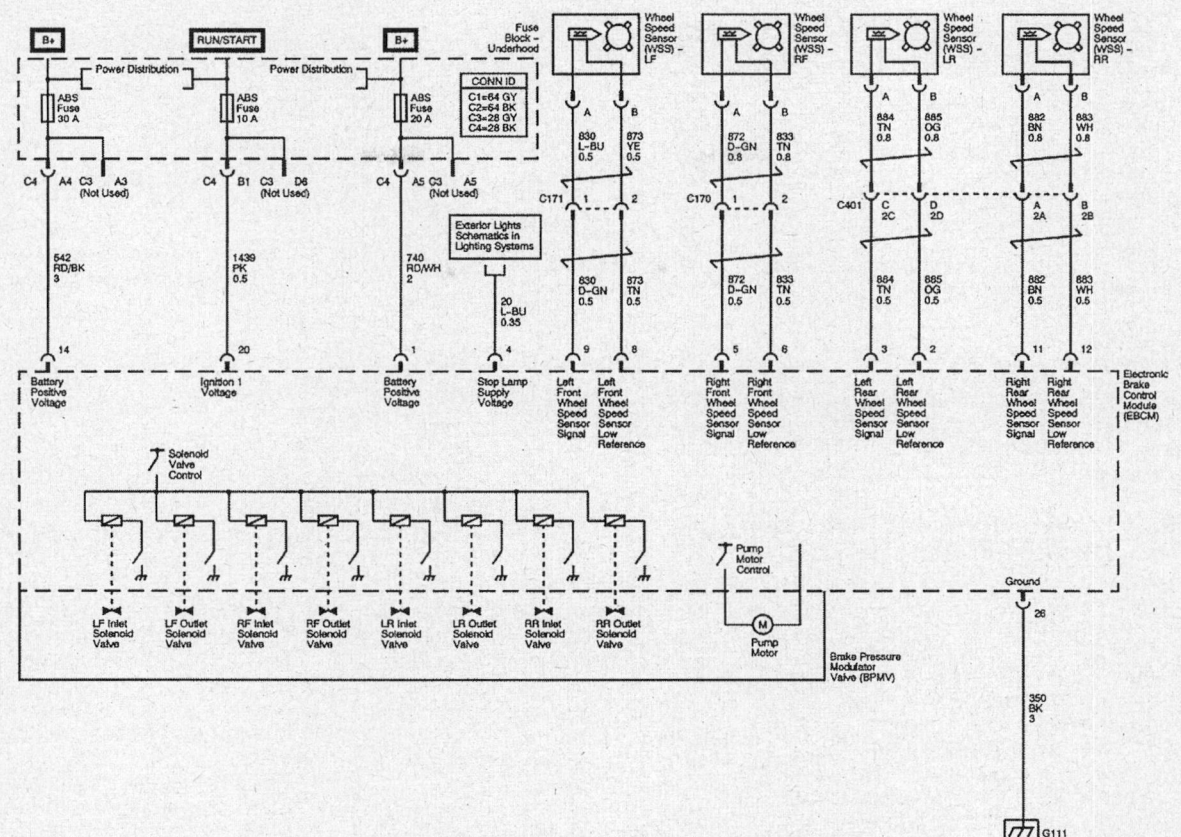

Fig. 6 Wiring diagram (Part 1 of 2)

case contacts battery voltage. **Do not contact control module metal case with battery voltage when servicing a control module, using battery booster cables or when charging vehicles battery.**

6. Disengage retaining tabs on sides of ECM and TCM bracket in order to remove ECM.
7. **On models equipped with automatic transmission,** remove transmission control module.
8. **On all models,** remove EBCM connector.
9. Remove brake pipe fittings.
10. Remove anti-lock brake control module assembly bracket bolt. Loosen but do not remove forward bolt.
11. Remove anti-lock brake control module assembly.
12. Remove EBCM.
13. Reverse procedure to install, noting the following:
    a. **Torque** anti-lock brake control module bolt to 89 inch lbs.
    b. **Torque** brake pipe fittings to 15 ft. lbs.

c. Program ECM using suitably programmed scan tool.
d. Install percentage of remaining engine oil using suitable scan tool.
e. Bleed BMPV as outlined in "ABS Automated Bleed Procedure."

BRAKE PRESSURE MODULATOR VALVE (BPMV) BRACKET

1. Remove brake pressure modulator valve as outlined in "Brake Pressure Modulator Valve (BPMV)."
2. Remove BPMV bolt.
3. Remove BPMV pins. **Insulators and pins are replaced as an assembly. Replace using new.**
4. Remove BPMV bracket.
5. Reverse procedure to install, noting the following:
    a. **Torque** BPMV pins to 89 inch lbs.
    b. **Torque** BPMV bolt to 97 inch lbs.
    c. Program ECM using suitably programmed scan tool.
    d. Install percentage of remaining engine oil using suitable scan tool.

e. Bleed BMPV as outlined in "ABS Automated Bleed Procedure."

ELECTRONIC BRAKE CONTROL MODULE (EBCM)

1. Remove brake pressure modulator valve as outlined in "Brake Pressure Modulator Valve (BPMV)."
2. Remove EBCM bolts.
3. Remove EBCM O-ring seal. **Do not reuse O-rings, replace with new.**
4. Remove EBCM.
5. Reverse procedure to install, noting the following:
    a. Clean mating surfaces between EBCM and BPMV using suitable denatured alcohol.
    b. **Torque** EBCM bolts to 20 inch lbs.
    c. Program ECM using suitably programmed scan tool.
    d. Install percentage of remaining engine oil using suitable scan tool.
    e. Bleed BMPV as outlined in "ABS Automated Bleed Procedure."

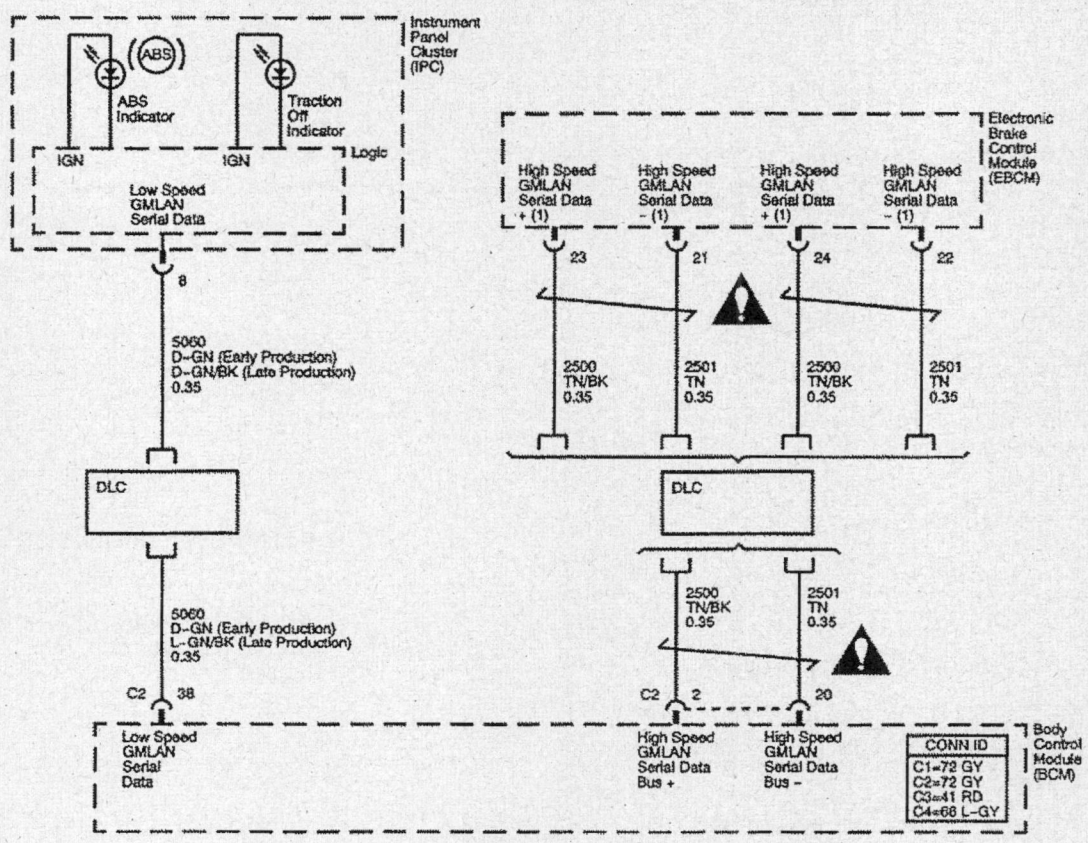

Fig. 6   Wiring diagram (Part 2 of 2)

LTV050000004656

DIAGNOSTIC CHART INDEX

Code	Description	Page No.	Fig. No.
—	Diagnostic System Check	5-82	7
—	ABS Indicator Always On	5-87	19
—	ABS Indicator Inoperative	5-87	20
C0035	Lefthand Front Wheel Speed Sensor Circuit Fault	5-82	8
C0040	Righthand Front Wheel Speed Sensor Circuit Fault	5-82	8
C0045	Lefthand Rear Wheel Speed Sensor Circuit Fault	5-82	8
C0050	Righthand Rear Wheel Speed Sensor Circuit Fault	5-82	8
C0110	Pump Motor Circuit Fault	5-83	9
C0131	ABS Pressure Circuit Fault	5-84	10
C0161	ABS/TCS Brake Switch Circuit Fault	5-84	11
C0201	Anti-Lock Brake System Enable Relay Contact Circuit	5-85	12
C0550	Electronic Control Unit Performance	5-85	13
C0551	Option Configuration Error/Variant Or VIN Not Programmed	5-85	14
C0561	System Disabled Information Stored	5-86	15
C0569	System Configuration Error No Additional Information	5-86	16
C0899	Device Voltage Low	5-86	17
C0900	Device Voltage High	5-87	18

1. Verify that none of the following preliminary inspections/tests reveal the cause of the vehicle concern before beginning diagnosis:
   - Ensure that the battery is fully charged.
   - Ensure that the battery cables are clean and tight.
   - Inspect for any open fuses.
   - Ensure that the grounds are clean, tight, and in the correct location.
   - Inspect the easily accessible systems or the visible system components for obvious damage or conditions that could cause the concern.
   - Inspect for aftermarket devices that could affect the operation of the system.
   - Search for applicable service bulletins.
   ⇒ If the preceding inspections/tests resolve the concern, go to Diagnostic Repair Verification .
2. Install a scan tool. Verify that the scan tool powers up.
   ⇒ If the scan tool does not power up, refer to Scan Tool Does Not Power Up .
3. Ignition ON, Engine OFF, verify communication with all of the control modules on the vehicle. Refer to Data Link References for information on the modules you should expect to communicate.
   ⇒ If the scan tool does not communicate with all of the expected control modules, refer to Data Link References .

Important: Open the drivers door to ensure retained accessory power mode (RAP) is inactive during this test. The engine may start during this test. Turn the engine OFF as soon as the crank power mode has been observed.

4. With a scan tool, access the body control module power mode data display list. Operate the ignition switch through all positions while observing the power mode data parameters. Verify that all the power mode parameters displayed correspond to the ignition key positions.
   ⇒ If any of the power mode parameters do not match in any ignition switch position, diagnose Power Mode Mismatch .
5. Ignition ON, view the security indicator. The security indicator should not remain illuminated after the vehicle bulb check has completed.
   ⇒ If the security indicator remains illuminated after the bulb check, refer to Diagnostic Trouble Code (DTC) List - Vehicle and diagnose any of the following theft deterrent DTCs set as

LTV0500000004663

Fig. 7 Diagnostic System Check (Part 1 of 2)

DTC Descriptors

DTC C0035 00 : Left Front Wheel Speed Sensor Circuit No Additional Information

DTC C0035 0F : Left Front Wheel Speed Sensor Circuit Erratic Signal

DTC C0035 18 : Left Front Wheel Speed Sensor Circuit Signal Amplitude Less Than Minimum

DTC C0040 00 : Right Front Wheel Speed Sensor Circuit No Additional Information

DTC C0040 0F : Right Front Wheel Speed Sensor Circuit Erratic Signal

DTC C0040 18 : Right Front Wheel Speed Sensor Circuit Signal Amplitude Less Than Minimum

DTC C0045 00 : Left Rear Wheel Speed Sensor Circuit No Additional Information

DTC C0045 0F : Left Rear Wheel Speed Sensor Circuit Erratic Signal

DTC C0045 18 : Left Rear Wheel Speed Sensor Circuit Signal Amplitude Less Than Minimum

DTC C0050 00 : Right Rear Wheel Speed Sensor Circuit No Additional Information

DTC C0050 0F : Right Rear Wheel Speed Sensor Circuit Erratic Signal

DTC C0050 18 : Right Rear Wheel Speed Sensor Circuit Signal Amplitude Less Than Minimum

Diagnostic Fault Information

Perform the Diagnostic System Check - Vehicle prior to using this diagnostic procedure.

Circuit	Short to Ground	Open/High Resistance	Short to Voltage	Signal Performance
Left Front Sensor Signal	C0035 00	C0035 00	C0035 00	C0035 0F, 18
Left Front Sensor Low Reference	C0035 00	C0035 00	C0035 00	C0035 0F, 18
Right Front Sensor Signal	C0040 00	C0040 00	C0040 00	C0040 0F, 18
Right Front Sensor Low Reference	C0040 00	C0040 00	C0040 00	C0040 0F, 18
Left Rear Sensor Signal	C0045 00	C0045 00	C0045 00	C0045 0F, 18

LTV0500000004665

Fig. 8 Codes C0035, C0040, C0045 & C0050: Wheel Speed Sensor Circuit Fault (Part 1 of 5)

current: B1000, B302A, B3031, B3055, B3060, B3935, B3976, P0513, P0633, P1629, P1631, or P1632.

6. Attempt to start the engine. Verify that the engine cranks.
   ⇒ If the engine does not crank, refer to Symptoms - Engine Electrical .
7. Attempt to start the engine. Verify the engine starts and runs.
   ⇒ If the engine does not start and run, refer to Engine Cranks but Does Not Run for the 2.2L (L61) engine or Engine Cranks but Does Not Run for the 2.4L engine.

Important: Do not clear any DTCs unless instructed to do so by a diagnostic procedure.

Important: If any DTCs are Powertrain related DTCs, select Capture Info in order to store the DTC information with the scan tool. If multiple Powertrain DTCs are stored, diagnose them in the following order:
1. Component level DTCs; such as sensor DTCs, solenoid DTCs, and relay DTCs.
2. System level DTCs; such as misfire DTCs, EVAP system DTCs, and fuel trim DTCs.

8. Advance to the List All DTCs screen on the scan tool selections to obtain DTCs from each of the vehicle modules. Verify there are no DTCs reported from any module.
   ⇒ If any DTCs are present, refer to Diagnostic Trouble Code (DTC) List - Vehicle and diagnose any current DTCs in the order the DTCs are displayed on the scan tool.
9. If the customer concern is related to inspection/maintenance (I/M) testing, refer to Inspection/Maintenance (I/M) System Check for the 2.2L (L61) engine or Inspection/Maintenance (I/M) System Check for the 2.4L engine.
   ⇒ If none of the previous tests or inspections addresses the concern, refer to Symptoms - Vehicle .

LTV0500000004664

Fig. 7 Diagnostic System Check (Part 2 of 2)

Left Rear Sensor Low Reference	C0045 00	C0045 00	C0045 00	C0045 0F, 18
Right Rear Sensor Signal	C0050 00	C0050 00	C0050 00	C0050 0F, 18
Right Rear Sensor Low Reference	C0050 00	C0050 00	C0050 00	C0050 0F, 18

Circuit/System Description

As the wheel spins, the wheel speed sensor produces an AC signal. The electronic brake control module (EBCM) uses the frequency of the AC signal to calculate the wheel speed.

Conditions for Running the DTC

C0035 - C0050 00

- The ignition is ON.
- Ignition voltage is greater than 8 volts.

C0035 - C0050 0F

- The ignition is ON.
- Ignition voltage is greater than 8 volts.
- The brake pedal is not pressed.
- A DTC is not set for the other wheel speed circuit on the same axle.

C0035 - C0050 18

- The ignition is ON.
- Ignition voltage is greater than 8 volts.
- The brake pedal is not pressed.
- No other wheel speed circuit DTCs are set.
- At least two other wheel speeds are not 0 km/h.

Conditions for Setting the DTC

C0035 - C0050 00

- An open is detected on the wheel speed sensor signal circuit.
- A short to ground is detected on the wheel speed sensor signal circuit.
- A short to voltage is detected on the wheel speed sensor signal circuit. C0035.

C0035 - C0050 0F

LTV0500000004666

Fig. 8 Codes C0035, C0040, C0045 & C0050: Wheel Speed Sensor Circuit Fault (Part 2 of 5)

The EBCM detects a rapid variation in the wheel speed. The wheel speed changes by 20 km/h (12 mph) or more in 0.01 second. The change must occur 3 times with no more than 0.2 seconds between occurrences.

C0035 - C0050 18

- One wheel speed is 2km/h (1.2 mph) .
- The remaining wheel speeds are greater than 10 km/h (6.2 mph).
- The difference between the remaining wheel speeds is less than 8 km/h (5 mph) from each other for 180 seconds.

OR

- The 2 wheel speed sensor inputs are 0 and DTCs are set.
- The 2 suspect wheel speeds equal zero for 6 seconds.
- The other wheel speeds are greater than 15 km/h (10 mph).
- The other wheel speeds are within 11 km/h (7 mph) of each other.

Action Taken When the DTC Sets

- The EBCM disables the Antilock Brake System (ABS)/Traction Control System (TCS) for the duration of the ignition cycle.
- The dynamic rear proportion (DRP) does not function optimally.
- The ABS indicator turns ON.
- The Traction Control indicator turns ON.

Conditions for Clearing the DTC

- The condition for setting the DTC is no longer present.
- The EBCM automatically clears the history DTC when a current DTC is not detected in 100 consecutive drive cycles.

Diagnostic Aids

If 2 or more wheel speed sensors are inoperative diagnose each wheel speed sensor individually.

If the customer comments that the ABS indicator is ON only during moist environmental conditions: rain, snow, vehicle wash, etc., inspect the wheel speed sensor wiring for signs of water intrusion. If the DTC is not current, clear all DTCs and simulate the effects of water intrusion by using the following procedure:

1. Spray the suspected area with a 5 percent saltwater solution. To create a 5 percent saltwater solution, add 2 teaspoons of salt to 8 FL oz of water (10 g of salt to 200 ml of water).
2. Test drive the vehicle over various road surfaces: bumps, turns, etc., above 40 km/h (25 mph) for

LTV0500000004667

Fig. 8   Codes C0035, C0040, C0045 & C0050: Wheel Speed Sensor Circuit Fault (Part 3 of 5)

⇒ If greater than 1350 ohms check for an open/high resistance in the circuit or faulty wheel speed sensor.

⇒ If less than 850 ohms check for a short between the circuits or faulty wheel speed sensor.

5. If all circuits test normal replace the EBCM.

Component Testing

1. Disconnect the wheel speed sensor connector.
2. With the ignition OFF, measure for 850-1350 ohms of resistance across the wheel speed sensor.
   ⇒ If the resistance is not between 850-1350 ohms replace the faulty wheel speed sensor.
3. Spin the wheel. Measure across the wheel speed sensor for 100 mV AC or greater.
   ⇒ If the AC voltage is less than 100 mV replace the wheel speed sensor.

Repair Instructions

Perform the Diagnostic Repair Verification after completing the diagnostic procedure.

- Wheel Bearing/Hub Replacement - Front
- Wheel Bearing/Hub Replacement - Rear
- Control Module References for EBCM replacement, setup, and programming

Repair Verification

Diagnostic Repair Verification

LTV0500000004669

Fig. 8   Codes C0035, C0040, C0045 & C0050: Wheel Speed Sensor Circuit Fault (Part 5 of 5)

Circuit/System Verification

With scan tool installed drive the vehicle in a straight line at a speed greater than 15 km/h (10 mph), all wheel speed sensors should read the same miles per hour.

Circuit/System Testing

It is recommended that Component Testing is performed before Circuit Testing when diagnosing wheel speed sensors.

1. With the ignition OFF, disconnect the EBCM connector.
2. With the ignition ON, measure for 0 volts between the sensor signal circuit or the low reference circuit and ground at the EBCM connector.
   ⇒ If over 0 volts, repair short to voltage in sensor signal circuit or the low reference circuit.
3. With the ignition OFF, Measure for infinite ohms of resistance between the wheel speed sensor signal or the low reference circuit and ground at the EBCM connector.
   ⇒ If less than infinite ohms, repair short to ground in the sensor signal or the low reference circuit.
4. Measure for 850-1350 ohms of resistance between the wheel speed sensor signal and low reference circuits at the EBCM connector.

LTV0500000004668

Fig. 8   Codes C0035, C0040, C0045 & C0050: Wheel Speed Sensor Circuit Fault (Part 4 of 5)

DTC Descriptors

DTC C0110 04: Pump Motor Circuit Open Circuit

DTC C0110 61: Pump Motor Circuit Actuator Stuck

Diagnostic Fault Information

Perform the Diagnostic System Check - Vehicle prior to using this diagnostic procedure.

Circuit/System Description

The pump motor is an integral part of the brake pressure modulator valve (BPMV), while the pump motor relay is integral to the electronic brake control module (EBCM). The pump motor relay is not engaged during normal system operation. When Antilock Brake System (ABS) or Traction Control System (TCS) operation is required the EBCM activates the pump motor relay and battery power is provided to the pump motor.

Conditions for Running the DTC

C0110 04

- The ignition switch is in the ON position.
- Initialization is complete.

C0110 61

- The test is initiated once per ignition cycle, when the vehicle speed is greater than 8 km/h (5 mph), and a fault was set on the last ignition cycle.
- The vehicle speed is greater than 20 km/h (13 mph), and the brake is not applied.
- The vehicle speed is greater than 40 km/h (26 mph).

Conditions for Setting the DTC

C0110 04

The EBCM detects a low voltage in the pump motor supply circuit when the feedback voltage is less than 6 volts for more than 1.8 seconds, and the pump motor is not activated. The ground circuit is open,

LTV0500000004670

Fig. 9   Code C0110: Pump Motor Circuit Fault (Part 1 of 3)

and the feedback voltage is greater than 0.93 volt for 1.8 seconds, the pump is not activated.

C00110 61

The pump motor continues to rotate briefly after activation creating a feedback voltage. The EBCM sets the code if the measured feedback voltage indicates a binding or stalled pump motor.

Action Taken When the DTC Sets

- The EBCM disables the ABS/TCS for the duration of the ignition cycle.
- The ABS indicator turns ON.
- The Traction Control indicator turns ON.

Conditions for Clearing the DTC

- The condition for the DTC is no longer present.
- The EBCM automatically clears the history DTC when a current DTC is not detected in 100 consecutive drive cycles.

Diagnostic Aids

The pump motor is integral to the BPMV. The pump motor is not serviceable. Inspect the power and ground circuits proper connections.

LTV0500000004671

Fig. 9   Code C0110: Pump Motor Circuit Fault (Part 2 of 3)

Scan Tool Data List for EBCM

Circuit/System Verification

With scan tool installed, clear the DTCs then drive the vehicle in a straight line at a speed greater than 20 km/h (13 mph). If the DTC did not set as a current DTC see diagnostic aids.

Circuit/System Testing

1. With the ignition OFF, disconnect the EBCM harness connector and connect a test lamp between the battery positive voltage circuit terminal going to the ABS pump motor, and to ground.
2. With the ignition ON, verify that the test lamp illuminates.
   ⇒ If the test lamp does not illuminate, repair the open or high resistance in the battery positive voltage circuit.
3. Connect a test lamp between the battery positive voltage circuit and pump motor ground circuit at the EBCM connector, verify that the test lamp illuminates.
   ⇒ If the test lamp does not illuminate, repair the open or high resistance in the pump motor ground circuit.
4. With ignition OFF, separate the electronic brake control module EBCM from the brake pressure modulator valve BPMV
5. Inspect the EBCM to BPMV connector for conditions such as damage, corrosion, or presence of brake fluid.
   ⇒ If connector corrosion or damage is evident, replace BPMV and/or EBCM as necessary.
   ⇒ If brake fluid is present, replace both BPMV and EBCM.
6. Connect the EBCM harness to the EBCM with the BPMV still separated.
7. Connect a test lamp between the pump motor circuits, the internal EBCM connector.
8. With ignition ON, use the scan tool to perform the Pump Motor Test.
   ⇒ If test lamp illuminates replace the BPMV.
   ⇒ If test lamp does not illuminate replace the EBCM, and BPMV.

Repair Instructions

Perform the Diagnostic Repair Verification after completing the diagnostic procedure.

- Brake Pressure Modulator Valve (BPMV) Replacement
- Electronic Brake Control Module Replacement
- Control Module References for EBCM replacement, setup, and programming

LTV0500000004672

Fig. 9   Code C0110: Pump Motor Circuit Fault (Part 3 of 3)

Circuit/System Verification

With scan tool installed, clear the DTCs then drive the vehicle in a straight line at a speed greater than 20 km/h (13 mph). If the DTC did not set as a current DTC see diagnostic aids.

Circuit/System Testing

Important: If DTC C0277 is set in Lighting Systems diagnose it first.

1. 1. Apply and release brake pedal. Verify brake lamps operate properly. If brake lamps do not operate properly, refer to Symptoms - Lighting Systems.
2. Replace the EBCM/BPMV assembly.

Repair Instructions

Perform the Diagnostic Repair Verification after completing the diagnostic procedure.

- Brake Pressure Modulator Valve (BPMV) Replacement
- Electronic Brake Control Module Replacement
- Control Module References for EBCM replacement, setup, and programming

LTV0500000004674

Fig. 10   Code C0131: ABS Pressure Circuit Fault (Part 2 of 2)

DTC Descriptors

DTC C0131 00: ABS Pressure Circuit No Additional Information

DTC C0131 4B: Pressure Circuit calibration not learned

DTC C0131 5A: Pressure Circuit calibration not learned plausibility failure

Diagnostic Fault Information

Perform the Diagnostic System Check - Vehicle prior to using this diagnostic procedure.

Circuit/System Description

The electronic brake control module (EBCM) uses input from the brake pressure sensor for more accurate control during a vehicle stability enhancement system (VSES) event.

Conditions for Running the DTC

- The ignition switch is in the ON position.
- Ignition voltage is greater than 8 volts.

Conditions for Setting the DTC

- Pressure signal does not correlate to estimated Pressure over time.
- Brake Signal does not correlate to Pressure Signal.
- Signal is erratic and changes faster than physically allowed.

Action Taken When the DTC Sets

- The EBCM disables the ABS/TCS for the duration of the ignition cycle.
- The Traction Control indicator turns ON.

Conditions for Clearing the DTC

- The condition for the DTC is no longer present and the DTC is cleared with a scan tool.
- The EBCM automatically clears the history DTC when a current DTC is not detected in 100 consecutive drive cycles.

LTV0500000004673

Fig. 10   Code C0131: ABS Pressure Circuit Fault (Part 1 of 2)

DTC Descriptor

DTC C0161 00: ABS/TCS Brake Switch Circuit Signal Malfunction No Additional Information

Diagnostic Fault Information

Perform the Diagnostic System Check - Vehicle prior to using this diagnostic procedure.

Circuit/System Description

The BCM illuminates the stop lamps by applying battery positive voltage to the stop lamp supply voltage circuit. The electronic brake control module (EBCM) receives a voltage input from the stop lamp supply voltage circuit to determine if the brake pedal is applied.

Conditions for Running the DTC

C0161 00

- The ignition is ON.
- The vehicle speed is greater than 20 km/h (12 mph).
- The ignition voltage is greater than 9 volts.

Conditions for Setting the DTC

C0161 11

- The brake pedal is sensed as applied for 6 minutes.
- The vehicle speed is greater than 20 km/h (12 mph).
- The EBCM does not receive a signal change from the stop lamp supply voltage circuit.
- Vehicle speed exceeds 40 km/h (25 mph) in four cycles, and decelerates to under 3 km/h (2 mph).

Action Taken When the DTC Sets

- The EBCM disables the engine drag control (EDC)/traction control system (TCS) for the duration of the ignition cycle.
- The Traction Control indicator turns ON.

LTV0500000004675

Fig. 11   Code C0161: ABS/TCS Brake Switch Circuit Fault (Part 1 of 2)

- The ABS remains functional.

Conditions for Clearing the DTC

- The condition for the DTC is no longer present and the DTC is cleared with a scan tool.
- The EBCM automatically clears the history DTC when a current DTC is not detected in 100 consecutive drive cycles.

Diagnostic Aids

The DTC C0161 00 can be set if the vehicle has been driven with the brake applied during acceleration.

Reference Information

Scan Tool Reference

Scan Tool Data List for EBCM

Circuit/System Verification

With the ignition ON, use a scan tool to display DTCs for the body control module (BCM).

⇒ If B codes are present, go to Diagnostic System Check - Vehicle .

⇒ If no DTCs are present, go to Diagnostic Aids.

Repair Verification

Diagnostic Repair Verification

LTV0500000004676

Fig. 11 Code C0161: ABS/TCS Brake Switch Circuit Fault (Part 2 of 2)

Circuit/System Verification

With the scan tool, access the ABS special functions menu and perform the ABS Motor test. The pump motor should function and no DTCs should be set.

Circuit/System Testing

Test for an open or a short to ground in the solenoid valve battery positive voltage circuit.

⇒ If battery positive voltage circuit tests normal, replace the EBCM/BPMV assembly.

Repair Instructions

Perform the Diagnostic Repair Verification after completing the diagnostic procedure.

Control Module References for EBCM replacement, setup, and programming

LTV0500000004678

Fig. 12 Code C0201: Anti-Lock Brake System Enable Relay Contact Circuit (Part 2 of 2)

DTC Descriptor

DTC C0550: Electronic Control Unit (ECU) Performance

Diagnostic Fault Information

Perform the Diagnostic System Check - Vehicle prior to using this diagnostic procedure.

Circuit/System Description

The electronic brake control module (EBCM) detects an internal malfunction.

Conditions for Running the DTC

The ignition switch is in the ON position.

Conditions for Setting the DTC

An internal EBCM malfunction exists.

Action Taken When the DTC Sets

One or more of the following actions may occur:

- The Antilock Brake System (ABS)/adaptive cruise control (ACC)/dynamic rear proportion (DRP)/engine drag control (EDC) are disabled.
- TCS is degraded.
- The ABS/TCS indicators turn ON.
- The red BRAKE Warning indicator turns ON.

Conditions for Clearing the DTC

The EBCM automatically clears the history DTC when a current DTC is not detected in 100 consecutive drive cycles.

Circuit/System Verification

Verify that the DTC will clear with a scan tool and does not reset.

⇒ If the DTC will not clear with a scan tool, replace the EBCM.

LTV0500000004679

Fig. 13 Code C0550: Electronic Control Unit Performance (Part 1 of 2)

DTC Descriptor

DTC C0201 04: Antilock Brake System (ABS) Enable Relay Contact Circuit

Diagnostic Fault Information

Perform the Diagnostic System Check - Vehicle prior to using this diagnostic procedure.

Circuit/System Description

The solenoid relay, located within the electronic brake control module (EBCM), supplies battery voltage to all of the valve solenoids.

Conditions for Running the DTC

- Ignition voltage is greater than 9.5 volts.
- The solenoid relay is commanded ON.

Conditions for Setting the DTC

One or more of the following conditions exists:

- The EBCM detects an open in the battery positive voltage circuit to the solenoid valve relay.
- The EBCM detects a stuck open solenoid valve relay or an open circuit between the solenoid valve relay and solenoid valves.

Action Taken When the DTC Sets

- The EBCM disables the ABS/DRP for the duration of the ignition cycle.
- The ABS indicator turns ON.
- The red brake warning indicator turns ON.

Conditions for Clearing the DTC

- The condition for setting the DTC is no longer present.
- The EBCM automatically clears the history DTC when a current DTC is not detected in 100 consecutive drive cycles.

LTV0500000004677

Fig. 12 Code C0201: Anti-Lock Brake System Enable Relay Contact Circuit (Part 1 of 2)

Repair Instructions

Perform the Diagnostic Repair Verification after completing the diagnostic procedure.

Control Module References for EBCM replacement, setup, and programming

Repair Verification

Diagnostic Repair Verification

LTV0500000004680

Fig. 13 Code C0550: Electronic Control Unit Performance (Part 2 of 2)

DTC Descriptors

DTC C0551 45: Option Configuration Error/Variant not programmed

DTC C0551 45: Option Configuration Error/Vin not programmed

Diagnostic Fault Information

Perform the Diagnostic System Check - Vehicle prior to using this diagnostic procedure.

Circuit/System Description

When the electronic brake control module (EBCM) is replaced, software and calibrations are flash programmed into the EBCM. The EBCM receives the vehicle powertrain options information from the powertrain control module (PCM) in order for the EBCM to automatically calibrate to the vehicle.

Conditions for Running the DTC

The ignition switch is in the ON position.

Conditions for Setting the DTC

C0551 45

The incorrect EBCM is installed on the vehicle.

C0551 47

The incorrect software or calibrations have been flash programmed into the EBCM.

Action Taken When the DTC Sets

One or more of the following actions may occur:

- The Antilock Brake System (ABS)/Traction Control System (TCS)/dynamic rear proportion (DRP) are disabled.
- The ABS/TCS indicators turn ON.
- The red BRAKE Warning indicator turns ON.

LTV0500000004681

Fig. 14 Code C0551: Option Configuration Error/ Variant Or VIN Not Programmed (Part 1 of 2)

Conditions for Clearing the DTC

- The condition for the DTC is no longer present and the DTC is cleared with a scan tool.
- The EBCM automatically clears the history DTC when a current DTC is not detected in 100 consecutive drive cycles.

Circuit/System Verification

1. Verify that the EBCM is the correct module for the vehicle:
   ⇒ If the EBCM is not correct, replace the EBCM.
   ⇒ Reprogram the EBCM.
2. With ignition OFF, separate the electronic brake control module EBCM from the brake pressure modulator valve brake pressure modulator valve (BPMV).

Repair Instructions

Perform the Diagnostic Repair Verification after completing the diagnostic procedure.

Control Module References for EBCM replacement, setup, and programming

LTV0500000004682

Fig. 14   Code C0551: Option Configuration Error/ Variant Or VIN Not Programmed (Part 2 of 2)

Circuit/System Verification

This DTC is for information only. As an aid to the technician, this DTC indicates that there are no problems in the ABS/TCS system.

Repair Verification

Diagnostic Repair Verification

LTV0500000004684

Fig. 15   Code C0561: System Disabled Information Stored (Part 2 of 2)

DTC Descriptor

DTC C0569 00: System Configuration Error No Additional Information

Diagnostic Fault Information

Perform the Diagnostic System Check - Vehicle prior to using this diagnostic procedure.

Circuit/System Description

The electronic brake control module (EBCM) receives a GMLAN message from each of the network modules. Each module contains its own unique identification (ID) code that must be learned into the EBCMs memory. Once all the IDs have been learned and vehicle speed is 25 mph, or greater, the EBCM continuously compares IDs in the GMLAN message to its learned Ids to determine if all the network modules are present.

Conditions for Running the DTC

The ignition is ON.

Conditions for Setting the DTC

The EBCM has not undergone the programming procedure.

Action Taken When the DTC Sets

The driver information center (DIC) displays the SERVICE ABS warning message.

Conditions for Clearing the DTC

A current DTC will clear when the EBCM has undergone the setup procedure.

Diagnostic Aids

A newly replaced EBCM will set DTC C0569 on its initial ignition ON cycle.

LTV0500000004685

Fig. 16   Code C0569: System Configuration Error No Additional Information (Part 1 of 2)

Special Tools Required

J-46079 Tire Pressure Monitor Diagnostic Tool

Repair Instructions

Perform the Diagnostic Repair Verification after completing the diagnostic procedure.

Electronic Brake Control Module Programming and Setup

LTV0500000004686

Fig. 16   Code C0569: System Configuration Error No Additional Information (Part 2 of 2)

DTC Descriptor

DTC C0561 71: System Disabled Information Stored

Diagnostic Fault Information

Perform the Diagnostic System Check - Vehicle prior to using this diagnostic procedure.

Circuit/System Description

The electronic brake control module (EBCM) disables the traction control when other electronic control modules set DTCs for components that effect the operation of the traction control system.

Conditions for Running the DTC

- The ignition switch is in the ON position.
- Ignition voltage is greater than 8 volts.

Conditions for Setting the DTC

The powertrain control module (PCM) or body control module (BCM) diagnosis a condition prevention the engine control portion of the traction control function and sends a serial data message to the EBCM indicating that torque reduction is not allowed. The PCM or BCM will typically set a DTC and the EBCM will set this DTC.

Action Taken When the DTC Sets

One or more of the following actions may occur:

- The EBCM disables the traction control system (TCS) until the DTC becomes a history DTC.
- The traction Off Indicator turns ON.
- The Antilock Brake System (ABS) remains functional.

Conditions for Clearing the DTC

- The condition for the DTC is no longer present and the DTC is cleared with a scan tool.
- The EBCM automatically clears the history DTC when a current DTC is not detected in 100 consecutive drive cycles.

Circuit/System Verification

LTV0500000004683

Fig. 15   Code C0561: System Disabled Information Stored (Part 1 of 2)

DTC Descriptor

DTC C0899: Device Voltage Low

Diagnostic Fault Information

Perform the Diagnostic System Check - Vehicle prior to using this diagnostic procedure.

Circuit	Short to Ground	Open/High Resistance	Short to Voltage	Signal Performance
EBCM Ground Circuit	-	C0899 00	-	-

Circuit/System Description

The electronic brake control module (EBCM) monitors the ignition voltage level available for system operation. A low voltage condition prevents the system from operating properly.

Conditions for Running the DTC

Ignition is ON.

Conditions for Setting the DTC

This fault will be set if the ignition voltage to EBCM is less than 9 volts for 100 msec.

Action Taken When the DTC Sets

- Traction Control System (TCS) indicator turns ON for the duration of the ignition cycle.
- The TCS indicator turns ON.

Conditions for Clearing the DTC

- The condition for the DTC is no longer present.
- The EBCM automatically clears the history DTC when a current DTC is not detected in 100 consecutive drive cycles.

Circuit/System Testing

1. Measure the voltage at the battery terminals.

LTV0500000004687

Fig. 17   Code C0899: Device Voltage Low (Part 1 of 2)

2. With scan tool, read the ignition voltage in the EBCM data list. Verify that battery terminal voltage, and ignition voltage readings do not differ more than 1 volt.
   ⇒ If more than 1 volt, test the ground circuit of the EBCM for high resistance. If the circuit test normal, test or replace the EBCM.
3. Refer to Battery Inspection/Test .

LTV0500000004688

Fig. 17   Code C0899: Device Voltage Low (Part 2 of 2)

Circuit Description

The instrument panel cluster (IPC) illuminates the ABS indicator by supplying ground to the lamp. The electronic brake control module (EBCM) sends serial data messages to the IPC to command the indicator ON or OFF.

Diagnostic Aids

The malfunction must be present during diagnosis in order to prevent unnecessary parts replacement. Always begin diagnosis with Diagnostic System Check - Vehicle .

Test Description

The number below refers to the step number on the diagnostic table.

3. This step tests if the IPC is able to turn OFF the ABS indicator.

Step	Action	Yes	No
Important: An ECE 13 response may cause the ABS indicator to remain ON when no DTCs are set. It is necessary to verify that ECE 13 is not causing the ABS indicator to remain illuminated, prior to performing this diagnostic. Refer to ABS Description and Operation for a complete description of the ECE 13 response.			
1	Did you perform the Diagnostic System Check - Vehicle?	Go to Step 2	Go to Diagnostic System Check - Vehicle
2	1. Turn OFF the ignition for 5 seconds. 2. Turn ON the ignition while observing the ABS indicator. Does the ABS indicator illuminate for approximately 2 seconds and then turn OFF?	Go to Diagnostic Aids	Go to Step 3
3	1. Select the Instrument Panel Cluster Special Functions menu on the scan tool. 2. Select Lamp Tests. 3. Command the IPC indicator lamps OFF. Does the ABS indicator turn OFF?	Go to Step 5	Go to Step 4

LTV0500000004690

Fig. 19   ABS Indicator Always On (Part 1 of 2)

4	Replace the instrument panel cluster (IPC). Did you complete the replacement?	Go to Step 6	--
5	Replace the electronic brake control module (EBCM). Did you complete the replacement?	Go to Step 6	--
6	1. Turn OFF the ignition for 5 seconds. 2. Turn ON the ignition while observing the ABS indicator. Does the ABS indicator illuminate for approximately 2 seconds and then turn OFF?	System OK	Go to Step 3

LTV0500000004691

Fig. 19   ABS Indicator Always On (Part 2 of 2)

DTC Descriptor

DTC C0900: Device Voltage High

Diagnostic Fault Information

Perform the Diagnostic System Check - Vehicle prior to using this diagnostic procedure.

Circuit	Short to Ground	Open/High Resistance	Short to Voltage	Signal Performance
EBCM Ignition Voltage High	-	-	-	C0900 00

Circuit/System Description

The electronic brake control module (EBCM) monitors the ignition voltage. If the voltage level is too high, damage may result in the system. When a high voltage condition is detected the EBCM turns OFF the system relay which removes battery voltage from the solenoid valves and pump motor.

Conditions for Running the DTC

Ignition is ON.

Conditions for Setting the DTC

The system voltage is greater than 16 volts for 100 msec.

Action Taken When the DTC Sets

- Traction Control System (TCS) disabled for the duration of the ignition cycle.
- ABS disabled if ignition voltage exceeds 19.5 volts.
- The TCS indicator turns ON.
- The Antilock Brake System (ABS) indicator turns ON if voltage exceeds 19.5 volts.

Conditions for Clearing the DTC

- The condition for the DTC is no longer present.
- The EBCM automatically clears the history DTC when a current DTC is not detected in 100 consecutive drive cycles.

LTV0500000004689

Fig. 18   Code C0900: Device Voltage High

Circuit Description

The instrument panel cluster (IPC) illuminates the ABS indicator by supplying ground to the lamp. The electronic brake control module (EBCM) sends class 2 serial data messages to the IPC in order to command the indicator ON or OFF.

Diagnostic Aids

Replace the Instrument Panel Cluster if the ABS indicator intermittently fails to operate during the bulb check.

Test Description

The number below refers to the step number on the diagnostic table.

2. This step tests if the IPC is able to illuminate the ABS indicator during the bulb check.

Step	Action	Yes	No
1	Did you perform the Diagnostic System Check - Vehicle?	Go to Step 2	Go to Diagnostic System Check
2	1. Turn OFF the ignition for 5 seconds. 2. Turn ON the ignition while observing the ABS indicator. Does the ABS indicator illuminate?	Go to Diagnostic Aids	Go to Step 3
3	Replace the instrument panel cluster (IPC). Did you complete the replacement?	Go to Step 4	--
4	1. Turn OFF the ignition for 5 seconds. 2. Turn ON the ignition while observing the ABS indicator. Does the ABS indicator illuminate?	System OK	Go to Step 3

LTV0500000004692

Fig. 20   ABS Indicator Inoperative

°C	°F	OHMS
Temperature vs Resistance Values (Approximate)		
150	302	47
140	284	60
130	266	77
120	248	100
110	230	132
100	212	177
90	194	241
80	176	332
70	158	467
60	140	667
50	122	973
45	113	1188
40	104	1459
35	95	1802
30	86	2238
25	77	2796
20	68	3520
15	59	4450
10	50	5670
5	41	7280
0	32	9420
-5	23	12300
-10	14	16180
-15	5	21450
-20	-4	28680
-30	-22	52700
-40	-40	100700

LTV0500000004693

Fig. 21   Temperature vs. resistance values

Delphi 7.0

NOTE: On Air Bag Equipped Models, Refer To "Air Bag System Precautions" Located In The Front Of This Manual For System Disarming & Arming Procedures.

NOTE: Electrical Symbol & Wire Color Code Identification Located In The Front Of This Manual May Be Used As An Aid When Using Wiring Circuits Found In This Section.

NOTE: Refer To "Computer Relearn Procedures" Located In The Front Of This Manual For Computer Relearn Procedures.

INDEX

	Page No.		Page No.		Page No.
Description	5-89	Symptom Tests	5-89	Hydraulic Brake System	
Diagnosis & Testing	5-89	Temperature Vs. Resistance	5-89	Bleeding – Pressure	5-90
Accessing Diagnostic Trouble		Wiring Diagrams	5-89	Component Replacement	5-90
Codes	5-89	**Diagnostic Chart Index**	5-93	Brake Pressure Modulator	
Clearing Diagnostic Trouble		**Precautions**	5-89	Valve (BPMV)	5-90
Codes	5-89	Air Bag Systems	5-89	Electronic Brake Control	
Connector Pin Identification	5-89	Battery Ground Cable	5-89	Module (EBCM)	5-90
Diagnostic Tests	5-89	**System Service**	5-89	Front Wheel Speed Sensor	5-91
Diagnostic Trouble Code		Brake System Bleed	5-89	Rear Wheel Speed Sensor	5-91
Interpretation	5-89	ABS Automated Bleed	5-89	Traction Control Switch	5-91
Intermittents & Poor		Hydraulic Brake System			
Connections	5-89	Bleeding – Manual	5-90		

PRECAUTIONS

Air Bag Systems

Refer to "Air Bag System Precautions" in the front of this manual for system disarming and arming procedures.

Battery Ground Cable

Prior to service disconnect battery ground cable and isolate as required.

DESCRIPTION

When wheel slip is detected during a brake application, the ABS enters anti-lock mode. During anti-lock braking, hydraulic pressure in the individual wheel circuits is controlled to prevent any wheel from slipping. A separate hydraulic line and specific solenoid valves are provided for each wheel. The ABS can decrease, hold, or increase hydraulic pressure to each wheel brake. The ABS cannot, however, increase hydraulic pressure above the amount which is transmitted by the master cylinder during braking.

During anti-lock braking, a series of rapid pulsations is felt in the brake pedal. These pulsations are caused by the rapid changes in position of the individual solenoid valves as the EBCM responds to wheel speed sensor inputs and attempts to prevent wheel slip. These pedal pulsations are present only during anti-lock braking and stop when normal braking is resumed or when the vehicle comes to a stop. A ticking or popping noise may also be heard as the solenoid valves cycle rapidly. During anti-lock braking on dry pavement, intermittent chirping noises may be heard as the tires approach slipping. These noises and pedal pulsations are considered normal during anti-lock operation.

Vehicles equipped with ABS may be stopped by applying normal force to the brake pedal. Brake pedal operation during normal braking is no different than that of previous non-ABS systems. Maintaining a constant force on the brake pedal provides the shortest stopping distance while maintaining vehicle stability.

DIAGNOSIS & TESTING

Accessing Diagnostic Trouble Codes

Connect a suitably programmed scan tool to Data Link Connector (DLC) and follow manufacturers instructions.

Diagnostic Trouble Code Interpretation

Refer to "Diagnostic Chart Index" for diagnostic trouble code interpretation.

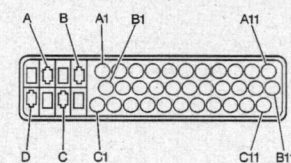

Connector Part Information	• 15336549 • 37-Way F Mixed Series (BLK)		
Pin	Wire Color	Circuit No.	Function
A1	BRN/WHT	1571	Traction Control Switch Signal
A2	--	--	Not Used
A3	BLK	884	Left Rear Wheel Speed Sensor Signal
A4	RED	885	Left Rear Wheel Speed Sensor Low Reference
A5	WHT	883	Right Rear Wheel Speed Sensor Low Reference
A6	BRN	882	Right Rear Wheel Speed Sensor Signal
A7	TAN	833	Right Front Wheel Speed Sensor Low Reference
A8	DK GRN	872	Right Front Wheel Speed Sensor Signal
A9	YEL	873	Left Front Wheel Speed Sensor Low Reference
A10	LT BLU	830	Left Front Wheel Speed Sensor Signal
A11	PNK	439	Ignition 1 Voltage
B1-B11	--	--	Not Used
C1	TAN/BLK	464	Delivered Torque Signal
C2-C6	--	--	Not Used
C7	WHT	17	Stop Lamp Switch Signal
C8	LT BLU	1122	ABS/TCS Class 2 Serial Data
C9	ORN/BLK	463	Requested Torque Signal
C10	--	--	Not Used
C11	--	--	Vent Tube
A	RED	102	Battery Positive Voltage
B	RED	302	Battery Positive Voltage
C	BLK	251	Ground
D	BLK	2050	Ground

LTV0500000004700

Fig. 1   Connector pin identification (EBCM)

Connector Pin Identification

Refer to **Figs. 1 through 5** for connector pin identification.

Wiring Diagrams

Refer to **Fig. 6** for wiring diagrams.

Diagnostic Tests

Refer to **Figs 7 through 25** for diagnostic test procedures.

Symptom Tests

Refer to **Figs 26 through 29** for symptom test procedures.

Temperature Vs. Resistance

Refer to **Fig. 30** for temperature vs. resistance values.

Intermittents & Poor Connections

Most Intermittents are caused by faulty electrical connections or wiring, although a sticking relay or solenoid can also cause an intermittent condition. Inspect wiring and connectors for the following:

1. Poor mating of connector halves, or terminals not fully seated in connector body.
2. Dirt or corrosion on terminals.
3. Damaged connector body.
4. Improperly formed or damaged terminals.
5. Poor terminal to wire connection.
6. Rubbed through wiring insulation.
7. Wiring broken inside insulation.

Clearing Diagnostic Trouble Codes

Connect a suitably programmed scan tool to Data Link Connector (DLC) and follow manufacturers instructions.

SYSTEM SERVICE

Brake System Bleed

ABS AUTOMATED BLEED

In most circumstances a base brake bleed is all that is required for most component replacements (such as wheel cylinders, calipers, brake tubes, and master cylinder) except for BPMV replacement.

The following automated ABS bleed procedure is required when one of the following occur: Manual bleeding at the wheel cylinders does not achieve the desired pedal height or feel. Brake Pressure Modulator Valve replacement (BPMV). Extreme loss of brake fluid has occurred. Air ingestion is suspected.

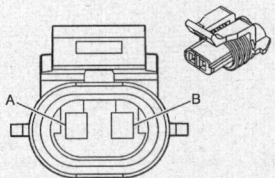

Connector Part Information	• 12052644		
	• 2-Way F Metric-Pack 150 Series (GRY)		
Pin	Wire Color	Circuit No.	Function
A	YEL	873	Left Front Wheel Speed Sensor Low Reference
B	LT BLU	830	Left Front Wheel Speed Sensor Signal

LTV0500000004701

Fig. 2 Connector pin identification (Lefthand front WSS)

Connector Part Information	• 12052644		
	• 2-Way F Metric-Pack 150 Series Sealed (GRY)		
Pin	Wire Color	Circuit No.	Function
A	BLK	884	Left Rear Wheel Speed Sensor Signal
B	WHT	885	Left Rear Wheel Speed Sensor Low Reference

LTV0500000004702

Fig. 3 Connector pin identification (Lefthand rear WSS)

If none of the above conditions apply use standard bleed procedures as outlined in "Hydraulic Brake System Bleeding – Manual" or "Hydraulic Brake System Bleeding – Pressure"

The "Automated Bleed Procedure" may be terminated at any time during the process by pressing the EXIT button. No further scan tool prompts pertaining to the "Automated Bleed Procedure" will be given. After exiting the bleed procedure, relieve bleed pressure and disconnect bleed equipment per manufacturers instructions. Failure to properly relieve pressure may result in spilled brake fluid causing damage to components and painted surfaces.

1. Preliminary Inspection:
   a. Inspect battery for full charge, repair battery and charging system as required.
   b. Connect a scan tool to Data Link Connector (DLC) and select current and history DTCs. Repair any DTCs prior to performing ABS bleed procedure.
   c. Inspect for visual damage and leaks and repair as required.
2. Preliminary Setup:
   a. Raise and support vehicle on a suitable lift.
   b. Turn ignition switch to Off position.
   c. Remove all four tires.
   d. Connect pressure bleeding tool according to manufacturer's instructions.
   e. Turn ignition switch to RUN position, engine off.
   f. Connect a scan tool and establish communications with ABS system.
   g. Pressurize bleeding tool to 30–35 psi.
3. Automated Bleed Procedure:
   a. With pressure bleeding tool at 30–35 psi, and all bleeder screws in closed position, select "Automated Bleed Procedure" on scan tool and follow instructions.
   b. First part of automated bleed procedure will cycle pump and front release valves for one minute. After cycling has stopped scan tool will enter a "cool down" mode and display a 3 minute timer. Auto bleed will not continue until this timer expired, and cannot be overridden.
   c. During next step, scan tool will request technician to open one of bleeder screws. Scan tool will then cycle respective release valve and pump motor for 1 minute.
   d. Scan tool will repeat step 3 for remaining bleeder screws.
   e. With bleeder tool still attached to vehicle and maintaining 35 psi, scan tool will instruct technician to independently open each bleeder screw for approximately 20 seconds. This should allow any remaining air to be purged from brake lines.
   f. When automated bleed procedure is completed scan tool will display appropriate message.
   g. Install all four tires.
   h. Remove pressure from pressure bleeding tool and then disconnect tool from vehicle.
   i. Depress brake pedal to gauge pedal height and feel. Repeat steps 1–8 until pedal is acceptable.
   j. Remove scan tool from DLC connector.
   k. Lower vehicle.
   l. Inspect brake fluid level in master cylinder.
   m. Road test vehicle while making sure brake pedal remains high and firm.
   n. If vehicle is equipped TCS scan tool will cycle both ABS and TCS solenoids valves. This bleed procedure is same as above.

HYDRAULIC BRAKE SYSTEM BLEEDING – MANUAL

Refer to "Continental Teves MK-70" section for bleed procedure.

HYDRAULIC BRAKE SYSTEM BLEEDING – PRESSURE

Refer to "Continental Teves MK-70" section for bleed procedure.

Component Replacement

ELECTRONIC BRAKE CONTROL MODULE (EBCM)

1. Turn ignition switch to Off position.
2. Remove air cleaner housing from engine compartment.
3. Disconnect EBCM harness connector.
4. Remove any dirt or debris from assembly.
5. Disconnect pump motor connector at bottom of EBCM.
6. Remove six EBCM to BPMV screws.
7. Separate EBCM from BPMV.
8. Reverse procedure to install, noting the following:
   a. Install new wave springs and screws to EBCM.
   b. **Torque** top four screws to 44 inch lbs., using a criss-cross pattern.
   c. **Torque** bottom two screws to 44 inch lbs.
   d. Turn ignition switch On position with engine Off and perform "Diagnostic System Check" as outlined in "Diagnostic Tests."

BRAKE PRESSURE MODULATOR VALVE (BPMV)

The Brake Pressure Modulator Valve (BPMV) must not be repaired; the complete unit must be replaced. With the exception of the EBCM/EBTCM, no screws may be loosened. If screws are loosened, it will not be possible to get the brake circuits leak-tight and personal injury may result.

1. Turn ignition switch to Off position.
2. Remove attaching bolts for cruise control module.
3. Place cruise control module off to side.
4. Remove air cleaner housing from engine compartment.
5. Disengage red locking tab from connector.
6. Push down lock tab and then move sliding connector cover to open position.
7. Disconnect EBCM harness connector.
8. Disconnect 4 wheel brake pipes from BPMV. **Note locations of brake pipes in order to aid in installation.**
9. Place four wheel brake pipes out of way only after covering open pipes to avoid dripping or being contaminated.
10. Disconnect master cylinder brake pipes from BPMV.
11. Loosen brake pipes, do not remove brake pipes from master cylinder.
12. Place two master cylinder brake pipes out of way only after covering open pipes to avoid dripping or being contaminated.

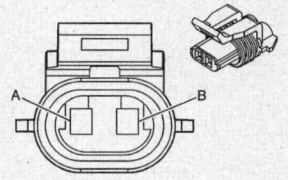

| Connector Part Information | • 12052644 | | |
| | • 2-Way F Metric-Pack 150 Series Sealed (GRY) | | |
Pin	Wire Color	Circuit No.	Function
A	TAN	833	Right Front Wheel Speed Sensor Low Reference
B	DK GRN	872	Right Front Wheel Speed Sensor Signal

LTV0500000004703

**Fig. 4   Connector pin identification
(Righthand front WSS)**

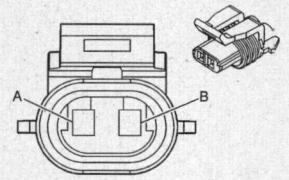

| Connector Part Information | • 12052644 | | |
| | • 2-Way F Metric-Pack 150 Series Sealed (GRY) | | |
Pin	Wire Color	Circuit No.	Function
A	BRN	882	Right Rear Wheel Speed Sensor Signal
B	WHT	883	Right Rear Wheel Speed Sensor Low Reference

LTV0500000004704

**Fig. 5   Connector pin identification
(Righthand rear WSS)**

13. Remove three BPMV mounting bracket nuts from inner wheel housing mount surface of strut tower.
14. Install top nut upside down on top stud.
15. Lightly tap on bottom of nut until stud has loosened up.
16. Disconnect ground strap between EBCM assembly and chassis.
17. Remove BPMV mounting bracket and EBCM assembly from vehicle.
18. Remove two bolts that connect BPMV to mounting bracket.
19. Remove EBCM, if replacing BPMV as outlined in "Electronic Brake Control Module (EBCM)."
20. Reverse procedure to install, noting the following:
   a. **Torque** two BPMV to mounting bracket bolts to 84 inch lbs.
   b. **Torque** three BPMV mounting bracket to strut tower bolts to 89 inch lbs.
   c. **Torque** master cylinder brake pipes to BPMV fittings to 18 ft. lbs.
   d. **Torque** wheel brake pipes to BPMV to 18 ft. lbs.
   e. Perform "ABS Automated Bleed" procedure.

FRONT WHEEL SPEED SENSOR

The front wheel speed sensors and rings are integral with the hub and bearing assemblies. If a speed sensor or a ring needs replacement, replace the entire hub and bearing assembly. Do not service the harness pigtail individually because the harness pigtail is part of the sensor.
1. Raise and support vehicle using a suitable lift.
2. Remove front tire and wheel assembly.
3. Remove front wheel speed sensor electrical connector from speed sensor connector.
4. Remove front hub and bearing assembly as outlined in appropriate chassis chapter.
5. Reverse procedure to install. Turn ignition switch On position with engine Off and perform "Diagnostic System Check" as outlined in "Diagnostic Tests."

REAR WHEEL SPEED SENSOR

The rear wheel speed sensors and rings are integral with the hub and bearing assemblies. If a speed sensor or a ring needs replacement, replace the entire hub and bearing assembly.
1. Raise and support vehicle using a suitable lift.
2. Remove rear tire and wheel assembly.
3. Remove rear wheel speed sensor electrical connector located next to rear strut.
4. Remove rear hub and bearing assembly as outlined in appropriate chassis chapter.
5. Reverse procedure to install. Turn ignition switch On position with engine Off and perform "Diagnostic System Check" as outlined in "Diagnostic Tests."

TRACTION CONTROL SWITCH

1. Remove instrument panel accessory trim plate.
2. Remove bolts and screws from switch bank to instrument panel.
3. Pull straight out from instrument panel in order to remove switch bank from instrument panel.
4. Disconnect electrical connectors.
5. Reverse procedure to install. **Torque** bolts and screws to switch bank to instrument panel to 22 inch lbs.

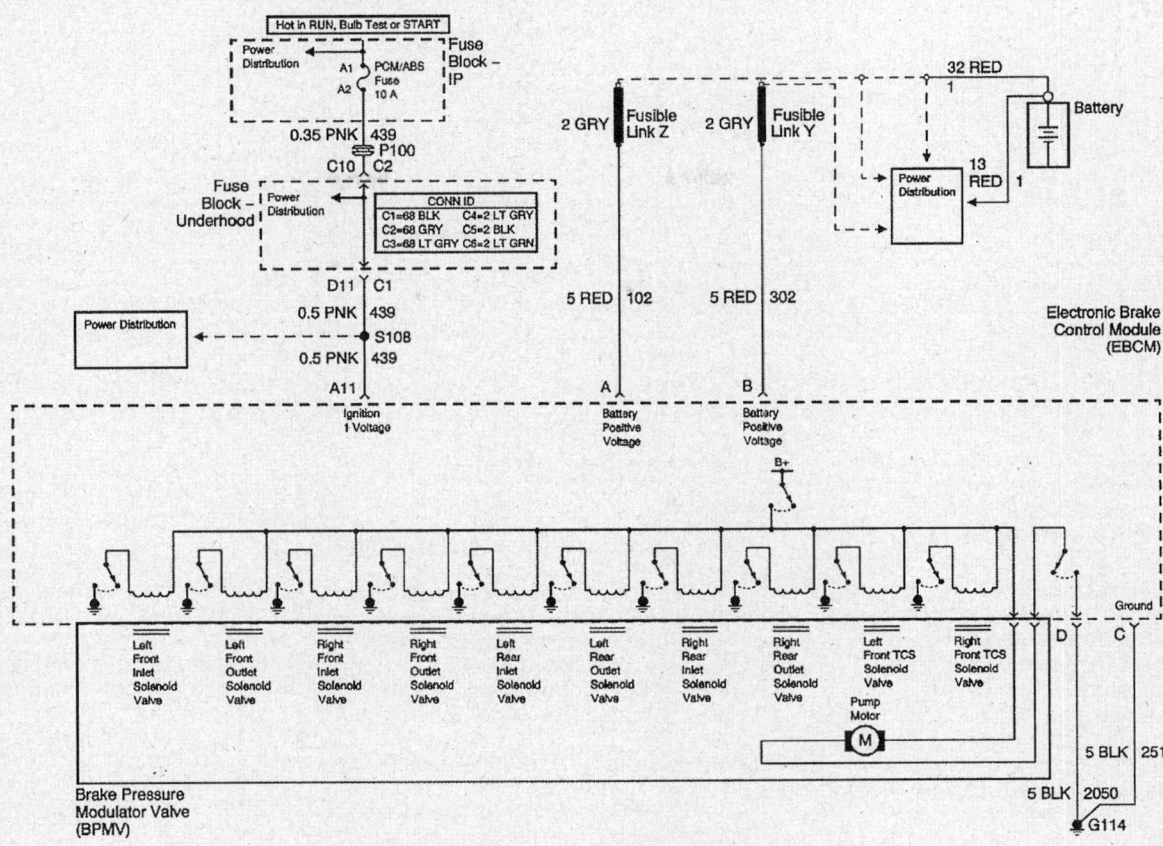

Fig. 6   Wiring diagram (Part 1 of 3)

LTV0500000004705

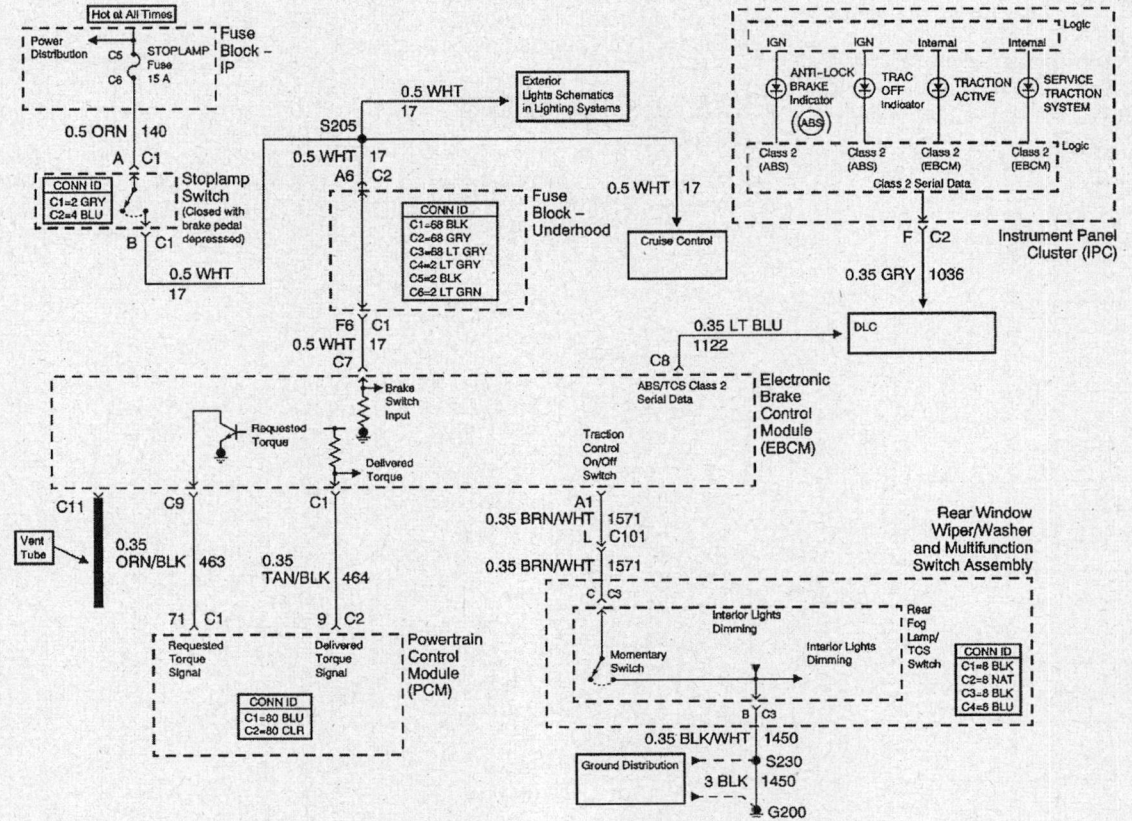

Fig. 6   Wiring diagram (Part 2 of 3)

LTV0500000004706

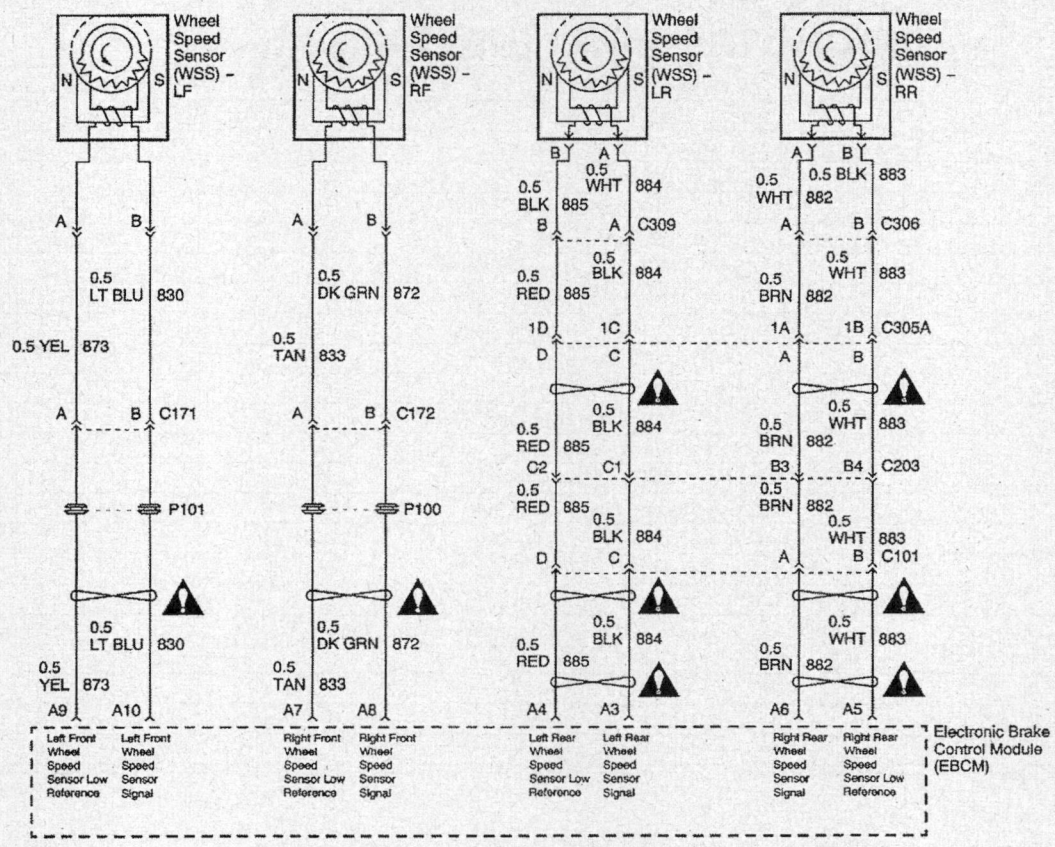

Fig. 6   Wiring diagram (Part 3 of 3)

LTV0500000004707

DIAGNOSTIC CHART INDEX

Code	Description	Page No.	Fig. No.
—	Diagnostic System Check	5-94	7
—	ABS Indicator Always On	5-107	26
—	ABS Indicator Inoperative	5-107	27
—	Traction Off Indicator Always On	5-107	28
—	Traction Off Indicator Inoperative	5-108	29
C1214	Solenoid Valve Relay Coil Or Contact Circuit Open	5-95	8
C1216	Valve Solenoid Release	5-95	9
C1217	Pump Motor Shorted to Ground	5-96	10
C1218	Pump Motor Circuit Short to Voltage or Motor Ground Open	5-96	11
C1221	Lefthand Front Wheel Speed Sensor Input Signal = 0	5-97	12
C1222	Righthand Front Wheel Speed Sensor Input Signal = 0	5-97	12
C1223	Lefthand Rear Wheel Speed Sensor Input Signal = 0	5-97	12
C1224	Righthand Rear Wheel Speed Sensor Input Signal = 0	5-97	12
C1225	Lefthand Front Excessive Wheel Speed Sensor Variation	5-97	12
C1226	Righthand Front Excessive Wheel Speed Sensor Variation	5-97	12
C1227	Lefthand Rear Excessive Wheel Speed Sensor Variation	5-97	12
C1228	Righthand Rear Excessive Wheel Speed Sensor Variation	5-97	12
C1232	Lefthand Front Wheel Speed Sensor Circuit Open or Shorted	5-97	12
C1233	Righthand Front Wheel Speed Sensor Circuit Open or Shorted	5-97	12
C1234	Lefthand Rear Wheel Speed Sensor Circuit Open or Shorted	5-97	12
C1235	Righthand Rear Wheel Speed Sensor Circuit Open or Shorted	5-97	12
C1236	System Supply Voltage Low	5-98	13
C1237	High System Supply Voltage	5-99	14
C1238	Brake Thermal Model Exceeded	5-99	15
C1242	Pump Motor Circuit Open	5-100	16
C1243	Pump Motor Stalled	5-100	16

Continued

DIAGNOSTIC CHART INDEX—Continued

Code	Description	Page No.	Fig. No.
C1254	Abnormal Shutdown Detected	5-101	17
C2155	Loss of Class 2 Communication	5-101	18
C1256	EBCM/EBTCM Internal Fault	5-101	18
C1261	Lefthand Front Inlet Valve Solenoid Fault	5-102	19
C1262	Lefthand Front Outlet Valve Solenoid Fault	5-102	19
C1263	Righthand Front Inlet Valve Solenoid Fault	5-102	19
C1264	Righthand Front Outlet Valve Solenoid Fault	5-102	19
C1265	Lefthand Rear Inlet Valve Solenoid Fault	5-102	19
C1266	Lefthand Rear Outlet Valve Solenoid Fault	5-102	19
C1267	Righthand Rear Inlet Valve Solenoid Fault	5-102	19
C1268	Righthand Rear Outlet Valve Solenoid Fault	5-102	19
C1272	Lefthand Front TCS Valve Solenoid Fault	5-102	19
C1274	Righthand Front TCS Valve Solenoid Fault	5-102	19
C1276	Delivered Torque Signal Circuit Fault	5-102	20
C1277	Requested Torque Signal Circuit Fault	5-103	21
C1278	TCS Temporarily Inhibited By PCM	5-104	22
C1291	Open Brake Lamp Switch Contacts During Deceleration	5-105	23
C1294	Brake Lamp Switch Circuit Always Active	5-105	24
C1295	Brake Lamp Switch Circuit Open	5-106	25
P1571	PCM Detects Torque Signal Fault	5-103	21
P1644	PCM Detects Torque Signal Fault	5-102	20
P1689	PCM Detects Torque Signal Fault	5-102	20

Circuit Description

The ABS Diagnostic System Check is an organized approach to identify problems associated with the EBCM. This check must be the starting point for any EBCM complaint, and will direct you to the next logical step in diagnosing the complaint. The EBCM is a very reliable component and is not likely the cause of the malfunction. Most system complaints are linked to faulty wiring, connectors, and occasionally to components. Understanding the ABS system and using the tables correctly will reduce diagnostic time and prevent unnecessary parts replacement.

Test Description

The numbers below refer to the step numbers on the diagnostic table.

2. Lack of communication may be due to a partial malfunction of the serial data circuit or due to a total malfunction of the serial data circuit. The specified procedure will determine the particular condition.

4. The presence of DTCs which begin with "U" indicate some other module is not communicating. The specified procedure will compile all the available information before tests are performed.

Step	Action	Yes	No
1	Install a scan tool. Does the scan tool power up?	Go to Step 2	Check Scan Tool Does Not Power Up
2	1. Turn ON the ignition, with the engine OFF. 2. Attempt to establish communication with the following control modules: - Electronic brake control module (EBCM) - Instrument panel cluster (IPC) - Powertrain control module (PCM) Does the scan tool communicate with all control modules?	Go to Step 3	Check Scan Tool Does Not Communicate with Class 2 Device

LTV0500000004708

Fig. 7 Diagnostic System Check (Part 1 of 2)

Step	Action		
3	Select the display DTCs function on the scan tool for the following control modules: - Electronic brake control module (EBCM) - Instrument panel cluster (IPC) - Powertrain control module (PCM) Does the scan tool display any DTCs?	Go to Step 4	Go to Symptoms
4	Does the scan tool display any DTCs which begin with a "U"?	Check Scan Tool Does Not Communicate with Class 2 Device	Go to Step 5
5	Does the scan tool display DTC B1000, or B1004?	Go to Diagnostic Trouble Code (DTC) List	Go to Diagnostic Trouble Code (DTC) List

LTV0500000004709

Fig. 7 Diagnostic System Check (Part 2 of 2)

Circuit Description

The system relay is energized when the ignition is ON. The system relay supplies voltage to the solenoid valves and the pump motor. This voltage is referred to as the system voltage.

The electronic brake control module (EBCM) controls each solenoid valve by grounding the solenoid.

The EBCM controls the pump motor by grounding the control circuit. The pump serves 2 purposes:

- Transfers brake fluid from the brake calipers to the master cylinder reservoir during pressure decrease events.
- Transfers brake fluid from the master cylinder reservoir to the brake calipers during pressure increase events.

Conditions for Running the DTC

- The ignition voltage is greater than 10.8 volts.
- The system relay is commanded ON.
- For Criteria 2, one of the following conditions exists:
  - The pump motor is OFF.
  - During initialization, the pump motor is ON.

Conditions for Setting the DTC

One of the following conditions exists for 0.23 seconds:

Criteria 1

The system voltage is less than 8 volts.

Criteria 2

The difference between the ignition voltage and system voltage is greater than 1.9 volts.

Action Taken When the DTC Sets

If equipped, the following actions occur:

- The EBCM disables the ABS/TCS for the duration of the ignition cycle.
- The DRP does not function optimally.
- The ABS indicator turns ON.
- The Traction Off indicator turns ON.
- The message center displays the Service Traction System message.

Conditions for Clearing the DTC

LTV0500000004710

Fig. 8 Code C1214: Solenoid Valve Relay Coil Or Contact Circuit Open (Part 1 of 3)

Step	Action	Value	Yes	No
1	Did you perform the ABS Diagnostic System Check?	--	Go to Step 2	Go to Diagnostic System Check
2	1. Install a scan tool. 2. Turn ON the ignition, with the engine OFF. 3. Use the scan tool in order to clear the DTCs. 4. With the scan tool, perform the Automated Test. Does the DTC reset as a current DTC?	--	Go to Step 3	Test for Intermittent and Poor Connections
3	1. Remove the EBCM from the BPMV. 2. Measure the resistance between each pump motor control circuit of the BPMV and the housing of the BPMV. Does the DMM display the specified value?	OL	Go to Step 5	Go to Step 4
4	Replace the EBCM and the BPMV. Did you complete the repair?	--	Go to Step 6	--
5	Replace the EBCM. Did you complete the repair?	--	Go to Step 6	--
6	1. Use the scan tool in order to clear the DTCs. 2. With the scan tool, perform the Automated Test. Does the DTC reset?	--	Go to Step 2	System OK

LTV0500000004712

Fig. 8 Code C1214: Solenoid Valve Relay Coil Or Contact Circuit Open (Part 3 of 3)

- The condition for the DTC is no longer present and the DTC is cleared with a scan tool.
- The electronic brake control module (EBCM) automatically clears the history DTC when a current DTC is not detected in 100 consecutive drive cycles.

Diagnostic Aids

The system relay is integral to the EBCM. The relay is not serviceable.

Test Description

The number below refers to the step number on the diagnostic table.

2. Determines whether the DTC is current.

LTV0500000004711

Fig. 8 Code C1214: Solenoid Valve Relay Coil Or Contact Circuit Open (Part 2 of 3)

Circuit Description

The EBCM monitors the On/Off state of each solenoid and recognizes when the ABS is in pressure decrease too long. This fault indicates that the EBCM was unable to decrease brake pressure enough to a certain wheel to prevent excessive wheel slip.

Conditions for Running the DTC

- The ABS is active.
- The wheel speed is less than 5 km/h (3 mph).

Conditions for Setting the DTC

The solenoid of the wheel is releasing for greater than 1 second.

Action Taken When the DTC Sets

If equipped, the following actions occur:

- The EBCM disables the ABS/TCS for the duration of the ignition cycle.
- The ABS indicator turns ON.
- The Traction Off indicator turns ON.
- The message center displays the Service Traction System message.

Conditions for Clearing the DTC

- The condition for the DTC is no longer present and the DTC is cleared with a scan tool.
- The electronic brake control module (EBCM) automatically clears the history DTC when a current DTC is not detected in 100 consecutive drive cycles.

Diagnostic Aids

Possible causes of this DTC are the following conditions:

- A contaminated hydraulic unit.
- An intermittent wheel speed sensor.
- A sticking solenoid.
- Excessive brake drag or high resistance in base brake system.
- Suspension system irregularities.

LTV0500000004713

Fig. 9 Code C1216: Valve Solenoid Release (Part 1 of 2)

Step	Action	Yes	No
1	Did you perform the ABS Diagnostic System Check?	Go to Step 2	Go to Diagnostic System Check
2	1. Install a scan tool. 2. Turn ON the ignition, with the ignition OFF. 3. With a scan tool, observe the DTC Information parameter in the ABS Diagnostic Trouble Codes (DTCs). Does the scan tool display any other ABS DTCs relating to wheel speed sensor or solenoid valve operation?	Go to Diagnostic Trouble Code (DTC) List	Go to Step 3
3	With a scan tool, monitor all of the wheel speed sensor in the ABS Data Display while decelerating the vehicle from 56 to 0 km/h (35 to 0 mph). Do any of the wheel speeds indicate erratic or intermittent operation?	Go to Diagnostic Trouble Code (DTC) List	Go to Step 4
4	Inspect the base brake system for the following conditions: • Brake fluid contamination. • Excessive brake drag. • Suspension system irregularities. Did you find and correct the condition?	Go to Step 7	Go to Step 5
5	1. Use the scan tool in order to clear the DTCs. 2. With the scan tool, perform the Automated Test. Does the DTC reset as a current DTC?	Go to Step 6	System OK
6	Replace the BPMV. Did you complete the repair?	Go to Step 7	--
7	1. Use the scan tool in order to clear the DTCs. 2. With the scan tool, perform the Automated Test. Does the DTC reset?	Go to Step 2	System OK

LTV0500000004714

Fig. 9   Code C1216: Valve Solenoid Release (Part 2 of 2)

Step	Action	Value	Yes	No
1	Did you perform the ABS Diagnostic System Check?	--	Go to Step 2	Go to Diagnostic System Check -
2	1. Turn OFF the ignition. 2. Disconnect the EBCM harness connector. 3. Connect the J 39700 100-pin breakout box using the J 39700-99 breakout box adapter to the EBCM harness connector only. 4. Test both ground circuits of the EBCM including the EBCM ground for a high resistance or an open. Did you find and correct the condition?	--	Go to Step 8	Go to Step 3
3	1. Remove the EBCM from the BPMV. 2. Measure the resistance from both pump motor control circuits of the BPMV to the housing of the BPMV. Does the resistance measure less than the specified value?	5 ohms	Go to Step 4	Go to Step 5
4	Inspect for poor connections at the connector of the BPMV. Did you find and correct the condition?	--	Go to Step 8	Go to Step 6
5	Inspect for poor connections at the harness connector of the EBCM. Did you find and correct the condition?	--	Go to Step 8	Go to Step 7
6	Replace the BPMV. Did you complete the repair?	--	Go to Step 8	--
7	Replace the EBCM. Did you complete the repair?	--	Go to Step 8	--
8	1. Use the scan tool in order to clear the DTCs. 2. With the scan tool, perform the Automated Test. Does the DTC reset?	--	Go to Step 2	System OK

LTV0500000004716

Fig. 10   Code C1217: Pump Motor Shorted to Ground (Part 2 of 2)

Circuit Description

The system relay is energized when the ignition is ON. The system relay supplies voltage to the solenoid valves and the pump motor. This voltage is referred to as the system voltage.

The electronic brake control module (EBCM) controls each solenoid valve by grounding the solenoid.

The EBCM controls the pump motor by grounding the control circuit. The pump serves 2 purposes:

- Transfers brake fluid from the brake calipers to the master cylinder reservoir during pressure decrease events.
- Transfers brake fluid from the master cylinder reservoir to the brake calipers during pressure increase events.

Conditions for Running the DTC

- The pump motor has been commanded OFF for 1 second.
- The system voltage is greater than 9.36 volts.

Conditions for Setting the DTC

One of the following conditions exists for 0.2 seconds:

- The voltage across the pump motor is greater than 10.2 volts.
- The pump motor low side voltage is less than 2.7 volts.

Action Taken When the DTC Sets

If equipped, the following actions occur:

- The EBCM disables the ABS/TCS for the duration of the ignition cycle.
- The ABS indicator turns ON.
- The Traction Off indicator turns ON.
- The message center displays the Service Traction System message.

Conditions for Clearing the DTC

- The condition for the DTC is no longer present and the DTC is cleared with a scan tool.
- The electronic brake control module (EBCM) automatically clears the history DTC when a current DTC is not detected in 100 consecutive drive cycles.

Diagnostic Aids

- This DTC determines if there is a short in the pump motor control circuit.
- The pump motor is integral to the BPMV. The pump motor is not serviceable.

Test Description

The number below refers to the step number on the diagnostic table.

3. Tests the pump motor circuits of the BPMV for a short to the housing of the BPMV.

LTV0500000004715

Fig. 10   Code C1217: Pump Motor Shorted to Ground (Part 1 of 2)

Circuit Description

The system relay is energized when the ignition is ON. The system relay supplies voltage to the solenoid valves and the pump motor. This voltage is referred to as the system voltage.

The electronic brake control module (EBCM) controls each solenoid valve by grounding the solenoid.

The EBCM controls the pump motor by grounding the control circuit. The pump serves 2 purposes:

- Transfers brake fluid from the brake calipers to the master cylinder reservoir during pressure decrease events.
- Transfers brake fluid from the master cylinder reservoir to the brake calipers during pressure increase events.

Conditions for Running the DTC

- The pump motor is commanded ON.
- The system voltage is greater than 8 volts.

Conditions for Setting the DTC

One of the following conditions exists for 0.16 seconds:

- With the commanded pump motor voltage less than the system voltage, the actual pump motor voltage is 3 volts less than the commanded voltage.
- With the commanded pump motor voltage greater than the system voltage, the actual pump motor voltage is less than 8 volts.

Action Taken When the DTC Sets

If equipped, the following actions occur:

- The EBCM disables the ABS/TCS for the duration of the ignition cycle.
- The ABS indicator turns ON.
- The Traction Off indicator turns ON.
- The message center displays the Service Traction System message.

Conditions for Clearing the DTC

- The condition for the DTC is no longer present and the DTC is cleared with a scan tool.
- The electronic brake control module (EBCM) automatically clears the history DTC when a current DTC is not detected in 100 consecutive drive cycles.

Diagnostic Aids

The pump motor is integral to the BPMV. The pump motor is not serviceable.

Test Description

The number below refers to the step number on the diagnostic table.

5. Tests the ability of the EBCM to control the pump motor. If the test lamp illuminates, the pump motor circuit within the EBCM is good.

LTV0500000004768

Fig. 11   Code C1218: Pump Motor Circuit Short to Voltage or Motor Ground Open (Part 1 of 3)

Step	Action	Yes	No
1	Did you perform the ABS Diagnostic System Check?	Go to Step 2	Go to Diagnostic System Check
2	1. Use the scan tool in order to clear the DTCs. 2. With the scan tool, perform the Automated Test. Does the DTC reset?	Go to Step 3	Test for Intermittent and Poor Connections
3	1. Turn the ignition OFF. 2. Remove the EBCM from the BPMV. Refer to Electronic Brake Control Module (EBCM) Replacement. 3. Inspect the EBCM to BPMV connector for conditions which could cause an intermittent, such as damage, corrosion, poor terminal contact, or presence of brake fluid. Is connector OK and cavity free of brake fluid?	Go to Step 5	Go to Step 4
4	1. If connector corrosion or damage is evident, replace BPMV and/or EBCM as necessary. 2. If brake fluid is present, replace both BPMV and EBCM. Did you complete the repair?	Go to Step 9	--
5	1. Connect the EBCM harness to the EBCM with the BPMV still separated. 2. Connect a test lamp between the pump motor circuits, internal EBCM side, using the J 35616-A GM terminal test kit. 3. Turn the ignition ON. 4. With the scan tool, perform the Automated Bleed. Does the test lamp illuminate?	Go to Step 8	Go to Step 6

LTV0500000004769

Fig. 11   Code C1218: Pump Motor Circuit Short to Voltage or Motor Ground Open (Part 2 of 3)

Circuit Description

As the wheel spins, the wheel speed sensor produces an AC signal. The electronic brake control module (EBCM) uses the frequency of the AC signal to calculate the wheel speed.

Conditions for Running the DTC

C1221 through C1228
- DTCs C1232 through C1235 are not set.
- The brake pedal is not pressed.
- The ABS is not active.

C1232 through C1235

The ignition is ON.

Conditions for Setting the DTC

C1221 through C1224

All of the following conditions exists for 2.5 seconds:

- The suspect wheel speed equals zero.
- The other wheel speeds are greater than 8 km/h (5 mph).
- The other wheel speeds are within 11 km/h (7 mph) of each other.

C1225 through C1228

The EBCM detects a rapid variation in the wheel speed. The wheel speed changes by 24 km/h (14.9 mph) or more in 0.01 second. The change must occur 5 times with no more than 1 second between occurrences.

C1232 through C1235

One of the following conditions exists for 0.02 seconds:

- A short to voltage - the wheel speed sensor signal circuit and wheel speed sensor return circuit voltages are both greater than 4.25 volts.
- A short to ground - the wheel speed sensor signal circuit and wheel speed sensor return circuit voltages are both less than 0.75 volts.
- An open - the wheel speed sensor signal circuit voltage is greater than 4.25 volts and wheel speed sensor return circuit voltage is less than 0.75 volts.

Action Taken When the DTC Sets

If equipped, the following actions occur:

LTV0500000004717

Fig. 12   Codes C1221–C1235: Wheel Speed Sensor (Part 1 of 4)

Step	Action	Yes	No
6	1. Turn OFF the ignition. 2. Disconnect the EBCM connector. 3. Connect the J 39700 100-pin breakout box using the J 39700-99 breakout box adapter to the EBCM harness connector only. 4. Test both ground circuits of the EBCM including the EBCM ground for a high resistance or an open. Did you find and correct the condition?	Go to Step 9	Go to Step 7
7	Replace the EBCM. Replacement. Did you complete the repair?	Go to Step 9	--
8	Replace the BPMV. Did you complete the repair?	Go to Step 9	--
9	1. Use the scan tool in order to clear the DTCs. 2. With the scan tool, perform the Automated Test. Does the DTC reset?	Go to Step 2	System OK

LTV0500000004770

Fig. 11   Code C1218: Pump Motor Circuit Short to Voltage or Motor Ground Open (Part 3 of 3)

- The EBCM disables the ABS/TCS for the duration of the ignition cycle.
- The ABS indicator turns ON.
- The Traction Off indicator turns ON.
- The message center displays the Service Traction System message.

Conditions for Clearing the DTC

- The condition for the DTC is no longer present and the DTC is cleared with a scan tool.
- The electronic brake control module (EBCM) automatically clears the history DTC when a current DTC is not detected in 100 consecutive drive cycles.

Diagnostic Aids

C1221 through C1224

Under the following conditions, 2 Wheel Speed Sensor Input is 0 DTCs are set:

- The 2 suspect wheel speeds equal zero for 20 seconds.
- The other wheel speeds are greater than 16 km/h (10 mph).
- The other wheel speeds are within 11 km/h (7 mph) of each other.

Diagnose each wheel speed sensor individually.

C1225 through C1228

A possible cause of this DTC is electrical noise on the wheel speed sensor harness wiring. Electrical noise could result from the wheel speed sensor wires being routed to close to high energy ignition system components, such as spark plug wires.

C1232 through C1235

If the customer comments that the ABS indicator is ON only during moist environmental conditions: rain, snow, vehicle wash, etc., inspect the wheel speed sensor wiring for signs of water intrusion. If the DTC is not current, clear all DTCs and simulate the effects of water intrusion by using the following procedure:

1. Spray the suspected area with a 5 percent saltwater solution. To create a 5 percent saltwater solution, add 2 teaspoons of salt to 8 fl oz of water (10 g of salt to 200 ml of water).
2. Test drive the vehicle over various road surfaces: bumps, turns, etc., above 40 km/h (25 mph) for at least 30 seconds.
3. If the DTC returns, replace the suspected wheel speed sensor or repair the wheel speed sensor wiring.
4. Rinse the area thoroughly when completed.

Test Description

The numbers below refer to the step numbers on the diagnostic table.

4. Measures the resistance of the wheel speed sensor in order to determine if the sensor has a valid resistance value.
5. Ensures that the wheel speed sensor is generating a valid AC voltage output.

LTV0500000004718

Fig. 12   Codes C1221–C1235: Wheel Speed Sensor (Part 2 of 4)

Step	Action	Value(s)	Yes	No
1	Did you perform the ABS Diagnostic System Check?	--	Go to Step 2	Go to Diagnostic System Check
2	1. Install a scan tool. 2. Turn ON the ignition. 3. Set up the scan tool snap shot feature to trigger for this DTC. 4. Drive the vehicle at a speed greater than the specified value. Does the scan tool indicate that this wheel speed DTC set?	8 km/h (5 mph)	Go to Step 3	Test for Intermittent and Poor Connections
3	1. Raise and support the vehicle. 2. Disconnect the wheel speed sensor connector. 3. Measure the resistance across the wheel speed sensor. Does the resistance measure within the specified range?	850-1350 ohms	Go to Step 4	Go to Step 8
4	1. Spin the wheel. 2. Measure the AC voltage across the wheel speed sensor. Does the AC voltage measure greater than the specified value?	100 mV	Go to Step 5	Go to Step 8
5	Inspect for poor connections at the harness connector of the wheel speed sensor. Did you find and correct the condition?	--	Go to Step 10	Go to Step 6
6	1. Disconnect the EBCM harness connector. 2. Install the J 39700 100-pin breakout box using the J 39700-99 breakout box adapter to the EBCM harness connector only. 3. Test the wheel speed sensor circuits for the following: - An open - A short to ground - A short to voltage - Shorted together Refer to Circuit Testing and Wiring Repairs in Wiring Systems. Did you find and correct the condition?	--	Go to Step 10	Go to Step 7

LTV0500000004719

Fig. 12 Codes C1221–C1235: Wheel Speed Sensor (Part 3 of 4)

Circuit Description

The electronic brake control module (EBCM) monitors the voltage level available for system operation. A low voltage condition prevents the system from operating properly.

Conditions for Running the DTC

- The vehicle speed is greater than 8 km/h (5 mph).
- The ignition voltage is less than 10.8 volts.
- The system relay is commanded ON.

Conditions for Setting the DTC

One of the following conditions exists for 0.72 seconds:

- During initialization or when the system is inactive, the system voltage is less than 10.8 volts.
- During the system operation, the system voltage is less than 9.36 volts.

Action Taken When the DTC Sets

If equipped, the following actions occur:

- The EBCM disables the ABS/TCS until the DTC becomes a history DTC.
- The ABS indicator turns ON.
- The Traction Off indicator turns ON.
- The message center displays the Service Traction System message.

Conditions for Clearing the DTC

- The condition for the DTC is no longer present and the DTC is cleared with a scan tool.
- The electronic brake control module (EBCM) automatically clears the history DTC when a current DTC is not detected in 100 consecutive drive cycles.

Diagnostic Aids

- Test the charging system.

- Possible causes of this DTC are the following conditions:
  - A charging system malfunction
  - An excessive battery draw
  - A weak battery
  - A faulty system ground

LTV0500000004761

Fig. 13 Code C1236: System Operation Low Voltage (Part 1 of 3)

Step	Action	Value(s)	Yes	No
7	Inspect for poor connections at the harness connector for the EBCM. Did you find and correct the condition?		Go to Step 10	Go to Step 9
8	Replace the wheel speed sensor. Did you complete the repair?		Go to Step 10	--
9	Replace the EBCM. Did you complete the repair?		Go to Step 10	--
10	1. Use the scan tool in order to clear the DTCs. 2. Operate the vehicle within the Conditions for Running the DTC as specified in the supporting text. Does the DTC reset?		Go to Step 2	System OK

LTV0500000004720

Fig. 12 Codes C1221–C1235: Wheel Speed Sensor (Part 4 of 4)

Test Description

2. Use the scan tool in order to inspect the voltage to the EBCM.

3. Use the scan tool in order to inspect the voltage to the instrument cluster. A low voltage value in multiple modules indicates a concern in the charging system.

5. Verifies that the condition is still present.

LTV0500000004762

Fig. 13 Code C1236: System Operation Low Voltage (Part 2 of 3)

Step	Action	Value(s)	Yes	No
1	Did you perform the ABS Diagnostic System Check?	--	Go to Step 2	Go to Diagnostic System Check
2	1. Install a scan tool. 2. Start the engine. 3. With a scan tool, observe the Switched Battery Voltage parameter in ABS data list. Does the scan tool indicate the voltage is greater than the specified value?	10.8 V	Go to Diagnostic Aids	Go to Step 3
3	With a scan tool, observe the Ignition 1 parameter in the Instrument Panel Cluster data list. Does the scan tool indicate the voltage is greater than the specified value?	10.8 V	Go to Step 4	Test for Intermittent and Poor Connections
4	1. Turn OFF the ignition. 2. Disconnect the EBCM harness connector. 3. Install the J 39700 100-pin breakout box using the J 39700-99 breakout box adaptor to the EBCM harness connector only. 4. Test the ground circuits of the EBCM including the EBCM ground for a high resistance or an open. Did you find and correct the condition?		Go to Step 7	Go to Step 5
5	1. Reconnect the EBCM harness connector. 2. Turn ON the ignition, with the engine OFF. 3. Use the scan tool in order to clear the DTCs. 4. Operate the vehicle within the Conditions for Running the DTC as specified in the supporting text. Does the DTC reset?	--	Go to Step 6	Go to Diagnostic Aids
6	Replace the EBCM. Did you complete the repair?	--	Go to Step 7	--
7	1. Use the scan tool in order to clear the DTCs. 2. Operate the vehicle within the Conditions for Running the DTC as specified in the supporting text. Does the DTC reset?	--	Go to Step 2	System OK

LTV0500000004763

Fig. 13 Code C1236: System Operation Low Voltage (Part 3 of 3)

Circuit Description

The electronic brake control module (EBCM) monitors the voltage level available for system operation. If the voltage level is too high, damage may result in the system. When the EBCM detects a high voltage condition, the EBCM turns OFF the system relay which removes battery voltage from the solenoid valves and pump motor.

Conditions for Running the DTC

The vehicle speed is greater than 8 km/h (5 mph).

Conditions for Setting the DTC

The system voltage is greater than 17 volts for 0.7 seconds.

Action Taken When the DTC Sets

If equipped, the following actions occur:

- The EBCM disables the ABS/TCS until the DTC becomes a history DTC.
- The ABS indicator turns ON.
- The Traction Off indicator turns ON.
- The message center displays the Service Traction System message.

Conditions for Clearing the DTC

- The condition for the DTC is no longer present and the DTC is cleared with a scan tool.
- The electronic brake control module (EBCM) automatically clears the history DTC when a current DTC is not detected in 100 consecutive drive cycles.

Diagnostic Aids

A possible cause of this DTC is overcharging.

Test Description

2. Use the scan tool in order to inspect the voltage to the EBCM.

3. Use the scan tool in order to inspect the voltage to the instrument cluster. A high voltage value in multiple modules indicates a concern in the charging system.

4. Verifies that the condition is still present.

LTV0500000004721

Fig. 14   Code C1237: System Operation High Voltage (Part 1 of 2)

Circuit Description

The EBCM monitors vehicle speed deceleration, system activation, and stoplamp switch active times in order to calculate an estimate of the brake rotor temperatures. If the EBCM calculates that the brake rotor temperatures have exceeded the thermal cutoff point, the EBCM will temporarily suspend the TCS function until the brake rotors cool. This feature is used to maintain braking effectiveness if normal base braking is required. An overly heated brake system could result in brake fade.

The EBCM continues calculating the brake rotor temperatures after the ignition is turned OFF. The EBCM remains awake until the EBCM calculates that the brake rotors cooled sufficiently. The cooling period may take up to 30 minutes.

Conditions for Running the DTC

The ABS conditions and the braking conditions are normal.

Conditions for Setting the DTC

This DTC sets when the estimated brake rotor temperature of either of the drive wheels exceeds 375°C (700°F). When the estimated brake rotor temperature of either of the drive wheels exceeds 375° (700°F) during normal braking or normal ABS operations, the DTC does not set until the next TCS activation. The brake rotor temperature can exceed 375°C (700°F) without setting the DTC if a TCS activation has not occurred. When the estimated brake rotor temperature of either of the drive wheels exceeds 375°C (700°F) during a TCS activation, the DTC sets immediately, but the EBCM does not disable TCS until the end of the TCS event.

Action Taken When the DTC Sets

- The EBCM disables the TCS until the DTC becomes a history DTC.
- The Traction Off indicator turns ON.
- The message center displays the Service Traction System message.
- The ABS remains functional.

Conditions for Clearing the DTC

- The current DTC becomes history when the estimated brake rotor temperatures of both drive wheels decreases below 275°C (530°F). The EBCM also enables TCS.
- The condition for the DTC is no longer present and you used the scan tool Clear DTC function.
- The EBCM automatically clears the history DTC when a current DTC is not detected in 100 consecutive drive cycles.

Diagnostic Aids

- With TCS temporarily disabled, the EBCM continues calculating the brake rotor temperatures after the ignition is turned OFF. Turning ON the ignition again while TCS is temporarily disabled will not re-enable TCS.
- The temperature is an estimate calculated by the EBCM.

LTV0500000004771

Fig. 15   Code C1238: Brake Rotor Temperature High (Part 1 of 3)

Step	Action	Value (s)	Yes	No
1	Did you perform the ABS Diagnostic System Check?	--	Go to Step 2	Go to Diagnostic System Check -
2	1. Turn OFF all of the accessories. 2. Install a scan tool. 3. Start the engine. 4. Run the engine at approximately 2000 RPM. 5. With a scan tool, observe the Switched Battery Voltage parameter in ABS data list. Does the scan tool indicate that the voltage is greater than the specified value?	17 V	Go to Step 3	Go to Diagnostic Aids
3	With a scan tool, observe the Ignition 1 parameter in the Instrument Panel Cluster data list. Does the scan tool indicate the voltage is greater than the specified value?	17 V	Go to Diagnostic System Check	Go to Step 4
4	1. Use the scan tool in order to clear the DTCs. 2. Operate the vehicle within the Conditions for Running the DTC as specified in the supporting text. Does the DTC reset?	--	Go to Step 5	Go to Diagnostic Aids
5	Replace the EBCM. Did you complete the repair?	--	Go to Step 6	--
6	1. Use the scan tool in order to clear the DTCs. 2. Operate the vehicle within the conditions for Running the DTC as specified in the supporting test. Does the DTC reset?	--	Go to Step 2	System OK

LTV0500000004722

Fig. 14   Code C1237: System Operation High Voltage (Part 2 of 2)

- Possible causes of this DTC are the following conditions:

  - The brake usage is excessive.

  - The TCS usage is excessive.

  - The stoplamp switch is misaligned or damaged.

Test Description

The number below refers to the step number on the diagnostic table.

4. Use the scan tool in order to verify that the Brake Thermal Model is exceeded.

LTV0500000004772

Fig. 15   Code C1238: Brake Rotor Temperature High (Part 2 of 3)

Step	Action	Yes	No
1	Did you perform the ABS Diagnostic System Check?	Go to Step 2	Go to Diagnostic System Check -
2	1. Install a scan tool. 2. Turn ON the ignition, with the engine OFF. 3. Select the display DTCs function on the scan tool for the EBCM. Does the scan tool display that this DTC is set current?	Go to Step 4	Go to Step 3
3	Since most occurrences of this DTC are caused by excessive braking, review with the customer to verify the conditions under which the DTC set. Did vehicle operation cause this DTC to set?	Go to Diagnostic Aids	Go to Step 4
4	1. Allow 30 minutes from the last time you drove the vehicle for the cooling of the brake rotors. 2. With a scan tool, observe the Brake Temp Status parameter in the ABS/TCS data list. Does the scan tool display Normal?	Go to Step 6	Go to Step 5
5	Inspect the alignment of the stop lamp switch. Did you find and correct the condition?	Go to Step 8	Go to Step 6
6	1. Use the scan tool in order to clear the DTCs. 2. Operate the vehicle within the Conditions for Running the DTC as specified in the supporting text. Does the DTC reset as a current DTC?	Go to Step 7	System OK
7	Replace the EBCM. Did you complete the repair?	Go to Step 8	--
8	1. Use the scan tool in order to clear the DTCs. 2. Operate the vehicle within the Conditions for Running the DTC as specified in the supporting text. Does the DTC reset?	Go to Step 2	System OK

LTV0500000004773

Fig. 15   Code C1238: Brake Rotor Temperature High (Part 3 of 3)

- The condition for the DTC is no longer present and the DTC is cleared with a scan tool.
- The electronic brake control module (EBCM) automatically clears the history DTC when a current DTC is not detected in 100 consecutive drive cycles.

Diagnostic Aids

The pump motor is integral to the BPMV. The pump motor is not serviceable.

Test Description

The number below refers to the step number on the diagnostic table.

5. Tests the ability of the EBCM to control the pump motor. If the test lamp illuminates, the pump motor circuit within the EBCM is good.

LTV0500000004724

Fig. 16   Codes C1242 Or C1243: System Voltage Is Greater Than 8 Volts Or Pump Motor Is On For .3 Seconds (Part 2 of 3)

Circuit Description

The system relay is energized when the ignition is ON. The system relay supplies voltage to the solenoid valves and the pump motor. This voltage is referred to as the system voltage.

The electronic brake control module (EBCM) controls each solenoid valve by grounding the solenoid.

The EBCM controls the pump motor by grounding the control circuit. The pump serves 2 purposes:

- Transfers brake fluid from the brake calipers to the master cylinder reservoir during pressure decrease events.
- Transfers brake fluid from the master cylinder reservoir to the brake calipers during pressure increase events.

Conditions for Running the DTC

C1242
- The system voltage is greater than 8.0 volts.
- The system relay is ON.
- The pump motor is commanded OFF.

C1243
- The pump motor is ON for at least 0.3 seconds.
- The system relay is ON.

Conditions for Setting the DTC

C1242

The voltage across the pump motor is between 1.7 - 10.2 volts for 2 seconds.

C1243

The pump motor is stalled or turning slowly.

Action Taken When the DTC Sets

If equipped, the following actions occur:

- The EBCM disables the ABS/TCS for the duration of the ignition cycle.
- The DRP does not function optimally.
- The ABS indicator turns ON.
- The Traction Off indicator turns ON.
- The message center displays the Service Traction System message.

Conditions for Clearing the DTC

LTV0500000004723

Fig. 16   Codes C1242 Or C1243: System Voltage Is Greater Than 8 Volts Or Pump Motor Is On For .3 Seconds (Part 1 of 3)

Step	Action	Yes	No
1	Did you perform the ABS Diagnostic System Check?	Go to Step 2	Go to Diagnostic System Check
2	1. Use the scan tool in order to clear the DTCs. 2. With the scan tool, perform the Automated Test. Does the DTC reset?	Go to Step 3	Test for Intermittent and Poor Connections
3	1. Remove the EBCM from the BPMV. 2. Inspect the EBCM to BPMV connector for conditions which could cause an intermittent, such as damage, corrosion, poor terminal contact, or presence of brake fluid. Is the connector OK and the cavity free of brake fluid?	Go to Step 5	Go to Step 4
4	1. If connector corrosion or damage is evident, replace BPMV and/or EBCM as necessary. 2. If brake fluid is present, replace both BPMV and EBCM. Did you complete the repair?	Go to Step 8	--
5	1. Connect the EBCM harness to the EBCM with the BPMV still separated. 2. Connect a test lamp between the pump motor circuits, internal EBCM side, using the J 35616-A GM terminal test kit. 3. With the scan tool, perform the Automated Bleed. Does the test lamp illuminate?	Go to Step 7	Go to Step 6
6	Replace the EBCM. Did you complete the repair?	Go to Step 8	--
7	Replace the BPMV. Did you complete the repair?	Go to Step 8	--
8	1. Use the scan tool in order to clear the DTCs. 2. With the scan tool, perform the Automated Test. Does the DTC reset?	Go to Step 2	System OK

LTV0500000004725

Fig. 16   Codes C1242 Or C1243: System Voltage Is Greater Than 8 Volts Or Pump Motor Is On For .3 Seconds (Part 3 of 3)

Circuit Description

The microprocessor contains a data storage area, keep alive memory, which can save pertinent data when the ignition is turned OFF. The keep alive memory (KAM) data is lost if battery power or module ground is removed from the module. The KAM area is an integral part of the microprocessor and cannot be serviced separately.

Conditions for Running the DTC

The ABS conditions and the braking conditions are normal.

Conditions for Setting the DTC

The microprocessor calculates a checksum on those areas of memory that hold critical operation data. This is done at a regular interval and is called the periodic checksum. The microprocessor also calculates a checksum on these memory locations when ever new data is written to them. This is called the running checksum.

To check the keep alive memory (KAM), the microprocessor compares the periodic checksum to the running checksum. If they do not match, the microprocessor sets the DTC.

Action Taken When the DTC Sets

If equipped, the following actions occur:

- The EBCM disables the ABS/TCS for the duration of the ignition cycle.
- The ABS indicator turns ON.
- The Traction Off indicator turns ON.
- The message center displays the Service Traction System message.
- The EBCM will not send serial data messages.
- The EBCM will not send the requested torque output to the PCM.

Conditions for Clearing the DTC

- The condition for the DTC is no longer present and the DTC is cleared with a scan tool.
- The electronic brake control module (EBCM) automatically clears the history DTC when a current DTC is not detected in 100 consecutive drive cycles.

Diagnostic Aids

Possible causes of this DTC are the following conditions:

- A loss of battery ground
- A disconnected battery
- A running reset A running reset is detected when the keep alive memory check sum is not updated properly.
- A sudden drop in the system voltage to less than 5 volts
- Long extended engine cranks that cause the battery voltage to drop

LTV0500000004726

Fig. 17 Code C1254: Periodic Checksum Different From Running Checksum (Part 1 of 3)

Step	Action	Yes	No
1	Did you perform the ABS Diagnostic System Check?	Go to Step 2	Go to Diagnostic System Check
2	1. Turn OFF the ignition. 2. Disconnect the EBCM harness connector. 3. Install the J 39700 100-pin breakout box using the J 39700-99 breakout box adapter to the EBCM harness connector only. 4. Test the module ground circuit of the EBCM for a high resistance or an open. Did you find and correct the condition?	Go to Step 8	Go to Step 3
3	Has the battery been disconnected recently?	Go to Step 8	Go to Step 4
4	Test the charging system. Did you find and correct the condition?	Go to Step 8	Go to Step 5
5	Inspect for poor connections at the harness connector of the EBCM. Did you find and correct the condition?	Go to Step 8	Go to Step 6
6	1. Use the scan tool in order to clear the DTCs. 2. With the scan tool, perform the Automated Test. Does the DTC reset?	Go to Step 7	Test for Intermittent and Poor Connections
7	Replace the EBCM. Did you complete the repair?	Go to Step 8	--
8	1. Use the scan tool in order to clear the DTCs. 2. With the scan tool, perform the Automated Test. Does the DTC reset?	Go to Step 2	System OK

LTV0500000004728

Fig. 17 Code C1254: Periodic Checksum Different From Running Checksum (Part 3 of 3)

- Poor power or ground connections
- An internal EBCM malfunction

Test Description

The numbers below refer to the step numbers on the diagnostic table.

2. Tests for an open in the ground circuits of the body control module.

4. Verifies the proper operation of the charging system.

6. Determines whether the DTC resets.

LTV0500000004727

Fig. 17 Code C1254: Periodic Checksum Different From Running Checksum (Part 2 of 3)

Circuit Description

This DTC identifies a malfunction within the electronic brake control module (EBCM).

Conditions for Running the DTC

The ABS conditions and the braking conditions are normal.

Conditions for Setting the DTC

An internal EBCM malfunction exists.

Action Taken When the DTC Sets

C1255

If equipped, the following actions occur:

- The EBCM disables the ABS/TCS for the duration of the ignition cycle.
- The ABS indicator turns ON.
- The Traction Off indicator turns ON.
- The message center displays the Service Traction System message.

C1256
- The ABS remains functional.
- The ABS indicator remains OFF.

Conditions for Clearing the DTC

- The condition for the DTC is no longer present and the DTC is cleared with a scan tool.
- The electronic brake control module (EBCM) automatically clears the history DTC when a current DTC is not detected in 100 consecutive drive cycles.

Diagnostic Aids

The scan tool displays 2 additional characters after the DTC. Take note of the 2 character code and any other DTCs that are set. The 2 character code is an engineering aid used in order to determine the cause of the internal malfunction.

Test Description

The number below refers to the step number on the diagnostic table.

2. Determines whether the DTC is current.

LTV0500000004729

Fig. 18 Codes C2155 Or C1256: EBCM Internal Fault (Part 1 of 2)

Step	Action	Yes	No
1	Did you perform the ABS Diagnostic System Check?	Go to Step 2	Go to Diagnostic System Check
2	1. Install a scan tool. 2. Turn ON the ignition, with the engine OFF. 3. Use the scan tool in order to clear the DTCs. 4. With the scan tool, perform the Automated Test. Does the DTC reset as a current DTC?	Go to Step 3	Test for Intermittent and Poor Connections
3	Replace the EBCM. Did you complete the repair?	Go to Step 4	--
4	1. Use the scan tool in order to clear the DTCs. 2. With the scan tool, perform the Automated Test. Does the DTC reset?	Go to Step 2	System OK

LTV0500000004730

Fig. 18 Codes C2155 Or C1256: EBCM Internal Fault (Part 2 of 2)

Circuit Description

The system relay is energized when the ignition is ON. The system relay supplies voltage to the valve solenoids and the pump motor. This voltage is referred to as the system voltage. The electronic brake control module (EBCM) microprocessor activates the valve solenoids by grounding the control circuit.

Conditions for Running the DTC

- The system voltage is greater than 8 volts.
- The ignition voltage is greater than 9 volts.

Conditions for Setting the DTC

The commanded state of the driver and the actual state of the control circuit do not match for 0.03 seconds.

Action Taken When the DTC Sets

If equipped, the following actions occur:

- The EBCM disables the ABS/TCS for the duration of the ignition cycle.
- The DRP does not function optimally.
- The ABS indicator turns ON.
- The Traction Off indicator turns ON.
- The message center displays the Service Traction System message.

Conditions for Clearing the DTC

- The condition for the DTC is no longer present and the DTC is cleared with a scan tool.
- The electronic brake control module (EBCM) automatically clears the history DTC when a current DTC is not detected in 100 consecutive drive cycles.

Diagnostic Aids

The solenoid valve circuit is internal to the EBCM. The solenoid valve circuit is not diagnosable external to the EBCM. The DTC sets when there is a malfunction in the solenoid circuit internal to the EBCM.

Test Description

The number below refers to the step number on the diagnostic table.

2. Determines whether the DTC is current.

LTV0500000004731

Fig. 19   Codes C1261–C1274: System Voltage Greater Than 8 Volts Or Ignition Voltage Greater Than 9 Volts (Part 1 of 2)

Circuit Description

The EBCM and the PCM simultaneously control the traction control. The PCM reduces the amount of torque supplied to the drive wheels by retarding spark timing and selectively turning off fuel injectors. The EBCM actively applies the brakes to the front wheels in order to reduce torque.

The EBCM sends a requested torque message via a pulse width modulated (PWM) signal to the PCM. The duty cycle of the signal is used to determine how much engine torque the EBCM is requesting the PCM to deliver. Normal values are between 10 and 90 percent duty cycle. The signal should be at 90 percent when traction control is not active and at lower values during traction control activations. The PCM supplies a pull up voltage of 5 volts that the EBCM switches to ground to create the signal.

The PCM sends a delivered torque message via a pulse width modulated (PWM) signal to the EBCM. The duty cycle of the signal is used to determine how much engine torque the PCM is delivering. Normal values are between 10 and 90 percent duty cycle. The signal should be at low values (around 10 percent) at idle and higher values under driving conditions. The EBCM supplies a pull up voltage of 12 volts that the PCM switches to ground to create the signal.

When certain PCM DTCs are set, the PCM will not be able to perform the torque reduction portion of traction control. A serial data message is sent to the EBCM indicating that traction control is not allowed.

Conditions for Running the DTC

The engine is running.

Conditions for Setting the DTC

C1276

One of the following conditions exists:

- The EBCM detects that delivered torque signal is out of the valid range.
- The EBCM does not receive the delivered torque signal.

P1644 or P1689

The PCM detects that the delivered torque signal voltage is invalid.

Action Taken When the DTC Sets

- The EBCM disables the TCS for the duration of the ignition cycle.
- The PCM will store conditions which were present when the DTC set as Fail Records data only.
- The Traction Off indicator turns ON.
- The message center displays the Service Traction System message.
- The ABS remains functional.

Conditions for Clearing the DTC

LTV0500000004733

Fig. 20   Codes C1276, P1644 Or P1689: EBCM Detects Torque Signal Fault Or PCM Detects Torque Signal Fault (Part 1 of 4)

Step	Action	Yes	No
1	Did you perform the ABS Diagnostic System Check?	Go to Step 2	Go to Diagnostic System Check
2	1. Install a scan tool. 2. Turn ON the ignition, with the engine OFF. 3. Use the scan tool in order to clear the DTCs. 4. With the scan tool, perform the Automated Test. Does the DTC reset as a current DTC?	Go to Step 3	Test for Intermittent and Poor Connections
3	Replace the EBCM. Did you complete the repair?	Go to Step 4	--
4	1. Use the scan tool in order to clear the DTCs. 2. With the scan tool, perform the Automated Test. Does the DTC reset?	Go to Step 2	System OK

LTV0500000004732

Fig. 19   Codes C1261–C1274: System Voltage Greater Than 8 Volts Or Ignition Voltage Greater Than 9 Volts (Part 2 of 2)

- The condition for the DTC is no longer present and you used the scan tool Clear DTC function.
- The EBCM automatically clears the history DTC when a current DTC is not detected in 100 consecutive drive cycles.
- The PCM automatically clears the history DTC when a current DTC is not detected in 40 consecutive warm-up cycles.

Diagnostic Aids

The following conditions can cause this concern:

- An open in the delivered torque circuit.
- An short to ground or voltage in the delivered torque circuit.
- A wiring problem, terminal corrosion, or poor connection in the delivered torque circuit.
- A communication frequency problem.
- A communication duty cycle problem.
- The EBCM is not receiving information from the PCM.
- Loose or corroded EBCM ground or PCM ground.

Test Description

The numbers below refer to the step numbers on the diagnostic table.

3. Use the scan tool in order to determine if the delivered torque signal has a valid duty cycle.

9. This vehicle is equipped with a PCM which uses an Electrically Erasable Programmable Read Only Memory (EEPROM). When replacing the PCM, the replacement PCM must be programmed.

LTV0500000004734

Fig. 20   Codes C1276, P1644 Or P1689: EBCM Detects Torque Signal Fault Or PCM Detects Torque Signal Fault (Part 2 of 4)

Step	Action	Value (s)	Yes	No
1	Did you perform the ABS Diagnostic System Check?	--	Go to Step 2	Go to Diagnostic System Check
2	Inspect the EBCM ground and PCM ground, making sure each ground is clean and torqued to the proper specification. Did you find and correct the condition?	--	Go to Step 11	Go to Step 3
3	1. Install a scan tool. 2. Start the engine. 3. With a scan tool, observe the PCM to EBTCM Delivered parameter in the TCS data list. Does the scan tool display the specified value?	90%	Go to Step 4	Test for Intermittent and Poor Connections
4	1. Turn OFF the ignition. 2. Disconnect the EBCM harness connector. 3. Install the J 39700 100-pin breakout box using the J 39700-99 breakout box adapter to the EBCM harness connector and the EBCM connector. 4. Disconnect the powertrain control module (PCM) harness connector. 5. Turn ON the ignition, with the engine OFF. 6. Measure the voltage from the delivered torque signal circuit to a good ground. Does the voltage measure near the specified value?	B+	Go to Step 5	Go to Step 6
5	1. Turn OFF the ignition. 2. Disconnect the J 39700-99 breakout box adapter from the EBCM connector. 3. Turn ON the ignition, with the engine OFF. 4. Test the delivered torque signal circuit for a short to voltage. Did you find and correct the condition?	--	Go to Step 11	Go to Step 7

LTV0500000004735

Fig. 20 Codes C1276, P1644 Or P1689: EBCM Detects Torque Signal Fault Or PCM Detects Torque Signal Fault (Part 3 of 4)

Step	Action		Yes	No

6	1. Turn OFF the ignition.
	 2. Disconnect the J 39700-99 breakout box adapter from the EBCM connector.
	 3. Test the delivered torque signal circuit for the following conditions:
	   - An open
	   - A short to ground
	   - A high resistance
	
	 Did you find and correct the condition?
			Go to Step 11	Go to Step 8

7	Inspect for poor connections the harness connector of the PCM. Did you find and correct the condition?		Go to Step 11	Go to Step 9
8	Inspect for poor connections the harness connector of the EBCM. Did you find and correct the condition?		Go to Step 11	Go to Step 10
9	**Important:** The replacement PCM must be programmed. Replace the PCM. Did you complete the repair?		Go to Step 11	--
10	Replace the EBCM. Did you complete the repair?		Go to Step 11	--
11	1. Use the scan tool in order to clear the DTCs. 2. Operate the vehicle within the Conditions for Running the DTC as specified in the supporting text. Does the DTC reset?		Go to Step 2	System OK

LTV0500000004736

Fig. 20 Codes C1276, P1644 Or P1689: EBCM Detects Torque Signal Fault Or PCM Detects Torque Signal Fault (Part 4 of 4)

Circuit Description

The EBCM and the PCM simultaneously control the traction control. The PCM reduces the amount of torque supplied to the drive wheels by retarding spark timing and selectively turning off fuel injectors. The EBCM actively applies the brakes to the front wheels in order to reduce torque.

The EBCM sends a requested torque message via a pulse width modulated (PWM) signal to the PCM. The duty cycle of the signal is used to determine how much engine torque the EBCM is requesting the PCM to deliver. Normal values are between 10 and 90 percent duty cycle. The signal should be at 90 percent when traction control is not active and at lower values during traction control activations. The PCM supplies a pull up voltage of 5 volts that the EBCM switches to ground to create the signal.

The PCM sends a delivered torque message via a pulse width modulated (PWM) signal to the EBCM. The duty cycle of the signal is used to determine how much engine torque the PCM is delivering. Normal values are between 10 and 90 percent duty cycle. The signal should be at low values (around 10 percent) at idle and higher values under driving conditions. The EBCM supplies a pull up voltage of 12 volts that the EBCM switches to ground to create the signal.

When certain PCM DTCs are set, the PCM will not be able to perform the torque reduction portion of traction control. A serial data message is sent to the EBCM indicating that traction control is not allowed.

Conditions for Running the DTC

The engine is running.

Conditions for Setting the DTC

C1277

The PCM diagnoses the requested torque signal circuit and sends a serial data message to the EBCM indicating a fault is present.

P1571

One of the following conditions exists:

- The PCM detects that requested torque signal is out of the valid range.
- The PCM does not receive the requested torque signal.

Action Taken When the DTC Sets

- The EBCM disables the TCS for the duration of the ignition cycle.
- The PCM will store conditions which were present when the DTC set as Fail Records data only.
- The Traction Off indicator turns ON.
- The message center displays the Service Traction System message.
- The ABS remains functional.

LTV0500000004737

Fig. 21 Codes C1277 Or P1571: PCM To EBCM Signal Fault Or PCM Detects Torque Signal Fault (Part 1 of 4)

Conditions for Clearing the DTC

- The condition for the DTC is no longer present and you used the scan tool Clear DTC function.
- The EBCM automatically clears the history DTC when a current DTC is not detected in 100 consecutive drive cycles.
- The PCM automatically clears the history DTC when a current DTC is not detected in 40 consecutive warm-up cycles.

Diagnostic Aids

The following conditions can cause this concern:

- An open in the delivered torque circuit.
- An short to ground or voltage in the delivered torque circuit.
- A wiring problem, terminal corrosion, or poor connection in the delivered torque circuit.
- A communication frequency problem.
- A communication duty cycle problem.
- The EBCM is not receiving information from the PCM.
- Loose or corroded EBCM ground or PCM ground.

Test Description

The numbers below refer to the step numbers on the diagnostic table.

3. Use the scan tool in order to determine if the requested torque signal has a valid duty cycle.

4. Measure the requested torque signal in order to determine if the signal has a valid duty cycle.

5. Measure the requested torque signal in order to determine if the signal has a valid frequency.

11. This vehicle is equipped with a PCM which uses an Electrically Erasable Programmable Read Only Memory (EEPROM). When replacing the PCM, the replacement PCM must be programmed

LTV0500000004738

Fig. 21 Codes C1277 Or P1571: PCM To EBCM Signal Fault Or PCM Detects Torque Signal Fault (Part 2 of 4)

Step	Action	Value (s)	Yes	No
1	Did you perform the ABS Diagnostic System Check?	--	Go to Step 2	Go to Diagnostic System Check
2	Inspect the EBCM ground and PCM ground, making sure each ground is clean and torqued to the proper specification. Did you find and correct the condition?	--	Go to Step 13	Go to Step 3
3	1. Install a scan tool. 2. Start the engine. 3. With the scan tool, observe the Torque Request Signal parameter in the Powertrain Control Module data list. Does the scan tool display less than the specified value?	100%	Test for Intermittent Conditions and Poor Connections	Go to Step 4
4	1. Turn OFF the ignition. 2. Disconnect the EBCM harness connector. 3. Install the J 39700 100-pin breakout box using the J 39700-99 breakout box adapter to the EBCM harness connector and the EBCM connector. 4. Start the engine. 5. Measure the DC duty cycle between the requested torque signal circuit and a good ground. Is the duty cycle within the specified range?	5-95%	Go to Step 5	Go to Step 6
5	Measure the DC Hz between the requested torque signal circuit and a good ground. Does the frequency measure within the specified range?	121-134 Hz	Go to Step 8	Go to Step 6
6	1. Turn OFF the ignition. 2. Disconnect the J 39700-99 cable adapter from the EBCM connector. **Important:** Disconnecting the EBCM connector and turning ON the ignition could cause other modules to set loss of communication DTCs (Uxxxx). Once the EBCM is reconnected, the EBCM may set DTC C1298. 3. Turn ON the ignition, with the engine OFF. 4. Measure the voltage from the requested torque signal circuit to a good ground. Does the voltage measure within the specified range?	4 - 6 V	Go to Step 10	Go to Step 7

LTV0500000004739

Fig. 21   Codes C1277 Or P1571: PCM To EBCM Signal Fault Or PCM Detects Torque Signal Fault (Part 3 of 4)

Circuit Description

The EBCM and the PCM simultaneously control the traction control. The PCM reduces the amount of torque supplied to the drive wheels by retarding spark timing and selectively turning off fuel injectors. The EBCM actively applies the brakes to the front wheels in order to reduce torque.

The EBCM sends a requested torque message via a pulse width modulated (PWM) signal to the PCM. The duty cycle of the signal is used to determine how much engine torque the EBCM is requesting the PCM to deliver. Normal values are between 10 and 90 percent duty cycle. The signal should be at 90 percent when traction control is not active and at lower values during traction control activations. The PCM supplies a pull up voltage of 5 volts that the EBCM switches to ground to create the signal.

The PCM sends a delivered torque message via a pulse width modulated (PWM) signal to the EBCM. The duty cycle of the signal is used to determine how much engine torque the PCM is delivering. Normal values are between 10 and 90 percent duty cycle. The signal should be at low values (around 10 percent) at idle and higher values under driving conditions. The EBCM supplies a pull up voltage of 12 volts that the PCM switches to ground to create the signal.

When certain PCM DTCs are set, the PCM will not be able to perform the torque reduction portion of traction control. A serial data message is sent to the EBCM indicating that traction control is not allowed.

Conditions for Running the DTC

The ignition is ON.

Conditions for Setting the DTC

The PCM diagnoses a condition preventing the engine control portion of the traction control function and sends a serial data message to the EBCM indicating that torque reduction is not allowed. The PCM will typically set a DTC and the EBCM will set this DTC.

Action Taken When the DTC Sets

- The EBCM disables the TCS for the duration of the ignition cycle.
- The Traction Off indicator turns ON.
- The message center displays the Service Traction System message.
- The ABS remains functional.

Conditions for Clearing the DTC

- The condition for the DTC is no longer present and the DTC is cleared with a scan tool.
- The electronic brake control module (EBCM) automatically clears the history DTC when a current DTC is not detected in 100 consecutive drive cycles.

Diagnostic Aids

This DTC is for information only. As an aid to the technician, this DTC indicates that there are no problems in the ABS/TCS system.

LTV0500000004741

Fig. 22   Code C1278: Invalid Message From PCM To EBCM Torque Reduction Not Allowed (Part 1 of 2)

Step	Action	Value (s)	Yes	No
7	1. Turn OFF the ignition. 2. Disconnect the powertrain control module (PCM) harness connector. 3. Test the requested torque signal circuit for the following conditions: - A short to voltage - A short to ground. Did you find and correct the condition?	-	Go to Step 13	Go to Step 10
8	1. Turn OFF the ignition. 2. Disconnect the powertrain control module (PCM) harness connector. 3. Test the requested torque signal circuit for the following conditions: - An open - A high resistance. Did you find and correct the condition?	-	Go to Step 13	Go to Step 9
9	Inspect for poor connections the harness connector of the PCM. Did you find and correct the condition?	-	Go to Step 13	Go to Step 11
10	Inspect for poor connections the harness connector of the EBCM. Did you find and correct the condition?	-	Go to Step 13	Go to Step 12
11	**Important:** The replacement PCM must be programmed. Replace the PCM. Did you complete the repair?	-	Go to Step 13	--
12	Replace the EBCM. Did you complete the repair?	-	Go to Step 13	--
13	1. Use the scan tool in order to clear the DTCs. 2. Operate the vehicle within the Conditions for Running the DTC as specified in the supporting text. Does the DTC reset?	-	Go to Step 2	System OK

LTV0500000004740

Fig. 21   Codes C1277 Or P1571: PCM To EBCM Signal Fault Or PCM Detects Torque Signal Fault (Part 4 of 4)

Step	Action	Value (s)	Yes	No
1	Did you perform the ABS Diagnostic System Check?	--	Go to Diagnostic System Check	Go to Diagnostic System Check

LTV0500000004742

Fig. 22   Code C1278: Invalid Message From PCM To EBCM Torque Reduction Not Allowed (Part 2 of 2)

Circuit Description

The stop lamp switch signal informs the electronic brake control module (EBCM) when the brake pedal is pressed.

Conditions for Running the DTC

The ABS conditions and the braking conditions are normal.

Conditions for Setting the DTC

- The stop lamp switch remains open for 3 deceleration cycles.
- A DTC C1291 was set in a previous ignition cycle.

Action Taken When the DTC Sets

- The EBCM disables the TCS for the duration of the ignition cycle.
- The Traction Off indicator turns ON.
- The message center displays the Service Traction System message.
- The ABS remains functional.

Conditions for Clearing the DTC

- The condition for the DTC is no longer present and the DTC is cleared with a scan tool.
- The electronic brake control module (EBCM) automatically clears the history DTC when a current DTC is not detected in 100 consecutive drive cycles.

Diagnostic Aids

- Diagnose any wheel speed sensor DTCs before continuing with the diagnosis of the DTC.
- A deceleration cycle consists of the following sequence:

1. The vehicle speed is greater than 24 km/h (15 mph).
2. The vehicle decelerates more than 8 km/h/second (5 mph/second) for 2 seconds.
3. The vehicle speed decelerates to less than 16 km/h (10 mph).

- Verify proper stop lamp switch operation using the data list of the scan tool. As the brake is applied, the data list displays the stop lamp switch on within 2.54 cm (1 in) of travel.
- Possible causes of this DTC are the following conditions:
  - An open stop lamp switch
  - The stop lamp switch is misadjusted
  - An open fuse
  - Circuit has a wiring problem, terminal corrosion, or poor connections
  - Erratic wheel speeds

LTV0500000004743

Fig. 23   Code C1291: Stop Lamp Switch Open For 3 Deceleration Cycles (Part 1 of 4)

Step	Action	Yes	No
1	Did you perform the ABS Diagnostic System Check?	Go to Step 2	Go to Diagnostic System Check -
2	Press the brake pedal. Do the brake lamps turn ON?	Go to Step 3	Go to Step 7
3	1. Press the brake pedal. 2. With a scan tool, observe the Brake Switch Status parameter in the ABS data list. Does the Brake Switch Status parameter change state?	Go to Diagnostic Aids	Go to Step 4
4	1. Turn OFF the ignition. 2. Inspect the stop lamp switch and adjust and/or calibrate if needed. Did you find and correct the condition?	Go to Step 14	Go to Step 5
5	1. Turn OFF the ignition. 2. Disconnect the stop lamp switch connector. 3. Connect a 3 amp fused jumper wire between the battery positive voltage circuit of the stop lamp switch and the signal circuit of the stop lamp switch. 4. Turn ON the ignition, with the engine OFF. 5. With a scan tool, observe the Brake Switch Status parameter. Does the scan tool display Applied?	Go to Step 11	Go to Step 6
6	Test the signal circuit of the stop lamp switch for an open between the splice pack of the stop lamp signal circuit and the EBCM. Did you find and correct the condition?	Go to Step 14	Go to Step 10
7	Test the battery positive voltage circuit of the stop lamp switch for a short to ground or an open. Did you find and correct the condition?	Go to Step 14	Go to Step 8

LTV0500000004745

Fig. 23   Code C1291: Stop Lamp Switch Open For 3 Deceleration Cycles (Part 3 of 4)

Test Description

The numbers below refer to the step numbers on the diagnostic table.

3. Tests the circuit for a change in states.

5. Tests for proper operation of the circuit by bypassing the stop lamp switch. If the fuse in the jumper opens when you perform this test, the signal circuit of the stop lamp switch is shorted to ground.

LTV0500000004744

Fig. 23   Code C1291: Stop Lamp Switch Open For 3 Deceleration Cycles (Part 2 of 4)

8	Test the signal circuit of the stop lamp switch for an open between the stop lamp switch and the splice of the stop lamp signal circuit. Did you find and correct the condition?	Go to Step 14	Go to Step 9
9	Test the signal circuit of the stop lamp switch for a short to ground. Did you find and correct the condition?	Go to Step 14	Go to Step 10
10	Inspect for poor connections at the harness connector of the EBCM. Did you find and correct the condition?	Go to Step 14	Go to Step 12
11	Inspect for poor connections at the harness connector of the stop lamp switch. Did you find and correct the condition?	Go to Step 14	Go to Step 13
12	Replace the EBCM. Did you complete the repair?	Go to Step 14	--
13	Replace the stop lamp switch. Did you complete the repair?	Go to Step 14	--
14	1. Use the scan tool in order to clear the DTCs. 2. Operate the vehicle within the Conditions for Running the DTC as specified in the supporting text. Does the DTC reset?	Go to Step 2	System OK

LTV0500000004746

Fig. 23   Code C1291: Stop Lamp Switch Open For 3 Deceleration Cycles (Part 4 of 4)

Circuit Description

The stop lamp switch signal informs the electronic brake control module (EBCM) when the brake pedal is pressed.

Conditions for Running the DTC

The vehicle speed is greater than 40 km/h (25 mph).

Conditions for Setting the DTC

The stop lamp switch input was active for 2 consecutive ignition cycles.

Action Taken When the DTC Sets

- The EBCM disables the TCS for the duration of the ignition cycle.
- The Traction Off indicator turns ON.
- The message center displays the Service Traction System message.
- The ABS remains functional.

Conditions for Clearing the DTC

- The condition for the DTC is no longer present and the DTC is cleared with a scan tool.
- The electronic brake control module (EBCM) automatically clears the history DTC when a current DTC is not detected in 100 consecutive drive cycles.

Diagnostic Aids

Possible causes of this DTC are the following conditions:

- The stop lamp switch circuit is shorted to voltage.
- The stop lamp switch is misadjusted.
- The stop lamp switch is stuck closed.
- A brake pedal that is binding.
- Both brake light bulbs are burned out.

Test Description

The number below refers to the step number on the diagnostic table.

2. Test for the current state of the brake lamp switch parameter.

LTV0500000004747

Fig. 24   Code C1294: Stop Lamp Switch Input Active For 2 Consecutive Ignition Cycles (Part 1 of 3)

Step	Action	Yes	No
1	Did you perform the ABS Diagnostic System Check?	Go to Step 2	Go to Diagnostic System Check
2	1. Install a scan tool. 2. Turn ON the ignition, with the engine OFF. 3. With a scan tool, observe the Brake Switch Status parameter in the ABS data list. Does the scan tool display Released?	Go to Step 3	Go to Step 4
3	1. Press the brake pedal. 2. With a scan tool, observe the Brake Switch Status parameter. Does the Brake Switch Status parameter change state?	Go to Diagnostic Aids	Go to Step 4
4	1. Turn OFF the ignition. 2. Inspect the stop lamp switch and adjust and/or calibrate if needed. Did you find and correct the condition?	Go to Step 11	Go to Step 5
5	1. Turn OFF the ignition. 2. Disconnect the stop lamp switch connector. 3. Turn ON the ignition, with the engine OFF. 4. With a scan tool, observe the Brake Switch Status parameter. Does the scan tool display Released?	Go to Step 8	Go to Step 6
6	Test the stop lamp switch signal circuit for a short to voltage. Did you find and correct the condition?	Go to Step 11	Go to Step 7

LTV0500000004748

Fig. 24 Code C1294: Stop Lamp Switch Input Active For 2 Consecutive Ignition Cycles (Part 2 of 3)

Circuit Description

The electronic brake control module (EBCM) sources 5 volts on the stop lamp switch signal circuit when the stop lamp switch is inactive. The voltage is supplied a ground path through the stop lamp bulbs.

Conditions for Running the DTC

The ignition is ON.

Conditions for Setting the DTC

The stop lamp switch input voltage is between 2.2 volts and 5.0 volts for 2 seconds.

Action Taken When the DTC Sets

- The EBCM disables the TCS for the duration of the ignition cycle.
- The Traction Off indicator turns ON.
- The message center displays the Service Traction System message.
- The ABS remains functional.

Conditions for Clearing the DTC

- The condition for the DTC is no longer present and the DTC is cleared with a scan tool.
- The electronic brake control module (EBCM) automatically clears the history DTC when a current DTC is not detected in 100 consecutive drive cycles.

Diagnostic Aids

Possible causes of this DTC are the following conditions:

- A signal circuit of the stop lamp switch is open.
- The stop lamp switch is misadjusted.
- Verify proper stop lamp switch operation using the data list of the scan tool. As the brake is applied, the data list displays the stop lamp switch ON within 2.54 cm (1 in) of travel.
- All brake lamps are open.
- All brake lamp grounds are open.
- Circuit has a wiring problem, terminal corrosion, or poor connections.
- Loose or corroded EBCM ground or ECM ground.
- An internal EBCM problem.

Test Description

The numbers below refer to the step numbers on the diagnostic table.

3. This DTC detects an open stop lamp switch signal circuit from the stop lamp side of the splice pack to the EBCM.
4. The EBCM sources 5 volts on the stop lamp switch signal circuit. This small voltage has a ground path through the stop lamp bulbs. This DTC sets if the path to ground is open.

LTV0500000004750

Fig. 25 Code C1295: Stop Lamp Switch Input Voltage Between 2.2 & 5.0 Volts For 2 Seconds (Part 1 of 3)

Step	Action	Yes	No
7	Inspect for poor connections at the harness connector of the EBCM. Did you find and correct the condition?	Go to Step 11	Go to Step 9
8	Inspect for poor connections at the harness connector of the stop lamp switch. Did you find and correct the condition?	Go to Step 11	Go to Step 10
9	Replace the EBCM. Did you complete the repair?	Go to Step 11	--
10	Replace the stop lamp switch. Did you complete the repair?	Go to Step 11	--
11	1. Use the scan tool in order to clear the DTCs. 2. Operate the vehicle within the Conditions for Running the DTC as specified in the supporting text. Does the DTC reset?	Go to Step 2	System OK

LTV0500000004749

Fig. 24 Code C1294: Stop Lamp Switch Input Active For 2 Consecutive Ignition Cycles (Part 3 of 3)

Step	Action	Yes	No
1	Did you perform the ABS Diagnostic System Check?	Go to Step 2	Go to Diagnostic System Check
2	1. Press the brake pedal. 2. With the scan tool, observe the Brake Switch Status parameter in the ABS data list. Does the Brake Switch Status parameter display Applied?	Go to Step 4	Go to Step 3
3	Test the signal circuit of the stop lamp switch for an open. Did you find and correct the condition?	Go to Step 9	Go to Step 7
4	Press the brake pedal. Are all of the stoplamps OFF?	Go to Step 5	Go to Diagnostic Aids
5	Test the feed circuit of the stop lamps for an open or high resistance. Did you find and correct the condition?	Go to Step 9	Go to Step 6
6	Test the ground circuit of the stop lamps for an open or high resistance. Did you find and correct the condition?	Go to Step 9	Go to Diagnostic

LTV0500000004751

Fig. 25 Code C1295: Stop Lamp Switch Input Voltage Between 2.2 & 5.0 Volts For 2 Seconds (Part 2 of 3)

Step	Action	Yes	No
7	Inspect for poor connections at the harness connector of the EBCM. Did you find and correct the condition?	Go to Step 9	Go to Step 8
8	Replace the EBCM. Did you complete the replacement?	Go to Step 9	--
9	1. Use the scan tool in order to clear the DTCs. 2. Operate the vehicle within the Conditions for Running the DTC as specified in the supporting text. Does the DTC reset?	Go to Step 2	System OK

LTV0500000004752

Fig. 25 Code C1295: Stop Lamp Switch Input Voltage Between 2.2 & 5.0 Volts For 2 Seconds (Part 3 of 3)

Circuit Description

The instrument cluster controls the operation of the ABS indicator. The electronic brake control module (EBCM) reports the desired status of the ABS indicator via serial data messages.

Test Description

The numbers below refer to the step numbers on the diagnostic table.

3. Use the scan tool to check the normal state of the ABS indicator control circuit.

4. Ensures that the instrument panel cluster (IPC) can operate the ABS indicator.

Step	Action	Yes	No
1	Did you perform the ABS Diagnostic System Check?	Go to Step 2	Go to Diagnostic System Check -
2	Inspect the EBCM ground, making sure the ground is clean and torqued to the proper specification. Did you find and correct the condition?	Go to Step 9	Go to Step 3
3	1. Install a scan tool. 2. Turn ON the ignition, with the engine OFF. 3. With a scan tool, observe the ABS Warning Lamp parameter in the ABS data list. Does the scan tool display Off?	Go to Step 4	Go to Step 5
4	1. Turn OFF the ignition. 2. Turn ON the ignition, with the engine OFF. 3. Observe the ABS indicator on the instrument panel cluster (IPC) during the displays test. Does the ABS indicator illuminate during the displays test and then turn OFF?	Test for Intermittent and Poor Connections	Go to Step 6
5	Inspect for poor connections at the harness connector of the EBCM. Did you find and correct the condition?	Go to Step 9	Go to Step 7

LTV0500000004753

Fig. 26 ABS Indicator Always On (Part 1 of 2)

Circuit Description

The instrument cluster controls the operation of the ABS indicator. The electronic brake control module (EBCM) reports the desired status of the ABS indicator via serial data messages.

Test Description

The numbers below refer to the step numbers on the diagnostic table.

3. Use the scan tool to check the normal state of the ABS indicator control circuit.

4. Ensures that the instrument panel cluster (IPC) can operate the ABS indicator.

Step	Action	Yes	No
1	Did you perform the ABS Diagnostic System Check?	Go to Step 2	Go to Diagnostic System Check -
2	Inspect the EBCM ground, making sure the ground is clean and torqued to the proper specification. Did you find and correct the condition?	Go to Step 9	Go to Step 3
3	1. Install a scan tool. 2. Turn ON the ignition, with the engine OFF. 3. With a scan tool, observe the ABS Warning Lamp parameter in the ABS data list. Does the scan tool display Off?	Go to Step 4	Go to Step 5
4	1. Turn OFF the ignition. 2. Turn ON the ignition, with the engine OFF. 3. Observe the ABS indicator on the instrument panel cluster (IPC) during the displays test. Does the ABS indicator illuminate during the displays test and then turn OFF?	Test for Intermittent and Poor Connections	Go to Step 6

LTV0500000004755

Fig. 27 ABS Indicator Inoperative (Part 1 of 2)

Step	Action	Yes	No
6	Inspect for poor connections at the harness connector of the IPC. Did you find and correct the condition?	Go to Step 9	Go to Step 8
7	Replace the EBCM. Did you complete the repair?	Go to Step 9	--
8	**Important** Perform the setup procedure for the replacement IPC. Replace the instrument panel cluster (IPC). Did you complete the repair?	Go to Step 9	--
9	Operate the system in order to verify the repair. Did you correct the condition?	System OK	Go to Step 2

LTV0500000004754

Fig. 26 ABS Indicator Always On (Part 2 of 2)

Step	Action	Yes	No
5	Inspect for poor connections at the harness connector of the EBCM. Did you find and correct the condition?	Go to Step 9	Go to Step 7
6	Inspect for poor connections at the harness connector of the IPC. Did you find and correct the condition?	Go to Step 9	Go to Step 8
7	Replace the EBCM. Did you complete the repair?	Go to Step 9	--
8	**Important** Perform the setup procedure for the replacement IPC. Replace the instrument panel cluster (IPC). Did you complete the repair?	Go to Step 9	--
9	Operate the system in order to verify the repair. Did you correct the condition?	System OK	Go to Step 2

LTV0500000004756

Fig. 27 ABS Indicator Inoperative (Part 2 of 2)

Circuit Description

The Traction Off indicator is controlled by the instrument cluster via serial data messages from the EBCM. When the EBCM sees the traction control switch input grounded through the momentary traction control switch, it then disables traction control and sends a serial data message to the instrument cluster to turn the Traction Off indicator ON. Each time the ignition is cycled from OFF to ON, the traction control system is enabled.

The following conditions will cause the Traction Off indicator to illuminate:

- The EBCM has disabled the TCS due to a DTC.
- The driver manually disabling the TCS via the traction control switch.
- The instrument cluster bulb check. When the ignition switch is turned to ON, the Traction Off indicator will turn on for approximately 3 seconds and then turn OFF.

Test Description

The numbers below refer to the step numbers on the diagnostic table.

2. Use the scan tool to check the normal state of the Traction Off indicator control.

3. Ensures that the instrument cluster can operate the Traction Off indicator.

Step	Action	Yes	No
1	Did you perform the ABS Diagnostic System Check?	Go to Step 2	Go to Diagnostic System Check - ABS
2	1. Install a scan tool. 2. Turn ON the ignition, with the engine OFF. 3. With a scan tool, observe the TCS Warning Lamp parameter in the TCS data list. Does the scan tool display Off?	Go to Step 3	Go to Step 4

LTV0500000004757

Fig. 28 Traction Off Indicator Always On (Part 1 of 3)

	Action		Yes	No
3	1. Turn OFF the ignition. 2. Turn ON the ignition, with the engine OFF. 3. Observe the Traction Off indicator on the instrument cluster (IPC) during the bulb check. Does the Traction Off indicator illuminate during the bulb check and then turn OFF?		Go to Step 4	Go to Step 13
4	1. Turn OFF the ignition. 2. Install a scan tool. 3. Turn ON the ignition, with the engine OFF. 4. With a scan tool, observe the TCS Enable Status parameter in the TCS data list. 5. Activate the traction control switch. Does the Traction Switch parameter change state?		Test for Intermittent and Poor Connections	Go to Step 5
5	Does the scan indicate that the TCS Enable Status parameter is Enabled?		Go to Step 6	Go to Step 7
6	1. Turn OFF the ignition. 2. Disconnect the traction control switch connector. 3. Turn ON the ignition, with the engine OFF. 4. With a scan tool, observe the TCS Enable Status parameter. Does the scan tool display Enabled?		Go to Step 11	Go to Step 8
7	1. Turn OFF the ignition. 2. Disconnect the traction control switch connector. 3. Connect a 3 amp fused jumper from the signal circuit of the traction control switch to the ground circuit of the traction control switch. 4. Turn ON the ignition, with the engine OFF. 5. With a scan tool, observe the TCS Enable Status parameter. Does the scan tool display Enabled?		Go to Step 11	Go to Step 9
8	Test the signal circuit of the traction control switch for a short to ground. Did you find and correct the condition?		Go to Step 17	Go to Step 12
9	Test the signal circuit of the traction control switch for an open or high resistance. Did you find and correct the condition?		Go to Step 17	Go to Step 10
10	Test the ground circuit of the traction control switch for an open or high resistance. Did you find and correct the condition?		Go to Step 17	Go to Step 12

LTV0500000004759

Fig. 28 Traction Off Indicator Always On (Part 2 of 3)

Circuit Description

The Traction Off indicator is controlled by the instrument cluster via serial data messages from the EBCM. When the EBCM sees the traction control switch input grounded through the momentary traction control switch, it then disables traction control and sends a serial data message to the instrument cluster to turn the Traction Off indicator ON. Each time the ignition is cycled from OFF to ON, the traction control system is enabled.

The following conditions will cause the Traction Off indicator to illuminate:

- The EBCM has disabled the TCS due to a DTC.
- The driver manually disabling the TCS via the traction control switch.
- The instrument cluster bulb check. When the ignition switch is turned to ON, the Traction Off indicator will turn on for approximately 3 seconds and then turn OFF.

Test Description

The numbers below refer to the step numbers on the diagnostic table.

2. Use the scan tool to check the normal state of the Traction Off indicator control.

3. Ensures that the instrument cluster can operate the Traction Off indicator.

Step	Action	Yes	No
1	Did you perform the ABS Diagnostic System Check?	Go to Step 2	Go to Diagnostic System Check
2	1. Install a scan tool. 2. Turn ON the ignition, with the engine OFF. 3. With a scan tool, observe the TCS Warning Lamp parameter in the TCS data list. Does the scan tool display Off?	Go to Step 3	Go to Step 12
3	1. Turn OFF the ignition. 2. Turn ON the ignition, with the engine OFF. 3. Observe the Traction Off indicator on the instrument cluster (IPC) during the bulb check. Does the Traction Off indicator illuminate during the bulb check and then turn OFF?	Go to Step 4	Go to Step 13

LTV0500000004765

Fig. 29 Traction Off Indicator Inoperative (Part 1 of 3)

	Action		Yes	No
11	Inspect for poor connections at the harness connector of the traction control switch. Did you find and correct the condition?		Go to Step 17	Go to Step 14
12	Inspect for poor connections at the harness connector of the EBCM. Did you find and correct the condition?		Go to Step 17	Go to Step 15
13	Inspect for poor connections at the harness connector of the instrument cluster (IPC). Did you find and correct the condition?		Go to Step 17	Go to Step 16
14	Replace the traction control switch. Did you complete the replacement?		Go to Step 17	--
15	Replace the EBCM. Did you complete the repair?		Go to Step 17	--
16	**Important** Perform the setup procedure for the replacement IPC. Replace the instrument cluster (IPC). Did you complete the repair?		Go to Step 17	--
17	Operate the system in order to verify the repair. Did you correct the condition?		System OK	Go to Step 2

LTV0500000004764

Fig. 28 Traction Off Indicator Always On (Part 3 of 3)

	Action		Yes	No
4	1. Turn OFF the ignition. 2. Install a scan tool. 3. Turn ON the ignition, with the engine OFF. 4. With a scan tool, observe the TCS Enable Status parameter in the TCS data list. 5. Activate the traction control switch. Does the Traction Switch parameter change state?		Test for Intermittent and Poor Connections	Go to Step 5
5	Does the scan indicate that the TCS Enable Status parameter is Enabled?		Go to Step 6	Go to Step 7
6	1. Turn OFF the ignition. 2. Disconnect the traction control switch connector. 3. Turn ON the ignition, with the engine OFF. 4. With a scan tool, observe the TCS Enable Status parameter. Does the scan tool display Enabled?		Go to Step 11	Go to Step 8
7	1. Turn OFF the ignition. 2. Disconnect the traction control switch connector. 3. Connect a 3 amp fused jumper from the signal circuit of the traction control switch to the ground circuit of the traction control switch. 4. Turn ON the ignition, with the engine OFF. 5. With a scan tool, observe the TCS Enable Status parameter. Does the scan tool display Enabled?		Go to Step 11	Go to Step 9
8	Test the signal circuit of the traction control switch for a short to ground. Did you find and correct the condition?		Go to Step 17	Go to Step 12
9	Test the signal circuit of the traction control switch for an open or high resistance. Did you find and correct the condition?		Go to Step 17	Go to Step 10
10	Test the ground circuit of the traction control switch for an open or high resistance. Did you find and correct the condition?		Go to Step 17	Go to Step 12
11	Inspect for poor connections at the harness connector of the traction control switch. Did you find and correct the condition?		Go to Step 17	Go to Step 14

LTV0500000004766

Fig. 29 Traction Off Indicator Inoperative (Part 2 of 3)

12	Inspect for poor connections at the harness connector of the EBCM. Did you find and correct the condition?	Go to Step 17	Go to Step 15
13	Inspect for poor connections at the harness connector of the instrument cluster (IPC). Did you find and correct the condition?	Go to Step 17	Go to Step 16
14	Replace the traction control switch. Did you complete the replacement?	Go to Step 17	--
15	Replace the EBCM. Did you complete the repair?	Go to Step 17	--
16	**Important** Perform the setup procedure for the replacement IPC. Replace the instrument cluster (IPC). Did you complete the repair?	Go to Step 17	--
17	Operate the system in order to verify the repair. Did you correct the condition?	System OK	Go to Step 2

LTV0500000004767

**Fig. 29 Traction Off Indicator Inoperative
(Part 3 of 3)**

°C	°F	OHMS
	Temperature vs Resistance Values (Approximate)	
150	302	47
140	284	60
130	266	77
120	248	100
110	230	132
100	212	177
90	194	241
80	176	332
70	158	467
60	140	667
50	122	973
45	113	1188
40	104	1459
35	95	1802
30	86	2238
25	77	2796
20	68	3520
15	59	4450
10	50	5670
5	41	7280
0	32	9420
-5	23	12300
-10	14	16180
-15	5	21450
-20	-4	28680
-30	-22	52700
-40	-40	100700

LTV0500000004760

Fig. 30 Temperature vs. resistance values

Delphi 7.2

NOTE: On Air Bag Equipped Models, Refer To "Air Bag System Precautions" Located In The Front Of This Manual For System Disarming & Arming Procedures.

NOTE: Electrical Symbol & Wire Color Code Identification Located In The Front Of This Manual May Be Used As An Aid When Using Wiring Circuits Found In This Section.

NOTE: Refer To "Computer Relearn Procedures" Located In The Front Of This Manual For Computer Relearn Procedures.

INDEX

	Page No.		Page No.		Page No.
Description	5-110	Symptom Tests	5-110	Valve (BPMV)	5-111
Diagnosis & Testing	5-110	Temperature Vs. Resistance	5-110	Electronic Brake Control	
Accessing Diagnostic Trouble		Wiring Diagrams	5-110	Module (EBCM)	5-111
Codes	5-110	**Diagnostic Chart Index**	5-116	Traction Control Switch	5-111
Clearing Diagnostic Trouble		**Precautions**	5-110	Yaw Rate Sensor/Lateral &	
Codes	5-111	Air Bag Systems	5-110	Longitudinal Accelerometer	5-112
Connector Pin Identification	5-110	Battery Ground Cable	5-110	Yaw Rate Sensor/Lateral	
Diagnostic Tests	5-110	**System Service**	5-111	Accelerometer	5-112
Diagnostic Trouble Code		Brake System Bleed	5-111		
Interpretation	5-110	Component Replacement	5-111		
Intermittents & Poor		Brake Fluid Pressure Sensor	5-111		
Connections	5-110	Brake Pressure Modulator			

PRECAUTIONS

Air Bag Systems

Refer to "Air Bag System Precautions" in the front of this manual for system disarming and arming procedures.

Battery Ground Cable

Prior to service disconnect battery ground cable and isolate as required.

DESCRIPTION

When wheel slip is detected during a brake application, the ABS enters anti-lock mode. During anti-lock braking, hydraulic pressure in the individual wheel circuits is controlled to prevent any wheel from slipping. A separate hydraulic line and specific solenoid valves are provided for each wheel. The ABS can decrease, hold, or increase hydraulic pressure to each wheel brake. The ABS cannot, however, increase hydraulic pressure above the amount which is transmitted by the master cylinder during braking.

During anti-lock braking, a series of rapid pulsations is felt in the brake pedal. These pulsations are caused by the rapid changes in position of the individual solenoid valves as the EBCM responds to wheel speed sensor inputs and attempts to prevent wheel slip. These pedal pulsations are present only during anti-lock braking and stop when normal braking is resumed or when the vehicle comes to a stop. A ticking or popping noise may also be heard as the solenoid valves cycle rapidly. During anti-lock braking on dry pavement, intermittent chirping noises may be heard as the tires approach slipping. These noises and pedal pulsations are considered normal during anti-lock operation.

Vehicles equipped with ABS may be stopped by applying normal force to the brake pedal. Brake pedal operation during normal braking is no different than that of previous non-ABS systems. Maintaining a constant force on the brake pedal provides the shortest stopping distance while maintaining vehicle stability.

DIAGNOSIS & TESTING

Accessing Diagnostic Trouble Codes

Connect a suitably programmed scan tool to Data Link Connector (DLC) and follow manufacturers instructions.

Diagnostic Trouble Code Interpretation

Refer to "Diagnostic Chart Index" for diagnostic trouble code interpretation.

Connector Pin Identification

Refer to **Fig. 1 through 10** for connector pin identification.

Wiring Diagrams

Refer to **Fig. 11** for wiring diagrams.

Diagnostic Tests

Refer to **Figs. 12 through 41** for diagnostic test procedures.

Symptom Tests

Refer to **Figs. 42 through 50** for symptom test procedures.

Temperature Vs. Resistance

Refer to **Fig. 51** for temperature vs. resistance values.

Intermittents & Poor Connections

Most Intermittents are caused by faulty electrical connections or wiring, although a sticking relay or solenoid can also cause an

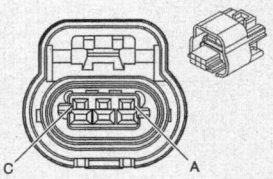

Connector Part Information	• 15393906		
	• 3-Way F GT 150 Series (BK)		
Pin	Wire Color	Circuit No.	Function
A	GY/BK	1337	5-Volt Reference
B	PU	5002	Brake Fluid Pressure Sensor Signal
C	L-GN/BK	1338	Low Reference

LTV0500000004774

Fig. 1 Connector pin identification (Brake fluid pressure sensor)

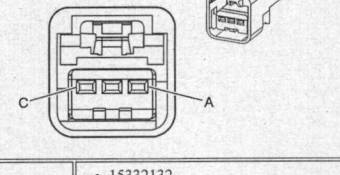

Connector Part Information	• 15332132		
	• 3-Way F GT 150 Series (BK)		
Pin	Wire Color	Circuit No.	Function
A	BN	5360	Low Reference
B	YE	5361	Brake Pedal Position Sensor Signal
C	WH	5359	5-Volt Reference

LTV0500000004775

Fig. 2 Connector pin identification (Brake pedal position sensor)

intermittent condition. Inspect wiring and connectors for the following:

1. Poor mating of connector halves, or terminals not fully seated in connector body.
2. Dirt or corrosion on terminals.
3. Damaged connector body.
4. Improperly formed or damaged terminals.
5. Poor terminal to wire connection.
6. Rubbed through wiring insulation.
7. Wiring broken inside insulation.

Clearing Diagnostic Trouble Codes

Connect a suitably programmed scan tool to Data Link Connector (DLC) and follow manufacturers instructions.

SYSTEM SERVICE

Brake System Bleed

Refer to "Continental Teves MK-70" system for brake system bleed procedures.

Component Replacement

ELECTRONIC BRAKE CONTROL MODULE (EBCM)

To prevent equipment damage, never connect or disconnect the wiring harness connection from the EBCM with the ignition switch in the On position.

1. Turn ignition to Off position.
2. Raise and support vehicle using a suitable lift.
3. Remove air deflector shield.
4. Remove righthand front wheelhouse liner.
5. Remove washer solvent container bracket.
6. Thoroughly clean all of contaminants from and around EBCM assembly.
7. Press retainer on EBCM electrical connector and rotate EBCM connector tab forward to unlocked position.
8. Disconnect EBCM electrical connector from EBCM and position out of way.

9. Remove and discard 4 EBCM to brake pressure modulator valve (BPMV) screws
10. Clean surface of EBCM/BPMV assembly.
11. Separate EBCM from BPMV. **EBCM cannot be repaired. If faulty, unit must be replaced.**
12. Reverse procedure to install, noting the following:
    a. **Torque** new screws connecting EBCM to BPMV to 44 inch lbs.
    b. Use scan tool to clear DTCs.
    c. Perform "Diagnostic System Check" as outlined in "Diagnostic Tests."

BRAKE PRESSURE MODULATOR VALVE (BPMV)

For safety reasons, the brake pressure modulator valve assembly must not be repaired, the complete unit must be replaced. With the exception of the EBCM, no screws on the brake pressure modulator valve assembly may be loosened. If screws are loosened, it will not be possible to get the brake circuits leak-tight and personal injury may result.

1. Turn ignition to Off position.
2. Thoroughly clean all contaminants from around EBCM.
3. Remove two master cylinder brake pipes from BPMV.
4. Clean any brake fluid spillage from BPMV.
5. Raise and support vehicle using a suitable lift.
6. Remove air deflector shield.
7. Remove front wheelhouse liner.
8. Remove washer solvent container bracket.
9. Remove four wheel brake pipes from BPMV.
10. Press retainer on EBCM electrical connector and rotate EBCM connector tab forward to unlocked position.
11. Disconnect EBCM electrical connector from EBCM and position out of way.
12. Remove front BPMV bracket nuts.
13. Remove EBCM/BPMV assembly from BPMV bracket.
14. Remove and discard four EBCM to BPMV screws.
15. Clean surface of EBCM/BPMV assembly.

16. Remove EBCM from BPMV.
17. Reverse procedure to install, noting the following:
    a. Use new EBCM/BPMV screws after separating EBCM from BPMV.
    b. **Torque** new screws connecting EBCM to BPMV to 44 inch lbs.
    c. **Torque** BPMV bracket nuts to 89 inch lbs.
    d. **Torque** wheel brake pipes to BPMV to 20 ft. lbs.
    e. **Torque** master cylinder brake pipes to BPMV to 20 ft. lbs.
    f. Perform "ABS Automated Bleed Procedure" as outlined in "Continental Teves MK-70" section.
    g. Perform "Diagnostic System Check" as outlined in "Diagnostic Tests."

BRAKE FLUID PRESSURE SENSOR

1. Thoroughly clean all contaminants from around EBCM.
2. Disconnect brake fluid pressure sensor electrical connector from brake fluid pressure sensor.
3. Remove brake fluid pressure sensor from EBCM.
4. Reverse procedure to install, noting the following:
    a. **Torque** brake fluid pressure sensor to EBCM to 13 ft. lbs.
    b. Fill and bleed hydraulic brake system.
    c. Perform "ABS Automated Bleed Procedure" as outlined in "Continental Teves MK-70" section.
    d. Perform "Diagnostic System Check" as outlined in "Diagnostic Tests."

TRACTION CONTROL SWITCH

1. Remove console shift lever bezel.
2. Disconnect traction control electrical connector.
3. Remove trim plate.
4. Remove two traction control mounting screws.
5. Remove traction control switch.
6. Reverse procedure to install. **Torque** traction control mounting screws to 18 inch lbs.

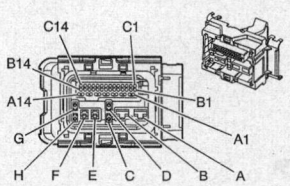

Connector Part Information	• 15411019		
	• 50-Way F Mixed Series (BK)		
Pin	Wire Color	Circuit No.	Function
A	RD/BK	342	Battery Positive Voltage
B	RD/BK	342	Battery Positive Voltage
C	PK	39	Ignition 1 Voltage
D	--	--	Not Used
E	BK	1150	Ground
F	BK	1150	Ground
G	GY	1787	Variable Effort Steering Actuator High Effort Control
H	WH	345	Variable Effort Steering Actuator Low Effort Control
A1	L-BU	830	Left Front Wheel Speed Sensor Signal
A2	YE	873	Left Front Wheel Speed Sensor Low Reference
A3	D-GN	872	Right Front Wheel Speed Sensor Signal
A4	TN	833	Right Front Wheel Speed Sensor Low Reference
A5	TN	884	Left Rear Wheel Speed Sensor Signal
A6	OG	885	Left Rear Wheel Speed Sensor Low Reference
A7	BN	882	Right Rear Wheel Speed Sensor Signal
A8	WH	883	Right Rear Wheel Speed Sensor Low Reference
A9	--	--	Not Used
A10	D-BU	1537	ABS Indicator Signal
A11	--	--	Not Used
A12	YE/BK	5270	Traction Control Data Signal
A13	PU	1807	Class 2 Serial Data

LTV0500000004776

Fig. 3   Connector pin identification (EBCM - Part 1 of 2)

A14	PU	1807	Class 2 Serial Data
B1	D-BU	5370	Long Accelerometer Signal
B2	--	--	Not Used
B3	YE	5361	5-Volt Reference
B4-B5	--	--	Not Used
B6	TN/BK	464	Delivered Torque Signal
B7	--	--	Not Used
B8	OG/BK	463	Requested Torque Signal
B9	--	--	Not Used
B10	GY	791	PWM Serial Data (F55)
B11	WH	790	PWM Serial Data (F55)
B12	--	--	Not Used
B13	L-GN/BK	1338	Yaw Rate Sensor Signal
B14	GY/BK	1337	5-Volt Reference
C1	--	--	Not Used
C2	YE/BK	2085	PWM Serial Data (F55)
C3	OG	5371	Stop Lamp Switch Signal
C4	--	--	Not Used
C5	GY	847	Extended Travel Brake Switch Signal
C6	L-BU	1764	Steering Wheel Position Signal B
C7	L-GN	1763	Steering Wheel Position Signal A
C8	D-BU	716	Yaw Rate Sensor Signal
C9	L-BU	715	Lateral Accelerometer Signal
C10	PU	5002	Brake Fluid Pressure Sensor Signal
C11	--	--	Not Used
C12	BN	5360	Low Reference
C13	WH	5359	Brake Pedal Position Sensor Signal
C14	--	--	Not Used

LTV0500000004777

Fig. 3   Connector pin identification (EBCM - Part 2 of 2)

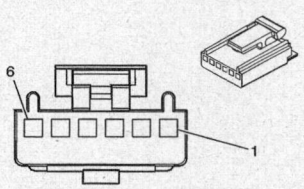

Connector Part Information	• 12064978		
	• 6-Way F Micro-Pack 100 Series (GY)		
Pin	Wire Color	Circuit No.	Function
1	GY/BK	1337	5-Volt reference
2	L-GN/BK	1338	Low Reference
3-4	--	--	Not Used
5	L-GN	1763	Steering Wheel Position Signal A
6	L-BU	1764	Steering Wheel Position Signal B

LTV0500000004778

Fig. 4   Connector pin identification (Steering angle sensor)

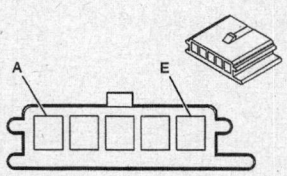

Connector Part Information	• 12059800		
	• 5-Way F Metri-Pack 150 Series (BK)		
Pin	Wire Color	Circuit No.	Function
A-B	--	--	Not Used
C	BN/WH	1571	Traction Control Switch Signal
D	BK	450	Ground
E	YE	1491	Backlight Lamps Control

LTV0500000004779

Fig. 5   Connector pin identification (Traction control switch)

YAW RATE SENSOR/ LATERAL ACCELEROMETER

1. Turn ignition to Off position.
2. To access yaw rate sensor/lateral accelerometer, move passenger seat rearward.
3. Carefully lift carpet by seam.
4. Remove two mounting nuts to yaw rate sensor/lateral accelerometer.
5. Disconnect electrical connector from accelerometer.
6. Remove accelerometer.
7. Reverse procedure to install, noting the following:
   a. **Torque** two nuts to accelerometer to 80 inch lbs.
   b. Perform "Diagnostic System Check" as outlined in "Diagnostic Tests."

YAW RATE SENSOR/ LATERAL & LONGITUDINAL ACCELEROMETER

1. Turn ignition to Off position.
2. To access yaw rate sensor/lateral and longitudinal accelerometer, move passenger seat rearward.
3. Carefully lift carpet by seam.
4. Remove two mounting nuts to accelerometer.
5. Disconnect electrical connector from accelerometer.
6. Remove accelerometer.
7. Reverse procedure to install, noting the following:
   a. **Torque** two nuts to accelerometer to 80 inch lbs.
   b. Perform "Diagnostic System Check" as outlined in "Diagnostic Tests."

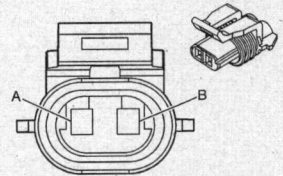

Connector Part Information		• 12052644 • 2-Way F Metri-Pack 150 Series, Sealed (GY)	
Pin	Wire Color	Circuit No.	Function
A	L-BU	830	Left Front Wheel Speed Sensor Signal
B	YE	873	Left Front Wheel Speed Sensor Low Reference

LTV0500000004780

Fig. 6 Connector pin identification (Lefthand front WSS)

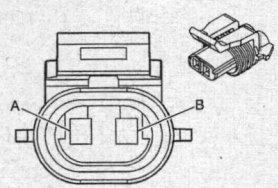

Connector Part Information		• 12052644 • 2-Way F Metri-Pack 150 Series, Sealed (GY)	
Pin	Wire Color	Circuit No.	Function
A	TN	884	Left Rear Wheel Speed Sensor Signal
B	OG	885	Left Rear Wheel Speed Sensor Low Reference

LTV0500000004781

Fig. 7 Connector pin identification (Lefthand rear WSS)

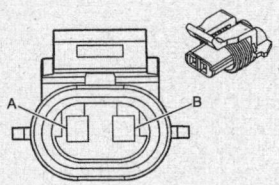

Connector Part Information		• 12052644 • 2-Way F Metri-Pack 150 Series, Sealed (GY)	
Pin	Wire Color	Circuit No.	Function
A	D-GN	872	Right Front Wheel Speed Sensor Signal
B	TN	833	Right Front Wheel Speed Sensor Low Reference

LTV0500000004782

Fig. 8 Connector pin identification (Righthand front WSS)

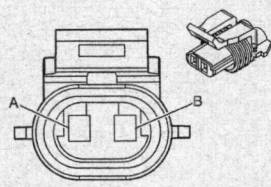

Connector Part Information		• 12052644 • 2-Way F Metri-Pack 150 Series, Sealed (GY)	
Pin	Wire Color	Circuit No.	Function
A	BN	882	Right Rear Wheel Speed Sensor Signal
B	WH	883	Right Rear Wheel Speed Sensor Low Reference

LTV0500000004783

Fig. 9 Connector pin identification (Righthand rear WSS)

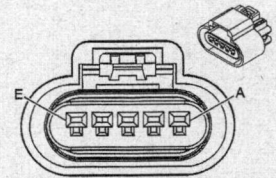

Connector Part Information		• 15326822 • 5-Way F GT 150 Series, Sealed (BK)	
Pin	Wire Color	Circuit No.	Function
A	D-BU	5370	Long Accelerometer Signal
B	GY/BK	1337	5-Volt Reference
C	D-BU	716	Yaw Rate Sensor Signal
D	L-GN/BK	1338	Low Reference
E	L-BU	715	Lateral Accelerometer Signal

LTV0500000004784

Fig. 10 Connector pin identification (Yaw & lateral long acceleration sensor)

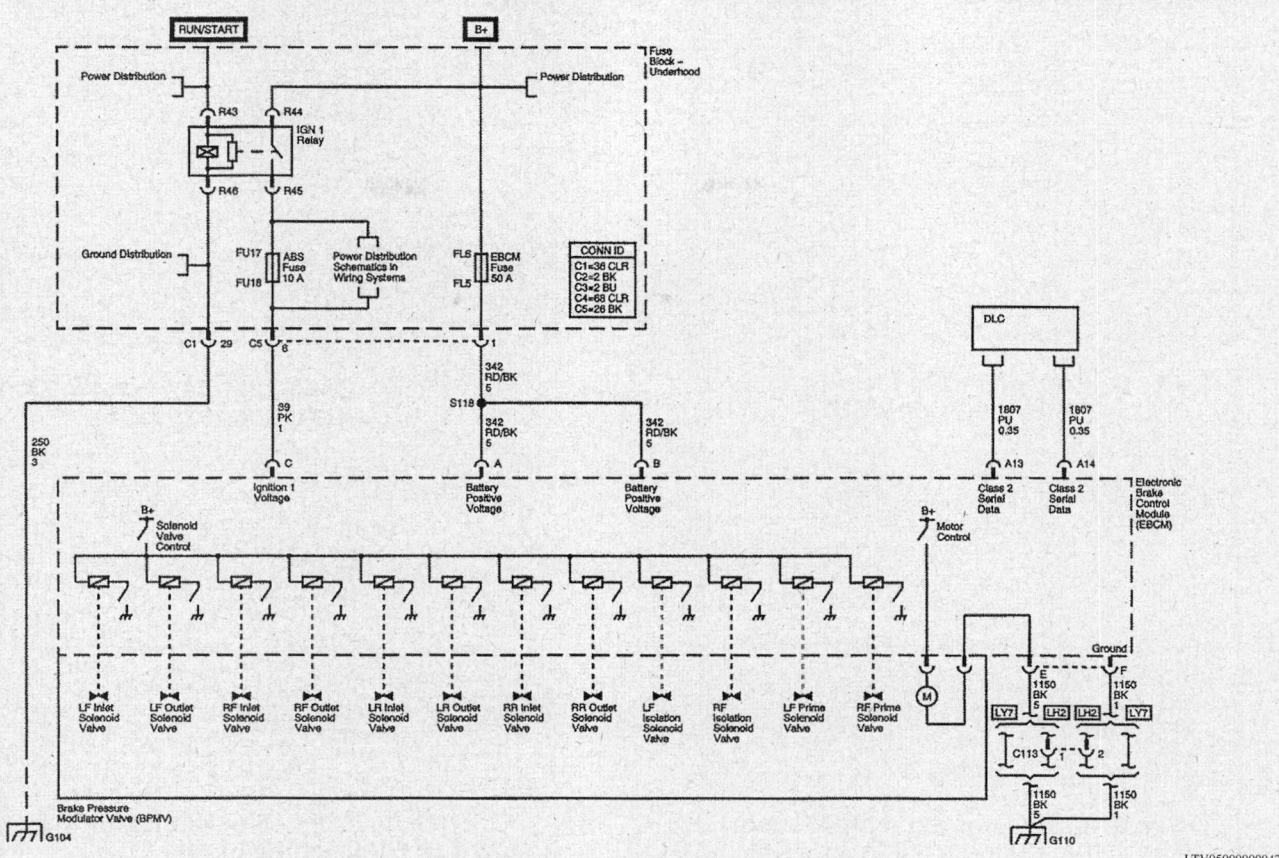

Fig. 11 Wiring diagram (Part 1 of 4)

LTV0500000004785

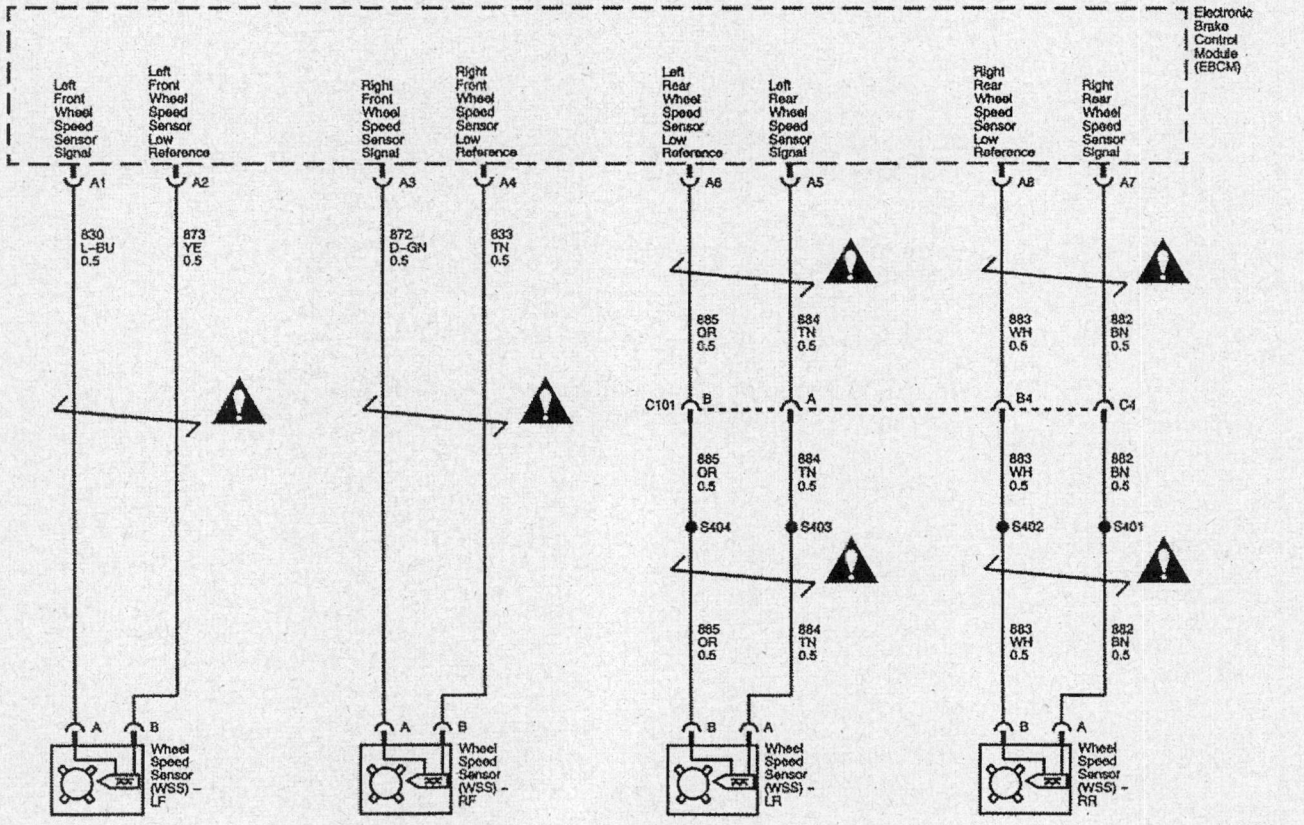

Fig. 11 Wiring diagram (Part 2 of 4)

LTV0500000004786

DELPHI 7.2

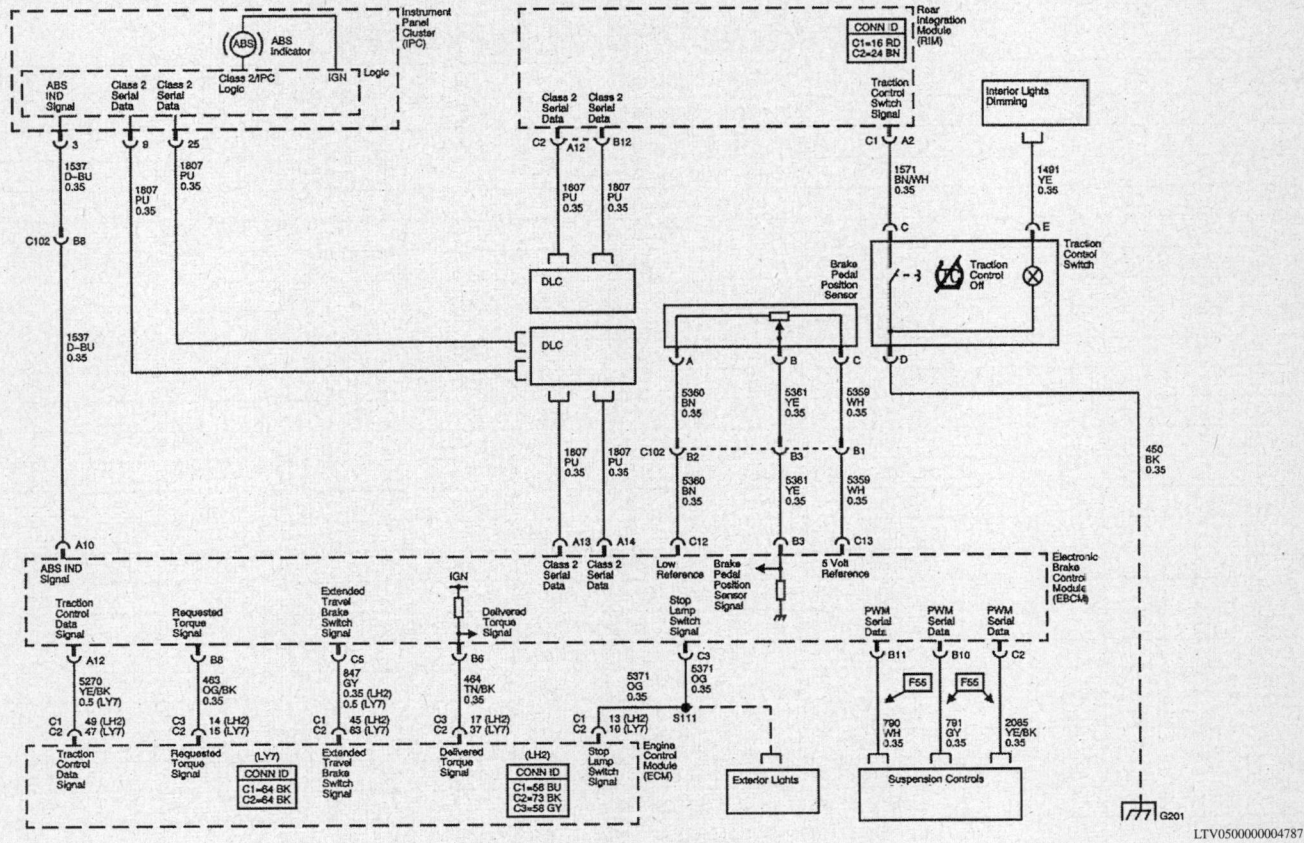

Fig. 11   Wiring diagram (Part 3 of 4)

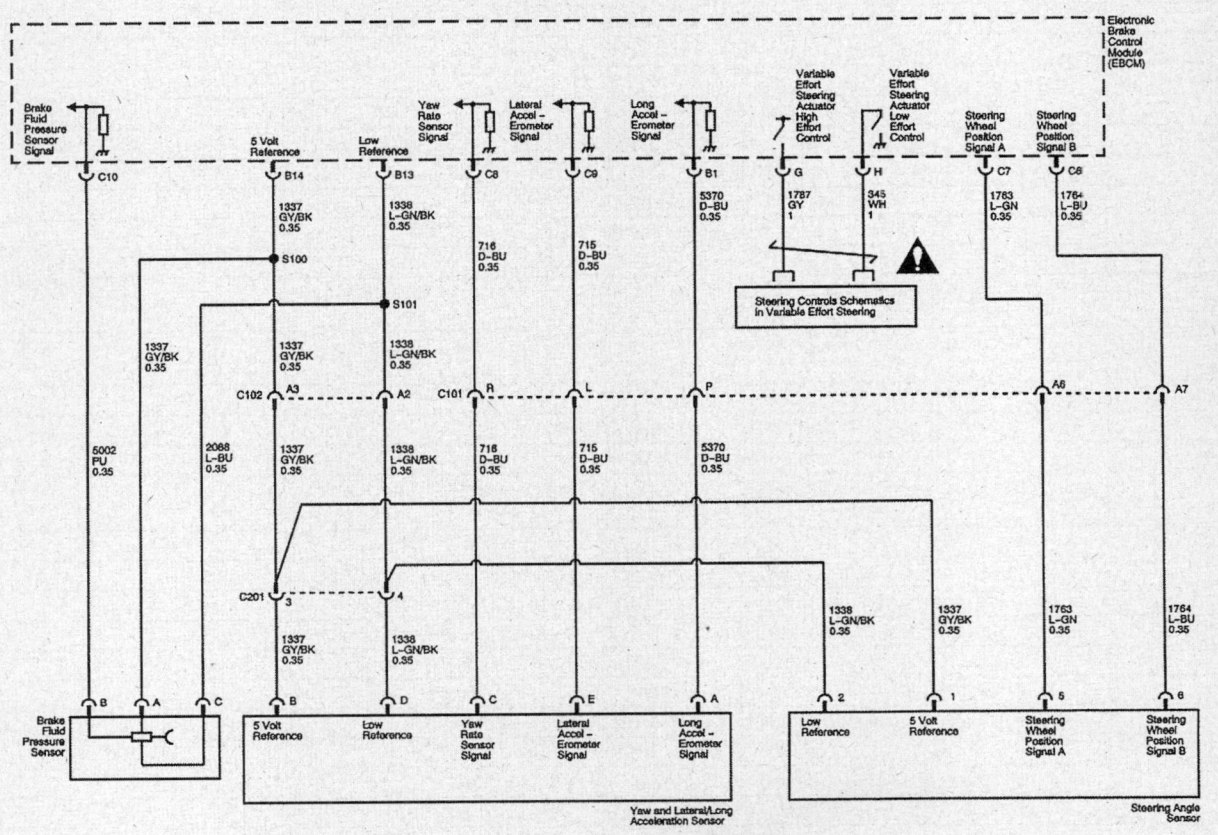

Fig. 11   Wiring diagram (Part 4 of 4)

DIAGNOSTIC CHART INDEX

Code	Description	Page No.	Fig. No.
—	Diagnostic System Check	5-117	12
—	ABS Indicator Always On	5-139	42
—	ABS Indicator Inoperative	5-139	43
—	Traction Control Indicator Always On	5-140	44
—	Traction Control Indicator Inoperative	5-140	45
—	Traction Off Indicator Always On	5-140	46
—	Traction Off Indicator Inoperative	5-141	47
—	Vehicle Stability Enhancement System Inoperative	5-142	48
—	Vehicle Stability Enhancement System Unwanted Activation	5-142	49
—	Vehicle Stability Enhancement System Excessive Brake Pulsation	5-143	50
B0665	Service Anti-Lock Brake System (ABS) Indicator Circuit	5-118	13
C0035	Lefthand Front Wheel Speed Sensor Circuit	5-118	14
C0036	Lefthand Front Wheel Speed Sensor Circuit Range/Performance	5-118	14
C0037	Lefthand Front Wheel Speed Sensor Circuit Low	5-118	14
C0038	Lefthand Front Wheel Speed Sensor Circuit High	5-118	14
C0039	Lefthand Front Wheel Speed Sensor Circuit Open	5-118	14
C0040	Righthand Front Wheel Speed Sensor Circuit	5-118	14
C0041	Righthand Front Wheel Speed Sensor Circuit Range/Performance	5-118	14
C0042	Righthand Front Wheel Speed Sensor Circuit Low	5-118	14
C0043	Righthand Front Wheel Speed Sensor Circuit High	5-118	14
C0044	Righthand Front Wheel Speed Sensor Circuit Open	5-118	14
C0045	Lefthand Rear Wheel Speed Sensor Circuit	5-118	14
C0046	Lefthand Rear Wheel Speed Sensor Circuit Range/Performance	5-118	14
C0047	Lefthand Rear Wheel Speed Sensor Circuit Low	5-118	14
C0048	Lefthand Rear Wheel Speed Sensor Circuit High	5-118	14
C0049	Lefthand Rear Wheel Speed Sensor Circuit Open	5-118	14
C0050	Righthand Rear Wheel Speed Sensor Circuit	5-118	14
C0051	Righthand Rear Wheel Speed Sensor Circuit Range/Performance	5-118	14
C0052	Righthand Rear Wheel Speed Sensor Circuit Low	5-118	14
C0113	Pump Motor Circuit High	5-119	15
C0114	Pump Motor Circuit Open	5-119	15
C0115	Pump Motor Performance	5-119	15
C0121	Valve Relay Circuit	5-120	16
C0136	Base Brake System Pressure Circuit	5-121	17
C0138	Base Brake System Pressure Circuit Low	5-122	18
C0139	Base Brake System Pressure Circuit High	5-122	18
C0163	Anti-Lock Brake System (ABS)/Traction Control System (TCS) Brake Switch/Sensor Circuit Low	5-123	19
C0164	Anti-Lock Brake System (ABS)/Traction Control System (TCS) Brake Switch/Sensor Circuit High	5-123	19
C0179	System Thermal High	5-124	20
C0186	Lateral Accelerometer Circuit	5-124	21
C0187	Lateral Accelerometer Circuit Range/Performance	5-124	21
C0192	All Wheel Drive (AWD)/Four Wheel Drive (4WD) Reference Accelerometer Circuit Range/Performance	5-125	22
C0196	Yaw Rate Circuit	5-126	23
C0220	Lefthand Front Anti-Lock Brake System (ABS) Channel In Release Too Long	5-127	24
C0221	Righthand Front Anti-Lock Brake System (ABS) Channel In Release Too Long	5-127	24
C0228	Lefthand Rear Anti-Lock Brake System (ABS) Channel In Release Too Long	5-127	24
C0229	Righthand Rear Anti-Lock Brake System (ABS) Channel In Release Too Long	5-127	24
C0241	Powertrain Control Module (PCM) Indicated Requested Torque Fault	5-128	25
C0242	Powertrain Control Module (PCM) Indicated TCS Fault	5-129	26
C0243	Engine Drag Control	5-129	27
C0244	Pulse Width Modulated (PWM) Delivered Torque	5-130	28
C0252	Vehicle Stability Enhancement System (VSES) Sensors Uncorrelated	5-130	29
C0253	Centering Error	5-131	30
C0254	Steering Sensor And/Or Lateral Accelerometer Bias	5-131	30
C0281	Dynamic Rear Proportioning (DRP) Performance	5-132	31

Continued

DIAGNOSTIC CHART INDEX—Continued

Code	Description	Page No.	Fig. No.
C0460	Steering Position Sensor	5-132	32
C0461	Steering Position Sensor Range/Performance	5-132	32
C0550	Electronic Control Unit (ECU) Performance	5-134	33
C0551	Option Configuration Error	5-134	34
C0561	System Disabled Information Stored	5-134	35
C0565	Vehicle Identification Number (VIN) Information Error	5-135	36
C0820	Device Ground Circuit	5-135	37
C0870	Device Voltage Performance Output Circuit	5-136	38
C0899	Device Voltage Low	5-137	39
C0900	Device Voltage High	5-137	40
P0856	Traction Control Torque Request Circuit	5-128	25
P1575	Extended Travel Brake Switch Circuit	5-138	41
P1689	Traction Control Delivered Torque Output Circuit	5-130	28

Circuit Description

The ABS Diagnostic System Check is an organized approach to identify problems associated with the EBCM. This check must be the starting point for any EBCM complaint, and will direct you to the next logical step in diagnosing the complaint. The EBCM is a very reliable component and is not likely the cause of the malfunction. Most system complaints are linked to faulty wiring, connectors, and occasionally to components. Understanding the ABS system and using the tables correctly will reduce diagnostic time and prevent unnecessary parts replacement.

Test Description

The numbers below refer to the step numbers on the diagnostic table.

2. Lack of communication may be due to a partial malfunction of the serial data circuit or due to a total malfunction of the serial data circuit. The specified procedure will determine the particular condition.

4. The presence of DTCs which begin with "U" indicate some other module is not communicating. The specified procedure will compile all the available information before tests are performed.

Step	Action	Yes	No
1	Install a scan tool. Does the scan tool power up?	Go to Step 2	Check Scan Tool Does Not Communicate with Class 2 Device
2	1. Turn ON the ignition, with the engine OFF. 2. Attempt to establish communication with the following control modules: - Dash integration module (DIM) - Electronic brake control module (EBCM) - Instrument panel cluster (IPC) - Powertrain control module (PCM) - Rear integration module (RIM) Does the scan tool communicate with all control modules?	Go to Step 3	Check Scan Tool Does Not Communicate with Class 2 Device

LTV0500000004789

Fig. 12 Diagnostic System Check (Part 1 of 2)

3	Select the display DTCs function on the scan tool for the following control modules: - Dash integration module (DIM) - Electronic brake control module (EBCM) - Instrument panel cluster (IPC) - Powertrain control module (PCM) - Rear integration module (RIM) Does the scan tool display any DTCs?	Go to Step 4	Go to Symptoms
4	Does the scan tool display any DTCs which begin with a "U"?		Go to Step 5
5	Does the scan tool display DTC B1000, B1004, B1007, B1009, or B1020?	Go to Diagnostic Trouble Code (DTC)	Go to Step 6
6	Does the scan tool display DTC B1327, B1328, B1513, or B1514?	Go to Diagnostic Trouble Code (DTC)	Go to Diagnostic Trouble Code (DTC) List

LTV0500000004790

Fig. 12 Diagnostic System Check (Part 2 of 2)

Circuit Description

The instrument cluster controls the operation of the ABS indicator. The electronic brake control module (EBCM) reports the desired status of the ABS indicator via serial data messages. The ABS indicator signal circuit is a back-up reporting circuit to the serial data messages. The EBCM supplies ground through the circuit when the ABS is operating properly. When there is a problem with ABS that should turn on the ABS indicator, the EBCM opens the ABS indicator signal circuit. If there is a problem with the ABS serial data messages, the instrument cluster uses the ABS indicator signal to determine if the ABS indicator should be illuminated. Using the serial data messages and back-up circuit, the instrument cluster decides whether to turn on the ABS indicator.

Conditions for Running the DTC

- The ignition is ON.
- Ignition voltage is greater than 8 volts.

Conditions for Setting the DTC

One of the following conditions exist for 0.3 seconds:

- The ABS indicator signal circuit voltage is greater than 9 volts when the ABS indicator is commanded ON.
- The ABS indicator signal circuit voltage is less than 3 volts when the ABS indicator is commanded OFF.

Action Taken When the DTC Sets

- The ABS remains functional.
- The ABS indicator remains OFF.

Conditions for Clearing the DTC

- The condition for the DTC is no longer present and the DTC is cleared with a scan tool.
- The electronic brake control module (EBCM) automatically clears the history DTC when a current DTC is not detected in 100 consecutive drive cycles.

Diagnostic Aids

The following conditions may cause this concern:

- Open, short to ground, or short to voltage.
- Internal EBCM failure.
- Internal IPC failure.

Test Description

The numbers below refer to the step numbers on the diagnostic table.

2. Use the scan tool to verify the normal state of the ABS indicator signal circuit.

3. Ensure that the instrument panel cluster can operate the ABS indicator.

LTV0500000004791

Fig. 13   Code B0665: Service Anti-Lock Brake System (ABS) Indicator Circuit (Part 1 of 3)

Step	Action	Yes	No
7	**Important** Perform the setup procedure for the EBCM. An unprogrammed EBCM will result in the following conditions: • Inoperative or poorly functioning system operations • The EBCM sets DTC C0281 and DTC C0550 Replace the EBCM. Did you complete the repair?	Go to Step 9	--
8	Replace the IPC. Did you complete the repair?	Go to Step 9	--
9	1. Use the scan tool in order to clear the DTCs. 2. Operate the vehicle within the Conditions for Running the DTC as specified in the supporting text. Does the DTC reset?	Go to Step 2	System OK

LTV0500000004793

Fig. 13   Code B0665: Service Anti-Lock Brake System (ABS) Indicator Circuit (Part 3 of 3)

Step	Action	Yes	No
1	Did you perform the ABS Diagnostic System Check?	Go to Step 2	Go to Diagnostic System Check -
2	1. Install a scan tool. 2. Turn ON the ignition, with the engine OFF. 3. With a scan tool, observe the ABS Warning Indicator parameter in the DRP/ABS/TCS/VSES data list. Does the scan tool display Off?	Go to Step 3	Go to Step 4
3	1. Turn OFF the ignition. 2. Turn ON the ignition, with the engine OFF. 3. Observe the ABS indicator on the instrument panel cluster (IPC) during the bulb check. Does the ABS indicator illuminate during the bulb check?	Go to Step 4	Go to Step 6
4	Test the ABS indicator signal circuit of the EBCM for the following conditions: • An open • A short to ground • A short to voltage Did you find and correct the condition?	Go to Step 9	Go to Step 5
5	Inspect for poor connections at the harness connector of the EBCM. Did you find and correct the condition?	Go to Step 9	Go to Step 7
6	Inspect for poor connections at the harness connector of the instrument panel cluster. Did you find and correct the condition?	Go to Step 9	Go to Step 8

LTV0500000004792

Fig. 13   Code B0665: Service Anti-Lock Brake System (ABS) Indicator Circuit (Part 2 of 3)

Circuit Description

As the wheel spins, the wheel speed sensor produces an AC signal. The electronic brake control module (EBCM) uses the frequency of the AC signal to calculate the wheel speed.

Conditions for Running the DTC

C0035, C0040, C0045, or C0050

The ignition is ON.

C0036, C0037, C0041, C0042, C0046, C0047, C0051, or C0052
- DTCs C0035, C0040, C0045, or C0050 are not set.
- The brake pedal is not pressed.
- The ABS is not active.

Conditions for Setting the DTC

C0035, C0040, C0045, or C0050

One of the following conditions exists for 0.02 seconds:

- A short to voltage - the wheel speed sensor signal circuit and wheel speed sensor return circuit voltages are both greater than 4.25 volts.
- A short to ground - the wheel speed sensor signal circuit and wheel speed sensor return circuit voltages are both less than 0.75 volts.
- An open - the wheel speed sensor signal circuit voltage is greater than 4.25 volts and wheel speed sensor return circuit voltage is less than 0.75 volts.

C0036, C0041, C0046, or C0051

The EBCM detects a rapid variation in the wheel speed. The wheel speed changes by 16 km/h (10 mph) or more in 0.01 second. The change must occur 3 times with no more than 0.2 seconds between occurrences.

C0037, C0042, C0047, or C0052

All of the following conditions exists for 2.5 seconds:

- The suspect wheel speed equals zero.
- The other wheel speeds are greater than 8 km/h (5 mph).
- The other wheel speeds are within 11 km/h (7 mph) of each other.

Action Taken When the DTC Sets

If equipped, the following actions occur:

LTV0500000004794

Fig. 14   Codes C0035–C0052: Wheel Speed Sensor Circuit Fault (Part 1 of 4)

- The EBCM disables the ABS/TCS/VSES for the duration of the ignition cycle.
- The DRP does not function optimally.
- The ABS indicator turns ON.
- The Traction Control indicator turns ON.
- The DIC displays the Service Stability System message.

Conditions for Clearing the DTC

- The condition for the DTC is no longer present and the DTC is cleared with a scan tool.
- The EBCM automatically clears the history DTC when a current DTC is not detected in 100 consecutive drive cycles.

Diagnostic Aids

C0035, C0040, C0045, or C0050

If the customer comments that the ABS indicator is ON only during moist environmental conditions (rain, snow, vehicle wash, etc.), inspect the wheel speed sensor wiring for signs of water intrusion. If the DTC is not current, clear all DTCs and simulate the effects of water intrusion by using the following procedure:

1. Spray the suspected area with a 5 percent saltwater solution. To create a 5 percent saltwater solution, add 2 teaspoons (9.9 ml) of salt to 354 ml (12 oz) of water.
2. Test drive the vehicle over various road surfaces (bumps, turns, etc.) above 40 km/h (25 mph) for at least 30 seconds.
3. If the DTC returns, replace the suspected wheel speed sensor or repair the wheel speed sensor wiring.
4. Rinse the area thoroughly when completed.

C0036, C0041, C0046, or C0051

A possible cause of this DTC is electrical noise on the wheel speed sensor harness wiring. Electrical noise could result from the wheel speed sensor wires being routed to close to high energy ignition system components, such as spark plug wires.

C0037, C0042, C0047, or C0052

One of the following conditions may exist:

- The wheel speed sensor inputs are shorted together.
- Internal malfunction of the wheel speed sensor.
- The other wheel speeds are within 11 km/h (7 mph) of each other.

Diagnose each wheel speed sensor individually.

Test Description

The numbers below refer to the step numbers on the diagnostic table.

3. Measure the resistance of the wheel speed sensor in order to determine if the sensor has a valid resistance value.

LTV0500000004795

Fig. 14 Codes C0035–C0052: Wheel Speed Sensor Circuit Fault (Part 2 of 4)

			Yes	No
7	Inspect for poor connections at the harness connector for the EBCM. Did you find and correct the condition?		Go to Step 10	Go to Step 9
8	Replace the wheel speed sensor. Did you complete the repair?		Go to Step 10	--
9	**Important:** Perform the setup procedure for the EBCM. An unprogrammed EBCM will result in the following conditions: • Inoperative or poorly functioning system operations • The EBCM sets DTC C0281 and DTC C0550 Replace the EBCM. Did you complete the repair?		Go to Step 10	--
10	1. Use the scan tool in order to clear the DTCs. 2. Operate the vehicle within the Conditions for Running the DTC as specified in the supporting text. Does the DTC reset?		Go to Step 2	System OK

LTV0500000004797

Fig. 14 Codes C0035–C0052: Wheel Speed Sensor Circuit Fault (Part 4 of 4)

Step	Action	Values	Yes	No
1	Did you perform the Diagnostic System Check - ABS?	--	Go to Step 2	Go to Diagnostic System Check -
2	1. Install a scan tool. 2. Turn ON the ignition. 3. Set up the scan tool snap shot feature to trigger for this DTC. 4. Drive the vehicle at a speed greater than the specified value. Does the scan tool indicate that this wheel speed DTC set?	8 km/h (5 mph)	Go to Step 3	Go to Diagnostic Aids
3	1. Raise and support the vehicle. 2. Disconnect the wheel speed sensor connector. 3. Measure the resistance across the wheel speed sensor. Does the resistance measure within the specified range?	850- 1350 ohms	Go to Step 4	Go to Step 8
4	1. Spin the wheel. 2. Measure the AC voltage across the wheel speed sensor. Does the AC voltage measure greater than the specified value?	100 mV	Go to Step 5	Go to Step 8
5	Inspect for poor connections at the harness connector of the wheel speed sensor. Did you find and correct the condition?	--	Go to Step 10	Go to Step 6
6	1. Disconnect the EBCM harness connector. 2. Install the J 39700 universal pinout box using the J 39700-300 cable adapter to the EBCM harness connector only. 3. Test the wheel speed sensor circuits for the following: - An open - A short to ground - A short to voltage - Shorted together Did you find and correct the condition?		Go to Step 10	Go to Step 7

LTV0500000004796

Fig. 14 Codes C0035–C0052: Wheel Speed Sensor Circuit Fault (Part 3 of 4)

Circuit Description

The system relay is energized when the ignition is ON. The system relay supplies voltage to the solenoid valves and the pump motor. This voltage is referred to as the system voltage.

The electronic brake control module (EBCM) controls each solenoid valve by grounding the solenoid.

The EBCM controls the pump motor by grounding the control circuit. The pump serves 2 purposes:

- Transfers brake fluid from the brake calipers to the master cylinder reservoir during pressure decrease events.
- Transfers brake fluid from the master cylinder reservoir to the brake calipers during pressure increase events.

Conditions for Running the DTC

- The pump motor is commanded ON.
- The system voltage is greater than 8 volts.

Conditions for Setting the DTC

One of the following conditions exists for 0.5 seconds:

- With the commanded pump motor voltage less than the system voltage, the actual pump motor voltage is 3 volts less than the commanded voltage.
- With the commanded pump motor voltage greater than the system voltage, the actual pump motor voltage is less than 8 volts.

Action Taken When the DTC Sets

If equipped, the following actions occur:

- The EBCM disables the ABS/TCS/VSES for the duration of the ignition cycle.
- The DRP does not function optimally.
- The ABS indicator turns ON.
- The Traction Control indicator turns ON.
- The DIC displays the Service Stability System message.

Conditions for Clearing the DTC

- The condition for the DTC is no longer present and the DTC is cleared with a scan tool.
- The EBCM automatically clears the history DTC when a current DTC is not detected in 100 consecutive drive cycles.

Diagnostic Aids

The pump motor is integral to the BPMV. The pump motor is not serviceable.

LTV0500000004798

Fig. 15 Codes C0113–C0115: Pump Motor Circuit Fault (Part 1 of 3)

Step	Action	Yes	No
1	Did you perform the Diagnostic System Check - ABS?	Go to Step 2	Go to Diagnostic System Check
2	1. Install a scan tool. 2. Turn ON the ignition, with the engine OFF. 3. Use the scan tool in order to clear the DTCs. 4. With the scan tool, perform the Automated Test. Does the DTC reset?	Go to Step 3	Test for Intermittent and Poor Connections
3	1. Turn OFF the ignition. 2. Disconnect the pump motor harness pigtail connector of the BPMV. 3. Connect a test lamp between the pump motor circuits at the pump motor connector of the EBCM using the J 35616-B connector test adapter kit. 4. Use the scan tool in order to clear the DTCs. 5. With the scan tool, perform the Pump Motor Test. Does the test lamp illuminate?	Go to Step 5	Go to Step 4
4	1. Turn OFF the ignition. 2. Disconnect the EBCM harness connector. 3. Connect the J 39700 universal pinout box using the J 39700-300 cable adapter to the EBCM harness connector only. 4. Test both ground circuits of the EBCM including the EBCM ground for a high resistance or an open. Did you find and correct the condition?	Go to Step 9	Go to Step 6
5	Inspect for poor connections at the pump motor harness pigtail connector of the BPMV. Did you find and correct the condition?	Go to Step 9	Go to Step 7

LTV0500000004799

Fig. 15 Codes C0113–C0115: Pump Motor Circuit Fault (Part 2 of 3)

Circuit Description

The system relay is energized when the ignition is ON. The system relay supplies voltage to the solenoid valves and the pump motor. This voltage is referred to as the system voltage.

The electronic brake control module (EBCM) controls each solenoid valve by grounding the solenoid.

The EBCM controls the pump motor by grounding the control circuit. The pump serves 2 purposes:

- Transfers brake fluid from the brake calipers to the master cylinder reservoir during pressure decrease events.
- Transfers brake fluid from the master cylinder reservoir to the brake calipers during pressure increase events.

Conditions for Running the DTC

- The ignition voltage is greater than 10.5 volts.
- The system relay is commanded ON.

Conditions for Setting the DTC

The system voltage is less than 8 volts for 0.23 seconds.

Action Taken When the DTC Sets

If equipped, the following actions occur:

- The EBCM disables the DRP/ABS/TCS/VSES for the duration of the ignition cycle.
- The ABS indicator turns ON.
- The Traction Control indicator turns ON.
- The DIC displays the Service Stability System message.
- The EBCM will also set DTC C0281.
- The red Brake warning indicator turns ON.

Conditions for Clearing the DTC

- The condition for the DTC is no longer present and the DTC is cleared with a scan tool.
- The EBCM automatically clears the history DTC when a current DTC is not detected in 100 consecutive drive cycles.

Diagnostic Aids

The system relay is integral to the EBCM. The relay is not serviceable.

Test Description

The number below refers to the step number on the diagnostic table.

2. Determines whether the DTC is current.

LTV0500000004801

Fig. 16 Code C0121: Valve Relay Circuit (Part 1 of 2)

Step	Action	Yes	No
6	Inspect for poor connections at the harness connector of the EBCM. Did you find and correct the condition?	Go to Step 9	Go to Step 8
7	Replace the BPMV. Did you complete the repair?	Go to Step 9	--
8	**Important** Perform the setup procedure for the EBCM. An unprogrammed EBCM will result in the following conditions: • Inoperative or poorly functioning system operations • The EBCM sets DTC C0281 and DTC C0550 Replace the EBCM. Did you complete the repair?	Go to Step 9	--
9	1. Use the scan tool in order to clear the DTCs. 2. With the scan tool, perform the Automated Test. Does the DTC reset?	Go to Step 2	System OK

LTV0500000004800

Fig. 15 Codes C0113–C0115: Pump Motor Circuit Fault (Part 3 of 3)

Step	Action	Values	Yes	No
1	Did you perform the Diagnostic System Check - ABS?	--	Go to Step 2	Go to Diagnostic System Check
2	1. Install a scan tool. 2. Turn ON the ignition, with the engine OFF. 3. Use the scan tool in order to clear the DTCs. 4. With the scan tool, perform the Automated Test. Does the DTC reset as a current DTC?	--	Go to Step 3	Test for Intermittent and Poor Connections
3	1. Disconnect the pump motor harness pigtail connector of the BPMV. 2. Measure the resistance between each pump motor control circuit and the housing of the BPMV at the pump motor harness pigtail connector of the BPMV. Does the DMM display the specified value?	OL	Go to Step 5	Go to Step 4
4	Replace the EBCM and the BPMV. Did you complete the repair?	--	Go to Step 6	--
5	Replace the EBCM. Did you complete the repair?	--	Go to Step 6	--
6	1. Use the scan tool in order to clear the DTCs. 2. With the scan tool, perform the Automated Test. Does the DTC reset?	--	Go to Step 2	System OK

LTV0500000005762

Fig. 16 Code C0121: Valve Relay Circuit (Part 2 of 2)

Circuit Description

The electronic brake control module (EBCM) uses the input from the brake fluid pressure sensor for more accurate braking control during vehicle stability enhancement system (VSES).

Conditions for Running the DTC

The ignition is ON for 1.0 second.

Conditions for Setting the DTC

One of the following conditions exists for 0.1 seconds.

- The brake fluid pressure sensor signal is greater than 4.9 volts.
- The brake fluid pressure sensor signal is less than 0.15 volts.

Action Taken When the DTC Sets

- The EBCM disables the VSES for the duration of the ignition cycle.
- ACC braking function disabled.
- TCS is degraded.
- The Traction Control and Active Handling indicator turns ON.
- The DIC displays the Service Active Handling message.

Conditions for Clearing the DTC

- The condition for the DTC is no longer present and the DTC is cleared with a scan tool.
- The electronic brake control module (EBCM) automatically clears the history DTC when a current DTC is not detected in 100 consecutive drive cycles.

Diagnostic Aids

- Find out from the driver under what conditions the DTC was set (when the DIC displayed the Service Stabilitrak message). This information will help to duplicate the failure.
- The Snapshot function on the scan tool can help find an intermittent DTC.
- A deceleration cycle consists of the following sequence:

1. The vehicle speed is greater than 24 km/h (15 mph).
2. The vehicle decelerates more than 8 km/h/second (5 mph/second) for 2 seconds.
3. The vehicle speed decelerates to less than 16 km/h (10 mph).

Test Description

The numbers below refer to the step numbers on the diagnostic table.

3. Tests for the proper operation of the circuit in the low voltage range.

LTV0500000005763

Fig. 17 Code C0136: Base Brake System Pressure Circuit (Part 1 of 5)

Step	Action	Values	Yes	No
1	Did you perform the Diagnostic System Check - ABS?	--	Go to Step 2	Go to Diagnostic System Check -
2	1. Install a scan tool. 2. Turn ON the ignition, with the engine OFF. 3. With a scan tool, observe the Brake Pressure Sensor parameter in the VSES data list. Does the scan tool display that the Brake Pressure Sensor parameter is within the specified range?	0.14-4.9 V	Go to Diagnostic Aids	Go to Step 3
3	1. Turn OFF the ignition. 2. Disconnect the brake fluid pressure sensor connector. 3. Turn ON the ignition, with the engine OFF. 4. With the scan tool, observe the Brake Pressure Sensor parameter. Does the scan tool indicate that the Brake Pressure Sensor parameter is less than the specified value?	0.14 V	Go to Step 4	Go to Step 10
4	1. Turn OFF the ignition. 2. Connect a 3-amp fused jumper wire between the 5-volt reference circuit of the brake fluid pressure sensor and the signal circuit of the brake fluid pressure sensor. 3. Turn ON the ignition, with the engine OFF. 4. With the scan tool, observe the Brake Pressure Sensor parameter. Does the scan tool indicate that the Brake Pressure Sensor parameter is greater than the specified value?	4.9 V	Go to Step 5	Go to Step 8
5	1. Disconnect the fused jumper wire. 2. Measure the voltage between the 5-volt reference circuit of the brake fluid pressure sensor and the low reference circuit of the brake fluid pressure sensor. Does the voltage measure less the specified value?	5 V	Go to Step 6	Go to Step 7

LTV0500000005765

Fig. 17 Code C0136: Base Brake System Pressure Circuit (Part 3 of 5)

4. Tests for the proper operation of the circuit in the high voltage range. If the fuse in the jumper opens when you perform this test, the signal circuit is shorted to ground.

5. Tests for a short to voltage in the 5-volt reference circuit.

6. Tests for a high resistance or an open in the low reference circuit.

LTV0500000005764

Fig. 17 Code C0136: Base Brake System Pressure Circuit (Part 2 of 5)

6	1. Turn OFF the ignition. 2. Disconnect the negative battery cable. 3. Measure the resistance from the low reference circuit of the brake fluid pressure sensor to a good ground. Does the resistance measure less than the specified value?	5 ohms	Go to Step 12	Go to Step 11
7	Test the 5-volt reference circuit of the brake fluid pressure sensor for a short to voltage. Did you find and correct the condition?	--	Go to Step 16	Go to Step 13
8	Test the 5-volt reference circuit of the brake fluid pressure sensor for the following conditions: • An open • A short to ground • A high resistance Did you find and correct the condition?	--	Go to Step 16	Go to Step 9
9	Test the signal circuit of the brake fluid pressure sensor for the following conditions: • An open • A short to ground • A high resistance Did you find and correct the condition?	--	Go to Step 16	Go to Step 13
10	Test the signal circuit of the brake fluid pressure sensor for a short to voltage. Did you find and correct the condition?	--	Go to Step 16	Go to Step 13
11	1. Disconnect the EBCM harness connector. 2. Install the J 39700 universal pinout box using the J 39700-300 cable adapter to the EBCM harness connector only. 3. Test the low reference circuit of the brake fluid pressure sensor for a high resistance or an open. Did you find and correct the condition?	--	Go to Step 16	Go to Step 13
12	Inspect for poor connections at the harness connector of the brake fluid pressure sensor. Did you find and correct the condition?	--	Go to Step 16	Go to Step 14

LTV0500000005766

Fig. 17 Code C0136: Base Brake System Pressure Circuit (Part 4 of 5)

13	Inspect for poor connections at the harness connector of the EBCM. Did you find and correct the condition?	--	Go to Step 16	Go to Step 15
14	Replace the brake fluid pressure sensor. Did you complete the repair?	--	Go to Step 16	--
15	Replace the EBCM. Did you complete the repair?	--	Go to Step 16	--
16	1. Clear the DTCs using the scan tool. 2. Operate the vehicle within the Conditions for Running the DTC as specified in the supporting text. Does the DTC reset?	--	Go to Step 2	System OK

LTV0500000005767

Fig. 17 Code C0136: Base Brake System Pressure Circuit (Part 5 of 5)

Circuit Description

Circuit Description

The electronic brake control module (EBCM) uses the input from the brake fluid pressure sensor for more accurate braking control during vehicle stability enhancement system (VSES).

Conditions for Running the DTC

DTC C0138
- The ignition is ON.
- Ignition voltage is greater than 8 volts.

DTC C0139
- The ignition is ON.
- Ignition voltage is greater than 8 volts.
- The vehicle speed is greater than 16 km/h (10 mph).

Conditions for Setting the DTC

DTC C0138

The vehicle speed exceeds 25 km/h (15 mph) then decelerates by 11.5 km/h (7 mph) per second and the brake pressure never increases.

DTC C0139

One of the following conditions occur:

- Brake pressure does not change after brake pedal has been applied twice.
- While brake pressure is greater than 50 psi, the vehicle speed exceeds 40 km/h (24 mph) and vehicle acceleration exceeds 8 km/h (5 mph) per second twice.

Action Taken When the DTC Sets

- The EBCM disables the PBA/TCS/VSES for the duration of the ignition cycle.
- The Traction Control and Active Handling indicator turns ON.
- The DIC displays the Service Stability System message.
- The ABS remains functional.

Conditions for Clearing the DTC

- The condition for the DTC is no longer present and the DTC is cleared with a scan tool.
- The EBCM automatically clears the history DTC when a current DTC is not detected in 100 consecutive drive cycles.

Diagnostic Aids

- Find out from the driver under what conditions the DTC was set (when the DIC displayed the Service Active Handling message). This information will help to duplicate the failure.

LTV0500000005768

Fig. 18 Codes C0138 Or C0139: Base Brake System Pressure Circuit Low Or Base Brake System Pressure Circuit High (Part 1 of 5)

Step	Action	Values	Yes	No
1	Did you perform the Diagnostic System Check - ABS?	--	Go to Step 2	Go to Diagnostic System Check -
2	1. Install a scan tool. 2. Turn ON the ignition, with the engine OFF. 3. With a scan tool, observe the Brake Fluid Pressure Sensor Input parameter in the VSES data list. Does the scan tool display that the Brake Fluid Pressure Sensor Input parameter is within the specified range?	0.14-4.9 V	Go to Diagnostic Aids	Go to Step 3
3	1. Turn OFF the ignition. 2. Disconnect the brake fluid pressure sensor connector. 3. Turn ON the ignition, with the engine OFF. 4. With the scan tool, observe the Brake Fluid Pressure Sensor Input parameter. Does the scan tool indicate that the Brake Fluid Pressure Sensor Input parameter is less than the specified value?	0.14 V	Go to Step 4	Go to Step 10
4	1. Turn OFF the ignition. 2. Connect a 3 amp fused jumper wire between the 5 volt reference circuit of the brake fluid pressure sensor and the signal circuit of the brake fluid pressure sensor. 3. Turn ON the ignition, with the engine OFF. 4. With the scan tool, observe the Brake Fluid Pressure Sensor Input parameter. Does the scan tool indicate that the Brake Fluid Pressure Sensor Input parameter is greater than the specified value?	4.9 V	Go to Step 5	Go to Step 8
5	1. Disconnect the fused jumper wire. 2. Measure the voltage between the 5 volt reference circuit of the brake fluid pressure sensor and the low reference circuit of the brake fluid pressure sensor. Does the voltage measure less the specified value?	5 V	Go to Step 6	Go to Step 7

LTV0500000005770

Fig. 18 Codes C0138 Or C0139: Base Brake System Pressure Circuit Low Or Base Brake System Pressure Circuit High (Part 3 of 5)

- The Snapshot function on the scan tool can help find an intermittent DTC.
- Brake pressure sensor internal malfunction.

Test Description

The numbers below refer to the step numbers on the diagnostic table.

3. Tests for the proper operation of the circuit in the low voltage range.

4. Tests for the proper operation of the circuit in the high voltage range. If the fuse in the jumper opens when you perform this test, the signal circuit is shorted to ground.

5. Tests for a short to voltage in the 5 volt reference circuit.

6. Tests for a high resistance or an open in the low reference circuit.

LTV0500000005769

Fig. 18 Codes C0138 Or C0139: Base Brake System Pressure Circuit Low Or Base Brake System Pressure Circuit High (Part 2 of 5)

	Action	Values	Yes	No
6	1. Turn OFF the ignition. 2. Disconnect the negative battery cable. 3. Measure the resistance from the low reference circuit of the brake fluid pressure sensor to a good ground. Does the resistance measure less than the specified value?	5 ohms	Go to Step 12	Go to Step 11
7	Test the 5 volt reference circuit of the brake fluid pressure sensor for a short to voltage. Did you find and correct the condition?	--	Go to Step 16	Go to Step 13
8	Test the 5 volt reference circuit of the brake fluid pressure sensor for the following conditions: - An open - A short to ground - A high resistance Did you find and correct the condition?	--	Go to Step 16	Go to Step 9
9	Test the signal circuit of the brake fluid pressure sensor for the following conditions: - An open - A short to ground - A high resistance Did you find and correct the condition?	--	Go to Step 16	Go to Step 13
10	Test the signal circuit of the brake fluid pressure sensor for a short to voltage. Did you find and correct the condition?	--	Go to Step 16	Go to Step 13
11	1. Disconnect the EBCM harness connector. 2. Install the J 39700 universal pinout box using the J 39700-300 cable adapter to the EBCM harness connector only. 3. Test the low reference circuit of the brake fluid pressure sensor for a high resistance or an open. Did you find and correct the condition?	--	Go to Step 16	Go to Step 13
12	Inspect for poor connections at the harness connector of the brake fluid pressure sensor. Did you find and correct the condition?	--	Go to Step 16	Go to Step 14

LTV0500000005771

Fig. 18 Codes C0138 Or C0139: Base Brake System Pressure Circuit Low Or Base Brake System Pressure Circuit High (Part 4 of 5)

	Action	Values	Yes	No
13	Inspect for poor connections at the harness connector of the EBCM. Did you find and correct the condition?	--	Go to Step 16	Go to Step 15
14	Replace the brake fluid pressure sensor. Did you complete the repair?	--	Go to Step 16	--
15	Replace the EBCM. Did you complete the repair?	--	Go to Step 16	--
16	1. Clear the DTCs using the scan tool. 2. Operate the vehicle within the Conditions for Running the DTC as specified in the supporting text. Does the DTC reset?	--	Go to Step 2	System OK

LTV0500000005772

Fig. 18 Codes C0138 Or C0139: Base Brake System Pressure Circuit Low Or Base Brake System Pressure Circuit High (Part 5 of 5)

Circuit Description

The brake pedal position sensor (BPP) is an input to the electronic brake control module (EBCM). The brake pedal position sensor is a potentiometer type sensor with a 5-volt reference circuit and a low reference circuit. The BCM supplies the 5-volt reference to the BPP.

Conditions for Running the DTC

DTC C0163

The ignition is ON.

DTC C0164

The vehicle speed is greater than 40 km/h (25 mph).

Conditions for Setting the DTC

DTC C0163

The brake pedal position sensor input voltage is between 1.87 volts and 5.03 volts for 2 seconds.

DTC C0164

The brake pedal position sensor input was active for 2 consecutive ignition cycles.

Action Taken When the DTC Sets

If equipped, the following actions occur:

- The EBCM disables the TCS/VSES for the duration of the ignition cycle.
- The Traction Control and Active Handling indicator turns ON.
- The DIC displays the following messages:
  - Service Traction System
  - Service Active Handling
- The ABS remains functional.

Conditions for Clearing the DTC

- The condition for the DTC is no longer present and the DTC is cleared with a scan tool.
- The EBCM automatically clears the history DTC when a current DTC is not detected in 100 consecutive drive cycles.

LTV0500000005773

Fig. 19 Codes C0163 Or C0164: Anti-Lock Brake System (ABS)/Traction Control System (TCS) Brake Switch/Sensor Circuit Low Or Anti-Lock Brake System (ABS)/Traction Control System (TCS) Brake Switch/Sensor Circuit High (Part 1 of 4)

Step	Action	Yes	No
1	Did you perform the ABS Diagnostic System Check?	Go to Step 2	Go to Diagnostic System Check -
2	1. Install a scan tool. 2. Turn ON the ignition, with the engine OFF. 3. With a scan tool, observe the BPP Sensor parameter in the TCS data list. Does the scan tool display Released?	Go to Step 3	Go to Step 4
3	1. Press the brake pedal. 2. With a scan tool, observe the BPP Sensor parameter. Does the BPP Sensor parameter change state?	Go to Diagnostic Aids	Go to Step 4
4	1. Turn OFF the ignition. 2. Inspect the brake pedal position sensor and adjust and/or calibrate if needed. Did you find and correct the condition?	Go to Step 11	Go to Step 5
5	1. Turn OFF the ignition. 2. Disconnect the brake pedal position sensor connector. 3. Turn ON the ignition, with the engine OFF. 4. With a scan tool, observe the BPP Sensor parameter. Does the scan tool display Released?	Go to Step 8	Go to Step 6
6	Test the brake pedal position sensor signal circuit for a short to voltage. Did you find and correct the condition?	Go to Step 11	Go to Step 7
7	Inspect for poor connections at the harness connector of the EBCM. Did you find and correct the condition?	Go to Step 11	Go to Step 9

LTV0500000005775

Fig. 19 Codes C0163 Or C0164: Anti-Lock Brake System (ABS)/Traction Control System (TCS) Brake Switch/Sensor Circuit Low Or Anti-Lock Brake System (ABS)/Traction Control System (TCS) Brake Switch/Sensor Circuit High (Part 3 of 4)

Diagnostic Aids

DTC C0163

Possible causes of this DTC are the following conditions:

- A signal circuit of the brake pedal position sensor is open.
- The BPP sensor needs calibration.
- All brake lamps are open.
- All brake lamp grounds are open.
- An internal EBCM problem.

DTC C0164

Possible causes of this DTC are the following conditions:

- The brake pedal position sensor circuit is shorted to voltage.
- The brake pedal position sensor is misadjusted.
- The brake pedal position sensor is stuck closed.
- A brake pedal that is binding.

Test Description

The number below refers to the step number on the diagnostic table.

2. Test for the current state of the BPP sensor.

LTV0500000005774

Fig. 19 Codes C0163 Or C0164: Anti-Lock Brake System (ABS)/Traction Control System (TCS) Brake Switch/Sensor Circuit Low Or Anti-Lock Brake System (ABS)/Traction Control System (TCS) Brake Switch/Sensor Circuit High (Part 2 of 4)

Step	Action	Yes	No
8	Inspect for poor connections at the harness connector of the brake pedal position sensor. Did you find and correct the condition?	Go to Step 11	Go to Step 10
9	Replace the EBCM. Did you complete the repair?	Go to Step 11	--
10	Replace the brake pedal position sensor. Did you complete the repair?	Go to Step 11	--
11	1. Use the scan tool in order to clear the DTCs. 2. Operate the vehicle within the Conditions for Running the DTC as specified in the supporting text. Does the DTC reset?	Go to Step 2	System OK

LTV0500000005776

Fig. 19 Codes C0163 Or C0164: Anti-Lock Brake System (ABS)/Traction Control System (TCS) Brake Switch/Sensor Circuit Low Or Anti-Lock Brake System (ABS)/Traction Control System (TCS) Brake Switch/Sensor Circuit High (Part 4 of 4)

Circuit Description

The electronic brake control module (EBCM) monitors vehicle speed deceleration, system activation, and brake pedal position sensor active times in order to calculate an estimate of the brake rotor temperatures. If the EBCM calculates that the brake rotor temperatures have exceeded the thermal cutoff point, the EBCM will temporarily suspend the traction control system (TCS) function until the brake rotors cool. This feature is used to maintain braking effectiveness if normal base braking is required. An overly heated brake system could result in brake fade.

The EBCM continues calculating the brake rotor temperatures after the ignition is turned OFF. The EBCM remains awake until the EBCM calculates that the brake rotors cooled sufficiently. The cooling period may take up to 30 minutes.

Conditions for Running the DTC

- The ignition is ON.
- Ignition voltage is greater than 8 volts.

Conditions for Setting the DTC

This DTC sets when the estimated brake rotor temperature exceeds 375°C (700°F). When the estimated brake rotor temperature exceeds 375°C (700°F) during normal braking or ABS operations, the DTC does not set until the next TCS activation. The EBCM does not disable TCS until the end of the TCS event.

Action Taken When the DTC Sets

- The EBCM disables the TCS until the DTC becomes a history DTC.
- The ABS remains functional.
- The Traction Control indicator turns ON.

Conditions for Clearing the DTC

- The current DTC becomes history when the estimated brake rotor temperatures of both drive wheels decreases below 275°C (530°F). The following actions also occur:
  - The EBCM enables TCS.
  - The DIC displays the Traction Ready message.
- The condition for the DTC is no longer present (the DTC is not current) and you used the scan tool Clear DTC function.
- The condition for the DTC is no longer present (the DTC is not current) and you used the On-Board Diagnostics Clear DTC function.
- The EBCM automatically clears the history DTC when a current DTC is not detected in 100 consecutive drive cycles.

LTV0500000005777

Fig. 20 Code C0179: System Thermal High (Part 1 of 4)

Step	Action	Yes	No
1	Did you perform the Diagnostic System Check - ABS?	Go to Step 2	Go to Diagnostic System Check -
2	1. Install a scan tool. 2. Turn ON the ignition, with the engine OFF. 3. Select the display DTCs function on the scan tool for the EBCM. Does the scan tool display that this DTC is set current?	Go to Step 4	Go to Step 3
3	Since most occurrences of this DTC are caused by excessive braking, review with the customer to verify the conditions under which the DTC set. Did vehicle operation cause this DTC to set?	Go to Diagnostic Aids	Go to Step 4
4	1. Allow 30 minutes from the last time you drove the vehicle for the cooling of the brake rotors. 2. With a scan tool, observe the Brake Temp Status parameter in the ABS data list. Does the scan tool display Normal?	Go to Step 6	Go to Step 5
5	Calibrate the brake pedal position sensor. Did you find and correct the condition?	Go to Step 8	Go to Step 6
6	1. Use the scan tool in order to clear the DTCs. 2. Operate the vehicle within the Conditions for Running the DTC as specified in the supporting text. Does the DTC reset as a current DTC?	Go to Step 7	System OK

LTV0500000005779

Fig. 20 Code C0179: System Thermal High (Part 3 of 4)

Diagnostic Aids

- With TCS temporarily disabled, the EBCM continues calculating the brake rotor temperatures after the ignition is turned OFF. Turning ON the ignition again while TCS is temporarily disabled will not re-enable TCS.
- The temperature is an estimate calculated by the EBCM.
- Possible causes of this DTC are the following conditions:
  - The brake usage is excessive.
  - The TCS usage is excessive.
  - The brake pedal position sensor is damaged or not calibrated.
  - The brake pressure sensor is damaged.

Test Description

The number below refers to the step number on the diagnostic table.

4. Use the scan tool in order to verify that the Brake Thermal Model is exceeded.

LTV0500000005778

Fig. 20 Code C0179: System Thermal High (Part 2 of 4)

	Important		
7	Perform the setup procedure for the EBCM. An unprogrammed EBCM will result in the following conditions: - Inoperative or poorly functioning system operations - The EBCM sets DTC C0281 and DTC C0550 Replace the EBCM. Did you complete the repair?	Go to Step 8	--
8	1. Use the scan tool in order to clear the DTCs. 2. Operate the vehicle within the Conditions for Running the DTC as specified in the supporting text. Does the DTC reset?	Go to Step 2	System OK

LTV0500000005780

Fig. 20 Code C0179: System Thermal High (Part 4 of 4)

Circuit Description

The electronic brake control module (EBCM) uses the lateral accelerometer signal to determine the lateral forces acting on a vehicle during a turn or a skid. The EBCM uses the signal from the lateral accelerometer as one of the inputs to operate the vehicle stability enhancement system (VSES).

DTC Descriptors

This diagnostic procedure supports the following DTCs:

- DTC C0186 Lateral Accelerometer Circuit
- DTC C0187 Lateral Accelerometer Circuit Range/Performance

Conditions for Running the DTC

C0186

Ignition voltage is greater than 8 volts.

C0187
- Ignition voltage is greater than 8 volts.
- No yaw rate DTCs are present.
- Vehicle yaw rate is centered.

Conditions for Setting the DTC

C0186

Lateral accelerometer signal voltage is less than 0.18 volt or above 4.84 volts.

C0187

The EBCM will set the DTC when one or more of the following conditions have occurred:

- The lateral acceleration signal changes to rapidly based on vehicle dynamics.
- The internal calibration in the lateral accelerometer is out of range.
- The lateral accelerometer has failed and internal self check test.

Action Taken When the DTC Sets

If equipped, the following actions will occur:

- The EBCM disables VSES for the duration of the ignition cycle.
- The driver information center (DIC) displays the Service Stability System message.

Conditions for Clearing the DTC

- The condition for the DTC is no longer present and the DTC is cleared with a scan tool.

LTV0500000005781

Fig. 21 Codes C0186 Or C0187: Lateral Accelerometer Circuit Or Lateral Accelerometer Circuit Range/Performance (Part 1 of 4)

- The EBCM automatically clears the history DTC when a current DTC is not detected in 100 consecutive drive cycles.

Diagnostic Aids

The lateral accelerometer is packaged with the yaw rate sensor as a single component.

Test Description

The numbers below refer to the step numbers on the diagnostic table.

2. Tests for the proper voltage output on the 5-volt reference circuit and the proper operation of the signal circuit.

3. Tests for possible low 5-volt reference output or a problem with the signal circuit.

4. Tests for a short to voltage on the 5-volt reference circuit. If a short to voltage exists, other DTCs may be set for the vehicle stability system.

8. Tests for a problem with the low reference circuit. If a short to voltage exists, other DTCs may be set for the vehicle stability system.

LTV0500000005782

Fig. 21 Codes C0186 Or C0187: Lateral Accelerometer Circuit Or Lateral Accelerometer Circuit Range/Performance (Part 2 of 4)

7	Test the lateral accelerometer signal circuit for a short to voltage.		
	Did you find and correct the condition?	Go to Step 12	Go to Step 11
8	Test the low reference circuit of the yaw and lateral acceleration sensor for the following conditions: • An open • A short to voltage • A high resistance		
	Did you find and correct the condition?	Go to Step 12	Go to Step 9
9	Inspect for poor connections at the harness connector of the yaw and lateral acceleration sensor.		
	Did you find and correct the condition?	Go to Step 12	Go to Step 10
10	Replace the yaw and lateral acceleration sensor.		
	Did you complete the replacement?	Go to Step 12	--
11	Replace the electronic brake control module (EBCM).		
	Did you complete the replacement?	Go to Step 12	--
12	1. Clear the DTCs using the scan tool. 2. Operate the vehicle within the Conditions for Running the DTC as specified in the supporting text. Does the DTC reset?	Go to Step 2	System OK

LTV0500000005784

Fig. 21 Codes C0186 Or C0187: Lateral Accelerometer Circuit Or Lateral Accelerometer Circuit Range/Performance (Part 4 of 4)

Step	Action	Values	Yes	No
1	Did you perform the ABS Diagnostic System Check?	--	Go to Step 2	Go to Diagnostic System Check - ABS
2	1. Turn OFF the ignition. 2. Disconnect the yaw and lateral acceleration sensor harness connector. 3. Connect a 3-amp fused jumper wire between the 5-volt reference circuit of the yaw and lateral acceleration sensor and the signal circuit of the yaw and lateral acceleration sensor. 4. Turn ON the ignition, with the engine OFF. 5. With the scan tool, observe the lateral acceleration signal voltage. Does the scan tool indicate that the lateral acceleration signal parameter is in between the specified voltage range?	4.5-5.5 V	Go to Step 8	Go to Step 3
3	With the 3-amp fused jumper wire still connected, does the scan tool indicate that the lateral acceleration sensor parameter is below the specified voltage value?	4.5 V	Go to Step 5	Go to Step 4
4	Test the 5-volt reference circuit of the yaw and lateral acceleration sensor for a short to voltage. Did you find and correct the condition?	--	Go to Step 12	Go to Step 7
5	Test the 5-volt reference circuit of the yaw and lateral acceleration sensor for the following conditions: • An open • A short to ground • A high resistance Did you find and correct the condition?	--	Go to Step 12	Go to Step 6
6	Test the lateral accelerometer signal circuit for the following conditions: • An open • A short to ground • A high resistance Did you find and correct the condition?	--	Go to Step 12	Go to Step 11

LTV0500000005783

Fig. 21 Codes C0186 Or C0187: Lateral Accelerometer Circuit Or Lateral Accelerometer Circuit Range/Performance (Part 3 of 4)

Circuit Description

The longitudinal accelerometer is used to determine straight-line acceleration. This information is us when calculating the desired Traction Control in AWD applications.

Conditions for Running the DTC

- The ignition is ON.
- Ignition voltage is greater than 8 volts.

Conditions for Setting the DTC

One of the following conditions exist:

- The yaw rate sensor input voltage is less than 0.15 volts.
- The yaw rate sensor input voltage is greater than 4.85 volts for 1 seconds.
- The longitudinal accelerometer bias exceeds 0.5 g.
- The longitudinal accelerometer signal is not increased by 0.5 volts during longitudinal accelerometer self test.

Action Taken When the DTC Sets

- TCS is degraded.
- The TCS indicators turn ON.
- The ABS remains funtional.

Conditions for Clearing the DTC

- The condition for the DTC is no longer present and the DTC is cleared with a scan tool.
- The electronic brake control module (EBCM) automatically clears the history DTC when a current DTC is not detected in 100 consecutive drive cycles.

Diagnostic Aids

The following conditions can cause this concern:

- The longitudinal accelerometer circuit is open, shorted to ground, or shorted to battery.
- Internal longitudinal accelerometer malfunction.
- Internal EBCM malfunction.

Test Description

The numbers below refer to the step numbers on the diagnostic table.

3. Tests for the proper operation of the circuit in the low voltage range.

4. Tests for the proper operation of the circuit in the high voltage range. If the fuse in the jumper opens when you perform this test, the signal circuit is shorted to ground.

5. Tests for a short to voltage in the 5-volt reference circuit.

6. Tests the bias voltage of the longitudinal accelerometer sensor.

LTV0500000005785

Fig. 22 Code C0192: All Wheel Drive (AWD)/Four Wheel Drive (4WD) Reference Accelerometer Circuit Range/Performance (Part 1 of 4)

Step	Action	Values	Yes	No
1	Did you perform the Diagnostic System Check - ABS?	--	Go to Step 2	Go to Diagnostic System Check
2	1. Install a scan tool. 2. Turn ON the ignition, with the engine OFF. 3. With a scan tool, observe the Longitudinal Accelerometer Sensor Input parameter in the VSES data list. Does the scan tool display within the specified range?	0.15-4.85 V	Go to Step 6	Go to Step 3
3	1. Turn OFF the ignition. 2. Disconnect the yaw rate/lateral/longitudinal accelerometer sensor connector. 3. Turn ON the ignition, with the engine OFF. 4. With the scan tool, observe the Longitudinal Accelerometer Sensor Input parameter. Does the scan tool display a voltage less than the specified value?	0.15 V	Go to Step 4	Go to Step 10
4	1. Turn OFF the ignition. 2. Connect a 3-amp fused jumper wire between the 5-volt reference circuit of the yaw rate/lateral/longitudinal accelerometer sensor and the signal circuit of the yaw rate/lateral/longitudinal accelerometer sensor. 3. Turn ON the ignition, with the engine OFF. 4. With the scan tool, observe the Longitudinal Accelerometer Sensor Input parameter. Does the scan tool display a voltage greater than the specified value?	4.85 V	Go to Step 5	Go to Step 8
5	1. Disconnect the fused jumper wire. 2. Use a DMM to measure the voltage between the 5-volt reference circuit of the yaw rate/lateral/longitudinal accelerometer sensor and the low reference circuit of the yaw rate/lateral/longitudinal accelerometer sensor. Does the voltage measure less the specified value?	5 V	Go to Step 12	Go to Step 7
6	Does the scan tool display that the Longitudinal Accelerometer Sensor Input parameter is within the specified range?	2.3-2.7 V	Go to Diagnostic Aids	Go to Step 11

LTV0500000005786

Fig. 22   Code C0192: All Wheel Drive (AWD)/Four Wheel Drive (4WD) Reference Accelerometer Circuit Range/Performance (Part 2 of 4)

Step	Action		Yes	No
12	Inspect for poor connections at the harness connector of the yaw rate/lateral/longitudinal accelerometer sensor. Did you find and correct the condition?	-	Go to Step 16	Go to Step 14
13	Inspect for poor connections at the harness connector of the EBCM. Did you find and correct the condition?	-	Go to Step 16	Go to Step 15
14	Replace the yaw rate/lateral/longitudinal accelerometer sensor Did you complete the repair?	-	Go to Step 16	--
15	Replace the EBCM. Did you complete the repair?	-	Go to Step 16	--
16	1. Clear the DTCs using the scan tool. 2. Operate the vehicle within the Conditions for Running the DTC as specified in the supporting text. Does the DTC reset?	-	Go to Step 2	System OK

LTV0500000005788

Fig. 22   Code C0192: All Wheel Drive (AWD)/Four Wheel Drive (4WD) Reference Accelerometer Circuit Range/Performance (Part 4 of 4)

Step	Action		Yes	No
7	Test the 5-volt reference circuit of the yaw rate/lateral/longitudinal accelerometer sensor for a short to voltage. Did you find and correct the condition?	-	Go to Step 16	Go to Step 13
8	Test the 5-volt reference circuit of the yaw rate/lateral/longitudinal accelerometer sensor for the following conditions: • An open • A short to ground • A high resistance Did you find and correct the condition?	-	Go to Step 16	Go to Step 9
9	Test the signal circuit of the yaw rate/lateral/longitudinal accelerometer sensor for the following conditions: • An open • A short to ground • A high resistance Did you find and correct the condition?	-	Go to Step 16	Go to Step 13
10	Test the signal circuit of the yaw rate/lateral/longitudinal accelerometer sensor for a short to voltage. Did you find and correct the condition?	-	Go to Step 16	Go to Step 13
11	Test the low reference circuit of the yaw rate/lateral/longitudinal accelerometer sensor for the following conditions: • An open • A high resistance Did you find and correct the condition?	-	Go to Step 16	Go to Step 12

LTV0500000005787

Fig. 22   Code C0192: All Wheel Drive (AWD)/Four Wheel Drive (4WD) Reference Accelerometer Circuit Range/Performance (Part 3 of 4)

Circuit Description

The electronic brake control module (EBCM) uses the yaw rate signal to determine the directional angle of the vehicle during a turn or a skid. The EBCM uses the signal from the yaw rate as one of the inputs to operate the vehicle stability enhancement system (VSES).

DTC Descriptor

This diagnostic procedure supports the following DTC:

DTC C0196 Yaw Rate Circuit

Conditions for Running the DTC

The ignition voltage is greater than 8 volts.

Conditions for Setting the DTC

The EBCM will set the DTC when one or more of the following conditions have occurred:

• The yaw rate signal is less than 0.18 volt or greater than 4.84 volts.
• The yaw rate signal changes to rapidly based on vehicle dynamics.
• The internal calibration in the yaw rate is out of range.
• The yaw and lateral acceleration sensor has failed and internal self check test.

Action Taken When the DTC Sets

If equipped, the following actions will occur:

• The EBCM disables VSES for the duration of the ignition cycle.
• The driver information center (DIC) displays the Service Stability System message.

Conditions for Clearing the DTC

• The condition for the DTC is no longer present and the DTC is cleared with a scan tool.
• The EBCM automatically clears the history DTC when a current DTC is not detected in 100 consecutive drive cycles.

Diagnostic Aids

The lateral accelerometer is packaged with the yaw rate sensor as a single component.

Test Description

The numbers below refer to the step numbers on the diagnostic table.

2. Tests for the proper voltage output on the 5-volt reference circuit and the proper operation of the signal circuit.

LTV0500000005789

Fig. 23   Code C0196: Yaw Rate Circuit (Part 1 of 4)

3. Tests for possible low 5-volt reference output or a problem with the signal circuit.

4. Tests for a short to voltage on the 5-volt reference circuit. If a short to voltage exists, other DTCs may be set for the vehicle stability system.

8. Tests for a problem with the low reference circuit. If a short to voltage exists, other DTCs may be set for the vehicle stability system.

LTV0500000005790

Fig. 23 Code C0196: Yaw Rate Circuit (Part 2 of 4)

	Action	Values	Yes	No
6	Test the yaw rate signal circuit for the following conditions: • An open • A short to ground • A high resistance Did you find and correct the condition?	-	Go to Step 12	Go to Step 11
7	Test the yaw rate signal circuit for a short to voltage. Did you find and correct the condition?	-	Go to Step 12	Go to Step 11
8	Test the low reference circuit of the yaw and lateral acceleration sensor for the following conditions: • An open • A short to voltage • A high resistance Did you find and correct the condition?	-	Go to Step 12	Go to Step 9
9	Inspect for poor connections at the harness connector of the yaw and lateral acceleration sensor. Did you find and correct the condition?	-	Go to Step 12	Go to Step 10
10	Replace the yaw and lateral acceleration sensor. Did you complete the replacement?	-	Go to Step 12	--
11	Replace the electronic brake control module (EBCM). Did you complete the replacement?	-	Go to Step 12	--
12	1. Clear the DTCs using the scan tool. 2. Operate the vehicle within the Conditions for Running the DTC as specified in the supporting text. Does the DTC reset?	-	Go to Step 2	System OK

LTV0500000005792

Fig. 23 Code C0196: Yaw Rate Circuit (Part 4 of 4)

Step	Action	Values	Yes	No
1	Did you perform the ABS Diagnostic System Check?	--	Go to Step 2	Go to Diagnostic System Check -
2	1. Turn OFF the ignition. 2. Disconnect the yaw and lateral acceleration sensor harness connector. 3. Connect a 3-amp fused jumper wire between the 5-volt reference circuit of the yaw and lateral acceleration sensor and the signal circuit of the yaw and lateral acceleration sensor. 4. Turn ON the ignition, with the engine OFF. 5. With the scan tool, observe the yaw rate signal voltage. Does the scan tool indicate that the yaw rate signal parameter is in between the specified voltage range?	4.5-5.5 V	Go to Step 8	Go to Step 3
3	With the 3-amp fused jumper wire still connected, does the scan tool indicate that the Yaw Rate Sensor parameter is below the specified voltage value?	4.5 V	Go to Step 5	Go to Step 4
4	Test the 5-volt reference circuit of the yaw and lateral acceleration sensor for a short to voltage. Did you find and correct the condition?	--	Go to Step 12	Go to Step 7
5	Test the 5-volt reference circuit of the yaw and lateral acceleration sensor for the following conditions: • An open • A short to ground • A high resistance Did you find and correct the condition?	--	Go to Step 12	Go to Step 6

LTV0500000005791

Fig. 23 Code C0196: Yaw Rate Circuit (Part 3 of 4)

Circuit Description

The system relay is energized when the ignition is ON. The system relay supplies voltage to the valve relay. The electronic brake control module (EBCM) activates the valve relay to supply voltage to the valve solenoids. This voltage is referred to as the system voltage. The EBCM microprocessor activates individual valve solenoids by grounding the valve solenoid control circuits.

Conditions for Running the DTC

• The ignition is ON.
• The vehicle is experiencing an ABS event.

Conditions for Setting the DTC

This code is set when the following criteria are met.

• The EBCM is commanding a valve solenoid to release brake pressure.
• The wheel that is commanded to release brake pressure has a speed below 5 km/h (3 mph) for 1.25 seconds.

Action Taken When the DTC Sets

If equipped, the following actions occur.

• The EBCM disables ABS/TCS.
• ACC Braking is degraded.
• VSES is disabled.
• The ABS indicator turns ON.
• The traction off indicator turns ON.

Conditions for Clearing the DTC

• The condition for the DTC is no longer present and the DTC is cleared with a scan tool.
• The electronic brake control module (EBCM) automatically clears the history DTC when a current DTC is not detected in 100 consecutive drive cycles.

Diagnostic Aids

The solenoid valve circuit is internal to the EBCM. The solenoid valve circuit is not diagnosable external to the EBCM. The DTC sets when there is a malfunction in the solenoid circuit internal to the EBCM.

Possible causes for this concern:

• Intermittent wheel speed sensor
• Wheel speed sensor is equal to 0 km/h (0 mph)
• Contaminated hydraulic unit

Test Description

The number below refers to the step number on the diagnostic table.

2. Determines whether the DTC is current.

LTV0500000005793

Fig. 24 Codes C0220–C0229: Anti-Lock Brake System (ABS) Channel in Release Too Long (Part 1 of 2)

Step	Action	Yes	No
1	Did you perform the Diagnostic System Check - ABS?	Go to Step 2	Go to Diagnostic System Check - ABS
2	1. Install a scan tool. 2. Turn ON the ignition, with the engine OFF. 3. Use the scan tool in order to clear the DTCs. 4. Use the scan tool to perform the Automated Test. Does the DTC reset as a current DTC?	Go to Step 3	Test for Intermittent and Poor Connections
3	Replace the EBCM. Did you complete the replacement?	Go to Step 4	--
4	1. Use the scan tool in order to clear the DTCs 2. With the scan tool, perform the Automated Test. Does the DTC reset?	Go to Step 3	System OK

LTV0500000005794

Fig. 24 Codes C0220–C0229: Anti-Lock Brake System (ABS) Channel in Release Too Long (Part 2 of 2)

The following conditions can cause this concern:

- An open in the delivered torque circuit.
- A short to ground or voltage in the delivered torque circuit.
- A wiring problem, terminal corrosion, or poor connection in the delivered torque circuit.
- A communication frequency problem.
- A communication duty cycle problem.
- The EBCM is not receiving information from the PCM.
- Loose or corroded EBCM ground or PCM ground.

Test Description

The numbers below refer to the step numbers on the diagnostic table.

2. Use the scan tool in order to determine if the requested torque signal has a valid duty cycle.

3. Measure the requested torque signal in order to determine if the signal has a valid duty cycle.

4. Measure the requested torque signal in order to determine if the signal has a valid frequency.

10. This vehicle is equipped with a ECM which uses an Electrically Erasable Programmable Read Only Memory (EEPROM). When replacing the ECM, the replacement ECM must be programmed.

LTV0500000005796

Fig. 25 Codes C0241 Or P0856: Powertrain Control Module (PCM) Indicated Requested Torque Fault Or Traction Control Torque Request Circuit (Part 2 of 5)

Circuit Description

The electronic brake control module (EBCM) and the engine control module (ECM) simultaneously control the traction control. The ECM reduces the amount of torque supplied to the drive wheels by retarding spark timing and selectively turning OFF fuel injectors. The EBCM actively applies the brakes to the front wheels in order to reduce torque.

The EBCM sends a requested torque message via a pulse width modulated (PWM) signal to the ECM. The duty cycle of the signal is used to determine how much engine torque the EBCM is requesting the ECM to deliver. Normal values are between 10-90 percent duty cycle. The signal should be at 90 percent when traction control is not active and at lower values during traction control activations. The ECM supplies a pull up voltage of 12 volts that the EBCM switches to ground to create the signal.

The ECM sends a delivered torque message via a PWM signal to the EBCM. The duty cycle of the signal is used to determine how much engine torque the ECM is delivering. Normal values are between 10-90 percent duty cycle. The signal should be at low values, around 10 percent, at idle and higher values under driving conditions. The EBCM supplies a pull up voltage of 12 volts that the ECM switches to ground to create the signal.

When certain ECM DTCs are set, the ECM will not be able to perform the torque reduction portion of traction control. A serial data message is sent to the EBCM indicating that traction control is not allowed.

Conditions for Running the DTC

The engine is running.

Conditions for Setting the DTC

The PCM diagnoses the requested torque signal circuit and sends a serial data message to the EBCM indicating that torque reduction is not allowed.

Action Taken When the DTC Sets

- The EBCM disables the EDC/TCS for the duration of the ignition cycle.
- The Traction Off indicator turns ON.
- The ABS remains functional.

Conditions for Clearing the DTC

- The condition for the DTC is no longer present and you used the scan tool Clear DTC function.
- The EBCM automatically clears the history DTC when a current DTC is not detected in 100 consecutive drive cycles.
- The PCM automatically clears the history DTC when a current DTC is not detected in 40 consecutive warm-up cycles.

LTV0500000005795

Fig. 25 Codes C0241 Or P0856: Powertrain Control Module (PCM) Indicated Requested Torque Fault Or Traction Control Torque Request Circuit (Part 1 of 5)

Step	Action	Value (s)	Yes	No
1	Did you perform the ABS Diagnostic System Check?	--	Go to Step 2	Go to Diagnostic System Check -
2	1. Install a scan tool. 2. Start the engine. 3. With a scan tool, observe the Torque Request Signal parameter in the Powertrain Control Module data list. Does the scan display less than the specified value?	100%	Test for Intermittent and Poor Connections	Go to Step 3
3	1. Turn OFF the ignition. 2. Disconnect the EBCM harness connector. 3. Install the J 39700 universal breakout box using the J 39700-300 cable adapter to the EBCM harness connector and the EBCM connector. 4. Start the engine. 5. Measure the DC duty cycle between the requested torque signal circuit and a good ground. Is the duty cycle within the specified range?	5-95%	Go to Step 4	Go to Step 5
4	Measure the DC frequency between the requested torque signal circuit and a good ground. Does the frequency measure within the specified range?	121-134 Hz	Go to Step 7	Go to Step 5
5	1. Turn OFF the ignition. 2. Disconnect the J 39700-300 cable adapter from the EBCM connector. 3. Turn ON the ignition, with the engine OFF. 4. Measure the voltage from the requested torque signal circuit to a good ground. Does the voltage measure near the specified value?	B+	Go to Step 9	Go to Step 6

LTV0500000005797

Fig. 25 Codes C0241 Or P0856: Powertrain Control Module (PCM) Indicated Requested Torque Fault Or Traction Control Torque Request Circuit (Part 3 of 5)

Step	Action		Yes	No
6	1. Turn OFF the ignition. 2. Disconnect the engine control module (ECM) harness connector. 3. Test the requested torque signal circuit for the following conditions: - A short to voltage - A short to ground Did you find and correct the condition?	-	Go to Step 12	Go to Step 9
7	1. Turn OFF the ignition. 2. Disconnect the engine control module (ECM) harness connector. 3. Test the requested torque signal circuit for the following conditions: - An open - A high resistance Did you find and correct the condition?	-	Go to Step 12	Go to Step 8
8	Inspect for poor connections the harness connector of the ECM. Did you find and correct the condition?	-	Go to Step 12	Go to Step 10
9	Inspect for poor connections the harness connector of the EBCM. Did you find and correct the condition?	-	Go to Step 12	Go to Step 11
10	**Important:** The replacement ECM must be programmed. Replace the ECM. Did you complete the repair?	-	Go to Step 12	--

LTV0500000005798

Fig. 25 Codes C0241 Or P0856: Powertrain Control Module (PCM) Indicated Requested Torque Fault Or Traction Control Torque Request Circuit (Part 4 of 5)

Circuit Description

The electronic brake control module (EBCM) and the powertrain control module (PCM) simultaneously control the traction control. The EBCM sends a serial data message to the PCM requesting torque reduction. When certain PCM DTCs are set, the PCM will not be able to perform the torque reduction for traction control. A serial data message is sent to the EBCM indicating that traction control is not allowed.

Conditions for Running the DTC

- The ignition is ON.
- Ignition voltage is greater than 8 volts.

Conditions for Setting the DTC

The PCM diagnoses a condition preventing the engine control portion of the traction control function and sends a serial data message to the EBCM indicating that torque reduction is not allowed. The PCM will typically set a DTC and the EBCM will set this DTC.

Action Taken When the DTC Sets

If equipped, the following actions occur:

- The EBCM disables the TCS/VSES for the duration of the ignition cycle.
- The Traction Control and Active Handling indicator turns ON.
- The DIC displays the following messages:
  - Service Traction System
  - Service Active Handling
- The ABS remains functional.

Conditions for Clearing the DTC

- The condition for the DTC is no longer present and the DTC is cleared with a scan tool.
- The electronic brake control module (EBCM) automatically clears the history DTC when a current DTC is not detected in 100 consecutive drive cycles.

Diagnostic Aids

This DTC is for information only. As an aid to the technician, this DTC indicates that there are no problems in the ABS/TCS system.

Step	Action	Yes	No
1	Did you perform the Diagnostic System Check - ABS?	--	Go to Diagnostic System Check -

LTV0500000005800

Fig. 26 Code C0242: Powertrain Control Module (PCM) Indicated TCS Fault

Step	Action		Yes	No
11	Replace the EBCM. Did you complete the repair?	-	Go to Step 12	--
12	1. Use the scan tool in order to clear the DTCs. 2. Operate the vehicle within the Conditions for Running the DTC as specified in the supporting text. Does the DTC reset?	-	Go to Step 2	System OK

LTV0500000005799

Fig. 25 Codes C0241 Or P0856: Powertrain Control Module (PCM) Indicated Requested Torque Fault Or Traction Control Torque Request Circuit (Part 5 of 5)

Circuit Description

The electronic brake control module (EBCM) sends an engine drag control (EDC) request via a dedicated data line. The engine control module (ECM) supplies a pull up voltage of 12 volts that the EBCM switches to ground to create the signal.

Conditions for Running the DTC

The engine is running.

Conditions for Setting the DTC

The EBCM receives a serial data message from the PCM indicating that the EDC circuit has failed.

Action Taken When the DTC Sets

- The EBCM disables the EDC for the duration of the ignition cycle.
- The DIC displays the Service Stability System message.
- The ABS/TCS remains functional.

Conditions for Clearing the DTC

- The condition for the DTC is no longer present and the DTC is cleared with a scan tool.
- The electronic brake control module (EBCM) automatically clears the history DTC when a current DTC is not detected in 100 consecutive drive cycles.

Diagnostic Aids

The following conditions can cause this concern:

- An open in the EDC control circuit.
- An short to ground or voltage in the EDC control circuit.
- A wiring problem, terminal corrosion, or poor connection in the EDC control circuit.

Test Description

The numbers below refer to the step numbers on the diagnostic table.

9. This vehicle is equipped with a ECM which uses an Electrically Erasable Programmable Read Only Memory (EEPROM). When replacing the ECM, the replacement ECM must be programmed.

LTV0500000005801

Fig. 27 Code C0243: Engine Drag Control (Part 1 of 3)

Step	Action	Value (s)	Yes	No
1	Did you perform the ABS Diagnostic System Check?	-	Go to Step 2	Go to Diagnostic System Check -
2	Inspect the EBCM ground and ECM ground, making sure each ground is clean and torqued to the proper specification. Did you find and correct the condition?	-	Go to Step 10	Go to Step 3
3	1. Disconnect the EBCM harness connector. 2. Install the J 39700 universal pinout box using the J 39700-300 cable adapter to the EBCM harness connector and the EBCM connector. 3. Disconnect the engine control module (ECM) harness connector. 4. Turn ON the ignition, with the engine OFF. 5. Measure the voltage from the engine drag control signal circuit to a good ground. Does the voltage measure near the specified value?	B+	Go to Step 4	Go to Step 5

LTV0500000005802

Fig. 27 Code C0243: Engine Drag Control (Part 2 of 3)

4	1. Turn OFF the ignition. 2. Disconnect the J 39700-300 cable adapter from the EBCM connector. 3. Turn ON the ignition, with the engine OFF. 4. Test the engine drag control signal circuit for a short to voltage. Did you find and correct the condition?	Go to Step 10	Go to Step 6

5	1. Turn OFF the ignition.
	2. Disconnect the J 39700-300 cable adapter from the EBCM connector.
	3. Test the engine drag control signal circuit for the following conditions:
	  - An open
	  - A short to ground
	  - A high resistance
	
	Did you find and correct the condition?
		Go to
		Step 10
			Go to
			Step 7

6	Inspect for poor connections the harness connector of the ECM. Did you find and correct the condition?	Go to Step 10	Go to Step 8
7	Inspect for poor connections the harness connector of the EBCM. Did you find and correct the condition?	Go to Step 10	Go to Step 9
8	**Important:** The replacement ECM must be programmed. Replace the ECM. Did you complete the repair?	Go to Step 10	--
9	Replace the EBCM. Did you complete the repair?	Go to Step 10	--
10	1. Use the scan tool in order to clear the DTCs. 2. Operate the vehicle within the Conditions for Running the DTC as specified in the supporting text. Does the DTC reset?	Go to Step 2	System OK

LTV0500000005803

Fig. 27 Code C0243: Engine Drag Control (Part 3 of 3)

Circuit/System Verification

Use a scan tool in order to clear the DTCs. Cycle the ignition to OFF and then start the engine. A current failure will set a DTC.

⇒ If DTC does not reset refer to Testing for Intermittent Conditions and Poor Connections.

Circuit/System Testing

1. Ignition OFF, disconnect the ECM harness connector. Ignition ON, measure for 10-12 volts on the delivered torque circuit at the ECM harness connector.
   ⇒ [rArr] If the voltage is below 10 volts, test for an open or short to ground on the requested torque circuit. If an open or short to ground cannot be found, replace the EBCM.
2. Connect one end of a test lamp to ground. With the DMM still connected to the PCM harness connector, touch the other end of the test lamp to the DMM lead connected to the PCM harness connector. The DMM voltage reading should drop below 0.5 volts.
   ⇒ [rArr] If the voltage does not drop to below 0.5 volts, check for a short to voltage on the requested torque circuit. If a short to voltage cannot be found, replace the EBCM.
3. If all circuits test normal replace the ECM.

Repair Instructions

- Engine Control Module (ECM) Replacement
- Electronic Brake Control Module Replacement

LTV0500000005805

Fig. 28 Codes C0244 Or P1689: Pulse Width Modulated (PWM) Delivered Torque Or Traction Control Delivered Torque Output Circuit (Part 2 of 2)

DTC Descriptor

DTC C0244: Pulse Width Modulated (PWM) Delivered Torque

DTC P1689: Traction Control Delivered Torque Output Circuit

Diagnostic Fault Information

Important: Always perform the Diagnostic System Check - ABS prior to using this diagnostic procedure.

Circuit/System Description

The electronic brake control module (EBCM) and the powertrain control module (PCM) simultaneously control the Traction Control System (TCS). The PCM sends a Delivered Torque message via a pulse width modulated (PWM) signal to the EBCM. The duty cycle of the signal is used to determine how much engine torque the PCM is delivering.

Conditions for Running the DTC

The ignition is ON and the engine is running.

Conditions for Setting the DTC

- Pulse signals from the Delivered Torque signal are not detected or are abnormal.
- The Duty Cycle is less than 5 percent or more than 95 percent

Action Taken When the DTC Sets

- The EBCM disables TCS and vehicle stability enhancement system (VSES) for the duration of the ignition cycle.
- The Stability Caution indicator turns ON.
- The driver information center (DIC) displays the TRACTION FAILED message.
- The DIC displays the SERVICE STAB SYS message.

Conditions for Clearing the DTC

- The condition for the DTC is no longer present and the DTC is cleared with a scan tool.
- The EBCM automatically clears the history DTC when a current DTC is not detected in 100 consecutive drive cycles.

LTV0500000005804

Fig. 28 Codes C0244 Or P1689: Pulse Width Modulated (PWM) Delivered Torque Or Traction Control Delivered Torque Output Circuit (Part 1 of 2)

Circuit Description

The vehicle stability enhancement system (VSES) is activated by the electronic brake control mdoule (EBCM) calculating the desired yaw rate and comparing it to the actual yaw rate input. The desired yaw rate is calculated from measured steering wheel position, vehicle speed, and lateral acceleration. The difference between the desired yaw rate and actual yaw rate is the yaw rate error, which is a measurement of oversteer or understeer. If the yaw rate error becomes too large, the EBCM will attempt to correct the vehicle's yaw motion by applying differential braking to the left or right front wheel.

The amount of differential braking applied to the left or right front wheel is based on both the yaw rate error and side slip rate error. The side slip rate error is a function of the lateral acceleration minus the product of the yaw rate and vehicle speed. The yaw rate error and side slip rate error are combined to produce the total delta velocity error. When the delta velocity error becomes too large and the VSES system activates, the drivers steering inputs combined with the differential braking will attempt to bring the delta velocity error toward zero.

The VSES activations generally occur during aggressive driving, in the turns or bumpy roads without much use of the accelerator pedal. When braking during VSES activation, the brake pedal will feel different than the ABS pedal pulsation. The brake pedal pulsates at a higher frequency during VSES activation.

Conditions for Running the DTC

- The steer angle has been centered.
- The VSES is active.
- The direction (understeer or oversteer) of the yaw rate error has not changed.
- The centered lateral acceleration value is less than 0.5 g.
- The yaw rate error is less than 6 degrees/second.
- The side slip error is greater than 1.8 meters/second*second.

Conditions for Setting the DTC

One of the following conditions exists:

- The yaw rate error is greater than 10 degrees/second with the vehicle speed less than 60 km/h (37 mph) and the acceleration pedal is pressed more than 25 percent of the pedal travel range for 1 second during the VSES activation.
- With the yaw rate less than 8 degrees/second, the side slip error is greater than 4.9 meters/second² for 5 seconds.

Action Taken When the DTC Sets

- The EBCM disables the VSES for the duration of the ignition cycle.
- The DIC displays the Service Stability System message.
- The ABS/TCS remains functional.

LTV0500000005806

Fig. 29 Code C0252: Vehicle Stability Enhancement System (VSES) Sensors Uncorrelated (Part 1 of 4)

- The condition for the DTC is no longer present and the DTC is cleared with a scan tool.
- The EBCM automatically clears the history DTC when a current DTC is not detected in 100 consecutive drive cycles.

Diagnostic Aids

The following conditions can cause this concern:

- Improper steering alignment.
- Open, short to ground, or short to voltage.
- Internal lateral accelerometer failure.
- EBCM internal failure.

Test Description

The numbers below refer to the step numbers on the diagnostic table.

2. Perform the Steering Position Sensor Test in order to verify that the steering wheel position sensor (SWPS) is operating properly.

3. Verify that the lateral accelerometer input parameter is within the valid range.

4. Verify that the yaw rate input parameter is within the valid range.

LTV0500000005807

Fig. 29 Code C0252: Vehicle Stability Enhancement System (VSES) Sensors Uncorrelated (Part 2 of 4)

7	Replace the steering wheel position sensor (SWPS). Did you complete the replacement?	-	Go to Step 9	--
8	Replace the yaw rate/lateral accelerometer sensor. Did you complete the replacement?	-	Go to Step 9	--
9	1. Use the scan tool in order to clear the DTCs. 2. Operate the vehicle within the Conditions for Running the DTC as specified in the supporting text. Does the DTC reset?	-	Go to Step 2	System OK

LTV0500000005809

Fig. 29 Code C0252: Vehicle Stability Enhancement System (VSES) Sensors Uncorrelated (Part 4 of 4)

Circuit Description

The electronic brake control module (EBCM) calibrates the steering sensor output so that the output reads zero when the steering wheel is centered. Using the yaw rate input, lateral accelerometer input, and the wheel speed sensor inputs, the initial steering center position is calculated after driving greater than 10 km/h (6 mph) for more than 10 seconds in a straight line on a level surface.

Conditions for Running the DTC

C0253
- The ignition is ON.
- Ignition voltage is greater than 8 volts.

C0254
- The ignition is ON.
- Ignition voltage is greater than 8 volts.
- The steer angle has been centered.

Conditions for Setting the DTC

C0253

The vehicle speed is greater than 40 km/h (25 mph) for 10 minutes without completing steer angle centering.

C0254

The steering sensor bias moves greater than 40 degrees after steer centering was accomplished.

Action Taken When the DTC Sets

- The EBCM disables the vehicle stability enhancement system (VSES) for the duration of the ignition cycle.
- The driver information center (DIC) displays the Service Stability System message.
- The ABS remains functional.

Conditions for Clearing the DTC

- The condition for the DTC is no longer present and the DTC is cleared with a scan tool.
- The electronic brake control module (EBCM) automatically clears the history DTC when a current DTC is not detected in 100 consecutive drive cycles.

Diagnostic Aids

- Check the vehicle for proper alignment. The car should not pull in either direction while driving straight on a level surface.
- The Snapshot function on the scan tool can help find an intermittent DTC.

LTV0500000005810

Fig. 30 Codes C0253 Or C0254: Centering Error Or Steering Sensor And/Or Lateral Accelerometer Bias (Part 1 of 4)

Step	Action	Values	Yes	No
1	Did you perform the ABS Diagnostic System Check?	--	Go to Step 2	Go to Diagnostic System Check
2	1. Install a scan tool. 2. Turn ON the ignition, with the engine OFF. 3. With the scan tool, perform the Steering Position Sensor Test. Did the SWPS pass the test?	--	Go to Step 3	Go to Step 7
3	With a scan tool, observe the Lateral Accelerometer Input parameter in the VSES data list. Does the scan tool display within the specified range?	2.3-2.7 V	Go to Step 4	Go to Step 8
4	With a scan tool, observe the Yaw Rate Sensor Input parameter in the VSES data list. Does the scan tool display within the specified range?	2.3-2.7 V	Go to Step 5	Go to Step 8
5	1. Use the scan tool in order to clear the DTCs. 2. Perform the Diagnostic Test Drive. Does the DTC reset?	--	Go to Step 6	Go to Diagnostic Aids
6	**Important** Perform the setup procedure for the EBCM. An unprogrammed EBCM will result in the following conditions: • Inoperative or poorly functioning system operations • The EBCM sets DTC C0281 and DTC C0550 Replace the EBCM. Did you complete the repair?	--	Go to Step 9	

LTV0500000005808

Fig. 29 Code C0252: Vehicle Stability Enhancement System (VSES) Sensors Uncorrelated (Part 3 of 4)

Test Description

The numbers below refer to the step numbers on the diagnostic table.

2. Perform the Steering Position Sensor Test in order to verify that the steering wheel position sensor (SWPS) is operating properly.

3. Verify that the lateral accelerometer input parameter is within the valid range.

4. Verify that the yaw rate input parameter is within the valid range.

LTV0500000005811

Fig. 30 Codes C0253 Or C0254: Centering Error Or Steering Sensor And/Or Lateral Accelerometer Bias (Part 2 of 4)

Step	Action	Values	Yes	No
1	Did you perform the ABS Diagnostic System Check?	--	Go to Step 2	Go to Diagnostic System Check
2	1. Install a scan tool. 2. Turn ON the ignition, with the engine OFF. 3. With the scan tool, perform the Steering Position Sensor Test. Did the SWPS pass the test?	--	Go to Step 3	Go to Step 7
3	With a scan tool, observe the Lateral Accelerometer Input parameter in the VSES data list. Does the scan tool display within the specified range?	2.3-2.7 V	Go to Step 4	Go to Step 8
4	With a scan tool, observe the Yaw Rate Sensor Input parameter in the VSES data list. Does the scan tool display within the specified range?	2.3-2.7 V	Go to Step 5	Go to Step 8
5	1. Use the scan tool in order to clear the DTCs. 2. Perform the Diagnostic Test Drive. Does the DTC reset?	--	Go to Step 6	Go to Diagnostic Aids
6	Replace the EBCM. Did you complete the repair?	--	Go to Step 9	--

LTV0500000005812

Fig. 30 Codes C0253 Or C0254: Centering Error Or Steering Sensor And/Or Lateral Accelerometer Bias (Part 3 of 4)

			Go to Step 9	--
7	Replace the steering wheel position sensor (SWPS). Did you complete the replacement?			
8	Replace the yaw rate/lateral accelerometer sensor. Did you complete the replacement?		Go to Step 9	--
9	1. Use the scan tool in order to clear the DTCs. 2. Operate the vehicle within the Conditions for Running the DTC as specified in the supporting text. Does the DTC reset?		Go to Step 2	System OK

LTV0500000005813

Fig. 30 Codes C0253 Or C0254: Centering Error Or Steering Sensor And/Or Lateral Accelerometer Bias (Part 4 of 4)

Step	Action	Yes	No
1	Did you perform the Diagnostic System Check - ABS?	Go to Step 2	Go to Diagnostic System Check
2	1. Install a scan tool. 2. Turn ON the ignition, with the engine OFF. 3. Select the display DTCs function on the scan tool for the EBCM. Does the scan tool display any ABS/TCS/VSES DTCs?	Go to Diagnostic System Check - ABS	Go to Step 3
3	1. Use the scan tool in order to clear the DTCs. 2. Operate the vehicle within the Conditions for Running the DTC as specified in the supporting text. Does the DTC reset?	Go to Step 2	Test for Intermittent and Poor Connections

LTV0500000005815

Fig. 31 Code C0281: Dynamic Rear Proportioning (DRP) Performance (Part 2 of 2)

Circuit Description

The steering wheel position sensor supplies 2 analog inputs, Phase A and Phase B, to the electronic brake control module (EBCM). The 2 input signals are approximately 90 degrees out of phase. By interpreting the relationship between the 2 inputs, the EBCM can determine the position of the steering wheel and the direction of the steering wheel rotation.

Conditions for Running the DTC

- The ignition is ON.
- Ignition voltage is greater than 8 volts.

Conditions for Setting the DTC

C0460

One of the following conditions exists:

- Both Phase A and Phase B are greater than 4.9 volts or less than 0.2 volts for 1.6 seconds.
- The changes in Phase A or Phase B is greater than 36 degrees between consecutive scans of the signal.

C0461

The difference in the phase angle between Phase A and Phase B is greater than 16 degrees continuously for 0.25 seconds.

Action Taken When the DTC Sets

- The EBCM disables the vehicle stability enhancement system (VSES) for the duration of the ignition cycle.
- The driver information center (DIC) displays the Service Stability System message.
- The ABS remains functional.

Conditions for Clearing the DTC

- The condition for the DTC is no longer present and the DTC is cleared with a scan tool.
- The electronic brake control module (EBCM) automatically clears the history DTC when a current DTC is not detected in 100 consecutive drive cycles.

Diagnostic Aids

- Check the vehicle for proper alignment. The car should not pull in either direction while driving straight on a level surface.
- The Snapshot function on the scan tool can help find an intermittent DTC.

LTV0500000005816

Fig. 32 Codes C0460 Or C0461: Steering Position Sensor Or Steering Position Sensor Range/ Performance (Part 1 of 6)

Circuit Description

The dynamic rear proportioning (DRP) is a control system that replaces the hydraulic proportioning function of the mechanical proportioning valve in the base brake system. The DRP control system is part of the operating software in the EBCM. The DRP uses active control with the existing ABS in order to regulate the vehicle's rear brake pressure.

Conditions for Running the DTC

One or more faults have been detected by the EBCM in the ABS/TCS systems.

Conditions for Setting the DTC

One of the following conditions exists:

- DTC C0121, C0113, C0114, C0115, C0900, or C0550 sets.
- Two wheel speed sensor DTCs on the same axle set.

Action Taken When the DTC Sets

- The EBCM disables the DRP for the duration of the ignition cycle.
- The red Brake warning indicator turns ON.

Conditions for Clearing the DTC

- The condition for the DTC is no longer present and the DTC is cleared with a scan tool.
- The electronic brake control module (EBCM) automatically clears the history DTC when a current DTC is not detected in 100 consecutive drive cycles.

Diagnostic Aids

This DTC is for information only. As an aid to the technician, this DTC indicates that another DTC exists that fails DRP.

Test Description

The number below refers to the step number on the diagnostic table.

2. Verifies whether other ABS/TCS/VSES DTCs are set.

LTV0500000005814

Fig. 31 Code C0281: Dynamic Rear Proportioning (DRP) Performance (Part 1 of 2)

Test Description

The numbers below refer to the step numbers on the diagnostic table.

2. Perform the Steering Position Sensor Test in order to verify if the steering wheel position sensor (SWPS) is operating properly.

3. Tests for the proper operation of the steering wheel position signal A circuit in the low voltage range.

4. Tests for the proper operation of the steering wheel position signal B circuit in the low voltage range.

5. Tests for the proper operation of the steering wheel position signal A circuit in the high voltage range. If the fuse in the jumper opens when you perform this test, the signal circuit is shorted to ground.

6. Tests for the proper operation of the steering wheel position signal B circuit in the high voltage range. If the fuse in the jumper opens when you perform this test, the signal circuit is shorted to ground.

7. Tests for a short to voltage in the 5-volt reference circuit.

8. Tests for a high resistance or an open in the low reference circuit.

LTV0500000005817

Fig. 32 Codes C0460 Or C0461: Steering Position Sensor Or Steering Position Sensor Range/ Performance (Part 2 of 6)

Step	Action	Values	Yes	No
1	Did you perform the Diagnostic System Check-ABS?	--	Go to Step 2	Go to Diagnostic System Check -
2	1. Install a scan tool. 2. Turn ON the ignition, with the engine OFF. 3. With the scan tool, perform the Steering Position Sensor Test. Did the SWPS pass the test?	--	Go to Diagnostic Aids	Go to Step 3
3	1. Turn OFF the ignition. 2. Disconnect the steering wheel position sensor (SWPS) connector. 3. Turn ON the ignition, with the engine OFF. 4. With the scan tool, observe the Dual Analog SWPS Input A parameter in the VSES data list. Does the scan tool indicate the Dual Analog SWPS Input A parameter is less than the specified value?	0.2 V	Go to Step 4	Go to Step 13
4	With the scan tool, observe the Dual Analog SWPS Input B parameter. Does the scan tool indicate the Dual Analog SWPS Input B parameter is less than the specified value?	0.2 V	Go to Step 5	Go to Step 14
5	1. Turn OFF the ignition. 2. Connect a 3-amp fused jumper wire between the 5-volt reference circuit of the steering wheel position sensor (SWPS) and the signal A circuit of the steering wheel position sensor (SWPS). 3. Turn ON the ignition, with the engine OFF. 4. With the scan tool, observe the Dual Analog SWPS Input A parameter. Does the scan tool indicate that the Dual Analog SWPS Input A parameter is greater than the specified value?	4.9 V	Go to Step 6	Go to Step 10

LTV0500000005818

Fig. 32 Codes C0460 Or C0461: Steering Position Sensor Or Steering Position Sensor Range/Performance (Part 3 of 6)

Step	Action	Values	Yes	No
12	Test the signal B circuit of the steering wheel position sensor (SWPS) for the following conditions: • An open • A short to ground • A high resistance Did you find and correct the condition?	--	Go to Step 20	Go to Step 17
13	Test the signal A circuit of the steering wheel position sensor (SWPS) for a short to voltage. Did you find and correct the condition?	--	Go to Step 20	Go to Step 17
14	Test the signal B circuit of the steering wheel position sensor (SWPS) for a short to voltage. Did you find and correct the condition?	--	Go to Step 20	Go to Step 17
15	1. Disconnect the EBCM harness connector. 2. Install the J 39700 universal pinout box using the J 39700-300 cable adapter to the EBCM harness connector only. 3. Test the low reference circuit of the steering wheel position sensor (SWPS) for a high resistance or an open. Did you find and correct the condition?	--	Go to Step 20	Go to Step 17
16	Inspect for poor connections at the harness connector of the steering wheel position sensor (SWPS). Did you find and correct the condition?	--	Go to Step 20	Go to Step 18
17	Inspect for poor connections at the harness connector of the EBCM. Did you find and correct the condition?	--	Go to Step 20	Go to Step 19

LTV0500000005820

Fig. 32 Codes C0460 Or C0461: Steering Position Sensor Or Steering Position Sensor Range/Performance (Part 5 of 6)

Step	Action	Values	Yes	No
6	1. Turn OFF the ignition. 2. Disconnect the fused jumper wire. 3. Connect a 3-amp fused jumper wire between the 5-volt reference circuit of the steering wheel position sensor (SWPS) and the signal B circuit of the steering wheel position sensor (SWPS). 4. Turn ON the ignition, with the engine OFF. 5. With the scan tool, observe the Dual Analog SWPS Input B parameter. Does the scan tool indicate that the Dual Analog SWPS Input B parameter is greater than the specified value?	4.9 V	Go to Step 7	Go to Step 10
7	1. Disconnect the fused jumper wire. 2. Measure the voltage between the 5-volt reference circuit of the steering wheel position sensor (SWPS) and the low reference circuit of the steering wheel position sensor (SWPS). Does the voltage measure less the specified value?	5 V	Go to Step 8	Go to Step 9
8	1. Turn OFF the ignition. 2. Disconnect the negative battery cable. 3. Measure the resistance from the low reference circuit of the steering wheel position sensor (SWPS) to a good ground. Does the resistance measure less than the specified value?	5 ohms	Go to Step 16	Go to Step 15
9	Test the 5-volt reference circuit of the steering wheel position sensor (SWPS) for a short to voltage. Did you find and correct the condition?	--	Go to Step 20	Go to Step 17
10	Test the 5-volt reference circuit of the steering wheel position sensor (SWPS) for the following conditions: • An open • A short to ground • A high resistance Did you find and correct the condition?	--	Go to Step 20	Go to Step 11
11	Test the signal A circuit of the steering wheel position sensor (SWPS) for the following conditions: • An open • A short to ground • A high resistance Did you find and correct the condition?	--	Go to Step 20	Go to Step 12

LTV0500000005819

Fig. 32 Codes C0460 Or C0461: Steering Position Sensor Or Steering Position Sensor Range/Performance (Part 4 of 6)

Step	Action	Values	Yes	No
18	Replace the steering wheel position sensor (SWPS). Did you complete the repair?	--	Go to Step 20	--
19	Replace the EBCM. Did you complete the repair?	--	Go to Step 20	--
20	1. Clear the DTCs using the scan tool. 2. Operate the vehicle within the Conditions for Running the DTC as specified in the supporting text. Does the DTC reset?	--	Go to Step 2	System OK

LTV0500000005821

Fig. 32 Codes C0460 Or C0461: Steering Position Sensor Or Steering Position Sensor Range/Performance (Part 6 of 6)

Circuit Description

The electronic brake control module (EBCM) detects an internal malfunction or loss of ground.

Conditions for Running the DTC

The ignition switch is in the ON position.

Conditions for Setting the DTC

- An internal EBCM malfunction exists.
- System voltage is less than half the ignition voltage continuously for 0.04 seconds.

Action Taken When the DTC Sets

If equipped, the following actions occur:

- The Antilock Brake System (ABS)/adaptive cruise control (ACC)/dynamic rear proportion (DRP)/engine drag control (EDC)/tire pressure monitor (TPM)/variable effort steering (VES)/Vehicle Stability Enhancement System (VSES) are disabled.
- Traction Control System (TCS) is degraded.
- The ABS/TCS indicators turn ON.
- The red BRAKE Warning indicator turns ON.

The driver information center (DIC) displays the following:

- Service ABS
- Service Traction System
- Service Stabilitrak
- Service Radar Cruise

Conditions for Clearing the DTC

- The condition for the DTC is no longer present and the DTC is cleared with a scan tool.
- The EBCM automatically clears the history DTC when a current DTC is not detected in 100 consecutive drive cycles.

Diagnostic Aids

When a EBCM has been replaced, but has not been programmed, DTC C0550 will set.

Possible causes of this DTC:

- Open ground at the EBCM
- Internal malfunction in the EBCM

Test Description

The number below refer to the step number on the diagnostic table.

LTV0500000005822

Fig. 33   Code C0550: Electronic Control Unit (ECU) Performance (Part 1 of 2)

Circuit Description

When the electronic brake control module (EBCM) is replaced, software and calibrations are flash programmed into the EBCM. The EBCM receives the vehicle powertrain options information from the powertrain control module (PCM) in order for the EBCM to automatically calibrate to the vehicle.

Conditions for Running the DTC

- The ignition is ON.
- Ignition voltage is greater than 8 volts.

Conditions for Setting the DTC

One or more of the following conditions are present:

- The incorrect EBCM is installed on the vehicle.
- The incorrect software or calibrations have been flash programmed into the EBCM.

Action Taken When the DTC Sets

If equipped, the following actions occur:

- The EDC/TCS are disabled.
- The TCS indicator turns ON.

The DIC displays the Service Traction System message.

Conditions for Clearing the DTC

- The condition for the DTC is no longer present and the DTC is cleared with a scan tool.
- The electronic brake control module (EBCM) automatically clears the history DTC when a current DTC is not detected in 100 consecutive drive cycles.

Diagnostic Aids

If the DTC was set after EBCM replacement, verify that the replacement EBCM and software are correct for the vehicle.

LTV0500000005824

Fig. 34   Code C0551: Option Configuration Error (Part 1 of 2)

Step	Action	Yes	No
1	Did you perform the Diagnostic System Check - Vehicle?	Go to Step 2	Go to Diagnostic System Check
2	Test both of the ground circuits of the electronic brake control module (EBCM) for a high resistance or an open. Did you find and correct the condition?	Go to Step 5	Go to Step 3
3	Inspect for poor connections at the harness connector of the EBCM. Did you find and correct the condition?	Go to Step 5	Go to Step 4
4	Replace the EBCM. Did you complete the replacement?	Go to Step 5	--
5	1. Use the scan tool to clear the DTCs. 2. Operate the vehicle within the Conditions for Running the DTC as specified in the supporting text. Does the DTC reset?	Go to Step 2	System OK

LTV0500000005823

Fig. 33   Code C0550: Electronic Control Unit (ECU) Performance (Part 2 of 2)

Step	Action	Yes	No
1	Did you perform the Diagnostic System Check - ABS?	Go to Step 2	Go to Diagnostic System Check
2	Is the EBCM the correct module for the vehicle?	Go to Step 4	Go to Step 3
3	Replace the EBCM. Did you complete the repair?	Go to Step 5	Go to Step 4
4	Reprogram the EBCM. Did you complete the repair?	Go to Step 5	--
5	1. Use the scan tool in order to clear the DTCs. 2. Turn ON the ignition. Does the DTC reset?	Go to Step 2	System OK

LTV0500000005825

Fig. 34   Code C0551: Option Configuration Error (Part 2 of 2)

Circuit Description

The electronic brake control module (EBCM) disables the traction control when other electronic control modules set DTCs for components that effect the operation of the traction control system.

Conditions for Running the DTC

- The ignition is ON.
- Ignition voltage is greater than 8 volts.

Conditions for Setting the DTC

The PCM or BCM diagnoses a condition preventing the engine control portion of the traction control function and sends a serial data message to the EBCM indicating that torque reduction is not allowed. The PCM or BCM will typically set a DTC and the EBCM will set this DTC.

Action Taken When the DTC Sets

- The EBCM disables the TCS until the DTC becomes a history DTC.
- The Traction Off indicator turns ON.
- The ABS remains functional.

Conditions for Clearing the DTC

- The condition for the DTC is no longer present and the DTC is cleared with a scan tool.
- The electronic brake control module (EBCM) automatically clears the history DTC when a current DTC is not detected in 100 consecutive drive cycles.

Diagnostic Aids

This DTC is for information only. As an aid to the technician, this DTC indicates that there are no problems in the ABS/TCS system.

Step	Action	Yes	No
1	Did you perform the Diagnostic System Check - ABS?	--	Go to Diagnostic System Check

LTV0500000005826

Fig. 35   Code C0561: System Disabled Information Stored

Circuit Description

When the electronic brake control module (EBCM) is replaced, software and calibrations are flash programmed into the EBCM. The EBCM receives the vehicle identification number information from the vehicle in order for the EBCM to automatically calibrate to the vehicle.

Conditions for Running the DTC

- The ignition is ON.
- Ignition voltage is greater than 8 volts.

Conditions for Setting the DTC

One or more of the following conditions are present:

- The incorrect EBCM is installed on the vehicle.
- The incorrect software or calibrations have been flash programmed into the EBCM.

Action Taken When the DTC Sets

If equipped, the following actions occur:

- The EDC/TCS are disabled.
- The TCS indicator turns ON.

The DIC displays the Service Traction System message.

Conditions for Clearing the DTC

- The condition for the DTC is no longer present and the DTC is cleared with a scan tool.
- The electronic brake control module (EBCM) automatically clears the history DTC when a current DTC is not detected in 100 consecutive drive cycles.

Diagnostic Aids

If the DTC was set after EBCM replacement, verify that the replacement EBCM and software are correct for the vehicle.

LTV0500000005827

Fig. 36 Code C0565: Vehicle Identification Number (VIN) Information Error (Part 1 of 2)

Circuit Description

The electronic brake control module (EBCM) monitors the voltage level of the EBCMs case. If the voltage level is too high, damage may result in the system. When the EBCM detects a high voltage condition, the EBCM turns OFF the system relay which removes battery voltage from the solenoid valves and pump motor.

Conditions for Running the DTC

The ignition is ON.

Conditions for Setting the DTC

The case voltage is greater than 2 volts for 0.1 seconds.

Action Taken When the DTC Sets

If equipped, the following actions occur:

- The EBCM disables the ABS/ACC/VSES for the duration of the ignition cycle.
- The DRP and TCS are degraded.
- The ABS indicator turns ON.
- The Traction Control indicator turns ON.
- The DIC displays the Service Stability System message.
- The red Brake warning indicator turns ON.

Conditions for Clearing the DTC

- The condition for the DTC is no longer present and the DTC is cleared with a scan tool.
- The electronic brake control module (EBCM) automatically clears the history DTC when a current DTC is not detected in 100 consecutive drive cycles.

Diagnostic Aids

Possible causes of this DTC are the following conditions:

- Internal short in the pump motor.
- External battery supply shorted to case.
- Internal EBCM battery supply shorted to case.

The pump motor is integral to the BPMV. The pump motor is not serviceable.

Test Description

The number below refers to the step number on the diagnostic table.

3. Tests the ability of the EBCM to control the pump motor. If the test lamp illuminates, the pump motor circuit within the EBCM is good.

LTV0500000005829

Fig. 37 Code C0820: Device Ground Circuit (Part 1 of 3)

Step	Action	Yes	No
1	Did you perform the Diagnostic System Check - ABS?	Go to Step 2	Go to Diagnostic System Check
2	Is the EBCM the correct module for the vehicle?	Go to Step 4	Go to Step 3
3	Replace the EBCM. Did you complete the repair?	Go to Step 5	Go to Step 4
4	Reprogram the EBCM. Did you complete the repair?	Go to Step 5	--
5	1. Use the scan tool in order to clear the DTCs. 2. Turn ON the ignition. Does the DTC reset?	Go to Step 2	System OK

LTV0500000005828

Fig. 36 Code C0565: Vehicle Identification Number (VIN) Information Error (Part 2 of 2)

Step	Action	Yes	No
1	Did you perform the Diagnostic System Check - ABS?	Go to Step 2	Go to Diagnostic System Check
2	1. Install a scan tool. 2. Turn ON the ignition, with the engine OFF. 3. Use the scan tool in order to clear the DTCs. 4. With the scan tool, perform the Automated Test. Does the DTC reset?	Go to Step 3	Test for Intermittent and Poor Connections
3	1. Turn OFF the ignition. 2. Disconnect the pump motor harness pigtail connector of the BPMV. 3. Connect a test lamp between the pump motor circuits at the pump motor connector of the EBCM using the J 35616-B Connector Test Adapter Kit. 4. Use the scan tool in order to clear the DTCs. 5. With the scan tool, perform the Pump Motor Test. Does the test lamp illuminate?	Go to Step 5	Go to Step 4
4	1. Turn OFF the ignition. 2. Disconnect the EBCM harness connector. 3. Connect the J 39700 Universal Pinout Box using the J 39700-300 Cable Adapter to the EBCM harness connector only. 4. Test both ground circuits of the EBCM including the EBCM ground for a high resistance or an open. Did you find and correct the condition?	Go to Step 9	Go to Step 6
5	Inspect for poor connections at the pump motor harness pigtail connector of the BPMV. Did you find and correct the condition?	Go to Step 9	Go to Step 7

LTV0500000005830

Fig. 37 Code C0820: Device Ground Circuit (Part 2 of 3)

Step	Action	Yes	No
6	Inspect for poor connections at the harness connector of the EBCM. Did you find and correct the condition?	Go to Step 9	Go to Step 8
7	Replace the BPMV. Did you complete the repair?	Go to Step 9	--
8	**Important** Perform the setup procedure for the EBCM. An unprogrammed EBCM will result in the following conditions: - Inoperative or poorly functioning system operations - The EBCM sets DTC C0281 and DTC C0550 Replace the EBCM. Did you complete the repair?	Go to Step 9	--
9	1. Use the scan tool in order to clear the DTCs. 2. With the scan tool, perform the Automated Test. Does the DTC reset?	Go to Step 2	System OK

LTV0500000005831

Fig. 37 Code C0820: Device Ground Circuit (Part 3 of 3)

Circuit Description

The electronic brake control module (EBCM) supplies voltage to the brake pressure sensor, steering angle sensor, and yaw rate/lateral accelerometer sensor. This voltage is monitored by the EBCM for an over or under voltage condition.

Conditions for Running the DTC

- The ignition is ON.
- Ignition voltage is greater than 8 volts.

Conditions for Setting the DTC

One of the follow conditions exists for 0.1 seconds:

- The sensor supply voltage is greater than 5.2 volts.
- The sensor supply voltage is less than 4.8 volts.

Action Taken When the DTC Sets

- The EBCM disables the VSES for the duration of the ignition cycle.
- ACC braking function disabled.
- TCS is degraded.
- The Traction Control and Active Handling indicator turns ON.
- The DIC displays the Service Active Handling message.

Conditions for Clearing the DTC

- The condition for the DTC is no longer present and the DTC is cleared with a scan tool.
- The electronic brake control module (EBCM) automatically clears the history DTC when a current DTC is not detected in 100 consecutive drive cycles.

Diagnostic Aids

The following conditions can cause this concern:

- The sensor supply circuit is open, shorted to ground, or shorted to battery.
- Internal sensor malfunction.
- Internal EBCM malfunction.

Test Description

The numbers below refer to the step numbers on the diagnostic table.

5. Tests for a short at the brake pressure sensor.

6. Tests for a short at the steering wheel position sensor.

7. Tests for a short at the yaw rate/lateral accelerometer sensor.

LTV0500000005832

Fig. 38   Code C0870: Device Voltage Performance Output Circuit (Part 1 of 4)

Step	Action	Values	Yes	No
6	1. Turn OFF the ignition. 2. Disconnect the steering wheel position sensor connector 3. Turn ON the ignition, with the engine OFF. 4. Using the DMM, measure the voltage between the 5 volt reference circuit and ground. Is the voltage within the specified value?	4.8-5.2 V	Go to Step 9	Go to Step 7
7	1. Turn OFF the ignition. 2. Disconnect the yaw rate/lateral accelerometer sensor connector 3. Turn ON the ignition, with the engine OFF. 4. Using the DMM, measure the voltage between the 5 volt reference circuit and ground. Is the voltage within the specified value?	4.8-5.2 V	Go to Step 10	Go to Step 11
8	Inspect for poor connections at the harness connector of the brake pressure sensor. Did you find and correct the condition?	--	Go to Step 16	Go to Step 12
9	Inspect for poor connections at the harness connector of the steering wheel position sensor. Did you find and correct the condition?	--	Go to Step 16	Go to Step 13
10	Inspect for poor connections at the harness connector of the yaw rate/lateral accelerometer sensor. Did you find and correct the condition?	--	Go to Step 16	Go to Step 14
11	Inspect for poor connections at the harness connector of the EBCM. Did you find and correct the condition?	--	Go to Step 16	Go to Step 15
12	Replace the brake pressure sensor. Did you complete the repair?	--	Go to Step 16	

LTV0500000005834

Fig. 38   Code C0870: Device Voltage Performance Output Circuit (Part 3 of 4)

Step	Action	Values	Yes	No
1	Did you perform the Diagnostic System Check - ABS?	--	Go to Step 2	Go to Diagnostic System Check -
2	Test the 5-volt reference circuit from the EBCM for the following conditions: • An open • A short to ground • A high resistance Did you find and correct the condition?	--	Go to Step 16	Go to Step 3
3	Test the 5-volt reference circuit from the EBCM for a short to voltage. Did you find and correct the condition?	--	Go to Step 16	Go to Step 4
4	1. Turn OFF the ignition. 2. Disconnect the EBCM. 3. Install the J 39700 Universal Pinout Box with the J 39700-530 Cable Adapter between the EBCM and the EBCM harness connector. 4. Turn ON the ignition, with the engine OFF. 5. Using the DMM, measure the voltage between the 5 volt reference circuit and ground. Is the voltage within the specified value?	4.8-5.2 V	Go to Diagnostic Aids	Go to Step 5
5	1. Turn OFF the ignition. 2. Disconnect the brake pressure sensor. 3. Turn ON the ignition, with the engine OFF. 4. Using the DMM, measure the voltage between the 5 volt reference circuit and ground. Is the voltage within the specified value?	4.8-5.2 V	Go to Step 8	Go to Step 6

LTV0500000005833

Fig. 38   Code C0870: Device Voltage Performance Output Circuit (Part 2 of 4)

Step	Action	Values	Yes	No
13	Replace the steering wheel position sensor. Did you complete the repair?	-	-	Go to Step 16
14	Replace the yaw rate/lateral accelerometer sensor. Did you complete the repair?	-	-	Go to Step 16
15	Replace the EBCM. Did you complete the repair?	-	-	Go to Step 16
16	1. Clear the DTCs using the scan tool. 2. Operate the vehicle within the Conditions for Running the DTC as specified in the supporting text. Does the DTC reset?	-	Go to Step 2	System OK

LTV0500000005835

Fig. 38   Code C0870: Device Voltage Performance Output Circuit (Part 4 of 4)

Circuit Description

The electronic brake control module (EBCM) monitors the voltage level available for system operation. A low voltage condition prevents the system from operating properly.

Conditions for Running the DTC

- The vehicle speed is greater than 8 km/h (5 mph).
- The system relay is commanded ON.

Conditions for Setting the DTC

One of the following conditions exists for 0.72 seconds:

- During initialization or when the system is inactive, the system voltage is less than 10.8 volts.
- During the system operation, the system voltage is less than 9.0 volts.

Action Taken When the DTC Sets

If equipped, the following actions occur:

- The EBCM disables the ABS/ACC/VES/VSES for the duration of the ignition cycle.
- The ABS indicator turns ON.
- The traction control indicator turns ON.
- The DIC displays the Service Stabilitrak and Service ABS messages.
- DRP and TCS are degraded.

Conditions for Clearing the DTC

- The condition for the DTC is no longer present and the DTC is cleared with a scan tool.
- The EBCM automatically clears the history DTC when a current DTC is not detected in 100 consecutive drive cycles.

Diagnostic Aids

- Test the charging system.
- Possible causes of this DTC are the following conditions:
  - A charging system malfunction
  - An excessive battery draw
  - A weak battery
  - A faulty system ground

Test Description

The numbers below refer to the step numbers on the diagnostic table.

LTV0500000005836

Fig. 39   Code C0899: Device Voltage Low
(Part 1 of 4)

Step	Action	Values	Yes	No
1	Did you perform the Diagnostic System Check - ABS?	--	Go to Step 2	Go to Diagnostic System Check -
2	1. Install a scan tool. 2. Start the engine. 3. With a scan tool, observe the Switched System Battery Voltage parameter in the ABS data list. Does the scan tool indicate the voltage is greater than the specified value?	10.5 V	Go to Diagnostic Aids	Go to Step 3
3	With a scan tool, observe the Battery Volts parameter in the body control module data list. Does the scan tool indicate the voltage is greater than the specified value?	10.5 V	Go to Step 4	Go to Diagnostic System Check -
4	1. Turn OFF the ignition. 2. Disconnect the EBCM harness connector. 3. Install the J 39700 Universal Pinout Box using the J 39700-300 Cable Adaptor to the EBCM harness connector only. 4. Test the ground circuits of the EBCM including the EBCM ground for a high resistance or an open. Did you find and correct the condition?	--	Go to Step 7	Go to Step 5

LTV0500000005838

Fig. 39   Code C0899: Device Voltage Low
(Part 3 of 4)

2. Use the scan tool in order to inspect the voltage to the EBCM.

3. Use the scan tool in order to inspect the voltage to the body control module (BCM). A low voltage value in multiple modules indicates a concern in the charging system.

5. Verifies that the condition is still present.

LTV0500000005837

Fig. 39   Code C0899: Device Voltage Low
(Part 2 of 4)

5	1. Connect the EBCM harness connector. 2. Turn ON the ignition, with the engine OFF. 3. Use the scan tool in order to clear the DTCs. 4. Operate the vehicle within the Conditions for Running the DTC as specified in the supporting text. Does the DTC reset?	--	Go to Step 6	Go to Diagnostic Aids
6	Replace the EBCM. Did you complete the repair?	--	Go to Step 7	--
7	1. Use the scan tool in order to clear the DTCs. 2. Operate the vehicle within the Conditions for Running the DTC as specified in the supporting text. Does the DTC reset?	--	Go to Step 2	System OK

LTV0500000005839

Fig. 39   Code C0899: Device Voltage Low
(Part 4 of 4)

Circuit Description

The electronic brake control module (EBCM) monitors the voltage level available for system operation. If the voltage level is too high, damage may result in the system. When the EBCM detects a high voltage condition, the EBCM turns OFF the system relay which removes battery voltage from the solenoid valves and pump motor.

Conditions for Running the DTC

The vehicle speed is greater than 8 km/h (5 mph).

Conditions for Setting the DTC

The system voltage is greater than 17 volts for 0.72 seconds.

Action Taken When the DTC Sets

If equipped, the following actions occur:

- The EBCM disables the ABS/TCS/VSES for the duration of the ignition cycle.
- The DRP does not function optimally.
- The ABS indicator turns ON.
- The Traction Control and Active Handling indicator turns ON.
- The DIC displays the following messages:
  - Service ABS
  - Service Traction System
  - Service Active Handling

Conditions for Clearing the DTC

- The condition for the DTC is no longer present and the DTC is cleared with a scan tool.
- The EBCM automatically clears the history DTC when a current DTC is not detected in 100 consecutive drive cycles.

Diagnostic Aids

A possible cause of this DTC is overcharging.

Test Description

The numbers below refer to the step numbers on the diagnostic table.

2. Use the scan tool in order to inspect the voltage to the EBCM.

3. Use the scan tool in order to inspect the voltage to the body control module (BCM). A high voltage value in multiple modules indicates a concern in the charging system.

4. Verifies that the condition is still present.

LTV0500000005840

Fig. 40   Code C0900: Device Voltage High
(Part 1 of 2)

Step	Action	Values	Yes	No
1	Did you perform the Diagnostic System Check - ABS?	--	Go to Step 2	Go to Diagnostic System Check -
2	1. Turn OFF all of the accessories. 2. Install a scan tool. 3. Start the engine 4. Run the engine at approximately 2,000 RPM. 5. With a scan tool, observe the Switched System Battery Voltage parameter in the ABS data list. Does the scan tool indicate that the voltage is greater than the specified value?	16.3 V	Go to Step 3	Go to Diagnostic Aids
3	With a scan tool, observe the Battery Volts parameter in body control module data list. Does the scan tool indicate the voltage is greater than the specified value?	16.3 V	Go to Diagnostic System Check -	Go to Step 4
4	1. Use the scan tool in order to clear the DTCs. 2. Operate the vehicle within the conditions for Running the DTC as specified in the supporting test. Does the DTC reset?	--	Go to Step 5	Go to Diagnostic Aids
5	Replace the EBCM. Did you complete the repair?	--	Go to Step 6	--
6	1. Use the scan tool in order to clear the DTCs. 2. Operate the vehicle within the conditions for Running the DTC as specified in the supporting test. Does the DTC reset?	--	Go to Step 2	System OK

LTV0500000005841

Fig. 40 Code C0900: Device Voltage High (Part 2 of 2)

Step	Action	Values	Yes	No
1	Did you perform the Diagnostic System Check - ABS?	--	Go to Step 2	Go to Diagnostic System Check -
2	Test the extended brake travel circuit of the EBCM for the following conditions: • An open • A short to ground • A short to battery Did you find and correct the condition?	--	Go to Step 9	Go to Step 3
3	1. Turn OFF the ignition. 2. Disconnect the EBCM harness connector. 3. Install the J 39700 Universal Pinout Box using the J 39700-300 Cable Adapter to the EBCM harness connector and the EBCM connector. 4. Turn ON the ignition, with the engine OFF. 5. With the brake pedal released, measure the voltage between the extended brake travel circuit and a good ground. Is the voltage greater than the specified value?	2 V	Go to Step 5	Go to Step 4
4	1. Install a scan tool. 2. Turn ON the ignition, with the engine OFF. 3. With the scan tool, observe the BPP Sensor Displacement parameter in the BPP System Data data list while applying pressure to the brake pedal. 4. With the BPP Sensor Displacement parameter reading 50 percent, measure the voltage between the extended brake travel circuit and a good ground. Is the voltage of the extended brake travel signal greater than the specified value?	0.8 V	Go to Step 6	Go to Step 5
5	Inspect for poor connections the harness connector of the EBCM. Did you find and correct the condition?	--	Go to Step 9	Go to Step 7

LTV0500000005843

Fig. 41 Code P1575: Extended Travel Brake Switch Circuit (Part 2 of 3)

Circuit Description

The EBCM uses the BPP Sensor to determine if an extended brake travel event has occured. If an extended brake travel condition exists, the EBCM will provide a 5 volt output via the extended brake travel circuit to the ECM.

Conditions for Running the DTC

- The ignition is ON.
- Ignition voltage is greater than 8 volts.

Conditions for Setting the DTC

One of the following conditions exist:

- The extended brake travel voltage is less than 0.8 volts when extended brake travel is ON.
- The extended brake travel voltage is greater than 2.0 volts when extended brake travel is OFF.

Action Taken When the DTC Sets

All systems remain functional.

Conditions for Clearing the DTC

- The condition for the DTC is no longer present and the DTC is cleared with a scan tool.
- The electronic brake control module (EBCM) automatically clears the history DTC when a current DTC is not detected in 100 consecutive drive cycles.

Diagnostic Aids

One of the following may cause this concern:

- An open in the extended brake travel circuit.
- A short to ground or voltage in the extended brake travel circuit.

Test Description

The numbers below refer to the step numbers on the diagnostic table.

3. Measure the extended brake travel circuit in order to determine if the extended brake travel signal has a valid voltage.

4. Measure the extended brake travel signal in order to determine if the EBCM is functioning properly.

8. This vehicle is equipped with a ECM which uses an electrically erasable programmable read only memory (EEPROM). When replacing the ECM, the replacement ECM must be programmed.

LTV0500000005842

Fig. 41 Code P1575: Extended Travel Brake Switch Circuit (Part 1 of 3)

Step	Action	Values	Yes	No
6	Inspect for poor connections the harness connector of the ECM. Did you find and correct the condition?	--	Go to Step 9	Go to Step 8
7	Important Perform the setup procedure for the EBCM. An unprogrammed EBCM will result in the following conditions: • Inoperative or poorly functioning system operations • The EBCM sets DTC C0281 and DTC C0550 Replace the EBCM. Did you complete the repair?	--	Go to Step 9	
8	Important The replacement ECM must be programmed. Replace the ECM. Did you complete the repair?	--	Go to Step 9	
9	1. Use the scan tool in order to clear the DTCs. 2. Operate the vehicle within the Conditions for Running the DTC as specified in the supporting text. Does the DTC reset?	--	Go to Step 2	System OK

LTV0500000005844

Fig. 41 Code P1575: Extended Travel Brake Switch Circuit (Part 3 of 3)

Circuit Description

The instrument cluster controls the operation of the ABS indicator. The electronic brake control module (EBCM) reports the desired status of the ABS indicator via serial data messages. The ABS indicator signal circuit is a back-up reporting circuit to the serial data messages. The EBCM supplies ground through the circuit when the ABS is operating properly. When there is a problem with ABS that should turn on the ABS indicator, the EBCM opens the ABS indicator signal circuit. If there is a problem with the ABS serial data messages, the instrument cluster uses the ABS indicator signal to determine if the ABS indicator should be illuminated. Using the serial data messages and back-up circuit, the instrument cluster decides whether to turn on the ABS indicator.

Test Description

The numbers below refer to the step numbers on the diagnostic table.

3. Use the scan tool to check the normal state of the ABS indicator control circuit.

4. Ensures that the instrument panel cluster (IPC) can operate the ABS indicator.

Step	Action	Value (s)	Yes	No
1	Did you perform the ABS Diagnostic System Check?	--	Go to Step 2	Go to Diagnostic System Check - ABS
2	Inspect the EBCM ground, making sure the ground is clean and torqued to the proper specification. Did you find and correct the condition?	--	Go to Step 9	Go to Step 3
3	1. Install a scan tool. 2. Turn ON the ignition, with the engine OFF. 3. With a scan tool, observe the ABS Warning Indicator parameter in the DRP/ABS/TCS data list. Does the scan tool display Off?	--	Go to Step 4	Go to Step 5

LTV0500000005845

Fig. 42 ABS Indicator Always On (Part 1 of 2)

	Action		Yes	No
4	1. Turn OFF the ignition. 2. Turn ON the ignition, with the engine OFF. 3. Observe the ABS indicator on the instrument panel cluster (IPC) during the displays test. Does the ABS indicator illuminate during the displays test and then turn OFF?		Test for Intermittent and Poor Connections	Go to Step 6
5	Inspect for poor connections at the harness connector of the EBCM. Did you find and correct the condition?		Go to Step 9	Go to Step 7
6	Inspect for poor connections at the harness connector of the IPC. Did you find and correct the condition?		Go to Step 9	Go to Step 8
7	Replace the EBCM. Did you complete the repair?		Go to Step 9	--
8	**Important** Perform the setup procedure for the replacement IPC. Replace the instrument panel cluster (IPC). Did you complete the repair?		Go to Step 9	--
9	Operate the system in order to verify the repair. Did you correct the condition?		System OK	Go to Step 2

LTV0500000005846

Fig. 42 ABS Indicator Always On (Part 2 of 2)

Circuit Description

The instrument cluster controls the operation of the ABS indicator. The electronic brake control module (EBCM) reports the desired status of the ABS indicator via serial data messages. The ABS indicator signal circuit is a back-up reporting circuit to the serial data messages. The EBCM supplies ground through the circuit when the ABS is operating properly. When there is a problem with ABS that should turn on the ABS indicator, the EBCM opens the ABS indicator signal circuit. If there is a problem with the ABS serial data messages, the instrument cluster uses the ABS indicator signal to determine if the ABS indicator should be illuminated. Using the serial data messages and back-up circuit, the instrument cluster decides whether to turn on the ABS indicator.

Test Description

The numbers below refer to the step numbers on the diagnostic table.

3. Use the scan tool to check the normal state of the ABS indicator control circuit.

4. Ensures that the instrument panel cluster (IPC) can operate the ABS indicator.

Step	Action	Value (s)	Yes	No
1	Did you perform the ABS Diagnostic System Check?	--	Go to Step 2	Go to Diagnostic System Check -
2	Inspect the EBCM ground, making sure the ground is clean and torqued to the proper specification. Did you find and correct the condition?	--	Go to Step 9	Go to Step 3
3	1. Install a scan tool. 2. Turn ON the ignition, with the engine OFF. 3. With a scan tool, observe the ABS Warning Indicator parameter in the DRP/ABS/TCS data list. Does the scan tool display Off?	--	Go to Step 4	Go to Step 5

LTV0500000005847

Fig. 43 ABS Indicator Inoperative (Part 1 of 2)

	Action		Yes	No
4	1. Turn OFF the ignition. 2. Turn ON the ignition, with the engine OFF. 3. Observe the ABS indicator on the instrument panel cluster (IPC) during the displays test. Does the ABS indicator illuminate during the displays test and then turn OFF?		Test for Intermittent and Poor Connections	Go to Step 6
5	Inspect for poor connections at the harness connector of the EBCM. Did you find and correct the condition?		Go to Step 9	Go to Step 7
6	Inspect for poor connections at the harness connector of the IPC. Did you find and correct the condition?		Go to Step 9	Go to Step 8
7	Replace the EBCM. Did you complete the repair?		Go to Step 9	--
8	**Important** Perform the setup procedure for the replacement IPC. Replace the instrument panel cluster (IPC). Did you complete the repair?		Go to Step 9	--
9	Operate the system in order to verify the repair. Did you correct the condition?		System OK	Go to Step 2

LTV0500000005848

Fig. 43 ABS Indicator Inoperative (Part 2 of 2)

Circuit Description

The Traction Control indicator is controlled by the instrument cluster (IPC) via serial data messages from the EBCM. The EBCM send a serial data message to the IPC to illuminate the Traction Control indicator when the EBCM has disabled TCS due to a DTC. The Traction Control indicator will also turn ON during the instrument cluster bulb check. When the ignition switch is turned to ON, the Traction Control indicator will turn ON for approximately 3 seconds and then turn OFF.

Test Description

The numbers below refer to the step numbers on the diagnostic table.

2. Use the scan tool to check the normal state of the Traction Control indicator control.

3. Ensures that the instrument cluster can operate the Traction Control indicator.

Step	Action	Yes	No
1	Did you perform the ABS Diagnostic System Check?	Go to Step 2	Go to Diagnostic System Check -
2	1. Install a scan tool. 2. Turn ON the ignition, with the engine OFF. 3. With a scan tool, observe the TCS Warning Indicator/Message parameter in the DRP/ABS/TCS data list. Does the scan tool display Off?	Go to Step 3	Go to Step 4
3	1. Turn OFF the ignition. 2. Turn ON the ignition, with the engine OFF. 3. Observe the Traction Control indicator on the instrument cluster (IPC) during the bulb check. Does the Traction Control indicator illuminate during the bulb check and then turn OFF?	Test for Intermittent and Poor Connections	Go to Step 5

LTV0500000005849

Fig. 44   Traction Control Indicator Always On (Part 1 of 2)

Circuit Description

The Traction Control indicator is controlled by the instrument cluster (IPC) via serial data messages from the EBCM. The EBCM send a serial data message to the IPC to illuminate the Traction Control indicator when the EBCM has disabled TCS due to a DTC. The Traction Control indicator will also turn ON during the instrument cluster bulb check. When the ignition switch is turned to ON, the Traction Control indicator will turn ON for approximately 3 seconds and then turn OFF.

Test Description

The numbers below refer to the step numbers on the diagnostic table.

2. Use the scan tool to check the normal state of the Traction Control indicator control.

3. Ensures that the instrument cluster can operate the Traction Control indicator.

Step	Action	Yes	No
1	Did you perform the ABS Diagnostic System Check?	Go to Step 2	Go to Diagnostic System Check -
2	1. Install a scan tool. 2. Turn ON the ignition, with the engine OFF. 3. With a scan tool, observe the TCS Warning Indicator/Message parameter in the DRP/ABS/TCS data list. Does the scan tool display Off?	Go to Step 3	Go to Step 4
3	1. Turn OFF the ignition. 2. Turn ON the ignition, with the engine OFF. 3. Observe the Traction Control indicator on the instrument cluster (IPC) during the bulb check. Does the Traction Control indicator illuminate during the bulb check and then turn OFF?		Go to Step 5

LTV0500000005851

Fig. 45   Traction Control Indicator Inoperative (Part 1 of 2)

4	Inspect for poor connections at the harness connector of the EBCM. Did you find and correct the condition?	Go to Step 8	Go to Step 6
5	Inspect for poor connections at the harness connector of the instrument cluster (IPC). Did you find and correct the condition?	Go to Step 8	Go to Step 7
6	Replace the EBCM. Did you complete the repair?	Go to Step 8	--
7	Replace the instrument cluster (IPC). Did you complete the repair?	Go to Step 8	--
8	Operate the system in order to verify the repair. Did you correct the condition?	System OK	Go to Step 2

LTV0500000005850

Fig. 44   Traction Control Indicator Always On (Part 2 of 2)

4	Inspect for poor connections at the harness connector of the EBCM. Did you find and correct the condition?	Go to Step 8	Go to Step 6
5	Inspect for poor connections at the harness connector of the instrument cluster (IPC). Did you find and correct the condition?	Go to Step 8	Go to Step 7
6	Replace the EBCM. Did you complete the repair?	Go to Step 8	--
7	Replace the instrument cluster (IPC). Did you complete the repair?	Go to Step 8	--
8	Operate the system in order to verify the repair. Did you correct the condition?	System OK	Go to Step 2

LTV0500000005852

Fig. 45   Traction Control Indicator Inoperative (Part 2 of 2)

Circuit Description

The Traction Off indicator is controlled by the instrument cluster via serial data messages from the EBCM. When the RIM sees the traction control switch input grounded through the momentary traction control switch, it sends a serial data message to the EBCM that tells the EBCM that the traction control switch has been pressed. The EBCM then disables traction control and sends a serial data message to the instrument cluster to turn on the Traction Off indicator on the instrument panel. Each time the ignition is cycled from OFF to ON, the traction control system is enabled.

Test Description

The numbers below refer to the step numbers on the diagnostic table.

2. Use the scan tool to check the normal state of the Traction Off indicator control.

3. Ensures that the instrument cluster can operate the Traction Off indicator.

Step	Action	Yes	No
1	Did you perform the ABS Diagnostic System Check?	Go to Step 2	Go to Diagnostic System Check -
2	1. Install a scan tool. 2. Turn ON the ignition, with the engine OFF. 3. With a scan tool, observe the TCS Warning Indicator/Message parameter in the DRP/AES/TCS data list. Does the scan tool display Off?	Go to Step 3	Go to Step 4
3	1. Turn OFF the ignition. 2. Turn ON the ignition, with the engine OFF. 3. Observe the Traction Off indicator on the instrument panel cluster (IPC) during the bulb check. Does the Traction Off indicator illuminate during the bulb check and then turn OFF?	Test for Intermittent and Poor Connections	Go to Step 5

LTV0500000005853

Fig. 46   Traction Off Indicator Always On (Part 1 of 2)

4	Inspect for poor connections at the harness connector of the EBCM. Did you find and correct the condition?	Go to Step 8	Go to Step 6
5	Inspect for poor connections at the harness connector of the instrument panel cluster (IPC). Did you find and correct the condition?	Go to Step 8	Go to Step 7
6	Replace the EBCM. Did you complete the repair?	Go to Step 8	--
7	Replace the instrument panel cluster (IPC). Did you complete the repair?	Go to Step 8	--
8	Operate the system in order to verify the repair. Did you correct the condition?	System OK	Go to Step 2

LTV0500000005854

**Fig. 46 Traction Off Indicator Always On
(Part 2 of 2)**

4	1. Turn OFF the ignition. 2. Install a scan tool. 3. Turn ON the ignition, with the engine OFF. 4. With a scan tool, observe the TCS On/Off Switch parameter in the Rear Integration Module data list. 5. Activate the traction control switch. Does the TCS On/Off Switch parameter change state?	Test for Intermittent and Poor Connections	Go to Step 5
5	1. Turn OFF the ignition. 2. Disconnect the traction control switch connector. 3. Connect a 3 amp fused jumper from the signal circuit of the traction control switch to the ground circuit of the traction control switch. 4. Turn ON the ignition, with the engine OFF. 5. With a scan tool, observe the TCS Switch State parameter. Does the scan tool display On?	Go to Step 9	Go to Step 6
6	Test the signal circuit of the traction control switch for an open or high resistance. Did you find and correct the condition?	Go to Step 16	Go to Step 7
7	Test the ground circuit of the traction control switch for an open or high resistance. Did you find and correct the condition?	Go to Step 16	Go to Step 8
8	Inspect for poor connections at the harness connector of the rear integration module (RIM). Did you find and correct the condition?	Go to Step 16	Go to Step 12
9	Inspect for poor connections at the harness connector of the traction control switch. Did you find and correct the condition?	Go to Step 16	Go to Step 13
10	Inspect for poor connections at the harness connector of the EBCM. Did you find and correct the condition?	Go to Step 16	Go to Step 14

LTV0500000005856

**Fig. 47 Traction Off Indicator Inoperative
(Part 2 of 3)**

Circuit Description

The Traction Off indicator is controlled by the instrument cluster via serial data messages from the EBCM. When the RIM sees the traction control switch input grounded through the momentary traction control switch, it sends a serial data message to the EBCM that tells the EBCM that the traction control switch has been pressed. The EBCM then disables traction control and sends a serial data message to the instrument cluster to turn on the Traction Off indicator on the instrument panel. Each time the ignition is cycled from OFF to ON, the traction control system is enabled.

Test Description

The numbers below refer to the step numbers on the diagnostic table.

2. Use the scan tool to check the normal state of the Traction Off control.

3. Ensures that the instrument cluster can operate the Traction Off inicator.

Step	Action	Yes	No
1	Did you perform the ABS Diagnostic System Check?	Go to Step 2	Go to Diagnostic System Check
2	1. Install a scan tool. 2. Turn ON the ignition, with the engine OFF. 3. With a scan tool, observe the TCS Warning Indicator/Message parameter in the DRP/ABS/TCS data list. Does the scan tool display Off?	Go to Step 3	Go to Step 10
3	1. Turn OFF the ignition. 2. Turn ON the ignition, with the engine OFF. 3. Observe the Traction Off indicator on the instrument panel cluster (IPC) during the bulb check. Does the Traction Off indicator illuminate during the bulb check and then turn OFF?	Go to Step 4	Go to Step 11

LTV0500000005855

**Fig. 47 Traction Off Indicator Inoperative
(Part 1 of 3)**

11	Inspect for poor connections at the harness connector of the instrument panel cluster (IPC). Did you find and correct the condition?	Go to Step 16	Go to Step 15
12	Replace the rear integration module (RIM). Did you complete the replacement?	Go to Step 16	--
13	Replace the traction control switch. Did you complete the replacement?	Go to Step 16	--
14	Replace the EBCM. Did you complete the repair?	Go to Step 16	--
15	Replace the instrument panel cluster (IPC). Did you complete the repair?	Go to Step 16	--
16	Operate the system in order to verify the repair. Did you correct the condition?	System OK	Go to Step 2

LTV0500000005857

**Fig. 47 Traction Off Indicator Inoperative
(Part 3 of 3)**

Circuit Description

The vehicle stability enhancement system (VSES) is activated by the electronic brake control module (EBCM) calculating the desired yaw rate and comparing it to the actual yaw rate input. The desired yaw rate is calculated from measured steering wheel position, vehicle speed, and lateral acceleration. The difference between the desired yaw rate and actual yaw rate is the yaw rate error, which is a measurement of oversteer or understeer. If the yaw rate error becomes too large, the EBCM will attempt to correct the vehicle's yaw motion by applying differential braking to the left or right front wheel.

Test Description

The numbers below refer to the step numbers on the diagnostic table.

3. Perform the Steering Position Sensor Test in order to verify if the steering wheel position sensor (SWPS) is operating properly.

4. Verify that the lateral accelerometer input parameter is within the valid range.

5. Verify that the yaw rate input parameter is within the valid range.

Step	Action	Value(s)	Yes	No
1	Did you perform the Diagnostic System Check - ABS?	--	Go to Step 2	Go to Diagnostic System Check - ABS
2	1. Install a scan tool. 2. Start the engine. 3. Observe the VSES Is Centered parameter in the VSES data list. 4. Perform the Diagnostic Test Drive. Did the scan tool display Yes within the specified value?	30 seconds	Test for Intermittent and Poor Connections	Go to Step 3
3	With the scan tool, perform the Steering Position Sensor Test. Did the SWPS pass the test?	--	Go to Step 4	Go to Step 7

LTV0500000005858

Fig. 48   Vehicle Stability Enhancement System Inoperative (Part 1 of 2)

Circuit Description

The vehicle stability enhancement system (VSES) is activated by the electronic brake control module (EBCM) calculating the desired yaw rate and comparing it to the actual yaw rate input. The desired yaw rate is calculated from measured steering wheel position, vehicle speed, and lateral acceleration. The difference between the desired yaw rate and actual yaw rate is the yaw rate error, which is a measurement of oversteer or understeer. If the yaw rate error becomes too large, the EBCM will attempt to correct the vehicle's yaw motion by applying differential braking to the left or right front wheel.

Test Description

The number below refers to the step number on the diagnostic table.

6. Perform the Steering Position Sensor Test in order to verify if the steering wheel position sensor (SWPS) is operating properly.

Step	Action	Value (s)	Yes	No
1	Did you perform the ABS Diagnostic System Check?	--	Go to Step 2	Go to Diagnostic System Check -
2	Inspect the mounting of the yaw rate/lateral accelerometer sensor. Did you find and correct the condition?	--	Go to Step 15	Go to Step 3
3	1. Install a scan tool. 2. Start the engine. 3. With a scan tool, observe the Yaw Rate Sensor Input parameter in the VSES data list. 4. Perform the Diagnostic Test Drive. Does the scan tool display suddenly increase or decrease without rapid turning of the vehicle?	--	Go to Step 4	Go to Step 5

LTV0500000005860

Fig. 49   Vehicle Stability Enhancement System Unwanted Activation (Part 1 of 3)

Step	Action	Value(s)	Yes	No
4	With a scan tool, observe the Lateral Accelerometer Input parameter in the VSES data list. Does the scan tool display within the specified range?	2.3-2.7 V	Go to Step 5	Go to Step 8
5	With a scan tool, observe the Yaw Rate Sensor Input parameter in the VSES data list. Does the scan tool display within the specified range?	2.3-2.7 V	Go to Step 6	Go to Step 8
6	Replace the EBCM. Did you complete the replacement?	--	Go to Step 9	--
7	Replace the steering wheel position sensor (SWPS). Did you complete the replacement?	--	Go to Step 9	--
8	Replace the yaw rate/lateral accelerometer sensor. Did you complete the replacement?	--	Go to Step 9	--
9	Operate the system in order to verify the repair. Did you correct the condition?	--	System OK	Go to Step 2

LTV0500000005859

Fig. 48   Vehicle Stability Enhancement System Inoperative (Part 2 of 2)

Step	Action	Value(s)	Yes	No
4	Perform the diagnosis for DTC C0252. Refer to DTC C0252. Did you find and correct the condition?	--	Go to Step 15	Go to Step 12
5	1. Straighten the front wheels. 2. Observe the Dual Analog SWPS Input A and Dual Analog SWPS Input B in the DRP/ABS/TCS data list. 3. Slowly rotate the steering wheel in both directions. Does the scan tool display change states as the steering wheel was rotated?	--	Go to Step 6	Go to Step 14
6	With the scan tool, perform the Steering Position Sensor Test. Did the SWPS pass the test?	--	Go to Step 7	Go to Step 14
7	1. Place the vehicle on a level surface. 2. With a scan tool, observe the Lateral Accelerometer Input parameter in the VSES data list. Does the scan tool display within the specified range?	2.3-2.7 V	Go to Step 9	Go to Step 8
8	Replace the yaw rate/lateral accelerometer sensor. Did you find and correct the condition?	--	Go to Step 15	Go to Step 9
9	Inspect the EBCM for the proper part number. Did you find the correct part number?	--	Go to Step 10	Go to Step 12
10	Inspect the power steering gear for the proper part number. Did you find the correct part number?	--	Go to Step 11	Go to Step 13

LTV0500000005861

Fig. 49   Vehicle Stability Enhancement System Unwanted Activation (Part 2 of 3)

Step	Action	Value(s)	Yes	No
11	Inspect the alignment of the vehicle. Did you find and correct the condition?	--	Go to Step 15	Test for Intermittent and Poor Connections
12	Replace the EBCM. Did you complete the repair?	--	Go to Step 15	--
13	Replace the power steering gear. Did you complete the repair?	--	Go to Step 15	--
14	Replace the steering wheel position sensor (SWPS). Did you complete the repair?	--	Go to Step 15	--
15	Operate the system in order to verify the repair. Did you correct the condition?	--	System OK	Go to Step 2

LTV0500000005862

Fig. 49   Vehicle Stability Enhancement System Unwanted Activation (Part 3 of 3)

Circuit Description

The vehicle stability enhancement system (VSES) is activated by the electronic brake control module (EBCM) calculating the desired yaw rate and comparing it to the actual yaw rate input. The desired yaw rate is calculated from measured steering wheel position, vehicle speed, and lateral acceleration. The difference between the desired yaw rate and actual yaw rate is the yaw rate error, which is a measurement of oversteer or understeer. If the yaw rate error becomes too large, the EBCM will attempt to correct the vehicle's yaw motion by applying differential braking to the left or right front wheel.

Test Description

The numbers below refer to the step numbers on the diagnostic table.

3. Perform the Steering Position Sensor Test in order to verify if the steering wheel position sensor (SWPS) is operating properly.

4. Verify that the lateral accelerometer input parameter is within the valid range.

5. Verify that the yaw rate input parameter is within the valid range.

Step	Action	Value(s)	Yes	No
1	Did you perform the Diagnostic System Check - ABS?	--	Go to Step 2	Go to Diagnostic System Check -
2	1. Install a scan tool. 2. Start the engine. 3. Observe the VSES Is Centered parameter in the VSES data list. 4. Perform the Diagnostic Test Drive. Did the scan tool display Yes within the specified value?	30 seconds		Go to Step 3
3	With the scan tool, perform the With the scan tool, perform the Steering Position Sensor Test. Did the SWPS pass the test?	--	Go to Step 4	Go to Step 7

LTV0500000005863

Fig. 50 Vehicle Stability Enhancement System Excessive Brake Pulsation (Part 1 of 2)

	Action	Value(s)	Yes	No
4	With a scan tool, observe the Lateral Accelerometer Input parameter in the VSES data list. Does the scan tool display within the specified range?	2.3-2.7 V	Go to Step 5	Go to Step 8
5	With a scan tool, observe the Yaw Rate Sensor Input parameter in the VSES data list. Does the scan tool display within the specified range?	2.3-2.7 V	Go to Step 6	Go to Step 8
6	Replace the EBCM. Did you complete the replacement?	--	Go to Step 9	--
7	Replace the steering wheel position sensor (SWPS). Did you complete the replacement?	--	Go to Step 9	--
8	Replace the yaw rate/lateral accelerometer sensor. Did you complete the replacement?	--	Go to Step 9	--
9	Operate the system in order to verify the repair. Did you correct the condition?	--	System OK	Go to Step 2

LTV0500000005864

Fig. 50 Vehicle Stability Enhancement System Excessive Brake Pulsation (Part 2 of 2)

°C	°F	OHMS
		Temperature vs Resistance Values (Approximate)
150	302	47
140	284	60
130	266	77
120	248	100
110	230	132
100	212	177
90	194	241
80	176	332
70	158	467
60	140	667
50	122	973
45	113	1188
40	104	1459
35	95	1802
30	86	2238
25	77	2796
20	68	3520
15	59	4450
10	50	5670
5	41	7280
0	32	9420
-5	23	12300
-10	14	16180
-15	5	21450
-20	-4	28680
-30	-22	52700
-40	-40	100700

LTV0500000005865

Fig. 51 Temperature vs. resistance values

Delphi 7.4

NOTE: On Air Bag Equipped Models, Refer To "Air Bag System Precautions" Located In The Front Of This Manual For System Disarming & Arming Procedures.

NOTE: Electrical Symbol & Wire Color Code Identification Located In The Front Of This Manual May Be Used As An Aid When Using Wiring Circuits Found In This Section.

NOTE: Refer To "Computer Relearn Procedures" Located In The Front Of This Manual For Computer Relearn Procedures.

INDEX

	Page No.		Page No.		Page No.
Description	5-144	Intermittents & Poor		Brake System Bleed	5-145
Diagnosis & Testing	5-144	Connections	5-144	Component Replacement	5-145
Accessing Diagnostic Trouble		Symptom Tests	5-144	Brake Pressure Modulator	
Codes	5-144	Temperature Vs. Resistance	5-144	Valve (BPMV)	5-145
Clearing Diagnostic Trouble		Wiring Diagrams	5-144	Electronic Brake Control	
Codes	5-145	**Diagnostic Chart Index**	5-149	Module (EBCM)	5-145
Connector Pin Identification	5-144	**Precautions**	5-144	Traction Control Switch	5-145
Diagnostic Tests	5-144	Air Bag Systems	5-144	Wheel Speed Sensor	5-145
Diagnostic Trouble Code		Battery Ground Cable	5-144	Yaw Rate Sensor/Lateral	
Interpretation	5-144	**System Service**	5-145	Accelerometer	5-145

PRECAUTIONS

Air Bag Systems

Refer to "Air Bag System Precautions" in the front of this manual for system disarming and arming procedures.

Battery Ground Cable

Prior to service disconnect battery ground cable and isolate as required.

DESCRIPTION

When wheel slip is detected during a brake application, the ABS enters anti-lock mode. During anti-lock braking, hydraulic pressure in the individual wheel circuits is controlled to prevent any wheel from slipping. A separate hydraulic line and specific solenoid valves are provided for each wheel. The ABS can decrease, hold, or increase hydraulic pressure to each wheel brake. The ABS cannot, however, increase hydraulic pressure above the amount which is transmitted by the master cylinder during braking.

During anti-lock braking, a series of rapid pulsations is felt in the brake pedal. These pulsations are caused by the rapid changes in position of the individual solenoid valves as the EBCM responds to wheel speed sensor inputs and attempts to prevent wheel slip. These pedal pulsations are present only during anti-lock braking and stop when normal braking is resumed or when the vehicle comes to a stop. A ticking or popping noise may also be heard as the solenoid valves cycle rapidly. During anti-lock braking on dry pavement, intermittent chirping noises may be heard as the tires approach slipping. These noises and pedal pulsations are considered normal during anti-lock operation.

Vehicles equipped with ABS may be stopped by applying normal force to the brake pedal. Brake pedal operation during normal braking is no different than that of previous non-ABS systems. Maintaining a constant force on the brake pedal provides the shortest stopping distance while maintaining vehicle stability.

DIAGNOSIS & TESTING

Accessing Diagnostic Trouble Codes

Connect a suitably programmed scan tool to Data Link Connector (DLC) and follow manufacturers instructions.

Diagnostic Trouble Code Interpretation

Refer to "Diagnostic Chart Index" for diagnostic trouble code interpretation.

Connector Pin Identification

Refer to **Figs. 1 through 7** for connector pin identification.

Wiring Diagrams

Refer to **Fig. 8** for wiring diagrams.

Diagnostic Tests

Refer to **Figs. 9 through 32** for diagnostic test procedures.

Symptom Tests

Refer to **Figs. 33 through 37** for symptom test procedures.

Temperature Vs. Resistance

Refer to **Fig. 38** for temperature vs. resistance values.

Intermittents & Poor Connections

Most Intermittents are caused by faulty electrical connections or wiring, although a sticking relay or solenoid can also cause an intermittent condition. Inspect wiring and connectors for the following:
1. Poor mating of connector halves, or terminals not fully seated in connector body.
2. Dirt or corrosion on terminals.
3. Damaged connector body.
4. Improperly formed or damaged terminals.
5. Poor terminal to wire connection.
6. Rubbed through wiring insulation.
7. Wiring broken inside insulation.

Clearing Diagnostic Trouble Codes

Connect a suitably programmed scan tool to Data Link Connector (DLC) and follow manufacturers instructions.

SYSTEM SERVICE

Brake System Bleed

Refer to "Delphi 7.0" system for brake bleed procedures.

Component Replacement

ELECTRONIC BRAKE CONTROL MODULE (EBCM)

Always connect or disconnect the wiring harness connector from the EBCM/EBTCM with the ignition switch in the Off position. Failure to observe this precaution could result in damage to the EBCM/EBTCM.
1. Turn ignition switch to Off position.
2. Remove air cleaner assembly from engine compartment.
3. Disconnect EBCM harness connector.
4. Brush off any dirt or debris that has accumulated on assembly.
5. Disconnect pump motor connector at bottom of EBCM.
6. Remove EBCM to BPMV screws.
7. Separate EBCM from BPMV by gently pulling apart until separated.
8. Reverse procedure to install, noting the following:
   a. **Torque** top four mounting screws to 44 inch lbs., in an X pattern.
   b. **Torque** bottom two mounting screws to 44 inch lbs.
   c. If a new EBCM was installed, EBCM must be programmed using a suitably programmed scan tool.
   d. Turn ignition switch to Run position, do not start engine.
   e. Perform "Diagnostic System Check" as outlined in "Diagnostic Tests."

BRAKE PRESSURE MODULATOR VALVE (BPMV)

For safety reasons, the Brake Pressure Modulator Valve (BPMV) must not be repaired; the complete unit must be replaced. With the exception of the EBCM/EBTCM, no screws may be loosened. If screws are loosened, it will not be possible to get the brake circuits leak-tight and personal injury may result.
1. Turn ignition switch to Off position.
2. Remove air cleaner assembly from engine compartment.
3. Disconnect EBCM harness connector.
4. Disconnect four wheel brake pipes and two master cylinder pipes from BPMV.
5. Cover open pipes to avoid dripping of brake fluid or contamination of brake system.

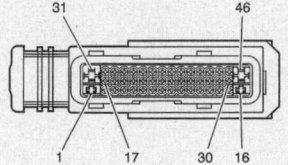

Connector Part Information

- OEM: 15487791
- Service: See Catalog
- Description: 46-Way F Receptacle 1.5, 2.8, 4.8 Series Sealed (BK)

Terminal Part Information

- Pins: 1, 12-16, 24-28, 39-43
- Terminal: 60012931/Tray 21
- Core/Insulation Crimp: Pins 1, 12-16: C/1
- Core/Insulation Crimp: Pins 24-28, 39-43: 2/1
- Release Tool/Test Probe: 12122378/J-35616-4A

- Pins: 5-11, 18-23, 29, 34-38, 44
- Terminal: 60000611/Tray 21
- Core/Insulation Crimp: 8/8
- Release Tool/Test Probe: 15314260/J-35616-2A

- Pins: 31, 46
- Terminal: 60040461/Tray 21
- Core/Insulation Crimp: D/3
- Release Tool/Test Probe: 12093647/J-35616-40

Electronic Brake Control Module (EBCM)

Pin	Wire Color	Circuit No.	Function
1	BK/WH	251	Ground
2-4	--	--	Not Used
5	D-GN/WH	2087	5-Volt Reference (JL4)
6	--	--	Not Used
7	L-BU	910	Yaw Rate Sensor Signal (JL4)
8-10	--	--	Not Used

LTV050000005866

Fig. 1   Connector pin identification (EBCM - Part 1 of 2)

6. Remove BPMV mounting bracket nuts from inner wheel housing mount surface of strut tower.
7. Reinstall top nut upside down on top stud.
8. Lightly tap on bottom of nut until stud has loosened up.
9. Remove BPMV mounting bracket and EBCM assembly from vehicle.
10. Remove bolt that connects BPMV to mounting bracket.
11. Lift BPMV off mounting bracket studs.
12. Remove EBCM, if replacing BPMV only.
13. Reverse procedure to install, noting the following:
   a. **Torque** BPMV assembly to the mounting bracket to 89 inch lbs.
   b. **Torque** three nuts to BPMV mounting bracket to strut tower 89 inch lbs.
   c. **Torque** master cylinder brake pipes into BPMV to 18 ft. lbs.
   d. **Torque** wheel brake pipes on BPMV to 18 ft. lbs.
   e. Perform "ABS Automated Bleed" as outlined in "Brake System Bleed."

WHEEL SPEED SENSOR

The wheel speed sensors and rings are integral with the hub and bearing assemblies. If a speed sensor or a ring needs replacement, replace the entire hub and bearing assembly.
1. Remove hub and bearing assembly as outlined in appropriate chassis chapter.
2. Reverse procedure to install, noting the following:

a. Install hub and bearing assembly to vehicle.
b. Turn ignition switch to On position, with engine Off.
c. Perform "Diagnostic System Check" as outlined in "Diagnostic Tests."

TRACTION CONTROL SWITCH

1. Remove instrument panel accessory trim panel.
2. Remove five instrument panel accessory trim panel clips.
3. Remove outlet assembly from instrument panel A/C center.
4. Remove driver information center display switch screw.
5. Remove traction control switch assembly.
6. Reverse procedure to install.

YAW RATE SENSOR/ LATERAL ACCELEROMETER

1. Remove front floor console reinforcement.
2. Disconnect electrical connector from yaw rate sensor.
3. Remove nuts retaining yaw rate sensor.
4. Remove yaw rate sensor from console bracket.
5. Reverse procedure to install. **Torque** yaw rate sensor nuts to 80 inch lbs.

11	L-BU	1122	Class 2 Serial Data
12	OG	885	Left Rear Wheel Speed Sensor Low Reference
13	TN	884	Left Rear Wheel Speed Sensor Signal
14-15	--	--	Not Used
16	PK	1039	Ignition 1 Voltage
17	--	--	Not Used
18	TN/BK	464	Delivered Torque Signal
19	D-GN	2087	5-Volt Reference (JL4)
20-22	--	--	Not Used
23	L-GN	1338	Lateral Accelerometer Signal (JL4)
24	TN	833	Right Front Wheel Speed Sensor Low Reference
25-26	--	--	Not Used
27	L-BU	830	Left Front Wheel Speed Sensor Signal
28	YE	873	Left Front Wheel Speed Sensor Low Reference
29	L-BU/WH	2088	Low Reference (JL4)
30	--	--	Not Used
31	BK/WH	251	Ground
32-33	--	--	Not Used
34	L-GN	1763	Steering Wheel Position Signal A (JL4)
35	L-BU	1764	Steering Wheel Position Signal B (JL4)
36-37	--	--	Not Used
38	OG/BK	463	Requested Torque Signal
39	D-GN	872	Right Front Wheel Speed Sensor Signal
40	--	--	Not Used
41	L-GN	526	Stop Lamp Supply Voltage
42	BN	882	Right Rear Wheel Speed Sensor Signal
43	WH	883	Right Rear Wheel Speed Sensor Low Reference
44	L-BU	2088	Low Reference (JL4)
45	--	--	Not Used
46	RD/BK	1442	Battery Positive Voltage

LTV0500000005867

Fig. 1 Connector pin identification (EBCM - Part 2 of 2)

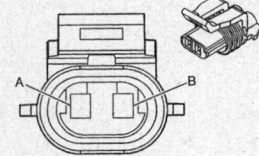

Connector Part Information

- OEM: 12052644
- Service: See Catalog
- Description: 2-Way F Metri-Pack 150 Series Sealed (GY)

Terminal Part Information

- Terminal: 12048074/Tray 2
- Core/Insulation Crimp: E/1
- Release Tool/Test Probe: 12094429/J-35616-2A

Pin	Wire Color	Circuit No.	Function
A	L-BU	830	Left Front Wheel Speed Sensor Signal
B	YE	873	Left Front Wheel Speed Sensor Low Reference

LTV0500000005869

Fig. 3 Connector pin identification (Lefthand front WSS)

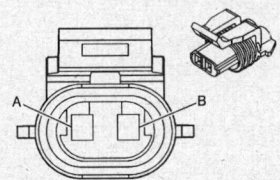

Connector Part Information

- OEM: 12052644
- Service: See Catalog
- Description: 2-Way F Metri-Pack 150 Series Sealed (GY)

Terminal Part Information

- Terminal: 12048074/Tray 2
- Core/Insulation Crimp: E/1
- Release Tool/Test Probe: 12094429/J-35616-2A

Pin	Wire Color	Circuit No.	Function
A	D-GN	872	Right Front Wheel Speed Sensor Signal
B	TN	833	Right Front Wheel Speed Sensor Low Reference

LTV0500000005871

Fig. 5 Connector pin identification (Righthand front WSS)

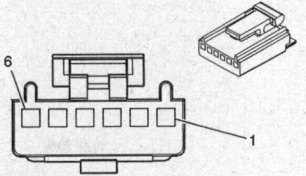

Connector Part Information

- OEM: 12064978
- Service: 12125678
- Description: 6-Way F Micro-Pack 100 Series (GY)

Terminal Part Information

- Terminal: 12144647/Tray 3
- Core/Insulation Crimp: See Terminal Repair Kit
- Release Tool/Test Probe: See Terminal Repair Kit

Pin	Wire Color	Circuit No.	Function
1	D-GN	2087	5-Volt Reference
2	L-BU	2088	Low Reference
3-4	--	--	Not Used
5	L-GN	1763	Steering Wheel Position Signal A
6	L-BU	1764	Steering Wheel Position Signal B

LTV0500000005868

Fig. 2 Connector pin identification (Steering wheel speed position sensor JL4)

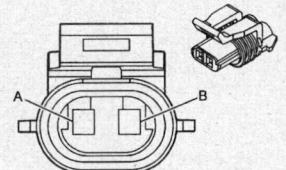

Connector Part Information

- OEM: 12052644
- Service: See Catalog
- Description: 2-Way F Metri-Pack 150 Series Sealed (GY)

Terminal Part Information

- Terminal: 12048074/Tray 2
- Core/Insulation Crimp: E/1
- Release Tool/Test Probe: 12094429/J-35616-2A

Pin	Wire Color	Circuit No.	Function
A	WH	883	Left Rear Wheel Speed Sensor Low Reference (F46)
A	BN	882	Left Rear Wheel Speed Sensor Signal (w/o F46)
B	BK	882	Left Rear Wheel Speed Sensor Signal (F46)
B	WH	883	Left Rear Wheel Speed Sensor Low Reference (w/o F46)

LTV0500000005870

Fig. 4 Connector pin identification (Lefthand rear WSS)

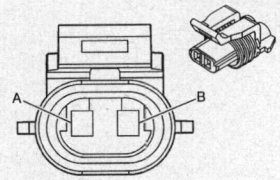

Connector Part Information

- OEM: 12052644
- Service: See Catalog
- Description: 2-Way F Metri-Pack 150 Series Sealed (GY)

Terminal Part Information

- Terminal: 12048074/Tray 2
- Core/Insulation Crimp: E/1
- Release Tool/Test Probe: 12094429/J-35616-2A

Pin	Wire Color	Circuit No.	Function
A	WH	883	Right Rear Wheel Speed Sensor Low Reference (F46)
A	BN	882	Right Rear Wheel Speed Sensor Signal (w/o F46)
B	BK	882	Right Rear Wheel Speed Sensor Signal (F46)
B	WH	883	Right Rear Wheel Speed Sensor Low Reference (w/o F46)

LTV0500000005872

Fig. 6 Connector pin identification (Righthand rear WSS)

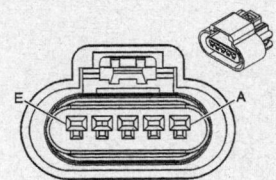

Connector Part Information

- OEM: 15326822
- Service: 88987186
- Description: 5-Way F GT 150 Series Sealed 4.0 (BK)

Terminal Part Information

- Terminal: 12191819/Tray 8
- Core/Insulation Crimp: See Terminal Repair Kit
- Release Tool/Test Probe: See Terminal Repair Kit

Yaw Rate and Lateral Acceleration Sensor (JL4)

Pin	Wire Color	Circuit No.	Function
A	--	--	Not Used
B	D-GN	2087	5-Volt Reference
C	L-BU	910	Yaw Rate Sensor Signal
D	L-BU	2088	Low Reference
E	L-GN/BK	1338	Lateral Accelerometer Signal

LTV0500000C05873

Fig. 7 Connector pin identification (Yaw rate & lateral acceleration sensor JL4)

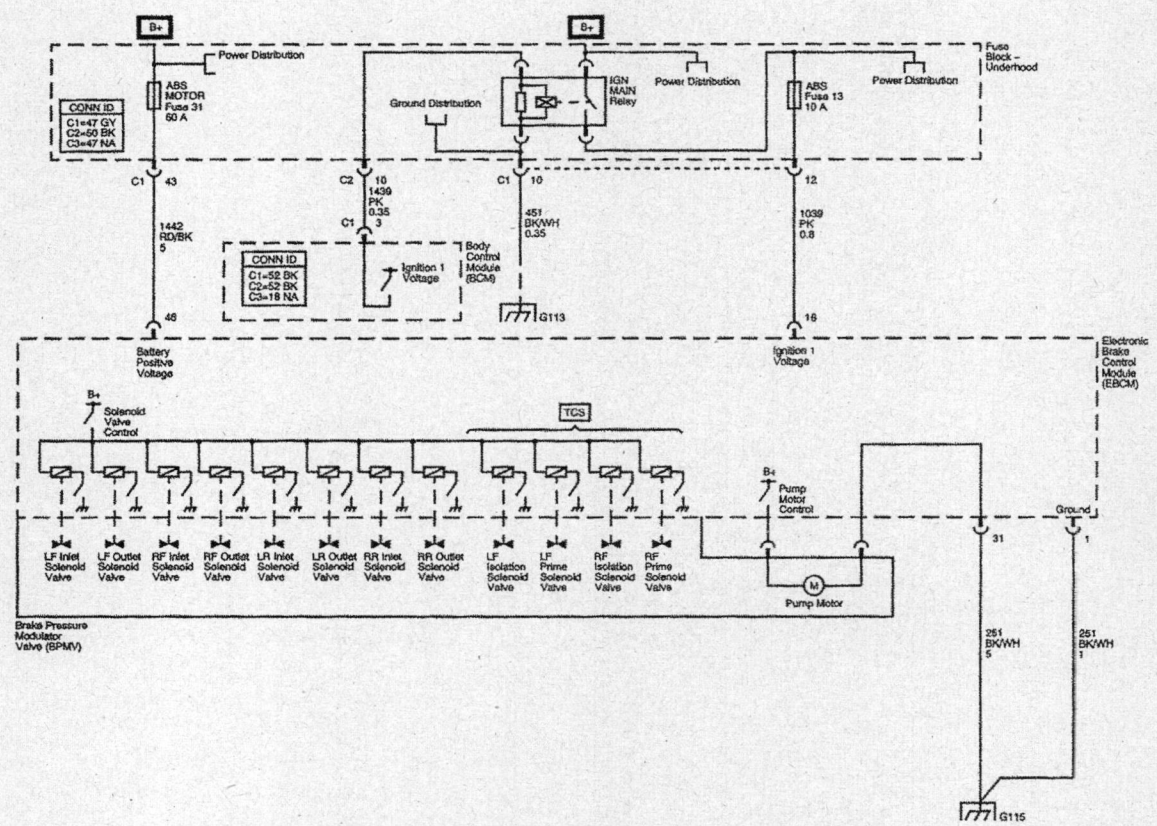

LTV0500000005874

Fig. 8 Wiring diagram (Part 1 of 4)

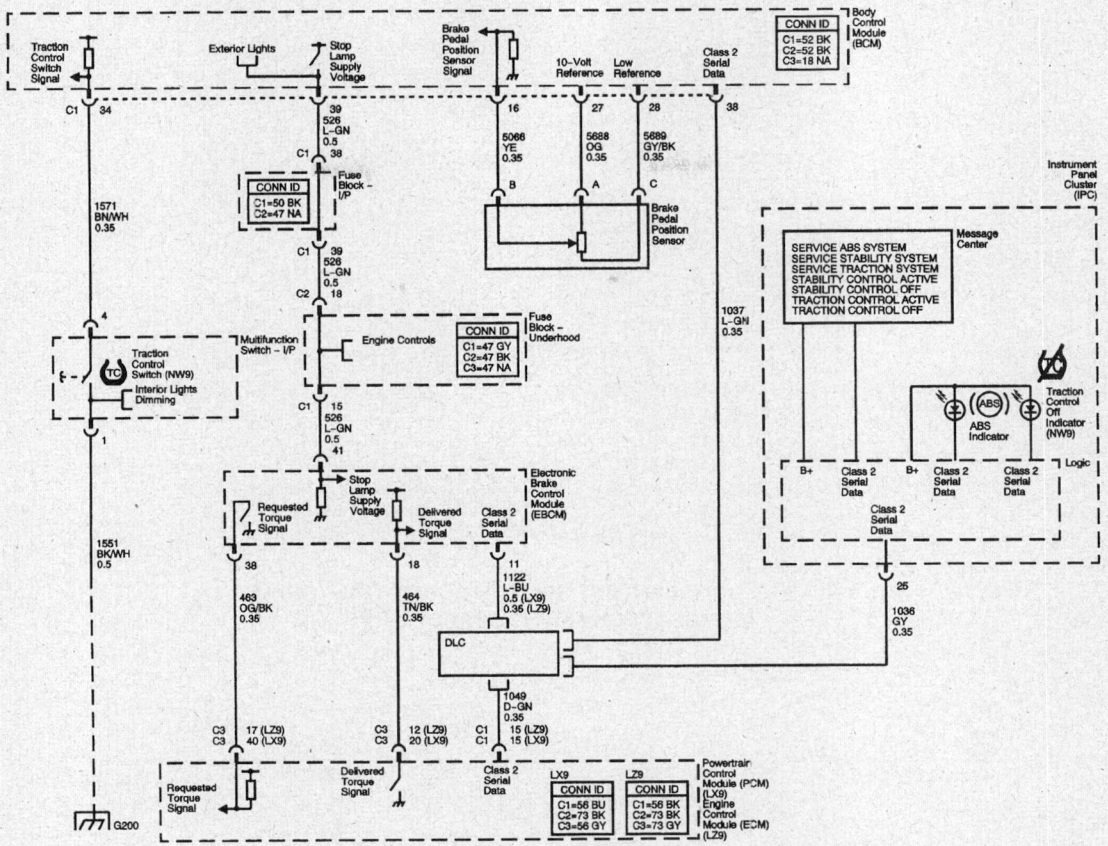

Fig. 8   Wiring diagram (Part 2 of 4)

LTV050000005875

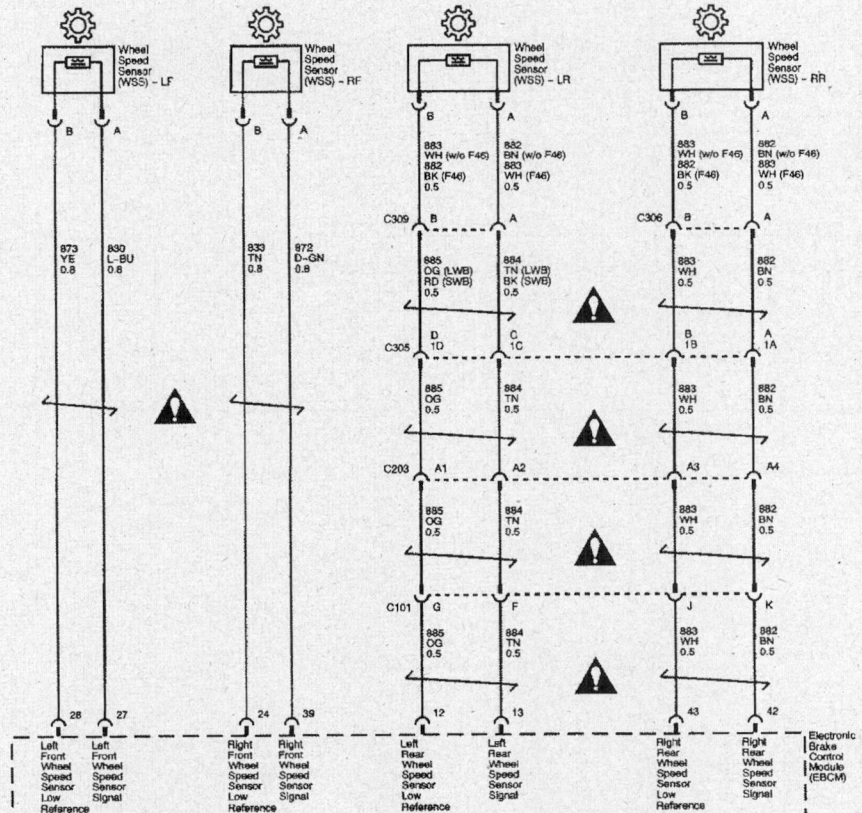

Fig. 8   Wiring diagram (Part 3 of 4)

LTV050000005876

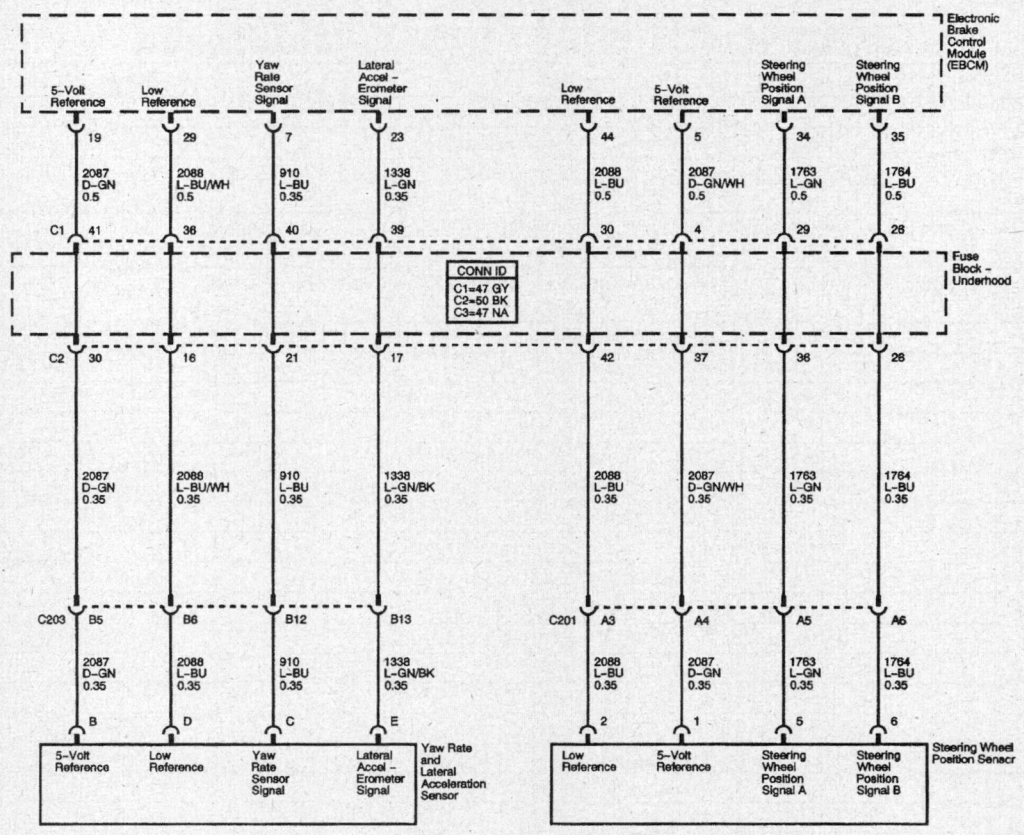

Fig. 8   Wiring diagram (Part 4 of 4)

LTV0500000005877

DIAGNOSTIC CHART INDEX

Code	Description	Page No.	Fig. No.
—	Diagnostic System Check	5-151	9
—	ABS Indicator Always On	5-167	33
—	ABS Indicator Inoperative	5-167	34
—	Traction Off Indicator Always On	5-167	35
—	Traction Off Indicator Inoperative	5-168	36
—	Vehicle Stability Enhancement System Poor Performance	5-168	37
C0035	Lefthand Front Wheel Speed Sensor Circuit	5-151	10
C0036	Lefthand Front Wheel Speed Sensor Circuit Range/Performance	5-151	10
C0037	Lefthand Front Wheel Speed Sensor Circuit Low	5-151	10
C0040	Righthand Front Wheel Speed Sensor Circuit	5-151	10
C0041	Righthand Front Wheel Speed Sensor Circuit Range/Performance	5-151	10
C0042	Righthand Front Wheel Speed Sensor Circuit Low	5-151	10
C0045	Lefthand Rear Wheel Speed Sensor Circuit	5-151	10
C0046	Lefthand Rear Wheel Speed Sensor Circuit Range/Performance	5-151	10
C0047	Lefthand Rear Wheel Speed Sensor Circuit Low	5-151	10
C0050	Righthand Rear Wheel Speed Sensor Circuit	5-151	10
C0051	Righthand Rear Wheel Speed Sensor Circuit Range/Performance	5-151	10
C0052	Righthand Rear Wheel Speed Sensor Circuit Low	5-151	10
C0111	Pump Motor Circuit Range/Performance	5-152	11
C0113	Pump Motor Circuit High	5-152	11
C0114	Pump Motor Circuit Open	5-152	11
C0115	Pump Motor Performance	5-152	11
C0120	Pump Motor Relay Circuit Open	5-152	11
C0121	Valve Relay Circuit	5-153	12
C0131	ABS Pressure Circuit	5-154	13
C0136	Brake System Pressure Circuit Sensor	5-154	13

Continued

DIAGNOSTIC CHART INDEX—Continued

Code	Description	Page No.	Fig. No.
C0138	Brake System Pressure Circuit Sensor Low	5-154	13
C0139	Brake System Pressure Circuit Sensor High	5-154	13
C0163	Anti-Lock Brake System (ABS)/Traction Control System (TCS) Brake Switch Sensor Circuit Low	5-155	14
C0164	Anti-Lock Brake System (ABS)/Traction Control System (TCS) Brake Switch Sensor Circuit High	5-155	14
C0165	Anti-Lock Brake System (ABS)/Traction Control System (TCS) Brake Switch Sensor Circuit Open	5-155	14
C0179	System Thermal High	5-155	15
C0186	Lateral Accelerometer Circuit	5-156	16
C0187	Lateral Accelerometer Circuit Range/Performance	5-156	16
C0196	Yaw Rate Circuit	5-157	17
C0220	Lefthand Front ABS Channel In Release Too Long	5-158	18
C0221	Righthand Front ABS Channel In Release Too Long	5-158	18
C0228	Lefthand Rear ABS Channel In Release Too Long	5-158	18
C0229	Righthand Rear ABS Channel In Release Too Long	5-158	18
C0241	PCM Indicated Requested Torque Fault	5-158	19
C0242	PCM Indicated TCS Fault	5-159	20
C0244	Pulse Width Modulated (PWM) Delivered Torque	5-159	21
C0252	Vehicle Speed Enhancement System (VSES) Sensor Uncorrelated	5-160	22
C0253	Centering Error	5-161	23
C0254	Steering Sensor Lateral Accelerometer Bias	5-161	23
C0281	Dynamic Rear Proportioning Performance	5-162	24
C0460	Steering Position Sensor	5-162	25
C0461	Steering Position Sensor Range/Performance	5-162	25
C0550	ECU Performance	5-163	26
C0561	System Disabled Information Stored	5-163	27
C0870	Device Voltage Reference Output Circuit	5-164	28
C0899	Device Voltage Low	5-164	29
C0900	Device Voltage High	5-165	30
C1100	Base Brake System Pressure Sensor 2	5-166	31
C1101	Base Brake System Pressure Sensor 2 Range	5-166	32
P0856	Traction Control Torque Request Circuit	5-158	19
P1689	Traction Control Delivered Torque Output Circuit	5-159	21

Test Description

The numbers below refer to the step numbers on the diagnostic table.

1. This step ensures that the battery, and the vehicle primary power and ground systems are functioning correctly.

3. Lack of communication may be due to a particular malfunction of a serial data circuit. The information in Scan Tool does not Communicate with Class 2 Device will provide a list of modules and the associated data network no communication diagnostic link.

4. A module that is operating in the incorrect power mode based on key position may cause other vehicle symptoms and/or DTCs to set. The information in Power Mode Mismatch will correct the condition before checking for module DTCs or symptoms.

8. This step ensures that all data link communication DTCs are diagnosed before system level DTCs.

9. This step ensures that all electronic control unit (ECU) internal DTCs are diagnosed before other system level DTCs.

10. This step ensures that all device voltage DTCs are diagnosed before other system level DTCs.

Step	Action	Yes	No
1	Perform the following preliminary inspections: • Ensure that the battery is fully charged. • Ensure that the battery cables are clean and tight. • Inspect for any open fuses. • Inspect the easily accessible systems or the visible system components for obvious damage or conditions that could cause the symptom. • Ensure that the grounds are clean, tight, and in the correct location. • Inspect for aftermarket devices that could affect the operation of the system. • Search for applicable service bulletins. Did you find and correct the condition?	System OK	Go to Step 2
2	Install a scan tool. Does the scan tool power up?	Go to Step 3	Diagnose Scan Tool Does Not Power Up

LTV0500000005878

Fig. 9   Diagnostic System Check (Part 1 of 3)

Step	Action	Yes	No
8	Does the scan tool display any DTCs that begin with a "U"?	Go to Diagnostic Trouble Code (DTC) List	Go to Step 9
9	**Important:** If any of these DTCs are displayed, diagnose them before diagnosing any other DTCs or symptoms. Does the scan tool display DTC B1000, B1001, B1004, B1007, B1009, B1013, B1290, C0550, P0601, P0602, P0603, P0604, P0606, P0607, P060D, P062F, P2107, P2108, or P2610?	Go to Diagnostic Trouble Code (DTC) List	Go to Step 10
10	**Important:** If any of these DTCs are displayed, diagnose them before diagnosing any other DTCs or symptoms. Does the scan tool display DTC B1327, B1328, B1370, B1390, B1420, C0899, C0900, P0560, P0562, or P0563?	Go to Diagnostic Trouble Code (DTC) List	Go to Step 11
11	**Important:** If any of the remaining DTCs are powertrain DTCs, select Capture Info in order to store the powertrain DTC information with a scan tool. If multiple DTCs are stored, diagnose the DTCs in the following order: 1. Component level DTCs, such as sensor DTCs, solenoid DTCs, and relay DTCs. 2. System level DTCs, such as misfire DTCs, evaporative emission (EVAP) system DTCs, and fuel trim DTCs. Diagnose the remaining DTCs.	Go to Diagnostic Trouble Code (DTC) List	--
12	Is the customers concern with inspection/maintenance (I/M) testing?	Go to Inspection/Maintenance (I/M) System Check	Go to Symptoms

LTV0500000005880

Fig. 9   Diagnostic System Check (Part 3 of 3)

Step	Action	Yes	No
3	1. Turn ON the ignition, with the engine OFF. 2. Attempt to establish communication with all of the control modules on the vehicle. Does the scan tool communicate with all of the expected vehicle control modules?	Go to Step 4	Check Scan Tool Does Not Communicate with Class 2 Device
4	**Important:** • To ensure that retained accessory power (RAP) mode is inactive, if equipped, open the drivers door during the following step. • The engine may start during the following step. Turn OFF the engine as soon as you have observed the crank power mode. 1. Access the Power Mode parameter on the scan tool. 2. Rotate the ignition switch, operate the ignition mode switch, through all positions while observing the Power Mode parameter. Does the Power Mode parameter reading on the scan tool match the ignition switch position for all switch positions?	Go to Step 5	Check Power Mode Mismatch
5	Attempt to start the engine. Does the engine crank?	Go to Step 6	Go to Symptoms
6	Attempt to start the engine. Does the engine start and idle?	Go to Step 7	Go to Engine Cranks but Does Not Run for
7	**Important:** Do not clear any DTCs unless instructed by a diagnostic procedure. Use the appropriate scan tool selections to obtain DTCs for each of the control modules. Does the scan tool display any DTCs?	Go to Step 8	Go to Step 12

LTV0500000005879

Fig. 9   Diagnostic System Check (Part 2 of 3)

Circuit Description

As the wheel spins, the wheel speed sensor produces an AC signal. The electronic brake control module (EBCM) uses the frequency of the AC signal to calculate the wheel speed.

DTC Descriptors

This diagnostic procedure supports the following DTCs:

• DTC C0035 Left Front Wheel Speed Sensor Circuit
• DTC C0036 Left Front Wheel Speed Sensor Circuit Range/Performance
• DTC C0037 Left Front Wheel Speed Sensor Circuit Low
• DTC C0040 Right Front Wheel Speed Sensor Circuit
• DTC C0041 Right Front Wheel Speed Sensor Circuit Range/Performance
• DTC C0042 Right Front Wheel Speed Sensor Circuit Low
• DTC C0045 Left Rear Wheel Speed Sensor Circuit
• DTC C0046 Left Rear Wheel Speed Sensor Circuit Range/Performance
• DTC C0047 Left Rear Wheel Speed Sensor Circuit Low
• DTC C0050 Right Rear Wheel Speed Sensor Circuit
• DTC C0051 Right Rear Wheel Speed Sensor Circuit Range/Performance
• DTC C0052 Right Rear Wheel Speed Sensor Circuit Low

Conditions for Running the DTC

C0035, C0040, C0045, or C0050

The ignition is ON.

C0036, C0037, C0041, C0042, C0046, C0047, C0051, or C0052

• DTCs C0035, C0040, C0045, or C0050 are not set.
• The brake pedal is not pressed.
• The ABS is not active.
• At least two wheel speeds are not 0 km/h.

LTV0500000005881

Fig. 10   Codes C0035–C0052: Wheel Speed Sensor Circuit (Part 1 of 5)

Conditions for Setting the DTC

C0035, C0040, C0045, or C0050

The EBCM detects an open, short to ground or a short to power on the wheel speed sensor signal circuit or the low reference circuit.

C0036, C0041, C0046, or C0051

The EBCM detects a rapid variation in the wheel speed. The wheel speed changes by 16 km/h (10 mph) or more in 0.01 second. The change must occur 3 times with no more than 0.2 seconds between occurrences.

C0037, C0042, C0047, or C0052

- The suspect wheel speed equals zero.
- The other wheel speeds are greater than 8 km/h (5 mph).
- The other wheel speeds are within 11 km/h (7 mph) of each other.

Action Taken When the DTC Sets

If equipped, the following actions occur:

- The EBCM disables the ABS/TCS/vehicle stability enhancement system (VSES) for the duration of the ignition cycle.
- The dynamic rear proportion (DRP) does not function optimally.
- The ABS indicator turns ON.
- The Traction Control indicator turns ON.
- The driver information center (DIC) displays the Service Stability System message.

Conditions for Clearing the DTC

- The condition for the DTC is no longer present and the DTC is cleared with a scan tool.
- The EBCM automatically clears the history DTC when a current DTC is not detected in 100 consecutive drive cycles.

Diagnostic Aids

C0035, C0037, C0040, C0042, C0045, C0047, C0050 or C0052

If the customer comments that the ABS indicator is ON only during moist environmental conditions (rain, snow, vehicle wash, etc.), inspect the wheel speed sensor wiring for signs of water intrusion. If the DTC is not current, clear all DTCs and simulate the effects of water intrusion by using the following procedure:

LTV0500000005882

Fig. 10   Codes C0035–C0052: Wheel Speed Sensor Circuit (Part 2 of 5)

1. Spray the suspected area with a 5 percent saltwater solution. To create a 5 percent saltwater solution, add 2 teaspoons (9.9 ml) of salt to 354 ml (12 oz) of water.
2. Test drive the vehicle over various road surfaces (bumps, turns, etc.) above 40 km/h (25 mph) for at least 30 seconds.
3. If the DTC returns, replace the suspected wheel speed sensor or repair the wheel speed sensor wiring.
4. Rinse the area thoroughly when completed.

C0036, C0041, C0046, or C0051

A possible cause of this DTC is electrical noise on the wheel speed sensor harness wiring. Electrical noise could result from the wheel speed sensor wires being routed to close to high energy ignition system components, such as spark plug wires.

Test Description

The numbers below refer to the step numbers on the diagnostic table.

3. Measure the resistance of the wheel speed sensor in order to determine if the sensor has a valid resistance value.

4. Ensures that the wheel speed sensor is generating a valid AC voltage output.

LTV0500000005883

Fig. 10   Codes C0035–C0052: Wheel Speed Sensor Circuit (Part 3 of 5)

7	Inspect for poor connections at the harness connector for the EBCM. Did you find and correct the condition?	-	Go to Step 10	Go to Step 9
8	Replace the wheel speed sensor. Did you complete the replacement?	-	Go to Step 10	--
9	Replace the EBCM. Did you complete the replacement?	-	Go to Step 10	--
10	1. Use the scan tool in order to clear the DTCs. 2. Operate the vehicle within the Conditions for Running the DTC as specified in the supporting text. Does the DTC reset?	-	Go to Step 2	System OK

LTV0500000005885

Fig. 10   Codes C0035–C0052: Wheel Speed Sensor Circuit (Part 5 of 5)

Circuit Description

The electronic brake control module (EBCM) supplies ground to activate the Antilock Brake System (ABS) pump motor. An internal system relay in the EBCM supplies battery positive voltage to the pump motor when the ignition is turned ON. The EBCM monitors pump motor feedback voltage after activation to detect a stalled or binding pump motor.

DTC Descriptors

This diagnostic procedure supports the following DTCs:

- DTC C0111 Pump Motor Circuit Range/Performance
- DTC C0113 Pump Motor Circuit High
- DTC C0114 Pump Motor Circuit Open
- DTC C0115 Pump Motor Performance
- DTC C0120 Pump Motor Relay Circuit Open

Conditions for Running the DTC

C0111

- The ignition voltage is greater than 8 volts.
- The pump motor has been commanded OFF for longer than 1.4 seconds and then commanded ON.
- Voltage to the pump motor is greater than 11 volts when the pump motor is commanded ON.

C0113

- The ignition voltage is between 9.2-17 volts.
- The system enable relay is ON.

C0114

- The system voltage is between 10.1-17 volts.
- The ignition voltage is between 9.2-17 volts.
- The system enable relay is ON.
- The pump motor has been commanded OFF for 1.4 seconds.

C0115

- The system and ignition voltage is greater than 8 volts.

Step	Action	Values	Yes	No
1	Did you perform the Diagnostic System Check - Vehicle?	--	Go to Step 2	Go to Diagnostic System Check
2	1. Install a scan tool. 2. Turn ON the ignition. 3. Set up the scan tool snap shot feature to trigger for this DTC. 4. Drive the vehicle at a speed greater than the specified value. Does the scan tool indicate that this wheel speed DTC set?	8 km/h (5 mph)	Go to Step 3	Go to Diagnostic Aids
3	1. Raise and support the vehicle. 2. Disconnect the wheel speed sensor connector. 3. Measure the resistance across the wheel speed sensor. Does the resistance measure within the specified range?	850-1350 ohms	Go to Step 4	Go to Step 8
4	1. Spin the wheel. 2. Measure the A/C voltage across the wheel speed sensor. Does the A/C voltage measure greater than the specified value?	100 mV	Go to Step 5	Go to Step 8
5	Inspect for poor connections at the harness connector of the wheel speed sensor. Did you find and correct the condition?	--	Go to Step 10	Go to Step 6
6	1. Disconnect the electronic brake control module (EBCM) harness connector. 2. Test the wheel speed sensor circuits for the following: - An open - A short to ground - A short to voltage - Shorted together Refer to Circuit Testing and Wiring Repairs in Wiring Systems. Did you find and correct the condition?	--	Go to Step 10	Go to Step 7

LTV0500000005884

Fig. 10   Codes C0035–C0052: Wheel Speed Sensor Circuit (Part 4 of 5)

LTV0500000005886

Fig. 11   Codes C0111, C0113, C0114, C0115 & C0120: Pump Motor (Part 1 of 5)

- The system enable relay is ON.
- The pump motor is commanded ON.
- No other pump motor faults have been detected

C0120

- The system and ignition voltage is greater than 8 volts.
- The system enable relay is ON.
- The pump motor is commanded ON.

Conditions for Setting the DTC

C0111

The EBCM excessive current draw from the pump motor.

C0113

The EBCM detects an open in the pump motor ground circuit.

C0114

This code sets for a possible open in the pump motor.

C0115

The EBCM monitors pump motor feedback voltage after activation

C0120

This code sets for a possible open in the internal EBCM pump motor relay circuit.

Action Taken When the DTC Sets

If equipped, the following actions occur:

- The EBCM disables the ABS/Traction Control System (TCS)/Vehicle Stability Enhancement System (VSES) for the duration of the ignition cycle.
- The dynamic rear proportion (DRP) is degraded.
- The ABS indicator turns ON.
- The stability OFF indicator turns ON.

LTV0500000005887

Fig. 11   Codes C0111, C0113, C0114, C0115 & C0120: Pump Motor (Part 2 of 5)

Step	Action	Yes	No
1	Did you perform the Diagnostic System Check - Vehicle?	Go to Step 2	Go to Diagnostic System Check
2	1. Use the scan tool in order to clear the DTCs. 2. Cycle the ignition to the OFF position. 3. Start the engine. 4. In park or neutral, release the brake. 5. Turn OFF the engine. Does the DTC reset?	Go to Step 3	Test for Intermittent and Poor Connections
3	1. Remove the electronic brake control module (EBCM) from the brake pressure modulator valve (BPMV). 2. Inspect the EBCM to BPMV connector for conditions which could cause an intermittent, such as damage, corrosion, poor terminal contact, or presence of brake fluid. Is the connector OK and the cavity free of brake fluid?	Go to Step 5	Go to Step 4
4	1. If connector corrosion or damage is evident, replace BPMV and/or EBCM as necessary. 2. If brake fluid is present, replace both BPMV and EBCM. Did you complete the repair?	Go to Step 8	--
5	1. Connect the EBCM harness to the EBCM with the BPMV still separated. 2. Connect a test lamp between the pump motor circuits, internal EBCM side, using the J 35616 GM Terminal Test Kit. 3. Cycle the ignition to the OFF position. 4. Start the engine. 5. In park or neutral, release the brake. Does the test lamp illuminate and then turn OFF?	Go to Step 7	Go to Step 6

LTV0500000005889

Fig. 11   Codes C0111, C0113, C0114, C0115 & C0120: Pump Motor (Part 4 of 5)

- The traction OFF indicator turns ON.

Conditions for Clearing the DTC

- The condition for the DTC is no longer present and the DTC is cleared with a scan tool.
- The EBCM automatically clears the history DTC when a current DTC is not detected in 100 consecutive drive cycles.

Diagnostic Aids

The pump motor is integral to the brake pressure modulator valve (BPMV). The pump motor is not serviceable.

Test Description

The number below refers to the step number on the diagnostic table.

5. Tests the ability of the EBCM to control the pump motor. If the test lamp illuminates, the pump motor circuit within the EBCM is good.

LTV0500000005888

Fig. 11   Codes C0111, C0113, C0114, C0115 & C0120: Pump Motor (Part 3 of 5)

6	Replace the EBCM. Did you complete the repair?	Go to Step 8	--
7	Replace the BPMV. Did you complete the repair?	Go to Step 8	--
8	1. Use the scan tool in order to clear the DTCs. 2. Operate the vehicle within the Conditions for Running the DTC as specified in the supporting text. Does the DTC reset?	Go to Step 2	System OK

LTV0500000005890

Fig. 11   Codes C0111, C0113, C0114, C0115 & C0120: Pump Motor (Part 5 of 5)

Circuit Description

An internal solenoid valve relay in the electronic brake control module (EBCM) supplies battery positive voltage to all solenoid valves. This voltage is referred to as system voltage. The EBCM activates the solenoid valve relay when the ignition is turned ON. Once the solenoid valve relay has been activated, The EBCM supplies ground to actuate individual solenoid valves.

DTC Descriptor

This diagnostic procedure supports the following DTC:

DTC C0121 Valve Relay Circuit

Conditions for Running the DTC

- The ignition is ON.
- Ignition voltage is greater than 8 volts.

Conditions for Setting the DTC

One of the following conditions exists for 0.23 second:

- The EBCM commands the solenoid valve relay on and battery voltage is less than 8 volts at the solenoid valves.
- An internal EBCM relay driver fault is not detected.

Action Taken When the DTC Sets

If equipped, the following actions occur:

- The EBCM disables the Antilock Brake System (ABS).
- The ABS indicator turns ON.
- Dynamic rear proportion (DRP) function is degraded (w/NW7 or JL4).
- DRP function is disabled (w/o NW7).
- The red brake warning turns ON (w/o NW7).
- The EBCM disables Traction Control System (TCS).
- The EBCM disables Vehicle Stability Enhancement System (VSES).

Conditions for Clearing the DTC

- The condition for the DTC is no longer present and the DTC is cleared with a scan tool.
- The EBCM automatically clears the history DTC when a current DTC is not detected in 100 consecutive drive cycles.

Diagnostic Aids

The solenoid valve relay is integral to the EBCM. The relay is not serviceable.

Test Description

The number below refers to the step number on the diagnostic table

LTV0500000005891

Fig. 12   Code C0121: Valve Relay Circuit (Part 1 of 2)

Step	Action	Yes	No
1	Did you perform the Diagnostic System Check - Vehicle?	Go to Step 2	Go to Diagnostic System Check
2	1. Use the scan tool in order to clear the DTCs. 2. Cycle the ignition to the OFF position. 3. Start the engine. 4. In park or neutral, release the brake. 5. Turn OFF the engine. Does the DTC reset?	Go to Step 3	Test for Intermittent and Poor Connections
3	Replace the electronic brake control module (EBCM). Did you complete the repair?	Go to Step 4	--
4	1. Use the scan tool in order to clear the DTCs. 2. Cycle the ignition to OFF and then ON. Does the DTC reset?	Go to Step 2	System OK

LTV0500000005892

Fig. 12   Code C0121: Valve Relay Circuit (Part 2 of 2)

Conditions for Setting the DTC

C0131

The 2 master cylinder pressure sensors do not correlate.

C0136

- The brake fluid pressure sensor signal is greater than 4.9 volts.
- The brake fluid pressure sensor signal is less than 0.15 volt.

C0138

This DTC is set when the vehicle decelerates and the brake pressure signal does not increase. The criteria to set this DTC is listed below:

- The vehicle decelerates from 25 km/h (16 mph) to 10 km/h (6 mph).
- The vehicle decelerates at a rate of 8 km/h (5 mph) per second.
- No increase in the brake pressure sensor signal is detected.

C0139

This DTC is set when the vehicle accelerates and the brake pressure signal is high. The criteria to set this DTC is listed below:

- The vehicle exceeds 40 km/h (25 mph).
- The vehicle accelerates at a rate of 8 km/h (5 mph) per second.
- The brake pressure sensor signal output is above 1034 kPa (150 psi).

Action Taken When the DTC Sets

If equipped, the following actions will occur:

- The EBCM disables the vehicle stability enhancement system (VSES) for the duration of the ignition cycle.
- The EBCM disables the traction control system (TCS) for the duration of the ignition cycle.
- The Traction Control Off indicator turns ON.
- The driver information center (DIC) displays the Service Stability System and Service Traction System message.

Conditions for Clearing the DTC

- The condition for the DTC is no longer present and the DTC is cleared with a scan tool.
- The EBCM automatically clears the history DTC when a current DTC is not detected in

LTV0500000005894

Fig. 13   Codes C0131, C0136, C0138 & C0139: Brake System Pressure (Part 2 of 4)

Circuit Description

The electronic brake control module (EBCM) uses an input from 2 brake fluid pressure sensors to enhance ABS braking and vehicle stability if equipped.

DTC Descriptors

This diagnostic procedure supports the following DTCs:

- DTC C0131 Antilock Brake System (ABS) Pressure Circuit
- DTC C0136 Base Brake System Pressure Circuit/Sensor
- DTC C0138 Base Brake System Pressure Circuit/Sensor Low
- DTC C0139 Base Brake System Pressure Circuit/Sensor High

Conditions for Running the DTC

C0131

- The braking system is not performing an antilock or traction control event.
- No other brake pressure sensor DTCs are set.

C0136

- The ignition is ON for 1 second and greater than 8 volts.
- The 5-volt reference to the brake pressure sensor is in range.

C0138

- The ignition is ON for 1 second and greater than 8 volts.
- The 5-volt reference to the brake pressure sensor is in range.
- DTC C0136 is not set.

C0139

- The ignition is ON for 1 second and greater than 8 volts.
- The 5-volt reference to the brake pressure sensor is in range.
- DTC C0136 is not set.
- Vehicle speed is above 16 km/h (10 mph).

LTV0500000005893

Fig. 13   Codes C0131, C0136, C0138 & C0139: Brake System Pressure (Part 1 of 4)

100 consecutive drive cycles.

Diagnostic Aids

The brake pressure sensor is mounted to the BPMV under the EBCM and cannot be diagnosed or replaced separately. If equipped, the brake pressure sensor 5-volt reference circuit and low reference circuit is shared with other components in the vehicle stability system. DTCs can set for other components that share circuits with the brake pressure sensor.

Test Description

The number below refers to the step number on the diagnostic table.

2. The EBCM supplies a 5-volt reference to several sensors. DTC C0870 is set if the 5-volt reference voltage is out of range.

LTV0500000005895

Fig. 13   Codes C0131, C0136, C0138 & C0139: Brake System Pressure (Part 3 of 4)

Step	Action	Yes	No
1	Did you perform the Diagnostic System Check - Vehicle?	Go to Step 2	Go to Diagnostic System Check
2	Is DTC C0870 set also?	Go to DTC C0870	Go to Step 3
3	Replace the electronic brake control module (EBCM) and the brake pressure modulator valve (BPMV). Did you complete the replacement?	Go to Step 4	--
4	1. Use the scan tool in order to clear the DTCs. 2. Operate the vehicle within normal driving conditions. Does the DTC reset?	Go to Step 1	System OK

LTV0500000005896

Fig. 13   Codes C0131, C0136, C0138 & C0139: Brake System Pressure (Part 4 of 4)

Circuit Description

The body control module (BCM) receives a signal from the brake pedal position (BPP) sensor. The BCM illuminates the stop lamps by applying battery positive voltage to the stop lamp supply voltage circuit. The electronic brake control module (EBCM) receives a voltage input from the stop lamp supply voltage circuit to determine if the brake pedal is applied.

DTC Descriptors

This diagnostic procedure supports the following DTCs:

- DTC C0163 Antilock Brake System (ABS)/Traction Control System (TCS) Brake Switch/Sensor Circuit Low
- DTC C0164 Antilock Brake System (ABS)/Traction Control System (TCS) Brake Switch/Sensor Circuit High
- DTC C0165 Antilock Brake System (ABS)/Traction Control System (TCS) Brake Switch/Sensor Circuit Open

Conditions for Running the DTCs

C0163, C0164 or C0165

The ignition voltage is greater than 8 volts.

Conditions for Setting the DTC

C0163

The DTC sets when the EBCM detects that the vehicle decelerates without a brake apply signal. All of the conditions below must be met 2 times before the DTC sets:

- The EBCM does not receive a voltage input from the stop lamp supply voltage circuit.
- ABS, vehicle stability enhancement system (VSES), and Traction Control System (TCS) is not active.
- Vehicle speed exceeds 24 km/h (15 mph) and decelerates greater than 12 km/h (7 mph) per second.
- Vehicle speed drops below 24 km/h (15 mph) during deceleration.

C0164

The DTC sets when the EBCM detects that the vehicle accelerates with a brake apply signal. All of the conditions below must be met 2 times before the DTC sets:

The EBCM receives a voltage input from the stop lamp supply voltage circuit.

LTV0500000005897

Fig. 14 Codes C0163–C0165: Anti-Lock Brake System (ABS)/Traction Control System (TCS) Brake Switch Sensor Circuit (Part 1 of 3)

- Vehicle speed exceeds 40 km/h (25 mph).
- Vehicle acceleration exceeds 8 km/h (5 mph) per second.

C0165

The DTC sets when the EBCM detects an open in the stop lamp supply voltage circuit. The EBCM determines an open circuit if the voltage at the stop lamp supply voltage circuit is between 75 percent and 40 percent of ignition voltage.

Action Taken When the DTC Sets

If equipped, the following actions will occur:

- The EBCM disables the VSES for the duration of the ignition cycle.
- The EBCM disables the TCS for the duration of the ignition cycle.
- The Traction Control Off indicator turns ON.
- The driver information center (DIC) displays the Service Stability System and Service Traction System message.

Conditions for Clearing the DTC

- The condition for the DTC is no longer present and the DTC is cleared with a scan tool.
- The EBCM automatically clears the history DTC when a current DTC is not detected in 100 consecutive drive cycles.

Diagnostic Aids

The DTC C0164 can be set if the vehicle has been driven with the brake applied during acceleration.

Test Description

The numbers below refer to the step numbers on the diagnostic table.

2. Symptoms in the stop lamp circuit can cause the DTC to set.

3. This step checks for a BPP DTC. BPP failure can cause the DTC to set.

4. This step Checks to see if the DTC will reset as current.

LTV0500000005898

Fig. 14 Codes C0163–C0165: Anti-Lock Brake System (ABS)/Traction Control System (TCS) Brake Switch Sensor Circuit (Part 2 of 3)

Step	Action	Yes	No
1	Did you perform the Diagnostic System Check - Vehicle?	Go to Step 2	Go to Diagnostic System Check
2	Are the stop lamps always ON or one or more inoperative?	Go to Symptoms	Go to Step 3
3	Use the scan tool to display DTCs for the body control module (BCM). Does the scan tool display DTC C0277 or C0278?	Go to Diagnostic Trouble Code (DTC)	Go to Step 4
4	Confirm that the brake pedal position (BPP) is adjusted to the correct position and perform the BPP calibration procedure. Operate the vehicle within the Conditions for Running the DTC as specified in the supporting text. Does the DTC reset?	Go to Step 5	Go to Step 6
5	Repair open or short in the center high mounted stop lamp (CHMSL) resistor. Did you find and correct the condition?	Go to Step 6	Go to Step 2
6	1. Use the scan tool in order to clear the DTCs. 2. Operate the vehicle within the Conditions for Running the DTC as specified in the supporting text. Does the DTC reset?	Go to Step 2	System OK

LTV0500000005899

Fig. 14 Codes C0163–C0165: Anti-Lock Brake System (ABS)/Traction Control System (TCS) Brake Switch Sensor Circuit (Part 3 of 3)

Circuit Description

The electronic brake control module (EBCM) monitors vehicle speed deceleration, antilock brake system (ABS) activation, traction control system (TCS) activation and brake pedal position in order to calculate an estimate of the brake rotor temperatures. In most cases high brake rotor tempreture is caused by extended TCS activation. If the EBCM calculates that the brake rotor temperatures are too high, the EBCM will temporarily suspend the TCS function until the brake rotors cool. The EBCM continues calculating the brake rotor temperatures after the ignition is turned OFF. The EBCM remains awake until the EBCM calculates that the brake rotors have cooled sufficiently. The cooling period may take up to 30 minutes.

DTC Descriptor

This diagnostic procedure supports the following DTC:

DTC C0179 System Thermal High

Conditions for Running the DTC

- The ignition is ON.
- Ignition voltage is greater than 8 volts.

Conditions for Setting the DTC

This DTC sets when the estimated brake rotor temperature exceeds 375°C (700°F). When the estimated brake rotor temperature exceeds 375°C (700°F) during normal braking or ABS operations, the DTC does not set until the next TCS activation. The EBCM does not disable TCS until the end of the TCS event.

Action Taken When the DTC Sets

- The EBCM disables the TCS until the DTC becomes a history DTC.
- The ABS remains functional.
- The Traction Control Off Indicator turns ON.

Conditions for Clearing the DTC

The current DTC becomes history when the estimated brake rotor temperatures of both drive wheels decreases below 275°C (530°F). The following actions also occur:

- The EBCM enables the TCS.
- The condition for the DTC is no longer present (the DTC is not current) and the DTC is cleared with the scan tool.
- The EBCM automatically clears the history DTC when a current DTC is not detected in 100 consecutive drive cycles.

LTV0500000005900

Fig. 15 Code C0179: System Thermal High (Part 1 of 3)

Diagnostic Aids

DTC C0179 does not indicate a malfunction has occurred. This DTC indicates that the EBCM has reacted to high brake rotor temperatures by temporarily suspending TCS.

Test Description

The number below refers to the step number on the diagnostic table.

2. This step tests if driving conditions caused DTC.

LTV0500000005901

Fig. 15   Code C0179: System Thermal High (Part 2 of 3)

Circuit Description

The electronic brake control module (EBCM) uses the lateral accelerometer signal to determine the lateral forces acting on a vehicle during a turn or a skid. The EBCM uses the signal from the lateral accelerometer as one of the inputs to operate the vehicle stability enhancement system (VSES).

DTC Descriptors

This diagnostic procedure supports the following DTCs:

- DTC C0186 Lateral Accelerometer Circuit
- DTC C0187 Lateral Accelerometer Circuit Range/Performance

Conditions for Running the DTC

C0186

Ignition voltage is greater than 8 volts.

C0187
- Ignition voltage is greater than 8 volts.
- No yaw rate DTCs are present.
- Vehicle yaw rate is centered.

Conditions for Setting the DTC

C0186

Lateral accelerometer signal voltage is less than 0.18 volt or above 4.84 volts.

C0187

The EBCM will set the DTC when one or more of the following conditions have occurred:

- The lateral acceleration signal changes to rapidly based on vehicle dynamics.
- The internal calibration in the lateral accelerometer is out of range.
- The lateral accelerometer has failed and internal self check test.

Action Taken When the DTC Sets

If equipped, the following actions will occur:

- The EBCM disables VSES for the duration of the ignition cycle.
- The driver information center (DIC) displays the Service Stability System message.

Conditions for Clearing the DTC

- The condition for the DTC is no longer present and the DTC is cleared with a scan tool.

LTV0500000005903

Fig. 16   Codes C0186 Or C0187: Lateral Accelerometer Circuit (Part 1 of 4)

- The EBCM automatically clears the history DTC when a current DTC is not detected in 100 consecutive drive cycles.

Diagnostic Aids

The lateral accelerometer is packaged with the yaw rate sensor as a single component.

Test Description

The numbers below refer to the step numbers on the diagnostic table.

2. Tests for the proper voltage output on the 5-volt reference circuit and the proper operation of the signal circuit.

3. Tests for possible low 5-volt reference output or a problem with the signal circuit.

4. Tests for a short to voltage on the 5-volt reference circuit. If a short to voltage exists, other DTCs may be set for the vehicle stability system.

8. Tests for a problem with the low reference circuit. If a short to voltage exists, other DTCs may be set for the vehicle stability system.

LTV0500000005904

Fig. 16   Codes C0186 Or C0187: Lateral Accelerometer Circuit (Part 2 of 4)

Step	Action	Yes	No
1	Did you perform the Diagnostic System Check - Vehicle?	Go to Step 2	Go to Diagnostic System Check
2	Most occurrences of this DTC are caused by excessive TCS activation or braking. Review with the customer to verify the conditions under which the DTC set. Did vehicle operation cause this DTC to set?	Go to Step 3	Go to Diagnostic Aids
3	1. Use the scan tool in order to clear the DTCs. 2. Operate the vehicle within normal driving conditions. Does the DTC reset?	Go to Step 1	System OK

LTV0500000005902

Fig. 15   Code C0179: System Thermal High (Part 3 of 3)

Step	Action	Values	Yes	No
.1	Did you perform the Diagnostic System Check - Vehicle?	--	Go to Step 2	Go to Diagnostic System Check
2	1. Turn OFF the ignition. 2. Disconnect the yaw and lateral acceleration sensor harness connector. 3. Connect a 3-amp fused jumper wire between the 5-volt reference circuit of the yaw and lateral acceleration sensor and the signal circuit of the yaw and lateral acceleration sensor. 4. Turn ON the ignition, with the engine OFF. 5. With the scan tool, observe the lateral acceleration signal voltage. Does the scan tool indicate that the lateral acceleration signal parameter is in between the specified voltage range?	4.5-5.5 V	Go to Step 8	Go to Step 3
3	With the 3-amp fused jumper wire still connected, does the scan tool indicate that the lateral acceleration sensor parameter is below the specified voltage value?	4.5 V	Go to Step 5	Go to Step 4
4	Test the 5-volt reference circuit of the yaw and lateral acceleration sensor for a short to voltage. Did you find and correct the condition?	--	Go to Step 12	Go to Step 7
5	Test the 5-volt reference circuit of the yaw and lateral acceleration sensor for the following conditions: • An open • A short to ground • A high resistance Did you find and correct the condition?	--	Go to Step 12	Go to Step 6
6	Test the lateral accelerometer signal circuit for the following conditions: • An open • A short to ground • A high resistance Did you find and correct the condition?	--	Go to Step 12	Go to Step 11

LTV0500000005905

Fig. 16   Codes C0186 Or C0187: Lateral Accelerometer Circuit (Part 3 of 4)

Step	Action	Values	Yes	No
7	Test the lateral accelerometer signal circuit for a short to voltage. Refer to Circuit Testing and Wiring Repairs in Wiring Systems. Did you find and correct the condition?	--	Go to Step 12	Go to Step 11
8	Test the low reference circuit of the yaw and lateral acceleration sensor for the following conditions: • An open • A short to voltage • A high resistance Did you find and correct the condition?	--	Go to Step 12	Go to Step 9
9	Inspect for poor connections at the harness connector of the yaw and lateral acceleration sensor. Did you find and correct the condition?	--	Go to Step 12	Go to Step 10
10	Replace the yaw and lateral acceleration sensor. Did you complete the replacement?	--	Go to Step 12	--
11	Replace the electronic brake control module (EBCM). Did you complete the replacement?	--	Go to Step 12	--
12	1. Clear the DTCs using the scan tool. 2. Operate the vehicle within the Conditions for Running the DTC as specified in the supporting text. Does the DTC reset?	--	Go to Step 2	System OK

LTV0500000005906

Fig. 16   Codes C0186 Or C0187: Lateral Accelerometer Circuit (Part 4 of 4)

3. Tests for possible low 5-volt reference output or a problem with the signal circuit.

4. Tests for a short to voltage on the 5-volt reference circuit. If a short to voltage exists, other DTCs may be set for the vehicle stability system.

8. Tests for a problem with the low reference circuit. If a short to voltage exists, other DTCs may be set for the vehicle stability system.

LTV0500000005908

Fig. 17   Code C0196: Yaw Rate Circuit (Part 2 of 4)

Circuit Description

The electronic brake control module (EBCM) uses the yaw rate signal to determine the directional angle of the vehicle during a turn or a skid. The EBCM uses the signal from the yaw rate as one of the inputs to operate the vehicle stability enhancement system (VSES).

DTC Descriptor

This diagnostic procedure supports the following DTC:

DTC C0196 Yaw Rate Circuit

Conditions for Running the DTC

The ignition voltage is greater than 8 volts.

Conditions for Setting the DTC

The EBCM will set the DTC when one or more of the following conditions have occurred:

• The yaw rate signal is less than 0.18 volt or greater than 4.84 volts.
• The yaw rate signal changes to rapidly based on vehicle dynamics.
• The internal calibration in the yaw rate is out of range.
• The yaw and lateral acceleration sensor has failed and internal self check test.

Action Taken When the DTC Sets

If equipped, the following actions will occur:

• The EBCM disables VSES for the duration of the ignition cycle.
• The driver information center (DIC) displays the Service Stability System message.

Conditions for Clearing the DTC

• The condition for the DTC is no longer present and the DTC is cleared with a scan tool.
• The EBCM automatically clears the history DTC when a current DTC is not detected in 100 consecutive drive cycles.

Diagnostic Aids

The lateral accelerometer is packaged with the yaw rate sensor as a single component.

Test Description

The numbers below refer to the step numbers on the diagnostic table.

2. Tests for the proper voltage output on the 5-volt reference circuit and the proper operation of the signal circuit.

LTV0500000005907

Fig. 17   Code C0196: Yaw Rate Circuit (Part 1 of 4)

Step	Action	Values	Yes	No
1	Did you perform the Diagnostic System Check - Vehicle?	--	Go to Step 2	Go to Diagnostic System Check
2	1. Turn OFF the ignition. 2. Disconnect the yaw and lateral acceleration sensor harness connector. 3. Connect a 3-amp fused jumper wire between the 5-volt reference circuit of the yaw and lateral acceleration sensor and the signal circuit of the yaw and lateral acceleration sensor. 4. Turn ON the ignition, with the engine OFF. 5. With the scan tool, observe the yaw rate signal voltage. Does the scan tool indicate that the yaw rate signal parameter is in between the specified voltage range?	4.5-5.5 V	Go to Step 8	Go to Step 3
3	With the 3-amp fused jumper wire still connected, does the scan tool indicate that the yaw rate sensor parameter is below the specified voltage value?	4.5 V	Go to Step 5	Go to Step 4
4	Test the 5-volt reference circuit of the yaw and lateral acceleration sensor for a short to voltage. Did you find and correct the condition?	--	Go to Step 12	Go to Step 7
5	Test the 5-volt reference circuit of the yaw and lateral acceleration sensor for the following conditions: • An open • A short to ground • A high resistance Did you find and correct the condition?	--	Go to Step 12	Go to Step 6

LTV0500000005909

Fig. 17   Code C0196: Yaw Rate Circuit (Part 3 of 4)

Step	Action	Values	Yes	No
6	Test the yaw rate signal circuit for the following conditions: • An open • A short to ground • A high resistance Did you find and correct the condition?	--	Go to Step 12	Go to Step 11
7	Test the yaw rate signal circuit for a short to voltage. Did you find and correct the condition?	--	Go to Step 12	Go to Step 11
8	Test the low reference circuit of the yaw and lateral acceleration sensor for the following conditions: • An open • A short to voltage • A high resistance Did you find and correct the condition?	--	Go to Step 12	Go to Step 9
9	Inspect for poor connections at the harness connector of the yaw and lateral acceleration sensor. Did you find and correct the condition?	--	Go to Step 12	Go to Step 10
10	Replace the yaw and lateral acceleration sensor. Did you complete the replacement?	--	Go to Step 12	--
11	Replace the electronic brake control module (EBCM). Did you complete the replacement?	--	Go to Step 12	--
12	1. Clear the DTCs using the scan tool. 2. Operate the vehicle within the Conditions for Running the DTC as specified in the supporting text. Does the DTC reset?	--	Go to Step 2	System OK

LTV0500000005910

Fig. 17   Code C0196: Yaw Rate Circuit (Part 4 of 4)

Circuit Description

The system relay is energized when the ignition is ON. The system relay supplies voltage to the valve relay. The electronic brake control module (EBCM) activates the valve relay to supply voltage to the valve solenoids. This voltage is referred to as the system voltage. The EBCM microprocessor activates individual valve solenoids by grounding the valve solenoid control circuits.

DTC Descriptors

This diagnostic procedure supports the following DTCs:

- DTC C0220 Left Front ABS Channel in Release Too Long
- DTC C0221 Right Front ABS Channel in Release Too Long
- DTC C0228 Left Rear ABS Channel in Release Too Long
- DTC C0229 Right Rear ABS Channel in Release Too Long

Conditions for Running the DTC

- Ignition voltage is greater than 8 volts.
- The system is in a ABS braking event.

Conditions for Setting the DTC

This code is set when the following criteria are met.

- The EBCM is commanding a valve solenoid to release brake pressure.
- The wheel that is commanded to release brake pressure has a speed below 5 km/h (3 mph) for 1.25 seconds.

Action Taken When the DTC Sets

If equipped, the following actions occur:

- The EBCM disables the ABS system.
- The ABS indicator turns ON.
- The driver information center (DIC) displays the Service ABS System message.
- The traction control system (TCS) is disabled.
- The DIC displays the Service Traction System Message.
- The vehicle stability enhancement system (VSES) is disabled.
- The DIC displays the Service Stability System Message.

Conditions for Clearing the DTC

- The condition for the DTC is no longer present and the DTC is cleared with a scan tool.
- The electronic brake control module (EBCM) automatically clears the history DTC when a current DTC is not detected in 100 consecutive drive cycles.

LTV0500000005911

Fig. 18 Codes C0220, C0221, C0228 & C0229: ABS Channel In Release (Part 1 of 3)

Circuit Description

The electronic brake control module (EBCM) and the powertrain control module (PCM) simultaneously control the Traction Control System (TCS). The EBCM sends a Requested Torque message via a pulse width modulated (PWM) signal to the PCM. The duty cycle of the signal is used to determine how much engine torque the EBCM is requesting the PCM to deliver. Normal values are between 10 and 90 percent duty cycle. The signal should be at 90 percent when traction control is not active and at lower values during traction control activations. The PCM supplies the pull up voltage that the EBCM switches to ground to create the signal.

DTC Descriptors

This diagnostic procedure supports the following DTCs:

- DTC C0241 Powertrain Control Module (PCM) Indicated Requested Torque Malfunction
- DTC P0856 Traction Control Torque Request Circuit

Conditions for Running the DTC

The engine is running.

Conditions for Setting the DTC

C0241

The EBCM has detected an open, short to power or short to ground on the requested torque signal circuit.

P0856

One of the following conditions exists:

- The PCM detects that requested torque signal is out of the valid range.
- The PCM does not receive the requested torque signal.

Action Taken When the DTC Sets

When the DTC sets the TCS can not reduce engine torque, however the brake intervention portion of the TCS System remains operational.

Conditions for Clearing the DTC

- The condition for the DTC is no longer present and you used the scan tool Clear DTC function.

LTV0500000005914

Fig. 19 Codes C0241 Or P0856: PCM Indicated Requested Torque Fault Or Traction Control Torque Request Circuit (Part 1 of 4)

Diagnostic Aids

Always diagnose and repair any wheel speed sensor failures prior to diagnosing DTCs C0220, C0221, C0228 or C0229. These DTCs in theory may be set on surfaces that are nearly impossible to get traction on. If the DTC sets within these conditions, diagnosis of the ABS system may not be necessary.

Test Description

The number below refers to the step number on the diagnostic table.

2. This step checks for DTCs that are wheel speed related. Wheel speed DTCs must be diagnosed first.

LTV0500000005912

Fig. 18 Codes C0220, C0221, C0228 & C0229: ABS Channel In Release (Part 2 of 3)

Step	Action	Yes	No
1	Did you perform the Diagnostic System Check - Vehicle?	Go to Step 2	Go to Diagnostic System Check
2	Are any wheel speed related DTCs set?	Go to Diagnostic Trouble Code (DTC)	Go to Step 3
3	1. Use the scan tool in order to clear the DTCs. 2. Use the scan tool and perform the solenoid test. Do the solenoids in question function normally?	Go to Diagnostic Aids	Go to Step 4
4	Replace the brake pressure modulator valve (BPMV). Did you complete the repair?	Go to Step 5	--
5	Use the scan tool and perform the solenoid test. Do the solenoids in question function normally?	System OK	Go to Step 2

LTV0500000005913

Fig. 18 Codes C0220, C0221, C0228 & C0229: ABS Channel In Release (Part 3 of 3)

- The EBCM automatically clears the history DTC when a current DTC is not detected in 100 consecutive drive cycles.
- The PCM automatically clears the history DTC when a current DTC is not detected in 40 consecutive warm-up cycles.

Diagnostic Aids

Check for poor or intermittent connections of the EBCM and the PCM.

Test Description

The numbers below refer to the step numbers on the diagnostic table.

4. This step tests for voltage supplied to the EBCM from the PCM.

5. This step tests for a shorted resistor in the PCM or a short to voltage within the requested torque signal circuit by verifying that a large voltage drop occurs when a test lamp is connected in parallel with the DMM.

LTV0500000005915

Fig. 19 Codes C0241 Or P0856: PCM Indicated Requested Torque Fault Or Traction Control Torque Request Circuit (Part 2 of 4)

Step	Action	Values	Yes	No
1	Did you perform the Diagnostic System Check - Vehicle?	--	Go to Step 2	Go to Diagnostic System Check
2	Is DTC P0856 set?	--	Go to Step 3	Go to Diagnostic Aids
3	1. Use a scan tool in order to clear the DTCs. 2. Start the engine. 3. Does DTC P0856 set?	--	Go to Step 4	Go to Diagnostic Aids
4	1. Turn OFF the ignition. 2. Disconnect from the electronic brake control module (EBCM), the harness connector containing the requested torque signal circuit. 3. Turn ON the ignition. 4. Use a DMM to measure the voltage between the requested torque signal circuit and a good ground. Does the voltage measure greater than the specified value?	4.75 V	Go to Step 5	Go to Step 6
5	1. With the DMM still connected to monitor the requested torque signal circuit, connect one end of a test lamp to a good ground. 2. Connect the other end of the test lamp to the positive lead of the DMM. Does the voltage measure less than the specified value?	0.15 V	Go to Step 9	Go to Step 7
6	Test the requested torque signal circuit for an open or a short to ground. Did you find and correct the condition?	--	Go to Step 12	Go to Step 8

LTV0500000005916

Fig. 19   Codes C0241 Or P0856: PCM Indicated Requested Torque Fault Or Traction Control Torque Request Circuit (Part 3 of 4)

Circuit Description

The electronic brake control module (EBCM) and the powertrain control module (PCM) simultaneously control the traction control. The EBCM sends a serial data message to the PCM requesting torque reduction. When certain PCM DTCs are set, the PCM will not be able to perform the torque reduction for traction control. A serial data message is sent to the EBCM indicating that traction control is not allowed.

DTC Descriptor

This diagnostic procedure supports the following DTC:

DTC C0242 PCM Indicated TCS Malfunction

Conditions for Running the DTC

- The ignition is ON.
- Ignition voltage is greater than 8 volts.

Conditions for Setting the DTC

The PCM diagnoses a condition preventing the engine control portion of the traction control function and sends a serial data message to the EBCM indicating that torque reduction is not allowed. The PCM will typically set a DTC and the EBCM will set this DTC.

Action Taken When the DTC Sets

If equipped, the following actions occur:

- The EBCM disables the Traction Control System (TCS) for the duration of the ignition cycle.
- The Traction Control indicator turns ON.
- The Antilock Brake System (ABS) remains functional.

Conditions for Clearing the DTC

- The condition for the DTC is no longer present and the DTC is cleared with a scan tool.
- The electronic brake control module (EBCM) automatically clears the history DTC when a current DTC is not detected in 100 consecutive drive cycles.

Diagnostic Aids

This DTC is for information only. As an aid to the technician, this DTC indicates that there are no problems in the ABS/TCS system.

Step	Action	Yes	No
1	Did you perform the Diagnostic System Check - Vehicle?	--	Go to Diagnostic System Check

LTV0500000005918

Fig. 20   Code C0242: PCM Indicated TCS Fault

Step	Action			Yes	No
7	Test the requested torque signal circuit for a short to voltage. Did you find and correct the condition?			Go to Step 12	Go to Step 10
8	Inspect for poor connections at the harness connector of the powertrain control module (PCM). Did you find and correct the condition?			Go to Step 12	Go to Step 10
9	Inspect for poor connections at the harness connector of the EBCM. Did you find and correct the condition?			Go to Step 12	Go to Step 11
10	Replace the PCM. Did you complete the replacement?			Go to Step 12	--
11	Replace the EBCM. Did you complete the replacement?			Go to Step 12	--
12	1. Use the scan tool in order to clear the DTCs. 2. Operate the vehicle within the Conditions for Running the DTC as specified in the supporting text. Does DTC P0856 reset?			Go to Step 4	System OK

LTV0500000005917

Fig. 19   Codes C0241 Or P0856: PCM Indicated Requested Torque Fault Or Traction Control Torque Request Circuit (Part 4 of 4)

Circuit Description

The electronic brake control module (EBCM) and the powertrain control module (PCM) simultaneously control the Traction Control System (TCS). The PCM sends a Delivered Torque message via a pulse width modulated (PWM) signal to the EBCM. The duty cycle of the signal is used to determine how much engine torque the PCM is delivering. Normal values are between 10 and 90 percent duty cycle. The EBCM supplies the pull up voltage that the PCM switches to ground to create the signal.

DTC Descriptors

This diagnostic procedure supports the following DTCs:

- DTC C0244 Pulse Width Modulated (PWM) Delivered Torque
- DTC P1689 Traction Control Delivered Torque Output Circuit

Conditions for Running the DTC

The engine is running.

Conditions for Setting the DTC

C0244

The EBCM has detected an open, short to power or short to ground on the delivered torque signal circuit.

P1689

One of the following conditions exists:

- The PCM detects that delivered torque signal is out of the valid range.
- The PCM does not receive the delivered torque signal.

Action Taken When the DTC Sets

When the DTC sets the TCS cannot reduce engine torque, however the brake intervention portion of the TCS system remains operational.

Conditions for Clearing the DTC

- The condition for the DTC is no longer present and you used the scan tool Clear DTC function.
- The EBCM automatically clears the history DTC when a current DTC is not detected in 100 consecutive drive cycles.

LTV0500000005919

Fig. 21   Codes C0244 Or P1689: Pulse Width Modulated (PWM) Delivered Torque Or Traction Control Delivered Torque Output Circuit (Part 1 of 4)

- The PCM automatically clears the history DTC when a current DTC is not detected in 40 consecutive warm-up cycles.

Diagnostic Aids

Check for poor or intermittent connections of the EBCM and the PCM.

Test Description

The numbers below refer to the step numbers on the diagnostic table.

3. This step tests for voltage supplied to the PCM from the EBCM.

4. This step tests for a shorted resistor in the EBCM or a short to voltage within the circuit, by verifying that a large voltage drop occurs in the circuit, when the test lamp is placed in parallel with the DMM. The PCM may be damaged, if either of these conditions are present.

LTV0500000005920

Fig. 21   Codes C0244 Or P1689: Pulse Width Modulated (PWM) Delivered Torque Or Traction Control Delivered Torque Output Circuit (Part 2 of 4)

	Action		Yes	No
8	Test the delivered torque signal circuit for a short to voltage. Did you find and correct the condition?	-	Go to Step 11	Go to Step 10
9	Inspect for poor connections at the harness connector of the PCM. Did you find and correct the condition?	-	Go to Step 11	Go to Step 10
10	Replace the PCM. Did you complete the replacement?	-	Go to Step 11	--
11	1. Use the scan tool to clear the DTCs. 2. Operate the vehicle within the Conditions for Running the DTC, as specified in the supporting text. Does the DTC reset?	-	Go to Step 3	System OK

LTV0500000005922

Fig. 21   Codes C0244 Or P1689: Pulse Width Modulated (PWM) Delivered Torque Or Traction Control Delivered Torque Output Circuit (Part 4 of 4)

Circuit Description

The Vehicle Stability Enhancement System (VSES) is activated by the electronic brake control module (EBCM) calculating the desired yaw rate and comparing it to the actual yaw rate input. The desired yaw rate is calculated from measured steering wheel position, vehicle speed, and lateral acceleration. The difference between the desired yaw rate and actual yaw rate is the yaw rate error, which is a measurement of oversteer or understeer. If the yaw rate error becomes too large, the EBCM will attempt to correct the vehicles yaw motion by applying differential braking to the left or right front wheel.

The amount of differential braking applied to the left or right front wheel is based on both the yaw rate error and side slip rate error. The side slip rate error is a function of the lateral acceleration minus the product of the yaw rate and vehicle speed. The yaw rate error and side slip rate error are combined to produce the total delta velocity error. When the delta velocity error becomes too large and the VSES system activates, the drivers steering inputs combined with the differential braking will attempt to bring the delta velocity error toward zero.

DTC Descriptor

This diagnostic procedure supports the following DTC:

DTC C0252 VSES Sensors Uncorrelated

Conditions for Running the DTC

- The steer angle has been centered.
- The VSES is active.
- The direction, understeer or oversteer, of the yaw rate error has not changed.
- The centered lateral acceleration value is less than 0.5 g.
- The yaw rate error is less than 6 degrees/second.
- The side slip error is greater than 1.8 meters/second².

Conditions for Setting the DTC

One of the following conditions exists:

- The yaw rate error is greater than 10 degrees/second with the vehicle speed less than 60 km/h (37 mph) and the acceleration pedal is pressed more than 25 percent of the pedal travel range for 1 second during the VSES activation.
- With the yaw rate less than 8 degrees/second, the side slip error is greater than 4.9 meters/second² for 5 seconds.

Action Taken When the DTC Sets

- The EBCM disables the VSES for the duration of the ignition cycle.
- The driver information center (DIC) displays the Service Stability message.
- The ABS/Traction Control System (TCS) remains functional.

LTV0500000005923

Fig. 22   Code C0252: Vehicle Speed Enhancement System (VSES) Sensor Uncorrelated (Part 1 of 4)

Step	Action	Values	Yes	No
1	Did you perform the Diagnostic System Check - Vehicle?	--	Go to Step 2	Go to Diagnostic System Check
2	1. Use a scan tool in order to clear the DTCs. 2. Turn OFF the ignition for 5 seconds. 3. Start the engine. Does the DTC set?	--	Go to Step 3	Go to Diagnostic Aids
3	1. Turn OFF the ignition. 2. Disconnect from the powertrain control module (PCM), the harness connector containing the delivered torque signal circuit. 3. Turn ON the ignition. 4. Use a DMM in order to measure the voltage between the delivered torque signal circuit and a good ground. Does the voltage measure greater than the specified value?	10 V	Go to Step 4	Go to Step 5
4	1. With the DMM still connected to monitor the delivered torque signal circuit, connect one end of a test lamp to a good ground. 2. Connect the other end of the test lamp to the positive lead of the DMM, while observing the DMM display. Does the voltage measure less than the specified value?	0.15 V	Go to Step 6	Go to Step 8
5	Test the delivered torque signal circuit for an open or a short to ground. Did you find and correct the condition?	--	Go to Step 11	Go to Step 9
6	Inspect for poor connections at the harness connector of the electronic brake control module (EBCM). Did you find and correct the condition?		Go to Step 11	Go to Step 7
7	Replace the EBCM. Did you complete the replacement?	--	Go to Step 11	--

LTV0500000005921

Fig. 21   Codes C0244 Or P1689: Pulse Width Modulated (PWM) Delivered Torque Or Traction Control Delivered Torque Output Circuit (Part 3 of 4)

Conditions for Clearing the DTC

- The condition for the DTC is no longer present and the DTC is cleared with a scan tool.
- The EBCM automatically clears the history DTC when a current DTC is not detected in 100 consecutive drive cycles.

Diagnostic Aids

The following conditions can cause this concern:

- Improper steering alignment
- Open, short to ground, or short to voltage
- Internal lateral accelerometer failure
- EBCM internal failure

Test Description

The numbers below refer to the step numbers on the diagnostic table.

2. Perform the Steering Position Sensor Test in order to verify that the steering wheel position sensor (SWPS) is operating properly.

3. Verify that the Lateral Accelerometer Signal parameter is within the valid range.

4. Verify that the Yaw Rate Signal parameter is within the valid range.

LTV0500000005924

Fig. 22   Code C0252: Vehicle Speed Enhancement System (VSES) Sensor Uncorrelated (Part 2 of 4)

Step	Action	Values	Yes	No
1	Did you perform the Diagnostic System Check - Vehicle?	--	Go to Step 2	Go to Diagnostic System Check
2	1. Install a scan tool. 2. Turn ON the ignition, with the engine OFF. 3. With the scan tool, perform the Steering Position Sensor Test. Did the SWPS pass the test?	--	Go to Step 3	Go to Step 7
3	With a scan tool, observe the Lateral Accelerometer Signal parameter in the Vehicle Stability Enhancement System (VSES) data list. Does the scan tool display within the specified range?	2.3-2.7 V	Go to Step 4	Go to Step 8
4	With a scan tool, observe the Yaw Rate Signal parameter in the VSES data list. Does the scan tool display within the specified range?	2.3-2.7 V	Go to Step 5	Go to Step 8
5	1. Use the scan tool in order to clear the DTCs. 2. Perform the Diagnostic Test Drive. Does the DTC reset?	--	Go to Step 6	Go to Diagnostic Aids
6	Replace the electronic brake control module (EBCM). Did you complete the replacement?	--	Go to Step 9	--
7	Replace the steering wheel position sensor (SWPS). Did you complete the replacement?	--	Go to Step 9	--

LTV0500000005925

Fig. 22   Code C0252: Vehicle Speed Enhancement System (VSES) Sensor Uncorrelated (Part 3 of 4)

Circuit Description

The Vehicle Stability Enhancement System (VSES) uses inputs from the steering wheel position sensor (SWPS) and the yaw/lateral acceleration sensor to determine if the vehicles steering is centered. The steering centered self calibration occurs when the vehicle travels in a straight path for greater than 10 seconds.

Variation of the SWPS alignment in the steering column is calibrated out by recording a bias value. The bias value is calculated by using inputs from the SWPS and the Yaw/Lateral acceleration sensor.

DTC Descriptors

This diagnostic procedure supports the following DTCs:

- DTC C0253 Centering Error
- DTC C0254 Steering Sensor and/or Lateral Accelerometer Bias

Conditions for Running the DTC

DTC C0253

All of the following conditions exists:

- Ignition voltage is greater than 8 volts.
- The vehicle has been driven in a straight path for greater than 10 seconds.

DTC C254

All of the following conditions exists:

- Ignition voltage is greater than 8 volts.
- The vehicle steering centered self calibration is successful.

Conditions for Setting the DTC

DTC C0253

All of the following conditions exists:

- The vehicle is traveling in a straight path greater than 40 km/h (25 mph).
- The vehicle fails to complete the steering centered self calibration in 60 seconds.

LTV0500000005927

Fig. 23   Codes C0253 Or C0254: Centering Error Or Steering Sensor Lateral Accelerometer Bias (Part 1 of 3)

Step	Action	Values	Yes	No
8	Replace the yaw rate/lateral accelerometer sensor. Did you complete the replacement?	--	Go to Step 9	--
9	1. Use the scan tool in order to clear the DTCs. 2. Operate the vehicle within the Conditions for Running the DTC as specified in the supporting text. Does the DTC reset?	--	Go to Step 2	System OK

LTV0500000005926

Fig. 22   Code C0252: Vehicle Speed Enhancement System (VSES) Sensor Uncorrelated (Part 4 of 4)

DTC C0254

If the bias value is greater than 40 degrees of steering wheel position the DTC will set.

Action Taken When the DTC Sets

- The EBCM disables the VSES for the duration of the ignition cycle.
- The driver information center (DIC) displays the Service Stability message.
- The ABS/Traction Control System (TCS) remains functional.

Conditions for Clearing the DTC

- The condition for the DTC is no longer present and the DTC is cleared with a scan tool.
- The EBCM automatically clears the history DTC when a current DTC is not detected in 100 consecutive drive cycles.

Diagnostic Aids

If present, diagnose any other VSES DTCs first. Wheel alignment issues should be corrected before diagnosis of this DTC.

Test Description

The numbers below refer to the step numbers on the diagnostic table.

2. Verify that the Lateral Acceleration and Yaw Rate Signal parameter is within the valid range.

3. Perform the Steering Position Sensor Test in order to verify that the SWPS is operating properly.

LTV0500000005928

Fig. 23   Codes C0253 Or C0254: Centering Error Or Steering Sensor Lateral Accelerometer Bias (Part 2 of 3)

Step	Action	Values	Yes	No
1	Did you perform the Diagnostic System Check - Vehicle?	--	Go to Step 2	Go to Diagnostic System Check
2	**Important:** If present, diagnose any other vehicle stability enhancement system (VSES) DTCs first. Wheel alignment issues should be corrected before diagnosis of this DTC. 1. Drive the vehicle on a straight and level path greater than 40 km/h (25 mph). 2. With a scan tool, observe the Lateral Accelerometer Signal and Yaw Rate Signal parameter in the VSES data list. Does the scan tool display both parameters within the specified range?	2.3-2.7 V	Go to Step 3	Go to Step 6
3	1. Position the steering wheel to the straight-ahead (centered) position. 2. Install a scan tool, ignition ON, engine OFF, and view SWPS Signal 1 and SWPS Signal 2. One of the signals should be approximately 2.5 volts and the other should be approximately 0 volts. 3. As the steering wheel is turned, each signal should travel smoothly between 0 and 5 volts. Did the steering wheel position sensor (SWPS) voltage travel between 0 and 5 volts?	--	Go to Step 4	Go to Step 5
4	Replace the electronic brake control module (EBCM). Did you complete the replacement?	--	Go to Step 7	--
5	Replace the SWPS. Did you complete the replacement?	--	Go to Step 7	--
6	Replace the yaw rate/lateral accelerometer sensor. Did you complete the replacement?	--	Go to Step 7	--
7	1. Use the scan tool in order to clear the DTCs. 2. Operate the vehicle within the Conditions for Running the DTC as specified in the supporting text. Does the DTC reset?	--	Go to Step 2	System OK

LTV0500000005929

Fig. 23   Codes C0253 Or C0254: Centering Error Or Steering Sensor Lateral Accelerometer Bias (Part 3 of 3)

Circuit Description

The dynamic rear proportioning (DRP) is a control system that replaces the hydraulic proportioning function of the mechanical proportioning valve in the base brake system. The DRP control system is part of the operating software in the EBCM. The DRP uses active control with the existing ABS in order to regulate the vehicle's rear brake pressure.

DTC Descriptor

This diagnostic procedure supports the following DTC:

DTC C0281 DRP Performance

Conditions for Running the DTC

One or more faults have been detected by the EBCM in the ABS/TCS systems.

Conditions for Setting the DTC

One of the following conditions exists:

- A DTC that fails the DRP is set.
- Two wheel speed sensor DTCs on the same axle set.

Action Taken When the DTC Sets

- The EBCM disables the DRP for the duration of the ignition cycle.
- The red Brake warning indicator turns ON.

Conditions for Clearing the DTC

- The condition for the DTC is no longer present and the DTC is cleared with a scan tool.
- The electronic brake control module (EBCM) automatically clears the history DTC when a current DTC is not detected in 100 consecutive drive cycles.

Diagnostic Aids

This DTC is for information only. As an aid to the technician, this DTC indicates that another DTC exists that fails DRP.

Test Description

The number below refers to the step number on the diagnostic table.

2. Verifies whether other ABS/TCS/VSES DTCs are set.

LTV0500000005930

Fig. 24   Code C0281: Dynamic Rear Proportioning Performance (Part 1 of 2)

Circuit Description

The steering wheel position sensor supplies 2 analog inputs, Phase A and Phase B, to the electronic brake control module (EBCM). The 2 input signals are approximately 90 degrees out of phase. By interpreting the relationship between the 2 inputs, the EBCM can determine the position of the steering wheel and the direction of the steering wheel rotation.

DTC Descriptors

This diagnostic procedure supports the following DTCs:

- DTC C0460 Steering Position Sensor
- DTC C0461 Steering Position Sensor Range/Performance

Conditions for Running the DTC

The ignition is ON.

Conditions for Setting the DTC

C0460

One of the following conditions exists:

- Both Phase A and Phase B are greater than 4.9 volts or less than 0.2 volt for 1.6 seconds.
- The angle change in Phase A or Phase B is greater than 36 degrees between 2 consecutive signal samples.

C0461

The difference in the phase angle between Phase A and Phase B is greater than 16 degrees continuously for 0.25 second.

Action Taken When the DTC Sets

If equipped, the following actions will occur:

- The EBCM disables vehicle stability enhancement system (VSES) for the duration of the ignition cycle.
- The driver information center (DIC) displays the Service Stability System message.

Conditions for Clearing the DTC

- A current DTC will clear when the malfunction is no longer present.
- A history DTC will clear after 100 consecutive malfunction free ignition cycles or when the scan tool Clear DTCs function is used.

LTV0500000005932

Fig. 25   Codes C0460 Or C0461: Steering Position Sensor Or Steering Position Sensor Range/Performance (Part 1 of 4)

Step	Action	Yes	No
1	Did you perform the Diagnostic System Check - Vehicle?	Go to Step 2	Go to Diagnostic System Check
2	1. Install a scan tool. 2. Turn ON the ignition, with the engine OFF. 3. Select the display DTCs function on the scan tool for the electronic brake control module (EBCM). Does the scan tool display any ABS/TCS/VSES DTCs?	Go to Diagnostic Trouble Code (DTC)	Go to Step 3
3	1. Use the scan tool in order to clear the DTCs. 2. Operate the vehicle within the Conditions for Running the DTC as specified in the supporting text. Does the DTC reset?	Go to Step 2	Test for Intermittent and Poor Connections

LTV0500000005931

Fig. 24   Code C0281: Dynamic Rear Proportioning Performance (Part 2 of 2)

Diagnostic Aids

Thoroughly inspect connections or circuitry that may cause an intermittent malfunction.

Test Description

The numbers below refer to the step numbers on the diagnostic table.

3. This step test the circuitry in the high voltage range.

4. This step test the circuitry in the low voltage range.

5. This step tests the low reference circuit of the steering wheel position sensor.

LTV0500000005933

Fig. 25   Codes C0460 Or C0461: Steering Position Sensor Or Steering Position Sensor Range/Performance (Part 2 of 4)

Step	Action	Values	Yes	No
1	Did you perform the Diagnostic System Check - Vehicle?	--	Go to Step 2	Go to Diagnostic System Check
2	1. Use the scan tool to clear the DTC. 2. Start the engine. 3. With the engine running, turn the steering wheel back and forth from lock to lock. Does the DTC reset?	--	Go to Step 3	Go to Diagnostic Aids
3	1. Turn OFF the ignition. 2. Disconnect the steering wheel position sensor harness connector. 3. Turn ON the ignition. 4. Select the VSES Data List on the scan tool. 5. Observe the Analog SWPS Signal parameter on the scan tool. Does the scan tool indicate that the Steering Wheel Position Sensor Data parameter is less than specified value?	0.2 V	Go to Step 4	Go to Step 9
4	1. Connect a 3-amp fused jumper wire between the steering wheel position 5-volt reference circuit and the analog steering signal circuit. 2. Observe the Analog SWPS Signal parameter on the scan tool. Does the scan tool indicate that the steering wheel position sensor data parameter is greater than specified value?	4.8 V	Go to Step 5	Go to Step 6
5	Use a DMM to measure the voltage between the steering wheel position 5-volt reference circuit and the steering wheel position low reference circuit. Does the voltage measure greater than the specified value?	4.8 V	Go to Step 10	Go to Step 8

LTV0500000005934

Fig. 25   Codes C0460 Or C0461: Steering Position Sensor Or Steering Position Sensor Range/Performance (Part 3 of 4)

			Go to	Go to
6	Test the 5-volt reference circuit of the steering wheel position sensor for an open. Did you find and correct the condition?		Go to Step 14	Go to Step 7
7	Test the signal circuit of the steering wheel position sensor for an open or a short to ground. Did you find and correct the condition?		Go to Step 14	Go to Step 11
8	Test the low reference circuit of the steering wheel position sensor for an open. Did you find and correct the condition?		Go to Step 14	Go to Step 11
9	Test the signal circuit of the steering wheel position sensor for a short to voltage. Did you find and correct the condition?		Go to Step 14	Go to Step 13
10	Inspect for poor connections at the harness connector of the steering wheel position sensor. Did you find and correct the condition?		Go to Step 14	Go to Step 12
11	Inspect for poor connections at the harness connector of the electronic brake control module (EBCM). Did you find and correct the condition?		Go to Step 14	Go to Step 13
12	Replace the steering wheel position sensor. Did you complete the replacement?		Go to Step 14	--
13	Replace the EBCM. Did you complete the replacement?		Go to Step 14	--
14	1. Use the scan tool to clear all DTCs from all modules. 2. Operate the vehicle within the conditions for running the DTC as specified in the supporting text. Does the DTC reset?		Go to Step 2	System OK

LTV0500000005935

Fig. 25   Codes C0460 Or C0461: Steering Position Sensor Or Steering Position Sensor Range/Performance (Part 4 of 4)

Step	Action	Yes	No
1	Did you perform the Diagnostic System Check - Vehicle?	Go to Step 2	Go to Diagnostic System Check
2	Use a scan tool in order to clear the DTCs. Can the DTC be cleared?	Go to Step 3	Go to Step 4
3	Test drive the vehicle. Does the DTC reset?	Go to Step 4	Go to Diagnostic Aids
4	Replace the electronic brake control module (EBCM). Did you complete the replacement?	Go to Step 5	--
5	1. Use the scan tool to clear the DTCs. 2. Turn OFF the ignition for 5 seconds. 3. Turn ON the ignition. 4. Operate the vehicle within the Conditions for Running the DTC as specified in the supporting text. Does the DTC reset?	Go to Step 3	System OK

LTV0500000005937

Fig. 26   Code C0550: ECU Performance (Part 2 of 2)

Circuit Description

The electronic brake control module (EBCM) performs several self-tests for internal problems which may affect proper operation.

DTC Descriptor

This diagnostic procedure supports the following DTC:

DTC C0550 Electronic Control Unit (ECU) Performance

Conditions for Running the DTC

The ignition is ON.

Conditions for Setting the DTC

The EBCM detects an internal malfunction.

Action Taken When the DTC Sets

One or more of the following actions may occur:

- The EBCM disables the ABS/dynamic rear proportioning (DRP)/TCS/vehicle stability enhancement system (VSES).
- The ABS indicator turns ON.
- The brake warning indicator turns ON.
- The message center displays the service stability system message.
- The traction off indicator turns ON.

Conditions for Clearing the DTC

Certain conditions that may cause this DTC to set cannot be cleared. Other conditions that may cause this DTC to set may be cleared, at least temporarily, by using the scan tool Clear DTCs function.

Diagnostic Aids

Replace the EBCM if this DTC continues to set intermittently.

LTV0500000005936

Fig. 26   Code C0550: ECU Performance (Part 1 of 2)

Circuit Description

The electronic brake control module (EBCM) disables the traction control when other electronic control modules set DTCs for components that effect the operation of the traction control system.

DTC Descriptor

This diagnostic procedure supports the following DTC:

DTC C0561 System Disabled Information Stored

Conditions for Running the DTC

- The ignition is ON.
- Ignition voltage is greater than 8 volts.

Conditions for Setting the DTC

The PCM or BCM diagnoses a condition preventing the engine control portion of the traction control function and sends a serial data message to the EBCM indicating that torque reduction is not allowed. The PCM or BCM will typically set a DTC and the EBCM will set this DTC.

Action Taken When the DTC Sets

Engine torque reduction traction control is disabled. The brake intervention traction remains operational.

Conditions for Clearing the DTC

- The condition for the DTC is no longer present and the DTC is cleared with a scan tool.
- The electronic brake control module (EBCM) automatically clears the history DTC when a current DTC is not detected in 100 consecutive drive cycles.

Diagnostic Aids

This DTC is for information only. As an aid to the technician, this DTC indicates that there are no problems in the ABS/TCS system.

Step	Action	Yes	No
1	Did you perform the Diagnostic System Check - Vehicle?	--	Go to Diagnostic System Check

LTV0500000005938

Fig. 27   Code C0561: System Disabled Information Stored

Circuit Description

The electronic brake control module (EBCM) supplies the 5-volt reference to the following sensors:

- The steering wheel position sensor (SWPS)
- The yaw rate and lateral acceleration sensor
- The master cylinder brake pressure sensors internal to the EBCM

DTC Descriptor

This diagnostic procedure supports the following DTC:

DTC C0870 Device Voltage Reference Output (Single or 1) Circuit

Conditions for Running the DTC

Ignition voltage is greater than 8 volts.

Conditions for Setting the DTC

One or more of the following conditions are met:

- When the EBCM commands the 5-volt reference ON, the output is less than 4.9 volts or greater than 5.1 volts.
- When the EBCM commands the 5-volt reference OFF, the output is greater than 0.5 volt.

Action Taken When the DTC Sets

If equipped, the following actions will occur:

- The EBCM disables the vehicle stability enhancement system (VSES) for the duration of the ignition cycle.
- The driver information center (DIC) displays the Service Stability System message.
- The EBCM disables the traction control system (TCS) for the duration of the ignition cycle.
- The DIC displays the Service Traction Control System message.

Conditions for Clearing the DTC

- The condition for the DTC is no longer present and the DTC is cleared with a scan tool.
- The EBCM automatically clears the history DTC when a current DTC is not detected in 100 consecutive drive cycles.

Diagnostic Aids

Multiple VSES DTCs can set if the 5-volt reference is shorted to ground or power.

LTV0500000005939

Fig. 28   Code C0870: Device Voltage Reference Output Circuit (Part 1 of 4)

Step	Action	Yes	No
1	Did you perform the Diagnostic System Check - Vehicle?	Go to Step 2	Go to Diagnostic System Check
2	Check for a short to ground or voltage on the 5-volt reference circuit of the following sensors: • The yaw rate and lateral acceleration sensor • The steering wheel position sensor (SWPS) Did you find and correct the condition?	Go to Step 8	Go to Step 3
3	1. Clear the DTCs with the scan tool. 2. Turn OFF the ignition. 3. Disconnect the yaw rate and lateral acceleration sensor. 4. Turn ON the ignition. Does DTC C0870 set?	Go to Step 4	Go to Step 5
4	1. Reconnect the yaw rate and lateral acceleration sensor. 2. Clear the DTCs with the scan tool. 3. Turn OFF the ignition. 4. Disconnect the SWPS. 5. Turn ON the ignition. Does DTC C0870 set?	Go to Step 7	Go to Step 6

LTV0500000005941

Fig. 28   Code C0870: Device Voltage Reference Output Circuit (Part 3 of 4)

Test Description

The numbers below refer to the step numbers on the diagnostic table.

2. This step tests for a short to ground or voltage on the 5-volt reference circuit.

3. This step tests for an internal short to ground in the yaw rate and lateral accelerometer sensor.

4. This step tests for an internal short to ground in the SWPS.

LTV0500000005940

Fig. 28   Code C0870: Device Voltage Reference Output Circuit (Part 2 of 4)

	Action		
5	Replace the yaw rate and lateral acceleration sensor. Did you complete the replacement?	Go to Step 8	--
6	Replace the SWPS. Did you complete the replacement?	Go to Step 8	--
7	Replace the electronic brake control module (EBCM). Did you complete the replacement?	Go to Step 8	--
8	1. Clear the DTCs using the scan tool. 2. Operate the vehicle within the Conditions for Running the DTC as specified in the supporting text. Does the DTC reset?	Go to Step 2	System OK

LTV0500000005942

Fig. 28   Code C0870: Device Voltage Reference Output Circuit (Part 4 of 4)

Circuit Description

The electronic brake control module (EBCM) monitors the voltage level available for system operation. A low voltage condition prevents the system from operating properly.

DTC Descriptor

This diagnostic procedure supports the following DTC:

DTC C0899 Device Voltage Low

Conditions for Running the DTC

The system relay is commanded ON.

If equipped, the following actions will occur:

- The EBCM disables vehicle stability enhancement system (VSES) for the duration of the ignition cycle.
- The driver information center (DIC) displays the Service Stability System message.

Conditions for Setting the DTC

One of the following conditions exists for 0.72 seconds:

- During initialization or when the system is inactive, the system voltage is less than 10.5 volts.
- During the system operation, the system voltage is less than 9 volts.

Action Taken When the DTC Sets

If equipped, the following actions will occur:

- The EBCM disables the ABS .
- Dynamic rear proportioning (DRP) is degraded when the code is current.
- The EBCM disables the traction control system (TCS).
- The EBCM disables the VSES.
- The ABS indicator turns ON.
- The DIC displays the Service Stability System message.
- The DIC displays the Service Traction System message.

LTV0500000005943

Fig. 29   Code C0899: Device Voltage Low (Part 1 of 3)

Conditions for Clearing the DTC

- The condition for the DTC is no longer present and the DTC is cleared with a scan tool.
- The EBCM automatically clears the history DTC when a current DTC is not detected in 100 consecutive drive cycles.

Diagnostic Aids

- Test the charging system.

- Possible causes of this DTC are the following conditions:
  - A charging system malfunction
  - An excessive battery draw
  - A weak battery
  - A faulty system ground

Test Description

The numbers below refer to the step numbers on the diagnostic table.

2. Use the scan tool in order to inspect the voltage to the EBCM.

5. This step verifies that the condition is still present.

LTV0500000005944

Fig. 29   Code C0899: Device Voltage Low
(Part 2 of 3)

Circuit Description

The electronic brake control module (EBCM) monitors the voltage level available for system operation. If the voltage level is too high, damage may result to the system. When the EBCM detects a high voltage condition, the EBCM disables the ABS system.

DTC Descriptor

This diagnostic procedure supports the following DTC:

DTC C0900 Device Voltage High

Conditions for Running the DTC

The vehicle speed is greater than 8 km/h (5 mph).

Conditions for Setting the DTC

The system voltage is greater than 17 volts.

Action Taken When the DTC Sets

If equipped, the following actions will occur:

- The EBCM disables the ABS .
- Dynamic rear proportioning (DRP) is degraded when the code is current.
- The EBCM disables the traction control system (TCS).
- The EBCM disables vehicle stability enhancement system (VSES).
- The ABS indicator turns ON.
- The driver information center (DIC) displays the Service Stability System message.
- The DIC displays the Service Traction System message.

Conditions for Clearing the DTC

- The condition for the DTC is no longer present and the DTC is cleared with a scan tool.
- The EBCM automatically clears the history DTC when a current DTC is not detected in 100 consecutive drive cycles.

Diagnostic Aids

A possible cause of this DTC is overcharging.

LTV0500000005946

Fig. 30   Code C0900: Device Voltage High
(Part 1 of 3)

Test Description

The numbers below refer to the step numbers on the diagnostic table.

2. Use the scan tool in order to inspect the voltage to the EBCM.

3. Use the scan tool in order to inspect the voltage to the body control module (BCM). A high voltage value in multiple modules indicates a concern in the charging system.

4. This step verifies that the condition is still present.

LTV0500000005947

Fig. 30   Code C0900: Device Voltage High
(Part 2 of 3)

Step	Action	Values	Yes	No
1	Did you perform the Diagnostic System Check - Vehicle?	--	Go to Step 2	Go to Diagnostic System Check
2	1. Install a scan tool. 2. Start the engine. 3. With a scan tool, observe the Switched Battery Voltage Signal parameter in the ABS data list. Does the scan tool indicate the voltage is greater than the specified value?	10.5 V	Go to Diagnostic Aids	Go to Step 3
3	With a scan tool, observe the Ignition Voltage Signal parameter in the ABS data list. Does the scan tool indicate the voltage is greater than the specified value?	10.5 V	Go to Step 4	Go to Diagnostic System Check
4	Test the ground circuits of the electronic brake control module (EBCM) including the EBCM ground for a high resistance or an open. Did you find and correct the condition?	--	Go to Step 7	Go to Step 5
5	1. Connect the EBCM harness connector. 2. Turn ON the ignition, with the engine OFF. 3. Use the scan tool in order to clear the DTCs. 4. Operate the vehicle within the Conditions for Running the DTC, as specified in the supporting text. Does the DTC reset?	--	Go to Step 6	Go to Diagnostic Aids
6	Replace the EBCM. Did you complete the repair?	--	Go to Step 7	--
7	1. Use the scan tool in order to clear the DTCs. 2. Operate the vehicle within the Conditions for Running the DTC, as specified in the supporting text. Does the DTC reset?	--	Go to Step 2	System OK

LTV0500000005945

Fig. 29   Code C0899: Device Voltage Low
(Part 3 of 3)

Step	Action	Values	Yes	No
1	Did you perform the Diagnostic System Check - Vehicle?	--	Go to Step 2	Go to Diagnostic System Check
2	1. Turn OFF all of the accessories. 2. Install a scan tool. 3. Start the engine 4. Run the engine at approximately 2,000 RPM. 5. With a scan tool, observe the Switched System Battery Voltage parameter in the ABS data list. Does the scan tool indicate that the voltage is greater than the specified value?	17 V	Go to Step 3	Go to Diagnostic Aids
3	With a scan tool, observe the Battery Volts parameter in Body Control Module (BCM) data list. Does the scan tool indicate the voltage is greater than the specified value?	17 V	Go to Diagnostic System Check	Go to Step 4
4	1. Use the scan tool in order to clear the DTCs. 2. Operate the vehicle within the conditions for Running the DTC, as specified in the supporting test. Does the DTC reset?	--	Go to Step 5	Go to Diagnostic Aids
5	Replace the electronic brake control module (EBCM). Did you complete the repair?	--	Go to Step 6	--
6	1. Use the scan tool in order to clear the DTCs. 2. Operate the vehicle within the conditions for Running the DTC, as specified in the supporting test. Does the DTC reset?	--	Go to Step 2	System OK

LTV0500000005948

Fig. 30   Code C0900: Device Voltage High
(Part 3 of 3)

DELPHI 7.4

5-165

DTC Descriptor

DTC C1100 : Base Brake System Pressure Sensor 2

Diagnostic Fault Information

Perform the Diagnostic System Check - Vehicle prior to using this diagnostic procedure.

Circuit/System Description

The electronic brake control module (EBCM) uses an input from 2 brake fluid pressure sensors to enhance Antilock Brake System (ABS) braking and vehicle stability if equipped.

Conditions for Running the DTC

- The ignition is ON for 1 second and greater than 8 volts.
- The 5-volt reference to the brake pressure sensor is in range.

Conditions for Setting the DTC

The 2 master cylinder pressure sensors do not correlate.

Action Taken When the DTC Sets

If equipped, the following actions will occur:

- The EBCM disables the Vehicle Stability Enhancement System (VSES) for the duration of the ignition cycle.
- The EBCM disables the Traction Control System (TCS) for the duration of the ignition cycle.
- The EBCM disables the TCS for the duration of the ignition cycle.
- The driver information center (DIC) displays the Service Stability System and Service Traction System message.

Conditions for Clearing the DTC

- The condition for the DTC is no longer present and the DTC is cleared with a scan tool.
- The EBCM automatically clears the history DTC when a current DTC is not detected in 100 consecutive drive cycles.

Diagnostic Aids

- The brake pressure sensors are internal to the EBCM assembly and cannot be diagnosed or replaced separately. If equipped, the primary and secondary brake pressure sensor 5-volt reference circuit and low reference is shared with other components in the vehicle stability system. DTCs can

LTV0500000005949

Fig. 31   Code C1100: Base Brake System Pressure Sensor 2 (Part 1 of 2)

Circuit Description

The electronic brake control module (EBCM) uses the input from the brake fluid pressure sensor 2 to enhance Antilock Brake System (ABS) braking and vehicle stability if equipped.

DTC Descriptor

This diagnostic procedure supports the following DTC:

DTC C1101 Base Brake System Pressure Sensor 2 Range

Conditions for Running the DTC

- The ignition is ON for 1 second and greater than 8 volts.
- The 5-volt reference to the secondary brake pressure sensor is in range.

Conditions for Setting the DTC

- The secondary brake fluid pressure sensor signal is greater than 4.9 volts.
- The secondary brake fluid pressure sensor signal is less than 0.15 volt.

Action Taken When the DTC Sets

If equipped, the following actions will occur:

- The EBCM disables the vehicle stability enhancement system (VSES) for the duration of the ignition cycle.
- The EBCM disables the traction control system (TCS) for the duration of the ignition cycle.
- The Traction Control Off indicator turns ON.
- The driver information center (DIC) displays the Service Stability System and Service Traction System message.

LTV0500000005951

Fig. 32   Code C1101: Base Brake System Pressure Sensor 2 Range (Part 1 of 3)

set for other components that share circuits with the secondary brake pressure sensor.

- DTC C0870 is set if the 5-volt reference voltage is out of range.

Reference Information

Schematic Reference
Antilock Brake System Schematics
Connector End View Reference
Antilock Brake System Connector End Views
Description and Operation
ABS Description and Operation
Electrical Information Reference

- Circuit Testing
- Connector Repairs
- Test for Intermittent Conditions and Poor Connections
- Wiring Repairs

Circuit/System Testing

Important: If DTC C0870 is set, diagnosis it before performing this diagnostic.

Verify DTC C1100 is not set.
⇒ If DTC is set, replace the EBCM and the Brake Pressure Modulator Valve.

Repair Instructions

Perform the Diagnostic Repair Verification after completing the diagnostic procedure.
- Brake Pressure Modulator Valve (BPMV) Replacement
- Control Module References for EBCM replacement, setup, and programming.

LTV0500000005950

Fig. 31   Code C1100: Base Brake System Pressure Sensor 2 (Part 2 of 2)

Conditions for Clearing the DTC

- The condition for the DTC is no longer present and the DTC is cleared with a scan tool.
- The EBCM automatically clears the history DTC when a current DTC is not detected in 100 consecutive drive cycles.

Diagnostic Aids

The brake pressure sensors are internal to the EBCM assembly and cannot be diagnosed or replaced separately. If equipped, the secondary brake pressure sensor 5-volt reference circuit and low reference circuit is shared with other components in the vehicle stability system. DTCs can set for other components that share circuits with the secondary brake pressure sensor.

Test Description

The number below refers to the step number on the diagnostic table.

2. The EBCM supplies a 5-volt reference to several sensors. DTC C0870 is set if the 5-volt reference voltage is out of range.

LTV0500000005952

Fig. 32   Code C1101: Base Brake System Pressure Sensor 2 Range (Part 2 of 3)

Step	Action	Yes	No
1	Did you perform the Diagnostic System Check - Vehicle?	Go to Step 2	Go to Diagnostic System Check
2	Is DTC C0870 set also?	Go to DTC C0870	Go to Step 3
3	Replace the electronic brake control module (EBCM). Did you complete the replacement?	Go to Step 4	--
4	1. Use the scan tool in order to clear the DTCs. 2. Operate the vehicle within normal driving conditions. Does the DTC reset?	Go to Step 1	System OK

LTV0500000005953

Fig. 32   Code C1101: Base Brake System Pressure Sensor 2 Range (Part 3 of 3)

Circuit Description

The instrument cluster controls the operation of the ABS indicator. The electronic brake control module (EBCM) reports the desired status of the ABS indicator via serial data messages.

Diagnostic Aids

The malfunction must be present during diagnosis in order to prevent unnecessary parts replacement. Always begin diagnosis with Diagnostic System Check - Vehicle .

Test Description

The number below refers to the step number on the diagnostic table.

3. This step tests if the instrument panel cluster (IPC) is able to turn OFF the ABS indicator.

Step	Action	Yes	No
1	Did you perform the Diagnostic System Check - Vehicle?	Go to Step 2	Go to Diagnostic System Check
2	1. Turn OFF the ignition for 5 seconds. 2. Turn ON the ignition while observing the ABS indicator. Does the ABS indicator illuminate for 2 seconds and then turn OFF?	Go to Diagnostic Aids	Go to Step 3
3	1. Install a scan tool. 2. Select the Instrument Panel Cluster Special Functions menu on the scan tool. 3. Command the instrument panel cluster (IPC) lamps OFF. Does the ABS indicator turn OFF?	Go to Step 5	Go to Step 4

LTV0500000005954

Fig. 33   ABS Indicator Always On (Part 1 of 2)

Circuit Description

The instrument cluster controls the operation of the ABS indicator. The electronic brake control module (EBCM) reports the desired status of the ABS indicator via serial data messages.

Diagnostic Aids

The malfunction must be present during diagnosis in order to prevent unnecessary parts replacement. Always begin diagnosis with Diagnostic System Check - Vehicle .

Test Description

The number below refers to the step number on the diagnostic table.

3. This step tests if the instrument panel cluster (IPC) is able to turn OFF the ABS indicator.

Step	Action	Yes	No
1	Did you perform the Diagnostic System Check - Vehicle?	Go to Step 2	Go to Diagnostic System Check
2	1. Turn OFF the ignition for 5 seconds. 2. Turn ON the ignition while observing the ABS indicator. Does the ABS indicator illuminate for 2 seconds and then turn OFF?	Go to Diagnostic Aids	Go to Step 3
3	1. Install a scan tool. 2. Select the Instrument Panel Cluster Special Functions menu on the scan tool. 3. Command the instrument panel cluster (IPC) lamps ON. Does the ABS indicator turn ON?	Go to Step 5	Go to Step 4

LTV0500000005956

Fig. 34   ABS Indicator Inoperative (Part 1 of 2)

4	Replace the IPC. Did you complete the replacement?	Go to Step 6	--
5	Replace the electronic brake control module (EBCM). Did you complete the replacement?	Go to Step 6	--
6	1. Turn OFF the ignition for 5 seconds. 2. Turn ON the ignition while observing the ABS indicator. Does the ABS indicator illuminate for 2 seconds and then turn OFF?	System OK	Go to Step 3

LTV0500000005957

Fig. 34   ABS Indicator Inoperative (Part 2 of 2)

4	Replace the IPC. Did you complete the replacement?	Go to Step 6	--
5	Replace the electronic brake control module (EBCM). Did you complete the replacement?	Go to Step 6	--
6	1. Turn OFF the ignition for 5 seconds. 2. Turn ON the ignition while observing the ABS indicator. Does the ABS indicator illuminate for 2 seconds and then turn OFF?	System OK	Go to Step 3

LTV0500000005955

Fig. 33   ABS Indicator Always On (Part 2 of 2)

Circuit Description

The Traction Off indicator is controlled by the instrument cluster via serial data messages from the body control module (BCM). When the traction control system (TCS) switch is pressed, the BCM commands the instrument cluster to turn ON the Traction Off indicator.

The Traction Off indicator will also turn ON during the instrument cluster bulb check. When the ignition switch is turned to ON, the Traction Off indicator will turn ON for approximately 3 seconds and then turn OFF.

Diagnostic Aids

The malfunction must be present during diagnosis in order to prevent unnecessary parts replacement. Always begin diagnosis with the Diagnostic System Check - Vehicle.

Test Description

The number below refers to the step number on the diagnostic table.

6. This step tests if the instrument panel cluster (IPC) is able to turn OFF the Traction Off indicator.

Step	Action	Yes	No
1	Did you perform the Diagnostic System Check - Vehicle?	Go to Step 2	Go to Diagnostic System Check
2	1. Turn OFF the ignition for 5 seconds. 2. Turn ON the ignition while observing the Traction Off indicator. Does the Traction Off indicator illuminate for 2 seconds and then turn OFF?	Go to Diagnostic Aids	Go to Step 3
3	1. Disconnect the harness connector of the traction control system (TCS) switch. 2. Momentarily ground the TCS switch signal circuit. Does the Traction Off indicator turn OFF and ON?	Go to Step 4	Go to Step 5

LTV0500000005958

Fig. 35   Traction Off Indicator Always On (Part 1 of 2)

4	Replace the TCS switch. Did you complete the replacement?	Go to Step 9	--
5	Test for a short to ground in the TCS switch signal circuit. Did you find and correct the condition?	Go to Step 9	Go to Step 6
6	1. Install a scan tool. 2. Select the Instrument Panel Cluster (IPC) Special Functions menu on the scan tool. 3. Command the IPC lamps OFF. Does the Traction Off indicator turn OFF?	Go to Step 8	Go to Step 7
7	Replace the IPC. Did you complete the replacement?	Go to Step 9	--
8	Replace the body control module (BCM). Did you complete the replacement?	Go to Step 9	--
9	1. Turn OFF the ignition for 5 seconds. 2. Turn ON the ignition while observing the Traction Off indicator. Does the Traction Off indicator illuminate for 2 seconds and then turn OFF?	System OK	Go to Step 2

LTV0500000005959

Fig. 35   Traction Off Indicator Always On (Part 2 of 2)

Circuit Description

The Traction Off indicator is controlled by the instrument cluster via serial data messages from the body control module (BCM). When the traction control system (TCS) switch is pressed, the BCM commands the instrument cluster to turn ON the Traction Off indicator.

The Traction Off indicator will also turn ON during the instrument cluster bulb check. When the ignition switch is turned to ON, the Traction Off indicator will turn ON for approximately 3 seconds and then turn OFF.

Diagnostic Aids

The malfunction must be present during diagnosis in order to prevent unnecessary parts replacement. Always begin diagnosis with the Diagnostic System Check - Vehicle.

Test Description

The number below refers to the step number on the diagnostic table.

6. This step tests if the instrument panel cluster (IPC) is able to turn ON the Traction Off indicator.

Step	Action	Yes	No
1	Did you perform the Diagnostic System Check - Vehicle?	Go to Step 2	Go to Diagnostic System Check
2	1. Turn OFF the ignition for 5 seconds. 2. Turn ON the ignition while observing the Traction Off indicator. Does the Traction Off indicator illuminate for 2 seconds and then turn OFF?	Go to Diagnostic Aids	Go to Step 3
3	1. Disconnect the harness connector of the traction control system (TCS) switch. 2. Ground the TCS signal circuit at the TCS harness connector. Does the Traction Off indicator illuminate?	Go to Step 4	Go to Step 5

LTV0500000005960

Fig. 36   Traction Off Indicator Inoperative (Part 1 of 2)

Circuit Description

Proper operation of the vehicle stability enhancement system (VSES) is highly dependent on the ability to apply brake pressure to a selected wheel, through the brake pressure modulator valve (BPMV), as commanded by the electronic brake control module (EBCM). The EBCM may not be able to detect certain mechanical failures that may cause the VSES to perform poorly. This diagnostic procedure is designed to help diagnose concerns of poor vehicle stability, that may occur without the presence of any DTCs, by verifying the following.

- The tires are the correct size, properly inflated and in acceptable condition.
- There are no mechanical problems in the steering system.
- There are no mechanical problems in the suspension system.
- There are no mechanical problems in the base brake system.
- All of the VSES related hydraulic controls within the BPMV are functioning correctly.

Step	Action	Yes	No
1	Did you review the system Description and Operation and the Diagnostic System Check - Vehicle?	Go to Step 2	Go to Symptoms
2	Inspect all four tires for the following. • Improper size • Incorrect air pressure • Uneven tread wear • Insufficient tread Did you find and correct a concern?	Go to Step 8	Go to Step 3
3	Inspect the vehicle for proper power steering operation. Did you find and correct a concern?	Go to Step 8	Go to Step 4

LTV0500000005962

Fig. 37   Vehicle Stability Enhancement System Poor Performance (Part 1 of 2)

	Action	Yes	No
4	Replace the TCS switch. Did you complete the replacement?	Go to Step 9	--
5	Test for an open in the TCS switch signal circuit. Did you find and correct the condition?	Go to Step 9	Go to Step 6
6	1. Install a scan tool. 2. Select the Instrument Panel Cluster (IPC) Special Functions menu on the scan tool. 3. Command the IPC lamps ON. Does the Traction Off indicator turn ON?	Go to Step 8	Go to Step 7
7	Replace the IPC. Did you complete the replacement?	Go to Step 9	--
8	Replace the body control module (BCM). Did you complete the replacement?	Go to Step 9	--
9	1. Turn OFF the ignition for 5 seconds. 2. Turn ON the ignition while observing the Traction Off indicator. Does the Traction Off indicator illuminate for 2 seconds and then turn OFF?	System OK	Go to Step 2

LTV0500000005961

Fig. 36   Traction Off Indicator Inoperative (Part 2 of 2)

	Action	Yes	No
4	Diagnose any suspension symptoms exhibited by the vehicle. Did you find and correct a concern?	Go to Step 8	Go to Step 5
5	1. Raise the vehicle so that all four wheels are about 15 cm (6 in) off of the floor. Refer to Lifting and Jacking the Vehicle in General Information. 2. With help from an assistant, verify that the brake at each wheel is applying and releasing properly when the brake pedal is applied and released. Did you find and correct a concern?	Go to Step 8	Go to Step 6
6	Diagnose any hydraulic brake symptoms exhibited by the vehicle. Did you find and correct a concern?	Go to Step 8	Go to Step 7
7	Replace the brake pressure modulator valve (BPMV). Did you complete the replacement?	Go to Step 8	--
8	Test drive the vehicle to verify that the stability concern has been corrected. Has the concern been corrected?	System OK	Go to Step 2

LTV0500000005963

Fig. 37   Vehicle Stability Enhancement System Poor Performance (Part 2 of 2)

°C	°F	OHMS
		Temperature vs Resistance Values (Approximate)
150	302	47
140	284	60
130	266	77
120	248	100
110	230	132
100	212	177
90	194	241
80	176	332
70	158	467
60	140	667
50	122	973
45	113	1188
40	104	1459
35	95	1802
30	86	2238
25	77	2796
20	68	3520
15	59	4450
10	50	5670
5	41	7280
0	32	9420
-5	23	12300
-10	14	16180
-15	5	21450
-20	-4	28680
-30	-22	52700
-40	-40	100700

LTV0500000005964

Fig. 38   Temperature vs. resistance values

Kelsey-Hayes

NOTE: On Air Bag Equipped Models, Refer To "Air Bag System Precautions" Located In The Front Of This Manual For System Disarming & Arming Procedures.

NOTE: Electrical Symbol & Wire Color Code Identification Located In The Front Of This Manual May Be Used As An Aid When Using Wiring Circuits Found In This Section.

NOTE: Refer To "Computer Relearn Procedures" Located In The Front Of This Manual For Computer Relearn Procedures.

INDEX

	Page No.
Description	5-169
Diagnosis & Testing	5-169
Accessing Diagnostic Trouble Codes	5-169
Clearing Diagnostic Trouble Codes	5-170
Connector Pin Identification	5-169
Diagnostic Tests	5-170
Astro, Blazer, Jimmy, Safari, Sonoma, SSR & S10	5-170
Avalanche, Escalade, Escalade EXT, Suburban, Tahoe & Yukon	5-170
Bravada, Envoy, Rainier & Trailblazer	5-170
Express & Savana	5-170
Sierra & Silverado	5-170
Diagnostic Trouble Code Interpretation	5-169

	Page No.
Intermittents & Poor Connections	5-170
Symptom Tests	5-170
Express & Savana	5-170
Astro, Blazer, Jimmy, Safari, Sonoma, SSR & S10	5-170
Avalanche, Escalade, Escalade EXT, Suburban, Tahoe & Yukon	5-170
Bravada, Envoy, Rainier & Trailblazer	5-170
Sierra & Silverado	5-170
Temperature Vs. Resistance	5-170
Wiring Diagrams	5-169
Astro, Blazer, Jimmy, Safari, Sonoma, SSR & S10	5-169
Avalanche, Escalade, Escalade EXT, Suburban, Tahoe & Yukon	5-169

	Page No.
Bravada, Envoy, Rainier & Trailblazer	5-170
Express & Savana	5-170
Sierra & Silverado	5-170
Diagnostic Chart Index	5-187
Precautions	5-169
Air Bag Systems	5-169
Battery Ground Cable	5-169
System Service	5-170
Brake System Bleed	5-170
Manual Bleed	5-171
Pressure Bleed	5-171
Component Replacement	5-171
Brake Pressure Modulator Valve (BPMV)	5-172
Electronic Brake Control Module (EBCM)	5-171
Front Wheel Speed Sensor	5-172

PRECAUTIONS

Air Bag Systems

Refer to "Air Bag System Precautions" in the front of this manual for system disarming and arming procedures.

Battery Ground Cable

Prior to service disconnect battery ground cable and isolate as required.

DESCRIPTION

When wheel slip is detected during a brake application, the ABS enters anti-lock mode. During anti-lock braking, hydraulic pressure in the individual wheel circuits is controlled to prevent any wheel from slipping. A separate hydraulic line and specific solenoid valves are provided for each wheel. The ABS can decrease, hold, or increase hydraulic pressure to each wheel brake. The ABS cannot, however, increase hydraulic pressure above the amount which is transmitted by the master cylinder during braking.

During anti-lock braking, a series of rapid pulsations is felt in the brake pedal. These pulsations are caused by the rapid changes in position of the individual solenoid valves as the EBCM responds to wheel speed sensor inputs and attempts to prevent wheel slip. These pedal pulsations are present only during anti-lock braking and stop when normal braking is resumed or when the vehicle comes to a stop. A ticking or popping noise may also be heard as the solenoid valves cycle rapidly. During anti-lock braking on dry pavement, intermittent chirping noises may be heard as the tires approach slipping. These noises and pedal pulsations are considered normal during anti-lock operation.

Vehicles equipped with ABS may be stopped by applying normal force to the brake pedal. Brake pedal operation during normal braking is no different than that of previous non-ABS systems. Maintaining a constant force on the brake pedal provides the shortest stopping distance while maintaining vehicle stability.

DIAGNOSIS & TESTING

Accessing Diagnostic Trouble Codes

Connect a suitably programmed scan tool to Data Link Connector (DLC) and follow manufacturers instructions.

Diagnostic Trouble Code Interpretation

Refer to "Diagnostic Chart Index" for trouble code identification.

Connector Pin Identification

Refer to **Figs. 1 through 9** for connector pin identification.

Wiring Diagrams

ASTRO, BLAZER, JIMMY, SAFARI, SONOMA, SSR & S10

Refer to **Figs. 10 through 12** for wiring diagrams.

AVALANCHE, ESCALADE, ESCALADE EXT, SUBURBAN, TAHOE & YUKON

Refer to **Figs. 13 and 14** for wiring diagrams.

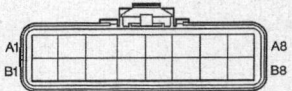

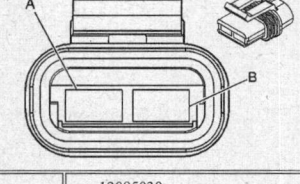

Connector Part Information	• 15356849	
	• 16-Way F Micro-Pack 100W Series (GRY)	
Pin	Wire Color	Circuit No.	Function
---	---	---	---
A1	BRN	441	Ignition 3 Voltage
A2	YEL	873	Left Front Wheel Speed Sensor Low Reference
A3	DK GRN	872	Right Front Wheel Speed Sensor Signal
A4-A8	--	--	Not Used
B1	YEL/BLK	1827	Vehicle Speed Signal
B2	LT BLU	830	Left Front Wheel Speed Sensor Signal
B3	TAN	833	Right Front Wheel Speed Sensor Low Reference
B4	--	--	Not Used
B5	PPL	420	TCC Brake Switch/Cruise Control Release Signal
B6	LT BLU	1122	ABS/TCS Class 2 Serial Data
B7	--	--	Not Used
B8	PPL	333	Brake Fluid Level Sensor Signal

LTV0500000005232

Fig. 1 Connector pin identification. Astro & Safari

Connector Part Information	• 12085030	
	• 2-Way F METRI PAC 630 Series Sealed (BLK)	
Pin	Wire Color	Circuit No.	Function
---	---	---	---
A	RED	442	Battery Positive Voltage
B	BLK	2150	Ground

LTV0500000005297

Fig. 2 Connector pin identification (Part 1 of 4). 2002 Avalanche, Escalade, Escalade EXT, Suburban, Tahoe & Yukon

BRAVADA, ENVOY, RAINIER & TRAILBLAZER

Refer to **Figs. 15 and 16** for wiring diagrams.

EXPRESS & SAVANA

Refer to **Figs. 17 and 18** for wiring diagrams.

SIERRA & SILVERADO

Refer to **Figs. 19 and 20** for wiring diagrams.

Diagnostic Tests

ASTRO, BLAZER, JIMMY, SAFARI, SONOMA, SSR & S10

Refer to **Figs. 21 through 37** for diagnostic test procedures.

AVALANCHE, ESCALADE, ESCALADE EXT, SUBURBAN, TAHOE & YUKON

2002

Refer to **Figs. 38 through 64** for diagnostic test procedures.

2003-06

Refer to **Figs. 65 through 107** for diagnostic test procedures.

BRAVADA, ENVOY, RAINIER & TRAILBLAZER

2002-03

Refer to **Figs. 108 through 125** for diagnostic test procedures.

2004-06

Refer to **Figs. 126 through 144** for diagnostic test procedures.

EXPRESS & SAVANA

2002

Refer to **Figs. 145 through 157** for diagnostic test procedures.

2003-06

Refer to **Figs. 158 through 178** for diagnostic test procedures.

SIERRA & SILVERADO

2002

Refer to "2002–03 Bravada, Envoy & Trailblazer" for diagnostic test procedures.

2003-06

Refer to **Figs. 179 through 207** for diagnostic test procedures.

Symptom Tests

ASTRO, BLAZER, JIMMY, SAFARI, SONOMA, SSR & S10

Refer to **Figs. 208 through 211** for symptom tests.

AVALANCHE, ESCALADE, ESCALADE EXT, SUBURBAN, TAHOE & YUKON

Refer to **Figs. 212 through 230** for symptom tests.

BRAVADA, ENVOY, RAINIER & TRAILBLAZER

Refer to **Figs. 231 through 241** for symptom tests.

EXPRESS & SAVANA

Refer to **Figs. 242 through 251** for symptom tests.

SIERRA & SILVERADO

2002

Refer to "2002–03 Bravada, Envoy & Trailblazer" for symptom test procedures.

2003-06

Refer to **Figs. 252 through 255** for symptoms test procedures.

Temperature Vs. Resistance

Refer to **Fig. 256** temperarature vs. resistance values.

Intermittents & Poor Connections

Most Intermittents are caused by faulty electrical connections or wiring, although a sticking relay or solenoid can also cause an intermittent condition. Inspect wiring and connectors for the following:
1. Poor mating of connector halves, or terminals not fully seated in connector body.
2. Dirt or corrosion on terminals.
3. Damaged connector body.
4. Improperly formed or damaged terminals.
5. Poor terminal to wire connection.
6. Rubbed through wiring insulation.
7. Wiring broken inside insulation.

Clearing Diagnostic Trouble Codes

Connect a suitably programmed scan tool to Data Link Connector (DLC) and follow manufacturers instructions.

SYSTEM SERVICE

Brake System Bleed

Gravity and vacuum bleeding procedures are not recommended for use with the anti-lock brake system. The manual bleed procedure is the preferred method, although pressure bleeding is

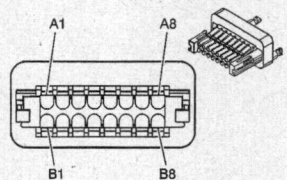

Connector Part Information	• 12193519	
	• 16-Way F Micro-Pack 100W (NAT)	
Pin	Wire Color	Circuit No.	Function
---	---	---	---
A1	BRN	441	Ignition 3 Voltage
A2	YEL	873	Wheel Speed Sensor - Return - Left Front
A3	DK GRN	872	Wheel Speed Sensor - Signal - Right Front
A4	TAN/BLK	464	Delivered Torque Signal
A5	--	--	Not Used
A6	WHT	1808	Service Traction Control Signal
A7	--	--	Not Used
A8	BLK/WHT	1695	Axle Switch Signal (W/O ETC)
A8	BRN/WHT	1571	Traction Control Switch Signal - W/ Auto Traction Control
B1	YEL/BLK	1827	Vehicle Speed Signal
B2	LT BLU	830	Wheel Speed Sensor - Signal - Left Front
B3	TAN	833	Wheel Speed Sensor - Return - Right Front
B4	ORN/BLK	463	Requested Torque Signal
B5	PPL	420	TCC Brake Switch Signal
B6	LT BLU	1122	ABS/TCS Class 2 Serial Data
B7	LT BLU	832	Traction Control Active Signal
B8	PPL	333	Brake Fluid Level Sensor Signal

LTV0500000005298

Fig. 2   Connector pin identification (Part 2 of 4). 2002 Avalanche, Escalade, Escalade EXT, Suburban, Tahoe & Yukon

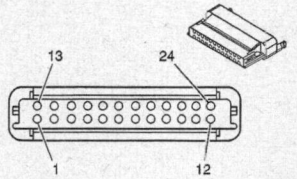

Connector Part Information	• 12129225	
	• 24-Way F Micro-Pack 100 series, sealed (NAT)	
Pin	Wire Color	Circuit No.	Function
---	---	---	---
1	YEL	873	Left Front Wheel Speed Sensor Low Reference
2	LT BLU	830	Left Front Wheel Speed Sensor Signal
3	BRN/WHT	2086	YAW Rate Signal
4	GRY	791	PWM Serial Data
5	YEL/BLK	1827	Vehicle Speed Signal
6	ORN/BLK	463	Requested Torque Signal
7	PPL	420	TCC Brake Switch Signal
8	-	-	Not Used
9	DK GRN	2087	Yaw Rate Sensor 5 Volt Reference
10-11	--	--	Not Used
12	BRN	441	Ignition 3 Voltage
13	TAN	833	Right Front Vehicle Speec Sensor Low Reference
14	WHT	790	PWM Serial Data
15	PPL/WHT	1699	Lateral Acceleration Signal
16	DK GRN	872	Right Front Wheel Speed Sensor Signal
17	ORN	2554	LED Signal
18	TAN/BLK	464	Delivered Torque Signal
19	PPL	333	Brake Fluid Level Sensor Signal
20	LT BLU	2206	VSES Mode
21	LT BLU	2088	Yaw Rate Sensor Low Reference
22-23	--	--	Not Used
24	LT BLU	1122	ABS/TCS CLass 2 Serial Data

LTV0500000005299

Fig. 2   Connector pin identification (Part 3 of 4). 2002 Avalanche, Escalade, Escalade EXT, Suburban, Tahoe & Yukon

also possible. Do not pump the brake pedal during the bleeding process, as fluid aeration may occur.

MANUAL BLEED

1. Raise and support vehicle, then connect a clear plastic tube to brake bleed screw at righthand rear wheel.
2. Place free end of tube in a glass jar partially filled with clean brake fluid. **Ensure end of tube remains submerged in fluid and master cylinder reservoir is kept full.**
3. Open bleed screw ½–1 full turn, then slowly depress brake pedal until it reaches bottom of travel.
4. With pedal held down, tighten bleed screw, then release brake pedal and wait 10–15 seconds.
5. Continue bleeding wheel hydraulic circuit until approximately one pint of fluid has been bled through, or until air bubbles no longer flow out through plastic tube.
6. **Inspect master cylinder reservoir brake fluid level after every four to six brake pedal strokes.**
7. Repeat preceding bleed steps for remaining wheel hydraulic circuits in following order: first lefthand rear, then righthand front and, finally, lefthand front wheel.
8. If any component is replaced which may have allowed air to enter Brake Pressure Modulator Valve (BPMV), proceed as follows:
   a. Set parking brake, then connect scan tool to diagnostic connector.

b. With brake pedal firmly applied, run scan tool "Function Test."
c. Bleed all four wheel hydraulic circuits using bleed procedure in preceding steps.
9. Ensure brake pedal feels firm and all bleed screws are tightened securely prior to test driving vehicle. Bleed system as many times as required to achieve proper operation.

PRESSURE BLEED

1. Install pressure bleeder using equipment manufacturer's instructions.
2. **On models equipped with metering portion of combination valve,** remove combination valve dust caps and install valve depressing tool No. J-39177, or equivalent on valve end.
3. **On all models,** bleed all four wheel hydraulic circuits. Bleed righthand rear wheel first, followed by lefthand rear, righthand front and, finally, lefthand front. **Leave bleed screws open until one pint of fluid has been bled out of each wheel.**
4. After all wheel hydraulic circuits have been bled, remove combination valve clip, then connect scan tool to diagnostic connector.
5. With brake pedal firmly applied, run four scan tool "Functional Tests," then repeat preceding steps.
6. Ensure brake pedal feels firm; bleed wheels as many times as required to achieve proper pedal feel. It is likely

that 2–3 quarts of brake fluid will be required to complete a thorough bleed procedure.

Component Replacement

ELECTRONIC BRAKE CONTROL MODULE (EBCM)

1. Raise and support vehicle.
2. Remove mounting nuts and Electro-Hydraulic Control Unit (EHCU) shield **Fig. 257.**
3. Disconnect EBCM electrical connectors.
4. Remove mounting bolts and EHCU from frame far enough to access EBCM **Fig. 258. Do not bend brake pipes.**
5. Remove mounting screws and separate EBCM from Brake Pressure Modulator Valve (BPMV). **Do not pry components to separate.**
6. Reverse procedure to install, noting the following:
   a. Install new EBCM gasket and mounting bolts. **Do not use any gasket sealant.**
   b. **Torque** EBCM to BPMV mounting screws to 39 inch lbs., in criss-cross pattern.
   c. **Torque** shield mounting nuts to 96 inch lbs.

Connector Part Information	• 12110293		
	• 3-Way M/P 150 Series Sealed (BLK)		
Pin	Wire Color	Circuit No.	Function
A	BLK	2552	Low Reference
B	RED	2549	Pressure Transducer Supply Voltage
C	DK GRN	2548	Pressure Transducer Sensor Signall

LTV0500000005300

Fig. 2 Connector pin identification (Part 4 of 4). 2002 Avalanche, Escalade, Escalade EXT, Suburban, Tahoe & Yukon

BRAKE PRESSURE MODULATOR VALVE (BPMV)

1. Raise and support vehicle.
2. Remove mounting nuts and Electro-Hydraulic Control Unit (EHCU) mounting shield **Fig. 257.**
3. Disconnect EBCM electrical connectors.
4. Disconnect combination valve electrical connector.
5. Remove front and rear brake pipes from combination valve.
6. Remove hydraulic lines from BPMV tube adapters.
7. Remove EHCU.
8. Remove mounting screws, then separate BPMV from EBCM. **Do not pry components to separate.**
9. Remove mounting bolts and combination valve.
10. Remove transfer tubes.
11. Reverse procedure to install, noting the following:
    a. Install new EBCM gasket, mounting bolts and transfer tubes.
    b. **Torque** combination valve bolts alternately to 72 inch lbs., then to 12 ft. lbs.
    c. **Torque** EBCM Torx bolts to 39 inch lbs., in X-pattern.
    d. **Torque** BPMV to bracket bolts to 84 inch lbs.
    e. **Torque** front brake pipe fittings to 16 ft. lbs.
    f. **Torque** rear brake pipe fittings to 22 ft. lbs.
    g. **Torque** hydraulic lines to 22 ft. lbs.
    h. **Torque** EHCU shield mounting nuts to 84 inch lbs.

FRONT WHEEL SPEED SENSOR

1. Raise and support vehicle, then remove wheel and tire assembly.

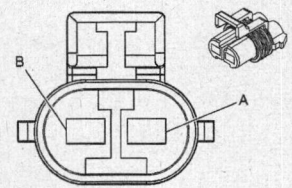

Connector Part Information

• OEM: 12052613
• Service: 12085212
• Description: 2-Way F Metri-Pack 480 Series Sealed (BK)

Pin	Wire Color	Circuit No.	Function
A	BK	2150	Ground
B	RD	442	Battery Positive Voltage

LTV0500000006211

Fig. 3 Connector pin identification (Part 1 of 4). 2003–06 Avalanche, Escalade, Escalade EXT, Suburban, Tahoe & Yukon

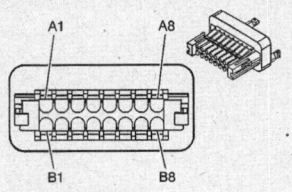

Connector Part Information

• OEM: 12193519
• Service: 88987916
• Description: 16-Way F Micro-Pack 100W (NA)

Pin	Wire Color	Circuit No.	Function
A1	BN	441	Ignition 3 Voltage
A2	YE	873	Left Front Wheel Speed Sensor Low Reference
A3	D-GN	872	Right Front Wheel Speed Sensor Signal
A4	TN/BK	464	Delivered Torque Signal
A5-A7	--	--	Not Used
A8	BK/WH	1695	Traction Control Switch Signal
B1	YE/BK	1827	Vehicle Speed Signal
B2	L-BU	830	Left Front Wheel Speed Sensor Signal
B3	TN	833	Right Front Wheel Speed Sensor Low Reference
B4	OG/BK	463	Requested Torque Signal
B5	PU	420	TCC Brake Switch/Cruise Control Release Signal
B6	L-BU	1122	ABS/TCS Class 2 Serial Data
B7	--	--	Not Used
B8	PU	333	Brake Pressure Sensor Signal (1500 Series)
B8	PU	333	Brake Fluid Level Sensor Signal (2500 Series)

LTV0500000006212

Fig. 3 Connector pin identification (Part 2 of 4). 2003–06 Avalanche, Escalade, Escalade EXT, Suburban, Tahoe & Yukon

2. Remove brake caliper as outlined under "Disc Brakes."
3. Remove hub and rotor assembly as outlined under "Disc Brakes."
4. Disconnect wheel sensor electrical connector.
5. Remove shock tower mounting bolt and washer, then upper control arm snap-in clip.
6. Drill out wheel speed sensor harness clip rivet with 3/16 inch bit.
7. Remove wheel speed sensor wire clip.
8. Remove sensor mounting bolts.
9. Remove mounting bolts, then the sensor and splash shield assembly.
10. Remove splash shield gasket.
11. Reverse procedure to install, noting the following:
    a. **Torque** splash shield mounting bolts to 12 ft. lbs.
    b. **Torque** speed sensor mounting bolts to 19 ft. lbs.
    c. **Torque** speed sensor harness clip mounting bolts to 11 ft. lbs.

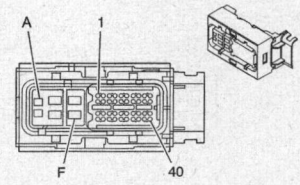

Connector Part Information

- OEM: 15405468
- Service: 89046639
- Description: 46-Way F GT 280 Series (BK)

Pin	Wire Color	Circuit No.	Function
1	D-GN	2087	Steering Wheel Position Sensor 5-Volt Reference
2-3	--	--	Not Used
4	L-BU	1122	ABS/TCS Class 2 Serial Data
5	L-BU	2088	Low Reference
6-10	--	--	Not Used
11	BN	441	Ignition 3 Voltage
12-13	--	--	Not Used
14	OG/BK	463	Requested Torque Signal
15	TN/BK	464	Delivered Torque Signal
16	--	--	Not Used
17	L-BU	715	Lateral Accelerometer Signal
18-20	--	--	Not Used
21	L-GN/BK	5352	Sensor Self Test Signal Circuit
22	PU	420	TCC Brake Switch/Cruise Control Release Signal
23	L-GN	1763	Steering Wheel Position Signal A
24	YE	5353	YAW Rate Frequency
25	--	--	Not Used
26	WH	1765	Steering Wheel Position Marker Pulse Signal
27	L-BU	1764	Steering Wheel Position Signal B
28	--	--	Not Used
29	L-BU	2206	Traction Control Preference Switch Signal
30	D-BU	716	Yaw Rate Sensor Signal
31	PU	333	Brake Fluid Level/Pressure Sensor Signal

LTV0500000006213

**Fig. 3 Connector pin identification (Part 3 of 4).
2003–06 Avalanche, Escalade, Escalade EXT,
Suburban, Tahoe & Yukon**

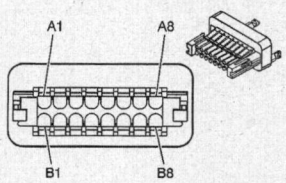

Connector Part Information			• 12193519
			• 16 Way F Micro-Pack 100 W Series (NAT)
Pin	Wire Color	Circuit No.	Function
A1	BRN	441	Ignition 3 Voltage
A1	BRN	441	Ignition 3 Voltage (w/L43)
A2	YEL	873	Left Front Wheel Speed Sensor Low Reference
A3	DK GRN	872	Right Front Wheel Speed Sensor Signal
A4-A7	--	--	Not Used
A8	BLK/WHT	1695	Axle Switch Signal
B1	YEL/BLK	1827	Vehicle Speed Signal
B2	LT BLU	830	Left Front Wheel Speed Sensor Signal
B3	TAN	833	Right Front Wheel Speed Sensor Low Reference
B4	--	--	Not Used
B5	PPL	420	TCC Brake Switch Signal
B6	LT BLU	1122	ABS/TCS Class 2 Serial Data
B7	--	--	Not Used
B8	PPL	333	Brake Fluid Level Sensor Signal

LTV0500000005233

Fig. 4 Connector pin identification. Blazer & Jimmy

32	YE/BK	1827	Vehicle Speed Signal
33	YE	873	Left Front Wheel Speed Sensor Low Reference
34	L-BU	830	Left Front Wheel Speed Sensor Signal
35	TN	833	Right Front Wheel Speed Sensor Low Reference
36	D-GN	872	Right Front Wheel Speed Sensor Signal
37	RD	885	Left Rear Wheel Speed Sensor Low Reference
38	BK	884	Left Rear Wheel Speed Sensor Signal
39	WH	883	Right Rear Wheel Speed Sensor Low Reference
40	BN	882	Right Rear Wheel Speed Sensor Signal
A	D-GN	2878	Precharge Motor Low
B	RD	4042	Battery Positive Voltage
C	BK	2150	Ground
D	D-BU	2877	Precharge Motor Hi
E	BK	2150	Ground
F	RD	442	Battery Positive Voltage

LTV0500000006214

**Fig. 3 Connector pin identification (Part 4 of 4).
2003–06 Avalanche, Escalade, Escalade EXT,
Suburban, Tahoe & Yukon**

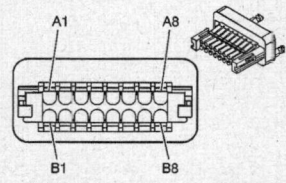

Connector Part Information			• 12193519
			• 16-Way F Micro-Pack 100W (BLK)
Pin	Wire Color	Circuit No.	Function
A1	BRN	441	Ignition 3 Voltage
A2	YEL	873	Left Front Wheel Speed Sensor Low Reference
A3	DK GRN	872	Right Front Wheel Speed Sensor Signal
A4	TAN/BLK	454	Delivered Torque Signal (w/NW7)
A5	--	--	Not Used

LTV0500000006344

**Fig. 5 Connector pin identification (Part 1 of 2).
Bravada, Envoy, Rainier, Sierra, Silverado &
Trailblazer**

A6	WHT	1808	Traction Control Off Indicator Control (w/NW7)
A7	--	--	Not Used
A8	BRN/WHT	1571	Traction Control Switch Signal (w/NW7)
B1	YEL/BLK	1827	Vehicle Speed Signal
B2	LT BLU	830	Left Front Wheel Speed Sensor Signal
B3	TAN	833	Right Front Wheel Speed Sensor Low Reference
B4	ORN/BLK	463	Requested Torque Signal (w/NW7)
B5	PPL	420	TCC Brake/Cruise Control Release Switch Signal
B6	LT BLU	1122	ABS/TCS Class 2 Serial Data
B7	LT BLU	832	Traction Control Active Indicator Control (w/NW7)
B8	PPL	333	Brake Fluid Level Sensor Signal

LTV0500000006345

**Fig. 5 Connector pin identification (Part 2 of 2).
Bravada, Envoy, Rainier, Sierra, Silverado &
Trailblazer**

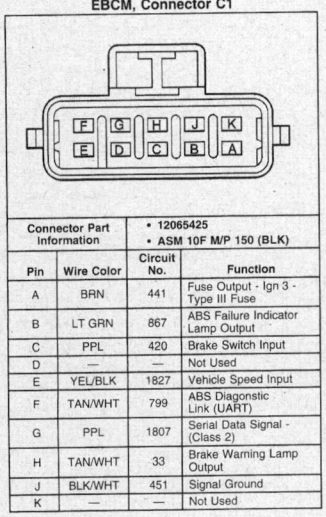

EBCM, Connector C1

Connector Part Information	• 12065425 • ASM 10F M/P 150 (BLK)		
Pin	**Wire Color**	**Circuit No.**	**Function**
A	BRN	441	Fuse Output - Ign 3 - Type III Fuse
B	LT GRN	867	ABS Failure Indicator Lamp Output
C	PPL	420	Brake Switch Input
D	—	—	Not Used
E	YEL/BLK	1827	Vehicle Speed Input
F	TAN/WHT	799	ABS Diagnostic Link (UART)
G	PPL	1807	Serial Data Signal - (Class 2)
H	TAN/WHT	33	Brake Warning Lamp Output
J	BLK/WHT	451	Signal Ground
K	—	—	Not Used

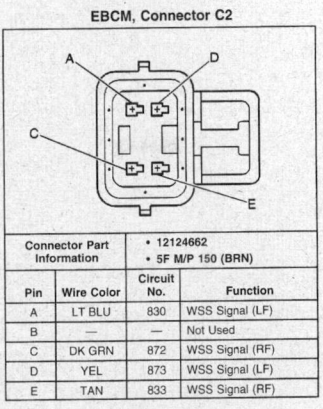

EBCM, Connector C2

Connector Part Information	• 12124662 • 5F M/P 150 (BRN)		
Pin	**Wire Color**	**Circuit No.**	**Function**
A	LT BLU	830	WSS Signal (LF)
B	—	—	Not Used
C	DK GRN	872	WSS Signal (RF)
D	YEL	873	WSS Signal (LF)
E	TAN	833	WSS Signal (RF)

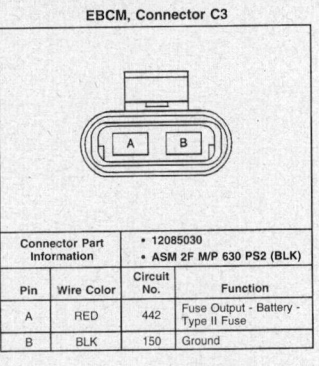

EBCM, Connector C3

Connector Part Information	• 12085030 • ASM 2F M/P 630 PS2 (BLK)		
Pin	**Wire Color**	**Circuit No.**	**Function**
A	RED	442	Fuse Output - Battery - Type II Fuse
B	BLK	150	Ground

GC4020051580010A

Fig. 6 Connector pin identification. 2002 Express & Savana

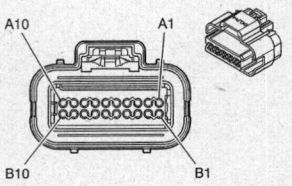

Connector Part Information	• 15339077 • 20-Way F MIC/P 100W (BLK)		
Pin	**Wire Color**	**Circuit No.**	**Function**
A1	YEL	873	Left Front Wheel Speed Sensor Low Reference
A2	DK GRN	872	Right Front Wheel Speed Sensor Signal
A3	PPL	420	TCC Brake Switch/Cruise Control Release Signal
A4-A9	--	--	Not Used
A10	PPL	333	Brake Fluid Level/Pressure Switch Signal

LTV0500000006555

Fig. 7 Connector pin identification (Part 1 of 4). 2003–06 Express & Savana

B1	LT BLU	830	Left Front Wheel Speed Sensor Signal
B2	TAN	833	Right Front Wheel Speed Sensor Low Reference
B3	YEL/BLK	1827	Vehicle Speed Signal
B4-B8	--	--	Not Used
B9	LT BLU	1122	Class 2 Serial Data
B10	BRN	441	Ignition 3 Voltage

LTV0500000006556

Fig. 7 Connector pin identification (Part 2 of 4). 2003–06 Express & Savana

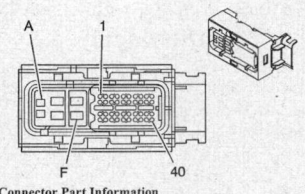

Connector Part Information
• OEM: 15405468
• Service: 89046639
• Description: 46-Way F Mixed 100W 480 Metri-Pack 280 GT Series Seal

Terminal Part Information
• Terminal/Tray: See Terminal Repair Kit
• Core/Insulation Crimp: See Terminal Repair Kit
• Release Tool/Test Probe: See Terminal Repair Kit

Pin	Wire Color	Circuit No.	Function
A	D-GN	2878	Precharge Motor Low
B	RD	4042	Battery Positive Voltage
C	BK	2851	Ground
D	D-BU	2877	Precharge Motor High
E	BK	2150	Ground
F	RD	442	Battery Positive Voltage
1	D-GN	2087	Yaw Rate Sensor 5-Volt Reference
2	GY	626	5-Volt Reference
3	--	--	Not Used
4	L-BU	1122	ABS/TCS Class 2 Serial Data
5	L-BU	2088	Yaw Rate Sensor Low Reference
6	OG/BK	556	Steering Wheel Position Sensor Low Reference
7-10	--	--	Not Used
11	BN	441	Ignition 3 Voltage
12-13	--	--	Not Used
14	OG/BK	463	Requested Torque Signal
15	TN/BK	464	Delivered Torque Signal
16	--	--	Not Used
17	L-BU	715	Lateral Accelerometer Signal

LTV0500000006557

Fig. 7 Connector pin identification (Part 3 of 4). 2003–06 Express & Savana

18-20	--	--	Not Used
21	L-GN/BK	5352	Sensor Self Test Signal Circuit
22	PU	420	TCC Brake Switch/Cruise Control Release Signal
23	L-GN	1763	Steering Wheel Position Signal A
24	YE	5353	Yaw Rate Frequency
25	L-BU	1059	Steering Wheel Position Sensor Signal 1
26	WH	1765	Steering Wheel Position Marker Pulse Signal
27	L-BU	1764	Steering Wheel Position Signal B
28	--	--	Not Used
29	L-BU	2206	Traction Control Preference Switch Signal
30	D-BU	716	Yaw Rate Sensor Signal
31	PU	333	Brake Level Switch Signal
32	YE/BK	1827	Vehicle Speed Signal
33	YE	873	Left Front Wheel Speed Sensor Low Reference
34	L-BU	830	Left Front Wheel Speed Sensor Signal
35	TN	833	Right Front Wheel Speed Sensor Low Reference
36	D-GN	872	Right Front Wheel Speed Sensor Signal
37	RD	885	Left Rear Wheel Speed Sensor Low Reference
38	BK	884	Left Rear Wheel Speed Sensor Signal
39	WH	883	Right Rear Wheel Speed Sensor Low Reference
40	BN	882	Right Rear Wheel Speed Sensor Signal

LTV0500000006558

Fig. 7 Connector pin identification (Part 4 of 4). 2003–06 Express & Savana

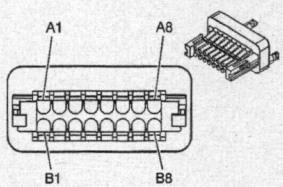

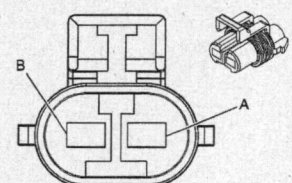

Connector Part Information	• 12193519		
	• 16 Way F Micro-Pack 100 W Series (NAT)		
Pin	Wire Color	Circuit No.	Function
A1	BRN	441	Ignition 3 Voltage
	BRN	441	Ignition 3 Voltage (w/L43)
A2	YEL	873	Left Front Wheel Speed Sensor Low Reference
A3	DK GRN	872	Right Front Wheel Speed Sensor Signal
A4-A7	--	--	Not Used
A8	BLK/WHT	1695	Axle Switch Signal
B1	YEL/BLK	1827	Vehicle Speed Signal
B2	LT BLU	830	Left Front Wheel Speed Sensor Signal
B3	TAN	833	Right Front Wheel Speed Sensor Low Reference
B4	--	--	Not Used
B5	PPL	420	TCC Brake Switch Signal
B6	LT BLU	1122	ABS/TCS Class 2 Serial Data
B7	--	--	Not Used
B8	PPL	333	Brake Fluid Level Sensor Signal

LTV0500000005234

Fig. 8   Connector pin identification. S10 & Sonoma

Connector Part Information

• OEM: 12052613
• Service: 12085212
• Description: 2-Way F Metri-Pack 480 Series Sealed (BK)

Pin	Wire Color	Circuit No.	Function
A	BK	1850	Ground
B	RD	642	Battery Positive Voltage

LTV0500000005235

Fig. 9   Connector pin identification (Part 1 of 2).
SSR

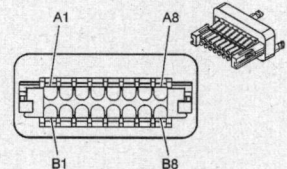

Connector Part Information

• OEM: 12193519
• Service: 88987916
• Description: 16-Way F Micro-Pack 100W Body (BK)/TPA (CL)

Pin	Wire Color	Circuit No.	Function
A1	BN	441	Ignition 3 Voltage
A2	YE	873	Left Front Wheel Speed Sensor Low Reference
A3	D-GN	872	Right Front Wheel Speed Sensor Signal
A4	TN/BK	464	Delivered Torque Signal
A5-A7	--	--	Not Used
A8	BN/WH	1571	Traction Control Switch Signal
B1	YE/BK	1827	Vehicle Speed Signal
B2	L-BU	830	Left Front Wheel Speed Sensor Signal
B3	TN	833	Right Front Wheel Speed Sensor Low Reference
B4	OG/BK	463	Requested Torque Signal
B5	PU	420	TCC Brake Switch/Cruise Control Release Signal
B6	L-BU	1122	ABS/TCS Class 2 Serial Data
B7	--	--	Not Used
B8	PU	333	Brake Fluid Level Sensor Signal

LTV0500000005236

Fig. 9   Connector pin identification (Part 2 of 2).
SSR

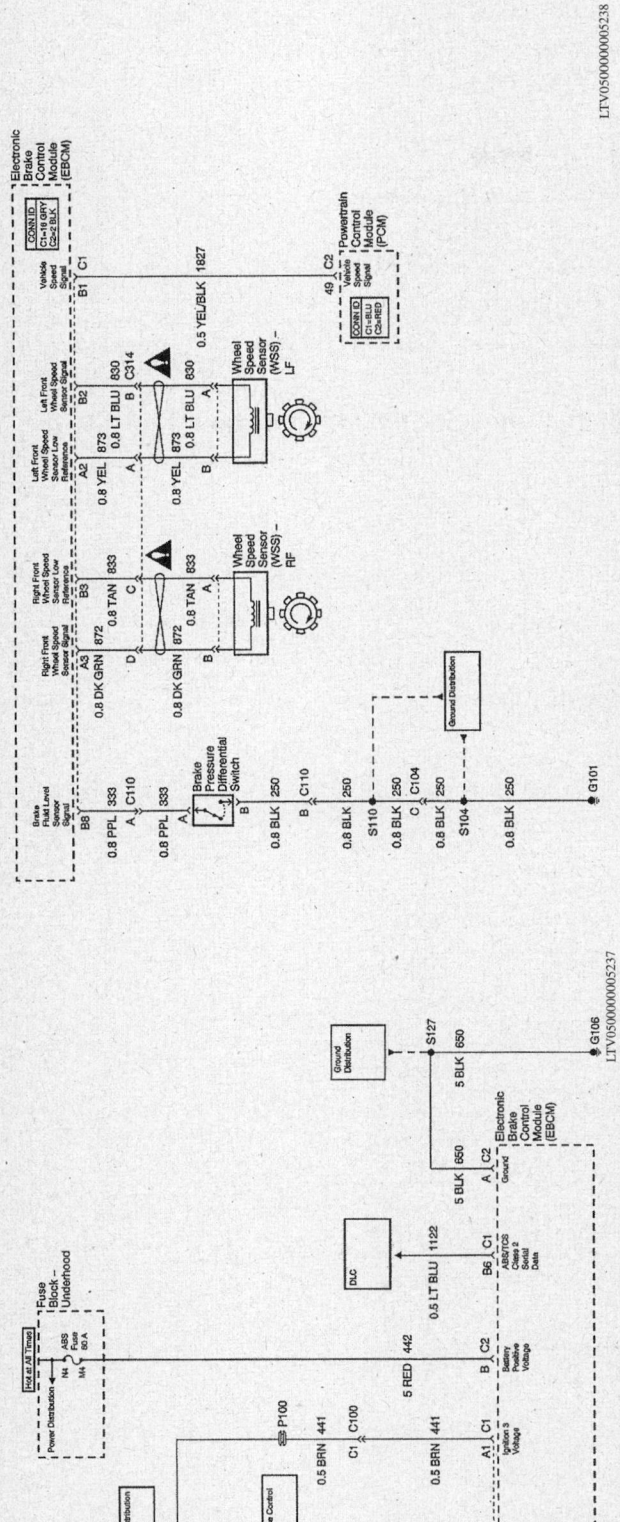

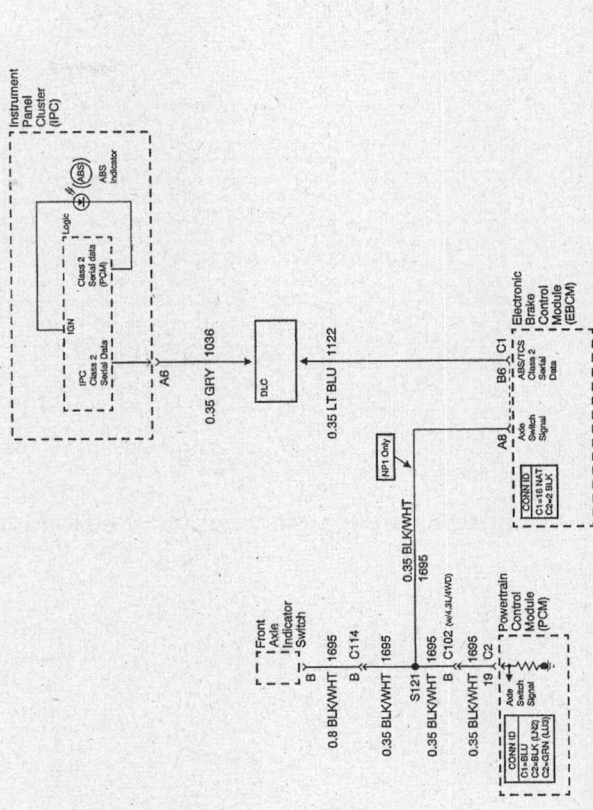

Fig. 10 Wiring diagram (Part 2 of 2). Astro & Safari

Fig. 10 Wiring diagram (Part 1 of 2). Astro & Safari

Fig. 11 Wiring diagram (Part 2 of 3). Blazer, Jimmy, S10 & Sonoma

Fig. 11 Wiring diagram (Part 1 of 3). Blazer, Jimmy, S10 & Sonoma

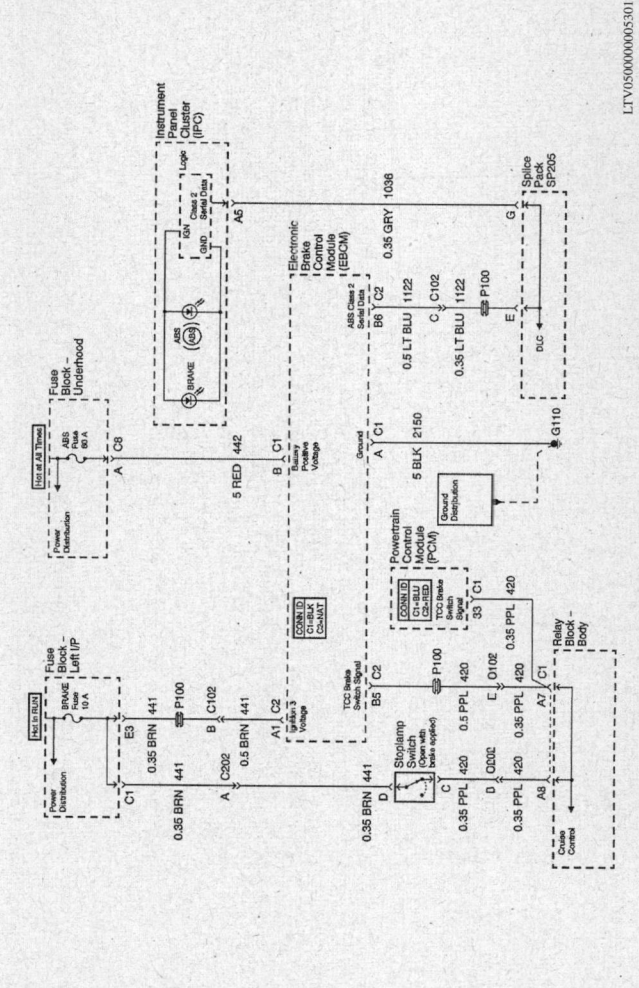

Fig. 12 Wiring diagram (Part 1 of 2). SSR

Fig. 13 Wiring diagram (Part 1 of 7). 2002 Avalanche, Escalade, Escalade EXT, Suburban, Tahoe & Yukon

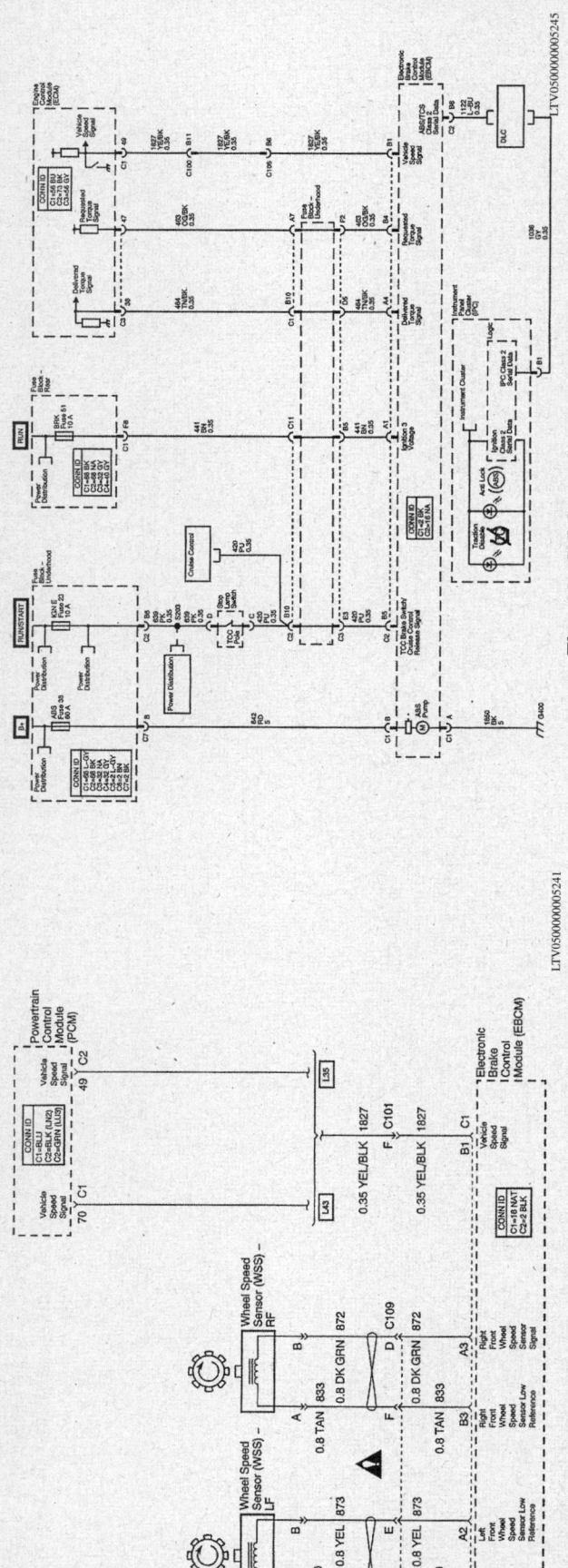

Fig. 11 Wiring diagram (Part 3 of 3). Blazer, Jimmy, S10 & Sonoma

Fig. 12 Wiring diagram (Part 2 of 2). SSR

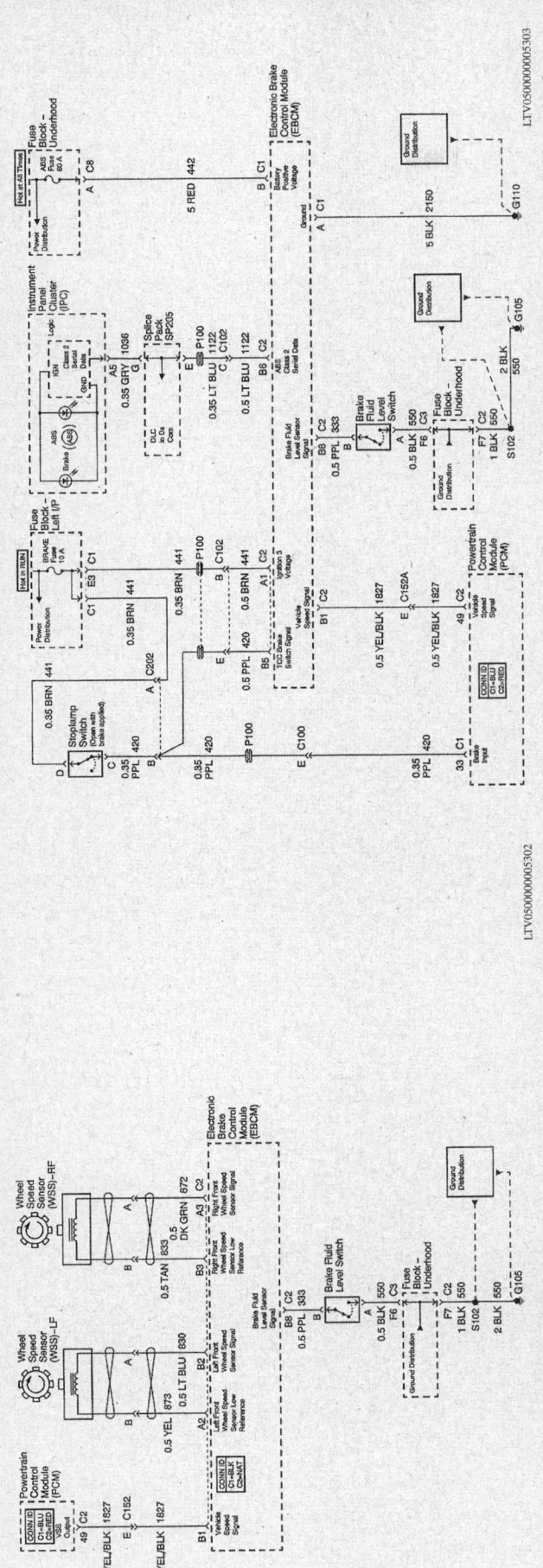

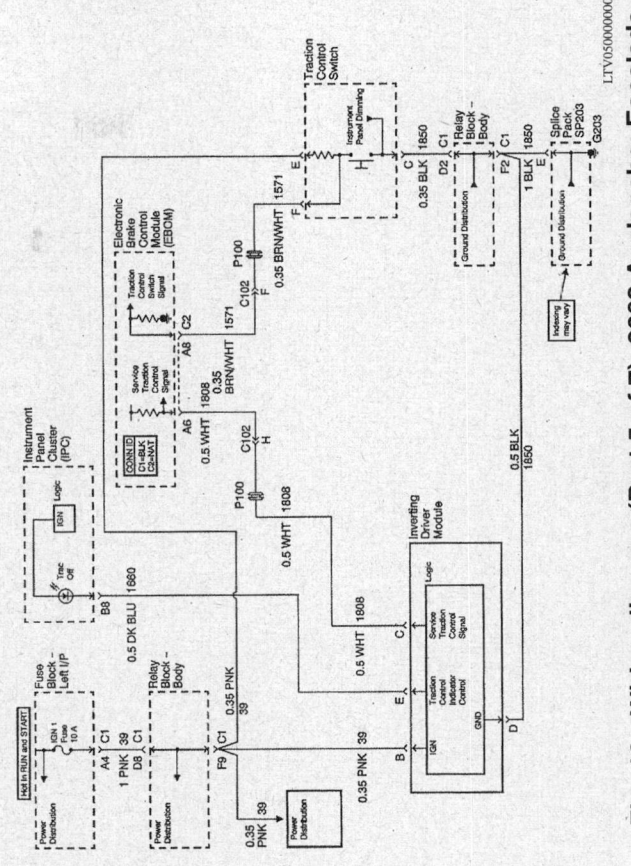

Fig. 13 Wiring diagram (Part 3 of 7). 2002 Avalanche, Escalade, Escalade EXT, Suburban, Tahoe & Yukon

Fig. 13 Wiring diagram (Part 5 of 7). 2002 Avalanche, Escalade, Escalade EXT, Suburban, Tahoe & Yukon

Fig. 13 Wiring diagram (Part 2 of 7). 2002 Avalanche, Escalade, Escalade EXT, Suburban, Tahoe & Yukon

Fig. 13 Wiring diagram (Part 4 of 7). 2002 Avalanche, Escalade, Escalade EXT, Suburban, Tahoe & Yukon

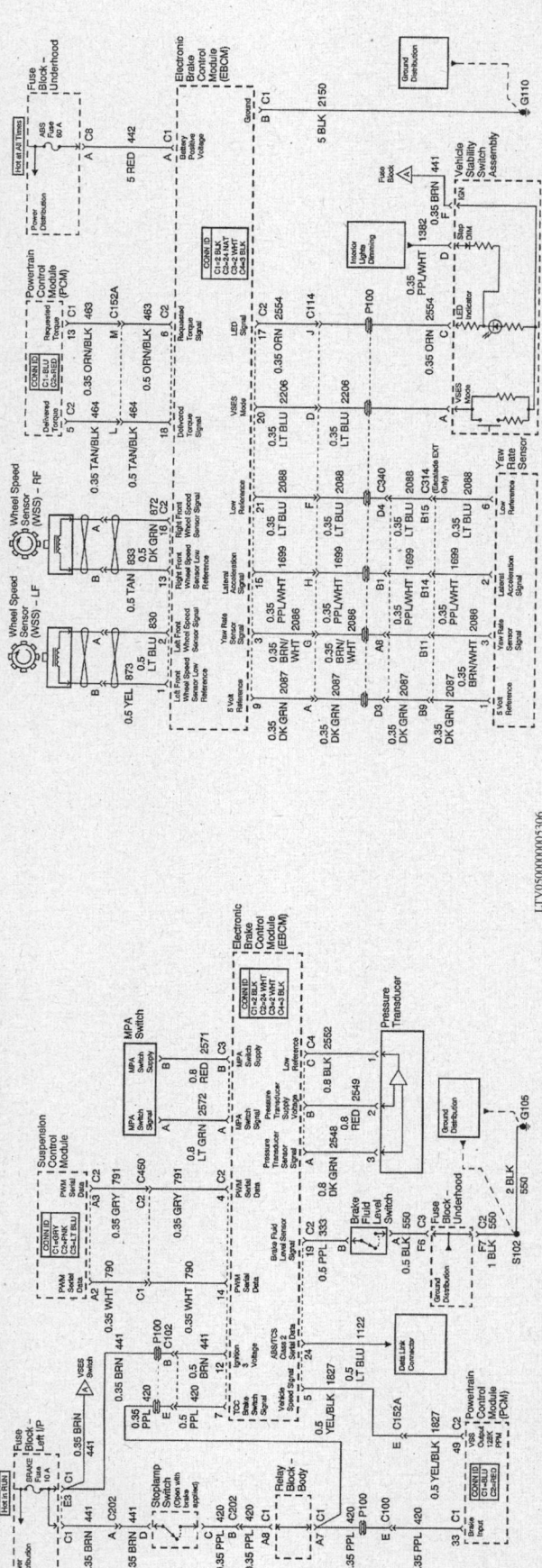

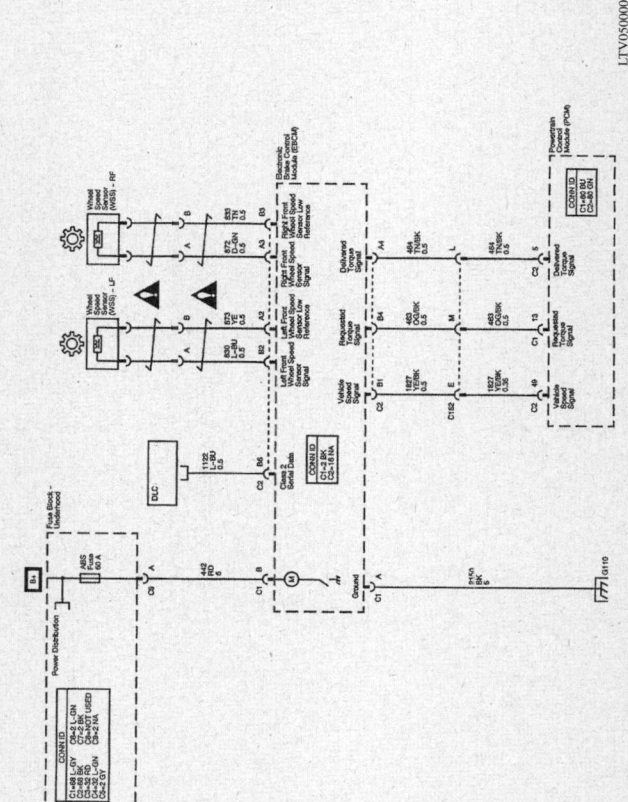

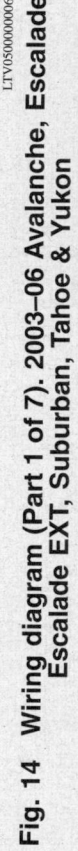

Fig. 13 Wiring diagram (Part 7 of 7). 2002 Avalanche, Escalade, Escalade EXT, Suburban, Tahoe & Yukon

Fig. 14 Wiring diagram (Part 2 of 7). 2003-06 Avalanche, Escalade, Escalade EXT, Suburban, Tahoe & Yukon

Fig. 13 Wiring diagram (Part 6 of 7). 2002 Avalanche, Escalade, Escalade EXT, Suburban, Tahoe & Yukon

Fig. 14 Wiring diagram (Part 1 of 7). 2003-06 Avalanche, Escalade, Escalade EXT, Suburban, Tahoe & Yukon

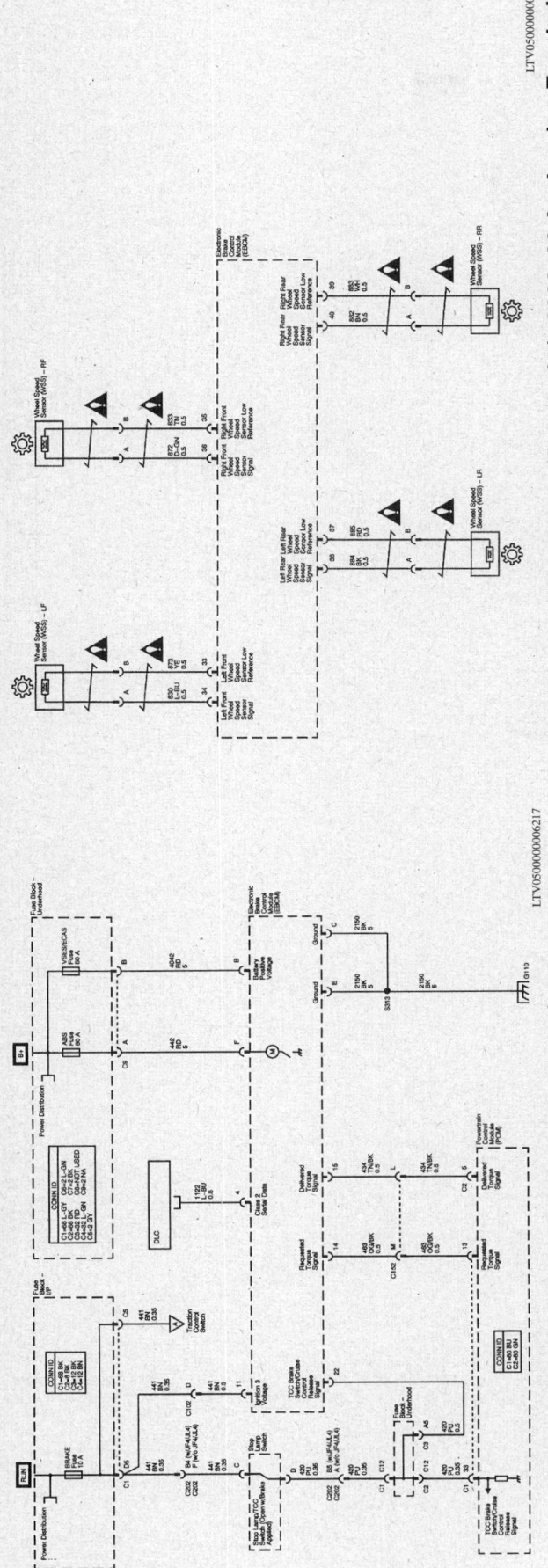

Fig. 14 Wiring diagram (Part 4 of 7). 2003–06 Avalanche, Escalade, Escalade EXT, Suburban, Tahoe & Yukon

Fig. 14 Wiring diagram (Part 6 of 7). 2003–06 Avalanche, Escalade, Escalade EXT, Suburban, Tahoe & Yukon

Fig. 14 Wiring diagram (Part 3 of 7). 2003–06 Avalanche, Escalade, Escalade EXT, Suburban, Tahoe & Yukon

Fig. 14 Wiring diagram (Part 5 of 7). 2003–06 Avalanche, Escalade, Escalade EXT, Suburban, Tahoe & Yukon

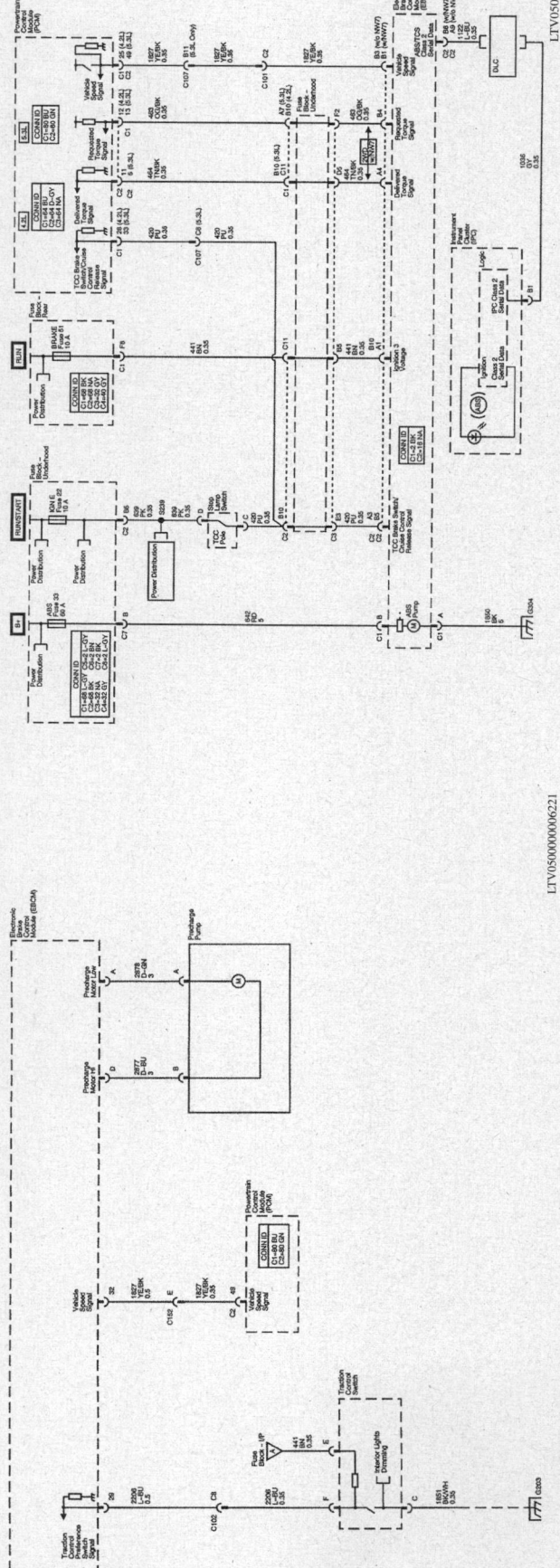

Fig. 14 Wiring diagram (Part 7 of 7). 2003–06 Avalanche, Escalade, Escalade EXT, Suburban, Tahoe & Yukon

Fig. 15 Wiring diagram (Part 1 of 3). 2002–05 Bravada, Envoy, Rainier & Trailblazer

Fig. 15 Wiring diagram (Part 2 of 3). 2002–05 Bravada, Envoy, Rainier & Trailblazer

Fig. 15 Wiring diagram (Part 3 of 3). 2002–05 Bravada, Envoy, Rainier & Trailblazer

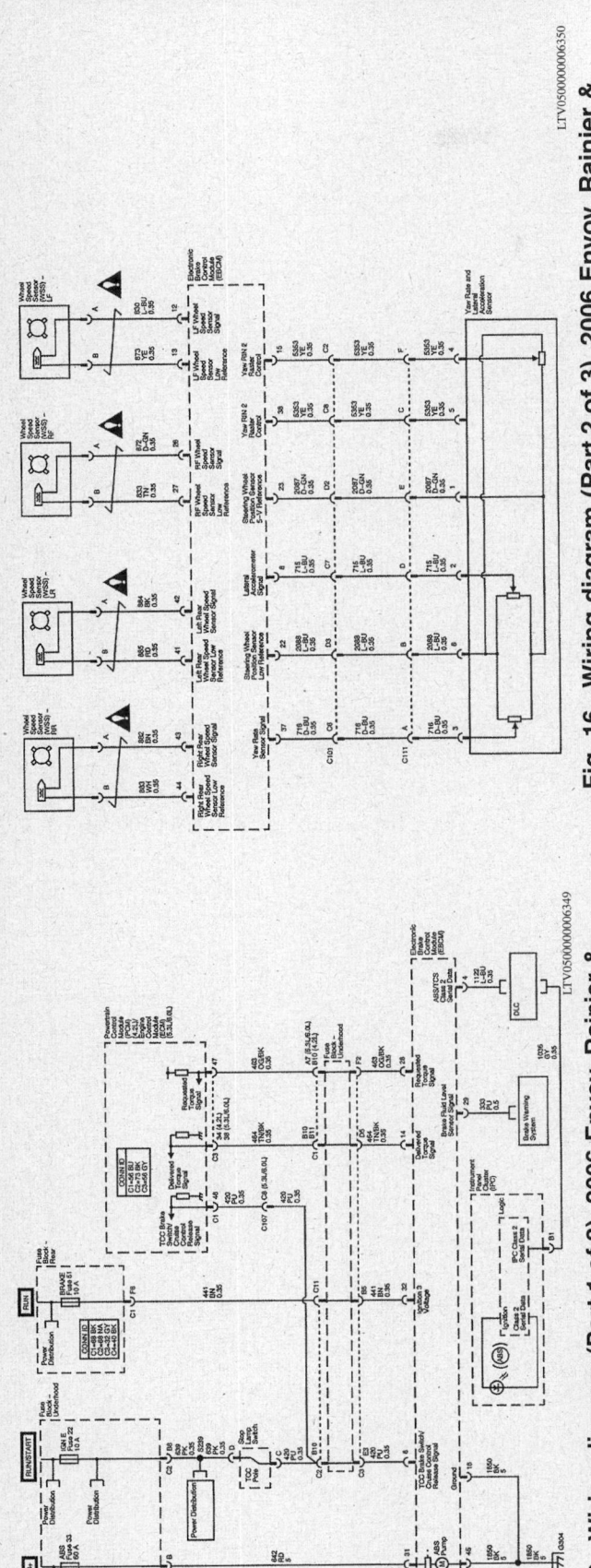

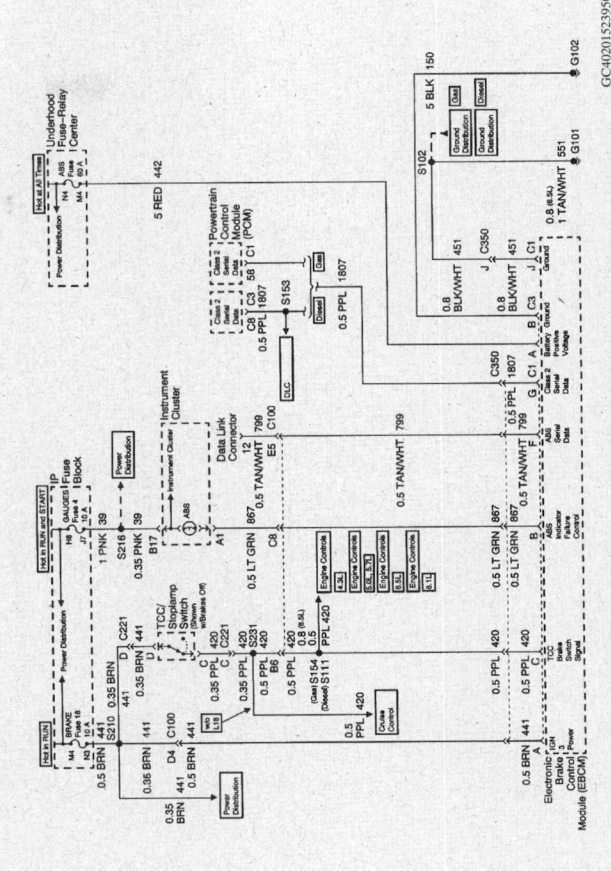

Fig. 16 Wiring diagram (Part 2 of 3). 2006 Envoy, Rainier & Trailblazer

Fig. 17 Wiring diagram (Part 1 of 2). 2002 Express & Savana

Fig. 16 Wiring diagram (Part 1 of 3). 2006 Envoy, Rainier & Trailblazer

Fig. 16 Wiring diagram (Part 3 of 3). 2006 Envoy, Rainier & Trailblazer

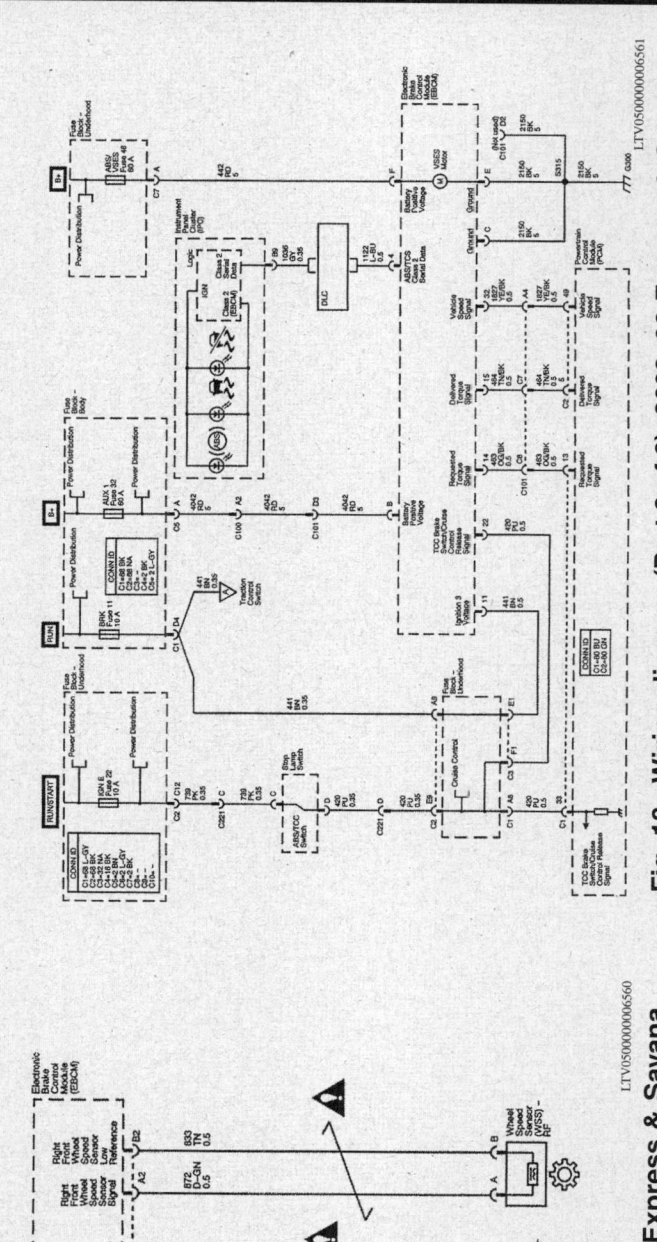

Fig. 18 Wiring diagram (Part 1 of 6). 2003-06 Express & Savana

Fig. 18 Wiring diagram (Part 3 of 6). 2003-06 Express & Savana

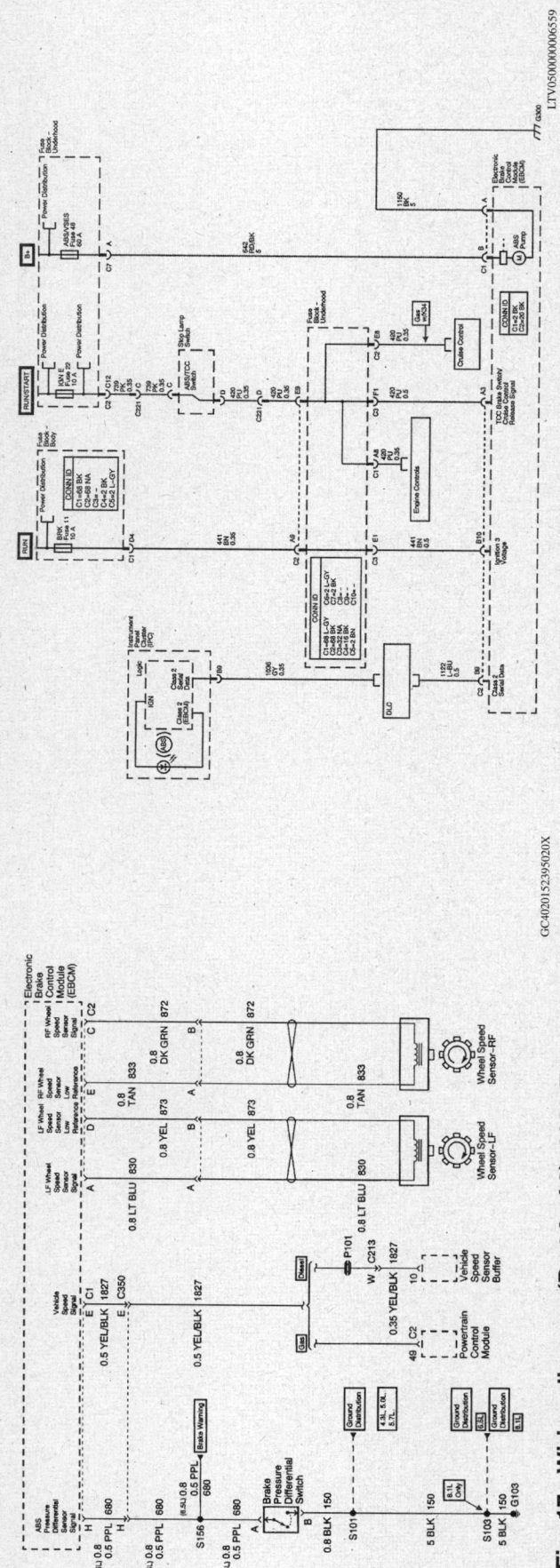

Fig. 17 Wiring diagram (Part 2 of 2). 2002 Express & Savana

Fig. 18 Wiring diagram (Part 2 of 6). 2003-06 Express & Savana

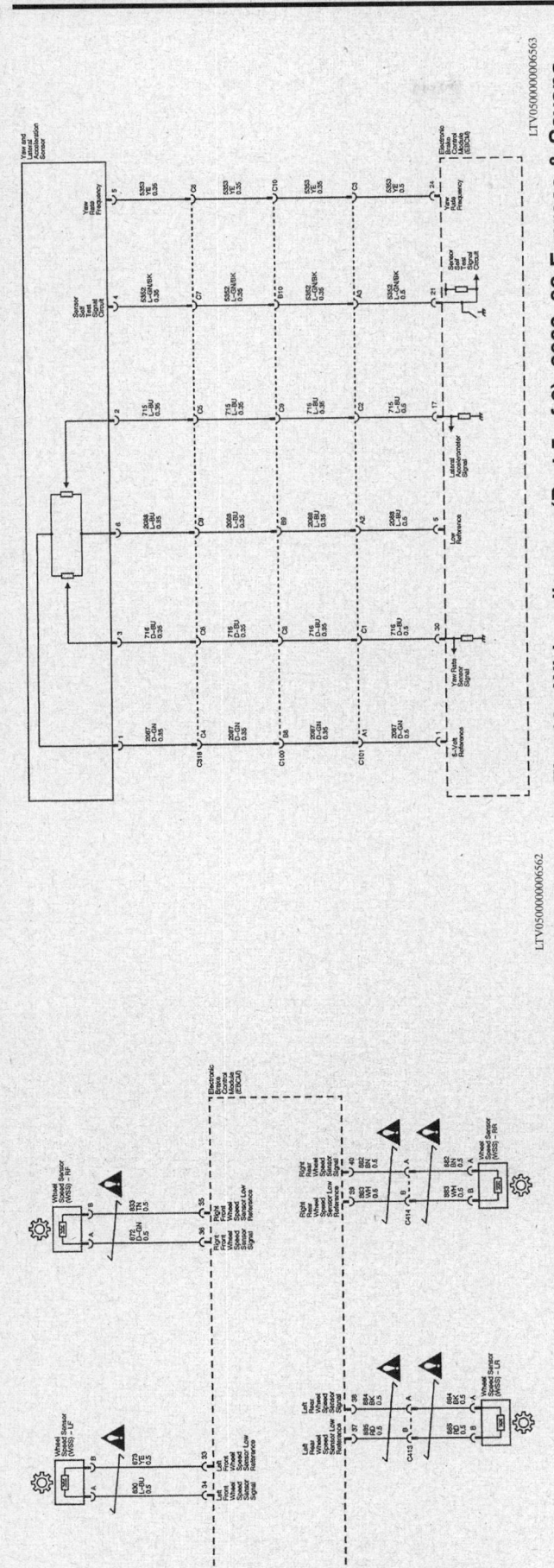

Fig. 18 Wiring diagram (Part 5 of 6). 2003–06 Express & Savana

Fig. 18 Wiring diagram (Part 4 of 6). 2003–06 Express & Savana

Fig. 19 Wiring diagram (Part 1 of 4). 2002 Sierra & Silverado

Fig. 18 Wiring diagram (Part 6 of 6). 2003–06 Express & Savana

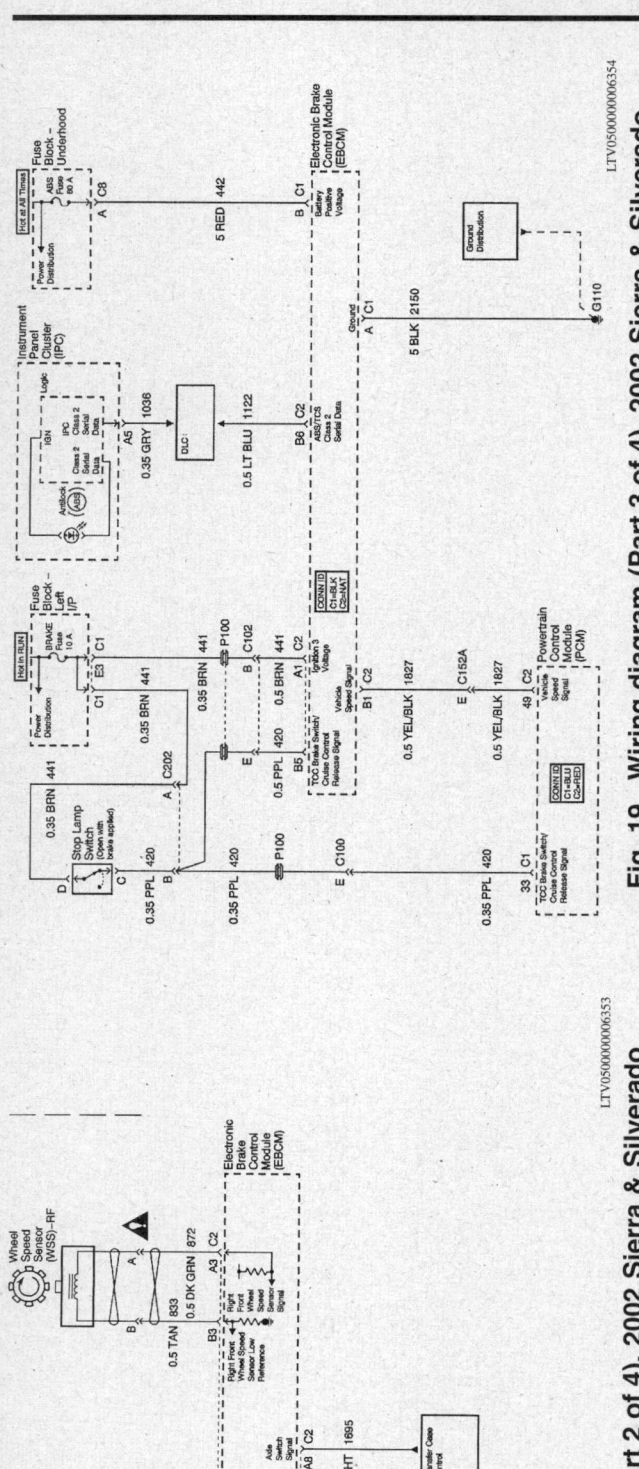

Fig. 19 Wiring diagram (Part 3 of 4). 2002 Sierra & Silverado

Fig. 19 Wiring diagram (Part 2 of 4). 2002 Sierra & Silverado

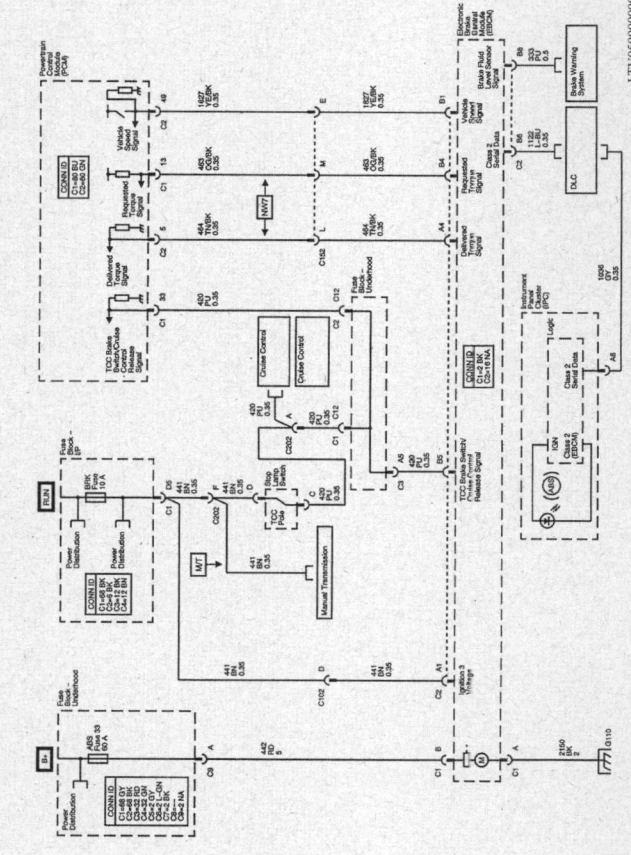

Fig. 20 Wiring diagram (Part 1 of 4). 2003–06 Sierra & Silverado

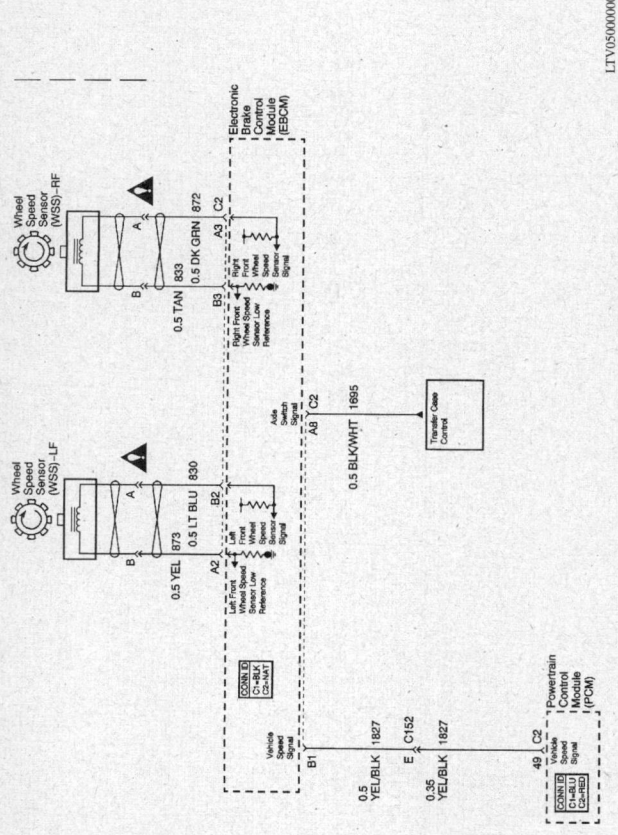

Fig. 19 Wiring diagram (Part 4 of 4). 2002 Sierra & Silverado

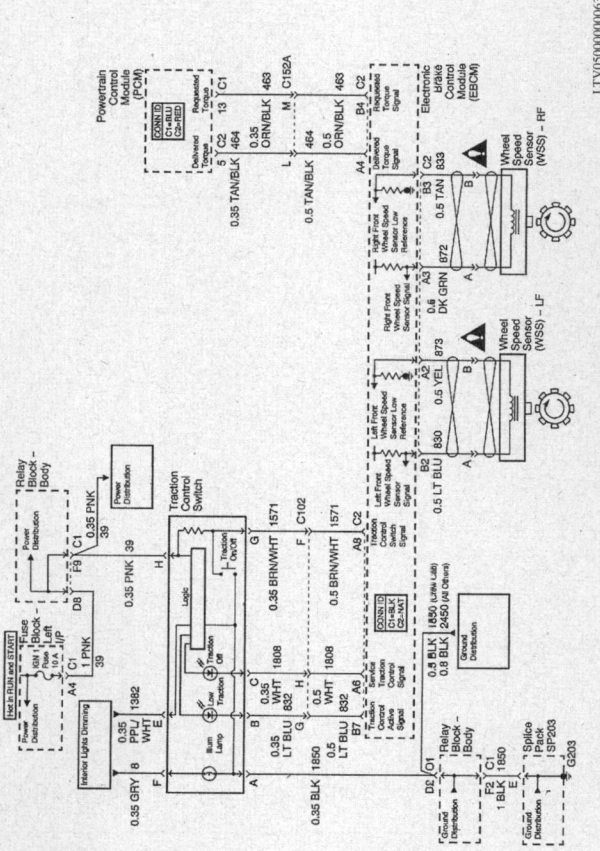

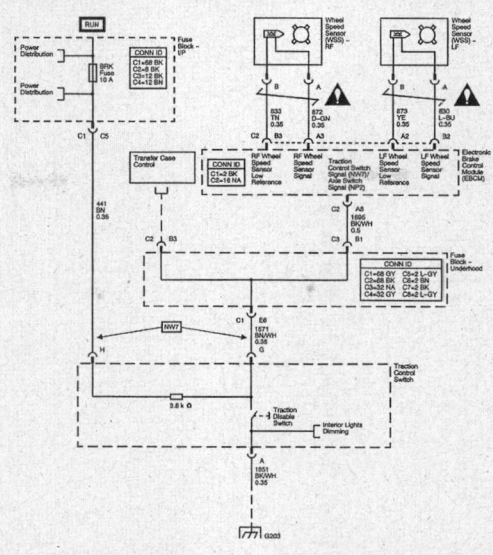

LTV0500000006473

Fig. 20   Wiring diagram (Part 2 of 4). 2003–06 Sierra & Silverado

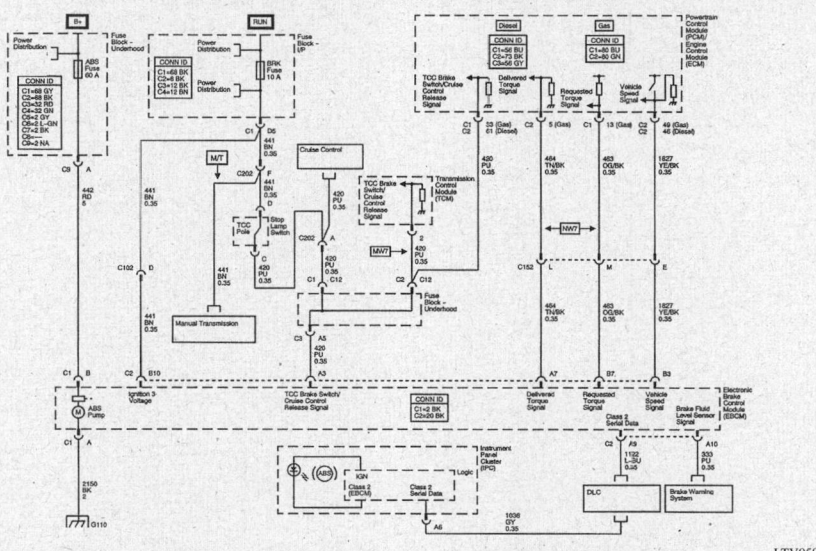

LTV0500000006474

Fig. 20   Wiring diagram (Part 3 of 4). 2003–06 Sierra & Silverado

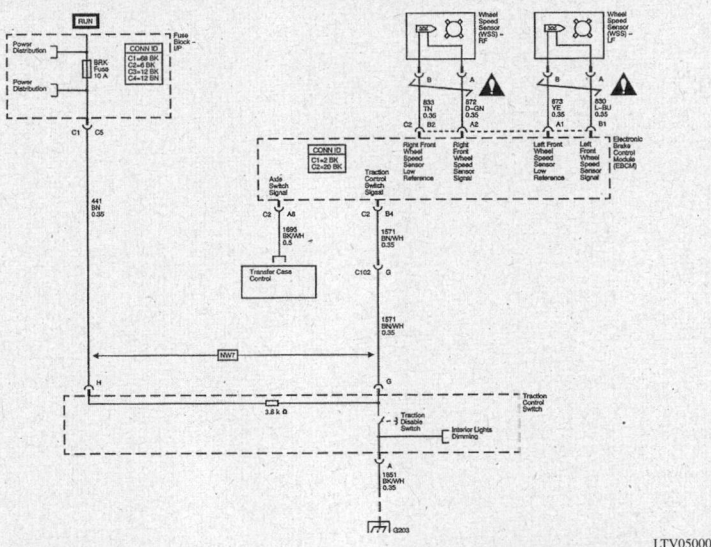

LTV0500000006475

Fig. 20   Wiring diagram (Part 4 of 4). 2003–06 Sierra & Silverado

DIAGNOSTIC CHART INDEX

Code	Description	Page No.	Fig. No.
ASTRO, BLAZER, JIMMY, SAFARI, SONOMA, SSR & S10			
—	ABS Indicator Always On	5-309	208
—	ABS Indicator Inoperative	5-309	209
—	Traction Off Indicator Always On	5-309	210
—	Traction Off Indicator Inoperative	5-309	211
—	Diagnostic System Check	5-196	21
C0221	Wheel Speed Sensor Circuit Fault	5-197	22
C0222	Wheel Speed Sensor Circuit Fault	5-197	22
C0223	Wheel Speed Sensor Circuit Fault	5-197	22
C0225	Wheel Speed Sensor Circuit Fault	5-197	22
C0226	Wheel Speed Sensor Circuit Fault	5-197	22
C0227	Wheel Speed Sensor Circuit Fault	5-197	22
C0229	Drop Out Of Front Wheel Speed Sensor Signals	5-198	23
C0235	Rear Wheel Speed Sensor Signal Fault	5-198	24
C0236	Rear Wheel Speed Sensor Signal Fault	5-198	24
C0237	Rear Wheel Speed Sensor Signal Fault	5-198	24
C0238	Wheel Speed Mismatch	5-199	25
C0241	EBCM Control Valve Circuit	5-200	26
C0242	EBCM Control Valve Circuit	5-200	26
C0243	EBCM Control Valve Circuit	5-200	26
C0244	EBCM Control Valve Circuit	5-200	26
C0245	EBCM Control Valve Circuit	5-200	26
C0246	EBCM Control Valve Circuit	5-200	26
C0247	EBCM Control Valve Circuit	5-200	26
C0248	EBCM Control Valve Circuit	5-200	26
C0251	EBCM Control Valve Circuit	5-200	26
C0252	EBCM Control Valve Circuit	5-200	26
C0253	EBCM Control Valve Circuit	5-200	26
C0254	EBCM Control Valve Circuit	5-200	26
C0265	EBCM Motor Relay Circuit	5-200	27
C0266	EBCM Motor Relay Circuit	5-200	27
C0267	Pump Motor Circuit Open Or Shorted	5-201	28
C0268	Pump Motor Circuit Open Or Shorted	5-201	28
C0269	Excessive Dump & Isolation Time	5-202	29
C0274	Excessive Dump & Isolation Time	5-202	29
C0273	EBCM Fault	5-202	30
C0273	EBCM Fault	5-202	30
C0284	EBCM Fault	5-202	30
C0279	Powertrain Configuration Not Valid	5-203	31
C0281	Stoplamp Switch Circuit	5-203	32
C0283	Mode Switch Circuit Fault	5-204	33
C0287	Delivered Torque Signal Fault	5-204	34
C0290	Data Link Fault	5-205	35
C0292	Data Link Fault	5-205	35
C0297	Powertrain Configuration Data Not Received	5-205	36
C0298	Powertrain Control Fault	5-206	37
P0609	Rear Wheel Speed Sensor Signal Fault	5-198	24
P0856	Powertrain Control Fault	5-206	37
P1664	Delivered Torque Signal Fault	5-204	34
P1689	Delivered Torque Signal Fault	5-204	34
2002 AVALANCHE, ESCALADE, ESCALADE EXT, SUBURBAN, TAHOE & YUKON			
—	ABS Indicator Always On	5-309	212
—	ABS Indicator Inoperative	5-310	213
—	Low Traction Indicator Always On	5-310	214
—	Low Traction Indicator Always On	5-310	215
—	Low Traction Indicator Inoperative	5-311	216
—	Low Traction Indicator Inoperative	5-311	217

Continued

DIAGNOSTIC CHART INDEX—Continued

Code	Description	Page No.	Fig. No.
2002 AVALANCHE, ESCALADE, ESCALADE EXT, SUBURBAN, TAHOE & YUKON			
—	Stability System Disabled Indicator Always On	5-312	218
—	Traction Off Indicator Always On	5-312	219
—	Traction Off Indicator Always On	5-313	220
—	Traction Off Indicator Inoperative	5-314	221
—	Traction Off Indicator Inoperative	5-315	222
—	Diagnostic System Check	5-207	38
C0205	Steering Wheel Position Circuit	5-207	39
C0206	Steering Wheel Position Circuit	5-207	39
C0207	Steering Wheel Position Circuit	5-207	39
C0208	Steering Wheel Position Circuit	5-207	39
C0209	Yaw Rate Sensor Circuit	5-208	40
C0210	Yaw Rate Sensor Circuit	5-208	40
C0211	Yaw Rate Sensor Circuit	5-208	40
C0212	Yaw Rate Sensor Circuit	5-208	40
C0213	Lateral Accelerometer Circuit	5-209	41
C0214	Lateral Accelerometer Circuit	5-209	41
C0215	Lateral Accelerometer Circuit	5-209	41
C0216	Lateral Accelerometer Circuit	5-209	41
C0217	Internal Longitudinal Sensor	5-210	42
C0218	Internal Longitudinal Sensor	5-210	42
C0219	Internal Longitudinal Sensor	5-210	42
C0220	Internal Longitudinal Sensor	5-210	42
C0221	Wheel Speed Sensor Circuit	5-211	43
C0222	Wheel Speed Sensor Circuit	5-211	43
C0223	Wheel Speed Sensor Circuit	5-211	43
C0225	Wheel Speed Sensor Circuit	5-211	43
C0226	Wheel Speed Sensor Circuit	5-211	43
C0227	Wheel Speed Sensor Circuit	5-211	43
C0229	Drop Out of Front Wheel Speed Signals	5-212	44
C0235	Rear Wheel Speed Sensor Circuit	5-212	45
C0236	Rear Wheel Speed Sensor Circuit	5-212	45
C0237	Rear Wheel Speed Sensor Circuit	5-212	45
C0238	Wheel Speed Sensor Mismatch	5-213	46
C0240	EBCM Internal Fault	5-213	47
C0241	EBCM Internal Fault	5-213	47
C0242	EBCM Internal Fault	5-213	47
C0243	EBCM Internal Fault	5-213	47
C0244	EBCM Internal Fault	5-213	47
C0245	EBCM Internal Fault	5-213	47
C0246	EBCM Internal Fault	5-213	47
C0247	EBCM Internal Fault	5-213	47
C0248	EBCM Internal Fault	5-213	47
C0249	EBCM Internal Fault	5-213	47
C0250	EBCM Internal Fault	5-213	47
C0251	EBCM Internal Fault	5-213	47
C0252	EBCM Internal Fault	5-213	47
C0253	EBCM Internal Fault	5-213	47
C0253	EBCM Internal Fault	5-213	47
C0255	EBCM Internal Fault	5-213	47
C0256	EBCM Internal Fault	5-213	47
C0257	EBCM Internal Fault	5-213	47
C0258	EBCM Internal Fault	5-213	47
C0259	EBCM Internal Fault	5-213	47
C0263	Brake Switch Circuit	5-214	48
C0265	EBCM Relay Circuit w/JL4	5-214	49
C0266	EBCM Relay Circuit w/JL4	5-214	49

Continued

DIAGNOSTIC CHART INDEX—Continued

Code	Description	Page No.	Fig. No.
2002 AVALANCHE, ESCALADE, ESCALADE EXT, SUBURBAN, TAHOE & YUKON			
C0265	EBCM Relay Circuit Less JL4	5-215	50
C0266	EBCM Relay Circuit Less JL4	5-215	50
C0267	Pump Motor Circuit Open/Short	5-215	51
C0268	Pump Motor Circuit Open/Short	5-215	51
C0269	Excessive Dump/Isolation Time	5-216	52
C0271	EBCM Fault	5-217	53
C0272	EBCM Fault	5-217	53
C0273	EBCM Fault	5-217	53
C0274	Excessive Dump/Isolation Time	5-216	52
C0275	VSES Internal Relay	5-217	54
C0276	VSES Internal Relay	5-217	54
C0279	Powertrain Configuration Not Valid	5-218	55
C0281	Brake Switch Circuit	5-218	56
C0282	MPA Switch Circuit	5-219	57
C0283	Traction Switch Shorted To Ground w/NW7	5-220	58
C0283	Traction Switch Shorted To Ground w/JL4	5-221	59
C0284	EBCM Fault	5-217	53
C0285	MPA Switch Circuit	5-219	57
C0286	MPA Switch Circuit	5-219	57
C0287	Delivered Torque Circuit	5-222	60
C0288	Brake Warning Lamp Circuit Shorted To B+	5-222	61
C0290	Lost Communication With PCM	5-223	62
C0292	Lost Communication With PCM	5-223	62
C0297	Powertrain Configuration Data Not Received	5-223	63
C0298	Traction Control Fault	5-224	64
P1504	Rear Wheel Speed Sensor Circuit	5-212	45
P1571	Traction Control Fault	5-224	64
P1644	Delivered Torque Circuit	5-222	60
P1689	Delivered Torque Circuit	5-222	60
2003–06 AVALANCHE, ESCALADE, ESCALADE EXT, SUBURBAN, TAHOE & YUKON			
—	ABS Indicator Always On	5-316	223
—	ABS Indicator Inoperative	5-316	224
—	Brake Pressure Modulator Valve Hydrualic Testing	5-319	230
—	Stability System Disabled Indicator Always On	5-316	225
—	Traction Off Indicator Always On	5-317	226
—	Traction Off Indicator Inoperative	5-317	227
—	Traction Control System Poor Performance	5-318	228
—	Vehicle Stability Enhancement System Poor Performance	5-318	229
—	Diagnostic System Check	5-225	65
C0035	Front Wheel Speed Sensor Circuit	5-225	66
C0040	Front Wheel Speed Sensor Circuit	5-225	66
C0045	Rear Wheel Speed Sensor Circuit	5-226	67
C0050	Rear Wheel Speed Sensor Circuit	5-226	67
C0110	Pump Motor Circuit	5-227	68
C0131	ABS/TCS Pressure Circuit	5-228	69
C0161	ABS/TCS Brake Switch	5-228	70
C0186	Lateral Accelerometer Circuit	5-229	71
C0196	Yaw Rate Circuit	5-230	72
C0201	ABS Enable Relay Contact Circuit	5-231	73
C0220	LH Front ABS Channel In Release Too Long	5-232	74
C0221	Wheel Speed Sensor Circuit Fault Less JL4	5-232	75
C0222	Wheel Speed Sensor Circuit Fault Less JL4	5-232	75
C0223	Wheel Speed Sensor Circuit Fault Less JL4	5-232	75
C0225	Wheel Speed Sensor Circuit Fault Less JL4	5-232	75
C0226	Wheel Speed Sensor Circuit Fault Less JL4	5-232	75
C0227	Wheel Speed Sensor Circuit Fault Less JL4	5-232	75

Continued

DIAGNOSTIC CHART INDEX—Continued

Code	Description	Page No.	Fig. No.
2003–06 AVALANCHE, ESCALADE, ESCALADE EXT, SUBURBAN, TAHOE & YUKON			
C0221	Wheel Speed Sensor Circuit Fault w/JL4	5-233	76
C0222	Wheel Speed Sensor Circuit Fault w/JL4	5-233	76
C0223	Wheel Speed Sensor Circuit Fault w/JL4	5-233	76
C0225	Wheel Speed Sensor Circuit Fault w/JL4	5-233	76
C0226	Wheel Speed Sensor Circuit Fault w/JL4	5-233	76
C0227	Wheel Speed Sensor Circuit Fault w/JL4	5-233	76
C0228	LH Rear ABS Channel In Release Too Long	5-234	77
C0229	RH Rear ABS Channel In Release Too Long w/JL4	5-234	78
C0229	Drop Out Of Both Front Speed Sensors Less JL4	5-234	79
C0235	Rear Wheel Speed Sensor Fault	5-235	80
C0236	Rear Wheel Speed Sensor Fault	5-235	80
C0237	Rear Wheel Speed Sensor Fault	5-235	80
C0238	Wheel Speed Mismatch	5-236	81
C0240	EBCM Fault	5-236	82
C0241	EBCM Control Valve Circuit	5-237	83
C0242	EBCM Control Valve Circuit	5-237	83
C0243	EBCM Control Valve Circuit	5-237	83
C0244	EBCM Control Valve Circuit Less JL4	5-237	84
C0244	Pulse Width Modulated Delivered Torque w/JL4	5-237	85
C0245	Wheel Speed Sensor Frequency Error w/JL4	5-238	86
C0245	EBCM Control Valve Circuit Less JL4	5-238	87
C0246	EBCM Control Valve Circuit	5-239	88
C0247	EBCM Control Valve Circuit	5-239	88
C0248	EBCM Control Valve Circuit	5-239	88
C0251	EBCM Control Valve Circuit	5-239	88
C0252	EBCM Control Valve Circuit	5-239	88
C0253	EBCM Control Valve Circuit	5-239	88
C0254	EBCM Control Valve Circuit	5-239	88
C0265	EBCM Motor Relay Circuit	5-239	89
C0266	EBCM Motor Relay Circuit	5-239	89
C0267	Pump Motor Circuit	5-240	90
C0268	Pump Motor Circuit	5-240	90
C0269	Excessive Dump/Isolation Time	5-241	91
C0271	EBCM Fault	5-241	92
C0272	EBCM Fault	5-241	92
C0273	EBCM Fault	5-241	92
C0274	Excessive Dump/Isolation Time	5-241	91
C0279	Powertrain Configuration Not Valid Less JL4	5-242	93
C0279	Pre-Charge Pump Circuit Performance w/JL4	5-242	94
C0281	Stoplamp Switch Circuit	5-243	95
C0283	Mode Switch Circuit Fault w/JL4	5-244	96
C0283	Mode Switch Circuit Fault Less JL4	5-244	97
C0284	EBCM Fault	5-241	92
C0287	Delivered Torque Signal Fault	5-245	98
C0290	Class 2 Data Link Fault Less JL4	5-246	99
C0290	Class 2 Data Link Fault w/JL4	5-246	100
C0291	Lost Communication With BCM	5-247	101
C0292	Class 2 Data Link Fault Less JL4	5-246	99
C0292	Class 2 Data Link Fault w/JL4	5-246	100
C0297	Powertrain Configuration Data Not Received	5-247	102
C0298	Powertrain Control Fault	5-248	103
C0455	Front Steering Position Sensor Circuit	5-249	104
C0472	Steering Hand Wheel Speed Sensor Circuit	5-250	105
C0473	Steering Hand Wheel Speed Sensor Circuit	5-250	105
C0550	ECU Performance	5-250	106
C0558	Calibration Data Not Programmed	5-251	107

Continued

DIAGNOSTIC CHART INDEX—Continued

Code	Description	Page No.	Fig. No.
2003–06 AVALANCHE, ESCALADE, ESCALADE EXT, SUBURBAN, TAHOE & YUKON			
P0609	Rear Wheel Speed Sensor Fault	5-235	80
P0856	Powertrain Control Fault	5-248	103
P1644	Delivered Torque Signal Fault	5-245	98
P1689	Delivered Torque Signal Fault	5-245	98
2002–03 BRAVADA, ENVOY & TRAILBLAZER			
—	ABS Indicator Always On	5-319	231
—	ABS Indicator Inoperative	5-319	232
—	Low Traction Indicator Always On	5-320	233
—	Low Traction Indicator Inoperative	5-320	234
—	Traction Off Indicator Always On	5-321	235
—	Traction Off Indicator Always On	5-322	236
—	Traction Off Indicator Inoperative	5-323	237
—	Diagnostic System Check	5-251	108
C0221	Front Wheel Speed Sensor Circuit	5-251	109
C0222	Front Wheel Speed Sensor Circuit	5-251	109
C0223	Front Wheel Speed Sensor Circuit	5-251	109
C0225	Front Wheel Speed Sensor Circuit	5-251	109
C0226	Front Wheel Speed Sensor Circuit	5-251	109
C0227	Front Wheel Speed Sensor Circuit	5-251	109
C0229	Drop Out of Front Wheel Speed Signals	5-252	110
C0235	Rear Wheel Speed Sensor Circuit	5-253	111
C0236	Rear Wheel Speed Sensor Circuit	5-253	111
C0237	Rear Wheel Speed Sensor Circuit	5-253	111
C0238	Wheel Speed Mismatch	5-253	112
C0241	EBCM Control Valve Circuit	5-254	113
C0242	EBCM Control Valve Circuit	5-254	113
C0243	EBCM Control Valve Circuit	5-254	113
C0244	EBCM Control Valve Circuit	5-254	113
C0245	EBCM Control Valve Circuit	5-254	113
C0246	EBCM Control Valve Circuit	5-254	113
C0247	EBCM Control Valve Circuit	5-254	113
C0248	EBCM Control Valve Circuit	5-254	113
C0251	EBCM Control Valve Circuit	5-254	113
C0252	EBCM Control Valve Circuit	5-254	113
C0253	EBCM Control Valve Circuit	5-254	113
C0254	EBCM Control Valve Circuit	5-254	113
C0265	EBCM Relay Circuit	5-254	114
C0266	EBCM Relay Circuit	5-254	114
C0267	Pump Motor Circuit Open/Short	5-255	115
C0268	Pump Motor Circuit Open/Short	5-255	115
C0269	Excessive Dump/Isolation Time	5-256	116
C0271	EBCM Fault	5-256	117
C0272	EBCM Fault	5-256	117
C0273	EBCM Fault	5-256	117
C0274	Excessive Dump/Isolation Time	5-256	116
C0279	Powertrain Configuration Not Valid	5-257	118
C0281	Brake Switch Circuit	5-257	119
C0283	Traction Switch Shorted To Ground	5-258	120
C0284	EBCM Fault	5-256	117
C0287	Delivered Torque Circuit	5-258	121
C0290	Lost Communication With PCM	5-259	122
C0291	Lost Communication With PCM	5-259	123
C0292	Lost Communication With PCM	5-259	122
C0297	Powertrain Configuration Data Not Received	5-259	124
C0298	Powertrain Indicated Traction Control Fault	5-260	125
P1504	Rear Wheel Speed Sensor Circuit	5-253	111

Continued

DIAGNOSTIC CHART INDEX—Continued

Code	Description	Page No.	Fig. No.
2002–03 BRAVADA, ENVOY & TRAILBLAZER			
P1571	Powertrain Indicated Traction Control Fault	5-260	125
P1644	Delivered Torque Circuit	5-258	121
P1689	Delivered Torque Circuit	5-258	121
2004–06 BRAVADA, ENVOY, RAINIER & TRAILBLAZER			
—	ABS Indicator Always On	5-325	238
—	ABS Indicator Inoperative	5-325	239
—	Traction Off Indicator Always On	5-326	240
—	Traction Off Indicator Inoperative	5-326	241
—	Diagnostic System Check	5-260	126
C0035	Front Wheel Speed Sensor Circuit	5-261	127
C0040	Front Wheel Speed Sensor Circuit	5-261	127
C0045	Rear Wheel Speed Sensor Circuit	5-262	128
C0050	Rear Wheel Speed Sensor Circuit	5-262	128
C0110	Pump Motor Circuit	5-263	129
C0131	ABS/TCS Pressure Circuit	5-263	130
C0161	ABS/TCS Brake Switch Circuit	5-264	131
C0186	Lateral Accelerometer Circuit	5-265	132
C0196	Yaw Rate Circuit	5-266	133
C0201	ABS Enable Relay Contact Circuit	5-267	134
C0240	EBCM Fault	5-267	135
C0241	PCM Indicated Requested Torque Fault	5-267	136
C0244	PWM Delivered Torque	5-268	137
C0245	Wheel Speed Sensor Frequency Error	5-269	138
C0283	Mode Switch Circuit	5-269	139
C0287	Longitudinal Accelerometer Circuit	5-270	140
C0290	Devise Voltage Reference Output Circuit	5-271	141
C0292	Devise Voltage Reference Output Circuit	5-271	141
C0455	Front Steering Position Sensor Circuit	5-271	142
C0550	ECU Performance	5-272	143
C0558	Calibration Data Not Programmed	5-273	144
P0856	PCM Indicated Requested Torque Fault	5-267	136
P1689	PWM Delivered Torque	5-268	137
2002 EXPRESS & SAVANA			
—	Anti-Lock Indicator Lamp Always On	5-327	242
—	Anti-Lock Indicator Lamp Off Always No DTC Set	5-328	243
—	Diagnostic System Check	5-273	145
C0221	Wheel Speed Sensor Fault	5-273	146
C0222	Wheel Speed Sensor Fault	5-273	146
C0223	Wheel Speed Sensor Fault	5-273	146
C0225	Wheel Speed Sensor Fault	5-273	146
C0226	Wheel Speed Sensor Fault	5-273	146
C0227	Wheel Speed Sensor Fault	5-273	146
C0229	Drop Out Of Front Wheel Speed Signal	5-274	147
C0235	Rear Wheel Speed Sensor Fault	5-274	148
C0236	Rear Wheel Speed Sensor Fault	5-274	148
C0237	Rear Wheel Speed Sensor Fault	5-274	148
C0238	Wheel Speed Mismatch	5-275	149
C0241	EBCM Control Valve Circuit	5-275	150
C0242	EBCM Control Valve Circuit	5-275	150
C0243	EBCM Control Valve Circuit	5-275	150
C0245	EBCM Control Valve Circuit	5-275	150
C0246	EBCM Control Valve Circuit	5-275	150
C0247	EBCM Control Valve Circuit	5-275	150
C0248	EBCM Control Valve Circuit	5-275	150
C0251	EBCM Control Valve Circuit	5-275	150
C0252	EBCM Control Valve Circuit	5-275	150

Continued

DIAGNOSTIC CHART INDEX—Continued

Code	Description	Page No.	Fig. No.
2002 EXPRESS & SAVANA			
C0253	EBCM Control Valve Circuit	5-275	150
C0254	EBCM Control Valve Circuit	5-275	150
C0265	EBCM Relay Circuit	5-275	151
C0266	EBCM Relay Circuit	5-275	151
C0267	Pump Motor Circuit Open Or Shorted	5-276	152
C0268	Pump Motor Circuit Open Or Shorted	5-276	152
C0269	Excessive Dump Isolation Time	5-276	153
C0274	Excessive Dump Isolation Time	5-276	153
C0271	EBCM Fault	5-276	154
C0272	EBCM Fault	5-276	154
C0273	EBCM Fault	5-276	154
C0281	Brake Switch Circuit	5-277	155
C0286	Anti-lock Indicator Lamp Shorted To B+	5-277	156
C0288	Brake Warning Lamp Shorted To B+	5-278	157
2003–06 EXPRESS & SAVANA			
—	ABS Indicator Always	5-329	244
—	ABS Indicator Inoperative	5-329	245
—	Stability System Caution Indicator Always On	5-330	246
—	Stability System Caution Indicator Inoperative	5-330	247
—	Stability System Not Ready Indicator Always On	5-331	248
—	Stability System Not Ready Indicator Inoperative	5-332	249
—	Vehicle Stability Enhancement System Poor Performance	5-333	250
—	Brake Pressure Modulator Valve Hydraulic Testing	5-334	251
—	Diagnostic System Check	5-278	158
C0035	Front Wheel Speed Sensor Circuit	5-279	159
C0040	Front Wheel Speed Sensor Circuit	5-279	159
C0045	Rear Wheel Speed Sensor Circuit	5-279	160
C0050	Rear Wheel Speed Sensor Circuit	5-279	160
C0055	Rear Wheel Speed Sensor Circuit	5-280	161
C0110	Pump Motor Circuit	5-281	162
C0131	ABS/TCS Pressure Circuit	5-282	163
C0161	ABS/TCS Brake Switch Circuit Less LJ4	5-282	164
C0161	ABS/TCS Brake Switch Circuit w/JL4	5-283	165
C0186	Lateral Accelerometer Circuit	5-284	166
C0196	Yaw Rate Circuit	5-285	167
C0201	ABS Enable Relay Contact Circuit	5-286	168
C0220	ABS Channel In Release Too Long Less JL4	5-286	169
C0221	ABS Channel In Release Too Long Less JL4	5-286	169
C0228	ABS Channel In Release Too Long Less JL4	5-286	169
C0229	ABS Channel In Release Too Long Less JL4	5-286	169
C0220	ABS Channel In Release Too Long w/JL4	5-287	170
C0221	ABS Channel In Release Too Long w/JL4	5-287	170
C0228	ABS Channel In Release Too Long w/JL4	5-287	170
C0229	ABS Channel In Release Too Long w/JL4	5-287	170
C0244	PWM Delivered Torque	5-287	171
C0245	Wheel Speed Sensor Frequency Error	5-288	172
C0279	Pre-Charge Pump Circuit Performance	5-289	173
C0283	Mode Switch Circuit Fault	5-290	174
C0290	Device Voltage Reference Circuit	5-290	175
C0292	Device Voltage Reference Circuit	5-290	175
C0455	Front Steering Position Sensor Circuit	5-291	176
C0550	ECU Performance	5-292	177
C0558	Calibration Data Not Programmed	5-293	178
P0609	Rear Wheel Speed Sensor Circuit	5-280	161
P1689	PWM Delivered Torque	5-287	171

Continued

DIAGNOSTIC CHART INDEX—Continued

Code	Description	Page No.	Fig. No.
2002 SIERRA & SILVERADO			
—	ABS Indicator Always On	5-319	231
—	ABS Indicator Inoperative	5-319	232
—	Low Traction Indicator Always On	5-320	233
—	Low Traction Indicator Inoperative	5-320	234
—	Traction Off Indicator Always On	5-321	235
—	Traction Off Indicator Always On	5-322	236
—	Traction Off Indicator Inoperative	5-323	237
—	Diagnostic System Check	5-251	108
C0221	Front Wheel Speed Sensor Circuit	5-251	109
C0222	Front Wheel Speed Sensor Circuit	5-251	109
C0223	Front Wheel Speed Sensor Circuit	5-251	109
C0225	Front Wheel Speed Sensor Circuit	5-251	109
C0226	Front Wheel Speed Sensor Circuit	5-251	109
C0227	Front Wheel Speed Sensor Circuit	5-251	109
C0229	Drop Out of Front Wheel Speed Signals	5-252	110
C0235	Rear Wheel Speed Sensor Circuit	5-253	111
C0236	Rear Wheel Speed Sensor Circuit	5-253	111
C0237	Rear Wheel Speed Sensor Circuit	5-253	111
C0238	Wheel Speed Mismatch	5-253	112
C0241	EBCM Control Valve Circuit	5-254	113
C0242	EBCM Control Valve Circuit	5-254	113
C0243	EBCM Control Valve Circuit	5-254	113
C0244	EBCM Control Valve Circuit	5-254	113
C0245	EBCM Control Valve Circuit	5-254	113
C0246	EBCM Control Valve Circuit	5-254	113
C0247	EBCM Control Valve Circuit	5-254	113
C0248	EBCM Control Valve Circuit	5-254	113
C0251	EBCM Control Valve Circuit	5-254	113
C0252	EBCM Control Valve Circuit	5-254	113
C0253	EBCM Control Valve Circuit	5-254	113
C0254	EBCM Control Valve Circuit	5-254	113
C0265	EBCM Relay Circuit	5-254	114
C0266	EBCM Relay Circuit	5-254	114
C0267	Pump Motor Circuit Open/Short	5-255	115
C0268	Pump Motor Circuit Open/Short	5-255	115
C0269	Excessive Dump/Isolation Time	5-256	116
C0271	EBCM Fault	5-256	117
C0272	EBCM Fault	5-256	117
C0273	EBCM Fault	5-256	117
C0274	Excessive Dump/Isolation Time	5-256	116
C0279	Powertrain Configuration Not Valid	5-257	118
C0281	Brake Switch Circuit	5-257	119
C0283	Traction Switch Shorted To Ground	5-258	120
C0284	EBCM Fault	5-256	117
C0287	Delivered Torque Circuit	5-258	121
C0290	Lost Communication With PCM	5-259	122
C0291	Lost Communication With PCM	5-259	123
C0292	Lost Communication With PCM	5-259	122
C0297	Powertrain Configuration Data Not Received	5-259	124
C0298	Powertrain Indicated Traction Control Fault	5-260	125
P1504	Rear Wheel Speed Sensor Circuit	5-253	111
P1571	Powertrain Indicated Traction Control Fault	5-260	125
P1644	Delivered Torque Circuit	5-258	121
P1689	Delivered Torque Circuit	5-258	121
2003–06 SIERRA & SILVERADO			
—	ABS Indicator Always On	5-334	252

Continued

DIAGNOSTIC CHART INDEX—Continued

Code	Description	Page No.	Fig. No.
2003–06 SIERRA & SILVERADO			
—	ABS Indicator Inoperative	5-335	253
—	Traction Off Indicator Always On	5-336	254
—	Traction Off Indicator Inoperative	5-337	255
—	Diagnostic System Check	5-293	179
C003D	Rear Wheel Speed Sensor Circuit	5-295	182
C0035	Front Wheel Speed Sensor	5-294	180
C0035	LH Front Wheel Speed Sensor Circuit	5-294	181
C0040	Front Wheel Speed Sensor	5-294	180
C0050	Rear Wheel Speed Sensor Circuit	5-295	182
C0078	Wheel Speed Sensor Frequency Error	5-301	193
C0110	Pump Motor Circuit	5-296	183
C0161	ABS/TCS Brake Switch	5-296	184
C0201	ABS Enable Relay Contact Circuit	5-297	185
C0221	Front Wheel Speed Sensor Circuit	5-297	186
C0222	Front Wheel Speed Sensor Circuit	5-297	186
C0223	Front Wheel Speed Sensor Circuit	5-297	186
C0225	Front Wheel Speed Sensor Circuit	5-297	186
C0226	Front Wheel Speed Sensor Circuit	5-297	186
C0227	Front Wheel Speed Sensor Circuit	5-297	186
C0228	LH Front ABS Channel In Release Too Long	5-298	187
C0229	Drop Out Of Both Front Speed Sensors	5-299	188
C0235	Rear Wheel Speed Sensor	5-299	189
C0236	Rear Wheel Speed Sensor	5-299	189
C0237	Rear Wheel Speed Sensor	5-299	189
C0238	Wheel Speed Mismatch	5-300	190
C0240	EBCM Fault	5-300	191
C0241	EBCM Control Valve Circuit	5-301	192
C0242	EBCM Control Valve Circuit	5-301	192
C0243	EBCM Control Valve Circuit	5-301	192
C0244	EBCM Control Valve Circuit	5-301	192
C0245	EBCM Control Valve Circuit	5-301	192
C0245	Wheel Speed Sensor Frequency Error	5-301	193
C0246	EBCM Control Valve Circuit	5-301	192
C0247	EBCM Control Valve Circuit	5-301	192
C0248	EBCM Control Valve Circuit	5-301	192
C0251	EBCM Control Valve Circuit	5-301	192
C0252	EBCM Control Valve Circuit	5-301	192
C0253	EBCM Control Valve Circuit	5-301	192
C0254	EBCM Control Valve Circuit	5-301	192
C0265	EBCM Motor Relay Circuit	5-301	194
C0266	EBCM Motor Relay Circuit	5-301	194
C0267	Pump Motor Circuit Open/Shorted	5-302	195
C0268	Pump Motor Circuit Open/Shorted	5-302	195
C0269	Excessive Dump/Isolation Time	5-303	196
C0271	EBCM Fault	5-304	197
C0272	EBCM Fault	5-304	197
C0273	EBCM Fault	5-304	197
C0274	Excessive Dump/Isolation Time	5-303	196
C0279	Powertrain Configuration Not Valid	5-304	198
C0281	Stoplamp Switch Circuit	5-304	199
C0283	Mode Switch Circuit Fault	5-305	200
C0284	EBCM Fault	5-304	197
C0287	Delivered Torque Signal Fault	5-306	201
C0290	Data Link Fault	5-306	202
C0291	BCM Configuration Not Valid	5-307	203
C0292	Data Link Fault	5-306	202

Continued

DIAGNOSTIC CHART INDEX—Continued

Code	Description	Page No.	Fig. No.
2003–06 SIERRA & SILVERADO			
C0297	Powertrain Configuration Data Not Received	5-307	204
C0298	Powertrain Control Fault	5-307	205
C0550	ECU Performance	5-308	206
C0558	Calibration Data Not Programmed	5-308	207
C0570	ECU Performance	5-308	206
P0609	Rear Wheel Speed Sensor	5-299	189
P0644	Delivered Torque Signal Fault	5-306	201
P0856	Powertrain Control Fault	5-307	205
P1689	Delivered Torque Signal Fault	5-306	201
U0415	LH Front Wheel Speed Sensor Circuit	5-294	181

Test Description

The numbers below refer to the step numbers on the diagnostic table.

1. This step insures that the battery, and the vehicle primary power and ground systems are functioning correctly.

3. Lack of communication may be due to a particular malfunction of a serial data circuit. The link to Scan Tool does not Communicate with Class 2 Device will provide a list of modules and the associated data network no communication diagnostic link.

4. A module that is operating in the incorrect power mode based on key position may cause other vehicle symptoms and/or DTCs to set. The link to Power Mode Mismatch will correct the condition before checking for module DTCs or symptoms.

8. This step insures that all data link communication DTCs are diagnosed before system level DTCs.

9. This step insures that all electronic control unit (ECU) internal DTCs are diagnosed before other system level DTCs.

10. This step insures that all device voltage DTCs are diagnosed before other system level DTCs.

LTV0500000005247

Fig. 21   Diagnostic System Check (Part 1 of 3). Astro, Blazer, Jimmy, Safari, Sonoma, SSR & S10

Step	Action	Yes	No
1	Perform the following preliminary inspections: • Ensure that the battery is fully charged. • Ensure that the battery cables are clean and tight. • Inspect for any open fuses. • Inspect the easily accessible systems or the visible system components for obvious damage or conditions that could cause the symptom. • Ensure that the grounds are clean, tight, and in the correct location. • Inspect for aftermarket devices that could affect the operation of the system. • Search for applicable service bulletins. Did you find and correct the condition?	System OK	Go to Step 2
2	Install a scan tool. Does the scan tool power up?	Go to Step 3	Check Scan Tool Does Not Power Up
3	1. Turn ON the ignition, with the engine OFF. 2. Attempt to establish communication with all of the control modules on the vehicle. Does the scan tool communicate with all of the expected vehicle control modules?	Go to Step 4	Check Scan Tool Does Not Communicate with Class 2 Device
4	**Important:** 1. To ensure that retained accessory power (RAP) mode is inactive (if equipped), open the drivers door during the following step. 2. The engine may start during the following step. Turn OFF the engine as soon as you have observed the crank power mode. 1. Access the Power Mode parameter on the scan tool. 2. Rotate the ignition switch (operate the ignition mode switch) through all positions while observing the Power Mode parameter. Does the Power Mode parameter reading on the scan tool match the ignition switch position for all switch positions?	Go to Step 5	Diagnose Power Mode Mismatch

LTV0500000005248

Fig. 21   Diagnostic System Check (Part 2 of 3). Astro, Blazer, Jimmy, Safari, Sonoma, SSR & S10

5	Attempt to start the engine. Does the engine crank?	Go to Step 6	Go to Symptoms
6	Attempt to start the engine. Does the engine start and idle?	Go to Step 7	Go to Engine Cranks but Does Not Run
7	**Important:** Do not clear any DTCs unless instructed by a diagnostic procedure. Use the appropriate scan tool selections to obtain DTCs for each of the control modules. Does the scan tool display any DTCs?	Go to Step 8	Go to Step 12
8	Does the scan tool display any DTCs that begin with a "U"?	Go to Diagnostic Trouble Code (DTC) List	Go to Step 9
9	**Important:** If any of these DTCs are displayed, diagnose them before diagnosing any other DTCs or symptoms. Does the scan tool display DTC B1000, B1001, C0550, P0601, P0602, P0604, P0606, or P2610?	Go to Diagnostic Trouble Code (DTC) List	Go to Step 10
10	**Important:** If any of these DTCs are displayed, diagnose them before diagnosing any other DTCs or symptoms. Does the scan tool display DTC B1367, B1477, B1478, P0562, or P0563?	Go to Diagnostic Trouble Code (DTC) List	Go to Step 11
11	**Important:** If any of the remaining DTCs are powertrain DTCs, select Capture Info in order to store the powertrain DTC information with a scan tool. If multiple DTCs are stored, diagnose the DTCs in the following order 1. Component level DTCs, such as sensor DTCs, solenoid DTCs, and relay DTCs. 2. System level DTCs, such as misfire DTCs, evaporative emission (EVAP) system DTCs, and fuel trim DTCs. Diagnose the remaining DTCs.	Go to Diagnostic Trouble Code (DTC) List	--
12	Is the customers concern with inspection/maintenance (I/M) testing?	Go to Inspection/Maintenance (I/M) System Check	Go to Symptoms -

LTV0500000005249

Fig. 21   Diagnostic System Check (Part 3 of 3). Astro, Blazer, Jimmy, Safari, Sonoma, SSR & S10

Action Taken When the DTC Sets

C0221, C0225

If equipped, the following actions occur:

- The EBCM disables the ABS/TCS.
- The ABS indicator turns ON.
- The TRACTION OFF indicator turns ON.

C0222, C0223, C0226, and C0227

If equipped, the following actions occur:

- The EBCM disables the ABS/TCS and may disable DRP.
- The ABS indicator turns ON.
- The TRACTION OFF indicator turns ON.
- The red Brake warning indicator may turn ON.

Conditions for Clearing the DTC

- Repair the condition responsible for setting the DTC.
- Use a scan tool in order to clear the DTC.
- After the DTC is cleared and the ignition is ON, the ABS indicator may remain ON until the EBCM completes a power-up self-test. This test concludes when the vehicle reaches a speed greater than 13 km/h (8 mph) and the wheel speeds are verified by the EBCM.

Diagnostic Aids

Operating the vehicle on extremely rough terrain can set DTC C0223, C0227 or C0229 even if the system is functioning normally.

Thoroughly inspect connections or circuitry that may cause an intermittent malfunction.

If the customer's concern is that the ABS indicator is on only during humid conditions such as rain, snow or vehicle wash, thoroughly inspect the wheel speed sensor circuits for signs of water intrusion. Use the following procedure in order to help isolate the problem area:

1. Spray the suspected area with a 5 percent salt water solution.
2. Drive the vehicle at a speed greater than 19 km/h (12 mph) for at least 30 seconds.

Repair or replace the suspect harness if the DTC sets.

Test Description

The numbers below refer to the step numbers on the diagnostic table.

3. Measure the resistance of the wheel speed sensor in order to determine if the sensor has a valid resistance value.

4. Ensures that the wheel speed sensor is generating a valid AC voltage

LTV0500000005251

Fig. 22   Codes C0221–C0227: Wheel Speed Sensor Circuit Fault (Part 2 of 4). Astro, Blazer, Jimmy, Safari, Sonoma, SSR & S10

Circuit Description

As the wheel spins, the wheel speed sensor produces an AC signal. The electronic brake control module (EBCM) uses the frequency of the AC signal to calculate the wheel speed.

DTC Descriptors

This diagnostic procedure supports the following DTCs:

- DTC C0221 Right Front Wheel Speed Sensor Circuit Open
- DTC C0222 Right Front Wheel Speed Signal Missing
- DTC C0223 Right Front Wheel Speed Signal Erratic
- DTC C0225 Left Front Wheel Speed Sensor Circuit Open
- DTC C0226 Left Front Wheel Speed Signal Missing
- DTC C0227 Left Front Wheel Speed Signal Erratic

Conditions for Running the DTC

C0221 and C0225

The ignition is ON.

C0222, C0223, C0226 and C0227

The vehicle speed is greater than 32 km/h (20 mph) when the brake is applied or 19 km/h (12 mph) when the brake is released.

Conditions for Setting the DTC

C0221 and C0225

The EBCM detects an open or shorted wheel speed sensor or wheel speed sensor circuit for 500 milliseconds.

C0222 and C0226

The corresponding wheel speed sensor signal is less than 6 km/h (4 mph) for 5 seconds, or 120 seconds in order to set both DTCs.

C0223 and C0227

The EBCM detects an erratic signal from the corresponding wheel speed sensor for 105 milliseconds.

LTV0500000005250

Fig. 22   Codes C0221–C0227: Wheel Speed Sensor Circuit Fault (Part 1 of 4). Astro, Blazer, Jimmy, Safari, Sonoma, SSR & S10

Step	Action	Values	Yes	No
	Important: If DTC C0229 is set, diagnose DTC C0229 before diagnosing any other wheel speed sensor DTCs.			
1	Did you perform the Diagnostic System Check - Vehicle?	--	Go to Step 2	Go to Diagnostic System Check
2	1. Use a scan tool in order to clear the DTCs. 2. Operate the vehicle at a speed greater than the specified value. Does the DTC set?	19 km/h (12 mph)	Go to Step 3	Go to Diagnostic Aids
3	1. Turn OFF the ignition. 2. Raise and support the vehicle. 3. Disconnect the wheel speed sensor connector. 4. Use a DMM in order to measure the resistance across the wheel speed sensor. Does the resistance measure within the specified range?	700-10,000 ohms	Go to Step 4	Go to Step 8
4	1. Spin the wheel by hand as fast as possible. 2. Use a DMM in order to measure the AC voltage across the wheel speed sensor as the wheel spins. Does the AC voltage measure greater than the specified value?	100 mV	Go to Step 5	Go to Step 8
5	Inspect for poor connections at the harness connector of the wheel speed sensor. Did you find and correct the condition?	--	Go to Step 10	Go to Step 6

LTV0500000005252

Fig. 22   Codes C0221–C0227: Wheel Speed Sensor Circuit Fault (Part 3 of 4). Astro, Blazer, Jimmy, Safari, Sonoma, SSR & S10

	Action		Go to Step 10	Go to Step 7
6	1. Disconnect the electronic brake control module (EBCM) harness connector. 2. Test the wheel speed sensor circuits for the following: – An open – A short to ground – A short to voltage – Shorted together Refer to Circuit Testing and to Wiring Repairs in Wiring Systems. Did you find and correct the condition?		Go to Step 10	Go to Step 7
7	Inspect for poor connections at the harness connector for the EBCM. Did you find and correct the condition?		Go to Step 10	Go to Step 9
8	Replace the wheel speed sensor. Did you complete the replacement?		Go to Step 10	--
9	Replace the EBCM. Did you complete the replacement?		Go to Step 10	--
10	1. Use the scan tool in order to clear the DTCs. 2. Operate the vehicle within the Conditions for Running the DTC as specified in the supporting text. Does the DTC reset?		Go to Step 2	System OK

LTV0500000005253

Fig. 22 Codes C0221–C0227: Wheel Speed Sensor Circuit Fault (Part 4 of 4). Astro, Blazer, Jimmy, Safari, Sonoma, SSR & S10

Step	Action	Yes	No
1	Did you perform the Diagnostic System Check - Vehicle?	Go to Step 2	Go to Diagnostic System Check
2	1. Use a scan tool in order to clear the DTCs. 2. Operate the vehicle within the Conditions for Running the DTC as specified in the supporting text. Does the DTC set?	Go to Step 3	Go to Diagnostic Aids
3	Inspect for poor connections at the harness connector of the electronic brake control module (EBCM). Did you find and correct the condition?	Go to Step 5	Go to Step 4
4	Replace the EBCM. Did you complete the replacement?	Go to Step 5	--
5	1. Use the scan tool in order to clear the DTCs. 2. Operate the vehicle within the Conditions for Running the DTC as specified in the supporting text. Does the DTC reset?	Go to Step 3	System OK

LTV0500000005255

Fig. 23 Code C0229: Drop Out Of Front Wheel Speed Sensor Signals (Part 2 of 2). Astro, Blazer, Jimmy, Safari, Sonoma, SSR & S10

Circuit Description

As the wheel spins, the wheel speed sensor produces an AC signal. The electronic brake control module (EBCM) uses the frequency of the AC signal to calculate the wheel speed.

DTC Descriptor

This diagnostic procedure supports the following DTC:

DTC C0229 Drop Out of Both Front Speed Sensors

Conditions for Running the DTC

- The ignition is ON.
- The vehicle speed is greater than 32 km/h (20 mph) when the brake is applied or 19 km/h (12 mph) when the brake is released.

Conditions for Setting the DTC

The EBCM detects an erratic signal from both front wheel speed sensors for 105 milliseconds.

Action Taken When the DTC Sets

If equipped, the following actions occur:

- The EBCM disables the ABS/TCS/DRP.
- The ABS indicator turns ON.
- The TRACTION OFF indicator turns ON.
- The red brake warning indicator turns ON.

Conditions for Clearing the DTC

- Repair the condition responsible for setting the DTC.
- Use a scan tool in order to clear the DTC.
- After the DTC is cleared and the ignition is ON, the ABS indicator may remain ON until the EBCM completes a power-up self-test. This test concludes when the vehicle reaches a speed greater than 13 km/h (8 mph) and the wheel speeds are verified by the EBCM.

Diagnostic Aids

Operating the vehicle on extremely rough terrain can set DTC C0223, C0227 or C0229 even if the system is functioning normally.

Thoroughly inspect connections or circuitry that may cause an intermittent malfunction.

If the customer's concern is that the ABS indicator is on only during humid conditions such as rain, snow or vehicle wash, thoroughly inspect the wheel speed sensor circuits for signs of water intrusion. Use the following procedure in order to help isolate the problem area:

1. Spray the suspected area with a 5 percent salt water solution.
2. Drive the vehicle at a speed greater than 19 km/h (12 mph) for at least 30 seconds.

LTV0500000005254

Fig. 23 Code C0229: Drop Out Of Front Wheel Speed Sensor Signals (Part 1 of 2). Astro, Blazer, Jimmy, Safari, Sonoma, SSR & S10

Circuit Description

The powertrain control module (PCM) converts the data from the vehicle speed sensor to a 128k pulses/mile signal. The electronic brake control module (EBCM) uses the vehicle speed signal from the PCM in order to calculate the rear wheel speed.

DTC Descriptors

This diagnostic procedure supports the following DTCs:

- DTC C0235 Rear Wheel Speed Signal Circuit Open
- DTC C0236 Rear Wheel Speed Signal Missing
- DTC C0237 Rear Wheel Speed Signal Erratic
- DTC P0609 Vehicle Speed Output Circuit 2

Conditions for Running the DTC

C0235

The ignition is ON.

C0236 and C0237

- The ignition is ON.
- The vehicle speed is greater than 32 km/h (20 mph) when the brake is applied or 19 km/h (12 mph) when the brake is released.

P1504

- The ignition is ON.
- The vehicle is not moving.

Conditions for Setting the DTC

C0235

The EBCM detects low voltage on the vehicle speed signal circuit for 500 milliseconds.

C0236

The rear wheel speed signal is less than 6 km/h (4 mph) for 5 seconds, or 120 seconds in order to set multiple missing sensor signal DTCs.

C0237

The EBCM detects an erratic rear wheel speed signal for 105 milliseconds.

P1504

The PCM detects low voltage on the vehicle speed signal circuit for 45 seconds.

Action Taken When the DTC Sets

LTV0500000005256

Fig. 24 Codes C0235–C0237 Or P0609: Rear Wheel Speed Sensor Signal Fault (Part 1 of 3). Astro, Blazer, Jimmy, Safari, Sonoma, SSR & S10

Action Taken When the DTC Sets

If equipped, the following actions occur:

- The EBCM disables the ABS/TCS/DRP.
- The ABS indicator turns ON.
- The TRACTION OFF indicator turns ON.
- The red brake warning indicator turns ON.

Conditions for Clearing the DTC

- Repair the condition responsible for setting the DTC.
- Use a scan tool in order to clear the DTC.
- After the DTC is cleared and the ignition is ON, the ABS indicator may remain ON until the EBCM completes a power-up self-test. This test concludes when the vehicle reaches a speed greater than 13 km/h (8 mph) and the wheel speeds are verified by the EBCM.

Diagnostic Aids

Thoroughly inspect connections or circuitry that may cause an intermittent malfunction.

Test Description

The numbers below refer to the step numbers on the diagnostic table:

3. This step tests for a voltage signal from the PCM.

4. This step tests for a missing or erratic vehicle speed signal from the PCM. An assistant may be required in order to perform this test.

Step	Action	Value(s)	Yes	No
1	Did you perform the Diagnostic System Check - Vehicle?	--	Go to Step 2	Go to Diagnostic System Check
2	1. Use a scan tool in order to clear the DTCs. 2. Operate the vehicle within the Conditions for Running the DTC as specified in the supporting text. Does the DTC set?	--	Go to Step 3	Go to Diagnostic Aids
3	1. Turn OFF the ignition. 2. Disconnect from the electronic brake control module (EBCM), the harness connector containing the vehicle speed signal circuit. 3. Turn ON the ignition. 4. Use a DMM in order to measure the DC voltage between the vehicle speed signal circuit and a good ground. Does the voltage measure greater than the specified value?	10 volts	Go to Step 4	Go to Step 7

LTV0500000005257

Fig. 24 Codes C0235–C0237 Or P0609: Rear Wheel Speed Sensor Signal Fault (Part 2 of 3). Astro, Blazer, Jimmy, Safari, Sonoma, SSR & S10

Circuit Description

As the front wheels spin, the wheel speed sensors (WSSs) produce an AC signal. The electronic brake control module (EBCM) uses the frequency of the AC signal to calculate the wheel speed. The powertrain control module (PCM) converts the data from the vehicle speed sensor (VSS) to a 128k pulses/mile signal. The EBCM uses the vehicle speed signal from the PCM in order to calculate the rear wheel speed.

DTC Descriptor

This diagnostic procedure supports the following DTC:

DTC C0238 Wheel Speed Mismatch

Conditions for Running the DTC

The ignition is ON and the vehicle speed is between 24 km/h (15 mph) and 80 km/h (50 mph).

Conditions for Setting the DTC

The EBCM detects that one wheel speed input is 10 percent greater than or 10 percent less than the other wheel speed inputs within 3.2 km (2 mi) of driving.

Action Taken When the DTC Sets

If equipped, the following actions occur:

- The EBCM disables the ABS/TCS/DRP.
- The ABS indicator turns ON.
- The TRACTION OFF indicator turns ON.
- The red brake warning indicator turns ON.

Conditions for Clearing the DTC

The conditions for setting the DTC are no longer present and you use the scan tool Clear DTCs function.

Diagnostic Aids

Installing one tire of significantly different size on the vehicle causes DTC C0238 to set. Operating the vehicle with a tire that has very low air pressure may also set this DTC. Inspect the vehicle for an incorrect or damaged wheel speed sensor or vehicle speed sensor if the tires and the EBCM and PCM calibrations are OK.

Test Description

The number below refers to the step number on the diagnostic table:

4. If the front tires are not the same size as the rear tires, the EBCM calibration must match the FRONT tire size and the PCM calibration must match the REAR tire size.

LTV0500000005259

Fig. 25 Code C0238: Wheel Speed Mismatch (Part 1 of 2). Astro, Blazer, Jimmy, Safari, Sonoma, SSR & S10

Step	Action	Value(s)	Yes	No
4	1. Raise and support the vehicle. 2. Place the transmission in neutral (N). 3. Set up the DMM in order to measure the DC voltage between the vehicle speed signal circuit and a good ground. 4. Spin the rear wheels as fast as possible by hand for at least 30 seconds and while ensuring the driveshaft is rotating, observe the DMM. Does the voltage measure within the specified range the entire time the driveshaft is rotating?	5-7 volts	Go to Step 5	Go to Step 7
5	Inspect for poor connections at the harness connector of the EBCM. Did you find and correct the condition?	--	Go to Step 10	Go to Step 6
6	Replace the EBCM. Did you complete the replacement?	--	Go to Step 10	--
7	Test the vehicle speed signal circuit for an open, a short to ground or a short to voltage. Did you find and correct the condition?	--	Go to Step 10	Go to Step 8
8	Inspect for poor connections at the harness connector of the powertrain control module (PCM). Did you find and correct the condition?	--	Go to Step 10	Go to Step 9
9	Replace the PCM. Did you complete the replacement?	--	Go to Step 10	--
10	1. Use the scan tool in order to clear the DTC. 2. Operate the vehicle within the Conditions for Running the DTC as specified in the supporting text. Does the DTC reset?	--	Go to Step 3	System OK

LTV0500000005258

Fig. 24 Codes C0235–C0237 Or P0609: Rear Wheel Speed Sensor Signal Fault (Part 3 of 3). Astro, Blazer, Jimmy, Safari, Sonoma, SSR & S10

Step	Action	Yes	No
1	Did you perform the Diagnostic System Check - Vehicle?	Go to Step 2	Go to Diagnostic System Check
2	Inspect both of the front tires on the vehicle to ensure that both tires are of equal size. Are both of the front tires of equal size?	Go to Step 3	Go to Diagnostic Aids
3	Inspect both of the rear tires on the vehicle to ensure that both tires are of equal size. Are both of the rear tires of equal size?	Go to Step 4	Go to Diagnostic Aids
4	Verify the electronic brake control module (EBCM) and the powertrain control module (PCM) both have the correct tire size calibration. Use the scan tool in order to view the EBCM tire size calibration or perform the Tire Size Calibration procedure and refer to Service Programming System (SPS) in Programming. Did you find and correct the condition?	Go to Step 5	Go to Diagnostic Aids
5	1. Use a scan tool in order to clear the DTCs. 2. Operate the vehicle for 3.2 km (2 mi) within the Conditions for Running the DTC as specified in the supporting text. Does the DTC reset?	Go to Step 2	System OK

LTV0500000005260

Fig. 25 Code C0238: Wheel Speed Mismatch (Part 2 of 2). Astro, Blazer, Jimmy, Safari, Sonoma, SSR & S10

Circuit Description

The ABS relay supplies battery voltage to 6 valve solenoids. The electronic brake control module (EBCM) microprocessor applies the grounds needed to activate each solenoid. The low side of each solenoid coil has a feedback circuit to the EBCM microprocessor. When a solenoid is commanded OFF, the feedback voltage is high. When a solenoid is commanded ON, the feedback voltage is low.

DTC Descriptors

This diagnostic procedure supports the following DTCs:

- DTC C0241 EBCM Control Valve Circuit
- DTC C0242 EBCM Control Valve Circuit
- DTC C0243 EBCM Control Valve Circuit
- DTC C0244 EBCM Control Valve Circuit
- DTC C0245 EBCM Control Valve Circuit
- DTC C0246 EBCM Control Valve Circuit
- DTC C0247 EBCM Control Valve Circuit
- DTC C0248 EBCM Control Valve Circuit
- DTC C0251 EBCM Control Valve Circuit
- DTC C0252 EBCM Control Valve Circuit
- DTC C0253 EBCM Control Valve Circuit
- DTC C0254 EBCM Control Valve Circuit

Conditions for Running the DTC

- The ignition is ON.
- The vehicle speed is greater than 6 km/h (4 mph).

Conditions for Setting the DTC

The EBCM detects an internal malfunction.

Action Taken When the DTC Sets

C0241, C0242, C0245, C0246, C0251, C0252, C0253, C0254

If equipped, the following actions occur:

- The EBCM disables the DRP/ABS.
- The ABS indicator turns ON.
- The red brake warning indicator turns ON.

C0243, C0244, C0247, C0248

If equipped, the following actions occur:

- The EBCM disables the ABS.
- The ABS indicator turns ON.

Conditions for Clearing the DTC

The conditions for setting the DTC are no longer present and you use the scan tool Clear DTCs function.

LTV050000005261

Fig. 26   Codes C0241–C0254: EBCM Control Valve Circuit (Part 1 of 2). Astro, Blazer, Jimmy, Safari, Sonoma, SSR & S10

Circuit Description

The ABS relay supplies battery voltage to 6 valve solenoids. The electronic brake control module (EBCM) microprocessor applies the grounds needed to activate each solenoid. The low side of each solenoid coil has a feedback circuit to the EBCM microprocessor. When a solenoid is commanded OFF, the feedback voltage is high. When a solenoid is commanded ON, the feedback voltage is low.

DTC Descriptors

This diagnostic procedure supports the following DTCs:

- DTC C0265 EBCM Motor Relay Circuit
- DTC C0266 EBCM Motor Relay Circuit

Conditions for Running the DTC

- The ignition is ON.
- The vehicle speed is greater than 6 km/h (4 mph).

Conditions for Setting the DTC

The EBCM detects an internal malfunction.

Action Taken When the DTC Sets

C0265

If equipped, the following actions occur:

- The EBCM disables the DRP/ABS.
- The ABS indicator turns ON.
- The brake warning indicator turns ON.

C0266

If equipped, the following actions occur:

- The EBCM disables the ABS.
- The ABS indicator turns ON.

Conditions for Clearing the DTC

The conditions for setting the DTC are no longer present and you use the scan tool Clear DTCs function.

LTV050000005263

Fig. 27   Codes C0265 Or C0266: EBCM Motor Relay Circuit (Part 1 of 4). Astro, Blazer, Jimmy, Safari, Sonoma, SSR & S10

Diagnostic Aids

An intermittent open/shorted solenoid DTC can be set by several different internal EBCM problems. Replace the EBCM if an open/shorted solenoid DTC continues to set intermittently.

Step	Action	Yes	No
1	Did you perform the Diagnostic System Check - Vehicle?	Go to Step 2	Go to Diagnostic System Check
2	1. Use a scan tool in order to clear the DTCs. 2. Operate the vehicle within the Conditions for Running the DTC as specified in the supporting text. Does the DTC set?	Go to Step 3	Go to Diagnostic Aids
3	Replace the electronic brake control module (EBCM). Did you complete the replacement?	Go to Step 4	
4	1. Use the scan tool in order to clear the DTCs. 2. Operate the vehicle within the Conditions for Running the DTC as specified in the supporting text. Does the DTC reset?	Go to Step 3	System OK

LTV050000005262

Fig. 26   Codes C0241–C0254: EBCM Control Valve Circuit (Part 2 of 2). Astro, Blazer, Jimmy, Safari, Sonoma, SSR & S10

Diagnostic Aids

Important

Whenever the EBCM is replaced for DTC C0265 or C0266, the ABS pump motor and motor circuitry must be tested for the proper resistance. Refer to steps 7 and 8 in the diagnostic table below for testing procedures and resistance values.

C0265

Thoroughly inspect connections and circuitry that may cause an intermittent malfunction.

C0266

Replace the EBCM if DTC C0266 continues to set intermittently.

Test Description

The numbers below refer to the step numbers on the diagnostic table.

4. This step tests if the battery positive voltage circuit can supply adequate power to the system relay.

7. A shorted ABS pump motor or shorted motor circuitry may damage the contacts within the system relay. Follow this step to prevent damage to a replacement EBCM.

Step	Action	Values	Yes	No
1	Did you perform the Diagnostic System Check - Vehicle?	--	Go to Step 2	Go to Diagnostic System Check
2	1. Use a scan tool in order to clear the DTCs. 2. Use the scan tool in order to perform an ABS Function Test. Does DTC C0266 set?	--	Go to Step 7	Go to Step 3

LTV050000005264

Fig. 27   Codes C0265 Or C0266: EBCM Motor Relay Circuit (Part 2 of 4). Astro, Blazer, Jimmy, Safari, Sonoma, SSR & S10

Step	Action	Values	Yes	No
3	Does DTC C0265 set?	--	Go to Step 4	Go to Diagnostic Aids
4	1. Turn OFF the ignition. 2. Disconnect from the electronic brake control module (EBCM), the harness connector containing the battery positive voltage circuit. 3. Connect a test lamp between the battery positive voltage circuit and a good ground. Does the test lamp illuminate?	--	Go to Step 6	Go to Step 5
5	Repair the open in the battery positive voltage circuit. Did you complete the repair?	--	Go to Step 11	--
6	Inspect for poor connections at the harness connector of the EBCM. Did you find and correct the condition?	--	Go to Step 11	Go to Step 7
7	**Important** It may be necessary to separate the EBCM from the brake pressure modulator valve (BPMV) to gain access to the pump motor pigtail connector. 1. Disconnect from the EBCM, the ABS pump motor pigtail connector. 2. Use a DMM in order to measure the resistance across the ABS pump motor. Does the resistance measure within the specified range?	0.3-1.0 ohms	Go to Step 8	Go to Step 10
8	Use a DMM in order to measure the resistance between the high side of the pump motor and a good ground. Does the resistance measure less than the specified value?	0L	Go to Step 10	Go to Step 9

LTV0500000005265

Fig. 27 Codes C0265 Or C0266: EBCM Motor Relay Circuit (Part 3 of 4). Astro, Blazer, Jimmy, Safari, Sonoma, SSR & S10

Circuit Description

The EBCM applies the ground needed for pump motor activation. The low side of the pump motor has a feedback circuit to the EBCM. When the pump motor is commanded OFF and at rest, feedback voltage is high. When the pump motor is winding down after being commanded ON and then OFF, feedback voltage is low. The EBCM monitors this feedback voltage in order to determine if the motor is functioning properly.

DTC Descriptors

This diagnostic procedure supports the following DTCs:

- DTC C0267 Pump Motor Circuit Open
- DTC C0268 Pump Motor Circuit Shorted

Conditions for Running the DTC

- The ignition is ON.
- The vehicle speed is greater than 6 km/h (4 mph).

Conditions for Setting the DTC

The EBCM detects any of the following conditions:

- An open or shorted pump motor
- An open or shorted pump motor driver circuit
- A seized pump motor

Action Taken When the DTC Sets

- The EBCM disables the ABS.
- The ABS indicator turns ON.

Conditions for Clearing the DTC

The conditions for setting the DTC are no longer present and you use the scan tool Clear DTCs function.

Diagnostic Aids

Thoroughly inspect connections or circuitry that may cause an intermittent malfunction.

LTV0500000005267

Fig. 28 Codes C0267 Or C0268: Pump Motor Circuit Open Or Shorted (Part 1 of 4). Astro, Blazer, Jimmy, Safari, Sonoma, SSR & S10

Step	Action	Values	Yes	No
9	Replace the EBCM. Did you complete the replacement?		Go to Step 11	--
10	**Important** Use the scan tool in order to perform the Tire Size Calibration procedure and the Trim Level Calibration procedure, if applicable. Replace the EBCM and the BPMV. Did you complete the replacements?		Go to Step 11	--
11	1. Use the scan tool in order to clear the DTCs. 2. Operate the vehicle within the Conditions for Running the DTC as specified in the supporting text. Does the DTC reset?		Go to Step 2	System OK

LTV0500000005266

Fig. 27 Codes C0265 Or C0266: EBCM Motor Relay Circuit (Part 4 of 4). Astro, Blazer, Jimmy, Safari, Sonoma, SSR & S10

Test Description

The numbers below refer to the step numbers on the diagnostic table.

2. It is imperative that the vehicle be driven to attempt to reset the DTC. Using the scan tool to perform a function test may not produce the same result, and therefore may cause misdiagnosis of the vehicle.

7. This step tests if the EBCM is capable of activating the ABS pump motor.

8. A shorted ABS pump motor may damage the EBCM. It is imperative that the steps in the table be followed in order to prevent damage to a replacement EBCM.

Step	Action	Values	Yes	No
1	Did you perform the Diagnostic System Check - Vehicle?	--	Go to Step 2	Go to Diagnostic System Check
2	1. Use a scan tool in order to clear the DTCs. 2. Operate the vehicle within the Conditions for Running the DTC as specified in the supporting text. Does DTC C0267 set?	--	Go to Step 6	Go to Step 3
3	Does DTC C0268 set?	--	Go to Step 4	Go to Diagnostic Aids
4	1. Turn OFF the ignition. 2. Disconnect from the electronic brake control module (EBCM), the 2-way harness connector which contains the battery positive voltage circuit and the ground circuit. **Caution: Before servicing any electrical component, the ignition key must be in the OFF or LOCK position and all electrical loads must be OFF, unless instructed otherwise in these procedures. If a tool or equipment could easily come in contact with a live exposed electrical terminal, also disconnect the negative battery cable. Failure to follow these precautions may cause personal injury and/or damage to the vehicle or its components.** 3. Disconnect the negative battery cable. 4. Disconnect the positive battery cable. 5. Place one lead of a DMM on the positive battery cable where the cable normally connects to the battery. 6. Place the other lead on the battery positive voltage circuit terminal within the 2-way EBCM harness connector. 7. Measure the total resistance between the positive battery cable and the EBCM. Does the resistance measure within the specified range?	0.0-0.2 ohms	Go to Step 5	Go to Step 10

LTV0500000005268

Fig. 28 Codes C0267 Or C0268: Pump Motor Circuit Open Or Shorted (Part 2 of 4). Astro, Blazer, Jimmy, Safari, Sonoma, SSR & S10

Step	Action	Value	Yes	No
5	Use a DMM to measure the resistance of the ground circuit. Does the resistance measure within the specified range?	0.0-0.2 ohms	Go to Step 7	Go to Step 11
6	**Important** On some applications, it may be necessary to separate the EBCM from the brake pressure modulator valve (BPMV) in order to perform this test. Also, DTC C0268 may set when this test is performed. 1. Turn OFF the ignition. 2. Disconnect from the EBCM, the ABS pump motor pigtail connector. For systems which have no pump motor pigtail, it is necessary to separate the EBCM from the BPMV in order to gain access to the pump motor connector of the EBCM. 3. Use a connector adapter test kit in order to connect a test lamp between the ABS pump motor power and ground circuits at the pump motor connector of the EBCM. 4. Turn ON the ignition. 5. Use the scan tool in order to clear the DTCs. 6. Use the scan tool in order to perform an ABS Function Test. Does DTC C0267 set?	—	Go to Step 12	Go to Step 9
7	**Important** On some applications, it may be necessary to separate the EBCM from the BPMV in order to perform this test. Also, DTC C0268 may set when this test is performed. 1. Reconnect both battery cables. 2. Disconnect from the EBCM, the ABS pump motor pigtail connector. For systems which have no pump motor pigtail, it is necessary to separate the EBCM from the BPMV in order to gain access to the pump motor connector of the EBCM. 3. Use a connector adapter test kit in order to connect a test lamp between the ABS pump motor power and ground circuits at the pump motor connector of the EBCM. 4. Turn ON the ignition. 5. Use the scan tool in order to clear the DTCs. 6. Use the scan tool in order to perform an ABS Function Test. Does the test lamp illuminate and then turn OFF when the Function Test is performed?	—	Go to Step 13	Go to Step 8
8	Use a DMM in order to measure the resistance across the ABS pump motor. Does the resistance measure within the specified range?	0.3-1.0 ohms	Go to Step 12	Go to Step 14
9	Inspect for poor connections at the pump motor pigtail connector. Did you find and correct the condition?	—	Go to Step 15	Go to Step 13
10	Repair the high resistance in the underhood electrical center or the battery positive voltage circuit. Did you complete the repair?	—	Go to Step 15	—

LTV0500000005269

Fig. 28   Codes C0267 Or C0268: Pump Motor Circuit Open Or Shorted (Part 3 of 4). Astro, Blazer, Jimmy, Safari, Sonoma, SSR & S10

Circuit Description

The system relay is energized when the ignition is ON. The system relay supplies voltage to the valve solenoids and the pump motor. This voltage is referred to as the system voltage. The electronic brake control module (EBCM) microprocessor activates the valve solenoids by grounding the control circuit.

DTC Descriptors

This diagnostic procedure supports the following DTCs:

- DTC C0269 Excessive Dump Time
- DTC C0274 Excessive Isolation Time

Conditions for Running the DTC

- The ignition is ON.
- The vehicle is experiencing an ABS event.

Conditions for Setting the DTC

C0269

The EBCM commands a dump solenoid ON for 9 consecutive seconds.

C0274

The EBCM commands an isolation solenoid ON for 255 consecutive seconds.

Action Taken When the DTC Sets

If equipped, the following actions may occur:

- The EBCM disables the ABS/TCS/DRP.
- The ABS indicator turns ON.
- The TRACTION OFF indicator turns ON.
- The red brake warning indicator turns ON.

Conditions for Clearing the DTC

The conditions for setting the DTC are no longer present and you use the scan tool Clear DTCs function.

Diagnostic Aids

The most likely cause of DTC C0269 or DTC C0274 is a mechanical failure that causes a wheel to lock and remain locked. The DTCs may also set, conceivably, when the ABS is activated on surfaces that are nearly impossible to get traction on. If the DTC sets within these conditions, diagnosis of the ABS system is not necessary.

Test Description

The number below refers to the step number on the diagnostic table:

2. Performing solenoid tests determines if there is a mechanical malfunction inside the brake pressure modulator valve (BPMV). Perform dump valve solenoid tests for DTC C0269 or isolation valve solenoid tests for DTC C0274.

LTV0500000005271

Fig. 29   Codes C0269 Or C0274: Excessive Dump & Isolation Time (Part 1 of 2). Astro, Blazer, Jimmy, Safari, Sonoma, SSR & S10

Step	Action	Yes	No
11	Repair the high resistance in the ground circuit. Did you complete the repair?	Go to Step 15	—
12	Replace the EBCM. Did you complete the replacement?	Go to Step 15	—
13	Replace the BPMV. Did you complete the replacement?	Go to Step 15	—
14	**Important** Following EBCM replacement, use the scan tool perform the Tire Size Calibration procedure and the Trim Level Calibration procedure, if applicable. Replace the EBCM and the BPMV. Did you complete the replacements?	Go to Step 15	—
15	1. Use a scan tool in order to clear the DTCs. 2. Operate the vehicle within the Conditions for Running the DTC as specified in the supporting text. Does the DTC reset?	Go to Step 3	System OK

LTV0500000005270

Fig. 28   Codes C0267 Or C0268: Pump Motor Circuit Open Or Shorted (Part 4 of 4). Astro, Blazer, Jimmy, Safari, Sonoma, SSR & S10

Step	Action	Yes	No
1	Did you perform the Diagnostic System Check - Vehicle?	Go to Step 2	Go to Diagnostic System Check
2	1. Use a scan tool in order to clear the DTCs. 2. Use the scan tool in order to perform the necessary Solenoid Tests. Refer to Scan Tool Output Controls . Do the Solenoid Tests show the system to be functioning normally?	Go to Diagnostic Aids	Go to Step 3
3	Replace the brake pressure modulator valve (BPMV). Did you complete the replacement?	Go to Step 4	—
4	Use the scan tool in order to perform the necessary Solenoid Tests. Do the Solenoid Tests show the system to be functioning normally?	System OK	Go to Step 3

LTV0500000005272

Fig. 29   Codes C0269 Or C0274: Excessive Dump & Isolation Time (Part 2 of 2). Astro, Blazer, Jimmy, Safari, Sonoma, SSR & S10

Circuit Description

This DTC identifies a malfunction within the electronic brake control module (EBCM).

DTC Descriptors

This diagnostic procedure supports the following DTCs:

- DTC C0271 EBCM Malfunction
- DTC C0273 EBCM Malfunction
- DTC C0284 EBCM Malfunction

Conditions for Running the DTC

The ignition is ON.

Conditions for Setting the DTC

The EBCM detects an internal malfunction.

Action Taken When the DTC Sets

If equipped, the following actions may occur:

- The EBCM disables the ABS/TCS/DRP.
- The ABS indicator turns ON.
- The TRACTION OFF indicator turns ON.
- The red brake warning indicator turns ON.

Conditions for Clearing the DTC

The conditions for setting the DTC are no longer present and you use the scan tool Clear DTCs function.

Diagnostic Aids

Replace the EBCM if DTC C0273 or DTC C0284 continues to set intermittently.

LTV0500000005273

Fig. 30   Codes C0271–C0273 & C0284: EBCM Fault (Part 1 of 2). Astro, Blazer, Jimmy, Safari, Sonoma, SSR & S10

Step	Action	Yes	No
1	Did you perform the Diagnostic System Check - Vehicle?	Go to Step 2	Go to Diagnostic System Check
2	Is DTC C0271 or DTC C0272 set in the electronic brake control module (EBCM) memory?	Go to Step 4	Go to Step 3
3	1. Use a scan tool in order to clear the DTCs. 2. Turn OFF the ignition for 5 seconds. 3. Turn ON the ignition. Does the DTC set?	Go to Step 4	Go to Diagnostic Aids
4	Replace the EBCM. Did you complete the replacement?	Go to Step 5	--
5	Use the scan tool in order to clear the DTCs. Operate the vehicle within the Conditions for Running the DTC as specified in the supporting text. Does the DTC reset?	Go to Step 2	System OK

LTV0500000005274

Fig. 30   Codes C0271–C0273 & C0284: EBCM Fault (Part 2 of 2). Astro, Blazer, Jimmy, Safari, Sonoma, SSR & S10

Step	Action	Yes	No
1	Did you perform the Diagnostic System Check - Vehicle?	Go to Step 2	Go to Diagnostic System Check
2	1. Use a scan tool in order to clear the DTCs. 2. Turn OFF the ignition for 5 seconds. 3. Turn ON the ignition and wait 10 seconds. Does the DTC set?	Go to Step 3	Go to Diagnostics Aids
3	Verify the correct powertrain control module (PCM) is installed in the vehicle. Does the vehicle have the correct PCM?	Go to Step 4	Go to Step 6
4	Use the scan tool in order to read the Calibration IDs of the PCM. Are the PCM calibration IDs correct?	Go to Diagnostics Aids	Go to Step 5
5	Perform the setup procedure for the PCM. Did you complete the action?	Go to Step 7	
6	Replace the PCM. Did you complete the replacement?	Go to Step 7	--
7	1. Use the scan tool in order to clear the DTCs. 2. Operate the vehicle within the Conditions for Running the DTC, as specified in the supporting text. Does the DTC reset?	Go to Step 3	System OK

LTV0500000005276

Fig. 31   Code C0279: Powertrain Configuration Not Valid (Part 2 of 2). SSR

Circuit Description

The stop lamp switch signal informs the electronic brake control module (EBCM) when the brake pedal is pressed.

DTC Descriptor

This diagnostic procedure supports the following DTC:

DTC C0281 Stoplamp Switch Circuit

Conditions for Running the DTC

Either of the following conditions will cause the DTC to run:

- The ignition is ON and the vehicle achieves at least 56 km/h (35 mph) before coming to a stop.
- The ignition is ON and the vehicle experiences an antilock brake system (ABS) event lasting at least 1 second.

Conditions for Setting the DTC

The EBCM detects an open or shorted brake switch or brake switch circuit.

Action Taken When the DTC Sets

This information-only DTC is stored in EBCM memory until it is cleared by using the specified procedure.

Conditions for Clearing the DTC

The conditions for setting the DTC are no longer present and you use the scan tool Clear DTCs function.

Diagnostic Aids

Thoroughly inspect connections or circuitry that may cause an intermittent malfunction.

Test Description

The numbers below refer to the step numbers on the diagnostic table.

4. This step tests for a shorted stop lamp switch.

5. This step tests for an open stop lamp switch.

LTV0500000005277

Fig. 32   Code C0281: Stoplamp Switch Circuit (Part 1 of 3). Astro, Blazer, Jimmy, Safari, Sonoma, SSR & S10

Circuit Description

The powertrain control module (PCM) sends engine/axle/tire IDs to the electronic brake control module (EBCM) via serial data communications immediately after the modules are powered up.

DTC Descriptor

This diagnostic procedure supports the following DTC:

DTC C0279 Powertrain Configuration Not Valid

Conditions for Running the DTC

The ignition is ON.

Conditions for Setting the DTC

The EBCM receives invalid information from the PCM.

Action Taken When the DTC Sets

If equipped, the following actions occur:

- The EBCM disables the traction control system (TCS).
- The traction off indicator turns ON.

Conditions for Clearing the DTC

The conditions for setting the DTC are no longer present and you use the scan tool Clear DTCs function.

Diagnostic Aids

- Diagnose other ABS or TCS related DTCs prior to diagnosing DTC C0279.
- If multiple TCS related DTCs are set, or the vehicle being serviced is not equipped with TCS, verify the correct EBCM is installed in the vehicle.

Test Description

The number below refers to the step number on the diagnostic table.

3. The PCM must have the correct part number for the specified application.

LTV0500000005275

Fig. 31   Code C0279: Powertrain Configuration Not Valid (Part 1 of 2). SSR

Step	Action	Yes	No
1	Did you perform the Diagnostic System Check - Vehicle?	Go to Step 2	Go to Diagnostic System Check
2	1. Install a scan tool. 2. Select the ABS Data Display function. 3. Observe the Brake Switch Status on the scan tool. Does the scan tool display Off?	Go to Step 3	Go to Step 5
3	1. Apply the brake. 2. Observe the Brake Switch Status on the scan tool. Does the scan tool display On?	Go to Diagnostic Aids	Go to Step 4
4	1. Turn OFF the ignition. 2. Disconnect the stop lamp switch. 3. Turn ON the ignition. 4. Observe the Brake Switch Status on the scan tool. Does the scan tool display On?	Go to Step 9	Go to Step 7
5	1. Turn OFF the ignition. 2. Disconnect the stop lamp switch. 3. Connect a fused jumper wire between the ignition 3 voltage circuit and the torque converter clutch (TCC) brake switch signal circuit at the stop lamp switch harness connector. 4. Turn ON the ignition. 5. Observe the Brake Switch Status on the scan tool. Does the scan tool display Off?	Go to Step 9	Go to Step 6
6	Test the ignition 3 voltage circuit and the TCC brake switch signal circuit for an open or a short to ground. Did you find and correct the condition?	Go to Step 12	Go to Step 8

LTV0500000005278

Fig. 32   Code C0281: Stoplamp Switch Circuit (Part 2 of 3). Astro, Blazer, Jimmy, Safari, Sonoma, SSR & S10

	Action	Yes	No
7	Test the TCC brake switch signal circuit for a short to voltage. Did you find and correct the condition?	Go to Step 12	Go to Step 8
8	Inspect for poor connections at the harness connector of the electronic brake control module (EBCM). Did you find and correct the condition?	Go to Step 12	Go to Step 10
9	Inspect for poor connections at the harness connector of the stop lamp switch. Did you find and correct the condition?	Go to Step 12	Go to Step 11
10	Replace the EBCM. Did you complete the replacement?	Go to Step 12	--
11	Replace the stop lamp switch. Did you complete the replacement?	Go to Step 12	--
12	1. Use the scan tool in order to clear the DTCs. 2. Operate the vehicle within the Conditions for Running the DTC as specified in the supporting text. Does the DTC reset?	Go to Step 2	System OK

LTV0500000005279

Fig. 32   Code C0281: Stoplamp Switch Circuit (Part 3 of 3). Astro, Blazer, Jimmy, Safari, Sonoma, SSR & S10

Step	Action	Yes	No
1	Did you perform the Diagnostic System Check - Vehicle?	Go to Step 2	Go to Diagnostic System Check - Vehicle
2	1. Use a scan tool in order to clear the DTCs. 2. Turn OFF the ignition for 5 seconds. 3. Start the engine and allow the engine to run for at least 20 seconds. Does the DTC set?	Go to Step 3	Go to Diagnostic Aids
3	1. Turn OFF the ignition. 2. Disconnect the traction control switch harness connector. 3. Turn ON the ignition. 4. Connect a test lamp between the ignition 1 voltage circuit and a good ground. Does the test lamp illuminate?	Go to Step 4	Go to Step 8
4	1. Use the scan tool in order to clear the DTCs. 2. Turn OFF the ignition. 3. Connect a fused jumper wire between the ignition 1 voltage circuit and the traction control switch signal circuit at the traction control switch harness connector. 4. Start the engine and allow the engine to run for at least 20 seconds. Does the DTC set?	Go to Step 5	Go to Step 9
5	Test the traction control switch signal circuit for an open or a short to ground. Did you find and correct the condition?	Go to Step 11	Go to Step 6
6	Inspect for poor connections at the harness connector of the electronic brake control module (EBCM). Did you find and correct the condition?	Go to Step 11	Go to Step 7

LTV0500000005281

Fig. 33   Code C0283: Mode Switch Circuit Fault (Part 2 of 3). SSR

	Action	Yes	No
7	Replace the EBCM. Did you complete the replacement?	Go to Step 11	--
8	Repair the open in the ignition 1 voltage circuit. Did you complete the repair?	Go to Step 11	--
9	Inspect for poor connections at the harness connector of the traction control switch. Did you find and correct the condition?	Go to Step 11	Go to Step 10
10	Replace the traction control switch. Did you complete the replacement?	Go to Step 11	--
11	1. Use the scan tool in order to clear the DTCs. 2. Operate the vehicle within the Conditions for Running the DTC, as specified in the supporting text. Does the DTC reset?	Go to Step 3	System OK

LTV0500000005282

Fig. 33   Code C0283: Mode Switch Circuit Fault (Part 3 of 3). SSR

Circuit Description

The traction control switch is a momentary-contact, normally-open switch that can be used to disable the traction control system (TCS). Each time the traction control switch is pressed, the TCS enabled/disabled status changes. When TCS is disabled, the electronic brake control module (EBCM) illuminates the traction off indicator by opening the service traction control signal circuit.

DTC Descriptor

This diagnostic procedure supports the following DTC:

DTC C0283 Mode Switch Circuit Malfunction

Conditions for Running the DTC

- The ignition is ON.
- The engine is running at a rate greater than 450 RPM.

Conditions for Setting the DTC

The EBCM detects low voltage on the traction control switch signal circuit for 10 seconds.

Action Taken When the DTC Sets

If equipped, the following actions occur:

- The EBCM disables the TCS.
- The traction off indicator turns ON.

Conditions for Clearing the DTC

The conditions for setting the DTC are no longer present and you use the scan tool Clear DTCs function.

Diagnostic Aids

Thoroughly inspect connections or circuitry that may cause an intermittent malfunction.

Test Description

The number below refers to the step number on the diagnostic table.

4. This step tests the traction control switch circuitry. If the fuse opens when you perform this test, the traction control switch signal circuit is shorted to ground.

LTV0500000005280

Fig. 33   Code C0283: Mode Switch Circuit Fault (Part 1 of 3). SSR

Circuit Description

The electronic brake control module (EBCM) supplies 5 VDC to the powertrain control module (PCM) on the delivered torque signal circuit. The PCM toggles this voltage to ground in order to create the delivered torque signal at the EBCM. A signal with a frequency of 128 Hz +/- 5 percent and a duty cycle of 25-95 percent is a valid delivered torque signal. The percentage of duty cycle is proportionate to the percentage of delivered torque.

DTC Descriptors

This diagnostic procedure supports the following DTCs:

- DTC C0287 Delivered Torque Signal Malfunction
- DTC P1644 Delivered Torque Circuit
- DTC P1689 Traction Control Delivered Torque Output Circuit

Conditions for Running the DTC

- The ignition is ON.
- The engine is running at a speed greater than 500 RPM for 1 second.

Conditions for Setting the DTC

C0287

The EBCM receives an invalid delivered torque signal for 300 milliseconds.

P1644 or P1689

The PCM detects the delivered torque signal voltage as being less than 4.75 volts or greater than 5.25 volts.

Action Taken When the DTC Sets

If equipped, the following actions occur:

- The EBCM disables the traction control system (TCS).
- The traction off indicator turns ON.

Conditions for Clearing the DTC

The conditions for setting the DTC are no longer present and you use the scan tool Clear DTCs function.

LTV0500000005283

Fig. 34   Codes C0287, P1664 Or P1689: Delivered Torque Signal Fault: (Part 1 of 3). SSR

Diagnostic Aids

Thoroughly inspect connections or circuitry that may cause an intermittent malfunction.

Test Description

The numbers below refer to the step numbers on the diagnostic table.

3. This step tests for voltage supplied to the PCM from the EBCM.

9. The PCM may be damaged if the delivered torque signal circuit is shorted to voltage.

Step	Action	Values	Yes	No
1	Did you perform the Diagnostic System Check - Vehicle?	--	Go to Step 2	Go to Diagnostic System Check - Vehicle
2	1. Use a scan tool in order to clear the DTCs. 2. Turn OFF the ignition for 5 seconds. 3. Start the engine. Does the DTC set?	--	Go to Step 3	Go to Diagnostic Aids
3	1. Turn OFF the ignition. 2. Disconnect from the powertrain control module (PCM), the harness connector containing the delivered torque signal circuit. 3. Turn ON the ignition. 4. Use a DMM in order to measure the voltage between the delivered torque signal circuit and a good ground. Does the voltage measure within the specified range?	4.75-5.25 V	Go to Step 5	Go to Step 4
4	Test the delivered torque signal circuit for an open, a short to voltage, or a short to ground. Did you find and correct the condition?	--	Go to Step 12	Go to Step 7

LTV0500000005284

Fig. 34   Codes C0287, P1664 Or P1689: Delivered Torque Signal Fault: (Part 2 of 3). SSR

Circuit Description

The powertrain control module (PCM) sends a state of health message to the EBCM within 5.5 seconds after the modules are powered up. This message is sent via serial data communications.

DTC Descriptors

This diagnostic procedure supports the following DTCs:

- DTC C0290 Class 2 Data Link Malfunction
- DTC C0292 Lost Communications With Engine Control System

Conditions for Running the DTC

The ignition is ON.

Conditions for Setting the DTC

The EBCM fails to receive serial data from the PCM.

Action Taken When the DTC Sets

If equipped, the following actions occur:

- The EBCM disables the TCS.
- The traction off indicator turns ON.

Conditions for Clearing the DTC

The conditions for setting the DTC are no longer present and you use the scan tool Clear DTCs function.

Step	Action	Yes	No
1	Did you perform the Diagnostic System Check - Vehicle?	Check Scan Tool Does Not Communicate with Class 2 Device	Go to Diagnostic System Check - Vehicle

LTV0500000005286

Fig. 35   Codes C0290 Or C0292: Data Link Fault. SSR

	Action	Values	Yes	No
5	1. Turn OFF the ignition. 2. Reconnect the PCM harness connector. 3. Start the engine. 4. Select the Traction Assist Data List on the scan tool. 5. Observe the Delivered Torque parameter on the scan tool. Does the scan tool display the duty cycle of the delivered torque signal is within the specified range?	25-95%	Go to Step 6	Go to Step 9
6	1. Turn OFF the ignition. 2. Install a J 39700 Universal Breakout Box and a J 39700-325 Adapter Cable. 3. Install the equipment between the electronic brake control module (EBCM) and the EBCM harness connector. 4. Start the engine. 5. Use a DMM in order to measure the Hz frequency of the delivered torque signal. Does the frequency of the delivered torque signal measure within the specified range?	121-134 Hz	Go to Step 7	Go to Step 9
7	1. Turn OFF the ignition. 2. Inspect for poor connections at the harness connector of the EBCM. Did you find and correct the condition?	--	Go to Step 12	Go to Step 8
8	Replace the EBCM. Did you complete the replacement?	--	Go to Step 12	--
9	1. Turn ON the ignition, with the engine OFF. 2. Test the delivered torque signal circuit for a short to voltage. Did you find and correct the condition?	--	Go to Step 12	Go to Step 10
10	Inspect for poor connections at the harness connector of the PCM. Did you find and correct the condition?	--	Go to Step 12	Go to Step 11
11	Replace the PCM. Did you complete the replacement?	--	Go to Step 12	--
12	1. Use the scan tool in order to clear the DTCs. 2. Operate the vehicle within the Conditions for Running the DTC, as specified in the supporting text. Does the DTC reset?	--	Go to Step 3	System OK

LTV0500000005285

Fig. 34   Codes C0287, P1664 Or P1689: Delivered Torque Signal Fault: (Part 3 of 3). SSR

Circuit Description

The PCM sends engine/axle/tire IDs to the EBCM via serial data communications immediately after the modules are powered up.

DTC Descriptor

This diagnostic procedure supports the following DTC:

DTC C0297 Powertrain Configuration Data Not Received

Conditions for Running the DTC

The ignition is ON.

Conditions for Setting the DTC

The EBCM fails to receive serial data from the PCM.

Action Taken When the DTC Sets

If equipped, the following actions occur:

- The EBCM disables the TCS.
- The traction off indicator turns ON.

Conditions for Clearing the DTC

The conditions for setting the DTC are no longer present and you use the scan tool Clear DTCs function.

Step	Action	Yes	No
1	Did you perform the Diagnostic System Check - Vehicle?	Check Scan Tool Does Not Communicate with Class 2 Device	Go to Diagnostic System Check - Vehicle

LTV0500000005287

Fig. 36   Code C0297: Powertrain Configuration Data Not Received. SSR

Circuit Description

C0298

The powertrain control module (PCM) and the electronic brake control module (EBCM) communicate on the serial data link whenever the ignition is ON.

P0856

The PCM supplies 5 volts through an internal resistor, to the EBCM on the requested torque signal circuit. The EBCM toggles this voltage to ground to create the requested torque signal at the PCM.

DTC Descriptors

This diagnostic procedure supports the following DTCs:

- DTC C0298 Powertrain Control Malfunction
- DTC P0856 Traction Control Torque Request Circuit

Conditions for Running the DTC

C0298

The ignition is ON.

P0856

- The ignition is ON.
- The engine is running at a speed greater than 450 RPM for 5-20 seconds.

Conditions for Setting the DTC

C0298

The EBCM receives a serial data message stating that the PCM has lost the ability to reduce engine torque.

P0856

The PCM receives an invalid requested torque signal for 3 seconds.

LTV0500000005288

Fig. 37 Codes C0298 Or P0856: Powertrain Control Fault (Part 1 of 4). SSR

Action Taken When the DTC Sets

C0298

- The EBCM disables the traction control system (TCS).
- The traction off indicator turns ON.

P0856

- The PCM sends a serial data message to the EBCM stating that the PCM has lost the ability to reduce engine torque.
- The EBCM sets DTC C0298 as a current DTC for as long as the malfunction is present.

Conditions for Clearing the DTC

C0298

The conditions for setting the DTC are no longer present and you use the scan tool Clear DTCs function.

P0856

- The conditions for setting the DTC are no longer present and you use the scan tool Clear DTCs function.
- A history DTC clears automatically after 40 consecutive warm-up cycles without a PCM detected failure.

Diagnostic Aids

C0298

A requested torque signal malfunction is only one possible cause for the PCM to lose the ability to perform traction control. DTC C0298 may set due to engine overheating, throttle actuator control failure, loss of ignition timing control by the PCM, etc. If DTC P0856 has not set, refer to link 30550 for the 6.0L engine in order to identify other possible causes of DTC C0298.

P0856

Thoroughly inspect connections or circuitry that may cause an intermittent malfunction. Refer to the following procedures:

- Testing for Electrical Intermittents
- Connector Repairs
- Testing for Intermittent Conditions and Poor Connections
- Wiring Repairs

Test Description

The numbers below refer to the step numbers on the diagnostic table.

4. This step tests for voltage supplied to the EBCM from the PCM.

LTV0500000005289

Fig. 37 Codes C0298 Or P0856: Powertrain Control Fault (Part 2 of 4). SSR

Step	Action	Values	Yes	No
1	Did you perform the Diagnostic System Check - Vehicle?	--	Go to Step 2	Go to Diagnostic System Check - Vehicle
2	Is DTC P0856 set?	--	Go to Step 3	Go to Diagnostic Aids
3	1. Use a scan tool in order to clear the DTCs. 2. Operate the vehicle within the Conditions for Running the DTC, as specified in the supporting text. Does DTC P0856 set?	--	Go to Step 4	Go to Diagnostic Aids
4	1. Turn OFF the ignition. 2. Disconnect from the electronic brake control module (EBCM), the harness connector containing the requested torque signal circuit. 3. Turn ON the ignition. 4. Use a DMM in order to measure the voltage between the requested torque signal circuit and a good ground. Does the voltage measure greater than the specified value?	4.75 V	Go to Step 5	Go to Step 8
5	1. With the DMM still connected to monitor the requested torque signal circuit, connect one end of a test lamp to a good ground. 2. Connect the other end of the test lamp to the positive lead of the DMM. Does the voltage measure less than the specified value?	0.15 V	Go to Step 6	Go to Step 9
6	1. Turn OFF the ignition. 2. Install a J 39700 Universal Breakout Box and a J 39700-325 Adapter Cable. Install the equipment between the EBCM and the EBCM harness connector. 3. Start the engine. 4. Use the DMM in order to measure the Hz frequency of the requested torque signal. Does the Hz frequency of the requested torque signal measure within the specified range?	121-134 Hz	Go to Step 7	Go to Step 11
7	Use the DMM in order to measure the duty cycle of the requested torque signal circuit. Does the duty cycle of the requested torque signal measure within the specified range?	40-95%	Go to Step 12	Go to Step 13

LTV0500000005290

Fig. 37 Codes C0298 Or P0856: Powertrain Control Fault (Part 3 of 4). SSR

	Action		Yes	No
8	Test the requested torque signal circuit for an open or a short to ground. Did you find and correct the condition?		Go to Step 14	Go to Step 10
9	Test the requested torque signal circuit for a short to voltage. Did you find and correct the condition?		Go to Step 14	Go to Step 12
10	Inspect for poor connections at the harness connector of the powertrain control module (PCM). Did you find and correct the condition?		Go to Step 14	Go to Step 12
11	Inspect for poor connections at the harness connector of the EBCM. Did you find and correct the condition?		Go to Step 14	Go to Step 13
12	Replace the PCM. Did you complete the replacement?		Go to Step 14	--
13	Replace the EBCM. Did you complete the replacement?		Go to Step 14	--
14	1. Use the scan tool in order to clear the DTCs. 2. Operate the vehicle within the Conditions for Running the DTC, as specified in the supporting text. Does DTC P0856 reset?		Go to Step 4	System OK

LTV0500000005291

Fig. 37 Codes C0298 Or P0856: Powertrain Control Fault (Part 4 of 4). SSR

Circuit Description

The ABS Diagnostic System Check is an organized approach to identifying problems associated with the ABS. This must be the starting point for any ABS related concern and will direct you to the next logical step in diagnosing a malfunction. Most system malfunctions are linked to faulty wiring, connections and occasionally, to components. Understanding the ABS system and using the diagnostic tables correctly will reduce diagnostic time and prevent unnecessary parts replacement.

Test Description

The numbers below refer to the step numbers in the diagnostic table.

2. Lack of communication may be due to partial or total malfunction of the class 2 serial data circuit. The specified procedure will determine the particular condition.

4. The presence of DTCs that begin with a "U" indicates that some other module is not communicating. The specified procedure will compile all of the available information before tests are performed. The electronic brake control module (EBCM) software does not support DTCs which begin with a "U". The EBCM may set DTC C0290, C0292 or C0297 to indicate a communication failure between the EBCM and the powertrain control module (PCM).

5. These DTCs may be set by the PCM and may effect the rear wheel speed input to the EBCM or indicate an internal failure within the PCM.

6. This DTC may be set by the instrument panel cluster (IPC) and effects the IPC's ability to illuminate indicators.

7. These DTCs may be set by the suspension control module (RTD) and may effect VSES system operation. These DTCs do not effect ABS systems on vehicles which are not equipped with JL4.

8. These DTCs may be set by the suspension control module (RTD) and may effect VSES system operation. These DTCs do not effect ABS systems on vehicles which are not equipped with JL4.

LTV0500000005308

Fig. 38 Diagnostic System Check (Part 1 of 2). 2002 Avalanche, Escalade, Escalade EXT, Suburban, Tahoe & Yukon

Circuit Description

The steering wheel position sensor produces 2 separate voltage signals to indicate steering wheel position to the real time damping (RTD) module. The RTD module converts each signal into a pulse width modulated (PWM) signal to indicate steering wheel position to the EBCM. The EBCM supplies 5 volts to the RTD module on each steering wheel position PWM serial data circuit. The RTD module toggles each of these voltages to ground in order to create the PWM signals. Each PWM signal must have a frequency of 121-134 Hz and a duty cycle of 9-91 percent in order to be a valid steering wheel position signal. With each 360 degree rotation of the steering wheel, each signal transitions from the minimum duty cycle to the maximum duty cycle and then back to the minimum duty cycle. The steering wheel position signals are spaced 90 degrees apart. Therefore, the duty cycles of the 2 signals usually differ, depending on steering wheel position.

Conditions for Running the DTC

C0205, C0206 and C0207

The ignition is ON.

C0208

The vehicle is driven straight forward at a speed greater than 19 km/h (12 mph) for more than 20 seconds.

Conditions for Setting the DTC

C0205

At least one of the steering wheel position PWM signals is out of range for 500 milliseconds.

C0206

The steering wheel position PWM signals indicate a sudden change in the steering wheel position which exceeds a physical limitation.

C0207

The steering wheel position PWM signals do not correlate with each other for 200 milliseconds.

LTV0500000005310

Fig. 39 Codes C0205–C0208: Steering Wheel Position Circuit (Part 1 of 5). 2002 Avalanche, Escalade, Escalade EXT, Suburban, Tahoe & Yukon

Step	Action	Yes	No
1	Install a scan tool. Does the scan tool power up?	Go to Step 2	Check Scan Tool Does Not Power Up
2	1. Turn the ignition ON. 2. Use the scan tool to attempt communication with the following control modules. • Powertrain • 4WAL 3 Sensor • RTD / EVO • Instrument Panel Cluster • Body Control Module Does the scan tool communicate with all of the control modules listed above?	Go to Step 3	Check Scan Tool Does Not Communicate with Class 2 Device
3	Use the scan tool in order to display DTCs for the following control modules: • Powertrain • 4WAL 3 Sensor • RTD / EVO • Instrument Panel Cluster • Body Control Module Does the scan tool display any DTCs for the control modules listed above?	Go to Step 4	Go to Symptoms
4	Does the scan tool display any DTCs that begin with a "U", DTC C0290, C0292 or C0297?	Check Scan Tool Does Not Communicate with Class 2 Device	Go to Step 5
5	Does the scan tool display DTC P0500, P0502, P0503, P0562, P0563, P0601-P0607, P1381, P1621, P1627 or P1683?	Go to Diagnostic Trouble Code (DTC)	Go to Step 6
6	Does the scan tool display DTC B1367?	Go to Diagnostic Trouble Code (DTC)	Go to Step 7
7	Does the scan tool display DTC C0470, C0506, C0521, or C0895?	Go to Diagnostic Trouble Code (DTC)	Go to Step 8
8	Does the scan tool display DTC C0550, C0551 or C0870?	Go to Diagnostic Trouble Code (DTC)	Go to Diagnostic Trouble Code (DTC) List

LTV0500000005309

Fig. 38 Diagnostic System Check (Part 2 of 2). Avalanche, Escalade, Escalade EXT, Suburban, Tahoe & Yukon

C0208

The steering wheel position that is indicated while driving the vehicle straight forward is at least 20 degrees greater or less than the steering wheel position that was indicated during the sensor initialization period.

Action Taken When the DTC Sets

- The EBCM disables the VSES.
- The message center displays the SERVICE STABILITY SYSTEM message.

Conditions for Clearing the DTC

The conditions for setting the DTC are no longer present and you use the scan tool Clear DTCs function.

Diagnostic Aids

Important

A malfunction between the steering wheel position sensor and the RTD module may be responsible for setting this DTC. When attempting to verify an intermittent malfunction, be sure to use the scan tool to send the Clear DTCs command to the RTD module. This enhances the RTD module's diagnostic capabilities so that the RTD module sets DTCs more readily. Do not cycle the ignition after sending the Clear DTCs command. Test drive the vehicle, making several turning maneuvers in both directions. If the service stability message is displayed due to DTC C0205, C0236, C0207 or C0208, use the scan tool to inspect for Current or History RTD DTCs. If the RTD module has set DTC C0470, C0506, C0521 or C0895, refer to the DTC list in Variable Effort Steering for diagnosis. If the RTD module has set DTC C0550, C0551 or C0870, refer to the DTC list in Real Time Damping for diagnosis.

- Inspect the vehicle for bent, worn or loose steering or suspension components.
- Inspect the vehicle for proper wheel alignment. The vehicle should not pull toward the left or right while driving straight forward on a level surface.
- Use the Snapshot function on the scan tool in order to assist you in locating an intermittent malfunction.
- Thoroughly inspect connections or circuitry that may cause an intermittent malfunction. Refer to Testing for Electrical Intermittents , Testing for Intermittent and Poor Connections , Wiring Repairs and Connector Repairs in Wiring Systems.

Test Description

The numbers below refer to the step numbers on the diagnostic table.

3. This step determines if there is a problem between the steering wheel position sensor and the RTD module.

5. This step tests for voltages supplied to the RTD module from the EBCM. A short to voltage is indicated if voltage on either circuit measures greater than 5.25 volts.

7. This step tests each steering wheel position PWM signal for a valid Hz frequency. Each measurement is made by backprobing one steering wheel position PWM signal circuit at the RTD module harness connector with one DMM lead and connecting the other DMM lead to a good ground.

8. This step tests each steering wheel position PWM signal for a valid duty cycle.

11. The RTD module may be damaged if either of the steering wheel position PWM serial data circuits is shorted to voltage.

LTV0500000005311

Fig. 39 Codes C0205–C0208: Steering Wheel Position Circuit (Part 2 of 5). 2002 Avalanche, Escalade, Escalade EXT, Suburban, Tahoe & Yukon

ANTI-LOCK BRAKES

Step	Action	Values	Yes	No
1	Did you perform the ABS Diagnostic System Check?	--	Go to Step 2	Go to Diagnostic System Check -
2	1. Use a scan tool in order to clear the DTCs. 2. Start the engine and allow the engine to idle. 3. Slowly turn the steering wheel back and forth, from lock to lock, several times. Does the DTC reset?	--	Go to Step 3	Go to Diagnostic Aids
3	**Important** Before proceeding with this diagnostic table, you must determine if a malfunction exists in the steering position signal input to the RTD module. Carefully perform the steps below to determine which diagnostic table you should continue using. 1. Start the engine and allow the engine to idle. 2. Select RTD/EVO DTC Information on the scan tool. **Important** Perform the action below even if no RTD DTCs are set. Sending the Clear DTCs command to the RTD module enhances the module's diagnostic capability, and allows the RTD module to set DTCs more readily. 3. Use the scan tool to send the Clear DTCs command to the RTD module. 4. Select the Display DTCs function on the scan tool to read Current RTD DTCs. 5. While observing the scan tool, slowly turn the steering wheel back and forth, from lock to lock, several times. Does the RTD module set DTC C0470, C0506, C0521 or C0895?	--	Go to Diagnostic Trouble Code (DTC)	Go to Step 4
4	Does the RTD module set DTC C0550, C0551, or C0870 during step 3?	--	Go to Diagnostic Trouble Code (DTC)	Go to Step 5

LTV0500000005312

Fig. 39   Codes C0205–C0208: Steering Wheel Position Circuit (Part 3 of 5). 2002 Avalanche, Escalade, Escalade EXT, Suburban, Tahoe & Yukon

Step	Action	Values	Yes	No
5	1. Turn OFF the ignition. 2. Disconnect from the RTD module, the harness connector containing the steering wheel position PWM serial data circuits. 3. Turn ON the ignition. 4. Use a DMM in order to measure the voltage between each steering wheel position PWM serial data circuit and a good ground. Do both voltages measure within the specified range?	4.75 V-5.25 V	Go to Step 7	Go to Step 6
6	Test the suspect steering wheel position PWM serial data circuit for an open, a short to ground or a short to voltage. Did you find and correct the condition?	--	Go to Step 14	Go to Step 9
7	1. Turn OFF the ignition. 2. Reconnect the RTD module harness connector. 3. Turn ON the ignition. 4. Use a DMM in order to measure the Hz frequency of each steering wheel position PWM signal by backprobing the RTD module harness connector, one circuit at a time. Do the frequencies of both steering wheel position signals measure within the specified range?	121-134 Hz	Go to Step 8	Go to Step 11
8	Use the DMM in order to measure the duty cycle of each steering wheel position PWM signal, one at a time. Do the duty cycles of both steering wheel position signals measure within the specified range?	9-91 %	Go to Step 10	Go to Step 11
9	Inspect for poor connections at the harness connector of the EBCM. Did you find and correct the condition?	--	Go to Step 14	Go to Step 10
10	**Important** Following EBCM replacement, use the scan tool to perform the Tire Size Calibration procedure. Replace the EBCM. Did you complete the replacement?		Go to Step 14	

LTV0500000005313

Fig. 39   Codes C0205–C0208: Steering Wheel Position Circuit (Part 4 of 5). 2002 Avalanche, Escalade, Escalade EXT, Suburban, Tahoe & Yukon

Step	Action	Values	Yes	No
11	Test the suspect steering wheel position PWM serial data circuit for a short to voltage. Did you find and correct the condition?		Go to Step 14	Go to Step 12
12	Inspect for poor connections at the harness connector of the RTD module. Did you find and correct the condition?		Go to Step 14	Go to Step 13
13	**Important** Perform the set up procedure for the RTD module. Replace the RTD module. Did you complete the replacement?		Go to Step 14	--
14	1. Use the scan tool in order to clear the DTCs. 2. Operate the vehicle within the Conditions for Running the DTC as specified in the supporting text. Does the DTC reset?		Go to Step 3	System OK

LTV0500000005314

Fig. 39   Codes C0205–C0208: Steering Wheel Position Circuit (Part 5 of 5). 2002 Avalanche, Escalade, Escalade EXT, Suburban, Tahoe & Yukon

Circuit Description

The vehicle stability enhancement system (VSES) is activated when the EBCM determines that the desired yaw rate does not match the actual yaw rate. The desired yaw rate is calculated from the measured steering wheel position, vehicle speed, and lateral acceleration.

The usable output voltage range is 0.15-4.85 volts for the following sensors:

- The yaw rate sensor
- The longitudinal accelerometer

The usable output voltage range is 0.4-4.6 volts for the lateral accelerometer.

With no sensor bias present, a 2.5 volt signal from these sensors is interpreted by the EBCM respectively as follows:

- Zero yaw rate
- Zero lateral acceleration
- Zero longitudinal acceleration

The sensor bias compensates, during VSES initialization, for sensor mounting alignment errors, electronic signal errors, temperature changes, and manufacturing differences.

Conditions for Running the DTC

C0209 and C0210

The ignition is ON.

C0211

The vehicle is driven straight forward at a speed greater than 19 km/h (12 mph) for more than 20 seconds.

C0212

The vehicle is driven straight forward at a speed greater than 19 km/h (12 mph) for at least 10 seconds prior to making a stable turning maneuver.

Conditions for Setting the DTC

C0209

The yaw rate sensor signal is less than 0.15 volts or greater than 4.85 volts for 20 milliseconds.

C0210

The yaw rate sensor signal indicates a sudden change in yaw rate which exceeds a physical limitation.

C0211

The yaw rate sensor signal indicates the yaw rate sensor bias voltage is out of normal operating range.

C0212

LTV0500000005315

Fig. 40   Codes C0209–C0212: Yaw Rate Sensor Circuit (Part 1 of 4). 2002 Avalanche, Escalade, Escalade EXT, Suburban, Tahoe & Yukon

Action Taken When the DTC Sets

- The EBCM disables the VSES.
- The message center displays the SERVICE STABILITY SYSTEM message.

Conditions for Clearing the DTC

The conditions for setting the DTC are no longer present and you use the scan tool Clear DTCs function.

Diagnostic Aids

- Inspect the vehicle for proper wheel alignment. Ensure the vehicle does not pull toward the left or right while driving straight forward on a level surface.
- Communicate with the customer to determine the conditions under which the message center displays the Service Stability System message. Learning the conditions under which the DTC sets may help you duplicate the failure.
- Use the Snapshot function on the scan tool in order to assist you in locating an intermittent malfunction.

Test Description

The numbers below refer to the step numbers on the diagnostic table.

3. This step tests the sensor circuitry in the high voltage range.

4. This step tests the sensor circuitry in the low voltage range. If the fuse in the jumper opens when you perform this test, the signal circuit is shorted to voltage.

5. This step tests the 5-volt reference circuit of the yaw rate sensor/lateral accelerometer.

Step	Action	Values	Yes	No
1	Did you perform the ABS Diagnostic System Check?	--	Go to Step 2	Go to Diagnostic System Check - ABS
2	1. Use the scan tool in order to clear the DTCs. 2. Operate the vehicle within the Conditions for running the DTC as specified in the supporting text. Does the DTC reset?	--	Go to Step 3	Go to Diagnostic Aids
3	1. Ensure the vehicle is parked on a level surface. 2. Turn OFF the ignition. 3. Disconnect the yaw rate sensor/lateral accelerometer harness connector. 4. Turn ON the ignition. 5. Select the VSES Data List on the scan tool. 6. Observe the Yaw Rate Sensor Input on the scan tool. Is the Yaw Rate Sensor Input greater than the specified value?	4.75 V	Go to Step 4	Go to Step 7

LTV0500000005316

Fig. 40 Codes C0209–C0212: Yaw Rate Sensor Circuit (Part 2 of 4). 2002 Avalanche, Escalade, Escalade EXT, Suburban, Tahoe & Yukon

Step	Action	Values	Yes	No
10	1. Inspect for poor connections at the harness connector of the yaw rate sensor/lateral accelerometer. 2. Ensure the yaw rate sensor/lateral accelerometer is mounted securely and that the mounting bracket is not bent or otherwise damaged. Did you find and correct the condition?	--	Go to Step 14	Go to Step 12
11	Inspect for poor connections at the harness connector of the EBCM. Did you find and correct the condition?	--	Go to Step 14	Go to Step 13
12	Replace the yaw rate sensor/lateral accelerometer. Did you complete the replacement?	--	Go to Step 14	--
13	**Important** Following EBCM replacement, use the scan tool to perform the Tire Size Calibration procedure. Replace the EBCM. Did you complete the replacement?	--	Go to Step 14	--
14	1. Use the scan tool in order to clear the DTCs. 2. Operate the vehicle within the Conditions for Running the DTC as specified in the supporting text. Does the DTC reset?	--	Go to Step 3	System OK

LTV0500000005318

Fig. 40 Codes C0209–C0212: Yaw Rate Sensor Circuit (Part 4 of 4). 2002 Avalanche, Escalade, Escalade EXT, Suburban, Tahoe & Yukon

Step	Action	Values	Yes	No
4	1. Turn OFF the ignition. 2. Connect a 3 amp fused jumper wire between the signal circuit of the yaw rate sensor and the low reference circuit of the yaw rate sensor/ lateral accelerometer. 3. Turn ON the ignition. 4. Observe the Yaw Rate Sensor Input on the scan tool. Is the Yaw Rate Sensor Input less than the specified value?	0.15 V	Go to Step 5	Go to Step 8
5	1. Disconnect the fused jumper wire. 2. Use a DMM in order to measure the voltage between the 5-volt reference circuit and the low reference circuit of the yaw rate sensor/lateral accelerometer. Does the voltage measure greater than the specified value?	4.75 V	Go to Step 10	Go to Step 6
6	Test the 5-volt reference circuit of the yaw rate sensor/lateral accelerometer for the following conditions. • An open • A high resistance Did you find and correct the condition?	--	Go to Step 14	Go to Step 11
7	Test the signal circuit of the yaw rate sensor for a short to ground. Did you find and correct the condition?	--	Go to Step 14	Go to Step 11
8	Test the signal circuit of the yaw rate sensor for the following conditions. • An open • A high resistance • A short to voltage Did you find and correct the condition?	--	Go to Step 14	Go to Step 9
9	Test the low reference circuit of the yaw rate sensor/lateral accelerometer for a high resistance or an open. Did you find and correct the condition?	--	Go to Step 14	Go to Step 11

LTV0500000005317

Fig. 40 Codes C0209–C0212: Yaw Rate Sensor Circuit (Part 3 of 4). 2002 Avalanche, Escalade, Escalade EXT, Suburban, Tahoe & Yukon

Circuit Description

The vehicle stability enhancement system (VSES) is activated when the EBCM determines that the desired yaw rate does not match the actual yaw rate. The desired yaw rate is calculated from the measured steering wheel position, vehicle speed, and lateral acceleration.

The usable output voltage range is 0.15-4.85 volts for the following sensors:

- The yaw rate sensor
- The longitudinal accelerometer

The usable output voltage range is 0.4-4.6 volts for the lateral accelerometer.

With no sensor bias present, a 2.5 volt signal from these sensors is interpreted by the EBCM respectively as follows:

- Zero yaw rate
- Zero lateral acceleration
- Zero longitudinal acceleration

The sensor bias compensates, during VSES initialization, for sensor mounting alignment errors, electronic signal errors, temperature changes, and manufacturing differences.

Conditions for Running the DTC

C0213, C0214

The ignition is ON.

C0215

The vehicle is driven straight at a speed greater than 19 km/h (12 mph) for more than 20 seconds.

C0216

The vehicle is driven straight forward at a speed greater than 19 km/h (12 mph) for at least 10 seconds prior to making a stable turning maneuver.

Conditions for Setting the DTC

C0213

The lateral accelerometer signal is less than 0.4 volts or greater than 4.6 volts for 200 milliseconds.

C0214

The lateral accelerometer signal indicates a sudden change in lateral acceleration which exceeds a physical limitation.

C0215

The lateral accelerometer signal indicates the lateral accelerometer bias voltage is out of normal operating range.

C0216

LTV0500000005319

Fig. 41 Codes C0213–C0216: Lateral Accelerometer Circuit (Part 1 of 4). 2002 Avalanche, Escalade, Escalade EXT, Suburban, Tahoe & Yukon

Action Taken When the DTC Sets

- The EBCM disables the VSES.
- The message center displays the SERVICE STABILITY SYSTEM message.

Conditions for Clearing the DTC

The conditions for setting the DTC are no longer present and you use the scan tool Clear DTCs function.

Diagnostic Aids

- Inspect the vehicle for proper wheel alignment. Ensure the vehicle does not pull toward the left or right while driving straight forward on a level surface.
- Communicate with the customer to determine the conditions under which the message center displays the Service Stability System message. Learning the conditions under which the DTC sets may help you duplicate the failure.
- Use the Snapshot function on the scan tool in order to assist you in locating an intermittent malfunction.

Test Description

The numbers below refer to the step numbers on the diagnostic table.

3. This step tests the sensor circuitry in the high voltage range.

4. This step tests the sensor circuitry in the low voltage range. If the fuse in the jumper opens when you perform this test, the signal circuit is shorted to voltage.

5. This step tests the 5-volt reference circuit of the yaw rate sensor/lateral accelerometer.

Step	Action	Values	Yes	No
1	Did you perform the ABS Diagnostic System Check?	--	Go to Step 2	Go to Diagnostic System Check - ABS
2	1. Use the scan tool in order to clear the DTCs. 2. Operate the vehicle within the Conditions for running the DTC as specified in the supporting text. Does the DTC reset?	--	Go to Step 3	Go to Diagnostic Aids
3	1. Ensure the vehicle is parked on a level surface. 2. Turn OFF the ignition. 3. Disconnect the yaw rate sensor/lateral accelerometer harness connector. 4. Turn ON the ignition. 5. Select the VSES Data List on the scan tool. 6. Observe the Lateral Accelerometer Sensor Input on the scan tool. Is the Lateral Accelerometer Sensor Input greater than the specified value?	4.75 V	Go to Step 4	Go to Step 7

LTV0500000005320

Fig. 41 Codes C0213–C0216: Lateral Accelerometer Circuit (Part 2 of 4). 2002 Avalanche, Escalade, Escalade EXT, Suburban, Tahoe & Yukon

Step	Action	Values	Yes	No
10	1. Inspect for poor connections at the harness connector of the yaw rate sensor/lateral accelerometer. 2. Ensure the yaw rate sensor/lateral accelerometer is mounted securely and that the mounting bracket is not bent or otherwise damaged. Did you find and correct the condition?	--	Go to Step 14	Go to Step 12
11	Inspect for poor connections at the harness connector of the EBCM. Did you find and correct the condition?	--	Go to Step 14	Go to Step 13
12	Replace the yaw rate sensor/lateral accelerometer. Did you complete the replacement?	--	Go to Step 14	--
13	**Important** Following EBCM replacement, use the scan tool to perform the Tire Size Calibration procedure. Replace the EBCM. Did you complete the replacement?	--	Go to Step 14	--
14	1. Use the scan tool in order to clear the DTCs. 2. Operate the vehicle within the Conditions for Running the DTC as specified in the supporting text. Does the DTC reset?	--	Go to Step 3	System OK

LTV0500000005322

Fig. 41 Codes C0213–C0216: Lateral Accelerometer Circuit (Part 4 of 4). 2002 Avalanche, Escalade, Escalade EXT, Suburban, Tahoe & Yukon

Step	Action	Values	Yes	No
4	1. Turn OFF the ignition. 2. Connect a 3 amp fused jumper wire between the signal circuit of the lateral accelerometer and the low reference circuit of the yaw rate sensor/ lateral accelerometer. 3. Turn ON the ignition. 4. Observe the Lateral Accelerometer Sensor Input on the scan tool. Is the Lateral Accelerometer Sensor Input less than the specified value?	0.15 V	Go to Step 5	Go to Step 8
5	1. Disconnect the fused jumper wire. 2. Use a DMM in order to measure the voltage between the 5-volt reference circuit and the low reference circuit of the yaw rate sensor/lateral accelerometer. Does the voltage measure greater than the specified value?	4.75 V	Go to Step 10	Go to Step 6
6	Test the 5-volt reference circuit of the yaw rate sensor/lateral accelerometer for the following conditions. • An open • A high resistance Did you find and correct the condition?	--	Go to Step 14	Go to Step 11
7	Test the signal circuit of the lateral accelerometer for a short to ground. Did you find and correct the condition?	--	Go to Step 14	Go to Step 11
8	Test the signal circuit of the lateral accelerometer for the following conditions. • An open • A high resistance • A short to voltage Did you find and correct the condition?	--	Go to Step 14	Go to Step 9
9	Test the low reference circuit of the yaw rate sensor/lateral accelerometer for a high resistance or an open. Did you find and correct the condition?	--	Go to Step 14	Go to Step 11

LTV0500000005321

Fig. 41 Codes C0213–C0216: Lateral Accelerometer Circuit (Part 3 of 4). 2002 Avalanche, Escalade, Escalade EXT, Suburban, Tahoe & Yukon

Circuit Description

The vehicle stability enhancement system (VSES) is activated when the EBCM determines that the desired yaw rate does not match the actual yaw rate. The desired yaw rate is calculated from the measured steering wheel position, vehicle speed, and lateral acceleration.

The usable output voltage range is 0.15-4.85 volts for the following sensors:

- The yaw rate sensor
- The longitudinal accelerometer

The usable output voltage range is 0.4-4.6 volts for the lateral accelerometer.

With no sensor bias present, a 2.5 volt signal from these sensors is interpreted by the EBCM respectively as follows:

- Zero yaw rate
- Zero lateral acceleration
- Zero longitudinal acceleration

The sensor bias compensates, during VSES initialization, for sensor mounting alignment errors, electronic signal errors, temperature changes, and manufacturing differences.

Conditions for Running the DTC

C0217, C0218, C0219

The ignition is ON.

C0220

- The ABS/VSES is not active.
- A rough road condition is not detected.
- The vehicle is not in reverse or neutral.
- The speed of the vehicle is greater than 5 km/h (3 mph).
- The vehicle is being driven in a relatively straight line, making no abrupt maneuvers.

Conditions for Setting the DTC

C0217

The signal voltage of the longitudinal accelerometer is less than 0.15 volts or greater than 4.85 volts for 200 milliseconds.

C0218

The longitudinal accelerometer signal indicates a sudden change in longitudinal acceleration which exceeds a physical limitation.

C0219

The longitudinal accelerometer signal indicates the longitudinal accelerometer bias voltage is out of normal operating range.

LTV0500000005323

Fig. 42 Codes C0217–C0220: Internal Longitudinal Sensor (Part 1 of 2). 2002 Avalanche, Escalade, Escalade EXT, Suburban, Tahoe & Yukon

C0220

The longitudinal accelerometer signal indicates a change in longitudinal acceleration which does not correlate with the signals from other sensors.

Action Taken When the DTC Sets

- The EBCM disables the VSES.
- The message center displays the SERVICE STABILITY SYSTEM message.

Conditions for Clearing the DTC

The conditions for setting the DTC are no longer present and you use the scan tool Clear DTCs function.

Diagnostic Aids

- Inspect the vehicle for proper wheel alignment. Ensure the vehicle does not pull toward the left or right while driving straight forward on a level surface.
- Communicate with the customer to determine the conditions under which the message center displays the Service Stability System message. Learning the conditions under which the DTC sets may help you duplicate the failure.
- Use the Snapshot function on the scan tool in order to assist you in locating an intermittent malfunction.

Step	Action	Yes	No
1	Did you perform the ABS Diagnostic System Check?	Go to Step 2	Go to Diagnostic System Check - ABS
2	1. Install a scan tool. 2. Turn ON the ignition. 3. Use the scan tool in order to clear the DTCs. 4. Operate the vehicle within the Conditions for Running the DTC. Does the DTC reset?	Go to Step 3	Go to Diagnostic Aids
3	**Important** Following EBCM replacement, use the scan tool to perform the Tire Size Calibration procedure. Replace the EBCM. Did you complete the replacement?	Go to Step 4	--
4	1. Use the scan tool in order to clear the DTCs. 2. Operate the vehicle within the Conditions for Running the DTC. Does the DTC reset?	Go to Step 2	System OK

LTV0500000005324

Fig. 42   Codes C0217–C0220: Internal Longitudinal Sensor (Part 2 of 2). 2002 Avalanche, Escalade, Escalade EXT, Suburban, Tahoe & Yukon

Conditions for Clearing the DTC

- Repair the condition responsible for setting the DTC.
- Use a scan tool in order to clear the DTC.
- After the DTC is cleared and the ignition is ON, the ABS indicator may remain ON until the EBCM completes a power-up self-test. This test concludes when the vehicle reaches a speed greater than 13 km/h (8 mph) and the wheel speeds are verified by the EBCM.

Diagnostic Aids

Operating the vehicle on extremely rough terrain can set DTC C0223, C0227 or C0229 even if the system is functioning normally.

Thoroughly inspect connections or circuitry that may cause an intermittent malfunction. Refer to Testing for Intermittent and Poor Connections , Connector Repairs , Testing for Electrical Intermittents and to Wiring Repairs in Wiring Systems.

If the customer's concern is that the ABS indicator is on only during humid conditions such as rain, snow or vehicle wash, thoroughly inspect the wheel speed sensor circuits for signs of water intrusion. Use the following procedure in order to help isolate the problem area:

1. Spray the suspected area with a 5 percent salt water solution.
2. Drive the vehicle at a speed greater than 19 km/h (12 mph) for at least 30 seconds.

Repair or replace the suspect harness if the DTC sets.

Test Description

The numbers below refer to the step numbers on the diagnostic table.

3. Measure the resistance of the wheel speed sensor in order to determine if the sensor has a valid resistance value.

4. Ensures that the wheel speed sensor is generating a valid AC voltage output.

Step	Action	Values	Yes	No
	Important: If DTC C0229 is set, diagnose DTC C0229 before diagnosing any other wheel speed sensor DTCs.			
1	Did you perform the ABS Diagnostic System Check?	---	Go to Step 2	Go to Diagnostic System Check - ABS
2	1. Use a scan tool in order to clear the DTCs. 2. Operate the vehicle at a speed greater than the specified value. Does the DTC set?	19 km/h (12 mph)	Go to Step 3	Go to Diagnostic Aids
3	1. Turn OFF the ignition. 2. Raise and support the vehicle. 3. Disconnect the wheel speed sensor connector. 4. Use a DMM in order to measure the resistance across the wheel speed sensor. Does the resistance measure within the specified range?	700-10,000 ohms	Go to Step 4	Go to Step 8

LTV0500000005326

Fig. 43   Codes C0221–C0227: Wheel Speed Sensor Circuit (Part 2 of 3). 2002 Avalanche, Escalade, Escalade EXT, Suburban, Tahoe & Yukon

Circuit Description

As the wheel spins, the wheel speed sensor produces an AC signal. The electronic brake control module (EBCM) uses the frequency of the AC signal to calculate the wheel speed.

Conditions for Running the DTC

C0221, C0223, C0225 and C0227

The ignition is ON.

C0222 and C0226

- The ignition is ON.
- The vehicle speed is greater than 13 km/h (8 mph).

Conditions for Setting the DTC

C0221 and C0225

The EBCM detects an open or shorted wheel speed sensor or wheel speed sensor circuit for 500 milliseconds.

C0222 and C0226

The corresponding wheel speed sensor signal is less than 6 km/h (4 mph) for 5 seconds, or 120 seconds in order to set both DTCs.

C0223 and C0227

The EBCM detects an erratic signal from the corresponding wheel speed sensor for 105 milliseconds.

Action Taken When the DTC Sets

C0221, C0225

If equipped, the following actions may occur:

- The EBCM disables the ABS/TCS/VSES.
- The ABS indicator turns ON.
- The TRACTION OFF indicator turns ON.
- The message center displays the SERVICE STABILITY SYSTEM message.

C0222, C0223, C0226, and C0227

If equipped, the following actions may occur:

- The EBCM disables the ABS/TCS/VSES/DRP.
- The ABS indicator turns ON.
- The TRACTION OFF indicator turns ON.
- The red brake warning indicator turns ON.
- The message center displays the SERVICE STABILITY SYSTEM message.

LTV0500000005325

Fig. 43   Codes C0221–C0227: Wheel Speed Sensor Circuit (Part 1 of 3). 2002 Avalanche, Escalade, Escalade EXT, Suburban, Tahoe & Yukon

Step	Action		Yes	No
4	1. Spin the wheel by hand as fast as possible. 2. Use a DMM in order to measure the AC voltage across the wheel speed sensor as the wheel spins. Does the AC voltage measure greater than the specified value?	100 mV	Go to Step 5	Go to Step 8
5	Inspect for poor connections at the harness connector of the wheel speed sensor. Did you find and correct the condition?	--	Go to Step 10	Go to Step 6
6	1. Disconnect the EBCM harness connector. 2. Test the wheel speed sensor circuits for the following: - An open - A short to ground - A short to voltage - Shorted together Refer to Circuit Testing and to Wiring Repairs in Wiring Systems. Did you find and correct the condition?	--	Go to Step 10	Go to Step 7
7	Inspect for poor connections at the harness connector for the EBCM. Did you find and correct the condition?	--	Go to Step 10	Go to Step 9
8	Replace the wheel speed sensor. Did you complete the replacement?	--	Go to Step 10	--
9	**Important:** Use the scan tool in order to perform the Tire Size Calibration procedure. Replace the EBCM. Did you complete the replacement?	--	Go to Step 10	--
10	1. Use the scan tool in order to clear the DTCs. 2. Operate the vehicle within the Conditions for Running the DTC as specified in the supporting text. Does the DTC reset?	--	Go to Step 2	System OK

LTV0500000005327

Fig. 43   Codes C0221–C0227: Wheel Speed Sensor Circuit (Part 3 of 3). 2002 Avalanche, Escalade, Escalade EXT, Suburban, Tahoe & Yukon

Circuit Description

As the wheel spins, the wheel speed sensor produces an AC signal. The electronic brake control module (EBCM) uses the frequency of the AC signal to calculate the wheel speed.

Conditions for Running the DTC

- The ignition is ON.
- The vehicle speed is greater than 32 km/h (20 mph) when the brake is applied or 19 km/h (12 mph) when the brake is released.

Conditions for Setting the DTC

The EBCM detects an erratic signal from both front wheel speed sensors for 105 milliseconds.

Action Taken When the DTC Sets

If equipped, the following actions may occur:

- The EBCM disables the ABS/TCS/VSES and DRP.
- The ABS indicator turns ON.
- The traction off indicator turns ON.
- The red brake warning indicator turns ON.
- The message center displays the SERVICE STABILITY SYSTEM message.

Conditions for Clearing the DTC

- Repair the condition responsible for setting the DTC.
- Use a scan tool in order to clear the DTC.
- After the DTC is cleared and the ignition is ON, the ABS indicator may remain ON until the EBCM completes a power-up self-test. This test concludes when the vehicle reaches a speed greater than 13 km/h (8 mph) and the wheel speeds are verified by the EBCM.

Diagnostic Aids

Operating the vehicle on extremely rough terrain can set DTC C0223, C0227 or C0229 even if the system is functioning normally.

Thoroughly inspect connections or circuitry that may cause an intermittent malfunction.

If the customer's concern is that the ABS indicator is on only during humid conditions such as rain, snow or vehicle wash, thoroughly inspect the wheel speed sensor circuits for signs of water intrusion. Use the following procedure in order to help isolate the problem area:

1. Spray the suspected area with a 5 percent salt water solution.
2. Drive the vehicle at a speed greater than 19 km/h (12 mph) for at least 30 seconds.

Repair or replace the suspect harness if the DTC sets.

LTV0500000005328

Fig. 44 Code C0229: Drop Out of Front Wheel Speed Signals (Part 1 of 2). 2002 Avalanche, Escalade, Escalade EXT, Suburban, Tahoe & Yukon

Circuit Description

The powertrain control module (PCM) converts the data from the vehicle speed sensor to a 128k pulses/mile signal. The electronic brake control module (EBCM) uses the vehicle speed signal from the PCM in order to calculate the rear wheel speed.

Conditions for Running the DTC

C0235

The ignition is ON.

C0236 and C0237

- The ignition is ON.
- The vehicle speed is greater than 32 km/h (20 mph) when the brake is applied or 19 km/h (12 mph) when the brake is released.

P1504

- The ignition is ON.
- The vehicle is not moving.

Conditions for Setting the DTC

C0235

The EBCM detects low voltage on the vehicle speed signal circuit for 500 milliseconds.

C0236

The rear wheel speed signal is less than 6 km/h (4 mph) for 5 seconds, or 120 seconds in order to set multiple missing sensor signal DTCs.

C0237

The EBCM detects an erratic rear wheel speed signal for 105 milliseconds.

P1504

The PCM detects low voltage on the vehicle speed signal circuit for 45 seconds.

Action Taken When the DTC Sets

If equipped, the following actions may occur:

- The EBCM disables the ABS/TCS/VSES and DRP.
- The ABS indicator turns ON.
- The traction off indicator turns ON.
- The red brake warning indicator turns ON.
- The message center displays the SERVICE STABILITY SYSTEM message.

LTV0500000005330

Fig. 45 Codes C0235–C0237 Or P1504: Rear Wheel Speed Sensor Circuit (Part 1 of 3). 2002 Avalanche, Escalade, Escalade EXT, Suburban, Tahoe & Yukon

Step	Action	Yes	No
1	Did you perform the ABS Diagnostic System Check?	Go to Step 2	Go to Diagnostic System Check - ABS
2	1. Use a scan tool in order to clear the DTCs. 2. Operate the vehicle within the Conditions for Running the DTC as specified in the supporting text. Does the DTC set?	Go to Step 3	Go to Diagnostic Aids
3	Inspect for poor connections at the harness connector of the EBCM. Did you find and correct the condition?	Go to Step 5	Go to Step 4
4	**Important** Following EBCM replacement, use the scan tool to perform the Tire Size Calibration procedure. Replace the EBCM. Did you complete the replacement?	Go to Step 5	--
5	1. Use the scan tool in order to clear the DTCs. 2. Operate the vehicle within the Conditions for Running the DTC as specified in the supporting text. Does the DTC reset?	Go to Step 3	System OK

LTV0500000005329

Fig. 44 Code C0229: Drop Out of Front Wheel Speed Signals (Part 2 of 2). 2002 Avalanche, Escalade, Escalade EXT, Suburban, Tahoe & Yukon

Conditions for Clearing the DTC

- Repair the condition responsible for setting the DTC.
- Use a scan tool in order to clear the DTC.
- After the DTC is cleared and the ignition is ON, the ABS indicator may remain ON until the EBCM completes a power-up self-test. This test concludes when the vehicle reaches a speed greater than 13 km/h (8 mph) and the wheel speeds are verified by the EBCM.

Diagnostic Aids

Thoroughly inspect connections or circuitry that may cause an intermittent malfunction.

Test Description

The numbers below refer to the step numbers on the diagnostic table:

3. This step tests for a voltage signal from the PCM.

4. This step tests for a missing or erratic vehicle speed signal from the PCM. An assistants may be required in order to perform this test.

Step	Action	Values	Yes	No
1	Did you perform the ABS Diagnostic System Check?	--	Go to Step 2	Go to Diagnostic System Check - ABS
2	1. Use a scan tool in order to clear the DTCs. 2. Operate the vehicle at a speed greater than the specified value. Does the DTC set?	19 km/h (12 mph)	Go to Step 3	Go to Diagnostic Aids
3	1. Turn OFF the ignition. 2. Disconnect from the EBCM, the harness connector containing the vehicle speed signal circuit. 3. Turn ON the ignition. 4. Use a DMM in order to measure the DC voltage between the vehicle speed signal circuit and a good ground. Does the voltage measure greater than the specified value?	10 V	Go to Step 4	Go to Step 7

LTV0500000005331

Fig. 45 Codes C0235–C0237 Or P1504: Rear Wheel Speed Sensor Circuit (Part 2 of 3). 2002 Avalanche, Escalade, Escalade EXT, Suburban, Tahoe & Yukon

Step	Action		Yes	No
4	1. Raise and support the vehicle. Refer to Lifting and Jacking the Vehicle in General Information. 2. Place the transmission in neutral (N). 3. Set up the DMM in order to measure the DC voltage between the vehicle speed signal circuit and a good ground. 4. Spin the rear wheels as fast as possible by hand for at least 30 seconds and while ensuring the driveshaft is rotating, observe the DMM. Does the voltage measure within the specified range the entire time the driveshaft is rotating?	5–7 V	Go to Step 5	Go to Step 7
5	Inspect for poor connections at the harness connector of the EBCM. Did you find and correct the condition?	—	Go to Step 10	Go to Step 6
6	**Important** Following EBCM replacement, use the scan tool to perform the Tire Size Calibration procedure. Replace the EBCM. Did you complete the replacement?	—	Go to Step 10	—
7	Test the vehicle speed signal circuit for an open, a short to ground or a short to voltage. Did you find and correct the condition?	—	Go to Step 10	Go to Step 8
8	Inspect for poor connections at the harness connector of the PCM. Did you find and correct the condition?	—	Go to Step 10	Go to Step 9
9	**Important** Perform the setup procedure for the PCM. Replace the PCM. Did you complete the replacement?	—	Go to Step 10	—
10	1. Use the scan tool in order to clear the DTCs. 2. Operate the vehicle within the Conditions for Running the DTC as specified in the supporting text. Does the DTC reset?	—	Go to Step 3	System OK

LTV0500000005332

Fig. 45 Codes C0235–C0237 Or P1504: Rear Wheel Speed Sensor Circuit (Part 3 of 3). 2002 Avalanche, Escalade, Escalade EXT, Suburban, Tahoe & Yukon

Step	Action	Yes	No
1	Did you perform the ABS Diagnostic System Check?	Go to Step 2	Go to Diagnostic System Check - ABS
2	Inspect both of the front tires on the vehicle to ensure that both tires are of equal size. Are both of the front tires of equal size?	Go to Step 3	Go to Diagnostic Aids
3	Inspect both of the rear tires on the vehicle to ensure that both tires are of equal size. Are both of the rear tires of equal size?	Go to Step 4	Go to Diagnostic Aids
4	Verify the EBCM and the PCM both have the correct tire size calibration. Use the scan tool in order to view the EBCM tire size calibration or perform the Tire Size Calibration procedure and refer to Powertrain Control Module (PCM) Programming. Did you find and correct the condition?	Go to Step 5	Go to Diagnostic Aids
5	1. Use a scan tool in order to clear the DTCs. 2. Operate the vehicle for 2 miles within the Conditions for Running the DTC as specified in the supporting text. Does the DTC reset?	Go to Step 2	System OK

LTV0500000005334

Fig. 46 Code C0238: Wheel Speed Sensor Mismatch (Part 2 of 2). 2002 Avalanche, Escalade, Escalade EXT, Suburban, Tahoe & Yukon

Circuit Description

As the front wheels spin, the wheel speed sensors (WSSs) produce an AC signal. The electronic brake control module (EBCM) uses the frequency of the AC signal to calculate the wheel speed. The powertrain control module (PCM) converts the data from the vehicle speed sensor (VSS) to a 128k pulses/mile signal. The EBCM uses the vehicle speed signal from the PCM in order to calculate the rear wheel speed.

Conditions for Running the DTC

The ignition is ON and the vehicle speed is between 24 km/h (15 mph) and 80 km/h (50 mph).

Conditions for Setting the DTC

The EBCM detects that one wheel speed input is 10 percent greater than or 10 percent less than the other wheel speed inputs within 3.2 km (2 mi) of driving.

Action Taken When the DTC Sets

If equipped, the following actions may occur:

- The EBCM disables the ABS/TCS/VSES and DRP.
- The ABS indicator turns ON.
- The traction off indicator turns ON.
- The red brake warning indicator turns ON.
- The message center displays the SERVICE STABILITY SYSTEM message.

Conditions for Clearing the DTC

The conditions for setting the DTC are no longer present and you use the scan tool Clear DTCs function.

Diagnostic Aids

Installing one tire of significantly different size on the vehicle causes DTC C0238 to set. Operating the vehicle with a tire that has very low air pressure may also set this DTC. Inspect the vehicle for an incorrect or damaged wheel speed sensor or vehicle speed sensor if the tires and the EBCM and PCM calibrations are OK.

Test Description

The number below refers to the step number on the diagnostic table:

4. If the front tires are not the same size as the rear tires, the EBCM calibration must match the FRONT tire size and the PCM calibration must match the REAR tire size.

LTV0500000005333

Fig. 46 Code C0238: Wheel Speed Sensor Mismatch (Part 1 of 2). 2002 Avalanche, Escalade, Escalade EXT, Suburban, Tahoe & Yukon

Circuit Description

The system relays are energized when the ignition is ON and the vehicle speed is greater than 6 km/h (4 mph). The system relay supplies voltage to the solenoid valves and to the pump motor. This voltage is referred to as the system voltage. The EBCM controls the solenoid valves by grounding the control circuit.

Conditions for Running the DTC

- The ignition is ON.
- The vehicle speed is greater than 6 km/h (4 mph).

Conditions for Setting the DTC

The EBCM detects an internal malfunction.

Action Taken When the DTC Sets

CC0240, C0249, C0250, C0255-C0259

If equipped, the following actions may occur:

- The EBCM disables the TCS/VSES.
- The traction off indicator turns ON.
- The message center displays the SERVICE STABILITY SYSTEM message.

C0241, C0242, C0245, C0246, C0251-C0254

If equipped, the following actions may occur:

- The EBCM disables the DRP/ABS/TCS/VSES.
- The ABS indicator turns ON.
- The brake warning indicator turns ON.
- The traction off indicator turns ON.
- The message center displays the SERVICE STABILITY SYSTEM message

C0243, C0244, C0247, C0248

If equipped, the following actions may occur:

- The EBCM disables the ABS/TCS/VSES.
- The ABS indicator turns ON.
- The traction off indicator turns ON.
- The message center displays the SERVICE STABILITY SYSTEM message.

Conditions for Clearing the DTC

The conditions for setting the DTC are no longer present and you use the scan tool Clear DTCs function.

Diagnostic Aids

An intermittent open/shorted solenoid DTC can be set by several different internal EBCM problems. Replace the EBCM if an open/shorted solenoid DTC continues to set intermittently.

LTV0500000005335

Fig. 47 Codes C0240–C0259: EBCM Internal Fault (Part 1 of 2). 2002 Avalanche, Escalade, Escalade EXT, Suburban, Tahoe & Yukon

Step	Action	Yes	No
1	Did you perform the ABS Diagnostic System Check?	Go to Step 2	Go to Diagnostic System Check - ABS
2	1. Use a scan tool in order to clear the DTCs. 2. Operate the vehicle within the Conditions for Running the DTC as specified in the supporting text. Does the DTC set?	Go to Step 3	Go to Diagnostic Aids
3	**Important** Following EBCM replacement, use the scan tool to perform the Tire Size Calibration procedure and the Trim Level Calibration procedure, if applicable. Replace the EBCM. Did you complete the replacement?	Go to Step 4	--
4	1. Use the scan tool in order to clear the DTCs. 2. Operate the vehicle within the Conditions for Running the DTC as specified in the supporting text. Does the DTC reset?	Go to Step 3	System OK

LTV0500000005336

Fig. 47   Codes C0240–C0259: EBCM Internal Fault (Part 2 of 2). 2002 Avalanche, Escalade, Escalade EXT, Suburban, Tahoe & Yukon

Step	Action	Values	Yes	No
1	Did you perform the ABS Diagnostic System Check?	--	Go to Step 2	Go to Diagnostic System Check - ABS
2	Drive the vehicle in order to verify that the brakes do not self-apply during turning maneuvers. Do the brakes self-apply during turning maneuvers?		Go to Symptoms -	Go to Step 3
3	1. Install a scan tool. 2. Turn ON the ignition. 3. Select the VSES data list on the scan tool. 4. Observe the Master Cylinder Pressure Sensor Input (psi) on the scan tool. Is the Master Cylinder Pressure Sensor Input within the specified range?	0-32 psi	Go to Step 4	Go to DTC C0201-C0204
4	Apply and release the brake several times while observing the Brake Switch Status on the scan tool. Is Brake Switch Status Off with the brake released and On with the brake applied?	--	Go to Diagnostic Aids	Go to DTC C0281

LTV0500000005338

Fig. 48   Code C0263: Brake Switch Circuit (Part 2 of 2). 2002 Avalanche, Escalade, Escalade EXT, Suburban, Tahoe & Yukon

Circuit Description

The ABS relay supplies battery voltage to 6 valve solenoids. The electronic brake control module (EBCM) microprocessor applies the grounds needed to activate each solenoid. The low side of each solenoid coil has a feedback circuit to the EBCM microprocessor. When a solenoid is commanded OFF, the feedback voltage is high. When a solenoid is commanded ON, the feedback voltage is low.

Conditions for Running the DTC

- The ignition is ON.
- The vehicle speed is greater than 6 km/h (4 mph).

Conditions for Setting the DTC

The EBCM detects an internal malfunction.

Action Taken When the DTC Sets

C0265

If equipped, the following actions may occur:

- The EBCM disables the DRP/ABS/TCS/VSES.
- The ABS indicator turns ON.
- The traction off indicator turns ON.
- The red brake warning indicator turns ON.
- The message center displays the SERVICE STABILITY SYSTEM message.

C0266

If equipped, the following actions may occur:

- The EBCM disables the ABS/TCS/VSES.
- The ABS indicator turns ON.
- The traction off indicator turns ON.
- The message center displays the SERVICE STABILITY SYSTEM message.

Conditions for Clearing the DTC

The conditions for setting the DTC are no longer present and you use the scan tool Clear DTCs function.

Diagnostic Aids

Important

Whenever the EBCM is replaced for DTC C0265 or C0266, the ABS pump motor and motor circuitry must be tested for the proper resistance. Refer to steps 3 and 4 in the diagnostic table below for testing procedures and resistance values.

Replace the EBCM if DTC C0265 or DTC C0266 continues to set intermittently.

Test Description

The number below refers to the step number on the diagnostic table.

LTV0500000005339

Fig. 49   Codes C0265 Or C0266: EBCM Relay Circuit (Part 1 of 2). 2002 Avalanche, Escalade, Escalade EXT, Suburban, Tahoe & Yukon w/JL4

Circuit Description

When the brake switch is closed (brake released), the master cylinder pressure sensor signal voltage is low. When the brake switch is open, the master cylinder pressure sensor signal voltage increases.

Conditions for Running the DTC

The ignition is ON.

Conditions for Setting the DTC

- The brake switch is detected as closed.
- The master cylinder pressure is detected as being above 862 kPa (125 psi) for 500 milliseconds.

Action Taken When the DTC Sets

- The EBCM disables the VSES.
- The message center displays the SERVICE STABILITY SYSTEM message.

Conditions for Clearing the DTC

- The conditions for setting the DTC are no longer present (the DTC is not current) and you use the scan tool Clear DTCs function.
- The current DTC clears when a DTC sets which directly indicates a brake switch or master cylinder pressure sensor malfunction.

Diagnostic Aids

Thoroughly inspect connections or circuitry that may cause an intermittent malfunction.

LTV0500000005337

Fig. 48   Code C0263: Brake Switch Circuit (Part 1 of 2). 2002 Avalanche, Escalade, Escalade EXT, Suburban, Tahoe & Yukon

Step	Action	Values	Yes	No
1	Did you perform the ABS Diagnostic System Check?	--	Go to Step 2	Go to Diagnostic System Check - ABS
2	1. Use a scan tool in order to clear the DTCs. 2. Use the scan tool in order to perform an ABS Function Test. Does the DTC set?	--	Go to Step 3	Go to Diagnostic Aids
3	1. Separate the EBCM from the BPMV. 2. Use a DMM in order to measure the resistance across the ABS pump motor. Does the resistance measure within the specified range?	0.3-1.0 ohms	Go to Step 4	Go to Step 6
4	Use a DMM in order to measure the resistance between the high side of the pump motor and a good ground. Does the resistance measure less than the specified value?	0L	Go to Step 6	Go to Step 5
5	**Important** Following EBCM replacement, use the scan tool to perform the Tire Size Calibration procedure. Replace the EBCM. Did you complete the replacement?	--	Go to Step 7	--
6	**Important** Following EBCM replacement, use the scan tool to perform the Tire Size Calibration procedure. Replace the EBCM and the BPMV. Did you complete the replacements?	--	Go to Step 7	--
7	1. Use the scan tool in order to clear the DTCs. 2. Operate the vehicle within the Conditions for Running the DTC as specified in the supporting text. Does the DTC reset?	--	Go to Step 3	System OK

LTV0500000005340

Fig. 49   Codes C0265 Or C0266: EBCM Relay Circuit (Part 2 of 2). 2002 Avalanche, Escalade, Escalade EXT, Suburban, Tahoe & Yukon w/JL4

Circuit Description

The ABS relay supplies battery voltage to 6 valve solenoids. The electronic brake control module (EBCM) microprocessor applies the grounds needed to activate each solenoid. The low side of each solenoid coil has a feedback circuit to the EBCM microprocessor. When a solenoid is commanded OFF, the feedback voltage is high. When a solenoid is commanded ON, the feedback voltage is low.

Conditions for Running the DTC

- The ignition is ON.
- The vehicle speed is greater than 6 km/h (4 mph).

Conditions for Setting the DTC

The EBCM detects an internal malfunction.

Action Taken When the DTC Sets

C0265

If equipped, the following actions occur:

- The EBCM disables the DRP/ABS.
- The ABS indicator turns ON.
- The brake warning indicator turns ON.

C0266

If equipped, the following actions occur:

- The EBCM disables the ABS.
- The ABS indicator turns ON.

Conditions for Clearing the DTC

The conditions for setting the DTC are no longer present and you use the scan tool Clear DTCs function.

LTV0500000005341

Fig. 50   Codes C0265 Or C0266: EBCM Relay Circuit (Part 1 of 3). 2002 Avalanche, Escalade, Escalade EXT, Suburban, Tahoe & Yukon Less JL4

Step	Action	Values	Yes	No
5	Repair the open in the battery positive voltage circuit. Did you complete the repair?	--	Go to Step 11	--
6	Inspect for poor connections at the harness connector of the EBCM. Did you find and correct the condition?	--	Go to Step 11	Go to Step 7
7	**Important** It may be necessary to separate the EBCM from the BPMV to gain access to the pump motor pigtail connector. 1. Disconnect from the EBCM, the ABS pump motor pigtail connector. 2. Use a DMM in order to measure the resistance across the ABS pump motor. Does the resistance measure within the specified range?	0.3-1.0 ohms	Go to Step 8	Go to Step 10
8	Use a DMM in order to measure the resistance between the high side of the pump motor and a good ground. Does the resistance measure less than the specified value?	0L	Go to Step 10	Go to Step 9
9	**Important** Use the scan tool in order to perform the Tire Size Calibration procedure and the Trim Level Calibration procedure, if applicable. Replace the EBCM. Replacement . Did you complete the replacement?	--	Go to Step 11	
10	**Important** Use the scan tool in order to perform the Tire Size Calibration procedure and the Trim Level Calibration procedure, if applicable. Replace the EBCM and the BPMV. Did you complete the replacements?	--	Go to Step 11	
11	1. Use the scan tool in order to clear the DTCs. 2. Operate the vehicle within the Conditions for Running the DTC as specified in the supporting text. Does the DTC reset?	--	Go to Step 2	System OK

LTV0500000005343

Fig. 50   Codes C0265 Or C0266: EBCM Relay Circuit (Part 3 of 3). 2002 Avalanche, Escalade, Escalade EXT, Suburban, Tahoe & Yukon Less JL4

Diagnostic Aids

Important

Whenever the EBCM is replaced for DTC C0265 or C0266, the ABS pump motor and motor circuitry must be tested for the proper resistance. Refer to steps 7 and 8 in the diagnostic table below for testing procedures and resistance values.

C0265

Thoroughly inspect connections and circuitry that may cause an intermittent malfunction.

C0266

Replace the EBCM if DTC C0266 continues to set intermittently.

Test Description

The numbers below refer to the step numbers on the diagnostic table.

4. This step tests if the battery positive voltage circuit can supply adequate power to the system relay.

7. A shorted ABS pump motor or shorted motor circuitry may damage the contacts within the system relay. Follow this step to prevent damage to a replacement EBCM.

Step	Action	Values	Yes	No
1	Did you perform the ABS Diagnostic System Check?	--	Go to Step 2	Go to Diagnostic System Check - ABS
2	1. Use a scan tool in order to clear the DTCs. 2. Use the scan tool in order to perform an ABS Function Test. Does DTC C0266 set?	--	Go to Step 7	Go to Step 3
3	Does DTC C0265 set?	--	Go to Step 4	Go to Diagnostic Aids
4	1. Turn OFF the ignition. 2. Disconnect from the EBCM, the harness connector containing the battery positive voltage circuit. 3. Connect a test lamp between the battery positive voltage circuit and a good ground. Does the test lamp illuminate?	--	Go to Step 6	Go to Step 5

LTV0500000005342

Fig. 50   Codes C0265 Or C0266: EBCM Relay Circuit (Part 2 of 3). 2002 Avalanche, Escalade, Escalade EXT, Suburban, Tahoe & Yukon Less JL4

Circuit Description

The EBCM applies the ground needed for pump motor activation. The low side of the pump motor has a feedback circuit to the EBCM. When the pump motor is commanded OFF and at rest, feedback voltage is high. When the pump motor is winding down after being commanded ON and then OFF, feedback voltage is low. The EBCM monitors this feedback voltage in order to determine if the motor is functioning properly.

Conditions for Running the DTC

- The ignition is ON.
- The vehicle speed is greater than 6 km/h (4 mph).

Conditions for Setting the DTC

The EBCM detects any of the following conditions:

- An open or shorted pump motor
- An open or shorted pump motor driver circuit
- A seized pump motor

Action Taken When the DTC Sets

If equipped, the following actions may occur:

- The EBCM disables the ABS/TCS/VSES.
- The ABS indicator turns ON.
- The traction off indicator turns ON.
- The message center displays the SERVICE STABILITY SYSTEM message.

Conditions for Clearing the DTC

The conditions for setting the DTC are no longer present and you use the scan tool Clear DTCs function.

Diagnostic Aids

Thoroughly inspect connections or circuitry that may cause an intermittent malfunction.

Test Description

The numbers below refer to the step numbers on the diagnostic table.

2. It is imperative that the vehicle be driven to attempt to reset the DTC. Using the scan tool to perform a function test may not produce the same result, and therefore may cause misdiagnosis of the vehicle.

7. This step tests if the EBCM is capable of activating the ABS pump motor.

8. A shorted ABS pump motor may damage the EBCM. It is imperative that the steps in the table be followed in order to prevent damage to a replacement EBCM.

LTV0500000005344

Fig. 51   Codes C0267 Or C0268: Pump Motor Circuit Open/Short (Part 1 of 4). 2002 Avalanche, Escalade, Escalade EXT, Suburban, Tahoe & Yukon

Step	Action	Values	Yes	No
1	Did you perform the ABS Diagnostic System Check?	--	Go to Step 2	Go to Diagnostic System Check - ABS
2	1. Use a scan tool in order to clear the DTCs. 2. Operate the vehicle within the Conditions for Running the DTC as specified in the supporting text. Does DTC C0267 set?	--	Go to Step 6	Go to Step 3
3	Does DTC C0268 set?	--	Go to Step 4	Go to Diagnostic Aids
4	1. Turn OFF the ignition. 2. Disconnect from the EBCM, the 2-way harness connector which contains the battery positive voltage circuit and the ground circuit. Caution: Before servicing any electrical component, the ignition key must be in the OFF or LOCK position and all electrical loads must be OFF, unless instructed otherwise in these procedures. If a tool or equipment could easily come in contact with a live exposed electrical terminal, also disconnect the negative battery cable. Failure to follow these precautions may cause personal injury and/or damage to the vehicle or its components. 3. Disconnect the negative battery cable. 4. Disconnect the positive battery cable. 5. Place one lead of a DMM on the positive battery cable where the cable normally connects to the battery. 6. Place the other lead on the battery positive voltage circuit terminal within the 2-way EBCM harness connector. 7. Measure the total resistance between the positive battery cable and the EBCM. Does the resistance measure within the specified range?	0.0-0.2 ohms	Go to Step 5	Go to Step 10
5	Use a DMM to measure the resistance of the ground circuit. Does the resistance measure within the specified range?	0.0-0.2 ohms	Go to Step 7	Go to Step 11

LTV0500000005345

Fig. 51   Codes C0267 Or C0268: Pump Motor Circuit Open/Short (Part 2 of 4). 2002 Avalanche, Escalade, Escalade EXT, Suburban, Tahoe & Yukon

Step	Action	Values	Yes	No
6	**Important** On some applications, it may be necessary to separate the EBCM from the BPMV in order to perform this test. Also, DTC C0268 may set when this test is performed. 1. Turn OFF the ignition. 2. Disconnect from the EBCM, the ABS pump motor pigtail connector. For systems which have no pump motor pigtail, it is necessary to separate the EBCM from the BPMV in order to gain access to the pump motor connector of the EBCM. 3. Use a connector adapter test kit in order to connect a test lamp between the ABS pump motor power and ground circuits at the pump motor connector of the EBCM. 4. Turn ON the ignition. 5. Use the scan tool in order to clear the DTCs. 6. Use the scan tool in order to perform an ABS Function Test. Does DTC C0267 set?	--	Go to Step 12	Go to Step 9
7	**Important** On some applications, it may be necessary to separate the EBCM from the BPMV in order to perform this test. Also, DTC C0268 may set when this test is performed. 1. Reconnect both battery cables. 2. Disconnect from the EBCM, the ABS pump motor pigtail connector. For systems which have no pump motor pigtail, it is necessary to separate the EBCM from the BPMV in order to gain access to the pump motor connector of the EBCM. 3. Use a connector adapter test kit in order to connect a test lamp between the ABS pump motor power and ground circuits at the pump motor connector of the EBCM. 4. Turn ON the ignition. 5. Use the scan tool in order to clear the DTCs. 6. Use the scan tool in order to perform an ABS Function Test. Does the test lamp illuminate and then turn OFF when the Function Test is performed?	--	Go to Step 13	Go to Step 8
8	Use a DMM in order to measure the resistance across the ABS pump motor. Does the resistance measure within the specified range?	0.3-1.0 ohms	Go to Step 12	Go to Step 14
9	Inspect for poor connections at the pump motor pigtail connector. Did you find and correct the condition?	--	Go to Step 15	Go to Step 13
10	Repair the high resistance in the underhood electrical center or the battery positive voltage circuit. Did you complete the repair?	--	Go to Step 15	--
11	Repair the high resistance in the ground circuit. Did you complete the repair?	--	Go to Step 15	--

LTV0500000005346

Fig. 51   Codes C0267 Or C0268: Pump Motor Circuit Open/Short (Part 3 of 4). 2002 Avalanche, Escalade, Escalade EXT, Suburban, Tahoe & Yukon

Step	Action	Values	Yes	No
12	**Important** Following EBCM replacement, use the scan tool to perform the Tire Size Calibration procedure and the Trim Level Calibration procedure, if applicable. Replace the EBCM. Did you complete the replacement?	--	Go to Step 15	--
13	Replace the BPMV. Did you complete the replacement?	--	Go to Step 15	--
14	**Important** Following EBCM replacement, use the scan tool perform the Tire Size Calibration procedure and the Trim Level Calibration procedure, if applicable. Replace the EBCM and the BPMV. Did you complete the replacements?	--	Go to Step 15	--
15	1. Use a scan tool in order to clear the DTCs. 2. Operate the vehicle within the Conditions for Running the DTC as specified in the supporting text. Does the DTC reset?	--	Go to Step 3	System OK

LTV0500000005347

Fig. 51   Codes C0267 Or C0268: Pump Motor Circuit Open/Short (Part 4 of 4). 2002 Avalanche, Escalade, Escalade EXT, Suburban, Tahoe & Yukon

Circuit Description

The ABS relay supplies battery voltage to 6 valve solenoids. The electronic brake control module (EBCM) microprocessor applies the grounds needed to activate each solenoid. The low side of each solenoid coil has a feedback circuit to the EBCM microprocessor. When a solenoid is commanded OFF, the feedback voltage is high. When a solenoid is commanded ON, the feedback voltage is low.

Conditions for Running the DTC

- The ignition is ON.
- The vehicle is experiencing an ABS event.

Conditions for Setting the DTC

C0269

The EBCM commands a dump solenoid ON for 9 consecutive seconds.

C0274

The EBCM commands an isolation solenoid ON for 255 consecutive seconds.

Action Taken When the DTC Sets

If equipped, the following actions may occur:

- The EBCM disables the ABS/TCS/VSES and DRP.
- The ABS indicator turns ON.
- The traction off indicator turns ON.
- The red brake warning indicator turns ON.
- The message center displays the SERVICE STABILITY SYSTEM message.

Conditions for Clearing the DTC

The conditions for setting the DTC are no longer present and you use the scan tool Clear DTCs function.

LTV0500000005348

Fig. 52   Codes C0269 Or C0274: Excessive Dump/ Isolation Time (Part 1 of 2). 2002 Avalanche, Escalade, Escalade EXT, Suburban, Tahoe & Yukon

Diagnostic Aids

The most likely cause of DTC C0269 or DTC C0274 is a mechanical failure that causes a wheel to lock and remain locked. The DTCs may also set, conceivably, when the ABS is activated on surfaces that are nearly impossible to get traction on. If the DTC sets within these conditions, diagnosis of the ABS system is not necessary.

Test Description

The number below refers to the step number on the diagnostic table:

2. Performing solenoid tests determines if there is a mechanical malfunction inside the BPMV. Perform dump valve solenoid tests for DTC C0269 or isolation valve solenoid tests for DTC C0274.

Step	Action	Yes	No
1	Did you perform the ABS Diagnostic System Check?	Go to Step 2	Go to Diagnostic System Check - ABS
2	1. Use a scan tool in order to clear the DTCs. 2. Use the scan tool in order to perform the necessary Solenoid Tests. Do the Solenoid Tests show the system to be functioning normally?	Go to Diagnostic Aids	Go to Step 3
3	Replace the BPMV. Did you complete the replacement?	Go to Step 4	--
4	Use the scan tool in order to perform the necessary Solenoid Tests. Do the Solenoid Tests show the system to be functioning normally?	System OK	Go to Step 3

LTV0500000005349

Fig. 52   Codes C0269 Or C0274: Excessive Dump/ Isolation Time (Part 2 of 2). 2002 Avalanche, Escalade, Escalade EXT, Suburban, Tahoe & Yukon

Step	Action	Yes	No
1	Did you perform the ABS Diagnostic System Check?	Go to Step 2	Go to Diagnostic System Check - ABS
2	Is DTC C0271 or DTC C0272 set in the EBCM memory?	Go to Step 4	Go to Step 3
3	1. Use a scan tool in order to clear the DTCs. 2. Turn OFF the ignition for 5 seconds. 3. Turn ON the ignition. Does the DTC set?	Go to Step 4	Go to Diagnostic Aids
4	Important Following EBCM replacement, use the scan tool to perform the Tire Size Calibration procedure and the Trim Level Calibration procedure, if applicable. Replace the EBCM. Did you complete the replacement?	Go to Step 5	--
5	Use the scan tool in order to clear the DTCs. Operate the vehicle within the Conditions for Running the DTC as specified in the supporting text. Does the DTC reset?	Go to Step 2	System OK

LTV0500000005351

Fig. 53   Codes C0271–C0273 & C0284: EBCM Fault (Part 2 of 2). 2002 Avalanche, Escalade, Escalade EXT, Suburban, Tahoe & Yukon

Circuit Description

This DTC identifies a malfunction within the electronic brake control module (EBCM).

Conditions for Running the DTC

The ignition is ON.

Conditions for Setting the DTC

The EBCM detects an internal malfunction.

Action Taken When the DTC Sets

If equipped, the following actions may occur:

- The EBCM disables the ABS/TCS/VSES and DRP.
- The ABS indicator turns ON.
- The traction off indicator turns ON.
- The red brake warning indicator turns ON.
- The message center displays the SERVICE STABILITY SYSTEM message.

Conditions for Clearing the DTC

The conditions for setting the DTC are no longer present and you use the scan tool Clear DTCs function.

Diagnostic Aids

Replace the EBCM if DTC C0273 or DTC C0284 continues to set intermittently.

LTV0500000005350

Fig. 53   Codes C0271–C0273 & C0284: EBCM Fault (Part 1 of 2). 2002 Avalanche, Escalade, Escalade EXT, Suburban, Tahoe & Yukon

Circuit Description

The YSC relay supplies battery voltage to 4 valve solenoids (priming, charging, supply and YSC). The EBCM microprocessor applies the grounds needed in order to activate each solenoid. The low side of each solenoid coil has a feedback circuit to the EBCM microprocessor. When a solenoid is commanded OFF, the feedback voltage is high. When a solenoid is commanded ON, the feedback voltage is low.

Conditions for Running the DTC

- The ignition is ON.
- The vehicle speed is greater than 6 km/h (4 mph).

Conditions for Setting the DTC

The EBCM detects an internal malfunction.

Action Taken When the DTC Sets

- The EBCM disables the VSES.
- The message center displays the SERVICE STABILITY SYSTEM message.

Conditions for Clearing the DTC

The conditions for setting the DTC are no longer present and you use the scan tool Clear DTCs function.

Diagnostic Aids

An intermittent open/shorted relay DTC can be set by several different internal EBCM problems. Replace the EBCM if an open/shorted relay DTC continues to set intermittently.

LTV0500000005352

Fig. 54   Codes C0275 Or C0276: VSES Internal Relay (Part 1 of 2). 2002 Avalanche, Escalade, Escalade EXT, Suburban, Tahoe & Yukon

Step	Action	Yes	No
1	Did you perform the ABS Diagnostic System Check?	Go to Step 2	Go to Diagnostic System Check - ABS
2	1. Use a scan tool in order to clear the DTCs. 2. Operate the vehicle within the Conditions for Running the DTC as specified in the supporting text. Does the DTC set?	Go to Step 3	Go to Diagnostic Aids
3	Important Following EBCM replacement, use the scan tool to perform the Tire Size Calibration procedure and the Trim Level Calibration procedure, if applicable. Replace the EBCM. Did you complete the replacement?	Go to Step 4	--
4	1. Use the scan tool in order to clear the DTCs. 2. Operate the vehicle within the Conditions for Running the DTC as specified in the supporting text. Does the DTC reset?	Go to Step 3	System OK

LTV0500000005353

Fig. 54   Codes C0275 Or C0276: VSES Internal Relay (Part 2 of 2). 2002 Avalanche, Escalade, Escalade EXT, Suburban, Tahoe & Yukon

Circuit Description

The PCM sends engine/axle/tire IDs to the EBCM via serial data communications immediately after the modules are powered up.

Conditions for Running the DTC

The ignition is ON.

Conditions for Setting the DTC

The EBCM receives invalid information from the PCM.

Action Taken When the DTC Sets

If equipped, the following actions occur:

- The EBCM disables the TCS.
- The traction off indicator turns ON.

Conditions for Clearing the DTC

The conditions for setting the DTC are no longer present and you use the scan tool Clear DTCs function.

Diagnostic Aids

Diagnose other ABS or TCS related DTCs prior to diagnosing DTC C0279.

If multiple TCS related DTCs are set, or the vehicle being serviced is not equipped with TCS, verify the correct EBCM is installed in the vehicle.

Test Description

The number below refers to the step number on the diagnostic table.

3. The PCM must have the correct part number for the specified application.

LTV0500000005354

Fig. 55   Code C0279: Powertrain Configuration Not Valid (Part 1 of 2). 2002 Avalanche, Escalade, Escalade EXT, Suburban, Tahoe & Yukon

Circuit Description

The stop lamp switch signal informs the electronic brake control module (EBCM) when the brake pedal is pressed.

Conditions for Running the DTC

Either of the following conditions will cause the DTC to run:

- The ignition is ON and the vehicle achieves at least 56 km/h (35 mph) before coming to a stop.
- The ignition is ON and the vehicle experiences an antilock brake system (ABS) event lasting at least 1 second.

Conditions for Setting the DTC

The EBCM detects an open or shorted brake switch or brake switch circuit.

Action Taken When the DTC Sets

- The EBCM disables the VSES.
- The message center displays the SERVICE STABILITY SYSTEM message.

Conditions for Clearing the DTC

The conditions for setting the DTC are no longer present and you use the scan tool Clear DTCs function.

Diagnostic Aids

Thoroughly inspect connections or circuitry that may cause an intermittent malfunction.

Test Description

The numbers below refer to the step numbers on the diagnostic table.

4. This step tests for a shorted stoplamp switch.

5. This step tests for an open stoplamp switch.

LTV0500000005356

Fig. 56   Code C0281: Brake Switch Circuit (Part 1 of 3). 2002 Avalanche, Escalade, Escalade EXT, Suburban, Tahoe & Yukon

Step	Action	Yes	No
1	Did you perform the ABS Diagnostic System Check?	Go to Step 2	Go to Diagnostic System Check - ABS
2	1. Use a scan tool in order to clear the DTCs. 2. Turn OFF the ignition for 5 seconds. 3. Turn ON the ignition and wait 10 seconds. Does the DTC set?	Go to Step 3	Go to Diagnostics Aids
3	Verify the correct PCM is installed in the vehicle. Does the vehicle have the correct PCM?	Go to Step 4	Go to Step 6
4	Use the scan tool in order to read the Calibration IDs of the PCM. Are the PCM Calibration IDs correct?	Go to Diagnostics Aids	Go to Step 5
5	Perform the set up procedure for the PCM. Did you complete the action?	Go to Step 7	--
6	**Important** Perform the set up procedure for the PCM. Replace the PCM. Did you complete the replacement?	Go to Step 7	--
7	1. Use the scan tool in order to clear the DTCs. 2. Operate the vehicle within the Conditions for Running the DTC as specified in the supporting text. Does the DTC reset?	Go to Step 3	System OK

LTV0500000005355

Fig. 55   Code C0279: Powertrain Configuration Not Valid (Part 2 of 2). 2002 Avalanche, Escalade, Escalade EXT, Suburban, Tahoe & Yukon

Step	Action	Yes	No
1	Did you perform the ABS Diagnostic System Check?	Go to Step 2	Go to Diagnostic System Check - ABS
2	1. Install a scan tool. 2. Select the 4WAL 3 Sensor Data Display function. 3. Observe the Brake Switch Status on the scan tool. Does the scan tool display Off?	Go to Step 3	Go to Step 5
3	1. Apply the brake. 2. Observe the Brake Switch Status on the scan tool. Does the scan tool display On?	Go to Diagnostic Aids	Go to Step 4
4	1. Turn OFF the ignition. 2. Disconnect the stop lamp switch. 3. Turn ON the ignition. 4. Observe the Brake Switch Status on the scan tool. Does the scan tool display On?	Go to Step 9	Go to Step 7
5	1. Turn OFF the ignition. 2. Disconnect the stop lamp switch. 3. Connect a fused jumper wire between the ignition 3 voltage circuit and the TCC brake switch signal circuit at the stop lamp switch harness connector. 4. Turn ON the ignition. 5. Observe the Brake Switch Status on the scan tool. Does the scan tool display Off?	Go to Step 9	Go to Step 6
6	Test the ignition 3 voltage circuit and the TCC brake switch signal circuit for an open or a short to ground. Did you find and correct the condition?	Go to Step 12	Go to Step 8

LTV0500000005357

Fig. 56   Code C0281: Brake Switch Circuit (Part 2 of 3). 2002 Avalanche, Escalade, Escalade EXT, Suburban, Tahoe & Yukon

7	Test the TCC brake switch signal circuit for a short to voltage. Did you find and correct the condition?	Go to Step 12	Go to Step 8
8	Inspect for poor connections at the harness connector of the EBCM. Did you find and correct the condition?	Go to Step 12	Go to Step 10
9	Inspect for poor connections at the harness connector of the stop lamp switch. Did you find and correct the condition?	Go to Step 12	Go to Step 11
10	**Important** Following EBCM replacement, use the scan tool to perform the Tire Size Calibration procedure. Replace the EBCM. Did you complete the replacement?	Go to Step 12	--
11	Replace the stop lamp switch. Did you complete the replacement?	Go to Step 12	--
12	1. Use the scan tool in order to clear the DTCs. 2. Operate the vehicle within the Conditions for Running the DTC as specified in the supporting text. Does the DTC reset?	Go to Step 2	System OK

LTV0500000005358

Fig. 56   Code C0281: Brake Switch Circuit (Part 3 of 3). 2002 Avalanche, Escalade, Escalade EXT, Suburban, Tahoe & Yukon

Ambient Temperature	Fault Timer
Greater than 0°C (32°F)	86 sec
Between -30°C and 0°C (-22°F and 32°F)	170 sec
Less than -30°C (-22°F)	230 sec

C0286

Any of the following conditions may cause DTC C0286 to set.

- The EBCM detects 2 fast MPA leakdowns during the system initialization period.
- The EBCM detects 3 fast MPA leakdowns after the system has initialized.
- The sum of the fast and slow MPA leakdowns detected after the system has initialized equals 7.

Action Taken When the DTC Sets

- The EBCM disables the VSES.
- The message center displays the SERVICE STABILITY SYSTEM message.

Conditions for Clearing the DTC

The conditions for setting the DTC are no longer present and you use the scan tool Clear DTCs function.

Diagnostic Aids

Thoroughly inspect the MPA switch jumper harness for any condition that may cause an intermittent malfunction.

An intermittent DTC may be difficult to verify since the DTC may take a substantial amount of time to set. If a DTC continues to set intermittently, remove the MPA switch and activate the switch by pressing and releasing the plunger. Ensure the plunger movement is smooth and that the plunger releases readily without sticking. Observe the MPA Switch input on the scan tool to verify that the status changes from Uncharged to Charged every time the switch is pressed. Replace the BPMV if no fault is found in the switch, circuitry or connections. Refer to Brake Pressure Modulator Valve (BPMV) Replacement.

Test Description

The numbers below refer to the step numbers on the diagnostic table.

4. This step simulates an open MPA switch.

5. This step simulates a closed MPA switch.

6. This step tests the MPA switch by closing the switch manually.

7. This step tests the MPA switch by ensuring the switch plunger is in the open position.

LTV0500000005360

Fig. 57   Codes C0282, C0285 Or C0286: MPA Switch Circuit (Part 2 of 4). 2002 Avalanche, Escalade, Escalade EXT, Suburban, Tahoe & Yukon

Circuit Description

The brake pressure modulator valve (BPMV) contains a medium pressure accumulator (MPA). The MPA provides pressure to the front brakes during certain VSES events. The MPA switch is included to monitor the status of the pressure accumulator. The MPA switch is open when the MPA is uncharged.

The integrity of the MPA switch is tested by the EBCM. The MPA is partially discharged during system initialization to open the switch, and then recharged to close the switch. The EBCM continues to monitor the switch to ensure the MPA remains charged. Provided the VSES is not activated, the MPA should remain charged for the entire ignition cycle. If the MPA switch opens within 5 minutes of closing, a fast leakdown condition is detected. If the MPA switch opens after 5 minutes has passed, a slow leakdown condition is detected.

Conditions for Running the DTC

C0282 and C0285

- The ignition is ON.
- The vehicle speed is greater than 12 km/h (8 mph).

C0286

- The ignition is ON.
- The MPA switch is closed.
- The diagnostic tests for DTC C0282 and C0285 have ran and passed.

Conditions for Setting the DTC

C0282

The MPA switch remains closed when the MPA is discharged for 1-2 seconds, depending on ambient temperature.

C0285

During the MPA charging period, the MPA switch does not close within the time indicated on the following table.

LTV0500000005359

Fig. 57   Codes C0282, C0285 Or C0286: MPA Switch Circuit (Part 1 of 4). 2002 Avalanche, Escalade, Escalade EXT, Suburban, Tahoe & Yukon

Step	Action	Yes	No
	Important		
	The introduction of air into the brakes' hydraulic system due to a BPMV replacement or for any other reason may cause DTC C0285 or C0286 to set. If it suspected that air may have been introduced to the hydraulic system, use the scan tool to perform the VSES Automated Bleed procedure and the Bleed MPA procedure before proceeding with this diagnostic table. You must refer to ABS Automated Bleed Procedure for complete system bleeding instructions.		
1	Did you perform the ABS Diagnostic System Check?	Go to Step 2	Go to Diagnostic System Check - ABS
2	1. Use a scan tool in order to clear the DTCs. 2. Operate the vehicle within the Conditions for Running the DTC as specified in the supporting text for 10 minutes or until the DTC resets. Does the DTC reset?	Go to Step 3	Go to Diagnostic Aids
3	1. Turn ON the ignition. 2. Select the VSES Data List on the scan tool. 3. Observe the MPA Switch input on the scan tool. Does the scan tool display Charged?	Go to Step 4	Go to Step 5
4	1. Turn OFF the ignition. 2. Disconnect the MPA switch harness connector. 3. Turn ON the ignition. 4. Observe the MPA Switch input on the scan tool. Does the scan tool display Uncharged?	Go to Step 7	Go to Step 9
5	1. Turn ON the ignition. 2. Disconnect the MPA switch harness connector. 3. Use a fused jumper wire to connect the MPA switch supply circuit to the MPA switch signal circuit. 4. Turn ON the ignition. 5. Observe the MPA Switch input on the scan tool. Does the scan tool display Charged?	Go to Step 6	Go to Step 8
6	1. Remove the MPA switch from the BPMV. 2. Reconnect the MPA switch harness connector. 3. Press and hold the MPA switch plunger. 4. Observe the MPA Switch input on the scan tool. Does the scan tool display Charged?	Go to Step 15	Go to Step 12

LTV0500000005361

Fig. 57   Codes C0282, C0285 Or C0286: MPA Switch Circuit (Part 3 of 4). 2002 Avalanche, Escalade, Escalade EXT, Suburban, Tahoe & Yukon

Step	Action		Yes	No
7	1. Remove the MPA switch from the BPMV. Replacement . 2. Reconnect the MPA switch harness connector. 3. Observe the MPA Switch input on the scan tool. Does the scan tool display Uncharged?		Go to Step 15	Go to Step 14
8	Test the MPA switch supply circuit for an open or a short to ground. Did you find and correct the condition?		Go to Step 16	Go to Step 10
9	Test the MPA switch signal circuit for a short to voltage. Did you find and correct the condition?		Go to Step 16	Go to Step 13
10	Test the MPA switch signal circuit for an open or a short to ground Did you find and correct the condition?		Go to Step 16	Go to Step 11
11	Inspect for poor connections at the harness connector of the EBCM. Did you find and correct the condition?		Go to Step 16	Go to Step 13
12	Inspect for poor connections at the harness connector of the MPA switch. Did you find and correct the condition?		Go to Step 16	Go to Step 14
13	**Important** Following EBCM replacement, use the scan tool to perform the Tire Size Calibration procedure. Replace the EBCM. Did you complete the replacement?		Go to Step 16	--
14	Replace the MPA switch. Did you complete the replacement?		Go to Step 16	--
15	**Important** DTC C0285 or C0286 may set after BPMV replacement if the VSES Automated Bleed procedure and the Bleed MPA Procedure are not performed exactly as specified in the service manual instructions. Replace the BPMV. Did you complete the replacement?		Go to Step 16	--
16	1. Use a scan tool in order to clear the DTCs. 2. Operate the vehicle within the Conditions for Running the DTC as specified in the supporting text for 10 minutes or until the DTC resets. Does the DTC reset?		Go to Step 3	System OK

LTV0500000006162

Fig. 57   Codes C0282, C0285 Or C0286: MPA Switch Circuit (Part 4 of 4). 2002 Avalanche, Escalade, Escalade EXT, Suburban, Tahoe & Yukon

Step	Action	Yes	No
1	Did you perform the antilock brake system (ABS) Diagnostic System Check?	Go to Step 2	Go to Diagnostic System Check
2	1. Use a scan tool in order to clear the DTCs. 2. Turn OFF the ignition for 5 seconds. 3. Start the engine and allow the engine to run for at least 20 seconds. Does the DTC set?	Go to Step 3	Go to Diagnostic Aids
3	1. Turn OFF the ignition. 2. Disconnect the traction control switch harness connector. 3. Turn ON the ignition. 4. Connect a test lamp between the ignition 1 voltage circuit and a good ground. Does the test lamp illuminate?	Go to Step 4	Go to Step 8
4	1. Use the scan tool in order to clear the DTCs. 2. Turn OFF the ignition. 3. Connect a fused jumper wire between the ignition 1 voltage circuit and the traction control switch signal circuit at the traction control switch harness connector. 4. Start the engine and allow the engine to run for at least 20 seconds. Does the DTC set?	Go to Step 5	Go to Step 9
5	Test the traction control switch signal circuit for an open or a short to ground. Did you find and correct the condition?	Go to Step 11	Go to Step 6

LTV0500000006164

Fig. 58   Code C0283: Traction Switch Shorted To Ground w/NW7(Part 2 of 3). 2002 Avalanche, Escalade, Escalade EXT, Suburban, Tahoe & Yukon w/NW7

Circuit Description

The traction control switch is a momentary-contact, normally-open switch that can be used to disable the traction control system (TCS). Each time the traction control switch is pressed, the TCS enabled/disabled status changes. When TCS is disabled, the electronic brake control module (EBCM) illuminates the traction off indicator by opening the service traction control signal circuit.

Conditions for Running the DTC

The ignition is ON.

Conditions for Setting the DTC

The EBCM detects low voltage on the traction control switch signal circuit for 10 seconds.

Action Taken When the DTC Sets

If equipped, the following actions occur:

- The EBCM disables the TCS.
- The traction off indicator turns ON.

Conditions for Clearing the DTC

The conditions for setting the DTC are no longer present and you use the scan tool Clear DTCs function.

Diagnostic Aids

Thoroughly inspect connections or circuitry that may cause an intermittent malfunction.

Test Description

The number below refers to the step number on the diagnostic table.

4. This step tests the traction control switch circuitry. If the fuse opens when you perform this test, the traction control switch signal circuit is shorted to ground.

LTV0500000006163

Fig. 58   Code C0283: Traction Switch Shorted To Ground w/NW7(Part 1 of 3). 2002 Avalanche, Escalade, Escalade EXT, Suburban, Tahoe & Yukon w/NW7

Step	Action	Yes	No
6	Inspect for poor connections at the harness connector of the electronic brake control module (EBCM). Did you find and correct the condition?	Go to Step 11	Go to Step 7
7	**Important** Following EBCM replacement, use the scan tool to perform the Tire Size Calibration procedure. Replace the EBCM. Did you complete the replacement?	Go to Step 11	--
8	Repair the open in the ignition 1 voltage circuit. Did you complete the repair?	Go to Step 11	--
9	Inspect for poor connections at the harness connector of the traction control switch. Did you find and correct the condition?	Go to Step 11	Go to Step 10
10	Replace the traction control switch. Did you complete the replacement?	Go to Step 11	--
11	1. Use the scan tool in order to clear the DTCs. 2. Operate the vehicle within the Conditions for Running the DTC as specified in the supporting text. Does the DTC reset?	Go to Step 3	System OK

LTV0500000006165

Fig. 58   Code C0283: Traction Switch Shorted To Ground w/NW7(Part 3 of 3). 2002 Avalanche, Escalade, Escalade EXT, Suburban, Tahoe & Yukon w/NW7

Circuit Description

The VSES mode switch is a momentary-contact switch that can be used to limit the VSES function. Each time the mode switch is pressed, the VSES full stability/limited status changes. When the VSES mode switch is released, voltage on the VSES mode switch signal circuit is approximately 4.5 volts. When the VSES mode switch is pressed, voltage on the VSES mode switch signal circuit is approximately 9 volts.

Conditions for Running the DTC

In order to detect a continuously low or high VSES mode switch signal:

The ignition is ON.

OR:

In order to detect a continuously pressed VSES mode switch:

- The ignition is ON.
- The engine speed is greater than 450 RPM.

Conditions for Setting the DTC

Either of the following conditions may cause DTC C0283 to set:

- The VSES mode switch signal is detected as excessively low or high for 200 milliseconds.
- The VSES mode switch is detected as pressed for 60 seconds.

Action Taken When the DTC Sets

- The EBCM disables the VSES.
- The message center displays the SERVICE STABILITY SYSTEM message.

Conditions for Clearing the DTC

The conditions for setting the DTC are no longer present and you use the scan tool Clear DTCs function.

LTV0500000006166

Fig. 59   Code C0283: Traction Switch Shorted To Ground w/JL4 (Part 1 of 4). 2002 Avalanche, Escalade, Escalade EXT, Suburban, Tahoe & Yukon w/JL4

	Action	Values	Yes	No
1	Turn OFF the ignition. 2. Reconnect the VSES mode switch harness connector. 3. Turn ON the ignition. 4. Backprobe the VSES mode switch harness connector in order to connect a DMM between the VSES mode switch signal circuit and a good ground. 5. Measure the DC voltage on the VSES mode switch signal circuit. Does the VSES mode switch signal measure within the specified range?	2-7 V	Go to Step 5	Go to Step 6
5	1. Press and hold the VSES mode switch. 2. Use a DMM in order to measure the DC voltage on the VSES mode switch signal circuit. Does the VSES mode switch signal measure within the specified range?	7-11 V	Go to Step 7	Go to Step 13
6	Test the VSES mode switch signal circuit for a short to ground or a short to voltage. Did you find and correct the condition?	--	Go to Step 14	Go to Step 12
7	1. Turn OFF the ignition. 2. Disconnect from the EBCM, the harness connector containing the VSES mode switch signal circuit. 3. Turn ON the ignition. 4. Use a DMM in order to measure the DC voltage on the VSES mode switch signal circuit. Does the VSES mode switch signal measure within the specified range?	2-7 V	Go to Step 9	Go to Step 8
8	Repair the open in the VSES mode switch signal circuit. Did you complete the repair?	--	Go to Step 14	--
9	Inspect for poor connections at the harness connector of the EBCM. Did you find and correct the condition?	--	Go to Step 14	Go to Step 10

LTV0500000006168

Fig. 59   Code C0283: Traction Switch Shorted To Ground w/JL4 (Part 3 of 4). 2002 Avalanche, Escalade, Escalade EXT, Suburban, Tahoe & Yukon w/JL4

Diagnostic Aids

Press and release the VSES mode switch several times while observing the message center in order to verify that the VSES full stability/limited status changes each time the switch is pressed and that DTC C0283 does not set. Using the scan tool in order to observe the Mode Switch Pressed or Released status may also be helpful in diagnosing an intermittent fault within the switch.

Thoroughly inspect connections or circuitry that may cause an intermittent malfunction. Refer to Testing for Electrical Intermittents , Testing for Intermittent and Poor Connections , Wiring Repairs and Connector Repairs in Wiring Systems.

Test Description

The number below refers to the step number on the diagnostic table.

4. This step tests for voltage on the VSES mode switch signal circuit indicating an unpressed VSES mode switch.

5. This step tests for voltage on the VSES mode switch signal circuit indicating a pressed VSES mode switch.

Step	Action	Values	Yes	No
1	Did you perform the ABS Diagnostic System Check?	--	Go to Step 2	Go to Diagnostic System Check
2	1. Use a scan tool in order to clear the DTCs. 2. Turn OFF the ignition for 5 seconds. 3. Start the engine. 4. Observe the scan tool for up to 60 seconds in order to verify the DTC resets. Does the DTC set?	--	Go to Step 3	Go to Diagnostic Aids
3	1. Turn OFF the ignition. 2. Disconnect the VSES mode switch harness connector. 3. Turn ON the ignition. 4. Connect a test lamp between the ignition 3 voltage circuit and a good ground. Does the test lamp illuminate?	--	Go to Step 4	Go to Step 11

LTV0500000006167

Fig. 59   Code C0283: Traction Switch Shorted To Ground w/JL4 (Part 2 of 4). 2002 Avalanche, Escalade, Escalade EXT, Suburban, Tahoe & Yukon w/JL4

	Important			
10	Following EBCM replacement, use the scan tool to perform the Tire Size Calibration procedure. Replace the EBCM. Did you complete the replacement?	--	--	Go to Step 14
11	Repair the open in the ignition 3 voltage circuit. Did you complete the repair?	--		Go to Step 14
12	Inspect for poor connections at the harness connector of the VSES mode switch. Did you find and correct the condition?	--	Go to Step 14	Go to Step 13
13	Replace the VSES mode switch. Did you complete the replacement?	--	Go to Step 14	--
14	1. Use the scan tool in order to clear the DTCs. 2. Operate the vehicle within the Conditions for Running the DTC as specified in the supporting text. Does the DTC reset?	--	Go to Step 3	System OK

LTV0500000006169

Fig. 59   Code C0283: Traction Switch Shorted To Ground w/JL4 (Part 4 of 4). 2002 Avalanche, Escalade, Escalade EXT, Suburban, Tahoe & Yukon w/JL4

Circuit Description

The EBCM supplies 5 VDC to the powertrain control module (PCM) on the delivered torque signal circuit. The PCM toggles this voltage to ground in order to create the delivered torque signal at the EBCM. A signal with a frequency of 128 Hz +/- 5 percent and a duty cycle of 25-95 percent is a valid delivered torque signal. The percentage of duty cycle is proportionate to the percentage of delivered torque.

Conditions for Running the DTC

- The ignition is ON.
- The engine is running at a speed greater than 500 RPM for 1 second.

Conditions for Setting the DTC

C0287

The EBCM receives an invalid delivered torque signal for 300 milliseconds.

P1644 or P1689

The PCM detects the delivered torque signal voltage as being less than 4.75 volts or greater than 5.25 volts.

Action Taken When the DTC Sets

If equipped, the following actions may occur:

- The EBCM disables the TCS/VSES.
- The traction off indicator turns ON.
- The message center displays the service stability system message.

Conditions for Clearing the DTC

The conditions for setting the DTC are no longer present and you use the scan tool Clear DTCs function.

LTV0500000006170

Fig. 60   Codes C0287, P1644 Or P1689: Delivered Torque Circuit (Part 1 of 3). 2002 Avalanche, Escalade, Escalade EXT, Suburban, Tahoe & Yukon

	Action	Values	Yes	No
6	1. Turn OFF the ignition. 　- For vehicles equipped with NW7, install a J 39700 100-pin breakout box using a J 39700-325 breakout box adaptor. Install the equipment between the EBCM and the EBCM harness connector. 　- For vehicles equipped with JL4, install a J 39700 100-pin breakout box using a J 39700-600 breakout box adaptor. Install the equipment between the EBCM and the EBCM harness connector. 2. Start the engine. 3. Use a DMM in order to measure the Hz frequency of the delivered torque signal. Does the frequency of the delivered torque signal measure within the specified range?	121-134 Hz	Go to Step 7	Go to Step 9
7	1. Turn OFF the ignition. 2. Inspect for poor connections at the harness connector of the EBCM. Did you find and correct the condition?	--	Go to Step 12	Go to Step 8
8	**Important:** Following EBCM replacement, use the scan tool to perform the Tire Size Calibration procedure. Replace the EBCM. Did you complete the replacement?	--	Go to Step 12	--
9	1. Turn ON the ignition. 2. Test the delivered torque signal circuit for a short to voltage. Did you find and correct the condition?	--	Go to Step 12	Go to Step 10
10	Inspect for poor connections at the harness connector of the PCM. Did you find and correct the condition?	--	Go to Step 12	Go to Step 11
11	**Important:** Perform the setup procedure for the PCM. Replace the PCM. Did you complete the replacement?	--	Go to Step 12	--
12	1. Use the scan tool in order to clear the DTCs. 2. Operate the vehicle within the Conditions for Running the DTC as specified in the supporting text. Does the DTC reset?	--	Go to Step 3	System OK

LTV0500000006172

Fig. 60   Codes C0287, P1644 Or P1689: Delivered Torque Circuit (Part 3 of 3). 2002 Avalanche, Escalade, Escalade EXT, Suburban, Tahoe & Yukon

Diagnostic Aids

Thoroughly inspect connections or circuitry that may cause an intermittent malfunction.

Test Description

The numbers below refer to the step numbers on the diagnostic table.

3. This step tests for voltage supplied to the PCM from the EBCM.

9. The PCM may be damaged if the delivered torque signal circuit is shorted to voltage.

Step	Action	Values	Yes	No
1	Did you perform the ABS Diagnostic System Check?	--	Go to Step 2	Go to Diagnostic System Check
2	1. Use the scan tool in order to clear the DTCs. 2. Operate the vehicle within the Conditions for Running the DTC as specified in the supporting text. Does the DTC set?	--	Go to Step 3	Go to Diagnostic Aids
3	1. Turn OFF the ignition. 2. Disconnect from the PCM, the harness connector containing the delivered torque signal circuit. 3. Turn ON the ignition. 4. Use a DMM in order to measure the voltage between the delivered torque signal circuit and a good ground. Does the voltage measure within the specified range?	4.75-5.25 V	Go to Step 5	Go to Step 4
4	Test the delivered torque signal circuit for an open, a short to voltage or a short to ground. Did you find and correct the condition?	--	Go to Step 12	Go to Step 7
5	1. Turn OFF the ignition. 2. Reconnect the PCM harness connector. 3. Start the engine. 4. Select the Traction Assist or VSES Data List on the scan tool. 5. Observe the Delivered Torque parameter on the scan tool. Is the duty cycle of the delivered torque signal is within the specified range?	25-95%	Go to Step 6	Go to Step 9

LTV0500000006171

Fig. 60   Codes C0287, P1644 Or P1689: Delivered Torque Circuit (Part 2 of 3). 2002 Avalanche, Escalade, Escalade EXT, Suburban, Tahoe & Yukon

Circuit Description

The EBCM supplies a reference voltage of 5 volts to the yaw rate sensor/lateral accelerometer and the master cylinder pressure sensor. The sensor supply voltage is monitored via an internal feedback circuit to the EBCM microprocessor.

Conditions for Running the DTC

The ignition is ON.

Conditions for Setting the DTC

The EBCM detects that the sensor supply voltage is less than 4.75 volts or greater than 5.25 volts for 200 milliseconds.

Action Taken When the DTC Sets

- The EBCM disables the VSES.
- The EBCM discontinues the output of the 5-volt reference signal to the external sensors.
- The message center displays the SERVICE STABILITY SYSTEM message.

Conditions for Clearing the DTC

The conditions for setting the DTC are no longer present and you use the scan tool Clear DTCs function.

Diagnostic Aids

Thoroughly inspect connections or circuitry that may cause an intermittent malfunction.

LTV0500000006173

Fig. 61   Code C0288: Brake Warning Lamp Circuit Shorted To B+ (Part 1 of 3). 2002 Avalanche, Escalade, Escalade EXT, Suburban, Tahoe & Yukon

Test Description

The numbers below refer to the step numbers on the diagnostic table.

3. This step tests for a shorted master cylinder pressure sensor.

4. This step tests for a shorted yaw rate sensor/lateral accelerometer.

Step	Action	Yes	No
1	Did you perform the ABS Diagnostic System Check?	Go to Step 2	Go to Diagnostic System Check
2	Use a scan tool in order to clear the DTCs. Does the DTC reset?	Go to Step 3	Go to Diagnostic Aids
3	1. Turn OFF the ignition. 2. Disconnect the master cylinder pressure sensor harness connector. 3. Turn ON the ignition. 4. Use a scan tool in order to clear the DTC. Does the DTC reset?	Go to Step 4	Go to Step 7
4	1. Turn OFF the ignition. 2. Reconnect the master cylinder pressure sensor harness connector. 3. Disconnect the yaw rate sensor/lateral accelerometer harness connector. 4. Turn ON the ignition. Does the DTC reset?	Go to Step 5	Go to Step 8
5	1. Turn OFF the ignition. 2. Disconnect from the EBCM, the harness connector containing both 5-volt reference circuits. 3. Test each 5-volt reference circuit for a short to ground. Did you find and correct the condition?	Go to Step 10	Go to Step 6

LTV0500000006174

Fig. 61   Code C0288: Brake Warning Lamp Circuit Shorted To B+ (Part 2 of 3). 2002 Avalanche, Escalade, Escalade EXT, Suburban, Tahoe & Yukon

Circuit Description

The powertrain control module (PCM) sends a state of health message to the EBCM within 5.5 seconds after the modules are powered up. This message is sent via serial data communications.

Conditions for Running the DTC

The ignition is ON.

Conditions for Setting the DTC

The EBCM fails to receive serial data from the PCM.

Action Taken When the DTC Sets

If equipped, the following actions may occur:

- The EBCM disables the TCS/VSES.
- The traction off indicator turns ON.
- The message center displays the service stability system message.

Conditions for Clearing the DTC

The conditions for setting the DTC are no longer present and you use the scan tool Clear DTCs function.

Step	Action	Yes	No
1	Did you perform the ABS Diagnostic System Check?	Check Scan Tool Does Not Communicate with Class 2 Device	Go to Diagnostic System Check

LTV0500000006176

Fig. 62   Codes C0290 Or C0292: Lost Communication With PCM. 2002 Avalanche, Escalade, Escalade EXT, Suburban, Tahoe & Yukon

Step	Action	Yes	No
6	1. Turn ON the ignition. 2. Test each 5-volt reference circuit for a short to voltage. Did you find and correct the condition?	Go to Step 10	Go to Step 9
7	Replace the master cylinder pressure sensor. Did you complete the replacement?	Go to Step 10	—
8	Replace the yaw rate sensor/lateral accelerometer. Did you complete the replacement?	Go to Step 10	—
9	**Important** Following EBCM replacement, use the scan tool to perform the Tire Size Calibration procedure. Replace the EBCM Did you complete the replacement?	Go to Step 10	—
10	1. Use the scan tool in order to clear the DTCs. 2. Operate the vehicle within the Conditions for Running the DTC as specified in the supporting text. Does the DTC reset?	Go to Step 3	System OK

LTV0500000006175

Fig. 61   Code C0288: Brake Warning Lamp Circuit Shorted To B+ (Part 3 of 3). 2002 Avalanche, Escalade, Escalade EXT, Suburban, Tahoe & Yukon

Circuit Description

The PCM sends engine/axle/tire IDs to the EBCM via serial data communications immediately after the modules are powered up.

Conditions for Running the DTC

The ignition is ON.

Conditions for Setting the DTC

The EBCM fails to receive serial data from the PCM.

Action Taken When the DTC Sets

If equipped, the following actions occur:

- The EBCM disables the TCS.
- The traction off indicator turns ON.

Conditions for Clearing the DTC

The conditions for setting the DTC are no longer present and you use the scan tool Clear DTCs function.

Step	Action	Yes	No
1	Did you perform the ABS Diagnostic System Check?	Check Scan Tool Does Not Communicate with Class 2 Device	Go to Diagnostic System Check

LTV0500000006177

Fig. 63   Code C0297: Powertrain Configuration Data Not Received. 2002 Avalanche, Escalade, Escalade EXT, Suburban, Tahoe & Yukon

Circuit Description

C0298

The powertrain control module (PCM) sends a state of health message to the EBCM via class 2 serial data communications.

P1571

The EBCM requests desired engine torque from the PCM via the requested torque signal circuit.

Conditions for Running the DTC

C0298

The ignition is ON.

P1571

- The ignition is ON.
- The engine is running at a speed greater than 500 RPM for 5-20 seconds.
- The EBCM has not set any current TCS related DTCs.

Conditions for Setting the DTC

C0298

The EBCM receives a state of health message informing the EBCM that the PCM has lost the ability to perform traction control.

P1571

The PCM receives an invalid requested torque signal for 3 seconds.

Action Taken When the DTC Sets

C0298

If equipped, the following actions may occur:

- The EBCM disables the TCS/VSES.
- The traction off indicator turns ON.
- The message center displays the SERVICE STABILITY SYSTEM message.

LTV0500000006178

Fig. 64 Codes C0298 Or P1571: Traction Control Fault (Part 1 of 4). 2002 Avalanche, Escalade, Escalade EXT, Suburban, Tahoe & Yukon

4	1. Turn OFF the ignition. 2. Disconnect from the EBCM, the harness connector containing the requested torque signal circuit. 3. Turn ON the ignition. 4. Use a DMM in order to measure the voltage between the requested torque signal circuit and a good ground. Does the voltage measure within the specified range?	4.75-5.25 V	Go to Step 5	Go to Step 7
5	1. Turn OFF the ignition. - For vehicles equipped with NW7, install a J 39700 100-pin breakout box using a J 39700-325 breakout box adaptor. Install the equipment between the EBCM and the EBCM harness connector. - For vehicles equipped with JL4, install a J 39700 100-pin breakout box using a J 39700-600 breakout box adaptor. Install the equipment between the EBCM and the EBCM harness connector. 2. Start the engine. 3. Use a DMM in order to measure the Hz frequency of the requested torque signal. Does the Hz frequency of the requested torque signal measure within the specified range?	121-134 Hz	Go to Step 6	Go to Step 9
6	Use the DMM in order to measure the duty cycle of the requested torque signal circuit. Does the duty cycle of the requested torque signal measure within the specified range?	40-95%	Go to Step 8	Go to Step 9
7	Test the requested torque signal circuit for an open, a short to ground or a short to voltage. Did you find and correct the condition?	--	Go to Step 12	Go to Step 8
8	Inspect for poor connections at the harness connector of the PCM. Did you find and correct the condition?	--	Go to Step 12	Go to Step 10
9	Inspect for poor connections at the harness connector of the EBCM. Did you find and correct the condition?	--	Go to Step 12	Go to Step 11

LTV0500000006180

Fig. 64 Codes C0298 Or P1571: Traction Control Fault (Part 3 of 4). 2002 Avalanche, Escalade, Escalade EXT, Suburban, Tahoe & Yukon

P1571

- The PCM sends a state of health message to the EBCM informing the EBCM that the PCM has lost the ability to perform traction control.
- The EBCM sets DTC C0298 as a current DTC for as long as the malfunction is present.

Conditions for Clearing the DTC

C0298

The conditions for setting the DTC are no longer present and you use the scan tool Clear DTCs function.

P1571

- The conditions for setting the DTC are no longer present and you use the scan tool Clear DTCs function.
- A history DTC clears automatically after 40 consecutive warm-up cycles without a PCM detected failure.

Diagnostic Aids

C0298

A requested torque signal malfunction is only one possible cause for the PCM to lose the ability to perform traction control. DTC C0298 may set due to engine overheating, throttle actuator control failure, loss of ignition timing control by the PCM, etc. If DTC P1571 has not set, refer to Diagnostic System Check - Engine Controls in Engine Controls

P1571

Thoroughly inspect connections or circuitry that may cause an intermittent malfunction.

Test Description

The numbers below refer to the step numbers on the diagnostic table.

4. This step tests for voltage supplied to the EBCM from the PCM.

5. This step verifies the EBCM is creating a requested torque signal with a valid Hz frequency.

6. This step verifies the EBCM is creating a requested torque signal with a valid duty cycle.

7. The EBCM may be damaged if the requested torque signal circuit is shorted to voltage.

Step	Action	Values	Yes	No
1	Did you perform the AES Diagnostic System Check?	--	Go to Step 2	Go to Diagnostic System Check
2	Is DTC P1571 set?	--	Go to Step 3	Go to Diagnostic Aids
3	1. Use a scan tool in order to clear the DTCs. 2. Operate the vehicle within the Conditions for Running DTC P1571 as specified in the supporting text. Do the DTCs set?	--	Go to Step 4	Go to Diagnostic Aids

LTV0500000006179

Fig. 64 Codes C0298 Or P1571: Traction Control Fault (Part 2 of 4). 2002 Avalanche, Escalade, Escalade EXT, Suburban, Tahoe & Yukon

10	**Important:** Perform the set up procedure for the PCM. Replace the PCM. Did you complete the replacement?	--	--	Go to Step 12
11	**Important:** Following EBCM replacement, use the scan tool to perform the Tire Size Calibration procedure. Replace the EBCM. Did you complete the replacement?	--	--	Go to Step 12
12	1. Use the scan tool in order to clear the DTCs. 2. Operate the vehicle within the Conditions for Running the DTC as specified in the supporting text. Do the DTCs reset?	--	Go to Step 4	System OK

LTV0500000006181

Fig. 64 Codes C0298 Or P1571: Traction Control Fault (Part 4 of 4). 2002 Avalanche, Escalade, Escalade EXT, Suburban, Tahoe & Yukon

Test Description

The numbers below refer to the step numbers on the diagnostic table.

1. This step ensures that the battery, the vehicle primary power, and the ground systems are functioning correctly.

3. Lack of communication may be due to a particular malfunction of a serial data circuit. The information in Scan Tool does not Communicate with Class 2 Device will provide a list of modules and the associated data network, no communication diagnostic link.

4. A module that is operating in the incorrect power mode based on key position may cause other vehicle symptoms and/or DTCs to set. The information in Power Mode Mismatch will correct the condition before checking for module DTCs or symptoms.

8. This step ensures that all data link communication DTCs are diagnosed before system level DTCs.

9. This step ensures that all ECU internal DTCs are diagnosed before other system level DTCs.

10. This step ensures that all device voltage DTCs are diagnosed before other system level DTCs.

Step	Action	Yes	No
1	Perform the following preliminary inspections: • Ensure that the battery is fully charged. • Ensure that the battery cables are clean and tight. • Inspect for any open fuses. • Inspect the easily accessible systems or the visible system components for obvious damage or conditions that could cause the symptom. • Ensure that the grounds are clean, tight, and in the correct location. • Inspect for aftermarket devices that could affect the operation of the system. • Search for applicable service bulletins. Did you find and correct the condition?	System OK	Go to Step 2

LTV0500000005242

Fig. 65   Diagnostic System Check (Part 1 of 3). 2003–06 Avalanche, Escalade, Escalade EXT, Suburban, Tahoe & Yukon

7	**Important:** Do not clear any DTCs unless instructed by a diagnostic procedure. Use the appropriate scan tool selections to obtain DTCs for each of the control modules. Does the scan tool display any DTCs?	Go to Step 8	Go to Step 12
8	Does the scan tool display any DTCs that begin with a "U"?	Go to Diagnostic Trouble Code (DTC) List	Go to Step 9
9	**Important:** If any of these DTCs are displayed, diagnose them before diagnosing any other DTCs or symptoms. Does the scan tool display DTC B1000, B1001, B1004, B1007, B1009, C0271, C0272, C0273, C0298, C0550, P0601, P0602, P0604, P0606, P2108, or P2610?	Go to Diagnostic Trouble Code (DTC) List	Go to Step 10
10	**Important:** If any of these DTCs are displayed, diagnose them before diagnosing any other DTCs or symptoms. Does the scan tool display DTC B1372, P0561, P0562, or P0563?	Go to Diagnostic Trouble Code (DTC) List	Go to Step 11
11	**Important:** If any of the remaining DTCs are powertrain DTCs, select Captured Info in order to store the powertrain DTC information with a scan tool. If multiple DTCs are stored, diagnose the DTCs in the following order 1. Component level DTCs, such as sensor DTCs, solenoid DTCs, and relay DTCs. 2. System level DTCs, such as misfire DTCs, EVAP system DTCs, and fuel trim DTCs. Diagnose the remaining DTCs.	Go to Diagnostic Trouble Code (DTC) List	--
12	Is the customers concern with inspection/maintenance (I/M) testing?	Go to Inspection/Maintenance (I/M) System Check	Go to Symptoms

LTV0500000005244

Fig. 65   Diagnostic System Check (Part 3 of 3). 2003–06 Avalanche, Escalade, Escalade EXT, Suburban, Tahoe & Yukon

2	Install a scan tool. Does the scan tool power up?	Go to Step 3	Check Scan Tool Does Not Power Up
3	1. Turn ON the ignition, with the engine OFF. 2. Attempt to establish communication with all of the control modules on the vehicle. Does the scan tool communicate with all of the expected vehicle control modules?	Go to Step 4	Check Scan Tool Does Not Communicate with Class 2 Device
4	**Important:** • To ensure that retained accessory power (RAP) mode is inactive, if equipped, open the driver door during the following step. • The engine may start during the following step. Turn OFF the engine as soon as you have observed the crank power mode. 1. Access the Power Mode parameter on the scan tool. 2. Rotate the ignition switch (operate the ignition mode switch) through all positions while observing the Power Mode parameter. Does the Power Mode parameter reading on the scan tool match the ignition switch position for all switch positions?	Go to Step 5	Check Power Mode Mismatch
5	Attempt to start the engine. Does the engine crank?	Go to Step 6	Go to Symptoms - Engine Electrical
6	Attempt to start the engine. Does the engine start and idle?	Go to Step 7	Go to Engine Cranks but Does Not Run

LTV0500000005243

Fig. 65   Diagnostic System Check (Part 2 of 3). 2003–06 Avalanche, Escalade, Escalade EXT, Suburban, Tahoe & Yukon

Circuit Description

As the wheels spin, each wheel speed sensor produces an AC signal. The electronic brake control module (EBCM) uses the frequency of the AC signals to calculate each wheel speed.

DTC Descriptors

This diagnostic procedure supports the following DTCs:

• DTC C0035 Left Front Wheel Speed Sensor Circuit

• DTC C0040 Right Front Wheel Speed Sensor Circuit

Conditions for Running the DTC

• The ignition is ON.

• The vehicle speed is greater than 13 km/h (8 mph).

Conditions for Setting the DTC

Any of the following conditions may cause the DTC to set:

• The EBCM detects an open wheel speed sensor circuit for 500 milliseconds.

• The EBCM detects a shorted wheel speed sensor circuit for 500 milliseconds.

• The EBCM detects the absence of a wheel speed sensor signal for 5 seconds. If more than one absent wheel speed sensor signal is detected, the condition must be present for 120 seconds to set DTCs.

• The EBCM detects an erratic wheel speed sensor signal for 200 milliseconds.

Action Taken When the DTC Sets

• The EBCM disables the ABS/traction control system (TCS)/vehicle stability enhancement system (VSES) and may disable the dynamic rear proportion (DRP), if more than one wheel speed sensor DTC is set.

• The ABS indicator turns ON.

• The traction off indicator turns ON.

• The message center displays the service stability system message.

• The brake warning indicator may turn ON.

• An ECE 13 response may occur. Refer to ABS Description and Operation for a complete description of ECE 13.

Conditions for Clearing the DTC

The Conditions for Setting the DTC are no longer present and you use the scan tool Clear DTCs function.

LTV0500000006222

Fig. 66   Codes C0035 Or C0040: Front Wheel Speed Sensor Circuit (Part 1 of 3). 2003–06 Avalanche, Escalade, Escalade EXT, Suburban, Tahoe & Yukon

Diagnostic Aids

Thoroughly inspect connections or circuitry that may cause an intermittent malfunction.

If the customer's concern is that the ABS indicator is ON only during humid conditions, such as rain, snow or vehicle wash, thoroughly inspect the wheel speed sensor circuits for signs of water intrusion. Use the following procedure in order to help isolate the problem area:

1. Spray the suspected area with a 5 percent salt water solution.
2. Operate the vehicle at a speed greater than 13 km/h (8 mph) for at least 30 seconds.

Repair or replace the suspect harness if the DTC sets.

Step	Action	Values	Yes	No
1	Did you perform the Diagnostic System Check - Vehicle?	--	Go to Step 2	Go to Diagnostic System Check
2	1. Use the scan tool to clear the DTCs. 2. Turn OFF the ignition for 5 seconds. 3. Turn ON the ignition. 4. Operate the vehicle within the Conditions for Running the DTC, as specified in the supporting text. Does the DTC reset?	13 km/h (8 mph)	Go to Step 3	Go to Diagnostic Aids
3	1. Turn OFF the ignition. 2. Raise and support the vehicle. 3. Disconnect the wheel speed sensor connector. 4. Use a DMM in order to measure the resistance across the wheel speed sensor. Does the resistance measure within the specified range?	700-10,000 ohms	Go to Step 4	Go to Step 8

LTV0500000006223

Fig. 66 Codes C0035 Or C0040: Front Wheel Speed Sensor Circuit (Part 2 of 3). 2003–06 Avalanche, Escalade, Escalade EXT, Suburban, Tahoe & Yukon

Circuit Description

As the wheel spins, the wheel speed sensor produces an AC signal. The electronic brake control module (EBCM) uses the frequency of the AC signal to calculate the wheel speed.

DTC Descriptors

This diagnostic procedure supports the following DTCs:

- DTC C0045 Left Rear Wheel Speed Sensor Circuit
- DTC C0050 Right Rear Wheel Speed Sensor Circuit

Conditions for Running the DTC

- The ignition is ON.
- The vehicle speed is greater than 13 km/h (8 mph).

Conditions for Setting the DTC

Any of the following conditions may cause the DTC to set:

- The EBCM detects an open wheel speed sensor circuit for 500 milliseconds.
- The EBCM detects a shorted wheel speed sensor circuit for 500 milliseconds.
- The EBCM detects the absence of a wheel speed sensor signal for 5 seconds. If more than one absent wheel speed sensor signal is detected, the condition must be present for 120 seconds to set DTCs.
- The EBCM detects an erratic wheel speed sensor signal for 200 milliseconds.

Action Taken When the DTC Sets

- The EBCM disables antilock brake system (ABS)/traction control system (TCS)/vehicle stability enhancement system (VSES) and may disable dynamic rear proportion (DRP) if more than one wheel speed sensor DTC is set.
- The ABS indicator turns ON.
- The traction OFF indicator turns ON.
- The message center displays the service stability system message.
- The brake warning indicator may turn ON.
- An ECE 13 response may occur. Refer to ABS Description and Operation for a complete description of ECE 13.

Conditions for Clearing the DTC

The Conditions for Setting the DTC are no longer present and you use the scan tool Clear DTCs function.

LTV0500000006225

Fig. 67 Codes C0045 Or C0050: Rear Wheel Speed Sensor Circuit (Part 1 of 3). 2003–06 Avalanche, Escalade, Escalade EXT, Suburban, Tahoe & Yukon

Step	Action	Values	Yes	No
4	1. Slowly spin the wheel by hand. 2. Use a DMM in order to measure the AC voltage across the wheel speed sensor as the wheel spins. Does the AC voltage measure greater than the specified value?	100 mV	Go to Step 5	Go to Step 8
5	Inspect for poor connections at the harness connector of the wheel speed sensor. Did you find and correct the condition?	--	Go to Step 10	Go to Step 6
6	1. Disconnect the electronic brake control module (EBCM) harness connector. 2. Test the wheel speed sensor circuits for the following: - An open - A short to ground - A short to voltage - Shorted together Did you find and correct the condition?	--	Go to Step 10	Go to Step 7
7	Inspect for poor connections at the harness connector for the EBCM. Did you find and correct the condition?	--	Go to Step 10	Go to Step 9
8	Replace the wheel speed sensor. Did you complete the replacement?	--	Go to Step 10	--
9	Replace the EBCM. Did you complete the replacement?	--	Go to Step 10	--
10	1. Use the scan tool Clear All Class 2 DTCs function to clear all of the DTCs from all modules. 2. Turn OFF the ignition for 5 seconds. 3. Turn ON the ignition. 4. Operate the vehicle within the Conditions for Running the DTC, as specified in the supporting text. Does the DTC reset?		Go to Step 2	System OK

LTV0500000006224

Fig. 66 Codes C0035 Or C0040: Front Wheel Speed Sensor Circuit (Part 3 of 3). 2003–06 Avalanche, Escalade, Escalade EXT, Suburban, Tahoe & Yukon

Diagnostic Aids

Thoroughly inspect connections or circuitry that may cause an intermittent malfunction.

If the customer's concern is that the ABS indicator is ON only during humid conditions, such as rain, snow or vehicle wash, thoroughly inspect the wheel speed sensor circuits for signs of water intrusion. Use the following procedure in order to help isolate the problem area:

1. Spray the suspected area with a 5 percent salt water solution.
2. Operate the vehicle at a speed greater than 13 km/h (8 mph) for at least 30 seconds.

Repair or replace the suspect harness if the DTC sets.

Step	Action	Values	Yes	No
1	Did you perform the Diagnostic System Check - Vehicle?	--	Go to Step 2	Go to Diagnostic System Check
2	1. Use the scan tool to clear the DTCs. 2. Turn OFF the ignition for 5 seconds. 3. Turn ON the ignition. 4. Operate the vehicle within the Conditions for Running the DTC, as specified in the supporting text. Does the DTC reset?	13 km/h (8 mph)	Go to Step 3	Go to Diagnostic Aids
3	1. Turn OFF the ignition. 2. Raise and support the vehicle. 3. Disconnect the wheel speed sensor connector. 4. Use a DMM in order to measure the resistance across the wheel speed sensor. Does the resistance measure within the specified range?	3,500-6,800 ohms	Go to Step 4	Go to Step 9
4	1. Slowly spin the wheel by hand. 2. Use a DMM in order to measure the AC voltage across the wheel speed sensor as the wheel spins. Does the AC voltage measure greater than the specified value?	100 mV	Go to Step 5	Go to Step 8

LTV0500000006226

Fig. 67 Codes C0045 Or C0050: Rear Wheel Speed Sensor Circuit (Part 2 of 3). 2003–06 Avalanche, Escalade, Escalade EXT, Suburban, Tahoe & Yukon

Step	Action		Yes	No
5	Inspect for poor connections at the harness connector of the wheel speed sensor. Did you find and correct the condition?		Go to Step 11	Go to Step 6

6	1. Disconnect the electronic brake control module (EBCM) harness connector.
	2. Test the wheel speed sensor circuits for the following:
	  – An open
	  – A short to ground
	  – A short to voltage
	  – Shorted together
	
	Refer to Circuit Testing and Wiring Repairs.
	
	Did you find and correct the condition?
			Go to Step 11	Go to Step 7

7	Inspect for poor connections at the harness connector for the EBCM. Did you find and correct the condition?		Go to Step 11	Go to Step 10
8	1. Remove the wheel speed sensor from the axle tube. 2. Inspect the wheel speed sensor tone ring, which is located on the axle, for damage. Did you find and correct the condition?		Go to Step 11	Go to Step 9
9	Replace the wheel speed sensor. Did you complete the replacement?		Go to Step 11	--
10	**Important:** Following EBCM replacement, perform the set-up procedure for the EBCM and perform the Yaw Rate Reference Table Reset Procedure. Use the scan tool to perform the Tire Size Calibration procedure. Replace the EBCM. Did you complete the replacement?		Go to Step 11	--
11	1. Use the scan tool Clear All Class 2 DTCs function to clear all of the DTCs from all modules. 2. Turn OFF the ignition for 5 seconds. 3. Turn ON the ignition. 4. Operate the vehicle within the Conditions for Running the DTC, as specified in the supporting text. Does the DTC reset?		Go to Step 2	System OK

LTV0500000006227

Fig. 67 Codes C0045 Or C0050: Rear Wheel Speed Sensor Circuit (Part 3 of 3). 2003–06 Avalanche, Escalade, Escalade EXT, Suburban, Tahoe & Yukon

Step	Action	Values	Yes	No
1	Did you perform the Diagnostic System Check - Vehicle?	--	Go to Step 2	Go to Diagnostic System Check -
2	1. Use a scan tool to clear the DTCs. 2. Turn OFF the ignition for 5 seconds. 3. Operate the vehicle within the Conditions for Running the DTC, as specified in the supporting text. Does the DTC set?	--	Go to Step 3	Go to Diagnostic Aids
3	1. Disconnect the electronic brake control module (EBCM) harness connector. 2. Connect a test lamp between the battery positive voltage circuit to the ABS pump motor, and a good ground. Does the test lamp illuminate?	--	Go to Step 4	Go to Step 5
4	**Important:** Using a test lamp other than that which is approved for performing diagnostic procedures on GM vehicles may cause an inaccurate result when performing this step. It is also imperative that the ground to which the test lamp is connected be clean and provide no resistance to battery ground. With the test lamp still connected and illuminated, use a DMM to measure the voltage between the high side of the test lamp and a good ground. Does the voltage measure greater than the specified value?	12 V	Go to Step 6	Go to Step 5
5	Repair the high resistance in the battery positive voltage circuit. Ensure that total circuit resistance is not greater than the specified value. Did you complete the repair?	0.2 ohms	Go to Step 13	--
6	Test the ABS motor ground circuit for an open or high resistance. Did you find and correct the condition?	--	Go to Step 13	Go to Step 7

LTV0500000006229

Fig. 68 Code C0110: Pump Motor Circuit (Part 2 of 3). 2003–06 Avalanche, Escalade, Escalade EXT, Suburban, Tahoe & Yukon

Circuit Description

Ground is continuously supplied to the low side of the ABS pump motor. The electronic brake control module (EBCM) activates the ABS pump by supplying battery voltage to the high side of the motor.

DTC Descriptor

This diagnostic procedure supports the following DTC:

DTC C0110 Pump Motor Circuit

Conditions for Running the DTC

- The ignition is ON.
- The vehicle speed is greater than 6 km/h (4 mph).

Conditions for Setting the DTC

The EBCM detects an open pump motor circuit, a shorted pump motor, or a seized pump motor or ABS pump.

Action Taken When the DTC Sets

- The EBCM disables the ABS/vehicle stability enhancement system (VSES).
- The traction control system (TCS) operates with engine torque reduction ability only.
- The ABS indicator turns ON.
- The message center displays the service stability system message.

Conditions for Clearing the DTC

The Conditions for Setting the DTC are no longer present and you use the scan tool Clear DTCs function.

Diagnostic Aids

Separate the EBCM from the brake pressure module (BPMV) in order to inspect for corrosion or any other condition that may cause a poor connection at the pump motor connector.

Test Description

The number below refers to the step number on the diagnostic table.

4. This step tests for high resistance in the battery positive voltage circuit by verifying that an excessive voltage drop does not occur in the circuit.

LTV0500000006228

Fig. 68 Code C0110: Pump Motor Circuit (Part 1 of 3). 2003–06 Avalanche, Escalade, Escalade EXT, Suburban, Tahoe & Yukon

Step	Action		Yes	No
7	1. Turn OFF the ignition. 2. Separate the EBCM from the brake pressure modulator valve (BPMV). 3. Connect a test lamp between the ABS pump motor power and ground circuits at the pump motor connector of the EBCM. 4. Turn ON the ignition. 5. Use the scan tool in order to clear the DTCs. Does the DTC clear and then remain cleared while the test lamp is connected?		Go to Step 8	Go to Step 10
8	1. Select the vehicle stability enhancement system (VSES) Special Functions menu on the scan tool. 2. Command the ABS Motor ON. Does the test lamp illuminate for 5 seconds and then turn OFF?		Go to Step 9	Go to Step 12
9	Inspect for poor connections at the pump motor connector. Did you find and correct the condition?		Go to Step 13	Go to Step 11
10	Replace the EBCM. Did you complete the replacement?		Go to Step 13	--
11	Replace the BPMV. Did you complete the replacement?		Go to Step 13	--
12	**Important:** Following EBCM replacement, perform the set-up procedure for the EBCM and perform the Yaw Rate Reference Table Reset Procedure. Use the scan tool to perform the Tire Size Calibration procedure. • Replace the EBCM. • Replace the BPMV. Did you complete the replacements?		Go to Step 13	--
13	1. Use the scan tool Clear All Class 2 DTCs function to clear all of the DTCs from all modules. 2. Turn OFF the ignition for 5 seconds. 3. Turn ON the ignition. 4. Operate the vehicle within the Conditions for Running the DTC, as specified in the supporting text. Does the DTC reset?		Go to Step 3	System OK

LTV0500000006230

Fig. 68 Code C0110: Pump Motor Circuit (Part 3 of 3). 2003–06 Avalanche, Escalade, Escalade EXT, Suburban, Tahoe & Yukon

Circuit Description

The master cylinder pressure sensor is a potentiometer located within the brake pedal modulator valve (BPMV). The master cylinder pressure sensor signal to the electronic brake control module (EBCM) increases as hydraulic pressure in the front brake circuit increases.

DTC Descriptor

This diagnostic procedure supports the following DTC:

DTC C0131 Antilock Brake System (ABS)/Traction Control System (TCS) Pressure Circuit

Conditions for Running the DTC

- The ignition is ON.
- The vehicle stability enhancement system (VSES) sensors have been successfully initialized or the message center has displayed the stability system disabled message due to an unsuccessful initialization attempt. Refer to ABS Description and Operation for a complete explanation of VSES sensor initialization.
- The vehicle is being driven relatively straight and level at a speed greater than 36 km/h (23 mph).
- The transmission is not shifted into NEUTRAL or low gear.
- The parking brake is released.

Conditions for Setting the DTC

Any of the following conditions may cause the DTC to set:

- The EBCM detects open master cylinder pressure sensor circuitry.
- The EBCM detects shorted master cylinder pressure sensor circuitry.
- The master cylinder pressure sensor self-test, which occurs at power-up, fails.
- The zero-pressure signal voltage is not within an acceptable range.
- The master cylinder pressure is not within an expected tolerance based on deceleration rate and other data available to the EBCM.

Action Taken When the DTC Sets

- The EBCM disables the VSES.
- The TCS operates with engine torque reduction only.
- The message center displays the service stability system message.

Conditions for Clearing the DTC

The conditions for setting the DTC are no longer present and you use the scan tool Clear DTCs function.

LTV0500000006231

Fig. 69   Code C0131: ABS/TCS Pressure Circuit (Part 1 of 3). 2003–06 Avalanche, Escalade, Escalade EXT, Suburban, Tahoe & Yukon

	Action		
5	1. Select the VSES Data Display function on the scan tool. 2. Observe the Brake Switch Status parameter while pressing and releasing the brake pedal. Does the Brake Switch Status change while pressing and releasing the brake?	Go to Step 6	Go to DTC C0161
6	1. Remove the electronic brake control module (EBCM) from the vehicle. 2. Inspect the master cylinder pressure sensor connector, within the EBCM, for damage or corrosion. Is there connector damage or corrosion present?	Go to Step 7	Go to Step 8
7	Replace the EBCM. Did you complete the replacement?	Go to Step 9	—
8	Important: Following EBCM replacement, perform the set-up procedure for the EBCM and perform the Yaw Rate Reference Table Reset Procedure. Use the scan tool to perform the Tire Size Calibration procedure. - Replace the EBCM. - Replace the brake pressure modulator valve (BPMV). Did you complete the replacements?	Go to Step 9	—
9	1. Use the scan tool Clear All Class 2 DTCs function to clear all of the DTCs from all modules. 2. Turn OFF the ignition for 5 seconds. 3. Turn ON the ignition. 4. Operate the vehicle within the Conditions for Running the DTC, as specified in the supporting text. Does the DTC reset?	Go to Step 2	System OK

LTV0500000006233

Fig. 69   Code C0131: ABS/TCS Pressure Circuit (Part 3 of 3). 2003–06 Avalanche, Escalade, Escalade EXT, Suburban, Tahoe & Yukon

Diagnostic Aids

Thoroughly inspect connections or circuitry that may cause an intermittent malfunction.

Test Description

The number below refers to the step number on the diagnostic table.

3. This step is required for vehicles equipped with a hydro-boost brake assist system only. If the vehicle being serviced has vacuum assisted brakes, proceed to step 4.

Step	Action	Yes	No
	Important: - Use the scan tool to read both current and history DTCs before proceeding. - If DTC C0292 is set, diagnose that DTC before proceeding with diagnostics for C0131. - If DTC C0161 is set, diagnose that DTC before proceeding with diagnostics for C0131.		
1	Did you perform the Diagnostic System Check - Vehicle?	Go to Step 2	Go to Diagnostic System Check
2	Inspect the vehicle for the following and ensure that there is no base brake failure: - Dragging brakes - Faulty parking brake switch - Brake fluid leakage - Air in the hydraulic system - Seized brake calipers - Swollen, kinked or otherwise damaged brake hoses Did you find and correct the condition?	Go to Step 9	Go to Step 3
3	Drive the vehicle in order to verify that the brakes do not self-apply during turning maneuvers. Do the brakes self-apply during turning maneuvers?	Go to Symptoms -	Go to Step 4
4	1. Use the scan tool to clear the DTCs. 2. Turn OFF the ignition for 5 seconds. 3. Turn ON the ignition. 4. Operate the vehicle within the Conditions for Running the DTC, as specified in the supporting text. Does the DTC reset?	Go to Step 5	Go to Diagnostic Aids

LTV0500000006232

Fig. 69   Code C0131: ABS/TCS Pressure Circuit (Part 2 of 3). 2003–06 Avalanche, Escalade, Escalade EXT, Suburban, Tahoe & Yukon

Circuit Description

The brake switch informs the electronic brake control module (EBCM) when the brake is depressed. The brake switch is normally closed, supplying 12 volts to the EBCM when the brake is released. When the brake pedal is pressed, voltage on the torque converter clutch (TCC) brake switch signal circuit is 0 volts.

DTC Descriptor

This diagnostic procedure supports the following DTC:

DTC C0161 Antilock Brake System (ABS)/Traction Control System (TCS) Brake Switch

Conditions for Running the DTC

Any of the following conditions may cause the DTC to run:

- The vehicle accelerates from 0 km/h (0 mph) to a speed greater than 56 km/h (35 mph).
- The vehicle experiences an ABS event involving all hydraulic circuits.
- The EBCM detects that the master cylinder pressure is greater than 1400 kPa (200 PSI) and that the vehicle is decelerating.

Conditions for Setting the DTC

Any of the following conditions may cause the DTC to set:

- Voltage on the TCC brake switch signal circuit is always low.
- Voltage on the TCC brake switch signal circuit is always high.
- Voltage on the TCC brake switch signal circuit is high for 0.5-4 seconds when voltage is expected to be low.

Action Taken When the DTC Sets

- The EBCM disables the vehicle stability enhancement system (VSES).
- The TCS operates with engine torque reduction capability only.
- The message center displays the service stability system message.

Conditions for Clearing the DTC

The Conditions for Setting the DTC are no longer present and you use the scan tool Clear DTCs function.

LTV0500000006234

Fig. 70   Code C0161: ABS/TCS Brake Switch (Part 1 of 3). 2003–06 Avalanche, Escalade, Escalade EXT, Suburban, Tahoe & Yukon

Diagnostic Aids

Thoroughly inspect connections or circuitry that may cause an intermittent malfunction.

Test Description

The numbers below refer to the step numbers on the diagnostic table.

4. This step tests for a shorted stop lamp switch.

5. This step tests for an open stop lamp switch.

Step	Action	Yes	No
1	Did you perform the Diagnostic System Check - Vehicle?	Go to Step 2	Go to Diagnostic System Check -
2	1. Select the ABS Data Display function on the scan tool. 2. Observe the Brake Switch Status on the scan tool. Does the scan tool display Off?	Go to Step 3	Go to Step 5
3	1. Apply the brake. 2. Observe the Brake Switch Status on the scan tool. Does the scan tool display On?	Go to Diagnostic Aids	Go to Step 4
4	1. Turn OFF the ignition. 2. Disconnect the stop lamp switch. 3. Turn ON the ignition. 4. Observe the Brake Switch Status on the scan tool. Does the scan tool display On?	Go to Step 9	Go to Step 7
5	1. Turn OFF the ignition. 2. Disconnect the stop lamp switch. 3. Connect a fused jumper wire between the ignition 3 voltage circuit and the torque converter clutch (TCC) brake switch signal circuit at the stop lamp switch harness connector. 4. Turn ON the ignition. 5. Observe the Brake Switch Status on the scan tool. Does the scan tool display Off?	Go to Step 9	Go to Step 6

LTV0500000006235

Fig. 70 Code C0161: ABS/TCS Brake Switch (Part 2 of 3). 2003–06 Avalanche, Escalade, Escalade EXT, Suburban, Tahoe & Yukon

Circuit Description

The electronic brake control module (EBCM) supplies 5 volts to the yaw rate sensor/lateral accelerometer. When the vehicle is not moving, or is being driven in a stable, straight line, lateral acceleration is 0 m/sec/sec (0 ft/sec/sec) and the lateral accelerometer signal voltage is very near 2.5 volts. This is referred to as lateral accelerometer bias voltage. Making a turning maneuver causes the lateral accelerometer signal voltage to increase, or decrease, depending on the direction of the turn. The sharper the turn, the greater the change in signal voltage.

DTC Descriptor

This diagnostic procedure supports the following DTC:

DTC C0186 Lateral Accelerometer Circuit

Conditions for Running the DTC

- The ignition is ON.
- The vehicle stability enhancement system (VSES) sensors have been successfully initialized or the message center has displayed the stability system disabled message due to an unsuccessful initialization attempt.
- The vehicle is being driven relatively straight and level at a speed greater than 11 km/h (7 mph), before performing a stable turning maneuver.

Conditions for Setting the DTC

Any of the following conditions may cause the DTC to set:

- Open lateral accelerometer circuitry is detected.
- Shorted lateral accelerometer circuitry is detected.
- An erratic lateral accelerometer signal is detected.
- The EBCM detects that the lateral accelerometer sensor signal does not correspond with signals from other sensors.

Action Taken When the DTC Sets

- The EBCM disables the VSES.
- The message center displays the service stability system message.

Conditions for Clearing the DTC

The conditions for setting the DTC are no longer present and you use the scan tool Clear DTCs function.

LTV0500000006237

Fig. 71 Code C0186: Lateral Accelerometer Circuit (Part 1 of 3). 2003–06 Avalanche, Escalade, Escalade EXT, Suburban, Tahoe & Yukon

Step	Action	Yes	No
6	Test the ignition 3 voltage circuit and the TCC brake switch signal circuit for an open or a short to ground. Did you find and correct the condition?	Go to Step 12	Go to Step 8
7	Test the TCC brake switch signal circuit for a short to voltage. Did you find and correct the condition?	Go to Step 12	Go to Step 8
8	Inspect for poor connections at the harness connector of the electronic brake control module (EBCM). Did you find and correct the condition?	Go to Step 12	Go to Step 10
9	Inspect for poor connections at the harness connector of the stop lamp switch. Did you find and correct the condition?	Go to Step 12	Go to Step 11
10	Replace the EBCM. Did you complete the replacement?	Go to Step 12	--
11	Replace the stop lamp switch. Did you complete the replacement?	Go to Step 12	--
12	1. Use the scan tool Clear All Class 2 DTCs function to clear all of the DTCs from all modules. 2. Turn OFF the ignition for 5 seconds. 3. Turn ON the ignition. 4. Operate the vehicle within the Conditions for Running the DTC, as specified in the supporting text. Does the DTC reset?	Go to Step 2	System OK

LTV0500000006236

Fig. 70 Code C0161: ABS/TCS Brake Switch (Part 3 of 3). 2003–06 Avalanche, Escalade, Escalade EXT, Suburban, Tahoe & Yukon

Diagnostic Aids

- Inspect the vehicle for proper wheel alignment. Ensure the vehicle does not pull toward the left or right while driving straight forward on a level surface.
- Communicate with the customer to determine the conditions under which the message center displays the Service Stability System message. Learning the conditions under which the DTC sets may help you duplicate the failure.
- Use the Snapshot function on the scan tool in order to assist you in locating an intermittent malfunction.

Test Description

The numbers below refer to the step numbers on the diagnostic table.

3. This step tests the sensor circuitry in the high voltage range.

4. This step tests the sensor circuitry in the low voltage range.

Step	Action	Values	Yes	No
Important:	• If DTC C0292 is set, diagnose C0292 before proceeding with diagnostics for C0186. • If DTC C0196 is set, diagnose C0196 before proceeding with diagnostics for C0186. • Always use connector test adapters when performing tests to avoid damage to delicate connector terminals. • Do not turn OFF the ignition during this diagnostic procedure unless the step in the table instructs you to do so. The scan tool may display some incorrect data if the ignition is cycled.			
1	Did you perform the Diagnostic System Check - Vehicle?	--	Go to Step 2	Go to Diagnostic System Check
2	1. Use the scan tool to clear the DTCs. 2. Turn OFF the ignition for 5 seconds. 3. Turn ON the ignition. 4. Operate the vehicle within the Conditions for Running the DTC, as specified in the supporting text. Does the DTC reset?	--	Go to Step 3	Go to Diagnostic Aids
3	1. Turn ON the ignition. 2. Disconnect the yaw rate sensor/lateral accelerometer harness connector. 3. Select the VSES Data Display function on the scan tool. 4. Connect a 3-amp fused jumper wire between the yaw rate sensor/lateral accelerometer 5-volt reference circuit and the lateral accelerometer signal circuit. 5. Observe the Lateral Accelerometer Sensor Input on the scan tool. Is the Lateral Accelerometer Sensor Input voltage greater than the specified value?	4.4 V	Go to Step 4	Go to Step 5

LTV0500000006238

Fig. 71 Code C0186: Lateral Accelerometer Circuit (Part 2 of 3). 2003–06 Avalanche, Escalade, Escalade EXT, Suburban, Tahoe & Yukon

Step	Action	Values	Yes	No
4	1. Remove the fused jumper wire from the yaw rate sensor/lateral accelerometer harness connector. 2. Observe the Lateral Accelerometer Sensor Input on the scan tool. Is the Lateral Accelerometer Sensor Input voltage less than the specified value?	0.6 V	Go to Step 6	Go to Step 9
5	Test the lateral accelerometer signal circuit for the following conditions: • An open • A high resistance • A short to ground Refer to Circuit Testing and Wiring Repairs . Did you find and correct the condition?	--	Go to Step 10	Go to Step 7
6	1. Inspect for poor connections at the harness connector of the yaw rate sensor/lateral accelerometer. 2. Ensure the yaw rate sensor/lateral accelerometer is mounted securely and that the mounting bracket is not bent or otherwise damaged. Did you find and correct the condition?	--	Go to Step 10	Go to Step 8
7	Inspect for poor connections at the harness connector of the electronic brake control module (EBCM). Did you find and correct the condition?	--	Go to Step 10	Go to Step 9
8	Important: The Yaw Rate Reference Table Reset Procedure must be performed when you are instructed to do so during the Yaw Rate Sensor/Lateral Accelerometer Replacement procedure. Replace the yaw rate sensor/lateral accelerometer. Did you complete the replacement?	--	Go to Step 10	--
9	Replace the EBCM. Did you complete the replacement?	--	Go to Step 10	--
10	1. Use the scan tool Clear All Class 2 DTCs function to clear all of the DTCs from all modules. 2. Turn OFF the ignition for 5 seconds. 3. Turn ON the ignition. 4. Operate the vehicle within the Conditions for Running the DTC, as specified in the supporting text. Does the DTC reset?	--	Go to Step 3	System OK

LTV0500000006239

Fig. 71   Code C0186: Lateral Accelerometer Circuit (Part 3 of 3). 2003–06 Avalanche, Escalade, Escalade EXT, Suburban, Tahoe & Yukon

Action Taken When the DTC Sets

• The EBCM disables the VSES.
• The message center displays the service stability system message.

Conditions for Clearing the DTC

The conditions for setting the DTC are no longer present and you use the scan tool Clear DTCs function.

Diagnostic Aids

• The following scenario may cause this DTC to set when no actual malfunction exists:
  - The vehicle is driven in a straight line in reverse at a speed greater than 13 km/h (8 mph).
  - The transmission is shifted into NEUTRAL while the vehicle continues to coast backward.
  - A turning maneuver is performed after the above conditions are met and the vehicle speed is still greater than 13 km/h (8 mph).
• This DTC may also set falsely if the yaw rate sensor is replaced without first following the diagnostic table below. Whenever a new yaw rate sensor is installed, the old sensor must be disconnected, the ignition turned ON for 5 seconds and then OFF, and then the new sensor connected.
• Inspect the vehicle for proper wheel alignment. Ensure the vehicle does not pull toward the left or right while driving straight forward on a level surface.
• Communicate with the customer to determine the conditions under which the message center displays the service stability system message. Learning the conditions under which the DTC sets may help you duplicate the failure.
• Use the Snapshot function on the scan tool in order to assist you in locating an intermittent malfunction.

Test Description

The number below refers to the step number on the diagnostic table.

12. This step tests for a shorted resistor in the EBCM or a short to voltage within the circuit, by verifying that a large voltage drop occurs in the circuit when the test lamp is placed in parallel with the DMM.

Step	Action	Values	Yes	No
Important:				
• If DTC C0292 is set, diagnose C0292 before proceeding with diagnostics for C0196.				
• Always use connector test adapters when performing tests to avoid damage to delicate connector terminals.				
• Do not turn OFF the ignition during this diagnostic procedure unless the step in the table instructs you to do so. The scan tool may display some incorrect data if the ignition is cycled.				

LTV0500000006241

Fig. 72   Code C0196: Yaw Rate Circuit (Part 2 of 5). 2003–06 Avalanche, Escalade, Escalade EXT, Suburban, Tahoe & Yukon

Circuit Description

The electronic brake control module (EBCM) supplies 5 volts to the yaw rate sensor/lateral accelerometer. When the vehicle is not moving, or is being driven in a stable, straight line, yaw rate is 0 degrees/second and the yaw rate sensor signal voltage is very near 2.5 volts. This is referred to as sensor bias voltage. Performing a turning maneuver causes the yaw rate sensor signal voltage to increase, or decrease, depending on the direction of the turn. The sharper the turn, the greater the change in signal voltage. Since the yaw rate signal is affected by temperature, the EBCM also monitors a Hz frequency signal from the yaw rate sensor/lateral accelerometer which is proportionate to the approximate temperature of the yaw rate sensor.

DTC Descriptor

This diagnostic procedure supports the following DTC:

DTC C0196 Yaw Rate Circuit

Conditions for Running the DTC

• The ignition is ON.
• The vehicle stability enhancement system (VSES) sensors have been successfully initialized or the message center has displayed the stability system disabled message due to an unsuccessful initialization attempt.
• The vehicle is being driven relatively straight and level at a speed greater than 11 km/h (7 mph), before performing a stable turning maneuver.

Conditions for Setting the DTC

Any of the following conditions may cause the DTC to set:

• Open yaw rate sensor circuitry is detected.
• Shorted yaw rate sensor circuitry is detected.
• An erratic yaw rate sensor signal is detected.
• The EBCM detects that the yaw rate sensor signal does not correspond with signals from other sensors.
• The EBCM detects that the yaw rate sensor frequency signal is not within the valid range.
• A voltage near 5 volts is detected on the yaw rate sensor test circuit at all times.
• A voltage near 0 volts is detected on the yaw rate sensor test circuit at all times.

LTV0500000006240

Fig. 72   Code C0196: Yaw Rate Circuit (Part 1 of 5). 2003–06 Avalanche, Escalade, Escalade EXT, Suburban, Tahoe & Yukon

	Action	Values	Yes	No
1	Did you perform the Diagnostic System Check - Vehicle?	--	Go to Step 2	Go to Diagnostic System Check
2	1. Use the scan tool to clear the DTCs. 2. Turn OFF the ignition for 5 seconds. 3. Turn ON the ignition. 4. Operate the vehicle within the Conditions for Running the DTC, as specified in the supporting text. Does the DTC reset?	--	Go to Step 3	Go to Diagnostic Aids
3	1. Turn ON the ignition. 2. Disconnect the yaw rate sensor/lateral accelerometer harness connector. 3. Select the VSES Data Display function on the scan tool. 4. Observe the Yaw Rate Sensor Input on the scan tool. Is the Yaw Rate Sensor Input less than the specified value?	0.6 V	Go to Step 4	Go to Step 19
4	1. Connect a fused jumper wire between the yaw rate sensor/lateral accelerometer 5-volt reference circuit and the yaw rate signal circuit. 2. Observe the Yaw Rate Sensor Input on the scan tool. Is the Yaw Rate Sensor Input greater than the specified value?	4.4 V	Go to Step 5	Go to Step 7
5	1. Disconnect the fused jumper wire. 2. Use a DMM to measure the voltage between the yaw rate sensor/lateral accelerometer 5-volt reference circuit and the yaw rate sensor/lateral accelerometer low reference circuit. Does the voltage measure greater than the specified value?	4.75 V	Go to Step 9	Go to Step 6
6	Test the yaw rate sensor/lateral accelerometer low reference circuit for an open. Did you find and correct the condition?	--	Go to Step 20	Go to Step 17

LTV0500000006242

Fig. 72   Code C0196: Yaw Rate Circuit (Part 3 of 5). 2003–06 Avalanche, Escalade, Escalade EXT, Suburban, Tahoe & Yukon

7	Test the yaw rate signal circuit for the following conditions: • An open • A high resistance • A short to ground Did you find and correct the condition?	—	Go to Step 20	Go to Step 8
8	Test the yaw rate sensor/lateral accelerometer 5-volt reference circuit for a high resistance or an open. Did you find and correct the condition?	—	Go to Step 20	Go to Step 17
9	Use a DMM to measure the voltage on the yaw rate frequency circuit. Does the voltage measure greater than the specified value?	4.75 V	Go to Step 10	Go to Step 13
10	Use a DMM to measure the voltage on the yaw rate sensor test circuit. Does the voltage measure greater than the specified value?	4.75 V	Go to Step 11	Go to Step 15
11	1. Turn OFF the ignition. 2. Reconnect the yaw rate sensor/lateral accelerometer harness connector. 3. Disconnect the electronic brake control module (EBCM) harness connector. 4. Install a J 39700 Universal Breakout Box and a J 39700-650 Adapter Cable. Install the equipment between the EBCM and the EBCM harness connector. 5. Turn ON the ignition. 6. At the breakout box, use a DMM to measure the Hz frequency between the yaw rate frequency circuit and a ground circuit. Does the HZ frequency signal measure within the specified range?	13.37–14.36 kHz	Go to Step 16	Go to Step 12
12	1. With the DMM still connected to monitor the yaw rate frequency circuit, set the DMM to measure DC voltage. 2. Connect one end of a test lamp to a good ground. 3. Connect the other end of the test lamp to the positive lead of the DMM. Does the voltage measure less than the specified value?	0.15 V	Go to Step 16	Go to Step 14
13	Test the yaw rate frequency circuit for an open or a short to ground. Did you find and correct the condition?	—	Go to Step 20	Go to Step 17
14	Test the yaw rate frequency circuit for a short to voltage. Did you find and correct the condition?	—	Go to Step 20	Go to Step 19
15	Test the yaw rate sensor test circuit for a short to ground. Did you find and correct the condition?	—	Go to Step 20	Go to Step 17

LTV0500000006243

Fig. 72   Code C0196: Yaw Rate Circuit (Part 4 of 5). 2003–06 Avalanche, Escalade, Escalade EXT, Suburban, Tahoe & Yukon

Circuit Description

The system relay, located within the electronic brake control module (EBCM), supplies battery voltage to all of the valve solenoids and to the precharge pump motor. When the relay contacts close, the EBCM monitors the voltage supplied to the valve solenoids and compares this voltage to monitored ignition voltage.

DTC Descriptor

This diagnostic procedure supports the following DTC:

DTC C0201 Antilock Brake System (ABS) Enable Relay Contact Circuit

Conditions for Running the DTC

The ignition is ON.

Conditions for Setting the DTC

Either of the following conditions may cause the DTC to set:

• The EBCM detects that the voltage supplied to the valve solenoids is less than 65 percent of monitored ignition voltage for 50 milliseconds.
• The EBCM detects that the relay contacts do not open when the relay is not energized.

Action Taken When the DTC Sets

• The EBCM disables the ABS/traction control system (TCS)/vehicle stability enhancement system (VSES)/dynamic rear proportion (DRP).
• The ABS indicator turns ON.
• The traction OFF indicator turns ON.
• The message center displays the service stability system message.
• The brake warning indicator turns ON.
• The message center displays the service brake system message.

Conditions for Clearing the DTC

The Conditions for Setting the DTC are no longer present and you use the scan tool Clear DTCs function.

Diagnostic Aids

Refer back to the diagnostic table, steps 3 through 7, if this DTC continues to set intermittently.

Test Description

The number below refers to the step number on the diagnostic table.

3. A shorted ABS pump motor may damage the contacts within the system relay. It is imperative that the steps in the table be followed to prevent damage to a replacement EBCM.

LTV0500000006245

Fig. 73   Code C0201: ABS Enable Relay Contact Circuit (Part 1 of 2). 2003–06 Avalanche, Escalade, Escalade EXT, Suburban, Tahoe & Yukon

16	1. Inspect for poor connections at the harness connector of the yaw rate sensor/lateral accelerometer. 2. Ensure the yaw rate sensor/lateral accelerometer is mounted securely and that the mounting bracket is not bent or otherwise damaged. Did you find and correct the condition?	—	Go to Step 20	Go to Step 18
17	Inspect for poor connections at the harness connector of the EBCM. Did you find and correct the condition?	—	Go to Step 20	Go to Step 19
18	**Important:** The Yaw Rate Reference Table Reset Procedure must be performed when you are instructed to do so, during the Yaw Rate Sensor/Lateral Accelerometer Replacement procedure. Replace the yaw rate sensor/lateral accelerometer. Did you complete the replacement?	—	Go to Step 20	—
19	Replace the EBCM. Did you complete the replacement?	—	Go to Step 20	—
20	1. Use the scan tool Clear All Class 2 DTCs function to clear all of the DTCs from all modules. 2. Turn OFF the ignition for 5 seconds. 3. Turn ON the ignition. 4. Operate the vehicle within the Conditions for Running the DTC, as specified in the supporting text. Does the DTC reset?	—	Go to Step 3	System OK

LTV0500000006244

Fig. 72   Code C0196: Yaw Rate Circuit (Part 5 of 5). 2003–06 Avalanche, Escalade, Escalade EXT, Suburban, Tahoe & Yukon

Step	Action	Values	Yes	No
1	Did you perform the Diagnostic System Check - Vehicle?	—	Go to Step 2	Go to Diagnostic System Check
2	1. Use the scan tool to clear the DTCs. 2. Turn OFF the ignition for 5 seconds. 3. Turn ON the ignition. Does the DTC reset?	—	Go to Step 3	Go to Diagnostic Aids
3	1. Separate the electronic brake control module (EBCM) from the brake pressure modulator valve (BPMV). 2. Use a DMM in order to measure the resistance across the ABS pump motor. Does the resistance measure within the specified range?	0.3–1 ohms	Go to Step 4	Go to Step 6
4	Use a DMM in order to measure the resistance between the high side of the pump motor and a good ground. Does the resistance measure less than the specified value?	OL	Go to Step 6	Go to Step 5
5	Replace the EBCM. Did you complete the replacement?	—	Go to Step 7	—
6	**Important:** Following EBCM replacement, perform the set-up procedure for the EBCM and perform the Yaw Rate Reference Table Reset Procedure. Use the scan tool to perform the Tire Size Calibration procedure. • Replace the EBCM. • Replace the BPMV. Did you complete the replacements?	—	Go to Step 7	—
7	1. Use the scan tool to clear the DTCs. 2. Turn OFF the ignition for 5 seconds. 3. Turn ON the ignition. Does the DTC reset?	—	Go to Step 3	System OK

LTV0500000006246

Fig. 73   Code C0201: ABS Enable Relay Contact Circuit (Part 2 of 2). 2003–06 Avalanche, Escalade, Escalade EXT, Suburban, Tahoe & Yukon

Circuit Description

The system relay is energized when the ignition is ON. The system relay supplies voltage to the valve solenoids and the pump motor. This voltage is referred to as the system voltage. The electronic brake control module (EBCM) microprocessor activates the valve solenoids by grounding the control circuit.

DTC Descriptor

This diagnostic procedure supports the following DTC:

DTC C0220 Left Front Antilock Brake System (ABS) Channel in Release Too Long

Conditions for Running the DTC

- The ignition is ON.
- The vehicle is experiencing an ABS event.

Conditions for Setting the DTC

The EBCM energizes the left, front dump valve for 9 consecutive seconds.

Action Taken When the DTC Sets

- The EBCM disables the ABS/dynamic rear proportion (DRP)/vehicle stability enhancement system (VSES).
- The traction control system (TCS) operates with engine torque reduction only.
- The ABS indicator turns ON.
- The brake warning indicator turns ON.
- The message center displays the service stability system message.

Conditions for Clearing the DTC

The conditions for setting the DTC are no longer present and you use the scan tool Clear DTCs function.

Diagnostic Aids

The most likely cause of this DTC is a mechanical failure that causes a wheel to lock and remain locked. The DTCs may also set, conceivably, when the ABS is activated on surfaces that are nearly impossible to get traction on. If the DTC sets within these conditions, diagnosis of the ABS system is not necessary.

Test Description

The number below refers to the step number on the diagnostic table:

2. Performing solenoid tests determines if there is a mechanical malfunction inside the brake pressure modulator valve (BPMV).

LTV0500000006247

Fig. 74 Code C0220: LH Front ABS Channel In Release Too Long (Part 1 of 2). 2003–06 Avalanche, Escalade, Escalade EXT, Suburban, Tahoe & Yukon

Circuit Description

As the wheel spins, the wheel speed sensor produces an AC signal. The electronic brake control module (EBCM) uses the frequency of the AC signal to calculate the wheel speed.

DTC Descriptors

This diagnostic procedure supports the following DTCs:

- DTC C0221 Right Front Wheel Speed Sensor Circuit Open
- DTC C0222 Right Front Wheel Speed Signal Missing
- DTC C0223 Right Front Wheel Speed Signal Erratic
- DTC C0225 Left Front Wheel Speed Signal Circuit Open
- DTC C0226 Left Front Wheel Speed Signal Missing
- DTC C0227 Left Front Wheel Speed Signal Erratic

Conditions for Running the DTC

C0221 and C0225

The ignition is ON.

C0222, C0223, C0226 and C0227

The vehicle speed is greater than 32 km/h (20 mph) when the brake is applied or 19 km/h (12 mph) when the brake is released.

Conditions for Setting the DTC

C0221 and C0225

The EBCM detects an open or shorted wheel speed sensor or wheel speed sensor circuit for 500 milliseconds.

C0222 and C0226

The corresponding wheel speed sensor signal is less than 6 km/h (4 mph) for 5 seconds, or 120 seconds in order to set both DTCs.

C0223 and C0227

The EBCM detects an erratic signal from the corresponding wheel speed sensor for 105 milliseconds.

LTV0500000006249

Fig. 75 Codes C0221–C0227: Wheel Speed Sensor Circuit Fault (Part 1 of 4). 2003–06 Avalanche, Escalade, Escalade EXT, Suburban, Tahoe & Yukon Less JL4

Step	Action	Yes	No
1	Did you perform the Diagnostic System Check - Vehicle?	Go to Step 2	Go to Diagnostic System Check
2	1. Use a scan tool in order to clear the DTCs. 2. Use the scan tool in order to perform the necessary Solenoid Tests. Refer to Scan Tool Output Controls. Do the Solenoid Tests show the system to be functioning normally?	Go to Diagnostic Aids	Go to Step 3
3	Replace the brake pressure modulator valve (BPMV). Did you complete the replacement?	Go to Step 4	--
4	Use the scan tool in order to perform the necessary Solenoid Tests. Do the Solenoid Tests show the system to be functioning normally?	System OK	Go to Step 3

LTV0500000006248

Fig. 74 Code C0220: LH Front ABS Channel In Release Too Long (Part 2 of 2). 2003–06 Avalanche, Escalade, Escalade EXT, Suburban, Tahoe & Yukon

Action Taken When the DTC Sets

C0221, C0225

If equipped, the following actions occur:

- The EBCM disables the ABS/TCS.
- The ABS indicator turns ON.
- The TRACTION OFF indicator turns ON.

C0222, C0223, C0226, and C0227

If equipped, the following actions occur:

- The EBCM disables the ABS/TCS and may disable DRP.
- The ABS indicator turns ON.
- The TRACTION OFF indicator turns ON.
- The red Brake warning indicator may turn ON.

Conditions for Clearing the DTC

- Repair the condition responsible for setting the DTC.
- Use a scan tool in order to clear the DTC.
- After the DTC is cleared and the ignition is ON, the ABS indicator may remain ON until the EBCM completes a power-up self-test. This test concludes when the vehicle reaches a speed greater than 13 km/h (8 mph) and the wheel speeds are verified by the EBCM.

Diagnostic Aids

Operating the vehicle on extremely rough terrain can set DTC C0223, C0227 or C0229 even if the system is functioning normally.

Thoroughly inspect connections or circuitry that may cause an intermittent malfunction.

If the customer's concern is that the ABS indicator is on only during humid conditions such as rain, snow or vehicle wash, thoroughly inspect the wheel speed sensor circuits for signs of water intrusion. Use the following procedure in order to help isolate the problem area:

1. Spray the suspected area with a 5 percent salt water solution.
2. Drive the vehicle at a speed greater than 19 km/h (12 mph) for at least 30 seconds.

Repair or replace the suspect harness if the DTC sets.

Test Description

The numbers below refer to the step numbers on the diagnostic table.

3. This step measures the resistance of the wheel speed sensor in order to determine if the sensor has a valid resistance value.

4. This step ensures that the wheel speed sensor is generating a valid AC voltage output.

LTV0500000006250

Fig. 75 Codes C0221–C0227: Wheel Speed Sensor Circuit Fault (Part 2 of 4). 2003–06 Avalanche, Escalade, Escalade EXT, Suburban, Tahoe & Yukon Less JL4

Important: If DTC C0229 is set, diagnose DTC C0229 before diagnosing any other wheel speed sensor DTCs.

Step	Action	Values	Yes	No
1	Did you perform the Diagnostic System Check - Vehicle?	--	Go to Step 2	Go to Diagnostic System Check -
2	1. Use a scan tool in order to clear the DTCs. 2. Operate the vehicle at a speed greater than the specified value. Does the DTC set?	19 km/h (12 mph)	Go to Step 3	Go to Diagnostic Aids
3	1. Turn OFF the ignition. 2. Raise and support the vehicle. Refer to Lifting and Jacking the Vehicle. 3. Disconnect the wheel speed sensor connector. 4. Use a DMM in order to measure the resistance across the wheel speed sensor. Does the resistance measure within the specified range?	700-10,000 ohms	Go to Step 4	Go to Step 8
4	1. Spin the wheel by hand as fast as possible. 2. Use a DMM in order to measure the AC voltage across the wheel speed sensor as the wheel spins. Does the AC voltage measure greater than the specified value?	100 mV	Go to Step 5	Go to Step 8
5	Inspect for poor connections at the harness connector of the wheel speed sensor. Did you find and correct the condition?	--	Go to Step 10	Go to Step 6

LTV0500000006251

Fig. 75 Codes C0221–C0227: Wheel Speed Sensor Circuit Fault (Part 3 of 4). 2003–06 Avalanche, Escalade, Escalade EXT, Suburban, Tahoe & Yukon Less JL4

Step	Action	Yes	No
6	1. Disconnect the electronic brake control module (EBCM) harness connector. 2. Test the wheel speed sensor circuits for the following: - An open - A short to ground - A short to voltage - Shorted together. Refer to Circuit Testing and to Wiring Repairs. Did you find and correct the condition?	Go to Step 10	Go to Step 7
7	Inspect for poor connections at the harness connector for the EBCM. Did you find and correct the condition?	Go to Step 10	Go to Step 9
8	Replace the wheel speed sensor. Did you complete the replacement?	Go to Step 10	--
9	Replace the EBCM. Did you complete the replacement?	Go to Step 10	--
10	1. Use the scan tool in order to clear the DTCs. 2. Operate the vehicle within the Conditions for Running the DTC, as specified in the supporting text. Does the DTC reset?	Go to Step 2	System OK

LTV0500000006252

Fig. 75 Codes C0221–C0227: Wheel Speed Sensor Circuit Fault (Part 4 of 4). 2003–06 Avalanche, Escalade, Escalade EXT, Suburban, Tahoe & Yukon Less JL4

Circuit Description

The system relay is energized when the ignition is ON. The system relay supplies voltage to the valve solenoids and the pump motor. This voltage is referred to as the system voltage. The electronic brake control module (EBCM) microprocessor activates the valve solenoids by grounding the control circuit.

DTC Descriptor

This diagnostic procedure supports the following DTC:

DTC C0224 Right Front Antilock Brake System (ABS) Channel in Release Too Long

Conditions for Running the DTC

- The ignition is ON.
- The vehicle is experiencing an ABS event.

Conditions for Setting the DTC

The EBCM energizes the right, front dump valve for 9 consecutive seconds.

Action Taken When the DTC Sets

- The EBCM disables the ABS/dynamic rear proportion (DRP)/vehicle stability enhancement system (VSES).
- The traction control system (TCS) operates with engine torque reduction only.
- The ABS indicator turns ON.
- The brake warning indicator turns ON.
- The message center displays the service stability system message.

Conditions for Clearing the DTC

The conditions for setting the DTC are no longer present and you use the scan tool Clear DTCs function.

LTV0500000006253

Fig. 76 Codes C0221–C0227: Wheel Speed Sensor Circuit Fault (Part 1 of 2). 2003–06 Avalanche, Escalade, Escalade EXT, Suburban, Tahoe & Yukon w/JL4

Diagnostic Aids

The most likely cause of this DTC is a mechanical failure that causes a wheel to lock and remain locked. The DTCs may also set, conceivably, when the ABS is activated on surfaces that are nearly impossible to get traction on. If the DTC sets within these conditions, diagnosis of the ABS system is not necessary.

Test Description

The number below refers to the step number on the diagnostic table:

2. Performing solenoid tests determines if there is a mechanical malfunction inside the brake pressure modulator valve (BPMV).

Step	Action	Yes	No
1	Did you perform the Diagnostic System Check - Vehicle?	Go to Step 2	Go to Diagnostic System Check
2	1. Use a scan tool in order to clear the DTCs. 2. Use the scan tool in order to perform the necessary Solenoid Tests. Do the Solenoid Tests show the system to be functioning normally?	Go to Diagnostic Aids	Go to Step 3
3	Replace the brake pressure modulator valve (BPMV). Did you complete the replacement?	Go to Step 4	--
4	Use the scan tool in order to perform the necessary Solenoid Tests. Do the Solenoid Tests show the system to be functioning normally?	System OK	Go to Step 3

LTV0500000006254

Fig. 76 Codes C0221–C0227: Wheel Speed Sensor Circuit Fault (Part 2 of 2). 2003–06 Avalanche, Escalade, Escalade EXT, Suburban, Tahoe & Yukon w/JL4

Circuit Description

The system relay is energized when the ignition is ON. The system relay supplies voltage to the valve solenoids and the pump motor. This voltage is referred to as the system voltage. The electronic brake control module (EBCM) microprocessor activates the valve solenoids by grounding the control circuit.

DTC Descriptor

This diagnostic procedure supports the following DTC:

DTC C0228 Left Rear Antilock Brake System (ABS) Channel in Release Too Long

Conditions for Running the DTC

- The ignition is ON.
- The vehicle is experiencing an ABS event.

Conditions for Setting the DTC

The EBCM energizes the left, rear dump valve for 9 consecutive seconds.

Action Taken When the DTC Sets

- The EBCM disables the ABS/dynamic rear proportion (DRP)/vehicle stability enhancement system (VSES).
- The TCS operates with engine torque reduction only.
- The ABS indicator turns ON.
- The brake warning indicator turns ON.
- The message center displays the service stability system message.

Conditions for Clearing the DTC

The conditions for setting the DTC are no longer present and you use the scan tool Clear DTCs function.

Diagnostic Aids

The most likely cause of this DTC is a mechanical failure that causes a wheel to lock and remain locked. The DTCs may also set, conceivably, when the ABS is activated on surfaces that are nearly impossible to get traction on. If the DTC sets within these conditions, diagnosis of the ABS system is not necessary.

LTV0500000006255

Fig. 77 Code C0228: LH Rear ABS Channel In Release Too Long (Part 1 of 2). 2003–06 Avalanche, Escalade, Escalade EXT, Suburban, Tahoe & Yukon

Circuit Description

The system relay is energized when the ignition is ON. The system relay supplies voltage to the valve solenoids and the pump motor. This voltage is referred to as the system voltage. The electronic brake control module (EBCM) microprocessor activates the valve solenoids by grounding the control circuit.

DTC Descriptor

This diagnostic procedure supports the following DTC:

DTC C0229 Right Rear Antilock Brake System (ABS) Channel in Release Too Long

Conditions for Running the DTC

- The ignition is ON.
- The vehicle is experiencing an ABS event.

Conditions for Setting the DTC

The EBCM energizes the right, rear dump valve for 9 consecutive seconds.

Action Taken When the DTC Sets

- The EBCM disables the ABS/dynamic rear proportion (DRP)/vehicle stability enhancement system (VSES).
- The TCS operates with engine torque reduction only.
- The ABS indicator turns ON.
- The brake warning indicator turns ON.
- The message center displays the service stability system message.

Conditions for Clearing the DTC

The conditions for setting the DTC are no longer present and you use the scan tool Clear DTCs function.

LTV0500000006257

Fig. 78 Code C0229: RH Rear ABS Channel In Release Too Long (Part 1 of 2). 2003–06 Avalanche, Escalade, Escalade EXT, Suburban, Tahoe & Yukon w/JL4

Test Description

The number below refers to the step number on the diagnostic table:

2. Performing solenoid tests determines if there is a mechanical malfunction inside the brake pressure modulator valve (BPMV).

Step	Action	Yes	No
1	Did you perform the Diagnostic System Check - Vehicle?	Go to Step 2	Go to Diagnostic System Check
2	1. Use a scan tool in order to clear the DTCs. 2. Use the scan tool in order to perform the necessary Solenoid Tests. Refer to Scan Tool Output Controls . Do the Solenoid Tests show the system to be functioning normally?	Go to Diagnostic Aids	Go to Step 3
3	Replace the brake pressure modulator valve (BPMV). Did you complete the replacement?	Go to Step 4	
4	Use the scan tool in order to perform the necessary Solenoid Tests. Do the Solenoid Tests show the system to be functioning normally?	System OK	Go to Step 3

LTV0500000006256

Fig. 77 Code C0228: LH Rear ABS Channel In Release Too Long (Part 2 of 2). 2003–06 Avalanche, Escalade, Escalade EXT, Suburban, Tahoe & Yukon

Diagnostic Aids

The most likely cause of this DTC is a mechanical failure that causes a wheel to lock and remain locked. The DTCs may also set, conceivably, when the ABS is activated on surfaces that are nearly impossible to get traction on. If the DTC sets within these conditions, diagnosis of the ABS system is not necessary.

Test Description

The number below refers to the step number on the diagnostic table:

2. Performing solenoid tests determines if there is a mechanical malfunction inside the brake pressure modulator valve (BPMV).

Step	Action	Yes	No
1	Did you perform the Diagnostic System Check - Vehicle?	Go to Step 2	Go to Diagnostic System Check - Vehicle
2	1. Use a scan tool in order to clear the DTCs. 2. Use the scan tool in order to perform the necessary Solenoid Tests. Do the Solenoid Tests show the system to be functioning normally?	Go to Diagnostic Aids	Go to Step 3
3	Replace the brake pressure modulator valve (BPMV). Did you complete the replacement?	Go to Step 4	--
4	Use the scan tool in order to perform the necessary Solenoid Tests. Do the Solenoid Tests show the system to be functioning normally?	System OK	Go to Step 3

LTV0500000006258

Fig. 78 Code C0229: RH Rear ABS Channel In Release Too Long (Part 2 of 2). 2003–06 Avalanche, Escalade, Escalade EXT, Suburban, Tahoe & Yukon w/JL4

Circuit Description

As the wheel spins, the wheel speed sensor produces an AC signal. The electronic brake control module (EBCM) uses the frequency of the AC signal to calculate the wheel speed.

DTC Descriptor

This diagnostic procedure supports the following DTC:

DTC C0229 Drop Out of Both Front Speed Sensors

Conditions for Running the DTC

- The ignition is ON.
- The vehicle speed is greater than 32 km/h (20 mph) when the brake is applied or 19 km/h (12 mph) when the brake is released.

Conditions for Setting the DTC

The EBCM detects an erratic signal from both front wheel speed sensors for 105 milliseconds.

Action Taken When the DTC Sets

If equipped, the following actions occur:

- The EBCM disables the ABS/TCS/DRP.
- The ABS indicator turns ON.
- The TRACTION OFF indicator turns ON.
- The red brake warning indicator turns ON.

Conditions for Clearing the DTC

- Repair the condition responsible for setting the DTC.
- Use a scan tool in order to clear the DTC.
- After the DTC is cleared and the ignition is ON, the ABS indicator may remain ON until the EBCM completes a power-up self-test. This test concludes when the vehicle reaches a speed greater than 13 km/h (8 mph) and the wheel speeds are verified by the EBCM.

LTV0500000006259

Fig. 79 Code C0229: Drop Out Of Both Front Speed Sensors (Part 1 of 2). 2003–06 Avalanche, Escalade, Escalade EXT, Suburban, Tahoe & Yukon Less JL4

Diagnostic Aids

Operating the vehicle on extremely rough terrain can set DTC C0223, C0227 or C0229 even if the system is functioning normally.

Thoroughly inspect connections or circuitry that may cause an intermittent malfunction. Refer to Testing for Intermittent and Poor Connections , Connector Repairs , Testing for Electrical Intermittents and to Wiring Repairs in Wiring Systems.

If the customer's concern is that the ABS indicator is on only during humid conditions such as rain, snow or vehicle wash, thoroughly inspect the wheel speed sensor circuits for signs of water intrusion. Use the following procedure in order to help isolate the problem area:

1. Spray the suspected area with a 5 percent salt water solution.
2. Drive the vehicle at a speed greater than 19 km/h (12 mph) for at least 30 seconds.

Repair or replace the suspect harness if the DTC sets.

Step	Action	Yes	No
1	Did you perform the Diagnostic System Check - Vehicle?	Go to Step 2	Go to Diagnostic System Check - Vehicle
2	1. Use a scan tool in order to clear the DTCs. 2. Operate the vehicle within the Conditions for Running the DTC as specified in the supporting text. Does the DTC set?	Go to Step 3	Go to Diagnostic Aids
3	Inspect for poor connections at the harness connector of the electronic brake control module (EBCM). Did you find and correct the condition?	Go to Step 5	Go to Step 4
4	Replace the EBCM. Did you complete the replacement?	Go to Step 5	--
5	1. Use the scan tool in order to clear the DTCs. 2. Operate the vehicle within the Conditions for Running the DTC as specified in the supporting text. Does the DTC reset?	Go to Step 3	System OK

LTV0500000006260

Fig. 79 Code C0229: Drop Out Of Both Front Speed Sensors (Part 2 of 2). 2003–06 Avalanche, Escalade, Escalade EXT, Suburban, Tahoe & Yukon Less JL4

P0609

The PCM detects low voltage on the vehicle speed signal circuit for 45 seconds.

Action Taken When the DTC Sets

If equipped, the following actions occur:

- The EBCM disables the ABS/TCS/DRP.
- The ABS indicator turns ON.
- The TRACTION OFF indicator turns ON.
- The red brake warning indicator turns ON.

Conditions for Clearing the DTC

- Repair the condition responsible for setting the DTC.
- Use a scan tool in order to clear the DTC.
- After the DTC is cleared and the ignition is ON, the ABS indicator may remain ON until the EBCM completes a power-up self-test. This test concludes when the vehicle reaches a speed greater than 13 km/h (8 mph) and the wheel speeds are verified by the EBCM.

LTV0500000006262

Fig. 80 Codes C0235–C0237 Or P0609: Rear Wheel Speed Sensor Fault (Part 2 of 4). 2003–06 Avalanche, Escalade, Escalade EXT, Suburban, Tahoe & Yukon

Circuit Description

The powertrain control module (PCM) converts the data from the vehicle speed sensor to a 128k pulses/mile signal. The electronic brake control module (EBCM) uses the vehicle speed signal from the PCM in order to calculate the rear wheel speed.

DTC Descriptors

This diagnostic procedure supports the following DTCs:

- DTC C0235 Rear Wheel Speed Signal Circuit Open
- DTC C0236 Rear Wheel Speed Signal Missing
- DTC C0237 Rear Wheel Speed Signal Erratic

Conditions for Running the DTC

C0235

The ignition is ON.

C0236 and C0237

- The ignition is ON.
- The vehicle speed is greater than 32 km/h (20 mph) when the brake is applied or 19 km/h (12 mph) when the brake is released.

P0609

- The ignition is ON.
- The vehicle is not moving.

Conditions for Setting the DTC

C0235

The EBCM detects low voltage on the vehicle speed signal circuit for 500 milliseconds.

C0236

The rear wheel speed signal is less than 6 km/h (4 mph) for 5 seconds, or 120 seconds in order to set multiple missing sensor signal DTCs.

C0237

The EBCM detects an erratic rear wheel speed signal for 105 milliseconds.

LTV0500000006261

Fig. 80 Codes C0235–C0237 Or P0609: Rear Wheel Speed Sensor Fault (Part 1 of 4). 2003–06 Avalanche, Escalade, Escalade EXT, Suburban, Tahoe & Yukon

Diagnostic Aids

Thoroughly inspect connections or circuitry that may cause an intermittent malfunction.

Test Description

The numbers below refer to the step numbers on the diagnostic table.

3. This step tests for a voltage signal from the PCM.

4. This step tests for a missing or erratic vehicle speed signal from the PCM. An assistant may be required to perform this test.

Step	Action	Values	Yes	No
1	Did you perform the Diagnostic System Check - Vehicle?	--	Go to Step 2	Go to Diagnostic System Check - Vehicle
2	1. Use a scan tool in order to clear the DTCs. 2. Operate the vehicle at a speed greater than the specified value. Does the DTC set?	19 km/h (12 mph)	Go to Step 3	Go to Diagnostic Aids
3	1. Turn OFF the ignition. 2. Disconnect from the electronic brake control module (EBCM), the harness connector containing the vehicle speed signal circuit. 3. Turn ON the ignition. 4. Use a DMM in order to measure the DC voltage between the vehicle speed signal circuit and a good ground. Does the voltage measure greater than the specified value?	10 V	Go to Step 4	Go to Step 7

LTV0500000006263

Fig. 80 Codes C0235–C0237 Or P0609: Rear Wheel Speed Sensor Fault (Part 3 of 4). 2003–06 Avalanche, Escalade, Escalade EXT, Suburban, Tahoe & Yukon

Step	Action		Yes	No
4	1. Raise and support the vehicle. Refer to Lifting and Jacking the Vehicle . 2. Place the transmission in neutral (N). 3. Set up the DMM in order to measure the DC voltage between the vehicle speed signal circuit and a good ground. 4. Spin the rear wheels as fast as possible by hand for at least 30 seconds and while ensuring the driveshaft is rotating, observe the DMM. Does the voltage measure within the specified range the entire time the driveshaft is rotating?	5–7 V	Go to Step 5	Go to Step 7
5	Inspect for poor connections at the harness connector of the EBCM. Did you find and correct the condition?	–	Go to Step 10	Go to Step 6
6	Replace the EBCM. Did you complete the replacement?	–	Go to Step 10	–
7	Test the vehicle speed signal circuit for an open, a short to ground or a short to voltage. Did you find and correct the condition?	–	Go to Step 10	Go to Step 8
8	Inspect for poor connections at the harness connector of the powertrain control module (PCM). Did you find and correct the condition?	–	Go to Step 10	Go to Step 9
9	Replace the PCM. Did you complete the replacement?	–	Go to Step 10	–
10	1. Use the scan tool in order to clear the DTCs. 2. Operate the vehicle within the Conditions for Running the DTC as specified in the supporting text. Does the DTC reset?		Go to Step 3	System OK

LTV0500000006264

Fig. 80   Codes C0235–C0237 Or P0609: Rear Wheel Speed Sensor Fault (Part 4 of 4). 2003–06 Avalanche, Escalade, Escalade EXT, Suburban, Tahoe & Yukon

Step	Action	Yes	No
1	Did you perform the Diagnostic System Check - Vehicle?	Go to Step 2	Go to Diagnostic System Check -
2	Inspect both of the front tires on the vehicle to ensure that both tires are of equal size. Are both of the front tires of equal size?	Go to Step 3	Go to Diagnostic Aids
3	Inspect both of the rear tires on the vehicle to ensure that both tires are of equal size. Are both of the rear tires of equal size?	Go to Step 4	Go to Diagnostic Aids
4	Verify the electronic brake control module (EBCM) and the powertrain control module (PCM) both have the correct tire size calibration. Use the scan tool in order to view the EBCM tire size calibration Did you find and correct the condition?	Go to Step 5	Go to Diagnostic Aids
5	1. Use a scan tool in order to clear the DTCs. 2. Operate the vehicle for at least 3 minutes within the Conditions for Running the DTC as specified in the supporting text. Does the DTC reset?	Go to Step 2	System OK

LTV0500000006266

Fig. 81   Code C0238: Wheel Speed Mismatch (Part 2 of 2). 2003–06 Avalanche, Escalade, Escalade EXT, Suburban, Tahoe & Yukon

Circuit Description

As the front wheels spin, the wheel speed sensors produce an AC signal. The electronic brake control module (EBCM) uses the frequency of the AC signal to calculate the wheel speed. The powertrain control module (PCM) converts the data from the wheel speed sensor to a 128k pulses/mile signal. The EBCM uses the vehicle speed signal from the PCM in order to calculate the rear wheel speed.

DTC Descriptor

This diagnostic procedure supports the following DTC:

DTC C0238 Wheel Speed Mismatch

Conditions for Running the DTC

The ignition is ON and the vehicle speed is between 24 km/h (15 mph) and 80 km/h (50 mph).

Conditions for Setting the DTC

The EBCM detects that one wheel speed input is 10 percent greater than or 10 percent less than the other wheel speed inputs within 3.2 km (2 mi) of driving.

Action Taken When the DTC Sets

If equipped, the following actions occur:

- The EBCM disables the ABS/TCS/DRP.
- The ABS indicator turns ON.
- The TRACTION OFF indicator turns ON.
- The red brake warning indicator turns ON.

Conditions for Clearing the DTC

The conditions for setting the DTC are no longer present and you use the scan tool Clear DTCs function.

Diagnostic Aids

Installing one tire of significantly different size on the vehicle causes DTC C0238 to set. Operating the vehicle with a tire that has very low air pressure may also set this DTC. Inspect the vehicle for an incorrect or damaged wheel speed sensor or vehicle speed sensor if the tires and the EBCM and PCM calibrations are OK.

Test Description

The number below refers to the step number on the diagnostic table.

4. If the front tires are not the same size as the rear tires, the EBCM calibration must match the FRONT tire size and the PCM calibration must match the REAR tire size.

LTV0500000006265

Fig. 81   Code C0238: Wheel Speed Mismatch (Part 1 of 2). 2003–06 Avalanche, Escalade, Escalade EXT, Suburban, Tahoe & Yukon

Circuit Description

The powertrain control module (PCM) and the electronic brake control module (EBCM) communicate on the serial data link whenever the ignition is ON.

DTC Descriptor

This diagnostic procedure supports the following DTC:

DTC C0240 EBCM Malfunction

Conditions for Running the DTC

- The ignition is ON.
- The engine is running at a speed greater than 450 RPM for 5-20 seconds.

Conditions for Setting the DTC

The EBCM receives a serial data message stating that the PCM has lost the ability to reduce engine torque.

Action Taken When the DTC Sets

- The EBCM disables the vehicle stability enhancement system (VSES).
- Engine torque reduction is disabled.
- The traction off indicator turns ON.
- The message center displays the service stability system or stability system disabled message.

Conditions for Clearing the DTC

The conditions for setting the DTC are no longer present and you use the scan tool Clear DTCs function.

Diagnostic Aids

A requested torque signal malfunction is only one possible cause for setting this DTC. DTC C0240 may set due to engine overheating, throttle actuator control failure, loss of ignition timing control by the PCM, etc. If DTC P0856 has not set, refer to Diagnostic System Check - Vehicle in order to identify other possible causes of DTC C0240.

Step	Action	Values	Yes	No
1	Did you perform the Diagnostic System Check - Vehicle?	–	Go to Step 2	Go to Diagnostic System Check - Vehicle
2	Is DTC P0856 set?	–	Go to DTC C0298 or P0856	Go to Diagnostic Aids

LTV0500000006267

Fig. 82   Code C0240: EBCM Fault. 2003–06 Avalanche, Escalade, Escalade EXT, Suburban, Tahoe & Yukon

Circuit Description

The ABS relay supplies battery voltage to 6 valve solenoids. The electronic brake control module (EBCM) microprocessor applies the grounds needed to activate each solenoid. The low side of each solenoid coil has a feedback circuit to the EBCM microprocessor. When a solenoid is commanded OFF, the feedback voltage is high. When a solenoid is commanded ON, the feedback voltage is low.

DTC Descriptors

This diagnostic procedure supports the following DTCs:

- DTC C0241 EBCM Control Valve Circuit
- DTC C0242 EBCM Control Valve Circuit
- DTC C0243 EBCM Control Valve Circuit

Conditions for Running the DTC

- The ignition is ON.
- The vehicle speed is greater than 6 km/h (4 mph).

Conditions for Setting the DTC

The EBCM detects an internal malfunction.

Action Taken When the DTC Sets

C0241 and C0242

If equipped, the following actions occur:

- The EBCM disables the dynamic rear proportion (DRP)/ABS.
- The ABS indicator turns ON.
- The red brake warning indicator turns ON.

C0243

If equipped, the following actions occur:

- The EBCM disables the ABS.
- The ABS indicator turns ON.

Conditions for Clearing the DTC

The conditions for setting the DTC are no longer present and you use the scan tool Clear DTCs function.

Diagnostic Aids

An intermittent open/shorted solenoid DTC can be set by several different internal EBCM problems. Replace the EBCM if an

LTV0500000006268

Fig. 83 Codes C0241–C0243: EBCM Control Valve Circuit (Part 1 of 2). 2003–06 Avalanche, Escalade, Escalade EXT, Suburban, Tahoe & Yukon

Circuit Description

The ABS relay supplies battery voltage to 6 valve solenoids. The electronic brake control module (EBCM) microprocessor applies the grounds needed to activate each solenoid. The low side of each solenoid coil has a feedback circuit to the EBCM microprocessor. When a solenoid is commanded OFF, the feedback voltage is high. When a solenoid is commanded ON, the feedback voltage is low.

DTC Descriptor

This diagnostic procedure supports the following DTC:

DTC C0244 EBCM Control Valve Circuit

Conditions for Running the DTC

- The ignition is ON.
- The vehicle speed is greater than 6 km/h (4 mph).

Conditions for Setting the DTC

The EBCM detects an internal malfunction.

Action Taken When the DTC Sets

- The EBCM disables the ABS.
- The ABS indicator turns ON.

Conditions for Clearing the DTC

The conditions for setting the DTC are no longer present and you use the scan tool Clear DTCs function.

Diagnostic Aids

An intermittent open/shorted solenoid DTC can be set by several different internal EBCM problems. Replace the EBCM if an open/shorted solenoid DTC continues to set intermittently.

LTV0500000006270

Fig. 84 Code C0244: EBCM Control Valve Circuit (Part 1 of 2). 2003–06 Avalanche, Escalade, Escalade EXT, Suburban, Tahoe & Yukon Less JL4

Step	Action	Yes	No
1	Did you perform the Diagnostic System Check - Vehicle?	Go to Step 2	Go to Diagnostic System Check - Vehicle
2	1. Use a scan tool in order to clear the DTCs. 2. Operate the vehicle within the Conditions for Running the DTC as specified in the supporting text. Does the DTC set?	Go to Step 3	Go to Diagnostic Aids
3	Replace the electronic brake control module (EBCM). Did you complete the replacement?	Go to Step 4	--
4	1. Use the scan tool in order to clear the DTCs. 2. Operate the vehicle within the Conditions for Running the DTC as specified in the supporting text. Does the DTC reset?	Go to Step 3	System OK

LTV0500000006269

Fig. 83 Codes C0241–C0243: EBCM Control Valve Circuit (Part 2 of 2). 2003–06 Avalanche, Escalade, Escalade EXT, Suburban, Tahoe & Yukon

Step	Action	Yes	No
1	Did you perform the Diagnostic System Check - Vehicle?	Go to Step 2	Go to Diagnostic System Check - Vehicle
2	1. Use a scan tool in order to clear the DTCs. 2. Operate the vehicle within the Conditions for Running the DTC as specified in the supporting text. Does the DTC set?	Go to Step 3	Go to Diagnostic Aids
3	Replace the electronic brake control module (EBCM). Did you complete the replacement?	Go to Step 4	--
4	1. Use the scan tool in order to clear the DTCs. 2. Operate the vehicle within the Conditions for Running the DTC as specified in the supporting text. Does the DTC reset?	Go to Step 3	System OK

LTV0500000006271

Fig. 84 Code C0244: EBCM Control Valve Circuit (Part 2 of 2). 2003–06 Avalanche, Escalade, Escalade EXT, Suburban, Tahoe & Yukon Less JL4

Circuit Description

The electronic brake control module (EBCM) supplies approximately 12 volts through an internal resistor to the powertrain control module (PCM) on the delivered torque signal circuit. The PCM toggles this voltage to ground in order to create the delivered torque signal at the EBCM. A signal with a frequency of 128 Hz +/- 5 percent and a duty cycle of 25-95 percent is a valid delivered torque signal. The percentage of duty cycle is proportionate to the percentage of delivered engine torque.

DTC Descriptor

This diagnostic procedure supports the following DTC:

DTC C0244 Pulse Width Modulated (PWM) Delivered Torque

Conditions for Running the DTC

- The ignition is ON.
- The engine is running at a speed greater than 450 RPM for 1 second.

Conditions for Setting the DTC

The EBCM receives an invalid delivered torque signal for 300 milliseconds.

Action Taken When the DTC Sets

- The EBCM disables the vehicle stability enhancement system (VSES).
- Engine torque reduction is disabled.
- The traction off indicator turns ON.
- The message center displays the service stability system message.

Conditions for Clearing the DTC

The conditions for setting the DTC are no longer present and you use the scan tool Clear DTCs function.

Diagnostic Aids

Thoroughly inspect connections or circuitry that may cause an intermittent malfunction.

Test Description

The numbers below refer to the step numbers on the diagnostic table.

3. This step tests for voltage supplied to the PCM from the EBCM.

4. This step tests for a shorted resistor in the EBCM or a short to voltage within the circuit, by verifying that a large voltage drop occurs in the circuit when the test lamp is placed in parallel with the DMM. The PCM may be damaged if either of these conditions is present.

LTV0500000006272

Fig. 85 Code C0244: Pulse Width Modulated Delivered Torque (Part 1 of 3). 2003–06 Avalanche, Escalade, Escalade EXT, Suburban, Tahoe & Yukon w/JL4

Step	Action	Values	Yes	No
1	Did you perform the Diagnostic System Check - Vehicle?	--	Go to Step 2	Go to Diagnostic System Check - Vehicle
2	1. Use a scan tool in order to clear the DTCs. 2. Turn OFF the ignition for 5 seconds. 3. Start the engine. Does the DTC set?	--	Go to Step 3	Go to Diagnostic Aids
3	1. Turn OFF the ignition. 2. Disconnect from the powertrain control module (PCM), the harness connector containing the delivered torque signal circuit. 3. Turn ON the ignition. 4. Use a DMM in order to measure the voltage between the delivered torque signal circuit and a good ground. Does the voltage measure greater than the specified value?	10 V	Go to Step 4	Go to Step 5
4	1. With the DMM still connected to monitor the delivered torque signal circuit, connect one end of a test lamp to a good ground. 2. Connect the other end of the test lamp to the positive lead of the DMM, while observing the DMM display. Does the voltage measure less than the specified value?	0.15 V	Go to Step 6	Go to Step 10
5	Test the delivered torque signal circuit for an open, or a short to ground. Did you find and correct the condition?	--	Go to Step 13	Go to Step 8
6	1. Turn OFF the ignition. 2. Reconnect the PCM harness connector. 3. Start the engine. 4. Select the VSES Data Display function on the scan tool. 5. Observe the Delivered Torque parameter on the scan tool. Does the scan tool display a duty cycle of the delivered torque signal within the specified range?	25-95%	Go to Step 7	Go to Step 11
7	1. Turn OFF the ignition. 2. Install a J 39700 Universal Breakout Box and a J 39700-650 Adapter Cable. Install the equipment between the electronic brake control module (EBCM) and the EBCM harness connector. 3. Start the engine. 4. Use a DMM in order to measure the Hz frequency between the delivered torque signal circuit and a ground circuit. Does the Hz frequency of the delivered torque signal measure within the specified range?	121-134 Hz	Go to Step 9	Go to Step 12

LTV0500000006273

Fig. 85   Code C0244: Pulse Width Modulated Delivered Torque (Part 2 of 3). 2003–06 Avalanche, Escalade, Escalade EXT, Suburban, Tahoe & Yukon w/JL4

Circuit Description

As the wheels spin, each wheel speed sensor produces an AC signal. The electronic brake control module (EBCM) uses the frequency of the AC signals to calculate each wheel speed.

DTC Descriptor

This diagnostic procedure supports the following DTC:

DTC C0245 Wheel Speed Sensor Frequency Error

Conditions for Running the DTC

- The ignition is ON.
- The vehicle speed is greater than 8 km/h (4 mph).
- No brake application or deceleration is detected.
- No wheel slip is detected.
- No turning maneuvers are detected.

Conditions for Setting the DTC

- At least one wheel speed sensor signal is 15 percent less than or greater than other wheel speed sensor signals.
- All of the Conditions for Running and Setting the DTC are present for a cumulative time of 3 minutes during a single ignition cycle.

Action Taken When the DTC Sets

- The EBCM disables the ABS/TCS/vehicle stability enhancement system (VSES)/dynamic rear proportion (DRP).
- The ABS indicator turns ON.
- The traction off indicator turns ON.
- The message center displays the service stability system message.
- The brake warning indicator turns ON.

Conditions for Clearing the DTC

The Conditions for Setting the DTC are no longer present and you use the scan tool Clear DTCs function.

Diagnostic Aids

Operating the vehicle with a tire that has very low air pressure may set this DTC.

LTV0500000006275

Fig. 86   Code C0245: Wheel Speed Sensor Frequency Error (Part 1 of 2). 2003–06 Avalanche, Escalade, Escalade EXT, Suburban, Tahoe & Yukon w/JL4

Step	Action		Yes	No
8	1. Turn OFF the ignition. 2. Inspect for poor connections at the harness connector of the EBCM. Did you find and correct the condition?		Go to Step 13	Go to Step 9
9	Replace the EBCM. Did you complete the replacement?		Go to Step 13	--
10	Test the delivered torque signal circuit for a short to voltage. Did you find and correct the condition?		Go to Step 13	Go to Step 12
11	Inspect for poor connections at the harness connector of the PCM. Did you find and correct the condition?		Go to Step 13	Go to Step 12
12	Replace the PCM. Did you complete the replacement?		Go to Step 13	--
13	1. Use the scan tool Clear All Class 2 DTCs function to clear all of the DTCs from all modules. 2. Turn OFF the ignition for 5 seconds. 3. Turn ON the ignition. 4. Operate the vehicle within the Conditions for Running the DTC as specified in the supporting text. Does the DTC reset?		Go to Step 3	System OK

LTV0500000006274

Fig. 85   Code C0244: Pulse Width Modulated Delivered Torque (Part 3 of 3). 2003–06 Avalanche, Escalade, Escalade EXT, Suburban, Tahoe & Yukon w/JL4

Step	Action	Yes	No
1	Did you perform the Diagnostic System Check - Vehicle?	Go to Step 2	Go to Diagnostic System Check - Vehicle
2	Inspect all of the tires on the vehicle to ensure that all of the tires are of equal size. Did you find and correct the condition?	Go to Step 4	Go to Step 3
3	Inspect the wheel speed sensors and tone rings for damage, incorrect application, or incorrect installation. Did you find and correct the condition?	Go to Step 4	Go to Diagnostic Aids
4	1. Use a scan tool in order to clear the DTCs. 2. Turn OFF the ignition for 5 seconds. 3. Turn ON the ignition. 4. Operate the vehicle for at least 3 minutes within the Conditions for Running the DTC as specified in the supporting text. Does the DTC reset?	Go to Step 2	System OK

LTV0500000006276

Fig. 86   Code C0245: Wheel Speed Sensor Frequency Error (Part 2 of 2). 2003–06 Avalanche, Escalade, Escalade EXT, Suburban, Tahoe & Yukon w/JL4

Circuit Description

The ABS relay supplies battery voltage to 6 valve solenoids. The electronic brake control module (EBCM) microprocessor applies the grounds needed to activate each solenoid. The low side of each solenoid coil has a feedback circuit to the EBCM microprocessor. When a solenoid is commanded OFF, the feedback voltage is high. When a solenoid is commanded ON, the feedback voltage is low.

DTC Descriptor

This diagnostic procedure supports the following DTC:

DTC C0245 EBCM Control Valve Circuit

Conditions for Running the DTC

- The ignition is ON.
- The vehicle speed is greater than 6 km/h (4 mph).

Conditions for Setting the DTC

The EBCM detects an internal malfunction.

Action Taken When the DTC Sets

- The EBCM disables the DRP/ABS.
- The ABS indicator turns ON.
- The red brake warning indicator turns ON.

Conditions for Clearing the DTC

The conditions for setting the DTC are no longer present and you use the scan tool Clear DTCs function.

LTV0500000006277

Fig. 87   Code C0245: EBCM Control Valve Circuit (Part 1 of 2). 2003–06 Avalanche, Escalade, Escalade EXT, Suburban, Tahoe & Yukon Less JL4

Diagnostic Aids

An intermittent open/shorted solenoid DTC can be set by several different internal EBCM problems. Replace the EBCM if an open/shorted solenoid DTC continues to set intermittently.

Step	Action	Yes	No
1	Did you perform the Diagnostic System Check - Vehicle?	Go to Step 2	Go to Diagnostic System Check - Vehicle
2	1. Use a scan tool in order to clear the DTCs. 2. Operate the vehicle within the Conditions for Running the DTC as specified in the supporting text. Does the DTC set?	Go to Step 3	Go to Diagnostic Aids
3	Replace the electronic brake control module (EBCM). Did you complete the replacement?	Go to Step 4	---
4	1. Use the scan tool in order to clear the DTCs. 2. Operate the vehicle within the Conditions for Running the DTC as specified in the supporting text. Does the DTC reset?	Go to Step 3	System OK

LTV0500000006278

Fig. 87 Code C0245: EBCM Control Valve Circuit (Part 2 of 2). 2003–06 Avalanche, Escalade, Escalade EXT, Suburban, Tahoe & Yukon Less JL4

Step	Action	Yes	No
1	Did you perform the Diagnostic System Check - Vehicle?	Go to Step 2	Go to Diagnostic System Check - Vehicle
2	1. Use a scan tool in order to clear the DTCs. 2. Operate the vehicle within the Conditions for Running the DTC as specified in the supporting text. Does the DTC set?	Go to Step 3	Go to Diagnostic Aids
3	Replace the electronic brake control module (EBCM). Did you complete the replacement?	Go to Step 4	---
4	1. Use the scan tool in order to clear the DTCs. 2. Operate the vehicle within the Conditions for Running the DTC as specified in the supporting text. Does the DTC reset?	Go to Step 3	System OK

LTV0500000006280

Fig. 88 Codes C0246–C0254: EBCM Control Valve Circuit (Part 2 of 2). 2003–06 Avalanche, Escalade, Escalade EXT, Suburban, Tahoe & Yukon

Circuit Description

The ABS relay supplies battery voltage to 6 valve solenoids. The electronic brake control module (EBCM) microprocessor applies the grounds needed to activate each solenoid. The low side of each solenoid coil has a feedback circuit to the EBCM microprocessor. When a solenoid is commanded OFF, the feedback voltage is high. When a solenoid is commanded ON, the feedback voltage is low.

DTC Descriptors

This diagnostic procedure supports the following DTCs:

- DTC C0265 EBCM Motor Relay Circuit
- DTC C0266 EBCM Motor Relay Circuit

Conditions for Running the DTC

- The ignition is ON.
- The vehicle speed is greater than 6 km/h (4 mph).

Conditions for Setting the DTC

The EBCM detects an internal malfunction.

Action Taken When the DTC Sets

C0265

If equipped, the following actions occur:

- The EBCM disables the DRP/ABS.
- The ABS indicator turns ON.
- The brake warning indicator turns ON.

C0266

If equipped, the following actions occur:

- The EBCM disables the ABS.
- The ABS indicator turns ON.

Conditions for Clearing the DTC

The conditions for setting the DTC are no longer present and you use the scan tool Clear DTCs function.

LTV0500000006281

Fig. 89 Codes C0265 Or C0266: EBCM Motor Relay Circuit (Part 1 of 3). 2003–06 Avalanche, Escalade, Escalade EXT, Suburban, Tahoe & Yukon

Circuit Description

The ABS relay supplies battery voltage to 6 valve solenoids. The electronic brake control module (EBCM) microprocessor applies the grounds needed to activate each solenoid. The low side of each solenoid coil has a feedback circuit to the EBCM microprocessor. When a solenoid is commanded OFF, the feedback voltage is high. When a solenoid is commanded ON, the feedback voltage is low.

DTC Descriptors

This diagnostic procedure supports the following DTCs:

- DTC C0246 EBCM Control Valve Circuit
- DTC C0247 EBCM Control Valve Circuit
- DTC C0248 EBCM Control Valve Circuit
- DTC C0251 EBCM Control Valve Circuit
- DTC C0252 EBCM Control Valve Circuit
- DTC C0253 EBCM Control Valve Circuit
- DTC C0254 EBCM Control Valve Circuit

Conditions for Running the DTC

- The ignition is ON.
- The vehicle speed is greater than 6 km/h (4 mph).

Conditions for Setting the DTC

The EBCM detects an internal malfunction.

Action Taken When the DTC Sets

C0246, C0251, C0252, C0253 and C0254

If equipped, the following actions occur:

- The EBCM disables the dynamic rear proportion (DRP)/ABS.
- The ABS indicator turns ON.
- The red brake warning indicator turns ON.

C0247 and C0248

If equipped, the following actions occur:

- The EBCM disables the ABS.
- The ABS indicator turns ON.

Conditions for Clearing the DTC

LTV0500000006279

Fig. 88 Codes C0246–C0254: EBCM Control Valve Circuit (Part 1 of 2). 2003–06 Avalanche, Escalade, Escalade EXT, Suburban, Tahoe & Yukon

Diagnostic Aids

Important

Whenever the EBCM is replaced for DTC C0265 or C0266, the ABS pump motor and motor circuitry must be tested for the proper resistance. Refer to steps 7 and 8 in the diagnostic table below for testing procedures and resistance values.

C0265

Thoroughly inspect connections and circuitry that may cause an intermittent malfunction.

C0266

Replace the EBCM if DTC C0266 continues to set intermittently.

Test Description

The numbers below refer to the step numbers on the diagnostic table.

4. This step tests if the battery positive voltage circuit can supply adequate power to the system relay.

7. A shorted ABS pump motor or shorted motor circuitry may damage the contacts within the system relay. Follow this step to prevent damage to a replacement EBCM.

Step	Action	Values	Yes	No
1	Did you perform the Diagnostic System Check - Vehicle?	---	Go to Step 2	Go to Diagnostic System Check - Vehicle
2	1. Use a scan tool in order to clear the DTCs. 2. Use the scan tool in order to perform an ABS Function Test. Does DTC C0266 set?	---	Go to Step 7	Go to Step 3
3	Does DTC C0265 set?	---	Go to Step 4	Go to Diagnostic Aids
4	1. Turn OFF the ignition. 2. Disconnect from the electronic brake control module (EBCM), the harness connector containing the battery positive voltage circuit. 3. Connect a test lamp between the battery positive voltage circuit and a good ground. Does the test lamp illuminate?	---	Go to Step 6	Go to Step 5

LTV0500000006282

Fig. 89 Codes C0265 Or C0266: EBCM Motor Relay Circuit (Part 2 of 3). 2003–06 Avalanche, Escalade, Escalade EXT, Suburban, Tahoe & Yukon

	Action	Values	Yes	No
5	Repair the open in the battery positive voltage circuit. Did you complete the repair?	--	Go to Step 11	--
6	Inspect for poor connections at the harness connector of the EBCM. Did you find and correct the condition?	--	Go to Step 11	Go to Step 7
7	**Important:** It may be necessary to separate the EBCM from the brake pressure modulator valve (BPMV) to gain access to the pump motor pigtail connector. 1. Disconnect from the EBCM, the ABS pump motor pigtail connector. 2. Use a DMM in order to measure the resistance across the ABS pump motor. Does the resistance measure within the specified range?	0.3-1 ohms	Go to Step 8	Go to Step 10
8	Use a DMM in order to measure the resistance between the high side of the pump motor and a good ground. Does the resistance measure less than the specified value?	0L	Go to Step 10	Go to Step 9
9	Replace the EBCM. Did you complete the replacement?	--	Go to Step 11	--
10	**Important:** Use the scan tool in order to perform the Tire Size Calibration procedure and the Trim Level Calibration procedure, if applicable. 1. Replace the EBCM. 2. Replace the BPMV. Did you complete the replacements?	--	Go to Step 11	--
11	1. Use the scan tool in order to clear the DTCs. 2. Operate the vehicle within the Conditions for Running the DTC, as specified in the supporting text. Does the DTC reset?	--	Go to Step 2	System OK

LTV0500000006283

Fig. 89   Codes C0265 Or C0266: EBCM Motor Relay Circuit (Part 3 of 3). 2003–06 Avalanche, Escalade, Escalade EXT, Suburban, Tahoe & Yukon

Step	Action	Values	Yes	No
1	Did you perform the Diagnostic System Check - Vehicle?	--	Go to Step 2	Go to Diagnostic System Check - Vehicle
2	1. Use a scan tool in order to clear the DTCs. 2. Operate the vehicle within the Conditions for Running the DTC, as specified in the supporting text. Does DTC C0267 set?	--	Go to Step 6	Go to Step 3
3	Does DTC C0268 set?	--	Go to Step 4	Go to Diagnostic Aids
4	1. Turn OFF the ignition. 2. Disconnect from the electronic brake control module (EBCM), the 2-way harness connector which contains the battery positive voltage circuit and the ground circuit. **Caution: Before servicing any electrical component, the ignition key must be in the OFF or LOCK position and all electrical loads must be OFF, unless instructed otherwise in these procedures. If a tool or equipment could easily come in contact with a live exposed electrical terminal, also disconnect the negative battery cable. Failure to follow these precautions may cause personal injury and/or damage to the vehicle or its components.** 3. Disconnect the negative battery cable. 4. Disconnect the positive battery cable. 5. Place one lead of a DMM on the positive battery cable where the cable normally connects to the battery. 6. Place the other lead on the battery positive voltage circuit terminal within the 2-way EBCM harness connector. 7. Measure the total resistance between the positive battery cable and the EBCM. Does the resistance measure within the specified range?	0.0-0.2 ohms	Go to Step 5	Go to Step 10

LTV0500000006285

Fig. 90   Codes C0267 Or C0268: Pump Motor Circuit (Part 2 of 4). 2003–06 Avalanche, Escalade, Escalade EXT, Suburban, Tahoe & Yukon

Circuit Description

The EBCM applies the ground needed for pump motor activation. The low side of the pump motor has a feedback circuit to the EBCM. When the pump motor is commanded OFF and at rest, feedback voltage is high. When the pump motor is winding down after being commanded ON and then OFF, feedback voltage is low. The EBCM monitors this feedback voltage in order to determine if the motor is functioning properly.

DTC Descriptors

This diagnostic procedure supports the following DTCs:

- DTC C0267 Pump Motor Circuit Open
- DTC C0268 Pump Motor Circuit Shorted

Conditions for Running the DTC

- The ignition is ON.
- The vehicle speed is greater than 6 km/h (4 mph).

Conditions for Setting the DTC

The EBCM detects any of the following conditions:

- An open or shorted pump motor
- An open or shorted pump motor driver circuit
- A seized pump motor

Action Taken When the DTC Sets

- The EBCM disables the ABS.
- The ABS indicator turns ON.

Conditions for Clearing the DTC

The conditions for setting the DTC are no longer present and you use the scan tool Clear DTCs function.

Diagnostic Aids

Thoroughly inspect connections or circuitry that may cause an intermittent malfunction.

Test Description

The numbers below refer to the step numbers on the diagnostic table.

2. It is imperative that the vehicle be driven to attempt to reset the DTC. Using the scan tool to perform a function test may not produce the same result, and therefore, may cause misdiagnosis of the vehicle.

7. This step tests if the EBCM is capable of activating the ABS pump motor.

8. A shorted ABS pump motor may damage the EBCM. It is imperative that the steps in the table be followed in order to prevent damage to a replacement EBCM.

LTV0500000006284

Fig. 90   Codes C0267 Or C0268: Pump Motor Circuit (Part 1 of 4). 2003–06 Avalanche, Escalade, Escalade EXT, Suburban, Tahoe & Yukon

	Action	Values	Yes	No
5	Use a DMM to measure the resistance of the ground circuit. Does the resistance measure within the specified range?	0.0-0.2 ohms	Go to Step 7	Go to Step 11
6	**Important:** On some applications, it may be necessary to separate the EBCM from the brake pressure modulator valve (BPMV) in order to perform this test. Also, DTC C0268 may set when this test is performed. 1. Turn OFF the ignition. 2. Disconnect from the EBCM, the ABS pump motor pigtail connector. For systems which have no pump motor pigtail, it is necessary to separate the EBCM from the BPMV in order to gain access to the pump motor connector of the EBCM. 3. Use a connector adapter test kit in order to connect a test lamp between the ABS pump motor power and ground circuits at the pump motor connector of the EBCM. 4. Turn ON the ignition. 5. Use the scan tool in order to clear the DTCs. 6. Use the scan tool in order to perform an ABS Function Test. Does DTC C0267 set?	--	Go to Step 12	Go to Step 9
7	**Important:** On some applications, it may be necessary to separate the EBCM from the BPMV in order to perform this test. Also, DTC C0268 may set when this test is performed. 1. Reconnect both battery cables. 2. Disconnect from the EBCM, the ABS pump motor pigtail connector. For systems which have no pump motor pigtail, it is necessary to separate the EBCM from the BPMV in order to gain access to the pump motor connector of the EBCM. 3. Use a connector adapter test kit in order to connect a test lamp between the ABS pump motor power and ground circuits at the pump motor connector of the EBCM. 4. Turn ON the ignition. 5. Use the scan tool in order to clear the DTCs. 6. Use the scan tool in order to perform an ABS Function Test. Does the test lamp illuminate and then turn OFF when the Function Test is performed?	--	Go to Step 13	Go to Step 8
8	Use a DMM in order to measure the resistance across the ABS pump motor. Does the resistance measure within the specified range?	0.3-1 ohms	Go to Step 12	Go to Step 14

LTV0500000006286

Fig. 90   Codes C0267 Or C0268: Pump Motor Circuit (Part 3 of 4). 2003–06 Avalanche, Escalade, Escalade EXT, Suburban, Tahoe & Yukon

Step	Action	Yes	No
9	Inspect for poor connections at the pump motor pigtail connector. Did you find and correct the condition?	Go to Step 15	Go to Step 13
10	Repair the high resistance in the underhood electrical center or the battery positive voltage circuit. Did you complete the repair?	Go to Step 15	--
11	Repair the high resistance in the ground circuit. Did you complete the repair?	Go to Step 15	--
12	Replace the EBCM. Did you complete the replacement?	Go to Step 15	--
13	Replace the BPMV. Did you complete the replacement?	Go to Step 15	--
14	Important: Following EBCM replacement, use the scan tool perform the Tire Size Calibration procedure and the Trim Level Calibration procedure, if applicable. 1. Replace the EBCM. 2. Replace the BPMV. Did you complete the replacements?	Go to Step 15	--
15	1. Use a scan tool in order to clear the DTCs. 2. Operate the vehicle within the Conditions for Running the DTC, as specified in the supporting text. Does the DTC reset?	Go to Step 3	System OK

LTV0500000006287

Fig. 90   Codes C0267 Or C0268: Pump Motor Circuit (Part 4 of 4). 2003–06 Avalanche, Escalade, Escalade EXT, Suburban, Tahoe & Yukon

Step	Action	Yes	No
1	Did you perform the Diagnostic System Check - Vehicle?	Go to Step 2	Go to Diagnostic System Check - Vehicle
2	1. Use a scan tool in order to clear the DTCs. 2. Use the scan tool in order to perform the necessary Solenoid Tests. Refer to Scan Tool Output Controls. Do the Solenoid Tests show the system to be functioning normally?	Go to Diagnostic Aids	Go to Step 3
3	Replace the brake pressure modulator valve (BPMV) Did you complete the replacement?	Go to Step 4	--
4	Use the scan tool in order to perform the necessary Solenoid Tests. Do the Solenoid Tests show the system to be functioning normally?	System OK	Go to Step 3

LTV0500000006289

Fig. 91   Codes C0269 Or C0274: Excessive Dump/ Isolation Time (Part 2 of 2). 2003–06 Avalanche, Escalade, Escalade EXT, Suburban, Tahoe & Yukon

Circuit Description

This DTC identifies a malfunction within the electronic brake control module (EBCM).

DTC Descriptors

This diagnostic procedure supports the following DTCs:

- DTC C0271 EBCM Malfunction
- DTC C0272 EBCM Malfunction
- DTC C0273 EBCM Malfunction
- DTC C0284 EBCM Malfunction

Conditions for Running the DTC

The ignition is ON.

Conditions for Setting the DTC

The EBCM detects an internal malfunction.

Action Taken When the DTC Sets

If equipped, the following actions may occur:

- The EBCM disables the ABS/TCS/DRP.
- The ABS indicator turns ON.
- The TRACTION OFF indicator turns ON.
- The red brake warning indicator turns ON.

Conditions for Clearing the DTC

The conditions for setting the DTC are no longer present and you use the scan tool Clear DTCs function.

Diagnostic Aids

Replace the EBCM if DTC C0273 or DTC C0284 continues to set intermittently.

LTV0500000006290

Fig. 92   Codes C0271–C0273, C0284: EBCM Fault (Part 1 of 2). 2003–06 Avalanche, Escalade, Escalade EXT, Suburban, Tahoe & Yukon

Circuit Description

The system relay is energized when the ignition is ON. The system relay supplies voltage to the valve solenoids and the pump motor. This voltage is referred to as the system voltage. The electronic brake control module (EBCM) microprocessor activates the valve solenoids by grounding the control circuit.

DTC Descriptors

This diagnostic procedure supports the following DTCs:

- DTC C0269 Excessive Dump Time
- DTC C0274 Excessive Isolation Time

Conditions for Running the DTC

- The ignition is ON.
- The vehicle is experiencing an ABS event.

Conditions for Setting the DTC

C0269

The EBCM commands a dump solenoid ON for 9 consecutive seconds.

C0274

The EBCM commands an isolation solenoid ON for 255 consecutive seconds.

Action Taken When the DTC Sets

If equipped, the following actions may occur:

- The EBCM disables the ABS/TCS/DRP.
- The ABS indicator turns ON.
- The TRACTION OFF indicator turns ON.
- The red brake warning indicator turns ON.

Conditions for Clearing the DTC

The conditions for setting the DTC are no longer present and you use the scan tool Clear DTCs function.

Diagnostic Aids

The most likely cause of DTC C0269 or DTC C0274 is a mechanical failure that causes a wheel to lock and remain locked. The DTCs may also set, conceivably, when the ABS is activated on surfaces that are nearly impossible to get traction on. If the DTC sets within these conditions, diagnosis of the ABS system is not necessary.

Test Description

The number below refers to the step number on the diagnostic table:

2. Performing solenoid tests determines if there is a mechanical malfunction inside the brake pressure modulator valve

LTV0500000006288

Fig. 91   Codes C0269 Or C0274: Excessive Dump/ Isolation Time (Part 1 of 2). 2003–06 Avalanche, Escalade, Escalade EXT, Suburban, Tahoe & Yukon

Step	Action	Yes	No
1	Did you perform the Diagnostic System Check - Vehicle?	Go to Step 2	Go to Diagnostic System Check - Vehicle
2	Is DTC C0271 or DTC C0272 set in the electronic brake control module (EBCM) memory?	Go to Step 4	Go to Step 3
3	1. Use a scan tool in order to clear the DTCs. 2. Turn OFF the ignition for 5 seconds. 3. Turn ON the ignition. Does the DTC set?	Go to Step 4	Go to Diagnostic Aids
4	Replace the EBCM. Did you complete the replacement?	Go to Step 5	--
5	Use the scan tool in order to clear the DTCs. Operate the vehicle within the Conditions for Running the DTC as specified in the supporting text. Does the DTC reset?	Go to Step 2	System OK

LTV0500000006291

Fig. 92   Codes C0271–C0273, C0284: EBCM Fault (Part 2 of 2). 2003–06 Avalanche, Escalade, Escalade EXT, Suburban, Tahoe & Yukon

Circuit Description

The PCM sends engine/axle/tire IDs to the EBCM via serial data communications immediately after the modules are powered up.

DTC Descriptor

This diagnostic procedure supports the following DTC:

DTC C0279 Powertrain Configuration Not Valid

Conditions for Running the DTC

The ignition is ON.

Conditions for Setting the DTC

The EBCM receives invalid information from the PCM.

Action Taken When the DTC Sets

If equipped, the following actions occur:

- The EBCM disables the TCS.
- The traction off indicator turns ON.

Conditions for Clearing the DTC

The conditions for setting the DTC are no longer present and you use the scan tool Clear DTCs function.

Diagnostic Aids

Diagnose other ABS or TCS related DTCs prior to diagnosing DTC C0279.

If multiple TCS related DTCs are set, or the vehicle being serviced is not equipped with TCS, verify the correct EBCM is installed in the vehicle.

Test Description

The number below refers to the step number on the diagnostic table.

3. The powertrain control module (PCM) must have the correct part number for the specified application.

LTV0500000006292

Fig. 93   Code C0279: Powertrain Configuration Not Valid (Part 1 of 2). 2003–06 Avalanche, Escalade, Escalade EXT, Suburban, Tahoe & Yukon Less JL4

Circuit Description

The electronic brake control module (EBCM) uses the precharge pump in conjunction with the ABS pump to build hydraulic pressure for brake application during a vehicle stability enhancement system (VSES) event. Power and ground are both switched ON by the EBCM to energize the precharge pump motor.

DTC Descriptor

This diagnostic procedure supports the following DTC:

DTC C0279 Pre-charge Pump Circuit Performance

Conditions for Running the DTC

- The ignition is ON.
- The precharge pump is activated during a VSES or traction control system (TCS) event or when the EBCM performs the power-up self-test. Refer to ABS Description and Operation for a complete description of the power-up self-test.

Conditions for Setting the DTC

- The EBCM detects open precharge pump circuitry.
- The EBCM detects shorted precharge pump circuitry.
- The master cylinder pressure sensor signal does not increase sufficiently during a pressure-build event.

Action Taken When the DTC Sets

- The EBCM disables the VSES.
- The TCS operates with engine torque reduction only.

Conditions for Clearing the DTC

The conditions for setting the DTC are no longer present and you use the scan tool Clear DTCs function.

Diagnostic Aids

Thoroughly inspect connections or circuitry that may cause an intermittent malfunction.

Test Description

The numbers below refer to the step numbers on the diagnostic table.

3. This step tests if the EBCM is detecting open or shorted precharge pump motor circuitry.

4. This step tests if the EBCM is capable of energizing the precharge pump motor.

LTV0500000006294

Fig. 94   Code C0279: Pre-Charge Pump Circuit Performance (Part 1 of 4). 2003–06 Avalanche, Escalade, Escalade EXT, Suburban, Tahoe & Yukon w/JL4

Step	Action	Yes	No
1	Did you perform the Diagnostic System Check - Vehicle?	Go to Step 2	Go to Diagnostic System Check - Vehicle
2	1. Use a scan tool in order to clear the DTCs. 2. Turn OFF the ignition for 5 seconds. 3. Turn ON the ignition and wait 10 seconds. Does the DTC set?	Go to Step 3	Go to Diagnostics Aids
3	Verify the correct powertrain control module (PCM) is installed in the vehicle. Does the vehicle have the correct PCM?	Go to Step 4	Go to Step 6
4	Use the scan tool in order to read the Calibration IDs of the PCM. Are the PCM Calibration IDs correct?	Go to Diagnostics Aids	Go to Step 5
5	Perform the set up procedure for the PCM. Did you complete the action?	Go to Step 7	--
6	Replace the PCM. Did you complete the replacement?	Go to Step 7	--
7	1. Use the scan tool in order to clear the DTCs. 2. Operate the vehicle within the Conditions for Running the DTC, as specified in the supporting text. Does the DTC reset?	Go to Step 3	System OK

LTV0500000006293

Fig. 93   Code C0279: Powertrain Configuration Not Valid (Part 2 of 2). 2003–06 Avalanche, Escalade, Escalade EXT, Suburban, Tahoe & Yukon Less JL4

Step	Action	Values	Yes	No
1	Did you perform the Diagnostic System Check - Vehicle?	--	Go to Step 2	Go to Diagnostic System Check - Vehicle
2	1. Use the scan tool to clear the DTCs. 2. Turn OFF the ignition for 5 seconds. 3. Turn ON the ignition. 4. Operate the vehicle within the Conditions for Running the DTC as specified in the supporting text. Does the DTC reset?	--	Go to Step 3	Go to Diagnostic Aids
3	1. Turn OFF the ignition. 2. Disconnect the precharge pump motor harness connector. 3. Use a connector test adapter kit to connect a test lamp between the precharge pump motor circuits. 4. Turn ON the ignition. Does the DTC reset?	--	Go to Step 9	Go to Step 4
4	1. With the test lamp still connected, select the VSES Special Functions menu on the scan tool. 2. Select and perform the Pre-Charge Bleed. Does the test lamp illuminate and then turn OFF when the Pre-Charge Bleed is performed?	--	Go to Step 5	Go to Step 11
5	Important: Always ensure that the master cylinder reservoir cap is in place and secure before turning ON the precharge pump. 1. Reconnect the precharge pump motor harness connector. 2. Use the scan tool to perform the Pre-Charge Bleed. Does the precharge pump motor run?	--	Go to Step 6	Go to Step 8
6	1. Observe the fluid in the master cylinder reservoir. 2. Use the scan tool to perform the Pre-Charge Bleed. When the precharge pump runs, can fluid be seen discharging back into the master cylinder reservoir?	--	Go to Step 13	Go to Step 7

LTV0500000006295

Fig. 94   Code C0279: Pre-Charge Pump Circuit Performance (Part 2 of 4). 2003–06 Avalanche, Escalade, Escalade EXT, Suburban, Tahoe & Yukon w/JL4

	Action		Yes	No
7	Inspect the master cylinder reservoir, the brake fluid supply hose to the precharge pump inlet and the precharge pump inlet port for any restriction that may cause the loss of fluid supply to the pump. Did you find and correct the condition?	—	Go to Step 16	Go to Step 15
8	Inspect for poor connections at the harness connectors of the precharge pump motor. Did you find and correct the condition?	—	Go to Step 16	Go to Step 15
9	**Important:** Turn ON the ignition when testing for a short to voltage. 1. Turn OFF the ignition. 2. Disconnect the electronic brake control module (EBCM) harness connector. 3. Test the precharge pump motor circuits for the following: – An open – A short to ground – A short to voltage – Shorted together Refer to Circuit Testing and Wiring Repairs. Did you find and correct the condition?	—	Go to Step 16	Go to Step 10
10	Inspect for poor connections at the harness connector of the EBCM. Did you find and correct the condition?	—	Go to Step 16	Go to Step 13
11	Use a DMM to measure the resistance value of the precharge pump motor. Does the resistance measure within the specified range?	0.3-1.0 ohms	Go to Step 12	Go to Step 14
12	Use the DMM to measure the resistance between the high side of the precharge pump motor and a good ground. Does the resistance measure less than the specified value?	OL	Go to Step 14	Go to Step 13
13	Replace the EBCM. Did you complete the replacement?	—	Go to Step 16	—

LTV0500000006296

Fig. 94 Code C0279: Pre-Charge Pump Circuit Performance (Part 3 of 4). 2003–06 Avalanche, Escalade, Escalade EXT, Suburban, Tahoe & Yukon

Circuit Description

The stop lamp switch signal informs the electronic brake control module (EBCM) when the brake pedal is pressed.

DTC Descriptor

This diagnostic procedure supports the following DTC:

DTC C0281 Stop Lamp Switch Circuit

Conditions for Running the DTC

Either of the following conditions will cause the DTC to run:

- The ignition is ON and the vehicle achieves at least 56 km/h (35 mph) before coming to a stop.
- The ignition is ON and the vehicle experiences an antilock brake system (ABS) event lasting at least 1 second.

Conditions for Setting the DTC

The EBCM detects an open or shorted brake switch or brake switch circuit.

Action Taken When the DTC Sets

This information-only DTC is stored in EBCM memory until it is cleared by using the specified procedure.

Conditions for Clearing the DTC

The conditions for setting the DTC are no longer present and you use the scan tool Clear DTCs function.

Diagnostic Aids

Thoroughly inspect connections or circuitry that may cause an intermittent malfunction.

Test Description

The numbers below refer to the step numbers on the diagnostic table.

4. This step tests for a shorted stop lamp switch.

5. This step tests for an open stop lamp switch.

LTV0500000006298

Fig. 95 Code C0281: Stoplamp Switch Circuit (Part 1 of 3). 2003–06 Avalanche, Escalade, Escalade EXT, Suburban, Tahoe & Yukon

	Action		Yes	No
14	**Important:** Following EBCM replacement, perform the set-up procedure for the EBCM and perform the Yaw Rate Reference Table Reset Procedure. Use the scan tool to perform the Tire Size Calibration procedure. 1. Replace the EBCM. 2. Replace the precharge pump assembly. Did you complete the replacements?		Go to Step 16	—
15	Replace the precharge pump assembly. Pump Replacement. Did you complete the replacement?		Go to Step 16	—
16	1. Use the scan tool Clear All Class 2 DTCs function to clear all of the DTCs from all modules. 2. Turn OFF the ignition for 5 seconds. 3. Turn ON the ignition. 4. Operate the vehicle within the Conditions for Running the DTC as specified in the supporting text. Does the DTC reset?		Go to Step 3	System OK

LTV0500000006297

Fig. 94 Code C0279: Pre-Charge Pump Circuit Performance (Part 4 of 4). 2003–06 Avalanche, Escalade, Escalade EXT, Suburban, Tahoe & Yukon

Step		Action	Yes	No
1		Did you perform the Diagnostic System Check - Vehicle?	Go to Step 2	Go to Diagnostic System Check - Vehicle
2		1. Install a scan tool. 2. Select the ABS Data Display function. 3. Observe the Brake Switch Status on the scan tool. Does the scan tool display Off?	Go to Step 3	Go to Step 5
3		1. Apply the brake. 2. Observe the Brake Switch Status on the scan tool. Does the scan tool display On?	Go to Diagnostic Aids	Go to Step 4
4		1. Turn OFF the ignition. 2. Disconnect the stop lamp switch. 3. Turn ON the ignition. 4. Observe the Brake Switch Status on the scan tool. Does the scan tool display On?	Go to Step 9	Go to Step 7
5		1. Turn OFF the ignition. 2. Disconnect the stop lamp switch. 3. Connect a fused jumper wire between the ignition 3 voltage circuit and the torque converter clutch (TCC) brake switch signal circuit at the stop lamp switch harness connector. 4. Turn ON the ignition. 5. Observe the Brake Switch Status on the scan tool. Does the scan tool display Off?	Go to Step 9	Go to Step 6
6		Test the ignition 3 voltage circuit and the TCC brake switch signal circuit for an open or a short to ground. Did you find and correct the condition?	Go to Step 12	Go to Step 8

LTV0500000006299

Fig. 95 Code C0281: Stoplamp Switch Circuit (Part 2 of 3). 2003–06 Avalanche, Escalade, Escalade EXT, Suburban, Tahoe & Yukon

	Action	Yes	No
7	Test the TCC brake switch signal circuit for a short to voltage. Did you find and correct the condition?	Go to Step 12	Go to Step 8
8	Inspect for poor connections at the harness connector of the electronic brake control module (EBCM). Did you find and correct the condition?	Go to Step 12	Go to Step 10
9	Inspect for poor connections at the harness connector of the stop lamp switch. Did you find and correct the condition?	Go to Step 12	Go to Step 11
10	Replace the EBCM. Did you complete the replacement?	Go to Step 12	—
11	Replace the stop lamp switch. Did you complete the replacement?	Go to Step 12	—
12	1. Use the scan tool in order to clear the DTCs. 2. Operate the vehicle within the Conditions for Running the DTC as specified in the supporting text. Does the DTC reset?	Go to Step 2	System OK

LTV0500000006300

Fig. 95 Code C0281: Stoplamp Switch Circuit (Part 3 of 3). 2003–06 Avalanche, Escalade, Escalade EXT, Suburban, Tahoe & Yukon

Circuit Description

The traction control switch is a momentary-contact, normally-open switch that can be used to disable the engine torque management function of the traction control system (TCS). On 2-wheel drive or all wheel drive vehicles, the traction control switch is directly monitored by the electronic brake control module (EBCM). On 4-wheel drive vehicles equipped with selectable 4 LO, the traction control switch is monitored by the transfer case shift control module (TCSCM), which sends the traction control switch status information to the EBCM on the serial data link. Each time the traction control switch is pressed, the vehicle stability enhancement system (VSES) and TCS enabled/disabled status changes. When TCS is disabled, the EBCM sends serial data messages to the instrument panel cluster (IPC) to turn ON the traction OFF indicator and display the stability system disabled message.

DTC Descriptor

This diagnostic procedure supports the following DTC:

DTC C0283 Mode Switch Circuit Malfunction

Conditions for Running the DTC

The ignition is ON.

Conditions for Setting the DTC

Two Wheel Drive or All Wheel Drive Vehicles

The EBCM detects low voltage on the traction control switch signal circuit for 8 seconds.

Four Wheel Drive Vehicles with Selectable 4 LO

The EBCM receives a serial data message from the TCSCM indicating that the VSES mode/transfer case shift control switch is detected as failed. The TCSCM sends this message 60 seconds after the TCSCM sets DTC B2725.

Action Taken When the DTC Sets

- The EBCM disables VSES and engine torque management.
- The traction OFF indicator turns ON.
- The message center displays the service stability system message.

LTV0500000006301

Fig. 96   Code C0283: Mode Switch Circuit Fault (Part 1 of 3). 2003–06 Avalanche, Escalade, Escalade EXT, Suburban, Tahoe & Yukon w/JL4

Step	Action		
4	1. Use the scan tool in order to clear the DTCs. 2. Turn OFF the ignition. 3. Connect a fused jumper wire between the ignition 3 voltage circuit and the traction control switch signal circuit at the traction control switch harness connector. 4. Turn ON the ignition for up to 20 seconds. Does the DTC set?	Go to Step 5	Go to Step 9
5	Test the traction control switch signal circuit for an open or a short to ground. Refer to Circuit Testing and Wiring Repairs . Did you find and correct the condition?	Go to Step 11	Go to Step 6
6	Inspect for poor connections at the harness connector of the electronic brake control module (EBCM). Did you find and correct the condition?	Go to Step 11	Go to Step 7
7	Replace the EBCM. Did you complete the replacement?	Go to Step 11	--
8	Repair the open in the ignition 3 voltage circuit. Did you complete the repair?	Go to Step 11	--
9	Inspect for poor connections at the harness connector of the traction control switch. Did you find and correct the condition?	Go to Step 11	Go to Step 10
10	Replace the traction control switch. Did you complete the replacement?	Go to Step 11	--
11	1. Use the scan tool to clear the DTCs. 2. Turn OFF the ignition for 5 seconds. 3. Turn ON the ignition. 4. Operate the vehicle within the Conditions for Running the DTC, as specified in the supporting text. Does the DTC reset?	Go to Step 3	System OK

LTV0500000006303

Fig. 96   Code C0283: Mode Switch Circuit Fault (Part 3 of 3). 2003–06 Avalanche, Escalade, Escalade EXT, Suburban, Tahoe & Yukon w/JL4

Conditions for Clearing the DTC

The conditions for setting the DTC are no longer present and you use the scan tool Clear DTCs function.

Diagnostic Aids

Thoroughly inspect connections or circuitry that may cause an intermittent malfunction. Refer to the following:

- Testing for Electrical Intermittents .
- Testing for Intermittent Conditions and Poor Connections
- Wiring Repairs
- Connector Repairs

Test Description

The number below refers to the step number on the diagnostic table.

4.   This step tests the traction control switch circuitry. If the fuse opens when you perform this test, the traction control switch signal circuit is shorted to ground.

Step	Action	Yes	No
1	Did you perform the Diagnostic System Check - Vehicle?	Go to Step 2	Go to Diagnostic System Check - Vehicle
2	1. Use a scan tool in order to clear the DTCs. 2. Turn OFF the ignition for 5 seconds. 3. Turn ON the ignition for up to 20 seconds. Does the DTC set?	Go to Step 3	Go to Diagnostic Aids
3	1. Turn OFF the ignition. 2. Disconnect the traction control switch harness connector. 3. Turn ON the ignition. 4. Connect a test lamp between the ignition 3 voltage circuit and a good ground. Does the test lamp illuminate?	Go to Step 4	Go to Step 8

LTV0500000006302

Fig. 96   Code C0283: Mode Switch Circuit Fault (Part 2 of 3). 2003–06 Avalanche, Escalade, Escalade EXT, Suburban, Tahoe & Yukon w/JL4

Circuit Description

The traction control switch is a momentary-contact, normally-open switch that can be used to disable the traction control system (TCS). Each time the traction control switch is pressed, the TCS enabled/disabled status changes. When TCS is disabled, the electronic brake control module (EBCM) illuminates the traction off indicator by opening the service traction control signal circuit.

DTC Descriptor

This diagnostic procedure supports the following DTC:

DTC C0283 Mode Switch Circuit Malfunction

Conditions for Running the DTC

The ignition is ON.

Conditions for Setting the DTC

The EBCM detects low voltage on the traction control switch signal circuit for 10 seconds.

Action Taken When the DTC Sets

If equipped, the following actions occur:

- The EBCM disables the TCS.
- The traction off indicator turns ON.

Conditions for Clearing the DTC

The conditions for setting the DTC are no longer present and you use the scan tool Clear DTCs function.

Diagnostic Aids

Thoroughly inspect connections or circuitry that may cause an intermittent malfunction.

Test Description

The number below refers to the step number on the diagnostic table.

4.   This step tests the traction control switch circuitry. If the fuse opens when you perform this test, the traction control switch signal circuit is shorted to ground.

LTV0500000006304

Fig. 97   Code C0283: Mode Switch Circuit Fault (Part 1 of 3). 2003–06 Avalanche, Escalade, Escalade EXT, Suburban, Tahoe & Yukon Less JL4

Step	Action	Yes	No
1	Did you perform the Diagnostic System Check - Vehicle?	Go to Step 2	Go to Diagnostic System Check - Vehicle
2	1. Use a scan tool in order to clear the DTCs. 2. Turn OFF the ignition for 5 seconds. 3. Start the engine and allow the engine to run for at least 20 seconds. Does the DTC set?	Go to Step 3	Go to Diagnostic Aids
3	1. Turn OFF the ignition. 2. Disconnect the traction control switch harness connector. 3. Turn ON the ignition. 4. Connect a test lamp between the ignition 1 voltage circuit and a good ground. Does the test lamp illuminate?	Go to Step 4	Go to Step 8
4	1. Use the scan tool in order to clear the DTCs. 2. Turn OFF the ignition. 3. Connect a fused jumper wire between the ignition 1 voltage circuit and the traction control switch signal circuit at the traction control switch harness connector. 4. Start the engine and allow the engine to run for at least 20 seconds. Does the DTC set?	Go to Step 5	Go to Step 9
5	Test the traction control switch signal circuit for an open or a short to ground. Did you find and correct the condition?	Go to Step 11	Go to Step 6
6	Inspect for poor connections at the harness connector of the electronic brake control module (EBCM). Did you find and correct the condition?	Go to Step 11	Go to Step 7

LTV0500000006305

Fig. 97 Code C0283: Mode Switch Circuit Fault (Part 2 of 3). 2003–06 Avalanche, Escalade, Escalade EXT, Suburban, Tahoe & Yukon Less LJ4

Step	Action	Yes	No
7	Replace the EBCM. Did you complete the replacement?	Go to Step 11	--
8	Repair the open in the ignition 1 voltage circuit. Did you complete the repair?	Go to Step 11	--
9	Inspect for poor connections at the harness connector of the traction control switch. Did you find and correct the condition?	Go to Step 11	Go to Step 10
10	Replace the traction control switch. Did you complete the replacement?	Go to Step 11	--
11	1. Use the scan tool in order to clear the DTCs. 2. Operate the vehicle within the Conditions for Running the DTC, as specified in the supporting text. Does the DTC reset?	Go to Step 3	System OK

LTV0500000006306

Fig. 97 Code C0283: Mode Switch Circuit Fault (Part 3 of 3). 2003–06 Avalanche, Escalade, Escalade EXT, Suburban, Tahoe & Yukon Less JL4

Circuit Description

The EBCM supplies 5 VDC to the powertrain control module (PCM) on the delivered torque signal circuit. The PCM toggles this voltage to ground in order to create the delivered torque signal at the EBCM. A signal with a frequency of 128 Hz +/- 5 percent and a duty cycle of 25-95 percent is a valid delivered torque signal. The percentage of duty cycle is proportionate to the percentage of delivered torque.

DTC Descriptor

This diagnostic procedure supports the following DTC:

DTC C0287 Delivered Torque Signal Malfunction

Conditions for Running the DTC

- The ignition is ON.
- The engine is running at a speed greater than 450 RPM for 1 second.

Conditions for Setting the DTC

C0287

The EBCM receives an invalid delivered torque signal for 300 milliseconds.

P1689

The PCM detects open or shorted delivered torque signal voltage as being less than 4.75 volts or greater than 5.25 volts.

Action Taken When the DTC Sets

- The EBCM disables the TCS.
- The traction off indicator turns ON.

LTV0500000006307

Fig. 98 Codes C0287, P1644 Or P1689: Delivered Torque Signal Fault (Part 1 of 4). 2003–06 Avalanche, Escalade, Escalade EXT, Suburban, Tahoe & Yukon

Conditions for Clearing the DTC

The conditions for setting the DTC are no longer present and you use the scan tool Clear DTCs function.

Diagnostic Aids

Thoroughly inspect connections or circuitry that may cause an intermittent malfunction.

Test Description

The numbers below refer to the step numbers on the diagnostic table.

4. This step tests for voltage supplied to the PCM from the EBCM.

5. This step tests for a shorted resistor in the EBCM or a short to voltage within the circuit, by verifying that a large voltage drop occurs in the circuit when the test lamp is placed in parallel with the DMM. The PCM may be damaged if either of these conditions is present.

Step	Action	Values	Yes	No
1	Did you perform the Diagnostic System Check - Vehicle?	--	Go to Step 2	Go to Diagnostic System Check - Vehicle
2	1. Use a scan tool in order to clear the DTCs. 2. Turn OFF the ignition for 5 seconds. 3. Start the engine. Does the DTC set?	--	Go to Step 3	Go to Diagnostic Aids
3	Is this vehicle equipped with vehicle stability enhancement system (VSES) (JL4)?	--	Go to DTC C0244	Go to Step 4

LTV0500000006308

Fig. 98 Codes C0287, P1644 Or P1689: Delivered Torque Signal Fault (Part 2 of 4). 2003–06 Avalanche, Escalade, Escalade EXT, Suburban, Tahoe & Yukon

Step	Action	Value	Yes	No
4	1. Turn OFF the ignition. 2. Disconnect from the powertrain control module (PCM), the harness connector containing the delivered torque signal circuit. 3. Turn ON the ignition. 4. Use a DMM in order to measure the voltage between the delivered torque signal circuit and a good ground. Does the voltage measure greater than the specified value?	4.75 V	Go to Step 5	Go to Step 6
5	1. With the DMM still connected to monitor the delivered torque signal circuit, connect one end of a test lamp to a good ground. 2. Connect the other end of the test lamp to the positive lead of the DMM. Does the voltage measure less than the specified value?	0.15 V	Go to Step 7	Go to Step 11
6	Test the delivered torque signal circuit for an open, or a short to ground. Did you find and correct the condition?	--	Go to Step 14	Go to Step 9
7	1. Turn OFF the ignition. 2. Reconnect the PCM harness connector. 3. Start the engine. 4. Select the Traction Assist Data List on the scan tool. 5. Observe the Delivered Torque parameter on the scan tool. Does the scan tool display a duty cycle of the delivered torque signal within the specified range?	25-95%	Go to Step 8	Go to Step 12
8	1. Turn OFF the ignition. 2. Install a J 39700 Universal Breakout Box and a J 39700-325 Adaptor Cable. Install the equipment between the electronic brake control module (EBCM) and the EBCM harness connector. 3. Start the engine. 4. Use a DMM in order to measure the Hz frequency between the delivered torque signal circuit and a ground circuit. Does the frequency of the delivered torque signal measure within the specified range?	121-134 Hz	Go to Step 10	Go to Step 13
9	1. Turn OFF the ignition. 2. Inspect for poor connections at the harness connector of the EBCM. Did you find and correct the condition?	--	Go to Step 14	Go to Step 10

LTV0500000006309

Fig. 98   Codes C0287, P1644 Or P1689: Delivered Torque Signal Fault (Part 3 of 4). 2003–06 Avalanche, Escalade, Escalade EXT, Suburban, Tahoe & Yukon

Step	Action	Yes	No
10	Replace the EBCM. Did you complete the replacement?	Go to Step 14	--
11	Test the delivered torque signal circuit for a short to voltage. Did you find and correct the condition?	Go to Step 14	Go to Step 13
12	Inspect for poor connections at the harness connector of the PCM. Did you find and correct the condition?	Go to Step 14	Go to Step 13
13	Replace the PCM. Did you complete the replacement?	Go to Step 14	--
14	1. Use the scan tool in order to clear the DTCs. 2. Operate the vehicle within the Conditions for Running the DTC, as specified in the supporting text. Does the DTC reset?	Go to Step 3	System OK

LTV0500000006310

Fig. 98   Codes C0287, P1644 Or P1689: Delivered Torque Signal Fault (Part 4 of 4). 2003–06 Avalanche, Escalade, Escalade EXT, Suburban, Tahoe & Yukon

Circuit Description

The powertrain control module (PCM) sends a state of health message to the EBCM within 5.5 seconds after the modules are powered up. This message is sent via serial data communications.

DTC Descriptors

This diagnostic procedure supports the following DTCs:

- DTC C0290 Class 2 Data Link Malfunction
- DTC C0292 Lost Communications with Engine Control System

Conditions for Running the DTC

The ignition is ON.

Conditions for Setting the DTC

The EBCM fails to receive serial data from the PCM.

Action Taken When the DTC Sets

If equipped, the following actions occur:

- The EBCM disables the TCS.
- The traction off indicator turns ON.

Conditions for Clearing the DTC

The conditions for setting the DTC are no longer present and you use the scan tool Clear DTCs function.

Step	Action	Yes	No
1	Did you perform the Diagnostic System Check - Vehicle?	Check Scan Tool Does Not Communicate with Class 2 Device	Go to Diagnostic System Check - Vehicle

LTV0500000006311

Fig. 99   Codes C0290 Or C0292: Class 2 Data Link Fault. 2003–06 Avalanche, Escalade, Escalade EXT, Suburban, Tahoe & Yukon Less JL4

Circuit Description

The EBCM supplies a reference voltage of 5 volts to the yaw rate sensor/lateral accelerometer and the master cylinder pressure sensor. The sensor supply voltage is monitored via an internal feedback circuit to the EBCM microprocessor.

DTC Descriptors

This diagnostic procedure supports the following DTCs:

- DTC C0290 Class 2 Data Link Malfunction
- DTC C0292 Lost Communications with Engine Control System

Conditions for Running the DTC

The ignition is ON.

Conditions for Setting the DTC

The electronic brake control module (EBCM) detects that the sensor supply voltage is less than 4.75 volts or greater than 5.25 volts for 30 milliseconds.

Action Taken When the DTC Sets

- The EBCM disables the vehicle stability enhancement system (VSES).
- The message center displays the service stability system message.

Conditions for Clearing the DTC

The conditions for setting the DTC are no longer present and you use the scan tool Clear DTCs function.

Diagnostic Aids

Thoroughly inspect connections or circuitry that may cause an intermittent malfunction

Test Description

The numbers below refer to the step numbers on the diagnostic table.

5. This step tests for a shorted yaw rate sensor/lateral accelerometer.

6. This step tests for a shorted master cylinder pressure sensor. The presence of DTC C0110 is normal during this step.

LTV0500000006312

Fig. 100   Codes C0290 Or C0292: Class 2 Data Link Fault (Part 1 of 3). 2003–06 Avalanche, Escalade, Escalade EXT, Suburban, Tahoe & Yukon w/JL4

Step	Action	Yes	No
	Important: Always use connector test adapters when performing tests to avoid damage to delicate connector terminals.		
1	Did you perform the Diagnostic System Check - Vehicle?	Go to Step 2	Go to Diagnostic System Check - Vehicle
2	1. Use the scan tool to clear the DTCs. 2. Turn OFF the ignition for 5 seconds. 3. Turn ON the ignition. Does the DTC reset?	Go to Step 3	Go to Diagnostic Aids
3	1. Turn OFF the ignition. 2. Disconnect the yaw rate sensor/lateral accelerometer harness connector. 3. Disconnect the electronic brake control module (EBCM) harness connector. 4. Test the yaw rate sensor/lateral accelerometer 5-volt reference circuit for a short to ground. Did you find and correct the condition?	Go to Step 10	Go to Step 4
4	1. Turn ON the ignition. 2. Test the following circuits for a short to voltage: - Yaw rate sensor/lateral accelerometer 5-volt reference circuit - Yaw rate sensor signal circuit - Lateral accelerometer signal circuit Refer to Circuit Testing and Wiring Repairs. Did you find and correct the condition?	Go to Step 10	Go to Step 5
5	1. Turn OFF the ignition. 2. Reconnect only the EBCM harness connector. 3. Turn ON the ignition. 4. Use the scan tool to clear any DTCs. Does the DTC reset?	Go to Step 6	Go to Step 8
6	1. Turn OFF the ignition. 2. Reconnect the yaw rate sensor/lateral accelerometer harness connector. 3. Separate the EBCM from the brake pressure modulator valve (BPMV), leaving the EBCM harness connector connected. 4. Turn ON the ignition. Does the DTC reset?	Go to Step 9	Go to Step 7

LTV0500000006313

Fig. 100   Codes C0290 Or C0292: Class 2 Data Link Fault (Part 2 of 3). 2003–06 Avalanche, Escalade, Escalade EXT, Suburban, Tahoe & Yukon w/JL4

Step	Action	Yes	No
7	Replace the BPMV. Did you complete the replacement?	Go to Step 10	--
8	**Important:** The Yaw Rate Reference Table Reset Procedure must be performed when you are instructed to do so during the Yaw Rate Sensor/Lateral Accelerometer Replacement procedure. Replace the yaw rate sensor/lateral accelerometer. Did you complete the replacement?	Go to Step 10	--
9	Replace the EBCM. Did you complete the replacement?	Go to Step 10	--
10	1. Use the scan tool Clear All Class 2 DTCs function to clear all of the DTCs from all modules. 2. Turn OFF the ignition for 5 seconds. 3. Turn ON the ignition. 4. Operate the vehicle within the Conditions for Running the DTC, as specified in the supporting text. Does the DTC reset?	Go to Step 3	System OK

LTV0500000006314

Fig. 100   Codes C0290 Or C0292: Class 2 Data Link Fault (Part 3 of 3). 2003–06 Avalanche, Escalade, Escalade EXT, Suburban, Tahoe & Yukon w/JL4

Circuit Description

The body control module (BCM) sends a state of health (SOH) serial data message to the electronic brake control module (EBCM) within 5.5 seconds after the ignition is turned ON.

DTC Descriptor

This diagnostic procedure supports the following DTC:

DTC C0291 Lost Communication with BCM

Conditions for Running the DTC

The ignition is ON.

Conditions for Setting the DTC

The EBCM fails to receive serial data from the BCM.

Action Taken When the DTC Sets

The EBCM sets this information-only DTC as a current DTC, for as long as the conditions for setting the DTC are present.

Conditions for Clearing the DTC

The conditions for setting the DTC are no longer present and you use the scan tool Clear DTCs function.

Step	Action	Yes	No
1	Did you perform the Diagnostic System Check - Vehicle?	Check Scan Tool Does Not Communicate with Class 2 Device	Go to Diagnostic System Check - Vehicle

LTV0500000006315

Fig. 101   Code C0291: Lost Communication With BCM. 2003–06 Avalanche, Escalade, Escalade EXT, Suburban, Tahoe & Yukon

Circuit Description

The PCM sends engine/axle/tire IDs to the EBCM via serial data communications immediately after the modules are powered up.

DTC Descriptor

This diagnostic procedure supports the following DTC:

DTC C0297 Powertrain Configuration Data Not Received

Conditions for Running the DTC

The ignition is ON.

Conditions for Setting the DTC

The EBCM fails to receive serial data from the PCM.

Action Taken When the DTC Sets

If equipped, the following actions occur:

- The EBCM disables the TCS.
- The traction off indicator turns ON.

Conditions for Clearing the DTC

The conditions for setting the DTC are no longer present and you use the scan tool Clear DTCs function.

Step	Action	Yes	No
1	Did you perform the Diagnostic System Check - Vehicle?	Check Scan Tool Does Not Communicate with Class 2 Device	Go to Diagnostic System Check - Vehicle

LTV0500000006316

Fig. 102   Code C0297: Powertrain Configuration Data Not Received. 2003–06 Avalanche, Escalade, Escalade EXT, Suburban, Tahoe & Yukon

Circuit Description

C0298

The powertrain control module (PCM) and the electronic brake control module (EBCM) communicate on the serial data line whenever the ignition is ON.

P0856

The PCM supplies 5 volts through an internal resistor, to the EBCM on the requested torque signal circuit. The EBCM toggles this voltage to ground to create the requested torque signal.

DTC Descriptor

This diagnostic procedure supports the following DTC:

DTC C0298 Powertrain Control Malfunction

Conditions for Running the DTC

C0298

The ignition is ON.

P0856

- The ignition is ON.
- The engine is running at a speed greater than 450 RPM for 5-20 seconds.

Conditions for Setting the DTC

C0298

The EBCM receives a serial data message stating that the PCM has lost the ability to reduce engine torque.

P0856

The PCM receives an invalid requested torque signal for 3 seconds.

LTV0500000006317

Fig. 103 Codes C0298 Or P0856: Powertrain Control Fault (Part 1 of 4). 2003–06 Avalanche, Escalade, Escalade EXT, Suburban, Tahoe & Yukon

Test Description

The numbers below refer to the step numbers on the diagnostic table.

4. This step tests for voltage supplied to the EBCM from the PCM.

5. This step tests for a shorted resistor in the PCM, or a short to voltage within the requested torque circuit, by verifying that a large voltage drop occurs when a test lamp is connected in parallel with the DMM.

Step	Action	Values	Yes	No
1	Did you perform the Diagnostic System Check - Vehicle?	--	Go to Step 2	Go to Diagnostic System Check - Vehicle
2	Is DTC P0856 set?	--	Go to Step 3	Go to Diagnostic Aids
3	1. Use the scan tool to clear the DTCs. 2. Turn OFF the ignition for 5 seconds. 3. Turn ON the ignition. 4. Operate the vehicle within the Conditions for Running the DTC, as specified in the supporting text. Does DTC P0856 reset?	--	Go to Step 4	Go to Diagnostic Aids
4	1. Turn OFF the ignition. 2. Disconnect from the electronic brake control module (EBCM), the harness connector containing the requested torque signal circuit. 3. Turn ON the ignition. 4. Use a DMM in order to measure the voltage between the requested torque signal circuit and a good ground. Does the voltage measure greater than the specified value?	4.75 V	Go to Step 5	Go to Step 8
5	1. With the DMM still connected to monitor the requested torque signal circuit, connect one end of a test lamp to a good ground. 2. Connect the other end of the test lamp to the positive lead of the DMM. Does the voltage measure less than the specified value?	0.15 V	Go to Step 6	Go to Step 9
6	1. Turn OFF the ignition. 2. Install a J 39700 Universal Breakout Box and a J 39700-325 (W/NW7) or a J 39700-650 (W/JL4) Adapter Cable. Install the equipment between the EBCM and the EBCM harness connector. 3. Start the engine. 4. Use the DMM in order to measure the Hz frequency of the requested torque signal. Does the Hz frequency of the requested torque signal measure within the specified range?	121-134 Hz	Go to Step 7	Go to Step 11
7	Use the DMM in order to measure the duty cycle of the requested torque signal circuit. Does the duty cycle of the requested torque signal measure within the specified range?	40-95%	Go to Step 12	Go to Step 13

LTV0500000006319

Fig. 103 Codes C0298 Or P0856: Powertrain Control Fault (Part 3 of 4). 2003–06 Avalanche, Escalade, Escalade EXT, Suburban, Tahoe & Yukon

Action Taken When the DTC Sets

C0298

- The EBCM disables the traction control system (TCS).
- The traction off indicator turns ON.

P0856

- The PCM sends a serial data message to the EBCM stating that the PCM has lost the ability to reduce engine torque.
- The EBCM sets DTC C0298 or DTC C0240 as a current DTC for as long as the malfunction is present.

Conditions for Clearing the DTC

C0298

The conditions for setting the DTC are no longer present and you use the scan tool Clear DTCs function.

P1571

- The conditions for setting the DTC are no longer present and you use the scan tool Clear DTCs function.
- A history DTC clears automatically after 40 consecutive warm-up cycles without a PCM detected failure.

Diagnostic Aids

C0298

A requested torque signal malfunction is only one possible cause for the PCM to lose the ability to perform traction control. DTC C0298 may set due to engine overheating, throttle actuator control failure, loss of ignition timing control by the PCM, etc. If DTC P1571 has not set, refer to Diagnostic System Check - Vehicle in order to identify other possible causes of DTC C0298.

P1571

Thoroughly inspect connections or circuitry that may cause an intermittent malfunction.

LTV0500000006318

Fig. 103 Codes C0298 Or P0856: Powertrain Control Fault (Part 2 of 4). 2003–06 Avalanche, Escalade, Escalade EXT, Suburban, Tahoe & Yukon

8	Test the requested torque signal circuit for an open or a short to ground. Did you find and correct the condition?		Go to Step 14	Go to Step 10
9	Test the requested torque signal circuit for a short to voltage Did you find and correct the condition?		Go to Step 14	Go to Step 12
10	Inspect for poor connections at the harness connector of the powertrain control module (PCM). Did you find and correct the condition?		Go to Step 14	Go to Step 12
11	Inspect for poor connections at the harness connector of the EBCM. Did you find and correct the condition?		Go to Step 14	Go to Step 13
12	Replace the powertrain control module (PCM). Did you complete the replacement?		Go to Step 14	--
13	Replace the EBCM. Did you complete the replacement?		Go to Step 14	--
14	1. Use the scan tool Clear All Class 2 DTCs function to clear all of the DTCs from all modules. 2. Turn OFF the ignition for 5 seconds. 3. Turn ON the ignition. 4. Operate the vehicle within the Conditions for Running the DTC, as specified in the supporting text. Does DTC P0856 reset?		Go to Step 4	System OK

LTV0500000006320

Fig. 103 Codes C0298 Or P0856: Powertrain Control Fault (Part 4 of 4). 2003–06 Avalanche, Escalade, Escalade EXT, Suburban, Tahoe & Yukon

Circuit Description

The electronic brake control module (EBCM) receives several inputs from the steering wheel position sensor. Three digital square wave signal inputs are wired directly to the EBCM harness connector, however, only signals A and B are used or monitored. The failure of the index pulse signal does not effect vehicle stability enhancement system (VSES) function. The body control module (BCM), which receives an analog steering position sensor input, transmits steering position data on the serial data line. The EBCM monitors the serial data information as an added fail-safe for the steering position sensor circuitry. Battery voltage is supplied to the digital portion of the steering wheel position sensor from the cruise control fuse. The analog portion of the steering wheel position sensor is supplied a 5-volt reference from the BCM. This circuit is also used for a lamp dimming function.

DTC Descriptor

This diagnostic procedure supports the following DTC:

DTC C0455 Front Steering Position Sensor Circuit

Conditions for Running the DTC

- The ignition is ON.
- The VSES sensors have been successfully initialized.

Conditions for Setting the DTC

Any of the following conditions may cause the DTC to set:

- The steering angle calculated by the EBCM does not correlate with the steering angle information which is being transmitted on the serial data line.
- When driven forward in a straight line, the centered steering angle differs by more than 30 degrees from the centered steering angle when the sensors are initialized.
- The EBCM detects an erratic signal from the steering wheel position signal A or signal B.
- The BCM detects an invalid steering wheel position sensor signal, sets a DTC, and therefore, cannot transmit valid serial data information. The BCM sends a serial data message to the EBCM, which causes the DTC to set.
- The EBCM detects an open or shorted steering wheel position signal A or signal B, after having received a valid signal during the same ignition.

LTV0500000006321

Fig. 104   Code C0455: Front Steering Position Sensor Circuit (Part 1 of 4). 2003–06 Avalanche, Escalade, Escalade EXT, Suburban, Tahoe & Yukon

Action Taken When the DTC Sets

- The EBCM disables the VSES.
- The message center displays the service stability system message.

Conditions for Clearing the DTC

The condition for setting the DTC is no longer present and you use the scan tool Clear DTCs function.

Diagnostic Aids

- DTC C0455 may be falsely set if you did not turn OFF the ignition for 5 seconds after clearing DTCs from the EBCM. This is why all diagnostic tables which apply to this system always instruct you to turn OFF the ignition for 5 seconds after clearing DTCs. If this DTC has set after you cleared DTCs from the EBCM, or used the scan tool to clear all DTCs from all modules, and you did not cycle the ignition afterward, it is likely that no actual malfunction exists.
- Whenever any one of the steering signals to the EBCM is lost, the scan tool displays a fixed steering wheel position, which indicates the last known steering wheel position. This can aid you in diagnosing an intermittent malfunction.
- If the DTC does not reset during step 2 or 3 of the diagnostic procedure, the stability system disabled message may be displayed due to an unsuccessful initialization. This occurs if the EBCM does not receive any signal from one or both of the digital inputs during the entire ignition cycle. If this occurs, refer to Stability System Disabled Indicator Always On for further diagnosis.
- Inspect the vehicle for proper wheel alignment. Ensure the vehicle does not pull toward the left or right while driving straight forward on a level surface.
- Communicate with the customer to determine the conditions under which the message center displays the service stability system message. Learning the conditions under which the DTC sets may help you duplicate the failure.
- Use the Snapshot function on the scan tool in order to assist you in locating an intermittent malfunction.

Test Description

The number below refers to the step number on the diagnostic table.

2. If the DTC sets without turning the steering wheel, or driving the vehicle, a malfunction exists in the analog steering wheel position signal to the BCM, and the BCM has set DTC C0472 or C0473.

LTV0500000006322

Fig. 104   Code C0455: Front Steering Position Sensor Circuit (Part 2 of 4). 2003–06 Avalanche, Escalade, Escalade EXT, Suburban, Tahoe & Yukon

Step	Action	Values	Yes	No
1	Did you perform the Diagnostic System Check - Vehicle?	--	Go to Step 2	Go to Diagnostic System Check - Vehicle
2	**Important:** Center the steering wheel before proceeding with this step. Do not rotate the steering wheel while performing this step. 1. Use the scan tool to clear the DTCs. 2. Turn OFF the ignition for 5 seconds. 3. Turn ON the ignition. 4. Wait approximately 5 seconds to verify whether or not the DTC sets. Does the DTC set?	--	Go to DTC C0472 or C0473	Go to Step 3
3	Operate the vehicle within the Conditions for Running the DTC, as specified in the supporting text. Does the DTC set?	--	Go to Step 4	Go to Diagnostic Aids
4	1. Select Body Control Module/Data Display/Data on the scan tool. 2. Center the steering wheel and verify that the front wheels are straight ahead. 3. Observe the Steering Wheel Sensor Signal parameter. Does the scan tool display an Steering Wheel Sensor Signal within the specified range?	2.3-2.7 V	Go to Step 5	Go to Step 9

LTV0500000006323

Fig. 104   Code C0455: Front Steering Position Sensor Circuit (Part 3 of 4). 2003–06 Avalanche, Escalade, Escalade EXT, Suburban, Tahoe & Yukon

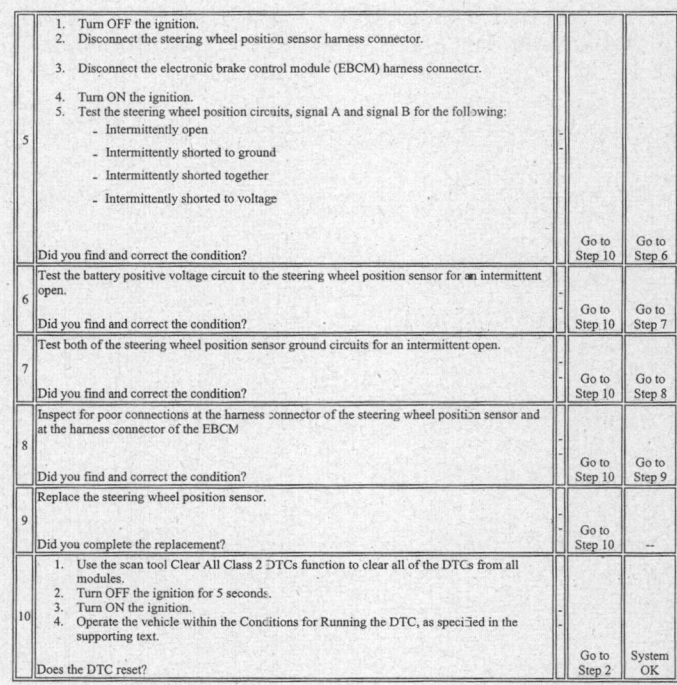

5	1. Turn OFF the ignition. 2. Disconnect the steering wheel position sensor harness connector. 3. Disconnect the electronic brake control module (EBCM) harness connector. 4. Turn ON the ignition. 5. Test the steering wheel position circuits, signal A and signal B for the following: - Intermittently open - Intermittently shorted to ground - Intermittently shorted together - Intermittently shorted to voltage Did you find and correct the condition?		Go to Step 10	Go to Step 6
6	Test the battery positive voltage circuit to the steering wheel position sensor for an intermittent open. Did you find and correct the condition?		Go to Step 10	Go to Step 7
7	Test both of the steering wheel position sensor ground circuits for an intermittent open. Did you find and correct the condition?		Go to Step 10	Go to Step 8
8	Inspect for poor connections at the harness connector of the steering wheel position sensor and at the harness connector of the EBCM Did you find and correct the condition?		Go to Step 10	Go to Step 9
9	Replace the steering wheel position sensor. Did you complete the replacement?		Go to Step 10	--
10	1. Use the scan tool Clear All Class 2 DTCs function to clear all of the DTCs from all modules. 2. Turn OFF the ignition for 5 seconds. 3. Turn ON the ignition. 4. Operate the vehicle within the Conditions for Running the DTC, as specified in the supporting text. Does the DTC reset?		Go to Step 2	System OK

LTV0500000006324

Fig. 104   Code C0455: Front Steering Position Sensor Circuit (Part 4 of 4). 2003–06 Avalanche, Escalade, Escalade EXT, Suburban, Tahoe & Yukon

Circuit Description

The steering wheel position sensor is a 0-5 volt device which is used to sense steering wheel position and turning speed. The valid signal voltage range of the sensor is 0.35-4.75 volts. The signal voltage will increase or decrease within the valid voltage range as the steering wheel is turned. The body control module (BCM) monitors the steering wheel position sensor signal voltage and transmits this data on the serial data line.

DTC Descriptors

This diagnostic procedure supports the following DTCs:

- DTC C0472 Steering Hand Wheel Speed Sensor Signal Circuit
- DTC C0473 Steering Hand Wheel Speed Sensor Signal Circuit

Conditions for Running the DTC

The ignition is ON.

Conditions for Setting the DTC

The BCM detects that the analog steering signal circuit is open, shorted to ground or shorted to voltage.

Action Taken When the DTC Sets

The BCM sends a serial data message reporting the failed steering signal.

Conditions for Clearing the DTC

- A current DTC will clear when the malfunction is no longer present.
- A history DTC will clear after 100 consecutive malfunction-free ignition cycles or when the scan tool Clear DTCs function is used.

Diagnostic Aids

Thoroughly inspect connections or circuitry that may cause an intermittent malfunction. Refer to the following:

- Testing for Electrical Intermittents
- Testing for Intermittent Conditions and Poor Connections
- Wiring Repairs
- Connector Repairs

LTV0500000006325

Fig. 105   Codes C0472 Or C0473: Steering Hand Wheel Speed Sensor Circuit (Part 1 of 3). 2003–06 Avalanche, Escalade, Escalade EXT, Suburban, Tahoe & Yukon

Test Description

The numbers below refer to the step numbers on the diagnostic table.

3. This step test the circuitry in the high voltage range.

4. This step test the circuitry in the low voltage range.

5. This step tests the low reference circuit of the steering wheel position sensor.

Step	Action	Values	Yes	No
1	Did you perform the Diagnostic System Check - Vehicle?	--	Go to Step 2	Go to Diagnostic System Check - Vehicle
2	1. Use the scan tool to clear the DTC. 2. Start the engine. 3. With the engine running, turn the steering wheel back and forth from lock to lock. Does the DTC reset?	--	Go to Step 3	Go to Diagnostic Aids
3	1. Turn OFF the ignition. 2. Disconnect the steering wheel position sensor harness connector. 3. Turn ON the ignition. 4. Select the Body Control Module (BCM) Data List on the scan tool. 5. Observe the Analog SWPS Signal parameter on the scan tool. Does the scan tool indicate that the steering wheel position sensor data parameter is less than specified value?	0.15 V	Go to Step 4	Go to Step 9
4	1. Connect a 3-amp fused jumper wire between the steering wheel position 5-volt reference circuit and the analog steering signal circuit. 2. Observe the Analog SWPS Signal parameter on the scan tool. Does the scan tool indicate that the steering wheel position sensor data parameter is greater than specified value?	4.75 V	Go to Step 5	Go to Step 6
5	Use a DMM to measure the voltage between the steering wheel position 5-volt reference circuit and the steering wheel position low reference circuit. Does the voltage measure greater than the specified value?	4.75 V	Go to Step 10	Go to Step 8

LTV0500000006326

Fig. 105   Codes C0472 Or C0473: Steering Hand Wheel Speed Sensor Circuit (Part 2 of 3). 2003–06 Avalanche, Escalade, Escalade EXT, Suburban, Tahoe & Yukon

Step	Action			
6	Test the 5-volt reference circuit of the steering wheel position sensor for an open. Did you find and correct the condition?		Go to Step 14	Go to Step 7
7	Test the signal circuit of the steering wheel position sensor for an open or a short to ground. Did you find and correct the condition?		Go to Step 14	Go to Step 11
8	Test the low reference circuit of the steering wheel position sensor for an open. Did you find and correct the condition?		Go to Step 14	Go to Step 11
9	Test the signal circuit of the steering wheel position sensor for a short to voltage. Did you find and correct the condition?		Go to Step 14	Go to Step 13
10	Inspect for poor connections at the harness connector of the steering wheel position sensor. Did you find and correct the condition?		Go to Step 14	Go to Step 12
11	Inspect for poor connections at the harness connector of the BCM. Did you find and correct the condition?		Go to Step 14	Go to Step 13
12	Replace the steering wheel position sensor. Did you complete the replacement?		Go to Step 14	--
13	Replace the BCM. Did you complete the replacement?		Go to Step 14	--
14	1. Use the scan tool to clear all DTCs from all modules. 2. Operate the vehicle within the conditions for running the DTC, as specified in the supporting text. Does the DTC reset?		Go to Step 2	System OK

LTV0500000006327

Fig. 105   Codes C0472 Or C0473: Steering Hand Wheel Speed Sensor Circuit (Part 3 of 3). 2003–06 Avalanche, Escalade, Escalade EXT, Suburban, Tahoe & Yukon

Circuit Description

The electronic brake control module (EBCM) performs several self-tests for internal problems, which may affect proper operation.

DTC Descriptor

This diagnostic procedure supports the following DTC:

DTC C0550 Electronic Control Unit (ECU) Performance

Conditions for Running the DTC

The ignition is ON.

Conditions for Setting the DTC

The EBCM detects an internal malfunction.

Action Taken When the DTC Sets

- The EBCM disables the ABS/dynamic rear proportion (DRP)/traction control system (TCS)/vehicle stability enhancement system (VSES).
- The ABS indicator turns ON.
- The brake warning indicator turns ON.
- The message center displays the service stability system message.
- The traction OFF indicator turns ON.

Conditions for Clearing the DTC

Certain conditions that may cause this DTC to set cannot be cleared. Other conditions that may cause this DTC to set may be cleared, at least temporarily, by using the scan tool Clear DTCs function.

Diagnostic Aids

Replace the EBCM if this DTC continues to set intermittently.

LTV0500000006328

Fig. 106   Code C0550: ECU Performance (Part 1 of 2). 2003–06 Avalanche, Escalade, Escalade EXT, Suburban, Tahoe & Yukon

Step	Action	Yes	No
1	Did you perform the Diagnostic System Check - Vehicle?	Go to Step 2	Go to Diagnostic System Check - Vehicle
2	Use a scan tool in order to clear the DTCs. Can the DTC be cleared?	Go to Step 3	Go to Step 4
3	1. Turn OFF the ignition. 2. Turn ON the ignition. Does the DTC reset?	Go to Step 4	Go to Diagnostic Aids
4	Replace the electronic brake control module (EBCM). Did you complete the replacement?	Go to Step 5	--
5	1. Use the scan tool to clear the DTCs. 2. Turn OFF the ignition for 5 seconds. 3. Turn ON the ignition. 4. Operate the vehicle within the Conditions for Running the DTC, as specified in the supporting text. Does the DTC reset?	Go to Step 3	System OK

LTV0500000006329

Fig. 106 Code C0550: ECU Performance (Part 2 of 2). 2003–06 Avalanche, Escalade, Escalade EXT, Suburban, Tahoe & Yukon

Circuit Description

The ABS Diagnostic System Check is an organized approach to identifying problems associated with the ABS. This must be the starting point for any ABS related concern and will direct you to the next logical step in diagnosing a malfunction. Most system malfunctions are linked to faulty wiring, connections and occasionally, to components. Understanding the ABS system and using the diagnostic tables correctly will reduce diagnostic time and prevent unnecessary parts replacement.

Test Description

The numbers below refer to the step numbers in the diagnostic table.

2. Lack of communication may be due to partial or total malfunction of the class 2 serial data circuit. The specified procedure will determine the particular condition.

4. The presence of DTCs that begin with a "U" indicates that some other module is not communicating. The specified procedure will compile all of the available information before tests are performed.

LTV0500000006356

Fig. 108 Diagnostic System Check. (Part 1 of 2). 2002–03 Bravada, Envoy & Trailblazer

Step	Action	Yes	No
1	Install a scan tool. Does the scan tool power up?	Go to Step 2	Check Scan Tool Does Not Power Up
2	1. Turn the ignition ON. 2. Use the scan tool in order to establish communication with the following modules: - 4WAL 3 Sensor - Powertrain - Instrument Panel Cluster - Body Control Module Does the scan tool communicate with all of the control modules listed above?	Go to Step 3	Check Scan Tool Does Not Communicate with Class 2 Device
3	Use the scan tool in order to display DTCs for the following control modules: - 4WAL 3 Sensor - Powertrain - Instrument Panel Cluster - Body Control Module Does the scan tool display any DTCs for the control modules listed above?	Go to Step 4	Go to Symptoms
4	Does the scan tool display any DTCs that begin with a "U", DTC C0290- C0292 or C0297?		Go to Step 5
5	Does the scan tool display DTC P0500, P0502, P0503, P0562, P0563, P0601-P0607, P1381, P1621, P1627 or P1683?	Go to Diagnostic Trouble Code (DTC) List	Go to Step 6
6	Does the scan tool display DTC B1372?	Go to Diagnostic Trouble Code (DTC) List	Go to Diagnostic Trouble Code (DTC) List

LTV0500000006357

Fig. 108 Diagnostic System Check. (Part 2 of 2). 2002–03 Bravada, Envoy & Trailblazer

Circuit Description

A replacement electronic brake control module (EBCM) is supplied with generic software and must be programmed to match the specific vehicle application.

DTC Descriptor

This diagnostic procedure supports the following DTC:

DTC C0558 Calibration Data Not Programmed

Conditions for Running the DTC

The ignition is ON.

Conditions for Setting the DTC

The EBCM is not programmed with complete software.

Action Taken When the DTC Sets

- The EBCM disables the ABS/dynamic rear proportion (DRP)/traction control system (TCS)/vehicle stability enhancement system (VSES).
- The ABS indicator turns ON.
- The brake warning indicator turns ON.
- The message center displays the service stability system message.
- The traction OFF indicator turns ON.

Conditions for clearing the DTC

The DTC clears when software programming is complete.

Step	Action	Yes	No
1	Did you perform the Diagnostic System Check - Vehicle?	Go to Step 2	Go to Diagnostic System Check - Vehicle
2	Perform the set-up procedure for the electronic brake control module (EBCM). Did you complete the action?	Go to Diagnostic System Check - Vehicle	--

LTV0500000006330

Fig. 107 Code C0558: Calibration Data Not Programmed. 2003–06 Avalanche, Escalade, Escalade EXT, Suburban, Tahoe & Yukon

Circuit Description

As the wheel spins, the wheel speed sensor produces an AC signal. The electronic brake control module (EBCM) uses the frequency of the AC signal to calculate the wheel speed.

Conditions for Running the DTC

C0221 and C0225

The ignition is ON.

C0222, C0223, C0226 and C0227

The vehicle speed is greater than 32 km/h (20 mph) when the brake is applied or 19 km/h (12 mph) when the brake is released.

Conditions for Setting the DTC

C0221 and C0225

The EBCM detects an open or shorted wheel speed sensor or wheel speed sensor circuit for 500 milliseconds.

C0222 and C0226

The corresponding wheel speed sensor signal is less than 6 km/h (4 mph) for 5 seconds, or 120 seconds in order to set both DTCs.

C0223 and C0227

The EBCM detects an erratic signal from the corresponding wheel speed sensor for 105 milliseconds.

Action Taken When the DTC Sets

C0221, C0225

If equipped, the following actions occur:

- The EBCM disables the ABS/TCS.
- The ABS indicator turns ON.
- The TRACTION OFF indicator turns ON.
- The DIC displays the SERVICE BRAKE SYSTEM message.

C0222, C0223, C0226, and C0227

If equipped, the following actions occur:

- The EBCM disables the ABS/TCS and may disable DRP.
- The ABS indicator turns ON.
- The TRACTION OFF indicator turns ON.
- The red Brake warning indicator may turn ON.
- The DIC displays the SERVICE BRAKE SYSTEM message.

LTV0500000006358

Fig. 109 Code C0221–C0227: Front Wheel Speed Sensor Circuit (Part 1 of 3). 2002–03 Bravada, Envoy & Trailblazer

Conditions for Clearing the DTC

- Repair the condition responsible for setting the DTC.
- Use a scan tool in order to clear the DTC.
- After the DTC is cleared and the ignition is ON, the ABS indicator may remain ON until the EBCM completes a power-up self-test. This test concludes when the vehicle reaches a speed greater than 13 km/h (8 mph) and the wheel speeds are verified by the EBCM.

Diagnostic Aids

Operating the vehicle on extremely rough terrain can set DTC C0223, C0227 or C0229 even if the system is functioning normally.

Thoroughly inspect connections or circuitry that may cause an intermittent malfunction.

If the customer's concern is that the ABS indicator is on only during humid conditions such as rain, snow or vehicle wash, thoroughly inspect the wheel speed sensor circuits for signs of water intrusion. Use the following procedure in order to help isolate the problem area:

1. Spray the suspected area with a 5 percent salt water solution.
2. Drive the vehicle at a speed greater than 19 km/h (12 mph) for at least 30 seconds.

Repair or replace the suspect harness if the DTC sets.

Test Description

The numbers below refer to the step numbers on the diagnostic table.

3. Measure the resistance of the wheel speed sensor in order to determine if the sensor has a valid resistance value.

4. Ensures that the wheel speed sensor is generating a valid AC voltage output.

Step	Action	Values	Yes	No
	Important: If DTC C0229 is set, diagnose DTC C0229 before diagnosing any other wheel speed sensor DTCs.			
1	Did you perform the ABS Diagnostic System Check?	--	Go to Step 2	Go to Diagnostic System Check - ABS
2	1. Use a scan tool in order to clear the DTCs. 2. Operate the vehicle at a speed greater than the specified value. Does the DTC set?	19 km/h (12 mph)	Go to Step 3	Go to Diagnostic Aids

LTV0500000006359

Fig. 109 Code C0221–C0227: Front Wheel Speed Sensor Circuit (Part 2 of 3). 2002–03 Bravada, Envoy & Trailblazer

Circuit Description

As the wheel spins, the wheel speed sensor produces an AC signal. The electronic brake control module (EBCM) uses the frequency of the AC signal to calculate the wheel speed.

Conditions for Running the DTC

- The ignition is ON.
- The vehicle speed is greater than 32 km/h (20 mph) when the brake is applied or 19 km/h (12 mph) when the brake is released.

Conditions for Setting the DTC

The EBCM detects an erratic signal from both front wheel speed sensors for 105 milliseconds.

Action Taken When the DTC Sets

If equipped, the following actions occur:

- The EBCM disables the ABS/TCS/DRP.
- The ABS indicator turns ON.
- The TRACTION OFF indicator turns ON.
- The red brake warning indicator turns ON.
- The DIC displays the SERVICE BRAKE SYSTEM message.

Conditions for Clearing the DTC

- Repair the condition responsible for setting the DTC.
- Use a scan tool in order to clear the DTC.
- After the DTC is cleared and the ignition is ON, the ABS indicator may remain ON until the EBCM completes a power-up self-test. This test concludes when the vehicle reaches a speed greater than 13 km/h (8 mph) and the wheel speeds are verified by the EBCM.

Diagnostic Aids

Operating the vehicle on extremely rough terrain can set DTC C0223, C0227 or C0229 even if the system is functioning normally.

Thoroughly inspect connections or circuitry that may cause an intermittent malfunction.

If the customer's concern is that the ABS indicator is on only during humid conditions such as rain, snow or vehicle wash, thoroughly inspect the wheel speed sensor circuits for signs of water intrusion. Use the following procedure in order to help isolate the problem area:

1. Spray the suspected area with a 5 percent salt water solution.
2. Drive the vehicle at a speed greater than 19 km/h (12 mph) for at least 30 seconds.

Repair or replace the suspect harness if the DTC sets.

LTV0500000006361

Fig. 110 Code C0229: Drop Out of Front Wheel Speed Signals (Part 1 of 2). 2002–03 Bravada, Envoy & Trailblazer

Step	Action	Values	Yes	No
3	1. Turn OFF the ignition. 2. Raise and support the vehicle. 3. Disconnect the wheel speed sensor connector. 4. Use a DMM in order to measure the resistance across the wheel speed sensor. Does the resistance measure within the specified range?	700-10,000 ohms	Go to Step 4	Go to Step 8
4	1. Spin the wheel by hand as fast as possible. 2. Use a DMM in order to measure the AC voltage across the wheel speed sensor as the wheel spins. Does the AC voltage measure greater than the specified value?	100 mV	Go to Step 5	Go to Step 8
5	Inspect for poor connections at the harness connector of the wheel speed sensor. Did you find and correct the condition?	--	Go to Step 10	Go to Step 6

6	1. Disconnect the EBCM harness connector.
	2. Test the wheel speed sensor circuits for the following:
	  – An open
	  – A short to ground
	  – A short to voltage
	  – Shorted together
	
	Did you find and correct the condition?
		--	Go to Step 10	Go to Step 7

7	Inspect for poor connections at the harness connector for the EBCM. Did you find and correct the condition?	--	Go to Step 10	Go to Step 9
8	Replace the wheel speed sensor. Did you complete the replacement?	--	Go to Step 10	
9	**Important:** Use the scan tool in order to perform the Tire Size Calibration procedure. Replace the EBCM. Did you complete the replacement?	--	Go to Step 10	
10	1. Use the scan tool in order to clear the DTCs. 2. Operate the vehicle within the Conditions for Running the DTC as specified in the supporting text. Does the DTC reset?	--	Go to Step 2	System OK

LTV0500000006360

Fig. 109 Code C0221–C0227: Front Wheel Speed Sensor Circuit (Part 3 of 3). 2002–03 Bravada, Envoy & Trailblazer

Step	Action	Yes	No
1	Did you perform the ABS Diagnostic System Check?	Go to Step 2	Go to Diagnostic System Check - ABS
2	1. Use a scan tool in order to clear the DTCs. 2. Operate the vehicle within the Conditions for Running the DTC as specified in the supporting text. Does the DTC set?	Go to Step 3	Go to Diagnostic Aids
3	Inspect for poor connections at the harness connector of the EBCM. Did you find and correct the condition?	Go to Step 5	Go to Step 4
4	**Important** Following EBCM replacement, use the scan tool to perform the Tire Size Calibration procedure. Replace the EBCM. Did you complete the replacement?	Go to Step 5	--
5	1. Use the scan tool in order to clear the DTCs. 2. Operate the vehicle within the Conditions for Running the DTC as specified in the supporting text. Does the DTC reset?	Go to Step 3	System OK

LTV0500000006362

Fig. 110 Code C0229: Drop Out of Front Wheel Speed Signals (Part 2 of 2). 2002–03 Bravada, Envoy & Trailblazer

Circuit Description

The powertrain control module (PCM) converts the data from the vehicle speed sensor to a 128k pulses/mile signal. The electronic brake control module (EBCM) uses the vehicle speed signal from the PCM in order to calculate the rear wheel speed.

Conditions for Running the DTC

C0235

The ignition is ON.

C0236 and C0237

- The ignition is ON.
- The vehicle speed is greater than 32 km/h (20 mph) when the brake is applied or 19 km/h (12 mph) when the brake is released.

P1504

- The ignition is ON.
- The vehicle is not moving.

Conditions for Setting the DTC

C0235

The EBCM detects low voltage on the vehicle speed signal circuit for 500 milliseconds.

C0236

The rear wheel speed signal is less than 6 km/h (4 mph) for 5 seconds, or 120 seconds in order to set multiple missing sensor signal DTCs.

C0237

The EBCM detects an erratic rear wheel speed signal for 105 milliseconds.

P1504

The PCM detects low voltage on the vehicle speed signal circuit for 45 seconds.

Action Taken When the DTC Sets

If equipped, the following actions occur:

- The EBCM disables the ABS/TCS/DRP.
- The ABS indicator turns ON.
- The TRACTION OFF indicator turns ON.
- The red brake warning indicator turns ON.
- The DIC displays the SERVICE BRAKE SYSTEM message.

LTV0500000006363

Fig. 111 Codes C0235–C0237 Or P1504: Rear Wheel Speed Sensor Circuit (Part 1 of 3). 2002–03 Bravada, Envoy & Trailblazer

Step	Action			
5	Inspect for poor connections at the harness connector of the EBCM. Did you find and correct the condition?	- -	Go to Step 10	Go to Step 6
6	**Important** Following EBCM replacement, use the scan tool to perform the Tire Size Calibration procedure. Replace the EBCM. Did you complete the replacement?	- -	Go to Step 10	--
7	Test the vehicle speed signal circuit for an open, a short to ground or a short to voltage Did you find and correct the condition?	- -	Go to Step 10	Go to Step 8
8	Inspect for poor connections at the harness connector of the PCM. Did you find and correct the condition?	- -	Go to Step 10	Go to Step 9
9	**Important** Perform the setup procedure for the PCM. Replace the PCM. Did you complete the replacement?	- -	Go to Step 10	--
10	1. Use the scan tool in order to clear the DTCs. 2. Operate the vehicle within the Conditions for Running the DTC as specified in the supporting text. Does the DTC reset?		Go to Step 3	System OK

LTV0500000006365

Fig. 111 Codes C0235–C0237 Or P1504: Rear Wheel Speed Sensor Circuit (Part 3 of 3). 2002–03 Bravada, Envoy & Trailblazer

Conditions for Clearing the DTC

- Repair the condition responsible for setting the DTC.
- Use a scan tool in order to clear the DTC.
- After the DTC is cleared and the ignition is ON, the ABS indicator may remain ON until the EBCM completes a power-up self-test. This test concludes when the vehicle reaches a speed greater than 13 km/h (8 mph) and the wheel speeds are verified by the EBCM.

Diagnostic Aids

Thoroughly inspect connections or circuitry that may cause an intermittent malfunction.

Test Description

The numbers below refer to the step numbers on the diagnostic table:

3. This step tests for a voltage signal from the PCM.

4. This step tests for a missing or erratic vehicle speed signal from the PCM. An assistant may be required to perform this test.

Step	Action	Values	Yes	No
1	Did you perform the ABS Diagnostic System Check?	--	Go to Step 2	Go to Diagnostic System Check - ABS
2	1. Use a scan tool in order to clear the DTCs. 2. Operate the vehicle at a speed greater than the specified value. Does the DTC set?	19 km/h (12 mph)	Go to Step 3	Go to Diagnostic Aids
3	1. Turn OFF the ignition. 2. Disconnect from the EBCM, the harness connector containing the vehicle speed signal circuit. 3. Turn ON the ignition. 4. Use a DMM in order to measure the DC voltage between the vehicle speed signal circuit and a good ground. Does the voltage measure greater than the specified value?	10 V	Go to Step 4	Go to Step 7
4	1. Raise and support the vehicle. 2. Place the transmission in neutral (N). 3. Set up the DMM in order to measure the DC voltage between the vehicle speed signal circuit and a good ground. 4. Spin the rear wheels as fast as possible by hand for at least 30 seconds and while ensuring the driveshaft is rotating, observe the DMM. Does the voltage measure within the specified range the entire time the driveshaft is rotating?	5-7 V	Go to Step 5	Go to Step 7

LTV0500000006364

Fig. 111 Codes C0235–C0237 Or P1504: Rear Wheel Speed Sensor Circuit (Part 2 of 3). 2002–03 Bravada, Envoy & Trailblazer

Circuit Description

As the front wheels spin, the wheel speed sensors (WSSs) produce an AC signal. The electronic brake control module (EBCM) uses the frequency of the AC signal to calculate the wheel speed. The powertrain control module (PCM) converts the data from the vehicle speed sensor (VSS) to a 128k pulses/mile signal. The EBCM uses the vehicle speed signal from the PCM in order to calculate the rear wheel speed.

Conditions for Running the DTC

The ignition is ON and the vehicle speed is between 24 km/h (15 mph) and 80 km/h (50 mph).

Conditions for Setting the DTC

The EBCM detects that one wheel speed input is 10 percent greater than or 10 percent less than the other wheel speed inputs within 3.2 km (2 mi) of driving.

Action Taken When the DTC Sets

If equipped, the following actions occur:

- The EBCM disables the ABS/TCS/DRP.
- The ABS indicator turns ON.
- The TRACTION OFF indicator turns ON.
- The red brake warning indicator turns ON.
- The DIC displays the SERVICE BRAKE SYSTEM message.

Conditions for Clearing the DTC

The conditions for setting the DTC are no longer present and you use the scan tool Clear DTCs function.

Diagnostic Aids

Installing one tire of significantly different size on the vehicle causes DTC C0238 to set. Operating the vehicle with a tire that has very low air pressure may also set this DTC. Inspect the vehicle for an incorrect or damaged wheel speed sensor or vehicle speed sensor if the tires and the EBCM and PCM calibrations are OK.

Test Description

The number below refers to the step number on the diagnostic table.

4. If the front tires are not the same size as the rear tires, the EBCM calibration must match the FRONT tire size and the PCM calibration must match the REAR tire size.

LTV0500000006366

Fig. 112 Code C0238: Wheel Speed Mismatch (Part 1 of 2). 2002–03 Bravada, Envoy & Trailblazer

Step	Action	Yes	No
1	Did you perform the ABS Diagnostic System Check?	Go to Step 2	Go to Diagnostic System Check - ABS .
2	Inspect both of the front tires on the vehicle to ensure that both tires are of equal size. Are both of the front tires of equal size?	Go to Step 3	Go to Diagnostic Aids
3	Inspect both of the rear tires on the vehicle to ensure that both tires are of equal size. Are both of the rear tires of equal size?	Go to Step 4	Go to Diagnostic Aids
4	Verify the EBCM and the PCM both have the correct tire size calibration. Use the scan tool in order to view the EBCM tire size calibration or perform the Tire Size Calibration procedure. Did you find and correct the condition?	Go to Step 5	Go to Diagnostic Aids
5	1. Use a scan tool in order to clear the DTCs. 2. Operate the vehicle for 3.2 km (2 mi) within the Conditions for Running the DTC as specified in the supporting text. Does the DTC reset?	Go to Step 2	System OK

LTV0500000006367

Fig. 112 Code C0238: Wheel Speed Mismatch (Part 2 of 2). 2002–03 Bravada, Envoy & Trailblazer

Step	Action	Yes	No
1	Did you perform the ABS Diagnostic System Check?	Go to Step 2	Go to Diagnostic System Check - ABS
2	1. Use a scan tool in order to clear the DTCs. 2. Operate the vehicle within the Conditions for Running the DTC as specified in the supporting text. Does the DTC set?	Go to Step 3	Go to Diagnostic Aids
3	**Important** Following EBCM replacement, use the scan tool to perform the Tire Size Calibration procedure and the Trim Level Calibration procedure, if applicable. Replace the EBCM. Did you complete the replacement?	Go to Step 4	--
4	1. Use the scan tool in order to clear the DTCs. 2. Operate the vehicle within the Conditions for Running the DTC as specified in the supporting text. Does the DTC reset?	Go to Step 3	System OK

LTV0500000006369

Fig. 113 Codes C0241–C0254: EBCM Control Valve Circuit (Part 2 of 2). 2002–03 Bravada, Envoy & Trailblazer

Circuit Description

The ABS relay supplies battery voltage to 6 valve solenoids. The electronic brake control module (EBCM) microprocessor applies the grounds needed to activate each solenoid. The low side of each solenoid coil has a feedback circuit to the EBCM microprocessor. When a solenoid is commanded OFF, the feedback voltage is high. When a solenoid is commanded ON, the feedback voltage is low.

Conditions for Running the DTC

- The ignition is ON.
- The vehicle speed is greater than 6 km/h (4 mph).

Conditions for Setting the DTC

The EBCM detects an internal malfunction.

Action Taken When the DTC Sets

C0265

If equipped, the following actions occur:

- The EBCM disables the DRP/ABS.
- The ABS indicator turns ON.
- The red Brake warning indicator turns ON.
- The DIC displays the SERVICE BRAKE SYSTEM message.

C0266

If equipped, the following actions occur:

- The EBCM disables the ABS.
- The ABS indicator turns ON.
- The DIC displays the SERVICE BRAKE SYSTEM message.

LTV0500000006370

Fig. 114 Codes C0265 Or C0266: EBCM Relay Circuit (Part 1 of 3). 2002–03 Bravada, Envoy & Trailblazer

Circuit Description

The system relays are energized when the ignition is ON and the vehicle speed is greater than 6 km/h (4 mph). The system relay supplies voltage to the solenoid valves and to the pump motor. This voltage is referred to as the system voltage. The EBCM controls the solenoid valves by grounding the control circuit.

Conditions for Running the DTC

- The ignition is ON.
- The vehicle speed is greater than 6 km/h (4 mph).

Conditions for Setting the DTC

The EBCM detects an internal malfunction.

Action Taken When the DTC Sets

C0241, C0242, C0245, C0246, C0251, C0252, C0253, C0254

If equipped, the following actions occur:

- The EBCM disables the DRP/ABS.
- The ABS indicator turns ON.
- The red Brake warning indicator turns ON.
- The DIC displays the SERVICE BRAKE SYSTEM message.

C0243, C0244, C0247, C0248

If equipped, the following actions occur:

- The EBCM disables the ABS.
- The ABS indicator turns ON.
- The DIC displays the SERVICE BRAKE SYSTEM message.

Conditions for Clearing the DTC

The conditions for setting the DTC are no longer present and you use the scan tool Clear DTCs function.

Diagnostic Aids

An intermittent open/shorted solenoid DTC can be set by several different internal EBCM problems. Replace the EBCM if an open/shorted solenoid DTC continues to set intermittently.

LTV0500000006368

Fig. 113 Codes C0241–C0254: EBCM Control Valve Circuit (Part 1 of 2). 2002–03 Bravada, Envoy & Trailblazer

Conditions for Clearing the DTC

The conditions for setting the DTC are no longer present and you use the scan tool Clear DTCs function.

Diagnostic Aids

Important

Whenever the EBCM is replaced for DTC C0265 or C0266, the ABS pump motor and motor circuitry must be tested for the proper resistance. Refer to steps 7 and 8 in the diagnostic table below for testing procedures and resistance values.

C0265

Thoroughly inspect connections and circuitry that may cause an intermittent malfunction.

C0266

Replace the EBCM if DTC C0266 continues to set intermittently.

Test Description

The numbers below refer to the step numbers on the diagnostic table.

4. This step tests if the battery positive voltage circuit can supply adequate power to the system relay.

7. A shorted ABS pump motor or shorted motor circuitry may damage the contacts within the system relay. Follow this step to prevent damage to a replacement EBCM.

Step	Action	Values	Yes	No
1	Did you perform the ABS Diagnostic System Check?	—	Go to Step 2	Go to Diagnostic System Check - ABS
2	1. Use a scan tool in order to clear the DTCs. 2. Use the scan tool in order to perform an ABS Function Test. Does DTC C0266 set?	—	Go to Step 7	Go to Step 3
3	Does DTC C0265 set?	—	Go to Step 4	Go to Diagnostic Aids

LTV0500000006371

Fig. 114 Codes C0265 Or C0266: EBCM Relay Circuit (Part 2 of 3). 2002–03 Bravada, Envoy & Trailblazer

Step	Action	Values	Yes	No
4	1. Turn OFF the ignition. 2. Disconnect from the EBCM, the harness connector containing the battery positive voltage circuit. 3. Connect a test lamp between the battery positive voltage circuit and a good ground. Does the test lamp illuminate?	--	Go to Step 6	Go to Step 5
5	Repair the open in the battery positive voltage circuit. Did you complete the repair?	--	Go to Step 11	--
6	Inspect for poor connections at the harness connector of the EBCM. Did you find and correct the condition?	--	Go to Step 11	Go to Step 7
7	Important It may be necessary to separate the EBCM from the BPMV to gain access to the pump motor pigtail connector. 1. Disconnect from the EBCM, the ABS pump motor pigtail connector. 2. Use a DMM in order to measure the resistance across the ABS pump motor. Does the resistance measure within the specified range?	0.3-1.0 ohms	Go to Step 8	Go to Step 10
8	Use a DMM in order to measure the resistance between the high side of the pump motor and a good ground. Does the resistance measure less than the specified value?	0L	Go to Step 10	Go to Step 9
9	Important Use the scan tool in order to perform the Tire Size Calibration procedure and the Trim Level Calibration procedure, if applicable. Replace the EBCM. Did you complete the replacement?	--	--	Go to Step 11
10	Important Use the scan tool in order to perform the Tire Size Calibration procedure and the Trim Level Calibration procedure, if applicable. Replace the EBCM and the BPMV. Did you complete the replacements?	--	--	Go to Step 11
11	1. Use the scan tool in order to clear the DTCs. 2. Operate the vehicle within the Conditions for Running the DTC as specified in the supporting text. Does the DTC reset?	--	Go to Step 2	System OK

LTV0500000006372

Fig. 114   Codes C0265 Or C0266: EBCM Relay Circuit (Part 3 of 3). 2002–03 Bravada, Envoy & Trailblazer

Step	Action	Values	Yes	No
1	Did you perform the ABS Diagnostic System Check?	--	Go to Step 2	Go to Diagnostic System Check - ABS
2	1. Use a scan tool in order to clear the DTCs. 2. Operate the vehicle within the Conditions for Running the DTC as specified in the supporting text. Does DTC C0267 set?	--	Go to Step 6	Go to Step 3
3	Does DTC C0268 set?	--	Go to Step 4	Go to Diagnostic Aids
4	1. Turn OFF the ignition. 2. Disconnect from the EBCM, the 2-way harness connector which contains the battery positive voltage circuit and the ground circuit. Caution: Before servicing any electrical component, the ignition key must be in the OFF or LOCK position and all electrical loads must be OFF, unless instructed otherwise in these procedures. If a tool or equipment could easily come in contact with a live exposed electrical terminal, also disconnect the negative battery cable. Failure to follow these precautions may cause personal injury and/or damage to the vehicle or its components. 3. Disconnect the negative battery cable. 4. Disconnect the positive battery cable. 5. Place one lead of a DMM on the positive battery cable where the cable normally connects to the battery. 6. Place the other lead on the battery positive voltage circuit terminal within the 2-way EBCM harness connector. 7. Measure the total resistance between the positive battery cable and the EBCM. Does the resistance measure within the specified range?	0.0-0.2 ohms	Go to Step 5	Go to Step 10

LTV0500000006374

Fig. 115   Codes C0267 Or C0268: Pump Motor Circuit Open/Short (Part 2 of 4). 2002–03 Bravada, Envoy & Trailblazer

Circuit Description

The EBCM applies the ground needed for pump motor activation. The low side of the pump motor has a feedback circuit to the EBCM. When the pump motor is commanded OFF and at rest, feedback voltage is high. When the pump motor is winding down after being commanded ON and then OFF, feedback voltage is low. The EBCM monitors this feedback voltage in order to determine if the motor is functioning properly.

Conditions for Running the DTC

- The ignition is ON.
- The vehicle speed is greater than 6 km/h (4 mph).

Conditions for Setting the DTC

The EBCM detects any of the following conditions:

- An open or shorted pump motor
- An open or shorted pump motor driver circuit
- A seized pump motor

Action Taken When the DTC Sets

If equipped, the following actions occur:

- The EBCM disables the ABS.
- The ABS indicator turns ON.
- The DIC displays the SERVICE BRAKE SYSTEM message.

Conditions for Clearing the DTC

The conditions for setting the DTC are no longer present and you use the scan tool Clear DTCs function.

Diagnostic Aids

Thoroughly inspect connections or circuitry that may cause an intermittent malfunction.

Test Description

The numbers below refer to the step numbers on the diagnostic table.

2. It is imperative that the vehicle be driven to attempt to reset the DTC. Using the scan tool to perform a function test may not produce the same result, and therefore may cause misdiagnosis of the vehicle.

7. This step tests if the EBCM is capable of activating the ABS pump motor.

8. A shorted ABS pump motor may damage the EBCM. It is imperative that the steps in the table be followed in order to prevent damage to a replacement EBCM.

LTV0500000006373

Fig. 115   Codes C0267 Or C0268: Pump Motor Circuit Open/Short (Part 1 of 4). 2002–03 Bravada, Envoy & Trailblazer

Step	Action	Values	Yes	No
5	Use a DMM to measure the resistance of the ground circuit. Does the resistance measure within the specified range?	0.0-0.2 ohms	Go to Step 7	Go to Step 11
6	Important On some applications, it may be necessary to separate the EBCM from the BPMV in order to perform this test. Also, DTC C0268 may set when this test is performed. 1. Turn OFF the ignition. 2. Disconnect from the EBCM, the ABS pump motor pigtail connector. For systems which have no pump motor pigtail, it is necessary to separate the EBCM from the BPMV in order to gain access to the pump motor connector of the EBCM. 3. Use a connector adapter test kit in order to connect a test lamp between the ABS pump motor power and ground circuits at the pump motor connector of the EBCM. 4. Turn ON the ignition. 5. Use the scan tool in order to clear the DTCs. 6. Use the scan tool in order to perform an ABS Function Test. Does DTC C0267 set?	--	Go to Step 12	Go to Step 9
7	Important On some applications, it may be necessary to separate the EBCM from the BPMV in order to perform this test. Also, DTC C0268 may set when this test is performed. 1. Reconnect both battery cables. 2. Disconnect from the EBCM, the ABS pump motor pigtail connector. For systems which have no pump motor pigtail, it is necessary to separate the EBCM from the BPMV in order to gain access to the pump motor connector of the EBCM. 3. Use a connector adapter test kit in order to connect a test lamp between the ABS pump motor power and ground circuits at the pump motor connector of the EBCM. 4. Turn ON the ignition. 5. Use the scan tool in order to clear the DTCs. 6. Use the scan tool in order to perform an ABS Function Test. Does the test lamp illuminate and then turn OFF when the Function Test is performed?	--	Go to Step 13	Go to Step 8
8	Use a DMM in order to measure the resistance across the ABS pump motor. Does the resistance measure within the specified range?	0.3-1.0 ohms	Go to Step 12	Go to Step 14
9	Inspect for poor connections at the pump motor pigtail connector. Did you find and correct the condition?	--	Go to Step 15	Go to Step 13
10	Repair the high resistance in the underhood electrical center or the battery positive voltage circuit. Did you complete the repair?	--	Go to Step 15	--

LTV0500000006375

Fig. 115   Codes C0267 Or C0268: Pump Motor Circuit Open/Short (Part 3 of 4). 2002–03 Bravada, Envoy & Trailblazer

		Go to Step 15	--
11	Repair the high resistance in the ground circuit. Did you complete the repair?		
12	**Important** Following EBCM replacement, use the scan tool to perform the Tire Size Calibration procedure and the Trim Level Calibration procedure, if applicable. Replace the EBCM. Did you complete the replacement?	Go to Step 15	--
13	Replace the BPMV. Did you complete the replacement?	Go to Step 15	--
14	**Important** Following EBCM replacement, use the scan tool perform the Tire Size Calibration procedure and the Trim Level Calibration procedure, if applicable. Replace the EBCM and the BPMV. Did you complete the replacements?	Go to Step 15	--
15	1. Use a scan tool in order to clear the DTCs. 2. Operate the vehicle within the Conditions for Running the DTC as specified in the supporting text. Does the DTC reset?	Go to Step 3	System OK

LTV0500000006376

Fig. 115 Codes C0267 Or C0268: Pump Motor Circuit Open/Short (Part 4 of 4). 2002–03 Bravada, Envoy & Trailblazer

Step	Action	Yes	No
1	Did you perform the ABS Diagnostic System Check?	Go to Step 2	Go to Diagnostic System Check - ABS
2	1. Use a scan tool in order to clear the DTCs. 2. Use the scan tool in order to perform the necessary Solenoid Tests. Do the Solenoid Tests show the system to be functioning normally?	Go to Diagnostic Aids	Go to Step 3
3	Replace the BPMV. Did you complete the replacement?	Go to Step 4	--
4	Use the scan tool in order to perform the necessary Solenoid Tests. Do the Solenoid Tests show the system to be functioning normally?	System OK	Go to Step 3

LTV0500000006378

Fig. 116 Codes C0269 Or C0274: Excessive Dump/ Isolation Time (Part 2 of 2). 2002–03 Bravada, Envoy & Trailblazer

Circuit Description

This DTC identifies a malfunction within the electronic brake control module (EBCM).

Conditions for Running the DTC

The ignition is ON.

Conditions for Setting the DTC

The EBCM detects an internal malfunction.

Action Taken When the DTC Sets

If equipped, the following actions may occur:

- The EBCM disables the ABS/TCS/DRP.
- The ABS indicator turns ON.
- The TRACTION OFF indicator turns ON.
- The red Brake warning indicator turns ON.
- The DIC displays the SERVICE BRAKE SYSTEM message.

Conditions for Clearing the DTC

The conditions for setting the DTC are no longer present and you use the scan tool Clear DTCs function.

Diagnostic Aids

Replace the EBCM if DTC C0273 or DTC C0284 continues to set intermittently.

LTV0500000006379

Fig. 117 Codes C0271–C0273 & C0284: EBCM Fault (Part 1 of 2). 2002–03 Bravada, Envoy & Trailblazer

Circuit Description

The system relay is energized when the ignition is ON. The system relay supplies voltage to the valve solenoids and the pump motor. This voltage is referred to as the system voltage. The electronic brake control module (EBCM) microprocessor activates the valve solenoids by grounding the control circuit.

Conditions for Running the DTC

- The ignition is ON.
- The vehicle is experiencing an ABS event.

Conditions for Setting the DTC

C0269

The EBCM commands a dump solenoid ON for 9 consecutive seconds.

C0274

The EBCM commands an isolation solenoid ON for 255 consecutive seconds.

Action Taken When the DTC Sets

If equipped, the following actions may occur:

- The EBCM disables the ABS/TCS/DRP.
- The ABS indicator turns ON.
- The TRACTION OFF indicator turns ON.
- The red Brake warning indicator turns ON.
- The DIC displays the SERVICE BRAKE SYSTEM message.

Conditions for Clearing the DTC

The conditions for setting the DTC are no longer present and you use the scan tool Clear DTCs function.

Diagnostic Aids

The most likely cause of DTC C0269 or DTC C0274 is a mechanical failure that causes a wheel to lock and remain locked. The DTCs may also set, conceivably, when the ABS is activated on surfaces that are nearly impossible to get traction on. If the DTC sets within these conditions, diagnosis of the ABS system is not necessary.

Test Description

The number below refers to the step number on the diagnostic table:

2. Performing solenoid tests determines if there is a mechanical malfunction inside the BPMV. Perform dump valve solenoid tests for DTC C0269 or isolation valve solenoid tests for DTC C0274.

LTV0500000006377

Fig. 116 Codes C0269 Or C0274: Excessive Dump/ Isolation Time (Part 1 of 2). 2002–03 Bravada, Envoy & Trailblazer

Step	Action	Yes	No
1	Did you perform the ABS Diagnostic System Check?	Go to Step 2	Go to Diagnostic System Check - ABS
2	Is DTC C0271 or DTC C0272 set in the EBCM memory?	Go to Step 4	Go to Step 3
3	1. Use a scan tool in order to clear the DTCs. 2. Turn OFF the ignition for 5 seconds. 3. Turn ON the ignition. Does the DTC set?	Go to Step 4	Go to Diagnostic Aids
4	**Important** Following EBCM replacement, use the scan tool to perform the Tire Size Calibration procedure and the Trim Level Calibration procedure, if applicable. Replace the EBCM. Did you complete the replacement?	Go to Step 5	--
5	Use the scan tool in order to clear the DTCs. Operate the vehicle within the Conditions for Running the DTC as specified in the supporting text. Does the DTC reset?	Go to Step 2	System OK

LTV0500000006380

Fig. 117 Codes C0271–C0273 & C0284: EBCM Fault (Part 2 of 2). 2002–03 Bravada, Envoy & Trailblazer

Circuit Description

The PCM sends engine/axle/tire IDs to the EBCM via serial data communications immediately after the modules are powered up.

Conditions for Running the DTC

The ignition is ON.

Conditions for Setting the DTC

The EBCM receives invalid information from the PCM.

Action Taken When the DTC Sets

If equipped, the following actions occur:

- The EBCM disables the TCS.
- The traction off indicator turns ON.

Conditions for Clearing the DTC

The conditions for setting the DTC are no longer present and you use the scan tool Clear DTCs function.

Diagnostic Aids

Diagnose other ABS or TCS related DTCs prior to diagnosing DTC C0279.

If multiple TCS related DTCs are set, or the vehicle being serviced is not equipped with TCS, verify the correct EBCM is installed in the vehicle.

Test Description

The number below refers to the step number on the diagnostic table:

3. The PCM must have the correct part number for the specified application.

LTV0500000006381

Fig. 118   Code C0279: Powertrain Configuration Not Valid (Part 1 of 2). 2002–03 Bravada, Envoy & Trailblazer

Circuit Description

The stop lamp switch signal informs the electronic brake control module (EBCM) when the brake pedal is pressed.

Conditions for Running the DTC

Either of the following conditions will cause the DTC to run:

- The ignition is ON and the vehicle achieves at least 56 km/h (35 mph) before coming to a stop.
- The ignition is ON and the vehicle experiences an antilock brake system (ABS) event lasting at least 1 second.

Conditions for Setting the DTC

The EBCM detects an open or shorted brake switch or brake switch circuit.

Action Taken When the DTC Sets

This information-only DTC is stored in EBCM memory until it is cleared by using the specified procedure.

Conditions for Clearing the DTC

The conditions for setting the DTC are no longer present and you use the scan tool Clear DTCs function.

Diagnostic Aids

Thoroughly inspect connections or circuitry that may cause an intermittent malfunction.

Test Description

The numbers below refer to the step numbers on the diagnostic table.

4. This step tests for a shorted stoplamp switch.

5. This step tests for an open stoplamp switch.

LTV0500000006383

Fig. 119   Code C0281: Brake Switch Circuit (Part 1 of 3). 2002–03 Bravada, Envoy & Trailblazer

Step	Action	Yes	No
1	Did you perform the ABS Diagnostic System Check?	Go to Step 2	Go to Diagnostic System Check - ABS
2	1. Use a scan tool in order to clear the DTCs. 2. Turn OFF the ignition for 5 seconds. 3. Turn ON the ignition and wait 10 seconds. Does the DTC set?	Go to Step 3	Go to Diagnostics Aids
3	Verify the correct PCM is installed in the vehicle. Does the vehicle have the correct PCM?	Go to Step 4	Go to Step 6
4	Use the scan tool in order to read the Calibration IDs of the PCM. Are the PCM Calibration IDs correct?	Go to Diagnostics Aids	Go to Step 5
5	Perform the set up procedure for the PCM. Did you complete the action?	Go to Step 7	--
6	**Important** Perform the set up procedure for the PCM. Replace the PCM. Did you complete the replacement?	Go to Step 7	--
7	1. Use the scan tool in order to clear the DTCs. 2. Operate the vehicle within the Conditions for Running the DTC as specified in the supporting text. Does the DTC reset?	Go to Step 3	System OK

LTV0500000006382

Fig. 118   Code C0279: Powertrain Configuration Not Valid (Part 2 of 2). 2002–03 Bravada, Envoy & Trailblazer

Step	Action	Yes	No
1	Did you perform the ABS Diagnostic System Check?	Go to Step 2	Go to Diagnostic System Check - ABS
2	1. Install a scan tool. 2. Select the 4WAL 3 Sensor Data Display function. 3. Observe the Brake Switch Status on the scan tool. Does the scan tool display Off?	Go to Step 3	Go to Step 5
3	1. Apply the brake. 2. Observe the Brake Switch Status on the scan tool. Does the scan tool display On?	Go to Diagnostic Aids	Go to Step 4
4	1. Turn OFF the ignition. 2. Disconnect the stop lamp switch. 3. Turn ON the ignition. 4. Observe the Brake Switch Status on the scan tool. Does the scan tool display On?	Go to Step 9	Go to Step 7
5	1. Turn OFF the ignition. 2. Disconnect the stop lamp switch. 3. Connect a fused jumper wire between the ignition 3 voltage circuit and the TCC brake switch signal circuit at the stop lamp switch harness connector. 4. Turn ON the ignition. 5. Observe the Brake Switch Status on the scan tool. Does the scan tool display Off?	Go to Step 9	Go to Step 6
6	Test the ignition 3 voltage circuit and the TCC brake switch signal circuit for an open or a short to ground. Did you find and correct the condition?	Go to Step 12	Go to Step 8
7	Test the TCC brake switch signal circuit for a short to voltage. Did you find and correct the condition?	Go to Step 12	Go to Step 8
8	Inspect for poor connections at the harness connector of the EBCM. Did you find and correct the condition?	Go to Step 12	Go to Step 10
9	Inspect for poor connections at the harness connector of the stop lamp switch. Did you find and correct the condition?	Go to Step 12	Go to Step 11

LTV0500000006384

Fig. 119   Code C0281: Brake Switch Circuit (Part 2 of 3). 2002–03 Bravada, Envoy & Trailblazer

10	**Important** Following EBCM replacement, use the scan tool to perform the Tire Size Calibration procedure. Replace the EBCM. Did you complete the replacement?			Go to Step 12		--
11	Replace the stop lamp switch. Did you complete the replacement?			Go to Step 12		--
12	1. Use the scan tool in order to clear the DTCs. 2. Operate the vehicle within the Conditions for Running the DTC as specified in the supporting text. Does the DTC reset?		Go to Step 2		System OK

LTV0500000006385

Fig. 119   Code C0281: Brake Switch Circuit (Part 3 of 3). 2002–03 Bravada, Envoy & Trailblazer

Step	Action	Yes	No
1	Did you perform the antilock brake system (ABS) Diagnostic System Check?	Go to Step 2	Go to Diagnostic System Check - ABS
2	1. Use a scan tool in order to clear the DTCs. 2. Turn OFF the ignition for 5 seconds. 3. Start the engine and allow the engine to run for at least 20 seconds. Does the DTC set?	Go to Step 3	Go to Diagnostic Aids
3	1. Turn OFF the ignition. 2. Disconnect the traction control switch harness connector. 3. Turn ON the ignition. 4. Connect a test lamp between the ignition 1 voltage circuit and a good ground. Does the test lamp illuminate?	Go to Step 4	Go to Step 8
4	1. Use the scan tool in order to clear the DTCs. 2. Turn OFF the ignition. 3. Connect a fused jumper wire between the ignition 1 voltage circuit and the traction control switch signal circuit at the traction control switch harness connector. 4. Start the engine and allow the engine to run for at least 20 seconds. Does the DTC set?	Go to Step 5	Go to Step 9
5	Test the traction control switch signal circuit for an open or a short to ground. Did you find and correct the condition?	Go to Step 11	Go to Step 6
6	Inspect for poor connections at the harness connector of the electronic brake control module (EBCM). Did you find and correct the condition?	Go to Step 11	Go to Step 7

LTV0500000006387

Fig. 120   Code C0283: Traction Switch Shorted To Ground (Part 2 of 3). 2002–03 Bravada, Envoy & Trailblazer

7	**Important** Following EBCM replacement, use the scan tool to perform the Tire Size Calibration procedure. Replace the EBCM. Did you complete the replacement?			Go to Step 11		--
8	Repair the open in the ignition 1 voltage circuit. Did you complete the repair?			Go to Step 11		--
9	Inspect for poor connections at the harness connector of the traction control switch. Did you find and correct the condition?		Go to Step 11		Go to Step 10
10	Replace the traction control switch. Did you complete the replacement?		Go to Step 11		--
11	1. Use the scan tool in order to clear the DTCs. 2. Operate the vehicle within the Conditions for Running the DTC as specified in the supporting text. Does the DTC reset?		Go to Step 3		System OK

LTV0500000006388

Fig. 120   Code C0283: Traction Switch Shorted To Ground (Part 3 of 3). 2002–03 Bravada, Envoy & Trailblazer

Circuit Description

The traction control switch is a momentary-contact, normally-open switch that can be used to disable the traction control system (TCS). Each time the traction control switch is pressed, the TCS enabled/disabled status changes. When TCS is disabled, the electronic brake control module (EBCM) illuminates the traction off indicator by opening the service traction control signal circuit.

Conditions for Running the DTC

The ignition is ON.

Conditions for Setting the DTC

The EBCM detects low voltage on the traction control switch signal circuit for 10 seconds.

Action Taken When the DTC Sets

If equipped, the following actions occur:

- The EBCM disables the TCS.
- The traction off indicator turns ON.

Conditions for Clearing the DTC

The conditions for setting the DTC are no longer present and you use the scan tool Clear DTCs function.

Diagnostic Aids

Thoroughly inspect connections or circuitry that may cause an intermittent malfunction.

Test Description

The number below refers to the step number on the diagnostic table.

4. This step tests the traction control switch circuitry. If the fuse opens when you perform this test, the traction control switch signal circuit is shorted to ground.

LTV0500000006386

Fig. 120   Code C0283: Traction Switch Shorted To Ground (Part 1 of 3). 2002–03 Bravada, Envoy & Trailblazer

Circuit Description

The EBCM supplies 5 VDC to the powertrain control module (PCM) on the delivered torque signal circuit. The PCM toggles this voltage to ground in order to create the delivered torque signal at the EBCM. A signal with a frequency of 128 Hz +/- 5 percent and a duty cycle of 25-95 percent is a valid delivered torque signal. The percentage of duty cycle is proportional to the percentage of delivered torque.

Conditions for Running the DTC

- The ignition is ON.
- The engine is running at a speed greater than 500 RPM for 1 second.

Conditions for Setting the DTC

C0287

The EBCM receives an invalid delivered torque signal for 300 milliseconds.

P1644 or P1689

The PCM detects the delivered torque signal voltage as being less than 4.75 volts or greater than 5.25 volts.

Action Taken When the DTC Sets

If equipped, the following actions occur:

- The EBCM disables the TCS.
- The traction off indicator turns ON.

Conditions for Clearing the DTC

The conditions for setting the DTC are no longer present and you use the scan tool Clear DTCs function.

Diagnostic Aids

Thoroughly inspect connections or circuitry that may cause an intermittent malfunction.

Test Description

The numbers below refer to the step numbers on the diagnostic table.

3. This step tests for voltage supplied to the PCM from the EBCM.

9. The PCM may be damaged if the delivered torque signal circuit is shorted to voltage.

LTV0500000006389

Fig. 121   Codes C0287, P1644 & P1689: Delivered Torque Circuit (Part 1 of 3). 2002–03 Bravada, Envoy & Trailblazer

Step	Action	Values	Yes	No
1	Did you perform the ABS Diagnostic System Check?	--	Go to Step 2	Go to Diagnostic System Check - ABS
2	1. Use a scan tool in order to clear the DTCs. 2. Turn OFF the ignition for 5 seconds. 3. Start the engine. Does the DTC set?	--	Go to Step 3	Go to Diagnostic Aids
3	1. Turn OFF the ignition. 2. Disconnect from the PCM, the harness connector containing the delivered torque signal circuit. 3. Turn ON the ignition. 4. Use a DMM in order to measure the voltage between the delivered torque signal circuit and a good ground. Does the voltage measure within the specified range?	4.75-5.25 V	Go to Step 5	Go to Step 4
4	Test the delivered torque signal circuit for an open, a short to voltage or a short to ground. Did you find and correct the condition?	--	Go to Step 12	Go to Step 7
5	1. Turn OFF the ignition. 2. Reconnect the PCM harness connector. 3. Start the engine. 4. Select the Traction Assist Data List on the scan tool. 5. Observe the Delivered Torque parameter on the scan tool. Does the scan tool display the duty cycle of the delivered torque signal is within the specified range?	25-95%	Go to Step 6	Go to Step 9
6	1. Turn OFF the ignition. 2. Install a J 39700 universal breakout box and a J 39700-325 adaptor cable. Install the equipment between the EBCM and the EBCM harness connector. 3. Start the engine. 4. Use a DMM in order to measure the Hz frequency of the delivered torque signal. Does the frequency of the delivered torque signal measure within the specified range?	121-134 Hz	Go to Step 7	Go to Step 9

LTV0500000006390

Fig. 121 Codes C0287, P1644 & P1689: Delivered Torque Circuit (Part 2 of 3). 2002–03 Bravada, Envoy & Trailblazer

Circuit Description

The powertrain control module (PCM) sends a state of health message to the EBCM within 5.5 seconds after the modules are powered up. This message is sent via serial data communications.

Conditions for Running the DTC

The ignition is ON.

Conditions for Setting the DTC

The EBCM fails to receive serial data from the PCM.

Action Taken When the DTC Sets

If equipped, the following actions occur:

- The EBCM disables the TCS.
- The traction off indicator turns ON.

Conditions for Clearing the DTC

The conditions for setting the DTC are no longer present and you use the scan tool Clear DTCs function.

Step	Action	Yes	No
1	Did you perform the ABS Diagnostic System Check?	Check Scan Tool Does Not Communicate with Class 2 Device	Go to Diagnostic System Check - ABS

LTV0500000006392

Fig. 122 Codes C0290 Or C0292: Lost Communication With PCM. 2002–03 Bravada, Envoy & Trailblazer

Step	Action		Yes	No
7	1. Turn OFF the ignition. 2. Inspect for poor connections at the harness connector of the EBCM. Did you find and correct the condition?		Go to Step 12	Go to Step 8
8	Replace the EBCM. **Important** Use the scan tool in order to perform the Tire Size Calibration procedure. Did you complete the replacement?		Go to Step 12	--
9	1. Turn ON the ignition with the engine OFF. 2. Test the delivered torque signal circuit for a short to voltage. Did you find and correct the condition?		Go to Step 12	Go to Step 10
10	Inspect for poor connections at the harness connector of the PCM. Did you find and correct the condition?		Go to Step 12	Go to Step 11
11	**Important** Perform the setup procedure for the PCM Replace the PCM. Did you complete the replacement?		Go to Step 12	--
12	1. Use the scan tool in order to clear the DTCs. 2. Operate the vehicle within the Conditions for Running the DTC as specified in the supporting text. Does the DTC reset?		Go to Step 3	System OK

LTV0500000006391

Fig. 121 Codes C0287, P1644 & P1689: Delivered Torque Circuit (Part 3 of 3). 2002–03 Bravada, Envoy & Trailblazer

Circuit Description

The body control module (BCM) sends a state of health serial data message to the electronic brake control module (EBCM) within 5.5 seconds after the ignition is turned ON.

Conditions for Running the DTC

The ignition is ON.

Conditions for Setting the DTC

The EBCM fails to receive serial data from the BCM.

Action Taken When the DTC Sets

The EBCM sets this information-only DTC as a current DTC for as long as the conditions for setting the DTC are present.

Conditions for Clearing the DTC

The conditions for setting the DTC are no longer present and you use the scan tool Clear DTCs function.

Step	Action	Yes	No
1	Did you perform the ABS Diagnostic System Check?	Check Scan Tool Does Not Communicate with Class 2 Device	Go to Diagnostic System Check - ABS

LTV0500000006393

Fig. 123 Code C0291: Lost Communication With PCM. 2002–03 Bravada, Envoy & Trailblazer

Circuit Description

The PCM sends engine/axle/tire IDs to the EBCM via serial data communications immediately after the modules are powered up.

Conditions for Running the DTC

The ignition is ON.

Conditions for Setting the DTC

The EBCM fails to receive serial data from the PCM.

Action Taken When the DTC Sets

If equipped, the following actions occur:

- The EBCM disables the TCS.
- The traction off indicator turns ON.

Conditions for Clearing the DTC

The conditions for setting the DTC are no longer present and you use the scan tool Clear DTCs function.

Step	Action	Yes	No
1	Did you perform the ABS Diagnostic System Check?	Check Scan Tool Does Not Communicate with Class 2 Device	Go to Diagnostic System Check - ABS

LTV0500000006394

Fig. 124 Code C0297: Powertrain Configuration Data Not Received. 2002–03 Bravada, Envoy & Trailblazer

Circuit Description

C0298

The powertrain control module (PCM) sends a state of health message to the EBCM via class 2 serial data communications.

P1571

The EBCM requests desired engine torque from the PCM via the requested torque signal circuit.

Conditions for Running the DTC

C0298

The ignition is ON.

P1571

- The ignition is ON.
- The engine is running at a speed greater than 500 RPM for 5-20 seconds.
- The EBCM has not set any current TCS related DTCs.

Conditions for Setting the DTC

C0298

The EBCM receives a state of health message informing the EBCM that the PCM has lost the ability to perform traction control.

P1571

The PCM receives an invalid requested torque signal for 3 seconds.

Action Taken When the DTC Sets

C0298

If equipped, the following actions occur:

- The EBCM disables the TCS.
- The TRACTION OFF indicator turns ON.

P1571

- The PCM sends a state of health message to the EBCM informing the EBCM that the PCM has lost the ability to perform traction control.
- The EBCM sets DTC C0298 as a current DTC for as long as the malfunction is present.

Conditions for Clearing the DTC

C0298

LTV0500000006395

Fig. 125 Code C0298 Or P1571: Powertrain Indicated Traction Control Fault (Part 1 of 3). 2002–03 Bravada, Envoy & Trailblazer

	Action	Values	Yes	No
1	Did you perform the ABS Diagnostic System Check?	--	Go to Step 2	Go to Diagnostic System Check - ABS
2	Is DTC P1571 set?	--	Go to Step 3	Go to Diagnostic Aids
3	1. Use a scan tool in order to clear the DTCs. 2. Operate the vehicle within the Conditions for Running the DTC as specified in the supporting text. 3. Does DTC P1571 set?		Go to Step 4	Go to Diagnostic Aids
4	1. Turn OFF the ignition. 2. Disconnect from the EBCM, the harness connector containing the requested torque signal circuit. 3. Turn ON the ignition. 4. Use a DMM in order to measure the voltage between the requested torque signal circuit and a good ground. Does the voltage measure within the specified range?	4.75-5.25 V	Go to Step 5	Go to Step 7

LTV0500000006396

Diagnostic Aids

C0298

A requested torque signal malfunction is only one possible cause for the PCM to lose the ability to perform traction control. DTC C0298 may set due to engine overheating, loss of ignition timing control by the PCM, etc. If DTC P1571 is not set, refer to Diagnostic Trouble Code (DTC) List in Engine Controls - 4.2L in order to identify other possible causes of DTC C0298.

P1571

Thoroughly inspect connections or circuitry that may cause an intermittent malfunction.

Test Description

The numbers below refer to the step numbers on the diagnostic table:

4. This step tests for voltage supplied to the EBCM from the PCM.

5. This step verifies the EBCM is creating a requested torque signal with a valid Hz frequency.

6. This step verifies the EBCM is creating a requested torque signal with a valid duty cycle.

7. The EBCM may be damaged if the requested torque signal circuit is shorted to voltage.

Fig. 125 Code C0298 Or P1571: Powertrain Indicated Traction Control Fault (Part 2 of 3). 2002–03 Bravada, Envoy & Trailblazer

	Action	Values	Yes	No
5	1. Turn OFF the ignition. 2. Install a J 39700 universal breakout box and a J 39700-325 adapter cable. Install the equipment between the EBCM and the EBCM harness connector. 3. Start the engine. 4. Use the DMM in order to measure the Hz frequency of the requested torque signal. Does the Hz frequency of the requested torque signal measure within the specified range?	121-134 Hz	Go to Step 6	Go to Step 9
6	Use the DMM in order to measure the duty cycle of the requested torque signal circuit. Does the duty cycle of the requested torque signal measure within the specified range?	40-95%	Go to Step 8	Go to Step 9
7	Test the requested torque signal circuit for an open, a short to ground or a short to voltage. Did you find and correct the condition?	--	Go to Step 12	Go to Step 8
8	Inspect for poor connections at the harness connector of the PCM. Did you find and correct the condition?	--	Go to Step 12	Go to Step 10
9	Inspect for poor connections at the harness connector of the EBCM. Did you find and correct the condition?	--	Go to Step 12	Go to Step 11
10	**Important** Perform the set up procedure for the PCM. Replace the PCM. Did you complete the replacement?	--	--	Go to Step 12
11	Replace the EBCM. **Important** Use the scan tool in order to perform the Tire Size Calibration procedure. Did you complete the replacement?	--	--	Go to Step 12
12	1. Use the scan tool in order to clear the DTCs. 2. Operate the vehicle within the Conditions for Running the DTC as specified in the supporting text. Does DTC P1571 reset?	--	Go to Step 4	System OK

LTV0500000006397

Fig. 125 Code C0298 Or P1571: Powertrain Indicated Traction Control Fault (Part 3 of 3). 2002–03 Bravada, Envoy & Trailblazer

Test Description

The numbers below refer to the step numbers on the diagnostic table.

1. This step ensures that the battery, and the vehicle primary power and ground systems are functioning correctly.

3. Lack of communication may be due to a particular malfunction of a serial data circuit. The information in Data Link References will provide a list of modules and the associated data network no communication diagnostic link.

4. A module that is operating in the incorrect power mode based on key position may cause other vehicle symptoms and/or DTCs to set. The information in Power Mode Mismatch will correct the condition before checking for module DTCs or symptoms.

8. This step ensures that all data link communication DTCs are diagnosed before system level DTCs.

9. This step ensures that all electronic control unit (ECU) internal DTCs are diagnosed before other system level DTCs.

10. This step ensures that all device voltage DTCs are diagnosed before other system level DTCs.

Step	Action	Yes	No
1	Perform the following preliminary inspections: • Ensure that the battery is fully charged. • Ensure that the battery cables are clean and tight. • Inspect for any open fuses. • Inspect the easily accessible systems or the visible system components for obvious damage or conditions that could cause the symptom. • Ensure that the grounds are clean, tight, and in the correct location. • Inspect for aftermarket devices that could affect the operation of the system. • Search for applicable service bulletins. Did you find and correct the condition?	System OK	Go to Step 2
2	Install a scan tool. Does the scan tool power up?	Go to Step 3	Check Scan Tool Does Not Power Up
3	1. Turn ON the ignition, with the engine OFF. 2. Attempt to establish communication with all of the control modules on the vehicle. Does the scan tool communicate with all of the expected vehicle control modules?	Go to Step 4	Go to Data Link References

LTV0500000006415

Fig. 126 Diagnostic System Check (Part 1 of 3). 2004–06 Bravada, Envoy, Rainier & Trailblazer

	Action		
4	**Important:** • To ensure that retained accessory power (RAP) mode is inactive, if equipped), open the driver door during the following step. • The engine may start during the following step. Turn OFF the engine as soon as you have observed the crank power mode. 1. Access the Power Mode parameter on the scan tool. 2. Rotate the ignition switch (operate the ignition mode switch) through all positions while observing the Power Mode parameter. Does the Power Mode parameter reading on the scan tool match the ignition switch position for all switch positions?	Go to Step 5	Check Power Mode Mismatch
5	Attempt to start the engine. Does the engine crank?	Go to Step 6	Go to Symptoms
6	Attempt to start the engine. Does the engine start and idle?	Go to Step 7	Go to Engine Cranks but Does Not Run
7	**Important:** Do not clear any DTCs unless instructed by a diagnostic procedure. Use the appropriate scan tool selections to obtain DTCs for each of the control modules. Does the scan tool display any DTCs?	Go to Step 8	Go to Step 12
8	Does the scan tool display any DTCs that begin with a "U"?	Go to Diagnostic Trouble Code (DTC) List - Vehicle	Go to Step 9

LTV0500000006416

Fig. 126   Diagnostic System Check (Part 2 of 3). 2004–06 Bravada, Envoy, Rainier & Trailblazer

Circuit Description

As the wheels spin, each wheel speed sensor produces an AC signal. The electronic brake control module (EBCM) uses the frequency of the AC signals to calculate each wheel speed.

DTC Descriptors

This diagnostic procedure supports the following DTCs:

• DTC C0035 Left Front Wheel Speed Sensor Circuit
• DTC C0040 Right Front Wheel Speed Sensor Circuit

Conditions for Running the DTC

• The ignition is ON.
• The vehicle speed is greater than 13 km/h (8 mph).

Conditions for Setting the DTC

Any of the following occurrences may cause the DTC to set.

• The EBCM detects an open or shorted wheel speed sensor circuit for 500 milliseconds.
• The EBCM detects the absence of a wheel speed sensor signal for 5 seconds. If more than one absent wheel speed sensor signal is detected, the condition must be present for 120 seconds to set DTCs.
• The EBCM detects an erratic wheel speed sensor signal for 200 milliseconds.

Action Taken When the DTC Sets

• The EBCM disables the ABS and may disable the dynamic rear proportion (DRP) if more than one wheel speed sensor DTC is set.
• The ABS indicator turns ON.
• The brake warning indicator may turn ON.

The actions above are maintained during subsequent ignition cycles until the EBCM completes a power up self-test. This test concludes when the vehicle achieves a speed greater than 13 km/h (8 mph) and the wheel speeds are verified by the EBCM.

Conditions for Clearing the DTC

The Conditions for Setting the DTC are no longer present and you use the scan tool Clear DTCs function.

LTV0500000006418

Fig. 127   Codes C0035 Or C0040: Front Wheel Speed Sensor Circuit (Part 1 of 3). 2004–06 Bravada, Envoy, Rainier & Trailblazer

	Action		
9	**Important:** If any of these DTCs are displayed, diagnose them before diagnosing any other DTCs or symptoms. Does the scan tool display DTC B1000, B1001, B1004, B1007, B1009, B2734, C0240, C0374, C0550, P0601, P0602, P0603, P0604, P0606, P0607, P062F, P1621, P1681, P2101, or P2610?	Go to Diagnostic Trouble Code (DTC) List - Vehicle	Go to Step 10
10	**Important:** If any of these DTCs are displayed, diagnose them before diagnosing any other DTCs or symptoms. Does the scan tool display DTC P0562 or P0563?	Go to Diagnostic Trouble Code (DTC) List - Vehicle	Go to Step 11
11	**Important:** If any of the remaining DTCs are powertrain DTCs, select Captured Info in order to store the powertrain DTC information with a scan tool. If multiple DTCs are stored, diagnose the DTCs in the following order 1. Component level DTCs, such as sensor DTCs, solenoid DTCs, and relay DTCs. 2. System level DTCs, such as misfire DTCs, evaporative emission (EVAP) system DTCs, and fuel trim DTCs. Diagnose the remaining DTCs.	Go to Diagnostic Trouble Code (DTC) List - Vehicle	—
12	Is the customers concern with inspection/maintenance (I/M) testing?	Go to Inspection/Maintenance (I/M) System Check	Go to Symptoms

LTV0500000006417

Fig. 126   Diagnostic System Check (Part 3 of 3). 2004–06 Bravada, Envoy, Rainier & Trailblazer

Diagnostic Aids

Thoroughly inspect connections or circuitry that may cause an intermittent malfunction. Refer to the following:

• Testing for Intermittent Conditions and Poor Connections
• Connector Repairs
• Testing for Electrical Intermittents
• Wiring Repairs

If the customer's concern is that the ABS indicator is on only during humid conditions such as rain, snow or vehicle wash, thoroughly inspect the wheel speed sensor circuits for signs of water intrusion. Use the following procedure in order to help isolate the problem area:

1. Spray the suspected area with a 5 percent salt water solution.
2. Operate the vehicle at a speed greater than 13 km/h (8 mph) for at least 30 seconds.

Repair or replace the suspect harness if the DTC sets.

Step	Action	Values	Yes	No
1	Did you perform the Diagnostic System Check - Vehicle?	--	Go to Step 2	Go to Diagnostic System Check - Vehicle
2	1. Use a scan tool in order to clear the DTCs. 2. Operate the vehicle at a speed greater than the specified value. Does the DTC set?	13 km/h (8 mph)	Go to Step 3	Go to Diagnostic Aids
3	1. Turn OFF the ignition. 2. Raise and support the vehicle. 3. Disconnect the wheel speed sensor connector. 4. Use a DMM in order to measure the resistance across the wheel speed sensor. Does the resistance measure within the specified range?	700-10,000 ohms	Go to Step 4	Go to Step 8

LTV0500000006419

Fig. 127   Codes C0035 Or C0040: Front Wheel Speed Sensor Circuit (Part 2 of 3). 2004–06 Bravada, Envoy, Rainier & Trailblazer

	Action	Values	Yes	No
4	1. Slowly spin the wheel by hand. 2. Use a DMM in order to measure the A/C voltage across the wheel speed sensor as the wheel spins. Does the A/C voltage measure greater than the specified value?	100 mV	Go to Step 5	Go to Step 8
5	Inspect for poor connections at the harness connector of the wheel speed sensor. Did you find and correct the condition?	—	Go to Step 10	Go to Step 6
6	1. Disconnect from the electronic brake control module (EBCM), the harness connector containing the wheel speed sensor circuits. 2. Test the wheel speed sensor circuits for the following: - An open - A short to ground - A short to voltage - Shorted together Did you find and correct the condition?	—	Go to Step 10	Go to Step 7
7	Inspect for poor connections at the harness connector for the EBCM. Did you find and correct the condition?	—	Go to Step 10	Go to Step 9
8	Replace the wheel speed sensor. Did you complete the replacement?	—	Go to Step 10	—
9	Replace the EBCM. Did you complete the replacement?	—	Go to Step 10	—
10	1. Use the scan tool in order to clear the DTCs. 2. Operate the vehicle within the Conditions for Running the DTC as specified in the supporting text. Does the DTC reset?	—	Go to Step 2	System OK

LTV0500000006420

Fig. 127 Codes C0035 Or C0040: Front Wheel Speed Sensor Circuit (Part 3 of 3). 2004–06 Bravada, Envoy, Rainier & Trailblazer

Diagnostic Aids

Thoroughly inspect connections or circuitry that may cause an intermittent malfunction. Refer to the following:

- Testing for Intermittent Conditions and Poor Connections
- Connector Repairs
- Testing for Electrical Intermittents
- Wiring Repairs

If the customer's concern is that the ABS indicator is on only during humid conditions such as rain, snow or vehicle wash, thoroughly inspect the wheel speed sensor circuits for signs of water intrusion. Use the following procedure in order to help isolate the problem area:

1. Spray the suspected area with a 5 percent salt water solution.
2. Operate the vehicle at a speed greater than 13 km/h (8 mph) for at least 30 seconds.

Repair or replace the suspect harness if the DTC sets.

Step	Action	Values	Yes	No
1	Did you perform the Diagnostic System Check - Vehicle?	—	Go to Step 2	Go to Diagnostic System Check - Vehicle
2	1. Use the scan tool to clear the DTCs. 2. Turn OFF the ignition for 5 seconds. 3. Turn ON the ignition. 4. Operate the vehicle within the Conditions for Running the DTC as specified in the supporting text. Does the DTC reset?	13 km/h (8 mph)	Go to Step 3	Go to Diagnostic Aids
3	1. Turn OFF the ignition. 2. Raise and support the vehicle. 3. Disconnect the wheel speed sensor connector. 4. Use a DMM in order to measure the resistance across the wheel speed sensor. Does the resistance measure within the specified range?	3,500-6,800 ohms	Go to Step 4	Go to Step 9

LTV0500000006422

Fig. 128 Codes C0045 Or C0050: Rear Wheel Speed Sensor Circuit (Part 2 of 3). 2004–06 Bravada, Envoy, Rainier & Trailblazer

Circuit Description

As the wheel spins, the wheel speed sensor produces an AC signal. The electronic brake control module (EBCM) uses the frequency of the AC signal to calculate the wheel speed.

DTC Descriptors

This diagnostic procedure supports the following DTCs:

- DTC C0045 Left Rear Wheel Speed Sensor Circuit
- DTC C0050 Right Rear Wheel Speed Sensor Circuit

Conditions for Running the DTC

- The ignition is ON.
- The vehicle speed is greater than 13 km/h (8 mph).

Conditions for Setting the DTC

Any of the following conditions may cause the DTC to set.

- The EBCM detects an open wheel speed sensor circuit for 500 milliseconds.
- The EBCM detects a shorted wheel speed sensor circuit for 500 milliseconds.
- The EBCM detects the absence of a wheel speed sensor signal for 5 seconds. If more than one absent wheel speed sensor signal is detected, the condition must be present for 120 seconds to set DTCs.
- The EBCM detects an erratic wheel speed sensor signal for 200 milliseconds.

Action Taken When the DTC Sets

- The EBCM disables antilock brake system (ABS)/traction control system (TCS)/vehicle stability enhancement system (VSES) and may disable dynamic rear proportion (DRP) if more than one wheel speed sensor DTC is set.
- The ABS indicator turns ON.
- The traction off indicator turns ON.
- The message center displays the service stability system message.
- The brake warning indicator may turn ON.
- An ECE 13 response may occur.

Conditions for Clearing the DTC

The Conditions for Setting the DTC are no longer present and you use the scan tool Clear DTCs function.

LTV0500000006421

Fig. 128 Codes C0045 Or C0050: Rear Wheel Speed Sensor Circuit (Part 1 of 3). 2004–06 Bravada, Envoy, Rainier & Trailblazer

	Action	Values	Yes	No
3	1. Slowly spin the wheel by hand. 2. Use a DMM in order to measure the AC voltage across the wheel speed sensor as the wheel spins. Does the AC voltage measure greater than the specified value?	100 mV	Go to Step 5	Go to Step 8
5	Inspect for poor connections at the harness connector of the wheel speed sensor. Did you find and correct the condition?	—	Go to Step 11	Go to Step 6
6	1. Disconnect the electronic brake control module (EBCM) harness connector. 2. Test the wheel speed sensor circuits for the following: - An open - A short to ground - A short to voltage - Shorted together Did you find and correct the condition?	—	Go to Step 11	Go to Step 7
7	Inspect for poor connections at the harness connector for the EBCM. Did you find and correct the condition?	—	Go to Step 11	Go to Step 10
8	1. Remove the wheel speed sensor from the axle tube. 2. Inspect the wheel speed sensor tone ring, which is located on the axle, for damage. Did you find and correct the condition?	—	Go to Step 11	Go to Step 9
9	Replace the wheel speed sensor. Did you complete the replacement?	—	Go to Step 11	—
10	**Important:** Following EBCM replacement, perform the set-up procedure for the EBCM and perform the Yaw Rate Reference Table Reset Procedure. Use the scan tool to perform the Tire Size Calibration procedure. Replace the EBCM. Did you complete the replacement?	—	Go to Step 11	—
11	1. Use the scan tool Clear All Class 2 DTCs function to clear all of the DTCs from all modules. 2. Turn OFF the ignition for 5 seconds. 3. Turn ON the ignition. 4. Operate the vehicle within the Conditions for Running the DTC as specified in the supporting text. Does the DTC reset?	—	Go to Step 2	System OK

LTV0500000006423

Fig. 128 Codes C0045 Or C0050: Rear Wheel Speed Sensor Circuit (Part 3 of 3). 2004–06 Bravada, Envoy, Rainier & Trailblazer

Circuit Description

Ground is continuously supplied to the low side of the ABS pump motor. The electronic brake control module (EBCM) activates the ABS pump by supplying battery voltage to the high side of the motor.

DTC Descriptor

This diagnostic procedure supports the following DTC:

DTC C0110 Pump Motor Circuit

Conditions for Running the DTC

- The ignition is ON.
- The vehicle speed is greater than 6 km/h (4 mph).

Conditions for Setting the DTC

The EBCM detects an open pump motor circuit, a shorted pump motor, or a seized pump motor or ABS pump.

Action Taken When the DTC Sets

- The EBCM disables the ABS/vehicle stability enhancement system (VSES).
- The traction control system (TCS) operates with engine torque reduction ability only.
- The ABS indicator turns ON.
- The stability indicator turns ON.
- An ECE 13 response may occur.

Conditions for Clearing the DTC

The Conditions for Setting the DTC are no longer present and you use the scan tool Clear DTCs function.

LTV0500000006424

Fig. 129 Code C0110: Pump Motor Circuit (Part 1 of 4). 2004–06 Bravada, Envoy, Rainier & Trailblazer

	Action	Values	Yes	No
4	**Important:** Using a test lamp other than that which is approved for performing diagnostic procedures on GM vehicles, may cause an inaccurate result when performing this step. It is also imperative that the ground to which the test lamp is connected be clean and provide no resistance to battery ground. With the test lamp still connected and illuminated, use a DMM to measure the voltage between the high side of the test lamp and a good ground. Does the voltage measure greater than the specified value?	12 V	Go to Step 6	Go to Step 5
5	Repair the high resistance in the battery positive voltage circuit. Ensure that total circuit resistance is not greater than the specified value. Did you complete the repair?	0.2 ohms	Go to Step 13	--
6	Test the ABS motor ground circuit for an open or high resistance. Did you find and correct the condition?	--	Go to Step 13	Go to Step 7
7	1. Turn OFF the ignition. 2. Separate the EBCM from the brake pressure modulator valve (BPMV). 3. Connect a test lamp between the ABS pump motor power and ground circuits at the pump motor connector of the EBCM. 4. Turn ON the ignition. 5. Use the scan tool in order to clear the DTCs. Does the DTC clear and then remain cleared while the test lamp is connected?	--	Go to Step 8	Go to Step 10
8	1. Select the vehicle stability enhancement system (VSES) Special Functions menu on the scan tool. 2. Command the ABS Motor ON. Does the test lamp illuminate for 5 seconds and then turn OFF?	--	Go to Step 9	Go to Step 12
9	Inspect for poor connections at the pump motor connector. Did you find and correct the condition?	--	Go to Step 13	Go to Step 11
10	**Important:** Following the EBCM replacement, perform the set-up procedure for the EBCM and perform the Yaw Rate Reference Table Reset Procedure. Use the scan tool to perform the Tire Size Calibration procedure. Replace the EBCM. Did you complete the replacement?	--	Go to Step 13	--
11	Replace the BPMV. Did you complete the replacement?	--	Go to Step 13	--

LTV0500000006426

Fig. 129 Code C0110: Pump Motor Circuit (Part 3 of 4). 2004–06 Bravada, Envoy, Rainier & Trailblazer

Diagnostic Aids

Separate the EBCM from the brake pressure modulator valve (BPMV) in order to inspect for corrosion or any other condition that may cause a poor connection at the pump motor connector.

Test Description

The number below refers to the step number on the diagnostic table.

4. This step tests for high resistance in the battery positive voltage circuit by verifying that an excessive voltage drop does not occur in the circuit.

Step	Action	Values	Yes	No
1	Did you perform the Diagnostic System Check - Vehicle?	--	Go to Step 2	Go to Diagnostic System Check - Vehicle
2	1. Use a scan tool to clear the DTCs. 2. Turn OFF the ignition for 5 seconds. 3. Operate the vehicle within the Conditions for Running the DTC as specified in the supporting text. Does the DTC set?	--	Go to Step 3	Go to Diagnostic Aids
3	1. Disconnect the electronic brake control module (EBCM) harness connector. 2. Connect a test lamp between the battery positive voltage circuit to the ABS pump motor, and a good ground. Does the test lamp illuminate?	--	Go to Step 4	Go to Step 5

LTV0500000006425

Fig. 129 Code C0110: Pump Motor Circuit (Part 2 of 4). 2004–06 Bravada, Envoy, Rainier & Trailblazer

12	**Important:** Following EBCM replacement, perform the set-up procedure for the EBCM and perform the Yaw Rate Reference Table Reset Procedure. Use the scan tool to perform the Tire Size Calibration procedure. Replace the EBCM and the BPMV. Did you complete the replacements?		Go to Step 13	--
13	1. Use the scan tool Clear All Class 2 DTCs function to clear all of the DTCs from all modules. 2. Turn OFF the ignition for 5 seconds. 3. Turn ON the ignition. 4. Operate the vehicle within the Conditions for Running the DTC as specified in the supporting text. Does the DTC reset?		Go to Step 3	System OK

LTV0500000006427

Fig. 129 Code C0110: Pump Motor Circuit (Part 4 of 4). 2004–06 Bravada, Envoy, Rainier & Trailblazer

Circuit Description

The master cylinder pressure sensor is located within the brake pressure modulator valve (BPMV). The master cylinder pressure sensor signal, to the electronic brake control module (EBCM), increases as hydraulic pressure in the front brake circuit increases.

DTC Descriptor

This diagnostic procedure supports the following DTC:

DTC C0131 Antilock Brake System (ABS)/Traction Control System (TCS) Pressure Circuit

Conditions for Running the DTC

- The ignition is ON.
- The vehicle stability enhancement system (VSES) sensors have been successfully initialized or the message center has displayed the stability system disabled message due to an unsuccessful initialization attempt.
- The vehicle is being driven relatively straight and level at a speed greater than 36 km/h (23 mph).
- The transmission is not shifted into neutral or low gear.
- The parking brake is released.

Conditions for Setting the DTC

Any of the following conditions may cause the DTC to set.

- The EBCM detects open master cylinder pressure sensor circuitry.
- The EBCM detects shorted master cylinder pressure sensor circuitry.
- The master cylinder pressure sensor self-test, which occurs at power-up, fails.
- The zero-pressure signal voltage is not within an acceptable range.
- The master cylinder pressure is not within an expected tolerance based on deceleration rate and other data available to the EBCM.

Action Taken When the DTC Sets

- The EBCM disables the VSES.
- The TCS operates with engine torque reduction only.
- The stability indicator turns ON.

Conditions for Clearing the DTC

The conditions for setting the DTC are no longer present and you use the scan tool Clear DTCs function.

LTV0500000006428

Fig. 130 Code C0131: ABS/TCS Pressure Circuit (Part 1 of 3). 2004–06 Bravada, Envoy, Rainier & Trailblazer

Diagnostic Aids

Thoroughly inspect connections or circuitry that may cause an intermittent malfunction.

Test Description

The number below refers to the step number on the diagnostic table.

3. This step is required for vehicles equipped with a hydro-boost brake assist system only. If the vehicle being serviced has vacuum assisted brakes, proceed to step 4.

Important: Use the scan tool to read both current and history DTCs before proceeding. If DTC C0292 is set, diagnose that DTC before proceeding with diagnostics for C0131.
If DTC C0161 is set, diagnose that DTC before proceeding with diagnostics for C0131.

Step	Action	Yes	No
1	Did you perform the Diagnostic System Check - Vehicle?	Go to Step 2	Go to Diagnostic System Check - Vehicle
2	Inspect the vehicle for the following and ensure that there is no base brake failure: • Dragging brakes • Faulty parking brake switch • Brake fluid leakage • Air in hydraulic system • Seized brake calipers • Swollen, kinked or otherwise damaged brake hoses Did you find and correct the condition?	Go to Step 9	Go to Step 3
3	Drive the vehicle in order to verify that the brakes do not self-apply during turning maneuvers. Do the brakes self-apply during turning maneuvers?	Go to Symptoms	Go to Step 4
4	1. Use the scan tool to clear the DTCs. 2. Turn OFF the ignition for 5 seconds. 3. Turn ON the ignition. 4. Operate the vehicle within the Conditions for Running the DTC as specified in the supporting text. Does the DTC reset?	Go to Step 5	Go to Diagnostic Aids

LTV0500000006429

Fig. 130   Code C0131: ABS/TCS Pressure Circuit (Part 2 of 3). 2004–06 Bravada, Envoy, Rainier & Trailblazer

Circuit Description

The brake switch informs the electronic brake control module (EBCM) when the brake is depressed. The brake switch is normally closed, supplying 12 volts to the EBCM when the brake is released. When the brake pedal is pressed, voltage on the torque converter clutch (TCC) brake switch signal circuit is 0 volts.

DTC Descriptor

This diagnostic procedure supports the following DTC:

DTC C0161 Antilock Brake System (ABS)/Traction Control System (TCS) Brake Switch Circuit

Conditions for Running the DTC

Any of the following conditions may cause the DTC to run.

• The vehicle accelerates from 0 km/h (0 mph) to a speed greater than 56 km/h (35 mph).
• The vehicle experiences an ABS event involving all hydraulic circuits.

Conditions for Setting the DTC

Any of the following conditions may cause the DTC to set:

• Voltage on the TCC brake switch signal circuit is always low.
• Voltage on the TCC brake switch signal circuit is always high.

Action Taken When the DTC Sets

The EBCM stores this information-only DTC for as long as the condition is present:

Conditions for Clearing the DTC

The Conditions for Setting the DTC are no longer present and you use the scan tool Clear DTCs function.

LTV0500000006431

Fig. 131   Code C0161: ABS/TCS Brake Switch Circuit (Part 1 of 3). 2004–06 Bravada, Envoy, Rainier & Trailblazer

Step	Action	Yes	No
5	1. Select the vehicle stability enhancement system (VSES) Data Display function on the scan tool. 2. Observe the Brake Switch Status parameter while pressing and releasing the brake pedal. Does the Brake Switch Status change while pressing and releasing the brake?	Go to Step 6	Go to DTC C0161
6	1. Remove the electronic brake control module (EBCM) from the vehicle. 2. Inspect the master cylinder pressure sensor connector within the EBCM for damage or corrosion. Is there connector damage or corrosion present?	Go to Step 7	Go to Step 8
7	**Important:** Following EBCM replacement, perform the set-up procedure for the EBCM. Use the scan tool to perform the Tire Size Calibration procedure. Replace the EBCM. Did you complete the replacement?	Go to Step 9	—
8	**Important:** Following EBCM replacement, perform the set-up procedure for the EBCM. Use the scan tool to perform the Tire Size Calibration procedure. Replace the EBCM and the brake pressure modulator valve (BPMV). Did you complete the replacements?	Go to Step 9	—
9	1. Use the scan tool Clear All Class 2 DTCs function to clear all of the DTCs from all modules. 2. Turn OFF the ignition for 5 seconds. 3. Turn ON the ignition. 4. Operate the vehicle within the Conditions for Running the DTC as specified in the supporting text. Does the DTC reset?	Go to Step 2	System OK

LTV0500000006430

Fig. 130   Code C0131: ABS/TCS Pressure Circuit (Part 3 of 3). 2004–06 Bravada, Envoy, Rainier & Trailblazer

Diagnostic Aids

Thoroughly inspect connections or circuitry that may cause an intermittent malfunction. Refer to the following:

• Testing for Intermittent Conditions and Poor Connections
• Connector Repairs
• Testing for Electrical Intermittents
• Wiring Repairs

Test Description

The numbers below refer to the step numbers on the diagnostic table.

4. This step tests for a shorted stop lamp switch.

5. This step tests for an open stop lamp switch.

Step	Action	Yes	No
1	Did you perform the Diagnostic System Check - Vehicle?	Go to Step 2	Go to Diagnostic System Check - Vehicle
2	1. Install a scan tool. 2. Select the 4WAL 3 Sensor Data Display function. 3. Observe the Brake Switch Status on the scan tool. Does the scan tool display Off?	Go to Step 3	Go to Step 5
3	1. Apply the brake. 2. Observe the Brake Switch Status on the scan tool. Does the scan tool display On?	Go to Diagnostic Aids	Go to Step 4
4	1. Turn OFF the ignition. 2. Disconnect the stop lamp switch. 3. Turn ON the ignition. 4. Observe the Brake Switch Status on the scan tool. Does the scan tool display On?	Go to Step 9	Go to Step 7
5	1. Turn OFF the ignition. 2. Disconnect the stop lamp switch. 3. Connect a fused jumper wire between the ignition 3 voltage circuit and the torque converter clutch (TCC) brake switch signal circuit at the stop lamp switch harness connector. 4. Turn ON the ignition. 5. Observe the Brake Switch Status on the scan tool. Does the scan tool display Off?	Go to Step 9	Go to Step 6

LTV0500000006432

Fig. 131   Code C0161: ABS/TCS Brake Switch Circuit (Part 2 of 3). 2004–06 Bravada, Envoy, Rainier & Trailblazer

		Yes	No
6	Test the ignition 3 voltage circuit and the TCC brake switch signal circuit for an open or a short to ground. Did you find and correct the condition?	Go to Step 12	Go to Step 8
7	Test the TCC brake switch signal circuit for a short to voltage. Did you find and correct the condition?	Go to Step 12	Go to Step 8
8	Inspect for poor connections at the harness connector of the electronic brake control module (EBCM). Did you find and correct the condition?	Go to Step 12	Go to Step 10
9	Inspect for poor connections at the harness connector of the stop lamp switch. Did you find and correct the condition?	Go to Step 12	Go to Step 11
10	**Important:** Following EBCM replacement, use the scan tool to perform the Tire Size Calibration procedure. Replace the EBCM. Did you complete the replacement?	Go to Step 12	--
11	Replace the stop lamp switch. Did you complete the replacement?	Go to Step 12	--
12	1. Use the scan tool in order to clear the DTCs. 2. Operate the vehicle within the Conditions for Running the DTC as specified in the supporting text. Does the DTC reset?	Go to Step 2	System OK

LTV0500000006433

Fig. 131   Code C0161: ABS/TCS Brake Switch Circuit (Part 3 of 3). 2004–06 Bravada, Envoy, Rainier & Trailblazer

Diagnostic Aids

- Inspect the vehicle for proper wheel alignment. Ensure the vehicle does not pull toward the left or right while driving straight forward on a level surface.
- Communicate with the customer to determine the conditions under which the message center displays the Service Stability System message. Learning the conditions under which the DTC sets may help you duplicate the failure.
- Use the Snapshot function on the scan tool in order to assist you in locating an intermittent malfunction.

Test Description

The numbers below refer to the step numbers on the diagnostic table.

3. This step tests the sensor circuitry in the high voltage range.

4. This step tests the sensor circuitry in the low voltage range.

Step	Action	Values	Yes	No
	Important: If DTC C0292 is set, diagnose C0292 before proceeding with diagnostics for C0186. If DTC C0196 is set, diagnose C0196 before proceeding with diagnostics for C0186. Always use connector test adapters when performing tests to avoid damage to delicate connector terminals. Do not turn OFF the ignition during this diagnostic procedure unless the step in the table instructs you to do so. The scan tool may display some incorrect data if the ignition is cycled.			
1	Did you perform the ABS Diagnostic System Check - Vehicle?	--	Go to Step 2	Go to Diagnostic System Check - Vehicle
2	1. Use the scan tool to clear the DTCs. 2. Turn OFF the ignition for 5 seconds. 3. Turn ON the ignition. 4. Operate the vehicle within the Conditions for Running the DTC as specified in the supporting text. Does the DTC reset?	--	Go to Step 3	Go to Diagnostic Aids
3	1. Turn OFF the ignition. 2. Disconnect the yaw rate sensor/lateral accelerometer harness connector. 3. Turn ON the ignition. 4. Select the vehicle stability enhancement system (VSES) Data Display function on the scan tool. 5. Connect a 3-amp fused jumper wire between the yaw rate sensor/lateral accelerometer 5-volt reference circuit and the lateral accelerometer signal circuit. 6. Observe the Lateral Accelerometer Sensor Input on the scan tool. Is the Lateral Accelerometer Sensor Input voltage greater than the specified value?	4.4 V	Go to Step 4	Go to Step 5

LTV0500000006435

Fig. 132   Code C0186: Lateral Accelerometer Circuit (Part 2 of 3). 2004–06 Bravada, Envoy, Rainier & Trailblazer

Circuit Description

The electronic brake control module (EBCM) supplies 5 volts to the yaw rate sensor/lateral accelerometer. When the vehicle is not moving, or is being driven in a stable, straight line, lateral acceleration is 0 m/sec/sec (0 ft/sec/sec) and the lateral accelerometer signal voltage is very near 2.5 volts. This is referred to as lateral accelerometer bias voltage. Making a turning maneuver causes the lateral accelerometer signal voltage to increase, or decrease, depending on the direction of the turn. The sharper the turn, the greater the change in signal voltage.

DTC Descriptor

This diagnostic procedure supports the following DTC:

DTC C0186 Lateral Accelerometer Circuit

Conditions for Running the DTC

- The ignition is ON.
- The vehicle stability enhancement system (VSES) sensors have been successfully initialized or the message center has displayed the stability system disabled message due to an unsuccessful initialization attempt. Refer to ABS Description and Operation for a complete explanation of VSES sensor initialization.
- The vehicle is being driven relatively straight and level at a speed greater than 11 km/h (7 mph), before performing a stable turning maneuver.

Conditions for Setting the DTC

Any of the following conditions may cause the DTC to set:

- Open lateral accelerometer circuitry is detected.
- Shorted lateral accelerometer circuitry is detected.
- An erratic lateral accelerometer signal is detected.
- The EBCM detects that the lateral accelerometer sensor signal does not correspond with signals from other sensors.

Action Taken When the DTC Sets

- The EBCM disables the VSES.
- The stability indicator turns ON.

Conditions for Clearing the DTC

The conditions for setting the DTC are no longer present and you use the scan tool Clear DTCs function.

LTV0500000006434

Fig. 132   Code C0186: Lateral Accelerometer Circuit (Part 1 of 3). 2004–06 Bravada, Envoy, Rainier & Trailblazer

		Values	Yes	No
4	1. Remove the fused jumper wire from the yaw rate sensor/lateral accelerometer harness connector. 2. Observe the Lateral Accelerometer Sensor Input on the scan tool. Is the Lateral Accelerometer Sensor Input voltage less than the specified value?	0.6 V	Go to Step 6	Go to Step 9
5	Test the lateral accelerometer signal circuit for the following conditions: • An open • A high resistance • A short to ground Did you find and correct the condition?	--	Go to Step 10	Go to Step 7
6	1. Inspect for poor connections at the harness connector of the yaw rate sensor/lateral accelerometer. 2. Ensure the yaw rate sensor/lateral accelerometer is mounted securely and that the mounting bracket is not bent or otherwise damaged. Did you find and correct the condition?	--	Go to Step 10	Go to Step 8
7	Inspect for poor connections at the harness connector of the electronic brake control module (EBCM). Did you find and correct the condition?	--	Go to Step 10	Go to Step 9
8	**Important:** Replace the EBCM and accelerometer sensor, Following EBCM replacement, perform the set-up procedure for the EBCM. Use the scan tool to perform the Tire Size Calibration procedure. Replace the yaw rate sensor/lateral accelerometer and EBCM. Did you complete the replacement?	--	Go to Step 10	--
9	**Important:** Following EBCM replacement, perform the set-up procedure for the EBCM. Use the scan tool to perform the Tire Size Calibration procedure. Replace the EBCM. Did you complete the replacement?	--	Go to Step 10	--
10	1. Use the scan tool Clear All Class 2 DTCs function to clear all of the DTCs from all modules. 2. Turn OFF the ignition for 5 seconds. 3. Turn ON the ignition. 4. Operate the vehicle within the Conditions for Running the DTC as specified in the supporting text. Does the DTC reset?		Go to Step 3	System OK

LTV0500000006436

Fig. 132   Code C0186: Lateral Accelerometer Circuit (Part 3 of 3). 2004–06 Bravada, Envoy, Rainier & Trailblazer

Circuit Description

The electronic brake control module (EBCM) supplies 5 volts to the yaw rate sensor/lateral accelerometer. When the vehicle is not moving, or is being driven in a stable, straight line, yaw rate is 0 degrees/second and the yaw rate sensor signal voltage is very near 2.5 volts. This is referred to as sensor bias voltage. Performing a turning maneuver causes the yaw rate sensor signal voltage to increase, or decrease, depending on the direction of the turn. The sharper the turn, the greater the change in signal voltage. Since the yaw rate signal is affected by temperature, the EBCM also monitors a Hz frequency signal from the yaw-rate sensor/lateral accelerometer which is proportionate to the approximate temperature of the yaw rate sensor.

DTC Descriptor

This diagnostic procedure supports the following DTC:

DTC C0196 Yaw Rate Circuit

Conditions for Running the DTC

- The ignition is ON.
- The vehicle stability enhancement system (VSES) sensors have been successfully initialized or the message center has displayed the stability system disabled message due to an unsuccessful initialization attempt.
- The vehicle is being driven relatively straight and level at a speed greater than 11 km/h (7 mph), before performing a stable turning maneuver.

Conditions for Setting the DTC

Any of the following conditions may cause the DTC to set:

- Open yaw rate sensor circuitry is detected.
- Shorted yaw rate sensor circuitry is detected.
- An erratic yaw rate sensor signal is detected.
- The EBCM detects that the yaw rate sensor signal does not correspond with signals from other sensors.
- The EBCM detects that the yaw rate sensor frequency signal is not within the valid range.
- A voltage near 5 volts is detected on the yaw rate sensor test circuit at all times.
- A voltage near 0 volts is detected on the yaw rate sensor test circuit at all times.

Action Taken When the DTC Sets

- The EBCM disables the VSES.
- The stability indicator turns ON.

Conditions for Clearing the DTC

The conditions for setting the DTC are no longer present and you use the scan tool Clear DTCs function.

LTV0500000006437

Fig. 133   Code C0196: Yaw Rate Circuit (Part 1 of 4). 2004–06 Bravada, Envoy, Rainier & Trailblazer

Diagnostic Aids

- The following scenario may cause this DTC to set when no actual malfunction exists:
  - The vehicle is driven in a straight line in reverse at a speed greater than 13 km/h (8 mph).
  - The transmission is shifted into neutral while the vehicle continues to coast backward.
  - A turning maneuver is performed after the above conditions are met and the vehicle speed is still greater than 13 km/h (8 mph).
- This DTC may also set falsely if the yaw rate sensor is replaced without first following the diagnostic table below. Whenever a new yaw rate sensor is installed, the old sensor must be disconnected, the ignition turned ON for 5 seconds and then OFF, and then the new sensor connected.
- Inspect the vehicle for proper wheel alignment. Ensure the vehicle does not pull toward the left or right while driving straight forward on a level surface.
- Communicate with the customer to determine the conditions under which the message center displays the service stability system message. Learning the conditions under which the DTC sets may help you duplicate the failure.
- Use the Snapshot function on the scan tool in order to assist you in locating an intermittent malfunction.

Test Description

The number below refers to the step number on the diagnostic table.

12. This step tests for a shorted resistor in the EBCM or a short to voltage within the circuit, by verifying that a large voltage drop occurs in the circuit when the test lamp is placed in parallel with the DMM.

Step	Action	Values	Yes	No
	Important: If DTC C0292 is set, diagnose C0292 before proceeding with diagnostics for C0196. Always use connector test adapters when performing tests to avoid damage to delicate connector terminals.			
1	Did you perform the Diagnostic System Check - Vehicle?	—	Go to Step 2	Go to Diagnostic System Check - Vehicle
2	1. Use the scan tool to clear the DTCs. 2. Turn OFF the ignition for 5 seconds. 3. Turn ON the ignition. 4. Operate the vehicle within the Conditions for Running the DTC as specified in the supporting text. Does the DTC reset?	—	Go to Step 3	Go to Diagnostic Aids

LTV0500000006438

Fig. 133   Code C0196: Yaw Rate Circuit (Part 2 of 4). 2004–06 Bravada, Envoy, Rainier & Trailblazer

Step	Action	Values	Yes	No
11	Ensure the yaw rate sensor/lateral accelerometer is mounted securely and that the mounting bracket is not bent or otherwise damaged. Did you find and correct the condition?	—	Go to Step 16	Go to Step 12
12	1. With the DMM connected to monitor the yaw rate frequency circuit, set the DMM to measure DC voltage. 2. Connect one end of a test lamp to a good ground. 3. Connect the other end of the test lamp to the positive lead of the DMM. Does the voltage measure less than the specified value?	0.15 V	Go to Step 16	Go to Step 14
13	Test the yaw rate frequency circuit for an open or a short to ground. Did you find and correct the condition?	—	Go to Step 20	Go to Step 17
14	Test the yaw rate frequency circuit for a short to voltage. Did you find and correct the condition?	—	Go to Step 20	Go to Step 19
15	Test the yaw rate sensor test circuit for a short to ground. Did you find and correct the condition?	—	Go to Step 20	Go to Step 17
16	Inspect for poor connections at the harness connector of the yaw rate sensor/lateral accelerometer. Did you find and correct the condition?	—	Go to Step 20	Go to Step 18
17	Inspect for poor connections at the harness connector of the EBCM. Did you find and correct the condition?	—	Go to Step 20	Go to Step 19
18	**Important:** Replace the EBCM and yaw rate sensor, Following EBCM replacement, perform the set-up procedure for the EBCM. Use the scan tool to perform the Tire Size Calibration procedure. Replace the yaw rate sensor/lateral accelerometer and EBCM. Did you complete the replacement?	—	Go to Step 20	—
19	**Important:** Following EBCM replacement, perform the set-up procedure for the EBCM and perform the . Use the scan tool to perform the Tire Size Calibration procedure. Replace the EBCM. Did you complete the replacement?	—	Go to Step 20	—
20	1. Use the scan tool Clear All Class 2 DTCs function to clear all of the DTCs from all modules. 2. Turn OFF the ignition for 5 seconds. 3. Turn ON the ignition. 4. Operate the vehicle within the Conditions for Running the DTC as specified in the supporting text. Does the DTC reset?	—	Go to Step 3	System OK

LTV0500000006440

Fig. 133   Code C0196: Yaw Rate Circuit (Part 4 of 4). 2004–06 Bravada, Envoy, Rainier & Trailblazer

Step	Action	Values	Yes	No
3	1. Turn OFF the ignition. 2. Disconnect the yaw rate sensor/lateral accelerometer harness connector. 3. Turn ON the ignition. 4. Select the vehicle stability enhancement system (VSES) Data Display function on the scan tool. 5. Observe the Yaw Rate Sensor Input on the scan tool. Is the Yaw Rate Sensor Input less than the specified value?	0.6 V	Go to Step 4	Go to Step 19
4	1. Connect a fused jumper wire between the yaw rate sensor/lateral accelerometer 5-volt reference circuit and the yaw rate signal circuit. 2. Observe the Yaw Rate Sensor Input on the scan tool. Is the Yaw Rate Sensor Input greater than the specified value?	4.4 V	Go to Step 5	Go to Step 7
5	1. Disconnect the fused jumper wire. 2. Use a DMM to measure the voltage between the yaw rate sensor/lateral accelerometer 5-volt reference circuit and the yaw rate sensor/lateral accelerometer low reference circuit. Does the voltage measure greater than the specified value?	4.75 V	Go to Step 9	Go to Step 6
6	Test the yaw rate sensor/lateral accelerometer low reference circuit for an open. Did you find and correct the condition?	—	Go to Step 20	Go to Step 17
7	Test the yaw rate signal circuit for the following conditions: - An open - A high resistance - A short to ground Refer to Circuit Testing and Wiring Repairs. Did you find and correct the condition?	—	Go to Step 20	Go to Step 8
8	Test the yaw rate sensor/lateral accelerometer 5-volt reference circuit for a high resistance or an open. Did you find and correct the condition?	—	Go to Step 20	Go to Step 17
9	Use a DMM to measure the voltage on the yaw rate frequency circuit. Does the voltage measure greater than the specified value?	4.75 V	Go to Step 10	Go to Step 13
10	Use a DMM to measure the voltage on the yaw rate sensor test circuit. Does the voltage measure greater than the specified value?	4.75 V	Go to Step 11	Go to Step 15

LTV0500000006439

Fig. 133   Code C0196: Yaw Rate Circuit (Part 3 of 4). 2004–06 Bravada, Envoy, Rainier & Trailblazer

Circuit Description

The system relay, located within the electronic brake control module (EBCM), supplies battery voltage to all of the valve solenoids and to the precharge pump motor. When the relay contacts close, the EBCM monitors the voltage supplied to the valve solenoids and compares this voltage to monitored ignition voltage.

DTC Descriptor

This diagnostic procedure supports the following DTC:

DTC C0201 Antilock Brake System (ABS) Enable Relay Contact Circuit

Conditions for Running the DTC

The ignition is ON.

Conditions for Setting the DTC

Either of the following conditions may cause the DTC to set:

- The EBCM detects that the voltage supplied to the valve solenoids is less than 65 percent of the monitored ignition voltage for 50 milliseconds.
- The EBCM detects that the relay contacts do not open when the relay is not energized.

Action Taken When the DTC Sets

If equipped, the following actions occur:

- The EBCM disables the ABS/traction control system (TCS)/vehicle stability enhancement system (VSES)/dynamic rear proportion (DRP).
- The ABS indicator turns ON.
- The stability indicator turns ON.
- The brake warning indicator turns ON.

Conditions for Clearing the DTC

The Conditions for Setting the DTC are no longer present and you use the scan tool Clear DTCs function.

Diagnostic Aids

Refer back to the diagnostic table, steps 3-7, if this DTC continues to set intermittently.

Test Description

The number below refers to the step number on the diagnostic table.

3. A shorted ABS pump motor may damage the contacts within the system relay. It is imperative that the steps in the table be followed to prevent

LTV050000006441

Fig. 134   Code C0201: ABS Enable Relay Contact Circuit (Part 1 of 2). 2004–06 Bravada, Envoy, Rainier & Trailblazer

Circuit Description

The powertrain control module (PCM) and the electronic brake control module (EBCM) communicate on the serial data link whenever the ignition is ON.

DTC Descriptor

This diagnostic procedure supports the following DTC:

DTC C0240 EBCM Malfunction

Conditions for Running the DTC

- The ignition is ON.
- The engine is running at a speed greater than 450 RPM for 5-20 seconds.

Conditions for Setting the DTC

The EBCM receives a serial data message stating that the PCM has lost the ability to reduce engine torque.

Action Taken When the DTC Sets

- The EBCM disables the vehicle stability enhancement system (VSES).
- Engine torque reduction is disabled.
- The traction off indicator turns ON.
- The message center displays the service stability system or stability system disabled message.

Conditions for Clearing the DTC

The conditions for setting the DTC are no longer present and you use the scan tool Clear DTCs function.

Diagnostic Aids

A requested torque signal malfunction is only one possible cause for setting this DTC. DTC C0240 may set due to engine overheating, throttle actuator control failure, loss of ignition timing control by the PCM, etc. If DTC P0856 has not set, refer to Diagnostic System Check - Vehicle in order to identify other possible causes of DTC C0240.

Step	Action	Values	Yes	No
1	Did you perform the Diagnostic System Check - Vehicle?	--	Go to Step 2	Go to Diagnostic System Check - Vehicle
2	Is DTC P0856 set?	--	Go to Symptoms	Go to Diagnostic Aids

LTV050000006443

Fig. 135   Code C0240: EBCM Fault. 2004–06 Bravada, Envoy, Rainier & Trailblazer

Step	Action	Values	Yes	No
1	Did you perform the Diagnostic System Check - Vehicle?	--	Go to Step 2	Go to Diagnostic System Check - Vehicle
2	1. Use the scan tool to clear the DTCs. 2. Turn OFF the ignition for 5 seconds. 3. Turn ON the ignition. Does the DTC reset?	--	Go to Step 3	Go to Diagnostic Aids
3	1. Separate the electronic brake control module (EBCM) from the brake pressure modulator valve (BPMV). 2. Use a DMM in order to measure the resistance across the ABS pump motor. Does the resistance measure within the specified range?	0.3-1 ohms	Go to Step 4	Go to Step 6
4	Use a DMM in order to measure the resistance between the high side of the pump motor and a good ground. Does the resistance measure less than the specified value?	OL	Go to Step 6	Go to Step 5
5	**Important:** Following the EBCM replacement, perform the set-up procedure for the EBCM. Use the scan tool to perform the Tire Size Calibration procedure. Replace the EBCM. Did you complete the replacement?	--	Go to Step 7	--
6	**Important:** Following the EBCM replacement, perform the set-up procedure for the EBCM. Use the scan tool to perform the Tire Size Calibration procedure. Replace the EBCM and the BPMV. Did you complete the replacements?	--	Go to Step 7	--
7	1. Use the scan tool to clear the DTCs. 2. Turn OFF the ignition for 5 seconds. 3. Turn ON the ignition. Does the DTC reset?	--	Go to Step 3	System OK

LTV050000006442

Fig. 134   Code C0201: ABS Enable Relay Contact Circuit (Part 2 of 2). 2004–06 Bravada, Envoy, Rainier & Trailblazer

Circuit Description

The EBCM and the PCM simultaneously control the traction control. The EBCM sends a Requested Torque message via a pulse width modulated (PWM) signal to the PCM. The duty cycle of the signal is used to determine how much engine torque the EBCM is requesting the PCM to deliver. Normal values are between 10 and 90 percent duty cycle. The signal should be at 90 percent when traction control is not active and at lower values during traction control activations. The PCM supplies the pull up voltage that the EBCM switches to ground to create the signal.

DTC Descriptors

This diagnostic procedure supports the following DTCs:

- DTC C0241 Powertrain Control Module (PCM) Indicated Requested Torque Malfunction
- DTC P0856 Traction Control Torque Request Circuit

Conditions for Running the DTC

The ignition is ON.

Conditions for Setting the DTC

The PCM diagnoses the requested torque PWM signal circuit and sends a class 2 serial data message to the EBCM indicating a fault is present. A fault exists in the circuit if the PCM detects one of the following conditions:

- The requested torque PWM signal is less than 5 percent duty cycle or greater than 95 percent duty cycle.
- The requested torque PWM signal is not present for 10 seconds.

Action Taken When the DTC Sets

If equipped, the following actions occur:

- The electronic brake control module (EBCM) disables the traction control system (TCS)/vehicle stability enhancement system (VSES) for the duration of the ignition cycle.
- A malfunction DTC will set.
- The Stability Off indicator turns ON.
- The antilock brake system (ABS) remains functional.

LTV050000006444

Fig. 136   Codes C0241 Or P0856: PCM Indicated Requested Torque Fault (Part 1 of 4). 2004–06 Bravada, Envoy, Rainier & Trailblazer

Conditions for Clearing the DTC

- The condition for the DTC is no longer present (the DTC is not current) and you used the scan tool Clear DTC function.
- The EBCM automatically clears the history DTC when a current DTC is not detected in 100 consecutive drive cycles.

Test Description

The numbers below refer to the step numbers on the diagnostic table.

3. Use the scan tool in order to determine if the requested torque signal has a valid duty cycle.

4. Measure the requested torque signal in order to determine if the signal has a valid duty cycle.

5. Measure the requested torque signal in order to determine if the signal has a valid frequency.

11. This vehicle is equipped with a powertrain control module (PCM) which uses an electrically erasable programmable read only memory (EEPROM). When replacing the PCM, the replacement PCM must be programmed.

Step	Action	Value (s)	Yes	No
1	Did you perform the Diagnostic System Check - Vehicle?	--	Go to Step 2	Go to Diagnostic System Check - Vehicle
2	Inspect the electronic brake control module (EBCM) ground and powertrain control module (PCM) ground, ensuring each ground is clean and torqued to the proper specification. Did you find and correct the condition?	--	Go to Step 13	Go to Step 3
3	1. Install a scan tool. 2. Start the engine. 3. With the scan tool, observe the Torque Request Signal parameter in the Powertrain Control Module data list. Does the scan tool display less than the specified value?	100%	Test for Intermittent Conditions and Poor Connections	Go to Step 4

LTV0500000006445

Fig. 136   Codes C0241 Or P0856: PCM Indicated Requested Torque Fault (Part 2 of 4). 2004–06 Bravada, Envoy, Rainier & Trailblazer

Step	Action	Value (s)	Yes	No
10	Inspect for poor connections at the harness connector of the EBCM. Did you find and correct the condition?	--	Go to Step 13	Go to Step 12
11	Replace the PCM. Did you complete the repair?	--	Go to Step 13	--
12	Replace the EBCM. Did you complete the repair?	--	Go to Step 13	--
13	1. Use the scan tool in order to clear the DTCs. 2. Operate the vehicle within the Conditions for Running the DTC as specified in the supporting text. Does the DTC reset?	--	Go to Step 2	System OK

LTV0500000006447

Fig. 136   Codes C0241 Or P0856: PCM Indicated Requested Torque Fault (Part 4 of 4). 2004–06 Bravada, Envoy, Rainier & Trailblazer

Circuit Description

Traction Control is simultaneously controlled by the electronic brake control module (EBCM) and the powertrain control module (PCM). The PCM sends a DELIVERED TORQUE message via a pulse width modulated (PWM) signal to the EBCM confirming the delivered torque level for proper Traction Control system operation. The EBCM supplies the pull up voltage.

DTC Descriptors

This diagnostic procedure supports the following DTCs:

- DTC C0244 Pulse Width Modulated (PWM) Delivered Torque
- DTC P1689 Traction Control Delivered Torque Output Circuit

Conditions for Running the DTC

- The ignition switch is ON.
- The DTC can be set after system initialization.

Conditions for Setting the DTC

DTC C0244 can be set anytime when ignition voltage is present. A malfunction exists, if the PWM signal is out of range, or no signal is received for a period of 2 seconds.

Action Taken When the DTC Sets

If equipped, the following actions occur:

- A malfunction DTC is stored.
- The traction control system (TCS) is disabled.
- The TRAC OFF indicator is turned on. The ABS remains functional.

Conditions for Clearing the DTC

- The condition for the DTC is no longer present and the DTC is cleared with a scan tool.
- The EBCM automatically clears the history DTC when a current DTC is not detected in 100 consecutive drive cycles.

LTV0500000006448

Fig. 137   Codes C0244 Or P1689: PWM Delivered Torque (Part 1 of 3). 2004–06 Bravada, Envoy, Rainier & Trailblazer

Step	Action	Value (s)	Yes	No
4	1. Turn OFF the ignition. 2. Disconnect the EBCM harness connector. 3. Install the J 39700 Universal Breakout Box using the J 39700-530 Cable Adapter to the EBCM harness connector and the EBCM connector. 4. Start the engine. 5. Measure the DC duty cycle between the requested torque signal circuit and a good ground. Is the duty cycle within the specified range?	5-95%	Go to Step 5	Go to Step 6
5	Measure the DC Hz between the requested torque signal circuit and a good ground. Does the frequency measure within the specified range?	121-134 Hz	Go to Step 8	Go to Step 6
6	1. Turn OFF the ignition. 2. Disconnect the cable adapter from the EBCM connector. **Important:** Disconnecting the EBCM connector and turning ON the ignition could cause other modules to set loss of communication DTCs (Uxxxx). Once the EBCM is reconnected, the EBCM may set DTC C0241. 3. Turn ON the ignition, with the engine OFF. 4. Measure the voltage from the requested torque signal circuit to a good ground. Does the voltage measure within the specified range?	4-6 V	Go to Step 10	Go to Step 7
7	1. Turn OFF the ignition. 2. Disconnect the PCM harness connector. 3. Test the requested torque signal circuit for the following conditions: - A short to voltage - A short to ground Refer to Circuit Testing and Wiring Repairs. Did you find and correct the condition?	--	Go to Step 13	Go to Step 10
8	1. Turn OFF the ignition. 2. Disconnect the PCM harness connector. 3. Test the requested torque signal circuit for the following conditions: - An open - A high resistance Refer to Circuit Testing and Wiring Repairs. Did you find and correct the condition?	--	Go to Step 13	Go to Step 9
9	Inspect for poor connections at the harness connector of the PCM. Did you find and correct the condition?	--	Go to Step 13	Go to Step 11

LTV0500000006446

Fig. 136   Codes C0241 Or P0856: PCM Indicated Requested Torque Fault (Part 3 of 4). 2004–06 Bravada, Envoy, Rainier & Trailblazer

Diagnostic Aids

- It is very important that a thorough inspection of the wiring and connectors be performed. Failure to carefully and fully inspect wiring and connectors may result in misdiagnosis, causing part replacement with reappearance of the malfunction.
- If an intermittent malfunction exists, refer to Checking Aftermarket Accessories.
- Possible causes for DTC C0244 to set:
  - An open in the torque delivered control circuit
  - Torque Delivered Control circuit shorted to ground or voltage
  - A communication frequency problem
  - A communication duty cycle problem
  - Torque delivered control circuit has a wiring problem, terminal corrosion, or poor connections
  - EBCM not receiving information from the PCM

Test Description

The numbers below refer to the step numbers on the diagnostic table.

3. Use the scan tool in order to determine if the delivered torque signal has a valid duty cycle.

9. This vehicle is equipped with a PCM which uses an electrically erasable programmable read only memory (EEPROM). When replacing the PCM, the replacement PCM must be programmed.

Step	Action	Value (s)	Yes	No
1	Did you perform the Diagnostic System Check - Vehicle?	--	Go to Step 2	Go to Diagnostic System Check - Vehicle
2	Inspect the electronic brake control module (EBCM) ground and powertrain control module (PCM) ground, making sure each ground is clean and torqued to the proper specification. Did you find and correct the condition?	--	Go to Step 11	Go to Step 3
3	1. Install a scan tool. 2. Start the engine. 3. With a scan tool, observe the PCM to EBCM Delivered parameter in the Powertrain Control Module data list. Does the scan tool display the specified value?	90%	Go to Step 4	Test for Intermittent Conditions and Poor Connections

LTV0500000006449

Fig. 137   Codes C0244 Or P1689: PWM Delivered Torque (Part 2 of 3). 2004–06 Bravada, Envoy, Rainier & Trailblazer

Step	Action		Yes	No
4	1. Turn OFF the ignition. 2. Disconnect the EBCM harness connector. 3. Install the J J 39700 Universal Breakout Box using the J J 39700-325 Cable Adapter to the EBCM harness connector and the EBCM connector. 4. Disconnect the PCM harness connector. 5. Turn ON the ignition, with the engine OFF. 6. Measure the voltage from the delivered torque signal circuit to a good ground. Does the voltage measure near the specified value?	B+	Go to Step 5	Go to Step 6
5	1. Turn OFF the ignition. 2. Disconnect the cable adapter from the EBCM connector. 3. Turn ON the ignition, with the engine OFF. 4. Test the delivered torque signal circuit for a short to voltage. Did you find and correct the condition?	--	Go to Step 11	Go to Step 7
6	1. Turn OFF the ignition. 2. Disconnect the J 39700-325 from the EBCM connector. 3. Test the delivered torque signal circuit for the following conditions: - An open - A short to ground - A high resistance Did you find and correct the condition?	--	Go to Step 11	Go to Step 8
7	Inspect for poor connections the harness connector of the PCM. Did you find and correct the condition?	--	Go to Step 11	Go to Step 9
8	Inspect for poor connections the harness connector of the EBCM. Did you find and correct the condition?	--	Go to Step 11	Go to Step 10
9	Important: The replacement PCM must be programmed. Replace the PCM. Did you complete the repair?	--	Go to Step 11	--
10	Replace the EBCM. Did you complete the repair?	--	Go to Step 11	--
11	1. Use the scan tool in order to clear the DTCs. 2. Operate the vehicle within the Conditions for Running the DTC as specified in the supporting text. Does the DTC reset?		Go to Step 2	System OK

LTV0500000006450

Fig. 137 Codes C0244 Or P1689: PWM Delivered Torque (Part 3 of 3). 2004–06 Bravada, Envoy, Rainier & Trailblazer

Step	Action	Yes	No
1	Did you perform the Diagnostic System Check - Vehicle?	Go to Step 2	Go to Diagnostic System Check - Vehicle
2	Inspect both of the front tires on the vehicle to ensure that both tires are of equal size. Are both of the front tires of equal size?	Go to Step 3	Go to Diagnostic Aids
3	Inspect both of the rear tires on the vehicle to ensure that both tires are of equal size. Are both of the rear tires of equal size?	Go to Step 4	Go to Diagnostic Aids
4	Verify the electronic brake control module (EBCM) and the powertrain control module (PCM) both have the correct tire size calibration. Use the scan tool in order to view the EBCM tire size calibration or perform the Tire Size Calibration procedure Did you find and correct the condition?	Go to Step 5	Go to Diagnostic Aids
5	1. Use a scan tool in order to clear the DTCs. 2. Operate the vehicle for at least 3 minutes within the Conditions for Running the DTC as specified in the supporting text. Does the DTC reset?	Go to Step 2	System OK

LTV0500000006452

Fig. 138 Code C0245: Wheel Speed Sensor Frequency Error (Part 2 of 2). 2004–06 Bravada, Envoy, Rainier & Trailblazer

Circuit Description

As the front wheels spin, each wheel speed sensor produces an AC signal. The electronic brake control module (EBCM) uses the frequency of the AC signals to calculate each wheel speed. The powertrain control module (PCM) converts the signal from the vehicle speed sensor (VSS) to a 128k pulses/mile signal. The EBCM uses the vehicle speed signal from the PCM to calculate the rear wheel speed.

DTC Descriptor

This diagnostic procedure supports the following DTC:

DTC C0245 Wheel Speed Sensor Frequency Error

Conditions for Running the DTC

- The ignition is ON.
- The vehicle speed is greater than 8 km/h (4 mph).
- No brake application or deceleration is detected.
- No wheel slip is detected.
- No turning maneuvers are detected.

Conditions for Setting the DTC

- At least one wheel speed sensor signal is 15 percent less than or greater than, other wheel speed sensor signals.
- All of the conditions for running and setting the DTC are present for a cumulative time of 3 minutes during a single ignition cycle.

Action Taken When the DTC Sets

- The EBCM disables the ABS/dynamic rear proportion (DRP).
- The ABS indicator turns ON.
- The brake warning indicator turns ON.

Conditions for Clearing the DTC

The Conditions for Setting the DTC are no longer present and you use the scan tool Clear DTCs function.

Diagnostic Aids

Installing one tire of significantly different size on the vehicle causes this DTC to set. Operating the vehicle with a tire that has very low air pressure may also set this DTC. Inspect the vehicle for an incorrect or damaged wheel speed sensor or VSS if the tires and the EBCM and PCM calibrations are OK.

Test Description

The number below refers to the step number on the diagnostic table.

4. If the front tires are not the same size as the rear tires, the EBCM calibration must match the FRONT tire size and the

LTV0500000006451

Fig. 138 Code C0245: Wheel Speed Sensor Frequency Error (Part 1 of 2). 2004–06 Bravada, Envoy, Rainier & Trailblazer

Step	Action	Yes	No
1	Did you perform the Diagnostic System Check - Vehicle?	Go to Step 2	Go to Diagnostic System Check - Vehicle
2	1. Use a scan tool in order to clear the DTCs. 2. Turn OFF the ignition for 5 seconds. 3. Turn ON the ignition for up to 20 seconds. Does the DTC set?	Go to Step 3	Go to Diagnostic Aids
3	1. Turn OFF the ignition. 2. Disconnect the mode switch harness connector. 3. Turn ON the ignition. 4. Connect a test lamp between the ignition 3 voltage circuit and a good ground. Does the test lamp illuminate?	Go to Step 4	Go to Step 8
4	1. Use the scan tool in order to clear the DTCs. 2. Turn OFF the ignition. 3. Connect a fused jumper wire between the ignition 3 voltage circuit and the traction control switch signal circuit at the mode switch harness connector. 4. Turn ON the ignition for up to 20 seconds. Does the DTC set?	Go to Step 5	Go to Step 9
5	Test the traction control switch signal circuit for an open or a short to ground. Did you find and correct the condition?	Go to Step 11	Go to Step 6

LTV0500000006453

Fig. 139 Code C0283: Mode Switch Circuit (Part 1 of 2). 2004–06 Bravada, Envoy, Rainier & Trailblazer

Step	Action		Values	Yes	No
6	Inspect for poor connections at the harness connector of the electronic brake control module (EBCM). Did you find and correct the condition?			Go to Step 11	Go to Step 7
7	**Important:** Following EBCM replacement, perform the set-up procedure for the EBCM. Use the scan tool to perform the Tire Size Calibration procedure. Replace the EBCM. Did you complete the replacement?			Go to Step 11	--
8	Repair the open in the ignition 3 voltage circuit. Did you complete the repair?			Go to Step 11	--
9	Inspect for poor connections at the harness connector of the mode switch. Did you find and correct the condition?			Go to Step 11	Go to Step 10
10	Replace the mode switch. Did you complete the replacement?			Go to Step 11	--
11	1. Use the scan tool to clear the DTCs. 2. Turn OFF the ignition for 5 seconds. 3. Turn ON the ignition. 4. Operate the vehicle within the Conditions for Running the DTC as specified in the supporting text. Does the DTC reset?			Go to Step 3	System OK

LTV0500000006454

Fig. 139   Code C0283: Mode Switch Circuit (Part 2 of 2). 2004–06 Bravada, Envoy, Rainier & Trailblazer

Diagnostic Aids

- Inspect the vehicle for proper wheel alignment. Ensure the vehicle does not pull toward the left or right while driving straight forward on a level surface.
- Communicate with the customer to determine the conditions under which the message center displays the Service Stability System message. Learning the conditions under which the DTC sets may help you duplicate the failure.
- Use the Snapshot function on the scan tool in order to assist you in locating an intermittent malfunction.

Test Description

The numbers below refer to the step numbers on the diagnostic table.

3. This step tests the sensor circuitry in the high voltage range.

4. This step tests the sensor circuitry in the low voltage range.

Step	Action	Values	Yes	No
	Important: If DTC C0292 is set, diagnose C0292 before proceeding with diagnostics for C0186. If DTC C0196 is set, diagnose C0196 before proceeding with diagnostics for C0186. Always use connector test adapters when performing tests to avoid damage to delicate connector terminals. Do not turn OFF the ignition during this diagnostic procedure unless the step in the table instructs you to do so. The scan tool may display some incorrect data if the ignition is cycled.			
1	Did you perform the ABS Diagnostic System Check - Vehicle?	--	Go to Step 2	Go to Diagnostic System Check - Vehicle
2	1. Use the scan tool to clear the DTCs. 2. Turn OFF the ignition for 5 seconds. 3. Turn ON the ignition. 4. Operate the vehicle within the Conditions for Running the DTC as specified in the supporting text. Does the DTC reset?	--	Go to Step 3	Go to Diagnostic Aids
3	1. Turn OFF the ignition. 2. Disconnect the yaw rate sensor/Longitudnal accelerometer harness connector. 3. Turn ON the ignition. 4. Select the vehicle stability enhancement system (VSES) Data Display function on the scan tool. 5. Connect a 3-amp fused jumper wire between the yaw rate sensor/Longitudnal accelerometer 5-volt reference circuit and the Longitudnal accelerometer signal circuit. 6. Observe the Longitudnal Accelerometer Sensor Input on the scan tool. Is the Longitudnal Accelerometer Sensor Input voltage greater than the specified value?	4.4 V	Go to Step 4	Go to Step 5
4	1. Remove the fused jumper wire from the yaw rate sensor/Longitudnal accelerometer harness connector. 2. Observe the Longitudnal Accelerometer Sensor Input on the scan tool. Is the Longitudnal Accelerometer Sensor Input voltage less than the specified value?	0.6 V	Go to Step 6	Go to Step 9

LTV0500000006456

Fig. 140   Code C0287: Longitudinal Accelerometer Circuit (Part 2 of 3). 2004–06 Bravada, Envoy, Rainier & Trailblazer

Circuit Description

The electronic brake control module (EBCM) provides power 5-volt reference to the longitudinal accelerometer. The longitudinal accelerometer converts the change in vehicle motion, or inertia, into a voltage signal. This signal is sent to the EBCM.

The voltage signal ranges, from 2.4-2.6 volts at zero speed change, constant motion, or stationary. The longitudinal accelerometer voltage signal drops when the vehicle is under acceleration. The longitudinal accelerometer voltage signal increases when the vehicle is under deceleration. The usable output voltage range for the longitudinal accelerometer is 0.48-4.82 volts. The longitudinal accelerometer sensor bias compensates for sensor mounting alignment errors and electronic signal errors.

DTC Descriptor

This diagnostic procedure supports the following DTC:

DTC C0287 Longitudnal Accelerometer Circuit

Conditions for Running the DTC

- The ignition is ON.
- The vehicle stability enhancement system (VSES) sensors have been successfully initialized or the message center has displayed the stability system disabled message due to an unsuccessful initialization attempt.
- The vehicle is being driven relatively straight and level at a speed greater than 11 km/h (7 mph), before performing a stable turning maneuver.

Conditions for Setting the DTC

Any of the following conditions may cause the DTC to set:

- Open Longitudnal accelerometer circuitry is detected.
- Shorted Longitudnal accelerometer circuitry is detected.
- An erratic Longitudnal accelerometer signal is detected.
- The EBCM detects that the Longitudnal accelerometer sensor signal does not correspond with signals from other sensors.

Action Taken When the DTC Sets

- The EBCM disables the VSES.
- The stability indicator turns ON.

Conditions for Clearing the DTC

The conditions for setting the DTC are no longer present and you use the scan tool Clear DTCs function.

LTV0500000006455

Fig. 140   Code C0287: Longitudinal Accelerometer Circuit (Part 1 of 3). 2004–06 Bravada, Envoy, Rainier & Trailblazer

Step	Action	Values	Yes	No
6	1. Inspect for poor connections at the harness connector of the yaw rate sensor/Longitudnal accelerometer. 2. Ensure the yaw rate sensor/Longitudnal accelerometer is mounted securely and that the mounting bracket is not bent or otherwise damaged. Did you find and correct the condition?		Go to Step 10	Go to Step 8
7	Inspect for poor connections at the harness connector of the electronic brake control module (EBCM). Did you find and correct the condition?		Go to Step 10	Go to Step 9
8	**Important:** Replace the EBCM and yaw rate sensor, Following EBCM replacement, perform the set-up procedure for the EBCM. Use the scan tool to perform the Tire Size Calibration procedure. Replace the yaw rate sensor/Longitudnal accelerometer. Did you complete the replacement?		Go to Step 10	--
9	**Important:** Following EBCM replacement, perform the set-up procedure for the EBCM. Use the scan tool to perform the Tire Size Calibration procedure. Replace the EBCM. Did you complete the replacement?		Go to Step 10	--
10	1. Use the scan tool Clear All Class 2 DTCs function to clear all of the DTCs from all modules. 2. Turn OFF the ignition for 5 seconds. 3. Turn ON the ignition. 4. Operate the vehicle within the Conditions for Running the DTC as specified in the supporting text. Does the DTC reset?		Go to Step 3	System OK

LTV0500000000313

Fig. 140   Code C0287: Longitudinal Accelerometer Circuit (Part 3 of 3). 2004–06 Bravada, Envoy, Rainier & Trailblazer

Circuit Description

The electronic brake control module (EBCM) supplies a reference voltage of 5 volts to the yaw rate sensor/lateral accelerometer, the steering wheel position sensor and the master cylinder pressure sensor. The sensor supply voltage is monitored via an internal feedback circuit to the EBCM microprocessor.

DTC Descriptors

This diagnostic procedure supports the following DTCs:

- DTC C0290 Devise Voltage Reference Output Circuit
- DTC C0292 Devise Voltage Reference Input Circuit

Conditions for Running the DTC

The ignition is ON.

Conditions for Setting the DTC

The EBCM detects that the sensor supply voltage is less than 4.75 volts or greater than 5.25 volts for 30 milliseconds.

Action Taken When the DTC Sets

- The EBCM disables the vehicle stability enhancement system (VSES).
- The stability system caution indicator turns ON.

Test Description

The numbers below refer to the step numbers on the diagnostic table.

5. This step tests for a shorted yaw rate sensor/lateral accelerometer or steering wheel position sensor.

6. This step tests for a shorted master cylinder pressure sensor. The presence of DTC C0110 is normal during this step.

LTV0500000006457

Fig. 141 Code C0290 Or C0292: Devise Voltage Reference Output Circuit (Part 1 of 3). 2004–06 Bravada, Envoy, Rainier & Trailblazer

	Action	Yes	No
7	Replace the BPMV.		
	Did you complete the replacement?	Go to Step 12	--
8	Reconnect the steering wheel position sensor harness connector.		
	Does the DTC reset?	Go to Step 10	Go to Step 9
9	**Important:** Replace the EBCM and yaw rate sensor, Following EBCM replacement, perform the set-up procedure for the EBCM. Use the scan tool to perform the Tire Size Calibration procedure. Replace the yaw rate sensor/lateral accelerometer.		
	Did you complete the replacement?	Go to Step 12	--
10	Replace the steering wheel position sensor.		
	Did you complete the replacement?	Go to Step 12	--
11	**Important:** Following EBCM replacement, perform the setup procedure for the EBCM. Use the scan tool to perform the Tire Size Calibration procedure. Replace the EBCM.		
	Did you complete the replacement?	Go to Step 12	--
12	1. Use the scan tool Clear All Class 2 DTCs function to clear all of the DTCs from all modules. 2. Turn OFF the ignition for 5 seconds. 3. Turn ON the ignition. 4. Operate the vehicle within the Conditions for Running the DTC as specified in the supporting text.		
	Does the DTC reset?	Go to Step 3	System OK

LTV0500000006459

Fig. 141 Code C0290 Or C0292: Devise Voltage Reference Output Circuit (Part 3 of 3). 2004–06 Bravada, Envoy, Rainier & Trailblazer

Step	Action	Yes	No
1	Did you perform the Diagnostic System Check - Vehicle?	Go to Step 2	Go to Diagnostic System Check - Vehicle
2	1. Use the scan tool to clear the DTCs. 2. Turn OFF the ignition for 5 seconds. 3. Turn ON the ignition. Does the DTC reset?	Go to Step 3	Go to Diagnostic Aids
3	1. Turn OFF the ignition. 2. Disconnect the yaw rate sensor/lateral accelerometer harness connector. 3. Disconnect the steering wheel position sensor harness connector. 4. Disconnect the electronic brake control module (EBCM) harness connector. Refer to . 5. Test the yaw rate sensor/lateral accelerometer 5-volt reference circuit and the steering wheel position sensor 5-volt reference circuit for a short to ground. Did you find and correct the condition?	Go to Step 12	Go to Step 4
4	1. Turn ON the ignition. 2. Test the following circuits for a short to voltage: - Yaw rate sensor/lateral accelerometer 5-volt reference circuit - Steering wheel position sensor 5-volt reference circuit - Yaw rate sensor signal circuit - Lateral accelerometer signal circuit Did you find and correct the condition?	Go to Step 12	Go to Step 5
5	1. Turn OFF the ignition. 2. Reconnect only the EBCM harness connector. 3. Turn ON the ignition. 4. Use the scan tool to clear any DTCs. Does the DTC reset?	Go to Step 6	Go to Step 8
6	1. Turn OFF the ignition. 2. Reconnect the yaw rate sensor/lateral accelerometer harness connector. 3. Reconnect the steering wheel position sensor harness connector. 4. Separate the EBCM from the brake pressure modulator valve (BPMV), leaving the EBCM harness connector connected. 5. Turn ON the ignition. Does the DTC reset?	Go to Step 11	Go to Step 7

LTV0500000006458

Fig. 141 Code C0290 Or C0292: Devise Voltage Reference Output Circuit (Part 2 of 3). 2004–06 Bravada, Envoy, Rainier & Trailblazer

Circuit Description

The electronic brake control module (EBCM) receives several inputs from the steering wheel position sensor. Three digital square wave signal inputs are wired directly to the EBCM harness connector, however, only signals A and B are used or monitored. The failure of the index pulse signal does not effect vehicle stability enhancement system (VSES) function. The EBCM also receives an analog steering wheel position input on the steering wheel position sensor signal 1 circuit. Ignition voltage is supplied to the digital portion of the steering wheel position sensor. The analog portion of the steering wheel position sensor is supplied a 5-volt reference from the EBCM.

DTC Descriptor

This diagnostic procedure supports the following DTC:

DTC C0455 Front Steering Position Sensor Circuit

Conditions for Running the DTC

- The ignition is ON.
- The VSES sensors have been successfully initialized.

Conditions for Setting the DTC

Any of the following conditions may cause the DTC to set:

- The analog steering wheel position signal does not correlate with the digital steering wheel position signals.
- When driven forward in a straight line, the centered steering angle differs by more than 30 degrees from the centered steering angle when the sensors are initialized.
- The EBCM detects an erratic signal from steering wheel position signal A or signal B.
- The EBCM detects an open or shorted steering wheel position analog signal.
- The EBCM detects an erratic steering wheel position analog signal.
- The EBCM detects an open or shorted steering wheel position signal A or signal B, after having received a valid signal during the same ignition.

Action Taken When the DTC Sets

- The EBCM disables the VSES.
- The stability system caution indicator is illuminated.

LTV0500000006460

Fig. 142 Code C0455: Front Steering Position Sensor Circuit (Part 1 of 5). 2004–06 Bravada, Envoy, Rainier & Trailblazer

Conditions for Clearing the DTC

The condition for setting the DTC is no longer present and you use the scan tool Clear DTCs function.

Diagnostic Aids

- DTC C0455 may be falsely set if you did not turn OFF the ignition for 5 seconds after clearing DTCs from the EBCM. This is why all diagnostic tables which apply to this system always instruct you to turn OFF the ignition for 5 seconds after clearing DTCs. If this DTC has set after you cleared DTCs from the EBCM or used the scan tool to clear all DTCs from all modules and you did not cycle the ignition afterward, it is likely that no actual malfunction exists.
- Whenever any one of the steering signals to the EBCM is lost, the scan tool displays a fixed steering wheel position, which indicates the last known steering wheel position. This can aid you in diagnosing an intermittent malfunction.
- If the DTC does not reset during step 2 or 3 of the diagnostic procedure, the stability system not ready indicator may be displayed due to an unsuccessful initialization. This occurs if the EBCM does not receive any signal from one or both of the digital inputs during the entire ignition cycle.
- Inspect the vehicle for proper wheel alignment. Ensure the vehicle does not pull toward the left or right while driving straight forward on a level surface.
- Communicate with the customer to determine the conditions under which the instrument panel cluster (IPC) illuminates the stability system caution indicator. Learning the conditions under which the DTC sets may help you duplicate the failure.
- Use the Snapshot function on the scan tool in order to assist you in locating an intermittent malfunction.

Test Description

The number below refers to the step number on the diagnostic table.

2. If the DTC sets without turning the steering wheel or driving the vehicle, a malfunction exists in the analog steering wheel position signal to the EBCM.

Step	Action	Values	Yes	No
1	Did you perform the Diagnostic System Check - Vehicle?	--	Go to Step 2	Go to Diagnostic System Check - Vehicle
2	**Important:** Center the steering wheel before proceeding with this step. Do not rotate the steering wheel while performing this step. 1. Use the scan tool to clear the DTCs. 2. Turn OFF the ignition for 5 seconds. 3. Turn ON the ignition. 4. Wait approximately 5 seconds to verify whether or not the DTC sets. Does the DTC set?	--	Go to Step 3	Go to Step 10

LTV0500000006461

Fig. 142   Code C0455: Front Steering Position Sensor Circuit (Part 2 of 5). 2004–06 Bravada, Envoy, Rainier & Trailblazer

Step	Action	Values	Yes	No
10	Operate the vehicle within the Conditions for Running the DTC as specified in the supporting text. Does the DTC set?	--	Go to Step 11	Go to Diagnostic Aids
11	1. Select the VSES Data Display on the scan tool. 2. Center the steering wheel and verify that the front wheels are straight ahead. 3. Observe the Analog SWPS Signal parameter. Does the scan tool display an Analog SWPS Signal within the specified range?	2.3-2.7 V	Go to Step 12	Go to Step 17
12	1. Turn OFF the ignition. 2. Disconnect the steering wheel position sensor harness connector. 3. Disconnect the electronic brake control module (EBCM) harness connector. Refer to Control Module References . 4. Turn ON the ignition. 5. Test the steering wheel position circuits, signal A and signal B for the following conditions: - Intermittently open - Intermittently shorted to ground - Intermittently shorted together - Intermittently shorted to voltage Did you find and correct the condition?	--	Go to Step 19	Go to Step 13
13	Test the battery positive voltage circuit to the steering wheel position sensor for an intermittent open. Did you find and correct the condition?	--	Go to Step 19	Go to Step 14
14	Test both of the steering wheel position sensor ground circuits for an intermittent open. Did you find and correct the condition?	--	Go to Step 19	Go to Step 15
15	Inspect for poor connections at the harness connector of the steering wheel position sensor. Did you find and correct the condition?	--	Go to Step 19	Go to Step 17
16	Inspect for poor connections at the harness connector of the EBCM. Did you find and correct the condition?	--	Go to Step 19	Go to Step 18

LTV0500000006463

Fig. 142   Code C0455: Front Steering Position Sensor Circuit (Part 4 of 5). 2004–06 Bravada, Envoy, Rainier & Trailblazer

Step	Action	Values	Yes	No
3	1. Turn OFF the ignition. 2. Disconnect the steering wheel position sensor harness connector. 3. Turn ON the ignition. 4. Select the vehicle stability enhancement system (VSES) Data Display on the scan tool. 5. Observe the Analog SWPS Signal parameter on the scan tool. Does the scan tool indicate that the steering wheel position sensor data parameter is less than specified value?	0.15 V	Go to Step 4	Go to Step 9
4	1. Connect a 3-amp fused jumper wire between the steering wheel position 5-volt reference circuit and the analog steering signal circuit. 2. Observe the Analog SWPS Signal parameter on the scan tool. Does the scan tool indicate that the steering wheel position sensor data parameter is greater than specified value?	4.75 V	Go to Step 5	Go to Step 6
5	Use a DMM to measure the voltage between the steering wheel position 5-volt reference circuit and the steering wheel position low reference circuit. Does the voltage measure greater than the specified value?	4.75 V	Go to Step 16	Go to Step 8
6	Test the 5-volt reference circuit of the steering wheel position sensor for an open. Did you find and correct the condition?	--	Go to Step 19	Go to Step 7
7	Test the signal circuit of the steering wheel position sensor for an open or a short to ground. Did you find and correct the condition?	--	Go to Step 19	Go to Step 16
8	Test the low reference circuit of the steering wheel position sensor for an open. Did you find and correct the condition?	--	Go to Step 19	Go to Step 16
9	Test the signal circuit of the steering wheel position sensor for a short to voltage. Did you find and correct the condition?	--	Go to Step 19	Go to Step 16

LTV0500000006462

Fig. 142   Code C0455: Front Steering Position Sensor Circuit (Part 3 of 5). 2004–06 Bravada, Envoy, Rainier & Trailblazer

Step	Action	Values	Yes	No
17	Replace the steering wheel position sensor. Did you complete the replacement?	--	Go to Step 19	--
18	**Important:** Following EBCM replacement, perform the setup procedure for the EBCM. Use the scan tool to perform the Tire Size Calibration procedure. Replace the EBCM. Did you complete the replacement?	--	Go to Step 19	--
19	1. Use the scan tool Clear All Class 2 DTCs function to clear all of the DTCs from all modules. 2. Turn OFF the ignition for 5 seconds. 3. Turn ON the ignition. 4. Operate the vehicle within the Conditions for Running the DTC as specified in the supporting text. Does the DTC reset?	--	Go to Step 2	System OK

LTV0500000006464

Fig. 142   Code C0455: Front Steering Position Sensor Circuit (Part 5 of 5). 2004–06 Bravada, Envoy, Rainier & Trailblazer

Circuit Description

The electronic brake control module (EBCM) performs several self-tests for any internal problems which may affect proper operation.

DTC Descriptor

This diagnostic procedure supports the following DTC:

DTC C0550 Electronic Control Unit (ECU) Performance

Conditions for Running the DTC

The ignition is ON.

Conditions for Setting the DTC

The EBCM detects an internal malfunction.

Action Taken When the DTC Sets

The following actions may occur:

- The EBCM disables the ABS/dynamic rear proportion (DRP).
- The ABS indicator turns ON.
- The brake warning indicator turns ON.

Conditions for Clearing the DTC

Certain failures that may cause this DTC to set cannot be cleared. Other failures that may cause this DTC to set may be cleared, at least temporarily, by using the scan tool Clear DTCs function.

Diagnostic Aids

Replace the EBCM if this DTC continues to set intermittently.

LTV0500000006465

Fig. 143   Code C0550: ECU Performance (Part 1 of 2). 2004–06 Bravada, Envoy, Rainier & Trailblazer

Step	Action	Yes	No
1	Did you perform the Diagnostic System Check - Vehicle?	Go to Step 2	Go to Diagnostic System Check - Vehicle
2	Use a scan tool in order to clear the DTCs. Can the DTC be cleared?	Go to Step 3	Go to Step 4
3	1. Turn OFF the ignition. 2. Turn ON the ignition. Does the DTC reset?	Go to Step 4	Go to Diagnostic Aids
4	**Important:** Following electronic brake control module (EBCM) replacement, use the scan tool to perform the Tire Size Calibration procedure. Replace the EBCM. Did you complete the replacement?	Go to Step 5	--
5	1. Use the scan tool in order to clear the DTCs. 2. Operate the vehicle within the Conditions for Running the DTC as specified in the supporting text. Does the DTC reset?	Go to Step 3	System OK

LTV0500000006466

Fig. 143   Code C0550: ECU Performance (Part 2 of 2). 2004–06 Bravada, Envoy, Rainier & Trailblazer

Step	Action	Value(s)	Yes	No
1	Install a scan tool. Does the scan tool power up?	—	Go to Step 2	Go to Scan Tool Does Not Power Up in Data Link Communications
2	1. Turn ON the ignition, with the engine OFF. 2. Attempt to establish communication with the following control modules. • 4WAL 3 Sensor • Powertrain Does the scan tool communicate with the control modules listed above?	—	Go to Step 3	Go to Scan Tool Does Not Communicate with UART Data Line (EBCM) or Scan Tool Does Not Communicate with Class 2 Device (PCM/VCM) in Data Link Communications
3	Select the display DTCs function on the scan tool for the following control modules. • 4WAL 3 Sensor • Powertrain Does the scan tool display any DTCs for the control modules listed above?	—	Go to Step 4	Go to Symptoms
4	Does the scan tool display any DTCs that begin with a "U"?	—	Go to Scan Tool Does Not Communicate with Class 2 Device in Data Link Communications	Go to Step 5
5	Does the scan tool display DTC P0500, P0601, P0602, P0603, P0604, P0605, P0606, P1381 or P1621?	—	Go to Diagnostic Trouble Code (DTC) List/Type	Go to Diagnostic Trouble Code (DTC) List/Type

GC4020152396000X

Fig. 145   Diagnostic System Check. 2002 Express & Savana

Circuit Description

A replacement electronic brake control module (EBCM) is supplied with generic software and must be programmed to match the specific vehicle application.

DTC Descriptor

This diagnostic procedure supports the following DTC:

DTC C0558 Calibration Data Not Programmed

Conditions for Running the DTC

The ignition is ON.

Conditions for Setting the DTC

The EBCM is not programmed with complete software.

Action Taken When the DTC Sets

• The EBCM disables the ABS/dynamic rear proportion (DRP)/vehicle stability enhancement system (VSES).
• The ABS indicator turns ON.
• The brake warning indicator turns ON.
• The stability indicator turns ON.

Conditions for Clearing the DTC

The DTC clears when software programming is complete.

Step	Action	Yes	No
1	Did you perform the Diagnostic System Check - Vehicle?	Go to Step 2	Go to Diagnostic System Check - Vehicle
2	Perform the set-up procedure for the electronic brake control module (EBCM). Did you complete the action?	Go to Diagnostic System Check - Vehicle	--

LTV0500000006467

Fig. 144   Code C0558: Calibration Data Not Programmed. 2004–06 Bravada, Envoy, Rainier & Trailblazer

Step	Action	Values	Yes	No
	Important If DTC C0229 is set, diagnose DTC C0229 before diagnosing any other wheel speed sensor DTCs.			
1	Did you perform the ABS Diagnostic System Check?	--	Go to Step 2	Go to A Diagnostic System Check
2	1. Use a scan tool in order to clear the DTCs. 2. Operate the vehicle at a speed greater than the specified value. Does the DTC set?	19 km/h (12 mph)	Go to Step 3	Go to Diagnostic Aids
3	1. Turn OFF the ignition. 2. Raise and support the vehicle. 3. Disconnect the wheel speed sensor connector. 4. Use a DMM in order to measure the resistance across the wheel speed sensor. Does the resistance measure within the specified range?	1980-3850 ohms	Go to Step 4	Go to Step 8
4	1. Spin the wheel by hand as fast as possible. 2. Use a DMM in order to measure the AC voltage across the wheel speed sensor as the wheel spins. Does the voltage measure greater than the specified value?	100 mV	Go to Step 5	Go to Step 8
5	Inspect for poor connections at the harness connector of the wheel speed sensor. Did you find and correct the condition?	--	Go to Step 10	Go to Step 6

GC4020152397010X

Fig. 146   Codes C0221–C0227: Wheel Speed Sensor Fault (Part 1 of 2). 2002 Express & Savana

Step	Action	Values	Yes	No
6	1. Disconnect the EBCM harness connector. 2. Test the wheel speed sensor circuits for the following: • An open • A short to ground • A short to voltage • Shorted together Did you find and correct the condition?	--	Go to Step 10	Go to Step 7
7	Inspect for poor connections at the harness connector of the EBCM. Did you find and correct the condition?	--	Go to Step 10	Go to Step 9
8	Replace the wheel speed sensor. Did you complete the replacement?	--	Go to Step 10	--
9	Replace the EBCM. **Important** Use the scan tool in order to perform the Tire Size Calibration procedure. Did you complete the replacement?	--	Go to Step 10	--
10	1. Use the scan tool in order to clear the DTCs. 2. Operate the vehicle within the Conditions for Running the DTC as specified in the supporting text. Does the DTC reset?	--	Go to Step 3	System OK

GC4020152397020X

Fig. 146   Codes C0221–C0227: Wheel Speed Sensor Fault (Part 2 of 2). 2002 Express & Savana

Step	Action	Yes	No
1	Did you perform the ABS Diagnostic System Check?	Go to Step 2	Go to A Diagnostic System Check
2	1. Use the scan tool in order to clear the DTCs. 2. Operate the vehicle under the conditions for running the DTC as specified in the supporting text. Does the DTC set?	Go to Step 3	Go to Diagnostic Aids
3	Inspect for poor connections at the 4-way harness connector of the EBCM. Did you find and correct the condition?	Go to Step 5	Go to Step 4
4	Replace the EBCM. **Important** Use the scan tool in order to perform the Tire Size Calibration procedure. Did you complete the replacement?	Go to Step 5	--
5	1. Use the scan tool in order to clear the DTC. 2. Operate the vehicle within the Conditions for Running the DTC as specified in the supporting text. Does the DTC reset?	Go to Step 3	System OK

GC4020152398000X

Fig. 147   Code C0229: Drop Out Of Front Wheel Speed Signal. 2002 Express & Savana

Step	Action	Values	Yes	No
6	Replace the EBCM. **Important** Use the scan tool in order to perform the Tire Size Calibration procedure. Did you complete the replacement?	--	Go to Step 10	--
7	Test the vehicle speed signal circuit for an open, a short to ground or a short to voltage. Did you find and correct the condition?	--	Go to Step 10	Go to Step 8
8	Inspect for poor connections at the harness connector of the PCM or vehicle speed sensor buffer (VSSB). Did you find and correct the condition?	--	Go to Step 10	Go to Step 9
9	**Important** Perform the setup procedure for the PCM (gas vehicles only). Replace the PCM or VSSB. Did you complete the replacement?	--	Go to Step 10	--
10	1. Use the scan tool in order to clear the DTC. 2. Operate the vehicle within the Conditions for Running the DTC as specified in the supporting text. Does the DTC reset?	--	Go to Step 3	System OK

GC4020152399020X

Fig. 148   Codes C0235–C0237: Rear Wheel Speed Sensor Fault (Part 2 of 2). 2002 Express & Savana

Step	Action	Values	Yes	No
1	Did you perform the ABS Diagnostic System Check?	--	Go to Step 2	Go to A Diagnostic System Check
2	1. Use a scan tool in order to clear the DTCs. 2. Operate the vehicle within the Conditions for Running the DTC as specified in the supporting text. Does the DTC set?	--	Go to Step 3	Go to Diagnostic Aids
3	1. Turn OFF the ignition. 2. Disconnect from the EBCM, the harness connector which contains the vehicle speed signal circuit. 3. Turn ON the ignition. 4. Use a DMM in order to measure the DC voltage between the vehicle speed signal circuit and a good ground. Does the voltage measure greater than the specified value?	10 volts	Go to Step 4	Go to Step 7
4	1. Raise and support the vehicle. 2. Place the transmission in neutral. 3. Set up the DMM in order to measure the DC voltage between the vehicle speed signal circuit and a good ground. 4. Spin the rear wheels as fast as possible by hand for at least 30 seconds and while ensuring the driveshaft is rotating, observe the DMM. Does the voltage measure within the specified range the entire time the driveshaft is rotating?	5-7 volts	Go to Step 5	Go to Step 7
5	Inspect for poor connections at the harness connector of the EBCM. Did you find and correct the condition?	--	Go to Step 10	Go to Step 6

GC4020152399010X

Fig. 148   Codes C0235–C0237: Rear Wheel Speed Sensor Fault (Part 1 of 2). 2002 Express & Savana

Step	Action	Yes	No
1	Did you perform the ABS Diagnostic System Check?	Go to Step 2	Go to A Diagnostic System Check
2	Inspect both of the front tires on the vehicle to ensure that both tires are of equal size. Are both of the front tires of equal size?	Go to Step 3	Go to Diagnostic Aids
3	Inspect both of the rear tires on the vehicle to ensure that both tires are of equal size. Are both of the rear tires of equal size?	Go to Step 4	Go to Diagnostic Aids
4	For vehicles equipped with gas engines, verify the EBCM and the PCM both have the correct tire size calibration. Use the scan tool in order to view the EBCM tire size calibration or perform the Tire Size Calibration procedure. For vehicles equipped with the 6.5L (L65) diesel engine, verify the correct VSSB is installed in the vehicle. Did you find and correct the condition?	Go to Step 5	Go to Diagnostic Aids
5	1. Use a scan tool in order to clear the DTCs. 2. Operate the vehicle for 2 miles within the Conditions for Running the DTC as specified in the supporting text. Does the DTC reset?	Go to Step 2	System OK

GC4020152402000X

Fig. 149   Code C0238: Wheel Speed Mismatch. 2002 Express & Savana

Step	Action	--	Yes	No
7	Replace the BPMV. Did you complete the replacement?	--	Go to Step 8	--
8	1. Use the scan tool in order to clear the DTCs. 2. Operate the vehicle within the Conditions for Running the DTC as specified in the supporting text. Does the DTC reset?	--	Go to Step 3	System OK

GC4020152401020X

Fig. 150   Codes C0241–C0254: EBCM Control Valve Circuit (Part 2 of 2). 2002 Express & Savana

Step	Action	Value	Yes	No
1	Did you perform the ABS Diagnostic System Check?	--	Go to Step 2	Go to A Diagnostic System Check
2	1. Use a scan tool in order to clear the DTCs. 2. Use the scan tool in order to perform an ABS Function Test. Does DTC C0266 set?	--	Go to Step 7	Go to Step 3
3	Does DTC C0265 set?	--	Go to Step 4	Go to Diagnostic Aids
4	1. Turn OFF the ignition. 2. Disconnect from the EBCM, the harness connector containing the battery positive voltage circuit. 3. Connect a test lamp between the battery positive voltage circuit and a good ground. Does the test lamp illuminate?	--	Go to Step 6	Go to Step 5
5	Repair the open in the battery positive voltage circuit. Did you find and correct the condition?	--	Go to Step 11	--
6	Inspect for poor connections at the harness connector of the EBCM. Did you find and correct the condition?	--	Go to Step 11	Go to Step 7
7	1. Disconnect from the EBCM, the ABS pump motor pigtail connector. 2. Use a DMM in order to measure the resistance across the ABS pump motor. Does the resistance measure within the specified range?	0.3-1.0 ohms	Go to Step 8	Go to Step 10

GC4020152402010X

Fig. 151   Codes C0265 & C0266: EBCM Relay Circuit (Part 1 of 2). 2002 Express & Savana

Step	Action	Values	Yes	No
1	Did you perform the ABS Diagnostic System Check?	--	Go to Step 2	Go to A Diagnostic System Check
2	1. Use a scan tool in order to clear the DTCs. 2. Use the scan tool in order to perform an ABS Function Test. Does the DTC set?	--	Go to Step 3	Go to Diagnostic Aids
3	Test the ground circuit (at connector C3 terminal B) for an open. Did you find and correct the condition?	--	Go to Step 8	Go to Step 4
4	1. Disconnect from the EBCM, the ABS pump motor pigtail connector. 2. Use a DMM in order to measure the resistance across the ABS pump motor. **Important** A shorted ABS pump motor may cause damage to the EBCM. Does the pump motor resistance measure within the specified range?	0.3-1.0 ohms	Go to Step 5	Go to Step 7
5	Inspect for poor connections at the harness connector of the EBCM. Did you find and correct the condition?	--	Go to Step 8	Go to Step 6
6	Replace the EBCM. **Important** Use the scan tool in order to perform the Tire Size Calibration procedure. Did you complete the replacement?	--	Go to Step 8	--

GC4020152401010X

Fig. 150   Codes C0241–C0254: EBCM Control Valve Circuit (Part 1 of 2). 2002 Express & Savana

Step	Action		Yes	No
8	Use a DMM in order to measure the resistance between the high side of the pump motor (the red wire at the pump motor pigtail connector) and a good ground. Does the resistance measure less than the specified value?	0L	Go to Step 10	Go to Step 9
9	Replace the EBCM. **Important** Use the scan tool in order to perform the Tire Size Calibration procedure and the Trim Level Calibration procedure (if applicable). Did you complete the replacement?	--	Go to Step 11	--
10	Replace the EBCM and the BPMV. **Important** Use the scan tool in order to perform the Tire Size Calibration procedure and the Trim Level Calibration procedure (if applicable). Did you complete the replacements?	--	Go to Step 11	--
11	1. Use the scan tool in order to clear the DTCs. 2. Operate the vehicle within the Conditions for Running the DTC as specified in the supporting text. Does the DTC reset?		Go to Step 2	System OK

GC4020152402020X

Fig. 151   Codes C0265 & C0266: EBCM Relay Circuit (Part 2 of 2). 2002 Express & Savana

Step	Action	Values	Yes	No
1	Did you perform the ABS Diagnostic System Check?	--	Go to Step 2	Go to A Diagnostic System Check
2	1. Use a scan tool in order to clear the DTCs. 2. Operate the vehicle within the Conditions for Running the DTC as specified in the supporting text. Does the DTC set?	--	Go to Step 3	Go to Diagnostic Aids
3	**Important** Replace the EBCM if DTC C0267 sets during this test. On some applications, it may be necessary to separate the EBCM from the BPMV in order to perform this test. 1. Turn OFF the ignition. 2. Disconnect from the EBCM, the ABS pump motor pigtail connector. For systems which have no pump motor pigtail, it is necessary to separate the EBCM from the BPMV in order to gain access to the pump motor connector of the EBCM. 3. Use a connector adapter test kit in order to connect a test lamp between the ABS pump motor power and ground circuits at the pump motor connector of the EBCM. 4. Turn ON the ignition. 5. Use the scan tool in order to clear the DTCs. 6. Use the scan tool in order to perform an ABS Function Test. Does the test lamp illuminate and then turn OFF when the Function Test is performed?	--	Go to Step 5	Go to Step 4
4	Use a DMM in order to measure the resistance across the ABS pump motor. Does the resistance measure within the specified range?	0.3-1.0 ohms	Go to Step 6	Go to Step 8

GC4020152403010X

Fig. 152 Codes C0267 & C0268: Pump Motor Circuit Open Or Shorted (Part 1 of 2). 2002 Express & Savana

Step	Action	Yes	No
1	Did you perform the ABS Diagnostic System Check?	Go to Step 2	Go to A Diagnostic System Check

2	1. Install a scan tool.
	2. Use the scan tool in order to clear the DTCs.
	3. Use the scan tool in order to perform an ABS Function Test while applying firm and steady pressure to the brake pedal. Observe the brake pedal and ensure the pedal reacts as follows (time values in the procedure below are approximate):
	  A. The pump motor activates (0.5 seconds).
	  B. The pedal drops to the floor (2 seconds).
	  C. The pedal pumps up (2 seconds).
	  D. The pedal drops approximately 1.25 cm (0.5 in) and then holds (1 second).
	  E. Steps 3.2, 3.3 and 3.4 repeat.
	  F. Steps 3.2, 3.3 and 3.4 repeat.
	  G. Step 3.2 repeats.
	  H. Step 3.3 repeats.
	  I. Step 3.2 repeats.
	  J. Step 3.3 repeats.
	
	Does the brake pedal react as described when the Function Test is performed?
		Go to Diagnostic Aids	Go to Step 3

3	Replace the BPMV. Did you complete the replacement?	Go to Step 4	--
4	Use the scan tool in order to perform an ABS Function Test while applying firm and steady pressure to the brake pedal. Observe the brake pedal and ensure the pedal reacts as described in step 2. Does the brake pedal react as described in step 2 when the Function Test is performed?	System OK	Go to Step 2

GC4020152404000X

Fig. 153 Codes C0269 & C0274: Excessive Dump Isolation Time. 2002 Express & Savana

Step	Action	Values	Yes	No
5	Inspect for poor connections at the pump motor pigtail connector. Did you find and correct the condition?	--	Go to Step 9	Go to Step 7
6	Replace the EBCM. **Important** Use the scan tool in order to perform the Tire Size Calibration procedure and the Trim Level Calibration procedure (if applicable). Did you complete the replacement?		Go to Step 9	--
7	Replace the BPMV. Did you complete the replacement?	--	Go to Step 9	
8	Replace the EBCM and the BPMV. **Important** Use the scan tool in order to perform the Tire Size Calibration procedure and the Trim Level Calibration procedure (if applicable). Did you complete the replacements?	--	Go to Step 9	
9	1. Use a scan tool in order to clear the DTCs. 2. Operate the vehicle within the Conditions for Running the DTC as specified in the supporting text. Does the DTC reset?	--	Go to Step 3	System OK

GC4020152403020X

Fig. 152 Codes C0267 & C0268: Pump Motor Circuit Open Or Shorted (Part 2 of 2). 2002 Express & Savana

Step	Action	Yes	No
1	Did you perform the ABS Diagnostic System Check?	Go to Step 2	Go to A Diagnostic System Check
2	Is DTC C0271 or DTC C0272 set in the EBCM memory?	Go to Step 4	Go to Step 3
3	1. Use a scan tool in order to clear the DTCs. 2. Turn OFF the ignition for 5 seconds. 3. Turn ON the ignition. Does the DTC set?	Go to Step 4	Go to Diagnostic Aids
4	Replace the EBCM. **Important** Use the scan tool in order to perform the Tire Size Calibration procedure and the Trim Level Calibration procedure (if applicable). Did you complete the replacement?	Go to Step 5	--
5	Use the scan tool in order to clear the DTCs. Operate the vehicle within the Conditions for Running the DTC as specified in the supporting text. Does the DTC reset?	Go to Step 2	System OK

GC4020152405000X

Fig. 154 Codes C0271–C0273: EBCM Fault. 2002 Express & Savana

Step	Action	Yes	No
1	Did you perform the ABS Diagnostic System Check?	Go to Step 2	Go to A Diagnostic System Check
2	1. Install a scan tool. 2. Select the 4WAL 3 Sensor Data Display function. 3. Observe the Brake Switch Status on the scan tool. Does the scan tool display Off?	Go to Step 3	Go to Step 5
3	1. Apply the brake. 2. Observe the Brake Switch Status on the scan tool. Does the scan tool display On?	Go to Diagnostic Aids	Go to Step 4
4	1. Turn OFF the ignition. 2. Disconnect the stoplamp switch. 3. Turn ON the ignition. 4. Observe the Brake Switch Status on the scan tool. Does the scan tool display On?	Go to Step 9	Go to Step 7
5	1. Turn OFF the ignition. 2. Disconnect the stoplamp switch. 3. Connect a fused jumper wire between the ignition 3 voltage circuit and the TCC brake switch signal circuit at the stoplamp switch harness connector. 4. Turn ON the ignition. 5. Observe the Brake Switch Status on the scan tool. Does the scan tool display Off?	Go to Step 9	Go to Step 6

GC4020152406010X

Fig. 155   Code C0281: Brake Switch Circuit (Part 1 of 2). 2002 Express & Savana

Step	Action	Yes	No
6	Test the ignition 3 voltage circuit and the TCC brake switch signal circuit for an open or a short to ground. Did you find and correct the condition?	Go to Step 12	Go to Step 8
7	Test the TCC brake switch signal circuit for a short to voltage. Did you find and correct the condition?	Go to Step 12	Go to Step 8
8	Inspect for poor connections at the harness connector of the EBCM. Did you find and correct the condition?	Go to Step 12	Go to Step 10
9	Inspect for poor connections at the harness connector of the stoplamp switch. Did you find and correct the condition?	Go to Step 12	Go to Step 11
10	Replace the EBCM. **Important** Use the scan tool in order to perform the Tire Size Calibration procedure. Did you complete the replacement?	Go to Step 12	--
11	Replace the stoplamp switch. Did you complete the replacement?	Go to Step 12	--
12	1. Use the scan tool in order to clear the DTCs. 2. Operate the vehicle within the Conditions for Running the DTC as specified in the supporting text. Does the DTC reset?	Go to Step 2	System OK

GC4020152406020X

Fig. 155   Code C0281: Brake Switch Circuit (Part 2 of 2). 2002 Express & Savana

Step	Action	Yes	No
1	Did you perform the ABS Diagnostic System Check?	Go to Step 2	Go to A Diagnostic System Check
2	1. Use a scan tool in order to clear the DTCs. 2. Turn OFF the ignition for 5 seconds. 3. Turn ON the ignition and observe the scan tool. Does the DTC set?	Go to Step 3	Go to Diagnostic Aids
3	1. Turn OFF the ignition. 2. Disconnect from the instrument panel cluster, the harness connector which contains the ABS failure control circuit. 3. Turn ON the ignition. 4. Use a scan tool in order to clear the DTC. 5. Turn OFF the ignition for 5 seconds. 6. Turn ON the ignition and observe the scan tool. Does the DTC set?	Go to Step 4	Go to Step 5
4	Test the ABS failure control circuit for a short to voltage. Did you find and correct the condition?	Go to Step 9	Go to Step 7
5	Inspect for poor connections at the harness connector of the instrument panel cluster. Did you find and correct the condition?	Go to Step 9	Go to Step 6
6	Replace the instrument panel cluster. Did you complete the replacement?	Go to Step 9	--
7	Inspect for poor connections at the harness connector of the EBCM. Did you find and correct the condition?	Go to Step 9	Go to Step 8

GC4020152407010X

Fig. 156   Code C0286: Anti-lock Indicator Lamp Shorted To B+ (Part 1 of 2). 2002 Express & Savana

Step	Action	Yes	No
8	Replace the EBCM. **Important** Use the scan tool in order to perform the Tire Size Calibration procedure. Did you complete the replacement?	Go to Step 9	--
9	1. Use the scan tool in order to clear the DTC. 2. Operate the vehicle within the Conditions for Running the DTC as specified in the supporting text. Does the DTC reset?	Go to Step 3	System OK

GC4020152407020X

Fig. 156   Code C0286: Anti-lock Indicator Lamp Shorted To B+ (Part 2 of 2). 2002 Express & Savana

Step	Action	Yes	No
1	Did you perform the ABS diagnostic system check?	Go to Step 2	Go to A Diagnostic System Check
2	1. Use a scan tool in order to clear the DTCs. 2. Turn OFF the ignition for 5 seconds. 3. Turn ON the ignition and observe the scan tool. Does the DTC set?	Go to Step 3	Go to Diagnostic Aids
3	1. Turn OFF the ignition. 2. Disconnect from the instrument panel cluster, the harness connector containing the brake warning indicator control circuit. 3. Turn ON the ignition. 4. Use a scan tool in order to clear the DTC. 5. Turn OFF the ignition for 5 seconds. 6. Turn ON the ignition and observe the scan tool. Does the DTC set?	Go to Step 4	Go to Step 5
4	Test the ABS pressure differential sensor signal circuit for a short to voltage. Did you find and correct the condition?	Go to Step 9	Go to Step 7
5	Inspect for poor connections at the harness connector of the instrument panel cluster. Did you find and correct the condition?	Go to Step 9	Go to Step 6
6	Replace the instrument panel cluster. Did you complete the replacement?	Go to Step 9	--
7	Inspect for poor connections at the harness connector of the EBCM. Did you find and correct the condition?	Go to Step 9	Go to Step 8

GC4020152408010X

Fig. 157 Code C0288: Brake Warning Lamp Shorted To B+ (Part 1 of 2). 2002 Express & Savana

Test Description

The numbers below refer to the step numbers on the diagnostic table.

1. This step ensures that the battery, and the vehicle primary power and ground systems are functioning correctly.

3. Lack of communication may be due to a particular malfunction of a serial data circuit. The information in Data Link References will provide a list of modules and the associated data network no communication diagnostic link.

4. A module that is operating in the incorrect power mode based on key position may cause other vehicle symptoms and/or DTCs to set. The information in Power Mode Mismatch will correct the condition before checking for module DTCs or symptoms.

8. This step ensures that all data link communication DTCs are diagnosed before system level DTCs.

9. This step ensures that all electronic control unit (ECU) internal DTCs are diagnosed before other system level DTCs.

10. This step ensures that all device voltage DTCs are diagnosed before other system level DTCs.

Step	Action	Yes	No
1	Perform the following preliminary inspections: • Ensure that the battery is fully charged. • Ensure that the battery cables are clean and tight. • Inspect for any open fuses. • Inspect the easily accessible systems or the visible system components for obvious damage or conditions that could cause the symptom. • Ensure that the grounds are clean, tight, and in the correct location. • Inspect for aftermarket devices that could affect the operation of the system. • Search for applicable service bulletins. Did you find and correct the condition?	System OK	Go to Step 2

LTV0500000006565

Fig. 158 Diagnostic System Check (Part 1 of 3). 2003–06 Express & Savana

8	Replace the EBCM **Important** Use the scan tool in order to perform the Tire Size Calibration procedure. Did you complete the replacement?	Go to Step 9	--
9	1. Use the scan tool in order to clear the DTC. 2. Operate the vehicle within the Conditions for Running the DTC as specified in the supporting text. Does the DTC reset?	Go to Step 3	System OK

GC4020152408020X

Fig. 157 Code C0288: Brake Warning Lamp Shorted To B+ (Part 2 of 2). 2002 Express & Savana

2	Install a scan tool. Does the scan tool power up?	Go to Step 3	Check Scan Tool Does Not Power Up
3	1. Turn ON the ignition, with the engine OFF. 2. Attempt to establish communication with all of the control modules on the vehicle. Does the scan tool communicate with all of the expected vehicle control modules?	Go to Step 4	Go to Data Link References
4	**Important:** 1. To ensure that RAP mode is inactive, if equipped, open the drivers door during the following step. 2. The engine may start during the following step. Turn OFF the engine as soon as you have observed the crank power mode. 1. Access the Power Mode parameter on the scan tool. 2. Rotate the ignition switch, operate the ignition mode switch, through all positions while observing the Power Mode parameter. Does the Power Mode parameter reading on the scan tool match the ignition switch position for all switch positions?	Go to Step 5	Go to Power Mode Mismatch
5	Attempt to start the engine. Does the engine crank?	Go to Step 6	Go to Symptoms
6	Attempt to start the engine. Does the engine start and idle?	Go to Step 7	Engine Cranks but Does Not Run

LTV0500000006566

Fig. 158 Diagnostic System Check (Part 2 of 3). 2003–06 Express & Savana

7	**Important:** Do not clear any DTCs unless instructed by a diagnostic procedure. Use the appropriate scan tool selections to obtain DTCs for each of the control modules. Does the scan tool display any DTCs?	Go to Step 8	Go to Step 12
8	Does the scan tool display any DTCs that begin with a "U"?	Go to Diagnostic Trouble Code (DTC) List - Vehicle	Go to Step 9
9	**Important:** If any of these DTCs are displayed, diagnose them before diagnosing any other DTCs or symptoms. Does the scan tool display DTC B1000, B1004, B1007, B1009, C0550, C0558, P0501, P0602, P0603, P0604, P0606, P061C, P062C, P052F, P064C, P160C, P2108, P2610, or P268A?	Go to Diagnostic Trouble Code (DTC) List - Vehicle	Go to Step 10
10	**Important:** If any of these DTCs are displayed, diagnose them before diagnosing any other DTCs or symptoms. Does the scan tool display DTC B1372, B1420, B1424, B1425, B1439, P0562, or P0563?	Go to Diagnostic Trouble Code (DTC) List - Vehicle	Go to Step 11
11	**Important:** If any of the remaining DTCs are powertrain DTCs, select Capture Info in order to store the powertrain DTC information with a scan tool. If multiple DTCs are stored, diagnose the DTCs in the following order 1. Component level DTCs, such as sensor DTCs, solenoid DTCs, and relay DTCs 2. System level DTCs, such as misfire DTCs, evaporative emission (EVAP) system DTCs, and fuel trim DTCs Diagnose the remaining DTCs.	Go to Diagnostic Trouble Code (DTC) List - Vehicle	
12	Is the customers concern with inspection/maintenance (I/M) testing?	Go to: Inspection/Maintenance (I/M) System Check	Go to Symptoms

LTV0500000006567

Fig. 158 Diagnostic System Check (Part 3 of 3). 2003–06 Express & Savana

Circuit Description

As the wheels spin, each wheel speed sensor produces an AC signal. The electronic brake control module (EBCM) uses the frequency of the AC signals to calculate each wheel speed.

DTC Descriptors

This diagnostic procedure supports the following DTCs:

- DTC C0035 Left Front Wheel Speed Sensor Circuit
- DTC C0040 Right Front Wheel Speed Sensor Circuit

Conditions for Running the DTC

Both of the conditions listed below may be required to set the DTC.

- The ignition is ON.
- The vehicle speed is greater than 13 km/h (8 mph).

Conditions for Setting the DTC

Any of the following occurrences may cause the DTC to set.

- The EBCM detects an open or shorted wheel speed sensor circuit for 500 milliseconds.
- The EBCM detects the absence of a wheel speed sensor signal for 5 seconds. If more than one absent wheel speed sensor signal is detected, the condition must be present for 120 seconds to set DTCs.
- The EBCM detects an erratic wheel speed sensor signal for 200 milliseconds.

Action Taken When the DTC Sets

If equipped, the following actions may occur.

- The EBCM disables the ABS/traction control system (TCS)/vehicle stability enhancement system (VSES) and may disable the dynamic rear proportion (DRP) if more than one wheel speed sensor DTC is set.
- The ABS indicator turns ON.
- The brake warning indicator may turn ON.
- The stability indicator turns ON.
- An ECE 13 response may occur.

Conditions for Clearing the DTC

The Conditions for Setting the DTC are no longer present and you use the scan tool Clear DTCs function.

LTV0500000006568

Fig. 159   Codes C0035 Or C0040: Front Wheel Speed Sensor Circuit (Part 1 of 3). 2003–06 Express & Savana

	Action	Values	Yes	No
5	Inspect for poor connections at the harness connector of the wheel speed sensor. Did you find and correct the condition?		Go to Step 10	Go to Step 6
6	1. Disconnect from the electronic brake control module (EBCM), the harness connector containing the wheel speed sensor circuits. 2. Test the wheel speed sensor circuits for the following conditions: - An open - A short to ground - A short to voltage - Shorted together Did you find and correct the condition?		Go to Step 10	Go to Step 7
7	Inspect for poor connections at the harness connector for the EBCM. Did you find and correct the condition?		Go to Step 10	Go to Step 9
8	Replace the wheel speed sensor. Did you complete the replacement?		Go to Step 10	--
9	**Important:** Use the scan tool in order to perform the Tire Size Calibration procedure. Replace the EBCM. Did you complete the replacement?		Go to Step 10	--
10	1. Use the scan tool in order to clear the DTCs. 2. Operate the vehicle within the Conditions for Running the DTC as specified in the supporting text. Does the DTC reset?		Go to Step 2	System OK

LTV0500000006570

Fig. 159   Codes C0035 Or C0040: Front Wheel Speed Sensor Circuit (Part 3 of 3). 2003–06 Express & Savana

Diagnostic Aids

Thoroughly inspect connections or circuitry that may cause an intermittent malfunction. Refer to Testing for Intermittent Conditions and Poor Connections , Connector Repairs , Testing for Electrical Intermittents and Wiring Repairs .

If the customer's concern is that the ABS indicator is on only during humid conditions such as rain, snow or vehicle wash, thoroughly inspect the wheel speed sensor circuits for signs of water intrusion. Use the following procedure in order to help isolate the problem area:

1. Spray the suspected area with a 5 percent salt water solution.
2. Operate the vehicle at a speed greater than 13 km/h (8 mph) for at least 30 seconds.

Repair or replace the suspect harness if the DTC sets.

Step	Action	Values	Yes	No
1	Did you perform the Diagnostic System Check - Vehicle?	--	Go to Step 2	Go to Diagnostic System Check - Vehicle
2	1. Use a scan tool in order to clear the DTCs. 2. Operate the vehicle within the Conditions for Running the DTC as specified in the supporting text. Does the DTC set?	--	Go to Step 3	Go to Diagnostic Aids
3	1. Turn OFF the ignition. 2. Raise and support the vehicle. 3. Disconnect the wheel speed sensor connector. 4. Use a DMM in order to measure the resistance across the wheel speed sensor. Does the resistance measure within the specified range?	700-10,000 ohms	Go to Step 4	Go to Step 8
4	1. Slowly spin the wheel by hand. 2. Use a DMM in order to measure the AC voltage across the wheel speed sensor as the wheel spins. Does the AC voltage measure greater than the specified value?	100 mV	Go to Step 5	Go to Step 8

LTV0500000006569

Fig. 159   Codes C0035 Or C0040: Front Wheel Speed Sensor Circuit (Part 2 of 3). 2003–06 Express & Savana

Circuit Description

As the wheel spins, the wheel speed sensor produces an AC signal. The electronic brake control module (EBCM) uses the frequency of the AC signal to calculate the wheel speed.

DTC Descriptors

This diagnostic procedure supports the following DTCs:

- DTC C0045 Left Rear Wheel Speed Sensor Circuit
- DTC C0050 Right Rear Wheel Speed Sensor Circuit

Conditions for Running the DTC

Both of the conditions listed below may be required to set the DTC.

- The ignition is ON.
- The vehicle speed is greater than 13 km/h (8 mph).

Conditions for Setting the DTC

Any of the following conditions may cause the DTC to set.

- The EBCM detects an open wheel speed sensor circuit for 500 milliseconds.
- The EBCM detects a shorted wheel speed sensor circuit for 500 milliseconds.
- The EBCM detects the absence of a wheel speed sensor signal for 5 seconds. If more than one absent wheel speed sensor signal is detected, the condition must be present for 120 seconds to set DTCs.
- The EBCM detects an erratic wheel speed sensor signal for 200 milliseconds.

Action Taken When the DTC Sets

If equipped, the following actions may occur.

- The EBCM disables the ABS/traction control system (TCS)/vehicle stability enhancement system (VSES) and may disable the dynamic rear proportion (DRP) if more than one wheel speed sensor DTC is set.
- The ABS indicator turns ON.
- The brake warning indicator may turn ON.
- The stability indicator turns ON.
- An ECE 13 response may occur. Refer to ABS Description and Operation for a complete description of ECE 13.

Conditions for Clearing the DTC

The Conditions for Setting the DTC are no longer present and you use the scan tool Clear DTCs function.

LTV0500000006571

Fig. 160   Codes C0045 Or C0050: Rear Wheel Speed Sensor Circuit (Part 1 of 3). 2003–06 Express & Savana

Diagnostic Aids

Thoroughly inspect connections or circuitry that may cause an intermittent malfunction.

If the customer concern is that the ABS indicator is ON only during humid conditions such as rain, snow, or vehicle wash, thoroughly inspect the wheel speed sensor circuits for signs of water intrusion. Use the following procedure in order to help isolate the problem area:

1. Spray the suspected area with a 5 percent salt water solution.
2. Operate the vehicle at a speed greater than 13 km/h (8 mph) for at least 30 seconds.
3. Repair or replace the suspect harness if the DTC sets.

Step	Action	Values	Yes	No
1	Did you perform the Diagnostic System Check - Vehicle?	--	Go to Step 2	Go to Diagnostic System Check - Vehicle
2	1. Use the scan tool to clear the DTCs. 2. Turn OFF the ignition for 5 seconds. 3. Turn ON the ignition. 4. Operate the vehicle within the Conditions for Running the DTC as specified in the supporting text. Does the DTC reset?	13 km/h (8 mph)	Go to Step 3	Go to Diagnostic Aids
3	1. Turn OFF the ignition. 2. Raise and support the vehicle. 3. Disconnect the wheel speed sensor connector. 4. Use a DMM in order to measure the resistance across the wheel speed sensor. Does the resistance measure within the specified range?	3,500-6,800 ohms	Go to Step 4	Go to Step 9
4	1. Slowly spin the wheel by hand. 2. Use a DMM in order to measure the AC voltage across the wheel speed sensor as the wheel spins. Does the AC voltage measure greater than the specified value?	100 mV	Go to Step 5	Go to Step 8

LTV0500000006572

Fig. 160 Codes C0045 Or C0050: Rear Wheel Speed Sensor Circuit (Part 2 of 3). 2003–06 Express & Savana

Step	Action	Values	Yes	No
5	Inspect for poor connections at the harness connector of the wheel speed sensor. Did you find and correct the condition?	--	Go to Step 11	Go to Step 6
6	1. Disconnect the electronic brake control module (EBCM) harness connector. 2. Test the wheel speed sensor circuits for the following conditions: - An open - A short to ground - A short to voltage - Shorted together Did you find and correct the condition?	--	Go to Step 11	Go to Step 7
7	Inspect for poor connections at the harness connector for the EBCM. Did you find and correct the condition?	--	Go to Step 11	Go to Step 10
8	1. Remove the wheel speed sensor from the axle tube. 2. Inspect the wheel speed sensor tone ring, which is located on the axle, for damage. Did you find and correct the condition?	--	Go to Step 11	Go to Step 9
9	Replace the wheel speed sensor. Did you complete the replacement?	--	Go to Step 11	--
10	**Important:** Following EBCM replacement, perform the set-up procedure for the EBCM and perform the Yaw Rate Reference Table Reset Procedure. Use the scan tool to perform the Tire Size Calibration procedure. Replace the EBCM. Did you complete the replacement?	--	Go to Step 11	--
11	1. Use the scan tool Clear All Class 2 DTCs function to clear all of the DTCs from all modules. 2. Turn OFF the ignition for 5 seconds. 3. Turn ON the ignition. 4. Operate the vehicle within the Conditions for Running the DTC as specified in the supporting text. Does the DTC reset?	--	Go to Step 2	System OK

LTV0500000006573

Fig. 160 Codes C0045 Or C0050: Rear Wheel Speed Sensor Circuit (Part 3 of 3). 2003–06 Express & Savana

Circuit Description

The powertrain control module (PCM) converts the signal from the vehicle speed sensor (VSS) to a 128k pulses/mile signal. The electronic brake control module (EBCM) uses the vehicle speed signal from the PCM to calculate the rear wheel speed.

DTC Descriptors

This diagnostic procedure supports the following DTCs:

- DTC C0055 Rear Wheel Speed Sensor (Both Wheels) Circuit
- DTC P0609 Rear Wheel Speed Sensor (Both Wheels) Circuit

Conditions for Running the DTC

C0055

Conditions for running as usual

- The ignition is ON.
- The vehicle speed is greater than 13 km/h (8 mph).

P0609

Conditions for running as usual

- The ignition is ON.
- The vehicle is not moving.

Conditions for Setting the DTC

C0055

Any of the following occurrences may cause the DTC to set:

- The EBCM detects an open or shorted vehicle speed signal circuit for 500 milliseconds.
- The EBCM detects the absence of the vehicle speed signal for 5 seconds. If more than one absent wheel speed sensor signal is detected, the condition must be present for 120 seconds to set DTCs.
- The EBCM detects an erratic vehicle speed signal for 200 milliseconds.

P0609

The PCM detects low voltage on the vehicle speed signal circuit for 45 seconds.

LTV0500000006574

Fig. 161 Codes C0055 Or P0609: Rear Wheel Speed Sensor Circuit (Part 1 of 3). 2003–06 Express & Savana

Action Taken When the DTC Sets

- The EBCM disables the ABS/dynamic rear proportion (DRP).
- The ABS indicator turns ON.
- The brake warning indicator turns ON.
- An ECE 13 response may occur. Refer to ABS Description and Operation for a complete description of ECE 13.

Conditions for Clearing the DTC

The Conditions for Setting the DTC are no longer present and you use the scan tool Clear DTCs function.

Diagnostic Aids

Thoroughly inspect connections or circuitry that may cause an intermittent malfunction.

Test Description

The numbers below refer to the step numbers on the diagnostic table.

3. This step tests for a voltage signal from the PCM.

4. This step tests for a missing or erratic vehicle speed signal from the PCM. An assistant may be required to perform this test.

Step	Action	Values	Yes	No
1	Did you perform the Diagnostic System Check - Vehicle?	--	Go to Step 2	Go to Diagnostic System Check - Vehicle
2	1. Use a scan tool in order to clear the DTCs. 2. Operate the vehicle at a speed greater than the specified value. Does the DTC set?	13 km/h (8 mph)	Go to Step 3	Go to Diagnostic Aids
3	1. Turn OFF the ignition. 2. Disconnect from the electronic brake control module (EBCM), the harness connector containing the vehicle speed signal circuit. 3. Turn ON the ignition. 4. Use a DMM in order to measure the DC voltage between the vehicle speed signal circuit and a good ground. Does the voltage measure greater than the specified value?	10 V	Go to Step 4	Go to Step 7

LTV0500000006575

Fig. 161 Codes C0055 Or P0609: Rear Wheel Speed Sensor Circuit (Part 2 of 3). 2003–06 Express & Savana

Step	Action	Values	Yes	No
4	1. Raise and support the vehicle. 2. Place the transmission in neutral (N). 3. Set up the DMM in order to measure the DC voltage between the vehicle speed signal circuit and a good ground. 4. Slowly spin the rear wheels by hand for at least 30 seconds and while ensuring the driveshaft is rotating, observe the DMM. Does the voltage measure within the specified range for the entire time that the driveshaft is rotating?	5-7 V	Go to Step 5	Go to Step 7
5	Inspect for poor connections at the harness connector of the EBCM. Did you find and correct the condition?	--	Go to Step 10	Go to Step 6
6	Important: Following EBCM replacement, use the scan tool to perform the Tire Size Calibration procedure. Replace the EBCM. Did you complete the replacement?	--	Go to Step 10	--
7	Test the vehicle speed signal circuit for an open, a short to ground, or a short to voltage. Did you find and correct the condition?	--	Go to Step 10	Go to Step 8
8	Inspect for poor connections at the harness connector of the powertrain control module (PCM). Did you find and correct the condition?	--	Go to Step 10	Go to Step 9
9	Important: Perform the setup procedure for the PCM. Replace the PCM. Did you complete the replacement?	--	Go to Step 10	--
10	1. Use the scan tool in order to clear the DTCs. 2. Operate the vehicle within the Conditions for Running the DTC as specified in the supporting text. Does the DTC reset?		Go to Step 3	System OK

LTV0500000006576

Fig. 161   Codes C0055 Or P0609: Rear Wheel Speed Sensor Circuit (Part 3 of 3). 2003–06 Express & Savana

Diagnostic Aids

Separate the EBCM from the brake pressure modulator valve (BPMV) in order to inspect for corrosion or any other condition that may cause a poor connection at the pump motor connector.

Test Description

The number below refers to the step number on the diagnostic table.

4. This step tests for high resistance in the battery positive voltage circuit by verifying that an excessive voltage drop does not occur in the circuit.

Step	Action	Values	Yes	No
1	Did you perform the Diagnostic System Check - Vehicle?	--	Go to Step 2	Go to Diagnostic System Check - Vehicle
2	1. Use a scan tool to clear the DTCs. 2. Turn OFF the ignition for 5 seconds. 3. Operate the vehicle within the Conditions for Running the DTC as specified in the supporting text. Does the DTC set?	--	Go to Step 3	Go to Diagnostic Aids
3	1. Disconnect the electronic brake control module (EBCM) harness connector. 2. Connect a test lamp between the battery positive voltage circuit to the ABS pump motor, and a good ground. Does the test lamp illuminate?	--	Go to Step 4	Go to Step 5
4	Important: Using a test lamp other than that which is approved for performing diagnostic procedures on GM vehicles, may cause an inaccurate result when performing this step. It is also imperative that the ground to which the test lamp is connected be clean and provide no resistance to battery ground. With the test lamp still connected and illuminated, use a DMM to measure the voltage between the high side of the test lamp and a good ground. Does the voltage measure greater than the specified value?	12 V	Go to Step 6	Go to Step 5

LTV0500000006578

Fig. 162   Code C0110: Pump Motor Circuit (Part 2 of 3). 2003–06 Express & Savana

Circuit Description

Ground is continuously supplied to the low side of the ABS pump motor. The electronic brake control module (EBCM) activates the ABS pump by supplying battery voltage to the high side of the motor.

DTC Descriptor

This diagnostic procedure supports the following DTC:

DTC C0110 Pump Motor Circuit

Conditions for Running the DTC

- The ignition is ON.
- The vehicle speed is greater than 6 km/h (4 mph).

Conditions for Setting the DTC

The EBCM detects an open pump motor circuit, a shorted pump motor, or a seized pump motor or ABS pump.

Action Taken When the DTC Sets

- The EBCM disables the ABS/vehicle stability enhancement system (VSES).
- The traction control system (TCS) operates with engine torque reduction ability only.
- The ABS indicator turns ON.
- The stability indicator turns ON.
- An ECE 13 response may occur.

Conditions for Clearing the DTC

The Conditions for Setting the DTC are no longer present and you use the scan tool Clear DTCs function.

LTV0500000006577

Fig. 162   Code C0110: Pump Motor Circuit (Part 1 of 3). 2003–06 Express & Savana

Step	Action	Values	Yes	No
5	Repair the high resistance in the battery positive voltage circuit. Ensure that total circuit Did you complete the repair?	0.2 ohms	Go to Step 13	--
6	Test the ABS motor ground circuit for an open or high resistance. Did you find and correct the condition?	--	Go to Step 13	Go to Step 7
7	1. Turn OFF the ignition. 2. Separate the EBCM from the brake pressure modulator valve (BPMV). 3. Connect a test lamp between the ABS pump motor power and ground circuits at the pump motor connector of the EBCM. 4. Turn ON the ignition. 5. Use the scan tool in order to clear the DTCs. Does the DTC clear and then remain cleared while the test lamp is connected?	--	Go to Step 8	Go to Step 10
8	1. Select the vehicle stability enhancement system (VSES) Special Functions menu on the scan tool. 2. Command the ABS Motor ON. Does the test lamp illuminate for 5 seconds and then turn OFF?	--	Go to Step 9	Go to Step 12
9	Inspect for poor connections at the pump motor connector. Did you find and correct the condition?	--	Go to Step 13	Go to Step 11
10	Important: Following the EBCM replacement, perform the set-up procedure for the EBCM and perform the Yaw Rate Reference Table Reset Procedure. Use the scan tool to perform the Tire Size Calibration procedure. Replace the EBCM. Did you complete the replacement?	--	Go to Step 13	--
11	Replace the BPMV. Did you complete the replacement?	--	Go to Step 13	--
12	Important: Following EBCM replacement, perform the set-up procedure for the EBCM and perform the Yaw Rate Reference Table Reset Procedure. Use the scan tool to perform the Tire Size Calibration procedure. Replace the EBCM and the BPMV. Did you complete the replacements?	--	Go to Step 13	--
13	1. Use the scan tool Clear All Class 2 DTCs function to clear all of the DTCs from all modules. 2. Turn OFF the ignition for 5 seconds. 3. Turn ON the ignition. 4. Operate the vehicle within the Conditions for Running the DTC as specified in the supporting text. Does the DTC reset?		Go to Step 3	System OK

LTV0500000006579

Fig. 162   Code C0110: Pump Motor Circuit (Part 3 of 3). 2003–06 Express & Savana

Circuit Description

The master cylinder pressure sensor is located within the brake pressure modulator valve (BPMV). The master cylinder pressure sensor signal, to the electronic brake control module (EBCM), increases as hydraulic pressure in the front brake circuit increases.

DTC Descriptor

This diagnostic procedure supports the following DTC:

DTC C0131 Antilock Brake System (ABS)/Traction Control System (TCS) Pressure Circuit

Conditions for Running the DTC

- The ignition is ON.
- The vehicle stability enhancement system (VSES) sensors have been successfully initialized or the message center has displayed the stability system disabled message due to an unsuccessful initialization attempt.
- The vehicle is being driven relatively straight and level at a speed greater than 36 km/h (23 mph).
- The transmission is not shifted into neutral or low gear.
- The parking brake is released.

Conditions for Setting the DTC

Any of the following conditions may cause the DTC to set:

- The EBCM detects open master cylinder pressure sensor circuitry.
- The EBCM detects shorted master cylinder pressure sensor circuitry.
- The master cylinder pressure sensor self-test, which occurs at power-up, fails.
- The zero-pressure signal voltage is not within an acceptable range.
- The master cylinder pressure is not within an expected tolerance based on deceleration rate and other data available to the EBCM.

Action Taken When the DTC Sets

- The EBCM disables the VSES.
- The TCS operates with engine torque reduction only.
- The stability indicator turns ON.

Conditions for Clearing the DTC

The conditions for setting the DTC are no longer present and you use the scan tool Clear DTCs function.

LTV0500000006580

Fig. 163   Code C0131: ABS/TCS Pressure Circuit (Part 1 of 3). 2003–06 Express & Savana

	Action	Yes	No
5	1. Select the vehicle stability enhancement system (VSES) Data Display function on the scan tool. 2. Observe the Brake Switch Status parameter while pressing and releasing the brake pedal. Does the Brake Switch Status change while pressing and releasing the brake?	Go to Step 6	Go to DTC C0161
6	1. Remove the electronic brake control module (EBCM) from the vehicle. 2. Inspect the master cylinder pressure sensor connector within the EBCM for damage or corrosion. Is there connector damage or corrosion present?	Go to Step 7	Go to Step 8
7	**Important:** Following EBCM replacement, perform the set-up procedure for the EBCM and perform the Yaw Rate Reference Table Reset Procedure. Use the scan tool to perform the Tire Size Calibration procedure. Replace the EBCM. Refer to Control Module References. Did you complete the replacement?	Go to Step 9	—
8	**Important:** Following EBCM replacement, perform the set-up procedure for the EBCM and perform the Yaw Rate Reference Table Reset Procedure. Use the scan tool to perform the Tire Size Calibration procedure. Replace the EBCM and the brake pressure modulator valve (BPMV). Did you complete the replacements?	Go to Step 9	—
9	1. Use the scan tool Clear All Class 2 DTCs function to clear all of the DTCs from all modules. 2. Turn OFF the ignition for 5 seconds. 3. Turn ON the ignition. 4. Operate the vehicle within the Conditions for Running the DTC as specified in the supporting text. Does the DTC reset?	Go to Step 2	System OK

LTV0500000006582

Fig. 163   Code C0131: ABS/TCS Pressure Circuit (Part 3 of 3). 2003–06 Express & Savana

Diagnostic Aids

Thoroughly inspect connections or circuitry that may cause an intermittent malfunction.

Test Description

The number below refers to the step number on the diagnostic table.

3. This step is required for vehicles equipped with a hydro-boost brake assist system only. If the vehicle being serviced has vacuum assisted brakes, proceed to step 4.

Step	Action	Yes	No
	Important: Use the scan tool to read both current and history DTCs before proceeding. If DTC C0292 is set, diagnose that DTC before proceeding with diagnostics for C0131. If DTC C0161 is set, diagnose that DTC before proceeding with diagnostics for C0131.		
1	Did you perform the Diagnostic System Check - Vehicle?	Go to Step 2	Go to Diagnostic System Check - Vehicle
2	Inspect the vehicle for the following and ensure that there is no base brake failure. - Dragging brakes - Faulty parking brake switch - Brake fluid leakage - Air in hydraulic system - Seized brake calipers - Swollen, kinked or otherwise damaged brake hoses Did you find and correct the condition?	Go to Step 9	Go to Step 3
3	Drive the vehicle in order to verify that the brakes do not self-apply during turning maneuvers. Do the brakes self-apply during turning maneuvers?	Go to Symptoms	Go to Step 4
4	1. Use the scan tool to clear the DTCs. 2. Turn OFF the ignition for 5 seconds. 3. Turn ON the ignition. 4. Operate the vehicle within the Conditions for Running the DTC as specified in the supporting text. Does the DTC reset?	Go to Step 5	Go to Diagnostic Aids

LTV0500000006581

Fig. 163   Code C0131: ABS/TCS Pressure Circuit (Part 2 of 3). 2003–06 Express & Savana

Circuit Description

The brake switch informs the electronic brake control module (EBCM) when the brake is depressed. The brake switch is normally closed, supplying 12 volts to the EBCM when the brake is released. When the brake pedal is pressed, voltage on the torque converter clutch (TCC) brake switch signal circuit is 0 volts.

DTC Descriptor

This diagnostic procedure supports the following DTC:

DTC C0161 Antilock Brake System (ABS)/Traction Control System (TCS) Brake Switch Circuit

Conditions for Running the DTC

Any of the following conditions may cause the DTC to run:

- The vehicle accelerates from 0 km/h (0 mph) to a speed greater than 56 km/h (35 mph).
- The vehicle experiences an ABS event involving all hydraulic circuits.

Conditions for Setting the DTC

Any of the following conditions may cause the DTC to set:

- Voltage on the TCC brake switch signal circuit is always low.
- Voltage on the TCC brake switch signal circuit is always high.

Action Taken When the DTC Sets

The EBCM stores this information-only DTC for as long as the condition is present:

Conditions for Clearing the DTC

The Conditions for Setting the DTC are no longer present and you use the scan tool Clear DTCs function.

LTV0500000006583

Fig. 164   Code C0161: ABS/TCS Brake Switch Circuit (Part 1 of 3). 2003–06 Express & Savana Less LJ4

Diagnostic Aids

Thoroughly inspect connections or circuitry that may cause an intermittent malfunction.

Test Description

The numbers below refer to the step numbers on the diagnostic table.

4. This step tests for a shorted stop lamp switch.

5. This step tests for an open stop lamp switch.

Step	Action	Yes	No
1	Did you perform the Diagnostic System Check - Vehicle?	Go to Step 2	Go to Diagnostic System Check - Vehicle
2	1. Install a scan tool. 2. Select the 4WAL 3 Sensor Data Display function. 3. Observe the Brake Switch Status on the scan tool. Does the scan tool display Off?	Go to Step 3	Go to Step 5
3	1. Apply the brake. 2. Observe the Brake Switch Status on the scan tool. Does the scan tool display On?	Go to Diagnostic Aids	Go to Step 4
4	1. Turn OFF the ignition. 2. Disconnect the stop lamp switch. Refer to Stop Lamp Switch Replacement . 3. Turn ON the ignition. 4. Observe the Brake Switch Status on the scan tool. Does the scan tool display On?	Go to Step 9	Go to Step 7
5	1. Turn OFF the ignition. 2. Disconnect the stop lamp switch 3. Connect a fused jumper wire between the ignition 3 voltage circuit and the torque converter clutch (TCC) brake switch signal circuit at the stop lamp switch harness connector. 4. Turn ON the ignition. 5. Observe the Brake Switch Status on the scan tool. Does the scan tool display Off?	Go to Step 9	Go to Step 6
6	Test the ignition 3 voltage circuit and the TCC brake switch signal circuit for an open or a short to ground. Did you find and correct the condition?	Go to Step 12	Go to Step 8

LTV0500000006584

Fig. 164   Code C0161: ABS/TCS Brake Switch Circuit (Part 2 of 3). 2003–06 Express & Savana Less JL4

Circuit Description

The brake switch informs the electronic brake control module (EBCM) when the brake is depressed. The brake switch is normally closed, supplying 12 volts to the EBCM when the brake is released. When the brake pedal is pressed, voltage on the torque converter clutch (TCC) brake switch signal circuit is 0 volts.

DTC Descriptor

This diagnostic procedure supports the following DTC:

DTC C0161 Antilock Brake System (ABS)/Traction Control System (TCS) Brake Switch Circuit

Conditions for Running the DTC

Any of the following conditions may cause the DTC to run:

• The vehicle accelerates from 0 km/h (0 mph) to a speed greater than 56 km/h (35 mph).
• The vehicle experiences an ABS event involving all hydraulic circuits.
• The EBCM detects that the master cylinder pressure is greater than 1 400 kPa (200 psi) and that the vehicle is decelerating.

Conditions for Setting the DTC

Any of the following conditions may cause the DTC to set:

• Voltage on the TCC brake switch signal circuit is always low.
• Voltage on the TCC brake switch signal circuit is always high.
• Voltage on the TCC brake switch signal circuit is high for 0.5-4 seconds when voltage is expected to be low.

Action Taken When the DTC Sets

• The EBCM disables the vehicle stability enhancement system (VSES).
• The TCS operates with engine torque reduction capability only.
• The stability indicator turns ON.

Conditions for Clearing the DTC

The Conditions for Setting the DTC are no longer present and you use the scan tool Clear DTCs function.

LTV0500000006586

Fig. 165   Code C0161: ABS/TCS Brake Switch Circuit (Part 1 of 3). 2003–06 Express & Savana w/JL4

Step	Action	Yes	No
7	Test the TCC brake switch signal circuit for a short to voltage. Did you find and correct the condition?	Go to Step 12	Go to Step 8
8	Inspect for poor connections at the harness connector of the electronic brake control module (EBCM). Did you find and correct the condition?	Go to Step 12	Go to Step 10
9	Inspect for poor connections at the harness connector of the stop lamp switch. Did you find and correct the condition?	Go to Step 12	Go to Step 11
10	**Important:** Following EBCM replacement, use the scan tool to perform the Tire Size Calibration procedure. Replace the EBCM. Did you complete the replacement?	Go to Step 12	--
11	Replace the stop lamp switch. Did you complete the replacement?	Go to Step 12	--
12	1. Use the scan tool in order to clear the DTCs. 2. Operate the vehicle within the Conditions for Running the DTC as specified in the supporting text. Does the DTC reset?	Go to Step 2	System OK

LTV0500000006585

Fig. 164   Code C0161: ABS/TCS Brake Switch Circuit (Part 3 of 3). 2003–06 Express & Savana Less JL4

Diagnostic Aids

Thoroughly inspect connections or circuitry that may cause an intermittent malfunction.

Test Description

The numbers below refer to the step numbers on the diagnostic table.

4. This step tests for a shorted stop lamp switch.

5. This step tests for an open stop lamp switch.

Step	Action	Yes	No
1	Did you perform the Diagnostic System Check - Vehicle?	Go to Step 2	Go to Diagnostic System Check - Vehicle
2	1. Select the ABS Data Display function on the scan tool. 2. Observe the Brake Switch Status on the scan tool. Does the scan tool display Off?	Go to Step 3	Go to Step 5
3	1. Apply the brake. 2. Observe the Brake Switch Status on the scan tool. Does the scan tool display On?	Go to Diagnostic Aids	Go to Step 4
4	1. Turn OFF the ignition. 2. Disconnect the stop lamp switch. 3. Turn ON the ignition. 4. Observe the Brake Switch Status on the scan tool. Does the scan tool display On?	Go to Step 9	Go to Step 7
5	1. Turn OFF the ignition. 2. Disconnect the stop lamp switch. 3. Connect a fused jumper wire between the ignition 3 voltage circuit and the torque converter clutch (TCC) brake switch signal circuit at the stop lamp switch harness connector. 4. Turn ON the ignition. 5. Observe the Brake Switch Status on the scan tool. Does the scan tool display Off?	Go to Step 9	Go to Step 6
6	Test the ignition 3 voltage circuit and the TCC brake switch signal circuit for an open or a short to ground. Did you find and correct the condition?	Go to Step 12	Go to Step 8

LTV0500000006587

Fig. 165   Code C0161: ABS/TCS Brake Switch Circuit (Part 2 of 3). 2003–06 Express & Savana w/JL4

7	Test the TCC brake switch signal circuit for a short to voltage. Did you find and correct the condition?		Go to Step 12	Go to Step 8
8	Inspect for poor connections at the harness connector of the electronic brake control module (EBCM). Did you find and correct the condition?		Go to Step 12	Go to Step 10
9	Inspect for poor connections at the harness connector of the stop lamp switch. Did you find and correct the condition?		Go to Step 12	Go to Step 11
10	**Important:** Following EBCM replacement, perform the set-up procedure for the EBCM and perform the Yaw Rate Reference Table Reset Procedure. Use the scan tool to perform the Tire Size Calibration procedure. Replace the EBCM. Did you complete the replacement?		Go to Step 12	--
11	Replace the stop lamp switch. Did you complete the replacement?		Go to Step 12	--
12	1. Use the scan tool Clear All Class 2 DTCs function to clear all of the DTCs from all modules. 2. Turn OFF the ignition for 5 seconds. 3. Turn ON the ignition. 4. Operate the vehicle within the Conditions for Running the DTC as specified in the supporting text. Does the DTC reset?		Go to Step 2	System OK

LTV0500000006588

Fig. 165   Code C0161: ABS/TCS Brake Switch Circuit (Part 3 of 3). 2003–06 Express & Savana w/JL4

Test Description

The numbers below refer to the step numbers on the diagnostic table.

3. This step tests the sensor circuitry in the high voltage range.

4. This step tests the sensor circuitry in the low voltage range.

Step	Action	Values	Yes	No
	Important: If DTC C0292 is set, diagnose C0292 before proceeding with diagnostics for C0186. If DTC C0196 is set, diagnose C0196 before proceeding with diagnostics for C0186. Always use connector test adapters when performing tests to avoid damage to delicate connector terminals. Do not turn OFF the ignition during this diagnostic procedure unless the step in the table instructs you to do so. The scan tool may display some incorrect data if the ignition is cycled.			
1	Did you perform the ABS Diagnostic System Check - Vehicle?	--	Go to Step 2	Go to Diagnostic System Check - Vehicle
2	1. Use the scan tool to clear the DTCs. 2. Turn OFF the ignition for 5 seconds. 3. Turn ON the ignition. 4. Operate the vehicle within the Conditions for Running the DTC as specified in the supporting text. Does the DTC reset?	--	Go to Step 3	Go to Diagnostic Aids
3	1. Turn OFF the ignition. 2. Disconnect the yaw rate sensor/lateral accelerometer harness connector. 3. Turn ON the ignition. 4. Select the vehicle stability enhancement system (VSES) Data Display function on the scan tool. 5. Connect a 3-amp fused jumper wire between the yaw rate sensor/lateral accelerometer 5-volt reference circuit and the lateral accelerometer signal circuit. 6. Observe the Lateral Accelerometer Sensor Input on the scan tool. Is the Lateral Accelerometer Sensor Input voltage greater than the specified value?	4.4 V	Go to Step 4	Go to Step 5
4	1. Remove the fused jumper wire from the yaw rate sensor/lateral accelerometer harness connector. 2. Observe the Lateral Accelerometer Sensor Input on the scan tool. Is the Lateral Accelerometer Sensor Input voltage less than the specified value?	0.6 V	Go to Step 6	Go to Step 9

LTV0500000006590

Fig. 166   Code C0186: Lateral Accelerometer Circuit (Part 2 of 3). 2003–06 Express & Savana

Circuit Description

The electronic brake control module (EBCM) supplies 5 volts to the yaw rate sensor/lateral accelerometer. When the vehicle is not moving, or is being driven in a stable, straight line, lateral acceleration is 0 m/sec/sec (0 ft/sec/sec) and the lateral accelerometer signal voltage is very near 2.5 volts. This is referred to as lateral accelerometer bias voltage. Making a turning maneuver causes the lateral accelerometer signal voltage to increase, or decrease, depending on the direction of the turn. The sharper the turn, the greater the change in signal voltage.

DTC Descriptor

This diagnostic procedure supports the following DTC:

DTC C0186 Lateral Accelerometer Circuit

Conditions for Running the DTC

- The ignition is ON.
- The vehicle stability enhancement system (VSES) sensors have been successfully initialized or the message center has displayed the stability system disabled message due to an unsuccessful initialization attempt.
- The vehicle is being driven relatively straight and level at a speed greater than 11 km/h (7 mph), before performing a stable turning maneuver.

Conditions for Setting the DTC

Any of the following conditions may cause the DTC to set:

- Open lateral accelerometer circuitry is detected.
- Shorted lateral accelerometer circuitry is detected.
- An erratic lateral accelerometer signal is detected.
- The EBCM detects that the lateral accelerometer sensor signal does not correspond with signals from other sensors.

Action Taken When the DTC Sets

- The EBCM disables the VSES.
- The stability indicator turns ON.

Conditions for Clearing the DTC

The conditions for setting the DTC are no longer present and you use the scan tool Clear DTCs function.

Diagnostic Aids

- Inspect the vehicle for proper wheel alignment. Ensure the vehicle does not pull toward the left or right while driving straight forward on a level surface.
- Communicate with the customer to determine the conditions under which the message center displays the Service Stability System message. Learning the conditions under which the DTC sets may help you duplicate the failure.
- Use the Snapshot function on the scan tool in order to assist you in locating an intermittent malfunction.

LTV0500000006589

Fig. 166   Code C0186: Lateral Accelerometer Circuit (Part 1 of 3). 2003–06 Express & Savana

5	Test the lateral accelerometer signal circuit for the following conditions: - An open - A high resistance - A short to ground Did you find and correct the condition?			Go to Step 10	Go to Step 7
6	1. Inspect for poor connections at the harness connector of the yaw rate sensor/lateral accelerometer. 2. Ensure the yaw rate sensor/lateral accelerometer is mounted securely and that the mounting bracket is not bent or otherwise damaged. Did you find and correct the condition?			Go to Step 10	Go to Step 8
7	Inspect for poor connections at the harness connector of the electronic brake control module (EBCM). Did you find and correct the condition?			Go to Step 10	Go to Step 9
8	**Important:** The Yaw Rate Reference Table Reset Procedure must be performed when you are instructed to do so during the Yaw Rate Sensor/Lateral Accelerometer Replacement procedure. Replace the yaw rate sensor/lateral accelerometer. Did you complete the replacement?			Go to Step 10	--
9	**Important:** Following EBCM replacement, perform the set-up procedure for the EBCM and perform the Yaw Rate Reference Table Reset Procedure. Use the scan tool to perform the Tire Size Calibration procedure. Replace the EBCM. Did you complete the replacement?			Go to Step 10	--
10	1. Use the scan tool Clear All Class 2 DTCs function to clear all of the DTCs from all modules. 2. Turn OFF the ignition for 5 seconds. 3. Turn ON the ignition. 4. Operate the vehicle within the Conditions for Running the DTC as specified in the supporting text. Does the DTC reset?			Go to Step 3	System OK

LTV0500000006591

Fig. 166   Code C0186: Lateral Accelerometer Circuit (Part 3 of 3). 2003–06 Express & Savana

Circuit Description

The electronic brake control module (EBCM) supplies 5 volts to the yaw rate sensor/lateral accelerometer. When the vehicle is not moving, or is being driven in a stable, straight line, yaw rate is 0 degrees/second and the yaw rate sensor signal voltage is very near 2.5 volts. This is referred to as sensor bias voltage. Performing a turning maneuver causes the yaw rate sensor signal voltage to increase, or decrease, depending on the direction of the turn. The sharper the turn, the greater the change in signal voltage. Since the yaw rate signal is affected by temperature, the EBCM also monitors a Hz frequency signal from the yaw rate sensor/lateral accelerometer which is proportionate to the approximate temperature of the yaw rate sensor.

DTC Descriptor

This diagnostic procedure supports the following DTC:

DTC C0196 Yaw Rate Circuit

Conditions for Running the DTC

- The ignition is ON.
- The vehicle stability enhancement system (VSES) sensors have been successfully initialized or the message center has displayed the stability system disabled message due to an unsuccessful initialization attempt.
- The vehicle is being driven relatively straight and level at a speed greater than 11 km/h (7 mph), before performing a stable turning maneuver.

Conditions for Setting the DTC

Any of the following conditions may cause the DTC to set:

- Open yaw rate sensor circuitry is detected.
- Shorted yaw rate sensor circuitry is detected.
- An erratic yaw rate sensor signal is detected.
- The EBCM detects that the yaw rate sensor signal does not correspond with signals from other sensors.
- The EBCM detects that the yaw rate sensor frequency signal is not within the valid range.
- A voltage near 5 volts is detected on the yaw rate sensor test circuit at all times.
- A voltage near 0 volts is detected on the yaw rate sensor test circuit at all times.

Action Taken When the DTC Sets

- The EBCM disables the VSES.
- The stability indicator turns ON.

Conditions for Clearing the DTC

The conditions for setting the DTC are no longer present and you use the scan tool Clear DTCs function.

LTV0500000006592

Fig. 167 Code C0196: Yaw Rate Circuit (Part 1 of 5). 2003–06 Express & Savana

Diagnostic Aids

- The following scenario may cause this DTC to set when no actual malfunction exists:
  - The vehicle is driven in a straight line in reverse at a speed greater than 13 km/h (8 mph).
  - The transmission is shifted into neutral while the vehicle continues to coast backward.
  - A turning maneuver is performed after the above conditions are met and the vehicle speed is still greater than 13 km/h (8 mph).
- This DTC may also set falsely if the yaw rate sensor is replaced without first following the diagnostic table below. Whenever a new yaw rate sensor is installed, the old sensor must be disconnected, the ignition turned ON for 5 seconds and then OFF, and then the new sensor connected.
- Inspect the vehicle for proper wheel alignment. Ensure the vehicle does not pull toward the left or right while driving straight forward on a level surface.
- Communicate with the customer to determine the conditions under which the message center displays the service stability system message. Learning the conditions under which the DTC sets may help you duplicate the failure.
- Use the Snapshot function on the scan tool in order to assist you in locating an intermittent malfunction.

Test Description

The number below refers to the step number on the diagnostic table.

12. This step tests for a shorted resistor in the EBCM or a short to voltage within the circuit, by verifying that a large voltage drop occurs in the circuit when the test lamp is placed in parallel with the DMM.

Step	Action	Values	Yes	No
	Important: If DTC C0292 is set, diagnose C0292 before proceeding with diagnostics for C0196. Always use connector test adapters when performing tests to avoid damage to delicate connector terminals.			
1	Did you perform the Diagnostic System Check - Vehicle?	--	Go to Step 2	Go to Diagnostic System Check - Vehicle
2	1. Use the scan tool to clear the DTCs. 2. Turn OFF the ignition for 5 seconds. 3. Turn ON the ignition. 4. Operate the vehicle within the Conditions for Running the DTC as specified in the supporting text. Does the DTC reset?	--	Go to Step 3	Go to Diagnostic Aids
3	1. Turn OFF the ignition. 2. Disconnect the yaw rate sensor/lateral accelerometer harness connector. 3. Turn ON the ignition. 4. Select the vehicle stability enhancement system (VSES) Data Display function on the scan tool. 5. Observe the Yaw Rate Sensor Input on the scan tool. Is the Yaw Rate Sensor Input less than the specified value?	0.6 V	Go to Step 4	Go to Step 19

LTV0500000006593

Fig. 167 Code C0196: Yaw Rate Circuit (Part 2 of 5). 2003–06 Express & Savana

Step	Action	Values	Yes	No
4	1. Connect a fused jumper wire between the yaw rate sensor/lateral accelerometer 5-volt reference circuit and the yaw rate signal circuit. 2. Observe the Yaw Rate Sensor Input on the scan tool. Is the Yaw Rate Sensor Input greater than the specified value?	4.4 V	Go to Step 5	Go to Step 7
5	1. Disconnect the fused jumper wire. 2. Use a DMM to measure the voltage between the yaw rate sensor/lateral accelerometer 5-volt reference circuit and the yaw rate sensor/lateral accelerometer low reference circuit. Does the voltage measure greater than the specified value?	4.75 V	Go to Step 9	Go to Step 6
6	Test the yaw rate sensor/lateral accelerometer low reference circuit for an open. Did you find and correct the condition?	--	Go to Step 20	Go to Step 17
7	Test the yaw rate signal circuit for the following conditions: • An open • A high resistance • A short to ground Did you find and correct the condition?	--	Go to Step 20	Go to Step 8
8	Test the yaw rate sensor/lateral accelerometer 5-volt reference circuit for a high resistance or an open. Did you find and correct the condition?	--	Go to Step 20	Go to Step 17
9	Use a DMM to measure the voltage on the yaw rate frequency circuit. Does the voltage measure greater than the specified value?	4.75 V	Go to Step 10	Go to Step 13
10	Use a DMM to measure the voltage on the yaw rate sensor test circuit. Does the voltage measure greater than the specified value?	4.75 V	Go to Step 11	Go to Step 15

LTV0500000006594

Fig. 167 Code C0196: Yaw Rate Circuit (Part 3 of 5). 2003–06 Express & Savana

Step	Action	Values	Yes	No
11	1. Turn OFF the ignition. 2. Reconnect the yaw rate sensor/lateral accelerometer harness connector. 3. Disconnect the electronic brake control module (EBCM) harness connector. 4. Install a J 39700 Universal Breakout Box and a J 39700-650 Adapter Cable Install the equipment between the EBCM and the EBCM harness connector 5. Turn ON the ignition. 6. At the breakout box, use a DMM to measure the Hz frequency between the yaw rate frequency circuit and a ground circuit. Does the HZ frequency signal measure within the specified range?	13.37-14.36 kHz	Go to Step 16	Go to Step 12
12	1. With the DMM still connected to monitor the yaw rate frequency circuit, set the DMM to measure DC voltage. 2. Connect one end of a test lamp to a good ground. 3. Connect the other end of the test lamp to the positive lead of the DMM. Does the voltage measure less than the specified value?	0.15 V	Go to Step 16	Go to Step 14
13	Test the yaw rate frequency circuit for an open or a short to ground. Did you find and correct the condition?	--	Go to Step 20	Go to Step 17
14	Test the yaw rate frequency circuit for a short to voltage. Did you find and correct the condition?	--	Go to Step 20	Go to Step 19
15	Test the yaw rate sensor test circuit for a short to ground. Did you find and correct the condition?	--	Go to Step 20	Go to Step 17
16	1. Inspect for poor connections at the harness connector of the yaw rate sensor/lateral accelerometer. 2. Ensure the yaw rate sensor/lateral accelerometer is mounted securely and that the mounting bracket is not bent or otherwise damaged. Did you find and correct the condition?	--	Go to Step 20	Go to Step 18
17	Inspect for poor connections at the harness connector of the EBCM. Did you find and correct the condition?	--	Go to Step 20	Go to Step 19

LTV0500000006595

Fig. 167 Code C0196: Yaw Rate Circuit (Part 4 of 5). 2003–06 Express & Savana

Step	Action	Values	Yes	No
18	**Important:** The Yaw Rate Reference Table Reset Procedure must be performed when you are instructed to do so during the Yaw Rate Sensor/Lateral Accelerometer Replacement procedure. Replace the yaw rate sensor/lateral accelerometer. Did you complete the replacement?	--	--	Go to Step 20
19	**Important:** Following EBCM replacement, perform the set-up procedure for the EBCM and perform the Yaw Rate Reference Table Reset Procedure. Use the scan tool to perform the Tire Size Calibration procedure. Replace the EBCM. Did you complete the replacement?	--	--	Go to Step 20
20	1. Use the scan tool Clear All Class 2 DTCs function to clear all of the DTCs from all modules. 2. Turn OFF the ignition for 5 seconds. 3. Turn ON the ignition. 4. Operate the vehicle within the Conditions for Running the DTC as specified in the supporting text. Does the DTC reset?	--	Go to Step 3	System OK

LTV0500000006596

Fig. 167 Code C0196: Yaw Rate Circuit (Part 5 of 5). 2003–06 Express & Savana

Step	Action	Values	Yes	No
1	Did you perform the Diagnostic System Check - Vehicle?	--	Go to Step 2	Go to Diagnostic System Check - Vehicle
2	1. Use the scan tool to clear the DTCs. 2. Turn OFF the ignition for 5 seconds. 3. Turn ON the ignition. Does the DTC reset?	--	Go to Step 3	Go to Diagnostic Aids
3	1. Separate the electronic brake control module (EBCM) from the brake pressure modulator valve (BPMV). 2. Use a DMM in order to measure the resistance across the ABS pump motor. Does the resistance measure within the specified range?	0.3-1 ohms	Go to Step 4	Go to Step 6
4	Use a DMM in order to measure the resistance between the high side of the pump motor and a good ground. Does the resistance measure less than the specified value?	OL	Go to Step 6	Go to Step 5
5	**Important:** Following the EBCM replacement, perform the set-up procedure for the EBCM and perform the Yaw Rate Reference Table Reset Procedure. Use the scan tool to perform the Tire Size Calibration procedure. Replace the EBCM. Did you complete the replacement?	--	Go to Step 7	--
6	**Important:** Following the EBCM replacement, perform the set-up procedure for the EBCM and perform the Yaw Rate Reference Table Reset Procedure. Use the scan tool to perform the Tire Size Calibration procedure. Replace the EBCM and the BPMV. Did you complete the replacements?	--	Go to Step 7	--
7	1. Use the scan tool to clear the DTCs. 2. Turn OFF the ignition for 5 seconds. 3. Turn ON the ignition. Does the DTC reset?	--	Go to Step 3	System OK

LTV0500000006598

Fig. 168 Codes C0201: ABS Enable Relay Contact Circuit (Part 2 of 2). 2003–06 Express & Savana

Circuit Description

The system relay, located within the electronic brake control module (EBCM), supplies battery voltage to all of the valve solenoids and to the precharge pump motor. When the relay contacts close, the EBCM monitors the voltage supplied to the valve solenoids and compares this voltage to monitored ignition voltage.

DTC Descriptor

This diagnostic procedure supports the following DTC:

DTC C0201 Antilock Brake System (ABS) Enable Relay Contact Circuit

Conditions for Running the DTC

The ignition is ON.

Conditions for Setting the DTC

Either of the following conditions may cause the DTC to set:

- The EBCM detects that the voltage supplied to the valve solenoids is less than 65 percent of the monitored ignition voltage for 50 milliseconds.
- The EBCM detects that the relay contacts do not open when the relay is not energized.

Action Taken When the DTC Sets

If equipped, the following actions occur:

- The EBCM disables the ABS/traction control system (TCS)/vehicle stability enhancement system (VSES)/dynamic rear proportion (DRP).
- The ABS indicator turns ON.
- The stability indicator turns ON.
- The brake warning indicator turns ON.

Conditions for Clearing the DTC

The Conditions for Setting the DTC are no longer present and you use the scan tool Clear DTCs function.

Diagnostic Aids

Refer back to the diagnostic table, steps 3-7, if this DTC continues to set intermittently.

Test Description

The number below refers to the step number on the diagnostic table.

3. A shorted ABS pump motor may damage the contacts within the system relay. It is imperative that the steps in the table be followed to prevent damage to a replacement EBCM.

LTV0500000006597

Fig. 168 Code C0201: ABS Enable Relay Contact Circuit (Part 1 of 2). 2003–06 Express & Savana

Circuit Description

During an ABS event, the electronic brake control modulator (EBCM) calculates the total time that a dump valve is energized while attempting to unlock a locked wheel.

DTC Descriptors

This diagnostic procedure supports the following DTCs:

DTC C0220-C0229 Antilock Brake System (ABS) Channel in Release Too Long

Conditions for Running the DTC

- The ignition is ON.
- The vehicle is experiencing an ABS event.

Conditions for Setting the DTC

The total dump time for any dump valve has exceeded 9 seconds and the EBCM has not received a wheel speed signal from the corresponding wheel during this activity.

Action Taken When the DTC Sets

- The EBCM disables the ABS/dynamic rear proportion (DRP).
- The ABS indicator turns ON.
- The brake warning indicator turns ON.

The actions above are maintained during subsequent ignition cycles until the EBCM completes a power up self-test. This test concludes when the vehicle achieves a speed greater than 13 km/h (8 mph) and the wheel speeds are verified by the EBCM.

Conditions for Clearing the DTC

The Conditions for Setting the DTC are no longer present and you use the scan tool Clear DTCs function.

Diagnostic Aids

The most likely cause of this DTC is a mechanical failure that causes a wheel to lock and remain locked. The DTC may also set, conceivably, when the ABS is activated on surfaces that are nearly impossible to get traction on. If the DTC sets within these conditions, diagnosis of the ABS system is not necessary.

Test Description

The number below refers to the step number on the diagnostic table.

2. Performing solenoid tests determines if there is a mechanical malfunction inside the brake pressure modulator valve (BPMV).

LTV0500000006599

Fig. 169 Codes C0220–C0229: ABS Channel In Release Too Long (Part 1 of 2). 2003–06 Express & Savana Less JL4

Step	Action	Yes	No
1	Did you perform the Diagnostic System Check - Vehicle?	Go to Step 2	Go to Diagnostic System Check - Vehicle
2	1. Use a scan tool in order to clear the DTCs. 2. Use the scan tool in order to perform the necessary solenoid tests. Refer to Scan Tool Output Controls . Do the solenoid tests show the system to be functioning normally?	Go to Diagnostic Aids	Go to Step 3
3	Replace the brake pressure modulator valve (BPMV). Did you complete the replacement?	Go to Step 4	--
4	Use the scan tool in order to perform the necessary solenoid tests. Do the solenoid tests show the system to be functioning normally?	System OK	Go to Step 3

LTV0500000006600

Fig. 169 Codes C0220–C0229: ABS Channel In Release Too Long (Part 2 of 2). 2003–06 Express & Savana Less JL4

Action Taken When the DTC Sets

- The EBCM disables the ABS/dynamic rear proportion (DRP).
- The ABS indicator turns ON.
- The brake warning indicator turns ON.

The actions above are maintained during subsequent ignition cycles until the EBCM completes a power up self-test. This test concludes when the vehicle achieves a speed greater than 13 km/h (8 mph) and the wheel speeds are verified by the EBCM.

Conditions for Clearing the DTC

The Conditions for Setting the DTC are no longer present and you use the scan tool Clear DTCs function.

Diagnostic Aids

The most likely cause of this DTC is a mechanical failure that causes a wheel to lock and remain locked. The DTC may also set, conceivably, when the ABS is activated on surfaces that are nearly impossible to get traction on. If the DTC sets within these conditions, diagnosis of the ABS system is not necessary.

Test Description

The number below refers to the step number on the diagnostic table.

2. Performing solenoid tests determines if there is a mechanical malfunction inside the brake pressure modulator valve (BPMV).

Step	Action	Yes	No
1	Did you perform the Diagnostic System Check - Vehicle?	Go to Step 2	Go to Diagnostic System Check - Vehicle
2	1. Use a scan tool in order to clear the DTCs. 2. Use the scan tool in order to perform the necessary solenoid tests. Refer to Scan Tool Output Controls . Do the solenoid tests show the system to be functioning normally?	Go to Diagnostic Aids	Go to Step 3
3	Replace the brake pressure modulator valve (BPMV). Did you complete the replacement?	Go to Step 4	--
4	Use the scan tool in order to perform the necessary solenoid tests. Do the solenoid tests show the system to be functioning normally?	System OK	Go to Step 3

LTV0500000006602

Fig. 170 Codes C0220–C0229: ABS Channel In Release Too Long (Part 2 of 2). 2003–06 Express & Savana w/JL4

Circuit Description

During an ABS event, the electronic brake control module (EBCM) calculates the total time that a dump valve is energized while attempting to unlock a locked wheel.

DTC Descriptors

This diagnostic procedure supports the following DTCs:

- DTC C0220 Left Front Antilock Brake System (ABS) Channel in Release Too Long
- DTC C0221 Right Front Antilock Brake System (ABS) Channel in Release Too Long
- DTC C0228 Left Rear Antilock Brake System (ABS) Channel in Release Too Long
- DTC C0229 Right Rear Antilock Brake System (ABS) Channel in Release Too Long

Conditions for Running the DTC

- The ignition is ON.
- The vehicle is experiencing an ABS event.

Conditions for Setting the DTC

C0220

The total dump valve ON time for the left front brake circuit has exceeded 9 seconds and the EBCM has not received a wheel speed signal from the left front wheel during this activity.

C0221

The total dump valve ON time for the right front brake circuit has exceeded 9 seconds and the EBCM has not received a wheel speed signal from the right front wheel during this activity.

C0228

The total dump valve ON time for the left rear brake circuit has exceeded 9 seconds and the EBCM has not received a wheel speed signal from the left rear wheel during this activity.

C0229

The total dump valve ON time for the right rear brake circuit has exceeded 9 seconds and the EBCM has not received a wheel speed signal from the right rear wheel during this activity.

LTV0500000006601

Fig. 170 Codes C0220–C0229: ABS Channel In Release Too Long (Part 1 of 2). 2003–06 Express & Savana w/JL4

Circuit Description

The electronic brake control module (EBCM) supplies approximately 12 volts through an internal resistor to the powertrain control module (PCM) on the delivered torque signal circuit. The PCM toggles this voltage to ground in order to create the delivered torque signal at the EBCM. A signal with a frequency of 128 Hz +/- 5 percent and a duty cycle of 25-95 percent is a valid delivered torque signal. The percentage of duty cycle is proportionate to the percentage of delivered engine torque.

DTC Descriptor

This diagnostic procedure supports the following DTC:

DTC C0244 or DTC P1689 Pulse Width Modulated (PWM) Delivered Torque

Conditions for Running the DTC

- The ignition is ON.
- The engine is running at a speed greater than 450 RPM for 1 second.

Conditions for Setting the DTC

C0244

The EBCM receives an invalid delivered torque signal for 300 milliseconds.

P1689

The PCM detects open or shorted delivered torque signal voltage as being less than 4.75 volts or greater than 5.25 volts.

Action Taken When the DTC Sets

- The EBCM disables the vehicle stability enhancement system (VSES).
- The stability indicator turns ON.

Conditions for Clearing the DTC

The conditions for setting the DTC are no longer present and you use the scan tool Clear DTCs function.

LTV0500000006603

Fig. 171 Codes C0244 Or P1689: PWM Delivered Torque (Part 1 of 4). 2003–06 Express & Savana

Diagnostic Aids

Thoroughly inspect connections or circuitry that may cause an intermittent malfunction.

Test Description

The numbers below refer to the step numbers on the diagnostic table.

3. This step tests for voltage supplied to the PCM from the EBCM.

4. This step tests for a shorted resistor in the EBCM or a short to voltage within the circuit, by verifying that a large voltage drop occurs in the circuit when the test lamp is placed in parallel with the DMM. The PCM may be damaged if either of these conditions is present.

Step	Action	Values	Yes	No
1	Did you performs the Diagnostic System Check - Vehicle?	--	Go to Step 2	Go to Diagnostic System Check - Vehicle
2	1. Use a scan tool in order to clear the DTCs. 2. Turn OFF the ignition for 5 seconds. 3. Start the engine. Does the DTC set?	--	Go to Step 3	Go to Diagnostic Aids
3	1. Turn OFF the ignition. 2. Disconnect from the powertrain control module (PCM), the harness connector containing the delivered torque signal circuit. 3. Turn ON the ignition. 4. Use a DMM in order to measure the voltage between the delivered torque signal circuit and a good ground. Does the voltage measure greater than the specified value?	10 V	Go to Step 4	Go to Step 5
4	1. With the DMM still connected to monitor the delivered torque signal circuit, connect one end of a test lamp to a good ground. 2. Connect the other end of the test lamp to the positive lead of the DMM, while observing the DMM display. Does the voltage measure less than the specified value?	0.15 V	Go to Step 6	Go to Step 10

LTV0500000006604

Fig. 171 Codes C0244 Or P1689: PWM Delivered Torque (Part 2 of 4). 2003–06 Express & Savana

Step	Action	Values	Yes	No
11	Inspect for poor connections at the harness connector of the PCM. Did you find and correct the condition?	--	Go to Step 13	Go to Step 12
12	**Important:** Perform the setup procedure for the PCM. Replace the PCM. Did you complete the replacement?	--	Go to Step 13	--
13	1. Use the scan tool Clear All Class 2 DTCs function to clear all of the DTCs from all modules. 2. Turn OFF the ignition for 5 seconds. 3. Turn ON the ignition. 4. Operate the vehicle within the Conditions for Running the DTC as specified in the supporting text. Does the DTC reset?	--	Go to Step 3	System OK

LTV0500000006606

Fig. 171 Codes C0244 Or P1689: PWM Delivered Torque (Part 4 of 4). 2003–06 Express & Savana

Step	Action	Values	Yes	No
5	Test the delivered torque signal circuit for an open or a short to ground. Did you find and correct the condition?	--	Go to Step 13	Go to Step 8
6	1. Turn OFF the ignition. 2. Reconnect the PCM harness connector. 3. Start the engine. 4. Select the vehicle stability enhancement system (VSES) Data Display function on the scan tool. 5. Observe the Delivered Torque parameter on the scan tool. Does the scan tool display a duty cycle of the delivered torque signal within the specified range?	25-95%	Go to Step 7	Go to Step 11
7	1. Turn OFF the ignition. 2. Install a J 39700 100-Pin Breakout Box and a J 39700-650 Adapter Cable. Install the equipment between the electronic brake control module (EBCM) and the EBCM harness connector. 3. Start the engine. 4. Use a DMM in order to measure the Hz frequency between the delivered torque signal circuit and a ground circuit. Does the Hz frequency of the delivered torque signal measure within the specified range?	121-134 Hz	Go to Step 9	Go to Step 12
8	1. Turn OFF the ignition. 2. Inspect for poor connections at the harness connector of the EBCM. Did you find and correct the condition?	--	Go to Step 13	Go to Step 9
9	**Important:** Following EBCM replacement, perform the set-up procedure for the EBCM and perform the Yaw Rate Reference Table Reset Procedure. Use the scan tool to perform the Tire Size Calibration procedure. Replace the EBCM. Did you complete the replacement?	--	Go to Step 13	--
10	Test the delivered torque signal circuit for a short to voltage. Did you find and correct the condition?	--	Go to Step 13	Go to Step 12

LTV0500000006605

Fig. 171 Codes C0244 Or P1689: PWM Delivered Torque (Part 3 of 4). 2003–06 Express & Savana

Circuit Description

As the front wheels spin, each wheel speed sensor produces an AC signal. The electronic brake control module (EBCM) uses the frequency of the AC signals to calculate each wheel speed. The powertrain control module (PCM) converts the signal from the vehicle speed sensor (VSS) to a 128k pulses/mile signal. The EBCM uses the vehicle speed signal from the PCM to calculate the rear wheel speed.

DTC Descriptor

This diagnostic procedure supports the following DTC:

DTC C0245 Wheel Speed Sensor Frequency Error

Conditions for Running the DTC

- The ignition is ON.
- The vehicle speed is greater than 8 km/h (4 mph).
- No brake application or deceleration is detected.
- No wheel slip is detected.
- No turning maneuvers are detected.

Conditions for Setting the DTC

- At least one wheel speed sensor signal is 15 percent less than or greater than, other wheel speed sensor signals.
- All of the conditions for running and setting the DTC are present for a cumulative time of 3 minutes during a single ignition cycle.

Action Taken When the DTC Sets

- The EBCM disables the ABS/dynamic rear proportion (DRP).
- The ABS indicator turns ON.
- The brake warning indicator turns ON.

Conditions for Clearing the DTC

The Conditions for Setting the DTC are no longer present and you use the scan tool Clear DTCs function.

Diagnostic Aids

Installing one tire of significantly different size on the vehicle causes this DTC to set. Operating the vehicle with a tire that has very low air pressure may also set this DTC. Inspect the vehicle for an incorrect or damaged wheel speed sensor or VSS if the tires and the EBCM and PCM calibrations are OK.

Test Description

The number below refers to the step number on the diagnostic table.

4. If the front tires are not the same size as the rear tires, the EBCM calibration must match the FRONT tire size and the

LTV0500000006607

Fig. 172 Code C0245: Wheel Speed Sensor Frequency Error (Part 1 of 2). 2003–06 Express & Savana

Step	Action	Yes	No
1	Did you perform the Diagnostic System Check - Vehicle?	Go to Step 2	Go to Diagnostic System Check - Vehicle
2	Inspect both of the front tires on the vehicle to ensure that both tires are of equal size. Are both of the front tires of equal size?	Go to Step 3	Go to Diagnostic Aids
3	Inspect both of the rear tires on the vehicle to ensure that both tires are of equal size. Are both of the rear tires of equal size?	Go to Step 4	Go to Diagnostic Aids
4	Verify the electronic brake control module (EBCM) and the powertrain control module (PCM) both have the correct tire size calibration. Use the scan tool in order to view the EBCM tire size calibration or perform the Tire Size Calibration procedure Did you find and correct the condition?	Go to Step 5	Go to Diagnostic Aids
5	1. Use a scan tool in order to clear the DTCs. 2. Operate the vehicle for at least 3 minutes within the Conditions for Running the DTC as specified in the supporting text. Does the DTC reset?	Go to Step 2	System OK

LTV0500000006608

Fig. 172   Code C0245: Wheel Speed Sensor Frequency Error (Part 2 of 2). 2003–06 Express & Savana

Test Description

The numbers below refer to the step numbers on the diagnostic table.

3. This step tests if the EBCM is detecting open or shorted precharge pump motor circuitry.

4. This step tests if the EBCM is capable of energizing the precharge pump motor.

Step	Action	Values	Yes	No
1	Did you perform the Diagnostic System Check - Vehicle?	—	Go to Step 2	Go to Diagnostic System Check - Vehicle
2	1. Use the scan tool to clear the DTCs. 2. Turn OFF the ignition for 5 seconds. 3. Turn ON the ignition. 4. Operate the vehicle within the Conditions for Running the DTC as specified in the supporting text. Does the DTC reset?	—	Go to Step 3	Go to Diagnostic Aids
3	1. Turn OFF the ignition. 2. Disconnect the precharge pump motor harness connector. 3. Use a connector test adapter kit to connect a test lamp between the precharge pump motor circuits. 4. Turn ON the ignition. Does the DTC reset?	—	Go to Step 9	Go to Step 4
4	1. With the test lamp still connected, select the vehicle stability enhancement system (VSES) Special Functions menu on the scan tool. 2. Select and perform the Pre-Charge Bleed. Does the test lamp illuminate and then turn OFF when the Pre-Charge Bleed is performed?	—	Go to Step 5	Go to Step 11

LTV0500000006610

Fig. 173   Code C0279: Pre-Charge Pump Circuit Performance (Part 2 of 4). 2003–06 Express & Savana

Step	Action			Yes	No
	Important: Always ensure that the master cylinder reservoir cap is in place and secure before turning ON the precharge pump.				
5	1. Reconnect the precharge pump motor harness connector. 2. Use the scan tool to perform the Pre-Charge Bleed. Does the precharge pump motor run?			Go to Step 6	Go to Step 8
6	1. Observe the fluid in the master cylinder reservoir. 2. Use the scan tool to perform the Pre-Charge Bleed. When the precharge pump runs, can fluid be seen discharging back into the master cylinder reservoir?			Go to Step 13	Go to Step 7
7	Inspect the master cylinder reservoir, the brake fluid supply hose to the precharge pump inlet, and the precharge pump inlet port for any restriction that may cause the loss of fluid supply to the pump. Did you find and correct the condition?			Go to Step 16	Go to Step 15
8	Inspect for poor connections at the harness connectors of the precharge pump motor. Did you find and correct the condition?			Go to Step 16	Go to Step 15
9	**Important:** Turn ON the ignition when testing for a short to voltage. 1. Turn OFF the ignition. 2. Disconnect the electronic brake control module (EBCM) harness connector. 3. Test the precharge pump motor circuits for the following conditions: • An open • A short to ground • A short to voltage • Shorted together Did you find and correct the condition?			Go to Step 16	Go to Step 10
10	Inspect for poor connections at the harness connector of the EBCM. Did you find and correct the condition?			Go to Step 16	Go to Step 13

LTV0500000006611

Fig. 173   Code C0279: Pre-Charge Pump Circuit Performance (Part 3 of 4). 2003–06 Express & Savana

Circuit Description

The electronic brake control module (EBCM) uses the precharge pump in conjunction with the ABS pump to build hydraulic pressure for brake application during a vehicle stability enhancement system (VSES) event. Power and ground are both switched ON by the EBCM to energize the precharge pump motor.

DTC Descriptor

This diagnostic procedure supports the following DTC:

DTC C0279 Pre-charge Pump Circuit Performance

Conditions for Running the DTC

- The ignition is ON.
- The precharge pump is activated during a VSES event or when the EBCM performs the power-up self-test. Refer to ABS Description and Operation for a complete description of the power-up self-test.

Conditions for Setting the DTC

- The EBCM detects open precharge pump circuitry.
- The EBCM detects shorted precharge pump circuitry.
- The master cylinder pressure sensor signal does not increase sufficiently during a pressure-build event.

Action Taken When the DTC Sets

- The EBCM disables the VSES.
- The stability indicator turns ON.

Conditions for Clearing the DTC

The conditions for setting the DTC are no longer present and you use the scan tool Clear DTCs function.

Diagnostic Aids

Thoroughly inspect connections or circuitry that may cause an intermittent malfunction.

LTV0500000006609

Fig. 173   Code C0279: Pre-Charge Pump Circuit Performance (Part 1 of 4). 2003–06 Express & Savana

Step	Action	Values	Yes	No
11	Use a DMM to measure the resistance value of the precharge pump motor. Does the resistance measure within the specified range?	0.3-1 ohms	Go to Step 12	Go to Step 14
12	Use the DMM to measure the resistance between the high side of the precharge pump motor and a good ground. Does the resistance measure less than the specified value?	OL	Go to Step 14	Go to Step 13
13	**Important:** Following EBCM replacement, perform the set-up procedure for the EBCM and perform the Yaw Rate Reference Table Reset Procedure. Use the scan tool to perform the Tire Size Calibration procedure. Replace the EBCM. Did you complete the replacement?	—	Go to Step 16	—
14	**Important:** Following EBCM replacement, perform the set-up procedure for the EBCM and perform the Yaw Rate Reference Table Reset Procedure. Use the scan tool to perform the Tire Size Calibration procedure. Replace the EBCM and the precharge pump assembly. Did you complete the replacements?	—	Go to Step 16	—
15	Replace the precharge pump assembly. Did you complete the replacement?	—	Go to Step 16	—
16	1. Use the scan tool Clear All Class 2 DTCs function to clear all of the DTCs from all modules. 2. Turn OFF the ignition for 5 seconds. 3. Turn ON the ignition. 4. Operate the vehicle within the Conditions for Running the DTC as specified in the supporting text. Does the DTC reset?		Go to Step 3	System OK

LTV0500000006612

Fig. 173   Code C0279: Pre-Charge Pump Circuit Performance (Part 4 of 4). 2003–06 Express & Savana

Circuit Description

The mode switch is a momentary-contact, normally-open switch that can be used to disable the vehicle stability enhancement system (VSES). The mode switch is directly monitored by the electronic brake control module (EBCM). Each time the mode switch is pressed, the VSES enabled/disabled status changes. When VSES is disabled, the EBCM sends serial data messages to the instrument panel cluster (IPC) to turn ON the stability indicator.

DTC Descriptor

This diagnostic procedure supports the following DTC:

DTC C0283 Mode Switch Circuit Malfunction

Conditions for Running the DTC

The ignition is ON.

Conditions for Setting the DTC

The EBCM detects low voltage on the traction control switch signal circuit for 8 seconds.

Action Taken When the DTC Sets

- The EBCM disables the VSES.
- The stability indicator turns ON.

Conditions for Clearing the DTC

The conditions for setting the DTC are no longer present and you use the scan tool Clear DTCs function.

LTV0500000006613

**Fig. 174   Code C0283: Mode Switch Circuit Fault
(Part 1 of 3). 2003–06 Express & Savana**

Step	Action	Yes	No
6	Inspect for poor connections at the harness connector of the electronic brake control module (EBCM). Did you find and correct the condition?	Go to Step 11	Go to Step 7
7	**Important:** Following EBCM replacement, perform the set-up procedure for the EBCM and perform the Yaw Rate Reference Table Reset Procedure. Use the scan tool to perform the Tire Size Calibration procedure. Replace the EBCM. Did you complete the replacement?	Go to Step 11	—
8	Repair the open in the ignition 3 voltage circuit. Did you complete the repair?	Go to Step 11	—
9	Inspect for poor connections at the harness connector of the mode switch. Did you find and correct the condition?	Go to Step 11	Go to Step 10
10	Replace the mode switch. Did you complete the replacement?	Go to Step 11	—
11	1. Use the scan tool to clear the DTCs. 2. Turn OFF the ignition for 5 seconds. 3. Turn ON the ignition. 4. Operate the vehicle within the Conditions for Running the DTC as specified in the supporting text. Does the DTC reset?	Go to Step 3	System OK

LTV0500000006615

**Fig. 174   Code C0283: Mode Switch Circuit Fault
(Part 3 of 3). 2003–06 Express & Savana**

Diagnostic Aids

Thoroughly inspect connections or circuitry that may cause an intermittent malfunction.

Test Description

The number below refers to the step number on the diagnostic table.

4. This step tests the traction control switch circuitry. If the fuse opens when you perform this test, the traction control switch signal circuit is shorted to ground.

Step	Action	Yes	No
1	Did you perform the Diagnostic System Check - Vehicle?	Go to Step 2	Go to Diagnostic System Check - Vehicle
2	1. Use a scan tool in order to clear the DTCs. 2. Turn OFF the ignition for 5 seconds. 3. Turn ON the ignition for up to 20 seconds. Does the DTC set?	Go to Step 3	Go to Diagnostic Aids
3	1. Turn OFF the ignition. 2. Disconnect the mode switch harness connector. 3. Turn ON the ignition. 4. Connect a test lamp between the ignition 3 voltage circuit and a good ground. Does the test lamp illuminate?	Go to Step 4	Go to Step 8
4	1. Use the scan tool in order to clear the DTCs. 2. Turn OFF the ignition. 3. Connect a fused jumper wire between the ignition 3 voltage circuit and the traction control switch signal circuit at the mode switch harness connector. 4. Turn ON the ignition for up to 20 seconds. Does the DTC set?	Go to Step 5	Go to Step 9
5	Test the traction control switch signal circuit for an open or a short to ground. Did you find and correct the condition?	Go to Step 11	Go to Step 6

LTV0500000006614

**Fig. 174   Code C0283: Mode Switch Circuit Fault
(Part 2 of 3). 2003–06 Express & Savana**

Circuit Description

The electronic brake control module (EBCM) supplies a reference voltage of 5 volts to the yaw rate sensor/lateral accelerometer, the steering wheel position sensor and the master cylinder pressure sensor. The sensor supply voltage is monitored via an internal feedback circuit to the EBCM microprocessor.

DTC Descriptors

This diagnostic procedure supports the following DTCs:

- DTC C0290 Devise Voltage Reference Output Circuit
- DTC C0292 Devise Voltage Reference Input Circuit

Conditions for Running the DTC

The ignition is ON.

Conditions for Setting the DTC

The EBCM detects that the sensor supply voltage is less than 4.75 volts or greater than 5.25 volts for 30 milliseconds.

Action Taken When the DTC Sets

- The EBCM disables the vehicle stability enhancement system (VSES).
- The stability system caution indicator turns ON.

Conditions for Clearing the DTC

The conditions for setting the DTC are no longer present and you use the scan tool Clear DTCs function.

Diagnostic Aids

Thoroughly inspect connections or circuitry that may cause an intermittent malfunction.

Test Description

The numbers below refer to the step numbers on the diagnostic table.

5. This step tests for a shorted yaw rate sensor/lateral accelerometer or steering wheel position sensor.

6. This step tests for a shorted master cylinder pressure sensor. The presence of DTC C0110 is normal during this step.

LTV0500000006616

**Fig. 175   Code C0290 &C0292: Device Voltage
Reference Circuit (Part 1 of 3). 2003–06 Express &
Savana**

Step	Action	Yes	No
1	Did you perform the Diagnostic System Check - Vehicle?	Go to Step 2	Go to Diagnostic System Check - Vehicle
2	1. Use the scan tool to clear the DTCs. 2. Turn OFF the ignition for 5 seconds. 3. Turn ON the ignition. Does the DTC reset?	Go to Step 3	Go to Diagnostic Aids
3	1. Turn OFF the ignition. 2. Disconnect the yaw rate sensor/lateral accelerometer harness connector. 3. Disconnect the steering wheel position sensor harness connector. Refer to CELL LINK . 4. Disconnect the electronic brake control module (EBCM) harness connector. 5. Test the yaw rate sensor/lateral accelerometer 5-volt reference circuit and the steering wheel position sensor 5-volt reference circuit for a short to ground. Refer to Circuit Testing and Wiring Repairs . Did you find and correct the condition?	Go to Step 12	Go to Step 4
4	1. Turn ON the ignition. 2. Test the following circuits for a short to voltage: - Yaw rate sensor/lateral accelerometer 5-volt reference circuit - Steering wheel position sensor 5-volt reference circuit - Yaw rate sensor signal circuit - Lateral accelerometer signal circuit Did you find and correct the condition?	Go to Step 12	Go to Step 5
5	1. Turn OFF the ignition. 2. Reconnect only the EBCM harness connector. 3. Turn ON the ignition. 4. Use the scan tool to clear any DTCs. Does the DTC reset?	Go to Step 6	Go to Step 8
6	1. Turn OFF the ignition. 2. Reconnect the yaw rate sensor/lateral accelerometer harness connector. 3. Reconnect the steering wheel position sensor harness connector. 4. Separate the EBCM from the brake pressure modulator valve (BPMV), leaving the EBCM harness connector connected. 5. Turn ON the ignition. Does the DTC reset?	Go to Step 11	Go to Step 7

LTV0500000006617

Fig. 175   Code C0290 &C0292: Device Voltage Reference Circuit (Part 2 of 3). 2003–06 Express & Savana

Circuit Description

The electronic brake control module (EBCM) receives several inputs from the steering wheel position sensor. Three digital square wave signal inputs are wired directly to the EBCM harness connector, however, only signals A and B are used or monitored. The failure of the index pulse signal does not effect vehicle stability enhancement system (VSES) function. The EBCM also receives an analog steering wheel position input on the steering wheel position sensor signal 1 circuit. Ignition voltage is supplied to the digital portion of the steering wheel position sensor. The analog portion of the steering wheel position sensor is supplied a 5-volt reference from the EBCM.

DTC Descriptor

This diagnostic procedure supports the following DTC:

DTC C0455 Front Steering Position Sensor Circuit

Conditions for Running the DTC

- The ignition is ON.
- The VSES sensors have been successfully initialized.

Conditions for Setting the DTC

Any of the following conditions may cause the DTC to set:

- The analog steering wheel position signal does not correlate with the digital steering wheel position signals.
- When driven forward in a straight line, the centered steering angle differs by more than 30 degrees from the centered steering angle when the sensors are initialized.
- The EBCM detects an erratic signal from steering wheel position signal A or signal B.
- The EBCM detects an open or shorted steering wheel position analog signal.
- The EBCM detects an erratic steering wheel position analog signal.
- The EBCM detects an open or shorted steering wheel position signal A or signal B, after having received a valid signal during the same ignition.

Action Taken When the DTC Sets

- The EBCM disables the VSES.
- The stability system caution indicator is illuminated.

Conditions for Clearing the DTC

The condition for setting the DTC is no longer present and you use the scan tool Clear DTCs function.

LTV0500000006619

Fig. 176   Code C0455: Front Steering Position Sensor Circuit (Part 1 of 5). 2003–06 Express & Savana

Step	Action	Yes	No
7	Replace the BPMV. Did you complete the replacement?	Go to Step 12	--
8	Reconnect the steering wheel position sensor harness connector. Does the DTC reset?	Go to Step 10	Go to Step 9
9	**Important:** The Yaw Rate Reference Table Reset Procedure must be performed when you are instructed to do so during the Yaw Rate Sensor/Lateral Accelerometer Replacement procedure. Replace the yaw rate sensor/lateral accelerometer. Did you complete the replacement?	Go to Step 12	--
10	Replace the steering wheel position sensor. Did you complete the replacement?	Go to Step 12	--
11	**Important:** Following EBCM replacement, perform the setup procedure for the EBCM and perform the Yaw Rate Reference Table Reset Procedure. Use the scan tool to perform the Tire Size Calibration procedure. Replace the EBCM. Did you complete the replacement?	Go to Step 12	--
12	1. Use the scan tool Clear All Class 2 DTCs function to clear all of the DTCs from all modules. 2. Turn OFF the ignition for 5 seconds. 3. Turn ON the ignition. 4. Operate the vehicle within the Conditions for Running the DTC as specified in the supporting text. Does the DTC reset?	Go to Step 3	System OK

LTV0500000006618

Fig. 175   Code C0290 &C0292: Device Voltage Reference Circuit (Part 3 of 3). 2003–06 Express & Savana

Diagnostic Aids

- DTC C0455 may be falsely set if you did not turn OFF the ignition for 5 seconds after clearing DTCs from the EBCM. This is why all diagnostic tables which apply to this system always instruct you to turn OFF the ignition for 5 seconds after clearing DTCs. If this DTC has set after you cleared DTCs from the EBCM or used the scan tool to clear all DTCs from all modules and you did not cycle the ignition afterward, it is likely that no actual malfunction exists.
- Whenever any one of the steering signals to the EBCM is lost, the scan tool displays a fixed steering wheel position, which indicates the last known steering wheel position. This can aid you in diagnosing an intermittent malfunction.
- If the DTC does not reset during step 2 or 3 of the diagnostic procedure, the stability system not ready indicator may be displayed due to an unsuccessful initialization. This occurs if the EBCM does not receive any signal from one or both of the digital inputs during the entire ignition cycle. If this occurs, refer to Stability System Not Ready Indicator Always On for further diagnosis.
- Inspect the vehicle for proper wheel alignment. Ensure the vehicle does not pull toward the left or right while driving straight forward on a level surface.
- Communicate with the customer to determine the conditions under which the instrument panel cluster (IPC) illuminates the stability system caution indicator. Learning the conditions under which the DTC sets may help you duplicate the failure.
- Use the Snapshot function on the scan tool in order to assist you in locating an intermittent malfunction.

Test Description

The number below refers to the step number on the diagnostic table.

2. If the DTC sets without turning the steering wheel or driving the vehicle, a malfunction exists in the analog steering wheel position signal to the EBCM.

Step	Action	Values	Yes	No
1	Did you perform the Diagnostic System Check - Vehicle?	--	Go to Step 2	Go to Diagnostic System Check - Vehicle

LTV0500000006620

Fig. 176   Code C0455: Front Steering Position Sensor Circuit (Part 2 of 5). 2003–06 Express & Savana

Step	Action	Value	Yes	No
2	**Important:** Center the steering wheel before proceeding with this step. Do not rotate the steering wheel while performing this step. 1. Use the scan tool to clear the DTCs. 2. Turn OFF the ignition for 5 seconds. 3. Turn ON the ignition. 4. Wait approximately 5 seconds to verify whether or not the DTC sets. Does the DTC set?	--	Go to Step 3	Go to Step 10
3	1. Turn OFF the ignition. 2. Disconnect the steering wheel position sensor harness connector. 3. Turn ON the ignition. 4. Select the vehicle stability enhancement system (VSES) Data Display on the scan tool. 5. Observe the Analog SWPS Signal parameter on the scan tool. Does the scan tool indicate that the steering wheel position sensor data parameter is less than specified value?	0.15 V	Go to Step 4	Go to Step 9
4	1. Connect a 3-amp fused jumper wire between the steering wheel position 5-volt reference circuit and the analog steering signal circuit. 2. Observe the Analog SWPS Signal parameter on the scan tool. Does the scan tool indicate that the steering wheel position sensor data parameter is greater than specified value?	4.75 V	Go to Step 5	Go to Step 6
5	Use a DMM to measure the voltage between the steering wheel position 5-volt reference circuit and the steering wheel position low reference circuit. Does the voltage measure greater than the specified value?	4.75 V	Go to Step 16	Go to Step 8
6	Test the 5-volt reference circuit of the steering wheel position sensor for an open. Did you find and correct the condition?	--	Go to Step 19	Go to Step 7
7	Test the signal circuit of the steering wheel position sensor for an open or a short to ground. Did you find and correct the condition?	--	Go to Step 19	Go to Step 16
8	Test the low reference circuit of the steering wheel position sensor for an open. Did you find and correct the condition?	--	Go to Step 19	Go to Step 16

LTV0500000006621

Fig. 176   Code C0455: Front Steering Position Sensor Circuit (Part 3 of 5). 2003–06 Express & Savana

Step	Action	Value	Yes	No
9	Test the signal circuit of the steering wheel position sensor for a short to voltage. Did you find and correct the condition?	--	Go to Step 19	Go to Step 16
10	Operate the vehicle within the Conditions for Running the DTC as specified in the supporting text. Does the DTC set?	--	Go to Step 11	Go to Diagnostic Aids
11	1. Select the VSES Data Display on the scan tool. 2. Center the steering wheel and verify that the front wheels are straight ahead. 3. Observe the Analog SWPS Signal parameter. Does the scan tool display an Analog SWPS Signal within the specified range?	2.3-2.7 V	Go to Step 12	Go to Step 17

12	1. Turn OFF the ignition.
	2. Disconnect the steering wheel position sensor harness connector.
	3. Disconnect the electronic brake control module (EBCM) harness connector.
	4. Turn ON the ignition.
	5. Test the steering wheel position circuits, signal A and signal B for the following conditions:
	  - Intermittently open
	  - Intermittently shorted to ground
	  - Intermittently shorted together
	  - Intermittently shorted to voltage
	
	Did you find and correct the condition?
		--	Go to Step 19	Go to Step 13

13	Test the battery positive voltage circuit to the steering wheel position sensor for an intermittent open. Did you find and correct the condition?	--	Go to Step 19	Go to Step 14
14	Test both of the steering wheel position sensor ground circuits for an intermittent open. Did you find and correct the condition?	--	Go to Step 19	Go to Step 15
15	Inspect for poor connections at the harness connector of the steering wheel position sensor. Did you find and correct the condition?	--	Go to Step 19	Go to Step 17

LTV0500000006622

Fig. 176   Code C0455: Front Steering Position Sensor Circuit (Part 4 of 5). 2003–06 Express & Savana

Step	Action	Value	Yes	No
16	Inspect for poor connections at the harness connector of the EBCM. Did you find and correct the condition?	--	Go to Step 19	Go to Step 18
17	Replace the steering wheel position sensor. Did you complete the replacement?	--	Go to Step 19	--
18	**Important:** Following EBCM replacement, perform the setup procedure for the EBCM and perform the Yaw Rate Reference Table Reset Procedure. Use the scan tool to perform the Tire Size Calibration procedure. Replace the EBCM. Did you complete the replacement?	--	Go to Step 19	--
19	1. Use the scan tool Clear All Class 2 DTCs function to clear all of the DTCs from all modules. 2. Turn OFF the ignition for 5 seconds. 3. Turn ON the ignition. 4. Operate the vehicle within the Conditions for Running the DTC as specified in the supporting text. Does the DTC reset?	--	Go to Step 2	System OK

LTV0500000006623

Fig. 176   Code C0455: Front Steering Position Sensor Circuit (Part 5 of 5). 2003–06 Express & Savana

Circuit Description

The electronic brake control module (EBCM) performs several self-tests for any internal problems which may affect proper operation.

DTC Descriptor

This diagnostic procedure supports the following DTC:

DTC C0550 Electronic Control Unit (ECU) Performance

Conditions for Running the DTC

The ignition is ON.

Conditions for Setting the DTC

The EBCM detects an internal malfunction.

Action Taken When the DTC Sets

The following actions may occur:

- The EBCM disables the ABS/dynamic rear proportion (DRP).
- The ABS indicator turns ON.
- The brake warning indicator turns ON.

Conditions for Clearing the DTC

Certain failures that may cause this DTC to set cannot be cleared. Other failures that may cause this DTC to set may be cleared, at least temporarily, by using the scan tool Clear DTCs function.

Diagnostic Aids

Replace the EBCM if this DTC continues to set intermittently.

LTV0500000006624

Fig. 177   Code C0550: ECU Performance (Part 1 of 2). 2003–06 Express & Savana

Step	Action	Yes	No
1	Did you perform the Diagnostic System Check - Vehicle?	Go to Step 2	Go to Diagnostic System Check - Vehicle
2	Use a scan tool in order to clear the DTCs. Can the DTC be cleared?	Go to Step 3	Go to Step 4
3	1. Turn OFF the ignition. 2. Turn ON the ignition. Does the DTC reset?	Go to Step 4	Go to Diagnostic Aids
4	**Important:** Following electronic brake control module (EBCM) replacement, use the scan tool to perform the Tire Size Calibration procedure. Replace the EBCM. Did you complete the replacement?	Go to Step 5	--
5	1. Use the scan tool in order to clear the DTCs. 2. Operate the vehicle within the Conditions for Running the DTC as specified in the supporting text. Does the DTC reset?	Go to Step 3	System OK

LTV0500000006625

Fig. 177   Code C0550: ECU Performance (Part 2 of 2). 2003–06 Express & Savana

Test Description

The numbers below refer to the step numbers on the diagnostic table.

1. This step insures that the battery, and the vehicle primary power and ground systems are functioning correctly.

3. Lack of communication may be due to a particular malfunction of a serial data circuit. The information in Data Link References will provide a list of modules and the associated data network no communication diagnostic link.

4. A module that is operating in the incorrect power mode based on key position may cause other vehicle symptoms and/or DTCs to set. The information in Power Mode Mismatch will correct the condition before checking for module DTCs or symptoms.

8. This step insures that all data link communication DTCs are diagnosed before system level DTCs.

9. This step insures that all electronic control unit (ECU) internal DTCs are diagnosed before other system level DTCs.

10. This step insures that all device voltage DTCs are diagnosed before other system level DTCs.

Step	Action	Yes	No
1	Perform the following preliminary inspections: • Ensure that the battery is fully charged. • Ensure that the battery cables are clean and tight. • Inspect for any open fuses. • Inspect the easily accessible systems or the visible system components for obvious damage or conditions that could cause the symptom. • Ensure that the grounds are clean, tight, and in the correct location. • Inspect for aftermarket devices that could affect the operation of the system. • Search for applicable service bulletins. Did you find and correct the condition?	System OK	Go to Step 2

LTV0500000006476

Fig. 179   Diagnostic System Check (Part 1 of 4). 2003–06 Sierra & Silverado

Step	Action	Yes	No
6	Attempt to start the engine. Does the engine start and idle?	Go to Step 7	Go to Engine Cranks but Does Not Run
7	**Important:** Do not clear any DTCs unless instructed by a diagnostic procedure. Use the appropriate scan tool selections to obtain DTCs for each of the control modules. Does the scan tool display any DTCs?	Go to Step 8	Go to Step 12
8	Does the scan tool display any DTCs that begin with a "U"?	Go to Diagnostic Trouble Code (DTC) List - Vehicle	Go to Step 9
9	**Important:** If any of these DTCs are displayed, diagnose them before diagnosing any other DTCs or symptoms. Does the scan tool display DTC B1000, B1001, B1004, B1007, B1009, C0240, C0271, C0272, C0273, C0284, C0298, C0374, C0550, C0564, C0570, P0601, P0602, P0604, P0606, P060B, P0613, P061C, P062C, P062F, P064C, P0A1D, P1A00, P1A01, P1A02, P1A03, P1A04, P1A05, P1A06, P1A08, P1658, P1687, P1A64, P1A65, P1A66, P1A67, P1A68, P1A69, P1A6A, P1A6C, P2101, P2108, or P2610?	Go to Diagnostic Trouble Code (DTC) List - Vehicle	Go to Step 10

LTV0500000006478

Fig. 179   Diagnostic System Check (Part 3 of 4). 2003–06 Sierra & Silverado

Circuit Description

A replacement electronic brake control module (EBCM) is supplied with generic software and must be programmed to match the specific vehicle application.

DTC Descriptor

This diagnostic procedure supports the following DTC:

DTC C0558 Calibration Data Not Programmed

Conditions for Running the DTC

The ignition is ON.

Conditions for Setting the DTC

The EBCM is not programmed with complete software.

Action Taken When the DTC Sets

• The EBCM disables the ABS/dynamic rear proportion (DRP)/vehicle stability enhancement system (VSES).
• The ABS indicator turns ON.
• The brake warning indicator turns ON.
• The stability indicator turns ON.

Conditions for Clearing the DTC

The DTC clears when software programming is complete.

Step	Action	Yes	No
1	Did you perform the Diagnostic System Check - Vehicle?	Go to Step 2	Go to Diagnostic System Check - Vehicle
2	Perform the set-up procedure for the electronic brake control module (EBCM). Did you complete the action?	Go to Diagnostic System Check - Vehicle	--

LTV0500000006626

Fig. 178   Code C0558: Calibration Data Not Programmed. 2003–06 Express & Savana

Step	Action	Yes	No
2	Install a scan tool. Does the scan tool power up?	Go to Step 3	Check Scan Tool Does Not Power Up
3	1. Turn ON the ignition, with the engine OFF. 2. Attempt to establish communication with all of the control modules on the vehicle. Does the scan tool communicate with all of the expected vehicle control modules?	Go to Step 4	Go to Data Link References
4	**Important:** 1. To ensure that retained accessory power (RAP) mode is inactive, if equipped, open the drivers door during the following step. 2. The engine may start during the following step. Turn OFF the engine as soon as you have observed the crank power mode. 1. Access the Power Mode parameter on the scan tool. 2. Rotate the ignition switch (operate the ignition mode switch) through all positions while observing the Power Mode parameter. Does the Power Mode parameter reading on the scan tool match the ignition switch position for all switch positions?	Go to Step 5	Check Power Mode Mismatch
5	Attempt to start the engine. Does the engine crank?	Go to Step 6	Go to Symptom

LTV0500000006477

Fig. 179   Diagnostic System Check (Part 2 of 4). 2003–06 Sierra & Silverado

Step	Action	Yes	No
10	**Important:** If any of these DTCs are displayed, diagnose them before diagnosing any other DTCs or symptoms. Does the scan tool display DTC B1372, B1422, B139A, P0561, P0562, P0563, P0880, P0881, P0882, P0883, P0A8B, P0A8E, P1A22, P1A23, P1A24, P1A26, P1A27, P1A28, P1A2A, P1A2B, P1A2D, P1A2E, P1A2F, P1A30, P1A31, P1A32, P1A34, P1A35, P1A36, or P1AB2?	Go to Diagnostic Trouble Code (DTC) List - Vehicle	Go to Step 11
11	**Important:** If any of the remaining DTCs are powertrain DTCs, select Captured Info in order to store the powertrain DTC information with a scan tool. If multiple DTCs are stored, diagnose the DTCs in the following order 1. Component level DTCs, such as sensor DTCs, solenoid DTCs, and relay DTCs. 2. System level DTCs, such as misfire DTCs, evaporative emission (EVAP) system DTCs, and fuel trim DTCs. Diagnose the remaining DTCs.	Go to Diagnostic Trouble Code (DTC) List - Vehicle	--
12	Is the customers concern with inspection/maintenance (I/M) testing?	Go to Inspection/Maintenance (I/M) System Check	Go to Symptoms

LTV0500000006479

Fig. 179   Diagnostic System Check (Part 4 of 4). 2003–06 Sierra & Silverado

Circuit Description

As the wheels spin, each wheel speed sensor produces an AC signal. The electronic brake control module (EBCM) uses the frequency of the AC signals to calculate each wheel speed.

DTC Descriptors

This diagnostic procedure supports the following DTCs:

- DTC C0035 Left Front Wheel Speed Sensor Circuit
- DTC C0040 Right Front Wheel Speed Sensor Circuit

Conditions for Running the DTC

- The ignition is ON.
- The vehicle speed is greater than 13 km/h (8 mph).

Conditions for Setting the DTC

Any of the following occurrences may cause the DTC to set.

- The EBCM detects an open or shorted wheel speed sensor circuit for 500 milliseconds.
- The EBCM detects the absence of a wheel speed sensor signal for 5 seconds. If more than one absent wheel speed sensor signal is detected, the condition must be present for 120 seconds to set DTCs.
- The EBCM detects an erratic wheel speed sensor signal for 200 milliseconds.

Action Taken When the DTC Sets

- The EBCM disables the ABS and may disable the dynamic rear proportion (DRP) if more than one wheel speed sensor DTC is set.
- The ABS indicator turns ON.
- The brake warning indicator may turn ON.

The actions above are maintained during subsequent ignition cycles until the EBCM completes a power up self-test. This test concludes when the vehicle achieves a speed greater than 13 km/h (8 mph) and the wheel speeds are verified by the EBCM.

Conditions for Clearing the DTC

The Conditions for Setting the DTC are no longer present and you use the scan tool Clear DTCs function.

LTV0500000006480

Fig. 180 Codes C0035 Or C0040: Front Wheel Speed Sensor (Part 1 of 3). 2003–06 Sierra & Silverado

4	1. Slowly spin the wheel by hand. 2. Use a DMM in order to measure the AC voltage across the wheel speed sensor as the wheel spins. Does the AC voltage measure greater than the specified value?	100 mV	Go to Step 5	Go to Step 8
5	Inspect for poor connections at the harness connector of the wheel speed sensor. Did you find and correct the condition?	--	Go to Step 10	Go to Step 6
6	1. Disconnect from the EBCM, the harness connector containing the wheel speed sensor circuits. 2. Test the wheel speed sensor circuits for the following: - An open - A short to ground - A short to voltage - Shorted together Did you find and correct the condition?	--	Go to Step 10	Go to Step 7
7	Inspect for poor connections at the harness connector for the EBCM. Did you find and correct the condition?	--	Go to Step 10	Go to Step 9
8	Replace the wheel speed sensor. Did you complete the replacement?	--	Go to Step 10	--
9	**Important:** Use the scan tool in order to perform the Tire Size Calibration procedure. Replace the EBCM. Did you complete the replacement?	--	Go to Step 10	--
10	1. Use the scan tool in order to clear the DTCs. 2. Operate the vehicle within the Conditions for Running the DTC as specified in the supporting text. Does the DTC reset?	--	Go to Step 2	System OK

LTV0500000006482

Fig. 180 Codes C0035 Or C0040: Front Wheel Speed Sensor (Part 3 of 3). 2003–06 Sierra & Silverado

Diagnostic Aids

Thoroughly inspect connections or circuitry that may cause an intermittent malfunction.

If the customer's concern is that the ABS indicator is on only during humid conditions such as rain, snow, or vehicle wash, thoroughly inspect the wheel speed sensor circuits for signs of water intrusion. Use the following procedure in order to help isolate the problem area:

1. Spray the suspected area with a 5 percent salt water solution.
2. Operate the vehicle at a speed greater than 13 km/h (8 mph) for at least 30 seconds.

Repair or replace the suspect harness if the DTC sets.

Step	Action	Values	Yes	No
1	Did you perform the ABS Diagnostic System Check?	--	Go to Step 2	Go to Diagnostic System Check - Vehicle
2	1. Use a scan tool in order to clear the DTCs. 2. Operate the vehicle at a speed greater than the specified value. Does the DTC set?	13 km/h (8 mph)	Go to Step 3	Go to Diagnostic Aids
3	1. Turn OFF the ignition. 2. Raise and support the vehicle. 3. Disconnect the wheel speed sensor connector. 4. Use a DMM in order to measure the resistance across the wheel speed sensor. Does the resistance measure within the specified range?	700-10,000 ohms	Go to Step 4	Go to Step 8

LTV0500000006481

Fig. 180 Codes C0035 Or C0040: Front Wheel Speed Sensor (Part 2 of 3). 2003–06 Sierra & Silverado

Circuit Description

As the wheels spin, each wheel speed sensor produces an AC signal. The electronic brake control module (EBCM) uses the frequency of the AC signals to calculate each wheel speed.

Conditions for Running the DTC

- The ignition is ON.
- The vehicle speed is greater than 13 km/h (8 mph).

DTC Descriptors

This diagnostic procedure supports the following DTCs:

- DTC C0035 Left Front Wheel Speed Sensor Circuit
- DTC U0415 Left Front Wheel Speed Sensor Circuit (PHT)

Conditions for Setting the DTC

Any of the following occurrences may cause the DTC to set:

- The EBCM detects an open or shorted wheel speed sensor circuit for 500 milliseconds.
- The EBCM detects the absence of a wheel speed sensor signal for 5 seconds. If more than one absent wheel speed sensor signal is detected, the condition must be present for 120 seconds to set DTCs.
- The EBCM detects an erratic wheel speed sensor signal for 200 milliseconds.

Action Taken When the DTC Sets

- The EBCM disables the ABS and may disable the dynamic rear proportion (DRP) if more than one wheel speed sensor DTC is set.
- The ABS indicator turns ON.
- The brake warning indicator may turn ON.

The actions above are maintained during subsequent ignition cycles until the EBCM completes a power up self-test. This test concludes when the vehicle achieves a speed greater than 13 km/h (8 mph) and the wheel speeds are verified by the EBCM.

Conditions for Clearing the DTC

The Conditions for Setting the DTC are no longer present and you use the scan tool Clear DTCs function.

LTV0500000006486

Fig. 181 Codes C0035 Or U0415: LH Front Wheel Speed Sensor Circuit (Part 1 of 3). 2003–06 Sierra & Silverado

Diagnostic Aids

Thoroughly inspect connections or circuitry that may cause an intermittent malfunction.

If the customer's concern is that the ABS indicator is on only during humid conditions such as rain, snow, or vehicle wash, thoroughly inspect the wheel speed sensor circuits for signs of water intrusion. Use the following procedure in order to help isolate the problem area:

1. Spray the suspected area with a 5 percent salt water solution.
2. Operate the vehicle at a speed greater than 13 km/h (8 mph) for at least 30 seconds.

Repair or replace the suspect harness if the DTC sets.

Step	Action	Values	Yes	No
1	Did you perform the ABS Diagnostic System Check?	--	Go to Step 2	Go to Diagnostic System Check - Vehicle
2	1. Use a scan tool in order to clear the DTCs. 2. Operate the vehicle at a speed greater than the specified value. Does the DTC set?	13 km/h (8 mph)	Go to Step 3	Go to Diagnostic Aids
3	1. Turn OFF the ignition. 2. Raise and support the vehicle. 3. Disconnect the wheel speed sensor connector. 4. Use a DMM in order to measure the resistance across the wheel speed sensor. Does the resistance measure within the specified range?	700-10,000 ohms	Go to Step 4	Go to Step 8
4	1. Slowly spin the wheel by hand. 2. Use a DMM in order to measure the AC voltage across the wheel speed sensor as the wheel spins. Does the AC voltage measure greater than the specified value?	100 mV	Go to Step 5	Go to Step 8

LTV0500000006487

Fig. 181 Codes C0035 Or U0415: LH Front Wheel Speed Sensor Circuit (Part 2 of 3). 2003–06 Sierra & Silverado

Circuit Description

The powertrain control module (PCM) converts the signal from the vehicle speed sensor (VSS) to a 128 k pulses/mile signal. The electronic brake control module (EBCM) uses the vehicle speed signal from the PCM to calculate the rear wheel speed.

DTC Descriptor

This diagnostic procedure supports the following DTCs:

- DTC C0055 Rear Wheel Speed Sensor (Both Wheels) Circuit
- DTC C003D Rear Wheel Speed Sensor (Both Wheels) Circuit (PHT)

Conditions for Running the DTC

- The ignition is ON.
- The vehicle speed is greater than 13 km/h (8 mph).

Conditions for Setting the DTC

- The EBCM detects an open or shorted vehicle speed signal circuit for 500 milliseconds.
- The EBCM detects the absence of the vehicle speed signal for 5 seconds. If more than one absent wheel speed sensor signal is detected, the condition must be present for 120 seconds to set DTCs.
- The EBCM detects an erratic vehicle speed signal for 200 milliseconds.

Action Taken When the DTC Sets

- The EBCM disables the ABS/dynamic rear proportion (DRP).
- The ABS indicator turns ON.
- The brake warning indicator turns ON.

The actions above are maintained during subsequent ignition cycles until the EBCM completes a power up self-test. This test concludes when the vehicle achieves a speed greater than 13 km/h (8 mph) and the wheel speeds are verified by the EBCM.

Conditions for Clearing the DTC

The Conditions for Setting the DTC are no longer present and you use the scan tool Clear DTCs function.

LTV0500000006489

Fig. 182 Codes C0050 Or C003D: Rear Wheel Speed Sensor Circuit (Part 1 of 3). 2003–06 Sierra & Silverado

Step	Action	Values	Yes	No
5	Inspect for poor connections at the harness connector of the wheel speed sensor. Did you find and correct the condition?	--	Go to Step 10	Go to Step 6
6	1. Disconnect from the EBCM, the harness connector containing the wheel speed sensor circuits. 2. Test the wheel speed sensor circuits for the following conditions: - An open - A short to ground - A short to voltage - Shorted together Did you find and correct the condition?	--	Go to Step 10	Go to Step 7
7	Inspect for poor connections at the harness connector for the EBCM. Did you find and correct the condition?	--	Go to Step 10	Go to Step 9
8	Replace the wheel speed sensor. Did you complete the replacement?	--	Go to Step 10	--
9	**Important:** Use the scan tool in order to perform the Tire Size Calibration procedure. Replace the EBCM. Did you complete the replacement?	--	Go to Step 10	--
10	1. Use the scan tool in order to clear the DTCs. 2. Operate the vehicle within the Conditions for Running the DTC as specified in the supporting text. Does the DTC reset?	--	Go to Step 2	System OK

LTV0500000006488

Fig. 181 Codes C0035 Or U0415: LH Front Wheel Speed Sensor Circuit (Part 3 of 3). 2003–06 Sierra & Silverado

Diagnostic Aids

Thoroughly inspect connections or circuitry that may cause an intermittent malfunction.

Test Description

The numbers below refer to the step numbers on the diagnostic table.

3. This step tests for a voltage signal from the PCM.

4. This step tests for a missing or erratic vehicle speed signal from the PCM. An assistant may be required to perform this test.

Step	Action	Values	Yes	No
1	Did you perform the Diagnostic System Check - Vehicle?	--	Go to Step 2	Go to Diagnostic System Check - Vehicle
2	1. Use a scan tool in order to clear the DTCs. 2. Operate the vehicle at a speed greater than the specified value. Does the DTC set?	13 km/h (8 mph)	Go to Step 3	Go to Diagnostic Aids
3	1. Turn OFF the ignition. 2. Disconnect from the electronic brake control module (EBCM), the harness connector containing the vehicle speed signal circuit. 3. Turn ON the ignition. 4. Use a DMM in order to measure the DC voltage between the vehicle speed signal circuit and a good ground. Does the voltage measure greater than the specified value?	10 V	Go to Step 4	Go to Step 7
4	1. Raise and support the vehicle. 2. Place the transmission in neutral (N). 3. Set up the DMM in order to measure the DC voltage between the vehicle speed signal circuit and a good ground. 4. Slowly spin the rear wheels by hand for at least 30 seconds and while ensuring the driveshaft is rotating, observe the DMM. Does the voltage measure within the specified range for the entire time that the driveshaft is rotating?	5-7 V	Go to Step 5	Go to Step 7
5	Inspect for poor connections at the harness connector of the electronic brake control module (EBCM). Did you find and correct the condition?	--	Go to Step 10	Go to Step 6
6	Replace the EBCM. Did you complete the replacement?	--	Go to Step 10	--
7	Test the vehicle speed signal circuit for an open, a short to ground, or a short to voltage. Did you find and correct the condition?	--	Go to Step 10	Go to Step 8

LTV0500000006490

Fig. 182 Codes C0050 Or C003D: Rear Wheel Speed Sensor Circuit (Part 2 of 3). 2003–06 Sierra & Silverado

Step	Action	Yes	No
8	Inspect for poor connections at the harness connector of the powertrain control module (PCM). Did you find and correct the condition?	Go to Step 10	Go to Step 9
9	Replace the PCM. Did you complete the replacement?	Go to Step 10	--
10	1. Use the scan tool in order to clear the DTCs. 2. Operate the vehicle within the Conditions for Running the DTC as specified in the supporting text. Does the DTC reset?	Go to Step 3	System OK

LTV0500000006491

Fig. 182   Codes C0050 Or C003D: Rear Wheel Speed Sensor Circuit (Part 3 of 3). 2003–06 Sierra & Silverado

Step	Action	Yes	No
1	Did you perform the Diagnostic System Check - Vehicle?	Go to Step 2	Go to Diagnostic System Check
2	Use a scan tool in order to clear the DTCs. Does the DTC reset?	Go to Step 3	Go to Diagnostic Aids
3	1. Separate the electronic brake control module (EBCM) from the brake pedal modulator valve (BPMV). 2. Inspect for poor connections at the pump motor connector. Did you find and correct the condition?	Go to Step 5	Go to Step 4
4	**Important:** Following EBCM replacement, use the scan tool to perform the Tire Size Calibration procedure. 1. Replace the EBCM 2. Replace the BPMV. Did you complete the replacements?	Go to Step 5	--
5	1. Use a scan tool in order to clear the DTCs. 2. Operate the vehicle within the Conditions for Running the DTC as specified in the supporting text. Does the DTC reset?	Go to Step 3	System OK

LTV0500000006493

Fig. 183   Code C0110: Pump Motor Circuit (Part 2 of 2). 2003–06 Sierra & Silverado

Circuit Description

The brake switch informs the electronic brake control module (EBCM) when the brake is depressed. The brake switch is normally closed, supplying 12 volts to the EBCM when the brake is released. When the brake pedal is pressed, voltage on the torque converter clutch (TCC) brake switch signal circuit is 0 volts.

DTC Descriptor

This diagnostic procedure supports the following DTC:

DTC C0161 Antilock Brake System (ABS)/Traction Control System (TCS) Brake Switch

Conditions for Running the DTC

Any of the following conditions may cause the diagnostic trouble code (DTC) to run.

- The vehicle accelerates from 0 km/h (0 mph) to a speed greater than 56 km/h (35 mph).
- The vehicle experiences an ABS event involving all hydraulic circuits.

Conditions for Setting the DTC

Any of the following conditions may cause the DTC to set.

- Voltage on the TCC brake switch signal circuit is always low.
- Voltage on the TCC brake switch signal circuit is always high.

Action Taken When the DTC Sets

The EBCM stores this information-only DTC for as long as the condition is present.

Conditions for Clearing the DTC

The Conditions for Setting the DTC are no longer present and you use the scan tool Clear DTCs function.

Diagnostic Aids

Thoroughly inspect connections or circuitry that may cause an intermittent malfunction.

Test Description

The numbers below refer to the step numbers on the diagnostic table.

4. This step tests for a shorted stop lamp switch.

5. This step tests for an open stop lamp switch.

LTV0500000006494

Fig. 184   Code C0161: ABS/TCS Brake Switch (Part 1 of 3). 2003–06 Sierra & Silverado

Circuit Description

Ground is continuously supplied to the low side of the Antilock Brake System (ABS) pump motor. The electronic brake control module (EBCM) activates the ABS pump by supplying battery voltage to the high side of the motor.

DTC Descriptor

This diagnostic procedure supports the following DTC:

DTC C0110 Pump Motor Circuit

Conditions for Running the DTC

The ignition is ON.

Conditions for Setting the DTC

The EBCM detects an open pump motor circuit, a shorted pump motor, or a seized pump motor or ABS pump.

Action Taken When the DTC Sets

- The EBCM disables the ABS.
- The ABS indicator turns ON.

Conditions for Clearing the DTC

The Conditions for Setting the DTC are no longer present and you use the scan tool Clear DTCs function.

Diagnostic Aids

Separate the EBCM from the brake pressure modulator valve (BPMV) in order to inspect for corrosion or any other condition that may cause a poor connection at the pump motor connector.

LTV0500000006492

Fig. 183   Code C0110: Pump Motor Circuit (Part 1 of 2). 2003–06 Sierra & Silverado

Step	Action	Yes	No
1	Did you perform the Diagnostic System Check - Vehicle?	Go to Step 2	Go to Diagnostic System Check
2	1. Install a scan tool. 2. Select the 4WAL 3 Sensor Data Display function. 3. Observe the Brake Switch Status on the scan tool. Does the scan tool display OFF?	Go to Step 3	Go to Step 5
3	1. Apply the brake. 2. Observe the Brake Switch Status on the scan tool. Does the scan tool display ON?	Go to Diagnostic Aids	Go to Step 4
4	1. Turn OFF the ignition. 2. Disconnect the stop lamp switch. 3. Turn ON the ignition. 4. Observe the Brake Switch Status on the scan tool. Does the scan tool display ON?	Go to Step 9	Go to Step 7
5	1. Turn OFF the ignition. 2. Disconnect the stop lamp switch. 3. Connect a fused jumper wire between the ignition 3 voltage circuit and the torque converter clutch (TCC) brake switch signal circuit at the stop lamp switch harness connector. 4. Turn ON the ignition. 5. Observe the Brake Switch Status on the scan tool. Does the scan tool display OFF?	Go to Step 9	Go to Step 6
6	Test the ignition 3 voltage circuit and the TCC brake switch signal circuit for an open or a short to ground. Did you find and correct the condition?	Go to Step 12	Go to Step 8
7	Test the TCC brake switch signal circuit for a short to voltage. Did you find and correct the condition?	Go to Step 12	Go to Step 8

LTV0500000006495

Fig. 184   Code C0161: ABS/TCS Brake Switch (Part 2 of 3). 2003–06 Sierra & Silverado

Step	Action	Yes	No
8	Inspect for poor connections at the harness connector of the electronic brake control module (EBCM). Did you find and correct the condition?	Go to Step 12	Go to Step 10
9	Inspect for poor connections at the harness connector of the stop lamp switch. Did you find and correct the condition?	Go to Step 12	Go to Step 11
10	Replace the EBCM. Did you complete the replacement?	Go to Step 12	--
11	Replace the stop lamp switch. Did you complete the replacement?	Go to Step 12	--
12	1. Use the scan tool in order to clear the DTCs. 2. Operate the vehicle within the Conditions for Running the DTC as specified in the supporting text. Does the DTC reset?	Go to Step 2	System OK

LTV0500000006496

Fig. 184   Code C0161: ABS/TCS Brake Switch (Part 3 of 3). 2003–06 Sierra & Silverado

Circuit Description

The system relay, located within the electronic brake control module (EBCM), supplies battery voltage to all of the valve solenoids and to the ABS pump motor. When the relay contacts close, the EBCM monitors the voltage supplied to the valve solenoids and compares this voltage to monitored ignition voltage.

DTC Descriptor

This diagnostic procedure supports the following DTC:

DTC C0201 Antilock Brake System (ABS) Enable Relay Contact Circuit

Conditions for Running the DTC

The ignition is ON.

Conditions for Setting the DTC

The EBCM detects that the voltage supplied to the valve solenoids is less than 80 percent of monitored ignition voltage for 50 milliseconds.

Action Taken When the DTC Sets

- The EBCM disables the ABS/DRP.
- The ABS indicator turns ON.
- The brake warning indicator turns ON.

Conditions for Clearing the DTC

The Conditions for Setting the DTC are no longer present and you use the scan tool Clear DTCs function.

Diagnostic Aids

Refer back to the diagnostic table, steps 3-7, if this DTC continues to set intermittently.

Test Description

The number below refers to the step number on the diagnostic table.

3. A shorted ABS pump motor may damage the contacts within the system relay. It is imperative that the steps in the table be followed to prevent damage to a replacement EBCM.

LTV0500000006497

Fig. 185 Code C0201: ABS Enable Relay Contact Circuit (Part 1 of 2). 2003–06 Sierra & Silverado

Circuit Description

As the wheel spins, the wheel speed sensor produces an AC signal. The electronic brake control module (EBCM) uses the frequency of the AC signal to calculate the wheel speed.

DTC Descriptors

This diagnostic procedure supports the following DTCs:

- DTC C0221 Right Front Wheel Speed Sensor Circuit Open
- DTC C0222 Right Front Wheel Speed Signal Missing
- DTC C0223 Right Front Wheel Speed Signal Erratic
- DTC C0225 Left Front Wheel Speed Sensor Circuit Open
- DTC C0226 Left Front Wheel Speed Signal Missing
- DTC C0227 Left Front Wheel Speed Signal Erratic

Conditions for Running the DTC

C0221 and C0225

The ignition is ON.

C0222, C0223, C0226 and C0227

The vehicle speed is greater than 32 km/h (20 mph) when the brake is applied or 19 km/h (12 mph) when the brake is released.

Conditions for Setting the DTC

C0221 and C0225

The EBCM detects an open or shorted wheel speed sensor or wheel speed sensor circuit for 500 milliseconds.

LTV0500000006499

Fig. 186 Codes C0221–C0227: Front Wheel Speed Sensor Circuit (Part 1 of 4). 2003–06 Sierra & Silverado

Step	Action	Values	Yes	No
1	Did you perform the Diagnostic System Check - Vehicle?	--	Go to Step 2	Go to Diagnostic System Check
2	1. Use a scan tool in order to clear the DTCs. 2. Use the scan tool in order to perform an ABS Function Test. Does the DTC set?	--	Go to Step 3	Go to Diagnostic Aids
3	1. Separate the electronic brake control module (EBCM) from the brake pressure 1 modulator valve (BPMV). 2. Use a DMM in order to measure the resistance across the ABS pump motor. Does the resistance measure within the specified range?	0.3-1.0 ohms	Go to Step 4	Go to Step 6
4	Use a DMM in order to measure the resistance between the high side of the pump motor and a good ground. Does the resistance measure less than the specified value?	0L	Go to Step 6	Go to Step 5
5	Replace the EBCM. Did you complete the replacement?	--	Go to Step 7	--
6	**Important:** Following EBCM replacement, use the scan tool to perform the Tire Size Calibration procedure. 1. Replace the EBCM 2. Replace the BPMV Did you complete the replacements?	--	Go to Step 7	--
7	1. Use the scan tool in order to clear the DTCs. 2. Operate the vehicle within the Conditions for Running the DTC as specified in the supporting text. Does the DTC reset?	--	Go to Step 3	System OK

LTV0500000006498

Fig. 185 Code C0201: ABS Enable Relay Contact Circuit (Part 2 of 2). 2003–06 Sierra & Silverado

C0222 and C0226

The corresponding wheel speed sensor signal is less than 6 km/h (4 mph) for 5 seconds, or 120 seconds in order to set both DTCs.

C0223 and C0227

The EBCM detects an erratic signal from the corresponding wheel speed sensor for 105 milliseconds.

Action Taken When the DTC Sets

C0221, C0225

If equipped, the following actions occur:

- The EBCM disables the ABS/TCS.
- The ABS indicator turns ON.
- The TRACTION OFF indicator turns ON.

C0222, C0223, C0226, and C0227

If equipped, the following actions occur:

- The EBCM disables the ABS/TCS and may disable DRP.
- The ABS indicator turns ON.
- The TRACTION OFF indicator turns ON.
- The red Brake warning indicator may turn ON.

Conditions for Clearing the DTC

- Repair the condition responsible for setting the DTC.
- Use a scan tool in order to clear the DTC.
- After the DTC is cleared and the ignition is ON, the ABS indicator may remain ON until the EBCM completes a power-up self-test. This test concludes when the vehicle reaches a speed greater than 13 km/h (8 mph) and the wheel speeds are verified by the EBCM.

Diagnostic Aids

Operating the vehicle on extremely rough terrain can set DTC C0223, C0227 or C0229 even if the system is functioning normally.

Thoroughly inspect connections or circuitry that may cause an intermittent malfunction. Refer to Testing for Intermittent and Poor Connections , Connector Repairs , Testing for Electrical Intermittents and to Wiring Repairs in Wiring Systems.

If the customer's concern is that the ABS indicator is on only during humid conditions such as rain, snow or vehicle wash, thoroughly inspect the wheel speed sensor circuits for signs of water intrusion. Use the following procedure in order to help isolate the problem area:

1. Spray the suspected area with a 5 percent salt water solution.
2. Drive the vehicle at a speed greater than 19 km/h (12 mph) for at least 30 seconds.

Repair or replace the suspect harness if the DTC sets.

LTV0500000006500

Fig. 186 Codes C0221–C0227: Front Wheel Speed Sensor Circuit (Part 2 of 4). 2003–06 Sierra & Silverado

Test Description

The numbers below refer to the step numbers on the diagnostic table.

3. Measure the resistance of the wheel speed sensor in order to determine if the sensor has a valid resistance value.

4. Ensures that the wheel speed sensor is generating a valid AC voltage output.

Step	Action	Values	Yes	No
Important: If DTC C0229 is set, diagnose DTC C0229 before diagnosing any other wheel speed sensor DTCs.				
1	Did you perform the Diagnostic System Check - Vehicle?	--	Go to Step 2	Go to Diagnostic System Check
2	1. Use a scan tool in order to clear the DTCs. 2. Operate the vehicle at a speed greater than the specified value. Does the DTC set?	19 km/h (12 mph)	Go to Step 3	Go to Diagnostic Aids
3	1. Turn OFF the ignition. 2. Raise and support the vehicle. 3. Disconnect the wheel speed sensor connector. 4. Use a DMM in order to measure the resistance across the wheel speed sensor. Does the resistance measure within the specified range?	700-10,000 ohms	Go to Step 4	Go to Step 8
4	1. Spin the wheel by hand as fast as possible. 2. Use a DMM in order to measure the A/C voltage across the wheel speed sensor as the wheel spins. Does the A/C voltage measure greater than the specified value?	100 mV	Go to Step 5	Go to Step 8
5	Inspect for poor connections at the harness connector of the wheel speed sensor. Did you find and correct the condition?	--	Go to Step 10	Go to Step 6

LTV0500000006501

Fig. 186   Codes C0221–C0227: Front Wheel Speed Sensor Circuit (Part 3 of 4). 2003–06 Sierra & Silverado

Circuit Description

During an ABS event, the electronic brake control module (EBCM) calculates the total time that a dump valve is energized while attempting to unlock a locked wheel.

DTC Descriptor

This diagnostic procedure supports the following DTC:

DTC C0228 Left Front Antilock Brake System (ABS) Channel in Release Too Long

Conditions for Running the DTC

- The ignition is ON.
- The vehicle is experiencing an ABS event.

Conditions for Setting the DTC

The total dump time for any dump valve has exceeded 9 seconds and the EBCM has not received a wheel speed signal from the corresponding wheel during this activity.

Action Taken When the DTC Sets

- The EBCM disables the ABS/DRP.
- The ABS indicator turns ON.
- The brake warning indicator turns ON.

The actions above are maintained during subsequent ignition cycles until the EBCM completes a power up self-test. This test concludes when the vehicle achieves a speed greater than 13 km/h (8 mph) and the wheel speeds are verified by the EBCM.

Conditions for Clearing the DTC

The Conditions for Setting the DTC are no longer present and you use the scan tool Clear DTCs function.

Diagnostic Aids

The most likely cause of this DTC is a mechanical failure that causes a wheel to lock and remain locked. The DTC may also set, conceivably, when the ABS is activated on surfaces that are nearly impossible to get traction on. If the DTC sets within these conditions, diagnosis of the ABS system is not necessary.

Test Description

The number below refers to the step number on the diagnostic table.

2. Performing Solenoid Tests determines if there is a mechanical malfunction inside the brake pressure modulator valve (BPMV).

LTV0500000006503

Fig. 187   Code C0228: LH Front ABS Channel In Release Too Long (Part 1 of 2). 2003–06 Sierra & Silverado

Step	Action		Yes	No
6	1. Disconnect the electronic brake control module (EBCM) harness connector. 2. Test the wheel speed sensor circuits for the following: - An open - A short to ground - A short to voltage - Shorted together Refer to Circuit Testing and to Wiring Repairs in Wiring Systems. Did you find and correct the condition?		Go to Step 10	Go to Step 7
7	Inspect for poor connections at the harness connector for the EBCM. Did you find and correct the condition?		Go to Step 10	Go to Step 9
8	Replace the wheel speed sensor. Did you complete the replacement?		Go to Step 10	--
9	Replace the EBCM. Did you complete the replacement?		Go to Step 10	--
10	1. Use the scan tool in order to clear the DTCs. 2. Operate the vehicle within the Conditions for Running the DTC as specified in the supporting text. Does the DTC reset?		Go to Step 2	System OK

LTV0500000006502

Fig. 186   Codes C0221–C0227: Front Wheel Speed Sensor Circuit (Part 4 of 4). 2003–06 Sierra & Silverado

Step	Action	Yes	No
1	Did you perform the Diagnostic System Check - Vehicle?	Go to Step 2	Go to Diagnostic System Check
2	1. Use a scan tool in order to clear the DTCs. 2. Use the scan tool in order to perform the necessary Solenoid Tests. Do the Solenoid Tests show the system to be functioning normally?	Go to Diagnostic Aids	Go to Step 3
3	Replace the brake pressure modulator valve (BPMV). Did you complete the replacement?	Go to Step 4	--
4	Use the scan tool in order to perform the necessary Solenoid Tests. Do the Solenoid Tests show the system to be functioning normally?	System OK	Go to Step 3

LTV0500000006504

Fig. 187   Code C0228: LH Front ABS Channel In Release Too Long (Part 2 of 2). 2003–06 Sierra & Silverado

Circuit Description

As the wheel spins, the wheel speed sensor produces an AC signal. The electronic brake control module (EBCM) uses the frequency of the AC signal to calculate the wheel speed.

DTC Descriptor

This diagnostic procedure supports the following DTC:

DTC C0229 Drop Out of Both Front Speed Sensors

Conditions for Running the DTC

- The ignition is ON.
- The vehicle speed is greater than 32 km/h (20 mph) when the brake is applied or 19 km/h (12 mph) when the brake is released.

Conditions for Setting the DTC

The EBCM detects an erratic signal from both front wheel speed sensors for 105 milliseconds.

Action Taken When the DTC Sets

If equipped, the following actions occur:

- The EBCM disables the ABS/TCS/DRP.
- The ABS indicator turns ON.
- The TRACTION OFF indicator turns ON.
- The red brake warning indicator turns ON.

Conditions for Clearing the DTC

- Repair the condition responsible for setting the DTC.
- Use a scan tool in order to clear the DTC.
- After the DTC is cleared and the ignition is ON, the ABS indicator may remain ON until the EBCM completes a power-up self-test. This test concludes when the vehicle reaches a speed greater than 13 km/h (8 mph) and the wheel speeds are verified by the EBCM.

Diagnostic Aids

Operating the vehicle on extremely rough terrain can set DTC C0223, C0227 or C0229 even if the system is functioning normally.

Thoroughly inspect connections or circuitry that may cause an intermittent malfunction.

If the customer's concern is that the ABS indicator is on only during humid conditions such as rain, snow or vehicle wash, thoroughly inspect the wheel speed sensor circuits for signs of water intrusion. Use the following procedure in order to help isolate the problem area:

1. Spray the suspected area with a 5 percent salt water solution.
2. Drive the vehicle at a speed greater than 19 km/h (12 mph) for at least 30 seconds.

LTV0500000006505

Fig. 188 Code C0229: Drop Out Of Both Front Speed Sensors (Part 1 of 2). 2003–06 Sierra & Silverado

Circuit Description

The powertrain control module (PCM) converts the data from the vehicle speed sensor to a 128k pulses/mile signal. The electronic brake control module (EBCM) uses the vehicle speed signal from the PCM in order to calculate the rear wheel speed.

DTC Descriptors

This diagnostic procedure supports the following DTCs:

- DTC C0235 Rear Wheel Speed Signal Circuit Open
- DTC C0236 Rear Wheel Speed Signal Missing
- DTC C0237 Rear Wheel Speed Signal Erratic
- DTC P0609 Vehicle Speed Output Circuit 2

Conditions for Running the DTC

C0235

The ignition is ON.

C0236 and C0237

- The ignition is ON.
- The vehicle speed is greater than 32 km/h (20 mph) when the brake is applied or 19 km/h (12 mph) when the brake is released.

P0609

- The ignition is ON.
- The vehicle is not moving.

Conditions for Setting the DTC

C0235

The EBCM detects low voltage on the vehicle speed signal circuit for 500 milliseconds.

LTV0500000006507

Fig. 189 Code C0235–C0237 Or P0609: Rear Wheel Speed Sensor (Part 1 of 3). 2003–06 Sierra & Silverado

Step	Action	Yes	No
1	Did you perform the Diagnostic System Check - Vehicle?	Go to Step 2	Go to Diagnostic System Check
2	1. Use a scan tool in order to clear the DTCs. 2. Operate the vehicle within the Conditions for Running the DTC as specified in the supporting text. Does the DTC set?	Go to Step 3	Go to Diagnostic Aids
3	Inspect for poor connections at the harness connector of the electronic brake control module (EBCM). Did you find and correct the condition?	Go to Step 5	Go to Step 4
4	Replace the EBCM. Did you complete the replacement?	Go to Step 5	—
5	1. Use the scan tool in order to clear the DTCs. 2. Operate the vehicle within the Conditions for Running the DTC as specified in the supporting text. Does the DTC reset?	Go to Step 3	System OK

LTV0500000006506

Fig. 188 Code C0229: Drop Out Of Both Front Speed Sensors (Part 2 of 2). 2003–06 Sierra & Silverado

C0236

The rear wheel speed signal is less than 6 km/h (4 mph) for 5 seconds, or 120 seconds in order to set multiple missing sensor signal DTCs.

C0237

The EBCM detects an erratic rear wheel speed signal for 105 milliseconds.

P0609

The PCM detects low voltage on the vehicle speed signal circuit for 45 seconds.

Action Taken When the DTC Sets

If equipped, the following actions occur:

- The EBCM disables the ABS/TCS/DRP.
- The ABS indicator turns ON.
- The TRACTION OFF indicator turns ON.
- The red brake warning indicator turns ON.

Conditions for Clearing the DTC

- Repair the condition responsible for setting the DTC.
- Use a scan tool in order to clear the DTC.
- After the DTC is cleared and the ignition is ON, the ABS indicator may remain ON until the EBCM completes a power-up self-test. This test concludes when the vehicle reaches a speed greater than 13 km/h (8 mph) and the wheel speeds are verified by the EBCM.

Diagnostic Aids

Thoroughly inspect connections or circuitry that may cause an intermittent malfunction.

Test Description

The numbers below refer to the step numbers on the diagnostic table.

3. This step tests for a voltage signal from the PCM.

4. This step tests for a missing or erratic vehicle speed signal from the PCM. An assistant may be required to perform this test.

Step	Action	Values	Yes	No
1	Did you perform the Diagnostic System Check - Vehicle	--	Go to Step 2	Go to Diagnostic System Check

LTV0500000006508

Fig. 189 Code C0235–C0237 Or P0609: Rear Wheel Speed Sensor (Part 2 of 3). 2003–06 Sierra & Silverado

	Action		Yes	No
2	1. Use a scan tool in order to clear the DTCs. 2. Operate the vehicle at a speed greater than the specified value. Does the DTC set?	19 km/h (12 mph)	Go to Step 3	Go to Diagnostic Aids
3	1. Turn OFF the ignition. 2. Disconnect from the electronic brake control module (EBCM), the harness connector containing the vehicle speed signal circuit. 3. Turn ON the ignition. 4. Use a DMM in order to measure the DC voltage between the vehicle speed signal circuit and a good ground. Does the voltage measure greater than the specified value?	10 V	Go to Step 4	Go to Step 7
4	1. Raise and support the vehicle. 2. Place the transmission in neutral (N). 3. Set up the DMM in order to measure the DC voltage between the vehicle speed signal circuit and a good ground. 4. Spin the rear wheels as fast as possible by hand for at least 30 seconds and while ensuring the driveshaft is rotating, observe the DMM. Does the voltage measure within the specified range the entire time the driveshaft is rotating?	5-7 V	Go to Step 5	Go to Step 7
5	Inspect for poor connections at the harness connector of the EBCM. Did you find and correct the condition?	--	Go to Step 10	Go to Step 6
6	Replace the EBCM. Did you complete the replacement?	--	Go to Step 10	--
7	Test the vehicle speed signal circuit for an open, a short to ground or a short to voltage. Did you find and correct the condition?	--	Go to Step 10	Go to Step 8
8	Inspect for poor connections at the harness connector of the powertrain control module (PCM). Did you find and correct the condition?	--	Go to Step 10	Go to Step 9
9	Replace the PCM. Did you complete the replacement?	--	Go to Step 10	--
10	1. Use the scan tool in order to clear the DTCs. 2. Operate the vehicle within the Conditions for Running the DTC as specified in the supporting text. Does the DTC reset?	--	Go to Step 3	System OK

LTV0500000006509

Fig. 189 Code C0235–C0237 Or P0609: Rear Wheel Speed Sensor (Part 3 of 3). 2003–06 Sierra & Silverado

Step	Action	Yes	No
1	Did you perform the Diagnostic System Check - Vehicle?	Go to Step 2	Go to Diagnostic System Check
2	Inspect both of the front tires on the vehicle to ensure that both tires are of equal size. Are both of the front tires of equal size?	Go to Step 3	Go to Diagnostic Aids
3	Inspect both of the rear tires on the vehicle to ensure that both tires are of equal size. Are both of the rear tires of equal size?	Go to Step 4	Go to Diagnostic Aids
4	Verify the electronic brake control module (EBCM) and the powertrain control module (PCM) both have the correct tire size calibration. Use the scan tool in order to view the EBCM tire size calibration or perform the Tire Size Calibration procedure Did you find and correct the condition?	Go to Step 5	Go to Diagnostic Aids
5	1. Use a scan tool in order to clear the DTCs. 2. Operate the vehicle for at least 3 minutes within the Conditions for Running the DTC as specified in the supporting text. Does the DTC reset?	Go to Step 2	System OK

LTV0500000006511

Fig. 190 Code C0238: Wheel Speed Mismatch (Part 2 of 2). 2003–06 Sierra & Silverado

Circuit Description

As the front wheels spin, the wheel speed sensors (WSSs) produce an AC signal. The electronic brake control module (EBCM) uses the frequency of the AC signal to calculate the wheel speed. The powertrain control module (PCM) converts the data from the vehicle speed sensor (VSS) to a 128k pulses/mile signal. The EBCM uses the vehicle speed signal from the PCM in order to calculate the rear wheel speed.

DTC Descriptor

This diagnostic procedure supports the following DTC:

DTC C0238 Wheel Speed Mismatch

Conditions for Running the DTC

The ignition is ON and the vehicle speed is between 24 km/h (15 mph) and 80 km/h (50 mph).

Conditions for Setting the DTC

The EBCM detects that one wheel speed input is 10 percent greater than or 10 percent less than the other wheel speed inputs within 3.2 km (2 mi) of driving.

Action Taken When the DTC Sets

If equipped, the following actions occur:

- The EBCM disables the ABS/TCS/DRP.
- The ABS indicator turns ON.
- The TRACTION OFF indicator turns ON.
- The red brake warning indicator turns ON.

Conditions for Clearing the DTC

The conditions for setting the DTC are no longer present and you use the scan tool Clear DTCs function.

Diagnostic Aids

Installing one tire of significantly different size on the vehicle causes DTC C0238 to set. Operating the vehicle with a tire that has very low air pressure may also set this DTC. Inspect the vehicle for an incorrect or damaged wheel speed sensor or vehicle speed sensor if the tires and the EBCM and PCM calibrations are OK.

Test Description

The number below refers to the step number on the diagnostic table.

4. If the front tires are not the same size as the rear tires, the EBCM calibration must match the FRONT tire size and the PCM calibration must match the REAR tire size.

LTV0500000006510

Fig. 190 Code C0238: Wheel Speed Mismatch (Part 1 of 2). 2003–06 Sierra & Silverado

Circuit Description

The powertrain control module (PCM) and the electronic brake control module (EBCM) communicate on the serial data link whenever the ignition is ON.

DTC Descriptor

This diagnostic procedure supports the following DTC:

DTC C0240 EBCM Malfunction

Conditions for Running the DTC

- The ignition is ON.
- The engine is running at a speed greater than 450 RPM for 5-20 seconds.

Conditions for Setting the DTC

The EBCM receives a serial data message stating that the PCM has lost the ability to reduce engine torque.

Action Taken When the DTC Sets

- The EBCM disables the vehicle stability enhancement system (VSES).
- Engine torque reduction is disabled.
- The traction off indicator turns ON.
- The message center displays the service stability system or stability system disabled message.

Conditions for Clearing the DTC

The conditions for setting the DTC are no longer present and you use the scan tool Clear DTCs function.

Diagnostic Aids

A requested torque signal malfunction is only one possible cause for setting this DTC. DTC C0240 may set due to engine overheating, throttle actuator control failure, loss of ignition timing control by the PCM, etc. If DTC P0856 has not set, refer to Diagnostic System Check - Vehicle in Vehicle DTC Information in order to identify other possible causes of DTC C0240.

Step	Action	Values	Yes	No
1	Did you perform the Diagnostic System Check - Vehicle?	--	Go to Step 2	Go to Diagnostic System Check
2	Is DTC P0856 set?	--	Go to DTC C0298 or P0856	Go to Diagnostic Aids

LTV0500000006512

Fig. 191 Code C0240: EBCM Fault. 2003–06 Sierra & Silverado

Circuit Description

The ABS relay supplies battery voltage to 6 valve solenoids. The electronic brake control module (EBCM) microprocessor applies the grounds needed to activate each solenoid. The low side of each solenoid coil has a feedback circuit to the EBCM microprocessor. When a solenoid is commanded OFF, the feedback voltage is high. When a solenoid is commanded ON, the feedback voltage is low.

DTC Descriptors

This diagnostic procedure supports the following DTCs:

- DTC C0241 EBCM Control Valve Circuit
- DTC C0242 EBCM Control Valve Circuit
- DTC C0243 EBCM Control Valve Circuit
- DTC C0244 EBCM Control Valve Circuit
- DTC C0245 EBCM Control Valve Circuit
- DTC C0246 EBCM Control Valve Circuit
- DTC C0247 EBCM Control Valve Circuit
- DTC C0248 EBCM Control Valve Circuit
- DTC C0251 EBCM Control Valve Circuit
- DTC C0252 EBCM Control Valve Circuit
- DTC C0253 EBCM Control Valve Circuit
- DTC C0254 EBCM Control Valve Circuit

Conditions for Running the DTC

- The ignition is ON.
- The vehicle speed is greater than 6 km/h (4 mph).

Conditions for Setting the DTC

The EBCM detects an internal malfunction.

Action Taken When the DTC Sets

C0241, C0242, C0245, C0246, C0251, C0252, C0253, C0254

If equipped, the following actions occur:

- The EBCM disables the DRP/ABS.
- The ABS indicator turns ON.
- The red brake warning indicator turns ON.

C0243, C0244, C0247, C0248

If equipped, the following actions occur:

LTV0500000006513

Fig. 192 Codes C0241–C0254: EBCM Control Valve Circuit (Part 1 of 2). 2003–06 Sierra & Silverado

Circuit Description

As the wheels spin, each wheel speed sensor produces an AC signal. The electronic brake control module (EBCM) uses the frequency of the AC signals to calculate each wheel speed.

DTC Descriptor

This diagnostic procedure supports the following DTCs:

- DTC C0245 Wheel Speed Sensor Frequency Error
- DTC C0078 Wheel Speed Sensor Frequency Error (PHT)

Conditions for Running the DTC

- The ignition is ON.
- The vehicle speed is greater than 8 km/h (4 mph).
- No brake application or deceleration is detected.
- No wheel slip is detected.
- No turning maneuvers are detected.

Conditions for Setting the DTC

- At least one wheel speed sensor signal is 15 percent less than or greater than other wheel speed sensor signals.
- All of the Conditions for Running and Setting the DTC are present for a cumulative time of 3 minutes during a single ignition cycle.

Action Taken When the DTC Sets

- The EBCM disables the ABS/traction control system (TCS)/vehicle stability enhancement system (VSES)/dynamic rear proportion (DRP).
- The ABS indicator turns ON.
- The traction off indicator turns ON.
- The message center displays the service stability system message.
- The brake warning indicator turns ON.

Conditions for Clearing the DTC

The Conditions for Setting the DTC are no longer present and you use the scan tool Clear DTCs function.

Diagnostic Aids

Operating the vehicle with a tire that has very low air pressure may set this DTC.

LTV0500000006515

Fig. 193 Code C0245 Or C0078: Wheel Speed Sensor Frequency Error (Part 1 of 2). 2003–06 Sierra & Silverado

Step	Action	Yes	No
1	Did you perform the Diagnostic System Check - Vehicle?	Go to Step 2	Go to Diagnostic System Check
2	1. Use a scan tool in order to clear the DTCs. 2. Operate the vehicle within the Conditions for Running the DTC as specified in the supporting text. Does the DTC set?	Go to Step 3	Go to Diagnostic Aids
3	Replace the electronic brake control module (EBCM). Did you complete the replacement?	Go to Step 4	--
4	1. Use the scan tool in order to clear the DTCs. 2. Operate the vehicle within the Conditions for Running the DTC as specified in the supporting text. Does the DTC reset?	Go to Step 3	System OK

LTV0500000006514

Fig. 192 Codes C0241–C0254: EBCM Control Valve Circuit (Part 2 of 2). 2003–06 Sierra & Silverado

Step	Action	Yes	No
1	Did you perform the Diagnostic System Check - Vehicle?	Go to Step 2	Go to Diagnostic System Check - Vehicle
2	Inspect all of the tires on the vehicle to ensure that all of the tires are of equal size. Did you find and correct the condition?	Go to Step 4	Go to Step 3
3	Inspect the wheel speed sensors and tone rings for damage, incorrect application, or incorrect installation. Did you find and correct the condition?	Go to Step 4	Go to Diagnostic Aids
4	1. Use a scan tool in order to clear the DTCs. 2. Turn OFF the ignition for 5 seconds. 3. Turn ON the ignition. 4. Operate the vehicle for at least 3 minutes within the Conditions for Running the DTC as specified in the supporting text. Does the DTC reset?	Go to Step 2	System OK

LTV0500000006516

Fig. 193 Code C0245 Or C0078: Wheel Speed Sensor Frequency Error (Part 2 of 2). 2003–06 Sierra & Silverado

Circuit Description

The ABS relay supplies battery voltage to 6 valve solenoids. The electronic brake control module (EBCM) microprocessor applies the grounds needed to activate each solenoid. The low side of each solenoid coil has a feedback circuit to the EBCM microprocessor. When a solenoid is commanded OFF, the feedback voltage is high. When a solenoid is commanded ON, the feedback voltage is low.

DTC Descriptors

This diagnostic procedure supports the following DTCs:

- DTC C0265 EBCM Motor Relay Circuit
- DTC C0266 EBCM Motor Relay Circuit

Conditions for Running the DTC

- The ignition is ON.
- The vehicle speed is greater than 6 km/h (4 mph).

Conditions for Setting the DTC

The EBCM detects an internal malfunction.

Action Taken When the DTC Sets

C0265

If equipped, the following actions occur:

- The EBCM disables the DRP/ABS.
- The ABS indicator turns ON.
- The brake warning indicator turns ON.

C0266

If equipped, the following actions occur:

- The EBCM disables the ABS.
- The ABS indicator turns ON.

Conditions for Clearing the DTC

The conditions for setting the DTC are no longer present and you use the scan tool Clear DTCs function.

LTV0500000006517

Fig. 194 Codes C0265 Or C0266: EBCM Motor Relay Circuit (Part 1 of 3). 2003–06 Sierra & Silverado

Diagnostic Aids

Important

Whenever the EBCM is replaced for DTC C0265 or C0266, the ABS pump motor and motor circuitry must be tested for the proper resistance. Refer to steps 7 and 8 in the diagnostic table below for testing procedures and resistance values.

C0265

Thoroughly inspect connections and circuitry that may cause an intermittent malfunction.

C0266

Replace the EBCM if DTC C0266 continues to set intermittently.

Test Description

The numbers below refer to the step numbers on the diagnostic table.

4. This step tests if the battery positive voltage circuit can supply adequate power to the system relay.

7. A shorted ABS pump motor or shorted motor circuitry may damage the contacts within the system relay. Follow this step to prevent damage to a replacement EBCM.

Step	Action	Values	Yes	No
1	Did you perform the Diagnostic System Check - Vehicle?	--	Go to Step 2	Go to Diagnostic System Check
2	1. Use a scan tool in order to clear the DTCs. 2. Use the scan tool in order to perform an ABS Function Test. Does DTC C0266 set?	--	Go to Step 7	Go to Step 3

LTV0500000006518

Fig. 194   Codes C0265 Or C0266: EBCM Motor Relay Circuit (Part 2 of 3). 2003–06 Sierra & Silverado

Circuit Description

The EBCM applies the ground needed for pump motor activation. The low side of the pump motor has a feedback circuit to the EBCM. When the pump motor is commanded OFF and at rest, feedback voltage is high. When the pump motor is winding down after being commanded ON and then OFF, feedback voltage is low. The EBCM monitors this feedback voltage in order to determine if the motor is functioning properly.

DTC Descriptors

This diagnostic procedure supports the following DTCs:

- DTC C0267 Pump Motor Circuit Open
- DTC C0268 Pump Motor Circuit Shorted

Conditions for Running the DTC

- The ignition is ON.
- The vehicle speed is greater than 6 km/h (4 mph).

Conditions for Setting the DTC

The EBCM detects any of the following conditions:

- An open or shorted pump motor
- An open or shorted pump motor driver circuit
- A seized pump motor

Action Taken When the DTC Sets

- The EBCM disables the ABS.
- The ABS indicator turns ON.

Conditions for Clearing the DTC

The conditions for setting the DTC are no longer present and you use the scan tool Clear DTCs function.

Diagnostic Aids

Thoroughly inspect connections or circuitry that may cause an intermittent malfunction.

LTV0500000006520

Fig. 195   Codes C0267 Or C0268: Pump Motor Circuit Open/Shorted (Part 1 of 4). 2003–06 Sierra & Silverado

	Action	Values	Yes	No
3	Does DTC C0265 set?	--	Go to Step 4	Go to Diagnostic Aids
4	1. Turn OFF the ignition. 2. Disconnect from the electronic brake control module (EBCM), the harness connector containing the battery positive voltage circuit. 3. Connect a test lamp between the battery positive voltage circuit and a good ground. Does the test lamp illuminate?	--	Go to Step 6	Go to Step 5
5	Repair the open in the battery positive voltage circuit. Did you complete the repair?	--	Go to Step 11	--
6	Inspect for poor connections at the harness connector of the EBCM. Did you find and correct the condition?	--	Go to Step 11	Go to Step 7
7	**Important:** It may be necessary to separate the EBCM from the brake pressure modulator valve (BPMV) to gain access to the pump motor pigtail connector. 1. Disconnect from the EBCM, the ABS pump motor pigtail connector. 2. Use a DMM in order to measure the resistance across the ABS pump motor. Does the resistance measure within the specified range?	0.3-1.0 ohms	Go to Step 8	Go to Step 10
8	Use a DMM in order to measure the resistance between the high side of the pump motor and a good ground. Does the resistance measure less than the specified value?	0L	Go to Step 10	Go to Step 9
9	Replace the EBCM. Did you complete the replacement?	--	Go to Step 11	--
10	**Important:** Use the scan tool in order to perform the Tire Size Calibration procedure and the Trim Level Calibration procedure, if applicable. 1. Replace the EBCM 2. Replace the brake pedal modulator valve (BPMV) Did you complete the replacements?	--	Go to Step 11	--
11	1. Use the scan tool in order to clear the DTCs. 2. Operate the vehicle within the Conditions for Running the DTC as specified in the supporting text. Does the DTC reset?	--	Go to Step 2	System OK

LTV0500000006519

Fig. 194   Codes C0265 Or C0266: EBCM Motor Relay Circuit (Part 3 of 3). 2003–06 Sierra & Silverado

Test Description

The numbers below refer to the step numbers on the diagnostic table.

2. It is imperative that the vehicle be driven to attempt to reset the DTC. Using the scan tool to perform a function test may not produce the same result, and therefore may cause misdiagnosis of the vehicle.

7. This step tests if the electronic brake control module (EBCM) is capable of activating the ABS pump motor.

8. A shorted ABS pump motor may damage the EBCM. It is imperative that the steps in the table be followed in order to prevent damage to a replacement EBCM.

Step	Action	Values	Yes	No
1	Did you perform the Diagnostic System Check - Vehicle?	--	Go to Step 2	Go to Diagnostic System Check
2	1. Use a scan tool in order to clear the DTCs. 2. Operate the vehicle within the Conditions for Running the DTC as specified in the supporting text. Does DTC C0267 set?	--	Go to Step 6	Go to Step 3
3	Does DTC C0268 set?	--	Go to Step 4	Go to Diagnostic Aids

LTV0500000006521

Fig. 195   Codes C0267 Or C0268: Pump Motor Circuit Open/Shorted (Part 2 of 4). 2003–06 Sierra & Silverado

Step	Action		Yes	No
4	1. Turn OFF the ignition. 2. Disconnect from the electronic brake control module (EBCM), the 2-way harness connector which contains the battery positive voltage circuit and the ground circuit. **Caution: Before servicing any electrical component, the ignition key must be in the OFF or LOCK position and all electrical loads must be OFF, unless instructed otherwise in these procedures. If a tool or equipment could easily come in contact with a live exposed electrical terminal, also disconnect the negative battery cable. Failure to follow these precautions may cause personal injury and/or damage to the vehicle or its components.** 3. Disconnect the negative battery cable. 4. Disconnect the positive battery cable. 5. Place one lead of a DMM on the positive battery cable where the cable normally connects to the battery. 6. Place the other lead on the battery positive voltage circuit terminal within the 2-way EBCM harness connector. 7. Measure the total resistance between the positive battery cable and the EBCM. Does the resistance measure within the specified range?	0.0-0.2 ohms	Go to Step 5	Go to Step 10
5	Use a DMM to measure the resistance of the ground circuit. Does the resistance measure within the specified range?	0.0-0.2 ohms	Go to Step 7	Go to Step 11
6	**Important:** On some applications, it may be necessary to separate the EBCM from the brake pressure modulator valve (BPMV) in order to perform this test. Also, DTC C0268 may set when this test is performed. 1. Turn OFF the ignition. 2. Disconnect from the EBCM, the ABS pump motor pigtail connector. For systems which have no pump motor pigtail, it is necessary to separate the EBCM from the BPMV in order to gain access to the pump motor connector of the EBCM. 3. Use a connector adapter test kit in order to connect a test lamp between the ABS pump motor power and ground circuits at the pump motor connector of the EBCM. 4. Turn ON the ignition. 5. Use the scan tool in order to clear the DTCs. 6. Use the scan tool in order to perform an ABS Function Test. Does DTC C0267 set?	--	Go to Step 12	Go to Step 9

LTV0500000006522

Fig. 195   Codes C0267 Or C0268: Pump Motor Circuit Open/Shorted (Part 3 of 4). 2003–06 Sierra & Silverado

Circuit Description

The system relay is energized when the ignition is ON. The system relay supplies voltage to the valve solenoids and the pump motor. This voltage is referred to as the system voltage. The electronic brake control module (EBCM) microprocessor activates the valve solenoids by grounding the control circuit.

DTC Descriptors

This diagnostic procedure supports the following DTCs:

- DTC C0269 Excessive Dump Time
- DTC C0274 Excessive Isolation Time

Conditions for Running the DTC

- The ignition is ON.
- The vehicle is experiencing an ABS event.

Conditions for Setting the DTC

C0269

The EBCM commands a dump solenoid ON for 9 consecutive seconds.

C0274

The EBCM commands an isolation solenoid ON for 255 consecutive seconds.

Action Taken When the DTC Sets

If equipped, the following actions may occur:

- The EBCM disables the ABS/TCS/DRP.
- The ABS indicator turns ON.
- The TRACTION OFF indicator turns ON.
- The red brake warning indicator turns ON.

Conditions for Clearing the DTC

The conditions for setting the DTC are no longer present and you use the scan tool Clear DTCs function.

Diagnostic Aids

The most likely cause of DTC C0269 or DTC C0274 is a mechanical failure that causes a wheel to lock and remain locked. The DTCs may also set, conceivably, when the ABS is activated on surfaces that are nearly impossible to get traction on. If the DTC sets within these conditions, diagnosis of the ABS system is not necessary.

Test Description

The number below refers to the step number on the diagnostic table:

2. Performing solenoid tests determines if there is a mechanical malfunction inside the BPMV. Perform dump valve

LTV0500000006524

Fig. 196   Codes C0269 Or C0274: Excessive Dump/Isolation Time (Part 1 of 2). 2003–06 Sierra & Silverado

Step	Action		Yes	No
7	**Important:** On some applications, it may be necessary to separate the EBCM from the BPMV in order to perform this test. Also, DTC C0268 may set when this test is performed. 1. Reconnect both battery cables. 2. Disconnect from the EBCM, the ABS pump motor pigtail connector. For systems which have no pump motor pigtail, it is necessary to separate the EBCM from the BPMV in order to gain access to the pump motor connector of the EBCM. 3. Use a connector adapter test kit in order to connect a test lamp between the ABS pump motor power and ground circuits at the pump motor connector of the EBCM. 4. Turn ON the ignition. 5. Use the scan tool in order to clear the DTCs. 6. Use the scan tool in order to perform an ABS Function Test. Does the test lamp illuminate and then turn OFF when the Function Test is performed?	--	Go to Step 13	Go to Step 8
8	Use a DMM in order to measure the resistance across the ABS pump motor. Does the resistance measure within the specified range?	0.3-1.0 ohms	Go to Step 12	Go to Step 14
9	Inspect for poor connections at the pump motor pigtail connector. Did you find and correct the condition?	--	Go to Step 15	Go to Step 13
10	Repair the high resistance in the underhood electrical center or the battery positive voltage circuit. Did you complete the repair?	--	Go to Step 15	--
11	Repair the high resistance in the ground circuit. Did you complete the repair?	--	Go to Step 15	--
12	Replace the EBCM. Did you complete the replacement?	--	Go to Step 15	--
13	Replace the BPMV. Did you complete the replacement?	--	Go to Step 15	--
14	**Important:** Following EBCM replacement, use the scan tool perform the Tire Size Calibration procedure and the Trim Level Calibration procedure, if applicable. 1. Replace the EBCM 2. Replace the BPMV, refer to Brake Pressure Modulator Valve (BPMV) Replacement. Did you complete the replacements?	--	Go to Step 15	
15	1. Use a scan tool in order to clear the DTCs. 2. Operate the vehicle within the Conditions for Running the DTC as specified in the supporting text. Does the DTC reset?	--	Go to Step 3	System OK

LTV0500000006523

Fig. 195   Codes C0267 Or C0268: Pump Motor Circuit Open/Shorted (Part 4 of 4). 2003–06 Sierra & Silverado

Step	Action	Yes	No
1	Did you perform the Diagnostic System Check - Vehicle?	Go to Step 2	Go to Diagnostic System Check -
2	1. Use a scan tool in order to clear the DTCs. 2. Use the scan tool in order to perform the necessary Solenoid Tests. Do the Solenoid Tests show the system to be functioning normally?	Go to Diagnostic Aids	Go to Step 3
3	Replace the BPMV. Did you complete the replacement?	Go to Step 4	--
4	Use the scan tool in order to perform the necessary Solenoid Tests. Do the Solenoid Tests show the system to be functioning normally?	System OK	Go to Step 3

LTV0500000006525

Fig. 196   Codes C0269 Or C0274: Excessive Dump/Isolation Time (Part 2 of 2). 2003–06 Sierra & Silverado

Circuit Description

This DTC identifies a malfunction within the electronic brake control module (EBCM).

DTC Descriptors

This diagnostic procedure supports the following DTCs:

- DTC C0271 EBCM Malfunction
- DTC C0272 EBCM Malfunction
- DTC C0273 EBCM Malfunction
- DTC C0284 EBCM Malfunction

Conditions for Running the DTC

The ignition is ON.

Conditions for Setting the DTC

The EBCM detects an internal malfunction.

Action Taken When the DTC Sets

If equipped, the following actions may occur:

- The EBCM disables the ABS/TCS/DRP.
- The ABS indicator turns ON.
- The TRACTION OFF indicator turns ON.
- The red brake warning indicator turns ON.

Conditions for Clearing the DTC

The conditions for setting the DTC are no longer present and you use the scan tool Clear DTCs function.

Diagnostic Aids

Replace the EBCM if DTC C0273 or DTC C0284 continues to set intermittently.

LTV0500000006526

Fig. 197   Codes C0271–C0273 & C0284: EBCM Fault (Part 1 of 2). 2003–06 Sierra & Silverado

Circuit Description

The PCM sends engine/axle/tire IDs to the EBCM via serial data communications immediately after the modules are powered up.

DTC Descriptor

This diagnostic procedure supports the following DTC:

DTC C0279 Powertrain Configuration Not Valid

Conditions for Running the DTC

The ignition is ON.

Conditions for Setting the DTC

The EBCM receives invalid information from the PCM.

Action Taken When the DTC Sets

If equipped, the following actions occur:

- The EBCM disables the TCS.
- The traction off indicator turns ON.

Conditions for Clearing the DTC

The conditions for setting the DTC are no longer present and you use the scan tool Clear DTCs function.

Diagnostic Aids

Diagnose other ABS or TCS related DTCs prior to diagnosing DTC C0279.

If multiple TCS related DTCs are set, or the vehicle being serviced is not equipped with TCS, verify the correct EBCM is installed in the vehicle.

Test Description

The number below refers to the step number on the diagnostic table.

3. The PCM must have the correct part number for the specified application.

LTV0500000006528

Fig. 198   Code C0279: Powertrain Configuration Not Valid (Part 1 of 2). 2003–06 Sierra & Silverado

Step	Action	Yes	No
1	Did you perform the Diagnostic System Check - Vehicle?	Go to Step 2	Go to Diagnostic System Check
2	Is DTC C0271 or DTC C0272 set in the EBCM memory?	Go to Step 4	Go to Step 3
3	1. Use a scan tool in order to clear the DTCs. 2. Turn OFF the ignition for 5 seconds. 3. Turn ON the ignition. Does the DTC set?	Go to Step 4	Go to Diagnostic Aids
4	Replace the electronic brake control module (EBCM). Did you complete the replacement?	Go to Step 5	--
5	Use the scan tool in order to clear the DTCs. Operate the vehicle within the Conditions for Running the DTC as specified in the supporting text. Does the DTC reset?	Go to Step 2	System OK

LTV0500000006527

Fig. 197   Codes C0271–C0273 & C0284: EBCM Fault (Part 2 of 2). 2003–06 Sierra & Silverado

Step	Action	Yes	No
1	Did you perform the Diagnostic System Check - Vehicle?	Go to Step 2	Go to Diagnostic System Check -
2	1. Use a scan tool in order to clear the DTCs. 2. Turn OFF the ignition for 5 seconds. 3. Turn ON the ignition and wait 10 seconds. Does the DTC set?	Go to Step 3	Go to Diagnostics Aids
3	Verify the correct powertrain control module (PCM) is installed in the vehicle. Does the vehicle have the correct PCM?	Go to Step 4	Go to Step 6
4	Use the scan tool in order to read the Calibration IDs of the PCM. Are the PCM Calibration IDs correct?	Go to Diagnostics Aids	Go to Step 5
5	Perform the set up procedure for the PCM. Did you complete the action?	Go to Step 7	--
6	Replace the PCM. Did you complete the replacement?	Go to Step 7	--
7	1. Use the scan tool in order to clear the DTCs. 2. Operate the vehicle within the Conditions for Running the DTC as specified in the supporting text. Does the DTC reset?	Go to Step 3	System OK

LTV0500000006529

Fig. 198   Code C0279: Powertrain Configuration Not Valid (Part 2 of 2). 2003–06 Sierra & Silverado

Circuit Description

The stop lamp switch signal informs the electronic brake control module (EBCM) when the brake pedal is pressed.

DTC Descriptor

This diagnostic procedure supports the following DTC:

DTC C0281 Stoplamp Switch Circuit

Conditions for Running the DTC

Either of the following conditions will cause the DTC to run:

- The ignition is ON and the vehicle achieves at least 56 km/h (35 mph) before coming to a stop.
- The ignition is ON and the vehicle experiences an antilock brake system (ABS) event lasting at least 1 second.

Conditions for Setting the DTC

The EBCM detects an open or shorted brake switch or brake switch circuit.

Action Taken When the DTC Sets

This information-only DTC is stored in EBCM memory until it is cleared by using the specified procedure.

Conditions for Clearing the DTC

The conditions for setting the DTC are no longer present and you use the scan tool Clear DTCs function.

Diagnostic Aids

Thoroughly inspect connections or circuitry that may cause an intermittent malfunction. Refer to Testing for Electrical Intermittents , Testing for Intermittent and Poor Connections , Wiring Repairs and Connector Repairs in Wiring Systems.

Test Description

The numbers below refer to the step numbers on the diagnostic table.

4. This step tests for a shorted stop lamp switch.

5. This step tests for an open stop lamp switch.

LTV0500000006530

Fig. 199   Code C0281: Stoplamp Switch Circuit (Part 1 of 3). 2003–06 Sierra & Silverado

Step	Action	Yes	No
1	Did you perform the Diagnostic System Check - Vehicle?	Go to Step 2	Go to Diagnostic System Check
2	1. Install a scan tool. 2. Select the 4WAL 3 Sensor Data Display function. 3. Observe the Brake Switch Status on the scan tool. Does the scan tool display OFF?	Go to Step 3	Go to Step 5
3	1. Apply the brake. 2. Observe the Brake Switch Status on the scan tool. Does the scan tool display ON?	Go to Diagnostic Aids	Go to Step 4
4	1. Turn OFF the ignition. 2. Disconnect the stop lamp switch. 3. Turn ON the ignition. 4. Observe the Brake Switch Status on the scan tool. Does the scan tool display ON?	Go to Step 9	Go to Step 7
5	1. Turn OFF the ignition. 2. Disconnect the stop lamp switch. 3. Connect a fused jumper wire between the ignition 3 voltage circuit and the torque converter clutch (TCC) brake switch signal circuit at the stop lamp switch harness connector. 4. Turn ON the ignition. 5. Observe the Brake Switch Status on the scan tool. Does the scan tool display OFF?	Go to Step 9	Go to Step 6
6	Test the ignition 3 voltage circuit and the TCC brake switch signal circuit for an open or a short to ground. Did you find and correct the condition?	Go to Step 12	Go to Step 8
7	Test the TCC brake switch signal circuit for a short to voltage. Did you find and correct the condition?	Go to Step 12	Go to Step 8

LTV0500000006531

Fig. 199 Code C0281: Stoplamp Switch Circuit (Part 2 of 3). 2003–06 Sierra & Silverado

Circuit Description

The traction control switch is a momentary-contact, normally-open switch that can be used to disable the traction control system (TCS). Each time the traction control switch is pressed, the TCS enabled/disabled status changes. When TCS is disabled, the electronic brake control module (EBCM) illuminates the traction off indicator by opening the service traction control signal circuit.

DTC Descriptor

This diagnostic procedure supports the following DTC:

DTC C0283 Mode Switch Circuit Malfunction

Conditions for Running the DTC

- The ignition is ON.
- The engine is running at a rate greater than 450 RPM.

Conditions for Setting the DTC

The EBCM detects low voltage on the traction control switch signal circuit for 10 seconds.

Action Taken When the DTC Sets

If equipped, the following actions occur:

- The EBCM disables the TCS.
- The traction off indicator turns ON.

Conditions for Clearing the DTC

The conditions for setting the DTC are no longer present and you use the scan tool Clear DTCs function.

Diagnostic Aids

Thoroughly inspect connections or circuitry that may cause an intermittent malfunction.

LTV0500000006533

Fig. 200 Code C0283: Mode Switch Circuit Fault (Part 1 of 3). 2003–06 Sierra & Silverado

Step	Action	Yes	No
8	Inspect for poor connections at the harness connector of the electronic brake control module (EBCM). Did you find and correct the condition?	Go to Step 12	Go to Step 10
9	Inspect for poor connections at the harness connector of the stop lamp switch. Did you find and correct the condition?	Go to Step 12	Go to Step 11
10	Replace the EBCM. Did you complete the replacement?	Go to Step 12	--
11	Replace the stop lamp switch. Did you complete the replacement?	Go to Step 12	--
12	1. Use the scan tool in order to clear the DTCs. 2. Operate the vehicle within the Conditions for Running the DTC as specified in the supporting text. Does the DTC reset?	Go to Step 2	System OK

LTV0500000006532

Fig. 199 Code C0281: Stoplamp Switch Circuit (Part 3 of 3). 2003–06 Sierra & Silverado

Test Description

The number below refers to the step number on the diagnostic table.

4. This step tests the traction control switch circuitry. If the fuse opens when you perform this test, the traction control switch signal circuit is shorted to ground.

Step	Action	Yes	No
1	Did you perform the Diagnostic System Check - Vehicle?	Go to Step 2	Go to Diagnostic System Check
2	1. Use a scan tool in order to clear the DTCs. 2. Turn OFF the ignition for 5 seconds. 3. Start the engine and allow the engine to run for at least 20 seconds. Does the DTC set?	Go to Step 3	Go to Diagnostic Aids
3	1. Turn OFF the ignition. 2. Disconnect the traction control switch harness connector. Refer to Traction Control Switch Replacement. 3. Turn ON the ignition. 4. Connect a test lamp between the ignition 1 voltage circuit and a good ground. Does the test lamp illuminate?	Go to Step 4	Go to Step 8
4	1. Use the scan tool in order to clear the DTCs. 2. Turn OFF the ignition. 3. Connect a fused jumper wire between the ignition 1 voltage circuit and the traction control switch signal circuit at the traction control switch harness connector. 4. Start the engine and allow the engine to run for at least 20 seconds. Does the DTC set?	Go to Step 5	Go to Step 9
5	Test the traction control switch signal circuit for an open or a short to ground. Did you find and correct the condition?	Go to Step 11	Go to Step 6
6	Inspect for poor connections at the harness connector of the electronic brake control module (EBCM). Did you find and correct the condition?	Go to Step 11	Go to Step 7

LTV0500000006534

Fig. 200 Code C0283: Mode Switch Circuit Fault (Part 2 of 3). 2003–06 Sierra & Silverado

Step	Action	Yes	No
7	Replace the EBCM. Did you complete the replacement?	Go to Step 11	--
8	Repair the open in the ignition 1 voltage circuit. Did you complete the repair?	Go to Step 11	--
9	Inspect for poor connections at the harness connector of the traction control switch. Did you find and correct the condition?	Go to Step 11	Go to Step 10
10	Replace the traction control switch. Did you complete the replacement?	Go to Step 11	--
11	1. Use the scan tool in order to clear the DTCs. 2. Operate the vehicle within the Conditions for Running the DTC as specified in the supporting text. Does the DTC reset?	Go to Step 3	System OK

LTV0500000006535

Fig. 200 Code C0283: Mode Switch Circuit Fault (Part 3 of 3). 2003–06 Sierra & Silverado

Circuit Description

The EBCM supplies 5 VDC to the powertrain control module (PCM) on the delivered torque signal circuit. The PCM toggles this voltage to ground in order to create the delivered torque signal at the EBCM. A signal with a frequency of 128 Hz +/- 5 percent and a duty cycle of 25-95 percent is a valid delivered torque signal. The percentage of duty cycle is proportionate to the percentage of delivered torque.

DTC Descriptors

This diagnostic procedure supports the following DTCs:

- DTC C0287 Delivered Torque Signal Malfunction
- DTC P1644 Traction Control Delivered Torque Output Circuit
- DTC P1689 Traction Control Delivered Torque Output Circuit

Conditions for Running the DTC

- The ignition is ON.
- The engine is running at a speed greater than 450 RPM for 1 second.

Conditions for Setting the DTC

C0287

The EBCM receives an invalid delivered torque signal for 300 milliseconds.

P1689

The PCM detects the delivered torque signal voltage as being less than 4.75 volts or greater than 5.25 volts.

Action Taken When the DTC Sets

- The EBCM disables the TCS.
- The traction off indicator turns ON.

Conditions for Clearing the DTC

The conditions for setting the DTC are no longer present and you use the scan tool Clear DTCs function.

Diagnostic Aids

Thoroughly inspect connections or circuitry that may cause an intermittent malfunction.

Test Description

The numbers below refer to the step numbers on the diagnostic table.

LTV0500000006536

Fig. 201 Codes C0287, P0644 Or P1689: Delivered Torque Signal Fault (Part 1 of 3). 2003–06 Sierra & Silverado

Step	Action	Values	Yes	No
6	1. Turn OFF the ignition. 2. Install a J 39700 100-pin breakout box using a J 39700-325 breakout box adaptor. Install the equipment between the EBCM and the EBCM harness connector. 3. Start the engine. 4. Use a DMM in order to measure the Hz frequency of the delivered torque signal. Does the frequency of the delivered torque signal measure within the specified range?	121-134 Hz	Go to Step 7	Go to Step 9
7	1. Turn OFF the ignition. 2. Inspect for poor connections at the harness connector of the electronic brake control module (EBCM). Did you find and correct the condition?	--	Go to Step 12	Go to Step 8
8	Replace the EBCM. Did you complete the replacement?	--	Go to Step 12	--
9	1. Turn ON the ignition. 2. Test the delivered torque signal circuit for a short to voltage. Did you find and correct the condition?	--	Go to Step 12	Go to Step 10
10	Inspect for poor connections at the harness connector of the PCM. Did you find and correct the condition?	--	Go to Step 12	Go to Step 11
11	Replace the PCM. Did you complete the replacement?	--	Go to Step 12	--
12	1. Use the scan tool in order to clear the DTCs. 2. Operate the vehicle within the Conditions for Running the DTC as specified in the supporting text. Does the DTC reset?	--	Go to Step 3	System OK

LTV0500000006538

Fig. 201 Codes C0287, P0644 Or P1689: Delivered Torque Signal Fault (Part 3 of 3). 2003–06 Sierra & Silverado

Step	Action	Values	Yes	No
1	Did you perform the Diagnostic System Check - Vehicle?	--	Go to Step 2	Go to Diagnostic System Check
2	1. Use the scan tool in order to clear the DTCs. 2. Operate the vehicle within the Conditions for Running the DTC as specified in the supporting text. Does the DTC set?		Go to Step 3	Go to Diagnostic Aids
3	1. Turn OFF the ignition. 2. Disconnect from the powertrain control module (PCM), the harness connector containing the delivered torque signal circuit. 3. Turn ON the ignition. 4. Use a DMM in order to measure the voltage between the delivered torque signal circuit and a good ground. Does the voltage measure within the specified range?	4.75-5.25 V	Go to Step 5	Go to Step 4
4	Test the delivered torque signal circuit for an open, a short to voltage or a short to ground. Did you find and correct the condition?	--	Go to Step 12	Go to Step 7
5	1. Turn OFF the ignition. 2. Reconnect the PCM harness connector. 3. Start the engine. 4. Select the Traction Assist Data Display on the scan tool. 5. Observe the Delivered Torque parameter on the scan tool. Is the duty cycle of the delivered torque signal is within the specified range?	25-95%	Go to Step 6	Go to Step 9

LTV0500000006537

Fig. 201 Codes C0287, P0644 Or P1689: Delivered Torque Signal Fault (Part 2 of 3). 2003–06 Sierra & Silverado

Circuit Description

The powertrain control module (PCM) sends a state of health message to the EBCM within 5.5 seconds after the modules are powered up. This message is sent via serial data communications.

DTC Descriptors

This diagnostic procedure supports the following DTC:

- DTC C0290 Class 2 Data Link Malfunction
- DTC C0292 Lost Communication With Engine Control System

Conditions for Running the DTC

The ignition is ON.

Conditions for Setting the DTC

The EBCM fails to receive serial data from the PCM.

Action Taken When the DTC Sets

If equipped, the following actions occur:

- The EBCM disables the TCS.
- The traction off indicator turns ON.

Conditions for Clearing the DTC

The conditions for setting the DTC are no longer present and you use the scan tool Clear DTCs function.

Step	Action	Yes	No
1	Did you perform the Diagnostic System Check - Vehicle?	Check Scan Tool Does Not Communicate with Class 2 Device	Go to Diagnostic System Check

LTV0500000006539

Fig. 202 Codes C0290 Or C0292: Data Link Fault. 2003–06 Sierra & Silverado

Circuit Description

The body control module (BCM) sends a state of health serial data message to the electronic brake control module (EBCM) within 5.5 seconds after the ignition is turned ON.

DTC Descriptor

This diagnostic procedure supports the following DTC:

DTC C0291 Body Control Module (BCM) Configuration Not Valid

Conditions for Running the DTC

The ignition is ON.

Conditions for Setting the DTC

The EBCM fails to receive serial data from the BCM.

Action Taken When the DTC Sets

The EBCM sets this information-only DTC as a current DTC for as long as the conditions for setting the DTC are present.

Conditions for Clearing the DTC

The conditions for setting the DTC are no longer present and you use the scan tool Clear DTCs function.

Step	Action	Yes	No
1	Did you perform the Diagnostic System Check - Vehicle?	Check Scan Tool Does Not Communicate with Class 2 Device	Go to Diagnostic System Check

LTV0500000006540

Fig. 203 Code C0291: BCM Configuration Not Valid. 2003–06 Sierra & Silverado

Circuit Description

C0298

The powertrain control module (PCM) and the electronic brake control module (EBCM) communicate on the serial data link whenever the ignition is ON.

P0856

The PCM supplies 5 volts through an internal resistor, to the EBCM on the requested torque signal circuit. The EBCM toggles this voltage to ground to create the requested torque signal at the PCM.

DTC Descriptors

This diagnostic procedure supports the following DTCs:

- DTC C0298 Powertrain Control Malfunction
- DTC P0856 Traction Control Torque Request Circuit

Conditions for Running the DTC

C0298

The ignition is ON.

P0856

- The ignition is ON.
- The engine is running at a speed greater than 450 RPM for 5-20 seconds.

LTV0500000006542

Fig. 205 Code C0298 Or P0856: Powertrain Control Fault (Part 1 of 4). 2003–06 Sierra & Silverado

Circuit Description

The PCM sends engine/axle/tire IDs to the EBCM via serial data communications immediately after the modules are powered up.

DTC Descriptor

This diagnostic procedure supports the following DTC:

DTC C0297 Powertrain Configuration Data Not Received

Conditions for Running the DTC

The ignition is ON.

Conditions for Setting the DTC

The EBCM fails to receive serial data from the PCM.

Action Taken When the DTC Sets

If equipped, the following actions occur:

- The EBCM disables the TCS.
- The traction off indicator turns ON.

Conditions for Clearing the DTC

The conditions for setting the DTC are no longer present and you use the scan tool Clear DTCs function.

Step	Action	Yes	No
1	Did you perform the Diagnostic System Check - Vehicle?	Check Scan Tool Does Not Communicate with Class 2 Device	Go to Diagnostic System Check

LTV0500000006541

Fig. 204 Code C0297: Powertrain Configuration Data Not Received. 2003–06 Sierra & Silverado

Conditions for Setting the DTC

C0298

The EBCM receives a serial data message stating that the PCM has lost the ability to reduce engine torque.

P0856

The PCM receives an invalid requested torque signal for 3 seconds.

Action Taken When the DTC Sets

C0298

- The EBCM disables the traction control system (TCS).
- The traction off indicator turns ON.

P0856

- The PCM sends a serial data message to the EBCM stating that the PCM has lost the ability to reduce engine torque.
- The EBCM sets DTC C0298 as a current DTC for as long as the malfunction is present.

Conditions for Clearing the DTC

C0298

The conditions for setting the DTC are no longer present and you use the scan tool Clear DTCs function.

P0856

- The conditions for setting the DTC are no longer present and you use the scan tool Clear DTCs function.
- A history DTC clears automatically after 40 consecutive warm-up cycles without a PCM detected failure.

Diagnostic Aids

C0298

A requested torque signal malfunction is only one possible cause for the PCM to lose the ability to perform traction control. DTC C0298 may set due to engine overheating, throttle actuator control failure, loss of ignition timing control by the PCM, etc. If DTC P0856 has not set, refer to Diagnostic System Check - Engine Controls in Engine Controls in order to identify other possible causes of DTC C0298.

P0856

Thoroughly inspect connections or circuitry that may cause an intermittent malfunction. Refer to following:

LTV0500000006543

Fig. 205 Code C0298 Or P0856: Powertrain Control Fault (Part 2 of 4). 2003–06 Sierra & Silverado

ANTI-LOCK BRAKES

Test Description

The numbers below refer to the step numbers on the diagnostic table.

4. This step tests for voltage supplied to the EBCM from the PCM.

5. This step tests for a shorted resistor in the PCM or a short to voltage within the requested torque circuit by verifying that a large voltage drop occurs when a test lamp is connected in parallel with the DMM.

Step	Action	Values	Yes	No
1	Did you perform the Diagnostic System Check - Vehicle?	--	Go to Step 2	Go to Diagnostic System Check - Vehicle
2	If DTCs set for the Parallel Hybrid Truck (PHT), C0035 or U0415, C0055 or C003D, C0245 or C0078, and C0550 or C0570, diagnose these DTC first. Is only DTC P0856 set?	--	Go to Step 3	Go to Diagnostic Aids
3	1. Use a scan tool in order to clear the DTCs. 2. Operate the vehicle within the Conditions for Running the DTC as specified in the supporting text. 3. Does DTC P0856 set?	--	Go to Step 4	Go to Diagnostic Aids
4	1. Turn OFF the ignition. 2. Disconnect from the electronic brake control module (EBCM), the harness connector containing the requested torque signal circuit. 3. Turn ON the ignition. 4. Use a DMM in order to measure the voltage between the requested torque signal circuit and a good ground. Does the voltage measure greater than the specified value?	4.75 V	Go to Step 5	Go to Step 8
5	1. With the DMM still connected to monitor the requested torque signal circuit, connect one end of a test lamp to a good ground. 2. Connect the other end of the test lamp to the positive lead of the DMM. Does the voltage measure less than the specified value?	0.15 V	Go to Step 6	Go to Step 9

LTV0500000006544

Fig. 205 Code C0298 Or P0856: Powertrain Control Fault (Part 3 of 4). 2003–06 Sierra & Silverado

Circuit Description

The electronic brake control module (EBCM) performs several self-tests for any internal problems which may affect proper operation.

DTC Descriptor

This diagnostic procedure supports the following DTCs:

- DTC C0550 Electronic Control Unit (ECU) Performance
- DTC C0570 Electronic Control Unit (ECU) Performance (PHT)

Conditions for Running the DTC

- The ignition is ON.
- The engine is running at a rate greater than 450 RPM.

Conditions for Setting the DTC

The EBCM detects an internal malfunction.

Action Taken When the DTC Sets

The following actions may occur:

- The EBCM disables the antilock brake system (ABS)/dynamic rear proportion (DRP).
- The ABS indicator turns ON.
- The brake warning indicator turns ON.

Conditions for Clearing the DTC

Certain failures that may cause this DTC to set cannot be cleared. Other failures that may cause this DTC to set may be cleared, at least temporarily, by using the scan tool Clear DTCs function.

Diagnostic Aids

Replace the EBCM if this DTC continues to set intermittently.

LTV0500000006546

Fig. 206 Codes C0550 Or C0570: ECU Performance (Part 1 of 2). 2003–06 Sierra & Silverado

Step	Action	Yes	No
1	Did you perform the Diagnostic System Check - Vehicle?	Go to Step 2	Go to Diagnostic System Check - Vehicle
2	Use a scan tool in order to clear the DTCs. Can the DTC be cleared?	Go to Step 3	Go to Step 4
3	Start the engine and allow the engine to idle. Does the DTC reset?	Go to Step 4	Go to Diagnostic Aids
4	Replace the electronic brake control module (EBCM). Did you complete the replacement?	Go to Step 5	--
5	1. Use the scan tool in order to clear the DTCs. 2. Operate the vehicle within the Conditions for Running the DTC as specified in the supporting text. Does the DTC reset?	Go to Step 3	System OK

LTV0500000006547

Fig. 206 Codes C0550 Or C0570: ECU Performance (Part 2 of 2). 2003–06 Sierra & Silverado

Step	Action	Values	Yes	No
6	1. Turn OFF the ignition. 2. Install a J 39700 Universal Breakout Box and a J 39700-325 Adapter Cable. Install the equipment between the EBCM and the EBCM harness connector. 3. Start the engine. 4. Use the DMM in order to measure the Hz frequency of the requested torque signal. Does the Hz frequency of the requested torque signal measure within the specified range?	121-134 Hz	Go to Step 7	Go to Step 11
7	Use the DMM in order to measure the duty cycle of the requested torque signal circuit. Does the duty cycle of the requested torque signal measure within the specified range?	40-95%	Go to Step 12	Go to Step 13
8	Test the requested torque signal circuit for an open or a short to ground. Did you find and correct the condition?	--	Go to Step 14	Go to Step 10
9	Test the requested torque signal circuit for a short to voltage. Did you find and correct the condition?	--	Go to Step 14	Go to Step 12
10	Inspect for poor connections at the harness connector of the powertrain control module (PCM). Did you find and correct the condition?	--	Go to Step 14	Go to Step 12
11	Inspect for poor connections at the harness connector of the EBCM. Did you find and correct the condition?	--	Go to Step 14	Go to Step 13
12	Replace the PCM. Did you complete the replacement?	--	Go to Step 14	
13	Replace the EBCM. Did you complete the replacement?	--	Go to Step 14	--
14	1. Use the scan tool in order to clear the DTCs. 2. Operate the vehicle within the Conditions for Running the DTC as specified in the supporting text. Does DTC P0856 reset?	--	Go to Step 4	System OK

LTV0500000006545

Fig. 205 Code C0298 Or P0856: Powertrain Control Fault (Part 4 of 4). 2003–06 Sierra & Silverado

Circuit Description

A replacement electronic brake control module (EBCM) is supplied with generic software and must be programmed to match the specific vehicle application.

DTC Descriptor

This diagnostic procedure supports the following DTC:

DTC C0558 Calibration Data Not Programmed

Conditions for Running the DTC

The ignition is ON.

Conditions for Setting the DTC

The EBCM is not programmed with complete software.

Action Taken When the DTC Sets

- The EBCM disables the AES/DRP/TCS/VSES.
- The ABS indicator turns ON.
- The brake warning indicator turns ON.
- The message center displays the service stability system message.
- The traction off indicator turns on.

Conditions for clearing the DTC

The DTC clears when software programming is complete.

Step	Action	Yes	No
1	Did you perform the Diagnostic System Check - Vehicle?	Go to Step 2	Go to Diagnostic System Check -
2	Perform the set-up procedure for the EBCM. Did you complete the action?	Go to Diagnostic System Check	--

LTV0500000006548

Fig. 207 Code C0558: Calibration Data Not Programmed. 2003–06 Sierra & Silverado

Circuit Description

The instrument panel cluster (IPC) illuminates the ABS indicator by supplying ground to the lamp. The electronic brake control module (EBCM) sends class 2 serial data messages to the IPC in order to command the indicator ON or OFF.

Diagnostic Aids

The malfunction must be present during diagnosis in order to prevent unnecessary parts replacement. Always begin diagnosis with Diagnostic System Check - Vehicle in Vehicle DTC Information.

Test Description

The number below refers to the step number on the diagnostic table.

3. This step tests if the IPC is able to turn OFF the ABS indicator.

Step	Action	Yes	No
	Important		
	After a wheel speed sensor DTC is cleared and the ignition is ON, the ABS indicator may remain ON until the electronic brake control module (EBCM) completes a power-up self test. This test concludes when the vehicle reaches a speed greater than 13 km/h (8 mph) and the wheel speeds are verified by the EBCM.		
1	Did you perform the Diagnostic System Check - Vehicle?	Go to Step 2	Go to Diagnostic System Check
2	1. Turn OFF the ignition for 5 seconds. 2. Turn ON the ignition while observing the ABS indicator. Does the ABS indicator illuminate for 2 seconds and then turn OFF?	Go to Diagnostic Aids	Go to Step 3

LTV0500000005292

Fig. 208 ABS Indicator Always On (Part 1 of 2). Astro, Blazer, Jimmy, Safari, Sonoma, SSR & S10

Circuit Description

The instrument panel cluster (IPC) illuminates the ABS indicator by supplying ground to the lamp. The electronic brake control module (EBCM) sends class 2 serial data messages to the IPC in order to command the indicator ON or OFF.

Diagnostic Aids

Replace the Instrument Panel Cluster if the ABS indicator intermittently fails to operate during the bulb check.

Test Description

The number below refers to the step number on the diagnostic table.

2. This step tests if the IPC is able to illuminate the ABS indicator during the bulb check.

Step	Action	Yes	No
1	Did you perform the Diagnostic System Check - Vehicle?	Go to Step 2	Go to Diagnostic System Check
2	1. Turn OFF the ignition for 5 seconds. 2. Turn ON the ignition while observing the ABS indicator. Does the ABS indicator illuminate?	Go to Diagnostic Aids	Go to Step 3
3	Replace the instrument panel cluster (IPC). Did you complete the replacement?	Go to Step 4	--
4	1. Turn OFF the ignition for 5 seconds. 2. Turn ON the ignition while observing the ABS indicator. Does the ABS indicator illuminate?	System OK	Go to Step 3

LTV0500000005294

Fig. 209 ABS Indicator Inoperative. Astro, Blazer, Jimmy, Safari, Sonoma, SSR & S10

Circuit Description

The instrument panel cluster (IPC) illuminates the traction Off indicator by supplying ground to the lamp. The electronic brake control module (EBCM) sends serial data messages to the IPC to command the indicator ON or OFF.

Diagnostic Aids

Replace the IPC if the traction Off indicator intermittently fails to illuminate during the bulb check.

Test Description

The number below refers to the step number on the diagnostic table.

2. This step tests if the IPC is able to illuminate the traction Off indicator during the bulb check.

Step	Action	Yes	No
1	Did you perform the Diagnostic System Check - Vehicle?	Go to Step 2	Go to Diagnostic System Check - Vehicle
2	1. Turn OFF the ignition for 5 seconds. 2. Turn ON the ignition while observing the traction Off indicator. Does the traction Off indicator illuminate?	Go to Diagnostic Aids	Go to Step 3
3	Replace the instrument panel cluster (IPC). Did you complete the replacement?	Go to Step 4	--
4	1. Turn OFF the ignition for 5 seconds. 2. Turn ON the ignition while observing the traction Off indicator. Does the traction Off indicator illuminate?	System OK	Go to Step 3

LTV0500000005296

Fig. 211 Traction Off Indicator Inoperative. SSR

Step	Action	Yes	No
3	1. Install a scan tool. 2. Select the Instrument Panel Cluster (IPC) Special Functions menu on the scan tool. 3. Command the ABS Lamp Off. Does the ABS indicator turn OFF?	Go to Step 5	Go to Step 4
4	Replace the IPC. Did you complete the replacement?	Go to Step 6	--
5	Replace the EBCM. Did you complete the replacement?	Go to Step 6	--
6	1. Turn OFF the ignition for 5 seconds. 2. Turn ON the ignition while observing the ABS indicator. Does the ABS indicator illuminate for 2 seconds and then turn OFF?	System OK	Go to Step 3

LTV0500000005293

Fig. 208 ABS Indicator Always On (Part 2 of 2). Astro, Blazer, Jimmy, Safari, Sonoma, SSR & S10

Circuit Description

The instrument panel cluster (IPC) illuminates the Traction Off indicator by supplying ground to the lamp. The electronic brake control module (EBCM) sends serial data messages to the IPC to command the indicator ON or OFF.

Diagnostic Aids

The malfunction must be present during diagnosis in order to prevent unnecessary parts replacement. Always begin diagnosis with Diagnostic System Check - Vehicle .

Test Description

The number below refers to the step number on the diagnostic table.

3. This step tests if the IPC is able to turn OFF the Traction Off indicator.

Step	Action	Yes	No
1	Did you perform the Diagnostic System Check - Vehicle?	Go to Step 2	Go to Diagnostic System Check - Vehicle
2	1. Turn OFF the ignition for 5 seconds. 2. Turn ON the ignition while observing the Traction Off indicator. Does the Traction Off indicator illuminate for approximately 2 seconds and then turn OFF?	Go to Diagnostic Aids	Go to Step 3
3	1. Select the Instrument Panel Cluster (IPC) Special Functions menu on the scan tool. 2. Select Lamp Tests. 3. Command the IPC indicator lamps OFF. Does the Traction Off indicator turn OFF?	Go to Step 5	Go to Step 4
4	Replace the IPC. Did you complete the replacement?	Go to Step 6	--
5	Replace the electronic brake control module (EBCM). Did you complete the replacement?	Go to Step 6	--
6	1. Turn OFF the ignition for 5 seconds. 2. Turn ON the ignition while observing the Traction Off indicator. Does the Traction Off indicator illuminate for approximately 2 seconds and then turn OFF?	System OK	Go to Step 3

LTV0500000005295

Fig. 210 Traction Off Indicator Always On. SSR

Circuit Description

The instrument panel cluster (IPC) illuminates the ABS indicator by supplying ground to the lamp. The electronic brake control module (EBCM) sends class 2 serial data messages to the IPC in order to command the indicator ON or OFF.

Diagnostic Aids

The malfunction must be present during diagnosis in order to prevent unnecessary parts replacement. Always begin diagnosis with Diagnostic System Check - ABS .

Test Description

The number below refers to the step number on the diagnostic table.

3. This step tests if the IPC is able to turn OFF the ABS indicator.

Step	Action	Yes	No
	Important		
	After a wheel speed sensor DTC is cleared and the ignition is ON, the ABS indicator may remain ON until the EBCM completes a power-up self test. This test concludes when the vehicle reaches a speed greater than 13 km/h (8 mph) and the wheel speeds are verified by the EBCM.		

LTV0500000006182

Fig. 212 ABS Indicator Always On (Part 1 of 2). 2002 Avalanche, Escalade, Escalade EXT, Suburban, Tahoe & Yukon

		Go to Step 2	Go to Diagnostic System Check
1	Did you perform the ABS Diagnostic System Check?		
2	1. Turn OFF the ignition for 5 seconds. 2. Turn ON the ignition while observing the ABS indicator. Does the ABS indicator illuminate for 2 seconds and then turn OFF?	Go to Diagnostic Aids	Go to Step 3
3	1. Install a scan tool. 2. Select the Instrument Panel Cluster Special Functions menu on the scan tool. 3. Command the ABS Lamp Off. Does the ABS indicator turn OFF?	Go to Step 5	Go to Step 4
4	Replace the instrument panel cluster. Did you complete the replacement?	Go to Step 6	--
5	**Important** Following EBCM replacement, use the scan tool to perform the Tire Size Calibration procedure. Replace the EBCM. Did you complete the replacement?	Go to Step 6	--
6	1. Turn OFF the ignition for 5 seconds. 2. Turn ON the ignition while observing the ABS indicator. Does the ABS indicator illuminate for 2 seconds and then turn OFF?	System OK	Go to Step 3

LTV0500000006183

Fig. 212   ABS Indicator Always On (Part 2 of 2). 2002 Avalanche, Escalade, Escalade EXT, Suburban, Tahoe & Yukon

Circuit Description

The ignition 1 voltage circuit supplies 12 volts to the traction control switch. The EBCM illuminates the low traction indicator by applying ground to the traction control active signal circuit.

Diagnostic Aids

Thoroughly inspect connections or circuitry that may cause an intermittent malfunction.

Test Description

The number below refers to the step number on the diagnostic table.

4.   This step tests for proper operation of the low traction indicator circuitry.

LTV0500000006185

Fig. 214   Low Traction Indicator Always On (Part 1 of 2). 2002 Avalanche, Suburban, Tahoe & Yukon

Step	Action	Yes	No
1	Did you perform the ABS Diagnostic System Check?	Go to Step 2	Go to Diagnostic System Check
2	1. Turn OFF the ignition for 5 seconds. 2. Turn ON the ignition while observing the low traction indicator. Does the low traction indicator illuminate for 3 seconds and then turn OFF?	Go to Diagnostic Aids	Go to Step 3
3	1. Select the Traction Assist Data Display function on the scan tool. 2. Observe the Low Traction Lamp Command. Does the scan tool display On?	Go to Step 7	Go to Step 4
4	**Important** The EBCM sets DTC C0283 during this step if the ignition is ON for greater than 10 seconds. 1. Turn OFF the ignition. 2. Disconnect the traction control switch harness connector. Refer to Traction Control Switch Replacement. 3. Connect a test lamp between the traction control active signal circuit and the ignition 1 voltage circuit. 4. Turn ON the ignition. Does the test lamp illuminate for 3 seconds and then turn OFF?	Go to Step 6	Go to Step 5
5	Test the traction control active signal circuit for a short to ground. Did you find and correct the condition?	Go to Step 8	Go to Step 7
6	Replace the traction control switch. Did you complete the replacement?	Go to Step 8	--
7	**Important** Following EBCM replacement, use the scan tool to perform the Tire Size Calibration procedure. Replace the EBCM. Did you complete the replacement?	Go to Step 8	--
8	1. Turn OFF the ignition for 5 seconds. 2. Turn ON the ignition while observing the low traction indicator. Does the low traction indicator illuminate for 3 seconds and then turn OFF?	System OK	Go to Step 3

LTV0500000006186

Fig. 214   Low Traction Indicator Always On (Part 2 of 2). 2002 Avalanche, Suburban, Tahoe & Yukon

Circuit Description

The instrument panel cluster (IPC) illuminates the ABS indicator by supplying ground to the lamp. The electronic brake control module (EBCM) sends class 2 serial data messages to the IPC in order to command the indicator ON or OFF.

Diagnostic Aids

Replace the Instrument Panel Cluster if the ABS indicator intermittently fails to operate during the bulb check.

Test Description

The number below refers to the step number on the diagnostic table.

2.   This step tests if the IPC is able to illuminate the ABS indicator during the bulb check.

Step	Action	Yes	No
1	Did you perform the ABS Diagnostic System Check?	Go to Step 2	Go to Diagnostic System Check
2	1. Turn OFF the ignition for 5 seconds. 2. Turn ON the ignition while observing the ABS indicator. Does the ABS indicator illuminate?	Go to Diagnostic Aids	Go to Step 3
3	Replace the instrument panel cluster. Did you complete the replacement?	Go to Step 4	--
4	1. Turn OFF the ignition for 5 seconds. 2. Turn ON the ignition while observing the ABS indicator. Does the ABS indicator illuminate?	System OK	Go to Step 3

LTV0500000006184

Fig. 213   ABS Indicator Inoperative. 2002 Avalanche, Escalade, Escalade EXT, Suburban, Tahoe & Yukon

Circuit Description

The EBCM illuminates the low traction indicator by applying ground to the traction control active signal circuit.

Diagnostic Aids

Thoroughly inspect connections or circuitry that may cause an intermittent malfunction.

Test Description

The number below refers to the step number on the diagnostic table.

4.   This step tests for proper operation of the low traction indicator circuitry.

LTV0500000006187

Fig. 215   Low Traction Indicator Always On (Part 1 of 2). 2002 Escalade & Escalade EXT

Step	Action	Yes	No
1	Did you perform the ABS Diagnostic System Check?	Go to Step 2	Go to Diagnostic System Check
2	1. Turn OFF the ignition for 5 seconds. 2. Turn ON the ignition while observing the low traction indicator. Does the low traction indicator illuminate for 3 seconds and then turn OFF?	Go to Diagnostic Aids	Go to Step 3
3	1. Select the Traction Assist Data Display function on the scan tool. 2. Observe the Low Traction Lamp Command. Does the scan tool display On?	Go to Step 7	Go to Step 4
4	1. Turn OFF the ignition. 2. Remove the instrument panel cluster. 3. Connect a test lamp between the ignition 1 voltage circuit and the traction control active signal circuit. 4. Turn ON the ignition. Does the test lamp illuminate for 3 seconds and then turn OFF?	Go to Step 6	Go to Step 5
5	Test the traction control active signal circuit for a short to ground. Did you find and correct the condition?	Go to Step 8	Go to Step 7
6	Replace the instrument panel cluster. Did you complete the replacement?	Go to Step 8	--
7	**Important** Following EBCM replacement, use the scan tool to perform the Tire Size Calibration procedure. Replace the EBCM. Did you complete the replacement?	Go to Step 8	--
8	1. Turn OFF the ignition for 5 seconds. 2. Turn ON the ignition while observing the low traction indicator. Does the low traction indicator illuminate for 3 seconds and then turn OFF?	System OK	Go to Step 3

LTV0500000006188

Fig. 215   Low Traction Indicator Always On (Part 2 of 2). 2002 Escalade & Escalade EXT

Circuit Description

The ignition 1 voltage circuit supplies 12 volts to the traction control switch. The EBCM illuminates the low traction indicator by applying ground to the traction control active signal circuit.

Diagnostic Aids

The traction control system can be controlled by the operator in the following ways:

- Through operation of the traction control switch.
- Through programming of the traction control system automatic engagement feature.

Depending on the programmed state, the operation of the traction control system, as well as the operation of the traction off and low traction indicators, differs.

Observe the data list parameters listed below in order to determine the status of the traction control system when it is unknown if the system is operational.

- Traction Control Enabled
- Traction Off Lamp Command

LTV0500000006189

Fig. 216 Low Traction Indicator Inoperative (Part 1 of 3). 2002 Avalanche, Suburban, Tahoe & Yukon

Step		Yes	No
4	**Important** Do not disconnect the traction control switch harness connector during this step. 1. Backprobe the traction control switch harness connector in order to connect a test lamp between the traction control active signal circuit and the ignition 1 voltage circuit at the traction control switch harness connector. 2. Use the scan tool in order to command the Low Trac Lamp On and Off. Does the test lamp turn ON and OFF with each command?	Go to Step 6	Go to Step 5
5	Test the traction control active signal circuit for a short to voltage or an open. Did you find and correct the condition?	Go to Step 11	Go to Step 7
6	Inspect for poor connections at the traction control switch. Did you find and correct the condition?	Go to Step 11	Go to Step 9
7	Inspect for poor connections at the harness connector of the EBCM. Did you find and correct the condition?	Go to Step 11	Go to Step 10
8	Repair the high resistance in the ignition 1 voltage circuit. Did you complete the repair?	Go to Step 11	--
9	Replace the traction control switch. Did you complete the replacement?	Go to Step 11	--
10	**Important** Following EBCM replacement, use the scan tool to perform the Tire Size Calibration procedure. Replace the EBCM. Refer to Electronic Brake Control Module (EBCM) Replacement. Did you complete the replacement?	Go to Step 11	--
11	Use the scan tool in order to command the Low Trac Lamp On and Off. Does the low traction indicator turn ON and OFF with each command?	System OK	Go to Step 3

LTV0500000006191

Fig. 216 Low Traction Indicator Inoperative (Part 3 of 3). 2002 Avalanche, Suburban, Tahoe & Yukon

Press the traction control switch and observe the scan tool in order to verify a change in the status of the data list parameters.

Thoroughly inspect connections or circuitry that may cause an intermittent malfunction.

Test Description

The numbers below refer to the step numbers on the diagnostic table.

3. This step verifies the ignition 1 voltage circuit can supply adequate power to the traction control switch.

4. This step verifies the EBCM is applying ground to the low traction indicator.

5. The EBCM may be damaged if the traction control active signal circuit is shorted to voltage.

Step	Action	Yes	No
1	Did you perform A Diagnostic System Check?	Go to Step 2	Go to Diagnostic System Check -
2	1. Select the Traction Assist Special Functions menu on the scan tool. 2. Command the Low Trac Lamp On and Off. Does the low traction indicator turn ON and OFF with each command?	Go to Diagnostic Aids	Go to Step 3
3	**Important** Do not disconnect the traction control switch harness connector during this step. 1. Turn OFF the ignition. 2. Access the traction control switch harness connector. 3. Turn ON the ignition. 4. Backprobe the traction control switch harness connector in order to connect a test lamp between the ignition 1 voltage circuit and a good ground. Does the test lamp illuminate?	Go to Step 4	Go to Step 8

LTV0500000006190

Fig. 216 Low Traction Indicator Inoperative (Part 2 of 3). 2002 Avalanche, Suburban, Tahoe & Yukon

Circuit Description

The EBCM illuminates the low traction indicator by applying ground to the traction control active signal circuit.

Diagnostic Aids

The traction control system can be controlled by the operator in the following ways:

- Through operation of the traction control switch.
- Through programming of the traction control system automatic engagement feature.

Depending on the programmed state, the operation of the traction control system, as well as the operation of the traction off and low traction indicators, differs. For a more detailed explanation of these operational characteristics, refer to Traction Control Indicator Lamps in ABS Description and Operation.

Observe the data list parameters listed below in order to determine the status of the traction control system when it is unknown if the system is operational.

- Traction Control Enabled
- Traction Off Lamp Command

Press the traction control switch and observe the scan tool in order to verify a change in the status of the data list parameters.

Thoroughly inspect connections or circuitry that may cause an intermittent malfunction.

Test Description

The numbers below refer to the step numbers on the diagnostic table.

3. This step verifies the EBCM is applying ground to the low traction indicator.

4. The EBCM may be damaged if the traction control active signal circuit is shorted to voltage.

LTV0500000006192

Fig. 217 Low Traction Indicator Inoperative (Part 1 of 2). 2002 Escalade & Escalade EXT

Step	Action	Yes	No
1	Did you perform A Diagnostic System Check?	Go to Step 2	Go to Diagnostic System Check
2	1. Select the Traction Assist Special Functions menu on the scan tool. 2. Command the Low Trac Lamp On and Off. Does the low traction indicator turn ON and OFF with each command?	Go to Diagnostic Aids	Go to Step 3
3	1. Turn OFF the ignition. 2. Remove the instrument panel cluster (IPC). 3. Connect a test lamp between the ignition 1 voltage circuit and the traction control active signal circuit. 4. Turn ON the ignition. Does the test lamp illuminate?	Go to Step 5	Go to Step 4
4	Test the traction control active signal circuit for a short to voltage or an open. Did you find and correct the condition?	Go to Step 9	Go to Step 6
5	Inspect for poor connections at the harness connector of the IPC. Did you find and correct the condition?	Go to Step 9	Go to Step 7
6	Inspect for poor connections at the harness connector of the EBCM. Did you find and correct the condition?	Go to Step 9	Go to Step 8
7	Replace the IPC. Did you complete the replacement?	Go to Step 9	--
8	**Important** Following EBCM replacement, use the scan tool to perform the Tire Size Calibration procedure. Replace the EBCM. Did you complete the replacement?	Go to Step 9	--
9	1. Turn ON the ignition. 2. Use the scan tool in order to command the Low Trac Lamp On and Off. Does the low traction indicator turn ON and OFF with each command?	System OK	Go to Step 3

LTV0500000006193

Fig. 217 Low Traction Indicator Inoperative (Part 2 of 2). 2002 Escalade, Escalade EXT

Test Description

The numbers below refer to the step numbers on the diagnostic table.

4. This step verifies that the yaw rate sensor signal voltage is within normal operating range. Voltage outside the specified range prevents VSES initialization.

5. This step verifies that the lateral accelerometer signal voltage is within normal operating range. Voltage outside the specified range prevents VSES initialization.

6. This step verifies that the master cylinder pressure sensor signal voltage is within normal operating range. Voltage outside the specified range prevents VSES initialization. If you completed steps 1 through 7 and did not locate the malfunction, you must have overlooked something.

Step	Action	Values	Yes	No
1	Did you perform the ABS Diagnostic System Check?	--	Go to Step 2	Go to Diagnostic System Check
2	Operate the vehicle at a speed greater than the specified value for approximately 3.2 km (2 mi). Does the message center display the Stability System Disabled message?	15 km/h (9 mph)	Go to Step 3	Go to Diagnostic Aids
3	Observe the brake warning indicator on the instrument panel cluster. Is the brake warning indicator always ON?	--	Go to Brake Warning Indicator Always On in Hydraulic Brakes	Go to Step 4
4	1. Ensure the vehicle is parked on a level surface. 2. Observe the Yaw Rate Sensor Input on the scan tool. Is the Yaw Rate Sensor Input within the specified range?	2.35-2.65 V	Go to Step 5	Go to Step 7
5	Observe the Lateral Accelerometer Sensor Input on the scan tool. Is the Lateral Accelerometer Sensor Input within the specified range?	2.0-3.0 V	Go to Step 6	Go to Step 8

LTV0500000006195

Fig. 218 Stability System Disabled Indicator Always On (Part 2 of 3). 2002 Avalanche, Escalade, Escalade EXT, Suburban, Tahoe & Yukon

Circuit Description

The 5 inputs to the EBCM which are used solely for vehicle stability enhancement are the longitudinal accelerometer, lateral accelerometer, yaw rate sensor, master cylinder pressure sensor and the steering wheel position PWM inputs. The EBCM must detect valid inputs from all 5 sources during the initialization period in order to enable the VSES. Initialization must occur during the first 3000 meters of vehicle travel or 1000 meters of straight vehicle travel. If initialization cannot be achieved during this time period, the VSES remains inactive and the message center displays the Stability System Disabled message. The EBCM does not attempt to reinitialize until the next ignition cycle.

During aggressive driving conditions which repeatedly activate the VSES, one or more of the solenoid coils may become overheated. The message center may display the Stability System Limited message at this time as the EBCM reduces VSES activation in an attempt to decrease the solenoid temperatures. If the temperature of any of the solenoids exceeds 275°C (527° F), the message center displays the Stability System Disabled message and the VSES becomes inactive. Coil temperatures are estimated by the EBCM based on ambient temperature and monitored solenoid activation and may not coincide with actual solenoid temperatures. The Stability System Disabled message turns OFF and VSES activity resumes when the EBCM determines the solenoids have cooled sufficiently.

Diagnostic Aids

If the customer's concern is that the Stability System Disabled message is displayed intermittently, communicate with the customer to determine what driving conditions are being experienced at the time the message is displayed. The EBCM may be unable to successfully initialize the system during operation on very winding roads. Initialization may also be unsuccessful if pressure is continuously applied to the brake pedal during the initialization period.

The VSES solenoid coils may overheat during aggressive driving. The Stability System Limited message is usually displayed prior to the Stability System Disabled message in the case of overheating solenoid coils.

A medium-low brake fluid level in the master cylinder reservoir may cause the Stability System Disabled message to be displayed during stopping or turning maneuvers. This condition will also cause the red brake warning indicator to turn ON. Ensure the master cylinder reservoir has an adequate brake fluid level.

If the message is displayed due to any of the above conditions, no diagnosis or repair of the VSES is required.

LTV0500000006194

Fig. 218 Stability System Disabled Indicator Always On (Part 1 of 3). 2002 Avalanche, Escalade, Escalade EXT, Suburban, Tahoe & Yukon

	Action		Yes	No
6	Observe the Master Cylinder Pressure Sensor Input on the scan tool. Is the Master Cylinder Pressure Sensor Input within the specified range?	0.0-0.5 V	Go to Step 1	Go to Step 9
7	Operate the vehicle within the Conditions for Running DTC C0211. Refer to DTC C0209-C0212. Does DTC C0211 set?	--	Go to DTC C0209-C0212	Go to Step 10
8	Operate the vehicle within the Conditions for Running DTC C0215. Refer to DTC C0213-C0215. Does DTC C0215 set?	--	Go to DTC C0201-C0204	Go to Step 10
9	Operate the vehicle within the Conditions for Running DTC C0203. Refer to DTC C0201-C0204. Does DTC C0203 set?	--	Go to DTC C0213-C0216	Go to Step 10
10	**Important** Following EBCM replacement, use the scan tool to perform the Tire Size Calibration procedure. Replace the EBCM. Did you complete the replacement?	--	Go to Step 11	--
11	Operate the vehicle at a speed greater than the specified value for approximately 3.2 km (2 mi). Does the message center display the Stability System Disabled message?	15 km/h (9 mph)	Go to Step 3	System OK

LTV0500000006196

Fig. 218 Stability System Disabled Indicator Always On (Part 3 of 3). 2002 Avalanche, Escalade, Escalade EXT, Suburban, Tahoe & Yukon

Circuit Description

The EBCM turns OFF the traction off indicator by applying ground to the service traction control signal circuit. When the inverting driver module detects the service traction control signal circuit is open, the inverting driver module applies ground to the traction off indicator control circuit in order to illuminate the traction off indicator.

Diagnostic Aids

The traction control system can be controlled by the operator in the following ways:

- Through operation of the traction control switch.
- Through programming of the traction control system automatic engagement feature.

Depending on the programmed state, the operation of the traction control system, as well as the operation of the traction off and low traction indicators, differs.

Observe the data list parameters listed below in order to determine the status of the traction control system when it is unknown if the system is operational.

- Traction Control Enabled
- Traction Off Lamp Command

Press the traction control switch and observe the scan tool in order to verify a change in the status of the data list parameters.

Thoroughly inspect connections or circuitry that may cause an intermittent malfunction.

LTV0500000006197

Fig. 219 Traction Off Indicator Always On (Part 1 of 4). 2002 Escalade & Escalade EXT

Test Description

The numbers below refer to the step numbers on the diagnostic table.

6. This step tests if the EBCM is commanding the inverting driver module to turn OFF the traction off indicator.

7. This step tests if the inverting driver module is receiving adequate power and ground in order to power up.

9. This step tests if the inverting driver module is falsely illuminating the traction off indicator.

10. This step tests the service traction control signal circuit for a short to ground by substituting the IPC with a test lamp.

11. This step simulates pressing and releasing a properly functioning traction control switch.

14. The traction control switch may be damaged if the traction control switch signal circuit is shorted to voltage.

Step	Action	Yes	No
1	Did you perform the ABS Diagnostic System Check?	Go to Step 2	Go to Diagnostic System Check
2	1. Turn OFF the ignition for 5 seconds. 2. Turn ON the ignition while observing the traction off indicator. Does the traction off indicator illuminate for 3 seconds and then turn OFF?	Go to Diagnostic Aids	Go to Step 3
3	Press and release the traction control switch. Does the traction off indicator turn OFF?	Go to Diagnostic Aids	Go to Step 4
4	1. Install a scan tool. 2. Select the Traction Assist Data Display function on the scan tool. 3. Press and release the traction control switch while observing the Traction Control Enabled status. Does the Traction Control Enabled status change?	Go to Step 5	Go to Step 11

LTV0500000006198

Fig. 219 Traction Off Indicator Always On (Part 2 of 4). 2002 Escalade & Escalade EXT

		Yes	No
12	Test the service traction control signal circuit for an open between the EBCM and the inverting driver module. Did you find and correct the condition?	Go to Step 23	Go to Step 18
13	Test the ground circuit of the traction control switch for an open. Did you find and correct the condition?	Go to Step 23	Go to Step 15
14	Test the traction control switch signal circuit for a short to voltage. Did you find and correct the condition?	Go to Step 23	Go to Step 19
15	Inspect for poor connections at the harness connector of the traction control switch. Did you find and correct the condition?	Go to Step 23	Go to Step 16
16	Replace the traction control switch. Did you complete the replacement?	Go to Step 23	—
17	Replace the IPC. Did you complete the replacement?	Go to Step 23	—
18	Inspect for poor connections at the harness connector of the EBCM. Did you find and correct the condition?	Go to Step 23	Go to Step 19
19	**Important** Following EBCM replacement, use the scan tool to perform the Tire Size Calibration procedure. Replace the EBCM. Did you complete the replacement?	Go to Step 23	—
20	Inspect for poor connections at the harness connector of the inverting driver module. Did you find and correct the condition?	Go to Step 23	Go to Step 21
21	Replace the inverting driver module. Did you complete the replacement?	Go to Step 23	—
22	Repair the short to ground in the traction off indicator control circuit. Did you complete the repair?	Go to Step 23	—
23	1. Turn ON the ignition. 2. Press and release the traction control switch several times. Does the traction off indicator turn ON and OFF each time the switch is pressed?	System OK	Go to Step 2

LTV0500000006200

Fig. 219 Traction Off Indicator Always On (Part 4 of 4). 2002 Escalade, Escalade EXT

		Yes	No
5	1. Turn ON the traction control system by verifying that the scan tool displays Traction Control Enabled - Yes. 2. Observe the Traction Off Lamp Command on the scan tool. Does the scan tool display Traction Off Lamp Command - On?	Go to Step 19	Go to Step 6
6	1. Access the inverting driver module harness connector. 2. Backprobe the inverting driver module harness connector in order to connect a test lamp between battery positive voltage and the service traction control signal circuit. Does the test lamp illuminate?	Go to Step 7	Go to Step 12
7	Backprobe the inverting driver module harness connector in order to connect a test lamp between the battery positive voltage circuit and the ground circuit of the inverting driver module. Does the test lamp illuminate?	Go to Step 9	Go to Step 8
8	Repair the open in the battery positive voltage circuit or the ground circuit of the inverting driver module. Did you complete the repair?	Go to Step 23	—
9	1. Turn OFF the ignition. 2. Remove the circuit board from the inverting driver module. 3. Turn ON the ignition. Does the traction off indicator turn OFF?	Go to Step 20	Go to Step 10
10	1. Turn OFF the ignition. 2. Remove the instrument panel cluster (IPC) 3. Connect a test lamp between the ignition 1 voltage circuit and the traction off indicator control circuit at the IPC harness connector. 4. Turn ON the ignition. Does the test lamp illuminate?	Go to Step 22	Go to Step 17
11	**Important** Do not disconnect the traction control switch harness connector during this step. 1. Access the traction control switch harness connector. 2. While observing the Traction Control Enabled status on the scan tool, backprobe the traction control switch harness connector with a test lamp connected to a good ground in order to momentarily contact the traction control switch signal circuit. Does the Traction Control Enabled status change?	Go to Step 13	Go to Step 14

LTV0500000006199

Fig. 219 Traction Off Indicator Always On (Part 3 of 4). 2002 Escalade & Escalade EXT

Circuit Description

The ignition 1 voltage circuit supplies 12 volts to the traction control switch. The EBCM turns OFF the traction off indicator by applying ground to the service traction control signal circuit.

Diagnostic Aids

The traction control system can be controlled by the operator in the following ways:

- Through operation of the traction control switch.
- Through programming of the traction control system automatic engagement feature.

Depending on the programmed state, the operation of the traction control system, as well as the operation of the traction off and low traction indicators, differs.

Observe the data list parameters listed below in order to determine the status of the traction control system when it is unknown if the system is operational.

- Traction Control Enabled
- Traction Off Lamp Command

Press the traction control switch and observe the scan tool in order to verify a change in the status of the data list parameters.

Thoroughly inspect connections or circuitry that may cause an intermittent malfunction.

Test Description

The numbers below refer to the step numbers on the diagnostic table.

7. This step simulates pressing and releasing a properly functioning traction control switch.

10. The traction control switch may be damaged if the traction control switch signal circuit is shorted to voltage.

LTV0500000006201

Fig. 220 Traction Off Indicator Always On (Part 1 of 3). 2002 Avalanche, Suburban, Tahoe & Yukon

Step	Action	Yes	No
1	Did you perform the ABS Diagnostic System Check?	Go to Step 2	Go to Diagnostic System Check
2	1. Turn OFF the ignition for 5 seconds. 2. Turn ON the ignition while observing the traction off indicator. Does the traction off indicator illuminate for 3 seconds and then turn OFF?	Go to Diagnostic Aids	Go to Step 3
3	Press and release the traction control switch. Does the traction off indicator turn OFF?	Go to Diagnostic Aids	Go to Step 4
4	1. Install a scan tool. 2. Select the Traction Assist Data Display function on the scan tool. 3. Press and release the traction control switch while observing the Traction Control Enabled status. Does the Traction Control Enabled status change?	Go to Step 5	Go to Step 7
5	1. Turn ON the traction control system by verifying the scan tool displays Traction Control Enabled - Yes. 2. Observe the Traction Off Lamp Command on the scan tool. Does the scan tool display Traction Off Lamp Command - On?	Go to Step 13	Go to Step 6
6	**Important** Do not disconnect the traction control switch harness connector during this step. Ensure the ignition is turned ON for the duration of this step. 1. Access the traction control switch harness connector. 2. Backprobe the traction control switch harness connector in order to connect a test lamp between the ignition 1 voltage circuit and the service traction control signal circuit. Does the test lamp illuminate?	Go to Step 9	Go to Step 8
7	**Important** Do not disconnect the traction control switch harness connector during this step. 1. Access the traction control switch harness connector. 2. While observing the Traction Control Enabled status on the scan tool, backprobe the traction control switch harness connector with a test lamp connected to a good ground in order to momentarily contact the traction control switch signal circuit. Does the Traction Control Enabled status change?	Go to Step 11	Go to Step 10

LTV0500000006202

Fig. 220   Traction Off Indicator Always On (Part 2 of 3). 2002 Avalanche, Suburban, Tahoe & Yukon

Circuit Description

The EBCM turns OFF the traction off indicator by applying ground to the service traction control signal circuit. When the inverting driver module detects the service traction control signal circuit is open, the inverting driver module applies ground to the traction off indicator control circuit in order to illuminate the traction off indicator.

Diagnostic Aids

The traction control system can be controlled by the operator in the following ways:

- Through operation of the traction control switch.
- Through programming of the traction control system automatic engagement feature.

Depending on the programmed state, the operation of the traction control system, as well as the operation of the traction off and low traction indicators, differs.

Observe the data list parameters listed below in order to determine the status of the traction control system when it is unknown if the system is operational.

- Traction Control Enabled
- Traction Off Lamp Command

Press the traction control switch and observe the scan tool in order to verify a change in the status of the data list parameters.

Thoroughly inspect connections or circuitry that may cause an intermittent malfunction.

Test Description

The numbers below refer to the step numbers on the diagnostic table.

5. This step tests if the EBCM is commanding the inverting driver module to turn OFF the traction off indicator.

6. This step tests if the inverting driver module is receiving adequate power and ground in order to power up.

7. This step tests the instrument panel cluster (IPC) and the traction off indicator control circuit for proper function.

10. This step simulates pressing and releasing a properly functioning traction control switch.

11. The traction control switch may be damaged if the traction control switch signal circuit is shorted to voltage.

12. This step tests the traction off indicator control circuit for faults by substituting the IPC with a test lamp.

LTV0500000006204

Fig. 221   Traction Off Indicator Inoperative (Part 1 of 4). 2002 Escalade & Escalade EXT

Step	Action	Yes	No
8	Test the service traction control signal circuit for an open. Did you find and correct the condition?	Go to Step 14	Go to Step 12
9	Inspect for poor connections at the harness connector of the traction control switch. Did you find and correct the condition?	Go to Step 14	Go to Step 11
10	Test the traction control switch signal circuit for a short to voltage. Did you find and correct the condition?	Go to Step 14	Go to Step 13
11	Replace the traction control switch. Did you complete the replacement?	Go to Step 14	—
12	Inspect for poor connections at the harness connector of the EBCM. Did you find and correct the condition?	Go to Step 14	Go to Step 13
13	**Important** Following EBCM replacement, use the scan tool to perform the Tire Size Calibration procedure. Replace the EBCM. Did you complete the replacement?	Go to Step 14	—
14	Press and release the traction control switch several times. Does the traction off indicator turn ON and OFF each time the switch is pressed?	System OK	Go to Step 2

LTV0500000006203

Fig. 220   Traction Off Indicator Always On (Part 3 of 3). 2002 Avalanche, Suburban, Tahoe & Yukon

Step	Action	Yes	No
1	Did you perform the ABS Diagnostic System Check?	Go to Step 2	Go to Diagnostic System Check -
2	1. Turn OFF the ignition for 5 seconds. 2. Turn ON the ignition while observing the traction off indicator. Does the traction off indicator illuminate for 3 seconds and then turn OFF?	Go to Step 3	Go to Step 5
3	Press and release the traction control switch. Does the traction off indicator turn ON?	Go to Diagnostic Aids	Go to Step 4
4	1. Install a scan tool. 2. Select the Traction Assist Data Display function on the scan tool. 3. Press and release the traction control switch while observing the Traction Control Enabled status. Does the Traction Control Enabled status change?	Go to Step 16	Go to Step 10
5	1. Turn OFF the ignition. 2. Disconnect from the EBCM, the harness connector containing the service traction control signal circuit. 3. Turn ON the ignition. Does the traction off indicator illuminate?	Go to Step 16	Go to Step 6
6	Backprobe the inverting driver module harness connector in order to connect a test lamp between the battery positive voltage circuit and the ground circuit of the inverting driver module. Does the test lamp illuminate?	Go to Step 7	Go to Step 9
7	1. Turn OFF the ignition. 2. Remove the circuit board from the inverting driver module. 3. Use a 3 amp fused jumper wire in order to connect the traction off indicator control circuit to a good ground. 4. Turn ON the ignition. Does the traction off indicator turn ON?	Go to Step 8	Go to Step 12

LTV0500000006205

Fig. 221   Traction Off Indicator Inoperative (Part 2 of 4). 2002 Escalade & Escalade EXT

Step	Action	Yes	No
8	Test the service traction control signal circuit for a short to ground. Did you find and correct the condition?	Go to Step 22	Go to Step 20
9	Repair the open in the battery positive voltage circuit or the ground circuit of the inverting driver module. Did you complete the repair?	Go to Step 22	--
10	**Important** Do not disconnect the traction control switch harness connector during this step. 1. Access the traction control switch harness connector. 2. While observing the Traction Control Enabled status on the scan tool, backprobe the traction control switch harness connector with a test lamp connected to a good ground in order to momentarily contact the traction control switch signal circuit. Does the Traction Control Enabled status change?	Go to Step 13	Go to Step 11
11	Test the traction control switch signal circuit for a short to voltage. Did you find and correct the condition?	Go to Step 22	Go to Step 16
12	1. Turn OFF the ignition. 2. Reinstall the inverting driver module circuit board. 3. Reconnect the EBCM harness connector. 4. Remove the instrument panel cluster (IPC). 5. Connect a test lamp between the ignition 1 voltage circuit and the traction off indicator control circuit at the IPC harness connector. 6. Turn ON the ignition. Does the test lamp illuminate?	Go to Step 18	Go to Step 17
13	Test the ground circuit of the traction control switch for an open. Did you find and correct the condition?	Go to Step 22	Go to Step 14
14	Inspect for poor connections at the harness connector of the traction control switch. Did you find and correct the condition?	Go to Step 22	Go to Step 15

LTV0500000006206

Fig. 221 Traction Off Indicator Inoperative (Part 3 of 4). 2002 Escalade & Escalade EXT

Circuit Description

The ignition 1 voltage circuit supplies 12 volts to the traction control switch. The EBCM turns OFF the traction off indicator by applying ground to the service traction control signal circuit.

Diagnostic Aids

The traction control system can be controlled by the operator in the following ways:

- Through operation of the traction control switch.
- Through programming of the traction control system automatic engagement feature.

Depending on the programmed state, the operation of the traction control system, as well as the operation of the traction off and low traction indicators, differs. For a more detailed explanation of these operational characteristics, refer to Traction Control Indicator Lamps in ABS Description and Operation.

Observe the data list parameters listed below in order to determine the status of the traction control system when it is unknown if the system is operational.

- Traction Control Enabled
- Traction Off Lamp Command

Press the traction control switch and observe the scan tool in order to verify a change in the status of the data list parameters.

Thoroughly inspect connections or circuitry that may cause an intermittent malfunction.

Test Description

The numbers below refer to the step numbers on the diagnostic table.

5. This step simulates pressing and releasing a properly functioning traction control switch.

6. The traction control switch may be damaged if the traction control switch signal circuit is shorted to voltage.

7. This step tests if the ignition 1 voltage circuit can supply adequate power to the traction control switch.

8. This step tests if the EBCM is commanding the traction off indicator OFF.

LTV0500000006208

Fig. 222 Traction Off Indicator Inoperative (Part 1 of 3). 2002 Avalanche, Suburban, Tahoe & Yukon

Step	Action	Yes	No
15	Replace the traction control switch. Did you complete the replacement?	Go to Step 22	--
16	**Important** Following EBCM replacement, use the scan tool to perform the Tire Size Calibration procedure. Replace the EBCM. Did you complete the replacement?	Go to Step 22	--
17	Repair the open or short to voltage in the traction off indicator control circuit. Did you complete the repair?	Go to Step 22	--
18	Inspect for poor connections at the harness connector of the IPC. Did you find and correct the condition?	Go to Step 22	Go to Step 19
19	Replace the IPC. Did you complete the replacement?	Go to Step 22	--
20	Inspect for poor connections at the harness connector of the inverting driver module. Did you find and correct the condition?	Go to Step 22	Go to Step 21
21	Replace the inverting driver module. Did you complete the replacement?	Go to Step 22	--
22	1. Turn ON the ignition. 2. Press and release the traction control switch several times. Does the traction off indicator turn ON and OFF each time the switch is pressed?	System OK	Go to Step 3

LTV0500000006207

Fig. 221 Traction Off Indicator Inoperative (Part 4 of 4). 2002 Escalade & Escalade EXT

Step	Action	Yes	No
1	Did you perform the ABS Diagnostic System Check?	Go to Step 2	Go to Diagnostic System Check -
2	1. Turn OFF the ignition for 5 seconds. 2. Turn ON the ignition while observing the traction off indicator. Does the traction off indicator illuminate for 3 seconds and then turn OFF?	Go to Step 3	Go to Step 7
3	Press and release the traction control switch. Does the traction off indicator turn ON?	Go to Diagnostic Aids	Go to Step 4
4	1. Install a scan tool. 2. Select the Traction Assist Data Display function on the scan tool. 3. Press and release the traction control switch while observing the Traction Control Enabled status. Does the Traction Control Enabled status change?	Go to Step 13	Go to Step 5
5	**Important** Do not disconnect the traction control switch harness connector during this step. 1. Access the traction control switch harness connector. 2. While observing the Traction Control Enabled status on the scan tool, backprobe the traction control switch harness connector with a test lamp connected to a good ground in order to momentarily contact the traction control switch signal circuit. Does the Traction Control Enabled status change?	Go to Step 12	Go to Step 6
6	Test the traction control switch signal circuit for a short to voltage. Did you find and correct the condition?	Go to Step 15	Go to Step 13
7	**Important** If the ignition is ON for more than 10 seconds, the EBCM sets DTC C0283. 1. Turn OFF the ignition. 2. Disconnect the traction control switch harness connector. 3. Connect a test lamp between the ignition 1 voltage circuit and a good ground. 4. Turn ON the ignition. Does the test lamp illuminate?	Go to Step 8	Go to Step 14

LTV0500000006209

Fig. 222 Traction Off Indicator Inoperative (Part 2 of 3). 2002 Avalanche, Suburban, Tahoe & Yukon

Step	Action	Yes	No
8	1. Turn OFF the ignition. 2. Reconnect the traction control switch harness connector. 3. Disconnect from the EBCM, the harness connector containing the service traction control signal circuit. 4. Turn ON the ignition. Does the traction off indicator illuminate?	Go to Step 13	Go to Step 9
9	Test the service traction control signal circuit for a short to ground or a short to voltage. Did you find and correct the condition?	Go to Step 15	Go to Step 10
10	Test the ground circuit of the traction control switch for an open. Did you find and correct the condition?	Go to Step 15	Go to Step 11
11	Inspect for poor connections at the harness connector of the traction control switch. Did you find and correct the condition?	Go to Step 15	Go to Step 12
12	Replace the traction control switch. Did you complete the replacement?	Go to Step 15	--
13	**Important** Following EBCM replacement, use the scan tool to perform the Tire Size Calibration procedure. Replace the EBCM. Did you complete the replacement?	Go to Step 15	--
14	Repair the high resistance in the ignition 1 voltage circuit. Did you complete the repair?	Go to Step 15	--
15	Press and release the traction control switch several times. Does the traction off indicator turn ON and OFF each time the switch is pressed?	System OK	Go to Step 2

LTV0500000006210

Fig. 222   Traction Off Indicator Inoperative (Part 3 of 3). 2002 Avalanche, Suburban, Tahoe & Yukon

Circuit Description

The instrument panel cluster (IPC) illuminates the ABS indicator by supplying ground to the lamp. The electronic brake control module (EBCM) sends class 2 serial data messages to the IPC in order to command the indicator ON or OFF.

Diagnostic Aids

Replace the Instrument Panel Cluster if the ABS indicator intermittently fails to operate during the bulb check.

Test Description

The number below refers to the step number on the diagnostic table.

2. This step tests if the IPC is able to illuminate the ABS indicator, during the bulb check.

Step	Action	Yes	No
1	Did you perform the Diagnostic System Check - Vehicle?	Go to Step 2	Go to Diagnostic System Check - Vehicle
2	1. Turn OFF the ignition for 5 seconds. 2. Turn ON the ignition while observing the ABS indicator. Does the ABS indicator illuminate?	Go to Diagnostic Aids	Go to Step 3
3	Replace the instrument panel cluster (IPC). Did you complete the replacement?	Go to Step 4	--
4	1. Turn OFF the ignition for 5 seconds. 2. Turn ON the ignition while observing the ABS indicator. Does the ABS indicator illuminate?	System OK	Go to Step 3

LTV0500000006332

Fig. 224   ABS Indicator Inoperative. 2003–06 Avalanche, Escalade, Escalade EXT, Suburban, Tahoe & Yukon

Circuit Description

The instrument panel cluster (IPC) illuminates the ABS indicator by supplying ground to the lamp. The electronic brake control module (EBCM) sends serial data messages to the IPC to command the indicator ON or OFF.

Diagnostic Aids

The malfunction must be present during diagnosis in order to prevent unnecessary parts replacement. Always begin diagnosis with Diagnostic System Check - Vehicle .

Test Description

The number below refers to the step number on the diagnostic table.

3. This step tests if the IPC is able to turn OFF the ABS indicator.

Step	Action	Yes	No
	Important: An ECE 13 response may cause the ABS indicator to remain ON when no DTCs are set. It is necessary to verify that ECE 13 is not causing the ABS indicator to remain illuminated, prior to performing this diagnostic. Refer to ABS Description and Operation for a complete description of the ECE 13 response.		
1	Did you perform the Diagnostic System Check - Vehicle?	Go to Step 2	Go to Diagnostic System Check - Vehicle
2	1. Turn OFF the ignition for 5 seconds. 2. Turn ON the ignition while observing the ABS indicator. Does the ABS indicator illuminate for approximately 2 seconds and then turn OFF?	Go to Diagnostic Aids	Go to Step 3
3	1. Select the Instrument Panel Cluster Special Functions menu on the scan tool. 2. Select Lamp Tests. 3. Command the IPC indicator lamps OFF. Does the ABS indicator turn OFF?	Go to Step 5	Go to Step 4
4	Replace the instrument panel cluster (IPC). Did you complete the replacement?	Go to Step 6	--
5	Replace the electronic brake control module (EBCM). Did you complete the replacement?	Go to Step 6	--
6	1. Turn OFF the ignition for 5 seconds. 2. Turn ON the ignition while observing the ABS indicator. Does the ABS indicator illuminate for approximately 2 seconds and then turn OFF?	System OK	Go to Step 3

LTV0500000006331

Fig. 223   ABS Indicator Always On. 2003–06 Avalanche, Escalade, Escalade EXT, Suburban, Tahoe & Yukon

Circuit Description

The 5 inputs to the electronic brake control module (EBCM) which are used solely for vehicle stability enhancement are the longitudinal accelerometer, lateral accelerometer, yaw rate sensor, master cylinder pressure sensor and the steering wheel position sensor. The EBCM must detect valid inputs from all 5 sources during the initialization period in order to enable the vehicle stability enhancement system (VSES). Initialization must occur during the first 3000 meters of vehicle travel or 1000 meters of straight vehicle travel. If initialization cannot be achieved during this time period, the VSES remains inactive and the stability system disabled message is displayed. The EBCM does not attempt to reinitialize until the next ignition cycle. One or more DTCs often set, shortly after an unsuccessful initialization attempt, indicating the root cause of the failure. If this occurs, the stability system disabled message is no longer displayed. The service stability system message is displayed instead.

During aggressive driving conditions which repeatedly activate the VSES or traction control system (TCS), one or more of the solenoid coils may become overheated. The stability system disabled message is displayed at this time and the EBCM disables all VSES and TCS brake pressure applications in an attempt to decrease the solenoid temperatures. Coil temperatures are estimated by the EBCM based on ambient temperature and monitored solenoid activation and may not coincide with actual solenoid temperatures. The stability system disabled message turns OFF and normal VSES/TCS activity resumes when the EBCM determines the solenoids have cooled sufficiently.

Diagnostic Aids

If the customer's concern is that the stability system disabled message is displayed intermittently, communicate with the customer to determine what driving conditions are being experienced at the time the message is displayed. The EBCM may be unable to successfully initialize the system during operation on very winding roads. Initialization may also be unsuccessful if pressure is continuously applied to the brake pedal during the initialization period.

The VSES solenoid coils may overheat during aggressive driving, causing the VSES to be disabled temporarily.

A medium-low brake fluid level in the master cylinder reservoir may cause the stability system disabled message to be displayed during stopping or turning maneuvers. This condition will also cause the red brake warning indicator to turn ON. Ensure the master cylinder reservoir has an adequate brake fluid level.

If the message is displayed due to any of the above conditions, no diagnosis or repair of the VSES is required.

Step	Action	Yes	No
1	Did you perform the Diagnostic System Check - Vehicle?	Go to Step 2	Go to Diagnostic System Check - Vehicle
2	1. Turn OFF the ignition for 5 seconds. 2. Turn ON the ignition. 3. Operate the vehicle at a speed greater than the specified value for approximately 3.2 km (2 mi). Is the stability system disabled message displayed?	Go to Step 3	Go to Diagnostic Aids
3	Observe the brake warning indicator on the instrument panel cluster. Is the brake warning indicator always ON?	Go to Brake Warning Indicator Always On	Go to Step 4

LTV0500000006333

Fig. 225   Stability System Disabled Indicator Always On (Part 1 of 3). 2003–06 Avalanche, Escalade, Escalade EXT, Suburban, Tahoe & Yukon

Step	Action	Yes	No
4	Use the scan tool to display VSES History DTCs. Are any of the following DTCs stored in History? • C0131 • C0186 • C0196 • C0550	Go to Step 5	Go to Step 6
5	Operate the vehicle within the Conditions for Running any History DTCs which may be the cause of unsuccessful initialization. Do any of the DTCs listed in step 4 set as a Current DTC?	Go to Diagnostic Trouble Code (DTC) List - Vehicle	Go to Step 6
6	1. Select the VSES data list on the scan tool. 2. Observe the Digital SWPS Phase A and the Digital SWPS Phase B parameters as you rotate the steering wheel. Do the Digital SWPS Phase A and the Digital SWPS Phase B parameters both transition from Low to High as the steering wheel is rotated?	Go to Step 1	Go to Step 7
7	1. Turn OFF the ignition. 2. Disconnect the steering wheel position sensor harness connector. 3. Turn ON the ignition. 4. Observe Digital SWPS Phase A and the Digital SWPS Phase B parameters on the scan tool. Does the scan tool display that both parameters are low?	Go to Step 8	Go to Step 14
8	1. Use a 3-amp fused jumper wire to connect the battery positive voltage circuit, at the steering wheel position sensor harness connector, to the steering wheel position signal A circuit. 2. Observe the Digital SWPS Phase A parameter on the scan tool. Does the scan tool display the Digital SWPS Phase A signal as being High?	Go to Step 11	Go to Step 9
9	Test the battery positive voltage circuit for an open. Did you find and correct the condition?	Go to Step 19	Go to Step 10
10	Test the steering wheel position signal A circuit for an open, a high resistance, or short to ground. Did you find and correct the condition?	Go to Step 19	Go to Step 16

LTV0500000006334

Fig. 225 Stability System Disabled Indicator Always On (Part 2 of 3). 2003–06 Avalanche, Escalade, Escalade EXT, Suburban, Tahoe & Yukon

Circuit Description

The instrument panel cluster (IPC) illuminates the traction OFF indicator by supplying ground to the lamp. The electronic brake control module (EBCM) sends serial data messages to the IPC to command the indicator ON or OFF.

Diagnostic Aids

The malfunction must be present during diagnosis in order to prevent unnecessary parts replacement. Always begin diagnosis with Diagnostic System Check - Vehicle .

Test Description

The number below refers to the step number on the diagnostic table.

3. This step tests if the IPC is able to turn OFF the traction OFF indicator.

LTV0500000006336

Fig. 226 Traction Off Indicator Always On (Part 1 of 2). 2003–06 Avalanche, Escalade, Escalade EXT, Suburban, Tahoe & Yukon

Step	Action	Yes	No
1	Did you perform the Diagnostic System Check - Vehicle?	Go to Step 2	Go to Diagnostic System Check - Vehicle
2	1. Turn OFF the ignition for 5 seconds. 2. Turn ON the ignition while observing the traction OFF indicator. Does the traction OFF indicator illuminate for approximately 2 seconds and then turn OFF?	Go to Diagnostic Aids	Go to Step 3
3	1. Select the Instrument Panel Cluster Special Functions menu on the scan tool. 2. Select Lamp Tests. 3. Command the instrument panel cluster (IPC) indicator lamps OFF. Does the traction off indicator turn OFF?	Go to Step 5	Go to Step 4
4	Replace the IPC. Did you complete the replacement?	Go to Step 6	--
5	Replace the electronic brake control module (EBCM). Did you complete the replacement?	Go to Step 6	--
6	1. Turn OFF the ignition for 5 seconds. 2. Turn ON the ignition while observing the traction off indicator. Does the traction OFF indicator illuminate for approximately 2 seconds and then turn OFF?	System OK	Go to Step 3

LTV0500000006337

Fig. 226 Traction Off Indicator Always On (Part 2 of 2). 2003–06 Avalanche, Escalade, Escalade EXT, Suburban, Tahoe & Yukon

Step	Action	Yes	No
11	1. Use a 3-amp fused jumper wire to connect the battery positive voltage circuit, at the steering wheel position sensor harness connector, to the steering wheel position signal B circuit. 2. Observe the Digital SWPS Phase B parameter on the scan tool . Does the scan tool display the Digital SWPS Phase B signal as being High?	Go to Step 13	Go to Step 12
12	Test the steering wheel position signal B circuit for an open, a high resistance, or short to ground. Did you find and correct the condition?	Go to Step 19	Go to Step 16
13	Test each ground circuit to the steering wheel position sensor for an open. Did you find and correct the condition?	Go to Step 19	Go to Step 15
14	Test each steering wheel position sensor signal circuit for a short to voltage. Did you find and correct the condition?	Go to Step 19	Go to Step 18
15	Inspect for poor connections at the harness connector of the steering wheel position sensor. Did you find and correct the condition?	Go to Step 19	Go to Step 17
16	Inspect for poor connections at the harness connector of the electronic brake control module (EBCM). Did you find and correct the condition?	Go to Step 19	Go to Step 18
17	Replace the steering wheel position sensor. Did you complete the replacement?	Go to Step 19	--
18	Replace the EBCM. Did you complete the replacement?	Go to Step 19	--
19	1. Use the scan tool to clear all DTCs from all modules. 2. Turn OFF the ignition for 5 seconds. 3. Turn ON the ignition. 4. Operate the vehicle at a speed greater than the specified value, for approximately 3.2 km (2 mi). Is the stability system disabled message displayed?	Go to Step 3	System OK

LTV0500000006335

Fig. 225 Stability System Disabled Indicator Always On (Part 3 of 3). 2003–06 Avalanche, Escalade, Escalade EXT, Suburban, Tahoe & Yukon

Circuit Description

The instrument panel cluster (IPC) illuminates the traction off indicator by supplying ground to the lamp. The electronic brake control module (EBCM) sends serial data messages to the IPC to command the indicator ON or OFF.

Diagnostic Aids

Replace the IPC if the traction off indicator intermittently fails to illuminate during the bulb check.

Test Description

The number below refers to the step number on the diagnostic table.

2. This step tests if the IPC is able to illuminate the traction off indicator during the bulb check.

Step	Action	Yes	No
1	Did you perform the Diagnostic System Check - Vehicle?	Go to Step 2	Go to Diagnostic System Check
2	1. Turn OFF the ignition for 5 seconds. 2. Turn ON the ignition while observing the traction off indicator. Does the traction off indicator illuminate?	Go to Diagnostic Aids	Go to Step 3
3	Replace the instrument panel cluster (IPC). Did you complete the replacement?	Go to Step 4	--
4	1. Turn OFF the ignition for 5 seconds. 2. Turn ON the ignition while observing the traction off indicator. Does the traction off indicator illuminate?	System OK	Go to Step 3

LTV0500000006338

Fig. 227 Traction Off Indicator Inoperative. 2003–06 Avalanche, Escalade, Escalade EXT, Suburban, Tahoe & Yukon

Circuit Description

Important: Information contained in this diagnostic procedure is intended for use when servicing vehicles equipped with RPO JL4. Do not use this information to address concerns on vehicles equipped with NW7.

Proper operation of the traction control system (TCS) is highly dependent on the ability to apply brake pressure to a selected wheel, through the brake pressure modulator valve (BPMV), as commanded by the electronic brake control module (EBCM). The EBCM may not be able to detect certain mechanical failures that may cause the TCS to perform poorly. This diagnostic procedure is designed to help diagnose concerns of excessive wheel slip or dragging brakes during acceleration, which may occur without the presence of any DTCs.

Step	Action	Yes	No
1	Did you review the system Description and Operation and perform the necessary inspections?	Go to Step 2	Go to Symptoms - Antilock Brake System
2	1. Raise the vehicle so that all four wheels are about 15 cm (6 in) off of the floor. 2. With help from an assistant, verify that the brake at each driven wheel is applying and releasing properly when the brake pedal is applied and released. Did you find and correct a concern?	Go to Step 8	Go to Step 3
3	Diagnose any hydraulic brake symptoms exhibited by the vehicle. Did you find and correct a concern?	Go to Step 8	Go to Step 4

LTV0500000006339

Fig. 228 Traction Control System Poor Performance (Part 1 of 2). 2003–06 Avalanche, Escalade, Escalade EXT, Suburban, Tahoe & Yukon

Step	Action	Yes	No
4	1. Install a scan tool. 2. Perform dump and isolation valve testing on all of the dump and isolation valves. Did any of the pressure dump or wheel isolation tests fail?	Go to Step 6	Go to Step 5
5	**Important:** For 2 wheel drive vehicles, it is not necessary to perform a front wheel apply if the only concern is TC poor performance. Perform brake pressure application testing. Did either of the TC isolation valve tests fail?	Go to Step 6	System OK
6	Replace the brake pressure modulator valve (BPMV). Did you complete the replacement?	Go to Step 7	--
7	Use the scan tool to perform all of the available BPMV hydraulic tests. Do the hydraulic tests show the system to be functioning normally?	Go to Step 8	Go to Step 2
8	Test drive the vehicle to verify that the concern has been corrected. Does the TCS operate normally?	System OK	Go to Step 2

LTV0500000006340

Fig. 228 Traction Control System Poor Performance (Part 2 of 2). 2003–06 Avalanche, Escalade, Escalade EXT, Suburban, Tahoe & Yukon

Circuit Description

Proper operation of the vehicle stability enhancement system (VSES) is highly dependent on the ability to apply brake pressure to a selected wheel, through the brake pressure modulator valve (BPMV), as commanded by the electronic brake control module (EBCM). The EBCM may not be able to detect certain mechanical failures that may cause the VSES to perform poorly. This diagnostic procedure is designed to help diagnose concerns of poor vehicle stability, that may occur without the presence of any DTCs, by verifying the following.

- The tires are the correct size, properly inflated and in acceptable condition.
- There are no mechanical problems in the steering system.
- There are no mechanical problems in the suspension system.
- There are no mechanical problems in the base brake system.
- All of the VSES related hydraulic controls within the BPMV are functioning correctly.

Step	Action	Yes	No
1	Did you review the system Description and Operation and perform the necessary inspections?	Go to Step 2	Go to Symptoms - Antilock Brake System
2	Inspect all 4 tires for the following: • Improper size • Incorrect air pressure • Uneven tread wear • Insufficient tread. Did you find and correct a concern?	Go to Step 11	Go to Step 3
3	Inspect the vehicle for following: • Worn, loose or binding steering linkage components • Proper power steering operation. Did you find and correct a concern?	Go to Step 11	Go to Step 4

LTV0500000006341

Fig. 229 Vehicle Stability Enhancement System Poor Performance (Part 1 of 2). 2003–06 Avalanche, Escalade, Escalade EXT, Suburban, Tahoe & Yukon

Step	Action	Yes	No
4	Diagnose any suspension symptoms exhibited by the vehicle. Did you find and correct a concern?	Go to Step 11	Go to Step 5
5	1. Raise the vehicle so that all 4 wheels are about 15 cm (6 in) off of the floor. 2. With help from an assistant, verify that the brake at each wheel is applying and releasing properly when the brake pedal is applied and released. Did you find and correct a concern?	Go to Step 11	Go to Step 6
6	Diagnose any hydraulic brake symptoms exhibited by the vehicle. Did you find and correct a concern?	Go to Step 11	Go to Step 7
7	1. Install a scan tool. 2. Perform the wheel isolation test procedure on all of the isolation valves. Did any of the wheel isolation tests fail?	Go to Step 9	Go to Step 8
8	Perform brake pressure application testing. Did either of the TC isolation valve tests fail?	Go to Step 9	System OK
9	Replace the brake pressure modulator valve (BPMV). Did you complete the replacement?	Go to Step 10	--
10	Use the scan tool to perform all of the available BPMV hydraulic tests. Do the hydraulic tests show the system to be functioning normally?	Go to Step 11	Go to Step 5
11	Test drive the vehicle to verify that the stability concern has been corrected. Has the concern been corrected?	System OK	Go to Step 2

LTV0500000006342

Fig. 229 Vehicle Stability Enhancement System Poor Performance (Part 2 of 2) . 2003–06 Avalanche, Escalade, Escalade EXT, Suburban, Tahoe & Yukon

Mechanical failures within the brake pressure modulator valve (BPMV) may cause improper operation of the ABS/DRP/TCS/VSES as well as possibly causing DTCs to set. The following diagnostic tests have been developed for use in diagnosing these concerns. Perform only the tests which apply for the DTC or symptom you are diagnosing.

Dump and Isolation Valve Testing

Pressure Dump Test Procedure

1. Apply the parking brake fully.
2. Start the engine and allow the engine to idle.
3. Select the desired Dump Valve Solenoid Test on the scan tool.
4. Apply the brake and maintain steady pressure on the brake pedal.
5. Command the solenoid On and verify that the brake pedal drops to the floor.

Wheel Isolation Test Procedure

1. Apply the parking brake fully.
2. Start the engine and allow the engine to idle.
3. Select the desired Isolation Valve Solenoid Test on the scan tool.
4. Apply the brake with very light pressure, only enough to open the brake switch.
5. Command the solenoid On and then immediately apply firm and steady pressure to the brake pedal.
6. The EBCM automatically de-energizes the solenoid after about 5 seconds. When this occurs, verify that the brake pedal drops about 2.2 cm (1 inch).

Brake Pressure Application Testing (W/JL4)

Important

Before performing the following tests, perform all of the isolation valve tests described in the wheel isolation test procedure. A malfunctioning isolation valve may cause pressure to be applied to multiple wheels, instead of to just one wheel as commanded.

If the brake being tested fails to apply, does not hold for the full 9 second period or releases slowly after the 9 second hold, the TC Isolation Valve Test has failed.

TC Isolation Valve Test Procedure

1. Turn OFF the ignition.
2. Disconnect the brake switch harness connector.
3. Raise the vehicle so that all four wheels are about 15 cm (6 in) off of the floor.
4. Ensure that the park brake is released.
5. Turn ON the ignition.
6. Ensure that the transmission is in neutral (N).
7. Select the VSES Special Functions menu on the scan tool.
8. Select either the Left Front Brake Apply or the Right Front Brake Apply, whichever wheel has the most convenient access for you.
9. Press the Apply key on the scan tool.
10. Listen for the precharge pump to activate for approximately 2 seconds.
11. Immediately verify brake activation at the wheel by attempting to turn the wheel by hand.
12. Continue attempting to turn the wheel by hand and ensure the wheel remains locked for 9 seconds after the precharge pump turns OFF.
13. Verify that the brake releases quickly when the 9 second pressure hold is terminated.
14. Select either the Left Rear Brake Apply or the Right Rear Brake Apply, whichever wheel has the most convenient access for you.
15. Repeat steps 11, 12 and 13 for the rear wheel being tested.
16. Turn OFF the ignition.
17. Reconnect the brake switch harness connector.

LTV0500000006343

Fig. 230   Brake Pressure Modulator Valve Hydraulic Testing. 2003–06 Avalanche, Escalade, Escalade EXT, Suburban, Tahoe & Yukon

	Action		
3	1. Install a scan tool. 2. Select the Instrument Panel Cluster Special Functions menu on the scan tool. 3. Command the ABS Lamp Off. Does the ABS indicator turn OFF?	Go to Step 5	Go to Step 4
4	Replace the instrument panel cluster. Did you complete the replacement?	Go to Step 6	--
5	**Important** Following EBCM replacement, use the scan tool to perform the Tire Size Calibration procedure. Replace the EBCM. Did you complete the replacement?	Go to Step 6	--
6	1. Turn OFF the ignition for 5 seconds. 2. Turn ON the ignition while observing the ABS indicator. Does the ABS indicator illuminate for 2 seconds and then turn OFF?	System OK	Go to Step 3

LTV0500000006399

Fig. 231   ABS Indicator Always On (Part 2 of 2). 2002–03 Bravada, Envoy & Trailblazer

Circuit Description

The instrument panel cluster (IPC) illuminates the ABS indicator by supplying ground to the lamp. The electronic brake control module (EBCM) sends class 2 serial data messages to the IPC in order to command the indicator ON or OFF.

Diagnostic Aids

The malfunction must be present during diagnosis in order to prevent unnecessary parts replacement. Always begin diagnosis with Diagnostic System Check - ABS .

Test Description

The number below refers to the step number on the diagnostic table.

3. This step tests if the IPC is able to turn OFF the ABS indicator.

Step	Action	Yes	No
Important			
After a wheel speed sensor DTC is cleared and the ignition is ON, the ABS indicator may remain ON until the EBCM completes a power-up self test. This test concludes when the vehicle reaches a speed greater than 13 km/h (8 mph) and the wheel speeds are verified by the EBCM.			
1	Did you perform the ABS Diagnostic System Check?	Go to Step 2	Go to Diagnostic System Check - ABS
2	1. Turn OFF the ignition for 5 seconds. 2. Turn ON the ignition while observing the ABS indicator. Does the ABS indicator illuminate for 2 seconds and then turn OFF?	Go to Diagnostic Aids	Go to Step 3

LTV0500000006398

Fig. 231   ABS Indicator Always On (Part 1 of 2). 2002–03 Bravada, Envoy & Trailblazer

Circuit Description

The instrument panel cluster (IPC) illuminates the ABS indicator by supplying ground to the lamp. The electronic brake control module (EBCM) sends class 2 serial data messages to the IPC in order to command the indicator ON or OFF.

Diagnostic Aids

Replace the Instrument Panel Cluster if the ABS indicator intermittently fails to operate during the bulb check.

Test Description

The number below refers to the step number on the diagnostic table.

2. This step tests if the IPC is able to illuminate the ABS indicator during the bulb check.

Step	Action	Yes	No
1	Did you perform the ABS Diagnostic System Check?	Go to Step 2	Go to Diagnostic System Check - ABS
2	1. Turn OFF the ignition for 5 seconds. 2. Turn ON the ignition while observing the ABS indicator. Does the ABS indicator illuminate?	Go to Diagnostic Aids	Go to Step 3
3	Replace the instrument panel cluster. Did you complete the replacement?	Go to Step 4	--
4	1. Turn OFF the ignition for 5 seconds. 2. Turn ON the ignition while observing the ABS indicator. Does the ABS indicator illuminate?	System OK	Go to Step 3

LTV0500000006400

Fig. 232   ABS Indicator Inoperative. 2002–03 Bravada, Envoy & Trailblazer

Circuit Description

The ignition 1 voltage circuit supplies 12 volts to the traction control switch. The EBCM illuminates the low traction indicator by applying ground to the traction control active signal circuit.

Diagnostic Aids

Thoroughly inspect connections or circuitry that may cause an intermittent malfunction. Refer to Testing for Electrical Intermittents , Testing for Intermittent and Poor Connections , Wiring Repairs and Connector Repairs in Wiring Systems.

Test Description

The number below refers to the step number on the diagnostic table.

4. This step tests for proper operation of the low traction indicator circuitry.

Step	Action	Yes	No
1	Did you perform the ABS Diagnostic System Check?	Go to Step 2	Go to Diagnostic System Check - ABS
2	1. Turn OFF the ignition for 5 seconds. 2. Turn ON the ignition while observing the low traction indicator. Does the low traction indicator illuminate for 3 seconds and then turn OFF?	Go to Diagnostic Aids	Go to Step 3

LTV0500000006401

Fig. 233 Low Traction Indicator Always On (Part 1 of 2). 2002–03 Bravada, Envoy & Trailblazer

Circuit Description

The ignition 1 voltage circuit supplies 12 volts to the traction control switch. The EBCM illuminates the low traction indicator by applying ground to the traction control active signal circuit.

Diagnostic Aids

The traction control system can be controlled by the operator in the following ways:

- Through operation of the traction control switch.
- Through programming of the traction control system automatic engagement feature.

Depending on the programmed state, the operation of the traction control system, as well as the operation of the traction off and low traction indicators, differs.

Observe the data list parameters listed below in order to determine the status of the traction control system when it is unknown if the system is operational.

- Traction Control Enabled
- Traction Off Lamp Command

Press the traction control switch and observe the scan tool in order to verify a change in the status of the data list parameters.

Thoroughly inspect connections or circuitry that may cause an intermittent malfunction.

Test Description

The numbers below refer to the step numbers on the diagnostic table.

3. This step verifies the ignition 1 voltage circuit can supply adequate power to the traction control switch.

4. This step verifies the EBCM is applying ground to the low traction indicator.

5. The EBCM may be damaged if the traction control active signal circuit is shorted to voltage.

LTV0500000006403

Fig. 234 Low Traction Indicator Inoperative (Part 1 of 3). 2002–03 Bravada, Envoy & Trailblazer

Step	Action	Yes	No
3	1. Select the Traction Assist Data Display function on the scan tool. 2. Observe the Low Traction Lamp Command. Does the scan tool display On?	Go to Step 7	Go to Step 4
4	**Important** The EBCM sets DTC C0283 during this step if the ignition is ON for greater than 10 seconds. 1. Turn OFF the ignition. 2. Disconnect the traction control switch harness connector. Refer to Traction Control Switch Replacement . 3. Connect a test lamp between the traction control active signal circuit and the ignition 1 voltage circuit. 4. Turn ON the ignition. Does the test lamp illuminate for 3 seconds and then turn OFF?	Go to Step 6	Go to Step 5
5	Test the traction control active signal circuit for a short to ground. Did you find and correct the condition?	Go to Step 8	Go to Step 7
6	Replace the traction control switch. Did you complete the replacement?	Go to Step 8	--
7	**Important** Following EBCM replacement, use the scan tool to perform the Tire Size Calibration procedure. Replace the EBCM. Did you complete the replacement?	Go to Step 8	
8	1. Turn OFF the ignition for 5 seconds. 2. Turn ON the ignition while observing the low traction indicator. Does the low traction indicator illuminate for 3 seconds and then turn OFF?	System OK	Go to Step 3

LTV0500000006402

Fig. 233 Low Traction Indicator Always On (Part 2 of 2). 2002–03 Bravada, Envoy & Trailblazer

Step	Action	Yes	No
1	Did you perform A Diagnostic System Check?	Go to Step 2	Go to Diagnostic System Check - ABS
2	1. Select the Traction Assist Special Functions menu on the scan tool. 2. Command the Low Trac Lamp On and Off. Does the low traction indicator turn ON and OFF with each command?	Go to Diagnostic Aids	Go to Step 3
3	**Important** Do not disconnect the traction control switch harness connector during this step. 1. Turn OFF the ignition. 2. Access the traction control switch harness connector. 3. Turn ON the ignition. 4. Backprobe the traction control switch harness connector in order to connect a test lamp between the ignition 1 voltage circuit and a good ground. Does the test lamp illuminate?	Go to Step 4	Go to Step 8
4	**Important** Do not disconnect the traction control switch harness connector during this step. 1. Backprobe the traction control switch harness connector in order to connect a test lamp between the traction control active signal circuit and the ignition 1 voltage circuit at the traction control switch harness connector. 2. Use the scan tool in order to command the Low Trac Lamp On and Off. Does the test lamp turn ON and OFF with each command?	Go to Step 6	Go to Step 5
5	Test the traction control active signal circuit for a short to voltage or an open. Did you find and correct the condition?	Go to Step 11	Go to Step 7
6	Inspect for poor connections at the traction control switch. Did you find and correct the condition?	Go to Step 11	Go to Step 9

LTV0500000006404

Fig. 234 Low Traction Indicator Inoperative (Part 2 of 3). 2002–03 Bravada, Envoy & Trailblazer

Step	Action	Yes	No
7	Inspect for poor connections at the harness connector of the EBCM. Did you find and correct the condition?	Go to Step 11	Go to Step 10
8	Repair the high resistance in the ignition 1 voltage circuit. Did you complete the repair?	Go to Step 11	--
9	Replace the traction control switch. Did you complete the replacement?	Go to Step 11	--
10	**Important** Following EBCM replacement, use the scan tool to perform the Tire Size Calibration procedure. Replace the EBCM. Did you complete the replacement?	Go to Step 11	--
11	Use the scan tool in order to command the Low Trac Lamp On and Off. Does the low traction indicator turn ON and OFF with each command?	System OK	Go to Step 3

LTV0500000006405

Fig. 234 Low Traction Indicator Inoperative (Part 3 of 3). 2002–03 Bravada, Envoy & Trailblazer

Step	Action	Yes	No
1	Did you perform the ABS Diagnostic System Check?	Go to Step 2	Go to Diagnostic System Check - ABS
2	1. Turn OFF the ignition for 5 seconds. 2. Turn ON the ignition while observing the traction off indicator. Does the traction off indicator illuminate for 3 seconds and then turn OFF?	Go to Diagnostic Aids	Go to Step 3
3	Press and release the traction control switch. Does the traction off indicator turn OFF?	Go to Diagnostic Aids	Go to Step 4
4	1. Install a scan tool. 2. Select the Traction Assist Data Display function on the scan tool. 3. Press and release the traction control switch while observing the Traction Control Enabled status. Does the Traction Control Enabled status change?	Go to Step 5	Go to Step 7
5	1. Turn ON the traction control system by verifying the scan tool displays Traction Control Enabled - Yes. 2. Observe the Traction Off Lamp Command on the scan tool. Does the scan tool display Traction Off Lamp Command - On?	Go to Step 13	Go to Step 6
6	**Important** Do not disconnect the traction control switch harness connector during this step. Ensure the ignition is turned ON for the duration of this step. 1. Access the traction control switch harness connector. 2. Backprobe the traction control switch harness connector in order to connect a test lamp between the ignition 1 voltage circuit and the service traction control signal circuit. Does the test lamp illuminate?	Go to Step 9	Go to Step 8

LTV0500000006407

Fig. 235 Traction Off Indicator Always On (Part 2 of 3). 2002–03 Envoy & Trailblazer

Circuit Description

The ignition 1 voltage circuit supplies 12 volts to the traction control switch. The EBCM turns OFF the traction off indicator by applying ground to the service traction control signal circuit.

Diagnostic Aids

The traction control system can be controlled by the operator in the following ways:

- Through operation of the traction control switch.
- Through programming of the traction control system automatic engagement feature.

Depending on the programmed state, the operation of the traction control system, as well as the operation of the traction off and low traction indicators, differs.

Observe the data list parameters listed below in order to determine the status of the traction control system when it is unknown if the system is operational.

- Traction Control Enabled
- Traction Off Lamp Command

Press the traction control switch and observe the scan tool in order to verify a change in the status of the data list parameters.

Thoroughly inspect connections or circuitry that may cause an intermittent malfunction.

Test Description

The numbers below refer to the step numbers on the diagnostic table.

7. This step simulates pressing and releasing a properly functioning traction control switch.

10. The traction control switch may be damaged if the traction control switch signal circuit is shorted to voltage.

LTV0500000006406

Fig. 235 Traction Off Indicator Always On (Part 1 of 3). 2003–03 Envoy & Trailblazer

	Action	Yes	No
7	**Important** Do not disconnect the traction control switch harness connector during this step. 1. Access the traction control switch harness connector. 2. While observing the Traction Control Enabled status on the scan tool, backprobe the traction control switch harness connector with a test lamp connected to a good ground in order to momentarily contact the traction control switch signal circuit. Does the Traction Control Enabled status change?	Go to Step 11	Go to Step 10
8	Test the service traction control signal circuit for an open. Did you find and correct the condition?	Go to Step 14	Go to Step 12
9	Inspect for poor connections at the harness connector of the traction control switch. Did you find and correct the condition?	Go to Step 14	Go to Step 11
10	Test the traction control switch signal circuit for a short to voltage. Did you find and correct the condition?	Go to Step 14	Go to Step 13
11	Replace the traction control switch. Did you complete the replacement?	Go to Step 14	--
12	Inspect for poor connections at the harness connector of the EBCM. Did you find and correct the condition?	Go to Step 14	Go to Step 13
13	**Important** Following EBCM replacement, use the scan tool to perform the Tire Size Calibration procedure. Replace the EBCM. Did you complete the replacement?	Go to Step 14	--
14	Press and release the traction control switch several times. Does the traction off indicator turn ON and OFF each time the switch is pressed?	System OK	Go to Step 2

LTV0500000006408

Fig. 235 Traction Off Indicator Always On (Part 3 of 3). 2002–03 Envoy & Trailblazer

Circuit Description

The LED dimming supply circuit supplies voltage to the traction control switch. The EBCM turns OFF the traction off indicator by applying ground to the service traction control signal circuit, which causes the inverting driver module to open the traction control system passive indicator control circuit.

Diagnostic Aids

The traction control system can be controlled by the operator in the following ways:

- Through operation of the traction control switch.
- Through programming of the traction control system automatic engagement feature.

Depending on the programmed state, the operation of the traction control system, as well as the operation of the traction off and low traction indicators, differs.

Observe the data list parameters listed below in order to determine the status of the traction control system when it is unknown if the system is operational.

- Traction Control Enabled
- Traction Off Lamp Command

Press the traction control switch and observe the scan tool in order to verify a change in the status of the data list parameters.

Thoroughly inspect connections or circuitry that may cause an intermittent malfunction.

Test Description

The numbers below refer to the step numbers on the diagnostic table.

11. This step simulates pressing and releasing a properly functioning traction control switch.

14. The traction control switch may be damaged if the traction control switch signal circuit is shorted to voltage.

LTV0500000006409

**Fig. 236 Traction Off Indicator Always On
(Part 1 of 3). 2002–03 Bravada**

Step	Action	Yes	No
1	Did you perform the ABS Diagnostic System Check?	Go to Step 2	Go to Diagnostic System Check - ABS
2	1. Turn OFF the ignition for 5 seconds. 2. Turn ON the ignition while observing the traction off indicator. Does the traction off indicator illuminate for 3 seconds and then turn OFF?	Go to Diagnostic Aids	Go to Step 3
3	Press and release the traction control switch. Does the traction off indicator turn OFF?	Go to Diagnostic Aids	Go to Step 4
4	1. Install a scan tool. 2. Select the Traction Assist Data Display function on the scan tool. 3. Press and release the traction control switch while observing the Traction Control Enabled status. Does the Traction Control Enabled status change?	Go to Step 5	Go to Step 11
5	1. Turn ON the traction control system by verifying the scan tool displays Traction Control Enabled - Yes. 2. Observe the Traction Off Lamp Command on the scan tool. Does the scan tool display Traction Off Lamp Command - On?	Go to Step 19	Go to Step 6
6	Remove the circuit board from the inverting driver module. Does the traction off indicator turn OFF?	Go to Step 8	Go to Step 7
7	Test the traction control system passive indicator control circuit for a short to ground. Did you find and correct the condition?	Go to Step 20	Go to Step 15
8	At the inverting driver module case, connect a test lamp between the ignition 1 voltage circuit and the ground circuit. Does the test lamp illuminate?	Go to Step 10	Go to Step 9
9	Test the igniton 1 voltage circuit and the ground circuit for opens and repair as necessary. Did you complete the repair?	Go to Step 20	—

LTV0500000006410

**Fig. 236 Traction Off Indicator Always On
(Part 2 of 3). 2002–03 Bravada**

10	At the inverting driver module case, connect a test lamp between the service traction control signal circuit and the ignition 1 circuit. Does the test lamp illuminate?	Go to Step 16	Go to Step 12
11	**Important:** Do not disconnect the traction control switch harness connector during this step. 1. Access the traction control switch harness connector. 2. While observing the Traction Control Enabled status on the scan tool, backprobe the traction control switch harness connector with a test lamp connected to a good ground in order to momentarily contact the traction control switch signal circuit. Does the Traction Control Enabled status change?	Go to Step 13	Go to Step 14
12	Test the service traction control signal circuit for an open. Did you find and correct the condition?	Go to Step 20	Go to Step 18
13	Inspect for poor connections at the harness connector of the traction control switch. Did you find and correct the condition?	Go to Step 20	Go to Step 15
14	Test the traction control switch signal circuit for a short to voltage. Did you find and correct the condition?	Go to Step 20	Go to Step 19
15	Replace the traction control switch. Did you complete the replacement?	Go to Step 20	--
16	Inspect for poor connections at the inverting driver module circuit board. Did you find and correct the condition?	Go to Step 20	Go to Step 17
17	Replace the inverting driver module. Did you complete the replacement?	Go to Step 20	--
18	Inspect for poor connections at the harness connector of the EBCM. Did you find and correct the condition?	Go to Step 20	Go to Step 19
19	**Important:** Following EBCM replacement, use the scan tool to perform the Tire Size Calibration procedure. Replace the EBCM. Did you complete the replacement?	Go to Step 20	--
20	Press and release the traction control switch several times. Does the traction off indicator turn ON and OFF each time the switch is pressed?	System OK	Go to Step 2

LTV0500000006411

Fig. 236 Traction Off Indicator Always On (Part 3 of 3). 2002–03 Bravada

Circuit Description

The ignition 1 voltage circuit supplies 12 volts to the traction control switch. The EBCM turns OFF the traction off indicator by applying ground to the service traction control signal circuit.

Diagnostic Aids

The traction control system can be controlled by the operator in the following ways:

- Through operation of the traction control switch.
- Through programming of the traction control system automatic engagement feature.

Depending on the programmed state, the operation of the traction control system, as well as the operation of the traction off and low traction indicators, differs.

Observe the data list parameters listed below in order to determine the status of the traction control system when it is unknown if the system is operational.

- Traction Control Enabled
- Traction Off Lamp Command

Press the traction control switch and observe the scan tool in order to verify a change in the status of the data list parameters.

Thoroughly inspect connections or circuitry that may cause an intermittent malfunction.

Test Description

The numbers below refer to the step numbers on the diagnostic table.

5. This step simulates pressing and releasing a properly functioning traction control switch.

6. The traction control switch may be damaged if the traction control switch signal circuit is shorted to voltage.

7. This step tests if the ignition 1 voltage circuit can supply adequate power to the traction control switch.

8. This step tests if the EBCM is commanding the traction off indicator OFF.

LTV0500000006412

Fig. 237 Traction Off Indicator Inoperative (Part 1 of 3). 2002–03 Bravada, Envoy & Trailblazer

Step	Action	Yes	No
1	Did you perform the ABS Diagnostic System Check?	Go to Step 2	Go to Diagnostic System Check - ABS
2	1. Turn OFF the ignition for 5 seconds. 2. Turn ON the ignition while observing the traction off indicator. Does the traction off indicator illuminate for 3 seconds and then turn OFF?	Go to Step 3	Go to Step 7
3	Press and release the traction control switch. Does the traction off indicator turn ON?	Go to Diagnostic Aids	Go to Step 4
4	1. Install a scan tool. 2. Select the Traction Assist Data Display function on the scan tool. 3. Press and release the traction control switch while observing the Traction Control Enabled status. Does the Traction Control Enabled status change?	Go to Step 13	Go to Step 5
5	**Important** Do not disconnect the traction control switch harness connector during this step. 1. Access the traction control switch harness connector. 2. While observing the Traction Control Enabled status on the scan tool, backprobe the traction control switch harness connector with a test lamp connected to a good ground in order to momentarily contact the traction control switch signal circuit. Does the Traction Control Enabled status change?	Go to Step 12	Go to Step 6
6	Test the traction control switch signal circuit for a short to voltage. Did you find and correct the condition?	Go to Step 15	Go to Step 13
7	**Important** If the ignition is ON for more than 10 seconds, the EBCM sets DTC C0283. 1. Turn OFF the ignition. 2. Disconnect the traction control switch harness connector. 3. Connect a test lamp between the ignition 1 voltage circuit and a good ground. 4. Turn ON the ignition. Does the test lamp illuminate?	Go to Step 8	Go to Step 14
8	1. Turn OFF the ignition. 2. Reconnect the traction control switch harness connector. 3. Disconnect from the EBCM, the harness connector containing the service traction control signal circuit. 4. Turn ON the ignition. Does the traction off indicator illuminate?	Go to Step 13	Go to Step 9

LTV0500000006413

**Fig. 237   Traction Off Indicator Inoperative
(Part 2 of 3). 2002–03 Bravada, Envoy & Trailblazer**

Step	Action	Yes	No
9	Test the service traction control signal circuit for a short to ground or a short to voltage. Did you find and correct the condition?	Go to Step 15	Go to Step 10
10	Test the ground circuit of the traction control switch for an open. Did you find and correct the condition?	Go to Step 15	Go to Step 11
11	Inspect for poor connections at the harness connector of the traction control switch. Did you find and correct the condition?	Go to Step 15	Go to Step 12
12	Replace the traction control switch. Did you complete the replacement?	Go to Step 15	--
13	**Important** Following EBCM replacement, use the scan tool to perform the Tire Size Calibration procedure. Replace the EBCM. Did you complete the replacement?	Go to Step 15	--
14	Repair the high resistance in the ignition 1 voltage circuit. Did you complete the repair?	Go to Step 15	--
15	Press and release the traction control switch several times. Does the traction off indicator turn ON and OFF each time the switch is pressed?	System OK	Go to Step 2

LTV0500000006414

**Fig. 237   Traction Off Indicator Inoperative
(Part 3 of 3). 2002–03 Bravada, Envoy & Trailblazer**

Circuit Description

The instrument panel cluster (IPC) illuminates the ABS indicator by supplying ground to the lamp. The electronic brake control module (EBCM) sends serial data messages to the IPC to command the indicator ON or OFF.

Diagnostic Aids

The malfunction must be present during diagnosis in order to prevent unnecessary parts replacement. Always begin diagnosis with Diagnostic System Check - Vehicle .

Test Description

The number below refers to the step number on the diagnostic table.

3. This step tests if the IPC is able to turn OFF the ABS indicator.

Step	Action	Yes	No
	Important: An ECE 13 response may cause the ABS indicator to remain ON when no DTCs are set. It is necessary to verify that ECE 13 is not causing the ABS indicator to remain illuminated, prior to performing this diagnostic. Refer to ABS Description and Operation for a complete description of the ECE 13 response.		
1	Did you perform the Diagnostic System Check - Vehicle?	Go to Step 2	Go to Diagnostic System Check - Vehicle
2	1. Turn OFF the ignition for 5 seconds. 2. Turn ON the ignition while observing the ABS indicator. Does the ABS indicator illuminate for approximately 2 seconds and then turn OFF?	Go to Diagnostic Aids	Go to Step 3
3	1. Select the Instrument Panel Cluster Special Functions menu on the scan tool. 2. Select Lamp Tests. 3. Command the IPC indicator lamps Off. Does the ABS indicator turn OFF?	Go to Step 5	Go to Step 4
4	Replace the instrument panel cluster (IPC). Did you complete the replacement?	Go to Step 6	--
5	Replace the electronic brake control module (EBCM). Did you complete the replacement?	Go to Step 6	--
6	1. Turn OFF the ignition for 5 seconds. 2. Turn ON the ignition while observing the ABS indicator. Does the ABS indicator illuminate for approximately 2 seconds and then turn OFF?	System OK	Go to Step 3

LTV0500000006468

Fig. 238 ABS Indicator Always On. 2004–06 Bravada, Envoy, Rainier & Trailblazer

Circuit Description

The instrument panel cluster (IPC) illuminates the ABS indicator by supplying ground to the lamp. The electronic brake control module (EBCM) sends class 2 serial data messages to the IPC in order to command the indicator ON or OFF.

Diagnostic Aids

Replace the Instrument Panel Cluster if the ABS indicator intermittently fails to operate during the bulb check.

Test Description

The number below refers to the step number on the diagnostic table.

2. This step tests if the IPC is able to illuminate the ABS indicator during the bulb check.

Step	Action	Yes	No
1	Did you perform the Diagnostic System Check - Vehicle?	Go to Step 2	Go to Diagnostic System Check - Vehicle
2	1. Turn OFF the ignition for 5 seconds. 2. Turn ON the ignition while observing the ABS indicator. Does the ABS indicator illuminate?	Go to Diagnostic Aids	Go to Step 3
3	Replace the instrument panel cluster (IPC). Did you complete the replacement?	Go to Step 4	--
4	1. Turn OFF the ignition for 5 seconds. 2. Turn ON the ignition while observing the ABS indicator. Does the ABS indicator illuminate?	System OK	Go to Step 3

LTV0500000006469

Fig. 239 ABS Indicator Inoperative. 2004–06 Bravada, Envoy, Rainier & Trailblazer

Circuit Description

The instrument panel cluster (IPC) illuminates the traction off indicator by supplying ground to the lamp. The electronic brake control module (EBCM) sends serial data messages to the IPC to command the indicator ON or OFF.

Diagnostic Aids

The malfunction must be present during diagnosis in order to prevent unnecessary parts replacement. Always begin diagnosis with Diagnostic System Check - Vehicle .

Test Description

The number below refers to the step number on the diagnostic table.

3. This step tests if the IPC is able to turn OFF the traction off indicator.

Step	Action	Yes	No
1	Did you perform the Diagnostic System Check - Vehicle?	Go to Step 2	Go to Diagnostic System Check - Vehicle
2	1. Turn OFF the ignition for 5 seconds. 2. Turn ON the ignition while observing the traction off indicator. Does the traction off indicator illuminate for approximately 2 seconds and then turn OFF?	Go to Diagnostic Aids	Go to Step 3
3	1. Select the Instrument Panel Cluster Special Functions menu on the scan tool. 2. Select Lamp Tests. 3. Command the instrument panel cluster (IPC) indicator lamps Off. Does the traction off indicator turn OFF?	Go to Step 5	Go to Step 4
4	Replace the IPC. Did you complete the replacement?	Go to Step 6	--
5	Replace the electronic brake control module (EBCM). Did you complete the replacement?	Go to Step 6	--
6	1. Turn OFF the ignition for 5 seconds. 2. Turn ON the ignition while observing the traction off indicator. Does the traction off indicator illuminate for approximately 2 seconds and then turn OFF?	System OK	Go to Step 3

LTV0500000006470

Fig. 240   Traction Off Indicator Always On. 2004–06 Bravada, Envoy, Rainier & Trailblazer

Circuit Description

The instrument panel cluster (IPC) illuminates the traction off indicator by supplying ground to the lamp. The electronic brake control module (EBCM) sends serial data messages to the IPC to command the indicator ON or OFF.

Diagnostic Aids

Replace the IPC if the traction off indicator intermittently fails to illuminate during the bulb check.

Test Description

The number below refers to the step number on the diagnostic table.

2. This step tests if the IPC is able to illuminate the traction off indicator during the bulb check.

Step	Action	Yes	No
1	Did you perform the Diagnostic System Check - Vehicle?	Go to Step 2	Go to Diagnostic System Check - Vehicle
2	1. Turn OFF the ignition for 5 seconds. 2. Turn ON the ignition while observing the traction off indicator. Does the traction off indicator illuminate?	Go to Diagnostic Aids	Go to Step 3
3	Replace the instrument panel cluster (IPC). Did you complete the replacement?	Go to Step 4	--
4	1. Turn OFF the ignition for 5 seconds. 2. Turn ON the ignition while observing the traction off indicator. Does the traction off indicator illuminate?	System OK	Go to Step 3

LTV0500000006471

Fig. 241   Traction Off Indicator Inoperative. 2004–06 Bravada, Envoy, Rainier & Trailblazer

Step	Action	Yes	No
1	Did you perform the ABS Diagnostic System Check?	Go to Step 2	Go to A Diagnostic System Check
2	1. Turn OFF the ignition for 5 seconds. 2. Turn ON the ignition while observing the ABS indicator. Does the ABS indicator illuminate for 2 seconds and then turn OFF?	Go to Diagnostic Aids	Go to Step 3
3	1. Turn OFF the ignition. 2. Disconnect the 10-way EBCM harness connector. 3. Turn ON the ignition. Does the ABS indicator illuminate?	Go to Step 4	Go to Step 6
4	1. Turn OFF the ignition. 2. Disconnect the Instrument Panel Cluster (IPC) harness connector. 3. Connect a test lamp between the ignition 1 voltage circuit and the ABS indicator failure control circuit. 4. Turn ON the ignition. Does the test lamp illuminate?	Go to Step 5	Go to Step 7
5	Repair the short to ground in the ABS indicator failure control circuit. Did you complete the repair?	Go to Step 10	--
6	Inspect for poor connections at the harness connector of the EBCM. Did you find and correct the condition?	Go to Step 10	Go to Step 9
7	Inspect for poor connections at the harness connector of the IPC. Did you find and correct the condition?	Go to Step 10	Go to Step 8

GC4020152409010X

Fig. 242   Anti-Lock Indicator Lamp Always On (Part 1 of 2). 2002 Express & Savana

Step	Action	Yes	No
8	Replace the Instrument Panel Cluster. Did you complete the replacement?	Go to Step 10	--
9	Replace the EBCM. **Important** Use the scan tool in order to perform the Tire Size Calibration procedure. Did you complete the replacement?	Go to Step 10	--
10	1. Turn OFF the ignition for 5 seconds. 2. Turn ON the ignition while observing the ABS indicator. Does the ABS indicator illuminate for 2 seconds and then turn OFF?	System OK	Go to Step 3

GC4020152409020X

Fig. 242   Anti-Lock Indicator Lamp Always On (Part 2 of 2). 2002 Express & Savana

Step	Action	Yes	No
1	Did you perform the ABS Diagnostic System Check?	Go to Step 2	Go to A Diagnostic System Check
2	1. Turn OFF the ignition for 5 seconds. 2. Turn ON the ignition while observing the ABS indicator. Does the ABS indicator illuminate?	Go to Diagnostic Aids	Go to Step 3
3	1. Turn OFF the ignition. 2. Disconnect from the EBCM, the 10-way EBCM harness connector. 3. Use a connector adapter test kit in order to connect the ABS indicator failure control circuit to a good ground. 4. Turn ON the ignition. Does the ABS indicator illuminate?	Go to Step 7	Go to Step 4
4	1. Turn OFF the ignition. 2. Reconnect the EBCM 10-way harness connector. 3. Disconnect the Instrument Panel Cluster (IPC) harness connector. 4. Connect a test lamp between the ignition 1 voltage circuit and the ABS indicator failure control circuit. 5. Turn ON the ignition. Does the test lamp illuminate?	Go to Step 6	Go to Step 5
5	Repair the open in the ABS indicator failure control circuit. Did you complete the repair?	Go to Step 12	--
6	Inspect the ABS indicator lamp for an open (burned out) filament. Did you find and correct the condition?	Go to Step 12	Go to Step 8

GC4020152410010X

Fig. 243   Anti-Lock Indicator Lamp Off Always No DTC Set (Part 1 of 2). 2002 Express & Savana

Step	Action	Yes	No
7	Inspect for poor connections at the harness connector of the EBCM. Did you find and correct the condition?	Go to Step 12	Go to Step 10
8	Inspect for poor connections at the harness connector of the IPC. Did you find and correct the condition?	Go to Step 12	Go to Step 9
9	Replace the Instrument Panel Cluster. Did you complete the replacement?	Go to Step 12	--
10	Replace the EBCM. **Important** Use the scan tool in order to perform the Tire Size Calibration procedure. Did you complete the replacement?	Go to Step 12	--
12	1. Turn OFF the ignition for 5 seconds. 2. Turn ON the ignition while observing the ABS indicator. Does the ABS indicator illuminate?	System OK	Go to Step 3

GC4020152410020X

Fig. 243   Anti-Lock Indicator Lamp Off Always No DTC Set (Part 2 of 2). 2002 Express & Savana

Circuit Description

The instrument panel cluster (IPC) illuminates the ABS indicator by supplying ground to the lamp. The electronic brake control module (EBCM) sends serial data messages to the IPC to command the indicator ON or OFF.

Diagnostic Aids

The malfunction must be present during diagnosis in order to prevent unnecessary parts replacement. Always begin diagnosis with Diagnostic System Check - Vehicle .

Test Description

The number below refers to the step number on the diagnostic table.

3. This step tests if the IPC is able to turn OFF the ABS indicator.

Step	Action	Yes	No
	Important: An ECE 13 response may cause the ABS indicator to remain ON when no DTCs are set. It is necessary to verify that ECE 13 is not causing the ABS indicator to remain illuminated, prior to performing this diagnostic. Refer to ABS Description and Operation for a complete description of the ECE 13 response.		
1	Did you perform the Diagnostic System Check - Vehicle?	Go to Step 2	Go to Diagnostic System Check - Vehicle
2	1. Turn OFF the ignition for 5 seconds. 2. Turn ON the ignition while observing the ABS indicator. Does the ABS indicator illuminate for approximately 2 seconds and then turn OFF?	Go to Diagnostic Aids	Go to Step 3
3	1. Select the Instrument Panel Cluster Special Functions menu on the scan tool. 2. Select Lamp Tests. 3. Command the instrument panel cluster (IPC) indicator lamps OFF. Does the ABS indicator turn OFF?	Go to Step 5	Go to Step 4
4	Replace the IPC. Did you complete the replacement?	Go to Step 6	--
5	**Important:** Following electronic brake control module (EBCM) replacement, perform the set-up procedure for the EBCM and use the scan tool to perform the Tire Size Calibration procedure. Replace the EBCM. Did you complete the replacement?	Go to Step 6	--
6	1. Turn OFF the ignition for 5 seconds. 2. Turn ON the ignition while observing the ABS indicator. Does the ABS indicator illuminate for approximately 2 seconds and then turn OFF?	System OK	Go to Step 3

LTV0500000006627

Fig. 244 ABS Indicator Always. 2003–06 Express & Savana

Circuit Description

The instrument panel cluster (IPC) illuminates the ABS indicator by supplying ground to the lamp. The electronic brake control module (EBCM) sends class 2 serial data messages to the IPC in order to command the indicator ON or OFF.

Diagnostic Aids

Replace the IPC if the ABS indicator intermittently fails to operate during the bulb check.

Test Description

The number below refers to the step number on the diagnostic table.

2. This step tests if the IPC is able to illuminate the ABS indicator during the bulb check.

Step	Action	Yes	No
1	Did you perform the Diagnostic System Check - Vehicle?	Go to Step 2	Go to Diagnostic System Check - Vehicle
2	1. Turn OFF the ignition for 5 seconds. 2. Turn ON the ignition while observing the ABS indicator. Does the ABS indicator illuminate?	Go to Diagnostic Aids	Go to Step 3
3	Replace the instrument panel cluster (IPC). Did you complete the replacement?	Go to Step 4	--
4	1. Turn OFF the ignition for 5 seconds. 2. Turn ON the ignition while observing the ABS indicator. Does the ABS indicator illuminate?	System OK	Go to Step 3

LTV0500000006628

Fig. 245 ABS Indicator Inoperative. 2003–06 Express & Savana

Circuit Description

The instrument panel cluster (IPC) illuminates the stability system caution indicator during the IPC bulb check or when the electronic brake control module (EBCM) sends a serial data message to the IPC commanding the indicator ON. The stability system caution indicator is used to indicate when the vehicle stability enhancement system (VSES) is disabled.

During aggressive driving conditions which repeatedly activate the VSES or traction control system (TCS), one or more of the solenoid coils may become overheated. The stability system caution indicator is displayed at this time and the EBCM disables all VSES/TCS brake pressure applications in an attempt to decrease the solenoid temperatures. Coil temperatures are estimated by the EBCM based on ambient temperature and monitored solenoid activation and may not coincide with actual solenoid temperatures. The stability system caution indicator turns OFF and normal VSES/TCS activity resumes when the EBCM determines that the solenoids have cooled sufficiently.

Diagnostic Aids

The VSES solenoid coils may overheat during aggressive driving, causing the VSES to be disabled temporarily.

A medium-low brake fluid level in the master cylinder reservoir may cause the stability system caution indicator to be illuminated during stopping or turning maneuvers. This condition will also cause the red brake warning indicator to turn ON. Ensure the master cylinder reservoir has an adequate brake fluid level.

If the stability system caution indicator turns ON due to any of the above conditions, no diagnosis or repair of the VSES is required.

Step	Action	Yes	No
1	Did you perform the Diagnostic System Check - Vehicle?	Go to Step 2	Go to Diagnostic System Check - Vehicle
2	Turn ON the ignition and observe the stability system caution indicator. Does the stability system caution indicator remain illuminated after the instrument panel cluster (IPC) bulb check is completed?	Go to Step 3	Go to Diagnostic

LTV0500000006629

Fig. 246   Stability System Caution Indicator Always On (Part 1 of 2). 2003–06 Express & Savana

Step	Action	Yes	No
3	Observe the brake warning indicator on the IPC. Is the brake warning indicator always ON?	Go to Brake Warning Indicator Always On	Go to Step 4
4	1. Select the Instrument Panel Cluster Special Functions menu on the scan tool. 2. Select Lamp Tests. 3. Command the IPC indicator lamps OFF. Does the stability system caution indicator turn OFF?	Go to Step 5	Go to Step 6
5	**Important:** Following the electronic brake control module (EBCM) replacement, perform the set-up procedure for the EBCM and use the scan tool to perform the Tire Size Calibration procedure. Replace the EBCM. Did you complete the replacement?	Go to Step 7	--
6	**Important:** Perform the set-up procedure for the IPC. Replace the IPC. Did you complete the replacement?	Go to Step 7	--
7	1. Use the scan tool to clear all DTCs from all modules. 2. Turn OFF the ignition for 5 seconds. 3. Turn ON the ignition and observe the stability system caution indicator. Does the stability system caution indicator remain illuminated after the IPC bulb check is completed?	Go to Step 3	System OK

LTV0500000006630

Fig. 246   Stability System Caution Indicator Always On (Part 2 of 2). 2003–06 Express & Savana

Circuit Description

The instrument panel cluster (IPC) illuminates the stability system caution indicator during the IPC bulb check or when the electronic brake control module (EBCM) sends a serial data message to the IPC commanding the indicator ON.

Diagnostic Aids

Replace the IPC if the stability system caution indicator intermittently fails to illuminate during the bulb check.

Test Description

The number below refers to the step number on the diagnostic table.

2. This step tests if the IPC is able to illuminate the stability system caution indicator during the bulb check.

Step	Action	Yes	No
1	Did you perform the Diagnostic System Check - Vehicle?	Go to Step 2	Go to Diagnostic System Check - Vehicle
2	1. Turn OFF the ignition for 5 seconds. 2. Turn ON the ignition while observing the stability system caution indicator. Does the stability system caution indicator illuminate?	Go to Diagnostic Aids	Go to Step 3
3	Replace the instrument panel cluster (IPC). Did you complete the replacement?	Go to Step 4	--
4	1. Turn OFF the ignition for 5 seconds. 2. Turn ON the ignition while observing the stability system caution indicator. Does the stability system caution indicator illuminate?	System OK	Go to Step 3

LTV0500000006631

Fig. 247   Stability System Caution Indicator Inoperative. 2003–06 Express & Savana

Circuit Description

The 5 inputs to the electronic brake control module (EBCM), which are used solely for vehicle stability enhancement, are the longitudinal accelerometer, lateral accelerometer, yaw rate sensor, master cylinder pressure sensor, and the steering wheel position sensor. The EBCM must detect valid inputs from all 5 sources during the initialization period in order to enable the vehicle stability enhancement system (VSES). Initialization must occur during the first 3000 meters of vehicle travel or 1000 meters of straight vehicle travel. If initialization cannot be achieved during this time period, the VSES remains inactive and the stability system not ready indicator is illuminated. The EBCM does not attempt to reinitialize until the next ignition cycle. One or more DTCs often set, shortly after an unsuccessful initialization attempt, indicating the root cause of the failure. If this occurs, the stability system not ready indicator is no longer illuminated. The stability system caution indicator is illuminated instead.

Diagnostic Aids

If the customer concern is that the stability system disabled message is displayed intermittently, communicate with the customer to determine what driving conditions are being experienced at the time the message is displayed. The EBCM may be unable to successfully initialize the system during operation on very winding roads. Initialization may also be unsuccessful if pressure is continuously applied to the brake pedal during the initialization period.

If the message is displayed due to any of the above conditions, no diagnosis or repair of the VSES is required.

Step	Action	Yes	No
1	Did you perform the Diagnostic System Check - Vehicle?	Go to Step 2	Go to Diagnostic System Check - Vehicle
2	1. Turn OFF the ignition for 5 seconds. 2. Turn ON the ignition. 3. Operate the vehicle at a speed greater than the specified value for approximately 3.2 km (2 mi), or until the stability system not ready indicator is displayed. Is the stability system not ready indicator illuminated?	Go to Step 3	Go to Diagnostic Aids

LTV0500000006632

Fig. 248   Stability System Not Ready Indicator Always On (Part 1 of 3). 2003–06 Express & Savana

3	Use the scan tool to display vehicle stability enhancement system (VSES) History DTCs. Are any of the following DTCs stored in History? • C0131 • C0186 • C0196 • C0550	Go to Step 4	Go to Step 5
4	Operate the vehicle within the conditions for running any history DTCs which may be the cause of unsuccessful initialization. Do any of the DTCs listed in step 4 set as a Current DTC?	Go to *(CELL LINK)*	Go to Step 5
5	1. Select the VSES data list on the scan tool. 2. Observe the Digital steering wheel position sensor (SWPS) Phase A and the Digital SWPS Phase B parameters as you rotate the steering wheel. Do the Digital SWPS Phase A and the Digital SWPS Phase B parameters both transition from Low to High as the steering wheel is rotated?	Go to Step 1	Go to Step 6
6	1. Turn OFF the ignition. 2. Disconnect the steering wheel position sensor harness connector. 3. Turn ON the ignition. 4. Observe Digital SWPS Phase A and the Digital SWPS Phase B parameters on the scan tool. Does the scan tool display that both parameters are low?	Go to Step 7	Go to Step 13
7	1. Use a 3-amp fused jumper wire to connect the battery positive voltage circuit, at the steering wheel position sensor harness connector, to the steering wheel position signal A circuit. 2. Observe the Digital SWPS Phase A parameter on the scan tool. Does the scan tool display the Digital SWPS Phase A signal as being High?	Go to Step 10	Go to Step 8
8	Test the battery positive voltage circuit for an open. Did you find and correct the condition?	Go to Step 18	Go to Step 9
9	Test the steering wheel position signal A circuit for an open, a high resistance, or short to ground. Did you find and correct the condition?	Go to Step 18	Go to Step 15

LTV0500000006633

Fig. 248   Stability System Not Ready Indicator Always On (Part 2 of 3). 2003–06 Express & Savana

Step	Action	Yes	No
10	1. Use a 3-amp fused jumper wire to connect the battery positive voltage circuit, at the steering wheel position sensor harness connector, to the steering wheel position signal B circuit. 2. Observe the Digital SWPS Phase B parameter on the scan tool . Does the scan tool display the Digital SWPS Phase B signal as being High?	Go to Step 12	Go to Step 11
11	Test the steering wheel position signal B circuit for an open, a high resistance, or short to ground. Did you find and correct the condition?	Go to Step 18	Go to Step 15
12	Test each ground circuit to the steering wheel position sensor for an open. Did you find and correct the condition?	Go to Step 18	Go to Step 14
13	Test each steering wheel position sensor signal circuit for a short to voltage. Did you find and correct the condition?	Go to Step 18	Go to Step 15
14	Inspect for poor connections at the harness connector of the steering wheel position sensor. Did you find and correct the condition?	Go to Step 18	Go to Step 16
15	Inspect for poor connections at the harness connector of the electronic brake control module (EBCM). Did you find and correct the condition?	Go to Step 18	Go to Step 17
16	Replace the steering wheel position sensor. Did you complete the replacement?	Go to Step 18	--
17	**Important:** Following the EBCM replacement, perform the set-up procedure for the EBCM and use the scan tool to perform the Tire Size Calibration procedure. Replace the EBCM. Did you complete the replacement?	Go to Step 18	--
18	1. Use the scan tool to clear all DTCs from all modules. 2. Turn OFF the ignition for 5 seconds. 3. Turn ON the ignition. 4. Operate the vehicle at a speed greater than the specified value for approximately 3.2 km (2 mi) , or until the stability system not ready indicator is displayed. Is the stability system not ready indicator illuminated?	Go to Step 3	System OK

LTV0500000006634

Fig. 248   Stability System Not Ready Indicator Always On (Part 3 of 3). 2003–06 Express & Savana

Circuit Description

The instrument panel cluster (IPC) illuminates the stability system not ready indicator during the IPC bulb check or when the electronic brake control module (EBCM) sends a serial data message to the IPC commanding the indicator ON.

Diagnostic Aids

Replace the IPC if the stability system not ready indicator intermittently fails to illuminate during the bulb check.

Test Description

The number below refers to the step number on the diagnostic table.

2. This step tests if the IPC is able to illuminate the stability system not ready indicator during the bulb check.

Step	Action	Yes	No
1	Did you perform the Diagnostic System Check - Vehicle?	Go to Step 2	Go to Diagnostic System Check - Vehicle
2	1. Turn OFF the ignition for 5 seconds. 2. Turn ON the ignition while observing the stability system not ready indicator. Does the stability system not ready indicator illuminate?	Go to Diagnostic Aids	Go to Step 3
3	Replace the instrument panel cluster (IPC). Did you complete the replacement?	Go to Step 4	--
4	1. Turn OFF the ignition for 5 seconds. 2. Turn ON the ignition while observing the stability system not ready indicator. Does the stability system not ready indicator illuminate?	System OK	Go to Step 3

LTV0500000006635

Fig. 249   Stability System Not Ready Indicator Inoperative. 2003–06 Express & Savana

Circuit Description

Proper operation of the vehicle stability enhancement system (VSES) is highly dependent on the ability to apply brake pressure to a selected wheel, through the brake pressure modulator valve (BPMV), as commanded by the electronic brake control module (EBCM). The EBCM may not be able to detect certain mechanical failures that may cause the VSES to perform poorly. This diagnostic procedure is designed to help diagnose concerns of poor vehicle stability, that may occur without the presence of any DTCs, by verifying the following:

- The tires are the correct size, properly inflated and in acceptable condition.
- There are no mechanical problems in the steering system.
- There are no mechanical problems in the suspension system.
- There are no mechanical problems in the base brake system.
- All of the VSES related hydraulic controls within the BPMV are functioning correctly.

Step	Action	Yes	No
1	Did you review the system Description and Operation and perform the necessary inspections?	Go to Step 2	Go to Symptoms - Antilock Brake System
2	Inspect all four tires for the following conditions: • Improper size • Incorrect air pressure • Uneven tread wear • Insufficient tread Did you find and correct a concern?	Go to Step 11	Go to Step 3
3	Inspect the vehicle for following conditions: • Worn, loose or binding steering linkage components. • Proper power steering operation. Did you find and correct a concern?	Go to Step 11	Go to Step 4
4	Diagnose any suspension symptoms exhibited by the vehicle. Did you find and correct a concern?	Go to Step 11	Go to Step 5
5	1. Raise the vehicle so that all 4 wheels are about 15 cm (6 in) off the floor. Refer to Lifting and Jacking the Vehicle. 2. With help from an assistant, verify that the brake at each wheel is applying and releasing properly when the brake pedal is applied and released. Did you find and correct a concern?	Go to Step 11	Go to Step 6

LTV0500000006636

Fig. 250 Vehicle Stability Enhancement System Poor Performance (Part 1 of 2). 2003–06 Express & Savana

6	Diagnose any hydraulic brake symptoms exhibited by the vehicle. Did you find and correct a concern?	Go to Step 11	Go to Step 7
7	1. Install a scan tool. 2. Perform the wheel isolation test procedure on all of the isolation valves. Did any of the wheel isolation tests fail?	Go to Step 9	Go to Step 8
8	Perform brake pressure application testing. Did either of the TC isolation valve tests fail?	Go to Step 9	System OK
9	Replace the BPMV. Did you complete the replacement?	Go to Step 10	--
10	Use the scan tool to perform all of the available BPMV hydraulic tests. Do the hydraulic tests show the system to be functioning normally?	Go to Step 11	Go to Step 5
11	Test drive the vehicle to verify that the stability concern has been corrected. Has the concern been corrected?	System OK	Go to Step 2

LTV0500000006637

Fig. 250 Vehicle Stability Enhancement System Poor Performance (Part 2 of 2). 2003–06 Express & Savana

Mechanical failures within the brake pressure modulator valve (BPMV) may cause improper operation of the ABS/dynamic rear proportion (DRP)/traction control system (TCS)/vehicle stability enhancement system (VSES) as well as possibly causing DTCs to set. The following diagnostic tests have been developed for use in diagnosing these concerns. Perform only the tests which apply for the DTC or symptom you are diagnosing.

Dump and Isolation Valve Testing

Pressure Dump Test Procedure

1. Apply the parking brake fully.
2. Start the engine and allow the engine to idle.
3. Select the desired Dump Valve Solenoid Test on the scan tool.
4. Apply the brake and maintain steady pressure on the brake pedal.
5. Command the solenoid ON and verify that the brake pedal drops to the floor.

Wheel Isolation Test Procedure

1. Apply the parking brake fully.
2. Start the engine and allow the engine to idle.
3. Select the desired Isolation Valve Solenoid Test on the scan tool.
4. Apply the brake with very light pressure, only enough to open the brake switch.
5. Command the solenoid ON and then immediately apply firm and steady pressure to the brake pedal.
6. The electronic brake control module (EBCM) automatically de-energizes the solenoid after about 5 seconds. When this occurs, verify that the brake pedal drops about 2.2 cm (1 in).

Brake Pressure Application Testing (W/JL4)

Important: Before performing the following tests, perform all of the isolation valve tests described in the wheel isolation test procedure. A malfunctioning isolation valve may cause pressure to be applied to multiple wheels, instead of to just one wheel as commanded.
If the brake being tested fails to apply, does not hold for the full 9 second period, or releases slowly after the 9 second hold, the TC Isolation Valve Test has failed.

LTV0500000006638

Fig. 251 Brake Pressure Modulator Valve Hydraulic Testing (Part 1 of 2). 2003–06 Express & Savana

TC Isolation Valve Test Procedure

1. Turn OFF the ignition.
2. Disconnect the brake switch harness connector.
3. Raise the vehicle so that all 4 wheels are about 15 cm (6 in) off of the floor. Refer to Lifting and Jacking the Vehicle in General Information.
4. Ensure that the park brake is released.
5. Turn ON the ignition.
6. Ensure that the transmission is in neutral (N).
7. Select the VSES Special Functions menu on the scan tool.
8. Select either the Left Front Brake Apply or the Right Front Brake Apply, whichever wheel has the most convenient access for you.
9. Press the Apply key on the scan tool.
10. Listen for the precharge pump to activate for approximately 2 seconds.
11. Immediately verify brake activation at the wheel by attempting to turn the wheel by hand.
12. Continue attempting to turn the wheel by hand and ensure the wheel remains locked for 9 seconds after the precharge pump turns OFF.
13. Verify that the brake releases quickly when the 9 second pressure hold is terminated.
14. Select either the Left Rear Brake Apply or the Right Rear Brake Apply, whichever wheel has the most convenient access for you.
15. Repeat steps 11, 12, and 13 for the rear wheel being tested.
16. Turn OFF the ignition.
17. Reconnect the brake switch harness connector.

LTV0500000006639

Fig. 251 Brake Pressure Modulator Valve Hydraulic Testing (Part 2 of 2). 2003–06 Express & Savana

Circuit Description

The instrument panel cluster (IPC) illuminates the ABS indicator by supplying ground to the lamp. The electronic brake control module (EBCM) sends class 2 serial data messages to the IPC in order to command the indicator ON or OFF.

Diagnostic Aids

The malfunction must be present during diagnosis in order to prevent unnecessary parts replacement. Always begin diagnosis with Diagnostic System Check - Vehicle in Vehicle DTC Information.

Test Description

The number below refers to the step number on the diagnostic table.

3. This step tests if the IPC is able to turn OFF the ABS indicator.

LTV0500000006549

Fig. 252 ABS Indicator Always On (Part 1 of 2). 2003–06 Sierra & Silverado

Step	Action	Yes	No
	Important: After a wheel speed sensor DTC is cleared and the ignition is ON, the antilock brake system (ABS) indicator may remain ON until the electronic brake control module (EBCM) completes a power-up self test. This test concludes when the vehicle reaches a speed greater than 13 km/h (8 mph) and the wheel speeds are verified by the EBCM.		
1	Did you perform the Diagnostic System Check - Vehicle?	Go to Step 2	Go to Diagnostic System Check
2	1. Turn OFF the ignition for 5 seconds. 2. Turn ON the ignition while observing the antilock brake system (ABS) indicator. Does the ABS indicator illuminate for 2 seconds and then turn OFF?	Go to Diagnostic Aids	Go to Step 3
3	1. Install a scan tool. 2. Select the instrument panel cluster (IPC) Special Functions menu on the scan tool. 3. Command the ABS Lamp OFF. Does the ABS indicator turn OFF?	Go to Step 5	Go to Step 4
4	Replace the IPC. Did you complete the replacement?	Go to Step 6	--
5	Replace the electronic brake control module (EBCM). Did you complete the replacement?	Go to Step 6	--
6	1. Turn OFF the ignition for 5 seconds. 2. Turn ON the ignition while observing the ABS indicator. Does the ABS indicator illuminate for 2 seconds and then turn OFF?	System OK	Go to Step 3

LTV0500000005550

Fig. 252 ABS Indicator Always On (Part 2 of 2). 2003–06 Sierra & Silverado

Circuit Description

The instrument panel cluster (IPC) illuminates the ABS indicator by supplying ground to the lamp. The electronic brake control module (EBCM) sends class 2 serial data messages to the IPC in order to command the indicator ON or OFF.

Diagnostic Aids

Replace the Instrument Panel Cluster if the ABS indicator intermittently fails to operate during the bulb check.

Test Description

The number below refers to the step number on the diagnostic table.

2. This step tests if the IPC is able to illuminate the ABS indicator during the bulb check.

Step	Action	Yes	No
1	Did you perform the Diagnostic System Check - Vehicle?	Go to Step 2	Go to Diagnostic System Check
2	1. Turn OFF the ignition for 5 seconds. 2. Turn ON the ignition while observing the antilock brake system (ABS) indicator. Does the ABS indicator illuminate?	Go to Diagnostic Aids	Go to Step 3
3	Replace the instrument panel cluster (IPC). Did you complete the replacement?	Go to Step 4	--
4	1. Turn OFF the ignition for 5 seconds. 2. Turn ON the ignition while observing the ABS indicator. Does the ABS indicator illuminate?	System OK	Go to Step 3

LTV0500000C06551

Fig. 253 ABS Indicator Inoperative. 2003–06 Sierra & Silverado

Circuit Description

The instrument panel cluster (IPC) illuminates the traction off indicator by supplying ground to the lamp. The electronic brake control module (EBCM) sends serial data messages to the IPC to command the indicator ON or OFF.

Diagnostic Aids

The malfunction must be present during diagnosis in order to prevent unnecessary parts replacement. Always begin diagnosis with Diagnostic System Check - Vehicle in Vehicle DTC Information.

Test Description

The number below refers to the step number on the diagnostic table.

3. This step tests if the IPC is able to turn OFF the traction off indicator.

LTV0500000006552

Fig. 254 Traction Off Indicator Always On (Part 1 of 2). 2003–06 Sierra & Silverado

Step	Action	Yes	No
1	Did you perform the Diagnostic System Check - Vehicle?	Go to Step 2	Go to Diagnostic System Check
2	1. Turn OFF the ignition for 5 seconds. 2. Turn ON the ignition while observing the traction off indicator. Does the traction off indicator illuminate for approximately 2 seconds and then turn OFF?	Go to Diagnostic Aids	Go to Step 3
3	1. Select the instrument panel cluster (IPC) Special Functions menu on the scan tool. 2. Select Lamp Tests. 3. Command the IPC indicator lamps Off. Does the traction off indicator turn OFF?	Go to Step 5	Go to Step 4
4	Replace the IPC. Did you complete the replacement?	Go to Step 6	--
5	Replace the electronic brake control module (EBCM). Did you complete the replacement?	Go to Step 6	--
6	1. Turn OFF the ignition for 5 seconds. 2. Turn ON the ignition while observing the traction off indicator. Does the traction off indicator illuminate for approximately 2 seconds and then turn OFF?	System OK	Go to Step 3

LTV0500000006553

Fig. 254 Traction Off Indicator Always On (Part 2 of 2). 2003–06 Sierra & Silverado

Circuit Description

The instrument panel cluster (IPC) illuminates the traction off indicator by supplying ground to the lamp. The electronic brake control module (EBCM) sends serial data messages to the IPC to command the indicator ON or OFF.

Diagnostic Aids

Replace the IPC if the traction off indicator intermittently fails to illuminate during the bulb check.

Test Description

The number below refers to the step number on the diagnostic table.

2. This step tests if the IPC is able to illuminate the traction off indicator during the bulb check.

Step	Action	Yes	No
1	Did you perform the Diagnostic System Check - Vehicle?	Go to Step 2	Go to Diagnostic System Check
2	1. Turn OFF the ignition for 5 seconds. 2. Turn ON the ignition while observing the traction off indicator. Does the traction off indicator illuminate?	Go to Diagnostic Aids	Go to Step 3
3	Replace the instrument panel cluster (IPC). Did you complete the replacement?	Go to Step 4	--
4	1. Turn OFF the ignition for 5 seconds. 2. Turn ON the ignition while observing the traction off indicator. Does the traction off indicator illuminate?	System OK	Go to Step 3

LTV0500000006554

Fig. 255   Traction Off Indicator Inoperative. 2003–06 Sierra & Silverado

°C	°F	Ohms
Temperature vs Resistance Values (Approximate)		
-40 to 4	-40 to 40	1575 to 2420
5 to 43	41 to 110	1980 to 2800
44 to 93	111 to 200	2250 to 3280
94 to 150	201 to 302	2750 to 3850

GC4029903668000X

Fig. 256   Temperature vs. resistance values

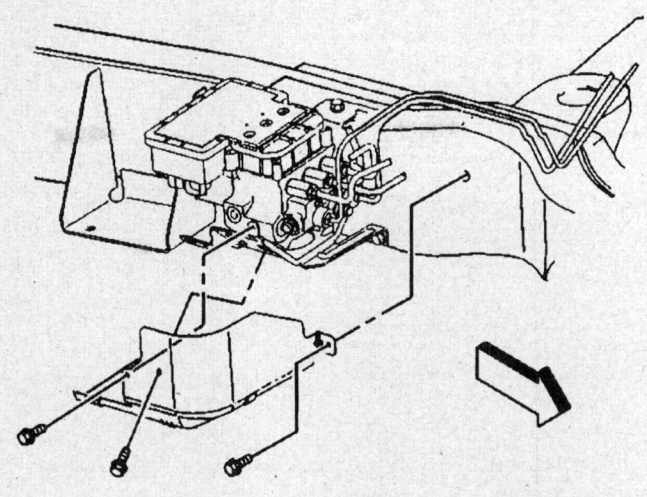

GC4029903715000X

Fig. 257   EHCU shield replacement

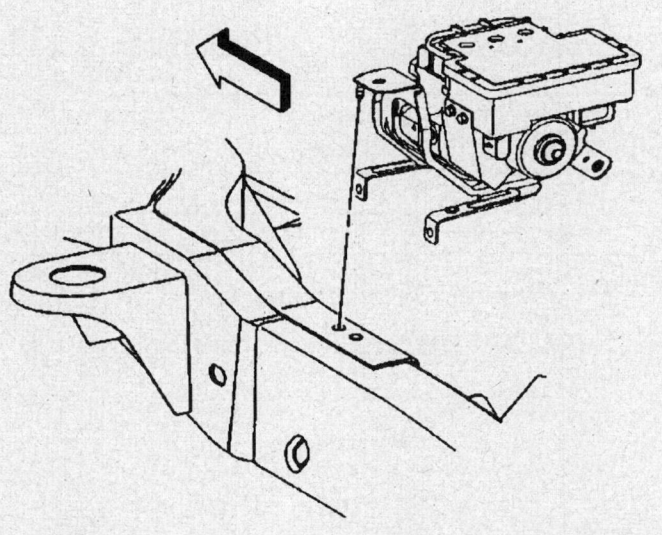

GC4029903716000X

Fig. 258   EHCU replacement

ACTIVE SUSPENSION SYSTEMS

TABLE OF CONTENTS

Page No.

APPLICATION CHART 6-1

AUTOMATIC LEVEL CONTROL
(ALC) 6-2

Page No.

ELECTRONIC SUSPENSION
CONTROL (ESC)/REAL TIME
DAMPING (RTD) 6-18

SELECTABLE RIDE (SR) 6-14

Application Chart

Model	Year	Type
Avalanche	2002–06	Electronic Suspension Control (ESC)/Real Time Damping (RTD)
Aztek	2002–06	Automatic Level Control (ALC)
Bravada	2002–04	Automatic Level Control (ALC)
Envoy	2002–06	Automatic Level Control (ALC)
Escalade	2002–06	Electronic Suspension Control (ESC)/Real Time Damping (RTD)
Hummer H2	2003–06	Automatic Level Control (ALC)
Montana	2002–05	Automatic Level Control (ALC)
Rainier	2004–06	Automatic Level Control (ALC)
Relay	2005–06	Automatic Level Control (ALC)
Rendezvous	2002–06	Automatic Level Control (ALC)
Sierra	2002–06	Selectable Ride (SR)
Silhouette	2002–04	Automatic Level Control (ALC)
Silverado	2002–06	Selectable Ride (SR)
SRX	2004–06	Electronic Suspension Control (ESC)/Real Time Damping (RTD)
Suburban	2002–06	Electronic Suspension Control (ESC)/Real Time Damping (RTD)
SV6	2005–06	Automatic Level Control (ALC)
Tahoe	2002–06	Electronic Suspension Control (ESC)/Real Time Damping (RTD)
Terraza	2005–06	Automatic Level Control (ALC)
Trailblazer	2002–06	Automatic Level Control (ALC)
Uplander	2005–06	Automatic Level Control (ALC)
Venture	2002–05	Automatic Level Control (ALC)
Yukon	2002–06	Electronic Suspension Control (ESC)/Real Time Damping (RTD)

Automatic Level Control (ALC)

NOTE: On Air Bag Equipped Models, Refer To "Air Bag System Precautions" Located In The Front Of This Manual For System Disarming & Arming Procedures.

NOTE: Refer To "Computer Relearn Procedures" Located In The Front Of This Manual When Battery Power To The Computer Has Been Interrupted.

NOTE: "Electrical Symbol & Wire Color Code Identification", Located In The Front Of This Manual, May Be Used As An Aid When Using Wiring Circuits Found In This Section.

INDEX

	Page No.		Page No.		Page No.
Adjustments	6-3	Bravada, Envoy, Rainier & Trailblazer	6-6	Hummer H2	6-4
Air Spring Sensor Calibration	6-4	Hummer H2	6-6	Clearing Diagnostic Trouble Codes	6-5
Bravada, Envoy, Rainier & Trailblazer	6-4	Automatic Level Control Air Dryer	6-6	Aztek, Bravada, Envoy, Montana, Rainier, Relay, Rendezvous, Silhouette,	
Automatic Level Control Sensor.	6-3	Relay, SV6, Terraza & Uplander	6-6	SV6, Terraza, Trailblazer,	
Aztek, Montana, Rendezvous, Silhouette & Venture	6-3	Compressor Head Assembly	6-6	Uplander & Venture	6-5
Component Replacement	6-5	Inflator Air Switch	6-7	Hummer H2	6-5
Accessory Fill Valve	6-6	Bravada, Envoy, Rainier & Trailblazer	6-7	Diagnostic Trouble Codes	6-4
Relay, SV6, Terraza & Uplander	6-6	Hummer H2	6-7	Aztek, Montana, Relay, Rendezvous, Silhouette,	
Air Compressor	6-5	Solenoid Valve Assembly	6-8	SV6, Terraza, Uplander & Venture	6-4
Aztek, Montana, Rendezvous, Silhouette & Venture	6-5	Aztek, Montana, Rendezvous, Silhouette & Venture	6-8	Bravada, Envoy, Rainier &	
Bravada, Envoy, Rainier & Trailblazer	6-5	Relay, SV6, Terraza & Uplander	6-8	Trailblazer	6-5
Hummer H2	6-5	Trim Height Sensor	6-8	Hummer H2	6-5
Relay, SV6, Terraza & Uplander	6-6	**Description**	6-3	Intermittents & Poor Connections	6-5
Air Inflator Relay	6-7	**Diagnosis & Testing**	6-4	Wiring Diagrams	6-4
Montana, Silhouette & Venture	6-7	Accessing Diagnostic Trouble Codes	6-4	**Precautions**	6-2
Air Inflator Switch	6-7	Aztek, Montana, Relay, Rendezvous, Silhouette,		Air Bag Systems	6-2
Aztek, Montana, Rendezvous, Silhouette & Venture	6-7	SV6, Terraza, Uplander & Venture	6-4	Air Suspension System Depressurization	6-2
Relay, SV6, Terraza & Uplander	6-7	Bravada, Envoy, Rainier & Trailblazer	6-4	Bravada, Envoy, Rainier & Trailblazer	6-2
Air Spring Leveling Sensor	6-6			Hummer H2	6-3
				Battery Ground Cable	6-2

PRECAUTIONS

Air Bag Systems

Refer to "Air Bag System Precautions" in the front of this manual for system disarming and arming procedures.

Battery Ground Cable

Prior to service, disconnect battery ground cable and isolate as required.

Air Suspension System Depressurization

BRAVADA, ENVOY, RAINIER & TRAILBLAZER

A sudden release of pressure may cause personal injury or damage to the vehicle. The air suspension system is under pressure until the air supply lines are disconnected. Always wear gloves, ear protection, and eye protection when performing repair procedures on the air suspension system. Wrap a clean cloth around the air supply lines. Depressurize the air suspension system only after the rear axle is supported and is set. Remove the air suspension system fuse before working on the rear suspension components or the rear axle. Failure to remove the air suspension system fuse could cause the calibration of the air suspension leveling sensor to change and the air suspension system not to function properly.

1. Remove air suspension system fuse. **Failure to remove air suspension system fuse could cause the calibration of the air suspension leveling sensor to change and the air suspension system not to function properly.**
2. Raise and support vehicle.
3. Support rear axle at designed height.
4. Remove air compressor mounting bolts from the frame and support air compressor.
5. Loosen both air supply line connections at air compressor to depressurize air springs.

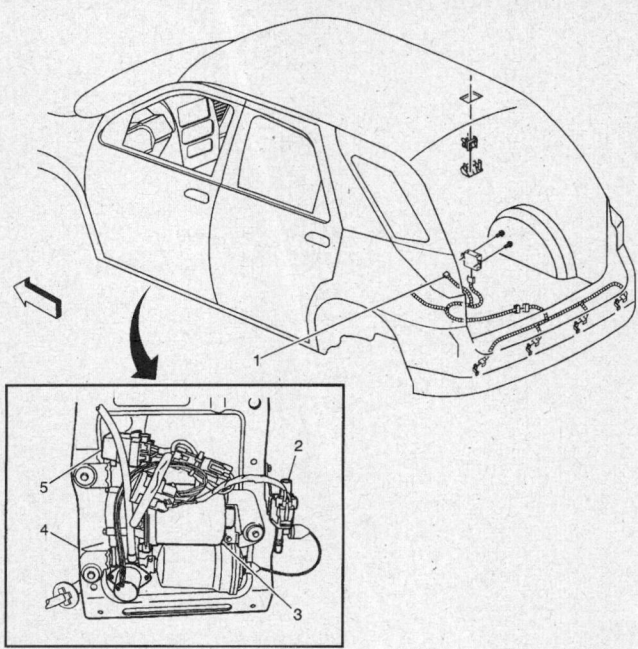

(1) Inflator Air Switch
(2) Inflator Soleniod
(3) Automatic Level Control (ALC) Compressor
(4) Exhaust Solenoid
(5) Automatic Level Control (ALC) Compressor Relay

LTV0500000000928

**Fig. 1   ALC component locations (Part 1 of 2).
Aztec & Rendezvous**

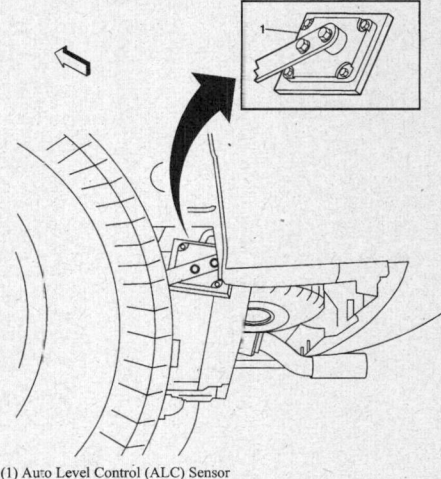

(1) Auto Level Control (ALC) Sensor

LTV0500000000929

**Fig. 1   ALC component locations
(Part 2 of 2).
Aztec & Rendezvous**

HUMMER H2

Connect a suitable scan tool to the Data Link Connector (DLC). Follow scan tool instructions to depressurize the air suspension system.

DESCRIPTION

The Automatic Level Control (ALC) system adjusts rear trim height in response to changes in vehicle loading. This system consists of an air compressor assembly, air dryer, exhaust solenoid, compressor relay, trim height sensor, air adjustable shocks and air tubing as shown in **Figs. 1 through 7.** The compressor is activated when the ignition is On and weight is added to the vehicle. The exhaust solenoid is connected directly to the positive side of the battery, allowing the system to exhaust when the ignition is Off and excess weight is removed.

When a load is added to the vehicle, the body is moved down causing the height sensor arm to rotate upward. This movement activates the internal timing circuit which, after a predetermined delay of 8–15 seconds, grounds the pin, thus completing the compressor relay circuit to ground. When the relay circuit is energized, the circuit allows the compressor to send pressurized air to the shocks.

As the shocks inflate, the vehicle body moves upward, causing the sensor arm to rotate downward. Once the body reaches its original height, the sensor opens the compressor relay circuit and shuts the compressor off.

When excess load is removed from the rear of the vehicle, the body rises upward, which causes the sensor arm to rotate downward. This movement activates the internal timing circuit which, after a predetermined delay of 8–15 seconds, allows the sensor to complete the exhaust solenoid circuit to ground. With the solenoid energized, air exhausts from the shocks back through the air dryer and exhaust solenoid valve.

As the vehicle body lowers, the height sensor arm is rotated upward until the vehicle reaches its original height. When this height is reached, the sensor opens the exhaust solenoid circuit which prevents air from escaping.

The height sensor position is checked when the ignition switch is turned On. If the height sensor indicates that it is not necessary to raise or lower the vehicle, the internal timer circuit is activated. After 40 seconds, the compressor will run for four seconds. This ensures the shocks are filled with the proper residual pressure (7–14 psi). If weight is added or removed from the vehicle during this 40 second delay, the air replenishment cycle will be overridden and the vehicle will raise or lower after normal delay.

When diagnostic procedures require that the vehicle be raised on a hoist, it is important that the rear axle assembly remains in the normal trim height position at all times. When a frame contact hoist is used, two additional jack stands should be used to support the rear axle or control arms in the normal trim height position.

ADJUSTMENTS

When repair or adjustment procedures require that the vehicle be raised on a hoist, it is important that the rear axle assembly remains in the normal trim height position at all times. When a frame contact hoist is used, two additional jack stands should be used to support the rear axle or control arms in the normal trim height position.

Automatic Level Control Sensor

AZTEK, MONTANA, RENDEZVOUS, SILHOUETTE & VENTURE

1. **On Montana, Silhouette and Venture models,** load rear passenger compartment with 400 lbs., or more to active compressor. Distribute weight evenly left to right.
2. **On Aztek and Rendezvous models,** load rear passenger compartment with 250–300 lbs. to active compressor. Distribute weight evenly left to right.
3. **On all models,** raise and support vehicle.
4. Inspect height sensor for damage.
5. Ensure height sensor link is properly attached to tie rod and height sensor arm.
6. Turn ignition switch to Run position.
7. Wait approximately one minute for arc to complete.
8. Measure rear axle ride height on both right and lefthand sides. Refer to "Wheel Alignment" in the appropriate chassis chapter for vehicle ride height specifications.
9. If ride height is within specifications, do not adjust. If ride height is not within specifications, proceed to next step.
10. Loosen height sensor arm adjustment bolt as shown in **Fig. 8.**
11. To raise vehicle, move height sensor arm plastic portion up.

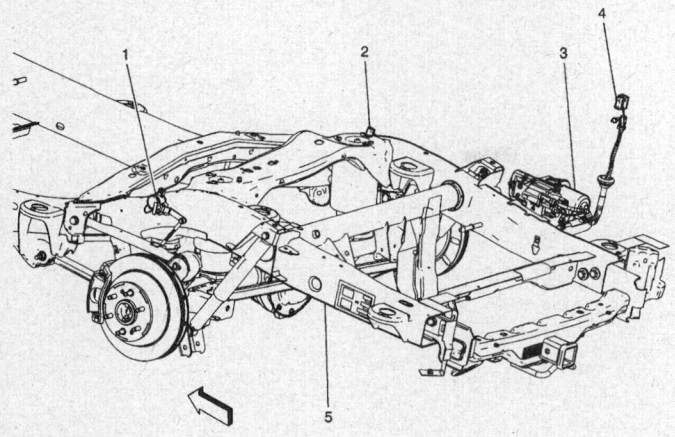

(1) Air Suspension Sensor - LR
(2) Air Suspension Sensor - RR
(3) Air Suspension Compressor Assembly
(4) Air Suspension Inflator Switch
(5) Frame

LTV0500000000937

Fig. 2   ALC component locations. Bravada, Envoy, Rainier & Trailblazer w/short wheelbase

(1) Air Suspension Compressor Assembly
(2) Air Suspension Inflator Switch
(3) Air Suspension Sensor - LR
(4) Air Suspension Sensor - RR
(5) Frame

LTV0500000000938

Fig. 3   ALC component locations. Bravada, Envoy, Rainier & Trailblazer w/long wheelbase

12. To lower vehicle, move height sensor arm plastic portion down.
13. Rotating plastic portion 1° will change ride height .16 inch.
14. **Torque** height sensor adjuster bolt to 44 inch lbs.

Air Spring Sensor Calibration

BRAVADA, ENVOY, RAINIER & TRAILBLAZER

1. Remove the air suspension system fuse.
2. Raise and support vehicle.
3. Raise and support rear axle, then remove rear tires and wheels.
4. Remove air compressor mounting bolts from frame and support air compressor.
5. Loosen both of air supply line connections at air compressor in order to depressurize air springs.
6. Support rear axle and set rear axle to proper height.
7. Loosen air spring level sensor to frame mounting bolts. **Failure to remove auto level control sensor locating pin before rear axle support is removed will cause damage to air suspension auto level control sensor.**
8. Install air spring level sensor locating pin, **Fig. 9**. **Do not remove air spring level sensor locating pin until air spring level sensor has been properly aligned and is at the proper height.**
9. **Torque** the air spring level sensor to frame mounting bolts to 71 inch lbs.
10. Remove air spring level sensor locating pin.
11. **Torque** air supply lines to air compressor to 20 inch lbs.
12. Install air compressor to frame mounting bolts and **torque** to 15 ft. lbs.

13. Install rear tires and wheels.
14. Remove rear axle support and lower vehicle.
15. Install air suspension system fuse, then start vehicle and run for approximately one minute to ensure air suspension system is functioning properly.

DIAGNOSIS & TESTING

Wiring Diagrams

Refer to **Figs. 10 through 18** for wiring diagrams.

Accessing Diagnostic Trouble Codes

AZTEK, MONTANA, RELAY, RENDEZVOUS, SILHOUETTE, SV6, TERRAZA, UPLANDER & VENTURE

Diagnostic Trouble Codes (DTC)s are displayed with a blink code on the accessory inflator switch LED. The diagnostic codes will flash after the completion of the self test. The self test is achieved by pressing the accessory inflator switch for three seconds. The self test will take 200 seconds to complete. The number of flashing pulses on the inflator switch LED represent the number of the DTC. The flashing pulses shall have a repetition rate of 0.5 seconds and each code digit shall be separated by a 1.0 second delay. Each code cycle shall be separated by a 3.0 second delay. All current failure codes shall be flashed in numerical order. All current failure codes shall be flashed until they are acknowledged by depressing the accessory inflator switch, or until the module enters asleep mode. The module will flash these codes with every

successive self test request until the failure is removed. The blink code shall take priority over other processes that have access to the accessory inflator switch LED.

BRAVADA, ENVOY, RAINIER & TRAILBLAZER

All the air suspensions diagnostic trouble codes are displayed with a blink code on the inflator switch LED. The air suspension compressor assembly shall begin to indicate the code when the condition to cause the code becomes current. The number of the fault code shall be represented by the number of flashing pulses on the inflator switch LED. The flashing pulses shall have a repetition rate of 0.5 seconds and each code is separated by a 3.0 second delay. All codes shall be flashed in the order of occurrence of the fault. The blink code shall take priority over other processes that have access to the inflator switch LED.

HUMMER H2

Connect a suitable scan tool to the Data Link Connector (DLC). Follow scan tool instructions to access Diagnostic Trouble Codes (DTC)s.

Diagnostic Trouble Codes

AZTEK, MONTANA, RELAY, RENDEZVOUS, SILHOUETTE, SV6, TERRAZA, UPLANDER & VENTURE

Refer to **Fig. 19** for Diagnostic Trouble Code (DTC) identification and description.

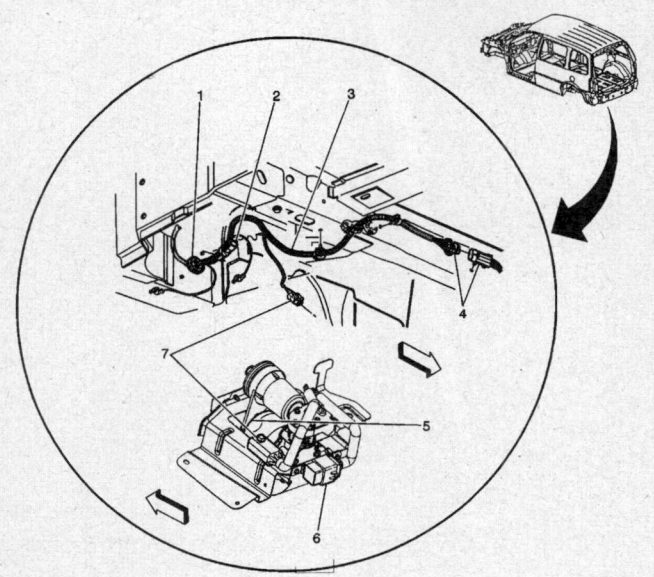

1. Pass Through P403
2. In-line Connector C407
3. Auto Level Control Harness
4. Auto Level Control (ALC) Sensor Connector
5. Auto Level Control (ALC) Air Compressor
6. Auto Level Control (ALC) Compressor Relay
7. Auto Level Control (ALC) Connector

GC2019900468000X

Fig. 4   ALC component locations. Montana, Silhouette & Venture

(1) Air Suspension Inlet Valve-LR
(2) Air Suspension Inlet Valve-RR
(3) Compressor Connector
(4) Air Suspension Air Dryer
(5) Air Suspension Compressor
(6) Air Suspension Module
(7) Air Suspension Exhaust Valve Connector
(8) C450
(9) C451
(10) Air Suspension Inlet Valve Connector-LR/RR
(11) Air Suspension Pressure Sensor
(12) Air Suspension Exhaust Valve

LTV0500000000943

Fig. 5   ALC component locations (Part 1 of 4). Hummer H2

BRAVADA, ENVOY, RAINIER & TRAILBLAZER

Refer to **Fig. 20** for Diagnostic Trouble Code (DTC) identification and description.

HUMMER H2

Refer to **Fig. 21** for Diagnostic Trouble Code (DTC) identification and description.

Intermittents & Poor Connections

Most intermittents are caused by faulty electrical connections or wiring, although a sticking relay or solenoid can also cause an intermittent condition. Check wiring and connectors for the following:
1. Poor mating of connector halves, or terminals not fully seated in connector body.
2. Dirt or corrosion on terminals.
3. Damaged connector body.
4. Improperly formed or damaged terminals.
5. Poor terminal to wire connection.
6. Rubbed through wiring insulation.
7. Wiring broken inside insulation.

Clearing Diagnostic Trouble Codes

AZTEK, BRAVADA, ENVOY, MONTANA, RAINIER, RELAY, RENDEZVOUS, SILHOUETTE, SV6, TERRAZA, TRAILBLAZER, UPLANDER & VENTURE

The air suspensions diagnostic trouble codes will clear when the ignition switch has been moved from off to on and the conditions that caused the code to set have been repaired.

HUMMER H2

Follow scan tool instructions to clear Diagnostic Trouble Codes (DTC)s.

COMPONENT REPLACEMENT

Air Compressor

AZTEK, MONTANA, RENDEZVOUS, SILHOUETTE & VENTURE

1. Raise and support vehicle.
2. Remove air compressor filter from underbody rail.
3. Disconnect air tube from air dryer.
4. Disconnect air compressor electrical connector.
5. Remove air compressor bracket bolts and nuts.
6. Remove air compressor, then the bracket.
7. Remove air dryer.
8. Remove air compressor bolts, then the air compressor from bracket.
9. Reverse procedure to install, noting the following:
   a. **Torque** air compressor bolts to bracket to 35 inch lbs.
   b. **Torque** air compressor bracket bolts and nuts to 89 inch lbs.

BRAVADA, ENVOY, RAINIER & TRAILBLAZER

1. Depressurize air suspension system as outlined under "Precautions."
2. Raise and support vehicle at ride height.
3. Remove air spring compressor to frame mounting bolts, **Figs. 2 and 3.**
4. Disconnect air inflator switch electrical connector and air spring compressor vent hose from compressor.
5. Disconnect compressor electrical connector.
6. Disconnect air supply lines from compressor. Ensure color on air supply lines matches color on air spring compressor for installation reference.
7. Remove compressor from vehicle.
8. Reverse procedure to install.

HUMMER H2

1. Depressurize air suspension system as outlined under "Precautions."
2. Raise and support vehicle.

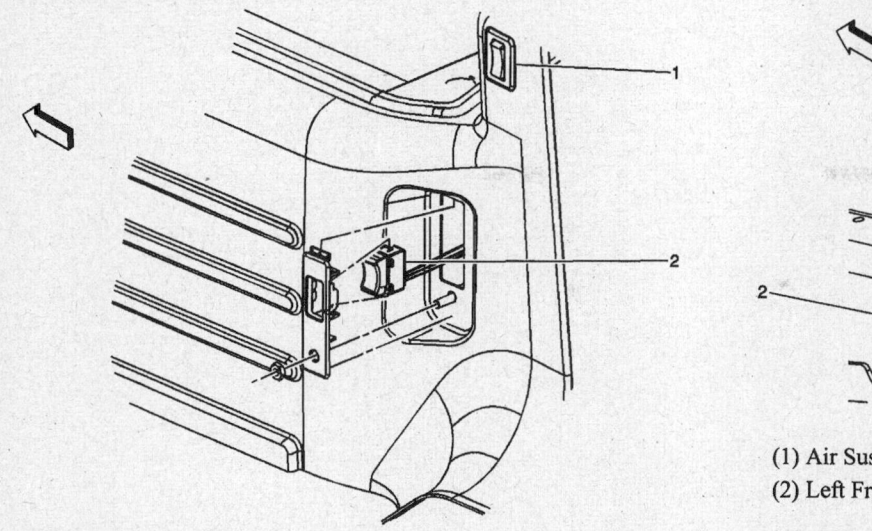

(1) Door Lock Switch-Rear
(2) Air Suspension Inflator Switch

LTV0500000000944

**Fig. 5   ALC component locations (Part 2 of 4).
Hummer H2**

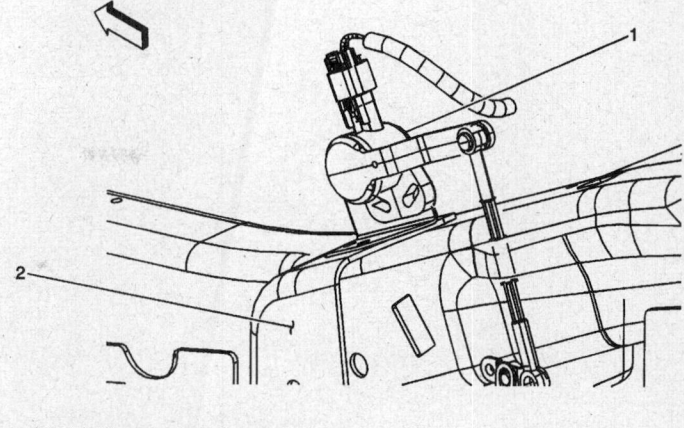

(1) Air Suspension Sensor-LR
(2) Left Frame Rail

LTV0500000000945

**Fig. 5   ALC component locations (Part 3 of 4).
Hummer H2**

3. Support compressor assembly with a suitable jack stand.
4. Disconnect air inflator switch and compressor electrical connectors, then the ground strap.
5. Remove rear and front compressor mounting bolts, **Fig. 5.**
6. Lower compressor assembly to access air lines, then disconnect air lines. Note port location of air lines for installation reference.
7. Remove compressor assembly from vehicle.
8. Set compressor assembly on a bench or suitable support.
9. Remove filter/air dryer from compressor assembly.
10. Disconnect electrical connector, then remove electrical harness from compressor assembly mounting bracket.
11. Remove compressor to bracket assembly mounting nuts and bolts.
12. Remove compressor from bracket assembly.
13. Reverse procedure to install.

RELAY, SV6, TERRAZA & UPLANDER

1. Remove electronic level control fuse.
2. Raise and support vehicle.
3. Squeeze clips on side of air compressor filter, then remove filter from underbody rail, **Fig. 7.**
4. Remove compressor bracket bolt and bracket nuts.
5. Allow compressor to hang from bracket hook.
6. Remove air line from air dryer, then disconnect air compressor electrical connector.
7. Rotate air compressor and bracket 90°, then disengage compressor bracket hook from vehicle.
8. Remove air compressor with air compressor bracket.
9. Remove air compressor dryer as outlined under "Automatic Level Control Air Dryer."
10. Remove air compressor relay from bracket.
11. Remove air compressor bolts, then the compressor from bracket.
12. Remove air compressor filter hose from air compressor.
13. Reverse procedure to install.

Air Spring Leveling Sensor

BRAVADA, ENVOY, RAINIER & TRAILBLAZER

1. Depressurize air suspension system as outlined under "Precautions."
2. Raise and support vehicle at ride height.
3. Remove rear tire and wheel.
4. Disconnect air spring level sensor link from upper control arm, **Figs. 2 and 3.**
5. Disconnect level sensor electrical connector.
6. Remove level sensor to frame mounting bolts, then the level sensor from vehicle.
7. Reverse procedure to install.

HUMMER H2

1. Raise and support vehicle, then remove tire and wheel.
2. Support rear axle at proper trim height.
3. Disconnect level sensor link from upper control arm.
4. Disconnect air spring level sensor electrical connector located on frame. Do not attempt to separate connector at sensor.
5. Remove level sensor to frame mounting bolts, then the level sensor from vehicle.
6. Reverse procedure to install.

Automatic Level Control Air Dryer

RELAY, SV6, TERRAZA & UPLANDER

1. Remove automatic level control air compressor from vehicle as outlined under "Air Compressor."
2. Clean area around air dryer to automatic level control air compressor head connection.
3. Rotate spring clip retaining dryer to air compressor 90°.
4. Remove air dryer from bracket and compressor.
5. Reverse procedure to install.

Compressor Head Assembly

1. Remove compressor as previously described.
2. Rotate dryer retainer spring 90°, then pull dryer and O-ring out of compressor head assembly.
3. Disconnect solenoid connector, **Fig. 22.**
4. Remove mounting bolts and head assembly.
5. Reverse procedure to install, noting the following:
   a. Install new O-ring.
   b. **Torque** head mounting bolts to 53 inch lbs., in sequence as shown in **Fig. 23.**

Accessory Fill Valve

RELAY, SV6, TERRAZA & UPLANDER

1. Remove rear seats.
2. Remove rear upper finish panel trim, then the rear seat belt escutcheons.
3. Remove rear seat belt anchor retainer bolts.
4. Remove upper cargo net retainers, then the liftgate sill plate.

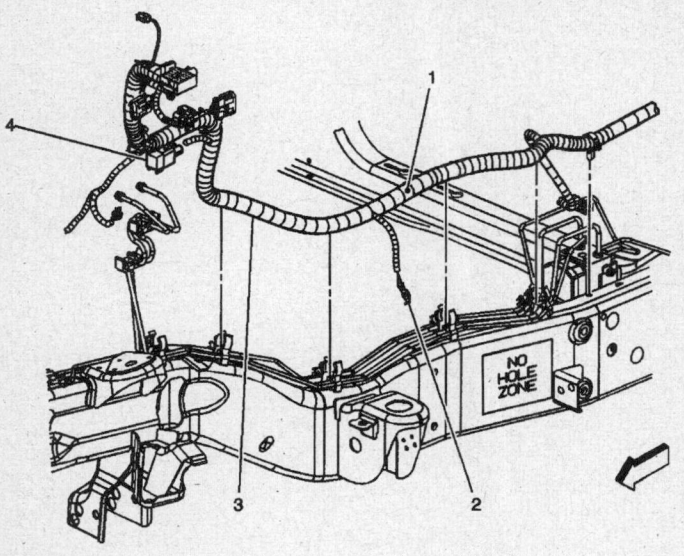

(1) S304
(2) G300
(3) Chassis Harness
(4) Electronically Controlled Air Suspension Relay

LTV0500000000946

**Fig. 5   ALC component locations (Part 4 of 4).
Hummer H2**

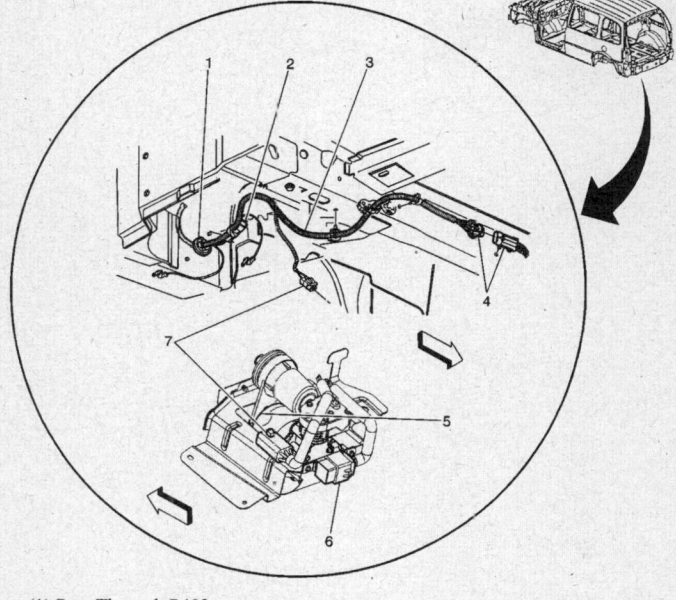

(1) Pass Through P403
(2) In-line Connector C407
(3) Auto Level Control Harness
(4) Auto Level Control (ALC) Sensor Connector
(5) Auto Level Control (ALC) Air Compressor
(6) Auto Level Control (ALC) Air Inflator Relay
(7) Auto Level Control (ALC) Connector

LTV0500000000951

**Fig. 6   ALC component locations (Part 1 of 3).
Montana, Silhouette & Venture**

5. Remove rear quarter trim panel retainers and feed seat belts through openings in trim panel.
6. Remove rear quarter trim panel from vehicle.
7. Disconnect solenoid electrical connector, **Fig. 7.**
8. Disconnect rear suspension strut air tube and air compressor tube.
9. Remove auto level control solenoid inflator valve opening cap.
10. Remove auto level control solenoid valve nut and washer.
11. Remove auto level control solenoid valve.
12. Reverse procedure to install. **Torque** solenoid valve nut to 25 inch lbs.

Air Inflator Relay

MONTANA, SILHOUETTE & VENTURE

1. Remove ALC fuse.
2. Remove inflator air valve opening cover by pulling lever inboard.
3. Remove inflator control panel retainers.
4. Remove mounting bolts.
5. Disconnect connector and remove relay.
6. Reverse procedure to install. **Torque** mounting bolts to 18 inch lbs.

Air Inflator Switch

AZTEK, MONTANA, RENDEZVOUS, SILHOUETTE & VENTURE

1. Remove inflator air valve opening cover by pulling lever inboard.

2. Remove inflator control access panel retainers.
3. Disconnect electrical connector.
4. Remove switch by depressing retainers.
5. Reverse procedure to install.

RELAY, SV6, TERRAZA & UPLANDER

1. Remove rear seat shoulder belt retractor opening trim cover.
2. Remove inflator access cover.
3. Access inflator switch through seat belt trim cover opening.
4. Disconnect inflator switch electrical connector.
5. Release inflator switch retainer and remove switch from rear quarter trim panel.
6. Reverse procedure to install.

Inflator Air Switch

BRAVADA, ENVOY, RAINIER & TRAILBLAZER

1. Raise and support vehicle.
2. Disconnect inflator air switch harness from air compressor.
3. Lower vehicle.
4. **On models equipped with long wheelbase,** proceed as follows:
   a. Remove cargo shelf, then tumble third row seats to cargo position.
   b. Remove left body side window rear and forward garnish moldings.
   c. Remove lift gate sill plate.

d. Remove left rear door sill panel.
e. Remove lower seat belt anchor bolt.
f. Release rear quarter trim panel to body attaching screws.
g. Remove rear quarter trim panel from vehicle.
5. **On models equipped with short wheelbase,** proceed as follows:
   a. Remove cargo shade/cover.
   b. Remove left body side upper trim panel.
   c. Remove liftgate sill plate and left rear door sill panel.
   d. Remove lower seat belt anchor bolt.
   e. Release left rear quarter trim panel to body retaining clips, then remove trim panel from vehicle.
6. **On all models,** remove inflator air switch from vehicle.
7. Reverse procedure to install.

HUMMER H2

1. Raise and support vehicle.
2. Disconnect air inflator switch harness and air line from air compressor.
3. Lower vehicle.
4. Remove inflator retaining nut.
5. Remove rear pillar trim panel.
6. Remove inflator nozzle retaining nut, then the inflator switch from bezel.
7. Remove inflator bezel.
8. Using a suitable flat bladed tool, press downward on door lock switch and rotate top of switch outward to disengage from trim panel.

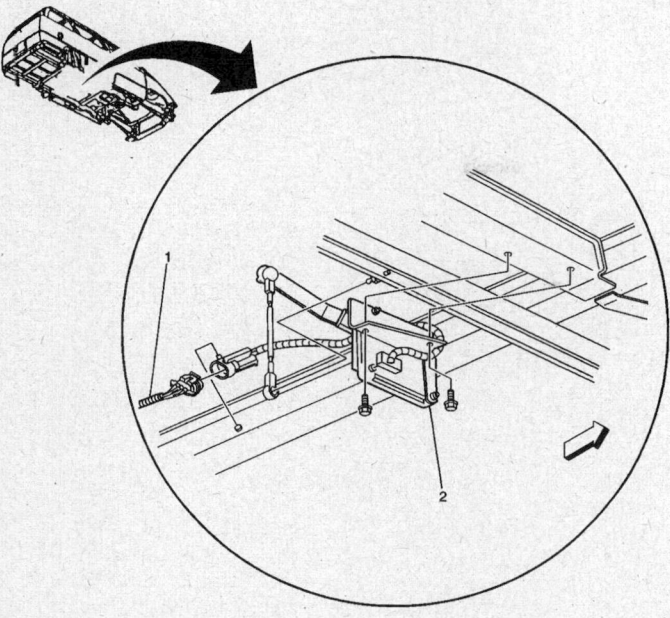

(1) Auto Level Control (ALC) Harness
(2) Auto Level Control (ALC) Sensor

LTV0500000000952

Fig. 6   ALC component locations (Part 2 of 3). Montana, Silhouette & Venture

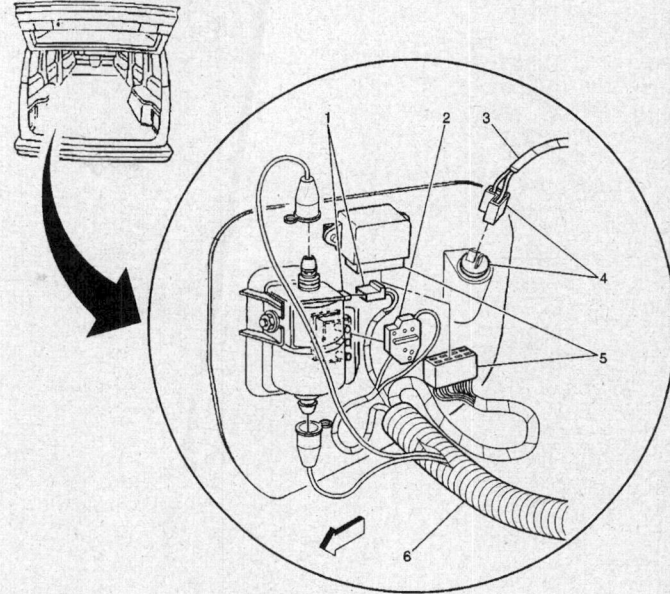

(1) Auto Level Control (ALC) Air Inflator Solenoid
(2) Air Inflator Switch
(3) Body Harness
(4) Auxiliary Power Outlet-Rear
(5) Auto Level Control (ALC) Air Inflator Relay
(6) Auto Level Control Harness

LTV0500000000953

Fig. 6   ALC component locations (Part 3 of 3). Montana, Silhouette & Venture

9. Remove Connector Position Assurance (CPA) pin and disconnect electrical connector from switch.
10. Remove lift gate sill plate.
11. Remove lock pillar trim panel.
12. Gently pull up on body side panel tray to disengage it from body panel.
13. Disconnect 12 volt power supply electrical connector.
14. Remove inflator nozzle from panel.
15. Gently pull front edge of body panel to disengage from retaining clips.
16. Remove right side body panel from vehicle.
17. Remove air inflator switch harness grommet from body.
18. Remove air inflator switch from vehicle.
19. Reverse procedure to install.

Solenoid Valve Assembly

AZTEK, MONTANA, RENDEZVOUS, SILHOUETTE & VENTURE

1. Remove ALC fuse.

2. Remove inflator air valve opening cover by pulling lever inboard.
3. Remove inflator control panel retainers.
4. Disconnect connector.
5. Remove inflator solenoid air lines.
6. Remove fill valve cap and nut.
7. Remove mounting nut and solenoid.
8. Reverse procedure to install. **Torque** mounting nuts to 27 inch lbs.

RELAY, SV6, TERRAZA & UPLANDER

1. Remove rear seat shoulder belt retractor opening trim cover.
2. Remove inflator solenoid fill valve nut.
3. Access solenoid through seat belt trim cover opening.
4. Disconnect inflator solenoid electrical connector.
5. Disconnect air lines from solenoid.
6. Remove inflator solenoid from rear quarter trim panel.

7. Reverse procedure to install.

Trim Height Sensor

1. Raise and support vehicle.
2. Disconnect ALC sensor connector.
3. Remove ALC sensor link from tie rod ball stud.
4. Remove mounting bolts, then the ALC sensor with bracket.
5. Remove ALC sensor to bracket bolts, then the sensor from bracket.
6. Reverse procedure to install, noting the following:
   a. **Torque** sensor mounting bolts to 35 inch lbs.
   b. **Torque** sensor bracket mounting bolts to 89 inch lbs.

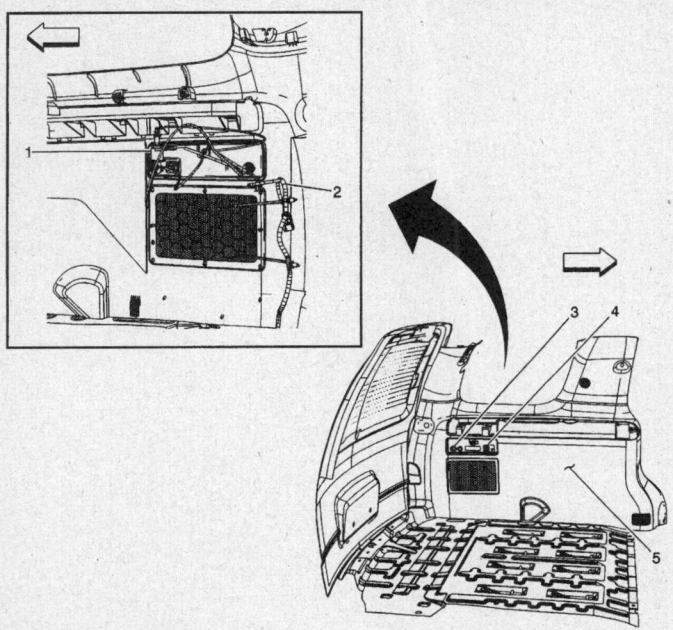

(1) Automatic Level Control (ALC) Solenoid Valve (G67 w/o Z10)
(2) ALC Harness (G67)
(3) Auxiliary Power Outlet - Rear
(4) Automatic Level Control (ALC) Inflator Air Switch (G67 w/o Z10)
(5) Left Rear Cargo Trim Panel

LTV0500000000934

Fig. 7 ALC component locations (Part 1 of 2). Relay, SV6, Terraza & Uplander

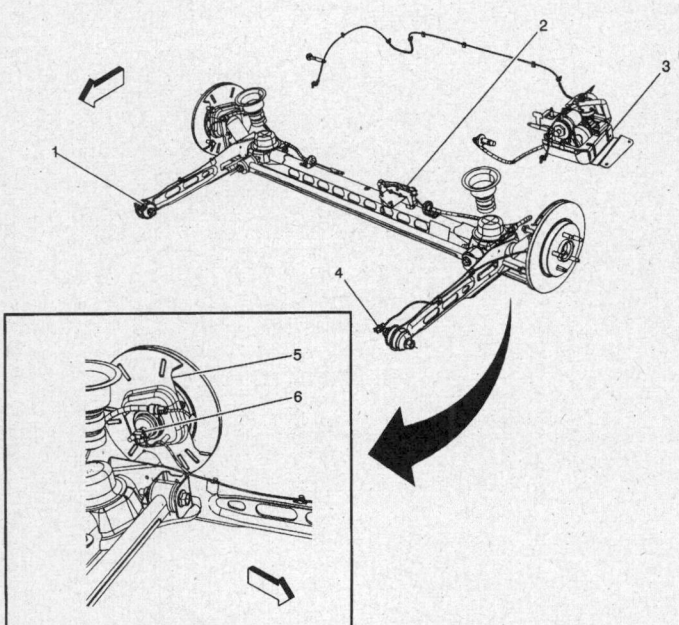

(1) C306 RR Wheel Speed Sensor Harness to Rear Cross-Car Jumper Harness
(2) Automatic Level Control (ALC) Sensor (G67)
(3) Automatic Level Control (ALC) Compressor (G67)
(4) C309 LR Wheel Speed Sensor Harness to Rear Cross-Car Jumper Harness
(5) Left Rear Hub
(6) Wheel Speed Sensor (WSS) - LR

LTV0500000000936

Fig. 7 ALC component locations (Part 2 of 2). Relay, SV6, Terraza & Uplander w/FWD

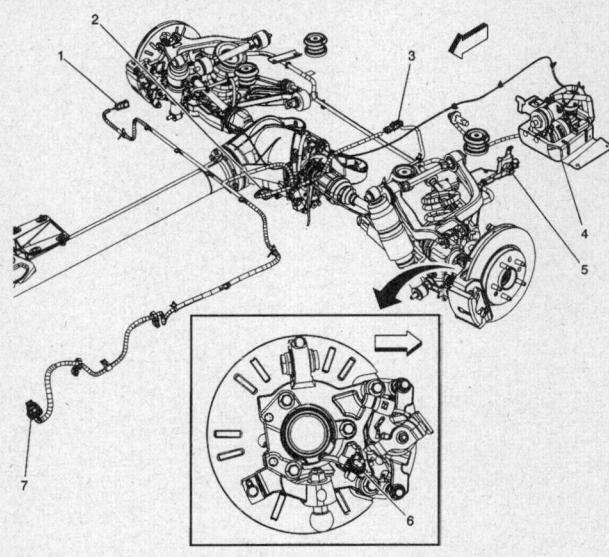

(1) C306 RR Wheel Speed Sensor Harness to Rear Cross-Car Jumper Harness
(2) Differential Clutch Pump Actuator Check Valve (M76)
(3) C309 LR Wheel Speed Sensor Harness to Rear Cross-Car Jumper Harness
(4) Automatic Level Control (ALC) Compressor (G67)
(5) Automatic Level Control (ALC) Sensor (G67)
(6) Wheel Speed Sensor (WSS) - LR
(7) C305 Rear Cross-Car Jumper Harness to Body Harness

LTV0500000000935

Fig. 7 ALC component locations (Part 2 of 2). Relay, SV6, Terraza & Uplander w/AWD

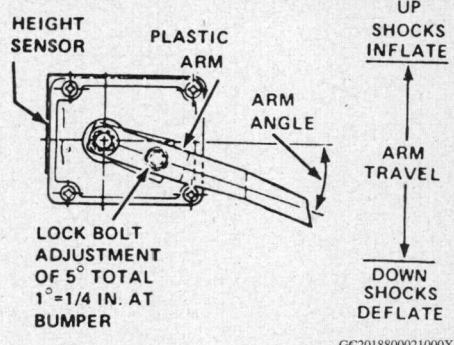

GC2018800021000X

Fig. 8 Height sensor adjustment. Aztek, Montana, Rendezvous, Silhouette & Venture

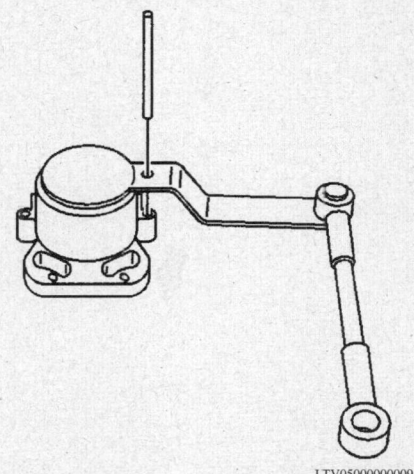

LTV0500000000942

Fig. 9 Auto level control sensor locating pin. Bravada, Envoy, Rainier & Trailblazer

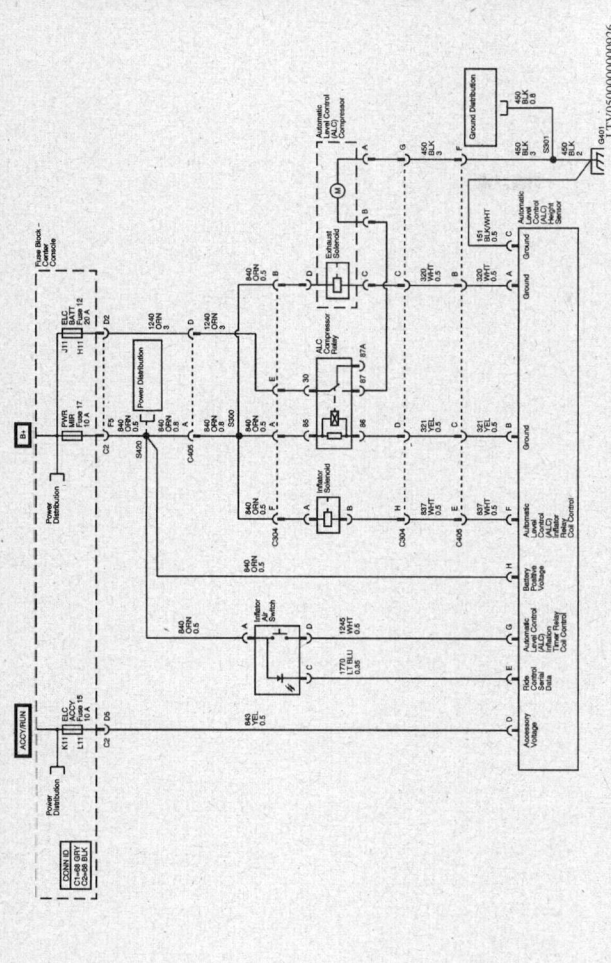

Fig. 11 Wiring diagram. 2003–06 Aztek & Rendezvous

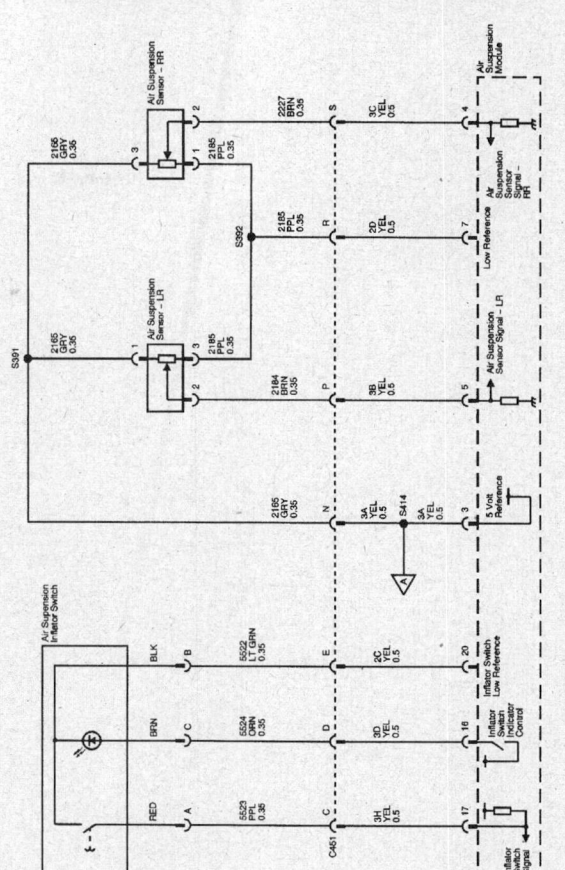

Fig. 12 Wiring diagrams (Part 2 of 3). Hummer H2

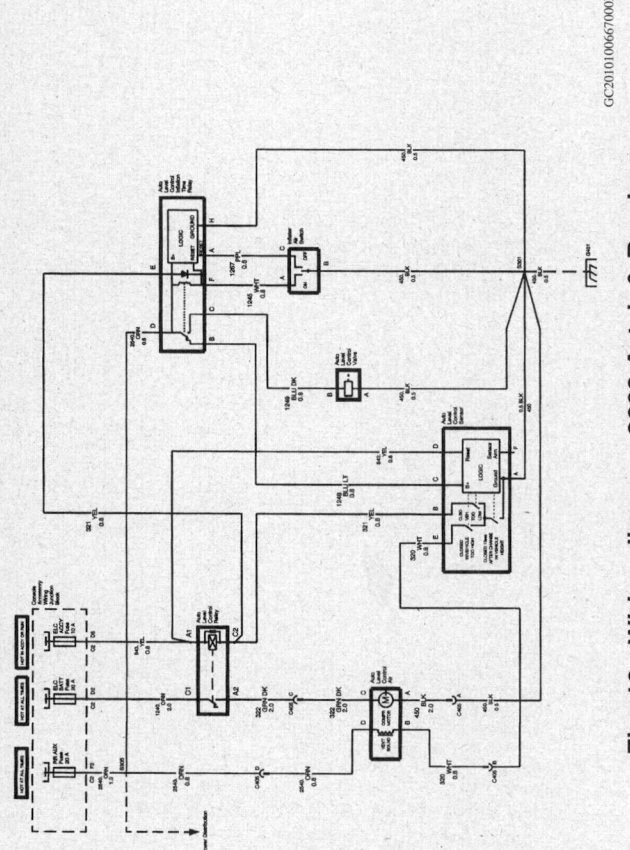

Fig. 10 Wiring diagram. 2002 Aztek & Rendezvous

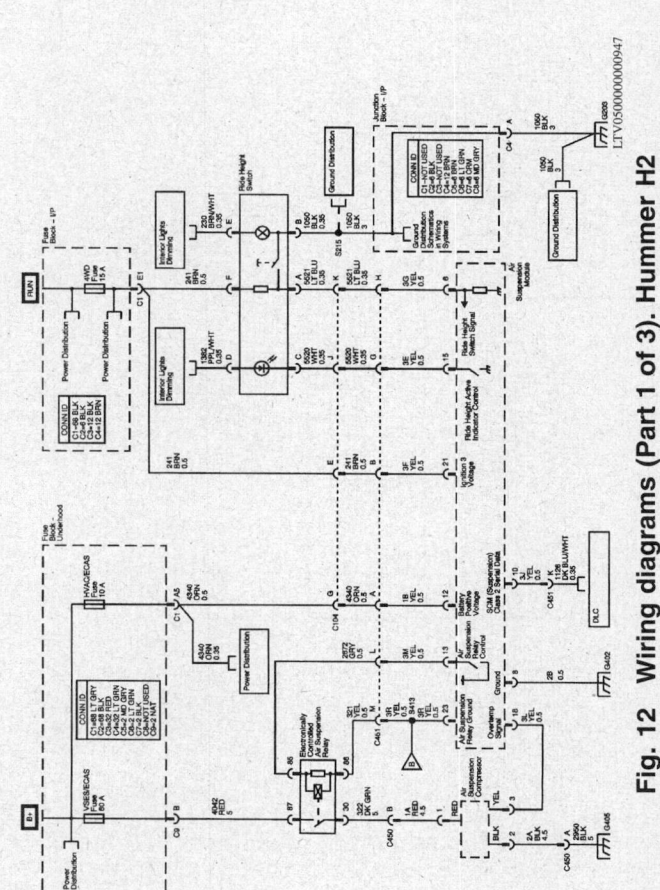

Fig. 12 Wiring diagrams (Part 1 of 3). Hummer H2

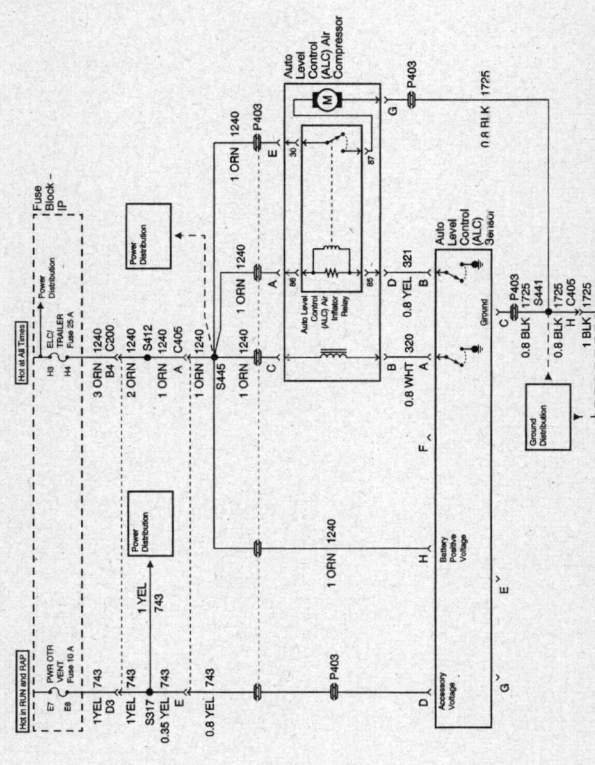

Fig. 13   Wiring diagram. 2002 Montana, Silhouette & Venture less Inflator

Fig. 15   Wiring diagram. 2003–05 Montana, Silhouette & Venture less Inflator

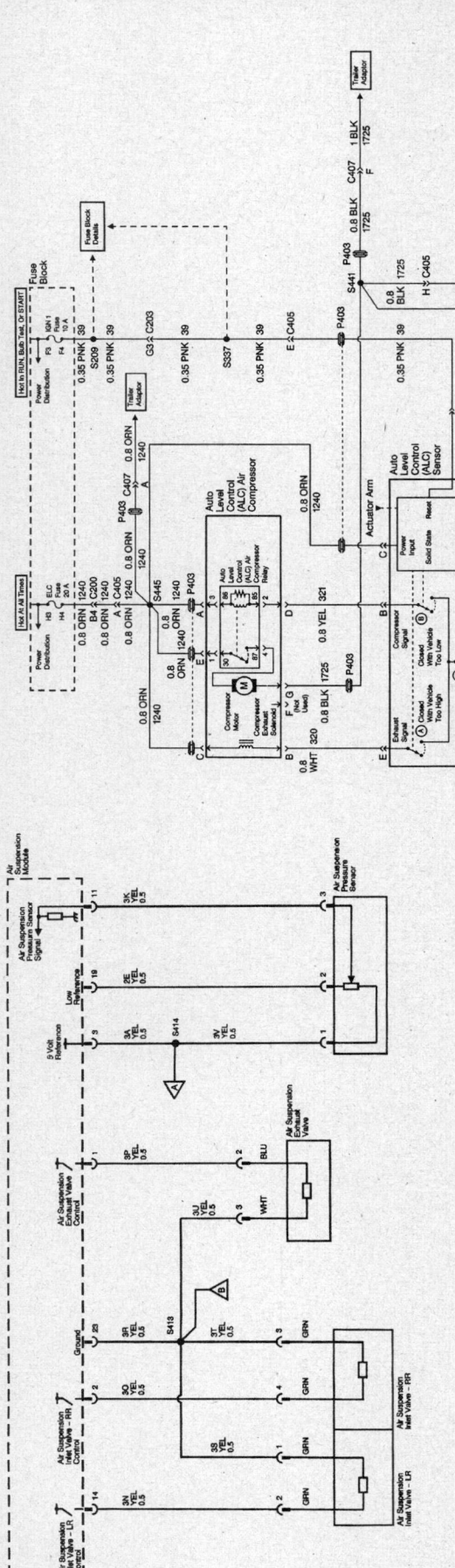

Fig. 12   Wiring diagrams (Part 3 of 3). Hummer H2

Fig. 14   Wiring diagram. 2002 Montana, Silhouette & Venture w/Inflator

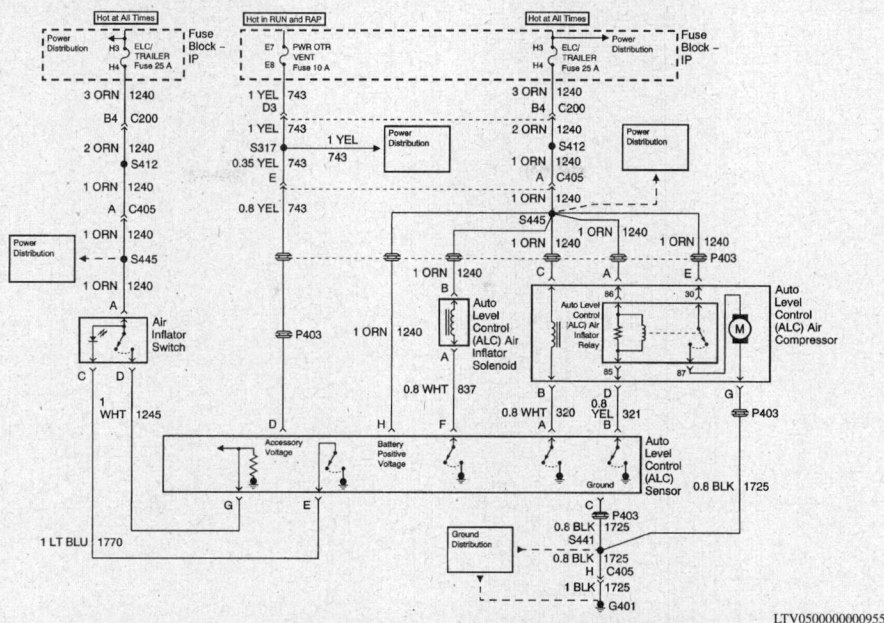

Fig. 16   Wiring diagram. 2003–05 Montana, Silhouette & Venture
w/Inflator

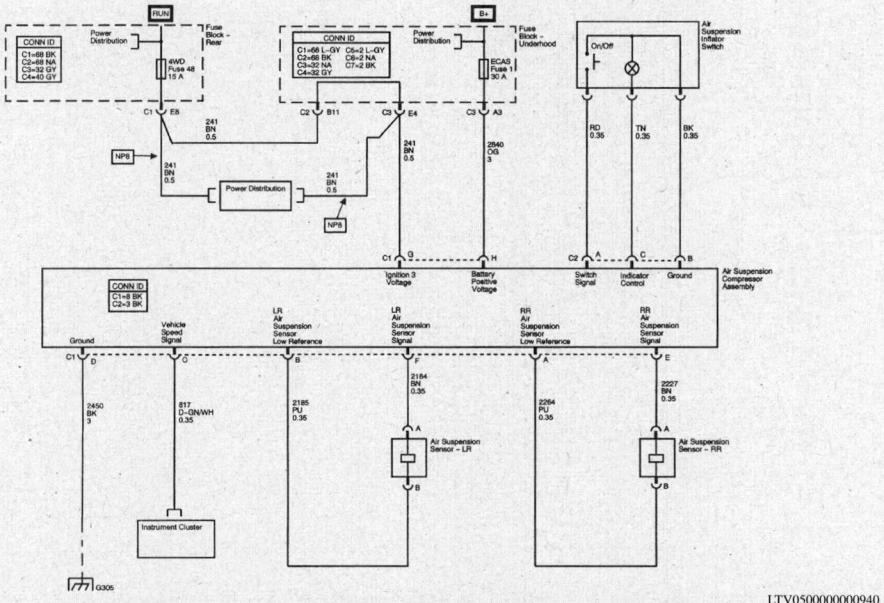

Fig. 17   Wiring diagram. Bravada, Envoy, Rainier & Trailblazer

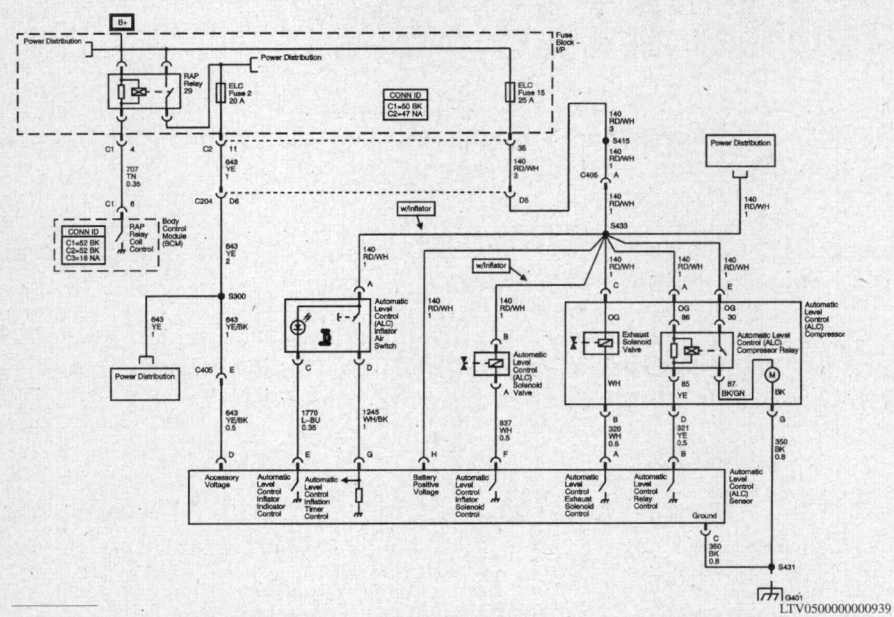

Fig. 18 Wiring diagram. Relay, SV6, Terraza & Uplander

Code	Description
011	Inflator Solenoid Circuit
012	No Faults Found
013	Height Sensor Internal Circuit
021	Compressor Relay Coil Control Circuit
022	Compressor Relay Coil Control Circuit
023	Compressor Has Been Running For 255 Seconds During a Leveling Function
031	Exhaust Solenoid Control Circuit
032	Exhaust Solenoid Control Circuit
033	Exhaust Valve Has Been On For 255 Seconds And Height Sensor Did Not Detect Downward Movement

Fig. 19 Diagnostic trouble codes. Aztek, Montana, Relay, Rendezvous, Silhouette, SV6, Terraza, Uplander & Venture

Code	Description
001	Invalid EPROM Checksum Or Internal Component Failure
002	Invalid Height Sensor Signal
003	Invalid Air Suspension Sensor Signal

Fig. 20 Diagnostic trouble codes. Bravada, Envoy, Rainier & Trailblazer

Code	Description
B2795	Ride Height Switch Signal Circuit Voltage Shorted To Ground Or Battery
C0563	EEPROM Test Failure
C0569	Height Sensor Voltage Out Of Range
C0626	Suspension Sensor Voltage Out Of Range
C0631	Suspension Sensor Voltage Out Of Range
C0660	Exhaust Valve Voltage Does Not Agree With Command State
C0696	Suspension Sensors Current Draw Out Of Range
C0702	General Valve Voltage Does Not Agree With Command State
C0707	Compressor Run Timer Has Exceeded 1 Hour Of Run Time
C0711	Air Pressure Sensor Signal Is Out Of Limits
C0712	Relay Circuity Voltage Does Not Agree With Command State
C0713	Compressor Overtemperature Condition
C0716	Inlet Valve Voltage Does Not Agree With Command State
C0717	Inlet Valve Voltage Does Not Agree With Command State

Fig. 21 Diagnostic trouble codes. Hummer H2

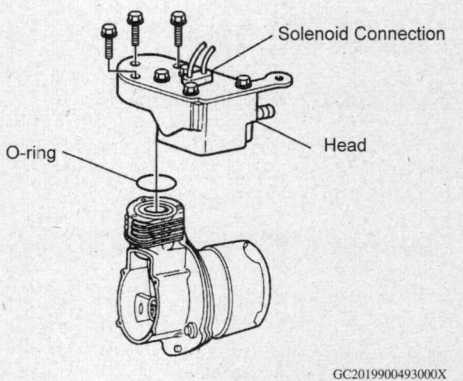

GC2019900493000X

Fig. 22 Compressor head removal

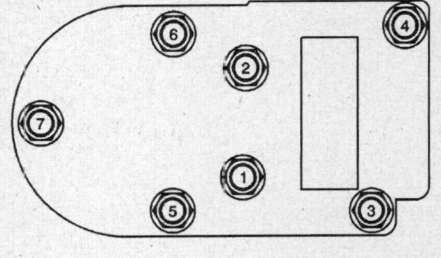

GC2019900494000X

Fig. 23 Compressor head tightening sequence

Selectable Ride (SR)

NOTE: On Air Bag Equipped Models, Refer To "Air Bag System Precautions" Located In The Front Of This Manual For System Disarming & Arming Procedures.

NOTE: Refer To "Computer Relearn Procedures" Located In The Front Of This Manual When Battery Power To The Computer Has Been Interrupted.

NOTE: Electrical Symbol & Wire Color Code Identification Located In The Front Of This Manual May Be Used As An Aid When Using Wiring Circuits Found In This Section.

INDEX

	Page No.		Page No.		Page No.
Component Replacement	6-17	Diagnostic Tests	6-14	**Diagnostic Chart Index**	6-15
Switch	6-17	Intermittents & Poor		**Precautions**	6-14
Description	6-14	Connections	6-14	Air Bag Systems	6-14
Diagnosis & Testing	6-14	Wiring Diagram	6-14	Battery Ground Cable	6-14

PRECAUTIONS

Air Bag Systems

Refer to "Air Bag System Precautions" in the front of this manual for system disarming and arming procedures.

Battery Ground Cable

Prior to service, disconnect battery ground cable and isolate as required.

DESCRIPTION

The Selectable Ride (SR) suspension system allows the drive to choose between two distinct damping levels within the shock absorbers in order to alter the vehicle's ride characteristics.

The SR shock absorbers are gas charged units which provide damping by forcing hydraulic fluid through internal orifices in order to resist suspension movement. Each unit contains an internal solenoid actuator that the SR switch controls. When the system is On, the voltage supplied to terminal A of the shocks provides firmer damping levels.

DIAGNOSIS & TESTING

Wiring Diagram

Refer to **Fig. 1** for wiring diagram.

Diagnostic Tests

Refer to **Figs. 2 through 6** for system diagnostic tests.

Intermittents & Poor Connections

Most intermittents are caused by faulty electrical connections or wiring, although a sticking relay or solenoid can also cause an intermittent condition. Check wiring and connectors for the following:
1. Poor mating of connector halves, or terminals not fully seated in connector body.
2. Dirt or corrosion on terminals.
3. Damaged connector body.
4. Improperly formed or damaged terminals.
5. Poor terminal to wire connection.
6. Rubbed through wiring insulation.
7. Wiring broken inside insulation.

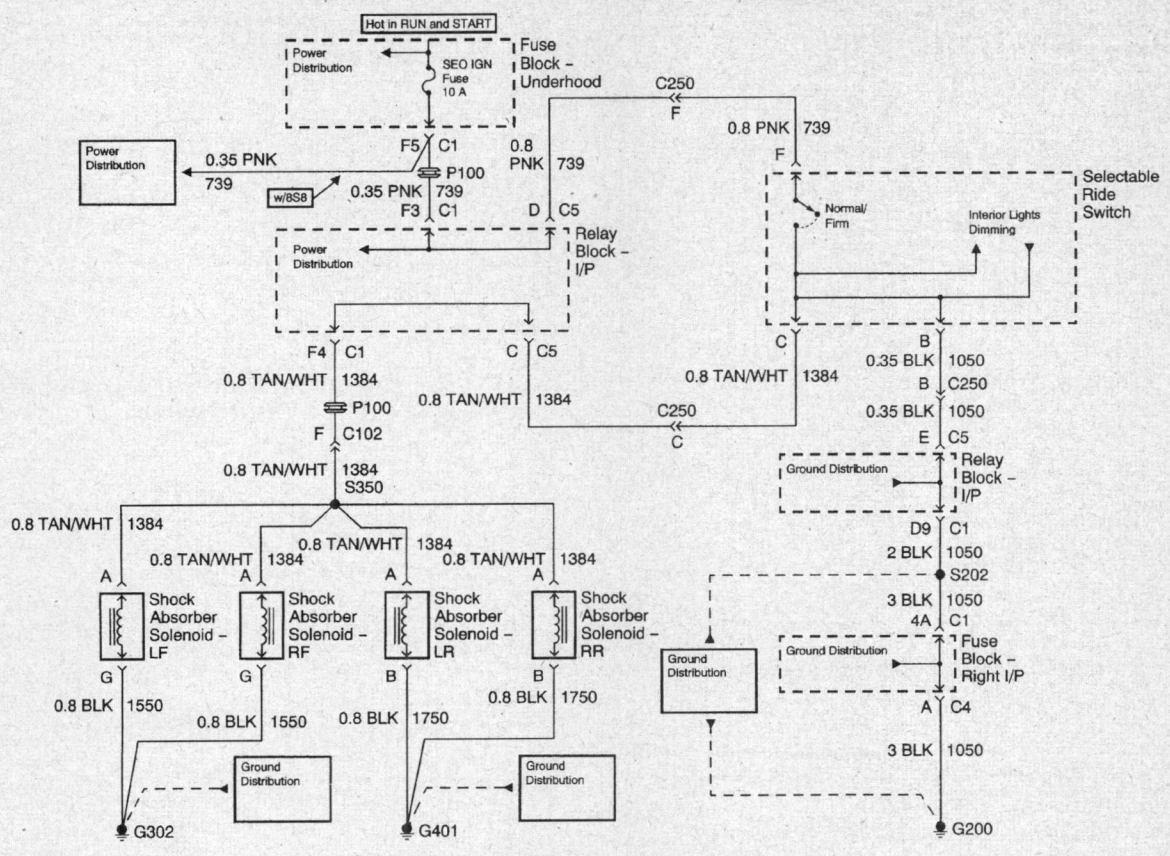

Fig. 1 Wiring diagram

DIAGNOSTIC CHART INDEX

Test	Page No.	Fig. No.
Selectable Ride Check	6-15	2
Selectable Ride Indicator Always On	6-15	3
Selectable Ride Indicator Inoperative	6-16	4
Ride Does Not Change When Switched On Or Off	6-16	5
One Shock Does Not Operate	6-17	6

Visual/Physical Inspection

- Inspect for aftermarket devices which could affect the operation of the Selectable Ride System.
- Inspect the easily accessible or visible system components for obvious damage or conditions which could cause the symptom.
- Inspect the SEO IGN fuse. If the fuse is open, locate the source of the overload and repair. Replace the fuse.
- Inspect grounds for front and rear shocks to be clean and tight.
- Inspect all inline connectors and the connectors at the shocks to be properly seated and free of corrosion.

Intermittent

Faulty electrical connections or wiring may be the cause of intermittent conditions.

Symptom List

Refer to a symptom diagnostic procedure from the following list in order to diagnose the symptom:

- Selectable Ride Indicator Always On
- Selectable Ride Indicator Inoperative
- Ride Does Not Change When Switched (ON - OFF)
- One Shock Does Not Operate

LTV0500000000957

Fig. 2 Selectable Ride Check

Step	Action	Yes	No
1	Did you review the system circuit description and perform the necessary inspections?	Go to Step 2	Go to Symptoms
2	1. Turn ON the ignition, with the engine OFF. 2. Press the RIDE CONTROL button several times to alternate from ON to OFF. Does the selectable ride switch indicator alternately turn ON and OFF?	Test for Electrical Intermittents	Go to Step 3
3	Replace the selectable ride switch. Did you complete the replacement?	Go to Step 4	--
4	Operate the system in order to verify the repair. Did you correct the condition?	System OK	Go to Step 2

LTV0500000000958

Fig. 3 Selectable Ride Indicator Always On

Step	Action	Yes	No
1	Did you review the system circuit description and perform the necessary inspections?	Go to Step 2	Go to Selectable Ride Check
2	Verify the fault is present. Does the system operate normally?	Test for Electrical Intermittents	Go to Step 3
3	1. Remove the selectable ride switch from the instrument panel. 2. Turn ON the ignition, with the engine OFF. 3. Ensure the selectable ride switch is in the ON or FIRM position. 4. Connect a test lamp and back probe between the selectable ride switch control circuit and a good ground. Does the test lamp illuminate?	Go to Step 5	Go to Step 4
4	Connect a test lamp and back probe, between the ignition 1 voltage circuit and a good ground. Does the test lamp illuminate?	Go to Step 8	Go to Step 6
5	1. Turn OFF the ignition. 2. Disconnect the selectable ride switch. 3. Connect a test lamp between the selectable ride switch indicator ground circuit and a battery positive voltage circuit. Does the test lamp illuminate?	Go to Step 6	Go to Step 7

LTV0500000000959

Fig. 4   Selectable Ride Indicator Inoperative (Part 1 of 2)

Step	Action	Yes	No
1	Did you review the system and circuit description and perform the necessary inspections?	Go to Step 2	Go to Selectable Ride Check
2	Verify the fault is present. Does the system operate normally?	Test for Electrical Intermittents	Go to Step 3
3	1. Turn OFF the ignition. 2. Disconnect the selectable ride switch. 3. Turn ON the ignition, with the engine OFF. 4. Connect a test lamp between the ignition 1 voltage circuit and a good ground. Does the test lamp illuminate?	Go to Step 4	Go to Step 8
4	Connect a test lamp between the selectable ride switch control circuit and a good ground. Does the test lamp illuminate?	Go to Step 10	Go to Step 5
5	1. Turn OFF the ignition. 2. Reconnect the selectable ride switch. 3. Connect a test lamp and back probe, between the selectable ride switch control circuit and a good ground. 4. Turn ON the ignition, with the engine OFF. 5. While back probing, turn the selectable ride switch from ON to OFF or FIRM to NORM. Does the test lamp illuminate in the ON position and off in the OFF position?	Go to Step 6	Go to Step 13
6	1. Ensure the selectable ride switch is in the ON or FIRM position and the ignition is in the ON position. 2. Gain access to connector at the Underhood Fuse Block. 3. Connect a test lamp and back probe, between the selective ride switch control circuit and a good ground. Does the test lamp illuminate?	Go to Step 7	Go to Step 11

LTV0500000000961

Fig. 5   Ride Does Not Change When Switched On Or Off (Part 1 of 2)

Step	Action	Yes	No
6	Repair the open in the ignition 1 voltage circuit between the selectable ride switch and Body Wiring Harness Junction Block. Did you complete the repair?	Go to Step 9	--
7	Repair the open selectable ride switch indicator ground circuit. Did you complete the repair?	Go to Step 9	--
8	Replace the selectable ride switch. Did you complete the replacement?	Go to Step 9	--
9	Operate the system in order to verify the repair. Did you correct the condition?	System OK	Go to Step 3

LTV0500000000960

Fig. 4   Selectable Ride Indicator Inoperative (Part 2 of 2)

Step	Action	Yes	No
7	1. Inspect the electrical connections at each shock. 2. Inspect the ground for both the front and the rear shocks to be clean and tight. 3. Ensure that all the connections are clean and tight and free of corrosion. Did you find the condition?	Go to Step 12	Go to One Shock Does Not Operate
8	Test the ignition 1 voltage circuit for an open or a short to ground. Did you find and correct the condition?	Go to Step 14	Go to Step 9
9	Repair the short to ground in the selectable ride switch control circuit. Did you complete the repair?	Go to Step 14	--
10	Repair the short to voltage in the selectable ride switch control circuit. Did you complete the repair?	Go to Step 14	--
11	Repair the open in the selectable ride switch control circuit between the switch and the Underhood Junction Block. Did you complete the repair?	Go to Step 14	--
12	Repair the conditions as necessary. Did you complete the repair?	Go to Step 14	--
13	Replace the selectable ride switch. Did you complete the replacement?	Go to Step 14	--
14	Operate the system in order to verify the repair. Did you correct the condition?	System OK	Go to Step 3

LTV0500000006722

Fig. 5   Ride Does Not Change When Switched On Or Off (Part 2 of 2)

Step	Action	Value(s)	Yes	No
1	Did you review the system circuit description and perform the necessary inspections?	--	Go to Step 2	Go to Selectable Ride Check
2	Verify the fault is present. Does the system operate normally?	--	Test for Electrical Intermittents	Go to Step 3
3	1. Disconnect the connector at the suspect shock. 2. Turn ON the ignition, with the engine OFF. 3. Ensure the selectable ride switch is in the ON or FIRM position. 4. Using the J 35616-A adapter, connect a test lamp between the selectable ride switch control circuit of the suspect shock to a good ground. Does the test lamp illuminate?	--	Go to Step 4	Go to Step 8
4	Using the J 35616-A adapter, connect a test lamp between ground of the suspect shock to a battery positive voltage circuit. Does the test lamp illuminate?	--	Go to Step 5	Go to Step 9
5	Important: Take care not to damage the pins in the connector. Using a J 39200 and J 35616-A , measure the resistance of the suspect shock. Front: the red probe to the center pin of the shock and the black probe to the rod of the shock. Rear: red probe to terminal A, black to terminal B. Does the resistance measure near the specified range?	11-21 ohms	Go to Step 6	Go to Step 7

LTV0500000006723

Fig. 6   One Shock Does Not Operate (Part 1 of 2)

COMPONENT REPLACEMENT

Switch

1. Move tilt steering wheel to lowest position.
2. Remove instrument cluster bezel by pulling gently to rear on clips.
3. Remove switch form lower switch plate pane opening as shown in **Fig. 7.**
4. Disconnect electrical connector.
5. Reverse procedure to install.

Step	Action		Yes	No
6	1. Inspect for corrosion within the shock connector. 2. Reconnect the shock connector. Did you find and correct the condition?		Go to Step 10	--
7	Replace the shock absorber. Did you complete the replacement?		Go to Step 10	--
8	Repair the open in the selectable ride switch control circuit between the shock and the Engine Wiring Harness Junction Block. Did you complete the repair?		Go to Step 10	--
9	Repair the open in the shock ground circuit. Did you complete the repair?		Go to Step 10	--
10	Operate the system in order to verify the repair. Did you correct the condition?		System OK	Go to Step 3

LTV0500000006724

Fig. 6   One Shock Does Not Operate (Part 2 of 2)

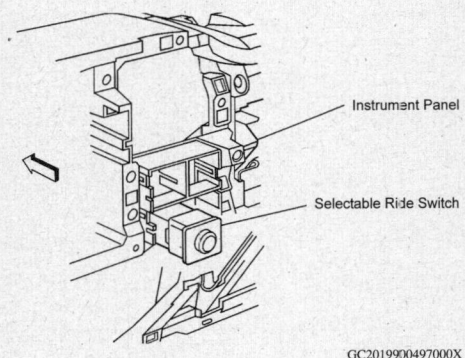

Instrument Panel

Selectable Ride Switch

GC2019900497000X

Fig. 7   Switch removal

Electronic Suspension Control (ESC)/Real Time Damping (RTD)

NOTE: On Air Bag Equipped Models, Refer To "Air Bag System Precautions" Located In The Front Of This Manual For System Disarming & Arming Procedures.

NOTE: Refer To "Computer Relearn Procedures" Located In The Front Of This Manual When Battery Power To The Computer Has Been Interrupted.

NOTE: Electrical Symbol & Wire Color Code Identification Located In The Front Of This Manual May Be Used As An Aid When Using Wiring Circuits Found In This Section.

INDEX

	Page No.		Page No.		Page No.
Component Replacement	6-18	Front/Rear Sensor Link	6-19	Interpretation	6-18
Air Compressor	6-18	Description	6-18	Intermittents & Poor	
Air Dryer/Pressure Sensor	6-18	Diagnosis & Testing	6-18	Connections	6-18
Control Module	6-19	Accessing Diagnostic Trouble		Wiring Diagrams	6-18
Avalanche, Escalade,		Codes	6-18	Precautions	6-18
Suburban, Tahoe & Yukon	6-19	Clearing Diagnostic Trouble		Air Bag Systems	6-18
SRX	6-19	Codes	6-18	Battery Ground Cable	6-18
Front/Rear Position Sensor	6-19	Diagnostic Trouble Code			

PRECAUTIONS

Air Bag Systems

Refer to "Air Bag System Precautions" in the front of this manual for system disarming and arming procedures.

Battery Ground Cable

Prior to service, disconnect battery ground cable and isolate as required.

DESCRIPTION

The Electronic Suspension Control (ESC)/Real Time Damping (RTD) system, **Figs. 1 through 4,** is fully automatic and uses a computer controller to continuously monitor vehicle speed, wheel to body position, lift/dive and steering position of the vehicle. The controller then sends signals to each damper to independently adjust the damping level. The ESC/RTD system consists of a control module, four dampers and four position sensors.

The ESC/RTD system has an integrated Automatic Level Control (ALC) system. The ALC consists of the rear automatic level control dampers and the automatic level control air compressor. The ESC/RTD system also interacts with the Tow/Haul switch. When engaged, the Tow/Haul mode will provide additional control of the dampers.

DIAGNOSIS & TESTING

Accessing Diagnostic Trouble Codes

Connect a suitably programmed scan tool to the Data Link Connector (DLC) and follow manufacturer instructions.

Diagnostic Trouble Code Interpretation

Refer to **Figs. 5 and 6** for Diagnostic Trouble Code (DTC) identification and description.

Wiring Diagrams

Refer to **Figs. 7 and 8** for wiring diagrams.

Intermittents & Poor Connections

Most intermittents are caused by faulty electrical connections or wiring, although a sticking relay or solenoid can also cause an intermittent condition. Check wiring and connectors for the following:
1. Poor mating of connector halves, or terminals not fully seated in connector body.
2. Dirt or corrosion on terminals.
3. Damaged connector body.
4. Improperly formed or damaged terminals.
5. Poor terminal to wire connection.
6. Rubbed through wiring insulation.
7. Wiring broken inside insulation.

Clearing Diagnostic Trouble Codes

Diagnostic Trouble Codes (DTCs) may be cleared by using a suitably programmed scan tool.

COMPONENT REPLACEMENT

Air Compressor

1. Raise and support vehicle.
2. Disconnect air tube from air dryer.
3. Disconnect electrical connector.
4. Remove air inlet and hose assembly.
5. Loosen air compressor mounting nuts, then slide air compressor rearward and remove from vehicle.**Fig. 9.**
6. Reverse procedure to install. **Torque** air compressor mounting nuts to 18 ft. lbs.

Air Dryer/Pressure Sensor

1. Remove air compressor as outlined previously in this section.
2. Disconnect electrical connectors.

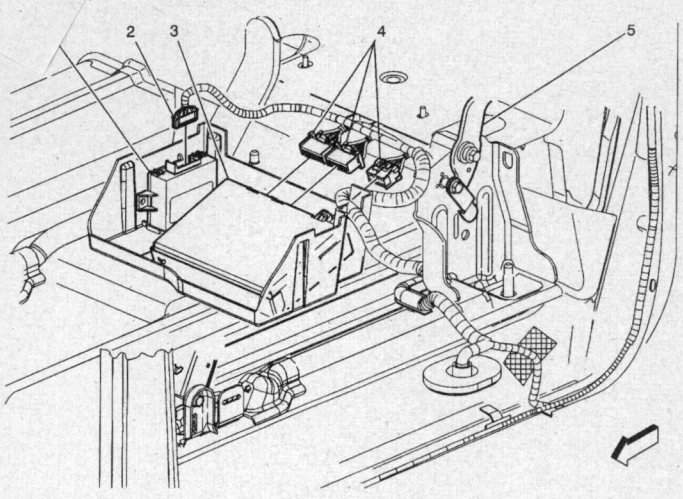

(1) Rear Object Sensor Control Module
(2) Rear Object Sensor Control Module Connector
(3) Electronic Suspension Control (ESC) Module
(4) Electronic Suspension Control (ESC) Module Connectors
(5) LR Passenger Seat Bracket

LTV0500000006727

**Fig. 1   Component locations
(passenger compartment).
Avalanche & Escalade EXT**

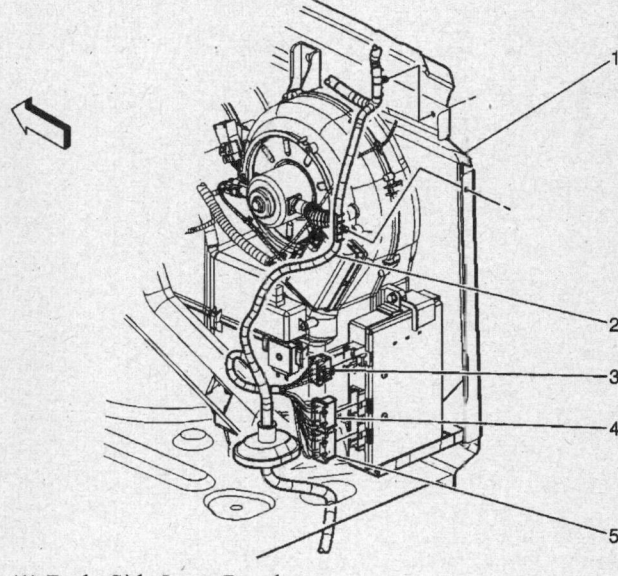

(1) Body Side Inner Panel
(2) Body Wiring Harness
(3) Electronic Suspension Control (ESC) Module Connector C1
(4) Electronic Suspension Control (ESC) Module Connector C2
(5) Electronic Suspension Control (ESC) Module Connector C3

LTV0500000006728

**Fig. 2   Component locations
(passenger compartment).
Escalade, Suburban, Tahoe & Yukon**

3. Remove air dryer/pressure sensor retaining screw.
4. Rotate air dryer/pressure sensor clockwise to remove from air compressor body.
5. Reverse procedure to install.

Control Module

AVALANCHE, ESCALADE, SUBURBAN, TAHOE & YUKON

1. Remove righthand side rear quarter interior trim panel.
2. Disconnect electrical connectors.
3. Remove control module mounting screw, then the control module from bracket.
4. Reverse procedure to install. **Torque** control module mounting screw to 14 inch lbs.

SRX

1. Remove seat belt retractor guide bolt and anchor bolt.

2. Remove garnish molding, then slide seat belt through garnish molding.
3. Remove right rear trim panel.
4. Disconnect control module electrical connectors.
5. Remove control module from bay board.
6. Reverse procedure to install.

Front/Rear Position Sensor

1. Raise and support vehicle.
2. Disconnect sensor harness connector at vehicle harness connector.
3. Remove wheel speed sensor wire at ESC/RTD sensor bracket.
4. Remove ESC/RTD sensor link bracket bolt at upper control arm.
5. Remove bolt, then the front/rear position sensor.

6. Reverse procedure to install, noting the following:
   a. **Torque** front position bolt to frame to 106 inch lbs.
   b. **Torque** sensor link bracket bolt 80 inch lbs.

Front/Rear Sensor Link

1. Remove ESC/RTD sensor as outlined previously in this section.
2. Twist link rod by hand, then remove from ball stud.
3. Remove link rod at mounting bracket ball stud.
4. Reverse procedure to install. Use tool No. J 38185, or equivalent to install link rod to ball stud.

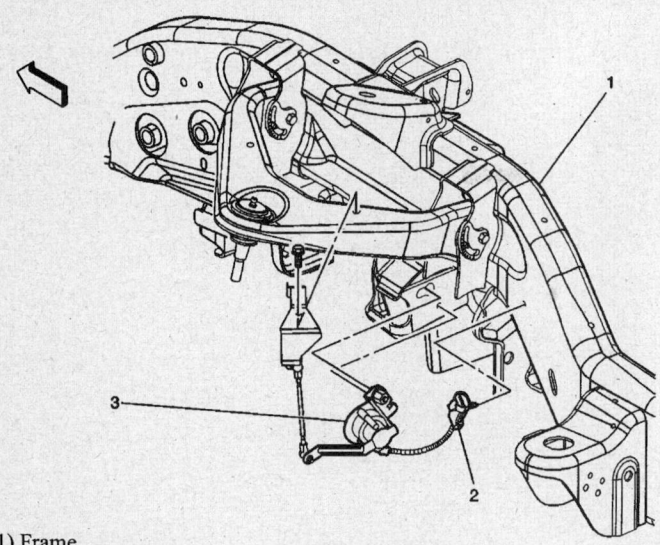

(1) Frame
(2) Suspension Position Sensor - LF Connector
(3) Suspension Position Sensor - LF

LTV0500000006729

Fig. 3   Component locations, chassis (Part 1 of 2). Avalanche, Escalade, Suburban, Tahoe & Yukon

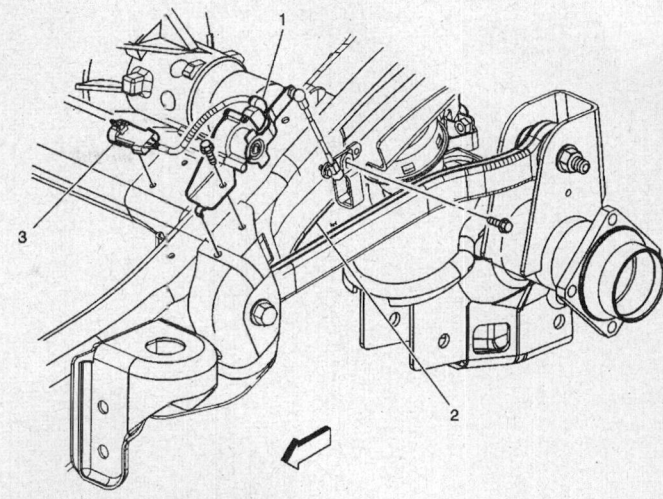

(1) Suspension Position Sensor - LR
(2) Frame
(3) Suspension Position Sensor - LR Connector

LTV0500000006730

Fig. 3   Component locations, chassis (Part 2 of 2). Avalanche, Escalade, Suburban, Tahoe & Yukon, 1500 series

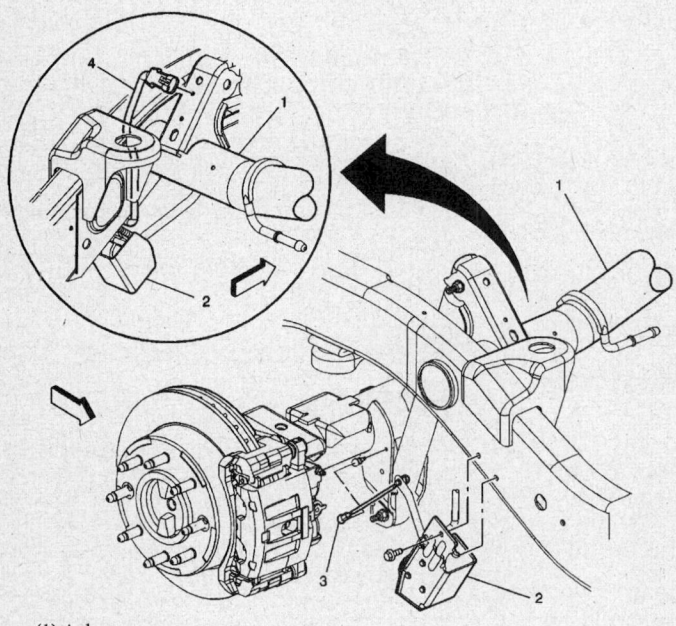

(1) Axle
(2) Suspension Position Sensor - RR
(3) Sensor Arm
(4) Suspension Position Sensor - RR Connector

LTV0500000006731

Fig. 3   Component locations, chassis (Part 2 of 2). Avalanche, Escalade, Suburban, Tahoe & Yukon, 2500 series

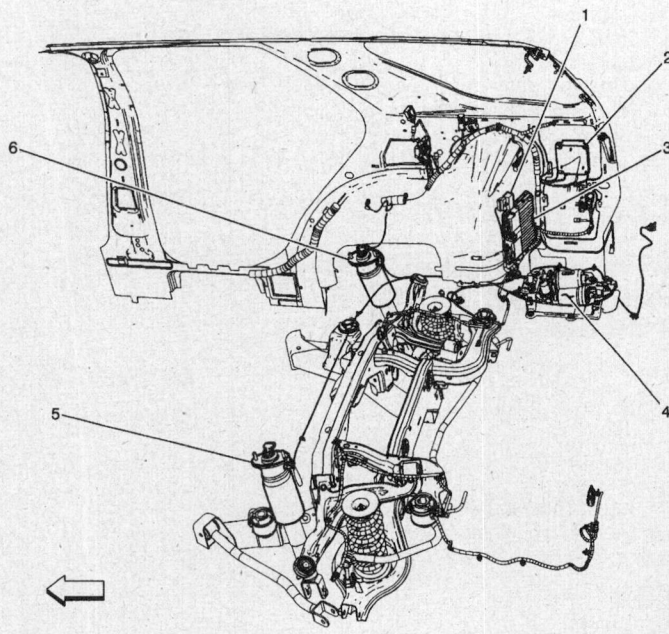

(1) Liftgate Lock/Unlock Relay
(2) Digital Radio Receiver (U2K)
(3) Electronic Suspension Control (ESC) Module
(4) Automatic Level Control (ALC) Compressor
(5) Suspension Damper - LR
(6) Suspension Damper - RR

LTV0500000006725

Fig. 4   Component locations (Part 1 of 2). SRX

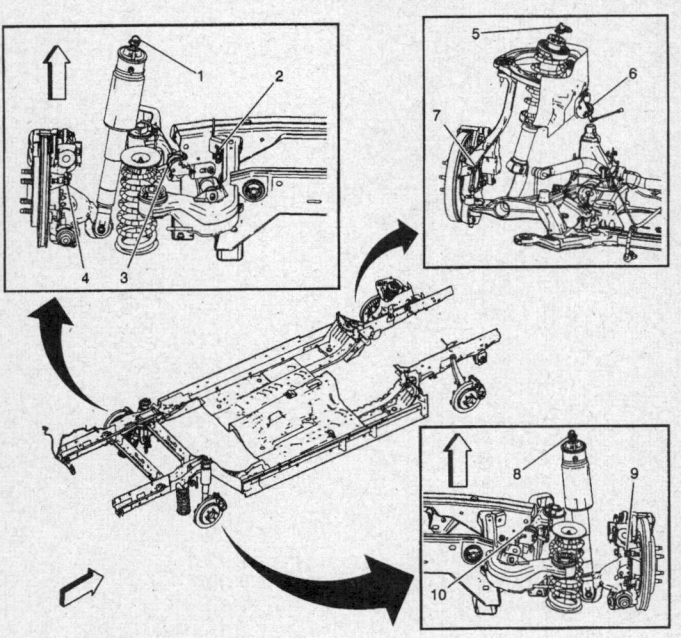

(1) Suspension Damper - LR
(2) Suspension Position Sensor Extension Harness Connector - LR
(3) Suspension Position Sensor - LR
(4) Wheel Speed Sensor (WSS) - LR
(5) Suspension Damper - LF, RF Similar
(6) Suspension Position Sensor - LF, RF Similar
(7) Wheel Speed Sensor (WSS) - LF, RF Similar
(8) Suspension Damper - RR
(9) Wheel Speed Sensor (WSS) - RR
(10) Suspension Position Sensor - RR

LTV0500000006726

Fig. 4   Component locations (Part 2 of 2). SRX

Code	Description
C0000	Vehicle Speed Information Circuit Fault
C0455	Steering Wheel Position Sensor Circuit Fault
C0550	ECU Fault
C0551	Option Configuration Error
C0575	Left Front Actuator Circuit Fault
C0580	Right Front Actuator Circuit Fault
C0585	Left Rear Actuator Circuit Fault
C0590	Right Rear Actuator Circuit Fault
C0615	Left Front Position Sensor Fault
C0620	Right Front Position Sensor Fault
C0625	Left Rear Position Sensor Fault
C0630	Right Rear Position Sensor Fault
C0655	Level Control Compressor Circuit Fault
C0660	Level Control Exhaust Valve Circuit Fault
C0665	Chassis Pitch Signal Circuit
C0690	Damper Control Relay Circuit Fault
C0711	Level Control Air Pressure Sensor Circuit Fault
C0870	Device Voltage Reference Output #1 Circuit Fault

Fig. 5   DTC interpretation. Avalanche, Escalade, Suburban, Tahoe & Yukon

Code	Description
C0249	Left Normal Force Error
C0250	Right Normal Force Error
C0550	ECU Fault
C0563	ECU Module Calibration Fault
C0577	Left Front Solenoid/Motor/Actuator Circuit Low
C0578	Left Front Solenoid/Motor/Actuator Circuit High
C0579	Left Front Solenoid/Motor/Actuator Circuit Open
C0582	Right Front Solenoid/Motor/Actuator Circuit Low
C0583	Right Front Solenoid/Motor/Actuator Circuit High
C0584	Right Front Solenoid/Motor/Actuator Circuit Open
C0587	Left Rear Solenoid/Motor/Actuator Circuit Low
C0588	Left Rear Solenoid/Motor/Actuator Circuit High
C0589	Left Rear Solenoid/Motor/Actuator Circuit Open
C0592	Right Rear Solenoid/Motor/Actuator Circuit Low
C0593	Right Rear Solenoid/Motor/Actuator Circuit High
C0594	Right Rear Solenoid/Motor/Actuator Circuit Open
C0615	Left Front Position Sensor Circuit
C0620	Right Front Position Sensor Circuit
C0625	Left Rear Position Sensor Fault
C0630	Right Rear Position Sensor Fault
C0635	Left Front Normal Force Circuit
C0638	Left Front Normal Force Circuit High
C0640	Right Front Normal Force Circuit
C0643	Right Front Normal Force Circuit High
C0665	Chassis Pitch Signal Circuit
C0690	Damper Control Relay Circuit Fault
C0691	Damper Control Relay Circuit Range/Performance
C0693	Damper Control Relay Circuit High
C0696	Position Sensor Overcurrent
C0710	Steering Position Signal
C0896	Device Voltage Range/Performance
P1652	Powertrain Induced Chassis Pitch Output Circuit

Fig. 6   DTC interpretation. SRX

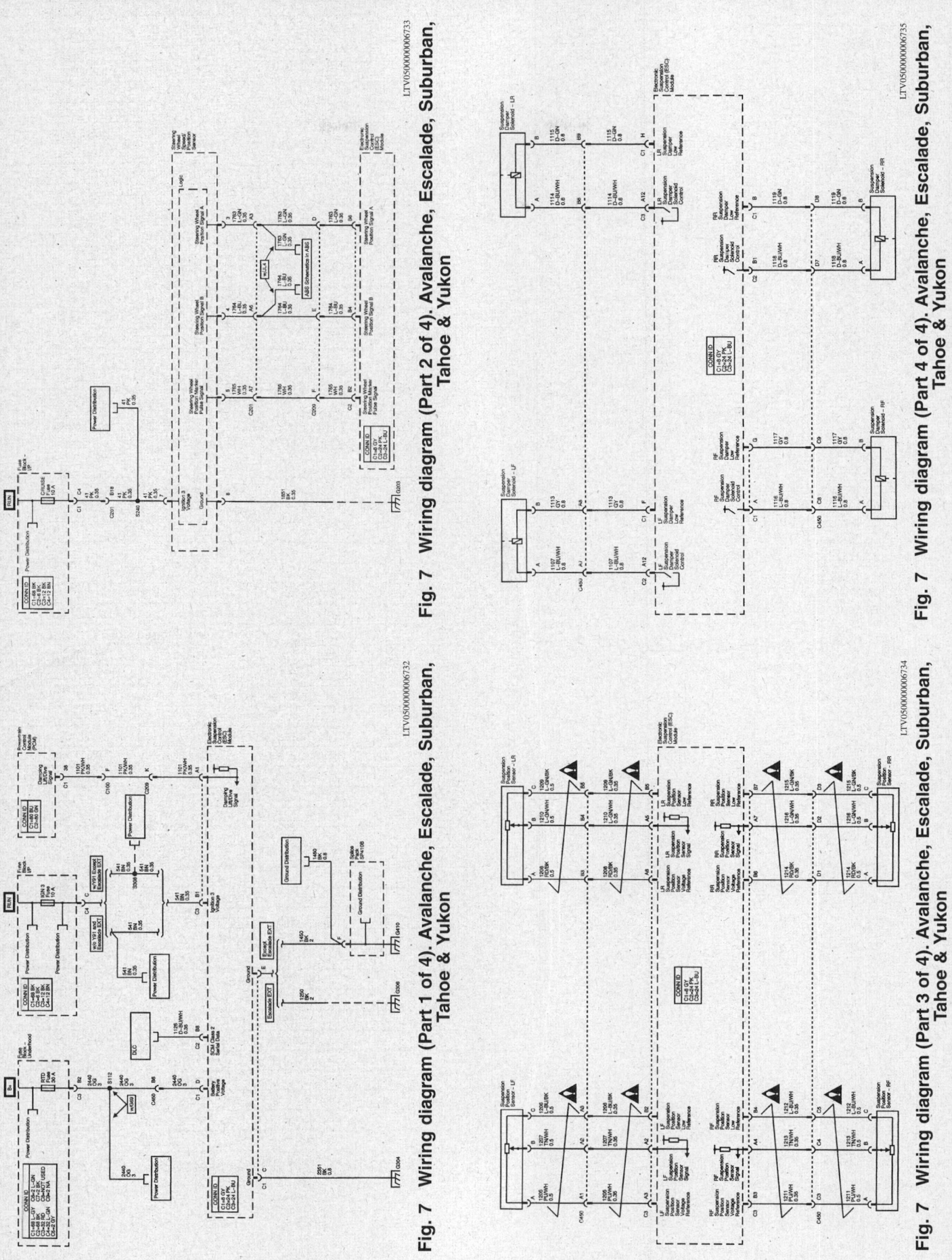

Fig. 7 Wiring diagram (Part 2 of 4). Avalanche, Escalade, Suburban, Tahoe & Yukon

Fig. 7 Wiring diagram (Part 4 of 4). Avalanche, Escalade, Suburban, Tahoe & Yukon

Fig. 7 Wiring diagram (Part 1 of 4). Avalanche, Escalade, Suburban, Tahoe & Yukon

Fig. 7 Wiring diagram (Part 3 of 4). Avalanche, Escalade, Suburban, Tahoe & Yukon

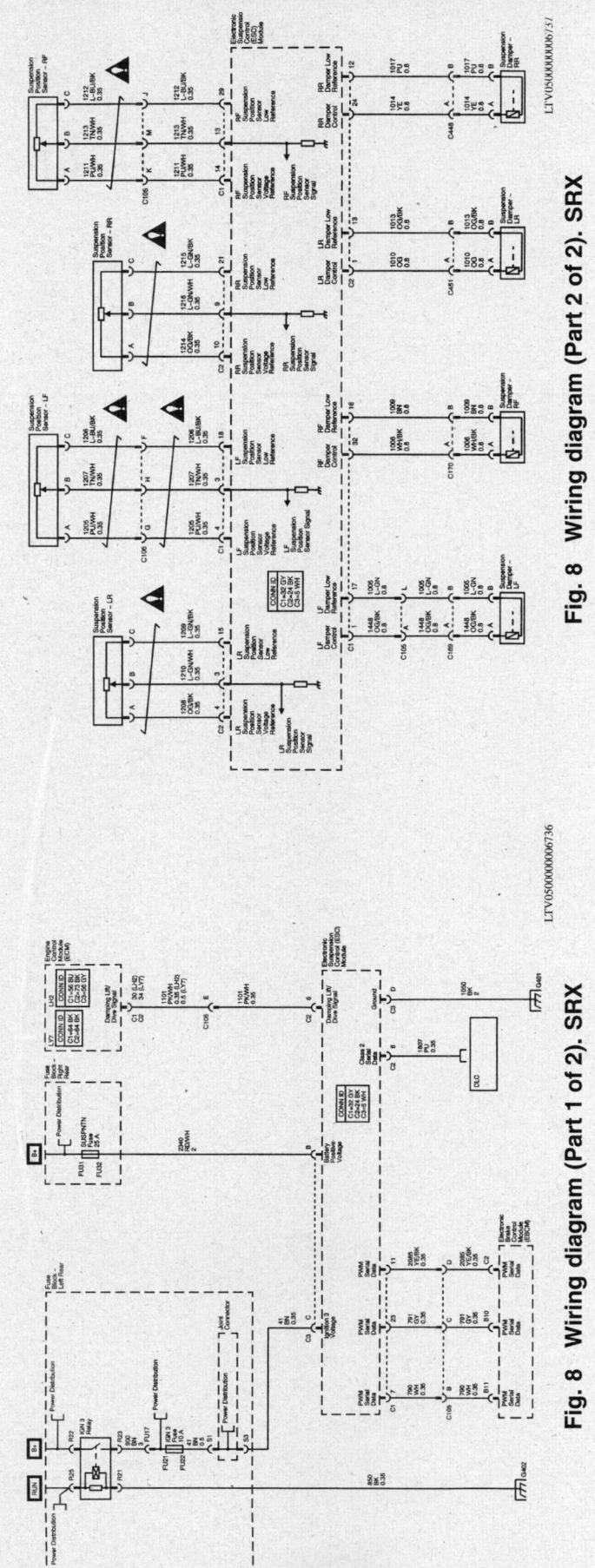

Fig. 8 Wiring diagram (Part 2 of 2). SRX

Fig. 8 Wiring diagram (Part 1 of 2). SRX

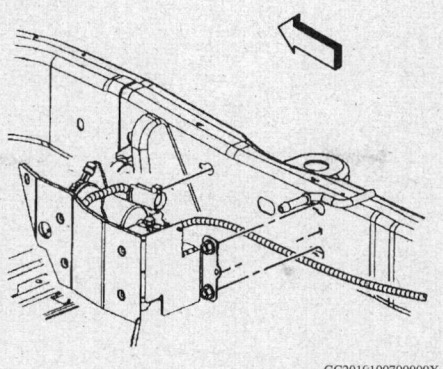

GC201©100700000X

Fig. 9   Air compressor removal

TIRE PRESSURE MONITORING SYSTEM

INDEX

	Page No.
Component Service	7-7
Pressure Monitor Sensor	
Programming	7-7
Avalanche, Escalade EXT,	
Sierra & Silverado	7-7
Aztek & Rendezvous	7-8
Envoy, Rainier & Trailblazer	7-7
Escalade, Escalade ESV,	
Suburban, Tahoe & Yukon	7-7
SRX	7-8
Pressure Monitor Sensor	
Replacement	7-8
Description	7-1
Diagnosis & Testing	7-1
Accessing Diagnostic Trouble	
Codes	7-1

	Page No.
Clearing Diagnostic Trouble	
Codes	7-1
Diagnostic Tests	7-1
Avalanche, Escalade EXT,	
Sierra & Silverado	7-1
Envoy, Rainier & Trailblazer	7-1
Escalade, Escalade ESV,	
Suburban, Tahoe & Yukon	7-1
SRX	7-1
Intermittent & Poor	
Connections	7-1
Intermittents	7-1
Poor Connections	7-2
Symptom Tests	7-1
Avalanche, Escalade EXT,	
Sierra & Silverado	7-1

	Page No.
Envoy, Rainier, Trailblazer	7-1
Escalade, Escalade ESV,	
Suburban, Tahoe & Yukon	7-1
Wiring Diagrams	7-1
Avalanche, Escalade EXT,	
Sierra & Silverado	7-1
Aztek	7-1
Escalade, Escalade ESV,	
Suburban, Tahoe & Yukon	7-1
Rendezvous	7-1
SRX	7-1
Diagnostic Chart Index	7-4
Precautions	7-1
Air Bag Systems	7-1
Battery Ground Cable	7-1
Tightening Specifications	7-8

PRECAUTIONS

Air Bag Systems

Refer to "Air Bag System Precautions" in the front of this manual for system disarming and arming procedures.

Battery Ground Cable

Prior to service, disconnect battery ground cable and isolate as required.

DESCRIPTION

The tire pressure monitor (TPM) system alerts the driver when a large change in the pressure of one tire exists. The system detects a tire pressure condition while the vehicle is in motion, once a tire pressure condition is detected, the system alerts the driver whenever the ignition is turned On.

The TPM system uses electronic brake control module, wheel speed sensors, data messages and instrument cluster to perform system functions as required.

DIAGNOSIS & TESTING

Accessing Diagnostic Trouble Codes

Connect a suitably programmed scan tool to Data Link Connector (DLC) and follow manufacturer's instructions.

Wiring Diagrams

AVALANCHE, ESCALADE EXT, SIERRA & SILVERADO

Refer to **Fig. 1** for wiring diagram.

AZTEK

Refer to **Fig. 2** for wiring diagram.

RENDEZVOUS

Refer to **Fig. 3** for wiring diagram.

ESCALADE, ESCALADE ESV, SUBURBAN, TAHOE & YUKON

Refer to **Fig. 4** for wiring diagram.

SRX

Refer to **Fig. 5** for wiring diagram.

Diagnostic Tests

AVALANCHE, ESCALADE EXT, SIERRA & SILVERADO

Refer to **Figs. 6 and 7** for diagnostic test procedures.

ESCALADE, ESCALADE ESV, SUBURBAN, TAHOE & YUKON

Refer to **Figs. 8 and 9** for diagnostic test procedures.

ENVOY, RAINIER & TRAILBLAZER

Refer to **Figs. 10 and 11** for diagnostic test procedures.

SRX

Refer to **Fig. 12** for diagnostic test procedures.

Symptom Tests

AVALANCHE, ESCALADE EXT, SIERRA & SILVERADO

Refer to **Figs. 13 and 14** for symptom tests.

ESCALADE, ESCALADE ESV, SUBURBAN, TAHOE & YUKON

Refer to **Figs. 15 and 16** for symptom tests.

ENVOY, RAINIER, TRAILBLAZER

Refer to **Figs. 17 and 18** for symptom tests.

Clearing Diagnostic Trouble Codes

Connect a suitably programmed scan tool to Data Link Connector (DLC), and follow manufacturer's instructions.

Intermittent & Poor Connections

INTERMITTENTS

Most intermittents are caused by faulty electrical connections or wiring. Inspect for the following:
1. Wiring broken inside insulation.
2. Poor connection between male and female terminal at connector.
3. Poor terminal to wire connection. Some conditions which fall under this are:

a. Poor crimps.
b. Poor solder joints.
c. Crimping over wire insulation rather than wire.
d. Corrosion in wire to terminal contact.

4. Wire insulation which is rubbed through. This causes an intermittent short as bare area touches other wiring or components.

POOR CONNECTIONS

1. It is important to test terminal contact at component and any inline connectors before replacing suspect component.
2. Mating terminals must be inspected to ensure good terminal contact.
3. Poor connection between male and female terminal at a connector may be result of contamination or deformation.
4. Contamination may be caused by:
   a. Connector halves being improperly connected.
   b. Missing or damaged seal.
   c. Damaged connector.
   d. Exposing terminals to moisture and dirt.
5. Deformation is caused by:
   a. Probing connector terminal mating side without proper adapter.
   b. Improperly joining connector halves.
   c. Repeatedly separating and joining connector halves.

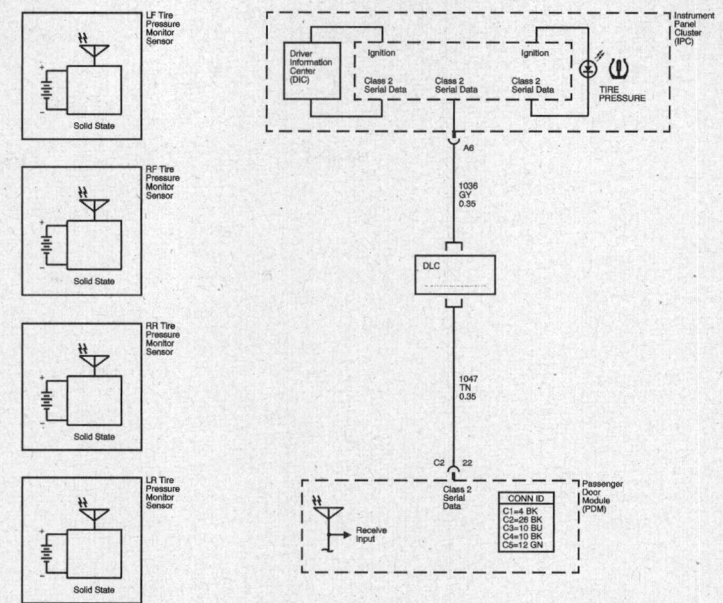

LTV0500000004339

Fig. 1   Wiring diagram. Avalanche, Escalade, Suburban, Tahoe & Yukon

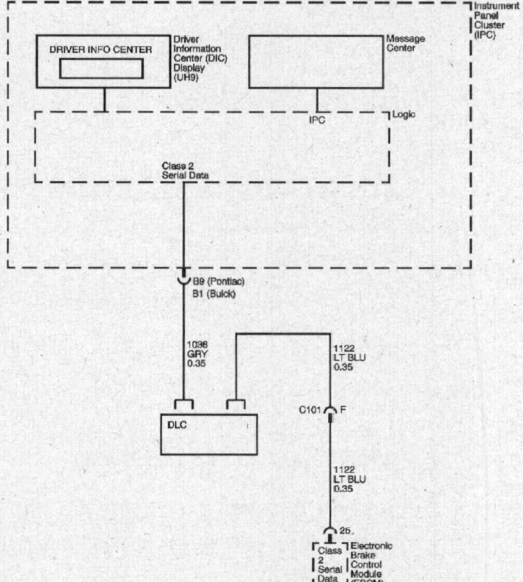

LTV0500000004342

Fig. 2   Wiring diagram. Aztek

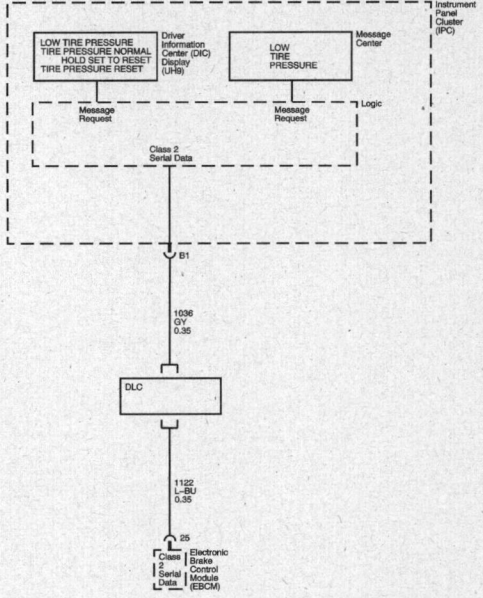

Fig. 3   Wiring diagram. Rendezvous

LTV0500000004338

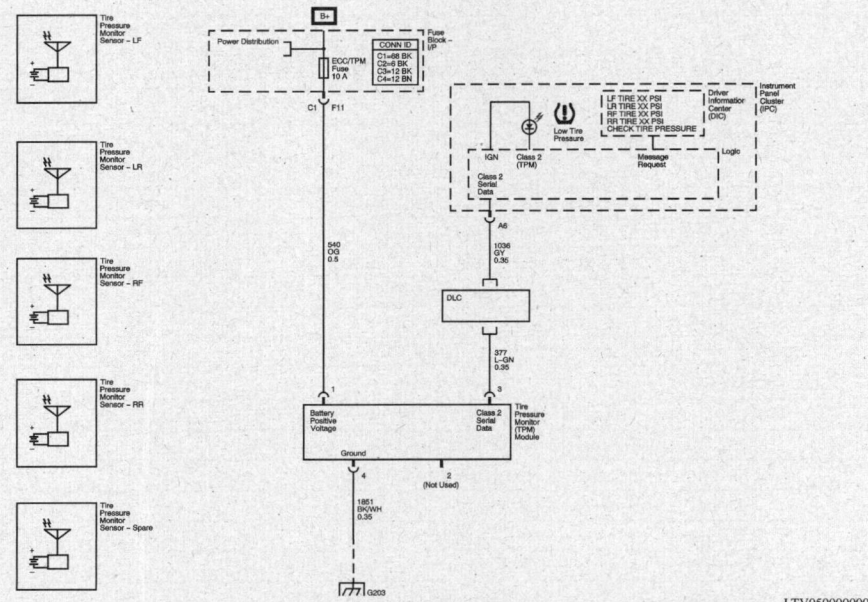

LTV0500000004341

Fig. 4   Wiring diagram. Escalade, Escalade ESV, Suburban, Tahoe & Yukon

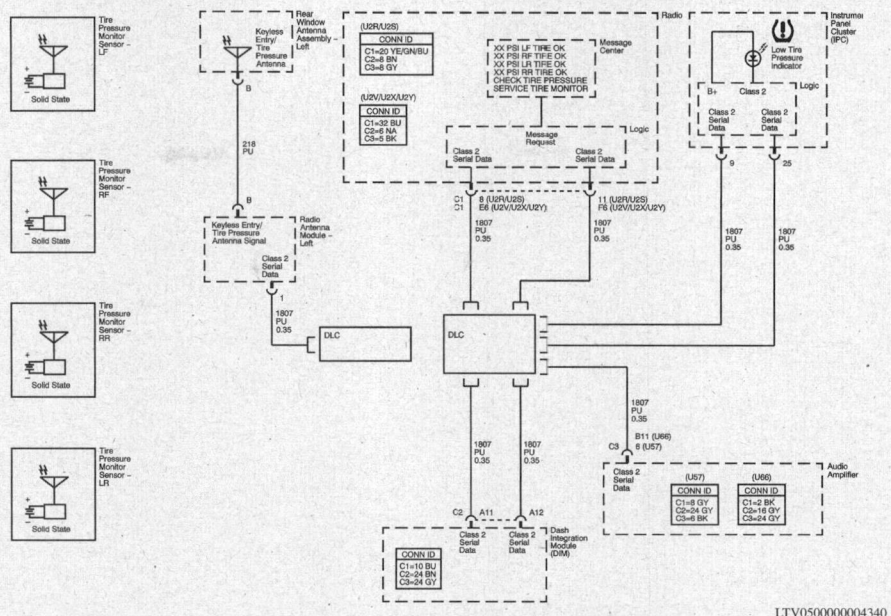

Fig. 5   Wiring diagram. SRX

LTV050000004340

DIAGNOSTIC CHART INDEX

Code	Description	Page No.	Fig. No.
AVALANCHE, ESCALADE EXT, SIERRA & SILVERADO			
—	Low Tire Pressure Indicator Always On	7-6	13
—	Low Tire Pressure Indicator Inoperative	7-6	14
C0750	Lefthand Front Low Tire Pressure Sensor	7-5	6
C0755	Righthand Front Low Tire Pressure Sensor	7-5	6
C0760	Lefthand Rear Low Tire Pressure Sensor	7-5	6
C0765	Righthand Rear Low Tire Pressure Sensor	7-5	6
C0775	Low Tire Pressure System Sensors Not Programmed	7-5	7
ENVOY, RAINIER & TRAILBLAZER			
—	Low Tire Pressure Indicator Always On	7-6	17
—	Low Tire Pressure Indicator Inoperative	7-7	18
C0750	Lefthand Front Low Tire Pressure Sensor	7-5	10
C0755	Righthand Front Low Tire Pressure Sensor	7-5	10
C0760	Lefthand Rear Low Tire Pressure Sensor	7-5	10
C0765	Righthand Rear Low Tire Pressure Sensor	7-5	10
C0775	Low Tire Pressure System Sensors Not Programmed	7-5	11
ESCALADE, ESCALADE ESV, SUBURBAN, TAHOE & YUKON			
—	Low Tire Pressure Indicator Always On	7-6	15
—	Low Tire Pressure Indicator Inoperative	7-6	16
C0750	Lefthand Front Low Tire Pressure Sensor	7-5	8
C0755	Righthand Front Low Tire Pressure Sensor	7-5	8
C0760	Lefthand Rear Low Tire Pressure Sensor	7-5	8
C0765	Righthand Rear Low Tire Pressure Sensor	7-5	8
C0775	Low Tire Pressure System Sensors Not Programmed	7-5	9
SRX			
C0750	Lefthand Front Low Tire Pressure Sensor	7-6	12
C0755	Righthand Front Low Tire Pressure Sensor	7-6	12
C0760	Lefthand Rear Low Tire Pressure Sensor	7-6	12
C0765	Righthand Rear Low Tire Pressure Sensor	7-6	12

Step	Action	Yes	No
1	Did you perform the Diagnostic System Check - Tire Pressure Monitoring?	Go to Step 2	Go to Diagnostic System Check
2	1. Install a scan tool. 2. Turn ON the ignition, with the engine OFF. 3. With a scan tool, observe the Suspect Pressure Sensor Mode Data parameter in Data Display. Does the scan tool indicate that the suspect Pressure Sensor Mode is Low Bat?	Go to Step 6	Go to Step 3
3	Since some occurrences of this DTC are caused by certain vehicle conditions. Review the tire pressure monitor (TPM) system with the customer to verify the conditions under which the DTC set. Did vehicle conditions cause this DTC to set?	Go to Diagnostic Aids	Go to Step 4
4	Learn the tire pressure sensors. Did a horn chirp sound when learning the suspect sensor?	Go to Step 5	Go to Step 6
5	1. Test drive the vehicle above 32 km/h (20 mph) for 10 seconds. 2. With the scan tool observe the Suspect Pressure Sensor Mode Data parameter. Does the Suspect Pressure Sensor Mode data parameter change from Wake to Drive above 32 km/h (20 mph)?	System OK	Go to Step 6
6	Replace the suspect tire pressure sensor. Did a horn chirp sound when learning the suspect sensor?	Go to Step 8	Go to Step 7
7	Replace the passenger door module (PDM) or remote control door lock receiver (RCDLR) module/switch assembly. Did you complete the replacement?	Go to Step 8	--
8	1. Use the scan tool in order to clear the DTCs. 2. Operate the vehicle within the conditions for running the DTC. Does the DTC reset?	Go to Step 2	System OK

LTV0500000005096

Fig. 6   Codes C0750, C0755, C0760 & C0765: Low Tire Pressure Sensor. Avalanche, Escalade EXT, Sierra & Silverado

Step	Action	Yes	No
1	Did you perform the Diagnostic System Check - Tire Pressure Monitoring?	Go to Step 2	Go to Diagnostic System Check
2	1. Install a scan tool. 2. Turn ON the ignition, with the engine OFF. 3. With a scan tool, observe the Suspect Pressure Sensor Mode Data parameter in Data Display. Does the scan tool indicate that the suspect Pressure Sensor Mode is Low Bat?	Go to Step 6	Go to Step 3
3	Since some occurrences of this DTC are caused by certain vehicle conditions. Review the tire pressure monitor (TPM) system with the customer to verify the conditions under which the DTC set. Did vehicle conditions cause this DTC to set?	Go to Diagnostic Aids	Go to Step 4
4	Learn the tire pressure sensors. Refer to Tire Pressure Sensor Learn. Did a horn chirp sound when learning the suspect sensor?	Go to Step 5	Go to Step 6
5	1. Test drive the vehicle above 32 km/h (20 mph) for 10 seconds. 2. With the scan tool observe the Suspect Pressure Sensor Mode Data parameter. Does the Suspect Pressure Sensor Mode data parameter change from Wake to Drive above 32 km/h (20 mph)?	System OK	Go to Step 6
6	Replace the suspect tire pressure sensor. Did a horn chirp sound when learning the suspect sensor?	Go to Step 8	Go to Step 7
7	Replace the passenger door module (PDM) or remote control door lock receiver (RCDLR) module/switch assembly. Did you complete the replacement?	Go to Step 8	--
8	1. Use the scan tool in order to clear the DTCs. 2. Operate the vehicle within the conditions for running the DTC. Does the DTC reset?	Go to Step 2	System OK

LTV0500000005098

Fig. 8   Codes C0750, C0755, C0760 & C0765: Low Tire Pressure Sensor. Escalade, Escalade ESV, Suburban, Tahoe & Yukon

Step	Action	Yes	No
1	Did you perform the Diagnostic System Check - Tire Pressure Monitoring?	Go to Step 2	Go to Diagnostic System Check
2	Learn the tire pressure sensors. Did you complete the procedure?	Go to Step 3	--
3	1. Use the scan tool in order to clear the DTCs. 2. Operate the vehicle within the Conditions for Running the DTC. Does the DTC reset?	Go to Step 2	System OK

LTV0500000005097

Fig. 7   Code C0775: Low Tire Pressure System Sensors Not Programmed. Avalanche, Escalade EXT, Sierra & Silverado

Step	Action	Yes	No
1	Did you perform the Diagnostic System Check - Tire Pressure Monitoring?	Go to Step 2	Go to Diagnostic System Check
2	Learn the tire pressure sensors. Did you complete the procedure?	Go to Step 3	--
3	1. Use the scan tool in order to clear the DTCs. 2. Operate the vehicle within the Conditions for Running the DTC. Does the DTC reset?	Go to Step 2	System OK

LTV0500000005099

Fig. 9   Code C0775: Low Tire Pressure System Sensors Not Programmed. Escalade, Escalade ESV, Suburban, Tahoe & Yukon

Step	Action	Yes	No
1	Did you perform the Diagnostic System Check - Vehicle?	Go to Step 2	Go to Diagnostic System Check
2	1. Install a scan tool. 2. Turn ON the ignition, with the engine OFF. 3. With a scan tool, observe the Suspect Pressure Sensor Mode Data parameter in Data Display. Does the scan tool indicate that the suspect Pressure Sensor Mode is Low Bat?	Go to Step 6	Go to Step 3
3	Since some occurrences of this DTC are caused by certain vehicle conditions. Review the tire pressure monitor (TPM) system with the customer to verify the conditions under which the DTC set. Did vehicle conditions cause this DTC to set?	Go to Diagnostic Aids	Go to Step 4
4	Learn the tire pressure sensors. Did a horn chirp sound when learning the suspect sensor?	Go to Step 5	Go to Step 6
5	1. Test drive the vehicle above 32 km/h (20 mph) for 10 seconds. 2. With the scan tool observe the Suspect Pressure Sensor Mode Data parameter. Does the Suspect Pressure Sensor Mode data parameter change from Wake to Drive above 32 km/h (20 mph)?	System OK	Go to Step 6
6	Replace the suspect tire pressure sensor. Did a horn chirp sound when learning the suspect sensor?	Go to Step 8	Go to Step 7
7	Replace the endgate module (EGM) or liftgate module (LGM) switch assembly. Did you complete the replacement?	Go to Step 8	--
8	1. Use the scan tool in order to clear the DTCs. 2. Operate the vehicle within the conditions for running the DTC. Does the DTC reset?	Go to Step 2	System OK

LTV0500000005100

Fig. 10   Codes C0750, C0755, C0760 & C0765: Low Tire Pressure Sensor. Envoy, Rainier & Trailblazer

Step	Action	Yes	No
1	Did you perform the Diagnostic System Check - Vehicle?	Go to Step 2	Go to Diagnostic System Check
2	Learn the tire pressure sensors. Did you complete the procedure?	Go to Step 3	--
3	1. Use the scan tool in order to clear the DTCs. 2. Operate the vehicle within the Conditions for Running the DTC. Does the DTC reset?	Go to Step 2	System OK

LTV0500000005101

Fig. 11   Code C0775: Low Tire Pressure System Sensors Not Programmed. Envoy, Rainier & Trailblazer

Step	Action	Yes	No
1	Did you perform the Diagnostic System Check - Vehicle?	Go to Step 2	Go to Diagnostic System Check
2	Using the J-46079 Tire Pressure Monitor Diagnostic Tool, activate each tire pressure sensor and record each sensor's transmission data and physical location on the repair order. Does the TPM diagnostic tool display each sensor's transmission data as an 8 digit ID number, accurate tire pressure +/- 2 psi, Learn Mode, good signal strength?	Go to Step 3	Go to Step 7
3	1. Turn ON the ignition, with the engine OFF. 2. Observe all 4 sensor IDs and their locations with a scan tool. Do the IDs and their locations observed on the scan tool match the IDs and locations recorded on the repair order?	Go to Step 4	Go to Step 5
4	1. Enable The TPM learn mode. 2. Using the TPM diagnostic tool in simulate mode, learn 4 simulated sensor transmissions into the driver antenna module's memory. 3. With the scan tool, observe all 4 sensor location, Ids and tire pressures. Does the scan tool display all 4 sensor locations, IDs, and tire pressures as specified?	Go to Step 5	Go to Step 8
5	Learn the tire pressure sensors. Did you complete the procedure?	Go to Step 6	--
6	1. Test drive the vehicle above 32 km/h (20 mph) for 10 seconds. 2. Observe the suspect Pressure Sensor Mode data parameter with the scan tool. Does the suspect Pressure Sensor Mode data parameter change from Wake to Drive above 32 km/h (20 mph)?	System OK	Go to Step 7
7	Replace the suspect tire pressure sensor. Did a horn chirp sound when learning the suspect sensor?	Go to Step 9	--
8	Replace the driver side antenna module. Did you complete the replacement?	Go to Step 9	--
9	1. Clear the DTCs with a scan tool. 2. Operate the vehicle within the Conditions for Running the DTC. Does the DTC reset?	Go to Step 2	System OK

LTV0500000005102

Fig. 12   Codes C0750, C0755, C0760 & C0765: Low Tire Pressure Sensor. SRX

Step	Action	Yes	No
1	Did you perform the Diagnostic System Check - Tire Pressure Monitoring?	Go to Step 2	Go to Diagnostic System Check
2	1. Turn OFF the ignition. 2. Turn ON the ignition, with the engine OFF. 3. Observe the low tire pressure indicator on the instrument panel cluster (IPC) during bulb check. Does the indicator illuminate during bulb check and then turn OFF?	Test for Intermittent Conditions and Poor Connections	Go to Step 3
3	Replace the IPC. Did you complete the replacement?	Go to Step 4	--
4	Operate the system in order to verify the repair. Did you correct the condition?	System OK	Go to Step 2

LTV0500000005104

Fig. 14   Low Tire Pressure Indicator Inoperative. Avalanche, Escalade EXT, Sierra & Silverado

Step	Action	Yes	No
1	Did you perform the Diagnostic System Check - Tire Pressure Monitoring?	Go to Step 2	Go to Diagnostic System Check
2	1. Turn OFF the ignition. 2. Turn ON the ignition, with the engine OFF. 3. Observe the low tire pressure indicator on the instrument panel cluster (IPC) during bulb check. Does the indicator illuminate during bulb check and then turn OFF?	Test for Intermittent Conditions and Poor Connections	Go to Step 3
3	Replace the IPC. Did you complete the replacement?	Go to Step 4	--
4	Operate the system in order to verify the repair. Did you correct the condition?	System OK	Go to Step 2

LTV0500000005106

Fig. 16   Low Tire Pressure Indicator Inoperative. Escalade, Escalade ESV, Suburban, Tahoe & Yukon

Step	Action	Yes	No
1	Did you perform the Diagnostic System Check - Tire Pressure Monitoring?	Go to Step 2	Go to Diagnostic System Check
2	1. Turn OFF the ignition. 2. Turn ON the ignition, with the engine OFF. 3. Observe the low tire pressure indicator on the instrument panel cluster (IPC) during bulb check. Does the indicator illuminate during bulb check and then turn OFF?	Test for Intermittent Conditions and Poor Connections	Go to Step 3
3	Inspect the tires for proper inflation pressure and inflate as needed. Did you find and correct the condition?	Go to Step 5	Go to Step 4
4	Replace the IPC. Did you complete the replacement?	Go to Step 5	--
5	Operate the system in order to verify the repair. Did you correct the condition?	System OK	Go to Step 2

LTV0500000005103

Fig. 13   Low Tire Pressure Indicator Always On. Avalanche, Escalade EXT, Sierra & Silverado

Step	Action	Yes	No
1	Did you perform the Diagnostic System Check - Tire Pressure Monitoring?	Go to Step 2	Go to Diagnostic System Check
2	1. Turn OFF the ignition. 2. Turn ON the ignition, with the engine OFF. 3. Observe the low tire pressure indicator on the instrument panel cluster (IPC) during bulb check. Does the indicator illuminate during bulb check and then turn OFF?	Test for Intermittent Conditions and Poor Connections	Go to Step 3
3	Inspect the tires for proper inflation pressure and inflate as needed. Did you find and correct the condition?	Go to Step 5	Go to Step 4
4	Replace the IPC. Did you complete the replacement?	Go to Step 5	--
5	Operate the system in order to verify the repair. Did you correct the condition?	System OK	Go to Step 2

LTV0500000005105

Fig. 15   Low Tire Pressure Indicator Always On. Escalade, Escalade ESV, Suburban, Tahoe & Yukon

Step	Action	Yes	No
1	Did you perform the Diagnostic System Check - Vehicle?	Go to Step 2	Go to Diagnostic System Check
2	1. Turn OFF the ignition. 2. Turn ON the ignition, with the engine OFF. 3. Observe the low tire pressure indicator on the instrument panel cluster (IPC) during bulb check. Does the indicator illuminate during bulb check and then turn OFF?	Test for Intermittent Conditions and Poor Connections	Go to Step 3
3	Inspect the tires for proper inflation pressure and inflate as needed. Did you find and correct the condition?	Go to Step 5	Go to Step 4
4	Replace the IPC. Did you complete the replacement?	Go to Step 5	--
5	Operate the system in order to verify the repair. Did you correct the condition?	System OK	Go to Step 2

LTV0500000005107

Fig. 17   Low Tire Pressure Indicator Always On. Envoy, Rainier, Trailblazer

COMPONENT SERVICE

Pressure Monitor Sensor Programming

AVALANCHE, ESCALADE EXT, SIERRA & SILVERADO

Learn mode will cancel if more than two minutes have passed and no sensor have been learned, or if more than five minutes has passed for entire procedure. If learn mode is canceled before any Ids are learned, PDM/RCDLR will remember all previously stored Ids and their locations. As soon as PDM/RCDLR learns first Id, all other Ids are erased from PDM/RCDLR's memory. Before proceeding with steps below, ensure that no other sensor learn procedure is being performed simultaneously, or that tire pressures are not being adjusted on a TPM equipped vehicle within close proximity.

1. Turn on ignition, with engine off.
2. Apply parking brake.
3. Cycle exterior lamp switch from off to parking lamps four times within four seconds. A double horn chirp will sound and low tire pressure indicator will begin to flash indicating learn mode has been enabled. **If learn mode cannot be enabled, ensure TPM system is enabled in PDM/RCDLR.**
4. Starting with lefthand front tire, hold antenna of tool no. J-46079 against tire sidewall close to wheel rim at valve stem location then press and release activate button and wait for a horn chirp, or increase/decrease tire pressure for 8-10 seconds then wait for a horn chirp. Horn chirp may occur before 8-10 second pressure increase/decrease time period has been reached, or up to 30 seconds after 8-10 second pressure increase/decrease time period has been reached. **Over inflating tires may cause personal injury or damage to tires and wheels. When increasing tire pressure do not exceed maximum inflation pressure as noted on tire sidewall.**
5. After horn chirp has sounded, proceed as in step 4 for the next three sensors in the following order:
   a. Righthand Front
   b. Righthand Rear
   c. Lefthand Rear
6. After lefthand rear sensor has been learned, turn off ignition to exit learn mode.
7. After learn mode has been exited, adjust all tire pressures to recommended psi.

ESCALADE, ESCALADE ESV, SUBURBAN, TAHOE & YUKON

Learn mode will cancel if more than two minutes have passed and no sensor have

Step	Action	Yes	No
1	Did you perform the Diagnostic System Check - Vehicle?	Go to Step 2	Go to Diagnostic System Check
2	1. Turn OFF the ignition. 2. Turn ON the ignition, with the engine OFF. 3. Observe the low tire pressure indicator on the instrument panel cluster (IPC) during bulb check. Does the indicator illuminate during bulb check and then turn OFF?	Test for Intermittent Conditions and Poor Connections	Go to Step 3
3	Replace the IPC. Did you complete the replacement?	Go to Step 4	--
4	Operate the system in order to verify the repair. Did you correct the condition?	System OK	Go to Step 2

LTV0500000005108

Fig. 18 Low Tire Pressure Indicator Inoperative. Envoy, Rainier, Trailblazer

been learned, or if more than five minutes has passed for entire procedure. If learn mode is canceled before any Ids are learned, PDM/RCDLR will remember all previously stored Ids and their locations. As soon as PDM/RCDLR learns first Id, all other Ids are erased from PDM/RCDLR's memory. Before proceeding with steps below, ensure that no other sensor learn procedure is being performed simultaneously, or that tire pressures are not being adjusted on a TPM equipped vehicle within close proximity.

1. Turn on ignition, with engine off.
2. Apply parking brake.
3. Cycle exterior lamp switch from off to parking lamps four times within four seconds. A double horn chirp will sound and low tire pressure indicator will begin to flash indicating learn mode has been enabled. **If learn mode cannot be enabled, ensure TPM system is enabled in PDM/RCDLR.**
4. Starting with lefthand front tire, hold antenna of tool no. J-46079 against tire sidewall close to wheel rim at valve stem location then press and release activate button and wait for a horn chirp, or increase/decrease tire pressure for 8-10 seconds then wait for a horn chirp. Horn chirp may occur before 8-10 second pressure increase/decrease time period has been reached, or up to 30 seconds after 8-10 second pressure increase/decrease time period has been reached. **Over inflating tires may cause personal injury or damage to tires and wheels. When increasing tire pressure do not exceed maximum inflation pressure as noted on tire sidewall.**
5. After horn chirp has sounded, proceed as in step 4 for the next three sensors in the following order:
   a. Righthand Front
   b. Righthand Rear
   c. Lefthand Rear
6. After lefthand rear sensor has been learned, turn off ignition to exit learn mode.
7. After learn mode has been exited, adjust all tire pressures to recommended psi.

ENVOY, RAINIER & TRAILBLAZER

Learn mode will cancel if more than two minutes have passed and no sensor have been learned, or if more than five minutes has passed for entire procedure. If learn mode is canceled before any Ids are learned, EGM/LGM will remember all previously stored Ids and their locations. As soon as EGM/LGM learns first Id, all other Ids are erased from EGM/LGM memory. Before proceeding with steps below, ensure that no other sensor learn procedure is being performed simultaneously, or that tire pressures are not being adjusted on a TPM equipped vehicle within close proximity.

1. Turn on ignition, with engine off.
2. Apply parking brake.
3. Cycle exterior lamp switch from off to parking lamps four times within four seconds. A double horn chirp will sound and low tire pressure indicator will begin to flash indicating learn mode has been enabled. **If learn mode cannot be enabled, ensure TPM system is enabled in the EGM/LGM.**
4. Starting with lefthand front tire, hold antenna of tool no. J-46079 against tire sidewall close to wheel rim at valve stem location then press and release activate button and wait for a horn chirp, or increase/decrease tire pressure for 8-10 seconds then wait for a horn chirp. Horn chirp may occur before the 8-10 second pressure increase/decrease time period has been reached, or up to 30 seconds after the 8-10 second pressure increase/decrease time period has been reached. **Over inflating tires may cause personal injury or damage to tires and wheels. When increasing tire pressure do not exceed maximum inflation pressure as noted on tire sidewall.**
5. After horn chirp has sounded, proceed as in step 4 for next three sensors in following order:
   a. Righthand Front
   b. Righthand Rear

  c. Lefthand Rear
6. After lefthand rear sensor has been learned, turn off ignition to exit learn mode.
7. After learn mode has been exited, adjust all tire pressures to recommended psi.

AZTEK & RENDEZVOUS

After resetting, tire pressure monitor system requires up to five miles of flat, smooth road, straight line driving in each of four speed ranges to complete calibration process.

1. Set all tire pressures to recommended psi.
2. Turn on ignition, with engine off.
3. Press mode button until "low tire pressure hold set to reset" is displayed.
4. Press and hold set button until a chime sounds and "tire pressure reset" is displayed and a chime sounds three times.
5. Release set button and "tire pressure normal" is displayed.

SRX

If using pressure increase/decrease method, following procedure must be completed within 15 minutes from when vehicle is stationary after being driven at 20 mph, or greater, for 10 seconds. Before proceeding with steps below, ensure that no other learn procedure is being performed simultaneously, or that no tire pressures are being adjusted on another TPM equipped vehicle within close proximity.

1. With ignition switch, select acc mode.
2. Simultaneously press keyless entry transmitter's lock and unlock buttons until a horn chirp sounds or use scan tool and select Special Functions/Sensor Learn Mode Enable/Enable soft key. A horn chirp will sound indicating mode has been enabled. When increasing tire pressure do not exceed maximum inflation pressure as noted on tire sidewall.
3. Starting with lefthand front tire, hold antenna of tool no. J-46079 against tire sidewall close to wheel rim at valve stem location then press and release activate button and wait for a horn chirp, or increase/decrease tire pressure for 5-8 seconds then wait for a horn chirp. Horn chirp may occur before the 5-8 second pressure increase/decrease time period has been reached, or up to 30 seconds after 5-8 second pressure increase/decrease time period has been reached.
4. After a horn chirp has sounded, proceed as in step three for next three sensors in the following order:
  a. Righthand Front
  b. Righthand Rear
  c. Lefthand Rear
5. After Lefthand Rear sensor has been learned a double horn chirp will sound indicating all sensors have been learned.
6. With ignition switch, select off mode to exit learn mode.
7. After learn mode has been exited, adjust all tire pressures to recommended pressure.

Pressure Monitor Sensor Replacement

1. Raise and support vehicle.
2. Remove tire/wheel assembly from vehicle.
3. Remove tire from the wheel. **Before tire is removed from wheel, note following items to avoid tire pressure sensor damage upon tire dismounting. Place sensors cap and valve on a dry clean surface after removal, cap is aluminum and valve is nickel plated to prevent corrosion and are not to be substituted with a cap or valve made of any other material. When separating tire bead from wheel, position bead breaking fixture 90° from valve stem. Position mounting/dismounting head so tire iron, or pry bar can be inserted slightly clockwise of sensor body when prying tire bead up and over mounting/dismounting head. Using tire machine, rotate tire/wheel assembly clockwise when transferring tire bead to out side of wheel rim. Repeat items for inner bead.**
4. Remove tire pressure sensor nut. **If any tire sealant is noted upon tire dismounting, remove all residual liquid sealant from inside of tire and wheel surfaces.**
5. Remove tire pressure sensor.
6. Reverse procedure to install.

TIGHTENING SPECIFICATIONS

Year	Component	Torque Ft. Lbs.
AZTEK, RENDEZVOUS & SRX		
2002–06	Tire Pressure Sensor	62①
	Wheel Lug Nuts	100
EXCEPT AZTEK, RENDEZVOUS & SRX		
2002–06	Tire Pressure Sensor	62①
	Wheel Lug Nuts	140

① — Inch lbs.

AAC: Auxilliary Air Control
AAV: Anti Afterburn Valve
ABS: Anti-Lock Brake System
A/C: Air Conditioning
A/C ATS: A/C Ambient Temperature Switch
ACC: Accessory Position
ACL: Air Cleaner
ACM: Air Bag Control Module
ACR-4: Air Conditioning Refrigerant, Recovery, Recycling, Recharging
ACT: Air Charge Temperature
A/D: Analog to Digital
AECM: Air Bag Electronic Control Module
A/F: Air/Fuel
AIR: Secondary Air Injection
AIRB: Secondary Air Injection Bypass
AIRD: Secondary Air Injection Diverter
AIS: Air Injection System
AIS: Automatic Idle Speed
ALDL: Assembly Line Diagnostic Link
AM1: Thermactor Air Management 1
AM2: Thermactor Air Management 2
AP: Accelerator Pedal
API: American Petroleum Institute
APP: Accelerator Pedal Position
APPS: Accelerator Pedal Position Sensor
ARS: Automatic Restraint System
ASD: Auto Shutdown Device
ASDM: Air Bag System Diagnostic Module
ASR: Automatic Slip Regulation
AT: Automatic Transmission
ATC: Active Transfer Case
ATDC: After Top Dead Center
AWD: All Wheel Drive
B+: Battery Positive Voltage
B-: Battery Negative Voltage
BAP: Barometric Atmosphere Pressure
BAR: Bureau Of Auto Repair
BARO: Barometric Pressure
BB: Barrel
BCDD: Boost Control Deceleration Device
BCI: Battery Council International
BCM: Body Control Module
BID: Breakerless Inductive Discharge
BOB: Breakout Box
BOO: Brake On/Off
BP: Barometric Pressure
BPA: Bypass Air
BPT: Backpressure Transducer
BTDC: Before Top Dead Center
BTS: Battery Temperature Sensor
BVSV: Bi-Metal Vacuum Switching Valve
BVT: Backpressure Variable Transducer
C: Continuous Memory
CA: California
CAA: Clean Air Act
CAB: Controller Anti-Lock Brakes
CAC: Charge Air Cooler
CALPAK: Device On FI To Allow Fuel Delivery In Event Of PROM Or ECM Malfunction
CANP: Canister Purge
CARB: California Air Resources Board
CAT: Catalytic Converter
CAT: Charge Air Temperature
CBD: Closed Bowl Distributor
CC: Catalytic Converter
CCA: Center Control Assembly
CCC: Computer Command Control
CCC: Converter Clutch Control Solenoid
CCCI: Computer Controlled Coil Ignition

CCD: Chrysler Collision Detection
CCD: Computer Controlled Dwell
CCD+: Chrysler Collision Detection Bus (+)
CCD−: Chrysler Collision Detection Bus (−)
CCECS: Computer Controlled Emission Control System
CCO: Converter Clutch Overdrive Solenoid
CCOT: Cycling Clutch Orifice Tube
CCP: Carbon Canister Purge
CCRM: Constant Control Relay Module
CEC: Computerized Emission Control System
CES: Clutch Engage Switch
CFI: Continuous Fuel Injection
CFRM: Condenser Fan Relay Module
CID: Cubic Inch Displacement
CID: Cylinder Identification
CIS: Constant Injection System
CIS-E: Constant Injection System Electronic
CKP: Crankshaft Position Sensor
CKT: Circuit
CL: Closed Loop
CLECS: Closed Loop Emission Control System
CLFCS: Closed Loop Fuel Control System
CMFI: Central Multi-Port Fuel Injection
CMP: Camshaft Position Sensor
CMTC: Compass/Mini-Trip Computer
CNG: Compressed Natural Gas
CO: Carbon Monoxide
COP: Coil On Plug
CO2: Carbon Dioxide
CP: Canister Purge
CPP: Clutch Pedal Position
CPS: Crankshaft Position Sensor
CPU: Central Processing Unit
CSF: Crankshaft Speed Fluctuation
CSFI: Central Sequential Fuel Injection
CTM: Central Timer Module
CTO: Coolant Temperature Override
CTOX: Continuous Trap Oxidizer
CTP: Closed Throttle Position
CTS: Coolant Temperature Sensor
CV: Constant Velocity
CVCC: Compound Vortex Controlled Combustion
CVVT: Continuous Variable Valve Timing
CYL: Cylinders
CYP: Cylinder Position
C3: Computer Command Control
C3I: Computer Controlled Computer Ignition
C-4: Computer Controlled Catalytic Convertor
DAB: Driver Air Bag
DCL: Data Communications Link
DCP: Duty Cycle Purge
DDS: Driveline Disengagement Switch
DEC: Diesel Engine Control
DERM: Diagnostic Energy Reserve Module
DFI: Direct Fuel Injection
DI: Distributor Ignition
DIC: Driver Information Center
DIS: Direct Or Distributorless Ignition System
DLC: Data Link Connector
DME: Digital Motor Electronics

DMIVA: Distributor Mounted Ignition Vacuum Advance
DOHC: Dual Overhead Camshaft
DPFE: Differential Pressure Feedback EGR
DPI: Dual Plug Ignition
DRB: Diagnostic Readout Box
DRB II: Diagnostic Readout Box II
DRB III: Diagnostic Readout Box III
DRL: Daytime Running Lamps
DS-I: Dura Spark I Ignition System
DS-II: Dura Spark II Ignition System
DSAS: Deceleration Spark Advance System
DTC: Diagnostic Trouble Code
DTM: Diagnostic Test Mode
DVOM: Digital Volt Ohm-Meter
EAT: Electronically Controlled Automatic Transaxle Or Transmission
EATXII: Electronic Automatic Transmission Controller 2nd Generation
EBCM: Engine Brake Control Module
EBL: Electric Back Lite
EBP: Exhaust Back Pressure
ECA: Electronic Control Assembly
ECCS: Electronic Concentrated Engine Control System
ECI: Electronic Control Injection
ECITS: Electronic Ignition Timing System
ECL: Engine Coolant Level
ECM: Engine Control Module
ECS: Evaporative Control System
ECT: Engine Coolant Temperature Sensor
ECTF: Cooling Fan Engine Coolant Temperature
ECU: Engine Control Unit
EDF: Electro Drive Fan
EDFI: Electronic Diesel Fuel Injection
EDI: Electronic Controlled Direct Ignition System
EDIS: Electronic Distributorless Ignition System
EDL: Engine Data Line
EEC: Electronic Engine Control
EEC-I: Electronic Engine Control I
EEC-II: Electronic Engine Control II
EEC-III: Electronic Engine Control III
EEC-IV: Electronic Engine Control IV
EEC-V: Electronic Engine Control V
EEGR: Electronic EGR Valve
EEPROM: Electronic Erasable Programmable Read Only Memory
EET: Electronic EGR Transducer
EETS: Electric EGR Transducer Solenoid
EFC: Electronic Fuel Control
EFE: Early Fuel Evaporation
EFI: Electronic Fuel Injection
EGO: Exhaust Gas Oxygen Sensor
EGR: Exhaust Gas Recirculation
EGRC: EGR Control
EGRT: EGR Temperature
EGRV: EGR Vent
EI: Electronic Ignition
EIC: Electronic Instrument Cluster
EICU: Electronic Ignition Control Unit
EITC: Electronic Ignition Timing Control
ELB: Electronic Lean Burn System
ELC: Electronic Level Control
ELCD: Evaporative Loss Control Device
ELD: Electric Load Detector

EM: Engine Modification
EMCC: Electronic Modulated Converter Clutch
EMI: Electromagnetic Interference
EMR: Electronic Module Retard
EOP: Engine Oil Pressure
EOT: Engine Oil Temperature
EPA: Environmental Protection Agency
EPC: Electronic Pressure Control
EPP: Engine Position Pulse
EPR: Exhaust Back Pressure Regulator
EPT: EGR Pressure Transducer
ESA: Electronic Spark Advance
ESC: Electronic Spark Control
ESS: Engine Speed Sensor
EST: Electronic Spark Timing
ETC: Electronic Temperature Control
ETCS-i: Electronic Throttle Control System-Intelligent
ETW: Equivalent Test Weight
EVAP: Evaporative Emission
EVIC: Electronic Vehicle Information Center
EVO: Electronic Variable Orifice
EVP: EGR Valve Position
EVR: Electronic Voltage Regulator
EVSV: Electronic Vacuum Switching Valve
EWL: Engine Warning Lamp
EWMA: Exponentially Weighted Moving Average
EZL: Electronic Ignition System With Variable Characteristics
FC: Fan Control
FDCS: Fuel Demand Command Signal
FED: Federal (49 State)
FEEPROM: Flash Electrically Erasable Programmable Read Only Memory
FEPROM: Flash Electrically Programmable Read Only Memory
FF: Flexible Fuel
FI: Fuel Injected Or Fuel Injection
FMEM: Failure Mode Effects Management
FMI: Failure Mode Identifiers
FPCM: Fuel Injection Pump Control Module
FPM: Fuel Pump Monitor
FPRC: Fuel Pressure Regulator Control
FR: Fillpipe Restrictor
FSS: Flexible Service System
FTP: Federal Test Procedure
FWD: Front Wheel Drive
GEN: Generator
GFD: Generic Field Data
GFP: Gaseous Fuel Prep
GPC: Glow Plug Control
GPL: Glow Plug Wait Lamp
GPM: Gallons Per Minute
gpm: Grams Per Million
GPR: Glow Plug Relay
GVW: Gross Vehicle Weight
GVWR: Gross Vehicle Weight Rating
HAI: Heated Air Intake
HC: Hydrocarbon
HCU: Hydraulic Control Unit
HD: Heavy Duty
HDC: Heavy Duty Emission Cycle
HE: Hall Effect
HEDF: High Electro Drive Fan
HEGO: Heated Exhaust Gas Oxygen Sensor
HEI: High Energy Ignition
HEUI: Hydraulically Actuated Electronically Controlled Unit Injectors
HF: High Fuel Economy
HFAN: High Speed Cooling Fan
HFC: High Fan Control

HFM: Hot Film Air Mass Sensor
Hg: Mercury
HIC: Hot Idle Compensation
HO: High Output
HO2S: Heated Oxygen Sensor
HPTBI: High Pressure TBI
HSC: High Swirl Combustion
HSIA: High Speed Inlet Air Conditioning
HVS: High Voltage Switch Ignition System
H2O: Water Column
IAC: Idle Air Control
IACV-AAC: Idle Air Control Valve-Auxilliary Air Control Valve
IAT: Intake Air Temperature
IC: Ignition Control
ICM: Ignition Control Module
ICP: Injector Control Pressure
ICS: Ignition Control System
ICTO: Ignition Coolant Temperature Overide
ID: Inner Diameter
IDI: Integrate Direct Ignition
IDM: Injector Driver Module
IDM: Ignition Diagnostic Monitor
IFI: Indirect Fuel Injection
IFS: Inertial Fuel Shutoff
ILC: Idle Load Compensator
ILEV: Inherently Low Emission Vehicle
I/M: Inspection & Maintenance Testing
IMRC: Intake Manifold Runner Control
IMT: Intake Manifold Temperature
IOD: Ignition Current Off Draw
IPR: Ignition Control Pressure Regulator
ISA: Idle Speed Actuator
ISC: Idle Speed Control
ISS: Integrated Idle Stabilization System
ITS: Idle Tracking Switch
IVS: Idle Validation Switch
JTEC: Combined Engine And Transmission Control Module
JTEC: Jeep Truck Powertrain Control Module System
KAM: Keep Alive Memory
KOEO: Key On Engine Off
KOER: Key On Engine Running
KS: Knock Sensor
L: Liter
LCD: Liquid Crystal Display
LD: Light Duty
LDP: Leak Detection Pump
LED: Light Emitting Diode
LEV: Low Emissions Vehicle
LFAN: Low Speed Cooling Fan
LH: Lefthand
LPG: Liquid Propane Gas
LPT: Light Pressure Turbo
LPTBI: Low Pressure TBI
LSIACV: Linear Solenoid Idle Air Control Valve
LTW: Low Tire Warning
LUS: Lock-Up Solenoid
LVW: Loaded Vehicle Weight
MAF: Mass Air Flow
MAP: Manifold Absolute Pressure
MAT: Manifold Absolute Temperature
MBEC: Multiple Board Engine Controller
MC: Mixture Control
MCC: Manifold Catalytic Converter
MCCA: Message Center Control Assembly
M/CCC: Modulated Converter Clutch Control
MCS: Mixture Control System
MCU: Microprocessor Control Unit
MC-VAF: Measuring Core Volume Air Flow

MDP: Manifold Differential Pressure
MDS2: Mopar Diagnostic System 2nd Generation
MEMCAL: Memory Calibration Unit
MFI: Multi-Point Fuel Injection
MIC: Mechanical Instrument Cluster
MID: Message Identifier
MIL: Malfunction Indicator Lamp
MLP: Manual Level Position
MLUS: Modulator Lock-Up Solenoid
MPFI: Multi-Point Fuel Injection
MPI: Multi-Port Injection
MST: Intake Manifold Surface Temperature
MT: Manual Transmission
MTA: Managed Thermactor Air
MTV: Manifold Tuning Valve
MUI: Mechanical Unit Injection
MUT II: Multi-Use Tool, Second Edition
MVLPS: Manual Valve Lever Position Switch (See Also PNP Switch)
MVZ: Manifold Vacuum Zone
NGC: Next Generation Controller
NGS: New Generation Star Tester
NGV: Natural Gas Vehicle
NOx: Oxides Of Nitrogen
NTC: Negative Temperature Coefficient
NVLD: Natural Vacuum Leak Detection
NVRAM: Non-Volatile Random Access Memory
O: Key On Engine Off
OBD: On-Board Diagnostic
OBD II: On-Board Diagnostic Class II
OC: Oxidation Catalytic Converter
OCC: Output Circuit Check
OD: Outer Diameter
ODM: Output Driver Module
ODO: Odometer
OHC: Overhead Cam
OL: Open Loop
ORVR: On Board Refueling Vapor Recovery
OSAC: Orifice Spark Advance Control
OSC: Output State Control
OSS: Output Shaft
OSS: Output Speed Sensor
OTIS: Overhead Travel Information System
OWL: Oil/Water Warning Lamp
O2: Oxygen Sensor
O2S: Oxygen Sensor (Left Sensor When Two Sensors Are Used)
O2SR: Right Oxygen Sensor
PAB: Passenger Air Bag
PAD: Passenger Air Bag Disable
PAG: Polyalkaline Glycol
PAIR: Pulse Secondary Air Injection
PCI: Programmable Communications Interface
PCM: Powertrain Control Module
PCV: Positive Crankcase Ventilation
PDC: Power Distribution Center
PEP: Peripheral Expansion Port
PFE: Pressure Feedback EGR
PG: Pulse Generator
PGM-FI: Programmed Fuel Injection
PGM-IG: Programmed Ignition
PID: Parameter Identifier
PIP: Profile Ignition Pickup
PNP: Park/Neutral Position
PPM: Parts Per Million
PPS: Proportional Purge Solenoid
PRC: Pressure Regulator Control

PROM: Programmable Read Only Memory
PSI: Pounds Per Square Inch
PSP: Power Steering Pressure
PTC: Positive Temperature Coefficient
PTEC: Powertrain Electronic Controller Management System
PTO: Power Take Off
PTOX: Periodic Trap Oxidizer
PVS: Ported Vacuum Switch
PWM: Pulse-Width Modulation
R: Key On Engine Running
RABS: Rear Anti-Locking Braking System
RAM: Random Access Memory
RAP: Retained Accessory Power
RDS: Radio Data System
REDOX: Reduction Oxydation Catalytic Converter
REGT: Recirculated Exhaust Gas Temperature
RFI: Radio Frequency Interference
RH: Righthand
RKE: Remote Keyless Entry
RM: Relay Module
ROM: Read Only Memory
RON: Research Octane Number
RPM: Revolutions Per Minute
RPS: Revolutions Per Second
RWAL: Rear Wheel Anti-Lock Brakes
RWD: Rear Wheel Drive
SAE: Society Of Automotive Engineers
SAS: Speed Adjusting Screw
SAW: Spark Angle Word
SBEC: Single Board Engine Controller (PCM)
SBEC II: Single Board Engine Controller II
SC: Supercharger
SCB: Supercharger Bypass
SCC: Spark Control Computer
SCCS: Speed Control Command Switches
SCI: Serial Communications Interface
SCS: Speed Controlled Spark
SCW: Similar Conditions Window
SFI: Sequential Multi-Port Fuel Injection
SFTP: Supplementary Federal Test Procedure
SHO: Super High Output
SID: Subsystem Identifier
SIL: Shift Indicator Lamp
SIR: Supplemental Inflatable Restraint
SKIM: Sentry Key Immobilizer Module
SKIS: Sentry Key Immobilizer System
SMEC: Single Module Engine Controller
SOHC: Single Overhead Camshaft
SO2: Sulfur Dioxide

SPCS: Spark Plug Switching Control System
SPI: Serial Peripheral Interface
SPK: Spark Control
SPL: Smoke Puff Limiter
SPOUT: Spark Output
SRI: Service Reminder Indicator
SRS: Supplemental Restraint System
SRT: System Readiness Test
SRV: Short Runner Valve
SS: Shift Solenoid
SSI: Solid State Ignition
SST: Special Service Tool
ST: Scan Tool
STAR: Self-Test Automatic Readout
STC: Spark Timing Control
STI: Self-Test Input
STO: Self-Test Output
SULEV: Super Ultra Low Emissions Vehicle
SVO: Special Vehicle Operations
SVT: Special Vehicle Team
TAB: Thermactor Air Bypass Vacuum Solenoid Valve
TAC: Thermal Air Control
TAD: Thermactor Air Diverter Valve
TBI: Throttle Body Injection
TC: Turbocharged
TCC: Torque Converter Clutch
TCM: Transmission Control Module
TCS: Transmission Controlled Spark
TDC: Top Dead Center
TFI-I: Thick Film I Ignition System
TFI-IV: Thick Film IV Ignition System
TFT: Transmission Fluid Temperature
TI: Transistor Ignition System
TLEV: Transitional Low Emission Vehicle
TOT: Transmission Oil Temperature
TP: Throttle Position
TPI: Tuned Port Injection
TPMS: Tire Pressure Monitoring System
TPOUT: Throttle Position Output
TPS: Throttle Position Sensor
TPT: Throttle Position Transducer
TR: Transmission Range
TRS: Transmission Range Sensor
TSB: Technical Service Bulletin
TSP: Throttle Solenoid Positioner
TSS: Transmission Speed Sensor
TSS: Turbine Speed Sensor
TTS: Transaxle Temperature Switch
TV: Throttle Valve
TVP: Throttle Valve Potentiometer
TVS: Thermal Vacuum Switch
TVSV: Thermal Vacuum Shutoff Valve
TVV: Thermal Vacuum Valve
TWC: Three-Way Catalyst

TWC: Three-Way Catalytic Converter
TWC+OC: Three-Way+Oxidation Catalytic Converter
UIC: Universal Integrated Circuit Ignition
ULEV: Ultra Low Emissions Vehicle
UVC: Under Valve Cover
V: Volt
VAF: Volume Air Flow
VANOS: Double Variable Camshaft Control
VAT: Vane Air Temperature
VCM: Vehicle Controll Module
VCRM: Variable Control Relay Module
VCV: Vacuum Control Valve
VDV: Vacuum Delay Valve
VECI: Vehicle Emission Control Information
VEPS: Vehicle Electronic Programming System
VFD: Vacuum Fluorescent Display
VIC: Vehicle Information Center
VICS: Variable Inertia Charging System
VIN: Vehicle Identification Number
VIT: Vehicle Interface Tool
VOM: Volt-Ohm Meter
VOTM: Vacuum Operated Throttle Modulator
VPM: Vehicle Personality Module
VP-20: Bosch VP-20 Diesel Engine Control System
VR: Voltage Regulator
VRE: Vehicle Retarder Enable
V-REF: Voltage Reference
VRV: Vacuum Regulator Valve
VSC: Vehicle Speed Control
VSS: Vehicle Speed Sensor
VTEC: Variable Valve Timing & Valve Lift Electronic Control
VTSS: Vehicle Theft Security System
VVTI: Variable Valve Timing With Intelligence
WAC: Wide Open Throttle A/C Cutoff
WOT: Wide Open Throttle
WOTPS: Wide Open Throttle Position Switch
WSS: Wheel Speed Sensor
WU-OC: Warm Up Oxidation Catalytic Converter
WU-TWC: Warm Up Three-Way Catalytic Converter
X: Equipped
ZEV: Zero Emissions Vehicle
2VH: 2 Valve Head
2WD: Two-Wheel Drive
4VH: 4 Valve Head
4WD: Four-Wheel Drive

NOTES

DECIMAL & MILLIMETER EQUIVALENTS

Inch	Inch	mm	Inch	Inch	mm	Inch	Inch	mm
1/64	.015625	.397	23/64	.359375	9.128	11/16	.6875	17.462
1/32	.03125	.794	3/8	.375	9.525	45/64	.703125	17.859
3/64	.046875	1.191	25/64	.390625	9.922	23/32	.71875	18.265
1/16	.0625	1.587	13/32	.40625	10.319	47/64	.734375	18.653
5/64	.078125	1.984	27/64	.421875	10.716	3/4	.75	19.505
3/32	.09375	2.381	7/16	.4375	11.113	49/64	.765625	19.447
7/64	.109375	2.778	29/64	.453125	11.509	25/32	.78125	19.884
1/8	.125	3.175	15/32	.46875	11.906	51/64	.796875	20.240
9/64	.140625	3.572	31/64	.484375	12.303	13/16	.8125	20.637
5/32	.15625	3.969	1/2	.5	12.700	53/64	.828125	21.034
11/64	.17185	4.366	33/64	.515625	13.097	27/32	.84375	21.431
3/16	.1875	4.762	17/32	.53125	13.494	55/64	.859375	21.828
13/64	.203125	5.159	35/64	.546875	13.890	7/8	.875	22.225
7/32	.21875	5.556	9/16	.5625	14.287	57/64	.890625	22.622
15/64	.234375	5.953	37/64	.578125	14.684	29/32	.90625	23.019
1/4	.25	6.350	19/32	.59375	15.081	59/64	.921875	23.415
17/64	.265626	6.747	39/64	.609375	15.478	15/16	.9375	23.812
9/32	.28125	7.144	5/8	.625	15.875	61/64	.953125	24.209
19/64	.296875	7.541	41/64	.640625	16.272	31/32	.96875	24.606
5/16	.3125	7.937	21/32	.65625	16.669	63/64	.984375	25.003
21/64	.328125	8.334	43/64	.671875	17.065	1	1	25.400
11/32	.34375	8.731						

Special Service Tools

Throughout this manual references are made to and illustrations may depict the use of special tools required to perform certain jobs. These special tools can generally be ordered through the dealers of the make vehicle being serviced. It is also suggested that you check with local automotive supply firms as they also supply tools manufactured by other firms that will assist in the performance of these jobs. The vehicle manufacturers special tools are supplied by:

Chrysler Corporation . . . . Miller Special Tools
OTC Division
28635 Mound Rd.
Warren, Michigan 48092-3499

Ford Motor Company . . . . SPX Corporation, OTC
ATTN: Ford Rotunda
28635 Mound Rd.
Warren, Michigan 48092-3499

General Motors Corporation . . . . Kent-Moore
SPX Corporation
28635 Mound Rd.
Warren, Michigan 48092-3499

Manual Information Locator

Front Wheel Drive Models

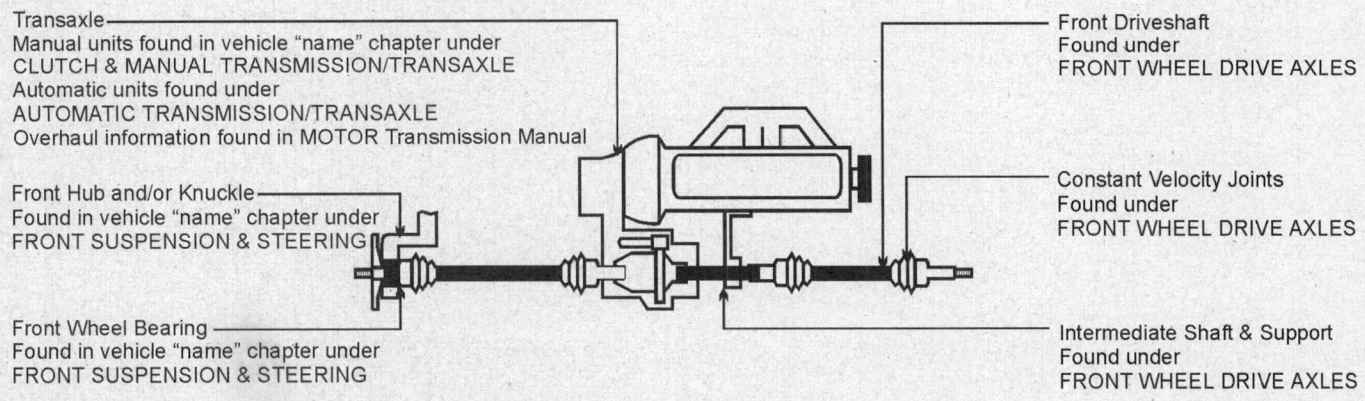

Transaxle
Manual units found in vehicle "name" chapter under
CLUTCH & MANUAL TRANSMISSION/TRANSAXLE
Automatic units found under
AUTOMATIC TRANSMISSION/TRANSAXLE
Overhaul information found in MOTOR Transmission Manual

Front Driveshaft
Found under
FRONT WHEEL DRIVE AXLES

Front Hub and/or Knuckle
Found in vehicle "name" chapter under
FRONT SUSPENSION & STEERING

Constant Velocity Joints
Found under
FRONT WHEEL DRIVE AXLES

Front Wheel Bearing
Found in vehicle "name" chapter under
FRONT SUSPENSION & STEERING

Intermediate Shaft & Support
Found under
FRONT WHEEL DRIVE AXLES

Four Wheel Drive Models

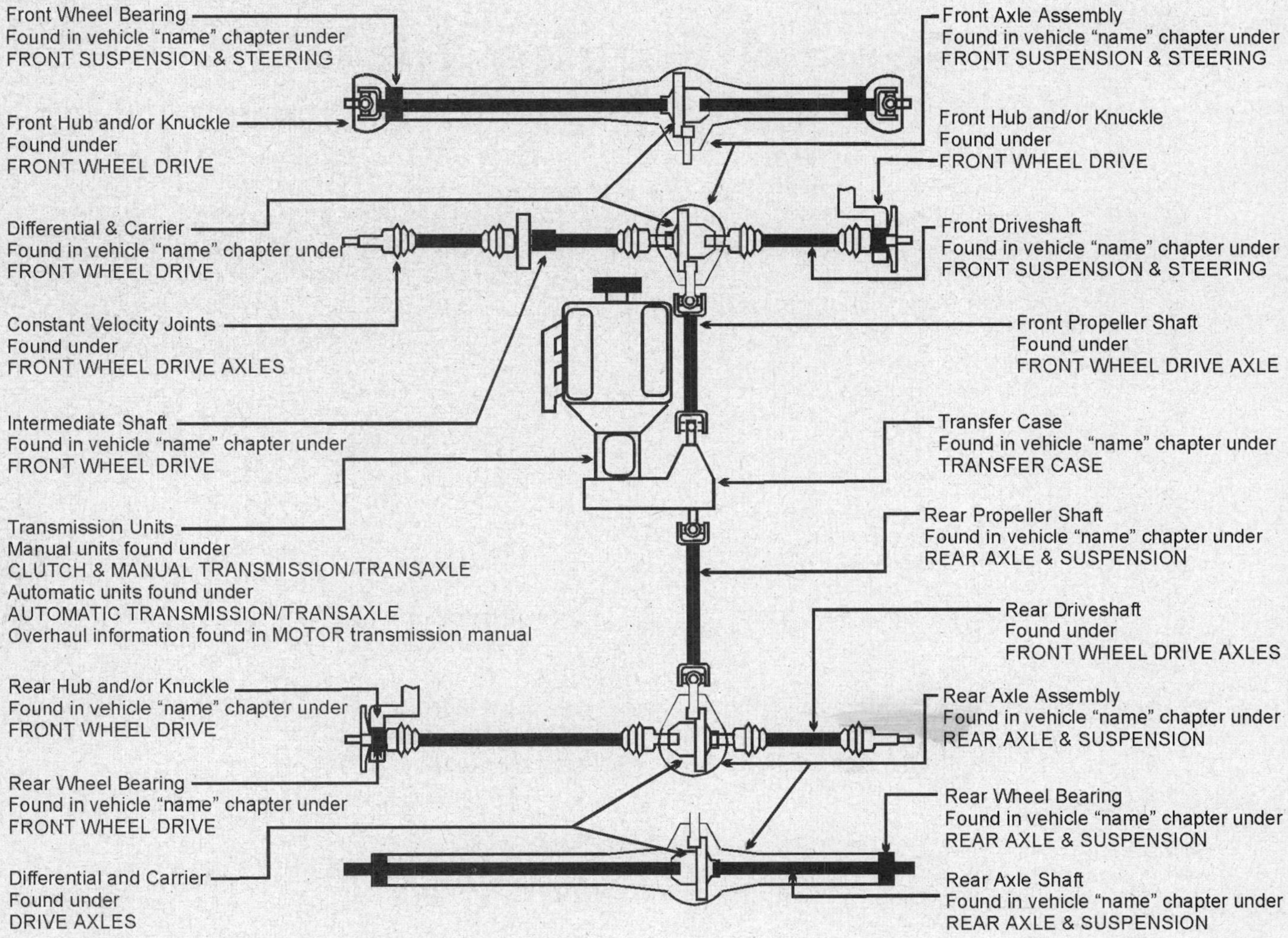

Front Wheel Bearing
Found in vehicle "name" chapter under
FRONT SUSPENSION & STEERING

Front Axle Assembly
Found in vehicle "name" chapter under
FRONT SUSPENSION & STEERING

Front Hub and/or Knuckle
Found under
FRONT WHEEL DRIVE

Front Hub and/or Knuckle
Found under
FRONT WHEEL DRIVE

Differential & Carrier
Found in vehicle "name" chapter under
FRONT WHEEL DRIVE

Front Driveshaft
Found in vehicle "name" chapter under
FRONT SUSPENSION & STEERING

Constant Velocity Joints
Found under
FRONT WHEEL DRIVE AXLES

Front Propeller Shaft
Found under
FRONT WHEEL DRIVE AXLE

Intermediate Shaft
Found in vehicle "name" chapter under
FRONT WHEEL DRIVE

Transfer Case
Found in vehicle "name" chapter under
TRANSFER CASE

Transmission Units
Manual units found under
CLUTCH & MANUAL TRANSMISSION/TRANSAXLE
Automatic units found under
AUTOMATIC TRANSMISSION/TRANSAXLE
Overhaul information found in MOTOR transmission manual

Rear Propeller Shaft
Found in vehicle "name" chapter under
REAR AXLE & SUSPENSION

Rear Driveshaft
Found under
FRONT WHEEL DRIVE AXLES

Rear Hub and/or Knuckle
Found in vehicle "name" chapter under
FRONT WHEEL DRIVE

Rear Axle Assembly
Found in vehicle "name" chapter under
REAR AXLE & SUSPENSION

Rear Wheel Bearing
Found in vehicle "name" chapter under
FRONT WHEEL DRIVE

Rear Wheel Bearing
Found in vehicle "name" chapter under
REAR AXLE & SUSPENSION

Differential and Carrier
Found under
DRIVE AXLES

Rear Axle Shaft
Found in vehicle "name" chapter under
REAR AXLE & SUSPENSION

Manual Information Locator

All Wheel Drive Models

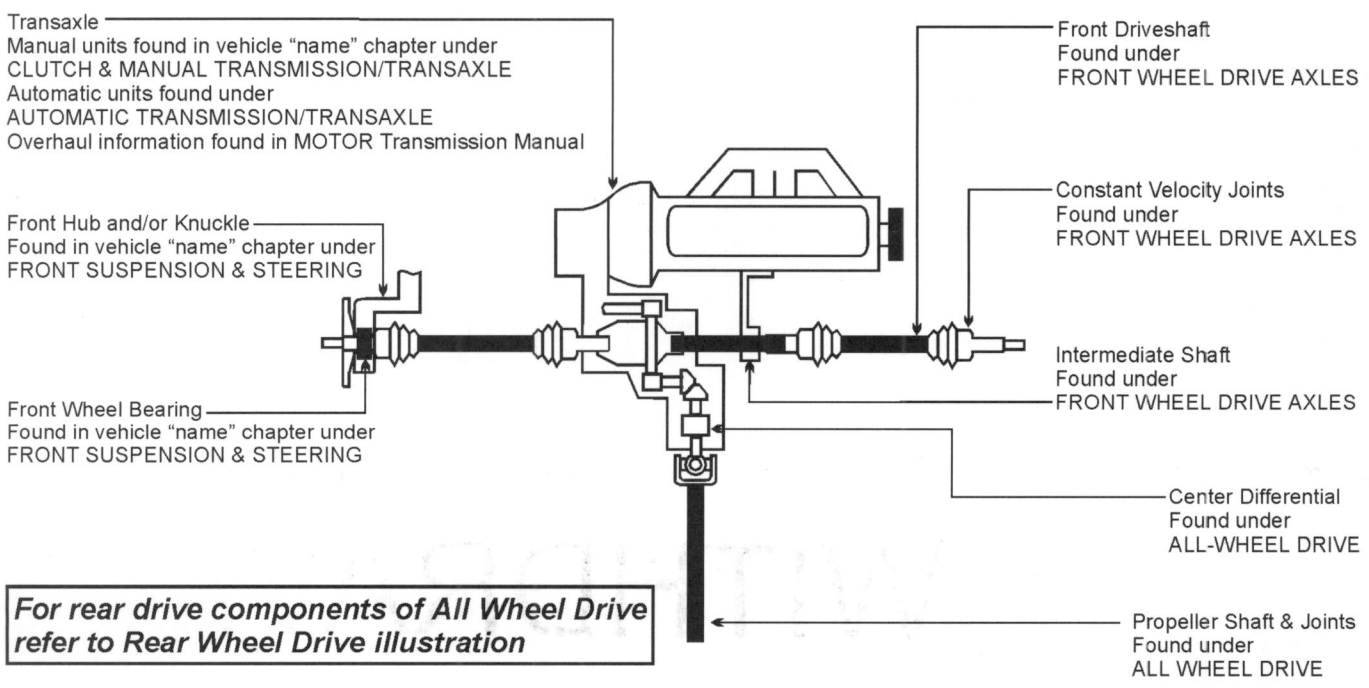

Transaxle
Manual units found in vehicle "name" chapter under
CLUTCH & MANUAL TRANSMISSION/TRANSAXLE
Automatic units found under
AUTOMATIC TRANSMISSION/TRANSAXLE
Overhaul information found in MOTOR Transmission Manual

Front Hub and/or Knuckle
Found in vehicle "name" chapter under
FRONT SUSPENSION & STEERING

Front Wheel Bearing
Found in vehicle "name" chapter under
FRONT SUSPENSION & STEERING

Front Driveshaft
Found under
FRONT WHEEL DRIVE AXLES

Constant Velocity Joints
Found under
FRONT WHEEL DRIVE AXLES

Intermediate Shaft
Found under
FRONT WHEEL DRIVE AXLES

Center Differential
Found under
ALL-WHEEL DRIVE

Propeller Shaft & Joints
Found under
ALL WHEEL DRIVE

For rear drive components of All Wheel Drive refer to Rear Wheel Drive illustration

Rear Wheel Drive Models

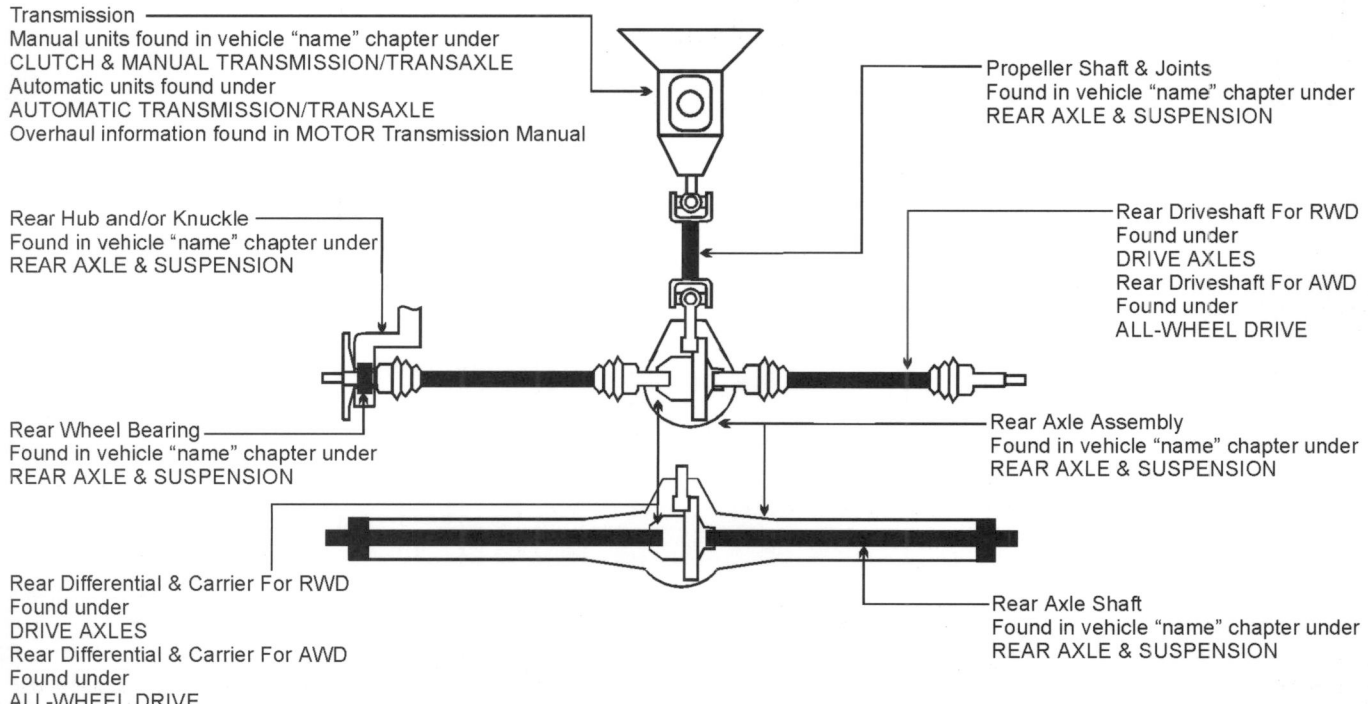

Transmission
Manual units found in vehicle "name" chapter under
CLUTCH & MANUAL TRANSMISSION/TRANSAXLE
Automatic units found under
AUTOMATIC TRANSMISSION/TRANSAXLE
Overhaul information found in MOTOR Transmission Manual

Rear Hub and/or Knuckle
Found in vehicle "name" chapter under
REAR AXLE & SUSPENSION

Rear Wheel Bearing
Found in vehicle "name" chapter under
REAR AXLE & SUSPENSION

Rear Differential & Carrier For RWD
Found under
DRIVE AXLES
Rear Differential & Carrier For AWD
Found under
ALL-WHEEL DRIVE

Propeller Shaft & Joints
Found in vehicle "name" chapter under
REAR AXLE & SUSPENSION

Rear Driveshaft For RWD
Found under
DRIVE AXLES
Rear Driveshaft For AWD
Found under
ALL-WHEEL DRIVE

Rear Axle Assembly
Found in vehicle "name" chapter under
REAR AXLE & SUSPENSION

Rear Axle Shaft
Found in vehicle "name" chapter under
REAR AXLE & SUSPENSION

Operation/Subject/Topic	Light Truck & Van Repair Manual Mechanical Repair	Light Truck & Van Repair Manual ABS/ Electrical	Engine Performance & Driveability Product
Air Bags	—	X	—
Air Bag System Precautions	X	X	X
Air Conditioning	X	—	—
AIR Systems	—	—	X
All-Wheel Drive Systems	X	—	—
Alternator Specifications	X	—	—
Alternator Systems	X	—	—
Anti-Lock Brake Systems	—	X	—
Automatic Seat Belts	—	X	—
Automatic Transaxle In-Vehicle Service	—	—	—
Automatic Transmission In-Vehicle Service	—	—	—
Axle Shaft Service	X	—	—
Back-Up Light Switch, Replace	X	—	—
Balance Shaft Service	X	—	—
Ball Joint Service	X	—	—
Belt Tension Data	X	—	—
Blower Motor, Replace	X	—	—
Brake Booster Service	X	—	—
Brake Service	X	—	—
Camber Adjustment	X	—	—
Camshaft Service	X	—	—
Capacity Data	X	—	—
Caster Adjustment	X	—	—
Catalytic Converters	—	—	X
Clutch Service	—	—	—
Clutch Start Switch, Replace	X	—	—
Coil Pack, Replace	X	—	X
Coil Spring, Replace	X	—	—
Compression Check	X	—	X
Compression Pressures	X	—	X
Computer Relearn Procedures	X	X	X
Computerized Engine Control Systems	—	—	X
Control Arm Service	X	—	—
Cooling System Bleed	X	—	—
Cooling System Data	X	—	—
Crankshaft Pulley, Replace	X	—	—
Crankshaft Rear Oil Seal Service	X	—	—
Cruise Control Systems	—	X	—
Cylinder Block Specifications	X	—	—
Cylinder Head Service	X	—	—
Cylinder Head Specifications	X	—	—
Cylinder Head, Replace	X	—	—
Cylinder Liner, Replace	X	—	—
Dash Panel Service	X	—	—
Differential Service	X	—	—
Dimmer Switch, Replace	X	—	—
Disc Brake Service	X	—	—
Distributor Service	—	—	X
Distributor, Replace	X	—	X
Distributorless Ignition Systems	—	—	X
Drive Axle Service	X	—	—
Drive Belt Tension Data	X	—	—
Drum Brake Service	X	—	—
EGR System	—	—	X
Electric Engine Cooling Fans	X	—	—
Electric Fuel Pumps	X	—	X
Electrical Symbol Identification	X	X	X
Electronic Fuel Injection	—	—	X
Electronic Ignition	—	—	X
Electronic Instrumentation	—	—	X
Electronic Level Controls	—	X	—

Operation/Subject/Topic	Light Truck & Van Repair Manual Mechanical Repair	Light Truck & Van Repair Manual ABS/ Electrical	Engine Performance & Driveability Product
Emission Control Application Charts	—	—	X
Emission Controls	—	—	X
Emission Vacuum Hose Routings	—	—	X
Engine Compartment Reference Diagrams	—	—	X
Engine Cooling Fans	X	—	—
Engine Control Module, Replace	—	—	X
Engine Control Unit, Replace	—	—	X
Engine Front Cover Service	X	—	—
Engine Mounts, Replace	X	—	—
Engine Oil Seal Service	X	—	—
Engine Rebuilding Specifications	X	—	—
Engine Repairs	X	—	—
Engine Sensor Location	—	—	X
Engine Sensor Replacement	—	—	X
Engine Sensor Specifications	—	—	X
Engine System Identification Charts	—	—	X
Engine Tightening Specifications	X	—	—
Engine, Replace	X	—	—
Evaporator Core, Replace	X	—	—
Exhaust Gas Recirculation (EGR) Systems	—	—	X
Exhaust Manifold, Replace	X	—	—
Fast Idle Speed Adjustment	—	—	X
Federal Air Quality Standards	—	—	X
Flasher Location	X	—	—
Front Drive Axle Service	X	—	—
Front Wheel Alignment	X	—	—
Fuel Control System Identification	—	—	X
Fuel Filter, Replace	X	—	—
Fuel Injection Systems	—	—	X
Fuel Injector Cleaning Procedures	—	—	X
Fuel Injector, Replace	—	—	X
Fuel Pump Pressure Specifications	X	—	X
Fuel Pump Pressure Test	—	—	X
Fuel Pump Relay Location	X	—	X
Fuel Pump Replacement	X	—	X
Fuse Panel Location	X	—	—
General Engine Specifications	X	—	—
Headlight Switch, Replace	X	—	—
Heated Air Cleaners	—	—	X
Heater Core, Replace	X	—	—
Hub & Bearing Assembly Service	X	—	—
Hydraulic Brake System Service	X	—	—
Hydraulic Engine Cooling Fans	X	—	—
Hydraulic Valve Lifter Service	X	—	—
Idle Mixture Adjustments	—	—	X
Idle Speed Adjustments	—	—	X
Ignition Lock, Replace	X	—	—
Ignition Switch, Replace	X	—	—
Ignition System Application	—	—	X
Ignition Timing Procedures	—	—	X
Instrument Cluster, Replace	X	—	—
Intake Manifold, Replace	X	—	—
Intermittent Malfunction Computer Diagnosis	—	—	X
Knock Sensor, Replace	—	—	X
Leaf Spring, Replace	X	—	—
Lift Point Illustrations	X	X	—
Locking Differential Service	X	—	—
Locking Hub Service	X	—	—
Lower Ball Joint, Replace	X	—	—